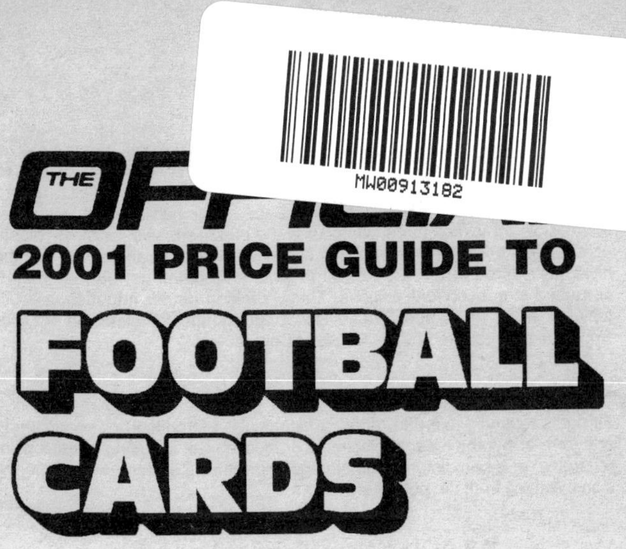

THE OFFICIAL 2001 PRICE GUIDE TO FOOTBALL CARDS

BY

DR. JAMES BECKETT

TWENTIETH EDITION

HOUSE OF COLLECTIBLES
THE CROWN PUBLISHING GROUP • NEW YORK

Important Notice: All of the information, including valuations, in this book has been compiled from the most reliable sources, and every effort has been made to eliminate errors and questionable data. Nevertheless, the possibility of error, in a work of such immense scope, always exists. The publisher will not be held responsible for losses that may occur in the purchase, sale, or other transaction of items because of information contained herein. Readers who feel they have discovered errors are invited to *write* and inform us, so they may be corrected in subsequent editions. Those seeking further information on the topics covered in this book are advised to refer to the complete line of *Official Price Guides* published by the House of Collectibles.

House of Collectibles and the HC colophon are trademarks of Random House, Inc.

Published by:
House of Collectibles
The Crown Publishing Group
New York, New York

Distributed by The Crown Publishing Group,
a division of Random House, Inc.,
New York, and simultaneously in Canada by
Random House of Canada Limited, Toronto.

www.randomhouse.com

Manufactured in the United States of America

ISSN: 0748-1365

ISBN: 0-676-60192-8

10 9 8 7 6 5 4 3 2 1

Twentieth Edition: October 2000

Table of Contents

About the Author

Jim Beckett, the leading authority on sport card values in the United States, maintains a wide range of activities in the world of sports. He possesses one of the finest collections of sports cards and autographs in the world, has made numerous appearances on radio and television, and has been frequently cited in many national publications. He was awarded the first "Special Achievement Award" for Contributions to the Hobby by the National Sports Collectors Convention in 1980, the "Jock-Jaspersen Award" for Hobby Dedication in 1983, and the "Buck Barker, Spirit of the Hobby" Award in 1991.

Dr. Beckett is the author of *Beckett Baseball Card Price Guide, The Official Price Guide to Baseball Cards, The Sport Americana Price Guide to Baseball Collectible, Beckett Almanac of Baseball Cards and Collectible, The Sport Americana Baseball Memorabilia and Autograph Price Guide, Beckett Football Card Price Guide, The Official Price Guide to Football Cards, Beckett Hockey Card Price Guide and Alphabetical Checklist, Beckett Basketball Card Price Guide, The Official Price Guide to Basketball Cards,* and *Beckett Baseball Card Alphabetical Checklist.* In addition, he is the founder, publisher, and editor of *Beckett Baseball Card Monthly, Beckett Basketball Card Monthly, Beckett Football Card Monthly, Beckett Hockey Collector, Beckett Sports Collectible and Autographs* and *Beckett Racing and Motorsports Marketplace.*

Jim Beckett received his Ph.D. in Statistics from Southern Methodist University in 1975. Prior to starting Beckett Publications in 1984, Dr. Beckett served as an Associate Professor of Statistics at Bowling Green State University and as a Vice President of a consulting firm in Dallas, Texas. He currently resides in Dallas.

How to Use This Book

Isn't it great? Every year this book gets bigger and bigger with all the new sets coming out. But even more exciting is that every year there are more attractive choices and, subsequently, more interest in the cards we love so much. This edition has been enhanced and expanded from the previous edition. The cards you collect — who appears on them, what they look like, where they are from, and (most important to most of you) what their current values are — are enumerated within. Many of the features contained in the other *Beckett Price Guides* have been incorporated into this volume since condition grading, terminology, and many other aspects of collecting are common to the card hobby in general. We hope you find the book both interesting and useful in your collecting pursuits.

The Beckett Guide has been successful where other attempts have failed because it is complete, current, and valid. This Price Guide contains not just one, but three prices by condition for all the football cards listed. These account for most of the football cards in existence. The prices were added to the card lists just prior to printing and reflect not the author's opinions or desires but the going retail prices for each card, based on the marketplace (sports memorabilia conventions and shows, sports card shops, hobby papers, current mail-order catalogs, local club meetings, auction results, and other firsthand reporting of actually realized prices).

What is the best price guide available on the market today? Of course card sellers will prefer the price guide with the highest prices, while card buyers will naturally prefer the one with the lowest prices. Accuracy, however, is the true test. Use the price guide used by more collectors and dealers than all the others combined. Look for the Beckett name. I won't put my name on anything I won't stake my reputation on. Not the lowest and not the highest — but the most accurate, with integrity.

To facilitate your use of this book, read the complete introductory section on the following pages before going to the pricing pages. Every collectible field has its own terminology; we've tried to capture most of these terms and definitions in our glossary. Please read carefully the section on grading and the condition of your cards, as you will not be able to determine which price column is appropriate for a given card without first knowing its condition.

Prices in This Guide

Prices found in this guide reflect current retail rates just prior to the printing of this book. They do not reflect the FOR SALE prices of the author, the publisher, the distributors, the advertisers, or any card dealers associated with this guide. No one is obligated in any way to buy, sell or trade his or her cards based on these prices. The price listings were compiled by the author from actual buy/sell transactions at sports conventions, sports card shops, buy/sell advertisements in the hobby papers, for sale prices from dealer catalogs and price lists, and discussions with leading hobbyists in the U.S. and Canada. All prices are in U.S. dollars.

Acknowledgments

A great deal of diligence, hard work, and dedicated effort went into this year's volume. The high standards to which we hold ourselves, however, could not have been met without the expert input and generous amount of time contributed by many people. Our sincere thanks are extended to each and every one of you.

A complete list of these invaluable contributors appears after the Price Guide section.

Introduction

Welcome to the exciting world of sports card collecting, one of America's most popular avocations. You have made a good choice in buying this book, since it will open up to you the entire panorama of this field in the simplest, most concise way.

The growth of *Beckett Baseball Card Monthly, Beckett Basketball Monthly, Beckett Football Card Monthly, Beckett Hockey Monthly, Sports Collectible & Beckett Racing Monthly* is an indication of the unprecedented popularity of sports cards. Founded in 1984 by Dr. James Beckett, the author of this Price Guide, *Beckett Baseball Card Monthly* contains the most extensive and accepted monthly Price Guide, collectible glossy superstar covers, colorful feature articles, "Hot List," Convention Calendar, tips for beginners, "Readers Write" letters to and responses from the editor, information on errors and varieties, autograph collecting tips and profiles of the sport's Hottest stars. Published every month, BBCM is the hobby's largest paid circulation periodical. The other five magazines were built on the success of BBCM.

So collecting sports cards — while still pursued as a hobby with youthful exuberance by kids in the neighborhood — has also taken on the trappings of an industry, with thousands of full- and part-time card dealers, as well as vendors of supplies, clubs and conventions. In fact, each year since 1980 thousands of hobbyists have assembled for a National Sports Collectors Convention, at which hundreds of dealers have displayed their wares, seminars have been conducted, autographs penned by sports notables, and millions of cards changed hands. The Beckett Guide is the best annual guide available to the exciting world of football cards. Read it and use it. May your enjoyment and your card collection increase in the coming months and years.

How to Collect

Each collection is personal and reflects the individuality of its owner. There are no set rules on how to collect cards. Since card collecting is a hobby or leisure pastime, what you collect, how much you collect, and how much time and money you spend collecting are entirely up to you. The funds you have available for collecting and your own personal taste should determine how you collect. The information and ideas presented here are intended to help you get the most enjoyment from this hobby.

It is impossible to collect every card ever produced. Therefore, beginners as well as intermediate and advanced collectors usually specialize in some way. One of the reasons this hobby is popular is that individual collectors can define and tailor their collecting methods to match their own tastes. To give you some ideas of the various approaches to collecting, we will list some of the more popular areas of specialization.

Many collectors select complete sets from particular years. For example, they may concentrate on assembling complete sets from all the years since their birth or since they became avid sports fans. They may try to collect a card for every player during that specified period of time. Many others wish to acquire only certain players. Usually such players are the superstars of the sport, but occasionally collectors will specialize in all the cards of players who attended a particular college or came from a certain town. Some collectors are only interested in the first cards or Rookie Cards of certain players.

Another fun way to collect cards is by team. Most fans have a favorite team, and it is natural for that loyalty to be translated into a desire for cards of the players on that favorite team. For most of the recent years, team sets (all the cards from a given team for that year) are readily available at a reasonable price. The Beckett Football Card Alphabetical Checklist will open up this field to the collector.

Obtaining Cards

Several avenues are open to card collectors. Cards still can be purchased in the traditional way: by the pack at the local discount, grocery or convenience stores. But there are also thousands of card shops across the country that specialize in selling cards individually or by the pack, box, or set. Another alternative is the thousands of card shows held each month around the country, which feature anywhere from five to 800 tables of sports cards and memorabilia for sale.

For many years, it has been possible to purchase complete sets of cards through mail-order advertisers found in traditional sports media publications, such as *The Sporting News, Football Digest, Street & Smith* yearbooks, and others. These sets also are advertised in the card collecting periodicals. Many collectors will begin by subscribing to at least one of the hobby periodicals, all with good up-to-date information. Another way of obtaining cards and information is through Beckett's website, www.beckett.com.

Most serious card collectors obtain old (and new) cards from one or more of several main sources: (1) trading or buying from other collectors or dealers; (2) responding to sale or auction ads in the hobby publications; (3) buying at a local hobby store; and/or (4) attending sports collectible shows or conventions.

We advise that you try all four methods since each has its own distinct advantages: (1) trading is a great way to make new friends; (2) hobby periodicals help you keep up with what's going on in the hobby (including when and where the conventions are happening); (3) stores provide the opportunity to enjoy personalized service and consider a great diversity of material in a relaxed sports-oriented atmosphere; and (4) shows allow you to choose from multiple dealers and thousands of cards under one roof in a competitive situation.

Preserving Your Cards

Cards are fragile. They must be handled properly in order to retain their value. Careless handling can easily result in creased or bent cards. It is, however, not recommended that tweezers or tongs be used to pick up your cards since such utensils might mar or indent card surfaces and thus reduce those cards' conditions and values. In general, your cards should be handled directly as little as possible. This is sometimes easier to say than to do.

Although there are still many who use custom boxes, storage trays, or even shoe boxes, plastic sheets are the preferred method of many collectors for storing cards. A collection stored in plastic pages in a three-ring album allows you to view your collection at any time without the need to touch the card itself. Cards can also be kept in single holders (of various types and thickness) designed for the enjoyment of each card individually. For a large collection, some collectors may use a combination of the above methods. When purchasing plastic sheets for your cards, be sure that you find the pocket size that fits the cards snugly. Don't put your 1951 Bowman in a sheet designed to fit 1981 Topps.

Most hobby and collectible shops and virtually all collectors' conventions will have these plastic pages available in quantity for the various sizes offered, or you can purchase them directly from the advertisers in this book. Also, remember that pocket size isn't the only factor to consider when looking for plastic sheets. Other factors such as safety, economy, appearance, availability, or personal preference also may indicate which types of sheets a collector may want to buy.

Damp, sunny and/or hot conditions — no, this is not a weather forecast — are three elements to avoid in extremes if you are interested in preserving your collection. Too much (or too little) humidity can cause gradual deterioration of a card. Direct, bright sun (or fluorescent light) over time will bleach out the color of a card. Extreme heat accelerates the decomposition of the card. On the other hand, many cards have lasted more than 50 years without much scientific intervention. So be cautious, even if the above factors typically present a problem only when present in the extreme. It never hurts to be prudent.

Collecting vs. Investing

Collecting individual players and collecting complete sets are both popular vehicles for investment and speculation. Most investors and speculators stock up on complete sets or on quantities of players they think have good investment potential.

There is obviously no guarantee in this book, or anywhere else for that matter, that cards will outperform the stock market or other investment alternatives in the future. After all, football cards do not pay quarterly dividends and cards cannot be sold at their "current values" as easily as stocks or bonds.

Nevertheless, investors have noticed a favorable long-term trend in the past performance of sports collectible, and certain cards and sets have outperformed just about any other investment in some years. Many hobbyists maintain that the best investment is and always will be the building of a collection, which traditionally has held up better than outright speculation.

Some of the obvious questions are: Which cards? When to buy? When to sell? The best investment you can make is in your own education. The more you know about your collection and the hobby, the more informed the decisions you will be able to make. We're not selling investment tips. We're selling information about the current value of football cards. It's up to you to use that information to your best advantage.

Terminology

Each hobby has its own language to describe its area of interest. The terminology traditionally used for trading cards is derived from the American Card Catalog, published in 1960 by Nostalgia Press. That catalog, written by Jefferson Burdick (who is called the "Father of Card Collecting" for his pioneering work), uses letter and number designations for each separate set of cards. The letter used in the ACC designation refers to the generic type of card. While both sport and non-sport issues are classified in the ACC, we shall confine ourselves to the sport issues. The following list defines the letters and their meanings as used by the American Card Catalog, as applied to football cards:

(none) or N - 19th Century U.S. Tobacco
F - Food Inserts
H - Advertising
M - Periodicals
N - 19th Century U.S. Tobacco
PC - Postcards
R - Recent Candy and Gum Cards, 1930 to Present
UO - Gas and Oil Inserts
V - Canadian Candy
W - Exhibits, Strip Cards, Team Cards

Following the letter prefix and an optional hyphen are one-, two-, or three-digit numbers, R(-)999. These typically represent the company or entity issuing the cards. In several cases, the ACC number is extended by an additional hyphen and another one- or two-digit numerical suffix. For example, the 1957 Topps regular-series football card issue carries an ACC designation of R415-5. The "R" indicates a Candy or Gum card produced since 1930. The "415" is the ACC designation for the 1957 regular issue (Topps fifth football set).

Like other traditional methods of identification, this system provides order to the process of cataloging cards; however, most serious collectors learn the ACC designation of the popular sets by repetition and familiarity, rather than by attempting to "figure out" what they might or should be. From 1948 forward, collectors and dealers commonly refer to all sets by their year, maker, type of issue, and any other distinguishing characteristic. For example, such a characteristic could be an unusual issue or one of several regular issues put out by a specific maker in a single year. Regional issues are usually referred to by year, maker, and sometimes by title or theme of the set.

Glossary/Legend

Our glossary defines terms frequently used in the card collecting hobby. Many of these terms are also common to other types of sports memorabilia collecting. Some terms may have several meanings depending on use and context.

ACC - Acronym for American Card Catalog.
ACETATE - A transparent plastic.
AFC - American Football Conference.
AFL - American Football League.
AS - All-Star.
ATG - All Time Great card.
AU(TO) - An autographed card.
BRICK - A group or "lot" or cards, usually 50 or more having common char-

acteristics, that is intended to be bought, sold, or traded as a unit.

C - Center.

CB - Cornerback.

CFL - Canadian Football League.

CL - Checklist card. A card that lists in order the cards and players in the set or series. Older checklist cards in Mint condition that have not been checked off are very desirable and command large premiums.

CO - Coach card.

COLLECTOR ISSUE - A set produced for the sake of the card itself, with no product or service sponsor. It derives its name from the fact that most of these sets are produced for sale directly to the hobby market.

COMBINATION CARD - A single card depicting two or more players (not including team cards).

COMMON CARD - The typical card of any set; it has no premium value accruing from subject matter, numerical scarcity, popular demand, or anomaly.

CONVENTION - A large gathering of dealers and collectors at a single location for the purpose of buying, selling, and sometimes trading sports memorabilia items. Conventions are open to the public and sometimes also feature autograph guests, door prizes, films, contests, etc. More commonly called "shows."

COR - Corrected card. A version of an error card that was fixed by the manufacturer.

DB - Defensive back.

DIE-CUT - A card with its stock partially cut. In some cases, after removal or appropriate folding, the remaining part of the card can be made to stand up.

DISC - A circular-shaped card.

DISPLAY SHEET - A clear, plastic page that is punched for insertion into a binder (with standard three-ring spacing) containing pockets for displaying cards. Many different styles of sheets exist with pockets of varying sizes to hold the many differing card formats. The vast majority of current cards measure 2 1/2 by 3 1/2 inches and fit in nine-pocket sheets.

DP - Double Print. A card that was printed in approximately double the quantity compared to other cards in the same series, or draft pick card.

DT - Defensive tackle or Dream Team.

DUFEX - A method of card manufacturing technology patented by Pinnacle Brands, Inc. It involves a refractive quality to a card with a foil coating.

EMBOSSED - A raised surface; features of a card that are projected from a flat background.

ERR - Error card. A card with erroneous information, spelling, or depiction on either side of the card. Most errors are never corrected by the producing card company.

ETCHED - Impressions within the surface of a card.

EXHIBIT - The generic name given to thick stock, postcard-size cards with single-color, obverse pictures. The name is derived from the Exhibit Supply Co. of Chicago, the principal manufacturer of this type of card. These are also known as Arcade cards since they were found in many arcades.

FB - Fullback.

FDP - First (round) draft pick.

FG - Field goal.

FOIL - A special type of sticker with a metallic-looking surface.

FULL-BLEED - A borderless card; a card containing a photo that encompasses the entire card.

FULL SHEET - A complete sheet of cards that has not been cut into individual cards by the manufacturer. Also called an uncut sheet.

G - Guard.

GLOSS- A card with luster; a shiny finish as in a card with UV coating.

HIGH NUMBER - The cards in the last series of number, in a year in which such higher-numbered cards were printed or distributed in significantly lesser amount than the lower-numbered cards. The high-number designation refers to a scarcity of the high-numbered cards.

HL - Highlight card, for example from the 1978 Topps subset.

HOF - Hall of Fame, or Hall of Famer (also abbreviated HOFer).

HOLOGRAM - A three-dimensional photographic image.

HOR - Horizontal pose on a card as opposed to the standard vertical orientation found on most cards.

IA - In Action card. A special type of card depicting a player in an action photo, such as the 1982 Topps cards.

IL - Inside linebacker.

INSERT - A card of a different type, e.g., a poster, or any other sports collectible contained and sold in the same package along with a card or cards of a major set.

INTERACTIVE - A concept that involves collector participation.

K - Kicker.

KARAT - A unit of measure for the fineness of gold; i.e. 24K.

KP - Kid Picture card.

LAYERING - The separation or peeling of one or more layers of the card stock, usually at the corner of the card. Also see the Condition Guide.

LB - Linebacker.

LID - A circular-shaped card (possibly with tab) that forms the top of the container for the product being promoted.

LL - League leader card. A card depicting the leader or leaders in a specific statistical category from the previous season. Not to be confused with team leader (TL).

LOGO - NFLPA logo on card.

MAJOR SET - A set produced by a national manufacturer of cards, containing a large number of cards. Usually 100 or more different cards comprise a major set.

MEM - Memorial.

METALLIC - A glossy design that enhances card features.

MINI - A small card or stamp (specifically the 1969 Topps Four-in-One football inserts or the 1987 Topps mini football set issued for the United Kingdom).

MVP - Most Valuable Player.

NFLPA - National Football League Players Association.

NO LOGO - No NFLPA logo on card.

NO TR - No trade reference on card.

NPO - No position.

NT - Nose tackle.

OFF - Officials cards.

O-ROY - Offensive Rookie of the Year.

OT - Offensive tackle.

P - Punter.

P1 - First Printing.

P2 - Second Printing.

PACKS - A means with which cards are issued in terms of pack type (wax, cello, foil, rack, etc.) and channels of distribution (hobby, retail, etc.).

PANEL - An extended card that is composed of multiple individual cards.

PARALLEL- A card that is similar in design to its counterpart from a basic set, but offers a distinguishing quality.

PB - Pro Bowl.

PLATINUM - A metallic element used in the process of creating a glossy card.

POY - Player of the Year.

PREMIUM - A card, sometimes on photographic stock, that is purchased or obtained in conjunction with (or redeemed for) another card or product. This term applies mainly to older products, as newer cards distributed in this manner are generally lumped together as peripheral sets.

PREMIUM CARDS - A class of products introduced recently, intended to have higher quality card stock and photography than regular cards, but more limited production and higher cost. Defining what is and isn't a premium card is somewhat subjective.

PRISMATIC/PRISM - A glossy or bright design that refracts or disperses light.

PROMOTIONAL SET - A set, usually containing a small number of cards, issued by a national card producer and distributed in limited quantities or to a select group of people, such as major show attendees or dealers with wholesale accounts. Presumably, the purpose of a promo set is to stir up demand for an upcoming set. Also called a preview, prototype or test set.

QB - Quarterback.

RARE - A card or series of cards of very limited availability. Unfortunately, "rare" is a subjective term sometimes used indiscriminately. Using the strict definitions, rare cards are harder to obtain than scarce cards.

RB - Record Breaker card or running back.

RC - Rookie Card. A player's first appearance on a regular issue card from one of the major card companies. Each company has only one regular issue set per season, and that is the widely available traditional set. With a few exceptions, each player has only one RC in any given set. A Rookie Card cannot be an All-Star, Highlight, In Action, league leader, Super Action or team leader card. It can, however, be a coach card or draft pick card.

REDEMPTION - A program established by manufacturers that allows collectors to mail in a special card (usually a random insert) in return for special cards, sets or other prizes not available through conventional channels.

REFRACTORS - A card that features a design element which enhances (distorts) its color/appearance through deflecting light.

REGIONAL - A card issued and distributed only in a limited geographical area of the country. The producer may or may not be a major, national producer of trading cards. The key is whether the set was distributed nationally in any form or not.

REPLICA - An identical copy or reproduction.

RET - Retired.

REV NEG - Reversed or flopped photo side of the card. This is a major type of error card, but only some are corrected.

ROY - Rookie of the Year.

S - Safety.

SB - Super Bowl.

SCARCE - A card or series of cards of limited availability. This subjective term is sometimes used indiscriminately to promote or hype value. Using strict definitions, scarce cards are easier to obtain than rare cards.

SEMI-HIGH - A card from the next-to-last series of a sequentially issued set. It has more value than an average card and generally less value than a high number. A card is not called a semi-high unless its next-to-last series has an additional premium attached to it.

SERIES - The entire set of cards issued by a particular producer in a particular year, e.g., the 1978 Topps series. Also, within a particular set, series can refer to a group of (consecutively numbered) cards printed at the same time, e.g., the first series of the 1948 Leaf set (#1 through #49).

SET - One each of an entire run of cards of the same type, produced by a particular manufacturer during a single season. In other words, if you have a complete set of 1975 Topps football cards, then you have every card from #1 up to and including #528; i.e., all the different cards that were produced.

SHEEN - Brightness or luster emitted by a card.

SKIP-NUMBERED - A set that has many unissued card numbers between the lowest number in the set and the highest number in the set, e.g., the 1949 Leaf football set contains 49 cards skip-numbered from number 1-144. A major set in which a few numbers were not printed is not considered to be skip-numbered.

SP - Single or Short Print. A card which was printed in lesser quantity compared to the other cards in the same series (also see DP). This term only can be used in a relative sense and in reference to one particular set. For instance, the 1989 Pro Set Pete Rozelle SP is less common than the other cards in that set, but it isn't necessarily scarcer than regular cards of any other set.

SPECIAL CARD - A card that portrays something other than a single player or team; for example, the 1990 Fleer Joe Montana/Jerry Rice Super Bowl MVPs card #397.

SR - Super Rookie.

STAMP - Adhesive-backed papers depicting a player. The stamp may be individual or in a sheet of many stamps. Moisture must be applied to the adhesive in order for the stamp to be attached to another surface.

STAR CARD - A card that portrays a player of some repute, usually determined by his ability, but sometimes referring to sheer popularity.

STICKER - A card-like item with a removable layer that can be affixed to another surface. Example: 1983 Topps inserts.

STOCK - The cardboard or paper on which the card is printed.

SUPERIMPOSED - To be affixed on top of something, i.e., a player photo over a solid background.

SUPERSTAR CARD - A card that portrays a superstar, e.g., a Hall of Fame member or a player whose current performance may eventually warrant serious Hall of Fame consideration.

TAB - A card portion set off from the rest of the card, usually with perforations, that may be removed without damaging the central character or event depicted by the card.

TC - Team card or team checklist card.

TEAM CARD - A card that depicts an entire team.

THREE-DIMENSIONAL (3D) - A visual image that provides an illusion of depth and perspective.

TL - Team leader card or Top Leader.

TOPICAL - a subset or group of cards that have a common theme, i.e., MVP award winners.

TR - Trade reference on card.

TRANSPARENT - Clear, see through.

TRIMMED - A card cut down from its original size. Trimmed cards are undesirable to most collectors, and are therefore less valuable than otherwise identical, untrimmed cards. Also see the Condition Guide.

UER - Uncorrected error card.

USFL - United States Football League.

UV - Ultraviolet, a glossy coating used in producing cards.

VAR - Variation card. One of two or more cards from the same series, with the same card number (or player with identical pose, if the series is unnumbered) differing from one another in some aspect, from the printing, stock or other feature of the card. This is often caused when the manufacturer of the cards notices an error in a particular card, corrects the error and then resumes the print run. In this case there will be two versions or variations of the same card. Sometimes one of the variations is relatively scarce. Variations also can result from accidental or deliberate design changes, information updates, photo substitutions, etc.

VERT - Vertical pose on a card.

WFL - World Football League.

WLAF - World League of American Football.

WR - Wide receiver.

XRC - Extended Rookie Card. A player's first appearance on a card, but issued in a set that was not distributed nationally nor in packs. In football sets, this term generally refers to the 1984 and 1985 Topps USFL sets.

Understanding Card Values

Determining Value

Why are some cards more valuable than others? Obviously, the economic laws of supply and demand are applicable to card collecting just as they are to any other field where a commodity is bought, sold or traded in a free, unregulated market.

Supply (the number of cards available on the market) is less than the total number of cards originally produced since attrition diminishes that original quantity. Each year a percentage of cards is typically thrown away, destroyed or otherwise lost to collectors. This percentage is much, much smaller today than it was in the past because more and more people have become increasingly aware of the value of their cards.

For those who collect only Mint condition cards, the supply of older cards can be quite small indeed. Until recently, collectors were not so conscious of the need to preserve the condition of their cards. For this reason, it is difficult to know exactly how many 1962 Topps are currently available, Mint or otherwise. It is generally accepted that there are fewer 1962 Topps available than 1972, 1982 or 1992 Topps cards. If demand were equal for each of these sets, the law of supply and demand would increase the price for the least available sets.

Demand, however, is never equal for all sets, so price correlations can be complicated. The demand for a card is influenced by many factors. These include: (1) the age of the card; (2) the number of cards printed; (3) the player(s) portrayed on the card; (4) the attractiveness and popularity of the set; and (5) the physical condition of the card.

In general, (1) the older the card, (2) the fewer the number of the cards printed, (3) the more famous, popular and talented the player, (4) the more attractive and popular the set, and (5) the better the condition of the card, the higher the value of the card will be. There are exceptions to all but one of these factors: the condition of the card. Given two cards similar in all respects except condition, the one in the better condition will always be valued higher.

While those guidelines help to establish the value of a card, the countless exceptions and peculiarities make any simple, direct mathematical formula to determine card values impossible.

Regional Variation

Since the market varies from region to region, card prices of local players may be higher. This is known as a regional premium. How significant the premium is — and if there is any premium at all — depends on the local popularity of the team and the player.

The largest regional premiums usually do not apply to superstars, who often are so well known nationwide that the prices of their key cards are too high for local dealers to realize a premium.

Lesser stars often command the strongest premiums. Their popularity is concentrated in their home region, creating local demand that greatly exceeds overall demand.

Regional premiums can apply to popular retired players and sometimes can be found in the areas where the players grew up or starred in college.

A regional discount is the converse of a regional premium. Regional discounts occur when a player has been so popular in his region for so long that local collectors and dealers have accumulated quantities of his cards. The abundant supply may make the cards available in that area at the lowest prices anywhere.

Set Prices

A somewhat paradoxical situation exists in the price of a complete set vs. the combined cost of the individual cards in the set. In nearly every case, the sum of the prices for the individual cards is higher than the cost for the complete set. This is prevalent especially in the cards of the past few years. The reasons for this apparent anomaly stem from the habits of collectors and from the carrying costs to dealers. Today, each card in a set normally is produced in the same quantity as all others in its set.

Many collectors pick up only stars, superstars and particular teams. As a result, the dealer is left with a shortage of certain player cards and an abundance of others. He therefore incurs an expense in simply "carrying" these less desirable cards in stock. On the other hand, if he sells a complete set, he gets rid of large numbers of cards at one time. For this reason, he generally is willing to receive less money for a complete set. By doing this, he recovers all of his costs and also makes a profit.

Set prices do not include rare card varieties, unless specifically stated. Of course, the prices for sets do include one example of each type for the given set, but this is the least expensive variety.

Scarce Series

Scarce series occur because cards issued before 1973 were made available to the public each year in several series of finite numbers of cards, rather than all cards of the set being available for purchase at one time. At some point during the season, interest in current year cards waned. Consequently, the manufacturers produced smaller numbers of these later-series cards. Nearly all nationwide issues from post World War II manufacturers (1948 to 1972) exhibit these series variations.

In the past, Topps, for example, may have issued series consisting of many different numbers of cards, including 55, 66, 80, 88, 110 and others. However, after 1968, the sheet size generally has been 132. Despite Topps' standardization of the sheet size, the company double-printed one sheet in 1983 and possibly in 1984 and 1985, too. This was apparently an effort to induce collectors to buy more packs.

We are always looking for information or photographs of printing sheets of cards for research. Each year, we try to update the hobby's knowledge of distribution anomalies. Please let us know at the address in this book if you have firsthand knowledge that would be helpful in this pursuit.

Grading Your Cards

Each hobby has its own grading terminology — stamps, coins, comic books, record collecting, etc. Collectors of sports cards are no exception. The one invariable criterion for determining the value of a card is its condition: the better the condition of the card, the more valuable it is. Condition grading, however, is subjective. Individual card dealers and collectors differ in the strictness of their grading, but the stated condition of a card should be determined without regard to whether it is being bought or sold.

No allowance is made for age. A 1952 card is judged by the same standards as a 1992 card. But there are specific sets and cards that are condition sensitive because of their border color, consistently poor centering, etc. Such cards and sets sometimes command premiums above the listed percentages in Mint condition.

Centering

Current centering terminology uses numbers representing the percentage of border on either side of the main design. Obviously, centering is diminished in importance for borderless cards such as Stadium Club.

Slightly Off-Center (60/40): A slightly off-center card is one that upon close inspection is found to have one border bigger than the opposite border. This degree once was offensive only to purists, but now some hobbyists try to avoid cards that are anything other than perfectly centered.

Off-Center (70/30): An offcenter card has one border that is noticeably more than twice as wide as the opposite border.

Badly Off-Center (80/20 or worse): A badly off-center card has virtually no border on one side of the card.

Miscut: A miscut card actually shows part of the adjacent card in its larger border and consequently a corresponding amount of its card is cut off.

Corner Wear

Corner wear is the most scrutinized grading criteria in the hobby. These are the major categories of corner wear:

Corner with a slight touch of wear: The corner still is sharp, but there is a slight touch of wear showing. On a dark-bordered card, this shows as a dot of white.

Fuzzy corner: The corner still comes to a point, but the point has just begun to fray. A slightly "dinged" corner is considered the same as a fuzzy corner.

Slightly rounded corner: The fraying of the corner has increased to where there is only a hint of a point. Mild layering may be evident. A "dinged" corner is considered the same as a slightly rounded corner.

Rounded corner: The point is completely gone. Some layering is noticeable.

Badly rounded corner: The corner is completely round and rough. Severe layering is evident.

Creases

A third common defect is the crease. The degree of creasing in a card is difficult to show in a drawing or picture. On giving the specific condition of an expensive card for sale, the seller should note any creases additionally. Creases can be categorized as to severity according to the following scale.

Light Crease: A light crease is a crease that is barely noticeable upon close inspection. In fact, when cards are in plastic sheets or holders, a light crease may not be seen (until the card is taken out of the holder). A light crease on the front is much more serious than a light crease on the card back only.

Medium Crease: A medium crease is noticeable when held and studied at arm's length by the naked eye, but does not overly detract from the appearance of the card. It is an obvious crease, but not one that breaks the picture surface of the card.

Heavy Crease: A heavy crease is one that has torn or broken through the card's picture surface, e.g., puts a tear in the photo surface.

Alterations

Deceptive Trimming: This occurs when someone alters the card in order (1) to shave off edge wear, (2) to improve the sharpness of the corners, or (3) to improve centering — obviously their objective is to falsely increase the perceived value of the card to an unsuspecting buyer. The shrinkage usually is evident only if the trimmed card is compared to an adjacent full-sized card or if the trimmed card is itself measured.

Obvious Trimming: Obvious trimming is noticeable and unfortunate. It is usually performed by non-collectors who give no thought to the present or future value of their cards.

Deceptively Retouched Borders: This occurs when the borders (especially on those cards with dark borders) are touched up on the edges and corners with magic marker or crayons of appropriate color in order to make the card appear to be Mint.

Categorization of Defects

Miscellaneous Flaws

The following are common minor flaws that, depending on severity, lower a card's condition by one to four grades and often render it no better than Excellent-Mint: bubbles (lumps in surface), gum and wax stains, diamond cutting (slanted borders), notching, off-centered backs, paper wrinkles, scratched-off cartoons or puzzles on back, rubber band marks, scratches, surface impressions and warping.

The following are common serious flaws that, depending on severity, lower a card's condition at least four grades and often render it no better than Good: chemical or sun fading, erasure marks, mildew, miscutting (severe off-centering), holes, bleached or retouched borders, tape marks, tears, trimming, water or coffee stains and writing.

Condition Guide

Grades

Mint (Mt) - A card with no flaws or wear. The card has four perfect corners, 60/40 or better centering from top to bottom and from left to right, original gloss, smooth edges and original color borders. A Mint card does not have print spots, color or focus imperfections.

Near Mint-Mint (NrMt-Mt) - A card with one minor flaw. Any one of the following would lower a Mint card to Near Mint-Mint: one corner with a slight touch of wear, barely noticeable print spots, color or focus imperfections. The card must have 60/40 or better centering in both directions, original gloss, smooth edges and original color borders.

Near Mint (NrMt) - A card with one minor flaw. Any one of the following would lower a Mint card to Near Mint: one fuzzy corner or two to four corners with slight touches of wear, 70/30 to 60/40 centering, slightly rough edges, minor print spots, color or focus imperfections. The card must have original gloss and original color borders.

Excellent-Mint (ExMt) - A card with two or three fuzzy, but not rounded, corners and centering no worse than 80/20. The card may have no more than two of the following: slightly rough edges, very slightly discolored borders, minor print spots, color or focus imperfections. The card must have original gloss.

Excellent (Ex) - A card with four fuzzy but definitely not rounded corners and centering no worse than 80/20. The card may have a small amount of original gloss lost, rough edges, slightly discolored borders and minor print spots, color or focus imperfections.

Very Good (Vg) - A card that has been handled but not abused: slightly rounded corners with slight layering, slight notching on edges, a significant amount of gloss lost from the surface but no scuffing and moderate discoloration of borders. The card may have a few light creases.

Good (G), **Fair (F)**, **Poor (P)** - A well-worn, mishandled or abused card: badly rounded and layered corners, scuffing, most or all original gloss missing, seriously discolored borders, moderate or heavy creases, and one or more serious flaws. The grade of Good, Fair or Poor depends on the severity of wear and flaws. Good, Fair and Poor cards generally are used only as fillers.

The most widely used grades are defined above. Obviously, many cards will not perfectly fit one of the definitions.

Therefore, categories between the major grades known as in-between grades are used, such as Good to Very Good (G-Vg), Very Good to Excellent (VgEx), and Excellent-Mint to Near Mint (ExMt-NrMt). Such grades indicate a card with all qualities of the lower category but with at least a few qualities of the higher category.

The Beckett Guide lists each card and set in three grades, with the middle grade valued at about 40-45% of the top grade, and the bottom grade valued at about 10-15% of the top grade.

The value of cards that fall between the listed columns can also be calculated using a percentage of the top grade. For example, a card that falls between the top and middle grades (Ex, ExMt or NrMt in most cases) will generally be valued at anywhere from 50% to 90% of the top grade.

Similarly, a card that falls between the middle and bottom grades (G-Vg, Vg or VgEx in most cases) will generally be valued at anywhere from 20% to 40% of the top grade.

There are also cases where cards are in better condition than the top grade or worse than the bottom grade. Cards that grade worse than the lowest grade are generally valued at 5-10% of the top grade.

When a card exceeds the top grade by one — such as NrMt-Mt when the top grade is NrMt, or Mint when the top grade is NrMt-Mt — a premium of up to 50% is possible, with 10-20% the usual norm.

When a card exceeds the top grade by two — such as Mint when the top grade is NrMt, or NrMt-Mt when the top grade is ExMt — a premium of 25-50% is the usual norm. But certain condition sensitive cards or sets, particularly those from the pre-war era, can bring premiums of up to 100% or even more.

Unopened packs, boxes and factory-collated sets are considered Mint in their unknown (and presumed perfect) state. Once opened, however, each card can be graded (and valued) in its own right by taking into account any defects that may be present in spite of the fact that the card has never been handled.

Centering

Well-centered

Slightly Off-centered

Off-centered

Badly Off-centered

Miscut

Selling Your Cards

Just about every collector sells cards or will sell cards eventually. Someday you may be interested in selling your duplicates or maybe even your whole collection. You may sell to other collectors, friends or dealers. You may even sell cards you purchased from a certain dealer back to that same dealer. In any event, it helps to know some of the mechanics of the typical transaction between buyer and seller.

Dealers will buy cards in order to resell them to other collectors who are interested in the cards. Dealers will always pay a higher percentage for items that (in their opinion) can be resold quickly, and a much lower percentage for those items that are perceived as having low demand and hence are slow moving. In either case, dealers must buy at a price that allows for the expense of doing business and a margin for profit.

If you have cards for sale, the best advice we can give is that you get several offers for your cards — either from card shops or at a card show — and take the best offer, all things considered. Note, the "best" offer may not be the one for the highest amount. And remember, if a dealer really wants your cards, he won't let you get away without making his best competitive offer. Another alternative is to place your cards in an auction as one or several lots.

Many people think nothing of going into a department store and paying $15 for an item of clothing for which the store paid $5. But if you were selling your $15 card to a dealer and he offered you $5 for it, you might think his markup unreasonable. To complete the analogy: most department stores (and card dealers) that consistently pay $10 for $15 items eventually go out of business. An exception is when the dealer has lined up a willing buyer for the item(s) you are attempting to sell, or if the cards are so Hot that it's likely he'll have to hold the cards for only a short period of time.

In those cases, an offer of up to 75 percent of book value still will allow the dealer to make a reasonable profit considering the short time he will need to hold the merchandise. In general, however, most cards and collections will bring offers in the range of 25 to 50 percent of retail price. Also consider that most material from the past five to 10 years is plentiful. If that's what you're selling, don't be surprised if your best offer is well below that range.

Interesting Notes

The first card numerically of an issue is the single card most likely to obtain excessive wear. Consequently, you typically will find the price on the #1 card (in NrMt or Mint condition) somewhat higher than might otherwise be the case. Similarly, but to a lesser extent (because normally the less important, reverse side of the card is the one exposed), the last card numerically in an issue also is prone to abnormal wear. This extra wear and tear occurs because the first and last cards are exposed to the elements (human element included) more than any other cards. They are generally end cards in any brick formations, rubber bandings, stackings on wet surfaces, and like activities.

Sports cards have no intrinsic value. The value of a card, like the value of other collectible, can be determined only by you and your enjoyment in viewing and possessing these cardboard treasures.

Remember, the buyer ultimately determines the price of each card. You are the determining price factor because you have the ability to say "No" to the price of any card by not exchanging your hard-earned money for a given card. When the cost of a trading card exceeds the enjoyment you will receive from it, your answer should be "No." We assess and report the prices. You set them!

We are always interested in receiving the price input of collectors and deal-

Corner Wear

The partial cards here have been photographed at 300%. This was done in order to magnify each card's corner wear to such a degree that differences could be shown on a printed page.

This 1985 Topps Fred Quillan card has a fuzzy corner. Notice the extremely slight fraying on the corner.

This 1985 Topps Fred Smerlas card has a slightly rounded corner. Notice that there is no longer a sharp corner but heavy wear.

This 1985 Topps Daryl Turner card has a rounded corner evident by the lack of a sharp point and heavy wear on both edges.

This 1985 Topps Kim Bokamper card displays a badly rounded corner. Notice a large portion of missing cardboard accompanied by heavy wear and excessive fraying.

This 1985 Topps Neil O'Donaghue card displays creases of varying degrees. Light creases (left side of the card) may not break the card's surface, while heavy creases (right side) will.

ers from around the country. We happily credit major contributors. We welcome your opinions, since your contributions assist us in ensuring a better guide each year. If you would like to join our survey list for the next editions of this book and others authored by Dr. Beckett, please send your name and address to Dr. James Beckett, 15850 Dallas Parkway, Dallas, Texas 75248.

History of Football Cards

Until the 1930s, the only set devoted exclusively to football players was the Mayo N302 set. The first bubblegum issue dedicated entirely to football players did not appear until the National Chicle issue of 1935. Before this, athletes from several sports were pictured in the multi-sport Goudey Sport Kings issue of 1933. In that set, football was represented by three legends whose fame has not diminished through the years: Red Grange, Knute Rockne and Jim Thorpe.

But it was not until 1948, and the post-war bubblegum boom, that the next football issues appeared. Bowman and Leaf Gum companies both issued football card sets in that year. From this point on, football cards have been issued annually by one company or another up to the present time, with Topps being the only major card producer until 1989, when Pro Set and Score debuted and sparked a football card boom.

Football cards depicting players from the Canadian Football League (CFL) did not appear until Parkhurst issued a 100-card set in 1952. Four years later, Parkhurst issued another CFL set with 50 small cards this time. Topps began issuing CFL sets in 1958 and continued annually until 1965, although from 1961 to 1965 these cards were printed in Canada by O-Pee-Chee. Post Cereal issued two CFL sets in 1962 and 1963; these cards formed the backs of boxes of Post Cereals distributed in Canada. The O-Pee-Chee company, which has maintained a working relationship with the Topps Gum Company, issued four CFL sets in the years 1968, 1970, 1971, and 1972. Since 1981, the JOGO Novelties Company has been producing a number of CFL sets depicting past and present players.

Returning to American football issues, Bowman resumed its football cards (by then with full-color fronts) from 1950 to 1955. The company twice increased the size of its card during that period. Bowman was unopposed during most of the early 1950s as the sole producer of cards featuring pro football players.

Topps issued its first football card set in 1950 with a group of very small, felt-back cards. In 1951 Topps issued what is referred to as the "Magic Football Card" set. This set of 75 has a scratch-off section on the back which answers a football quiz. Topps did not issue another football set until 1955 when its All-American Football set paid tribute to past college football greats. In January of 1956, Topps Gum Company (of Brooklyn) purchased the Bowman Company (of Philadelphia).

After the purchase, Topps issued sets of National Football League (NFL) players up until 1963. The 1961 Topps football set also included American Football League (AFL) players in the high number series (133-198). Topps sets from 1964 to 1967 contained AFL players only. From 1968 to the present, Topps has issued a major set of football cards each year.

When the AFL was founded in 1960, Fleer produced a 132-card set of AFL players and coaches. In 1961, Fleer issued a 220-card set (even larger than the Topps issue of that year) featuring players from both the NFL and AFL. Apparently, for that one year, Topps and Fleer tested a reciprocal arrangement, trading the card printing rights to each other's contracted players. The 1962 and 1963 Fleer sets feature only AFL players. Both sets are relatively small at 88 cards each.

Post Cereal issued a 200-card set of National League football players in 1962 which contains numerous scarcities, namely those players appearing on unpopular varieties of Post Cereal. From 1964 to 1967, the Philadelphia Gum company issued four 198-card NFL player sets.

In 1984 and 1985, Topps produced a set for the now defunct United States Football League, in addition to its annual NFL set. The 1984 set in particular is quite scarce, due to both low distribution and the high demand for the extended Rookie Cards of current NFL superstars Jim Kelly and Reggie White, among others.

In 1986, the McDonald's Restaurants generated the most excitement in football cards in many years. McDonald's created a nationwide football card promotion in which customers could receive a card or two per food purchase, upon request. However, the cards distributed were only of the local team, or of the "McDonald's All-Stars" for areas not near NFL cities. Also, each set was produced with four possible color tabs: blue, black, gold, and green. The tab color distributed depended on the week of the promotion. In general, cards with blue tabs are the scarcest, although for some teams the cards with black tabs are the hardest to find. The tabs were intended to be scratched off and removed by customers to be redeemed for food and other prizes, but among collectors, cards with scratched or removed tabs are categorized as having a major defect, and therefore are valued considerably less.

The entire set, including four color tabs for all 29 subsets, totals over 2800 different cards. The hoopla over the McDonald's cards fell off precipitously after 1988, as collector interest shifted to the new 1989 Score and Pro Set issues.

The popularity of football cards has continued to grow since 1986. Topps introduced "Super Rookie" cards in 1987. Card companies other than Topps noticed the burgeoning interest in football cards, resulting in the two landmark 1989 football sets: a 330-card Score issue, and a 440-card Pro Set release. Score later produced a self-contained 110-card supplemental set, while Pro Set printed 100 Series II cards and a 21-card "Final Update" set. Topps, Pro Set and Score all improved card quality and increased the size of their sets for 1990. That season also marked Fleer's return to football cards and Action Packed's first major set.

In 1991, Pacific, Pro Line, Upper Deck and Wild Card joined a market that is now at least as competitive as the baseball card market. And the premium card trend that began in baseball cards spilled over to the gridiron in the form of Fleer Ultra, Pro Set Platinum, Score Pinnacle, and Topps Stadium Club sets.

The year 1992 brought even more growth with the debuts of All World, Collectors Edge, GameDay, Playoff, Pro Set Power, SkyBox Impact and SkyBox Primetime.

The football card market stabilized somewhat in 1993 thanks to an agreement between the long-feuding NFL licensing bodies, NFL Properties and the NFL Players Association. Also helping the stabilization was the emergence of several promising rookies, including Drew Bledsoe, Jerome Bettis and Rick Mirer. Limited production became the industry buzzword in sports cards, and football was no exception. The result was the success of three new product lines: 1993 Playoff Contenders, 1993 Select and 1993 SP.

The year 1994 brought further stabilization and limited production. Pro Set and Wild Card dropped out, while no new card companies joined the ranks. However, several new NFL sets were added to the mix by existing manufacturers: Classic NFL Experience, Collector's Choice, Excalibur, Finest and Sportflics. The new trend centered around multi-level parallel sets and interactive game inserts with parallel prizes. Another strong rookie crop and reported production cutbacks contributed to strong football card sales throughout 1994.

The football card market continued to grow between 1995 and 1998. Many new sets were released by the major manufacturers and a few new players entered the hobby. Companies continued to push the limits of printing technology with issues printed on plastic, leather, cloth and various metals. Rookie Cards once more came into vogue and the "1-of-1" insert card was born. There are more choices than ever before for the football card collector - most like it that way. In the last couple of years, more changes have occured in the football card market. The Rookie Card popularity continued but with a twist. Since 1998, many Rookie Cards have been sequentially numbered and/or printed to a shorter supply than other cards in the set they are in.

Also, many companies have begun to issued "game worn jerseys" or certified autographed cards of leading players, both active and retired.

In addition, graded cards, old and new, have revitalized the card market. Many collectors and dealers have been able to trade over Internet services such as eBay or the many different ways cards are available on beckett.com.

While some collectors are frustrated by the changing hobby, others are thrilled because there are more choices than ever for the football card collector - and many of the collectors like it that way.

Additional Reading

Each year Beckett Publications produces comprehensive annual price guides for each of the four major sports: *Beckett Baseball Card Price Guide, Beckett Football Card Price Guide, Beckett Basketball Card Price Guide*, and *Beckett Hockey Card Price Guide*. The aim of these annual guides is to provide information and accurate pricing on a wide array of sports cards, ranging from main issues by the major card manufacturers to various regional, promotional, and food issues. Also other alphabetical checklists, such as *The Beckett Baseball Card Alphabetical, The Beckett Football Card Alphabetical, The Beckett Basketball Card Alphabetical,* and *The Beckett Hockey Card Price Guide and Alphabetical*, are published to assist the collector in identifying all the cards of any particular player. Our website beckett.com was created to allow our readers with Internet access an avenue for buying and selling cards as well as participating in online auctions and interactive Price Guides. The seasoned collector will find these tools valuable sources of information that will enable him to pursue his hobby interests.

In addition, abridged editions of the Beckett Price Guides have been published for each of the three major sports as part of the House of Collectible series: *The Official Price Guide to Baseball Cards, The Official Price Guide to Football Cards,* and *The Official Price Guide to Basketball Cards*. Published in a convenient mass-market paperback format, these price guides provide information and accurate pricing on all the main issues by the major card manufacturers.

1998 Aurora

	MINT	NRMT
COMPLETE SET (200)	70.00	32.00
COMMON CARD (1-200)	.20	.09
SEMISTARS	.40	.18
UNLISTED STARS	.75	.35
COMMON ROOKIE	1.50	.70
ROOKIE SEMISTARS	2.50	1.10

❑ 1 Rob Moore	.40	.18
❑ 2 Jake Plummer	2.50	1.10
❑ 3 Frank Sanders	.40	.18
❑ 4 Eric Swann	.20	.09
❑ 5 Jamal Anderson	.75	.35
❑ 6 Chris Chandler	.40	.18
❑ 7 Byron Hanspard	.40	.18
❑ 8 Terance Mathis	.40	.18
❑ 9 O.J. Santiago	.20	.09
❑ 10 Chuck Smith	.20	.09
❑ 11 Jessie Tuggle	.20	.09
❑ 12 Jay Graham	.20	.09
❑ 13 Jim Harbaugh	.40	.18
❑ 14 Michael Jackson	.20	.09
❑ 15 Pat Johnson RC	1.50	.70
❑ 16 Jermaine Lewis	.40	.18
❑ 17 Errict Rhett	.40	.18
❑ 18 Rod Woodson	.40	.18
❑ 19 Quinn Early	.20	.09
❑ 20 Andre Reed	.40	.18
❑ 21 Antowain Smith	.75	.35
❑ 22 Bruce Smith	.40	.18
❑ 23 Thurman Thomas	.75	.35
❑ 24 Ted Washington	.20	.09
❑ 25 Michael Bates	.20	.09
❑ 26 Rae Carruth	.40	.18
❑ 27 Kerry Collins	.40	.18
❑ 28 Fred Lane	.40	.18
❑ 29 Wesley Walls	.40	.18
❑ 30 Edgar Bennett	.20	.09
❑ 31 Curtis Conway	.40	.18
❑ 32 Curtis Enis RC	3.00	1.35
❑ 33 Walt Harris	.20	.09
❑ 34 Erik Kramer	.20	.09
❑ 35 Barry Minter	.20	.09
❑ 36 Jeff Blake	.40	.18
❑ 37 Corey Dillon	1.25	.55
❑ 38 Carl Pickens	.75	.35
❑ 39 Darnay Scott	.40	.18
❑ 40 Troy Aikman	2.00	.90
❑ 41 Michael Irvin	.75	.35
❑ 42 Deion Sanders	.75	.35
❑ 43 Emmitt Smith	3.00	1.35
❑ 44 Chris Warren	.40	.18
❑ 45 Terrell Davis	3.00	1.35
❑ 46 John Elway	4.00	1.80
❑ 47 Brian Griese RC	5.00	2.20
❑ 48 Ed McCaffrey	.40	.18
❑ 49 John Mobley	.20	.09
❑ 50 Shannon Sharpe	.40	.18
❑ 51 Neil Smith	.40	.18
❑ 52 Rod Smith WR	.40	.18
❑ 53 Stephen Boyd	.20	.09
❑ 54 Scott Mitchell	.40	.18
❑ 55 Herman Moore	.75	.35
❑ 56 Johnnie Morton	.40	.18
❑ 57 Robert Porcher	.20	.09
❑ 58 Barry Sanders	4.00	1.80
❑ 59 Robert Brooks	.40	.18
❑ 60 Mark Chmura	.40	.18
❑ 61 Brett Favre	4.00	1.80
❑ 62 Antonio Freeman	.75	.35
❑ 63 Vonnie Holliday RC	2.50	1.10
❑ 64 Dorsey Levens	.75	.35
❑ 65 Ross Verba	.20	.09
❑ 66 Reggie White	.75	.35
❑ 67 Elijah Alexander	.20	.09
❑ 68 Ken Dilger	.20	.09
❑ 69 Marshall Faulk	.75	.35
❑ 70 Marvin Harrison	.40	.18
❑ 71 Peyton Manning RC	15.00	6.75
❑ 72 Bryan Barker	.20	.09
❑ 73 Mark Brunell	1.50	.70
❑ 74 Keenan McCardell	.40	.18
❑ 75 Jimmy Smith	.40	.18
❑ 76 James Stewart	.40	.18
❑ 77 Derrick Alexander WR	.40	.18
❑ 78 Kimble Anders	.40	.18
❑ 79 Donnell Bennett	.20	.09
❑ 80 Elvis Grbac	.40	.18
❑ 81 Andre Rison	.40	.18
❑ 82 Rashaan Shehee RC	2.50	1.10
❑ 83 Derrick Thomas	.40	.18
❑ 84 Karim Abdul-Jabbar	.75	.35
❑ 85 Trace Armstrong	.20	.09
❑ 86 Charles Jordan	.20	.09
❑ 87 Dan Marino	4.00	1.80
❑ 88 O.J. McDuffie	.40	.18
❑ 89 Zach Thomas	.20	.09
❑ 90 Cris Carter	.75	.35
❑ 91 Charles Evans	.20	.09
❑ 92 Andrew Glover	.20	.09
❑ 93 Brad Johnson	.75	.35
❑ 94 Randy Moss RC	15.00	6.75
❑ 95 John Randle	.40	.18
❑ 96 Jake Reed	.40	.18
❑ 97 Robert Smith	.75	.35
❑ 98 Bruce Armstrong	.20	.09
❑ 99 Drew Bledsoe	1.50	.70
❑ 100 Ben Coates	.40	.18
❑ 101 Robert Edwards RC	2.50	1.10
❑ 102 Terry Glenn	.75	.35
❑ 103 Willie McGinest	.20	.09
❑ 104 Sedrick Shaw	.20	.09
❑ 105 Tony Simmons RC	2.50	1.10
❑ 106 Chris Slade	.20	.09
❑ 107 Billy Joe Hobert	.20	.09
❑ 108 Qadry Ismail	.20	.09
❑ 109 Heath Shuler	.20	.09
❑ 110 Lamar Smith	.20	.09
❑ 111 Ray Zellars	.20	.09
❑ 112 Tiki Barber	.40	.18
❑ 113 Chris Calloway	.20	.09
❑ 114 Ike Hilliard	.40	.18
❑ 115 Joe Jurevicius RC	2.50	1.10
❑ 116 Danny Kanell	.40	.18
❑ 117 Amani Toomer	.40	.18
❑ 118 Charles Way	.20	.09
❑ 119 Tyrone Wheatley	.40	.18
❑ 120 Wayne Chrebet	.75	.35
❑ 121 John Elliott	.20	.09
❑ 122 Glenn Foley	.40	.18
❑ 123 Scott Frost	.40	.18
❑ 124 Aaron Glenn	.20	.09
❑ 125 Keyshawn Johnson	.75	.35
❑ 126 Curtis Martin	.75	.35
❑ 127 Vinny Testaverde	.40	.18
❑ 128 Tim Brown	.75	.35
❑ 129 Rickey Dudley	.20	.09
❑ 130 Jeff George	.40	.18
❑ 131 James Jett	.40	.18
❑ 132 Napoleon Kaufman	.75	.35
❑ 133 Darrell Russell	.20	.09
❑ 134 Charles Woodson RC	3.00	1.35
❑ 135 James Darling RC	.20	.09
❑ 136 Koy Detmer	.75	.35
❑ 137 Irving Fryar	.40	.18
❑ 138 Charlie Garner	.20	.09
❑ 139 Bobby Hoying	.40	.18
❑ 140 Chad Lewis	.20	.09
❑ 141 Duce Staley	1.25	.55
❑ 142 Kevin Turner	.20	.09
❑ 143 Jerome Bettis	.75	.35
❑ 144 Will Blackwell	.20	.09
❑ 145 Mark Bruener	.20	.09
❑ 146 Dermontti Dawson	.20	.09
❑ 147 Charles Johnson	.20	.09
❑ 148 Levon Kirkland	.20	.09
❑ 149 Tim Lester	.20	.09
❑ 150 Kordell Stewart	.75	.35
❑ 151 Tony Banks	.40	.18
❑ 152 Isaac Bruce	.75	.35
❑ 153 Robert Holcombe RC	1.50	.70
❑ 154 Eddie Kennison	.40	.18
❑ 155 Amp Lee	.20	.09
❑ 156 Jerald Moore	.20	.09
❑ 157 Charlie Jones	.20	.09
❑ 158 Freddie Jones	.20	.09
❑ 159 Ryan Leaf RC	2.50	1.10
❑ 160 Natrone Means	.75	.35
❑ 161 Junior Seau	.40	.18
❑ 162 Bryan Still	.20	.09
❑ 163 Marc Edwards	.20	.09
❑ 164 Merton Hanks	.20	.09
❑ 165 Garrison Hearst	.75	.35
❑ 166 Terrell Owens	.75	.35
❑ 167 Jerry Rice	2.00	.90
❑ 168 J.J. Stokes	.40	.18
❑ 169 Bryant Young	.20	.09
❑ 170 Steve Young	1.25	.55
❑ 171 Chad Brown	.20	.09
❑ 172 Joey Galloway	.75	.35
❑ 173 Walter Jones	.20	.09
❑ 174 Cortez Kennedy	.20	.09
❑ 175 Jon Kitna	2.00	.90
❑ 176 James McKnight	.20	.09
❑ 177 Warren Moon	.75	.35
❑ 178 Michael Sinclair	.20	.09
❑ 179 Mike Alstott	.75	.35
❑ 180 Reidel Anthony	.40	.18
❑ 181 Derrick Brooks	.20	.09
❑ 182 Trent Dilfer	.75	.35
❑ 183 Warrick Dunn	1.25	.55
❑ 184 Hardy Nickerson	.20	.09
❑ 185 Warren Sapp	.40	.18
❑ 186 Willie Davis	.20	.09
❑ 187 Eddie George	1.50	.70
❑ 188 Steve McNair	.75	.35
❑ 189 Jon Runyan	.20	.09
❑ 190 Chris Sanders	.20	.09
❑ 191 Frank Wycheck	.20	.09
❑ 192 Stephen Alexander RC	2.50	1.10
❑ 193 Terry Allen	.75	.35
❑ 194 Stephen Davis	.20	.09
❑ 195 Cris Dishman	.20	.09
❑ 196 Gus Frerotte	.20	.09
❑ 197 Darrell Green	.40	.18
❑ 198 Skip Hicks RC	2.50	1.10
❑ 199 Dana Stubblefield	.20	.09
❑ 200 Michael Westbrook	.40	.18
❑ S1 Warrick Dunn Sample	2.00	.90

1998 Aurora Championship Fever

	MINT	NRMT
COMP.GOLD SET (50)	50.00	22.00
COMMON CARD (1-50)	.50	.23
SEMISTARS	.75	.35

OVERALL ODDS ONE PER PACK
*COPPER CARDS: 30X TO 80X HI COL.
COPPER PRINT RUN 20 SERIAL #'d SETS

COPPERS RANDOM INSERTS IN HOBBY PACKS
*PLATINUM BLUES: 8X TO 20X HI COL.
PLAT.BLUE PRINT RUN 100 SERIAL #'d SETS
PLAT.BLUES RANDOM INSERTS IN HOB/RET
*REDS: 1.25X TO 3X HI COL. ......
RED STATED ODDS 4:25 SPECIAL RETAIL
*SILVER CARDS: 5X TO 10X HI COL.
SILVER PRINT RUN 250 SERIAL #'d SETS
SILVERS RANDOM INSERTS IN RETAIL PACKS

❑ 1 Jake Plummer	2.50	1.10
❑ 2 Antowain Smith	1.00	.45
❑ 3 Bruce Smith	.75	.35
❑ 4 Kerry Collins	.75	.35
❑ 5 Kevin Greene	.75	.35
❑ 6 Jeff Blake	.75	.35
❑ 7 Corey Dillon	1.25	.55
❑ 8 Carl Pickens	1.00	.45
❑ 9 Troy Aikman	2.50	1.10
❑ 10 Michael Irvin	1.00	.45
❑ 11 Deion Sanders	1.00	.45
❑ 12 Emmitt Smith	4.00	1.80
❑ 13 Terrell Davis	4.00	1.80
❑ 14 John Elway	5.00	2.20
❑ 15 Shannon Sharpe	.75	.35
❑ 16 Herman Moore	1.00	.45
❑ 17 Barry Sanders	5.00	2.20
❑ 18 Brett Favre	5.00	2.20
❑ 19 Antonio Freeman	1.00	.45
❑ 20 Dorsey Levens	1.00	.45
❑ 21 Marshall Faulk	1.00	.45
❑ 22 Peyton Manning	6.00	2.70
❑ 23 Mark Brunell	2.00	.90
❑ 24 Elvis Grbac	.75	.35
❑ 25 Andre Rison	.75	.35
❑ 26 Rashaan Shehee	.75	.35
❑ 27 Derrick Thomas	.75	.35
❑ 28 Dan Marino	5.00	2.20
❑ 29 Cris Carter	1.00	.45
❑ 30 Robert Smith	1.00	.45
❑ 31 Drew Bledsoe	2.00	.90
❑ 32 Robert Edwards	.75	.35
❑ 33 Terry Glenn	1.00	.45
❑ 34 Danny Kanell	.75	.35
❑ 35 Keyshawn Johnson	1.00	.45
❑ 36 Tim Brown	1.00	.45
❑ 37 Napoleon Kaufman	1.00	.45
❑ 38 Bobby Hoying	.75	.35
❑ 39 Jerome Bettis	1.00	.45
❑ 40 Kordell Stewart	.75	.35
❑ 41 Ryan Leaf	.75	.35
❑ 42 Jerry Rice	2.50	1.10
❑ 43 Steve Young	1.50	.70
❑ 44 Joey Galloway	1.00	.45
❑ 45 Mike Alstott	1.00	.45
❑ 46 Trent Dilfer	1.00	.45
❑ 47 Warrick Dunn	1.25	.55
❑ 47AU Warrick Dunn AUTO	60.00	27.00
❑ 48 Eddie George	2.00	.90
❑ 49 Steve McNair	1.00	.45
❑ 50 Gus Frerotte	.50	.23

1998 Aurora Cubes

	MINT	NRMT
COMPLETE SET (20)	150.00	70.00
COMMON CARD (1-20)	4.00	1.80
ONE PER HOBBY BOX		
❑ 1 Corey Dillon	5.00	2.20
❑ 2 Troy Aikman	10.00	4.50
❑ 3 Emmitt Smith	15.00	6.75
❑ 4 Terrell Davis	15.00	6.75
❑ 5 John Elway	20.00	9.00
❑ 6 Barry Sanders	20.00	9.00
❑ 7 Brett Favre	20.00	9.00
❑ 8 Dorsey Levens	4.00	1.80
❑ 9 Peyton Manning	25.00	11.00
❑ 10 Mark Brunell	8.00	3.60
❑ 11 Dan Marino	20.00	9.00
❑ 12 Drew Bledsoe	8.00	3.60
❑ 13 Napoleon Kaufman	4.00	1.80
❑ 14 Jerome Bettis	4.00	1.80
❑ 15 Kordell Stewart	4.00	1.80
❑ 16 Ryan Leaf	4.00	1.80
❑ 17 Jerry Rice	10.00	4.50
❑ 18 Steve Young	6.00	2.70
❑ 19 Warrick Dunn	5.00	2.20
❑ 20 Eddie George	8.00	3.60

1998 Aurora Face Mask Cel Fusions

	MINT	NRMT
COMPLETE SET (20)	250.00	110.00
COMMON CARD (1-20)	8.00	3.60
STATED ODDS 1:73		
❑ 1 Corey Dillon	10.00	4.50
❑ 2 Troy Aikman	15.00	6.75
❑ 3 Emmitt Smith	25.00	11.00
❑ 4 Terrell Davis	25.00	11.00
❑ 5 John Elway	30.00	13.50
❑ 6 Barry Sanders	30.00	13.50
❑ 7 Brett Favre	30.00	13.50
❑ 8 Antonio Freeman	10.00	4.50
❑ 9 Peyton Manning	30.00	13.50
❑ 10 Mark Brunell	12.00	5.50
❑ 11 Dan Marino	30.00	13.50
❑ 12 Drew Bledsoe	12.00	5.50
❑ 13 Napoleon Kaufman	10.00	4.50
❑ 14 Jerome Bettis	10.00	4.50
❑ 15 Kordell Stewart	8.00	3.60
❑ 16 Ryan Leaf	8.00	3.60
❑ 17 Jerry Rice	15.00	6.75
❑ 18 Steve Young	12.00	5.50
❑ 19 Warrick Dunn	12.00	5.50
❑ 20 Eddie George	12.00	5.50

1998 Aurora Gridiron Laser Cuts

	MINT	NRMT
COMPLETE SET (20)	120.00	55.00
COMMON CARD (1-20)	3.00	1.35
STATED ODDS 4:37 HOBBY		
❑ 1 Jake Plummer	8.00	3.60
❑ 2 Corey Dillon	4.00	1.80
❑ 3 Troy Aikman	8.00	3.60
❑ 4 Emmitt Smith	12.00	5.50
❑ 5 Terrell Davis	12.00	5.50
❑ 6 John Elway	15.00	6.75
❑ 7 Barry Sanders	15.00	6.75
❑ 8 Brett Favre	15.00	6.75
❑ 9 Peyton Manning	20.00	9.00
❑ 10 Mark Brunell	6.00	2.70

❑ 11 Dan Marino	15.00	6.75
❑ 12 Drew Bledsoe	6.00	2.70
❑ 13 Jerome Bettis	3.00	1.35
❑ 14 Kordell Stewart	3.00	1.35
❑ 15 Ryan Leaf	3.00	1.35
❑ 16 Jerry Rice	8.00	3.60
❑ 17 Steve Young	5.00	2.20
❑ 18 Warrick Dunn	4.00	1.80
❑ 19 Eddie George	6.00	2.70
❑ 20 Steve McNair	3.00	1.35

1998 Aurora NFL Command

	MINT	NRMT
COMPLETE SET (10)	600.00	275.00
COMMON CARD (1-10)	30.00	13.50
STATED ODDS 1:361		
❑ 1 Terrell Davis	80.00	36.00
❑ 2 John Elway	100.00	45.00
❑ 3 Barry Sanders	100.00	45.00
❑ 4 Brett Favre	100.00	45.00

❑ 5 Peyton Manning	80.00	36.00
❑ 6 Mark Brunell	40.00	18.00
❑ 7 Dan Marino	100.00	45.00
❑ 8 Drew Bledsoe	40.00	18.00
❑ 9 Ryan Leaf	30.00	13.50
❑ 10 Warrick Dunn	30.00	13.50

1999 Aurora

	MINT	NRMT
COMPLETE SET (150)	50.00	22.00
COMMON CARD (1-150)	.15	.07
SEMISTARS	.25	.11
UNLISTED STARS	.50	.23
COMMON ROOKIE	1.50	.70
COMP.PINSTRIPE SET (50)	40.00	18.00

*PINSTRIPES: SAME PRICE AS BASE

Card	MINT	NRMT
❑ 1 David Boston RC	2.50	1.10
❑ 2 Larry Centers	.15	.07
❑ 3 Rob Moore	.25	.11
❑ 4 Adrian Murrell	.25	.11
❑ 5 Jake Plummer	1.00	.45
❑ 6 Jamal Anderson	.50	.23
❑ 7 Chris Chandler	.25	.11
❑ 8 Tim Dwight	.50	.23
❑ 9 Terance Mathis	.25	.11
❑ 10 O.J. Santiago	.15	.07
❑ 11 Priest Holmes	.50	.23
❑ 12 Michael Jackson	.15	.07
❑ 13 Jermaine Lewis	.25	.11
❑ 14 Ray Lewis	.15	.07
❑ 15 Michael McCrary	.15	.07
❑ 16 Doug Flutie	.60	.25
❑ 17 Eric Moulds	.50	.23
❑ 18 Peerless Price RC	2.50	1.10
❑ 19 Antowain Smith	.50	.23
❑ 20 Bruce Smith	.25	.11
❑ 21 Steve Beuerlein	.15	.07
❑ 22 Tim Biakabutuka	.25	.11
❑ 23 Kevin Greene	.15	.07
❑ 24 Muhsin Muhammad	.25	.11
❑ 25 Wesley Walls	.25	.11
❑ 26 Curtis Conway	.25	.11
❑ 27 Bobby Engram	.25	.11
❑ 28 Curtis Enis	.50	.23
❑ 29 Erik Kramer	.15	.07
❑ 30 Cade McNown RC	5.00	2.20
❑ 31 Jeff Blake	.25	.11
❑ 32 Corey Dillon	.50	.23
❑ 33 Carl Pickens	.25	.11
❑ 34 Darnay Scott	.15	.07
❑ 35 Akili Smith RC	3.00	1.35
❑ 36 Tim Couch RC	8.00	3.60
❑ 37 Ty Detmer	.25	.11
❑ 38 Kevin Johnson RC	4.00	1.80
❑ 39 Terry Kirby	.15	.07
❑ 40 Troy Aikman	1.25	.55
❑ 41 Michael Irvin	.25	.11
❑ 42 Rocket Ismail	.25	.11
❑ 43 Deion Sanders	.50	.23
❑ 44 Emmitt Smith	1.25	.55
❑ 45 Bubby Brister	.15	.07
❑ 46 Terrell Davis	1.25	.55
❑ 47 Brian Griese	1.00	.45
❑ 48 Ed McCaffrey	.25	.11
❑ 49 Shannon Sharpe	.25	.11
❑ 50 Rod Smith	.25	.11
❑ 51 Charlie Batch	1.00	.45
❑ 52 Sedrick Irvin RC	.50	.23
❑ 53 Herman Moore	.50	.23
❑ 54 Johnnie Morton	.25	.11
❑ 55 Barry Sanders	2.00	.90
❑ 56 Robert Brooks	.25	.11
❑ 57 Brett Favre	2.00	.90
❑ 58 Antonio Freeman	.50	.23
❑ 59 Dorsey Levens	.50	.23
❑ 60 Derrick Mayes	.15	.07
❑ 61 Marvin Harrison	.50	.23
❑ 62 Edgerrin James RC	12.00	5.50
❑ 63 Peyton Manning	2.00	.90
❑ 64 Jerome Pathon	.15	.07
❑ 65 Tavian Banks	.15	.07
❑ 66 Mark Brunell	.75	.35
❑ 67 Keenan McCardell	.25	.11
❑ 68 Jimmy Smith	.25	.11
❑ 69 Fred Taylor	1.25	.55
❑ 70 Derrick Alexander	.25	.11
❑ 71 Kimble Anders	.25	.11
❑ 72 Mike Cloud RC	1.50	.70
❑ 73 Elvis Grbac	.25	.11
❑ 74 Andre Rison	.25	.11
❑ 75 Karim Abdul-Jabbar	.25	.11
❑ 76 James Johnson RC	2.00	.90
❑ 77 Dan Marino	2.00	.90
❑ 78 O.J. McDuffie	.25	.11
❑ 79 Lamar Thomas	.15	.07
❑ 80 Cris Carter	.50	.23
❑ 81 Daunte Culpepper RC	5.00	2.20
❑ 82 Randall Cunningham	.50	.23
❑ 83 Randy Moss	2.00	.90
❑ 84 John Randle	.25	.11
❑ 85 Robert Smith	.50	.23
❑ 86 Drew Bledsoe	.75	.35
❑ 87 Ben Coates	.25	.11
❑ 88 Kevin Faulk RC	2.00	.90
❑ 89 Terry Glenn	.50	.23
❑ 90 Ty Law	.15	.07
❑ 91 Cam Cleeland	.15	.07
❑ 92 Andre Hastings	.15	.07
❑ 93 Billy Joe Hobert	.15	.07
❑ 94 Ricky Williams RC	8.00	3.60
❑ 95 Tiki Barber	.15	.07
❑ 96 Kent Graham	.15	.07
❑ 97 Ike Hilliard	.15	.07
❑ 98 Charles Way	.15	.07
❑ 99 Wayne Chrebet	.25	.11
❑ 100 Keyshawn Johnson	.50	.23
❑ 101 Curtis Martin	.50	.23
❑ 102 Vinny Testaverde	.25	.11
❑ 103 Dedric Ward	.15	.07
❑ 104 Tim Brown	.50	.23
❑ 105 Rickey Dudley	.15	.07
❑ 106 James Jett	.25	.11
❑ 107 Napoleon Kaufman	.50	.23
❑ 108 Charles Woodson	.50	.23
❑ 109 Jeff Graham	.15	.07
❑ 110 Charles Johnson	.15	.07
❑ 111 Donovan McNabb RC	5.00	2.20
❑ 112 Duce Staley	.50	.23
❑ 113 Jerome Bettis	.50	.23
❑ 114 Troy Edwards RC	2.50	1.10
❑ 115 Courtney Hawkins	.15	.07
❑ 116 Kordell Stewart	.50	.23
❑ 117 Amos Zereoue RC		
❑ 118 Isaac Bruce	.50	.23
❑ 119 Marshall Faulk	.50	.23
❑ 120 Joe Germaine RC		
❑ 121 Torry Holt RC	4.00	1.80
❑ 122 Amp Lee	.15	.07
❑ 123 Charlie Jones	.15	.07
❑ 124 Ryan Leaf	.50	.23
❑ 125 Natrone Means	.25	.11
❑ 126 Junior Seau	.25	.11
❑ 127 Garrison Hearst	.25	.11
❑ 128 Terrell Owens	.50	.23
❑ 129 Jerry Rice	1.25	.55
❑ 130 J.J. Stokes	.25	.11
❑ 131 Steve Young	.75	.35
❑ 132 Chad Brown	.15	.07
❑ 133 Joey Galloway	.50	.23
❑ 134 Brock Huard RC	2.00	.90
❑ 135 Jon Kitna	.60	.25
❑ 136 Ricky Watters	.25	.11
❑ 137 Mike Alstott	.50	.23
❑ 138 Reidel Anthony	.25	.11
❑ 139 Trent Dilfer	.25	.11
❑ 140 Warrick Dunn	.50	.23
❑ 141 Jacquez Green	.25	.11
❑ 142 Shaun King RC	5.00	2.20
❑ 143 Eddie George	.60	.25
❑ 144 Steve McNair	.50	.23
❑ 145 Yancey Thigpen	.15	.07
❑ 146 Frank Wycheck	.15	.07
❑ 147 Champ Bailey RC	2.00	.90
❑ 148 Skip Hicks	.50	.23
❑ 149 Brad Johnson	.50	.23
❑ 150 Michael Westbrook	.25	.11
❑ AU1 Terrell Owens AUTO/197	50.00	22.00

1999 Aurora Premiere Date

	MINT	NRMT
COMMON CARD (1-150)	6.00	2.70

*PREM.DATE STARS: 15X TO 40X HI COL.
*PREM.DATE YOUNG STARS: 12X TO 30X
*PREMIERE DATE RCs: 4X TO 10X
*PINSTRIPE PD STARS: 15X TO 40X BASE CARD HI
*PINSTRIPE PD YOUNG STARS: 12X TO 30X BASE CARD HI
*PINSTRIPE PD RC'S: 4X TO 10X BASE CARD HI
PREMIERE DATE STATED ODDS 1:25 HOB
PREMIERE DATE PRINT RUN 77 SER.#'d SETS

1999 Aurora Canvas Creations

	MINT	NRMT
COMPLETE SET (10)	250.00	110.00
COMMON CARD (1-10)	15.00	6.75

STATED ODDS 1:193

Card	MINT	NRMT
❑ 1 Troy Aikman	30.00	13.50
❑ 2 Terrell Davis	30.00	13.50
❑ 3 Barry Sanders	50.00	22.00
❑ 4 Brett Favre	50.00	22.00
❑ 5 Peyton Manning	40.00	18.00
❑ 6 Dan Marino	50.00	22.00
❑ 7 Randy Moss	40.00	18.00
❑ 8 Drew Bledsoe	20.00	9.00
❑ 9 Steve Young	20.00	9.00
❑ 10 Jon Kitna	15.00	6.75

1999 Aurora Championship Fever

	MINT	NRMT
COMPLETE SET (20)	40.00	18.00
COMMON CARD (1-20)	1.00	.45

STATED ODDS 4:25
*COPPERS: 20X TO 50X HI COL.
COPPERS PRINT RUN 20 SER.#'d SETS
COPPERS INSERTED IN HOBBY PACKS
*PLATINUM BLUES: 6X TO 15X HI COL.
PLAT.BLUES PRINT RUN 100 SER.#'d SETS
PLAT.BLUES INSERTED IN HOB.AND RET.PACKS
*SILVERS: 3X TO 8X HI COL.
SILVERS PRINT RUN 250 SER.#'d SETS
SILVERS INSERTED IN RETAIL PACKS

Card	MINT	NRMT
❑ 1 Jake Plummer	2.00	.90
❑ 2 Jamal Anderson	1.00	.45
❑ 3 Tim Couch	3.00	1.35
❑ 4 Troy Aikman	2.50	1.10
❑ 5 Emmitt Smith	2.50	1.10
❑ 6 Terrell Davis	2.50	1.10
❑ 7 Barry Sanders	4.00	1.80
❑ 8 Brett Favre	4.00	1.80
❑ 9 Peyton Manning	3.00	1.35
❑ 10 Fred Taylor	2.00	.90
❑ 11 Dan Marino	4.00	1.80
❑ 12 Randy Moss	3.00	1.35
❑ 13 Drew Bledsoe	1.50	.70
❑ 14 Ricky Williams	3.00	1.35
❑ 15 Keyshawn Johnson	1.00	.45
❑ 16 Terrell Owens	1.00	.45
❑ 17 Jerry Rice	2.50	1.10
❑ 18 Steve Young	1.50	.70
❑ 19 Jon Kitna	1.25	.55
❑ 20 Eddie George	1.25	.55

1999 Aurora Complete Players

	MINT	NRMT
COMPLETE SET (10)	120.00	55.00
COMMON CARD (1-10)	10.00	4.50

STATED PRINT RUN 299 SERIAL #'d SETS
10-CARDS EACH IN HOBBY AND RETAIL PACKS
*HOLOGOLDS: 4X TO 10X HI COL.
HOLOGOLDS PRINT RUN 25 SER.#'d SETS
HOLOGOLDS INSERTED IN HOB/RET PACKS

	MINT	NRMT
❑ 1 Troy Aikman	15.00	6.75
❑ 2 Terrell Davis	15.00	6.75
❑ 3 Barry Sanders	25.00	11.00
❑ 4 Brett Favre	25.00	11.00
❑ 5 Peyton Manning	20.00	9.00
❑ 6 Dan Marino	25.00	11.00
❑ 7 Randy Moss	20.00	9.00
❑ 8 Drew Bledsoe	10.00	4.50
❑ 9 Jerry Rice	15.00	6.75
❑ 10 Steve Young	10.00	4.50

1999 Aurora Leather Bound

	MINT	NRMT
COMPLETE SET (20)	100.00	45.00
COMMON CARD (1-20)	2.50	1.10

STATED ODDS 2:25 HOBBY

	MINT	NRMT
❑ 1 Jake Plummer	5.00	2.20
❑ 2 Jamal Anderson	2.50	1.10
❑ 3 Tim Couch	10.00	4.50
❑ 4 Troy Aikman	6.00	2.70
❑ 5 Emmitt Smith	6.00	2.70
❑ 6 Terrell Davis	6.00	2.70
❑ 7 Barry Sanders	10.00	4.50
❑ 8 Brett Favre	10.00	4.50
❑ 9 Peyton Manning	8.00	3.60
❑ 10 Fred Taylor	5.00	2.20
❑ 11 Dan Marino	10.00	4.50
❑ 12 Randy Moss	8.00	3.60
❑ 13 Drew Bledsoe	4.00	1.80
❑ 14 Ricky Williams	10.00	4.50
❑ 15 Curtis Martin	2.50	1.10
❑ 16 Jerome Bettis	2.50	1.10
❑ 17 Jerry Rice	6.00	2.70
❑ 18 Steve Young	4.00	1.80
❑ 19 Jon Kitna	3.00	1.35
❑ 20 Eddie George	3.00	1.35

1999 Aurora Styrotechs

	MINT	NRMT
COMPLETE SET (20)	120.00	55.00
COMMON CARD (1-20)	3.00	1.35

STATED ODDS 1:25

	MINT	NRMT
❑ 1 Jake Plummer	6.00	2.70
❑ 2 Jamal Anderson	3.00	1.35
❑ 3 Tim Couch	12.00	5.50
❑ 4 Troy Aikman	8.00	3.60
❑ 5 Emmitt Smith	8.00	3.60
❑ 6 Terrell Davis	8.00	3.60
❑ 7 Barry Sanders	12.00	5.50
❑ 8 Brett Favre	12.00	5.50
❑ 9 Peyton Manning	10.00	4.50
❑ 10 Fred Taylor	6.00	2.70
❑ 11 Dan Marino	12.00	5.50
❑ 12 Randy Moss	10.00	4.50
❑ 13 Drew Bledsoe	5.00	2.20
❑ 14 Ricky Williams	12.00	5.50
❑ 15 Curtis Martin	3.00	1.35
❑ 16 Jerry Rice	8.00	3.60
❑ 17 Steve Young	5.00	2.20
❑ 18 Joey Galloway	3.00	1.35
❑ 19 Jon Kitna	4.00	1.80
❑ 20 Eddie George	4.00	1.80

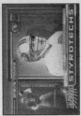

1997 Black Diamond

	MINT	NRMT
COMPLETE SET (180)	300.00	135.00
COMP.SERIES 1 (90)	25.00	11.00
COMMON CARD (1-90)	.20	.09
SEMISTARS SINGLE	.40	.18
UNLISTED STARS SINGLE	.75	.35
COMMON DOUBLE (91-150)	1.25	.55
SEMISTARS DOUBLE	2.00	.90
UNLISTED STARS DOUBLE	3.00	1.35
DOUBLE STATED ODDS 1:4		
COMMON TRIPLE (151-180)	5.00	2.20
SEMISTARS TRIPLE	8.00	3.60
TRIPLE STATED ODDS 1:30		

	MINT	NRMT
❑ 1 Alfred Williams	.20	.09
❑ 2 Alvin Harper	.20	.09
❑ 3 Andre Hastings	.20	.09
❑ 4 Andre Reed	.40	.18
❑ 5 Anthony Johnson	.20	.09
❑ 6 Anthony Miller	.20	.09
❑ 7 Byron Bam Morris	.20	.09
❑ 8 Bobby Hebert	.20	.09
❑ 9 Bobby Taylor	.20	.09
❑ 10 Boomer Esiason	.40	.18
❑ 11 Brett Perriman	.20	.09
❑ 12 Brian Blades	.20	.09
❑ 13 Bryan Cox	.20	.09
❑ 14 Bryant Young	.20	.09
❑ 15 Bryce Paup	.20	.09
❑ 16 Carnell Lake	.20	.09
❑ 17 Cedric Jones	.20	.09
❑ 18 Chad Brown	.20	.09
❑ 19 Charlie Garner	.20	.09
❑ 20 Chris Chandler	.40	.18
❑ 21 Cornelius Bennett	.20	.09
❑ 22 Cortez Kennedy	.20	.09
❑ 23 Cris Carter	.75	.35
❑ 24 Dale Carter	.20	.09
❑ 25 Daryl Gardener	.20	.09
❑ 26 Derrick Alexander WR	.40	.18
❑ 27 Derrick Mayes	.40	.18
❑ 28 Don Beebe	.20	.09
❑ 29 Eric Allen	.20	.09
❑ 30 Eric Moulds	.75	.35
❑ 31 Errict Rhett	.20	.09
❑ 32 Frank Sanders	.40	.18
❑ 33 Glyn Milburn	.20	.09
❑ 34 Henry Ellard	.20	.09
❑ 35 Jamal Anderson	1.25	.55
❑ 36 James O. Stewart	.40	.18
❑ 37 Jason Dunn	.20	.09
❑ 38 Jerry Rice	3.00	1.35
❑ 39 Jim Everett	.20	.09
❑ 40 Jim Kelly	.75	.35
❑ 41 Joey Galloway	1.25	.55
❑ 42 John Carney	.20	.09
❑ 43 John Elway	5.00	2.20
❑ 44 John Randle	.20	.09
❑ 45 Karim Abdul-Jabbar	.75	.35
❑ 46 Keenan McCardell	.40	.18
❑ 47 Ken Dilger	.20	.09
❑ 48 Ken Norton	.20	.09
❑ 49 Ki-Jana Carter	.20	.09
❑ 50 Kordell Stewart	1.25	.55
❑ 51 Lawrence Phillips	.20	.09
❑ 52 Leslie O'Neal	.20	.09
❑ 53 Mark Chmura	.40	.18
❑ 54 Marshall Faulk	.75	.35
❑ 55 Michael Haynes	.20	.09
❑ 56 Michael Irvin	.75	.35
❑ 57 Michael Jackson	.40	.18
❑ 58 Michael Westbrook	.40	.18
❑ 59 Mike Tomczak	.20	.09
❑ 60 Napoleon Kaufman	.75	.35
❑ 61 Neil O'Donnell	.40	.18
❑ 62 Neil Smith	.40	.18
❑ 63 O.J. McDuffie	.40	.18
❑ 64 Orlando Thomas	.20	.09
❑ 65 Rashaan Salaam	.20	.09
❑ 66 Regan Upshaw	.20	.09
❑ 67 Rick Mirer	.20	.09
❑ 68 Rob Moore	.40	.18
❑ 69 Ronnie Harmon	.20	.09
❑ 70 Sam Mills	.20	.09
❑ 71 Sean Dawkins	.20	.09
❑ 72 Shawn Jefferson	.20	.09
❑ 73 Stan Humphries	.40	.18
❑ 74 Stepfret Williams	.20	.09
❑ 75 Stephen Davis	2.00	.90
❑ 76 Steve Atwater	.20	.09
❑ 77 Terance Mathis	.40	.18
❑ 78 Terrell Fletcher	.20	.09
❑ 79 Terry Glenn	.75	.35
❑ 80 Terry McDaniel	.20	.09
❑ 81 Tony McGee	.20	.09
❑ 82 Trent Dilfer	.75	.35
❑ 83 Troy Drayton	.20	.09
❑ 84 Ty Detmer	.40	.18
❑ 85 Tyrone Hughes	.20	.09
❑ 86 Walt Harris	.20	.09
❑ 87 Wayne Chrebet	.75	.35
❑ 88 Wesley Walls	.40	.18
❑ 89 Willie Davis	.20	.09
❑ 90 Willie McGinest	.20	.09
❑ 91 Adrian Murrell	3.00	1.35
❑ 92 Alex Molden	1.25	.55
❑ 93 Alex Van Dyke	2.00	.90
❑ 94 Andre Coleman	1.25	.55
❑ 95 Ben Coates	3.00	1.35
❑ 96 Bobby Engram	2.00	.90
❑ 97 Bruce Smith	3.00	1.35
❑ 98 Charles Johnson	3.00	1.35
❑ 99 Chris Sanders	3.00	1.35
❑ 100 Chris T. Jones	3.00	1.35
❑ 101 Chris Warren	2.00	.90
❑ 102 Darnay Scott	3.00	1.35
❑ 103 Dave Brown	2.00	.90
❑ 104 Derrick Thomas	3.00	1.35
❑ 105 Drew Bledsoe	10.00	4.50
❑ 106 Edgar Bennett	3.00	1.35
❑ 107 Emmitt Smith	15.00	6.75

		MINT	NRMT
❑ 108	Eric Bjornson	1.25	.55
❑ 109	Eric Metcalf	3.00	1.35
❑ 110	Garrison Hearst	2.00	.90
❑ 111	Gus Frerotte	2.00	.90
❑ 112	Hardy Nickerson	1.25	.55
❑ 113	Herman Moore	3.00	1.35
❑ 114	Hugh Douglas	1.25	.55
❑ 115	Irving Fryar	2.00	.90
❑ 116	J.J. Stokes	2.00	.90
❑ 117	Jake Reed	2.00	.90
❑ 118	Jeff Hostetler	2.00	.90
❑ 119	Jeff Lewis	2.00	.90
❑ 120	Jim Harbaugh	2.00	.90
❑ 121	Johnnie Morton	2.00	.90
❑ 122	Jonathan Ogden	1.25	.55
❑ 123	Kevin Carter	1.25	.55
❑ 124	Kevin Greene	2.00	.90
❑ 125	Kevin Hardy	2.00	.90
❑ 126	Leeland McElroy	2.00	.90
❑ 127	Mike Alstott	3.00	1.35
❑ 128	Muhsin Muhammad	3.00	1.35
❑ 129	Natrone Means	3.00	1.35
❑ 130	Quentin Coryatt	1.25	.55
❑ 131	Ray Lewis	1.25	.55
❑ 132	Ray Zellars	1.25	.55
❑ 133	Rickey Dudley	2.00	.90
❑ 134	Ricky Watters	2.00	.90
❑ 135	Robert Smith	2.00	.90
❑ 136	Scott Mitchell	2.00	.90
❑ 137	Sean Gilbert	1.25	.55
❑ 138	Shannon Sharpe	2.00	.90
❑ 139	Simeon Rice	2.00	.90
❑ 140	Stanley Pritchett	1.25	.55
❑ 141	Steve McNair	5.00	2.20
❑ 142	Steve Young	8.00	3.60
❑ 143	Tamarick Vanover	2.00	.90
❑ 144	Terry Allen	2.00	.90
❑ 145	Thurman Thomas	3.00	1.35
❑ 146	Tony Banks	3.00	1.35
❑ 147	Tony Martin	2.00	.90
❑ 148	Tyrone Wheatley	2.00	.90
❑ 149	Vinny Testaverde	2.00	.90
❑ 150	Zach Thomas	3.00	1.35
❑ 151	Amani Toomer	8.00	3.60
❑ 152	Barry Sanders	30.00	13.50
❑ 153	Bobby Hoying	8.00	3.60
❑ 154	Brett Favre	30.00	13.50
❑ 155	Carl Pickens	8.00	3.60
❑ 156	Curtis Conway	8.00	3.60
❑ 157	Curtis Martin	12.00	5.50
❑ 158	Dan Marino	30.00	13.50
❑ 159	Deion Sanders	8.00	3.60
❑ 160	Eddie George	15.00	6.75
❑ 161	Eddie Kennison	8.00	3.60
❑ 162	Elvis Grbac	5.00	2.20
❑ 163	Isaac Bruce	8.00	3.60
❑ 164	Jeff Blake	8.00	3.60
❑ 165	Jerome Bettis	8.00	3.60
❑ 166	Junior Seau	8.00	3.60
❑ 167	Kerry Collins	5.00	2.20
❑ 168	Keyshawn Johnson	8.00	3.60
❑ 169	Larry Centers	5.00	2.20
❑ 170	Marcus Allen	8.00	3.60
❑ 171	Mark Brunell	15.00	6.75
❑ 172	Marvin Harrison	8.00	3.60
❑ 173	Reggie White	8.00	3.60
❑ 174	Rodney Hampton	5.00	2.20
❑ 175	Terrell Davis	25.00	11.00
❑ 176	Tim Brown	5.00	2.20
❑ 177	Todd Collins	5.00	2.20
❑ 178	Troy Aikman	15.00	6.75
❑ 179	Tim Biakabutuka	8.00	3.60
❑ 180	Warren Moon	5.00	2.20
❑ BD1	Troy Aikman Promo	2.00	.90

1997 Black Diamond Gold

	MINT	NRMT
COMPLETE SET (180)	2500.00	1100.00
COMP.SERIES 1 (90)	200.00	90.00

*SINGLE STARS: 3X TO 7X HI COL.
SINGLE GOLD STATED ODDS 1:15
*DOUBLE STARS: 2X TO 4X HI COL.
DOUBLE GOLD ODDS 1:46 ....

*TRIPLE STARS: 3X TO 6X HI COL.
TRIPLE GOLD STATED PRINT RUN 50 SETS

1997 Black Diamond Title Quest

	MINT	NRMT
COMPLETE SET (20)	800.00	350.00
COMMON CARD (1-20)	12.00	5.50
SEMISTARS	20.00	9.00
UNLISTED STARS	30.00	13.50

STATED PRINT RUN 100 SERIAL #'d SETS

		MINT	NRMT
❑ 1	Dan Marino	120.00	55.00
❑ 2	Jerry Rice	60.00	27.00
❑ 3	Drew Bledsoe	60.00	27.00
❑ 4	Emmitt Smith	100.00	45.00
❑ 5	Troy Aikman	60.00	27.00
❑ 6	Steve Young	50.00	22.00
❑ 7	Brett Favre	120.00	55.00
❑ 8	John Elway	120.00	55.00
❑ 9	Barry Sanders	120.00	55.00
❑ 10	Jerome Bettis	30.00	13.50
❑ 11	Deion Sanders	30.00	13.50
❑ 12	Karim Abdul-Jabbar	12.00	5.50
❑ 13	Terrell Davis	120.00	55.00
❑ 14	Marshall Faulk	30.00	13.50
❑ 15	Curtis Martin	40.00	18.00
❑ 16	Eddie George	50.00	22.00
❑ 17	Steve McNair	40.00	18.00
❑ 18	Terry Glenn	20.00	9.00
❑ 19	Joey Galloway	30.00	13.50
❑ 20	Keyshawn Johnson	30.00	13.50

1998 Black Diamond

	MINT	NRMT
COMPLETE SET (150)	40.00	18.00
COMMON CARD (1-150)	.20	.09
SEMISTARS	.40	.18
UNLISTED STARS	.75	.35
COMP.DOUBLE SET (150)	100.00	45.00

*DOUBLE STARS: 1X TO 2X HI COL.
*DOUBLE YOUNG STARS: .75X TO 1.5X
DOUBLE DIAMOND CARDS ONE PER PACK

	MINT	NRMT
COMP.TRIPLE SET (150)	300.00	135.00

*TRIPLE STARS: 2.5X TO 6X HI COL.
*TRIPLE YOUNG STARS: 2X TO 5X
TRIPLE DIAMOND STATED ODDS 1:5

	MINT	NRMT
COMMON QUADRUPLE	15.00	6.75

*QUAD STARS: 20X TO 50X HI COL.
*QUAD YOUNG STARS: 15X TO 40X
QUAD DIAMOND PRINT RUN 50 SETS

		MINT	NRMT
❑ 1	Kent Graham	.20	.09
❑ 2	Darrell Russell	.20	.09
❑ 3	Jim Harbaugh	.40	.18
❑ 4	Cornelius Bennett	.20	.09
❑ 5	Troy Vincent	.20	.09
❑ 6	Natrone Means	.75	.35
❑ 7	Michael Jackson	.20	.09
❑ 8	Will Blackwell	.20	.09
❑ 9	Greg Hill	.20	.09
❑ 10	Andre Reed	.40	.18
❑ 11	Darren Bennett	.20	.09
❑ 12	Dan Marino	4.00	1.80
❑ 13	Tim Biakabutuka	.40	.18
❑ 14	Terrell Owens	.75	.35
❑ 15	Cris Carter	.75	.35
❑ 16	Darnell Autry	.20	.09
❑ 17	Joey Galloway	.75	.35
❑ 18	Terry Glenn	.75	.35
❑ 19	Ki-Jana Carter	.20	.09
❑ 20	Isaac Bruce	.75	.35
❑ 21	Shawn Jefferson	.20	.09
❑ 22	Michael Irvin	.75	.35
❑ 23	Warren Sapp	.40	.18
❑ 24	Dave Brown	.20	.09
❑ 25	Terrell Davis	3.00	1.35
❑ 26	Frank Wycheck	.20	.09
❑ 27	Neil O'Donnell	.40	.18
❑ 28	Scott Mitchell	.40	.18
❑ 29	Michael Westbrook	.40	.18
❑ 30	Tim Brown	.75	.35
❑ 31	Antonio Freeman	.75	.35
❑ 32	Jake Plummer	2.50	1.10
❑ 33	Irving Fryar	.40	.18
❑ 34	Quentin Coryatt	.20	.09
❑ 35	Jamal Anderson	.75	.35
❑ 36	Jerome Bettis	.75	.35
❑ 37	Keenan McCardell	.40	.18
❑ 38	Derrick Alexander WR	.40	.18
❑ 39	Stan Humphries	.20	.09
❑ 40	Andre Rison	.40	.18
❑ 41	Bruce Smith	.40	.18
❑ 42	Garrison Hearst	.75	.35
❑ 43	Zach Thomas	.20	.09
❑ 44	Rae Carruth	.40	.18
❑ 45	Kevin Greene	.40	.18
❑ 46	Robert Smith	.75	.35
❑ 47	Curtis Conway	.40	.18
❑ 48	Christian Fauria	.20	.09
❑ 49	Curtis Martin	.75	.35
❑ 50	Dan Wilkinson	.20	.09
❑ 51	Eddie Kennison	.40	.18
❑ 52	Mark Fields	.20	.09
❑ 53	Anthony Miller	.20	.09
❑ 54	Mike Alstott	.75	.35
❑ 55	Tiki Barber	.40	.18
❑ 56	Neil Smith	.40	.18
❑ 57	Gus Frerotte	.20	.09
❑ 58	Adrian Murrell	.40	.18
❑ 59	Johnnie Morton	.40	.18
❑ 60	O.J. McDuffie	.40	.18
❑ 61	Napoleon Kaufman	.75	.35
❑ 62	Robert Brooks	.40	.18
❑ 63	Byron Hanspard	.40	.18
❑ 64	Ty Detmer	.40	.18

	MINT	NRMT
❑ 65 Mark Brunell	1.50	.70
❑ 66 Byron Bam Morris	.20	.09
❑ 67 Kordell Stewart	.75	.35
❑ 68 Elvis Grbac	.40	.18
❑ 69 Antowain Smith	.75	.35
❑ 70 Junior Seau	.40	.18
❑ 71 Tony Gonzalez	.20	.09
❑ 72 Anthony Johnson	.20	.09
❑ 73 Steve Young	1.25	.55
❑ 74 Brian Manning	.20	.09
❑ 75 Erik Kramer	.20	.09
❑ 76 Warren Moon	.75	.35
❑ 77 Torrian Gray	.20	.09
❑ 78 Carl Pickens	.75	.35
❑ 79 Tony Banks	.40	.18
❑ 80 Willie McGinest	.20	.09
❑ 81 Deion Sanders	.75	.35
❑ 82 Warrick Dunn	1.25	.55
❑ 83 Danny Wuerffel	.40	.18
❑ 84 Rod Smith WR	.40	.18
❑ 85 Steve McNair	.75	.35
❑ 86 Danny Kanell	.40	.18
❑ 87 Herman Moore	.75	.35
❑ 88 Brian Mitchell	.20	.09
❑ 89 James Farrior	.20	.09
❑ 90 Reggie White	.75	.35
❑ 91 Simeon Rice	.40	.18
❑ 92 James Jett	.40	.18
❑ 93 Marshall Faulk	.75	.35
❑ 94 Chris Chandler	.40	.18
❑ 95 Mike Mamula	.20	.09
❑ 96 Jimmy Smith	.40	.18
❑ 97 Jamie Sharper	.20	.09
❑ 98 Carnell Lake	.20	.09
❑ 99 Marcus Allen	.75	.35
❑ 100 Thurman Thomas	.75	.35
❑ 101 Freddie Jones	.20	.09
❑ 102 Karim Abdul-Jabbar	.75	.35
❑ 103 Kerry Collins	.40	.18
❑ 104 Jerry Rice	2.00	.90
❑ 105 Brad Johnson	.75	.35
❑ 106 Raymont Harris	.20	.09
❑ 107 Lamar Smith	.20	.09
❑ 108 Drew Bledsoe	1.50	.70
❑ 109 Corey Dillon	1.25	.55
❑ 110 Lawrence Phillips	.20	.09
❑ 111 Heath Shuler	.20	.09
❑ 112 Emmitt Smith	3.00	1.35
❑ 113 Reidel Anthony	.40	.18
❑ 114 Ike Hilliard	.40	.18
❑ 115 Shannon Sharpe	.40	.18
❑ 116 Chris Sanders	.20	.09
❑ 117 Keyshawn Johnson	.75	.35
❑ 118 Barry Sanders	4.00	1.80
❑ 119 Cris Dishman	.20	.09
❑ 120 Jeff George	.40	.18
❑ 121 Dorsey Levens	.75	.35
❑ 122 Rob Moore	.40	.18
❑ 123 Ricky Watters	.40	.18
❑ 124 Marvin Harrison	.40	.18
❑ 125 Vinny Testaverde	.40	.18
❑ 126 Charles Johnson	.20	.09
❑ 127 Renaldo Wynn	.20	.09
❑ 128 Todd Collins QB	.20	.09
❑ 129 Tony Martin	.40	.18
❑ 130 Derrick Thomas	.40	.18
❑ 131 Wesley Walls	.40	.18
❑ 132 Rod Woodson	.40	.18
❑ 133 Troy Drayton	.20	.09
❑ 134 Bryan Cox	.20	.09
❑ 135 Shawn Springs	.20	.09
❑ 136 Jake Reed	.40	.18
❑ 137 Jeff Blake	.40	.18
❑ 138 Craig Heyward	.20	.09
❑ 139 Ben Coates	.40	.18
❑ 140 Troy Aikman	2.00	.90
❑ 141 Trent Dilfer	.75	.35
❑ 142 Troy Davis	.20	.09
❑ 143 John Elway	4.00	1.80
❑ 144 Eddie George	1.50	.70
❑ 145 Rodney Hampton	.40	.18
❑ 146 Ed McCaffrey	.40	.18
❑ 147 Terry Allen	.75	.35
❑ 148 Wayne Chrebet	.75	.35
❑ 149 Brett Favre	4.00	1.80
❑ 150 Daryl Johnston	.40	.18

1998 Black Diamond Premium Cut

	MINT	NRMT
COMPLETE SET (30)	200.00	90.00
COMMON CARD (PC1-PC30)	5.00	2.20
SEMISTARS	6.00	2.70
UNLISTED STARS	8.00	3.60

SINGLE DIAMOND STATED ODDS 1:7
*DOUBLE DIAMONDS: .6X TO 1.5X HI COL.
DOUBLE DIAMOND STATED ODDS 1:15
*TRIPLE DIAMONDS: .8X TO 2X HI COL.
TRIPLE DIAMOND STATED ODDS 1:30
*QUAD VERTICALS: 2.5X TO 6X HI COL.
QUAD VERTICAL STATED ODDS 1:180

	MINT	NRMT
❑ PC1 Karim Abdul-Jabbar	8.00	3.60
❑ PC2 Troy Aikman	12.00	5.50
❑ PC3 Kerry Collins	5.00	2.20
❑ PC4 Drew Bledsoe	10.00	4.50
❑ PC5 Barry Sanders	25.00	11.00
❑ PC6 Marcus Allen	8.00	3.60
❑ PC7 John Elway	25.00	11.00
❑ PC8 Adrian Murrell	6.00	2.70
❑ PC9 Junior Seau	6.00	2.70
❑ PC10 Eddie George	10.00	4.50
❑ PC11 Antowain Smith	8.00	3.60
❑ PC12 Reggie White	8.00	3.60
❑ PC13 Dan Marino	25.00	11.00
❑ PC14 Joey Galloway	8.00	3.60
❑ PC15 Kordell Stewart	8.00	3.60
❑ PC16 Terry Allen	8.00	3.60
❑ PC17 Napoleon Kaufman	8.00	3.60
❑ PC18 Curtis Martin	8.00	3.60
❑ PC19 Steve Young	10.00	4.50
❑ PC20 Rod Smith WR	6.00	2.70
❑ PC21 Mark Brunell	10.00	4.50
❑ PC22 Emmitt Smith	20.00	9.00
❑ PC23 Rae Carruth	5.00	2.20
❑ PC24 Brett Favre	25.00	11.00
❑ PC25 Jeff George	6.00	2.70
❑ PC26 Terry Glenn	8.00	3.60
❑ PC27 Warrick Dunn	10.00	4.50
❑ PC28 Herman Moore	8.00	3.60
❑ PC29 Cris Carter	8.00	3.60
❑ PC30 Terrell Davis	20.00	9.00

1998 Black Diamond Premium Cut Quadruple Horizontal

	MINT	NRMT
COMP.SHORT SET (26)	1500.00	700.00
COMMON TIER 1 (PC1-PC30)	15.00	6.75
UNLISTED STARS TIER 1	20.00	9.00
COMMON TIER 2 (PC1-PC30)	30.00	13.50

1/3/8/9/11/12/14/20/23/25 ODDS 1:30H
6/10/16/17/18/21/26/28-30 ODDS 1:90H
4/5/15/19/22/24 ODDS 1:1500 HOBBY
7/27 STATED ODDS 1:11,250 HOBBY
2/13 STATED ODDS 1:22,500 HOBBY
TOUGHEST TWO CARDS NOT YET PRICED

	MINT	NRMT
❑ PC1 Karim Abdul-Jabbar	20.00	9.00
❑ PC2 Troy Aikman		
❑ PC3 Kerry Collins	20.00	9.00
❑ PC4 Drew Bledsoe	120.00	55.00
❑ PC5 Barry Sanders	300.00	135.00
❑ PC6 Marcus Allen	40.00	18.00
❑ PC7 John Elway	800.00	350.00
❑ PC8 Adrian Murrell	15.00	6.75
❑ PC9 Junior Seau	15.00	6.75
❑ PC10 Eddie George	60.00	27.00
❑ PC11 Antowain Smith	30.00	13.50
❑ PC12 Reggie White	20.00	9.00
❑ PC13 Dan Marino		
❑ PC14 Joey Galloway	20.00	9.00
❑ PC15 Kordell Stewart	60.00	27.00
❑ PC16 Terry Allen	40.00	18.00
❑ PC17 Napoleon Kaufman	40.00	18.00
❑ PC18 Curtis Martin	30.00	13.50
❑ PC19 Steve Young	100.00	45.00
❑ PC20 Rod Smith WR	15.00	6.75
❑ PC21 Mark Brunell	60.00	27.00
❑ PC22 Emmitt Smith	250.00	110.00
❑ PC23 Rae Carruth	15.00	6.75
❑ PC24 Brett Favre	300.00	135.00
❑ PC25 Jeff George	15.00	6.75
❑ PC26 Terry Glenn	40.00	18.00
❑ PC27 Warrick Dunn	500.00	220.00
❑ PC28 Herman Moore	40.00	18.00
❑ PC29 Cris Carter	40.00	18.00
❑ PC30 Terrell Davis	100.00	45.00

1998 Black Diamond Rookies

	MINT	NRMT
COMPLETE SET (120)	100.00	45.00
COMMON CARD (1-90)	.15	.07
SEMISTARS	.30	.14
UNLISTED STARS	.60	.25
COMMON ROOKIE (91-120)	1.50	.70
ROOKIE SEMISTARS	2.50	1.10
ROOKIE UNLISTED STARS	4.00	1.80

ROOKIE SUBSET STATED ODDS 1:4
*DOUBLE STARS: 1.25X TO 3X HI COL.
*DOUBLE YOUNG STARS: 1X TO 2.5X
*DOUBLE RCs: .6X TO 1.5X
DOUBLE VETERAN PRINT RUN 3000 SETS
DOUBLE ROOKIES PRINT RUN 2500 SETS
*TRIPLE STARS: 2.5X TO 6X HI COL.
*TRIPLE YOUNG STARS: 2X TO 5X
*TRIPLE RCs: 1X TO 2.5X
TRIPLE VETERAN PRINT RUN 1500 SETS
TRIPLE ROOKIES PRINT RUN 1000 SETS

COMMON QUADRUPLE	4.00	1.80

*QUAD.STARS: 10X TO 25X HI COL.
*QUAD.YOUNG STARS: 8X TO 20X
*QUADRUPLE RCs: 2.5X TO 6X..
QUAD VETS STATED PRINT RUN 150 SETS
QUAD ROOKIES STATED PRINT RUN 100
NOTE THAT MANY QUADS WERE MISNUMBERED DURING THE PRINTING PROCESS
WE'VE LISTED STATED PRINT RUNS

❑ 1 Jake Plummer	1.50	.70
❑ 2 Adrian Murrell	.30	.14
❑ 3 Frank Sanders	.30	.14
❑ 4 Jamal Anderson	.60	.25
❑ 5 Chris Chandler	.30	.14
❑ 6 Tony Martin	.30	.14
❑ 7 Jim Harbaugh	.30	.14
❑ 8 Errict Rhett	.30	.14
❑ 9 Michael Jackson	.15	.07
❑ 10 Rob Johnson	.30	.14
❑ 11 Antowain Smith	.60	.25
❑ 12 Thurman Thomas	.60	.25
❑ 13 Fred Lane	.30	.14
❑ 14 Kerry Collins	.15	.07
❑ 15 Rae Carruth	.30	.14
❑ 16 Erik Kramer	.15	.07
❑ 17 Edgar Bennett	.15	.07
❑ 18 Curtis Conway	.30	.14
❑ 19 Corey Dillon	1.00	.45
❑ 20 Neil O'Donnell	.30	.14
❑ 21 Carl Pickens	.60	.25
❑ 22 Troy Aikman	1.50	.70
❑ 23 Emmitt Smith	2.50	1.10
❑ 24 Deion Sanders	.60	.25
❑ 25 John Elway	3.00	1.35
❑ 26 Terrell Davis	2.50	1.10
❑ 27 Rod Smith	.30	.14
❑ 28 Barry Sanders	3.00	1.35
❑ 29 Johnnie Morton	.30	.14
❑ 30 Herman Moore	.60	.25
❑ 31 Brett Favre	3.00	1.35
❑ 32 Antonio Freeman	.60	.25
❑ 33 Dorsey Levens	.60	.25
❑ 34 Marshall Faulk	.60	.25
❑ 35 Marvin Harrison	.30	.14
❑ 36 Zack Crockett	.15	.07
❑ 37 Mark Brunell	1.25	.55
❑ 38 Jimmy Smith	.30	.14
❑ 39 Keenan McCardell	.30	.14
❑ 40 Elvis Grbac	.30	.14
❑ 41 Andre Rison	.30	.14
❑ 42 Derrick Alexander	.30	.14
❑ 43 Dan Marino	3.00	1.35
❑ 44 Karim Abdul-Jabbar	.60	.25
❑ 45 Zach Thomas	.15	.07
❑ 46 Brad Johnson	.60	.25
❑ 47 Cris Carter	.60	.25
❑ 48 Robert Smith	.60	.25
❑ 49 Drew Bledsoe	1.25	.55
❑ 50 Terry Glenn	.60	.25
❑ 51 Ben Coates	.30	.14
❑ 52 Danny Wuerffel	.30	.14
❑ 53 Lamar Smith	.15	.07
❑ 54 Sean Dawkins	.15	.07
❑ 55 Danny Kanell	.30	.14
❑ 56 Tiki Barber	.30	.14
❑ 57 Ike Hilliard	.30	.14
❑ 58 Curtis Martin	.60	.25
❑ 59 Vinny Testaverde	.30	.14
❑ 60 Keyshawn Johnson	.60	.25
❑ 61 Napoleon Kaufman	.60	.25
❑ 62 Jeff George	.30	.14
❑ 63 Tim Brown	.60	.25
❑ 64 Bobby Hoying	.30	.14
❑ 65 Charlie Garner	.15	.07
❑ 66 Duce Staley	1.00	.45
❑ 67 Kordell Stewart	.60	.25
❑ 68 Jerome Bettis	.60	.25
❑ 69 Charles Johnson	.15	.07
❑ 70 Tony Banks	.30	.14
❑ 71 Isaac Bruce	.60	.25
❑ 72 Eddie Kennison	.30	.14
❑ 73 Natrone Means	.60	.25
❑ 74 Bryan Still	.15	.07
❑ 75 Junior Seau	.30	.14
❑ 76 Steve Young	1.00	.45
❑ 77 Jerry Rice	1.50	.70
❑ 78 Garrison Hearst	.60	.25
❑ 79 Ricky Watters	.30	.14
❑ 80 Joey Galloway	.60	.25
❑ 81 Warren Moon	.15	.07
❑ 82 Warrick Dunn	1.00	.45
❑ 83 Trent Dilfer	.60	.25
❑ 84 Bert Emanuel	.30	.14
❑ 85 Steve McNair	.60	.25
❑ 86 Eddie George	1.25	.55
❑ 87 Yancey Thigpen	.15	.07
❑ 88 Leslie Shepherd	.15	.07
❑ 89 Terry Allen	.60	.25
❑ 90 Michael Westbrook	.30	.14
❑ 91 Peyton Manning RC	20.00	9.00
❑ 92 Jacquez Green RC	4.00	1.80
❑ 93 Fred Taylor RC	12.00	5.50
❑ 94 Terry Fair RC	2.50	1.10
❑ 95 Pat Johnson RC	4.00	1.80
❑ 96 Corey Chavous RC	1.50	.70
❑ 97 Randy Moss RC	20.00	9.00
❑ 98 Curtis Enis RC	5.00	2.20
❑ 99 Rashaan Shehee RC	2.50	1.10
❑ 100 Kevin Dyson RC	4.00	1.80
❑ 101 Shaun Williams RC	1.50	.70
❑ 102 Grant Wistrom RC	1.50	.70
❑ 103 John Avery RC	4.00	1.80
❑ 104 Brian Griese RC	8.00	3.60
❑ 105 Ryan Leaf RC	4.00	1.80
❑ 106 Jerome Pathon RC	2.50	1.10
❑ 107 Sam Cowart RC	1.50	.70
❑ 108 Germane Crowell RC	5.00	2.20
❑ 109 Ahman Green RC	4.00	1.80
❑ 110 Greg Ellis RC	1.50	.70
❑ 111 Robert Holcombe RC	4.00	1.80
❑ 112 Marcus Nash RC	4.00	1.80
❑ 113 Duane Starks RC	1.50	.70
❑ 114 Andre Wadsworth RC	2.50	1.10
❑ 115 Takeo Spikes RC	2.50	1.10
❑ 116 Eric Brown RC	1.50	.70
❑ 117 Robert Edwards RC	4.00	1.80
❑ 118 Charlie Batch RC	8.00	3.60
❑ 119 Mikhael Ricks RC	2.50	1.10
❑ 120 Charles Woodson RC	5.00	2.20
❑ S13 Dan Marino SAMPLE	2.00	.90

1998 Black Diamond Rookies Sheer Brilliance

	MINT	NRMT
COMPLETE SET (30)	200.00	90.00
COMMON CARD (B1-B30)	2.50	1.10
SEMISTARS	3.00	1.35

RANDOM INSERTS IN PACKS....

❑ B1 Dan Marino/1300	15.00	6.75
❑ B2 Troy Aikman/800	12.00	5.50
❑ B3 Brett Favre/400	30.00	13.50
❑ B4 Ryan Leaf/1600	8.00	3.60
❑ B5 Peyton Manning/1800	40.00	18.00
❑ B6 Barry Sanders/2000	12.00	5.50
❑ B7 Emmitt Smith/2200	10.00	4.50
❑ B8 John Elway/700	25.00	11.00
❑ B9 Steve Young/800	8.00	3.60
❑ B10 Steve McNair/900	6.00	2.70
❑ B11 Antowain Smith/2300	3.00	1.35
❑ B12 Corey Dillon/2800	2.50	1.10
❑ B13 Terrell Davis/3000	6.00	2.70
❑ B14 Mark Brunell/800	10.00	4.50
❑ B15 Charles Woodson/2400	6.00	2.70
❑ B16 Brian Griese/1400	12.00	5.50
❑ B17 Curtis Martin/2800	3.00	1.35
❑ B18 Keyshawn Johnson/1900	3.00	1.35
❑ B19 Kordell Stewart/1000	6.00	2.70
❑ B20 Eddie George/2700	4.00	1.80
❑ B21 Drew Bledsoe/1100	10.00	4.50
❑ B22 Jake Plummer/1600	8.00	3.60
❑ B23 Warren Moon/100	20.00	9.00
❑ B24 Curtis Enis/3900	5.00	2.20
❑ B25 John Avery/2000	3.00	1.35
❑ B26 Randy Moss/1800	40.00	18.00
❑ B27 Rob Johnson/1100	4.00	1.80
❑ B28 Warrick Dunn/2800	5.00	2.20
❑ B29 Terry Allen/2100	3.00	1.35
❑ B30 Robert Smith/2600	3.00	1.35

1998 Black Diamond Rookies Extreme Brilliance

	MINT	NRMT
COMMON CARD (B1-B30)	60.00	27.00
SEMISTARS	80.00	36.00

EXTREMES SER.#'d TO PLAYER'S JERSEY NO.
CARDS NUMBERED UNDER 12 NOT PRICED

❑ B1 Dan Marino/13	800.00	350.00
❑ B2 Troy Aikman/8		
❑ B3 Brett Favre/4		
❑ B4 Ryan Leaf/16	150.00	70.00
❑ B5 Peyton Manning/18	500.00	220.00
❑ B6 Barry Sanders/20	500.00	220.00
❑ B7 Emmitt Smith/22	350.00	160.00
❑ B8 John Elway/7		
❑ B9 Steve Young/8		
❑ B10 Steve McNair/9		
❑ B11 Antowain Smith/23	80.00	36.00
❑ B12 Corey Dillon/28	100.00	45.00
❑ B13 Terrell Davis/30	300.00	135.00
❑ B14 Mark Brunell/8		
❑ B15 Charles Woodson/24	100.00	45.00
❑ B16 Brian Griese/14	250.00	110.00
❑ B17 Curtis Martin/28	80.00	36.00
❑ B18 Keyshawn Johnson19	100.00	45.00
❑ B19 Kordell Stewart/10		
❑ B20 Eddie George/27	150.00	70.00
❑ B21 Drew Bledsoe/11	300.00	135.00
❑ B22 Jake Plummer/16	250.00	110.00
❑ B23 Warren Moon/1		
❑ B24 Curtis Enis/39	60.00	27.00
❑ B25 John Avery/20	80.00	36.00
❑ B26 Randy Moss/18	500.00	220.00
❑ B27 Rob Johnson/11		
❑ B28 Warrick Dunn/28	80.00	36.00
❑ B29 Terry Allen/21	80.00	36.00
❑ B30 Robert Smith/26	80.00	36.00

1998 Black Diamond Rookies White Onyx

	MINT	NRMT
COMPLETE SET (30)	200.00	90.00

COMMON CARD (ON1-ON30)	2.50	1.10
SEMISTARS	4.00	1.80
STATED PRINT RUN 2250 SERIAL #'d SETS		

❑ ON1 Peyton Manning	40.00	18.00
❑ ON2 Corey Dillon	6.00	2.70
❑ ON3 Jerome Bettis	5.00	2.20
❑ ON4 Brett Favre	20.00	9.00
❑ ON5 Napoleon Kaufman	5.00	2.20
❑ ON6 Joey Galloway	5.00	2.20
❑ ON7 John Elway	20.00	9.00
❑ ON8 Troy Aikman	10.00	4.50
❑ ON9 Robert Smith	5.00	2.20
❑ ON10 Kordell Stewart	4.00	1.80
❑ ON11 Garrison Hearst	5.00	2.20
❑ ON12 Curtis Enis	8.00	3.60
❑ ON13 Dan Marino	20.00	9.00
❑ ON14 Jimmy Smith	2.50	1.10
❑ ON15 Steve Young	6.00	2.70
❑ ON16 Ryan Leaf	8.00	3.60
❑ ON17 Steve McNair	5.00	2.20
❑ ON18 Randy Moss	40.00	18.00
❑ ON19 Curtis Martin	5.00	2.20
❑ ON20 Barry Sanders	20.00	9.00
❑ ON21 Rob Johnson	4.00	1.80
❑ ON22 Emmitt Smith	15.00	6.75
❑ ON23 Jake Plummer	10.00	4.50
❑ ON24 Antonio Freeman	5.00	2.20
❑ ON25 Mark Brunell	8.00	3.60
❑ ON26 Warrick Dunn	6.00	2.70
❑ ON27 Eddie George	8.00	3.60
❑ ON28 Jerry Rice	10.00	4.50
❑ ON29 Drew Bledsoe	8.00	3.60
❑ ON30 Terrell Davis	15.00	6.75

1999 Black Diamond

	MINT	NRMT
COMPLETE SET (150)	120.00	55.00
COMP.SET w/o SPs (110)	20.00	9.00
COMMON CARD (1-110)	.20	.09
SEMISTARS	.40	.18
UNLISTED STARS	.75	.35
COMMON ROOKIE (111-150)	2.00	.90
ROOKIE SEMISTARS	3.00	1.35
ROOKIE UNL.STARS	4.00	1.80
ROOKIE SUBSET STATED ODDS 1:4		

❑ 1 Adrian Murrell	.40	.18
❑ 2 Jake Plummer	1.50	.70
❑ 3 Rob Moore	.40	.18
❑ 4 Frank Sanders	.40	.18
❑ 5 Jamal Anderson	.75	.35
❑ 6 Terance Mathis	.40	.18
❑ 7 Chris Chandler	.40	.18
❑ 8 Tim Dwight	.75	.35
❑ 9 Jermaine Lewis	.40	.18
❑ 10 Priest Holmes	.75	.35
❑ 11 Peter Boulware	.20	.09
❑ 12 Doug Flutie	1.00	.45
❑ 13 Antowain Smith	.75	.35
❑ 14 Eric Moulds	.75	.35
❑ 15 Bruce Smith	.40	.18
❑ 16 Rae Carruth	.40	.18
❑ 17 Muhsin Muhammad	.40	.18
❑ 18 Wesley Walls	.40	.18
❑ 19 Tim Biakabutuka	.40	.18
❑ 20 Curtis Enis	.75	.35
❑ 21 Curtis Conway	.40	.18
❑ 22 Bobby Engram	.40	.18
❑ 23 Damay Scott	.20	.09
❑ 24 Corey Dillon	.75	.35
❑ 25 Jeff Blake	.40	.18
❑ 26 Ty Detmer	.40	.18
❑ 27 Terry Kirby	.20	.09
❑ 28 Leslie Shepherd	.20	.09
❑ 29 Emmitt Smith	2.00	.90
❑ 30 Troy Aikman	2.00	.90
❑ 31 Michael Irvin	.40	.18
❑ 32 Rocket Ismail	.40	.18
❑ 33 Brian Griese	1.50	.70
❑ 34 Terrell Davis	2.00	.90
❑ 35 Shannon Sharpe	.40	.18
❑ 36 Rod Smith	.40	.18
❑ 37 Barry Sanders	3.00	1.35
❑ 38 Herman Moore	.75	.35
❑ 39 Charlie Batch	1.50	.70
❑ 40 Johnnie Morton	.40	.18
❑ 41 Brett Favre	3.00	1.35
❑ 42 Dorsey Levens	.75	.35
❑ 43 Antonio Freeman	.75	.35
❑ 44 Mark Chmura	.20	.09
❑ 45 Peyton Manning	3.00	1.35
❑ 46 Jerome Pathon	.20	.09
❑ 47 Marvin Harrison	.75	.35
❑ 48 Fred Taylor	2.00	.90
❑ 49 Mark Brunell	1.25	.55
❑ 50 Jimmy Smith	.40	.18
❑ 51 Keenan McCardell	.40	.18
❑ 52 Andre Rison	.40	.18
❑ 53 Elvis Grbac	.40	.18
❑ 54 Derrick Alexander WR	.40	.18
❑ 55 Tony Gonzalez	.40	.18
❑ 56 Dan Marino	3.00	1.35
❑ 57 Oronde Gadsden	.20	.09
❑ 58 O.J. McDuffie	.40	.18
❑ 59 Randy Moss	3.00	1.35
❑ 60 Randall Cunningham	.75	.35
❑ 61 Cris Carter	.75	.35
❑ 62 Robert Smith	.75	.35
❑ 63 Drew Bledsoe	1.25	.55
❑ 64 Terry Glenn	.75	.35
❑ 65 Ben Coates	.40	.18
❑ 66 Billy Joe Hobert	.20	.09
❑ 67 Eddie Kennison	.40	.18
❑ 68 Cam Cleeland	.20	.09
❑ 69 Gary Brown	.20	.09
❑ 70 Ike Hilliard	.20	.09
❑ 71 Amani Toomer	.20	.09
❑ 72 Vinny Testaverde	.40	.18
❑ 73 Keyshawn Johnson	.75	.35
❑ 74 Curtis Martin	.75	.35
❑ 75 Wayne Chrebet	.40	.18
❑ 76 Tim Brown	.75	.35
❑ 77 Rickey Dudley	.20	.09
❑ 78 Napoleon Kaufman	.75	.35
❑ 79 Charles Woodson	.75	.35
❑ 80 Duce Staley	.75	.35
❑ 81 Doug Pederson	.20	.09
❑ 82 Charles Johnson	.20	.09
❑ 83 Kordell Stewart	.75	.35
❑ 84 Jerome Bettis	.75	.35
❑ 85 Courtney Hawkins	.20	.09
❑ 86 Isaac Bruce	.75	.35
❑ 87 Marshall Faulk	.75	.35
❑ 88 Trent Green	.40	.18
❑ 89 Jim Harbaugh	.40	.18
❑ 90 Junior Seau	.40	.18
❑ 91 Natrone Means	.40	.18
❑ 92 Lawrence Phillips	.40	.18
❑ 93 Steve Young	1.25	.55
❑ 94 Terrell Owens	.75	.35
❑ 95 Jerry Rice	2.00	.90
❑ 96 Jon Kitna	1.00	.45
❑ 97 Ricky Watters	.40	.18
❑ 98 Joey Galloway	.75	.35
❑ 99 Shawn Springs	.20	.09
❑ 100 Warrick Dunn	.75	.35
❑ 101 Trent Dilfer	.40	.18
❑ 102 Reidel Anthony	.40	.18
❑ 103 Mike Alstott	.75	.35
❑ 104 Steve McNair	.75	.35
❑ 105 Eddie George	1.00	.45
❑ 106 Kevin Dyson	.40	.18
❑ 107 Yancey Thigpen	.20	.09
❑ 108 Michael Westbrook	.40	.18
❑ 109 Brad Johnson	.75	.35
❑ 110 Skip Hicks	.75	.35
❑ 111 Tim Couch RC	20.00	9.00
❑ 112 Akili Smith RC	8.00	3.60
❑ 113 Ricky Williams RC	20.00	9.00
❑ 114 Donovan McNabb RC	12.00	5.50
❑ 115 Edgerrin James RC	30.00	13.50
❑ 116 Cade McNown RC	12.00	5.50
❑ 117 Daunte Culpepper RC	12.00	5.50
❑ 118 Shaun King RC	12.00	5.50
❑ 119 Brock Huard RC	5.00	2.20
❑ 120 Joe Germaine RC	4.00	1.80
❑ 121 Troy Edwards RC	6.00	2.70
❑ 122 Champ Bailey RC	5.00	2.20
❑ 123 Kevin Faulk RC	5.00	2.20
❑ 124 David Boston RC	6.00	2.70
❑ 125 Kevin Johnson RC	10.00	4.50
❑ 126 Torry Holt RC	10.00	4.50
❑ 127 James Johnson RC	5.00	2.20
❑ 128 Peerless Price RC	6.00	2.70
❑ 129 D'Wayne Bates RC	3.00	1.35
❑ 130 Cecil Collins RC	4.00	1.80
❑ 131 Na Brown RC	4.00	1.80
❑ 132 Rob Konrad RC	4.00	1.80
❑ 133 Joel Makovicka RC	4.00	1.80
❑ 134 Dameane Douglas RC	3.00	1.35
❑ 135 Scott Covington RC	3.00	1.35
❑ 136 Daylon McCutcheon RC	2.00	.90
❑ 137 Chris Claiborne RC	3.00	1.35
❑ 138 Karsten Bailey RC	3.00	1.35
❑ 139 Mike Cloud RC	4.00	1.80
❑ 140 Sean Bennett RC	4.00	1.80
❑ 141 Jermaine Fazande RC	3.00	1.35
❑ 142 Chris McAlister RC	3.00	1.35
❑ 143 Ebenezer Ekuban RC	3.00	1.35
❑ 144 Jeff Paulk RC	3.00	1.35
❑ 145 Jim Kleinsasser RC	4.00	1.80
❑ 146 Bobby Collins RC	4.00	1.80
❑ 147 Andy Katzenmoyer RC	4.00	1.80
❑ 148 Jevon Kearse RC	8.00	3.60
❑ 149 Amos Zereoue RC	4.00	1.80
❑ 150 Sedrick Irvin RC	4.00	1.80
❑ WPBD Walter Payton (Game Jersey AUTO/34)	2000.00	900.00

1999 Black Diamond Diamond Cut

	MINT	NRMT
COMPLETE SET (150)	200.00	90.00
*DIAMOND CUT STARS: 1.5X TO 4X HI COL.		
*DIAMOND CUT YOUNG STARS: 1.2X TO 3X		
1-110 STATED ODDS 1:7		
*DIAMOND CUT RCs: .5X TO 1.2X		
111-150 STATED ODDS 1:12		

1999 Black Diamond Final Cut

	MINT	NRMT
COMMON CARD (1-110)	5.00	2.20
*FINAL CUT STARS: 10X TO 25X		
*FINAL CUT YOUNG STARS: 8X TO 20X		
1-110 FINAL CUT PRINT RUN 100 SER.#'d SETS		
COMMON ROOKIE (111-150)	12.00	5.50

*DIAMOND CUT RCs: 2.5X TO 6X
111-150 FINAL CUT PRINT RUN 50 SER.#'d SETS

1999 Black Diamond A Piece of History

	MINT	NRMT
COMPLETE SET (26)	1200.00	550.00
COMMON CARD	25.00	11.00

H STATED ODDS 1:179 HOBBY..
HR STATED ODDS 1:359 HOB/RET
*DOUBLE DIAMONDS: .8X TO 2X HI COL.
DOUBLE H STATED ODDS 1:1079 HOBBY
DOUBLE HR ODDS 1:1079 HOB/RET

	MINT	NRMT
❑ AS Akili Smith H	50.00	22.00
❑ BF Brett Favre H/R	80.00	36.00
❑ BG Brian Griese H	40.00	18.00
❑ BH Brock Huard H	40.00	18.00
❑ CB Charlie Batch H/R	30.00	13.50
❑ CM Cade McNown H/R	50.00	22.00
❑ DC Daunte Culpepper H/R	50.00	22.00
❑ DF Doug Flutie H/R	50.00	22.00
❑ DM Dan Marino H/R	80.00	36.00
❑ EJ Edgerrin James H	120.00	55.00
❑ ES Emmitt Smith H	60.00	27.00
❑ HM Herman Moore H	25.00	11.00
❑ JP Jake Plummer H	50.00	22.00
❑ JR Jerry Rice H/R	50.00	22.00
❑ RM Randy Moss H	80.00	36.00
❑ RW Ricky Williams H/R	80.00	36.00
❑ SY Steve Young H/R	40.00	18.00
❑ TA Troy Aikman H/R	50.00	22.00
❑ TB Tim Brown H/R	25.00	11.00
❑ TC Tim Couch H	80.00	36.00
❑ TD Terrell Davis H	50.00	22.00
❑ TH Torry Holt H/R	40.00	18.00
❑ WD Warrick Dunn H	25.00	11.00
❑ DBL Drew Bledsoe H	40.00	18.00
❑ DBO David Boston H	30.00	13.50
❑ DMC Donovan McNabb H/R	50.00	22.00

1999 Black Diamond Diamonation

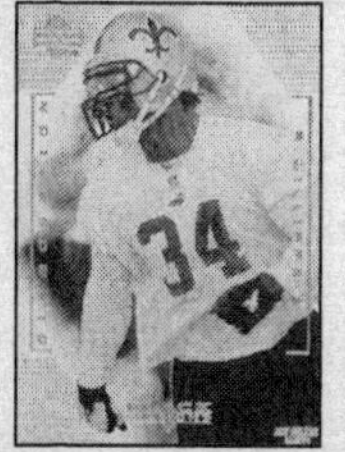

	MINT	NRMT
COMPLETE SET (20)	60.00	27.00
COMMON CARD (D1-D20)	2.00	.90

STATED ODDS 1:6

	MINT	NRMT
❑ D1 Brett Favre	8.00	3.60
❑ D2 Eddie George	2.50	1.10
❑ D3 Terrell Davis	5.00	2.20
❑ D4 Jerome Bettis	2.00	.90
❑ D5 Randall Cunningham	2.00	.90
❑ D6 Jon Kitna	2.50	1.10
❑ D7 Troy Aikman	5.00	2.20
❑ D8 Marshall Faulk	2.00	.90
❑ D9 Steve Young	3.00	1.35
❑ D10 Warrick Dunn	2.00	.90
❑ D11 Jake Plummer	4.00	1.80
❑ D12 Fred Taylor	4.00	1.80
❑ D13 Antonio Freeman	2.00	.90
❑ D14 Peyton Manning	6.00	2.70
❑ D15 Randy Moss	6.00	2.70
❑ D16 Steve McNair	2.00	.90
❑ D17 Emmitt Smith	5.00	2.20
❑ D18 Terrell Owens	2.00	.90
❑ D19 Kordell Stewart	2.00	.90
❑ D20 Ricky Williams	10.00	4.50

1999 Black Diamond Gallery

	MINT	NRMT
COMPLETE SET (10)	60.00	27.00
COMMON CARD (G1-G10)	3.00	1.35

STATED ODDS 1:14

	MINT	NRMT
❑ G1 Akili Smith	5.00	2.20
❑ G2 Barry Sanders	12.00	5.50
❑ G3 Curtis Martin	3.00	1.35
❑ G4 Drew Bledsoe	5.00	2.20
❑ G5 Emmitt Smith	8.00	3.60
❑ G6 Keyshawn Johnson	3.00	1.35
❑ G7 Jerry Rice	8.00	3.60
❑ G8 Tim Couch	12.00	5.50
❑ G9 Terrell Owens	3.00	1.35
❑ G10 Troy Aikman	8.00	3.60

1999 Black Diamond Might

	MINT	NRMT
COMPLETE SET (10)	25.00	11.00
COMMON CARD (DM1-DM10)	2.00	.90

STATED ODDS 1:12

	MINT	NRMT
❑ DM1 Antowain Smith	2.00	.90
❑ DM2 Steve McNair	2.00	.90
❑ DM3 Corey Dillon	2.00	.90
❑ DM4 Dan Marino	8.00	3.60
❑ DM5 Eddie George	2.50	1.10
❑ DM6 Jerome Bettis	2.00	.90
❑ DM7 Jerry Rice	5.00	2.20
❑ DM8 Randall Cunningham	2.00	.90
❑ DM9 Brian Griese	3.00	1.35
❑ DM10 Joey Galloway	2.00	.90

1999 Black Diamond Myriad

	MINT	NRMT
COMPLETE SET (10)	60.00	27.00
COMMON CARD (M1-M10)	3.00	1.35

STATED ODDS 1:29

	MINT	NRMT
❑ M1 Barry Sanders	12.00	5.50
❑ M2 Randy Moss	10.00	4.50
❑ M3 Terrell Davis	8.00	3.60
❑ M4 Brett Favre	12.00	5.50
❑ M5 Jamal Anderson	3.00	1.35
❑ M6 Mark Brunell	5.00	2.20
❑ M7 Donovan McNabb	8.00	3.60
❑ M8 Steve Young	5.00	2.20
❑ M9 Ricky Williams	12.00	5.50
❑ M10 Warrick Dunn	3.00	1.35

1999 Black Diamond Skills

	MINT	NRMT
COMPLETE SET (10)	80.00	36.00
COMMON CARD (S1-S10)	3.00	1.35

STATED ODDS 1:29

	MINT	NRMT
❑ S1 Drew Bledsoe	5.00	2.20
❑ S2 Fred Taylor	6.00	2.70
❑ S3 Dan Marino	12.00	5.50
❑ S4 Jake Plummer	6.00	2.70
❑ S5 Kurt Warner	30.00	13.50
❑ S6 Marshall Faulk		
❑ S7 Randy Moss	10.00	4.50
❑ S8 Peyton Manning	10.00	4.50
❑ S9 Keyshawn Johnson		
❑ S10 Tim Couch	12.00	5.50

1948 Bowman

	NRMT	VG-E
COMPLETE SET (108)	6000.00	2700.00
COMMON 1/4/7/-/-/-	20.00	9.00
SEMISTARS 1/4/7/-/-/-	25.00	11.00
COMMON 2/5/8/-/-/-	25.00	11.00
SEMISTARS 2/5/8 /-/-/-	30.00	13.50
COMMON SP 3/6/9 /-/-/-	100.00	45.00
SEMISTARS SP 3/6/9/-/-/-	110.00	50.00
CARDS PRICED IN NM CONDITION		

Card	NRMT	VG-E
❑ 1 Joe Tereshinski RC !	150.00	38.00
❑ 2 Larry Olsonoski	25.00	11.00
❑ 3 John Lujack SP RC	325.00	145.00
❑ 4 Ray Poole	20.00	9.00
❑ 5 Bill DeCorrevont	25.00	11.00
❑ 6 Paul Briggs SP	100.00	45.00
❑ 7 Steve Van Buren RC	150.00	70.00
❑ 8 Kenny Washington RC	60.00	27.00
❑ 9 Nolan Luhn SP	100.00	45.00
❑ 10 Chris Iversen	20.00	9.00
❑ 11 Jack Wiley	25.00	11.00
❑ 12 Charley Conerly RC SP	325.00	145.00
❑ 13 Hugh Taylor RC	25.00	11.00
❑ 14 Frank Seno	25.00	11.00
❑ 15 Gil Bouley SP	100.00	45.00
❑ 16 Tommy Thompson RC	35.00	16.00
❑ 17 Charley Trippi RC	100.00	45.00
❑ 18 Vince Banonis SP	100.00	45.00
❑ 19 Art Faircloth	20.00	9.00
❑ 20 Clyde Goodnight	25.00	11.00
❑ 21 Bill Chipley SP	100.00	45.00
❑ 22 Sammy Baugh RC	500.00	220.00
❑ 23 Don Kindt	25.00	11.00
❑ 24 John Koniszewski SP	100.00	45.00
❑ 25 Pat McHugh	20.00	9.00
❑ 26 Bob Waterfield RC	200.00	90.00
❑ 27 Tony Compagno SP	100.00	45.00
❑ 28 Paul Governali RC	25.00	11.00
❑ 29 Pat Harder RC	50.00	22.00
❑ 30 Vic Lindskog SP	100.00	45.00
❑ 31 Salvatore Rosato	20.00	9.00
❑ 32 John Mastrangelo	25.00	11.00
❑ 33 Fred Gehrke SP	100.00	45.00
❑ 34 Bosh Pritchard	20.00	9.00
❑ 35 Mike Micka	25.00	11.00
❑ 36 Bulldog Turner RC SP	250.00	110.00
❑ 37 Len Younce	20.00	9.00
❑ 38 Pat West	25.00	11.00
❑ 39 Russ Thomas SP	100.00	45.00
❑ 40 James Peebles	20.00	9.00
❑ 41 Bob Skoglund	25.00	11.00
❑ 42 Walt Stickle SP	100.00	45.00
❑ 43 Whitey Wistert RC	25.00	11.00
❑ 44 Paul Christman RC	50.00	22.00
❑ 45 Jay Rhodemyre SP	100.00	45.00
❑ 46 Tony Minisi	20.00	9.00
❑ 47 Bob Mann	25.00	11.00
❑ 48 Mal Kutner RC SP	110.00	50.00
❑ 49 Dick Poillon	20.00	9.00
❑ 50 Charles Cherundolo	25.00	11.00
❑ 51 Gerald Cowhig SP	100.00	45.00
❑ 52 Neill Armstrong RC	25.00	11.00
❑ 53 Frank Maznicki	25.00	11.00
❑ 54 John Sanchez SP	100.00	45.00
❑ 55 Frank Reagan	20.00	9.00
❑ 56 Jim Hardy	25.00	11.00
❑ 57 John Badaczewski SP	100.00	45.00
❑ 58 Robert Nussbaumer	20.00	9.00
❑ 59 Marvin Pregulman	25.00	11.00
❑ 60 Elbert Nickel RC SP	125.00	55.00
❑ 61 Alex Wojciechowicz RC	100.00	45.00
❑ 62 Walt Schlinkman	25.00	11.00
❑ 63 Pete Pihos RC SP	225.00	100.00
❑ 64 Joseph Sulaitis	20.00	9.00
❑ 65 Mike Holovak RC	50.00	22.00
❑ 66 Cecil Souders SP	100.00	45.00
❑ 67 Paul McKee	20.00	9.00
❑ 68 Bill Moore	25.00	11.00
❑ 69 Frank Minini SP	100.00	45.00
❑ 70 Jack Ferrante	20.00	9.00
❑ 71 Les Horvath RC	50.00	22.00
❑ 72 Ted Fritsch Sr. RC SP	110.00	50.00
❑ 73 Tex Coulter RC	25.00	11.00
❑ 74 Boley Dancewicz	25.00	11.00
❑ 75 Dante Mangani SP	100.00	45.00
❑ 76 James Hefti	20.00	9.00
❑ 77 Paul Sarringhaus	25.00	11.00
❑ 78 Joe Scott SP	100.00	45.00
❑ 79 Bucko Kilroy RC	25.00	11.00
❑ 80 Bill Dudley RC	100.00	45.00
❑ 81 Marshall Goldberg RC SP	110.00	50.00
❑ 82 John Cannady	20.00	9.00
❑ 83 Perry Moss	25.00	11.00
❑ 84 Harold Crisler RC SP	110.00	50.00
❑ 85 Bill Gray	20.00	9.00
❑ 86 John Clement	25.00	11.00
❑ 87 Dan Sandifer SP	100.00	45.00
❑ 88 Ben Kish	20.00	9.00
❑ 89 Herbert Banta	25.00	11.00
❑ 90 Bill Garnaas SP	100.00	45.00
❑ 91 Jim White	20.00	9.00
❑ 92 Frank Barzilauskas	25.00	11.00
❑ 93 Vic Sears SP	100.00	45.00
❑ 94 John Adams	20.00	9.00
❑ 95 George McAfee RC	100.00	45.00
❑ 96 Ralph Heywood SP	100.00	45.00
❑ 97 Joe Muha	20.00	9.00
❑ 98 Fred Enke	25.00	11.00
❑ 99 Harry Gilmer RC SP	175.00	80.00
❑ 100 Bill Miklich	20.00	9.00
❑ 101 Joe Gottlieb	25.00	11.00
❑ 102 Bud Angsman SP RC	110.00	50.00
❑ 103 Tom Farmer	20.00	9.00
❑ 104 Bruce Smith RC	60.00	27.00
❑ 105 Bob Cifers SP	100.00	45.00
❑ 106 Ernie Steele	20.00	9.00
❑ 107 Sid Luckman RC	250.00	110.00
❑ 108 Buford Ray SP RC	350.00	90.00

1950 Bowman

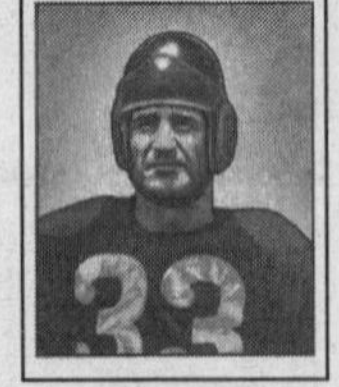

	NRMT	VG-E
COMPLETE SET (144)	4000.00	1800.00
COMMON CARD (1-144)	25.00	11.00
SEMISTARS	30.00	13.50
UNLISTED STARS	40.00	18.00
CARDS PRICED IN NM CONDITION		

Card	NRMT	VG-E
❑ 1 Doak Walker	180.00	45.00
❑ 2 John Greene	25.00	11.00
❑ 3 Bob Nowasky	25.00	11.00
❑ 4 Jonathan Jenkins	25.00	11.00
❑ 5 Y.A. Tittle RC	250.00	110.00
❑ 6 Lou Groza RC	175.00	80.00
❑ 7 Alex Agase RC	30.00	13.50
❑ 8 Mac Speedie RC	50.00	22.00
❑ 9 Tony Canadeo RC	90.00	40.00
❑ 10 Larry Craig	25.00	11.00
❑ 11 Ted Fritsch Sr.	30.00	13.50
❑ 12 Joe Goldring	25.00	11.00
❑ 13 Martin Ruby	25.00	11.00
❑ 14 George Taliaferro	30.00	13.50
❑ 15 Tank Younger RC	50.00	22.00
❑ 16 Glenn Army Davis RC	125.00	55.00
❑ 17 Bob Waterfield	125.00	55.00
❑ 18 Val Jansante	25.00	11.00
❑ 19 Joe Geri	25.00	11.00
❑ 20 Jerry Nuzum	25.00	11.00
❑ 21 Elmer Bud Angsman	25.00	11.00
❑ 22 Billy Dewell	25.00	11.00
❑ 23 Steve Van Buren	90.00	40.00
❑ 24 Cliff Patton	25.00	11.00
❑ 25 Bosh Pritchard	25.00	11.00
❑ 26 John Lujack	75.00	34.00
❑ 27 Sid Luckman	100.00	45.00
❑ 28 Bulldog Turner	60.00	27.00
❑ 29 Bill Dudley	60.00	27.00
❑ 30 Hugh Taylor	30.00	13.50
❑ 31 George Thomas	25.00	11.00
❑ 32 Ray Poole	25.00	11.00
❑ 33 Travis Tidwell	25.00	11.00
❑ 34 Gail Bruce	25.00	11.00
❑ 35 Joe Perry RC	175.00	80.00
❑ 36 Frankie Albert RC	40.00	18.00
❑ 37 Bobby Layne	200.00	90.00
❑ 38 Leon Hart	40.00	18.00
❑ 39 Bob Hoernschemeyer RC	30.00	13.50
❑ 40 Dick Barwegan RC	25.00	11.00
❑ 41 Adrian Burk RC	30.00	13.50
❑ 42 Barry French	25.00	11.00
❑ 43 Marion Motley RC	200.00	90.00
❑ 44 Jim Martin	30.00	13.50
❑ 45 Otto Graham RC	450.00	200.00
❑ 46 Al Baldwin	25.00	11.00
❑ 47 Larry Coutre	25.00	11.00
❑ 48 John Rauch	25.00	11.00
❑ 49 Sam Tamburo	25.00	11.00
❑ 50 Mike Swistowicz	25.00	11.00
❑ 51 Tom Fears RC	125.00	55.00
❑ 52 Elroy Hirsch RC	175.00	80.00
❑ 53 Dick Huffman	25.00	11.00
❑ 54 Bob Gage	25.00	11.00
❑ 55 Buddy Tinsley	25.00	11.00
❑ 56 Bill Blackburn	25.00	11.00
❑ 57 John Cochran	25.00	11.00
❑ 58 Bill Fischer	25.00	11.00
❑ 59 Whitey Wistert	30.00	13.50
❑ 60 Clyde Scott	25.00	11.00
❑ 61 Walter Barnes	25.00	11.00
❑ 62 Bob Perina	25.00	11.00
❑ 63 Bill Wightkin	25.00	11.00
❑ 64 Bob Goode	25.00	11.00
❑ 65 Al Demao	25.00	11.00
❑ 66 Harry Gilmer	30.00	13.50
❑ 67 Bill Austin	25.00	11.00
❑ 68 Joe Scott	25.00	11.00
❑ 69 Tex Coulter	30.00	13.50
❑ 70 Paul Salata	25.00	11.00
❑ 71 Emil Sitko RC	30.00	13.50
❑ 72 Bill Johnson	25.00	11.00
❑ 73 Don Doll RC	25.00	11.00
❑ 74 Dan Sandifer	25.00	11.00
❑ 75 John Panelli	25.00	11.00
❑ 76 Bill Leonard	25.00	11.00
❑ 77 Bob Kelly	25.00	11.00
❑ 78 Dante Lavelli RC	110.00	50.00
❑ 79 Tony Adamle	30.00	13.50
❑ 80 Dick Wildung	25.00	11.00
❑ 81 Tobin Rote RC	40.00	18.00
❑ 82 Paul Burris	25.00	11.00
❑ 83 Lowell Tew	25.00	11.00
❑ 84 Barney Poole	25.00	11.00
❑ 85 Fred Naumetz	25.00	11.00
❑ 86 Dick Hoerner	25.00	11.00
❑ 87 Bob Reinhard	25.00	11.00
❑ 88 Howard Hartley RC	25.00	11.00
❑ 89 Darrell Hogan RC	25.00	11.00
❑ 90 Jerry Shipkey	25.00	11.00
❑ 91 Frank Tripucka	30.00	13.50
❑ 92 Garrard Ramsey RC	25.00	11.00
❑ 93 Pat Harder	30.00	13.50
❑ 94 Vic Sears	25.00	11.00
❑ 95 Tommy Thompson	30.00	13.50
❑ 96 Bucko Kilroy	30.00	13.50
❑ 97 George Connor	45.00	20.00

Card	NRMT	VG-E
❑ 98 Fred Morrison	25.00	11.00
❑ 99 Jim Keane	25.00	11.00
❑ 100 Sammy Baugh	250.00	110.00
❑ 101 Harry Ulinski	25.00	11.00
❑ 102 Frank Spaniel	25.00	11.00
❑ 103 Charley Conerly	90.00	40.00
❑ 104 Dick Hensley	25.00	11.00
❑ 105 Eddie Price	25.00	11.00
❑ 106 Ed Carr	25.00	11.00
❑ 107 Leo Nomellini	75.00	34.00
❑ 108 Verl Lillywhite	25.00	11.00
❑ 109 Wallace Triplett	25.00	11.00
❑ 110 Joe Watson	25.00	11.00
❑ 111 Cloyce Box RC	30.00	13.50
❑ 112 Billy Stone	25.00	11.00
❑ 113 Earl Murray	25.00	11.00
❑ 114 Chet Mutryn RC	30.00	13.50
❑ 115 Ken Carpenter	30.00	13.50
❑ 116 Lou Rymkus RC	30.00	13.50
❑ 117 Dub Jones RC	30.00	13.50
❑ 118 Clayton Tonnemaker	25.00	11.00
❑ 119 Walt Schlinkman	25.00	11.00
❑ 120 Billy Grimes	25.00	11.00
❑ 121 George Ratterman RC	30.00	13.50
❑ 122 Bob Mann	25.00	11.00
❑ 123 Buddy Young RC	40.00	18.00
❑ 124 Jack Zilly	25.00	11.00
❑ 125 Tom Kalmanir	25.00	11.00
❑ 126 Frank Sinkovitz	25.00	11.00
❑ 127 Elbert Nickel	30.00	13.50
❑ 128 Jim Finks RC	50.00	22.00
❑ 129 Charley Trippi	60.00	27.00
❑ 130 Tom Wham	25.00	11.00
❑ 131 Ventan Yablonski	25.00	11.00
❑ 132 Chuck Bednarik	100.00	45.00
❑ 133 Joe Muha	25.00	11.00
❑ 134 Pete Pihos	60.00	27.00
❑ 135 Washington Serini	25.00	11.00
❑ 136 George Gulyanics	25.00	11.00
❑ 137 Ken Kavanaugh	30.00	13.50
❑ 138 Howie Livingston	25.00	11.00
❑ 139 Joe Tereshinski	25.00	11.00
❑ 140 Jim White	25.00	11.00
❑ 141 Gene Roberts	25.00	11.00
❑ 142 Bill Swiacki	30.00	13.50
❑ 143 Norm Standlee	25.00	11.00
❑ 144 Knox Ramsey RC !	100.00	25.00

1951 Bowman

	NRMT	VG-E
COMPLETE SET (144)	3500.00	1600.00
COMMON CARD (1-144)	20.00	9.00
SEMISTARS	25.00	11.00
UNLISTED STARS	35.00	16.00
CARDS PRICED IN NM CONDITION		

Card	NRMT	VG-E
❑ 1 Weldon Humble RC !	75.00	19.00
❑ 2 Otto Graham	200.00	90.00
❑ 3 Mac Speedie	35.00	16.00
❑ 4 Norm Van Brocklin RC	275.00	125.00
❑ 5 Woodley Lewis RC	25.00	11.00
❑ 6 Tom Fears	50.00	22.00
❑ 7 George Musacco	20.00	9.00
❑ 8 George Taliaferro	25.00	11.00
❑ 9 Barney Poole	20.00	9.00
❑ 10 Steve Van Buren	60.00	27.00
❑ 11 Whitey Wistert	25.00	11.00
❑ 12 Chuck Bednarik	80.00	36.00
❑ 13 Bulldog Turner	50.00	22.00
❑ 14 Bob Williams	20.00	9.00
❑ 15 John Lujack	60.00	27.00
❑ 16 Roy Rebel Steiner	20.00	9.00
❑ 17 Jug Girard	25.00	11.00
❑ 18 Bill Neal	20.00	9.00
❑ 19 Travis Tidwell	20.00	9.00
❑ 20 Tom Landry RC	525.00	240.00
❑ 21 Arnie Weinmeister RC	60.00	27.00
❑ 22 Joe Geri	20.00	9.00
❑ 23 Bill Walsh RC	25.00	11.00
❑ 24 Fran Rogel	20.00	9.00
❑ 25 Doak Walker	60.00	27.00
❑ 26 Leon Hart	35.00	16.00
❑ 27 Thurman McGraw	20.00	9.00
❑ 28 Buster Ramsey	20.00	9.00
❑ 29 Frank Tripucka	35.00	16.00
❑ 30 Don Paul	20.00	9.00
❑ 31 Alex Loyd	20.00	9.00
❑ 32 Y.A. Tittle	135.00	60.00
❑ 33 Verl Lillywhite	20.00	9.00
❑ 34 Sammy Baugh	175.00	80.00
❑ 35 Chuck Drazenovich	20.00	9.00
❑ 36 Bob Goode	20.00	9.00
❑ 37 Horace Gillom	20.00	9.00
❑ 38 Lou Rymkus	25.00	11.00
❑ 39 Ken Carpenter	20.00	9.00
❑ 40 Bob Waterfield	75.00	34.00
❑ 41 Vitamin Smith RC	25.00	11.00
❑ 42 Glenn Army Davis	60.00	27.00
❑ 43 Dan Edwards	20.00	9.00
❑ 44 John Rauch	20.00	9.00
❑ 45 Zollie Toth	20.00	9.00
❑ 46 Pete Pihos	60.00	27.00
❑ 47 Russ Craft	20.00	9.00
❑ 48 Walter Barnes	20.00	9.00
❑ 49 Fred Morrison	20.00	9.00
❑ 50 Ray Bray	20.00	9.00
❑ 51 Ed Sprinkle RC	25.00	11.00
❑ 52 Floyd Reid	20.00	9.00
❑ 53 Billy Grimes	20.00	9.00
❑ 54 Ted Fritsch Sr.	25.00	11.00
❑ 55 Al DeRogatis	25.00	11.00
❑ 56 Charley Conerly	70.00	32.00
❑ 57 Jon Baker	20.00	9.00
❑ 58 Tom McWilliams	20.00	9.00
❑ 59 Jerry Shipkey	20.00	9.00
❑ 60 Lynn Chandnois RC	25.00	11.00
❑ 61 Don Doll	20.00	9.00
❑ 62 Lou Creekmur	45.00	20.00
❑ 63 Bob Hoernschemeyer	25.00	11.00
❑ 64 Tom Wham	20.00	9.00
❑ 65 Bill Fischer	20.00	9.00
❑ 66 Robert Nussbaumer	20.00	9.00
❑ 67 Gordy Soltau RC	20.00	9.00
❑ 68 Visco Grgich	20.00	9.00
❑ 69 John Strzykalski RC	20.00	9.00
❑ 70 Pete Stout	20.00	9.00
❑ 71 Paul Lipscomb	20.00	9.00
❑ 72 Harry Gilmer	35.00	16.00
❑ 73 Dante Lavelli	50.00	22.00
❑ 74 Dub Jones	25.00	11.00
❑ 75 Lou Groza	75.00	34.00
❑ 76 Elroy Hirsch	75.00	34.00
❑ 77 Tom Kalmanir	20.00	9.00
❑ 78 Jack Zilly	20.00	9.00
❑ 79 Bruce Alford	20.00	9.00
❑ 80 Art Weiner	20.00	9.00
❑ 81 Brad Ecklund	20.00	9.00
❑ 82 Bosh Pritchard	20.00	9.00
❑ 83 John Green	20.00	9.00
❑ 84 Ebert Van Buren	20.00	9.00
❑ 85 Julie Rykovich	20.00	9.00
❑ 86 Fred Davis	20.00	9.00
❑ 87 John Hoffman	20.00	9.00
❑ 88 Tobin Rote	25.00	11.00
❑ 89 Paul Burris	20.00	9.00
❑ 90 Tony Canadeo	45.00	20.00
❑ 91 Emlen Tunnell RC	100.00	45.00
❑ 92 Otto Schnellbacher RC	20.00	9.00
❑ 93 Ray Poole	20.00	9.00
❑ 94 Darrell Hogan	20.00	9.00
❑ 95 Frank Sinkovitz	20.00	9.00
❑ 96 Ernie Stautner	75.00	34.00
❑ 97 Elmer Bud Angsman	20.00	9.00
❑ 98 Jack Jennings	20.00	9.00
❑ 99 Jerry Groom	20.00	9.00
❑ 100 John Prchlik	20.00	9.00
❑ 101 J. Robert Smith	20.00	9.00
❑ 102 Bobby Layne	135.00	60.00
❑ 103 Frankie Albert	35.00	16.00
❑ 104 Gail Bruce	20.00	9.00
❑ 105 Joe Perry	70.00	32.00
❑ 106 Leon Heath	20.00	9.00
❑ 107 Ed Quirk	20.00	9.00
❑ 108 Hugh Taylor	25.00	11.00
❑ 109 Marion Motley	100.00	45.00
❑ 110 Tony Adamle	20.00	9.00
❑ 111 Alex Agase	25.00	11.00
❑ 112 Tank Younger	35.00	16.00
❑ 113 Bob Boyd	20.00	9.00
❑ 114 Jerry Williams	20.00	9.00
❑ 115 Joe Golding	20.00	9.00
❑ 116 Sherman Howard	20.00	9.00
❑ 117 John Wozniak	20.00	9.00
❑ 118 Frank Reagan	20.00	9.00
❑ 119 Vic Sears	20.00	9.00
❑ 120 Clyde Scott	20.00	9.00
❑ 121 George Gulyanics	20.00	9.00
❑ 122 Bill Wightkin	20.00	9.00
❑ 123 Chuck Hunsinger	20.00	9.00
❑ 124 Jack Cloud	20.00	9.00
❑ 125 Abner Wimberly	20.00	9.00
❑ 126 Dick Wildung	20.00	9.00
❑ 127 Eddie Price	20.00	9.00
❑ 128 Joe Scott	20.00	9.00
❑ 129 Jerry Nuzum	20.00	9.00
❑ 130 Jim Finks	35.00	16.00
❑ 131 Bob Gage	20.00	9.00
❑ 132 Bill Swiacki	25.00	11.00
❑ 133 Joe Watson	20.00	9.00
❑ 134 Ollie Cline	20.00	9.00
❑ 135 Jack Lininger	20.00	9.00
❑ 136 Fran Polsfoot	20.00	9.00
❑ 137 Charley Trippi	45.00	20.00
❑ 138 Ventan Yablonski	20.00	9.00
❑ 139 Emil Sitko	20.00	9.00
❑ 140 Leo Nomellini	55.00	25.00
❑ 141 Norm Standlee	20.00	9.00
❑ 142 Eddie Saenz	20.00	9.00
❑ 143 Al Demao	20.00	9.00
❑ 144 Bill Dudley	150.00	38.00
❑ NNO Johnny Lujack Proof	300.00	135.00
❑ NNO Darrell Hogan Proof	125.00	55.00
❑ NNO Bob Gage Proof	125.00	55.00

1952 Bowman Large

	NRMT	VG-E
COMPLETE SET (144)	12500.00	5600.00
COMMON CARD (1-72)	35.00	16.00
SEMISTARS 1-72	45.00	20.00
UNLISTED STARS 1-72	50.00	22.00
COMMON CARD (73-144)	40.00	18.00
SEMISTARS 73-144	50.00	22.00
UNLISTED STARS 73-144	60.00	27.00
SP (9/54/55/64)	75.00	34.00
SP (91/109/118/136)	100.00	45.00
SP (73/81/90/100/117)	150.00	70.00
CARDS PRICED IN NM CONDITION !		

Card	NRMT	VG-E
❑ 1 Norm Van Brocklin	500.00	125.00
❑ 2 Otto Graham	300.00	135.00

❑ 3 Doak Walker 75.00 34.00
❑ 4 Steve Owen CO RC 75.00 34.00
❑ 5 Frankie Albert 50.00 22.00
❑ 6 Laurie Niemi 35.00 16.00
❑ 7 Chuck Hunsinger........... 35.00 16.00
❑ 8 Ed Modzelewski 50.00 22.00
❑ 9 Joe Spencer SP 75.00 34.00
❑ 10 Chuck Bednarik SP.... 300.00 135.00
❑ 11 Barney Poole............... 35.00 16.00
❑ 12 Charley Trippi 75.00 34.00
❑ 13 Tom Fears.................. 75.00 34.00
❑ 14 Paul Brown CO RC 250.00 110.00
❑ 15 Leon Hart 50.00 22.00
❑ 16 Frank Gifford RC 500.00 220.00
❑ 17 Y.A. Tittle................... 275.00 125.00
❑ 18 Charlie Justice SP...... 175.00 80.00
❑ 19 George Connor SP 175.00 80.00
❑ 20 Lynn Chandnois 45.00 20.00
❑ 21 Billy Howton RC 50.00 22.00
❑ 22 Kenneth Snyder 35.00 16.00
❑ 23 Gino Marchetti RC...... 225.00 100.00
❑ 24 John Karras.................. 35.00 16.00
❑ 25 Tank Younger 50.00 22.00
❑ 26 Tommy Thompson LB.. 35.00 16.00
❑ 27 Bob Miller SP RC 300.00 135.00
❑ 28 Kyle Rote RC SP........ 175.00 80.00
❑ 29 Hugh McElhenny RC.. 250.00 110.00
❑ 30 Sammy Baugh........... 350.00 160.00
❑ 31 Jim Dooley RC 45.00 20.00
❑ 32 Ray Mathews 35.00 16.00
❑ 33 Fred Cone.................. 35.00 16.00
❑ 34 Al Pollard..................... 35.00 16.00
❑ 35 Brad Ecklund............... 35.00 16.00
❑ 36 John Lee Hancock SP RC 350.00160.00
❑ 37 Elroy Hirsch SP.......... 200.00 90.00
❑ 38 Keever Jankovich 35.00 16.00
❑ 39 Emlen Tunnell 75.00 34.00
❑ 40 Steve Dowden............. 35.00 16.00
❑ 41 Claude Hipps............... 35.00 16.00
❑ 42 Norm Standlee 35.00 16.00
❑ 43 Dick Todd CO 35.00 16.00
❑ 44 Babe Parilli 50.00 22.00
❑ 45 Steve Van Buren SP .. 300.00 135.00
❑ 46 Art Donovan RC SP .. 350.00 160.00
❑ 47 Bill Fischer.................... 35.00 16.00
❑ 48 George Halas CO RC 275.00 125.00
❑ 49 Jerrell Price 35.00 16.00
❑ 50 John Sandusky RC 35.00 16.00
❑ 51 Ray Beck...................... 35.00 16.00
❑ 52 Jim Martin 45.00 20.00
❑ 53 Joe Bach CO UER 35.00 16.00
(Misspelled Back)
❑ 54 Glen Christian SP 75.00 34.00
❑ 55 Andy Davis SP 75.00 34.00
❑ 56 Tobin Rote.................... 45.00 20.00
❑ 57 Wayne Millner CO RC.. 90.00 40.00
❑ 58 Zollie Toth 35.00 16.00
❑ 59 Jack Jennings 35.00 16.00
❑ 60 Bill McColl 35.00 16.00
❑ 61 Les Richter RC 45.00 20.00
❑ 62 Walt Michaels RC 45.00 20.00
❑ 63 Charley Conerly SP.... 500.00 220.00
❑ 64 Howard Hartley SP 75.00 34.00
❑ 65 Jerome Smith 35.00 16.00
❑ 66 James Clark 35.00 16.00
❑ 67 Dick Logan 35.00 16.00
❑ 68 Wayne Robinson.......... 35.00 16.00
❑ 69 James Hammond 35.00 16.00
❑ 70 Gene Schroeder 35.00 16.00
❑ 71 Tex Coulter 45.00 20.00
❑ 72 John Schweder SP RC 525.00 240.00
❑ 73 Vitamin Smith SP 150.00 70.00
❑ 74 Joe Campanella RC 40.00 18.00
❑ 75 Joe Kuharich CO RC.... 50.00 22.00
❑ 76 Herman Clark 40.00 18.00
❑ 77 Dan Edwards............... 40.00 18.00
❑ 78 Bobby Layne............... 250.00 110.00
❑ 79 Bob Hoernschemeyer .. 50.00 22.00
❑ 80 John Carr Blount.......... 40.00 18.00
❑ 81 John Kastan RC SP .. 150.00 70.00
❑ 82 Harry Minarik RC SP.. 150.00 70.00
❑ 83 Joe Perry.................. 100.00 45.00
❑ 84 Ray(Buddy) Parker CO RC 50.00 22.00
❑ 85 Andy Robustelli RC 200.00 90.00
❑ 86 Dub Jones.................... 50.00 22.00
❑ 87 Mal Cook...................... 40.00 18.00
❑ 88 Billy Stone 40.00 18.00
❑ 89 George Taliaferro 50.00 22.00
❑ 90 Thomas Johnson RC SP 150.00 70.00
❑ 91 Leon Heath SP 100.00 45.00
❑ 92 Pete Pihos.................... 90.00 40.00
❑ 93 Fred Benners 40.00 18.00
❑ 94 George Tarasovic 40.00 18.00
❑ 95 Lawr. (Buck) Shaw CO RC 40.00 18.00
❑ 96 Bill Wightkin.................. 40.00 18.00
❑ 97 John Wozniak 40.00 18.00
❑ 98 Bobby Dillon RC 50.00 22.00
❑ 99 Joe Stydahar CO SP RC 650.00 300.00
❑ 100 Dick Alban RC SP.... 150.00 70.00
❑ 101 Arnie Weinmeister...... 60.00 27.00
❑ 102 Bobby Cross 40.00 18.00
❑ 103 Don Paul 40.00 18.00
❑ 104 Buddy Young............. 60.00 27.00
❑ 105 Lou Groza 100.00 45.00
❑ 106 Ray Pelfrey 40.00 18.00
❑ 107 Maurice Nipp............. 40.00 18.00
❑ 108 Hubert Johnston SP RC 650.00 300.00
❑ 109 Volney Quinlan RC SP 100.00 45.00
❑ 110 Jack Simmons........... 40.00 18.00
❑ 111 George Ratterman 50.00 22.00
❑ 112 John Badaczewski 40.00 18.00
❑ 113 Bill Reichardt............. 40.00 18.00
❑ 114 Art Weiner.................. 40.00 18.00
❑ 115 Keith Flowers 40.00 18.00
❑ 116 Russ Craft.................. 40.00 18.00
❑ 117 Jim O'Donahue RC SP 150.00 70.00
❑ 118 Darrell Hogan SP 100.00 45.00
❑ 119 Frank Ziegler............. 40.00 18.00
❑ 120 Deacon Dan Towler .. 60.00 27.00
❑ 121 Fred Williams 40.00 18.00
❑ 122 Jimmy Phelan CO 40.00 18.00
❑ 123 Eddie Price 40.00 18.00
❑ 124 Chet Ostrowski 40.00 18.00
❑ 125 Leo Nomellini 100.00 45.00
❑ 126 Steve Romanik SP RC 300.00 135.00
❑ 127 Ollie Matson RC SP 300.00 135.00
❑ 128 Dante Lavelli 90.00 40.00
❑ 129 Jack Christiansen RC 150.00 70.00
❑ 130 Dom Moselle 40.00 18.00
❑ 131 John Rapacz 40.00 18.00
❑ 132 Chuck Ortmann UER 40.00 18.00
(Avg. gain 9.4,
should be 4.8)
❑ 133 Bob Williams 40.00 18.00
❑ 134 Chuck Ulrich 40.00 18.00
❑ 135 Gene Ronzani CO SP RC 650.00 300.00
❑ 136 Bert Rechichar SP.... 100.00 45.00
❑ 137 Bob Waterfield.......... 125.00 55.00
❑ 138 Bobby Walston RC 50.00 22.00
❑ 139 Jerry Shipkey 40.00 18.00
❑ 140 Yale Lary RC............ 175.00 80.00
❑ 141 Gordy Soltau 40.00 18.00
❑ 142 Tom Landry............. 600.00 275.00
❑ 143 John Papit.................. 40.00 18.00
❑ 144 Jim Lansford SP RC 3000.00 750.00

1952 Bowman Small

	NRMT	VG-E
COMPLETE SET (144)	5000.00	2200.00
COMMON CARD (1-72)	25.00	11.00
SEMISTARS 1-72..................	30.00	13.50
UNLISTED STARS 1-72.........	35.00	16.00
COMMON CARD (73-144)......	30.00	13.50
SEMISTARS 73-144................	35.00	16.00
UNLISTED STARS 73-144......	40.00	18.00

CARDS PRICED IN NM CONDITION

❑ 1 Norm Van Brocklin 300.00 75.00
❑ 2 Otto Graham 175.00 80.00
❑ 3 Doak Walker 60.00 27.00
❑ 4 Steve Owen CO RC 60.00 27.00
❑ 5 Frankie Albert 35.00 16.00
❑ 6 Laurie Niemi 25.00 11.00
❑ 7 Chuck Hunsinger........... 25.00 11.00
❑ 8 Ed Modzelewski 30.00 13.50
❑ 9 Joe Spencer 25.00 11.00
❑ 10 Chuck Bednarik........... 75.00 34.00
❑ 11 Barney Poole............... 25.00 11.00
❑ 12 Charley Trippi 60.00 27.00
❑ 13 Tom Fears.................. 60.00 27.00
❑ 14 Paul Brown CO RC 150.00 70.00
❑ 15 Leon Hart 35.00 16.00
❑ 16 Frank Gifford RC 400.00 180.00
❑ 17 Y.A. Tittle................... 125.00 55.00
❑ 18 Charlie Justice............. 45.00 20.00
❑ 19 George Connor 35.00 16.00
❑ 20 Lynn Chandnois 25.00 11.00
❑ 21 Billy Howton RC 40.00 18.00
❑ 22 Kenneth Snyder 25.00 11.00
❑ 23 Gino Marchetti RC...... 125.00 55.00
❑ 24 John Karras.................. 25.00 11.00
❑ 25 Tank Younger 35.00 16.00
❑ 26 Tommy Thompson 25.00 11.00
❑ 27 Bob Miller 25.00 11.00
❑ 28 Kyle Rote RC 50.00 22.00
❑ 29 Hugh McElhenny RC.. 175.00 80.00
❑ 30 Sammy Baugh........... 250.00 110.00
❑ 31 Jim Dooley RC 30.00 13.50
❑ 32 Ray Mathews 25.00 11.00
❑ 33 Fred Cone.................. 25.00 11.00
❑ 34 Al Pollard..................... 25.00 11.00
❑ 35 Brad Ecklund............... 25.00 11.00
❑ 36 John Lee Hancock 25.00 11.00
❑ 37 Elroy Hirsch................. 60.00 27.00
❑ 38 Keever Jankovich 25.00 11.00
❑ 39 Emlen Tunnell 50.00 22.00
❑ 40 Steve Dowden............. 25.00 11.00
❑ 41 Claude Hipps............... 25.00 11.00
❑ 42 Norm Standlee 25.00 11.00
❑ 43 Dick Todd CO 25.00 11.00
❑ 44 Babe Parilli 35.00 16.00
❑ 45 Steve Van Buren.......... 75.00 34.00
❑ 46 Art Donovan RC 175.00 80.00
❑ 47 Bill Fischer.................... 25.00 11.00
❑ 48 George Halas CO RC 175.00 80.00
❑ 49 Jerrell Price 25.00 11.00
❑ 50 John Sandusky RC 25.00 11.00
❑ 51 Ray Beck...................... 25.00 11.00
❑ 52 Jim Martin 30.00 13.50
❑ 53 Joe Bach CO UER 25.00 11.00
(Misspelled Back)
❑ 54 Glen Christian 25.00 11.00
❑ 55 Andy Davis 25.00 11.00
❑ 56 Tobin Rote................... 30.00 13.50
❑ 57 Wayne Millner CO RC.. 50.00 22.00
❑ 58 Zollie Toth 25.00 11.00
❑ 59 Jack Jennings 25.00 11.00
❑ 60 Bill McColl 25.00 11.00
❑ 61 Les Richter RC 30.00 13.50
❑ 62 Walt Michaels RC 30.00 13.50
❑ 63 Charley Conerly 60.00 27.00
❑ 64 Howard Hartley 25.00 11.00
❑ 65 Jerome Smith 25.00 11.00
❑ 66 James Clark 25.00 11.00
❑ 67 Dick Logan 25.00 11.00
❑ 68 Wayne Robinson.......... 25.00 11.00
❑ 69 James Hammond 25.00 11.00
❑ 70 Gene Schroeder 25.00 11.00
❑ 71 Tex Coulter 30.00 13.50
❑ 72 John Schweder 25.00 11.00
❑ 73 Vitamin Smith 35.00 16.00
❑ 74 Joe Campanella RC 30.00 13.50
❑ 75 Joe Kuharich CO RC.... 35.00 16.00
❑ 76 Herman Clark 30.00 13.50
❑ 77 Dan Edwards............... 30.00 13.50
❑ 78 Bobby Layne.............. 150.00 70.00
❑ 79 Bob Hoernschemeyer .. 35.00 16.00
❑ 80 John Carr Blount.......... 30.00 13.50

❑ 81 John Kastan RC	30.00	13.50
❑ 82 Harry Minarik	30.00	13.50
❑ 83 Joe Perry	75.00	34.00
❑ 84 Ray(Buddy) Parker CO RC	35.00	16.00
❑ 85 Andy Robustelli RC	125.00	55.00
❑ 86 Dub Jones	35.00	16.00
❑ 87 Mal Cook	30.00	13.50
❑ 88 Billy Stone	30.00	13.50
❑ 89 George Taliaferro	35.00	16.00
❑ 90 Thomas Johnson RC	30.00	13.50
❑ 91 Leon Heath	30.00	13.50
❑ 92 Pete Pihos	50.00	22.00
❑ 93 Fred Benners	30.00	13.50
❑ 94 George Tarasovic	30.00	13.50
❑ 95 Lawr. (Buck) Shaw CO RC	30.00	13.50
❑ 96 Bill Wightkin	30.00	13.50
❑ 97 John Wozniak	30.00	13.50
❑ 98 Bobby Dillon RC	35.00	16.00
❑ 99 Joe Stydahar CO RC	45.00	20.00
❑ 100 Dick Alban RC	30.00	13.50
❑ 101 Arnie Weinmeister	40.00	18.00
❑ 102 Bobby Cross	30.00	13.50
❑ 103 Don Paul	30.00	13.50
❑ 104 Buddy Young	40.00	18.00
❑ 105 Lou Groza	65.00	29.00
❑ 106 Ray Pelfrey	30.00	13.50
❑ 107 Maurice Nipp	30.00	13.50
❑ 108 Hubert Johnston	30.00	13.50
❑ 109 Volney Quinlan RC	30.00	13.50
❑ 110 Jack Simmons	30.00	13.50
❑ 111 George Ratterman	35.00	16.00
❑ 112 John Badaczewski	30.00	13.50
❑ 113 Bill Reichardt	30.00	13.50
❑ 114 Art Weiner	30.00	13.50
❑ 115 Keith Flowers	30.00	13.50
❑ 116 Russ Craft	30.00	13.50
❑ 117 Jim O'Donahue RC	30.00	13.50
❑ 118 Darrell Hogan	30.00	13.50
❑ 119 Frank Ziegler	30.00	13.50
❑ 120 Deacon Dan Towler	40.00	18.00
❑ 121 Fred Williams	30.00	13.50
❑ 122 Jimmy Phelan CO	30.00	13.50
❑ 123 Eddie Price	30.00	13.50
❑ 124 Chet Ostrowski	30.00	13.50
❑ 125 Leo Nomellini	75.00	34.00
❑ 126 Steve Romanik	30.00	13.50
❑ 127 Ollie Matson RC	125.00	55.00
❑ 128 Dante Lavelli	60.00	27.00
❑ 129 Jack Christiansen RC	80.00	36.00
❑ 130 Dom Moselle	30.00	13.50
❑ 131 John Rapacz	30.00	13.50
❑ 132 Chuck Ortmann UER (Avg. gain 9.4, should be 4.8)	30.00	13.50
❑ 133 Bob Williams	30.00	13.50
❑ 134 Chuck Ulrich	30.00	13.50
❑ 135 Gene Ronzani CO RC	30.00	13.50
❑ 136 Bert Rechichar	35.00	16.00
❑ 137 Bob Waterfield	75.00	34.00
❑ 138 Bobby Walston RC	35.00	16.00
❑ 139 Jerry Shipkey	30.00	13.50
❑ 140 Yale Lary RC	80.00	36.00
❑ 141 Gordy Soltau	30.00	13.50
❑ 142 Tom Landry	400.00	180.00
❑ 143 John Papit	30.00	13.50
❑ 144 Jim Lansford RC !	160.00	40.00

1953 Bowman

	NRMT	VG-E
COMPLETE SET (96)	3400.00	1500.00
COMMON CARD (1-96)	30.00	13.50
SEMISTARS	35.00	16.00
UNLISTED STARS	40.00	18.00
SP (39/41/44/45/47/49)	45.00	20.00
SP (54/55/57/58/64/66)	45.00	20.00
SP (67/68/70/75/77/81/87)	45.00	20.00
CARDS PRICED IN NM CONDITION !		

❑ 1 Eddie LeBaron RC !	120.00	30.00
❑ 2 John Dottley	30.00	13.50
❑ 3 Babe Parilli	35.00	16.00
❑ 4 Bucko Kilroy	35.00	16.00
❑ 5 Joe Tereshinski	30.00	13.50
❑ 6 Doak Walker	60.00	27.00
❑ 7 Fran Polsfoot	30.00	13.50
❑ 8 Sisto Averno	30.00	13.50
❑ 9 Marion Motley	75.00	34.00
❑ 10 Pat Brady	30.00	13.50
❑ 11 Norm Van Brocklin	125.00	55.00
❑ 12 Bill McColl	30.00	13.50
❑ 13 Jerry Groom	30.00	13.50
❑ 14 Al Pollard	30.00	13.50
❑ 15 Dante Lavelli	50.00	22.00
❑ 16 Eddie Price	30.00	13.50
❑ 17 Charley Trippi	50.00	22.00
❑ 18 Elbert Nickel	35.00	16.00
❑ 19 George Taliaferro	35.00	16.00
❑ 20 Charley Conerly	60.00	27.00
❑ 21 Bobby Layne	125.00	55.00
❑ 22 Elroy Hirsch	75.00	34.00
❑ 23 Jim Finks	40.00	18.00
❑ 24 Chuck Bednarik	75.00	34.00
❑ 25 Kyle Rote	40.00	18.00
❑ 26 Otto Graham	175.00	80.00
❑ 27 Harry Gilmer	35.00	16.00
❑ 28 Tobin Rote	35.00	16.00
❑ 29 Billy Stone	30.00	13.50
❑ 30 Buddy Young	40.00	18.00
❑ 31 Leon Hart	40.00	18.00
❑ 32 Hugh McElhenny	75.00	34.00
❑ 33 Dale Samuels	30.00	13.50
❑ 34 Lou Creekmur	50.00	22.00
❑ 35 Tom Catlin	30.00	13.50
❑ 36 Tom Fears	60.00	27.00
❑ 37 George Connor	40.00	18.00
❑ 38 Bill Walsh C	30.00	13.50
❑ 39 Leo Sanford SP	45.00	20.00
❑ 40 Horace Gillom	30.00	13.50
❑ 41 John Schweder SP	45.00	20.00
❑ 42 Tom O'Connell	30.00	13.50
❑ 43 Frank Gifford SP	450.00	200.00
❑ 44 Frank Continetti SP	45.00	20.00
❑ 45 John Olszewski SP	45.00	20.00
❑ 46 Dub Jones	35.00	16.00
❑ 47 Don Paul SP	45.00	20.00
❑ 48 Gerald Weatherly	30.00	13.50
❑ 49 Fred Bruney SP	45.00	20.00
❑ 50 Jack Scarbath	30.00	13.50
❑ 51 John Karras	30.00	13.50
❑ 52 Al Conway	30.00	13.50
❑ 53 Emlen Tunnell SP	125.00	55.00
❑ 54 Gern Nagler SP	45.00	20.00
❑ 55 Kenneth Snyder SP	45.00	20.00
❑ 56 Y.A. Tittle	125.00	55.00
❑ 57 John Rapacz SP	45.00	20.00
❑ 58 Harley Sewell SP	45.00	20.00
❑ 59 Don Bingham	30.00	13.50
❑ 60 Darrell Hogan	30.00	13.50
❑ 61 Tony Curcillo	30.00	13.50
❑ 62 Ray Renfro RC SP	50.00	22.00
❑ 63 Leon Heath	30.00	13.50
❑ 64 Tex Coulter SP	45.00	20.00
❑ 65 Dewayne Douglas	30.00	13.50
❑ 66 J. Robert Smith SP	45.00	20.00
❑ 67 Bob McChesney SP	45.00	20.00
❑ 68 Dick Alban SP	45.00	20.00
❑ 69 Andy Kozar	30.00	13.50
❑ 70 Merwin Hodel SP	45.00	20.00
❑ 71 Thurman McGraw	30.00	13.50
❑ 72 Cliff Anderson	30.00	13.50
❑ 73 Pete Pihos	50.00	22.00
❑ 74 Julie Rykovich	30.00	13.50
❑ 75 John Kreamcheck SP	45.00	20.00
❑ 76 Lynn Chandnois	35.00	16.00
❑ 77 Cloyce Box SP	45.00	20.00
❑ 78 Ray Mathews	30.00	13.50
❑ 79 Bobby Walston	35.00	16.00
❑ 80 Jim Dooley	30.00	13.50
❑ 81 Pat Harder SP	45.00	20.00
❑ 82 Jerry Shipkey	30.00	13.50
❑ 83 Bobby Thomason RC	30.00	13.50
❑ 84 Hugh Taylor	35.00	16.00
❑ 85 George Ratterman	35.00	16.00
❑ 86 Don Stonesifer	30.00	13.50
❑ 87 John Williams SP	45.00	20.00
❑ 88 Leo Nomellini	50.00	22.00
❑ 89 Frank Ziegler	30.00	13.50
❑ 90 Don Paul UER (19th in punt returns, should be 9th) Chicago Cardinals	30.00	13.50
❑ 91 Tom Dublinski	30.00	13.50
❑ 92 Ken Carpenter	30.00	13.50
❑ 93 Ted Marchibroda RC	40.00	18.00
❑ 94 Chuck Drazenovich	30.00	13.50
❑ 95 Lou Groza SP	125.00	55.00
❑ 96 William Cross SP RC	100.00	25.00

1954 Bowman

	NRMT	VG-E
COMPLETE SET (128)	1700.00	750.00
COMMON CARD (1-64)	5.00	2.20
SEMISTARS (1-64/97-128)	8.00	3.60
UNLISTED STARS	15.00	6.75
COMMON SP (65-96)	25.00	11.00
SEMISTARS SP (65-96)	30.00	13.50
COMMON CARD (97-128)	5.00	2.20
CARDS PRICED IN NM CONDITION !		

❑ 1 Ray Mathews	30.00	7.50
❑ 2 John Huzvar	5.00	2.20
❑ 3 Jack Scarbath	5.00	2.20
❑ 4 Doug Atkins RC	50.00	22.00
❑ 5 Bill Stits	5.00	2.20
❑ 6 Joe Perry	30.00	13.50
❑ 7 Kyle Rote	15.00	6.75
❑ 8 Norm Van Brocklin	50.00	22.00
❑ 9 Pete Pihos	20.00	9.00
❑ 10 Babe Parilli	8.00	3.60
❑ 11 Zeke Bratkowski RC	25.00	11.00
❑ 12 Ollie Matson	25.00	11.00
❑ 13 Pat Brady	5.00	2.20
❑ 14 Fred Enke	5.00	2.20
❑ 15 Harry Ulinski	5.00	2.20
❑ 16 Bob Garrett	5.00	2.20
❑ 17 Bill Bowman	5.00	2.20
❑ 18 Leo Rucka	5.00	2.20
❑ 19 John Cannady	5.00	2.20
❑ 20 Tom Fears	25.00	11.00
❑ 21 Norm Willey	5.00	2.20
❑ 22 Floyd Reid	5.00	2.20
❑ 23 George Blanda RC	175.00	80.00
❑ 24 Don Doheney	5.00	2.20
❑ 25 John Schweder	5.00	2.20
❑ 26 Bert Rechichar	5.00	2.20
❑ 27 Harry Dowda	5.00	2.20
❑ 28 John Sandusky	5.00	2.20
❑ 29 Les Bingaman RC	15.00	6.75
❑ 30 Joe Arenas	5.00	2.20
❑ 31 Ray Wietecha RC	5.00	2.20
❑ 32 Elroy Hirsch	30.00	13.50

- ❑ 33 Harold Giancanelli 5.00 2.20
- ❑ 34 Billy Howton 8.00 3.60
- ❑ 35 Fred Morrison 5.00 2.20
- ❑ 36 Bobby Cavazos 5.00 2.20
- ❑ 37 Darrell Hogan 5.00 2.20
- ❑ 38 Buddy Young 8.00 3.60
- ❑ 39 Charlie Justice 20.00 9.00
- ❑ 40 Otto Graham 75.00 34.00
- ❑ 41 Doak Walker 30.00 13.50
- ❑ 42 Y.A. Tittle 60.00 27.00
- ❑ 43 Buford Long 5.00 2.20
- ❑ 44 Volney Quinlan 5.00 2.20
- ❑ 45 Bobby Thomason 5.00 2.20
- ❑ 46 Fred Cone 5.00 2.20
- ❑ 47 Gerald Weatherly 5.00 2.20
- ❑ 48 Don Stonesifer 5.00 2.20
- ❑ 49 Lynn Chandnois 5.00 2.20
- ❑ 50 George Taliaferro 5.00 2.20
- ❑ 51 Dick Alban 5.00 2.20
- ❑ 52 Lou Groza 30.00 13.50
- ❑ 53 Bobby Layne 60.00 27.00
- ❑ 54 Hugh McElhenny 40.00 18.00
- ❑ 55 Frank Gifford UER 100.00 45.00 (Avg. gain 7.83, should be 3.1)
- ❑ 56 Leon McLaughlin 5.00 2.20
- ❑ 57 Chuck Bednarik 40.00 18.00
- ❑ 58 Art Hunter 5.00 2.20
- ❑ 59 Bill McColl 5.00 2.20
- ❑ 60 Charley Trippi 20.00 9.00
- ❑ 61 Jim Finks 15.00 6.75
- ❑ 62 Bill Lange 5.00 2.20
- ❑ 63 Laurie Niemi 5.00 2.20
- ❑ 64 Ray Renfro 8.00 3.60
- ❑ 65 Dick Chapman 25.00 11.00
- ❑ 66 Bob Hantla 25.00 11.00
- ❑ 67 Ralph Starkey 25.00 11.00
- ❑ 68 Don Paul 25.00 11.00
- ❑ 69 Kenneth Snyder 25.00 11.00
- ❑ 70 Tobin Rote 30.00 13.50
- ❑ 71 Art DeCarlo 25.00 11.00
- ❑ 72 Tom Keane 25.00 11.00
- ❑ 73 Hugh Taylor 30.00 13.50
- ❑ 74 Warren Lahr RC 25.00 11.00
- ❑ 75 Jim Neal 25.00 11.00
- ❑ 76 Leo Nomellini 60.00 27.00
- ❑ 77 Dick Yelvington 25.00 11.00
- ❑ 78 Les Richter 30.00 13.50
- ❑ 79 Bucko Kilroy 30.00 13.50
- ❑ 80 John Martinkovic 25.00 11.00
- ❑ 81 Dale Dodrill RC 25.00 11.00
- ❑ 82 Ken Jackson 25.00 11.00
- ❑ 83 Paul Lipscomb 25.00 11.00
- ❑ 84 John Bauer 25.00 11.00
- ❑ 85 Lou Creekmur 50.00 22.00
- ❑ 86 Eddie Price 25.00 11.00
- ❑ 87 Kenneth Farragut 25.00 11.00
- ❑ 88 Dave Hanner RC 30.00 13.50
- ❑ 89 Don Boll 25.00 11.00
- ❑ 90 Chet Hanulak 25.00 11.00
- ❑ 91 Thurman McGraw 25.00 11.00
- ❑ 92 Don Heinrich RC 30.00 13.50
- ❑ 93 Dan McKown 25.00 11.00
- ❑ 94 Bob Fleck 25.00 11.00
- ❑ 95 Jerry Hilgenberg 25.00 11.00
- ❑ 96 Bill Walsh 25.00 11.00
- ❑ 97A Tom Finnin ERR 60.00 27.00
- ❑ 97B Tom Finnan COR 8.00 3.60
- ❑ 98 Paul Barry 5.00 2.20
- ❑ 99 Chick Jagade 5.00 2.20
- ❑ 100 Jack Christiansen 20.00 9.00
- ❑ 101 Gordy Soltau 5.00 2.20
- ❑ 102 Emlen Tunnell 20.00 9.00
- ❑ 103 Stan West 5.00 2.20
- ❑ 104 Jerry Williams 5.00 2.20
- ❑ 105 Veryl Switzer 5.00 2.20
- ❑ 106 Billy Stone 5.00 2.20
- ❑ 107 Jerry Watford 5.00 2.20
- ❑ 108 Elbert Nickel 8.00 3.60
- ❑ 109 Ed Sharkey 5.00 2.20
- ❑ 110 Steve Meilinger 5.00 2.20
- ❑ 111 Dante Lavelli 20.00 9.00
- ❑ 112 Leon Hart 15.00 6.75
- ❑ 113 Charley Conerly 30.00 13.50
- ❑ 114 Richard Lemmon 5.00 2.20
- ❑ 115 Al Carmichael 5.00 2.20
- ❑ 116 George Connor 15.00 6.75
- ❑ 117 John Olszewski 5.00 2.20
- ❑ 118 Ernie Stautner 25.00 11.00
- ❑ 119 Ray Smith 5.00 2.20
- ❑ 120 Neil Worden 5.00 2.20
- ❑ 121 Jim Dooley 5.00 2.20
- ❑ 122 Arnold Galiffa 5.00 2.20
- ❑ 123 Kline Gilbert 5.00 2.20
- ❑ 124 Bob Hoernschemeyer 8.00 3.60
- ❑ 125 Wilford Whizzer White RC 15.00 6.75 (not the Supreme Court Justice)
- ❑ 126 Art Spinney 5.00 2.20
- ❑ 127 Joe Koch 5.00 2.20
- ❑ 128 John Lattner RC ! 80.00 20.00

1955 Bowman

	NRMT	VG-E
COMPLETE SET (160)	1600.00	700.00
COMMON CARD (1-64)	5.00	2.20
SEMISTARS 1-64	8.00	3.60
UNLISTED STARS 1-64	12.00	5.50
COMMON CARD (65-160)	8.00	3.60
SEMISTARS 65-160	12.00	5.50
UNLISTED STARS 65-160	15.00	6.75

CARDS PRICED IN NM CONDITION !

- ❑ 1 Doak Walker 60.00 15.00
- ❑ 2 Mike McCormack RC 30.00 13.50
- ❑ 3 John Olszewski 5.00 2.20
- ❑ 4 Dorne Dibble 5.00 2.20
- ❑ 5 Lindon Crow 5.00 2.20
- ❑ 6 Hugh Taylor UER 8.00 3.60 (First word in bio should be Bones)
- ❑ 7 Frank Gifford 75.00 34.00
- ❑ 8 Alan Ameche RC 30.00 13.50
- ❑ 9 Don Stonesifer 5.00 2.20
- ❑ 10 Pete Pihos 15.00 6.75
- ❑ 11 Bill Austin 5.00 2.20
- ❑ 12 Dick Alban 5.00 2.20
- ❑ 13 Bobby Walston 8.00 3.60
- ❑ 14 Len Ford RC 35.00 16.00
- ❑ 15 Jug Girard 5.00 2.20
- ❑ 16 Charley Conerly 25.00 11.00
- ❑ 17 Volney Peters 5.00 2.20
- ❑ 18 Max Boydston 5.00 2.20
- ❑ 19 Leon Hart 12.00 5.50
- ❑ 20 Bert Rechichar 5.00 2.20
- ❑ 21 Lee Riley 5.00 2.20
- ❑ 22 Johnny Carson 5.00 2.20
- ❑ 23 Harry Thompson 5.00 2.20
- ❑ 24 Ray Wietecha 5.00 2.20
- ❑ 25 Ollie Matson 25.00 11.00
- ❑ 26 Eddie LeBaron 15.00 6.75
- ❑ 27 Jack Simmons 5.00 2.20
- ❑ 28 Jack Christiansen 15.00 6.75
- ❑ 29 Bucko Kilroy 8.00 3.60
- ❑ 30 Tom Keane 5.00 2.20
- ❑ 31 Dave Leggett 5.00 2.20
- ❑ 32 Norm Van Brocklin 35.00 16.00
- ❑ 33 Harlon Hill RC 8.00 3.60
- ❑ 34 Robert Haner 5.00 2.20
- ❑ 35 Veryl Switzer 5.00 2.20
- ❑ 36 Dick Stanfel RC 12.00 5.50
- ❑ 37 Lou Groza 25.00 11.00
- ❑ 38 Tank Younger 12.00 5.50
- ❑ 39 Dick Flanagan 5.00 2.20
- ❑ 40 Jim Dooley 5.00 2.20
- ❑ 41 Ray Collins 5.00 2.20
- ❑ 42 John Henry Johnson RC 40.00 18.00
- ❑ 43 Tom Fears 15.00 6.75
- ❑ 44 Joe Perry 25.00 11.00
- ❑ 45 Gene Brito RC 5.00 2.20
- ❑ 46 Bill Johnson 5.00 2.20
- ❑ 47 Deacon Dan Towler 12.00 5.50
- ❑ 48 Dick Moegle 8.00 3.60
- ❑ 49 Kline Gilbert 5.00 2.20
- ❑ 50 Les Gobel 5.00 2.20
- ❑ 51 Ray Krouse 5.00 2.20
- ❑ 52 Pat Summerall RC 75.00 34.00
- ❑ 53 Ed Brown RC 12.00 5.50
- ❑ 54 Lynn Chandnois 5.00 2.20
- ❑ 55 Joe Heap 5.00 2.20
- ❑ 56 John Hoffman 5.00 2.20
- ❑ 57 Howard Ferguson 5.00 2.20
- ❑ 58 Bobby Watkins 5.00 2.20
- ❑ 59 Charlie Ane 5.00 2.20
- ❑ 60 Ken MacAfee E RC 8.00 3.60
- ❑ 61 Ralph Guglielmi RC 8.00 3.60
- ❑ 62 George Blanda 60.00 27.00
- ❑ 63 Kenneth Snyder 5.00 2.20
- ❑ 64 Chet Ostrowski 5.00 2.20
- ❑ 65 Buddy Young 15.00 6.75
- ❑ 66 Gordy Soltau 8.00 3.60
- ❑ 67 Eddie Bell 8.00 3.60
- ❑ 68 Ben Agajanian RC 12.00 5.50
- ❑ 69 Tom Dahms 8.00 3.60
- ❑ 70 Jim Ringo RC 50.00 22.00
- ❑ 71 Bobby Layne 75.00 34.00
- ❑ 72 Y.A. Tittle 75.00 34.00
- ❑ 73 Bob Gaona 8.00 3.60
- ❑ 74 Tobin Rote 12.00 5.50
- ❑ 75 Hugh McElhenny 30.00 13.50
- ❑ 76 John Kreamcheck 8.00 3.60
- ❑ 77 Al Dorow 12.00 5.50
- ❑ 78 Bill Wade 15.00 6.75
- ❑ 79 Dale Dodrill 8.00 3.60
- ❑ 80 Chuck Drazenovich 8.00 3.60
- ❑ 81 Billy Wilson RC 12.00 5.50
- ❑ 82 Les Richter 12.00 5.50
- ❑ 83 Pat Brady 8.00 3.60
- ❑ 84 Bob Hoernschemeyer 12.00 5.50
- ❑ 85 Joe Arenas 8.00 3.60
- ❑ 86 Len Szafaryn UER 8.00 3.60 (Listed as Ben on front)
- ❑ 87 Rick Casares RC 20.00 9.00
- ❑ 88 Leon McLaughlin 8.00 3.60
- ❑ 89 Charley Toogood 8.00 3.60
- ❑ 90 Tom Bettis 8.00 3.60
- ❑ 91 John Sandusky 8.00 3.60
- ❑ 92 Bill Wightkin 8.00 3.60
- ❑ 93 Darrel Brewster 8.00 3.60
- ❑ 94 Marion Campbell 15.00 6.75
- ❑ 95 Floyd Reid 8.00 3.60
- ❑ 96 Chick Jagade 8.00 3.60
- ❑ 97 George Taliaferro 8.00 3.60
- ❑ 98 Carlton Massey 8.00 3.60
- ❑ 99 Fran Rogel 8.00 3.60
- ❑ 100 Alex Sandusky 8.00 3.60
- ❑ 101 Bob St. Clair RC 35.00 16.00
- ❑ 102 Al Carmichael 8.00 3.60
- ❑ 103 Carl Taseff RC 8.00 3.60
- ❑ 104 Leo Nomellini 25.00 11.00
- ❑ 105 Tom Scott 8.00 3.60
- ❑ 106 Ted Marchibroda 15.00 6.75
- ❑ 107 Art Spinney 8.00 3.60
- ❑ 108 Wayne Robinson 8.00 3.60
- ❑ 109 Jim Ricca 8.00 3.60
- ❑ 110 Lou Ferry 8.00 3.60
- ❑ 111 Roger Zatkoff 8.00 3.60
- ❑ 112 Lou Creekmur 15.00 6.75
- ❑ 113 Kenny Konz 8.00 3.60
- ❑ 114 Doug Eggers 8.00 3.60
- ❑ 115 Bobby Thomason 8.00 3.60
- ❑ 116 Bill McPeak 8.00 3.60
- ❑ 117 William Brown 8.00 3.60
- ❑ 118 Royce Womble 8.00 3.60
- ❑ 119 Frank Gatski RC 30.00 13.50
- ❑ 120 Jim Finks 15.00 6.75
- ❑ 121 Andy Robustelli 25.00 11.00
- ❑ 122 Bobby Dillon 8.00 3.60
- ❑ 123 Leo Sanford 8.00 3.60
- ❑ 124 Elbert Nickel 12.00 5.50

Card	MINT	NRMT
❑ 125 Wayne Hansen	8.00	3.60
❑ 126 Buck Lansford	8.00	3.60
❑ 127 Gern Nagler	8.00	3.60
❑ 128 Jim Salsbury	8.00	3.60
❑ 129 Dale Atkeson RC	8.00	3.60
❑ 130 John Schweder	8.00	3.60
❑ 131 Dave Hanner	12.00	5.50
❑ 132 Eddie Price	8.00	3.60
❑ 133 Vic Janowicz	20.00	9.00
❑ 134 Ernie Stautner	25.00	11.00
❑ 135 James Parmer	8.00	3.60
❑ 136 Emlen Tunnell UER (Misspelled Tunnel on card front)	20.00	9.00
❑ 137 Kyle Rote UER (Longest gain 1.8 yards, should be 18 yards)	15.00	6.75
❑ 138 Norm Willey	8.00	3.60
❑ 139 Charley Trippi	20.00	9.00
❑ 140 Billy Howton	12.00	5.50
❑ 141 Bobby Clatterbuck	8.00	3.60
❑ 142 Bob Boyd	8.00	3.60
❑ 143 Bob Toneff RC UER (name misspelled Toneoff)	12.00	5.50
❑ 144 Jerry Helluin	8.00	3.60
❑ 145 Adrian Burk	8.00	3.60
❑ 146 Walt Michaels	12.00	5.50
❑ 147 Zollie Toth	8.00	3.60
❑ 148 Frank Varrichione RC	8.00	3.60
❑ 149 Dick Bielski	8.00	3.60
❑ 150 George Ratterman	12.00	5.50
❑ 151 Mike Jarmoluk	8.00	3.60
❑ 152 Tom Landry	200.00	90.00
❑ 153 Ray Renfro	12.00	5.50
❑ 154 Zeke Bratkowski	12.00	5.50
❑ 155 Jerry Norton	8.00	3.60
❑ 156 Maurice Bassett	8.00	3.60
❑ 157 Volney Quinlan	8.00	3.60
❑ 158 Chuck Bednarik	30.00	13.50
❑ 159 Don Colo	8.00	3.60
❑ 160 L.G. Dupre RC !	40.00	10.00

1991 Bowman

	MINT	NRMT
COMPLETE SET (561)	12.00	5.50
COMP.FACT.SET (561)	15.00	6.75
COMMON CARD (1-561)	.04	.02
SEMISTARS	.10	.05
UNLISTED STARS	.25	.11

Card	MINT	NRMT
❑ 1 Jeff George RS	.25	.11
❑ 2 Richmond Webb RS	.04	.02
❑ 3 Emmitt Smith RS	1.00	.45
❑ 4 Mark Carrier DB RS UER (Chambers was rookie in '73, not '74)	.04	.02
❑ 5 Steve Christie RS	.04	.02
❑ 6 Keith Sims RS	.04	.02
❑ 7 Rob Moore RS UER (Yards misspelled as yarders on back)	.25	.11
❑ 8 Johnny Johnson RS	.04	.02
❑ 9 Eric Green RS	.04	.02
❑ 10 Ben Smith RS	.04	.02
❑ 11 Tory Epps RS	.04	.02
❑ 12 Andre Rison	.10	.05
❑ 13 Shawn Collins	.04	.02
❑ 14 Chris Hinton	.04	.02
❑ 15 Deion Sanders UER (Bio says he played for Georgia, College listed should be Florida State)	.40	.18
❑ 16 Darion Conner	.04	.02
❑ 17 Michael Haynes	.25	.11
❑ 18 Chris Miller	.10	.05
❑ 19 Jessie Tuggle	.04	.02
❑ 20 Scott Fulhage	.04	.02
❑ 21 Bill Fralic	.04	.02
❑ 22 Floyd Dixon	.04	.02
❑ 23 Oliver Barnett	.04	.02
❑ 24 Mike Rozier	.04	.02
❑ 25 Tory Epps	.04	.02
❑ 26 Tim Green	.04	.02
❑ 27 Steve Broussard	.04	.02
❑ 28 Bruce Pickens RC	.04	.02
❑ 29 Mike Pritchard RC	.25	.11
❑ 30 Andre Reed	.10	.05
❑ 31 Darryl Talley	.04	.02
❑ 32 Nate Odomes	.04	.02
❑ 33 Jamie Mueller	.04	.02
❑ 34 Leon Seals	.04	.02
❑ 35 Keith McKeller	.04	.02
❑ 36 Al Edwards	.04	.02
❑ 37 Butch Rolle	.04	.02
❑ 38 Jeff Wright RC	.04	.02
❑ 39 Will Wolford	.04	.02
❑ 40 James Williams	.04	.02
❑ 41 Kent Hull	.04	.02
❑ 42 James Lofton	.10	.05
❑ 43 Frank Reich	.10	.05
❑ 44 Bruce Smith	.25	.11
❑ 45 Thurman Thomas	.25	.11
❑ 46 Leonard Smith	.04	.02
❑ 47 Shane Conlan	.04	.02
❑ 48 Steve Tasker	.10	.05
❑ 49 Ray Bentley	.04	.02
❑ 50 Cornelius Bennett	.10	.05
❑ 51 Stan Thomas	.04	.02
❑ 52 Shaun Gayle	.04	.02
❑ 53 Wendell Davis	.04	.02
❑ 54 James Thornton	.04	.02
❑ 55 Mark Carrier DB	.10	.05
❑ 56 Richard Dent	.10	.05
❑ 57 Ron Morris	.04	.02
❑ 58 Mike Singletary	.10	.05
❑ 59 Jay Hilgenberg	.04	.02
❑ 60 Donnell Woolford	.04	.02
❑ 61 Jim Covert	.04	.02
❑ 62 Jim Harbaugh	.25	.11
❑ 63 Neal Anderson	.10	.05
❑ 64 Brad Muster	.04	.02
❑ 65 Kevin Butler	.04	.02
❑ 66 Trace Armstrong UER (Bio says 80 tackles in '90, stats say 82)	.04	.02
❑ 67 Ron Cox	.04	.02
❑ 68 Peter Tom Willis	.04	.02
❑ 69 Johnny Bailey	.04	.02
❑ 70 Mark Bortz UER (Bio has 6th round, but was 8th round)	.04	.02
❑ 71 Chris Zorich RC	.25	.11
❑ 72 Lamar Rogers RC	.04	.02
❑ 73 David Grant UER (Listed as DE, but should be NT)	.04	.02
❑ 74 Lewis Billups	.04	.02
❑ 75 Harold Green	.10	.05
❑ 76 Ickey Woods	.04	.02
❑ 77 Eddie Brown	.04	.02
❑ 78 David Fulcher	.04	.02
❑ 79 Anthony Munoz	.10	.05
❑ 80 Carl Zander	.04	.02
❑ 81 Rodney Holman	.04	.02
❑ 82 James Brooks	.10	.05
❑ 83 Tim McGee	.04	.02
❑ 84 Boomer Esiason	.10	.05
❑ 85 Leon White	.04	.02
❑ 86 James Francis UER (Ron is CB, card says he's LB)	.04	.02
❑ 87 Mitchell Price RC	.04	.02
❑ 88 Ed King RC	.04	.02
❑ 89 Eric Turner RC	.10	.05
❑ 90 Rob Burnett RC	.04	.02
❑ 91 Leroy Hoard	.10	.05
❑ 92 Kevin Mack UER (Height 6-2, should be 6-0)	.04	.02
❑ 93 Thane Gash UER (Comma omitted after name in bio)	.04	.02
❑ 94 Gregg Rakoczy	.04	.02
❑ 95 Clay Matthews	.10	.05
❑ 96 Eric Metcalf	.10	.05
❑ 97 Stephen Braggs	.04	.02
❑ 98 Frank Minnifield	.04	.02
❑ 99 Reggie Langhorne	.04	.02
❑ 100 Mike Johnson	.04	.02
❑ 101 Brian Brennan	.04	.02
❑ 102 Anthony Pleasant	.04	.02
❑ 103 Godfrey Myles RC UER (Vertical misspelled as verticle)	.04	.02
❑ 104 Russell Maryland RC	.25	.11
❑ 105 James Washington RC	.04	.02
❑ 106 Nate Newton	.10	.05
❑ 107 Jimmie Jones	.04	.02
❑ 108 Jay Novacek	.25	.11
❑ 109 Alexander Wright	.04	.02
❑ 110 Jack Del Rio	.04	.02
❑ 111 Jim Jeffcoat	.04	.02
❑ 112 Mike Saxon	.04	.02
❑ 113 Troy Aikman	.75	.35
❑ 114 Issiac Holt	.04	.02
❑ 115 Ken Norton	.25	.11
❑ 116 Kelvin Martin	.04	.02
❑ 117 Emmitt Smith	2.00	.90
❑ 118 Ken Willis	.04	.02
❑ 119 Daniel Stubbs	.04	.02
❑ 120 Michael Irvin	.25	.11
❑ 121 Danny Noonan	.04	.02
❑ 122 Alvin Harper RC UER (Drafted in first round, not second)	.25	.11
❑ 123 Reggie Johnson RC	.04	.02
❑ 124 Vance Johnson	.04	.02
❑ 125 Steve Atwater	.04	.02
❑ 126 Greg Kragen	.04	.02
❑ 127 John Elway	1.25	.55
❑ 128 Simon Fletcher	.04	.02
❑ 129 Wymon Henderson	.04	.02
❑ 130 Ricky Nattiel	.04	.02
❑ 131 Shannon Sharpe	.50	.23
❑ 132 Ron Holmes	.04	.02
❑ 133 Karl Mecklenburg	.04	.02
❑ 134 Bobby Humphrey	.04	.02
❑ 135 Clarence Kay	.04	.02
❑ 136 Dennis Smith	.04	.02
❑ 137 Jim Juriga	.04	.02
❑ 138 Melvin Bratton	.04	.02
❑ 139 Mark Jackson UER (Apostrophe placed in front of longest)	.04	.02
❑ 140 Michael Brooks	.04	.02
❑ 141 Alton Montgomery	.04	.02
❑ 142 Mike Croel RC	.04	.02
❑ 143 Mel Gray	.10	.05
❑ 144 Michael Cofer	.04	.02
❑ 145 Jeff Campbell	.04	.02
❑ 146 Dan Owens	.04	.02
❑ 147 Robert Clark UER (Drafted in '87, not '89)	.04	.02
❑ 148 Jim Arnold	.04	.02
❑ 149 William White	.04	.02
❑ 150 Rodney Peete	.10	.05
❑ 151 Jerry Ball	.04	.02
❑ 152 Bennie Blades	.04	.02
❑ 153 Barry Sanders UER (Drafted in '89, not '88)	1.50	.70
❑ 154 Andre Ware	.10	.05
❑ 155 Lomas Brown	.04	.02
❑ 156 Chris Spielman	.10	.05
❑ 157 Kelvin Pritchett RC	.10	.05
❑ 158 Herman Moore RC	2.00	.90
❑ 159 Chris Jacke	.04	.02
❑ 160 Tony Mandarich	.04	.02

❑	161	Perry Kemp	.04	.02
❑	162	Johnny Holland	.04	.02
❑	163	Mark Lee	.04	.02
❑	164	Anthony Dilweg	.04	.02
❑	165	Scott Stephen RC	.04	.02
❑	166	Ed West	.04	.02
❑	167	Mark Murphy	.04	.02
❑	168	Darrell Thompson	.04	.02
❑	169	James Campen RC	.04	.02
❑	170	Jeff Query	.04	.02
❑	171	Brian Noble	.04	.02
❑	172	Sterling Sharpe UER	.25	.11
		(Card says he gained 3314 yards in 1990)		
❑	173	Robert Brown	.04	.02
❑	174	Tim Harris	.04	.02
❑	175	LeRoy Butler	.10	.05
❑	176	Don Majkowski	.04	.02
❑	177	Vinnie Clark RC	.04	.02
❑	178	Esera Tuaolo RC	.04	.02
❑	179	Lorenzo White UER	.04	.02
		(Bio says 3rd year, actually 4th year)		
❑	180	Warren Moon	.25	.11
❑	181	Sean Jones	.10	.05
❑	182	Curtis Duncan	.04	.02
❑	183	Al Smith	.04	.02
❑	184	Richard Johnson RC	.04	.02
❑	185	Tony Jones	.10	.05
❑	186	Bubba McDowell	.04	.02
❑	187	Bruce Matthews	.10	.05
❑	188	Ray Childress	.04	.02
❑	189	Haywood Jeffires	.10	.05
❑	190	Ernest Givins	.10	.05
❑	191	Mike Munchak	.04	.02
❑	192	Greg Montgomery	.04	.02
❑	193	Cody Carlson RC	.04	.02
❑	194	Johnny Meads	.04	.02
❑	195	Drew Hill UER	.04	.02
		(Age listed as 24, should be 34)		
❑	196	Mike Dumas RC	.04	.02
❑	197	Darryll Lewis RC	.10	.05
❑	198	Rohn Stark	.04	.02
❑	199	Clarence Verdin UER	.04	.02
		(Played 2 seasons in USFL, not one)		
❑	200	Mike Prior	.04	.02
❑	201	Eugene Daniel	.04	.02
❑	202	Dean Biasucci	.04	.02
❑	203	Jeff Herrod	.04	.02
❑	204	Keith Taylor	.04	.02
❑	205	Jon Hand	.04	.02
❑	206	Pat Beach	.04	.02
❑	207	Duane Bickett	.04	.02
❑	208	Jessie Hester UER	.04	.02
		(Bio confuses Hester's NFL history)		
❑	209	Chip Banks	.04	.02
❑	210	Ray Donaldson	.04	.02
❑	211	Bill Brooks	.04	.02
❑	212	Jeff George	.25	.11
❑	213	Tony Siragusa RC	.04	.02
❑	214	Albert Bentley	.04	.02
❑	215	Joe Valerio	.04	.02
❑	216	Chris Martin	.04	.02
❑	217	Christian Okoye	.04	.02
❑	218	Stephone Paige	.04	.02
❑	219	Percy Snow	.04	.02
❑	220	David Szott	.04	.02
❑	221	Derrick Thomas	.25	.11
❑	222	Todd McNair	.04	.02
❑	223	Albert Lewis	.04	.02
❑	224	Neil Smith	.25	.11
❑	225	Barry Word	.04	.02
❑	226	Robb Thomas	.04	.02
❑	227	John Alt	.04	.02
❑	228	Jonathan Hayes	.04	.02
❑	229	Kevin Ross	.04	.02
❑	230	Nick Lowery	.04	.02
❑	231	Tim Grunhard	.04	.02
❑	232	Dan Saleaumua	.04	.02
❑	233	Steve DeBerg	.04	.02
❑	234	Harvey Williams RC	.25	.11
❑	235	Nick Bell RC UER	.04	.02
		(Lives in Nevada, not California)		
❑	236	Mervyn Fernandez UER	.04	.02
		(Drafted in '83, not FA '87 as on card)		
❑	237	Howie Long	.10	.05
❑	238	Marcus Allen	.25	.11
❑	239	Eddie Anderson	.04	.02
❑	240	Ethan Horton	.04	.02
❑	241	Lionel Washington	.04	.02
❑	242	Steve Wisniewski UER	.04	.02
		(Drafted, should be traded to)		
❑	243	Bo Jackson UER	.25	.11
		(Drafted by Raiders, should say drafted by Tampa Bay in '86)		
❑	244	Greg Townsend	.04	.02
❑	245	Jeff Jaeger	.04	.02
❑	246	Aaron Wallace	.04	.02
❑	247	Garry Lewis	.04	.02
❑	248	Steve Smith	.04	.02
❑	249	Willie Gault UER	.04	.02
		('90 stats 839 yards, should be 985)		
❑	250	Scott Davis	.04	.02
❑	251	Jay Schroeder	.04	.02
❑	252	Don Mosebar	.04	.02
❑	253	Todd Marinovich RC	.04	.02
❑	254	Irv Pankey	.04	.02
❑	255	Flipper Anderson	.04	.02
❑	256	Tom Newberry	.04	.02
❑	257	Kevin Greene	.25	.11
❑	258	Mike Wilcher	.04	.02
❑	259	Bern Brostek	.04	.02
❑	260	Buford McGee	.04	.02
❑	261	Cleveland Gary	.04	.02
❑	262	Jackie Slater	.04	.02
❑	263	Henry Ellard	.10	.05
❑	264	Alvin Wright	.04	.02
❑	265	Darryl Henley RC	.04	.02
❑	266	Damone Johnson RC	.04	.02
❑	267	Frank Stams	.04	.02
❑	268	Jerry Gray	.04	.02
❑	269	Jim Everett	.10	.05
❑	270	Pat Terrell	.04	.02
❑	271	Todd Lyght RC	.04	.02
❑	272	Aaron Cox	.04	.02
❑	273	Barry Sanders LL	.60	.25
		Rushing Leader		
❑	274	Jerry Rice LL	.40	.18
		Receiving Leader		
❑	275	Derrick Thomas LL	.25	.11
		Sack Leader		
❑	276	Mark Carrier DB LL	.10	.05
		Interception Leader		
❑	277	Warren Moon LL	.25	.11
		Passing Yardage Leader		
❑	278	Randall Cunningham LL	.10	.05
		Rushing Average Leader		
❑	279	Nick Lowery LL	.04	.02
		Scoring Leader		
❑	280	Clarence Verdin LL	.04	.02
		Punt Return Leader		
❑	281	Thurman Thomas LL	.25	.11
		Yards From Scrimmage Leader		
❑	282	Mike Horan LL	.04	.02
		Punting Average Leader		
❑	283	Flipper Anderson LL	.04	.02
		Receiving Average Leader		
❑	284	John Offerdahl	.04	.02
❑	285	Dan Marino UER	1.25	.55
		(2637 yards gained, should be 3563)		
❑	286	Mark Clayton	.10	.05
❑	287	Tony Paige	.04	.02
❑	288	Keith Sims	.04	.02
❑	289	Jeff Cross	.04	.02
❑	290	Pete Stoyanovich	.04	.02
❑	291	Ferrell Edmunds	.04	.02
❑	292	Reggie Roby	.04	.02
❑	293	Louis Oliver	.04	.02
❑	294	Jarvis Williams	.04	.02
❑	295	Sammie Smith	.04	.02
❑	296	Richmond Webb	.04	.02
❑	297	J.B. Brown	.04	.02
❑	298	Jim C.Jensen	.04	.02
❑	299	Mark Duper	.10	.05
❑	300	David Griggs	.04	.02
❑	301	Randal Hill RC	.10	.05
❑	302	Aaron Craver RC	.04	.02
		(See also 320)		
❑	303	Keith Millard	.04	.02
❑	304	Steve Jordan	.04	.02
❑	305	Anthony Carter	.10	.05
❑	306	Mike Merriweather	.04	.02
❑	307	Audray McMillian RC UER		.04
	.02	(Front Audray, back Audrey)		
❑	308	Randall McDaniel	.04	.02
❑	309	Gary Zimmerman	.04	.02
❑	310	Carl Lee	.04	.02
❑	311	Reggie Rutland	.04	.02
❑	312	Hassan Jones	.04	.02
❑	313	Kirk Lowdermilk UER	.04	.02
		(Reversed negative)		
❑	314	Herschel Walker	.10	.05
❑	315	Chris Doleman	.04	.02
❑	316	Joey Browner	.04	.02
❑	317	Wade Wilson	.10	.05
❑	318	Henry Thomas	.04	.02
❑	319	Rich Gannon	.04	.02
❑	320	Al Noga UER	.04	.02
		(Numbered incorrectly as 302 on card)		
❑	321	Pat Harlow RC	.04	.02
❑	322	Bruce Armstrong	.04	.02
❑	323	Maurice Hurst	.04	.02
❑	324	Brent Williams	.04	.02
❑	325	Chris Singleton	.04	.02
❑	326	Jason Staurovsky	.04	.02
❑	327	Marvin Allen	.04	.02
❑	328	Hart Lee Dykes	.04	.02
❑	329	Johnny Rembert	.04	.02
❑	330	Andre Tippett	.04	.02
❑	331	Greg McMurtry	.04	.02
❑	332	John Stephens	.04	.02
❑	333	Ray Agnew	.04	.02
❑	334	Tommy Hodson	.04	.02
❑	335	Ronnie Lippett	.04	.02
❑	336	Marv Cook	.04	.02
❑	337	Tommy Barnhardt RC	.04	.02
❑	338	Dalton Hilliard	.04	.02
❑	339	Sam Mills	.04	.02
❑	340	Morten Andersen	.04	.02
❑	341	Stan Brock	.04	.02
❑	342	Brett Maxie	.04	.02
❑	343	Steve Walsh	.04	.02
❑	344	Vaughan Johnson	.04	.02
❑	345	Rickey Jackson	.04	.02
❑	346	Renaldo Turnbull	.04	.02
❑	347	Joel Hilgenberg	.04	.02
❑	348	Toi Cook RC	.04	.02
❑	349	Robert Massey	.04	.02
❑	350	Pat Swilling	.10	.05
❑	351	Eric Martin	.04	.02
❑	352	Rueben Mayes UER	.04	.02
		(Bio says 2nd round, should be 3rd)		
❑	353	Vince Buck	.04	.02
❑	354	Brett Perriman	.25	.11
❑	355	Wesley Carroll RC	.04	.02
❑	356	Jarrod Bunch RC	.04	.02
❑	357	Pepper Johnson	.04	.02
❑	358	Dave Meggett	.10	.05
❑	359	Mark Collins	.04	.02
❑	360	Sean Landeta	.04	.02
❑	361	Maurice Carthon	.04	.02
❑	362	Mike Fox UER	.04	.02
		(Listed as DE, should say DT)		
❑	363	Jeff Hostetler	.10	.05
❑	364	Phil Simms	.10	.05
❑	365	Leonard Marshall	.04	.02
❑	366	Gary Reasons	.04	.02
❑	367	Rodney Hampton	.25	.11
❑	368	Greg Jackson RC	.04	.02
❑	369	Jumbo Elliott	.04	.02
❑	370	Bob Kratch RC	.04	.02
❑	371	Lawrence Taylor	.25	.11
❑	372	Erik Howard	.04	.02

❑ 373 Carl Banks .04 .02
❑ 374 Stephen Baker .04 .02
❑ 375 Mark Ingram .10 .05
❑ 376 Browning Nagle RC .04 .02
❑ 377 Jeff Lageman .04 .02
❑ 378 Ken O'Brien .04 .02
❑ 379 Al Toon .10 .05
❑ 380 Joe Prokop .04 .02
❑ 381 Tony Stargell .04 .02
❑ 382 Blair Thomas .04 .02
❑ 383 Erik McMillan .04 .02
❑ 384 Dennis Byrd .04 .02
❑ 385 Freeman McNeil .04 .02
❑ 386 Brad Baxter .04 .02
❑ 387 Mark Boyer .04 .02
❑ 388 Terance Mathis .10 .05
❑ 389 Jim Sweeney .04 .02
❑ 390 Kyle Clifton .04 .02
❑ 391 Pat Leahy .04 .02
❑ 392 Rob Moore .25 .11
❑ 393 James Hasty .04 .02
❑ 394 Blaise Bryant .04 .02
❑ 395A Jesse Campbell RC ERR 1.00 .45
(Photo actually
Dan McGwire; see 509)
❑ 395B Jesse Campbell RC COR .04
.02
❑ 396 Keith Jackson .10 .05
❑ 397 Jerome Brown .04 .02
❑ 398 Keith Byars .04 .02
❑ 399 Seth Joyner .10 .05
❑ 400 Mike Bellamy .04 .02
❑ 401 Fred Barnett .25 .11
❑ 402 Reggie Singletary RC .04 .02
❑ 403 Reggie White .25 .11
❑ 404 Randall Cunningham .25 .11
❑ 405 Byron Evans .04 .02
❑ 406 Wes Hopkins .04 .02
❑ 407 Ben Smith .04 .02
❑ 408 Roger Ruzek .04 .02
❑ 409 Eric Allen UER .04 .02
(Comparative misspelled
as comparate)
❑ 410 Anthony Toney UER .04 .02
(Heath Sherman was
rookie in '89, not '90)
❑ 411 Clyde Simmons .04 .02
❑ 412 Andre Waters .04 .02
❑ 413 Calvin Williams .10 .05
❑ 414 Eric Swann RC .25 .11
❑ 415 Eric Hill .04 .02
❑ 416 Tim McDonald .04 .02
❑ 417 Luis Sharpe .04 .02
❑ 418 Ernie Jones UER .04 .02
(Photo actually
Steve Jordan)
❑ 419 Ken Harvey .10 .05
❑ 420 Ricky Proehl .04 .02
❑ 421 Johnny Johnson .04 .02
❑ 422 Anthony Bell .04 .02
❑ 423 Timm Rosenbach .04 .02
❑ 424 Rich Camarillo .04 .02
❑ 425 Walter Reeves .04 .02
❑ 426 Freddie Joe Nunn .04 .02
❑ 427 Anthony Thompson UER .04 .02
(40 touchdowns, sic)
❑ 428 Bill Lewis .04 .02
❑ 429 Jim Wahler RC .04 .02
❑ 430 Cedric Mack .04 .02
❑ 431 Michael Jones RC .04 .02
❑ 432 Ernie Mills RC .10 .05
❑ 433 Tim Worley .04 .02
❑ 434 Greg Lloyd .25 .11
❑ 435 Dermontti Dawson .04 .02
❑ 436 Louis Lipps .04 .02
❑ 437 Eric Green .04 .02
❑ 438 Donald Evans .04 .02
❑ 439 D.J. Johnson .04 .02
❑ 440 Tunch Ilkin .04 .02
❑ 441 Bubby Brister .04 .02
❑ 442 Chris Calloway .04 .02
❑ 443 David Little .04 .02
❑ 444 Thomas Everett .04 .02
❑ 445 Carnell Lake .04 .02
❑ 446 Rod Woodson .25 .11
❑ 447 Gary Anderson K .04 .02
❑ 448 Merril Hoge .04 .02
❑ 449 Gerald Williams .04 .02
❑ 450 Eric Moten RC .04 .02
❑ 451 Marion Butts .10 .05
❑ 452 Leslie O'Neal .10 .05
❑ 453 Ronnie Harmon .04 .02
❑ 454 Gill Byrd .04 .02
❑ 455 Junior Seau .25 .11
❑ 456 Nate Lewis RC .04 .02
❑ 457 Leo Goeas .04 .02
❑ 458 Burt Grossman .04 .02
❑ 459 Courtney Hall .04 .02
❑ 460 Anthony Miller .10 .05
❑ 461 Gary Plummer .04 .02
❑ 462 Billy Joe Tolliver .04 .02
❑ 463 Lee Williams .04 .02
❑ 464 Arthur Cox .04 .02
❑ 465 John Kidd UER .04 .02
(Stron gleg, sic)
❑ 466 Frank Cornish .04 .02
❑ 467 John Carney .04 .02
❑ 468 Eric Bieniemy RC .04 .02
❑ 469 Don Griffin .04 .02
❑ 470 Jerry Rice .75 .35
❑ 471 Keith DeLong .04 .02
❑ 472 John Taylor .10 .05
❑ 473 Brent Jones .25 .11
❑ 474 Pierce Holt .04 .02
❑ 475 Kevin Fagan .04 .02
❑ 476 Bill Romanowski .04 .02
❑ 477 Dexter Carter .04 .02
❑ 478 Guy McIntyre .04 .02
❑ 479 Joe Montana 1.25 .55
❑ 480 Charles Haley .10 .05
❑ 481 Mike Cofer .04 .02
❑ 482 Jesse Sapolu .04 .02
❑ 483 Eric Davis .04 .02
❑ 484 Mike Sherrard .04 .02
❑ 485 Steve Young .75 .35
❑ 486 Darryl Pollard .04 .02
❑ 487 Tom Rathman .04 .02
❑ 488 Michael Carter .04 .02
❑ 489 Ricky Watters RC 1.50 .70
❑ 490 John Johnson RC .04 .02
❑ 491 Eugene Robinson .04 .02
❑ 492 Andy Heck .04 .02
❑ 493 John L. Williams .04 .02
❑ 494 Norm Johnson .04 .02
❑ 495 David Wyman .04 .02
❑ 496 Derrick Fenner UER .04 .02
(Drafted in '88,
should be '89)
❑ 497 Rick Donnelly .04 .02
❑ 498 Tony Woods .04 .02
❑ 499 Derek Loville RC UER .04 .02
(Ahmad Rashad is
misspelled Ahmed)
❑ 500 Dave Krieg .10 .05
❑ 501 Joe Nash .04 .02
❑ 502 Brian Blades .10 .05
❑ 503 Cortez Kennedy .25 .11
❑ 504 Jeff Bryant .04 .02
❑ 505 Tommy Kane .04 .02
❑ 506 Travis McNeal .04 .02
❑ 507 Terry Wooden .04 .02
❑ 508 Chris Warren .25 .11
❑ 509A Dan McGwire RC ERR .04 .02
(Photo actually Jesse
Campbell; see 395)
❑ 509B Dan McGwire COR RC .04 .02
❑ 510 Mark Robinson .04 .02
❑ 511 Ron Hall .04 .02
❑ 512 Paul Gruber .04 .02
❑ 513 Harry Hamilton .04 .02
❑ 514 Keith McCants .04 .02
❑ 515 Reggie Cobb .04 .02
❑ 516 Steve Christie UER .04 .02
(Listed as Californian,
should be Canadian)
❑ 517 Broderick Thomas .04 .02
❑ 518 Mark Carrier WR .25 .11
❑ 519 Vinny Testaverde .10 .05
❑ 520 Ricky Reynolds .04 .02
❑ 521 Jesse Anderson .04 .02
❑ 522 Reuben Davis .04 .02
❑ 523 Wayne Haddix .04 .02
❑ 524 Gary Anderson RB UER .04 .02
(Photo actually
Don Mosebar)
❑ 525 Bruce Hill .04 .02
❑ 526 Kevin Murphy .04 .02
❑ 527 Lawrence Dawsey RC .10 .05
❑ 528 Ricky Ervins RC .10 .05
❑ 529 Charles Mann .04 .02
❑ 530 Jim Lachey .04 .02
❑ 531 Mark Rypien UER .10 .05
(No stat for percentage;
2,0703 yards, sic)
❑ 532 Darrell Green .04 .02
❑ 533 Stan Humphries .25 .11
❑ 534 Jeff Bostic UER .04 .02
(Age listed as 32 in
stats and 33 in bio)
❑ 535 Earnest Byner .04 .02
❑ 536 Art Monk UER .10 .05
(Bio says 718 recep-
tions, should be 730)
❑ 537 Don Warren .04 .02
❑ 538 Darryl Grant .04 .02
❑ 539 Wilber Marshall .04 .02
❑ 540 Kurt Gouveia RC .04 .02
❑ 541 Markus Koch .04 .02
❑ 542 Andre Collins .04 .02
❑ 543 Chip Lohmiller .04 .02
❑ 544 Alvin Walton .04 .02
❑ 545 Gary Clark .25 .11
❑ 546 Ricky Sanders .04 .02
❑ 547 Redskins vs. Eagles .04 .02
(Gary Clark)
❑ 548 Bengals vs. Oilers .04 .02
(Cody Carlson)
❑ 549 Dolphins vs. Chiefs .04 .02
(Mark Clayton)
❑ 550 Bears vs. Saints UER .04 .02
(Neal Anderson;
Name misspelled
Andersen on back)
❑ 551 Bills vs. Dolphins .10 .05
(Thurman Thomas)
❑ 552 49ers vs. Redskins .04 .02
(Line play)
❑ 553 Giants vs. Bears .04 .02
(Ottis Anderson)
❑ 554 Raiders vs. Bengals .10 .05
(Bo Jackson)
❑ 555 AFC Championship .04 .02
(Andre Reed)
❑ 556 NFC Championship .04 .02
(Jeff Hostetler)
❑ 557 Super Bowl XXV .04 .02
(Ottis Anderson)
❑ 558 Checklist 1-140 .04 .02
❑ 559 Checklist 141-280 .04 .02
❑ 560 Checklist 281-420 UER .04 .02
(301 Randall Hill)
❑ 561 Checklist 421-561 UER .04 .02

1992 Bowman

	MINT	NRMT
COMPLETE SET (573)	120.00	55.00
COMMON CARD (1-573)	.25	.11
SEMISTARS	.50	.23
UNLISTED STARS	1.00	.45

COMMON FOILS .50 .23
FOIL SEMISTARS 1.00 .45
FOIL SP (27/68/126/137/168) .. 1.50 .70
FOIL SP (216/365/374/393) 1.50 .70
FOIL SP (401/461/487/494) 1.50 .70
FOIL SP (505/519/528) 1.50 .70
FOIL SP SEMISTARS 2.00 .90
ONE FOIL CARD PER PACK ......
SIX FOIL CARDS PER 90-CARD CARTON

❑ 1 Reggie White 1.00 .45
❑ 2 Johnny Meads .25 .11
❑ 3 Chip Lohmiller .25 .11
❑ 4 James Lofton .50 .23
❑ 5 Ray Horton .25 .11
❑ 6 Rich Moran .25 .11
❑ 7 Howard Cross .25 .11
❑ 8 Mike Horan .25 .11
❑ 9 Erik Kramer .50 .23
❑ 10 Steve Wisniewski .25 .11
❑ 11 Michael Haynes .50 .23
❑ 12 Donald Evans .25 .11
❑ 13 Michael Irvin FOIL 1.00 .45
❑ 14 Gary Zimmerman .25 .11
❑ 15 John Friesz .50 .23
❑ 16 Mark Carrier WR 1.00 .45
❑ 17 Mark Duper .25 .11
❑ 18 James Thornton .25 .11
❑ 19 Jon Hand .25 .11
❑ 20 Sterling Sharpe 1.00 .45
❑ 21 Jacob Green .25 .11
❑ 22 Wesley Carroll .25 .11
❑ 23 Clay Matthews .50 .23
❑ 24 Kevin Greene 1.00 .45
❑ 25 Brad Baxter .25 .11
❑ 26 Don Griffin .25 .11
❑ 27 Robert Delpino FOIL SP 1.50 .70
❑ 28 Lee Johnson .25 .11
❑ 29 Jim Wahler .25 .11
❑ 30 Leonard Russell .50 .23
❑ 31 Eric Moore .25 .11
❑ 32 Dino Hackett .25 .11
❑ 33 Simon Fletcher .25 .11
❑ 34 Al Edwards .25 .11
❑ 35 Brad Edwards .25 .11
❑ 36 James Joseph .25 .11
❑ 37 Rodney Peete .50 .23
❑ 38 Ricky Reynolds .25 .11
❑ 39 Eddie Anderson .25 .11
❑ 40 Ken Clarke .25 .11
❑ 41 Tony Bennett FOIL .50 .23
❑ 42 Larry Brown DB .25 .11
❑ 43 Ray Childress .25 .11
❑ 44 Mike Kenn .25 .11
❑ 45 Vestee Jackson .25 .11
❑ 46 Neil O'Donnell 1.00 .45
❑ 47 Bill Brooks .25 .11
❑ 48 Kevin Butler .25 .11
❑ 49 Joe Phillips .25 .11
❑ 50 Cortez Kennedy .50 .23
❑ 51 Rickey Jackson .25 .11
❑ 52 Vinnie Clark .25 .11
❑ 53 Michael Jackson .50 .23
❑ 54 Ernie Jones .25 .11
❑ 55 Tom Newberry .25 .11
❑ 56 Pat Harlow .25 .11
❑ 57 Craig Taylor .25 .11
❑ 58 Joe Prokop .25 .11
❑ 59 Warren Moon FOIL SP .. 2.00 .90
❑ 60 Jeff Lageman .25 .11
❑ 61 Neil Smith .50 .23
❑ 62 Jim Jeffcoat .25 .11
❑ 63 Bill Fralic .25 .11
❑ 64 Mark Schlereth RC .25 .11
❑ 65 Keith Byars .25 .11
❑ 66 Jeff Hostetler .50 .23
❑ 67 Joey Browner .25 .11
❑ 68 Bobby Hebert FOIL SP .. 1.50 .70
❑ 69 Keith Sims .25 .11
❑ 70 Warren Moon 1.00 .45
❑ 71 Pio Sagapolutele RC .25 .11
❑ 72 Cornelius Bennett .50 .23
❑ 73 Greg Davis .25 .11
❑ 74 Ronnie Harmon .25 .11
❑ 75 Ron Hall .25 .11
❑ 76 Howie Long .50 .23
❑ 77 Greg Lewis .25 .11
❑ 78 Carnell Lake .25 .11
❑ 79 Ray Crockett .25 .11
❑ 80 Tom Waddle .25 .11
❑ 81 Vincent Brown .25 .11
❑ 82 Bill Brooks FOIL .50 .23
❑ 83 John L. Williams .25 .11
❑ 84 Floyd Turner .25 .11
❑ 85 Scott Radecic .25 .11
❑ 86 Anthony Munoz .50 .23
❑ 87 Lonnie Young .25 .11
❑ 88 Dexter Carter .25 .11
❑ 89 Tony Zendejas .25 .11
❑ 90 Tim Jorden .25 .11
❑ 91 LeRoy Butler .25 .11
❑ 92 Richard Brown RC .25 .11
❑ 93 Erric Pegram .50 .23
❑ 94 Sean Landeta .25 .11
❑ 95 Clyde Simmons .25 .11
❑ 96 Martin Mayhew .25 .11
❑ 97 Jarvis Williams .25 .11
❑ 98 Barry Word .25 .11
❑ 99 John Taylor FOIL .50 .23
❑ 100 Emmitt Smith 12.00 5.50
❑ 101 Leon Seals .25 .11
❑ 102 Marion Butts .25 .11
❑ 103 Mike Merriweather .25 .11
❑ 104 Ernest Givins .50 .23
❑ 105 Wymon Henderson .25 .11
❑ 106 Robert Wilson .25 .11
❑ 107 Bobby Hebert .25 .11
❑ 108 Terry McDaniel .25 .11
❑ 109 Jerry Ball .25 .11
❑ 110 John Taylor .50 .23
❑ 111 Rob Moore .50 .23
❑ 112 Thurman Thomas FOIL 1.00 .45
❑ 113 Checklist 1-115 .25 .11
❑ 114 Brian Blades .50 .23
❑ 115 Larry Kelm .25 .11
❑ 116 James Francis .25 .11
❑ 117 Rod Woodson 1.00 .45
❑ 118 Trace Armstrong .25 .11
❑ 119 Eugene Daniel .25 .11
❑ 120 Andre Tippett .25 .11
❑ 121 Chris Jacke .25 .11
❑ 122 Jessie Tuggle .25 .11
❑ 123 Chris Chandler 1.00 .45
❑ 124 Tim Johnson .25 .11
❑ 125 Mark Collins .25 .11
❑ 126 Aeneas Williams FOIL SP 1.50 .70
❑ 127 James Jones .25 .11
❑ 128 George Jamison .25 .11
❑ 129 Deron Cherry .25 .11
❑ 130 Mark Clayton .50 .23
❑ 131 Keith DeLong .25 .11
❑ 132 Marcus Allen 1.00 .45
❑ 133 Joe Walter RC .25 .11
❑ 134 Reggie Rutland .25 .11
❑ 135 Kent Hull .25 .11
❑ 136 Jeff Feagles .25 .11
❑ 137 Ronnie Lott FOIL SP .... 2.00 .90
❑ 138 Henry Rolling .25 .11
❑ 139 Gary Anderson RB .25 .11
❑ 140 Morten Andersen .25 .11
❑ 141 Cris Dishman .25 .11
❑ 142 David Treadwell .25 .11
❑ 143 Kevin Gogan .25 .11
❑ 144 James Hasty .25 .11
❑ 145 Robert Delpino .25 .11
❑ 146 Patrick Hunter .25 .11
❑ 147 Gary Anderson K .25 .11
❑ 148 Chip Banks .25 .11
❑ 149 Dan Fike .25 .11
❑ 150 Chris Miller .50 .23
❑ 151 Hugh Millen .25 .11
❑ 152 Courtney Hall .25 .11
❑ 153 Gary Clark .50 .23
❑ 154 Michael Brooks .25 .11
❑ 155 Jay Hilgenberg .25 .11
❑ 156 Tim McDonald .25 .11
❑ 157 Andre Tippett FOIL .50 .23
❑ 158 Doug Riesenberg .25 .11
❑ 159 Bill Maas .25 .11
❑ 160 Fred Barnett .50 .23
❑ 161 Pierce Holt .25 .11
❑ 162 Brian Noble .25 .11
❑ 163 Harold Green .25 .11
❑ 164 Joel Hilgenberg .25 .11
❑ 165 Mervyn Fernandez .25 .11
❑ 166 John Offerdahl .25 .11
❑ 167 Shane Conlan .25 .11
❑ 168 Mark Higgs FOIL SP .... 1.50 .70
❑ 169 Bubba McDowell .25 .11
❑ 170 Barry Sanders 10.00 4.50
❑ 171 Larry Roberts .25 .11
❑ 172 Herschel Walker .50 .23
❑ 173 Steve McMichael .50 .23
❑ 174 Kelly Stouffer .25 .11
❑ 175 Louis Lipps .25 .11
❑ 176 Jim Everett .50 .23
❑ 177 Tony Tolbert .25 .11
❑ 178 Mike Baab .25 .11
❑ 179 Eric Swann .50 .23
❑ 180 Emmitt Smith FOIL SP 20.00 9.00
❑ 181 Tim Brown 1.00 .45
❑ 182 Dennis Smith .25 .11
❑ 183 Moe Gardner .25 .11
❑ 184 Derrick Walker .25 .11
❑ 185 Reyna Thompson .25 .11
❑ 186 Esera Tuaolo .25 .11
❑ 187 Jeff Wright .25 .11
❑ 188 Mark Rypien .25 .11
❑ 189 Quinn Early .50 .23
❑ 190 Christian Okoye .25 .11
❑ 191 Keith Jackson .50 .23
❑ 192 Doug Smith .25 .11
❑ 193 John Elway FOIL 12.00 5.50
❑ 194 Reggie Cobb .25 .11
❑ 195 Reggie Roby .25 .11
❑ 196 Clarence Verdin .25 .11
❑ 197 Jim Breech .25 .11
❑ 198 Jim Sweeney .25 .11
❑ 199 Marv Cook .25 .11
❑ 200 Ronnie Lott .50 .23
❑ 201 Mel Gray .50 .23
❑ 202 Maury Buford .25 .11
❑ 203 Lorenzo Lynch .25 .11
❑ 204 Jesse Sapolu .25 .11
❑ 205 Steve Jordan .25 .11
❑ 206 Don Majkowski .25 .11
❑ 207 Flipper Anderson .25 .11
❑ 208 Ed King .25 .11
❑ 209 Tony Woods .25 .11
❑ 210 Ron Heller .25 .11
❑ 211 Greg Kragen .25 .11
❑ 212 Scott Case .25 .11
❑ 213 Tommy Barnhardt .25 .11
❑ 214 Charles Mann .25 .11
❑ 215 David Griggs .25 .11
❑ 216 Kenneth Davis FOIL SP 1.50 .70
❑ 217 Lamar Lathon .25 .11
❑ 218 Nate Odomes .25 .11
❑ 219 Vinny Testaverde .50 .23
❑ 220 Rod Bernstine .25 .11
❑ 221 Barry Sanders FOIL .. 15.00 6.75
❑ 222 Carlton Haselrig RC .25 .11
❑ 223 Steve Beuerlein .25 .11
❑ 224 John Alt .25 .11
❑ 225 Pepper Johnson .25 .11
❑ 226 Checklist 116-230 .25 .11
❑ 227 Irv Eatman .25 .11
❑ 228 Greg Townsend .25 .11
❑ 229 Mark Jackson .25 .11
❑ 230 Robert Blackmon .25 .11
❑ 231 Terry Allen 2.00 .90
❑ 232 Bennie Blades .25 .11
❑ 233 Sam Mills FOIL 1.00 .45
❑ 234 Richmond Webb .25 .11
❑ 235 Richard Dent .50 .23
❑ 236 Alonzo Mitz RC .25 .11
❑ 237 Steve Young 6.00 2.70
❑ 238 Pat Swilling .50 .23
❑ 239 James Campen .25 .11
❑ 240 Earnest Byner .25 .11
❑ 241 Pat Terrell .25 .11
❑ 242 Carwell Gardner .25 .11
❑ 243 Charles McRae .25 .11
❑ 244 Vince Newsome .25 .11
❑ 245 Eric Hill .25 .11
❑ 246 Steve Young FOIL 6.00 2.70
❑ 247 Nate Lewis .25 .11
❑ 248 William Fuller .50 .23

☐ 249 Andre Waters .25 .11
☐ 250 Dean Biasucci .25 .11
☐ 251 Andre Rison .50 .23
☐ 252 Brent Williams .25 .11
☐ 253 Todd McNair .25 .11
☐ 254 Jeff Davidson RC .25 .11
☐ 255 Art Monk .50 .23
☐ 256 Kirk Lowdermilk .25 .11
☐ 257 Bob Golic .25 .11
☐ 258 Michael Irvin 1.00 .45
☐ 259 Eric Green .25 .11
☐ 260 David Fulcher FOIL .50 .23
☐ 261 Damone Johnson .25 .11
☐ 262 Marc Spindler .25 .11
☐ 263 Alfred Williams .25 .11
☐ 264 Donnie Elder .25 .11
☐ 265 Keith McKeller .25 .11
☐ 266 Steve Bono RC 1.50 .70
☐ 267 Jumbo Elliott .25 .11
☐ 268 Randy Hilliard RC .25 .11
☐ 269 Rufus Porter .25 .11
☐ 270 Neal Anderson .25 .11
☐ 271 Dalton Hilliard .25 .11
☐ 272 Michael Zordich RC .25 .11
☐ 273 Cornelius Bennett FOIL .50 .23
☐ 274 Louie Aguiar RC .25 .11
☐ 275 Aaron Craver .25 .11
☐ 276 Tony Bennett .25 .11
☐ 277 Terry Wooden .25 .11
☐ 278 Mike Munchak .25 .11
☐ 279 Chris Hinton .25 .11
☐ 280 John Elway 8.00 3.60
☐ 281 Randall McDaniel .25 .11
☐ 282 Brad Baxter FOIL .50 .23
☐ 283 Wes Hopkins .25 .11
☐ 284 Scott Davis .25 .11
☐ 285 Mark Tuinei .25 .11
☐ 286 Broderick Thompson .25 .11
☐ 287 Henry Ellard .50 .23
☐ 288 Adrian Cooper .25 .11
☐ 289 Don Warren .25 .11
☐ 290 Rodney Hampton 1.00 .45
☐ 291 Kevin Ross .25 .11
☐ 292 Mark Carrier DB .25 .11
☐ 293 Ian Beckles .25 .11
☐ 294 Gene Atkins .25 .11
☐ 295 Mark Rypien FOIL .50 .23
☐ 296 Eric Metcalf .50 .23
☐ 297 Howard Ballard .25 .11
☐ 298 Nate Newton .50 .23
☐ 299 Dan Owens .25 .11
☐ 300 Tim McGee .25 .11
☐ 301 Greg McMurtry .25 .11
☐ 302 Walter Reeves .25 .11
☐ 303 Jeff Herrod .25 .11
☐ 304 Darren Comeaux .25 .11
☐ 305 Pete Stoyanovich .25 .11
☐ 306 Johnny Holland .25 .11
☐ 307 Jay Novacek .50 .23
☐ 308 Steve Broussard .25 .11
☐ 309 Darrell Green .25 .11
☐ 310 Sam Mills .25 .11
☐ 311 Tim Barnett .25 .11
☐ 312 Steve Atwater .25 .11
☐ 313 Tom Waddle FOIL .50 .23
☐ 314 Felix Wright .25 .11
☐ 315 Sean Jones .50 .23
☐ 316 Jim Harbaugh 1.00 .45
☐ 317 Eric Allen .25 .11
☐ 318 Don Mosebar .25 .11
☐ 319 Rob Taylor .25 .11
☐ 320 Terance Mathis .50 .23
☐ 321 Leroy Hoard .50 .23
☐ 322 Kenneth Davis .25 .11
☐ 323 Guy McIntyre .25 .11
☐ 324 Deron Cherry FOIL .50 .23
☐ 325 Tunch Ilkin .25 .11
☐ 326 Willie Green .25 .11
☐ 327 Darryl Henley .25 .11
☐ 328 Shawn Jefferson .25 .11
☐ 329 Greg Jackson .25 .11
☐ 330 John Roper .25 .11
☐ 331 Bill Lewis .25 .11
☐ 332 Rodney Holman .25 .11
☐ 333 Bruce Armstrong .25 .11
☐ 334 Robb Thomas .25 .11
☐ 335 Alvin Harper .50 .23
☐ 336 Brian Jordan .50 .23
☐ 337 Morten Andersen FOIL .50 .23
☐ 338 Dermontti Dawson .25 .11
☐ 339 Checklist 231-345 .25 .11
☐ 340 Louis Oliver .25 .11
☐ 341 Paul McJulien RC .25 .11
☐ 342 Karl Mecklenburg .25 .11
☐ 343 Lawrence Dawsey .50 .23
☐ 344 Kyle Clifton .25 .11
☐ 345 Jeff Bostic .25 .11
☐ 346 Cris Carter 2.00 .90
☐ 347 Al Smith .25 .11
☐ 348 Mark Kelso .25 .11
☐ 349 Art Monk FOIL 1.00 .45
☐ 350 Michael Carter .25 .11
☐ 351 Ethan Horton .25 .11
☐ 352 Andy Heck .25 .11
☐ 353 Gill Fenerty .25 .11
☐ 354 David Brandon RC .25 .11
☐ 355 Anthony Johnson 1.00 .45
☐ 356 Mike Golic .25 .11
☐ 357 Ferrell Edmunds .25 .11
☐ 358 Dennis Gibson .25 .11
☐ 359 Gill Byrd .25 .11
☐ 360 Todd Lyght .25 .11
☐ 361 Jayice Pearson RC .25 .11
☐ 362 John Rade .25 .11
☐ 363 Keith Van Horne .25 .11
☐ 364 John Kasay .25 .11
☐ 365 Broderick Thomas FOIL SP 1.50 .70
☐ 366 Ken Harvey .25 .11
☐ 367 Rich Gannon .25 .11
☐ 368 Darrell Thompson .25 .11
☐ 369 Jon Vaughn .25 .11
☐ 370 Jesse Solomon .25 .11
☐ 371 Erik McMillan .25 .11
☐ 372 Bruce Matthews .25 .11
☐ 373 Wilber Marshall .25 .11
☐ 374 Brian Blades FOIL SP 1.50 .70
☐ 375 Vance Johnson .25 .11
☐ 376 Eddie Brown .25 .11
☐ 377 Don Beebe .25 .11
☐ 378 Brent Jones .50 .23
☐ 379 Matt Bahr .25 .11
☐ 380 Dwight Stone .25 .11
☐ 381 Tony Casillas .25 .11
☐ 382 Jay Schroeder .25 .11
☐ 383 Byron Evans .25 .11
☐ 384 Dan Saleaumua .25 .11
☐ 385 Wendell Davis .25 .11
☐ 386 Ron Holmes .25 .11
☐ 387 George Thomas RC .25 .11
☐ 388 Ray Berry .25 .11
☐ 389 Eric Martin .25 .11
☐ 390 Kevin Mack .25 .11
☐ 391 Natu Tuatagaloa RC .25 .11
☐ 392 Bill Romanowski .25 .11
☐ 393 Nick Bell FOIL SP 1.50 .70
☐ 394 Grant Feasel .25 .11
☐ 395 Eugene Lockhart .25 .11
☐ 396 Lorenzo White .25 .11
☐ 397 Mike Farr .25 .11
☐ 398 Eric Bieniemy .25 .11
☐ 399 Kevin Murphy .25 .11
☐ 400 Luis Sharpe .25 .11
☐ 401 Jessie Tuggle FOIL SP 1.50 .70
☐ 402 Cleveland Gary .25 .11
☐ 403 Tony Mandarich .25 .11
☐ 404 Bryan Cox .50 .23
☐ 405 Marvin Washington .25 .11
☐ 406 Fred Stokes .25 .11
☐ 407 Duane Bickett .25 .11
☐ 408 Leonard Marshall .25 .11
☐ 409 Barry Foster .50 .23
☐ 410 Thurman Thomas 1.00 .45
☐ 411 Willie Gault .50 .23
☐ 412 Vinson Smith RC .25 .11
☐ 413 Mark Bortz .25 .11
☐ 414 Johnny Johnson .25 .11
☐ 415 Rodney Hampton FOIL 1.00 .45
☐ 416 Steve Wallace .25 .11
☐ 417 Fuad Reveiz .25 .11
☐ 418 Derrick Thomas .50 .23
☐ 419 Jackie Harris RC 1.00 .45
☐ 420 Derek Russell .25 .11
☐ 421 David Grant .25 .11
☐ 422 Tommy Kane .25 .11
☐ 423 Stan Brock .25 .11
☐ 424 Haywood Jeffires .50 .23
☐ 425 Broderick Thomas .25 .11
☐ 426 John Kidd .25 .11
☐ 427 Shawn McCarthy FOIL RC .50 .23
☐ 428 Jim Arnold .25 .11
☐ 429 Scott Fulhage .25 .11
☐ 430 Jackie Slater .25 .11
☐ 431 Scott Galbraith RC .25 .11
☐ 432 Roger Ruzek .25 .11
☐ 433 Irving Fryar .50 .23
☐ 434A Derrick Thomas FOIL ERR 1.00 .45
(Misnumbered 494)
☐ 434B Derrick Thomas FOIL COR 1.00 .45
(Numbered 434)
☐ 435 D.J. Johnson .25 .11
☐ 436 Jim C.Jensen .25 .11
☐ 437 James Washington .25 .11
☐ 438 Phil Hansen .25 .11
☐ 439 Rohn Stark .25 .11
☐ 440 Jarrod Bunch .25 .11
☐ 441 Todd Marinovich .25 .11
☐ 442 Brett Perriman 1.00 .45
☐ 443 Eugene Robinson .25 .11
☐ 444 Robert Massey .25 .11
☐ 445 Nick Lowery .25 .11
☐ 446 Rickey Dixon .25 .11
☐ 447 Jim Lachey .25 .11
☐ 448 Johnny Hector FOIL .50 .23
☐ 449 Gary Plummer .25 .11
☐ 450 Robert Brown .25 .11
☐ 451 Gaston Green .25 .11
☐ 452 Checklist 346-459 .25 .11
☐ 453 Darion Conner .25 .11
☐ 454 Mike Cofer .25 .11
☐ 455 Craig Heyward .50 .23
☐ 456 Anthony Carter .50 .23
☐ 457 Pat Coleman RC .25 .11
☐ 458 Jeff Bryant .25 .11
☐ 459 Mark Gunn RC .25 .11
☐ 460 Stan Thomas .25 .11
☐ 461 Simon Fletcher FOIL SP 1.50 .70
☐ 462 Ray Agnew .25 .11
☐ 463 Jessie Hester .25 .11
☐ 464 Rob Burnett .25 .11
☐ 465 Mike Croel .25 .11
☐ 466 Mike Pitts .25 .11
☐ 467 Darryl Talley .25 .11
☐ 468 Rich Camarillo .25 .11
☐ 469 Reggie White FOIL 1.00 .45
☐ 470 Nick Bell .25 .11
☐ 471 Tracy Hayworth RC .25 .11
☐ 472 Eric Thomas .25 .11
☐ 473 Paul Gruber .25 .11
☐ 474 David Richards .25 .11
☐ 475 T.J. Turner .25 .11
☐ 476 Mark Ingram .25 .11
☐ 477 Tim Grunhard .25 .11
☐ 478 Marion Butts FOIL .50 .23
☐ 479 Tom Rathman .25 .11
☐ 480 Brian Mitchell .50 .23
☐ 481 Bryce Paup 1.00 .45
☐ 482 Mike Pritchard .50 .23
☐ 483 Ken Norton Jr. .50 .23
☐ 484 Roman Phifer .25 .11
☐ 485 Greg Lloyd 1.00 .45
☐ 486 Brett Maxie .25 .11
☐ 487 Richard Dent FOIL SP 1.50 .70
☐ 488 Curtis Duncan .25 .11
☐ 489 Chris Burkett .25 .11
☐ 490 Travis McNeal .25 .11
☐ 491 Carl Lee .25 .11
☐ 492 Clarence Kay .25 .11
☐ 493 Tom Thayer .25 .11
☐ 494 Erik Kramer FOIL SP 2.00 .90
(See also 434A)
☐ 495 Perry Kemp .25 .11
☐ 496 Jeff Jaeger .25 .11
☐ 497 Eric Sanders .25 .11
☐ 498 Burt Grossman .25 .11
☐ 499 Ben Smith .25 .11
☐ 500 Keith McCants .25 .11
☐ 501 John Stephens .25 .11

❑ 502	John Rienstra	.25	.11
❑ 503	Jim Ritcher	.25	.11
❑ 504	Harris Barton	.25	.11
❑ 505	Andre Rison FOIL SP	2.00	.90
❑ 506	Chris Martin	.25	.11
❑ 507	Freddie Joe Nunn	.25	.11
❑ 508	Mark Higgs	.25	.11
❑ 509	Norm Johnson	.25	.11
❑ 510	Stephen Baker	.25	.11
❑ 511	Ricky Sanders	.25	.11
❑ 512	Ray Donaldson	.25	.11
❑ 513	David Fulcher	.25	.11
❑ 514	Gerald Williams	.25	.11
❑ 515	Toi Cook	.25	.11
❑ 516	Chris Warren	1.00	.45
❑ 517	Jeff Gossett	.25	.11
❑ 518	Ken Lanier	.25	.11
❑ 519	Haywood Jeffires FOIL SP	2.00	.90
❑ 520	Kevin Glover	.25	.11
❑ 521	Mo Lewis	.25	.11
❑ 522	Bern Brostek	.25	.11
❑ 523	Bo Orlando RC	.25	.11
❑ 524	Mike Saxon	.25	.11
❑ 525	Seth Joyner	.50	.23
❑ 526	John Carney	.25	.11
❑ 527	Jeff Cross	.25	.11
❑ 528	Gary Anderson K FOIL SP	1.50	.70
❑ 529	Chuck Cecil	.25	.11
❑ 530	Tim Green	.25	.11
❑ 531	Kevin Porter	.25	.11
❑ 532	Chris Spielman	.50	.23
❑ 533	Willie Drewrey	.25	.11
❑ 534	Chris Singleton UER (Card has wrong score for Super Bowl XX)	.25	.11
❑ 535	Matt Stover	.25	.11
❑ 536	Andre Collins	.25	.11
❑ 537	Erik Howard	.25	.11
❑ 538	Steve Tasker	.50	.23
❑ 539	Anthony Thompson	.25	.11
❑ 540	Charles Haley	.50	.23
❑ 541	Mike Merriweather FOIL	.50	.23
❑ 542	Henry Thomas	.25	.11
❑ 543	Scott Stephen	.25	.11
❑ 544	Bruce Kozerski	.25	.11
❑ 545	Tim McKyer	.25	.11
❑ 546	Chris Doleman	.25	.11
❑ 547	Riki Ellison	.25	.11
❑ 548	Mike Prior	.25	.11
❑ 549	Dwayne Harper	.25	.11
❑ 550	Bubby Brister	.25	.11
❑ 551	Dave Meggett	.50	.23
❑ 552	Greg Montgomery	.25	.11
❑ 553	Kevin Mack FOIL	.50	.23
❑ 554	Mark Stepnoski	.50	.23
❑ 555	Kenny Walker	.25	.11
❑ 556	Eric Moten	.25	.11
❑ 557	Michael Stewart	.25	.11
❑ 558	Calvin Williams	.50	.23
❑ 559	Johnny Hector	.25	.11
❑ 560	Tony Paige	.25	.11
❑ 561	Tim Newton	.25	.11
❑ 562	Brad Muster	.25	.11
❑ 563	Aeneas Williams	.50	.23
❑ 564	Herman Moore	8.00	3.60
❑ 565	Checklist 460-573	.25	.11
❑ 566	Jerome Henderson	.25	.11
❑ 567	Danny Copeland	.25	.11
❑ 568	Alexander Wright FOIL	.50	.23
❑ 569	Tim Harris	.25	.11
❑ 570	Jonathan Hayes	.25	.11
❑ 571	Tony Jones	.25	.11
❑ 572	Carlton Bailey RC	.50	.23
❑ 573	Vaughan Johnson	.25	.11

1993 Bowman

	MINT	NRMT
COMPLETE SET (423)	60.00	27.00
COMMON CARD (1-423)	.20	.09
COMMON FOIL	.40	.18
SEMISTARS	.40	.18
UNLISTED STARS	.75	.35

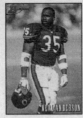

ONE FOIL CARD PER PACK ......
TWO FOIL CARDS PER JUMBO PACK

❑ 1	Troy Aikman FOIL	3.00	1.35
❑ 2	John Parrella RC	.20	.09
❑ 3	Dana Stubblefield RC	.75	.35
❑ 4	Mark Higgs	.20	.09
❑ 5	Tom Carter RC	.40	.18
❑ 6	Nate Lewis	.20	.09
❑ 7	Vaughn Hebron RC	.20	.09
❑ 8	Ernest Givins	.40	.18
❑ 9	Vince Buck	.20	.09
❑ 10	Levon Kirkland	.20	.09
❑ 11	J.J. Birden	.20	.09
❑ 12	Steve Jordan	.20	.09
❑ 13	Simon Fletcher	.20	.09
❑ 14	Willie Green	.20	.09
❑ 15	Pepper Johnson	.20	.09
❑ 16	Roger Harper RC	.20	.09
❑ 17	Rob Moore	.40	.18
❑ 18	David Lang	.20	.09
❑ 19	David Klingler	.20	.09
❑ 20	Garrison Hearst FOIL RC	5.00	2.20
❑ 21	Anthony Johnson	.40	.18
❑ 22	Eric Curry FOIL RC	.20	.09
❑ 23	Nolan Harrison	.20	.09
❑ 24	Earl Dotson RC	.20	.09
❑ 25	Leonard Russell	.40	.18
❑ 26	Doug Riesenberg	.20	.09
❑ 27	Dwayne Harper	.20	.09
❑ 28	Richard Dent	.40	.18
❑ 29	Victor Bailey RC	.20	.09
❑ 30	Junior Seau	.75	.35
❑ 31	Steve Tasker	.40	.18
❑ 32	Kurt Gouveia	.20	.09
❑ 33	Renaldo Turnbull UER (Listed as wide receiver)	.20	.09
❑ 34	Dale Carter	.20	.09
❑ 35	Russell Maryland	.20	.09
❑ 36	Dana Hall	.20	.09
❑ 37	Marco Coleman	.20	.09
❑ 38	Greg Montgomery	.20	.09
❑ 39	Deon Figures RC	.40	.18
❑ 40	Troy Drayton RC	.40	.18
❑ 41	Eric Metcalf	.40	.18
❑ 42	Michael Husted RC	.20	.09
❑ 43	Harry Newsome	.20	.09
❑ 44	Kelvin Pritchett	.20	.09
❑ 45	Andre Rison FOIL	.35	.16
❑ 46	John Copeland RC	.40	.18
❑ 47	Greg Biekert RC	.20	.09
❑ 48	Johnny Johnson	.20	.09
❑ 49	Chuck Cecil	.20	.09
❑ 50	Rick Mirer FOIL RC	2.00	.90
❑ 51	Rod Bernstine	.20	.09
❑ 52	Steve McMichael	.40	.18
❑ 53	Roosevelt Potts RC	.20	.09
❑ 54	Mike Sherrard	.20	.09
❑ 55	Terrell Buckley	.20	.09
❑ 56	Eugene Chung	.20	.09
❑ 57	Kimble Anders RC	1.25	.55
❑ 58	Daryl Johnston	.75	.35
❑ 59	Harris Barton	.20	.09
❑ 60	Thurman Thomas FOIL	.75	.35
❑ 61	Eric Martin	.20	.09
❑ 62	Reggie Brooks FOIL RC	.40	.18
❑ 63	Eric Bieniemy	.20	.09
❑ 64	John Offerdahl	.20	.09
❑ 65	Wilber Marshall	.20	.09
❑ 66	Mark Carrier WR	.40	.18
❑ 67	Merril Hoge	.20	.09
❑ 68	Cris Carter	1.25	.55
❑ 69	Marty Thompson RC	.20	.09
❑ 70	Randall Cunningham FOIL	.75	.35
❑ 71	Winston Moss	.20	.09
❑ 72	Doug Pelfrey RC	.20	.09
❑ 73	Jackie Slater	.20	.09
❑ 74	Pierce Holt	.20	.09
❑ 75	Hardy Nickerson	.40	.18
❑ 76	Chris Burkett	.20	.09
❑ 77	Michael Brandon	.20	.09
❑ 78	Tom Waddle	.20	.09
❑ 79	Walter Reeves	.20	.09
❑ 80	Lawrence Taylor FOIL	.75	.35
❑ 81	Wayne Simmons RC	.20	.09
❑ 82	Brent Williams	.20	.09
❑ 83	Shannon Sharpe	.75	.35
❑ 84	Robert Blackmon	.20	.09
❑ 85	Keith Jackson	.40	.18
❑ 86	A.J. Johnson	.20	.09
❑ 87	Ryan McNeil RC	.20	.09
❑ 88	Michael Dean Perry	.40	.18
❑ 89	Russell Copeland RC	.40	.18
❑ 90	Sam Mills	.20	.09
❑ 91	Courtney Hall	.20	.09
❑ 92	Gino Torretta RC	.40	.18
❑ 93	Artie Smith RC	.20	.09
❑ 94	David Whitmore	.20	.09
❑ 95	Charles Haley	.40	.18
❑ 96	Rod Woodson	.75	.35
❑ 97	Lorenzo White	.20	.09
❑ 98	Tom Scott RC	.20	.09
❑ 99	Tyji Armstrong	.20	.09
❑ 100	Boomer Esiason	.40	.18
❑ 101	Rocket Ismail FOIL	.40	.18
❑ 102	Mark Carrier DB	.20	.09
❑ 103	Broderick Thompson	.20	.09
❑ 104	Bob Whitfield	.20	.09
❑ 105	Ben Coleman RC	.20	.09
❑ 106	Jon Vaughn	.20	.09
❑ 107	Marcus Buckley RC	.20	.09
❑ 108	Cleveland Gary	.20	.09
❑ 109	Ashley Ambrose	.20	.09
❑ 110	Reggie White FOIL	.75	.35
❑ 111	Arthur Marshall RC	.20	.09
❑ 112	Greg McMurtry	.20	.09
❑ 113	Mike Johnson	.20	.09
❑ 114	Tim McGee	.20	.09
❑ 115	John Carney	.20	.09
❑ 116	Neil Smith	.75	.35
❑ 117	Mark Stepnoski	.20	.09
❑ 118	Don Beebe	.20	.09
❑ 119	Scott Mitchell	.75	.35
❑ 120	Randall McDaniel	.20	.09
❑ 121	Chidi Ahanotu RC	.20	.09
❑ 122	Ray Childress	.20	.09
❑ 123	Tony McGee RC	.40	.18
❑ 124	Marc Boutte	.20	.09
❑ 125	Ronnie Lott	.40	.18
❑ 126	Jason Elam RC	.75	.35
❑ 127	Martin Harrison RC	.20	.09
❑ 128	Leonard Renfro RC	.20	.09
❑ 129	Jessie Armstead RC	.20	.09
❑ 130	Quentin Coryatt	.40	.18
❑ 131	Luis Sharpe	.20	.09
❑ 132	Bill Maas	.20	.09
❑ 133	Jesse Solomon	.20	.09
❑ 134	Kevin Greene	.75	.35
❑ 135	Derek Brown RBK RC	.40	.18
❑ 136	Greg Townsend	.20	.09
❑ 137	Neal Anderson	.20	.09
❑ 138	John L. Williams	.20	.09
❑ 139	Vincent Brisby RC	.75	.35
❑ 140	Barry Sanders FOIL	6.00	2.70
❑ 141	Charles Mann	.20	.09
❑ 142	Ken Norton	.40	.18
❑ 143	Eric Moten	.20	.09
❑ 144	John Alt	.20	.09
❑ 145	Dan Footman RC	.20	.09
❑ 146	Bill Brooks	.20	.09
❑ 147	James Thornton	.20	.09
❑ 148	Martin Mayhew	.20	.09
❑ 149	Andy Harmon	.40	.18

❑ 150 Dan Marino FOIL 6.00 2.70
❑ 151 Micheal Barrow .20 .09
❑ 152 Flipper Anderson .20 .09
❑ 153 Jackie Harris .20 .09
❑ 154 Todd Kelly RC .20 .09
❑ 155 Dan Williams RC .20 .09
❑ 156 Harold Green .20 .09
❑ 157 David Treadwell .20 .09
❑ 158 Chris Doleman .20 .09
❑ 159 Eric Hill .20 .09
❑ 160 Lincoln Kennedy RC .20 .09
❑ 161 Devon McDonald RC .20 .09
❑ 162 Natrone Means RC 4.00 1.80
❑ 163 Rick Hamilton RC .20 .09
❑ 164 Kelvin Martin .20 .09
❑ 165 Jeff Hostetler .40 .18
❑ 166 Mark Brunell RC 12.00 5.50
❑ 167 Tim Barnett .20 .09
❑ 168 Ray Crockett .20 .09
❑ 169 William Perry .40 .18
❑ 170 Michael Irvin .75 .35
❑ 171 Marvin Washington .20 .09
❑ 172 Irving Fryar .40 .18
❑ 173 Scott Sisson RC .20 .09
❑ 174 Gary Anderson K .20 .09
❑ 175 Bruce Smith .75 .35
❑ 176 Clyde Simmons .20 .09
❑ 177 Russell White RC .40 .18
❑ 178 Irv Smith RC .20 .09
❑ 179 Mark Wheeler .20 .09
❑ 180 Warren Moon .75 .35
❑ 181 Del Speer RC .20 .09
❑ 182 Henry Thomas .20 .09
❑ 183 Keith Kartz .20 .09
❑ 184 Ricky Ervins .20 .09
❑ 185 Phil Simms .40 .18
❑ 186 Tim Brown .75 .35
❑ 187 Willis Peguese .20 .09
❑ 188 Rich Moran .20 .09
❑ 189 Robert Jones .20 .09
❑ 190 Craig Heyward .40 .18
❑ 191 Ricky Watters .75 .35
❑ 192 Stan Humphries .75 .35
❑ 193 Larry Webster .20 .09
❑ 194 Brad Baxter .20 .09
❑ 195 Randal Hill .20 .09
❑ 196 Robert Porcher .20 .09
❑ 197 Patrick Robinson RC .20 .09
❑ 198 Ferrell Edmunds .20 .09
❑ 199 Melvin Jenkins .20 .09
❑ 200 Joe Montana FOIL 6.00 2.70
❑ 201 Marv Cook .20 .09
❑ 202 Henry Ellard .40 .18
❑ 203 Calvin Williams .40 .18
❑ 204 Craig Erickson .40 .18
❑ 205 Steve Atwater .20 .09
❑ 206 Najee Mustafaa .20 .09
❑ 207 Darryl Talley .20 .09
❑ 208 Jarrod Bunch .20 .09
❑ 209 Tim McDonald .20 .09
❑ 210 Patrick Bates RC .20 .09
❑ 211 Sean Jones .20 .09
❑ 212 Leslie O'Neal .40 .18
❑ 213 Mike Golic .20 .09
❑ 214 Mark Clayton .20 .09
❑ 215 Leonard Marshall .20 .09
❑ 216 Curtis Conway RC 2.50 1.10
❑ 217 Andre Hastings RC .75 .35
❑ 218 Barry Word .20 .09
❑ 219 Will Wolford .20 .09
❑ 220 Desmond Howard .40 .18
❑ 221 Rickey Jackson .20 .09
❑ 222 Alvin Harper .40 .18
❑ 223 William White .20 .09
❑ 224 Steve Broussard .20 .09
❑ 225 Aeneas Williams .20 .09
❑ 226 Michael Brooks .20 .09
❑ 227 Reggie Cobb .20 .09
❑ 228 Derrick Walker .20 .09
❑ 229 Marcus Allen .75 .35
❑ 230 Jerry Ball .20 .09
❑ 231 J.B. Brown .20 .09
❑ 232 Terry McDaniel .20 .09
❑ 233 LeRoy Butler .20 .09
❑ 234 Kyle Clifton .20 .09
❑ 235 Henry Jones .20 .09
❑ 236 Shane Conlan .20 .09
❑ 237 Michael Bates RC .20 .09
❑ 238 Vincent Brown .20 .09
❑ 239 William Fuller .20 .09
❑ 240 Ricardo McDonald .20 .09
❑ 241 Gary Zimmerman .20 .09
❑ 242 Fred Barnett .40 .18
❑ 243 Elvis Grbac RC 4.00 1.80
❑ 244 Myron Baker RC .20 .09
❑ 245 Steve Emtman .20 .09
❑ 246 Mike Compton RC .20 .09
❑ 247 Mark Jackson .20 .09
❑ 248 Santo Stephens RC .20 .09
❑ 249 Tommie Agee .20 .09
❑ 250 Broderick Thomas .20 .09
❑ 251 Fred Baxter RC .20 .09
❑ 252 Andre Collins .20 .09
❑ 253 Ernest Dye RC .20 .09
❑ 254 Raylee Johnson RC .20 .09
❑ 255 Rickey Dixon .20 .09
❑ 256 Ron Heller .20 .09
❑ 257 Joel Steed .20 .09
❑ 258 Everett Lindsay RC .20 .09
❑ 259 Tony Smith .20 .09
❑ 260 Sterling Sharpe UER .75 .35
(Edgar Bennett is pictured on front)
❑ 261 Tommy Vardell .20 .09
❑ 262 Morten Andersen .20 .09
❑ 263 Eddie Robinson .20 .09
❑ 264 Jerome Bettis RC 5.00 2.20
❑ 265 Alonzo Spellman .20 .09
❑ 266 Harvey Williams .40 .18
❑ 267 Jason Belser RC .20 .09
❑ 268 Derek Russell .20 .09
❑ 269 Derrick Lassic RC .20 .09
❑ 270 Steve Young FOIL 3.00 1.35
❑ 271 Adrian Murrell RC 4.00 1.80
❑ 272 Lewis Tillman .20 .09
❑ 273 O.J. McDuffie RC 4.00 1.80
❑ 274 Marty Carter .20 .09
❑ 275 Ray Seals .20 .09
❑ 276 Earnest Byner .20 .09
❑ 277 Marion Butts .20 .09
❑ 278 Chris Spielman .40 .18
❑ 279 Carl Pickens .75 .35
❑ 280 Drew Bledsoe FOIL RC 12.00 5.50
❑ 281 Mark Kelso .20 .09
❑ 282 Eugene Robinson .20 .09
❑ 283 Eric Allen .20 .09
❑ 284 Ethan Horton .20 .09
❑ 285 Greg Lloyd .75 .35
❑ 286 Anthony Carter .40 .18
❑ 287 Edgar Bennett .75 .35
❑ 288 Bobby Hebert .20 .09
❑ 289 Haywood Jeffires .40 .18
❑ 290 Glyn Milburn RC .75 .35
❑ 291 Bernie Kosar .40 .18
❑ 292 Jumbo Elliott .20 .09
❑ 293 Jessie Hester .20 .09
❑ 294 Brent Jones .40 .18
❑ 295 Carl Banks .20 .09
❑ 296 Brian Washington .20 .09
❑ 297 Steve Beuerlein .20 .09
❑ 298 John Lynch RC .20 .09
❑ 299 Troy Vincent .20 .09
❑ 300 Emmitt Smith FOIL 5.00 2.20
❑ 301 Chris Zorich .20 .09
❑ 302 Wade Wilson .20 .09
❑ 303 Darrien Gordon RC .20 .09
❑ 304 Fred Stokes .20 .09
❑ 305 Nick Lowery .20 .09
❑ 306 Rodney Peete .20 .09
❑ 307 Chris Warren .40 .18
❑ 308 Herschel Walker .40 .18
❑ 309 Aundray Bruce .20 .09
❑ 310 Barry Foster FOIL .40 .18
❑ 311 George Teague RC .40 .18
❑ 312 Darryl Williams .20 .09
❑ 313 Thomas Smith RC .40 .18
❑ 314 Dennis Brown .20 .09
❑ 315 Marvin Jones FOIL RC .40 .18
❑ 316 Andre Tippett .20 .09
❑ 317 Demetrius DuBose RC .20 .09
❑ 318 Kirk Lowdermilk .20 .09
❑ 319 Shane Dronett .20 .09
❑ 320 Terry Kirby RC .75 .35
❑ 321 Qadry Ismail RC 2.00 .90
❑ 322 Lorenzo Lynch .20 .09
❑ 323 Willie Drewrey .20 .09
❑ 324 Jessie Tuggle .20 .09
❑ 325 Leroy Hoard .40 .18
❑ 326 Mark Collins .20 .09
❑ 327 Darrell Green .20 .09
❑ 328 Anthony Miller .40 .18
❑ 329 Brad Muster .20 .09
❑ 330 Jim Kelly FOIL .75 .35
❑ 331 Sean Gilbert .40 .18
❑ 332 Tim McKyer .20 .09
❑ 333 Scott Mersereau .20 .09
❑ 334 Willie Davis .75 .35
❑ 335 Brett Favre FOIL 6.00 2.70
❑ 336 Kevin Gogan .20 .09
❑ 337 Jim Harbaugh .75 .35
❑ 338 James Trapp RC .20 .09
❑ 339 Pete Stoyanovich .20 .09
❑ 340 Jerry Rice FOIL 3.00 1.35
❑ 341 Gary Anderson RB .20 .09
❑ 342 Carlton Gray RC .20 .09
❑ 343 Dermontti Dawson .20 .09
❑ 344 Ray Buchanan RC .20 .09
❑ 345 Derrick Fenner .20 .09
❑ 346 Dennis Smith .20 .09
❑ 347 Todd Rucci RC .20 .09
❑ 348 Seth Joyner .20 .09
❑ 349 Jim McMahon .20 .09
❑ 350 Rodney Hampton .75 .35
❑ 351 Al Smith .20 .09
❑ 352 Steve Everitt RC .20 .09
❑ 353 Vinnie Clark .20 .09
❑ 354 Eric Swann .40 .18
❑ 355 Brian Mitchell .40 .18
❑ 356 Will Shields RC .20 .09
❑ 357 Cornelius Bennett .40 .18
❑ 358 Darrin Smith RC .40 .18
❑ 359 Chris Mims .20 .09
❑ 360 Blair Thomas .20 .09
❑ 361 Dennis Gibson .20 .09
❑ 362 Santana Dotson .40 .18
❑ 363 Mark Ingram .20 .09
❑ 364 Don Mosebar .20 .09
❑ 365 Ty Detmer .75 .35
❑ 366 Bob Christian RC .20 .09
❑ 367 Adrian Hardy .20 .09
❑ 368 Vaughan Johnson .20 .09
❑ 369 Jim Everett .40 .18
❑ 370 Ricky Sanders .20 .09
❑ 371 Jonathan Hayes .20 .09
❑ 372 Bruce Matthews .20 .09
❑ 373 Darren Drozdov RC .75 .35
❑ 374 Scott Brumfield RC .20 .09
❑ 375 Cortez Kennedy .40 .18
❑ 376 Tim Harris .20 .09
❑ 377 Neil O'Donnell .75 .35
❑ 378 Robert Smith RC 5.00 2.20
❑ 379 Mike Caldwell RC .20 .09
❑ 380 Burt Grossman .20 .09
❑ 381 Corey Miller .20 .09
❑ 382 Kevin Williams FOIL RC .40 .18
❑ 383 Ken Harvey .20 .09
❑ 384 Greg Robinson RC .20 .09
❑ 385 Harold Alexander RC .20 .09
❑ 386 Andre Reed .40 .18
❑ 387 Reggie Langhorne .20 .09
❑ 388 Courtney Hawkins .20 .09
❑ 389 James Hasty .20 .09
❑ 390 Pat Swilling .20 .09
❑ 391 Chris Slade RC .40 .18
❑ 392 Keith Byars .20 .09
❑ 393 Dalton Hilliard .20 .09
❑ 394 David Williams .20 .09
❑ 395 Terry Obee RC .20 .09
❑ 396 Heath Sherman .20 .09
❑ 397 John Taylor .40 .18
❑ 398 Irv Eatman .20 .09
❑ 399 Johnny Holland .20 .09
❑ 400 John Elway FOIL 6.00 2.70
❑ 401 Clay Matthews .40 .18
❑ 402 Dave Meggett .20 .09
❑ 403 Eric Green .20 .09
❑ 404 Bryan Cox .20 .09
❑ 405 Jay Novacek .40 .18
❑ 406 Kenneth Davis .20 .09

❑ 407	Lamar Thomas RC	.20	.09
❑ 408	Lance Gunn RC	.20	.09
❑ 409	Audray McMillian	.20	.09
❑ 410	Derrick Thomas FOIL	.75	.35
❑ 411	Rufus Porter	.20	.09
❑ 412	Coleman Rudolph RC	.20	.09
❑ 413	Mark Rypien	.20	.09
❑ 414	Duane Bickett	.20	.09
❑ 415	Chris Singleton	.20	.09
❑ 416	Mitch Lyons RC	.20	.09
❑ 417	Bill Fralic	.20	.09
❑ 418	Gary Plummer	.20	.09
❑ 419	Ricky Proehl	.20	.09
❑ 420	Howie Long	.40	.18
❑ 421	Willie Roaf FOIL RC	.75	.35
❑ 422	Checklist 1-212	.20	.09
❑ 423	Checklist 213-423	.20	.09

1994 Bowman

	MINT	NRMT
COMPLETE SET (390)	60.00	27.00
COMMON CARD (1-390)	.20	.09
SEMISTARS	.40	.18
UNLISTED STARS	.75	.35
ONE FOIL CARD PER PACK		

❑ 1	Dan Wilkinson RC	.40	.18
❑ 2	Marshall Faulk RC	20.00	9.00
❑ 3	Heath Shuler RC	.75	.35
❑ 4	Willie McGinest RC	.75	.35
❑ 5	Trent Dilfer RC	4.00	1.80
❑ 6	Brent Jones	.40	.18
❑ 7	Sam Adams RC	.40	.18
❑ 8	Randy Baldwin	.20	.09
❑ 9	Jamir Miller RC	.20	.09
❑ 10	John Thierry RC	.20	.09
❑ 11	Aaron Glenn RC	.40	.18
❑ 12	Joe Johnson RC	.20	.09
❑ 13	Bernard Williams RC	.20	.09
❑ 14	Wayne Gandy RC	.20	.09
❑ 15	Aaron Taylor RC	.20	.09
❑ 16	Charles Johnson RC	.75	.35
❑ 17	Dewayne Washington RC	.40	.18
❑ 18	Bernie Kosar	.40	.18
❑ 19	Johnnie Morton RC	2.00	.90
❑ 20	Rob Fredrickson RC	.40	.18
❑ 21	Shante Carver RC	.20	.09
❑ 22	Thomas Lewis RC	.40	.18
❑ 23	Greg Hill RC	1.50	.70
❑ 24	Cris Dishman	.20	.09
❑ 25	Jeff Burris RC	.40	.18
❑ 26	Isaac Davis RC	.20	.09
❑ 27	Bert Emanuel RC	1.50	.70
❑ 28	Allen Aldridge RC	.20	.09
❑ 29	Kevin Lee RC	.20	.09
❑ 30	Chris Brantley RC	.20	.09
❑ 31	Rich Braham RC	.20	.09
❑ 32	Ricky Watters	.75	.35
❑ 33	Quentin Coryatt	.20	.09
❑ 34	Hardy Nickerson	.40	.18
❑ 35	Johnny Johnson	.20	.09
❑ 36	Ken Harvey	.20	.09
❑ 37	Chris Zorich	.20	.09
❑ 38	Chris Warren	.40	.18
❑ 39	David Palmer RC	1.50	.70
❑ 40	Chris Miller	.20	.09
❑ 41	Ken Ruettgers	.20	.09
❑ 42	Joe Panos RC	.20	.09
❑ 43	Mario Bates RC	.75	.35
❑ 44	Harry Colon	.20	.09
❑ 45	Barry Foster	.20	.09
❑ 46	Steve Tasker	.40	.18
❑ 47	Richmond Webb	.20	.09
❑ 48	James Folston RC	.20	.09
❑ 49	Erik Williams	.20	.09
❑ 50	Rodney Hampton	.75	.35
❑ 51	Derek Russell	.20	.09
❑ 52	Greg Montgomery	.20	.09
❑ 53	Anthony Phillips	.20	.09
❑ 54	Andre Coleman RC	.20	.09
❑ 55	Gary Brown	.20	.09
❑ 56	Neil Smith	.75	.35
❑ 57	Myron Baker	.20	.09
❑ 58	Sean Dawkins RC	.75	.35
❑ 59	Marvin Washington	.20	.09
❑ 60	Steve Beuerlein	.20	.09
❑ 61	Brenston Buckner RC	.20	.09
❑ 62	William Gaines RC	.20	.09
❑ 63	LeShon Johnson RC	.40	.18
❑ 64	Errict Rhett RC	4.00	1.80
❑ 65	Jim Everett	.40	.18
❑ 66	Desmond Howard	.40	.18
❑ 67	Jack Del Rio	.20	.09
❑ 68	Isaac Bruce RC	20.00	9.00
❑ 69	Van Malone RC	.20	.09
❑ 70	Jim Kelly	.75	.35
❑ 71	Leon Lett	.20	.09
❑ 72	Greg Robinson	.20	.09
❑ 73	Ryan Yarborough RC	.20	.09
❑ 74	Terry Wooden	.20	.09
❑ 75	Eric Allen	.20	.09
❑ 76	Ernest Givins	.40	.18
❑ 77	Marcus Spears RC	.20	.09
❑ 78	Thomas Randolph RC	.20	.09
❑ 79	Willie Clark RC	.20	.09
❑ 80	John Elway	5.00	2.20
❑ 81	Aubrey Beavers RC	.20	.09
❑ 82	Jeff Cothran RC	.20	.09
❑ 83	Norm Johnson	.20	.09
❑ 84	Donnell Bennett RC	.75	.35
❑ 85	Phillippi Sparks	.20	.09
❑ 86	Scott Mitchell	.75	.35
❑ 87	Bucky Brooks RC	.20	.09
❑ 88	Courtney Hawkins	.20	.09
❑ 89	Kevin Greene	.75	.35
❑ 90	Doug Nussmeier RC	.20	.09
❑ 91	Floyd Turner	.20	.09
❑ 92	Anthony Newman	.20	.09
❑ 93	Vinny Testaverde	.40	.18
❑ 94	Ronnie Lott	.40	.18
❑ 95	Troy Aikman	2.50	1.10
❑ 96	John Taylor	.40	.18
❑ 97	Henry Ellard	.40	.18
❑ 98	Carl Lee	.20	.09
❑ 99	Terry McDaniel	.20	.09
❑ 100	Joe Montana	5.00	2.20
❑ 101	David Klingler	.20	.09
❑ 102	Bruce Walker RC	.20	.09
❑ 103	Rick Cunningham RC	.20	.09
❑ 104	Robert Delpino	.20	.09
❑ 105	Mark Ingram	.20	.09
❑ 106	Leslie O'Neal	.20	.09
❑ 107	Darrell Thompson	.20	.09
❑ 108	Dave Meggett	.20	.09
❑ 109	Chris Gardocki	.20	.09
❑ 110	Andre Rison	.40	.18
❑ 111	Kelvin Martin	.20	.09
❑ 112	Marcus Robertson	.20	.09
❑ 113	Jason Gildon RC	.20	.09
❑ 114	Mel Gray	.20	.09
❑ 115	Tommy Vardell	.20	.09
❑ 116	Dexter Carter	.20	.09
❑ 117	Scottie Graham RC	.40	.18
❑ 118	Horace Copeland	.20	.09
❑ 119	Cornelius Bennett	.40	.18
❑ 120	Chris Maumalanga RC	.20	.09
❑ 121	Mo Lewis	.20	.09
❑ 122	Toby Wright RC	.20	.09
❑ 123	George Hegamin RC	.20	.09
❑ 124	Chip Lohmiller	.20	.09
❑ 125	Calvin Jones RC	.20	.09
❑ 126	Steve Shine	.20	.09
❑ 127	Chuck Levy RC	.20	.09
❑ 128	Sam Mills	.20	.09
❑ 129	Terance Mathis	.40	.18
❑ 130	Randall Cunningham	.75	.35
❑ 131	John Fina	.20	.09
❑ 132	Reggie White	.75	.35
❑ 133	Tom Waddle	.20	.09
❑ 134	Chris Calloway	.20	.09
❑ 135	Kevin Mawae RC	.20	.09
❑ 136	Lake Dawson RC	.75	.35
❑ 137	Alai Kalaniubalu	.20	.09
❑ 138	Tom Nalen	.20	.09
❑ 139	Cody Carlson	.20	.09
❑ 140	Dan Marino	5.00	2.20
❑ 141	Harris Barton	.20	.09
❑ 142	Don Mosebar	.20	.09
❑ 143	Romeo Bandison	.20	.09
❑ 144	Bruce Smith	.75	.35
❑ 145	Warren Moon	.75	.35
❑ 146	David Lutz	.20	.09
❑ 147	Dermontti Dawson	.20	.09
❑ 148	Ricky Proehl	.20	.09
❑ 149	Lou Benfatti RC	.20	.09
❑ 150	Craig Erickson	.20	.09
❑ 151	Sean Gilbert	.20	.09
❑ 152	Zefross Moss	.20	.09
❑ 153	Darnay Scott RC	2.00	.90
❑ 154	Courtney Hall	.20	.09
❑ 155	Brian Mitchell	.20	.09
❑ 156	Joe Burch RC UER	.20	.09
❑ 157	Terry Mickens	.20	.09
❑ 158	Jay Novacek	.40	.18
❑ 159	Chris Gedney	.20	.09
❑ 160	Bruce Matthews	.20	.09
❑ 161	Mario Perry RC	.20	.09
❑ 162	Vince Buck	.20	.09
❑ 163	Michael Bates	.20	.09
❑ 164	Willie Davis	.40	.18
❑ 165	Mike Pritchard	.20	.09
❑ 166	Doug Riesenberg	.20	.09
❑ 167	Herschel Walker	.40	.18
❑ 168	Tim Ruddy RC	.20	.09
❑ 169	William Floyd RC	.75	.35
❑ 170	John Randle	.20	.09
❑ 171	Winston Moss	.20	.09
❑ 172	Thurman Thomas	.75	.35
❑ 173	Eric England RC	.20	.09
❑ 174	Vincent Brisby	.75	.35
❑ 175	Greg Lloyd	.75	.35
❑ 176	Paul Gruber	.20	.09
❑ 177	Brad Ottis RC	.20	.09
❑ 178	George Teague	.20	.09
❑ 179	Willie Jackson RC	.75	.35
❑ 180	Barry Sanders	5.00	2.20
❑ 181	Brian Washington	.20	.09
❑ 182	Michael Jackson	.40	.18
❑ 183	Jason Mathews RC	.20	.09
❑ 184	Chester McGlockton	.20	.09
❑ 185	Tydus Winans RC	.20	.09
❑ 186	Michael Haynes	.40	.18
❑ 187	Erik Kramer	.40	.18
❑ 188	Chris Doleman	.20	.09
❑ 189	Haywood Jeffires	.40	.18
❑ 190	Larry Whigham RC	.20	.09
❑ 191	Shawn Jefferson	.20	.09
❑ 192	Pete Stoyanovich	.20	.09
❑ 193	Rod Bernstine	.20	.09
❑ 194	William Thomas	.20	.09
❑ 195	Marcus Allen	.75	.35
❑ 196	Dave Brown	.40	.18
❑ 197	Harold Bishop RC	.20	.09
❑ 198	Lorenzo Lynch	.20	.09
❑ 199	Dwight Stone	.20	.09
❑ 200	Jerry Rice	2.50	1.10
❑ 201	Rocket Ismail	.40	.18
❑ 202	LeRoy Butler	.20	.09
❑ 203	Glenn Parker	.20	.09
❑ 204	Bruce Armstrong	.20	.09
❑ 205	Shane Conlan	.20	.09
❑ 206	Russell Maryland	.20	.09
❑ 207	Herman Moore	.75	.35
❑ 208	Eric Martin	.20	.09
❑ 209	John Friesz	.40	.18
❑ 210	Boomer Esiason	.40	.18
❑ 211	Jim Harbaugh	.75	.35
❑ 212	Harold Green	.20	.09
❑ 213	Perry Klein RC	.20	.09

❑ 214 Eric Metcalf .40 .18
❑ 215 Steve Everitt .20 .09
❑ 216 Victor Bailey .20 .09
❑ 217 Lincoln Kennedy .20 .09
❑ 218 Glyn Milburn .40 .18
❑ 219 John Copeland .20 .09
❑ 220 Drew Bledsoe 3.00 1.35
❑ 221 Kevin Williams .40 .18
❑ 222 Roosevelt Potts .20 .09
❑ 223 Troy Drayton .20 .09
❑ 224 Terry Kirby .75 .35
❑ 225 Ronald Moore .20 .09
❑ 226 Tyrone Hughes .40 .18
❑ 227 Wayne Simmons .20 .09
❑ 228 Tony McGee .20 .09
❑ 229 Derek Brown RBK .20 .09
❑ 230 Jason Elam .20 .09
❑ 231 Qadry Ismail .75 .35
❑ 232 O.J. McDuffie .75 .35
❑ 233 Mike Caldwell .20 .09
❑ 234 Reggie Brooks .40 .18
❑ 235 Rick Mirer .75 .35
❑ 236 Steve Tovar .20 .09
❑ 237 Patrick Robinson .20 .09
❑ 238 Tom Carter .20 .09
❑ 239 Ben Coates .75 .35
❑ 240 Jerome Bettis .75 .35
❑ 241 Garrison Hearst .75 .35
❑ 242 Natrone Means .75 .35
❑ 243 Dana Stubblefield .75 .35
❑ 244 Willie Roaf .20 .09
❑ 245 Cortez Kennedy .40 .18
❑ 246 Todd Steussie RC .40 .18
❑ 247 Pat Coleman .20 .09
❑ 248 David Wyman .20 .09
❑ 249 Jeremy Lincoln .20 .09
❑ 250 Carlester Crumpler .20 .09
❑ 251 Dale Carter .20 .09
❑ 252 Corey Raymond RC .20 .09
❑ 253 Bryan Cox .20 .09
❑ 254 Charlie Garner RC 4.00 1.80
❑ 255 Jeff Hostetler .40 .18
❑ 256 Shane Bonham RC .20 .09
❑ 257 Thomas Everett .20 .09
❑ 258 John Jackson .20 .09
❑ 259 Terry Irving RC .20 .09
❑ 260 Corey Sawyer .20 .09
❑ 261 Rob Waldrop .20 .09
❑ 262 Curtis Conway .75 .35
❑ 263 Winfred Tubbs RC .40 .18
❑ 264 Sean Jones .20 .09
❑ 265 James Washington .20 .09
❑ 266 Lonnie Johnson RC .20 .09
❑ 267 Rob Moore .40 .18
❑ 268 Flipper Anderson .20 .09
❑ 269 Jon Hand .20 .09
❑ 270 Joe Patton RC .20 .09
❑ 271 Howard Ballard .20 .09
❑ 272 Fernando Smith RC .20 .09
❑ 273 Jessie Tuggle .20 .09
❑ 274 John Alt .20 .09
❑ 275 Corey Miller .20 .09
❑ 276 Gus Frerotte RC 1.50 .70
❑ 277 Jeff Cross .20 .09
❑ 278 Kevin Smith .20 .09
❑ 279 Corey Louchiey RC .20 .09
❑ 280 Micheal Barrow .20 .09
❑ 281 Jim Flanigan RC .40 .18
❑ 282 Calvin Williams .40 .18
❑ 283 Jeff Jaeger .20 .09
❑ 284 John Reece RC .20 .09
❑ 285 Jason Hanson .20 .09
❑ 286 Kurt Haws RC .20 .09
❑ 287 Eric Davis .20 .09
❑ 288 Maurice Hurst .20 .09
❑ 289 Kirk Lowdermilk .20 .09
❑ 290 Rod Woodson .75 .35
❑ 291 Andre Reed .40 .18
❑ 292 Vince Workman .20 .09
❑ 293 Wayne Martin .20 .09
❑ 294 Keith Lyle RC .20 .09
❑ 295 Brett Favre 5.00 2.20
❑ 296 Doug Brien RC .20 .09
❑ 297 Junior Seau .75 .35
❑ 298 Randall McDaniel .20 .09
❑ 299 Johnny Mitchell .20 .09
❑ 300 Emmitt Smith 4.00 1.80
❑ 301 Michael Brooks .20 .09
❑ 302 Steve Jackson .20 .09
❑ 303 Jeff George .75 .35
❑ 304 Irving Fryar .40 .18
❑ 305 Derrick Thomas .75 .35
❑ 306 Dante Jones .20 .09
❑ 307 Darrell Green .20 .09
❑ 308 Mark Bavaro .20 .09
❑ 309 Eugene Robinson .20 .09
❑ 310 Shannon Sharpe .40 .18
❑ 311 Michael Timpson .20 .09
❑ 312 Kevin Mitchell RC .20 .09
❑ 313 Stevon Moore .20 .09
❑ 314 Eric Swann .40 .18
❑ 315 James Bostic RC .75 .35
❑ 316 Robert Brooks .75 .35
❑ 317 Pete Pierson RC .20 .09
❑ 318 Jim Sweeney .20 .09
❑ 319 Anthony Smith .20 .09
❑ 320 Rohn Stark .20 .09
❑ 321 Gary Anderson K .20 .09
❑ 322 Robert Porcher .20 .09
❑ 323 Darryl Talley .20 .09
❑ 324 Stan Humphries .75 .35
❑ 325 Shelly Hammonds RC .20 .09
❑ 326 Jim McMahon .20 .09
❑ 327 Lamont Warren RC .20 .09
❑ 328 Chris Penn RC .20 .09
❑ 329 Tony Woods .20 .09
❑ 330 Raymont Harris RC .75 .35
❑ 331 Mitch Davis RC .20 .09
❑ 332 Michael Irvin .75 .35
❑ 333 Kent Graham .40 .18
❑ 334 Brian Blades .40 .18
❑ 335 Lomas Brown .20 .09
❑ 336 Willie Drewrey .20 .09
❑ 337 Russell Freeman .20 .09
❑ 338 Eric Zomalt RC .20 .09
❑ 339 Santana Dotson .40 .18
❑ 340 Sterling Sharpe .40 .18
❑ 341 Ray Crittenden RC .20 .09
❑ 342 Perry Carter RC .20 .09
❑ 343 Austin Robbins .20 .09
❑ 344 Mike Wells RC .20 .09
❑ 345 Toddrick McIntosh RC .20 .09
❑ 346 Mark Carrier WR .40 .18
❑ 347 Eugene Daniel .20 .09
❑ 348 Tre Johnson RC .20 .09
❑ 349 D.J. Johnson .20 .09
❑ 350 Steve Young 2.00 .90
❑ 351 Jim Pyne RC .20 .09
❑ 352 Jocelyn Borgella RC .20 .09
❑ 353 Pat Carter .20 .09
❑ 354 Sam Rogers RC .20 .09
❑ 355 Jason Sehorn RC .20 .09
❑ 356 Darren Carrington .20 .09
❑ 357 Lamar Smith RC .75 .35
❑ 358 James Burton RC .20 .09
❑ 359 Darrin Smith .20 .09
❑ 360 Marco Coleman .20 .09
❑ 361 Webster Slaughter .20 .09
❑ 362 Lewis Tillman .20 .09
❑ 363 David Alexander .20 .09
❑ 364 Bradford Banta RC .20 .09
❑ 365 Erric Pegram .20 .09
❑ 366 Mike Fox .20 .09
❑ 367 Jeff Lageman .20 .09
❑ 368 Kurt Gouveia .20 .09
❑ 369 Tim Brown .75 .35
❑ 370 Seth Joyner .20 .09
❑ 371 Irv Eatman .20 .09
❑ 372 Dorsey Levens RC 15.00 6.75
❑ 373 Anthony Pleasant .20 .09
❑ 374 Henry Jones .20 .09
❑ 375 Cris Carter 1.25 .55
❑ 376 Morten Andersen .20 .09
❑ 377 Neil O'Donnell .75 .35
❑ 378 Tyronne Drakeford RC .20 .09
❑ 379 John Carney .20 .09
❑ 380 Vincent Brown .20 .09
❑ 381 J.J. Birden .20 .09
❑ 382 Chris Spielman .40 .18
❑ 383 Mark Bortz .20 .09
❑ 384 Ray Childress .20 .09
❑ 385 Carlton Bailey .20 .09
❑ 386 Charles Haley .40 .18
❑ 387 Shane Dronett .20 .09
❑ 388 Jon Vaughn .20 .09
❑ 389 Checklist 1-195 .20 .09
❑ 390 Checklist 196-390 .20 .09

1995 Bowman

	MINT	NRMT
COMPLETE SET (357)	125.00	55.00
COMMON CARD (1-357)	.15	.07
EXPANSION FOILS (221-247)	.40	.18
SEMISTARS	.30	.14
UNLISTED STARS	.60	.25

*FIRST ROUND STAMPED: 1X TO 2X HI COL.
FR STAMPED: STATED ODDS 1:12
*EXPANSION TEAM GOLDS: 1.5X TO 3X HI
EXP.TEAM GOLD: STATED ODDS 1:12

❑ 1 Ki-Jana Carter RC .60 .25
❑ 2 Tony Boselli RC .30 .14
❑ 3 Steve McNair RC 10.00 4.50
❑ 4 Michael Westbrook RC 6.00 2.70
❑ 5 Kerry Collins RC 4.00 1.80
❑ 6 Kevin Carter RC .60 .25
❑ 7 Mike Mamula RC .30 .14
❑ 8 Joey Galloway RC 10.00 4.50
❑ 9 Kyle Brady RC .60 .25
❑ 10 J.J. Stokes RC 3.00 1.35
❑ 11 Derrick Alexander DE RC .15 .07
❑ 12 Warren Sapp RC 1.50 .70
❑ 13 Mark Fields RC .15 .07
❑ 14 Ruben Brown RC .15 .07
❑ 15 Ellis Johnson RC .15 .07
❑ 16 Hugh Douglas RC .30 .14
❑ 17 Mike Pelton RC .15 .07
❑ 18 Napoleon Kaufman RC 8.00 3.60
❑ 19 James O. Stewart RC 8.00 3.60
❑ 20 Luther Elliss RC .15 .07
❑ 21 Rashaan Salaam RC .60 .25
❑ 22 Tyrone Poole RC .30 .14
❑ 23 Ty Law RC .30 .14
❑ 24 Korey Stringer RC .15 .07
❑ 25 Billy Milner RC .15 .07
❑ 26 Devin Bush RC .15 .07
❑ 27 Mark Bruener RC .30 .14
❑ 28 Derrick Brooks RC .15 .07
❑ 29 Blake Brockermeyer RC .15 .07
❑ 30 Alundis Brice RC .15 .07
❑ 31 Trezelle Jenkins RC .15 .07
❑ 32 Craig Newsome RC .15 .07
❑ 33 Fred Barnett .30 .14
❑ 34 Ray Childress .15 .07
❑ 35 Chris Miller .15 .07
❑ 36 Charles Haley .30 .14
❑ 37 Ray Crittenden .15 .07
❑ 38 Gus Frerotte .60 .25
❑ 39 Jeff George .30 .14
❑ 40 Dan Marino 3.00 1.35
❑ 41 Shawn Lee .15 .07
❑ 42 Herman Moore .60 .25
❑ 43 Chris Calloway .15 .07
❑ 44 Jeff Graham .15 .07
❑ 45 Ray Buchanan .15 .07
❑ 46 Doug Pelfrey .15 .07
❑ 47 Lake Dawson .30 .14
❑ 48 Glenn Parker .15 .07
❑ 49 Terry McDaniel .15 .07

❑ 50 Rod Woodson .30 .14	❑ 136 Carl Pickens .60 .25	❑ 222 Derrick Graham FOIL .40 .18
❑ 51 Santana Dotson .15 .07	❑ 137 Mike Verstegen RC .15 .07	❑ 223 Mike Hollis FOIL .40 .18
❑ 52 Anthony Miller .30 .14	❑ 138 Chris Mims .15 .07	❑ 224 Darion Conner FOIL .40 .18
❑ 53 Bo Orlando .15 .07	❑ 139 Darryl Pounds RC .15 .07	❑ 225 Steve Beuerlein FOIL .40 .18
❑ 54 David Palmer .30 .14	❑ 140 Emmitt Smith 2.50 1.10	❑ 226 Rod Smith DB FOIL .40 .18
❑ 55 William Floyd .60 .25	❑ 141 Mike Frederick RC .15 .07	❑ 227 James Williams FOIL .40 .18
❑ 56 Edgar Bennett .30 .14	❑ 142 Henry Ellard .30 .14	❑ 228 Bob Christian FOIL .40 .18
❑ 57 Jeff Blake RC 4.00 1.80	❑ 143 Willie McGinest .30 .14	❑ 229 Jeff Lageman FOIL .40 .18
❑ 58 Anthony Pleasant .15 .07	❑ 144 Michael Roan RC .15 .07	❑ 230 Frank Reich FOIL .40 .18
❑ 59 Quinn Early .30 .14	❑ 145 Chris Spielman .30 .14	❑ 231 Harry Colon FOIL .40 .18
❑ 60 Bobby Houston .15 .07	❑ 146 Darryl Talley .15 .07	❑ 232 Carlton Bailey FOIL .40 .18
❑ 61 Terrell Fletcher RC .15 .07	❑ 147 Randall Cunningham .60 .25	❑ 233 Mickey Washington FOIL .40 .18
❑ 62 Gary Brown .15 .07	❑ 148 Andrew Greene RC .15 .07	❑ 234 Shawn Bouwens FOIL .40 .18
❑ 63 Dwayne Sabb .15 .07	❑ 149 George Teague .15 .07	❑ 235 Don Beebe FOIL .40 .18
❑ 64 Roman Phifer .15 .07	❑ 150 Tyrone Hughes .30 .14	❑ 236 Kelvin Pritchett FOIL .40 .18
❑ 65 Sherman Williams RC .15 .07	❑ 151 Ron Davis RC .15 .07	❑ 237 Tommy Barnhardt FOIL .40 .18
❑ 66 Roosevelt Potts .15 .07	❑ 152 Stevon Moore .15 .07	❑ 238 Mike Dumas FOIL .40 .18
❑ 67 Darnay Scott .60 .25	❑ 153 Merton Hanks .15 .07	❑ 239 Brett Maxie FOIL .40 .18
❑ 68 Charlie Garner .30 .14	❑ 154 Darren Perry .15 .07	❑ 240 Desmond Howard FOIL .40 .18
❑ 69 Bert Emanuel .60 .25	❑ 155 Dave Brown .30 .14	❑ 241 Sam Mills FOIL .40 .18
❑ 70 Herschel Walker .30 .14	❑ 156 Mike Morton RC .15 .07	❑ 242 Keith Goganious FOIL .40 .18
❑ 71 Lorenzo Styles RC .15 .07	❑ 157 Seth Joyner .15 .07	❑ 243 Bubba McDowell FOIL .40 .18
❑ 72 Andre Coleman .15 .07	❑ 158 Bryan Cox .15 .07	❑ 244 Vinnie Clark FOIL .40 .18
❑ 73 Tyronne Drakeford .15 .07	❑ 159 Corey Fuller RC .15 .07	❑ 245 Lamar Lathon FOIL .40 .18
❑ 74 Jay Novacek .30 .14	❑ 160 John Elway 3.00 1.35	❑ 246 Bryan Barker FOIL .40 .18
❑ 75 Raymont Harris .15 .07	❑ 161 Dewayne Washington .30 .14	❑ 247 Darren Carrington FOIL .40 .18
❑ 76 Tamarick Vanover RC .60 .25	❑ 162 Chris Warren .30 .14	❑ 248 Jay Barker RC .15 .07
❑ 77 Tom Carter .15 .07	❑ 163 Jeff Kopp RC .15 .07	❑ 249 Eric Davis .15 .07
❑ 78 Eric Green .15 .07	❑ 164 Sean Dawkins .30 .14	❑ 250 Heath Shuler .60 .25
❑ 79 Patrick Hunter .15 .07	❑ 165 Mark Carrier DB .15 .07	❑ 251 Donta Jones RC .15 .07
❑ 80 Jeff Hostetler .30 .14	❑ 166 Andre Hastings .30 .14	❑ 252 LeRoy Butler .15 .07
❑ 81 Robert Blackmon .15 .07	❑ 167 Derek West RC .15 .07	❑ 253 Michael Zordich .15 .07
❑ 82 Anthony Cook RC .15 .07	❑ 168 Glenn Montgomery .15 .07	❑ 254 Cortez Kennedy .30 .14
❑ 83 Craig Erickson .15 .07	❑ 169 Trent Dilfer .60 .25	❑ 255 Brian DeMarco RC .30 .14
❑ 84 Glyn Milburn .15 .07	❑ 170 Rob Johnson RC 6.00 2.70	❑ 256 Randal Hill .15 .07
❑ 85 Greg Lloyd .30 .14	❑ 171 Todd Scott .15 .07	❑ 257 Michael Irvin .60 .25
❑ 86 Brent Jones .15 .07	❑ 172 Charles Johnson .30 .14	❑ 258 Natrone Means .60 .25
❑ 87 Barrett Brooks RC .15 .07	❑ 173 Kez McCorvey RC .15 .07	❑ 259 Linc Harden RC .15 .07
❑ 88 Alvin Harper .15 .07	❑ 174 Rob Fredrickson .15 .07	❑ 260 Jerome Bettis .60 .25
❑ 89 Sean Jones .15 .07	❑ 175 Corey Sawyer .15 .07	❑ 261 Tony Bennett .15 .07
❑ 90 Cris Carter .60 .25	❑ 176 Brett Perriman .30 .14	❑ 262 Dameian Jeffries RC .15 .07
❑ 91 Russell Copeland .15 .07	❑ 177 Ken Dilger RC .30 .14	❑ 263 Cornelius Bennett .30 .14
❑ 92 Frank Sanders RC 4.00 1.80	❑ 178 Dana Stubblefield .60 .25	❑ 264 Chris Zorich .15 .07
❑ 93 Mo Lewis .15 .07	❑ 179 Eric Allen .15 .07	❑ 265 Bobby Taylor RC .30 .14
❑ 94 Michael Haynes .30 .14	❑ 180 Drew Bledsoe 1.50 .70	❑ 266 Terrell Buckley .15 .07
❑ 95 Andre Rison .30 .14	❑ 181 Tyrone Davis RC .15 .07	❑ 267 Troy Dumas RC .15 .07
❑ 96 Jesse James RC .15 .07	❑ 182 Reggie Brooks .30 .14	❑ 268 Rodney Hampton .30 .14
❑ 97 Stan Humphries .30 .14	❑ 183 Dale Carter .30 .14	❑ 269 Steve Everitt .15 .07
❑ 98 James Hasty .15 .07	❑ 184 William Henderson RC .15 .07	❑ 270 Mel Gray .15 .07
❑ 99 Ricardo McDonald .15 .07	❑ 185 Reggie White .60 .25	❑ 271 Antonio Armstrong RC .15 .07
❑ 100 Jerry Rice 1.50 .70	❑ 186 Lorenzo White .15 .07	❑ 272 Jim Harbaugh .30 .14
❑ 101 Chris Hudson RC .15 .07	❑ 187 Leslie O'Neal .30 .14	❑ 273 Gary Clark .15 .07
❑ 102 Dave Meggett .15 .07	❑ 188 Stoney Case RC 1.25 .55	❑ 274 Tau Pupua RC .15 .07
❑ 103 Brian Mitchell .15 .07	❑ 189 Jeff Burris .15 .07	❑ 275 Warren Moon .30 .14
❑ 104 Mike Johnson .15 .07	❑ 190 Leroy Hoard .15 .07	❑ 276 Corey Croom .15 .07
❑ 105 Kordell Stewart RC 10.00 4.50	❑ 191 Thomas Randolph .15 .07	❑ 277 Tony Berti RC .15 .07
❑ 106 Michael Brooks .15 .07	❑ 192 Rodney Thomas RC .60 .25	❑ 278 Shannon Sharpe .30 .14
❑ 107 Steve Walsh .15 .07	❑ 193 Quentin Coryatt .30 .14	❑ 279 Boomer Esiason .30 .14
❑ 108 Eric Metcalf .30 .14	❑ 194 Terry Wooden .15 .07	❑ 280 Aeneas Williams .15 .07
❑ 109 Ricky Watters .60 .25	❑ 195 David Sloan RC .30 .14	❑ 281 Lethon Flowers RC .15 .07
❑ 110 Brett Favre 3.00 1.35	❑ 196 Bernie Parmalee .30 .14	❑ 282 Derek Brown TE .15 .07
❑ 111 Aubrey Beavers .15 .07	❑ 197 Zack Crockett RC .15 .07	❑ 283 Charlie Williams .15 .07
❑ 112 Brian Williams LB RC .15 .07	❑ 198 Troy Aikman 1.50 .70	❑ 284 Dan Wilkinson .30 .14
❑ 113 Eugene Robinson .15 .07	❑ 199 Bruce Smith .60 .25	❑ 285 Mike Sherrard .15 .07
❑ 114 Matt O'Dwyer RC .15 .07	❑ 200 Eric Zeier RC 1.25 .55	❑ 286 Evan Pilgrim RC .15 .07
❑ 115 Micheal Barrow .15 .07	❑ 201 Anthony Smith .15 .07	❑ 287 Kimble Anders .30 .14
❑ 116 Rocket Ismail .30 .14	❑ 202 Jake Reed .30 .14	❑ 288 Greg Jefferson RC .15 .07
❑ 117 Scott Gragg RC .15 .07	❑ 203 Hardy Nickerson .15 .07	❑ 289 Ken Norton .30 .14
❑ 118 Leon Lett .15 .07	❑ 204 Patrick Riley RC .15 .07	❑ 290 Terance Mathis .30 .14
❑ 119 Reggie Roby .15 .07	❑ 205 Bruce Matthews .15 .07	❑ 291 Torey Hunter RC .15 .07
❑ 120 Marshall Faulk 1.00 .45	❑ 206 Larry Centers .30 .14	❑ 292 Ken Harvey .15 .07
❑ 121 Jack Jackson RC .15 .07	❑ 207 Troy Drayton .15 .07	❑ 293 Irving Fryar .30 .14
❑ 122 Keith Byars .15 .07	❑ 208 John Burrough RC .15 .07	❑ 294 Michael Reed RC .15 .07
❑ 123 Eric Hill .15 .07	❑ 209 Jason Elam .15 .07	❑ 295 Andre Reed .30 .14
❑ 124 Todd Sauerbrun RC .15 .07	❑ 210 Donnell Woolford .15 .07	❑ 296 Vencie Glenn .15 .07
❑ 125 Dexter Carter .15 .07	❑ 211 Sam Shade RC .15 .07	❑ 297 Corey Swinson .15 .07
❑ 126 Vinny Testaverde .30 .14	❑ 212 Kevin Greene .30 .14	❑ 298 Harvey Williams .15 .07
❑ 127 Shane Conlan .15 .07	❑ 213 Ronald Moore .15 .07	❑ 299 Willie Davis .30 .14
❑ 128 Terrance Shaw RC .15 .07	❑ 214 Shane Hannah RC .15 .07	❑ 300 Barry Sanders 3.00 1.35
❑ 129 Willie Roaf .15 .07	❑ 215 Jim Everett .15 .07	❑ 301 Curtis Martin RC 10.00 4.50
❑ 130 Jim Kelly .60 .25	❑ 216 Scott Mitchell .30 .14	❑ 302 Johnny Mitchell .15 .07
❑ 131 Neil O'Donnell .30 .14	❑ 217 Antonio Freeman RC 10.00 4.50	❑ 303 Daryl Johnston .30 .14
❑ 132 Ray McElroy RC .15 .07	❑ 218 Tony McGee .15 .07	❑ 304 Lorenzo Lynch .15 .07
❑ 133 Ed McDaniel .15 .07	❑ 219 Clay Matthews .30 .14	❑ 305 Christian Fauria RC .15 .07
❑ 134 Brian Gelzheiser RC .30 .14	❑ 220 Neil Smith .30 .14	❑ 306 Sean Gilbert .30 .14
❑ 135 Marcus Allen .60 .25	❑ 221 Mark Williams FOIL .40 .18	❑ 307 Ray Zellars RC .30 .14

	Player	Mint	Nrmt
❑ 308	William Strong RC	.15	.07
❑ 309	Jack Del Rio	.15	.07
❑ 310	Junior Seau	.60	.25
❑ 311	Justin Armour RC	.15	.07
❑ 312	Eric Bjornson RC	.30	.14
❑ 313	Vincent Brown	.15	.07
❑ 314	Darius Holland RC	.15	.07
❑ 315	Chad May RC	.15	.07
❑ 316	Simon Fletcher	.15	.07
❑ 317	Roell Preston RC	1.00	.45
❑ 318	John Thierry	.15	.07
❑ 319	Orlando Thomas RC	.15	.07
❑ 320	Zach Wiegert RC	.15	.07
❑ 321	Derrick Alexander WR	.60	.25
❑ 322	Chris Cowart RC	.15	.07
❑ 323	Chris Sanders RC	.60	.25
❑ 324	Robert Brooks	.60	.25
❑ 325	Todd Collins RC	.60	.25
❑ 326	Ken Irvin RC	.15	.07
❑ 327	Erric Pegram	.30	.14
❑ 328	Damien Covington RC	.15	.07
❑ 329	Brendan Stai RC	.15	.07
❑ 330	James A.Stewart RC	.15	.07
❑ 331	Jessie Tuggle	.15	.07
❑ 332	Marco Coleman	.15	.07
❑ 333	Steve Young	1.25	.55
❑ 334	Greg Hill	.30	.14
❑ 335	Darryl Williams	.15	.07
❑ 336	Calvin Williams	.30	.14
❑ 337	Cris Dishman	.15	.07
❑ 338	Anthony Morgan	.15	.07
❑ 339	Renaldo Turnbull	.15	.07
❑ 340	Rick Mirer	.60	.25
❑ 341	Tim Brown	.60	.25
❑ 342	Dennis Gibson	.15	.07
❑ 343	Brad Baxter	.15	.07
❑ 344	Henry Jones	.15	.07
❑ 345	Johnny Bailey	.15	.07
❑ 346	Rocket Ismail	.30	.14
❑ 347	Richmond Webb	.15	.07
❑ 348	Robert Jones	.15	.07
❑ 349	Garrison Hearst	.60	.25
❑ 350	Errict Rhett	.60	.25
❑ 351	Steve Atwater	.15	.07
❑ 352	Joe Cain	.15	.07
❑ 353	Ben Coates	.30	.14
❑ 354	Aaron Glenn	.15	.07
❑ 355	Antonio Langham	.15	.07
❑ 356	Eugene Daniel	.15	.07
❑ 357	Tim Bowens	.15	.07

1998 Bowman

	MINT	NRMT
COMPLETE SET (220)	60.00	27.00
COMMON CARD (1-220)	.15	.07
SEMISTARS	.30	.14
UNLISTED STARS	.60	.25
COMMON ROOKIES	1.50	.70
ROOKIE SEMISTARS	2.00	.90
ROOKIE UNLISTED STARS	2.50	1.10
COMP.INTERSTATE (220)	250.00	110.00

*INTERSTATE STARS: 1.5X TO 3X HI COL.
*INTERSTATE YOUNG STARS: 1X TO 2X
*INTERSTATE RCs: .6X TO 1.5X
INTERSTATES ONE PER PACK..

	MINT	NRMT
COMMON GOLDEN ANN.	15.00	6.75

*GOLDEN ANN.STARS: 30X TO 80X HI COL.
*GOLDEN ANN.YOUNG STARS: 25X TO 60X
*GOLDEN ANN.RCs: 7.5X TO 15X
GOLDEN ANNIVERSARY STATED ODDS 1:180
GOLDEN ANN.PRINT RUN 50 SER.#'d SETS

	Player	Mint	Nrmt
❑ 1	Peyton Manning RC	20.00	9.00
❑ 2	Keith Brooking RC	2.00	.90
❑ 3	Duane Starks RC	1.50	.70
❑ 4	Takeo Spikes RC	2.00	.90
❑ 5	Andre Wadsworth RC	2.00	.90
❑ 6	Greg Ellis RC	1.50	.70
❑ 7	Brian Griese RC	8.00	3.60
❑ 8	Germane Crowell RC	4.00	1.80
❑ 9	Jerome Pathon RC	2.00	.90
❑ 10	Ryan Leaf RC	3.00	1.35
❑ 11	Fred Taylor RC	12.00	5.50
❑ 12	Robert Edwards RC	2.50	1.10
❑ 13	Grant Wistrom RC	1.50	.70
❑ 14	Robert Holcombe RC	2.50	1.10
❑ 15	Tim Dwight RC	3.00	1.35
❑ 16	Jacquez Green RC	3.00	1.35
❑ 17	Marcus Nash RC	2.50	1.10
❑ 18	Jason Peter RC	1.50	.70
❑ 19	Anthony Simmons RC	1.50	.70
❑ 20	Curtis Enis RC	4.00	1.80
❑ 21	John Avery RC	2.50	1.10
❑ 22	Pat Johnson RC	2.00	.90
❑ 23	Joe Jurevicius RC	2.00	.90
❑ 24	Brian Simmons RC	1.50	.70
❑ 25	Kevin Dyson RC	3.00	1.35
❑ 26	Skip Hicks RC	3.00	1.35
❑ 27	Hines Ward RC	2.00	.90
❑ 28	Tavian Banks RC	2.00	.90
❑ 29	Ahman Green RC	2.50	1.10
❑ 30	Tony Simmons RC	2.00	.90
❑ 31	Charles Johnson	.15	.07
❑ 32	Freddie Jones	.15	.07
❑ 33	Joey Galloway	.60	.25
❑ 34	Tony Banks	.30	.14
❑ 35	Jake Plummer	2.00	.90
❑ 36	Reidel Anthony	.30	.14
❑ 37	Steve McNair	.60	.25
❑ 38	Michael Westbrook	.30	.14
❑ 39	Chris Sanders	.15	.07
❑ 40	Isaac Bruce	.60	.25
❑ 41	Charlie Garner	.15	.07
❑ 42	Wayne Chrebet	.60	.25
❑ 43	Michael Strahan	.15	.07
❑ 44	Brad Johnson	.60	.25
❑ 45	Mike Alstott	.60	.25
❑ 46	Tony Gonzalez	.15	.07
❑ 47	Johnnie Morton	.30	.14
❑ 48	Darnay Scott	.30	.14
❑ 49	Rae Carruth	.30	.14
❑ 50	Terrell Davis	2.50	1.10
❑ 51	Jermaine Lewis	.30	.14
❑ 52	Frank Sanders	.30	.14
❑ 53	Byron Hanspard	.30	.14
❑ 54	Gus Frerotte	.15	.07
❑ 55	Terry Glenn	.60	.25
❑ 56	J.J. Stokes	.30	.14
❑ 57	Will Blackwell	.15	.07
❑ 58	Keyshawn Johnson	.60	.25
❑ 59	Tiki Barber	.30	.14
❑ 60	Dorsey Levens	.60	.25
❑ 61	Zach Thomas	.15	.07
❑ 62	Corey Dillon	1.00	.45
❑ 63	Antowain Smith	.60	.25
❑ 64	Michael Sinclair	.15	.07
❑ 65	Rod Smith	.30	.14
❑ 66	Trent Dilfer	.60	.25
❑ 67	Warren Sapp	.30	.14
❑ 68	Charles Way	.15	.07
❑ 69	Tamarick Vanover	.15	.07
❑ 70	Drew Bledsoe	1.25	.55
❑ 71	John Mobley	.15	.07
❑ 72	Kerry Collins	.30	.14
❑ 73	Peter Boulware	.15	.07
❑ 74	Simeon Rice	.30	.14
❑ 75	Eddie George	1.25	.55
❑ 76	Fred Lane	.30	.14
❑ 77	Jamal Anderson	.60	.25
❑ 78	Antonio Freeman	.60	.25
❑ 79	Jason Sehorn	.15	.07
❑ 80	Curtis Martin	.60	.25
❑ 81	Bobby Hoying	.30	.14
❑ 82	Garrison Hearst	.60	.25
❑ 83	Glenn Foley	.30	.14
❑ 84	Danny Kanell	.30	.14
❑ 85	Kordell Stewart	.60	.25
❑ 86	O.J. McDuffie	.30	.14
❑ 87	Marvin Harrison	.30	.14
❑ 88	Bobby Engram	.30	.14
❑ 89	Chris Slade	.15	.07
❑ 90	Warrick Dunn	1.00	.45
❑ 91	Ricky Watters	.30	.14
❑ 92	Rickey Dudley	.15	.07
❑ 93	Terrell Owens	.60	.25
❑ 94	Karim Abdul-Jabbar	.60	.25
❑ 95	Napoleon Kaufman	.60	.25
❑ 96	Darrell Green	.30	.14
❑ 97	Levon Kirkland	.15	.07
❑ 98	Jeff George	.30	.14
❑ 99	Andre Hastings	.15	.07
❑ 100	John Elway	3.00	1.35
❑ 101	John Randle	.30	.14
❑ 102	Andre Rison	.30	.14
❑ 103	Keenan McCardell	.30	.14
❑ 104	Marshall Faulk	.60	.25
❑ 105	Emmitt Smith	2.50	1.10
❑ 106	Robert Brooks	.30	.14
❑ 107	Scott Mitchell	.30	.14
❑ 108	Shannon Sharpe	.30	.14
❑ 109	Deion Sanders	.60	.25
❑ 110	Jerry Rice	1.50	.70
❑ 111	Erik Kramer	.15	.07
❑ 112	Michael Jackson	.15	.07
❑ 113	Aeneas Williams	.15	.07
❑ 114	Terry Allen	.60	.25
❑ 115	Steve Young	1.00	.45
❑ 116	Warren Moon	.60	.25
❑ 117	Junior Seau	.30	.14
❑ 118	Jerome Bettis	.60	.25
❑ 119	Irving Fryar	.30	.14
❑ 120	Barry Sanders	3.00	1.35
❑ 121	Tim Brown	.60	.25
❑ 122	Chad Brown	.15	.07
❑ 123	Ben Coates	.30	.14
❑ 124	Robert Smith	.60	.25
❑ 125	Brett Favre	3.00	1.35
❑ 126	Derrick Thomas	.30	.14
❑ 127	Reggie White	.60	.25
❑ 128	Troy Aikman	1.50	.70
❑ 129	Jeff Blake	.30	.14
❑ 130	Mark Brunell	1.25	.55
❑ 131	Curtis Conway	.30	.14
❑ 132	Wesley Walls	.30	.14
❑ 133	Thurman Thomas	.60	.25
❑ 134	Chris Chandler	.30	.14
❑ 135	Dan Marino	3.00	1.35
❑ 136	Larry Centers	.15	.07
❑ 137	Shawn Jefferson	.15	.07
❑ 138	Andre Reed	.30	.14
❑ 139	Jake Reed	.30	.14
❑ 140	Cris Carter	.60	.25
❑ 141	Elvis Grbac	.30	.14
❑ 142	Mark Chmura	.30	.14
❑ 143	Michael Irvin	.60	.25
❑ 144	Carl Pickens	.60	.25
❑ 145	Herman Moore	.60	.25
❑ 146	Marvin Jones	.15	.07
❑ 147	Terance Mathis	.30	.14
❑ 148	Rob Moore	.30	.14
❑ 149	Bruce Smith	.30	.14
❑ 150	Rob Johnson CL	.15	.07
❑ 151	Leslie Shepherd	.15	.07
❑ 152	Chris Spielman	.15	.07
❑ 153	Tony McGee	.15	.07
❑ 154	Kevin Smith	.15	.07
❑ 155	Bill Romanowski	.15	.07
❑ 156	Stephen Boyd	.15	.07
❑ 157	James Stewart	.30	.14
❑ 158	Jason Taylor	.15	.07
❑ 159	Troy Drayton	.15	.07
❑ 160	Mark Fields	.15	.07
❑ 161	Jessie Armstead	.15	.07
❑ 162	James Jett	.30	.14
❑ 163	Bobby Taylor	.15	.07
❑ 164	Kimble Anders	.30	.14
❑ 165	Jimmy Smith	.30	.14
❑ 166	Quentin Coryatt	.15	.07
❑ 167	Bryant Westbrook	.15	.07

❑ 168	Neil Smith	.30	.14
❑ 169	Darren Woodson	.15	.07
❑ 170	Ray Buchanan	.15	.07
❑ 171	Earl Holmes	.15	.07
❑ 172	Ray Lewis	.15	.07
❑ 173	Steve Broussard	.15	.07
❑ 174	Derrick Brooks	.15	.07
❑ 175	Ken Harvey	.15	.07
❑ 176	Darryll Lewis	.15	.07
❑ 177	Derrick Rodgers	.15	.07
❑ 178	James McKnight	.15	.07
❑ 179	Cris Dishman	.15	.07
❑ 180	Hardy Nickerson	.15	.07
❑ 181	Charles Woodson RC	4.00	1.80
❑ 182	Randy Moss RC	20.00	9.00
❑ 183	Stephen Alexander RC	2.00	.90
❑ 184	Samari Rolle RC	1.50	.70
❑ 185	Jamie Duncan RC	1.50	.70
❑ 186	Lance Schulters RC	1.50	.70
❑ 187	Tony Parrish RC	1.50	.70
❑ 188	Corey Chavous RC	1.50	.70
❑ 189	Jammi German RC	1.50	.70
❑ 190	Sam Cowart RC	1.50	.70
❑ 191	Donald Hayes RC	2.00	.90
❑ 192	R.W. McQuarters RC	1.50	.70
❑ 193	Az-Zahir Hakim RC	3.00	1.35
❑ 194	Chris Fuamatu-Ma'Afala RC	2.00	.90
❑ 195	Allen Rossum RC	2.00	.90
❑ 196	Jon Ritchie RC	2.00	.90
❑ 197	Blake Spence RC	1.50	.70
❑ 198	Brian Alford RC	2.00	.90
❑ 199	Fred Weary RC	1.50	.70
❑ 200	Rod Rutledge RC	1.50	.70
❑ 201	Michael Myers RC	1.50	.70
❑ 202	Rashaan Shehee RC	2.00	.90
❑ 203	Donovin Darius RC	1.50	.70
❑ 204	E.G. Green RC	2.00	.90
❑ 205	Vonnie Holliday RC	2.00	.90
❑ 206	Charlie Batch RC	8.00	3.60
❑ 207	Michael Pittman RC	2.00	.90
❑ 208	Artrell Hawkins RC	1.50	.70
❑ 209	Jonathan Quinn RC	2.00	.90
❑ 210	Kailee Wong RC	1.50	.70
❑ 211	DeShea Townsend RC	1.50	.70
❑ 212	Patrick Surtain RC	1.50	.70
❑ 213	Brian Kelly RC	1.50	.70
❑ 214	Tebucky Jones RC	1.50	.70
❑ 215	Pete Gonzalez RC	1.50	.70
❑ 216	Shaun Williams RC	1.50	.70
❑ 217	Scott Frost RC	2.00	.90
❑ 218	Leonard Little RC	1.50	.70
❑ 219	Alonzo Mayes RC	1.50	.70
❑ 220	Cordell Taylor RC	1.50	.70

1998 Bowman Rookie Autographs

	MINT	NRMT
COMP.BLUE SET (11)	800.00	350.00
COMMON BLUE (A1-A11)	30.00	13.50
BLUE STATED ODDS 1:360		
*GOLD FOILS: 1X TO 2.5X BLUE		
GOLD STATED ODDS 1:7202		
*SILVER FOILS: .6X TO 1.5X BLUE		
SILVER STATED ODDS 1:2401		

❑ A1	Peyton Manning	200.00	90.00
❑ A2	Andre Wadsworth	30.00	13.50
❑ A3	Brian Griese	60.00	27.00
❑ A4	Ryan Leaf	40.00	18.00
❑ A5	Fred Taylor	80.00	36.00
❑ A6	Robert Edwards	30.00	13.50
❑ A7	Randy Moss	200.00	90.00
❑ A8	Curtis Enis	40.00	18.00
❑ A9	Kevin Dyson	30.00	13.50
❑ A10	Charles Woodson	50.00	22.00
❑ A11	Tim Dwight	40.00	18.00

1998 Bowman Chrome Preview

	MINT	NRMT
COMPLETE SET (10)	50.00	22.00
COMMON CARD (BCP1-BCP10)	4.00	1.80
STATED ODDS 1:12		
REFRACTORS: .75X TO 2X HI COL.		
REFRACTOR STATED ODDS 1:48		

❑ BCP1	Peyton Manning	15.00	6.75
❑ BCP2	Curtis Enis	5.00	2.20
❑ BCP3	Kevin Dyson	4.00	1.80
❑ BCP4	Robert Edwards	4.00	1.80
❑ BCP5	Ryan Leaf	5.00	2.20
❑ BCP6	Brett Favre	10.00	4.50
❑ BCP7	John Elway	10.00	4.50
❑ BCP8	Barry Sanders	10.00	4.50
❑ BCP9	Kordell Stewart	4.00	1.80
❑ BCP10	Terrell Davis	8.00	3.60

1998 Bowman Scout's Choice

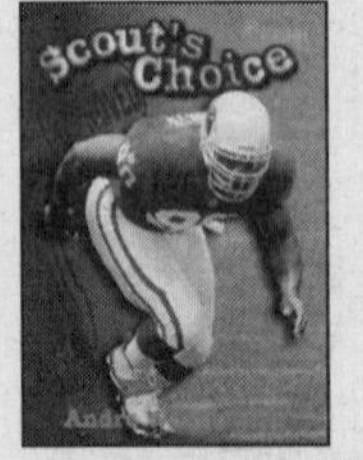

	MINT	NRMT
COMPLETE SET (14)	60.00	27.00
COMMON CARD (SC1-SC14)	2.00	.90
SEMISTARS	3.00	1.35
UNLISTED STARS	4.00	1.80
STATED ODDS 1:12		

❑ SC1	Peyton Manning	15.00	6.75
❑ SC2	John Avery	4.00	1.80
❑ SC3	Grant Wistrom	2.00	.90
❑ SC4	Kevin Dyson	4.00	1.80
❑ SC5	Andre Wadsworth	3.00	1.35
❑ SC6	Joe Jurevicius	3.00	1.35
❑ SC7	Charles Woodson	5.00	2.20
❑ SC8	Takeo Spikes	3.00	1.35
❑ SC9	Fred Taylor	8.00	3.60
❑ SC10	Ryan Leaf	5.00	2.20
❑ SC11	Robert Edwards	4.00	1.80
❑ SC12	Randy Moss	15.00	6.75
❑ SC13	Pat Johnson	3.00	1.35
❑ SC14	Curtis Enis	5.00	2.20

1999 Bowman

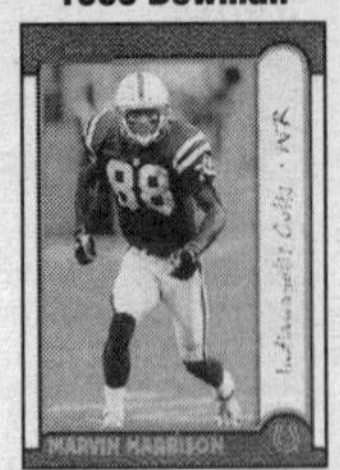

	MINT	NRMT
COMPLETE SET (220)	60.00	27.00
COMMON CARD (1-150)	.15	.07
SEMISTARS	.30	.14
UNLISTED STARS	.60	.25
COMMON ROOKIE (151-220)	.75	.35
ROOKIE SEMISTARS	1.50	.70
ROOKIE UNL.STARS	2.00	.90

❑ 1	Dan Marino	2.50	1.10
❑ 2	Michael Westbrook	.30	.14
❑ 3	Yancey Thigpen	.15	.07
❑ 4	Tony Martin	.30	.14
❑ 5	Michael Strahan	.15	.07
❑ 6	Dedric Ward	.15	.07
❑ 7	Joey Galloway	.60	.25
❑ 8	Bobby Engram	.30	.14
❑ 9	Frank Sanders	.30	.14
❑ 10	Jake Plummer	1.25	.55
❑ 11	Eddie Kennison	.30	.14
❑ 12	Curtis Martin	.60	.25
❑ 13	Chris Spielman	.15	.07
❑ 14	Trent Dilfer	.30	.14
❑ 15	Tim Biakabutuka	.30	.14
❑ 16	Elvis Grbac	.30	.14
❑ 17	Charlie Batch	1.25	.55
❑ 18	Takeo Spikes	.15	.07
❑ 19	Tony Banks	.30	.14
❑ 20	Doug Flutie	.75	.35
❑ 21	Ty Law	.15	.07
❑ 22	Isaac Bruce	.60	.25
❑ 23	James Jett	.30	.14
❑ 24	Kent Graham	.15	.07
❑ 25	Derrick Mayes	.15	.07
❑ 26	Amani Toomer	.15	.07
❑ 27	Ray Lewis	.15	.07
❑ 28	Shawn Springs	.15	.07
❑ 29	Warren Sapp	.15	.07
❑ 30	Jamal Anderson	.60	.25
❑ 31	Byron Bam Morris	.15	.07
❑ 32	Johnnie Morton	.15	.07
❑ 33	Terance Mathis	.15	.07
❑ 34	Terrell Davis	1.50	.70
❑ 35	John Randle	.30	.14
❑ 36	Vinny Testaverde	.15	.07
❑ 37	Junior Seau	.30	.14
❑ 38	Reidel Anthony	.30	.14
❑ 39	Brad Johnson	.15	.07
❑ 40	Emmitt Smith	1.50	.70
❑ 41	Mo Lewis	.15	.07
❑ 42	Terry Glenn	.60	.25
❑ 43	Dorsey Levens	.60	.25
❑ 44	Thurman Thomas	.30	.14
❑ 45	Rob Moore	.30	.14
❑ 46	Corey Dillon	.60	.25
❑ 47	Jessie Armstead	.15	.07
❑ 48	Marshall Faulk	.60	.25
❑ 49	Charles Woodson	.15	.07
❑ 50	John Elway	2.50	1.10

❑ 51 Kevin Dyson	.30	.14
❑ 52 Tony Simmons	.15	.07
❑ 53 Keenan McCardell	.30	.14
❑ 54 O.J. Santiago	.15	.07
❑ 55 Jermaine Lewis	.30	.14
❑ 56 Herman Moore	.60	.25
❑ 57 Gary Brown	.15	.07
❑ 58 Jim Harbaugh	.30	.14
❑ 59 Mike Alstott	.60	.25
❑ 60 Brett Favre	2.50	1.10
❑ 61 Tim Brown	.60	.25
❑ 62 Steve McNair	.60	.25
❑ 63 Ben Coates	.30	.14
❑ 64 Jerome Pathon	.15	.07
❑ 65 Ray Buchanan	.15	.07
❑ 66 Troy Aikman	1.50	.70
❑ 67 Andre Reed	.30	.14
❑ 68 Bubby Brister	.15	.07
❑ 69 Karim Abdul-Jabbar	.30	.14
❑ 70 Peyton Manning	2.50	1.10
❑ 71 Charles Johnson	.15	.07
❑ 72 Natrone Means	.30	.14
❑ 73 Michael Sinclair	.15	.07
❑ 74 Skip Hicks	.30	.14
❑ 75 Derrick Alexander	.30	.14
❑ 76 Wayne Chrebet	.30	.14
❑ 77 Rod Smith	.30	.14
❑ 78 Carl Pickens	.30	.14
❑ 79 Adrian Murrell	.30	.14
❑ 80 Fred Taylor	1.50	.70
❑ 81 Eric Moulds	.60	.25
❑ 82 Lawrence Phillips	.30	.14
❑ 83 Marvin Harrison	.60	.25
❑ 84 Cris Carter	.60	.25
❑ 85 Ike Hilliard	.15	.07
❑ 86 Hines Ward	.15	.07
❑ 87 Terrell Owens	.60	.25
❑ 88 Ricky Proehl	.15	.07
❑ 89 Bert Emanuel	.30	.14
❑ 90 Randy Moss	2.50	1.10
❑ 91 Aaron Glenn	.15	.07
❑ 92 Robert Smith	.60	.25
❑ 93 Andre Hastings	.15	.07
❑ 94 Jake Reed	.30	.14
❑ 95 Curtis Enis	.60	.25
❑ 96 Andre Wadsworth	.15	.07
❑ 97 Ed McCaffrey	.30	.14
❑ 98 Zach Thomas	.30	.14
❑ 99 Kerry Collins	.30	.14
❑ 100 Drew Bledsoe	1.00	.45
❑ 101 Germane Crowell	.30	.14
❑ 102 Bryan Still	.15	.07
❑ 103 Chad Brown	.15	.07
❑ 104 Jacquez Green	.15	.07
❑ 105 Garrison Hearst	.30	.14
❑ 106 Napoleon Kaufman	.60	.25
❑ 107 Ricky Watters	.30	.14
❑ 108 O.J. McDuffie	.30	.14
❑ 109 Keyshawn Johnson	.60	.25
❑ 110 Jerome Bettis	.60	.25
❑ 111 Duce Staley	.60	.25
❑ 112 Curtis Conway	.30	.14
❑ 113 Chris Chandler	.30	.14
❑ 114 Marcus Nash	.30	.14
❑ 115 Stephen Alexander	.15	.07
❑ 116 Darnay Scott	.15	.07
❑ 117 Bruce Smith	.30	.14
❑ 118 Priest Holmes	.60	.25
❑ 119 Mark Brunell	1.00	.45
❑ 120 Jerry Rice	1.50	.70
❑ 121 Randall Cunningham	.60	.25
❑ 122 Scott Mitchell	.15	.07
❑ 123 Antonio Freeman	.60	.25
❑ 124 Kordell Stewart	.60	.25
❑ 125 Jon Kitna	.75	.35
❑ 126 Ahman Green	.30	.14
❑ 127 Warrick Dunn	.60	.25
❑ 128 Robert Brooks	.30	.14
❑ 129 Derrick Thomas	.30	.14
❑ 130 Steve Young	1.00	.45
❑ 131 Peter Boulware	.15	.07
❑ 132 Michael Irvin	.30	.14
❑ 133 Shannon Sharpe	.15	.07
❑ 134 Jimmy Smith	.30	.14
❑ 135 John Avery	.30	.14
❑ 136 Fred Lane	.30	.14
❑ 137 Trent Green	.30	.14
❑ 138 Andre Rison	.30	.14
❑ 139 Antowain Smith	.15	.07
❑ 140 Eddie George	.75	.35
❑ 141 Jeff Blake	.30	.14
❑ 142 Rocket Ismail	.30	.14
❑ 143 Rickey Dudley	.15	.07
❑ 144 Courtney Hawkins	.15	.07
❑ 145 Mikhael Ricks	.15	.07
❑ 146 J.J. Stokes	.30	.14
❑ 147 Levon Kirkland	.15	.07
❑ 148 Deion Sanders	.60	.25
❑ 149 Barry Sanders	2.50	1.10
❑ 150 Tiki Barber	.15	.07
❑ 151 David Boston RC	3.00	1.35
❑ 152 Chris McAlister RC	1.50	.70
❑ 153 Peerless Price RC	3.00	1.35
❑ 154 D'Wayne Bates RC	1.50	.70
❑ 155 Cade McNown RC	6.00	2.70
❑ 156 Akili Smith RC	4.00	1.80
❑ 157 Kevin Johnson RC	5.00	2.20
❑ 158 Tim Couch RC	10.00	4.50
❑ 159 Sedrick Irvin RC	2.00	.90
❑ 160 Chris Claiborne RC	1.50	.70
❑ 161 Edgerrin James RC	15.00	6.75
❑ 162 Mike Cloud RC	2.00	.90
❑ 163 Cecil Collins RC	2.00	.90
❑ 164 James Johnson RC	2.50	1.10
❑ 165 Rob Konrad RC	2.00	.90
❑ 166 Daunte Culpepper RC	6.00	2.70
❑ 167 Kevin Faulk RC	2.50	1.10
❑ 168 Donovan McNabb RC	6.00	2.70
❑ 169 Troy Edwards RC	3.00	1.35
❑ 170 Amos Zereoue RC	2.00	.90
❑ 171 Karsten Bailey RC	1.50	.70
❑ 172 Brock Huard RC	2.50	1.10
❑ 173 Joe Germaine RC	2.00	.90
❑ 174 Torry Holt RC	5.00	2.20
❑ 175 Shaun King RC	6.00	2.70
❑ 176 Jevon Kearse RC	4.00	1.80
❑ 177 Champ Bailey RC	2.50	1.10
❑ 178 Ebenezer Ekuban RC	1.50	.70
❑ 179 Andy Katzenmoyer	2.00	.90
❑ 180 Antoine Winfield RC	1.50	.70
❑ 181 Jermaine Fazande RC	1.50	.70
❑ 182 Ricky Williams RC	10.00	4.50
❑ 183 Joel Makovicka RC	2.00	.90
❑ 184 Reginald Kelly RC	.75	.35
❑ 185 Brandon Stokley RC	1.50	.70
❑ 186 L.C. Stevens RC	.75	.35
❑ 187 Marty Booker RC	1.50	.70
❑ 188 Jerry Azumah	2.00	.90
❑ 189 Ted White RC	.75	.35
❑ 190 Scott Covington RC	1.50	.70
❑ 191 Tim Alexander RC	.75	.35
❑ 192 Darrin Chiaverini RC	1.50	.70
❑ 193 Dat Nguyen RC	2.00	.90
❑ 194 Wane McGarity RC	1.50	.70
❑ 195 Al Wilson RC	2.00	.90
❑ 196 Travis McGriff RC	2.00	.90
❑ 197 Stacey Mack RC	1.50	.70
❑ 198 Antuan Edwards RC	.75	.35
❑ 199 Aaron Brooks RC	2.00	.90
❑ 200 De'Mond Parker RC	2.00	.90
❑ 201 Jed Weaver RC	.75	.35
❑ 202 Madre Hill RC	.75	.35
❑ 203 Jim Kleinsasser RC	2.00	.90
❑ 204 Michael Bishop RC	2.50	1.10
❑ 205 Michael Basnight RC	1.50	.70
❑ 206 Sean Bennett RC	2.00	.90
❑ 207 Dameane Douglas RC	1.50	.70
❑ 208 Na Brown RC	2.00	.90
❑ 209 Patrick Kerney RC	.75	.35
❑ 210 Malcolm Johnson RC	1.50	.70
❑ 211 Dre Bly RC	1.50	.70
❑ 212 Terry Jackson RC	1.50	.70
❑ 213 Eugene Baker RC	.75	.35
❑ 214 Autry Denson RC	2.00	.90
❑ 215 Darnell McDonald	2.00	.90
❑ 216 Charlie Rogers RC	1.50	.70
❑ 217 Joe Montgomery RC	2.00	.90
❑ 218 Cecil Martin RC	1.50	.70
❑ 219 Larry Parker RC	1.50	.70
❑ 220 Mike Peterson RC	2.00	.90

1999 Bowman Gold

	MINT	NRMT
COMMON CARD (1-150)	3.00	1.35
*GOLD STARS: 10X TO 25X HI COL.		
*GOLD YOUNG STARS: 8X TO 20X		
COMMON ROOKIE (151-220)	10.00	4.50
*GOLD RCs: 4X TO 10X		
STATED PRINT RUN 99 SER.#'d SETS		

1999 Bowman Interstate

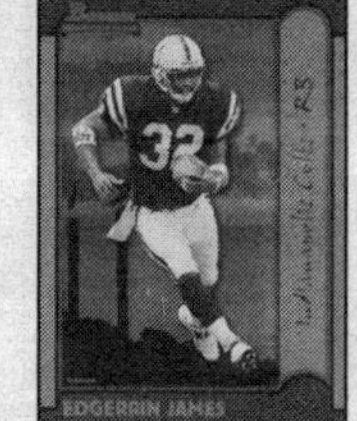

	MINT	NRMT
COMPLETE SET (220)	200.00	90.00
COMMON CARD (1-150)	.50	.23
*INTERSTATE STARS: 1.2X TO 3X HI COL.		
*INTERSTATE YOUNG STARS: 1X TO 2.5X		
COMMON ROOKIE (151-220)	1.50	.70
*INTERSTATE RCs: .6X TO 1.5X		
ONE INTERSTATE PER PACK		

1999 Bowman Autographs

	MINT	NRMT
COMPLETE SET (32)	1000.00	450.00
COMMON GOLD (A1-A6)	60.00	27.00
GOLD STATED ODDS 1:850		
COMMON SILVER (A7-A21)	20.00	9.00
SEMISTARS SILVER	30.00	13.50
SILVER STATED ODDS 1:212		
COMMON BLUE (A22-A32)	15.00	6.75
SEMISTARS BLUE	20.00	9.00
BLUE STATED ODDS 1:180		
TRADE CARD EXPIRATION: 4/30/2000		
❑ A1 Randy Moss G	120.00	55.00
❑ A2 Akili Smith G	80.00	36.00
❑ A3 Edgerrin James G	200.00	90.00
❑ A4 Ricky Williams G	120.00	55.00
❑ A5 Torry Holt G	60.00	27.00
❑ A6 Daunte Culpepper G	80.00	36.00
❑ A7 Donovan McNabb S	60.00	27.00
❑ A8 Tim Couch S	100.00	45.00
❑ A9 Champ Bailey S	30.00	13.50
❑ A10 David Boston S	40.00	18.00
❑ A11 Chris Claiborne S	20.00	9.00
❑ A12 Chris McAlister S	20.00	9.00
❑ A13 Rob Konrad S	30.00	13.50
❑ A14 Mike Cloud S	30.00	13.50

Card	MINT	NRMT
❑ A15 Jermaine Fazande S	20.00	9.00
❑ A16 Brock Huard S	30.00	13.50
❑ A17 Joe Germaine S	30.00	13.50
❑ A18 Sedrick Irvin S	30.00	13.50
❑ A19 Cecil Collins S	30.00	13.50
❑ A20 Karsten Bailey S	20.00	9.00
❑ A21 Antoine Winfield S	20.00	9.00
❑ A22 Cade McNown B	50.00	22.00
❑ A23 Troy Edwards B	30.00	13.50
❑ A24 Jevon Kearse B	40.00	18.00
❑ A25 Andy Katzenmoyer B	20.00	9.00
❑ A26 Kevin Johnson B	50.00	22.00
❑ A27 James Johnson B	25.00	11.00
❑ A28 Kevin Faulk B	25.00	11.00
❑ A29 Shaun King B	50.00	22.00
❑ A30 Peerless Price B	30.00	13.50
❑ A31 D'Wayne Bates B	15.00	6.75
❑ A32 Amos Zereoue B	20.00	9.00

1999 Bowman Late Bloomers/Early Risers

	MINT	NRMT
COMPLETE SET (10)	25.00	11.00
COMMON CARD (U1-U10)	1.50	.70
SEMISTARS	1.50	.70
STATED ODDS 1:12		

Card	MINT	NRMT
❑ U1 Fred Taylor	4.00	1.80
❑ U2 Peyton Manning	5.00	2.20
❑ U3 Dan Marino	6.00	2.70
❑ U4 Barry Sanders	6.00	2.70
❑ U5 Randy Moss	5.00	2.20
❑ U6 Mark Brunell	2.50	1.10
❑ U7 Jamal Anderson	1.50	.70
❑ U8 Curtis Martin	1.50	.70
❑ U9 Wayne Chrebet	1.50	.70
❑ U10 Terrell Davis	4.00	1.80

1999 Bowman Scout's Choice

	MINT	NRMT
COMPLETE SET (21)	50.00	22.00
COMMON CARD (SC1-SC21)	1.00	.45
SEMISTARS	1.50	.70
STATED ODDS 1:12		

Card	MINT	NRMT
❑ SC1 David Boston	2.50	1.10
❑ SC2 Champ Bailey	2.00	.90
❑ SC3 Edgerrin James	12.00	5.50
❑ SC4 Mike Cloud	1.50	.70
❑ SC5 Kevin Faulk	2.00	.90
❑ SC6 Troy Edwards	2.50	1.10
❑ SC7 Cecil Collins	1.50	.70
❑ SC8 Peerless Price	2.50	1.10
❑ SC9 Torry Holt	4.00	1.80
❑ SC10 Rob Konrad	1.50	.70
❑ SC11 Akili Smith	3.00	1.35
❑ SC12 Daunte Culpepper	5.00	2.20
❑ SC13 D'Wayne Bates	1.00	.45
❑ SC14 Donovan McNabb	5.00	2.20
❑ SC15 James Johnson	2.00	.90
❑ SC16 Cade McNown	5.00	2.20
❑ SC17 Kevin Johnson	4.00	1.80
❑ SC18 Ricky Williams	8.00	3.60
❑ SC19 Karsten Bailey	1.00	.45
❑ SC20 Tim Couch	8.00	3.60
❑ SC21 Shaun King	5.00	2.20

1998 Bowman Chrome

	MINT	NRMT
COMPLETE SET (220)	250.00	110.00
COMMON CARD (1-220)	.25	.11
SEMISTARS	.50	.23
UNLISTED STARS	1.00	.45
COMMON ROOKIE	3.00	1.35
ROOKIE SEMISTARS	5.00	2.20
ROOKIE UNLISTED STARS	8.00	3.60
COMP.INTERSTATE (220)	800.00	350.00
*INTERSTATE STARS: 1X TO 2.5X HI COL.		
*INTERSTATE YOUNG STARS: .8X TO 2X		
*INTERSTATE RCs: .5X TO 1X....		
INTERSTATE STATED ODDS 1:4		
COMMON INTER.REFRACT.	2.00	.90
*INTERSTATE REF.STARS: 3X TO 8X HI COL.		
*INTERSTATE REF.YOUNG STARS: 2.5X TO 6X		
*INTERSTATE REF.RCs: 1.5X TO 4X		
INTERSTATE REFRACTOR ODDS 1:24		
COMP.REFRACT.SET (220)	1500.00	700.00
*REFRACTOR STARS: 2X TO 5X HI COL.		
*REFRACTOR YOUNG STARS: 1.5X TO 4X		
*REFRACTOR RCs: 1X TO 2.5X..		
REFRACTOR STATED ODDS 1:12		

Card	MINT	NRMT
❑ 1 Peyton Manning RC	60.00	27.00
❑ 2 Keith Brooking RC	5.00	2.20
❑ 3 Duane Starks RC	3.00	1.35
❑ 4 Takeo Spikes RC	5.00	2.20
❑ 5 Andre Wadsworth RC	5.00	2.20
❑ 6 Greg Ellis RC	3.00	1.35
❑ 7 Brian Griese RC	15.00	6.75
❑ 8 Germane Crowell RC	12.00	5.50
❑ 9 Jerome Pathon RC	5.00	2.20
❑ 10 Ryan Leaf RC	12.00	5.50
❑ 11 Fred Taylor RC	25.00	11.00
❑ 12 Robert Edwards RC	8.00	3.60
❑ 13 Grant Wistrom RC	3.00	1.35
❑ 14 Robert Holcombe RC	8.00	3.60
❑ 15 Tim Dwight RC	12.00	5.50
❑ 16 Jacquez Green RC	10.00	4.50
❑ 17 Marcus Nash RC	8.00	3.60
❑ 18 Jason Peter RC	3.00	1.35
❑ 19 Anthony Simmons RC	3.00	1.35
❑ 20 Curtis Enis RC	12.00	5.50
❑ 21 John Avery RC	8.00	3.60
❑ 22 Pat Johnson RC	5.00	2.20
❑ 23 Joe Jurevicius RC	5.00	2.20
❑ 24 Brian Simmons RC	3.00	1.35
❑ 25 Kevin Dyson RC	12.00	5.50
❑ 26 Skip Hicks RC	8.00	3.60
❑ 27 Hines Ward RC	5.00	2.20
❑ 28 Tavian Banks RC	5.00	2.20
❑ 29 Ahman Green RC	8.00	3.60
❑ 30 Tony Simmons RC	5.00	2.20
❑ 31 Charles Johnson	.25	.11
❑ 32 Freddie Jones	.25	.11
❑ 33 Joey Galloway	1.00	.45
❑ 34 Tony Banks	.50	.23
❑ 35 Jake Plummer	3.00	1.35
❑ 36 Reidel Anthony	.50	.23
❑ 37 Steve McNair	1.00	.45
❑ 38 Michael Westbrook	.50	.23
❑ 39 Chris Sanders	.25	.11
❑ 40 Isaac Bruce	.25	.11
❑ 41 Charlie Garner	.25	.11
❑ 42 Wayne Chrebet	1.00	.45
❑ 43 Michael Strahan	.25	.11
❑ 44 Brad Johnson	1.00	.45
❑ 45 Mike Alstott	.25	.11
❑ 46 Tony Gonzalez	.25	.11
❑ 47 Johnnie Morton	.50	.23
❑ 48 Darnay Scott	.50	.23
❑ 49 Rae Carruth	.50	.23
❑ 50 Terrell Davis	4.00	1.80
❑ 51 Jermaine Lewis	.50	.23
❑ 52 Frank Sanders	.50	.23
❑ 53 Byron Hanspard	.50	.23
❑ 54 Gus Frerotte	.25	.11
❑ 55 Terry Glenn	1.00	.45
❑ 56 J.J. Stokes	.50	.23
❑ 57 Will Blackwell	.25	.11
❑ 58 Keyshawn Johnson	1.00	.45
❑ 59 Tiki Barber	.50	.23
❑ 60 Dorsey Levens	1.00	.45
❑ 61 Zach Thomas	.25	.11
❑ 62 Corey Dillon	1.50	.70
❑ 63 Antowain Smith	1.00	.45
❑ 64 Michael Sinclair	.25	.11
❑ 65 Rod Smith	.50	.23
❑ 66 Trent Dilfer	1.00	.45
❑ 67 Warren Sapp	.50	.23
❑ 68 Charles Way	.25	.11
❑ 69 Tamarick Vanover	.25	.11
❑ 70 Drew Bledsoe	2.00	.90
❑ 71 John Mobley	.25	.11
❑ 72 Kerry Collins	.50	.23
❑ 73 Peter Boulware	.25	.11
❑ 74 Simeon Rice	.50	.23
❑ 75 Eddie George	2.00	.90
❑ 76 Fred Lane	.50	.23
❑ 77 Jamal Anderson	1.00	.45
❑ 78 Antonio Freeman	1.00	.45
❑ 79 Jason Sehorn	.25	.11
❑ 80 Curtis Martin	1.00	.45
❑ 81 Bobby Hoying	.50	.23
❑ 82 Garrison Hearst	1.00	.45
❑ 83 Glenn Foley	.50	.23
❑ 84 Danny Kanell	.50	.23
❑ 85 Kordell Stewart	1.00	.45
❑ 86 O.J. McDuffie	.50	.23
❑ 87 Marvin Harrison	.50	.23
❑ 88 Bobby Engram	.50	.23
❑ 89 Chris Slade	.25	.11
❑ 90 Warrick Dunn	1.50	.70
❑ 91 Ricky Watters	.50	.23
❑ 92 Rickey Dudley	.25	.11
❑ 93 Terrell Owens	1.00	.45
❑ 94 Karim Abdul-Jabbar	1.00	.45
❑ 95 Napoleon Kaufman	1.00	.45
❑ 96 Darrell Green	.50	.23
❑ 97 Levon Kirkland	.25	.11
❑ 98 Jeff George	.50	.23
❑ 99 Andre Hastings	.25	.11
❑ 100 John Elway	5.00	2.20
❑ 101 John Randle	.50	.23
❑ 102 Andre Rison	.50	.23
❑ 103 Keenan McCardell	.50	.23
❑ 104 Marshall Faulk	1.00	.45
❑ 105 Emmitt Smith	4.00	1.80
❑ 106 Robert Brooks	.50	.23
❑ 107 Scott Mitchell	.50	.23
❑ 108 Shannon Sharpe	.50	.23
❑ 109 Deion Sanders	1.00	.45
❑ 110 Jerry Rice	2.50	1.10
❑ 111 Erik Kramer	.25	.11
❑ 112 Michael Jackson	.25	.11
❑ 113 Aeneas Williams	.25	.11
❑ 114 Terry Allen	1.00	.45
❑ 115 Steve Young	1.50	.70
❑ 116 Warren Moon	1.00	.45
❑ 117 Junior Seau	.50	.23
❑ 118 Jerome Bettis	1.00	.45
❑ 119 Irving Fryar	.50	.23
❑ 120 Barry Sanders	5.00	2.20
❑ 121 Tim Brown	.25	.11
❑ 122 Chad Brown	.25	.11
❑ 123 Ben Coates	.50	.23
❑ 124 Robert Smith	1.00	.45

		MINT	NRMT
❑ 125	Brett Favre	5.00	2.20
❑ 126	Derrick Thomas	.50	.23
❑ 127	Reggie White	1.00	.45
❑ 128	Troy Aikman	2.50	1.10
❑ 129	Jeff Blake	.50	.23
❑ 130	Mark Brunell	2.00	.90
❑ 131	Curtis Conway	.50	.23
❑ 132	Wesley Walls	.50	.23
❑ 133	Thurman Thomas	1.00	.45
❑ 134	Chris Chandler	.50	.23
❑ 135	Dan Marino	5.00	2.20
❑ 136	Larry Centers	.25	.11
❑ 137	Shawn Jefferson	.25	.11
❑ 138	Andre Reed	.50	.23
❑ 139	Jake Reed	.50	.23
❑ 140	Cris Carter	1.00	.45
❑ 141	Elvis Grbac	.50	.23
❑ 142	Mark Chmura	.50	.23
❑ 143	Michael Irvin	1.00	.45
❑ 144	Carl Pickens	1.00	.45
❑ 145	Herman Moore	1.00	.45
❑ 146	Marvin Jones	.25	.11
❑ 147	Terance Mathis	.50	.23
❑ 148	Rob Moore	.50	.23
❑ 149	Bruce Smith	.50	.23
❑ 150	Rob Johnson CL	.25	.11
❑ 151	Leslie Shepherd	.25	.11
❑ 152	Chris Spielman	.25	.11
❑ 153	Tony McGee	.25	.11
❑ 154	Kevin Smith	.25	.11
❑ 155	Bill Romanowski	.25	.11
❑ 156	Stephen Boyd	.25	.11
❑ 157	James Stewart	.50	.23
❑ 158	Jason Taylor	.25	.11
❑ 159	Troy Drayton	.25	.11
❑ 160	Mark Fields	.25	.11
❑ 161	Jessie Armstead	.25	.11
❑ 162	James Jett	.50	.23
❑ 163	Bobby Taylor	.25	.11
❑ 164	Kimble Anders	.50	.23
❑ 165	Jimmy Smith	.50	.23
❑ 166	Quentin Coryatt	.25	.11
❑ 167	Bryant Westbrook	.25	.11
❑ 168	Neil Smith	.50	.23
❑ 169	Darren Woodson	.25	.11
❑ 170	Ray Buchanan	.25	.11
❑ 171	Earl Holmes	.25	.11
❑ 172	Ray Lewis	.25	.11
❑ 173	Steve Broussard	.25	.11
❑ 174	Derrick Brooks	.25	.11
❑ 175	Ken Harvey	.25	.11
❑ 176	Darryll Lewis	.25	.11
❑ 177	Derrick Rodgers	.25	.11
❑ 178	James McKnight	.25	.11
❑ 179	Cris Dishman	.25	.11
❑ 180	Hardy Nickerson	.25	.11
❑ 181	Charles Woodson RC	12.00	5.50
❑ 182	Randy Moss RC	60.00	27.00
❑ 183	Stephen Alexander RC	5.00	2.20
❑ 184	Samari Rolle RC	3.00	1.35
❑ 185	Jamie Duncan RC	3.00	1.35
❑ 186	Lance Schulters RC	3.00	1.35
❑ 187	Tony Parrish RC	3.00	1.35
❑ 188	Corey Chavous RC	3.00	1.35
❑ 189	Jammi German RC	3.00	1.35
❑ 190	Sam Cowart RC	3.00	1.35
❑ 191	Donald Hayes RC	5.00	2.20
❑ 192	R.W. McQuarters RC	3.00	1.35
❑ 193	Az-Zahir Hakim RC	10.00	4.50
❑ 194	C. Fuamatu-Ma'afala RC	5.00	2.20
❑ 195	Allen Rossum RC	3.00	1.35
❑ 196	Jon Ritchie RC	5.00	2.20
❑ 197	Blake Spence RC	3.00	1.35
❑ 198	Brian Alford RC	5.00	2.20
❑ 199	Fred Weary RC	3.00	1.35
❑ 200	Rod Rutledge RC	3.00	1.35
❑ 201	Michael Myers RC	3.00	1.35
❑ 202	Rashaan Shehee RC	5.00	2.20
❑ 203	Donovin Darius RC	3.00	1.35
❑ 204	E.G. Green RC	5.00	2.20
❑ 205	Vonnie Holliday RC	5.00	2.20
❑ 206	Charlie Batch RC	15.00	6.75
❑ 207	Michael Pittman RC	5.00	2.20
❑ 208	Artrell Hawkins RC	3.00	1.35
❑ 209	Jonathan Quinn RC	5.00	2.20
❑ 210	Kailee Wong RC	3.00	1.35
❑ 211	Deshea Townsend RC	3.00	1.35
❑ 212	Patrick Surtain RC	3.00	1.35
❑ 213	Brian Kelly RC	3.00	1.35
❑ 214	Tebucky Jones RC	3.00	1.35
❑ 215	Pete Gonzalez RC	3.00	1.35
❑ 216	Shaun Williams RC	3.00	1.35
❑ 217	Scott Frost RC	5.00	2.20
❑ 218	Leonard Little RC	3.00	1.35
❑ 219	Alonzo Mayes RC	3.00	1.35
❑ 220	Cordell Taylor RC	3.00	1.35

1998 Bowman Chrome Golden Anniversary

	MINT	NRMT
COMMON CARD (1-220)	15.00	6.75
*GOLD.ANN.STARS: 20X TO 50X HI COL.		
*GOLD.ANN.YOUNG STARS: 15X TO 40X		
*GOLD.ANN.RCs: 2X TO 4X		
STATED ODDS 1:138		
STATED PRINT RUN 50 SERIAL #'d SETS		
REFRACTOR STATED ODDS 1:1072		
REF.STATED PRINT RUN 5 SERIAL #'d SETS		

1999 Bowman Chrome

	MINT	NRMT
COMPLETE SET (220)	250.00	110.00
COMMON CARD (1-220)	.25	.11
SEMISTARS	.50	.23
UNLISTED STARS	1.00	.45
COMMON ROOKIE	2.00	.90
ROOKIE SEMISTARS	3.00	1.35
ROOKIE UNL.STARS	4.00	1.80

		MINT	NRMT
❑ 1	Dan Marino	4.00	1.80
❑ 2	Michael Westbrook	.50	.23
❑ 3	Yancey Thigpen	.25	.11
❑ 4	Tony Martin	.50	.23
❑ 5	Michael Strahan	.25	.11
❑ 6	Dedric Ward	.25	.11
❑ 7	Joey Galloway	1.00	.45
❑ 8	Bobby Engram	.50	.23
❑ 9	Frank Sanders	.50	.23
❑ 10	Jake Plummer	1.50	.70
❑ 11	Eddie Kennison	.50	.23
❑ 12	Curtis Martin	1.00	.45
❑ 13	Chris Spielman	.25	.11
❑ 14	Trent Dilfer	.50	.23
❑ 15	Tim Biakabutuka	.50	.23
❑ 16	Elvis Grbac	.50	.23
❑ 17	Charlie Batch	2.00	.90
❑ 18	Takeo Spikes	.25	.11
❑ 19	Tony Banks	.50	.23
❑ 20	Doug Flutie	1.25	.55
❑ 21	Ty Law	.25	.11
❑ 22	Isaac Bruce	1.00	.45
❑ 23	James Jett	.50	.23
❑ 24	Kent Graham	.25	.11
❑ 25	Derrick Mayes	.25	.11
❑ 26	Amani Toomer	.25	.11
❑ 27	Ray Lewis	.25	.11
❑ 28	Shawn Springs	.25	.11
❑ 29	Warren Sapp	.25	.11
❑ 30	Jamal Anderson	1.00	.45
❑ 31	Byron Bam Morris	.25	.11
❑ 32	Johnnie Morton	.25	.11
❑ 33	Terance Mathis	.25	.11
❑ 34	Terrell Davis	2.50	1.10
❑ 35	John Randle	.50	.23
❑ 36	Vinny Testaverde	.25	.11
❑ 37	Junior Seau	.50	.23
❑ 38	Reidel Anthony	.50	.23
❑ 39	Brad Johnson	.25	.11
❑ 40	Emmitt Smith	2.50	1.10
❑ 41	Mo Lewis	.25	.11
❑ 42	Terry Glenn	1.00	.45
❑ 43	Dorsey Levens	1.00	.45
❑ 44	Thurman Thomas	.50	.23
❑ 45	Rob Moore	.50	.23
❑ 46	Corey Dillon	1.00	.45
❑ 47	Jessie Armstead	.25	.11
❑ 48	Marshall Faulk	1.00	.45
❑ 49	Charles Woodson	.25	.11
❑ 50	John Elway	4.00	1.80
❑ 51	Kevin Dyson	.50	.23
❑ 52	Tony Simmons	.25	.11
❑ 53	Keenan McCardell	.50	.23
❑ 54	O.J. Santiago	.25	.11
❑ 55	Jermaine Lewis	.50	.23
❑ 56	Herman Moore	.25	.11
❑ 57	Gary Brown	.25	.11
❑ 58	Jim Harbaugh	.50	.23
❑ 59	Mike Alstott	1.00	.45
❑ 60	Brett Favre	4.00	1.80
❑ 61	Tim Brown	1.00	.45
❑ 62	Steve McNair	.25	.11
❑ 63	Ben Coates	.50	.23
❑ 64	Jerome Pathon	.25	.11
❑ 65	Ray Buchanan	.25	.11
❑ 66	Troy Aikman	2.50	1.10
❑ 67	Andre Reed	.50	.23
❑ 68	Bubby Brister	.25	.11
❑ 69	Karim Abdul-Jabbar	.50	.23
❑ 70	Peyton Manning	4.00	1.80
❑ 71	Charles Johnson	.25	.11
❑ 72	Natrone Means	.50	.23
❑ 73	Michael Sinclair	.25	.11
❑ 74	Skip Hicks	.50	.23
❑ 75	Derrick Alexander	.25	.11
❑ 76	Wayne Chrebet	.50	.23
❑ 77	Rod Smith	.50	.23
❑ 78	Carl Pickens	.50	.23
❑ 79	Adrian Murrell	.50	.23
❑ 80	Fred Taylor	2.50	1.10
❑ 81	Eric Moulds	1.00	.45
❑ 82	Lawrence Phillips	.50	.23
❑ 83	Marvin Harrison	1.00	.45
❑ 84	Cris Carter	1.00	.45
❑ 85	Ike Hilliard	.25	.11
❑ 86	Hines Ward	.25	.11
❑ 87	Terrell Owens	1.00	.45
❑ 88	Ricky Proehl	.25	.11
❑ 89	Bert Emanuel	.50	.23
❑ 90	Randy Moss	4.00	1.80
❑ 91	Aaron Glenn	.25	.11
❑ 92	Robert Smith	1.00	.45
❑ 93	Andre Hastings	.25	.11
❑ 94	Jake Reed	.50	.23
❑ 95	Curtis Enis	1.00	.45
❑ 96	Andre Wadsworth	.25	.11
❑ 97	Ed McCaffrey	.50	.23
❑ 98	Zach Thomas	.50	.23
❑ 99	Kerry Collins	.50	.23
❑ 100	Drew Bledsoe	1.50	.70
❑ 101	Germane Crowell	.50	.23
❑ 102	Bryan Still	.25	.11
❑ 103	Chad Brown	.25	.11
❑ 104	Jacquez Green	.25	.11
❑ 105	Garrison Hearst	.50	.23
❑ 106	Napoleon Kaufman	1.00	.45
❑ 107	Ricky Watters	.50	.23
❑ 108	O.J. McDuffie	.50	.23
❑ 109	Keyshawn Johnson	1.00	.45
❑ 110	Jerome Bettis	1.00	.45
❑ 111	Duce Staley	1.00	.45
❑ 112	Curtis Conway	.50	.23
❑ 113	Chris Chandler	.50	.23
❑ 114	Marcus Nash	.50	.23
❑ 115	Stephen Alexander	.25	.11
❑ 116	Darnay Scott	.50	.23
❑ 117	Bruce Smith	.50	.23

	No.	Player	MINT	NRMT
❑	118	Priest Holmes	1.00	.45
❑	119	Mark Brunell	1.50	.70
❑	120	Jerry Rice	2.50	1.10
❑	121	Randall Cunningham	1.00	.45
❑	122	Scott Mitchell	.25	.11
❑	123	Antonio Freeman	1.00	.45
❑	124	Kordell Stewart	1.00	.45
❑	125	Jon Kitna	1.25	.55
❑	126	Ahman Green	.50	.23
❑	127	Warrick Dunn	1.00	.45
❑	128	Robert Brooks	.50	.23
❑	129	Derrick Thomas	.50	.23
❑	130	Steve Young	1.50	.70
❑	131	Peter Boulware	.25	.11
❑	132	Michael Irvin	.50	.23
❑	133	Shannon Sharpe	.50	.23
❑	134	Jimmy Smith	.50	.23
❑	135	John Avery	.50	.23
❑	136	Fred Lane	.50	.23
❑	137	Trent Green	.50	.23
❑	138	Andre Rison	.50	.23
❑	139	Antowain Smith	1.00	.45
❑	140	Eddie George	1.25	.55
❑	141	Jeff Blake	.50	.23
❑	142	Rocket Ismail	.50	.23
❑	143	Rickey Dudley	.25	.11
❑	144	Courtney Hawkins	.25	.11
❑	145	Mikhael Ricks	.25	.11
❑	146	J.J. Stokes	.50	.23
❑	147	Levon Kirkland	.25	.11
❑	148	Deion Sanders	1.00	.45
❑	149	Barry Sanders	4.00	1.80
❑	150	Tiki Barber	.25	.11
❑	151	David Boston RC	8.00	3.60
❑	152	Chris McAlister RC	3.00	1.35
❑	153	Peerless Price RC	8.00	3.60
❑	154	D'Wayne Bates RC	3.00	1.35
❑	155	Cade McNown RC	15.00	6.75
❑	156	Akili Smith RC	10.00	4.50
❑	157	Kevin Johnson RC	12.00	5.50
❑	158	Tim Couch RC	25.00	11.00
❑	159	Sedrick Irvin RC	4.00	1.80
❑	160	Chris Claiborne RC	3.00	1.35
❑	161	Edgerrin James RC	40.00	18.00
❑	162	Mike Cloud RC	4.00	1.80
❑	163	Cecil Collins RC	4.00	1.80
❑	164	James Johnson RC	6.00	2.70
❑	165	Rob Konrad RC	4.00	1.80
❑	166	Daunte Culpepper RC	15.00	6.75
❑	167	Kevin Faulk RC	6.00	2.70
❑	168	Donovan McNabb RC	15.00	6.75
❑	169	Troy Edwards RC	8.00	3.60
❑	170	Amos Zereoue RC	4.00	1.80
❑	171	Karsten Bailey RC	3.00	1.35
❑	172	Brock Huard RC	6.00	2.70
❑	173	Joe Germaine RC	4.00	1.80
❑	174	Torry Holt RC	12.00	5.50
❑	175	Shaun King RC	15.00	6.75
❑	176	Jevon Kearse RC	10.00	4.50
❑	177	Champ Bailey RC	6.00	2.70
❑	178	Ebenezer Ekuban RC	3.00	1.35
❑	179	Andy Katzenmoyer RC	4.00	1.80
❑	180	Antoine Winfield RC	3.00	1.35
❑	181	Jermaine Fazande RC	3.00	1.35
❑	182	Ricky Williams RC	25.00	11.00
❑	183	Joel Makovicka RC	4.00	1.80
❑	184	Reginald Kelly RC	3.00	1.35
❑	185	Brandon Stokley RC	3.00	1.35
❑	186	L.C. Stevens RC	2.00	.90
❑	187	Marty Booker RC	3.00	1.35
❑	188	Jerry Azumah RC	3.00	1.35
❑	189	Ted White RC	3.00	1.35
❑	190	Scott Covington RC	3.00	1.35
❑	191	Tim Alexander RC	2.00	.90
❑	192	Darrin Chiaverini RC	3.00	1.35
❑	193	Dat Nguyen RC	4.00	1.80
❑	194	Wane McGarity RC	3.00	1.35
❑	195	Al Wilson RC	4.00	1.80
❑	196	Travis McGriff RC	3.00	1.35
❑	197	Stacey Mack RC	3.00	1.35
❑	198	Antuan Edwards RC	2.00	.90
❑	199	Aaron Brooks RC	4.00	1.80
❑	200	De'Mond Parker RC	4.00	1.80
❑	201	Jed Weaver RC	2.00	.90
❑	202	Madre Hill RC	3.00	1.35
❑	203	Jim Kleinsasser RC	4.00	1.80
❑	204	Michael Bishop RC	6.00	2.70
❑	205	Michael Basnight RC	3.00	1.35
❑	206	Sean Bennett RC	3.00	1.35
❑	207	Dameane Douglas RC	3.00	1.35
❑	208	Na Brown RC	4.00	1.80
❑	209	Patrick Kerney RC	3.00	1.35
❑	210	Malcolm Johnson RC	3.00	1.35
❑	211	Dre Bly RC	3.00	1.35
❑	212	Terry Jackson RC	3.00	1.35
❑	213	Eugene Baker RC	2.00	.90
❑	214	Autry Denson RC	4.00	1.80
❑	215	Darnell McDonald RC	4.00	1.80
❑	216	Charlie Rogers RC	3.00	1.35
❑	217	Joe Montgomery RC	4.00	1.80
❑	218	Cecil Martin RC	3.00	1.35
❑	219	Larry Parker RC	3.00	1.35
❑	220	Mike Peterson RC	3.00	1.35

1999 Bowman Chrome Gold

	MINT	NRMT
COMPLETE SET (220)	1000.00	450.00
COMMON CARD (1-150)	2.00	.90
*STARS: 3X TO 8X HI COL.		
*YOUNG STARS: 2.5X TO 6X		
COMMON ROOKIE (151-220)	5.00	2.20
*RCs: 1X TO 2.5X		
STATED ODDS 1:24		

1999 Bowman Chrome Gold Refractors

	MINT	NRMT
COMPLETE SET (220)	3000.00	1350.00
COMMON CARD (1-220)	15.00	6.75
*STARS: 25X TO 60X HI COL.		
*YOUNG STARS: 20X TO 50X		
COMMON ROOKIE	15.00	6.75
*RCs: 2.5X TO 6X		
STATED ODDS 1:253		
STATED PRINT RUN 25 SER.#'d SETS		

1999 Bowman Chrome Interstate

	MINT	NRMT
COMPLETE SET (220)	400.00	180.00
COMMON CARD (1-220)	.75	.35
*STARS: 1.2X TO 3X HI COL.		
*YOUNG STARS: 1X TO 2.5X		
COMMON ROOKIE	2.50	1.10
*RCs: .5X TO 1.2X		
STATED ODDS 1:4		

1999 Bowman Chrome Interstate Refractors

	MINT	NRMT
COMPLETE SET (220)	2000.00	900.00
COMMON CARD (1-220)	5.00	2.20
*STARS: 8X TO 20X HI COL.		
*YOUNG STARS: 6X TO 15X		
COMMON ROOKIE	6.00	2.70
*RCs: 1.2X TO 3X		
STATED ODDS 1:63		
STATED PRINT RUN 100 SER.#'d SETS		

1999 Bowman Chrome Refractors

	MINT	NRMT
COMPLETE SET (220)	800.00	350.00
COMMON CARD (1-220)	1.50	.70
*STARS: 2.5X TO 6X HI COL.		
*YOUNG STARS: 2X TO 5X		
COMMON ROOKIE	4.00	1.80
*RCs: .8X TO 2X		
STATED ODDS 1:12		

1999 Bowman Chrome Scout's Choice

	MINT	NRMT
COMPLETE SET (21)	50.00	22.00
COMMON CARD (SC1-SC21)	1.25	.55
SEMISTARS	1.50	.70
STATED ODDS 1:12		
*REFRACTORS: 1X TO 2.5X HI COL.		
REFRACTOR STATED ODDS 1:60		

	No.	Player	MINT	NRMT
❑	SC1	David Boston	2.50	1.10
❑	SC2	Champ Bailey	2.00	.90
❑	SC3	Edgerrin James	15.00	6.75
❑	SC4	Mike Cloud	1.50	.70
❑	SC5	Kevin Faulk	2.00	.90
❑	SC6	Troy Edwards	2.50	1.10
❑	SC7	Cecil Collins	1.50	.70

		MINT	NRMT
❑ SC8	Peerless Price	2.50	1.10
❑ SC9	Torry Holt	4.00	1.80
❑ SC10	Rob Konrad	1.50	.70
❑ SC11	Akili Smith	3.00	1.35
❑ SC12	Daunte Culpepper	5.00	2.20
❑ SC13	D'Wayne Bates	1.25	.55
❑ SC14	Donovan McNabb	5.00	2.20
❑ SC15	James Johnson	2.00	.90
❑ SC16	Cade McNown	5.00	2.20
❑ SC17	Kevin Johnson	4.00	1.80
❑ SC18	Ricky Williams	8.00	3.60
❑ SC19	Karsten Bailey	1.50	.70
❑ SC20	Tim Couch	8.00	3.60
❑ SC21	Shaun King	5.00	2.20

1999 Bowman Chrome Stock in the Game

	MINT	NRMT
COMPLETE SET (18)	40.00	18.00
COMMON CARD (S1-S18)	2.00	.90
SEMISTARS	2.50	1.10
STATED ODDS 1:21		
*REFRACTORS: 1X TO 2.5X HI COL.		
REFRACTOR STATED ODDS 1:105		

		MINT	NRMT
❑ S1	Joe Germaine	2.50	1.10
❑ S2	Jevon Kearse	3.00	1.35
❑ S3	Sedrick Irvin	2.50	1.10
❑ S4	Brock Huard	2.50	1.10
❑ S5	Amos Zereoue	2.00	.90
❑ S6	Andy Katzenmoyer	2.00	.90
❑ S7	Randy Moss	6.00	2.70
❑ S8	Jake Plummer	3.00	1.35
❑ S9	Keyshawn Johnson	2.50	1.10
❑ S10	Fred Taylor	4.00	1.80
❑ S11	Eddie George	3.00	1.35
❑ S12	Peyton Manning	6.00	2.70
❑ S13	Dan Marino	8.00	3.60
❑ S14	Terrell Davis	5.00	2.20
❑ S15	Brett Favre	8.00	3.60
❑ S16	Jamal Anderson	2.50	1.10
❑ S17	Steve Young	3.00	1.35
❑ S18	Jerry Rice	5.00	2.20

1995 Bowman's Best

	MINT	NRMT
COMPLETE SET (180)	200.00	90.00
COMMON BLUE CARD (R1-R90)	.30	.14
COMMON BLACK CARD (V1-V90)	.30	.14
SEMISTARS	.60	.25
UNLISTED STARS	1.25	.55
COMP.REFRACT.SET (180)	800.00	350.00
*REF.STARS: 2X TO 5X HI COL.		
*REF.RC's: 1.25X TO 3X HI		
REF.STATED ODDS: 1:6		

		MINT	NRMT
❑ R1	Ki-Jana Carter RC	1.25	.55
❑ R2	Tony Boselli RC	.60	.25
❑ R3	Steve McNair RC	20.00	9.00
❑ R4	Michael Westbrook RC	12.00	5.50
❑ R5	Kerry Collins RC	6.00	2.70
❑ R6	Kevin Carter	1.25	.55
❑ R7	Mike Mamula	.60	.25
❑ R8	Joey Galloway RC	20.00	9.00
❑ R9	Kyle Brady RC	1.25	.55
❑ R10	Ray McElroy	.30	.14
❑ R11	Derrick Alexander DE	.30	.14
❑ R12	Warren Sapp RC	3.00	1.35
❑ R13	Mark Fields	.30	.14
❑ R14	Ruben Brown RC	.30	.14
❑ R15	Ellis Johnson RC	.30	.14
❑ R16	Hugh Douglas RC	.60	.25
❑ R17	Alundis Brice	.30	.14
❑ R18	Napoleon Kaufman RC	15.00	6.75
❑ R19	James O. Stewart RC	12.00	5.50
❑ R20	Luther Elliss	.30	.14
❑ R21	Rashaan Salaam RC	1.25	.55
❑ R22	Tyrone Poole	.60	.25
❑ R23	Ty Law	.60	.25
❑ R24	Korey Stringer	.30	.14
❑ R25	Billy Milner	.30	.14
❑ R26	Roell Preston RC	1.50	.70
❑ R27	Mark Bruener RC	.60	.25
❑ R28	Derrick Brooks	.30	.14
❑ R29	Blake Brockermeyer	.30	.14
❑ R30	Mike Frederick	.30	.14
❑ R31	Trezelle Jenkins	.30	.14
❑ R32	Craig Newsome	.30	.14
❑ R33	Matt O'Dwyer	.30	.14
❑ R34	Terrance Shaw RC	.30	.14
❑ R35	Anthony Cook	.30	.14
❑ R36	Darick Holmes RC	.60	.25
❑ R37	Cory Raymer	.30	.14
❑ R38	Zach Wiegert	.30	.14
❑ R39	Sam Shade	.30	.14
❑ R40	Brian DeMarco	.60	.25
❑ R41	Ron Davis	.30	.14
❑ R42	Orlando Thomas	.30	.14
❑ R43	Derek West	.30	.14
❑ R44	Ray Zellars RC	.60	.25
❑ R45	Todd Collins RC	1.25	.55
❑ R46	Linc Harden	.30	.14
❑ R47	Frank Sanders RC	6.00	2.70
❑ R48	Ken Dilger RC	.60	.25
❑ R49	Barrett Robbins RC	.30	.14
❑ R50	Bobby Taylor RC	.60	.25
❑ R51	Terrell Fletcher RC	.30	.14
❑ R52	Jack Jackson	.30	.14
❑ R53	Jeff Kopp	.30	.14
❑ R54	Brendan Stai	.30	.14
❑ R55	Corey Fuller	.30	.14
❑ R56	Todd Sauerbrun	.30	.14
❑ R57	Dameian Jeffries	.30	.14
❑ R58	Troy Dumas	.30	.14
❑ R59	Charlie Williams	.30	.14
❑ R60	Kordell Stewart RC	20.00	9.00
❑ R61	Jay Barker RC	.30	.14
❑ R62	Jesse James	.30	.14
❑ R63	Shane Hannah	.30	.14
❑ R64	Rob Johnson RC	15.00	6.75
❑ R65	Darius Holland	.30	.14
❑ R66	William Henderson	.30	.14
❑ R67	Chris Sanders RC	1.25	.55
❑ R68	Darryl Pounds	.30	.14
❑ R69	Melvin Tuten	.30	.14
❑ R70	David Sloan RC	.60	.25
❑ R71	Chris Hudson	.30	.14
❑ R72	William Strong	.30	.14
❑ R73	Brian Williams LB	.30	.14
❑ R74	Curtis Martin RC	20.00	9.00
❑ R75	Mike Verstegen	.30	.14
❑ R76	Justin Armour RC	.30	.14
❑ R77	Lorenzo Styles	.30	.14
❑ R78	Oliver Gibson	.30	.14
❑ R79	Zack Crockett RC	.30	.14
❑ R80	Tau Pupua	.30	.14
❑ R81	Tamarick Vanover RC	1.25	.55
❑ R82	Steve McLaughlin	.30	.14
❑ R83	Sean Harris	.30	.14
❑ R84	Eric Zeier RC	2.50	1.10
❑ R85	Rodney Young	.30	.14
❑ R86	Chad May RC	.30	.14
❑ R87	Evan Pilgrim	.30	.14
❑ R88	James A.Stewart RC	.30	.14
❑ R89	Torey Hunter	.30	.14
❑ R90	Antonio Freeman RC	20.00	9.00
❑ V1	Rob Moore	.30	.14
❑ V2	Craig Heyward	.60	.25
❑ V3	Jim Kelly	1.25	.55
❑ V4	John Kasay	.30	.14
❑ V5	Jeff Graham	.30	.14
❑ V6	Jeff Blake RC	5.00	2.20
❑ V7	Antonio Langham	.30	.14
❑ V8	Troy Aikman	3.00	1.35
❑ V9	Simon Fletcher	.30	.14
❑ V10	Barry Sanders	6.00	2.70
❑ V11	Edgar Bennett	.60	.25
❑ V12	Ray Childress	.30	.14
❑ V13	Ray Buchanan	.30	.14
❑ V14	Desmond Howard	.60	.25
❑ V15	Dale Carter	.60	.25
❑ V16	Troy Vincent	.30	.14
❑ V17	David Palmer	.60	.25
❑ V18	Ben Coates	.60	.25
❑ V19	Derek Brown TE	.30	.14
❑ V20	Dave Brown	.60	.25
❑ V21	Mo Lewis	.30	.14
❑ V22	Harvey Williams	.30	.14
❑ V23	Randall Cunningham	1.25	.55
❑ V24	Kevin Greene	.60	.25
❑ V25	Junior Seau	1.25	.55
❑ V26	Merton Hanks	.30	.14
❑ V27	Cortez Kennedy	.60	.25
❑ V28	Troy Drayton	.30	.14
❑ V29	Hardy Nickerson	.30	.14
❑ V30	Brian Mitchell	.30	.14
❑ V31	Raymont Harris	.30	.14
❑ V32	Keith Goganious	.30	.14
❑ V33	Andre Reed	.60	.25
❑ V34	Terance Mathis	.60	.25
❑ V35	Garrison Hearst	1.25	.55
❑ V36	Glyn Milburn	.30	.14
❑ V37	Emmitt Smith	5.00	2.20
❑ V38	Vinny Testaverde	.60	.25
❑ V39	Darnay Scott	1.25	.55
❑ V40	Mickey Washington	.30	.14
❑ V41	Craig Erickson	.30	.14
❑ V42	Chris Chandler	1.25	.55
❑ V43	Brett Favre	6.00	2.70
❑ V44	Scott Mitchell	.60	.25
❑ V45	Chris Slade	.60	.25
❑ V46	Warren Moon	.60	.25
❑ V47	Dan Marino	6.00	2.70
❑ V48	Greg Hill	.60	.25
❑ V49	Rocket Ismail	.60	.25
❑ V50	Bobby Houston	.30	.14
❑ V51	Rodney Hampton	.60	.25
❑ V52	Jim Everett	.30	.14
❑ V53	Rick Mirer	1.25	.55
❑ V54	Steve Young	2.50	1.10
❑ V55	Dennis Gibson	.30	.14
❑ V56	Rod Woodson	.60	.25
❑ V57	Calvin Williams	.60	.25
❑ V58	Tom Carter	.30	.14
❑ V59	Trent Dilfer	1.25	.55
❑ V60	Shane Conlan	.30	.14
❑ V61	Cornelius Bennett	.60	.25
❑ V62	Eric Metcalf	.60	.25
❑ V63	Frank Reich	.30	.14
❑ V64	Eric Hill	.30	.14
❑ V65	Erik Kramer	.30	.14
❑ V66	Michael Irvin	1.25	.55
❑ V67	Tony McGee	.30	.14
❑ V68	Andre Rison	.60	.25
❑ V69	Shannon Sharpe	.60	.25
❑ V70	Quentin Coryatt	.60	.25
❑ V71	Robert Brooks	1.25	.55
❑ V72	Steve Beuerlein	.30	.14
❑ V73	Herman Moore	1.25	.55
❑ V74	Jack Del Rio	.30	.14

❑ V75 Dave Meggett	.30	.14
❑ V76 Pete Stoyanovich	.30	.14
❑ V77 Neil Smith	.60	.25
❑ V78 Corey Miller	.30	.14
❑ V79 Tim Brown	1.25	.55
❑ V80 Tyrone Hughes	.60	.25
❑ V81 Boomer Esiason	.60	.25
❑ V82 Natrone Means	1.25	.55
❑ V83 Chris Warren	.60	.25
❑ V84 Byron Bam Morris	.60	.25
❑ V85 Jerry Rice	3.00	1.35
❑ V86 Michael Zordich	.30	.14
❑ V87 Errict Rhett	1.25	.55
❑ V88 Henry Ellard	.60	.25
❑ V89 Chris Miller	.30	.14
❑ V90 John Elway	6.00	2.70

1995 Bowman's Best Mirror Images Draft Picks

	MINT	NRMT
COMPLETE SET (15)	25.00	11.00
COMMON CARD (1-15)	1.25	.55
SEMISTARS	2.00	.90

STATED ODDS 1:4
*REFRACTORS: 2.5X TO 5X HI COLUMN
REFRACTOR STATED ODDS 1:36

❑ 1 Ki-Jana Carter Dan Wilkinson	2.00	.90
❑ 2 Marshall Faulk Tony Boselli	3.00	1.35
❑ 3 Steve McNair Heath Shuler	8.00	3.60
❑ 4 Michael Westbrook Willie McGinest	4.00	1.80
❑ 5 Kerry Collins Trev Alberts	3.00	1.35
❑ 6 Trent Dilfer Kevin Carter	2.00	.90
❑ 7 Bryant Young Mike Mamula	2.00	.90
❑ 8 Joey Galloway Sam Adams	8.00	3.60
❑ 9 Antonio Langham Kyle Brady	1.25	.55
❑ 10 J.J.Stokes Jamir Miller	3.00	1.35
❑ 11 John Thierry Derrick Alexander DE	2.00	.90
❑ 12 Aaron Glenn Warren Sapp	1.25	.55
❑ 13 Joe Johnson Mark Fields	1.25	.55
❑ 14 Bernard Williams Ruben Brown	1.25	.55
❑ 15 Wayne Gandy Ellis Johnson	1.25	.55

1996 Bowman's Best

	MINT	NRMT
COMPLETE SET (180)	80.00	36.00
COMMON CARD (1-180)	.20	.09
SEMISTARS	.40	.18
UNLISTED STARS	.75	.35
COMP.ATOMIC REF.(180)	1200.00	550.00

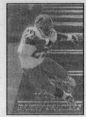

*ATOMIC REF.STARS: 5X TO 12X HI COL.
*ATOMIC REF.RCs: 2X TO 5X
STATED ODDS 1:48 HOBBY, 1:80 RETAIL

COMP.REFRACTOR (180)	600.00	275.00

*REF.STARS: 1.5X TO 4X HI COLUMN
*REF.RCs: 1.2X TO 3X HI
STATED ODDS 1:12 HOBBY, 1:20 RETAIL

❑ 1 Emmitt Smith	3.00	1.35
❑ 2 Kordell Stewart	1.25	.55
❑ 3 Mark Chmura	.40	.18
❑ 4 Sean Dawkins	.20	.09
❑ 5 Steve Young	1.50	.70
❑ 6 Tamarick Vanover	.40	.18
❑ 7 Scott Mitchell	.40	.18
❑ 8 Aaron Hayden	.20	.09
❑ 9 William Thomas	.20	.09
❑ 10 Dan Marino	4.00	1.80
❑ 11 Curtis Conway	.75	.35
❑ 12 Steve Atwater	.20	.09
❑ 13 Derrick Brooks	.20	.09
❑ 14 Rick Mirer	.40	.18
❑ 15 Mark Brunell	2.00	.90
❑ 16 Garrison Hearst	.40	.18
❑ 17 Eric Turner	.20	.09
❑ 18 Mark Carrier WR	.20	.09
❑ 19 Darnay Scott	.40	.18
❑ 20 Steve McNair	1.25	.55
❑ 21 Jim Everett	.20	.09
❑ 22 Wayne Chrebet	1.00	.45
❑ 23 Ben Coates	.40	.18
❑ 24 Harvey Williams	.20	.09
❑ 25 Michael Westbrook	.75	.35
❑ 26 Kevin Carter	.20	.09
❑ 27 Dave Brown	.20	.09
❑ 28 Jake Reed	.40	.18
❑ 29 Thurman Thomas	.75	.35
❑ 30 Jeff George	.40	.18
❑ 31 Carnell Lake	.20	.09
❑ 32 J.J. Stokes	.75	.35
❑ 33 Jay Novacek	.20	.09
❑ 34 Brett Perriman	.20	.09
❑ 35 Robert Brooks	.75	.35
❑ 36 Neil Smith	.20	.09
❑ 37 Chris Zorich	.20	.09
❑ 38 Micheal Barrow	.20	.09
❑ 39 Quentin Coryatt	.20	.09
❑ 40 Kerry Collins	.75	.35
❑ 41 Aeneas Williams	.20	.09
❑ 42 James O.Stewart	.40	.18
❑ 43 Warren Moon	.40	.18
❑ 44 Willie McGinest	.20	.09
❑ 45 Rodney Hampton	.40	.18
❑ 46 Jeff Hostetler	.20	.09
❑ 47 Darrell Green	.20	.09
❑ 48 Warren Sapp	.20	.09
❑ 49 Troy Drayton	.20	.09
❑ 50 Junior Seau	.40	.18
❑ 51 Mike Mamula	.20	.09
❑ 52 Antonio Langham	.20	.09
❑ 53 Eric Metcalf	.20	.09
❑ 54 Adrian Murrell	.75	.35
❑ 55 Joey Galloway	1.25	.55
❑ 56 Anthony Miller	.40	.18
❑ 57 Carl Pickens	.75	.35
❑ 58 Bruce Smith	.40	.18
❑ 59 Merton Hanks	.20	.09
❑ 60 Troy Aikman	2.00	.90
❑ 61 Erik Kramer	.20	.09
❑ 62 Tyrone Poole	.20	.09
❑ 63 Michael Jackson	.40	.18
❑ 64 Rob Moore	.40	.18
❑ 65 Marcus Allen	.75	.35
❑ 66 Orlando Thomas	.20	.09
❑ 67 Dave Meggett	.20	.09
❑ 68 Trent Dilfer	.75	.35
❑ 69 Herman Moore	.75	.35
❑ 70 Brett Favre	4.00	1.80
❑ 71 Blaine Bishop	.20	.09
❑ 72 Eric Allen	.20	.09
❑ 73 Bernie Parmalee	.20	.09
❑ 74 Kyle Brady	.20	.09
❑ 75 Terry McDaniel	.20	.09
❑ 76 Rodney Peete	.20	.09
❑ 77 Yancey Thigpen	.40	.18
❑ 78 Stan Humphries	.40	.18
❑ 79 Craig Heyward	.20	.09
❑ 80 Rashaan Salaam	.75	.35
❑ 81 Shannon Sharpe	.40	.18
❑ 82 Jim Harbaugh	.40	.18
❑ 83 Vinnie Clark	.20	.09
❑ 84 Steve Bono	.20	.09
❑ 85 Drew Bledsoe	2.00	.90
❑ 86 Ken Norton	.20	.09
❑ 87 Brian Mitchell	.20	.09
❑ 88 Hardy Nickerson	.20	.09
❑ 89 Todd Lyght	.20	.09
❑ 90 Barry Sanders	4.00	1.80
❑ 91 Robert Blackmon	.20	.09
❑ 92 Larry Centers	.40	.18
❑ 93 Jim Kelly	.75	.35
❑ 94 Lamar Lathon	.20	.09
❑ 95 Cris Carter	.75	.35
❑ 96 Hugh Douglas	.20	.09
❑ 97 Michael Strahan	.20	.09
❑ 98 Lee Woodall	.20	.09
❑ 99 Michael Irvin	.75	.35
❑ 100 Marshall Faulk	.75	.35
❑ 101 Terance Mathis	.20	.09
❑ 102 Eric Zeier	.20	.09
❑ 103 Marty Carter	.20	.09
❑ 104 Steve Tovar	.20	.09
❑ 105 Isaac Bruce	.75	.35
❑ 106 Tony Martin	.40	.18
❑ 107 Dale Carter	.20	.09
❑ 108 Terry Kirby	.40	.18
❑ 109 Tyrone Hughes	.20	.09
❑ 110 Bryce Paup	.20	.09
❑ 111 Errict Rhett	.40	.18
❑ 112 Ricky Watters	.40	.18
❑ 113 Chris Chandler	.40	.18
❑ 114 Edgar Bennett	.40	.18
❑ 115 John Elway	4.00	1.80
❑ 116 Sam Mills	.20	.09
❑ 117 Seth Joyner	.20	.09
❑ 118 Jeff Lageman	.20	.09
❑ 119 Chris Calloway	.20	.09
❑ 120 Curtis Martin	1.25	.55
❑ 121 Ken Harvey	.20	.09
❑ 122 Eugene Daniel	.20	.09
❑ 123 Tim Brown	.75	.35
❑ 124 Mo Lewis	.20	.09
❑ 125 Jeff Blake	.75	.35
❑ 126 Jessie Tuggle	.20	.09
❑ 127 Vinny Testaverde	.40	.18
❑ 128 Chris Warren	.40	.18
❑ 129 Terrell Davis	5.00	2.20
❑ 130 Greg Lloyd	.40	.18
❑ 131 Deion Sanders	1.00	.45
❑ 132 Derrick Thomas	.40	.18
❑ 133 Darryll Lewis UER back Daryl Lewis	.20	.09
❑ 134 Reggie White	.75	.35
❑ 135 Jerry Rice	2.00	.90
❑ 136 Tony Banks RC	5.00	2.20
❑ 137 Derrick Mayes RC	3.00	1.35
❑ 138 Leeland McElroy RC	1.25	.55
❑ 139 Bryan Still RC	.75	.35
❑ 140 Tim Biakabutuka RC	5.00	2.20
❑ 141 Rickey Dudley RC	.75	.35
❑ 142 Tory James RC	.20	.09
❑ 143 Lawyer Milloy RC	.20	.09
❑ 144 Mike Ulufale RC	.20	.09

❑ 145 Bobby Engram RC .... .75 .35
❑ 146 Willie Anderson RC .... .20 .09
❑ 147 Terrell Owens RC 15.00 6.75
❑ 148 Jonathan Ogden RC ...... .20 .09
❑ 149 Darrius Johnson RC ...... .20 .09
❑ 150 Kevin Hardy RC .... .75 .35
❑ 151 Simeon Rice RC .... .75 .35
❑ 152 Alex Molden RC .... .20 .09
❑ 153 Cedric Jones RC .... .20 .09
❑ 154 Duane Clemons RC ...... .20 .09
❑ 155 Karim Abdul-Jabbar RC 3.00 1.35
❑ 156 Dedric Mathis RC .... .20 .09
❑ 157 John Michels RC .... .20 .09
❑ 158 Winslow Oliver RC .... .20 .09
❑ 159 Stepfret Williams RC ...... .40 .18
❑ 160 Eddie Kennison RC .... .75 .35
❑ 161 Marcus Coleman RC ...... .20 .09
❑ 162 Tedy Bruschi RC .... .20 .09
❑ 163 Detron Smith RC .... .20 .09
❑ 164 Ray Lewis RC .... .20 .09
❑ 165 Marvin Harrison RC 15.00 6.75
❑ 166 Je'rod Cherry RC .... .20 .09
❑ 167 Jerris McPhail RC .... .20 .09
❑ 168 Eric Moulds RC 10.00 4.50
❑ 169 Walt Harris RC .... .20 .09
❑ 170 Eddie George RC 20.00 9.00
❑ 171 Jermaine Lewis RC 2.50 1.10
❑ 172 Jeff Lewis RC 2.50 1.10
❑ 173 Ray Mickens RC .... .20 .09
❑ 174 Amani Toomer RC .... .75 .35
❑ 175 Zach Thomas RC 2.50 1.10
❑ 176 Lawrence Phillips RC .. 2.50 1.10
❑ 177 John Mobley RC .... .20 .09
❑ 178 Anthony Dorsett RC ...... .20 .09
❑ 179 DeRon Jenkins .... .20 .09
❑ 180 Keyshawn Johnson RC 15.00 6.75

1996 Bowman's Best Bets

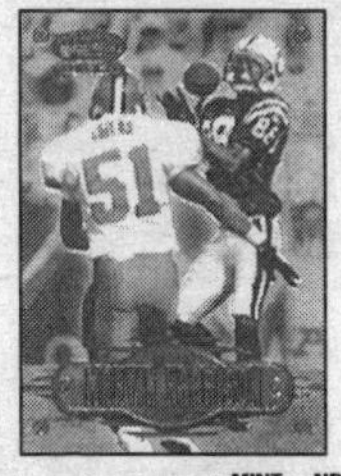

	MINT	NRMT
COMPLETE SET (9)	30.00	13.50

STATED ODDS 1:12 HOBBY, 1:20 RETAIL
*ATOMIC REF: 1X TO 2.5X BASE CARD HI
ATOMIC ODDS 1:96 HOB, 1:160 RET
*REFRACTORS: .6X TO 1.5X BASE CARD HI
REFRACTOR ODDS 1:48 HOB, 1:80 RET

❑ 1 Keyshawn Johnson 10.00 4.50
❑ 2 Lawrence Phillips .... 1.50 .70
❑ 3 Tim Biakabutuka 3.00 1.35
❑ 4 Eddie George 12.00 5.50
❑ 5 John Mobley .... .10 .05
❑ 6 Eddie Kennison .... .50 .23
❑ 7 Marvin Harrison 10.00 4.50
❑ 8 Amani Toomer .... .50 .23
❑ 9 Bobby Engram .... .50 .23

1996 Bowman's Best Cuts

	MINT	NRMT
COMPLETE SET (15)	100.00	45.00

STATED ODDS 1:24 HOBBY, 1:40 RETAIL
*ATOMIC REF: 3X TO 7.5X BASE CARD HI
ATOMIC ODDS 1:96 HOB, 1:160 RET
*REFRACTORS: 2X TO 5X BASE CARD HI

REFRACTOR ODDS 1:48 HOB. 1:96 RET

❑ 1 Dan Marino 12.00 5.50
❑ 2 Emmitt Smith 10.00 4.50
❑ 3 Rashaan Salaam 2.50 1.10
❑ 4 Herman Moore 2.50 1.10
❑ 5 Brett Favre 12.00 5.50
❑ 6 Marshall Faulk 2.50 1.10
❑ 7 John Elway 12.00 5.50
❑ 8 Curtis Martin 4.00 1.80
❑ 9 Deion Sanders 3.00 1.35
❑ 10 Jerry Rice 6.00 2.70
❑ 11 Terrell Davis 15.00 6.75
❑ 12 Kerry Collins 2.50 1.10
❑ 13 Steve Young 5.00 2.20
❑ 14 Troy Aikman 6.00 2.70
❑ 15 Barry Sanders 12.00 5.50

1996 Bowman's Best Mirror Images

	MINT	NRMT
COMPLETE SET (9)	100.00	45.00
COMMON CARD (1-9)	5.00	2.20
SEMISTARS	8.00	3.60

STATED ODDS 1:48 HOBBY, 1:80 RETAIL
*ATOMIC REFRACT: 1X TO 2.5X HI COL.
ATOMIC ODDS 1:192 HOB, 1:320 RET
*REFRACTORS: .6X TO 1.5X HI COLUMN
REFRACTOR ODDS 1:96 HOB, 1:160 RET

❑ 1 Steve Young 25.00 11.00
Kerry Collins
Dan Marino
Mark Brunell
❑ 2 Brett Favre 25.00 11.00
Elvis Grbac
John Elway
Drew Bledsoe
❑ 3 Troy Aikman 12.00 5.50
Gus Frerotte
Jim Harbaugh
Jeff Blake
❑ 4 Emmitt Smith 20.00 9.00
Errict Rhett
Chris Warren
Curtis Martin
❑ 5 Barry Sanders 25.00 11.00
Rashaan Salaam
Thurman Thomas
Terrell Davis
❑ 6 Rodney Hampton 8.00 3.60
Lawrence Phillips
Marcus Allen
Marshall Faulk
❑ 7 Jerry Rice 12.00 5.50
Isaac Bruce
Tim Brown
Joey Galloway
❑ 8 Cris Carter 8.00 3.60
Curtis Conway
Carl Pickens
Keyshawn Johnson
❑ 9 Robert Brooks 5.00 2.20
Michael Westbrook
Anthony Miller
O.J. McDuffie

1997 Bowman's Best

	MINT	NRMT
COMPLETE SET (125)	40.00	18.00
COMMON CARD (1-125)	.20	.09
SEMISTARS	.40	.18
UNLISTED STARS	.75	.35
COMP.ATOMIC REF.(125)	1000.00	450.00

*ATOMIC REF.STARS: 3X TO 8X HI
*ATOMIC REF.RCs: 1.5X TO 4X ..
ATOMIC REF.STATED ODDS 1:24

COMP.REFRACTOR (125) ..	600.00	275.00

*REFRACTOR STARS: 2X TO 5X HI COL.
*REFRACTOR RCs: 1.25X TO 3X
REFRACTOR STATED ODDS 1:12

❑ 1 Brett Favre 4.00 1.80
❑ 2 Larry Centers .... .40 .18
❑ 3 Trent Dilfer .... .75 .35
❑ 4 Rodney Hampton .... .40 .18
❑ 5 Wesley Walls .... .40 .18
❑ 6 Jerome Bettis .... .75 .35
❑ 7 Keyshawn Johnson .... .75 .35
❑ 8 Keenan McCardell .... .40 .18
❑ 9 Terry Allen .... .75 .35
❑ 10 Troy Aikman .... 2.00 .90
❑ 11 Tony Banks .... .40 .18
❑ 12 Ty Detmer .... .40 .18
❑ 13 Chris Chandler .... .40 .18
❑ 14 Marshall Faulk .... .75 .35
❑ 15 Heath Shuler .... .20 .09
❑ 16 Stan Humphries .... .40 .18
❑ 17 Bryan Cox .... .20 .09
❑ 18 Chris Spielman .... .20 .09
❑ 19 Derrick Thomas .... .40 .18
❑ 20 Steve Young .... 1.25 .55
❑ 21 Desmond Howard .... .40 .18
❑ 22 Jeff Blake .... .40 .18
❑ 23 Michael Jackson .... .40 .18
❑ 24 Cris Carter .... .75 .35
❑ 25 Joey Galloway .... 1.00 .45
❑ 26 Simeon Rice .... .40 .18
❑ 27 Reggie White .... .75 .35
❑ 28 Dave Brown .... .20 .09
❑ 29 Mike Alstott .... .75 .35
❑ 30 Emmitt Smith 3.00 1.35
❑ 31 Anthony Johnson .... .20 .09
❑ 32 Mark Brunell .... 2.00 .90
❑ 33 Ricky Watters .... .40 .18
❑ 34 Terrell Davis 3.00 1.35

❑ 35 Ben Coates	.40	.18
❑ 36 Gus Frerotte	.20	.09
❑ 37 Andre Reed	.40	.18
❑ 38 Isaac Bruce	.75	.35
❑ 39 Junior Seau	.40	.18
❑ 40 Eddie George	2.00	.90
❑ 41 Adrian Murrell	.40	.18
❑ 42 Jake Reed	.40	.18
❑ 43 Karim Abdul-Jabbar	.75	.35
❑ 44 Scott Mitchell	.40	.18
❑ 45 Ki-Jana Carter	.20	.09
❑ 46 Curtis Conway	.40	.18
❑ 47 Jim Harbaugh	.40	.18
❑ 48 Tim Brown	.75	.35
❑ 49 Mario Bates	.20	.09
❑ 50 Jerry Rice	2.00	.90
❑ 51 Byron Bam Morris	.20	.09
❑ 52 Marcus Allen	.75	.35
❑ 53 Errict Rhett	.20	.09
❑ 54 Steve McNair	1.00	.45
❑ 55 Kerry Collins	.40	.18
❑ 56 Bert Emanuel	.40	.18
❑ 57 Curtis Martin	1.00	.45
❑ 58 Bryce Paup	.20	.09
❑ 59 Brad Johnson	1.00	.45
❑ 60 John Elway	4.00	1.80
❑ 61 Natrone Means	.75	.35
❑ 62 Deion Sanders	.75	.35
❑ 63 Tony Martin	.40	.18
❑ 64 Michael Westbrook	.40	.18
❑ 65 Chris Calloway	.20	.09
❑ 66 Antonio Freeman	1.00	.45
❑ 67 Rob Johnson	.75	.35
❑ 68 Kent Graham	.20	.09
❑ 69 O.J. McDuffie	.40	.18
❑ 70 Barry Sanders	4.00	1.80
❑ 71 Chris Warren	.40	.18
❑ 72 Kordell Stewart	1.00	.45
❑ 73 Thurman Thomas	.75	.35
❑ 74 Marvin Harrison	.75	.35
❑ 75 Carl Pickens	.75	.35
❑ 76 Brent Jones	.40	.18
❑ 77 Irving Fryar	.40	.18
❑ 78 Neil O'Donnell	.40	.18
❑ 79 Elvis Grbac	.40	.18
❑ 80 Drew Bledsoe	2.00	.90
❑ 81 Shannon Sharpe	.40	.18
❑ 82 Vinny Testaverde	.40	.18
❑ 83 Chris Sanders	.20	.09
❑ 84 Herman Moore	.75	.35
❑ 85 Jeff George	.40	.18
❑ 86 Bruce Smith	.40	.18
❑ 87 Robert Smith	.40	.18
❑ 88 Kevin Hardy	.20	.09
❑ 89 Kevin Greene	.40	.18
❑ 90 Dan Marino	4.00	1.80
❑ 91 Michael Irvin	.75	.35
❑ 92 Garrison Hearst	.40	.18
❑ 93 Lake Dawson	.20	.09
❑ 94 Lawrence Phillips	.20	.09
❑ 95 Terry Glenn	.75	.35
❑ 96 Jake Plummer RC	10.00	4.50
❑ 97 Byron Hanspard RC	2.50	1.10
❑ 98 Bryant Westbrook RC	.20	.09
❑ 99 Troy Davis RC	.75	.35
❑ 100 Danny Wuerffel RC	2.50	1.10
❑ 101 Tony Gonzalez RC	4.00	1.80
❑ 102 Jim Druckenmiller RC	1.50	.70
❑ 103 Kevin Lockett RC	.40	.18
❑ 104 Renaldo Wynn RC	.20	.09
❑ 105 James Farrior RC	.20	.09
❑ 106 Rae Carruth RC	.75	.35
❑ 107 Tom Knight RC	.20	.09
❑ 108 Corey Dillon RC	5.00	2.20
❑ 109 Kenny Holmes RC	.20	.09
❑ 110 Orlando Pace RC	.20	.09
❑ 111 Reidel Anthony RC	2.00	.90
❑ 112 Chad Scott RC	.20	.09
❑ 113 Antowain Smith RC	3.00	1.35
❑ 114 David LaFleur RC	1.50	.70
❑ 115 Yatil Green RC	.40	.18
❑ 116 Darrell Russell RC	.20	.09
❑ 117 Joey Kent RC	.75	.35
❑ 118 Darnell Autry RC	.40	.18
❑ 119 Peter Boulware RC	.40	.18
❑ 120 Shawn Springs RC	.40	.18
❑ 121 Ike Hilliard RC	2.50	1.10
❑ 122 Dwayne Rudd RC	.20	.09
❑ 123 Reinard Wilson RC	.20	.09
❑ 124 Michael Booker RC	.20	.09
❑ 125 Warrick Dunn RC	4.00	1.80

1997 Bowman's Best Autographs

	MINT	NRMT
COMPLETE SET (10)	250.00	110.00
COMMON CARD	20.00	9.00
SEMISTARS	25.00	11.00

BASE AUTOGRAPH STATED ODDS 1:131
*ATOMIC REFRACTORS: 1.5X TO 4X
ATOMIC REFRACTOR ODDS 1:4733
*REFRACTORS: .75X TO 2X........
REFRACTOR STATED ODDS 1:1578

❑ 22 Jeff Blake	25.00	11.00
❑ 44 Scott Mitchell	25.00	11.00
❑ 47 Jim Harbaugh	25.00	11.00
❑ 99 Troy Davis	25.00	11.00
❑ 102 Jim Druckenmiller	25.00	11.00
❑ 113 Antowain Smith	30.00	13.50
❑ 114 David LaFleur	25.00	11.00
❑ 120 Shawn Springs	20.00	9.00
❑ 121 Ike Hilliard	25.00	11.00
❑ 125 Warrick Dunn	50.00	22.00

1997 Bowman's Best Cuts

	MINT	NRMT
COMPLETE SET (20)	100.00	45.00

STATED ODDS 1:24
*ATO. REF. STARS: 3X TO 7.5X BASE CARD HI
*ATO. REF. ROOKIES: 1.5X TO 4X BASE CARD HI
ATOMIC REF.STATED ODDS 1:96
*REFRACTOR STARS: 2X TO 5X BASE CARD HI
*REFRACTOR ROOKIES: 1X TO 2.5X BASE CARD HI
REFRACTOR STATED ODDS 1:48

❑ BC1 Orlando Pace	.30	.14
❑ BC2 Eddie George	6.00	2.70
❑ BC3 John Elway	12.00	5.50
❑ BC4 Tony Gonzalez	6.00	2.70
❑ BC5 Brett Favre	12.00	5.50
❑ BC6 Shawn Springs	.60	.25
❑ BC7 Warrick Dunn	6.00	2.70
❑ BC8 Troy Aikman	6.00	2.70
❑ BC9 Terry Glenn	2.50	1.10
❑ BC10 Dan Marino	12.00	5.50
❑ BC11 Jake Plummer	15.00	6.75
❑ BC12 Ike Hilliard	4.00	1.80
❑ BC13 Emmitt Smith	10.00	4.50
❑ BC14 Steve Young	4.00	1.80
❑ BC15 Barry Sanders	12.00	5.50
❑ BC16 Jim Druckenmiller	2.50	1.10
❑ BC17 Drew Bledsoe	6.00	2.70
❑ BC18 Antowain Smith	5.00	2.20
❑ BC19 Mark Brunell	6.00	2.70
❑ BC20 Jerry Rice	6.00	2.70

1997 Bowman's Best Mirror Images

	MINT	NRMT
COMPLETE SET (10)	120.00	55.00
COMMON CARD (MI1-MI10)	4.00	1.80

STATED ODDS 1:48
*ATOMIC REFRACT: 1X TO 2.5X BASIC INSERTS
ATOMIC REF.STATED ODDS 1:192
*REFRACTORS: .6X TO 1.5X BASIC INSERTS
REFRACTOR STATED ODDS 1:96

❑ MI1 Brett Favre Gus Frerotte John Elway Mark Brunell	25.00	11.00
❑ MI2 Steve Young Tony Banks Dan Marino Drew Bledsoe	25.00	11.00
❑ MI3 Troy Aikman Kerry Collins Vinny Testaverde Kordell Stewart	15.00	6.75
❑ MI4 Emmitt Smith Dorsey Levens Marcus Allen Eddie George	20.00	9.00
❑ MI5 Barry Sanders Errict Rhett Thurman Thomas Curtis Martin	25.00	11.00
❑ MI6 Ricky Watters Jamal Anderson Chris Warren Terrell Davis	20.00	9.00
❑ MI7 Jerry Rice Isaac Bruce Tony Martin Marvin Harrison	15.00	6.75
❑ MI8 Herman Moore Curtis Conway Tim Brown Terry Glenn	5.00	2.20
❑ MI9 Michael Irvin Eddie Kennison Carl Pickens Keyshawn Johnson	4.00	1.80
❑ MI10 Wesley Walls Jason Dunn Shannon Sharpe Rickey Dudley	4.00	1.80

1998 Bowman's Best

	MINT	NRMT
COMPLETE SET (125)	100.00	45.00
COMMON CARD (1-100)	.20	.09
SEMISTARS	.40	.18
UNLISTED STARS	.75	.35
COMMON ROOKIE (101-125)	2.00	.90
ROOKIE SEMISTARS	3.00	1.35
ROOKIE SUBSET ODDS 1:2		
COMMON ATOMIC REF.	5.00	2.20

*ATOMIC REF.STARS: 12X TO 30X HI COL.
*ATOMIC REF.YOUNG STARS: 10X TO 25X
*ATOMIC REF.RCs: 3X TO 8X
ATOMIC REFRACTOR STATED ODDS 1:103
STATED PRINT RUN 100 SERIAL #'d SETS

	MINT	NRMT
COMP.REFRACT.SET (125)	500.00	220.00

*REFRACTOR STARS: 3X TO 8X HI COL.
*REFRACTOR YOUNG STARS: 2.5X TO 6X
*REFRACTOR RCs: 1.2X TO 3X..
REFRACTOR STATED ODDS 1:25
STATED PRINT RUN 400 SERIAL #'d SETS

Card	MINT	NRMT
❑ 1 Emmitt Smith	3.00	1.35
❑ 2 Reggie White	.75	.35
❑ 3 Jake Plummer	2.50	1.10
❑ 4 Ike Hilliard	.20	.09
❑ 5 Isaac Bruce	.20	.09
❑ 6 Trent Dilfer	.75	.35
❑ 7 Ricky Watters	.40	.18
❑ 8 Jeff George	.40	.18
❑ 9 Wayne Chrebet	.75	.35
❑ 10 Brett Favre	4.00	1.80
❑ 11 Terry Allen	.75	.35
❑ 12 Bert Emanuel	.20	.09
❑ 13 Andre Reed	.40	.18
❑ 14 Andre Rison	.40	.18
❑ 15 Jeff Blake	.40	.18
❑ 16 Steve McNair	.75	.35
❑ 17 Joey Galloway	.75	.35
❑ 18 Irving Fryar	.40	.18
❑ 19 Dorsey Levens	.75	.35
❑ 20 Jerry Rice	2.00	.90
❑ 21 Kerry Collins	.40	.18
❑ 22 Michael Jackson	.20	.09
❑ 23 Kordell Stewart	.75	.35
❑ 24 Junior Seau	.40	.18
❑ 25 Jimmy Smith	.40	.18
❑ 26 Michael Westbrook	.40	.18
❑ 27 Eddie George	1.50	.70
❑ 28 Cris Carter	.75	.35
❑ 29 Jason Sehorn	.20	.09
❑ 30 Warrick Dunn	1.25	.55
❑ 31 Garrison Hearst	.75	.35
❑ 32 Erik Kramer	.20	.09
❑ 33 Chris Chandler	.40	.18
❑ 34 Michael Irvin	.75	.35
❑ 35 Marshall Faulk	.75	.35
❑ 36 Warren Moon	.75	.35
❑ 37 Rickey Dudley	.20	.09
❑ 38 Drew Bledsoe	1.50	.70
❑ 39 Antowain Smith	.75	.35
❑ 40 Terrell Davis	3.00	1.35
❑ 41 Gus Frerotte	.20	.09
❑ 42 Robert Brooks	.40	.18
❑ 43 Tony Banks	.40	.18
❑ 44 Terrell Owens	.75	.35
❑ 45 Edgar Bennett	.20	.09
❑ 46 Rob Moore	.40	.18
❑ 47 J.J. Stokes	.40	.18
❑ 48 Yancey Thigpen	.20	.09
❑ 49 Elvis Grbac	.40	.18
❑ 50 John Elway	4.00	1.80
❑ 51 Charles Johnson	.20	.09
❑ 52 Karim Abdul-Jabbar	.75	.35
❑ 53 Carl Pickens	.75	.35
❑ 54 Peter Boulware	.20	.09
❑ 55 Chris Warren	.20	.09
❑ 56 Terance Mathis	.40	.18
❑ 57 Andre Hastings	.20	.09
❑ 58 Jake Reed	.40	.18
❑ 59 Mike Alstott	.20	.09
❑ 60 Mark Brunell	1.50	.70
❑ 61 Herman Moore	.75	.35
❑ 62 Troy Aikman	2.00	.90
❑ 63 Fred Lane	.40	.18
❑ 64 Rod Smith	.40	.18
❑ 65 Terry Glenn	.75	.35
❑ 66 Jerome Bettis	.75	.35
❑ 67 Derrick Thomas	.40	.18
❑ 68 Marvin Harrison	.40	.18
❑ 69 Adrian Murrell	.20	.09
❑ 70 Curtis Martin	.75	.35
❑ 71 Bobby Hoying	.40	.18
❑ 72 Darrell Green	.40	.18
❑ 73 Sean Dawkins	.20	.09
❑ 74 Robert Smith	.75	.35
❑ 75 Antonio Freeman	.75	.35
❑ 76 Scott Mitchell	.40	.18
❑ 77 Curtis Conway	.40	.18
❑ 78 Rae Carruth	.40	.18
❑ 79 Jamal Anderson	.75	.35
❑ 80 Dan Marino	4.00	1.80
❑ 81 Brad Johnson	.75	.35
❑ 82 Danny Kanell	.40	.18
❑ 83 Charlie Garner	.20	.09
❑ 84 Rob Johnson	.40	.18
❑ 85 Natrone Means	.75	.35
❑ 86 Tim Brown	.75	.35
❑ 87 Keyshawn Johnson	.75	.35
❑ 88 Ben Coates	.40	.18
❑ 89 Derrick Alexander	.40	.18
❑ 90 Steve Young	1.25	.55
❑ 91 Shannon Sharpe	.40	.18
❑ 92 Corey Dillon	1.25	.55
❑ 93 Bruce Smith	.40	.18
❑ 94 Errict Rhett	.40	.18
❑ 95 Jim Harbaugh	.20	.09
❑ 96 Napoleon Kaufman	.75	.35
❑ 97 Glenn Foley	.40	.18
❑ 98 Tony Gonzalez	.20	.09
❑ 99 Keenan McCardell	.40	.18
❑ 100 Barry Sanders	4.00	1.80
❑ 101 Charles Woodson RC	6.00	2.70
❑ 102 Tim Dwight RC	5.00	2.20
❑ 103 Marcus Nash RC	4.00	1.80
❑ 104 Joe Jurevicius RC	3.00	1.35
❑ 105 Jacquez Green RC	5.00	2.20
❑ 106 Kevin Dyson RC	5.00	2.20
❑ 107 Keith Brooking RC	3.00	1.35
❑ 108 Andre Wadsworth RC	3.00	1.35
❑ 109 Randy Moss RC	25.00	11.00
❑ 110 Robert Edwards RC	3.00	1.35
❑ 111 Pat Johnson RC	3.00	1.35
❑ 112 Peyton Manning RC	25.00	11.00
❑ 113 Duane Starks RC	2.00	.90
❑ 114 Grant Wistrom RC	2.00	.90
❑ 115 Anthony Simmons RC	2.00	.90
❑ 116 Takeo Spikes RC	3.00	1.35
❑ 117 Tony Simmons RC	3.00	1.35
❑ 118 Jerome Pathon RC	3.00	1.35
❑ 119 Ryan Leaf RC	5.00	2.20
❑ 120 Skip Hicks RC	5.00	2.20
❑ 121 Curtis Enis RC	6.00	2.70
❑ 122 Germane Crowell RC	6.00	2.70
❑ 123 John Avery RC	3.00	1.35
❑ 124 Hines Ward RC	3.00	1.35
❑ 125 Fred Taylor RC	15.00	6.75

1998 Bowman's Best Autographs

	MINT	NRMT
COMPLETE SET (20)	400.00	180.00

	MINT	NRMT
COMMON CARD (1A-10B)	15.00	6.75
SEMISTARS	25.00	11.00

*A/B CARDS SAME PRICE
STATED ODDS 1:158
*ATOMIC REFRACTORS: 1.25X TO 3X HI COL.
ATOMIC REFRACTOR STATED ODDS 1:2521
*REFRACTORS: .75X TO 2X HI COL.
REFRACTOR STATED ODDS 1:840

Card	MINT	NRMT
❑ 1A Jake Plummer	50.00	22.00
❑ 1B Jake Plummer	75.00	34.00
❑ 2A Jason Sehorn	15.00	6.75
❑ 2B Jason Sehorn	15.00	6.75
❑ 3A Corey Dillon	25.00	11.00
❑ 3B Corey Dillon	25.00	11.00
❑ 4A Tim Brown	25.00	11.00
❑ 4B Tim Brown	25.00	11.00
❑ 5A Keenan McCardell	25.00	11.00
❑ 5B Keenan McCardell	25.00	11.00
❑ 6A Kordell Stewart	30.00	13.50
❑ 6B Kordell Stewart	60.00	27.00
❑ 7A Peyton Manning	120.00	55.00
❑ 7B Peyton Manning	120.00	55.00
❑ 8A Danny Kanell	25.00	11.00
❑ 8B Danny Kanell	25.00	11.00
❑ 9A Fred Taylor (The Ryan Leaf trade card was redeemed for a Fred Taylor autograph)	60.00	27.00
❑ 9B Fred Taylor (Ryan Leaf trade card was redeemed for a Fred Taylor autograph)	50.00	22.00
❑ 10A Curtis Enis	40.00	18.00
❑ 10B Curtis Enis	40.00	18.00

1998 Bowman's Best Mirror Image Fusion

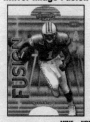

	MINT	NRMT
COMPLETE SET (20)	150.00	70.00
COMMON CARD (MI1-MI20)	3.00	1.35
SEMISTARS	4.00	1.80
UNLISTED STARS	5.00	2.20

STATED ODDS 1:48
*ATOMIC REFRACTORS: 5X TO 12X HI COL.
ATOMIC REFRACTOR STATED ODDS 1:2521
STATED PRINT RUN 25 SERIAL #'d SETS
*REFRACTORS: 1.5X TO 4X HI COL.
REFRACTOR STATED ODDS 1:630
STATED PRINT RUN 100 SERIAL #'d SETS

Card	MINT	NRMT
❑ MI1 Terrell Davis John Avery	15.00	6.75
❑ MI2 Emmitt Smith Curtis Enis	15.00	6.75
❑ MI3 Barry Sanders Skip Hicks	20.00	9.00
❑ MI4 Eddie George Robert Edwards	6.00	2.70
❑ MI5 Jerome Bettis Fred Taylor	10.00	4.50
❑ MI6 Mark Brunell Ryan Leaf	8.00	3.60
❑ MI7 John Elway Brian Griese	20.00	9.00
❑ MI8 Dan Marino Peyton Manning	25.00	11.00
❑ MI9 Brett Favre Charlie Batch	20.00	9.00
❑ MI10 Drew Bledsoe Jonathan Quinn	8.00	3.60
❑ MI11 Tim Brown Kevin Dyson	5.00	2.20
❑ MI12 Herman Moore Germane Crowell	4.00	1.80
❑ MI13 Joey Galloway Jerome Pathon	4.00	1.80
❑ MI14 Cris Carter Jacquez Green	5.00	2.20
❑ MI15 Jerry Rice Randy Moss	25.00	11.00
❑ MI16 Junior Seau Takeo Spikes	4.00	1.80
❑ MI17 John Randle Jason Peter	3.00	1.35
❑ MI18 Reggie White Andre Wadsworth	4.00	1.80
❑ MI19 Peter Boulware Anthony Simmons	3.00	1.35
❑ MI20 Derrick Thomas Brian Simmons	3.00	1.35

1998 Bowman's Best Performers

	MINT	NRMT
COMPLETE SET (10)	40.00	18.00
COMMON CARD (BP1-BP10)	2.00	.90
SEMISTARS	3.00	1.35
STATED ODDS 1:12		

*ATOMIC REFRACTORS: 5X TO 12X
ATOMIC REFRACTOR STATED ODDS 1:2521
STATED PRINT RUN 50 SERIAL #'d SETS
*REFRACTORS: 1.5X TO 4X HI COL.
REFRACTOR STATED ODDS 1:630
STATED PRINT RUN 200 SERIAL #'d SETS

Card	MINT	NRMT
❑ BP1 Peyton Manning	15.00	6.75
❑ BP2 Charles Woodson	4.00	1.80
❑ BP3 Skip Hicks	3.00	1.35
❑ BP4 Andre Wadsworth	3.00	1.35
❑ BP5 Randy Moss	15.00	6.75
❑ BP6 Marcus Nash	3.00	1.35
❑ BP7 Ahman Green	3.00	1.35
❑ BP8 Anthony Simmons	2.00	.90
❑ BP9 Tavian Banks	3.00	1.35
❑ BP10 Ryan Leaf	3.00	1.35

1999 Bowman's Best

	MINT	NRMT
COMPLETE SET (133)	80.00	36.00
COMMON CARD (1-100)	.20	.09
SEMISTARS	.40	.18
UNLISTED STARS	.75	.35
COMMON ROOKIE (101-133)	1.50	.70
ROOKIE SEMISTARS	2.00	.90

ROOKIE CLASS INSERT STATED ODDS 1:100

Card	MINT	NRMT
❑ 1 Randy Moss	3.00	1.35
❑ 2 Skip Hicks	.40	.18
❑ 3 Robert Smith	.75	.35
❑ 4 Drew Bledsoe	1.25	.55
❑ 5 Tim Brown	.75	.35
❑ 6 Marshall Faulk	.75	.35
❑ 7 Terance Mathis	.40	.18
❑ 8 Sean Dawkins	.20	.09
❑ 9 Ed McCaffrey	.40	.18
❑ 10 Jamal Anderson	.75	.35
❑ 11 Antonio Freeman	.75	.35
❑ 12 Terry Kirby	.40	.18
❑ 13 Vinny Testaverde	.40	.18
❑ 14 Eddie George	1.00	.45
❑ 15 Ricky Watters	.40	.18
❑ 16 Johnnie Morton	.40	.18
❑ 17 Natrone Means	.40	.18
❑ 18 Terry Glenn	.75	.35
❑ 19 Michael Westbrook	.40	.18
❑ 20 Doug Flutie	1.00	.45
❑ 21 Jake Plummer	1.25	.55
❑ 22 Darnay Scott	.40	.18
❑ 23 Andre Rison	.40	.18
❑ 24 Jon Kitna	1.00	.45
❑ 25 Dan Marino	3.00	1.35
❑ 26 Ike Hilliard	.40	.18
❑ 27 Warrick Dunn	.75	.35
❑ 28 Jerome Bettis	.75	.35
❑ 29 Curtis Conway	.40	.18
❑ 30 Emmitt Smith	2.00	.90
❑ 31 Jimmy Smith	.40	.18
❑ 32 Isaac Bruce	.75	.35
❑ 33 Jerry Rice	2.00	.90
❑ 34 Curtis Martin	.75	.35
❑ 35 Steve McNair	.75	.35
❑ 36 Jeff Blake	.40	.18
❑ 37 Rob Moore	.40	.18
❑ 38 Dorsey Levens	.75	.35
❑ 39 Terrell Davis	2.00	.90
❑ 40 John Elway	3.00	1.35
❑ 41 Trent Dilfer	.40	.18
❑ 42 Joey Galloway	.75	.35
❑ 43 Keyshawn Johnson	.75	.35
❑ 44 O.J. McDuffie	.40	.18
❑ 45 Fred Taylor	2.00	.90
❑ 46 Andre Reed	.40	.18
❑ 47 Frank Sanders	.40	.18
❑ 48 Keenan McCardell	.40	.18
❑ 49 Elvis Grbac	.40	.18
❑ 50 Barry Sanders	3.00	1.35
❑ 51 Terrell Owens	.75	.35
❑ 52 Trent Green	.40	.18
❑ 53 Brad Johnson	.75	.35
❑ 54 Rich Gannon	.40	.18
❑ 55 Randall Cunningham	.75	.35
❑ 56 Tony Martin	.40	.18
❑ 57 Rod Smith	.40	.18
❑ 58 Eric Moulds	.75	.35
❑ 59 Yancey Thigpen	.20	.09
❑ 60 Brett Favre	3.00	1.35
❑ 61 Cris Carter	.75	.35
❑ 62 Marvin Harrison	.75	.35
❑ 63 Chris Chandler	.40	.18
❑ 64 Antowain Smith	.75	.35
❑ 65 Carl Pickens	.40	.18
❑ 66 Shannon Sharpe	.40	.18
❑ 67 Mike Alstott	.75	.35
❑ 68 J.J. Stokes	.40	.18
❑ 69 Ben Coates	.40	.18
❑ 70 Peyton Manning	3.00	1.35
❑ 71 Duce Staley	.75	.35
❑ 72 Michael Irvin	.40	.18
❑ 73 Tim Biakabutuka	.40	.18
❑ 74 Priest Holmes	.75	.35
❑ 75 Steve Young	1.25	.55
❑ 76 Jerome Pathon	.40	.18
❑ 77 Wayne Chrebet	.75	.35
❑ 78 Bert Emanuel	.20	.09
❑ 79 Curtis Enis	.75	.35
❑ 80 Mark Brunell	1.25	.55
❑ 81 Herman Moore	.75	.35
❑ 82 Corey Dillon	.75	.35
❑ 83 Jim Harbaugh	.40	.18
❑ 84 Gary Brown	.20	.09
❑ 85 Kordell Stewart	.75	.35
❑ 86 Garrison Hearst	.40	.18
❑ 87 Rocket Ismail	.40	.18
❑ 88 Charlie Batch	1.50	.70
❑ 89 Napoleon Kaufman	.75	.35
❑ 90 Troy Aikman	2.00	.90
❑ 91 Brett Favre BP	1.50	.70
❑ 92 Randy Moss BP	1.50	.70
❑ 93 Terrell Davis BP	1.00	.45
❑ 94 Barry Sanders BP	1.50	.70
❑ 95 Peyton Manning BP	1.50	.70
❑ 96 Troy Edwards BP	1.00	.45
❑ 97 Cade McNown BP	2.00	.90
❑ 98 Edgerrin James BP	6.00	2.70
❑ 99 Torry Holt BP	1.25	.55
❑ 100 Tim Couch BP	3.00	1.35
❑ 101 Chris Claiborne RC	2.00	.90
❑ 102 Brock Huard RC	2.50	1.10
❑ 103 Amos Zereoue RC	2.00	.90
❑ 104 Sedrick Irvin RC	2.00	.90
❑ 105 Kevin Faulk RC	2.50	1.10
❑ 106 Ebenezer Ekuban RC	1.50	.70
❑ 107 Daunte Culpepper RC	6.00	2.70
❑ 108 Rob Konrad RC	2.00	.90
❑ 109 James Johnson RC	2.50	1.10
❑ 110 Kurt Warner RC	25.00	11.00
❑ 111 Mike Cloud RC	2.00	.90
❑ 112 Andy Katzenmoyer RC	2.00	.90
❑ 113 Jevon Kearse RC	3.00	1.35
❑ 114 Akili Smith RC	4.00	1.80
❑ 115 Edgerrin James RC	15.00	6.75
❑ 116 Cecil Collins RC	1.50	.70
❑ 117 Chris McAlister RC	1.50	.70
❑ 118 Donovan McNabb RC	6.00	2.70
❑ 119 Kevin Johnson RC	5.00	2.20
❑ 120 Torry Holt RC	4.00	1.80
❑ 121 Antoine Winfield RC	1.50	.70
❑ 122 Michael Bishop RC	2.50	1.10
❑ 123 Joe Germaine RC	2.00	.90
❑ 124 David Boston RC	3.00	1.35
❑ 125 D'Wayne Bates RC	1.50	.70
❑ 126 Champ Bailey RC	2.50	1.10
❑ 127 Cade McNown RC	6.00	2.70
❑ 128 Shaun King RC	6.00	2.70
❑ 129 Peerless Price RC	3.00	1.35
❑ 130 Troy Edwards RC	3.00	1.35
❑ 131 Karsten Bailey RC	2.00	.90
❑ 132 Tim Couch RC	10.00	4.50
❑ 133 Ricky Williams RC	10.00	4.50
❑ C1 Rookie Class Photo	10.00	4.50

1999 Bowman's Best Atomic Refractors

	MINT	NRMT
COMPLETE SET (133)	1200.00	550.00
COMMON CARD (1-100)	4.00	1.80
*STARS: 8X TO 20X HI COL.		

*YOUNG STARS: 6X TO 15X ......
COMMON ROOKIE (101-133) 12.00 5.50
*RCs: 3X TO 8X ......
STATED ODDS 1:69 ......
STATED PRINT RUN 100 SER.#'d SETS
ROOKIE CLASS ATOMIC REF.ODDS 1:26,880
ROOKIE CLASS ATOMIC REF.PRINT RUN 35

❑ C1 Rookie Class Photo .. 200.00 90.00

1999 Bowman's Best Refractors

	MINT	NRMT
COMPLETE SET (133)	500.00	220.00
COMMON CARD (1-100)	1.50	.70
*STARS: 3X TO 8X HI COL.		
*YOUNG STARS: 2.5X TO 6X		
COMMON ROOKIE (101-133) ..	6.00	2.70
*RCs: 1.5X TO 4X		
STATED ODDS 1:17		
STATED PRINT RUN 400 SER.#'d SETS		
ROOKIE CLASS REF.STATED ODDS 1:7429		
ROOKIE CLASS REF.PRINT RUN 125-CARDS		
❑ C1 Rookie Class Photo	80.00	36.00

1999 Bowman's Best Autographs

	MINT	NRMT
COMPLETE SET (3)	225.00	100.00
COMMON AUTO	40.00	18.00
A1-A2 STATED ODDS 1:915		
ROY1 STATED ODDS 1:9129		
TRADE CARD EXPIRATION: 9/30/2000		
❑ A1 Fred Taylor	50.00	22.00
❑ A2 Jake Plummer	40.00	18.00
❑ ROY1 Randy Moss ROY	150.00	70.00

1999 Bowman's Best Franchise Best

	MINT	NRMT
COMPLETE SET (9)	50.00	22.00
COMMON CARD (FB1-FB9)	4.00	1.80
STATED ODDS 1:20		
❑ FB1 Dan Marino	12.00	5.50
❑ FB2 Fred Taylor	6.00	2.70
❑ FB3 Emmitt Smith	8.00	3.60
❑ FB4 Terrell Davis	8.00	3.60
❑ FB5 Brett Favre	12.00	5.50
❑ FB6 Tim Couch	12.00	5.50
❑ FB7 Peyton Manning	10.00	4.50
❑ FB8 Eddie George	4.00	1.80
❑ FB9 Randy Moss	10.00	4.50

1999 Bowman's Best Franchise Favorites

	MINT	NRMT
COMPLETE SET (2)	25.00	11.00
COMMON CARD (F1-F2)	10.00	4.50
STATED ODDS 1:153		
❑ F1 Tony Dorsett ...... Roger Staubach	10.00	4.50
❑ F2 Randy Moss ...... Fran Tarkenton	20.00	9.00

1999 Bowman's Best Franchise Favorites Autographs

	MINT	NRMT
COMPLETE SET (6)	600.00	275.00
COMMON CARD (FA1-FA6) ..	60.00	27.00
FA1 STATED ODDS 1:4599		
FA2/FA5 COMBINED STATED ODDS 1:1017		
FA3/FA6 COMBINED STATED ODDS 1:9129		
FA4 STATED ODDS 1:9129		
OVERALL STATED ODDS 1:703		
❑ FA1 Tony Dorsett	60.00	27.00
❑ FA2 Roger Staubach	100.00	45.00
❑ FA3 Tony Dorsett ...... Roger Staubach	150.00	70.00
❑ FA4 Randy Moss	150.00	70.00
❑ FA5 Fran Tarkenton	60.00	27.00
❑ FA6 Randy Moss ...... Fran Tarkenton	200.00	90.00

1999 Bowman's Best Future Foundations

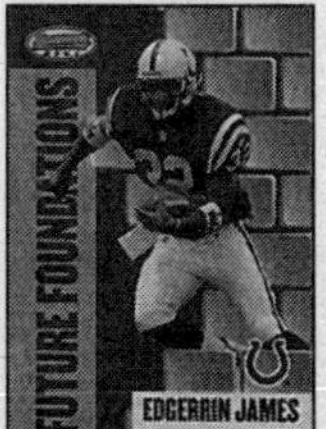

	MINT	NRMT
COMPLETE SET (18)	50.00	22.00
COMMON CARD (FF1-FF18) ..	1.25	.55
SEMISTARS	1.50	.70
STATED ODDS 1:20		
❑ FF1 Tim Couch	8.00	3.60
❑ FF2 David Boston	2.50	1.10
❑ FF3 Donovan McNabb	5.00	2.20
❑ FF4 Troy Edwards	2.50	1.10
❑ FF5 Ricky Williams	8.00	3.60
❑ FF6 Daunte Culpepper	5.00	2.20
❑ FF7 Torry Holt	4.00	1.80
❑ FF8 Cade McNown	5.00	2.20
❑ FF9 Akili Smith	3.00	1.35
❑ FF10 Edgerrin James	15.00	6.75
❑ FF11 Cecil Collins	1.50	.70
❑ FF12 Peerless Price	2.50	1.10
❑ FF13 Kevin Johnson	4.00	1.80
❑ FF14 Champ Bailey	2.00	.90
❑ FF15 Mike Cloud	1.50	.70
❑ FF16 D'Wayne Bates	1.25	.55
❑ FF17 Shaun King	5.00	2.20
❑ FF18 James Johnson	2.00	.90

1999 Bowman's Best Honor Roll

	MINT	NRMT
COMPLETE SET (8)	40.00	18.00
COMMON CARD (H1-H8)	3.00	1.35
STATED ODDS 1:40		
❑ H1 Peyton Manning	12.00	5.50
❑ H2 Drew Bledsoe	5.00	2.20
❑ H3 Doug Flutie	4.00	1.80
❑ H4 Tim Couch	12.00	5.50
❑ H5 Charles Woodson	3.00	1.35
❑ H6 Ricky Williams	12.00	5.50
❑ H7 Tim Brown	3.00	1.35
❑ H8 Eddie George	4.00	1.80

1999 Bowman's Best Legacy

	MINT	NRMT
COMPLETE SET (3)	30.00	13.50
COMMON CARD (L1-L3)	10.00	4.50
STATED ODDS 1:102		
❑ L1 Ricky Williams	12.00	5.50
❑ L2 Earl Campbell	10.00	4.50
❑ L3 Ricky Williams ...... Earl Campbell	15.00	6.75

1999 Bowman's Best Legacy Autographs

	MINT	NRMT
COMPLETE SET (3)	400.00	180.00
COMMON CARD (LA1-LA3) ..	60.00	27.00
LA1 STATED ODDS 1:4599		
LA2 STATED ODDS 1:2040		
LA3 STATED ODDS 1:18,108		
OVERALL STATED ODDS 1:1311		

	Card	Mint	Nrmt
❑ LA1	Ricky Williams	100.00	45.00
❑ LA2	Earl Campbell	60.00	27.00
❑ LA3	Ricky Williams Earl Campbell	250.00	110.00

1999 Bowman's Best Rookie Locker Room Autographs

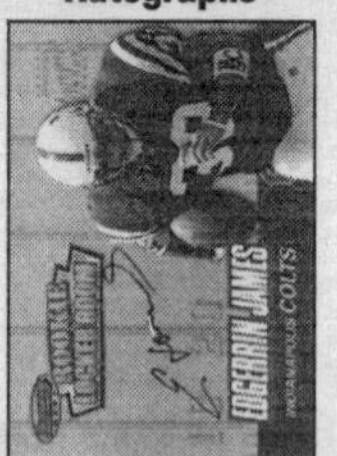

	MINT	NRMT
COMPLETE SET (5)	350.00	160.00
COMMON CARD (RA1-RA5)	25.00	11.00

RA1/RA4/RA5 STATED OODS 1:305
RA2/RA3 STATED OODS 1:915
TRADE CARD EXPIRATION: 9/30/2000

	Card	Mint	Nrmt
❑ RA1	Tim Couch	80.00	36.00
❑ RA2	Donovan McNabb Trade	60.00	27.00
❑ RA3	Edgerrin James	150.00	70.00
❑ RA4	David Boston	25.00	11.00
❑ RA5	Torry Holt	30.00	13.50

1999 Bowman's Best Rookie Locker Room Jerseys

	MINT	NRMT
COMPLETE SET (4)	200.00	90.00
COMMON CARD	30.00	13.50

STATED ODDS 1:229
TRADE CARD EXPIRATION: 9/30/2000

	Card	Mint	Nrmt
❑ RU1	Ricky Williams	100.00	45.00
❑ RU2	Donovan McNabb	50.00	22.00
❑ RU3	Kevin Faulk	30.00	13.50
❑ RU5	Torry Holt	50.00	22.00

1994 Collector's Choice

	MINT	NRMT
COMPLETE SET (384)	20.00	9.00
COMMON CARD (1-384)	.05	.02
EXPANSION TEAMS (379-380)	.15	.07
SEMISTARS	.10	.05
UNLISTED STARS	.25	.11
COMP.GOLD SET (384)	500.00	220.00

*GOLD STARS: 10 to 25X HI COL.
*GOLD RCS: 6X to 15X HI
GOLD STATED ODDS 1:36

	MINT	NRMT
COMP.SILVER SET (384)	80.00	36.00

*SILVER STARS 1.2X TO 3X HI COL.
*SILVER RCS: 1X to 2X HI
ONE GOLD OR SILVER PER FOIL PACK
THREE GOLD OR SILVER PER JUMBO PACK
TWO SILVER OR GOLD PER SPEC.RET.PACK

	Card	Mint	Nrmt
❑ 1	Antonio Langham RC	.10	.05
❑ 2	Aaron Glenn RC	.10	.05
❑ 3	Sam Adams RC	.10	.05
❑ 4	Dewayne Washington RC	.10	.05
❑ 5	Dan Wilkinson RC	.10	.05
❑ 6	Bryant Young RC	.25	.11
❑ 7	Aaron Taylor RC	.05	.02
❑ 8	Willie McGinest RC	.10	.05
❑ 9	Trev Alberts RC	.10	.05
❑ 10	Jamir Miller RC	.05	.02
❑ 11	John Thierry RC	.05	.02
❑ 12	Heath Shuler RC	.25	.11
❑ 13	Trent Dilfer RC	1.50	.70
❑ 14	Marshall Faulk RC	4.00	1.80
❑ 15	Greg Hill RC	.50	.23
❑ 16	William Floyd RC	.25	.11
❑ 17	Chuck Levy RC	.05	.02
❑ 18	Charlie Garner RC	1.50	.70
❑ 19	Mario Bates RC	.25	.11
❑ 20	Donnell Bennett RC	.25	.11
❑ 21	LeShon Johnson RC	.10	.05
❑ 22	Calvin Jones RC	.05	.02
❑ 23	Darnay Scott RC	.75	.35
❑ 24	Charles Johnson RC	.25	.11
❑ 25	Johnnie Morton RC	.25	.11
❑ 26	Shante Carver RC	.05	.02
❑ 27	Derrick Alexander WR RC	.50	.23
❑ 28	David Palmer RC	.50	.23
❑ 29	Ryan Yarborough RC	.05	.02
❑ 30	Errict Rhett RC	1.50	.70
❑ 31	James Washington I93	.05	.02
❑ 32	Sterling Sharpe I93	.05	.02
❑ 33	Drew Bledsoe I93	.40	.18
❑ 34	Eric Allen I93	.05	.02
❑ 35	Jerome Bettis I93	.10	.05
❑ 36	Joe Montana I93	.60	.25
❑ 37	John Carney I93	.05	.02
❑ 38	Emmitt Smith I93	.50	.23
❑ 39	Chris Warren I93	.25	.11
❑ 40	Reggie Brooks I93	.05	.02
❑ 41	Gary Brown I93	.05	.02
❑ 42	Tim Brown I93	.10	.05
❑ 43	Erric Pegram I93	.05	.02
❑ 44	Ronald Moore I93	.05	.02
❑ 45	Jerry Rice I93	.40	.18
❑ 46	Ricky Watters TE	.25	.11
❑ 47	Joe Montana TE	.60	.25
❑ 48	Reggie Brooks TE	.05	.02
❑ 49	Rick Mirer TE	.25	.11
❑ 50	Rocket Ismail TE	.10	.05
❑ 51	Curtis Conway TE	.10	.05
❑ 52	Junior Seau TE	.25	.11
❑ 53	Mark Carrier DB TE	.05	.02
❑ 54	Ronnie Lott TE	.10	.05
❑ 55	Marcus Allen TE	.25	.11
❑ 56	Michael Irvin TE	.25	.11
❑ 57	Bennie Blades	.05	.02
❑ 58	Randal Hill	.05	.02
❑ 59	Brian Blades	.10	.05
❑ 60	Russell Maryland	.05	.02
❑ 61	Jim Kelly	.25	.11
❑ 62	Arthur Marshall	.05	.02
❑ 63	Webster Slaughter	.05	.02
❑ 64	Dave Krieg	.10	.05
❑ 65	Steve Jordan	.05	.02
❑ 66	Neil O'Donnell	.25	.11
❑ 67	Andre Reed	.10	.05
❑ 68	Mike Croel	.05	.02
❑ 69	Al Smith	.05	.02
❑ 70	Joe Montana	1.50	.70
❑ 71	Randall McDaniel	.05	.02
❑ 72	Greg Lloyd	.25	.11
❑ 73	Thomas Smith	.05	.02
❑ 74	Glyn Milburn	.10	.05
❑ 75	Lorenzo White	.05	.02
❑ 76	Neil Smith	.25	.11
❑ 77	John Randle	.05	.02
❑ 78	Rod Woodson	.25	.11
❑ 79	Russell Maryland	.05	.02
❑ 80	Rodney Peete	.05	.02
❑ 81	Jackie Harris	.05	.02
❑ 82	James Jett	.05	.02
❑ 83	Rodney Hampton	.25	.11
❑ 84	Bill Romanowski	.05	.02
❑ 85	Ken Norton Jr.	.10	.05
❑ 86	Barry Sanders	1.50	.70
❑ 87	Johnny Holland	.05	.02
❑ 88	Terry McDaniel	.05	.02
❑ 89	Greg Jackson	.05	.02
❑ 90	Dana Stubblefield	.25	.11
❑ 91	Jay Novacek	.10	.05
❑ 92	Chris Spielman	.10	.05
❑ 93	Ken Ruettgers	.05	.02
❑ 94	Greg Robinson	.05	.02
❑ 95	Mark Jackson	.05	.02
❑ 96	John Taylor	.10	.05
❑ 97	Roger Harper	.05	.02
❑ 98	Jerry Ball	.05	.02
❑ 99	Keith Byars	.05	.02
❑ 100	Morten Andersen	.05	.02
❑ 101	Eric Allen	.05	.02
❑ 102	Marion Butts	.05	.02
❑ 103	Michael Haynes	.10	.05
❑ 104	Rob Burnett	.05	.02
❑ 105	Marco Coleman	.05	.02
❑ 106	Derek Brown RBK	.05	.02
❑ 107	Andy Harmon	.05	.02
❑ 108	Darren Carrington	.05	.02
❑ 109	Bobby Hebert	.05	.02
❑ 110	Mark Carrier WR	.10	.05
❑ 111	Bryan Cox	.05	.02
❑ 112	Toi Cook	.05	.02
❑ 113	Tim Harris	.05	.02
❑ 114	John Friesz	.10	.05
❑ 115	Neal Anderson	.05	.02
❑ 116	Jerome Bettis	.25	.11
❑ 117	Bruce Armstrong	.05	.02
❑ 118	Brad Baxter	.05	.02
❑ 119	Johnny Bailey	.05	.02
❑ 120	Brian Blades	.10	.05
❑ 121	Mark Carrier DB	.05	.02
❑ 122	Shane Conlan	.05	.02
❑ 123	Drew Bledsoe	.75	.35
❑ 124	Chris Burkett	.05	.02
❑ 125	Steve Beuerlein	.05	.02
❑ 126	Ferrell Edmunds	.05	.02
❑ 127	Curtis Conway	.25	.11
❑ 128	Troy Drayton	.05	.02
❑ 129	Vincent Brown	.05	.02
❑ 130	Boomer Esiason	.10	.05
❑ 131	Larry Centers	.25	.11
❑ 132	Carlton Gray	.05	.02
❑ 133	Chris Miller	.05	.02
❑ 134	Eric Metcalf	.10	.05
❑ 135	Mark Higgs	.05	.02
❑ 136	Tyrone Hughes	.10	.05
❑ 137	Randall Cunningham	.25	.11
❑ 138	Ronnie Harmon	.05	.02
❑ 139	Andre Rison	.10	.05
❑ 140	Eric Turner	.05	.02
❑ 141	Terry Kirby	.25	.11
❑ 142	Eric Martin	.05	.02
❑ 143	Seth Joyner	.05	.02
❑ 144	Stan Humphries	.25	.11
❑ 145	Deion Sanders	.40	.18
❑ 146	Vinny Testaverde	.10	.05
❑ 147	Dan Marino	1.50	.70
❑ 148	Renaldo Turnbull	.05	.02
❑ 149	Herschel Walker	.10	.05
❑ 150	Anthony Miller	.10	.05
❑ 151	Richard Dent	.10	.05
❑ 152	Jim Everett	.10	.05
❑ 153	Ben Coates	.25	.11
❑ 154	Jeff Lageman	.05	.02
❑ 155	Garrison Hearst	.25	.11
❑ 156	Kelvin Martin	.05	.02
❑ 157	Dante Jones	.05	.02
❑ 158	Sean Gilbert	.05	.02
❑ 159	Leonard Russell	.05	.02
❑ 160	Ronnie Lott	.10	.05
❑ 161	Randal Hill	.05	.02
❑ 162	Rick Mirer	.25	.11
❑ 163	Alonzo Spellman	.05	.02
❑ 164	Todd Lyght	.05	.02

❑ 165 Chris Slade .05 .02
❑ 166 Johnny Mitchell .05 .02
❑ 167 Ronald Moore .05 .02
❑ 168 Eugene Robinson .05 .02
❑ 169 Chris Hinton .05 .02
❑ 170 Dan Footman .05 .02
❑ 171 Keith Jackson .05 .02
❑ 172 Rickey Jackson .05 .02
❑ 173 Heath Sherman .05 .02
❑ 174 Chris Mims .05 .02
❑ 175 Erric Pegram .05 .02
❑ 176 Leroy Hoard .05 .02
❑ 177 O.J. McDuffie .25 .11
❑ 178 Wayne Martin .05 .02
❑ 179 Clyde Simmons .05 .02
❑ 180 Leslie O'Neal .05 .02
❑ 181 Mike Pritchard .05 .02
❑ 182 Michael Jackson .10 .05
❑ 183 Scott Mitchell .25 .11
❑ 184 Lorenzo Neal .05 .02
❑ 185 William Thomas .05 .02
❑ 186 Junior Seau UER .25 .11
(Career tackles 322, but add up to 451)
❑ 187 Chris Gedney .05 .02
❑ 188 Tim Lester .05 .02
❑ 189 Sam Gash .05 .02
❑ 190 Johnny Johnson .05 .02
❑ 191 Chuck Cecil .05 .02
❑ 192 Cortez Kennedy .10 .05
❑ 193 Jim Harbaugh .25 .11
❑ 194 Roman Phifer .05 .02
❑ 195 Pat Harlow .05 .02
❑ 196 Rob Moore .10 .05
❑ 197 Gary Clark .10 .05
❑ 198 Jon Vaughn .05 .02
❑ 199 Craig Heyward .10 .05
❑ 200 Michael Stewart .05 .02
❑ 201 Greg McMurtry .05 .02
❑ 202 Brian Washington .05 .02
❑ 203 Ken Harvey .05 .02
❑ 204 Chris Warren .10 .05
❑ 205 Bruce Smith .25 .11
❑ 206 Tom Rouen .05 .02
❑ 207 Cris Dishman .05 .02
❑ 208 Keith Cash .05 .02
❑ 209 Carlos Jenkins .05 .02
❑ 210 Levon Kirkland .05 .02
❑ 211 Pete Metzelaars .05 .02
❑ 212 Shannon Sharpe .10 .05
❑ 213 Cody Carlson .05 .02
❑ 214 Derrick Thomas .25 .11
❑ 215 Emmitt Smith 1.25 .55
❑ 216 Robert Porcher .05 .02
❑ 217 Sterling Sharpe .10 .05
❑ 218 Anthony Smith .05 .02
❑ 219 Mike Sherrard .05 .02
❑ 220 Tom Rathman .05 .02
❑ 221 Nate Newton .05 .02
❑ 222 Pat Swilling .05 .02
❑ 223 George Teague .05 .02
❑ 224 Greg Townsend .05 .02
❑ 225 Eric Guliford RC .05 .02
❑ 226 Leroy Thompson .05 .02
❑ 227 Thurman Thomas .25 .11
❑ 228 Dan Williams .05 .02
❑ 229 Bubba McDowell .05 .02
❑ 230 Tracy Simien .05 .02
❑ 231 Scottie Graham RC .10 .05
❑ 232 Eric Green .05 .02
❑ 233 Phil Simms .10 .05
❑ 234 Ricky Watters .25 .11
❑ 235 Kevin Williams .10 .05
❑ 236 Brett Perriman .10 .05
❑ 237 Reggie White .25 .11
❑ 238 Steve Wisniewski .05 .02
❑ 239 Mark Collins .05 .02
❑ 240 Steve Young .75 .35
❑ 241 Steve Tovar .05 .02
❑ 242 Jason Belser .05 .02
❑ 243 Ray Seals .05 .02
❑ 244 Earnest Byner .05 .02
❑ 245 Ricky Proehl .05 .02
❑ 246 Rich Miano .05 .02
❑ 247 Alfred Williams .05 .02
❑ 248 Ray Buchanan UER .05 .02
(Buchannan on front)
❑ 249 Hardy Nickerson .10 .05
❑ 250 Brad Edwards .05 .02
❑ 251 Jerrol Williams .05 .02
❑ 252 Marvin Washington .05 .02
❑ 253 Tony McGee .05 .02
❑ 254 Jeff George .25 .11
❑ 255 Ron Hall .05 .02
❑ 256 Tim Johnson .05 .02
❑ 257 Willie Roaf .05 .02
❑ 258 Corwin Brown RC .05 .02
❑ 259 Ricardo McDonald .05 .02
❑ 260 Jeff Herrod .05 .02
❑ 261 Demetrius DuBose .05 .02
❑ 262 Ricky Sanders .05 .02
❑ 263 John L. Williams .05 .02
❑ 264 John Lynch .05 .02
❑ 265 Lance Gunn .05 .02
❑ 266 Jessie Hester .05 .02
❑ 267 Mark Wheeler .05 .02
❑ 268 Chip Lohmiller .05 .02
❑ 269 Eric Swann .10 .05
❑ 270 Byron Evans .05 .02
❑ 271 Gary Plummer .05 .02
❑ 272 Roger Duffy RC .05 .02
❑ 273 Irv Smith .05 .02
❑ 274 Todd Collins .05 .02
❑ 275 Robert Blackmon .05 .02
❑ 276 Reggie Roby .05 .02
❑ 277 Russell Copeland .05 .02
❑ 278 Simon Fletcher .05 .02
❑ 279 Ernest Givins .10 .05
❑ 280 Tim Barnett .05 .02
❑ 281 Chris Doleman .05 .02
❑ 282 Jeff Graham .05 .02
❑ 283 Kenneth Davis .05 .02
❑ 284 Vance Johnson .05 .02
❑ 285 Haywood Jeffires .10 .05
❑ 286 Todd McNair .05 .02
❑ 287 Daryl Johnston .10 .05
❑ 288 Ryan McNeil .05 .02
❑ 289 Terrell Buckley .05 .02
❑ 290 Ethan Horton .05 .02
❑ 291 Corey Miller .05 .02
❑ 292 Marc Logan .05 .02
❑ 293 Lincoln Coleman RC .05 .02
❑ 294 Derrick Moore .05 .02
❑ 295 LeRoy Butler .05 .02
❑ 296 Jeff Hostetler .10 .05
❑ 297 Qadry Ismail .25 .11
❑ 298 Andre Hastings .10 .05
❑ 299 Henry Jones .05 .02
❑ 300 John Elway 1.50 .70
❑ 301 Warren Moon .25 .11
❑ 302 Willie Davis .10 .05
❑ 303 Vencie Glenn .05 .02
❑ 304 Kevin Greene .25 .11
❑ 305 Marcus Buckley .05 .02
❑ 306 Tim McDonald .05 .02
❑ 307 Michael Irvin .25 .11
❑ 308 Herman Moore .25 .11
❑ 309 Brett Favre 1.50 .70
❑ 310 Rocket Ismail .10 .05
❑ 311 Jarrod Bunch .05 .02
❑ 312 Don Beebe .05 .02
❑ 313 Steve Atwater .05 .02
❑ 314 Gary Brown .05 .02
❑ 315 Marcus Allen .25 .11
❑ 316 Terry Allen .10 .05
❑ 317 Chad Brown .05 .02
❑ 318 Cornelius Bennett .10 .05
❑ 319 Rod Bernstine .05 .02
❑ 320 Greg Montgomery .05 .02
❑ 321 Kimble Anders .10 .05
❑ 322 Charles Haley .10 .05
❑ 323 Mel Gray .05 .02
❑ 324 Edgar Bennett .25 .11
❑ 325 Eddie Anderson .05 .02
❑ 326 Derek Brown TE .05 .02
❑ 327 Steve Bono .10 .05
❑ 328 Alvin Harper .10 .05
❑ 329 Willie Green .05 .02
❑ 330 Robert Brooks .25 .11
❑ 331 Patrick Bates .05 .02
❑ 332 Anthony Carter .10 .05
❑ 333 Barry Foster .05 .02
❑ 334 Bill Brooks .05 .02
❑ 335 Jason Elam .05 .02
❑ 336 Ray Childress .05 .02
❑ 337 J.J. Birden .05 .02
❑ 338 Cris Carter .40 .18
❑ 339 Deon Figures .05 .02
❑ 340 Carlton Bailey .05 .02
❑ 341 Brent Jones .10 .05
❑ 342 Troy Aikman UER .75 .35
(Stats on back has 60 Int., should be 66)
❑ 343 Rodney Holman .05 .02
❑ 344 Tony Bennett .05 .02
❑ 345 Tim Brown .25 .11
❑ 346 Michael Brooks .05 .02
❑ 347 Martin Harrison .05 .02
❑ 348 Jerry Rice .75 .35
❑ 349 John Copeland .05 .02
❑ 350 Kerry Cash .05 .02
❑ 351 Reggie Cobb .05 .02
❑ 352 Brian Mitchell .05 .02
❑ 353 Derrick Fenner .05 .02
❑ 354 Roosevelt Potts .05 .02
❑ 355 Courtney Hawkins .05 .02
❑ 356 Carl Banks .05 .02
❑ 357 Harold Green .05 .02
❑ 358 Steve Emtman .05 .02
❑ 359 Santana Dotson .10 .05
❑ 360 Reggie Brooks .10 .05
❑ 361 Terry Obee .05 .02
❑ 362 David Klingler .05 .02
❑ 363 Quentin Coryatt .05 .02
❑ 364 Craig Erickson .05 .02
❑ 365 Desmond Howard .10 .05
❑ 366 Carl Pickens .25 .11
❑ 367 Lawrence Dawsey .05 .02
❑ 368 Henry Ellard .10 .05
❑ 369 Shaun Gayle .05 .02
❑ 370 David Lang .05 .02
❑ 371 Anthony Johnson .10 .05
❑ 372 Darnell Walker RC .05 .02
❑ 373 Pepper Johnson .05 .02
❑ 374 Kurt Gouveia .05 .02
❑ 375 Louis Oliver .05 .02
❑ 376 Lincoln Kennedy .05 .02
❑ 377 Anthony Pleasant .05 .02
❑ 378 Irving Fryar .10 .05
❑ 379 Carolina Panthers .25 .11
Expansion Team Card
❑ 380 Jacksonville Jaguars .05 .02
Expansion Team Card
❑ 381 Checklist UER .10 .05
Sterling Sharpe
(Front has 193-288 and back has Sharp; should be Sharpe)
❑ 382 Dan Marino ART .25 .11
Checklist Card
❑ 383 Jerry Rice ART UER .25 .11
Checklist Card
(Front has 289-384)
❑ 384 Joe Montana ART UER .25 .11
Checklist Card
(Front has 1-96)
Joe Montana
❑ P19 Joe Montana Promo 2.00 .90

1994 Collector's Choice Crash the Game

	MINT	NRMT
COMP.BLUE SET (30)	75.00	34.00
COMP.GREEN SET (30)	75.00	34.00
COMMON BLUE/GRN (C1-C30)	1.00	.45
SEMISTARS	1.50	.70

BLUE FOIL INSERTED IN HOBBY PACKS
GREEN FOIL INSERTED IN RETAIL PACKS
UNLESS NOTED BLUE/GREEN SAME PRICE

COMP.BRONZE SET (30)	12.00	5.50

*BRONZE CARDS: .1X to .2X HI COLUMN
ONE SET PER BRONZE WINNER CARD

COMP.SILVER SET (30)	16.00	7.25

*SILVER CARDS: .15X to .3X HI COLUMN
ONE SET PER SILVER WINNER CARD

COMP.GOLD SET (30)	25.00	11.00

*GOLD CARDS: .25X to .5X HI COLUMN

ONE SET PER GOLD WINNER CARD

❑ C1B Steve Young WIN G 3.00 1.35
❑ C1G Steve Young WIN G .. 5.00 2.20
❑ C2B Troy Aikman WIN S 3.00 1.35
❑ C2G Troy Aikman WIN B 6.00 2.70
❑ C3B Rick Mirer WIN B .... 1.50 .70
❑ C3G Rick Mirer WIN B .... 1.50 .70
❑ C4B Trent Dilfer WIN B ...... 2.00 .90
❑ C4G Trent Dilfer NO WIN.... 2.00 .90
❑ C5B Dan Marino WIN G...... 5.00 2.20
❑ C5G Dan Marino WIN S.... 10.00 4.50
❑ C6B John Elway WIN S 5.00 2.20
❑ C6G John Elway WIN S 5.00 2.20
❑ C7B Heath Shuler WIN S.... 1.50 .70
❑ C7G Heath Shuler NO WIN 1.50 .70
❑ C8B Joe Montana WIN G.... 5.00 2.20
❑ C8G Joe Montana WIN S.... 8.00 3.60
❑ C9B D.Bledsoe WIN G UER 3.00 1.35
❑ C9G D.Bledsoe WIN G UER 10.00 4.50
❑ C10B Warren Moon WIN S 1.50 .70
❑ C10G Warren Moon WIN S 1.50 .70
❑ C11B Marshall Faulk WIN B 4.00 1.80
❑ C11G Marshall Faulk WIN S 10.00 4.50
❑ C12B T.Thomas WIN B ...... 1.50 .70
❑ C12G T.Thomas WIN B ...... 1.50 .70
❑ C13B Barry Foster WIN B .. 1.00 .45
❑ C13G Barry Foster WIN B .. 1.00 .45
❑ C14B Gary Brown NO WIN 1.00 .45
❑ C14G Gary Brown NO WIN 1.00 .45
❑ C15B Emmitt Smith WIN G 6.00 2.70
❑ C15G Emmitt Smith WIN G 10.00 4.50
❑ C16B Barry Sanders WIN B 5.00 2.20
❑ C16G Barry Sanders WIN B 6.00 2.70
❑ C17B R.Hampton WIN B .... 1.50 .70
❑ C17G R.Hampton WIN B .... 1.50 .70
❑ C18B Jerome Bettis WIN B 4.00 1.80
❑ C18G Jerome Bettis NO WIN 4.00 1.80
❑ C19B Ricky Watters WIN B 1.50 .70
❑ C19G Ricky Watters NO WIN 1.50 .70
❑ C20B Ronald Moore WIN B 1.50 .70
❑ C20G Ronald Moore WIN B 1.50 .70
❑ C21B Jerry Rice WIN G 3.00 1.35
❑ C21G Jerry Rice NO WIN .. 3.00 1.35
❑ C22B Andre Rison WIN G .. 1.50 .70
❑ C22G Andre Rison WIN B .. 1.50 .70
❑ C23B Michael Irvin NO WIN 1.50 .70
❑ C23G Michael Irvin WIN S .. 1.50 .70
❑ C24B Sterling Sharpe WIN S 1.50 .70
❑ C24G Sterling Sharpe WIN B 1.50 .70
❑ C25B Sh.Sharpe NO WIN .. 1.50 .70
❑ C25G Sh.Sharpe NO WIN .. 1.50 .70
❑ C26B Darnay Scott NO WIN 1.50 .70
❑ C26G Darnay Scott WIN B.. 1.50 .70
❑ C27B Andre Reed WIN S.... 1.50 .70
❑ C27G Andre Reed WIN B .. 1.50 .70
❑ C28B Tim Brown NO WIN .. 1.50 .70
❑ C28G Tim Brown WIN S .... 1.50 .70
❑ C29B Charles Johnson WIN B 1.50 .70
❑ C29G C.Johnson NO WIN .. 1.00 .45
❑ C30B Irving Fryar NO WIN.. 1.00 .45
❑ C30G Irving Fryar NO WIN 1.00 .45

1994 Collector's Choice Then and Now

MINT NRMT
COMPLETE SET (8) 10.00 4.50

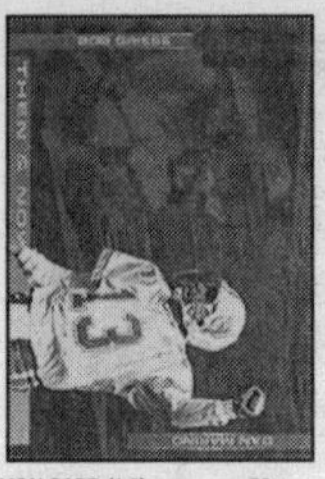

COMMON CARD (1-8) .... .75 .35
JOE MONTANA HEADER (NNO) 2.50 1.10
ERIC DICKERSON CL (NNO) .... .75 .35
ONE SET PER TRADE CARD BY MAIL

❑ 1 Eric Dickerson .... .75 .35
Jerome Bettis
❑ 2 Fred Biletnikoff .... .75 .35
Tim Brown
❑ 3 Len Dawson .... 2.00 .90
Joe Montana
❑ 4 Joe Montana 2.50 1.10
Steve Young
❑ 5 Bob Griese 4.00 1.80
Dan Marino
❑ 6 Jim Zorn .... .75 .35
Rick Mirer
❑ NNO Joe Montana 2.50 1.10
Header Card
❑ NNO Then/Now Exch. Card.. .30 .14

1995 Collector's Choice

MINT NRMT
COMPLETE SET (348) 20.00 9.00
COMMON CARD (1-348) .... .05 .02
SEMISTARS .... .10 .05
UNLISTED STARS .... .25 .11
MARINO CHRONICLES (10) .. 15.00 6.75
MONTANA CHRONICLES (10) 15.00 6.75
CHRONICLES:ONE PER SPECIAL RETAIL PACK
COMP.PLAYER'S CLUB (348) 50.00 22.00
*PC STARS: 1X to 2.5X HI COLUMN
*PC RCS: .75X to 2X HI ....
PLAY.CLUB ODDS 1:1HOB/RET, 6:1JUM
COMP. PC PLAT.SET (348) 500.00 220.00
*PC PLATINUM STARS: 8X TO 20X HI
*PC PLATINUM RCS: 4X TO 10X
PLAY.CLUB ODDS 1:35 HOB/RET,1:12 JUM

❑ 1 Ki-Jana Carter RC .... .25 .11
❑ 2 Tony Boselli RC .... .10 .05
❑ 3 Steve McNair RC 2.50 1.10
❑ 4 Michael Westbrook RC .... 1.25 .55
❑ 5 Kerry Collins RC .... .75 .35
❑ 6 Kevin Carter RC .... .25 .11
❑ 7 Mike Mamula RC............... .10 .05
❑ 8 Joey Galloway RC........... 2.50 1.10
❑ 9 Kyle Brady RC.................... .25 .11
❑ 10 J.J. Stokes RC .... .60 .25
❑ 11 Derrick Alexander DE RC .05 .02
❑ 12 Warren Sapp RC .... .40 .18
❑ 13 Mark Fields RC .... .05 .02
❑ 14 Tyrone Wheatley RC...... 1.00 .45
❑ 15 Napoleon Kaufman RC .. 1.50 .70
❑ 16 James O. Stewart RC .. 1.50 .70
❑ 17 Luther Elliss RC .... .05 .02
❑ 18 Rashaan Salaam RC ...... .25 .11
❑ 19 Ty Law RC .... .10 .05
❑ 20 Mark Bruener RC .... .10 .05
❑ 21 Derrick Brooks RC .... .05 .02
❑ 22 Christian Fauria RC.......... .05 .02
❑ 23 Ray Zellars RC .... .10 .05
❑ 24 Todd Collins RC .... .25 .11
❑ 25 Sherman Williams RC...... .05 .02
❑ 26 Frank Sanders RC .... .75 .35
❑ 27 Rodney Thomas RC .... .25 .11
❑ 28 Rob Johnson RC........... 1.25 .55
❑ 29 Steve Stenstrom RC .... .05 .02
❑ 30 James A.Stewart RC ...... .05 .02
❑ 31 Barry Sanders DYK.......... .60 .25
❑ 32 Marshall Faulk DYK .... .25 .11
❑ 33 Darnay Scott DYK............ .25 .11
❑ 34 Joe Montana DYK............ .60 .25
❑ 35 Michael Irvin DYK .... .10 .05
❑ 36 Jerry Rice DYK .... .40 .18
❑ 37 Errict Rhett DYK .... .25 .11
❑ 38 Drew Bledsoe DYK .... .40 .18
❑ 39 Dan Marino DYK .... .60 .25
❑ 40 Terance Mathis DYK........ .05 .02
❑ 41 Natrone Means DYK .... .25 .11
❑ 42 Tim Brown DYK................ .10 .05
❑ 43 Steve Young DYK .... .30 .14
❑ 44 Mel Gray DYK .... .05 .02
❑ 45 Jerome Bettis DYK .... .25 .11
❑ 46 Aeneas Williams DYK ...... .05 .02
❑ 47 Charlie Garner DYK .... .10 .05
❑ 48 Deion Sanders DYK .... .25 .11
❑ 49 Ken Harvey DYK .... .05 .02
❑ 50 Emmitt Smith DYK .... .50 .23
❑ 51 Andre Reed...................... .10 .05
❑ 52 Sean Dawkins .... .10 .05
❑ 53 Irving Fryar .... .10 .05
❑ 54 Vincent Brisby .... .05 .02
❑ 55 Rob Moore .... .05 .02
❑ 56 Carl Pickens .... .25 .11
❑ 57 Vinny Testaverde .... .10 .05
❑ 58 Webster Slaughter .... .05 .02
❑ 59 Eric Green .... .05 .02
❑ 60 Anthony Miller .... .10 .05
❑ 61 Lake Dawson .... .10 .05
❑ 62 Tim Brown .... .25 .11
❑ 63 Stan Humphries .... .10 .05
❑ 64 Rick Mirer .... .25 .11
❑ 65 Gary Clark .... .05 .02
❑ 66 Troy Aikman .... .75 .35
❑ 67 Mike Sherrard .... .05 .02
❑ 68 Fred Barnett .... .10 .05
❑ 69 Henry Ellard .... .10 .05
❑ 70 Terry Allen .... .10 .05
❑ 71 Jeff Graham .... .05 .02
❑ 72 Herman Moore .... .25 .11
❑ 73 Brett Favre .... 1.50 .70
❑ 74 Trent Dilfer .... .25 .11
❑ 75 Derek Brown RBK .... .05 .02
❑ 76 Andre Rison .... .10 .05
❑ 77 Flipper Anderson.............. .05 .02
❑ 78 Jerry Rice UER .... .75 .35
Career totals are all wrong
❑ 79 Thurman Thomas .... .25 .11
❑ 80 Marshall Faulk.................. .40 .18
❑ 81 O.J. McDuffie .... .25 .11
❑ 82 Ben Coates .... .10 .05
❑ 83 Johnny Mitchell .... .05 .02
❑ 84 Darnay Scott .... .25 .11
❑ 85 Derrick Alexander WR...... .25 .11
❑ 86 Micheal Barrow UER........ .05 .02
Name spelled Michael on both sides
❑ 87 Charles Johnson .... .10 .05
❑ 88 John Elway .... 1.50 .70
❑ 89 Willie Davis .... .10 .05
❑ 90 James Jett........................ .10 .05
❑ 91 Mark Seay......................... .10 .05
❑ 92 Brian Blades .... .10 .05
❑ 93 Ricky Proehl .... .05 .02
❑ 94 Charles Haley .... .10 .05
❑ 95 Chris Calloway .... .05 .02
❑ 96 Calvin Williams .... .10 .05

❑ 97 Ethan Horton .05 .02
❑ 98 Cris Carter .25 .11
❑ 99 Curtis Conway .25 .11
❑ 100 Lomas Brown .05 .02
❑ 101 Edgar Bennett .10 .05
❑ 102 Craig Erickson .05 .02
❑ 103 Jim Everett .05 .02
❑ 104 Terance Mathis .10 .05
❑ 105 Wayne Gandy .05 .02
❑ 106 Brent Jones .05 .02
❑ 107 Bruce Smith .25 .11
❑ 108 Roosevelt Potts .05 .02
❑ 109 Dan Marino 1.50 .70
❑ 110 Michael Timpson .05 .02
❑ 111 Boomer Esiason .10 .05
❑ 112 David Klingler .10 .05
❑ 113 Eric Metcalf .10 .05
❑ 114 Lorenzo White .05 .02
❑ 115 Neil O'Donnell .10 .05
❑ 116 Shannon Sharpe .10 .05
❑ 117 Joe Montana 1.50 .70
❑ 118 Jeff Hostetler .10 .05
❑ 119 Ronnie Harmon .05 .02
❑ 120 Chris Warren .10 .05
❑ 121 Randal Hill .05 .02
❑ 122 Alvin Harper .05 .02
❑ 123 Dave Brown .10 .05
❑ 124 Randall Cunningham .25 .11
❑ 125 Heath Shuler .25 .11
❑ 126 Jake Reed .10 .05
❑ 127 Donnell Woolford .05 .02
❑ 128 Scott Mitchell .10 .05
❑ 129 Reggie White .25 .11
❑ 130 Lawrence Dawsey .05 .02
❑ 131 Michael Haynes .10 .05
❑ 132 Bert Emanuel .25 .11
❑ 133 Troy Drayton .05 .02
❑ 134 Merton Hanks .05 .02
❑ 135 Jim Kelly .25 .11
❑ 136 Tony Bennett .05 .02
❑ 137 Terry Kirby .10 .05
❑ 138 Drew Bledsoe .75 .35
❑ 139 Johnny Johnson .05 .02
❑ 140 Dan Wilkinson .10 .05
❑ 141 Leroy Hoard .05 .02
❑ 142 Gary Brown .05 .02
❑ 143 Barry Foster .10 .05
❑ 144 Shane Dronett .05 .02
❑ 145 Marcus Allen .25 .11
❑ 146 Harvey Williams .05 .02
❑ 147 Tony Martin .10 .05
❑ 148 Rod Stephens .05 .02
❑ 149 Ronald Moore .05 .02
❑ 150 Michael Irvin .25 .11
❑ 151 Rodney Hampton .10 .05
❑ 152 Herschel Walker .10 .05
❑ 153 Reggie Brooks .10 .05
❑ 154 Qadry Ismail .10 .05
❑ 155 Chris Zorich .05 .02
❑ 156 Barry Sanders 1.50 .70
❑ 157 Sean Jones .05 .02
❑ 158 Errict Rhett .25 .11
❑ 159 Tyrone Hughes .10 .05
❑ 160 Jeff George .10 .05
❑ 161 Chris Miller .05 .02
❑ 162 Steve Young .60 .25
❑ 163 Cornelius Bennett .10 .05
❑ 164 Trev Alberts .05 .02
❑ 165 J.B. Brown .05 .02
❑ 166 Marion Butts .05 .02
❑ 167 Aaron Glenn .05 .02
❑ 168 James Francis .05 .02
❑ 169 Eric Turner .05 .02
❑ 170 Darryll Lewis .05 .02
❑ 171 John L. Williams .05 .02
❑ 172 Simon Fletcher .05 .02
❑ 173 Neil Smith .10 .05
❑ 174 Chester McGlockton .10 .05
❑ 175 Natrone Means .25 .11
❑ 176 Michael Sinclair .05 .02
❑ 177 Larry Centers .10 .05
❑ 178 Daryl Johnston .10 .05
❑ 179 Dave Meggett .05 .02
❑ 180 Greg Jackson .05 .02
❑ 181 Ken Harvey .05 .02
❑ 182 Warren Moon .10 .05
❑ 183 Steve Walsh .05 .02
❑ 184 Chris Spielman .10 .05
❑ 185 Bryce Paup .25 .11
❑ 186 Courtney Hawkins .05 .02
❑ 187 Willie Roaf .05 .02
❑ 188 Chris Doleman .05 .02
❑ 189 Jerome Bettis .25 .11
❑ 190 Ricky Watters .25 .11
❑ 191 Henry Jones .05 .02
❑ 192 Quentin Coryatt .10 .05
❑ 193 Bryan Cox .05 .02
❑ 194 Kevin Turner .05 .02
❑ 195 Siupeli Malamala .05 .02
❑ 196 Louis Oliver .05 .02
❑ 197 Rob Burnett .05 .02
❑ 198 Cris Dishman .05 .02
❑ 199 Byron Bam Morris .10 .05
❑ 200 Ray Crockett .05 .02
❑ 201 Jon Vaughn .05 .02
❑ 202 Nolan Harrison .05 .02
❑ 203 Leslie O'Neal .10 .05
❑ 204 Sam Adams .05 .02
❑ 205 Eric Swann .10 .05
❑ 206 Jay Novacek .10 .05
❑ 207 Keith Hamilton .05 .02
❑ 208 Charlie Garner .10 .05
❑ 209 Tom Carter .05 .02
❑ 210 Henry Thomas .05 .02
❑ 211 Lewis Tillman .05 .02
❑ 212 Pat Swilling .05 .02
❑ 213 Terrell Buckley .05 .02
❑ 214 Hardy Nickerson .05 .02
❑ 215 Mario Bates .25 .11
❑ 216 D.J. Johnson .05 .02
❑ 217 Robert Young .05 .02
❑ 218 Dana Stubblefield .25 .11
❑ 219 Jeff Burris .05 .02
❑ 220 Floyd Turner .05 .02
❑ 221 Troy Vincent .05 .02
❑ 222 Willie McGinest .10 .05
❑ 223 James Hasty .05 .02
❑ 224 Jeff Blake RC .75 .35
❑ 225 Stevon Moore .05 .02
❑ 226 Ernest Givins .05 .02
❑ 227 Greg Lloyd .10 .05
❑ 228 Steve Atwater .05 .02
❑ 229 Dale Carter .10 .05
❑ 230 Terry McDaniel .05 .02
❑ 231 John Carney .05 .02
❑ 232 Cortez Kennedy .10 .05
❑ 233 Clyde Simmons .05 .02
❑ 234 Emmitt Smith 1.25 .55
❑ 235 Thomas Lewis .10 .05
❑ 236 William Fuller .05 .02
❑ 237 Ricky Ervins .05 .02
❑ 238 John Randle .05 .02
❑ 239 John Thierry .05 .02
❑ 240 Mel Gray .05 .02
❑ 241 George Teague .05 .02
❑ 242 Charles Wilson Bucs .05 .02
see '95 Coll.Choice Update #U170
❑ 243 Joe Johnson .05 .02
❑ 244 Chuck Smith .05 .02
❑ 245 Sean Gilbert .10 .05
❑ 246 Bryant Young .10 .05
❑ 247 Bucky Brooks .05 .02
❑ 248 Ray Buchanan .05 .02
❑ 249 Tim Bowens .05 .02
❑ 250 Vincent Brown .05 .02
❑ 251 Marcus Turner .05 .02
❑ 252 Derrick Fenner .05 .02
❑ 253 Antonio Langham .05 .02
❑ 254 Cody Carlson .05 .02
❑ 255 Kevin Greene .10 .05
❑ 256 Leonard Russell .05 .02
❑ 257 Donnell Bennett .10 .05
❑ 258 Rocket Ismail .10 .05
❑ 259 Alfred Pupunu RC .05 .02
❑ 260 Eugene Robinson .05 .02
❑ 261 Seth Joyner .05 .02
❑ 262 Darren Woodson .10 .05
❑ 263 Phillippi Sparks .05 .02
❑ 264 Andy Harmon .05 .02
❑ 265 Brian Mitchell .05 .02
❑ 266 Fuad Reveiz .05 .02
❑ 267 Mark Carrier DB .05 .02
❑ 268 Johnnie Morton .10 .05
❑ 269 LeShon Johnson .10 .05
❑ 270 Eric Curry .05 .02
❑ 271 Quinn Early .10 .05
❑ 272 Elbert Shelley .05 .02
❑ 273 Roman Phifer .05 .02
❑ 274 Ken Norton Jr. .10 .05
❑ 275 Steve Tasker .10 .05
❑ 276 Jim Harbaugh .10 .05
❑ 277 Aubrey Beavers .05 .02
❑ 278 Chris Slade .10 .05
❑ 279 Mo Lewis .05 .02
❑ 280 Alfred Williams .05 .02
❑ 281 Michael Dean Perry UER .05 .02
misspelled Micheal
❑ 282 Marcus Robertson .05 .02
❑ 283 Rod Woodson .10 .05
❑ 284 Glyn Milburn .05 .02
❑ 285 Greg Hill .10 .05
❑ 286 Rob Fredrickson .05 .02
❑ 287 Junior Seau .25 .11
❑ 288 Rick Tuten .05 .02
❑ 289 Aeneas Williams .05 .02
❑ 290 Darrin Smith .05 .02
❑ 291 John Booty .05 .02
❑ 292 Eric Allen .05 .02
❑ 293 Reggie Roby .05 .02
❑ 294 David Palmer .10 .05
❑ 295 Trace Armstrong .05 .02
❑ 296 Dave Krieg UER .05 .02
misspelled Kreig on front
❑ 297 Robert Brooks .25 .11
❑ 298 Brad Culpepper .05 .02
❑ 299 Wayne Martin .05 .02
❑ 300 Craig Heyward .10 .05
❑ 301 Isaac Bruce .40 .18
❑ 302 Deion Sanders .40 .18
❑ 303 Matt Darby .05 .02
❑ 304 Kirk Lowdermilk .05 .02
❑ 305 Bernie Parmalee .10 .05
❑ 306 Leroy Thompson .05 .02
❑ 307 Ronnie Lott .10 .05
❑ 308 Steve Tovar .05 .02
❑ 309 Michael Jackson .10 .05
❑ 310 Al Smith .05 .02
❑ 311 Chad Brown .10 .05
❑ 312 Elijah Alexander .05 .02
❑ 313 Kimble Anders .10 .05
❑ 314 Anthony Smith .05 .02
❑ 315 Andre Coleman .05 .02
❑ 316 Terry Wooden .05 .02
❑ 317 Garrison Hearst .25 .11
❑ 318 Russell Maryland .05 .02
❑ 319 Michael Brooks .05 .02
❑ 320 Bernard Williams .05 .02
❑ 321 Andre Collins .05 .02
❑ 322 Dewayne Washington .10 .05
❑ 323 Raymont Harris .05 .02
❑ 324 Brett Perriman .10 .05
❑ 325 LeRoy Butler .05 .02
❑ 326 Santana Dotson .05 .02
❑ 327 Irv Smith .05 .02
❑ 328 Ron George .05 .02
❑ 329 Marquez Pope .05 .02
❑ 330 William Floyd .25 .11
❑ 331 Mickey Washington .05 .02
❑ 332 Keith Goganious .05 .02
❑ 333 Derek Brown TE .05 .02
❑ 334 Steve Beuerlein UER .05 .02
Name spelled Beuerlien on front
❑ 335 Reggie Cobb .05 .02
❑ 336 Jeff Lageman .05 .02
❑ 337 Kelvin Martin .05 .02
❑ 338 Darren Carrington .05 .02
❑ 339 Mark Carrier WR .10 .05
❑ 340 Willie Green .05 .02
❑ 341 Frank Reich .05 .02
❑ 342 Don Beebe .05 .02
❑ 343 Lamar Lathon .05 .02
❑ 344 Tim McKyer .05 .02
❑ 345 Pete Metzelaars .05 .02
❑ 346 Vernon Turner .05 .02
❑ 347 Dan Marino .25 .11
Checklist 1-174
❑ 348 Joe Montana .25 .11

Checklist 175-348
❑ PC1 Joe Montana Promo.... 1.00 .45
(Crash the Game promo)
❑ P1 Joe Montana Promo ...... 1.00 .45

1995 Collector's Choice Crash The Game

	MINT	NRMT
COMPLETE SILVER SET (90)	50.00	22.00
SILVER ODDS 1:5 HOB/RET, 1:1 JUM		
*GOLD STARS: 2X TO 4X BASE CARD HI		
*GOLD ROOKIES: .75X TO 1.5X BASE CARD HI		
GOLD ODDS 1:50 HOB/RET		
COMP.SILVER REDEMPT.(30)	8.00	3.60
*SILVER TD REDEMPT.CARDS: 1X TO 2X		
COMP.GOLD REDEMPT.(30)	40.00	18.00
*GOLD REDEMPT.CARDS: 1X TO 2X		
*GOLD TD REDEMPT.CARDS: 3X TO 6X		

❑ C1A Dan Marino 9/10 W .... 2.00 .90
❑ C1B Dan Marino 10/8 W .... 2.00 .90
❑ C1C Dan Marino 11/20 W .. 2.00 .90
❑ C2A John Elway 9/3 L .... 2.00 .90
❑ C2B John Elway 11/12 W .. 2.00 .90
❑ C2C John Elway 11/19 W .. 2.00 .90
❑ C3A Kerry Collins 10/1 W .... .40 .18
❑ C3B Kerry Collins 10/29 W .. .40 .18
❑ C3C Kerry Collins 11/12 W .. .40 .18
❑ C4A Stan Humphries 9/3 W .. .10 .05
❑ C4B Stan Humphries 10/9 W .10 .05
❑ C4C Stan Humphries 11/5 W .10 .05
❑ C5A Steve Young 9/10 W .... .75 .35
❑ C5B Steve Young 10/15 W .. .75 .35
❑ C5C Steve Young 11/5 L ...... .75 .35
❑ C6A Brett Favre 9/17 W ...... 2.00 .90
❑ C6B Brett Favre 9/24 W ...... 2.00 .90
❑ C6C Brett Favre 10/29 W ...... 2.00 .90
❑ C7A Troy Aikman 9/4 W ...... 1.00 .45
❑ C7B Troy Aikman 10/1 L .... 1.00 .45
❑ C7C Troy Aikman 11/12 L .. 1.00 .45
❑ C8A Warren Moon 9/3 W ...... .10 .05
❑ C8B Warren Moon 10/8 W .... .10 .05
❑ C8C Warren Moon 11/23 W .. .10 .05
❑ C9A Drew Bledsoe 9/10 L .. 1.00 .45
❑ C9B Drew Bledsoe 9/17 L .. 1.00 .45
❑ C9C Drew Bledsoe 10/23 W 1.00 .45
❑ C10A Steve McNair 10/1 L.. 1.25 .55
❑ C10B Steve McNair 10/29 L 1.25 .55
❑ C10C Steve McNair 11/19 L 1.25 .55
❑ C11A Chris Warren 10/22 W .10 .05
❑ C11B Chris Warren 11/12 W .10 .05
❑ C11C Chris Warren 11/26 L.. .10 .05
❑ C12A Natrone Means 10/1 W .30 .14
❑ C12B Natrone Means 10/9 W .30 .14
❑ C12C Natrone Means 11/27 L .30 .14
❑ C13A T.Thomas 9/17 W........ .30 .14
❑ C13B T.Thomas 10/22 L ...... .30 .14
❑ C13C T.Thomas 12/3 L .... .30 .14
❑ C14A Barry Sanders 9/25 L 2.00 .90
❑ C14B Barry Sanders 10/22 L 2.00 .90
❑ C14C Barry Sanders 11/23 W 2.00 .90
❑ C15A Emmitt Smith 9/10 W 1.50 .70
❑ C15B Emmitt Smith 10/29 W 1.50 .70
❑ C15C Emmitt Smith 11/19 W 1.50 .70
❑ C16A Jerome Bettis 9/10 L .. .30 .14
❑ C16B Jerome Bettis 10/22 L .30 .14
❑ C16C Jerome Bettis 11/19 L .30 .14
❑ C17A Ki-Jana Carter 9/10 L .. .15 .07
❑ C17B Ki-Jana Carter 10/1 L .. .15 .07
❑ C17C Ki-Jana Carter 11/12 L .15 .07
❑ C18A N.Kaufman 10/8 L ...... .75 .35
❑ C18B N.Kaufman 11/5 L ...... .75 .35
❑ C18C N.Kaufman 12/3 L ...... .75 .35
❑ C19A Marshall Faulk 9/3 L .... .50 .23
❑ C19B Marshall Faulk 10/1 W .50 .23
❑ C19C Marshall Faulk 11/5 W .50 .23
❑ C20A Errict Rhett 10/8 W...... .30 .14
❑ C20B Errict Rhett 10/22 W .... .30 .14
❑ C20C Errict Rhett 11/19 W .... .30 .14
❑ C21A Cris Carter 9/17 W ...... .30 .14
❑ C21B Cris Carter 10/30 L...... .30 .14
❑ C21C Cris Carter 11/19 W .... .30 .14
❑ C22A Jerry Rice 9/3 W........ 1.00 .45
❑ C22B Jerry Rice 10/1 W...... 1.00 .45
❑ C22C Jerry Rice 11/26 W .. 1.00 .45
❑ C23A Tim Brown 10/1 W ...... .30 .14
❑ C23B Tim Brown 10/16 L ...... .30 .14
❑ C23C Tim Brown 11/27 L ...... .30 .14
❑ C24A Andre Reed 9/10 L ...... .10 .05
❑ C24B Andre Reed 10/29 L .... .10 .05
❑ C24C Andre Reed 11/26 L .... .10 .05
❑ C25A Andre Rison 9/3 L ...... .10 .05
❑ C25B Andre Rison 10/2 L .... .10 .05
❑ C25C Andre Rison 10/22 L .. .10 .05
❑ C26A Ben Coates 10/8 L ...... .10 .05
❑ C26B Ben Coates 10/29 L .... .10 .05
❑ C26C Ben Coates 11/19 L .... .10 .05
❑ C27A Michael Irvin 9/17 W .... .30 .14
❑ C27B Michael Irvin 10/15 L .. .30 .14
❑ C27C Michael Irvin 11/6 W .. .30 .14
❑ C28B Terance Mathis 10/1 L .10 .05
❑ C28C Terance Mathis 10/12 L .10 .05
❑ C29A M.Westbrook 9/24 L .. 1.50 .70
❑ C29B M.Westbrook 10/22 L 1.50 .70
❑ C29C M.Westbrook 11/19 W 1.50 .70
❑ C30A Herman Moore 9/10 W .30 .14
❑ C30B Herman Moore 10/15 W .30 .14
❑ C30C Herman Moore 11/12 L .30 .14

1995 Collector's Choice Update

	MINT	NRMT
COMPLETE SET (225)	18.00	8.00
COMMON CARD (U1-U225)	.05	.02
DAN MARINO CL (U224-U225) ..	.50	.23
SEMISTARS	.10	.05
UNLISTED STARS	.25	.11
COMPLETE SILVER SET (90)	50.00	22.00
*SILVER STARS: 1.25X TO 3X HI COLUMN		
*SILVER RCs: 1X TO 2.5X HI		
SILVER ODDS 1:3		
COMPLETE GOLD SET (90)	400.00	180.00
*GOLD STARS: 7.5X TO 20X HI COLUMN		
*GOLD RCs: 5X TO 12X		
GOLD ODDS 1:35		

❑ U1 Roell Preston RC .... .05 .02
❑ U2 Lorenzo Styles RC .... .05 .02
❑ U3 Todd Collins .... .25 .11
❑ U4 Darick Holmes RC .... .10 .05
❑ U5 Justin Armour RC .... .05 .02
❑ U6 Tony Cline RC .... .05 .02
❑ U7 Tyrone Poole .... .10 .05
❑ U8 Kerry Collins .... .60 .25
❑ U9 Sean Harris .... .05 .02
❑ U10 Steve Stenstrom .... .05 .02
❑ U11 Rashaan Salaam .... .25 .11
❑ U12 Ki-Jana Carter .... .25 .11
❑ U13 Craig Powell .... .05 .02
❑ U14 Eric Zeier RC .... .40 .18
❑ U15 Ernest Hunter .... .05 .02
❑ U16 Sherman Williams.......... .05 .02
❑ U17 Terrell Davis RC 10.00 4.50
❑ U18 Luther Elliss .... .05 .02
❑ U19 Craig Newsome .... .05 .02
❑ U20 Steve McNair .... 1.25 .55
❑ U21 Chris Sanders RC.......... .25 .11
❑ U22 Rodney Thomas .... .25 .11
❑ U23 Ellis Johnson .... .05 .02
❑ U24 Ken Dilger RC............... .10 .05
❑ U25 Zack Crockett RC .... .05 .02
❑ U26 Tony Boselli .... .10 .05
❑ U27 Rob Johnson .... .75 .35
❑ U28 James O. Stewart .... 1.00 .45
❑ U29 Tamarick Vanover RC .. .25 .11
❑ U30 Napoleon Kaufman...... 1.00 .45
❑ U31 Kevin Carter .... .25 .11
❑ U32 Steve McLaughlin .... .05 .02
❑ U33 Lovell Pinkney .... .05 .02
❑ U34 Pete Mitchell RC............ .25 .11
❑ U35 James A.Stewart .... .05 .02
❑ U36 Chad May RC .... .05 .02
❑ U37 Derrick Alexander DE .... .05 .02
❑ U38 Curtis Martin RC 2.50 1.10
❑ U39 Will Moore RC .... .05 .02
❑ U40 Ty Law .... .10 .05
❑ U41 Ray Zellars .... .10 .05
❑ U42 Mark Fields .... .05 .02
❑ U43 Tyrone Wheatley .... .25 .11
❑ U44 Kyle Brady .... .25 .11
❑ U45 Mike Mamula .... .10 .05
❑ U46 Bobby Taylor RC .... .10 .05
❑ U47 Chris T.Jones RC .... .25 .11
❑ U48 Frank Sanders .... .60 .25
❑ U49 Stoney Case RC............ .40 .18
❑ U50 Mark Bruener .... .10 .05
❑ U51 Kordell Stewart RC 2.50 1.10
❑ U52 Jimmy Oliver.................. .05 .02
❑ U53 Terrance Shaw RC .... .05 .02
❑ U54 Terrell Fletcher RC .... .05 .02
❑ U55 J.J. Stokes .... .50 .23
❑ U56 Christian Fauria .... .05 .02
❑ U57 Joey Galloway .... 1.25 .55
❑ U58 Warren Sapp .... .10 .05
❑ U59 Derrick Brooks .... .05 .02
❑ U60 Michael Westbrook .... .75 .35
❑ U61 Emmitt Smith K............. .75 .35
❑ U62 Barry Sanders K .... 1.00 .45
❑ U63 Marshall Faulk K............ .30 .14
❑ U64 Troy Aikman K .... .50 .23
❑ U65 Steve Young K .... .40 .18
❑ U66 Junior Seau K .... .25 .11
❑ U67 John Elway K .... 1.00 .45
❑ U68 Dan Marino K .... 1.00 .45
❑ U69 Drew Bledsoe K .... .50 .23
❑ U70 Errict Rhett K .... .25 .11
❑ U71 Natrone Means K .... .25 .11
❑ U72 Deion Sanders K .... .30 .14
❑ U73 Brett Favre K .... 1.00 .45
❑ U74 Cris Carter K.................. .25 .11
❑ U75 Ben Coates K .... .10 .05
❑ U76 Jerome Bettis K .... .25 .11
❑ U77 Reggie White K.............. .25 .11
❑ U78 Stan Humphries K .... .05 .02
❑ U79 Michael Westbrook K .... .25 .11
❑ U80 Steve McNair K.............. .75 .35
❑ U81 Kevin Greene K .... .10 .05
❑ U82 Joey Galloway K............ .75 .35
❑ U83 Napoleon Kaufman K .... .60 .25
❑ U84 Jerry Rice K .... .50 .23
❑ U85 Andre Rison K .... .10 .05
❑ U86 Eric Metcalf K .... .10 .05
❑ U87 Kerry Collins K .... .25 .11
❑ U88 Chris Warren K.............. .10 .05
❑ U89 Irving Fryar K .... .10 .05
❑ U90 Michael Irvin K .... .25 .11
❑ U91 Don Beebe .... .05 .02
❑ U92 Pete Metzelaars .... .05 .02
❑ U93 Mark Carrier .... .05 .02
❑ U94 Frank Reich .... .05 .02

❑ U95 Randy Baldwin .05 .02
❑ U96 Bob Christian .05 .02
❑ U97 John Kasay .05 .02
❑ U98 Lamar Lathon .05 .02
❑ U99 Sam Mills .10 .05
❑ U100 Carlton Bailey .05 .02
❑ U101 Darion Conner .05 .02
❑ U102 Blake Brockermeyer .05 .02
❑ U103 Gerald Williamss .05 .02
❑ U104 Willie Green .05 .02
❑ U105 Derrick Moore .05 .02
❑ U106 Desmond Howard .10 .05
❑ U107 Harry Colon .05 .02
❑ U108 Steve Beuerlein .05 .02
❑ U109 Reggie Cobb .05 .02
❑ U110 Jeff Lageman .05 .02
❑ U111 Mark Brunell UER 1.25 .55
name spelled Brunnell on front
❑ U112 Darren Carrington .05 .02
❑ U113 Brian DeMarco .10 .05
❑ U114 Ernest Givins .05 .02
❑ U115 Le'shai Maston .05 .02
❑ U116 Willie Jackson .10 .05
❑ U117 Keith Goganious .05 .02
❑ U118 Kelvin Pritchett .05 .02
❑ U119 Ryan Christopherson .05 .02
❑ U120 Bryan Schwartz .05 .02
❑ U121 Dave Krieg UER .05 .02
name spelled Kreig on front
❑ U122 Darryl Talley .05 .02
❑ U123 Bryce Paup .25 .11
❑ U124 Anthony Johnson .10 .05
❑ U125 Eric Bieniemy .05 .02
❑ U126 Andre Rison .10 .05
❑ U127 Rodney Peete .05 .02
❑ U128 Aaron Craver .05 .02
❑ U129 Henry Thomas .05 .02
❑ U130 Antonio Freeman RC 2.50 1.10
❑ U131 Chris Chandler .10 .05
❑ U132 Craig Erickson .05 .02
❑ U133 Roell Preston .05 .02
❑ U134 Brian Washington .05 .02
❑ U135 Eric Green .05 .02
❑ U136 Broderick Thomas .05 .02
❑ U137 Dave Meggett .05 .02
❑ U138 Eric Allen .05 .02
❑ U139 Herschel Walker .10 .05
❑ U140 Dexter Carter .05 .02
❑ U141 Kerry Cash .05 .02
❑ U142 Kelvin Martin .05 .02
❑ U143 Erric Pegram .10 .05
❑ U144 Bo Orlando .05 .02
❑ U145 Ricky Ervins .05 .02
❑ U146 John Friesz .10 .05
❑ U147 Alexander Wright .05 .02
❑ U148 Alvin Harper .05 .02
❑ U149 Gus Frerotte .25 .11
❑ U150 Duval Love .05 .02
❑ U151 Eric Metcalf .10 .05
❑ U152 Ruben Brown RC .05 .02
❑ U153 Marty Carter .05 .02
❑ U154 James Joseph .05 .02
❑ U155 Hugh Douglas RC .10 .05
❑ U156 Wade Wilson .05 .02
❑ U157 Britt Hager .05 .02
❑ U158 Mark Schlereth .05 .02
❑ U159 Cory Schlesinger UER .05 .02
(name spelled Corey)
❑ U160 Mark Ingram .05 .02
❑ U161 Mark Stepnoski .05 .02
❑ U162 Flipper Anderson .05 .02
❑ U163 Donta Jones .05 .02
❑ U164 James Hasty .05 .02
❑ U165 Gary Clark .05 .02
❑ U166 David Sloan RC .10 .05
❑ U167 Jeff Dellenbach .05 .02
❑ U168 Rufus Porter .05 .02
❑ U169 Mike Croel .05 .02
❑ U170 Charles Wilson Jets UER .05 .02
Card number 242
see '95 Coll.Choice #242
❑ U171 Pat Swilling .05 .02
❑ U172 Kurt Gouveia .05 .02
❑ U173 Norm Johnson .05 .02
❑ U174 Shaun Gayle .05 .02
❑ U175 Marquez Pope .05 .02
❑ U176 Tyronne Stowe .05 .02
❑ U177 Anthony Parker .05 .02
❑ U178 Kenneth Gant .05 .02
❑ U179 James Washington .05 .02
❑ U180 Rob Moore .05 .02
❑ U181 Alundis Brice .05 .02
❑ U182 Lamont Warren .05 .02
❑ U183 Michael Timpson .05 .02
❑ U184 Lorenzo White .05 .02
❑ U185 Charlie Williams .05 .02
❑ U186 Ed McCaffrey .10 .05
❑ U187 James Jones .05 .02
❑ U188 Derrick Fenner .05 .02
❑ U189 Mel Gray .05 .02
❑ U190 James Williams LB .05 .02
❑ U191 Jeff Criswell .05 .02
❑ U192 Randal Hill .05 .02
❑ U193 Terry Allen .10 .05
❑ U194 Joel Smeenge .05 .02
❑ U195 Ricky Watters .25 .11
❑ U196 Don Sasa .05 .02
❑ U197 Steve Bono .10 .05
❑ U198 Steve Broussard .05 .02
❑ U199 Carlos Jenkins .05 .02
❑ U200 Reggie Roby .05 .02
❑ U201 Stanley Richard .05 .02
❑ U202 Vince Workman .05 .02
❑ U203 Eric Guliford .05 .02
❑ U204 Lionel Washington .05 .02
❑ U205 Brian Williams LB .05 .02
❑ U206 Ronnie Lott .10 .05
❑ U207 Corey Harris .05 .02
❑ U208 Harlon Barnett .05 .02
❑ U209 Bubby Brister .05 .02
❑ U210 Darren Bennett .10 .05
❑ U211 Winston Moss .05 .02
❑ U212 Leonard Russell .05 .02
❑ U213 Ron Davis .05 .02
❑ U214 Curtis Whitley .05 .02
❑ U215 Webster Slaughter .05 .02
❑ U216 Korey Stringer .05 .02
❑ U217 Don Davey .05 .02
❑ U218 Mark Rypien .05 .02
❑ U219 Chad Cota .05 .02
❑ U220 Tim Ruddy .05 .02
❑ U221 Corey Fuller .05 .02
❑ U222 Mike Dumas .05 .02
❑ U223 Eddie Murray .05 .02
❑ U224 Checklist (U1-U114) .50 .23
Dan Marino
❑ U225 Checklist (U115-U225) UER .50 .23
(front reads U115-U228)
Dan Marino
❑ P1 Michael Westbrook Promo .75 .35
Numbered CUS1
❑ P2 Dan Marino Promo 1.00 .45
Stick-um card, blankbacked
❑ P3 Dan Marino Promo .75 .35
Michael Westbrook
Tim Brown
Stick-um card, blankbacked

1995 Collector's Choice Update Crash the Playoffs

	MINT	NRMT
COMPLETE SET (18)	20.00	9.00
COMMON CARD (CP1-CP18)	.50	.23
SEMISTARS	.75	.35
SILVER ODDS 1:5		
*GOLD CARDS: 1.5X TO 3X HI COLUMN		
GOLD ODDS 1:50		

❑ CP1 AFC East QB 3.00 1.35
Drew Bledsoe
Dan Marino
Boomer Esiason
Jim Kelly
❑ CP2 AFC Central QB 1.50 .70
Steve Beuerlein
Jeff Blake
Steve McNair
Neil O'Donnell
Vinny Testaverde
❑ CP3 AFC West QB 2.50 1.10
Steve Bono
John Elway
Jeff Hostetler
Stan Humphries
Rick Mirer
❑ CP4 NFC East QB 1.50 .70
Troy Aikman
Dave Brown
Randall Cunningham
Dave Krieg
Heath Shuler
❑ CP5 NFC Central QB 3.00 1.35
Trent Dilfer
Brett Favre
Erik Krmaer
Scott Mitchell
Warren Moon
❑ CP6 NFC West QB 1.50 .70
Kerry Collins
Jim Everett
Jeff George
Chris Miller
Steve Young
❑ CP7 AFC East RB 2.00 .90
Brad Baxter
Marshall Faulk
Darick Holmes
Terry Kirby
Curtis Martin
❑ CP8 AFC Central RB .50 .23
Gary Brown
Harold Green
Leroy Hoard
Bam Morris
James O. Stewart
❑ CP9 AFC West RB 3.00 1.35
Terrell Davis
Greg Hill
Napoleon Kaufman
Natrone Means
Chris Warren
❑ CP10 NFC East RB .75 .35
Terry Allen
Rodney Hampton
Garrison Hearst
Emmitt Smith
Ricky Watters
❑ CP11 NFC Central WR .50 .23
Robert Brooks
Cris Carter
Jeff Graham
Alvin Harper
Herman Moore
❑ CP12 NFC West RB .50 .23
Randy Baldwin
Mario Bates
Jerome Bettis
William Floyd
Craig Heyward
❑ CP13 AFC East WR .50 .23
Kyle Brady
Ben Coates
Sean Dawkins
Irving Fryar
Andre Reed
❑ CP14 AFC Central WR .50 .23
Desmond Howard
Haywood Jeffires
Charles Johnson
Andre Rison
Darnay Scott
❑ CP15 AFC West WR 1.25 .55
Tim Brown
Willie Davis
Joey Galloway
Tony Martin
Shannon Sharpe
❑ CP16 NFC East WR .75 .35
Fred Barnett
Michael Irvin
Rob Moore
Mike Sherrard
Michael Westbrook

❑ CP17 NFC Central RB 3.00 1.35
Edgar Bennett
Errict Rhett
Rashaan Salaam
Barry Sanders
Robert Smith
❑ CP18 NFC West WR .... 1.50 .70
Isaac Bruce
Mark Carrier
Michael Haynes
Terance Mathis
Jerry Rice

1995 Collector's Choice Update Post Season Heroics

	MINT	NRMT
COMPLETE SET (20)	12.00	5.50

*GOLD CARDS: 6X TO 12X BASE CARD HI
PRIZE SET FOR CRASH THE PLAYOFFS

❑ 1 Stan Humphries .... .20 .09
❑ 2 Natrone Means .... 1.00 .45
❑ 3 Tony Martin .... 1.00 .45
❑ 4 Neil O'Donnell .... .40 .18
❑ 5 Byron Bam Morris .... .20 .09
❑ 6 Charles Johnson .... .40 .18
❑ 7 Jim Harbaugh .... 1.00 .45
❑ 8 Darick Holmes.................... .40 .18
❑ 9 Sean Dawkins .... .20 .09
❑ 10 Steve Young .... 1.50 .70
❑ 11 Craig Heyward .... .20 .09
❑ 12 Jerry Rice .... 2.00 .90
❑ 13 Brett Favre 4.00 1.80
❑ 14 Edgar Bennett .... .40 .18
❑ 15 Robert Brooks .... .40 .18
❑ 16 Troy Aikman .... 2.00 .90
❑ 17 Emmitt Smith................. 3.00 1.35
❑ 18 Michael Irvin .... 1.00 .45
❑ 19 Byron Bam Morris .... .20 .09
❑ 20 Larry Brown...................... .20 .09

1995 Collector's Choice Update Stick-Ums

	MINT	NRMT
COMPLETE SET (90)	12.00	5.50
COMMON CARD (1-90).............	.10	.05
SEMISTARS...............................	.15	.07
UNLISTED STARS.......................	.25	.11

ONE PER HOB.PACK/TWO PER RET.PACK

❑ 1 Jeff George .... .25 .11
❑ 2 Kerry Collins .... .25 .11
❑ 3 Jerome Bettis .... .25 .11
❑ 4 Mario Bates .... .15 .07
❑ 5 Steve Young .... .40 .18
❑ 6 Rashaan Salaam.................. .25 .11
❑ 7 Barry Sanders .... 1.00 .45
❑ 8 Brett Favre .... 1.00 .45
❑ 9 Warren Moon .... .25 .11
❑ 10 Errict Rhett .... .15 .07
❑ 11 Emmitt Smith....................... .75 .35
❑ 12 Rodney Hampton .... .15 .07
❑ 13 Ricky Watters .... .25 .11
❑ 14 Garrison Hearst................... .25 .11
❑ 15 Michael Westbrook .... .25 .11
❑ 16 Jim Kelly .... .25 .11
❑ 17 Marshall Faulk.................... .25 .11
❑ 18 Dan Marino .... 1.00 .45
❑ 19 Drew Bledsoe .... .50 .23
❑ 20 Kyle Brady........................... .15 .07
❑ 21 Ki-Jana Carter.................... .15 .07
❑ 22 Andre Rison .... .15 .07
❑ 23 Steve McNair....................... .50 .23
❑ 24 James O. Stewart .... .25 .11
❑ 25 Byron Bam Morris .... .15 .07
❑ 26 John Elway .... 1.00 .45
❑ 27 Marcus Allen .... .25 .11
❑ 28 Tim Brown .... .25 .11
❑ 29 Natrone Means .... .25 .11
❑ 30 Chris Warren........................ .15 .07
❑ 31 Terence Mathis .... .15 .07
Mark Carrier WR
Chris Miller
Jim Everett
❑ 32 Bert Emanuel .... .25 .11
Pete Metzelaars
Isaac Bruce
Dana Stubblefield
❑ 33 Chris Doleman .... .30 .14
Frank Reich
Derek Brown RBK
Jerry Rice
❑ 34 Jesse Tuggle....................... .30 .14
Roman Phifer
Tyrone Hughes
Steve Young
❑ 35 Sam Mills............................ .10 .05
Kevin Carter
Michael Haynes
Brent Jones
❑ 36 Falcons Helmet .... .10 .05
Eric Metcalf
Tyrone Poole
Lovell Pinkney
❑ 37 Panthers Helmet .... .10 .05
Morten Andersen UER
(Morton on front)
John Kasay
Troy Drayton
❑ 38 Rams Helmet .... .25 .11
Sean Gilbert
Mark Fields
J.J.Stokes
❑ 39 Saints Helmet .... .10 .05
Bob Christian
Willie Roaf
Ken Norton
❑ 40 49ers Helmet...................... .10 .05
Craig Heyward
Renaldo Turnbull
William Floyd
❑ 41 Raymont Harris .... .25 .11
Herman Moore
Edgar Bennett
Cris Carter
❑ 42 Jeff Graham .... .25 .11
Henry Thomas
Reggie White
Trent Dilfer
❑ 43 Curtis Conway.................... .25 .11
Scott Mitchell
Robert Smith
Alvin Harper
❑ 44 Steve Walsh .... .10 .05
Sean Jones
Qadry Ismail
Hardy Nickerson
❑ 45 Bennie Blades .... .10 .05
John Jurkovic
John Randle
Courtney Hawkins
❑ 46 Bears Helmet .... .10 .05
John Thierry
Luther Elliss
Leroy Butler
❑ 47 Lions Helmet .... .25 .11
Johnnie Morton
Robert Brooks
Jake Reed
❑ 48 Packers Helmet................. .10 .05
LeShon Johnson
Dewayne Washington
Jackie Harris
❑ 49 Vikings Helmet .... .10 .05
Donnell Woolford
James A.Stewart
Eric Curry
❑ 50 Buccaneers Helmet.......... .10 .05
Mark Carrier DB
Chris Spielman
Warren Sapp
❑ 51 Troy Aikman .... .30 .14
Mike Sherrard
Fred Barnett
Dave Krieg
❑ 52 Michael Irvin .... .15 .07
Chris Calloway
Calvin Williams
Henry Ellard
❑ 53 Sherman Williams .... .25 .11
Dave Brown
Rob Moore
Heath Shuler
❑ 54 Charles Haley .... .15 .07
Randall Cunningham
Eric Swann
Ken Harvey
❑ 55 Thomas Lewis.................. .10 .05
Charlie Garner
Clyde Simmons
Tom Carter
❑ 56 Cowboys Helmet............... .15 .07
Tyrone Wheatley
Bobby Taylor
Daryl Johnston
❑ 57 Giants Helmet .... .10 .05
Mike Croel
Byron Evans
Aeneas Williams
❑ 58 Eagles Helmet.................. .10 .05
Mike Mamula
Larry Centers
Brian Mitchell
❑ 59 Cardinals Helmet.............. .25 .11
Jay Novacek
Frank Sanders
Terry Allen
❑ 60 Redskins Helmet.............. .25 .11
Deion Sanders
Herschel Walker
Sterling Palmer
❑ 61 Henry Jones .... .10 .05
Craig Erickson
Terry Kirby
Ben Coates
❑ 62 Andre Reed....................... .15 .07
Flipper Anderson
Irving Fryar
Johnny Mitchell
❑ 63 Russell Copeland .... .15 .07
Sean Dawkins
Vincent Brisby
Boomer Esiason
❑ 64 Bruce Smith....................... .25 .11
O.J.McDuffie
Willie McGinest
Ryan Yarborough
❑ 65 Roosevelt Potts .... .50 .23

Keith Byars
Curtis Martin
Brad Baxter
❑ 66 Bills Helmet .... .10 .05
Cornelius Bennett
Ray Buchanan
Marco Coleman
❑ 67 Colts Helmet .... .10 .05
Quentin Coryatt
Bryan Cox
Chris Slade
❑ 68 Dolphins Helmet .... .10 .05
Eric Green
Ty Law
Marvin Washington
❑ 69 Patriots Helmet .... .10 .05
Todd Collins
Vincent Brown
Ronald Moore
❑ 70 Jets Helmet .... .10 .05
Jeff Burris
Floyd Turner
Aaron Glenn
❑ 71 Carl Pickens .... .25 .11
Vinny Testaverde
Haywood Jeffires
Desmond Howard
❑ 72 Darnay Scott .... .15 .07
Eric Turner
Gary Brown
Neil O'Donnell
❑ 73 David Klingler .... .15 .07
Leroy Hoard
Tony Boselli
Charles Johnson
❑ 74 Steve Tovar .... .10 .05
Al Smith
Derek Brown TE
John L.Williams
❑ 75 Lorenzo White .... .15 .07
Rodney Thomas
Steve Beuerlein
Kevin Greene
❑ 76 Bengals Helmet .... .25 .11
Jeff Blake
Derrick Alexander WR
Ray Childress
❑ 77 Browns Helmet .... .10 .05
Eric Zeier
Mel Gray
Reggie Cobb
❑ 78 Oilers Helmet .... .15 .07
Todd McNair
Jeff Lageman
Greg Lloyd
❑ 79 Jaguars Helmet .... .25 .11
Dan Wilkinson
Rob Johnson
Rod Woodson
❑ 80 Steelers Helmet .... .10 .05
Eric Bieniemy
Antonio Langham
Mark Bruener
❑ 81 Shannon Sharpe .... .25 .11
Willie Davis
Jeff Hostetler
Stan Humphries
❑ 82 Rod Bernstine .... .15 .07
Ronnie Lott
Harvey Williams
Rick Mirer
❑ 83 Anthony Miller .... .15 .07
Neil Smith
Junior Seau
Brian Blades
❑ 84 Mike Pritchard .... .15 .07
Napoleon Kaufman
Leslie O'Neal
Sam Adams
❑ 85 Greg Hill .... .15 .07
Rocket Ismail
Alfred Pupunu
Cortez Kennedy
❑ 86 Broncos Helmet .... .15 .07
Steve Atwater
Tamarick Vanover
Chester McGlockton
❑ 87 Chiefs Helmet .... .15 .07
Steve Bono
Rob Fredrickson
Tony Martin
❑ 88 Raiders Helmet .... .10 .05
Terry McDaniel
Jimmy Oliver
Christian Fauria
❑ 89 Chargers Helmet .... .40 .18
Glen Milburn
John Carney
Joey Galloway
❑ 90 Seahawks Helmet .... .10 .05
Terrell Fletcher
Keith Cash
Eugene Robinson

1996 Collector's Choice

	MINT	NRMT
COMPLETE SET (375)	25.00	11.00
COMP.FACT.SET (395)	30.00	13.50
COMMON CARD (1-375)	.10	.05
SEMISTARS	.20	.09
UNLISTED STARS	.30	.14
COMP.MARINO CUT ABOVE (10) 6.75		15.00
ONE PER SPECIAL RETAIL PACK		

❑ 1 Keyshawn Johnson RC .... 2.00 .90
❑ 2 Kevin Hardy RC .... .30 .14
❑ 3 Simeon Rice RC .... .30 .14
❑ 4 Jonathan Ogden RC .... .10 .05
❑ 5 Cedric Jones RC .... .10 .05
❑ 6 Lawrence Phillips RC .... .50 .23
❑ 7 Tim Biakabutuka RC .... .75 .35
❑ 8 Terry Glenn RC .... 1.25 .55
❑ 9 Rickey Dudley RC .... .30 .14
❑ 10 Regan Upshaw RC .... .10 .05
❑ 11 Walt Harris RC .... .10 .05
❑ 12 Eddie George RC 2.50 1.10
❑ 13 John Mobley RC .... .10 .05
❑ 14 Duane Clemons RC .... .10 .05
❑ 15 Marvin Harrison RC .... 2.00 .90
❑ 16 Daryl Gardener RC .... .10 .05
❑ 17 Pete Kendall RC .... .10 .05
❑ 18 Marcus Jones RC .... .10 .05
❑ 19 Eric Moulds RC .... 1.50 .70
❑ 20 Ray Lewis RC .... .10 .05
❑ 21 Alex Van Dyke RC .... .20 .09
❑ 22 Leeland McElroy RC .... .30 .14
❑ 23 Mike Alstott RC .... 1.25 .55
❑ 24 Lawyer Milloy RC .... .10 .05
❑ 25 Marco Battaglia RC .... .10 .05
❑ 26 Je'rod Cherry RC .... .10 .05
❑ 27 Israel Ifeanyi RC .... .10 .05
❑ 28 Bobby Engram RC .... .30 .14
❑ 29 Jason Dunn RC .... .20 .09
❑ 30 Derrick Mayes RC .... .60 .25
❑ 31 Stepfret Williams RC .... .20 .09
❑ 32 Bobby Hoying RC .... .50 .23
❑ 33 Karim Abdul-Jabbar RC .. .50 .23
❑ 34 Danny Kanell RC .... .30 .14
❑ 35 Chris Darkins RC .... .10 .05
❑ 36 Charlie Jones RC .... .30 .14
❑ 37 Tedy Bruschi RC .... .10 .05
❑ 38 Stanley Pritchett RC .... .20 .09
❑ 39 Donnie Edwards RC .... .10 .05
❑ 40 Jeff Lewis RC .... .50 .23
❑ 41 Stephen Davis RC 2.50 1.10
❑ 42 Winslow Oliver RC .... .10 .05
❑ 43 Mercury Hayes RC .... .10 .05
❑ 44 Jon Runyan RC .... .10 .05
❑ 45 Steve Taneyhill RC .... .10 .05
❑ 46 Eric Metcalf SR .... .10 .05
❑ 47 Bryce Paup SR .... .10 .05
❑ 48 Kerry Collins SR .... .30 .14
❑ 49 Rashaan Salaam SR .... .20 .09
❑ 50 Carl Pickens SR .... .30 .14
❑ 51 Emmitt Smith SR .... .50 .23
❑ 52 Michael Irvin SR .... .20 .09
❑ 53 Troy Aikman SR .... .40 .18
❑ 54 Terrell Davis SR .... 1.00 .45
❑ 55 John Elway SR .... .75 .35
❑ 56 Herman Moore SR .... .30 .14
❑ 57 Brett Favre SR .... .75 .35
❑ 58 Rodney Thomas SR .... .10 .05
❑ 59 Jim Harbaugh SR .... .20 .09
❑ 60 Mark Brunell SR .... .40 .18
❑ 61 Marcus Allen SR .... .30 .14
❑ 62 Tamarick Vanover SR .... .20 .09
❑ 63 Steve Bono SR .... .10 .05
❑ 64 Dan Marino SR .... .75 .35
❑ 65 Warren Moon SR .... .10 .05
❑ 66 Curtis Martin SR .... .30 .14
❑ 67 Tyrone Hughes SR .... .10 .05
❑ 68 Rodney Hampton SR .... .10 .05
❑ 69 Hugh Douglas SR .... .10 .05
❑ 70 Tim Brown SR .... .20 .09
❑ 71 Ricky Watters SR .... .20 .09
❑ 72 Kordell Stewart SR .... .30 .14
❑ 73 Andre Coleman SR .... .10 .05
❑ 74 Jerry Rice SR .... .40 .18
❑ 75 Joey Galloway SR .... .30 .14
❑ 76 Isaac Bruce SR .... .30 .14
❑ 77 Errict Rhett SR .... .20 .09
❑ 78 Michael Westbrook SR .... .30 .14
❑ 79 Brian Mitchell SR .... .10 .05
❑ 80 Aeneas Williams .... .10 .05
❑ 81 Andre Reed .... .20 .09
❑ 82 Brett Maxie .... .10 .05
❑ 83 Jim Flanigan .... .10 .05
❑ 84 Jeff Blake .... .30 .14
❑ 85 Mike Frederick .... .10 .05
❑ 86 Michael Irvin .... .30 .14
❑ 87 Aaron Craver .... .10 .05
❑ 88 Barry Sanders .... 1.50 .70
❑ 89 Travis Jervey RC .... .30 .14
❑ 90 Chris Sanders .... .20 .09
❑ 91 Marshall Faulk .... .30 .14
❑ 92 Bryan Schwartz .... .10 .05
❑ 93 Tamarick Vanover .... .20 .09
❑ 94 Troy Vincent .... .10 .05
❑ 95 Robert Smith .... .20 .09
❑ 96 Drew Bledsoe .... .75 .35
❑ 97 Quinn Early .... .10 .05
❑ 98 Wayne Chrebet .... .20 .09
❑ 99 Tim Brown .... .30 .14
❑ 100 Charlie Garner .... .10 .05
❑ 101 Yancey Thigpen .... .20 .09
❑ 102 Isaac Bruce .... .30 .14
❑ 103 Natrone Means .... .30 .14
❑ 104 Jerry Rice .... .75 .35
❑ 105 Chris Warren .... .20 .09
❑ 106 Errict Rhett .... .20 .09
❑ 107 Heath Shuler .... .20 .09
❑ 108 Eric Swann .... .10 .05
❑ 109 Jeff George .... .20 .09
❑ 110 Steve Tasker .... .10 .05
❑ 111 Sam Mills .... .10 .05
❑ 112 Jeff Graham .... .10 .05
❑ 113 Carl Pickens .... .30 .14
❑ 114 Vinny Testaverde .... .20 .09
❑ 115 Emmitt Smith .... 1.25 .55
❑ 116 John Elway .... 1.50 .70
❑ 117 Henry Thomas .... .10 .05
❑ 118 LeRoy Butler .... .10 .05
❑ 119 Blaine Bishop .... .10 .05
❑ 120 Floyd Turner .... .10 .05
❑ 121 Jeff Lageman .... .10 .05
❑ 122 Kimble Anders .... .20 .09
❑ 123 Bryan Cox .... .10 .05
❑ 124 Qadry Ismail .... .10 .05

❑	125	Ted Johnson RC	.10	.05
❑	126	Wesley Walls	.20	.09
❑	127	Rodney Hampton	.20	.09
❑	128	Adrian Murrell	.30	.14
❑	129	Daryl Hobbs RC	.10	.05
❑	130	Ricky Watters	.20	.09
❑	131	Carnell Lake	.10	.05
❑	132	Toby Wright	.10	.05
❑	133	Darren Bennett	.10	.05
❑	134	J.J. Stokes	.30	.14
❑	135	Eugene Robinson	.10	.05
❑	136	Eric Curry	.10	.05
❑	137	Tom Carter	.10	.05
❑	138	Dave Krieg	.10	.05
❑	139	Eric Metcalf	.10	.05
❑	140	Bill Brooks	.10	.05
❑	141	Pete Metzelaars	.10	.05
❑	142	Kevin Butler	.10	.05
❑	143	John Copeland	.10	.05
❑	144	Keenan McCardell	.30	.14
❑	145	Larry Brown	.10	.05
❑	146	Jason Elam	.10	.05
❑	147	Willie Clay	.10	.05
❑	148	Robert Brooks	.30	.14
❑	149	Chris Chandler	.20	.09
❑	150	Quentin Coryatt	.10	.05
❑	151	Pete Mitchell	.20	.09
❑	152	Martin Bayless	.10	.05
❑	153	Pete Stoyanovich	.10	.05
❑	154	Cris Carter	.30	.14
❑	155	Jimmy Hitchcock	.10	.05
❑	156	Mario Bates	.20	.09
❑	157	Mike Sherrard	.10	.05
❑	158	Boomer Esiason	.20	.09
❑	159	Chester McGlockton	.10	.05
❑	160	Bobby Taylor	.10	.05
❑	161	Kordell Stewart	.50	.23
❑	162	Kevin Carter	.10	.05
❑	163	Junior Seau	.20	.09
❑	164	Derek Loville	.10	.05
❑	165	Brian Blades	.10	.05
❑	166	Jackie Harris	.10	.05
❑	167	Michael Westbrook	.30	.14
❑	168	Rob Moore	.20	.09
❑	169	Jessie Tuggle	.10	.05
❑	170	Darick Holmes	.10	.05
❑	171	Tim McKyer	.10	.05
❑	172	Erik Kramer	.10	.05
❑	173	Harold Green	.10	.05
❑	174	Stevon Moore	.10	.05
❑	175	Deion Sanders	.40	.18
❑	176	Anthony Miller	.20	.09
❑	177	Herman Moore	.30	.14
❑	178	Brett Favre	1.50	.70
❑	179	Rodney Thomas	.10	.05
❑	180	Ken Dilger	.20	.09
❑	181	Mark Brunell	.75	.35
❑	182	Marcus Allen	.30	.14
❑	183	Dan Marino	1.50	.70
❑	184	John Randle	.10	.05
❑	185	Ben Coates	.20	.09
❑	186	Tyrone Hughes	.10	.05
❑	187	Dave Brown	.10	.05
❑	188	Johnny Mitchell	.10	.05
❑	189	Harvey Williams	.10	.05
❑	190	Andy Harmon	.10	.05
❑	191	Kevin Greene	.20	.09
❑	192	D'Marco Farr	.10	.05
❑	193	Andre Coleman	.10	.05
❑	194	Bryant Young	.20	.09
❑	195	Rick Mirer	.20	.09
❑	196	Horace Copeland	.10	.05
❑	197	Leslie Shepherd	.10	.05
❑	198	Jamir Miller	.10	.05
❑	199	Bert Emanuel	.20	.09
❑	200	Steve Christie	.10	.05
❑	201	Kerry Collins	.30	.14
❑	202	Rashaan Salaam	.30	.14
❑	203	Steve Tovar	.10	.05
❑	204	Michael Jackson	.20	.09
❑	205	Kevin Williams	.10	.05
❑	206	Glyn Milburn	.10	.05
❑	207	Johnnie Morton	.20	.09
❑	208	Antonio Freeman	.50	.23
❑	209	Cris Dishman	.10	.05
❑	210	Ellis Johnson	.10	.05
❑	211	Cedric Tillman	.10	.05
❑	212	Steve Bono	.10	.05
❑	213	Eric Green	.10	.05
❑	214	David Palmer	.10	.05
❑	215	Vincent Brisby	.10	.05
❑	216	Michael Haynes	.10	.05
❑	217	Chris Calloway	.10	.05
❑	218	Kyle Brady	.10	.05
❑	219	Terry McDaniel	.10	.05
❑	220	Calvin Williams	.10	.05
❑	221	Greg Lloyd	.20	.09
❑	222	Jerome Bettis	.30	.14
❑	223	Stan Humphries	.20	.09
❑	224	Lee Woodall	.10	.05
❑	225	Robert Blackmon	.10	.05
❑	226	Warren Sapp	.10	.05
❑	227	Brian Mitchell	.10	.05
❑	228	Garrison Hearst	.20	.09
❑	229	Terance Mathis	.10	.05
❑	230	Bryce Paup	.10	.05
❑	231	Derrick Moore	.10	.05
❑	232	Curtis Conway	.30	.14
❑	233	Darnay Scott	.20	.09
❑	234	Andre Rison	.20	.09
❑	235	Jay Novacek	.10	.05
❑	236	Terrell Davis	2.00	.90
❑	237	David Sloan	.10	.05
❑	238	Reggie White	.30	.14
❑	239	Todd McNair	.10	.05
❑	240	Ray Buchanan	.10	.05
❑	241	Steve Beuerlein	.10	.05
❑	242	Dan Saleaumua	.10	.05
❑	243	Bernie Parmalee	.10	.05
❑	244	Warren Moon	.20	.09
❑	245	Ty Law	.10	.05
❑	246	Torrance Small	.10	.05
❑	247	Phillippi Sparks	.10	.05
❑	248	Mo Lewis	.10	.05
❑	249	Jeff Hostetler	.10	.05
❑	250	Rodney Peete	.10	.05
❑	251	Byron Bam Morris	.20	.09
❑	252	Chris Miller	.10	.05
❑	253	Tony Martin	.20	.09
❑	254	Eric Davis	.10	.05
❑	255	Joey Galloway	.50	.23
❑	256	Derrick Brooks	.10	.05
❑	257	Ken Harvey	.10	.05
❑	258	Frank Sanders	.20	.09
❑	259	Morten Andersen	.10	.05
❑	260	Marlon Kerner	.10	.05
❑	261	Mark Carrier WR	.10	.05
❑	262	Mark Carrier DB	.10	.05
❑	263	Tony McGee	.10	.05
❑	264	Eric Zeier	.10	.05
❑	265	Darren Woodson	.20	.09
❑	266	Shannon Sharpe	.20	.09
❑	267	Brett Perriman	.10	.05
❑	268	Edgar Bennett	.20	.09
❑	269	Darryll Lewis	.10	.05
❑	270	Jim Harbaugh	.20	.09
❑	271	Desmond Howard	.20	.09
❑	272	Derrick Thomas	.20	.09
❑	273	Irving Fryar	.20	.09
❑	274	Jake Reed	.20	.09
❑	275	Curtis Martin	.50	.23
❑	276	Eric Allen	.10	.05
❑	277	Thomas Lewis	.10	.05
❑	278	Hugh Douglas	.10	.05
❑	279	Pat Swilling	.10	.05
❑	280	William Thomas	.10	.05
❑	281	Norm Johnson	.10	.05
❑	282	Roman Phifer	.10	.05
❑	283	Chris Mims	.10	.05
❑	284	Steve Young	.60	.25
❑	285	Cortez Kennedy	.10	.05
❑	286	Trent Dilfer	.30	.14
❑	287	Terry Allen	.20	.09
❑	288	Clyde Simmons	.10	.05
❑	289	Craig Heyward	.10	.05
❑	290	Jim Kelly	.30	.14
❑	291	Tyrone Poole	.10	.05
❑	292	Chris Zorich	.10	.05
❑	293	Dan Wilkinson	.10	.05
❑	294	Antonio Langham	.10	.05
❑	295	Troy Aikman	.75	.35
❑	296	Steve Atwater	.10	.05
❑	297	Scott Mitchell	.20	.09
❑	298	Mark Chmura	.20	.09
❑	299	Steve McNair	.50	.23
❑	300	Tony Bennett	.10	.05
❑	301	Willie Jackson	.10	.05
❑	302	Neil Smith	.10	.05
❑	303	Terry Kirby	.20	.09
❑	304	Orlando Thomas	.10	.05
❑	305	Willie McGinest	.10	.05
❑	306	Wayne Martin	.10	.05
❑	307	Michael Brooks	.10	.05
❑	308	Marvin Washington	.10	.05
❑	309	Nolan Harrison	.10	.05
❑	310	William Fuller	.10	.05
❑	311	Willie Williams	.10	.05
❑	312	Troy Drayton	.10	.05
❑	313	Shawn Lee	.10	.05
❑	314	Ken Norton	.10	.05
❑	315	Terry Wooden	.10	.05
❑	316	Hardy Nickerson	.10	.05
❑	317	Gus Frerotte	.30	.14
❑	318	Oscar McBride	.10	.05
❑	319	Merton Hanks	.10	.05
❑	320	Justin Armour	.10	.05
❑	321	Willie Green	.10	.05
❑	322	Roger Jones RC	.10	.05
❑	323	Leroy Hoard	.10	.05
❑	324	Chris Boniol	.10	.05
❑	325	Jason Hanson	.10	.05
❑	326	Sean Jones	.10	.05
❑	327	Roosevelt Potts	.10	.05
❑	328	Greg Hill	.20	.09
❑	329	O.J. McDuffie	.20	.09
❑	330	Amp Lee	.10	.05
❑	331	Chris Slade	.10	.05
❑	332	Jim Everett	.10	.05
❑	333	Tyrone Wheatley	.20	.09
❑	334	Charles Wilson	.10	.05
❑	335	Napoleon Kaufman	.40	.18
❑	336	Fred Barnett	.10	.05
❑	337	Neil O'Donnell	.20	.09
❑	338	Sean Gilbert	.10	.05
❑	339	Aaron Hayden RC	.10	.05
❑	340	Brent Jones	.10	.05
❑	341	Christian Fauria	.10	.05
❑	342	Alvin Harper	.10	.05
❑	343	Henry Ellard	.10	.05
❑	344	Willie Davis	.10	.05
❑	345	Charles Haley	.20	.09
❑	346	Chris Jacke	.10	.05
❑	347	Allen Aldridge	.10	.05
❑	348	Jeff Herrod	.10	.05
❑	349	Rocket Ismail	.10	.05
❑	350	Leslie O'Neal	.10	.05
❑	351	Marquez Pope	.10	.05
❑	352	Brock Marion	.10	.05
❑	353	Ernie Mills	.10	.05
❑	354	Larry Centers	.20	.09
❑	355	Chris Doleman	.10	.05
❑	356	Bruce Smith	.20	.09
❑	357	John Kasay	.10	.05
❑	358	Donnell Woolford	.10	.05
❑	359	David Dunn	.10	.05
❑	360	Eric Turner	.10	.05
❑	361	Sherman Williams	.10	.05
❑	362	Chris Spielman	.10	.05
❑	363	Craig Newsome	.10	.05
❑	364	Sean Dawkins	.10	.05
❑	365	James O. Stewart	.20	.09
❑	366	Dale Carter	.10	.05
❑	367	Marco Coleman	.10	.05
❑	368	Dave Meggett	.10	.05
❑	369	Irv Smith	.10	.05
❑	370	Mike Mamula	.10	.05
❑	371	Erric Pegram	.10	.05
❑	372	Dana Stubblefield	.20	.09
❑	373	Terrance Shaw	.10	.05
❑	374	Jerry Rice CL	.30	.14
❑	375	Dan Marino CL	.40	.18
❑	P1	Jerry Rice Promo Base brand card #801	1.00	.45
❑	P2	Dan Marino Promo Crash the Game April 1	1.50	.70

1996 Collector's Choice A Cut Above

	MINT	NRMT
COMPLETE SET (10)	12.00	5.50
ONE PER SPECIAL RETAIL PACK		
*UDA JUMBO CARDS: .75X TO 1.5X BASE CARD HI		
❑ 1 Troy Aikman	1.25	.55
❑ 2 Tim Biakabutuka	1.25	.55
❑ 3 Drew Bledsoe	1.25	.55
❑ 4 Emmitt Smith	2.00	.90
❑ 5 Marshall Faulk	.50	.23
❑ 6 Brett Favre	2.50	1.10
❑ 7 Keyshawn Johnson	3.00	1.35
❑ 8 Deion Sanders	.60	.25
❑ 9 Lawrence Phillips	.75	.35
❑ 10 Jerry Rice	1.25	.55

1996 Collector's Choice Crash The Game

	MINT	NRMT
COMPLETE SET (90)	75.00	34.00
SILVER STATED ODDS 1:5		
COMP.GOLD SET (90)	300.00	135.00
*GOLD STARS: 4X TO 8X BASE CARD HI		
*GOLD ROOKIES: 2X TO 4X BASE CARD HI		
GOLD STATED ODDS 1:50		
THREE GAME DATES PER PLAYER		
COMP.GOLD REDEMPT.(22)	225.00	100.00
*GOLD RED. STARS: 10X TO 20X BASE CARD HI		
*GOLD RED. ROOKIES: 5X TO 10X BASE CARD HI		
COMP.SILVER REDEMPT.(22)	75.00	34.00
*SILVER RED. STARS: 3X TO 6X BASE CARD HI		
*SILVER RED. ROOKIES: 1.5X TO 3X BASE CARD HI		
ONE PRIZE CARD VIA MAIL PER WINNER		
❑ CG1A Dan Marino 9/23 L	3.00	1.35
❑ CG1B Dan Marino 10/27 W	3.00	1.35
❑ CG1C Dan Marino 11/25 W	3.00	1.35
❑ CG2A John Elway 10/6 W	3.00	1.35
❑ CG2B John Elway 10/27 W	3.00	1.35
❑ CG2C John Elway 12/24 W	3.00	1.35
❑ CG3A Jeff Blake 9/29 W	.60	.25
❑ CG3B Jeff Blake 10/20 W	.60	.25
❑ CG3C Jeff Blake 12/1 W	.60	.25
❑ CG4A Drew Bledsoe 9/22 W	1.50	.70
❑ CG4B Drew Bledsoe 10/13 L	1.50	.70
❑ CG4C Drew Bledsoe 12/1 W	1.50	.70
❑ CG5A Steve Young 9/29 L	1.25	.55
❑ CG5B Steve Young 10/14 L	1.25	.55
❑ CG5C Steve Young 12/8 W	1.25	.55
❑ CG6A Brett Favre 10/6 W	3.00	1.35
❑ CG6B Brett Favre 11/3 W	3.00	1.35
❑ CG6C Brett Favre 11/24 W	3.00	1.35
❑ CG7A Jim Kelly 9/22 L	.60	.25
❑ CG7B Jim Kelly 10/27 W	.60	.25
❑ CG7C Jim Kelly 11/10 W	.60	.25
❑ CG8A Scott Mitchell 10/6 W	.40	.18
❑ CG8B Scott Mitchell 10/27 W	.40	.18
❑ CG8C Scott Mitchell 11/11 L	.40	.18
❑ CG9A Jeff George 9/22 W	.40	.18
❑ CG9B Jeff George 10/20 L	.40	.18
❑ CG9C Jeff George 11/17 L	.40	.18
❑ CG10A Erik Kramer 9/29 L	.20	.09
❑ CG10B Erik Kramer 10/28 L	.20	.09
❑ CG10C Erik Kramer 11/24 L	.20	.09
❑ CG11A Jerry Rice 9/22 L	1.50	.70
❑ CG11B Jerry Rice 10/27 L	1.50	.70
❑ CG11C Jerry Rice 11/17 W	1.50	.70
❑ CG12A Michael Irvin 9/30 L	.60	.25
❑ CG12B Michael Irvin 10/13 L	.60	.25
❑ CG12C Michael Irvin 11/10 L	.60	.25
❑ CG13A J.Galloway 9/22 L	1.00	.45
❑ CG13B J.Galloway 10/27 L	1.00	.45
❑ CG13C J.Galloway 11/24 L	1.00	.45
❑ CG14A Cris Carter 9/29 L	.60	.25
❑ CG14B Cris Carter 11/3 W	.60	.25
❑ CG14C Cris Carter 12/1 W	.60	.25
❑ CG15A Carl Pickens 10/6 L	.60	.25
❑ CG15B Carl Pickens 10/27 W	.60	.25
❑ CG15C Carl Pickens 11/17 W	.60	.25
❑ CG16A H.Moore 9/22 L	.60	.25
❑ CG16B H.Moore 10/13 W	.60	.25
❑ CG16C H.Moore 11/28 L	.60	.25
❑ CG17A Isaac Bruce 10/13 L	.60	.25
❑ CG17B Isaac Bruce 11/10 W	.60	.25
❑ CG17C Isaac Bruce 11/24 W	.60	.25
❑ CG18A Tim Brown 9/22 W	.60	.25
❑ CG18B Tim Brown 10/21L	.60	.25
❑ CG18C Tim Brown 11/24 L	.60	.25
❑ CG19A Keyshawn Johnson 10/6 L	2.00	.90
❑ CG19B Keyshawn Johnson 11/10 L	2.00	.90
❑ CG19C Keyshawn Johnson 12/1 W	2.00	.90
❑ CG20A Terry Glenn 10/13 L	1.25	.55
❑ CG20B Terry Glenn 11/10 W	1.25	.55
❑ CG20C Terry Glenn 12/1 W	1.25	.55
❑ CG21A E.Smith 9/22 W	2.50	1.10
❑ CG21B E.Smith 11/3 W	2.50	1.10
❑ CG21C E.Smith 11/28 W	2.50	1.10
❑ CG22A E.Bennett 10/6 L	.40	.18
❑ CG22B E.Bennett 11/3 L	.40	.18
❑ CG22C E.Bennett 11/18 L	.40	.18
❑ CG23A Chris Warren 10/6 L	.40	.18
❑ CG23B Chris Warren 10/27 W	.40	.18
❑ CG23C Chris Warren 11/17 L	.40	.18
❑ CG24A M.Faulk 9/23 L	.60	.25
❑ CG24B M.Faulk 11/3 L	.60	.25
❑ CG24C M.Faulk 11/24 L	.60	.25
❑ CG25A Curtis Martin 9/22 W	1.00	.45
❑ CG25B Curtis Martin 10/20 W	1.00	.45
❑ CG25C Curtis Martin 12/1 L	1.00	.45
❑ CG26A B.Sanders 9/29 L	3.00	1.35
❑ CG26B B.Sanders 10/17 W	3.00	1.35
❑ CG26C B.Sanders 11/17 W	3.00	1.35
❑ CG27A R.Salaam 9/22 L	.60	.25
❑ CG27B R.Salaam 10/28 W	.60	.25
❑ CG27C R.Salaam 11/17 L	.60	.25
❑ CG28A L.McElroy 9/29 L	.30	.14
❑ CG28B L.McElroy 10/27 L	.30	.14
❑ CG28C L.McElroy 11/17 L	.30	.14
❑ CG29A T.Biakabutuka 9/22 L	.75	.35
❑ CG29B T.Biakabutuka 10/13 L	.75	.35
❑ CG29C T.Biakabutuka 11/3 L	.75	.35
❑ CG30A L.Phillips 9/29 L	.50	.23
❑ CG30B L.Phillips 10/20 L	.50	.23
❑ CG30C L.Phillips 10/27 L	.50	.23

1996 Collector's Choice MVPs

	MINT	NRMT
COMPLETE SET (45)	10.00	4.50
STATED ODDS 1:1 HOBBY, 2:1 SPEC.RET		
*GOLD STARS: 5X TO 12X BASE CARD HI		
TEN GOLDS PER FACTORY SET		
GOLD STATED ODDS 1:35		
❑ M1 Larry Centers	.30	.14
❑ M2 Jeff George	.30	.14
❑ M3 Jim Kelly	.50	.23
❑ M4 Bryce Paup	.15	.07
❑ M5 Kerry Collins	.50	.23
❑ M6 Erik Kramer	.15	.07
❑ M7 Rashaan Salaam	.50	.23
❑ M8 Jeff Blake	.50	.23
❑ M9 Carl Pickens	.50	.23
❑ M10 Vinny Testaverde	.30	.14
❑ M11 Michael Irvin	.50	.23
❑ M12 Emmitt Smith	2.00	.90
❑ M13 John Elway	2.50	1.10
❑ M14 Terrell Davis	3.00	1.35
❑ M15 Herman Moore	.50	.23
❑ M16 Barry Sanders	2.50	1.10
❑ M17 Brett Favre	2.50	1.10
❑ M18 Edgar Bennett	.30	.14
❑ M19 Rodney Thomas	.15	.07
❑ M20 Jim Harbaugh	.30	.14
❑ M21 Marshall Faulk	.50	.23
❑ M22 Mark Brunell	1.25	.55
❑ M23 Steve Bono	.15	.07
❑ M24 Marcus Allen	.50	.23
❑ M25 Dan Marino	2.50	1.10
❑ M26 Bryan Cox	.15	.07
❑ M27 Cris Carter	.50	.23
❑ M28 Curtis Martin	.75	.35
❑ M29 Drew Bledsoe	1.25	.55
❑ M30 Jim Everett	.15	.07
❑ M31 Rodney Hampton	.30	.14
❑ M32 Adrian Murrell	.50	.23
❑ M33 Tim Brown	.50	.23
❑ M34 Rodney Peete	.15	.07
❑ M35 Ricky Watters	.30	.14
❑ M36 Yancey Thigpen	.30	.14
❑ M37 Greg Lloyd	.30	.14
❑ M38 Isaac Bruce	.50	.23
❑ M39 Tony Martin	.30	.14
❑ M40 Junior Seau	.30	.14
❑ M41 Steve Young	1.00	.45
❑ M42 Jerry Rice	1.25	.55
❑ M43 Chris Warren	.30	.14
❑ M44 Errict Rhett	.30	.14
❑ M45 Brian Mitchell	.15	.07

1996 Collector's Choice Stick-Ums

	MINT	NRMT
COMPLETE SET (30)	12.00	5.50
STATED ODDS 1:3		
TEN PER FACTORY SET		
❑ S1 Dan Marino	2.50	1.10
❑ S2 Mike Mamula	.15	.07
❑ S3 Errict Rhett	.30	.14

Card	MINT	NRMT
❑ S4 Drew Bledsoe	1.25	.55
❑ S5 Anthony Smith	.15	.07
❑ S6 Brett Favre UER named spelled Farve	2.50	1.10
❑ S7 Morten Andersen	.15	.07
❑ S8 Deion Sanders	.60	.25
❑ S9 Jeff George	.30	.14
❑ S10 Erik Kramer	.15	.07
❑ S11 Jerry Rice	1.25	.55
❑ S12 Michael Irvin	.50	.23
❑ S13 Greg Lloyd	.30	.14
❑ S14 Cris Carter	.50	.23
❑ S15 Ken Norton	.15	.07
❑ S16 Natrone Means	.50	.23
❑ S17 Robert Brooks	.50	.23
❑ S18 Bomb/Blitz	.15	.07
❑ S19 Kordell Stewart	.75	.35
❑ S20 Referee	.15	.07
❑ S21 Emmitt Smith	2.00	.90
❑ S22 Reggie White	.50	.23
❑ S23 Eric Metcalf	.15	.07
❑ S24 Jesse Sapolu	.15	.07
❑ S25 Curtis Martin	.75	.35
❑ S26 Neil Smith	.15	.07
❑ S27 Junior Seau	.30	.14
❑ S28 TD	.15	.07
❑ S29 Yardmarkers	.15	.07
❑ S30 Terry McDaniel	.15	.07

1996 Collector's Choice Update

	MINT	NRMT
COMPLETE SET (200)	15.00	6.75
COMMON CARD (U1-U200)	.10	.05
SEMISTARS	.20	.09
UNLISTED STARS	.30	.14

Card	MINT	NRMT
❑ U1 Zach Thomas RC	.50	.23
❑ U2 Simeon Rice	.20	.09
❑ U3 Jonathan Ogden	.10	.05
❑ U4 Eric Moulds	.30	.14
❑ U5 Tim Biakabutuka	.50	.23
❑ U6 Walt Harris	.10	.05
❑ U7 Willie Anderson	.10	.05
❑ U8 Ricky Whittle	.10	.05
❑ U9 John Mobley	.10	.05
❑ U10 Reggie Brown	.10	.05
❑ U11 John Michels	.10	.05
❑ U12 Eddie George	1.50	.70
❑ U13 Marvin Harrison	1.25	.55
❑ U14 Kevin Hardy	.20	.09
❑ U15 Kavika Pittman	.10	.05
❑ U16 Daryl Gardener	.10	.05
❑ U17 Duane Clemons	.10	.05
❑ U18 Terry Glenn	.60	.25
❑ U19 Alex Molden RC	.10	.05
❑ U20 Cedric Jones	.10	.05
❑ U21 Keyshawn Johnson	1.00	.45
❑ U22 Rickey Dudley	.30	.14
❑ U23 Jason Dunn	.10	.05
❑ U24 Jamain Stephens	.10	.05
❑ U25 Lawrence Phillips	.30	.14
❑ U26 Bryan Still RC	.30	.14
❑ U27 Israel Ifeanyi	.10	.05
❑ U28 Pete Kendall	.10	.05
❑ U29 Regan Upshaw	.10	.05
❑ U30 Andre Johnson	.10	.05
❑ U31 Leeland McElroy	.30	.14
❑ U32 Ray Lewis	.10	.05
❑ U33 Sean Moran	.10	.05
❑ U34 Muhsin Muhammad RC	.50	.23
❑ U35 Bobby Engram	.30	.14
❑ U36 Marco Battaglia	.10	.05
❑ U37 Stepfret Williams	.10	.05
❑ U38 Jeff Lewis	.20	.09
❑ U39 Derrick Mayes	.20	.09
❑ U40 Reggie Tongue	.10	.05
❑ U41 Tory James	.10	.05
❑ U42 Tony Banks RC	1.00	.45
❑ U43 Tedy Bruschi	.10	.05
❑ U44 Mike Alstott	.60	.25
❑ U45 Anthony Dorsett	.10	.05
❑ U46 Tony Brackens RC	.20	.09
❑ U47 Bryant Mix	.10	.05
❑ U48 Karim Abdul-Jabbar	.40	.18
❑ U49 Moe Williams RC	.20	.09
❑ U50 Lawyer Milloy	.10	.05
❑ U51 Je'rod Cherry	.10	.05
❑ U52 Amani Toomer RC	.30	.14
❑ U53 Alex Van Dyke	.20	.09
❑ U54 Lance Johnstone	.10	.05
❑ U55 Bobby Hoying	.30	.14
❑ U56 Jon Witman RC	.20	.09
❑ U57 Eddie Kennison RC	.30	.14
❑ U58 Brian Roche	.10	.05
❑ U59 Terrell Owens RC	2.00	.90
❑ U60 Stephen Davis	1.50	.70
❑ U61 Jeff George FP	.20	.09
❑ U62 Darick Holmes FP	.10	.05
❑ U63 Kerry Collins FP	.30	.14
❑ U64 Rashaan Salaam FP	.20	.09
❑ U65 Jeff Blake FP	.20	.09
❑ U66 Emmitt Smith FP	.75	.35
❑ U67 Troy Aikman FP	.50	.23
❑ U68 John Elway FP	1.00	.45
❑ U69 Terrell Davis FP	1.25	.55
❑ U70 Barry Sanders FP	1.00	.45
❑ U71 Herman Moore FP	.30	.14
❑ U72 Brett Favre FP	1.00	.45
❑ U73 Robert Brooks FP	.20	.09
❑ U74 Steve McNair FP	.50	.23
❑ U75 Marshall Faulk FP	.20	.09
❑ U76 Marcus Allen FP	.30	.14
❑ U77 Dan Marino FP	1.00	.45
❑ U78 Warren Moon FP	.10	.05
❑ U79 Drew Bledsoe FP	.50	.23
❑ U80 Curtis Martin FP	.50	.23
❑ U81 Mario Bates FP	.20	.09
❑ U82 Tim Brown FP	.20	.09
❑ U83 Charlie Garner FP	.10	.05
❑ U84 Kordell Stewart FP	.50	.23
❑ U85 Isaac Bruce FP	.30	.14
❑ U86 Tony Martin FP	.10	.05
❑ U87 Jerry Rice FP	.50	.23
❑ U88 J.J. Stokes FP	.30	.14
❑ U89 Joey Galloway FP	.50	.23
❑ U90 Errict Rhett FP	.20	.09
❑ U91 Mike Pritchard	.10	.05
❑ U92 Jerome Bettis	.30	.14
❑ U93 Winslow Oliver	.10	.05
❑ U94 David Klingler	.10	.05
❑ U95 Lawrence Dawsey	.10	.05
❑ U96 Charlie Jones	.20	.09
❑ U97 Dave Krieg	.10	.05
❑ U98 Chris Spielman	.10	.05
❑ U99 Stanley Pritchett	.10	.05
❑ U100 Sean Gilbert	.10	.05
❑ U101 Tommy Vardell	.10	.05
❑ U102 DeRon Jenkins	.10	.05
❑ U103 Larry Bowie	.10	.05
❑ U104 Kyle Wachholtz	.10	.05
❑ U105 Brady Smith	.10	.05
❑ U106 Steve Walsh	.10	.05
❑ U107 Wesley Walls	.20	.09
❑ U108 Kevin Ross	.10	.05
❑ U109 Willie Clay	.10	.05
❑ U110 Olanda Truitt	.10	.05
❑ U111 Calvin Williams	.10	.05
❑ U112 Chris Doleman	.10	.05
❑ U113 Irving Fryar	.20	.09
❑ U114 Jimmy Spencer	.10	.05
❑ U115 Reggie Barlow RC	.10	.05
❑ U116 Reggie Brown	.10	.05
❑ U117 Dixon Edwards	.10	.05
❑ U118 Haywood Jeffires	.10	.05
❑ U119 Santana Dotson	.10	.05
❑ U120 Herschel Walker	.20	.09
❑ U121 Darryl Williams	.10	.05
❑ U122 Bryan Cox	.10	.05
❑ U123 Lamar Thomas	.10	.05
❑ U124 Hendrick Lusk	.10	.05
❑ U125 Jahine Arnold	.10	.05
❑ U126 Boomer Esiason	.20	.09
❑ U127 Willie Davis	.10	.05
❑ U128 Pete Stoyanovich	.10	.05
❑ U129 Bill Romanowski	.10	.05
❑ U130 Tim McKyer	.10	.05
❑ U131 Patrick Sapp	.10	.05
❑ U132 Natrone Means	.30	.14
❑ U133 Quinn Early	.10	.05
❑ U134 Leslie O'Neal	.10	.05
❑ U135 Mark Seay	.10	.05
❑ U136 Pete Metzelaars	.10	.05
❑ U137 Jay Leeuwenburg UER name misspelled ...berg	.10	.05
❑ U138 Buster Owens	.10	.05
❑ U139 Todd McNair	.10	.05
❑ U140 Eugene Robinson	.10	.05
❑ U141 Sean Salisbury	.10	.05
❑ U142 Eddie Robinson	.10	.05
❑ U143 Jerris McPhail	.10	.05
❑ U144 Ray Farmer RC	.10	.05
❑ U145 Garrison Hearst	.20	.09
❑ U146 Leonard Russell	.10	.05
❑ U147 Roy Barker	.10	.05
❑ U148 Larry Brown	.10	.05
❑ U149 Webster Slaughter	.10	.05
❑ U150 Roman Oben	.10	.05
❑ U151 LeShon Johnson	.10	.05
❑ U152 Patrick Bates	.10	.05
❑ U153 I.Uwaezuoke RC UER Uwaezoke on back	.30	.14
❑ U154 Scott Slutzker	.10	.05
❑ U155 John Jurkovic	.10	.05
❑ U156 Brian Milne	.10	.05
❑ U157 Mike Sherrard	.10	.05
❑ U158 Neil O'Donnell	.20	.09
❑ U159 Roger Harper	.10	.05
❑ U160 Desmond Howard	.20	.09
❑ U161 Alfred Williams	.10	.05
❑ U162 Ronnie Harmon	.10	.05
❑ U163 Sammie Burroughs RC	.10	.05
❑ U164 Keenan McCardell	.30	.14
❑ U165 Shane Dronett	.10	.05
❑ U166 Jeff Graham	.10	.05
❑ U167 Bill Brooks	.10	.05
❑ U168 Shawn Jefferson	.10	.05
❑ U169 Detron Smith	.10	.05
❑ U170 Danny Kanell	.30	.14
❑ U171 Jevon Langford	.10	.05
❑ U172 Russell Maryland	.10	.05
❑ U173 Scott Milanovich	.10	.05
❑ U174 Eric Davis	.10	.05
❑ U175 Ernie Conwell	.10	.05
❑ U176 Kurt Gouveia	.10	.05
❑ U177 Andre Rison	.20	.09
❑ U178 Harold Green	.10	.05
❑ U179 Frank Reich	.10	.05
❑ U180 Glyn Milburn	.10	.05
❑ U181 Nilo Silvan	.10	.05
❑ U182 Cornelius Bennett	.10	.05

❑ U183 Freddie Solomon	.10	.05
❑ U184 Pat Terrell	.10	.05
❑ U185 Miles Macik	.10	.05
❑ U186 Bo Orlando	.10	.05
❑ U187 Kelvin Martin	.10	.05
❑ U188 Todd Kinchen	.10	.05
❑ U189 Reggie Brooks	.10	.05
❑ U190 Steve Beuerlein UER .. name misspelled Beurlein	.10	.05
❑ U191 Marco Coleman	.10	.05
❑ U192 Johnny Johnson	.10	.05
❑ U193 Dedric Mathis	.10	.05
❑ U194 Leon Searcy	.10	.05
❑ U195 Kevin Greene	.20	.09
❑ U196 Daniel Stubbs	.10	.05
❑ U197 Ray Mickens	.10	.05
❑ U198 Devin Wyman	.10	.05
❑ U199 Lorenzo Lynch	.10	.05
❑ U200 Checklist Card Jerry Rice and Dan Marino ghosted images	.30	.14

1996 Collector's Choice Update Record Breaking Trio

	MINT	NRMT
COMPLETE SET (4)	80.00	36.00
COMMON CARD (1-4)	15.00	6.75
STATED ODDS 1:100		

❑ 1 Joe Montana	15.00	6.75
❑ 2 Dan Marino	30.00	13.50
❑ 3 Jerry Rice	15.00	6.75
❑ 4 Joe Montana Dan Marino Jerry Rice	25.00	11.00

1996 Collector's Choice Update Stick-Ums

	MINT	NRMT
COMPLETE SET (30)	15.00	6.75
STICKER STATED ODDS 1:4		
*MYSTERY BASE: .5X TO 1X BASE CARD HI		
MYSTERY STATED ODDS 1:4		

❑ S1 Jeff George	.40	.18
❑ S2 Darren Bennett	.20	.09
❑ S3 Marcus Allen	.60	.25
❑ S4 Brett Favre	2.00	.90
❑ S5 Carl Pickens	.40	.18
❑ S6 Troy Aikman	1.00	.45
❑ S7 John Elway	2.00	.90
❑ S8 Steve Young	1.00	.45
❑ S9 Norm Johnson	.20	.09
❑ S10 Kordell Stewart	1.00	.45
❑ S11 Drew Bledsoe	1.00	.45
❑ S12 Jim Kelly	.60	.25
❑ S13 Dan Marino	2.00	.90
❑ S14 Joey Galloway	1.00	.45
❑ S15 Lawrence Phillips	.60	.25
❑ S16 Reggie White	.60	.25
❑ S17 Kevin Hardy	.40	.18
❑ S18 Isaac Bruce	.60	.25
❑ S19 Keyshawn Johnson	2.00	.90
❑ S20 Barry Sanders	2.00	.90
❑ S21 Deion Sanders	.60	.25
❑ S22 Emmitt Smith	1.50	.70
❑ S23 Chris Warren	.40	.18
❑ S24 Tim Biakabutuka	1.00	.45
❑ S25 Terry Glenn	1.25	.55
❑ S26 Marshall Faulk	.40	.18
❑ S27 Tamarick Vanover	.20	.09
❑ S28 Curtis Martin	1.00	.45
❑ S29 Terrell Davis	2.50	1.10
❑ S30 Jerry Rice	1.00	.45

1996 Collector's Choice Update You Make The Play

	MINT	NRMT
COMPLETE SET (90)	20.00	9.00
ONE PER PACK		

❑ Y1 Norm Johnson Kick Good	.20	.09
❑ Y2 Jerry Rice Touchdown	1.00	.45
❑ Y3 Dan Marino 9 Yards	2.00	.90
❑ Y4 Marshall Faulk 3 Yards	.40	.18
❑ Y5 Neil Smith Sack - 5 Yards	.20	.09
❑ Y6 Herman Moore 1st Down	.60	.25
❑ Y7 Brett Favre 8 Yards	2.00	.90
❑ Y8 Curtis Martin 5 Yards	1.00	.45
❑ Y9 Reggie White Sack - 8 Yards	.60	.25
❑ Y10 Cris Carter 12 Yards	.60	.25
❑ Y11 Rick Tuten Kick Good	.20	.09
❑ Y12 Steve Young 6 Yards	.75	.35
❑ Y13 Barry Sanders 6 Yards	2.00	.90
❑ Y14 Deion Sanders Interception	.60	.25
❑ Y15 Isaac Bruce 11 Yards	.60	.25
❑ Y16 Troy Aikman 6 Yards	1.00	.45
❑ Y17 Emmitt Smith 7 Yards	1.50	.70
❑ Y18 Junior Seau Fumble	.60	.25
❑ Y19 Joey Galloway 17 Yards	1.00	.45
❑ Y20 Drew Bledsoe 4 Yards	1.00	.45
❑ Y21 Jason Elam Kick No Good	.20	.09
❑ Y22 Edgar Bennett 3 Yards	.40	.18
❑ Y23 Greg Lloyd Fumble	.20	.09
❑ Y24 Tamarick Vanover 13 Yards	.20	.09
❑ Y25 John Elway 5 Yards	2.00	.90
❑ Y26 Larry Centers 4 Yards	.40	.18
❑ Y27 Derrick Thomas Sack - 7 Yards	.60	.25
❑ Y28 Michael Irvin 12 Yards	.60	.25
❑ Y29 Jeff George 3 Yards	.40	.18
❑ Y30 Thurman Thomas 3 Yards	.60	.25
❑ Y31 Darren Bennett Kick Good	.20	.09
❑ Y32 Ken Norton Fumble	.20	.09
❑ Y33 Carl Pickens 14 Yards	.60	.25
❑ Y34 Jeff Blake 10 Yards	.40	.18
❑ Y35 Craig Heyward 3 Yards	.40	.18
❑ Y36 Aeneas Williams No Gain	.20	.09
❑ Y37 Terance Mathis 10 Yards	.40	.18
❑ Y38 Jim Kelly 7 Yards	.60	.25
❑ Y39 Marcus Allen 5 Yards	.60	.25
❑ Y40 Tim McDonald 1 Yard	.20	.09
❑ Y41 Jason Hanson Kick No Good	.20	.09
❑ Y42 Scott Mitchell 4 Yards	.40	.18
❑ Y43 Tim Brown 16 Yards	.40	.18
❑ Y44 Kordell Stewart 3 Yards	1.00	.45
❑ Y45 Eric Metcalf 4 Yards	.40	.18
❑ Y46 Norm Johnson Kick Good	.20	.09
❑ Y47 Jerry Rice 1st Down	1.00	.45
❑ Y48 Dan Marino 1st Down	2.00	.90
❑ Y49 Marshall Faulk 8 Yards	.40	.18
❑ Y50 Neil Smith 2 Yards	.20	.09
❑ Y51 Herman Moore 14 Yards	.60	.25
❑ Y52 Brett Favre 1st Down	2.00	.90
❑ Y53 Curtis Martin 6 Yards	1.00	.45
❑ Y54 Reggie White 2 Yards	.60	.25
❑ Y55 Cris Carter 1st Down	.60	.25
❑ Y56 Rick Tuten Kick No Good	.20	.09
❑ Y57 Steve Young 1st Down	.75	.35
❑ Y58 Barry Sanders 4 Yards	2.00	.90

Y59 Deion Sanders 1 Yard	.60	.25
Y60 Isaac Bruce 1st Down	.60	.25
Y61 Troy Aikman 1st Down	1.00	.45
Y62 Emmitt Smith Touchdown	1.50	.70
Y63 Junior Seau -2 Yards	.60	.25
Y64 Joey Galloway 1st Down	1.00	.45
Y65 Drew Bledsoe 1st Down	1.00	.45
Y66 Jason Elam Kick Good	.20	.09
Y67 Edgar Bennett 4 Yards	.40	.18
Y68 Greg Lloyd -4 Yards	.20	.09
Y69 Tamarick Vanover 15 Yards	.20	.09
Y70 John Elway 1st Down	2.00	.90
Y71 Larry Centers 7 Yards	.40	.18
Y72 Derrick Thomas No Gain	.60	.25
Y73 Michael Irvin 1st Down	.60	.25
Y74 Jeff George 12 Yards	.40	.18
Y75 Thurman Thomas 5 Yards	.60	.25
Y76 Darren Bennett Kick No Good	.20	.09
Y77 Ken Norton -3 Yards	.20	.09
Y78 Carl Pickens 1st Down	.60	.25
Y79 Jeff Blake 1st Down	.40	.18
Y80 Craig Heyward 5 Yards	.40	.18
Y81 Aeneas Williams -3 Yards	.20	.09
Y82 Terance Mathis 14 Yards	.40	.18
Y83 Jim Kelly 1st Down	.60	.25
Y84 Marcus Allen 6 Yards	.60	.25
Y85 Tim McDonald No Gain	.20	.09
Y86 Jason Hanson Kick Good	.20	.09
Y87 Scott Mitchell 7 Yards	.40	.18
Y88 Tim Brown 1st Down	.40	.18
Y89 Kordell Stewart 7 Yards	1.00	.45
Y90 Eric Metcalf 7 Yards	.40	.18

1997 Collector's Choice

	MINT	NRMT
COMPLETE SET (565)	35.00	16.00
COMP.SERIES 1 (310)	20.00	9.00
COMP.FACT.SER.1(330)	30.00	13.50
COMP.SERIES 2 (255)	15.00	6.75
COMMON CARD (1-565)	.10	.05
SEMISTARS	.20	.09
UNLISTED STARS	.40	.18
1 Orlando Pace RC	.10	.05
2 Darrell Russell RC	.10	.05
3 Shawn Springs RC	.20	.09
4 Peter Boulware RC	.20	.09
5 Bryant Westbrook RC	.10	.05
6 Tom Knight RC	.10	.05
7 Ike Hilliard RC	.75	.35
8 James Farrior RC	.10	.05
9 Chris Naeole RC	.10	.05
10 Michael Booker RC	.10	.05
11 Warrick Dunn RC UER (no card number on back)	1.25	.55
12 Tony Gonzalez RC	1.25	.55
13 Reinard Wilson RC	.10	.05
14 Yatil Green RC	.20	.09
15 Reidel Anthony RC	.75	.35
16 Kenard Lang RC	.10	.05
17 Kenny Holmes RC	.10	.05
18 Tarik Glenn RC	.10	.05
19 Dwayne Rudd RC	.10	.05
20 Renaldo Wynn RC	.10	.05
21 David LaFleur RC	.20	.09
22 Antowain Smith RC	1.00	.45
23 Jim Druckenmiller RC	.60	.25
24 Rae Carruth RC	.40	.18
25 Jared Tomich RC	.10	.05
26 Chris Canty RC	.10	.05
27 Jake Plummer RC	3.00	1.35
28 Troy Davis RC	.40	.18
29 Sedrick Shaw RC	.40	.18
30 Jamie Sharper RC	.10	.05
31 Tiki Barber RC	.60	.25
32 Byron Hanspard RC	.75	.35
33 Darnell Autry RC	.20	.09
34 Corey Dillon RC	1.50	.70
35 Joey Kent RC	.40	.18
36 Nathan Davis RC	.10	.05
37 Will Blackwell RC	.40	.18
38 Kim Herring RC	.10	.05
39 Pat Barnes RC	.40	.18
40 Kevin Lockett RC	.20	.09
41 Trevor Pryce RC	.10	.05
42 Matt Russell RC	.10	.05
43 Greg Jones RC	.10	.05
44 Antonio Anderson RC	.10	.05
45 George Jones RC	.20	.09
46 Steve Young NG	.40	.18
47 Jerry Rice NG	.50	.23
48 Curtis Conway NG	.10	.05
49 Jeff Blake NG	.20	.09
50 Carl Pickens NG	.20	.09
51 Bruce Smith NG	.10	.05
52 John Elway NG	1.00	.45
53 Terrell Davis NG	.75	.35
54 Shannon Sharpe NG	.10	.05
55 Junior Seau NG	.10	.05
56 Darren Bennett NG	.10	.05
57 Jim Harbaugh NG	.20	.09
58 Marshall Faulk NG	.40	.18
59 Emmitt Smith NG	.75	.35
60 Troy Aikman NG	.50	.23
61 Deion Sanders NG	.40	.18
62 Dan Marino NG	1.00	.45
63 Ricky Watters NG	.10	.05
64 Mark Brunell NG	.50	.23
65 Keenan McCardell NG	.10	.05
66 Keyshawn Johnson NG	.40	.18
67 Barry Sanders NG	1.00	.45
68 Herman Moore NG	.20	.09
69 Eddie George NG	.50	.23
70 Steve McNair NG	.40	.18
71 Brett Favre NG	1.00	.45
72 Reggie White NG	.20	.09
73 Edgar Bennett NG	.10	.05
74 Kerry Collins NG	.20	.09
75 Kevin Greene NG	.10	.05
76 Drew Bledsoe NG	.50	.23
77 Terry Glenn NG	.20	.09
78 Curtis Martin NG	.40	.18
79 Jeff Hostetler NG	.10	.05
80 Napoleon Kaufman NG	.40	.18
81 Isaac Bruce NG	.40	.18
82 Terry Allen NG	.20	.09
83 Joey Galloway NG	.40	.18
84 Kordell Stewart NG	.40	.18
85 Jerome Bettis NG	.40	.18
86 Dana Stubblefield	.10	.05
87 Merton Hanks	.10	.05
88 Terrell Owens	.40	.18
89 Brent Jones	.20	.09
90 Ken Norton Jr.	.10	.05
91 Jerry Rice	1.00	.45
92 Terry Kirby	.20	.09
93 Bryant Young	.10	.05
94 Raymont Harris	.10	.05
95 Jeff Jaeger	.10	.05
96 Curtis Conway	.20	.09
97 Walt Harris	.10	.05
98 Bobby Engram	.20	.09
99 Donnell Woolford	.10	.05
100 Rashaan Salaam	.10	.05
101 Jeff Blake	.20	.09
102 Tony McGee	.10	.05
103 Ashley Ambrose	.10	.05
104 Dan Wilkinson	.10	.05
105 Jevon Langford	.10	.05
106 Darnay Scott	.20	.09
107 David Dunn	.10	.05
108 Eric Moulds	.40	.18
109 Darick Holmes	.10	.05
110 Thurman Thomas	.40	.18
111 Quinn Early	.10	.05
112 Jim Kelly	.40	.18
113 Bryce Paup	.10	.05
114 Bruce Smith	.20	.09
115 Todd Collins	.10	.05
116 Tory James	.10	.05
117 Anthony Miller	.10	.05
118 Terrell Davis	1.50	.70
119 Tyrone Braxton	.10	.05
120 John Mobley	.10	.05
121 Bill Romanowski	.10	.05
122 Vaughn Hebron	.10	.05
123 Mike Alstott	.40	.18
124 Errict Rhett	.10	.05
125 Trent Dilfer	.40	.18
126 Courtney Hawkins	.10	.05
127 Hardy Nickerson	.10	.05
128 Donnie Abraham RC	.10	.05
129 Regan Upshaw	.10	.05
130 Kent Graham	.10	.05
131 Rob Moore	.20	.09
132 Simeon Rice	.20	.09
133 LeShon Johnson	.10	.05
134 Frank Sanders	.20	.09
135 Leeland McElroy	.10	.05
136 Seth Joyner	.10	.05
137 Andre Coleman	.10	.05
138 Stan Humphries	.20	.09
139 Charlie Jones	.20	.09
140 Junior Seau	.20	.09
141 Rodney Harrison	.10	.05
142 Darrien Gordon	.10	.05
143 Terrell Fletcher	.10	.05
144 Tamarick Vanover	.20	.09
145 Greg Hill	.10	.05
146 Marcus Allen	.40	.18
147 Lake Dawson	.10	.05
148 Dale Carter	.10	.05
149 Kimble Anders	.20	.09
150 Chris Penn	.10	.05
151 Sean Dawkins	.10	.05
152 Ken Dilger	.10	.05
153 Marvin Harrison	.40	.18
154 Jeff Herrod	.10	.05
155 Jim Harbaugh	.20	.09
156 Cary Blanchard	.10	.05
157 Aaron Bailey	.10	.05
158 Deion Sanders	.40	.18
159 Jim Schwantz RC	.10	.05
160 Michael Irvin	.40	.18
161 Herschel Walker	.20	.09
162 Emmitt Smith	1.50	.70
163 Chris Boniol	.10	.05

❑ 164 Eric Bjornson .10 .05
❑ 165 Karim Abdul-Jabbar .40 .18
❑ 166 O.J. McDuffie .20 .09
❑ 167 Troy Drayton .10 .05
❑ 168 Zach Thomas .20 .09
❑ 169 Irving Spikes .10 .05
❑ 170 Shane Burton .10 .05
❑ 171 Stanley Pritchett .10 .05
❑ 172 Ty Detmer .20 .09
❑ 173 Chris T. Jones .10 .05
❑ 174 Troy Vincent .10 .05
❑ 175 Brian Dawkins .10 .05
❑ 176 Irving Fryar .20 .09
❑ 177 Charlie Garner .10 .05
❑ 178 Bobby Taylor .10 .05
❑ 179 Jamal Anderson .60 .25
❑ 180 Terance Mathis .20 .09
❑ 181 Craig Heyward .10 .05
❑ 182 Cornelius Bennett .10 .05
❑ 183 Jessie Tuggle .10 .05
❑ 184 Devin Bush .10 .05
❑ 185 Dave Brown .10 .05
❑ 186 Danny Kanell .20 .09
❑ 187 Rodney Hampton .20 .09
❑ 188 Tyrone Wheatley .20 .09
❑ 189 Amani Toomer .20 .09
❑ 190 Phillippi Sparks .10 .05
❑ 191 Thomas Lewis .10 .05
❑ 192 Jimmy Smith .20 .09
❑ 193 Pete Mitchell .10 .05
❑ 194 Natrone Means .40 .18
❑ 195 Mark Brunell 1.00 .45
❑ 196 Kevin Hardy .10 .05
❑ 197 Tony Brackens .10 .05
❑ 198 Aaron Beasley .10 .05
❑ 199 Chris Hudson .10 .05
❑ 200 Wayne Chrebet .40 .18
❑ 201 Keyshawn Johnson .40 .18
❑ 202 Adrian Murrell .20 .09
❑ 203 Neil O'Donnell .20 .09
❑ 204 Hugh Douglas .10 .05
❑ 205 Mo Lewis .10 .05
❑ 206 Glenn Foley .10 .05
❑ 207 Aaron Glenn .10 .05
❑ 208 Johnnie Morton .20 .09
❑ 209 Reggie Brown LB .20 .09
❑ 210 Barry Sanders 2.00 .90
❑ 211 Glyn Milburn .10 .05
❑ 212 Bennie Blades .10 .05
❑ 213 Steve McNair .50 .23
❑ 214 Frank Wycheck .10 .05
❑ 215 Chris Sanders .10 .05
❑ 216 Blaine Bishop .10 .05
❑ 217 Willie Davis .10 .05
❑ 218 Darryll Lewis .10 .05
❑ 219 Marcus Robertson .10 .05
❑ 220 Robert Brooks .20 .09
❑ 221 Antonio Freeman .50 .23
❑ 222 Keith Jackson .10 .05
❑ 223 Mark Chmura .20 .09
❑ 224 Brett Favre 2.00 .90
❑ 225 Sean Jones .10 .05
❑ 226 Reggie White .40 .18
❑ 227 LeRoy Butler .10 .05
❑ 228 Craig Newsome .10 .05
❑ 229 Wesley Walls .20 .09
❑ 230 Mark Carrier WR .10 .05
❑ 231 Muhsin Muhammad .20 .09
❑ 232 John Kasay .10 .05
❑ 233 Anthony Johnson .10 .05
❑ 234 Kerry Collins .20 .09
❑ 235 Kevin Greene .20 .09
❑ 236 Sam Mills .10 .05
❑ 237 Ben Coates .20 .09
❑ 238 Terry Glenn .40 .18
❑ 239 Willie McGinest .10 .05
❑ 240 Ted Johnson .10 .05
❑ 241 Lawyer Milloy .10 .05
❑ 242 Drew Bledsoe 1.00 .45
❑ 243 Willie Clay .10 .05
❑ 244 Chris Slade .10 .05
❑ 245 Tim Brown .40 .18
❑ 246 Daryl Hobbs .10 .05
❑ 247 Rickey Dudley .20 .09
❑ 248 Joe Aska .10 .05
❑ 249 Chester McGlockton .10 .05
❑ 250 Rob Fredrickson .10 .05
❑ 251 Terry McDaniel .10 .05
❑ 252 Tony Banks .20 .09
❑ 253 Lawrence Phillips .10 .05
❑ 254 Isaac Bruce .40 .18
❑ 255 Eddie Kennison .20 .09
❑ 256 Kevin Carter .10 .05
❑ 257 Roman Phifer .10 .05
❑ 258 Keith Lyle .10 .05
❑ 259 Vinny Testaverde .20 .09
❑ 260 Derrick Alexander WR .20 .09
❑ 261 Ray Lewis .10 .05
❑ 262 Jermaine Lewis .40 .18
❑ 263 Byron Bam Morris .10 .05
❑ 264 Stevon Moore .10 .05
❑ 265 Antonio Langham .10 .05
❑ 266 Brian Mitchell .10 .05
❑ 267 Henry Ellard .10 .05
❑ 268 Leslie Shepherd .10 .05
❑ 269 Michael Westbrook .20 .09
❑ 270 Jamie Asher .10 .05
❑ 271 Ken Harvey .10 .05
❑ 272 Gus Frerotte .10 .05
❑ 273 Michael Haynes .10 .05
❑ 274 Ray Zellars .10 .05
❑ 275 Jim Everett .10 .05
❑ 276 Tyrone Hughes .10 .05
❑ 277 Joe Johnson .10 .05
❑ 278 Eric Allen .10 .05
❑ 279 Brady Smith .10 .05
❑ 280 Mario Bates .10 .05
❑ 281 Torrance Small .10 .05
❑ 282 John Friesz .10 .05
❑ 283 Brian Blades .10 .05
❑ 284 Chris Warren .20 .09
❑ 285 Joey Galloway .50 .23
❑ 286 Michael Sinclair .10 .05
❑ 287 Lamar Smith .10 .05
❑ 288 Mike Pritchard .10 .05
❑ 289 Jerome Bettis .40 .18
❑ 290 Charles Johnson .20 .09
❑ 291 Mike Tomczak .10 .05
❑ 292 Levon Kirkland .10 .05
❑ 293 Carnell Lake .10 .05
❑ 294 Erric Pegram .10 .05
❑ 295 Kordell Stewart .50 .23
❑ 296 Greg Lloyd .10 .05
❑ 297 Dixon Edwards .10 .05
❑ 298 Cris Carter .40 .18
❑ 299 Brad Johnson .50 .23
❑ 300 Qadry Ismail .20 .09
❑ 301 John Randle .10 .05
❑ 302 Orlanda Thomas .10 .05
❑ 303 Dewayne Washington .10 .05
❑ 304 Jake Reed .20 .09
❑ 305 Derrick Alexander DE .10 .05
❑ 306 Eddie George CL .40 .18
❑ 307 Dan Marino CL .40 .18
❑ 308 Curtis Martin CL .20 .09
❑ 309 Troy Aikman CL .40 .18
❑ 310 Marcus Allen CL .40 .18
❑ 311 Jim Druckenmiller .40 .18
❑ 312 Greg Clark RC .10 .05
❑ 313 Darnell Autry .20 .09
❑ 314 Reinard Wilson .10 .05
❑ 315 Corey Dillon .75 .35
❑ 316 Antowain Smith .50 .23
❑ 317 Trevor Pryce .10 .05
❑ 318 Warrick Dunn .50 .23
❑ 319 Reidel Anthony .50 .23
❑ 320 Jake Plummer 1.50 .70
❑ 321 Tom Knight .10 .05
❑ 322 Freddie Jones RC .20 .09
❑ 323 Tony Gonzalez .50 .23
❑ 324 Pat Barnes .20 .09
❑ 325 Kevin Lockett .20 .09
❑ 326 Tarik Glenn .10 .05
❑ 327 David LaFleur .20 .09
❑ 328 Antonio Anderson .10 .05
❑ 329 Yatil Green .20 .09
❑ 330 Jason Taylor RC .10 .05
❑ 331 Brian Manning RC .10 .05
❑ 332 Michael Booker .10 .05
❑ 333 Byron Hanspard .40 .18
❑ 334 Ike Hilliard .40 .18
❑ 335 Tiki Barber .40 .18
❑ 336 Renaldo Wynn .10 .05
❑ 337 Damon Jones RC .10 .05
❑ 338 James Farrior .10 .05
❑ 339 Dedric Ward RC .75 .35
❑ 340 Bryant Westbrook .10 .05
❑ 341 Joey Kent .40 .18
❑ 342 Kenny Holmes .10 .05
❑ 343 Darren Sharper RC .10 .05
❑ 344 Rae Carruth .20 .09
❑ 345 Chris Canty .10 .05
❑ 346 Darrell Russell .10 .05
❑ 347 Orlando Pace .10 .05
❑ 348 Peter Boulware .20 .09
❑ 349 Kenard Lang .10 .05
❑ 350 Danny Wuerffel RC .60 .25
❑ 351 Troy Davis .40 .18
❑ 352 Shawn Springs .20 .09
❑ 353 Walter Jones RC .10 .05
❑ 354 Will Blackwell .40 .18
❑ 355 Dwayne Rudd .10 .05
❑ 356 49ers BB .10 .05
Jerry Rice
Steve Young
Ken Norton
Jim Druckenmiller
Bryant Young
❑ 357 Bears BB .10 .05
Bobby Engram
Rick Mirer
Raymont Harris
Curtis Conway
Bryan Cox
❑ 358 Bengals BB .10 .05
Ki-Jana Carter
Jeff Blake
Carl Pickens
Dan Wilkinson
Darnay Scott
❑ 359 Bills BB .10 .05
Thurman Thomas
Todd Collins
Antowain Smith
Bruce Smth
Chris Spielman
❑ 360 Broncos BB .10 .05
Terrell Davis
John Elway
Shannon Sharpe
Neil Smith
Rod Smith WR
❑ 361 Buccaneers BB .10 .05
Warrick Dunn
Trent Dilfer
Errict Rhett
Hardy Nickerson
Reidel Anthony
❑ 362 Cardinals BB .10 .05
Frank Sanders
Eric Swann
Jake Plummer
Kent Graham
Rob Moore
❑ 363 Chargers BB .10 .05
Tony Martin
Stan Humphries
Junior Seau
Eric Metcalf
Freddie Jones
❑ 364 Chiefs BB .10 .05
Marcus Allen
Kevin Lockett
Tony Gonzalez
Pat Barnes
Elvis Grbac
Derrick Thomas
Eric Hill
❑ 365 Colts BB .10 .05
Marvin Harrison
Jim Harbaugh
Marshall Faulk
Quentin Coryatt
Sean Dawkins
❑ 366 Cowboys BB .10 .05
Emmitt Smith
Troy Aikman
Deion Sanders

Michael Irvin
David LaFleur
❑ 367 Dolphins BB .10 .05
Dan Marino
Troy Drayton
Karim Abdul-Jabbar
Zach Thomas
O.J. McDuffie
❑ 368 Eagles BB .10 .05
Chris T. Jones
Ricky Watters
Ty Detmer
Irving Fryar
Mike Mamula
❑ 369 Falcons BB .10 .05
Byron Hanspard
Jamal Anderson
Cornelius Bennett
Ray Buchanan
Terence Mathis
❑ 370 Giants BB .10 .05
Ike Hilliard
Dave Brown
Rodney Hampton
Tyrone Wheatley
Phillippi Sparks
❑ 371 Jaguars BB .10 .05
Keenan McCardell
Mark Brunell
Kevin Hardy
Renaldo Wynn
Natrone Means
❑ 372 Jets BB .10 .05
Keyshawn Johnson
Neil O'Donnell
James Farrior
Adrian Murrell
Wayne Chrebet
❑ 373 Lions BB .10 .05
Barry Sanders
Bryant Westbrook
Herman Moore
Johnnie Morton
Scott Mitchell
❑ 374 Oilers BB .10 .05
Eddie George
Steve McNair
Joey Kent
Chris Sanders
Blaine Bishop
❑ 375 Packers BB .40 .18
Robert Brooks
Brett Favre
Reggie White
Dorsey Levens
Derrick Mayes
❑ 376 Panthers BB .10 .05
Tim Biakabutuka
Kerry Collins
Rae Carruth
Sam Mills
Anthony Johnson
❑ 377 Patriots BB .10 .05
Terry Glenn
Drew Bledsoe
Curtis Martin
Willie McGinest
Ben Coates
❑ 378 Raiders BB .10 .05
Tim Brown
Jeff George
Napoleon Kaufman
Darrell Russell
Desmond Howard
❑ 379 Rams BB .10 .05
Eddie Kennison
Tony Banks
Isaac Bruce
Orlando Pace
Lawrence Phillips
❑ 380 Ravens BB .10 .05
Vinny Testaverde
Peter Boulware
Michael Jackson
Byron Bam Morris
Derrick Alexander WR

❑ 381 Redskins BB .10 .05
Brian Mitchell
Gus Frerotte
Terry Allen
Sean Gilbert
Michael Westbrook
❑ 382 Saints BB .10 .05
Heath Shuler
Daryl Hobbs
Troy Davis
Wayne Martin
Mario Bates
❑ 383 Seahawks BB .10 .05
Joey Galloway
Chris Warren
Shawn Springs
Cortez Kennedy
Warren Moon
❑ 384 Steelers BB .10 .05
Jerome Bettis
Kordell Stewart
Greg Lloyd
Charles Johnson
Will Blackwell
❑ 385 Vikings BB .10 .05
Jake Reed
Cris Carter
Brad Johnson
Robert Smith
John Randle
❑ 386 William Floyd .20 .09
❑ 387 Steve Young .60 .25
❑ 388 Lee Woodall .10 .05
❑ 389 J.J. Stokes .20 .09
❑ 390 Marc Edwards .10 .05
❑ 391 Rod Woodson .20 .09
❑ 392 Jim Schwantz .10 .05
❑ 393 Garrison Hearst .20 .09
❑ 394 Rick Mirer .10 .05
❑ 395 Alonzo Spellman .10 .05
❑ 396 Tom Carter .10 .05
❑ 397 Bryan Cox .10 .05
❑ 398 John Allred RC .10 .05
❑ 399 Ricky Proehl .10 .05
❑ 400 Tyrone Hughes .10 .05
❑ 401 Carl Pickens .40 .18
❑ 402 Tremain Mack RC .10 .05
❑ 403 Boomer Esiason .20 .09
❑ 404 Ki-Jana Carter .10 .05
❑ 405 Steve Tovar .10 .05
❑ 406 Billy Joe Hobert .20 .09
❑ 407 Andre Reed .20 .09
❑ 408 Marcelius Wiley RC .10 .05
❑ 409 Steve Tasker .10 .05
❑ 410 Chris Spielman .10 .05
❑ 411 Alfred Williams .10 .05
❑ 412 John Elway 2.00 .90
❑ 413 Shannon Sharpe .20 .09
❑ 414 Steve Atwater .10 .05
❑ 415 Neil Smith .20 .09
❑ 416 Darrien Gordon .10 .05
❑ 417 Jeff Lewis .10 .05
❑ 418 Flipper Anderson .10 .05
❑ 419 Willie Green .10 .05
❑ 420 Jackie Harris .10 .05
❑ 421 Steve Walsh .10 .05
❑ 422 Anthony Parker .10 .05
❑ 423 Ronde Barber RC .10 .05
❑ 424 Warren Sapp .20 .09
❑ 425 Aeneas Williams .10 .05
❑ 426 Larry Centers .20 .09
❑ 427 Eric Swann .10 .05
❑ 428 Kevin Williams .10 .05
❑ 429 Darren Bennett .10 .05
❑ 430 Tony Martin .20 .09
❑ 431 John Carney .10 .05
❑ 432 Jim Everett .10 .05
❑ 433 William Fuller .10 .05
❑ 434 Latario Rachal RC .10 .05
❑ 435 Erric Pegram .10 .05
❑ 436 Eric Metcalf .20 .09
❑ 437 Jerome Woods .10 .05
❑ 438 Derrick Thomas .20 .09
❑ 439 Elvis Grbac .20 .09
❑ 440 Terry Wooden .10 .05
❑ 441 Andre Rison .20 .09

❑ 442 Brett Perriman .10 .05
❑ 443 Paul Justin .10 .05
❑ 444 Robert Blackmon .10 .05
❑ 445 Carlton Gray .10 .05
❑ 446 Chris Gardocki .10 .05
❑ 447 Marshall Faulk .40 .18
❑ 448 Sammie Burroughs .10 .05
❑ 449 Quentin Coryatt .10 .05
❑ 450 Troy Aikman 1.00 .45
❑ 451 Daryl Johnston .20 .09
❑ 452 Tony Tolbert .10 .05
❑ 453 Brock Marion .10 .05
❑ 454 Billy Davis RC .10 .05
❑ 455 Stepfret Williams .10 .05
❑ 456 Anthony Miller .10 .05
❑ 457 Dan Marino 2.00 .90
❑ 458 Jerris McPhail .10 .05
❑ 459 Terrell Buckley .10 .05
❑ 460 Daryl Gardener .10 .05
❑ 461 George Teague .10 .05
❑ 462 Derrick Rodgers RC .10 .05
❑ 463 Fred Barnett .10 .05
❑ 464 Darrin Smith .10 .05
❑ 465 Michael Timpson .10 .05
❑ 466 Jon Harris .10 .05
❑ 467 Jason Dunn .10 .05
❑ 468 Bobby Hoying .20 .09
❑ 469 Ricky Watters .20 .09
❑ 470 Derrick Witherspoon .10 .05
❑ 471 Chris Chandler .20 .09
❑ 472 Ray Buchanan .10 .05
❑ 473 Michael Haynes .10 .05
❑ 474 O.J. Santiago RC .40 .18
❑ 475 Morten Andersen .10 .05
❑ 476 Bert Emanuel .20 .09
❑ 477 Chris Calloway .10 .05
❑ 478 Jason Sehorn .20 .09
❑ 479 John Jurkovic .10 .05
❑ 480 Keenan McCardell .20 .09
❑ 481 James O. Stewart .20 .09
❑ 482 Rob Johnson .40 .18
❑ 483 Mike Logan RC .10 .05
❑ 484 Deon Figures .10 .05
❑ 485 Kyle Brady .10 .05
❑ 486 Alex Van Dyke .10 .05
❑ 487 Jeff Graham .10 .05
❑ 488 Jason Hanson .10 .05
❑ 489 Herman Moore .40 .18
❑ 490 Scott Mitchell .20 .09
❑ 491 Tommy Vardell .10 .05
❑ 492 Derrick Mason RC .10 .05
❑ 493 Rodney Thomas .10 .05
❑ 494 Ronnie Harmon .10 .05
❑ 495 Eddie George 1.00 .45
❑ 496 Edgar Bennett .20 .09
❑ 497 William Henderson .10 .05
❑ 498 Dorsey Levens .40 .18
❑ 499 Gilbert Brown .10 .05
❑ 500 Steve Bono .20 .09
❑ 501 Derrick Mayes .20 .09
❑ 502 Fred Lane RC .60 .25
❑ 503 Ernie Mills .10 .05
❑ 504 Tim Biakabutuka .20 .09
❑ 505 Michael Bates .10 .05
❑ 506 Winslow Oliver .10 .05
❑ 507 Ty Law .10 .05
❑ 508 Shawn Jefferson .10 .05
❑ 509 Vincent Brisby .10 .05
❑ 510 Henry Thomas .10 .05
❑ 511 Tedy Bruschi .10 .05
❑ 512 Curtis Martin .50 .23
❑ 513 Jeff George .20 .09
❑ 514 Desmond Howard .20 .09
❑ 515 Napoleon Kaufman .40 .18
❑ 516 Kenny Shedd RC .10 .05
❑ 517 Russell Maryland .10 .05
❑ 518 Lance Johnstone .10 .05
❑ 519 Eric Turner .10 .05
❑ 520 Dexter McLeon RC .10 .05
❑ 521 Craig Heyward .10 .05
❑ 522 Ryan McNeil .10 .05
❑ 523 Mark Rypien .10 .05
❑ 524 Mike Jones LB .10 .05
❑ 525 Jamie Sharper .10 .05
❑ 526 Tony Siragusa .10 .05
❑ 527 Michael Jackson .20 .09

❑ 528 Floyd Turner .10 .05
❑ 529 Eric Green .10 .05
❑ 530 Michael McCrary .10 .05
❑ 531 Jay Graham RC .40 .18
❑ 532 Terry Allen .40 .18
❑ 533 Sean Gilbert .10 .05
❑ 534 Scott Turner .10 .05
❑ 535 Cris Dishman .10 .05
❑ 536 Darrell Green .20 .09
❑ 537 Stephen Davis .50 .23
❑ 538 Alvin Harper .10 .05
❑ 539 Daryl Hobbs .10 .05
❑ 540 Wayne Martin .10 .05
❑ 541 Heath Shuler .10 .05
❑ 542 Andre Hastings .10 .05
❑ 543 Jared Tomich .10 .05
❑ 544 Nicky Savoie RC .10 .05
❑ 545 Cortez Kennedy .10 .05
❑ 546 Warren Moon .40 .18
❑ 547 Chad Brown .10 .05
❑ 548 Willie Williams .10 .05
❑ 549 Bennie Blades .10 .05
❑ 550 Darren Perry .10 .05
❑ 551 Mark Bruener .10 .05
❑ 552 Yancey Thigpen .20 .09
❑ 553 Courtney Hawkins .10 .05
❑ 554 Chad Scott .10 .05
❑ 555 George Jones .20 .09
❑ 556 Robert Tate RC .10 .05
❑ 557 Torrian Gray RC .10 .05
❑ 558 Robert Griffith .10 .05
❑ 559 Leroy Hoard .10 .05
❑ 560 Robert Smith .20 .09
❑ 561 Randall Cunningham .40 .18
❑ 562 Darrell Russell CL .10 .05
❑ 563 Troy Aikman CL .40 .18
❑ 564 Dan Marino CL .40 .18
❑ 565 Jim Druckenmiller CL .40 .18

1997 Collector's Choice Crash the Game

	MINT	NRMT
COMPLETE SET (90)	60.00	27.00
COMP.SHORT SET (30)	20.00	9.00

STATED ODDS 1:5 SERIES 1
THREE GAME DATES PER PLAYER

COMP.PRIZE SET (19)	30.00	13.50

*PRIZE STARS: 1X TO 2.5X BASE CARD HI
*PRIZE ROOKIES: .5X TO 1X BASE CARD HI

❑ 1A Troy Aikman 10/13 W 1.50 .70
❑ 1B Troy Aikman 11/2 W 1.50 .70
❑ 1C Troy Aikman 11/27 W 1.50 .70
❑ 2A Dan Marino 9/21 W 3.00 1.35
❑ 2B Dan Marino 11/17 W 3.00 1.35
❑ 2C Dan Marino 11/30 W 3.00 1.35
❑ 3A Steve Young 9/29 W 1.00 .45
❑ 3B Steve Young 11/2 L 1.00 .45
❑ 3C Steve Young 11/23 W 1.00 .45
❑ 4A Brett Favre 10/5 W 3.00 1.35
❑ 4B Brett Favre 10/27 W 3.00 1.35
❑ 4C Brett Favre 12/1 W 3.00 1.35
❑ 5A Drew Bledsoe 10/6 W 1.50 .70
❑ 5B Drew Bledsoe 11/9 W 1.50 .70
❑ 5C Drew Bledsoe 11/23 L 1.50 .70
❑ 6A Jeff Blake 9/28 W .30 .14
❑ 6B Jeff Blake 10/19 L .30 .14
❑ 6C Jeff Blake 11/30 L .30 .14
❑ 7A Mark Brunell 9/22 W 1.50 .70
❑ 7B Mark Brunell 10/19 W 1.50 .70
❑ 7C Mark Brunell 11/16 W 1.50 .70
❑ 8A John Elway 10/6 W 3.00 1.35
❑ 8B John Elway 11/9 W 3.00 1.35
❑ 8C John Elway 11/30 W 3.00 1.35
❑ 9A Vinny Testaverde 9/28 W .30 .14
❑ 9B Vinny Testaverde 10/19 W .30 .14
❑ 9C Vinny Testaverde 11/9 L .30 .14
❑ 10A Steve McNair 10/12 W .75 .35
❑ 10B Steve McNair 10/26 W .75 .35
❑ 10C Steve McNair 11/27 W .75 .35
❑ 11A Jerry Rice 9/29 L 1.50 .70
❑ 11B Jerry Rice 10/12 L 1.50 .70
❑ 11C Jerry Rice 11/10 L 1.50 .70
❑ 12A Terry Glenn 10/12 L .60 .25
❑ 12B Terry Glenn 10/27 L .60 .25
❑ 12C Terry Glenn 11/16 L .60 .25
❑ 13A Michael Jackson 10/5 L .30 .14
❑ 13B Michael Jackson 11/9 L .30 .14
❑ 13C Michael Jackson 11/23 L .30 .14
❑ 14A Tony Martin 9/21 L .30 .14
❑ 14B Tony Martin 10/16 L .30 .14
❑ 14C Tony Martin 11/16 L .30 .14
❑ 15A Isaac Bruce 9/28 L .60 .25
❑ 15B Isaac Bruce 10/12 L .60 .25
❑ 15C Isaac Bruce 11/16 L .60 .25
❑ 16A Cris Carter 9/28 W .60 .25
❑ 16B Cris Carter 11/16 L .60 .25
❑ 16C Cris Carter 12/1 L .60 .25
❑ 17A Shannon Sharpe 10/19 L .30 .14
❑ 17B Shannon Sharpe 11/2 L .30 .14
❑ 17C Shannon Sharpe 11/30 L .30 .14
❑ 18A Rae Carruth 9/29 W .30 .14
❑ 18B Rae Carruth 10/26 L .30 .14
❑ 18C Rae Carruth 11/9 L .30 .14
❑ 19A Ike Hilliard 10/5 L .60 .25
❑ 19B Ike Hilliard 10/19 L .60 .25
❑ 19C Ike Hilliard 11/23 L .60 .25
❑ 20A Yatil Green 9/21 L .15 .07
❑ 20B Yatil Green 10/5 L .15 .07
❑ 20C Yatil Green 11/17 L .15 .07
❑ 21A Terry Allen 10/5 W .60 .25
❑ 21B Terry Allen 10/13 L .60 .25
❑ 21C Terry Allen 11/23 L .60 .25
❑ 22A Emmitt Smith 10/19 W 2.50 1.10
❑ 22B Emmitt Smith 11/16 L 2.50 1.10
❑ 22C Emmitt Smith 11/23 W 2.50 1.10
❑ 23A Karim Abdul-Jabbar 10/12 W .60 .25
❑ 23B Karim Abdul-Jabbar 11/17 W .60 .25
❑ 23C Karim Abdul-Jabbar 11/30 W .60 .25
❑ 24A Barry Sanders 9/24 W 3.00 1.35
❑ 24B Barry Sanders 11/9 W 3.00 1.35
❑ 24C Barry Sanders 11/27 W 3.00 1.35
❑ 25A Terrell Davis 9/21 W 2.50 1.10
❑ 25B Terrell Davis 11/16 L 2.50 1.10
❑ 25C Terrell Davis 11/24 W 2.50 1.10
❑ 26A Jerome Bettis 9/22 L .60 .25
❑ 26B Jerome Bettis 11/3 L .60 .25
❑ 26C Jerome Bettis 11/16 L .60 .25
❑ 27A Ricky Watters 9/28 L .30 .14
❑ 27B Ricky Watters 10/26 L .30 .14
❑ 27C Ricky Watters 11/10 L .30 .14
❑ 28A Curtis Martin 10/12 W .75 .35
❑ 28B Curtis Martin 10/27 L .75 .35
❑ 28C Curtis Martin 11/16 L .75 .35
❑ 29A Byron Hanspard 9/28 L .60 .25
❑ 29B Byron Hanspard 10/26 L .60 .25
❑ 29C Byron Hanspard 11/23 L .60 .25
❑ 30A Warrick Dunn 9/21 W 1.00 .45
❑ 30B Warrick Dunn 10/5 W 1.00 .45
❑ 30C Warrick Dunn 11/16 L 1.00 .45

1997 Collector's Choice Mini-Standee

	MINT	NRMT
COMPLETE SET (30)	25.00	11.00

STATED ODDS 1:5 SERIES 2

❑ ST1 Jerry Rice 1.50 .70

❑ ST2 Rashaan Salaam .15 .07
❑ ST3 Jeff Blake .30 .14
❑ ST4 Antowain Smith 1.50 .70
❑ ST5 John Elway 3.00 1.35
❑ ST6 Errict Rhett .15 .07
❑ ST7 Jake Plummer 5.00 2.20
❑ ST8 Junior Seau .30 .14
❑ ST9 Marcus Allen .60 .25
❑ ST10 Marvin Harrison .60 .25
❑ ST11 Emmitt Smith 2.50 1.10
❑ ST12 Dan Marino 3.00 1.35
❑ ST13 Ricky Watters .30 .14
❑ ST14 Jamal Anderson 1.00 .45
❑ ST15 Rodney Hampton .30 .14
❑ ST16 Mark Brunell 1.50 .70
❑ ST17 Keyshawn Johnson .60 .25
❑ ST18 Barry Sanders 3.00 1.35
❑ ST19 Eddie George 1.50 .70
❑ ST20 Brett Favre 3.00 1.35
❑ ST21 Kerry Collins .30 .14
❑ ST22 Drew Bledsoe 1.50 .70
❑ ST23 Napoleon Kaufman .60 .25
❑ ST24 Tony Banks .30 .14
❑ ST25 Vinny Testaverde .30 .14
❑ ST26 Terry Allen .60 .25
❑ ST27 Mario Bates .15 .07
❑ ST28 Joey Galloway .75 .35
❑ ST29 Jerome Bettis .60 .25
❑ ST30 Robert Smith .30 .14

1997 Collector's Choice Star Quest

	MINT	NRMT
COMPLETE SET (90)	300.00	135.00
COMP.SERIES 1 (45)	10.00	4.50
COMMON CARD (SQ1-SQ45)	.25	.11
SEMISTARS SQ1-SQ45	.40	.18
UNLISTED STARS SQ1-SQ45	.75	.35
SQ1-SQ45 STATED ODDS 1:1 SERIES 2		
COMMON CARD (SQ46-SQ65)	2.00	.90
SEMISTARS SQ46-SQ65	3.00	1.35
SQ46-SQ65 STATED ODDS 1:21 SER.2		
COMMON CARD (SQ66-SQ80)	5.00	2.20
SEMISTARS (SQ66-SQ80)	8.00	3.60
SQ66-SQ80 STATED ODDS 1:71 SER.2		
SQ81-SQ90 STATED ODDS 1:145 SER.2		

❑ SQ1 Frank Sanders .40 .18
❑ SQ2 Jamal Anderson 1.00 .45

❑ SQ3 Byron Bam Morris .... .25 .11
❑ SQ4 Thurman Thomas.......... .75 .35
❑ SQ5 Muhsin Muhammad ...... .40 .18
❑ SQ6 Bobby Engram .... .40 .18
❑ SQ7 Carl Pickens.................. .75 .35
❑ SQ8 Deion Sanders .... .75 .35
❑ SQ9 Shannon Sharpe .... .40 .18
❑ SQ10 Herman Moore............ .75 .35
❑ SQ11 Robert Brooks .... .40 .18
❑ SQ12 Steve McNair .... .75 .35
❑ SQ13 Marshall Faulk .... .75 .35
❑ SQ14 Keenan McCardell ...... .40 .18
❑ SQ15 Tamarick Vanover ...... .40 .18
❑ SQ16 Fred Barnett................ .25 .11
❑ SQ17 Orlanda Thomas .... .25 .11
❑ SQ18 Drew Bledsoe........... 1.50 .70
❑ SQ19 Mario Bates .... .25 .11
❑ SQ20 Keyshawn Johnson .... .75 .35
❑ SQ21 Rodney Hampton........ .40 .18
❑ SQ22 Darrell Russell .... .25 .11
❑ SQ23 Irving Fryar.................. .40 .18
❑ SQ24 Charles Johnson .... .40 .18
❑ SQ25 Stan Humphries .... .40 .18
❑ SQ26 Terrell Owens.............. .75 .35
❑ SQ27 Chris Warren .... .40 .18
❑ SQ28 Isaac Bruce .... .75 .35
❑ SQ29 Warrick Dunn .... 1.50 .70
❑ SQ30 Gus Frerotte................ .25 .11
❑ SQ31 Rocket Ismail .... .40 .18
❑ SQ32 Natrone Means .... .75 .35
❑ SQ33 Chris Sanders .... .25 .11
❑ SQ34 Vinny Testaverde........ .40 .18
❑ SQ35 Ken Norton Jr. .... .25 .11
❑ SQ36 Tim Biakabutuka .... .40 .18
❑ SQ37 Marcus Allen .... .75 .35
❑ SQ38 Zach Thomas .... .40 .18
❑ SQ39 Derrick Thomas .... .40 .18
❑ SQ40 Tyrone Wheatley .... .40 .18
❑ SQ41 Dorsey Levens............ .75 .35
❑ SQ42 Darnay Scott .... .40 .18
❑ SQ43 Scott Mitchell .... .40 .18
❑ SQ44 Marvin Harrison .... .75 .35
❑ SQ45 Eddie Kennison .... .40 .18
❑ SQ46 Jake Reed 3.00 1.35
❑ SQ47 Andre Reed 3.00 1.35
❑ SQ48 Neil Smith.................. 3.00 1.35
❑ SQ49 Anthony Johnson ...... 2.00 .90
❑ SQ50 Napoleon Kaufman .. 4.00 1.80
❑ SQ51 Terance Mathis 3.00 1.35
❑ SQ52 Tony Martin 3.00 1.35
❑ SQ53 Adrian Murrell............ 3.00 1.35
❑ SQ54 Glyn Milburn.............. 2.00 .90
❑ SQ55 Errict Rhett................ 2.00 .90
❑ SQ56 Kerry Collins.............. 3.00 1.35
❑ SQ57 Curtis Conway 3.00 1.35
❑ SQ58 Eric Swann................ 2.00 .90
❑ SQ59 Michael Jackson 3.00 1.35
❑ SQ60 Ty Detmer 3.00 1.35
❑ SQ61 Michael Irvin.............. 4.00 1.80
❑ SQ62 Terrell Fletcher.......... 2.00 .90
❑ SQ63 Brian Mitchell .... 2.00 .90
❑ SQ64 Tony Banks 3.00 1.35
❑ SQ65 Eddie George.......... 10.00 4.50
❑ SQ66 Kordell Stewart........ 10.00 4.50
❑ SQ67 Greg Hill.................... 5.00 2.20
❑ SQ68 Karim Abdul-Jabbar .. 5.00 2.20
❑ SQ69 Cris Carter 10.00 4.50
❑ SQ70 Terry Glenn 8.00 3.60
❑ SQ71 Emmitt Smith 25.00 11.00
❑ SQ72 Jim Harbaugh............ 8.00 3.60
❑ SQ73 Jeff Blake 8.00 3.60
❑ SQ74 Rashaan Salaam 5.00 2.20
❑ SQ75 Ricky Watters............ 8.00 3.60
❑ SQ76 Joey Galloway 10.00 4.50
❑ SQ77 Junior Seau 8.00 3.60
❑ SQ78 Dave Brown 5.00 2.20
❑ SQ79 Tim Brown 10.00 4.50
❑ SQ80 Troy Aikman.......... 20.00 9.00
❑ SQ81 Dan Marino 40.00 18.00
❑ SQ82 Brett Favre............ 40.00 18.00
❑ SQ83 John Elway............ 40.00 18.00
❑ SQ84 Steve Young 15.00 6.75
❑ SQ85 Mark Brunell.......... 25.00 11.00
❑ SQ86 Barry Sanders 50.00 22.00
❑ SQ87 Jerome Bettis 12.00 5.50
❑ SQ88 Terrell Davis.......... 40.00 18.00
❑ SQ89 Curtis Martin.......... 15.00 6.75
❑ SQ90 Jerry Rice.............. 25.00 11.00

1997 Collector's Choice Stick-Ums

	MINT	NRMT
COMPLETE SET (30)	10.00	4.50
STATED ODDS 1:3 SERIES 1		

❑ S1 Kerry Collins .... .15 .07
❑ S2 Troy Aikman .... .75 .35
❑ S3 Steve Young .... .50 .23
❑ S4 Ricky Watters .... .15 .07
❑ S5 Cris Carter .... .30 .14
❑ S6 Terry Allen .... .30 .14
❑ S7 Bobby Engram .... .15 .07
❑ S8 Larry Centers .... .15 .07
❑ S9 Mike Alstott...................... .30 .14
❑ S10 Rodney Hampton .... .15 .07
❑ S11 Eddie Kennison.............. .15 .07
❑ S12 Jamal Anderson .... .50 .23
❑ S13 Jim Everett .... .10 .05
❑ S14 Curtis Martin .... .40 .18
❑ S15 Keenan McCardell .... .15 .07
❑ S16 Kordell Stewart .... .40 .18
❑ S17 John Elway .... 1.50 .70
❑ S18 Terrell Davis .... 1.25 .55
❑ S19 Thurman Thomas .... .30 .14
❑ S20 Marshall Faulk .... .30 .14
❑ S21 Marcus Allen.................. .30 .14
❑ S22 Tony Martin.................... .15 .07
❑ S23 Dan Marino .... 1.50 .70
❑ S24 Karim Abdul-Jabbar ...... .30 .14
❑ S25 Carl Pickens .... .30 .14
❑ S26 Eddie George .... .75 .35
❑ S27 Joey Galloway .... .40 .18
❑ S28 Napoleon Kaufman........ .30 .14
❑ S29 Vinny Testaverde .... .15 .07
❑ S30 Keyshawn Johnson........ .30 .14

1997 Collector's Choice Turf Champions

	MINT	NRMT
COMPLETE SET (90)	400.00	180.00
COMP.SERIES 1 (30)	6.00	2.70
COMMON CARD (TC1-TC30)	.20	.09
SEMISTARS (TC1-TC30)	.30	.14
UNLISTED STARS (TC1-TC30)	.50	.23
TC1-TC30 STATED ODDS 1:1H, 2:1R SER.1		
COMMON CARD (TC31-TC60)	2.50	1.10
SEMISTARS (TC31-TC60)	4.00	1.80
UNLISTED STARS (TC31-TC60)	6.00	2.70
TC31-TC60 STATED ODDS 1:21 SER.1		
COMMON CARD (TC61-TC90)	5.00	2.20
SEMISTARS (TC61-TC90)	8.00	3.60
UNLISTED STARS (TC61-TC90)	12.00	5.50
TC61-TC80 STATED ODDS 1:71 SER.1		
TC81-TC90 STATED ODDS 1:145 SER.1		

❑ TC1 Kerry Collins .... .30 .14
❑ TC2 Scott Mitchell .... .30 .14
❑ TC3 Jim Schwantz .... .20 .09
❑ TC4 Orlando Pace .... .20 .09
❑ TC5 Troy Davis .... .50 .23
❑ TC6 Vinny Testaverde .... .30 .14
❑ TC7 Rocket Ismail .... .30 .14
❑ TC8 Henry Ellard .... .20 .09
❑ TC9 Kevin Turner.................. .20 .09
❑ TC10 Bobby Engram .... .30 .14
❑ TC11 Keyshawn Johnson .... .50 .23
❑ TC12 Trent Dilfer .... .50 .23
❑ TC13 Elvis Grbac.................. .30 .14
❑ TC14 Trev Alberts .... .20 .09
❑ TC15 Kevin Hardy .... .20 .09
❑ TC16 Warren Sapp .... .30 .14
❑ TC17 Chris Hudson .... .20 .09
❑ TC18 Antonio Langham........ .20 .09
❑ TC19 Jonathan Ogden.......... .20 .09
❑ TC20 Bruce Smith .... .30 .14
❑ TC21 Marcus Allen................ .50 .23
❑ TC22 Desmond Howard........ .30 .14
❑ TC23 Eric Metcalf.................. .30 .14
❑ TC24 Terance Mathis............ .30 .14
❑ TC25 LeShon Johnson .... .20 .09
❑ TC26 Kevin Greene .... .30 .14
❑ TC27 Alex Van Dyke .... .20 .09
❑ TC28 Jeff Jaeger .... .20 .09
❑ TC29 Jason Elam.................. .20 .09
❑ TC30 Thomas Lewis .... .20 .09
❑ TC31 Rick Mirer 2.50 1.10
❑ TC32 Warren Moon 6.00 2.70
❑ TC33 Jim Kelly.................. 6.00 2.70
❑ TC34 Junior Seau 4.00 1.80
❑ TC35 Jeff Hostetler 2.50 1.10
❑ TC36 Neil O'Donnell.......... 4.00 1.80
❑ TC37 Jeff Blake 4.00 1.80
❑ TC38 Kordell Stewart........ 12.00 5.50
❑ TC39 Terry Glenn 6.00 2.70
❑ TC40 Simeon Rice............ 4.00 1.80
❑ TC41 Jimmy Smith............ 4.00 1.80
❑ TC42 Natrone Means........ 6.00 2.70
❑ TC43 Tony Martin 4.00 1.80
❑ TC44 Charles Johnson 4.00 1.80
❑ TC45 Napoleon Kaufman.... 6.00 2.70
❑ TC46 Dale Carter.............. 2.50 1.10
❑ TC47 Brett Perriman 2.50 1.10
❑ TC48 Cortez Kennedy 2.50 1.10
❑ TC49 Bryce Paup.............. 2.50 1.10
❑ TC50 Greg Lloyd 2.50 1.10
❑ TC51 Bryant Young 2.50 1.10
❑ TC52 Steve McNair 6.00 2.70
❑ TC53 Garrison Hearst 4.00 1.80
❑ TC54 John Copeland.......... 2.50 1.10
❑ TC55 Eric Curry 2.50 1.10
❑ TC56 Reggie White 6.00 2.70
❑ TC57 Rod Woodson.......... 6.00 2.70
❑ TC58 Andre Rison 4.00 1.80
❑ TC59 Herschel Walker........ 4.00 1.80
❑ TC60 John Kasay.............. 2.50 1.10
❑ TC61 Emmitt Smith 30.00 13.50
❑ TC62 Dan Marino............ 40.00 18.00
❑ TC63 Michael Irvin 12.00 5.50
❑ TC64 Drew Bledsoe........ 20.00 9.00
❑ TC65 Mark Brunell 20.00 9.00
❑ TC66 Jim Harbaugh.......... 8.00 3.60
❑ TC67 Herman Moore 12.00 5.50
❑ TC68 Rashaan Salaam 5.00 2.20
❑ TC69 Ty Detmer................ 8.00 3.60
❑ TC70 Cris Carter 12.00 5.50
❑ TC71 Chris Warren 8.00 3.60
❑ TC72 Thurman Thomas.... 12.00 5.50
❑ TC73 Ricky Watters 8.00 3.60
❑ TC74 Tim Brown 12.00 5.50

- ❑ TC75 Marshall Faulk 12.00 5.50
- ❑ TC76 Jerome Bettis 12.00 5.50
- ❑ TC77 Karim Abdul-Jabbar 12.00 5.50
- ❑ TC78 Deion Sanders 12.00 5.50
- ❑ TC79 Ben Coates 8.00 3.60
- ❑ TC80 Andre Reed 8.00 3.60
- ❑ TC81 Brett Favre 40.00 18.00
- ❑ TC82 Terrell Davis 30.00 13.50
- ❑ TC83 Troy Aikman 20.00 9.00
- ❑ TC84 Carl Pickens 12.00 5.50
- ❑ TC85 Barry Sanders 40.00 18.00
- ❑ TC86 Jerry Rice 20.00 9.00
- ❑ TC87 Curtis Martin 12.00 5.50
- ❑ TC88 Steve Young 15.00 6.75
- ❑ TC89 Eddie George 20.00 9.00
- ❑ TC90 John Elway 40.00 18.00

1992 Collector's Edge

	MINT	NRMT
COMPLETE SET (250)	25.00	11.00
COMP.SERIES 1 (175)	15.00	6.75
COMP.FACT.SER.1 (175)	20.00	9.00
COMP.SERIES 2 (75)	10.00	4.50
COMP.FACT.SER.2 (75)	12.00	5.50
COMMON CARD (1-250)	.10	.05
SEMISTARS	.20	.09
UNLISTED STARS	.40	.18

- ❑ 1 Chris Miller .20 .09
- ❑ 2 Steve Broussard .10 .05
- ❑ 3 Mike Pritchard .20 .09
- ❑ 4 Tim Green .10 .05
- ❑ 5 Andre Rison .20 .09
- ❑ 6 Deion Sanders 1.00 .45
- ❑ 7 Jim Kelly .40 .18
- ❑ 8 James Lofton .20 .09
- ❑ 9 Andre Reed .20 .09
- ❑ 10 Bruce Smith .40 .18
- ❑ 11 Thurman Thomas .40 .18
- ❑ 12 Cornelius Bennett .20 .09
- ❑ 13 Jim Harbaugh .40 .18
- ❑ 14 William Perry .20 .09
- ❑ 15 Mike Singletary .20 .09
- ❑ 16 Mark Carrier DB .10 .05
- ❑ 17 Kevin Butler .10 .05
- ❑ 18 Tom Waddle .10 .05
- ❑ 19 Boomer Esiason .20 .09
- ❑ 20 David Fulcher .10 .05
- ❑ 21 Anthony Munoz .20 .09
- ❑ 22 Tim McGee .10 .05
- ❑ 23 Harold Green .10 .05
- ❑ 24 Rickey Dixon .10 .05
- ❑ 25 Bernie Kosar .20 .09
- ❑ 26 Michael Dean Perry .20 .09
- ❑ 27 Mike Baab .10 .05
- ❑ 28 Brian Brennan .10 .05
- ❑ 29 Michael Jackson .20 .09
- ❑ 30 Eric Metcalf .20 .09
- ❑ 31 Troy Aikman 2.50 1.10
- ❑ 32 Emmitt Smith 5.00 2.20
- ❑ 33 Michael Irvin .40 .18
- ❑ 34 Jay Novacek .20 .09
- ❑ 35 Issac Holt .10 .05
- ❑ 36 Ken Norton .40 .18
- ❑ 37 John Elway 4.00 1.80
- ❑ 38 Gaston Green .10 .05
- ❑ 39 Charles Dimry .10 .05
- ❑ 40 Vance Johnson .10 .05
- ❑ 41 Dennis Smith .10 .05
- ❑ 42 David Treadwell .10 .05
- ❑ 43 Michael Young .10 .05
- ❑ 44 Bennie Blades .10 .05
- ❑ 45 Mel Gray .20 .09
- ❑ 46 Andre Ware .10 .05
- ❑ 47 Rodney Peete .20 .09
- ❑ 48 Toby Caston RC .10 .05
- ❑ 49 Herman Moore 2.00 .90
- ❑ 50 Brian Noble .10 .05
- ❑ 51 Sterling Sharpe .40 .18
- ❑ 52 Mike Tomczak .10 .05
- ❑ 53 Vinnie Clark .10 .05
- ❑ 54 Tony Mandarich .10 .05
- ❑ 55 Ed West .10 .05
- ❑ 56 Warren Moon .40 .18
- ❑ 57 Ray Childress .10 .05
- ❑ 58 Haywood Jeffires .20 .09
- ❑ 59 Al Smith .10 .05
- ❑ 60 Cris Dishman .10 .05
- ❑ 61 Ernest Givins .20 .09
- ❑ 62 Richard Johnson .10 .05
- ❑ 63 Eric Dickerson .20 .09
- ❑ 64 Jessie Hester .10 .05
- ❑ 65 Rohn Stark .10 .05
- ❑ 66 Clarence Verdin .10 .05
- ❑ 67 Dean Biasucci .10 .05
- ❑ 68 Duane Bickett .10 .05
- ❑ 69 Jeff George .40 .18
- ❑ 70 Christian Okoye .10 .05
- ❑ 71 Derrick Thomas .40 .18
- ❑ 72 Stephone Paige .10 .05
- ❑ 73 Dan Saleaumua .10 .05
- ❑ 74 Deron Cherry .10 .05
- ❑ 75 Kevin Ross .10 .05
- ❑ 76 Barry Word .10 .05
- ❑ 77 Ronnie Lott .20 .09
- ❑ 78 Greg Townsend .10 .05
- ❑ 79 Willie Gault .20 .09
- ❑ 80 Howie Long .20 .09
- ❑ 81 Winston Moss .10 .05
- ❑ 82 Steve Smith .10 .05
- ❑ 83 Jay Schroeder .10 .05
- ❑ 84 Jim Everett .20 .09
- ❑ 85 Flipper Anderson .10 .05
- ❑ 86 Henry Ellard .20 .09
- ❑ 87 Tony Zendejas .10 .05
- ❑ 88 Robert Delpino .10 .05
- ❑ 89 Pat Terrell .10 .05
- ❑ 90 Dan Marino 4.00 1.80
- ❑ 91 Mark Clayton .20 .09
- ❑ 92 Jim C.Jensen .10 .05
- ❑ 93 Reggie Roby .10 .05
- ❑ 94 Sammie Smith .10 .05
- ❑ 95 Tony Martin .40 .18
- ❑ 96 Jeff Cross .10 .05
- ❑ 97 Anthony Carter .20 .09
- ❑ 98 Chris Doleman .10 .05
- ❑ 99 Wade Wilson .20 .09
- ❑ 100 Cris Carter .75 .35
- ❑ 101 Mike Merriweather .10 .05
- ❑ 102 Gary Zimmerman .10 .05
- ❑ 103 Chris Singleton .10 .05
- ❑ 104 Bruce Armstrong .10 .05
- ❑ 105 Marv Cook .10 .05
- ❑ 106 Andre Tippett .10 .05
- ❑ 107 Tommy Hodson .10 .05
- ❑ 108 Greg McMurtry .10 .05
- ❑ 109 Jon Vaughn .10 .05
- ❑ 110 Vaughan Johnson .10 .05
- ❑ 111 Craig Heyward .20 .09
- ❑ 112 Floyd Turner .10 .05
- ❑ 113 Pat Swilling .20 .09
- ❑ 114 Rickey Jackson .10 .05
- ❑ 115 Steve Walsh .10 .05
- ❑ 116 Phil Simms .20 .09
- ❑ 117 Carl Banks .10 .05
- ❑ 118 Mark Ingram .10 .05
- ❑ 119 Bart Oates .10 .05
- ❑ 120 Lawrence Taylor .40 .18
- ❑ 121 Jeff Hostetler .20 .09
- ❑ 122 Rob Moore .20 .09
- ❑ 123 Ken O'Brien .10 .05
- ❑ 124 Bill Pickel .10 .05
- ❑ 125 Irv Eatman .10 .05
- ❑ 126 Browning Nagle .10 .05
- ❑ 127 Al Toon .20 .09
- ❑ 128 Randall Cunningham .40 .18
- ❑ 129 Eric Allen .10 .05
- ❑ 130 Mike Golic .10 .05
- ❑ 131 Fred Barnett .40 .18
- ❑ 132 Keith Byars .10 .05
- ❑ 133 Calvin Williams .20 .09
- ❑ 134 Randal Hill .10 .05
- ❑ 135 Ricky Proehl .10 .05
- ❑ 136 Lance Smith .10 .05
- ❑ 137 Ernie Jones .10 .05
- ❑ 138 Timm Rosenbach .10 .05
- ❑ 139 Anthony Thompson .10 .05
- ❑ 140 Bubby Brister .10 .05
- ❑ 141 Merril Hoge .10 .05
- ❑ 142 Louis Lipps .10 .05
- ❑ 143 Eric Green .10 .05
- ❑ 144 Gary Anderson K .10 .05
- ❑ 145 Neil O'Donnell .40 .18
- ❑ 146 Rod Bernstine .10 .05
- ❑ 147 John Friesz .20 .09
- ❑ 148 Anthony Miller .20 .09
- ❑ 149 Junior Seau .40 .18
- ❑ 150 Leslie O'Neal .20 .09
- ❑ 151 Nate Lewis .10 .05
- ❑ 152 Steve Young 2.00 .90
- ❑ 153 Kevin Fagan .10 .05
- ❑ 154 Charles Haley .20 .09
- ❑ 155 Tom Rathman .10 .05
- ❑ 156 Jerry Rice 2.50 1.10
- ❑ 157 John Taylor .20 .09
- ❑ 158 Brian Blades .20 .09
- ❑ 159 Patrick Hunter .10 .05
- ❑ 160 Cortez Kennedy .20 .09
- ❑ 161 Vann McElroy .10 .05
- ❑ 162 Dan McGwire .10 .05
- ❑ 163 John L. Williams .10 .05
- ❑ 164 Gary Anderson RB .10 .05
- ❑ 165 Broderick Thomas .10 .05
- ❑ 166 Vinny Testaverde .20 .09
- ❑ 167 Lawrence Dawsey .20 .09
- ❑ 168 Paul Gruber .10 .05
- ❑ 169 Keith McCants .10 .05
- ❑ 170 Mark Rypien .10 .05
- ❑ 171 Gary Clark .40 .18
- ❑ 172 Earnest Byner .10 .05
- ❑ 173 Brian Mitchell .20 .09
- ❑ 174 Monte Coleman .10 .05
- ❑ 175 Joe Jacoby .10 .05
- ❑ 176 Tommy Vardell RC .20 .09
- ❑ 177 Troy Vincent RC .20 .09
- ❑ 178 Robert Jones RC .10 .05
- ❑ 179 Marc Boutte RC .10 .05
- ❑ 180 Marco Coleman RC .20 .09
- ❑ 181 Chris Mims RC .20 .09
- ❑ 182 Tony Casillas .10 .05
- ❑ 182X Ray Roberts 10.00 4.50
  Large X on front
- ❑ 183 Shane Dronett RC .10 .05
- ❑ 184 Sean Gilbert RC .40 .18
- ❑ 185 Siran Stacy RC .10 .05
- ❑ 186 Tommy Maddox RC .10 .05
- ❑ 187 Steve Israel RC .10 .05
- ❑ 188 Brad Muster .10 .05
- ❑ 188X Casey Weldon 10.00 4.50
  large X on front
- ❑ 189 Shane Collins RC .10 .05
- ❑ 190 Terrell Buckley RC .10 .05
- ❑ 191 Eugene Chung RC .10 .05
- ❑ 192 Leon Searcy RC .20 .09
- ❑ 193 Chuck Smith RC .10 .05
- ❑ 194 Patrick Rowe RC .10 .05
- ❑ 195 Bill Johnson RC .10 .05
- ❑ 196 Gerald Dixon RC .10 .05
- ❑ 197 Robert Porcher RC .20 .09
- ❑ 198 Tracy Scroggins RC .10 .05
- ❑ 199 Jason Hanson RC .20 .09
- ❑ 200 Corey Harris RC .10 .05
- ❑ 201 Eddie Robinson RC .10 .05
- ❑ 202 Steve Emtman RC .10 .05
- ❑ 203 Ashley Ambrose RC .20 .09
- ❑ 204 Greg Skrepenak RC .10 .05
- ❑ 205 Todd Collins RC .10 .05
- ❑ 206 Derek Brown TE RC .10 .05
- ❑ 207 Kurt Barber RC .10 .05

❑ 208 Tony Sacca RC .10 .05
❑ 209 Mark Wheeler RC .10 .05
❑ 210 Kevin Smith RC .40 .18
❑ 211 John Fina RC .10 .05
❑ 212 Johnny Mitchell RC .10 .05
❑ 213 Dale Carter RC .40 .18
❑ 214 Bob Spitulski RC .10 .05
❑ 215 Phillippi Sparks RC .10 .05
❑ 216 Levon Kirkland RC .10 .05
❑ 217 Mike Sherrard .10 .05
❑ 218 Marquez Pope RC .10 .05
❑ 219 Courtney Hawkins RC .20 .09
❑ 220 Tyji Armstrong RC .10 .05
❑ 221 Keith Jackson .20 .09
❑ 222 Clayton Holmes RC .10 .05
❑ 223 Quentin Coryatt RC .40 .18
❑ 224 Troy Auzenne RC .10 .05
❑ 225 David Klingler RC .20 .09
❑ 226 Darryl Williams RC .10 .05
❑ 227 Carl Pickens RC 1.25 .55
❑ 228 Jimmy Smith RC 3.00 1.35
❑ 229 Chester McGlockton RC .40 .18
❑ 230 Robert Brooks RC 2.00 .90
❑ 231 Alonzo Spellman RC .20 .09
❑ 232 Darren Woodson RC .40 .18
❑ 233 Lewis Billups .10 .05
❑ 234 Edgar Bennett RC .75 .35
❑ 235 Vaughn Dunbar RC .10 .05
❑ 236 Steve Bono RC .40 .18
❑ 237 Clarence Kay .10 .05
❑ 238 Chris Hinton .10 .05
❑ 239 Jimmie Jones .10 .05
❑ 240 Vai Sikahema .10 .05
❑ 241 Russell Maryland .20 .09
❑ 241X Bobby Humphrey 10.00 4.50
large X on front
❑ 242 Neal Anderson .10 .05
❑ 242X Mark Bavaro 10.00 4.50
large X on front
❑ 243 Charles Mann .10 .05
❑ 244 Hugh Millen .10 .05
❑ 245 Roger Craig .20 .09
❑ 246 Rich Gannon .10 .05
❑ 247 Ricky Ervins .10 .05
❑ 247X Marion Butts 10.00 4.50
large X on front
❑ 248 Leonard Marshall .10 .05
❑ 249 Eric Dickerson .20 .09
❑ 250 Joe Montana 4.00 1.80
❑ RU1 Terrell Buckley 4.00 1.80
Prototype
❑ RU2 Tommy Maddox 4.00 1.80
Prototype
❑ AU37 John Elway 80.00 36.00
(2,500 signed)
❑ AU77 Ronnie Lott Bonus 15.00 6.75
(2,500 signed)
❑ AU123 Ken O'Brien 8.00 3.60
(2,500 signed)

1993 Collector's Edge

	MINT	NRMT
COMPLETE SET (325)	20.00	9.00
COMP.SERIES 1 (250)	10.00	4.50
COMP.SERIES 2 (75)	10.00	4.50
COMMON CARD (1-325)	.05	.02
SEMISTARS	.10	.05
UNLISTED STARS	.25	.11
COMPLETE CHECKLISTS (5)	2.00	.90

CHECKLISTS: RANDOM INS.IN PACKS
COMP.ELWAY PRISM E (5) 4.00 1.80
*ELWAY S PREFIX SERIAL NUMB: 2X to 3X
ELWAY S PREFIX: RAND.INS.IN EARLY PACKS

❑ 1 Falcons Team Photo .05 .02
❑ 2 Michael Haynes .10 .05
❑ 3 Chris Miller .10 .05
❑ 4 Mike Pritchard .10 .05
❑ 5 Andre Rison .10 .05
❑ 6 Deion Sanders .50 .23
❑ 7 Chuck Smith .05 .02
❑ 8 Drew Hill .05 .02
❑ 9 Bobby Hebert .05 .02
❑ 10 Bills Team Photo .05 .02
❑ 11 Matt Darby .05 .02
❑ 12 John Fina .05 .02
❑ 13 Jim Kelly .25 .11
❑ 14 Marvcus Patton RC .05 .02
❑ 15 Andre Reed .10 .05
❑ 16 Thurman Thomas .25 .11
❑ 17 James Lofton .10 .05
❑ 18 Bruce Smith .25 .11
❑ 19 Bears Team Photo .05 .02
❑ 20 Neal Anderson .05 .02
❑ 21 Troy Auzenne .05 .02
❑ 22 Jim Harbaugh .25 .11
❑ 23 Alonzo Spellman .05 .02
❑ 24 Tom Waddle .05 .02
❑ 25 Darren Lewis .05 .02
❑ 26 Wendell Davis .05 .02
❑ 27 Will Furrer .05 .02
❑ 28 Bengals Team Photo .05 .02
❑ 29 David Klingler .05 .02
❑ 30 Ricardo McDonald .05 .02
❑ 31 Carl Pickens .25 .11
❑ 32 Harold Green .05 .02
❑ 33 Anthony Munoz .10 .05
❑ 34 Darryl Williams .05 .02
❑ 35 Browns Team Photo .05 .02
❑ 36 Michael Jackson .10 .05
❑ 37 Pio Sagapolutele .05 .02
❑ 38 Tommy Vardell .05 .02
❑ 39 Bernie Kosar .10 .05
❑ 40 Michael Dean Perry .10 .05
❑ 41 Bill Johnson .05 .02
❑ 42 Vinny Testaverde .10 .05
❑ 43 Cowboys Team Photo .05 .02
❑ 44 Troy Aikman .75 .35
❑ 45 Alvin Harper .10 .05
❑ 46 Michael Irvin .25 .11
❑ 47 Russell Maryland .05 .02
❑ 48 Emmitt Smith 1.50 .70
❑ 49 Kenneth Gant .05 .02
❑ 50 Jay Novacek .10 .05
❑ 51 Robert Jones .05 .02
❑ 52 Clayton Holmes .05 .02
❑ 53 Broncos Team Photo .05 .02
❑ 54 Mike Croel .05 .02
❑ 55 Shane Dronett .05 .02
❑ 56 Kenny Walker .05 .02
❑ 57 Tommy Maddox .05 .02
❑ 58 Dennis Smith .05 .02
❑ 59 John Elway 1.50 .70
❑ 60 Karl Mecklenburg .05 .02
❑ 61 Steve Atwater .05 .02
❑ 62 Vance Johnson .05 .02
❑ 63 Lions Team Photo .05 .02
❑ 64 Barry Sanders 1.50 .70
❑ 65 Andre Ware .05 .02
❑ 66 Pat Swilling .05 .02
❑ 67 Jason Hanson .05 .02
❑ 68 Willie Green .05 .02
❑ 69 Herman Moore .50 .23
❑ 70 Rodney Peete .05 .02
❑ 71 Erik Kramer .10 .05
❑ 72 Robert Porcher .05 .02
❑ 73 Packers Team Photo .05 .02
❑ 74 Terrell Buckley .05 .02
❑ 75 Reggie White .25 .11
❑ 76 Brett Favre 2.00 .90
❑ 77 Don Majkowski .05 .02
❑ 78 Edgar Bennett .25 .11
❑ 79 Ty Detmer .25 .11
❑ 80 Sanjay Beach .05 .02
❑ 81 Sterling Sharpe .25 .11
❑ 82 Oilers Team Photo .05 .02
❑ 83 Gary Brown .05 .02
❑ 84 Ernest Givins .10 .05
❑ 85 Haywood Jeffires .10 .05
❑ 86 Corey Harris .05 .02
❑ 87 Warren Moon .25 .11
❑ 88 Eddie Robinson .05 .02
❑ 89 Lorenzo White .05 .02
❑ 90 Bo Orlando .05 .02
❑ 91 Colts Team Photo .05 .02
❑ 92 Quentin Coryatt .10 .05
❑ 93 Steve Emtman .05 .02
❑ 94 Jeff George .25 .11
❑ 95 Jessie Hester .05 .02
❑ 96 Rohn Stark .05 .02
❑ 97 Ashley Ambrose .05 .02
❑ 98 John Baylor .05 .02
❑ 99 Chiefs Team Photo .05 .02
❑ 100 Tim Barnett .05 .02
❑ 101 Derrick Thomas .25 .11
❑ 102 Barry Word .05 .02
❑ 103 Dale Carter .05 .02
❑ 104 Jayice Pearson .05 .02
❑ 105 Tracy Simien .05 .02
❑ 106 Harvey Williams .10 .05
❑ 107 Dave Krieg .10 .05
❑ 108 Christian Okoye .05 .02
❑ 109 Joe Montana 1.50 .70
❑ 110 Dolphins Team Photo .05 .02
❑ 111 J.B. Brown .05 .02
❑ 112 Marco Coleman .05 .02
❑ 113 Dan Marino 1.50 .70
❑ 114 Mark Clayton .05 .02
❑ 115 Mark Higgs .05 .02
❑ 116 Bryan Cox .05 .02
❑ 117 Chuck Klingbeil .05 .02
❑ 118 Troy Vincent .05 .02
❑ 119 Keith Jackson .10 .05
❑ 120 Bruce Alexander .05 .02
❑ 121 Vikings Team Photo .05 .02
❑ 122 Terry Allen .25 .11
❑ 123 Rich Gannon .05 .02
❑ 124 Todd Scott .05 .02
❑ 125 Cris Carter .50 .23
❑ 126 Sean Salisbury .05 .02
❑ 127 Jack Del Rio .05 .02
❑ 128 Chris Doleman .05 .02
❑ 129 Anthony Carter .10 .05
❑ 130 Patriots Team Photo .05 .02
❑ 131 Eugene Chung .05 .02
❑ 132 Todd Collins .05 .02
❑ 133 Tommy Hodson .05 .02
❑ 134 Leonard Russell .10 .05
❑ 135 Jon Vaughn .05 .02
❑ 136 Andre Tippett .05 .02
❑ 137 Saints Team Photo .05 .02
❑ 138 Wesley Carroll .05 .02
❑ 139 Richard Cooper .05 .02
❑ 140 Vaughn Dunbar .05 .02
❑ 141 Fred McAfee .05 .02
❑ 142 Torrance Small .05 .02
❑ 143 Steve Walsh .05 .02
❑ 144 Vaughan Johnson .05 .02
❑ 145 Giants Team Photo .05 .02
❑ 146 Jarrod Bunch .05 .02
❑ 147 Phil Simms .10 .05
❑ 148 Carl Banks .05 .02
❑ 149 Lawrence Taylor .25 .11
❑ 150 Rodney Hampton .25 .11
❑ 151 Phillippi Sparks .05 .02
❑ 152 Derek Brown TE .05 .02
❑ 153 Jets Team Photo .05 .02
❑ 154 Boomer Esiason .10 .05
❑ 155 Johnny Mitchell .05 .02
❑ 156 Rob Moore .10 .05
❑ 157 Ronnie Lott .10 .05
❑ 158 Browning Nagle .05 .02
❑ 159 Johnny Johnson .05 .02
❑ 160 Dwayne White .05 .02
❑ 161 Blair Thomas .05 .02
❑ 162 Eagles Team Photo .05 .02
❑ 163 Randall Cunningham .25 .11
❑ 164 Fred Barnett .10 .05
❑ 165 Siran Stacy .05 .02

❑ 166 Keith Byars .05 .02
❑ 167 Calvin Williams .10 .05
❑ 168 Jeff Sydner .05 .02
❑ 169 Tommy Jeter .05 .02
❑ 170 Andre Waters .05 .02
❑ 171 Phoenix Team Photo .05 .02
❑ 172 Steve Beuerlein .05 .02
❑ 173 Randal Hill .05 .02
❑ 174 Timm Rosenbach .05 .02
❑ 175 Ed Cunningham .05 .02
❑ 176 Walter Reeves .05 .02
❑ 177 Michael Zordich .05 .02
❑ 178 Gary Clark .10 .05
❑ 179 Ken Harvey .05 .02
❑ 180 Steelers Team Photo .05 .02
❑ 181 Barry Foster .10 .05
❑ 182 Neil O'Donnell .25 .11
❑ 183 Leon Searcy .05 .02
❑ 184 Bubby Brister .05 .02
❑ 185 Merril Hoge .05 .02
❑ 186 Joel Steed .05 .02
❑ 187 Raiders Team Photo .05 .02
❑ 188 Nick Bell .05 .02
❑ 189 Eric Dickerson .10 .05
❑ 190 Nolan Harrison .05 .02
❑ 191 Todd Marinovich .05 .02
❑ 192 Greg Skrepenak .05 .02
❑ 193 Howie Long .10 .05
❑ 194 Jay Schroeder .05 .02
❑ 195 Chester McGlockton .10 .05
❑ 196 Rams Team Photo .05 .02
❑ 197 Jim Everett .10 .05
❑ 198 Sean Gilbert .10 .05
❑ 199 Steve Israel .05 .02
❑ 200 Marc Boutte .05 .02
❑ 201 Joe Milinichik .05 .02
❑ 202 Henry Ellard .10 .05
❑ 203 Jackie Slater .05 .02
❑ 204 Chargers Team Photo .05 .02
❑ 205 Eric Bieniemy .05 .02
❑ 206 Marion Butts .05 .02
❑ 207 Nate Lewis .05 .02
❑ 208 Junior Seau .25 .11
❑ 209 Steve Hendrickson .05 .02
❑ 210 Chris Mims .05 .02
❑ 211 Harry Swayne .05 .02
❑ 212 Marquez Pope .05 .02
❑ 213 Donald Frank .05 .02
❑ 214 Anthony Miller .10 .05
❑ 215 Seahawks Team Photo .05 .02
❑ 216 Cortez Kennedy .10 .05
❑ 217 Dan McGwire .05 .02
❑ 218 Kelly Stouffer .05 .02
❑ 219 Chris Warren .10 .05
❑ 220 Brian Blades .10 .05
❑ 221 Rod Stephens RC .05 .02
❑ 222 49ers Team Photo .05 .02
❑ 223 Jerry Rice 1.00 .45
❑ 224 Ricky Watters .25 .11
❑ 225 Steve Young .75 .35
❑ 226 Tom Rathman .05 .02
❑ 227 Dana Hall .05 .02
❑ 228 Amp Lee .05 .02
❑ 229 Brian Bollinger .05 .02
❑ 230 Keith DeLong .05 .02
❑ 231 John Taylor .10 .05
❑ 232 Buccaneers Team Photo .05 .02
❑ 233 Tyji Armstrong .05 .02
❑ 234 Lawrence Dawsey .05 .02
❑ 235 Mark Wheeler .05 .02
❑ 236 Vince Workman .05 .02
❑ 237 Reggie Cobb .05 .02
❑ 238 Tony Mayberry .05 .02
❑ 239 Marty Carter .05 .02
❑ 240 Courtney Hawkins .05 .02
❑ 241 Ray Seals .05 .02
❑ 242 Mark Carrier WR .10 .05
❑ 243 Redskins Team Photo .05 .02
❑ 244 Mark Rypien .05 .02
❑ 245 Ricky Ervins .05 .02
❑ 246 Gerald Riggs .05 .02
❑ 247 Art Monk .10 .05
❑ 248 Mark Schlereth .05 .02
❑ 249 Monte Coleman .05 .02
❑ 250 Wilber Marshall .05 .02
❑ 251 Ben Coleman RC .05 .02
❑ 252 Curtis Conway RC .50 .23
❑ 253 Ernest Dye RC .05 .02
❑ 254 Todd Kelly RC .05 .02
❑ 255 Patrick Bates RC .05 .02
❑ 256 George Teague RC .10 .05
❑ 257 Mark Brunell RC 3.00 1.35
❑ 258 Adrian Hardy .05 .02
❑ 259 Dana Stubblefield RC .25 .11
❑ 260 William Roaf RC .10 .05
❑ 261 Irv Smith RC .05 .02
❑ 262 Drew Bledsoe RC 3.00 1.35
❑ 263 Dan Williams RC .05 .02
❑ 264 Jerry Ball .05 .02
❑ 265 Mark Clayton .05 .02
❑ 266 John Stephens .05 .02
❑ 267 Reggie White .25 .11
❑ 268 Jeff Hostetler .10 .05
❑ 269 Boomer Esiason .10 .05
❑ 270 Wade Wilson .05 .02
❑ 271 Steve Beuerlein .05 .02
❑ 272 Tim McDonald .05 .02
❑ 273 Craig Heyward .10 .05
❑ 274 Everson Walls .05 .02
❑ 275 Stan Humphries .25 .11
❑ 276 Carl Banks .05 .02
❑ 277 Brad Muster .05 .02
❑ 278 Tim Harris .05 .02
❑ 279 Gary Clark .10 .05
❑ 280 Joe Milinichik .05 .02
❑ 281 Leonard Marshall .05 .02
❑ 282 Joe Montana 1.50 .70
❑ 283 Rod Bernstine .05 .02
❑ 284 Mark Carrier WR .10 .05
❑ 285 Michael Brooks .05 .02
❑ 286 Marvin Jones RC .05 .02
❑ 287 John Copeland RC .10 .05
❑ 288 Eric Curry RC .05 .02
❑ 289 Steve Everitt RC .05 .02
❑ 290 Tom Carter RC .10 .05
❑ 291 Deon Figures RC .10 .05
❑ 292A Leonard Renfro RC .05 .02
❑ 292B Leonard Renfro RC .05 .02
❑ 293 Thomas Smith RC .10 .05
❑ 294 Carlton Gray RC .05 .02
❑ 295 Demetrius DuBose RC .05 .02
❑ 296 Coleman Rudolph RC .05 .02
❑ 297 John Parrella RC .05 .02
❑ 298 Glyn Milburn RC .25 .11
❑ 299 Reggie Brooks RC .10 .05
❑ 300 Garrison Hearst RC 1.25 .55
❑ 301 John Elway 1.50 .70
❑ 302 Brad Hopkins RC .05 .02
❑ 303 Darrien Gordon RC UER .05 .02
Card states he was drafted 12th instead of 22nd
❑ 304 Robert Smith RC 1.25 .55
❑ 305 Chris Slade RC .10 .05
❑ 306 Ryan McNeil RC .05 .02
❑ 307 Micheal Barrow .05 .02
❑ 308 Roosevelt Potts RC .05 .02
❑ 309 Qadry Ismail RC .25 .11
❑ 310 Reggie Freeman RC .05 .02
❑ 311 Vincent Brisby RC .25 .11
❑ 312 Rick Mirer RC .50 .23
❑ 313 Billy Joe Hobert RC .25 .11
❑ 314 Natrone Means RC 1.00 .45
❑ 315 Gary Zimmerman .05 .02
❑ 316 Bobby Hebert .05 .02
❑ 317 Don Beebe .05 .02
❑ 318 Wilber Marshall .05 .02
❑ 319 Marcus Allen .25 .11
❑ 320 Ronnie Lott .10 .05
❑ 321 Ricky Sanders .05 .02
❑ 322 Charles Mann .05 .02
❑ 323 Simon Fletcher .05 .02
❑ 324 Johnny Johnson .05 .02
❑ 325 Gary Plummer .05 .02
❑ 326 Carolina Panthers 25.00 11.00
Insert
❑ M326 Carolina Panthers 4.00 1.80
Send Away
❑ M327 Jacksonville Jaguars 4.00 1.80
Send Away
❑ PRO1 John Elway AU/3000 60.00 27.00
❑ NNO Factory Set Redemption 1.00 .45
Card (Expired)

1993 Collector's Edge Rookies FX

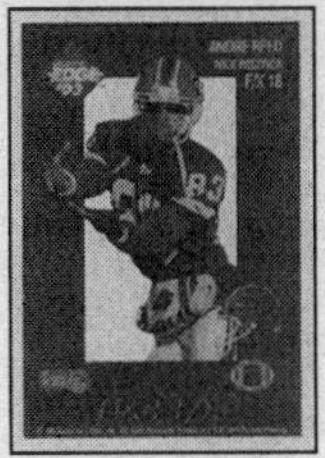

	MINT	NRMT
COMPLETE SET (25)	16.00	7.25

ONE PER ROOKIE/UPDATE PACK
*GOLD STARS: 6X TO 15X BASE CARD HI
*GOLD ROOKIES: 3X TO 8X BASE CARD HI

❑ 1 Garrison Hearst 1.25 .55
❑ 2 Glyn Milburn .25 .11
❑ 3 Demetrius DuBose .05 .02
❑ 4 Joe Montana 3.00 1.35
❑ 5 Thomas Smith .10 .05
❑ 6 Mark Clayton .10 .05
❑ 7 Curtis Conway .50 .23
❑ 8 Drew Bledsoe 3.00 1.35
❑ 9 Todd Kelly .05 .02
❑ 10 Stan Humphries .50 .23
❑ 11 John Elway 3.00 1.35
❑ 12 Troy Aikman 1.50 .70
❑ 13 Marion Butts .10 .05
❑ 14 Alvin Harper .20 .09
❑ 15 Drew Hill .10 .05
❑ 16 Michael Irvin .50 .23
❑ 17 Warren Moon .50 .23
❑ 18 Andre Reed .20 .09
❑ 19 Andre Rison .20 .09
❑ 20 Emmitt Smith 3.00 1.35
❑ 21 Thurman Thomas .50 .23
❑ 22 Ricky Watters .50 .23
❑ 23 Calvin Williams .20 .09
❑ 24 Steve Young 1.50 .70
❑ 25 Howie Long .20 .09
❑ P1A Drew Bledsoe Prototype 3.00 1.35
(Gray checkered border)
❑ P1B Drew Bledsoe Prototype 3.00 1.35
Red border
❑ P2 Drew Bledsoe Prototype 3.00 1.35
(Red border)
❑ P3 Drew Bledsoe Prototype 3.00 1.35
(Gray checkered border)
❑ P4 Drew Bledsoe Prototype 3.00 1.35
(Red border)
❑ P5 Drew Bledsoe Prototype 3.00 1.35
(Red border)

1994 Collector's Edge

	MINT	NRMT
COMPLETE SET (200)	15.00	6.75
COMMON CARD (1-200)	.05	.02
SEMISTARS	.10	.05
UNLISTED STARS	.25	.11
*GOLD CARDS: .75X to 1.5X HI COLUMN		
*SILVER CARDS: .6X to 1.25X HI COLUMN		
*POP WARNER CARDS: SAME VALUE		
*POP WARNER 22K GOLDS: 2.5X to 5X HI		
RANDOM INSERTS IN PACKS		

Card	MINT	NRMT
❑ 1 Mike Pritchard	.05	.02
❑ 2 Erric Pegram	.05	.02
❑ 3 Michael Haynes	.10	.05
❑ 4 Bobby Hebert	.05	.02
❑ 5 Deion Sanders	.50	.23
❑ 6 Andre Rison	.10	.05
❑ 7 Don Beebe	.05	.02
❑ 8 Mark Kelso	.05	.02
❑ 9 Darryl Talley	.05	.02
❑ 10 Cornelius Bennett	.10	.05
❑ 11 Jim Kelly	.25	.11
❑ 12 Andre Reed	.10	.05
❑ 13 Bruce Smith	.25	.11
❑ 14 Thurman Thomas	.25	.11
❑ 15 Craig Heyward	.10	.05
❑ 16 Chris Zorich	.05	.02
❑ 17 Alonzo Spellman	.05	.02
❑ 18 Tom Waddle	.05	.02
❑ 19 Neal Anderson	.05	.02
❑ 20 Kevin Butler	.05	.02
❑ 21 Curtis Conway	.25	.11
❑ 22 Richard Dent	.10	.05
❑ 23 Jim Harbaugh	.25	.11
❑ 24 Derrick Fenner	.05	.02
❑ 25 Harold Green	.05	.02
❑ 26 David Klingler	.05	.02
❑ 27 Daniel Stubbs	.05	.02
❑ 28 Alfred Williams	.05	.02
❑ 29 John Copeland	.05	.02
❑ 30 Mark Carrier WR	.10	.05
❑ 31 Michael Jackson	.10	.05
❑ 32 Eric Metcalf	.10	.05
❑ 33 Vinny Testaverde	.10	.05
❑ 34 Tommy Vardell	.05	.02
❑ 35 Alvin Harper	.10	.05
❑ 36 Ken Norton Jr.	.10	.05
❑ 37 Tony Casillas	.05	.02
❑ 38 Leon Lett	.05	.02
❑ 39 Jay Novacek	.10	.05
❑ 40 Kevin Smith	.05	.02
❑ 41 Troy Aikman	1.00	.45
❑ 42 Michael Irvin	.25	.11
❑ 43 Russell Maryland	.05	.02
❑ 44 Emmitt Smith	1.50	.70
❑ 45 Robert Delpino	.05	.02
❑ 46 Simon Fletcher	.05	.02
❑ 47 Greg Kragen	.05	.02
❑ 48 Arthur Marshall	.05	.02
❑ 49 Steve Atwater	.05	.02
❑ 50 Rod Bernstine	.05	.02
❑ 51 John Elway	2.00	.90
❑ 52 Glyn Milburn	.10	.05
❑ 53 Shannon Sharpe	.10	.05
❑ 54 Bennie Blades	.05	.02
❑ 55 Mel Gray	.05	.02
❑ 56 Herman Moore	.25	.11
❑ 57 Pat Swilling	.05	.02
❑ 58 Chris Spielman	.10	.05
❑ 59 Rodney Peete	.05	.02
❑ 60 Andre Ware	.05	.02
❑ 61 Brett Perriman	.10	.05
❑ 62 Erik Kramer	.10	.05
❑ 63 Barry Sanders	2.00	.90
❑ 64 Mark Clayton	.05	.02
❑ 65 Chris Jacke	.05	.02
❑ 66 Terrell Buckley	.05	.02
❑ 67 Ty Detmer	.10	.05
❑ 68 Sanjay Beach	.05	.02
❑ 69 Brian Noble	.05	.02
❑ 70 Edgar Bennett	.25	.11
❑ 71 Brett Favre	2.00	.90
❑ 72 Sterling Sharpe	.10	.05
❑ 73 Reggie White	.25	.11
❑ 74 Ernest Givins	.10	.05
❑ 75 Al Del Greco	.05	.02
❑ 76 Cris Dishman	.05	.02
❑ 77 Curtis Duncan	.05	.02
❑ 78 Webster Slaughter	.05	.02
❑ 79 Spencer Tillman	.05	.02
❑ 80 Warren Moon	.25	.11
❑ 81 Wilber Marshall	.05	.02
❑ 82 Haywood Jeffires	.10	.05
❑ 83 Lorenzo White	.05	.02
❑ 84 Gary Brown	.05	.02
❑ 85 Reggie Langhorne	.05	.02
❑ 86 Dean Biasucci	.05	.02
❑ 87 Steve Emtman	.05	.02
❑ 88 Jessie Hester	.05	.02
❑ 89 Quentin Coryatt	.05	.02
❑ 90 Roosevelt Potts	.05	.02
❑ 91 Jeff George	.25	.11
❑ 92 Nick Lowery	.05	.02
❑ 93 Willie Davis	.10	.05
❑ 94 Joe Montana	2.00	.90
❑ 95 Neil Smith	.25	.11
❑ 96 Marcus Allen	.25	.11
❑ 97 Derrick Thomas	.25	.11
❑ 98 Greg Townsend	.05	.02
❑ 99 Willie Gault	.05	.02
❑ 100 Ethan Horton	.05	.02
❑ 101 Jeff Hostetler	.10	.05
❑ 102 Tim Brown	.25	.11
❑ 103 Rocket Ismail	.10	.05
❑ 104 Shane Conlan	.05	.02
❑ 105 Henry Ellard	.10	.05
❑ 106 T.J. Rubley	.05	.02
❑ 107 Sean Gilbert	.05	.02
❑ 108 Troy Drayton	.05	.02
❑ 109 Jerome Bettis	.25	.11
❑ 110 Terry Kirby	.25	.11
❑ 111 Mark Ingram	.05	.02
❑ 112 John Offerdahl	.05	.02
❑ 113 Louis Oliver	.05	.02
❑ 114 Irving Fryar	.10	.05
❑ 115 Dan Marino	2.00	.90
❑ 116 Keith Jackson	.05	.02
❑ 117 O.J. McDuffie	.25	.11
❑ 118 Jim McMahon	.05	.02
❑ 119 Sean Salisbury	.05	.02
❑ 120 Randall McDaniel	.05	.02
❑ 121 Jack Del Rio	.05	.02
❑ 122 Cris Carter	.50	.23
❑ 123 Chris Doleman	.05	.02
❑ 124 John Randle	.05	.02
❑ 125 Vincent Brisby	.25	.11
❑ 126 Greg McMurtry	.05	.02
❑ 127 Drew Bledsoe	1.00	.45
❑ 128 Leonard Russell	.05	.02
❑ 129 Michael Brooks	.05	.02
❑ 130 Mark Jackson	.05	.02
❑ 131 Pepper Johnson	.05	.02
❑ 132 Doug Riesenberg	.05	.02
❑ 133 Phil Simms	.10	.05
❑ 134 Rodney Hampton	.25	.11
❑ 135 Leonard Marshall	.05	.02
❑ 136 Rob Moore	.10	.05
❑ 137 Chris Burkett	.05	.02
❑ 138 Boomer Esiason	.10	.05
❑ 139 Johnny Johnson	.05	.02
❑ 140 Ronnie Lott	.10	.05
❑ 141 Brad Muster	.05	.02
❑ 142 Renaldo Turnbull	.05	.02
❑ 143 Willie Roaf	.05	.02
❑ 144 Rickey Jackson	.05	.02
❑ 145 Morten Andersen	.05	.02
❑ 146 Vaughn Dunbar	.05	.02
❑ 147 Wade Wilson	.05	.02
❑ 148 Eric Martin	.05	.02
❑ 149 Seth Joyner	.05	.02
❑ 150 Calvin Williams	.10	.05
❑ 151 Vai Sikahema	.05	.02
❑ 152 Herschel Walker	.10	.05
❑ 153 Eric Allen	.05	.02
❑ 154 Fred Barnett	.10	.05
❑ 155 Randall Cunningham	.25	.11
❑ 156 Steve Beuerlein	.05	.02
❑ 157 Gary Clark	.10	.05
❑ 158 Anthony Edwards	.05	.02
❑ 159 Randal Hill	.05	.02
❑ 160 Freddie Joe Nunn	.05	.02
❑ 161 Garrison Hearst	.25	.11
❑ 162 Ricky Proehl	.05	.02
❑ 163 Eric Green	.05	.02
❑ 164 Levon Kirkland	.05	.02
❑ 165 Joel Steed	.05	.02
❑ 166 Deon Figures	.05	.02
❑ 167 Leroy Thompson	.05	.02
❑ 168 Barry Foster	.05	.02
❑ 169 Neil O'Donnell	.25	.11
❑ 170 Junior Seau	.25	.11
❑ 171 Leslie O'Neal	.05	.02
❑ 172 Stan Humphries	.25	.11
❑ 173 Marion Butts	.05	.02
❑ 174 Anthony Miller	.10	.05
❑ 175 Natrone Means	.25	.11
❑ 176 Odessa Turner	.05	.02
❑ 177 Dana Stubblefield	.25	.11
❑ 178 John Taylor	.10	.05
❑ 179 Ricky Watters	.25	.11
❑ 180 Steve Young	.75	.35
❑ 181 Jerry Rice	1.00	.45
❑ 182 Tom Rathman	.05	.02
❑ 183 Brian Blades	.10	.05
❑ 184 Patrick Hunter	.05	.02
❑ 185 Rick Mirer	.25	.11
❑ 186 Chris Warren	.10	.05
❑ 187 Cortez Kennedy	.10	.05
❑ 188 Reggie Cobb	.05	.02
❑ 189 Craig Erickson	.05	.02
❑ 190 Hardy Nickerson	.10	.05
❑ 191 Lawrence Dawsey	.05	.02
❑ 192 Broderick Thomas	.05	.02
❑ 193 Ricky Sanders	.05	.02
❑ 194 Carl Banks	.05	.02
❑ 195 Ricky Ervins	.05	.02
❑ 196 Darrell Green	.05	.02
❑ 197 Mark Rypien	.05	.02
❑ 198 Desmond Howard	.10	.05
❑ 199 Art Monk	.10	.05
❑ 200 Reggie Brooks	.10	.05
❑ P1 Sh.Sharpe Prototype Numbered 53	1.00	.45

1994 Collector's Edge Boss Rookies

	MINT	NRMT
COMPLETE SET (19)	12.00	5.50
COMMON CARD (1-19)	.30	.14
SEMISTARS	.50	.23
UNLISTED STARS	.75	.35
STATED ODDS 1:2 ALL EDGE PACK TYPES		

Card	MINT	NRMT
❑ 1 Isaac Bruce	4.00	1.80
❑ 2 Jeff Burris	.30	.14
❑ 3 Shante Carver	.30	.14
❑ 4 Lake Dawson	.50	.23
❑ 5 Bert Emanuel	.75	.35
❑ 6 William Floyd	.50	.23
❑ 7 Wayne Gandy	.30	.14
❑ 8 Aaron Glenn	.30	.14
❑ 9 Chris Maumalanga	.30	.14
❑ 10 David Palmer	.75	.35
❑ 11 Errict Rhett	1.50	.70
❑ 12 Heath Shuler	.75	.35
❑ 13 Dewayne Washington	.30	.14
❑ 14 Bryant Young	.50	.23
❑ 15 Dan Wilkinson	.50	.23
❑ 16 Rob Fredrickson	.30	.14

		MINT	NRMT
❑ 17	Calvin Jones	.30	.14
❑ 18	James Folston	.30	.14
❑ 19	Marshall Faulk	4.00	1.80

1994 Collector's Edge Boss Rookies Update

	MINT	NRMT
COMPLETE FACT.SET (25)	30.00	13.50
COMMON CARD (1-25)	.75	.35
SEMISTARS	1.25	.55
UNLISTED STARS	2.00	.90

AVAILABLE VIA MAIL REDEMPTION
*DIAMOND CARDS: 1.5X to 2.5X HI COLUMN
ONE SET PER MAIL REDEMPTION CARD
*GREEN CARDS: .4X TO .75X HI COLUMN
STATED ODDS 1:3 POP WARNER

		MINT	NRMT
❑ 1	Trent Dilfer	3.00	1.35
❑ 2	Jeff Burris	.75	.35
❑ 3	Shante Carver	.75	.35
❑ 4	Lake Dawson	1.25	.55
❑ 5	Bert Emanuel	2.00	.90
❑ 6	Marshall Faulk	8.00	3.60
❑ 7	William Floyd	1.25	.55
❑ 8	Charlie Garner	1.25	.55
❑ 9	Rob Fredrickson	.75	.35
❑ 10	Wayne Gandy	.75	.35
❑ 11	Aaron Glenn	.75	.35
❑ 12	Greg Hill	1.25	.55
❑ 13	Isaac Bruce	8.00	3.60
❑ 14	Charles Johnson	2.00	.90
❑ 15	Johnnie Morton	2.00	.90
❑ 16	Calvin Jones	.75	.35
❑ 17	Tim Bowens	.75	.35
❑ 18	David Palmer	2.00	.90
❑ 19	Errict Rhett	2.00	.90
❑ 20	Darnay Scott	2.50	1.10
❑ 21	Heath Shuler	2.00	.90
❑ 22	John Thierry	.75	.35
❑ 23	Bernard Williams	.75	.35
❑ 24	Dan Wilkinson	.75	.35
❑ 25	Bryant Young	1.25	.55

1994 Collector's Edge Boss Squad

	MINT	NRMT
COMPLETE SET (25)	15.00	6.75

STATED ODDS 1:2 ALL EDGE PACK TYPES
*SILVERS: 1X TO 2X BASE CARD HI
STATED ODDS 1:2 POP WARNER
*BRONZE EQII: 1X TO 2X BASE CARD HI
ONE SET PER EDGEQUEST REDEMPTION
*GOLD HELMETS: 1X TO 2X BASE CARD HI
ONE SET PER POP WARN.EDGEQUEST RED.

		MINT	NRMT
❑ 1	John Elway W/2	4.00	1.80
❑ 2	Joe Montana	4.00	1.80
❑ 3	Vinny Testaverde	.20	.09
❑ 4	Boomer Esiason	.20	.09
❑ 5	Steve Young W/1	1.50	.70
❑ 6	Troy Aikman	2.00	.90
❑ 7	Phil Simms	.20	.09
❑ 8	Bobby Hebert	.10	.05
❑ 9	Thurman Thomas	.50	.23
❑ 10	Leonard Russell	.10	.05
❑ 11	Chris Warren W/2	.20	.09
❑ 12	Gary Brown	.10	.05
❑ 13	Emmitt Smith	3.00	1.35
❑ 14	Jerome Bettis	.50	.23
❑ 15	Erric Pegram	.10	.05
❑ 16	Barry Sanders W/1	4.00	1.80
❑ 17	Reggie Langhorne	.10	.05
❑ 18	Anthony Miller	.20	.09
❑ 19	Shannon Sharpe	.20	.09
❑ 20	Tim Brown	.50	.23
❑ 21	Sterling Sharpe W/2	.20	.09
❑ 22	Jerry Rice W/1	2.00	.90
❑ 23	Michael Irvin	.50	.23
❑ 24	Andre Rison	.20	.09
❑ 25	Checklist	.10	.05

1994 Collector's Edge FX

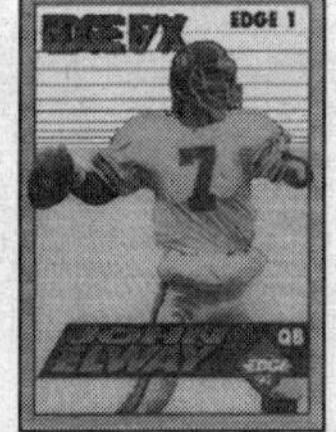

	MINT	NRMT
COMPLETE SET (7)	20.00	9.00

CARDS ARE CLEAR WITH NO FOIL
STATED ODDS 1:7 GOLD
*GOLD SHIELDS: 3X to 8X BASE CARD HI
STATED ODDS 1:200 GOLD
*WHITE BACKS: 1.5X TO 4X BASE CARD HI
STATED ODDS 1:7 RETAIL/JUMBO
*SILVER SHIELDS: 8X to 20X BASE CARD HI
STATED ODDS 1:200 RETAIL/JUMBO
*SILVER BACKS: .8X TO 2X BASE CARD HI
STATED ODDS 1:7 SILVER
*GOLD BACKS: 5X to 12X BASE CARD HI
STATED ODDS 1:200 SILVER
*SILVER LETTERS: 2X TO 4X BASE CARD HI
STATED ODDS 1:7 POP WARNER
*GOLD LETTERS: 3X to 8X BASE CARD HI
STATED ODDS 1:200 POP WARNER
*RED LETTERS: 1.2X to 3X BASE CARD HI
ONE SET PER EDGEQUEST REDEMPTION

		MINT	NRMT
❑ 1	John Elway	8.00	3.60
❑ 2	Joe Montana	8.00	3.60
❑ 3	Troy Aikman	4.00	1.80
❑ 4	Emmitt Smith	6.00	2.70
❑ 5	Jerome Bettis	1.00	.45
❑ 6	Anthony Miller	.40	.18
❑ 7	Sterling Sharpe	.40	.18

1995 Collector's Edge

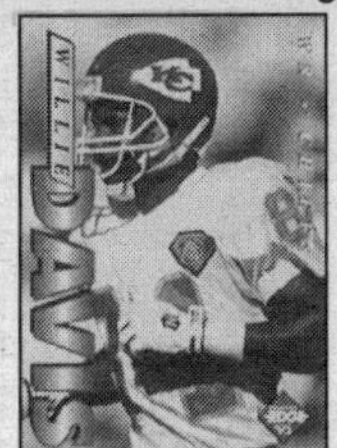

	MINT	NRMT
COMPLETE SET (205)	20.00	9.00
COMMON CARD (1-205)	.05	.02
SEMISTARS	.10	.05
UNLISTED STARS	.25	.11

*BLACK LABEL CARDS: SAME VALUE
CARDS FOUND IN BLACK LABEL PACKS
*GOLD LOGO CARDS: SAME VALUE
INSERTS IN EDGE HOBBY/RETAIL PACKS

	MINT	NRMT
COMP.DIE CUT SET (205)	120.00	55.00

*DIE CUT STARS: 2X TO 5X HI COL.
STATED ODDS 1:24 HOB/RET

	MINT	NRMT
COMP.22K GOLD SET (205)	800.00	350.00

*22K GOLD STARS: 12X TO 30X HI COL.
STATED ODDS 1:200 RETAIL

	MINT	NRMT
COMP.BL SIL.DIE CUT (205)	250.00	110.00

*BL SILV.DIE CUT STARS: 4X TO 10X
STATED ODDS 1:24 BLACK LABEL

	MINT	NRMT
COMP.BL 22K GOLD (205)	800.00	350.00

*BL 22K GOLD STARS: 12X TO 30X HI
STATED ODDS 1:200 BLACK LABEL

	MINT	NRMT
COMP.NITRO 22K SET (205)	300.00	135.00

*NITRO 22K STARS: 5X TO ,12X HI COL.
INS.IN NITRO BOXES AND MAIL REDEM.

		MINT	NRMT
❑ 1	Anthony Edwards	.05	.02
❑ 2	Garrison Hearst	.25	.11
❑ 3	Seth Joyner	.05	.02
❑ 4	Dave Krieg	.05	.02
❑ 5	Chuck Levy	.05	.02
❑ 6	Rob Moore	.05	.02
❑ 7	J.J. Birden	.05	.02
❑ 8	Jeff George	.10	.05
❑ 9	Craig Heyward	.10	.05
❑ 10	Norm Johnson	.05	.02
❑ 11	Terance Mathis	.10	.05
❑ 12	Eric Metcalf	.10	.05
❑ 13	Chuck Smith	.05	.02
❑ 14	Darryl Talley	.05	.02
❑ 15	Cornelius Bennett	.10	.05
❑ 16	Steve Christie	.05	.02
❑ 17	Kenneth Davis	.05	.02
❑ 18	Phil Hansen	.05	.02
❑ 19	Jim Kelly	.25	.11
❑ 20	Bryce Paup	.25	.11
❑ 21	Andre Reed	.10	.05
❑ 22	Bruce Smith	.25	.11
❑ 23	Eric Ball	.05	.02
❑ 24	Don Beebe	.05	.02
❑ 25	Mark Carrier WR	.10	.05
❑ 26	Tim McKyer	.05	.02
❑ 27	Pete Metzelaars	.05	.02
❑ 28	Sam Mills	.10	.05
❑ 29	Jack Trudeau	.05	.02
❑ 30	Mark Carrier DB	.05	.02
❑ 31	Curtis Conway	.25	.11
❑ 32	Erik Kramer	.05	.02
❑ 33	Lewis Tillman	.05	.02
❑ 34	Michael Timpson	.05	.02
❑ 35	Steve Walsh	.05	.02
❑ 36	Chris Zorich	.05	.02
❑ 37	Jeff Blake RC	.75	.35
❑ 38	Harold Green	.05	.02
❑ 39	David Klingler	.10	.05
❑ 40	Carl Pickens	.25	.11
❑ 41	Tom Waddle	.05	.02

Card	MINT	NRMT
❑ 42 Dan Wilkinson	.10	.05
❑ 43 Leroy Hoard	.05	.02
❑ 44 Michael Jackson	.10	.05
❑ 45 Antonio Langham	.05	.02
❑ 46 Andre Rison	.10	.05
❑ 47 Vinny Testaverde	.10	.05
❑ 48 Eric Turner	.05	.02
❑ 49 Tommy Vardell	.05	.02
❑ 50 Troy Aikman	1.00	.45
❑ 51 Charles Haley	.10	.05
❑ 52 Michael Irvin	.25	.11
❑ 53 Daryl Johnston	.10	.05
❑ 54 Leon Lett	.05	.02
❑ 55 Jay Novacek	.10	.05
❑ 56 Emmitt Smith	1.50	.70
❑ 57 Kevin Williams WR	.10	.05
❑ 58 Steve Atwater	.05	.02
❑ 59 John Elway	2.00	.90
❑ 60 Simon Fletcher	.05	.02
❑ 61 Glyn Milburn	.05	.02
❑ 62 Anthony Miller	.10	.05
❑ 63 Leonard Russell	.05	.02
❑ 64 Shannon Sharpe	.10	.05
❑ 65 Scott Mitchell	.10	.05
❑ 66 Herman Moore	.25	.11
❑ 67 Johnnie Morton	.10	.05
❑ 68 Brett Perriman	.10	.05
❑ 69 Barry Sanders	2.00	.90
❑ 70 Edgar Bennett	.10	.05
❑ 71 Brett Favre	2.00	.90
❑ 72 Mark Ingram	.05	.02
❑ 73 Chris Jacke	.05	.02
❑ 74 Guy McIntyre	.05	.02
❑ 75 Reggie White	.25	.11
❑ 76 Gary Brown	.05	.02
❑ 77 Ernest Givins	.05	.02
❑ 78 Mel Gray	.05	.02
❑ 79 Haywood Jeffires	.05	.02
❑ 80 Webster Slaughter	.05	.02
❑ 81 Craig Erickson	.05	.02
❑ 82 Marshall Faulk	.40	.18
❑ 83 Jim Harbaugh	.10	.05
❑ 84 Roosevelt Potts	.05	.02
❑ 85 Floyd Turner	.05	.02
❑ 86 Steve Beuerlein	.05	.02
❑ 87 Reggie Cobb	.05	.02
❑ 88 Jeff Lageman	.05	.02
❑ 89 Mazio Royster	.05	.02
❑ 90 Marcus Allen	.25	.11
❑ 91 Steve Bono	.10	.05
❑ 92 Willie Davis	.10	.05
❑ 93 Lake Dawson	.10	.05
❑ 94 Ronnie Lott	.10	.05
❑ 95 Eric Martin	.05	.02
❑ 96 Chris Penn	.05	.02
❑ 97 Tim Brown	.25	.11
❑ 98 Derrick Fenner	.05	.02
❑ 99 Rob Fredrickson	.05	.02
❑ 100 Nolan Harrison	.05	.02
❑ 101 Jeff Hostetler	.10	.05
❑ 102 Rocket Ismail	.10	.05
❑ 103 James Jett	.10	.05
❑ 104 Chester McGlockton	.10	.05
❑ 105 Anthony Smith	.05	.02
❑ 106 Harvey Williams	.05	.02
❑ 107 Jerome Bettis	.25	.11
❑ 108 Troy Drayton	.05	.02
❑ 109 Chris Miller	.05	.02
❑ 110 Robert Young	.05	.02
❑ 111 Keith Byars	.05	.02
❑ 112 Gary Clark	.05	.02
❑ 113 Bryan Cox	.05	.02
❑ 114 Jeff Cross	.05	.02
❑ 115 Irving Fryar	.10	.05
❑ 116 Randal Hill	.05	.02
❑ 117 Terry Kirby	.10	.05
❑ 118 Dan Marino	2.00	.90
❑ 119 O.J. McDuffie	.25	.11
❑ 120 Bernie Parmalee	.10	.05
❑ 121 Terry Allen	.10	.05
❑ 122 Cris Carter	.25	.11
❑ 123 Qadry Ismail	.10	.05
❑ 124 Warren Moon	.10	.05
❑ 125 John Randle	.05	.02
❑ 126 Jake Reed	.10	.05
❑ 127 Fuad Reveiz	.05	.02
❑ 128 Broderick Thomas	.05	.02
❑ 129 Drew Bledsoe	1.00	.45
❑ 130 Vincent Brisby	.05	.02
❑ 131 Ben Coates	.10	.05
❑ 132 Dave Meggett	.05	.02
❑ 133 Chris Slade	.10	.05
❑ 134 Leroy Thompson	.05	.02
❑ 135 Eric Allen	.05	.02
❑ 136 Mario Bates	.25	.11
❑ 137 Quinn Early	.05	.02
❑ 138 Jim Everett	.05	.02
❑ 139 Michael Haynes	.10	.05
❑ 140 Torrance Small	.05	.02
❑ 141 Dave Brown	.10	.05
❑ 142 Chris Calloway	.05	.02
❑ 143 Keith Hamilton	.05	.02
❑ 144 Rodney Hampton	.10	.05
❑ 145 Mike Sherrard	.05	.02
❑ 146 David Treadwell	.05	.02
❑ 147 Herschel Walker	.10	.05
❑ 148 Boomer Esiason	.10	.05
❑ 149 Erik Howard	.05	.02
❑ 150 Johnny Johnson	.05	.02
❑ 151 Mo Lewis	.05	.02
❑ 152 Johnny Mitchell	.05	.02
❑ 153 Fred Barnett	.10	.05
❑ 154 Randall Cunningham	.25	.11
❑ 155 William Fuller	.05	.02
❑ 156 Charlie Garner	.10	.05
❑ 157 Greg Jackson	.05	.02
❑ 158 Ricky Watters	.25	.11
❑ 159 Calvin Williams	.10	.05
❑ 160 Barry Foster	.10	.05
❑ 161 Kevin Greene	.10	.05
❑ 162 Greg Lloyd	.10	.05
❑ 163 Byron Bam Morris	.10	.05
❑ 164 Neil O'Donnell	.10	.05
❑ 165 Erric Pegram	.10	.05
❑ 166 John L. Williams	.05	.02
❑ 167 Rod Woodson	.10	.05
❑ 168 John Carney	.05	.02
❑ 169 Stan Humphries	.10	.05
❑ 170 Natrone Means	.25	.11
❑ 171 Chris Mims	.05	.02
❑ 172 Leslie O'Neal	.10	.05
❑ 173 Alfred Pupunu RC	.05	.02
❑ 174 Junior Seau	.25	.11
❑ 175 Mark Seay	.10	.05
❑ 176 William Floyd	.25	.11
❑ 177 Jerry Rice	1.00	.45
❑ 178 Deion Sanders	.60	.25
❑ 179 Dana Stubblefield	.25	.11
❑ 180 John Taylor	.05	.02
❑ 181 Steve Young	.75	.35
❑ 182 Bryant Young	.10	.05
❑ 183 Brian Blades	.10	.05
❑ 184 Cortez Kennedy	.10	.05
❑ 185 Kelvin Martin	.05	.02
❑ 186 Rick Mirer	.25	.11
❑ 187 Ricky Proehl	.05	.02
❑ 188 Michael Sinclair	.05	.02
❑ 189 Chris Warren	.10	.05
❑ 190 Trent Dilfer	.25	.11
❑ 191 Alvin Harper	.05	.02
❑ 192 Jackie Harris	.05	.02
❑ 193 Hardy Nickerson	.05	.02
❑ 194 Errict Rhett	.25	.11
❑ 195 Reggie Roby	.05	.02
❑ 196 Henry Ellard	.10	.05
❑ 197 Ricky Ervins	.05	.02
❑ 198 Darrell Green	.05	.02
❑ 199 Brian Mitchell	.05	.02
❑ 200 Heath Shuler	.25	.11
❑ 201 Checklist	.05	.02
❑ 202 Checklist	.05	.02
❑ 203 Checklist	.05	.02
❑ 204 Checklist	.05	.02
❑ 205 Checklist	.05	.02
❑ P1 Natrone Means Promo	.50	.23
❑ P2 Chris Warren Promo	.50	.23

1995 Collector's Edge EdgeTech

	MINT	NRMT
COMPLETE SET (37)	40.00	18.00

STATED ODDS 1:12 HOB/RET....
*BLACK LABEL: .75X TO 1.5X BASE CARD HI
STATED ODDS 1:12 BLACK LABEL
*BLACK LABEL 22K: 2X TO 5X BASE CARD HI
BL 22K STATED ODDS 1:120 BLACK LABEL
*22K GOLDS: 4X TO 10X BASE CARD HI
STATED ODDS 1:120 RETAIL ....
*QUANTUMS: 8X TO 20X BASE CARD HI
STATED ODDS 1:120 BLACK LABEL
*QUANT.DIE CUTS: 12X TO 30X BASE CARD HI
RANDOM INSERTS IN BLACK LABEL PACKS
*CIRCULAR PRISMS: 1.5X TO 3X BASE CARD HI
CIRC.PRISMS: ONE PER JUMBO

Card	MINT	NRMT
❑ 1 Dan Marino	6.00	2.70
❑ 2 Steve Young	2.50	1.10
❑ 3 Rick Mirer	.75	.35
❑ 4 Emmitt Smith	5.00	2.20
❑ 5 John Elway	6.00	2.70
❑ 6 Neil O'Donnell	.30	.14
❑ 7 Marshall Faulk	1.25	.55
❑ 8 Deion Sanders	2.00	.90
❑ 9 Terance Mathis	.30	.14
❑ 10 Kevin Greene	.30	.14
❑ 11 Ricky Watters	.75	.35
❑ 12 Tim Brown	.75	.35
❑ 13 Antonio Langham	.15	.07
❑ 14 Lake Dawson	.30	.14
❑ 15 Jay Novacek	.30	.14
❑ 16 Herman Moore	.75	.35
❑ 17 Mark Seay	.30	.14
❑ 18 Bernie Parmalee	.30	.14
❑ 19 Drew Bledsoe	3.00	1.35
❑ 20 Troy Aikman	3.00	1.35
❑ 21 Brett Favre	6.00	2.70
❑ 22 Jerry Rice	3.00	1.35
❑ 23 Barry Sanders	6.00	2.70
❑ 24 Heath Shuler	.75	.35
❑ 25 Errict Rhett	.75	.35
❑ 26 Cris Carter	.75	.35
❑ 27 Jerome Bettis	.75	.35
❑ 28 Reggie White	.75	.35
❑ 29 Chris Warren	.30	.14
❑ 30 Ben Coates	.30	.14
❑ 31 Bryant Young	.30	.14
❑ 32 Mel Gray	.15	.07
❑ 33 Darryl Talley	.15	.07
❑ 34 Mike Sherrard	.15	.07
❑ 35 William Floyd	.75	.35
❑ 36 Alvin Harper	.15	.07
❑ 37 Checklist (1-36)	.15	.07

1995 Collector's Edge Rookies

	MINT	NRMT
COMPLETE SET (25)	40.00	18.00
COMMON CARD (1-25)	.60	.25
SEMISTARS	1.00	.45
UNLISTED STARS	1.50	.70

STATED ODDS 1:4 RETAIL ....
*22K GOLD CARDS: 1.25X TO 3X HI COLUMN

22K GOLD ODDS 1:40 RETAIL....
*BLACK LABEL CARDS: SAME VALUE

❑ 1 Derrick Alexander DE .... .60 .25
❑ 2 Tony Boselli.................... 1.00 .45
❑ 3 Ki-Jana Carter................. 1.50 .70
❑ 4 Kevin Carter .... 1.00 .45
❑ 5 Kerry Collins .... 2.00 .90
❑ 6 Steve McNair.................. 5.00 2.20
❑ 7 Billy Milner........................ .60 .25
❑ 8 Rashaan Salaam............. 1.50 .70
❑ 9 Warren Sapp.................. 1.00 .45
❑ 10 James O. Stewart .... 1.00 .45
❑ 11 J.J.Stokes .... 2.00 .90
❑ 12 Bobby Taylor................ 1.00 .45
❑ 13 Tyrone Wheatley UER .. 2.50 1.10
❑ 14 Derrick Brooks................ .60 .25
❑ 15 Reuben Brown .... .60 .25
❑ 16 Mark Bruener .... 1.00 .45
❑ 17 Joey Galloway.............. 5.00 2.20
❑ 18 Napoleon Kaufman 4.00 1.80
❑ 19 Ty Law.......................... 1.00 .45
❑ 20 Craig Newsome............. 1.00 .45
❑ 21 Kordell Stewart 5.00 2.20
❑ 22 Korey Stringer .... .60 .25
❑ 23 Zach Wiegert.................... .60 .25
❑ 24 Michael Westbrook 3.00 1.35
❑ 25 Checklist .... .60 .25

1995 Collector's Edge TimeWarp

	MINT	NRMT
COMPLETE SET (21)	60.00	27.00
COMMON CARD (1-20)...........	2.50	1.10
SEMISTARS...........................	4.00	1.80

STATED ODDS 1:400 HOB/RET,1:200 JUM
*22K GOLDS: 2X TO 4X HI COLUMN
22K GOLD ODDS 1:4000 HOB/RET
*PRISM CARDS: SAME VALUE ..
*BLACK LABEL VERSIONS:SAME VALUE
BL ODDS 1:200 BLACK LABEL PACKS

❑ 1 Emmitt Smith.................. 12.00 5.50
Dick Butkus
❑ 2 Troy Aikman 8.00 3.60
Gino Marchetti
❑ 3 Natrone Means 2.50 1.10
Ray Nitschke
❑ 4 Chris Zorich..................... 2.50 1.10
Steve Van Buren
❑ 5 Barry Sanders 12.00 5.50
Deacon Jones
❑ 6 Kevin Greene 4.00 1.80
Paul Hornung
❑ 7 Charles Haley 2.50 1.10
Len Dawson
❑ 8 Marshall Faulk................. 4.00 1.80
Willie Lanier
❑ 9 Ronnie Lott 4.00 1.80
Gale Sayers
❑ 10 Cris Carter...................... 2.50 1.10
Jack Ham
❑ 11 Junior Seau.................... 4.00 1.80
Gale Sayers
❑ 12 Reggie White.................. 4.00 1.80
Otto Graham
❑ 13 Leslie O'Neal................. 2.50 1.10
Y.A.Tittle
❑ 14 Drew Bledsoe 8.00 3.60
Ted Hendricks
❑ 15 Heath Shuler 4.00 1.80
Bob Lilly
❑ 16 Ricky Watters 4.00 1.80
Daryl Lamonica
❑ 17 Marshall Faulk............... 4.00 1.80
Dick Butkus
❑ 18 Deion Sanders 5.00 2.20
Raymond Berry
❑ 19 Steve Young 6.00 2.70
Jack Youngblood
❑ 20 Bruce Smith................... 4.00 1.80
Sammy Baugh
❑ NNO Checklist .... 2.00 .90
❑ TW1 Gale Sayers................. 2.00 .90
Junior Seau
Dick Butkus
Promo card

1996 Collector's Edge

	MINT	NRMT
COMPLETE SET (250)	20.00	9.00
COMMON CARD (1-250)...........	.10	.05
SEMISTARS............................	.20	.09
UNLISTED STARS....................	.40	.18
COMP.DIE CUT SET (250)	80.00	36.00

*DC STARS: 1.25X TO 3X HI COLUMN
DCs:ONE PER SPECIAL RETAIL PACK

COMP.HOLO.SET (250)	1200.00	550.00

*HOLO.STARS: 25X TO 60X HI COLUMN
HOLOFOILS 1:48 1996 EDGE PACKS
HOLOFOILS 1:33 1997 COWBOYBILIA PLUS
....

❑ 1 Larry Centers .... .20 .09
❑ 2 Garrison Hearst................ .20 .09
❑ 3 Dave Krieg .... .10 .05
❑ 4 Rob Moore .... .20 .09
❑ 5 Frank Sanders.................. .20 .09
❑ 6 Eric Swann .... .10 .05
❑ 7 Morten Andersen.............. .10 .05
❑ 8 Chris Doleman .... .10 .05
❑ 9 Bert Emanuel .... .20 .09
❑ 10 Jeff George .... .20 .09
❑ 11 Craig Heyward .... .10 .05
❑ 12 Terance Mathis .... .10 .05
❑ 13 Clay Matthews................. .10 .05
❑ 14 Eric Metcalf .... .10 .05
❑ 15 Bill Brooks .... .10 .05
❑ 16 Todd Collins .... .20 .09
❑ 17 Russell Copeland .... .10 .05
❑ 18 Jim Kelly .... .40 .18
❑ 19 Bryce Paup .... .10 .05
❑ 20 Andre Reed..................... .20 .09
❑ 21 Bruce Smith..................... .20 .09
❑ 22 Mark Carrier WR .... .10 .05
❑ 23 Kerry Collins .... .40 .18
❑ 24 Willie Green..................... .10 .05
❑ 25 Eric Guliford .... .10 .05
❑ 26 Brett Maxie .... .10 .05
❑ 27 Tim McKyer .... .10 .05
❑ 28 Derrick Moore .... .10 .05
❑ 29 Curtis Conway................. .40 .18
❑ 30 Jim Flanigan .... .10 .05
❑ 31 Jeff Graham .... .10 .05
❑ 32 Robert Green .... .10 .05
❑ 33 Erik Kramer...................... .10 .05
❑ 34 Rashaan Salaam.............. .40 .18
❑ 35 Alonzo Spellman .... .10 .05
❑ 36 Donnell Woolford.............. .10 .05
❑ 37 Chris Zorich...................... .10 .05
❑ 38 Eric Bieniemy .... .10 .05
❑ 39 Jeff Blake .... .40 .18
❑ 40 Ki-Jana Carter.................. .20 .09
❑ 41 John Copeland .... .10 .05
❑ 42 Harold Green.................... .10 .05
❑ 43 Tony McGee .... .10 .05
❑ 44 Carl Pickens .... .40 .18
❑ 45 Darnay Scott .... .20 .09
❑ 46 Bracey Walker.................. .10 .05
❑ 47 Dan Wilkinson .... .10 .05
❑ 48 Rob Burnett...................... .10 .05
❑ 49 Leroy Hoard .... .10 .05
❑ 50 Ernest Hunter .... .10 .05
❑ 51 Michael Jackson .... .20 .09
❑ 52 Stevon Moore .... .10 .05
❑ 53 Anthony Pleasant .... .10 .05
❑ 54 Andre Rison .... .20 .09
❑ 55 Vinny Testaverde .... .20 .09
❑ 56 Eric Zeier.......................... .10 .05
❑ 57 Troy Aikman .... 1.00 .45
❑ 58 Bill Bates .... .20 .09
❑ 59 Shante Carver.................. .10 .05
❑ 60 Michael Irvin .... .40 .18
❑ 61 Daryl Johnston .... .20 .09
❑ 62 Jay Novacek .... .10 .05
❑ 63 Deion Sanders .... .60 .25
❑ 64 Emmitt Smith................. 1.50 .70
❑ 65 Sherman Williams .... .10 .05
❑ 66 Terrell Davis 2.50 1.10
❑ 67 John Elway .... 2.00 .90
❑ 68 Ed McCaffrey .... .20 .09
❑ 69 Glyn Milburn .... .10 .05
❑ 70 Anthony Miller .... .20 .09
❑ 71 Michael Dean Perry........... .10 .05
❑ 72 Shannon Sharpe .... .20 .09
❑ 73 Willie Clay .... .10 .05
❑ 74 Scott Mitchell..................... .20 .09
❑ 75 Herman Moore .... .40 .18
❑ 76 Johnnie Morton .... .20 .09
❑ 77 Brett Perriman.................... .10 .05
❑ 78 Barry Sanders .... 2.00 .90
❑ 79 Tracy Scroggins .... .10 .05
❑ 80 Edgar Bennett.................... .20 .09
❑ 81 Robert Brooks .... .40 .18
❑ 82 Brett Favre .... 2.00 .90
❑ 83 Dorsey Levens .... .50 .23
❑ 84 Craig Newsome................. .10 .05
❑ 85 Wayne Simmons .... .10 .05
❑ 86 Reggie White..................... .40 .18
❑ 87 Chris Chandler .... .20 .09
❑ 88 Anthony Cook .... .10 .05
❑ 89 Mel Gray .... .10 .05
❑ 90 Haywood Jeffires............... .10 .05
❑ 91 Darryll Lewis .... .10 .05
❑ 92 Steve McNair..................... .75 .35
❑ 93 Todd McNair .... .10 .05
❑ 94 Rodney Thomas .... .10 .05
❑ 95 Trev Alberts....................... .10 .05
❑ 96 Tony Bennett...................... .10 .05
❑ 97 Quentin Coryatt.................. .10 .05
❑ 98 Sean Dawkins .... .10 .05

Card	MINT	NRMT
❑ 99 Ken Dilger	.20	.09
❑ 100 Marshall Faulk	.40	.18
❑ 101 Jim Harbaugh	.20	.09
❑ 102 Ronald Humphrey	.10	.05
❑ 103 Floyd Turner	.10	.05
❑ 104 Steve Beuerlein	.10	.05
❑ 105 Tony Boselli	.10	.05
❑ 106 Mark Brunell	1.00	.45
❑ 107 Willie Jackson	.10	.05
❑ 108 Jeff Lageman	.10	.05
❑ 109 James O. Stewart	.20	.09
❑ 110 Cedric Tillman	.10	.05
❑ 111 Marcus Allen	.40	.18
❑ 112 Kimble Anders	.20	.09
❑ 113 Steve Bono	.10	.05
❑ 114 Dale Carter	.10	.05
❑ 115 Willie Davis	.10	.05
❑ 116 Lake Dawson	.10	.05
❑ 117 Dan Saleaumua	.10	.05
❑ 118 Neil Smith	.10	.05
❑ 119 Derrick Thomas	.20	.09
❑ 120 Tamarick Vanover	.20	.09
❑ 121 Marco Coleman	.10	.05
❑ 122 Bryan Cox	.10	.05
❑ 123 Steve Emtman	.10	.05
❑ 124 Irving Fryar	.20	.09
❑ 125 Eric Green	.10	.05
❑ 126 Terry Kirby	.20	.09
❑ 127 Dan Marino	2.00	.90
❑ 128 O.J. McDuffie	.20	.09
❑ 129 Bernie Parmalee	.10	.05
❑ 130 Troy Vincent	.10	.05
❑ 131 Cris Carter	.40	.18
❑ 132 Jack Del Rio	.10	.05
❑ 133 Qadry Ismail	.10	.05
❑ 134 Amp Lee	.10	.05
❑ 135 Warren Moon	.20	.09
❑ 136 John Randle	.10	.05
❑ 137 Jake Reed	.20	.09
❑ 138 Robert Smith	.20	.09
❑ 139 Drew Bledsoe	1.00	.45
❑ 140 Vincent Brisby	.10	.05
❑ 141 Ben Coates	.20	.09
❑ 142 Curtis Martin	.75	.35
❑ 143 Dave Meggett	.10	.05
❑ 144 Will Moore	.10	.05
❑ 145 Chris Slade	.10	.05
❑ 146 Mario Bates	.20	.09
❑ 147 Quinn Early	.10	.05
❑ 148 Jim Everett	.10	.05
❑ 149 Michael Haynes	.10	.05
❑ 150 Tyrone Hughes	.10	.05
❑ 151 Wayne Martin	.10	.05
❑ 152 Renaldo Turnbull	.10	.05
❑ 153 Dave Brown	.10	.05
❑ 154 Chris Calloway	.10	.05
❑ 155 Rodney Hampton	.20	.09
❑ 156 Mike Sherrard	.10	.05
❑ 157 Michael Strahan	.10	.05
❑ 158 Herschel Walker	.20	.09
❑ 159 Tyrone Wheatley	.20	.09
❑ 160 Kyle Brady	.10	.05
❑ 161 Wayne Chrebet	.20	.09
❑ 162 Hugh Douglas	.10	.05
❑ 163 Adrian Murrell	.40	.18
❑ 164 Todd Scott	.10	.05
❑ 165 Charles Wilson	.10	.05
❑ 166 Tim Brown	.40	.18
❑ 167 Aundray Bruce	.10	.05
❑ 168 Andrew Glover	.10	.05
❑ 169 Jeff Hostetler	.10	.05
❑ 170 Napoleon Kaufman	.50	.23
❑ 171 Terry McDaniel	.10	.05
❑ 172 Chester McGlockton	.10	.05
❑ 173 Pat Swilling	.10	.05
❑ 174 Harvey Williams	.10	.05
❑ 175 Fred Barnett	.10	.05
❑ 176 Randall Cunningham	.40	.18
❑ 177 William Fuller	.10	.05
❑ 178 Charlie Garner	.10	.05
❑ 179 Andy Harmon	.10	.05
❑ 180 Rodney Peete	.10	.05
❑ 181 Ricky Watters	.20	.09
❑ 182 Calvin Williams	.10	.05
❑ 183 Chad Brown	.10	.05
❑ 184 Kevin Greene	.20	.09
❑ 185 Greg Lloyd	.20	.09
❑ 186 Byron Bam Morris	.20	.09
❑ 187 Neil O'Donnell	.20	.09
❑ 188 Erric Pegram	.10	.05
❑ 189 Kordell Stewart	.75	.35
❑ 190 Yancey Thigpen	.20	.09
❑ 191 Rod Woodson	.20	.09
❑ 192 Darren Bennett	.10	.05
❑ 193 Ronnie Harmon	.10	.05
❑ 194 Stan Humphries	.20	.09
❑ 195 Tony Martin	.20	.09
❑ 196 Natrone Means	.40	.18
❑ 197 Leslie O'Neal	.10	.05
❑ 198 Junior Seau	.20	.09
❑ 199 Mark Seay	.10	.05
❑ 200 William Floyd	.20	.09
❑ 201 Merton Hanks	.10	.05
❑ 202 Brent Jones	.10	.05
❑ 203 Derek Loville	.10	.05
❑ 204 Ken Norton, Jr.	.10	.05
❑ 205 Gary Plummer	.10	.05
❑ 206 Jerry Rice	1.00	.45
❑ 207 J.J. Stokes	.40	.18
❑ 208 Dana Stubblefield	.20	.09
❑ 209 John Taylor	.10	.05
❑ 210 Bryant Young	.20	.09
❑ 211 Steve Young	.75	.35
❑ 212 Brian Blades	.10	.05
❑ 213 Joey Galloway	.75	.35
❑ 214 Carlton Gray	.10	.05
❑ 215 Cortez Kennedy	.10	.05
❑ 216 Rick Mirer	.20	.09
❑ 217 Chris Warren	.20	.09
❑ 218 Jerome Bettis	.40	.18
❑ 219 Isaac Bruce	.40	.18
❑ 220 Troy Drayton	.10	.05
❑ 221 D'Marco Farr	.10	.05
❑ 222 Sean Gilbert	.10	.05
❑ 223 Chris Miller	.10	.05
❑ 224 Roman Phifer	.10	.05
❑ 225 Trent Dilfer	.40	.18
❑ 226 Santana Dotson	.10	.05
❑ 227 Alvin Harper	.10	.05
❑ 228 Jackie Harris	.10	.05
❑ 229 John Lynch	.10	.05
❑ 230 Hardy Nickerson	.10	.05
❑ 231 Errict Rhett	.20	.09
❑ 232 Warren Sapp	.10	.05
❑ 233 Terry Allen	.20	.09
❑ 234 Henry Ellard	.10	.05
❑ 235 Gus Frerotte	.40	.18
❑ 236 Ken Harvey	.10	.05
❑ 237 Brian Mitchell	.10	.05
❑ 238 Heath Shuler	.20	.09
❑ 239 James Washington	.10	.05
❑ 240 Michael Westbrook	.40	.18
❑ 241 Checklist	.10	.05
❑ 242 Checklist	.10	.05
❑ 243 Checklist	.10	.05
❑ 244 Checklist	.10	.05
❑ 245 Checklist	.10	.05
❑ 246 Checklist	.10	.05
❑ 247 Checklist	.10	.05
❑ 248 Checklist	.10	.05
❑ 249 Checklist	.10	.05
❑ 250 Checklist	.10	.05
❑ PR1 Eddie George Promo die cut Crucibles promo	3.00	1.35

1996 Collector's Edge Big Easy

	MINT	NRMT
COMPLETE SET (19)	60.00	27.00
CL (NNO)	1.50	.70
STATED ODDS 1:72		
STATED PRINT RUN 2000 SERIAL #'d SETS		
GOLD FOILS: 1.25X TO 3X BASE CARD HI		
GOLDS PRINT RUN 3100 SERIAL #'d SETS		
GOLD FOILS ISSUED VIA DIRECT MAIL OFFER		

Card	MINT	NRMT
❑ 1 Kerry Collins	2.50	1.10
❑ 2 Rashaan Salaam	2.50	1.10
❑ 3 Troy Aikman	6.00	2.70
❑ 4 Deion Sanders	4.00	1.80
❑ 5 Emmitt Smith	10.00	4.50
❑ 6 Terrell Davis	15.00	6.75
❑ 7 Barry Sanders	12.00	5.50
❑ 8 Brett Favre	12.00	5.50
❑ 9 Marshall Faulk	2.50	1.10
❑ 10 Tamarick Vanover	1.25	.55
❑ 11 Dan Marino	12.00	5.50
❑ 12 Drew Bledsoe	6.00	2.70
❑ 13 Curtis Martin	5.00	2.20
❑ 14 J.J.Stokes	2.50	1.10
❑ 15 Joey Galloway	5.00	2.20
❑ 16 Isaac Bruce	2.50	1.10
❑ 17 Errict Rhett	1.25	.55
❑ 18 Carl Pickens	2.50	1.10
❑ NNO Checklist Card	.60	.25
❑ P1 Errict Rhett Promo	1.00	.45

1996 Collector's Edge Cowboybilia

	MINT	NRMT
COMPLETE SET (25)	20.00	9.00
COMMON CARD (Q1-Q25)	.50	.23
SEMISTARS	.75	.35
UNLISTED STARS	1.50	.70
TWO PER 1997 COWBOYBILIA PLUS		

Card	MINT	NRMT
❑ Q1 Chris Boniol	.50	.23
❑ Q2 John Jett	.50	.23
❑ Q3 Sherman Williams	.50	.23
❑ Q4 Chad Hennings	.50	.23
❑ Q5 Larry Allen	.50	.23
❑ Q6 Jason Garrett	.75	.35
❑ Q7 Tony Tolbert	.50	.23
❑ Q8 Kevin Williams	.50	.23
❑ Q9 Mark Tuinei	.50	.23
❑ Q10 Larry Brown/4000 MVP gold foil	.50	.23
❑ Q11 Kevin Smith	.50	.23
❑ Q12 Darrin Smith	.50	.23
❑ Q13 Robert Jones	.50	.23
❑ Q14 Nate Newton	.50	.23
❑ Q15 Darren Woodson	.75	.35
❑ Q16 Leon Lett	.75	.35
❑ Q17 Russell Maryland	.50	.23
❑ Q18 Erik Williams	.50	.23
❑ Q19 Bill Bates	.75	.35
❑ Q20 Daryl Johnston	.75	.35
❑ Q21 Jay Novacek	.75	.35
❑ Q22 Charles Haley	.75	.35
❑ Q23 Troy Aikman	3.00	1.35
❑ Q24 Michael Irvin	1.50	.70
❑ Q25 Emmitt Smith	5.00	2.20

1996 Collector's Edge Cowboybilia Autographs

	MINT	NRMT
COMPLETE SET (25)	500.00	220.00
COMMONS (DCA1-DCA25)	10.00	4.50
SEMISTARS	15.00	6.75
STARS NUMBERED OF 2300	20.00	9.00

STATED ODDS 1:2.5 COWBOYBILIA
AND 1:1.5 1997 COWBOYBILIA PLUS
STAU/PEAR ODDS 1:192 COWBOYBILIA
AND 1:134 1997 COWBOYBILIA PLUS

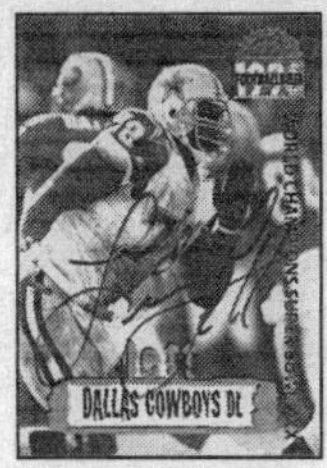

		MINT	NRMT
❑ DCA1	Chris Boniol/4000	10.00	4.50
❑ DCA2	John Jett/4000	10.00	4.50
❑ DCA3	Sherman Williams/4000	10.00	4.50
❑ DCA4	Chad Hennings/4000	15.00	6.75
❑ DCA5	Larry Allen/4000	10.00	4.50
❑ DCA6	Jason Garrett/4000	10.00	4.50
❑ DCA7	Tony Tolbert/4000	10.00	4.50
❑ DCA8	Kevin Williams/4000	10.00	4.50
❑ DCA9	Mark Tuinei/4000	10.00	4.50
❑ DCA10	Larry Brown/4000	10.00	4.50
	MVP gold foil		
❑ DCA11	Kevin Smith/4000	15.00	6.75
❑ DCA12	Darrin Smith/4000	10.00	4.50
❑ DCA13	Robert Jones/4000	10.00	4.50
❑ DCA14	Nate Newton/4000	10.00	4.50
❑ DCA15	D.Woodson/4000	15.00	6.75
❑ DCA16	Leon Lett/4000	15.00	6.75
❑ DCA17	R.Maryland/4000	10.00	4.50
❑ DCA18	Erik Williams/4000	10.00	4.50
❑ DCA19	Bill Bates/4000	15.00	6.75
❑ DCA20	Daryl Johnston/2300	20.00	9.00
❑ DCA21	Jay Novacek/2300	20.00	9.00
❑ DCA22	Charles Haley/2300	20.00	9.00
❑ DCA23	Troy Aikman/600	60.00	27.00
	all cards unsigned		
❑ DCA24	Michael Irvin/500	80.00	36.00
❑ DCA25	Emmitt Smith/500	200.00	90.00
❑ NNO	Roger Staubach	120.00	55.00
	Drew Pearson		
	Hail Mary Pass		
	numbered of 1000		

1996 Collector's Edge Cowboybilia 24K Holofoil

	MINT	NRMT
COMPLETE SET (4)	200.00	90.00

STATED ODDS 1:48 1996 COWBOYBILIA AND 1:32.5 1997 COWBOYBILIA PLUS

		MINT	NRMT
❑ CB57	Troy Aikman	75.00	34.00
❑ CB60	Michael Irvin	30.00	13.50
❑ CB63	Deion Sanders	50.00	22.00
❑ CB64	Emmitt Smith	150.00	70.00

1996 Collector's Edge Draft Day Redemption

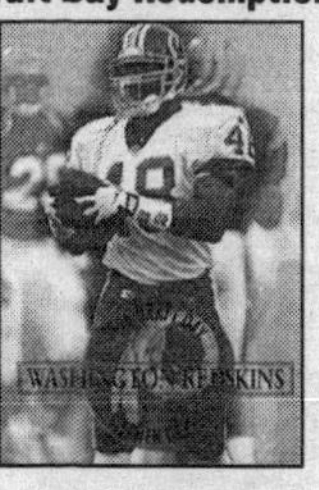

	MINT	NRMT
COMPLETE SET (30)	100.00	45.00
COMMON CARD (1-30)	1.25	.55
SEMISTARS	2.00	.90
UNLISTED STARS	3.00	1.35

CARDS AVAIL.VIA MAIL REDEMPTION

		MINT	NRMT
❑ 1	Simeon Rice	1.25	.55
❑ 2	Richard Huntley	1.25	.55
❑ 3	Jonathan Ogden	1.25	.55
❑ 4	Eric Moulds	3.00	1.35
❑ 5	Tim Biakabutuka	4.00	1.80
❑ 6	Walt Harris	1.25	.55
❑ 7	Marco Battaglia	1.25	.55
❑ 8	Stepfret Williams	1.25	.55
❑ 9	John Mobley	1.25	.55
❑ 10	Reggie Brown LB	1.25	.55
❑ 11	Derrick Mayes	2.00	.90
❑ 12	Eddie George	10.00	4.50
❑ 13	Marvin Harrison	8.00	3.60
❑ 14	Kevin Hardy	1.25	.55
❑ 15	Jerome Woods	1.25	.55
❑ 16	Karim Abdul-Jabbar	2.00	.90
❑ 17	Duane Clemons	1.25	.55
❑ 18	Terry Glenn	3.00	1.35
❑ 19	Ricky Whittle	1.25	.55
❑ 20	Amani Toomer	1.25	.55
❑ 21	Keyshawn Johnson	3.00	1.35
❑ 22	Rickey Dudley	2.00	.90
❑ 23	Bobby Hoying	2.00	.90
❑ 24	Jahine Arnold	1.25	.55
❑ 25	Tony Banks	2.00	.90
❑ 26	Bryan Still	1.25	.55
❑ 27	Terrell Owens	8.00	3.60
❑ 28	Reggie Brown RB	1.25	.55
❑ 29	Mike Alstott	3.00	1.35
❑ 30	Stephen Davis	10.00	4.50

1996 Collector's Edge Proteges

	MINT	NRMT
COMPLETE SET (13)	120.00	55.00
COMMON CARD (1-12)	6.00	2.70
CL (NNO)	2.00	.90
SEMISTARS	8.00	3.60
UNLISTED STARS	12.00	5.50

STATED ODDS 1:164

		MINT	NRMT
❑ 1	Eric Metcalf	8.00	3.60
	Joey Galloway		
❑ 2	Herman Moore	8.00	3.60
	Michael Westbrook		
❑ 3	Emmitt Smith	25.00	11.00
	Errict Rhett		
❑ 4	Kordell Stewart	30.00	13.50
	John Elway		
❑ 5	Terrell Davis	35.00	16.00
	Marshall Faulk		
❑ 6	Rashaan Salaam	8.00	3.60
	Marcus Allen		
❑ 7	Dan Marino	30.00	13.50
	Drew Bledsoe		
❑ 8	Brett Favre	30.00	13.50
	Kerry Collins		
❑ 9	Tim Brown	8.00	3.60
	Isaac Bruce		
❑ 10	Cris Carter	6.00	2.70
	Chris Sanders		
❑ 11	Curtis Martin	12.00	5.50
	Chris Warren		
❑ 12	Tamarick Vanover	8.00	3.60
	Brian Mitchell		
❑ NNO	Checklist Card	2.00	.90
❑ P1	Rashaan Salaam Promo	2.00	.90
	Terry Kirby		

1996 Collector's Edge Quantum Motion

	MINT	NRMT
COMPLETE SET (25)	150.00	70.00
CL (NNO)	1.00	.45

STATED ODDS 1:36 1996 EDGE PACKS
STATED ODDS 1:50 1997 COWBOYBILIA
*FOIL CARDS: SAME PRICE

		MINT	NRMT
❑ 1	Troy Aikman	10.00	4.50
❑ 2	Marcus Allen	4.00	1.80
❑ 3	Drew Bledsoe	10.00	4.50
❑ 4	Tim Brown	4.00	1.80
❑ 5	Isaac Bruce	4.00	1.80
❑ 6	Mark Brunell	10.00	4.50
❑ 7	Kerry Collins	4.00	1.80
❑ 8	John Elway	20.00	9.00
❑ 9	Marshall Faulk	4.00	1.80
❑ 10	Brett Favre	20.00	9.00
❑ 11	Jeff George	2.00	.90
❑ 12	Terry Kirby	2.00	.90
❑ 13	Dan Marino	20.00	9.00
❑ 14	Natrone Means	4.00	1.80
❑ 15	Carl Pickens	4.00	1.80
❑ 16	Errict Rhett	2.00	.90
❑ 17	Rashaan Salaam	4.00	1.80
❑ 18	Deion Sanders	6.00	2.70
❑ 19	Barry Sanders	20.00	9.00
❑ 20	Emmitt Smith	15.00	6.75
❑ 21	Kordell Stewart	8.00	3.60
❑ 22	Tamarick Vanover	2.00	.90
❑ 23	Michael Westbrook	4.00	1.80
❑ 24	Steve Young	8.00	3.60
❑ NNO	Checklist Card	1.00	.45
❑ QM1	Rashaan Salaam Promo	2.00	.90

1996 Collector's Edge Ripped

	MINT	NRMT
COMP.SERIES 1 (19)	50.00	22.00

STATED ODDS 1:12 1996 EDGE PACKS
STATED ODDS 1:6 1997 COWBOYBILIA
*DIE CUTS: 2.5X TO 5X BASE CARD HI
DIE CUTS PRINT RUN 500 SERIAL #'d SETS
DIE CUTS: AVAIL.VIA DIRECT MAIL OFFER

Card	MINT	NRMT
❑ 1 Jeff Blake	2.00	.90
❑ 2 Steve Bono	.50	.23
❑ 3 Terrell Davis	12.00	5.50
❑ 4 John Elway	10.00	4.50
❑ 6 Brett Favre	10.00	4.50
❑ 8 Erik Kramer	.50	.23
❑ 9 Dan Marino	10.00	4.50
❑ 10 Natrone Means	2.00	.90
❑ 11 Eric Metcalf	.50	.23
❑ 12 Anthony Miller	1.00	.45
❑ 13 Herman Moore	2.00	.90
❑ 14 Errict Rhett	1.00	.45
❑ 15 Andre Rison	1.00	.45
❑ 16 Joey Galloway	4.00	1.80
❑ 17 Yancey Thigpen	1.00	.45
❑ 18 Michael Westbrook	2.00	.90
❑ CK1 Checklist Series 1	.50	.23
❑ R1 Jeff Blake Promo	2.00	.90

1996 Collector's Edge Too Cool Rookies

	MINT	NRMT
COMPLETE SET (25)	50.00	22.00

STATED ODDS 1:8 1996 EDGE PACKS
STATED ODDS 1:5 1997 COWBOYBILIA

Card	MINT	NRMT
❑ 1 Tony Boselli	.60	.25
❑ 2 Kyle Brady	.60	.25
❑ 3 Ki-Jana Carter	1.25	.55
❑ 4 Kerry Collins	2.50	1.10
❑ 5 Todd Collins	1.25	.55
❑ 6 Terrell Davis	15.00	6.75
❑ 7 Hugh Douglas	.60	.25
❑ 8 Joey Galloway	5.00	2.20
❑ 9 Darius Holland	.60	.25
❑ 10 Napoleon Kaufman	3.00	1.35
❑ 11 Mike Mamula	2.50	1.10
❑ 12 Curtis Martin	5.00	2.20
❑ 13 Steve McNair	5.00	2.20
❑ 14 Billy Milner	.60	.25
❑ 15 Rashaan Salaam	2.50	1.10
❑ 16 Frank Sanders	1.25	.55
❑ 17 Warren Sapp	.60	.25
❑ 18 James O. Stewart	1.25	.55
❑ 19 J.J. Stokes	2.50	1.10
❑ 20 Tamarick Vanover	1.25	.55
❑ 21 Michael Westbrook	2.50	1.10
❑ 22 Tyrone Wheatley	1.25	.55
❑ 23 Kordell Stewart	5.00	2.20
❑ 24 Sherman Williams	.60	.25
❑ 25 Eric Zeier	.60	.25
❑ TC1 M.Westbrook Promo	2.00	.90

1996 Collector's Edge Advantage

	MINT	NRMT
COMPLETE SET (150)	25.00	11.00

	MINT	NRMT
COMMON CARD (1-150)	.15	.07
SEMISTARS	.25	.11
UNLISTED STARS	.50	.23
COMP.FOIL SET (150)	150.00	70.00

FOIL STARS: 3X TO 6X HI COLUMN
FOIL RCs: 1.5X TO 3X HI
FOIL STATED ODDS 1:2

Card	MINT	NRMT
❑ 1 Drew Bledsoe	1.25	.55
❑ 2 Chris Warren	.25	.11
❑ 3 Eddie George RC	4.00	1.80
❑ 4 Barry Sanders	2.50	1.10
❑ 5 Scott Mitchell	.25	.11
❑ 6 Carl Pickens	.50	.23
❑ 7 Tim Brown	.50	.23
❑ 8 John Elway	2.50	1.10
❑ 9 Michael Westbrook	.50	.23
❑ 10 Cris Carter	.50	.23
❑ 11 Troy Aikman	1.25	.55
❑ 12 Ben Coates	.25	.11
❑ 13 Brett Favre	2.50	1.10
❑ 14 Marshall Faulk	.50	.23
❑ 15 Steve Young	1.00	.45
❑ 16 Terrell Davis	3.00	1.35
❑ 17 Keyshawn Johnson RC	3.00	1.35
❑ 18 Mario Bates	.25	.11
❑ 19 Steve McNair	1.00	.45
❑ 20 Kerry Collins	.50	.23
❑ 21 Natrone Means	.50	.23
❑ 22 Kordell Stewart	1.00	.45
❑ 23 Jeff George	.25	.11
❑ 24 Rick Mirer	.25	.11
❑ 25 Herman Moore	.50	.23
❑ 26 Rodney Peete	.15	.07
❑ 27 Isaac Bruce	.50	.23
❑ 28 Errict Rhett	.25	.11
❑ 29 Jerry Rice	1.25	.55
❑ 30 Rashaan Salaam	.50	.23
❑ 31 Eric Metcalf	.15	.07
❑ 32 Jim Kelly	.50	.23
❑ 33 Jerome Bettis	.50	.23
❑ 34 Deion Sanders	.75	.35
❑ 35 J.J. Stokes	.50	.23
❑ 36 Neil O'Donnell	.25	.11
❑ 37 Marcus Allen	.50	.23
❑ 38 Thurman Thomas	.50	.23
❑ 39 Dan Marino	2.50	1.10
❑ 40 Rickey Dudley RC	.50	.23
❑ 41 Napoleon Kaufman	.75	.35
❑ 42 Kyle Brady	.15	.07
❑ 43 Emmitt Smith	2.00	.90
❑ 44 Tyrone Wheatley	.25	.11
❑ 45 Jeff Blake	.50	.23
❑ 46 Reggie White	.50	.23
❑ 47 Joey Galloway	1.00	.45
❑ 48 Antonio Langham	.15	.07
❑ 49 Craig Heyward	.15	.07
❑ 50 Curtis Martin	1.00	.45
❑ 51 Karim Abdul-Jabbar RC	.75	.35
❑ 52 Antonio Freeman	1.00	.45
❑ 53 Ki-Jana Carter	.25	.11
❑ 54 Willie Davis	.15	.07
❑ 55 Jim Everett	.15	.07
❑ 56 Gus Frerotte	.50	.23
❑ 57 Daryl Gardener RC	.15	.07
❑ 58 Charles Haley	.25	.11
❑ 59 Michael Irvin	.50	.23
❑ 60 Keith Jackson	.15	.07
❑ 61 Cortez Kennedy	.15	.07
❑ 62 Greg Lloyd	.25	.11
❑ 63 Tony Martin	.25	.11
❑ 64 Ken Norton Jr.	.15	.07
❑ 65 Bobby Hoying RC	.75	.35
❑ 66 Bryce Paup	.15	.07
❑ 67 Jake Reed	.25	.11
❑ 68 Frank Sanders	.25	.11
❑ 69 Vinny Testaverde	.25	.11
❑ 70 Regan Upshaw RC	.15	.07
❑ 71 Tamarick Vanover	.25	.11
❑ 72 Walt Harris RC	.15	.07
❑ 73 John Randle	.15	.07
❑ 74 Ricky Watters	.25	.11
❑ 75 Terry Allen	.25	.11
❑ 76 Edgar Bennett	.25	.11
❑ 77 Larry Centers	.25	.11
❑ 78 Chris Penn	.15	.07
❑ 79 Bobby Engram RC	.50	.23
❑ 80 Irving Fryar	.25	.11
❑ 81 Charlie Garner	.15	.07
❑ 82 Rodney Hampton	.25	.11
❑ 83 Michael Jackson	.25	.11
❑ 84 O.J. McDuffie	.25	.11
❑ 85 Shannon Sharpe	.25	.11
❑ 86 Aaron Hayden	.15	.07
❑ 87 Muhsin Muhammad RC	1.00	.45
❑ 88 Rod Woodson	.25	.11
❑ 89 Levon Kirkland	.15	.07
❑ 90 Chad Brown	.15	.07
❑ 91 Junior Seau	.25	.11
❑ 92 Terry Kirby	.25	.11
❑ 93 Zach Thomas RC	.75	.35
❑ 94 Harvey Williams	.15	.07
❑ 95 Robert Brooks	.50	.23
❑ 96 Darrell Green	.15	.07
❑ 97 Chester McGlockton	.15	.07
❑ 98 Neil Smith	.15	.07
❑ 99 Eric Swann	.15	.07
❑ 100 Mike Alstott RC	1.50	.70
❑ 101 Tim Biakabutuka RC	1.00	.45
❑ 102 Mark Brunell	1.25	.55
❑ 103 Chris Doleman	.15	.07
❑ 104 Sean Gilbert	.15	.07
❑ 105 Jim Harbaugh	.25	.11
❑ 106 Chris T. Jones	.25	.11
❑ 107 Tyrone Hughes	.15	.07
❑ 108 Amani Toomer RC	.50	.23
❑ 109 Larry Brown	.15	.07
❑ 110 Kevin Greene	.25	.11
❑ 111 John Mobley	.15	.07
❑ 112 Danny Kanell RC	.50	.23
❑ 113 Kevin Hardy RC	.50	.23
❑ 114 Brett Perriman	.15	.07
❑ 115 Simeon Rice RC	.50	.23
❑ 116 Chris Sanders	.25	.11
❑ 117 Dave Brown	.15	.07
❑ 118 Bryan Cox	.15	.07
❑ 119 Yancey Thigpen	.25	.11
❑ 120 Terance Mathis	.15	.07
❑ 121 Warren Moon	.25	.11
❑ 122 Derrick Thomas	.25	.11
❑ 123 Trent Dilfer	.50	.23
❑ 124 Terry Glenn RC	1.50	.70
❑ 125 Jeff Hostetler	.15	.07
❑ 126 Leeland McElroy RC	.50	.23
❑ 127 Hardy Nickerson	.15	.07
❑ 128 Steve Bono	.15	.07
❑ 129 Stanley Pritchett RC	.25	.11
❑ 130 Dana Stubblefield	.25	.11
❑ 131 Andre Coleman	.15	.07
❑ 132 Anthony Miller	.25	.11
❑ 133 Stan Humphries	.25	.11
❑ 134 Robert Smith	.25	.11
❑ 135 Curtis Conway	.50	.23
❑ 136 Darick Holmes	.15	.07
❑ 137 Pat Swilling	.15	.07
❑ 138 Andre Rison	.25	.11
❑ 139 Erik Kramer	.15	.07
❑ 140 Jason Dunn RC	.25	.11
❑ 141 Torrance Small	.15	.07
❑ 142 Cedric Jones RC	.15	.07
❑ 143 Derek Loville	.15	.07
❑ 144 Brian Mitchell	.15	.07
❑ 145 Eric Moulds RC	2.00	.90
❑ 146 James O.Stewart	.25	.11

❑ 147 Bruce Smith .25 .11
❑ 148 Keenan McCardell .50 .23
❑ 149 Warren Sapp .15 .07
❑ 150 Marvin Harrison RC 3.00 1.35

1996 Collector's Edge Advantage Crystal Cuts

	MINT	NRMT
COMPLETE SET (25)	100.00	45.00

STATED ODDS 1:8
STATED PRINT RUN 5000 SERIAL #'d SETS
*SILVER FOILS: SAME PRICE
*SILVER STARS: 2.5X TO 5X BASE CARD HI
*SILVER ROOKIES: 1.25X TO 2.5X BASE CARD HI
SILVERS PRINT RUN 3100 SERIAL #'d SETS
SILVERS: AVAIL.VIA DIRECT MAIL

❑ CC1 Barry Sanders 12.00 5.50
❑ CC2 Eddie George 10.00 4.50
❑ CC3 Curtis Martin 5.00 2.20
❑ CC4 J.J. Stokes 2.50 1.10
❑ CC5 Kyle Brady .75 .35
❑ CC6 Chris Warren 1.25 .55
❑ CC7 Jerry Rice 6.00 2.70
❑ CC8 Ben Coates 1.25 .55
❑ CC9 Terrell Davis 15.00 6.75
❑ CC10 Marcus Allen 2.50 1.10
❑ CC11 John Elway 12.00 5.50
❑ CC12 Joey Galloway 5.00 2.20
❑ CC13 Dan Marino 12.00 5.50
❑ CC14 Napoleon Kaufman 4.00 1.80
❑ CC15 Emmitt Smith 10.00 4.50
❑ CC16 Eric Metcalf .75 .35
❑ CC17 Kerry Collins 2.50 1.10
❑ CC18 Troy Aikman 6.00 2.70
❑ CC19 Rickey Dudley 1.25 .55
❑ CC20 Steve McNair 5.00 2.20
❑ CC21 Steve Young 5.00 2.20
❑ CC22 Isaac Bruce 2.50 1.10
❑ CC23 Kordell Stewart 5.00 2.20
❑ CC24 LeShon Johnson 1.25 .55
❑ CC25 Scott Mitchell 1.25 .55

1996 Collector's Edge Advantage Video

	MINT	NRMT
COMPLETE SET (25)	200.00	90.00

STATED ODDS 1:36
STATED PRINT RUN 2000 SERIAL #'d SETS
*DIE CUT STARS: 20X TO 40X BASE CARD HI
*DIE CUT ROOKIES: 7.5X TO 15X BASE CARD HI
DIE CUT PRINT RUN 300 SERIAL #'d SETS
DIE CUTS: AVAIL.VIA DIRECT MAIL OFFER

❑ V1 Brett Favre 30.00 13.50
❑ V2 Keyshawn Johnson 15.00 6.75
❑ V3 Deion Sanders 10.00 4.50
❑ V4 Marcus Allen 6.00 2.70
❑ V5 Rashaan Salaam 6.00 2.70
❑ V6 Thurman Thomas 6.00 2.70
❑ V7 Emmitt Smith 25.00 11.00
❑ V8 Isaac Bruce 6.00 2.70
❑ V9 Michael Westbrook 6.00 2.70
❑ V10 Cris Carter 6.00 2.70
❑ V11 Marshall Faulk 6.00 2.70
❑ V12 Jerry Rice 15.00 6.75
❑ V13 Tim Brown 6.00 2.70
❑ V14 Steve Young 12.00 5.50
❑ V15 Eric Metcalf 2.00 .90
❑ V16 Chris Warren 3.00 1.35
❑ V17 Drew Bledsoe 15.00 6.75
❑ V18 Barry Sanders 30.00 13.50
❑ V19 Herman Moore 6.00 2.70
❑ V20 Rodney Peete 2.00 .90
❑ V21 Troy Aikman 15.00 6.75
❑ V22 Jerome Bettis 6.00 2.70
❑ V23 Errict Rhett 3.00 1.35
❑ V24 Dan Marino 30.00 13.50
❑ V25 Natrone Means 6.00 2.70

1996 Collector's Edge Advantage Game Ball

	MINT	NRMT
COMPLETE SET (37)	1000.00	450.00
CL (NNO)	1.00	.45

STATED ODDS 1:72
RICE AUTO ODDS 1:12,000 98 CE MASTERS

❑ G1 Kordell Stewart 30.00 13.50
❑ G2 Emmitt Smith 80.00 36.00
❑ G3 Brett Favre 100.00 45.00
❑ G4 Steve Young 40.00 18.00
❑ G5 Barry Sanders 100.00 45.00
❑ G6 John Elway 100.00 45.00
❑ G7 Drew Bledsoe 50.00 22.00
❑ G8 Dan Marino 100.00 45.00
❑ G9 Keyshawn Johnson 40.00 18.00
❑ G10 Eddie George 50.00 22.00
❑ G11 Kevin Hardy 6.00 2.70
❑ G12 Terry Glenn 20.00 9.00
❑ G13 Michael Westbrook 15.00 6.75
❑ G14 Joey Galloway 30.00 13.50
❑ G15 John Mobley 5.00 2.20
❑ G16 Curtis Martin 30.00 13.50
❑ G17 Rashaan Salaam 15.00 6.75
❑ G18 J.J. Stokes 15.00 6.75
❑ G19 Kerry Collins 15.00 6.75
❑ G20 Deion Sanders 30.00 13.50
❑ G21 Shannon Sharpe 10.00 4.50
❑ G22 Terry Allen 10.00 4.50
❑ G23 Ricky Watters 10.00 4.50
❑ G24 Marshall Faulk 20.00 9.00
❑ G25 Tim Biakabutuka 12.00 5.50
❑ G26 Troy Aikman 50.00 22.00
❑ G27 Jerry Rice 50.00 22.00
❑ G28 Chris Warren 10.00 4.50
❑ G29 Jeff Blake 15.00 6.75
❑ G30 Carl Pickens 20.00 9.00
❑ G31 Isaac Bruce 20.00 9.00
❑ G32 Terrell Davis 100.00 45.00
❑ G33 Mark Brunell 50.00 22.00
❑ G34 Karim Abdul-Jabbar 10.00 4.50
❑ G35 Herman Moore 20.00 9.00
❑ G36 Cris Carter 20.00 9.00
❑ NNO Checklist Card 6.00 2.70
❑ G27AU Jerry Rice AUTO/50 350.00 160.00

1996 Collector's Edge Advantage Role Models

	MINT	NRMT
COMPLETE SET (13)	50.00	22.00
CL (NNO)	1.00	.45

STATED ODDS 1:12

❑ RM1 John Elway 12.00 5.50
❑ RM2 Dan Marino 12.00 5.50
❑ RM3 Jerry Rice 6.00 2.70
❑ RM4 Emmitt Smith 10.00 4.50
❑ RM5 Chris Warren 1.25 .55
❑ RM6 Tim Brown 2.50 1.10
❑ RM7 Jeff George 1.25 .55
❑ RM8 Tyrone Wheatley 1.25 .55
❑ RM9 Steve Bono .75 .35
❑ RM10 Kerry Collins 2.50 1.10
❑ RM11 Jerome Bettis 2.50 1.10
❑ RM12 Steve Beuerlein 2.50 1.10
❑ NNO Checklist Card .75 .35

1996 Collector's Edge Advantage Super Bowl Game Ball

	MINT	NRMT
COMPLETE SET (36)	1200.00	550.00

STATED ODDS 1:164

❑ SB1 Emmitt Smith 120.00 55.00
❑ SB2 Troy Aikman 80.00 36.00
❑ SB3 Michael Irvin 30.00 13.50
❑ SB4 Deion Sanders 50.00 22.00
❑ SB5 John Elway 150.00 70.00
❑ SB6 Dan Marino 150.00 70.00
❑ SB7 Marcus Allen 30.00 13.50
❑ SB8 Kordell Stewart 50.00 22.00
❑ SB9 Steve Young 60.00 27.00
❑ SB10 Ricky Watters 15.00 6.75
❑ SB11 Jerry Rice 80.00 36.00
❑ SB12 Jim Kelly 30.00 13.50
❑ SB13 Thurman Thomas 30.00 13.50
❑ SB14 Bruce Smith 15.00 6.75
❑ SB15 Stan Humphries 15.00 6.75
❑ SB16 Junior Seau 15.00 6.75
❑ SB17 Natrone Means 30.00 13.50
❑ SB18 Neil O'Donnell 15.00 6.75
❑ SB19 Rod Woodson 15.00 6.75
❑ SB20 Andre Reed 30.00 13.50
❑ SB21 Jeff Hostetler 10.00 4.50
❑ SB22 Dave Meggett 15.00 6.75
❑ SB23 Greg Lloyd 15.00 6.75
❑ SB24 Kevin Greene 15.00 6.75

Card	MINT	NRMT
❑ SB25 Yancey Thigpen	12.00	5.50
❑ SB26 Charles Haley	15.00	6.75
❑ SB27 Byron Bam Morris	10.00	4.50
❑ SB28 Alvin Harper	10.00	4.50
❑ SB29 Ken Norton Jr.	10.00	4.50
❑ SB30 William Floyd	15.00	6.75
❑ SB31 Leslie O'Neal	10.00	4.50
❑ SB32 Jay Novacek	15.00	6.75
❑ SB33 Irving Fryar	15.00	6.75
❑ SB34 Leon Lett	10.00	4.50
❑ SB35 Tony Martin	15.00	6.75
❑ SB36 Mark Collins	10.00	4.50

1998 Collector's Edge Advantage

	MINT	NRMT
COMPLETE SET (200)	80.00	36.00
COMP.SHORT SET (180)	60.00	27.00
COMMON CARD (1-180)	.30	.14
SEMISTARS	.50	.23
UNLISTED STARS	1.00	.45
COMMON ROOKIE (181-200)	.25	.11
ROOKIE SEMISTARS	.50	.23
ROOKIES INSERTED IN LATE RETAIL BOXES		
COMP.GOLD SET (180)	300.00	135.00
*GOLD STARS: 2.5X TO 5X HI COL.		
*GOLD YOUNG STARS: 2X TO 4X		
COMP.50-POINT SET (180)	150.00	70.00
*50-POINT STARS: 1.25X TO 2.5X HI COL.		
*50-POINT YOUNG STARS: 1X TO 2X		
50-POINT STATED ODDS ONE PER PACK		
COMP.SILVER SET (180)	250.00	110.00
*SILVER STARS: 2X TO 4X HI COL.		
*SILVER YOUNG STARS: 1.5X TO 3X		
SILVER STATED ODDS 1:2		

Card	MINT	NRMT
❑ 1 Larry Centers	.30	.14
❑ 2 Kent Graham	.30	.14
❑ 3 LeShon Johnson	.30	.14
❑ 4 Leeland McElroy	.30	.14
❑ 5 Jake Plummer	3.00	1.35
❑ 6 Jamal Anderson	1.00	.45
❑ 7 Chris Chandler	.50	.23
❑ 8 Bert Emanuel	.50	.23
❑ 9 Byron Hanspard	.50	.23
❑ 10 O.J. Santiago	.30	.14
❑ 11 Derrick Alexander WR	.50	.23
❑ 12 Peter Boulware	.30	.14
❑ 13 Eric Green	.30	.14
❑ 14 Michael Jackson	.30	.14
❑ 15 Byron Bam Morris	.30	.14
❑ 16 Vinny Testaverde	.50	.23
❑ 17 Todd Collins	.30	.14
❑ 18 Quinn Early	.30	.14
❑ 19 Jim Kelly	1.00	.45
❑ 20 Andre Reed	.50	.23
❑ 21 Antowain Smith	1.00	.45
❑ 22 Steve Tasker	.30	.14
❑ 23 Thurman Thomas	1.00	.45
❑ 24 Steve Beuerlein	.30	.14
❑ 25 Rae Carruth	.50	.23
❑ 26 Kerry Collins	.50	.23
❑ 27 Anthony Johnson	.30	.14
❑ 28 Ernie Mills	.30	.14
❑ 29 Wesley Walls	.50	.23
❑ 30 Curtis Conway	.50	.23
❑ 31 Bobby Engram	.50	.23
❑ 32 Raymont Harris	.30	.14
❑ 33 Erik Kramer	.30	.14
❑ 34 Rick Mirer	.30	.14
❑ 35 Darnay Scott	.50	.23
❑ 36 Tony McGee	.30	.14
❑ 37 Jeff Blake	.50	.23
❑ 38 Corey Dillon	1.50	.70
❑ 39 Carl Pickens	1.00	.45
❑ 40 Troy Aikman	2.50	1.10
❑ 41 Billy Davis	.30	.14
❑ 42 David LaFleur	.30	.14
❑ 43 Anthony Miller	.30	.14
❑ 44 Emmitt Smith	4.00	1.80
❑ 45 Herschel Walker	.50	.23
❑ 46 Sherman Williams	.30	.14
❑ 47 Flipper Anderson	.30	.14
❑ 48 Terrell Davis	4.00	1.80
❑ 49 Jason Elam	.30	.14
❑ 50 John Elway	5.00	2.20
❑ 51 Darrien Gordon	.30	.14
❑ 52 Ed McCaffrey	.50	.23
❑ 53 Shannon Sharpe	.50	.23
❑ 54 Neil Smith	.50	.23
❑ 55 Rod Smith WR	.50	.23
❑ 56 Maa Tanuvasa	.30	.14
❑ 57 Glyn Milburn	.30	.14
❑ 58 Scott Mitchell	.50	.23
❑ 59 Herman Moore	1.00	.45
❑ 60 Johnnie Morton	.50	.23
❑ 61 Barry Sanders	5.00	2.20
❑ 62 Tommy Vardell	.30	.14
❑ 63 Bryant Westbrook	.30	.14
❑ 64 Robert Brooks	.50	.23
❑ 65 Mark Chmura	.50	.23
❑ 66 Brett Favre	5.00	2.20
❑ 67 Antonio Freeman	1.00	.45
❑ 68 Dorsey Levens	1.00	.45
❑ 69 Bill Schroeder RC	4.00	1.80
❑ 70 Marshall Faulk	1.00	.45
❑ 71 Jim Harbaugh	.50	.23
❑ 72 Marvin Harrison	.50	.23
❑ 73 Derek Brown TE	.30	.14
❑ 74 Mark Brunell	2.00	.90
❑ 75 Rob Johnson	.50	.23
❑ 76 Keenan McCardell	.50	.23
❑ 77 Natrone Means	1.00	.45
❑ 78 Jimmy Smith	.50	.23
❑ 79 James O.Stewart	.50	.23
❑ 80 Marcus Allen	1.00	.45
❑ 81 Pat Barnes	.30	.14
❑ 82 Tony Gonzalez	.30	.14
❑ 83 Elvis Grbac	.50	.23
❑ 84 Greg Hill	.30	.14
❑ 85 Kevin Lockett	.30	.14
❑ 86 Andre Rison	.50	.23
❑ 87 Karim Abdul-Jabbar	1.00	.45
❑ 88 Fred Barnett	.30	.14
❑ 89 Troy Drayton	.30	.14
❑ 90 Dan Marino	5.00	2.20
❑ 91 Irving Spikes	.30	.14
❑ 92 Cris Carter	1.00	.45
❑ 93 Matthew Hatchette	.30	.14
❑ 94 Brad Johnson	1.00	.45
❑ 95 Jake Reed	.50	.23
❑ 96 Robert Smith	1.00	.45
❑ 97 Drew Bledsoe	2.00	.90
❑ 98 Keith Byars	.30	.14
❑ 99 Ben Coates	.50	.23
❑ 100 Terry Glenn	1.00	.45
❑ 101 Shawn Jefferson	.30	.14
❑ 102 Curtis Martin	1.00	.45
❑ 103 Dave Meggett	.30	.14
❑ 104 Troy Davis	.30	.14
❑ 105 Danny Wuerffel	.50	.23
❑ 106 Ray Zellars	.30	.14
❑ 107 Tiki Barber	.50	.23
❑ 108 Rodney Hampton	.50	.23
❑ 109 Ike Hilliard	.50	.23
❑ 110 Danny Kanell	.50	.23
❑ 111 Tyrone Wheatley	.50	.23
❑ 112 Kyle Brady	.30	.14
❑ 113 Wayne Chrebet	1.00	.45
❑ 114 Aaron Glenn	.30	.14
❑ 115 Jeff Graham	.30	.14
❑ 116 Keyshawn Johnson	1.00	.45
❑ 117 Adrian Murrell	.50	.23
❑ 118 Neil O'Donnell	.50	.23
❑ 119 Heath Shuler	.30	.14
❑ 120 Tim Brown	1.00	.45
❑ 121 Rickey Dudley	.30	.14
❑ 122 Jeff George	.50	.23
❑ 123 Desmond Howard	.50	.23
❑ 124 James Jett	.50	.23
❑ 125 Napoleon Kaufman	1.00	.45
❑ 126 Chad Levitt RC	.30	.14
❑ 127 Darrell Russell	.30	.14
❑ 128 Ty Detmer	.50	.23
❑ 129 Irving Fryar	.50	.23
❑ 130 Charlie Garner	.30	.14
❑ 131 Kevin Turner	.30	.14
❑ 132 Ricky Watters	.50	.23
❑ 133 Jerome Bettis	1.00	.45
❑ 134 Will Blackwell	.30	.14
❑ 135 Mark Bruener	.30	.14
❑ 136 Charles Johnson	.30	.14
❑ 137 George Jones	.30	.14
❑ 138 Kordell Stewart	1.00	.45
❑ 139 Yancey Thigpen	.30	.14
❑ 140 Gary Brown	.30	.14
❑ 141 Jim Everett	.30	.14
❑ 142 Terrell Fletcher	.30	.14
❑ 143 Stan Humphries	.30	.14
❑ 144 Freddie Jones	.30	.14
❑ 145 Tony Martin	.50	.23
❑ 146 Jim Druckenmiller	.50	.23
❑ 147 Garrison Hearst	1.00	.45
❑ 148 Brent Jones	.30	.14
❑ 149 Terrell Owens	1.00	.45
❑ 150 Jerry Rice	2.50	1.10
❑ 151 J.J. Stokes	.50	.23
❑ 152 Steve Young	1.50	.70
❑ 153 Steve Broussard	.30	.14
❑ 154 Joey Galloway	1.00	.45
❑ 155 Jon Kitna	2.50	1.10
❑ 156 Warren Moon	1.00	.45
❑ 157 Shawn Springs	.30	.14
❑ 158 Chris Warren	.50	.23
❑ 159 Tony Banks	.50	.23
❑ 160 Isaac Bruce	1.00	.45
❑ 161 Eddie Kennison	.50	.23
❑ 162 Orlando Pace	.30	.14
❑ 163 Lawrence Phillips	.30	.14
❑ 164 Mike Alstott	1.00	.45
❑ 165 Reidel Anthony	.50	.23
❑ 166 Horace Copeland	.30	.14
❑ 167 Trent Dilfer	1.00	.45
❑ 168 Warrick Dunn	1.50	.70
❑ 169 Hardy Nickerson	.30	.14
❑ 170 Karl Williams	.30	.14
❑ 171 Eddie George	2.00	.90
❑ 172 Ronnie Harmon	.30	.14
❑ 173 Joey Kent	.50	.23
❑ 174 Steve McNair	1.00	.45
❑ 175 Chris Sanders	.30	.14
❑ 176 Terry Allen	1.00	.45
❑ 177 Jamie Asher	.30	.14
❑ 178 Stephen Davis	.30	.14
❑ 179 Gus Frerotte	.30	.14
❑ 180 Leslie Shepherd	.30	.14
❑ 181 Victor Riley RC	.25	.11
❑ 182 Curtis Enis RC	1.50	.70
❑ 183 Brian Griese RC	2.50	1.10
❑ 184 Eric Brown RC	.25	.11
❑ 185 Jacquez Green RC	1.00	.45
❑ 186 Andre Wadsworth RC	.50	.23
❑ 187 Ryan Leaf RC	1.25	.55
❑ 188 Rashaan Shehee RC	.50	.23
❑ 189 Peyton Manning RC	8.00	3.60
❑ 190 Flozell Adams RC	.25	.11
❑ 191 Fred Taylor RC	4.00	1.80
❑ 192 Charlie Batch RC	2.50	1.10
❑ 193 Kevin Dyson RC	1.25	.55
❑ 194 Charles Woodson RC	1.50	.70
❑ 195 Ahman Green RC	.50	.23
❑ 196 Randy Moss RC	8.00	3.60
❑ 197 Robert Edwards RC	.50	.23
❑ 198 Reidel Anthony	.50	.23
❑ 199 Jerome Pathon RC	.50	.23
❑ 200 Samari Rolle RC	.25	.11

1998 Collector's Edge Advantage Livin' Large

	MINT	NRMT
COMPLETE SET (22)	150.00	70.00
COMMON CARD (1-22)	2.50	1.10
SEMISTARS	4.00	1.80
UNLISTED STARS	5.00	2.20
STATED ODDS 1:12		
HOLOFOILS: 4X TO 8X BASE INSERT		
HOLOFOIL STATED PRINT RUN 100 SETS		

Card	MINT	NRMT
❑ 1 Leeland McElroy	2.50	1.10
❑ 2 Jamal Anderson	5.00	2.20
❑ 3 Antowain Smith	5.00	2.20
❑ 4 Emmitt Smith	20.00	9.00
❑ 5 John Elway	25.00	11.00
❑ 6 Barry Sanders	25.00	11.00

- ❑ 7 Elvis Grbac 4.00 1.80
- ❑ 8 Dan Marino 25.00 11.00
- ❑ 9 Cris Carter 5.00 2.20
- ❑ 10 Drew Bledsoe 10.00 4.50
- ❑ 11 Curtis Martin 5.00 2.20
- ❑ 12 Troy Davis 2.50 1.10
- ❑ 13 Ike Hilliard 4.00 1.80
- ❑ 14 Adrian Murrell 4.00 1.80
- ❑ 15 Tim Brown 5.00 2.20
- ❑ 16 Kordell Stewart 5.00 2.20
- ❑ 17 Jerry Rice 12.00 5.50
- ❑ 18 Tony Banks 4.00 1.80
- ❑ 19 Mike Alstott 5.00 2.20
- ❑ 20 Trent Dilfer 5.00 2.20
- ❑ 21 Eddie George 10.00 4.50
- ❑ 22 Steve McNair 5.00 2.20

1998 Collector's Edge Advantage Memorable Moments

	MINT	NRMT
COMPLETE SET (12)	400.00	180.00
COMMON CARD (1-12)	20.00	9.00
SEMISTARS	30.00	13.50

STATED PRINT 200 SERIAL #'d SETS
STATED ODDS 1:360

- ❑ 1 Carl Pickens 100.00 45.00
- ❑ 2 Terrell Davis 80.00 36.00
- ❑ 3 Herman Moore 100.00 45.00
- ❑ 4 Antonio Freeman 40.00 18.00
- ❑ 5 Jimmy Smith 20.00 9.00
- ❑ 6 Marcus Allen 100.00 45.00
- ❑ 7 Cris Carter 100.00 45.00
- ❑ 8 Curtis Martin 40.00 18.00
- ❑ 9 Napoleon Kaufman 100.00 45.00
- ❑ 10 Joey Galloway 100.00 45.00
- ❑ 11 Warrick Dunn 30.00 13.50
- ❑ 12 Eddie George 60.00 27.00

1998 Collector's Edge Advantage Personal Victory

	MINT	NRMT
COMPLETE SET (6)	800.00	350.00
COMMON CARD (1-6)	80.00	36.00

STATED PRINT 200 SERIAL #'d SETS
STATED ODDS 1:675

- ❑ 1 John Elway 200.00 90.00
- ❑ 2 Barry Sanders 200.00 90.00
- ❑ 3 Brett Favre 200.00 90.00
- ❑ 4 Mark Brunell 80.00 36.00
- ❑ 5 Drew Bledsoe 80.00 36.00
- ❑ 6 Jerry Rice 100.00 45.00

1998 Collector's Edge Advantage Prime Connection

	MINT	NRMT
COMPLETE SET (25)	500.00	220.00
COMMON CARD (1-25)	6.00	2.70
SEMISTARS	10.00	4.50
UNLISTED STARS	12.00	5.50

STATED ODDS 1:36

- ❑ 1 LeShon Johnson 6.00 2.70
  Leeland McElroy
- ❑ 2 Peter Boulware 10.00 4.50
  Michael Jackson
- ❑ 3 Andre Reed 12.00 5.50
  Antowain Smith
- ❑ 4 Rae Carruth 10.00 4.50
  Anthony Johnson
- ❑ 5 Herschel Walker 50.00 22.00
  Emmitt Smith
- ❑ 6 Terrell Davis 40.00 18.00
  John Elway
- ❑ 7 Ed McCaffrey 10.00 4.50
  Shannon Sharpe
- ❑ 8 Herman Moore 60.00 27.00
  Barry Sanders
- ❑ 9 Brett Favre 60.00 27.00
  Antonio Freeman
- ❑ 10 Mark Brunell 25.00 11.00
  James O. Stewart
- ❑ 11 Marcus Allen 12.00 5.50
  Elvis Grbac
- ❑ 12 Karim Abdul-Jabbar 60.00 27.00
  Dan Marino
- ❑ 13 Drew Bledsoe 25.00 11.00
  Ben Coates
- ❑ 14 Terry Glenn 15.00 6.75
  Curtis Martin
- ❑ 15 Troy Davis 10.00 4.50
  Danny Wuerffel
- ❑ 16 Ike Hilliard 10.00 4.50
  Danny Kanell
- ❑ 17 Aaron Glenn 10.00 4.50
  Adrian Murrell
- ❑ 18 Tim Brown 12.00 5.50
  Napoleon Kaufman
- ❑ 19 Mark Bruener 12.00 5.50
  Jerome Bettis
- ❑ 20 Jim Druckenmiller 12.00 5.50
  Terrell Owens
- ❑ 21 Garrison Hearst 25.00 11.00
  Steve Young
- ❑ 22 Tony Banks 12.00 5.50
  Eddie Kennison
- ❑ 23 Mike Alstott 15.00 6.75
  Reidel Anthony
- ❑ 24 Hardy Nickerson 20.00 9.00
  Warrick Dunn
- ❑ 25 Eddie George 25.00 11.00
  Steve McNair

1998 Collector's Edge Advantage Showtime

	MINT	NRMT
COMPLETE SET (23)	200.00	90.00
COMMON CARD (1-23)	4.00	1.80
SEMISTARS	6.00	2.70
UNLISTED STARS	10.00	4.50

STATED ODDS 1:18
*HOLOFOILS: 2X TO 4X BASE INSERT
HOLOFOIL STATED PRINT RUN 100 SETS

- ❑ 1 LeShon Johnson 4.00 1.80
- ❑ 2 Peter Boulware 4.00 1.80
- ❑ 3 Jim Kelly 10.00 4.50
- ❑ 4 Rae Carruth 6.00 2.70
- ❑ 5 Kerry Collins 6.00 2.70
- ❑ 6 Troy Aikman 20.00 9.00
- ❑ 7 Terrell Davis 30.00 13.50
- ❑ 8 Shannon Sharpe 6.00 2.70
- ❑ 9 Brett Favre 40.00 18.00
- ❑ 10 Mark Brunell 15.00 6.75
- ❑ 11 Keenan McCardell 6.00 2.70
- ❑ 12 Marcus Allen 10.00 4.50
- ❑ 13 Terry Glenn 10.00 4.50
- ❑ 14 Danny Wuerffel 6.00 2.70
- ❑ 15 Danny Kanell 6.00 2.70
- ❑ 16 Aaron Glenn 4.00 1.80
- ❑ 17 Napoleon Kaufman 10.00 4.50
- ❑ 18 Mark Bruener 4.00 1.80
- ❑ 19 Jim Druckenmiller 6.00 2.70
- ❑ 20 Terrell Owens 10.00 4.50
- ❑ 21 Steve Young 12.00 5.50
- ❑ 22 Reidel Anthony 6.00 2.70
- ❑ 23 Warrick Dunn 12.00 5.50

1999 Collector's Edge Advantage

	MINT	NRMT
COMPLETE SET (190)	50.00	22.00
COMMON CARD (1-190)	.15	.07
SEMISTARS	.30	.14
UNLISTED STARS	.60	.25
COMMON ROOKIE (151-188)	.75	.35

ROOKIE SEMISTARS .... 1.25 .55
ROOKIE UNL.STARS .... 1.50 .70
ROOKIES WERE SHORT PRINTED
COMP.GOLD INGOT (190) 80.00 36.00
*GOLD INGOT STARS: .75X TO 2X HI COL.
*GOLD INGOT YOUNG STARS: .6X TO 1.5X
*GOLD INGOT RCs: .6X TO 1.5X
GOLD INGOTS ONE PER PACK..
COMP.GALVANIZED (190) .. 300.00 135.00
*GALVANIZED STARS: 2.5X TO 6X HI COL.
*GALVANIZED YOUNG STARS: 2.X TO 5X
*GALVANIZED RCs: 2.5X TO 6X..
GALVANIZED VETS SERIAL #'d OF 500
GALVANIZED ROOKIES SERIAL #'d OF 200

❑ 1 Larry Centers .... .15 .07
❑ 2 Rob Moore .... .30 .14
❑ 3 Adrian Murrell .... .30 .14
❑ 4 Jake Plummer .... 1.25 .55
❑ 5 Frank Sanders .... .30 .14
❑ 6 Jamal Anderson .... .60 .25
❑ 7 Chris Chandler .... .30 .14
❑ 8 Tim Dwight .... .60 .25
❑ 9 Tony Martin .... .30 .14
❑ 10 Terance Mathis .... .30 .14
❑ 11 O.J. Santiago .... .15 .07
❑ 12 Jim Harbaugh .... .30 .14
❑ 13 Priest Holmes .... .60 .25
❑ 14 Jermaine Lewis .... .30 .14
❑ 15 Rod Woodson .... .30 .14
❑ 16 Eric Zeier .... .30 .14
❑ 17 Doug Flutie .... .75 .35
❑ 18 Sam Gash .... .15 .07
❑ 19 Rob Johnson .... .30 .14
❑ 20 Eric Moulds .... .60 .25
❑ 21 Andre Reed .... .30 .14
❑ 22 Antowain Smith .... .60 .25
❑ 23 Bruce Smith .... .30 .14
❑ 24 Thurman Thomas .... .30 .14
❑ 25 Steve Beuerlein .... .30 .14
❑ 26 Kevin Greene .... .30 .14
❑ 27 Rocket Ismail .... .30 .14
❑ 28 Fred Lane .... .30 .14
❑ 29 Muhsin Muhammad .... .30 .14
❑ 30 Edgar Bennett .... .15 .07
❑ 31 Curtis Conway .... .30 .14
❑ 32 Bobby Engram .... .30 .14
❑ 33 Curtis Enis .... .60 .25
❑ 34 Erik Kramer .... .30 .14
❑ 35 Jeff Blake .... .30 .14
❑ 36 Corey Dillon .... .60 .25
❑ 37 Neil O'Donnell .... .30 .14
❑ 38 Carl Pickens .... .30 .14
❑ 39 Takeo Spikes .... .15 .07
❑ 40 Troy Aikman .... 1.50 .70
❑ 41 Billy Davis .... .15 .07
❑ 42 Michael Irvin .... .30 .14
❑ 43 Deion Sanders .... .60 .25
❑ 44 Emmitt Smith .... 1.50 .70
❑ 45 Darren Woodson .... .15 .07
❑ 46 Bubby Brister .... .30 .14
❑ 47 Terrell Davis .... 1.50 .70
❑ 48 John Elway 2.50 1.10
❑ 49 Ed McCaffrey .... .30 .14
❑ 50 Bill Romanowski .... .15 .07
❑ 51 Shannon Sharpe .... .30 .14
❑ 52 Rod Smith .... .30 .14
❑ 53 Charlie Batch .... 1.25 .55
❑ 54 Germane Crowell .... .30 .14
❑ 55 Herman Moore .... .60 .25
❑ 56 Johnnie Morton .... .30 .14
❑ 57 Barry Sanders 2.50 1.10
❑ 58 Robert Brooks .... .30 .14
❑ 59 Brett Favre 2.50 1.10
❑ 60 Antonio Freeman .... .60 .25
❑ 61 Darick Holmes .... .15 .07
❑ 62 Dorsey Levens .... .60 .25
❑ 63 Roell Preston .... .15 .07
❑ 64 Marshall Faulk .... .60 .25
❑ 65 E.G.Green .... .15 .07
❑ 66 Marvin Harrison .... .60 .25
❑ 67 Peyton Manning 2.50 1.10
❑ 68 Jerome Pathon .... .15 .07
❑ 69 Mark Brunell .... 1.00 .45
❑ 70 Kevin Hardy .... .15 .07
❑ 71 Keenan McCardell .... .30 .14
❑ 72 Jimmy Smith .... .30 .14
❑ 73 Fred Taylor .... 1.50 .70
❑ 74 Alvis Whitted .... .15 .07
❑ 75 Kimble Anders .... .30 .14
❑ 76 Donnell Bennett .... .15 .07
❑ 77 Rich Gannon .... .30 .14
❑ 78 Elvis Grbac .... .30 .14
❑ 79 Byron Bam Morris .... .15 .07
❑ 80 Andre Rison .... .30 .14
❑ 81 Karim Abdul-Jabbar .... .30 .14
❑ 82 John Avery .... .15 .07
❑ 83 Oronde Gadsden .... .15 .07
❑ 84 Sam Madison .... .15 .07
❑ 85 Dan Marino 2.50 1.10
❑ 86 O.J. McDuffie .... .30 .14
❑ 87 Zach Thomas .... .15 .07
❑ 88 Cris Carter .... .60 .25
❑ 89 Randall Cunningham .... .60 .25
❑ 90 Brad Johnson .... .60 .25
❑ 91 Randy Moss 2.50 1.10
❑ 92 John Randle .... .30 .14
❑ 93 Jake Reed .... .30 .14
❑ 94 Robert Smith .... .60 .25
❑ 95 Drew Bledsoe .... 1.00 .45
❑ 96 Ben Coates .... .30 .14
❑ 97 Robert Edwards .... .30 .14
❑ 98 Terry Glenn .... .60 .25
❑ 99 Ty Law .... .15 .07
❑ 100 Cam Cleeland .... .15 .07
❑ 101 Kerry Collins .... .30 .14
❑ 102 Gary Brown .... .15 .07
❑ 103 Kent Graham .... .15 .07
❑ 104 Ike Hilliard .... .30 .14
❑ 105 Joe Jurevicius .... .15 .07
❑ 106 Danny Kanell .... .15 .07
❑ 107 Wayne Chrebet .... .30 .14
❑ 108 Aaron Glenn .... .15 .07
❑ 109 Keyshawn Johnson .... .60 .25
❑ 110 Curtis Martin .... .60 .25
❑ 111 Vinny Testaverde .... .30 .14
❑ 112 Tim Brown .... .60 .25
❑ 113 Jeff George .... .30 .14
❑ 114 James Jett .... .30 .14
❑ 115 Napoleon Kaufman .... .60 .25
❑ 116 Charles Woodson .... .60 .25
❑ 117 Koy Detmer .... .15 .07
❑ 118 Duce Staley .... .60 .25
❑ 119 Jerome Bettis .... .60 .25
❑ 120 Charles Johnson .... .30 .14
❑ 121 Kordell Stewart .... .60 .25
❑ 122 Tony Banks .... .30 .14
❑ 123 Isaac Bruce .... .60 .25
❑ 124 June Henley RC .... .15 .07
❑ 125 Ryan Leaf .... .60 .25
❑ 126 Natrone Means .... .30 .14
❑ 127 Mikhael Ricks .... .15 .07
❑ 128 Craig Whelihan .... .15 .07
❑ 129 Garrison Hearst .... .30 .14
❑ 130 Terrell Owens .... .60 .25
❑ 131 Jerry Rice .... 1.50 .70
❑ 132 J.J.Stokes .... .30 .14
❑ 133 Steve Young .... 1.00 .45
❑ 134 Joey Galloway .... .60 .25
❑ 135 Ahman Green .... .30 .14
❑ 136 Jon Kitna .... .75 .35
❑ 137 Ricky Watters .... .30 .14
❑ 138 Mike Alstott .... .60 .25
❑ 139 Reidel Anthony .... .30 .14
❑ 140 Trent Dilfer .... .30 .14
❑ 141 Warrick Dunn .... .60 .25
❑ 142 Jacquez Green .... .30 .14
❑ 143 Kevin Dyson .... .30 .14
❑ 144 Eddie George .... .75 .35
❑ 145 Steve McNair .... .60 .25
❑ 146 Yancey Thigpen .... .15 .07
❑ 147 Terry Allen .... .30 .14
❑ 148 Trent Green .... .30 .14
❑ 149 Skip Hicks .... .60 .25
❑ 150 Michael Westbrook .... .30 .14
❑ 151 Rahim Abdullah RC .... 1.25 .55
❑ 152 Champ Bailey RC .... 2.00 .90
❑ 153 Marlon Barnes RC .... 1.25 .55
❑ 154 D'Wayne Bates RC .... 1.25 .55
❑ 155 Michael Bishop RC .... 2.00 .90
❑ 156 Dre' Bly RC .... 1.25 .55
❑ 157 David Boston RC 2.50 1.10
❑ 158 Chris Claiborne RC .... 1.25 .55
❑ 159 Tim Couch RC 8.00 3.60
❑ 160 Daunte Culpepper RC .. 5.00 2.20
❑ 161 Autry Denson RC .... 1.50 .70
❑ 162 Jared DeVries RC .... 1.25 .55
❑ 163 Troy Edwards RC 2.50 1.10
❑ 164 Kris Farris RC .... .75 .35
❑ 165 Kevin Faulk RC .... 2.00 .90
❑ 166 Martin Gramatica RC .... .75 .35
❑ 167 Torry Holt RC 3.00 1.35
❑ 168 Brock Huard RC .... 2.00 .90
❑ 169 Sedrick Irvin RC .... 1.50 .70
❑ 170 Edgerrin James RC 12.00 5.50
❑ 171 James Johnson RC .... 2.00 .90
❑ 172 Kevin Johnson RC 4.00 1.80
❑ 173 Andy Katzenmoyer RC 1.50 .70
❑ 174 Jevon Kearse RC 2.50 1.10
❑ 175 Shaun King RC 5.00 2.20
❑ 176 Rob Konrad RC .... 1.25 .55
❑ 177 Chris McAlister RC .... 1.25 .55
❑ 178 Darnell McDonald RC .. 1.50 .70
❑ 179 Donovan McNabb RC .. 5.00 2.20
❑ 180 Cade McNown RC 5.00 2.20
❑ 181 Dat Nguyen RC .... 1.50 .70
❑ 182 Peerless Price RC 2.50 1.10
❑ 183 Akili Smith RC 3.00 1.35
❑ 184 Tai Streets RC .... 1.25 .55
❑ 185 Cuncho Brown RC UER 1.25 .55
(Photo is actually Courtney Brown)
❑ 186 Ricky Williams RC 8.00 3.60
❑ 187 Craig Yeast RC .... 1.25 .55
❑ 188 Amos Zereoue RC .... 1.50 .70
❑ 189 Checklist .... .15 .07
❑ 190 Checklist .... .15 .07

1999 Collector's Edge Advantage HoloGold

	MINT	NRMT
COMMON HOLOGOLD (1-190)	8.00	3.60

*HOLOGOLD STARS: 30X TO 70X HI COL.
*HOLOGOLD YOUNG STARS: 25X TO 60X
*HOLOGOLD RCs: 10X TO 25X ..
HOLOGOLD VETS SERIAL #'d OF 50
HOLOGOLD ROOKIES SERIAL #'d OF 20

1999 Collector's Edge Advantage Rookie Autographs

	MINT	NRMT
COMPLETE SET (34)	600.00	275.00
COMMON CARD (151-188)	8.00	3.60
SEMISTARS	10.00	4.50
UNLISTED STARS	12.00	5.50
STATED ODDS 1:24		

*BLUE SER.#'d AUTOGRAPHS: 1.25X TO 3X
MOST BLUE AUTOS SERIAL #'d OF 40
KRIS FARRIS BLUE SERIAL #'d OF 80
JAMES/COUCH/WILLIAMS BLUES NOT SER.#'d
UNPRICED REDS PRINT RUN 10 SER.#'d SETS

	MINT	NRMT
❑ 151 Rahim Abdullah	10.00	4.50
❑ 152 Champ Bailey	15.00	6.75
❑ 153 Marlon Barnes	10.00	4.50
❑ 154 D'Wayne Bates	10.00	4.50
❑ 155 Michael Bishop	15.00	6.75
❑ 156 Dre' Bly	8.00	3.60
❑ 157 David Boston	20.00	9.00
❑ 158 Chris Claiborne	10.00	4.50
❑ 159 Tim Couch	60.00	27.00
❑ 160 Daunte Culpepper	25.00	11.00
❑ 162 Jared DeVries	10.00	4.50
❑ 163 Troy Edwards	20.00	9.00
❑ 164 Kris Farris	8.00	3.60
❑ 165 Kevin Faulk	15.00	6.75
❑ 166 Martin Gramatica	8.00	3.60
❑ 168 Brock Huard	15.00	6.75
❑ 169 Sedrick Irvin	12.00	5.50
❑ 170 Edgerrin James Blue	100.00	45.00
❑ 171 James Johnson	15.00	6.75
❑ 172 Kevin Johnson	25.00	11.00
❑ 174 Jevon Kearse	20.00	9.00
❑ 175 Shaun King	30.00	13.50
❑ 176 Rob Konrad	10.00	4.50
❑ 177 Chris McAlister	10.00	4.50
❑ 178 Darnell McDonald	12.00	5.50
❑ 179 Donovan McNabb	30.00	13.50
❑ 180 Cade McNown	30.00	13.50
❑ 181 Dat Nguyen	12.00	5.50
❑ 182 Peerless Price	20.00	9.00
❑ 183 Akili Smith	20.00	9.00
❑ 184 Tai Streets	10.00	4.50
❑ 186 Ricky Williams Blue	60.00	27.00
❑ 187 Craig Yeast	10.00	4.50
❑ 188 Amos Zereoue	12.00	5.50

1999 Collector's Edge Advantage Jumpstarters

	MINT	NRMT
COMPLETE SET (10)	70.00	32.00
COMMON CARD (JS1-JS10)	4.00	1.80

STATED PRINT RUN 500 SERIAL #'d SETS

	MINT	NRMT
❑ JS1 Champ Bailey	4.00	1.80
❑ JS2 David Boston	5.00	2.20
❑ JS3 Tim Couch	15.00	6.75
❑ JS4 Daunte Culpepper	10.00	4.50
❑ JS5 Torry Holt	8.00	3.60
❑ JS6 Donovan McNabb	10.00	4.50
❑ JS7 Cade McNown	10.00	4.50
❑ JS8 Peerless Price	5.00	2.20
❑ JS9 Brock Huard	4.00	1.80
❑ JS10 Ricky Williams	15.00	6.75

1999 Collector's Edge Advantage Memorable Moments

	MINT	NRMT
COMPLETE SET (10)	80.00	36.00
COMMON CARD (MM1-MM10)	4.00	1.80
STATED ODDS 1:24		
❑ MM1 Terrell Davis	10.00	4.50
❑ MM2 Randy Moss	12.00	5.50
❑ MM3 Peyton Manning	12.00	5.50
❑ MM4 Emmitt Smith	10.00	4.50
❑ MM5 Keyshawn Johnson	4.00	1.80
❑ MM6 Dan Marino	15.00	6.75
❑ MM7 John Elway	15.00	6.75
❑ MM8 Doug Flutie	5.00	2.20
❑ MM9 Jerry Rice	10.00	4.50
❑ MM10 Steve Young	6.00	2.70

1999 Collector's Edge Advantage Overture

	MINT	NRMT
COMPLETE SET (10)	100.00	45.00
COMMON CARD (1-10)	4.00	1.80
STATED ODDS 1:24		
❑ 1 Jamal Anderson	4.00	1.80
❑ 2 Terrell Davis	10.00	4.50
❑ 3 John Elway	15.00	6.75
❑ 4 Brett Favre	15.00	6.75
❑ 5 Peyton Manning	12.00	5.50
❑ 6 Dan Marino	15.00	6.75
❑ 7 Randy Moss	12.00	5.50
❑ 8 Jerry Rice	10.00	4.50
❑ 9 Barry Sanders	15.00	6.75
❑ 10 Emmitt Smith	10.00	4.50

1999 Collector's Edge Advantage Prime Connection

	MINT	NRMT
COMPLETE SET (20)	60.00	27.00
COMMON CARD (PC1-PC20)	1.50	.70
STATED ODDS 1:4		
❑ PC1 Ricky Williams	8.00	3.60
❑ PC2 Fred Taylor	3.00	1.35
❑ PC3 Tim Couch	8.00	3.60
❑ PC4 Peyton Manning	4.00	1.80
❑ PC5 Daunte Culpepper	5.00	2.20
❑ PC6 Drew Bledsoe	2.50	1.10
❑ PC7 Torry Holt	4.00	1.80
❑ PC8 Keyshawn Johnson	2.50	1.10
❑ PC9 Champ Bailey	1.80	.70
❑ PC10 Charles Woodson	1.80	.70
❑ PC11 Brock Huard	1.80	.70
❑ PC12 Jake Plummer	3.00	1.35
❑ PC13 Donovan McNabb	5.00	2.20
❑ PC14 Steve Young	2.50	1.10
❑ PC15 Edgerrin James	12.00	5.50
❑ PC16 Jamal Anderson	1.80	.70
❑ PC17 Cade McNown	5.00	2.20
❑ PC18 Mark Brunell	2.50	1.10
❑ PC19 Peerless Price	2.50	1.10
❑ PC20 Randy Moss	4.00	1.80

1999 Collector's Edge Advantage Shockwaves

	MINT	NRMT
COMPLETE SET (20)	100.00	45.00
COMMON CARD (SW1-SW20)	4.00	1.80
STATED ODDS 1:12		
❑ SW1 Jamal Anderson	4.00	1.80
❑ SW2 Jake Plummer	8.00	3.60
❑ SW3 Eric Moulds	4.00	1.80
❑ SW4 Troy Aikman	10.00	4.50
❑ SW5 Emmitt Smith	10.00	4.50
❑ SW6 Marshall Faulk	4.00	1.80
❑ SW7 John Elway	15.00	6.75
❑ SW8 Barry Sanders	15.00	6.75
❑ SW9 Brett Favre	15.00	6.75
❑ SW10 Peyton Manning	12.00	5.50
❑ SW11 Mark Brunell	6.00	2.70

Card	Mint	NRMT
❑ SW12 Fred Taylor	8.00	3.60
❑ SW13 Randall Cunningham	4.00	1.80
❑ SW14 Randy Moss	12.00	5.50
❑ SW15 Drew Bledsoe	6.00	2.70
❑ SW16 Keyshawn Johnson	4.00	1.80
❑ SW17 Curtis Martin	4.00	1.80
❑ SW18 Steve Young	6.00	2.70
❑ SW19 Warrick Dunn	4.00	1.80
❑ SW20 Eddie George	5.00	2.20

1999 Collector's Edge Advantage Showtime

	MINT	NRMT
COMPLETE SET (15)	100.00	45.00
COMMON CARD (ST1-ST15)	4.00	1.80

STATED PRINT RUN 500 SERIAL #'d SETS

Card	Mint	NRMT
❑ ST1 Troy Aikman	10.00	4.50
❑ ST2 Jamal Anderson	4.00	1.80
❑ ST3 Mark Brunell	6.00	2.70
❑ ST4 Terrell Davis	10.00	4.50
❑ ST5 Warrick Dunn	4.00	1.80
❑ ST6 Brett Favre	15.00	6.75
❑ ST7 Doug Flutie	5.00	2.20
❑ ST8 Eddie George	5.00	2.20
❑ ST9 Keyshawn Johnson	4.00	1.80
❑ ST10 Peyton Manning	12.00	5.50
❑ ST11 Dan Marino	15.00	6.75
❑ ST12 Randy Moss	12.00	5.50
❑ ST13 Jake Plummer	8.00	3.60
❑ ST14 Jerry Rice	10.00	4.50
❑ ST15 Barry Sanders	15.00	6.75

2000 Collector's Edge EG

	MINT	NRMT
COMPLETE SET (148)	120.00	55.00
COMMON CARD (1-150)	.25	.11
SEMISTARS	.50	.23
UNLISTED STARS	1.00	.45
COMMON ROOKIE (80-109)	1.50	.70
ROOKIE SEMISTARS	2.00	.90

CARDS 93, 110 NOT RELEASED

Card	Mint	NRMT
❑ 1 Marcus Robinson	1.00	.45
❑ 2 Adrian Murrell	.50	.23
❑ 3 Qadry Ismail	.25	.11
❑ 4 Tim Biakabutuka	.50	.23
❑ 5 Jamal Anderson	1.00	.45
❑ 6 Dorsey Levens	1.00	.45
❑ 7 Robert Smith	1.00	.45
❑ 8 Tony Banks	.50	.23
❑ 9 Yancey Thigpen	.25	.11
❑ 10 Elvis Grbac	.50	.23
❑ 11 Sedrick Irvin	.25	.11
❑ 12 Rob Johnson	.50	.23
❑ 13 Frank Sanders	.50	.23
❑ 14 Rich Gannon	.50	.23
❑ 15 Steve Beuerlein	.50	.23
❑ 16 James Stewart	.50	.23
❑ 17 Ricky Watters	.50	.23
❑ 18 Curtis Enis	1.00	.45
❑ 19 Eddie Kennison	.25	.11
❑ 20 Kerry Collins	.50	.23
❑ 21 Ray Lucas	1.00	.45
❑ 22 Carl Pickens	.50	.23
❑ 23 Natrone Means	.25	.11
❑ 24 Daunte Culpepper	1.50	.70
❑ 25 Karim Abdul-Jabbar	.50	.23
❑ 26 David Boston	1.00	.45
❑ 27 Rocket Ismail	.50	.23
❑ 28 Jacquez Green	.50	.23
❑ 29 Kevin Dyson	.50	.23
❑ 30 Chris Chandler	.50	.23
❑ 31 Brian Griese	1.25	.55
❑ 32 Charlie Garner	.50	.23
❑ 33 Wayne Chrebet	.50	.23
❑ 34 Mike Alstott	1.00	.45
❑ 35 Germane Crowell	.50	.23
❑ 36 Michael Cloud	.25	.11
❑ 37 Antowain Smith	1.00	.45
❑ 38 Jeff George	.50	.23
❑ 39 Antonio Freeman	1.00	.45
❑ 40 Champ Bailey		
❑ 41 Terrence Wilkins	1.00	.45
❑ 42 Junior Seau	.50	.23
❑ 43 Jimmy Smith	.50	.23
❑ 44 Greg Hill	.25	.11
❑ 45 Tyrone Wheatley	.50	.23
❑ 46 Tony Gonzalez	.50	.23
❑ 47 Rod Smith	.50	.23
❑ 48 Damon Huard	1.00	.45
❑ 49 Jerome Bettis	1.00	.45
❑ 50 Cris Carter	1.00	.45
❑ 51 Darnay Scott	.50	.23
❑ 52 Ike Hilliard	.50	.23
❑ 53 Errict Rhett	.50	.23
❑ 54 Tim Brown	1.00	.45
❑ 55 Terry Glenn	1.00	.45
❑ 56 Jeff Blake	.50	.23
❑ 57 Terance Mathis	.50	.23
❑ 58 Duce Staley	1.00	.45
❑ 59 Amani Toomer	.25	.11
❑ 60 Terry Allen	.50	.23
❑ 61 Corey Dillon	1.00	.45
❑ 62 Kordell Stewart	1.00	.45
❑ 63 Az-Zahir Hakim	.50	.23
❑ 64 Jim Harbaugh	.50	.23
❑ 65 Bill Schroeder	.50	.23
❑ 66 O.J. McDuffie	.50	.23
❑ 67 Keenan McCardell	.50	.23
❑ 68 Terrell Owens	1.00	.45
❑ 69 Joey Galloway	1.00	.45
❑ 70 Derrick Alexander	.50	.23
❑ 71 Ed McCaffrey	.50	.23
❑ 72 Reidel Anthony	.25	.11
❑ 73 Michael Irvin	.50	.23
❑ 74 Herman Moore	1.00	.45
❑ 75 Joe Montgomery	.25	.11
❑ 76 Muhsin Muhammad	.50	.23
❑ 77 Charles Johnson	.25	.11
❑ 78 Michael Westbrook	.50	.23
❑ 79 Jevon Kearse	1.00	.45
❑ 80 Courtney Brown RC	4.00	1.80
❑ 81 Shaun Alexander RC	6.00	2.70
❑ 82 R.Jay Soward RC	2.50	1.10
❑ 83 Sylvester Morris RC	2.50	1.10
❑ 84 Giovanni Carmazzi RC	4.00	1.80
❑ 85 J.R. Redmond RC	3.00	1.35
❑ 86 Sherrod Gideon RC	1.50	.70
❑ 87 Tee Martin RC	3.00	1.35
❑ 88 Dennis Northcutt RC	2.50	1.10
❑ 89 Troy Walters RC	2.00	.90
❑ 90 Joe Hamilton RC	2.00	.90
❑ 91 Reuben Droughns RC	2.50	1.10
❑ 92 Trung Canidate RC	2.00	.90
❑ 94 Tim Rattay RC	2.50	1.10
❑ 95 Jerry Porter RC	2.50	1.10
❑ 96 Michael Wiley RC	2.50	1.10
❑ 97 Anthony Lucas RC	2.00	.90
❑ 98 Danny Farmer RC	2.00	.90
❑ 99 Travis Prentice RC	2.50	1.10
❑ 100 Dez White RC	2.50	1.10
❑ 101 Chad Pennington RC	8.00	3.60
❑ 102 Chris Redman RC	3.00	1.35
❑ 103 Thomas Jones RC	6.00	2.70
❑ 104 Ron Dayne RC	10.00	4.50
❑ 105 Jamal Lewis RC	6.00	2.70
❑ 106 Shyrone Stith RC	1.50	.70
❑ 107 Peter Warrick RC	10.00	4.50
❑ 108 Plaxico Burress RC	5.00	2.20
❑ 109 Travis Taylor RC	4.00	1.80
❑ 111 Terrell Davis	2.50	1.10
❑ 112 Dan Marino	4.00	1.80
❑ 113 Brad Johnson	1.00	.45
❑ 114 Isaac Bruce	1.00	.45
❑ 115 Eric Moulds	1.00	.45
❑ 116 Olandis Gary	1.00	.45
❑ 117 Drew Bledsoe	1.50	.70
❑ 118 Steve Young	1.50	.70
❑ 119 Keyshawn Johnson	1.00	.45
❑ 120 Emmitt Smith	2.50	1.10
❑ 121 Warrick Dunn	1.00	.45
❑ 122 Doug Flutie	1.25	.55
❑ 123 Troy Edwards	1.00	.45
❑ 124 Brett Favre	4.00	1.80
❑ 125 Charlie Batch	1.00	.45
❑ 126 Curtis Martin	1.00	.45
❑ 127 Stephen Davis	1.00	.45
❑ 128 Troy Aikman	2.50	1.10
❑ 129 Fred Taylor	1.50	.70
❑ 130 Jerry Rice	2.50	1.10
❑ 131 Jon Kitna	1.00	.45
❑ 132 Steve McNair	1.00	.45
❑ 133 Jake Plummer	1.00	.45
❑ 134 Donovan McNabb	1.50	.70
❑ 135 Ricky Williams	2.50	1.10
❑ 136 Torry Holt	1.00	.45
❑ 137 James Johnson	.50	.23
❑ 138 Kevin Johnson	1.00	.45
❑ 139 Akili Smith	1.25	.55
❑ 140 Cade McNown	1.50	.70
❑ 141 Eddie George	1.25	.55
❑ 142 Shaun King	1.50	.70
❑ 143 Marshall Faulk	1.00	.45
❑ 144 Kurt Warner	5.00	2.20
❑ 145 Randy Moss	3.00	1.35
❑ 146 Mark Brunell	1.50	.70
❑ 147 Marvin Harrison	1.00	.45
❑ 148 Edgerrin James	4.00	1.80
❑ 149 Tim Couch	2.50	1.10
❑ 150 Peyton Manning	3.00	1.35

2000 Collector's Edge EG Brilliant Graded

	MINT	NRMT
COMMON CARD Gem Mt	30.00	13.50
COMMON CARD Mint	15.00	6.75

STATED PRINT RUN 500 SERIAL #'d SETS

Card	Mint	NRMT
❑ 101 C.Pennington Gem Mt		
❑ 101 C.Pennington Mint		
❑ 102 C.Redman Gem Mt	50.00	22.00
❑ 102 C.Redman Mint	25.00	11.00
❑ 103 T.Jones Gem Mt	100.00	45.00
❑ 103 T.Jones Mint	50.00	22.00
❑ 104 R.Dayne Gem Mt	200.00	90.00
❑ 104 R.Dayne Mint	80.00	36.00
❑ 105 J.Lewis Gem Mt	100.00	45.00
❑ 105 J.Lewis Mint	50.00	22.00
❑ 106 S.Stith Gem Mt		
❑ 106 S.Stith Mint	30.00	13.50
❑ 107 P.Warrick Gem Mt	200.00	90.00
❑ 107 P.Warrick Mint	80.00	36.00
❑ 108 P.Burress Gem Mt	80.00	36.00
❑ 108 P.Burress Mint	40.00	18.00
❑ 109 T.Taylor Gem Mt		
❑ 109 T.Taylor Mint	30.00	13.50
❑ 111 T.Davis Gem Mt	50.00	22.00
❑ 111 T.Davis Mint	25.00	11.00
❑ 112 D.Marino Gem Mt	80.00	36.00
❑ 112 D.Marino Mint	40.00	18.00
❑ 113 B.Johnson Gem Mt	30.00	13.50
❑ 113 B.Johnson Mint	15.00	6.75
❑ 114 I.Bruce Gem Mt	30.00	13.50
❑ 114 I.Bruce Mint	15.00	6.75
❑ 115 E.Moulds Gem Mt	30.00	13.50
❑ 115 E.Moulds Mint	15.00	6.75
❑ 116 O.Gary Gem Mt	30.00	13.50
❑ 116 O.Gary Mint	15.00	6.75
❑ 117 D.Bledsoe Gem Mt	40.00	18.00
❑ 117 D.Bledsoe Mint	20.00	9.00
❑ 118 S.Young Gem Mt	40.00	18.00
❑ 118 S.Young Mint	20.00	9.00
❑ 119 Key.Johnson Gem Mt		

❑ 119 Key.Johnson Mint 15.00 6.75
❑ 120 E.Smith Gem Mt 50.00 22.00
❑ 120 E.Smith Mint 25.00 11.00
❑ 121 W.Dunn Gem Mt 30.00 13.50
❑ 121 W.Dunn Mint 15.00 6.75
❑ 122 D.Flutie Gem Mt 40.00 18.00
❑ 122 D.Flutie Mint 20.00 9.00
❑ 123 T.Edwards Gem Mt 30.00 13.50
❑ 123 T.Edwards Mint 15.00 6.75
❑ 124 B.Favre Gem Mt ....
❑ 124 B.Favre Mint 40.00 18.00
❑ 125 C.Batch Gem Mt 30.00 13.50
❑ 125 C.Batch Mint 15.00 6.75
❑ 126 C.Martin Gem Mt........ 30.00 13.50
❑ 126 C.Martin Mint.............. 15.00 6.75
❑ 127 S.Davis Gem Mt 30.00 13.50
❑ 127 S.Davis Mint 15.00 6.75
❑ 128 T.Aikman Gem Mt ....
❑ 128 T.Aikman Mint 25.00 11.00
❑ 129 F.Taylor Gem Mt 40.00 18.00
❑ 129 F.Taylor Mint 20.00 9.00
❑ 130 J.Rice Gem Mt 50.00 22.00
❑ 130 J.Rice Mint 25.00 11.00
❑ 131 J.Kitna Gem Mt 30.00 13.50
❑ 131 J.Kitna Mint 15.00 6.75
❑ 132 S.McNair Gem Mt 30.00 13.50
❑ 132 S.McNair Mint 15.00 6.75
❑ 133 J.Plummer Gem Mt 30.00 13.50
❑ 133 J.Plummer Mint 15.00 6.75
❑ 134 D.McNabb Gem Mt 40.00 18.00
❑ 134 D.McNabb Mint 20.00 9.00
❑ 135 R.Williams Gem Mt ....
❑ 135 R.Williams Mint ....
❑ 136 T.Holt Gem Mt..................
❑ 136 T.Holt Mint.......................
❑ 137 J.Johnson Gem Mt ....
❑ 137 J.Johnson Mint 15.00 6.75
❑ 138 Kev.Johnson Gem Mt ......
❑ 138 Kev.Johnson Mint 15.00 6.75
❑ 139 A.Smith Gem Mt ....
❑ 139 A.Smith Mint 15.00 6.75
❑ 140 C.McNown Gem Mt..........
❑ 140 C.McNown Mint.......... 20.00 9.00
❑ 141 E.George Gem Mt...... 40.00 18.00
❑ 141 E.George Mint............ 20.00 9.00
❑ 142 S.King Gem Mt 40.00 18.00
❑ 142 S.King Mint 20.00 9.00
❑ 143 M.Faulk Gem Mt 30.00 13.50
❑ 143 M.Faulk Mint 15.00 6.75
❑ 144 K.Warner Gem Mt 80.00 36.00
❑ 144 K.Warner Mint 40.00 18.00
❑ 145 R.Moss Gem Mt 60.00 27.00
❑ 145 R.Moss Mint 30.00 13.50
❑ 146 M.Brunell Gem Mt ....
❑ 146 M.Brunell Mint 20.00 9.00
❑ 147 M.Harrison Gem Mt..........
❑ 147 M.Harrison Mint................
❑ 148 E.James Gem Mt ....
❑ 148 E.James Mint 30.00 13.50
❑ 149 T.Couch Gem Mt........ 50.00 22.00
❑ 149 T.Couch Mint.............. 25.00 11.00
❑ 150 P.Manning Gem Mt ....
❑ 150 P.Manning Mint.......... 30.00 13.50

2000 Collector's Edge EG Edge Gems

	MINT	NRMT
COMPLETE SET (50)	400.00	180.00
COMMON CARD (E1-E50)	4.00	1.80

STATED PRINT RUN 500 SERIAL #'d SETS

❑ E1 Doug Flutie 5.00 2.20
❑ E2 Cade McNown 5.00 2.20
❑ E3 Akili Smith...................... 4.00 1.80
❑ E4 Tim Couch 8.00 3.60
❑ E5 Kevin Johnson 4.00 1.80
❑ E6 Troy Aikman 10.00 4.50
❑ E7 Emmitt Smith 10.00 4.50
❑ E8 Terrell Davis 10.00 4.50
❑ E9 Brett Favre 15.00 6.75
❑ E10 Marvin Harrison 4.00 1.80
❑ E11 Edgerrin James............ 12.00 5.50
❑ E12 Peyton Manning 12.00 5.50
❑ E13 Mark Brunell 6.00 2.70
❑ E14 Dan Marino 15.00 6.75
❑ E15 Randy Moss 12.00 5.50
❑ E16 Drew Bledsoe 6.00 2.70
❑ E17 Ricky Williams.............. 8.00 3.60
❑ E18 Keyshawn Johnson...... 4.00 1.80
❑ E19 Curtis Martin 4.00 1.80
❑ E20 Donovan McNabb 5.00 2.20
❑ E21 Marshall Fauk 4.00 1.80
❑ E22 Torry Holt 4.00 1.80
❑ E23 Kurt Warner 15.00 6.75
❑ E24 Jerry Rice 10.00 4.50
❑ E25 Steve Young 6.00 2.70
❑ E26 Jon Kitna...................... 4.00 1.80
❑ E27 Shaun King 5.00 2.20
❑ E28 Eddie George 5.00 2.20
❑ E29 Stephen Davis 4.00 1.80
❑ E30 Brad Johnson 4.00 1.80
❑ E31 Chad Pennington 25.00 11.00
❑ E32 Chris Redman............ 10.00 4.50
❑ E33 Tim Rattay 8.00 3.60
❑ E34 Tee Martin.................. 10.00 4.50
❑ E35 Thomas Jones 20.00 9.00
❑ E36 Ron Dayne 30.00 13.50
❑ E37 Jamal Lewis 20.00 9.00
❑ E38 J.R. Redmond............ 10.00 4.50
❑ E39 Travis Prentice 8.00 3.60
❑ E40 Shaun Alexander 20.00 9.00
❑ E41 Michael Wiley 8.00 3.60
❑ E42 Quinton Spotwood 5.00 2.20
❑ E43 Peter Warrick 30.00 13.50
❑ E44 Plaxico Burress.......... 15.00 6.75
❑ E45 Travis Taylor.............. 12.00 5.50
❑ E46 Troy Walters 6.00 2.70
❑ E47 R.Jay Soward 8.00 3.60
❑ E48 Dez White 8.00 3.60
❑ E50 Courtney Brown 12.00 5.50

2000 Collector's Edge EG Golden Edge

	MINT	NRMT
COMPLETE SET (50)	200.00	90.00
COMMON CARD (GE1-GE50)	1.50	.70

STATED PRINT RUN 2000 SERIAL #'d SETS

❑ GE1 Jake Plummer 2.50 1.10
❑ GE2 Qadry Ismail................ 1.50 .70
❑ GE3 Doug Flutie.................. 3.00 1.35
❑ GE4 Muhsin Muhammad .... 1.50 .70
❑ GE5 Cade McNown 3.00 1.35
❑ GE6 Marcus Robinson........ 2.50 1.10
❑ GE7 Akili Smith 2.50 1.10
❑ GE8 Tim Couch 5.00 2.20
❑ GE9 Kevin Johnson 2.50 1.10
❑ GE10 Troy Aikman.............. 6.00 2.70
❑ GE11 Emmitt Smith 6.00 2.70
❑ GE12 Terrell Davis.............. 6.00 2.70
❑ GE13 Charlie Batch 2.50 1.10
❑ GE14 Brett Favre 10.00 4.50
❑ GE15 Marvin Harrison 2.50 1.10
❑ GE16 Edgerrin James 8.00 3.60
❑ GE17 Peyton Manning 8.00 3.60
❑ GE18 Mark Brunell.............. 4.00 1.80
❑ GE19 Fred Taylor................ 4.00 1.80
❑ GE20 Dan Marino 10.00 4.50
❑ GE21 Randy Moss.............. 8.00 3.60
❑ GE22 Drew Bledsoe............ 4.00 1.80
❑ GE23 Ricky Williams 5.00 2.20
❑ GE24 Curtis Martin.............. 2.50 1.10
❑ GE25 Donovan McNabb 3.00 1.35
❑ GE26 Isaac Bruce 2.50 1.10
❑ GE27 Marshall Faulk 2.50 1.10
❑ GE28 Torry Holt 2.50 1.10
❑ GE29 Kurt Warner 10.00 4.50
❑ GE30 Jerry Rice.................. 6.00 2.70
❑ GE31 Jon Kitna 2.50 1.10
❑ GE32 Eddie George............ 3.00 1.35
❑ GE33 Steve McNair 2.50 1.10
❑ GE34 Stephen Davis 2.50 1.10
❑ GE35 Brad Johnson............ 2.50 1.10
❑ GE36 Travis Prentice 4.00 1.80
❑ GE37 Dez White 4.00 1.80
❑ GE38 Chad Pennington 12.00 5.50
❑ GE39 Chris Redman 5.00 2.20
❑ GE40 Thomas Jones 10.00 4.50
❑ GE41 Ron Dayne.............. 15.00 6.75
❑ GE42 Jamal Lewis 10.00 4.50
❑ GE43 Shyrone Stith .... 1.50 .70
❑ GE44 Peter Warrick 15.00 6.75
❑ GE45 Plaxico Burress 8.00 3.60
❑ GE46 Travis Taylor 6.00 2.70
❑ GE48 Shaun Alexander 10.00 4.50
❑ GE49 R.Jay Soward............ 4.00 1.80
❑ GE50 Sylvester Morris 4.00 1.80

2000 Collector's Edge EG Impeccable

	MINT	NRMT
COMPLETE SET (20)	80.00	36.00
COMMON CARD (I1-I20)	2.50	1.10

STATED PRINT RUN 2000 SERIAL #'d SETS

❑ I1 Cade McNown 3.00 1.35
❑ I2 Tim Couch 5.00 2.20
❑ I3 Troy Aikman.................... 6.00 2.70
❑ I4 Emmitt Smith 6.00 2.70
❑ I5 Terrell Davis.................... 6.00 2.70
❑ I6 Brett Favre 10.00 4.50
❑ I7 Edgerrin James 8.00 3.60
❑ I8 Peyton Manning 8.00 3.60
❑ I9 Mark Brunell.................... 4.00 1.80
❑ I10 Fred Taylor.................... 4.00 1.80
❑ I11 Dan Marino.................. 10.00 4.50
❑ I12 Randy Moss.................. 8.00 3.60
❑ I13 Drew Bledsoe................ 4.00 1.80
❑ I14 Ricky Williams 5.00 2.20
❑ I15 Curtis Martin.................. 2.50 1.10
❑ I16 Marshall Faulk 2.50 1.10
❑ I17 Kurt Warner 10.00 4.50
❑ I18 Eddie George................ 3.00 1.35
❑ I19 Steve McNair 2.50 1.10
❑ I20 Stephen Davis 2.50 1.10

2000 Collector's Edge EG Making the Grade

	MINT	NRMT
COMPLETE SET (29)	100.00	45.00
COMMON CARD (M1-M29)	2.50	1.10

STATED PRINT RUN 2000 SERIAL #'d SETS

❑ M1 Shaun Alexander 10.00 4.50
❑ M2 R.Jay Soward.............. 4.00 1.80

❑ M3 Sylvester Morris	4.00	1.80
❑ M4 Corey Simon	3.00	1.35
❑ M5 J.R. Redmond	5.00	2.20
❑ M6 Sherrod Gideon	2.50	1.10
❑ M7 Tee Martin	5.00	2.20
❑ M8 Dennis Northcutt	4.00	1.80
❑ M9 Courtney Brown	6.00	2.70
❑ M10 Joe Hamilton	3.00	1.35
❑ M11 Reuben Droughns	4.00	1.80
❑ M12 Trung Canidate	3.00	1.35
❑ M14 Brian Urlacher	4.00	1.80
❑ M15 Jerry Porter	4.00	1.80
❑ M16 Ron Dugans	3.00	1.35
❑ M17 Anthony Becht	3.00	1.35
❑ M18 Danny Farmer	3.00	1.35
❑ M19 Travis Prentice	4.00	1.80
❑ M20 Dez White	4.00	1.80
❑ M21 Chad Pennington	12.00	5.50
❑ M22 Chris Redman	5.00	2.20
❑ M23 Thomas Jones	10.00	4.50
❑ M24 Ron Dayne	15.00	6.75
❑ M25 Jamal Lewis	10.00	4.50
❑ M26 Todd Pinkston	3.00	1.35
❑ M27 Peter Warrick	15.00	6.75
❑ M28 Plaxico Burress	8.00	3.60
❑ M29 Travis Taylor	6.00	2.70

2000 Collector's Edge EG Rookie Leatherbacks

	MINT	NRMT
COMMON CARD		

STATED PRINT RUN 12 SERIAL #'d SETS
NOT PRICED DUE TO SCARCITY

❑ AB Anthony Becht
❑ BF Bubba Franks
❑ BU Brian Urlacher
❑ CK Curtis Keaton
❑ CP Chad Pennington
❑ CR Chris Redman
❑ CS Corey Simon
❑ DF Danny Farmer
❑ DN Dennis Northcutt
❑ DW Dez White
❑ JH Joe Hamilton
❑ JL Jamal Lewis
❑ JP Jerry Porter
❑ JR J.R. Redmond
❑ LC Laveranues Coles
❑ PB Plaxico Burress
❑ PW Peter Warrick
❑ RD Ron Dayne
❑ RD Reuben Droughns
❑ RD Ron Dugans
❑ RS R.Jay Soward
❑ SA Shaun Alexander
❑ SM Sylvester Morris
❑ TC Trung Canidate
❑ TJ Thomas Jones
❑ TM Tee Martin
❑ TP Travis Prentice
❑ TP Todd Pinkston
❑ TT Travis Taylor

2000 Collector's Edge EG Supreme PSA Redemption

	MINT	NRMT
COMMON CARD	25.00	11.00

RANDOM INSERTS IN PACKS ....
REDEEMABLE FOR PSA 9 OR 10
EXPIRATION DATE: 12/31/2000 ..

❑ U151 Sylvester Morris	30.00	13.50
❑ U152 Peter Warrick	100.00	45.00
❑ U153 Chad Pennington	80.00	36.00
❑ U154 Courtney Brown	50.00	22.00
❑ U155 Thomas Jones	60.00	27.00
❑ U156 Chris Redman	40.00	18.00
❑ U157 R.Jay Soward	30.00	13.50
❑ U159 Shaun Alexander	60.00	27.00
❑ U160 Travis Taylor	50.00	22.00
❑ U161 Ron Dayne	100.00	45.00
❑ U162 Travis Prentice	30.00	13.50
❑ U163 Plaxico Burress	50.00	22.00
❑ U164 J.R. Redmond	40.00	18.00
❑ U166 Dez White	30.00	13.50
❑ U169 Ron Dugans	25.00	11.00
❑ U170 Laveranues Coles	25.00	11.00
❑ U172 Todd Pinkston	25.00	11.00
❑ U175 Bubba Franks	30.00	13.50
❑ U180 Dennis Northcutt	30.00	13.50
❑ U188 Todd Husak	25.00	11.00
❑ U189 Jerry Porter	30.00	13.50

2000 Collector's Edge EG Uncirculated Graded

	MINT	NRMT
COMMON CARD Gem Mt	15.00	6.75
COMMON CARD Mint	8.00	3.60

STATED PRINT RUN 5000 SERIAL #'d SETS

Card		
❑ 101 C.Pennington Gem Mt	60.00	27.00
❑ 101 C.Pennington Mint	30.00	13.50
❑ 102 C.Redman Gem Mt	25.00	11.00
❑ 102 C.Redman Mint	12.00	5.50
❑ 103 T.Jones Gem Mt	50.00	22.00
❑ 103 T.Jones Mint	25.00	11.00
❑ 104 R.Dayne Gem Mt	80.00	36.00
❑ 104 R.Dayne Mint	40.00	18.00
❑ 105 J.Lewis Gem Mt	50.00	22.00
❑ 105 J.Lewis Mint	25.00	11.00
❑ 106 S.Stith Gem Mt	15.00	6.75
❑ 106 S.Stith Mint	8.00	3.60
❑ 107 P.Warrick Gem Mt	80.00	36.00
❑ 107 P.Warrick Mint	40.00	18.00
❑ 108 P.Burress Gem Mt	40.00	18.00
❑ 108 P.Burress Mint	20.00	9.00
❑ 109 T.Taylor Gem Mt	30.00	13.50
❑ 109 T.Taylor Mint	15.00	6.75
❑ 111 T.Davis Gem Mt		
❑ 111 T.Davis Mint	12.00	5.50
❑ 112 D.Marino Gem Mt	40.00	18.00
❑ 112 D.Marino Mint	20.00	9.00
❑ 113 B.Johnson Gem Mt	15.00	6.75
❑ 113 B.Johnson Mint	8.00	3.60
❑ 114 I.Bruce Gem Mt	15.00	6.75
❑ 114 I.Bruce Mint	8.00	3.60
❑ 115 E.Moulds Gem Mt	15.00	6.75
❑ 115 E.Moulds Mint	8.00	3.60
❑ 116 O.Gary Gem Mt	15.00	6.75
❑ 116 O.Gary Mint	8.00	3.60
❑ 117 D.Bledsoe Gem Mt	20.00	9.00
❑ 117 D.Bledsoe Mint	10.00	4.50
❑ 118 S.Young Gem Mt	20.00	9.00
❑ 118 S.Young Mint	10.00	4.50
❑ 119 Key.Johnson Gem Mt	15.00	6.75
❑ 119 Key.Johnson Mint	8.00	3.60
❑ 120 E.Smith Gem Mt	25.00	11.00
❑ 120 E.Smith Mint	12.00	5.50
❑ 121 W.Dunn Gem Mt	15.00	6.75
❑ 121 W.Dunn Mint	8.00	3.60
❑ 122 D.Flutie Gem Mt	20.00	9.00
❑ 122 D.Flutie Mint	10.00	4.50
❑ 123 T.Edwards Gem Mt	15.00	6.75
❑ 123 T.Edwards Mint	8.00	3.60
❑ 124 B.Favre Gem Mt		
❑ 124 B.Favre Mint	20.00	9.00
❑ 125 C.Batch Gem Mt		
❑ 125 C.Batch Mint	8.00	3.60
❑ 126 C.Martin Gem Mt	15.00	6.75
❑ 126 C.Martin Mint	8.00	3.60
❑ 127 S.Davis Gem Mt	15.00	6.75
❑ 127 S.Davis Mint	8.00	3.60
❑ 128 T.Aikman Gem Mt	25.00	11.00
❑ 128 T.Aikman Mint	12.00	5.50
❑ 129 F.Taylor Gem Mt	20.00	9.00
❑ 129 F.Taylor Mint	10.00	4.50
❑ 130 J.Rice Gem Mt	25.00	11.00
❑ 130 J.Rice Mint	12.00	5.50
❑ 131 J.Kitna Gem Mt	15.00	6.75
❑ 131 J.Kitna Mint	8.00	3.60
❑ 132 S.McNair Gem Mt	15.00	6.75
❑ 132 S.McNair Mint	8.00	3.60
❑ 133 J.Plummer Gem Mt	15.00	6.75
❑ 133 J.Plummer Mint	8.00	3.60
❑ 134 D.McNabb Gem Mt	20.00	9.00
❑ 134 D.McNabb Mint	10.00	4.50
❑ 135 R.Williams Gem Mt		
❑ 135 R.Williams Mint	12.00	5.50
❑ 136 T.Holt Gem Mt	15.00	6.75
❑ 136 T.Holt Mint	8.00	3.60
❑ 137 J.Johnson Gem Mt	15.00	6.75
❑ 137 J.Johnson Mint	8.00	3.60
❑ 138 Kev.Johnson Gem Mt	15.00	6.75
❑ 138 Kev.Johnson Mint	8.00	3.60
❑ 139 A.Smith Gem Mt	15.00	6.75
❑ 139 A.Smith Mint	8.00	3.60
❑ 140 C.McNown Gem Mt	20.00	9.00
❑ 140 C.McNown Mint	10.00	4.50
❑ 141 E.George Gem Mt	20.00	9.00
❑ 141 E.George Mint	10.00	4.50
❑ 142 S.King Gem Mt	20.00	9.00
❑ 142 S.King Mint	10.00	4.50
❑ 143 M.Faulk Gem Mt	15.00	6.75
❑ 143 M.Faulk Mint	8.00	3.60
❑ 144 K.Warner Gem Mt	40.00	18.00
❑ 144 K.Warner Mint	20.00	9.00
❑ 145 R.Moss Gem Mt	30.00	13.50
❑ 145 R.Moss Mint	15.00	6.75
❑ 146 M.Brunell Gem Mt	20.00	9.00
❑ 146 M.Brunell Mint	10.00	4.50
❑ 147 M.Harrison Gem Mt	15.00	6.75
❑ 147 M.Harrison Mint	8.00	3.60
❑ 148 E.James Gem Mt	30.00	13.50
❑ 148 E.James Mint	15.00	6.75
❑ 149 T.Couch Gem Mt	25.00	11.00
❑ 149 T.Couch Mint	12.00	5.50
❑ 150 P.Manning Gem Mt	30.00	13.50
❑ 150 P.Manning Mint	15.00	6.75

1997 Collector's Edge Extreme

	MINT	NRMT
COMPLETE SET (180)	20.00	9.00
COMMON CARD (1-180)	.10	.05
SEMISTARS	.20	.09
UNLISTED STARS	.40	.18

*SILVER STARS: 1.25X TO 2.5X HI COL.
*SILVER RCs: .5X TO 1X
SILVER STATED ODDS 1:2
*GOLD STARS: 2.5X TO 5X HI COL.

*GOLD RCs: 1X TO 2X ....
GOLD STATED ODDS 1:12..........
*DIE CUT STARS: 7.5X TO 15X HI COL.
*DIE CUT RCs: 3X TO 6X ....
DIE CUT STATED ODDS 1:36......

Card	MINT	NRMT
❑ 1 Larry Centers	.20	.09
❑ 2 Leeland McElroy	.10	.05
❑ 3 Jake Plummer RC	3.00	1.35
❑ 4 Simeon Rice	.20	.09
❑ 5 Eric Swann	.10	.05
❑ 6 Jamal Anderson	.60	.25
❑ 7 Bert Emanuel	.20	.09
❑ 8 Byron Hanspard RC	.75	.35
❑ 9 Derrick Alexander WR UER (Derek on back)	.20	.09
❑ 10 Peter Boulware RC	.20	.09
❑ 11 Michael Jackson	.20	.09
❑ 12 Ray Lewis	.10	.05
❑ 13 Vinny Testaverde	.20	.09
❑ 14 Todd Collins	.10	.05
❑ 15 Eric Moulds	.40	.18
❑ 16 Bryce Paup UER (numbered 122 on back)	.10	.05
❑ 17 Andre Reed	.20	.09
❑ 18 Bruce Smith	.20	.09
❑ 19 Antowain Smith RC	1.00	.45
❑ 20 Chris Spielman	.10	.05
❑ 21 Thurman Thomas	.40	.18
❑ 22 Tim Biakabutuka	.20	.09
❑ 23 Rae Carruth RC	.40	.18
❑ 24 Kerry Collins	.20	.09
❑ 25 Anthony Johnson	.10	.05
❑ 26 Lamar Lathon	.10	.05
❑ 27 Muhsin Muhammad	.20	.09
❑ 28 Darnell Autry RC	.20	.09
❑ 29 Curtis Conway	.20	.09
❑ 30 Bryan Cox	.10	.05
❑ 31 Bobby Engram	.20	.09
❑ 32 Walt Harris	.10	.05
❑ 33 Erik Kramer	.10	.05
❑ 34 Rashaan Salaam	.10	.05
❑ 35 Jeff Blake	.20	.09
❑ 36 Ki-Jana Carter	.10	.05
❑ 37 Corey Dillon RC	1.50	.70
❑ 38 Carl Pickens	.40	.18
❑ 39 Troy Aikman	1.00	.45
❑ 40 Dexter Coakley RC	.10	.05
❑ 41 Michael Irvin	.40	.18
❑ 42 Daryl Johnston	.20	.09
❑ 43 David LaFleur RC	.20	.09
❑ 44 Anthony Miller	.10	.05
❑ 45 Deion Sanders	.40	.18
❑ 46 Emmitt Smith	1.50	.70
❑ 47 Broderick Thomas	.10	.05
❑ 48 Terrell Davis	1.50	.70
❑ 49 John Elway	2.00	.90
❑ 50 John Mobley	.10	.05
❑ 51 Shannon Sharpe	.20	.09
❑ 52 Neil Smith	.20	.09
❑ 53 Checklist	.10	.05
❑ 54 Scott Mitchell	.20	.09
❑ 55 Herman Moore	.40	.18
❑ 56 Barry Sanders	2.00	.90
❑ 57 Edgar Bennett	.20	.09
❑ 58 Robert Brooks	.20	.09
❑ 59 Mark Chmura	.20	.09
❑ 60 Brett Favre	2.00	.90
❑ 61 Antonio Freeman	.50	.23
❑ 62 Dorsey Levens	.40	.18
❑ 63 Reggie White	.40	.18
❑ 64 Eddie George	1.00	.45
❑ 65 Darryll Lewis	.10	.05
❑ 66 Steve McNair	.50	.23
❑ 67 Chris Sanders	.10	.05
❑ 68 Marshall Faulk	.40	.18
❑ 69 Jim Harbaugh	.20	.09
❑ 70 Marvin Harrison	.40	.18
❑ 71 Tony Brackens	.10	.05
❑ 72 Mark Brunell	1.00	.45
❑ 73 Kevin Hardy	.10	.05
❑ 74 Rob Johnson	.40	.18
❑ 75 Keenan McCardell	.20	.09
❑ 76 Natrone Means	.40	.18
❑ 77 Jimmy Smith	.20	.09
❑ 78 Marcus Allen	.40	.18
❑ 79 Pat Barnes RC	.40	.18
❑ 80 Tony Gonzalez RC UER (Gonzalez on back)	1.25	.55
❑ 81 Elvis Grbac	.20	.09
❑ 82 Brett Perriman	.10	.05
❑ 83 Andre Rison	.20	.09
❑ 84 Derrick Thomas	.20	.09
❑ 85 Tamarick Vanover	.20	.09
❑ 86 Karim Abdul-Jabbar	.40	.18
❑ 87 Fred Barnett	.10	.05
❑ 88 Terrell Buckley	.10	.05
❑ 89 Yatil Green RC	.20	.09
❑ 90 Dan Marino	2.00	.90
❑ 91 O.J. McDuffie	.20	.09
❑ 92 Jason Taylor	.10	.05
❑ 93 Zach Thomas	.20	.09
❑ 94 Cris Carter	.40	.18
❑ 95 Brad Johnson	.50	.23
❑ 96 John Randle	.10	.05
❑ 97 Jake Reed	.20	.09
❑ 98 Robert Smith	.20	.09
❑ 99 Drew Bledsoe	1.00	.45
❑ 100 Chris Canty RC	.10	.05
❑ 101 Ben Coates	.20	.09
❑ 102 Terry Glenn	.40	.18
❑ 103 Ty Law	.10	.05
❑ 104 Curtis Martin	.50	.23
❑ 105 Willie McGinest	.10	.05
❑ 106 Troy Davis RC	.40	.18
❑ 107 Wayne Martin	.10	.05
❑ 108 Heath Shuler	.10	.05
❑ 109 Danny Wuerffel RC	.60	.25
❑ 110 Ray Zellars	.10	.05
❑ 111 Tiki Barber RC	.60	.25
❑ 112 Dave Brown	.10	.05
❑ 113 Checklist	.10	.05
❑ 114 Ike Hilliard RC	.75	.35
❑ 115 Jason Sehorn	.20	.09
❑ 116 Amani Toomer	.20	.09
❑ 117 Tyrone Wheatley	.20	.09
❑ 118 Hugh Douglas	.10	.05
❑ 119 Aaron Glenn	.10	.05
❑ 120 Jeff Graham	.10	.05
❑ 121 Keyshawn Johnson	.40	.18
❑ 122 Adrian Murrell	.20	.09
❑ 123 Neil O'Donnell	.20	.09
❑ 124 Tim Brown	.40	.18
❑ 125 Jeff George	.20	.09
❑ 126 Desmond Howard	.20	.09
❑ 127 Napoleon Kaufman	.40	.18
❑ 128 Chester McGlockton	.10	.05
❑ 129 Darrell Russell RC	.10	.05
❑ 130 Ty Detmer	.20	.09
❑ 131 Irving Fryar	.20	.09
❑ 132 Chris T. Jones	.10	.05
❑ 133 Ricky Watters	.20	.09
❑ 134 Jerome Bettis	.40	.18
❑ 135 Charles Johnson	.20	.09
❑ 136 George Jones RC	.20	.09
❑ 137 Greg Lloyd	.10	.05
❑ 138 Kordell Stewart	.50	.23
❑ 139 Yancey Thigpen	.20	.09
❑ 140 Jim Everett	.10	.05
❑ 141 Stan Humphries	.20	.09
❑ 142 Tony Martin	.20	.09
❑ 143 Eric Metcalf	.20	.09
❑ 144 Junior Seau	.20	.09
❑ 145 Jim Druckenmiller RC	.60	.25
❑ 146 Kevin Greene	.20	.09
❑ 147 Garrison Hearst	.20	.09
❑ 148 Terry Kirby	.20	.09
❑ 149 Terrell Owens	.40	.18
❑ 150 Jerry Rice	1.00	.45
❑ 151 Dana Stubblefield	.10	.05
❑ 152 Rod Woodson	.20	.09
❑ 153 Bryant Young	.10	.05
❑ 154 Steve Young	.60	.25
❑ 155 Chad Brown	.10	.05
❑ 156 John Friesz	.10	.05
❑ 157 Joey Galloway	.50	.23
❑ 158 Cortez Kennedy	.10	.05
❑ 159 Warren Moon	.40	.18
❑ 160 Shawn Springs RC	.20	.09
❑ 161 Chris Warren	.20	.09
❑ 162 Tony Banks	.20	.09
❑ 163 Isaac Bruce	.40	.18
❑ 164 Eddie Kennison	.20	.09
❑ 165 Keith Lyle	.10	.05
❑ 166 Orlando Pace RC	.10	.05
❑ 167 Lawrence Phillips	.10	.05
❑ 168 Checklist	.10	.05
❑ 169 Mike Alstott	.40	.18
❑ 170 Reidel Anthony RC	.75	.35
❑ 171 Warrick Dunn RC	1.25	.55
❑ 172 Hardy Nickerson	.10	.05
❑ 173 Errict Rhett	.10	.05
❑ 174 Warren Sapp	.20	.09
❑ 175 Terry Allen	.40	.18
❑ 176 Gus Frerotte	.10	.05
❑ 177 Sean Gilbert	.10	.05
❑ 178 Ken Harvey	.10	.05
❑ 179 Jeff Hostetler	.10	.05
❑ 180 Michael Westbrook	.20	.09

1997 Collector's Edge Extreme Finesse

	MINT	NRMT
COMPLETE SET (25)	250.00	110.00
STATED ODDS 1:60		
❑ 1 Troy Aikman	20.00	9.00
❑ 2 Marcus Allen	8.00	3.60
❑ 3 Ben Coates	4.00	1.80
❑ 4 Tony Banks	4.00	1.80
❑ 5 Jeff Blake	4.00	1.80
❑ 6 Tim Brown	8.00	3.60
❑ 7 Mark Brunell	20.00	9.00
❑ 8 Todd Collins	2.00	.90
❑ 9 Terrell Davis	30.00	13.50
❑ 10 Jim Druckenmiller	6.00	2.70
❑ 11 John Elway	40.00	18.00
❑ 12 Marshall Faulk	8.00	3.60
❑ 13 Brett Favre	40.00	18.00
❑ 14 Antonio Freeman	10.00	4.50
❑ 15 Joey Galloway	10.00	4.50
❑ 16 Eddie George	20.00	9.00
❑ 17 Terry Glenn	8.00	3.60
❑ 18 Marvin Harrison	8.00	3.60
❑ 19 Garrison Hearst	4.00	1.80
❑ 20 Warrick Dunn	12.00	5.50
❑ 21 Muhsin Muhammad	4.00	1.80
❑ 22 Jerry Rice	20.00	9.00
❑ 23 Barry Sanders	40.00	18.00
❑ 24 Emmitt Smith	30.00	13.50
❑ 25 Shawn Springs	2.00	.90

1997 Collector's Edge Extreme Force

	MINT	NRMT
COMPLETE SET (25)	60.00	27.00
STATED ODDS 1:8		

	MINT	NRMT
❑ 1 Marcus Allen	2.50	1.10
❑ 2 Chris Canty	.30	.14
❑ 3 Jerome Bettis	2.50	1.10
❑ 4 Carl Pickens	2.50	1.10
❑ 5 Drew Bledsoe	6.00	2.70
❑ 6 Robert Brooks	1.25	.55
❑ 7 Shannon Sharpe	1.25	.55
❑ 8 Tim Brown	2.50	1.10
❑ 9 Mark Brunell	6.00	2.70
❑ 10 Ben Coates	1.25	.55
❑ 11 Todd Collins	.60	.25
❑ 12 Terrell Davis	10.00	4.50
❑ 13 John Elway	12.00	5.50
❑ 14 Brett Favre	12.00	5.50
❑ 15 Antonio Freeman	3.00	1.35
❑ 16 Joey Galloway	3.00	1.35
❑ 17 Warrick Dunn	4.00	1.80
❑ 18 Terry Glenn	2.50	1.10
❑ 19 Marvin Harrison	2.50	1.10
❑ 20 Dan Marino	12.00	5.50
❑ 21 Jerry Rice	6.00	2.70
❑ 22 Junior Seau	1.25	.55
❑ 23 Tony Banks	1.25	.55
❑ 24 Emmitt Smith	10.00	4.50
❑ 25 Napoleon Kaufman	2.50	1.10

1997 Collector's Edge Extreme Forerunners

	MINT	NRMT
COMPLETE SET (25)	150.00	70.00
STATED PRINT RUN 1500 SERIAL #'d SETS		

	MINT	NRMT
❑ 1 Karim Abdul-Jabbar	6.00	2.70
❑ 2 Marcus Allen	6.00	2.70
❑ 3 Jerome Bettis	6.00	2.70
❑ 4 Drew Bledsoe	15.00	6.75
❑ 5 Robert Brooks	3.00	1.35
❑ 6 Mark Brunell	15.00	6.75
❑ 7 Todd Collins	1.50	.70
❑ 8 Terrell Davis	25.00	11.00
❑ 9 John Elway	30.00	13.50
❑ 10 Brett Favre	30.00	13.50
❑ 11 Joey Galloway	8.00	3.60
❑ 12 Eddie George	15.00	6.75
❑ 13 Terry Glenn	6.00	2.70
❑ 14 Marvin Harrison	6.00	2.70
❑ 15 Keyshawn Johnson	6.00	2.70
❑ 16 Rob Johnson	6.00	2.70
❑ 17 Eddie Kennison	3.00	1.35
❑ 18 Dorsey Levens	6.00	2.70
❑ 19 Dan Marino	30.00	13.50
❑ 20 Steve McNair	8.00	3.60
❑ 21 Terrell Owens	6.00	2.70
❑ 22 Carl Pickens	6.00	2.70
❑ 23 Jerry Rice	15.00	6.75
❑ 24 Emmitt Smith	25.00	11.00
❑ 25 Kordell Stewart	8.00	3.60

1997 Collector's Edge Extreme Fury

	MINT	NRMT
COMPLETE SET (18)	200.00	90.00
STATED ODDS 1:48		

	MINT	NRMT
❑ 1 Jerome Bettis	8.00	3.60
❑ 2 Terry Glenn	8.00	3.60
❑ 3 Drew Bledsoe	20.00	9.00
❑ 4 Mark Brunell	20.00	9.00
❑ 5 Terrell Davis	30.00	13.50
❑ 6 Troy Davis	8.00	3.60
❑ 7 Marshall Faulk	8.00	3.60
❑ 8 Brett Favre	40.00	18.00
❑ 9 Antonio Freeman	10.00	4.50
❑ 10 Joey Galloway	10.00	4.50
❑ 11 Eddie George	20.00	9.00
❑ 12 Eddie Kennison	4.00	1.80
❑ 13 Errict Rhett	2.00	.90
❑ 14 Rashaan Salaam	2.00	.90
❑ 15 Emmitt Smith	30.00	13.50
❑ 16 Kordell Stewart	10.00	4.50
❑ 17 Danny Wuerffel	12.00	5.50
❑ 18 Steve Young	12.00	5.50

1997 Collector's Edge Extreme Game Gear Quads

	MINT	NRMT
COMMON BALL/SHOE	25.00	11.00
SEMISTARS BALL/SHOE	30.00	13.50
UNL.STARS BALL/SHOE	40.00	18.00
COMMON JERS/PANT	25.00	11.00
SEMISTARS JERS/PANT	30.00	13.50
UNL.STARS JERS/PANT	40.00	18.00
STATED ODDS 1:360		

	MINT	NRMT
❑ 1A Marcus Allen B	40.00	18.00
❑ 1B Marcus Allen J	40.00	18.00
❑ 2A Mike Alstott B	40.00	18.00
❑ 2B Mike Alstott J	40.00	18.00
❑ 2C Mike Alstott P	40.00	18.00
❑ 2D Mike Alstott S	40.00	18.00
❑ 3A Drew Bledsoe B	80.00	36.00
❑ 3B Drew Bledsoe J	80.00	36.00
❑ 4A Tim Brown B	40.00	18.00
❑ 4B Tim Brown J	40.00	18.00
❑ 5A Mark Brunell B	60.00	27.00
❑ 5B Mark Brunell J	60.00	27.00
❑ 5C Mark Brunell P	60.00	27.00
❑ 5D Mark Brunell S	60.00	27.00
❑ 6A Kerry Collins B	25.00	11.00
❑ 6B Kerry Collins J	25.00	11.00
❑ 7A Terrell Davis B	80.00	36.00
❑ 7B Terrell Davis J	100.00	45.00
❑ 7C Terrell Davis P	100.00	45.00
❑ 7D Terrell Davis S	100.00	45.00
❑ 8A Jim Druckenmiller B	30.00	13.50
❑ 8B Jim Druckenmiller J	30.00	13.50
❑ 9A Warrick Dunn B	40.00	18.00
❑ 9B Warrick Dunn J	40.00	18.00
❑ 9C Warrick Dunn P	40.00	18.00
❑ 9D Warrick Dunn S	40.00	18.00
❑ 10A John Elway B	120.00	55.00
❑ 10B John Elway J	150.00	70.00
❑ 10C John Elway P	150.00	70.00
❑ 10D John Elway S	150.00	70.00
❑ 11A Brett Favre B	150.00	70.00
❑ 11B Brett Favre J	150.00	70.00
❑ 12A Eddie George B	80.00	36.00
❑ 12B Eddie George J	80.00	36.00
❑ 12C Eddie George P	80.00	36.00
❑ 12D Eddie George S	80.00	36.00
❑ 13A Terry Glenn B	30.00	13.50
❑ 13B Terry Glenn J	40.00	18.00
❑ 14A Leeland McElroy B	25.00	11.00
❑ 15A Adrian Murrell B	25.00	11.00
❑ 15B Adrian Murrell J	25.00	11.00
❑ 15C Adrian Murrell P	25.00	11.00
❑ 15D Adrian Murrell S	25.00	11.00
❑ 16A Carl Pickens B	40.00	18.00
❑ 16B Carl Pickens J	40.00	18.00
❑ 17A Kordell Stewart B	50.00	22.00
❑ 17B Kordell Stewart J	50.00	22.00
❑ 18A Danny Wuerffel B	25.00	11.00
❑ 18B Danny Wuerffel J	25.00	11.00

1998 Collector's Edge First Place

	MINT	NRMT
COMPLETE SET (250)	60.00	27.00
COMMON CARD (1-250)	.15	.07
SEMISTARS	.30	.14
UNLISTED STARS	.60	.25
COMMON ROOKIE	.75	.35
ROOKIE SEMISTARS	1.00	.45
ROOKIE UNLISTED STARS	2.00	.90
COMMON CL (CK1-CK9)	.10	.05

COMP.50-POINT SET (250) 300.00 135.00
*50-POINT STARS: 2X TO 4X HI COL.
*50-POINT YOUNG STARS: 1.5X TO 3X
*50-POINT RCs: .8X TO 2X
50-POINT STATED ODDS ONE PER PACK
COMMON 50-P.SILVER 8.00 3.60
*50-P.SILVER STARS: 12X TO 30X HI COL.
*50-P.SILVER YOUNG STARS: 10X TO 25X
*50-P.SILVER RCs: 4X TO 10X
50-POINT SILVER STATED ODDS 1:24
50-P.SILVER PRINT RUN 125 SERIAL #'d SETS
COMP.LEAF SET (5) 15.00 6.75
RYAN LEAF INSERT STATED ODDS 1:24
COMP.MANNING SET (5) 25.00 11.00
P.MANNING INSERT STATED ODDS 1:24

❑ 1 Karim Abdul-Jabbar .60 .25
❑ 2 Flozell Adams RC .75 .35
❑ 3 Troy Aikman 1.50 .70
❑ 4 Robert Smith .60 .25
❑ 5 Stephen Alexander RC 1.00 .45
❑ 6 Harold Shaw RC 1.00 .45
❑ 7 Marcus Allen .60 .25
❑ 8 Terry Allen .60 .25
❑ 9 Mike Alstott .60 .25
❑ 10 Jamal Anderson .60 .25
❑ 11 Reidel Anthony .30 .14
❑ 12 Jamie Asher .15 .07
❑ 13 Darnell Autry .15 .07
❑ 14 Phil Savoy RC 1.00 .45
❑ 15 Jon Ritchie RC 1.00 .45
❑ 16 Tony Banks .30 .14
❑ 17 Tiki Barber .30 .14
❑ 18 Pat Barnes .15 .07
❑ 19 Charlie Batch RC 4.00 1.80
❑ 20 Mikhael Ricks RC 1.00 .45
❑ 21 Jerome Bettis .60 .25
❑ 22 Tim Biakabutuka .30 .14
❑ 23 Roosevelt Blackmon RC .75 .35
❑ 24 Jeff Blake .30 .14
❑ 25 Drew Bledsoe 1.25 .55
❑ 26 Tony Boselli .15 .07
❑ 27 Peter Boulware .15 .07
❑ 28 Tony Brackens .15 .07
❑ 29 Corey Bradford RC 5.00 2.20
❑ 30 Michael Pittman RC 1.00 .45
❑ 31 Keith Brooking RC 1.00 .45
❑ 32 Robert Brooks .30 .14
❑ 33 Derrick Brooks .15 .07
❑ 34 Ken Oxendine RC .75 .35
❑ 35 R.W. McQuarters RC .75 .35
❑ 36 Tim Brown .60 .25
❑ 37 Chad Brown .15 .07
❑ 38 Isaac Bruce .60 .25
❑ 39 Mark Brunell 1.25 .55
❑ 40 Chris Canty .15 .07
❑ 41 Mark Carrier .15 .07
❑ 42 Rae Carruth .30 .14
❑ 43 Ki-Jana Carter .15 .07
❑ 44 Cris Carter .60 .25
❑ 45 Larry Centers .15 .07
❑ 46 Corey Chavous RC .75 .35
❑ 47 Mark Chmura .30 .14
❑ 48 Cameron Cleeland RC 1.00 .45
❑ 49 Dexter Coakley .15 .07
❑ 50 Ben Coates .30 .14
❑ 51 Jonathan Linton RC 2.50 1.10
❑ 52 Todd Collins .15 .07
❑ 53 Kerry Collins .30 .14
❑ 54 Tebucky Jones RC .75 .35
❑ 55 Curtis Conway .30 .14
❑ 56 Sam Cowart RC .75 .35
❑ 57 Bryan Cox .15 .07
❑ 58 Randall Cunningham .60 .25
❑ 59 Terrell Davis 2.50 1.10
❑ 60 Troy Davis .15 .07
❑ 61 Pat Johnson RC 1.00 .45
❑ 62 Trent Dilfer .60 .25
❑ 63 Vonnie Holliday RC 1.00 .45
❑ 64 Corey Dillon 1.00 .45
❑ 65 Hugh Douglas .15 .07
❑ 66 Jim Druckenmiller .30 .14
❑ 67 Warrick Dunn 1.00 .45
❑ 68 Robert Edwards RC 2.00 .90
❑ 69 Greg Ellis RC .75 .35
❑ 70 John Elway 3.00 1.35
❑ 71 Bert Emanuel .30 .14
❑ 72 Bobby Engram .30 .14
❑ 73 Curtis Enis RC 3.00 1.35
❑ 74 Marshall Faulk .60 .25
❑ 75 Brett Favre 3.00 1.35
❑ 76 Doug Flutie .60 .25
❑ 77 Glenn Foley .30 .14
❑ 78 Antonio Freeman .60 .25
❑ 79 Gus Frerotte .15 .07
❑ 80 John Friesz .15 .07
❑ 81 Irving Fryar .30 .14
❑ 82 Joey Galloway .60 .25
❑ 83 Rich Gannon .15 .07
❑ 84 Charlie Garner .15 .07
❑ 85 Jeff George .30 .14
❑ 86 Eddie George 1.25 .55
❑ 87 Sean Gilbert .15 .07
❑ 88 Terry Glenn .60 .25
❑ 89 Aaron Glenn .15 .07
❑ 90 Tony Gonzalez .15 .07
❑ 91 Jeff Graham .15 .07
❑ 92 Elvis Grbac .30 .14
❑ 93 Jacquez Green RC 2.50 1.10
❑ 94 Kevin Greene .30 .14
❑ 95 Brian Griese RC UER 4.00 1.80
❑ 96 Byron Hanspard .30 .14
❑ 97 Jim Harbaugh .30 .14
❑ 98 Kevin Hardy .15 .07
❑ 99 Walt Harris .15 .07
❑ 100 Marvin Harrison .30 .14
❑ 101 Rodney Harrison .30 .14
❑ 102 Jeff Hartings RC .75 .35
❑ 103 Ken Harvey .15 .07
❑ 104 Garrison Hearst .60 .25
❑ 105 Ike Hilliard .30 .14
❑ 106 Jeff Hostetler .15 .07
❑ 107 Bobby Hoying .30 .14
❑ 108 Michael Jackson .15 .07
❑ 109 Anthony Johnson .15 .07
❑ 110 Brad Johnson .60 .25
❑ 111 Keyshawn Johnson .60 .25
❑ 112 Charles Johnson .15 .07
❑ 113 Daryl Johnston .30 .14
❑ 114 Chris Jones .15 .07
❑ 115 George Jones .15 .07
❑ 116 Donald Hayes RC 1.00 .45
❑ 117 Danny Kanell .30 .14
❑ 118 Napoleon Kaufman .60 .25
❑ 119 Cortez Kennedy .15 .07
❑ 120 Eddie Kennison .30 .14
❑ 121 Levon Kirkland .15 .07
❑ 122 Jon Kitna 2.00 .90
❑ 123 Erik Kramer .15 .07
❑ 124 David LaFleur .15 .07
❑ 125 Lamar Lathon .15 .07
❑ 126 Ty Law .15 .07
❑ 127 Ryan Leaf RC 2.50 1.10
❑ 128 Dorsey Levens .60 .25
❑ 129 Ray Lewis .15 .07
❑ 130 Darryll Lewis .15 .07
❑ 131 Matt Hasselbeck RC 8.00 3.60
❑ 132 Greg Lloyd .15 .07
❑ 133 Kevin Lockett .15 .07
❑ 134 Keith Lyle .15 .07
❑ 135 Peyton Manning RC 12.00 5.50
❑ 136 Dan Marino 3.00 1.35
❑ 137 Wayne Martin .15 .07
❑ 138 Ahman Green RC 2.00 .90
❑ 139 Tony Martin .30 .14
❑ 140 E.G. Green RC 1.00 .45
❑ 141 Derrick Mayes .30 .14
❑ 142 Ed McCaffrey .30 .14
❑ 143 Keenan McCardell .30 .14
❑ 144 O.J. McDuffie .30 .14
❑ 145 Leeland McElroy .15 .07
❑ 146 Willie McGinest .15 .07
❑ 147 Chester McGlockton .15 .07
❑ 148 Steve McNair .60 .25
❑ 149 Natrone Means .60 .25
❑ 150 Eric Metcalf .15 .07
❑ 151 Anthony Miller .15 .07
❑ 152 Rick Mirer .15 .07
❑ 153 Scott Mitchell .30 .14
❑ 154 John Mobley .15 .07
❑ 155 Warren Moon .60 .25
❑ 156 Herman Moore .60 .25
❑ 157 Randy Moss RC 12.00 5.50
❑ 158 Eric Moulds .60 .25
❑ 159 Muhsin Muhammad .30 .14
❑ 160 Adrian Murrell .30 .14
❑ 161 Marcus Nash RC 2.00 .90
❑ 162 Hardy Nickerson .15 .07
❑ 163 Ken Norton .15 .07
❑ 164 Neil O'Donnell .30 .14
❑ 165 Terrell Owens .60 .25
❑ 166 Orlando Pace .15 .07
❑ 167 Jammi German RC .75 .35
❑ 168 Erric Pegram .15 .07
❑ 169 Jason Peter RC .75 .35
❑ 170 Carl Pickens .60 .25
❑ 171 Jake Plummer 2.00 .90
❑ 172 John Randle .30 .14
❑ 173 Andre Reed .30 .14
❑ 174 Jake Reed .30 .14
❑ 175 Errict Rhett .30 .14
❑ 176 Simeon Rice .30 .14
❑ 177 Jerry Rice 1.50 .70
❑ 178 Andre Rison .30 .14
❑ 179 Darrell Russell .15 .07
❑ 180 Rashaan Salaam .15 .07
❑ 181 Deion Sanders .60 .25
❑ 182 Barry Sanders 3.00 1.35
❑ 183 Chris Sanders .15 .07
❑ 184 Warren Sapp .30 .14
❑ 185 Junior Seau .30 .14
❑ 186 Jason Sehorn .15 .07
❑ 187 Shannon Sharpe .30 .14
❑ 188 Sedrick Shaw .15 .07
❑ 189 Heath Shuler .15 .07
❑ 190 Chris Floyd RC .75 .35
❑ 191 Terry Fair RC 1.00 .45
❑ 192 Kevin Dyson RC 2.50 1.10
❑ 193 Torrance Small .15 .07
❑ 194 Antowain Smith .60 .25
❑ 195 Bruce Smith .30 .14
❑ 196 Tarik Smith RC 1.00 .45
❑ 197 Emmitt Smith 2.50 1.10
❑ 198 Neil Smith .30 .14
❑ 199 Jimmy Smith .30 .14
❑ 200 Chris Spielman .15 .07
❑ 201 Danny Wuerffel .30 .14
❑ 202 Irving Spikes .15 .07
❑ 203 Shawn Springs .15 .07
❑ 204 Duane Starks RC .75 .35
❑ 205 Kordell Stewart .60 .25
❑ 206 J.J. Stokes .30 .14
❑ 207 Eric Swann .15 .07
❑ 208 Steve Tasker .15 .07
❑ 209 Tim Dwight RC 2.50 1.10
❑ 210 Jason Taylor .15 .07
❑ 211 Vinny Testaverde .30 .14
❑ 212 Thurman Thomas .60 .25
❑ 213 Broderick Thomas .15 .07
❑ 214 Derrick Thomas .30 .14
❑ 215 Zach Thomas .15 .07
❑ 216 Germane Crowell RC 3.00 1.35
❑ 217 Amani Toomer .30 .14
❑ 218 Tamarick Vanover .15 .07
❑ 219 Ross Verba .15 .07
❑ 220 Andre Wadsworth RC 1.00 .45
❑ 221 Ray Zellars .15 .07
❑ 222 Chris Warren .30 .14
❑ 223 Steve Young 1.00 .45
❑ 224 Tyrone Wheatley .30 .14
❑ 225 Reggie White .60 .25
❑ 226 John Avery RC 2.00 .90
❑ 227 Charles Woodson RC 3.00 1.35
❑ 228 Takeo Spikes RC 1.00 .45
❑ 229 Bryant Young .15 .07
❑ 230 Tavian Banks RC .30 .14
❑ 231 Fred Beasley RC .75 .35
❑ 232 Chris Ruhman RC .75 .35
❑ CK1A Broncos Logo CL .10 .05
❑ CK1B Steelers Logo CL .10 .05
❑ CK2A 49ers Logo CL .10 .05
❑ CK2B Panthers Logo CL .10 .05
❑ CK3A Giants Logo CL .10 .05
❑ CK3B Packers Logo CL .10 .05
❑ CK4A Colts Logo CL .10 .05
❑ CK4B Dolphins Logo CL .10 .05
❑ CK5A Chargers Logo CL .10 .05
❑ CK5B Vikings Logo Cl .10 .05

	MINT	NRMT
❑ CK6A Patriots Logo Cl	.10	.05
❑ CK6B Raiders Logo CL	.10	.05
❑ CK7A Buccaneers Logo CL	.10	.05
❑ CK7B Cowboys Logo CL	.10	.05
❑ CK8A Bills Logo CL	.10	.05
❑ CK8B Lions Logo CL	.10	.05
❑ CK9A Chiefs Logo CL	.10	.05
❑ CK9B Seahawks Logo CL	.10	.05

1998 Collector's Edge First Place Game Gear Jersey

	MINT	NRMT
COMPLETE SET (2)	125.00	55.00
COMMON CARD (1-2)	40.00	18.00
STATED ODDS 1:480		

	MINT	NRMT
❑ 1 Peyton Manning	100.00	45.00
❑ 2 Ryan Leaf	40.00	18.00
❑ P1 Peyton Manning (No Jersey Swatch Promo)	10.00	4.50
❑ P2 Ryan Leaf (No Jersey Swatch Promo)	4.00	1.80

1998 Collector's Edge First Place Markers

	MINT	NRMT
COMPLETE SET (30)	100.00	45.00
COMMON CARD (1-30)	1.25	.55
SEMISTARS	2.00	.90
UNLISTED STARS	3.00	1.35
STATED ODDS 1:24		

	MINT	NRMT
❑ 1 Michael Pittman	2.00	.90
❑ 2 Andre Wadsworth	2.00	.90
❑ 3 Keith Brooking	2.00	.90
❑ 4 Pat Johnson	2.00	.90
❑ 5 Jonathan Linton	2.00	.90
❑ 6 Donald Hayes	2.00	.90
❑ 7 Mark Chmura	2.00	.90
❑ 8 Terry Allen	3.00	1.35
❑ 9 Brian Griese	8.00	3.60
❑ 10 Marcus Nash	3.00	1.35
❑ 11 Germane Crowell	5.00	2.20
❑ 12 Roosevelt Blackmon	1.25	.55
❑ 13 Peyton Manning	25.00	11.00
❑ 14 Tavian Banks	2.00	.90
❑ 15 Fred Taylor	12.00	5.50
❑ 16 Jim Druckenmiller	2.00	.90
❑ 17 John Avery	3.00	1.35
❑ 18 Randy Moss	25.00	11.00
❑ 19 Robert Edwards	3.00	1.35
❑ 20 Cameron Cleeland	2.00	.90
❑ 21 Joe Jurevicius	2.00	.90
❑ 22 Charles Woodson	5.00	2.20
❑ 23 Terry Allen	3.00	1.35
❑ 24 Ryan Leaf	4.00	1.80
❑ 25 Chris Ruhman	1.25	.55
❑ 26 Ahman Green	3.00	1.35
❑ 27 Jerome Pathon	2.00	.90
❑ 28 Jacquez Green	4.00	1.80
❑ 29 Kevin Dyson	4.00	1.80
❑ 30 Skip Hicks	2.00	.90

1998 Collector's Edge First Place Rookie Ink

	MINT	NRMT
COMP.BLUE SET (31)	800.00	350.00
COMMON BLUE INK (1-31)	10.00	4.50
BLUE SEMISTARS	15.00	6.75
BLUE UNLISTED STARS	20.00	9.00

BLUE INK STATED ODDS 1:24....
*RED SIGNATURES: 1X TO 2.5X HI COL.
RED INK PRINT RUN 40-50 SERIAL #'d SETS

	MINT	NRMT
❑ 1 Terry Allen	20.00	9.00
❑ 2 Mike Alstott	20.00	9.00
❑ 3 Reidel Anthony	15.00	6.75
❑ 4 Justin Armour	10.00	4.50
❑ 5 Tavian Banks	15.00	6.75
❑ 6 Tiki Barber	15.00	6.75
❑ 7 Charlie Batch	40.00	18.00
❑ 8 Mark Bruener	10.00	4.50
❑ 9 Cris Carter	25.00	11.00
❑ 10 Stephen Davis	10.00	4.50
❑ 11 Jim Druckenmiller	15.00	6.75
❑ 12 Tim Dwight	25.00	11.00
❑ 13 Ahman Green	20.00	9.00
❑ 14 Jacquez Green	25.00	11.00
❑ 15 Kevin Greene	15.00	6.75
❑ 16 Brian Griese	40.00	18.00
❑ 17 Marvin Harrison	15.00	6.75
❑ 18 Skip Hicks	15.00	6.75
❑ 19 Robert Holcombe	20.00	9.00
❑ 20 Joe Jurevicius	15.00	6.75
❑ 21 Fred Lane	20.00	9.00
❑ 22 Ryan Leaf	25.00	11.00
❑ 23 Peyton Manning	120.00	55.00
❑ 24 Derrick Mayes	15.00	6.75
❑ 25 Randy Moss	120.00	55.00
❑ 26 Adrian Murrell	15.00	6.75
❑ 27 Marcus Nash	20.00	9.00
❑ 28 Jeremy Newberry	10.00	4.50
❑ 29 Terrell Owens	20.00	9.00
❑ 30 Fred Taylor	60.00	27.00
❑ 31 Hines Ward	15.00	6.75

1998 Collector's Edge First Place Successors

	MINT	NRMT
COMPLETE SET (25)	70.00	32.00
COMMON CARD (1-25)	1.50	.70
STATED ODDS 1:8		

	MINT	NRMT
❑ 1 Troy Aikman	4.00	1.80
❑ 2 Jerome Bettis	2.50	1.10
❑ 3 Drew Bledsoe	3.00	1.35
❑ 4 Tim Brown	2.50	1.10
❑ 5 Mark Brunell	3.00	1.35
❑ 6 Cris Carter	2.50	1.10
❑ 7 Terrell Davis	6.00	2.70
❑ 8 Robert Edwards	1.50	.70
❑ 9 John Elway	8.00	3.60
❑ 10 Brett Favre	8.00	3.60
❑ 11 Eddie George	3.00	1.35
❑ 12 Brian Griese	3.00	1.35
❑ 13 Napoleon Kaufman	2.50	1.10
❑ 14 Ryan Leaf	2.50	1.10
❑ 15 Dorsey Levens	2.50	1.10
❑ 16 Peyton Manning	10.00	4.50
❑ 17 Dan Marino	8.00	3.60
❑ 18 Jim Druckenmiller	2.00	.90
❑ 19 Herman Moore	2.50	1.10
❑ 20 Randy Moss	10.00	4.50
❑ 21 Jake Plummer	4.00	1.80
❑ 22 Barry Sanders	8.00	3.60
❑ 23 Emmitt Smith	6.00	2.70
❑ 24 Rod Smith	2.00	.90
❑ 25 Fred Taylor	5.00	2.20

1998 Collector's Edge First Place Triple Threat

	MINT	NRMT
COMPLETE SET (40)	150.00	70.00
COMMON CARD (1-30)	2.50	1.10
SEMISTARS 1-30	2.50	1.10
UNLISTED STARS 1-30	3.00	1.35
1-15/26-30 BRONZE STATED ODDS 1:12		
16-25 SILVER STATED ODDS 1:24		
COMMON GOLD (31-40)	4.00	1.80
31-40 GOLD STATED ODDS 1:36		

	MINT	NRMT
❑ 1 Robert Brooks	2.50	1.10
❑ 2 Troy Aikman	8.00	3.60
❑ 3 Randy Moss	15.00	6.75
❑ 4 Tim Brown	3.00	1.35
❑ 5 Brad Johnson	3.00	1.35
❑ 6 Kevin Dyson	3.00	1.35
❑ 7 Mark Chmura	2.50	1.10
❑ 8 Joey Galloway	3.00	1.35
❑ 9 Eddie George	6.00	2.70
❑ 10 Napoleon Kaufman	3.00	1.35
❑ 11 Dan Marino	15.00	6.75
❑ 12 Ed McCaffrey	2.50	1.10
❑ 13 Herman Moore	3.00	1.35
❑ 14 Carl Pickens	3.00	1.35
❑ 15 Emmitt Smith	12.00	5.50
❑ 16 Drew Bledsoe	6.00	2.70
❑ 17 Keith Brooking	2.50	1.10
❑ 18 Mark Brunell	6.00	2.70
❑ 19 Terrell Davis	12.00	5.50
❑ 20 Antonio Freeman	3.00	1.35
❑ 21 Peyton Manning	15.00	6.75
❑ 22 Jerry Rice	8.00	3.60
❑ 23 Terry Allen	3.00	1.35
❑ 24 Danny Wuerffel	2.50	1.10
❑ 25 Jerome Bettis	3.00	1.35

❑ 26 Fred Taylor	8.00	3.60
❑ 27 Andre Wadsworth	2.50	1.10
❑ 28 Charles Woodson	4.00	1.80
❑ 29 Steve Young	5.00	2.20
❑ 30 Mark Chmura	2.50	1.10
❑ 31 Cris Carter	5.00	2.20
❑ 32 Jim Druckenmiller	4.00	1.80
❑ 33 Warrick Dunn	5.00	2.20
❑ 34 John Elway	12.00	5.50
❑ 35 Brett Favre	20.00	9.00
❑ 36 Ryan Leaf	4.00	1.80
❑ 37 Dorsey Levens	5.00	2.20
❑ 38 Terrell Owens	5.00	2.20
❑ 39 Barry Sanders	20.00	9.00
❑ 40 Kordell Stewart	4.00	1.80

1998 Collector's Edge First Place Triumph

	MINT	NRMT
COMPLETE SET (25)	80.00	36.00
COMMON CARD (1-25)	2.00	.90
STATED ODDS 1:12		

❑ 1 Troy Aikman	5.00	2.20
❑ 2 Jerome Bettis	2.50	1.10
❑ 3 Drew Bledsoe	4.00	1.80
❑ 4 Tim Brown	2.50	1.10
❑ 5 Mark Brunell	4.00	1.80
❑ 6 Cris Carter	2.50	1.10
❑ 7 Terrell Davis	8.00	3.60
❑ 8 Jim Druckenmiller	2.00	.90
❑ 9 Robert Edwards	3.00	1.35
❑ 10 John Elway	10.00	4.50
❑ 11 Brett Favre	10.00	4.50
❑ 12 Eddie George	4.00	1.80
❑ 13 Brian Griese	4.00	1.80
❑ 14 Napoleon Kaufman	2.50	1.10
❑ 15 Ryan Leaf	3.00	1.35
❑ 16 Dorsey Levens	2.50	1.10
❑ 17 Peyton Manning	12.00	5.50
❑ 18 Dan Marino	10.00	4.50
❑ 19 Herman Moore	2.50	1.10
❑ 20 Randy Moss	12.00	5.50
❑ 21 Jake Plummer	5.00	2.20
❑ 22 Barry Sanders	10.00	4.50
❑ 23 Emmitt Smith	8.00	3.60
❑ 24 Rod Smith	2.00	.90
❑ 25 Fred Taylor	6.00	2.70

1999 Collector's Edge First Place

	MINT	NRMT
COMPLETE SET (200)	50.00	22.00
COMMON CARD (1-201)	.15	.07
SEMISTARS	.30	.14
UNLISTED STARS	.60	.25
COMMON ROOKIE (151-200)	.60	.25
ROOKIE SEMISTARS	1.00	.45
ROOKIE UNL.STARS	1.25	.55

❑ 1 Adrian Murrell	.30	.14
❑ 2 Rob Moore	.30	.14
❑ 3 Jake Plummer	1.25	.55
❑ 4 Simeon Rice	.15	.07
❑ 5 Frank Sanders	.30	.14
❑ 6 Jamal Anderson	.60	.25
❑ 7 Chris Calloway	.15	.07
❑ 8 Chris Chandler	.30	.14
❑ 9 Tim Dwight	.60	.25
❑ 10 Terance Mathis	.30	.14
❑ 11 Jessie Tuggle	.15	.07
❑ 12 Tony Banks	.30	.14
❑ 13 Priest Holmes	.60	.25
❑ 14 Jermaine Lewis	.30	.14
❑ 15 Scott Mitchell	.15	.07
❑ 16 Doug Flutie	.75	.35
❑ 17 Eric Moulds	.60	.25
❑ 18 Andre Reed	.30	.14
❑ 19 Antowain Smith	.60	.25
❑ 20 Bruce Smith	.30	.14
❑ 21 Thurman Thomas	.30	.14
❑ 22 Steve Beuerlein	.15	.07
❑ 23 Tim Biakabutuka	.30	.14
❑ 24 Kevin Greene	.15	.07
❑ 25 Muhsin Muhammad	.30	.14
❑ 26 Edgar Bennett	.15	.07
❑ 27 Curtis Conway	.30	.14
❑ 28 Bobby Engram	.30	.14
❑ 29 Curtis Enis	.60	.25
❑ 30 Erik Kramer	.15	.07
❑ 31 Jeff Blake	.30	.14
❑ 32 Corey Dillon	.60	.25
❑ 33 Carl Pickens	.30	.14
❑ 34 Darnay Scott	.15	.07
❑ 35 Takeo Spikes	.15	.07
❑ 36 Ty Detmer	.15	.07
❑ 37 Terry Kirby	.15	.07
❑ 38 Leslie Shepherd	.15	.07
❑ 39 Chris Spielman	.15	.07
❑ 40 Troy Aikman	1.50	.70
❑ 41 Michael Irvin	.30	.14
❑ 42 Rocket Ismail	.30	.14
❑ 43 Ernie Mills	.15	.07
❑ 44 Deion Sanders	.60	.25
❑ 45 Emmitt Smith	1.50	.70
❑ 46 Chris Warren	.15	.07
❑ 47 Bubba Brister	.15	.07
❑ 48 Terrell Davis	1.50	.70
❑ 49 Brian Griese	1.25	.55
❑ 50 Ed McCaffrey	.30	.14
❑ 51 Shannon Sharpe	.30	.14
❑ 52 Rod Smith	.30	.14
❑ 53 Charlie Batch	1.25	.55
❑ 54 Terry Fair	.15	.07
❑ 55 Herman Moore	.60	.25
❑ 56 Johnnie Morton	.30	.14
❑ 57 Barry Sanders	2.50	1.10
❑ 58 Santana Dotson	.15	.07
❑ 59 Brett Favre	2.50	1.10
❑ 60 Mark Chmura	.15	.07
❑ 61 Antonio Freeman	.60	.25
❑ 62 Dorsey Levens	.60	.25
❑ 63 Derrick Mayes	.30	.14
❑ 64 Marvin Harrison	.60	.25
❑ 65 Peyton Manning	2.50	1.10
❑ 66 Jerome Pathon	.15	.07
❑ 67 Mark Brunell	1.00	.45
❑ 68 Keenan McCardell	.30	.14
❑ 69 Jimmy Smith	.30	.14
❑ 70 Fred Taylor	1.50	.70
❑ 71 Derrick Alexander WR	.30	.14
❑ 72 Kimble Anders	.30	.14
❑ 73 Elvis Grbac	.30	.14
❑ 74 Warren Moon	.60	.25
❑ 75 Byron Bam Morris	.15	.07
❑ 76 Andre Rison	.30	.14
❑ 77 Karim Abdul-Jabbar	.30	.14
❑ 78 Dan Marino	2.50	1.10
❑ 79 Tony Martin	.30	.14
❑ 80 O.J. McDuffie	.30	.14
❑ 81 Zach Thomas	.30	.14
❑ 82 Cris Carter	.60	.25
❑ 83 Randall Cunningham	.60	.25
❑ 84 Jeff George	.30	.14
❑ 85 Randy Moss	2.50	1.10
❑ 86 Jake Reed	.30	.14
❑ 87 Robert Smith	.60	.25
❑ 88 Drew Bledsoe	1.00	.45
❑ 89 Ben Coates	.30	.14
❑ 90 Terry Glenn	.60	.25
❑ 91 Ty Law	.15	.07
❑ 92 Shawn Jefferson	.15	.07
❑ 93 Cameron Cleeland	.15	.07
❑ 94 Andre Hastings	.15	.07
❑ 95 Billy Joe Hobert	.15	.07
❑ 96 Eddie Kennison	.30	.14
❑ 97 Gary Brown	.15	.07
❑ 98 Kerry Collins	.30	.14
❑ 99 Kent Graham	.15	.07
❑ 100 Ike Hilliard	.15	.07
❑ 101 Joe Jurevicius	.15	.07
❑ 102 Wayne Chrebet	.30	.14
❑ 103 Aaron Glenn	.15	.07
❑ 104 Keyshawn Johnson	.60	.25
❑ 105 Mo Lewis	.15	.07
❑ 106 Curtis Martin	.60	.25
❑ 107 Vinny Testaverde	.30	.14
❑ 108 Tim Brown	.60	.25
❑ 109 Rich Gannon	.30	.14
❑ 110 James Jett	.30	.14
❑ 111 Napoleon Kaufman	.60	.25
❑ 112 Charles Woodson	.60	.25
❑ 113 Koy Detmer	.15	.07
❑ 114 Charles Johnson	.15	.07
❑ 115 Duce Staley	.60	.25
❑ 116 Jerome Bettis	.60	.25
❑ 117 Courtney Hawkins	.15	.07
❑ 118 Levon Kirkland	.15	.07
❑ 119 Kordell Stewart	.60	.25
❑ 120 Isaac Bruce	.60	.25
❑ 121 Marshall Faulk	.60	.25
❑ 122 Trent Green	.30	.14
❑ 123 Amp Lee	.15	.07
❑ 124 Jim Harbaugh	.30	.14
❑ 125 Bryan Still	.15	.07
❑ 126 Freddie Jones	.15	.07
❑ 127 Mikhael Ricks	.15	.07
❑ 128 Natrone Means	.30	.14
❑ 129 Junior Seau	.30	.14
❑ 130 Lawrence Phillips	.30	.14
❑ 131 Terrell Owens	.60	.25
❑ 132 Jerry Rice	1.50	.70
❑ 133 J.J. Stokes	.30	.14
❑ 134 Steve Young	1.00	.45
❑ 135 Joey Galloway	.60	.25
❑ 136 Jon Kitna	.75	.35
❑ 137 Ricky Watters	.30	.14
❑ 138 Mike Alstott	.60	.25
❑ 139 Reidel Anthony	.30	.14
❑ 140 Trent Dilfer	.30	.14
❑ 141 Warrick Dunn	.60	.25
❑ 142 Kevin Dyson	.30	.14
❑ 143 Eddie George	.75	.35
❑ 144 Steve McNair	.60	.25
❑ 145 Frank Wycheck	.15	.07
❑ 146 Skip Hicks	.60	.25
❑ 147 Brad Johnson	.60	.25
❑ 148 Michael Westbrook	.30	.14
❑ 149 Checklist Card	.15	.07
❑ 150 Checklist Card	.15	.07
❑ 151 David Boston RC	2.00	.90
❑ 152 Patrick Kerney RC	.60	.25
❑ 153 Chris McAlister RC	1.00	.45
❑ 154 Peerless Price RC	2.00	.90
❑ 155 Antoine Winfield RC	1.00	.45
❑ 156 D'Wayne Bates RC	1.00	.45
❑ 157 Cade McNown RC	4.00	1.80
❑ 158 Akili Smith RC	2.50	1.10
❑ 159 Rahim Abdullah RC	1.00	.45

❑ 160 Tim Couch RC	6.00	2.70
❑ 161 Kevin Johnson RC	3.00	1.35
❑ 162 Ebenezer Ekuban RC	1.00	.45
❑ 163 Dat Nguyen RC	1.25	.55
❑ 164 Al Wilson RC	1.00	.45
❑ 165 Chris Claiborne RC	1.00	.45
❑ 166 Sedrick Irvin RC	1.25	.55
❑ 167 Antuan Edwards RC	1.00	.45
❑ 168 Aaron Brooks RC	1.25	.55
❑ 169 De'Mond Parker RC	1.25	.55
❑ 170 Edgerrin James RC	10.00	4.50
❑ 171 Fernando Bryant RC	1.00	.45
❑ 172 Mike Cloud RC	1.25	.55
❑ 173 John Tait RC	.60	.25
❑ 174 Cecil Collins RC	1.25	.55
❑ 175 James Johnson RC	1.50	.70
❑ 176 Rob Konrad RC	1.25	.55
❑ 177 Daunte Culpepper RC	4.00	1.80
❑ 178 Jim Kleinsasser RC	1.25	.55
❑ 179 Brock Huard RC	1.50	.70
❑ 180 Michael Bishop RC	1.50	.70
❑ 181 Kevin Faulk RC	1.50	.70
❑ 182 Andy Katzenmoyer RC	1.25	.55
❑ 183 Ricky Williams RC	6.00	2.70
❑ 184 Joe Montgomery RC	1.25	.55
❑ 185 Donovan McNabb RC	4.00	1.80
❑ 186 Troy Edwards RC	2.00	.90
❑ 187 Amos Zereoue RC	1.25	.55
❑ 188 Joe Germaine RC	1.25	.55
❑ 189 Torry Holt RC	3.00	1.35
❑ 190 Jermaine Fazande RC	1.00	.45
❑ 191 Reggie McGrew RC	1.00	.45
❑ 192 Karsten Bailey RC	1.00	.45
❑ 193 Lamar King RC	.60	.25
❑ 194 Autry Denson RC	1.25	.55
❑ 195 Martin Gramatica RC	.60	.25
❑ 196 Shaun King RC	4.00	1.80
❑ 197 Darnell McDonald RC	1.25	.55
❑ 198 Anthony McFarland RC	1.25	.55
❑ 199 Jevon Kearse RC	2.50	1.10
❑ 200 Champ Bailey RC	1.50	.70
❑ 201 Kurt Warner /500 RC	400.00	180.00
❑ 201P Kurt Warner Promo	10.00	4.50

1999 Collector's Edge First Place Galvanized

	MINT	NRMT
COMPLETE SET (200)	400.00	180.00

*GALVANIZED STARS: 2X TO 5X HI COL.
*GALVANIZED YOUNG STARS: 1.5X TO 4X
*GALVANIZED RCs: 3X TO 8X
GALV.VETS PRINT RUN 500 SER.#'d SETS
GALV.RCs PRINT RUN 100 SER.#'d SETS

1999 Collector's Edge First Place Gold Ingot

	MINT	NRMT
COMPLETE SET (200)	80.00	36.00

*GOLD INGOT STARS: .8X TO 2X HI COL.
*GOLD INGOT YOUNG STARS: .6X TO 1.5X
*GOLD INGOT RCs: .6X TO 1.5X
ONE GOLD INGOT PER PACK

1999 Collector's Edge First Place HoloGold

	MINT	NRMT
COMPLETE SET (200)	2500.00	1100.00

*HOLOGOLD STARS: 25X TO 60X HI COL.
*HOLOGOLD YOUNG STARS: 20X TO 50X
*HOLOGOLD RCs: 20X TO 50X
HOLOGOLD VETS PRINT RUN 50 SER.#'d SETS
HOLOGOLD RCs PRINT RUN 10 SER.#'d SETS

1999 Collector's Edge First Place Adrenalin

	MINT	NRMT
COMPLETE SET (20)	100.00	45.00
COMMON CARD (A1-A20)	4.00	1.80

STATED PRINT RUN 1000 SERIAL #'d SETS

❑ A1 Jake Plummer	8.00	3.60
❑ A2 Jamal Anderson	4.00	1.80
❑ A3 Eric Moulds	4.00	1.80
❑ A4 Emmitt Smith	10.00	4.50
❑ A5 Terrell Davis	10.00	4.50
❑ A6 Barry Sanders	15.00	6.75
❑ A7 Brett Favre	15.00	6.75
❑ A8 Antonio Freeman	4.00	1.80
❑ A9 Peyton Manning	12.00	5.50
❑ A10 Mark Brunell	6.00	2.70
❑ A11 Fred Taylor	8.00	3.60
❑ A12 Dan Marino	15.00	6.75
❑ A13 Cris Carter	4.00	1.80
❑ A14 Randy Moss	12.00	5.50
❑ A15 Keyshawn Johnson	4.00	1.80
❑ A16 Curtis Martin	4.00	1.80
❑ A17 Jerome Bettis	4.00	1.80
❑ A18 Terrell Owens	4.00	1.80
❑ A19 Joey Galloway	4.00	1.80
❑ A20 Eddie George	5.00	2.20

1999 Collector's Edge First Place Excalibur

	MINT	NRMT
COMPLETE SET (9)	50.00	22.00
COMMON CARD	4.00	1.80

STATED ODDS 1:24

❑ S1 Uncut Sheet	150.00	70.00
❑ X2 Torry Holt	6.00	2.70
❑ X5 Edgerrin James	15.00	6.75
❑ X6 Brett Favre	12.00	5.50
❑ X13 Peyton Manning	10.00	4.50
❑ X17 Randy Moss	10.00	4.50
❑ X19 Terrell Davis	8.00	3.60
❑ X20 Mark Brunell	5.00	2.20
❑ X22 Eddie George	4.00	1.80
❑ X24 Doug Flutie	4.00	1.80

1999 Collector's Edge First Place Future Legends

	MINT	NRMT
COMPLETE SET (20)	40.00	18.00
COMMON CARD (FL1-FL20)	1.00	.45
SEMISTARS	1.50	.70

STATED ODDS 1:6

❑ FL1 Tim Couch	8.00	3.60
❑ FL2 Donovan McNabb	5.00	2.20
❑ FL3 Akili Smith	3.00	1.35
❑ FL4 Edgerrin James	12.00	5.50
❑ FL5 Ricky Williams	8.00	3.60
❑ FL6 Torry Holt	4.00	1.80
❑ FL7 Champ Bailey	2.00	.90
❑ FL8 David Boston	2.50	1.10
❑ FL9 Daunte Culpepper	5.00	2.20
❑ FL10 Cade McNown	5.00	2.20
❑ FL11 Troy Edwards	2.50	1.10
❑ FL12 Chris Claiborne	1.00	.45
❑ FL13 Jevon Kearse	3.00	1.35
❑ FL14 Shaun King	5.00	2.20
❑ FL15 Kevin Faulk	2.00	.90
❑ FL16 James Johnson	2.00	.90
❑ FL17 Peerless Price	2.50	1.10
❑ FL18 Kevin Johnson	4.00	1.80
❑ FL19 Brock Huard	2.00	.90
❑ FL20 Joe Germaine	1.50	.70

1999 Collector's Edge First Place Loud and Proud

	MINT	NRMT
COMPLETE SET (20)	50.00	22.00
COMMON CARD (LP1-LP20)	2.00	.90

STATED ODDS 1:12 ....

❑ LP1 Jamal Anderson	2.00	.90
❑ LP2 Emmitt Smith	5.00	2.20
❑ LP3 Terrell Davis	5.00	2.20
❑ LP4 Barry Sanders	8.00	3.60
❑ LP5 Fred Taylor	4.00	1.80
❑ LP6 Randy Moss	6.00	2.70
❑ LP7 Antonio Freeman	2.00	.90
❑ LP8 Curtis Martin	2.00	.90
❑ LP9 Terrell Owens	2.00	.90
❑ LP10 Eddie George	2.50	1.10
❑ LP11 Dan Marino	8.00	3.60
❑ LP12 Brett Favre	8.00	3.60
❑ LP13 Jerry Rice	5.00	2.20
❑ LP14 Steve Young	3.00	1.35
❑ LP15 Doug Flutie	2.50	1.10
❑ LP16 Jake Plummer	4.00	1.80
❑ LP17 Troy Aikman	5.00	2.20
❑ LP18 Mark Brunell	3.00	1.35
❑ LP19 Jon Kitna	2.50	1.10
❑ LP20 Charlie Batch	3.00	1.35

1999 Collector's Edge First Place Pro Signature Authentics

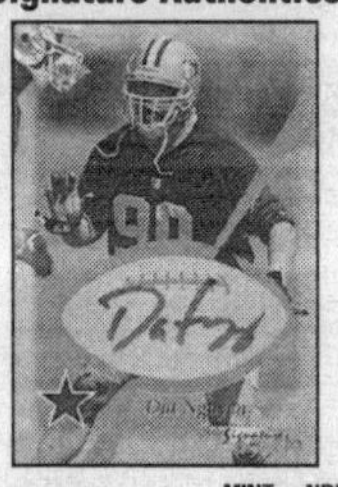

	MINT	NRMT
COMPLETE SET (29)	400.00	180.00
COMMON CARD (1-29)	8.00	3.60
SEMISTARS	10.00	4.50
UNLISTED STARS	12.00	5.50

STATED ODDS 1:24 ....
*BLUE AUTOS: 1.2X TO 3X HI COL.
BLUE AUTOS PRINT RUN 40 SER.#'d SETS
UNPRICED REDS PRINT RUN 10 SER.#'d SETS ....

Card	MINT	NRMT
❑ 1 Rahim Abdullah	10.00	4.50
❑ 2 Kimble Anders	12.00	5.50
❑ 3 Dre Bly	10.00	4.50
❑ 4 David Boston	20.00	9.00
❑ 5 Cuncho Brown	10.00	4.50
❑ 6 Gary Brown	12.00	5.50
❑ 7 Ray Buchanan	10.00	4.50
❑ 8 Tim Couch	60.00	27.00
❑ 9 Autry Denson	12.00	5.50
❑ 10 Jared DeVries	8.00	3.60
❑ 11 Bobby Engram	12.00	5.50
❑ 12 Terry Fair	10.00	4.50
❑ 13 Kevin Faulk	15.00	6.75
❑ 14 Joey Galloway	20.00	9.00
❑ 15 Rich Gannon	15.00	6.75
❑ 16 Marvin Harrison	20.00	9.00
❑ 17 Andre Hastings	12.00	5.50
❑ 18 Courtney Hawkins	12.00	5.50
❑ 19 Brock Huard	15.00	6.75
❑ 20 Edgerrin James	100.00	45.00
❑ 21 Chris McAlister	10.00	4.50
❑ 22 Keenan McCardell	15.00	6.75
❑ 23 Eric Moulds	15.00	6.75
❑ 24 Dat Nguyen	12.00	5.50
❑ 25 Andre Reed	15.00	6.75
❑ 26 Jimmy Smith	15.00	6.75
❑ 27 Akili Smith	20.00	9.00
❑ 28 Duce Staley	20.00	9.00
❑ 29 Craig Yeast	10.00	4.50

1999 Collector's Edge First Place Rookie Game Gear

	MINT	NRMT
COMPLETE SET (10)	200.00	90.00
COMMON CARD (RG1-RG10)	12.00	5.50

STATED PRINT RUN 500 SERIAL #'d SETS

Card	MINT	NRMT
❑ RG1 Tim Couch	50.00	22.00
❑ RG2 Donovan McNabb	30.00	13.50
❑ RG3 Akili Smith	20.00	9.00
❑ RG4 Daunte Culpepper	30.00	13.50
❑ RG5 Ricky Williams	50.00	22.00
❑ RG6 Kevin Johnson	25.00	11.00
❑ RG7 Cade McNown	30.00	13.50
❑ RG8 Torry Holt	30.00	13.50
❑ RG9 Champ Bailey	12.00	5.50
❑ RG10 David Boston	15.00	6.75

1999 Collector's Edge First Place Successors

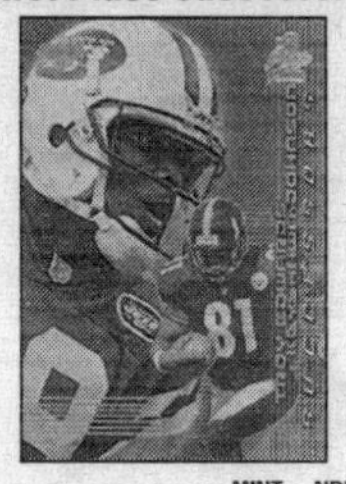

	MINT	NRMT
COMPLETE SET (15)	60.00	27.00
COMMON CARD (S1-S15)	3.00	1.35

STATED ODDS 1:12 ....

Card	MINT	NRMT
❑ S1 David Boston Cris Carter	4.00	1.80
❑ S2 Peerless Price Eric Moulds	3.00	1.35
❑ S3 Cade McNown Brett Favre	8.00	3.60
❑ S4 Akili Smith Charlie Batch	5.00	2.20
❑ S5 Tim Couch Peyton Manning	12.00	5.50
❑ S6 Kevin Johnson Joey Galloway	3.00	1.35
❑ S7 Edgerrin James Emmitt Smith	12.00	5.50
❑ S8 James Johnson C.Martin	4.00	1.80
❑ S9 Daunte Culpepper Dan Marino	8.00	3.60
❑ S10 Kevin Faulk Barry Sanders	8.00	3.60
❑ S11 Rickey Williams Marshall Faulk	8.00	3.60
❑ S12 Donovan McNabb Steve Young	6.00	2.70
❑ S13 Troy Edwards Keyshawn Johnson	4.00	1.80
❑ S14 Torry Holt Jerry Rice	5.00	2.20
❑ S15 Shaun King Jake Plummer	4.00	1.80

1999 Collector's Edge Fury

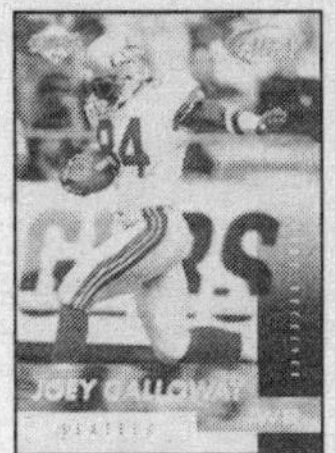

	MINT	NRMT
COMPLETE SET (200)	40.00	18.00
COMMON CARD (1-200)	.15	.07
SEMISTARS	.30	.14
UNLISTED STARS	.60	.25
COMMON ROOKIE	.50	.23
ROOKIE SEMISTARS	1.00	.45
ROOKIE UNL.STARS	1.50	.70

ROOKIES INSERTED ONE PER PACK
COMP.GOLD INGOT (200) .. 100.00 45.00
*GOLD INGOT STARS: .75X TO 2X HI COL.
*GOLD INGOT YOUNG STARS: .6X TO 1.5X
*GOLD INGOT RCs: .6X TO 1.5X
GOLD INGOTS ONE PER PACK..
COMP.GALVANIZED (200) .. 400.00 180.00
*GALVANIZED STARS: 2.5X TO 6X HI COL.
*GALVANIZED YOUNG STARS: 2X TO 5X
*GALVANIZED RCs: 4X TO 8X ....
GALVANIZED VETS SERIAL #'d OF 500
GALVANIZED ROOKIES SER.#'d OF 100

Card	MINT	NRMT
❑ 1 Checklist Card 1	.15	.07
❑ 2 Checklist Card 2	.15	.07
❑ 3 Karim Abdul-Jabbar	.30	.14
❑ 4 Troy Aikman	1.50	.70
❑ 5 Derrick Alexander WR	.30	.14
❑ 6 Mike Alstott	.60	.25
❑ 7 Jamal Anderson	.60	.25
❑ 8 Reidel Anthony	.30	.14
❑ 9 Tiki Barber	.15	.07
❑ 10 Charlie Batch	1.25	.55
❑ 11 Edgar Bennett	.15	.07
❑ 12 Jerome Bettis	.60	.25
❑ 13 Steve Beuerlein	.15	.07
❑ 14 Tim Biakabutuka	.30	.14
❑ 15 Jeff Blake	.30	.14
❑ 16 Drew Bledsoe	1.00	.45
❑ 17 Bubby Brister	.15	.07
❑ 18 Robert Brooks	.30	.14
❑ 19 Gary Brown	.15	.07
❑ 20 Tim Brown	.60	.25
❑ 21 Isaac Bruce	.60	.25
❑ 22 Mark Brunell	1.00	.45
❑ 23 Chris Calloway	.15	.07
❑ 24 Cris Carter	.60	.25
❑ 25 Larry Centers	.15	.07
❑ 26 Chris Chandler	.30	.14
❑ 27 Wayne Chrebet	.30	.14
❑ 28 Cam Cleeland	.15	.07
❑ 29 Kerry Collins	.30	.14
❑ 30 Curtis Conway	.30	.14
❑ 31 Germane Crowell	.30	.14
❑ 32 Randall Cunningham	.60	.25
❑ 33 Terrell Davis	1.50	.70
❑ 34 Koy Detmer	.15	.07
❑ 35 Ty Detmer	.30	.14
❑ 36 Trent Dilfer	.30	.14
❑ 37 Corey Dillon	.60	.25
❑ 38 Warrick Dunn	.60	.25
❑ 39 Tim Dwight	.60	.25
❑ 40 Kevin Dyson	.30	.14
❑ 41 John Elway	2.50	1.10
❑ 42 Bobby Engram	.30	.14
❑ 43 Curtis Enis	.60	.25
❑ 44 Terry Fair	.15	.07
❑ 45 Marshall Faulk	.60	.25
❑ 46 Brett Favre	2.50	1.10
❑ 47 Doug Flutie	.75	.35
❑ 48 Antonio Freeman	.60	.25
❑ 49 Joey Galloway	.60	.25
❑ 50 Rich Gannon	.30	.14
❑ 51 Eddie George	.75	.35

❑ 52 Jeff George .30 .14
❑ 53 Terry Glenn .60 .25
❑ 54 Elvis Grbac .30 .14
❑ 55 Ahman Green .30 .14
❑ 56 Jacquez Green .15 .07
❑ 57 Trent Green .30 .14
❑ 58 Kevin Greene .15 .07
❑ 59 Brian Griese 1.25 .55
❑ 60 Az-Zahir Hakim .15 .07
❑ 61 Jim Harbaugh .30 .14
❑ 62 Marvin Harrison .60 .25
❑ 63 Courtney Hawkins .15 .07
❑ 64 Garrison Hearst .30 .14
❑ 65 Ike Hilliard .15 .07
❑ 66 Billy Joe Hobert .15 .07
❑ 67 Priest Holmes .60 .25
❑ 68 Michael Irvin .30 .14
❑ 69 Rocket Ismail .30 .14
❑ 70 Shawn Jefferson .15 .07
❑ 71 James Jett .30 .14
❑ 72 Brad Johnson .60 .25
❑ 73 Charles Johnson .15 .07
❑ 74 Keyshawn Johnson .60 .25
❑ 75 Pat Johnson .15 .07
❑ 76 Joe Jurevicius .15 .07
❑ 77 Napoleon Kaufman .60 .25
❑ 78 Eddie Kennison .30 .14
❑ 79 Terry Kirby .15 .07
❑ 80 Jon Kitna .75 .35
❑ 81 Erik Kramer .15 .07
❑ 82 Fred Lane .30 .14
❑ 83 Ty Law .15 .07
❑ 84 Ryan Leaf .60 .25
❑ 85 Amp Lee .15 .07
❑ 86 Dorsey Levens .60 .25
❑ 87 Jermaine Lewis .30 .14
❑ 88 Sam Madison .15 .07
❑ 89 Peyton Manning 2.50 1.10
❑ 90 Dan Marino 2.50 1.10
❑ 91 Curtis Martin .60 .25
❑ 92 Tony Martin .30 .14
❑ 93 Terance Mathis .30 .14
❑ 94 Ed McCaffrey .30 .14
❑ 95 Keenan McCardell .30 .14
❑ 96 O.J. McDuffie .30 .14
❑ 97 Steve McNair .60 .25
❑ 98 Natrone Means .30 .14
❑ 99 Herman Moore .60 .25
❑ 100 Rob Moore .30 .14
❑ 101 Byron Bam Morris .15 .07
❑ 102 Johnnie Morton .15 .07
❑ 103 Randy Moss 2.50 1.10
❑ 104 Eric Moulds .60 .25
❑ 105 Muhsin Muhammad .30 .14
❑ 106 Adrian Murrell .30 .14
❑ 107 Terrell Owens .60 .25
❑ 108 Jerome Pathon .15 .07
❑ 109 Carl Pickens .30 .14
❑ 110 Jake Plummer 1.25 .55
❑ 111 Andre Reed .30 .14
❑ 112 Jake Reed .30 .14
❑ 113 Jerry Rice 1.50 .70
❑ 114 Mikhael Ricks .15 .07
❑ 115 Andre Rison .30 .14
❑ 116 Barry Sanders 2.50 1.10
❑ 117 Deion Sanders .60 .25
❑ 118 Frank Sanders .30 .14
❑ 119 O.J. Santiago .15 .07
❑ 120 Darnay Scott .15 .07
❑ 121 Junior Seau .30 .14
❑ 122 Shannon Sharpe .30 .14
❑ 123 Leslie Shepherd .15 .07
❑ 124 Antowain Smith .60 .25
❑ 125 Bruce Smith .30 .14
❑ 126 Emmitt Smith 1.50 .70
❑ 127 Jimmy Smith .30 .14
❑ 128 Robert Smith .60 .25
❑ 129 Rod Smith .30 .14
❑ 130 Chris Spielman .15 .07
❑ 131 Takeo Spikes .15 .07
❑ 132 Duce Staley .60 .25
❑ 133 Kordell Stewart .60 .25
❑ 134 Bryan Still .15 .07
❑ 135 J.J. Stokes .30 .14
❑ 136 Fred Taylor 1.50 .70
❑ 137 Vinny Testaverde .30 .14
❑ 138 Yancey Thigpen .15 .07
❑ 139 Thurman Thomas .30 .14
❑ 140 Zach Thomas .30 .14
❑ 141 Amani Toomer .15 .07
❑ 142 Hines Ward .15 .07
❑ 143 Chris Warren .15 .07
❑ 144 Ricky Watters .30 .14
❑ 145 Michael Westbrook .30 .14
❑ 146 Alvis Whitted .15 .07
❑ 147 Charles Woodson .60 .25
❑ 148 Rod Woodson .30 .14
❑ 149 Frank Wycheck .15 .07
❑ 150 Steve Young 1.00 .45
❑ 151 Rahim Abdullah RC 1.00 .45
❑ 152 Champ Bailey RC 2.00 .90
❑ 153 D'Wayne Bates RC 1.00 .45
❑ 154 Michael Bishop RC 2.00 .90
❑ 155 Dre' Bly RC 1.00 .45
❑ 156 David Boston RC 2.50 1.10
❑ 157 Fernando Bryant RC 1.00 .45
❑ 158 Chris Claiborne RC 1.00 .45
❑ 159 Mike Cloud RC 1.50 .70
❑ 160 Cecil Colliins RC 1.50 .70
❑ 161 Tim Couch RC 8.00 3.60
❑ 162 Daunte Culpepper RC 5.00 2.20
❑ 163 Antuan Edwards RC .50 .23
❑ 164 Troy Edwards RC 2.50 1.10
❑ 165 Ebenezer Ekuban RC 1.00 .45
❑ 166 Kevin Faulk RC 2.00 .90
❑ 167 Joe Germaine RC 1.50 .70
❑ 168 Aaron Gibson RC .50 .23
❑ 169 Martin Gramatica RC .50 .23
❑ 170 Torry Holt RC 4.00 1.80
❑ 171 Brock Huard RC 2.00 .90
❑ 172 Sedrick Irvin RC 1.50 .70
❑ 173 Edgerrin James RC 12.00 5.50
❑ 174 James Johnson RC 2.00 .90
❑ 175 Kevin Johnson RC 4.00 1.80
❑ 176 Andy Katzenmoyer RC 1.50 .70
❑ 177 Jevon Kearse RC 3.00 1.35
❑ 178 Patrick Kerney RC .50 .23
❑ 179 Lamar King RC .50 .23
❑ 180 Shaun King RC 5.00 2.20
❑ 181 Jim Kleinsasser RC 1.50 .70
❑ 182 Rob Konrad RC 1.00 .45
❑ 183 Chris McAlister RC 1.00 .45
❑ 184 Anthony McFarland RC 1.50 .70
❑ 185 Karsten Bailey RC 1.00 .45
❑ 186 Donovan McNabb RC 5.00 2.20
❑ 187 Cade McNown RC 5.00 2.20
❑ 188 Joe Montgomery RC 1.50 .70
❑ 189 Dat Nguyen RC 1.50 .70
❑ 190 Luke Petitgout RC .50 .23
❑ 191 Peerless Price RC 2.50 1.10
❑ 192 Akili Smith RC 3.00 1.35
❑ 193 Matt Stinchcomb RC .50 .23
❑ 194 John Tait RC .50 .23
❑ 195 Jermaine Fazande RC 1.00 .45
❑ 196 Ricky Williams RC 8.00 3.60
❑ 197 Al Wilson RC 1.00 .45
❑ 198 Antoine Winfield RC 1.00 .45
❑ 199 Damien Woody RC .50 .23
❑ 200 Amos Zereoue RC 1.50 .70

1999 Collector's Edge Fury HoloGold

	MINT	NRMT
COMMON HOLOGOLD	8.00	3.60

*HOLOGOLD STARS: 30X TO 70X HI COL.
*HOLOGOLD YOUNG STARS: 25X TO 60X
*HOLOGLD RC's: 20X TO 50X
HOLOGOLD VETS PRINT RUN 50 SER.#'d SETS
HOLOGOLD ROOK.PRINT RUN 10 SER.#'d SETS

1999 Collector's Edge Fury Extreme Team

	MINT	NRMT
COMPLETE SET (10)	60.00	27.00
COMMON CARD (E1-E10)	4.00	1.80
STATED ODDS 1:24		
❑ E1 Keyshawn Johnson	4.00	1.80
❑ E2 Emmitt Smith	10.00	4.50
❑ E3 John Elway	15.00	6.75
❑ E4 Doug Flutie	5.00	2.20
❑ E5 Jamal Anderson	4.00	1.80
❑ E6 Brett Favre	15.00	6.75
❑ E7 Peyton Manning	12.00	5.50
❑ E8 Fred Taylor	8.00	3.60
❑ E9 Dan Marino	15.00	6.75
❑ E10 Randy Moss	12.00	5.50

1999 Collector's Edge Fury Fast and Furious

	MINT	NRMT
COMPLETE SET (25)	100.00	45.00
COMMON CARD (1-25)	2.00	.90
SEMISTARS	4.00	1.80
STATED PRINT RUN 500 SERIAL #'d SETS		
❑ 1 Jake Plummer	8.00	3.60
❑ 2 Jamal Anderson	5.00	2.20
❑ 3 Eric Moulds	5.00	2.20
❑ 4 Curtis Enis	5.00	2.20
❑ 5 Emmitt Smith	10.00	4.50
❑ 6 Deion Sanders	5.00	2.20
❑ 7 Terrell Davis	10.00	4.50
❑ 8 Barry Sanders	15.00	6.75
❑ 9 Herman Moore	5.00	2.20
❑ 10 Charlie Batch	6.00	2.70
❑ 11 Marshall Faulk	5.00	2.20
❑ 12 Mark Brunell	6.00	2.70
❑ 13 Fred Taylor	8.00	3.60
❑ 14 Randy Moss	12.00	5.50

		MINT	NRMT
❑ 15	Cris Carter	5.00	2.20
❑ 16	Robert Edwards	2.00	.90
❑ 17	Keyshawn Johnson	5.00	2.20
❑ 18	Curtis Martin	5.00	2.20
❑ 19	Charles Woodson	5.00	2.20
❑ 20	Jerome Bettis	5.00	2.20
❑ 21	Kordell Stewart	5.00	2.20
❑ 22	Steve Young	6.00	2.70
❑ 23	Jerry Rice	10.00	4.50
❑ 24	Warrick Dunn	5.00	2.20
❑ 25	Eddie George	5.00	2.20

1999 Collector's Edge Fury Forerunners

	MINT	NRMT
COMPLETE SET (15)	50.00	22.00
COMMON CARD (F1-F15)	1.50	.70
SEMISTARS	3.00	1.35
STATED ODDS 1:8		

		MINT	NRMT
❑ F1	Jamal Anderson	3.00	1.35
❑ F2	Curtis Enis	3.00	1.35
❑ F3	Corey Dillon	3.00	1.35
❑ F4	Emmitt Smith	8.00	3.60
❑ F5	Barry Sanders	12.00	5.50
❑ F6	Terrell Davis	8.00	3.60
❑ F7	Marshall Faulk	3.00	1.35
❑ F8	Fred Taylor	6.00	2.70
❑ F9	Robert Smith	3.00	1.35
❑ F10	Curtis Martin	3.00	1.35
❑ F11	Jerome Bettis	3.00	1.35
❑ F12	Garrison Hearst	1.50	.70
❑ F13	Warrick Dunn	3.00	1.35
❑ F14	Eddie George	4.00	1.80
❑ F15	Ricky Watters	1.50	.70

1999 Collector's Edge Fury Game Ball

	MINT	NRMT
COMPLETE SET (43)	600.00	275.00
COMMON CARD	8.00	3.60
SEMISTARS	15.00	6.75
STATED ODDS 1:24		

		MINT	NRMT
❑ AF	Antonio Freeman	12.00	5.50
❑ AM	Adrian Murrell	8.00	3.60
❑ AS	Antowain Smith	12.00	5.50
❑ BF	Brett Favre	50.00	22.00
❑ BS	Barry Sanders	50.00	22.00
❑ CB	Charlie Batch	20.00	9.00
❑ CC	Cris Carter	12.00	5.50
❑ CD	Corey Dillon	12.00	5.50
❑ CE	Curtis Enis	12.00	5.50
❑ CM	Curtis Martin	12.00	5.50
❑ CP	Carl Pickens	8.00	3.60
❑ DL	Dorsey Levens	12.00	5.50
❑ DS	Deion Sanders	12.00	5.50
❑ EG	Eddie George	20.00	9.00
❑ ES	Emmitt Smith	30.00	13.50
❑ FT	Fred Taylor	25.00	11.00
❑ GH	Garrison Hearst	8.00	3.60
❑ HM	Herman Moore	12.00	5.50
❑ JB	Jerome Bettis	12.00	5.50
❑ JE	John Elway	50.00	22.00
❑ JG	Joey Galloway	12.00	5.50
❑ JP	Jake Plummer	30.00	13.50
❑ JR	Jerry Rice	30.00	13.50
❑ KS	Kordell Stewart	12.00	5.50
❑ MA	Mike Alstott	12.00	5.50
❑ MB	Mark Brunell	20.00	9.00
❑ MF	Marshall Faulk	12.00	5.50
❑ MI	Michael Irvin	15.00	6.75
❑ NK	Napoleon Kaufman	12.00	5.50
❑ NM	Natrone Means	8.00	3.60
❑ PM	Peyton Manning	40.00	18.00
❑ RJ	Rob Johnson	8.00	3.60
❑ RL	Ryan Leaf	12.00	5.50
❑ RM	Randy Moss	40.00	18.00
❑ RS	Rod Smith	8.00	3.60
❑ SM	Steve McNair	12.00	5.50
❑ SS	Shannon Sharpe	8.00	3.60
❑ SY	Steve Young	20.00	9.00
❑ TA	Troy Aikman	30.00	13.50
❑ TD	Terrell Davis	30.00	13.50
❑ TO	Terrell Owens	12.00	5.50
❑ WD	Warrick Dunn	12.00	5.50
❑ WM	Warren Moon	12.00	5.50

1999 Collector's Edge Fury Heir Force

	MINT	NRMT
COMPLETE SET (20)	50.00	22.00
COMMON CARD (HF1-HF20)	1.25	.55
SEMISTARS	1.50	.70
STATED ODDS 1:6		

		MINT	NRMT
❑ HF1	Rahim Abdullah	1.25	.55
❑ HF2	Champ Bailey	2.00	.90
❑ HF3	D'Wayne Bates	1.25	.55
❑ HF4	Michael Bishop	2.00	.90
❑ HF5	David Boston	2.50	1.10
❑ HF6	Chris Claiborne	1.25	.55
❑ HF7	Tim Couch	8.00	3.60
❑ HF8	Daunte Culpepper	5.00	2.20
❑ HF9	Kevin Faulk	2.00	.90
❑ HF10	Torry Holt	4.00	1.80
❑ HF11	Brock Huard	2.00	.90
❑ HF12	Edgerrin James	12.00	5.50
❑ HF13	Andy Katzenmoyer	1.50	.70
❑ HF14	Shaun King	5.00	2.20
❑ HF15	Rob Konrad	1.50	.70
❑ HF16	Donovan McNabb	5.00	2.20
❑ HF17	Cade McNown	5.00	2.20
❑ HF18	Peerless Price	2.50	1.10
❑ HF19	Akili Smith	3.00	1.35
❑ HF20	Ricky Williams	8.00	3.60

1999 Collector's Edge Fury Xplosive

	MINT	NRMT
COMPLETE SET (20)	100.00	45.00
COMMON CARD (1-20)	1.50	.70
SEMISTARS	3.00	1.35
STATED ODDS 1:12		

		MINT	NRMT
❑ 1	Jake Plummer	8.00	3.60
❑ 2	Doug Flutie	5.00	2.20
❑ 3	Eric Moulds	3.00	1.35
❑ 4	Troy Aikman	10.00	4.50
❑ 5	John Elway	15.00	6.75
❑ 6	Charlie Batch	6.00	2.70
❑ 7	Herman Moore	3.00	1.35
❑ 8	Brett Favre	15.00	6.75
❑ 9	Antonio Freeman	3.00	1.35
❑ 10	Peyton Manning	12.00	5.50
❑ 11	Mark Brunell	6.00	2.70
❑ 12	Dan Marino	15.00	6.75
❑ 13	Randy Moss	12.00	5.50
❑ 14	Drew Bledsoe	6.00	2.70
❑ 15	Keyshawn Johnson	3.00	1.35
❑ 16	Vinny Testaverde	1.50	.70
❑ 17	Kordell Stewart	3.00	1.35
❑ 18	Terrell Owens	3.00	1.35
❑ 19	Jerry Rice	10.00	4.50
❑ 20	Steve Young	6.00	2.70

1997 Collector's Edge Masters

	MINT	NRMT
COMPLETE SET (270)	40.00	18.00
COMMON CARD (1-270)	.20	.09
SEMISTARS	.40	.18
UNLISTED STARS	.75	.35
COMMON FLAG	.50	.23
FLAG STATED ODDS 1:3		
FOILS/NON-FOILS SAME PRICE		
COMP.NITRO SET (36)	80.00	36.00
*NITRO CARDS: 2X TO 4X HI COL.		
NITRO STATED ODDS 1:8		

		MINT	NRMT
❑ 1	Cardinals Flag	.50	.23
❑ 2	Larry Centers	.40	.18
❑ 3	Rob Moore	.40	.18
❑ 4	Frank Sanders	.40	.18
❑ 5	Eric Swann	.20	.09

❑ 6 Falcons Flag .50 .23
❑ 7 Morten Andersen UER .20 .09
misspelled Morton
❑ 8 Bert Emanuel .40 .18
❑ 9 Jeff George .40 .18
❑ 10 Craig Heyward .20 .09
❑ 11 Terance Mathis .40 .18
❑ 12 Clay Matthews .20 .09
❑ 13 Eric Metcalf .40 .18
❑ 14 Ravens Flag .50 .23
❑ 15 Rob Burnett .20 .09
❑ 16 Leroy Hoard .20 .09
❑ 17 Ernest Hunter .20 .09
❑ 18 Michael Jackson .40 .18
❑ 19 Stevon Moore .20 .09
❑ 20 Anthony Pleasant .20 .09
❑ 21 Vinny Testaverde .40 .18
❑ 22 Eric Zeier .40 .18
❑ 23 Bills Flag .50 .23
❑ 24 Todd Collins .20 .09
❑ 25 Russell Copeland .20 .09
❑ 26 Quinn Early .20 .09
❑ 27 Jim Kelly .75 .35
❑ 28 Bryce Paup .20 .09
❑ 29 Andre Reed .40 .18
❑ 30 Bruce Smith .40 .18
❑ 31 Panthers Flag .50 .23
❑ 32 Steve Beuerlein .20 .09
❑ 33 Mark Carrier WR .20 .09
❑ 34 Kerry Collins .40 .18
❑ 35 Willie Green .20 .09
❑ 36 Kevin Greene .40 .18
❑ 37 Eric Guliford .20 .09
❑ 38 Brett Maxie .20 .09
❑ 39 Tim McKyer .20 .09
❑ 40 Derrick Moore .20 .09
❑ 41 Bears Flag .50 .23
❑ 42 Curtis Conway .40 .18
❑ 43 Bryan Cox .20 .09
❑ 44 Jim Flanigan .20 .09
❑ 45 Robert Green .20 .09
❑ 46 Erik Kramer .20 .09
❑ 47 Dave Krieg .20 .09
❑ 48 Rashaan Salaam .20 .09
❑ 49 Alonzo Spellman .20 .09
❑ 50 Donnell Woolford .20 .09
❑ 51 Chris Zorich .20 .09
❑ 52 Bengals Flag .50 .23
❑ 53 Eric Bieniemy .20 .09
❑ 54 Jeff Blake .40 .18
❑ 55 Ki-Jana Carter .20 .09
❑ 56 John Copeland .20 .09
❑ 57 Garrison Hearst .40 .18
❑ 58 Tony McGee .20 .09
❑ 59 Carl Pickens .75 .35
❑ 60 Darnay Scott .40 .18
❑ 61 Bracey Walker .20 .09
❑ 62 Dan Wilkinson .20 .09
❑ 63 Cowboys Flag .50 .23
❑ 64 Troy Aikman 2.00 .90
❑ 65 Bill Bates .40 .18
❑ 66 Shante Carver .20 .09
❑ 67 Michael Irvin .75 .35
❑ 68 Daryl Johnston .40 .18
❑ 69 Jay Novacek .20 .09
❑ 70 Deion Sanders .75 .35
❑ 71 Emmitt Smith 3.00 1.35
❑ 72 Herschel Walker .40 .18
❑ 73 Sherman Williams .20 .09
❑ 74 Broncos Flag .50 .23
❑ 75 Terrell Davis 3.00 1.35
❑ 76 John Elway 4.00 1.80
❑ 77 Ed McCaffrey .40 .18
❑ 78 Anthony Miller .20 .09
❑ 79 Michael Dean Perry .20 .09
❑ 80 Shannon Sharpe .40 .18
❑ 81 Mike Sherrard .20 .09
❑ 82 Lions Flag .50 .23
❑ 83 Scott Mitchell .40 .18
❑ 84 Glyn Milburn .20 .09
❑ 85 Herman Moore .75 .35
❑ 86 Johnnie Morton .40 .18
❑ 87 Brett Perriman .20 .09
❑ 88 Barry Sanders 4.00 1.80
❑ 89 Tracy Scroggins .20 .09
❑ 90 Packers Flag .50 .23
❑ 91 Edgar Bennett .40 .18
❑ 92 Robert Brooks .40 .18
❑ 93 Santana Dotson .20 .09
❑ 94 Brett Favre 4.00 1.80
❑ 95 Dorsey Levens .75 .35
❑ 96 Craig Newsome .20 .09
❑ 97 Wayne Simmons .20 .09
❑ 98 Reggie White .75 .35
❑ 99 Oilers Flag .50 .23
❑ 100 Chris Chandler .40 .18
❑ 101 Anthony Cook .20 .09
❑ 102 Willie Davis .20 .09
❑ 103 Mel Gray .20 .09
❑ 104 Ronnie Harmon .20 .09
❑ 105 Darryll Lewis .20 .09
❑ 106 Steve McNair 1.25 .55
❑ 107 Todd McNair .20 .09
❑ 108 Rodney Thomas .20 .09
❑ 109 Colts Flag .50 .23
❑ 110 Trev Alberts .20 .09
❑ 111 Tony Bennett .20 .09
❑ 112 Quentin Coryatt .20 .09
❑ 113 Sean Dawkins .20 .09
❑ 114 Ken Dilger .20 .09
❑ 115 Marshall Faulk .75 .35
❑ 116 Jim Harbaugh UER .40 .18
numbered 115 on back
❑ 117 Ronald Humphrey .20 .09
❑ 118 Floyd Turner .20 .09
❑ 119 Jaguars Flag .50 .23
❑ 120 Tony Boselli .20 .09
❑ 121 Mark Brunell 2.00 .90
❑ 122 Willie Jackson .20 .09
❑ 123 Jeff Lageman .20 .09
❑ 124 Natrone Means .75 .35
❑ 125 Andre Rison .40 .18
❑ 126 James O.Stewart .40 .18
❑ 127 Cedric Tillman .20 .09
❑ 128 Chiefs Flag .50 .23
❑ 129 Marcus Allen .75 .35
❑ 130 Kimble Anders .40 .18
❑ 131 Steve Bono .40 .18
❑ 132 Dale Carter .20 .09
❑ 133 Lake Dawson .20 .09
❑ 134 Dan Saleaumua .20 .09
❑ 135 Neil Smith .40 .18
❑ 136 Derrick Thomas .40 .18
❑ 137 Tamarick Vanover .40 .18
❑ 138 Dolphins Flag .50 .23
❑ 139 Fred Barnett .20 .09
❑ 140 Steve Emtman .20 .09
❑ 141 Eric Green .20 .09
❑ 142 Dan Marino 4.00 1.80
❑ 143 O.J. McDuffie .40 .18
❑ 144 Bernie Parmalee .20 .09
❑ 145 Vikings Flag .50 .23
❑ 146 Cris Carter .75 .35
❑ 147 Jack Del Rio .20 .09
❑ 148 Qadry Ismail .40 .18
❑ 149 Amp Lee .20 .09
❑ 150 Warren Moon .75 .35
❑ 151 John Randle .20 .09
❑ 152 Jake Reed .40 .18
❑ 153 Robert Smith .40 .18
❑ 154 Patriots Flag .50 .23
❑ 155 Drew Bledsoe 2.00 .90
❑ 156 Vincent Brisby .20 .09
❑ 157 Willie Clay .20 .09
❑ 158 Ben Coates .40 .18
❑ 159 Curtis Martin 1.25 .55
❑ 160 Dave Meggett .20 .09
❑ 161 Will Moore .20 .09
❑ 162 Chris Slade .20 .09
❑ 163 Saints Flag .50 .23
❑ 164 Mario Bates .20 .09
❑ 165 Jim Everett .20 .09
❑ 166 Michael Haynes .20 .09
❑ 167 Tyrone Hughes .20 .09
❑ 168 Haywood Jeffires .20 .09
❑ 169 Wayne Martin .20 .09
❑ 170 Renaldo Turnbull .20 .09
❑ 171 Giants Flag .50 .23
❑ 172 Dave Brown .20 .09
❑ 173 Chris Calloway .20 .09
❑ 174 Rodney Hampton .40 .18
see card 259
❑ 175 Michael Strahan .20 .09
❑ 176 Tyrone Wheatley .40 .18
❑ 177 Jets Flag .50 .23
❑ 178 Kyle Brady .20 .09
❑ 179 Wayne Chrebet .75 .35
❑ 180 Hugh Douglas .20 .09
❑ 181 Jeff Graham .20 .09
❑ 182 Adrian Murrell .40 .18
❑ 183 Neil O'Donnell .40 .18
❑ 184 Raiders Flag .50 .23
❑ 185 Tim Brown .75 .35
❑ 186 Aundray Bruce .20 .09
❑ 187 Andrew Glover .20 .09
❑ 188 Jeff Hostetler .20 .09
❑ 189 Napoleon Kaufman .75 .35
❑ 190 Terry McDaniel .20 .09
❑ 191 Chester McGlockton .20 .09
❑ 192 Pat Swilling .20 .09
❑ 193 Harvey Williams .20 .09
❑ 194 Eagles Flag .50 .23
❑ 195 Randall Cunningham .75 .35
❑ 196 Irving Fryar .40 .18
❑ 197 William Fuller .20 .09
❑ 198 Charlie Garner .20 .09
❑ 199 Andy Harmon .20 .09
❑ 200 Rodney Peete .20 .09
❑ 201 Mark Seay .20 .09
❑ 202 Troy Vincent .20 .09
❑ 203 Ricky Watters .40 .18
❑ 204 Calvin Williams .20 .09
❑ 205 Steelers Flag .50 .23
❑ 206 Jerome Bettis .75 .35
❑ 207 Chad Brown .20 .09
❑ 208 Greg Lloyd .20 .09
❑ 209 Byron Bam Morris .20 .09
❑ 210 Erric Pegram .20 .09
❑ 211 Kordell Stewart 1.25 .55
❑ 212 Yancey Thigpen .40 .18
❑ 213 Rod Woodson .40 .18
❑ 214 Chargers Flag .50 .23
❑ 215 Darren Bennett .20 .09
❑ 216 Marco Coleman .20 .09
❑ 217 Stan Humphries .40 .18
❑ 218 Tony Martin .40 .18
❑ 219 Junior Seau .40 .18
❑ 220 49ers Flag .50 .23
❑ 221 Chris Doleman .20 .09
❑ 222 William Floyd .40 .18
❑ 223 Merton Hanks .20 .09
❑ 224 Brent Jones .40 .18
❑ 225 Terry Kirby .40 .18
❑ 226 Derek Loville .20 .09
❑ 227 Ken Norton Jr. .20 .09
❑ 228 Gary Plummer .20 .09
❑ 229 Jerry Rice 2.00 .90
❑ 230 J.J. Stokes .40 .18
❑ 231 Dana Stubblefield .20 .09
❑ 232 John Taylor .20 .09
❑ 233 Bryant Young .20 .09
❑ 234 Steve Young 1.50 .70
❑ 235 Seahawks Flag .50 .23
❑ 236 Brian Blades .20 .09
❑ 237 Joey Galloway 1.25 .55
❑ 238 Carlton Gray .20 .09
❑ 239 Cortez Kennedy .20 .09
❑ 240 Rick Mirer .20 .09
❑ 241 Chris Warren .40 .18
❑ 242 Rams Flag .50 .23
❑ 243 Isaac Bruce .75 .35
❑ 244 Troy Drayton .20 .09
❑ 245 D'Marco Farr .20 .09
❑ 246 Harold Green .20 .09
❑ 247 Chris Miller .20 .09
❑ 248 Leslie O'Neal .20 .09
❑ 249 Roman Phifer .20 .09
❑ 250 Buccaneers Flag .50 .23
❑ 251 Trent Dilfer .75 .35
❑ 252 Alvin Harper .20 .09
❑ 253 Jackie Harris .20 .09
❑ 254 John Lynch .20 .09
❑ 255 Hardy Nickerson .20 .09
❑ 256 Errict Rhett .20 .09
❑ 257 Warren Sapp .40 .18
❑ 258 Todd Scott .20 .09
❑ 259 Charles Wilson UER .20 .09
numbered 174 on back

❑ 260 Redskins Flag .50 .23
❑ 261 Terry Allen .75 .35
❑ 262 Bill Brooks .20 .09
❑ 263 Henry Ellard .20 .09
❑ 264 Gus Frerotte .20 .09
❑ 265 Sean Gilbert .20 .09
❑ 266 Ken Harvey .20 .09
❑ 267 Brian Mitchell .20 .09
❑ 268 Heath Shuler .20 .09
❑ 269 James Washington .20 .09
❑ 270 Michael Westbrook .40 .18

1997 Collector's Edge Masters Crucibles

	MINT	NRMT
COMPLETE SET (25)	60.00	27.00
COMMON CARD (1-25)	1.00	.45
SEMISTARS	1.50	.70
UNLISTED STARS	2.50	1.10

STATED ODDS 1:6 HOBBY
STATED PRINT RUN 3000 SERIAL #'d SETS

❑ 1 Jake Plummer 10.00 4.50
❑ 2 Byron Hanspard 2.50 1.10
❑ 3 Peter Boulware 1.50 .70
❑ 4 Jay Graham 2.50 1.10
❑ 5 Antowain Smith 3.00 1.35
❑ 6 Rae Carruth 1.50 .70
❑ 7 Darnell Autry 1.50 .70
❑ 8 Corey Dillon 5.00 2.20
❑ 9 Bryant Westbrook 1.00 .45
❑ 10 Joey Kent 2.50 1.10
❑ 11 Kevin Lockett 1.50 .70
❑ 12 Pat Barnes 1.50 .70
❑ 13 Tony Gonzalez 4.00 1.80
❑ 14 Yatil Green 1.50 .70
❑ 15 Danny Wuerffel 1.50 .70
❑ 16 Troy Davis 2.50 1.10
❑ 17 Tiki Barber 2.50 1.10
❑ 18 Ike Hilliard 2.50 1.10
❑ 19 Leon Johnson 1.00 .45
❑ 20 Darrell Russell 1.00 .45
❑ 21 Jim Druckenmiller 2.50 1.10
❑ 22 Shawn Springs 1.50 .70
❑ 23 Orlando Pace 1.00 .45
❑ 24 Warrick Dunn 4.00 1.80
❑ 25 Reidel Anthony 2.50 1.10

1997 Collector's Edge Masters Night Games

	MINT	NRMT
COMPLETE SET (25)	250.00	110.00

STATED ODDS 1:20
STATED PRINT RUN 1500 SERIAL #'d SETS
*PRISMS: 12.5X TO 25X BASE CARD HI
PRISMS STATED ODDS 1:60
PRISMS PRINT RUN 250 SERIAL #'d SETS

❑ 1 Terry Glenn 6.00 2.70
❑ 2 Eddie George 15.00 6.75
❑ 3 Ricky Watters 3.00 1.35
❑ 4 Barry Sanders 30.00 13.50
❑ 5 Curtis Martin 10.00 4.50
❑ 6 Brett Favre 30.00 13.50
❑ 7 Emmitt Smith 25.00 11.00

❑ 8 John Elway 30.00 13.50
❑ 9 Keyshawn Johnson 6.00 2.70
❑ 10 Kordell Stewart 10.00 4.50
❑ 11 Vinny Testaverde 3.00 1.35
❑ 12 Kerry Collins 3.00 1.35
❑ 13 Terrell Davis 25.00 11.00
❑ 14 Karim Abdul-Jabbar 6.00 2.70
❑ 15 Drew Bledsoe 15.00 6.75
❑ 16 Antonio Freeman 8.00 3.60
❑ 17 Tony Banks 6.00 2.70
❑ 18 Jerry Rice 15.00 6.75
❑ 19 Mark Brunell 15.00 6.75
❑ 20 Mike Alstott 6.00 2.70
❑ 21 Napoleon Kaufman 6.00 2.70
❑ 22 Herman Moore 6.00 2.70
❑ 23 Terry Allen 6.00 2.70
❑ 24 Jerome Bettis 6.00 2.70
❑ 25 Dorsey Levens 6.00 2.70

1997 Collector's Edge Masters 1996 Rookies

	MINT	NRMT
COMPLETE SET (25)	60.00	27.00
COMMON CARD (1-25)	2.00	.90
SEMISTARS	3.00	1.35
UNLISTED STARS	4.00	1.80

STATED ODDS 1:8 RETAIL
STATED PRINT RUN 2000 SERIAL #'d SETS

❑ 1 Simeon Rice 3.00 1.35
❑ 2 Jonathan Ogden 2.00 .90
❑ 3 Eric Moulds 5.00 2.20
❑ 4 Tim Biakabutuka 3.00 1.35
❑ 5 Walt Harris 2.00 .90
❑ 6 John Mobley 2.00 .90
❑ 7 Stephen Davis 10.00 4.50
❑ 8 Derrick Mayes 3.00 1.35
❑ 9 Eddie George 10.00 4.50
❑ 10 Marvin Harrison 6.00 2.70
❑ 11 Kevin Hardy 2.00 .90
❑ 12 Jerome Woods 2.00 .90
❑ 13 Karim Abdul-Jabbar 4.00 1.80
❑ 14 Duane Clemons 2.00 .90
❑ 15 Terry Glenn 5.00 2.20
❑ 16 Ricky Whittle 2.00 .90
❑ 17 Amani Toomer 3.00 1.35
❑ 18 Keyshawn Johnson 6.00 2.70
❑ 19 Rickey Dudley 3.00 1.35
❑ 20 Bobby Hoying 3.00 1.35
❑ 21 Tony Banks 3.00 1.35
❑ 22 Bryan Still 2.00 .90
❑ 23 Terrell Owens 6.00 2.70
❑ 24 Reggie Brown RB 2.00 .90
❑ 25 Mike Alstott 4.00 1.80

1997 Collector's Edge Masters Packers Super Bowl XXXI

	MINT	NRMT
COMPLETE SET (25)	20.00	9.00
COMMON CARD (1-25)	.20	.09

SET AVAILABLE VIA MAIL REDEMPTION
STATED PRINT RUN 5000 SERIAL #'d SETS
*GOLD FOILS: .75X TO 1.5X BASE CARD HI
GOLDS PRINT RUN 1000 SERIAL #'d SETS

❑ 1 Edgar Bennett .40 .18
❑ 2 Mark Chmura .20 .09
❑ 3 Brett Favre 4.00 1.80
❑ 4 Dorsey Levens .75 .35
❑ 5 Wayne Simmons .20 .09
❑ 6 Robert Brooks .40 .18
❑ 7 Sean Jones .20 .09
❑ 8 George Koonce .20 .09
❑ 9 Craig Newsome .20 .09
❑ 10 Reggie White .75 .35
❑ 11 Desmond Howard .40 .18
❑ 12 Antonio Freeman 2.00 .90
❑ 13 Brett Favre 4.00 1.80
❑ 14 Keith Jackson .40 .18
❑ 15 Andre Rison .40 .18
❑ 16 Eugene Robinson .20 .09
❑ 17 LeRoy Butler .20 .09
❑ 18 Don Beebe .40 .18
❑ 19 Derrick Mayes .20 .09
❑ 20 Gilbert Brown .20 .09
❑ 21 Santana Dotson .20 .09
❑ 22 Brett Favre 4.00 1.80
❑ 23 Reggie White .75 .35
❑ 24 Desmond Howard .40 .18
❑ 25 Antonio Freeman 2.00 .90

1997 Collector's Edge Masters Playoff Game Ball

	MINT	NRMT
COMPLETE SET (19)	800.00	350.00
COMMON CARD (1-19)	15.00	6.75

SEMISTARS	25.00	11.00
STATED ODDS 1:72		
UNPRICED GOLDS SER.#'d OF 1		

❑ 1 Natrone Means Thurman Thomas	25.00	11.00
❑ 2 Tony Boselli Bruce Smith	25.00	11.00
❑ 3 Jerome Bettis Marshall Faulk	25.00	11.00
❑ 4 Kordell Stewart Jim Harbaugh	40.00	18.00
❑ 5 Natrone Means Terrell Davis	100.00	45.00
❑ 6 Mark Brunell John Elway	100.00	45.00
❑ 7 Curtis Martin Jerome Bettis	40.00	18.00
❑ 8 Drew Bledsoe Mark Brunell	60.00	27.00
❑ 9 Terry Glenn Keenan McCardell	25.00	11.00
❑ 10 Ricky Watters Terry Kirby	15.00	6.75
❑ 11 Kevin Greene Reggie White	25.00	11.00
❑ 12 Jerry Rice Irving Fryar	50.00	22.00
❑ 13 Dorsey Levens Terry Kirby	25.00	11.00
❑ 14 Brett Favre Steve Young	100.00	45.00
❑ 15 Andre Rison Jerry Rice	50.00	22.00
❑ 16 Reggie White Ken Norton Jr.	25.00	11.00
❑ 17 Kerry Collins Troy Aikman	50.00	22.00
❑ 18 Kerry Collins Brett Favre	80.00	36.00
❑ 19 Mark Carrier WR Antonio Freeman	30.00	13.50

1997 Collector's Edge Masters Radical Rivals

	MINT	NRMT
COMPLETE SET (13)	200.00	90.00
COMMON CARD (1-12)	8.00	3.60
TITLE CARD (NNO)	1.00	.45
STATED ODDS 1:30 HOBBY		
STATED PRINT RUN 1000 SERIAL #'d SETS		

❑ 1 Emmitt Smith Eddie George	30.00	13.50
❑ 2 Brett Favre Kerry Collins	30.00	13.50
❑ 3 Jerry Rice Antonio Freeman	25.00	11.00
❑ 4 Ricky Watters Napoleon Kaufman	10.00	4.50
❑ 5 Herman Moore Keyshawn Johnson	8.00	3.60
❑ 6 Dan Marino John Elway	30.00	13.50
❑ 7 Jerome Bettis Karim Abdul-Jabbar	8.00	3.60
❑ 8 Isaac Bruce Carl Pickens	8.00	3.60
❑ 9 Barry Sanders Terry Allen	30.00	13.50
❑ 10 Terry Glenn Joey Galloway	12.00	5.50
❑ 11 Mark Brunell Steve Young	15.00	6.75
❑ 12 Terrell Davis Curtis Martin	30.00	13.50
❑ NNO Title Card CL	1.00	.45

1997 Collector's Edge Masters Ripped

	MINT	NRMT
COMPLETE SET (19)	150.00	70.00
CL (NNO)	1.00	.45
STATED ODDS 1:24 RET		

❑ 19 Troy Aikman	15.00	6.75
❑ 20 Drew Bledsoe	15.00	6.75
❑ 21 Tim Brown	6.00	2.70
❑ 22 Mark Brunell	15.00	6.75
❑ 23 Cris Carter	6.00	2.70
❑ 24 Kerry Collins	3.00	1.35
❑ 25 Barry Sanders	30.00	13.50
❑ 26 Eddie George	6.00	2.70
❑ 27 Karim Abdul-Jabbar	6.00	2.70
❑ 28 Curtis Martin	10.00	4.50
❑ 29 Carl Pickens	6.00	2.70
❑ 30 Marshall Faulk	6.00	2.70
❑ 31 Rashaan Salaam	1.50	.70
❑ 32 Deion Sanders	6.00	2.70
❑ 33 Emmitt Smith	25.00	11.00
❑ 34 Herman Moore	6.00	2.70
❑ 35 Ricky Watters	3.00	1.35
❑ 36 Terry Allen	6.00	2.70
❑ NNO Checklist Card	1.50	.70

1997 Collector's Edge Masters Super Bowl Game Ball

	MINT	NRMT
COMPLETE SET (6)	500.00	220.00
COMMON CARD (1-6)	40.00	18.00
SEMISTARS	60.00	27.00
STATED ODDS 1:350 RETAIL		
STATED PRINT RUN 250 SETS		
SILVER PARALLEL EXISTS/UNPRICED		

❑ 1 Brett Favre Drew Bledsoe	250.00	110.00
❑ 2 Dorsey Levens Curtis Martin	100.00	45.00
❑ 3 Desmond Howard Dave Meggett	40.00	18.00
❑ 4 Antonio Freeman Terry Glenn	100.00	45.00
❑ 5 Keith Jackson Ben Coates	40.00	18.00
❑ 6 Willie McGinest Reggie White	60.00	27.00

1998 Collector's Edge Masters

	MINT	NRMT
COMPLETE SET (199)	250.00	110.00
COMMON CARD (1-200)	.30	.14
SEMISTARS	.60	.25
UNLISTED STARS	1.25	.55
STATED PRINT RUN 5000 SERIAL #'d SETS		
COMMON ROOKIE	1.50	.70
ROOKIE SEMISTARS	4.00	1.80
COMP.50-POINT SET (199)	400.00	180.00
*50-POINT CARDS: .5X TO 1.2X HI COL.		
ONE 50-POINT PER PACK		
STATED PRINT RUN 3000 SERIAL #'d SETS		
COMP.50-POINT GOLD (199)	1500.00	700.00
*50-POINT GOLD STARS: 5X TO 12X HI COL.		
*50-POINT GOLD YOUNG STARS: 4X TO 10X		
*50-POINT GOLD RCs: 1.25X TO 3X		
STATED ODDS 1:20		
STATED PRINT RUN 150 SERIAL #'d SETS		
COMMON HOLOGOLD	30.00	13.50
*HOLOGOLD STARS: 40X TO 100X HI COL.		
*HOLOGOLD YOUNG STARS: 30X TO 80X		
*HOLOGOLD RCs: 6X TO 15X		
STATED ODDS 1:300		
STATED PRINT RUN 10 SERIAL #'d SETS		
COMP.GOLD REDEMP. (199)	500.00	220.00
*GOLD REDEMP.STARS: 1.5X TO 4X HI COL.		
*GOLD REDEMP.YOUNG STARS: 1.2X TO 3X		
*GOLD REDEMPTION RCs: .5X TO 1.2X		
GOLD REDEMPTION SET ISSUED VIA MAIL RED.		
GOLD REDEMP.PRINT RUN 500 SER.#'d SETS		
CARD #28 WAS NEVER PRODUCED		

❑ 1 Rob Moore	.60	.25
❑ 2 Adrian Murrell	.60	.25
❑ 3 Jake Plummer	4.00	1.80
❑ 4 Michael Pittman RC	4.00	1.80
❑ 5 Frank Sanders	.60	.25
❑ 6 Andre Wadsworth RC	4.00	1.80
❑ 7 Jamal Anderson	1.25	.55
❑ 8 Chris Chandler	.60	.25
❑ 9 Tim Dwight RC	6.00	2.70
❑ 10 Tony Martin	.60	.25
❑ 11 Terance Mathis	.60	.25
❑ 12 Ken Oxendine RC	1.50	.70
❑ 13 Jim Harbaugh	.60	.25
❑ 14 Priest Holmes RC	10.00	4.50
❑ 15 Michael Jackson	.30	.14
❑ 16 Pat Johnson RC	4.00	1.80
❑ 17 Jermaine Lewis	.60	.25
❑ 18 Eric Zeier	.60	.25

Card		MINT	NRMT
❑ 19	Doug Flutie	1.50	.70
❑ 20	Rob Johnson	.60	.25
❑ 21	Eric Moulds	1.25	.55
❑ 22	Andre Reed	.60	.25
❑ 23	Antowain Smith	1.25	.55
❑ 24	Bruce Smith	.60	.25
❑ 25	Thurman Thomas	1.25	.55
❑ 26	Steve Beuerlein	.30	.14
❑ 27	Kevin Greene	.60	.25
❑ 29	Rocket Ismail	.30	.14
❑ 30	Fred Lane	.60	.25
❑ 31	Muhsin Muhammad	.60	.25
❑ 32	Edgar Bennett	.30	.14
❑ 33	Curtis Conway	.60	.25
❑ 34	Bobby Engram	.60	.25
❑ 35	Curtis Enis RC	8.00	3.60
❑ 36	Erik Kramer	.30	.14
❑ 37	Chris Penn	.30	.14
❑ 38	Jeff Blake	.60	.25
❑ 39	Corey Dillon	2.00	.90
❑ 40	Neil O'Donnell	.60	.25
❑ 41	Carl Pickens	1.25	.55
❑ 42	Darnay Scott	.60	.25
❑ 43	Damon Gibson RC	1.50	.70
❑ 44	Troy Aikman	3.00	1.35
❑ 45	Billy Davis	.30	.14
❑ 46	Michael Irvin	1.25	.55
❑ 47	Ernie Mills	.30	.14
❑ 48	Deion Sanders	1.25	.55
❑ 49	Emmitt Smith	5.00	2.20
❑ 50	Chris Warren	.60	.25
❑ 51	Bubby Brister	.30	.14
❑ 52	Terrell Davis	5.00	2.20
❑ 53	John Elway	6.00	2.70
❑ 54	Brian Griese RC	10.00	4.50
❑ 55	Ed McCaffrey	.60	.25
❑ 56	Marcus Nash RC	4.00	1.80
❑ 57	Shannon Sharpe	.60	.25
❑ 58	Rod Smith	.60	.25
❑ 59	Charlie Batch RC	10.00	4.50
❑ 60	Germane Crowell RC	8.00	3.60
❑ 61	Scott Mitchell	.60	.25
❑ 62	Johnnie Morton	.60	.25
❑ 63	Herman Moore	1.25	.55
❑ 64	Barry Sanders	6.00	2.70
❑ 65	Robert Brooks	.60	.25
❑ 66	Brett Favre	6.00	2.70
❑ 67	Antonio Freeman	1.25	.55
❑ 68	Raymont Harris	.30	.14
❑ 69	Dorsey Levens	1.25	.55
❑ 70	Reggie White	1.25	.55
❑ 71	Marshall Faulk	1.25	.55
❑ 72	Marvin Harrison	.60	.25
❑ 73	Peyton Manning RC	25.00	11.00
❑ 74	Jerome Pathon RC	4.00	1.80
❑ 75	Tavian Banks RC	4.00	1.80
❑ 76	Mark Brunell	2.50	1.10
❑ 77	Keenan McCardell	.60	.25
❑ 78	Jimmy Smith	.60	.25
❑ 79	Fred Taylor RC	15.00	6.75
❑ 80	Derrick Alexander	.60	.25
❑ 81	Donnell Bennett	.30	.14
❑ 82	Rich Gannon	.30	.14
❑ 83	Elvis Grbac	.60	.25
❑ 84	Andre Rison	.60	.25
❑ 85	Rashaan Shehee RC	4.00	1.80
❑ 86	Karim Abdul-Jabbar	1.25	.55
❑ 87	John Avery RC	4.00	1.80
❑ 88	Oronde Gadsden RC	4.00	1.80
❑ 89	Dan Marino	6.00	2.70
❑ 90	O.J. McDuffie	.60	.25
❑ 91	Zach Thomas	.30	.14
❑ 92	Cris Carter	1.25	.55
❑ 93	Randall Cunningham	1.25	.55
❑ 94	Brad Johnson	1.25	.55
❑ 95	Randy Moss RC	25.00	11.00
❑ 96	Jake Reed	.60	.25
❑ 97	Robert Smith	1.25	.55
❑ 98	Drew Bledsoe	2.50	1.10
❑ 99	Ben Coates	.60	.25
❑ 100	Robert Edwards RC	4.00	1.80
❑ 101	Terry Glenn	1.25	.55
❑ 102	Shawn Jefferson	.30	.14
❑ 103	Ty Law	.30	.14
❑ 104	Cameron Cleeland RC	4.00	1.80
❑ 105	Kerry Collins	.60	.25
❑ 106	Sean Dawkins	.30	.14
❑ 107	Andre Hastings	.30	.14
❑ 108	Lamar Smith	.30	.14
❑ 109	Danny Wuerffel	.60	.25
❑ 110	Gary Brown	.30	.14
❑ 111	Chris Calloway	.30	.14
❑ 112	Ike Hilliard	.60	.25
❑ 113	Joe Jurevicius RC	4.00	1.80
❑ 114	Danny Kanell	.60	.25
❑ 115	Wayne Chrebet	1.25	.55
❑ 116	Glenn Foley	.60	.25
❑ 117	Keyshawn Johnson	1.25	.55
❑ 118	Leon Johnson	.30	.14
❑ 119	Curtis Martin	1.25	.55
❑ 120	Vinny Testaverde	.60	.25
❑ 121	Tim Brown	1.25	.55
❑ 122	Jeff George	.60	.25
❑ 123	James Jett	.60	.25
❑ 124	Napoleon Kaufman	1.25	.55
❑ 125	Charles Woodson RC	8.00	3.60
❑ 126	Irving Fryar	.60	.25
❑ 127	Jeff Graham	.30	.14
❑ 128	Bobby Hoying	.60	.25
❑ 129	Duce Staley	2.00	.90
❑ 130	Jerome Bettis	1.25	.55
❑ 131	C.Fuamatu-Ma'afala RC	4.00	1.80
❑ 132	Courtney Hawkins	.30	.14
❑ 133	Charles Johnson	.30	.14
❑ 134	Kordell Stewart	1.25	.55
❑ 135	Hines Ward RC	4.00	1.80
❑ 136	Tony Banks	.60	.25
❑ 137	Isaac Bruce	1.25	.55
❑ 138	Robert Holcombe RC	4.00	1.80
❑ 139	Eddie Kennison	.60	.25
❑ 140	Ryan Leaf RC	6.00	2.70
❑ 141	Natrone Means	1.25	.55
❑ 142	Mikhael Ricks RC	4.00	1.80
❑ 143	Junior Seau	.60	.25
❑ 144	Bryan Still	.30	.14
❑ 145	Garrison Hearst	1.25	.55
❑ 146	R.W. McQuarters RC	1.50	.70
❑ 147	Terrell Owens	1.25	.55
❑ 148	Jerry Rice	3.00	1.35
❑ 149	J.J. Stokes	.60	.25
❑ 150	Steve Young	2.00	.90
❑ 151	Joey Galloway	1.25	.55
❑ 152	Ahman Green RC	4.00	1.80
❑ 153	Warren Moon	1.25	.55
❑ 154	Shawn Springs	.30	.14
❑ 155	Ricky Watters	.60	.25
❑ 156	Mike Alstott	1.25	.55
❑ 157	Reidel Anthony	.60	.25
❑ 158	Trent Dilfer	1.25	.55
❑ 159	Warrick Dunn	2.00	.90
❑ 160	Jacquez Green RC	5.00	2.20
❑ 161	Kevin Dyson RC	6.00	2.70
❑ 162	Eddie George	2.50	1.10
❑ 163	Steve McNair	1.25	.55
❑ 164	Yancey Thigpen	.30	.14
❑ 165	Frank Wycheck	.30	.14
❑ 166	Terry Allen	1.25	.55
❑ 167	Gus Frerotte	.30	.14
❑ 168	Trent Green	1.50	.70
❑ 169	Skip Hicks RC	5.00	2.20
❑ 170	Michael Westbrook	.60	.25
❑ 171	Jamal Anderson SM	1.25	.55
❑ 172	Carl Pickens SM	1.25	.55
❑ 173	Deion Sanders SM	1.25	.55
❑ 174	Emmitt Smith SM	3.00	1.35
❑ 175	Terrell Davis SM	3.00	1.35
❑ 176	John Elway SM	4.00	1.80
❑ 177	Charlie Batch SM	6.00	2.70
❑ 178	Herman Moore SM	1.25	.55
❑ 179	Barry Sanders SM	4.00	1.80
❑ 180	Brett Favre SM	4.00	1.80
❑ 181	Antonio Freeman SM	.60	.25
❑ 182	Marshall Faulk SM	1.25	.55
❑ 183	Peyton Manning SM	15.00	6.75
❑ 184	Mark Brunell SM	1.25	.55
❑ 185	Dan Marino SM	4.00	1.80
❑ 186	Randy Moss SM	15.00	6.75
❑ 187	Drew Bledsoe SM	1.25	.55
❑ 188	Robert Edwards SM	1.25	.55
❑ 189	Curtis Martin SM	1.25	.55
❑ 190	Charles Woodson SM	3.00	1.35
❑ 191	Jerome Bettis SM	1.25	.55
❑ 192	Robert Holcombe SM	1.25	.55
❑ 193	Ryan Leaf SM	2.50	1.10
❑ 194	Natrone Means SM	1.25	.55
❑ 195	Jerry Rice SM	2.00	.90
❑ 196	Steve Young SM	1.25	.55
❑ 197	Warrick Dunn SM	1.25	.55
❑ 198	Eddie George SM	1.25	.55
❑ 199	Peyton Manning CL	8.00	3.60
❑ 200	Ryan Leaf CL	2.50	1.10

1998 Collector's Edge Masters Main Event

	MINT	NRMT
COMPLETE SET (20)	150.00	70.00
COMMON CARD (ME1-ME20)	3.00	1.35
STATED ODDS 1:16		
STATED PRINT RUN 2000 SERIAL #'d SETS		

Card		MINT	NRMT
❑ ME1	Troy Aikman	8.00	3.60
❑ ME2	Jamal Anderson	3.00	1.35
❑ ME3	Charlie Batch	10.00	4.50
❑ ME4	Jerome Bettis	3.00	1.35
❑ ME5	Mark Brunell	6.00	2.70
❑ ME6	Terrell Davis	12.00	5.50
❑ ME7	Warrick Dunn	4.00	1.80
❑ ME8	Robert Edwards	3.00	1.35
❑ ME9	John Elway	15.00	6.75
❑ ME10	Brett Favre	15.00	6.75
❑ ME11	Doug Flutie	4.00	1.80
❑ ME12	Eddie George	6.00	2.70
❑ ME13	Dan Marino	15.00	6.75
❑ ME14	Curtis Martin	3.00	1.35
❑ ME15	Randy Moss	30.00	13.50
❑ ME16	Carl Pickens	3.00	1.35
❑ ME17	Jake Plummer	8.00	3.60
❑ ME18	Barry Sanders	15.00	6.75
❑ ME19	Emmitt Smith	12.00	5.50
❑ ME20	Fred Taylor	15.00	6.75

1998 Collector's Edge Masters Legends

	MINT	NRMT
COMPLETE SET (30)	80.00	36.00
COMMON CARD (ML1-ML30)	2.50	1.10
STATED ODDS 1:8		
STATED PRINT RUN 2500 SERIAL #'d SETS		

Card		MINT	NRMT
❑ ML1	Jake Plummer	6.00	2.70

❑ ML2 Doug Flutie	3.00	1.35
❑ ML3 Corey Dillon	2.50	1.10
❑ ML4 Carl Pickens	2.50	1.10
❑ ML5 Troy Aikman	6.00	2.70
❑ ML6 Deion Sanders	2.50	1.10
❑ ML7 Emmitt Smith	10.00	4.50
❑ ML8 Terrell Davis	10.00	4.50
❑ ML9 John Elway	12.00	5.50
❑ ML10 Herman Moore	2.50	1.10
❑ ML11 Barry Sanders	12.00	5.50
❑ ML12 Brett Favre	12.00	5.50
❑ ML13 Antonio Freeman	2.50	1.10
❑ ML14 Marshall Faulk	2.50	1.10
❑ ML15 Mark Brunell	5.00	2.20
❑ ML16 Dan Marino	12.00	5.50
❑ ML17 Cris Carter	2.50	1.10
❑ ML18 Drew Bledsoe	5.00	2.20
❑ ML19 Keyshawn Johnson	2.50	1.10
❑ ML20 Curtis Martin	2.50	1.10
❑ ML21 Napoleon Kaufman	2.50	1.10
❑ ML22 Jerome Bettis	2.50	1.10
❑ ML23 Kordell Stewart	2.50	1.10
❑ ML24 Natrone Means	2.50	1.10
❑ ML25 Jerry Rice	6.00	2.70
❑ ML26 Steve Young	4.00	1.80
❑ ML27 Joey Galloway	2.50	1.10
❑ ML28 Warrick Dunn	4.00	1.80
❑ ML29 Eddie George	5.00	2.20
❑ ML30 Terry Allen	2.50	1.10

1998 Collector's Edge Masters Rookie Masters

	MINT	NRMT
COMPLETE SET (30)	120.00	55.00
COMMON CARD (RM1-RM30)	1.25	.55
SEMISTARS	2.00	.90
UNLISTED STARS	3.00	1.35
STATED ODDS 1:8		
STATED PRINT RUN 2500 SERIAL #'d SETS		
❑ RM1 Peyton Manning	25.00	11.00
❑ RM2 Ryan Leaf	4.00	1.80
❑ RM3 Charlie Batch	10.00	4.50
❑ RM4 Brian Griese	10.00	4.50
❑ RM5 Randy Moss	25.00	11.00
❑ RM6 Jacquez Green	4.00	1.80
❑ RM7 Kevin Dyson	5.00	2.20
❑ RM8 Mikhael Ricks	2.00	.90
❑ RM9 Jerome Pathon	2.00	.90
❑ RM10 Joe Jurevicius	2.00	.90
❑ RM11 Germane Crowell	6.00	2.70
❑ RM12 Tim Dwight	4.00	1.80
❑ RM13 Pat Johnson	2.00	.90
❑ RM14 Hines Ward	2.00	.90
❑ RM15 Marcus Nash	3.00	1.35
❑ RM16 Damon Gibson	1.25	.55
❑ RM17 Robert Edwards	3.00	1.35
❑ RM18 Robert Holcombe	3.00	1.35
❑ RM19 Tavian Banks	2.00	.90
❑ RM20 Fred Taylor	15.00	6.75
❑ RM21 Skip Hicks	2.00	.90
❑ RM22 Curtis Enis	6.00	2.70
❑ RM23 Ahman Green	3.00	1.35
❑ RM24 John Avery	3.00	1.35
❑ RM25 C.Fuamatu-Ma'afala	2.00	.90
❑ RM26 Rashaan Shehee	2.00	.90
❑ RM27 Cameron Cleeland	2.00	.90
❑ RM28 Charles Woodson	6.00	2.70
❑ RM29 R.W. McQuarters	1.25	.55
❑ RM30 Andre Wadsworth	2.00	.90

1998 Collector's Edge Masters Sentinels

	MINT	NRMT
COMPLETE SET (10)	200.00	90.00
COMMON CARD (S1-S10)	10.00	4.50
STATED ODDS 1:120		
STATED PRINT RUN 500 SERIAL #'d SETS		
❑ S1 John Elway	25.00	11.00
❑ S2 Brett Favre	25.00	11.00
❑ S3 Barry Sanders	25.00	11.00
❑ S4 Terrell Davis	20.00	9.00
❑ S5 Dan Marino	25.00	11.00
❑ S6 Emmitt Smith	20.00	9.00
❑ S7 Randy Moss	40.00	18.00
❑ S8 Peyton Manning	40.00	18.00
❑ S9 Robert Edwards	10.00	4.50
❑ S10 Fred Taylor	25.00	11.00

1998 Collector's Edge Masters Super Masters

	MINT	NRMT
COMPLETE SET (23)	60.00	27.00
COMMON CARD (SM1-SM30)	1.50	.70
SEMISTARS	2.50	1.10
STATED ODDS 1:10		
STATED PRINT RUN 2000 SERIAL #'d SETS		
PRINT RUN OF SIGNED RET.PLAYERS VARIES		
❑ SM1 Terrell Davis	10.00	4.50
❑ SM2 John Elway	12.00	5.50
❑ SM3 Shannon Sharpe	2.50	1.10
❑ SM4 Rod Smith	2.50	1.10
❑ SM5 Brett Favre	12.00	5.50
❑ SM6 Antonio Freeman	2.50	1.10
❑ SM7 Robert Brooks	2.50	1.10
❑ SM8 Edgar Bennett	1.50	.70
❑ SM9 Reggie White	2.50	1.10
❑ SM10 Troy Aikman	6.00	2.70
❑ SM11 Michael Irvin	2.50	1.10
❑ SM12 Deion Sanders	2.50	1.10
❑ SM13 Emmitt Smith	10.00	4.50
❑ SM14 Steve Young	4.00	1.80
❑ SM15 Jerry Rice	6.00	2.70
❑ SM16 Bart Starr	12.00	5.50
❑ SM16AU Bart Starr AUTO SP	250.00	110.00
❑ SM17 Johnny Unitas	10.00	4.50
❑ SM17AU J.Unitas AUTO SP	200.00	90.00
❑ SM18 Roger Craig	2.50	1.10
❑ SM18AU Roger Craig AUTO	15.00	6.75
❑ SM19 Drew Pearson	2.50	1.10
❑ SM19AU Drew Pearson AUTO (Trade card)	15.00	6.75
❑ SM20 Jack Ham	2.50	1.10
❑ SM20AU Jack Ham AUTO	20.00	9.00
❑ SM21AU Len Dawson AUTO	60.00	27.00
❑ SM23 Dwight Clark	2.50	1.10
❑ SM23AU Dwight Clark AUTO (Trade card)	15.00	6.75
❑ SM29 John Stallworth	2.50	1.10
❑ SM29AU J.Stallworth AUTO	15.00	6.75
❑ SM30 Butch Johnson AUTO	10.00	4.50

1999 Collector's Edge Masters

	MINT	NRMT
COMPLETE SET (200)	500.00	220.00
COMMON CARD (1-200)	.25	.11
SEMISTARS	.50	.23
UNLISTED STARS	1.00	.45
STATED PRINT RUN 5000 SERIAL #'d SETS		
COMMON ROOKIE	4.00	1.80
ROOKIE SEMISTARS	6.00	2.70
ROOKIE UNL.STARS	8.00	3.60
UNLESS NOTED RCs ARE SER.#'d OF 2000		
❑ 1 David Boston RC	12.00	5.50
❑ 2 Mac Cody RC	6.00	2.70
❑ 3 Chris Greisen RC	10.00	4.50
❑ 4 Joel Makovicka RC	8.00	3.60
❑ 5 Adrian Murrell	.50	.23
❑ 6 Jake Plummer	1.50	.70
❑ 7 Frank Sanders	.50	.23
❑ 8 Jamal Anderson	1.00	.45
❑ 9 Chris Chandler	.50	.23
❑ 10 Reginald Kelly RC	6.00	2.70
❑ 11 Patrick Kerney RC	6.00	2.70
❑ 12 Terance Mathis	.50	.23
❑ 13 Jeff Paulk RC	6.00	2.70
❑ 14 Stoney Case	.25	.11
❑ 15 Qadry Ismail	.25	.11
❑ 16 Chris McAlister RC	6.00	2.70
❑ 17 Errict Rhett	.25	.11
❑ 18 Brandon Stokley RC	6.00	2.70
❑ 19 Doug Flutie	1.25	.55
❑ 20 Kamil Loud RC	6.00	2.70
❑ 21 Eric Moulds	1.00	.45
❑ 22 Peerless Price RC	12.00	5.50
❑ 23 Andre Reed	.50	.23
❑ 24 Antowain Smith	1.00	.45
❑ 25 Antoine Winfield RC	6.00	2.70
❑ 26 Steve Beuerlein	.50	.23
❑ 27 Tim Biakabutuka	.50	.23
❑ 28 Dameyune Craig RC	8.00	3.60
❑ 29 Patrick Jeffers RC	25.00	11.00
❑ 30 Muhsin Muhammad	.50	.23
❑ 31 D'Wayne Bates RC	6.00	2.70
❑ 32 Marty Booker RC	8.00	3.60
❑ 33 Bobby Engram	.25	.11
❑ 34 Curtis Enis	1.00	.45
❑ 35 Ty Hallock RC	6.00	2.70
❑ 36 Shane Matthews	1.00	.45
❑ 37 Cade McNown RC	25.00	11.00
❑ 38 Marcus Robinson	2.00	.90
❑ 39 Scott Covington RC	8.00	3.60
❑ 40 Corey Dillon	1.00	.45
❑ 41 Damon Griffin RC	8.00	3.60
❑ 42 Carl Pickens	.50	.23
❑ 43 Darnay Scott	.50	.23
❑ 44 Akili Smith RC	15.00	6.75
❑ 45 Craig Yeast RC	6.00	2.70
❑ 46 Darrin Chiaverini RC	8.00	3.60
❑ 47 Tim Couch RC	40.00	18.00
❑ 48 Phil Dawson RC	6.00	2.70
❑ 49 Kevin Johnson RC	20.00	9.00
❑ 50 Terry Kirby	.25	.11
❑ 51 Wali Rainer RC	8.00	3.60
❑ 52 Troy Aikman	2.50	1.10
❑ 53 Ebenezer Ekuban RC	6.00	2.70
❑ 54 Michael Irvin	.50	.23

❑ 55 Rocket Ismail	.50	.23
❑ 56 Wane McGarity RC	6.00	2.70
❑ 57 Dat Nguyen RC	8.00	3.60
❑ 58 Deion Sanders	1.00	.45
❑ 59 Emmitt Smith	2.50	1.10
❑ 60 Byron Chamberlain	.50	.23
❑ 61 Andre Cooper RC	6.00	2.70
❑ 62 Terrell Davis	2.50	1.10
❑ 63 Olandis Gary RC	25.00	11.00
❑ 64 Brian Griese	2.00	.90
❑ 65 Ed McCaffrey	.50	.23
❑ 66 Travis McGriff RC	6.00	2.70
❑ 67 Shannon Sharpe	.50	.23
❑ 68 Rod Smith	.50	.23
❑ 69 Al Wilson RC	8.00	3.60
❑ 70 Charlie Batch	2.00	.90
❑ 71 Chris Claiborne RC	6.00	2.70
❑ 72 Germane Crowell	.50	.23
❑ 73 Greg Hill	.25	.11
❑ 74 Sedrick Irvin RC	8.00	3.60
❑ 75 Herman Moore	1.00	.45
❑ 76 Johnnie Morton	.50	.23
❑ 77 Barry Sanders	4.00	1.80
❑ 78 Aaron Brooks RC	8.00	3.60
❑ 79 Antuan Edwards RC	6.00	2.70
❑ 80 Brett Favre	4.00	1.80
❑ 81 Antonio Freeman	1.00	.45
❑ 82 Dorsey Levens	1.00	.45
❑ 83 Bill Schroeder	1.00	.45
❑ 84 E.G. Green	.25	.11
❑ 85 Marvin Harrison	1.00	.45
❑ 86 Edgerrin James RC	60.00	27.00
❑ 87 Peyton Manning	4.00	1.80
❑ 88 Mark Brunell	1.50	.70
❑ 89 Jay Fiedler RC	8.00	3.60
❑ 90 Keenan McCardell	.50	.23
❑ 91 Jimmy Smith	.50	.23
❑ 92 James Stewart	.50	.23
❑ 93 Fred Taylor	2.50	1.10
❑ 94 Derrick Alexander WR	.50	.23
❑ 95 Mike Cloud RC	8.00	3.60
❑ 96 Elvis Grbac	.50	.23
❑ 97 Byron Bam Morris	.25	.11
❑ 98 Andre Rison	.50	.23
❑ 99 Cecil Collins RC	8.00	3.60
❑ 100 Damon Huard	2.50	1.10
❑ 101 James Johnson RC	10.00	4.50
❑ 102 Rob Konrad RC	8.00	3.60
❑ 103 Dan Marino	4.00	1.80
❑ 104 O.J. McDuffie	.50	.23
❑ 105 Cris Carter	1.00	.45
❑ 106 Daunte Culpepper RC	25.00	11.00
❑ 107 Randall Cunningham	1.00	.45
❑ 108 Jeff George	.50	.23
❑ 109 Jim Kleinsasser RC	8.00	3.60
❑ 110 Randy Moss	4.00	1.80
❑ 111 Robert Smith	1.00	.45
❑ 112 Terry Allen	.50	.23
❑ 113 Michael Bishop RC	10.00	4.50
❑ 114 Drew Bledsoe	1.50	.70
❑ 115 Kevin Faulk RC	10.00	4.50
❑ 116 Terry Glenn	1.00	.45
❑ 117 Andy Katzenmoyer RC	8.00	3.60
❑ 118 Billy Joe Hobert	.25	.11
❑ 119 Eddie Kennison	.50	.23
❑ 120 Ricky Williams RC	40.00	18.00
❑ 121 Tiki Barber	.50	.23
❑ 122 Sean Bennett RC	6.00	2.70
❑ 123 Gary Brown	.25	.11
❑ 124 Kent Graham	.25	.11
❑ 125 Ike Hilliard	.25	.11
❑ 126 Joe Montgomery RC	8.00	3.60
❑ 127 Amani Toomer	.25	.11
❑ 128 Wayne Chrebet	1.00	.45
❑ 129 Keyshawn Johnson	1.00	.45
❑ 130 Curtis Martin	1.00	.45
❑ 131 Ray Lucas RC	10.00	4.50
❑ 132 Vinny Testaverde	.50	.23
❑ 133 Tim Brown	1.00	.45
❑ 134 Tony Bryant RC	6.00	2.70
❑ 135 Scott Dreisbach RC	8.00	3.60
❑ 136 Rich Gannon	.50	.23
❑ 137 Tyrone Wheatley	1.00	.45
❑ 138 Charles Woodson	1.00	.45
❑ 139 Na Brown RC	8.00	3.60
❑ 140 Charles Johnson	.25	.11
❑ 141 Cecil Martin RC	6.00	2.70
❑ 142 Donovan McNabb RC	25.00	11.00
❑ 143 Doug Pederson	.25	.11
❑ 144 Duce Staley	1.00	.45
❑ 145 Jerome Bettis	1.00	.45
❑ 146 Kris Brown RC	6.00	2.70
❑ 147 Troy Edwards RC	12.00	5.50
❑ 148 Kordell Stewart	1.00	.45
❑ 149 Hines Ward	.25	.11
❑ 150 Amos Zereoue RC	8.00	3.60
❑ 151 Dre' Bly RC	6.00	2.70
❑ 152 Isaac Bruce	1.00	.45
❑ 153 Marshall Faulk	1.00	.45
❑ 154 Joe Germaine RC	8.00	3.60
❑ 155 Az-Zahir Hakim	.25	.11
❑ 156 Torry Holt RC	20.00	9.00
❑ 157 Kurt Warner RC	100.00	45.00
❑ 158 Justin Watson RC	6.00	2.70
❑ 159 Jermaine Fazande RC	6.00	2.70
❑ 160 Jeff Graham	.25	.11
❑ 161 Jim Harbaugh	.50	.23
❑ 162 Steve Heiden RC	4.00	1.80
❑ 163 Erik Kramer	.25	.11
❑ 164 Natrone Means	.50	.23
❑ 165 Mikhael Ricks	.25	.11
❑ 166 Junior Seau	.50	.23
❑ 167 Jeff Garcia RC	15.00	6.75
❑ 168 Charlie Garner	.50	.23
❑ 169 Terry Jackson RC	6.00	2.70
❑ 170 Terrell Owens	1.00	.45
❑ 171 Jerry Rice	2.50	1.10
❑ 172 Steve Young	1.50	.70
❑ 173 Karsten Bailey RC	8.00	3.60
❑ 174 Joey Galloway	1.00	.45
❑ 175 Brock Huard RC	8.00	3.60
❑ 176 Jon Kitna	1.25	.55
❑ 177 Derrick Mayes	.50	.23
❑ 178 Charlie Rogers RC	6.00	2.70
❑ 179 Ricky Watters	.50	.23
❑ 180 Rabih Abdullah RC	6.00	2.70
❑ 181 Mike Alstott	1.00	.45
❑ 182 Reidel Anthony	.50	.23
❑ 183 Trent Dilfer	.50	.23
❑ 184 Warrick Dunn	1.00	.45
❑ 185 Martin Gramatica RC	4.00	1.80
❑ 186 Shaun King RC	25.00	11.00
❑ 187 Darnell McDonald RC	6.00	2.70
❑ 188 Yo Murphy RC	6.00	2.70
❑ 189 Kevin Daft RC	8.00	3.60
❑ 190 Kevin Dyson	.50	.23
❑ 191 Eddie George	1.25	.55
❑ 192 Jevon Kearse RC	15.00	6.75
❑ 193 Steve McNair	1.00	.45
❑ 194 Yancey Thigpen	.25	.11
❑ 195 Champ Bailey RC	10.00	4.50
❑ 196 Albert Connell	.25	.11
❑ 197 Stephen Davis	1.00	.45
❑ 198 Skip Hicks	.50	.23
❑ 199 Brad Johnson	1.00	.45
❑ 200 Michael Westbrook	.50	.23

1999 Collector's Edge Masters HoloGold

	MINT	NRMT
COMMON CARD (1-200)	12.00	5.50
*HOLOGOLD STARS: 20X TO 50X HI COL.		
*HOLOGOLD YOUNG STARS: 15X TO 40X		
COMMON ROOKIE	15.00	6.75
*HOLOGOLD RCs: 1.5X TO 4X....		
HOLOGOLD PRINT RUN 25 SER.#'d SETS		

1999 Collector's Edge Masters HoloSilver

	MINT	NRMT
COMPLETE SET (200)	250.00	110.00
COMMON CARD (1-200)	.40	.18
*HOLOSILVER STARS: .6X TO 1.5X HI COL.		
*HOLOSILVER YOUNG STARS: .5X TO 1.2X		
COMMON ROOKIE	1.50	.70
*HOLOSILVER ROOKIES/2000: .15X TO .4X		

*HOLOSILVER ROOKIES/5000: .3X TO .8X
HOLOSILVER PRINT RUN 3500 SER.#'d SETS

1999 Collector's Edge Masters Excalibur

	MINT	NRMT
COMPLETE SET (8)	40.00	18.00
COMMON CARD	2.50	1.10
STATED PRINT RUN 5000 SER.#'d SETS		
❑ X3 Dan Marino	10.00	4.50
❑ X6 Brett Favre	10.00	4.50
❑ X7 Barry Sanders	10.00	4.50
❑ X10 Champ Bailey	2.50	1.10
❑ X12 Akili Smith	5.00	2.20
❑ X14 Tim Couch	10.00	4.50
❑ X18 Steve Young	4.00	1.80
❑ X25 Curtis Martin	2.50	1.10

1999 Collector's Edge Masters Main Event

	MINT	NRMT
COMPLETE SET (10)	50.00	22.00
COMMON CARD (ME1-ME10)	4.00	1.80
STATED PRINT RUN 1000 SER.#'d SETS		
❑ ME1 Randy Moss Jamal Anderson	12.00	5.50
❑ ME2 Mark Brunell Eddie George	6.00	2.70
❑ ME3 Terrell Davis Cecil Collins	8.00	3.60
❑ ME4 Rocket Ismail Stephen Davis	4.00	1.80
❑ ME5 Troy Edwards Kevin Johnson	8.00	3.60
❑ ME6 Antonio Freeman Charlie Batch	6.00	2.70
❑ ME7 Terry Glenn Marvin Harrison	4.00	1.80
❑ ME8 Keyshawn Johnson Doug Flutie	6.00	2.70
❑ ME9 Cade McNown Ricky Williams	15.00	6.75
❑ ME10 Steve Young Marshall Faulk	6.00	2.70

1999 Collector's Edge Masters Majestic

	MINT	NRMT
COMPLETE SET (30)	100.00	45.00
COMMON CARD (M1-M30)	1.25	.55
SEMISTARS	2.50	1.10
STATED PRINT RUN 3000 SER. #'d SETS		
❑ M1 Jake Plummer	4.00	1.80
❑ M2 David Boston	3.00	1.35
❑ M3 Doug Flutie	3.00	1.35
❑ M4 Eric Moulds	2.50	1.10
❑ M5 Peerless Price	3.00	1.35
❑ M6 Tim Biakabutuka	1.25	.55
❑ M7 Troy Aikman	6.00	2.70
❑ M8 Olandis Gary	6.00	2.70

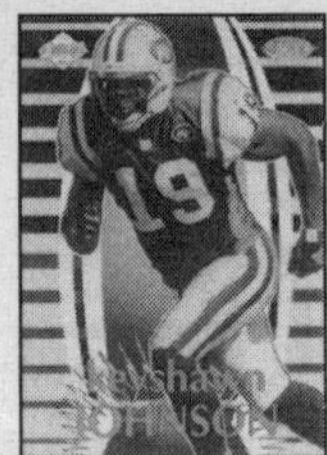

❑ M9 Brian Griese	4.00	1.80
❑ M10 Charlie Batch	4.00	1.80
❑ M11 Antonio Freeman	2.50	1.10
❑ M12 Peyton Manning	8.00	3.60
❑ M13 Edgerrin James	15.00	6.75
❑ M14 Marvin Harrison	2.50	1.10
❑ M15 Fred Taylor	5.00	2.20
❑ M16 Daunte Culpepper	6.00	2.70
❑ M17 Terry Glenn	2.50	1.10
❑ M18 Keyshawn Johnson	2.50	1.10
❑ M19 Curtis Martin	2.50	1.10
❑ M20 Donovan McNabb	6.00	2.70
❑ M21 Kordell Stewart	2.50	1.10
❑ M22 Torry Holt	5.00	2.20
❑ M23 Marshall Faulk	2.50	1.10
❑ M24 Kurt Warner	40.00	18.00
❑ M25 Jerry Rice	6.00	2.70
❑ M26 Jon Kitna	3.00	1.35
❑ M27 Eddie George	3.00	1.35
❑ M28 Champ Bailey	2.50	1.10
❑ M29 Brad Johnson	2.50	1.10
❑ M30 Stephen Davis	2.50	1.10

1999 Collector's Edge Masters Master Legends

	MINT	NRMT
COMPLETE SET (20)	150.00	70.00
COMMON CARD (ML1-ML20)	4.00	1.80
STATED PRINT RUN 1000 SER.#'d SETS		

❑ ML1 Doug Flutie	5.00	2.20
❑ ML2 Troy Aikman	10.00	4.50
❑ ML3 Emmitt Smith	10.00	4.50
❑ ML4 Terrell Davis	10.00	4.50
❑ ML5 Charlie Batch	6.00	2.70
❑ ML6 Barry Sanders	15.00	6.75
❑ ML7 Brett Favre	15.00	6.75
❑ ML8 Antonio Freeman	4.00	1.80
❑ ML9 Peyton Manning	12.00	5.50
❑ ML10 Mark Brunell	6.00	2.70
❑ ML11 Fred Taylor	8.00	3.60
❑ ML12 Dan Marino	15.00	6.75
❑ ML13 Randy Moss	12.00	5.50
❑ ML14 Drew Bledsoe	6.00	2.70
❑ ML15 Kurt Warner	40.00	18.00
❑ ML16 Marshall Faulk	4.00	1.80
❑ ML17 Steve Young	6.00	2.70
❑ ML18 Jerry Rice	10.00	4.50
❑ ML19 Jon Kitna	5.00	2.20
❑ ML20 Eddie George	5.00	2.20

1999 Collector's Edge Masters Pro Signature Authentics

	MINT	NRMT
COMPLETE SET (2)	250.00	110.00
COMMON CARD	100.00	45.00
STATED PRINT RUN 500 SER.#'d SETS		
MANNING 1B/C/D ISSUED AS MAIL REDEMP.		

❑ 1A Peyton Manning/500	100.00	45.00
❑ 1B Peyton Manning/445	100.00	45.00
❑ 1C Peyton Manning/40	175.00	80.00
❑ 1D Peyton Manning/10 Red		
❑ 2 Kurt Warner	175.00	80.00

1999 Collector's Edge Masters Quest

	MINT	NRMT
COMPLETE SET (20)	40.00	18.00
COMMON CARD (Q1-Q20)	1.25	.55
SEMISTARS	2.50	1.10
STATED PRINT RUN 3000 SER.#'d SETS		

❑ Q1 Jake Plummer	4.00	1.80
❑ Q2 Eric Moulds	2.50	1.10
❑ Q3 Curtis Enis	2.50	1.10
❑ Q4 Emmitt Smith	6.00	2.70
❑ Q5 Brian Griese	4.00	1.80
❑ Q6 Dorsey Levens	2.50	1.10
❑ Q7 Marvin Harrison	2.50	1.10
❑ Q8 Mark Brunell	4.00	1.80
❑ Q9 Fred Taylor	5.00	2.20
❑ Q10 Cris Carter	2.50	1.10
❑ Q11 Terry Glenn	2.50	1.10
❑ Q12 Keyshawn Johnson	2.50	1.10
❑ Q13 Isaac Bruce	2.50	1.10
❑ Q14 Terrell Owens	2.50	1.10
❑ Q15 Jon Kitna	3.00	1.35
❑ Q16 Natrone Means	1.25	.55
❑ Q17 Warrick Dunn	2.50	1.10
❑ Q18 Steve McNair	2.50	1.10
❑ Q19 Brad Johnson	2.50	1.10
❑ Q20 Stephen Davis	2.50	1.10

1999 Collector's Edge Masters Rookie Masters

	MINT	NRMT
COMPLETE SET (30)	80.00	36.00
COMMON CARD (RM1-RM30)	1.50	.70
SEMISTARS	2.00	.90
STATED PRINT RUN 3000 SER.#'d SETS		

❑ RM1 David Boston	3.00	1.35
❑ RM2 Chris McAlister	1.50	.70
❑ RM3 Peerless Price	3.00	1.35
❑ RM4 D'Wayne Bates	3.00	1.35
❑ RM5 Cade McNown	6.00	2.70
❑ RM6 Akili Smith	4.00	1.80
❑ RM7 Tim Couch	10.00	4.50
❑ RM8 Kevin Johnson	5.00	2.20

❑ RM9 Wane McGarity	1.50	.70
❑ RM10 Chris Claiborne	1.50	.70
❑ RM11 Sedrick Irvin	2.50	1.10
❑ RM12 Edgerrin James	15.00	6.75
❑ RM13 Mike Cloud	2.00	.90
❑ RM14 Cecil Collins	2.00	.90
❑ RM15 James Johnson	2.50	1.10
❑ RM16 Rob Konrad	2.00	.90
❑ RM17 Daunte Culpepper	6.00	2.70
❑ RM18 Kevin Faulk	2.50	1.10
❑ RM19 Andy Katzenmoyer	2.00	.90
❑ RM20 Ricky Williams	10.00	4.50
❑ RM21 Donovan McNabb	6.00	2.70
❑ RM22 Troy Edwards	3.00	1.35
❑ RM23 Amos Zereoue	2.00	.90
❑ RM24 Joe Germaine	2.00	.90
❑ RM25 Torry Holt	5.00	2.20
❑ RM26 Karsten Bailey	2.00	.90
❑ RM27 Brock Huard	2.50	1.10
❑ RM28 Shaun King	6.00	2.70
❑ RM29 Jevon Kearse	4.00	1.80
❑ RM30 Champ Bailey	2.50	1.10

1999 Collector's Edge Masters Sentinels

	MINT	NRMT
COMPLETE SET (20)	250.00	110.00
COMMON CARD (S1-S20)	6.00	2.70
STATED PRINT RUN 500 SER.#'d SETS		

❑ S1 Troy Aikman	15.00	6.75
❑ S2 Emmitt Smith	15.00	6.75
❑ S3 Terrell Davis	15.00	6.75
❑ S4 Barry Sanders	25.00	11.00
❑ S5 Brett Favre	25.00	11.00
❑ S6 Peyton Manning	20.00	9.00
❑ S7 Dan Marino	25.00	11.00
❑ S8 Randy Moss	20.00	9.00
❑ S9 Drew Bledsoe	10.00	4.50
❑ S10 Isaac Bruce	6.00	2.70
❑ S11 Kurt Warner	50.00	22.00
❑ S12 David Boston	6.00	2.70
❑ S13 Cade McNown	12.00	5.50
❑ S14 Akili Smith	8.00	3.60
❑ S15 Tim Couch	20.00	9.00
❑ S16 Edgerrin James	30.00	13.50
❑ S17 Ricky Williams	20.00	9.00
❑ S18 Donovan McNabb	12.00	5.50
❑ S19 Troy Edwards	6.00	2.70
❑ S20 Torry Holt	10.00	4.50

1998 Collector's Edge Odyssey

	MINT	NRMT
COMPLETE SET (250)	400.00	180.00
COMMON CARD (1-150)	.10	.05
SEMISTARS 1-150	.20	.09
UNLISTED STARS 1-150	.40	.18
COMMON ROOKIE	2.00	.90
COMMON CARD (151-200)	.60	.25
151-200 STATED ODDS 1:1.5		
COMMON CARD (201-230)	.75	.35
201-230 STATED ODDS 1:3		
COMMON CARD (231-250)	2.50	1.10
231-250 STATED ODDS 1:18		

❑ 1 Terance Mathis .20 .09
❑ 2 Tony Martin .20 .09
❑ 3 Chris Chandler .20 .09
❑ 4 Jamal Anderson .40 .18
❑ 5 Jake Plummer 1.00 .45
❑ 6 Adrian Murrell .20 .09
❑ 7 Rob Moore .20 .09
❑ 8 Frank Sanders .20 .09
❑ 9 Larry Centers .10 .05
❑ 10 Andre Wadsworth RC 2.00 .90
❑ 11 Jim Harbaugh .20 .09
❑ 12 Errict Rhett .20 .09
❑ 13 Jermaine Lewis .20 .09
❑ 14 Michael Jackson .10 .05
❑ 15 Eric Zeier .20 .09
❑ 16 Rob Johnson .20 .09
❑ 17 Antowain Smith .40 .18
❑ 18 Andre Reed .20 .09
❑ 19 Bruce Smith .20 .09
❑ 20 Doug Flutie .40 .18
❑ 21 Thurman Thomas .40 .18
❑ 22 Kerry Collins .20 .09
❑ 23 Fred Lane .20 .09
❑ 24 Muhsin Muhammad .20 .09
❑ 25 Rae Carruth .20 .09
❑ 26 Rocket Ismail .10 .05
❑ 27 Kevin Greene .20 .09
❑ 28 Curtis Enis RC 3.00 1.35
❑ 29 Curtis Conway .20 .09
❑ 30 Erik Kramer .10 .05
❑ 31 Edgar Bennett .10 .05
❑ 32 Neil O'Donnell .20 .09
❑ 33 Jeff Blake .20 .09
❑ 34 Carl Pickens .40 .18
❑ 35 Corey Dillon .50 .23
❑ 36 Troy Aikman 1.00 .45
❑ 37 Jason Garrett .10 .05
❑ 38 Emmitt Smith 1.50 .70
❑ 39 Deion Sanders .40 .18
❑ 40 Michael Irvin .40 .18
❑ 41 Chris Warren .20 .09
❑ 42 John Elway 2.00 .90
❑ 43 Terrell Davis 1.50 .70
❑ 44 Shannon Sharpe .20 .09
❑ 45 Rod Smith WR .20 .09
❑ 46 Marcus Nash RC 2.00 .90
❑ 47 Brian Griese RC 4.00 1.80
❑ 48 Barry Sanders 2.00 .90
❑ 49 Herman Moore .40 .18
❑ 50 Scott Mitchell .20 .09
❑ 51 Johnnie Morton .20 .09
❑ 52 Rashaan Shehee RC 2.00 .90
❑ 53 Charlie Batch RC 4.00 1.80
❑ 54 Brett Favre 2.00 .90
❑ 55 Dorsey Levens .40 .18
❑ 56 Antonio Freeman .40 .18
❑ 57 Reggie White .40 .18
❑ 58 Robert Brooks .20 .09
❑ 59 Raymont Harris .10 .05
❑ 60 Peyton Manning RC 12.00 5.50
❑ 61 Marshall Faulk .40 .18
❑ 62 Jerome Pathon RC 2.00 .90
❑ 63 Marvin Harrison .20 .09
❑ 64 Mark Brunell .75 .35
❑ 65 Fred Taylor RC 6.00 2.70
❑ 66 Jimmy Smith .20 .09
❑ 67 James Stewart .20 .09
❑ 68 Keenan McCardell .20 .09
❑ 69 Andre Rison .20 .09
❑ 70 Elvis Grbac .20 .09
❑ 71 Donnell Bennett .10 .05
❑ 72 Rich Gannon .10 .05
❑ 73 Derrick Thomas .20 .09
❑ 74 Dan Marino 2.00 .90
❑ 75 Karim Abdul-Jabbar UER .40 .18
no first name on cardfront
❑ 76 John Avery RC 2.00 .90
UER photo Karim Abdul-Jabbar
❑ 77 O.J. McDuffie .20 .09
❑ 78 Oronde Gadsden RC 2.00 .90
❑ 79 Zach Thomas .10 .05
❑ 80 Randy Moss RC 12.00 5.50
❑ 81 Cris Carter .40 .18
❑ 82 Jake Reed .20 .09
❑ 83 Robert Smith .40 .18
❑ 84 Brad Johnson .40 .18
❑ 85 Drew Bledsoe .75 .35
❑ 86 Robert Edwards RC 2.00 .90
❑ 87 Terry Glenn .40 .18
❑ 88 Troy Brown .10 .05
❑ 89 Shawn Jefferson .10 .05
❑ 90 Danny Wuerffel .20 .09
❑ 91 Dana Stubblefield .10 .05
❑ 92 Derrick Alexander .20 .09
❑ 93 Ray Zellars .10 .05
❑ 94 Andre Hastings .10 .05
❑ 95 Danny Kanell .20 .09
❑ 96 Tiki Barber .20 .09
❑ 97 Ike Hilliard .20 .09
❑ 98 Charles Way .10 .05
❑ 99 Chris Calloway .10 .05
❑ 100 Curtis Martin .40 .18
❑ 101 Glenn Foley .20 .09
❑ 102 Vinny Testaverde .20 .09
❑ 103 Keyshawn Johnson .40 .18
❑ 104 Wayne Chrebet .40 .18
❑ 105 Leon Johnson .10 .05
❑ 106 Jeff George .20 .09
❑ 107 Charles Woodson RC 3.00 1.35
❑ 108 Tim Brown .40 .18
❑ 109 James Jett .20 .09
❑ 110 Napoleon Kaufman .40 .18
❑ 111 Charlie Garner .10 .05
❑ 112 Bobby Hoying .20 .09
❑ 113 Duce Staley .75 .35
❑ 114 Irving Fryar .20 .09
❑ 115 Kordell Stewart .40 .18
❑ 116 Jerome Bettis .40 .18
❑ 117 Charles Johnson .10 .05
❑ 118 Randall Cunningham .40 .18
❑ 119 Courtney Hawkins .10 .05
❑ 120 Tony Banks .20 .09
❑ 121 Isaac Bruce .40 .18
❑ 122 Robert Holcombe RC 2.00 .90
❑ 123 Eddie Kennison .20 .09
❑ 124 Ryan Leaf RC 2.50 1.10
❑ 125 Mikhael Ricks RC 2.00 .90
❑ 126 Natrone Means .40 .18
❑ 127 Junior Seau .20 .09
❑ 128 Jerry Rice 1.00 .45
❑ 129 Terrell Owens .40 .18
❑ 130 Garrison Hearst .40 .18
❑ 131 Steve Young .50 .23
❑ 132 J.J. Stokes .20 .09
❑ 133 Warren Moon .40 .18
❑ 134 Joey Galloway .40 .18
❑ 135 Ricky Watters .20 .09
❑ 136 Ahman Green RC 2.00 .90
❑ 137 Trent Dilfer .40 .18
❑ 138 Mike Alstott .40 .18
❑ 139 Warrick Dunn .50 .23
❑ 140 Reidel Anthony .20 .09
❑ 141 Jacquez Green RC 2.50 1.10
❑ 142 Steve McNair .40 .18
❑ 143 Eddie George .75 .35
❑ 144 Yancey Thigpen .10 .05
❑ 145 Kevin Dyson RC 2.50 1.10
❑ 146 Trent Green .60 .25
❑ 147 Gus Frerotte .10 .05
❑ 148 Terry Allen .40 .18
❑ 149 Michael Westbrook .20 .09
❑ 150 Jim Druckenmiller .20 .09
❑ 151 Jake Plummer 2Q 1.50 .70
❑ 152 Adrian Murrell 2Q .60 .25
❑ 153 Rob Johnson 2Q .60 .25
❑ 154 Antowain Smith 2Q .60 .25
❑ 155 Kerry Collins 2Q .60 .25
❑ 156 Curtis Enis 2Q 5.00 2.20
❑ 157 Carl Pickens 2Q .60 .25
❑ 158 Corey Dillon 2Q .75 .35
❑ 159 Troy Aikman 2Q 1.50 .70
❑ 160 Emmitt Smith 2Q 2.00 .90
❑ 161 Deion Sanders 2Q .60 .25
❑ 162 Michael Irvin 2Q .60 .25
❑ 163 John Elway 2Q 3.00 1.35
❑ 164 Terrell Davis 2Q 2.00 .90
❑ 165 Shannon Sharpe 2Q .60 .25
❑ 166 Rod Smith 2Q .60 .25
❑ 167 Barry Sanders 2Q 3.00 1.35
❑ 168 Herman Moore 2Q .60 .25
❑ 169 Brett Favre 2Q 3.00 1.35
❑ 170 Dorsey Levens 2Q .60 .25
❑ 171 Antonio Freeman 2Q .60 .25
❑ 172 Peyton Manning 2Q 15.00 6.75
❑ 173 Marshall Faulk 2Q .60 .25
❑ 174 Mark Brunell 2Q 1.00 .45
❑ 175 Fred Taylor 2Q 8.00 3.60
❑ 176 Dan Marino 2Q 3.00 1.35
❑ 177 Randy Moss 2Q 15.00 6.75
❑ 178 Cris Carter 2Q .60 .25
❑ 179 Drew Bledsoe 2Q 1.00 .45
❑ 180 Robert Edwards 2Q 2.00 .90
❑ 181 Curtis Martin 2Q .60 .25
❑ 182 Napoleon Kaufman 2Q .60 .25
❑ 183 Kordell Stewart 2Q .60 .25
❑ 184 Jerome Bettis 2Q .60 .25
❑ 185 Tony Banks 2Q .60 .25
❑ 186 Isaac Bruce 2Q .60 .25
❑ 187 Ryan Leaf 2Q 5.00 2.20
❑ 188 Natrone Means 2Q .60 .25
❑ 189 Jerry Rice 2Q 1.50 .70
❑ 190 Terrell Owens 2Q .60 .25
❑ 191 Garrison Hearst 2Q .60 .25
❑ 192 Steve Young 2Q .75 .35
❑ 193 Warren Moon 2Q .60 .25
❑ 194 Joey Galloway 2Q .60 .25
❑ 195 Trent Dilfer 2Q .60 .25
❑ 196 Mike Alstott 2Q .60 .25
❑ 197 Warrick Dunn 2Q .75 .35
❑ 198 Steve McNair 2Q .60 .25
❑ 199 Eddie George 2Q 1.00 .45
❑ 200 Terry Allen 2Q .60 .25
❑ 201 Jake Plummer 3Q 2.00 .90
❑ 202 Curtis Enis 3Q 6.00 2.70
❑ 203 Carl Pickens 3Q .75 .35
❑ 204 Corey Dillon 3Q 1.00 .45
❑ 205 Troy Aikman 3Q 2.00 .90
❑ 206 Emmitt Smith 3Q 3.00 1.35
❑ 207 John Elway 3Q 4.00 1.80
❑ 208 Terrell Davis 3Q 3.00 1.35
❑ 209 Barry Sanders 3Q 4.00 1.80
❑ 210 Brett Favre 3Q 4.00 1.80
❑ 211 Antonio Freeman 3Q .75 .35
❑ 212 Peyton Manning 3Q 20.00 9.00
❑ 213 Mark Brunell 3Q 1.50 .70
❑ 214 Fred Taylor 3Q 10.00 4.50
❑ 215 Dan Marino 3Q 4.00 1.80
❑ 216 Randy Moss 3Q 20.00 9.00
❑ 217 Drew Bledsoe 3Q 1.50 .70
❑ 218 Robert Edwards 3Q 2.50 1.10
❑ 219 Curtis Martin 3Q .75 .35
❑ 220 Kordell Stewart 3Q .75 .35
❑ 221 Jerome Bettis 3Q .75 .35
❑ 222 Tony Banks 3Q .75 .35
❑ 223 Ryan Leaf 3Q 6.00 2.70
❑ 224 Jerry Rice 3Q 2.00 .90
❑ 225 Steve Young 3Q 1.00 .45
❑ 226 Warren Moon 3Q .75 .35
❑ 227 Trent Dilfer 3Q .75 .35
❑ 228 Warrick Dunn 3Q 1.00 .45
❑ 229 Steve McNair 3Q .75 .35
❑ 230 Eddie George 3Q 1.50 .70
❑ 231 Curtis Enis 4Q 10.00 4.50
❑ 232 Carl Pickens 4Q 2.50 1.10
❑ 233 Troy Aikman 4Q 6.00 2.70
❑ 234 Emmitt Smith 4Q 10.00 4.50
❑ 235 John Elway 4Q 12.00 5.50
❑ 236 Terrell Davis 4Q 10.00 4.50
❑ 237 Barry Sanders 4Q 12.00 5.50
❑ 238 Brett Favre 4Q 12.00 5.50

	MINT	NRMT
❑ 239 Peyton Manning 4Q	30.00	13.50
❑ 240 Fred Taylor 4Q	15.00	6.75
❑ 241 Dan Marino 4Q	12.00	5.50
❑ 242 Randy Moss 4Q	30.00	13.50
❑ 243 Drew Bledsoe 4Q	5.00	2.20
❑ 244 Kordell Stewart 4Q	2.50	1.10
❑ 245 Jerome Bettis 4Q	2.50	1.10
❑ 246 Ryan Leaf 4Q	10.00	4.50
❑ 247 Jerry Rice 4Q	6.00	2.70
❑ 248 Steve Young 4Q	4.00	1.80
❑ 249 Warren Moon 4Q	2.50	1.10
❑ 250 Eddie George 4Q	5.00	2.20

1998 Collector's Edge Odyssey Level 1 Galvanized

	MINT	NRMT
COMPLETE SET (250)	800.00	350.00
COMMON GALVAN. (1-150)	.30	.14

*STARS 1-150: 1.25X TO 3X HI COL.
*YOUNG STARS 1-150: 1X TO 2.5X
*RCs 1-150: .6X TO 1.5X
GALVANIZED 1-150 STATED ODDS 1:3

COMMON GALVAN.(151-200)	2.00	.90

*STARS 151-200: 1.5X TO 4X HI COL.
*YOUNG STARS 151-200: 1.25X TO 3X
*ROOKIES 151-200: .75X TO 2X..
GALVANIZED 151-200 STATED ODDS 1:15

COMMON GALVAN.(201-230)	2.00	.90

*STARS 201-230: 1.5X TO 3X HI COL.
*YOUNG STARS 201-230: 1.25X TO 2.5X
*ROOKIES 201-230: .6X TO 1.5X
GALVANIZED 201-230 STATED ODDS 1:29

COMMON GALVAN.(231-250)	5.00	2.20

*STARS 231-250: .75X TO 2X HI COL.
*ROOKIES 231-250: .5X TO 1X....
GALVANIZED 231-250 STATED ODDS 1:59
GALVANIZED CARDS HAVE "G" ON BACK

1998 Collector's Edge Odyssey Level 2 HoloGold

	MINT	NRMT
COMMON HOLOGOLD (1-150)	3.00	1.35

*STARS 1-150: 12.5X TO 30X HI COL.
*YOUNG STARS 1-150: 10X TO 25X
*ROOKIES 1-150: 4X TO 10X ......
HOLO.GOLD 1-150 STATED ODDS 1:34
HOLO.GOLD 1-150 PRINT RUN 150 SETS

COMMON HOLOGOLD (151-200)	30.00	13.50

*STARS 151-200: 20X TO 50X HI COL.
*YOUNG STARS 151-200: 15X TO 40X
*RCs 151-200: 6X TO 15X ....
HOLO.GOLD 151-200 STATED ODDS 1:307
HOLO.GOLD 151-200 PRINT RUN 50 SETS

COMMON HOLOGOLD (201-230)	60.00	27.00

*STARS 201-230: 35X TO 80X HI COL.
*YOUNG STARS 201-230: 25X TO 60X
*RCs 201-230: 10X TO 25X ....
HOLO.GOLD 201-230 STATED ODDS 1:840
HOLO.GOLD 201-230 PRINT RUN 30 SETS

COMMON HOLO.GOLD (231-250)	100.00	45.00

*STARS 231-250: 15X TO 40X HI COL.
*RCs 231-250: 5X TO 12X ....
HOLO.GOLD 231-250 STATED ODDS 1:1920
HOLO.GOLD 231-250 PRINT RUN 20 SETS
HOLOFOIL GOLDS HAVE "H" ON BACK

1998 Collector's Edge Odyssey Double Edge

	MINT	NRMT
COMPLETE SET (12)	80.00	36.00
COMMON CARD (1-12)	4.00	1.80
SEMISTARS	6.00	2.70
STATED ODDS 1:15		

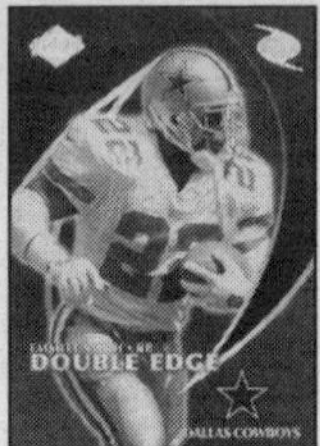

	MINT	NRMT
❑ 1 Jerry Rice Randy Moss	25.00	11.00
❑ 2 Brett Favre Ryan Leaf	15.00	6.75
❑ 3 Dan Marino Bobby Hoying	12.00	5.50
❑ 4 Deion Sanders Charles Woodson	4.00	1.80
❑ 5 Terrell Davis Curtis Enis	12.00	5.50
❑ 6 Barry Sanders Fred Taylor	15.00	6.75
❑ 7 Emmitt Smith Robert Edwards	10.00	4.50
❑ 8 John Elway Brian Griese	15.00	6.75
❑ 9 Reggie White Andre Wadsworth	4.00	1.80
❑ 10 Drew Bledsoe Charlie Batch	10.00	4.50
❑ 11 Doug Flutie Glenn Foley	4.00	1.80
❑ 12 Napoleon Kaufman Warrick Dunn	4.00	1.80

1998 Collector's Edge Odyssey Game Ball Redemption

	MINT	NRMT
COMPLETE SET (9)	400.00	180.00
COMMON CARD (1-12)	25.00	11.00
STATED ODDS 1:360		
❑ 1 Troy Aikman	40.00	18.00
❑ 4 Cris Carter	25.00	11.00
❑ 5 Terrell Davis	60.00	27.00
❑ 6 John Elway	80.00	36.00
❑ 7 Peyton Manning	100.00	45.00
❑ 8 Herman Moore	25.00	11.00
❑ 10 Barry Sanders	80.00	36.00
❑ 11 Emmitt Smith	40.00	18.00
❑ 12 Fred Taylor	50.00	22.00

1998 Collector's Edge Odyssey Leading Edge

	MINT	NRMT
COMPLETE SET (30)	80.00	36.00
COMMON CARD (1-30)	1.00	.45
STATED ODDS 1:7		
❑ 1 Jake Plummer	2.50	1.10
❑ 2 Rob Johnson	1.00	.45
❑ 3 Curtis Enis	3.00	1.35
❑ 4 Carl Pickens	1.00	.45
❑ 5 Troy Aikman	3.00	1.35
❑ 6 Emmitt Smith	5.00	2.20
❑ 7 John Elway	6.00	2.70
❑ 8 Terrell Davis	5.00	2.20
❑ 9 Shannon Sharpe	1.00	.45
❑ 10 Barry Sanders	6.00	2.70
❑ 11 Brett Favre	6.00	2.70
❑ 12 Antonio Freeman	1.00	.45
❑ 13 Peyton Manning	12.00	5.50
❑ 14 Marshall Faulk	1.00	.45
❑ 15 Mark Brunell	2.50	1.10
❑ 16 Dan Marino	6.00	2.70
❑ 17 Randy Moss	12.00	5.50
❑ 18 Cris Carter	1.00	.45
❑ 19 Robert Edwards	1.25	.55
❑ 20 Curtis Martin	1.00	.45
❑ 21 Ryan Leaf	2.50	1.10
❑ 22 Terrell Owens	1.00	.45
❑ 23 Garrison Hearst	1.00	.45
❑ 24 Steve Young	2.00	.90
❑ 25 Joey Galloway	1.00	.45
❑ 26 Mike Alstott	1.00	.45
❑ 27 Warrick Dunn	2.00	.90
❑ 28 Eddie George	2.50	1.10
❑ 29 Kevin Dyson	2.50	1.10
❑ 30 Terry Allen	1.00	.45

1998 Collector's Edge Odyssey Prodigies

	MINT	NRMT
COMPLETE SET (31)	800.00	350.00
COMMON CARD (1-31)	10.00	4.50
SEMISTARS	15.00	6.75
UNLISTED STARS	20.00	9.00
STATED ODDS 1:24		

*RED SIGNATURES: .75X TO 2X HI COL.
RED INK PRINT RUN 50-80 SER.#'d SETS
ELWAY RED INK PRINT RUN 13
T.DAVIS RED INK PRINT RUN 10
SET PRICE EXCLUDES ELWAY AND DAVIS!
ELWAY/T.DAVIS INSERTS IN 98 CE MASTERS

	MINT	NRMT
❑ 1 Tavian Banks	15.00	6.75
❑ 2 Charlie Batch	40.00	18.00
❑ 3 Blaine Bishop	10.00	4.50
❑ 4 Robert Brooks	40.00	18.00
❑ 5 Tim Brown	80.00	36.00
❑ 6 Mark Brunell	100.00	45.00
❑ 7 Wayne Chrebet	25.00	11.00
❑ 8 Terrell Davis Blue/40	200.00	90.00
❑ 9 Jim Druckenmiller	15.00	6.75
❑ 10 Robert Edwards	20.00	9.00
❑ 11 John Elway Blue/40	350.00	160.00
❑ 12 Doug Flutie	50.00	22.00
❑ 13 Oronde Gadsden	15.00	6.75
❑ 14 Joey Galloway	20.00	9.00
❑ 15 Garrison Hearst	20.00	9.00
❑ 16 Robert Holcombe	20.00	9.00
❑ 17 Joey Kent	15.00	6.75
❑ 18 Jon Kitna	25.00	11.00
❑ 19 Ryan Leaf	40.00	18.00
❑ 20 Peyton Manning	120.00	55.00
❑ 21 Herman Moore	40.00	18.00

	MINT	NRMT
❑ 22 Randy Moss	100.00	45.00
❑ 23 Terrell Owens	20.00	9.00
❑ 24 Mikhael Ricks	15.00	6.75
❑ 25 Antowain Smith	25.00	11.00
❑ 26 Emmitt Smith	150.00	70.00
❑ 27 Robert Smith	20.00	9.00
❑ 28 Rod Smith	15.00	6.75
❑ 29 J.J. Stokes	15.00	6.75
❑ 30 Fred Taylor	50.00	22.00
❑ 31 Derrick Thomas	40.00	18.00
❑ 32 Chris Warren	15.00	6.75
❑ 33 Eric Zeier	15.00	6.75

1998 Collector's Edge Odyssey S.L. Edge

	MINT	NRMT
COMPLETE SET (12)	150.00	70.00
COMMON CARD (1-12)	8.00	3.60
STATED ODDS 1:99		
❑ 1 Emmitt Smith	20.00	9.00
❑ 2 Deion Sanders	8.00	3.60
❑ 3 John Elway	25.00	11.00
❑ 4 Brett Favre	25.00	11.00
❑ 5 Antonio Freeman	8.00	3.60
❑ 6 Peyton Manning	25.00	11.00
❑ 7 Mark Brunell	10.00	4.50
❑ 8 Dan Marino	25.00	11.00
❑ 9 Randy Moss	25.00	11.00
❑ 10 Joey Galloway	8.00	3.60
❑ 11 Mike Alstott	8.00	3.60
❑ 12 Eddie George	10.00	4.50

1999 Collector's Edge Odyssey

	MINT	NRMT
COMPLETE SET (193)	150.00	70.00
COMP.SET w/o SP's (148)	40.00	18.00
COMMON CARD (1-149)	.15	.07
SEMISTARS	.30	.14
UNLISTED STARS	.60	.25
COMMON ROOKIE	.75	.35
ROOKIE SEMISTARS	1.00	.45
COMMON CARD (151-170)	1.00	.45
SEMISTARS 151-170	1.25	.55
151-170 STATED ODDS 1:4		
COMMON CARD (171-185)	3.00	1.35
171-185 STATED ODDS 1:8		
COMMON CARD (186-195)	5.00	2.20
186-195 STATED ODDS 1:24		
CARDS 21 AND 55 NOT ISSUED		

	MINT	NRMT
❑ 1 Checklist Card	.15	.07
❑ 2 Checklist Card	.15	.07
❑ 3 David Boston RC	1.50	.70
❑ 4 Rob Moore	.30	.14
❑ 5 Adrian Murrell	.30	.14
❑ 6 Jake Plummer	1.00	.45
❑ 7 Frank Sanders	.30	.14
❑ 8 Jamal Anderson	.60	.25
❑ 9 Chris Calloway	.15	.07
❑ 10 Chris Chandler	.30	.14
❑ 11 Tim Dwight	.60	.25
❑ 12 Terance Mathis	.30	.14
❑ 13 Tony Banks	.30	.14
❑ 14 Priest Holmes	.60	.25
❑ 15 Jermaine Lewis	.30	.14
❑ 16 Chris McAlister RC	.75	.35
❑ 17 Scott Mitchell	.30	.14
❑ 18 Doug Flutie	.75	.35
❑ 19 Eric Moulds	.60	.25
❑ 20 Peerless Price RC	1.50	.70
❑ 22 Antowain Smith	.60	.25
❑ 23 Antoine Winfield RC	.75	.35
❑ 24 Steve Beuerlein	.30	.14
❑ 25 Tim Biakabutuka	.30	.14
❑ 26 Rae Carruth	.15	.07
❑ 27 Muhsin Muhammad	.30	.14
❑ 28 D'Wayne Bates RC	.75	.35
❑ 29 Bobby Engram	.30	.14
❑ 30 Curtis Enis	.60	.25
❑ 31 Shane Matthews	.60	.25
❑ 32 Cade McNown RC	3.00	1.35
❑ 33 Jeff Blake	.30	.14
❑ 34 Corey Dillon	.60	.25
❑ 35 Carl Pickens	.30	.14
❑ 36 Darnay Scott	.30	.14
❑ 37 Akili Smith RC	2.00	.90
❑ 38 Tim Couch RC	5.00	2.20
❑ 39 Kevin Johnson RC	2.50	1.10
❑ 40 Terry Kirby	.30	.14
❑ 41 Leslie Shepherd	.15	.07
❑ 42 Troy Aikman	1.50	.70
❑ 43 Michael Irvin	.30	.14
❑ 44 Rocket Ismail	.30	.14
❑ 45 Deion Sanders	.60	.25
❑ 46 Emmitt Smith	1.50	.70
❑ 47 Bubby Brister	.30	.14
❑ 48 Terrell Davis	1.50	.70
❑ 49 Brian Griese	1.25	.55
❑ 50 Ed McCaffrey	.30	.14
❑ 51 Shannon Sharpe	.30	.14
❑ 52 Rod Smith	.30	.14
❑ 53 Charlie Batch	1.25	.55
❑ 54 Chris Claiborne RC	1.00	.45
❑ 56 Herman Moore	.60	.25
❑ 57 Johnnie Morton	.30	.14
❑ 58 Ron Rivers	.15	.07
❑ 59 Brett Favre	2.50	1.10
❑ 60 Mark Chmura	.30	.14
❑ 61 Antonio Freeman	.60	.25
❑ 62 Dorsey Levens	.60	.25
❑ 63 E.G. Green	.15	.07
❑ 64 Marvin Harrison	.60	.25
❑ 65 Edgerrin James RC	10.00	4.50
❑ 66 Peyton Manning	2.50	1.10
❑ 67 Mark Brunell	1.00	.45
❑ 68 Keenan McCardell	.30	.14
❑ 69 Jimmy Smith	.30	.14
❑ 70 Fred Taylor	1.50	.70
❑ 71 Derrick Alexander WR	.30	.14
❑ 72 Kimble Anders	.30	.14
❑ 73 Mike Cloud RC	1.00	.45
❑ 74 Elvis Grbac	.30	.14
❑ 75 Andre Rison	.30	.14
❑ 76 Karim Abdul-Jabbar	.30	.14
❑ 77 Cecil Collins RC	.75	.35
❑ 78 James Johnson RC	1.25	.55
❑ 79 Rob Konrad RC	1.00	.45
❑ 80 Dan Marino	2.50	1.10
❑ 81 O.J. McDuffie	.30	.14
❑ 82 Cris Carter	.60	.25
❑ 83 Daunte Culpepper RC	3.00	1.35
❑ 84 Randall Cunningham	.60	.25
❑ 85 Randy Moss	2.50	1.10
❑ 86 Jake Reed	.30	.14
❑ 87 Robert Smith	.60	.25
❑ 88 Terry Allen	.30	.14
❑ 89 Drew Bledsoe	1.00	.45
❑ 90 Ben Coates	.15	.07
❑ 91 Kevin Faulk RC	1.25	.55
❑ 92 Terry Glenn	.60	.25
❑ 93 Andy Katzenmoyer RC	1.00	.45
❑ 94 Cameron Cleeland	.15	.07
❑ 95 Billy Joe Hobert	.15	.07
❑ 96 Eddie Kennison	.30	.14
❑ 97 Ricky Williams RC	5.00	2.20
❑ 98 Sean Bennett RC	1.00	.45
❑ 99 Gary Brown	.15	.07
❑ 100 Kerry Collins	.30	.14
❑ 101 Kent Graham	.15	.07
❑ 102 Ike Hilliard	.30	.14
❑ 103 Wayne Chrebet	.60	.25
❑ 104 Keyshawn Johnson	.60	.25
❑ 105 Curtis Martin	.60	.25
❑ 106 Rick Mirer	.30	.14
❑ 107 Tim Brown	.60	.25
❑ 108 Rich Gannon	.30	.14
❑ 109 Napoleon Kaufman	.60	.25
❑ 110 Charles Woodson	.60	.25
❑ 111 Charles Johnson	.15	.07
❑ 112 Donovan McNabb RC	3.00	1.35
❑ 113 Doug Pederson	.30	.14
❑ 114 Duce Staley	.60	.25
❑ 115 Jerome Bettis	.60	.25
❑ 116 Troy Edwards RC	1.50	.70
❑ 117 Kordell Stewart	.60	.25
❑ 118 Amos Zereoue RC	1.00	.45
❑ 119 Isaac Bruce	.60	.25
❑ 120 Marshall Faulk	.60	.25
❑ 121 Joe Germaine RC	1.00	.45
❑ 122 Torry Holt RC	2.50	1.10
❑ 123 Kurt Warner RC	20.00	9.00
❑ 124 Jim Harbaugh	.30	.14
❑ 125 Erik Kramer	.15	.07
❑ 126 Natrone Means	.30	.14
❑ 127 Junior Seau	.30	.14
❑ 128 Terrell Owens	.60	.25
❑ 129 Lawrence Phillips	.30	.14
❑ 130 Jerry Rice	1.50	.70
❑ 131 J.J. Stokes	.30	.14
❑ 132 Steve Young	1.00	.45
❑ 133 Karsten Bailey RC	1.00	.45
❑ 134 Joey Galloway	.60	.25
❑ 135 Brock Huard RC	1.25	.55
❑ 136 Jon Kitna	.75	.35
❑ 137 Ricky Watters	.30	.14
❑ 138 Reidel Anthony	.15	.07
❑ 139 Trent Dilfer	.30	.14
❑ 140 Warrick Dunn	.60	.25
❑ 141 Shaun King RC	3.00	1.35
❑ 142 Jevon Kearse RC	2.00	.90
❑ 143 Kevin Dyson	.30	.14
❑ 144 Eddie George	.75	.35
❑ 145 Steve McNair	.60	.25
❑ 146 Champ Bailey RC	1.25	.55
❑ 147 Stephen Davis	.60	.25
❑ 148 Skip Hicks	.30	.14
❑ 149 Brad Johnson	.60	.25
❑ 150 Michael Westbrook	.30	.14
❑ 151 Chris McAlister 2Q	1.00	.45
❑ 152 Peerless Price 2Q	2.00	.90
❑ 153 Antoine Winfield 2Q	1.00	.45
❑ 154 D'Wayne Bates 2Q	1.00	.45
❑ 155 Kevin Johnson 2Q	3.00	1.35
❑ 156 Chris Claiborne 2Q	1.00	.45
❑ 157 Sedrick Irvin 2Q	.15	.07
❑ 158 Mike Cloud 2Q	1.25	.55
❑ 159 Cecil Collins 2Q	.15	.07
❑ 160 James Johnson 2Q	1.50	.70
❑ 161 Rob Konrad 2Q	1.25	.55
❑ 162 Daunte Culpepper 2Q	4.00	1.80
❑ 163 Andy Katzenmoyer 2Q	1.25	.55
❑ 164 Amos Zereoue 2Q	1.25	.55
❑ 165 Joe Germaine 2Q	1.25	.55
❑ 166 Karsten Bailey 2Q	1.25	.55
❑ 167 Brock Huard 2Q	1.50	.70
❑ 168 Shaun King 2Q	4.00	1.80
❑ 169 Jevon Kearse 2Q	2.50	1.10
❑ 170 Champ Bailey 2Q	1.50	.70
❑ 171 Jake Plummer 3Q	3.00	1.35
❑ 172 Doug Flutie 3Q	3.00	1.35
❑ 173 Troy Aikman 3Q	5.00	2.20
❑ 174 Emmitt Smith 3Q	5.00	2.20
❑ 175 Terrell Davis 3Q	5.00	2.20
❑ 176 Barry Sanders 3Q	8.00	3.60
❑ 177 Brett Favre 3Q	8.00	3.60
❑ 178 Peyton Manning 3Q	8.00	3.60
❑ 179 Mark Brunell 3Q	3.00	1.35
❑ 180 Fred Taylor 3Q	5.00	2.20
❑ 181 Dan Marino 3Q	8.00	3.60
❑ 182 Randy Moss 3Q	8.00	3.60
❑ 183 Drew Bledsoe 3Q	3.00	1.35
❑ 184 Jerry Rice 3Q	5.00	2.20
❑ 185 Steve Young 3Q	3.00	1.35
❑ 186 David Boston 4Q	6.00	2.70
❑ 187 Cade McNown 4Q	12.00	5.50

		MINT	NRMT
❑ 188	Akili Smith 4Q	8.00	3.60
❑ 189	Tim Couch 4Q	20.00	9.00
❑ 190	Edgerrin James 4Q	30.00	13.50
❑ 191	Kevin Faulk 4Q	5.00	2.20
❑ 192	Ricky Williams 4Q	20.00	9.00
❑ 193	Donovan McNabb 4Q	12.00	5.50
❑ 194	Troy Edwards 4Q	6.00	2.70
❑ 195	Torry Holt 4Q	10.00	4.50

1999 Collector's Edge Odyssey Two Minute Warning

	MINT	NRMT
COMMON CARD (151-170)	3.00	1.35
*151-170 ROOKIES: 1.2X TO 3X HI COL.		
151-170 STATED PRINT RUN 600 SER.#'d SETS		
COMMON CARD (171-185)	8.00	3.60
*171-185 STARS: 1X TO 2.5X HI COL.		
171-185 STATED PRINT RUN 300 SER.#'d SETS		
COMMON CARD (186-195)	20.00	9.00
*186-195 ROOKIES: 1.5X TO 4X HI COL.		
186-195 STATED PRINT RUN 100 SER.#'d SETS		

1999 Collector's Edge Odyssey Overtime

	MINT	NRMT
COMMON CARD (151-170)	25.00	11.00
*151-170 ROOKIES: 8X TO 20X HI COL.		
151-170 STATED PRINT RUN 60 SER.#'d SETS		
COMMON CARD (171-185)	80.00	36.00
*171-185 STARS: 12X TO 30X HI COL.		
171-185 STATED PRINT RUN 30 SER.#'d SETS		
COMMON CARD (186-195)	100.00	45.00
*186-195 ROOKIES: 8X TO 20X HI COL.		
186-195 STATED PRINT RUN 10 SER.#'d SETS		

1999 Collector's Edge Odyssey Cut 'n' Ripped

	MINT	NRMT
COMPLETE SET (15)	20.00	9.00
COMMON CARD (CR1-CR15)	1.00	.45
SEMISTARS	1.25	.55
STATED ODDS 1:12		

		MINT	NRMT
❑ CR1	Chris McAlister	1.00	.45
❑ CR2	Kevin Johnson	3.00	1.35
❑ CR3	Chris Claiborne	1.00	.45
❑ CR4	Sedrick Irvin	1.25	.55
❑ CR5	Edgerrin James	10.00	4.50
❑ CR6	Mike Cloud	1.25	.55
❑ CR7	James Johnson	1.50	.70
❑ CR8	Rob Konrad	1.25	.55
❑ CR9	Daunte Culpepper	4.00	1.80
❑ CR10	Andy Katzenmoyer	1.25	.55
❑ CR11	Amos Zereoue	1.25	.55
❑ CR12	Torry Holt	3.00	1.35
❑ CR13	Shaun King	4.00	1.80
❑ CR14	Jevon Kearse	2.50	1.10
❑ CR15	Champ Bailey	1.50	.70

1999 Collector's Edge Odyssey Cutting Edge

	MINT	NRMT
COMPLETE SET (10)	30.00	13.50
COMMON CARD (CE1-CE10)	3.00	1.35
STATED ODDS 1:18		

		MINT	NRMT
❑ CE1	Akili Smith	3.00	1.35
❑ CE2	Tim Couch	6.00	2.70
❑ CE3	Brian Griese	3.00	1.35
❑ CE4	Charlie Batch	3.00	1.35
❑ CE5	Brett Favre	8.00	3.60
❑ CE6	Peyton Manning	6.00	2.70
❑ CE7	Mark Brunell	3.00	1.35
❑ CE8	Dan Marino	8.00	3.60
❑ CE9	Drew Bledsoe	3.00	1.35
❑ CE10	Steve Young	3.00	1.35

1999 Collector's Edge Odyssey Excalibur

	MINT	NRMT
COMPLETE SET (8)	30.00	13.50
COMMON CARD	4.00	1.80
STATED ODDS 1:24		

		MINT	NRMT
❑ X1	David Boston	4.00	1.80
❑ X4	Cade McNown	6.00	2.70
❑ X8	Troy Edwards	4.00	1.80
❑ X9	Daunte Culpepper	6.00	2.70
❑ X11	Ricky Williams	8.00	3.60
❑ X15	Donovan McNabb	6.00	2.70
❑ X16	Troy Aikman	8.00	3.60
❑ X21	Emmitt Smith	8.00	3.60

1999 Collector's Edge Odyssey End Zone

	MINT	NRMT
COMPLETE SET (20)	30.00	13.50
COMMON CARD (EZ1-EZ20)	1.00	.45
SEMISTARS	2.00	.90
STATED ODDS 1:9		

		MINT	NRMT
❑ EZ1	Jamal Anderson	2.00	.90
❑ EZ2	Priest Holmes	2.00	.90
❑ EZ3	Doug Flutie	2.50	1.10
❑ EZ4	Eric Moulds	2.00	.90
❑ EZ5	Charlie Batch	3.00	1.35
❑ EZ6	Barry Sanders	8.00	3.60
❑ EZ7	Antonio Freeman	2.00	.90
❑ EZ8	Fred Taylor	4.00	1.80
❑ EZ9	Cris Carter	2.00	.90
❑ EZ10	Randy Moss	6.00	2.70
❑ EZ11	Keyshawn Johnson	2.00	.90
❑ EZ12	Curtis Martin	2.00	.90
❑ EZ13	Vinny Testaverde	1.00	.45
❑ EZ14	Kordell Stewart	2.00	.90
❑ EZ15	Jerry Rice	5.00	2.20
❑ EZ16	Terrell Owens	2.00	.90
❑ EZ17	Jon Kitna	2.50	1.10
❑ EZ18	Warrick Dunn	2.00	.90
❑ EZ19	Eddie George	2.50	1.10
❑ EZ20	Steve McNair	2.00	.90

1999 Collector's Edge Odyssey Game Gear

	MINT	NRMT
COMPLETE SET (8)	250.00	110.00
COMMON CARD (GG1-GG8)	20.00	9.00
STATED ODDS 1:360		

		MINT	NRMT
❑ GG1	Terrell Davis/500	30.00	13.50
❑ GG2	Curtis Enis/338	20.00	9.00
❑ GG3	Marshall Faulk/247	30.00	13.50
❑ GG4	Brian Griese/500	30.00	13.50
❑ GG5	Skip Hicks/315	20.00	9.00
❑ GG6	Randy Moss/415	50.00	22.00
❑ GG7	Lawrence Phillips/406	25.00	11.00
❑ GG8	Fred Taylor/85	80.00	36.00

1999 Collector's Edge Odyssey Old School

	MINT	NRMT
COMPLETE SET (25)	50.00	22.00
COMMON CARD (OS1-OS25)	1.25	.55
SEMISTARS	1.50	.70
STATED ODDS 1:8		

		MINT	NRMT
❑ OS1	David Boston	2.50	1.10
❑ OS2	Chris McAlister	1.25	.55
❑ OS3	Peerless Price	2.50	1.10
❑ OS4	D'Wayne Bates	1.25	.55

Card	MINT	NRMT
❑ OS5 Cade McNown	5.00	2.20
❑ OS6 Akili Smith	3.00	1.35
❑ OS7 Tim Couch	8.00	3.60
❑ OS8 Kevin Johnson	4.00	1.80
❑ OS9 Chris Claiborne	1.25	.55
❑ OS10 Sedrick Irvin	1.50	.70
❑ OS11 Edgerrin James	12.00	5.50
❑ OS12 Mike Cloud	1.50	.70
❑ OS13 James Johnson	2.00	.90
❑ OS14 Rob Konrad	1.50	.70
❑ OS15 Daunte Culpepper	5.00	2.20
❑ OS16 Kevin Faulk	2.00	.90
❑ OS17 Donovan McNabb	5.00	2.20
❑ OS18 Troy Edwards	2.50	1.10
❑ OS19 Amos Zereoue	1.50	.70
❑ OS20 Joe Germaine	1.50	.70
❑ OS21 Torry Holt	4.00	1.80
❑ OS22 Karsten Bailey	1.25	.55
❑ OS23 Shaun King	5.00	2.20
❑ OS24 Jevon Kearse	3.00	1.35
❑ OS25 Champ Bailey	2.00	.90

1999 Collector's Edge Odyssey Pro Signature Authentics

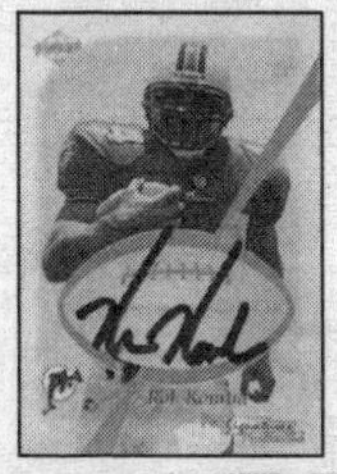

	MINT	NRMT
COMPLETE SET (18)	400.00	180.00
COMMON CARD	10.00	4.50
SEMISTARS	15.00	6.75
STATED ODDS 1:36		

Card	MINT	NRMT
❑ 1 D'Wayne Bates/1450	10.00	4.50
❑ 2 Michael Bishop/2200	15.00	6.75
❑ 3 Chris Claiborne/1120	10.00	4.50
❑ 4 Daunte Culpepper/450	40.00	18.00
❑ 5 Jared DeVries/290	10.00	4.50
❑ 6 Jeff Garcia/2110	20.00	9.00
❑ 7 Martin Gramatica/1950	10.00	4.50
❑ 8 Torry Holt/1115	25.00	11.00
❑ 9 Brock Huard/350	20.00	9.00
❑ 10 Sedrick Irvin/1240	15.00	6.75
❑ 11 Edgerrin James/435	120.00	55.00
❑ 12 Kevin Johnson/1920	25.00	11.00
❑ 13 Shaun King/920	40.00	18.00
❑ 14 Rob Konrad/1420	15.00	6.75
❑ 15 Darnell McDonald/2435	10.00	4.50
❑ 16 Peerless Price/825	25.00	11.00
❑ 17 Akili Smith/111	100.00	45.00
❑ 18 Amos Zereoue1450	15.00	6.75

1999 Collector's Edge Odyssey Super Limited Edge

	MINT	NRMT
COMPLETE SET (30)	100.00	45.00
COMMON CARD (SLE1-SLE30)	3.00	1.35
STATED PRINT RUN 1000 SER.#'d SETS		

Card	MINT	NRMT
❑ SLE1 Jake Plummer	5.00	2.20
❑ SLE2 Jamal Anderson	3.00	1.35
❑ SLE3 Doug Flutie	4.00	1.80
❑ SLE4 Eric Moulds	3.00	1.35
❑ SLE5 Troy Aikman	8.00	3.60
❑ SLE6 Emmitt Smith	8.00	3.60
❑ SLE7 Terrell Davis	8.00	3.60
❑ SLE8 Charlie Batch	5.00	2.20
❑ SLE9 Herman Moore	3.00	1.35
❑ SLE10 Barry Sanders	12.00	5.50
❑ SLE11 Brett Favre	12.00	5.50
❑ SLE12 Antonio Freeman	3.00	1.35
❑ SLE13 Dorsey Levens	3.00	1.35
❑ SLE14 Peyton Manning	10.00	4.50
❑ SLE15 Mark Brunell	5.00	2.20
❑ SLE16 Fred Taylor	6.00	2.70
❑ SLE17 Dan Marino	12.00	5.50
❑ SLE18 Cris Carter	3.00	1.35
❑ SLE19 Randall Cunningham	3.00	1.35
❑ SLE20 Randy Moss	10.00	4.50
❑ SLE21 Drew Bledsoe	5.00	2.20
❑ SLE22 Ricky Williams	12.00	5.50
❑ SLE23 Keyshawn Johnson	3.00	1.35
❑ SLE24 Curtis Martin	3.00	1.35
❑ SLE25 Jerome Bettis	3.00	1.35
❑ SLE26 Jerry Rice	8.00	3.60
❑ SLE27 Terrell Owens	3.00	1.35
❑ SLE28 Jon Kitna	4.00	1.80
❑ SLE29 Eddie George	4.00	1.80
❑ SLE30 Steve Young	5.00	2.20

1998 CE Supreme Season Review

	MINT	NRMT
COMPLETE SET (200)	70.00	32.00
COMP.SET w/o SPs (200)	25.00	11.00
COMMON CARD (1-200)	.25	.11
SEMISTARS	.50	.23
UNLISTED STARS	1.00	.45
COMMON TEAM DRAFT	.10	.05
TEAM DRAFT REDEMPT.EXPIRED: 3/31/99		
COMMON DRAFT PRIZE	1.00	.45
DRAFT PRIZE SEMISTARS	1.50	.70
COMP.GOLD INGOT (200)	400.00	180.00
*GOLD INGOT STARS: 2X TO 4X HI		
*GOLD INGOT YOUNG STARS: 1.5X TO 3X		
*GOLD INGOT RCs: .6X TO 1.5X		
GOLD INGOTS ONE PER PACK..		

Card	MINT	NRMT
❑ 1 Larry Centers	.25	.11
❑ 2 Jake Plummer	2.50	1.10
❑ 3 Simeon Rice	.50	.23
❑ 4 Cardinals Draft Pick	.10	.05
❑ 4A Andre Wadsworth RC	1.50	.70
❑ 4B Michael Pittman RC	1.50	.70
❑ 5 Jamal Anderson	1.00	.45
❑ 6 Bert Emanuel	.50	.23
❑ 7 Byron Hanspard	.50	.23
❑ 8 Falcons Draft Pick	.10	.05
❑ 8A Jammi German RC	1.00	.45
❑ 8B Keith Brooking RC	1.50	.70
❑ 9 Derrick Alexander WR	.50	.23
❑ 10 Peter Boulware	.25	.11
❑ 11 Michael Jackson	.25	.11
❑ 12 Ray Lewis	.25	.11
❑ 13 Vinny Testaverde	.50	.23
❑ 14 Ravens Draft Pick	.10	.05
❑ 14A Duane Starks RC	1.00	.45
❑ 14B Pat Johnson RC	1.50	.70
❑ 15 Todd Collins	.25	.11
❑ 16 Jim Kelly	1.00	.45
❑ 17 Andre Reed	.50	.23
❑ 18 Antowain Smith	1.00	.45
❑ 19 Bruce Smith	.50	.23
❑ 20 Thurman Thomas	1.00	.45
❑ 21 Bills Draft Pick	.10	.05
❑ 21A Jonathan Linton RC	2.00	.90
❑ 22 Tim Biakabutuka	.50	.23
❑ 23 Rae Carruth	.50	.23
❑ 24 Kerry Collins	.50	.23
❑ 25 Anthony Johnson	.25	.11
❑ 26 Lamar Lathon	.25	.11
❑ 27 Panthers Draft Pick	.10	.05
❑ 27A Jason Peters RC	1.50	.70
❑ 27B Donald Hayes RC	1.50	.70
❑ 28 Curtis Conway	.50	.23
❑ 29 Bryan Cox	.25	.11
❑ 30 Bobby Engram	.50	.23
❑ 31 Erik Kramer	.25	.11
❑ 32 Rick Mirer	.25	.11
❑ 33 Rashaan Salaam	.25	.11
❑ 34 Bears Draft Pick	.10	.05
❑ 34A Curtis Enis RC	3.00	1.35
❑ 35 Jeff Blake	.50	.23
❑ 36 Ki-Jana Carter	.25	.11
❑ 37 Corey Dillon	1.25	.55
❑ 38 Carl Pickens	1.00	.45
❑ 39 Bengals Draft Pick	.10	.05
❑ 39A Takeo Spikes RC	1.50	.70
❑ 39B Brian Simmons RC	1.00	.45
❑ 40 Troy Aikman	2.00	.90
❑ 41 Daryl Johnston	.50	.23
❑ 42 David LaFleur	.25	.11
❑ 43 Anthony Miller	.25	.11
❑ 44 Deion Sanders	1.00	.45
❑ 45 Emmitt Smith	3.00	1.35
❑ 46 Broderick Thomas	.25	.11
❑ 47 Cowboys Draft Pick	.10	.05
❑ 47A Greg Ellis RC	1.00	.45
❑ 48 Terrell Davis	3.00	1.35
❑ 49 John Elway	4.00	1.80
❑ 50 Ed McCaffrey	.50	.23
❑ 51 John Mobley	.25	.11
❑ 52 Bill Romanowski	.25	.11
❑ 53 Shannon Sharpe	.50	.23
❑ 54 Neil Smith	.50	.23
❑ 55 Rod Smith WR	.50	.23
❑ 56 Maa Tanuvasa	.25	.11
❑ 57 Broncos Draft Pick	.10	.05
❑ 57A Marcus Nash RC	2.00	.90
❑ 57B Brian Griese RC	4.00	1.80
❑ 58 Scott Mitchell	.50	.23
❑ 59 Herman Moore	1.00	.45
❑ 60 Barry Sanders	4.00	1.80
❑ 61 Lions Draft Pick	.10	.05
❑ 61A Jamaal Alexander RC	1.00	.45

❑ 61B	Chris Liwienski RC	1.00	.45
❑ 61C	Terry Fair RC	1.00	.45
❑ 61D	Germane Crowell RC	3.00	1.35
❑ 61E	Charlie Batch RC	4.00	1.80
❑ 62	Robert Brooks	.50	.23
❑ 63	Mark Chmura	.50	.23
❑ 64	Brett Favre	4.00	1.80
❑ 65	Antonio Freeman	1.00	.45
❑ 66	Dorsey Levens	1.00	.45
❑ 67	Derrick Mayes	.50	.23
❑ 68	Ross Verba	.25	.11
❑ 69	Reggie White	1.00	.45
❑ 70	Packers Draft Pick	.50	.23
❑ 70A	Vonnie Holliday RC	1.50	.70
❑ 70B	Roosevelt Blackmon RC	1.00	.45
❑ 71	Marshall Faulk	1.00	.45
❑ 72	Jim Harbaugh	.50	.23
❑ 73	Marvin Harrison	.50	.23
❑ 74	Colts Draft Pick	.10	.05
❑ 74A	E.G. Green RC	2.00	.90
❑ 74B	Peyton Manning RC	15.00	6.75
❑ 75	Tony Brackens	.25	.11
❑ 76	Mark Brunell	1.50	.70
❑ 77	Rob Johnson	.50	.23
❑ 78	Keenan McCardell	.50	.23
❑ 79	Natrone Means	1.00	.45
❑ 80	Jimmy Smith	.50	.23
❑ 81	Jaguars Draft Pick	.10	.05
❑ 81A	Tavian Banks RC	2.00	.90
❑ 82	Marcus Allen	1.00	.45
❑ 83	Tony Gonzalez	.25	.11
❑ 84	Elvis Grbac	.50	.23
❑ 85	Derrick Thomas	.50	.23
❑ 86	Tamarick Vanover	.25	.11
❑ 87	Chiefs Draft Pick	.10	.05
❑ 87A	Rashaan Shehee RC	2.00	.90
❑ 88	Karim Abdul-Jabbar	1.00	.45
❑ 89	Fred Barnett	.25	.11
❑ 90	Dan Marino	4.00	1.80
❑ 91	O.J. McDuffie	.50	.23
❑ 92	Brett Perriman	.25	.11
❑ 93	Irving Spikes	.25	.11
❑ 94	Zach Thomas	.25	.11
❑ 95	Dolphins Draft Pick	.10	.05
❑ 95A	John Avery RC	1.50	.70
❑ 96	Cris Carter	1.00	.45
❑ 97	Brad Johnson	1.00	.45
❑ 98	John Randle	.50	.23
❑ 99	Jake Reed	.50	.23
❑ 100	Robert Smith	1.00	.45
❑ 101	Vikings Draft Pick	.10	.05
❑ 101A	Randy Moss RC	15.00	6.75
❑ 102	Drew Bledsoe	1.50	.70
❑ 103	Chris Canty	.25	.11
❑ 104	Ben Coates	.50	.23
❑ 105	Terry Glenn	1.00	.45
❑ 106	Curtis Martin	1.00	.45
❑ 107	Willie McGinest	.25	.11
❑ 108	Sedrick Shaw	.25	.11
❑ 109	Patriots Draft Pick	.10	.05
❑ 109A	Chris Floyd RC	1.00	.45
❑ 109B	Tebucky Jones RC	1.00	.45
❑ 109C	Harold Shaw RC	1.50	.70
❑ 110	Mario Bates	.50	.23
❑ 111	Heath Shuler	.25	.11
❑ 112	Danny Wuerffel	.50	.23
❑ 113	Saints Draft Pick	.10	.05
❑ 113A	Cameron Cleeland RC	1.50	.70
❑ 114	Ray Zellars	.25	.11
❑ 115	Tiki Barber	.50	.23
❑ 116	Dave Brown	.25	.11
❑ 117	Ike Hilliard	.50	.23
❑ 118	Danny Kanell	.50	.23
❑ 119	Jason Sehorn	.25	.11
❑ 120	Amani Toomer	.50	.23
❑ 121	Giants Draft Pick	.10	.05
❑ 121A	Shaun Williams RC	1.00	.45
❑ 121B	Joe Jurevicius RC	2.00	.90
❑ 121C	Brian Alford RC	1.50	.70
❑ 122	Wayne Chrebet	1.00	.45
❑ 123	Hugh Douglas	.25	.11
❑ 124	Jeff Graham	.25	.11
❑ 125	Keyshawn Johnson	1.00	.45
❑ 126	Adrian Murrell	.50	.23
❑ 127	Neil O'Donnell	.50	.23
❑ 128	Jets Draft Pick	.10	.05
❑ 128A	Scott Frost RC	1.50	.70
❑ 129	Tim Brown	1.00	.45
❑ 130	Jeff George	.50	.23
❑ 131	Desmond Howard	.50	.23
❑ 132	Napoleon Kaufman	1.00	.45
❑ 133	Darrell Russell	.25	.11
❑ 134	Raiders Draft Pick	.10	.05
❑ 134A	Charles Woodson RC	3.00	1.35
❑ 135	Ty Detmer	.50	.23
❑ 136	Irving Fryar	.50	.23
❑ 137	Bobby Hoying	.50	.23
❑ 138	Chris T. Jones	.25	.11
❑ 139	Ricky Watters	.50	.23
❑ 140	Eagles Draft Pick	.10	.05
❑ 140A	Allen Rossum RC	1.00	.45
❑ 141	Jerome Bettis	1.00	.45
❑ 142	Charles Johnson	.25	.11
❑ 143	George Jones	.25	.11
❑ 144	Greg Lloyd	.25	.11
❑ 145	Kordell Stewart	1.00	.45
❑ 146	Yancey Thigpen	.25	.11
❑ 147	Steelers Draft Pick	.10	.05
❑ 147A	C.Fuamatu-Ma'afala RC	1.50	.70
❑ 148	Stan Humphries	.25	.11
❑ 149	Tony Martin	.50	.23
❑ 150	Eric Metcalf	.25	.11
❑ 151	Junior Seau	.50	.23
❑ 152	Chargers Draft Pick	.10	.05
❑ 152A	Ryan Leaf RC	2.50	1.10
❑ 153	Jim Druckenmiller	.50	.23
❑ 154	William Floyd	.25	.11
❑ 155	Kevin Greene	.50	.23
❑ 156	Garrison Hearst	1.00	.45
❑ 157	Ken Norton	.25	.11
❑ 158	Terrell Owens	1.00	.45
❑ 159	Jerry Rice	2.00	.90
❑ 160	J.J. Stokes	.50	.23
❑ 161	Dana Stubblefield	.25	.11
❑ 162	Rod Woodson	.50	.23
❑ 163	Bryant Young	.25	.11
❑ 164	Steve Young	1.25	.55
❑ 165	49ers Draft Pick	.25	.11
❑ 165A	Fred Beasley RC	1.00	.45
❑ 165B	R.W. McQuarters RC	1.00	.45
❑ 165C	Chris Ruhman RC	1.00	.45
❑ 166	Steve Broussard	.25	.11
❑ 167	Chad Brown	.25	.11
❑ 168	Joey Galloway	1.00	.45
❑ 169	Jon Kitna	2.50	1.10
❑ 170	Warren Moon	1.00	.45
❑ 171	Chris Warren	.50	.23
❑ 172	Seahawks Draft Pick	.10	.05
❑ 172A	Ahman Green RC	2.00	.90
❑ 173	Tony Banks	.50	.23
❑ 174	Isaac Bruce	1.00	.45
❑ 175	Eddie Kennison	.50	.23
❑ 176	Keith Lyle	.25	.11
❑ 177	Lawrence Phillips	.25	.11
❑ 178	Rams Draft Pick	.10	.05
❑ 178A	Robert Holcombe RC	2.00	.90
❑ 179	Mike Alstott	1.00	.45
❑ 180	Reidel Anthony	.50	.23
❑ 181	Trent Dilfer	1.00	.45
❑ 182	Warrick Dunn	1.25	.55
❑ 183	Hardy Nickerson	.25	.11
❑ 184	Errict Rhett	.50	.23
❑ 185	Warren Sapp	.50	.23
❑ 186	Bucs Draft Pick	.10	.05
❑ 186A	Jacquez Green RC	2.00	.90
❑ 187	Eddie George	1.50	.70
❑ 188	Darryll Lewis	.25	.11
❑ 189	Steve McNair	1.00	.45
❑ 190	Chris Sanders	.25	.11
❑ 191	Oilers Draft Pick	.10	.05
❑ 191A	Kevin Dyson RC	2.50	1.10
❑ 192	Terry Allen	1.00	.45
❑ 193	Jamie Asher	.25	.11
❑ 194	Stephen Davis	.25	.11
❑ 195	Gus Frerotte	.25	.11
❑ 196	Sean Gilbert	.25	.11
❑ 197	Ken Harvey	.25	.11
❑ 198	Jeff Hostetler	.25	.11
❑ 199	Michael Westbrook	.50	.23
❑ 200	Redskins Draft Pick	.10	.05
❑ 200A	Stephen Alexander RC	2.00	.90
❑ 200B	Mike Sellers RC	1.00	.45

1998 CE Supreme Season Review Markers

	MINT	NRMT
COMPLETE SET (30)	250.00	110.00
COMMON CARD (1-30)	5.00	2.20
SEMISTARS	8.00	3.60
STATED ODDS 1:24		
❑ 1 Jamal Anderson	10.00	4.50
❑ 2 Corey Dillon	12.00	5.50
❑ 3 Emmitt Smith	25.00	11.00
❑ 4 Terrell Davis	30.00	13.50
❑ 5 John Elway	30.00	13.50
❑ 6 Rod Smith	8.00	3.60
❑ 7 Herman Moore	10.00	4.50
❑ 8 Barry Sanders	30.00	13.50
❑ 9 Robert Brooks	8.00	3.60
❑ 10 Brett Favre	30.00	13.50
❑ 11 Antonio Freeman	10.00	4.50
❑ 12 Dorsey Levens	10.00	4.50
❑ 13 Marshall Faulk	10.00	4.50
❑ 14 Mark Brunell	12.00	5.50
❑ 15 Karim Abdul-Jabbar	10.00	4.50
❑ 16 Dan Marino	30.00	13.50
❑ 17 Cris Carter	10.00	4.50
❑ 18 Drew Bledsoe	12.00	5.50
❑ 19 Curtis Martin	10.00	4.50
❑ 20 Adrian Murrell	8.00	3.60
❑ 21 Tim Brown	10.00	4.50
❑ 22 Jeff George	8.00	3.60
❑ 23 Napoleon Kaufman	10.00	4.50
❑ 24 Jerome Bettis	10.00	4.50
❑ 25 Kordell Stewart	8.00	3.60
❑ 26 Yancey Thigpen	5.00	2.20
❑ 27 Garrison Hearst	10.00	4.50
❑ 28 Steve Young	10.00	4.50
❑ 29 Joey Galloway	10.00	4.50
❑ 30 Eddie George	12.00	5.50

1998 CE Supreme Season Review Pro-Signature Authentic

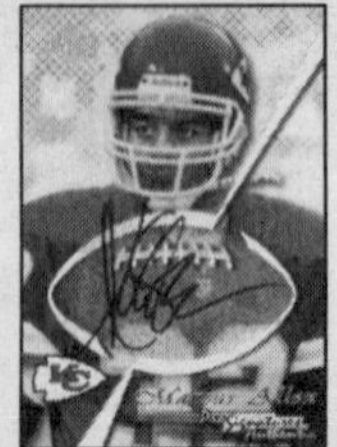

	MINT	NRMT
COMPLETE SET (10)	1800.00	800.00
COMMON CARD (1-10)	60.00	27.00
1-5 STATED ODDS 1:2300		
VETERANS STATED PRINT RUN 50		

ROOKIE REDEMPTION ODDS 1:800
ROOKIES STATED PRINT RUN 500
EMMITT SMITH INSERTED IN 98 CE MASTERS

Card	MINT	NRMT
❑ 1 Troy Aikman	300.00	135.00
❑ 2 Marcus Allen	150.00	70.00
❑ 3 Terrell Davis	400.00	180.00
❑ 4 Desmond Howard	80.00	36.00
❑ 6 Ryan Leaf/500	60.00	27.00
❑ 7 Peyton Manning/500	150.00	70.00
❑ 8 Jerry Rice	300.00	135.00
❑ 9 Emmitt Smith	300.00	135.00
❑ 10 Rookie Redemption (Ryan Leaf or Peyton Manning trade card)	120.00	55.00

1998 CE Supreme Season Review T3

	MINT	NRMT
COMPLETE SET (30)	200.00	90.00
COMMON WR (1-30)	2.50	1.10
SEMISTARS WR	3.00	1.35
COMMON RB (1-30)	4.00	1.80
COMMON QB (1-30)	5.00	2.20

STATED ODDS 1:36 QB/1:24 RB/1:12 WR

Card	MINT	NRMT
❑ 1 Rae Carruth	3.00	1.35
❑ 2 Carl Pickens	4.00	1.80
❑ 3 Troy Aikman	12.00	5.50
❑ 4 Emmitt Smith	12.00	5.50
❑ 5 Terrell Davis	15.00	6.75
❑ 6 John Elway	25.00	11.00
❑ 7 Herman Moore	4.00	1.80
❑ 8 Barry Sanders	20.00	9.00
❑ 9 Robert Brooks	3.00	1.35
❑ 10 Brett Favre	25.00	11.00
❑ 11 Antonio Freeman	4.00	1.80
❑ 12 Dorsey Levens	4.00	1.80
❑ 13 Rob Johnson	5.00	2.20
❑ 14 Jerry Rice	8.00	3.60
❑ 15 Dan Marino	25.00	11.00
❑ 16 Cris Carter	4.00	1.80
❑ 17 Drew Bledsoe	10.00	4.50
❑ 18 Curtis Martin	4.00	1.80
❑ 19 Adrian Murrell	4.00	1.80
❑ 20 Tim Brown	4.00	1.80
❑ 21 Napoleon Kaufman	4.00	1.80
❑ 22 Jerome Bettis	4.00	1.80
❑ 23 Kordell Stewart	5.00	2.20
❑ 24 Joey Galloway	4.00	1.80
❑ 25 Jim Druckenmiller	5.00	2.20
❑ 26 Terrell Owens	4.00	1.80
❑ 27 Jake Plummer	12.00	5.50
❑ 28 Warrick Dunn	5.00	2.20
❑ 29 Eddie George	8.00	3.60
❑ 30 Steve McNair	5.00	2.20

1999 Collector's Edge Supreme

	MINT	NRMT
COMPLETE SET (170)	300.00	135.00
COMP.SET w/o #166 (169)	100.00	45.00
COMMON CARD (1-130)	.15	.07
SEMISTARS	.30	.14
UNLISTED STARS	.60	.25

	MINT	NRMT
COMMON ROOKIE (131-170)	1.00	.45
ROOKIE SEMISTARS	1.50	.70
ROOKIE UNLISTED STARS	2.50	1.10

SOME RCs REDEMPTION CARDS AS WELL
COMP.GALVANIZED (167) .. 800.00 350.00
*GALVANIZED STARS: 2.5X TO 6X HI COL.
*GALVANIZED YOUNG STARS: 2.5X TO 6X
*GALVANIZED RCs: 2X TO 5X ....
GALVANIZED VETS PRINT RUN 500 SETS
GALVANIZED RCs PRINT RUN 250 SETS
COMP.GOLD INGOT (167) .. 300.00 135.00
*GOLD INGOT STARS: .75X TO 2X HI COL.
*GOLD INGOT YOUNG STARS: .75X TO 2X
*GOLD INGOT RCs: .6X TO 1.5X
GOLD INGOTS ONE PER PACK..
CARDS 1/2/166 WEREN'T MADE FOR PARALLELS

Card	MINT	NRMT
❑ 1 Randy Moss CL	1.25	.55
❑ 2 Peyton Manning CL	.60	.25
❑ 3 Rob Moore	.30	.14
❑ 4 Adrian Murrell	.30	.14
❑ 5 Jake Plummer	1.25	.55
❑ 6 Andre Wadsworth	.15	.07
❑ 7 Jamal Anderson	.60	.25
❑ 8 Chris Chandler	.30	.14
❑ 9 Tony Martin	.30	.14
❑ 10 Terence Mathis	.30	.14
❑ 11 Jim Harbaugh	.30	.14
❑ 12 Priest Holmes	.60	.25
❑ 13 Jermaine Lewis	.30	.14
❑ 14 Eric Zeier	.15	.07
❑ 15 Doug Flutie	.60	.25
❑ 16 Eric Moulds	.60	.25
❑ 17 Andre Reed	.30	.14
❑ 18 Antowain Smith	.60	.25
❑ 19 Steve Beuerlein	.15	.07
❑ 20 Kevin Greene	.15	.07
❑ 21 Rocket Ismail	.30	.14
❑ 22 Fred Lane	.15	.07
❑ 23 Edgar Bennett	.15	.07
❑ 24 Curtis Conway	.30	.14
❑ 25 Curtis Enis	.60	.25
❑ 26 Erik Kramer	.15	.07
❑ 27 Corey Dillon	.60	.25
❑ 28 Neil O'Donnell	.15	.07
❑ 29 Carl Pickens	.30	.14
❑ 30 Darnay Scott	.15	.07
❑ 31 Troy Aikman	1.50	.70
❑ 32 Michael Irvin	.30	.14
❑ 33 Deion Sanders	.60	.25
❑ 34 Emmitt Smith	1.50	.70
❑ 35 Chris Warren	.15	.07
❑ 36 Terrell Davis	1.50	.70
❑ 37 John Elway	2.50	1.10
❑ 38 Ed McCaffrey	.30	.14
❑ 39 Shannon Sharpe	.30	.14
❑ 40 Rod Smith	.30	.14
❑ 41 Charlie Batch	1.25	.55
❑ 42 Herman Moore	.60	.25
❑ 43 Johnnie Morton	.15	.07
❑ 44 Barry Sanders	2.50	1.10
❑ 45 Robert Brooks	.30	.14
❑ 46 Brett Favre	2.50	1.10
❑ 47 Antonio Freeman	.60	.25
❑ 48 Darick Holmes	.15	.07
❑ 49 Dorsey Levens	.60	.25
❑ 50 Reggie White	.15	.07
❑ 51 Marshall Faulk	.60	.25
❑ 52 Marvin Harrison	.60	.25
❑ 53 Peyton Manning	2.50	1.10
❑ 54 Jerome Pathon	.15	.07
❑ 55 Tavian Banks	.15	.07
❑ 56 Mark Brunell	1.00	.45
❑ 57 Keenan McCardell	.30	.14
❑ 58 Fred Taylor	1.50	.70
❑ 59 Derrick Alexander	.15	.07
❑ 60 Donnell Bennett	.15	.07
❑ 61 Rich Gannon	.30	.14
❑ 62 Andre Rison	.30	.14
❑ 63 Karim Abdul-Jabbar	.30	.14
❑ 64 John Avery	.30	.14
❑ 65 Oronde Gadsden	.15	.07
❑ 66 Dan Marino	2.50	1.10
❑ 67 O.J. McDuffie	.30	.14
❑ 68 Cris Carter	.60	.25
❑ 69 Randall Cunningham	.60	.25
❑ 70 Brad Johnson	.60	.25
❑ 71 Randy Moss	3.00	1.35
❑ 72 Jake Reed	.30	.14
❑ 73 Robert Smith	.60	.25
❑ 74 Drew Bledsoe	1.00	.45
❑ 75 Ben Coates	.30	.14
❑ 76 Robert Edwards	.30	.14
❑ 77 Terry Glenn	.60	.25
❑ 78 Cameron Cleeland	.15	.07
❑ 79 Kerry Collins	.30	.14
❑ 80 Sean Dawkins	.15	.07
❑ 81 Lamar Smith	.15	.07
❑ 82 Gary Brown	.15	.07
❑ 83 Chris Calloway	.15	.07
❑ 84 Danny Kanell	.15	.07
❑ 85 Ike Hilliard	.15	.07
❑ 86 Wayne Chrebet	.30	.14
❑ 87 Keyshawn Johnson	.60	.25
❑ 88 Curtis Martin	.60	.25
❑ 89 Vinny Testaverde	.30	.14
❑ 90 Tim Brown	.60	.25
❑ 91 Jeff George	.30	.14
❑ 92 Napoleon Kaufman	.60	.25
❑ 93 Charles Woodson	.60	.25
❑ 94 Irving Fryar	.30	.14
❑ 95 Bobby Hoying	.30	.14
❑ 96 Duce Staley	.60	.25
❑ 97 Jerome Bettis	.60	.25
❑ 98 Courtney Hawkins	.15	.07
❑ 99 Charles Johnson	.15	.07
❑ 100 Kordell Stewart	.60	.25
❑ 101 Hines Ward	.30	.14
❑ 102 Tony Banks	.30	.14
❑ 103 Isaac Bruce	.60	.25
❑ 104 Robert Holcombe	.30	.14
❑ 105 Ryan Leaf	.60	.25
❑ 106 Natrone Means	.30	.14
❑ 107 Mikhael Ricks	.15	.07
❑ 108 Junior Seau	.30	.14
❑ 109 Garrison Hearst	.30	.14
❑ 110 Terrell Owens	.60	.25
❑ 111 Jerry Rice	1.50	.70
❑ 112 J.J. Stokes	.30	.14
❑ 113 Steve Young	1.00	.45
❑ 114 Joey Galloway	.60	.25
❑ 115 Jon Kitna	.75	.35
❑ 116 Warren Moon	.60	.25
❑ 117 Ricky Watters	.30	.14
❑ 118 Mike Alstott	.60	.25
❑ 119 Reidel Anthony	.30	.14
❑ 120 Warrick Dunn	.60	.25
❑ 121 Trent Dilfer	.30	.14
❑ 122 Jacquez Green	.30	.14
❑ 123 Kevin Dyson	.30	.14
❑ 124 Eddie George	.75	.35
❑ 125 Steve McNair	.60	.25
❑ 126 Frank Wycheck	.15	.07
❑ 127 Terry Allen	.30	.14
❑ 128 Trent Green	.30	.14
❑ 129 Skip Hicks	.60	.25
❑ 130 Michael Westbrook	.30	.14
❑ 131 Rahim Abdullah RC	1.50	.70
❑ 132 Champ Bailey RC	2.50	1.10
❑ 133 Marlon Barnes RC	1.50	.70
❑ 134 D'Wayne Bates RC	1.50	.70
❑ 135 Michael Bishop RC	2.50	1.10
❑ 136 Dre' Bly RC	1.50	.70
❑ 137 David Boston RC	3.00	1.35

	Card	MINT	NRMT
❑ 138	Cuncho Brown RC UER (Photo is actually Courtney Brown)	1.50	.70
❑ 139	Na Brown RC	2.50	1.10
❑ 140	Tony Bryant RC	1.50	.70
❑ 141	Tim Couch RC ERR (text on back reads "already sent")	70.00	32.00
❑ 141TC	Tim Couch RC COR (card number reads "TC")	20.00	9.00
❑ 142	Chris Claiborne RC	1.50	.70
❑ 143	Daunte Culpepper RC	6.00	2.70
❑ 144	Jared DeVries RC	1.50	.70
❑ 145	Troy Edwards RC UER	3.00	1.35
❑ 146	Kris Farris RC	1.00	.45
❑ 147	Kevin Faulk RC	2.50	1.10
❑ 148	Joe Germaine RC	2.50	1.10
❑ 149	Aaron Gibson RC	1.00	.45
❑ 150	Torry Holt RC	5.00	2.20
❑ 151	Brock Huard RC	2.50	1.10
❑ 152	Sedrick Irvin RC	2.50	1.10
❑ 153	James Johnson RC	2.50	1.10
❑ 154	Kevin Johnson RC	5.00	2.20
❑ 155	Andy Katzenmoyer RC	2.50	1.10
❑ 156	Jevon Kearse RC	4.00	1.80
❑ 157	Shaun King RC	6.00	2.70
❑ 158	Rob Konrad RC	1.50	.70
❑ 159	Chris McAlister RC	1.50	.70
❑ 160	Darnell McDonald RC	2.50	1.10
❑ 161	Donovan McNabb RC	6.00	2.70
❑ 162	Cade McNown RC	6.00	2.70
❑ 163	Peerless Price RC	3.00	1.35
❑ 164	Akili Smith RC	4.00	1.80
❑ 165	Matt Stinchcomb RC	1.00	.45
❑ 166A	Michael Wiley (pink tint on cardfront)	400.00	180.00
❑ 166B	Edgerrin James RC (issue via mail redemption)	100.00	45.00
❑ 167	Ricky Williams RC	10.00	4.50
❑ 168	Antoine Winfield RC	1.50	.70
❑ 169	Craig Yeast RC	1.50	.70
❑ 170	Amos Zereoue RC	2.50	1.10

1999 Collector's Edge Supreme Future

		MINT	NRMT
COMPLETE SET (10)		60.00	27.00
COMMON CARD (SF1-SF10)		3.00	1.35
STATED ODDS 1:24			
❑ SF1	Ricky Williams	12.00	5.50
❑ SF2	Tim Couch	12.00	5.50
❑ SF3	Daunte Culpepper	8.00	3.60
❑ SF4	Torry Holt	6.00	2.70
❑ SF5	Edgerrin James	20.00	9.00
❑ SF6	Brock Huard	3.00	1.35
❑ SF7	Donovan McNabb	8.00	3.60
❑ SF8	Joe Germaine	3.00	1.35
❑ SF9	Cade McNown	8.00	3.60
❑ SF10	Michael Bishop	5.00	2.20

1999 Collector's Edge Supreme Homecoming

		MINT	NRMT
COMPLETE SET (20)		60.00	27.00
COMMON CARD (H1-H20)		1.50	.70
SEMISTARS		2.50	1.10
STATED ODDS 1:12			
❑ H1	Ricky Williams / Priest Holmes	8.00	3.60
❑ H2	Andy Katzenmoyer / Eddie George	4.00	1.80
❑ H3	Daunte Culpepper / Shawn Jefferson	6.00	2.70
❑ H4	Torry Holt / Eric Kramer	5.00	2.20
❑ H5	Edgerrin James / Vinny Testaverde	12.00	5.50
❑ H6	Chris Claiborne / Junior Seau	2.50	1.10
❑ H7	Brock Huard / Mark Brunell	3.00	1.35
❑ H8	Champ Bailey / Terrell Davis	5.00	2.20
❑ H9	Donovan McNabb / Rob Moore	6.00	2.70
❑ H10	David Boston / Joey Galloway	3.00	1.35
❑ H11	Cade McNown / Troy Aikman	8.00	3.60
❑ H12	Kevin Faulk / Eddie Kennison	2.50	1.10
❑ H13	Sedrick Irvin / Andre Rison	2.50	1.10
❑ H14	Rob Konrad / Daryl Johnston	1.50	.70
❑ H15	Amos Zereoue / Adrian Murrell	3.00	1.35
❑ H16	Peerless Price / Peyton Manning	8.00	3.60
❑ H17	Kevin Johnson / Marvin Harrison	4.00	1.80
❑ H18	Jevon Kearse / Emmitt Smith	6.00	2.70
❑ H19	Antoine Winfield / Shawn Springs	1.50	.70
❑ H20	Tony Bryant / Andre Wadsworth	1.50	.70

1999 Collector's Edge Supreme Markers

		MINT	NRMT
COMPLETE SET (15)		70.00	32.00
COMMON CARD (M1-M15)		3.00	1.35
STATED PRINT RUN 5000 SERIAL #'d SETS			
❑ M1	Terrell Davis	8.00	3.60
❑ M2	John Elway	10.00	4.50
❑ M3	Dan Marino	10.00	4.50
❑ M4	Peyton Manning	8.00	3.60
❑ M5	Barry Sanders	10.00	4.50
❑ M6	Emmitt Smith	8.00	3.60
❑ M7	Randy Moss	10.00	4.50
❑ M8	Jake Plummer	6.00	2.70
❑ M9	Cris Carter	3.00	1.35
❑ M10	Brett Favre	10.00	4.50
❑ M11	Drew Bledsoe	5.00	2.20
❑ M12	Charlie Batch	5.00	2.20
❑ M13	Curtis Martin	3.00	1.35
❑ M14	Mark Brunell	5.00	2.20
❑ M15	Jamal Anderson	3.00	1.35

1999 Collector's Edge Supreme PSA10 Redemption

		MINT	NRMT
COMPLETE SET (3)		200.00	90.00
COMMON CARD		50.00	22.00
1/4/10 STATED PRINT RUN 1999 SETS			
❑ 1	Tim Couch	80.00	36.00
❑ 4	Daunte Culpepper	50.00	22.00
❑ 10	Ricky Williams	80.00	36.00

1999 Collector's Edge Supreme Route XXXIII

		MINT	NRMT
COMPLETE SET (10)		50.00	22.00
COMMON CARD (R1-R10)		3.00	1.35
STATED PRINT RUN 1000 SERIAL #'d SETS			
❑ R1	Randy Moss	10.00	4.50
❑ R2	Jamal Anderson	3.00	1.35
❑ R3	Jake Plummer	5.00	2.20
❑ R4	Steve Young	5.00	2.20
❑ R5	Fred Taylor	6.00	2.70
❑ R6	Dan Marino	12.00	5.50
❑ R7	Keyshawn Johnson	3.00	1.35
❑ R8	Curtis Martin	3.00	1.35
❑ R9	John Elway	12.00	5.50
❑ R10	Terrell Davis	8.00	3.60

1999 Collector's Edge Supreme Supremacy

		MINT	NRMT
COMPLETE SET (5)		40.00	18.00
COMMON CARD (S1-S5)		4.00	1.80
STATED PRINT RUN 500 SERIAL #'d SETS			
❑ S1	John Elway	20.00	9.00
❑ S2	Terrell Davis	12.00	5.50
❑ S3	Ed McCaffrey	7.00	1.80
❑ S4	Jamal Anderson	6.00	2.70
❑ S5	Chris Chandler	7.00	1.80

1999 Collector's Edge Supreme T3

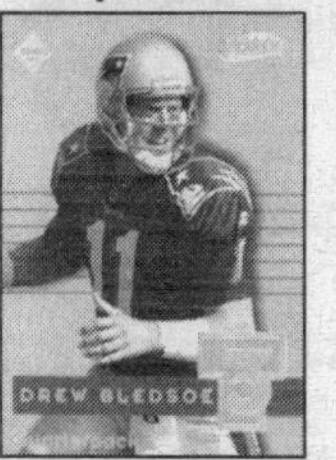

	MINT	NRMT
COMPLETE SET (30)	100.00	45.00
COMMON QB (T1-T10)	4.00	1.80
QB STATED ODDS 1:24		
COMMON RB (T11-T20)	1.25	.55
SEMISTARS RB	2.00	.90
RB STATED ODDS 1:12		
COMMON WR (T21-T30)	1.00	.45
SEMISTARS WR	1.50	.70
WR STATED ODDS 1:8		

❑ T1 Doug Flutie	4.00	1.80
❑ T2 Troy Aikman	8.00	3.60
❑ T3 John Elway	12.00	5.50
❑ T4 Jake Plummer	6.00	2.70
❑ T5 Brett Favre	12.00	5.50
❑ T6 Mark Brunell	5.00	2.20
❑ T7 Peyton Manning	12.00	5.50
❑ T8 Dan Marino	12.00	5.50
❑ T9 Drew Bledsoe	5.00	2.20
❑ T10 Steve Young	5.00	2.20
❑ T11 Jamal Anderson	2.00	.90
❑ T12 Emmitt Smith	5.00	2.20
❑ T13 Terrell Davis	5.00	2.20
❑ T14 Barry Sanders	8.00	3.60
❑ T15 Robert Smith	1.25	.55
❑ T16 Robert Edwards	1.25	.55
❑ T17 Curtis Martin	2.00	.90
❑ T18 Jerome Bettis	2.00	.90
❑ T19 Fred Taylor	5.00	2.20
❑ T20 Eddie George	2.50	1.10
❑ T21 Michael Irvin	1.50	.70
❑ T22 Eric Moulds	1.50	.70
❑ T23 Herman Moore	1.50	.70
❑ T24 Reidel Anthony	1.00	.45
❑ T25 Randy Moss	6.00	2.70
❑ T26 Cris Carter	4.00	1.80
❑ T27 Keyshawn Johnson	1.50	.70
❑ T28 Jacquez Green	1.00	.45
❑ T29 Jerry Rice	3.00	1.35
❑ T30 Terrell Owens	1.50	.70

2000 Collector's Edge Supreme

	MINT	NRMT
COMPLETE SET (190)	200.00	90.00
COMP.SET w/o SP's (150)	20.00	9.00
COMMON CARD (1-150)	.10	.05
SEMISTARS	.20	.09
UNLISTED STARS	.50	.23
COMMON ROOKIE (151-190)	5.00	2.20
ROOKIE SEMISTARS	6.00	2.70

151-190 ROOKIES PRINT RUN 2000 SER.#'d SETS
SOME RCs ISSUED VIA MAIL REDEMPTION
RC REDEMPTION EXPIRATION: 3/31/2001

❑ 1 David Boston	.50	.23
❑ 2 Adrian Murrell	.20	.09
❑ 3 Michael Pittman	.10	.05
❑ 4 Jake Plummer	.50	.23
❑ 5 Frank Sanders	.20	.09
❑ 6 Jamal Anderson	.50	.23
❑ 7 Chris Chandler	.20	.09
❑ 8 Terance Mathis	.20	.09
❑ 9 Justin Armour	.10	.05
❑ 10 Tony Banks	.20	.09
❑ 11 Qadry Ismail	.10	.05
❑ 12 Errict Rhett	.20	.09
❑ 13 Doug Flutie	.60	.25
❑ 14 Eric Moulds	.50	.23
❑ 15 Peerless Price	.50	.23
❑ 16 Andre Reed	.20	.09
❑ 17 Antowain Smith	.50	.23
❑ 18 Steve Beuerlein	.20	.09
❑ 19 Tim Biakabutuka	.20	.09
❑ 20 Muhsin Muhammad	.20	.09
❑ 21 Wesley Walls	.10	.05
❑ 22 Bobby Engram	.10	.05
❑ 23 Curtis Enis	.50	.23
❑ 24 Shane Matthews	.20	.09
❑ 25 Cade McNown	.75	.35
❑ 26 Jim Miller	.10	.05
❑ 27 Marcus Robinson	.50	.23
❑ 28 Corey Dillon	.50	.23
❑ 29 Carl Pickens	.20	.09
❑ 30 Darnay Scott	.20	.09
❑ 31 Akili Smith	.60	.25
❑ 32 Karim Abdul-Jabbar	.20	.09
❑ 33 Tim Couch	1.25	.55
❑ 34 Kevin Johnson	.50	.23
❑ 35 Troy Aikman	1.25	.55
❑ 36 Michael Irvin	.20	.09
❑ 37 Rocket Ismail	.20	.09
❑ 38 Deion Sanders	.50	.23
❑ 39 Emmitt Smith	1.25	.55
❑ 40 Terrell Davis	1.25	.55
❑ 41 Olandis Gary	.60	.25
❑ 42 Brian Griese	.60	.25
❑ 43 Ed McCaffrey	.20	.09
❑ 44 Rod Smith	.20	.09
❑ 45 Charlie Batch	.50	.23
❑ 46 Germane Crowell	.20	.09
❑ 47 Greg Hill	.10	.05
❑ 48 Sedrick Irvin	.10	.05
❑ 49 Herman Moore	.50	.23
❑ 50 Johnnie Morton	.20	.09
❑ 51 Corey Bradford	.20	.09
❑ 52 Brett Favre	2.00	.90
❑ 53 Antonio Freeman	.50	.23
❑ 54 Dorsey Levens	.50	.23
❑ 55 Bill Schroeder	.20	.09
❑ 56 E.G. Green	.10	.05
❑ 57 Marvin Harrison	.50	.23
❑ 58 Edgerrin James	2.00	.90
❑ 59 Peyton Manning	1.50	.70
❑ 60 Terrence Wilkins	.50	.23
❑ 61 Mark Brunell	.75	.35
❑ 62 Keenan McCardell	.20	.09
❑ 63 Jimmy Smith	.20	.09
❑ 64 James Stewart	.20	.09
❑ 65 Fred Taylor	.75	.35
❑ 66 Derrick Alexander	.20	.09
❑ 67 Donnell Bennett	.10	.05
❑ 68 Mike Cloud	.10	.05
❑ 69 Tony Gonzalez	.20	.09
❑ 70 Elvis Grbac	.20	.09
❑ 71 Damon Huard	.50	.23
❑ 72 James Johnson	.20	.09
❑ 73 Rob Konrad	.10	.05
❑ 74 Dan Marino	2.00	.90
❑ 75 Tony Martin	.20	.09
❑ 76 O.J. McDuffie	.20	.09
❑ 77 Cris Carter	.50	.23
❑ 78 Daunte Culpepper	.75	.35
❑ 79 Jeff George	.20	.09
❑ 80 Randy Moss	1.50	.70
❑ 81 Robert Smith	.50	.23
❑ 82 Terry Allen	.20	.09
❑ 83 Drew Bledsoe	.75	.35
❑ 84 Kevin Faulk	.20	.09
❑ 85 Terry Glenn	.50	.23
❑ 86 Shawn Jefferson	.10	.05
❑ 87 Billy Joe Hobert	.10	.05
❑ 88 Eddie Kennison	.20	.09
❑ 89 Billy Joe Tolliver	.10	.05
❑ 90 Ricky Williams	1.25	.55
❑ 91 Tiki Barber	.20	.09
❑ 92 Gary Brown	.10	.05
❑ 93 Kent Graham	.10	.05
❑ 94 Ike Hilliard	.20	.09
❑ 95 Amani Toomer	.10	.05
❑ 96 Wayne Chrebet	.20	.09
❑ 97 Keyshawn Johnson	.50	.23
❑ 98 Ray Lucas	.50	.23
❑ 99 Curtis Martin	.50	.23
❑ 100 Vinny Testaverde	.20	.09
❑ 101 Tim Brown	.50	.23
❑ 102 Rich Gannon	.20	.09
❑ 103 James Jett	.10	.05
❑ 104 Napoleon Kaufman	.50	.23
❑ 105 Tyrone Wheatley	.20	.09
❑ 106 Charles Johnson	.10	.05
❑ 107 Donovan McNabb	.75	.35
❑ 108 Duce Staley	.50	.23
❑ 109 Jerome Bettis	.50	.23
❑ 110 Troy Edwards	.50	.23
❑ 111 Kordell Stewart	.50	.23
❑ 112 Hines Ward	.10	.05
❑ 113 Isaac Bruce	.50	.23
❑ 114 Marshall Faulk	.50	.23
❑ 115 Az-Zahir Hakim	.20	.09
❑ 116 Torry Holt	.50	.23
❑ 117 Kurt Warner	2.50	1.10
❑ 118 Jeff Graham	.10	.05
❑ 119 Jim Harbaugh	.20	.09
❑ 120 Freddie Jones	.10	.05
❑ 121 Natrone Means	.10	.05
❑ 122 Junior Seau	.20	.09
❑ 123 Jeff Garcia	.50	.23
❑ 124 Charlie Garner	.20	.09
❑ 125 Terrell Owens	.50	.23
❑ 126 Jerry Rice	1.25	.55
❑ 127 Steve Young	.75	.35
❑ 128 Sean Dawkins	.10	.05
❑ 129 Joey Galloway	.50	.23
❑ 130 Jon Kitna	.50	.23
❑ 131 Derrick Mayes	.20	.09
❑ 132 Ricky Watters	.20	.09
❑ 133 Mike Alstott	.50	.23
❑ 134 Reidel Anthony	.10	.05
❑ 135 Trent Dilfer	.20	.09
❑ 136 Warrick Dunn	.50	.23
❑ 137 Jacquez Green	.20	.09
❑ 138 Shaun King	.75	.35
❑ 139 Kevin Dyson	.20	.09
❑ 140 Eddie George	.60	.25
❑ 141 Jevon Kearse	.50	.23
❑ 142 Steve McNair	.50	.23
❑ 143 Yancey Thigpen	.10	.05
❑ 144 Champ Bailey	.20	.09
❑ 145 Albert Connell	.10	.05
❑ 146 Stephen Davis	.50	.23
❑ 147 Brad Johnson	.50	.23
❑ 148 Michael Westbrook	.20	.09
❑ 149 Checklist	.10	.05
❑ 150 Checklist	.10	.05
❑ 151 Rookie Trade Card	10.00	4.50
❑ 152 Peter Warrick RC	40.00	18.00
❑ 153 Chad Pennington RC	30.00	13.50
❑ 154 Courtney Brown RC	15.00	6.75
❑ 155 Thomas Jones RC	25.00	11.00
❑ 156 Chris Redman RC	12.00	5.50
❑ 157 R.Jay Soward RC	8.00	3.60
❑ 158 Jamal Lewis RC	25.00	11.00
❑ 159 Shaun Alexander RC	25.00	11.00
❑ 160 Travis Taylor RC	15.00	6.75
❑ 161 Ron Dayne RC	40.00	18.00
❑ 162 Travis Prentice RC	8.00	3.60

❑ 163 Plaxico Burress RC 20.00 9.00
❑ 164 J.R. Redmond RC 12.00 5.50
❑ 165 Sherrod Gideon RC 5.00 2.20
❑ 166 Dez White RC 8.00 3.60
❑ 167 Chafie Fields RC 5.00 2.20
❑ 168 Rookie Trade Card 10.00 4.50
❑ 169 Reuben Droughns RC 8.00 3.60
❑ 170 Trung Canidate RC 6.00 2.70
❑ 171 Rookie Trade Card 10.00 4.50
❑ 172 Rookie Trade Card 10.00 4.50
❑ 173 Shyrone Stith RC 5.00 2.20
❑ 174 Michael Wiley RC 8.00 3.60
❑ 175 Bubba Franks RC 8.00 3.60
❑ 176 Tom Brady RC 6.00 2.70
❑ 177 Anthony Lucas RC 6.00 2.70
❑ 178 Danny Farmer RC 6.00 2.70
❑ 179 Rob Morris RC 5.00 2.20
❑ 180 Dennis Northcutt RC 8.00 3.60
❑ 181 Troy Walters RC 6.00 2.70
❑ 182 Giovanni Carmazzi RC 15.00 6.75
❑ 183 Tee Martin RC 12.00 5.50
❑ 184 Joe Hamilton RC 6.00 2.70
❑ 185 Tim Rattay RC 8.00 3.60
❑ 186 Sebastian Janikowski RC 5.00 2.20
❑ 187 Na'il Diggs RC 5.00 2.20
❑ 188 Todd Husak RC 6.00 2.70
❑ 189 Jerry Porter RC 8.00 3.60
❑ 190 Rookie Trade Card 10.00 4.50
❑ 59A Peyton Manning AUTO/300 70.00 32.00

2000 Collector's Edge Supreme Hologold

MINT NRMT
COMMON CARD (1-150) 1.00 .45
*HOLOGOLD STARS: 4X TO 10X HI COL.
*HOLOGOLD YOUNG STARS: 3X TO 8X
1-150 PRINT RUN 200 SERIAL #'d SETS
COMMON ROOKIE (151-190) 25.00 11.00
*HOLOGOLD RCs: 2X TO 5X
151-190 ROOKIES PRINT RUN 20 SER.#'d SETS

❑ 59 Peyton Manning AUTO 80.00 36.00

2000 Collector's Edge Supreme EdgeTech

MINT NRMT
COMPLETE SET (49) 600.00 275.00
COMMON CARD (ET1-ET50) 8.00 3.60
STATED PRINT RUN 100 SERIAL #'D SETS

❑ ET1 Doug Flutie 10.00 4.50
❑ ET2 Cade McNown 10.00 4.50
❑ ET3 Akili Smith 8.00 3.60
❑ ET4 Tim Couch 15.00 6.75
❑ ET5 Kevin Johnson 8.00 3.60
❑ ET6 Troy Aikman 20.00 9.00
❑ ET7 Emmitt Smith 20.00 9.00
❑ ET8 Terrell Davis 20.00 9.00
❑ ET9 Brett Favre 30.00 13.50
❑ ET10 Marvin Harrison 8.00 3.60
❑ ET11 Edgerrin James 25.00 11.00
❑ ET12 Peyton Manning 25.00 11.00
❑ ET13 Mark Brunell 12.00 5.50
❑ ET14 Dan Marino 30.00 13.50
❑ ET15 Randy Moss 25.00 11.00
❑ ET16 Drew Bledsoe 12.00 5.50
❑ ET17 Ricky Williams 15.00 6.75
❑ ET18 Keyshawn Johnson 8.00 3.60
❑ ET19 Curtis Martin 8.00 3.60
❑ ET20 Donovan McNabb 10.00 4.50
❑ ET21 Marshall Faulk 8.00 3.60
❑ ET22 Torry Holt 8.00 3.60
❑ ET23 Kurt Warner 40.00 18.00
❑ ET24 Jerry Rice 20.00 9.00
❑ ET25 Steve Young 12.00 5.50
❑ ET26 Jon Kitna 8.00 3.60
❑ ET27 Shaun King 10.00 4.50
❑ ET28 Eddie George 10.00 4.50
❑ ET29 Stephen Davis 8.00 3.60
❑ ET30 Brad Johnson 8.00 3.60
❑ ET31 Chad Pennington 40.00 18.00
❑ ET32 Chris Redman 15.00 6.75
❑ ET33 Tim Rattay 12.00 5.50
❑ ET34 Tee Martin 15.00 6.75
❑ ET35 Thomas Jones 30.00 13.50
❑ ET36 Ron Dayne 50.00 22.00
❑ ET37 Jamal Lewis 30.00 13.50
❑ ET38 J.R. Redmond 15.00 6.75
❑ ET39 Travis Prentice 12.00 5.50
❑ ET40 Shaun Alexander 30.00 13.50
❑ ET41 Michael Wiley 12.00 5.50
❑ ET42 Shyrone Stith 10.00 4.50
❑ ET43 Peter Warrick 50.00 22.00
❑ ET44 Plaxico Burress 25.00 11.00
❑ ET45 Travis Taylor 20.00 9.00
❑ ET46 Jerry Porter 12.00 5.50
❑ ET47 R.Jay Soward 12.00 5.50
❑ ET48 Dez White 12.00 5.50
❑ ET49 To be announced
❑ ET50 Courtney Brown 20.00 9.00

2000 Collector's Edge Supreme Future

MINT NRMT
COMPLETE SET (9) 150.00 70.00
COMMON CARD (SF1-SF9) 12.00 5.50
STATED PRINT RUN 100 SERIAL #'D SETS

❑ SF1 Peter Warrick 50.00 22.00
❑ SF2 Plaxico Burress 25.00 11.00
❑ SF3 R.Jay Soward 12.00 5.50
❑ SF4 Ron Dayne 50.00 22.00
❑ SF5 Thomas Jones 30.00 13.50
❑ SF6 Shaun Alexander 30.00 13.50
❑ SF7 Chad Pennington 40.00 18.00
❑ SF8 Chris Redman 15.00 6.75
❑ SF9 Travis Prentice 12.00 5.50

2000 Collector's Edge Supreme Monday Knights

MINT NRMT
COMPLETE SET (20) 25.00 11.00
COMMON CARD (MK1-MK20) 1.25 .55
STATED ODDS 1:8

❑ MK1 Jake Plummer 1.25 .55

❑ MK2 Doug Flutie 1.50 .70
❑ MK3 Cade McNown 1.50 .70
❑ MK4 Akili Smith 1.25 .55
❑ MK5 Tim Couch 2.50 1.10
❑ MK6 Kevin Johnson 1.25 .55
❑ MK7 Troy Aikman 3.00 1.35
❑ MK8 Emmitt Smith 3.00 1.35
❑ MK9 Terrell Davis 3.00 1.35
❑ MK10 Charlie Batch 1.25 .55
❑ MK11 Brett Favre 5.00 2.20
❑ MK12 Cris Carter 1.25 .55
❑ MK13 Drew Bledsoe 2.00 .90
❑ MK14 Ricky Williams 2.50 1.10
❑ MK15 Curtis Martin 1.25 .55
❑ MK16 Jerry Rice 3.00 1.35
❑ MK17 Jon Kitna 1.25 .55
❑ MK18 Shaun King 1.50 .70
❑ MK19 Eddie George 1.50 .70
❑ MK20 Brad Johnson 1.25 .55

2000 Collector's Edge Supreme Pro Signature Authentics

MINT NRMT
COMMON CARD 12.00 5.50
STATED ODDS 1:197
RED AUTOS SERIAL #'d OF 10 NOT PRICED

❑ CM1 C.McNown/650 Black 30.00 13.50
❑ CM2 C.McNown/325 Red 40.00 18.00
❑ DM1 D.McDonald/230 Black 15.00 6.75
❑ DM2 D.McDonald/40 Blue 30.00 13.50
❑ DM3 D.McDonald/10 Red
❑ JJ1 J.Johnson/1450 Black 12.00 5.50
❑ JJ2 J.Johnson/42 Blue 40.00 18.00
❑ JJ3 J.Johnson/10 Red
❑ PM P.Manning/1000 Black 50.00 22.00
❑ RM R.Moss/150 Blue 100.00 45.00
❑ RW1 R.Williams/230 Black 60.00 27.00
❑ RW2 R.Williams/39 Blue 120.00 55.00
❑ RW3 R.Williams/10 Red
❑ TC T.Couch/650 Black 50.00 22.00

2000 Collector's Edge Supreme PSA Redemption

MINT NRMT
COMPLETE SET (9) 600.00 275.00
COMMON CARD (1-9) 40.00 18.00
STATED PRINT RUN 100 SETS

❑ 1 Peter Warrick 150.00 70.00
❑ 2 Plaxico Burress 80.00 36.00
❑ 3 R. Jay Soward 40.00 18.00
❑ 4 Ron Dayne 120.00 55.00
❑ 5 Thomas Jones 100.00 45.00
❑ 6 Shaun Alexander 100.00 45.00
❑ 7 Chad Pennington 120.00 55.00
❑ 8 Chris Redman 50.00 22.00
❑ 9 Travis Prentice 40.00 18.00
❑ 10 To be announced

2000 Collector's Edge Supreme Route XXXIV

	MINT	NRMT
COMPLETE SET (10)	20.00	9.00
COMMON CARD (R1-R10)	1.25	.55
STATED ODDS 1:16		

Card	MINT	NRMT
❑ R1 Peyton Manning	4.00	1.80
❑ R2 Edgerrin James	4.00	1.80
❑ R3 Warrick Dunn	1.25	.55
❑ R4 Dan Marino	5.00	2.20
❑ R5 Steve McNair	1.25	.55
❑ R6 Mark Brunell	2.00	.90
❑ R7 Kurt Warner	6.00	2.70
❑ R8 Marshall Faulk	1.25	.55
❑ R9 Randy Moss	4.00	1.80
❑ R10 Stephen Davis	1.25	.55

2000 Collector's Edge Supreme Team

	MINT	NRMT
COMPLETE SET (20)	30.00	13.50
COMMON CARD (ST1-ST20)	1.25	.55
STATED ODDS 1:8		

Card	MINT	NRMT
❑ ST1 Peyton Manning	4.00	1.80
❑ ST2 Kurt Warner	6.00	2.70
❑ ST3 Tim Couch	2.50	1.10
❑ ST4 Cade McNown	1.50	.70
❑ ST5 Akili Smith	1.25	.55
❑ ST6 Donovan McNabb	1.50	.70
❑ ST7 Edgerrin James	4.00	1.80
❑ ST8 Stephen Davis	1.25	.55
❑ ST9 Mark Brunell	2.00	.90
❑ ST10 Brett Favre	5.00	2.20
❑ ST11 Marvin Harrison	1.25	.55
❑ ST12 Isaac Bruce	1.25	.55
❑ ST13 Terrell Davis	3.00	1.35
❑ ST14 Ricky Williams	2.50	1.10
❑ ST15 Keyshawn Johnson	1.25	.55
❑ ST16 Randy Moss	4.00	1.80
❑ ST17 Kevin Johnson	1.25	.55
❑ ST18 Torry Holt	1.25	.55
❑ ST19 Dan Marino	5.00	2.20
❑ ST20 Troy Aikman	3.00	1.35

1999 Collector's Edge Triumph

	MINT	NRMT
COMPLETE SET (180)	60.00	27.00
COMMON CARD (1-140)	.15	.07
SEMISTARS	.30	.14
UNLISTED STARS	.60	.25
COMMON ROOKIES (141-180)	.50	.23
ROOKIE SEMISTARS	1.00	.45
ROOKIE UNL.STARS	1.50	.70
ONE ROOKIE SUBSET PER PACK		

Card	MINT	NRMT
❑ 1 Jamal Anderson	.60	.25
❑ 2 Jerome Bettis	.60	.25
❑ 3 Terrell Davis	1.50	.70
❑ 4 Corey Dillon	.60	.25
❑ 5 Warrick Dunn	.60	.25
❑ 6 Marshall Faulk	.60	.25
❑ 7 Eddie George	.75	.35
❑ 8 Garrison Hearst	.30	.14
❑ 9 Skip Hicks	.60	.25
❑ 10 Napoleon Kaufman	.60	.25
❑ 11 Dorsey Levens	.60	.25
❑ 12 Curtis Martin	.60	.25
❑ 13 Natrone Means	.30	.14
❑ 14 Adrian Murrell	.30	.14
❑ 15 Barry Sanders	2.50	1.10
❑ 16 Antowain Smith	.60	.25
❑ 17 Emmitt Smith	1.50	.70
❑ 18 Robert Smith	.60	.25
❑ 19 Fred Taylor	1.50	.70
❑ 20 Ricky Watters	.30	.14
❑ 21 Cameron Cleeland	.15	.07
❑ 22 Ben Coates	.30	.14
❑ 23 Shannon Sharpe	.30	.14
❑ 24 Frank Wycheck	.15	.07
❑ 25 Derrick Alexander WR	.30	.14
❑ 26 Reidel Anthony	.30	.14
❑ 27 Robert Brooks	.30	.14
❑ 28 Tim Brown	.60	.25
❑ 29 Cris Carter	.60	.25
❑ 30 Wayne Chrebet	.30	.14
❑ 31 Curtis Conway	.30	.14
❑ 32 Tim Dwight	.60	.25
❑ 33 Kevin Dyson	.30	.14
❑ 34 Antonio Freeman	.60	.25
❑ 35 Joey Galloway	.60	.25
❑ 36 Terry Glenn	.60	.25
❑ 37 Marvin Harrison	.60	.25
❑ 38 Ike Hilliard	.15	.07
❑ 39 Michael Irvin	.30	.14
❑ 40 Keyshawn Johnson	.60	.25
❑ 41 Jermaine Lewis	.30	.14
❑ 42 Terance Mathis	.30	.14
❑ 43 Ed McCaffrey	.30	.14
❑ 44 Keenan McCardell	.30	.14
❑ 45 O.J. McDuffie	.30	.14
❑ 46 Herman Moore	.60	.25
❑ 47 Rob Moore	.30	.14
❑ 48 Randy Moss	2.50	1.10
❑ 49 Eric Moulds	.60	.25
❑ 50 Muhsin Muhammad	.30	.14
❑ 51 Terrell Owens	.60	.25
❑ 52 Jerome Pathon	.15	.07
❑ 53 Carl Pickens	.30	.14
❑ 54 Andre Reed	.30	.14
❑ 55 Jake Reed	.30	.14
❑ 56 Jerry Rice	1.50	.70
❑ 57 Andre Rison	.30	.14
❑ 58 Jimmy Smith	.30	.14
❑ 59 Rod Smith WR	.30	.14
❑ 60 Michael Westbrook	.30	.14
❑ 61 Morten Andersen	.15	.07
❑ 62 Gary Anderson	.15	.07
❑ 63 Doug Brien	.15	.07
❑ 64 Chris Boniol	.15	.07
❑ 65 John Carney	.15	.07
❑ 66 Steve Christie	.15	.07
❑ 67 Richie Cunningham	.15	.07
❑ 68 Brad Daluiso	.15	.07
❑ 69 AL Del Greco	.15	.07
❑ 70 Jason Elam	.15	.07
❑ 71 John Hall	.15	.07
❑ 72 Jason Hanson	.15	.07
❑ 73 Mike Hollis	.15	.07
❑ 74 Norm Johnson	.15	.07
❑ 75 Olindo Mare	.15	.07
❑ 76 Doug Pelfrey	.15	.07
❑ 77 Wade Richey	.15	.07
❑ 78 Pete Stoyanovich	.15	.07
❑ 79 Mike Vanderjagt	.15	.07
❑ 80 Adam Vinatieri	.15	.07
❑ 81 Ray Buchanan	.15	.07
❑ 82 Jim Flanigan	.15	.07
❑ 83 Darrell Green	.15	.07
❑ 84 Kevin Greene	.15	.07
❑ 85 Ty Law	.15	.07
❑ 86 Ken Norton Jr.	.15	.07
❑ 87 John Randle	.30	.14
❑ 88 Bill Romanowski	.15	.07
❑ 89 Deion Sanders	.60	.25
❑ 90 Junior Seau	.30	.14
❑ 91 Michael Sinclair	.15	.07
❑ 92 Bruce Smith	.30	.14
❑ 93 Takeo Spikes	.15	.07
❑ 94 Michael Strahan	.15	.07
❑ 95 Derrick Thomas	.30	.14
❑ 96 Zach Thomas	.30	.14
❑ 97 Andre Wadsworth	.15	.07
❑ 98 Charles Woodson	.60	.25
❑ 99 Checklist Card	.15	.07
❑ 100 Checklist Card	.15	.07
❑ 101 Troy Aikman	1.50	.70
❑ 102 Tony Banks	.30	.14
❑ 103 Charlie Batch	1.25	.55
❑ 104 Steve Beuerlein	.15	.07
❑ 105 Jeff Blake	.30	.14
❑ 106 Drew Bledsoe	1.00	.45
❑ 107 Bubby Brister	.15	.07
❑ 108 Mark Brunell	1.00	.45
❑ 109 Chris Chandler	.30	.14
❑ 110 Kerry Collins	.30	.14
❑ 111 Randall Cunningham	.60	.25
❑ 112 Koy Detmer	.15	.07
❑ 113 Ty Detmer	.15	.07
❑ 114 Trent Dilfer	.30	.14
❑ 115 John Elway	2.50	1.10
❑ 116 Brett Favre	2.50	1.10
❑ 117 Doug Flutie	.75	.35
❑ 118 Rich Gannon	.30	.14
❑ 119 Jeff Garcia RC**/C	4.00	1.80
❑ 120 Jeff George	.30	.14
❑ 121 Jon Kitna	.75	.35
❑ 122 Elvis Grbac	.30	.14
❑ 123 Brian Griese	1.25	.55
❑ 124 Trent Green	.30	.14
❑ 125 Jim Harbaugh	.30	.14
❑ 126 Billy Joe Hobert	.15	.07
❑ 127 Brad Johnson	.60	.25
❑ 128 Rob Johnson	.30	.14
❑ 129 Jon Kitna	.75	.35
❑ 130 Erik Kramer	.15	.07
❑ 131 Ryan Leaf	.60	.25
❑ 132 Peyton Manning	2.50	1.10
❑ 133 Dan Marino	2.50	1.10
❑ 134 Steve McNair	.60	.25
❑ 135 Scott Mitchell	.15	.07
❑ 136 Warren Moon	.60	.25
❑ 137 Jake Plummer	1.25	.55
❑ 138 Kordell Stewart	.60	.25
❑ 139 Vinny Testaverde	.30	.14
❑ 140 Steve Young	1.00	.45
❑ 141 Champ Bailey RC	2.00	.90
❑ 142 Karsten Bailey RC	1.00	.45
❑ 143 D'Wayne Bates RC	1.50	.70
❑ 144 David Boston RC	2.50	1.10
❑ 145 Cuncho Brown RC	1.00	.45
❑ 146 Dat Nguyen RC	1.50	.70
❑ 147 Chris Claiborne RC	1.00	.45
❑ 148 Mike Cloud RC	1.50	.70
❑ 149 Cecil Collins RC	1.50	.70
❑ 150 Tim Couch RC	8.00	3.60
❑ 151 Daunte Culpepper RC	5.00	2.20
❑ 152 Autry Denson RC	1.50	.70
❑ 153 Troy Edwards RC	2.50	1.10
❑ 154 Ebenezer Ekuban RC	1.00	.45
❑ 155 Kevin Faulk RC	2.00	.90
❑ 156 Jermaine Fazande RC	1.00	.45
❑ 157 Joe Germaine RC	1.50	.70
❑ 158 Martin Gramatica RC	.50	.23
❑ 159 Torry Holt RC	4.00	1.80

		MINT	NRMT
❑ 160	Brock Huard RC	2.00	.90
❑ 161	Sedrick Irvin RC	1.50	.70
❑ 162	Edgerrin James RC	12.00	5.50
❑ 163	James Johnson RC	2.00	.90
❑ 164	Kevin Johnson RC	4.00	1.80
❑ 165	Andy Katzenmoyer RC	1.50	.70
❑ 166	Jevon Kearse RC	3.00	1.35
❑ 167	Patrick Kerney RC	.50	.23
❑ 168	Shaun King RC	5.00	2.20
❑ 169	Jim Kleinsasser RC	1.50	.70
❑ 170	Rob Konrad RC	1.50	.70
❑ 171	Chris McAlister RC	1.00	.45
❑ 172	Donovan McNabb RC	5.00	2.20
❑ 173	Cade McNown RC	5.00	2.20
❑ 174	Joe Montgomery RC	1.50	.70
❑ 175	Peerless Price RC	2.50	1.10
❑ 176	Akili Smith RC	3.00	1.35
❑ 177	Ricky Williams RC	8.00	3.60
❑ 178	Larry Parker RC	1.00	.45
❑ 179	Antoine Winfield RC	1.00	.45
❑ 180	Amos Zereoue RC	1.50	.70

1999 Collector's Edge Triumph Commissioner's Choice

	MINT	NRMT
COMPLETE SET (10)	50.00	22.00
COMMON CARD (CC1-CC10)	2.50	1.10
STATED ODDS 1:15		
*GOLDS: .75X TO 2X HI COL.		
GOLD PRINT RUN 500 SER.#'d SETS		

❑ CC1	Tim Couch	10.00	4.50
❑ CC2	Donovan McNabb	6.00	2.70
❑ CC3	Cade McNown	6.00	2.70
❑ CC4	Daunte Culpepper	6.00	2.70
❑ CC5	Akili Smith	4.00	1.80
❑ CC6	Ricky Williams	10.00	4.50
❑ CC7	Edgerrin James	15.00	6.75
❑ CC8	Torry Holt	5.00	2.20
❑ CC9	David Boston	3.00	1.35
❑ CC10	Champ Bailey	2.50	1.10

1999 Collector's Edge Triumph Fantasy Team

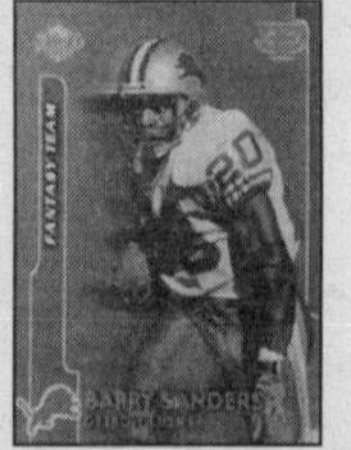

	MINT	NRMT
COMPLETE SET (10)	40.00	18.00
COMMON CARD (FT1-FT10)	4.00	1.80
STATED ODDS 1:10		

❑ FT1	Terrell Davis	5.00	2.20
❑ FT2	John Elway	8.00	3.60
❑ FT3	Brett Favre	8.00	3.60
❑ FT4	Peyton Manning	6.00	2.70
❑ FT5	Dan Marino	8.00	3.60
❑ FT6	Randy Moss	6.00	2.70
❑ FT7	Jake Plummer	4.00	1.80
❑ FT8	Barry Sanders	8.00	3.60
❑ FT9	Emmitt Smith	5.00	2.20
❑ FT10	Fred Taylor	4.00	1.80

1999 Collector's Edge Triumph Future Fantasy Team

	MINT	NRMT
COMPLETE SET (20)	40.00	18.00
COMMON CARD (FFT1-FFT20)	.75	.35
SEMISTARS	1.25	.55
UNLISTED STARS	1.50	.70
STATED ODDS 1:6		

❑ FFT1	Champ Bailey	1.50	.70
❑ FFT2	D'Wayne Bates	.75	.35
❑ FFT3	David Boston	2.00	.90
❑ FFT4	Tim Couch	6.00	2.70
❑ FFT5	Daunte Culpepper	4.00	1.80
❑ FFT6	Troy Edwards	2.00	.90
❑ FFT7	Kevin Faulk	1.50	.70
❑ FFT8	Torry Holt	3.00	1.35
❑ FFT9	Brock Huard	1.50	.70
❑ FFT10	Sedrick Irvin	1.25	.55
❑ FFT11	Edgerrin James	10.00	4.50
❑ FFT12	James Johnson	1.25	.55
❑ FFT13	Kevin Johnson	3.00	1.35
❑ FFT14	Rob Konrad	1.25	.55
❑ FFT15	Donovan McNabb	4.00	1.80
❑ FFT16	Cade McNown	4.00	1.80
❑ FFT17	Peerless Price	2.00	.90
❑ FFT18	Akili Smith	2.50	1.10
❑ FFT19	Ricky Williams	6.00	2.70
❑ FFT20	Amos Zereoue	1.25	.55

1999 Collector's Edge Triumph Heir Supply

	MINT	NRMT
COMPLETE SET (15)	30.00	13.50
COMMON CARD (HS1-HS15)	.75	.35
SEMISTARS	1.00	.45
UNLISTED STARS	1.25	.55
STATED ODDS 1:3		

❑ HS1	Ricky Williams	5.00	2.20
❑ HS2	Tim Couch	5.00	2.20
❑ HS3	Cade McNown	3.00	1.35
❑ HS4	Donovan McNabb	3.00	1.35
❑ HS5	Akili Smith	2.00	.90
❑ HS6	Daunte Culpepper	3.00	1.35
❑ HS7	Torry Holt	2.50	1.10
❑ HS8	Edgerrin James	8.00	3.60
❑ HS9	David Boston	1.50	.70
❑ HS10	Troy Edwards	1.50	.70
❑ HS11	Peerless Price	1.50	.70
❑ HS12	Champ Bailey	1.25	.55
❑ HS13	D'Wayne Bates	.75	.35
❑ HS14	Kevin Faulk	1.25	.55
❑ HS15	Amos Zereoue	1.00	.45

1999 Collector's Edge Triumph K-Klub Y3K

	MINT	NRMT
COMPLETE SET (50)	120.00	55.00
COMMON CARD (KK1-KK50)	1.50	.70
SEMISTARS	3.00	1.35
STATED PRINT RUN 1000 SERIAL #'d SETS		

❑ KK1	Karim Abdul-Jabbar	1.50	.70
❑ KK2	Jamal Anderson	2.50	1.10
❑ KK3	Jerome Bettis	2.50	1.10
❑ KK4	Isaac Bruce	2.50	1.10
❑ KK5	Cris Carter	2.50	1.10
❑ KK6	Terrell Davis	8.00	3.60
❑ KK7	Corey Dillon	2.50	1.10
❑ KK8	Warrick Dunn	2.50	1.10
❑ KK9	Curtis Enis	2.50	1.10
❑ KK10	Marshall Faulk	2.50	1.10
❑ KK11	Antonio Freeman	2.50	1.10
❑ KK12	Joey Galloway	2.50	1.10
❑ KK13	Eddie George	4.00	1.80
❑ KK14	Terry Glenn	2.50	1.10
❑ KK15	Garrison Hearst	1.50	.70
❑ KK16	Keyshawn Johnson	2.50	1.10
❑ KK17	Napoleon Kaufman	2.50	1.10
❑ KK18	Curtis Martin	2.50	1.10
❑ KK19	Rob Moore	1.50	.70
❑ KK20	Herman Moore	2.50	1.10
❑ KK21	Eric Moulds	2.50	1.10
❑ KK22	Randy Moss	10.00	4.50
❑ KK23	Adrian Murrell	1.50	.70
❑ KK24	Carl Pickens	1.50	.70
❑ KK25	Jerry Rice	8.00	3.60
❑ KK26	Barry Sanders	12.00	5.50
❑ KK27	Antowain Smith	2.50	1.10
❑ KK28	Emmitt Smith	8.00	3.60
❑ KK29	Fred Taylor	6.00	2.70
❑ KK30	Ricky Watters	1.50	.70
❑ KK31	Troy Aikman	8.00	3.60
❑ KK32	Charlie Batch	5.00	2.20
❑ KK33	Drew Bledsoe	5.00	2.20
❑ KK34	Mark Brunell	5.00	2.20
❑ KK35	Chris Chandler	1.50	.70
❑ KK36	Randall Cunningham	2.50	1.10
❑ KK37	Trent Dilfer	1.50	.70

❑ KK38	John Elway	12.00	5.50
❑ KK39	Brett Favre	12.00	5.50
❑ KK40	Doug Flutie	4.00	1.80
❑ KK41	Brad Johnson	2.50	1.10
❑ KK42	Jon Kitna	4.00	1.80
❑ KK43	Ryan Leaf	2.50	1.10
❑ KK44	Peyton Manning	10.00	4.50
❑ KK45	Dan Marino	12.00	5.50
❑ KK46	Steve McNair	2.50	1.10
❑ KK47	Jake Plummer	6.00	2.70
❑ KK48	Kordell Stewart	2.50	1.10
❑ KK49	Vinny Testaverde	1.50	.70
❑ KK50	Steve Young	5.00	2.20

1999 Collector's Edge Triumph Pack Warriors

	MINT	NRMT
COMPLETE SET (15)	30.00	13.50
COMMON CARD (PW1-PW15)	1.25	.55
STATED ODDS 1:4		

❑ PW1	Jamal Anderson	1.25	.55
❑ PW2	Jake Plummer	2.50	1.10
❑ PW3	Emmitt Smith	3.00	1.35
❑ PW4	Troy Aikman	3.00	1.35
❑ PW5	Terrell Davis	3.00	1.35
❑ PW6	John Elway	5.00	2.20
❑ PW7	Barry Sanders	5.00	2.20
❑ PW8	Brett Favre	5.00	2.20
❑ PW9	Peyton Manning	4.00	1.80
❑ PW10	Dan Marino	5.00	2.20
❑ PW11	Randy Moss	4.00	1.80
❑ PW12	Keyshawn Johnson	1.25	.55
❑ PW13	Fred Taylor	2.50	1.10
❑ PW14	Jerry Rice	3.00	1.35
❑ PW15	Jerome Bettis	1.25	.55

1999 Collector's Edge Triumph Signed, Sealed, Delivered

	MINT	NRMT
COMPLETE SET (39)	600.00	275.00
COMMON CARD	6.00	2.70
SEMISTARS	8.00	3.60
UNLISTED STARS	10.00	4.50
STATED ODDS 1:32		

*BLUE AUTOS: 1.25X TO 3X HI COL.
BLUE AUTOS PRINT RUN 40 SER.#'d SETS
UNPRICED REDS PRINT RUN 10 SER.#'d SETS

❑ AD	Autry Denson	10.00	4.50
❑ AS	Akili Smith	20.00	9.00
❑ AW	Antoine Winfield	8.00	3.60
❑ AZ	Amos Zereoue	10.00	4.50
❑ BH	Brock Huard	12.00	5.50
❑ CB	Cuncho Brown	8.00	3.60
❑ CB1	Champ Bailey	12.00	5.50
❑ CC	Chris Claiborne	8.00	3.60
❑ CC1	Cecil Collins	10.00	4.50
❑ CM	Chris McAlister	8.00	3.60
❑ CM1	Cade McNown	30.00	13.50
❑ DB	D'Wayne Bates	8.00	3.60
❑ DB1	David Boston	15.00	6.75
❑ DC	Daunte Culpepper	30.00	13.50
❑ DM	Donovan McNabb	30.00	13.50
❑ DN	Dat Nguyen	10.00	4.50
❑ EE	Ebenezer Ekuban	8.00	3.60
❑ EJ	Edgerrin James	100.00	45.00
❑ JF	Jermaine Fazande	8.00	3.60
❑ JG	Joe Germaine	10.00	4.50
❑ JJ	James Johnson	12.00	5.50
❑ JK	Jevon Kearse	20.00	9.00
❑ JK1	Jim Kleinsasser	10.00	4.50
❑ JM	Joe Montgomery	10.00	4.50
❑ KB	Karsten Bailey	8.00	3.60
❑ KF	Kevin Faulk	12.00	5.50
❑ KJ	Kevin Johnson	25.00	11.00
❑ LP	Larry Parker	8.00	3.60
❑ MC	Mike Cloud	10.00	4.50
❑ MG	Martin Gramatica	6.00	2.70
❑ PK	Patrick Kerney	6.00	2.70
❑ PP	Peerless Price	15.00	6.75
❑ RK	Rob Konrad	10.00	4.50
❑ RW	Ricky Williams	60.00	27.00
❑ SI	Sedrick Irvin	10.00	4.50
❑ SK	Shaun King	30.00	13.50
❑ TC	Tim Couch	60.00	27.00
❑ TE	Troy Edwards	15.00	6.75
❑ TH	Torry Holt	25.00	11.00

1995 Crown Royale

	MINT	NRMT
COMPLETE SET (144)	80.00	36.00
COMMON CARD (1-144)	.40	.18
SEMISTARS	.75	.35
UNLISTED STARS	1.50	.70
COMP.COPPER SET (144)	600.00	275.00

*COPPER STARS: 2X TO 5X HI COLUMN
*COPPER RCs: 1X TO 2.5X HI
COPPER: STATED ODDS 4:25 HOBBY

COMP.BLUE HOLO. (144)	1000.00	450.00

*BLUE HOLOFOIL STARS: 3X TO 8X HI COL.
*BLUE HOLOFOIL RCs: 1.5X TO 4X HI
BLUE HOLO: STATED ODDS 4:25 RETAIL

❑ 1	Lake Dawson	.75	.35
❑ 2	Steve Beuerlein	.40	.18
❑ 3	Jake Reed	.75	.35
❑ 4	Jim Everett	.40	.18
❑ 5	Sean Dawkins	.75	.35
❑ 6	Jeff Hostetler	.75	.35
❑ 7	Marshall Faulk	2.50	1.10
❑ 8	Jeff Blake RC	4.00	1.80
❑ 9	Dave Brown	.75	.35
❑ 10	Frank Reich	.40	.18
❑ 11	Rocket Ismail	.75	.35
❑ 12	Jerry Jones OWN UER Built is spelled bulit	1.50	.70
❑ 13	Dan Marino	8.00	3.60
❑ 14	Ricky Watters	1.50	.70
❑ 15	Herman Moore	1.50	.70
❑ 16	Daryl Johnston	.75	.35
❑ 17	Craig Erickson	.40	.18
❑ 18	Alexander Wright	.40	.18
❑ 19	Reggie White	1.50	.70
❑ 20	Andre Rison	.75	.35
❑ 21	Fred Barnett	.75	.35
❑ 22	Tyrone Wheatley RC	5.00	2.20
❑ 23	Charles Johnson	.75	.35
❑ 24	Rashaan Salaam RC	1.50	.70
❑ 25	Mark Brunell	4.00	1.80
❑ 26	Derek Loville	.40	.18
❑ 27	Garrison Hearst	1.50	.70
❑ 28	Ken Norton Jr.	.75	.35
❑ 29	Kerry Collins RC	4.00	1.80
❑ 30	Isaac Bruce	2.50	1.10
❑ 31	Andre Reed	.75	.35
❑ 32	Leon Lett	.40	.18
❑ 33	Deion Sanders	2.50	1.10
❑ 34	Terance Mathis	.75	.35
❑ 35	Tim Bowens	.40	.18
❑ 36	Shannon Sharpe	.75	.35
❑ 37	Quinn Early	.75	.35
❑ 38	Jerry Rice	4.00	1.80
❑ 39	Bruce Smith	1.50	.70
❑ 40	Drew Bledsoe	4.00	1.80
❑ 41	Alvin Harper	.40	.18
❑ 42	Jim Kelly	1.50	.70
❑ 43	Napoleon Kaufman RC	8.00	3.60
❑ 44	Errict Rhett	1.50	.70
❑ 45	Henry Ellard	.75	.35
❑ 46	Barry Sanders	8.00	3.60
❑ 47	Vincent Brisby	.40	.18
❑ 48	Chris Zorich	.40	.18
❑ 49	Zack Crockett RC	.40	.18
❑ 50	Haywood Jeffires	.40	.18
❑ 51	Byron Bam Morris	.75	.35
❑ 52	John Kasay	.40	.18
❑ 53	Scott Mitchell	.75	.35
❑ 54	Boomer Esiason	.75	.35
❑ 55	Eric Metcalf	.75	.35
❑ 56	Kevin Greene	.75	.35
❑ 57	Courtney Hawkins	.40	.18
❑ 58	Johnny Johnson	.40	.18
❑ 59	Larry Centers	.75	.35
❑ 60	Leroy Hoard	.40	.18
❑ 61	Lorenzo White	.40	.18
❑ 62	Chris Spielman	.75	.35
❑ 63	Carl Pickens	1.50	.70
❑ 64	Steve Young	3.00	1.35
❑ 65	Trent Dilfer	1.50	.70
❑ 66	Erik Kramer	.40	.18
❑ 67	Cortez Kennedy	.75	.35
❑ 68	Ray Childress	.40	.18
❑ 69	Rick Mirer	1.50	.70
❑ 70	Kevin Williams WR	.75	.35
❑ 71	Joey Galloway RC	10.00	4.50
❑ 72	Dan Wilkinson	.75	.35
❑ 73	Antonio Freeman RC	10.00	4.50
❑ 74	Curtis Conway	1.50	.70
❑ 75	Troy Aikman	4.00	1.80
❑ 76	Natrone Means	1.50	.70
❑ 77	Jeff George	.75	.35
❑ 78	Curtis Martin RC	10.00	4.50
❑ 79	William Floyd	1.50	.70
❑ 80	Anthony Miller	.75	.35
❑ 81	Greg Hill	.75	.35
❑ 82	Craig Heyward	.75	.35
❑ 83	Brian Mitchell	.40	.18
❑ 84	Anthony Carter	.75	.35
❑ 85	Jerome Bettis	1.50	.70
❑ 86	Jim Harbaugh	.75	.35
❑ 87	Harvey Williams	.40	.18
❑ 88	Tony Martin	.75	.35
❑ 89	Rob Moore	.40	.18
❑ 90	Neil O'Donnell	.75	.35
❑ 91	Cris Carter	1.50	.70
❑ 92	Warren Sapp RC	2.50	1.10
❑ 93	Terry Allen	.75	.35
❑ 94	Michael Irvin	1.50	.70

❑ 95 Heath Shuler	1.50	.70
❑ 96 Cornelius Bennett	.75	.35
❑ 97 Randy Baldwin	.40	.18
❑ 98 Vince Workman	.40	.18
❑ 99 Irving Fryar	.75	.35
❑ 100 Randall Cunningham	1.50	.70
❑ 101 James O. Stewart RC	8.00	3.60
❑ 102 Stan Humphries	.75	.35
❑ 103 Mario Bates	1.50	.70
❑ 104 Ben Coates	.75	.35
❑ 105 Charlie Garner	.75	.35
❑ 106 Todd Collins RC	1.50	.70
❑ 107 Tim Brown	1.50	.70
❑ 108 Edgar Bennett	.75	.35
❑ 109 J.J. Stokes RC	3.00	1.35
❑ 110 Michael Timpson	.40	.18
❑ 111 Junior Seau	1.50	.70
❑ 112 Bernie Parmalee	.75	.35
❑ 113 Willie McGinest	.75	.35
❑ 114 David Dunn	.40	.18
❑ 115 Kyle Brady RC	1.50	.70
❑ 116 Vinny Testaverde	.75	.35
❑ 117 Ernest Givins	.40	.18
❑ 118 Eric Zeier RC	2.00	.90
❑ 119 Michael Jackson	.75	.35
❑ 120 Chad May RC	.40	.18
❑ 121 Dave Krieg	.40	.18
❑ 122 Rodney Hampton	.75	.35
❑ 123 Darnay Scott	1.50	.70
❑ 124 Chris Miller	.40	.18
❑ 125 Emmitt Smith	6.00	2.70
❑ 126 Steve McNair RC	10.00	4.50
❑ 127 Warren Moon	.75	.35
❑ 128 Robert Brooks	1.50	.70
❑ 129 Bert Emanuel	1.50	.70
❑ 130 John Elway	8.00	3.60
❑ 131 Chris Warren	.75	.35
❑ 132 Herschel Walker	.75	.35
❑ 133 Terry Kirby	.75	.35
❑ 134 Michael Westbrook RC	6.00	2.70
❑ 135 Kordell Stewart RC	10.00	4.50
❑ 136 Terrell Davis RC	30.00	13.50
❑ 137 Desmond Howard	.75	.35
❑ 138 Rodney Thomas RC	1.50	.70
❑ 139 Brett Favre	8.00	3.60
❑ 140 Ray Zellars RC	.75	.35
❑ 141 Marcus Allen	1.50	.70
❑ 142 Gus Frerotte	1.50	.70
❑ 143 Steve Bono	.75	.35
❑ 144 Aaron Craver	.40	.18
❑ P144 Natrone Means Promo Jumbo card 7" by 9 3/4"	2.00	.90

1995 Crown Royale Cramer's Choice Jumbos

	MINT	NRMT
COMPLETE SET (6)	250.00	110.00
STATED ODDS 1:16 BOXES		
❑ CC1 Rashaan Salaam	25.00	11.00
❑ CC2 Emmitt Smith	100.00	45.00
❑ CC3 Marshall Faulk	40.00	18.00
❑ CC4 Jerry Rice	60.00	27.00
❑ CC5 Deion Sanders	40.00	18.00
❑ CC6 Steve Young	50.00	22.00

1995 Crown Royale Pride of the NFL

	MINT	NRMT
COMPLETE SET (36)	180.00	80.00
STATED ODDS 3:25		
❑ PN1 Jim Kelly	3.00	1.35
❑ PN2 Kerry Collins	5.00	2.20
❑ PN3 Darnay Scott	3.00	1.35
❑ PN4 Jeff Blake	5.00	2.20
❑ PN5 Terry Allen	1.50	.70
❑ PN6 Emmitt Smith	12.00	5.50
❑ PN7 Michael Irvin	3.00	1.35
❑ PN8 Troy Aikman	8.00	3.60
❑ PN9 John Elway	15.00	6.75
❑ PN10 Napoleon Kaufman	10.00	4.50
❑ PN11 Barry Sanders	15.00	6.75
❑ PN12 Brett Favre	15.00	6.75
❑ PN13 Michael Westbrook	8.00	3.60
❑ PN14 Marcus Allen	3.00	1.35
❑ PN15 Tim Brown	3.00	1.35
❑ PN16 Bernie Parmalee	1.50	.70
❑ PN17 Dan Marino	15.00	6.75
❑ PN18 Cris Carter	3.00	1.35
❑ PN19 Drew Bledsoe	8.00	3.60
❑ PN20 Mario Bates	3.00	1.35
❑ PN21 Rodney Hampton	1.50	.70
❑ PN22 Ben Coates	1.50	.70
❑ PN23 Charles Johnson	1.50	.70
❑ PN24 Byron Bam Morris	1.50	.70
❑ PN25 Stan Humphries	1.50	.70
❑ PN26 Rashaan Salaam	2.00	.90
❑ PN27 Jerry Rice	8.00	3.60
❑ PN28 Ricky Watters	3.00	1.35
❑ PN29 Steve Young	6.00	2.70
❑ PN30 Natrone Means	3.00	1.35
❑ PN31 William Floyd	3.00	1.35
❑ PN32 Chris Warren	1.50	.70
❑ PN33 Rick Mirer	3.00	1.35
❑ PN34 Jerome Bettis	3.00	1.35
❑ PN35 Errict Rhett	3.00	1.35
❑ PN36 Heath Shuler	3.00	1.35

1995 Crown Royale Pro Bowl Die Cuts

	MINT	NRMT
COMPLETE SET (20)	400.00	180.00
ALL CARDS CONDITION SENSITIVE!		
STATED ODDS 1:25		
❑ PB1 Drew Bledsoe	30.00	13.50
❑ PB2 Ben Coates	6.00	2.70
❑ PB3 John Elway	60.00	27.00
❑ PB4 Marshall Faulk	20.00	9.00
❑ PB5 Dan Marino	60.00	27.00
❑ PB6 Natrone Means	12.00	5.50
❑ PB7 Junior Seau	12.00	5.50
❑ PB8 Chris Warren	6.00	2.70
❑ PB9 Rod Woodson	3.00	1.35
❑ PB10 Tim Brown	12.00	5.50
❑ PB11 Troy Aikman	30.00	13.50
❑ PB12 Jerome Bettis	12.00	5.50
❑ PB13 Michael Irvin	12.00	5.50
❑ PB14 Jerry Rice	30.00	13.50
❑ PB15 Barry Sanders	60.00	27.00
❑ PB16 Deion Sanders	20.00	9.00
❑ PB17 Emmitt Smith	50.00	22.00
❑ PB18 Steve Young	25.00	11.00
❑ PB19 Reggie White	12.00	5.50
❑ PB20 Cris Carter	12.00	5.50

1996 Crown Royale

	MINT	NRMT
COMPLETE SET (144)	100.00	45.00
COMMON CARD (1-144)	.60	.25
SEMISTARS	1.00	.45
UNLISTED STARS	2.00	.90
COMP.BLUE SET (144)	600.00	275.00
*BLUE STARS: 2.5X TO 5X HI COLUMN		
*BLUE RCs: 1.5X TO 3X HI		
BLUE ODDS 4:25 HOBBY		
COMP.SILVER SET (144)	800.00	350.00
*SILVER STARS: 3X TO 6X HI COLUMN		
*SILVER RCs: 2X TO 4X HI		
SILVER ODDS 4:25 RETAIL		
❑ 1 Dan Marino	10.00	4.50
❑ 2 Frank Sanders	1.00	.45
❑ 3 Bobby Engram RC	2.00	.90
❑ 4 Cornelius Bennett	.60	.25
❑ 5 Steve Bono	.60	.25
❑ 6 Aaron Hayden RC	.60	.25
❑ 7 Leroy Hoard	.60	.25
❑ 8 Brett Perriman	.60	.25
❑ 9 Irv Smith	.60	.25
❑ 10 Jim Kelly	2.00	.90
❑ 11 Rodney Thomas	.60	.25
❑ 12 Eric Bieniemy	.60	.25
❑ 13 Darnay Scott	1.00	.45
❑ 14 Ki-Jana Carter	1.00	.45
❑ 15 Kerry Collins	2.00	.90
❑ 16 Shannon Sharpe	1.00	.45
❑ 17 Michael Westbrook	2.00	.90
❑ 18 Steve McNair	4.00	1.80
❑ 19 Tony Banks RC	5.00	2.20
❑ 20 Rashaan Salaam	2.00	.90
❑ 21 Terrell Fletcher	.60	.25
❑ 22 Michael Timpson	.60	.25
❑ 23 Bobby Hoying RC	3.00	1.35
❑ 24 Quinn Early	.60	.25
❑ 25 Warren Moon	1.00	.45
❑ 26 Tommy Vardell	.60	.25
❑ 27 Marvin Harrison RC	12.00	5.50
❑ 28 Lake Dawson	.60	.25
❑ 29 Karim Abdul-Jabbar RC	4.00	1.80

	MINT	NRMT
❑ 30 Chris Warren	1.00	.45
❑ 31 Heath Shuler	1.00	.45
❑ 32 Bert Emanuel	1.00	.45
❑ 33 Howard Griffith RC	.60	.25
❑ 34 Alex Van Dyke RC	1.00	.45
❑ 35 Isaac Bruce	2.00	.90
❑ 36 Mark Brunell	5.00	2.20
❑ 37 Winslow Oliver RC	.60	.25
❑ 38 O.J. McDuffie	1.00	.45
❑ 39 Terrell Owens RC	12.00	5.50
❑ 40 Jerry Rice	5.00	2.20
❑ 41 Henry Ellard	.60	.25
❑ 42 Chris Sanders	1.00	.45
❑ 43 Craig Heyward	.60	.25
❑ 44 Eddie Kennison RC	2.00	.90
❑ 45 Terrell Davis	10.00	4.50
❑ 46 Rodney Hampton	1.00	.45
❑ 47 Bryan Still RC	2.00	.90
❑ 48 Tim Brown	2.00	.90
❑ 49 Keyshawn Johnson RC	12.00	5.50
❑ 50 Barry Sanders	10.00	4.50
❑ 51 Terry Allen	1.00	.45
❑ 52 Sean Dawkins	.60	.25
❑ 53 Bryce Paup	.60	.25
❑ 54 Brett Favre	10.00	4.50
❑ 55 Deion Sanders	3.00	1.35
❑ 56 Kevin Hardy RC	2.00	.90
❑ 57 Kevin Williams	.60	.25
❑ 58 Jeff George	1.00	.45
❑ 59 Tim Biakabutuka RC	6.00	2.70
❑ 60 Drew Bledsoe	5.00	2.20
❑ 61 Michael Jackson	1.00	.45
❑ 62 James O. Stewart	1.00	.45
❑ 63 Mario Bates	1.00	.45
❑ 64 Daryl Johnston	1.00	.45
❑ 65 Herman Moore	2.00	.90
❑ 66 Ben Coates	1.00	.45
❑ 67 Terry Glenn RC	6.00	2.70
❑ 68 Robert Smith	1.00	.45
❑ 69 Irving Fryar	1.00	.45
❑ 70 Napoleon Kaufman	3.00	1.35
❑ 71 Rickey Dudley RC	2.00	.90
❑ 72 Bernie Parmalee	.60	.25
❑ 73 Kyle Brady	.60	.25
❑ 74 Neil O'Donnell	1.00	.45
❑ 75 Lawrence Phillips RC	3.00	1.35
❑ 76 Hardy Nickerson	.60	.25
❑ 77 John Elway	10.00	4.50
❑ 78 Pete Mitchell	1.00	.45
❑ 79 Jason Dunn RC	1.00	.45
❑ 80 Reggie White	2.00	.90
❑ 81 J.J. Stokes	2.00	.90
❑ 82 Jake Reed	1.00	.45
❑ 83 Yancey Thigpen	1.00	.45
❑ 84 Jonathan Ogden RC	.60	.25
❑ 85 Larry Centers	1.00	.45
❑ 86 Scott Mitchell	1.00	.45
❑ 87 Eric Zeier	.60	.25
❑ 88 Anthony Miller	1.00	.45
❑ 89 Brian Blades	.60	.25
❑ 90 Cris Carter	2.00	.90
❑ 91 Kordell Stewart	4.00	1.80
❑ 92 Charles Way RC	2.00	.90
❑ 93 Jeff Hostetler	.60	.25
❑ 94 Brad Johnson	5.00	2.20
❑ 95 Marcus Allen	2.00	.90
❑ 96 Errict Rhett	1.00	.45
❑ 97 Stan Humphries	1.00	.45
❑ 98 Michael Haynes	.60	.25
❑ 99 Curtis Martin	4.00	1.80
❑ 100 Troy Aikman	5.00	2.20
❑ 101 Earnest Byner	.60	.25
❑ 102 Vincent Brisby	.60	.25
❑ 103 Zack Crockett	.60	.25
❑ 104 Haywood Jeffires	.60	.25
❑ 105 Joey Galloway	4.00	1.80
❑ 106 Carl Pickens	2.00	.90
❑ 107 Leeland McElroy RC	2.50	1.10
❑ 108 Adrian Murrell	2.00	.90
❑ 109 Joe Horn RC/C	.60	.25
❑ 110 Steve Young	4.00	1.80
❑ 111 Andre Rison	1.00	.45
❑ 112 Jim Everett	.60	.25
❑ 113 Jamie Asher RC	1.00	.45
❑ 114 Steve Walsh	.60	.25
❑ 115 Robert Brooks	2.00	.90
❑ 116 Eric Moulds RC	8.00	3.60
❑ 117 Edgar Bennett	1.00	.45
❑ 118 Greg Lloyd	1.00	.45
❑ 119 Jerris McPhail RC	.60	.25
❑ 120 Marshall Faulk	2.00	.90
❑ 121 Dave Brown	.60	.25
❑ 122 Harvey Williams	.60	.25
❑ 123 Trent Dilfer	2.00	.90
❑ 124 Eddie George RC	15.00	6.75
❑ 125 Jeff Blake	2.00	.90
❑ 126 Mark Chmura	1.00	.45
❑ 127 Boomer Esiason	1.00	.45
❑ 128 Jim Harbaugh	1.00	.45
❑ 129 Bryan Cox	.60	.25
❑ 130 Ricky Watters	1.00	.45
❑ 131 Amani Toomer RC	2.00	.90
❑ 132 Jim Miller	.60	.25
❑ 133 Cortez Kennedy	.60	.25
❑ 134 Courtney Hawkins	.60	.25
❑ 135 Junior Seau	1.00	.45
❑ 136 Tamarick Vanover	1.00	.45
❑ 137 Jerome Bettis	2.00	.90
❑ 138 Chris Calloway	.60	.25
❑ 139 Rick Mirer	1.00	.45
❑ 140 Thurman Thomas	2.00	.90
❑ 141 Sheddrick Wilson RC	.60	.25
❑ 142 Charlie Garner	.60	.25
❑ 143 Erik Kramer	.60	.25
❑ 144 Emmitt Smith	8.00	3.60

1996 Crown Royale Cramer's Choice Jumbos

	MINT	NRMT
COMPLETE SET (10)	750.00	350.00
STATED ODDS 1:385		
❑ 1 John Elway	120.00	55.00
❑ 2 Brett Favre	120.00	55.00
❑ 3 Keyshawn Johnson *	150.00	70.00
❑ 4 Dan Marino	120.00	55.00
❑ 5 Curtis Martin *	50.00	22.00
❑ 6 Jerry Rice	60.00	27.00
❑ 7 Barry Sanders *	120.00	55.00
❑ 8 Emmitt Smith	100.00	45.00
❑ 9 Kordell Stewart *	50.00	22.00
❑ 10 Reggie White *	25.00	11.00

1996 Crown Royale Field Force

	MINT	NRMT
COMPLETE SET (20)	500.00	220.00
STATED ODDS 1:49		
❑ 1 Troy Aikman	25.00	11.00
❑ 2 Karim Abdul-Jabbar	12.00	5.50
❑ 3 Jeff Blake	10.00	4.50
❑ 4 Drew Bledsoe	25.00	11.00
❑ 5 Lawrence Phillips	10.00	4.50
❑ 6 Kerry Collins	10.00	4.50
❑ 7 Terrell Davis	50.00	22.00
❑ 8 John Elway	50.00	22.00
❑ 9 Brett Favre	50.00	22.00
❑ 10 Eddie George	50.00	22.00
❑ 11 Dan Marino	50.00	22.00
❑ 12 Curtis Martin	20.00	9.00
❑ 13 Jerry Rice	25.00	11.00
❑ 14 Rashaan Salaam	10.00	4.50
❑ 15 Barry Sanders	50.00	22.00
❑ 16 Deion Sanders	15.00	6.75
❑ 17 Emmitt Smith	40.00	18.00
❑ 18 Kordell Stewart	20.00	9.00
❑ 19 Chris Warren	5.00	2.20
❑ 20 Steve Young	20.00	9.00

1996 Crown Royale NFL Regime

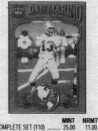

	MINT	NRMT
COMPLETE SET (110)	25.00	11.00
COMMON CARD (1-110)	.15	.07
SEMISTARS	.20	.09
UNLISTED STARS	.40	.18
ONE PER PACK		
❑ 1 Steve Young	1.00	.45
❑ 2 Jamir Miller	.15	.07
❑ 3 Tyrone Brown	.15	.07
❑ 4 Chris Shelling	.15	.07
❑ 5 Warren Moon	.20	.09
❑ 6 Shane Bonham	.15	.07
❑ 7 Gary Brown T	.15	.07
❑ 8 Chris Chandler	.20	.09
❑ 9 Bradford Banta	.15	.07
❑ 10 John Elway	2.50	1.10
❑ 11 Tom McManus	.15	.07
❑ 12 Alfred Jackson	.15	.07
❑ 13 Jay Barker	.15	.07
❑ 14 Kirk Botkin	.15	.07
❑ 15 Jim Kelly	.40	.18
❑ 16 Lou Benfatti	.15	.07
❑ 17 Billy Joe Hobert	.20	.09
❑ 18 John Jackson	.15	.07
❑ 19 Torin Dorn	.15	.07
❑ 20 Drew Bledsoe	1.25	.55
❑ 21 Gale Gilbert	.15	.07
❑ 22 James Atkins	.15	.07
❑ 23 John Lynch	.15	.07
❑ 24 James Jenkins	.15	.07
❑ 25 Kerry Collins	.40	.18
❑ 26 Eric Swann	.15	.07
❑ 27 Dan Stryzinski	.15	.07
❑ 28 Mike Groh	.15	.07
❑ 29 Tim Tindale	.15	.07
❑ 30 Kordell Stewart	1.00	.45
❑ 31 Frank Garcia	.15	.07
❑ 32 Mill Coleman	.15	.07
❑ 33 Bracey Walker	.15	.07
❑ 34 Ryan McNeil	.15	.07
❑ 35 Rodney Hampton	.20	.09
❑ 36 John Mobley	.15	.07
❑ 37 Derek Russell	.15	.07
❑ 38 Jeff George	.20	.09
❑ 39 Steve Morrison	.15	.07
❑ 40 Rashaan Salaam	.40	.18
❑ 41 Ryan Christopherson	.15	.07
❑ 42 Darren Anderson	.15	.07
❑ 43 Ronnie Williams	.15	.07
❑ 44 Scottie Graham	.15	.07
❑ 45 Thurman Thomas	.40	.18
❑ 46 Corwin Brown	.15	.07
❑ 47 Lee DeRamus	.15	.07

❑ 48	Ray Agnew	.15	.07
❑ 49	Erik Howard	.15	.07
❑ 50	Emmitt Smith	2.00	.90
❑ 51	Dan Land	.15	.07
❑ 52	Vinny Testaverde	.20	.09
❑ 53	Myron Bell	.15	.07
❑ 54	Keith Lyle	.15	.07
❑ 55	Aaron Hayden	.15	.07
❑ 56	Jeff Brohm	.15	.07
❑ 57	Ronnie Harris	.15	.07
❑ 58	Trent Dilfer	.40	.18
❑ 59	Browning Nagle	.15	.07
❑ 60	Jeff Blake	.40	.18
❑ 61	Rich Owens	.15	.07
❑ 62	Anthony Edwards	.15	.07
❑ 63	Orlando Brown	.15	.07
❑ 64	Matthew Campbell	.15	.07
❑ 65	Ricky Watters	.20	.09
❑ 66	Travis Hannah	.15	.07
❑ 67	Melvin Tuten	.15	.07
❑ 68	Aaron Taylor	.15	.07
❑ 69	Dale Hellestrae	.15	.07
❑ 70	Marshall Faulk	.40	.18
❑ 71	Gary Anderson	.15	.07
❑ 72	David Williams	.15	.07
❑ 73	Jim Harbaugh	.20	.09
❑ 74	Ray Hall	.15	.07
❑ 75	Dan Marino	2.50	1.10
❑ 76	Chris Mims	.15	.07
❑ 77	Matt Blundin	.15	.07
❑ 78	Roy Barker	.15	.07
❑ 79	John Burke	.15	.07
❑ 80	Troy Aikman	1.25	.55
❑ 81	Ed King	.15	.07
❑ 82	Stan White	.15	.07
❑ 83	Vance Joseph	.15	.07
❑ 84	David Klingler	.15	.07
❑ 85	Terrell Davis	3.00	1.35
❑ 86	Bobby Hoying	.40	.18
❑ 87	Lethon Flowers	.15	.07
❑ 88	Dwayne White	.15	.07
❑ 89	Vaughn Parker	.15	.07
❑ 90	Jerry Rice	1.25	.55
❑ 91	Casey Weldon	.15	.07
❑ 92	Rick Mirer	.20	.09
❑ 93	Jim Pyne	.15	.07
❑ 94	Matt Turk	.15	.07
❑ 95	Marcus Allen	.40	.18
❑ 96	Rob Moore	.20	.09
❑ 97	Ruben Brown	.15	.07
❑ 98	Zach Thomas	.40	.18
❑ 99	Carwell Gardner	.15	.07
❑ 100	Barry Sanders	2.50	1.10
❑ 101	Ben Coleman	.15	.07
❑ 102	Steve Rhem	.15	.07
❑ 103	Everett McIver	.15	.07
❑ 104	Cole Ford	.15	.07
❑ 105	Dave Krieg	.15	.07
❑ 106	Anthony Parker	.15	.07
❑ 107	Michael Brandon	.15	.07
❑ 108	Michael McCrary	.15	.07
❑ 109	Chad Fann	.15	.07
❑ 110	Brett Favre	2.50	1.10

1996 Crown Royale Pro Bowl Die Cuts

	MINT	NRMT
COMPLETE SET (20)	300.00	135.00
STATED ODDS 1:25		

❑ 1	Jeff Blake	10.00	4.50
❑ 2	Mark Chmura	5.00	2.20
❑ 3	Marshall Faulk	10.00	4.50
❑ 4	Brett Favre	50.00	22.00
❑ 5	Charles Haley	3.00	1.35
❑ 6	Merton Hanks	3.00	1.35
❑ 7	Greg Lloyd	5.00	2.20
❑ 8	Dan Marino	50.00	22.00
❑ 9	Curtis Martin	20.00	9.00
❑ 10	Anthony Miller	5.00	2.20
❑ 11	Herman Moore	10.00	4.50
❑ 12	Bryce Paup	3.00	1.35
❑ 13	Jerry Rice	25.00	11.00
❑ 14	Barry Sanders	50.00	22.00
❑ 15	Junior Seau	5.00	2.20
❑ 16	Emmitt Smith	40.00	18.00
❑ 17	Yancey Thigpen	5.00	2.20
❑ 18	Chris Warren	5.00	2.20
❑ 19	Ricky Watters	5.00	2.20
❑ 20	Steve Young	20.00	9.00

1996 Crown Royale Triple Crown Die Cuts

	MINT	NRMT
COMPLETE SET (10)	350.00	160.00
STATED ODDS 1:73		

❑ 1	Troy Aikman	30.00	13.50
❑ 2	John Elway	60.00	27.00
❑ 3	Brett Favre	60.00	27.00
❑ 4	Keyshawn Johnson	30.00	13.50
❑ 5	Dan Marino	60.00	27.00
❑ 6	Curtis Martin	25.00	11.00
❑ 7	Jerry Rice	30.00	13.50
❑ 8	Barry Sanders	60.00	27.00
❑ 9	Emmitt Smith	50.00	22.00
❑ 10	Steve Young	25.00	11.00

1997 Crown Royale

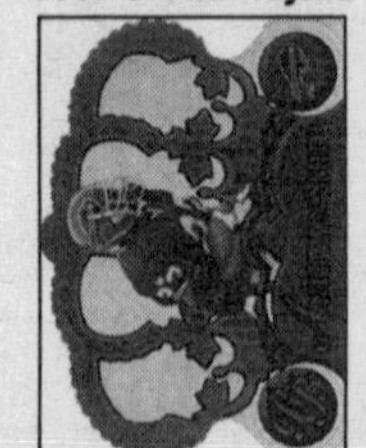

	MINT	NRMT
COMPLETE SET (144)	150.00	70.00
COMMON CARD (1-144)	.50	.23
SEMISTARS	.75	.35
UNLISTED STARS	1.50	.70
COMMON BLUE HOLO.	5.00	2.20
*BLUE HOLO.STARS: 6X TO 15X HI COL.		
*BLUE HOLO.RCs: 2.5X TO 6X HI		
BLUE HOLO.STATED ODDS 1:25		
COMP.GOLD HOLO (144)	600.00	275.00
*GOLD HOLO.STARS: 2X TO 5X HI COL.		
*GOLD HOLO.RCs: 1X TO 2.5X HI		
GOLD HOLO.STATED ODDS 4:25		

❑ 1	Larry Centers	.75	.35
❑ 2	Kent Graham	.50	.23
❑ 3	LeShon Johnson	.50	.23
❑ 4	Leeland McElroy	.50	.23
❑ 5	Jake Plummer RC	15.00	6.75
❑ 6	Jamal Anderson	2.50	1.10
❑ 7	Chris Chandler	.75	.35
❑ 8	Byron Hanspard RC	4.00	1.80
❑ 9	O.J. Santiago RC	2.00	.90
❑ 10	Derrick Alexander WR	.75	.35
❑ 11	Jay Graham RC	1.50	.70
❑ 12	Michael Jackson	.75	.35
❑ 13	Vinny Testaverde	.75	.35
❑ 14	Todd Collins	.50	.23
❑ 15	Jay Riemersma RC	.50	.23
❑ 16	Antowain Smith RC	5.00	2.20
❑ 17	Steve Tasker	.50	.23
❑ 18	Thurman Thomas	1.50	.70
❑ 19	Rae Carruth RC	1.50	.70
❑ 20	Kerry Collins	.75	.35
❑ 21	Anthony Johnson	.50	.23
❑ 22	Fred Lane RC	2.00	.90
❑ 23	Muhsin Muhammad	.75	.35
❑ 24	Wesley Walls	.75	.35
❑ 25	Darnell Autry RC	.75	.35
❑ 26	Raymont Harris	.50	.23
❑ 27	Erik Kramer	.50	.23
❑ 28	Rick Mirer	.50	.23
❑ 29	Rashaan Salaam	.50	.23
❑ 30	Jeff Blake	.75	.35
❑ 31	Ki-Jana Carter	.50	.23
❑ 32	Corey Dillon RC	8.00	3.60
❑ 33	Carl Pickens	1.50	.70
❑ 34	Troy Aikman	4.00	1.80
❑ 35	Michael Irvin	1.50	.70
❑ 36	Daryl Johnston	.75	.35
❑ 37	David LaFleur RC	2.00	.90
❑ 38	Deion Sanders	1.50	.70
❑ 39	Emmitt Smith	6.00	2.70
❑ 40	Terrell Davis	6.00	2.70
❑ 41	John Elway	8.00	3.60
❑ 42	Ed McCaffrey	.75	.35
❑ 43	Shannon Sharpe	.75	.35
❑ 44	Neil Smith	.75	.35
❑ 45	Scott Mitchell	.75	.35
❑ 46	Herman Moore	1.50	.70
❑ 47	Johnnie Morton	.75	.35
❑ 48	Barry Sanders	8.00	3.60
❑ 49	Robert Brooks	.75	.35
❑ 50	Mark Chmura	.75	.35
❑ 51	Brett Favre	8.00	3.60
❑ 52	Antonio Freeman	2.50	1.10
❑ 53	Dorsey Levens	1.50	.70
❑ 54	Reggie White	1.50	.70
❑ 55	Ken Dilger	.50	.23
❑ 56	Marshall Faulk	1.50	.70
❑ 57	Jim Harbaugh	.75	.35
❑ 58	Marvin Harrison	1.50	.70
❑ 59	Mark Brunell	4.00	1.80
❑ 60	Rob Johnson	1.50	.70
❑ 61	Keenan McCardell	.75	.35
❑ 62	Natrone Means	1.50	.70
❑ 63	Jimmy Smith	.75	.35
❑ 64	Marcus Allen	1.50	.70
❑ 65	Tony Gonzalez RC	6.00	2.70
❑ 66	Elvis Grbac	.75	.35
❑ 67	Greg Hill	.50	.23
❑ 68	Tamarick Vanover	.75	.35
❑ 69	Karim Abdul-Jabbar	1.50	.70
❑ 70	Fred Barnett	.50	.23
❑ 71	Dan Marino	8.00	3.60
❑ 72	O.J. McDuffie	.75	.35
❑ 73	Jerris McPhail	.50	.23
❑ 74	Cris Carter	1.50	.70
❑ 75	Randall Cunningham	1.50	.70
❑ 76	Brad Johnson	1.50	.70
❑ 77	Jake Reed	.75	.35

❑ 78 Robert Smith	.75	.35
❑ 79 Drew Bledsoe	4.00	1.80
❑ 80 Ben Coates	.75	.35
❑ 81 Terry Glenn	1.50	.70
❑ 82 Curtis Martin	2.50	1.10
❑ 83 Troy Davis RC	1.50	.70
❑ 84 Heath Shuler	.50	.23
❑ 85 Irv Smith	.50	.23
❑ 86 Danny Wuerffel RC	2.50	1.10
❑ 87 Tiki Barber RC	2.00	.90
❑ 88 Dave Brown	.50	.23
❑ 89 Rodney Hampton	.75	.35
❑ 90 Ike Hilliard RC	4.00	1.80
❑ 91 Amani Toomer	.75	.35
❑ 92 Wayne Chrebet	1.50	.70
❑ 93 Keyshawn Johnson	1.50	.70
❑ 94 Adrian Murrell	.75	.35
❑ 95 Neil O'Donnell	.75	.35
❑ 96 Dedric Ward RC	3.00	1.35
❑ 97 Tim Brown	1.50	.70
❑ 98 Jeff George	.75	.35
❑ 99 Desmond Howard	.75	.35
❑ 100 Napoleon Kaufman	1.50	.70
❑ 101 Ty Detmer	.75	.35
❑ 102 Irving Fryar	.75	.35
❑ 103 Bobby Hoying	.75	.35
❑ 104 Ricky Watters	.75	.35
❑ 105 Jerome Bettis	1.50	.70
❑ 106 Will Blackwell RC	1.50	.70
❑ 107 Charles Johnson	.75	.35
❑ 108 George Jones RC	.75	.35
❑ 109 Kordell Stewart	2.50	1.10
❑ 110 Tony Banks	.75	.35
❑ 111 Isaac Bruce	1.50	.70
❑ 112 Eddie Kennison	.75	.35
❑ 113 Lawrence Phillips	.50	.23
❑ 114 Jim Everett	.50	.23
❑ 115 Stan Humphries	.75	.35
❑ 116 Freddie Jones	.75	.35
❑ 117 Tony Martin	.75	.35
❑ 118 Junior Seau	.75	.35
❑ 119 Jim Druckenmiller RC	2.00	.90
❑ 120 Garrison Hearst	.75	.35
❑ 121 Brent Jones	.75	.35
❑ 122 Terrell Owens	1.50	.70
❑ 123 Jerry Rice	4.00	1.80
❑ 124 Steve Young	3.00	1.35
❑ 125 Chad Brown	.50	.23
❑ 126 Joey Galloway	2.50	1.10
❑ 127 Jon Kitna RC	40.00	18.00
❑ 128 Warren Moon	1.50	.70
❑ 129 Chris Warren	.75	.35
❑ 130 Mike Alstott	1.50	.70
❑ 131 Reidel Anthony RC	4.00	1.80
❑ 132 Trent Dilfer	1.50	.70
❑ 133 Warrick Dunn RC	6.00	2.70
❑ 134 Karl Williams RC	1.50	.70
❑ 135 Willie Davis	.50	.23
❑ 136 Eddie George	4.00	1.80
❑ 137 Joey Kent RC	1.50	.70
❑ 138 Steve McNair	2.50	1.10
❑ 139 Chris Sanders	.50	.23
❑ 140 Terry Allen	1.50	.70
❑ 141 Jamie Asher	.50	.23
❑ 142 Stephen Davis	4.00	1.80
❑ 143 Henry Ellard	.50	.23
❑ 144 Gus Frerotte	.50	.23
❑ S1 Mark Brunell Sample	1.00	.45

1997 Crown Royale Cel-Fusion

	MINT	NRMT
COMPLETE SET (20)	250.00	110.00
STATED ODDS 1:49		
❑ 1 Antowain Smith	10.00	4.50
❑ 2 Troy Aikman	15.00	6.75
❑ 3 Emmitt Smith	25.00	11.00
❑ 4 Terrell Davis	25.00	11.00
❑ 5 John Elway	30.00	13.50
❑ 6 Barry Sanders	30.00	13.50
❑ 7 Brett Favre	30.00	13.50
❑ 8 Mark Brunell	15.00	6.75
❑ 9 Elvis Grbac	3.00	1.35

❑ 10 Karim Abdul-Jabbar	6.00	2.70
❑ 11 Dan Marino	30.00	13.50
❑ 12 Drew Bledsoe	15.00	6.75
❑ 13 Curtis Martin	10.00	4.50
❑ 14 Danny Wuerffel	5.00	2.20
❑ 15 Tiki Barber	4.00	1.80
❑ 16 Jeff George	3.00	1.35
❑ 17 Kordell Stewart	10.00	4.50
❑ 18 Tony Banks	3.00	1.35
❑ 19 Jerry Rice	15.00	6.75
❑ 20 Steve Young	12.00	5.50

1997 Crown Royale Chalk Talk

	MINT	NRMT
COMPLETE SET (20)	600.00	275.00
STATED ODDS 1:73		
❑ 1 Kerry Collins	6.00	2.70
❑ 2 Troy Aikman	30.00	13.50
❑ 3 Emmitt Smith	50.00	22.00
❑ 4 Terrell Davis	50.00	22.00
❑ 5 John Elway	60.00	27.00
❑ 6 Barry Sanders	60.00	27.00
❑ 7 Brett Favre	60.00	27.00
❑ 8 Mark Brunell	30.00	13.50
❑ 9 Marcus Allen	12.00	5.50
❑ 10 Dan Marino	60.00	27.00
❑ 11 Drew Bledsoe	30.00	13.50
❑ 12 Curtis Martin	20.00	9.00
❑ 13 Troy Davis	5.00	2.20
❑ 14 Napoleon Kaufman	12.00	5.50
❑ 15 Jerome Bettis	12.00	5.50
❑ 16 Jim Druckenmiller	6.00	2.70
❑ 17 Jerry Rice	30.00	13.50
❑ 18 Steve Young	25.00	11.00
❑ 19 Warrick Dunn	20.00	9.00
❑ 20 Eddie George	30.00	13.50

1997 Crown Royale Cramer's Choice Jumbos

	MINT	NRMT
COMPLETE SET (10)	80.00	36.00
ONE PER BOX		
❑ 1 Deion Sanders	4.00	1.80
❑ 2 Emmitt Smith	15.00	6.75
❑ 3 Terrell Davis	15.00	6.75
❑ 4 John Elway	20.00	9.00
❑ 5 Barry Sanders	20.00	9.00
❑ 6 Brett Favre	20.00	9.00
❑ 7 Mark Brunell	10.00	4.50
❑ 8 Drew Bledsoe	10.00	4.50
❑ 9 Jim Druckenmiller	2.50	1.10
❑ 10 Eddie George	10.00	4.50

1997 Crown Royale Firestone on Football

	MINT	NRMT
COMPLETE SET (21)	300.00	135.00
STATED ODDS 1:25		
❑ 1 Kerry Collins	3.00	1.35
❑ 2 Troy Aikman	15.00	6.75
❑ 3 Deion Sanders	6.00	2.70
❑ 4 Emmitt Smith	25.00	11.00
❑ 5 Terrell Davis	25.00	11.00
❑ 6 John Elway	30.00	13.50
❑ 7 Barry Sanders	30.00	13.50
❑ 8 Brett Favre	30.00	13.50
❑ 9 Reggie White	6.00	2.70
❑ 10 Mark Brunell	15.00	6.75
❑ 11 Marcus Allen	6.00	2.70
❑ 12 Dan Marino	30.00	13.50
❑ 13 Drew Bledsoe	15.00	6.75
❑ 14 Terry Glenn	6.00	2.70
❑ 15 Curtis Martin	10.00	4.50
❑ 16 Jerome Bettis	6.00	2.70
❑ 17 Jerry Rice	15.00	6.75
❑ 18 Steve Young	12.00	5.50
❑ 19 Eddie George	15.00	6.75
❑ 20 Gus Frerotte	2.00	.90
❑ 21 Roy Firestone	2.00	.90

1997 Crown Royale Pro Bowl Die Cuts

	MINT	NRMT
COMPLETE SET (20)	200.00	90.00
STATED ODDS 1:25		
❑ 1 Kerry Collins	3.00	1.35
❑ 2 Troy Aikman	15.00	6.75
❑ 3 Deion Sanders	6.00	2.70
❑ 4 Terrell Davis	25.00	11.00

❑ 5 John Elway	30.00	13.50
❑ 6 Shannon Sharpe	3.00	1.35
❑ 7 Barry Sanders	30.00	13.50
❑ 8 Brett Favre	30.00	13.50
❑ 9 Reggie White	6.00	2.70
❑ 10 Mark Brunell	15.00	6.75
❑ 11 Derrick Thomas	6.00	2.70
❑ 12 Drew Bledsoe	15.00	6.75
❑ 13 Ben Coates	3.00	1.35
❑ 14 Curtis Martin	10.00	4.50
❑ 15 Jerome Bettis	6.00	2.70
❑ 16 Isaac Bruce	6.00	2.70
❑ 17 Jerry Rice	15.00	6.75
❑ 18 Steve Young	12.00	5.50
❑ 19 Terry Allen	6.00	2.70
❑ 20 Gus Frerotte	2.00	.90

1998 Crown Royale

	MINT	NRMT
COMPLETE SET (144)	120.00	55.00
COMMON CARD (1-144)	.40	.18
SEMISTARS	.75	.35
UNLISTED STARS	1.50	.70
COMMON ROOKIE	1.50	.70
ROOKIE SEMISTARS	2.50	1.10
ROOKIE UNLISTED STARS	3.00	1.35
COMMON LIMITED SERIES	8.00	3.60

*LIMITED SER.STARS: 6X TO 15X HI COL.
*LIMITED SER.YOUNG STARS: 5X TO 12X
*LIMITED SER.RCs: 2X TO 5X ....
LIMITED SERIES PRINT RUN 99 SETS

❑ 1 Larry Centers	.40	.18
❑ 2 Rob Moore	.75	.35
❑ 3 Adrian Murrell	.75	.35
❑ 4 Jake Plummer	4.00	1.80
❑ 5 Jamal Anderson	1.50	.70
❑ 6 Chris Chandler	.75	.35
❑ 7 Tim Dwight RC	4.00	1.80
❑ 8 Tony Martin	.75	.35
❑ 9 Jay Graham	.40	.18
❑ 10 Pat Johnson RC	2.50	1.10
❑ 11 Jermaine Lewis	.75	.35
❑ 12 Eric Zeier	.75	.35
❑ 13 Rob Johnson	.75	.35
❑ 14 Eric Moulds	1.50	.70
❑ 15 Antowain Smith	1.50	.70
❑ 16 Bruce Smith	.75	.35
❑ 17 Steve Beuerlein	.40	.18
❑ 18 Anthony Johnson	.40	.18
❑ 19 Fred Lane	.75	.35
❑ 20 Muhsin Muhammad	.75	.35
❑ 21 Curtis Conway	.75	.35
❑ 22 Curtis Enis RC	6.00	2.70
❑ 23 Erik Kramer	.40	.18
❑ 24 Tony Parrish RC	1.50	.70
❑ 25 Corey Dillon	2.50	1.10
❑ 26 Neil O'Donnell	.75	.35
❑ 27 Carl Pickens	1.50	.70
❑ 28 Takeo Spikes RC	2.50	1.10
❑ 29 Troy Aikman	4.00	1.80
❑ 30 Michael Irvin	1.50	.70
❑ 31 Deion Sanders	1.50	.70
❑ 32 Emmitt Smith	6.00	2.70
❑ 33 Chris Warren	.75	.35
❑ 34 Terrell Davis	6.00	2.70
❑ 35 John Elway	8.00	3.60
❑ 36 Brian Griese RC	10.00	4.50
❑ 37 Ed McCaffrey	.75	.35
❑ 38 Shannon Sharpe	.75	.35
❑ 39 Rod Smith WR	.75	.35
❑ 40 Charlie Batch RC	10.00	4.50
❑ 41 Herman Moore	1.50	.70
❑ 42 Johnnie Morton	.75	.35
❑ 43 Barry Sanders	8.00	3.60
❑ 44 Bryant Westbrook	.40	.18
❑ 45 Robert Brooks	.75	.35
❑ 46 Brett Favre	8.00	3.60
❑ 47 Antonio Freeman	1.50	.70
❑ 48 Raymont Harris	.40	.18
❑ 49 Vonnie Holliday RC	2.50	1.10
❑ 50 Reggie White	1.50	.70
❑ 51 Marshall Faulk	1.50	.70
❑ 52 E.G. Green RC	2.50	1.10
❑ 53 Marvin Harrison	.75	.35
❑ 54 Peyton Manning RC	25.00	11.00
❑ 55 Jerome Pathon RC	4.00	1.80
❑ 56 Tavian Banks RC	.75	.35
❑ 57 Mark Brunell	3.00	1.35
❑ 58 Keenan McCardell	.75	.35
❑ 59 Jimmy Smith	.75	.35
❑ 60 Fred Taylor RC	12.00	5.50
❑ 61 Derrick Alexander WR	.75	.35
❑ 62 Tony Gonzalez	.40	.18
❑ 63 Elvis Grbac	.75	.35
❑ 64 Andre Rison	.75	.35
❑ 65 Rashaan Shehee RC	2.50	1.10
❑ 66 Derrick Thomas	.75	.35
❑ 67 Karim Abdul-Jabbar	1.50	.70
❑ 68 John Avery RC	3.00	1.35
❑ 69 Oronde Gadsden RC	2.50	1.10
❑ 70 Dan Marino	8.00	3.60
❑ 71 O.J. McDuffie	.75	.35
❑ 72 Cris Carter	1.50	.70
❑ 73 Randall Cunningham	1.50	.70
❑ 74 Brad Johnson	1.50	.70
❑ 75 Randy Moss RC	25.00	11.00
❑ 76 John Randle	.75	.35
❑ 77 Jake Reed	.75	.35
❑ 78 Robert Smith	1.50	.70
❑ 79 Drew Bledsoe	3.00	1.35
❑ 80 Robert Edwards RC	3.00	1.35
❑ 81 Terry Glenn	1.50	.70
❑ 82 Tebucky Jones RC	1.50	.70
❑ 83 Tony Simmons RC	2.50	1.10
❑ 84 Mark Fields	.40	.18
❑ 85 Andre Hastings	.40	.18
❑ 86 Danny Wuerffel	.75	.35
❑ 87 Ray Zellars	.40	.18
❑ 88 Tiki Barber	.75	.35
❑ 89 Ike Hilliard	.75	.35
❑ 90 Joe Jurevicius RC	2.50	1.10
❑ 91 Danny Kanell	.75	.35
❑ 92 Wayne Chrebet	1.50	.70
❑ 93 Glenn Foley	.75	.35
❑ 94 Keyshawn Johnson	1.50	.70
❑ 95 Leon Johnson	.40	.18
❑ 96 Curtis Martin	1.50	.70
❑ 97 Tim Brown	1.50	.70
❑ 98 Jeff George	.75	.35
❑ 99 Napoleon Kaufman	1.50	.70
❑ 100 Jon Ritchie RC	2.50	1.10
❑ 101 Charles Woodson RC	6.00	2.70
❑ 102 Irving Fryar	.75	.35
❑ 103 Bobby Hoying	.75	.35
❑ 104 Allen Rossum RC	1.50	.70
❑ 105 Duce Staley	2.50	1.10
❑ 106 Jerome Bettis	1.50	.70
❑ 107 Chris Fuamatu-Ma'afala RC	2.50	1.10
❑ 108 Charles Johnson	.40	.18
❑ 109 Levon Kirkland	.40	.18
❑ 110 Kordell Stewart	1.50	.70
❑ 111 Hines Ward RC	2.50	1.10
❑ 112 Tony Banks	.75	.35
❑ 113 Tony Horne RC	1.50	.70
❑ 114 Eddie Kennison	.75	.35
❑ 115 Amp Lee	.40	.18
❑ 116 Freddie Jones	.40	.18
❑ 117 Ryan Leaf RC	4.00	1.80
❑ 118 Natrone Means	1.50	.70
❑ 119 Mikhael Ricks RC	2.50	1.10
❑ 120 Bryan Still	.40	.18
❑ 121 Marc Edwards	.40	.18
❑ 122 Garrison Hearst	1.50	.70
❑ 123 Terrell Owens	1.50	.70
❑ 124 Jerry Rice	4.00	1.80
❑ 125 J.J. Stokes	.75	.35
❑ 126 Steve Young	2.50	1.10
❑ 127 Joey Galloway	1.50	.70
❑ 128 Ahman Green RC	4.00	1.80
❑ 129 Warren Moon	1.50	.70
❑ 130 Ricky Watters	.75	.35
❑ 131 Mike Alstott	1.50	.70
❑ 132 Trent Dilfer	1.50	.70
❑ 133 Warrick Dunn	2.50	1.10
❑ 134 Jacquez Green RC	4.00	1.80
❑ 135 Warren Sapp	.75	.35
❑ 136 Kevin Dyson RC	4.00	1.80
❑ 137 Eddie George	3.00	1.35
❑ 138 Steve McNair	1.50	.70
❑ 139 Yancey Thigpen	.40	.18
❑ 140 Stephen Alexander RC	2.50	1.10
❑ 141 Terry Allen	1.50	.70
❑ 142 Trent Green	2.00	.90
❑ 143 Skip Hicks RC	4.00	1.80
❑ 144 Michael Westbrook	.75	.35

1998 Crown Royale Cramer's Choice Jumbos

	MINT	NRMT
COMPLETE SET (10)	120.00	55.00
COMMON CARD (1-10)	8.00	3.60

OVERALL STATED ODDS 1 PER BOX
*DARK BLUES: 5X TO 12X HI COL.
DARK BLUE PRINT RUN 35 SERIAL #'d SETS
*GOLDS: 15X TO 30X HI COL. ....
GOLD PRINT RUN 10 SERIAL #'d SETS
*GREENS: 6X TO 15X HI COL. ....
GREEN PRINT RUN 30 SERIAL #'d SETS
*LIGHT BLUES: 10X TO 20X HI COL.
LIGHT BLUE PRINT RUN 20 SERIAL #'d SETS
*REDS: 8X TO 18X HI COL. ....
RED PRINT RUN 25 SERIAL #'d SETS

❑ 1 Terrell Davis	15.00	6.75
❑ 2 John Elway	20.00	9.00
❑ 3 Barry Sanders	20.00	9.00
❑ 4 Brett Favre	20.00	9.00
❑ 5 Peyton Manning	20.00	9.00
❑ 6 Mark Brunell	8.00	3.60
❑ 7 Dan Marino	20.00	9.00
❑ 8 Randy Moss	20.00	9.00
❑ 9 Jerry Rice	10.00	4.50
❑ 10 Warrick Dunn	8.00	3.60

1998 Crown Royale Living Legends

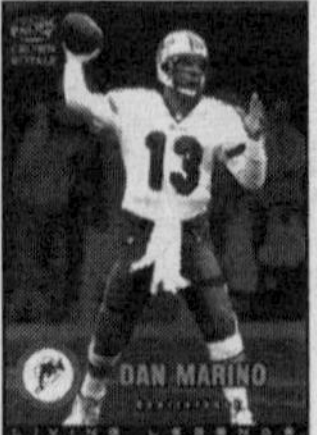

	MINT	NRMT
COMPLETE SET (10)	200.00	90.00
COMMON CARD (1-10)	15.00	6.75

STATED PRINT RUN 375 SERIAL #'d SETS

❑ 1 Troy Aikman	20.00	9.00
❑ 2 Emmitt Smith	30.00	13.50
❑ 3 Terrell Davis	30.00	13.50
❑ 4 John Elway	40.00	18.00
❑ 5 Barry Sanders	40.00	18.00

	MINT	NRMT
❏ 6 Brett Favre	40.00	18.00
❏ 7 Mark Brunell	15.00	6.75
❏ 8 Dan Marino	40.00	18.00
❏ 9 Drew Bledsoe	15.00	6.75
❏ 10 Jerry Rice	20.00	9.00

1998 Crown Royale Master Performers

	MINT	NRMT
COMPLETE SET (20)	100.00	45.00
COMMON CARD (1-20)	2.50	1.10
STATED ODDS 2:25 HOBBY		
❏ 1 Corey Dillon	2.50	1.10
❏ 2 Troy Aikman	6.00	2.70
❏ 3 Emmitt Smith	10.00	4.50
❏ 4 Terrell Davis	10.00	4.50
❏ 5 John Elway	12.00	5.50
❏ 6 Charlie Batch	5.00	2.20
❏ 7 Barry Sanders	12.00	5.50
❏ 8 Brett Favre	12.00	5.50
❏ 9 Peyton Manning	12.00	5.50
❏ 10 Mark Brunell	5.00	2.20
❏ 11 Fred Taylor	8.00	3.60
❏ 12 Dan Marino	12.00	5.50
❏ 13 Randy Moss	12.00	5.50
❏ 14 Drew Bledsoe	5.00	2.20
❏ 15 Curtis Martin	2.50	1.10
❏ 16 Kordell Stewart	2.50	1.10
❏ 17 Ryan Leaf	3.00	1.35
❏ 18 Jerry Rice	6.00	2.70
❏ 19 Steve Young	3.00	1.35
❏ 20 Warrick Dunn	3.00	1.35

1998 Crown Royale Pillars of the Game

	MINT	NRMT
COMPLETE SET (25)	30.00	13.50
COMMON CARD (1-25)	.50	.23
STATED ODDS 1:1 HOBBY		
❏ 1 Antowain Smith	.50	.23
❏ 2 Corey Dillon	.75	.35
❏ 3 Troy Aikman	1.25	.55
❏ 4 Emmitt Smith	2.00	.90
❏ 5 Terrell Davis	2.00	.90
❏ 6 John Elway	2.50	1.10
❏ 7 Charlie Batch	4.00	1.80
❏ 8 Barry Sanders	2.50	1.10
❏ 9 Brett Favre	2.50	1.10
❏ 10 Antonio Freeman	.50	.23
❏ 11 Peyton Manning	8.00	3.60
❏ 12 Mark Brunell	1.00	.45
❏ 13 Dan Marino	2.50	1.10
❏ 14 Randy Moss	8.00	3.60
❏ 15 Drew Bledsoe	1.00	.45
❏ 16 Curtis Martin	.50	.23
❏ 17 Napoleon Kaufman	.50	.23
❏ 18 Jerome Bettis	.50	.23
❏ 19 Kordell Stewart	.50	.23
❏ 20 Ryan Leaf	1.50	.70
❏ 21 Jerry Rice	1.25	.55
❏ 22 Steve Young	.75	.35
❏ 23 Ricky Watters	.50	.23
❏ 24 Eddie George	1.00	.45
❏ 25 Warrick Dunn	.75	.35

1998 Crown Royale Pivotal Players

	MINT	NRMT
COMPLETE SET (25)	30.00	13.50
COMMON CARD (1-25)	.50	.23
STATED ODDS 1:1 HOBBY		
❏ 1 Jake Plummer	1.00	.45
❏ 2 Antowain Smith	.50	.23
❏ 3 Corey Dillon	.75	.35
❏ 4 Troy Aikman	1.25	.55
❏ 5 Deion Sanders	.50	.23
❏ 6 Emmitt Smith	2.00	.90
❏ 7 Terrell Davis	2.00	.90
❏ 8 John Elway	2.50	1.10
❏ 9 Charlie Batch	3.00	1.35
❏ 10 Barry Sanders	2.50	1.10
❏ 11 Brett Favre	2.50	1.10
❏ 12 Peyton Manning	8.00	3.60
❏ 13 Mark Brunell	1.00	.45
❏ 14 Fred Taylor	5.00	2.20
❏ 15 Dan Marino	2.50	1.10
❏ 16 Randy Moss	8.00	3.60
❏ 17 Drew Bledsoe	1.00	.45
❏ 18 Curtis Martin	.50	.23
❏ 19 Napoleon Kaufman	.50	.23
❏ 20 Jerome Bettis	.50	.23
❏ 21 Kordell Stewart	.50	.23
❏ 22 Ryan Leaf	1.50	.70
❏ 23 Jerry Rice	1.25	.55
❏ 24 Eddie George	1.00	.45
❏ 25 Warrick Dunn	.75	.35

1998 Crown Royale Rookie Paydirt

	MINT	NRMT
COMPLETE SET (20)	150.00	70.00
COMMON CARD (1-20)	4.00	1.80
SEMISTARS	4.00	1.80
STATED ODDS 1:25 HOBBY		
❏ 1 Curtis Enis	8.00	3.60
❏ 2 Marcus Nash	5.00	2.20
❏ 3 Charlie Batch	12.00	5.50
❏ 4 Vonnie Holliday	4.00	1.80
❏ 5 E.G. Green	4.00	1.80

	MINT	NRMT
❏ 6 Peyton Manning	30.00	13.50
❏ 7 Jerome Pathon	4.00	1.80
❏ 8 Tavian Banks	4.00	1.80
❏ 9 Fred Taylor	20.00	9.00
❏ 10 Rashaan Shehee	4.00	1.80
❏ 11 John Avery	5.00	2.20
❏ 12 Randy Moss	30.00	13.50
❏ 13 Robert Edwards	5.00	2.20
❏ 14 Charles Woodson	8.00	3.60
❏ 15 Hines Ward	4.00	1.80
❏ 16 Ryan Leaf	6.00	2.70
❏ 17 Mikhael Ricks	4.00	1.80
❏ 18 Ahman Green	4.00	1.80
❏ 19 Jacquez Green	5.00	2.20
❏ 20 Kevin Dyson	5.00	2.20

1999 Crown Royale

	MINT	NRMT
COMPLETE SET (144)	150.00	70.00
COMMON CARD (1-144)	.40	.18
SEMISTARS	.75	.35
UNLISTED STARS	1.50	.70
COMMON ROOKIE	3.00	1.35
ROOKIE SEMISTARS	4.00	1.80
❏ 1 David Boston RC	6.00	2.70
❏ 2 Chris Greisen RC	5.00	2.20
❏ 3 Rob Moore	.75	.35
❏ 4 Jake Plummer	3.00	1.35
❏ 5 Frank Sanders	.75	.35
❏ 6 Jamal Anderson	1.50	.70
❏ 7 Chris Chandler	.75	.35
❏ 8 Tim Dwight	1.50	.70
❏ 9 Byron Hanspard	.75	.35
❏ 10 Stoney Case	.40	.18
❏ 11 Priest Holmes	1.50	.70
❏ 12 Jermaine Lewis	.75	.35
❏ 13 Chris McAlister RC	3.00	1.35
❏ 14 Brandon Stokley RC	3.00	1.35
❏ 15 Doug Flutie	2.00	.90
❏ 16 Eric Moulds	1.50	.70
❏ 17 Peerless Price RC	6.00	2.70
❏ 18 Antowain Smith	1.50	.70
❏ 19 Steve Beuerlein	.40	.18
❏ 20 Tim Biakabutuka	.75	.35
❏ 21 Muhsin Muhammad	.75	.35
❏ 22 Curtis Conway	.75	.35
❏ 23 Curtis Enis	1.50	.70
❏ 24 Shane Matthews	.75	.35
❏ 25 Cade McNown RC	12.00	5.50

Card	Mint	NRMT
☐ 26 Marcus Robinson	3.00	1.35
☐ 27 Jeff Blake	.75	.35
☐ 28 Scott Covington RC	3.00	1.35
☐ 29 Corey Dillon	1.50	.70
☐ 30 Damon Griffin RC	4.00	1.80
☐ 31 Carl Pickens	.75	.35
☐ 32 Akili Smith RC	8.00	3.60
☐ 33 Tim Couch RC	20.00	9.00
☐ 34 Kevin Johnson RC	10.00	4.50
☐ 35 Terry Kirby	.40	.18
☐ 36 Leslie Shepherd	.40	.18
☐ 37 Troy Aikman	4.00	1.80
☐ 38 Rocket Ismail	.40	.18
☐ 39 Wane McGarity RC	3.00	1.35
☐ 40 Deion Sanders	1.50	.70
☐ 41 Emmitt Smith	4.00	1.80
☐ 42 Terrell Davis	4.00	1.80
☐ 43 Brian Griese	3.00	1.35
☐ 44 Ed McCaffrey	.75	.35
☐ 45 Shannon Sharpe	.75	.35
☐ 46 Rod Smith	.75	.35
☐ 47 Charlie Batch	3.00	1.35
☐ 48 Germane Crowell	.75	.35
☐ 49 Sedrick Irvin RC		
☐ 50 Herman Moore	1.50	.70
☐ 51 Barry Sanders	6.00	2.70
☐ 52 Brett Favre	6.00	2.70
☐ 53 Antonio Freeman	1.50	.70
☐ 54 Matt Hasselbeck	1.50	.70
☐ 55 Dorsey Levens	1.50	.70
☐ 56 Basil Mitchell RC	3.00	1.35
☐ 57 E.G. Green	.40	.18
☐ 58 Marvin Harrison	1.50	.70
☐ 59 Edgerrin James RC	30.00	13.50
☐ 60 Peyton Manning	6.00	2.70
☐ 61 Terrence Wilkins RC	10.00	4.50
☐ 62 Mark Brunell	2.50	1.10
☐ 63 Keenan McCardell	.75	.35
☐ 64 Jimmy Smith	.75	.35
☐ 65 Fred Taylor	4.00	1.80
☐ 66 Derrick Alexander WR	.75	.35
☐ 67 Elvis Grbac	.75	.35
☐ 68 Warren Moon	.40	.18
☐ 69 Larry Parker RC	3.00	1.35
☐ 70 Andre Rison	.75	.35
☐ 71 Cecil Collins RC	3.00	1.25
☐ 72 Damon Huard	4.00	1.80
☐ 73 James Johnson RC	5.00	2.20
☐ 74 Rob Konrad RC	4.00	1.80
☐ 75 Dan Marino	6.00	2.70
☐ 76 O.J. McDuffie	.75	.35
☐ 77 Cris Carter	1.50	.70
☐ 78 Daunte Culpepper RC	12.00	5.50
☐ 79 Randall Cunningham	1.50	.70
☐ 80 Randy Moss	6.00	2.70
☐ 81 Robert Smith UER (card actually #80)	.40	.18
☐ 82 Michael Bishop RC	5.00	2.20
☐ 83 Drew Bledsoe	2.50	1.10
☐ 84 Ben Coates	.75	.35
☐ 85 Kevin Faulk RC	5.00	2.20
☐ 86 Terry Glenn	1.50	.70
☐ 87 Billy Joe Hobert	.40	.18
☐ 88 Eddie Kennison	.75	.35
☐ 89 Keith Poole	.40	.18
☐ 90 Ricky Williams RC	20.00	9.00
☐ 91 Sean Bennett RC	4.00	1.80
☐ 92 Kerry Collins	.75	.35
☐ 93 Pete Mitchell	.40	.18
☐ 94 Amani Toomer	.40	.18
☐ 95 Wayne Chrebet	.75	.35
☐ 96 Keyshawn Johnson	1.50	.70
☐ 97 Curtis Martin	1.50	.70
☐ 98 Tim Brown	1.50	.70
☐ 99 Scott Dreisbach RC	4.00	1.80
☐ 100 Rich Gannon	.75	.35
☐ 101 Napoleon Kaufman	1.50	.70
☐ 102 Tyrone Wheatley	.75	.35
☐ 103 Duce Staley	1.50	.70
☐ 104 Charles Johnson	.40	.18
☐ 105 Donovan McNabb RC	12.00	5.50
☐ 106 Torrance Small	.40	.18
☐ 107 Jed Weaver RC	3.00	1.35
☐ 108 Jerome Bettis	1.50	.70
☐ 109 Troy Edwards RC	6.00	2.70
☐ 110 Kordell Stewart	1.50	.70
☐ 111 Amos Zereoue RC	4.00	1.80
☐ 112 Isaac Bruce	1.50	.70
☐ 113 Marshall Faulk	1.50	.70
☐ 114 Joe Germaine RC	4.00	1.80
☐ 115 Torry Holt RC	10.00	4.50
☐ 116 Kurt Warner RC	30.00	13.50
☐ 117 Jim Harbaugh	.75	.35
☐ 118 Erik Kramer	.40	.18
☐ 119 Natrone Means	.75	.35
☐ 120 Junior Seau	.75	.35
☐ 121 Jeff Garcia RC	8.00	3.60
☐ 122 Terrell Owens	1.50	.70
☐ 123 Jerry Rice	4.00	1.80
☐ 124 J.J. Stokes	.75	.35
☐ 125 Steve Young	2.50	1.10
☐ 126 Sean Dawkins	.40	.18
☐ 127 Brock Huard RC	5.00	2.20
☐ 128 Jon Kitna	2.00	.90
☐ 129 Derrick Mayes	.75	.35
☐ 130 Charlie Rogers RC	3.00	1.35
☐ 131 Ricky Watters	.75	.35
☐ 132 Mike Alstott	1.50	.70
☐ 133 Trent Dilfer	.75	.35
☐ 134 Warrick Dunn	1.50	.70
☐ 135 Eric Zeier	.75	.35
☐ 136 Kevin Daft RC	3.00	1.35
☐ 137 Kevin Dyson	.75	.35
☐ 138 Eddie George	2.00	.90
☐ 139 Steve McNair	1.50	.70
☐ 140 Neil O'Donnell	.75	.35
☐ 141 Champ Bailey RC	5.00	2.20
☐ 142 Albert Connell	.40	.18
☐ 143 Stephen Davis	1.50	.70
☐ 144 Brad Johnson	1.50	.70

1999 Crown Royale Limited Series

	MINT	NRMT
COMMON CARD (1-144)	6.00	2.70
*STARS: 6X TO 15X HI COL.		
*YOUNG STARS: 5X TO 12X		
*RCs: 1.25X TO 3X		
STATED PRINT RUN 99 SER.#'d SETS		

1999 Crown Royale Premiere Date

	MINT	NRMT
COMMON CARD (1-144)	6.00	2.70
*STARS: 6X TO 15X HI COL.		
*YOUNG STARS: 5X TO 12X		
*RCs: 2X TO 5X		
STATED ODDS 1:25		
STATED PRINT RUN 68 SER.#'d SETS		

1999 Crown Royale Card Supials

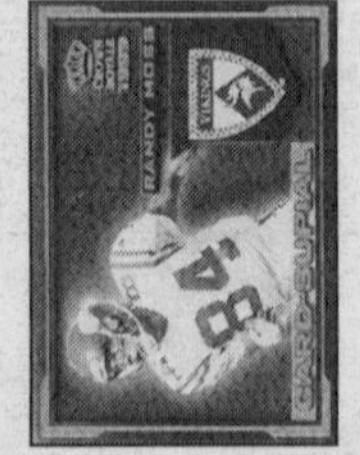

	MINT	NRMT
COMPLETE SET (20)	100.00	45.00
COMMON CARD (1-20)	2.50	1.10
*SMALL CARDS: .3X TO .8X LARGE		
STATED ODDS 2:25		

Card	Mint	NRMT
☐ 1 Cade McNown	6.00	2.70
☐ 2 Tim Couch	10.00	4.50
☐ 3 Troy Aikman	6.00	2.70
☐ 4 Emmitt Smith	6.00	2.70
☐ 5 Barry Sanders	10.00	4.50
☐ 6 Brett Favre	10.00	4.50
☐ 7 Edgerrin James	15.00	6.75
☐ 8 Peyton Manning	8.00	3.60
☐ 9 Mark Brunell	4.00	1.80
☐ 10 Fred Taylor	5.00	2.20
☐ 11 Damon Huard	5.00	2.20
☐ 12 Dan Marino	10.00	4.50
☐ 13 Randy Moss	8.00	3.60
☐ 14 Drew Bledsoe	4.00	1.80
☐ 15 Ricky Williams	10.00	4.50
☐ 16 Jerome Bettis	2.50	1.10
☐ 17 Kurt Warner	15.00	6.75
☐ 18 Terrell Owens	2.50	1.10
☐ 19 Jerry Rice	6.00	2.70
☐ 20 Jon Kitna	3.00	1.35

1999 Crown Royale Century 21

	MINT	NRMT
COMPLETE SET (10)	100.00	45.00
COMMON CARD (1-10)	8.00	3.60
STATED PRINT RUN 375 SER.#'d SETS		

Card	Mint	NRMT
☐ 1 Jake Plummer	10.00	4.50
☐ 2 Tim Couch	15.00	6.75
☐ 3 Terrell Davis	12.00	5.50
☐ 4 Peyton Manning	15.00	6.75
☐ 5 Mark Brunell	8.00	3.60
☐ 6 Fred Taylor	10.00	4.50
☐ 7 Randy Moss	15.00	6.75
☐ 8 Drew Bledsoe	8.00	3.60
☐ 9 Ricky Williams	15.00	6.75
☐ 10 Kurt Warner	40.00	18.00

1999 Crown Royale Cramers Choice Jumbos

	MINT	NRMT
COMPLETE SET (10)	80.00	36.00
COMMON CARD (1-10)	5.00	2.20
OVERALL STATED ODDS ONE PER BOX		
*DARK BLUES: 3X TO 8X HI COL.		
DARK BLUE PRINT RUN 35 SER.#'d SETS		
*GOLDS: 10X TO 25X HI COL.		
GOLD PRINT RUN 10 SER.#'d SETS		

*GREENS: 3X TO 8X HI COL. ......
GREEN PRINT RUN 30 SER.#'d SETS
*LIGHT BLUES: 5X TO 12X HI COL.
LIGHT BLUE PRINT RUN 20 SER.#'d SETS
UNPRICED PURPLES SERIAL #'d OF 1
*REDS: 4X TO 10X HI COL. ....
RED PRINT RUN 25 SER.#'d SETS

❑ 1 Cade McNown	8.00	3.60
❑ 2 Tim Couch	12.00	5.50
❑ 3 Emmitt Smith	12.00	5.50
❑ 4 Edgerrin James	20.00	9.00
❑ 5 Mark Brunell	8.00	3.60
❑ 6 Fred Taylor	10.00	4.50
❑ 7 Randy Moss	15.00	6.75
❑ 8 Kurt Warner	25.00	11.00
❑ 9 Jon Kitna	6.00	2.70
❑ 10 Eddie George	5.00	2.20

1999 Crown Royale Franchise Glory

	MINT	NRMT
COMPLETE SET (25)	40.00	18.00
COMMON CARD (1-25)	1.25	.55
ONE PER PACK		

❑ 1 Doug Flutie	1.50	.70
❑ 2 Corey Dillon	1.25	.55
❑ 3 Troy Aikman	3.00	1.35
❑ 4 Emmitt Smith	3.00	1.35
❑ 5 Terrell Davis	3.00	1.35
❑ 6 Herman Moore	1.25	.55
❑ 7 Barry Sanders	5.00	2.20
❑ 8 Brett Favre	5.00	2.20
❑ 9 Antonio Freeman	1.25	.55
❑ 10 Peyton Manning	4.00	1.80
❑ 11 Mark Brunell	2.00	.90
❑ 12 Fred Taylor	2.50	1.10
❑ 13 Dan Marino	5.00	2.20
❑ 14 Randy Moss	4.00	1.80
❑ 15 Drew Bledsoe	2.00	.90
❑ 16 Keyshawn Johnson	1.25	.55
❑ 17 Jerome Bettis	1.25	.55
❑ 18 Marshall Faulk	1.25	.55
❑ 19 Kurt Warner	20.00	9.00
❑ 20 Terrell Owens	1.25	.55
❑ 21 Jerry Rice	3.00	1.35
❑ 22 Steve Young	2.00	.90
❑ 23 Warrick Dunn	1.25	.55
❑ 24 Eddie George	1.50	.70
❑ 25 Brad Johnson	1.25	.55

1999 Crown Royale Gold Crown Die Cuts

	MINT	NRMT
COMPLETE SET (6)	60.00	27.00
COMMON CARD (1-6)	6.00	2.70
STATED PRINT RUN 976 SER.#'d SETS		

❑ 1 Tim Couch	15.00	6.75
❑ 2 Troy Aikman	10.00	4.50
❑ 3 Emmitt Smith	10.00	4.50
❑ 4 Damon Huard	6.00	2.70
❑ 5 Randy Moss	12.00	5.50
❑ 6 Kurt Warner	25.00	11.00

1999 Crown Royale Rookie Gold

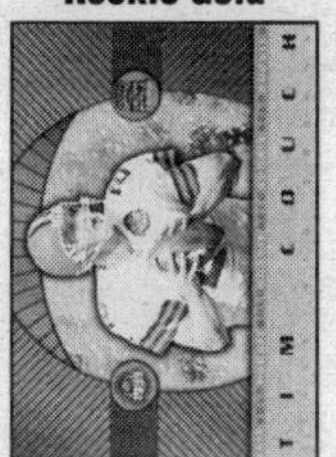

	MINT	NRMT
COMPLETE SET (25)	50.00	22.00
COMMON CARD (1-25)	1.00	.45
SEMISTARS	1.25	.55
ONE PER PACK		
*DIE CUTS: 15X TO 40X HI COL.		
DIE CUTS PRINT RUN 10 SER.#'d SETS		

❑ 1 David Boston	2.00	.90
❑ 2 Brandon Stokley	1.00	.45
❑ 3 Cade McNown	4.00	1.80
❑ 4 Akili Smith	2.50	1.10
❑ 5 Tim Couch	6.00	2.70
❑ 6 Kevin Johnson	3.00	1.35
❑ 7 Wane McGarity	1.00	.45
❑ 8 Edgerrin James	10.00	4.50
❑ 9 Terrence Wilkins	3.00	1.35
❑ 10 Cecil Collins	1.25	.55
❑ 11 Rob Konrad	1.25	.55
❑ 12 James Johnson	1.50	.70
❑ 13 Daunte Culpepper	4.00	1.80
❑ 14 Michael Bishop	1.50	.70
❑ 15 Kevin Faulk	1.50	.70
❑ 16 Ricky Williams	6.00	2.70
❑ 17 Scott Dreisbach	1.25	.55
❑ 18 Donovan McNabb	4.00	1.80
❑ 19 Troy Edwards	2.00	.90
❑ 20 Amos Zereoue	1.25	.55
❑ 21 Joe Germaine	1.25	.55
❑ 22 Torry Holt	3.00	1.35
❑ 23 Brock Huard	1.50	.70
❑ 24 Charlie Rogers	1.00	.45
❑ 25 Champ Bailey	1.50	.70

1999 Crown Royale Test of Time

	MINT	NRMT
COMPLETE SET (10)	60.00	27.00
COMMON CARD (1-10)	3.00	1.35
STATED ODDS 1:25		

❑ 1 Tim Couch	12.00	5.50
❑ 2 Emmitt Smith	8.00	3.60
❑ 3 Terrell Davis	8.00	3.60
❑ 4 Barry Sanders	12.00	5.50
❑ 5 Brett Favre	12.00	5.50
❑ 6 Antonio Freeman	3.00	1.75
❑ 7 Edgerrin James	20.00	9.00
❑ 8 Mark Brunell	5.00	2.20
❑ 9 Dan Marino	12.00	5.50
❑ 10 Jerry Rice	8.00	3.60

2000 Crown Royale

	MINT	NRMT
COMPLETE SET (144)	120.00	55.00
COMMON CARD (1-108)	.20	.09
SEMISTARS	.40	.18
UNLISTED STARS	.75	.35
COMMON ROOKIE (109-144)	1.25	.55
ROOKIE SEMISTARS	2.00	.90
ROOKIE UNLISTED STARS	2.50	1.10

❑ 1 Rob Moore	.40	.18
❑ 2 Jake Plummer	.75	.35
❑ 3 Frank Sanders	.40	.18
❑ 4 Jamal Anderson	.75	.35
❑ 5 Chris Chandler	.40	.18
❑ 6 Tim Dwight	.75	.35
❑ 7 Tony Banks	.40	.18
❑ 8 Priest Holmes	.40	.18
❑ 9 Qadry Ismail	.20	.09
❑ 10 Doug Flutie	1.00	.45
❑ 11 Rob Johnson	.40	.18
❑ 12 Eric Moulds	.75	.35
❑ 13 Peerless Price	.75	.35
❑ 14 Steve Beuerlein	.40	.18
❑ 15 Patrick Jeffers	.75	.35
❑ 16 Muhsin Muhammad	.40	.18
❑ 17 Curtis Enis	.75	.35
❑ 18 Cade McNown	1.25	.55
❑ 19 Marcus Robinson	.75	.35
❑ 20 Corey Dillon	.75	.35
❑ 21 Darnay Scott	.40	.18
❑ 22 Akili Smith	1.00	.45
❑ 23 Karim Abdul-Jabbar	.40	.18
❑ 24 Tim Couch	2.00	.90
❑ 25 Kevin Johnson	.75	.35
❑ 26 Troy Aikman	2.00	.90
❑ 27 Joey Galloway	.75	.35
❑ 28 Emmitt Smith	2.00	.90
❑ 29 Terrell Davis	2.00	.90
❑ 30 Olandis Gary	1.00	.45
❑ 31 Brian Griese	1.00	.45
❑ 32 Ed McCaffrey	.40	.18
❑ 33 Charlie Batch	.75	.35
❑ 34 Herman Moore	.75	.35
❑ 35 Barry Sanders	2.50	1.10
❑ 36 James Stewart	.40	.18
❑ 37 Brett Favre	3.00	1.35
❑ 38 Antonio Freeman	.75	.35
❑ 39 Dorsey Levens	.75	.35
❑ 40 Marvin Harrison	.75	.35
❑ 41 Edgerrin James	3.00	1.35
❑ 42 Peyton Manning	2.50	1.10
❑ 43 Mark Brunell	1.25	.55
❑ 44 Keenan McCardell	.40	.18
❑ 45 Jimmy Smith	.40	.18
❑ 46 Fred Taylor	1.25	.55
❑ 47 Derrick Alexander	.40	.18
❑ 48 Tony Gonzalez	.40	.18
❑ 49 Elvis Grbac	.40	.18
❑ 50 Damon Huard	.75	.35
❑ 51 James Johnson	.40	.18

Card	MINT	NRMT
❑ 52 Dan Marino	3.00	1.35
❑ 53 O.J. McDuffie	.40	.18
❑ 54 Cris Carter	.75	.35
❑ 55 Daunte Culpepper	1.25	.55
❑ 56 Jeff George	.40	.18
❑ 57 Randy Moss	2.50	1.10
❑ 58 Robert Smith	.75	.35
❑ 59 Drew Bledsoe	1.25	.55
❑ 60 Terry Glenn	.75	.35
❑ 61 Lawyer Milloy	.20	.09
❑ 62 Jeff Blake	.40	.18
❑ 63 Keith Poole	.20	.09
❑ 64 Ricky Williams	2.00	.90
❑ 65 Kerry Collins	.40	.18
❑ 66 Ike Hilliard	.40	.18
❑ 67 Amani Toomer	.20	.09
❑ 68 Wayne Chrebet	.40	.18
❑ 69 Keyshawn Johnson	.75	.35
❑ 70 Ray Lucas	.75	.35
❑ 71 Curtis Martin	.75	.35
❑ 72 Vinny Testaverde	.40	.18
❑ 73 Tim Brown	.75	.35
❑ 74 Rich Gannon	.40	.18
❑ 75 Napoleon Kaufman	.75	.35
❑ 76 Tyrone Wheatley	.40	.18
❑ 77 Donovan McNabb	1.25	.55
❑ 78 Torrance Small	.20	.09
❑ 79 Duce Staley	.75	.35
❑ 80 Jerome Bettis	.75	.35
❑ 81 Troy Edwards	.75	.35
❑ 82 Kordell Stewart	.75	.35
❑ 83 Issac Bruce	.75	.35
❑ 84 Marshall Faulk	.75	.35
❑ 85 Torry Holt	.75	.35
❑ 86 Kurt Warner	4.00	1.80
❑ 87 Jim Harbaugh	.40	.18
❑ 88 Jermaine Fazande	.20	.09
❑ 89 Junior Seau	.40	.18
❑ 90 Charlie Garner	.40	.18
❑ 91 Terrell Owens	.75	.35
❑ 92 Jerry Rice	2.00	.90
❑ 93 Steve Young	1.25	.55
❑ 94 Sean Dawkins	.20	.09
❑ 95 Jon Kitna	.75	.35
❑ 96 Derrick Mayes	.40	.18
❑ 97 Ricky Watters	.40	.18
❑ 98 Mike Alstott	.75	.35
❑ 99 Warrick Dunn	.75	.35
❑ 100 Jacquez Green	.40	.18
❑ 101 Shaun King	1.25	.55
❑ 102 Kevin Dyson	.40	.18
❑ 103 Eddie George	1.00	.45
❑ 104 Jevon Kearse	.75	.35
❑ 105 Steve McNair	.75	.35
❑ 106 Stephen Davis	.75	.35
❑ 107 Brad Johnson	.75	.35
❑ 108 Michael Westbrook	.40	.18
❑ 109 Shaun Alexander RC	8.00	3.60
❑ 110 Tom Brady RC	2.50	1.10
❑ 111 Marc Bulger RC	2.50	1.10
❑ 112 Plaxico Burress RC	6.00	2.70
❑ 113 Giovanni Carmazzi RC	5.00	2.20
❑ 114 Kwame Cavil RC	2.00	.90
❑ 115 Chris Cole RC	2.00	.90
❑ 116 Chris Coleman RC	1.25	.55
❑ 117 Laveranues Coles RC	2.50	1.10
❑ 118 Ron Dayne RC	12.00	5.50
❑ 119 Reuben Droughns RC	3.00	1.35
❑ 120 Ron Dugans RC	2.50	1.10
❑ 121 Danny Farmer RC	2.50	1.10
❑ 122 Chafie Fields RC	2.00	.90
❑ 123 Joe Hamilton RC	2.50	1.10
❑ 124 Todd Husak RC	2.50	1.10
❑ 125 Darrell Jackson RC	2.50	1.10
❑ 126 Thomas Jones RC	8.00	3.60
❑ 127 Jamal Lewis RC	8.00	3.60
❑ 128 Tee Martin RC	4.00	1.80
❑ 129 Rondell Mealey RC	2.00	.90
❑ 130 Sylvester Morris RC	3.00	1.35
❑ 131 Chad Morton RC	2.00	.90
❑ 132 Dennis Northcutt RC	3.00	1.35
❑ 133 Chad Pennington RC	10.00	4.50
❑ 134 Travis Prentice RC	3.00	1.35
❑ 135 Tim Rattay RC	3.00	1.35
❑ 136 Chris Redman RC	4.00	1.80
❑ 137 J.R. Redmond RC	4.00	1.80
❑ 138 R.Jay Soward RC	3.00	1.35
❑ 139 Shyrone Stith RC	2.00	.90
❑ 140 Travis Taylor RC	5.00	2.20
❑ 141 Troy Walters RC	2.50	1.10
❑ 142 Peter Warrick RC	12.00	5.50
❑ 143 Dez White RC	3.00	1.35
❑ 144 Michael Wiley RC	3.00	1.35
❑ S1 Jon Kitna Sample	1.50	.70

2000 Crown Royale Draft Picks 499

	MINT	NRMT
COMPLETE SET (35)	200.00	90.00
COMMON CARD (109-144)	2.50	1.10

*SERIAL NUMBERED: .8X TO 2X BASE ROOKIES
STATED PRINT RUN 499 SERIAL #'d SETS

2000 Crown Royale Limited Series

	MINT	NRMT
COMMON CARD (1-108)	2.00	.90
*LIMITED STARS: 4X TO 10X HI COL		
*LIMITED YOUNG STARS: 3X TO 8X		
COMMON ROOKIE (109-144)	5.00	2.20
*LIMITED ROOKIES: 1.5X TO 4X HI COL		
STATED PRINT RUN 144 SERIAL #'d SETS		

2000 Crown Royale Premiere Date

	MINT	NRMT
COMMON CARD (1-108)	2.00	.90
*PREMIERE DATE STARS: 4X TO 10X HI COL.		
*PREMIERE DATE YOUNG STARS: 3X TO 8X		
COMMON ROOKIE (109-144)	5.00	2.20
*PREM.DATE ROOKIES: 1.5X TO 4X		
STATED PRINT RUN 145 SERIAL #'d SETS		

2000 Crown Royale Autographs

	MINT	NRMT
COMMON CARD	10.00	4.50
SEMISTARS	15.00	6.75
UNLISTED STARS	20.00	9.00
RANDOM INSERTS IN PACKS		
SP STATED PRINT RUN 100 AUTOS EACH		

Card	MINT	NRMT
❑ 109 Shaun Alexander	40.00	18.00
❑ 110 Tom Brady	15.00	6.75
❑ 111 Marc Bulger	15.00	6.75
❑ 112 Plaxico Burress	30.00	13.50
❑ 113 Giovanni Carmazzi	25.00	11.00
❑ 114 Kwame Cavil	10.00	4.50
❑ 115 Chris Cole	10.00	4.50
❑ 116 Chris Coleman	10.00	4.50
❑ 117 Laveranues Coles	15.00	6.75
❑ 118 Ron Dayne SP		
❑ 119 Reuben Droughns	20.00	9.00
❑ 120 Ron Dugans	15.00	6.75
❑ 121 Danny Farmer		
❑ 122 Chafie Fields	10.00	4.50
❑ 123 Joe Hamilton	15.00	6.75
❑ 124 Todd Husak	15.00	6.75
❑ 125 Darrell Jackson	15.00	6.75
❑ 126 Thomas Jones	40.00	18.00
❑ 127 Jamal Lewis		
❑ 128 Tee Martin	25.00	11.00
❑ 129 Rondell Mealey	10.00	4.50
❑ 130 Sylvester Morris	20.00	9.00
❑ 131 Chad Morton	10.00	4.50
❑ 132 Dennis Northcutt	20.00	9.00
❑ 133 Chad Pennington SP	80.00	36.00
❑ 134 Travis Prentice		
❑ 135 Tim Rattay	20.00	9.00
❑ 136 Chris Redman SP	30.00	13.50
❑ 137 J.R. Redmond	25.00	11.00
❑ 138 R.Jay Soward	20.00	9.00
❑ 139 Shyrone Stith	10.00	4.50
❑ 140 Travis Taylor		
❑ 141 Troy Walters	15.00	6.75
❑ 142 Peter Warrick SP	100.00	45.00
❑ 143 Dez White	20.00	9.00
❑ 144 Michael Wiley	20.00	9.00

2000 Crown Royale Cramers Choice Jumbos

	MINT	NRMT
COMPLETE SET (10)	40.00	18.00
COMMON CARD (1-10)	2.50	1.10

STATED ODDS ONE PER HOBBY BOX
*DARK BLUES: 3X TO 8X HI COL.
DARK BLUE PRINT RUN 35 SER.#'d SETS
*GOLD: 10X TO 25X HI COL
GOLD PRINT RUN 10 SER.#'d SETS
*GREEN: 3X TO 8X HI COL
GREEN PRINT RUN 30 SER.#'d SETS
*LIGHT BLUE: 5X TO 12X HI COL
LIGHT BLUE PRINT RUN 20 SER.#'d SETS
UNPRICED PURPLE SERIAL #'d OF 1
*RED: 4X TO 10X HI COL
RED PRINT RUN 25 SER.#'d SETS

Card	MINT	NRMT
❑ 1 Tim Couch	5.00	2.20
❑ 2 Emmitt Smith	6.00	2.70
❑ 3 Edgerrin James	8.00	3.60
❑ 4 Damon Huard	2.50	1.10
❑ 5 Randy Moss	8.00	3.60
❑ 6 Kurt Warner	10.00	4.50
❑ 7 Jon Kitna	2.50	1.10
❑ 8 Eddie George	3.00	1.35
❑ 9 Chad Pennington	10.00	4.50
❑ 10 Peter Warrick	12.00	5.50

2000 Crown Royale Fifth Anniversary Jumbos

	MINT	NRMT
COMPLETE SET (6)	30.00	13.50
COMMON CARD (1-6)	2.50	1.10

STATED ODDS 6:10 BOXES

Card	MINT	NRMT
❑ 1 Terrell Davis	6.00	2.70
❑ 2 Eddie George	3.00	1.35
❑ 3 Jon Kitna	2.50	1.10
❑ 4 Randy Moss	8.00	3.60
❑ 5 Kurt Warner	10.00	4.50
❑ 6 Peter Warrick	12.00	5.50

2000 Crown Royale First and Ten

	MINT	NRMT
COMPLETE SET (10)	60.00	27.00
COMMON CARD (1-10)	6.00	2.70

STATED PRINT RUN 375 SERIAL #'d SETS

Card	MINT	NRMT
❑ 1 Tim Couch	6.00	2.70
❑ 2 Troy Aikman	8.00	3.60
❑ 3 Emmitt Smith	8.00	3.60
❑ 4 Terrell Davis	8.00	3.60
❑ 5 Brett Favre	12.00	5.50
❑ 6 Edgerrin James	10.00	4.50
❑ 7 Peyton Manning	10.00	4.50

	MINT	NRMT
❑ 8 Randy Moss	10.00	4.50
❑ 9 Kurt Warner	12.00	5.50
❑ 10 Jerry Rice	8.00	3.60

2000 Crown Royale Game Worn Jerseys

	MINT	NRMT
COMPLETE SET (9)	350.00	160.00
COMMON CARD (1-9)	20.00	9.00
RANDOM INSERTS IN PACKS		
❑ 1 Eric Moulds	30.00	13.50
❑ 2 Brett Favre	100.00	45.00
❑ 3 Antonio Freeman	30.00	13.50
❑ 4 Ricky Williams	60.00	27.00
❑ 5 Tiki Barber	20.00	9.00
❑ 6 Charles Woodson	25.00	11.00
❑ 7 Isaac Bruce	25.00	11.00
❑ 8 Kurt Warner	100.00	45.00
❑ 9 Tim Couch	60.00	27.00

2000 Crown Royale In the Pocket

	MINT	NRMT
COMPLETE SET (20)	80.00	36.00
COMMON CARD (1-20)	2.00	.90
*MINIS: .3X TO .6X HI COL		
STATED ODDS 2:25		
❑ 1 Tim Couch	4.00	1.80
❑ 2 Troy Aikman	5.00	2.20
❑ 3 Emmitt Smith	5.00	2.20
❑ 4 Charlie Batch	2.00	.90
❑ 5 Edgerrin James	6.00	2.70
❑ 6 Peyton Manning	6.00	2.70
❑ 7 Mark Brunell	3.00	1.35
❑ 8 Randy Moss	6.00	2.70
❑ 9 Drew Bledsoe	3.00	1.35
❑ 10 Donovan McNabb	2.50	1.10
❑ 11 Kurt Warner	8.00	3.60
❑ 12 Jon Kitna	2.00	.90
❑ 13 Eddie George	2.50	1.10
❑ 14 Steve McNair	2.00	.90
❑ 15 Brad Johnson	2.00	.90
❑ 16 Plaxico Burress	6.00	2.70
❑ 17 Ron Dayne	12.00	5.50
❑ 18 Thomas Jones	8.00	3.60
❑ 19 Chad Pennington	10.00	4.50
❑ 20 Peter Warrick	12.00	5.50

2000 Crown Royale In Your Face

	MINT	NRMT
COMPLETE SET (25)	20.00	9.00
COMMON CARD (1-25)	.60	.25
STATED ODDS 1:1H/1:2R		
*RAINBOW: 25X TO 60X HI COL		
RAINBOW PRINT RUN 20 SER.#'d SETS		
RAINBOW FOUND ONLY IN HOBBY PACKS		
❑ 1 Jake Plummer	.60	.25
❑ 2 Cade McNown	.75	.35
❑ 3 Marcus Robinson	.60	.25
❑ 4 Corey Dillon	.60	.25
❑ 5 Tim Couch	1.25	.55
❑ 6 Emmitt Smith	1.50	.70
❑ 7 Terrell Davis	1.50	.70
❑ 8 Barry Sanders	2.00	.90
❑ 9 Marvin Harrison	.60	.25
❑ 10 Edgerrin James	2.00	.90
❑ 11 Mark Brunell	1.00	.45
❑ 12 Fred Taylor	1.00	.45
❑ 13 Dan Marino	2.50	1.10
❑ 14 Randy Moss	2.00	.90
❑ 15 Drew Bledsoe	1.00	.45
❑ 16 Ricky Williams	1.25	.55
❑ 17 Curtis Martin	.60	.25
❑ 18 Isaac Bruce	.60	.25
❑ 19 Marshall Faulk	.60	.25
❑ 20 Kurt Warner	2.50	1.10
❑ 21 Jerry Rice	1.50	.70
❑ 22 Jon Kitna	.60	.25
❑ 23 Shaun King	.75	.35
❑ 24 Eddie George	.75	.35
❑ 25 Stephen Davis	.60	.25

2000 Crown Royale Productions

	MINT	NRMT
COMPLETE SET (20)	80.00	36.00
COMMON CARD (1-20)	2.50	1.10
STATED ODDS 1:25		
❑ 1 Cade McNown	3.00	1.35
❑ 2 Tim Couch	5.00	2.20
❑ 3 Emmitt Smith	6.00	2.70
❑ 4 Olandis Gary	2.50	1.10
❑ 5 Barry Sanders	8.00	3.60
❑ 6 Brett Favre	10.00	4.50
❑ 7 Edgerrin James	8.00	3.60
❑ 8 Peyton Manning	8.00	3.60
❑ 9 Fred Taylor	4.00	1.80
❑ 10 Damon Huard	2.50	1.10
❑ 11 Dan Marino	10.00	4.50
❑ 12 Randy Moss	8.00	3.60
❑ 13 Drew Bledsoe	4.00	1.80
❑ 14 Ricky Williams	5.00	2.20
❑ 15 Marshall Faulk	2.50	1.10
❑ 16 Kurt Warner	10.00	4.50
❑ 17 Jerry Rice	6.00	2.70
❑ 18 Shaun King	3.00	1.35
❑ 19 Eddie George	3.00	1.35
❑ 20 Stephen Davis	2.50	1.10

2000 Crown Royale Rookie Royalty

	MINT	NRMT
COMPLETE SET (25)	30.00	13.50
COMMON CARD (1-25)	.75	.35
STATED ODDS 1:1H/1:2R		
*DIE CUTS: 20X TO 50X HI COL.		
DIE CUTS PRINT RUN 10 SER.#'d SETS		
DIE CUTS FOUND ONLY IN HOBBY PACKS		
❑ 1 Shaun Alexander	3.00	1.35
❑ 2 Tom Brady	1.00	.45
❑ 3 Plaxico Burress	2.50	1.10
❑ 4 Ron Dayne	5.00	2.20
❑ 5 Reuben Droughns	1.25	.55
❑ 6 Danny Farmer	1.00	.45

	MINT	NRMT
❑ 7 Chafie Fields	.75	.35
❑ 8 Joe Hamilton	1.00	.45
❑ 9 Todd Husak	1.00	.45
❑ 10 Thomas Jones	3.00	1.35
❑ 11 Jamal Lewis	3.00	1.35
❑ 12 Tee Martin	1.50	.70
❑ 13 Sylvester Morris	1.25	.55
❑ 14 Dennis Northcutt	1.25	.55
❑ 15 Chad Pennington	4.00	1.80
❑ 16 Travis Prentice	1.25	.55
❑ 17 Tim Rattay	1.25	.55
❑ 18 Chris Redman	1.50	.70
❑ 19 J.R. Redmond	1.50	.70
❑ 20 R.Jay Soward	1.25	.55
❑ 21 Shyrone Stith	.75	.35
❑ 22 Travis Taylor	2.00	.90
❑ 23 Troy Walters	1.00	.45
❑ 24 Peter Warrick	5.00	2.20
❑ 25 Dez White	1.25	.55

1996 Donruss

	MINT	NRMT
COMPLETE SET (240)	20.00	9.00
COMMON CARD (1-240)	.10	.05
SEMISTARS	.20	.09
UNLISTED STARS	.40	.18
COMP.PRESS PROOF (240)	300.00	135.00
*PRESS PROOF STARS: 5X TO 12X HI		
*PRESS PROOF RCs: 2.5X TO 6X HI		
PPs: STATED ODDS 1:5		
STATED PRINT RUN 2000 SETS		
❑ 1 Barry Sanders	2.00	.90
❑ 2 Flipper Anderson	.10	.05
❑ 3 Ben Coates	.20	.09
❑ 4 Rob Johnson	.40	.18
❑ 5 Rodney Hampton	.20	.09
❑ 6 Desmond Howard	.20	.09
❑ 7 Craig Heyward	.10	.05
❑ 8 Alvin Harper	.10	.05
❑ 9 Todd Collins	.20	.09
❑ 10 Ken Norton Jr.	.10	.05
❑ 11 Stan Humphries	.20	.09
❑ 12 Aeneas Williams	.10	.05
❑ 13 Jeff Hostetler	.10	.05
❑ 14 Frank Sanders	.20	.09
❑ 15 J.J. Birden	.10	.05
❑ 16 Bryce Paup	.10	.05
❑ 17 Bill Brooks	.10	.05
❑ 18 Kevin Williams	.10	.05

❑ 19 Boomer Esiason .20 .09
❑ 20 O.J. McDuffie .20 .09
❑ 21 Eric Swann .10 .05
❑ 22 Neil Smith .10 .05
❑ 23 Charlie Garner .10 .05
❑ 24 Greg Lloyd .20 .09
❑ 25 Willie Jackson .10 .05
❑ 26 Shawn Jefferson .10 .05
❑ 27 Rodney Peete .10 .05
❑ 28 Michael Westbrook .40 .18
❑ 29 J.J. Stokes .40 .18
❑ 30 Troy Aikman 1.00 .45
❑ 31 Sean Dawkins .10 .05
❑ 32 Larry Centers .20 .09
❑ 33 Herschel Walker .20 .09
❑ 34 Stoney Case .10 .05
❑ 35 Kevin Greene .20 .09
❑ 36 Quinn Early .10 .05
❑ 37 Fred Barnett .10 .05
❑ 38 Andre Coleman .10 .05
❑ 39 Mark Chmura .20 .09
❑ 40 Adrian Murrell .40 .18
❑ 41 Roosevelt Potts .10 .05
❑ 42 Jay Novacek .10 .05
❑ 43 Derrick Alexander WR .20 .09
❑ 44 Ken Dilger .20 .09
❑ 45 Rob Moore .20 .09
❑ 46 Cris Carter .40 .18
❑ 47 Jeff Blake .40 .18
❑ 48 Derek Loville .10 .05
❑ 49 Tyrone Wheatley .20 .09
❑ 50 Terrell Fletcher .10 .05
❑ 51 Sherman Williams .10 .05
❑ 52 Justin Armour .10 .05
❑ 53 Kordell Stewart .75 .35
❑ 54 Tim Brown .40 .18
❑ 55 Kevin Carter .10 .05
❑ 56 Andre Rison .20 .09
❑ 57 James O.Stewart .20 .09
❑ 58 Brent Jones .10 .05
❑ 59 Erik Kramer .10 .05
❑ 60 Floyd Turner .10 .05
❑ 61 Ricky Watters .20 .09
❑ 62 Hardy Nickerson .10 .05
❑ 63 Aaron Craver .10 .05
❑ 64 Dave Krieg .10 .05
❑ 65 Warren Moon .20 .09
❑ 66 Wayne Chrebet .20 .09
❑ 67 Napoleon Kaufman .50 .23
❑ 68 Terance Mathis .10 .05
❑ 69 Chad May .10 .05
❑ 70 Andre Reed .20 .09
❑ 71 Reggie White .40 .18
❑ 72 Brett Favre 2.00 .90
❑ 73 Chris Zorich .10 .05
❑ 74 Kerry Collins .75 .35
❑ 75 Herman Moore .40 .18
❑ 76 Yancey Thigpen .20 .09
❑ 77 Glenn Foley .20 .09
❑ 78 Quentin Coryatt .10 .05
❑ 79 Terry Kirby .20 .09
❑ 80 Edgar Bennett .20 .09
❑ 81 Mark Brunell 1.00 .45
❑ 82 Heath Shuler .20 .09
❑ 83 Gus Frerotte .40 .18
❑ 84 Deion Sanders .60 .25
❑ 85 Calvin Williams .10 .05
❑ 86 Junior Seau .20 .09
❑ 87 Jim Kelly .40 .18
❑ 88 Daryl Johnston .20 .09
❑ 89 Irving Fryar .20 .09
❑ 90 Brian Blades .10 .05
❑ 91 Willie Davis .10 .05
❑ 92 Jerome Bettis .40 .18
❑ 93 Marcus Allen .40 .18
❑ 94 Jeff Graham .10 .05
❑ 95 Rick Mirer .20 .09
❑ 96 Harvey Williams .10 .05
❑ 97 Steve Atwater .10 .05
❑ 98 Carl Pickens .40 .18
❑ 99 Darick Holmes .10 .05
❑ 100 Bruce Smith .20 .09
❑ 101 Vinny Testaverde .20 .09
❑ 102 Thurman Thomas .40 .18
❑ 103 Drew Bledsoe 1.00 .45
❑ 104 Bernie Parmalee .10 .05
❑ 105 Greg Hill .20 .09
❑ 106 Steve McNair .75 .35
❑ 107 Andre Hastings .10 .05
❑ 108 Eric Metcalf .10 .05
❑ 109 Kimble Anders .20 .09
❑ 110 Steve Tasker .10 .05
❑ 111 Mark Carrier WR .10 .05
❑ 112 Jerry Rice 1.00 .45
❑ 113 Joey Galloway .75 .35
❑ 114 Robert Smith .20 .09
❑ 115 Hugh Douglas .10 .05
❑ 116 Willie McGinest .10 .05
❑ 117 Terrell Davis 2.50 1.10
❑ 118 Cortez Kennedy .10 .05
❑ 119 Marshall Faulk .40 .18
❑ 120 Michael Haynes .10 .05
❑ 121 Isaac Bruce .40 .18
❑ 122 Brian Mitchell .10 .05
❑ 123 Bryan Cox .10 .05
❑ 124 Tamarick Vanover .20 .09
❑ 125 William Floyd .20 .09
❑ 126 Chris Chandler .20 .09
❑ 127 Carnell Lake .10 .05
❑ 128 Aaron Bailey .10 .05
❑ 129 Darnay Scott .20 .09
❑ 130 Darren Woodson .20 .09
❑ 131 Ernie Mills .10 .05
❑ 132 Charles Haley .20 .09
❑ 133 Rocket Ismail .10 .05
❑ 134 Bert Emanuel .20 .09
❑ 135 Lake Dawson .10 .05
❑ 136 Jake Reed .20 .09
❑ 137 Dave Brown .10 .05
❑ 138 Steve Bono .10 .05
❑ 139 Terry Allen .20 .09
❑ 140 Erict Rhett .20 .09
❑ 141 Rod Woodson .20 .09
❑ 142 Charles Johnson .10 .05
❑ 143 Emmitt Smith 1.50 .70
❑ 144 Ki-Jana Carter .20 .09
❑ 145 Garrison Hearst .20 .09
❑ 146 Rashaan Salaam .40 .18
❑ 147 Tony Boselli .10 .05
❑ 148 Derrick Thomas .20 .09
❑ 149 Mark Seay .10 .05
❑ 150 Derrick Alexander DE .10 .05
❑ 151 Christian Fauria .10 .05
❑ 152 Aaron Hayden .10 .05
❑ 153 Chris Warren .20 .09
❑ 154 Dave Meggett .10 .05
❑ 155 Jeff George .20 .09
❑ 156 Jackie Harris .10 .05
❑ 157 Michael Irvin .40 .18
❑ 158 Scott Mitchell .20 .09
❑ 159 Trent Dilfer .40 .18
❑ 160 Kyle Brady .10 .05
❑ 161 Dan Marino 2.00 .90
❑ 162 Curtis Martin .75 .35
❑ 163 Mario Bates .20 .09
❑ 164 Erric Pegram .10 .05
❑ 165 Eric Zeier .10 .05
❑ 166 Rodney Thomas .10 .05
❑ 167 Neil O'Donnell .20 .09
❑ 168 Warren Sapp .10 .05
❑ 169 Jim Harbaugh .20 .09
❑ 170 Henry Ellard .10 .05
❑ 171 Anthony Miller .20 .09
❑ 172 Derrick Moore .10 .05
❑ 173 John Elway 2.00 .90
❑ 174 Vincent Brisby .10 .05
❑ 175 Antonio Freeman .75 .35
❑ 176 Chris Sanders .20 .09
❑ 177 Steve Young .75 .35
❑ 178 Shannon Sharpe .20 .09
❑ 179 Brett Perriman .10 .05
❑ 180 Orlando Thomas .10 .05
❑ 181 Eric Bjornson .10 .05
❑ 182 Natrone Means .40 .18
❑ 183 Jim Everett .10 .05
❑ 184 Curtis Conway .40 .18
❑ 185 Robert Brooks .40 .18
❑ 186 Tony Martin .20 .09
❑ 187 Mark Carrier DB .10 .05
❑ 188 LeShon Johnson .10 .05
❑ 189 Bernie Kosar .10 .05
❑ 190 Ray Zellars .10 .05
❑ 191 Steve Walsh .10 .05
❑ 192 Craig Erickson .10 .05
❑ 193 Tommy Maddox .10 .05
❑ 194 Leslie O'Neal .10 .05
❑ 195 Harold Green .10 .05
❑ 196 Steve Beuerlein .10 .05
❑ 197 Ronald Moore .10 .05
❑ 198 Leslie Shepherd .10 .05
❑ 199 Leroy Hoard .10 .05
❑ 200 Michael Jackson .20 .09
❑ 201 Will Moore .10 .05
❑ 202 Ricky Ervins .10 .05
❑ 203 Keith Jennings .10 .05
❑ 204 Eric Green .10 .05
❑ 205 Mark Rypien .10 .05
❑ 206 Torrance Small .10 .05
❑ 207 Sean Gilbert .10 .05
❑ 208 Mike Alstott RC 1.50 .70
❑ 209 Willie Anderson RC .10 .05
❑ 210 Alex Molden RC .10 .05
❑ 211 Jonathan Ogden RC .10 .05
❑ 212 Stepfret Williams RC .20 .09
❑ 213 Jeff Lewis RC .60 .25
❑ 214 Regan Upshaw RC .10 .05
❑ 215 Daryl Gardener RC .10 .05
❑ 216 Danny Kanell RC .50 .23
❑ 217 John Mobley RC .10 .05
❑ 218 Reggie Brown LB RC .10 .05
❑ 219 Muhsin Muhammad RC .75 .35
❑ 220 Kevin Hardy RC .40 .18
❑ 221 Stanley Pritchett RC .20 .09
❑ 222 Cedric Jones RC .10 .05
❑ 223 Marco Battaglia RC .10 .05
❑ 224 Duane Clemons RC .10 .05
❑ 225 Jerald Moore RC .40 .18
❑ 226 Simeon Rice RC .40 .18
❑ 227 Chris Darkins RC .10 .05
❑ 228 Bobby Hoying RC .60 .25
❑ 229 Stephen Davis RC 2.50 1.10
❑ 230 Walt Harris RC .10 .05
❑ 231 Jermane Mayberry RC .10 .05
❑ 232 Tony Brackens RC .20 .09
❑ 233 Eric Moulds RC 2.00 .90
❑ 234 Alex Van Dyke RC .20 .09
❑ 235 Marvin Harrison RC 2.00 .90
❑ 236 Rickey Dudley RC .50 .23
❑ 237 Terrell Owens RC 2.50 1.10
❑ 238 Jerry Rice .40 .18
Checklist Card
❑ 239 Dan Marino .40 .18
Checklist Card
❑ 240 Emmitt Smith .40 .18
Checklist Card

1996 Donruss Elite

	MINT	NRMT
COMPLETE SET (20)	100.00	45.00

STAT.PRINT RUN 10,000 SER.#'d SETS
*GOLD STARS: .8X TO 2X SILVERS
GOLD STAT.PRINT RUN 2000 SER.#'d SETS

❑ 1 Emmitt Smith 12.00 5.50
❑ 2 Barry Sanders 15.00 6.75
❑ 3 Marshall Faulk 3.00 1.35
❑ 4 Curtis Martin 6.00 2.70
❑ 5 Junior Seau 1.50 .70
❑ 6 Troy Aikman 8.00 3.60

	Player	MINT	NRMT
❑ 7	Steve Young	6.00	2.70
❑ 8	Dan Marino	15.00	6.75
❑ 9	Brett Favre	15.00	6.75
❑ 10	John Elway	15.00	6.75
❑ 11	Kerry Collins	6.00	2.70
❑ 12	Drew Bledsoe	8.00	3.60
❑ 13	Jerry Rice	8.00	3.60
❑ 14	Keyshawn Johnson	6.00	2.70
❑ 15	Deion Sanders	5.00	2.20
❑ 16	Isaac Bruce	3.00	1.35
❑ 17	Rashaan Salaam	3.00	1.35
❑ 18	Tim Biakabutuka	3.00	1.35
❑ 19	Lawrence Phillips	2.50	1.10
❑ 20	Robert Brooks	3.00	1.35

1996 Donruss Hit List

	MINT	NRMT
COMPLETE SET (20)	100.00	45.00

STATED PRINT RUN 10,000 SERIAL #'d SETS

	Player	MINT	NRMT
❑ 1	Bruce Smith	1.25	.55
❑ 2	Barry Sanders	12.00	5.50
❑ 3	Kevin Hardy	2.50	1.10
❑ 4	Greg Lloyd	1.25	.55
❑ 5	Brett Favre	12.00	5.50
❑ 6	Emmitt Smith	10.00	4.50
❑ 7	Kerry Collins	5.00	2.20
❑ 8	Ken Norton Jr.	.60	.25
❑ 9	Steve Atwater	.60	.25
❑ 10	Curtis Martin	5.00	2.20
❑ 11	Chris Warren	1.25	.55
❑ 12	Steve Young	5.00	2.20
❑ 13	Marshall Faulk	2.50	1.10
❑ 14	Junior Seau	1.25	.55
❑ 15	Lawrence Phillips	8.00	3.60
❑ 16	Troy Aikman	6.00	2.70
❑ 17	Jerry Rice	6.00	2.70
❑ 18	Dan Marino	12.00	5.50
❑ 19	Reggie White	2.50	1.10
❑ 20	John Elway	12.00	5.50

1996 Donruss Rated Rookies

	MINT	NRMT
COMPLETE SET (10)	30.00	13.50
COMMON CARD (1-10)	2.00	.90
SEMISTARS	3.00	1.35

RANDOM INSERTS IN PACKS....

	Player	MINT	NRMT
❑ 1	Keyshawn Johnson	6.00	2.70
❑ 2	Terry Glenn	4.00	1.80
❑ 3	Tim Biakabutuka	4.00	1.80
❑ 4	Bobby Engram	2.00	.90
❑ 5	Leeland McElroy	2.00	.90
❑ 6	Eddie George	8.00	3.60
❑ 7	Lawrence Phillips	3.00	1.35
❑ 8	Derrick Mayes	2.00	.90
❑ 9	Karim Abdul-Jabbar	3.00	1.35
❑ 10	Eddie Kennison	3.00	1.35

1996 Donruss Stop Action

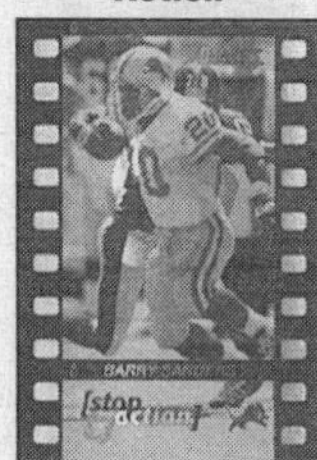

	MINT	NRMT
COMPLETE SET (10)	80.00	36.00

STATED PRINT RUN 4000 SERIAL #'d SETS
RANDOM INSERTS IN JUMBO PACKS

	Player	MINT	NRMT
❑ 1	Deion Sanders	5.00	2.20
❑ 2	Troy Aikman	8.00	3.60
❑ 3	Brett Favre	15.00	6.75
❑ 4	Steve Young	6.00	2.70
❑ 5	Joey Galloway	6.00	2.70
❑ 6	Dan Marino	15.00	6.75
❑ 7	Jerry Rice	8.00	3.60
❑ 8	Emmitt Smith	12.00	5.50
❑ 9	Isaac Bruce	3.00	1.35
❑ 10	Barry Sanders	15.00	6.75

1996 Donruss What If?

	MINT	NRMT
COMPLETE SET (10)	100.00	45.00

RANDOM INSERTS IN HOBBY PACKS
STATED PRINT RUN 5000 SERIAL #'d SETS

	Player	MINT	NRMT
❑ 1	Troy Aikman	8.00	3.60
❑ 2	Jerry Rice	8.00	3.60
❑ 3	Barry Sanders	15.00	6.75
❑ 4	Drew Bledsoe	8.00	3.60
❑ 5	Deion Sanders	5.00	2.20
❑ 6	Brett Favre	15.00	6.75
❑ 7	Dan Marino	15.00	6.75
❑ 8	Steve Young	6.00	2.70
❑ 9	Emmitt Smith	12.00	5.50
❑ 10	John Elway	15.00	6.75

1996 Donruss Will To Win

	MINT	NRMT
COMPLETE SET (10)	80.00	36.00

RANDOM INSERTS IN RETAIL PACKS
STATED PRINT RUN 5000 SERIAL #'d SETS

	Player	MINT	NRMT
❑ 1	Emmitt Smith	12.00	5.50
❑ 2	Brett Favre	15.00	6.75
❑ 3	Curtis Martin	6.00	2.70
❑ 4	Jerry Rice	8.00	3.60
❑ 5	Barry Sanders	15.00	6.75
❑ 6	Errict Rhett	1.50	.70
❑ 7	Troy Aikman	8.00	3.60
❑ 8	Dan Marino	15.00	6.75
❑ 9	Steve Young	6.00	2.70
❑ 10	John Elway	15.00	6.75

1997 Donruss

	MINT	NRMT
COMPLETE SET (230)	20.00	9.00
COMMON CARD (1-230)	.10	.05
SEMISTARS	.20	.09
UNLISTED STARS	.30	.14
COMP.PRESS PROOF SILV.	500.00	220.00

*PP SILVER STARS: 3X TO 8X....
*PP SILVER RCs: 2.5X TO 6X......
SILVER PRINT RUN 1500 SERIAL #'d SETS

	MINT	NRMT
COMP.PRE.PROOF GOLD	1200.00	550.00

*PP GOLD STARS: 8X TO 20X ....
*PP GOLD RCs: 5X TO 12X ....
GOLD PRINT RUN 500 SERIAL #'d SETS

	Player	MINT	NRMT
❑ 1	Dan Marino	2.00	.90
❑ 2	Brett Favre	2.00	.90
❑ 3	Emmitt Smith	1.50	.70
❑ 4	Eddie George	1.00	.45
❑ 5	Karim Abdul-Jabbar	.30	.14
❑ 6	Terrell Davis	1.50	.70
❑ 7	Curtis Martin	.50	.23
❑ 8	Drew Bledsoe	1.00	.45
❑ 9	Jerry Rice	1.00	.45
❑ 10	Troy Aikman	1.00	.45
❑ 11	Barry Sanders	2.00	.90
❑ 12	Mark Brunell	1.00	.45
❑ 13	Kerry Collins	.20	.09
❑ 14	Steve Young	.60	.25
❑ 15	Kordell Stewart	.50	.23

❑ 16 Eddie Kennison .20 .09
❑ 17 Terry Glenn .30 .14
❑ 18 John Elway 2.00 .90
❑ 19 Joey Galloway .50 .23
❑ 20 Deion Sanders .30 .14
❑ 21 Keyshawn Johnson .30 .14
❑ 22 Lawrence Phillips .10 .05
❑ 23 Ricky Watters .20 .09
❑ 24 Marvin Harrison .30 .14
❑ 25 Bobby Engram .20 .09
❑ 26 Marshall Faulk .30 .14
❑ 27 Carl Pickens .30 .14
❑ 28 Isaac Bruce .30 .14
❑ 29 Herman Moore .30 .14
❑ 30 Jerome Bettis .30 .14
❑ 31 Rashaan Salaam .10 .05
❑ 32 Errict Rhett .10 .05
❑ 33 Tim Biakabutuka .20 .09
❑ 34 Robert Brooks .20 .09
❑ 35 Antonio Freeman .50 .23
❑ 36 Steve McNair .50 .23
❑ 37 Jeff Blake .20 .09
❑ 38 Tony Banks .20 .09
❑ 39 Terrell Owens .30 .14
❑ 40 Eric Moulds .30 .14
❑ 41 Leeland McElroy .10 .05
❑ 42 Chris Sanders .10 .05
❑ 43 Thurman Thomas .30 .14
❑ 44 Bruce Smith .20 .09
❑ 45 Reggie White .30 .14
❑ 46 Chris Warren .20 .09
❑ 47 J.J. Stokes .20 .09
❑ 48 Ben Coates .20 .09
❑ 49 Tim Brown .30 .14
❑ 50 Marcus Allen .30 .14
❑ 51 Michael Irvin .30 .14
❑ 52 William Floyd .20 .09
❑ 53 Ken Dilger .10 .05
❑ 54 Bobby Taylor .10 .05
❑ 55 Keenan McCardell .20 .09
❑ 56 Raymont Harris .10 .05
❑ 57 Keith Byars .10 .05
❑ 58 O.J. McDuffie .20 .09
❑ 59 Robert Smith .20 .09
❑ 60 Bert Emanuel .20 .09
❑ 61 Rick Mirer .10 .05
❑ 62 Vinny Testaverde .20 .09
❑ 63 Kyle Brady .10 .05
❑ 64 Mark Bruener .10 .05
❑ 65 Neil O'Donnell .20 .09
❑ 66 Anthony Johnson .10 .05
❑ 67 Ken Norton .10 .05
❑ 68 Warren Sapp .20 .09
❑ 69 Amani Toomer .20 .09
❑ 70 Simeon Rice .20 .09
❑ 71 Kevin Hardy .10 .05
❑ 72 Junior Seau .20 .09
❑ 73 Neil Smith .20 .09
❑ 74 LeShon Johnson .10 .05
❑ 75 Quinn Early .10 .05
❑ 76 Andre Reed .20 .09
❑ 77 Jake Reed .20 .09
❑ 78 Elvis Grbac .20 .09
❑ 79 Tyrone Wheatley .20 .09
❑ 80 Adrian Murrell .20 .09
❑ 81 Fred Barnett .10 .05
❑ 82 Darrell Green .20 .09
❑ 83 Stan Humphries .20 .09
❑ 84 Troy Drayton .10 .05
❑ 85 Steve Atwater .10 .05
❑ 86 Quentin Coryatt .10 .05
❑ 87 Dan Wilkinson .10 .05
❑ 88 Scott Mitchell .20 .09
❑ 89 Willie McGinest .10 .05
❑ 90 Kevin Smith .10 .05
❑ 91 Gus Frerotte .10 .05
❑ 92 Byron Bam Morris .10 .05
❑ 93 Darick Holmes .10 .05
❑ 94 Zach Thomas .20 .09
❑ 95 Tom Carter .10 .05
❑ 96 Cortez Kennedy .10 .05
❑ 97 Kevin Williams .10 .05
❑ 98 Michael Haynes .10 .05
❑ 99 Lamont Warren .10 .05
❑ 100 Jeff Graham .10 .05
❑ 101 Alex Van Dyke .10 .05
❑ 102 Jim Everett .10 .05
❑ 103 Chris Chandler .20 .09
❑ 104 Qadry Ismail .20 .09
❑ 105 Ray Zellars .10 .05
❑ 106 Chris T. Jones .10 .05
❑ 107 Charlie Garner .10 .05
❑ 108 Bobby Hoying .20 .09
❑ 109 Mark Chmura .20 .09
❑ 110 Cris Carter .30 .14
❑ 111 Darnay Scott .20 .09
❑ 112 Anthony Miller .10 .05
❑ 113 Desmond Howard .20 .09
❑ 114 Terance Mathis .20 .09
❑ 115 Rodney Hampton .20 .09
❑ 116 Napoleon Kaufman .30 .14
❑ 117 Jim Harbaugh .20 .09
❑ 118 Shannon Sharpe .20 .09
❑ 119 Irving Fryar .20 .09
❑ 120 Garrison Hearst .20 .09
❑ 121 Terry Allen .30 .14
❑ 122 Larry Centers .20 .09
❑ 123 Sean Dawkins .10 .05
❑ 124 Jeff George .20 .09
❑ 125 Tony Martin .20 .09
❑ 126 Mike Alstott .30 .14
❑ 127 Rickey Dudley .20 .09
❑ 128 Kevin Carter .10 .05
❑ 129 Derrick Alexander WR .20 .09
❑ 130 Greg Lloyd .10 .05
❑ 131 Bryce Paup .10 .05
❑ 132 Derrick Thomas .20 .09
❑ 133 Greg Hill .10 .05
❑ 134 Jamal Anderson .60 .25
❑ 135 Curtis Conway .20 .09
❑ 136 Frank Sanders .20 .09
❑ 137 Brett Perriman .10 .05
❑ 138 Edgar Bennett .20 .09
❑ 139 Wayne Chrebet .30 .14
❑ 140 Natrone Means .30 .14
❑ 141 Eric Metcalf .20 .09
❑ 142 Trent Dilfer .30 .14
❑ 143 Terry Kirby .20 .09
❑ 144 Johnnie Morton .20 .09
❑ 145 Dale Carter .10 .05
❑ 146 Michael Westbrook .20 .09
❑ 147 Stanley Pritchett .10 .05
❑ 148 Todd Collins .10 .05
❑ 149 Tamarick Vanover .20 .09
❑ 150 Kevin Greene .20 .09
❑ 151 Lamar Lathon .10 .05
❑ 152 Muhsin Muhammad .20 .09
❑ 153 Dorsey Levens .30 .14
❑ 154 Rod Woodson .20 .09
❑ 155 Brent Jones .20 .09
❑ 156 Michael Jackson .20 .09
❑ 157 Shawn Jefferson .10 .05
❑ 158 Kimble Anders .20 .09
❑ 159 Sean Gilbert .10 .05
❑ 160 Carnell Lake .10 .05
❑ 161 Darren Woodson .10 .05
❑ 162 Dave Meggett .10 .05
❑ 163 Henry Ellard .10 .05
❑ 164 Eric Swann .10 .05
❑ 165 Tony Boselli .10 .05
❑ 166 Daryl Johnston .20 .09
❑ 167 Willie Jackson .10 .05
❑ 168 Wesley Walls .20 .09
❑ 169 Mario Bates .10 .05
❑ 170 Lake Dawson .10 .05
❑ 171 Mike Mamula .10 .05
❑ 172 Ed McCaffrey .20 .09
❑ 173 Tony Brackens .10 .05
❑ 174 Craig Heyward .10 .05
❑ 175 Harvey Williams .10 .05
❑ 176 Dave Brown .10 .05
❑ 177 Aaron Glenn .10 .05
❑ 178 Jeff Hostetler .10 .05
❑ 179 Alvin Harper .10 .05
❑ 180 Ty Detmer .20 .09
❑ 181 James Jett .20 .09
❑ 182 James O.Stewart .20 .09
❑ 183 Warren Moon .30 .14
❑ 184 Herschel Walker .20 .09
❑ 185 Ki-Jana Carter .10 .05
❑ 186 Leslie O'Neal .10 .05
❑ 187 Danny Kanell .20 .09
❑ 188 Eric Bjornson .10 .05
❑ 189 Alex Molden .10 .05
❑ 190 Bryant Young .10 .05
❑ 191 Merton Hanks .10 .05
❑ 192 Heath Shuler .10 .05
❑ 193 Brian Blades .10 .05
❑ 194 Steve Bono .20 .09
❑ 195 Wayne Simmons .10 .05
❑ 196 Warrick Dunn RC 1.25 .55
❑ 197 Peter Boulware RC .20 .09
❑ 198 David LaFleur RC .20 .09
❑ 199 Shawn Springs RC .20 .09
❑ 200 Reidel Anthony RC .75 .35
❑ 201 Jim Druckenmiller RC .50 .23
❑ 202 Orlando Pace RC .10 .05
❑ 203 Yatil Green RC .20 .09
❑ 204 Bryant Westbrook RC .10 .05
❑ 205 Tiki Barber RC .50 .23
❑ 206 James Farrior RC .10 .05
❑ 207 Rae Carruth RC .30 .14
❑ 208 Danny Wuerffel RC .60 .25
❑ 209 Corey Dillon RC 1.50 .70
❑ 210 Ike Hilliard RC .75 .35
❑ 211 Tony Gonzalez RC 1.25 .55
❑ 212 Antowain Smith RC 1.00 .45
❑ 213 Pat Barnes RC .30 .14
❑ 214 Troy Davis RC .30 .14
❑ 215 Byron Hanspard RC .75 .35
❑ 216 Joey Kent RC .30 .14
❑ 217 Jake Plummer RC 3.00 1.35
❑ 218 Kenny Holmes RC .10 .05
❑ 219 Darnell Autry RC .20 .09
❑ 220 Darrell Russell RC .10 .05
❑ 221 Walter Jones RC .10 .05
❑ 222 Dwayne Rudd RC .10 .05
❑ 223 Tom Knight RC .10 .05
❑ 224 Kevin Lockett RC .20 .09
❑ 225 Will Blackwell RC .30 .14
❑ 226 Dan Marino .40 .18
Checklist back
❑ 227 Brett Favre .40 .18
Checklist back
❑ 228 Emmitt Smith .30 .14
Checklist back
❑ 229 Barry Sanders .30 .14
Checklist back
❑ 230 Jerry Rice .25 .11
Checklist back
❑ P1 Drew Bledsoe 1.00 .45
(Ad back promo)
❑ P2 Mark Brunell 1.00 .45
(Ad back promo)
❑ P3 Barry Sanders 1.50 .70
(Ad back promo)

1997 Donruss Elite

	MINT	NRMT
COMPLETE SET (20)	120.00	55.00

SILVER STATED PRINT RUN 5000 #'d SETS
*GOLD CARDS: 5X TO 12X BASE CARD HI
GOLD STATED PRINT RUN 2000 #'d SETS
RANDOM INSERTS IN PACKS ....

❑ 1 Emmitt Smith 12.00 5.50
❑ 2 Dan Marino 15.00 6.75
❑ 3 Brett Favre 15.00 6.75
❑ 4 Curtis Martin 4.00 1.80

Card	MINT	NRMT
❑ 5 Terrell Davis	12.00	5.50
❑ 6 Barry Sanders	15.00	6.75
❑ 7 Drew Bledsoe	8.00	3.60
❑ 8 Mark Brunell	8.00	3.60
❑ 9 Troy Aikman	8.00	3.60
❑ 10 Jerry Rice	8.00	3.60
❑ 11 Steve McNair	4.00	1.80
❑ 12 Kerry Collins	1.50	.70
❑ 13 John Elway	15.00	6.75
❑ 14 Eddie George	8.00	3.60
❑ 15 Karim Abdul-Jabbar	2.50	1.10
❑ 16 Kordell Stewart	4.00	1.80
❑ 17 Jerome Bettis	2.50	1.10
❑ 18 Terry Glenn	2.50	1.10
❑ 19 Errict Rhett	.75	.35
❑ 20 Carl Pickens	2.50	1.10

1997 Donruss Legends of the Fall

	MINT	NRMT
COMPLETE SET (10)	100.00	45.00

STATED PRINT RUN 10,000 #'d SETS
*CANVAS CARDS: 7.5X TO 20X BASE CARD HI
CANVAS PRINT RUN FIRST 500 SETS
RANDOM INSERTS IN PACKS....

Card	MINT	NRMT
❑ 1 Troy Aikman	10.00	4.50
❑ 2 Barry Sanders	20.00	9.00
❑ 3 John Elway	20.00	9.00
❑ 4 Dan Marino	20.00	9.00
❑ 5 Emmitt Smith	15.00	6.75
❑ 6 Jerry Rice	10.00	4.50
❑ 7 Deion Sanders	3.00	1.35
❑ 8 Brett Favre	20.00	9.00
❑ 9 Marcus Allen	3.00	1.35
❑ 10 Steve Young	6.00	2.70

1997 Donruss Passing Grade

	MINT	NRMT
COMPLETE SET (16)	120.00	55.00

STATED PRINT RUN 3000 #'d SETS
RANDOM INSERTS IN HOBBY PACKS

Card	MINT	NRMT
❑ 1 Steve Young	6.00	2.70
❑ 2 Drew Bledsoe	10.00	4.50
❑ 3 Mark Brunell	10.00	4.50
❑ 4 Kerry Collins	2.00	.90
❑ 5 Steve McNair	5.00	2.20
❑ 6 John Elway	20.00	9.00
❑ 7 Ty Detmer	2.00	.90
❑ 8 Jeff Blake	2.00	.90
❑ 9 Dan Marino	20.00	9.00
❑ 10 Kordell Stewart	5.00	2.20
❑ 11 Tony Banks	2.00	.90
❑ 12 Brett Favre	20.00	9.00
❑ 13 Gus Frerotte	1.00	.45
❑ 14 Troy Aikman	10.00	4.50
❑ 15 Jeff George	2.00	.90
❑ 16 Brad Johnson	3.00	1.35

1997 Donruss Rated Rookies

	MINT	NRMT
COMPLETE SET (10)	40.00	18.00

*MEDALISTS: 12X TO 30X BASE CARD HI
RANDOM INSERTS IN PACKS....

Card	MINT	NRMT
❑ 1 Ike Hilliard	4.00	1.80
❑ 2 Warrick Dunn	6.00	2.70
❑ 3 Yatil Green	1.00	.45
❑ 4 Jim Druckenmiller	2.50	1.10
❑ 5 Rae Carruth	1.50	.70
❑ 6 Antowain Smith	5.00	2.20
❑ 7 Tiki Barber	2.50	1.10
❑ 8 Byron Hanspard	4.00	1.80
❑ 9 Reidel Anthony	4.00	1.80
❑ 10 Jake Plummer	15.00	6.75

1997 Donruss Zoning Commission

	MINT	NRMT
COMPLETE SET (20)	120.00	55.00

RANDOM INSERTS IN RETAIL PACKS
STATED PRINT RUN 5000 #'d SETS

Card	MINT	NRMT
❑ 1 Brett Favre	15.00	6.75
❑ 2 Jerry Rice	8.00	3.60
❑ 3 Jerome Bettis	2.50	1.10
❑ 4 Troy Aikman	8.00	3.60
❑ 5 Drew Bledsoe	8.00	3.60
❑ 6 Natrone Means	2.50	1.10
❑ 7 Steve Young	5.00	2.20
❑ 8 John Elway	15.00	6.75
❑ 9 Barry Sanders	15.00	6.75
❑ 10 Emmitt Smith	12.00	5.50
❑ 11 Curtis Martin	4.00	1.80
❑ 12 Terry Allen	2.50	1.10
❑ 13 Dan Marino	15.00	6.75
❑ 14 Mark Brunell	8.00	3.60
❑ 15 Terry Glenn	2.50	1.10
❑ 16 Herman Moore	2.50	1.10
❑ 17 Ricky Watters	1.50	.70
❑ 18 Terrell Davis	12.00	5.50
❑ 19 Isaac Bruce	2.50	1.10
❑ 20 Curtis Conway	1.50	.70

1999 Donruss

	MINT	NRMT
COMPLETE SET (200)	150.00	70.00
COMP.SET w/o SP's (150)	20.00	9.00
COMMON CARD (1-200)	.15	.07
SEMISTARS	.25	.11
UNLISTED STARS	.50	.23
COMMON ROOKIE (141-190)	2.00	.90
ROOKIE SEMISTARS	2.50	1.10

ROOKIE SUBSET STATED ODDS 1:4

Card	MINT	NRMT
❑ 1 Jake Plummer	.75	.35
❑ 2 Rob Moore	.25	.11
❑ 3 Adrian Murrell	.25	.11
❑ 4 Frank Sanders	.25	.11
❑ 5 Jamal Anderson	.50	.23
❑ 6 Tim Dwight	.25	.11
❑ 7 Terance Mathis	.25	.11
❑ 8 Chris Chandler	.25	.11
❑ 9 Byron Hanspard	.25	.11
❑ 10 Priest Holmes	.50	.23
❑ 11 Jermaine Lewis	.25	.11
❑ 12 Errict Rhett	.25	.11
❑ 13 Doug Flutie	.60	.25
❑ 14 Eric Moulds	.50	.23
❑ 15 Antowain Smith	.50	.23
❑ 16 Thurman Thomas	.25	.11
❑ 17 Andre Reed	.25	.11
❑ 18 Bruce Smith	.25	.11
❑ 19 Tim Biakabutuka	.25	.11
❑ 20 Rae Carruth	.25	.11
❑ 21 Muhsin Muhammad	.25	.11
❑ 22 Curtis Enis	.50	.23
❑ 23 Curtis Conway	.25	.11
❑ 24 Bobby Engram	.25	.11
❑ 25 Corey Dillon	.50	.23
❑ 26 Carl Pickens	.25	.11
❑ 27 Jeff Blake	.25	.11
❑ 28 Darnay Scott	.25	.11
❑ 29 Ty Detmer	.25	.11
❑ 30 Leslie Shepherd	.15	.07
❑ 31 Emmitt Smith	1.25	.55
❑ 32 Troy Aikman	1.25	.55
❑ 33 Michael Irvin	.25	.11
❑ 34 Deion Sanders	.50	.23
❑ 35 Rocket Ismail	.25	.11
❑ 36 John Elway	2.00	.90
❑ 37 Terrell Davis	1.25	.55
❑ 38 Ed McCaffrey	.25	.11
❑ 39 Shannon Sharpe	.25	.11
❑ 40 Rod Smith	.25	.11
❑ 41 Bubby Brister	.15	.07
❑ 42 Brian Griese	1.00	.45
❑ 43 Barry Sanders	2.00	.90
❑ 44 Charlie Batch	1.00	.45
❑ 45 Herman Moore	.50	.23
❑ 46 Germane Crowell	.25	.11
❑ 47 Johnnie Morton	.25	.11
❑ 48 Ron Rivers	.15	.07
❑ 49 Brett Favre	2.00	.90
❑ 50 Antonio Freeman	.50	.23
❑ 51 Dorsey Levens	.50	.23
❑ 52 Mark Chmura	.15	.07
❑ 53 Corey Bradford	.50	.23
❑ 54 Bill Schroeder	.50	.23
❑ 55 Peyton Manning	2.00	.90
❑ 56 Marvin Harrison	.50	.23
❑ 57 E.G. Green	.15	.07
❑ 58 Fred Taylor	1.25	.55
❑ 59 Mark Brunell	.75	.35
❑ 60 Tavian Banks	.15	.07
❑ 61 Jimmy Smith	.25	.11
❑ 62 Keenan McCardell	.25	.11

❑ 63 Warren Moon .50 .23
❑ 64 Derrick Alexander WR .25 .11
❑ 65 Byron Bam Morris .15 .07
❑ 66 Elvis Grbac .25 .11
❑ 67 Andre Rison .25 .11
❑ 68 Dan Marino 2.00 .90
❑ 69 Karim Abdul-Jabbar .25 .11
❑ 70 O.J. McDuffie .25 .11
❑ 71 Tony Martin .15 .07
❑ 72 Randy Moss 2.00 .90
❑ 73 Cris Carter .50 .23
❑ 74 Randall Cunningham .50 .23
❑ 75 Robert Smith .50 .23
❑ 76 Jeff George .25 .11
❑ 77 Jake Reed .25 .11
❑ 78 Terry Allen .25 .11
❑ 79 Drew Bledsoe .75 .35
❑ 80 Terry Glenn .50 .23
❑ 81 Ben Coates .25 .11
❑ 82 Tony Simmons .15 .07
❑ 83 Cam Cleeland .15 .07
❑ 84 Eddie Kennison .25 .11
❑ 85 Kerry Collins .15 .07
❑ 86 Ike Hilliard .15 .07
❑ 87 Gary Brown .15 .07
❑ 88 Joe Jurevicius .15 .07
❑ 89 Kent Graham .15 .07
❑ 90 Wayne Chrebet .25 .11
❑ 91 Keyshawn Johnson .50 .23
❑ 92 Curtis Martin .50 .23
❑ 93 Vinny Testaverde .25 .11
❑ 94 Tim Brown .50 .23
❑ 95 Napoleon Kaufman .50 .23
❑ 96 Charles Woodson .50 .23
❑ 97 Tyrone Wheatley .25 .11
❑ 98 Rich Gannon .25 .11
❑ 99 Charles Johnson .15 .07
❑ 100 Duce Staley .50 .23
❑ 101 Kordell Stewart .50 .23
❑ 102 Jerome Bettis .50 .23
❑ 103 Hines Ward .15 .07
❑ 104 Ryan Leaf .50 .23
❑ 105 Natrone Means .25 .11
❑ 106 Jim Harbaugh .25 .11
❑ 107 Junior Seau .25 .11
❑ 108 Mikhael Ricks .15 .07
❑ 109 Jerry Rice 1.25 .55
❑ 110 Steve Young .75 .35
❑ 111 Garrison Hearst .25 .11
❑ 112 Terrell Owens .50 .23
❑ 113 Lawrence Phillips .25 .11
❑ 114 J.J. Stokes .25 .11
❑ 115 Sean Dawkins .15 .07
❑ 116 Derrick Mayes .15 .07
❑ 117 Joey Galloway .50 .23
❑ 118 Jon Kitna .60 .25
❑ 119 Ahman Green .25 .11
❑ 120 Ricky Watters .25 .11
❑ 121 Isaac Bruce .50 .23
❑ 122 Marshall Faulk .50 .23
❑ 123 Az-Zahir Hakim .15 .07
❑ 124 Warrick Dunn .50 .23
❑ 125 Mike Alstott .50 .23
❑ 126 Trent Dilfer .25 .11
❑ 127 Reidel Anthony .25 .11
❑ 128 Jacquez Green .25 .11
❑ 129 Warren Sapp .25 .11
❑ 130 Eddie George .60 .25
❑ 131 Steve McNair .50 .23
❑ 132 Kevin Dyson .25 .11
❑ 133 Yancey Thigpen .15 .07
❑ 134 Frank Wycheck .15 .07
❑ 135 Stephen Davis .50 .23
❑ 136 Brad Johnson .50 .23
❑ 137 Skip Hicks .25 .11
❑ 138 Michael Westbrook .25 .11
❑ 139 Darrell Green .15 .07
❑ 140 Albert Connell .15 .07
❑ 141 Tim Couch RC 12.00 5.50
❑ 142 Donovan McNabb RC 8.00 3.60
❑ 143 Akili Smith RC 5.00 2.20
❑ 144 Edgerrin James RC 20.00 9.00
❑ 145 Ricky Williams RC 12.00 5.50
❑ 146 Torry Holt RC 6.00 2.70
❑ 147 Champ Bailey RC 3.00 1.35
❑ 148 David Boston RC 4.00 1.80
❑ 149 Andy Katzenmoyer RC 2.50 1.10
❑ 150 Chris McAlister RC 2.50 1.10
❑ 151 Daunte Culpepper RC 8.00 3.60
❑ 152 Cade McNown RC 8.00 3.60
❑ 153 Troy Edwards RC 4.00 1.80
❑ 154 Kevin Johnson RC 6.00 2.70
❑ 155 James Johnson RC 3.00 1.35
❑ 156 Rob Konrad RC 2.50 1.10
❑ 157 Jim Kleinsasser RC 2.50 1.10
❑ 158 Kevin Faulk RC 3.00 1.35
❑ 159 Joe Montgomery RC 2.50 1.10
❑ 160 Shaun King RC 8.00 3.60
❑ 161 Peerless Price RC 4.00 1.80
❑ 162 Mike Cloud RC 2.50 1.10
❑ 163 Jermaine Fazande RC 2.50 1.10
❑ 164 D'Wayne Bates RC 2.50 1.10
❑ 165 Brock Huard RC 3.00 1.35
❑ 166 Marty Booker RC 2.50 1.10
❑ 167 Karsten Bailey RC 2.50 1.10
❑ 168 Shawn Bryson RC 2.50 1.10
❑ 169 Jeff Paulk RC 2.50 1.10
❑ 170 Travis McGriff RC 2.50 1.10
❑ 171 Amos Zereoue RC 2.50 1.10
❑ 172 Craig Yeast RC 2.50 1.10
❑ 173 Joe Germaine RC 2.50 1.10
❑ 174 Dameane Douglas RC 2.50 1.10
❑ 175 Brandon Stokley RC 2.50 1.10
❑ 176 Larry Parker RC 2.50 1.10
❑ 177 Joel Makovicka RC 2.50 1.10
❑ 178 Wane McGarity RC 2.50 1.10
❑ 179 Na Brown RC 2.50 1.10
❑ 180 Cecil Collins RC 2.50 1.10
❑ 181 Nick Williams RC 2.50 1.10
❑ 182 Charlie Rogers RC 2.50 1.10
❑ 183 Darrin Chiaverini RC 2.50 1.10
❑ 184 Terry Jackson RC 2.50 1.10
❑ 185 De'Mond Parker RC 2.50 1.10
❑ 186 Sedrick Irvin RC 2.50 1.10
❑ 187 MarTay Jenkins RC 2.50 1.10
❑ 188 Kurt Warner RC 30.00 13.50
❑ 189 Michael Bishop RC 3.00 1.35
❑ 190 Sean Bennett RC 2.50 1.10
❑ 191 Jamal Anderson CL .15 .07
❑ 192 Eric Moulds CL .15 .07
❑ 193 Terrell Davis CL .50 .23
❑ 194 John Elway CL .75 .35
❑ 195 Barry Sanders CL .75 .35
❑ 196 Peyton Manning CL .75 .35
❑ 197 Fred Taylor CL .50 .23
❑ 198 Dan Marino CL .75 .35
❑ 199 Randy Moss CL .75 .35
❑ 200 Terrell Owens CL .15 .07

1999 Donruss Career Stat Line

	MINT	NRMT
COMMON CARD/400-589	1.50	.70
SEMISTARS/400-589	2.00	.90
UNL.STARS/400-589	3.00	1.35
COMMON CARD/300-399	2.00	.90
SEMISTARS/300-399	2.50	1.10
UNL.STARS/300-399	4.00	1.80
COMMON CARD/226-299	2.50	1.10
SEMISTARS/226-299	3.00	1.35
UNL.STARS/226-299	5.00	2.20
COMMON CARD/176-225	3.00	1.35
SEMISTARS/176-225	4.00	1.80
UNL.STARS/176-225	6.00	2.70
COMMON CARD/131-175	4.00	1.80
SEMISTARS/131-175	5.00	2.20
UNL.STARS/131-175	8.00	3.60
COMMON CARD/100-130	5.00	2.20
SEMISTARS/100-130	6.00	2.70
UNL.STARS/100-130	10.00	4.50
COMMON CARD/80-99	6.00	2.70
SEMISTARS/80-99	8.00	3.60
UNL.STARS/80-99	12.00	5.50
COMMON CARD/65-79	10.00	4.50
SEMISTARS/65-79	15.00	6.75
COMMON CARD/45-64	8.00	3.60
SEMISTARS/45-64	12.00	5.50
UNL.STARS/45-64	20.00	9.00

RANDOM INSERTS IN PACKS

❑ 1 Jake Plummer/481 5.00 2.20
❑ 2 Rob Moore/274 3.00 1.35
❑ 3 Adrian Murrell/145 5.00 2.20
❑ 4 Frank Sanders/285 3.00 1.35
❑ 5 Jamal Anderson/410 3.00 1.35
❑ 6 Tim Dwight/263 5.00 2.20
❑ 7 Terance Mathis/78 10.00 4.50
❑ 8 Chris Chandler/118 6.00 2.70
❑ 9 Byron Hanspard/335 2.50 1.10
❑ 10 Priest Holmes/233 5.00 2.20
❑ 11 Jermaine Lewis/96 8.00 3.60
❑ 12 Errict Rhett/305 2.50 1.10
❑ 13 Doug Flutie/368 5.00 2.20
❑ 14 Eric Moulds/116 10.00 4.50
❑ 15 Antowain Smith/188 6.00 2.70
❑ 16 Thurman Thomas/168 5.00 2.20
❑ 17 Andre Reed/205 4.00 1.80
❑ 18 Bruce Smith/164 5.00 2.20
❑ 19 Tim Biakabutuka/247 3.00 1.35
❑ 20 Rae Carruth/52 8.00 3.60
❑ 21 Muhsin Muhammad/120 6.00 2.70
❑ 22 Curtis Enis/133 8.00 3.60
❑ 23 Curtis Conway/285 3.00 1.35
❑ 24 Bobby Engram/142 5.00 2.20
❑ 25 Corey Dillon/182 6.00 2.70
❑ 26 Carl Pickens/352 2.50 1.10
❑ 27 Jeff Blake/224 4.00 1.80
❑ 28 Darnay Scott/261 3.00 1.35
❑ 29 Ty Detmer/113 5.00 2.20
❑ 30 Leslie Shepherd/277 2.50 1.10
❑ 31 Emmitt Smith/134 25.00 11.00
❑ 32 Troy Aikman/141 25.00 11.00
❑ 33 Michael Irvin/374 2.50 1.10
❑ 34 Deion Sanders/152 8.00 3.60
❑ 35 Rocket Ismail/205 4.00 1.80
❑ 36 John Elway/300 20.00 9.00
❑ 37 Terrell Davis/372 10.00 4.50
❑ 38 Ed McCaffrey/299 3.00 1.35
❑ 39 Shannon Sharpe/106 6.00 2.70
❑ 40 Rod Smith/178 4.00 1.80
❑ 41 Bubby Brister/81 8.00 3.60
❑ 42 Brian Griese/33 60.00 27.00
❑ 43 Barry Sanders/99 60.00 27.00
❑ 44 Charlie Batch/229 8.00 3.60
❑ 45 Herman Moore/93 12.00 5.50
❑ 46 Germane Crowell/68 15.00 6.75
❑ 47 Johnnie Morton/98 8.00 3.60
❑ 48 Ron Rivers/427 1.50 .70
❑ 49 Brett Favre/89 60.00 27.00
❑ 50 Antonio Freeman/229 5.00 2.20
❑ 51 Dorsey Levens/160 8.00 3.60
❑ 52 Mark Chmura/183 4.00 1.80
❑ 53 Corey Bradford/27 40.00 18.00
❑ 54 Bill Schroeder/452 3.00 1.35
❑ 55 Peyton Manning/326 15.00 6.75
❑ 56 Marvin Harrison/177 6.00 2.70
❑ 57 E.G. Green/177 3.00 1.35
❑ 58 Fred Taylor/264 10.00 4.50
❑ 59 Mark Brunell/250 8.00 3.60
❑ 60 Tavian Banks/133 4.00 1.80
❑ 61 Jimmy Smith/265 3.00 1.35
❑ 62 Keenan McCardell/138 5.00 2.20
❑ 63 Warren Moon/81 15.00 6.75
❑ 64 Derrick Alexander WR/244 3.00 1.35
❑ 65 Byron Bam Morris/198 3.00 1.35
❑ 66 Elvis Grbac/250 3.00 1.35
❑ 67 Andre Rison/78 10.00 4.50
❑ 68 Dan Marino/87 60.00 27.00
❑ 69 Karim Abdul-Jabbar/198 4.00 1.80

❑ 70 O.J. McDuffie/358 2.50 1.10
❑ 71 Tony Martin/463 1.50 .70
❑ 72 Randy Moss/18 250.00 110.00
❑ 73 Cris Carter/101 15.00 6.75
❑ 74 Randall Cunningham/190 6.00 2.70
❑ 75 Robert Smith/158 8.00 3.60
❑ 76 Jeff George/124 6.00 2.70
❑ 77 Jake Reed/342 2.50 1.10
❑ 78 Terry Allen/392 2.50 1.10
❑ 79 Drew Bledsoe/128 20.00 9.00
❑ 80 Terry Glenn/167 8.00 3.60
❑ 81 Ben Coates/290 2.50 1.10
❑ 82 Tony Simmons/474 1.50 .70
❑ 83 Cam Cleeland/54 8.00 3.60
❑ 84 Eddie Kennison/103 5.00 2.20
❑ 85 Kerry Collins/89 6.00 2.70
❑ 86 Ike Hilliard/53 12.00 5.50
❑ 87 Gary Brown/144 4.00 1.80
❑ 88 Joe Jurevicius/146 4.00 1.80
❑ 89 Kent Graham/87 6.00 2.70
❑ 90 Wayne Chrebet/283 3.00 1.35
❑ 91 Keyshawn Johnson/216 6.00 2.70
❑ 92 Curtis Martin/280 5.00 2.20
❑ 93 Vinny Testaverde/204 4.00 1.80
❑ 94 Tim Brown/304 4.00 1.80
❑ 95 Napoleon Kaufman/83 12.00 5.50
❑ 96 Charles Woodson/61 20.00 9.00
❑ 97 Tyrone Wheatley/218 4.00 1.80
❑ 98 Rich Gannon/262 3.00 1.35
❑ 99 Charles Johnson/247 2.50 1.10
❑ 100 Duce Staley/265 5.00 2.20
❑ 101 Kordell Stewart/223 6.00 2.70
❑ 102 Jerome Bettis/128 10.00 4.50
❑ 103 Hines Ward/246 2.50 1.10
❑ 104 Ryan Leaf/245 5.00 2.20
❑ 105 Natrone Means/252 3.00 1.35
❑ 106 Jim Harbaugh/111 6.00 2.70
❑ 107 Junior Seau/200 4.00 1.80
❑ 108 Mikhael Ricks/130 5.00 2.20
❑ 109 Jerry Rice/175 20.00 9.00
❑ 110 Steve Young/229 8.00 3.60
❑ 111 Garrison Hearst/124 6.00 2.70
❑ 112 Terrell Owens/162 8.00 3.60
❑ 113 Lawrence Phillips/194 4.00 1.80
❑ 114 J.J. Stokes/177 4.00 1.80
❑ 115 Sean Dawkins/304 2.00 .90
❑ 116 Derrick Mayes/150 5.00 2.20
❑ 117 Joey Galloway/261 5.00 2.20
❑ 118 Jon Kitna/217 8.00 3.60
❑ 119 Ahman Green/209 3.00 1.35
❑ 120 Ricky Watters/353 2.50 1.10
❑ 121 Isaac Bruce/312 4.00 1.80
❑ 122 Marshall Faulk/306 4.00 1.80
❑ 123 Az-Zahir Hakim/247 2.50 1.10
❑ 124 Warrick Dunn/469 3.00 1.35
❑ 125 Mike Alstott/150 8.00 3.60
❑ 126 Trent Dilfer/130 6.00 2.70
❑ 127 Reidel Anthony/127 5.00 2.20
❑ 128 Jacquez Green/251 2.50 1.10
❑ 129 Warren Sapp/133 5.00 2.20
❑ 130 Eddie George/130 12.00 5.50
❑ 131 Steve McNair/220 6.00 2.70
❑ 132 Kevin Dyson/263 3.00 1.35
❑ 133 Yancey Thigpen/260 2.50 1.10
❑ 134 Frank Wycheck/249 2.50 1.10
❑ 135 Stephen Davis/397 4.00 1.80
❑ 136 Brad Johnson/233 5.00 2.20
❑ 137 Skip Hicks/433 2.00 .90
❑ 138 Michael Westbrook/146 5.00 2.20
❑ 139 Darrell Green/234 3.00 1.35
❑ 140 Albert Connell/589 1.50 .70
❑ 141 Tim Couch/142 80.00 36.00
❑ 142 Donovan McNabb/465 20.00 9.00
❑ 143 Akili Smith/323 15.00 6.75
❑ 144 Edgerrin James/212 100.00 45.00
❑ 145 Ricky Williams/75 120.00 55.00
❑ 146 Torry Holt/191 15.00 6.75
❑ 147 Champ Bailey/560 6.00 2.70
❑ 148 David Boston/191 12.00 5.50
❑ 149 Andy Katzenmoyer/193 8.00 3.60
❑ 150 Chris McAlister/243 4.00 1.80
❑ 151 Daunte Culpepper/108 50.00 22.00
❑ 152 Cade McNown C 25.00 11.00
❑ 153 Troy Edwards/280 10.00 4.50
❑ 154 Kevin Johnson/126 50.00 22.00
❑ 155 James Johnson/300 10.00 4.50
❑ 156 Rob Konrad/295 6.00 2.70
❑ 157 Jim Kleinsasser/87 15.00 6.75
❑ 158 Kevin Faulk/318 10.00 4.50
❑ 159 Joe Montgomery/216 8.00 3.60
❑ 160 Shaun King/353 25.00 11.00
❑ 161 Peerless Price/147 25.00 11.00
❑ 162 Mike Cloud/156 15.00 6.75
❑ 163 Jermaine Fazande/187 5.00 2.20
❑ 164 D'Wayne Bates/210 5.00 2.20
❑ 165 Brock Huard/422 6.00 2.70
❑ 166 Marty Booker/178 5.00 2.20
❑ 167 Karsten Bailey/150 6.00 2.70
❑ 168 Shawn Bryson/505 3.00 1.35
❑ 169 Jeff Paulk/554 3.00 1.35
❑ 170 Travis McGriff/123 10.00 4.50
❑ 171 Amos Zereoue/252 6.00 2.70
❑ 172 Craig Yeast/208 5.00 2.20
❑ 173 Joe Germaine/151 15.00 6.75
❑ 174 Dameane Douglas/195 5.00 2.20
❑ 175 Brandon Stokley/241 4.00 1.80
❑ 176 Larry Parker/78 12.00 5.50
❑ 177 Joel Makovicka/247 6.00 2.70
❑ 178 Wane McGarity/102 10.00 4.50
❑ 179 Na Brown/165 10.00 4.50
❑ 180 Cecil Collins/100 15.00 6.75
❑ 181 Nick Williams/289 4.00 1.80
❑ 182 Charlie Rogers/220 4.00 1.80
❑ 183 Darrin Chiaverini/97 10.00 4.50
❑ 184 Terry Jackson/321 5.00 2.20
❑ 185 De'Mond Parker/132 20.00 9.00
❑ 186 Sedrick Irvin/336 8.00 3.60
❑ 187 MarTay Jenkins/102 8.00 3.60
❑ 188 Kurt Warner/165 120.00 55.00
❑ 189 Michael Bishop/130 15.00 6.75
❑ 190 Sean Bennett/240 6.00 2.70
❑ 191 Jamal Anderson CL/203 4.00 1.80
❑ 192 Eric Moulds CL/240 3.00 1.35
❑ 193 Terrell Davis CL/167 20.00 9.00
❑ 194 John Elway CL/336 15.00 6.75
❑ 195 Barry Sanders CL/185 30.00 13.50
❑ 196 Peyton Manning CL/357 12.00 5.50
❑ 197 Fred Taylor CL/162 20.00 9.00
❑ 198 Dan Marino CL/355 15.00 6.75
❑ 199 Randy Moss CL/190 30.00 13.50

1999 Donruss Season Stat Line

	MINT	NRMT
COMMON CARD/45-64	8.00	3.60
SEMISTARS/45-64	12.00	5.50
COMMON CARD/30-44	10.00	4.50
SEMISTARS/30-44	15.00	6.75
UNL.STARS/30-44	30.00	13.50
COMMON CARD/20-29	12.00	5.50
SEMISTARS/20-29	20.00	9.00
UNL.STARS/20-29	40.00	18.00
COMMON CARD/11-19	15.00	6.75
SEMISTARS/11-19	25.00	11.00
UNL.STARS/11-19	50.00	22.00

RANDOM INSERTS IN PACKS
CARDS SER.#d UNDER 12 NOT PRICED

❑ 1 Jake Plummer/21 60.00 27.00
❑ 2 Rob Moore/43 15.00 6.75
❑ 3 Adrian Murrell/18 25.00 11.00
❑ 4 Frank Sanders/13 25.00 11.00
❑ 5 Jamal Anderson/14 50.00 22.00
❑ 6 Tim Dwight/27 40.00 18.00
❑ 7 Terance Mathis/11 25.00 11.00
❑ 8 Chris Chandler/27 20.00 9.00
❑ 9 Byron Hanspard/25 20.00 9.00
❑ 10 Priest Holmes/7
❑ 11 Jermaine Lewis/13 25.00 11.00
❑ 12 Errict Rhett/46 12.00 5.50
❑ 13 Doug Flutie/21 50.00 22.00
❑ 14 Eric Moulds/20 40.00 18.00
❑ 15 Antowain Smith/30 30.00 13.50
❑ 16 Thurman Thomas/17 25.00 11.00
❑ 17 Andre Reed/5
❑ 18 Bruce Smith/10
❑ 19 Tim Biakabutuka/17 15.00 6.75
❑ 20 Rae Carruth/15 15.00 6.75
❑ 21 Muhsin Muhammad/6
❑ 22 Curtis Enis/29 40.00 18.00
❑ 23 Curtis Conway/29 20.00 9.00
❑ 24 Bobby Engram/15 25.00 11.00
❑ 25 Corey Dillon/41 30.00 13.50
❑ 26 Carl Pickens/5
❑ 27 Jeff Blake/8
❑ 28 Darnay Scott/16 25.00 11.00
❑ 29 Ty Detmer/36 10.00 4.50
❑ 30 Leslie Shepherd/9
❑ 31 Emmitt Smith/27 100.00 45.00
❑ 32 Troy Aikman/12 150.00 70.00
❑ 33 Michael Irvin/14 25.00 11.00
❑ 34 Deion Sanders/16 50.00 22.00
❑ 35 Rocket Ismail/8
❑ 36 John Elway/22 200.00 90.00
❑ 37 Terrell Davis/21 120.00 55.00
❑ 38 Ed McCaffrey/10
❑ 39 Shannon Sharpe/12 25.00 11.00
❑ 40 Rod Smith/10
❑ 41 Bubby Brister/10
❑ 42 Brian Griese/2
❑ 43 Barry Sanders/8
❑ 44 Charlie Batch/12 100.00 45.00
❑ 45 Herman Moore/10
❑ 46 Germane Crowell/12 25.00 11.00
❑ 47 Johnnie Morton/11 25.00 11.00
❑ 48 Ron Rivers/19 15.00 6.75
❑ 49 Brett Favre/31 150.00 70.00
❑ 50 Antonio Freeman/13 50.00 22.00
❑ 51 Dorsey Levens/20 40.00 18.00
❑ 52 Mark Chmura/12 25.00 11.00
❑ 53 Corey Bradford/17
❑ 54 Bill Schroeder/46
❑ 55 Peyton Manning/24 150.00 70.00
❑ 56 Marvin Harrison/13 50.00 22.00
❑ 57 E.G. Green/25 12.00 5.50
❑ 58 Fred Taylor/14 100.00 45.00
❑ 59 Mark Brunell/21 80.00 36.00
❑ 60 Tavian Banks/27 12.00 5.50
❑ 61 Jimmy Smith/12 25.00 11.00
❑ 62 Keenan McCardell/14 25.00 11.00
❑ 63 Warren Moon/12 60.00 27.00
❑ 64 Derrick Alexander WR/12 25.00 11.00
❑ 65 Byron Bam Morris/29 12.00 5.50
❑ 66 Elvis Grbac/12 25.00 11.00
❑ 67 Andre Rison/11 25.00 11.00
❑ 68 Dan Marino/26 150.00 70.00
❑ 69 Karim Abdul-Jabbar/21 20.00 9.00
❑ 70 O.J. McDuffie/7
❑ 71 Tony Martin/18 15.00 6.75
❑ 72 Randy Moss/18 250.00 110.00
❑ 73 Cris Carter/12 60.00 27.00
❑ 74 Randall Cunningham/34 30.00 13.50
❑ 75 Robert Smith/10
❑ 76 Jeff George/15 25.00 11.00
❑ 77 Jake Reed/14 25.00 11.00
❑ 78 Terry Allen/27 20.00 9.00
❑ 79 Drew Bledsoe/20 80.00 36.00
❑ 80 Terry Glenn/16 50.00 22.00
❑ 81 Ben Coates/36 10.00 4.50
❑ 82 Tony Simmons/21 12.00 5.50
❑ 83 Cam Cleeland/53 8.00 3.60
❑ 84 Eddie Kennison/10
❑ 85 Kerry Collins/20 12.00 5.50
❑ 86 Ike Hilliard/14 15.00 6.75
❑ 87 Gary Brown/45 8.00 3.60
❑ 88 Joe Jurevicius/16 15.00 6.75
❑ 89 Kent Graham/7
❑ 90 Wayne Chrebet/14 50.00 22.00
❑ 91 Keyshawn Johnson/11 50.00 22.00
❑ 92 Curtis Martin/9
❑ 93 Vinny Testaverde/29 20.00 9.00
❑ 94 Tim Brown/9
❑ 95 Napoleon Kaufman/25 40.00 18.00
❑ 96 Charles Woodson/24 40.00 18.00
❑ 97 Tyrone Wheatley/16 50.00 22.00
❑ 98 Rich Gannon/18 50.00 22.00
❑ 99 Charles Johnson/43 10.00 4.50
❑ 100 Duce Staley/6
❑ 101 Kordell Stewart/14 50.00 22.00
❑ 102 Jerome Bettis/42 30.00 13.50
❑ 103 Hines Ward/16 15.00 6.75
❑ 104 Ryan Leaf/25 40.00 18.00
❑ 105 Natrone Means/22 20.00 9.00
❑ 106 Jim Harbaugh/27 20.00 9.00
❑ 107 Junior Seau/29 20.00 9.00
❑ 108 Mikhael Ricks/30 15.00 6.75

- ❑ 109 Jerry Rice/14 .... 150.00 70.00
- ❑ 110 Steve Young/24 .... 80.00 36.00
- ❑ 111 Garrison Hearst/39 .... 15.00 6.75
- ❑ 112 Terrell Owens/14 .... 50.00 22.00
- ❑ 113 Lawrence Phillips/14 .. 25.00 11.00
- ❑ 114 J.J. Stokes/33 .... 15.00 6.75
- ❑ 115 Sean Dawkins/16 ...... 15.00 6.75
- ❑ 116 Derrick Mayes/30 ...... 15.00 6.75
- ❑ 117 Joey Galloway/16 ...... 50.00 22.00
- ❑ 118 Jon Kitna/21 .... 40.00 18.00
- ❑ 119 Ahman Green/27 .... 12.00 5.50
- ❑ 120 Ricky Watters/39 .... 15.00 6.75
- ❑ 121 Isaac Bruce/21 .... 40.00 18.00
- ❑ 122 Marshall Faulk/10 ....
- ❑ 123 Az-Zahir Hakim/20 .... 20.00 9.00
- ❑ 124 Warrick Dunn/42 .... 30.00 13.50
- ❑ 125 Mike Alstott/22 .... 40.00 18.00
- ❑ 126 Trent Dilfer/21 .... 20.00 9.00
- ❑ 127 Reidel Anthony/35 ...... 10.00 4.50
- ❑ 128 Jacquez Green/18 ...... 15.00 6.75
- ❑ 129 Warren Sapp/42 .... 15.00 6.75
- ❑ 130 Eddie George/37 .... 40.00 18.00
- ❑ 131 Steve McNair/15 .... 60.00 27.00
- ❑ 132 Kevin Dyson/21 .... 20.00 9.00
- ❑ 133 Yancey Thigpen/20 .... 20.00 9.00
- ❑ 134 Frank Wycheck/38 .... 10.00 4.50
- ❑ 135 Stephen Davis/21 ...... 40.00 18.00
- ❑ 136 Brad Johnson/28 .... 40.00 18.00
- ❑ 137 Skip Hicks/28 .... 20.00 9.00
- ❑ 138 Michael Westbrook/17 25.00 11.00
- ❑ 139 Darrell Green/19 .... 15.00 6.75
- ❑ 140 Albert Connell/28 .... 12.00 5.50
- ❑ 141 Tim Couch/1 ....
- ❑ 142 Donovan McNabb/2 ....
- ❑ 143 Akili Smith/3 ....
- ❑ 144 Edgerrin James/4 ....
- ❑ 145 Ricky Williams/5 ....
- ❑ 146 Torry Holt/6 ....
- ❑ 147 Champ Bailey/7 ....
- ❑ 148 David Boston/8 ....
- ❑ 149 Andy Katzenmoyer/9 ....
- ❑ 150 Chris McAlister/10 ....
- ❑ 151 Daunte Culpepper/11 150.00 70.00
- ❑ 152 Cade McNown/12 .... 200.00 90.00
- ❑ 153 Troy Edwards/13 ...... 100.00 45.00
- ❑ 154 Kevin Johnson/32 ...... 80.00 36.00
- ❑ 155 James Johnson/39 .... 30.00 13.50
- ❑ 156 Rob Konrad/43 .... 25.00 11.00
- ❑ 157 Jim Kleinsasser/44 .... 25.00 11.00
- ❑ 158 Kevin Faulk/46 .... 25.00 11.00
- ❑ 159 Joe Montgomery/49 .. 20.00 9.00
- ❑ 160 Shaun King/50 .... 60.00 27.00
- ❑ 161 Peerless Price/53 ...... 30.00 13.50
- ❑ 162 Mike Cloud/54 .... 20.00 9.00
- ❑ 163 Jermaine Fazande/60 12.00 5.50
- ❑ 164 D'Wayne Bates/71 ...... 12.00 5.50
- ❑ 165 Brock Huard/77 .... 20.00 9.00
- ❑ 166 Marty Booker/78 .... 12.00 5.50
- ❑ 167 Karsten Bailey/82 ...... 10.00 4.50
- ❑ 168 Shawn Bryson/86 ...... 10.00 4.50
- ❑ 169 Jeff Paulk/92 .... 15.00 6.75
- ❑ 170 Travis McGriff/93 .... 15.00 6.75
- ❑ 171 Amos Zereoue/95 ...... 15.00 6.75
- ❑ 172 Craig Yeast/98 .... 10.00 4.50
- ❑ 173 Joe Germaine/101 ...... 12.00 5.50
- ❑ 174 Dameane Douglas/102 8.00 3.60
- ❑ 175 Brandon Stokley/105 .... 8.00 3.60
- ❑ 176 Larry Parker/108 .... 8.00 3.60
- ❑ 177 Joel Makovicka/116 .... 12.00 5.50
- ❑ 178 Wane McGarity/118 .... 8.00 3.60
- ❑ 179 Na Brown/130 .... 6.00 2.70
- ❑ 180 Cecil Collins/134 .... 10.00 4.50
- ❑ 181 Nick Williams/135 .... 6.00 2.70
- ❑ 182 Charlie Rogers/152 ...... 6.00 2.70
- ❑ 183 Darrin Chiaverini/148 10.00 4.50
- ❑ 184 Terry Jackson/157 .... 6.00 2.70
- ❑ 185 De'Mond Parker/159 .. 12.00 5.50
- ❑ 186 Sedrick Irvin/103 .... 12.00 5.50
- ❑ 187 MarTay Jenkins/193 .... 5.00 2.20
- ❑ 188 Kurt Warner/15 .... 500.00 220.00
- ❑ 189 Michael Bishop/227 .... 12.00 5.50
- ❑ 190 Sean Bennett/112 ...... 12.00 5.50
- ❑ 191 Jamal Anderson CL/8 ......
- ❑ 192 Eric Moulds CL/32 ...... 15.00 6.75
- ❑ 193 Terrell Davis CL/31 .... 80.00 36.00
- ❑ 194 John Elway CL/18 .... 200.00 90.00
- ❑ 195 Barry Sanders CL/67 .. 80.00 36.00
- ❑ 196 Peyton Manning CL/27 150.00 70.00
- ❑ 197 Fred Taylor CL/13 .... 100.00 45.00
- ❑ 198 Dan Marino CL/4 ....
- ❑ 199 Randy Moss CL/38 .. 120.00 55.00
- ❑ 200 Terrell Owens CL/28 .. 20.00 9.00

1999 Donruss All-Time Gridiron Kings

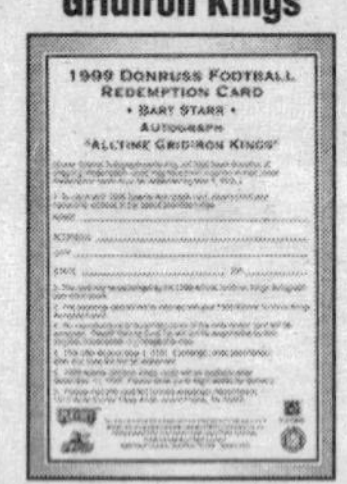

	MINT	NRMT
COMPLETE SET (5)	60.00	27.00
COMMON CARD (AGK1-AGK5)	12.00	5.50
STATED PRINT RUN 1000 SER.#'d SETS		

- ❑ AGK1 Bart Starr 20.00 9.00
- ❑ AGK2 Johnny Unitas 20.00 9.00
- ❑ AGK3 Earl Campbell 12.00 5.50
- ❑ AGK4 Walter Payton 25.00 11.00
- ❑ AGK5 Jim Brown 20.00 9.00

1999 Donruss All-Time Gridiron Kings Autographs

	MINT	NRMT
COMPLETE SET (5)	600.00	275.00
COMMON CARD (AGK1-AGK5)	60.00	27.00
FIRST 500 CARDS SIGNED ON CANVAS STOCK		

- ❑ AGK1 Bart Starr Trade 120.00 55.00
- ❑ AGK2 Johnny Unitas 100.00 45.00
- ❑ AGK3 Earl Campbell 60.00 27.00
- ❑ AGK4 Walter Payton 250.00 110.00
- ❑ AGK5 Jim Brown 120.00 55.00

1999 Donruss Elite Inserts

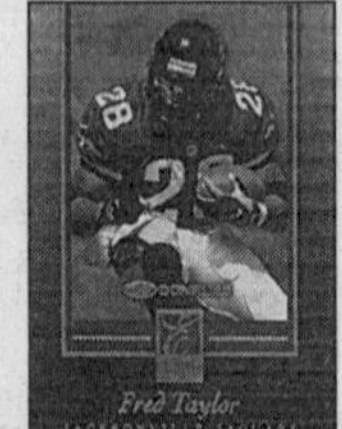

	MINT	NRMT
COMPLETE SET (20)	80.00	36.00
COMMON CARD (EL1-EL20)	2.50	1.10
STATED PRINT RUN 2500 SER.#'d SETS		

- ❑ EL1 Cris Carter 2.50 1.10
- ❑ EL2 Jerry Rice 6.00 2.70
- ❑ EL3 Mark Brunell 4.00 1.80
- ❑ EL4 Brett Favre 10.00 4.50
- ❑ EL5 Keyshawn Johnson 2.50 1.10
- ❑ EL6 Eddie George 3.00 1.35
- ❑ EL7 John Elway 10.00 4.50
- ❑ EL8 Troy Aikman 6.00 2.70
- ❑ EL9 Marshall Faulk 2.50 1.10
- ❑ EL10 Antonio Freeman 2.50 1.10
- ❑ EL11 Drew Bledsoe 4.00 1.80
- ❑ EL12 Steve Young 4.00 1.80
- ❑ EL13 Dan Marino 10.00 4.50
- ❑ EL14 Emmitt Smith 6.00 2.70
- ❑ EL15 Fred Taylor 5.00 2.20
- ❑ EL16 Jake Plummer 4.00 1.80
- ❑ EL17 Terrell Davis 6.00 2.70
- ❑ EL18 Peyton Manning 8.00 3.60
- ❑ EL19 Randy Moss 8.00 3.60
- ❑ EL20 Barry Sanders 10.00 4.50

1999 Donruss Executive Producers

	MINT	NRMT
COMPLETE SET (45)	100.00	45.00
COMMON CARD (EP1-EP15)	1.50	.70
COMMON CARD (EP16-EP30)	2.50	1.10
SEMISTARS EP16-EP30	3.00	1.35
COMMON CARD (EP31-EP45)	2.00	.90
SEMISTARS EP31-EP45	2.50	1.10
RANDOM INSERTS IN PACKS		

- ❑ EP1 Dan Marino/3497 .... 6.00 2.70
- ❑ EP2 John Elway/2806 .... 8.00 3.60
- ❑ EP3 Kordell Stewart/2560 .. 1.50 .70
- ❑ EP4 Troy Aikman/2330 ...... 5.00 2.20
- ❑ EP5 Steve Young/4170 ...... 2.50 1.10
- ❑ EP6 Doug Flutie/2711 .... 2.50 1.10
- ❑ EP7 Drew Bledsoe/3633 .... 2.50 1.10
- ❑ EP8 Jon Kitna/1177 .... 3.00 1.35
- ❑ EP9 Steve McNair/3228 ...... 1.50 .70
- ❑ EP10 Mark Brunell/2601 .... 3.00 1.35
- ❑ EP11 R.Cunningham/3704 1.50 .70
- ❑ EP12 Jake Plummer/3737 .. 3.00 1.35
- ❑ EP13 Charlie Batch/2178 .... 4.00 1.80
- ❑ EP14 Peyton Manning/3739 5.00 2.20
- ❑ EP15 Brett Favre/4212 .... 6.00 2.70
- ❑ EP16 Terrell Davis/2008 .... 5.00 2.20
- ❑ EP17 Fred Taylor/1223 ...... 5.00 2.20
- ❑ EP18 Eddie George/1294 .. 3.00 1.35
- ❑ EP19 Corey Dillon/1130 ...... 2.50 1.10
- ❑ EP20 Jamal Anderson/1846 2.50 1.10
- ❑ EP21 Curtis Martin/1287 .... 2.50 1.10
- ❑ EP22 Dorsey Levens/378 .. 3.00 1.35
- ❑ EP23 Karim Abdul-Jabbar/960 2.50 1.10
- ❑ EP24 Curtis Enis/497 .... 3.00 1.35
- ❑ EP25 Mike Alstott/846 .... 2.50 1.10
- ❑ EP26 Natrone Means/883 .. 2.50 1.10
- ❑ EP27 Jerome Bettis/1185 .. 2.50 1.10
- ❑ EP28 Warrick Dunn/1026 .... 2.50 1.10
- ❑ EP29 Emmitt Smith/1332 .... 6.00 2.70
- ❑ EP30 Barry Sanders/1491 10.00 4.50
- ❑ EP31 Jerry Rice/1157 .... 6.00 2.70
- ❑ EP32 Randy Moss/1313 .... 8.00 3.60
- ❑ EP33 K.Johnson/1131 .... 2.50 1.10
- ❑ EP34 Isaac Bruce/457 .... 3.00 1.35
- ❑ EP35 Antonio Freeman/1424 2.50 1.10
- ❑ EP36 Eric Moulds/1368 ...... 2.50 1.10
- ❑ EP37 Tim Dwight/94 .... 10.00 4.50
- ❑ EP38 Herman Moore/983 .. 2.50 1.10
- ❑ EP39 Tim Brown/1012 .... 2.50 1.10
- ❑ EP40 Marshall Faulk/1319 .. 2.50 1.10

❑ EP41 Terry Glenn/792 .... 2.50 1.10
❑ EP42 Joey Galloway/1047 .. 2.50 1.10
❑ EP43 Carl Pickens/1023 .... 2.00 .90
❑ EP44 Terrell Owens/1097 .. 2.50 1.10
❑ EP45 Cris Carter/1011 .... 2.50 1.10

1999 Donruss Fan Club

	MINT	NRMT
COMPLETE SET (20)	50.00	22.00
COMMON CARD (FC1-FC20) ..	1.50	.70

STATED PRINT RUN 5000 SER.#'d SETS

❑ FC1 Troy Aikman 5.00 2.20
❑ FC2 Ricky Williams 8.00 3.60
❑ FC3 Jerry Rice 5.00 2.20
❑ FC4 Brett Favre 8.00 3.60
❑ FC5 Terrell Davis 5.00 2.20
❑ FC6 Doug Flutie 2.50 1.10
❑ FC7 John Elway 8.00 3.60
❑ FC8 Steve Young 3.00 1.35
❑ FC9 Steve McNair .... 2.00 .90
❑ FC10 Kordell Stewart .... 2.00 .90
❑ FC11 Drew Bledsoe 3.00 1.35
❑ FC12 Donovan McNabb 5.00 2.20
❑ FC13 Dan Marino 8.00 3.60
❑ FC14 Cade McNown 5.00 2.20
❑ FC15 Vinny Testaverde ...... 2.00 .90
❑ FC16 Jake Plummer 3.00 1.35
❑ FC17 Randall Cunningham 2.00 .90
❑ FC18 Peyton Manning 6.00 2.70
❑ FC19 Keyshawn Johnson .. 2.00 .90
❑ FC20 Barry Sanders 8.00 3.60

1999 Donruss Gridiron Kings

	MINT	NRMT
COMPLETE SET (20)	100.00	45.00
COMMON CARD (GK1-GK20)..	3.00	1.35

STATED PRINT RUN 5000 SER.#'d SETS
*CANVAS CARDS: 1X TO 2.5X HI COL.
FIRST 500 CARDS ON CANVAS STOCK

❑ GK1 Randy Moss 10.00 4.50
❑ GK2 Fred Taylor 6.00 2.70
❑ GK3 Doug Flutie 4.00 1.80
❑ GK4 Brett Favre 12.00 5.50
❑ GK5 Mark Brunell 5.00 2.20
❑ GK6 Troy Aikman 8.00 3.60
❑ GK7 John Elway 12.00 5.50
❑ GK8 Jerry Rice 8.00 3.60
❑ GK9 Drew Bledsoe 5.00 2.20
❑ GK10 Eddie George 4.00 1.80
❑ GK11 Randall Cunningham 3.00 1.35
❑ GK12 Emmitt Smith 8.00 3.60
❑ GK13 Dan Marino 12.00 5.50
❑ GK14 Jake Plummer 5.00 2.20
❑ GK15 Jamal Anderson 3.00 1.35
❑ GK16 Terrell Davis 8.00 3.60
❑ GK17 Steve Young 5.00 2.20
❑ GK18 Peyton Manning 10.00 4.50
❑ GK19 Jerome Bettis 3.00 1.35
❑ GK20 Barry Sanders 12.00 5.50

1999 Donruss Private Signings

	MINT	NRMT
COMPLETE SET (32)	1000.00	450.00
COMMON CARD (1-32)	15.00	6.75
SEMISTARS	20.00	9.00
UNLISTED STARS	25.00	11.00

RANDOM INSERTS IN PACKS ....
TRADE CARD EXPIRATION: 5/1/2000
REPORTED PRINT RUNS: 50-600 CARDS

❑ 1 Terrell Davis 50.00 22.00
❑ 2 Cris Carter 30.00 13.50
❑ 3 Thurman Thomas 25.00 11.00
❑ 4 Derrick Thomas 40.00 18.00
❑ 5 Priest Holmes 25.00 11.00
❑ 6 Corey Dillon 20.00 9.00
❑ 7 Antonio Freeman 30.00 13.50
❑ 8 Duce Staley 20.00 9.00
❑ 9 Jerome Bettis 20.00 9.00
❑ 10 Natrone Means 20.00 9.00
❑ 11 Mike Alstott 30.00 13.50
❑ 12 Eddie George 40.00 18.00
❑ 13 Terrell Owens 25.00 11.00
❑ 14 Curtis Enis 25.00 11.00
❑ 15 Wesley Walls 15.00 6.75
❑ 16 Neil Smith 15.00 6.75
❑ 17 Doug Flutie 40.00 18.00
❑ 18 Tim Brown 30.00 13.50
❑ 19 Randy Moss 135.00 60.00
❑ 20 Ricky Williams SP 120.00 55.00
❑ 21 Skip Hicks 20.00 9.00
❑ 22 Isaac Bruce 25.00 11.00
❑ 23 Barry Sanders 175.00 80.00
❑ 24 Fred Taylor 40.00 18.00
❑ 25 Steve Young 50.00 22.00
❑ 26 Vinny Testaverde 20.00 9.00
❑ 27 Randall Cunningham 25.00 11.00
❑ 28 Jake Plummer 50.00 22.00
❑ 29 Jerry Rice 135.00 60.00
❑ 30 Eric Moulds 25.00 11.00
❑ 31 Kordell Stewart 25.00 11.00
❑ 32 Brian Griese 40.00 18.00

1999 Donruss Rated Rookies

	MINT	NRMT
COMPLETE SET (20)	80.00	36.00
COMMON CARD (RR1-RR20)..	2.50	1.10

STATED PRINT RUN 5000 SER.#'d SETS

*MEDALISTS: 1.2X TO 3X HI COL.
MEDALISTS PRINT RUN FIRST 250 CARDS

❑ RR1 Tim Couch 12.00 5.50
❑ RR2 Peerless Price 4.00 1.80
❑ RR3 Ricky Williams 12.00 5.50
❑ RR4 Torry Holt 6.00 2.70
❑ RR5 Champ Bailey 3.00 1.35
❑ RR6 Rob Konrad 2.50 1.10
❑ RR7 Donovan McNabb 8.00 3.60
❑ RR8 Edgerrin James 20.00 9.00
❑ RR9 David Boston 4.00 1.80
❑ RR10 Akili Smith 5.00 2.20
❑ RR11 Cecil Collins 2.50 1.10
❑ RR12 Troy Edwards 4.00 1.80
❑ RR13 Daunte Culpepper 8.00 3.60
❑ RR14 Kevin Faulk 3.00 1.35
❑ RR15 Kevin Johnson 6.00 2.70
❑ RR16 Cade McNown 8.00 3.60
❑ RR17 Shaun King 8.00 3.60
❑ RR18 Brock Huard 3.00 1.35
❑ RR19 James Johnson 3.00 1.35
❑ RR20 Sedrick Irvin 2.50 1.10

1999 Donruss Rookie Gridiron Kings

	MINT	NRMT
COMPLETE SET (10)	60.00	27.00
COMMON CARD (RGK1-RGK10)	3.00	1.35

STATED PRINT RUN 5000 SER.#'d SETS
*CANVAS CARDS: 1X TO 2.5X HI COL.
FIRST 500 CARDS PRINTED ON CANVAS STOCK

❑ RGK1 Ricky Williams 12.00 5.50
❑ RGK2 Donovan McNabb 8.00 3.60
❑ RGK3 Daunte Culpepper 8.00 3.60
❑ RGK4 Edgerrin James 20.00 9.00
❑ RGK5 David Boston 4.00 1.80
❑ RGK6 Champ Bailey 3.00 1.35
❑ RGK7 Torry Holt 6.00 2.70
❑ RGK8 Cade McNown 8.00 3.60
❑ RGK9 Akili Smith 5.00 2.20
❑ RGK10 Tim Couch 12.00 5.50

1999 Donruss Zoning Commission

	MINT	NRMT
COMPLETE SET (25)	60.00	27.00
COMMON CARD (1-25)	2.00	.90
STATED PRINT RUN 1000 SER.#'d SETS		

Card	MINT	NRMT
❑ 1 Eric Moulds	2.00	.90
❑ 2 Steve Young	3.00	1.35
❑ 3 Brad Johnson	2.00	.90
❑ 4 Peyton Manning	6.00	2.70
❑ 5 Randy Moss	6.00	2.70
❑ 6 Brett Favre	8.00	3.60
❑ 7 Emmitt Smith	5.00	2.20
❑ 8 Mark Brunell	3.00	1.35
❑ 9 Keyshawn Johnson	2.00	.90
❑ 10 Dan Marino	8.00	3.60
❑ 11 Eddie George	2.50	1.10
❑ 12 Drew Bledsoe	3.00	1.35
❑ 13 Terrell Davis	5.00	2.20
❑ 14 Terrell Owens	2.00	.90
❑ 15 Barry Sanders	8.00	3.60
❑ 16 Curtis Martin	2.00	.90
❑ 17 John Elway	8.00	3.60
❑ 18 Jake Plummer	3.00	1.35
❑ 19 Jerry Rice	5.00	2.20
❑ 20 Fred Taylor	4.00	1.80
❑ 21 Antonio Freeman	2.00	.90
❑ 22 Marshall Faulk	2.00	.90
❑ 23 Dorsey Levens	2.00	.90
❑ 24 Steve McNair	2.00	.90
❑ 25 Cris Carter	2.00	.90

1999 Donruss Zoning Commission Red

	MINT	NRMT
COMMON CARD (1-25)	50.00	22.00
RANDOM INSERTS IN PACKS		
CARDS SER.#'d UNDER 10 NOT PRICED		

Card	MINT	NRMT
❑ 1 Eric Moulds/8		
❑ 2 Steve Young/36	50.00	22.00
❑ 3 Brad Johnson/7		
❑ 4 Peyton Manning/26	150.00	70.00
❑ 5 Randy Moss/17	250.00	110.00
❑ 6 Brett Favre/31	150.00	70.00
❑ 7 Emmitt Smith/13	150.00	70.00
❑ 8 Mark Brunell/20	80.00	36.00
❑ 9 Keyshawn Johnson/10	120.00	55.00
❑ 10 Dan Marino/23	150.00	70.00
❑ 11 Eddie George/5		
❑ 12 Drew Bledsoe/20	80.00	36.00
❑ 13 Terrell Davis/21	120.00	55.00
❑ 14 Terrell Owens/14	50.00	22.00
❑ 15 Barry Sanders/4		
❑ 16 Curtis Martin/8		
❑ 17 John Elway/22	200.00	90.00
❑ 18 Jake Plummer/17	80.00	36.00
❑ 19 Jerry Rice/9		
❑ 20 Fred Taylor/14	100.00	45.00
❑ 21 Antonio Freeman/14	60.00	27.00
❑ 22 Marshall Faulk/10	120.00	55.00
❑ 23 Dorsey Levens/1		
❑ 24 Steve McNair/15	60.00	27.00
❑ 25 Cris Carter/12	60.00	27.00

1999 Donruss Elite

	MINT	NRMT
COMPLETE SET (200)	200.00	90.00
COMP.SET w/o SP's (160)	30.00	13.50
COMMON CARD (1-100)	.25	.11
SEMISTARS 1-100	.50	.23
UNL.STARS 1-100	1.00	.45
COMMON CARD (101-200)	.50	.23
SEMISTARS 101-200	1.00	.45
UNL.STARS 101-200	2.00	.90
COMMON ROOKIE (161-200)	3.00	1.35
ROOKIE SEMISTARS	4.00	1.80
ROOKIE UNL.STARS	5.00	2.20
101-200 STATED ODDS ONE PER PACK		

Card	MINT	NRMT
❑ 1 Warren Moon	1.00	.45
❑ 2 Terry Allen	.50	.23
❑ 3 Jeff George	.50	.23
❑ 4 Brett Favre	4.00	1.80
❑ 5 Rob Moore	.50	.23
❑ 6 Bubby Brister	.25	.11
❑ 7 John Elway	4.00	1.80
❑ 8 Troy Aikman	2.50	1.10
❑ 9 Steve McNair	1.00	.45
❑ 10 Charlie Batch	2.00	.90
❑ 11 Elvis Grbac	.50	.23
❑ 12 Trent Dilfer	.50	.23
❑ 13 Kerry Collins	.50	.23
❑ 14 Neil O'Donnell	.25	.11
❑ 15 Tony Simmons	.25	.11
❑ 16 Ryan Leaf	1.00	.45
❑ 17 Bobby Hoying	.50	.23
❑ 18 Marvin Harrison	1.00	.45
❑ 19 Keyshawn Johnson	1.00	.45
❑ 20 Cris Carter	1.00	.45
❑ 21 Deion Sanders	1.00	.45
❑ 22 Emmitt Smith	2.50	1.10
❑ 23 Antowain Smith	1.00	.45
❑ 24 Terry Fair	.25	.11
❑ 25 Robert Holcombe	.50	.23
❑ 26 Napoleon Kaufman	1.00	.45
❑ 27 Eddie George	1.25	.55
❑ 28 Corey Dillon	1.00	.45
❑ 29 Adrian Murrell	.50	.23
❑ 30 Charles Way	.25	.11
❑ 31 Amp Lee	.25	.11
❑ 32 Ricky Watters	.50	.23
❑ 33 Gary Brown	.25	.11
❑ 34 Thurman Thomas	.50	.23
❑ 35 Pat Johnson	.25	.11
❑ 36 Jerome Bettis	1.00	.45
❑ 37 Muhsin Muhammad	.50	.23
❑ 38 Kimble Anders	.50	.23
❑ 39 Curtis Enis	1.00	.45
❑ 40 Mike Alstott	1.00	.45
❑ 41 Charles Johnson	.25	.11
❑ 42 Chris Warren	.25	.11
❑ 43 Tony Banks	.50	.23
❑ 44 Leroy Hoard	.25	.11
❑ 45 Chris Fuamatu-Ma'afala	.25	.11
❑ 46 Michael Irvin	1.00	.45
❑ 47 Robert Edwards	.50	.23
❑ 48 Hines Ward	.25	.11
❑ 49 Trent Green	.50	.23
❑ 50 Eric Zeier	.25	.11
❑ 51 Sean Dawkins	.25	.11
❑ 52 Yancey Thigpen	.25	.11
❑ 53 Jacquez Green	.50	.23
❑ 54 Zach Thomas	.50	.23
❑ 55 Junior Seau	.50	.23
❑ 56 Darnay Scott	.25	.11
❑ 57 Kent Graham	.25	.11
❑ 58 O.J. Santiago	.25	.11
❑ 59 Tony Gonzalez	.50	.23
❑ 60 Ty Detmer	.25	.11
❑ 61 Albert Connell	.25	.11
❑ 62 James Jett	.50	.23
❑ 63 Bert Emanuel	.50	.23
❑ 64 Derrick Alexander WR	.50	.23
❑ 65 Wesley Walls	.50	.23
❑ 66 Jake Reed	.50	.23
❑ 67 Randall Cunningham	1.00	.45
❑ 68 Leslie Shepherd	.25	.11
❑ 69 Mark Chmura	.25	.11
❑ 70 Bobby Engram	.50	.23
❑ 71 Rickey Dudley	.25	.11
❑ 72 Darick Holmes	.25	.11
❑ 73 Andre Reed	.50	.23
❑ 74 Az-Zahir Hakim	.25	.11
❑ 75 Cameron Cleeland	.25	.11
❑ 76 Lamar Thomas	.25	.11
❑ 77 Oronde Gadsden	.25	.11
❑ 78 Ben Coates	.50	.23
❑ 79 Bruce Smith	.50	.23
❑ 80 Jerry Rice	2.50	1.10
❑ 81 Tim Brown	1.00	.45
❑ 82 Michael Westbrook	.50	.23
❑ 83 J.J. Stokes	.50	.23
❑ 84 Shannon Sharpe	.50	.23
❑ 85 Reidel Anthony	.50	.23
❑ 86 Antonio Freeman	1.00	.45
❑ 87 Keenan McCardell	.50	.23
❑ 88 Terry Glenn	1.00	.45
❑ 89 Andre Rison	.50	.23
❑ 90 Neil Smith	.50	.23
❑ 91 Terrance Mathis	.50	.23
❑ 92 Rocket Ismail	.50	.23
❑ 93 Byron Bam Morris	.25	.11
❑ 94 Ike Hilliard	.25	.11
❑ 95 Eddie Kennison	.50	.23
❑ 96 Tavian Banks	.50	.23
❑ 97 Yatil Green	.25	.11
❑ 98 Frank Wycheck	.25	.11
❑ 99 Warren Sapp	.25	.11
❑ 100 Germane Crowell	.50	.23
❑ 101 Curtis Martin	2.00	.90
❑ 102 John Avery	1.00	.45
❑ 103 Eric Moulds	2.00	.90
❑ 104 Randy Moss	10.00	4.50
❑ 105 Terrell Owens	2.00	.90
❑ 106 Vinny Testaverde	1.00	.45
❑ 107 Doug Flutie	2.50	1.10
❑ 108 Mark Brunell	3.00	1.35
❑ 109 Isaac Bruce	2.00	.90
❑ 110 Kordell Stewart	2.00	.90
❑ 111 Drew Bledsoe	3.00	1.35
❑ 112 Chris Chandler	1.00	.45
❑ 113 Dan Marino	8.00	3.60
❑ 114 Brian Griese	3.00	1.35
❑ 115 Carl Pickens	1.00	.45
❑ 116 Jake Plummer	4.00	1.80
❑ 117 Natrone Means	1.00	.45
❑ 118 Peyton Manning	10.00	4.50
❑ 119 Garrison Hearst	2.00	.90
❑ 120 Barry Sanders	8.00	3.60
❑ 121 Steve Young	3.00	1.35
❑ 122 Rashaan Shehee	.50	.23
❑ 123 Ed McCaffrey	1.00	.45
❑ 124 Charles Woodson	2.00	.90
❑ 125 Dorsey Levens	2.00	.90
❑ 126 Robert Smith	2.00	.90
❑ 127 Greg Hill	.50	.23
❑ 128 Fred Taylor	5.00	2.20
❑ 129 Marcus Nash	1.00	.45
❑ 130 Terrell Davis	5.00	2.20
❑ 131 Ahman Green	1.00	.45
❑ 132 Jamal Anderson	2.00	.90
❑ 133 Karim Abdul-Jabbar	1.00	.45
❑ 134 Jermaine Lewis	1.00	.45
❑ 135 Jerome Pathon	1.00	.45
❑ 136 Brad Johnson	2.00	.90
❑ 137 Herman Moore	2.00	.90
❑ 138 Tim Dwight	2.00	.90
❑ 139 Johnnie Morton	.50	.23
❑ 140 Marshall Faulk	2.00	.90
❑ 141 Frank Sanders	1.00	.45
❑ 142 Kevin Dyson	1.00	.45
❑ 143 Curtis Conway	1.00	.45
❑ 144 Derrick Mayes	.50	.23
❑ 145 O.J. McDuffie	1.00	.45
❑ 146 Joe Jurevicius	.50	.23
❑ 147 Jon Kitna	2.50	1.10
❑ 148 Joey Galloway	2.00	.90
❑ 149 Jimmy Smith	1.00	.45
❑ 150 Skip Hicks	1.00	.45
❑ 151 Rod Smith	1.00	.45
❑ 152 Duce Staley	2.00	.90
❑ 153 James Stewart	.50	.23
❑ 154 Rob Johnson	1.00	.45
❑ 155 Mikhael Ricks	.50	.23

❑ 156 Wayne Chrebet 1.00 .45
❑ 157 Robert Brooks 1.00 .45
❑ 158 Tim Biakabutuka 1.00 .45
❑ 159 Priest Holmes 2.00 .90
❑ 160 Warrick Dunn 2.00 .90
❑ 161 Champ Bailey RC 6.00 2.70
❑ 162 D'Wayne Bates RC 4.00 1.80
❑ 163 Michael Bishop RC 6.00 2.70
❑ 164 David Boston RC 8.00 3.60
❑ 165 Na Brown RC 5.00 2.20
❑ 166 Chris Claiborne RC 4.00 1.80
❑ 167 Joe Montgomery RC 5.00 2.20
❑ 168 Mike Cloud RC 5.00 2.20
❑ 169 Travis McGriff RC 5.00 2.20
❑ 170 Tim Couch RC 25.00 11.00
❑ 171 Daunte Culpepper RC 15.00 6.75
❑ 172 Autry Denson RC 5.00 2.20
❑ 173 Jermaine Fazande RC 4.00 1.80
❑ 174 Troy Edwards RC 8.00 3.60
❑ 175 Kevin Faulk RC 6.00 2.70
❑ 176 Dee Miller RC 4.00 1.80
❑ 177 Brock Huard RC 6.00 2.70
❑ 178 Torry Holt RC 12.00 5.50
❑ 179 Sedrick Irvin RC 5.00 2.20
❑ 180 Edgerrin James RC 40.00 18.00
❑ 181 Joe Germaine RC 5.00 2.20
❑ 182 James Johnson RC 5.00 2.20
❑ 183 Kevin Johnson RC 12.00 5.50
❑ 184 Andy Katzenmoyer RC 5.00 2.20
❑ 185 Jevon Kearse RC 10.00 4.50
❑ 186 Shaun King RC 15.00 6.75
❑ 187 Rob Konrad RC 5.00 2.20
❑ 188 Jim Kleinsasser RC 5.00 2.20
❑ 189 Chris McAlister RC 4.00 1.80
❑ 190 Donovan McNabb RC 15.00 6.75
❑ 191 Cade McNown RC 15.00 6.75
❑ 192 De'Mond Parker RC 2.00 .90
❑ 193 Craig Yeast RC 4.00 1.80
❑ 194 Shawn Bryson RC 3.00 1.35
❑ 195 Peerless Price RC 8.00 3.60
❑ 196 Darnell McDonald RC 5.00 2.20
❑ 197 Akili Smith RC 10.00 4.50
❑ 198 Tai Streets RC 4.00 1.80
❑ 199 Ricky Williams RC 25.00 11.00
❑ 200 Amos Zereoue RC 5.00 2.20

1999 Donruss Elite Aspirations

	MINT	NRMT
COMMON 80-99 (1-200)	5.00	2.20
SEMISTARS 80-99	8.00	3.60
UNLISTED STARS 80-99	15.00	6.75
COMMON 65-79	6.00	2.70
SEMISTARS 65-79	10.00	4.50
UNLISTED STARS 65-79	20.00	9.00
COMMON 45-64	8.00	3.60
SEMISTARS 45-64	12.00	5.50
UNLISTED STARS 45-64	25.00	11.00
COMMON 20-29	25.00	11.00
SEMISTARS 20-29	50.00	22.00
COMMON 10-19	20.00	9.00
SEMISTARS 10-19	30.00	13.50
UNLISTED STARS 10-19	60.00	27.00

CARDS #'d UNDER 10 NOT PRICED

❑ 1 Warren Moon/99 15.00 6.75
❑ 2 Terry Allen/79 10.00 4.50
❑ 3 Jeff George/97 8.00 3.60
❑ 4 Brett Favre/96 80.00 36.00
❑ 5 Rob Moore/15 30.00 13.50
❑ 6 Bubby Brister/94 8.00 3.60
❑ 7 John Elway/93 80.00 36.00
❑ 8 Troy Aikman/92 50.00 22.00
❑ 9 Steve McNair/91 15.00 6.75
❑ 10 Charlie Batch/90 40.00 18.00
❑ 11 Elvis Grbac/89 8.00 3.60
❑ 12 Trent Dilfer/88 8.00 3.60
❑ 13 Kerry Collins/87 8.00 3.60
❑ 14 Neil O'Donnell/88 8.00 3.60
❑ 15 Tony Simmons/19 20.00 9.00
❑ 16 Ryan Leaf/84 15.00 6.75
❑ 17 Bobby Hoying/93 8.00 3.60
❑ 18 Marvin Harrison/12 60.00 27.00
❑ 19 Keyshawn Johnson/81 15.00 6.75
❑ 20 Cris Carter/20 50.00 22.00
❑ 21 Deion Sanders/79 20.00 9.00
❑ 22 Emmitt Smith/78 60.00 27.00
❑ 23 Antowain Smith/77 20.00 9.00
❑ 24 Terry Fair/77 6.00 2.70
❑ 25 Robert Holcombe/75 6.00 2.70
❑ 26 Napoleon Kaufman/74 20.00 9.00
❑ 27 Eddie George/73 30.00 13.50
❑ 28 Corey Dillon/72 20.00 9.00
❑ 29 Adrian Murrell/71 10.00 4.50
❑ 30 Charles Way/70 6.00 2.70
❑ 31 Amp Lee/69 6.00 2.70
❑ 32 Ricky Watters/68 10.00 4.50
❑ 33 Gary Brown/67 6.00 2.70
❑ 34 Thurman Thomas/66 20.00 9.00
❑ 35 Patrick Johnson/15 20.00 9.00
❑ 36 Jerome Bettis/64 25.00 11.00
❑ 37 Muhsin Muhammad/13 30.00 13.50
❑ 38 Kimble Anders/62 12.00 5.50
❑ 39 Curtis Enis/61 25.00 11.00
❑ 40 Mike Alstott/60 25.00 11.00
❑ 41 Charles Johnson/19 20.00 9.00
❑ 42 Chris Warren/58 8.00 3.60
❑ 43 Tony Banks/88 8.00 3.60
❑ 44 Leroy Hoard/56 8.00 3.60
❑ 45 Chris Fuamatu-Ma'afala/55 8.00 3.60
❑ 46 Michael Irvin/12 30.00 13.50
❑ 47 Robert Edwards/53 12.00 5.50
❑ 48 Hines Ward/14 20.00 9.00
❑ 49 Trent Green/90 8.00 3.60
❑ 50 Eric Zeier/90 8.00 3.60
❑ 51 Sean Dawkins/14 20.00 9.00
❑ 52 Yancey Thigpen/18 20.00 9.00
❑ 53 Jacquez Green/19 20.00 9.00
❑ 54 Zach Thomas/46 12.00 5.50
❑ 55 Junior Seau/45 12.00 5.50
❑ 56 Darnay Scott/14 30.00 13.50
❑ 57 Kent Graham/90 5.00 2.20
❑ 58 O.J. Santiago/12 20.00 9.00
❑ 59 Tony Gonzalez/12 30.00 13.50
❑ 60 Ty Detmer/89 5.00 2.20
❑ 61 Albert Connell/17 25.00 11.00
❑ 62 James Jett/18 20.00 9.00
❑ 63 Bert Emanuel/13 30.00 13.50
❑ 64 Derrick Alexander WR/18 30.00 13.50
❑ 65 Wesley Walls/15 30.00 13.50
❑ 66 Jake Reed/14 30.00 13.50
❑ 67 Randall Cunningham/93 15.00 6.75
❑ 68 Leslie Shepherd/14 20.00 9.00
❑ 69 Mark Chmura/11 20.00 9.00
❑ 70 Bobby Engram/19 20.00 9.00
❑ 71 Rickey Dudley/17 25.00 11.00
❑ 72 Darick Holmes/78 6.00 2.70
❑ 73 Andre Reed/17 30.00 13.50
❑ 74 Az-Zahir Hakim/19 30.00 13.50
❑ 75 Cameron Cleeland/15 20.00 9.00
❑ 76 Lamar Thomas/15 20.00 9.00
❑ 77 Oronde Gadsden/14 20.00 9.00
❑ 78 Ben Coates/13 30.00 13.50
❑ 79 Bruce Smith/22 50.00 22.00
❑ 80 Jerry Rice/20 150.00 70.00
❑ 81 Tim Brown/19 60.00 27.00
❑ 82 Michael Westbrook/18 30.00 13.50
❑ 83 J.J. Stokes/17 30.00 13.50
❑ 84 Shannon Sharpe/16 30.00 13.50
❑ 85 Reidel Anthony/15 20.00 9.00
❑ 86 Antonio Freeman/14 60.00 27.00
❑ 87 Keenan McCardell/13 30.00 13.50
❑ 88 Terry Glenn/12 60.00 27.00
❑ 89 Andre Rison/11 30.00 13.50
❑ 90 Neil Smith/10 20.00 9.00
❑ 91 Terrance Mathis/19 30.00 13.50
❑ 92 Rocket Ismail/19 30.00 13.50
❑ 93 Byron Bam Morris/61 8.00 3.60
❑ 94 Ike Hilliard/12 20.00 9.00
❑ 95 Eddie Kennison/12 20.00 9.00
❑ 96 Tavian Banks/78 6.00 2.70
❑ 97 Yatil Green/13 20.00 9.00
❑ 98 Frank Wycheck/11 20.00 9.00
❑ 99 Warren Sapp/1
❑ 100 Germane Crowell/18 60.00 27.00
❑ 101 Curtis Martin/72 20.00 9.00
❑ 102 John Avery/80 8.00 3.60
❑ 103 Eric Moulds/20 50.00 22.00
❑ 104 Randy Moss/16 300.00 135.00
❑ 105 Terrell Owens/19 60.00 27.00
❑ 106 Vinny Testaverde/84 8.00 3.60
❑ 107 Doug Flutie/93 25.00 11.00
❑ 108 Mark Brunell/92 35.00 16.00
❑ 109 Isaac Bruce/20 50.00 22.00
❑ 110 Kordell Stewart/90 25.00 11.00
❑ 111 Drew Bledsoe/89 35.00 16.00
❑ 112 Chris Chandler/88 8.00 3.60
❑ 113 Dan Marino/87 80.00 36.00
❑ 114 Brian Griese/86 40.00 18.00
❑ 115 Carl Pickens/19 30.00 13.50
❑ 116 Jake Plummer/84 60.00 27.00
❑ 117 Natrone Means/80 8.00 3.60
❑ 118 Peyton Manning/82 80.00 36.00
❑ 119 Garrison Hearst/80 15.00 6.75
❑ 120 Barry Sanders/80 100.00 45.00
❑ 121 Steve Young/92 35.00 16.00
❑ 122 Rashaan Shehee/78 6.00 2.70
❑ 123 Ed McCaffrey/13 30.00 13.50
❑ 124 Charles Woodson/76 20.00 9.00
❑ 125 Dorsey Levens/75 20.00 9.00
❑ 126 Robert Smith/74 20.00 9.00
❑ 127 Greg Hill/73 6.00 2.70
❑ 128 Fred Taylor/72 50.00 22.00
❑ 129 Marcus Nash/18 20.00 9.00
❑ 130 Terrell Davis/70 60.00 27.00
❑ 131 Ahman Green/70 10.00 4.50
❑ 132 Jamal Anderson/68 20.00 9.00
❑ 133 Karim Abdul-Jabbar/67 10.00 4.50
❑ 134 Jermaine Lewis/16 30.00 13.50
❑ 135 Jerome Pathon/14 20.00 9.00
❑ 136 Brad Johnson/86 15.00 6.75
❑ 137 Herman Moore/16 60.00 27.00
❑ 138 Tim Dwight/17 60.00 27.00
❑ 139 Johnnie Morton/13 30.00 13.50
❑ 140 Marshall Faulk/72 20.00 9.00
❑ 141 Frank Sanders/19 30.00 13.50
❑ 142 Kevin Dyson/13 30.00 13.50
❑ 143 Curtis Conway/17 30.00 13.50
❑ 144 Derrick Mayes/20 50.00 22.00
❑ 145 O.J. McDuffie/19 30.00 13.50
❑ 146 Joe Jurevicius/14 20.00 9.00
❑ 147 Jon Kitna/93 30.00 13.50
❑ 148 Joey Galloway/16 60.00 27.00
❑ 149 Jimmy Smith/18 30.00 13.50
❑ 150 Skip Hicks/80 15.00 6.75
❑ 151 Rod Smith/20 50.00 22.00
❑ 152 Duce Staley/78 20.00 9.00
❑ 153 James Stewart/67 10.00 4.50
❑ 154 Rob Johnson/89 8.00 3.60
❑ 155 Mikhael Ricks/90 5.00 2.20
❑ 156 Wayne Chrebet/20 50.00 22.00
❑ 157 Robert Brooks/13 20.00 9.00
❑ 158 Tim Biakabutuka/79 10.00 4.50
❑ 159 Priest Holmes/67 20.00 9.00
❑ 160 Warrick Dunn/72 20.00 9.00
❑ 161 Champ Bailey/96 20.00 9.00
❑ 162 D'Wayne Bates/95 15.00 6.75
❑ 163 Michael Bishop/93 20.00 9.00
❑ 164 David Boston/91 30.00 13.50
❑ 165 Na Brown/81 15.00 6.75
❑ 166 Chris Claiborne/45 25.00 11.00
❑ 167 Joe Montgomery/67 20.00 9.00
❑ 168 Mike Cloud/79 20.00 9.00
❑ 169 Travis McGriff/97 15.00 6.75
❑ 170 Tim Couch/98 80.00 36.00
❑ 171 Daunte Culpepper/92 50.00 22.00
❑ 172 Autry Denson/67 20.00 9.00
❑ 173 Jermaine Fazande/70 10.00 4.50
❑ 174 Troy Edwards/84 40.00 18.00

Card	MINT	NRMT
❑ 175 Kevin Faulk/97	20.00	9.00
❑ 176 Dee Miller/85	8.00	3.60
❑ 177 Brock Huard/93	20.00	9.00
❑ 178 Torry Holt/19	120.00	55.00
❑ 179 Sedrick Irvin/67	25.00	11.00
❑ 180 Edgerrin James/95	150.00	70.00
❑ 181 Joe Germaine/93	15.00	6.75
❑ 182 James Johnson/78	25.00	11.00
❑ 183 Kevin Johnson/88	40.00	18.00
❑ 184 Andy Katzenmoyer/55	25.00	11.00
❑ 185 Jevon Kearse/58	50.00	22.00
❑ 186 Shaun King/90	50.00	22.00
❑ 187 Rob Konrad/56	25.00	11.00
❑ 188 Jim Kleinsasser/18	30.00	13.50
❑ 189 Chris McAlister/89	15.00	6.75
❑ 190 Donovan McNabb/95	50.00	22.00
❑ 191 Cade McNown/82	60.00	27.00
❑ 192 De'Mond Parker/67	20.00	9.00
❑ 193 Craig Yeast/97	15.00	6.75
❑ 194 Shawn Bryson/76	10.00	4.50
❑ 195 Peerless Price/63	40.00	18.00
❑ 196 Darnell McDonald/20	60.00	27.00
❑ 197 Akili Smith/89	30.00	13.50
❑ 198 Tai Streets/14	20.00	9.00
❑ 199 Ricky Williams/66	150.00	70.00
❑ 200 Amos Zereoue/80	25.00	11.00

1999 Donruss Elite Status

	MINT	NRMT
COMMON 80-99 (1-200)	5.00	2.20
SEMISTARS 80-99	8.00	3.60
UNLISTED STARS 80-99	15.00	6.75
COMMON 65-79	6.00	2.70
COMMON 45-64	8.00	3.60
SEMISTARS 45-64	12.00	5.50
UNLISTED STARS 45-64	25.00	11.00
COMMON 30-44	10.00	4.50
SEMISTARS 30-44	20.00	9.00
UNLISTED STARS 30-44	40.00	18.00
COMMON 20-29	15.00	6.75
SEMISTARS 20-29	30.00	13.50
UNLISTED STARS 20-29	50.00	22.00
COMMON 10-19	20.00	9.00
SEMISTARS 10-19	40.00	18.00
UNLISTED STARS 10-19	60.00	27.00

CARDS #'d UNDER 10 NOT PRICED

Card	MINT	NRMT
❑ 1 Warren Moon/1		
❑ 2 Terry Allen/21	30.00	13.50
❑ 3 Jeff George/3		
❑ 4 Brett Favre/4		
❑ 5 Rob Moore/85	8.00	3.60
❑ 6 Bubby Brister/6		
❑ 7 John Elway/7		
❑ 8 Troy Aikman/8		
❑ 9 Steve McNair/9		
❑ 10 Charlie Batch/10	120.00	55.00
❑ 11 Elvis Grbac/11	20.00	9.00
❑ 12 Trent Dilfer/12	40.00	18.00
❑ 13 Kerry Collins/13	40.00	18.00
❑ 14 Neil O'Donnell/12	20.00	9.00
❑ 15 Tony Simmons/81	5.00	2.20
❑ 16 Ryan Leaf/16	60.00	27.00
❑ 17 Bobby Hoying/7		
❑ 18 Marvin Harrison/88	15.00	6.75
❑ 19 Keyshawn Johnson/19	60.00	27.00
❑ 20 Cris Carter/80	15.00	6.75
❑ 21 Deion Sanders/21	50.00	22.00
❑ 22 Emmitt Smith/22	150.00	70.00
❑ 23 Antowain Smith/23	50.00	22.00
❑ 24 Terry Fair/23	15.00	6.75
❑ 25 Robert Holcombe/25	15.00	6.75
❑ 26 Napoleon Kaufman/26	50.00	22.00
❑ 27 Eddie George/27	60.00	27.00
❑ 28 Corey Dillon/28	50.00	22.00
❑ 29 Adrian Murrell/29	30.00	13.50
❑ 30 Charles Way/30	10.00	4.50
❑ 31 Amp Lee/31	10.00	4.50
❑ 32 Ricky Watters/32	20.00	9.00
❑ 33 Gary Brown/33	10.00	4.50
❑ 34 Thurman Thomas/34	40.00	18.00
❑ 35 Patrick Johnson/85	5.00	2.20
❑ 36 Jerome Bettis/36	40.00	18.00
❑ 37 Muhsin Muhammad/87	8.00	3.60
❑ 38 Kimble Anders/38	10.00	4.50
❑ 39 Curtis Enis/39	40.00	18.00
❑ 40 Mike Alstott/40	40.00	18.00
❑ 41 Charles Johnson/81	8.00	3.60
❑ 42 Chris Warren/42	10.00	4.50
❑ 43 Tony Banks/12	40.00	18.00
❑ 44 Leroy Hoard/44	10.00	4.50
❑ 45 Chris Fuamatu-Ma'afala/45	8.00	3.60
❑ 46 Michael Irvin/88	15.00	6.75
❑ 47 Robert Edwards/47	12.00	5.50
❑ 48 Hines Ward/86	8.00	3.60
❑ 49 Trent Green/10	40.00	18.00
❑ 50 Eric Zeier/10	40.00	18.00
❑ 51 Sean Dawkins/86	5.00	2.20
❑ 52 Yancey Thigpen/82	5.00	2.20
❑ 53 Jacquez Green/81	5.00	2.20
❑ 54 Zach Thomas/54	12.00	5.50
❑ 55 Junior Seau/55	12.00	5.50
❑ 56 Darnay Scott/86	8.00	3.60
❑ 57 Kent Graham/10	20.00	9.00
❑ 58 O.J. Santiago/88	5.00	2.20
❑ 59 Tony Gonzalez/88	8.00	3.60
❑ 60 Ty Detmer/11	20.00	9.00
❑ 61 Albert Connell/83	5.00	2.20
❑ 62 James Jett/82	8.00	3.60
❑ 63 Bert Emanuel/87	5.00	2.20
❑ 64 Derrick Alexander WR/82	8.00	3.60
❑ 65 Wesley Walls/85	8.00	3.60
❑ 66 Jake Reed/86	8.00	3.60
❑ 67 Randall Cunningham/7		
❑ 68 Leslie Shepherd/86	5.00	2.20
❑ 69 Mark Chmura/89	5.00	2.20
❑ 70 Bobby Engram/81	5.00	2.20
❑ 71 Rickey Dudley/83	5.00	2.20
❑ 72 Darick Holmes/22	15.00	6.75
❑ 73 Andre Reed/83	8.00	3.60
❑ 74 Az-Zahir Hakim/81	8.00	3.60
❑ 75 Cameron Cleeland/85	5.00	2.20
❑ 76 Lamar Thomas/85	5.00	2.20
❑ 77 Oronde Gadsden/86	5.00	2.20
❑ 78 Ben Coates/87	8.00	3.60
❑ 79 Bruce Smith/78	6.00	2.70
❑ 80 Jerry Rice/80	60.00	27.00
❑ 81 Tim Brown/81	15.00	6.75
❑ 82 Michael Westbrook/82	8.00	3.60
❑ 83 J.J. Stokes/83	8.00	3.60
❑ 84 Shannon Sharpe/84	8.00	3.60
❑ 85 Reidel Anthony/85	8.00	3.60
❑ 86 Antonio Freeman/86	15.00	6.75
❑ 87 Keenan McCardell/87	8.00	3.60
❑ 88 Terry Glenn/88	15.00	6.75
❑ 89 Andre Rison/89	8.00	3.60
❑ 90 Neil Smith/90	5.00	2.20
❑ 91 Terrance Mathis/81	8.00	3.60
❑ 92 Rocket Ismail/81	8.00	3.60
❑ 93 Byron Bam Morris/39	10.00	4.50
❑ 94 Ike Hilliard/88	8.00	3.60
❑ 95 Eddie Kennison/88	8.00	3.60
❑ 96 Tavian Banks/22	30.00	13.50
❑ 97 Yatil Green/87	5.00	2.20
❑ 98 Frank Wycheck/89	5.00	2.20
❑ 99 Warren Sapp/99	5.00	2.20
❑ 100 Germane Crowell/82	8.00	3.60
❑ 101 Curtis Martin/28	50.00	22.00
❑ 102 John Avery/20	15.00	6.75
❑ 103 Eric Moulds/80	15.00	6.75
❑ 104 Randy Moss/84	100.00	45.00
❑ 105 Terrell Owens/81	15.00	6.75
❑ 106 Vinny Testaverde/16	40.00	18.00
❑ 107 Doug Flutie/7		
❑ 108 Mark Brunell/8		
❑ 109 Isaac Bruce/80	15.00	6.75
❑ 110 Kordell Stewart/10	60.00	27.00
❑ 111 Drew Bledsoe/11	120.00	55.00
❑ 112 Chris Chandler/12	40.00	18.00
❑ 113 Dan Marino/13	300.00	135.00
❑ 114 Brian Griese/14	150.00	70.00
❑ 115 Carl Pickens/81	8.00	3.60
❑ 116 Jake Plummer/16	150.00	70.00
❑ 117 Natrone Means/20	30.00	13.50
❑ 118 Peyton Manning/18	250.00	110.00
❑ 119 Garrison Hearst/20	50.00	22.00
❑ 120 Barry Sanders/20	250.00	110.00
❑ 121 Steve Young/8		
❑ 122 Rashaan Shehee/22	15.00	6.75
❑ 123 Ed McCaffrey/87	8.00	3.60
❑ 124 Charles Woodson/24	50.00	22.00
❑ 125 Dorsey Levens/25	50.00	22.00
❑ 126 Robert Smith/26	50.00	22.00
❑ 127 Greg Hill/27	15.00	6.75
❑ 128 Fred Taylor/28	100.00	45.00
❑ 129 Marcus Nash/82	8.00	3.60
❑ 130 Terrell Davis/30	175.00	80.00
❑ 131 Ahman Green/30	20.00	9.00
❑ 132 Jamal Anderson/32	40.00	18.00
❑ 133 Karim Abdul-Jabbar/33	20.00	9.00
❑ 134 Jermaine Lewis/84	8.00	3.60
❑ 135 Jerome Pathon/86	5.00	2.20
❑ 136 Brad Johnson/14	60.00	27.00
❑ 137 Herman Moore/84	15.00	6.75
❑ 138 Tim Dwight/83	20.00	9.00
❑ 139 Johnnie Morton/87	8.00	3.60
❑ 140 Marshall Faulk/28	50.00	22.00
❑ 141 Frank Sanders/81	8.00	3.60
❑ 142 Kevin Dyson/87	8.00	3.60
❑ 143 Curtis Conway/83	8.00	3.60
❑ 144 Derrick Mayes/80	8.00	3.60
❑ 145 O.J. McDuffie/81	8.00	3.60
❑ 146 Joe Jurevicius/86	5.00	2.20
❑ 147 Jon Kitna/7		
❑ 148 Joey Galloway/84	15.00	6.75
❑ 149 Jimmy Smith/82	8.00	3.60
❑ 150 Skip Hicks/20	30.00	13.50
❑ 151 Rod Smith/80	8.00	3.60
❑ 152 Duce Staley/22	50.00	22.00
❑ 153 James Stewart/33	20.00	9.00
❑ 154 Rob Johnson/11	40.00	18.00
❑ 155 Mikhael Ricks/10	20.00	9.00
❑ 156 Wayne Chrebet/80	15.00	6.75
❑ 157 Robert Brooks/87	8.00	3.60
❑ 158 Tim Biakabutuka/21	30.00	13.50
❑ 159 Priest Holmes/33	40.00	18.00
❑ 160 Warrick Dunn/28	50.00	22.00
❑ 161 Champ Bailey/4		
❑ 162 D'Wayne Bates/5		
❑ 163 Michael Bishop/7		
❑ 164 David Boston/9		
❑ 165 Na Brown/18	40.00	18.00
❑ 166 Chris Claiborne/55	25.00	11.00
❑ 167 Joe Montgomery/33	40.00	18.00
❑ 168 Mike Cloud/21	50.00	22.00
❑ 169 Travis McGriff/3		
❑ 170 Tim Couch/2		
❑ 171 Daunte Culpepper/8		
❑ 172 Autry Denson/23	50.00	22.00
❑ 173 Jermaine Fazande/30	20.00	9.00
❑ 174 Troy Edwards/16	100.00	45.00
❑ 175 Kevin Faulk/3		
❑ 176 Dee Miller/15	40.00	18.00
❑ 177 Brock Huard/7		
❑ 178 Torry Holt/81	30.00	13.50
❑ 179 Sedrick Irvin/33	50.00	22.00
❑ 180 Edgerrin James/5		
❑ 181 Joe Germaine/7		
❑ 182 James Johnson/22	60.00	27.00
❑ 183 Kevin Johnson/12	150.00	70.00
❑ 184 Andy Katzenmoyer/45	30.00	13.50
❑ 185 Jevon Kearse/42	60.00	27.00
❑ 186 Shaun King/10	200.00	90.00
❑ 187 Rob Konrad/44	40.00	18.00
❑ 188 Jim Kleinsasser/82	15.00	6.75
❑ 189 Chris McAlister/11	20.00	9.00
❑ 190 Donovan McNabb/5		
❑ 191 Cade McNown/18	200.00	90.00
❑ 192 De'Mond Parker/33	40.00	18.00
❑ 193 Craig Yeast/3		
❑ 194 Shawn Bryson/24	30.00	13.50
❑ 195 Peerless Price/37	60.00	27.00
❑ 196 Darnell McDonald/80	20.00	9.00
❑ 197 Akili Smith/11	120.00	55.00
❑ 198 Tai Streets/86	8.00	3.60
❑ 199 Ricky Williams/34	400.00	180.00
❑ 200 Amos Zereoue/20	60.00	27.00

1999 Donruss Elite Common Threads

	MINT	NRMT
COMPLETE SET (18)	2500.00	1100.00
COMMON CARD (1-18)	60.00	27.00

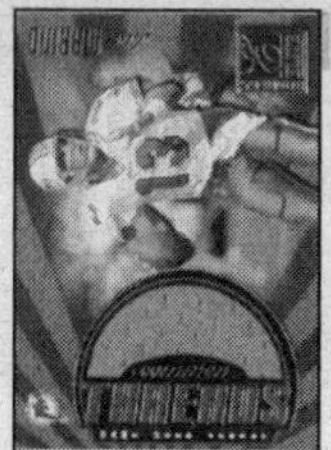

SEMISTARS 80.00 36.00
MULTI-COLORED SWATCHES: .6X TO 1.5X
STATED PRINT RUN 150 SERIAL #'d SETS

❑ 1 Randy Moss 250.00 110.00
Randall Cunningham
❑ 2 Randy Moss 200.00 90.00
❑ 3 Randall Cunningham 80.00 36.00
❑ 4 John Elway 250.00 110.00
Terrell Davis
❑ 5 John Elway 200.00 90.00
❑ 6 Terrell Davis 150.00 70.00
❑ 7 Jerry Rice 200.00 90.00
Steve Young
❑ 8 Jerry Rice 150.00 70.00
❑ 9 Steve Young 120.00 55.00
❑ 10 Mark Brunell 120.00 55.00
Fred Taylor
❑ 11 Mark Brunell 100.00 45.00
❑ 12 Fred Taylor 100.00 45.00
❑ 13 Kordell Stewart 100.00 45.00
Jerome Bettis
❑ 14 Kordell Stewart 80.00 36.00
❑ 15 Jerome Bettis 80.00 36.00
❑ 16 Dan Marino 250.00 110.00
Karim Abdul-Jabbar
❑ 17 Dan Marino 200.00 90.00
❑ 18 Karim Abdul-Jabbar 60.00 27.00

1999 Donruss Elite Field of Vision

MINT NRMT
COMMON CARD (1A-12C) 5.00 2.20
RANDOM INSERTS IN PACKS
CARDS SERIAL #'d TO A 1998 SEASON STAT

❑ 1A Dan Marino/1712 10.00 4.50
❑ 1B Dan Marino/834 15.00 6.75
❑ 1C Dan Marino/951 15.00 6.75
❑ 2A Emmitt Smith/640 12.00 5.50
❑ 2B Emmitt Smith/202 20.00 9.00
❑ 2C Emmitt Smith/490 12.00 5.50
❑ 3A Jake Plummer/1165 8.00 3.60
❑ 3B Jake Plummer/624 10.00 4.50
❑ 3C Jake Plummer/1948 5.00 2.20
❑ 4A Brett Favre/1408 10.00 4.50
❑ 4B Brett Favre/983 15.00 6.75
❑ 4C Brett Favre/1820 10.00 4.50
❑ 5A Fred Taylor/486 10.00 4.50
❑ 5B Fred Taylor/400 10.00 4.50
❑ 5C Fred Taylor/337 12.00 5.50
❑ 6A Drew Bledsoe/1355 5.00 2.20
❑ 6B Drew Bledsoe/689 8.00 3.60
❑ 6C Drew Bledsoe/1589 5.00 2.20
❑ 7A Terrell Davis/1283 8.00 3.60
❑ 7B Terrell Davis/306 15.00 6.75
❑ 7C Terrell Davis/419 12.00 5.50
❑ 8A Jerry Rice/611 10.00 4.50
❑ 8B Jerry Rice/234 20.00 9.00
❑ 8C Jerry Rice/312 15.00 6.75
❑ 9A Randy Moss/639 20.00 9.00
❑ 9B Randy Moss/16 300.00 135.00
❑ 9C Randy Moss/658 20.00 9.00
❑ 10A John Elway/1320 12.00 5.50
❑ 10B John Elway/615 15.00 6.75
❑ 10C John Elway/871 15.00 6.75
❑ 11A Peyton Manning/1141 12.00 5.50
❑ 11B Peyton Manning/1020 12.00 5.50
❑ 11C Peyton Manning/1578 10.00 4.50
❑ 12A Barry Sanders/556 15.00 6.75
❑ 12B Barry Sanders/373 20.00 9.00
❑ 12C Barry Sanders/562 15.00 6.75

1999 Donruss Elite Field of Vision Die Cuts

MINT NRMT
COMMON CARD (1A-12C) 15.00 6.75
RANDOM INSERTS IN PACKS
CARDS SERIAL #'d TO A 1998 SEASON STAT

❑ 1A Dan Marino/164 40.00 18.00
❑ 1B Dan Marino/56 100.00 45.00
❑ 1C Dan Marino/90 60.00 27.00
❑ 2A Emmitt Smith/158 20.00 9.00
❑ 2B Emmitt Smith/64 60.00 27.00
❑ 2C Emmitt Smith/97 30.00 13.50
❑ 3A Jake Plummer/89 25.00 11.00
❑ 3B Jake Plummer/44 50.00 22.00
❑ 3C Jake Plummer/191 15.00 6.75
❑ 4A Brett Favre/112 50.00 22.00
❑ 4B Brett Favre/67 100.00 45.00
❑ 4C Brett Favre/168 40.00 18.00
❑ 5A Fred Taylor/103 25.00 11.00
❑ 5B Fred Taylor/79 30.00 13.50
❑ 5C Fred Taylor/82 30.00 13.50
❑ 6A Drew Bledsoe/90 20.00 9.00
❑ 6B Drew Bledsoe/48 30.00 13.50
❑ 6C Drew Bledsoe/125 15.00 6.75
❑ 7A Terrell Davis/217 20.00 9.00
❑ 7B Terrell Davis/66 60.00 27.00
❑ 7C Terrell Davis/109 30.00 13.50
❑ 8A Jerry Rice/50 60.00 27.00
❑ 8B Jerry Rice/11
❑ 8C Jerry Rice/21 120.00 55.00
❑ 9A Randy Moss/34 200.00 90.00
❑ 9B Randy Moss/2
❑ 9C Randy Moss/33 200.00 90.00
❑ 10A John Elway/98 60.00 27.00
❑ 10B John Elway/35 150.00 70.00
❑ 10C John Elway/77 80.00 36.00
❑ 11A Peyton Manning/110 40.00 18.00
❑ 11B Peyton Manning/79 50.00 22.00
❑ 11C Peyton Manning/137 25.00 11.00
❑ 12A Barry Sanders/137 40.00 18.00
❑ 12B Barry Sanders/83 80.00 36.00
❑ 12C Barry Sanders/123 50.00 22.00

1999 Donruss Elite Passing the Torch

MINT NRMT
COMPLETE SET (18) 150.00 70.00
COMMON CARD (1-18) 5.00 2.20
TOTAL PRINT RUN 1500 SERIAL #'d SETS
FIRST 100-CARDS WERE SIGNED

❑ 1 Johnny Unitas 15.00 6.75
Peyton Manning
❑ 2 Johnny Unitas 10.00 4.50
❑ 3 Peyton Manning 15.00 6.75
❑ 4A Walter Payton 25.00 11.00
Barry Sanders
❑ 4B Emmitt Smith 12.00 5.50
Fred Taylor

❑ 5A Walter Payton 15.00 6.75
❑ 5B Emmitt Smith 10.00 4.50
❑ 6A Barry Sanders 15.00 6.75
❑ 6B Fred Taylor 10.00 4.50
❑ 7A Earl Campbell 20.00 9.00
Ricky Williams
❑ 7B Earl Campbell ERR 20.00 9.00
Ricky Williams ERR
(Rams listed as Williams' team)
❑ 7C Earl Campbell ERR 20.00 9.00
Ricky Williams ERR
(Redskins listed as Williams' team)
❑ 8 Earl Campbell 5.00 2.20
❑ 9A Ricky Williams COR 15.00 6.75
❑ 9B Ricky Williams ERR 15.00 6.75
(Rams listed as team)
❑ 9C Ricky Williams ERR 15.00 6.75
(Redskins listed as team)
❑ 10 Jim Brown 12.00 5.50
Terrell Davis
❑ 11 Jim Brown 10.00 4.50
❑ 12 Terrell Davis 10.00 4.50
❑ 16 Cris Carter 15.00 6.75
Randy Moss
❑ 17 Cris Carter 5.00 2.20
❑ 18 Randy Moss 15.00 6.75

1999 Donruss Elite Passing the Torch Autographs

MINT NRMT
COMPLETE SET (18) 5000.00 2200.00
COMMON CARD (1-18) 100.00 45.00
FIRST 100-CARDS OF PRINT RUN
SOME CARDS TRADE/REDEMPTION ONLY
TRADE CARD EXPIRATION 5/1/2000

❑ 1 Johnny Unitas 400.00 180.00
Peyton Manning
❑ 2 Johnny Unitas 200.00 90.00
❑ 3 Peyton Manning 200.00 90.00
❑ 4A Walter Payton 1000.00 450.00
Barry Sanders
❑ 4B Emmitt Smith 300.00 135.00
Fred Taylor
❑ 5A Walter Payton 400.00 180.00
❑ 5B Emmitt Smith 250.00 110.00
❑ 6A Barry Sanders 500.00 220.00
❑ 6B Fred Taylor 120.00 55.00

❑ 7 Earl Campbell Ricky Williams	400.00	180.00
❑ 8 Earl Campbell	100.00	45.00
❑ 9 Ricky Williams	300.00	135.00
❑ 10 Jim Brown Terrell Davis	400.00	180.00
❑ 11 Jim Brown	200.00	90.00
❑ 12 Terrell Davis	250.00	110.00
❑ 16 Cris Carter Randy Moss	400.00	180.00
❑ 17 Cris Carter	100.00	45.00
❑ 18 Randy Moss	250.00	110.00

1999 Donruss Elite Power Formulas

	MINT	NRMT
COMPLETE SET (30)	100.00	45.00
COMMON CARD (1-30)	1.50	.70
SEMISTARS	2.50	1.10

STATED PRINT RUN 3500 SERIAL #'d SETS

❑ 1 Randy Moss	10.00	4.50
❑ 2 Terrell Davis	6.00	2.70
❑ 3 Brett Favre	10.00	4.50
❑ 4 Dan Marino	10.00	4.50
❑ 5 Barry Sanders	10.00	4.50
❑ 6 Peyton Manning	10.00	4.50
❑ 7 John Elway	10.00	4.50
❑ 8 Fred Taylor	5.00	2.20
❑ 9 Emmitt Smith	6.00	2.70
❑ 10 Steve Young	4.00	1.80
❑ 11 Jerry Rice	6.00	2.70
❑ 12 Jake Plummer	5.00	2.20
❑ 13 Kordell Stewart	2.50	1.10
❑ 14 Mark Brunell	4.00	1.80
❑ 15 Drew Bledsoe	4.00	1.80
❑ 16 Eddie George	3.00	1.35
❑ 17 Troy Aikman	6.00	2.70
❑ 18 Warrick Dunn	2.50	1.10
❑ 19 Keyshawn Johnson	2.50	1.10
❑ 20 Jamal Anderson	2.50	1.10
❑ 21 Randall Cunningham	2.50	1.10
❑ 22 Doug Flutie	3.00	1.35
❑ 23 Jerome Bettis	2.50	1.10
❑ 24 Garrison Hearst	2.50	1.10
❑ 25 Curtis Martin	2.50	1.10
❑ 26 Corey Dillon	1.50	.70
❑ 27 Antowain Smith	2.50	1.10
❑ 28 Antonio Freeman	2.50	1.10
❑ 29 Terrell Owens	2.50	1.10
❑ 30 Carl Pickens	2.50	1.10

1999 Donruss Elite Primary Colors

	MINT	NRMT
COMPLETE SET (40)	150.00	70.00
COMMON YELLOW (1-40)	2.50	1.10

YELLOW PRINT RUN 1875 SER.#'d SETS
*BLUE CARDS: .6X TO 1.5X YELLOW
BLUE PRINT RUN 950 SERIAL #'d SET
*RED STARS: 10X TO 25X YELLOWS
*RED ROOKIES: 6X TO 15X YELLOWS
RED PRINT RUN 25 SERIAL #'d SET
*BLUE DIE CUT STARS: 5X TO 12X YELL.

*BLUE DIE CUT ROOKIES: 4X TO 10X
BLUE DIE CUT PRINT RUN 50 SER.#'d SETS
*RED DIE CUT STARS: 4X TO 10X YELLOWS
*RED DIE CUT ROOKIES: 2.5X TO 6X
RED DIE CUT PRINT RUN 75 SER.#'d SETS
*YELLOW DIE CUT STARS: 8X TO 20X
*YELLOW DIE CUT ROOKIES: 5X TO 12X
YELLOW DIE CUT PRINT RUN 25 SER.#'d SETS

❑ 1 Herman Moore	2.50	1.10
❑ 2 Marshall Faulk	2.50	1.10
❑ 3 Dorsey Levens	2.50	1.10
❑ 4 Napoleon Kaufman	2.50	1.10
❑ 5 Jamal Anderson	2.50	1.10
❑ 6 Edgerrin James	20.00	9.00
❑ 7 Troy Aikman	6.00	2.70
❑ 8 Cris Carter	2.50	1.10
❑ 9 Eddie George	3.00	1.35
❑ 10 Donovan McNabb	8.00	3.60
❑ 11 Drew Bledsoe	4.00	1.80
❑ 12 Daunte Culpepper	8.00	3.60
❑ 13 Mark Brunell	4.00	1.80
❑ 14 Corey Dillon	2.50	1.10
❑ 15 Kordell Stewart	2.50	1.10
❑ 16 Curtis Martin	2.50	1.10
❑ 17 Jake Plummer	5.00	2.20
❑ 18 Charlie Batch	4.00	1.80
❑ 19 Jerry Rice	6.00	2.70
❑ 20 Antonio Freeman	2.50	1.10
❑ 21 Steve Young	4.00	1.80
❑ 22 Steve McNair	2.50	1.10
❑ 23 Emmitt Smith	6.00	2.70
❑ 24 Terrell Owens	2.50	1.10
❑ 25 Fred Taylor	5.00	2.20
❑ 26 Joey Galloway	2.50	1.10
❑ 27 John Elway	10.00	4.50
❑ 28 Ryan Leaf	2.50	1.10
❑ 29 Barry Sanders	10.00	4.50
❑ 30 Ricky Williams	12.00	5.50
❑ 31 Dan Marino	10.00	4.50
❑ 32 Tim Couch	12.00	5.50
❑ 33 Brett Favre	10.00	4.50
❑ 34 Eric Moulds	2.50	1.10
❑ 35 Peyton Manning	10.00	4.50
❑ 36 Deion Sanders	2.50	1.10
❑ 37 Terrell Davis	6.00	2.70
❑ 38 Tim Brown	2.50	1.10
❑ 39 Randy Moss	10.00	4.50
❑ 40 Mike Alstott	2.50	1.10

2000 Donruss Elite

	MINT	NRMT
COMPLETE SET (200)	500.00	220.00
COMP.SET w/o SP's (100)	12.00	5.50
COMMON CARD (1-100)	.20	.09
SEMISTARS 1-100	.40	.18
UNL.STARS 1-100	.75	.35
COMMON CARD (101-125)	1.00	.45
SEMISTARS 101-125	2.00	.90
101-125 STATED ODDS 1:17		
COMMON ROOKIE (126-200)	5.00	2.20
ROOKIE SEMISTARS	8.00	3.60
ROOKIE UNLISTED STARS	10.00	4.50

ROOKIE STATED PRINT RUN 2000 SER.#'d SETS
ROOKIE REDEMPT.EXPIRATION: 5/31/2001

❑ 1 Jake Plummer	.75	.35
❑ 2 David Boston	.75	.35
❑ 3 Rob Moore	.40	.18
❑ 4 Chris Chandler	.40	.18
❑ 5 Tim Dwight	.75	.35
❑ 6 Terance Mathis	.40	.18
❑ 7 Jamal Anderson	.75	.35
❑ 8 Priest Holmes	.40	.18
❑ 9 Tony Banks	.40	.18
❑ 10 Shannon Sharpe	.40	.18
❑ 11 Qadry Ismail	.20	.09
❑ 12 Eric Moulds	.75	.35
❑ 13 Doug Flutie	1.00	.45
❑ 14 Antowain Smith	.75	.35
❑ 15 Peerless Price	.75	.35
❑ 16 Muhsin Muhammad	.40	.18
❑ 17 Tim Biakabutuka	.40	.18
❑ 18 Patrick Jeffers	.75	.35
❑ 19 Steve Beuerlein	.40	.18
❑ 20 Wesley Walls	.20	.09
❑ 21 Curtis Enis	.75	.35
❑ 22 Marcus Robinson	.75	.35
❑ 23 Carl Pickens	.40	.18
❑ 24 Corey Dillon	.75	.35
❑ 25 Akili Smith	1.00	.45
❑ 26 Darnay Scott	.40	.18
❑ 27 Kevin Johnson	.75	.35
❑ 28 Errict Rhett	.40	.18
❑ 29 Emmitt Smith	2.00	.90
❑ 30 Deion Sanders	.75	.35
❑ 31 Troy Aikman	2.00	.90
❑ 32 Joey Galloway	.75	.35
❑ 33 Michael Irvin	.40	.18
❑ 34 Rocket Ismail	.40	.18
❑ 35 Jason Tucker	.40	.18
❑ 36 Ed McCaffrey	.40	.18
❑ 37 Rod Smith	.40	.18
❑ 38 Brian Griese	1.00	.45
❑ 39 Terrell Davis	2.00	.90
❑ 40 Olandis Gary	1.00	.45
❑ 41 Charlie Batch	.75	.35
❑ 42 Johnnie Morton	.40	.18
❑ 43 Herman Moore	.75	.35
❑ 44 James Stewart	.40	.18
❑ 45 Dorsey Levens	.75	.35
❑ 46 Antonio Freeman	.75	.35
❑ 47 Brett Favre	3.00	1.35
❑ 48 Bill Schroeder	.40	.18
❑ 49 Peyton Manning	2.50	1.10
❑ 50 Keenan McCardell	.40	.18
❑ 51 Fred Taylor	1.25	.55
❑ 52 Jimmy Smith	.40	.18
❑ 53 Elvis Grbac	.40	.18
❑ 54 Tony Gonzalez	.40	.18
❑ 55 Derrick Alexander	.40	.18
❑ 56 Dan Marino	3.00	1.35
❑ 57 Tony Martin	.40	.18
❑ 58 James Johnson	.40	.18
❑ 59 Damon Huard	.75	.35
❑ 60 Thurman Thomas	.40	.18
❑ 61 Robert Smith	.75	.35
❑ 62 Randall Cunningham	.75	.35
❑ 63 Jeff George	.40	.18
❑ 64 Terry Glenn	.75	.35
❑ 65 Drew Bledsoe	1.25	.55
❑ 66 Jeff Blake	.40	.18
❑ 67 Amani Toomer	.20	.09
❑ 68 Kerry Collins	.40	.18
❑ 69 Joe Montgomery	.20	.09
❑ 70 Vinny Testaverde	.40	.18
❑ 71 Ray Lucas	.75	.35

❑ 72	Keyshawn Johnson	.75	.35
❑ 73	Wayne Chrebet	.40	.18
❑ 74	Napoleon Kaufman	.75	.35
❑ 75	Tim Brown	.75	.35
❑ 76	Rich Gannon	.40	.18
❑ 77	Duce Staley	.75	.35
❑ 78	Kordell Stewart	.75	.35
❑ 79	Jerome Bettis	.75	.35
❑ 80	Troy Edwards	.75	.35
❑ 81	Natrone Means	.20	.09
❑ 82	Curtis Conway	.40	.18
❑ 83	Jim Harbaugh	.40	.18
❑ 84	Junior Seau	.40	.18
❑ 85	Jermaine Fazande	.20	.09
❑ 86	Terrell Owens	.75	.35
❑ 87	Charlie Garner	.40	.18
❑ 88	Steve Young	1.25	.55
❑ 89	Jeff Garcia	.75	.35
❑ 90	Derrick Mayes	.40	.18
❑ 91	Ricky Watters	.40	.18
❑ 92	Az-Zahir Hakim	.40	.18
❑ 93	Torry Holt	.75	.35
❑ 94	Warren Sapp	.40	.18
❑ 95	Mike Alstott	.75	.35
❑ 96	Warrick Dunn	.75	.35
❑ 97	Kevin Dyson	.40	.18
❑ 98	Bruce Smith	.40	.18
❑ 99	Albert Connell	.20	.09
❑ 100	Michael Westbrook	.40	.18
❑ 101	Cade McNown	3.00	1.35
❑ 102	Tim Couch	5.00	2.20
❑ 103	John Elway	8.00	3.60
❑ 104	Barry Sanders	6.00	2.70
❑ 105	Germane Crowell	1.00	.45
❑ 106	Marvin Harrison	2.00	.90
❑ 107	Edgerrin James	8.00	3.60
❑ 108	Mark Brunell	3.00	1.35
❑ 109	Randy Moss	6.00	2.70
❑ 110	Cris Carter	2.00	.90
❑ 111	Daunte Culpepper	3.00	1.35
❑ 112	Ricky Williams	5.00	2.20
❑ 113	Curtis Martin	2.00	.90
❑ 114	Donovan McNabb	3.00	1.35
❑ 115	Jerry Rice	5.00	2.20
❑ 116	Jon Kitna	2.00	.90
❑ 117	Isaac Bruce	2.00	.90
❑ 118	Marshall Faulk	2.00	.90
❑ 119	Kurt Warner	10.00	4.50
❑ 120	Shaun King	3.00	1.35
❑ 121	Eddie George	2.50	1.10
❑ 122	Steve McNair	2.00	.90
❑ 123	Jevon Kearse	2.00	.90
❑ 124	Stephen Davis	2.00	.90
❑ 125	Brad Johnson	2.00	.90
❑ 126	Redemption Card	10.00	4.50
❑ 127	Peter Warrick RC	50.00	22.00
❑ 128	Courtney Brown RC	20.00	9.00
❑ 129	Plaxico Burress RC	25.00	11.00
❑ 130	Corey Simon RC	10.00	4.50
❑ 131	Thomas Jones RC	30.00	13.50
❑ 132	Travis Taylor RC	20.00	9.00
❑ 133	Shaun Alexander RC	30.00	13.50
❑ 134	Deon Grant RC	8.00	3.60
❑ 135	Chris Redman RC	15.00	6.75
❑ 136	Chad Pennington RC	40.00	18.00
❑ 137	Jamal Lewis RC	30.00	13.50
❑ 138	Brian Urlacher RC	12.00	5.50
❑ 139	Keith Bulluck RC	10.00	4.50
❑ 140	Bubba Franks RC	12.00	5.50
❑ 141	Dez White RC	12.00	5.50
❑ 142	Na'il Diggs RC	8.00	3.60
❑ 143	Ahmed Plummer RC	8.00	3.60
❑ 144	Ron Dayne RC	50.00	22.00
❑ 145	Shaun Ellis RC	8.00	3.60
❑ 146	Sylvester Morris RC	12.00	5.50
❑ 147	Deltha O'Neal RC	8.00	3.60
❑ 148	Raynoch Thompson RC	8.00	3.60
❑ 149	R.Jay Soward RC	12.00	5.50
❑ 150	Mario Edwards RC	5.00	2.20
❑ 151	John Engelberger RC	5.00	2.20
❑ 152	D.Goodrich RC Trade	10.00	4.50
❑ 153	Sherrod Gideon RC	8.00	3.60
❑ 154	John Abraham RC	8.00	3.60
❑ 155	Ben Kelly RC Trade	10.00	4.50
❑ 156	Travis Prentice RC	12.00	5.50
❑ 157	Darrell Jackson RC	10.00	4.50
❑ 158	Giovanni Carmazzi RC	20.00	9.00
❑ 159	Anthony Lucas RC	10.00	4.50
❑ 160	Danny Farmer RC	10.00	4.50
❑ 161	Dennis Northcutt RC	12.00	5.50
❑ 162	Troy Walters RC	10.00	4.50
❑ 163	Laveranues Coles RC	10.00	4.50
❑ 164	Tee Martin RC	15.00	6.75
❑ 165	J.R. Redmond RC	15.00	6.75
❑ 166	Tim Rattay RC	12.00	5.50
❑ 167	Jerry Porter RC	12.00	5.50
❑ 168	Sebastian Janikowski RC	8.00	3.60
❑ 169	Michael Wiley RC	12.00	5.50
❑ 170	Reuben Droughns RC	12.00	5.50
❑ 171	Trung Canidate RC	10.00	4.50
❑ 172	Shyrone Stith RC	8.00	3.60
❑ 173	Chris Hovan RC	8.00	3.60
❑ 174	Redemption Card	10.00	4.50
❑ 175	Redemption Card	10.00	4.50
❑ 176	Trevor Gaylor RC	8.00	3.60
❑ 177	Chris Cole RC	8.00	3.60
❑ 178	Hank Poteat RC	8.00	3.60
❑ 179	Darren Howard RC	8.00	3.60
❑ 180	Rob Morris RC	8.00	3.60
❑ 181	Redemption Card	10.00	4.50
❑ 182	Marc Bulger RC	10.00	4.50
❑ 183	Tom Brady RC	10.00	4.50
❑ 184	Todd Husak RC	10.00	4.50
❑ 185	Gari Scott RC	10.00	4.50
❑ 186	Erron Kinney RC	8.00	3.60
❑ 187	Redemption Card	10.00	4.50
❑ 188	Sammy Morris RC	10.00	4.50
❑ 189	Rondell Mealey RC	8.00	3.60
❑ 190	D.Chapman RC Trade	10.00	4.50
❑ 191	Ron Dugans RC	10.00	4.50
❑ 192	Deon Dyer RC	8.00	3.60
❑ 193	Fred Robbins RC	5.00	2.20
❑ 194	Redemption Card	10.00	4.50
❑ 195	Mareno Philyaw RC	8.00	3.60
❑ 196	T.Hamner RC Trade	10.00	4.50
❑ 197	Jarious Jackson RC	10.00	4.50
❑ 198	Anthony Becht RC	10.00	4.50
❑ 199	Joe Hamilton RC	10.00	4.50
❑ 200	Todd Pinkston RC	10.00	4.50

2000 Donruss Elite Aspirations

	MINT	NRMT
COMMON CARD/80-99	6.00	2.70
SEMISTARS/80-99	12.00	5.50
COMMON CARD/65-79	5.00	2.20
SEMISTARS/65-79	8.00	3.60
UNLISTED STARS/65-79	15.00	6.75
COMMON CARD/45-64	10.00	4.50
SEMISTARS/45-64	20.00	9.00
COMMON CARD/20-29	10.00	4.50
SEMISTARS/20-29	20.00	9.00
UNLISTED STARS/20-29	40.00	18.00
COMMON CARD/10-19	15.00	6.75
SEMISTARS/10-19	30.00	13.50
UNLISTED STARS/10-19	60.00	27.00

CARDS #'d UNDER 10 NOT PRICED

❑ 1	Jake Plummer/84	12.00	5.50
❑ 2	David Boston/11	60.00	27.00
❑ 3	Rob Moore/15	30.00	13.50
❑ 4	Chris Chandler/88	6.00	2.70
❑ 5	Tim Dwight/17	60.00	27.00
❑ 6	Terance Mathis/19	30.00	13.50
❑ 7	Jamal Anderson/68	15.00	6.75
❑ 8	Priest Holmes/67	15.00	6.75
❑ 9	Tony Banks/88	6.00	2.70
❑ 10	Shannon Sharpe/16	30.00	13.50
❑ 11	Qadry Ismail/13	15.00	6.75
❑ 12	Eric Moulds/20	40.00	18.00
❑ 13	Doug Flutie/93	20.00	9.00
❑ 14	Antowain Smith/77	15.00	6.75
❑ 15	Peerless Price/19	60.00	27.00
❑ 16	Muhsin Muhammad/13	30.00	13.50
❑ 17	Tim Biakabutuka/79	8.00	3.60
❑ 18	Patrick Jeffers/17	60.00	27.00
❑ 19	Steve Beuerlein/93	6.00	2.70
❑ 20	Wesley Walls/15	15.00	6.75
❑ 21	Curtis Enis/56	20.00	9.00
❑ 22	Marcus Robinson/12	60.00	27.00
❑ 23	Carl Pickens/19	30.00	13.50
❑ 24	Corey Dillon/72	15.00	6.75
❑ 25	Akili Smith/89	12.00	5.50
❑ 26	Darnay Scott/14	30.00	13.50
❑ 27	Kevin Johnson/14	60.00	27.00
❑ 28	Errict Rhett/68	5.00	2.20
❑ 29	Emmitt Smith/78	50.00	22.00
❑ 30	Deion Sanders/79	15.00	6.75
❑ 31	Troy Aikman/92	40.00	18.00
❑ 32	Joey Galloway/16	60.00	27.00
❑ 33	Michael Irvin/12	30.00	13.50
❑ 34	Rocket Ismail/19	30.00	13.50
❑ 35	Jason Tucker/13	30.00	13.50
❑ 36	Ed McCaffrey/13	60.00	27.00
❑ 37	Rod Smith/20	20.00	9.00
❑ 38	Brian Griese/86	20.00	9.00
❑ 39	Terrell Davis/70	50.00	22.00
❑ 40	Olandis Gary/78	15.00	6.75
❑ 41	Charlie Batch/90	12.00	5.50
❑ 42	Johnnie Morton/13	30.00	13.50
❑ 43	Herman Moore/16	60.00	27.00
❑ 44	James Stewart/67	8.00	3.60
❑ 45	Dorsey Levens/75	15.00	6.75
❑ 46	Antonio Freeman/14	60.00	27.00
❑ 47	Brett Favre/96	60.00	27.00
❑ 48	Bill Schroeder/16	30.00	13.50
❑ 49	Peyton Manning/82	50.00	22.00
❑ 50	Keenan McCardell/13	30.00	13.50
❑ 51	Fred Taylor/72	30.00	13.50
❑ 52	Jimmy Smith/18	30.00	13.50
❑ 53	Elvis Grbac/82	6.00	2.70
❑ 54	Tony Gonzalez/12	30.00	13.50
❑ 55	Derrick Alexander/18	30.00	13.50
❑ 56	Dan Marino/87	60.00	27.00
❑ 57	Tony Martin/20	10.00	4.50
❑ 58	James Johnson/68	8.00	3.60
❑ 59	Damon Huard/89	12.00	5.50
❑ 60	Thurman Thomas/66	15.00	6.75
❑ 61	Robert Smith/74	15.00	6.75
❑ 62	Randall Cunningham/93	12.00	5.50
❑ 63	Jeff George/97	6.00	2.70
❑ 64	Terry Glenn/12	60.00	27.00
❑ 65	Drew Bledsoe/89	25.00	11.00
❑ 66	Jeff Blake/92	6.00	2.70
❑ 67	Amani Toomer/19	15.00	6.75
❑ 68	Kerry Collins/95	6.00	2.70
❑ 69	Joe Montgomery/75	5.00	2.20
❑ 70	Vinny Testaverde/84	12.00	5.50
❑ 71	Ray Lucas/94	12.00	5.50
❑ 72	Keyshawn Johnson/81	12.00	5.50
❑ 73	Wayne Chrebet/20	20.00	9.00
❑ 74	Napoleon Kaufman/74	15.00	6.75
❑ 75	Tim Brown/19	60.00	27.00
❑ 76	Rich Gannon/88	6.00	2.70
❑ 77	Duce Staley/78	15.00	6.75
❑ 78	Kordell Stewart/90	12.00	5.50
❑ 79	Jerome Bettis/64	20.00	9.00
❑ 80	Troy Edwards/19	60.00	27.00
❑ 81	Natrone Means/80	6.00	2.70
❑ 82	Curtis Conway/20	20.00	9.00
❑ 83	Jim Harbaugh/96	6.00	2.70
❑ 84	Junior Seau/45	10.00	4.50
❑ 85	Jermaine Fazande/65	5.00	2.20
❑ 86	Terrell Owens/19	60.00	27.00
❑ 87	Charlie Garner/75	8.00	3.60
❑ 88	Steve Young/92	25.00	11.00
❑ 89	Jeff Garcia/95	12.00	5.50
❑ 90	Derrick Mayes/13	30.00	13.50
❑ 91	Ricky Watters/68	8.00	3.60
❑ 92	Az-Zahir Hakim/19	15.00	6.75
❑ 93	Torry Holt/12	60.00	27.00
❑ 94	Warren Sapp/1		
❑ 95	Mike Alstott/60	20.00	9.00
❑ 96	Warrick Dunn/72	15.00	6.75
❑ 97	Kevin Dyson/13	30.00	13.50
❑ 98	Bruce Smith/22	10.00	4.50
❑ 99	Albert Connell/17	15.00	6.75
❑ 100	Michael Westbrook/18	30.00	13.50
❑ 101	Cade McNown/92	20.00	9.00
❑ 102	Tim Couch/98	30.00	13.50
❑ 103	John Elway/93	60.00	27.00
❑ 104	Barry Sanders/80	50.00	22.00
❑ 105	Germane Crowell/18	30.00	13.50
❑ 106	Marvin Harrison/12	60.00	27.00
❑ 107	Edgerrin James/68	60.00	27.00
❑ 108	Mark Brunell/92	25.00	11.00

❑ 109 Randy Moss/16 .... 150.00 70.00
❑ 110 Cris Carter/20 .... 40.00 18.00
❑ 111 Daunte Culpepper/88 20.00 9.00
❑ 112 Ricky Williams/66 ...... 40.00 18.00
❑ 113 Curtis Martin/72 .... 15.00 6.75
❑ 114 Donovan McNabb/95 20.00 9.00
❑ 115 Jerry Rice/20 .... 120.00 55.00
❑ 116 Jon Kitna/93 .... 12.00 5.50
❑ 117 Isaac Bruce/20 .... 40.00 18.00
❑ 118 Marshall Faulk/72 ...... 15.00 6.75
❑ 119 Kurt Warner/87 .... 80.00 36.00
❑ 120 Shaun King/90 .... 20.00 9.00
❑ 121 Eddie George/73 .... 25.00 11.00
❑ 122 Steve McNair/91 .... 12.00 5.50
❑ 123 Jevon Kearse/10 .... 60.00 27.00
❑ 124 Stephen Davis/52 ...... 20.00 9.00
❑ 125 Brad Johnson/86 .... 12.00 5.50
❑ 126 Redemption Card ....
❑ 127 Peter Warrick/91 ...... 100.00 45.00
❑ 128 Courtney Brown/14 .. 120.00 55.00
❑ 129 Plaxico Burress/96 .... 50.00 22.00
❑ 130 Corey Simon/47 .... 30.00 13.50
❑ 131 Thomas Jones/94 ...... 60.00 27.00
❑ 132 Travis Taylor/81 .... 40.00 18.00
❑ 133 Shaun Alexander/63 .. 60.00 27.00
❑ 134 Deon Grant/93 .... 15.00 6.75
❑ 135 Chris Redman/93 ...... 30.00 13.50
❑ 136 Chad Pennington/90 .. 80.00 36.00
❑ 137 Jamal Lewis/69 .... 80.00 36.00
❑ 138 Brian Urlacher/56 ...... 40.00 18.00
❑ 139 Keith Bulluck/67 .... 25.00 11.00
❑ 140 Bubba Franks/12 .... 80.00 36.00
❑ 141 Dez White/78 .... 30.00 13.50
❑ 142 Na'il Diggs/68 .... 20.00 9.00
❑ 143 Ahmed Plummer/81 .. 15.00 6.75
❑ 144 Ron Dayne/67 .... 100.00 45.00
❑ 145 Shaun Ellis/7 ....
❑ 146 Sylvester Morris/15 .... 80.00 36.00
❑ 147 Deltha O'Neal/92 .... 15.00 6.75
❑ 148 Raynoch Thompson/54 25.00 11.00
❑ 149 R.Jay Soward/82 .... 25.00 11.00
❑ 150 Mario Edwards/85 ...... 12.00 5.50
❑ 151 John Engelberger/4 ....
❑ 152 Dwayne Goodrich Trade ..
❑ 153 Sherrod Gideon/89 .... 15.00 6.75
❑ 154 John Abraham/5 ....
❑ 155 Ben Kelly Trade ....
❑ 156 Travis Prentice/59 ...... 40.00 18.00
❑ 157 Darrell Jackson/91 .... 20.00 9.00
❑ 158 Giovanni Carmazzi/81 40.00 18.00
❑ 159 Anthony Lucas/20 ...... 50.00 22.00
❑ 160 Danny Farmer/13 ...... 60.00 27.00
❑ 161 Dennis Northcutt/92 .. 25.00 11.00
❑ 162 Troy Walters/95 .... 20.00 9.00
❑ 163 Laveranues Coles/93 20.00 9.00
❑ 164 Tee Martin/83 .... 30.00 13.50
❑ 165 J.R. Redmond/79 ...... 40.00 18.00
❑ 166 Tim Rattay/87 .... 25.00 11.00
❑ 167 Jerry Porter/99 .... 25.00 11.00
❑ 168 Sebastian Janikowski/62 25.00 11.00
❑ 169 Michael Wiley/95 .... 25.00 11.00
❑ 170 Reuben Droughns/78 30.00 13.50
❑ 171 Trung Canidate/70 .... 25.00 11.00
❑ 172 Shyrone Stith/62 .... 25.00 11.00
❑ 173 Chris Hovan/5 ....
❑ 174 Redemption Card ....
❑ 175 Redemption Card ....
❑ 176 Trevor Gaylor/91 .... 15.00 6.75
❑ 177 Chris Cole/20 .... 40.00 18.00
❑ 178 Hank Poteat/69 .... 20.00 9.00
❑ 179 Darren Howard/51 ...... 25.00 11.00
❑ 180 Rob Morris/56 .... 25.00 11.00
❑ 181 Redemption Card ....
❑ 182 Marc Bulger/90 .... 20.00 9.00
❑ 183 Tom Brady/90 .... 20.00 9.00
❑ 184 Todd Husak/93 .... 20.00 9.00
❑ 185 Gari Scott/14 .... 60.00 27.00
❑ 186 Erron Kinney/12 .... 60.00 27.00
❑ 187 Redemption Card ....
❑ 188 Sammy Morris/95 ...... 20.00 9.00
❑ 189 Rondell Mealey/93 .... 15.00 6.75
❑ 190 Doug Chapman Trade......
❑ 191 Ron Dugans/20 .... 50.00 22.00
❑ 192 Fred Robbins/10 .... 30.00 13.50
❑ 192 Deon Dyer/62 .... 25.00 11.00
❑ 194 Redemption Card ....
❑ 195 Mareno Philyaw/92 .... 15.00 6.75
❑ 196 Thomas Hamner Trade ....
❑ 197 Jarious Jackson/93 .... 20.00 9.00
❑ 198 Anthony Becht/18 ...... 60.00 27.00
❑ 199 Joe Hamilton/86 .... 20.00 9.00
❑ 200 Todd Pinkston/20 ...... 50.00 22.00

2000 Donruss Elite Rookie Die Cuts

	MINT	NRMT
COMMON CARD (126-200)	8.00	3.60

*DIE CUTS: .6X TO 1.5X BASE ROOKIE CARD

2000 Donruss Elite Status

	MINT	NRMT
COMMON CARD 80-99	4.00	1.80
SEMISTARS 80-99	6.00	2.70
UNLISTED STARS 80-99	12.00	5.50
COMMON CARD 65-79	5.00	2.20
COMMON CARD 45-64	10.00	4.50
SEMISTARS 45-64	20.00	9.00
COMMON CARD 30-44	8.00	3.60
SEMISTARS 30-44	15.00	6.75
UNLISTED STARS 30-44	30.00	13.50
COMMON CARD 20-29	10.00	4.50
SEMISTARS 20-29	20.00	9.00
UNLISTED STARS 20-29	40.00	18.00
COMMON CARD 10-19	30.00	13.50
SEMISTARS 10-19	60.00	27.00

CARDS #'d UNDER 10 NOT PRICED

❑ 1 Jake Plummer/16 .... 50.00 22.00
❑ 2 David Boston/89 .... 12.00 5.50
❑ 3 Rob Moore/85 .... 6.00 2.70
❑ 4 Chris Chandler/12 .... 30.00 13.50
❑ 5 Tim Dwight/83 .... 12.00 5.50
❑ 6 Terance Mathis/81 .... 6.00 2.70
❑ 7 Jamal Anderson/32 .... 30.00 13.50
❑ 8 Priest Holmes/33 .... 15.00 6.75
❑ 9 Tony Banks/12 .... 30.00 13.50
❑ 10 Shannon Sharpe/84 ...... 6.00 2.70
❑ 11 Qadry Ismail/87 .... 4.00 1.80
❑ 12 Eric Moulds/80 .... 12.00 5.50
❑ 13 Doug Flutie/7 ....
❑ 14 Antowain Smith/23 ...... 40.00 18.00
❑ 15 Peerless Price/81 .... 12.00 5.50
❑ 16 Muhsin Muhammad/87 .. 6.00 2.70
❑ 17 Tim Biakabutuka/21 .... 20.00 9.00
❑ 18 Patrick Jeffers/83 .... 12.00 5.50
❑ 19 Steve Beuerlein/7 ....
❑ 20 Wesley Walls/85 .... 4.00 1.80
❑ 21 Curtis Enis/44 .... 30.00 13.50
❑ 22 Marcus Robinson/88 .... 12.00 5.50
❑ 23 Carl Pickens/81 .... 6.00 2.70
❑ 24 Corey Dillon/28 .... 40.00 18.00
❑ 25 Akili Smith/11 .... 50.00 22.00
❑ 26 Darnay Scott/86 .... 6.00 2.70
❑ 27 Kevin Johnson/86 .... 12.00 5.50
❑ 28 Errict Rhett/32 .... 8.00 3.60
❑ 29 Emmitt Smith/22 .... 100.00 45.00
❑ 30 Deion Sanders/21 .... 40.00 18.00
❑ 31 Troy Aikman/8 ....
❑ 32 Joey Galloway/84 .... 12.00 5.50
❑ 33 Michael Irvin/88 .... 12.00 5.50
❑ 34 Rocket Ismail/81 .... 6.00 2.70
❑ 35 Jason Tucker/87 .... 6.00 2.70
❑ 36 Ed McCaffrey/87 .... 6.00 2.70
❑ 37 Rod Smith/80 .... 6.00 2.70
❑ 38 Brian Griese/14 .... 60.00 27.00
❑ 39 Terrell Davis/30 .... 80.00 36.00
❑ 40 Olandis Gary/22 .... 40.00 18.00
❑ 41 Charlie Batch/10 .... 50.00 22.00
❑ 42 Johnnie Morton/87 .... 4.00 1.80
❑ 43 Herman Moore/84 .... 12.00 5.50
❑ 44 James Stewart/33 .... 15.00 6.75
❑ 45 Dorsey Levens/25 .... 40.00 18.00
❑ 46 Antonio Freeman/86 .... 12.00 5.50
❑ 47 Brett Favre/4 ....
❑ 48 Bill Schroeder/84 .... 6.00 2.70
❑ 49 Peyton Manning/18 .... 200.00 90.00
❑ 50 Keenan McCardell/87 .... 6.00 2.70
❑ 51 Fred Taylor/28 .... 60.00 27.00
❑ 52 Jimmy Smith/82 .... 6.00 2.70
❑ 53 Elvis Grbac/18 .... 30.00 13.50
❑ 54 Tony Gonzalez/88 .... 6.00 2.70
❑ 55 Derrick Alexander/82 ...... 6.00 2.70
❑ 56 Dan Marino/13 .... 250.00 110.00
❑ 57 Tony Martin/80 .... 4.00 1.80
❑ 58 James Johnson/32 ...... 15.00 6.75
❑ 59 Damon Huard/11 .... 50.00 22.00
❑ 60 Thurman Thomas/34 .... 30.00 13.50
❑ 61 Robert Smith/26 .... 40.00 18.00
❑ 62 Randall Cunningham/7 ......
❑ 63 Jeff George/3 ....
❑ 64 Terry Glenn/88 .... 12.00 5.50
❑ 65 Drew Bledsoe/11 .... 100.00 45.00
❑ 66 Jeff Blake/8 ....
❑ 67 Amani Toomer/81 .... 4.00 1.80
❑ 68 Kerry Collins/5 ....
❑ 69 Joe Montgomery/25 .... 10.00 4.50
❑ 70 Vinny Testaverde/16 .... 30.00 13.50
❑ 71 Ray Lucas/6 ....
❑ 72 Keyshawn Johnson/19 50.00 22.00
❑ 73 Wayne Chrebet/80 .... 6.00 2.70
❑ 74 Napoleon Kaufman/26 40.00 18.00
❑ 75 Tim Brown/81 .... 12.00 5.50
❑ 76 Rich Gannon/12 .... 30.00 13.50
❑ 77 Duce Staley/22 .... 40.00 18.00
❑ 78 Kordell Stewart/10 .... 50.00 22.00
❑ 79 Jerome Bettis/36 .... 30.00 13.50
❑ 80 Troy Edwards/81 .... 12.00 5.50
❑ 81 Natrone Means/20 .... 20.00 9.00
❑ 82 Curtis Conway/80 .... 6.00 2.70
❑ 83 Jim Harbaugh/4 ....
❑ 84 Junior Seau/55 .... 10.00 4.50
❑ 85 Jermaine Fazande/35 .... 8.00 3.60
❑ 86 Terrell Owens/81 .... 12.00 5.50
❑ 87 Charlie Garner/25 .... 20.00 9.00
❑ 88 Steve Young/8 ....
❑ 89 Jeff Garcia/5 ....
❑ 90 Derrick Mayes/87 .... 6.00 2.70
❑ 91 Ricky Watters/32 .... 15.00 6.75
❑ 92 Az-Zahir Hakim/81 .... 4.00 1.80
❑ 93 Torry Holt/88 .... 12.00 5.50
❑ 94 Warren Sapp/99 .... 6.00 2.70
❑ 95 Mike Alstott/40 .... 30.00 13.50
❑ 96 Warrick Dunn/28 .... 40.00 18.00
❑ 97 Kevin Dyson/87 .... 6.00 2.70
❑ 98 Bruce Smith/78 .... 5.00 2.20
❑ 99 Albert Connell/83 .... 4.00 1.80
❑ 100 Michael Westbrook/82.. 6.00 2.70
❑ 101 Cade McNown/8 ....
❑ 102 Tim Couch/2 ....

❑ 103 John Elway/7
❑ 104 Barry Sanders/20 .... 150.00 70.00
❑ 105 Germane Crowell/82 .... 6.00 2.70
❑ 106 Marvin Harrison/88 .... 12.00 5.50
❑ 107 Edgerrin James/32 .. 100.00 45.00
❑ 108 Mark Brunell/8
❑ 109 Randy Moss/84 .... 50.00 22.00
❑ 110 Cris Carter/80 .... 12.00 5.50
❑ 111 Daunte Culpepper/12 80.00 36.00
❑ 112 Ricky Williams/34 ...... 60.00 27.00
❑ 113 Curtis Martin/28.......... 40.00 18.00
❑ 114 Donovan McNabb/5
❑ 115 Jerry Rice/80.............. 40.00 18.00
❑ 116 Jon Kitna/7
❑ 117 Isaac Bruce/80 .... 12.00 5.50
❑ 118 Marshall Faulk/28 ...... 40.00 18.00
❑ 119 Kurt Warner/13 .... 300.00 135.00
❑ 120 Shaun King/10............ 80.00 36.00
❑ 121 Eddie George/27 .... 30.00 13.50
❑ 122 Steve McNair/9
❑ 123 Jevon Kearse/90 .... 12.00 5.50
❑ 124 Stephen Davis/48 ...... 20.00 9.00
❑ 125 Brad Johnson/14......... 50.00 22.00
❑ 126 Redemption Card
❑ 127 Peter Warrick/9
❑ 128 Courtney Brown/86 .... 40.00 18.00
❑ 129 Plaxico Burress/4
❑ 130 Corey Simon/53 .... 30.00 13.50
❑ 131 Thomas Jones/6
❑ 132 Travis Taylor/19 ...... 120.00 55.00
❑ 133 Shaun Alexander/37 150.00 70.00
❑ 134 Deon Grant/7
❑ 135 Chris Redman/7
❑ 136 Chad Pennington/10 350.00 160.00
❑ 137 Jamal Lewis/31 .... 150.00 70.00
❑ 138 Brian Urlacher/44 ...... 50.00 22.00
❑ 139 Keith Bulluck/33 .... 40.00 18.00
❑ 140 Bubba Franks/88........ 25.00 11.00
❑ 141 Dez White/22.............. 60.00 27.00
❑ 142 Na'il Diggs/32 .... 30.00 13.50
❑ 143 Ahmed Plummer/19 .. 60.00 27.00
❑ 144 Ron Dayne/33 .... 250.00 110.00
❑ 145 Shaun Ellis/93 .... 15.00 6.75
❑ 146 Sylvester Morris/85 .... 25.00 11.00
❑ 147 Deltha O'Neal/8
❑ 148 Raynoch Thompson/46 25.00 11.00
❑ 149 R.Jay Soward/18.......... 80.00 36.00
❑ 150 Mario Edwards/15 ...... 30.00 13.50
❑ 151 John Engelberger/96.. 12.00 5.50
❑ 152 Dwayne Goodrich Trade
❑ 153 Sherrod Gideon/11 .... 60.00 27.00
❑ 154 John Abraham/95 ...... 15.00 6.75
❑ 155 Ben Kelly Trade
❑ 156 Travis Prentice/41 ...... 50.00 22.00
❑ 157 Darrell Jackson/9
❑ 158 Giovanni Carmazzi/19 120.00 55.00
❑ 159 Anthony Lucas/80 ...... 20.00 9.00
❑ 160 Danny Farmer/87 ...... 20.00 9.00
❑ 161 Dennis Northcutt/8
❑ 162 Troy Walters/5
❑ 163 Laveranues Coles/7
❑ 164 Tee Martin/17 .... 100.00 45.00
❑ 165 J.R. Redmond/21 ...... 80.00 36.00
❑ 166 Tim Rattay/13 .... 80.00 36.00
❑ 167 Jerry Porter/1
❑ 168 Sebastian Janikowski/38 30.00 13.50
❑ 169 Michael Wiley/5
❑ 170 Reuben Droughns/22 60.00 27.00
❑ 171 Trung Canidate/30 .... 40.00 18.00
❑ 172 Shyrone Stith/38 .... 30.00 13.50
❑ 173 Chris Hovan/95 .... 15.00 6.75
❑ 174 Redemption Card
❑ 175 Redemption Card
❑ 176 Trevor Gaylor/9
❑ 177 Chris Cole/80 .... 15.00 6.75
❑ 178 Hank Poteat/31 .... 30.00 13.50
❑ 179 Darren Howard/49...... 25.00 11.00
❑ 180 Rob Morris/44 .... 30.00 13.50
❑ 181 Redemption Card
❑ 182 Marc Bulger/10 .... 60.00 27.00
❑ 183 Tom Brady/10 .... 60.00 27.00
❑ 184 Todd Husak/7
❑ 185 Gari Scott/86.............. 20.00 9.00
❑ 186 Erron Kinney/88 .... 15.00 6.75
❑ 187 Redemption Card
❑ 188 Sammy Morris/5
❑ 189 Rondell Mealey/7
❑ 190 Doug Chapman Trade
❑ 191 Ron Dugans/80.......... 20.00 9.00
❑ 192 Deon Dyer/38 .... 30.00 13.50
❑ 193 Fred Robbins/90 .... 12.00 5.50
❑ 194 Redemption Card
❑ 195 Mareno Philyaw/8
❑ 196 Thomas Hamner Trade
❑ 197 Jarious Jackson/7
❑ 198 Anthony Becht/82 ...... 20.00 9.00
❑ 199 Joe Hamilton/14 .... 60.00 27.00
❑ 200 Todd Pinkston/80 ...... 20.00 9.00

2000 Donruss Elite Craftsmen

	MINT	NRMT
COMPLETE SET (40)	80.00	36.00
COMMON CARD (C1-C40)	1.50	.70

STATED PRINT RUN 2500 SERIAL #'d SETS
*MASTERS VETS: 5X TO 12X BASIC INSERTS
*MASTERS ROOKIES: 3X TO 8X BASIC INS.
MASTERS PRINT RUN 50 SERIAL #'d SETS

❑ C1 Dan Marino.................... 6.00 2.70
❑ C2 Edgerrin James 5.00 2.20
❑ C3 Peyton Manning 5.00 2.20
❑ C4 Drew Bledsoe 2.50 1.10
❑ C5 Doug Flutie.................... 2.00 .90
❑ C6 Curtis Martin.................. 1.50 .70
❑ C7 Eddie George .... 2.00 .90
❑ C8 Steve McNair .... 1.50 .70
❑ C9 Fred Taylor.................... 2.50 1.10
❑ C10 Mark Brunell 2.50 1.10
❑ C11 Tim Couch 3.00 1.35
❑ C12 Corey Dillon .... 1.50 .70
❑ C13 Terrell Davis 4.00 1.80
❑ C14 Jon Kitna...................... 1.50 .70
❑ C15 Emmitt Smith 4.00 1.80
❑ C16 Troy Aikman 4.00 1.80
❑ C17 Stephen Davis .... 1.50 .70
❑ C18 Brad Johnson .... 1.50 .70
❑ C19 Jake Plummer.............. 1.50 .70
❑ C20 Brett Favre 6.00 2.70
❑ C21 Barry Sanders.............. 5.00 2.20
❑ C22 Marshall Faulk .... 1.50 .70
❑ C23 Kurt Warner 8.00 3.60
❑ C24 Ricky Williams.............. 3.00 1.35
❑ C25 Steve Young................ 2.50 1.10
❑ C26 Randy Moss 5.00 2.20
❑ C27 John Elway.................. 6.00 2.70
❑ C28 Jerry Rice 4.00 1.80
❑ C29 Tim Brown .... 1.50 .70
❑ C30 Cris Carter .... 1.50 .70
❑ C31 Antonio Freeman .... 1.50 .70
❑ C32 Joey Galloway .... 1.50 .70
❑ C33 Terry Glenn.................. 1.50 .70
❑ C34 Marvin Harrison .... 1.50 .70
❑ C35 Keyshawn Johnson .... 1.50 .70
❑ C36 Eric Moulds.................. 1.50 .70
❑ C37 Isaac Bruce.................. 1.50 .70
❑ C38 Peter Warrick 12.00 5.50
❑ C39 Plaxico Burress............ 6.00 2.70
❑ C40 Thomas Jones 8.00 3.60

2000 Donruss Elite Down and Distance

	MINT	NRMT
COMMON CARD (1A-12D)	4.00	1.80

CARD BACKS CARRY DD PREFIX
A,B,C,D FOR 1ST,2ND,3RD,4TH DOWN
CARDS SERIAL #'d TO A 1999 SEASON STAT
CARDS #'d UNDER 10 NOT PRICED

❑ 1A Randy Moss/611.......... 12.00 5.50
❑ 1B Randy Moss/493.......... 15.00 6.75
❑ 1C Randy Moss/263.......... 20.00 9.00
❑ 1D Randy Moss/46............ 40.00 18.00
❑ 2A Brett Favre/1386.......... 12.00 5.50
❑ 2B Brett Favre/1543.......... 10.00 4.50
❑ 2C Brett Favre/1139.......... 12.00 5.50
❑ 2D Brett Favre/23............ 100.00 45.00
❑ 3A Dan Marino/1023 .... 12.00 5.50
❑ 3B Dan Marino/855 .... 15.00 6.75
❑ 3C Dan Marino/505 .... 20.00 9.00
❑ 3D Dan Marino/65 .... 50.00 22.00
❑ 4A Peyton Manning/1857.... 8.00 3.60
❑ 4B Peyton Manning/1219.. 10.00 4.50
❑ 4C Peyton Manning/1029.. 10.00 4.50
❑ 4D Peyton Manning/30...... 80.00 36.00
❑ 5A Emmitt Smith/832 .... 10.00 4.50
❑ 5B Emmitt Smith/506 .... 12.00 5.50
❑ 5C Emmitt Smith/55 .... 30.00 13.50
❑ 5D Emmitt Smith/4
❑ 6A Jerry Rice/391.............. 12.00 5.50
❑ 6B Jerry Rice/238.............. 15.00 6.75
❑ 6C Jerry Rice/176 .... 15.00 6.75
❑ 6D Jerry Rice/25 .... 60.00 27.00
❑ 7A Mark Brunell/1066.......... 5.00 2.20
❑ 7B Mark Brunell/1112.......... 5.00 2.20
❑ 7C Mark Brunell/878 .... 6.00 2.70
❑ 7D Mark Brunell/4
❑ 8A Eddie George/716.......... 5.00 2.20
❑ 8B Eddie George/487.......... 6.00 2.70
❑ 8C Eddie George/98 .... 10.00 4.50
❑ 8D Eddie George/3
❑ 9A Marshall Faulk/762 .... 4.00 1.80
❑ 9B Marshall Faulk/512 .... 5.00 2.20
❑ 9C Marshall Faulk/101 .... 8.00 3.60
❑ 9D Marshall Faulk/6
❑ 10A Kurt Warner/1682 ...... 12.00 5.50
❑ 10B Kurt Warner/1336 ...... 15.00 6.75
❑ 10C Kurt Warner/1307 ...... 15.00 6.75
❑ 10D Kurt Warner/28 .... 120.00 55.00
❑ 11A Edgerrin James/894 .. 12.00 5.50
❑ 11B Edgerrin James/531 .. 15.00 6.75
❑ 11C Edgerrin James/126 .. 25.00 11.00
❑ 11D Edgerrin James/2
❑ 12A Tim Couch/940 .... 8.00 3.60
❑ 12B Tim Couch/908 .... 8.00 3.60
❑ 12C Tim Couch/564 .... 10.00 4.50
❑ 12D Tim Couch/35 .... 60.00 27.00

2000 Donruss Elite Down and Distance Die Cuts

	MINT	NRMT
COMMON CARD (1A-12D)	8.00	3.60

SERIAL #'d TO A 1999 SEASON STAT

CARDS #'d UNDER 10 NOT PRICED

Card		
❑ 1A Randy Moss/34	80.00	36.00
❑ 1B Randy Moss/30	80.00	36.00
❑ 1C Randy Moss/14	120.00	55.00
❑ 1D Randy Moss/2		
❑ 2A Brett Favre/133	30.00	13.50
❑ 2B Brett Favre/119	30.00	13.50
❑ 2C Brett Favre/88	40.00	18.00
❑ 2D Brett Favre/1		
❑ 3A Dan Marino/82	40.00	18.00
❑ 3B Dan Marino/77	40.00	18.00
❑ 3C Dan Marino/42	50.00	22.00
❑ 3D Dan Marino/3		
❑ 4A Peyton Manning/121	25.00	11.00
❑ 4B Peyton Manning/118	25.00	11.00
❑ 4C Peyton Manning/91	30.00	13.50
❑ 4D Peyton Manning/3		
❑ 5A Emmitt Smith/175	15.00	6.75
❑ 5B Emmitt Smith/121	20.00	9.00
❑ 5C Emmitt Smith/29	60.00	27.00
❑ 5D Emmitt Smith/4		
❑ 6A Jerry Rice/24	60.00	27.00
❑ 6B Jerry Rice/24	60.00	27.00
❑ 6C Jerry Rice/16	80.00	36.00
❑ 6D Jerry Rice/3		
❑ 7A Mark Brunell/81	15.00	6.75
❑ 7B Mark Brunell/100	12.00	5.50
❑ 7C Mark Brunell/77	15.00	6.75
❑ 7D Mark Brunell/1		
❑ 8A Eddie George/171	8.00	3.60
❑ 8B Eddie George/119	10.00	4.50
❑ 8C Eddie George/29	25.00	11.00
❑ 8D Eddie George/1		
❑ 9A Marshall Faulk/138	8.00	3.60
❑ 9B Marshall Faulk/94	10.00	4.50
❑ 9C Marshall Faulk/20	25.00	11.00
❑ 9D Marshall Faulk/1		
❑ 10A Kurt Warner/129	40.00	18.00
❑ 10B Kurt Warner/106	40.00	18.00
❑ 10C Kurt Warner/87	50.00	22.00
❑ 10D Kurt Warner/3		
❑ 11A Edgerrin James/220	15.00	6.75
❑ 11B Edgerrin James/130	25.00	11.00
❑ 11C Edgerrin James/17	120.00	55.00
❑ 11D Edgerrin James/2		
❑ 12A Tim Couch/83	20.00	9.00
❑ 12B Tim Couch/81	20.00	9.00
❑ 12C Tim Couch/56	30.00	13.50
❑ 12D Tim Couch/3		

2000 Donruss Elite Passing the Torch

	MINT	NRMT
COMPLETE SET (18)	200.00	90.00
COMMON CARD (PT1-PT18)	5.00	2.20

PRINT RUN 1-12 SERIAL #'d TO 1500
PRINT RUN 13-18 SERIAL #'d TO 500
FIRST 150-CARDS 1-12 WERE SIGNED
FIRST 50-CARDS 13-18 WERE SIGNED

Card		
❑ PT1 Jerry Rice	8.00	3.60
❑ PT2 Randy Moss	10.00	4.50
❑ PT3 Dan Marino	12.00	5.50
❑ PT4 Kurt Warner	15.00	6.75
❑ PT5 Joe Montana	20.00	9.00
❑ PT6 Steve Young	5.00	2.20
❑ PT7 Bart Starr	12.00	5.50
❑ PT8 Brett Favre	12.00	5.50
❑ PT9 Roger Staubach	10.00	4.50
❑ PT10 Troy Aikman	8.00	3.60
❑ PT11 Gale Sayers	8.00	3.60
❑ PT12 Edgerrin James	12.00	5.50
❑ PT13 Jerry Rice / Randy Moss	12.00	5.50
❑ PT14 Dan Marino / Kurt Warner	20.00	9.00
❑ PT15 Joe Montana / Steve Young	25.00	11.00
❑ PT16 Bart Starr / Brett Favre	15.00	6.75
❑ PT17 Roger Staubach / Troy Aikman	12.00	5.50
❑ PT18 Gale Sayers / Edgerrin James	15.00	6.75

2000 Donruss Elite Passing the Torch Autographs

	MINT	NRMT
COMMON CARD (PT1-PT18)	60.00	27.00

1-12 FIRST 100-CARDS OF PRINT RUN
13-18 FIRST 50-CARDS OF PRINT RUN

Card		
❑ PT1 Jerry Rice	150.00	70.00
❑ PT2 Randy Moss Trade	150.00	70.00
❑ PT3 Dan Marino	250.00	110.00
❑ PT4 Kurt Warner	200.00	90.00
❑ PT5 Joe Montana	300.00	135.00
❑ PT6 Steve Young	100.00	45.00
❑ PT7 Bart Starr Trade	200.00	90.00
❑ PT8 Brett Favre Trade	250.00	110.00
❑ PT9 Roger Staubach	175.00	80.00
❑ PT10 Troy Aikman	120.00	55.00
❑ PT11 Gale Sayers	60.00	27.00
❑ PT12 Edgerrin James	175.00	80.00
❑ PT13 Jerry Rice / Randy Moss	250.00	110.00
❑ PT14 Dan Marino / Kurt Warner	350.00	160.00
❑ PT15 Joe Montana / Steve Young	500.00	220.00
❑ PT16 Bart Starr / Brett Favre	400.00	180.00
❑ PT17 Roger Staubach / Troy Aikman	250.00	110.00
❑ PT18 Gale Sayers / Edgerrin James	300.00	135.00

2000 Donruss Elite Throwback Threads

	MINT	NRMT
COMMON CARD (TT1-TT45)	60.00	27.00

SINGLE JERSEYS #'d TO 100
DOUBLE JERSEYS #'d TO 50

❑ TT1 Joe Namath AUTO	500.00	220.00
❑ TT2 Dan Marino	150.00	70.00
❑ TT3 Walter Payton	300.00	135.00
❑ TT4 Barry Sanders	120.00	55.00
❑ TT5 Joe Montana/50	300.00	135.00
❑ TT5A Joe Montana AUTO/50 (Trade card)	500.00	220.00
❑ TT6 Steve Young	80.00	36.00
❑ TT7 Eric Dickerson/50	60.00	27.00
❑ TT7A E.Dickerson AUTO/50	175.00	80.00
❑ TT8 Edgerrin James	150.00	70.00
❑ TT9 Johnny Unitas/75	200.00	90.00
❑ TT10 Peyton Manning	175.00	80.00
❑ TT11 Bart Starr	200.00	90.00
❑ TT12 Brett Favre	150.00	70.00
❑ TT13 Terry Bradshaw/50	200.00	90.00
❑ TT13A T.Bradshaw AUTO/50	450.00	200.00
❑ TT14 Kurt Warner	150.00	70.00
❑ TT15 Dan Fouts/50	80.00	36.00
❑ TT15A Dan Fouts AUTO/50	175.00	80.00
❑ TT16 Drew Bledsoe	80.00	36.00
❑ TT17 Earl Campbell/75	120.00	55.00
❑ TT17A E.Campbell AUTO/25 Trade card	200.00	90.00
❑ TT18 Eddie George	80.00	36.00
❑ TT19 Jim Brown	200.00	90.00
❑ TT20 Terrell Davis	100.00	45.00
❑ TT21 Marcus Allen	80.00	36.00
❑ TT22 Emmitt Smith	120.00	55.00
❑ TT23 Bob Griese/75	80.00	36.00
❑ TT24 Brian Griese	80.00	36.00
❑ TT25 Don Meredith AUTO	150.00	70.00
❑ TT26 Troy Aikman	100.00	45.00
❑ TT27 Ken Stabler/75	120.00	55.00
❑ TT27 Ken Stabler AUTO/75 (Trade card)	300.00	135.00
❑ TT28 Jake Plummer	60.00	27.00
❑ TT29 Fran Tarkenton/75	150.00	70.00
❑ TT29 F.Tarkenton AUTO/25	300.00	135.00
❑ TT30 Mark Brunell	80.00	36.00
❑ TT31 Joe Namath / Dan Marino	1000.00	450.00
❑ TT32 Walter Payton / Barry Sanders	600.00	275.00
❑ TT33 Joe Montana / Steve Young	500.00	220.00
❑ TT34 Eric Dickerson / Edgerrin James	200.00	90.00
❑ TT35 Johnny Unitas / Peyton Manning	400.00	180.00
❑ TT36 Bart Starr / Brett Favre	400.00	180.00
❑ TT37 Terry Bradshaw / Kurt Warner	250.00	110.00
❑ TT38 Dan Fouts / Drew Bledsoe	120.00	55.00
❑ TT39 Earl Campbell / Eddie George	150.00	70.00
❑ TT40 Jim Brown / Terrell Davis	300.00	135.00
❑ TT41 Marcus Allen / Emmitt Smith	175.00	80.00
❑ TT42 Bob Griese / Brian Griese	150.00	70.00
❑ TT43 Don Meredith / Troy Aikman	200.00	90.00
❑ TT44 Ken Stabler / Jake Plummer	150.00	70.00
❑ TT45 Fran Tarkenton / Mark Brunell	200.00	90.00

2000 Donruss Elite Turn of the Century

	MINT	NRMT
COMPLETE SET (60)	200.00	90.00
COMMON CARD (TC1-TC60)	1.25	.55
SEMISTARS	2.50	1.10

STATED PRINT RUN 1000 SERIAL #'d SETS
*GOLD DC STARS: 6X TO 15X BASIC INSERTS
*GOLD DC ROOKIES: 6X TO 15X BASIC INSERTS
GOLD DIE CUT PRINT RUN 21 SER.#'d CARDS

Card	MINT	NRMT
❑ TC1 Dan Marino	10.00	4.50
❑ TC2 Edgerrin James	8.00	3.60
❑ TC3 Peyton Manning	8.00	3.60
❑ TC4 Drew Bledsoe	4.00	1.80
❑ TC5 Doug Flutie	3.00	1.35
❑ TC6 Curtis Martin	2.50	1.10
❑ TC7 Eddie George	2.50	1.10
❑ TC8 Steve McNair	2.50	1.10
❑ TC9 Fred Taylor	1.25	.55
❑ TC10 Mark Brunell	1.25	.55
❑ TC11 Tim Couch	5.00	2.20
❑ TC12 Peter Warrick	15.00	6.75
❑ TC13 Terrell Davis	6.00	2.70
❑ TC14 Jon Kitna	2.50	1.10
❑ TC15 Emmitt Smith	6.00	2.70
❑ TC16 Troy Aikman	6.00	2.70
❑ TC17 Stephen Davis	2.50	1.10
❑ TC18 Brad Johnson	2.50	1.10
❑ TC19 Jake Plummer	2.50	1.10
❑ TC20 Brett Favre	10.00	4.50
❑ TC21 Barry Sanders	8.00	3.60
❑ TC22 Marshall Faulk	2.50	1.10
❑ TC23 Kurt Warner	12.00	5.50
❑ TC24 Ricky Williams	5.00	2.20
❑ TC25 Steve Young	4.00	1.80
❑ TC26 Randy Moss	8.00	3.60
❑ TC27 John Elway	10.00	4.50
❑ TC28 Jerry Rice	6.00	2.70
❑ TC29 Plaxico Burress	8.00	3.60
❑ TC30 Cris Carter	2.50	1.10
❑ TC31 Antonio Freeman	2.50	1.10
❑ TC32 Thomas Jones	10.00	4.50
❑ TC33 Travis Taylor	6.00	2.70
❑ TC34 Marvin Harrison	2.50	1.10
❑ TC35 Keyshawn Johnson	2.50	1.10
❑ TC36 Shaun Alexander	10.00	4.50
❑ TC37 Isaac Bruce	2.50	1.10
❑ TC38 Ricky Watters	1.25	.55
❑ TC39 Ron Dayne	15.00	6.75
❑ TC40 Brian Griese	3.00	1.35
❑ TC41 Charlie Batch	1.25	.55
❑ TC42 Jamal Lewis	10.00	4.50
❑ TC43 Jamal Anderson	2.50	1.10
❑ TC44 Dorsey Levens	2.50	1.10
❑ TC45 Chris Redman	5.00	2.20
❑ TC46 Robert Smith	2.50	1.10
❑ TC47 Chad Pennington	12.00	5.50
❑ TC48 Terrell Owens	2.50	1.10
❑ TC49 Deion Sanders	2.50	1.10
❑ TC50 Duce Staley	2.50	1.10
❑ TC51 Dez White	4.00	1.80
❑ TC52 Jimmy Smith	1.25	.55
❑ TC53 Cade McNown	3.00	1.35
❑ TC54 Daunte Culpepper	3.00	1.35
❑ TC55 Akili Smith	2.50	1.10
❑ TC56 Torry Holt	1.25	.55
❑ TC57 Kevin Johnson	2.50	1.10
❑ TC58 Shaun King	3.00	1.35
❑ TC59 Olandis Gary	2.50	1.10
❑ TC60 Donovan McNabb	3.00	1.35

1997 Donruss Preferred

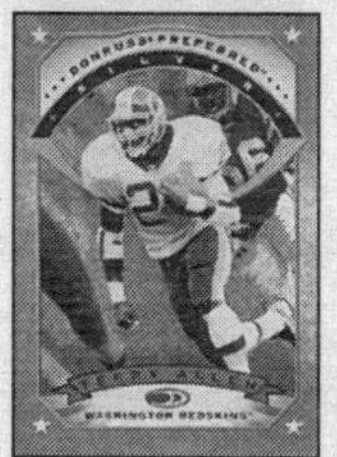

	MINT	NRMT
COMPLETE SET (150)	400.00	180.00
COMP.BRONZE SET (80)	30.00	13.50
COMMON BRONZE	.30	.14
BRONZE SEMISTARS	.50	.23
BRONZE UNLISTED STARS	.75	.35
COMMON SILVER	2.50	1.10
SILVER SEMISTARS	4.00	1.80
SILVER STATED ODDS 1:5		
COMMON GOLD	4.00	1.80
GOLD SEMISTARS	6.00	2.70
GOLD STATED ODDS 1:17		
PLATINUM STATED ODDS 1:48		

Card	MINT	NRMT
❑ 1 Emmitt Smith P	25.00	11.00
❑ 2 Steve Young G	10.00	4.50
❑ 3 Cris Carter S	4.00	1.80
❑ 4 Tim Biakabutuka B	.50	.23
❑ 5 Brett Favre P	30.00	13.50
❑ 6 Troy Aikman G	12.00	5.50
❑ 7 Eddie Kennison S	4.00	1.80
❑ 8 Ben Coates B	.50	.23
❑ 9 Dan Marino P	30.00	13.50
❑ 10 Deion Sanders G	8.00	3.60
❑ 11 Curtis Conway S	4.00	1.80
❑ 12 Jeff George B	.50	.23
❑ 13 Barry Sanders P	30.00	13.50
❑ 14 Kerry Collins G	.50	.23
❑ 15 Marvin Harrison S	4.00	1.80
❑ 16 Bobby Engram B	.50	.23
❑ 17 Jerry Rice P	20.00	9.00
❑ 18 Kordell Stewart G	10.00	4.50
❑ 19 Tony Banks S	4.00	1.80
❑ 20 Jim Harbaugh B	.50	.23
❑ 21 Mark Brunell P	15.00	6.75
❑ 22 Steve McNair G	10.00	4.50
❑ 23 Terrell Owens S	8.00	3.60
❑ 24 Raymont Harris B	.30	.14
❑ 25 Curtis Martin P	12.00	5.50
❑ 26 Karim Abdul-Jabbar G	8.00	3.60
❑ 27 Joey Galloway S	6.00	2.70
❑ 28 Bobby Hoying B	.50	.23
❑ 29 Terrell Davis P	25.00	11.00
❑ 30 Terry Glenn G	6.00	2.70
❑ 31 Antonio Freeman S	6.00	2.70
❑ 32 Brad Johnson B	1.00	.45
❑ 33 Drew Bledsoe P	15.00	6.75
❑ 34 John Elway G	25.00	11.00
❑ 35 Herman Moore G	8.00	3.60
❑ 36 Robert Brooks S	4.00	1.80
❑ 37 Rod Smith B	.75	.35
❑ 38 Eddie George P	15.00	6.75
❑ 39 Keyshawn Johnson G	8.00	3.60
❑ 40 Greg Hill S	2.50	1.10
❑ 41 Scott Mitchell B	.50	.23
❑ 42 Muhsin Muhammad B	.50	.23
❑ 43 Isaac Bruce G	8.00	3.60
❑ 44 Jeff Blake S	4.00	1.80
❑ 45 Neil O'Donnell B	.50	.23
❑ 46 Jimmy Smith B	.50	.23
❑ 47 Jerome Bettis G	8.00	3.60
❑ 48 Terry Allen S	4.00	1.80
❑ 49 Andre Reed B	.50	.23
❑ 50 Frank Sanders B	.50	.23
❑ 51 Tim Brown G	8.00	3.60
❑ 52 Thurman Thomas S	4.00	1.80
❑ 53 Heath Shuler B	.30	.14
❑ 54 Vinny Testaverde B	.50	.23
❑ 55 Marcus Allen S	4.00	1.80
❑ 56 Napoleon Kaufman B	.75	.35
❑ 57 Derrick Alexander WR B	.50	.23
❑ 58 Carl Pickens G	6.00	2.70
❑ 59 Marshall Faulk S	4.00	1.80
❑ 60 Mike Alstott B	.75	.35
❑ 61 Jamal Anderson B	2.00	.90
❑ 62 Ricky Watters G	6.00	2.70
❑ 63 Dorsey Levens S	4.00	1.80
❑ 64 Todd Collins B	.30	.14
❑ 65 Trent Dilfer B	.75	.35
❑ 66 Natrone Means S	4.00	1.80
❑ 67 Gus Frerotte B	.30	.14
❑ 68 Irving Fryar B	.50	.23
❑ 69 Adrian Murrell S	4.00	1.80
❑ 70 Rodney Hampton B	.50	.23
❑ 71 Garrison Hearst B	.50	.23
❑ 72 Reggie White S	4.00	1.80
❑ 73 Anthony Johnson B	.30	.14
❑ 74 Tony Martin B	.50	.23
❑ 75 Chris Sanders S	2.50	1.10
❑ 76 O.J. McDuffie B	.50	.23
❑ 77 Leeland McElroy B	.30	.14
❑ 78 Ki-Jana Carter S	4.00	1.80
❑ 79 Anthony Miller B	.30	.14
❑ 80 Johnnie Morton B	.50	.23
❑ 81 Robert Smith S	.50	.23
❑ 82 Brett Perriman B	.30	.14
❑ 83 Errict Rhett B	.30	.14
❑ 84 Michael Irvin S	4.00	1.80
❑ 85 Darnay Scott B	.50	.23
❑ 86 Shannon Sharpe B	.50	.23
❑ 87 Lawrence Phillips S	4.00	1.80
❑ 88 Bruce Smith B	.50	.23
❑ 89 James O.Stewart B	.50	.23
❑ 90 J.J. Stokes B	.50	.23
❑ 91 Chris Warren B	.50	.23
❑ 92 Daryl Johnston B	.50	.23
❑ 93 Andre Rison B	.50	.23
❑ 94 Rashaan Salaam B	.30	.14
❑ 95 Amani Toomer B	.50	.23
❑ 96 Warrick Dunn G RC	20.00	9.00
❑ 97 Tiki Barber S RC	4.00	1.80
❑ 98 Peter Boulware B RC	.50	.23
❑ 99 Ike Hilliard G RC	12.00	5.50
❑ 100 Antowain Smith S RC	8.00	3.60
❑ 101 Yatil Green S RC	4.00	1.80
❑ 102 Tony Gonzalez B RC	5.00	2.20
❑ 103 Reidel Anthony G RC	12.00	5.50
❑ 104 Troy Davis S RC	4.00	1.80
❑ 105 Rae Carruth S RC	2.50	1.10
❑ 106 David LaFleur B RC	.75	.35
❑ 107 Jim Druckenmiller G RC	8.00	3.60
❑ 108 Joey Kent S RC	6.00	2.70
❑ 109 Byron Hanspard S RC	6.00	2.70
❑ 110 Darrell Russell B RC	.30	.14
❑ 111 Danny Wuerffel S RC	4.00	1.80
❑ 112 Jake Plummer S RC	20.00	9.00
❑ 113 Jay Graham B RC	.75	.35
❑ 114 Corey Dillon S RC	10.00	4.50
❑ 115 Orlando Pace B RC	.30	.14
❑ 116 Pat Barnes S RC	4.00	1.80
❑ 117 Shawn Springs B RC	.50	.23
❑ 118 Troy Aikman NT B	2.00	.90
❑ 119 Drew Bledsoe NT B	2.00	.90
❑ 120 Mark Brunell NT B	2.00	.90
❑ 121 Kerry Collins NT B	.50	.23
❑ 122 Terrell Davis NT B	3.00	1.35
❑ 123 Jerome Bettis NT B	.75	.35
❑ 124 Brett Favre NT B	4.00	1.80
❑ 125 Eddie George NT B	2.00	.90
❑ 126 Terry Glenn NT B	.75	.35
❑ 127 Karim Abdul-Jabbar NT B	.75	.35
❑ 128 Keyshawn Johnson NT B	.75	.35
❑ 129 Dan Marino NT B	4.00	1.80
❑ 130 Curtis Martin NT B	1.00	.45

- ❑ 131 Natrone Means NT B .... .75 .35
- ❑ 132 Herman Moore NT S 4.00 1.80
- ❑ 133 Jerry Rice NT B .... 2.00 .90
- ❑ 134 Barry Sanders NT B 4.00 1.80
- ❑ 135 Deion Sanders NT B ...... .75 .35
- ❑ 136 Emmitt Smith NT B 3.00 1.35
- ❑ 137 Kordell Stewart NT B.... 1.25 .55
- ❑ 138 Steve Young NT B ...... 1.50 .70
- ❑ 139 Carl Pickens NT S........ 4.00 1.80
- ❑ 140 Isaac Bruce NT S 4.00 1.80
- ❑ 141 Steve McNair NT S 5.00 2.20
- ❑ 142 John Elway NT S........ 10.00 4.50
- ❑ 143 Cris Carter NT B .... .50 .23
- ❑ 144 Tim Brown NT B .... .50 .23
- ❑ 145 Ricky Watters NT B........ .30 .14
- ❑ 146 Robert Brooks NT B ...... .50 .23
- ❑ 147 Jeff Blake NT B .... .50 .23
- ❑ 148 Tiki Barber CL B .... .50 .23
- ❑ 149 Jim Druckenmiller CL B.. .75 .35
- ❑ 150 Warrick Dunn CL B ...... 1.00 .45

1997 Donruss Preferred Cut To The Chase

	MINT	NRMT
COMPLETE SET (150)	2500.00	1100.00
COMP.BRONZE SET (80)	300.00	135.00

*BRONZE STARS: 4X TO 8X HI COL.
*BRONZE RCs: 2X TO 4X ....
*SILVER STARS: 2X TO 4X HI COL.
*SILVER RCs: 1.25X TO 2.5X ......
*GOLD STARS: 1X TO 2.5X HI COL.
*GOLD RCs: .8X TO 2X ....
*PLATINUM STARS: 1X TO 2.5X HI COL.
RANDOM INSERTS IN PACKS ....

1997 Donruss Preferred Chain Reaction

	MINT	NRMT
COMPLETE SET (24)	250.00	110.00

STATED PRINT RUN 3000 SERIAL #'d SETS

- ❑ 1A Dan Marino 40.00 18.00
- ❑ 1B Karim Abdul-Jabbar 15.00 6.75
- ❑ 2A Troy Aikman 15.00 6.75
- ❑ 2B Emmitt Smith 30.00 13.50
- ❑ 3A Steve McNair 15.00 6.75
- ❑ 3B Eddie George 15.00 6.75
- ❑ 4A Brett Favre 40.00 18.00
- ❑ 4B Robert Brooks.................. 8.00 3.60
- ❑ 5A John Elway 30.00 13.50
- ❑ 5B Terrell Davis 30.00 13.50
- ❑ 6A Drew Bledsoe 15.00 6.75
- ❑ 6B Curtis Martin 15.00 6.75
- ❑ 7A Steve Young 15.00 6.75
- ❑ 7B Jerry Rice 15.00 6.75
- ❑ 8A Mark Brunell 15.00 6.75
- ❑ 8B Natrone Means 15.00 6.75
- ❑ 9A Barry Sanders.............. 40.00 18.00
- ❑ 9B Herman Moore 15.00 6.75
- ❑ 10A Kordell Stewart 15.00 6.75
- ❑ 10B Jerome Bettis 15.00 6.75
- ❑ 11A Jeff Blake 8.00 3.60
- ❑ 11B Carl Pickens 15.00 6.75
- ❑ 12A Lawrence Phillips 6.00 2.70
- ❑ 12B Isaac Bruce................ 15.00 6.75

1997 Donruss Preferred Double-Wide Tins

	MINT	NRMT
COMPLETE SET (12)	12.00	5.50
COMMON TIN (1-12)	.50	.23

PRICES BELOW REFER TO OPENED TINS

- ❑ 1 Emmitt Smith .... 1.50 .70
  Terrell Davis
- ❑ 2 Troy Aikman .... 1.00 .45
  Kerry Collins
- ❑ 3 Herman Moore .... .50 .23
  Carl .Pickens
- ❑ 4 Brett Favre .... 2.00 .90
  Mark Brunell
- ❑ 5 Deion Sanders .... 1.00 .45
  Kordell Stewart
- ❑ 6 Barry Sanders .... 1.50 .70
  Karim Abdul-Jabbar
- ❑ 7 Jerry Rice .... 1.00 .45
  Terry Glenn
- ❑ 8 Dan Marino .... 2.00 .90
  Drew Bledsoe
- ❑ 9 John Elway .... 2.00 .90
  Steve Young
- ❑ 10 Curtis Martin .... 1.00 .45
  Warrick Dunn
- ❑ 11 Eddie George .... 1.00 .45
  Tim Brown
- ❑ 12 Keyshawn Johnson.......... .50 .23
  Ike Hilliard

1997 Donruss Preferred Precious Metals

	MINT	NRMT
COMPLETE SET (15)	1200.00	550.00
COMMON CARD (1-15)..........	40.00	18.00

STATED PRINT RUN 100 SERIAL #'d SETS
ONE GRAM OF METAL PER CARD

- ❑ 1 Drew Bledsoe 80.00 36.00
- ❑ 2 Curtis Martin 60.00 27.00
- ❑ 3 Troy Aikman 80.00 36.00
- ❑ 4 Eddie George 80.00 36.00
- ❑ 5 Warrick Dunn 50.00 22.00
- ❑ 6 Brett Favre 150.00 70.00
- ❑ 7 John Elway 150.00 70.00
- ❑ 8 Barry Sanders 150.00 70.00
- ❑ 9 Emmitt Smith................ 120.00 55.00
- ❑ 10 Terrell Davis 150.00 70.00
- ❑ 11 Mark Brunell 80.00 36.00
- ❑ 12 Jerry Rice 80.00 36.00
- ❑ 13 Dan Marino 150.00 70.00
- ❑ 14 Terry Glenn 40.00 18.00
- ❑ 15 Tiki Barber.................... 40.00 18.00

1997 Donruss Preferred Staremasters

	MINT	NRMT
COMPLETE SET (24)	500.00	220.00

STATED PRINT RUN 1500 SERIAL #'d SETS

- ❑ 1 Tim Brown 6.00 2.70

- ❑ 2 Mark Brunell 25.00 11.00
- ❑ 3 Kerry Collins 6.00 2.70
- ❑ 4 Brett Favre 50.00 22.00
- ❑ 5 Eddie George 25.00 11.00
- ❑ 6 Terry Glenn 10.00 4.50
- ❑ 7 Dan Marino 50.00 22.00
- ❑ 8 Curtis Martin 12.00 5.50
- ❑ 9 Jerry Rice 25.00 11.00
- ❑ 10 Barry Sanders 50.00 22.00
- ❑ 11 Deion Sanders 10.00 4.50
- ❑ 12 Emmitt Smith................. 40.00 18.00
- ❑ 13 Drew Bledsoe 25.00 11.00
- ❑ 14 Troy Aikman 25.00 11.00
- ❑ 15 Tiki Barber......................... 6.00 2.70
- ❑ 16 Terrell Davis 40.00 18.00
- ❑ 17 Karim Abdul-Jabbar 10.00 4.50
- ❑ 18 Warrick Dunn 12.00 5.50
- ❑ 19 John Elway 50.00 22.00
- ❑ 20 Yatil Green 6.00 2.70
- ❑ 21 Ike Hilliard 6.00 2.70
- ❑ 22 Kordell Stewart 15.00 6.75
- ❑ 23 Ricky Watters 4.00 1.80
- ❑ 24 Steve Young 20.00 9.00

1997 Donruss Preferred Tins

	MINT	NRMT
COMP.BLUE PACK SET (24)	20.00	9.00

*SILVER PACK TINS: 5X TO 10X BLUES
STATED PRINT RUN 1200 SETS
*BLUE BOX TINS: 3X TO 6X BLUE PACKS
STATED PRINT RUN 1200 SETS
*GOLD PACK TINS: 10X TO 20X BLUE PACKS
STATED PRINT RUN 300 SETS ..
*GOLD BOX TINS: 8X TO 16X BLUE PACKS
STATED PRINT RUN 300 SETS ..
PRICES BELOW REFER TO OPENED TINS

- ❑ 1 Mark Brunell .... 1.00 .45
- ❑ 2 Karim Abdul-Jabbar .... .40 .18
- ❑ 3 Terry Glenn .... .40 .18
- ❑ 4 Brett Favre .... 2.00 .90
- ❑ 5 Troy Aikman .... 1.00 .45
- ❑ 6 Eddie George .... 1.00 .45
- ❑ 7 John Elway .... 2.00 .90
- ❑ 8 Steve Young .... .75 .35
- ❑ 9 Terrell Davis .... 1.50 .70
- ❑ 10 Kordell Stewart .... .60 .25
- ❑ 11 Drew Bledsoe .... 1.00 .45

	MINT	NRMT
❑ 12 Kerry Collins	.25	.11
❑ 13 Dan Marino	2.00	.90
❑ 14 Tim Brown	.25	.11
❑ 15 Carl Pickens	.40	.18
❑ 16 Warrick Dunn	.50	.23
❑ 17 Herman Moore	.40	.18
❑ 18 Curtis Martin	.50	.23
❑ 19 Ike Hilliard	.40	.18
❑ 20 Barry Sanders	2.00	.90
❑ 21 Deion Sanders	.40	.18
❑ 22 Emmitt Smith	1.50	.70
❑ 23 Keyshawn Johnson	.40	.18
❑ 24 Jerry Rice	1.00	.45

1999 Donruss Preferred QBC

	MINT	NRMT
COMPLETE SET (120)	150.00	70.00
COMP.BRONZE SET (45)	25.00	11.00
COMMON BRONZE (1-45)	.15	.07
SEMISTARS BRONZE	.30	.14
UNL.STARS BRONZE	.60	.25
COMMON SILVER (46-80)	.50	.23
SEMISTARS SILVER	1.00	.45
SILVER STATED ODDS 1:1		
COMMON GOLD (81-105)	1.00	.45
SEMISTARS GOLD	2.00	.90
GOLD STATED ODDS 1:4		
COMMON PLATINUM (106-120)	3.00	1.35
PLATINUM STATED ODDS 1:8		

	MINT	NRMT
❑ 1 Troy Aikman B	1.50	.70
❑ 2 Tony Banks B	.30	.14
❑ 3 Jeff Blake B	.30	.14
❑ 4 Drew Bledsoe B	1.00	.45
❑ 5 Bubby Brister B	.15	.07
❑ 6 Chris Chandler B	.30	.14
❑ 7 Kerry Collins B	.30	.14
❑ 8 Randall Cunningham B	.60	.25
❑ 9 Terrell Davis B	1.50	.70
❑ 10 Trent Dilfer B	.30	.14
❑ 11 John Elway B	2.50	1.10
❑ 12 Boomer Esiason B	.15	.07
❑ 13 Jim Everett B	.15	.07
❑ 14 Brett Favre B	2.50	1.10
❑ 15 Doug Flutie B	.60	.25
❑ 16 Gus Frerotte B	.15	.07
❑ 17 Jeff George B	.30	.14
❑ 18 Elvis Grbac B	.30	.14
❑ 19 Jim Harbaugh B	.30	.14
❑ 20 Michael Irvin B	.30	.14
❑ 21 Brad Johnson B	.60	.25
❑ 22 Keyshawn Johnson B	.60	.25
❑ 23 Danny Kanell B	.15	.07
❑ 24 Jim Kelly B	.15	.07
❑ 25 Bernie Kosar B	.15	.07
❑ 26 Erik Kramer B	.15	.07
❑ 27 Ryan Leaf B	.60	.25
❑ 28 Peyton Manning B	2.50	1.10
❑ 29 Dan Marino B	2.50	1.10
❑ 30 Donovan McNabb B RC	4.00	1.80
❑ 31 Steve McNair B	.60	.25
❑ 32 Cade McNown B RC	4.00	1.80
❑ 33 Scott Mitchell B	.15	.07
❑ 34 Warren Moon B	.60	.25
❑ 35 Neil O'Donnell B	.30	.14
❑ 36 Jake Plummer B	1.25	.55
❑ 37 Jerry Rice B	1.50	.70
❑ 38 Barry Sanders B	2.50	1.10
❑ 39 Junior Seau B	.30	.14
❑ 40 Phil Simms B	.15	.07
❑ 41 Kordell Stewart B	.60	.25
❑ 42 Vinny Testaverde B	.30	.14
❑ 43 Ricky Williams B RC	6.00	2.70
❑ 44 Steve Young B	1.00	.45
❑ 45 Dan Marino B Brett Favre B John Elway B	3.00	1.35
❑ 46 Troy Aikman S	2.50	1.10
❑ 47 Tony Banks S	.30	.14
❑ 48 Drew Bledsoe S	1.50	.70
❑ 49 Bubby Brister S	.15	.07
❑ 50 Chris Chandler S	.30	.14
❑ 51 Kerry Collins S	.30	.14
❑ 52 Randall Cunningham S	1.00	.45
❑ 53 Terrell Davis S	2.50	1.10
❑ 54 Trent Dilfer S	.30	.14
❑ 55 John Elway S	4.00	1.80
❑ 56 Boomer Esiason S	.15	.07
❑ 57 Brett Favre S	4.00	1.80
❑ 58 Doug Flutie S	1.25	.55
❑ 59 Elvis Grbac S	.30	.14
❑ 60 Jim Harbaugh S	1.00	.45
❑ 61 Michael Irvin S	.30	.14
❑ 62 Brad Johnson S	1.00	.45
❑ 63 Keyshawn Johnson S	1.00	.45
❑ 64 Jim Kelly S	1.00	.45
❑ 65 Ryan Leaf S	1.00	.45
❑ 66 Peyton Manning S	4.00	1.80
❑ 67 Dan Marino S	4.00	1.80
❑ 68 Donovan McNabb S	6.00	2.70
❑ 69 Steve McNair S	1.00	.45
❑ 70 Cade McNown S	6.00	2.70
❑ 71 Warren Moon S	1.00	.45
❑ 72 Jake Plummer S	2.00	.90
❑ 73 Jerry Rice S	2.50	1.10
❑ 74 Barry Sanders S	4.00	1.80
❑ 75 Junior Seau S	.30	.14
❑ 76 Phil Simms S	.15	.07
❑ 77 Kordell Stewart S	1.00	.45
❑ 78 Vinny Testaverde S	.30	.14
❑ 79 Ricky Williams S	10.00	4.50
❑ 80 Steve Young S	1.50	.70
❑ 81 Troy Aikman G	5.00	2.20
❑ 82 Drew Bledsoe G	3.00	1.35
❑ 83 Bubby Brister G	.15	.07
❑ 84 Chris Chandler G	.30	.14
❑ 85 Randall Cunningham G	2.00	.90
❑ 86 Terrell Davis G	6.00	2.70
❑ 87 John Elway G	8.00	3.60
❑ 88 Brett Favre G	8.00	3.60
❑ 89 Doug Flutie G	2.50	1.10
❑ 90 Brad Johnson G	2.00	.90
❑ 91 Keyshawn Johnson G	2.00	.90
❑ 92 Ryan Leaf G	2.00	.90
❑ 93 Peyton Manning G	8.00	3.60
❑ 94 Dan Marino G	8.00	3.60
❑ 95 Donovan McNabb G	12.00	5.50
❑ 96 Steve McNair G	2.00	.90
❑ 97 Cade McNown G	12.00	5.50
❑ 98 Warren Moon G	2.00	.90
❑ 99 Jake Plummer G	4.00	1.80
❑ 100 Jerry Rice G	5.00	2.20
❑ 101 Barry Sanders G	8.00	3.60
❑ 102 Kordell Stewart G	2.00	.90
❑ 103 Vinny Testaverde G	.30	.14
❑ 104 Ricky Williams G	20.00	9.00
❑ 105 Steve Young G	3.00	1.35
❑ 106 Troy Aikman P	8.00	3.60
❑ 107 Drew Bledsoe P	5.00	2.20
❑ 108 Terrell Davis P	8.00	3.60
❑ 109 John Elway P	12.00	5.50
❑ 110 Brett Favre P	12.00	5.50
❑ 111 Keyshawn Johnson P	3.00	1.35
❑ 112 Peyton Manning P	12.00	5.50
❑ 113 Dan Marino P	12.00	5.50
❑ 114 Donovan McNabb P	15.00	6.75
❑ 115 Cade McNown P	15.00	6.75
❑ 116 Jake Plummer P	6.00	2.70
❑ 117 Jerry Rice P	8.00	3.60
❑ 118 Barry Sanders P	12.00	5.50
❑ 119 Kordell Stewart P	3.00	1.35
❑ 120 Ricky Williams P	25.00	11.00

1999 Donruss Preferred QBC Power

	MINT	NRMT
COMMON BRONZE (1-45)	.75	.35

*POWER BRONZE STARS: 2X TO 5X HI COL.
*POWER BRONZE YOUNG STARS: 1.5X TO 4X
*POWER BRONZE RCs: 1.2X TO 3X
POWER BRONZE PRINT RUN 500 SER.#'d SETS
*POWER SILVER STARS: 2X TO 5X HI COL.
*POWER SILVER YOUNG STARS: 1.5X TO 4X
*POWER SILVER ROOKIES: 1.2X TO 3X
POWER SILVER PRINT RUN 300 SER.#'d SETS
*POWER GOLD STARS: 2.5X TO 6X HI COL.
*POWER GOLD YOUNG STARS: 2X TO 5X
*POWER GOLD ROOKIES: 1.2X TO 3X
POWER GOLD PRINT RUN 150 SER.#'d SETS
*POWER PLATINUM STARS: 3X TO 8X HI COL.
*POWER PLATINUM YOUNG STARS: 2.5X TO 6X
*POWER PLATINUM ROOKIES: 1.5X TO 4X
POWER PLAT.PRINT RUN 50 SER.#'d SETS

1999 Donruss Preferred QBC Autographs

	MINT	NRMT
COMPLETE SET (15)	800.00	350.00
COMMON CARD (1-15)	20.00	9.00
SEMISTARS	40.00	18.00
RANDOM INSERTS IN PACKS		
TRADE CARD EXPIRATION: 5/1/2000		

	MINT	NRMT
❑ 1 Steve Young	60.00	27.00
❑ 2 Ricky Williams	100.00	45.00
❑ 3 Jerry Rice	100.00	45.00
❑ 4 Jake Plummer	60.00	27.00
❑ 5 Peyton Manning	100.00	45.00
❑ 6 Michael Irvin	40.00	18.00
❑ 7 Dan Marino	150.00	70.00
❑ 8 Randall Cunningham	40.00	18.00
❑ 9 Troy Aikman	80.00	36.00
❑ 10 Terrell Davis	80.00	36.00
❑ 11 Vinny Testaverde	20.00	9.00
❑ 12 Chris Chandler	20.00	9.00
❑ 13 Kordell Stewart	40.00	18.00
❑ 14 Bubby Brister	20.00	9.00
❑ 15 Steve McNair	40.00	18.00

1999 Donruss Preferred QBC Chain Reaction

	MINT	NRMT
COMPLETE SET (20)	60.00	27.00
COMMON CARD (1A-10B)	1.00	.45
SEMISTARS	2.00	.90
STATED PRINT RUN 5000 SERIAL #'d SETS		

	MINT	NRMT
❑ 1A Terrell Davis	5.00	2.20
❑ 1B Ricky Williams	8.00	3.60
❑ 2A Donovan McNabb	5.00	2.20
❑ 2B Cade McNown	5.00	2.20
❑ 3A Brett Favre	8.00	3.60
❑ 3B Barry Sanders	8.00	3.60
❑ 4A Jerry Rice	5.00	2.20
❑ 4B Steve Young	3.00	1.35
❑ 5A John Elway	8.00	3.60

❑ 5B Chris Chandler	1.00	.45
❑ 6A Dan Marino	8.00	3.60
❑ 6B Drew Bledsoe	3.00	1.35
❑ 7A Keyshawn Johnson	2.00	.90
❑ 7B Vinny Testaverde	1.00	.45
❑ 8A Warren Moon	2.00	.90
❑ 8B Steve McNair	2.00	.90
❑ 9A Jake Plummer	4.00	1.80
❑ 9B Kordell Stewart	2.00	.90
❑ 10A Troy Aikman	5.00	2.20
❑ 10B Peyton Manning	6.00	2.70

1999 Donruss Preferred QBC Hard Hats

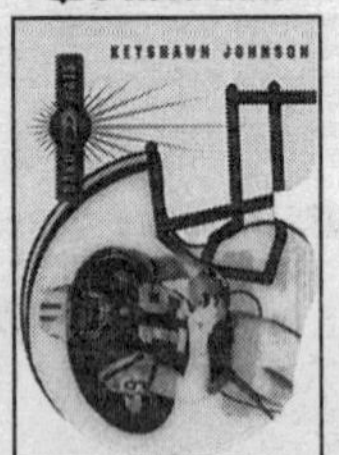

	MINT	NRMT
COMPLETE SET (30)	120.00	55.00
COMMON CARD (1-30)	1.50	.70
SEMISTARS	3.00	1.35

STATED PRINT RUN 3000 SER.#'d SETS

❑ 1 Brett Favre	12.00	5.50
❑ 2 Keyshawn Johnson	3.00	1.35
❑ 3 John Elway	12.00	5.50
❑ 4 Drew Bledsoe	5.00	2.20
❑ 5 Chris Chandler	3.00	1.35
❑ 6 Terrell Davis	8.00	3.60
❑ 7 Ryan Leaf	1.50	.70
❑ 8 Ricky Williams	12.00	5.50
❑ 9 Cade McNown	8.00	3.60
❑ 10 Barry Sanders	12.00	5.50
❑ 11 Donovan McNabb	8.00	3.60
❑ 12 Peyton Manning	10.00	4.50
❑ 13 Troy Aikman	8.00	3.60
❑ 14 Steve Young	5.00	2.20
❑ 15 Vinny Testaverde	3.00	1.35
❑ 16 Dan Marino	12.00	5.50
❑ 17 Steve McNair	3.00	1.35
❑ 18 Kordell Stewart	3.00	1.35
❑ 19 Michael Irvin	1.50	.70
❑ 20 Jake Plummer	6.00	2.70
❑ 21 Jerry Rice	8.00	3.60
❑ 22 Brad Johnson	3.00	1.35
❑ 23 Phil Simms	1.50	.70
❑ 24 Jim Kelly	3.00	1.35
❑ 25 Trent Dilfer	3.00	1.35
❑ 26 Kerry Collins	3.00	1.35
❑ 27 Warren Moon	3.00	1.35
❑ 28 Bubby Brister	1.50	.70
❑ 29 Randall Cunningham	3.00	1.35
❑ 30 Doug Flutie	4.00	1.80

1999 Donruss Preferred QBC Materials

	MINT	NRMT
COMPLETE SET (21)	2500.00	1100.00
COMMON CARD (1-20)	50.00	22.00

JERSEY PRINT RUN 300 SER. #'d SETS
SHOE PRINT RUN 300 SER. #'d SETS
HELMET PRINT RUN 120 SER. #'d SETS
CARD #13 NEVER RELEASED....
RANDOM INSERTS IN PACKS....

❑ 1 Dan Marino J	120.00	55.00
❑ 2 John Elway J	120.00	55.00
❑ 3 Drew Bledsoe J	60.00	27.00
❑ 4 Jake Plummer J	60.00	27.00
❑ 5A Doug Flutie White	60.00	27.00
❑ 5H Doug Flutie Blue	60.00	27.00
❑ 6 Peyton Manning J	120.00	55.00
❑ 7A Jerry Rice White/150	250.00	110.00
❑ 7H Jerry Rice Red	100.00	45.00
❑ 8 Brett Favre J	120.00	55.00
❑ 9 Jim Kelly J	50.00	22.00
❑ 10 Barry Sanders J	120.00	55.00
❑ 11 Keyshawn Johnson S	50.00	22.00
❑ 12 Brett Favre S	150.00	70.00
❑ 14 Troy Aikman S	80.00	36.00
❑ 15 Terrell Davis S	80.00	36.00
❑ 16 Dan Marino H	250.00	110.00
❑ 17 Troy Aikman H	150.00	70.00
❑ 18 Brett Favre H	250.00	110.00
❑ 19 Jerry Rice H	175.00	80.00
❑ 20 Terrell Davis H	150.00	70.00

1999 Donruss Preferred QBC National Treasures

	MINT	NRMT
COMPLETE SET (44)	150.00	70.00
COMMON CARD (1-44)	1.00	.45
SEMISTARS	2.00	.90
UNLISTED STARS	4.00	1.80

STATED PRINT RUN 2000 SERIAL #'d SETS

❑ 1 Jake Plummer	8.00	3.60
❑ 2 Chris Chandler	2.00	.90
❑ 3 Danny Kanell	1.00	.45
❑ 4 Tony Banks	2.00	.90
❑ 5 Scott Mitchell	1.00	.45
❑ 6 Doug Flutie	5.00	2.20
❑ 7 Jim Kelly	4.00	1.80
❑ 8 Erik Kramer	1.00	.45
❑ 9 Cade McNown	10.00	4.50
❑ 10 Jeff Blake	2.00	.90
❑ 11 Boomer Esiason	2.00	.90
❑ 12 Bernie Kosar	1.00	.45
❑ 13 Troy Aikman	10.00	4.50
❑ 14 Michael Irvin	2.00	.90
❑ 15 Bubby Brister	1.00	.45
❑ 16 Terrell Davis	10.00	4.50
❑ 17 John Elway	15.00	6.75
❑ 18 Gus Frerotte	2.00	.90
❑ 19 Barry Sanders	15.00	6.75
❑ 20 Brett Favre	15.00	6.75
❑ 21 Peyton Manning	12.00	5.50
❑ 22 Elvis Grbac	2.00	.90
❑ 23 Warren Moon	4.00	1.80
❑ 24 Dan Marino	15.00	6.75
❑ 25 Randall Cunningham	4.00	1.80
❑ 26 Jeff George	2.00	.90
❑ 27 Drew Bledsoe	6.00	2.70
❑ 28 Ricky Williams	15.00	6.75
❑ 29 Kerry Collins	2.00	.90
❑ 30 Phil Simms	2.00	.90
❑ 31 Keyshawn Johnson	4.00	1.80
❑ 32 Vinny Testaverde	2.00	.90
❑ 33 Donovan McNabb	10.00	4.50
❑ 34 Kordell Stewart	4.00	1.80
❑ 35 Jim Harbaugh	2.00	.90
❑ 36 Ryan Leaf	1.00	.45
❑ 37 Junior Seau	2.00	.90
❑ 38 Jerry Rice	10.00	4.50
❑ 39 Steve Young	6.00	2.70
❑ 40 Jim Everett	1.00	.45
❑ 41 Trent Dilfer	2.00	.90
❑ 42 Steve McNair	4.00	1.80
❑ 43 Brad Johnson	4.00	1.80
❑ 44 Neil O'Donnell	2.00	.90

1999 Donruss Preferred QBC Passing Grade

	MINT	NRMT
COMPLETE SET (20)	150.00	70.00
COMMON CARD (1-20)	2.50	1.10
SEMISTARS	5.00	2.20

STATED PRINT RUN 1500 SERIAL #'d SETS

❑ 1 Steve Young	8.00	3.60
❑ 2 Dan Marino	20.00	9.00
❑ 3 Kordell Stewart	5.00	2.20
❑ 4 Trent Dilfer	2.50	1.10
❑ 5 Doug Flutie	6.00	2.70
❑ 6 Vinny Testaverde	2.50	1.10
❑ 7 Donovan McNabb	12.00	5.50
❑ 8 Brad Johnson	5.00	2.20
❑ 9 Troy Aikman	12.00	5.50
❑ 10 Brett Favre	20.00	9.00
❑ 11 Steve McNair	5.00	2.20
❑ 12 Peyton Manning	15.00	6.75
❑ 13 John Elway	20.00	9.00
❑ 14 Chris Chandler	2.50	1.10
❑ 15 Randall Cunningham	5.00	2.20
❑ 16 Cade McNown	12.00	5.50
❑ 17 Ryan Leaf	2.50	1.10
❑ 18 Drew Bledsoe	8.00	3.60
❑ 19 Jake Plummer	10.00	4.50
❑ 20 Warren Moon	5.00	2.20

1999 Donruss Preferred QBC Precious Metals

	MINT	NRMT
COMMON CARD (1-30)	50.00	22.00
SEMISTARS	80.00	36.00

STATED PRINT RUN 25 SER.#'d SETS

❑ 1 Troy Aikman G	175.00	80.00
❑ 2 Drew Bledsoe G	120.00	55.00
❑ 3 Terrell Davis G	150.00	70.00
❑ 4 John Elway P	200.00	90.00
❑ 5 Brett Favre P	200.00	90.00
❑ 6 Keyshawn Johnson G	80.00	36.00
❑ 7 Peyton Manning G	200.00	90.00
❑ 8 Dan Marino P	200.00	90.00
❑ 9 Donovan McNabb G	150.00	70.00
❑ 10 Cade McNown G	150.00	70.00
❑ 11 Jake Plummer G	120.00	55.00
❑ 12 Jerry Rice P	175.00	80.00
❑ 13 Barry Sanders P	200.00	90.00
❑ 14 Kordell Stewart G	80.00	36.00
❑ 15 Ricky Williams P	300.00	135.00
❑ 16 Bubby Brister S	50.00	22.00
❑ 17 Chris Chandler S	80.00	36.00
❑ 18 Randall Cunningham S	80.00	36.00
❑ 19 Doug Flutie S	100.00	45.00
❑ 20 Brad Johnson S	80.00	36.00
❑ 21 Ryan Leaf S	50.00	22.00
❑ 22 Steve McNair S	80.00	36.00

Card	MINT	NRMT
❑ 23 Warren Moon S	80.00	36.00
❑ 24 Vinny Testaverde S	80.00	36.00
❑ 25 Steve Young S	120.00	55.00
❑ 26 Kerry Collins S	80.00	36.00
❑ 27 Trent Dilfer S	80.00	36.00
❑ 28 Boomer Esiason S	50.00	22.00
❑ 29 Jim Kelly S	50.00	22.00
❑ 30 Phil Simms S	50.00	22.00

1999 Donruss Preferred QBC Staremasters

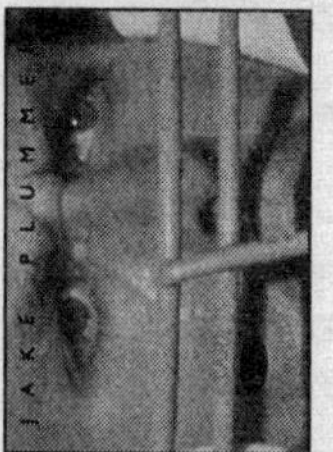

	MINT	NRMT
COMPLETE SET (20)	200.00	90.00
COMMON CARD (1-20)	2.50	1.10
SEMISTARS	5.00	2.20

STATED PRINT RUN 1000 SERIAL #'d SETS

Card	MINT	NRMT
❑ 1 Jake Plummer	8.00	3.60
❑ 2 Doug Flutie	6.00	2.70
❑ 3 Cade McNown	12.00	5.50
❑ 4 Troy Aikman	12.00	5.50
❑ 5 Michael Irvin	2.50	1.10
❑ 6 Terrell Davis	12.00	5.50
❑ 7 John Elway	20.00	9.00
❑ 8 Barry Sanders	20.00	9.00
❑ 9 Brett Favre	20.00	9.00
❑ 10 Peyton Manning	15.00	6.75
❑ 11 Dan Marino	20.00	9.00
❑ 12 Randall Cunningham	5.00	2.20
❑ 13 Drew Bledsoe	8.00	3.60
❑ 14 Ricky Williams	20.00	9.00
❑ 15 Keyshawn Johnson	10.00	4.50
❑ 16 Donovan McNabb	12.00	5.50
❑ 17 Kordell Stewart	10.00	4.50
❑ 18 Ryan Leaf	5.00	2.20
❑ 19 Steve Young	8.00	3.60
❑ 20 Jerry Rice	12.00	5.50

1999 Donruss Preferred QBC X-Ponential Power

	MINT	NRMT
COMPLETE SET (20)	150.00	70.00
COMMON CARD (1-20)	4.00	1.80

STATED PRINT RUN 2500 SERIAL #'d SETS

Card	MINT	NRMT
❑ 1A Troy Aikman	10.00	4.50
❑ 1B Cade McNown	10.00	4.50
❑ 2A Kordell Stewart	4.00	1.80
❑ 2B Steve McNair	10.00	4.50
❑ 3A Donovan McNabb	10.00	4.50
❑ 3B Ricky Williams	15.00	6.75
❑ 4A Barry Sanders	15.00	6.75
❑ 4B Terrell Davis	10.00	4.50
❑ 5A Dan Marino	15.00	6.75
❑ 5B Peyton Manning	12.00	5.50
❑ 6A Jerry Rice	10.00	4.50
❑ 6B Keyshawn Johnson	4.00	1.80
❑ 7A Doug Flutie	5.00	2.20
❑ 7B Jim Kelly	4.00	1.80
❑ 8A Brett Favre	15.00	6.75
❑ 8B Steve Young	6.00	2.70
❑ 9A Drew Bledsoe	6.00	2.70
❑ 9B Ryan Leaf	4.00	1.80
❑ 10A John Elway	15.00	6.75
❑ 10B Jake Plummer	8.00	3.60

1997 E-X2000

	MINT	NRMT
COMPLETE SET (60)	60.00	27.00
COMMON CARD (1-60)	.30	.14
SEMISTARS	.60	.25
UNLISTED STARS	1.25	.55
CONDITION SENSITIVE SET !		
COMP.ESSEN.CRED.(60)	800.00	350.00

*ESS.CRED.STARS: 7.5X TO 20X HI COL.
*ESS.CRED.RCs: 2.5X TO 6X
STATED PRINT RUN 100 SERIAL #'D SETS

Card	MINT	NRMT
❑ 1 Jake Plummer RC	25.00	11.00
❑ 2 Jamal Anderson	2.00	.90
❑ 3 Rae Carruth RC	1.25	.55
❑ 4 Kerry Collins	.60	.25
❑ 5 Darnell Autry RC	.60	.25
❑ 6 Rashaan Salaam	.30	.14
❑ 7 Troy Aikman	3.00	1.35
❑ 8 Deion Sanders	1.25	.55
❑ 9 Emmitt Smith	5.00	2.20
❑ 10 Herman Moore	1.25	.55
❑ 11 Barry Sanders	6.00	2.70
❑ 12 Mark Chmura	.60	.25
❑ 13 Brett Favre	6.00	2.70
❑ 14 Antonio Freeman	2.00	.90
❑ 15 Reggie White	1.25	.55
❑ 16 Cris Carter	1.25	.55
❑ 17 Brad Johnson	1.50	.70
❑ 18 Troy Davis RC	1.25	.55
❑ 19 Danny Wuerffel RC	3.00	1.35
❑ 20 Dave Brown	.30	.14
❑ 21 Ike Hilliard RC	4.00	1.80
❑ 22 Ty Detmer	.60	.25
❑ 23 Ricky Watters	.60	.25
❑ 24 Tony Banks	.60	.25
❑ 25 Eddie Kennison	.60	.25
❑ 26 Jim Druckenmiller RC	2.00	.90
❑ 27 Jerry Rice	3.00	1.35
❑ 28 Steve Young	2.00	.90
❑ 29 Trent Dilfer	1.25	.55
❑ 30 Warrick Dunn RC	8.00	3.60
❑ 31 Terry Allen	1.25	.55
❑ 32 Gus Frerotte	.30	.14
❑ 33 Vinny Testaverde	.60	.25
❑ 34 Antowain Smith RC	5.00	2.20
❑ 35 Thurman Thomas	1.25	.55
❑ 36 Jeff Blake	.60	.25
❑ 37 Carl Pickens	1.25	.55
❑ 38 Terrell Davis	5.00	2.20
❑ 39 John Elway	6.00	2.70
❑ 40 Eddie George	3.00	1.35
❑ 41 Steve McNair	2.00	.90
❑ 42 Marshall Faulk	1.25	.55
❑ 43 Marvin Harrison	1.25	.55
❑ 44 Mark Brunell	3.00	1.35
❑ 45 Marcus Allen	1.25	.55
❑ 46 Elvis Grbac	.60	.25
❑ 47 Karim Abdul-Jabbar	1.25	.55
❑ 48 Dan Marino	6.00	2.70
❑ 49 Drew Bledsoe	3.00	1.35
❑ 50 Terry Glenn	1.25	.55
❑ 51 Curtis Martin	2.00	.90
❑ 52 Keyshawn Johnson	1.25	.55
❑ 53 Tim Brown	1.25	.55
❑ 54 Jeff George	.60	.25
❑ 55 Jerome Bettis	1.25	.55
❑ 56 Kordell Stewart	2.00	.90
❑ 57 Stan Humphries	.60	.25
❑ 58 Junior Seau	.60	.25
❑ 59 Joey Galloway	2.00	.90
❑ 60 Chris Warren	.60	.25

1997 E-X2000 A Cut Above

	MINT	NRMT
COMPLETE SET (10)	300.00	135.00

STATED ODDS 1:288

Card	MINT	NRMT
❑ 1 Barry Sanders	50.00	22.00
❑ 2 Brett Favre	50.00	22.00
❑ 3 Dan Marino	50.00	22.00
❑ 4 Eddie George	25.00	11.00
❑ 5 Emmitt Smith	40.00	18.00
❑ 6 Jerry Rice	25.00	11.00
❑ 7 Joey Galloway	15.00	6.75
❑ 8 John Elway	50.00	22.00
❑ 9 Mark Brunell	25.00	11.00
❑ 10 Terrell Davis	40.00	18.00

1997 E-X2000 Fleet of Foot

	MINT	NRMT
COMPLETE SET (20)	100.00	45.00

STATED ODDS 1:20

Card	MINT	NRMT
❑ 1 Antonio Freeman	8.00	3.60
❑ 2 Barry Sanders	25.00	11.00
❑ 3 Carl Pickens	8.00	3.60
❑ 4 Chris Warren	6.00	2.70
❑ 5 Curtis Martin	8.00	3.60
❑ 6 Deion Sanders	8.00	3.60
❑ 7 Emmitt Smith	20.00	9.00
❑ 8 Jerry Rice	12.00	5.50
❑ 9 Joey Galloway	8.00	3.60
❑ 10 Karim Abdul-Jabbar	5.00	2.20
❑ 11 Kordell Stewart	8.00	3.60
❑ 12 Lawrence Phillips	1.25	.55
❑ 13 Mark Brunell	12.00	5.50
❑ 14 Marvin Harrison	8.00	3.60
❑ 15 Rae Carruth	6.00	2.70
❑ 16 Ricky Watters	6.00	2.70
❑ 17 Steve Young	10.00	4.50
❑ 18 Terrell Davis	25.00	11.00

Card	MINT	NRMT
❑ 19 Terry Glenn	8.00	3.60
❑ 20 Shawn Springs	6.00	2.70

1997 E-X2000 Star Date 2000

	MINT	NRMT
COMPLETE SET (15)	40.00	18.00
COMMON CARD (1-15)	1.25	.55
SEMISTARS	2.00	.90
UNLISTED STARS	3.00	1.35
STATED ODDS 1:9		

Card	MINT	NRMT
❑ 1 Curtis Martin	3.00	1.35
❑ 2 Darnell Autry	2.00	.90
❑ 3 Darrell Russell	1.25	.55
❑ 4 Eddie Kennison	2.00	.90
❑ 5 Jim Druckenmiller	3.00	1.35
❑ 6 Karim Abdul-Jabbar	3.00	1.35
❑ 7 Kerry Collins	2.00	.90
❑ 8 Keyshawn Johnson	3.00	1.35
❑ 9 Marvin Harrison	3.00	1.35
❑ 10 Orlando Pace	1.25	.55
❑ 11 Pat Barnes	3.00	1.35
❑ 12 Reidel Anthony	3.00	1.35
❑ 13 Tim Biakabutuka	2.00	.90
❑ 14 Warrick Dunn	4.00	1.80
❑ 15 Yatil Green	2.00	.90

1998 E-X2001

	MINT	NRMT
COMPLETE SET (60)	90.00	40.00
COMMON CARD (1-60)	.20	.09
SEMISTARS	.40	.18
UNLISTED STARS	.75	.35
COMMON ROOKIE	2.00	.90
ROOKIE SEMISTARS	4.00	1.80

Card	MINT	NRMT
❑ 1 Kordell Stewart	.75	.35
❑ 2 Steve Young	2.00	.90
❑ 3 Mark Brunell	2.50	1.10
❑ 4 Brett Favre	6.00	2.70
❑ 5 Barry Sanders	6.00	2.70
❑ 6 Warrick Dunn	2.00	.90
❑ 7 Jerry Rice	3.00	1.35
❑ 8 Dan Marino	6.00	2.70
❑ 9 Emmitt Smith	5.00	2.20
❑ 10 John Elway	6.00	2.70
❑ 11 Eddie George	2.50	1.10
❑ 12 Jake Plummer	4.00	1.80
❑ 13 Terrell Davis	5.00	2.20
❑ 14 Curtis Martin	.75	.35
❑ 15 Troy Aikman	3.00	1.35
❑ 16 Terry Glenn	.75	.35
❑ 17 Mike Alstott	.75	.35
❑ 18 Drew Bledsoe	2.50	1.10
❑ 19 Keyshawn Johnson	.75	.35
❑ 20 Dorsey Levens	.75	.35
❑ 21 Elvis Grbac	.40	.18
❑ 22 Ricky Watters	.40	.18
❑ 23 Robert Smith	.75	.35
❑ 24 Trent Dilfer	.75	.35
❑ 25 Joey Galloway	.75	.35
❑ 26 Rob Moore	.40	.18
❑ 27 Steve McNair	.75	.35
❑ 28 Jim Harbaugh	.40	.18
❑ 29 Troy Davis	.20	.09
❑ 30 Rob Johnson	.40	.18
❑ 31 Shannon Sharpe	.40	.18
❑ 32 Jerome Bettis	.75	.35
❑ 33 Tim Brown	.75	.35
❑ 34 Kerry Collins	.40	.18
❑ 35 Garrison Hearst	.75	.35
❑ 36 Antonio Freeman	.75	.35
❑ 37 Charlie Garner	.20	.09
❑ 38 Glenn Foley	.40	.18
❑ 39 Yatil Green	.20	.09
❑ 40 Tiki Barber	.40	.18
❑ 41 Bobby Hoying	.40	.18
❑ 42 Corey Dillon	2.00	.90
❑ 43 Antowain Smith	.75	.35
❑ 44 Robert Edwards RC	4.00	1.80
❑ 45 Jammi German RC	2.00	.90
❑ 46 Ahman Green RC	5.00	2.20
❑ 47 Hines Ward RC	4.00	1.80
❑ 48 Skip Hicks RC	6.00	2.70
❑ 49 Brian Griese RC	10.00	4.50
❑ 50 Charlie Batch RC	10.00	4.50
❑ 51 Jacquez Green RC	6.00	2.70
❑ 52 John Avery RC	.40	.18
❑ 53 Kevin Dyson RC	6.00	2.70
❑ 54 Peyton Manning RC	25.00	11.00
❑ 55 Randy Moss RC	25.00	11.00
❑ 56 Ryan Leaf RC	8.00	3.60
❑ 57 Curtis Enis RC	8.00	3.60
❑ 58 Charles Woodson RC	8.00	3.60
❑ 59 Robert Holcombe RC	.40	.18
❑ 60 Fred Taylor RC	15.00	6.75
❑ NNO Checklist Card 1	.20	.09
❑ NNO Checklist Card 2	.20	.09

1998 E-X2001 Essential Credentials Future

	MINT	NRMT
COMMON CARD (1-60)	60.00	27.00
SEMISTARS	80.00	36.00

RANDOM INSERTS IN PACKS....
CARDS 49-60 NOT PRICED DUE TO SCARCITY
PRINT RUNS IN PARENTHESES BELOW

Card	MINT	NRMT
❑ 1 Kordell Stewart (60)	80.00	36.00
❑ 2 Steve Young (59)	100.00	45.00
❑ 3 Mark Brunell (58)	100.00	45.00
❑ 4 Brett Favre (57)	200.00	90.00
❑ 5 Barry Sanders (56)	200.00	90.00
❑ 6 Warrick Dunn (55)	80.00	36.00
❑ 7 Jerry Rice (54)	150.00	70.00
❑ 8 Dan Marino (53)	200.00	90.00
❑ 9 Emmitt Smith (52)	200.00	90.00
❑ 10 John Elway (51)	200.00	90.00
❑ 11 Eddie George (50)	100.00	45.00
❑ 12 Jake Plummer (49)	120.00	55.00
❑ 13 Terrell Davis (48)	200.00	90.00
❑ 14 Curtis Martin (47)	80.00	36.00
❑ 15 Troy Aikman (46)	120.00	55.00
❑ 16 Terry Glenn (45)	80.00	36.00
❑ 17 Mike Alstott (44)	80.00	36.00
❑ 18 Drew Bledsoe (43)	120.00	55.00
❑ 19 Keyshawn Johnson (42)	80.00	36.00
❑ 20 Dorsey Levens (41)	80.00	36.00
❑ 21 Elvis Grbac (40)	60.00	27.00
❑ 22 Ricky Watters (39)	60.00	27.00
❑ 23 Robert Smith (38)	60.00	27.00
❑ 24 Trent Dilfer (37)	80.00	36.00
❑ 25 Joey Galloway (36)	100.00	45.00
❑ 26 Rob Moore (35)	80.00	36.00
❑ 27 Steve McNair (34)	120.00	55.00
❑ 28 Jim Harbaugh (33)	80.00	36.00
❑ 29 Troy Davis (32)	60.00	27.00
❑ 30 Rob Johnson (31)	80.00	36.00
❑ 31 Shannon Sharpe (30)	80.00	36.00
❑ 32 Jerome Bettis (29)	150.00	70.00
❑ 33 Tim Brown (28)	150.00	70.00
❑ 34 Kerry Collins (27)	80.00	36.00
❑ 35 Garrison Hearst (26)	150.00	70.00
❑ 36 Antonio Freeman (25)	150.00	70.00
❑ 37 Charlie Garner (24)	80.00	36.00
❑ 38 Glenn Foley (23)	80.00	36.00
❑ 39 Yatil Green (22)	80.00	36.00
❑ 40 Tiki Barber (21)	80.00	36.00
❑ 41 Bobby Hoying (20)	80.00	36.00
❑ 42 Corey Dillon (19)	200.00	90.00
❑ 43 Antowain Smith (18)	150.00	70.00
❑ 44 Robert Edwards (17)	150.00	70.00
❑ 45 Jammi German (16)	100.00	45.00
❑ 46 Ahman Green (15)	150.00	70.00
❑ 47 Hines Ward (14)	80.00	36.00
❑ 48 Skip Hicks (13)	200.00	90.00
❑ 49 Brian Griese (12)		
❑ 50 Charlie Batch (11)		
❑ 51 Jacquez Green (10)		
❑ 52 John Avery (9)		
❑ 53 Kevin Dyson (8)		
❑ 54 Peyton Manning (7)		
❑ 55 Randy Moss (6)		
❑ 56 Ryan Leaf (5)		
❑ 57 Curtis Enis (4)		
❑ 58 Charles Woodson (3)		
❑ 59 Robert Holcombe (2)		
❑ 60 Fred Taylor (1)		

1998 E-X2001 Essential Credentials Now

	MINT	NRMT
COMMON CARD (1-60)	50.00	22.00
SEMISTARS	60.00	27.00

RANDOM INSERTS IN PACKS....
CARDS 1-12 NOT PRICED DUE TO SCARCITY
PRINT RUNS IN PARENTHESES BELOW

Card	MINT	NRMT
❑ 1 Kordell Stewart (1)		
❑ 2 Steve Young (2)		
❑ 3 Mark Brunell (3)		
❑ 4 Brett Favre (4)		
❑ 5 Barry Sanders (5)		
❑ 6 Warrick Dunn (6)		
❑ 7 Jerry Rice (7)		
❑ 8 Dan Marino (8)		
❑ 9 Emmitt Smith (9)		
❑ 10 John Elway (10)		
❑ 11 Eddie George (11)		
❑ 12 Jake Plummer (12)		
❑ 13 Terrell Davis (13)	800.00	350.00
❑ 14 Curtis Martin (14)	250.00	110.00
❑ 15 Troy Aikman (15)	400.00	180.00
❑ 16 Terry Glenn (16)	120.00	55.00
❑ 17 Mike Alstott (17)	120.00	55.00
❑ 18 Drew Bledsoe (18)	250.00	110.00
❑ 19 Keyshawn Johnson (19)	120.00	55.00
❑ 20 Dorsey Levens (20)	120.00	55.00
❑ 21 Elvis Grbac (21)	60.00	27.00
❑ 22 Ricky Watters (22)	60.00	27.00
❑ 23 Robert Smith (23)	100.00	45.00
❑ 24 Trent Dilfer (24)	60.00	27.00
❑ 25 Joey Galloway (25)	120.00	55.00
❑ 26 Rob Moore (26)	60.00	27.00
❑ 27 Steve McNair (27)	120.00	55.00
❑ 28 Jim Harbaugh (28)	60.00	27.00
❑ 29 Troy Davis (29)	50.00	22.00
❑ 30 Rob Johnson (30)	60.00	27.00
❑ 31 Shannon Sharpe (31)	60.00	27.00
❑ 32 Jerome Bettis (32)	100.00	45.00
❑ 33 Tim Brown (33)	100.00	45.00
❑ 34 Kerry Collins (34)	60.00	27.00
❑ 35 Garrison Hearst (35)	100.00	45.00
❑ 36 Antonio Freeman (36)	100.00	45.00
❑ 37 Charlie Garner (37)	50.00	22.00

❑ 38 Glenn Foley (38) 50.00 22.00
❑ 39 Yatil Green (39).......... 50.00 22.00
❑ 40 Tiki Barber (40) 50.00 22.00
❑ 41 Bobby Hoying (41) 50.00 22.00
❑ 42 Corey Dillon (42) 80.00 36.00
❑ 43 Antowain Smith (43) 60.00 27.00
❑ 44 Robert Edwards (44).... 60.00 27.00
❑ 45 Jammi German (45) 50.00 22.00
❑ 46 Ahman Green (46) 60.00 27.00
❑ 47 Hines Ward (47) 50.00 22.00
❑ 48 Skip Hicks (48) 50.00 22.00
❑ 49 Brian Griese (49)......... 80.00 36.00
❑ 50 Charlie Batch (50) 80.00 36.00
❑ 51 Jacquez Green (51) 60.00 27.00
❑ 52 John Avery (52)........... 50.00 22.00
❑ 53 Kevin Dyson (53).......... 50.00 22.00
❑ 54 Peyton Manning (54).. 250.00 110.00
❑ 55 Randy Moss (55)........ 250.00 110.00
❑ 56 Ryan Leaf (56) 60.00 27.00
❑ 57 Curtis Enis (57) 60.00 27.00
❑ 58 Charles Woodson (58) 60.00 27.00
❑ 59 Robert Holcombe (59).. 60.00 27.00
❑ 60 Fred Taylor (60) 120.00 55.00

1998 E-X2001 Destination Honolulu

	MINT	NRMT
COMPLETE SET (10)	600.00	275.00
COMMON CARD (1-10)..........	25.00	11.00
STATED ODDS 1:720 HOBBY		

❑ 1 Peyton Manning 120.00 55.00
❑ 2 Terrell Davis 100.00 45.00
❑ 3 Corey Dillon................... 25.00 11.00
❑ 4 Eddie George 50.00 22.00
❑ 5 Emmitt Smith................ 100.00 45.00
❑ 6 Warrick Dunn 50.00 22.00
❑ 7 Brett Favre 120.00 55.00
❑ 8 Antowain Smith 40.00 18.00
❑ 9 Barry Sanders 120.00 55.00
❑ 10 Ryan Leaf 25.00 11.00

1998 E-X2001 Helmet Heroes

	MINT	NRMT
COMPLETE SET (20)	150.00	70.00
COMMON CARD (1-20)...........	2.50	1.10
SEMISTARS...........................	4.00	1.80
STATED ODDS 1:24 HOBBY		

❑ 1 Barry Sanders 20.00 9.00
❑ 2 Emmitt Smith................. 15.00 6.75
❑ 3 Brett Favre 20.00 9.00
❑ 4 Mark Brunell 8.00 3.60
❑ 5 Jerry Rice 10.00 4.50
❑ 6 Steve Young 6.00 2.70
❑ 7 Warrick Dunn 4.00 1.80
❑ 8 Kordell Stewart 4.00 1.80
❑ 9 John Elway 20.00 9.00
❑ 10 Troy Aikman 10.00 4.50
❑ 11 Dan Marino 20.00 9.00
❑ 12 Curtis Martin 4.00 1.80
❑ 13 Dorsey Levens 4.00 1.80
❑ 14 Jake Plummer 10.00 4.50
❑ 15 Corey Dillon................. 5.00 2.20
❑ 16 Yancey Thigpen 2.50 1.10
❑ 17 Randy Moss 25.00 11.00
❑ 18 Curtis Enis.................... 5.00 2.20
❑ 19 Charles Woodson 6.00 2.70
❑ 20 Fred Taylor 10.00 4.50

1998 E-X2001 Star Date 2001

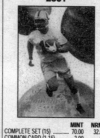

	MINT	NRMT
COMPLETE SET (15)	70.00	32.00
COMMON CARD (1-15)...........	2.00	.90
SEMISTARS...........................	3.00	1.35
UNLISTED STARS..................	4.00	1.80
STATED PDDS 1:12 HOBBY........		

❑ 1 Randy Moss 20.00 9.00
❑ 2 Fred Taylor 10.00 4.50
❑ 3 Corey Dillon.................... 4.00 1.80
❑ 4 Jake Plummer 8.00 3.60
❑ 5 Antowain Smith 4.00 1.80
❑ 6 Wilmont Perry .... 2.00 .90
❑ 7 Donald Hayes .... 2.00 .90
❑ 8 Tavian Banks 3.00 1.35
❑ 9 John Dutton..................... 2.00 .90
❑ 10 Kevin Dyson 4.00 1.80
❑ 11 Germane Crowell 5.00 2.20
❑ 12 Bobby Hoying 3.00 1.35
❑ 13 Jerome Pathon 3.00 1.35
❑ 14 Ryan Leaf 4.00 1.80
❑ 15 Peyton Manning 20.00 9.00

1999 E-X Century

	MINT	NRMT
COMPLETE SET (90)	150.00	70.00
COMP.SET w/o SP's (60)........	40.00	18.00
COMMON CARD (1-60)	.25	.11
SEMISTARS...........................	.50	.23
UNLISTED STARS..................	1.00	.45
COMMON ROOKIE (61-90)......	2.00	.90
ROOKIE SEMISTARS	3.00	1.35
ROOKIE UNL.STARS	4.00	1.80
ROOKIE SUBSET ODDS 1:4.......		

❑ 1 Keyshawn Johnson.......... 1.00 .45
❑ 2 Natrone Means .... .50 .23
❑ 3 Antonio Freeman............. 1.00 .45
❑ 4 Muhsin Muhammad........... .50 .23
❑ 5 Curtis Martin .... 1.00 .45
❑ 6 Chris Chandler .... .50 .23
❑ 7 Priest Holmes .... 1.00 .45
❑ 8 Vinny Testaverde .... .50 .23
❑ 9 Tim Brown........................ 1.00 .45
❑ 10 Eddie George .... 1.25 .55
❑ 11 Brad Johnson .... 1.00 .45
❑ 12 Mike Alstott .... 1.00 .45
❑ 13 Dorsey Levens .... 1.00 .45
❑ 14 Jamal Anderson .... 1.00 .45
❑ 15 Herman Moore .... 1.00 .45
❑ 16 Brett Favre 4.00 1.80
❑ 17 John Elway 4.00 1.80
❑ 18 Steve Young .... 1.50 .70
❑ 19 Warrick Dunn .... 1.00 .45
❑ 20 Fred Taylor 2.50 1.10
❑ 21 Charlie Batch.................. 2.00 .90
❑ 22 Jimmy Smith .... .50 .23
❑ 23 Steve McNair.................. 1.00 .45
❑ 24 Jerry Rice 2.50 1.10
❑ 25 Dan Marino 4.00 1.80
❑ 26 Jake Plummer .... 2.00 .90
❑ 27 Marshall Faulk................. 1.00 .45
❑ 28 Garrison Hearst................ .50 .23
❑ 29 Terrell Davis 2.50 1.10
❑ 30 Barry Sanders 4.00 1.80
❑ 31 Carl Pickens .... .50 .23
❑ 32 Jerome Bettis .... 1.00 .45
❑ 33 Scott Mitchell................... .25 .11
❑ 34 Duce Staley..................... 1.00 .45
❑ 35 Robert Smith.................... 1.00 .45
❑ 36 Wayne Chrebet .... .50 .23
❑ 37 Steve Beuerlein................ .25 .11
❑ 38 Elvis Grbac .... .50 .23
❑ 39 Troy Aikman 2.50 1.10
❑ 40 Emmitt Smith................... 2.50 1.10
❑ 41 Joey Galloway................. 1.00 .45
❑ 42 Ryan Leaf .... 1.00 .45
❑ 43 Skip Hicks .... 1.00 .45
❑ 44 Cris Carter...................... 1.00 .45
❑ 45 Shannon Sharpe .... .50 .23
❑ 46 Mark Brunell .... 1.50 .70
❑ 47 Kerry Collins .... .50 .23
❑ 48 Corey Dillon.................... 1.00 .45
❑ 49 Kordell Stewart .... 1.00 .45
❑ 50 Randy Moss 4.00 1.80
❑ 51 Jon Kitna .... 1.25 .55
❑ 52 Deion Sanders .... 1.00 .45
❑ 53 Rod Smith .... .50 .23
❑ 54 Drew Bledsoe .... 1.50 .70
❑ 55 Terrell Owens .... 1.00 .45
❑ 56 Napoleon Kaufman .... 1.00 .45
❑ 57 Trent Green....................... .50 .23
❑ 58 Ricky Watters .... .50 .23
❑ 59 Randall Cunningham...... 1.00 .45
❑ 60 Peyton Manning 4.00 1.80
❑ 61 Tim Couch RC............... 20.00 9.00
❑ 62 Amos Zereoue RC 4.00 1.80
❑ 63 Cade McNown RC 12.00 5.50
❑ 64 Donovan McNabb RC .. 12.00 5.50
❑ 65 Ricky Williams RC........ 20.00 9.00
❑ 66 Daunte Culpepper RC.. 12.00 5.50
❑ 67 Troy Edwards RC 6.00 2.70
❑ 68 Peerless Price RC.......... 6.00 2.70
❑ 69 Edgerrin James RC....... 35.00 16.00
❑ 70 Champ Bailey RC 5.00 2.20
❑ 71 Akili Smith RC 8.00 3.60
❑ 72 Kevin Johnson RC 10.00 4.50
❑ 73 Cecil Collins RC 4.00 1.80
❑ 74 David Boston RC............ 6.00 2.70
❑ 75 Torry Holt RC 10.00 4.50

Card	MINT	NRMT
❑ 76 James Johnson RC	5.00	2.20
❑ 77 Na Brown RC	4.00	1.80
❑ 78 Rob Konrad RC	3.00	1.35
❑ 79 Mike Cloud RC	4.00	1.80
❑ 80 Craig Yeast RC	3.00	1.35
❑ 81 Brock Huard RC	5.00	2.20
❑ 82 Chris McAlister RC	3.00	1.35
❑ 83 Shaun King RC	12.00	5.50
❑ 84 Wane McGarity RC	3.00	1.35
❑ 85 Joe Germaine RC	4.00	1.80
❑ 86 D'Wayne Bates RC	4.00	1.80
❑ 87 Kevin Faulk RC	5.00	2.20
❑ 88 Antoine Winfield RC	3.00	1.35
❑ 89 Reginald Kelly RC	2.00	.90
❑ 90 Antuan Edwards RC	2.00	.90
❑ P1 Jake Plummer Promo	2.00	.90

1999 E-X Century Essential Credentials Future

	MINT	NRMT
COMMON CARD/70-90	8.00	3.60
SEMISTARS/70-90	15.00	6.75
UNL.STARS/70-90	20.00	9.00
COMMON CARD/60-69	10.00	4.50
SEMISTARS/60-69	20.00	9.00
COMMON CARD/50-59	15.00	6.75
SEMISTARS/50-59	25.00	11.00
COMMON CARD/40-49	20.00	9.00
COMMON CARD/30-39	30.00	13.50

RANDOM INSERTS IN PACKS ....
CARDS #'d UNDER 16 NOT PRICED

Card	MINT	NRMT
❑ 1 Keyshawn Johnson/90	15.00	6.75
❑ 2 Natrone Means/89	8.00	3.60
❑ 3 Antonio Freeman/88	15.00	6.75
❑ 4 Muhsin Muhammad/87	8.00	3.60
❑ 5 Curtis Martin/86	15.00	6.75
❑ 6 Chris Chandler/85	8.00	3.60
❑ 7 Priest Holmes/84	15.00	6.75
❑ 8 Vinny Testaverde/83	8.00	3.60
❑ 9 Tim Brown/82	15.00	6.75
❑ 10 Eddie George/81	25.00	11.00
❑ 11 Brad Johnson/80	20.00	9.00
❑ 12 Mike Alstott/79	20.00	9.00
❑ 13 Dorsey Levens/78	20.00	9.00
❑ 14 Jamal Anderson/77	20.00	9.00
❑ 15 Herman Moore/76	20.00	9.00
❑ 16 Brett Favre/75	80.00	36.00
❑ 17 John Elway/74	80.00	36.00
❑ 18 Steve Young/73	30.00	13.50
❑ 19 Warrick Dunn/72	20.00	9.00
❑ 20 Fred Taylor/71	50.00	22.00
❑ 21 Charlie Batch/70	40.00	18.00
❑ 22 Jimmy Smith/69	10.00	4.50
❑ 23 Steve McNair/68	20.00	9.00
❑ 24 Jerry Rice/67	80.00	36.00
❑ 25 Dan Marino/66	100.00	45.00
❑ 26 Jake Plummer/65	40.00	18.00
❑ 27 Marshall Faulk/64	20.00	9.00
❑ 28 Garrison Hearst/63	20.00	9.00
❑ 29 Terrell Davis/62	80.00	36.00
❑ 30 Barry Sanders/61	100.00	45.00
❑ 31 Carl Pickens/60	10.00	4.50
❑ 32 Jerome Bettis/59	25.00	11.00
❑ 33 Scott Mitchell/58	15.00	6.75
❑ 34 Duce Staley/57	25.00	11.00
❑ 35 Robert Smith/56	15.00	6.75
❑ 36 Wayne Chrebet/55	25.00	11.00
❑ 37 Steve Beuerlein/54	15.00	6.75
❑ 38 Elvis Grbac/53	15.00	6.75
❑ 39 Troy Aikman/52	80.00	36.00
❑ 40 Emmitt Smith/51	80.00	36.00
❑ 41 Joey Galloway/50	40.00	18.00
❑ 42 Ryan Leaf/49	30.00	13.50
❑ 43 Skip Hicks/48	25.00	11.00
❑ 44 Cris Carter/47	40.00	18.00
❑ 45 Shannon Sharpe/46	20.00	9.00
❑ 46 Mark Brunell/45	60.00	27.00
❑ 47 Kerry Collins/44	20.00	9.00
❑ 48 Corey Dillon/43	40.00	18.00
❑ 49 Kordell Stewart/42	40.00	18.00
❑ 50 Randy Moss/41	150.00	70.00
❑ 51 Jon Kitna/40	60.00	27.00
❑ 52 Deion Sanders/39	50.00	22.00
❑ 53 Rod Smith/38	30.00	13.50
❑ 54 Drew Bledsoe/37	80.00	36.00
❑ 55 Terrell Owens/36	50.00	22.00
❑ 56 Napoleon Kaufman/35	50.00	22.00
❑ 57 Trent Green/34	30.00	13.50
❑ 58 Ricky Watters/33	30.00	13.50
❑ 59 Randall Cunningham/32	50.00	22.00
❑ 60 Peyton Manning/31	175.00	80.00
❑ 61 Tim Couch/30	200.00	90.00
❑ 62 Amos Zereoue/29	50.00	22.00
❑ 63 Cade McNown/28	120.00	55.00
❑ 64 Donovan McNabb/27	120.00	55.00
❑ 65 Ricky Williams/26	200.00	90.00
❑ 66 Daunte Culpepper/25	120.00	55.00
❑ 67 Troy Edwards/24	80.00	36.00
❑ 68 Peerless Price/23	80.00	36.00
❑ 69 Edgerrin James/22	450.00	200.00
❑ 70 Champ Bailey/21	60.00	27.00
❑ 71 Akili Smith/20	100.00	45.00
❑ 72 Kevin Johnson/19	100.00	45.00
❑ 73 Cecil Collins/18	60.00	27.00
❑ 74 David Boston/17	80.00	36.00
❑ 75 Torry Holt/16	120.00	55.00
❑ 76 James Johnson/15		
❑ 77 Na Brown/14		
❑ 78 Rob Konrad/13		
❑ 79 Mike Cloud/12		
❑ 80 Craig Yeast/11		
❑ 81 Brock Huard/10		
❑ 82 Chris McAlister/9		
❑ 83 Shaun King/8		
❑ 84 Wane McGarity/7		
❑ 85 Joe Germaine/6		
❑ 86 D'Wayne Bates/5		
❑ 87 Kevin Faulk/4		
❑ 88 Antoine Winfield/3		
❑ 89 Reginald Kelly/2		
❑ 90 Antuan Edwards/1		

1999 E-X Century Essential Credentials Now

	MINT	NRMT
COMMON CARD/75-90	8.00	3.60
SEMISTARS/75-90	15.00	6.75
UNL.STARS/75-90	20.00	9.00
COMMON CARD/50-60	15.00	6.75
SEMISTARS/50-60	25.00	11.00
COMMON CARD/40-49	20.00	9.00
SEMISTARS/40-49	30.00	13.50
COMMON CARD/30-39	20.00	9.00
SEMISTARS/30-39	30.00	13.50

RANDOM INSERTS IN PACKS ....
CARDS #'d UNDER 10 NOT PRICED

Card	MINT	NRMT
❑ 1 Keyshawn Johnson/1		
❑ 2 Natrone Means/2		
❑ 3 Antonio Freeman/3		
❑ 4 Muhsin Muhammad/4		
❑ 5 Curtis Martin/5		
❑ 6 Chris Chandler/6		
❑ 7 Priest Holmes/7		
❑ 8 Vinny Testaverde/8		
❑ 9 Tim Brown/9		
❑ 10 Eddie George/10	120.00	55.00
❑ 11 Brad Johnson/11	120.00	55.00
❑ 12 Mike Alstott/12	100.00	45.00
❑ 13 Dorsey Levens/13	100.00	45.00
❑ 14 Jamal Anderson/14	100.00	45.00
❑ 15 Herman Moore/15	100.00	45.00
❑ 16 Brett Favre/16	300.00	135.00
❑ 17 John Elway/17	300.00	135.00
❑ 18 Steve Young/18	100.00	45.00
❑ 19 Warrick Dunn/19	80.00	36.00
❑ 20 Fred Taylor/20	150.00	70.00
❑ 21 Charlie Batch/21	100.00	45.00
❑ 22 Jimmy Smith/22	40.00	18.00
❑ 23 Steve McNair/23	80.00	36.00
❑ 24 Jerry Rice/24	150.00	70.00
❑ 25 Dan Marino/25	200.00	90.00
❑ 26 Jake Plummer/26	80.00	36.00
❑ 27 Marshall Faulk/27	60.00	27.00
❑ 28 Garrison Hearst/28	40.00	18.00
❑ 29 Terrell Davis/29	120.00	55.00
❑ 30 Barry Sanders/30	200.00	90.00
❑ 31 Carl Pickens/31	30.00	13.50
❑ 32 Jerome Bettis/32	60.00	27.00
❑ 33 Scott Mitchell/33	30.00	13.50
❑ 34 Duce Staley/34	40.00	18.00
❑ 35 Robert Smith/35	30.00	13.50
❑ 36 Wayne Chrebet/36	40.00	18.00
❑ 37 Steve Beuerlein/37	20.00	9.00
❑ 38 Elvis Grbac/38	20.00	9.00
❑ 39 Troy Aikman/39	100.00	45.00
❑ 40 Emmitt Smith/40	100.00	45.00
❑ 41 Joey Galloway/41	40.00	18.00
❑ 42 Ryan Leaf/42	30.00	13.50
❑ 43 Skip Hicks/43	30.00	13.50
❑ 44 Cris Carter/44	40.00	18.00
❑ 45 Shannon Sharpe/45	20.00	9.00
❑ 46 Mark Brunell/46	60.00	27.00
❑ 47 Kerry Collins/47	20.00	9.00
❑ 48 Corey Dillon/48	40.00	18.00
❑ 49 Kordell Stewart/49	40.00	18.00
❑ 50 Randy Moss/50	100.00	45.00
❑ 51 Jon Kitna/51	30.00	13.50
❑ 52 Deion Sanders/52	30.00	13.50
❑ 53 Rod Smith/53	15.00	6.75
❑ 54 Drew Bledsoe/54	50.00	22.00
❑ 55 Terrell Owens/55	25.00	11.00
❑ 56 Napoleon Kaufman/56	25.00	11.00
❑ 57 Trent Green/57	15.00	6.75
❑ 58 Ricky Watters/58	15.00	6.75
❑ 59 Randall Cunningham/59	25.00	11.00
❑ 60 Peyton Manning/60	100.00	45.00
❑ 61 Tim Couch/61	150.00	70.00
❑ 62 Amos Zereoue/62	30.00	13.50
❑ 63 Cade McNown/63	80.00	36.00
❑ 64 Donovan McNabb/64	80.00	36.00
❑ 65 Ricky Williams/65	150.00	70.00
❑ 66 Daunte Culpepper/66	60.00	27.00
❑ 67 Troy Edwards/67	40.00	18.00
❑ 68 Peerless Price/68	40.00	18.00
❑ 69 Edgerrin James/69	250.00	110.00
❑ 70 Champ Bailey/70	30.00	13.50
❑ 71 Akili Smith/71	60.00	27.00
❑ 72 Kevin Johnson/72	60.00	27.00
❑ 73 Cecil Collins/73	30.00	13.50
❑ 74 David Boston/74	40.00	18.00
❑ 75 Torry Holt/75	50.00	22.00
❑ 76 James Johnson/76	25.00	11.00
❑ 77 Na Brown/77	15.00	6.75
❑ 78 Rob Konrad/78	20.00	9.00
❑ 79 Mike Cloud/79	20.00	9.00
❑ 80 Craig Yeast/80	15.00	6.75
❑ 81 Brock Huard/81	25.00	11.00
❑ 82 Chris McAlister/82	15.00	6.75
❑ 83 Shaun King/83	50.00	22.00
❑ 84 Wane McGarity/84	15.00	6.75
❑ 85 Joe Germaine/85	20.00	9.00
❑ 86 D'Wayne Bates/86	20.00	9.00
❑ 87 Kevin Faulk/87	25.00	11.00
❑ 88 Antoine Winfield/88	15.00	6.75
❑ 89 Reginald Kelly/89	8.00	3.60
❑ 90 Antuan Edwards/90	8.00	3.60

1999 E-X Century Authen-Kicks

	MINT	NRMT
COMPLETE SET (12)	800.00	350.00
COMMON CARD (1AK-12AK)	40.00	18.00

RANDOM INSERTS IN PACKS ....

Card	MINT	NRMT
❑ 1AK Travis McGriff/235	40.00	18.00
❑ 2AK Trent Green/190	40.00	18.00
❑ 3AK Brock Huard/280	50.00	22.00
❑ 4AK Randall Cunningham/290	50.00	22.00
❑ 5AK Donovan McNabb/210	100.00	45.00
❑ 6AK Torry Holt/285	70.00	32.00
❑ 7AK Joe Germaine/280	40.00	18.00
❑ 8AK Cade McNown/260	100.00	45.00
❑ 9AK Doug Flutie/215	50.00	22.00
❑ 10AK O.J. McDuffie/285	40.00	18.00
❑ 11AK Ricky Williams/215	150.00	70.00
❑ 12AK Dan Marino/285	150.00	70.00

1999 E-X Century Bright Lites

	MINT	NRMT
COMPLETE SET (20)	150.00	70.00
COMMON CARD (1BL-20BL)	4.00	1.80
STATED ODDS 1:24		
*ORANGE CARDS: 1.2X TO 3X GREENS		

	MINT	NRMT
❑ 1BL Randy Moss	12.00	5.50
❑ 2BL Tim Couch	15.00	6.75
❑ 3BL Eddie George	5.00	2.20
❑ 4BL Brett Favre	15.00	6.75
❑ 5BL Steve Young	6.00	2.70
❑ 6BL Barry Sanders	15.00	6.75
❑ 7BL Troy Aikman	10.00	4.50
❑ 8BL Jake Plummer	8.00	3.60
❑ 9BL Edgerrin James	25.00	11.00
❑ 10BL Terrell Davis	10.00	4.50
❑ 11BL Warrick Dunn	5.00	2.20
❑ 12BL Jerry Rice	10.00	4.50
❑ 13BL Fred Taylor	8.00	3.60
❑ 14BL Mark Brunell	6.00	2.70
❑ 15BL Emmitt Smith	10.00	4.50
❑ 16BL Ricky Williams	15.00	6.75
❑ 17BL Charlie Batch	6.00	2.70
❑ 18BL Jamal Anderson	4.00	1.80
❑ 19BL Peyton Manning	12.00	5.50
❑ 20BL Dan Marino	15.00	6.75

1999 E-X Century E-Xtraordinary

	MINT	NRMT
COMPLETE SET (15)	80.00	36.00
COMMON CARD (1XT-15XT)	2.50	1.10
STATED ODDS 1:9		

	MINT	NRMT
❑ 1XT Ricky Williams	10.00	4.50
❑ 2XT Corey Dillon	2.50	1.10
❑ 3XT Charlie Batch	4.00	1.80
❑ 4XT Terrell Davis	6.00	2.70
❑ 5XT Edgerrin James	15.00	6.75
❑ 6XT Jake Plummer	5.00	2.20
❑ 7XT Tim Couch	10.00	4.50
❑ 8XT Warrick Dunn	2.50	1.10
❑ 9XT Akili Smith	4.00	1.80
❑ 10XT Randy Moss	8.00	3.60
❑ 11XT Cade McNown	6.00	2.70
❑ 12XT Fred Taylor	5.00	2.20
❑ 13XT Donovan McNabb	6.00	2.70
❑ 14XT Torry Holt	5.00	2.20
❑ 15XT Peyton Manning	8.00	3.60

1994 Excalibur

	MINT	NRMT
COMPLETE SET (75)	25.00	11.00
COMMON CARD (1-75)	.25	.11
SEMISTARS	.50	.23
UNLISTED STARS	.75	.35

	MINT	NRMT
❑ 1 Bobby Hebert	.25	.11
❑ 2 Deion Sanders	1.25	.55
❑ 3 Andre Rison	.50	.23
❑ 4 Cornelius Bennett	.50	.23
❑ 5 Jim Kelly	.75	.35
❑ 6 Andre Reed	.50	.23
❑ 7 Bruce Smith	.75	.35
❑ 8 Thurman Thomas	.75	.35
❑ 9 Curtis Conway	.75	.35
❑ 10 Richard Dent	.50	.23
❑ 11 Jim Harbaugh	.75	.35
❑ 12 Troy Aikman	2.50	1.10
❑ 13 Michael Irvin	.75	.35
❑ 14 Russell Maryland	.25	.11
❑ 15 Emmitt Smith	4.00	1.80
❑ 16 Steve Atwater	.25	.11
❑ 17 Rod Bernstine	.25	.11
❑ 18 John Elway	5.00	2.20
❑ 19 Glyn Milburn	.50	.23
❑ 20 Shannon Sharpe	.50	.23
❑ 21 Barry Sanders	5.00	2.20
❑ 22 Edgar Bennett	.75	.35
❑ 23 Brett Favre	5.00	2.20
❑ 24 Sterling Sharpe	.50	.23
❑ 25 Reggie White	.75	.35
❑ 26 Warren Moon	.75	.35
❑ 27 Wilber Marshall	.25	.11
❑ 28 Haywood Jeffires	.50	.23
❑ 29 Lorenzo White	.25	.11
❑ 30 Quentin Coryatt	.25	.11
❑ 31 Roosevelt Potts	.25	.11
❑ 32 Jeff George	.75	.35
❑ 33 Joe Montana	5.00	2.20
❑ 34 Neil Smith	.75	.35
❑ 35 Marcus Allen	.75	.35
❑ 36 Derrick Thomas	.75	.35
❑ 37 Jeff Hostetler	.50	.23
❑ 38 Tim Brown	.75	.35
❑ 39 Rocket Ismail	.50	.23
❑ 40 Randall Cunningham	.75	.35
❑ 41 Jerome Bettis	.75	.35
❑ 42 Dan Marino	5.00	2.20
❑ 43 Keith Jackson	.25	.11
❑ 44 O.J. McDuffie	.75	.35
❑ 45 Drew Bledsoe	2.50	1.10
❑ 46 Leonard Russell	.25	.11
❑ 47 Wade Wilson	.25	.11
❑ 48 Eric Martin	.25	.11
❑ 49 Phil Simms	.50	.23
❑ 50 Gary Brown RB	.75	.35
❑ 51 Rodney Hampton	.75	.35
❑ 52 Boomer Esiason	.50	.23
❑ 53 Johnny Johnson	.25	.11
❑ 54 Ronnie Lott	.50	.23
❑ 55 Fred Barnett	.50	.23
❑ 56 Leroy Thompson	.25	.11
❑ 57 Barry Foster	.25	.11
❑ 58 Neil O'Donnell	.75	.35
❑ 59 Stan Humphries	.75	.35
❑ 60 Marion Butts	.25	.11
❑ 61 Anthony Miller	.50	.23
❑ 62 Natrone Means	.75	.35
❑ 63 Dana Stubblefield	.75	.35
❑ 64 John Taylor	.50	.23
❑ 65 Ricky Watters	.75	.35
❑ 66 Steve Young	2.00	.90
❑ 67 Jerry Rice	2.50	1.10
❑ 68 Tom Rathman	.25	.11
❑ 69 Rick Mirer	.75	.35
❑ 70 Chris Warren	.50	.23
❑ 71 Cortez Kennedy	.50	.23
❑ 72 Mark Rypien	.25	.11
❑ 73 Desmond Howard	.50	.23
❑ 74 Art Monk	.50	.23
❑ 75 Reggie Brooks	.50	.23

1994 Excalibur FX

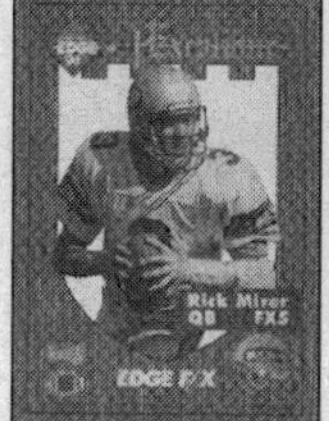

	MINT	NRMT
COMPLETE SET (7)	25.00	11.00
STATED ODDS 1:7		
*FX GOLD SHIELDS: 5X to 10X BASE CARD HI		
STATED ODDS 1:170		
*EQ GOLD SHIELDS: SAME VALUE		
ONE SET PER EDGEQUEST REDEMPTION		
*EQ SILVER SHIELDS: SAME VALUE		
ONE SET PER EDGEQUEST REDEMPTION		

	MINT	NRMT
❑ 1 Emmitt Smith	10.00	4.50
❑ 2 Rodney Hampton	2.00	.90
❑ 3 Jerome Bettis	2.00	.90
❑ 4 Steve Young	5.00	2.20
❑ 5 Rick Mirer	2.00	.90
❑ 6 John Elway	12.00	5.50
❑ 7 Troy Aikman UER (RB on front)	6.00	2.70

1994 Excalibur 22K

	MINT	NRMT
COMPLETE SET (25)	40.00	18.00
STATED ODDS 1:2		

	MINT	NRMT
❑ 1 Troy Aikman	4.00	1.80
❑ 2 Michael Irvin	1.25	.55
❑ 3 Emmitt Smith	6.00	2.70
❑ 4 Edgar Bennett	1.25	.55

Card	MINT	NRMT
❑ 5 Brett Favre	8.00	3.60
❑ 6 Sterling Sharpe	.75	.35
❑ 7 Rodney Hampton	1.25	.55
❑ 8 Jerome Bettis	1.25	.55
❑ 9 Jerry Rice	4.00	1.80
❑ 10 Steve Young	3.00	1.35
❑ 11 Ricky Watters	1.25	.55
❑ 12 Thurman Thomas	1.25	.55
❑ 13 John Elway	8.00	3.60
❑ 14 Shannon Sharpe	.75	.35
❑ 15 Joe Montana	8.00	3.60
❑ 16 Marcus Allen	1.25	.55
❑ 17 Tim Brown	1.25	.55
❑ 18 Rocket Ismail	.75	.35
❑ 19 Barry Foster	.40	.18
❑ 20 Natrone Means	1.25	.55
❑ 21 Rick Mirer	1.25	.55
❑ 22 Dan Marino	8.00	3.60
❑ 23 AFC Card	.40	.18
❑ 24 NFC Card	.40	.18
❑ 25 Excalibur Card	.40	.18
❑ NNO Uncut Sheet	25.00	11.00

1995 Excalibur

	MINT	NRMT
COMPLETE SET (150)	30.00	13.50
COMP.SERIES 1 (75)	15.00	6.75
COMP.SERIES 2 (75)	15.00	6.75
COMMON CARD (1-150)	.15	.07
SEMISTARS	.30	.14
UNLISTED STARS	.50	.23
COMP.DIE CUT SET (150)	300.00	135.00
COMP.DC SERIES 1 (75)	150.00	70.00
COMP.DC SERIES 2 (75)	150.00	70.00

*DC STARS: 2.5X to 6X HI COLUMN
DIE CUTS: STATED ODDS 1:9 ....

Card	MINT	NRMT
❑ 1 Gary Clark	.15	.07
❑ 2 Randal Hill	.15	.07
❑ 3 Anthony Edwards	.15	.07
❑ 4 Terance Mathis	.30	.14
❑ 5 Erric Pegram	.30	.14
❑ 6 Jeff George	.30	.14
❑ 7 Pete Metzelaars	.15	.07
❑ 8 Jim Kelly	.50	.23
❑ 9 Andre Reed	.30	.14
❑ 10 Lewis Tillman	.15	.07
❑ 11 Curtis Conway	.50	.23
❑ 12 Steve Walsh	.15	.07
❑ 13 Derrick Fenner	.15	.07
❑ 14 Harold Green	.15	.07
❑ 15 Michael Jackson	.30	.14
❑ 16 Eric Metcalf	.30	.14
❑ 17 Antonio Langham	.15	.07
❑ 18 Troy Aikman	2.00	.90
❑ 19 Alvin Harper	.15	.07
❑ 20 Jay Novacek	.30	.14
❑ 21 John Elway	4.00	1.80
❑ 22 Glyn Milburn	.15	.07
❑ 23 Steve Atwater	.15	.07
❑ 24 Mel Gray	.15	.07
❑ 25 Herman Moore	.50	.23
❑ 26 Scott Mitchell	.30	.14
❑ 27 Guy McIntyre	.15	.07
❑ 28 Edgar Bennett	.30	.14
❑ 29 Sterling Sharpe	.30	.14
❑ 30 Gary Brown	.15	.07
❑ 31 Haywood Jeffires	.15	.07
❑ 32 Marshall Faulk	.75	.35
❑ 33 Roosevelt Potts	.15	.07
❑ 34 Marcus Allen	.50	.23
❑ 35 Willie Davis	.30	.14
❑ 36 Lake Dawson	.30	.14
❑ 37 Jeff Hostetler	.30	.14
❑ 38 Rocket Ismail	.30	.14
❑ 39 Troy Drayton	.15	.07
❑ 40 Jerome Bettis	.50	.23
❑ 41 Dan Marino	4.00	1.80
❑ 42 Mark Ingram	.15	.07
❑ 43 O.J. McDuffie	.50	.23
❑ 44 Warren Moon	.30	.14
❑ 45 Qadry Ismail	.30	.14
❑ 46 Jake Reed	.30	.14
❑ 47 Ben Coates	.30	.14
❑ 48 Vincent Brisby	.15	.07
❑ 49 Michael Timpson	.15	.07
❑ 50 Brad Daluiso	.15	.07
❑ 51 Rodney Hampton	.30	.14
❑ 52 Chris Calloway	.15	.07
❑ 53 Rob Moore	.15	.07
❑ 54 Boomer Esiason	.30	.14
❑ 55 Michael Haynes	.30	.14
❑ 56 Vaughn Dunbar	.15	.07
❑ 57 Calvin Williams	.30	.14
❑ 58 Herschel Walker	.30	.14
❑ 59 Charlie Garner	.30	.14
❑ 60 Neil O'Donnell	.30	.14
❑ 61 Deon Figures	.15	.07
❑ 62 Byron Bam Morris	.30	.14
❑ 63 Junior Seau	.50	.23
❑ 64 Leslie O'Neal	.30	.14
❑ 65 Natrone Means	.50	.23
❑ 66 Jerry Rice	2.00	.90
❑ 67 Deion Sanders	1.25	.55
❑ 68 William Floyd	.50	.23
❑ 69 Chris Warren	.30	.14
❑ 70 Cortez Kennedy	.30	.14
❑ 71 Hardy Nickerson	.15	.07
❑ 72 Craig Erickson	.15	.07
❑ 73 Heath Shuler	.50	.23
❑ 74 Reggie Brooks	.30	.14
❑ 75 Henry Ellard	.30	.14
❑ 76 Garrison Hearst	.50	.23
❑ 77 Steve Beuerlein	.15	.07
❑ 78 Seth Joyner	.15	.07
❑ 79 Andre Rison	.30	.14
❑ 80 Norm Johnson	.15	.07
❑ 81 Craig Heyward	.30	.14
❑ 82 Darryl Talley	.15	.07
❑ 83 Kenneth Davis	.15	.07
❑ 84 Bruce Smith	.50	.23
❑ 85 Tom Waddle	.15	.07
❑ 86 Erik Kramer	.15	.07
❑ 87 Carl Pickens	.50	.23
❑ 88 Dan Wilkinson	.30	.14
❑ 89 Jeff Blake RC	1.00	.45
❑ 90 Vinny Testaverde	.30	.14
❑ 91 Tommy Vardell	.15	.07
❑ 92 Leroy Hoard	.15	.07
❑ 93 Emmitt Smith	3.00	1.35
❑ 94 Michael Irvin	.50	.23
❑ 95 Daryl Johnston	.30	.14
❑ 96 Shannon Sharpe	.30	.14
❑ 97 Anthony Miller	.30	.14
❑ 98 Leonard Russell	.15	.07
❑ 99 Barry Sanders	4.00	1.80
❑ 100 Brett Perriman	.30	.14
❑ 101 Johnnie Morton	.30	.14
❑ 102 Brett Favre	4.00	1.80
❑ 103 Bryce Paup	.50	.23
❑ 104 Ernest Givins	.15	.07
❑ 105 Webster Slaughter	.15	.07
❑ 106 Jim Harbaugh	.30	.14
❑ 107 Joe Montana	4.00	1.80
❑ 108 J.J. Birden	.15	.07
❑ 109 Steve Bono	.30	.14
❑ 110 James Jett	.30	.14
❑ 111 Tim Brown	.50	.23
❑ 112 Rob Fredrickson	.15	.07
❑ 113 Chris Miller	.15	.07
❑ 114 Bernie Parmalee	.30	.14
❑ 115 Terry Kirby	.30	.14
❑ 116 Bryan Cox	.15	.07
❑ 117 Irving Fryar	.30	.14
❑ 118 Terry Allen	.30	.14
❑ 119 Cris Carter	.50	.23
❑ 120 Fuad Reveiz	.15	.07
❑ 121 Drew Bledsoe	2.00	.90
❑ 122 Greg McMurtry	.20	.09
❑ 123 Dave Brown	.30	.14
❑ 124 Dave Meggett	.15	.07
❑ 125 Johnny Johnson	.15	.07
❑ 126 Ronnie Lott	.30	.14
❑ 127 Johnny Mitchell	.15	.07
❑ 128 Eric Martin	.15	.07
❑ 129 Jim Everett	.15	.07
❑ 130 Randall Cunningham	.50	.23
❑ 131 Eric Allen	.15	.07
❑ 132 Fred Barnett	.30	.14
❑ 133 Barry Foster	.30	.14
❑ 134 Kevin Greene	.30	.14
❑ 135 Eric Green	.15	.07
❑ 136 Stan Humphries	.30	.14
❑ 137 Mark Seay	.30	.14
❑ 138 Alfred Pupunu RC	.15	.07
❑ 139 Steve Young	1.50	.70
❑ 140 John Taylor	.15	.07
❑ 141 Ricky Watters	.50	.23
❑ 142 Brian Blades	.30	.14
❑ 143 Rick Mirer	.50	.23
❑ 144 Cortez Kennedy	.30	.14
❑ 145 Jackie Harris	.15	.07
❑ 146 Errict Rhett	.50	.23
❑ 147 Trent Dilfer	.50	.23
❑ 148 Brian Mitchell	.15	.07
❑ 149 Ricky Ervins	.15	.07
❑ 150 Darrell Green	.15	.07

1995 Excalibur Challengers Draft Day Rookie Redemption

	MINT	NRMT
COMPLETE SILVER SET (31)	30.00	13.50
COMMON SILVER (DD1-DD31)	1.00	.45
SEMISTARS SILVER	1.50	.70
UNLISTED STARS SILVER	2.00	.90

ONE SILV.CARD PER TEAM LOGO REDEMP.
*GOLD CARDS: SAME VALUE ....
ONE GOLD SET/EDGEQUEST STONE REDEMP.

Card	MINT	NRMT
❑ DD1 Derrick Alexander	1.00	.45
❑ DD2 Tony Boselli	1.50	.70
❑ DD3 Kyle Brady	1.50	.70
❑ DD4 Mark Bruener	1.50	.70
❑ DD5 Jamie Brown	1.00	.45
❑ DD6 Ruben Brown	1.00	.45
❑ DD7 Devin Bush	1.00	.45
❑ DD8 Kevin Carter	1.50	.70
❑ DD9 Ki-Jana Carter	2.00	.90
❑ DD10 Kerry Collins	2.50	1.10
❑ DD11 Kordell Stewart	6.00	2.70
❑ DD12 Mark Fields	1.00	.45
❑ DD13 Joey Galloway	6.00	2.70
❑ DD14 Trezelle Jenkins	1.00	.45
❑ DD15 Ellis Johnson	1.00	.45
❑ DD16 Napoleon Kaufman	5.00	2.20
❑ DD17 Ty Law	1.50	.70
❑ DD18 Mike Mamula	1.00	.45
❑ DD19 Steve McNair	6.00	2.70

		MINT	NRMT
DD20	Billy Milner	1.00	.45
DD21	Craig Newsome	1.50	.70
DD22	Craig Powell	1.00	.45
DD23	Rashaan Salaam	2.00	.90
DD24	Frank Sanders	2.50	1.10
DD25	Warren Sapp	1.50	.70
DD26	Terrance Shaw	1.00	.45
DD27	J.J.Stokes	2.00	.90
DD28	Michael Westbrook	4.00	1.80
DD29	Tyrone Wheatley	3.00	1.35
DD30	Sherman Williams	1.50	.70
DD31	Cover Card Checklist back	1.00	.45

1995 Excalibur Dragon Slayers

	MINT	NRMT
COMPLETE SET (14)	30.00	13.50
STATED ODDS 1:12 STONE		

		MINT	NRMT
1	Troy Aikman	4.00	1.80
2	Jerome Bettis	1.00	.45
3	Drew Bledsoe	4.00	1.80
4	Marshall Faulk	1.50	.70
5	Natrone Means	1.00	.45
6	Joe Montana	8.00	3.60
7	Byron Bam Morris	.60	.25
8	Errict Rhett	1.00	.45
9	Jerry Rice	4.00	1.80
10	Barry Sanders	8.00	3.60
11	Deion Sanders	2.50	1.10
12	Junior Seau	1.00	.45
13	Emmitt Smith	6.00	2.70
14	Ricky Watters	1.00	.45

1995 Excalibur EdgeTech

	MINT	NRMT
COMPLETE SET (12)	80.00	36.00
STATED ODDS 1:75 SWORD		

		MINT	NRMT
1	Emmitt Smith	20.00	9.00
2	Errict Rhett	3.00	1.35
3	Steve Young	10.00	4.50
4	Jerry Rice	12.00	5.50
5	Ben Coates	2.00	.90
6	Marcus Allen	3.00	1.35
7	John Elway	25.00	11.00
8	Keith Jackson	1.00	.45
9	Garrison Hearst	3.00	1.35
10	Natrone Means	3.00	1.35
11	Michael Haynes	2.00	.90
12	Byron Bam Morris	2.00	.90

1995 Excalibur Rookie Roundtable

	MINT	NRMT
COMPLETE SET (25)	18.00	8.00
COMP.SERIES 1 (13)	6.00	2.70
COMP.SERIES 2 (12)	12.00	5.50
1-13 STATED ODDS 1:9 SWORD		
14-25 STATED ODDS 1:9 STONE		

		MINT	NRMT
1	Sam Adams	.50	.23
2	Joe Johnson	.50	.23
3	Tim Bowens	.50	.23
4	Bryant Young	.50	.23
5	Aubrey Beavers	.50	.23
6	Willie McGinest	.50	.23
7	Rob Fredrickson	.50	.23
8	Lee Woodall	.50	.23
9	Antonio Langham	.50	.23
10	Dewayne Washington	.50	.23
11	Darryl Morrison	.50	.23
12	Keith Lyle	.50	.23
13	Antonio Langham	.50	.23
14	Darnay Scott	.50	.23
15	Derrick Alexander WR	1.00	.45
16	Todd Steussie	.50	.23
17	Larry Allen	.50	.23
18	Anthony Redmon	.50	.23
19	Joe Panos	.50	.23
20	Kevin Mawae	.50	.23
21	Andrew Jordan	1.00	.45
22	Heath Shuler	1.50	.70
23	Marshall Faulk	2.50	1.10
24	Errict Rhett	1.50	.70
25	Marshall Faulk POY	2.50	1.10

1995 Excalibur TekTech

	MINT	NRMT
COMPLETE SET (12)	70.00	32.00
SER.2 STATED ODDS 1:75 STONE		

		MINT	NRMT
1	Troy Aikman	12.00	5.50
2	Jerome Bettis	3.00	1.35
3	Drew Bledsoe	12.00	5.50
4	Tim Brown	3.00	1.35
5	Marshall Faulk	5.00	2.20
6	Haywood Jeffires	1.00	.45
7	Dan Marino	25.00	11.00
8	Barry Sanders	25.00	11.00
9	Deion Sanders	8.00	3.60
10	Junior Seau	3.00	1.35
11	Darryl Talley	1.00	.45
12	Ricky Watters	3.00	1.35

1995 Excalibur 22K

	MINT	NRMT
COMPLETE SET (50)	250.00	110.00
COMP.SWORD SER.1 (25)	120.00	55.00
COMP.STONE SER.2 (25)	150.00	70.00

*PRISM CARDS: 5X to 12X BASE CARD HI
PRISMS HAVE A RAINDROP PRISM LOOK
1SW-25SW STATED ODDS 1:36 SWORD
1ST-25ST STATED ODDS 1:36 STONE

		MINT	NRMT
1SW	Steve Young	12.00	5.50
2SW	Barry Sanders	30.00	13.50
3SW	John Elway	30.00	13.50
4SW	Warren Moon	2.50	1.10
5SW	Chris Warren	2.50	1.10
6SW	William Floyd	4.00	1.80
7SW	Jim Kelly	4.00	1.80
8SW	Troy Aikman	15.00	6.75
9SW	Jerome Bettis	4.00	1.80
10SW	Terance Mathis	2.50	1.10
11SW	Marcus Allen	4.00	1.80
12SW	Antonio Langham	1.25	.55
13SW	Sterling Sharpe	2.50	1.10
14SW	Leonard Russell	1.25	.55
15SW	Drew Bledsoe	15.00	6.75
16SW	Rodney Hampton	2.50	1.10
17SW	Herschel Walker	2.50	1.10
18SW	Jim Everett	1.25	.55
19SW	Terry Allen	2.50	1.10
20SW	Junior Seau	4.00	1.80
21SW	Natrone Means	4.00	1.80
22SW	Deion Sanders	10.00	4.50
23SW	Charlie Garner	2.50	1.10
24SW	Marshall Faulk	6.00	2.70
25SW	Ben Coates	2.50	1.10
1ST	Emmitt Smith	25.00	11.00
2ST	Jerry Rice	15.00	6.75
3ST	Stan Humphries	2.50	1.10
4ST	Joe Montana	30.00	13.50
5ST	Steve Atwater	1.25	.55
6ST	Eric Metcalf	2.50	1.10
7ST	Andre Rison	2.50	1.10
8ST	Brett Favre	30.00	13.50
9ST	Dan Marino	30.00	13.50
10ST	Byron Bam Morris	2.50	1.10
11ST	Heath Shuler	4.00	1.80
12ST	Trent Dilfer	4.00	1.80
13ST	Errict Rhett	4.00	1.80
14ST	Herman Moore	4.00	1.80
15ST	Eric Allen	1.25	.55
16ST	Cris Carter	4.00	1.80
17ST	Ronnie Lott	2.50	1.10
18ST	Randall Cunningham	4.00	1.80
19ST	Barry Foster	2.50	1.10
20ST	John Taylor	1.25	.55
21ST	Rick Mirer	4.00	1.80

Card	MINT	NRMT
❑ 22ST Tim Brown	4.00	1.80
❑ 23ST Michael Irvin	4.00	1.80
❑ 24ST Ricky Watters	4.00	1.80
❑ 25ST Jay Novacek	2.50	1.10

1997 Excalibur

	MINT	NRMT
COMPLETE SET (150)	60.00	27.00
COMMON CARD (1-150)	.25	.11
SEMISTARS	.50	.23
UNLISTED STARS	1.00	.45
COMP.NO-FOIL SET (150)	15.00	6.75
COMMON NO-FOIL	.05	.02

*NO-FOIL CARDS: .1X TO .25X FOILS

Card	MINT	NRMT
❑ 1 Larry Centers	.50	.23
❑ 2 Leeland McElroy	.25	.11
❑ 3 Simeon Rice	.50	.23
❑ 4 Eric Swann	.25	.11
❑ 5 Jamal Anderson	2.00	.90
❑ 6 Bert Emanuel	.50	.23
❑ 7 Eric Metcalf	.50	.23
❑ 8 Ray Lewis	.25	.11
❑ 9 Derrick Alexander WR	.50	.23
❑ 10 Michael Jackson	.50	.23
❑ 11 Vinny Testaverde	.50	.23
❑ 12 Todd Collins	.25	.11
❑ 13 Jim Kelly	1.00	.45
❑ 14 Eric Moulds	1.00	.45
❑ 15 Andre Reed	.50	.23
❑ 16 Bruce Smith	.50	.23
❑ 17 Thurman Thomas	1.00	.45
❑ 18 Tim Biakabutuka	.50	.23
❑ 19 Kerry Collins	.50	.23
❑ 20 Kevin Greene	.50	.23
❑ 21 Anthony Johnson	.25	.11
❑ 22 Lamar Lathon	.25	.11
❑ 23 Muhsin Muhammad	.50	.23
❑ 24 Curtis Conway	.50	.23
❑ 25 Bryan Cox	.25	.11
❑ 26 Walt Harris	.25	.11
❑ 27 Erik Kramer	.25	.11
❑ 28 Rick Mirer	.25	.11
❑ 29 Rashaan Salaam	.25	.11
❑ 30 Jeff Blake	.50	.23
❑ 31 Ki-Jana Carter	.25	.11
❑ 32 Carl Pickens	1.00	.45
❑ 33 Troy Aikman	3.00	1.35
❑ 34 Michael Irvin	1.00	.45
❑ 35 Daryl Johnston	.50	.23
❑ 36 Emmitt Smith	5.00	2.20
❑ 37 Broderick Thomas	.25	.11
❑ 38 Terrell Davis	5.00	2.20
❑ 39 John Elway	6.00	2.70
❑ 40 Anthony Miller	.25	.11
❑ 41 John Mobley	.25	.11
❑ 42 Shannon Sharpe	.50	.23
❑ 43 Neil Smith	.50	.23
❑ 44 Scott Mitchell	.50	.23
❑ 45 Herman Moore	1.00	.45
❑ 46 Brett Perriman	.25	.11
❑ 47 Barry Sanders	6.00	2.70
❑ 48 Edgar Bennett	.50	.23
❑ 49 Robert Brooks	.50	.23
❑ 50 Brett Favre	6.00	2.70
❑ 51 Antonio Freeman	1.50	.70
❑ 52 Dorsey Levens	1.00	.45
❑ 53 Reggie White	1.00	.45
❑ 54 Eddie George	4.00	1.80
❑ 55 Darryll Lewis	.25	.11
❑ 56 Steve McNair	1.50	.70
❑ 57 Chris Sanders	.25	.11
❑ 58 Marshall Faulk	1.00	.45
❑ 59 Jim Harbaugh	.50	.23
❑ 60 Marvin Harrison	1.00	.45
❑ 61 Jimmy Smith	.50	.23
❑ 62 Tony Brackens	.25	.11
❑ 63 Mark Brunell	3.00	1.35
❑ 64 Kevin Hardy	.25	.11
❑ 65 Keenan McCardell	.50	.23
❑ 66 Natrone Means	1.00	.45
❑ 67 Marcus Allen	1.00	.45
❑ 68 Elvis Grbac	.50	.23
❑ 69 Derrick Thomas	.50	.23
❑ 70 Tamarick Vanover	.50	.23
❑ 71 Karim Abdul-Jabbar	1.00	.45
❑ 72 Terrell Buckley	.25	.11
❑ 73 Irving Fryar	.50	.23
❑ 74 Dan Marino	6.00	2.70
❑ 75 O.J. McDuffie	.50	.23
❑ 76 Zach Thomas	.50	.23
❑ 77 Terry Kirby	.50	.23
❑ 78 Cris Carter	1.00	.45
❑ 79 Brad Johnson	1.25	.55
❑ 80 John Randle	.25	.11
❑ 81 Jake Reed	.50	.23
❑ 82 Robert Smith	.50	.23
❑ 83 Drew Bledsoe	3.00	1.35
❑ 84 Ben Coates	.50	.23
❑ 85 Terry Glenn	1.00	.45
❑ 86 Ty Law	.25	.11
❑ 87 Curtis Martin	1.50	.70
❑ 88 Willie McGinest	.25	.11
❑ 89 Mario Bates	.25	.11
❑ 90 Jim Everett	.25	.11
❑ 91 Wayne Martin	.25	.11
❑ 92 Heath Shuler	.25	.11
❑ 93 Torrance Small	.25	.11
❑ 94 Ray Zellars	.25	.11
❑ 95 Dave Brown	.25	.11
❑ 96 Jason Sehorn	.50	.23
❑ 97 Amani Toomer	.50	.23
❑ 98 Tyrone Wheatley	.50	.23
❑ 99 Hugh Douglas	.25	.11
❑ 100 Aaron Glenn	.25	.11
❑ 101 Jeff Graham	.25	.11
❑ 102 Keyshawn Johnson	1.00	.45
❑ 103 Adrian Murrell	.50	.23
❑ 104 Neil O'Donnell	.50	.23
❑ 105 Tim Brown	1.00	.45
❑ 106 Jeff George	.50	.23
❑ 107 Jeff Hostetler	.25	.11
❑ 108 Napoleon Kaufman	1.50	.70
❑ 109 Chester McGlockton	.25	.11
❑ 110 Fred Barnett	.25	.11
❑ 111 Ty Detmer	.50	.23
❑ 112 Chris T. Jones	.25	.11
❑ 113 Ricky Watters	.50	.23
❑ 114 Bobby Engram	.50	.23
❑ 115 Jerome Bettis	1.00	.45
❑ 116 Charles Johnson	.50	.23
❑ 117 Greg Lloyd	.25	.11
❑ 118 Kordell Stewart	1.50	.70
❑ 119 Yancey Thigpen	.50	.23
❑ 120 Rod Woodson	.50	.23
❑ 121 Stan Humphries	.50	.23
❑ 122 Tony Martin	.50	.23
❑ 123 Leonard Russell	.25	.11
❑ 124 Junior Seau	.50	.23
❑ 125 Chad Brown	.25	.11
❑ 126 John Friesz	.25	.11
❑ 127 Joey Galloway	1.50	.70
❑ 128 Cortez Kennedy	.25	.11
❑ 129 Warren Moon	1.00	.45
❑ 130 Chris Warren	.50	.23
❑ 131 Garrison Hearst	.50	.23
❑ 132 Terrell Owens	1.00	.45
❑ 133 Jerry Rice	3.00	1.35
❑ 134 Dana Stubblefield	.25	.11
❑ 135 Bryant Young	.25	.11
❑ 136 Steve Young	2.00	.90
❑ 137 Tony Banks	.50	.23
❑ 138 Isaac Bruce	1.00	.45
❑ 139 Eddie Kennison	.50	.23
❑ 140 Keith Lyle	.25	.11
❑ 141 Lawrence Phillips	.25	.11
❑ 142 Mike Alstott	1.00	.45
❑ 143 Hardy Nickerson	.25	.11
❑ 144 Errict Rhett	.25	.11
❑ 145 Warren Sapp	.50	.23
❑ 146 Gus Frerotte	.25	.11
❑ 147 Sean Gilbert	.25	.11
❑ 148 Ken Harvey	.25	.11
❑ 149 Terry Allen	1.00	.45
❑ 150 Michael Westbrook	.50	.23

1997 Excalibur Crusaders

	MINT	NRMT
COMPLETE SET (25)	150.00	70.00

STATED ODDS 1:30

STATED PRINT RUN 750 SERIAL #'d SETS

Card	MINT	NRMT
❑ 1 Brett Favre	40.00	18.00
❑ 2 Mark Brunell	20.00	9.00
❑ 3 Jim Kelly	6.00	2.70
❑ 4 Michael Westbrook	3.00	1.35
❑ 5 Emmitt Smith	30.00	13.50
❑ 6 Marshall Faulk	6.00	2.70
❑ 7 Kerry Collins	3.00	1.35
❑ 8 Jeff Hostetler	1.50	.70
❑ 9 Rashaan Salaam	1.50	.70
❑ 10 Garrison Hearst	3.00	1.35
❑ 11 Tamarick Vanover	3.00	1.35
❑ 12 Rodney Hampton	6.00	2.70
❑ 13 Leeland McElroy	1.50	.70
❑ 14 Tony Banks	3.00	1.35
❑ 15 Deion Sanders	6.00	2.70
❑ 16 Errict Rhett	1.50	.70
❑ 17 Thurman Thomas	6.00	2.70
❑ 18 Chris Warren	3.00	1.35
❑ 19 Andre Reed	3.00	1.35
❑ 20 Napoleon Kaufman	10.00	4.50
❑ 21 Terry Allen	6.00	2.70
❑ 22 Carl Pickens	6.00	2.70
❑ 23 Marvin Harrison	6.00	2.70
❑ 24 Lawrence Phillips	1.50	.70
❑ 25 Troy Aikman	20.00	9.00

1997 Excalibur Game Helmets

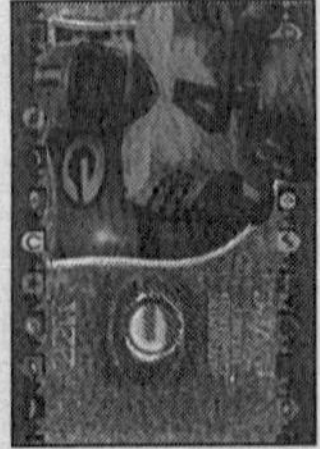

	MINT	NRMT
COMP.UNSIGNED SET (23)	600.00	275.00
COMMON CARD (1-25)	15.00	6.75
SEMISTARS	20.00	9.00
UNLISTED STARS	30.00	13.50

UNSIGNED CARDS STATED ODDS 1:60
STATED PRINT RUN 249 UNSIGNED SETS
UNSIGNED BETTIS STATED PRINT RUN 40
SIGNED CARDS STATED ODDS 1:350
BETTIS AUTO ISSUED AS DEALER PREMIUM

	MINT	NRMT
❑ 1 Brett Favre	80.00	36.00
❑ 2AU Mark Brunell	60.00	27.00
AUTO/700		
❑ 3 Barry Sanders	80.00	36.00
❑ 4 John Elway	80.00	36.00
❑ 5 Emmitt Smith	80.00	36.00
❑ 6 Drew Bledsoe	50.00	22.00
❑ 7 Troy Aikman	50.00	22.00
❑ 8 Dan Marino	80.00	36.00
❑ 9 Eddie George	40.00	18.00
❑ 10 Terry Glenn	20.00	9.00
❑ 11 Keyshawn Johnson	30.00	13.50
❑ 12AU Terrell Davis	120.00	55.00
AUTO/500		
❑ 13 Curtis Martin	30.00	13.50
❑ 14 Steve McNair	30.00	13.50
❑ 15 Muhsin Muhammad	20.00	9.00
❑ 16 Antonio Freeman	40.00	18.00
❑ 17 Ricky Watters	20.00	9.00
❑ 18 Jerome Bettis SP	100.00	45.00
❑ 18AU Jerome Bettis	120.00	55.00
AUTO/100		
(released as dealer premium only)		
❑ 19 Herman Moore	30.00	13.50
❑ 20 Isaac Bruce	30.00	13.50
❑ 21 Deion Sanders	30.00	13.50
❑ 22 Cris Carter	30.00	13.50
❑ 23 Tim Biakabutuka	15.00	6.75
❑ 24 Karim Abdul-Jabbar	30.00	13.50
❑ 25 Mike Alstott	30.00	13.50
❑ 26 Jamal Anderson	120.00	55.00
AUTO/100		
❑ 27 Kevin Greene	60.00	27.00
AUTO/100		
❑ 28 Tim Brown AUTO/100	120.00	55.00

1997 Excalibur Gridiron Wizards Draft

	MINT	NRMT
COMPLETE SET (25)	120.00	55.00
COMMON CARD (1-25)	3.00	1.35
SEMISTARS	5.00	2.20

STATED ODDS 1:20

	MINT	NRMT
❑ 1 Orlando Pace	3.00	1.35
❑ 2 Peter Boulware	5.00	2.20
❑ 3 Darrell Russell	3.00	1.35
❑ 4 Shawn Springs	5.00	2.20
❑ 5 Yatil Green	5.00	2.20
❑ 6 Jim Druckenmiller	6.00	2.70
❑ 7 Bryant Westbrook	3.00	1.35
❑ 8 Dwayne Rudd	3.00	1.35
❑ 9 David LaFleur	5.00	2.20
❑ 10 Rae Carruth	5.00	2.20
❑ 11 Corey Dillon	10.00	4.50
❑ 12 Antowain Smith	6.00	2.70
❑ 13 Tiki Barber	5.00	2.20
❑ 14 Marcus Harris	3.00	1.35
❑ 15 Warrick Dunn	8.00	3.60
❑ 16 Chris Canty	3.00	1.35
❑ 17 Tony Gonzalez	8.00	3.60
❑ 18 Danny Wuerffel	5.00	2.20
❑ 19 Ike Hilliard	5.00	2.20
❑ 20 James Farrior	3.00	1.35
❑ 21 Reidel Anthony	5.00	2.20
❑ 22 Jake Plummer	20.00	9.00
❑ 23 Troy Davis	5.00	2.20
❑ 24 Pat Barnes	5.00	2.20
❑ 25 Darnell Autry	5.00	2.20

1997 Excalibur Marauders

	MINT	NRMT
COMPLETE SET (25)	225.00	100.00
COMMON CARD (1-25)	2.50	1.10
SEMISTARS	4.00	1.80
UNLISTED STARS	6.00	2.70

STATED ODDS 1:20
*SUPREME EDGE: 2X TO 5X HI COL.
SUP.EDGE CARDS IN '98 CE
SUP.SEAS.REVIEW
SUPREME EDGE STATED PRINT RUN 50 SETS

❑ 1 Tony Banks	10.00	4.50
Antonio Freeman		
❑ 2 Tim Biakabutuka	2.50	1.10
Heath Shuler		
❑ 3 Eddie Kennison	30.00	13.50
Brett Favre		
❑ 4 Todd Collins	6.00	2.70
Marcus Allen		
❑ 5 Shannon Sharpe	30.00	13.50
Dan Marino		
❑ 6 Napoleon Kaufman	6.00	2.70
Desmond Howard		
❑ 7 Mushin Muhammad	4.00	1.80
Dorsey Levens		
❑ 8 Mike Alstott	20.00	9.00
Drew Bledsoe		
❑ 9 Michael Westbrook	25.00	11.00
Emmitt Smith		
❑ 10 Marvin Harrison	4.00	1.80
Heath Shuler		
❑ 11 Marshall Faulk	4.00	1.80
Jeff Blake		
❑ 12 Lawrence Phillips	2.50	1.10
Jeff George		
❑ 13 Edgar Bennett	2.50	1.10
Tony Martin		
❑ 14 Karim Abdul-Jabbar	15.00	6.75
Jerry Rice		
❑ 15 Terrell Owens	10.00	4.50
Jim Harbaugh		
❑ 16 Isaac Bruce	30.00	13.50
John Elway		
❑ 17 Eric Metcalf	2.50	1.10
Dave Brown		
❑ 18 Eddie Kennison	4.00	1.80
Junior Seau		
❑ 19 Eddie George	15.00	6.75
Mark Brunell		
❑ 20 Deion Sanders	8.00	3.60
Cris Carter		
❑ 21 Eric Moulds	12.00	5.50
Steve Young		
❑ 22 Chris Warren	4.00	1.80
Ben Coates		
❑ 23 Carl Pickens	6.00	2.70
Robert Brooks		
❑ 24 Bobby Engram	6.00	2.70
Tim Brown		
❑ 25 Ben Coates	15.00	6.75
Troy Aikman		

1997 Excalibur Overlords

	MINT	NRMT
COMPLETE SET (25)	250.00	110.00

STATED ODDS 1:30
STATED PRINT RUN 750 SERIAL #'d SETS
CASTLES: SAME PRICE AS OVERLORDS
CASTLE PRINT RUN 750 SERIAL #'d SETS

	MINT	NRMT
❑ 1 Jeff Blake	4.00	1.80
❑ 2 Mark Brunell	25.00	11.00
❑ 3 Bobby Engram	4.00	1.80
❑ 4 Joey Galloway	12.00	5.50
❑ 5 Eddie Kennison	4.00	1.80
❑ 6 Terrell Davis	40.00	18.00
❑ 7 Chris Calloway	4.00	1.80
❑ 8 Hardy Nickerson	2.00	.90
❑ 9 Errict Rhett	2.00	.90
❑ 10 Emmitt Smith	40.00	18.00
❑ 11 Kordell Stewart	12.00	5.50
❑ 12 Steve Young	15.00	6.75
❑ 13 Marcus Allen	8.00	3.60
❑ 14 Edgar Bennett	4.00	1.80
❑ 15 Robert Brooks	4.00	1.80
❑ 16 Kerry Collins	4.00	1.80
❑ 17 Todd Collins	2.00	.90
❑ 18 Brett Favre	50.00	22.00
❑ 19 Gus Frerotte	2.00	.90
❑ 20 Elvis Grbac	4.00	1.80
❑ 21 Jeff Hostetler	2.00	.90
❑ 22 Tony Martin	4.00	1.80
❑ 23 Terrell Owens	8.00	3.60
❑ 24 Dorsey Levens	8.00	3.60
❑ 25 Thurman Thomas	8.00	3.60

1997 Excalibur 22K Knights

	MINT	NRMT
COMPLETE SET (25)	200.00	90.00

STATED ODDS 1:20
STATED PRINT RUN 2000 SERIAL #'d SETS
*BLACK MAGNUMS: 6X TO 12X BASE CARD HI
BL STATED ODDS 1:75 SUPER PREM.HOBBY
BL STATED PRINT RUN 250 SERIAL #'d SETS
*SUPREME EDGE: 10X TO 20X BASE CARD HI
SUP.EDGE CARDS IN '98 CE
SUP.SEAS.REVIEW
SUPREME EDGE STATED PRINT RUN 50 SETS

	MINT	NRMT
❑ 1 Troy Aikman	12.00	5.50
❑ 2 John Elway	25.00	11.00
❑ 3 Brett Favre	25.00	11.00
❑ 4 Dan Marino	25.00	11.00

❑	5 Barry Sanders	25.00	11.00
❑	6 Emmitt Smith	20.00	9.00
❑	7 Mark Brunell	12.00	5.50
❑	8 Jerry Rice	12.00	5.50
❑	9 Terrell Davis	20.00	9.00
❑	10 Natrone Means	4.00	1.80
❑	11 Joey Galloway	6.00	2.70
❑	12 Keyshawn Johnson	4.00	1.80
❑	13 Curtis Martin	6.00	2.70
❑	14 Herman Moore	4.00	1.80
❑	15 Eddie George	15.00	6.75
❑	16 Terry Glenn	4.00	1.80
❑	17 Steve McNair	6.00	2.70
❑	18 Warren Moon	4.00	1.80
❑	19 Ricky Watters	2.00	.90
❑	20 Karim Abdul-Jabbar	4.00	1.80
❑	21 Gus Frerotte	1.00	.45
❑	22 Terry Allen	4.00	1.80
❑	23 Andre Reed	2.00	.90
❑	24 Jerome Bettis	4.00	1.80
❑	25 Tim Brown	4.00	1.80

1994 Finest

	MINT	NRMT
COMPLETE SET (220)	60.00	27.00
COMMON CARD (1-220)	.40	.18
SEMISTARS	.75	.35
UNLISTED STARS	1.50	.70
COMP.REFRACT.SET (220)	1200.00	550.00

*REFRACTORS: 2.5X TO 6X HI COL.
REFRACT.RANDOM INSERTS IN PACKS

❑	1 Emmitt Smith	8.00	3.60
❑	2 Calvin Williams	.75	.35
❑	3 Mark Collins	.40	.18
❑	4 Steve McMichael	.75	.35
❑	5 Jim Kelly	1.50	.70
❑	6 Michael Dean Perry	.75	.35
❑	7 Wayne Simmons	.40	.18
❑	8 Rocket Ismail	.75	.35
❑	9 Mark Rypien	.40	.18
❑	10 Brian Blades	.75	.35
❑	11 Barry Word	.40	.18
❑	12 Jerry Rice	5.00	2.20
❑	13 Derrick Fenner	.40	.18
❑	14 Karl Mecklenburg	.40	.18
❑	15 Reggie Cobb	.40	.18
❑	16 Eric Swann	.75	.35
❑	17 Neil Smith	1.50	.70
❑	18 Barry Foster	.40	.18
❑	19 Willie Roaf	.40	.18
❑	20 Troy Drayton	.40	.18
❑	21 Warren Moon	1.50	.70
❑	22 Richmond Webb	.40	.18
❑	23 Anthony Miller	.75	.35
❑	24 Chris Slade	.40	.18
❑	25 Mel Gray	.40	.18
❑	26 Ronnie Lott	.75	.35
❑	27 Andre Rison	.75	.35
❑	28 Jeff George	1.50	.70
❑	29 John Copeland	.40	.18
❑	30 Derrick Thomas	1.50	.70
❑	31 Sterling Sharpe	.75	.35
❑	32 Chris Doleman	.40	.18
❑	33 Monte Coleman	.40	.18
❑	34 Mark Bavaro	.40	.18
❑	35 Kevin Williams	.75	.35
❑	36 Eric Metcalf	.75	.35
❑	37 Brent Jones	.75	.35
❑	38 Steve Tasker	.75	.35
❑	39 Dave Meggett	.40	.18
❑	40 Howie Long	.75	.35
❑	41 Rick Mirer	1.50	.70
❑	42 Jerome Bettis	2.50	1.10
❑	43 Marion Butts	.40	.18
❑	44 Barry Sanders	10.00	4.50
❑	45 Jason Elam	.40	.18
❑	46 Broderick Thomas	.40	.18
❑	47 Derek Brown RBK	.40	.18
❑	48 Lorenzo White	.40	.18
❑	49 Neil O'Donnell	1.50	.70
❑	50 Chris Burkett	.40	.18
❑	51 John Offerdahl	.40	.18
❑	52 Rohn Stark	.40	.18
❑	53 Neal Anderson	.40	.18
❑	54 Steve Beuerlein	.40	.18
❑	55 Bruce Armstrong	.40	.18
❑	56 Lincoln Kennedy	.40	.18
❑	57 Darrell Green	.40	.18
❑	58 Ricardo McDonald	.40	.18
❑	59 Chris Warren	.75	.35
❑	60 Mark Jackson	.40	.18
❑	61 Pepper Johnson	.40	.18
❑	62 Chris Spielman	.75	.35
❑	63 Marcus Allen	1.50	.70
❑	64 Jim Everett	.75	.35
❑	65 Greg Townsend	.40	.18
❑	66 Cris Carter	2.00	.90
❑	67 Don Beebe	.40	.18
❑	68 Reggie Langhorne	.40	.18
❑	69 Randall Cunningham	1.50	.70
❑	70 Johnny Holland	.40	.18
❑	71 Morten Andersen	.40	.18
❑	72 Leonard Marshall	.40	.18
❑	73 Keith Jackson	.40	.18
❑	74 Leslie O'Neal	.40	.18
❑	75 Hardy Nickerson	.75	.35
❑	76 Dan Williams	.40	.18
❑	77 Steve Young	4.00	1.80
❑	78 Deon Figures	.40	.18
❑	79 Michael Irvin	1.50	.70
❑	80 Luis Sharpe	.40	.18
❑	81 Andre Tippett	.40	.18
❑	82 Ricky Sanders	.40	.18
❑	83 Erric Pegram	.40	.18
❑	84 Albert Lewis	.40	.18
❑	85 Anthony Blaylock	.40	.18
❑	86 Pat Swilling	.40	.18
❑	87 Duane Bickett	.40	.18
❑	88 Myron Guyton	.40	.18
❑	89 Clay Matthews	.40	.18
❑	90 Jim McMahon	.40	.18
❑	91 Bruce Smith	1.50	.70
❑	92 Reggie White	1.50	.70
❑	93 Shannon Sharpe	.75	.35
❑	94 Rickey Jackson	.40	.18
❑	95 Ronnie Harmon	.40	.18
❑	96 Terry McDaniel	.40	.18
❑	97 Bryan Cox	.40	.18
❑	98 Webster Slaughter	.40	.18
❑	99 Boomer Esiason	.75	.35
❑	100 Tim Krumrie	.40	.18
❑	101 Cortez Kennedy	.75	.35
❑	102 Henry Ellard	.75	.35
❑	103 Clyde Simmons	.40	.18
❑	104 Craig Erickson	.40	.18
❑	105 Eric Green	.40	.18
❑	106 Gary Clark	.75	.35
❑	107 Jay Novacek	.75	.35
❑	108 Dana Stubblefield	1.50	.70
❑	109 Mike Johnson	.40	.18
❑	110 Ray Crockett	.40	.18
❑	111 Leonard Russell	.40	.18
❑	112 Robert Smith	2.50	1.10
❑	113 Art Monk	.75	.35
❑	114 Ray Childress	.40	.18
❑	115 O.J. McDuffie	1.50	.70
❑	116 Tim Brown	1.50	.70
❑	117 Kevin Ross	.40	.18
❑	118 Richard Dent	.75	.35
❑	119 John Elway	10.00	4.50
❑	120 James Hasty	.40	.18
❑	121 Gary Plummer	.40	.18
❑	122 Pierce Holt	.40	.18
❑	123 Eric Martin	.40	.18
❑	124 Brett Favre	10.00	4.50
❑	125 Cornelius Bennett	.75	.35
❑	126 Jessie Hester	.40	.18
❑	127 Lewis Tillman	.40	.18
❑	128 Qadry Ismail	1.50	.70
❑	129 Jay Schroeder	.40	.18
❑	130 Curtis Conway	1.50	.70
❑	131 Santana Dotson	.75	.35
❑	132 Nick Lowery	.40	.18
❑	133 Lomas Brown	.40	.18
❑	134 Reggie Roby	.40	.18
❑	135 John L. Williams	.40	.18
❑	136 Vinny Testaverde	.75	.35
❑	137 Seth Joyner	.40	.18
❑	138 Ethan Horton	.40	.18
❑	139 Jackie Slater	.40	.18
❑	140 Rod Bernstine	.40	.18
❑	141 Rob Moore	.75	.35
❑	142 Dan Marino	10.00	4.50
❑	143 Ken Harvey	.40	.18
❑	144 Ernest Givins	.75	.35
❑	145 Russell Maryland	.40	.18
❑	146 Drew Bledsoe	6.00	2.70
❑	147 Kevin Greene	1.50	.70
❑	148 Bobby Hebert	.40	.18
❑	149 Junior Seau	1.50	.70
❑	150 Tim McDonald	.40	.18
❑	151 Thurman Thomas	1.50	.70
❑	152 Phil Simms	.75	.35
❑	153 Terrell Buckley	.40	.18
❑	154 Sam Mills	.40	.18
❑	155 Anthony Carter	.75	.35
❑	156 Kelvin Martin	.40	.18
❑	157 Shane Conlan	.40	.18
❑	158 Irving Fryar	.75	.35
❑	159 Demetrius DuBose	.40	.18
❑	160 David Klingler	.40	.18
❑	161 Herman Moore	1.50	.70
❑	162 Jeff Hostetler	.75	.35
❑	163 Tommy Vardell	.40	.18
❑	164 Craig Heyward	.75	.35
❑	165 Wilber Marshall	.40	.18
❑	166 Quentin Coryatt	.40	.18
❑	167 Glyn Milburn	.75	.35
❑	168 Fred Barnett	.75	.35
❑	169 Charles Haley	.75	.35
❑	170 Carl Banks	.40	.18
❑	171 Ricky Proehl	.40	.18
❑	172 Joe Montana	10.00	4.50
❑	173 Johnny Mitchell	.40	.18
❑	174 Andre Reed	.75	.35
❑	175 Marco Coleman	.40	.18
❑	176 Vaughan Johnson	.40	.18
❑	177 Carl Pickens	1.50	.70
❑	178 Dwight Stone	.40	.18
❑	179 Ricky Watters	1.50	.70
❑	180 Michael Haynes	.75	.35
❑	181 Roger Craig	.75	.35
❑	182 Cleveland Gary	.40	.18
❑	183 Steve Emtman	.40	.18
❑	184 Patrick Bates	.40	.18
❑	185 Mark Carrier WR	.75	.35
❑	186 Brad Hopkins	.40	.18
❑	187 Dennis Smith	.40	.18
❑	188 Natrone Means	1.50	.70
❑	189 Michael Jackson	.75	.35
❑	190 Ken Norton Jr.	.75	.35

		MINT	NRMT
❑ 191	Carlton Gray	.40	.18
❑ 192	Edgar Bennett	1.50	.70
❑ 193	Lawrence Taylor	1.50	.70
❑ 194	Marv Cook	.40	.18
❑ 195	Eric Curry	.40	.18
❑ 196	Victor Bailey	.40	.18
❑ 197	Ryan McNeil	.40	.18
❑ 198	Rod Woodson	1.50	.70
❑ 199	Earnest Byner	.40	.18
❑ 200	Marvin Jones	.40	.18
❑ 201	Thomas Smith	.40	.18
❑ 202	Troy Aikman	5.00	2.20
❑ 203	Audray McMillian	.40	.18
❑ 204	Wade Wilson	.40	.18
❑ 205	George Teague	.40	.18
❑ 206	Deion Sanders	2.50	1.10
❑ 207	Will Shields	.40	.18
❑ 208	John Taylor	.75	.35
❑ 209	Jim Harbaugh	1.50	.70
❑ 210	Micheal Barrow	.40	.18
❑ 211	Harold Green	.40	.18
❑ 212	Steve Everitt	.40	.18
❑ 213	Flipper Anderson	.40	.18
❑ 214	Rodney Hampton	1.50	.70
❑ 215	Steve Atwater	.40	.18
❑ 216	James Trapp	.40	.18
❑ 217	Terry Kirby	1.50	.70
❑ 218	Garrison Hearst	2.50	1.10
❑ 219	Jeff Bryant	.40	.18
❑ 220	Roosevelt Potts	.40	.18

1994 Finest Rookie Jumbos

	MINT	NRMT
COMPLETE SET (37)	120.00	55.00

ONE JUMBO CARD PER SEALED BOX

		MINT	NRMT
❑ 7	Wayne Simmons	1.50	.70
❑ 19	Willie Roaf	1.50	.70
❑ 20	Troy Drayton	1.50	.70
❑ 24	Chris Slade	1.50	.70
❑ 29	John Copeland	1.50	.70
❑ 35	Kevin Williams	3.00	1.35
❑ 41	Rick Mirer	6.00	2.70
❑ 42	Jerome Bettis	10.00	4.50
❑ 45	Jason Elam	1.50	.70
❑ 47	Derek Brown RBK	1.50	.70
❑ 56	Lincoln Kennedy	1.50	.70
❑ 78	Deon Figures	1.50	.70
❑ 108	Dana Stubblefield	6.00	2.70
❑ 112	Robert Smith	10.00	4.50
❑ 115	O.J. McDuffie	6.00	2.70
❑ 128	Qadry Ismail	6.00	2.70
❑ 130	Curtis Conway	6.00	2.70
❑ 146	Drew Bledsoe	25.00	11.00
❑ 159	Demetrius DuBose	1.50	.70
❑ 167	Glyn Milburn	3.00	1.35
❑ 184	Patrick Bates	1.50	.70
❑ 186	Brad Hopkins	1.50	.70
❑ 188	Natrone Means	6.00	2.70
❑ 191	Carlton Gray	1.50	.70
❑ 195	Eric Curry	1.50	.70
❑ 196	Victor Bailey	1.50	.70
❑ 197	Ryan McNeil	1.50	.70
❑ 200	Marvin Jones	1.50	.70
❑ 201	Thomas Smith	1.50	.70
❑ 205	George Teague	1.50	.70
❑ 207	Will Shields	1.50	.70
❑ 210	Micheal Barrow	1.50	.70
❑ 212	Steve Everitt	1.50	.70
❑ 216	James Trapp	1.50	.70
❑ 217	Terry Kirby	6.00	2.70
❑ 218	Garrison Hearst	10.00	4.50
❑ 220	Roosevelt Potts	1.50	.70

1995 Finest

	MINT	NRMT
COMPLETE SET (275)	100.00	45.00
COMP.SERIES 1 (165)	20.00	9.00
COMP.SERIES 2 (110)	80.00	36.00
COMMON CARD (1-275)	.25	.11
SEMISTARS	.60	.25
UNLISTED STARS	1.25	.55
COMP.REFRACT.SET (275)	600.00	275.00
COMP.REFRACT.SER.1	200.00	90.00
COMP.REFRACT.SER.2	400.00	180.00

*REFRACTOR STARS: 2.5X TO 6X HI COL.
*REFRACTOR RCs: 1.5X TO 4X HI
REFRACTOR STATED ODDS 1:12

		MINT	NRMT
❑ 1	Natrone Means	1.25	.55
❑ 2	Dave Meggett	.25	.11
❑ 3	Tim Bowens	.25	.11
❑ 4	Jay Novacek	.60	.25
❑ 5	Michael Jackson	.60	.25
❑ 6	Calvin Williams	.60	.25
❑ 7	Neil Smith	.60	.25
❑ 8	Chris Gardocki	.25	.11
❑ 9	Jeff Burris	.25	.11
❑ 10	Warren Moon	.60	.25
❑ 11	Gary Anderson K	.25	.11
❑ 12	Bert Emanuel	1.25	.55
❑ 13	Rick Tuten	.25	.11
❑ 14	Steve Wallace	.25	.11
❑ 15	Marion Butts	.25	.11
❑ 16	Johnnie Morton	.60	.25
❑ 17	Rob Moore	.25	.11
❑ 18	Wayne Gandy	.25	.11
❑ 19	Quentin Coryatt	.60	.25
❑ 20	Richmond Webb	.25	.11
❑ 21	Errict Rhett	1.25	.55
❑ 22	Joe Johnson	.25	.11
❑ 23	Gary Brown	.25	.11
❑ 24	Jeff Hostetler	.60	.25
❑ 25	Larry Centers	.60	.25
❑ 26	Tom Carter	.25	.11
❑ 27	Steve Atwater	.25	.11
❑ 28	Doug Pelfrey	.25	.11
❑ 29	Bryce Paup	1.25	.55
❑ 30	Erik Williams	.25	.11
❑ 31	Henry Jones	.25	.11
❑ 32	Stanley Richard	.25	.11
❑ 33	Marcus Allen	1.25	.55
❑ 34	Antonio Langham	.25	.11
❑ 35	Lewis Tillman	.25	.11
❑ 36	Thomas Randolph	.25	.11
❑ 37	Byron Bam Morris	.60	.25
❑ 38	David Palmer	.60	.25
❑ 39	Ricky Watters	1.25	.55
❑ 40	Brett Perriman	.60	.25
❑ 41	Will Wolford	.25	.11
❑ 42	Burt Grossman	.25	.11
❑ 43	Vincent Brisby	.25	.11
❑ 44	Ronnie Lott	.60	.25
❑ 45	Brian Blades	.60	.25
❑ 46	Brent Jones	.25	.11
❑ 47	Anthony Newman	.25	.11
❑ 48	Willie Roaf	.25	.11
❑ 49	Paul Gruber	.25	.11
❑ 50	Jeff George	.60	.25
❑ 51	Jamir Miller	.25	.11
❑ 52	Anthony Miller	.60	.25
❑ 53	Darrell Green	.25	.11
❑ 54	Steve Wisniewski	.25	.11
❑ 55	Dan Wilkinson	.60	.25
❑ 56	Brett Favre	5.00	2.20
❑ 57	Leslie O'Neal	.60	.25
❑ 58	Keith Byars	.25	.11
❑ 59	James Washington	.25	.11
❑ 60	Andre Reed	.60	.25
❑ 61	Ken Norton Jr.	.60	.25
❑ 62	John Randle	.25	.11
❑ 63	Lake Dawson	.60	.25
❑ 64	Greg Montgomery	.25	.11
❑ 65	Erric Pegram	.60	.25
❑ 66	Steve Everitt	.25	.11
❑ 67	Chris Brantley	.25	.11
❑ 68	Rod Woodson	.60	.25
❑ 69	Eugene Robinson	.25	.11
❑ 70	Dave Brown	.60	.25
❑ 71	Ricky Reynolds	.25	.11
❑ 72	Rohn Stark	.25	.11
❑ 73	Randal Hill	.25	.11
❑ 74	Brian Washington	.25	.11
❑ 75	Heath Shuler	1.25	.55
❑ 76	Darion Conner	.25	.11
❑ 77	Terry McDaniel	.25	.11
❑ 78	Al Del Greco	.25	.11
❑ 79	Allen Aldridge	.25	.11
❑ 80	Trace Armstrong	.25	.11
❑ 81	Darnay Scott	1.25	.55
❑ 82	Charlie Garner	.60	.25
❑ 83	Harold Bishop	.25	.11
❑ 84	Reggie White	1.25	.55
❑ 85	Shawn Jefferson	.25	.11
❑ 86	Irving Spikes	.60	.25
❑ 87	Mel Gray	.25	.11
❑ 88	D.J. Johnson	.25	.11
❑ 89	Daryl Johnston	.60	.25
❑ 90	Joe Montana	5.00	2.20
❑ 91	Michael Strahan	.25	.11
❑ 92	Robert Blackmon	.25	.11
❑ 93	Ryan Yarborough	.60	.25
❑ 94	Terry Allen	.60	.25
❑ 95	Michael Haynes	.60	.25
❑ 96	Jim Harbaugh	.60	.25
❑ 97	Micheal Barrow	.25	.11
❑ 98	John Thierry	.25	.11
❑ 99	Seth Joyner	.25	.11
❑ 100	Deion Sanders	2.00	.90
❑ 101	Eric Turner	.25	.11
❑ 102	LeShon Johnson	.60	.25
❑ 103	John Copeland	.25	.11
❑ 104	Cornelius Bennett	.60	.25
❑ 105	Sean Gilbert	.60	.25
❑ 106	Herschel Walker	.60	.25
❑ 107	Henry Ellard	.60	.25
❑ 108	Neil O'Donnell	.60	.25
❑ 109	Charles Wilson	.25	.11
❑ 110	Willie McGinest	.60	.25
❑ 111	Tim Brown	1.25	.55
❑ 112	Simon Fletcher	.25	.11
❑ 113	Broderick Thomas	.25	.11
❑ 114	Tom Waddle	.25	.11
❑ 115	Jessie Tuggle	.25	.11
❑ 116	Maurice Hurst	.25	.11
❑ 117	Aubrey Beavers	.25	.11
❑ 118	Donnell Bennett	.60	.25
❑ 119	Shante Carver	.25	.11
❑ 120	Eric Metcalf	.60	.25
❑ 121	John Carney	.25	.11
❑ 122	Thomas Lewis	.60	.25
❑ 123	Johnny Mitchell	.25	.11
❑ 124	Trent Dilfer	1.25	.55
❑ 125	Marshall Faulk	2.50	1.10
❑ 126	Ernest Givins	.25	.11
❑ 127	Aeneas Williams	.25	.11
❑ 128	Bucky Brooks	.25	.11
❑ 129	Todd Steussie	.25	.11
❑ 130	Randall Cunningham	1.25	.55

Card	Player	Mint	NrMt
❑ 131	Reggie Brooks	.60	.25
❑ 132	Morten Andersen	.25	.11
❑ 133	James Jett	.60	.25
❑ 134	George Teague	.25	.11
❑ 135	John Taylor	.25	.11
❑ 136	Charles Johnson	.60	.25
❑ 137	Isaac Bruce	2.50	1.10
❑ 138	Jason Elam	.25	.11
❑ 139	Carl Pickens	1.25	.55
❑ 140	Chris Warren	.60	.25
❑ 141	Bruce Armstrong	.25	.11
❑ 142	Mark Carrier DB	.25	.11
❑ 143	Irving Fryar	.60	.25
❑ 144	Van Malone	.25	.11
❑ 145	Charles Haley	.60	.25
❑ 146	Chris Calloway	.25	.11
❑ 147	J.J. Birden	.25	.11
❑ 148	Tony Bennett	.25	.11
❑ 149	Lincoln Kennedy	.25	.11
❑ 150	Stan Humphries	.60	.25
❑ 151	Hardy Nickerson	.25	.11
❑ 152	Randall McDaniel	.25	.11
❑ 153	Marcus Robertson	.25	.11
❑ 154	Ronald Moore	.25	.11
❑ 155	Thurman Thomas	1.25	.55
❑ 156	Tommy Vardell	.25	.11
❑ 157	Ken Ruettgers	.25	.11
❑ 158	Rob Fredrickson	.25	.11
❑ 159	Johnny Bailey	.25	.11
❑ 160	Greg Lloyd	.60	.25
❑ 161	David Alexander	.25	.11
❑ 162	Kevin Mawae	.25	.11
❑ 163	Derek Brown RBK	.25	.11
❑ 164	William Floyd	1.25	.55
❑ 165	Aaron Glenn	.25	.11
❑ 166	Joey Galloway RC	15.00	6.75
❑ 167	Troy Drayton	.25	.11
❑ 168	Dermontti Dawson	.60	.25
❑ 169	Ronald Moore	.25	.11
❑ 170	Dan Marino	5.00	2.20
❑ 171	Dennis Gibson	.25	.11
❑ 172	Raymont Harris	.25	.11
❑ 173	Shannon Sharpe	.60	.25
❑ 174	Kevin Williams	.60	.25
❑ 175	Jim Everett	.25	.11
❑ 176	Rocket Ismail	.60	.25
❑ 177	Mark Fields	.25	.11
❑ 178	George Koonce	.25	.11
❑ 179	Chris Hudson	.25	.11
❑ 180	Jerry Rice	2.50	1.10
❑ 181	Dewayne Washington	.60	.25
❑ 182	Dale Carter	.60	.25
❑ 183	Pete Stoyanovich	.25	.11
❑ 184	Blake Brockermeyer	.25	.11
❑ 185	Troy Aikman	2.50	1.10
❑ 186	Jeff Blake RC	4.00	1.80
❑ 187	Troy Vincent	.25	.11
❑ 188	Lamar Lathon	.25	.11
❑ 189	Tony Boselli	.60	.25
❑ 190	Emmitt Smith	4.00	1.80
❑ 191	Bobby Houston	.25	.11
❑ 192	Edgar Bennett	.60	.25
❑ 193	Derrick Brooks	.25	.11
❑ 194	Ricky Proehl	.25	.11
❑ 195	Rodney Hampton	.60	.25
❑ 196	Dave Krieg	.25	.11
❑ 197	Vinny Testaverde	.60	.25
❑ 198	Erik Kramer	.25	.11
❑ 199	Ben Coates	.60	.25
❑ 200	Steve Young	2.00	.90
❑ 201	Glyn Milburn	.25	.11
❑ 202	Bryan Cox	.25	.11
❑ 203	Luther Elliss	.25	.11
❑ 204	Mark McMillian	.25	.11
❑ 205	Jerome Bettis	1.25	.55
❑ 206	Craig Heyward	.60	.25
❑ 207	Ray Buchanan	.25	.11
❑ 208	Kimble Anders	.60	.25
❑ 209	Kevin Greene	.60	.25
❑ 210	Eric Allen	.25	.11
❑ 211	Ricardo McDonald	.25	.11
❑ 212	Ruben Brown RC	.25	.11
❑ 213	Harvey Williams	.25	.11
❑ 214	Broderick Thomas	.25	.11
❑ 215	Frank Reich	.25	.11
❑ 216	Frank Sanders RC UER Plays Wide Receiver Defensive Record on Back	6.00	2.70
❑ 217	Craig Newsome	.25	.11
❑ 218	Merton Hanks	.25	.11
❑ 219	Chris Miller	.25	.11
❑ 220	John Elway	5.00	2.20
❑ 221	Ernest Givins	.25	.11
❑ 222	Boomer Esiason	.60	.25
❑ 223	Reggie Roby	.25	.11
❑ 224	Qadry Ismail	.60	.25
❑ 225	Ki-Jana Carter RC	1.25	.55
❑ 226	Leon Lett	.25	.11
❑ 227	Eric Hill	.25	.11
❑ 228	Scott Mitchell	.60	.25
❑ 229	Craig Erickson	.25	.11
❑ 230	Drew Bledsoe	2.50	1.10
❑ 231	Sean Landeta	.25	.11
❑ 232	Barrett Brooks	.25	.11
❑ 233	Brian Mitchell	.25	.11
❑ 234	Tyrone Poole	.60	.25
❑ 235	Desmond Howard	.60	.25
❑ 236	Wayne Simmons	.25	.11
❑ 237	Michael Westbrook RC	10.00	4.50
❑ 238	Quinn Early	.60	.25
❑ 239	Willie Davis	.60	.25
❑ 240	Rashaan Salaam RC	1.25	.55
❑ 241	Devin Bush	.25	.11
❑ 242	Dana Stubblefield	1.25	.55
❑ 243	Dexter Carter	.25	.11
❑ 244	Shane Conlan	.25	.11
❑ 245	Keith Elias	.25	.11
❑ 246	Robert Brooks	1.25	.55
❑ 247	Garrison Hearst	1.25	.55
❑ 248	Eric Zeier RC	2.00	.90
❑ 249	Nate Newton	.60	.25
❑ 250	Barry Sanders	5.00	2.20
❑ 251	Dave Meggett	.25	.11
❑ 252	Courtney Hawkins	.25	.11
❑ 253	Cortez Kennedy	.60	.25
❑ 254	Mario Bates	1.25	.55
❑ 255	Junior Seau	1.25	.55
❑ 256	Brian Washington	.25	.11
❑ 257	Darius Holland	.25	.11
❑ 258	Jeff Graham	.25	.11
❑ 259	Rob Moore	.25	.11
❑ 260	Andre Rison	.60	.25
❑ 261	Kerry Collins RC	6.00	2.70
❑ 262	Roosevelt Potts	.25	.11
❑ 263	Cris Carter	1.25	.55
❑ 264	Curtis Martin RC	15.00	6.75
❑ 265	Rick Mirer	1.25	.55
❑ 266	Mo Lewis	.25	.11
❑ 267	Mike Sherrard	.25	.11
❑ 268	Herman Moore	1.25	.55
❑ 269	Eric Metcalf	.60	.25
❑ 270	Ray Childress	.25	.11
❑ 271	Chris Slade	.60	.25
❑ 272	Michael Irvin	1.25	.55
❑ 273	Jim Kelly	1.25	.55
❑ 274	Terance Mathis	.60	.25
❑ 275	LeRoy Butler	.25	.11

1995 Finest Fan Favorites

	MINT	NRMT
COMPLETE SET (25)	80.00	36.00
STATED ODDS 1:12 SER.1		

Card	Player	Mint	NrMt
❑ FF1	Drew Bledsoe	5.00	2.20
❑ FF2	Jerome Bettis	2.50	1.10
❑ FF3	Rick Mirer	2.50	1.10
❑ FF4	Andre Rison	1.25	.55
❑ FF5	Troy Aikman	5.00	2.20
❑ FF6	Cortez Kennedy	1.25	.55
❑ FF7	Emmitt Smith	8.00	3.60
❑ FF8	Sterling Sharpe	1.25	.55
❑ FF9	Junior Seau	2.50	1.10
❑ FF10	Michael Irvin	2.50	1.10
❑ FF11	Jim Kelly	2.50	1.10
❑ FF12	Steve Young	4.00	1.80
❑ FF13	John Elway	10.00	4.50
❑ FF14	Jerry Rice	5.00	2.20
❑ FF15	Barry Sanders	10.00	4.50
❑ FF16	Dan Marino	10.00	4.50
❑ FF17	Dan Wilkinson	1.25	.55
❑ FF18	Reggie White	2.50	1.10
❑ FF19	Deion Sanders	4.00	1.80
❑ FF20	Willie McGinest	1.25	.55
❑ FF21	Stan Humphries	1.25	.55
❑ FF22	Heath Shuler	2.50	1.10
❑ FF23	Natrone Means	2.50	1.10
❑ FF24	Warren Moon	1.25	.55
❑ FF25	Marshall Faulk	5.00	2.20

1996 Finest

	MINT	NRMT
COMPLETE SET (359)	700.00	325.00
COMP.SERIES 1 (191)	400.00	180.00
COMP.SERIES 2 (168)	300.00	135.00
COMP.BRONZE SER.1 (110)	40.00	18.00
COMP.BRONZE SER.2 (110)	40.00	18.00
COMMON BRONZE	.30	.14
SEMISTARS BRONZE	.60	.25
UNL.STARS BRONZE	1.00	.45
COMMON GOLD	2.00	.90
SEMISTARS GOLD	4.00	1.80
UNL.STARS GOLD	6.00	2.70
GOLD STATED ODDS 1:24		
COMMON SILVER	.75	.35
SEMISTARS SILVER	1.50	.70
UNL.STARS SILVER	3.00	1.35
SILVER STATED ODDS 1:4		

Card	Player	Mint	NrMt
❑ B2	Jay Novacek B	.60	.25
❑ B3	Ray Buchanan B	.30	.14
❑ B5	Phil Hansen B	.30	.14
❑ B6	Mike Mamula B	.30	.14
❑ B9	Bernie Parmalee B	.30	.14
❑ B10	Herman Moore B	1.00	.45
❑ B11	Shawn Jefferson B	.30	.14
❑ B12	Chris Doleman B	.30	.14
❑ B13	Erik Kramer B	.60	.25
❑ B15	Orlando Thomas B	.30	.14
❑ B16	Terrell Davis B	10.00	4.50
❑ B18	Roman Phifer B	.30	.14
❑ B19	Trent Dilfer B	.60	.25
❑ B21	Darnay Scott B	.60	.25
❑ B22	Steve McNair B	5.00	2.20
❑ B23	Lamar Lathon B	.30	.14
❑ B26	Thomas Randolph B	.30	.14
❑ B27	Michael Jackson B	.60	.25
❑ B28	Seth Joyner B	.30	.14
❑ B29	Jeff Lageman B	.30	.14
❑ B30	Darryl Williams B	.30	.14
❑ B32	Erric Pegram B	.60	.25

❑ B34 Sean Dawkins B .60 .25
❑ B38 Dan Saleaumua B UER .30 .14
card misnumbered 28
❑ B39 Henry Thomas B .30 .14
❑ B43 Pat Swilling B .30 .14
❑ B44 Marty Carter B .30 .14
❑ B45 Anthony Miller B .60 .25
❑ B48 Chris Warren B .60 .25
❑ B49 Derek Brown RBK B .30 .14
❑ B51 Blaine Bishop B .30 .14
❑ B52 Jake Reed B .60 .25
❑ B55 Vencie Glenn B .30 .14
❑ B58 Derrick Alexander WR B .60 .25
❑ B64 Jessie Tuggle B .30 .14
❑ B65 Terrance Shaw B .30 .14
❑ B66 David Sloan B .60 .25
❑ B68 Brent Jones B .30 .14
❑ B70 William Thomas B .30 .14
❑ B71 Robert Smith B .60 .25
❑ B72 Wayne Simmons B .30 .14
❑ B73 Jim Harbaugh B .60 .25
❑ B76 Wayne Chrebet B 1.25 .55
❑ B77 Chris Hudson B .30 .14
❑ B79 Stevon Moore B .30 .14
❑ B80 Chris Calloway B .30 .14
❑ B81 Tom Carter B .30 .14
❑ B82 Dave Meggett B .30 .14
❑ B83 Sam Mills B .60 .25
❑ B86 Renaldo Turnbull B .30 .14
❑ B87 Derrick Brooks B .30 .14
❑ B89 Eugene Robinson B .30 .14
❑ B91 Rodney Thomas B .30 .14
❑ B92 Dan Wilkinson B .30 .14
❑ B93 Mark Fields B .30 .14
❑ B94 Warren Sapp B .30 .14
❑ B95 Curtis Martin B 5.00 2.20
❑ B97 Ray Crockett B .30 .14
❑ B98 Ed McDaniel B .30 .14
❑ B101 Craig Heyward B .30 .14
❑ B102 Ellis Johnson B .30 .14
❑ B104 O.J. McDuffie B .60 .25
❑ B105 J.J. Stokes B 1.00 .45
❑ B106 Mo Lewis B .30 .14
❑ B108 Rob Moore B .30 .14
❑ B110 Tyrone Wheatley B .60 .25
❑ B111 Ken Harvey B .30 .14
❑ B113 Willie Green B .30 .14
❑ B114 Willie Davis B .60 .25
❑ B115 Andy Harmon B .30 .14
❑ B117 Bryan Cox B .30 .14
❑ B119 Bert Emanuel B .60 .25
❑ B120 Greg Lloyd B .60 .25
❑ B122 Willie Jackson B .60 .25
❑ B123 Lorenzo Lynch B .30 .14
❑ B124 Pepper Johnson B .30 .14
❑ B128 Tyrone Poole B .30 .14
❑ B129 Neil Smith B .60 .25
❑ B130 Eddie Robinson B .30 .14
❑ B131 Bryce Paup B .60 .25
❑ B134 Troy Aikman B 5.00 2.20
❑ B136 Chris Sanders B .60 .25
❑ B138 Jim Everett B .30 .14
❑ B139 Frank Sanders B .60 .25
❑ B141 Cortez Kennedy B .60 .25
❑ B143 Derrick Alexander DE B .30 .14
❑ B144 Rob Fredrickson B .30 .14
❑ B145 Chris Zorich B .30 .14
❑ B146 Devin Bush B .30 .14
❑ B149 Troy Vincent B .30 .14
❑ B151 Deion Sanders B 2.50 1.10
❑ B152 James O. Stewart B .60 .25
❑ B156 Lawrence Dawsey B .30 .14
❑ B157 Robert Brooks B 1.00 .45
❑ B158 Rashaan Salaam B 1.00 .45
❑ B161 Tim Brown B .60 .25
❑ B162 Brendan Stai B .30 .14
❑ B163 Sean Gilbert B .30 .14
❑ B169 Calvin Williams B .60 .25
❑ B171 Ruben Brown B .30 .14
❑ B172 Eric Green B .30 .14
❑ B175 Jerry Rice B 5.00 2.20
❑ B176 Bruce Smith B 1.00 .45
❑ B177 Mark Bruener B .30 .14
❑ B179 Lamont Warren B .30 .14
❑ B180 Tamarick Vanover B 1.00 .45
❑ B182 Scott Mitchell B .60 .25
❑ B186 Terry Wooden B .30 .14
❑ B187 Ken Norton B .60 .25
❑ B188 Jeff Herrod B .30 .14
❑ B192 Gus Frerotte B 1.00 .45
❑ B194 Brett Maxie B .30 .14
❑ B198 Eddie Kennison B RC 1.00 .45
❑ B201 Marcus Jones B RC .30 .14
❑ B202 Terry Allen B .60 .25
❑ B203 Leroy Hoard B .30 .14
❑ B205 Reggie White B 1.00 .45
❑ B206 Larry Centers B .60 .25
❑ B208 Vincent Brisby B .30 .14
❑ B209 Michael Timpson B .30 .14
❑ B211 John Mobley B RC .30 .14
❑ B212 Clay Matthews B .60 .25
❑ B213 Shannon Sharpe B .60 .25
❑ B214 Tony Bennett B .30 .14
❑ B216 Mickey Washington B .30 .14
❑ B217 Fred Barnett B .60 .25
❑ B218 Michael Haynes B .60 .25
❑ B219 Stan Humphries B .60 .25
❑ B221 Winston Moss B .30 .14
❑ B222 Tim Biakabutuka B RC 4.00 1.80
❑ B223 Leeland McElroy B RC 1.25 .55
❑ B224 Vinnie Clark B .30 .14
❑ B225 Keyshawn Johnson B RC 10.00 4.50
❑ B228 Tony Woods B .30 .14
❑ B231 Anthony Pleasant B .30 .14
❑ B232 Jeff George B .60 .25
❑ B233 Curtis Conway B 1.00 .45
❑ B235 Jeff Lewis B RC 2.50 1.10
❑ B236 Edgar Bennett B .60 .25
❑ B237 Regan Upshaw B RC .30 .14
❑ B238 William Fuller B .30 .14
❑ B241 Willie Anderson B RC .30 .14
❑ B242 Derrick Thomas B .60 .25
❑ B243 Marvin Harrison B RC 10.00 4.50
❑ B244 Darion Conner B .30 .14
❑ B245 Antonio Langham B .30 .14
❑ B246 Rodney Peete B .30 .14
❑ B247 Tim McDonald B .30 .14
❑ B248 Robert Jones B .30 .14
❑ B251 Mark Carrier DB B .30 .14
❑ B252 Stephen Grant B .30 .14
❑ B254 Jeff Hostetler B .60 .25
❑ B255 Darrell Green B .30 .14
❑ B261 Eric Swann B .60 .25
❑ B263 Irv Smith B .30 .14
❑ B264 Tim McKyer B .30 .14
❑ B266 Sean Jones B .30 .14
❑ B271 Yancey Thigpen B .60 .25
❑ B273 Quentin Coryatt B .30 .14
❑ B274 Hardy Nickerson B .30 .14
❑ B275 Ricardo McDonald B .30 .14
❑ B277 Robert Blackmon B .30 .14
❑ B279 Alonzo Spellman B .30 .14
❑ B281 Rickey Dudley B RC 1.00 .45
❑ B282 Joe Cain B .30 .14
❑ B284 John Randle B .30 .14
❑ B286 Vinny Testaverde B .60 .25
❑ B289 Henry Jones B .30 .14
❑ B290 Simeon Rice B RC 1.00 .45
❑ B295 Leslie O'Neal B .30 .14
❑ B297 Greg Hill B .60 .25
❑ B301 Eric Metcalf B .60 .25
❑ B303 Jerome Woods B RC .30 .14
❑ B306 Anthony Smith B .30 .14
❑ B307 Darren Perry B .30 .14
❑ B311 James Hasty B .30 .14
❑ B312 Cris Carter B 1.00 .45
❑ B314 Lawrence Phillips B RC 2.50 1.10
❑ B317 Aeneas Williams B .30 .14
❑ B318 Eric Hill B .30 .14
❑ B319 Kevin Hardy B RC 1.00 .45
❑ B321 Chris Chandler B .60 .25
❑ B322 Rocket Ismail B .60 .25
❑ B323 Anthony Parker B .30 .14
❑ B324 John Thierry B .30 .14
❑ B325 Micheal Barrow B .30 .14
❑ B326 Henry Ford B .30 .14
❑ B327 Aaron Hayden B RC .30 .14
❑ B328 Terance Mathis B .30 .14
❑ B329 Kirk Pointer B RC .30 .14
❑ B330 Ray Mickens B RC .30 .14
❑ B331 Jermane Mayberry B RC .30 .14
❑ B332 Mario Bates B .60 .25
❑ B333 Carlton Gray B .30 .14
❑ B334 Derek Loville B .30 .14
❑ B335 Mike Alstott B RC 6.00 2.70
❑ B336 Eric Guliford B .30 .14
❑ B337 Marvcus Patton B .30 .14
❑ B338 Terrell Owens B RC 12.00 5.50
❑ B339 Lance Johnstone B RC .30 .14
❑ B340 Lake Dawson B .60 .25
❑ B341 Winslow Oliver B RC .30 .14
❑ B342 Adrian Murrell B .60 .25
❑ B343 Jason Belser B .30 .14
❑ B344 Brian Dawkins B RC .30 .14
❑ B345 Reggie Brown B RC .30 .14
❑ B346 Shaun Gayle B .30 .14
❑ B347 Tony Brackens B RC 1.25 .55
❑ B348 Thomas Lewis B .30 .14
❑ B349 Kelvin Pritchett B .30 .14
❑ B350 Bobby Engram B RC 1.00 .45
❑ B351 Moe Williams B RC .60 .25
❑ B352 Thomas Smith B .30 .14
❑ B353 Dexter Carter B .30 .14
❑ B354 Qadry Ismail B .60 .25
❑ B355 Marco Battaglia B RC .30 .14
❑ B356 Levon Kirkland B .30 .14
❑ B357 Eric Allen B .30 .14
❑ B358 Bobby Hoying B RC 2.50 1.10
❑ B359 Checklist B .30 .14
❑ G1 Kordell Stewart G 12.00 5.50
❑ G7 Kimble Anders G 2.00 .90
❑ G8 Merton Hanks G 2.00 .90
❑ G17 Rick Mirer G 4.00 1.80
❑ G33 Craig Newsome G 2.00 .90
❑ G36 Bryce Paup G 4.00 1.80
❑ G40 Dan Marino G 25.00 11.00
❑ G42 Andre Coleman G 2.00 .90
❑ G47 Kevin Carter G 2.00 .90
❑ G60 Mark Brunell G 15.00 6.75
❑ G61 David Palmer G 4.00 1.80
❑ G75 Carnell Lake G 2.00 .90
❑ G96 Joey Galloway G 12.00 5.50
❑ G112 Melvin Tuten G 2.00 .90
❑ G121 Aaron Glenn G 2.00 .90
❑ G132 Brett Favre G 25.00 11.00
❑ G133 Ken Dilger G 4.00 1.80
❑ G140 Barry Sanders G 25.00 11.00
❑ G142 Glyn Milburn G 2.00 .90
❑ G148 Brett Perriman G 4.00 1.80
❑ G160 Kerry Collins G 6.00 2.70
❑ G164 Lee Woodall G 2.00 .90
❑ G173 Marshall Faulk G 6.00 2.70
❑ G178 Troy Aikman G 15.00 6.75
❑ G190 Drew Bledsoe G 15.00 6.75
❑ G191 Checklist G 2.00 .90
❑ G193 Michael Irvin G 6.00 2.70
❑ G196 Warren Moon G 4.00 1.80
❑ G200 Steve Young G 12.00 5.50
❑ G207 Alex Van Dyke G RC 4.00 1.80
❑ G220 Cris Carter G 6.00 2.70
❑ G230 John Elway G 25.00 11.00
❑ G234 Charles Haley G 4.00 1.80
❑ G240 Jim Kelly G 6.00 2.70
❑ G250 Rodney Hampton G 4.00 1.80
❑ G256 Errict Rhett G 4.00 1.80
❑ G257 Alex Molden G 2.00 .90
❑ G260 Kevin Hardy G 4.00 1.80
❑ G267 Bryant Young G 4.00 1.80
❑ G268 Jeff Blake G 6.00 2.70
❑ G270 Keyshawn Johnson G 12.00 5.50
❑ G278 Junior Seau G 6.00 2.70
❑ G285 Terry Kirby G 4.00 1.80
❑ G293 Hugh Douglas G 2.00 .90
❑ G296 Reggie White G 6.00 2.70
❑ G298 Elvis Grbac G 6.00 2.70
❑ G300 Emmitt Smith G 20.00 9.00
❑ G309 Ricky Watters G 4.00 1.80
❑ S4 Brett Favre S 15.00 6.75
❑ S14 Chester McGlockton S .75 .35
❑ S20 Tyrone Hughes S .75 .35
❑ S24 Ty Law S .75 .35
❑ S25 Brian Mitchell S .75 .35
❑ S31 Darren Woodson S 1.50 .70
❑ S35 Brian Mitchell S .75 .35
❑ S37 Dana Stubblefield S 1.50 .70
❑ S41 Kerry Collins S 3.00 1.35
❑ S46 Orlando Thomas S .75 .35

❑ S50 Jerry Rice S 8.00 3.60
❑ S53 Willie McGinest S .75 .35
❑ S54 Blake Brockermeyer S .75 .35
❑ S56 Michael Westbrook S 3.00 1.35
❑ S57 Garrison Hearst S 3.00 1.35
❑ S59 Kyle Brady S 1.50 .70
❑ S62 Tim Brown S 1.50 .70
❑ S63 Jeff Graham S .75 .35
❑ S67 Dan Marino S 15.00 6.75
❑ S69 Tamarick Vanover S 3.00 1.35
❑ S74 Daryl Johnston S 1.50 .70
❑ S78 Frank Sanders S 1.50 .70
❑ S84 Darryll Lewis S .75 .35
❑ S85 Carl Pickens S 3.00 1.35
❑ S88 Jerome Bettis S 3.00 1.35
❑ S90 Terrell Davis S 15.00 6.75
❑ S99 Napoleon Kaufman S 6.00 2.70
❑ S100 Rashaan Salaam S 3.00 1.35
❑ S103 Barry Sanders S 15.00 6.75
❑ S107 Tony Boselli S 1.50 .70
❑ S109 Eric Zeier S 1.50 .70
❑ S116 Bruce Smith S 3.00 1.35
❑ S118 Zack Crockett S .75 .35
❑ S125 Joey Galloway S 8.00 3.60
❑ S126 Heath Shuler S 3.00 1.35
❑ S127 Curtis Martin S 8.00 3.60
❑ S135 Greg Lloyd S 1.50 .70
❑ S137 Marshall Faulk S 3.00 1.35
❑ S147 Tyrone Poole S .75 .35
❑ S150 J.J. Stokes S 3.00 1.35
❑ S153 Drew Bledsoe S 8.00 3.60
❑ S154 Terry McDaniel S .75 .35
❑ S155 Terrell Fletcher S .75 .35
❑ S159 Dave Brown S .75 .35
❑ S165 Jim Harbaugh S 1.50 .70
❑ S166 Larry Brown S .75 .35
❑ S167 Neil Smith S 1.50 .70
❑ S168 Herman Moore S 3.00 1.35
❑ S170 Deion Sanders S 5.00 2.20
❑ S174 Mark Chmura S 1.50 .70
❑ S181 Chris Warren S 1.50 .70
❑ S183 Robert Brooks S 3.00 1.35
❑ S184 Steve McNair S 8.00 3.60
❑ S185 Kordell Stewart S 8.00 3.60
❑ S189 Charlie Garner S .75 .35
❑ S195 Harvey Williams S .75 .35
❑ S197 Jeff George S 1.50 .70
❑ S199 Ricky Watters S 1.50 .70
❑ S204 Steve Bono S 1.50 .70
❑ S210 Jeff Blake S 3.00 1.35
❑ S215 Phillippi Sparks S .75 .35
❑ S226 William Floyd S 1.50 .70
❑ S227 Troy Drayton S .75 .35
❑ S229 Rodney Hampton S 1.50 .70
❑ S239 Duane Clemons S RC .75 .35
❑ S249 Curtis Conway S 3.00 1.35
❑ S253 John Mobley S .75 .35
❑ S258 Chris Slade S .75 .35
❑ S259 Derrick Thomas S 1.50 .70
❑ S262 Eric Metcalf S 1.50 .70
❑ S265 Emmitt Smith S 12.00 5.50
❑ S269 Jeff Hostetler S 1.50 .70
❑ S272 Thurman Thomas S 3.00 1.35
❑ S276 Steve Atwater S .75 .35
❑ S280 Isaac Bruce S 3.00 1.35
❑ S283 Neil O'Donnell S 1.50 .70
❑ S287 Jim Kelly S 3.00 1.35
❑ S288 Lawrence Phillips S 4.00 1.80
❑ S291 Terance Mathis S .75 .35
❑ S292 Errict Rhett S 1.50 .70
❑ S294 Santo Stephens S .75 .35
❑ S299 Walt Harris S RC .75 .35
❑ S302 Jamir Miller S .75 .35
❑ S304 Ben Coates S 1.50 .70
❑ S305 Marcus Allen S 3.00 1.35
❑ S308 Jonathan Ogden S RC .75 .35
❑ S310 John Elway S 15.00 6.75
❑ S313 Irving Fryar S 1.50 .70
❑ S315 Junior Seau S 3.00 1.35
❑ S316 Alex Molden S RC .75 .35
❑ S320 Steve Young S 6.00 2.70

1996 Finest Refractors

	MINT	NRMT
COMPLETE SET (359)	5000.00	2200.00
COMPLETE SER.1 (191)	3000.00	1350.00
COMPLETE SER.2 (168)	2000.00	900.00
COMP.BRONZE SET (220)	1000.00	450.00
COMP.BRONZE SER.1 (110)	500.00	220.00
COMP.BRONZE SER.2 (110)	500.00	220.00

*BRONZE REF.STARS: 4X TO 10X HI COL.
*BRONZE REF.RCs: 1.5X TO 4X
BRONZE REF.STATED ODDS 1:12
*GOLD REFRACTORS: 1X TO 2.5X HI COL.
GOLD REF.STATED ODDS 1:288
*SILVER REF.STARS: 2.5X TO 6X HI COL.
SILVER REF.STATED ODDS 1:48

1997 Finest

	MINT	NRMT
COMPLETE SET (350)	800.00	350.00
COMP.SERIES 1 SET (175)	400.00	180.00
COMP.SERIES 2 SET (175)	400.00	180.00
COMP.BRONZE SER.1 (100)	30.00	13.50
COMP.BRONZE SER.2 (100)	50.00	22.00
COMMON BRONZE	.30	.14
BRONZE SEMISTARS	.60	.25
BRONZE UNLISTED STARS	1.25	.55
COMMON SILVER	.75	.35
SILVER SEMISTARS	1.50	.70
SILVER UNLISTED STARS	3.00	1.35
SILVER STATED ODDS 1:4		
COMMON GOLD	2.00	.90
GOLD SEMISTARS	4.00	1.80
GOLD UNLISTED STARS	6.00	2.70
GOLD STATED ODDS 1:24		

❑ 1 Mark Brunell B 4.00 1.80
❑ 2 Chris Slade B .30 .14
❑ 3 Chris Doleman B .30 .14
❑ 4 Chris Hudson B .30 .14
❑ 5 Karim Abdul-Jabbar B 1.25 .55
❑ 6 Darren Perry B .30 .14
❑ 7 Daryl Johnston B .60 .25
❑ 8 Rob Moore B UER .60 .25
listed as uncommon
❑ 9 Robert Smith B .60 .25
❑ 10 Terry Allen B 1.25 .55
❑ 11 Jason Dunn B .30 .14
❑ 12 Henry Thomas B .30 .14
❑ 13 Rod Stephens B .30 .14
❑ 14 Ray Mickens B .30 .14
❑ 15 Ty Detmer B .60 .25
❑ 16 Fred Barnett B .30 .14
❑ 17 Derrick Alexander WR B .60 .25
❑ 18 Marcus Robertson B .30 .14
❑ 19 Robert Blackmon B .30 .14
❑ 20 Isaac Bruce B 1.25 .55
❑ 21 Chester McGlockton B .30 .14
❑ 22 Stan Humphries B .60 .25
❑ 23 Lonnie Marts B .30 .14
❑ 24 Jason Sehorn B .60 .25
❑ 25 Bobby Engram B UER .60 .25
listed as uncommon
❑ 26 Brett Perriman B UER .30 .14
listed as uncommon
❑ 27 Stevon Moore B .30 .14
❑ 28 Jamal Anderson B 2.00 .90
❑ 29 Wayne Martin B .30 .14
❑ 30 Michael Irvin B UER 1.25 .55
listed as uncommon
❑ 31 Thomas Smith B .30 .14
❑ 32 Tony Brackens B .30 .14
❑ 33 Eric Davis B .30 .14
❑ 34 James O.Stewart B .60 .25
❑ 35 Ki-Jana Carter B .30 .14
❑ 36 Ken Norton B .30 .14
❑ 37 William Thomas B .30 .14
❑ 38 Tim Brown B 1.25 .55
❑ 39 Lawrence Phillips B .30 .14
❑ 40 Ricky Watters B .60 .25
❑ 41 Tony Bennett B .30 .14
❑ 42 Jessie Armstead B .30 .14
❑ 43 Trent Dilfer B 1.25 .55
❑ 44 Rodney Hampton B .60 .25
❑ 45 Sam Mills B .30 .14
❑ 46 Rodney Harrison B .30 .14
❑ 47 Rob Fredrickson B .30 .14
❑ 48 Eric Hill B .30 .14
❑ 49 Bennie Blades B .30 .14
❑ 50 Eddie George B 4.00 1.80
❑ 51 Dave Brown B .30 .14
❑ 52 Raymont Harris B .30 .14
❑ 53 Steve Tovar B .30 .14
❑ 54 Thurman Thomas B 1.25 .55
❑ 55 Leeland McElroy B .30 .14
❑ 56 Brian Mitchell B UER .30 .14
listed as uncommon
❑ 57 Eric Allen B .30 .14
❑ 58 Vinny Testaverde B .60 .25
❑ 59 Marvin Washington B .30 .14
❑ 60 Junior Seau B .60 .25
❑ 61 Bert Emanuel B .60 .25
❑ 62 Kevin Carter B .30 .14
❑ 63 Mark Carrier DB B .30 .14
❑ 64 Andre Coleman B .30 .14
❑ 65 Chris Warren B .60 .25
❑ 66 Aeneas Williams B .30 .14
❑ 67 Eugene Robinson B .30 .14
❑ 68 Darren Woodson B .30 .14
❑ 69 Anthony Johnson B .30 .14
❑ 70 Terry Glenn B 1.25 .55
❑ 71 Troy Vincent B .30 .14
❑ 72 John Copeland B .30 .14
❑ 73 Warren Sapp B .60 .25
❑ 74 Bobby Hebert B .30 .14
❑ 75 Jeff Hostetler B .30 .14
❑ 76 Willie Davis B .30 .14
❑ 77 Mickey Washington B .30 .14
❑ 78 Cortez Kennedy B .30 .14
❑ 79 Michael Strahan B .30 .14
❑ 80 Jerome Bettis B 1.25 .55
❑ 81 Andre Hastings B UER .30 .14
listed as uncommon
❑ 82 Simeon Rice B .60 .25
❑ 83 Cornelius Bennett B .30 .14
❑ 84 Napoleon Kaufman B 2.00 .90
❑ 85 Jim Harbaugh B .60 .25
❑ 86 Aaron Hayden B .30 .14
❑ 87 Gus Frerotte B .30 .14
❑ 88 Jeff Blake B .60 .25
❑ 89 Anthony Miller B UER .30 .14
listed as uncommon
❑ 90 Deion Sanders B 1.25 .55
❑ 91 Curtis Conway B .60 .25
❑ 92 William Floyd B .60 .25
❑ 93 Eric Moulds B UER 1.25 .55
listed as uncommon
❑ 94 Mel Gray B .30 .14
❑ 95 Andre Rison B UER .60 .25
listed as uncommon
❑ 96 Eugene Daniel B .30 .14
❑ 97 Jason Belser B .30 .14
❑ 98 Mike Mamula B .30 .14
❑ 99 Jim Everett B .30 .14
❑ 100 Checklist B .30 .14
❑ 101 Drew Bledsoe S 8.00 3.60
❑ 102 Shannon Sharpe S 1.50 .70
❑ 103 Ken Harvey S .75 .35
❑ 104 Isaac Bruce S 3.00 1.35
❑ 105 Terry Allen S 3.00 1.35
❑ 106 Lawyer Milloy S .75 .35
❑ 107 Ashley Ambrose S .75 .35
❑ 108 Alfred Williams S .75 .35

- ❑ 109 Hugh Douglas S .75 .35
- ❑ 110 Junior Seau S 1.50 .70
- ❑ 111 Kordell Stewart S 6.00 2.70
- ❑ 112 Adrian Murrell S 1.50 .70
- ❑ 113 Byron Bam Morris S .75 .35
- ❑ 114 Terrell Buckley S .75 .35
- ❑ 115 Dan Marino S 15.00 6.75
- ❑ 116 Willie Clay S .75 .35
- ❑ 117 Neil Smith S 1.50 .70
- ❑ 118 Blaine Bishop S .75 .35
- ❑ 119 John Mobley S .75 .35
- ❑ 120 Herman Moore S 3.00 1.35
- ❑ 121 Keyshawn Johnson S 3.00 1.35
- ❑ 122 Boomer Esiason S 1.50 .70
- ❑ 123 Marshall Faulk S 3.00 1.35
- ❑ 124 Keith Jackson S .75 .35
- ❑ 125 Ricky Watters S 1.50 .70
- ❑ 126 Carl Pickens S 1.50 .70
- ❑ 127 Cris Carter S 3.00 1.35
- ❑ 128 Mike Alstott S 3.00 1.35
- ❑ 129 Simeon Rice S 1.50 .70
- ❑ 130 Troy Aikman S 8.00 3.60
- ❑ 131 Tamarick Vanover S 1.50 .70
- ❑ 132 Marquez Pope S .75 .35
- ❑ 133 Winslow Oliver S .75 .35
- ❑ 134 Edgar Bennett S 1.50 .70
- ❑ 135 Dave Meggett S .75 .35
- ❑ 136 Marcus Allen S 3.00 1.35
- ❑ 137 Jerry Rice S 8.00 3.60
- ❑ 138 Steve Atwater S .75 .35
- ❑ 139 Tim McDonald S .75 .35
- ❑ 140 Barry Sanders S 15.00 6.75
- ❑ 141 Eddie George S 10.00 4.50
- ❑ 142 Wesley Walls S .75 .35
- ❑ 143 Jerome Bettis S 3.00 1.35
- ❑ 144 Kevin Greene S 1.50 .70
- ❑ 145 Terrell Davis S 15.00 6.75
- ❑ 146 Gus Frerotte S 1.50 .70
- ❑ 147 Joey Galloway S 6.00 2.70
- ❑ 148 Vinny Testaverde S 1.50 .70
- ❑ 149 Hardy Nickerson S .75 .35
- ❑ 150 Brett Favre S 15.00 6.75
- ❑ 151 Desmond Howard G 2.00 .90
- ❑ 152 Keyshawn Johnson G 6.00 2.70
- ❑ 153 Tony Banks G 6.00 2.70
- ❑ 154 Chris Spielman G 2.00 .90
- ❑ 155 Reggie White G 6.00 2.70
- ❑ 156 Zach Thomas G 6.00 2.70
- ❑ 157 Carl Pickens G 4.00 1.80
- ❑ 158 Karim Abdul-Jabbar G 6.00 2.70
- ❑ 159 Chad Brown G 2.00 .90
- ❑ 160 Kerry Collins G 4.00 1.80
- ❑ 161 Marvin Harrison G 6.00 2.70
- ❑ 162 Steve Young G 10.00 4.50
- ❑ 163 Deion Sanders G 6.00 2.70
- ❑ 164 Trent Dilfer G 6.00 2.70
- ❑ 165 Barry Sanders G 25.00 11.00
- ❑ 166 Cris Carter G 6.00 2.70
- ❑ 167 Keenan McCardell G 4.00 1.80
- ❑ 168 Terry Glenn G 6.00 2.70
- ❑ 169 Emmitt Smith G 20.00 9.00
- ❑ 170 John Elway G 25.00 11.00
- ❑ 171 Jerry Rice G 12.00 5.50
- ❑ 172 Troy Aikman G 12.00 5.50
- ❑ 173 Curtis Martin G 10.00 4.50
- ❑ 174 Darrell Green G 2.00 .90
- ❑ 175 Mark Brunell G 12.00 5.50
- ❑ 176 Corey Dillon B RC 8.00 3.60
- ❑ 177 Tyrone Poole B .30 .14
- ❑ 178 Anthony Pleasant B .30 .14
- ❑ 179 Frank Sanders B .60 .25
- ❑ 180 Troy Aikman B 3.00 1.35
- ❑ 181 Bill Romanowski B .30 .14
- ❑ 182 Ty Law B .30 .14
- ❑ 183 Orlando Thomas B .30 .14
- ❑ 184 Quentin Coryatt B .30 .14
- ❑ 185 Kenny Holmes B RC .30 .14
- ❑ 186 Bryant Young B .30 .14
- ❑ 187 Michael Sinclair B .30 .14
- ❑ 188 Mike Tomczak B .30 .14
- ❑ 189 Bobby Taylor B .30 .14
- ❑ 190 Brett Favre B 6.00 2.70
- ❑ 191 Kent Graham B .30 .14
- ❑ 192 Jessie Tuggle B .30 .14
- ❑ 193 Jimmy Smith B .60 .25
- ❑ 194 Greg Hill B .30 .14
- ❑ 195 Yatil Green B RC .60 .25
- ❑ 196 Mark Fields B .30 .14
- ❑ 197 Phillippi Sparks B .30 .14
- ❑ 198 Aaron Glenn B .30 .14
- ❑ 199 Pat Swilling B .30 .14
- ❑ 200 Barry Sanders B 6.00 2.70
- ❑ 201 Mark Chmura B .60 .25
- ❑ 202 Marco Coleman B .30 .14
- ❑ 203 Merton Hanks B .30 .14
- ❑ 204 Brian Blades B .30 .14
- ❑ 205 Errict Rhett B .30 .14
- ❑ 206 Henry Ellard B .30 .14
- ❑ 207 Andre Reed B .60 .25
- ❑ 208 Bryan Cox B .30 .14
- ❑ 209 Darnay Scott B .60 .25
- ❑ 210 John Elway B 6.00 2.70
- ❑ 211 Glyn Milburn B .30 .14
- ❑ 212 Don Beebe B .30 .14
- ❑ 213 Kevin Lockett B RC .60 .25
- ❑ 214 Dorsey Levens B 1.25 .55
- ❑ 215 Kordell Stewart B 2.00 .90
- ❑ 216 Larry Centers B .60 .25
- ❑ 217 Cris Carter B 1.25 .55
- ❑ 218 Willie McGinest B .30 .14
- ❑ 219 Renaldo Wynn B RC .30 .14
- ❑ 220 Jerry Rice B 3.00 1.35
- ❑ 221 Reidel Anthony B RC 4.00 1.80
- ❑ 222 Mark Carrier WR B .30 .14
- ❑ 223 Quinn Early B .30 .14
- ❑ 224 Chris Sanders B .30 .14
- ❑ 225 Shawn Springs B RC .60 .25
- ❑ 226 Kevin Smith B .30 .14
- ❑ 227 Ben Coates B .60 .25
- ❑ 228 Tyrone Wheatley B .60 .25
- ❑ 229 Antonio Freeman B 2.00 .90
- ❑ 230 Dan Marino B 6.00 2.70
- ❑ 231 Dwayne Rudd B RC .30 .14
- ❑ 232 Leslie O'Neal B .30 .14
- ❑ 233 Brent Jones B .60 .25
- ❑ 234 Jake Plummer B RC 15.00 6.75
- ❑ 235 Kerry Collins B .60 .25
- ❑ 236 Rashaan Salaam B .30 .14
- ❑ 237 Tyrone Braxton B .30 .14
- ❑ 238 Herman Moore B 1.25 .55
- ❑ 239 Keyshawn Johnson B 1.25 .55
- ❑ 240 Drew Bledsoe B 3.00 1.35
- ❑ 241 Rickey Dudley B .60 .25
- ❑ 242 Antowain Smith B RC 5.00 2.20
- ❑ 243 Jeff Lageman B .30 .14
- ❑ 244 Chris T. Jones B .30 .14
- ❑ 245 Steve Young B 2.00 .90
- ❑ 246 Eddie Robinson B .30 .14
- ❑ 247 Chad Cota B .30 .14
- ❑ 248 Michael Jackson B .60 .25
- ❑ 249 Robert Porcher B .30 .14
- ❑ 250 Reggie White B 1.25 .55
- ❑ 251 Carnell Lake B .30 .14
- ❑ 252 Chris Calloway B .30 .14
- ❑ 253 Terance Mathis B .60 .25
- ❑ 254 Carl Pickens B 1.25 .55
- ❑ 255 Curtis Martin B 2.00 .90
- ❑ 256 Jeff Graham B .30 .14
- ❑ 257 Regan Upshaw B RC .30 .14
- ❑ 258 Sean Gilbert B .30 .14
- ❑ 259 Will Blackwell B RC 1.25 .55
- ❑ 260 Emmitt Smith B 5.00 2.20
- ❑ 261 Reinard Wilson B RC .30 .14
- ❑ 262 Darrell Russell B RC .30 .14
- ❑ 263 Wayne Chrebet B .60 .25
- ❑ 264 Kevin Hardy B .30 .14
- ❑ 265 Shannon Sharpe B .60 .25
- ❑ 266 Harvey Williams B .30 .14
- ❑ 267 John Randle B .30 .14
- ❑ 268 Tim Bowens B .30 .14
- ❑ 269 Tony Gonzalez B RC 6.00 2.70
- ❑ 270 Warrick Dunn B RC 6.00 2.70
- ❑ 271 Sean Dawkins B .30 .14
- ❑ 272 Darryll Lewis B .30 .14
- ❑ 273 Alonzo Spellman B .30 .14
- ❑ 274 Mark Collins B .30 .14
- ❑ 275 Checklist Card B .30 .14
- ❑ 276 Pat Barnes S RC 4.00 1.80
- ❑ 277 Dana Stubblefield S 1.50 .70
- ❑ 278 Dan Wilkinson S .75 .35
- ❑ 279 Bryce Paup S .75 .35
- ❑ 280 Kerry Collins S 1.50 .70
- ❑ 281 Derrick Brooks S .75 .35
- ❑ 282 Walter Jones S .75 .35
- ❑ 283 Terry McDaniel S .75 .35
- ❑ 284 James Farrior S RC .75 .35
- ❑ 285 Curtis Martin S 6.00 2.70
- ❑ 286 O.J. McDuffie S 1.50 .70
- ❑ 287 Natrone Means S 3.00 1.35
- ❑ 288 Bryant Westbrook S RC .75 .35
- ❑ 289 Peter Boulware S RC 1.50 .70
- ❑ 290 Emmitt Smith S 12.00 5.50
- ❑ 291 Joey Kent S RC 3.00 1.35
- ❑ 292 Eddie Kennison S 1.50 .70
- ❑ 293 LeRoy Butler S .75 .35
- ❑ 294 Dale Carter S .75 .35
- ❑ 295 Jim Druckenmiller S RC 4.00 1.80
- ❑ 296 Byron Hanspard S RC 8.00 3.60
- ❑ 297 Jeff Blake S 1.50 .70
- ❑ 298 Levon Kirkland S .75 .35
- ❑ 299 Michael Westbrook S 1.50 .70
- ❑ 300 John Elway S 15.00 6.75
- ❑ 301 Lamar Lathon S .75 .35
- ❑ 302 Ray Lewis S .75 .35
- ❑ 303 Steve McNair S 6.00 2.70
- ❑ 304 Shawn Springs S 1.50 .70
- ❑ 305 Karim Abdul-Jabbar S 1.50 .70
- ❑ 306 Orlando Pace S RC .75 .35
- ❑ 307 Scott Mitchell S .75 .35
- ❑ 308 Walt Harris S .75 .35
- ❑ 309 Bruce Smith S 1.50 .70
- ❑ 310 Reggie White S 3.00 1.35
- ❑ 311 Eric Swann S .75 .35
- ❑ 312 Derrick Thomas S 1.50 .70
- ❑ 313 Tony Martin S 1.50 .70
- ❑ 314 Darrell Russell S RC .75 .35
- ❑ 315 Mark Brunell S 8.00 3.60
- ❑ 316 Trent Dilfer S 3.00 1.35
- ❑ 317 Irving Fryar S .75 .35
- ❑ 318 Amani Toomer S 1.50 .70
- ❑ 319 Jake Reed S 1.50 .70
- ❑ 320 Steve Young S 6.00 2.70
- ❑ 321 Troy Davis S RC 1.50 .70
- ❑ 322 Jim Harbaugh S 1.50 .70
- ❑ 323 Neil O'Donnell S .75 .35
- ❑ 324 Terry Glenn S 3.00 1.35
- ❑ 325 Deion Sanders S 3.00 1.35
- ❑ 326 Gus Frerotte G 4.00 1.80
- ❑ 327 Tom Knight G RC 2.00 .90
- ❑ 328 Peter Boulware G 4.00 1.80
- ❑ 329 Jerome Bettis G 6.00 2.70
- ❑ 330 Orlando Pace G 2.00 .90
- ❑ 331 Darnell Autry G RC 2.00 .90
- ❑ 332 Ike Hilliard G RC 15.00 6.75
- ❑ 333 David LaFleur G RC 4.00 1.80
- ❑ 334 Jim Harbaugh G 4.00 1.80
- ❑ 335 Eddie George G 15.00 6.75
- ❑ 336 Vinny Testaverde G 4.00 1.80
- ❑ 337 Terry Allen G 4.00 1.80
- ❑ 338 Jim Druckenmiller G 6.00 2.70
- ❑ 339 Ricky Watters G 4.00 1.80
- ❑ 340 Brett Favre G 25.00 11.00
- ❑ 341 Simeon Rice G 4.00 1.80
- ❑ 342 Shannon Sharpe G 4.00 1.80
- ❑ 343 Kordell Stewart G 10.00 4.50
- ❑ 344 Isaac Bruce G 6.00 2.70
- ❑ 345 Drew Bledsoe G 12.00 5.50
- ❑ 346 Jeff Blake G 4.00 1.80
- ❑ 347 Herman Moore G 6.00 2.70
- ❑ 348 Junior Seau G 4.00 1.80
- ❑ 349 Rae Carruth G RC 6.00 2.70
- ❑ 350 Dan Marino G 25.00 11.00
- ❑ P5 K.Abdul-Jabbar Promo 4.00 1.80
- ❑ P32 Tony Brackens Promo 1.00 .45
- ❑ P45 Sam Mills Promo 1.00 .45
- ❑ P70 Terry Glenn Promo 4.00 1.80
- ❑ P87 Gus Frerotte Promo 2.00 .90

1997 Finest Embossed

	MINT	NRMT
COMPLETE SET (150)	1000.00	450.00
COMP.SERIES 1 (75)	400.00	180.00
COMP.SERIES 2 (75)	600.00	275.00

*SILVER STARS: .75X TO 2X HI COL.
*SILVER RCs: .6X TO 1.5X
SILVER STATED ODDS 1:16
*GOLD STARS: .5X TO 1.25X HI COL.

*GOLD RCs: SAME PRICE ....
GOLD STATED ODDS 1:96.........

1997 Finest Embossed Refractors

	MINT	NRMT
COMMON SILVER....................	8.00	3.60
*SILVER STARS: 2X TO 5X HI COL.		
*SILVER RCs: 1X TO 2.5X...........		
SILVER STATED ODDS 1:192		
COMMON GOLD DIE CUT	25.00	11.00
*GOLD DC STARS: 2.5X TO 6X HI COL.		
*GOLD DC RCs: 1.2X TO 3X........		
GOLD STATED ODDS 1:1152......		

1997 Finest Refractors

	MINT	NRMT
COMPLETE SET (350)	3500.00	1600.00
COMP.SERIES 1 (175)	1500.00	700.00
COMP.SERIES 2 (175)	2000.00	900.00
COMP.BRONZE SER.1 (100)	400.00	180.00
COMP.BRONZE SER.2 (100)	600.00	275.00
*BRONZE STARS: 3X TO 8X HI ..		
*BRONZE RCs: 2X TO 5X		
BRONZE REF.STATED ODDS 1:12		
*SILVER STARS: 1.2X TO 3X HI..		
*SILVER RCs: 1X TO 2.5X...........		
SILVER REF.STATED ODDS 1:48		
*GOLD STARS: 1.5X TO 4X HI COL.		
*GOLD RCs: 1X TO 2.5X		
GOLD REF.STATED ODDS 1:288		

1998 Finest

	MINT	NRMT
COMPLETE SET (270)	150.00	70.00
COMP.SERIES 1 (150)	100.00	45.00
COMP.SERIES 2 (120)	50.00	22.00
COMMON CARD (1-120/151-270)	.25	.11
SEMISTARS...........................	.50	.23
UNLISTED STARS................	1.00	.45
COMMON ROOKIE (121-150) ..	2.00	.90
ROOKIE SEMISTARS	3.00	1.35
ROOKIE UNLISTED STARS	4.00	1.80
COMP.NO-PROT.SET (270)	300.00	135.00
*NP STARS: 1.25X TO 3X HI COL.		
*NO-PROTECTOR RCs: .5X TO 1.2X		
NO-PROTECTOR ODDS 1:2H/R, 1:1J		

1-120 NO-PROTECTORS IN SERIES 1 PACKS
121-270 NO-PROTECTORS IN SERIES 2 PACKS

Card	MINT	NRMT
❑ 1 John Elway	5.00	2.20
❑ 2 Terance Mathis	.50	.23
❑ 3 Jermaine Lewis	.50	.23
❑ 4 Fred Lane	.50	.23
❑ 5 Simeon Rice	.50	.23
❑ 6 David Dunn	.25	.11
❑ 7 Dexter Coakley	.25	.11
❑ 8 Carl Pickens	1.00	.45
❑ 9 Antonio Freeman	1.00	.45
❑ 10 Herman Moore	1.00	.45
❑ 11 Kevin Hardy	.25	.11
❑ 12 Tony Gonzalez	.25	.11
❑ 13 O.J. McDuffie	.50	.23
❑ 14 David Palmer	.25	.11
❑ 15 Lawyer Milloy	.25	.11
❑ 16 Danny Kanell	.50	.23
❑ 17 Randal Hill	.25	.11
❑ 18 Chris Slade	.25	.11
❑ 19 Charlie Garner	.25	.11
❑ 20 Mark Brunell	2.00	.90
❑ 21 Donnell Woolford	.25	.11
❑ 22 Freddie Jones	.25	.11
❑ 23 Ken Norton	.25	.11
❑ 24 Tony Banks	.50	.23
❑ 25 Isaac Bruce	1.00	.45
❑ 26 Willie Davis	.25	.11
❑ 27 Cris Dishman	.25	.11
❑ 28 Aeneas Williams	.25	.11
❑ 29 Michael Booker	.25	.11
❑ 30 Cris Carter	1.00	.45
❑ 31 Michael McCrary	.25	.11
❑ 32 Eric Moulds	1.00	.45
❑ 33 Rae Carruth	.50	.23
❑ 34 Bobby Engram	.50	.23
❑ 35 Jeff Blake	.50	.23
❑ 36 Deion Sanders	1.00	.45
❑ 37 Rod Smith	.50	.23
❑ 38 Bryant Westbrook	.25	.11
❑ 39 Mark Chmura	.50	.23
❑ 40 Tim Brown	1.00	.45
❑ 41 Bobby Taylor	.25	.11
❑ 42 James Stewart	.50	.23
❑ 43 Kimble Anders	.50	.23
❑ 44 Karim Abdul-Jabbar	1.00	.45
❑ 45 Willie McGinest	.25	.11
❑ 46 Jessie Armstead	.25	.11
❑ 47 Brad Johnson	1.00	.45
❑ 48 Greg Lloyd	.25	.11
❑ 49 Stephen Davis	.25	.11
❑ 50 Jerome Bettis	1.00	.45
❑ 51 Warren Sapp	.50	.23
❑ 52 Horace Copeland	.25	.11
❑ 53 Chad Brown	.25	.11
❑ 54 Chris Canty	.25	.11
❑ 55 Robert Smith	1.00	.45
❑ 56 Pete Mitchell	.25	.11
❑ 57 Aaron Bailey	.25	.11
❑ 58 Robert Porcher	.25	.11
❑ 59 John Mobley	.25	.11
❑ 60 Tony Martin	.50	.23
❑ 61 Michael Irvin	1.00	.45
❑ 62 Charles Way	.25	.11
❑ 63 Raymont Harris	.25	.11
❑ 64 Chuck Smith	.25	.11
❑ 65 Larry Centers	.25	.11
❑ 66 Greg Hill	.25	.11
❑ 67 Kenny Holmes	.25	.11
❑ 68 John Lynch	.25	.11
❑ 69 Michael Sinclair	.25	.11
❑ 70 Steve Young	1.50	.70
❑ 71 Michael Strahan	.25	.11
❑ 72 Levon Kirkland	.25	.11
❑ 73 Rickey Dudley	.25	.11
❑ 74 Marcus Allen	1.00	.45
❑ 75 John Randle	.50	.23
❑ 76 Erik Kramer	.25	.11
❑ 77 Neil Smith	.50	.23
❑ 78 Byron Hanspard	.50	.23
❑ 79 Quinn Early	.25	.11
❑ 80 Warren Moon	1.00	.45
❑ 81 William Thomas	.25	.11
❑ 82 Ben Coates	.50	.23
❑ 83 Lake Dawson	.25	.11
❑ 84 Steve McNair	1.00	.45
❑ 85 Gus Frerotte	.25	.11
❑ 86 Rodney Harrison	.50	.23
❑ 87 Reggie White	1.00	.45
❑ 88 Derrick Thomas	.50	.23
❑ 89 Dale Carter	.25	.11
❑ 90 Warrick Dunn	1.50	.70
❑ 91 Will Blackwell	.25	.11
❑ 92 Troy Vincent	.25	.11
❑ 93 Johnnie Morton	.50	.23
❑ 94 David LaFleur	.25	.11
❑ 95 Tony McGee	.25	.11
❑ 96 Lonnie Johnson	.25	.11
❑ 97 Thurman Thomas	1.00	.45
❑ 98 Chris Chandler	.50	.23
❑ 99 Jamal Anderson	1.00	.45
❑ 100 Checklist	.25	.11
❑ 101 Marshall Faulk	1.00	.45
❑ 102 Chris Calloway	.25	.11
❑ 103 Chris Spielman	.25	.11
❑ 104 Zach Thomas	.25	.11
❑ 105 Jeff George	.50	.23
❑ 106 Darrell Russell	.25	.11
❑ 107 Darryll Lewis	.25	.11
❑ 108 Reidel Anthony	.50	.23
❑ 109 Terrell Owens	1.00	.45
❑ 110 Rob Moore	.50	.23
❑ 111 Darrell Green	.50	.23
❑ 112 Merton Hanks	.25	.11
❑ 113 Shawn Jefferson	.25	.11
❑ 114 Chris Sanders	.25	.11
❑ 115 Scott Mitchell	.50	.23
❑ 116 Vaughn Hebron	.25	.11
❑ 117 Ed McCaffrey	.50	.23
❑ 118 Bruce Smith	.50	.23
❑ 119 Peter Boulware	.25	.11
❑ 120 Brett Favre	5.00	2.20
❑ 121 Peyton Manning RC	30.00	13.50
❑ 122 Brian Griese RC	10.00	4.50
❑ 123 Tavian Banks RC	3.00	1.35
❑ 124 Duane Starks RC	2.00	.90
❑ 125 Robert Holcombe RC	4.00	1.80
❑ 126 Brian Simmons RC	2.00	.90
❑ 127 Skip Hicks RC	6.00	2.70
❑ 128 Keith Brooking RC	3.00	1.35
❑ 129 Ahman Green RC	6.00	2.70
❑ 130 Jerome Pathon RC	3.00	1.35
❑ 131 Curtis Enis RC	8.00	3.60
❑ 132 Grant Wistrom RC	2.00	.90
❑ 133 Germane Crowell RC	8.00	3.60
❑ 134 Jacquez Green RC	6.00	2.70
❑ 135 Randy Moss RC	30.00	13.50
❑ 136 Jason Peter RC	2.00	.90
❑ 137 John Avery RC	4.00	1.80
❑ 138 Takeo Spikes RC	3.00	1.35
❑ 139 Pat Johnson RC	3.00	1.35
❑ 140 Andre Wadsworth RC	3.00	1.35
❑ 141 Fred Taylor RC	15.00	6.75
❑ 142 Charles Woodson RC	8.00	3.60
❑ 143 Marcus Nash RC	6.00	2.70
❑ 144 Robert Edwards RC	4.00	1.80
❑ 145 Kevin Dyson RC	6.00	2.70
❑ 146 Joe Jurevicius RC	3.00	1.35
❑ 147 Anthony Simmons RC	2.00	.90
❑ 148 Hines Ward RC	3.00	1.35
❑ 149 Greg Ellis RC	2.00	.90
❑ 150 Ryan Leaf RC	6.00	2.70
❑ 151 Jerry Rice	2.50	1.10

❑ 152	Tony Martin	.50	.23
❑ 153	Checklist	.25	.11
❑ 154	Rob Johnson	.50	.23
❑ 155	Shannon Sharpe	.50	.23
❑ 156	Bert Emanuel	.50	.23
❑ 157	Eric Metcalf	.25	.11
❑ 158	Natrone Means	1.00	.45
❑ 159	Derrick Alexander	.50	.23
❑ 160	Emmitt Smith	4.00	1.80
❑ 161	Jeff Burris	.25	.11
❑ 162	Chris Warren	.50	.23
❑ 163	Corey Fuller	.25	.11
❑ 164	Courtney Hawkins	.25	.11
❑ 165	James McKnight	.25	.11
❑ 166	Shawn Springs	.25	.11
❑ 167	Wayne Martin	.25	.11
❑ 168	Michael Westbrook	.50	.23
❑ 169	Michael Jackson	.25	.11
❑ 170	Dan Marino	5.00	2.20
❑ 171	Amp Lee	.25	.11
❑ 172	James Jett	.50	.23
❑ 173	Ty Law	.25	.11
❑ 174	Kerry Collins	.50	.23
❑ 175	Robert Brooks	.50	.23
❑ 176	Blaine Bishop	.25	.11
❑ 177	Stephen Boyd	.25	.11
❑ 178	Keyshawn Johnson	1.00	.45
❑ 179	Deon Figures	.25	.11
❑ 180	Allen Aldridge	.25	.11
❑ 181	Corey Miller	.25	.11
❑ 182	Chad Lewis	.25	.11
❑ 183	Derrick Rodgers	.25	.11
❑ 184	Troy Drayton	.25	.11
❑ 185	Darren Woodson	.25	.11
❑ 186	Ken Dilger	.25	.11
❑ 187	Elvis Grbac	.50	.23
❑ 188	Terrell Fletcher	.25	.11
❑ 189	Frank Sanders	.50	.23
❑ 190	Curtis Martin	1.00	.45
❑ 191	Derrick Brooks	.25	.11
❑ 192	Darrien Gordon	.25	.11
❑ 193	Andre Reed	.50	.23
❑ 194	Darnay Scott	.50	.23
❑ 195	Curtis Conway	.50	.23
❑ 196	Tim McDonald	.25	.11
❑ 197	Sean Dawkins	.25	.11
❑ 198	Napoleon Kaufman	1.00	.45
❑ 199	Willie Clay	.25	.11
❑ 200	Terrell Davis	4.00	1.80
❑ 201	Wesley Walls	.50	.23
❑ 202	Santana Dotson	.25	.11
❑ 203	Frank Wycheck	.25	.11
❑ 204	Wayne Chrebet	1.00	.45
❑ 205	Andre Rison	.50	.23
❑ 206	Jason Sehorn	.25	.11
❑ 207	Jessie Tuggle	.25	.11
❑ 208	Kevin Turner	.25	.11
❑ 209	Jason Taylor	.25	.11
❑ 210	Yancey Thigpen	.25	.11
❑ 211	Jake Reed	.50	.23
❑ 212	Carnell Lake	.25	.11
❑ 213	Joey Galloway	1.00	.45
❑ 214	Andre Hastings	.25	.11
❑ 215	Terry Allen	1.00	.45
❑ 216	Jim Harbaugh	.50	.23
❑ 217	Tony Banks	.50	.23
❑ 218	Greg Clark	.25	.11
❑ 219	Corey Dillon	1.50	.70
❑ 220	Troy Aikman	2.50	1.10
❑ 221	Antowain Smith	1.00	.45
❑ 222	Steve Atwater	.25	.11
❑ 223	Trent Dilfer	1.00	.45
❑ 224	Junior Seau	.50	.23
❑ 225	Garrison Hearst	1.00	.45
❑ 226	Eric Allen	.25	.11
❑ 227	Chad Cota	.25	.11
❑ 228	Vinny Testaverde	.50	.23
❑ 229	Duce Staley	1.50	.70
❑ 230	Drew Bledsoe	2.00	.90
❑ 231	Charles Johnson	.25	.11
❑ 232	Jake Plummer	3.00	1.35
❑ 233	Errict Rhett	.50	.23
❑ 234	Doug Evans	.25	.11
❑ 235	Phillippi Sparks	.25	.11
❑ 236	Ashley Ambrose	.25	.11
❑ 237	Bryan Cox	.25	.11
❑ 238	Kevin Smith	.25	.11
❑ 239	Hardy Nickerson	.25	.11
❑ 240	Terry Glenn	1.00	.45
❑ 241	Lee Woodall	.25	.11
❑ 242	Andre Coleman	.25	.11
❑ 243	Michael Bates	.25	.11
❑ 244	Mark Fields	.25	.11
❑ 245	Eddie Kennison	.50	.23
❑ 246	Dana Stubblefield	.25	.11
❑ 247	Bobby Hoying	.50	.23
❑ 248	Mo Lewis	.25	.11
❑ 249	Derrick Mayes	.50	.23
❑ 250	Eddie George	2.00	.90
❑ 251	Mike Alstott	1.00	.45
❑ 252	J.J. Stokes	.50	.23
❑ 253	Adrian Murrell	.50	.23
❑ 254	Kevin Greene	.50	.23
❑ 255	LeRoy Butler	.25	.11
❑ 256	Glenn Foley	.50	.23
❑ 257	Jimmy Smith	.50	.23
❑ 258	Tiki Barber	.50	.23
❑ 259	Irving Fryar	.50	.23
❑ 260	Ricky Watters	.50	.23
❑ 261	Jeff Graham	.25	.11
❑ 262	Kordell Stewart	1.00	.45
❑ 263	Rod Woodson	.50	.23
❑ 264	Leslie Shepherd	.25	.11
❑ 265	Ryan McNeil	.25	.11
❑ 266	Ike Hilliard	.50	.23
❑ 267	Keenan McCardell	.50	.23
❑ 268	Marvin Harrison	.50	.23
❑ 269	Dorsey Levens	1.00	.45
❑ 270	Barry Sanders	5.00	2.20

1998 Finest Refractors

	MINT	NRMT
COMP.REFRACT.SET (270)	1000.00	450.00

*REFRACT.STARS: .4X TO 10X HI COL.
*REFRACT.YOUNG STARS: 3X TO 8X
*REFRACTOR RCs: 1.2X TO 3X..
REFRACTOR ODDS 1:12H/R, 1:5J
1-120 REFRACTORS IN SERIES 1 PACKS
121-270 REFRACTORS SERIES 2 PACKS

COMP.NP.REF.SET (270)..	1800.00	800.00

*NP.REFRACT.STARS: 8X TO 20X HI COL.
*NP.REFRACT.YOUNG STARS: 6X TO 15X
*NP.REFRACT.RCs: 2X TO 5X ....
*NO-PROT.REF.ODDS 1:24H/R, 1:10J
NO-PROT.REFRACTORS HAVE FOIL REF.BACKS

1998 Finest Centurions

	MINT	NRMT
COMPLETE SET (20)	400.00	180.00
COMMON CARD (C1-C20)	10.00	4.50
SEMISTARS	15.00	6.75
UNLISTED STARS	20.00	9.00

STATED ODDS 1:125H/R, 1:58J ..
STATED PRINT RUN 500 SERIAL #'d SETS
*REFRACTORS: .75X TO 2X HI COL.
REFRACT.STATED ODDS 1:831H/R, 1:383J
REF.STATED PRINT RUN 75 SERIAL #'d SETS

❑ C1	Brett Favre	80.00	36.00
❑ C2	Eddie George	30.00	13.50
❑ C3	Antonio Freeman	20.00	9.00
❑ C4	Napoleon Kaufman	20.00	9.00
❑ C5	Terrell Davis	50.00	22.00
❑ C6	Keyshawn Johnson	20.00	9.00
❑ C7	Peter Boulware	10.00	4.50
❑ C8	Mike Alstott	20.00	9.00
❑ C9	Jake Plummer	40.00	18.00
❑ C10	Mark Brunell	30.00	13.50
❑ C11	Marvin Harrison	20.00	9.00
❑ C12	Antowain Smith	20.00	9.00
❑ C13	Dorsey Levens	15.00	6.75
❑ C14	Terry Glenn	15.00	6.75
❑ C15	Warrick Dunn	20.00	9.00
❑ C16	Joey Galloway	20.00	9.00
❑ C17	Steve McNair	20.00	9.00
❑ C18	Corey Dillon	30.00	13.50
❑ C19	Drew Bledsoe	30.00	13.50
❑ C20	Kordell Stewart	20.00	9.00

1998 Finest Future's Finest

	MINT	NRMT
COMPLETE SET (20)	250.00	110.00
COMMON CARD (F1-F20)	12.00	5.50

STATED ODDS 1:83
STATED PRINT RUN 500 SERIAL #'d SETS
*REFRACTORS: 1X TO 2.5X HI COL.
REFRACTOR STATED ODDS 1:557
REF.STATED PRINT RUN 75 SERIAL #'d SETS

❑ F1	Peyton Manning	50.00	22.00
❑ F2	Napoleon Kaufman	15.00	6.75
❑ F3	Jake Plummer	25.00	11.00
❑ F4	Terry Glenn	15.00	6.75
❑ F5	Ryan Leaf	15.00	6.75
❑ F6	Drew Bledsoe	20.00	9.00
❑ F7	Dorsey Levens	12.00	5.50
❑ F8	Andre Wadsworth	12.00	5.50
❑ F9	Joey Galloway	15.00	6.75
❑ F10	Curtis Enis	15.00	6.75
❑ F11	Warrick Dunn	15.00	6.75
❑ F12	Kordell Stewart	12.00	5.50
❑ F13	Randy Moss	50.00	22.00
❑ F14	Robert Edwards	12.00	5.50
❑ F15	Eddie George	20.00	9.00
❑ F16	Fred Taylor	25.00	11.00
❑ F17	Corey Dillon	12.00	5.50
❑ F18	Brett Favre	50.00	22.00
❑ F19	Kevin Dyson	15.00	6.75
❑ F20	Terrell Davis	40.00	18.00

1998 Finest Jumbos 1

	MINT	NRMT
COMPLETE SET (8)	100.00	45.00
COMMON CARD (1-8)	6.00	2.70

STATED ODDS 1:3 BOXES
*REFRACTORS: .75X TO 2X HI COL.
REFRACTOR ODDS 1:12 BOXES

❑ 1	John Elway	25.00	11.00
❑ 2	Peyton Manning	40.00	18.00
❑ 3	Mark Brunell	10.00	4.50
❑ 4	Curtis Enis	12.00	5.50
❑ 5	Jerome Bettis	6.00	2.70
❑ 6	Ryan Leaf	10.00	4.50
❑ 7	Warrick Dunn	10.00	4.50
❑ 8	Brett Favre	25.00	11.00

1998 Finest Jumbos 2

	MINT	NRMT
COMPLETE SET (7)	80.00	36.00
COMMON CARD	6.00	2.70

STATED ODDS 1:3 BOXES
*REFRACTORS: .75X TO 2X HI COL.
REFRACTOR STATED ODDS 1:12 BOXES

		MINT	NRMT
151	Jerry Rice	12.00	5.50
160	Emmitt Smith	20.00	9.00
170	Dan Marino	25.00	11.00
213	Joey Galloway	6.00	2.70
230	Drew Bledsoe	10.00	4.50
250	Eddie George	10.00	4.50
270	Barry Sanders	25.00	11.00

1998 Finest Mystery Finest 1

	MINT	NRMT
COMPLETE SET (50)	600.00	275.00
COMMON CARD (M1-M50)	8.00	3.60

STATED ODDS 1:36H/R, 1:15J
*REFRACTORS: .6X TO 1.5X HI COL.
REFRACT.STATED ODDS 1:144H/R, 1:64J

		MINT	NRMT
M1	Brett Favre Mark Brunell	25.00	11.00
M2	Brett Favre Jake Plummer	25.00	11.00
M3	Brett Favre Steve Young	25.00	11.00
M4	Brett Favre Brett Favre	30.00	13.50
M5	Mark Brunell Steve Young	10.00	4.50
M6	Mark Brunell Mark Brunell	12.00	5.50
M7	Jake Plummer Mark Brunell	12.00	5.50
M8	Jake Plummer Jake Plummer	15.00	6.75
M9	Steve Young Jake Plummer	10.00	4.50
M10	Steve Young Steve Young	10.00	4.50
M11	John Elway Drew Bledsoe	25.00	11.00
M12	John Elway Troy Aikman	25.00	11.00
M13	John Elway Dan Marino	30.00	13.50
M14	John Elway John Elway	30.00	13.50
M15	Drew Bledsoe Troy Aikman	15.00	6.75
M16	Drew Bledsoe Drew Bledsoe	12.00	5.50
M17	Troy Aikman Dan Marino	25.00	11.00
M18	Troy Aikman Troy Aikman	15.00	6.75
M19	Dan Marino Drew Bledsoe	25.00	11.00
M20	Dan Marino Dan Marino	30.00	13.50
M21	Kordell Stewart Corey Dillon	8.00	3.60
M22	Kordell Stewart Tim Brown	8.00	3.60
M23	Kordell Stewart Barry Sanders	25.00	11.00
M24	Kordell Stewart Kordell Stewart	8.00	3.60
M25	Corey Dillon Tim Brown	12.00	5.50
M26	Corey Dillon Corey Dillon	12.00	5.50
M27	Tim Brown Barry Sanders	25.00	11.00
M28	Tim Brown Tim Brown	8.00	3.60
M29	Barry Sanders Corey Dillon	25.00	11.00
M30	Barry Sanders Barry Sanders	30.00	13.50
M31	Terrell Davis Emmitt Smith	25.00	11.00
M32	Terrell Davis Jerome Bettis	20.00	9.00
M33	Terrell Davis Eddie George	20.00	9.00
M34	Terrell Davis Terrell Davis	25.00	11.00
M35	Emmitt Smith Eddie George	20.00	9.00
M36	Emmitt Smith Emmitt Smith	25.00	11.00
M37	Jerome Bettis Emmitt Smith	20.00	9.00
M38	Jerome Bettis Jerome Bettis	10.00	4.50
M39	Eddie George Jerome Bettis	10.00	4.50
M40	Eddie George Eddie George	15.00	6.75
M41	Herman Moore Jerry Rice	15.00	6.75
M42	Herman Moore Herman Moore	8.00	3.60
M43	Warrick Dunn Herman Moore	8.00	3.60
M44	Warrick Dunn Jerry Rice	15.00	6.75
M45	Warrick Dunn Dorsey Levens	8.00	3.60
M46	Warrick Dunn Warrick Dunn	12.00	5.50
M47	Jerry Rice Dorsey Levens	15.00	6.75
M48	Jerry Rice Jerry Rice	20.00	9.00
M49	Dorsey Levens Herman Moore	8.00	3.60
M50	Dorsey Levens Dorsey Levens	8.00	3.60

1998 Finest Mystery Finest 2

	MINT	NRMT
COMPLETE SET (40)	400.00	180.00
COMMON CARD (M1-M40)	5.00	2.20
SEMISTARS	6.00	2.70
UNLISTED STARS	8.00	3.60

STATED ODDS 1:36
*REFRACTORS: .6X TO 1.5X HI COL.
REFRACTOR STATED ODDS 1:144

		MINT	NRMT
M1	Brett Favre Dan Marino	25.00	11.00
M2	Brett Favre Peyton Manning	30.00	13.50
M3	Brett Favre Ryan Leaf	15.00	6.75
M4	Dan Marino Peyton Manning	30.00	13.50
M5	Dan Marino Ryan Leaf	15.00	6.75
M6	Peyton Manning Ryan Leaf	15.00	6.75
M7	Barry Sanders Emmitt Smith	25.00	11.00
M8	Barry Sanders Curtis Enis	15.00	6.75
M9	Barry Sanders Fred Taylor	20.00	9.00
M10	Emmitt Smith Curtis Enis	12.00	5.50
M11	Emmitt Smith Fred Taylor	15.00	6.75
M12	Curtis Enis Fred Taylor	10.00	4.50
M13	John Elway Jerry Rice	20.00	9.00
M14	John Elway Randy Moss	30.00	13.50
M15	John Elway Charles Woodson	15.00	6.75
M16	Jerry Rice Randy Moss	30.00	13.50
M17	Jerry Rice Charles Woodson	10.00	4.50
M18	Randy Moss Charles Woodson	25.00	11.00
M19	Terrell Davis Kordell Stewart	15.00	6.75
M20	Terrell Davis Ricky Watters	12.00	5.50
M21	Terrell Davis Kevin Dyson	10.00	4.50
M22	Kordell Stewart Ricky Watters	8.00	3.60
M23	Kordell Stewart Kevin Dyson	8.00	3.60
M24	Ricky Watters Kevin Dyson	5.00	2.20
M25	Warrick Dunn Eddie George	10.00	4.50
M26	Warrick Dunn Curtis Martin	5.00	2.20
M27	Warrick Dunn Robert Edwards	8.00	3.60
M28	Eddie George Curtis Martin	8.00	3.60
M29	Eddie George Robert Edwards	8.00	3.60
M30	Curtis Martin Robert Edwards	8.00	3.60
M31	Peyton Manning Peyton Manning	30.00	13.50
M32	Ryan Leaf Ryan Leaf	8.00	3.60
M33	Curtis Enis Curtis Enis	8.00	3.60
M34	Fred Taylor Fred Taylor	12.00	5.50
M35	Randy Moss Randy Moss	30.00	13.50
M36	Charles Woodson Charles Woodson	8.00	3.60
M37	Ricky Watters Ricky Watters	5.00	2.20
M38	Kevin Dyson Kevin Dyson	6.00	2.70
M39	Curtis Martin Curtis Martin	6.00	2.70
M40	Robert Edwards Robert Edwards	8.00	3.60

1998 Finest Mystery Finest Jumbos 2

	MINT	NRMT
COMPLETE SET (3)	50.00	22.00
COMMON CARD (M3-M16)	15.00	6.75

STATED ODDS 1:4 BOXES
*REFRACTORS: .75X TO 2X HI COL.
REFRACTOR STATED ODDS 1:17 BOXES

❑ M3 Brett Favre Ryan Leaf	15.00	6.75
❑ M8 Barry Sanders Curtis Enis	15.00	6.75
❑ M16 Jerry Rice Randy Moss	25.00	11.00

1998 Finest Stadium Stars

	MINT	NRMT
COMPLETE SET (20)	100.00	45.00
COMMON CARD (S1-S20)	3.00	1.35

STATED ODDS 1:45

❑ S1 Barry Sanders	15.00	6.75
❑ S2 Steve Young	5.00	2.20
❑ S3 Emmitt Smith	12.00	5.50
❑ S4 Mark Brunell	6.00	2.70
❑ S5 Curtis Martin	4.00	1.80
❑ S6 Kordell Stewart	3.00	1.35
❑ S7 Jerry Rice	8.00	3.60
❑ S8 Warrick Dunn	4.00	1.80
❑ S9 Peyton Manning	20.00	9.00
❑ S10 Brett Favre	15.00	6.75
❑ S11 Terrell Davis	12.00	5.50
❑ S12 Cris Carter	4.00	1.80
❑ S13 Herman Moore	4.00	1.80
❑ S14 Troy Aikman	8.00	3.60
❑ S15 Tim Brown	4.00	1.80
❑ S16 Dan Marino	15.00	6.75
❑ S17 Drew Bledsoe	6.00	2.70
❑ S18 Jerome Bettis	4.00	1.80
❑ S19 Ryan Leaf	5.00	2.20
❑ S20 John Elway	15.00	6.75

1998 Finest Stadium Stars Jumbos

	MINT	NRMT
COMPLETE SET (6)	80.00	36.00
COMMON CARD	5.00	2.20

STATED ODDS 1:12 BOXES

❑ SS9 Peyton Manning	25.00	11.00
❑ SS10 Brett Favre	25.00	11.00
❑ SS11 Terrell Davis	20.00	9.00
❑ SS18 Jerome Bettis	5.00	2.20
❑ SS19 Ryan Leaf	6.00	2.70
❑ SS20 John Elway	25.00	11.00

1998 Finest Undergrads

	MINT	NRMT
COMPLETE SET	120.00	55.00
COMMON CARD (U1-U20)	2.50	1.10
SEMISTARS	4.00	1.80
UNLISTED STARS	6.00	2.70

STATED ODDS 1:72H/R, 1:32J
*REFRACTORS: .6X TO 1.5X HI COL.
REFRACT.STATED ODDS 1:216H/R, 1:96J

❑ U1 Warrick Dunn	6.00	2.70
❑ U2 Tony Gonzalez	2.50	1.10
❑ U3 Antowain Smith	6.00	2.70
❑ U4 Jake Plummer	20.00	9.00
❑ U5 Peter Boulware	2.50	1.10
❑ U6 Derrick Rodgers	2.50	1.10
❑ U7 Freddie Jones	2.50	1.10
❑ U8 Reidel Anthony	4.00	1.80
❑ U9 Bryant Westbrook	2.50	1.10
❑ U10 Corey Dillon	10.00	4.50
❑ U11 Curtis Enis	8.00	3.60
❑ U12 Andre Wadsworth	4.00	1.80
❑ U13 Fred Taylor	20.00	9.00
❑ U14 Greg Ellis	2.50	1.10
❑ U15 Ryan Leaf	6.00	2.70
❑ U16 Robert Edwards	6.00	2.70
❑ U17 Germane Crowell	8.00	3.60
❑ U18 Brian Griese	12.00	5.50
❑ U19 Kevin Dyson	6.00	2.70
❑ U20 Peyton Manning	30.00	13.50

1999 Finest

	MINT	NRMT
COMPLETE SET (175)	120.00	55.00
COMP.SET w/o SPs (124)	30.00	13.50
COMMON CARD (1-124)	.20	.09
SEMISTARS	.40	.18
UNLISTED STARS	.75	.35
COMMON CARD (125-146)	1.25	.55
COMMON ROOKIE (147-175)	3.00	1.35
ROOKIE SEMISTARS	4.00	1.80

SUBSETS 125-175 1:1 HOB, 1:2 HTA

❑ 1 Peyton Manning	3.00	1.35
❑ 2 Priest Holmes	.75	.35
❑ 3 Kordell Stewart	.75	.35
❑ 4 Shannon Sharpe	.40	.18
❑ 5 Andre Rison	.40	.18
❑ 6 Rickey Dudley	.20	.09
❑ 7 Duce Staley	.75	.35
❑ 8 Randall Cunningham	.75	.35
❑ 9 Warrick Dunn	.75	.35
❑ 10 Dan Marino	3.00	1.35
❑ 11 Kevin Greene	.20	.09
❑ 12 Garrison Hearst	.40	.18
❑ 13 Eric Moulds	.75	.35
❑ 14 Marvin Harrison	.75	.35
❑ 15 Eddie George	1.00	.45
❑ 16 Vinny Testaverde	.40	.18
❑ 17 Brad Johnson	.75	.35
❑ 18 Derrick Thomas	.40	.18
❑ 19 Chris Chandler	.40	.18
❑ 20 Troy Aikman	2.00	.90
❑ 21 Terance Mathis	.40	.18
❑ 22 Terrell Owens	.75	.35
❑ 23 Junior Seau	.40	.18
❑ 24 Cris Carter	.75	.35
❑ 25 Fred Taylor	2.00	.90
❑ 26 Adrian Murrell	.40	.18
❑ 27 Terry Glenn	.75	.35
❑ 28 Rod Smith	.40	.18
❑ 29 Darnay Scott	.40	.18
❑ 30 Brett Favre	3.00	1.35
❑ 31 Cam Cleeland	.20	.09
❑ 32 Ricky Watters	.40	.18
❑ 33 Derrick Alexander	.40	.18
❑ 34 Bruce Smith	.40	.18
❑ 35 Steve McNair	.75	.35
❑ 36 Wayne Chrebet	.40	.18
❑ 37 Herman Moore	.75	.35
❑ 38 Bert Emanuel	.40	.18
❑ 39 Michael Irvin	.40	.18
❑ 40 Steve Young	1.25	.55
❑ 41 Napoleon Kaufman	.75	.35
❑ 42 Tim Biakabutuka	.40	.18
❑ 43 Isaac Bruce	.75	.35
❑ 44 J.J. Stokes	.40	.18
❑ 45 Antonio Freeman	.75	.35
❑ 46 John Randle	.40	.18
❑ 47 Frank Sanders	.40	.18
❑ 48 O.J. McDuffie	.40	.18
❑ 49 Keenan McCardell	.40	.18
❑ 50 Randy Moss	3.00	1.35
❑ 51 Ed McCaffrey	.40	.18
❑ 52 Yancey Thigpen	.20	.09
❑ 53 Curtis Conway	.40	.18
❑ 54 Mike Alstott	.75	.35
❑ 55 Deion Sanders	.75	.35
❑ 56 Dorsey Levens	.75	.35
❑ 57 Joey Galloway	.75	.35
❑ 58 Natrone Means	.40	.18
❑ 59 Tim Brown	.75	.35
❑ 60 Jerry Rice	2.00	.90
❑ 61 Robert Smith	.75	.35
❑ 62 Carl Pickens	.40	.18
❑ 63 Ben Coates	.40	.18
❑ 64 Jerome Bettis	.75	.35
❑ 65 Corey Dillon	.75	.35
❑ 66 Curtis Martin	.75	.35
❑ 67 Jimmy Smith	.40	.18
❑ 68 Keyshawn Johnson	.75	.35
❑ 69 Charlie Batch	1.50	.70
❑ 70 Jamal Anderson	.75	.35
❑ 71 Mark Brunell	1.25	.55
❑ 72 Antowain Smith	.75	.35
❑ 73 Aeneas Williams	.20	.09
❑ 74 Wesley Walls	.40	.18
❑ 75 Jake Plummer	1.50	.70
❑ 76 Oronde Gadsden	.20	.09
❑ 77 Gary Brown	.20	.09
❑ 78 Peter Boulware	.20	.09
❑ 79 Stephen Alexander	.20	.09
❑ 80 Barry Sanders	3.00	1.35
❑ 81 Warren Sapp	.40	.18
❑ 82 Michael Sinclair	.20	.09
❑ 83 Freddie Jones	.20	.09
❑ 84 Ike Hilliard	.20	.09
❑ 85 Jake Reed	.40	.18
❑ 86 Tim Dwight	.75	.35
❑ 87 Johnnie Morton	.40	.18
❑ 88 Robert Brooks	.40	.18
❑ 89 Rocket Ismail	.40	.18
❑ 90 Emmitt Smith	2.00	.90
❑ 91 Ricky Proehl	.20	.09
❑ 92 James Jett	.40	.18
❑ 93 Karim Abdul-Jabbar	.40	.18
❑ 94 Mark Chmura	.20	.09
❑ 95 Andre Reed	.40	.18
❑ 96 Michael Westbrook	.40	.18
❑ 97 Michael Strahan	.20	.09
❑ 98 Chad Brown	.20	.09

❑ 99 Trent Dilfer .... .40 .18
❑ 100 Terrell Davis .... 2.00 .90
❑ 101 Aaron Glenn .... .20 .09
❑ 102 Skip Hicks .... .40 .18
❑ 103 Tony Gonzalez .... .40 .18
❑ 104 Ty Law.......................... .20 .09
❑ 105 Jermaine Lewis .... .40 .18
❑ 106 Ray Lewis .... .20 .09
❑ 107 Zach Thomas .... .40 .18
❑ 108 Reidel Anthony .... .40 .18
❑ 109 Levon Kirkland .... .20 .09
❑ 110 Drew Bledsoe .... 1.25 .55
❑ 111 Bobby Engram .... .40 .18
❑ 112 Jerome Pathon .... .20 .09
❑ 113 Muhsin Muhammad........ .40 .18
❑ 114 Vonnie Holliday .... .20 .09
❑ 115 Bill Romanowski .... .20 .09
❑ 116 Marshall Faulk.............. .75 .35
❑ 117 Ty Detmer .... .40 .18
❑ 118 Mo Lewis....................... .20 .09
❑ 119 Charles Woodson .... .75 .35
❑ 120 Doug Flutie .... 1.00 .45
❑ 121 Jon Kitna .... 1.00 .45
❑ 122 Courtney Hawkins.......... .20 .09
❑ 123 Trent Green.................... .40 .18
❑ 124 John Elway 3.00 1.35
❑ 125 Barry Sanders GM 5.00 2.20
❑ 126 Brett Favre GM 5.00 2.20
❑ 127 Curtis Martin GM.......... 1.25 .55
❑ 128 Dan Marino GM............ 5.00 2.20
❑ 129 Eddie George GM........ 1.50 .70
❑ 130 Emmitt Smith GM 5.00 2.20
❑ 131 Jamal Anderson GM .... 1.25 .55
❑ 132 Jerry Rice GM............. 3.00 1.35
❑ 133 John Elway GM........... 5.00 2.20
❑ 134 Terrell Davis GM.......... 3.00 1.35
❑ 135 Troy Aikman GM.......... 3.00 1.35
❑ 136 Skip Hicks SN .... .75 .35
❑ 137 Charles Woodson SN .... .75 .35
❑ 138 Charlie Batch SN.......... 2.50 1.10
❑ 139 Curtis Enis SN............. 1.25 .55
❑ 140 Fred Taylor SN 3.00 1.35
❑ 141 Jake Plummer SN 2.50 1.10
❑ 142 Peyton Manning SN 5.00 2.20
❑ 143 Randy Moss SN 5.00 2.20
❑ 144 Corey Dillon SN........... 1.25 .55
❑ 145 Priest Holmes SN .... 1.25 .55
❑ 146 Warrick Dunn SN .... 1.25 .55
❑ 147 Jevon Kearse RC 8.00 3.60
❑ 148 Chris Claiborne RC 4.00 1.80
❑ 149 Akili Smith RC 8.00 3.60
❑ 150 Brock Huard RC 5.00 2.20
❑ 151 Daunte Culpepper RC 12.00 5.50
❑ 152 Edgerrin James RC.... 30.00 13.50
❑ 153 Cecil Collins RC 5.00 2.20
❑ 154 Kevin Faulk RC 5.00 2.20
❑ 155 Amos Zereoue RC 5.00 2.20
❑ 156 James Johnson RC...... 5.00 2.20
❑ 157 Sedrick Irvin RC 5.00 2.20
❑ 158 Ricky Williams RC...... 20.00 9.00
❑ 159 Mike Cloud RC 4.00 1.80
❑ 160 Chris McAlister 3.00 1.35
❑ 161 Rob Konrad RC............ 4.00 1.80
❑ 162 Champ Bailey RC 5.00 2.20
❑ 163 Ebenezer Ekuban RC .. 4.00 1.80
❑ 164 Tim Couch RC........... 20.00 9.00
❑ 165 Cade McNown RC 12.00 5.50
❑ 166 Donovan McNabb RC 12.00 5.50
❑ 167 Joe Germaine RC 5.00 2.20
❑ 168 Shaun King RC 12.00 5.50
❑ 169 Peerless Price RC........ 6.00 2.70
❑ 170 Kevin Johnson RC 10.00 4.50
❑ 171 Troy Edwards RC 6.00 2.70
❑ 172 Karsten Bailey RC........ 3.00 1.35
❑ 173 David Boston RC.......... 6.00 2.70
❑ 174 D'Wayne Bates RC 4.00 1.80
❑ 175 Torry Holt RC 10.00 4.50

1999 Finest Gold Refractors

	MINT	NRMT
COMMON CARD (1-175)..........	8.00	3.60

*STARS: 15X TO 35X HI COL. ....
*YOUNG STARS: 12X TO 30X HI COL.

*GEMS: 8X TO 20X HI COL. ....
*SENSATIONS: 6X TO 15X HI COL.
*RCs: 3X TO 8X HI COL. ....
STATED ODDS 1:72 H/R, 1:33 HTA
STATED PRINT RUN 100 SERIAL #'d SETS

1999 Finest Refractors

	MINT	NRMT
COMMON CARD (1-175)..........	1.50	.70

*STARS: 3X TO 8X HI COL. ....
*YOUNG STARS: 2.5X TO 6X HI COL.
*GEMS: 2.5X TO 6X HI COL.........
*SENSATIONS: 2X TO 5X HI COL.
*RCs: 1.2X TO 3X HI COL. ....
STATED ODDS 1:12 H/R, 1:5 HTA

1999 Finest Double Team

	MINT	NRMT
COMPLETE SET (7)	25.00	11.00
COMMON CARD (DT1-DT7)	3.00	1.35

*RIGHT/LEFT REF.VARIATIONS EQUAL VALUE
STATED ODDS 1:50 H/R, 1:24 HTA
*DUAL REFRACTORS: .75X TO 2X HI COL.
DUAL REFRACTOR ODDS 1:150H/R, 1:72HTA

❑ DT1 Akili Smith.................... 5.00 2.20
Carl Pickens
❑ DT2 Cade McNown 6.00 2.70
Curtis Enis
❑ DT3 Doug Flutie................. 4.00 1.80
Eric Moulds
❑ DT4 Mark Brunell 4.00 1.80
Fred Taylor
❑ DT5 Kordell Stewart 3.00 1.35
Jerome Bettis
❑ DT6 Jon Kitna 3.00 1.35
Joey Galloway
❑ DT7 Warrick Dunn 3.00 1.35
Mike Alstott

1999 Finest Future's Finest

	MINT	NRMT
COMPLETE SET (10)	120.00	55.00
COMMON CARD (1-10)...........	6.00	2.70

STATED ODDS 1:253 H/R, 1:117 HTA
STATED PRINT RUN 500 SER.#'d SETS
*REFRACTORS: 1X TO 2.5X HI COL.
REFRACTOR ODDS 1:1262 H/R, 1:583 HTA
REFRACTOR PRINT RUN 100 SER.#'d SETS

❑ F1 Akili Smith.................... 10.00 4.50
❑ F2 Cade McNown 15.00 6.75
❑ F3 Champ Bailey 6.00 2.70
❑ F4 Daunte Culpepper....... 15.00 6.75
❑ F5 David Boston................. 8.00 3.60
❑ F6 Donovan McNabb 15.00 6.75
❑ F7 Edgerrin James........... 50.00 22.00
❑ F8 Ricky Williams.............. 30.00 13.50
❑ F9 Tim Couch.................... 30.00 13.50
❑ F10 Torry Holt 12.00 5.50

1999 Finest Leading Indicators

	MINT	NRMT
COMPLETE SET (10)	30.00	13.50
COMMON CARD (L1-L10)........	1.50	.70
SEMISTARS..............................	3.00	1.35

STATED ODDS 1:30 H/R, 1:14 HTA

❑ L1 Jamal Anderson 3.00 1.35
❑ L2 Doug Flutie 4.00 1.80
❑ L3 Drew Bledsoe 5.00 2.20
❑ L4 Eddie George 4.00 1.80
❑ L5 Emmitt Smith................. 8.00 3.60
❑ L6 John Elway 12.00 5.50
❑ L7 Keyshawn Johnson........ 3.00 1.35
❑ L8 Steve Young 5.00 2.20
❑ L9 Terrell Owens 3.00 1.35
❑ L10 Vinny Testaverde .... 1.50 .70

1999 Finest Main Attractions

	MINT	NRMT
COMPLETE SET (7)	40.00	18.00
COMMON CARD (MA1-MA7) ..	3.00	1.35

*RIGHT/LEFT REF.VARIATIONS SAME VALUE
STATED ODDS 1:50 H/R, 1:24 HTA
*DUAL REFRACTORS: .75X TO 2X HI COL.
DUAL REFRACTOR ODDS 1:150H/R, 1:72HTA

❑ MA1 Champ Bailey 4.00 1.80
Deion Sanders

		MINT	NRMT
❑ MA2	Daunte Culpepper / Steve McNair	8.00	3.60
❑ MA3	Donovan McNabb / Kordell Stewart	8.00	3.60
❑ MA4	Edgerrin James / Marshall Faulk	15.00	6.75
❑ MA5	Kevin Faulk / Warrick Dunn	5.00	2.20
❑ MA6	Joe Germaine / Troy Aikman	8.00	3.60
❑ MA7	Rob Konrad / Mike Alstott	3.00	1.35

1999 Finest Prominent Figures

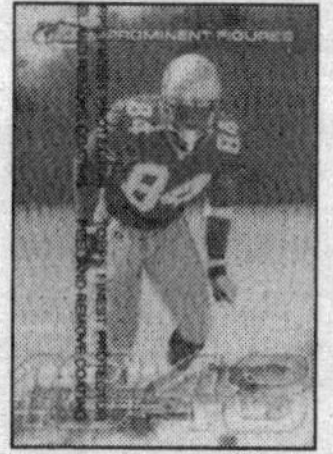

	MINT	NRMT
COMMON QB-YD (PF1-PF10)	1.25	.55
SEMISTARS PF1-PF10	2.50	1.10
QB-YARDAGE PRINT RUN 5084 SER.#'d SETS		
QB-YARDAGE STATED ODDS 1:25H/R,1:11HTA		
COMMON QB-TDs (PF11-PF20)	20.00	9.00
SEMISTARS PF11-PF20	40.00	18.00
QB-TDs PRINT RUN 48 SER.#'d SETS		
QB-TOUCHDOWNS ODDS 1:2634H/R,1:1220HTA		
COMMON RB-TDs (PF21-PF30)	60.00	27.00
SEMISTARS PF21-PF30	80.00	36.00
RB-TDs PRINT RUN 25 SER.#'d SETS		
RB-TOUCHDOWNS ODDS 1:5099H/R,1:2333HTA		
COMMON RB-YD (PF31-PF40)	5.00	2.20
SEMISTARS PF31-PF40	6.00	2.70
RB-YARDAGE PRINT RUN 2105 SER.#'d SETS		
RB-YARDAGE STATED ODDS 1:60H/R,1:28HTA		
COMMON WR-TDs (PF41-PF50)	60.00	27.00
WR-TDs PRINT RUN 22 SER.#'d SETS		
WR-TDs STATED ODDS 1:5779H/R,1:2660HTA		
COMMON WR-YD (PF51-PF60)	2.50	1.10
SEMISTARS PF51-PF60	5.00	2.20
WR-YARDAGE PRINT RUN 1848 SER.#'d SETS		
WR-YARDAGE ODDS 1:68H/R, 1:32HTA		

		MINT	NRMT
❑ PF1	Brett Favre	10.00	4.50
❑ PF2	Dan Marino	10.00	4.50
❑ PF3	Drew Bledsoe	4.00	1.80
❑ PF4	Jake Plummer	5.00	2.20
❑ PF5	Mark Brunell	4.00	1.80
❑ PF6	Peyton Manning	8.00	3.60
❑ PF7	Randall Cunningham	2.50	1.10
❑ PF8	Steve Young	4.00	1.80
❑ PF9	Tim Couch	12.00	5.50
❑ PF10	Vinny Testaverde	1.25	.55
❑ PF11	Brett Favre	150.00	70.00
❑ PF12	Dan Marino	150.00	70.00
❑ PF13	Drew Bledsoe	60.00	27.00
❑ PF14	Jake Plummer	80.00	36.00
❑ PF15	Mark Brunell	60.00	27.00
❑ PF16	Peyton Manning	120.00	55.00
❑ PF17	Randall Cunningham	40.00	18.00
❑ PF18	Steve Young	60.00	27.00
❑ PF19	Tim Couch	150.00	70.00
❑ PF20	Vinny Testaverde	2.50	1.10
❑ PF21	Barry Sanders	250.00	110.00
❑ PF22	Curtis Martin	60.00	27.00
❑ PF23	Eddie George	100.00	45.00
❑ PF24	Emmitt Smith	150.00	70.00
❑ PF25	Fred Taylor	120.00	55.00
❑ PF26	Garrison Hearst	60.00	27.00
❑ PF27	Jamal Anderson	60.00	27.00
❑ PF28	Marshall Faulk	60.00	27.00
❑ PF29	Ricky Williams	250.00	110.00
❑ PF30	Terrell Davis	150.00	70.00
❑ PF31	Barry Sanders	20.00	9.00
❑ PF32	Curtis Martin	5.00	2.20
❑ PF33	Eddie George	8.00	3.60
❑ PF34	Emmitt Smith	12.00	5.50
❑ PF35	Fred Taylor	10.00	4.50
❑ PF36	Garrison Hearst	5.00	2.20
❑ PF37	Jamal Anderson	5.00	2.20
❑ PF38	Marshall Faulk	5.00	2.20
❑ PF39	Ricky Williams	25.00	11.00
❑ PF40	Terrell Davis	12.00	5.50
❑ PF41	Antonio Freeman	60.00	27.00
❑ PF42	David Boston	60.00	27.00
❑ PF43	Cris Carter	60.00	27.00
❑ PF44	Jerry Rice	150.00	70.00
❑ PF45	Joey Galloway	60.00	27.00
❑ PF46	Keyshawn Johnson	60.00	27.00
❑ PF47	Randy Moss	200.00	90.00
❑ PF48	Terrell Owens	60.00	27.00
❑ PF49	Tim Brown	60.00	27.00
❑ PF50	Torry Holt	80.00	36.00
❑ PF51	Antonio Freeman	5.00	2.20
❑ PF52	David Boston	6.00	2.70
❑ PF53	Eric Moulds	5.00	2.20
❑ PF54	Jerry Rice	12.00	5.50
❑ PF55	Joey Galloway	5.00	2.20
❑ PF56	Keyshawn Johnson	5.00	2.20
❑ PF57	Randy Moss	15.00	6.75
❑ PF58	Terrell Owens	5.00	2.20
❑ PF59	Jimmy Smith	5.00	2.20
❑ PF60	Torry Holt	10.00	4.50

1999 Finest Salute

	MINT	NRMT
COMPLETE SET (3)	250.00	110.00
STATED ODDS 1:53 HOB, 1:25 HTA		
REFRACTOR ODDS 1:1900 HOB,1:790 HTA		
GOLD REF.ODDS 1:12,384 HOB,1:5782 HTA		
GOLD REFRACTOR PRINT RUN 100 CARDS		

		MINT	NRMT
❑ FS	Terrell Davis / John Elway / Randy Moss	12.00	5.50
❑ FSR	Terrell Davis / John Elway / Randy Moss (Refractor version)	50.00	22.00
❑ FSGR	Terrell Davis / John Elway / Randy Moss (Gold Refractor version)	200.00	90.00

1999 Finest Team Finest

	MINT	NRMT
COMPLETE SET (10)	100.00	45.00
COMMON CARD (T1-T10)	4.00	1.80
BLUE PRINT RUN 1500 SER.#'d SETS		

BLUE STATED ODDS 1:84HOB, 1:39 HTA
*BLUE REFRACTORS: 1.5X TO 4X BLUES
BLUE REF.PRINT RUN 150 SER.#'d SETS
BLUE REF.STATED ODDS 1:843HOB,1:389HTA
*GOLDS: 1.2X TO 3X BLUES
GOLD PRINT RUN 250 SER.#'d SETS
GOLD STATED ODDS 1:57 HTA..
*GOLD REFRACTORS: 6X TO 15X BLUES
GOLD REF.PRINT RUN 25 SER. #'d SETS
GOLD REF.STATED ODDS 1:573 HTA
*REDS: .75X TO 2X BLUES
RED PRINT RUN 500 SER.#'d SETS
RED STATED ODDS 1:29 HTA
*RED REFRACTORS: 3X TO 8X BLUES
RED REF.PRINT RUN 50 SER.#'d SETS
RED REF.STATED ODDS 1:285 HTA

		MINT	NRMT
❑ T1	Barry Sanders	15.00	6.75
❑ T2	Brett Favre	15.00	6.75
❑ T3	Dan Marino	15.00	6.75
❑ T4	Drew Bledsoe	6.00	2.70
❑ T5	Jamal Anderson	4.00	1.80
❑ T6	John Elway	15.00	6.75
❑ T7	Peyton Manning	12.00	5.50
❑ T8	Randy Moss	12.00	5.50
❑ T9	Terrell Davis	10.00	4.50
❑ T10	Troy Aikman	10.00	4.50

1995 Flair

	MINT	NRMT
COMPLETE SET (220)	30.00	13.50
COMMON CARD (1-220)	.20	.09
SEMISTARS	.40	.18
UNLISTED STARS	.75	.35

		MINT	NRMT
❑ 1	Larry Centers	.40	.18
❑ 2	Garrison Hearst	.75	.35
❑ 3	Seth Joyner	.20	.09
❑ 4	Dave Krieg	.20	.09
❑ 5	Rob Moore	.20	.09
❑ 6	Frank Sanders RC / Wearing 18 on front / Wearing 81 on back	1.50	.70
❑ 7	Eric Swann	.40	.18
❑ 8	Devin Bush	.20	.09
❑ 9	Chris Doleman	.20	.09
❑ 10	Bert Emanuel	.75	.35
❑ 11	Jeff George	.40	.18
❑ 12	Craig Heyward	.40	.18

❑ 13 Terance Mathis .40 .18
❑ 14 Eric Metcalf .40 .18
❑ 15 Cornelius Bennett .40 .18
❑ 16 Jeff Burris .20 .09
❑ 17 Todd Collins RC .75 .35
❑ 18 Russell Copeland .20 .09
❑ 19 Jim Kelly .75 .35
❑ 20 Andre Reed .40 .18
❑ 21 Bruce Smith .75 .35
❑ 22 Don Beebe .20 .09
❑ 23 Mark Carrier .40 .18
❑ 24 Kerry Collins RC 1.50 .70
❑ 25 Barry Foster .40 .18
❑ 26 Pete Metzelaars .20 .09
❑ 27 Tyrone Poole .40 .18
❑ 28 Frank Reich .20 .09
❑ 29 Curtis Conway .75 .35
❑ 30 Chris Gedney .20 .09
❑ 31 Jeff Graham .20 .09
❑ 32 Raymont Harris .20 .09
❑ 33 Erik Kramer .20 .09
❑ 34 Rashaan Salaam RC .75 .35
❑ 35 Lewis Tillman .20 .09
❑ 36 Michael Timpson .20 .09
❑ 37 Jeff Blake RC 1.50 .70
❑ 38 Ki-Jana Carter RC .75 .35
❑ 39 Tony McGee .20 .09
❑ 40 Carl Pickens .75 .35
❑ 41 Corey Sawyer .20 .09
❑ 42 Darnay Scott .75 .35
❑ 43 Dan Wilkinson .40 .18
❑ 44 Derrick Alexander .75 .35
❑ 45 Leroy Hoard .20 .09
❑ 46 Michael Jackson .40 .18
❑ 47 Antonio Langham .20 .09
❑ 48 Andre Rison .40 .18
❑ 49 Vinny Testaverde .40 .18
❑ 50 Eric Turner .20 .09
❑ 51 Troy Aikman 2.00 .90
❑ 52 Charles Haley .40 .18
❑ 53 Michael Irvin .75 .35
❑ 54 Daryl Johnston .40 .18
❑ 55 Leon Lett .20 .09
❑ 56 Jay Novacek .40 .18
❑ 57 Emmitt Smith 3.00 1.35
❑ 58 Kevin Williams WR .40 .18
❑ 59 Steve Atwater .20 .09
❑ 60 Rod Bernstine .20 .09
❑ 61 John Elway 4.00 1.80
❑ 62 Glyn Milburn .20 .09
❑ 63 Anthony Miller .40 .18
❑ 64 Mike Pritchard .20 .09
❑ 65 Shannon Sharpe .40 .18
❑ 66 Scott Mitchell .40 .18
❑ 67 Herman Moore .75 .35
❑ 68 Johnnie Morton .40 .18
❑ 69 Brett Perriman .40 .18
❑ 70 Barry Sanders 4.00 1.80
❑ 71 Chris Spielman .40 .18
❑ 72 Edgar Bennett .40 .18
❑ 73 Robert Brooks .75 .35
❑ 74 Brett Favre 4.00 1.80
❑ 75 LeShon Johnson .40 .18
❑ 76 Sean Jones .20 .09
❑ 77 George Teague .20 .09
❑ 78 Reggie White .75 .35
❑ 79 Micheal Barrow .20 .09
❑ 80 Gary Brown .20 .09
❑ 81 Mel Gray .20 .09
❑ 82 Haywood Jeffires .20 .09
❑ 83 Steve McNair RC 4.00 1.80
❑ 84 Rodney Thomas RC .75 .35
❑ 85 Trev Alberts .20 .09
❑ 86 Flipper Anderson .20 .09
❑ 87 Tony Bennett .20 .09
❑ 88 Quentin Coryatt .40 .18
❑ 89 Sean Dawkins .40 .18
❑ 90 Craig Erickson .20 .09
❑ 91 Marshall Faulk 1.25 .55
❑ 92 Steve Beuerlein .20 .09
❑ 93 Tony Boselli RC .40 .18
❑ 94 Reggie Cobb .20 .09
❑ 95 Ernest Givins .20 .09
❑ 96 Desmond Howard .40 .18
❑ 97 Jeff Lageman .20 .09
❑ 98 James O. Stewart RC 3.00 1.35
❑ 99 Marcus Allen .75 .35
❑ 100 Steve Bono .40 .18
❑ 101 Dale Carter .40 .18
❑ 102 Willie Davis .40 .18
❑ 103 Lake Dawson .40 .18
❑ 104 Greg Hill .40 .18
❑ 105 Neil Smith .40 .18
❑ 106 Tim Bowens .20 .09
❑ 107 Bryan Cox .20 .09
❑ 108 Irving Fryar .40 .18
❑ 109 Eric Green .20 .09
❑ 110 Terry Kirby .40 .18
❑ 111 Dan Marino 4.00 1.80
❑ 112 O.J. McDuffie .75 .35
❑ 113 Bernie Parmalee .40 .18
❑ 114 Derrick Alexander RC .20 .09
❑ 115 Cris Carter .75 .35
❑ 116 Qadry Ismail .40 .18
❑ 117 Warren Moon .40 .18
❑ 118 Jake Reed .40 .18
❑ 119 Robert Smith .75 .35
❑ 120 Dewayne Washington .40 .18
❑ 121 Drew Bledsoe 2.00 .90
❑ 122 Vincent Brisby .20 .09
❑ 123 Ben Coates .40 .18
❑ 124 Curtis Martin RC 4.00 1.80
❑ 125 Willie McGinest .40 .18
❑ 126 Dave Meggett .20 .09
❑ 127 Chris Slade UER 126 .40 .18
❑ 128 Eric Allen .20 .09
❑ 129 Mario Bates .75 .35
❑ 130 Jim Everett .20 .09
❑ 131 Michael Haynes .40 .18
❑ 132 Tyrone Hughes .40 .18
❑ 133 Renaldo Turnbull .20 .09
❑ 134 Ray Zellars RC .40 .18
❑ 135 Michael Brooks .20 .09
❑ 136 Dave Brown .40 .18
❑ 137 Rodney Hampton .40 .18
❑ 138 Thomas Lewis .40 .18
❑ 139 Mike Sherrard .20 .09
❑ 140 Herschel Walker .40 .18
❑ 141 Tyrone Wheatley RC 2.00 .90
❑ 142 Kyle Brady RC .75 .35
❑ 143 Boomer Esiason .40 .18
❑ 144 Aaron Glenn .20 .09
❑ 145 Mo Lewis .20 .09
❑ 146 Johnny Mitchell .20 .09
❑ 147 Ronald Moore .20 .09
❑ 148 Joe Aska .40 .18
❑ 149 Tim Brown .75 .35
❑ 150 Jeff Hostetler .40 .18
❑ 151 Rocket Ismail .40 .18
❑ 152 Napoleon Kaufman RC 3.00 1.35
❑ 153 Chester McGlockton .40 .18
❑ 154 Harvey Williams .20 .09
❑ 155 Fred Barnett .40 .18
❑ 156 Randall Cunningham .75 .35
❑ 157 Charlie Garner .40 .18
❑ 158 Mike Mamula RC .40 .18
❑ 159 Kevin Turner .20 .09
❑ 160 Ricky Watters .75 .35
❑ 161 Calvin Williams .40 .18
❑ 162 Mark Bruener RC .40 .18
❑ 163 Kevin Greene .40 .18
❑ 164 Charles Johnson .40 .18
❑ 165 Greg Lloyd .40 .18
❑ 166 Byron Bam Morris .40 .18
❑ 167 Neil O'Donnell .40 .18
❑ 168 Kordell Stewart RC 4.00 1.80
❑ 169 John L. Williams .20 .09
❑ 170 Rod Woodson .40 .18
❑ 171 Jerome Bettis .75 .35
❑ 172 Isaac Bruce 1.25 .55
❑ 173 Kevin Carter RC .75 .35
❑ 174 Troy Drayton .20 .09
❑ 175 Sean Gilbert .40 .18
❑ 176 Carlos Jenkins .20 .09
❑ 177 Todd Lyght .20 .09
❑ 178 Chris Miller .20 .09
❑ 179 Andre Coleman .20 .09
❑ 180 Stan Humphries .40 .18
❑ 181 Shawn Jefferson .20 .09
❑ 182 Natrone Means .75 .35
❑ 183 Leslie O'Neal .40 .18
❑ 184 Junior Seau .75 .35
❑ 185 Mark Seay .40 .18
❑ 186 William Floyd .75 .35
❑ 187 Merton Hanks .20 .09
❑ 188 Brent Jones .20 .09
❑ 189 Ken Norton .40 .18
❑ 190 Jerry Rice 2.00 .90
❑ 191 Deion Sanders 1.00 .45
❑ 192 J.J. Stokes RC 1.25 .55
❑ 193 Dana Stubblefield .75 .35
❑ 194 Steve Young 1.50 .70
❑ 195 Sam Adams .20 .09
❑ 196 Brian Blades .40 .18
❑ 197 Joey Galloway RC 4.00 1.80
❑ 198 Cortez Kennedy .40 .18
❑ 199 Rick Mirer .75 .35
❑ 200 Chris Warren .40 .18
❑ 201 Derrick Brooks .20 .09
❑ 202 Lawrence Dawsey .20 .09
❑ 203 Trent Dilfer .75 .35
❑ 204 Alvin Harper .20 .09
❑ 205 Jackie Harris .20 .09
❑ 206 Courtney Hawkins .20 .09
❑ 207 Hardy Nickerson .20 .09
❑ 208 Errict Rhett .75 .35
❑ 209 Warren Sapp RC 1.00 .45
❑ 210 Terry Allen .40 .18
❑ 211 Tom Carter .20 .09
❑ 212 Henry Ellard .40 .18
❑ 213 Darrell Green .20 .09
❑ 214 Brian Mitchell .20 .09
❑ 215 Heath Shuler .75 .35
❑ 216 Michael Westbrook RC 2.50 1.10
❑ 217 Tydus Winans .20 .09
❑ 218 Checklist .20 .09
❑ 219 Checklist .20 .09
❑ 220 Checklist .40 .18
❑ S1 Michael Irvin Sample .75 .35

1995 Flair Hot Numbers

	MINT	NRMT
COMPLETE SET (10)	30.00	13.50
STATED ODDS 1:6		

❑ 1 Jeff Blake 2.00 .90
❑ 2 Tim Brown 2.00 .90
❑ 3 Drew Bledsoe 6.00 2.70
❑ 4 Ben Coates 1.25 .55
❑ 5 Trent Dilfer 2.00 .90
❑ 6 Brett Favre 12.00 5.50
❑ 7 Dan Marino 12.00 5.50
❑ 8 Byron Bam Morris 1.25 .55
❑ 9 Ricky Watters 2.00 .90
❑ 10 Steve Young 5.00 2.20

1995 Flair TD Power

	MINT	NRMT
COMPLETE SET (10)	20.00	9.00
STATED ODDS 1:12		

❑ 1 Marshall Faulk 2.50 1.10
❑ 2 Natrone Means 1.50 .70
❑ 3 William Floyd 1.50 .70
❑ 4 Byron Bam Morris .75 .35
❑ 5 Errict Rhett 1.50 .70
❑ 6 Andre Rison .75 .35
❑ 7 Jerry Rice 4.00 1.80

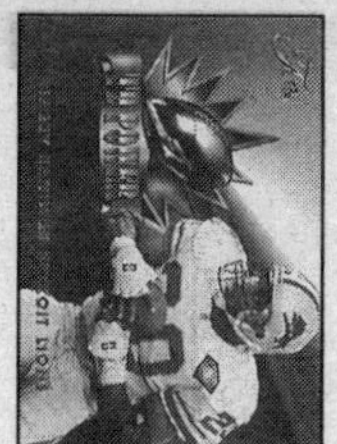

❑ 8 Barry Sanders	8.00	3.60
❑ 9 Emmitt Smith	6.00	2.70
❑ 10 Chris Warren	.75	.35

1995 Flair Wave of the Future

	MINT	NRMT
COMPLETE SET (9)	70.00	32.00
COMMON CARD (1-9)	2.50	1.10
SEMISTARS	4.00	1.80
UNLISTED STARS	6.00	2.70
STATED ODDS 1:37		

❑ 1 Kyle Brady	2.50	1.10
❑ 2 Ki-Jana Carter	6.00	2.70
❑ 3 Kerry Collins	8.00	3.60
❑ 4 Joey Galloway	20.00	9.00
❑ 5 Steve McNair	20.00	9.00
❑ 6 Rashaan Salaam	6.00	2.70
❑ 7 James O. Stewart	12.00	5.50
❑ 8 Michael Westbrook	12.00	5.50
❑ 9 Tyrone Wheatley	10.00	4.50

1997 Flair Showcase Row 2

	MINT	NRMT
COMPLETE SET (120)	60.00	27.00
COMMON CARD (1-40)	.20	.09
SEMISTARS 1-40	.40	.18
UNLISTED STARS 1-40	.75	.35
ROW 2 1-40 ODDS 1.5:1		
COMMON CARD (41-80)	.25	.11
SEMISTARS 41-80	.50	.23
UNLISTED STARS 41-80	1.00	.45
ROW 2 41-80 ODDS 1:1.5		
COMMON CARD (81-120)	.20	.09
SEMISTARS 81-120	.40	.18
UNLISTED STARS 81-120	.75	.35
ROW 2 81-120 ODDS 1:1		
AKA FLAIR SHOWCASE STYLE		

❑ 1 Jerry Rice	2.00	.90
❑ 2 Mark Brunell	2.00	.90
❑ 3 Eddie Kennison	.40	.18
❑ 4 Brett Favre	4.00	1.80
❑ 5 Karim Abdul-Jabbar	.75	.35
❑ 6 David LaFleur RC	.75	.35
❑ 7 John Elway	4.00	1.80
❑ 8 Troy Aikman	2.00	.90
❑ 9 Steve McNair	1.25	.55
❑ 10 Kordell Stewart	1.25	.55
❑ 11 Drew Bledsoe	2.00	.90
❑ 12 Kerry Collins	.40	.18
❑ 13 Dan Marino	4.00	1.80
❑ 14 Steve Young	1.25	.55
❑ 15 Marvin Harrison	.75	.35
❑ 16 Lawrence Phillips	.20	.09
❑ 17 Jeff Blake	.40	.18
❑ 18 Yatil Green RC	.40	.18
❑ 19 Jake Plummer RC	10.00	4.50
❑ 20 Barry Sanders	4.00	1.80
❑ 21 Deion Sanders	.75	.35
❑ 22 Emmitt Smith	3.00	1.35
❑ 23 Rae Carruth RC	.75	.35
❑ 24 Chris Warren	.40	.18
❑ 25 Terry Glenn	.75	.35
❑ 26 Jim Druckenmiller RC	1.25	.55
❑ 27 Eddie George	2.50	1.10
❑ 28 Curtis Martin	1.25	.55
❑ 29 Warrick Dunn RC	4.00	1.80
❑ 30 Terrell Davis	3.00	1.35
❑ 31 Rashaan Salaam	.20	.09
❑ 32 Marcus Allen	.75	.35
❑ 33 Jeff George	.40	.18
❑ 34 Thurman Thomas	.75	.35
❑ 35 Keyshawn Johnson	.75	.35
❑ 36 Jerome Bettis	.75	.35
❑ 37 Larry Centers	.40	.18
❑ 38 Tony Banks	.40	.18
❑ 39 Marshall Faulk	.75	.35
❑ 40 Mike Alstott	.75	.35
❑ 41 Elvis Grbac	.40	.18
❑ 42 Errict Rhett	.20	.09
❑ 43 Edgar Bennett	.40	.18
❑ 44 Jim Harbaugh	.40	.18
❑ 45 Antonio Freeman	1.50	.70
❑ 46 Tiki BarbeR RC	2.00	.90
❑ 47 Tim Biakabutuka	.40	.18
❑ 48 Joey Galloway	1.50	.70
❑ 49 Tony Gonzalez RC	4.00	1.80
❑ 50 Keenan McCardell	.40	.18
❑ 51 Darnay Scott	.40	.18
❑ 52 Brad Johnson	1.50	.70
❑ 53 Herman Moore	.75	.35
❑ 54 Reidel Anthony RC	2.50	1.10
❑ 55 Junior Seau	.40	.18
❑ 56 Ricky Watters	.40	.18
❑ 57 Amani Toomer	.40	.18
❑ 58 Andre Reed	.40	.18
❑ 59 Antowain Smith RC	3.00	1.35
❑ 60 Ike Hilliard RC	2.50	1.10
❑ 61 Byron Hanspard RC	2.50	1.10
❑ 62 Robert Smith	.40	.18
❑ 63 Gus Frerotte	.20	.09
❑ 64 Charles Way	.40	.18
❑ 65 Trent Dilfer	.75	.35
❑ 66 Adrian Murrell	.40	.18
❑ 67 Stan Humphries	.40	.18
❑ 68 Robert Brooks	.40	.18
❑ 69 Jamal Anderson	2.50	1.10
❑ 70 Natrone Means	.75	.35
❑ 71 John Friesz	.20	.09
❑ 72 Ki-Jana Carter	.20	.09
❑ 73 Marc Edwards RC	.20	.09
❑ 74 Michael Westbrook	.40	.18
❑ 75 Neil O'Donnell	.40	.18
❑ 76 Scott Mitchell	.40	.18
❑ 77 Wesley Walls	.40	.18
❑ 78 Bruce Smith	.40	.18
❑ 79 Corey Dillon RC	6.00	2.70
❑ 80 Wayne Chrebet	.75	.35
❑ 81 Tony Martin	.40	.18
❑ 82 Jimmy Smith	.40	.18
❑ 83 Terry Allen	.75	.35
❑ 84 Shannon Sharpe	.40	.18
❑ 85 Derrick Alexander WR	.40	.18
❑ 86 Garrison Hearst	.40	.18
❑ 87 Tamarick Vanover	.40	.18
❑ 88 Michael Irvin	.75	.35
❑ 89 Mark Chmura	.40	.18
❑ 90 Bert Emanuel	.40	.18
❑ 91 Eric Metcalf	.40	.18
❑ 92 Reggie White	.75	.35
❑ 93 Carl Pickens	.75	.35
❑ 94 Chris Sanders	.20	.09
❑ 95 Frank Sanders	.40	.18
❑ 96 Desmond Howard	.40	.18
❑ 97 Michael Jackson	.40	.18
❑ 98 Tim Brown	.75	.35
❑ 99 O.J. McDuffie	.40	.18
❑ 100 Mario Bates	.20	.09
❑ 101 Warren Moon	.75	.35
❑ 102 Curtis Conway	.40	.18
❑ 103 Irving Fryar	.40	.18
❑ 104 Isaac Bruce	.75	.35
❑ 105 Cris Carter	.75	.35
❑ 106 Chris Chandler	.40	.18
❑ 107 Charles Johnson	.40	.18
❑ 108 Kevin Lockett RC	.75	.35
❑ 109 Rob Moore	.40	.18
❑ 110 Napoleon Kaufman	.75	.35
❑ 111 Henry Ellard	.20	.09
❑ 112 Vinny Testaverde	.40	.18
❑ 113 Rick Mirer	.20	.09
❑ 114 Ty Detmer	.40	.18
❑ 115 Todd Collins	.20	.09
❑ 116 Jake Reed	.40	.18
❑ 117 Dave Brown	.20	.09
❑ 118 Dedric Ward RC	2.50	1.10
❑ 119 Heath Shuler	.20	.09
❑ 120 Ben Coates	.40	.18
❑ S1 Rae Carruth Sample (three card strip)	1.00	.45

1997 Flair Showcase Row 1

	MINT	NRMT
COMPLETE SET (120)	120.00	55.00
*STARS 1-40: 1X TO 2X ROW 2		
*RCs 1-40: .5X TO 1.2X ROW 2		
ROW 1 1-40 ODDS 1:2.5		
*STARS 41-80: .6X TO 1.2X ROW 2		
*RCs 41-80: .6X TO 1.2X ROW 2		
ROW 1 41-80 ODDS 1:2		
*STARS 81-120: 1.5X TO 3X ROW 2		
*RCs 81-120: 1X TO 2X ROW 2		
ROW 1 81-120 ODDS 1:3		
AKA FLAIR SHOWCASE GRACE		

1997 Flair Showcase Row 0

	MINT	NRMT
COMPLETE SET (120)	1200.00	550.00
*STARS 1-40: 5X TO 12X ROW 2		
*RCs 1-40: 3X TO 8X ROW 2		
ROW 0 1-40 ODDS 1:24		
*STARS 41-80: 3X TO 8X ROW 2		
*RCs 41-80: 2X TO 5X ROW 2		
ROW 0 41-80 ODDS 1:12		
*STARS 81-120: 2X TO 5X ROW 2		
*RCs 81-120: 1.25X TO 3X ROW 2		
ROW 0 81-120 ODDS 1:5		
AKA FLAIR SHOWCASE SHOWCASE		

1997 Flair Showcase Legacy Collection

	MINT	NRMT
COMMON CARD (A1-C360) ..	10.00	4.50
*STARS 1-40: 12X TO 30X HI COL.		
*RCs 1-40: 6X TO 15X		
*STARS 41-80: 8X TO 20X HI COL.		
*RCs 41-80: 6X TO 15X		
*STARS 81-120: 12X TO 30X HI COL.		
*RCs 81-120: 5X TO 12X		
STATED PRINT RUN 100 SERIAL #'d SETS		
THREE CARDS PER PLAYER/SAME PRICE		
UNPRICED MASTERPIECES SERIAL #'d TO 1		

1997 Flair Showcase Hot Hands

	MINT	NRMT
COMPLETE SET (12)	300.00	135.00
COMMON CARD (HH1-HH12)..	6.00	2.70
STATED ODDS 1:90		
❑ HH1 Kerry Collins................	6.00	2.70
❑ HH2 Emmitt Smith	30.00	13.50
❑ HH3 Terrell Davis.............	30.00	13.50
❑ HH4 Brett Favre	40.00	18.00
❑ HH5 Eddie George............	25.00	11.00
❑ HH6 Marvin Harrison	8.00	3.60
❑ HH7 Mark Brunell.............	20.00	9.00
❑ HH8 Dan Marino	40.00	18.00
❑ HH9 Curtis Martin.............	12.00	5.50
❑ HH10 Terry Glenn	8.00	3.60
❑ HH11 Keyshawn Johnson ..	8.00	3.60
❑ HH12 Jerry Rice................	20.00	9.00

1997 Flair Showcase Midas Touch

	MINT	NRMT
COMPLETE SET (12)	80.00	36.00
STATED ODDS 1:20		
❑ MT1 Troy Aikman.............	12.00	5.50
❑ MT2 John Elway...............	25.00	11.00
❑ MT3 Barry Sanders	25.00	11.00
❑ MT4 Marshall Faulk	5.00	2.20
❑ MT5 Karim Abdul-Jabbar	5.00	2.20
❑ MT6 Drew Bledsoe...........	12.00	5.50
❑ MT7 Ricky Watters.............	2.50	1.10
❑ MT8 Kordell Stewart...........	8.00	3.60
❑ MT9 Tony Martin	2.50	1.10
❑ MT10 Steve Young	8.00	3.60
❑ MT11 Joey Galloway	10.00	4.50
❑ MT12 Isaac Bruce	5.00	2.20

1997 Flair Showcase Now and Then

	MINT	NRMT
COMPLETE SET (4)	150.00	70.00
COMMON CARD (NT1-NT4) ..	30.00	13.50
STATED ODDS 1:400		
❑ NT1 Dan Marino...............	50.00	22.00
John Elway		
Darrell Green		
❑ NT2 Troy Aikman	50.00	22.00
Barry Sanders		
Deion Sanders		
❑ NT3 Emmitt Smith	30.00	13.50
Chris Warren		
Junior Seau		
❑ NT4 Brett Favre	30.00	13.50
Herman Moore		
Ricky Watters		

1997 Flair Showcase Wave of the Future

	MINT	NRMT
COMPLETE SET (25)	30.00	13.50
COMMON CARD (WF1-WF25) ..	.75	.35
SEMISTARS................................	1.25	.55
UNLISTED STARS...................	2.00	.90
STATED ODDS 1:4		
❑ WF1 Mike Adams..................	.75	.35
❑ WF2 John Allred....................	.75	.35
❑ WF3 Pat Barnes.................	2.00	.90
❑ WF4 Kenny Bynum	.75	.35
❑ WF5 Will Blackwell.............	2.00	.90
❑ WF6 Peter Boulware	1.25	.55
❑ WF7 Greg Clark	.75	.35
❑ WF8 Troy Davis	2.00	.90
❑ WF9 Albert Connell	4.00	1.80
❑ WF10 Jay Graham.............	2.00	.90
❑ WF11 Leon Johnson	.75	.35
❑ WF12 Damon Jones	.75	.35
❑ WF13 Freddie Jones	1.25	.55
❑ WF14 George Jones	1.25	.55
❑ WF15 Chad Levitt	.75	.35
❑ WF16 Joey Kent.................	2.00	.90
❑ WF17 Danny Wuerffel	1.25	.55
❑ WF18 Orlando Pace.............	.75	.35
❑ WF19 Darnell Autry	1.25	.55
❑ WF20 Sedrick Shaw............	2.00	.90
❑ WF21 Shawn Springs	1.25	.55
❑ WF22 Duce Staley	10.00	4.50
❑ WF23 Darrell Russell	.75	.35
❑ WF24 Bryant Westbrook	.75	.35
❑ WF25 Antwuan Wyatt	.75	.35

1998 Flair Showcase Row 3

	MINT	NRMT
COMPLETE SET (80)	70.00	32.00
COMMON CARD (1-40)............	.20	.09
SEMISTARS 1-40.......................	.40	.18
UNLISTED STARS 1-40.............	.75	.35
ROW 3 FLAIR 1-20 STATED ODDS 1:0.9		
COMMON ROOKIE 1-40	1.00	.45
ROOKIE SEMISTARS	1.50	.70
ROW 3 FLAIR 21-40 STATED ODDS 1:1.1		
COMMON CARD (41-60)............	.30	.14
SEMISTARS 41-60......................	.50	.23

UNLISTED STARS 41-60	1.00	.45
ROW 3 FLAIR 41-60 STATED ODDS 1:1.4		
COMMON CARD (61-80)	.40	.18
SEMISTARS 61-80	.75	.35
UNLISTED STARS 61-80	1.50	.70
ROW 3 FLAIR 61-80 STATED ODDS 1:1.8		
AKA FLAIR SHOWCASE FLAIR ..		

❑ 1 Brett Favre	3.00	1.35
❑ 2 Emmitt Smith	2.50	1.10
❑ 3 Peyton Manning RC	12.00	5.50
❑ 4 Mark Brunell	1.25	.55
❑ 5 Randy Moss RC	12.00	5.50
❑ 6 Jerry Rice	1.50	.70
❑ 7 John Elway	3.00	1.35
❑ 8 Troy Aikman	1.50	.70
❑ 9 Warrick Dunn	1.00	.45
❑ 10 Kordell Stewart	.75	.35
❑ 11 Drew Bledsoe	1.25	.55
❑ 12 Eddie George	1.25	.55
❑ 13 Dan Marino	3.00	1.35
❑ 14 Antowain Smith	.75	.35
❑ 15 Curtis Enis RC	2.50	1.10
❑ 16 Jake Plummer	2.00	.90
❑ 17 Steve Young	1.00	.45
❑ 18 Ryan Leaf RC	2.00	.90
❑ 19 Terrell Davis	2.50	1.10
❑ 20 Barry Sanders	3.00	1.35
❑ 21 Corey Dillon	1.00	.45
❑ 22 Fred Taylor RC	8.00	3.60
❑ 23 Herman Moore	.75	.35
❑ 24 Marshall Faulk	.75	.35
❑ 25 John Avery RC	.40	.18
❑ 26 Terry Glenn	.75	.35
❑ 27 Keyshawn Johnson	.75	.35
❑ 28 Charles Woodson RC	2.50	1.10
❑ 29 Garrison Hearst	.75	.35
❑ 30 Steve McNair	.75	.35
❑ 31 Deion Sanders	.75	.35
❑ 32 Robert Holcombe RC	.40	.18
❑ 33 Jerome Bettis	.75	.35
❑ 34 Robert Edwards RC	1.50	.70
❑ 35 Skip Hicks RC	2.00	.90
❑ 36 Marcus Nash RC	2.00	.90
❑ 37 Fred Lane	.40	.18
❑ 38 Kevin Dyson RC	2.00	.90
❑ 39 Dorsey Levens	.75	.35
❑ 40 Jacquez Green RC	2.00	.90
❑ 41 Shannon Sharpe	.50	.23
❑ 42 Michael Irvin	1.00	.45
❑ 43 Jim Harbaugh	.50	.23
❑ 44 Curtis Martin	1.00	.45
❑ 45 Bobby Hoying	.50	.23
❑ 46 Trent Dilfer	1.00	.45
❑ 47 Yancey Thigpen	.30	.14
❑ 48 Warren Moon	1.00	.45
❑ 49 Danny Kanell	.50	.23
❑ 50 Rob Johnson	.50	.23
❑ 51 Carl Pickens	1.00	.45
❑ 52 Scott Mitchell	.50	.23
❑ 53 Tim Brown	1.00	.45
❑ 54 Tony Banks	1.00	.45
❑ 55 Jamal Anderson	1.00	.45
❑ 56 Kerry Collins	.50	.23
❑ 57 Elvis Grbac	.50	.23
❑ 58 Mike Alstott	1.00	.45
❑ 59 Glenn Foley	.50	.23
❑ 60 Brad Johnson	1.00	.45
❑ 61 Robert Brooks	.75	.35
❑ 62 Irving Fryar	.75	.35
❑ 63 Natrone Means	1.50	.70
❑ 64 Rae Carruth	.75	.35
❑ 65 Isaac Bruce	1.50	.70
❑ 66 Andre Rison	.75	.35
❑ 67 Jeff George	.75	.35
❑ 68 Charles Way	.40	.18
❑ 69 Derrick Alexander	.75	.35
❑ 70 Michael Jackson	.40	.18
❑ 71 Rob Moore	.75	.35
❑ 72 Ricky Watters	.75	.35
❑ 73 Curtis Conway	.75	.35
❑ 74 Antonio Freeman	1.50	.70
❑ 75 Jimmy Smith	.75	.35
❑ 76 Troy Davis	.40	.18
❑ 77 Robert Smith	1.50	.70
❑ 78 Terry Allen	1.50	.70
❑ 79 Joey Galloway	1.50	.70
❑ 80 Charles Johnson	.40	.18
❑ NNO Checklist Card	.20	.09

1998 Flair Showcase Row 2

	MINT	NRMT
COMPLETE SET (80)	120.00	55.00
*STARS 1-20: 1X TO 2.5X ROW 3		
*ROOKIES 1-20: .5X TO 1.2X ROW 3		
ROW 2 STYLE 1-20 STATED ODDS 1:3		
*STARS 21-40: .75X TO 2X ROW 3		
*ROOKIES 21-40: .6X TO 1.5X ROW 3		
ROW 2 STYLE 21-40 STATED ODDS 1:2.5		
*STARS 41-60: 1X TO 2.5X ROW 3		
ROW 2 STYLE 41-60 STATED ODDS 1:4		
*STARS 61-80: .6X TO 1.5X ROW 3		
ROW 2 STYLE 61-80 STATED ODDS 1:3.4		
AKA FLAIR SHOWCASE STYLE..		

1998 Flair Showcase Row 1

	MINT	NRMT
COMPLETE SET (80)	500.00	220.00
*STARS 1-20: 3X TO 8X ROW 3 ..		
*ROOKIES 1-20: 1.5X TO 4X ROW 3		
ROW 1 GRACE 1-20 STATED ODDS 1:16		
*STARS 21-40: 4X TO 10X ROW 3		
*ROOKIES 21-40: 2X TO 5X ROW 3		
ROW 1 GRACE 21-40 STATED ODDS 1:24		
*STARS 41-60: 1.25X TO 3X ROW 3		
ROW 1 GRACE 41-60 STATED ODDS 1:6		
*STARS 61-80: 1.25X TO 3X ROW 3		
ROW 1 GRACE 61-80 STATED ODDS 1:9.6		
AKA FLAIR SHOWCASE GRACE		

1998 Flair Showcase Row 0

	MINT	NRMT
COMPLETE SET (80)	3000.00	1350.00
*STARS 1-20: 12.5X TO 30X ROW 3		
*ROOKIES 1-20: 4X TO 10X ROW 3		
ROW 0 SHOWCASE 1-20 PRINT RUN 250		
*STARS 21-40: 8X TO 20X ROW 3		
*ROOKIES 21-40: 3X TO 7X ROW 3		
ROW 0 SHOWCASE 21-40 PRINT RUN 500		
*STARS 41-60: 6X TO 15X ROW 3		
ROW 0 SHOWCASE 41-60 PRINT RUN 1000		
*STARS 61-80: 3X TO 8X ROW 3		
ROW 0 SHOWCASE 61-80 PRINT RUN 2000		
AKA FLAIR SHOWCASE SHOWCASE		

1998 Flair Showcase Legacy Collection

	MINT	NRMT
COMMON CARD (1-80)	15.00	6.75
*STARS 1-40: 15X TO 40X ROW 3 HI		
*YOUNG STARS 1-40: 12X TO 30X ROW 3		
*RCs 1-40: 6X TO 12X ROW 3		
*STARS 41-60: 12.5X TO 30X ROW 3 HI		
*STARS 61-80: 10X TO 25X ROW 3 HI		
STATED PRINT RUN 100 SERIAL #'d SETS		
FOUR CARDS PER PLAYER/SAME PRICE		
UNPRICED MASTERPIECES SERIAL #'d TO 1		

1998 Flair Showcase Feature Film

	MINT	NRMT
COMPLETE SET (10)	150.00	70.00
COMMON CARD (1-10)	10.00	4.50
STATED ODDS 1:60		
UNPRICED MASTERS SERIAL #'d TO 1		

❑ 1 Terrell Davis	25.00	11.00
❑ 2 Brett Favre	30.00	13.50
❑ 3 Antowain Smith	10.00	4.50
❑ 4 Emmitt Smith	25.00	11.00
❑ 5 Dan Marino	30.00	13.50
❑ 6 Kordell Stewart	15.00	6.75
❑ 7 Warrick Dunn	20.00	9.00
❑ 8 Barry Sanders	30.00	13.50
❑ 9 Peyton Manning	25.00	11.00
❑ 10 Ryan Leaf	10.00	4.50

1999 Flair Showcase

	MINT	NRMT
COMPLETE SET (192)	800.00	350.00
COMP.SET w/o SPs (160)	50.00	22.00
COMMON CARD (1-161)	.20	.09
SEMISTARS	.40	.18
UNLISTED STARS	.75	.35
COMMON ROOKIE (162-192)	12.00	5.50
ROOKIE SEMISTARS	15.00	6.75

161-192 STATED PRINT RUN 1999 SER.#'d SETS ....

Card	MINT	NRMT
❑ 1 Troy Aikman PW	2.00	.90
❑ 2 Jamal Anderson PW	.20	.09
❑ 3 Charlie Batch PW	1.50	.70
❑ 4 Jerome Bettis PW	.20	.09
❑ 5 Drew Bledsoe PW	1.25	.55
❑ 6 Mark Brunell PW	1.25	.55
❑ 7 Randall Cunningham PW	.75	.35
❑ 8 Terrell Davis PW	2.00	.90
❑ 9 Corey Dillon PW	.75	.35
❑ 10 Warrick Dunn PW	.75	.35
❑ 11 Curtis Enis PW	.75	.35
❑ 12 Marshall Faulk PW	.75	.35
❑ 13 Brett Favre PW	3.00	1.35
❑ 14 Doug Flutie PW	1.00	.45
❑ 15 Eddie George PW	1.00	.45
❑ 16 Brian Griese PW	1.50	.70
❑ 17 Keyshawn Johnson PW	.75	.35
❑ 18 Peyton Manning PW	3.00	1.35
❑ 19 Dan Marino PW	3.00	1.35
❑ 20 Curtis Martin PW	.75	.35
❑ 21 Steve McNair PW	.75	.35
❑ 22 Randy Moss PW	3.00	1.35
❑ 23 Terrell Owens PW	.75	.35
❑ 24 Jake Plummer PW	1.50	.70
❑ 25 Jerry Rice PW	2.00	.90
❑ 26 Barry Sanders PW	3.00	1.35
❑ 27 Antowain Smith PW	.75	.35
❑ 28 Emmitt Smith PW	2.00	.90
❑ 29 Kordell Stewart PW	.75	.35
❑ 30 J.J. Stokes PW	.40	.18
❑ 31 Fred Taylor PW	2.00	.90
❑ 32 Steve Young PW	1.25	.55
❑ 33 Troy Aikman PN	2.00	.90
❑ 34 Mike Alstott PN	.75	.35
❑ 35 Jamal Anderson PN	.75	.35
❑ 36 Charlie Batch PN	1.50	.70
❑ 37 Jerome Bettis PN	.75	.35
❑ 38 Drew Bledsoe PN	1.25	.55
❑ 39 Mark Brunell PN	1.25	.55
❑ 40 Cris Carter PN	.75	.35
❑ 41 Mark Chmura PN	.20	.09
❑ 42 Wayne Chrebet PN	.40	.18
❑ 43 Kerry Collins PN	.20	.09
❑ 44 Randall Cunningham PN	.75	.35
❑ 45 Terrell Davis PN	2.00	.90
❑ 46 Trent Dilfer PN	.40	.18
❑ 47 Corey Dillon PN	.75	.35
❑ 48 Warrick Dunn PN	.75	.35
❑ 49 Kevin Dyson PN	.40	.18
❑ 50 Curtis Enis PN	.75	.35
❑ 51 Marshall Faulk PN	.75	.35
❑ 52 Brett Favre PN	3.00	1.35
❑ 53 Doug Flutie PN	1.00	.45
❑ 54 Antonio Freeman PN	.75	.35
❑ 55 Eddie George PN	1.00	.45
❑ 56 Terry Glenn PN	.75	.35
❑ 57 Tony Gonzalez PN	.40	.18
❑ 58 Elvis Grbac PN	.40	.18
❑ 59 Jacquez Green PN	.40	.18
❑ 60 Brian Griese PN	1.50	.70
❑ 61 Marvin Harrison PN	.75	.35
❑ 62 Garrison Hearst PN	.40	.18
❑ 63 Skip Hicks PN	.40	.18
❑ 64 Priest Holmes PN	.75	.35
❑ 65 Michael Irvin PN	.40	.18
❑ 66 Brad Johnson PN	.40	.18
❑ 67 Keyshawn Johnson PN	.75	.35
❑ 68 Napoleon Kaufman PN	.75	.35
❑ 69 Dorsey Levens PN	.75	.35
❑ 70 Peyton Manning PN	3.00	1.35
❑ 71 Dan Marino PN	3.00	1.35
❑ 72 Curtis Martin PN	.75	.35
❑ 73 Ed McCaffrey PN	.40	.18
❑ 74 Keenan McCardell PN	.40	.18
❑ 75 O.J. McDuffie PN	.40	.18
❑ 76 Steve McNair PN	.75	.35
❑ 77 Scott Mitchell PN	.20	.09
❑ 78 Randy Moss PN	3.00	1.35
❑ 79 Eric Moulds PN	.75	.35
❑ 80 Terrell Owens PN	.75	.35
❑ 81 Lawrence Phillips PN	.40	.18
❑ 82 Jake Plummer PN	1.50	.70
❑ 83 Jerry Rice PN	2.00	.90
❑ 84 Andre Rison PN	.40	.18
❑ 85 Barry Sanders PN	3.00	1.35
❑ 86 Shannon Sharpe PN	.40	.18
❑ 87 Antowain Smith PN	.75	.35
❑ 88 Emmitt Smith PN	2.00	.90
❑ 89 Rod Smith PN	.40	.18
❑ 90 Duce Staley PN	.75	.35
❑ 91 Kordell Stewart PN	.75	.35
❑ 92 J.J. Stokes PN	.40	.18
❑ 93 Fred Taylor PN	2.00	.90
❑ 94 Vinny Testaverde PN	.40	.18
❑ 95 Ricky Watters PN	.40	.18
❑ 96 Steve Young PN	1.25	.55
❑ 97 Mike Alstott	.75	.35
❑ 98 Jamal Anderson	.75	.35
❑ 99 Charlie Batch	1.50	.70
❑ 100 Jerome Bettis	.75	.35
❑ 101 Tim Biakabutuka	.40	.18
❑ 102 Drew Bledsoe	1.25	.55
❑ 103 Tim Brown	.75	.35
❑ 104 Mark Brunell	1.25	.55
❑ 105 Cris Carter	.75	.35
❑ 106 Chris Chandler	.40	.18
❑ 107 Mark Chmura	.20	.09
❑ 108 Wayne Chrebet	.40	.18
❑ 109 Ben Coates	.40	.18
❑ 110 Kerry Collins	.40	.18
❑ 111 Randall Cunningham	.75	.35
❑ 112 Trent Dilfer	.40	.18
❑ 113 Corey Dillon	.75	.35
❑ 114 Warrick Dunn	.75	.35
❑ 115 Kevin Dyson	.40	.18
❑ 116 Curtis Enis	.75	.35
❑ 117 Marshall Faulk	.75	.35
❑ 118 Doug Flutie	1.00	.45
❑ 119 Antonio Freeman	.75	.35
❑ 120 Joey Galloway	.75	.35
❑ 121 Rich Gannon	.40	.18
❑ 122 Eddie George	1.00	.45
❑ 123 Terry Glenn	.75	.35
❑ 124 Tony Gonzalez	.40	.18
❑ 125 Elvis Grbac	.40	.18
❑ 126 Jacquez Green	.40	.18
❑ 127 Brian Griese	1.50	.70
❑ 128 Marvin Harrison	.75	.35
❑ 129 Garrison Hearst	.40	.18
❑ 130 Skip Hicks	.40	.18
❑ 131 Priest Holmes	.75	.35
❑ 132 Michael Irvin	.40	.18
❑ 133 Brad Johnson	.40	.18
❑ 134 Napoleon Kaufman	.75	.35
❑ 135 Terry Kirby	.20	.09
❑ 136 Dorsey Levens	.75	.35
❑ 137 Curtis Martin	.75	.35
❑ 138 Ed McCaffrey	.40	.18
❑ 139 Keenan McCardell	.40	.18
❑ 140 O.J. McDuffie	.40	.18
❑ 141 Steve McNair	.75	.35
❑ 142 Natrone Means	.40	.18
❑ 143 Scott Mitchell	.20	.09
❑ 144 Herman Moore	.75	.35
❑ 145 Eric Moulds	.75	.35
❑ 146 Terrell Owens	.75	.35
❑ 147 Lawrence Phillips	.40	.18
❑ 148 Jerry Rice	2.00	.90
❑ 149 Andre Rison	.40	.18
❑ 150 Deion Sanders	.75	.35
❑ 151 Shannon Sharpe	.40	.18
❑ 152 Antowain Smith	.75	.35
❑ 153 Rod Smith	.40	.18
❑ 154 Duce Staley	.75	.35
❑ 155 Kordell Stewart	.75	.35
❑ 156 J.J. Stokes	.40	.18
❑ 157 Vinny Testaverde	.40	.18
❑ 158 Yancey Thigpen	.20	.09
❑ 159 Ricky Watters	.40	.18
❑ 160 Steve Young	1.25	.55
❑ 161 Troy Aikman SP	12.00	5.50
❑ 162 Champ Bailey RC	20.00	9.00
❑ 163 Karsten Bailey RC	12.00	5.50
❑ 164 D'Wayne Bates RC	12.00	5.50
❑ 165 David Boston RC	25.00	11.00
❑ 166 Mike Cloud RC	15.00	6.75
❑ 167 Cecil Collins RC	15.00	6.75
❑ 168 Tim Couch RC	150.00	70.00
❑ 169 Daunte Culpepper RC	60.00	27.00
❑ 170 Terrell Davis SP	12.00	5.50
❑ 171 Troy Edwards RC	25.00	11.00
❑ 172 Kevin Faulk RC	20.00	9.00
❑ 173 Brett Favre SP	20.00	9.00
❑ 174 Torry Holt RC	40.00	18.00
❑ 175 Sedrick Irvin RC	15.00	6.75
❑ 176 Edgerrin James RC	225.00	100.00
❑ 177 James Johnson RC	20.00	9.00
❑ 178 Kevin Johnson RC	40.00	18.00
❑ 179 Keyshawn Johnson SP	5.00	2.20
❑ 180 Peyton Manning SP	20.00	9.00
❑ 181 Dan Marino SP	20.00	9.00
❑ 182 Donovan McNabb RC	60.00	27.00
❑ 183 Cade McNown RC	60.00	27.00
❑ 184 Joe Montgomery RC	15.00	6.75
❑ 185 Randy Moss SP	20.00	9.00
❑ 186 Jake Plummer SP	10.00	4.50
❑ 187 Peerless Price RC	25.00	11.00
❑ 188 Barry Sanders SP	20.00	9.00
❑ 189 Akili Smith RC	50.00	22.00
❑ 190 Emmitt Smith SP	12.00	5.50
❑ 191 Fred Taylor SP	12.00	5.50
❑ 192 Ricky Williams RC	125.00	55.00

1999 Flair Showcase Legacy Collection

	MINT	NRMT
COMMON CARD (1-192)	5.00	2.20

*STARS: 10X TO 25X HI COL. ....
*SP STARS: 3X TO 8X HI COL.....
*YOUNG STARS: 8X TO 20X ......
*RCs: .6X TO 1.5X ....
STATED PRINT RUN 99 SERIAL #'d SETS
UNPRICED MASTERPIECES SER.#'d TO 1

1999 Flair Showcase Class of '99

	MINT	NRMT
COMPLETE SET (15)	250.00	110.00
COMMON CARD (1-15)	8.00	3.60
SEMISTARS	10.00	4.50

STATED PRINT RUN 500 SETS ..

Card	MINT	NRMT
❑ 1 Tim Couch	40.00	18.00
❑ 2 Donovan McNabb	25.00	11.00
❑ 3 Akili Smith	15.00	6.75
❑ 4 Cade McNown	25.00	11.00
❑ 5 Daunte Culpepper	25.00	11.00
❑ 6 Ricky Williams	40.00	18.00
❑ 7 Edgerrin James	60.00	27.00
❑ 8 Kevin Faulk	10.00	4.50
❑ 9 Torry Holt	20.00	9.00
❑ 10 David Boston	12.00	5.50
❑ 11 Sedrick Irvin	8.00	3.60
❑ 12 Peerless Price	12.00	5.50
❑ 13 Joe Germaine	10.00	4.50
❑ 14 Brock Huard	10.00	4.50
❑ 15 Shaun King	25.00	11.00

1999 Flair Showcase Feel The Game

	MINT	NRMT
COMPLETE SET (10)	750.00	350.00

COMMON CARD (1FG-10FG)	30.00	13.50
STATED ODDS 1:168		

❑ 1FG Edgerrin James Glove	225.00	100.00
❑ 2FG Antowain Smith Shorts	40.00	18.00
❑ 3FG Peyton Manning Jersey	150.00	70.00
❑ 4FG Cecil Collins Shoe	40.00	18.00
❑ 5FG Brett Favre Jersey	120.00	55.00
❑ 6FG Jake Plummer Shoe	50.00	22.00
❑ 7FG Dan Marino Jersey	120.00	55.00
❑ 8FG Sean Dawkins Shoes	30.00	13.50
❑ 9FG Torry Holt Shoe	60.00	27.00
❑ 10FG Marshall Faulk Jersey	60.00	27.00

1999 Flair Showcase First Rounders

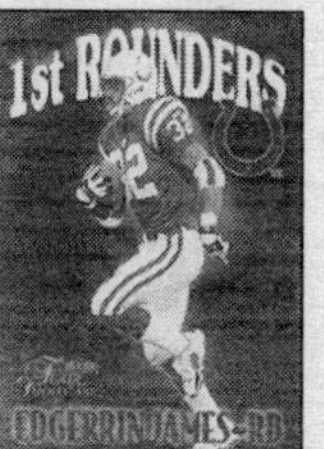

	MINT	NRMT
COMPLETE SET (10)	40.00	18.00
COMMON CARD (1FR-10FR)	2.50	1.10
STATED ODDS 1:10		

❑ 1FR Tim Couch	8.00	3.60
❑ 2FR Donovan McNabb	5.00	2.20
❑ 3FR Akili Smith	3.00	1.35
❑ 4FR Cade McNown	5.00	2.20
❑ 5FR Daunte Culpepper	5.00	2.20
❑ 6FR David Boston	2.50	1.10
❑ 7FR Torry Holt	4.00	1.80
❑ 8FR Ricky Williams	8.00	3.60
❑ 9FR Edgerrin James	12.00	5.50
❑ 10FR Troy Edwards	2.50	1.10

1999 Flair Showcase Shrine Time

	MINT	NRMT
COMPLETE SET (15)	100.00	45.00
COMMON CARD (1-15)	4.00	1.80
STATED PRINT RUN 1500 SER.#'d SETS		

❑ 1 Peyton Manning	12.00	5.50
❑ 2 Fred Taylor	8.00	3.60
❑ 3 Terrell Owens	4.00	1.80
❑ 4 Charlie Batch	6.00	2.70
❑ 5 Jerry Rice	10.00	4.50
❑ 6 Randy Moss	12.00	5.50
❑ 7 Warrick Dunn	4.00	1.80
❑ 8 Mark Brunell	6.00	2.70
❑ 9 Emmitt Smith	10.00	4.50
❑ 10 Eddie George	5.00	2.20
❑ 11 Barry Sanders	15.00	6.75
❑ 12 Terrell Davis	10.00	4.50
❑ 13 Dan Marino	15.00	6.75
❑ 14 Troy Aikman	10.00	4.50
❑ 15 Brett Favre	15.00	6.75

1960 Fleer

	NRMT	VG-E
COMPLETE SET (132)	750.00	350.00
COMMON CARD (1-132)	3.50	1.55
SEMISTARS	5.00	2.20
UNLISTED STARS	6.00	2.70
CARDS PRICED IN NM CONDITION !		

❑ 1 Harvey White RC !	20.00	5.00
❑ 2 Tom Corky Tharp	3.50	1.55
❑ 3 Dan McGrew	3.50	1.55
❑ 4 Bob White	3.50	1.55
❑ 5 Dick Jamieson	3.50	1.55
❑ 6 Sam Salerno	3.50	1.55
❑ 7 Sid Gillman CO RC	20.00	9.00
❑ 8 Ben Preston	3.50	1.55
❑ 9 George Blanch	3.50	1.55
❑ 10 Bob Stransky	3.50	1.55
❑ 11 Fran Curci	3.50	1.55
❑ 12 George Shirkey	3.50	1.55
❑ 13 Paul Larson	3.50	1.55
❑ 14 John Stolte	3.50	1.55
❑ 15 Serafino(Foge) Fazio RC	5.00	2.20
❑ 16 Tom Dimitroff	3.50	1.55
❑ 17 Elbert Dubenion RC	12.00	5.50
❑ 18 Hogan Wharton	3.50	1.55
❑ 19 Tom O'Connell	3.50	1.55
❑ 20 Sammy Baugh CO	45.00	20.00
❑ 21 Tony Sardisco	3.50	1.55
❑ 22 Alan Cann	3.50	1.55
❑ 23 Mike Hudock	3.50	1.55
❑ 24 Bill Atkins	3.50	1.55
❑ 25 Charlie Jackson	3.50	1.55
❑ 26 Frank Tripucka	6.00	2.70
❑ 27 Tony Teresa	3.50	1.55
❑ 28 Joe Amstutz	3.50	1.55
❑ 29 Bob Fee	3.50	1.55
❑ 30 Jim Baldwin	3.50	1.55
❑ 31 Jim Yates	3.50	1.55
❑ 32 Don Flynn	3.50	1.55
❑ 33 Ken Adamson	3.50	1.55
❑ 34 Ron Drzewiecki	3.50	1.55
❑ 35 J.W. Slack	3.50	1.55
❑ 36 Bob Yates	3.50	1.55
❑ 37 Gary Cobb	3.50	1.55
❑ 38 Jacky Lee RC	5.00	2.20
❑ 39 Jack Spikes RC	5.00	2.20
❑ 40 Jim Padgett	3.50	1.55
❑ 41 Jack Larscheid RC	3.50	1.55
❑ 42 Bob Reifsnyder RC	3.50	1.55
❑ 43 Fran Rogel	3.50	1.55
❑ 44 Ray Moss	3.50	1.55
❑ 45 Tony Banfield RC	5.00	2.20
❑ 46 George Herring	3.50	1.55
❑ 47 Willie Smith	3.50	1.55
❑ 48 Buddy Allen	3.50	1.55
❑ 49 Bill Brown	3.50	1.55
❑ 50 Ken Ford	3.50	1.55
❑ 51 Billy Kinard	3.50	1.55
❑ 52 Buddy Mayfield	3.50	1.55
❑ 53 Bill Krisher	3.50	1.55
❑ 54 Frank Bernardi	3.50	1.55
❑ 55 Lou Saban CO RC	5.00	2.20
❑ 56 Gene Cockrell	3.50	1.55
❑ 57 Sam Sanders	3.50	1.55
❑ 58 George Blanda	50.00	22.00
❑ 59 Sherrill Headrick RC	5.00	2.20
❑ 60 Carl Larpenter	3.50	1.55
❑ 61 Gene Prebola	3.50	1.55
❑ 62 Dick Chorovich	3.50	1.55
❑ 63 Bob McNamara	3.50	1.55
❑ 64 Tom Saidock	3.50	1.55
❑ 65 Willie Evans	3.50	1.55
❑ 66 Billy Cannon RC UER (Hometown: Istruma, should be Istrouma)	18.00	8.00
❑ 67 Sam McCord	3.50	1.55
❑ 68 Mike Simmons	3.50	1.55
❑ 69 Jim Swink RC	5.00	2.20
❑ 70 Don Hitt	3.50	1.55
❑ 71 Gerhard Schwedes	3.50	1.55
❑ 72 Thurlow Cooper	3.50	1.55
❑ 73 Abner Haynes RC	18.00	8.00
❑ 74 Billy Shoemake	3.50	1.55
❑ 75 Marv Lasater	3.50	1.55
❑ 76 Paul Lowe RC	15.00	6.75
❑ 77 Bruce Hartman	3.50	1.55
❑ 78 Blanche Martin	3.50	1.55
❑ 79 Gene Grabosky	3.50	1.55
❑ 80 Lou Rymkus CO	5.00	2.20
❑ 81 Chris Burford RC	8.00	3.60
❑ 82 Don Allen	3.50	1.55
❑ 83 Bob Nelson	3.50	1.55
❑ 84 Jim Woodard	3.50	1.55
❑ 85 Tom Rychlec	3.50	1.55
❑ 86 Bob Cox	3.50	1.55
❑ 87 Jerry Cornelison	3.50	1.55
❑ 88 Jack Work	3.50	1.55
❑ 89 Sam DeLuca	3.50	1.55
❑ 90 Rommie Loudd	3.50	1.55
❑ 91 Teddy Edmondson	3.50	1.55
❑ 92 Buster Ramsey CO	3.50	1.55
❑ 93 Doug Asad	3.50	1.55
❑ 94 Jimmy Harris	3.50	1.55
❑ 95 Larry Cundiff	3.50	1.55
❑ 96 Richie Lucas RC	6.00	2.70
❑ 97 Don Norwood	3.50	1.55
❑ 98 Larry Grantham RC	5.00	2.20
❑ 99 Bill Mathis RC	6.00	2.70
❑ 100 Mel Branch RC	5.00	2.20
❑ 101 Marvin Terrell	3.50	1.55
❑ 102 Charlie Flowers	3.50	1.55
❑ 103 John McMullan	3.50	1.55
❑ 104 Charlie Kaaihue	3.50	1.55
❑ 105 Joe Schaffer	3.50	1.55
❑ 106 Al Day	3.50	1.55
❑ 107 Johnny Carson	3.50	1.55
❑ 108 Alan Goldstein	3.50	1.55
❑ 109 Doug Cline	3.50	1.55
❑ 110 Al Carmichael	3.50	1.55
❑ 111 Bob Dee	3.50	1.55
❑ 112 John Bredice	3.50	1.55
❑ 113 Don Floyd	3.50	1.55
❑ 114 Ronnie Cain	3.50	1.55
❑ 115 Stan Flowers	3.50	1.55
❑ 116 Hank Stram CO RC	50.00	22.00
❑ 117 Bob Dougherty	3.50	1.55
❑ 118 Ron Mix RC	30.00	13.50
❑ 119 Roger Ellis	3.50	1.55
❑ 120 Elvin Caldwell	3.50	1.55
❑ 121 Bill Kimber	3.50	1.55
❑ 122 Jim Matheny	3.50	1.55
❑ 123 Curley Johnson RC	3.50	1.55
❑ 124 Jack Kemp RC	275.00	125.00
❑ 125 Ed Denk	3.50	1.55
❑ 126 Jerry McFarland	3.50	1.55
❑ 127 Dan Lanphear	3.50	1.55
❑ 128 Paul Maguire RC	18.00	8.00
❑ 129 Ray Collins	3.50	1.55
❑ 130 Ron Burton RC	6.00	2.70
❑ 131 Eddie Erdelatz CO	3.50	1.55
❑ 132 Ron Beagle RC !	15.00	3.70

1961 Fleer

	NRMT	VG-E
COMPLETE SET (220)	1600.00	700.00
COMMON CARD (1-132)	4.00	1.80
SEMISTARS 1-132	6.00	2.70
UNLISTED STARS 1-132	7.00	3.10
COMMON CARD (133-220)	6.00	2.70
SEMISTARS 133-220	8.00	3.60
UNLISTED STARS 133-220	10.00	4.50
CARDS PRICED IN NM CONDITION		

❑	Card	NRMT	VG-E
❑	1 Ed Brown	15.00	3.70
❑	2 Rick Casares	6.00	2.70
❑	3 Willie Galimore	6.00	2.70
❑	4 Jim Dooley	4.00	1.80
❑	5 Harlon Hill	4.00	1.80
❑	6 Stan Jones	7.00	3.10
❑	7 J.C. Caroline	4.00	1.80
❑	8 Joe Fortunato	4.00	1.80
❑	9 Doug Atkins	8.00	3.60
❑	10 Milt Plum	6.00	2.70
❑	11 Jim Brown	125.00	55.00
❑	12 Bobby Mitchell	10.00	4.50
❑	13 Ray Renfro	6.00	2.70
❑	14 Gern Nagler	4.00	1.80
❑	15 Jim Shofner	4.00	1.80
❑	16 Vince Costello	4.00	1.80
❑	17 Galen Fiss	4.00	1.80
❑	18 Walt Michaels	6.00	2.70
❑	19 Bob Gain	4.00	1.80
❑	20 Mal Hammack	4.00	1.80
❑	21 Frank Mestnick	4.00	1.80
❑	22 Bobby Joe Conrad	6.00	2.70
❑	23 John David Crow	6.00	2.70
❑	24 Sonny Randle RC	6.00	2.70
❑	25 Don Gillis	4.00	1.80
❑	26 Jerry Norton	4.00	1.80
❑	27 Bill Stacy	4.00	1.80
❑	28 Leo Sugar	4.00	1.80
❑	29 Frank Fuller	4.00	1.80
❑	30 John Unitas	60.00	27.00
❑	31 Alan Ameche	7.00	3.10
❑	32 Lenny Moore	15.00	6.75
❑	33 Raymond Berry	15.00	6.75
❑	34 Jim Mutscheller	4.00	1.80
❑	35 Jim Parker	7.00	3.10
❑	36 Bill Pellington	4.00	1.80
❑	37 Gino Marchetti	10.00	4.50
❑	38 Gene Lipscomb	7.00	3.10
❑	39 Art Donovan	15.00	6.75
❑	40 Eddie LeBaron	6.00	2.70
❑	41 Don Meredith RC	150.00	70.00
❑	42 Don McIlhenny	4.00	1.80
❑	43 L.G. Dupre	4.00	1.80
❑	44 Fred Dugan	4.00	1.80
❑	45 Billy Howton	6.00	2.70
❑	46 Duane Putnam	4.00	1.80
❑	47 Gene Cronin	4.00	1.80
❑	48 Jerry Tubbs	4.00	1.80
❑	49 Clarence Peaks	4.00	1.80
❑	50 Ted Dean RC	4.00	1.80
❑	51 Tommy McDonald	7.00	3.10
❑	52 Bill Barnes	4.00	1.80
❑	53 Pete Retzlaff	6.00	2.70
❑	54 Bobby Walston	4.00	1.80
❑	55 Chuck Bednarik	12.00	5.50
❑	56 Maxie Baughan RC	6.00	2.70
❑	57 Bob Pellegrini	4.00	1.80
❑	58 Jesse Richardson	4.00	1.80
❑	59 John Brodie RC	50.00	22.00
❑	60 J.D. Smith RB	6.00	2.70
❑	61 Ray Norton RC	4.00	1.80
❑	62 Monty Stickles RC	4.00	1.80
❑	63 Bob St. Clair	7.00	3.10
❑	64 Dave Baker	4.00	1.80
❑	65 Abe Woodson	4.00	1.80
❑	66 Matt Hazeltine	4.00	1.80
❑	67 Leo Nomellini	10.00	4.50
❑	68 Charley Conerly	10.00	4.50
❑	69 Kyle Rote	7.00	3.10
❑	70 Jack Stroud	4.00	1.80
❑	71 Roosevelt Brown	7.00	3.10
❑	72 Jim Patton	4.00	1.80
❑	73 Erich Barnes	4.00	1.80
❑	74 Sam Huff	15.00	6.75
❑	75 Andy Robustelli	10.00	4.50
❑	76 Dick Modzelewski	4.00	1.80
❑	77 Roosevelt Grier	7.00	3.10
❑	78 Earl Morrall	7.00	3.10
❑	79 Jim Ninowski	4.00	1.80
❑	80 Nick Pietrosante RC	6.00	2.70
❑	81 Howard Cassady	6.00	2.70
❑	82 Jim Gibbons	4.00	1.80
❑	83 Gail Cogdill RC	6.00	2.70
❑	84 Dick Lane	7.00	3.10
❑	85 Yale Lary	7.00	3.10
❑	86 Joe Schmidt	8.00	3.60
❑	87 Darris McCord	4.00	1.80
❑	88 Bart Starr	60.00	27.00
❑	89 Jim Taylor	50.00	22.00
❑	90 Paul Hornung	55.00	25.00
❑	91 Tom Moore RC	8.00	3.60
❑	92 Boyd Dowler RC	15.00	6.75
❑	93 Max McGee	7.00	3.10
❑	94 Forrest Gregg	8.00	3.60
❑	95 Jerry Kramer	10.00	4.50
❑	96 Jim Ringo	8.00	3.60
❑	97 Bill Forester	6.00	2.70
❑	98 Frank Ryan	6.00	2.70
❑	99 Ollie Matson	12.00	5.50
❑	100 Jon Arnett	6.00	2.70
❑	101 Dick Bass RC	6.00	2.70
❑	102 Jim Phillips	4.00	1.80
❑	103 Del Shofner	6.00	2.70
❑	104 Art Hunter	4.00	1.80
❑	105 Lindon Crow	4.00	1.80
❑	106 Les Richter	6.00	2.70
❑	107 Lou Michaels	4.00	1.80
❑	108 Ralph Guglielmi	4.00	1.80
❑	109 Don Bosseler	4.00	1.80
❑	110 John Olszewski	4.00	1.80
❑	111 Bill Anderson	4.00	1.80
❑	112 Joe Walton	4.00	1.80
❑	113 Jim Schrader	4.00	1.80
❑	114 Gary Glick	4.00	1.80
❑	115 Ralph Felton	4.00	1.80
❑	116 Bob Toneff	4.00	1.80
❑	117 Bobby Layne	35.00	16.00
❑	118 John Henry Johnson	7.00	3.10
❑	119 Tom Tracy	6.00	2.70
❑	120 Jimmy Orr RC	7.00	3.10
❑	121 John Nisby	4.00	1.80
❑	122 Dean Derby	4.00	1.80
❑	123 John Reger	4.00	1.80
❑	124 George Tarasovic	4.00	1.80
❑	125 Ernie Stautner	10.00	4.50
❑	126 George Shaw	4.00	1.80
❑	127 Hugh McElhenny	12.00	5.50
❑	128 Dick Haley	4.00	1.80
❑	129 Dave Middleton	4.00	1.80
❑	130 Perry Richards	4.00	1.80
❑	131 Gene Johnson	4.00	1.80
❑	132 Don Joyce	4.00	1.80
❑	133 Johnny Green	8.00	3.60
❑	134 Wray Carlton RC	8.00	3.60
❑	135 Richie Lucas	8.00	3.60
❑	136 Elbert Dubenion	8.00	3.60
❑	137 Tom Rychlec	6.00	2.70
❑	138 Mack Yoho	6.00	2.70
❑	139 Phil Blazer	6.00	2.70
❑	140 Dan McGrew	6.00	2.70
❑	141 Bill Atkins	6.00	2.70
❑	142 Archie Matsos RC	6.00	2.70
❑	143 Gene Grabosky	6.00	2.70
❑	144 Frank Tripucka	10.00	4.50
❑	145 Al Carmichael	6.00	2.70
❑	146 Bob McNamara	6.00	2.70
❑	147 Lionel Taylor RC	15.00	6.75
❑	148 Eldon Danenhauer	6.00	2.70
❑	149 Willie Smith	6.00	2.70
❑	150 Carl Larpenter	6.00	2.70
❑	151 Ken Adamson	6.00	2.70
❑	152 Goose Gonsoulin RC	10.00	4.50
❑	153 Joe Young	6.00	2.70
❑	154 Gordy Molz	6.00	2.70
❑	155 Jack Kemp	200.00	90.00
❑	156 Charlie Flowers	6.00	2.70
❑	157 Paul Lowe	10.00	4.50
❑	158 Don Norton	6.00	2.70
❑	159 Howard Clark	6.00	2.70
❑	160 Paul Maguire	15.00	6.75
❑	161 Ernie Wright RC	8.00	3.60
❑	162 Ron Mix	15.00	6.75
❑	163 Fred Cole	6.00	2.70
❑	164 Jim Sears	6.00	2.70
❑	165 Volney Peters	6.00	2.70
❑	166 George Blanda	45.00	20.00
❑	167 Jacky Lee	8.00	3.60
❑	168 Bob White	6.00	2.70
❑	169 Doug Cline	6.00	2.70
❑	170 Dave Smith	6.00	2.70
❑	171 Billy Cannon	15.00	6.75
❑	172 Bill Groman	6.00	2.70
❑	173 Al Jamison	6.00	2.70
❑	174 Jim Norton	6.00	2.70
❑	175 Dennit Morris	6.00	2.70
❑	176 Don Floyd	6.00	2.70
❑	177 Butch Songin	6.00	2.70
❑	178 Billy Lott	6.00	2.70
❑	179 Ron Burton	10.00	4.50
❑	180 Jim Colclough	6.00	2.70
❑	181 Charley Leo	6.00	2.70
❑	182 Walt Cudzik	6.00	2.70
❑	183 Fred Bruney	6.00	2.70
❑	184 Ross O'Hanley	6.00	2.70
❑	185 Tony Sardisco	6.00	2.70
❑	186 Harry Jacobs	6.00	2.70
❑	187 Bob Dee	6.00	2.70
❑	188 Tom Flores RC	30.00	13.50
❑	189 Jack Larscheid	6.00	2.70
❑	190 Dick Christy	6.00	2.70
❑	191 Alan Miller RC	6.00	2.70
❑	192 James Smith	6.00	2.70
❑	193 Gerald Burch	6.00	2.70
❑	194 Gene Prebola	6.00	2.70
❑	195 Alan Goldstein	6.00	2.70
❑	196 Don Manoukian	6.00	2.70
❑	197 Jim Otto RC	60.00	27.00
❑	198 Wayne Crow	6.00	2.70
❑	199 Cotton Davidson RC	8.00	3.60
❑	200 Randy Duncan RC*/C	8.00	3.60
❑	201 Jack Spikes	8.00	3.60
❑	202 Johnny Robinson RC	15.00	6.75
❑	203 Abner Haynes	15.00	6.75
❑	204 Chris Burford	8.00	3.60
❑	205 Bill Krisher	6.00	2.70
❑	206 Marvin Terrell	6.00	2.70
❑	207 Jimmy Harris	6.00	2.70
❑	208 Mel Branch	8.00	3.60
❑	209 Paul Miller	6.00	2.70
❑	210 Al Dorow	6.00	2.70
❑	211 Dick Jamieson	6.00	2.70
❑	212 Pete Hart	6.00	2.70
❑	213 Bill Shockley	6.00	2.70
❑	214 Dewey Bohling	6.00	2.70
❑	215 Don Maynard RC	80.00	36.00
❑	216 Bob Mischak	6.00	2.70
❑	217 Mike Hudock	6.00	2.70
❑	218 Bob Reifsnyder	6.00	2.70
❑	219 Tom Saidock	6.00	2.70
❑	220 Sid Youngelman	20.00	5.00

1962 Fleer

	NRMT	VG-E
COMPLETE SET (88)	900.00	400.00
COMMON CARD (1-88)	7.00	3.10
SEMISTARS	8.00	3.60
UNLISTED STARS	10.00	4.50
CARDS PRICED IN NM CONDITION !		

❑ 1 Billy Lott 16.00 4.00
❑ 2 Ron Burton 10.00 4.50
❑ 3 Gino Cappelletti RC 15.00 6.75
❑ 4 Babe Parilli 10.00 4.50
❑ 5 Jim Colclough 7.00 3.10
❑ 6 Tony Sardisco 7.00 3.10
❑ 7 Walt Cudzik 7.00 3.10
❑ 8 Bob Dee 7.00 3.10
❑ 9 Tommy Addison RC 8.00 3.60
❑ 10 Harry Jacobs 7.00 3.10
❑ 11 Ross O'Hanley 7.00 3.10
❑ 12 Art Baker 7.00 3.10
❑ 13 Johnny Green 7.00 3.10
❑ 14 Elbert Dubenion 10.00 4.50
❑ 15 Tom Rychlec 7.00 3.10
❑ 16 Billy Shaw RC 18.00 8.00
❑ 17 Ken Rice 7.00 3.10
❑ 18 Bill Atkins 7.00 3.10
❑ 19 Richie Lucas 8.00 3.60
❑ 20 Archie Matsos 7.00 3.10
❑ 21 Laverne Torczon 7.00 3.10
❑ 22 Warren Rabb 7.00 3.10
❑ 23 Jack Spikes 8.00 3.60
❑ 24 Cotton Davidson 8.00 3.60
❑ 25 Abner Haynes 15.00 6.75
❑ 26 Jimmy Saxton 7.00 3.10
❑ 27 Chris Burford 8.00 3.60
❑ 28 Bill Miller 7.00 3.10
❑ 29 Sherrill Headrick 8.00 3.60
❑ 30 E.J. Holub RC 8.00 3.60
❑ 31 Jerry Mays RC 10.00 4.50
❑ 32 Mel Branch 8.00 3.60
❑ 33 Paul Rochester 7.00 3.10
❑ 34 Frank Tripucka 10.00 4.50
❑ 35 Gene Mingo 7.00 3.10
❑ 36 Lionel Taylor 12.00 5.50
❑ 37 Ken Adamson 7.00 3.10
❑ 38 Eldon Danenhauer 7.00 3.10
❑ 39 Goose Gonsoulin 10.00 4.50
❑ 40 Gordy Holz 7.00 3.10
❑ 41 Bud McFadin 8.00 3.60
❑ 42 Jim Stinnette 7.00 3.10
❑ 43 Bob Hudson 7.00 3.10
❑ 44 George Herring 7.00 3.10
❑ 45 Charley Tolar RC 7.00 3.10
❑ 46 George Blanda 50.00 22.00
❑ 47 Billy Cannon 15.00 6.75
❑ 48 Charlie Hennigan RC 15.00 6.75
❑ 49 Bill Groman 7.00 3.10
❑ 50 Al Jamison 7.00 3.10
❑ 51 Tony Banfield 7.00 3.10
❑ 52 Jim Norton 7.00 3.10
❑ 53 Dennit Morris 7.00 3.10
❑ 54 Don Floyd 7.00 3.10
❑ 55 Ed Husmann UER 7.00 3.10
(Misspelled Hussman on both sides)
❑ 56 Robert Brooks 7.00 3.10
❑ 57 Al Dorow 7.00 3.10
❑ 58 Dick Christy 7.00 3.10
❑ 59 Don Maynard 50.00 22.00
❑ 60 Art Powell 10.00 4.50
❑ 61 Mike Hudock 7.00 3.10
❑ 62 Bill Mathis 8.00 3.60
❑ 63 Butch Songin 7.00 3.10
❑ 64 Larry Grantham 7.00 3.10
❑ 65 Nick Mumley 7.00 3.10
❑ 66 Tom Saidock 7.00 3.10
❑ 67 Alan Miller 7.00 3.10
❑ 68 Tom Flores 15.00 6.75
❑ 69 Bob Coolbaugh 7.00 3.10
❑ 70 George Fleming 7.00 3.10
❑ 71 Wayne Hawkins RC 8.00 3.60
❑ 72 Jim Otto 35.00 16.00
❑ 73 Wayne Crow 7.00 3.10
❑ 74 Fred Williamson RC 25.00 11.00
❑ 75 Tom Louderback 7.00 3.10
❑ 76 Volney Peters 7.00 3.10
❑ 77 Charley Powell 7.00 3.10
❑ 78 Don Norton 7.00 3.10
❑ 79 Jack Kemp 250.00 110.00
❑ 80 Paul Lowe 10.00 4.50
❑ 81 Dave Kocourek 7.00 3.10
❑ 82 Ron Mix 15.00 6.75
❑ 83 Ernie Wright 10.00 4.50
❑ 84 Dick Harris 7.00 3.10
❑ 85 Bill Hudson 7.00 3.10
❑ 86 Ernie Ladd RC 25.00 11.00
❑ 87 Earl Faison RC 8.00 3.60
❑ 88 Ron Nery 18.00 4.50

1963 Fleer

	NRMT	VG-E
COMPLETE SET (88)	1800.00	800.00
COMMON CARD (1-88)	8.00	3.60
SEMISTARS	10.00	4.50
UNLISTED STARS	12.00	5.50

CARDS PRICED IN NM CONDITION

❑ 1 Larry Garron RC ! 20.00 5.00
❑ 2 Babe Parilli 10.00 4.50
❑ 3 Ron Burton 12.00 5.50
❑ 4 Jim Colclough 8.00 3.60
❑ 5 Gino Cappelletti 12.00 5.50
❑ 6 Charles Long RC SP 150.00 70.00
❑ 7 Bill Neighbors RC 8.00 3.60
❑ 8 Dick Felt 8.00 3.60
❑ 9 Tommy Addison 8.00 3.60
❑ 10 Nick Buoniconti RC 65.00 29.00
❑ 11 Larry Eisenhauer RC 8.00 3.60
❑ 12 Bill Mathis 8.00 3.60
❑ 13 Lee Grosscup RC 10.00 4.50
❑ 14 Dick Christy 8.00 3.60
❑ 15 Don Maynard 50.00 22.00
❑ 16 Alex Kroll RC 8.00 3.60
❑ 17 Bob Mischak 8.00 3.60
❑ 18 Dainard Paulson 8.00 3.60
❑ 19 Lee Riley 8.00 3.60
❑ 20 Larry Grantham 10.00 4.50
❑ 21 Hubert Bobo 8.00 3.60
❑ 22 Nick Mumley 8.00 3.60
❑ 23 Cookie Gilchrist RC**/C 45.00 20.00
❑ 24 Jack Kemp 250.00 110.00
❑ 25 Wray Carlton 8.00 3.60
❑ 26 Elbert Dubenion 10.00 4.50
❑ 27 Ernie Warlick 8.00 3.60
❑ 28 Billy Shaw 12.00 5.50
❑ 29 Ken Rice 8.00 3.60
❑ 30 Booker Edgerson 8.00 3.60
❑ 31 Ray Abruzzese 8.00 3.60
❑ 32 Mike Stratton RC 12.00 5.50
❑ 33 Tom Sestak RC 10.00 4.50
❑ 34 Charley Tolar 8.00 3.60
❑ 35 Dave Smith 8.00 3.60
❑ 36 George Blanda 55.00 25.00
❑ 37 Billy Cannon 15.00 6.75
❑ 38 Charlie Hennigan 10.00 4.50
❑ 39 Bob Talamini RC 8.00 3.60
❑ 40 Jim Norton 8.00 3.60
❑ 41 Tony Banfield 8.00 3.60
❑ 42 Doug Cline 8.00 3.60
❑ 43 Don Floyd 8.00 3.60
❑ 44 Ed Husmann 8.00 3.60
❑ 45 Curtis McClinton RC 15.00 6.75
❑ 46 Jack Spikes 10.00 4.50
❑ 47 Len Dawson RC 225.00 100.00
❑ 48 Abner Haynes 15.00 6.75
❑ 49 Chris Burford 10.00 4.50
❑ 50 Fred Arbanas RC 12.00 5.50
❑ 51 Johnny Robinson 10.00 4.50
❑ 52 E.J. Holub 10.00 4.50
❑ 53 Sherrill Headrick 10.00 4.50
❑ 54 Mel Branch 10.00 4.50
❑ 55 Jerry Mays 10.00 4.50
❑ 56 Cotton Davidson 10.00 4.50
❑ 57 Clem Daniels RC 15.00 6.75
❑ 58 Bo Roberson 8.00 3.60
❑ 59 Art Powell 12.00 5.50
❑ 60 Bob Coolbaugh 8.00 3.60
❑ 61 Wayne Hawkins 8.00 3.60
❑ 62 Jim Otto 30.00 13.50
❑ 63 Fred Williamson 12.00 5.50
❑ 64 Bob Dougherty SP 160.00 70.00
❑ 65 Dalva Allen 8.00 3.60
❑ 66 Chuck McMurtry 8.00 3.60
❑ 67 Gerry McDougall 8.00 3.60
❑ 68 Tobin Rote 10.00 4.50
❑ 69 Paul Lowe 12.00 5.50
❑ 70 Keith Lincoln RC 40.00 18.00
❑ 71 Dave Kocourek 8.00 3.60
❑ 72 Lance Alworth RC 200.00 90.00
❑ 73 Ron Mix 25.00 11.00
❑ 74 Charley McNeil RC 8.00 3.60
❑ 75 Emil Karas 8.00 3.60
❑ 76 Ernie Ladd 20.00 9.00
❑ 77 Earl Faison 8.00 3.60
❑ 78 Jim Stinnette 8.00 3.60
❑ 79 Frank Tripucka 12.00 5.50
❑ 80 Don Stone 8.00 3.60
❑ 81 Bob Scarpitto 8.00 3.60
❑ 82 Lionel Taylor 12.00 5.50
❑ 83 Jerry Tarr 8.00 3.60
❑ 84 Eldon Danenhauer 8.00 3.60
❑ 85 Goose Gonsoulin 10.00 4.50
❑ 86 Jim Fraser 8.00 3.60
❑ 87 Chuck Gavin 8.00 3.60
❑ 88 Bud McFadin 20.00 5.00
❑ NNO Checklist Card SP ! 375.00 95.00

1990 Fleer

	MINT	NRMT
COMPLETE SET (400)	7.50	3.40
COMMON CARD (1-400)	.04	.02
SEMISTARS	.10	.05
UNLISTED STARS	.25	.11

❑ 1 Harris Barton .04 .02
❑ 2 Chet Brooks .04 .02
❑ 3 Michael Carter .04 .02
❑ 4 Mike Cofer UER .04 .02
(FGA and FGM columns switched)
❑ 5 Roger Craig .10 .05
❑ 6 Kevin Fagan RC .04 .02
❑ 7 Charles Haley UER .10 .05
(Fumble recoveries should be 2 in '86 and 5 career, card says 1 and 4)
❑ 8 Pierce Holt RC .04 .02
❑ 9 Ronnie Lott .10 .05
❑ 10A Joe Montana ERR 1.25 .55
(31,054 TD's)
❑ 10B Joe Montana COR 1.25 .55
(216 TD's)
❑ 11 Bubba Paris .04 .02
❑ 12 Tom Rathman .04 .02
❑ 13 Jerry Rice .75 .35
❑ 14 John Taylor .25 .11
❑ 15 Keena Turner .04 .02
❑ 16 Michael Walter .04 .02

❑ 17 Steve Young .50 .23
❑ 18 Steve Atwater .04 .02
❑ 19 Tyrone Braxton .04 .02
❑ 20 Michael Brooks RC .04 .02
❑ 21 John Elway 1.25 .55
❑ 22 Simon Fletcher .04 .02
❑ 23 Bobby Humphrey .04 .02
❑ 24 Mark Jackson .04 .02
❑ 25 Vance Johnson .04 .02
❑ 26 Greg Kragen .04 .02
❑ 27 Ken Lanier RC .04 .02
❑ 28 Karl Mecklenburg .04 .02
❑ 29 Orson Mobley RC .04 .02
❑ 30 Steve Sewell .04 .02
❑ 31 Dennis Smith .04 .02
❑ 32 David Treadwell .04 .02
❑ 33 Flipper Anderson .04 .02
❑ 34 Greg Bell .04 .02
❑ 35 Henry Ellard .10 .05
❑ 36 Jim Everett .10 .05
❑ 37 Jerry Gray .04 .02
❑ 38 Kevin Greene .25 .11
❑ 39 Pete Holohan .04 .02
❑ 40 LeRoy Irvin .04 .02
❑ 41 Mike Lansford .04 .02
❑ 42 Buford McGee RC .04 .02
❑ 43 Tom Newberry .04 .02
❑ 44 Vince Newsome RC .04 .02
❑ 45 Jackie Slater .04 .02
❑ 46 Mike Wilcher .04 .02
❑ 47 Matt Bahr .04 .02
❑ 48 Brian Brennan .04 .02
❑ 49 Thane Gash RC .04 .02
❑ 50 Mike Johnson .04 .02
❑ 51 Bernie Kosar .10 .05
❑ 52 Reggie Langhorne .04 .02
❑ 53 Tim Manoa .04 .02
❑ 54 Clay Matthews .10 .05
❑ 55 Eric Metcalf .25 .11
❑ 56 Frank Minnifield .04 .02
❑ 57 Gregg Rakoczy RC UER .04 .02
(First line of text
calls him Greg)
❑ 58 Webster Slaughter .10 .05
❑ 59 Bryan Wagner .04 .02
❑ 60 Felix Wright .04 .02
❑ 61 Raul Allegre .04 .02
❑ 62 Ottis Anderson UER .10 .05
(Stats say 9.317 yards,
should be 9,317)
❑ 63 Carl Banks .04 .02
❑ 64 Mark Bavaro .04 .02
❑ 65 Maurice Carthon .04 .02
❑ 66 Mark Collins UER .04 .02
(Total fumble recoveries
should be 5, not 3)
❑ 67 Jeff Hostetler RC .25 .11
❑ 68 Erik Howard .04 .02
❑ 69 Pepper Johnson .04 .02
❑ 70 Sean Landeta .04 .02
❑ 71 Lionel Manuel .04 .02
❑ 72 Leonard Marshall .04 .02
❑ 73 Dave Meggett .10 .05
❑ 74 Bart Oates .04 .02
❑ 75 Doug Riesenberg RC .04 .02
❑ 76 Phil Simms .10 .05
❑ 77 Lawrence Taylor .25 .11
❑ 78 Eric Allen .04 .02
❑ 79 Jerome Brown .04 .02
❑ 80 Keith Byars .04 .02
❑ 81 Cris Carter .50 .23
❑ 82A Byron Evans RC ERR .15 .07
(should be 83
according to checklist)
❑ 82B Randall Cunningham .15 .07
❑ 83A Ron Heller RC ERR .15 .07
(should be 84
according to checklist)
❑ 83B Byron Evans COR RC .15 .07
❑ 84 Ron Heller RC .04 .02
❑ 85 Terry Hoage RC .04 .02
❑ 86 Keith Jackson .10 .05
❑ 87 Seth Joyner .10 .05
❑ 88 Mike Quick .04 .02
❑ 89 Mike Schad .04 .02
❑ 90 Clyde Simmons .04 .02
❑ 91 John Teltschik .04 .02
❑ 92 Anthony Toney .04 .02
❑ 93 Reggie White .25 .11
❑ 94 Ray Berry .04 .02
❑ 95 Joey Browner .04 .02
❑ 96 Anthony Carter .10 .05
❑ 97 Chris Doleman .04 .02
❑ 98 Rick Fenney .04 .02
❑ 99 Rich Gannon RC .75 .35
❑ 100 Hassan Jones .04 .02
❑ 101 Steve Jordan .04 .02
❑ 102 Rich Karlis .04 .02
❑ 103 Andre Ware RC .25 .11
❑ 104 Kirk Lowdermilk .04 .02
❑ 105 Keith Millard .04 .02
❑ 106 Scott Studwell .04 .02
❑ 107 Herschel Walker .10 .05
❑ 108 Wade Wilson .10 .05
❑ 109 Gary Zimmerman .04 .02
❑ 110 Don Beebe .10 .05
❑ 111 Cornelius Bennett .10 .05
❑ 112 Shane Conlan .04 .02
❑ 113 Jim Kelly .25 .11
❑ 114 Scott Norwood UER .04 .02
(FGA and FGM columns
switched)
❑ 115 Mark Kelso UER .04 .02
(Some stats added wrong
on back)
❑ 116 Larry Kinnebrew .04 .02
❑ 117 Pete Metzelaars .04 .02
❑ 118 Scott Radecic .04 .02
❑ 119 Andre Reed .25 .11
❑ 120 Jim Ritcher RC .04 .02
❑ 121 Bruce Smith .25 .11
❑ 122 Leonard Smith .04 .02
❑ 123 Art Still .04 .02
❑ 124 Thurman Thomas .25 .11
❑ 125 Steve Brown .04 .02
❑ 126 Ray Childress .04 .02
❑ 127 Ernest Givins .10 .05
❑ 128 John Grimsley .04 .02
❑ 129 Alonzo Highsmith .04 .02
❑ 130 Drew Hill .04 .02
❑ 131 Bruce Matthews .10 .05
❑ 132 Johnny Meads .04 .02
❑ 133 Warren Moon UER .25 .11
(186 completions in '87
and 1341 career, should
be 184 and 1339)
❑ 134 Mike Munchak .04 .02
❑ 135 Mike Rozier .04 .02
❑ 136 Dean Steinkuhler .04 .02
❑ 137 Lorenzo White .04 .02
❑ 138 Tony Zendejas .04 .02
❑ 139 Gary Anderson K .04 .02
❑ 140 Bubby Brister .04 .02
❑ 141 Thomas Everett .04 .02
❑ 142 Derek Hill .04 .02
❑ 143 Merril Hoge .04 .02
❑ 144 Tim Johnson .04 .02
❑ 145 Louis Lipps .10 .05
❑ 146 David Little .04 .02
❑ 147 Greg Lloyd .25 .11
❑ 148 Mike Mularkey .04 .02
❑ 149 John Rienstra RC .04 .02
❑ 150 Gerald Williams RC UER .04 .02
(Tackles and fumble
recovery headers
are switched)
❑ 151 Keith Willis UER .04 .02
(Tackles and fumble
recovery headers
are switched)
❑ 152 Rod Woodson .25 .11
❑ 153 Tim Worley .04 .02
❑ 154 Gary Clark .25 .11
❑ 155 Darryl Grant .04 .02
❑ 156 Darrell Green .10 .05
❑ 157 Joe Jacoby .04 .02
❑ 158 Jim Lachey .04 .02
❑ 159 Chip Lohmiller .04 .02
❑ 160 Charles Mann .04 .02
❑ 161 Wilber Marshall .04 .02
❑ 162 Mark May .04 .02
❑ 163 Ralf Mojsiejenko .04 .02
❑ 164 Art Monk UER .10 .05
(No explanation of
How Acquired)
❑ 165 Gerald Riggs .10 .05
❑ 166 Mark Rypien .10 .05
❑ 167 Ricky Sanders .04 .02
❑ 168 Don Warren .04 .02
❑ 169 Robert Brown RC .04 .02
❑ 170 Blair Bush .04 .02
❑ 171 Brent Fullwood .04 .02
❑ 172 Tim Harris .04 .02
❑ 173 Chris Jacke .04 .02
❑ 174 Perry Kemp .04 .02
❑ 175 Don Majkowski .04 .02
❑ 176 Tony Mandarich .04 .02
❑ 177 Mark Murphy .04 .02
❑ 178 Brian Noble .04 .02
❑ 179 Ken Ruettgers .04 .02
❑ 180 Sterling Sharpe .25 .11
❑ 181 Ed West RC .04 .02
❑ 182 Keith Woodside .04 .02
❑ 183 Morten Andersen .04 .02
❑ 184 Stan Brock .04 .02
❑ 185 Jim Dombrowski RC .04 .02
❑ 186 John Fourcade .04 .02
❑ 187 Bobby Hebert .04 .02
❑ 188 Craig Heyward .10 .05
❑ 189 Dalton Hilliard .04 .02
❑ 190 Rickey Jackson .10 .05
❑ 191 Buford Jordan .04 .02
❑ 192 Eric Martin .04 .02
❑ 193 Robert Massey .04 .02
❑ 194 Sam Mills .10 .05
❑ 195 Pat Swilling .10 .05
❑ 196 Jim Wilks .04 .02
❑ 197 John Alt RC .04 .02
❑ 198 Walker Lee Ashley .04 .02
❑ 199 Steve DeBerg .04 .02
❑ 200 Leonard Griffin .04 .02
❑ 201 Albert Lewis .04 .02
❑ 202 Nick Lowery .04 .02
❑ 203 Bill Maas .04 .02
❑ 204 Pete Mandley .04 .02
❑ 205 Chris Martin RC .04 .02
❑ 206 Christian Okoye .04 .02
❑ 207 Stephone Paige .04 .02
❑ 208 Kevin Porter RC .04 .02
❑ 209 Derrick Thomas .25 .11
❑ 210 Lewis Billups .04 .02
❑ 211 James Brooks .10 .05
❑ 212 Jason Buck .04 .02
❑ 213 Rickey Dixon RC .04 .02
❑ 214 Boomer Esiason .10 .05
❑ 215 David Fulcher .04 .02
❑ 216 Rodney Holman .04 .02
❑ 217 Lee Johnson .04 .02
❑ 218 Tim Krumrie .04 .02
❑ 219 Tim McGee .04 .02
❑ 220 Anthony Munoz .10 .05
❑ 221 Bruce Reimers RC .04 .02
❑ 222 Leon White .04 .02
❑ 223 Ickey Woods .04 .02
❑ 224 Harvey Armstrong RC .04 .02
❑ 225 Michael Ball RC .04 .02
❑ 226 Chip Banks .04 .02
❑ 227 Pat Beach .04 .02
❑ 228 Duane Bickett .04 .02
❑ 229 Bill Brooks .04 .02
❑ 230 Jon Hand .04 .02
❑ 231 Andre Rison .25 .11
❑ 232 Rohn Stark .04 .02
❑ 233 Donnell Thompson .04 .02
❑ 234 Jack Trudeau .04 .02
❑ 235 Clarence Verdin .04 .02
❑ 236 Mark Clayton .10 .05
❑ 237 Jeff Cross .04 .02
❑ 238 Jeff Dellenbach RC .04 .02
❑ 239 Mark Duper .10 .05
❑ 240 Ferrell Edmunds .04 .02
❑ 241 Hugh Green UER .04 .02
(Back says Traded '86,
should be '85)
❑ 242 E.J. Junior .04 .02
❑ 243 Marc Logan .04 .02
❑ 244 Dan Marino 1.25 .55
❑ 245 John Offerdahl .04 .02

❑ 246 Reggie Roby .04 .02
❑ 247 Sammie Smith .04 .02
❑ 248 Pete Stoyanovich .04 .02
❑ 249 Marcus Allen .25 .11
❑ 250 Eddie Anderson RC .04 .02
❑ 251 Steve Beuerlein .10 .05
❑ 252 Mike Dyal .04 .02
❑ 253 Mervyn Fernandez .04 .02
❑ 254 Bob Golic .04 .02
❑ 255 Mike Harden .04 .02
❑ 256 Bo Jackson .25 .11
❑ 257 Howie Long UER .10 .05
(Born Sommerville, should be Somerville)
❑ 258 Don Mosebar .04 .02
❑ 259 Jay Schroeder .04 .02
❑ 260 Steve Smith .04 .02
❑ 261 Greg Townsend .04 .02
❑ 262 Lionel Washington .04 .02
❑ 263 Brian Blades .10 .05
❑ 264 Jeff Bryant .04 .02
❑ 265 Grant Feasel RC .04 .02
❑ 266 Jacob Green .04 .02
❑ 267 James Jefferson .04 .02
❑ 268 Norm Johnson .04 .02
❑ 269 Dave Krieg UER .10 .05
(Misspelled Kreig on card front)
❑ 270 Travis McNeal .04 .02
❑ 271 Joe Nash .04 .02
❑ 272 Rufus Porter .04 .02
❑ 273 Kelly Stouffer .04 .02
❑ 274 John L. Williams .04 .02
❑ 275 Jim Arnold .04 .02
❑ 276 Jerry Ball .04 .02
❑ 277 Bennie Blades .04 .02
❑ 278 Lomas Brown .04 .02
❑ 279 Michael Cofer .04 .02
❑ 280 Bob Gagliano .04 .02
❑ 281 Richard Johnson .04 .02
❑ 282 Eddie Murray .04 .02
❑ 283 Rodney Peete .10 .05
❑ 284 Barry Sanders 2.50 1.10
❑ 285 Eric Sanders .04 .02
❑ 286 Chris Spielman .25 .11
❑ 287 Eric Williams RC .04 .02
❑ 288 Neal Anderson .10 .05
❑ 289A Kevin Butler ERR/ERR .25 .11
(Listed as Punter on front and back)
❑ 289B Kevin Butler COR/ERR .25 .11
(Listed as Placekicker on front and Punter on back)
❑ 289C Kevin Butler ERR/COR .25 .11
(Listed as Punter on front and Placekicker on back)
❑ 289D Kevin Butler COR/COR .04 .02
(Listed as Placekicker on front and back)
❑ 290 Jim Covert .04 .02
❑ 291 Richard Dent .10 .05
❑ 292 Dennis Gentry .04 .02
❑ 293 Jim Harbaugh .25 .11
❑ 294 Jay Hilgenberg .04 .02
❑ 295 Vestee Jackson .04 .02
❑ 296 Steve McMichael .10 .05
❑ 297 Ron Morris .04 .02
❑ 298 Brad Muster .04 .02
❑ 299 Mike Singletary .10 .05
❑ 300 James Thornton UER .04 .02
(Missing birthdate)
❑ 301 Mike Tomczak .10 .05
❑ 302 Keith Van Horne .04 .02
❑ 303 Chris Bahr UER .04 .02
('86 FGA and FGM stats are reversed)
❑ 304 Martin Bayless RC .04 .02
❑ 305 Marion Butts .10 .05
❑ 306 Gill Byrd .04 .02
❑ 307 Arthur Cox .04 .02
❑ 308 Burt Grossman .04 .02
❑ 309 Jamie Holland .04 .02
❑ 310 Jim McMahon .10 .05
❑ 311 Anthony Miller .25 .11
❑ 312 Leslie O'Neal .10 .05
❑ 313 Billy Ray Smith .04 .02
❑ 314 Tim Spencer .04 .02
❑ 315 Broderick Thompson RC .04 .02
❑ 316 Lee Williams .04 .02
❑ 317 Bruce Armstrong .04 .02
❑ 318 Tim Goad RC .04 .02
❑ 319 Steve Grogan .10 .05
❑ 320 Roland James .04 .02
❑ 321 Cedric Jones .04 .02
❑ 322 Fred Marion .04 .02
❑ 323 Stanley Morgan .04 .02
❑ 324 Robert Perryman .04 .02
(Back says Robert, front says Bob)
❑ 325 Johnny Rembert .04 .02
❑ 326 Ed Reynolds .04 .02
❑ 327 Kenneth Sims .04 .02
❑ 328 John Stephens .04 .02
❑ 329 Danny Villa RC .04 .02
❑ 330 Robert Awalt .04 .02
❑ 331 Anthony Bell .04 .02
❑ 332 Rich Camarillo .04 .02
❑ 333 Earl Ferrell .04 .02
❑ 334 Roy Green .10 .05
❑ 335 Gary Hogeboom .04 .02
❑ 336 Cedric Mack .04 .02
❑ 337 Freddie Joe Nunn .04 .02
❑ 338 Luis Sharpe .04 .02
❑ 339 Vai Sikahema .04 .02
❑ 340 J.T. Smith .04 .02
❑ 341 Tom Tupa RC .04 .02
❑ 342 Percy Snow RC .04 .02
❑ 343 Mark Carrier WR .25 .11
❑ 344 Randy Grimes .04 .02
❑ 345 Paul Gruber .04 .02
❑ 346 Ron Hall .04 .02
❑ 347 Jeff George RC 1.00 .45
❑ 348 Bruce Hill UER .04 .02
(Photo on back is actually Jerry Bell)
❑ 349 William Howard UER .04 .02
(Yards rec. says 284, should be 285)
❑ 350 Donald Igwebuike .04 .02
❑ 351 Chris Mohr RC .04 .02
❑ 352 Winston Moss RC .04 .02
❑ 353 Ricky Reynolds .04 .02
❑ 354 Mark Robinson .04 .02
❑ 355 Lars Tate .04 .02
❑ 356 Vinny Testaverde .10 .05
❑ 357 Broderick Thomas .04 .02
❑ 358 Troy Benson .04 .02
❑ 359 Jeff Criswell RC .04 .02
❑ 360 Tony Eason .04 .02
❑ 361 James Hasty .04 .02
❑ 362 Johnny Hector .04 .02
❑ 363 Bobby Humphery UER .04 .02
(Photo on back is actually Bobby Humphrey)
❑ 364 Pat Leahy .04 .02
❑ 365 Erik McMillan .04 .02
❑ 366 Freeman McNeil .04 .02
❑ 367 Ken O'Brien .04 .02
❑ 368 Ron Stallworth .04 .02
❑ 369 Al Toon .10 .05
❑ 370 Blair Thomas RC .04 .02
❑ 371 Aundray Bruce .04 .02
❑ 372 Tony Casillas .04 .02
❑ 373 Shawn Collins .04 .02
❑ 374 Evan Cooper .04 .02
❑ 375 Bill Fralic .04 .02
❑ 376 Scott Funhage .04 .02
❑ 377 Mike Gann .04 .02
❑ 378 Ron Heller .04 .02
❑ 379 Keith Jones .04 .02
❑ 380 Mike Kenn .04 .02
❑ 381 Chris Miller .25 .11
❑ 382 Deion Sanders UER .50 .23
(Stats say no '89 fumble recoveries, should be 1)
❑ 383 John Settle .04 .02
❑ 384 Troy Aikman .75 .35
❑ 385 Bill Bates .10 .05
❑ 386 Willie Broughton .04 .02
❑ 387 Steve Folsom .04 .02
❑ 388 Ray Horton UER .04 .02
(Extra line after career totals)
❑ 389 Michael Irvin .25 .11
❑ 390 Jim Jeffcoat .04 .02
❑ 391 Eugene Lockhart .04 .02
❑ 392 Kelvin Martin RC .04 .02
❑ 393 Nate Newton .10 .05
❑ 394 Mike Saxon UER .04 .02
(6 career blocked kicks, stats add up to 4)
❑ 395 Derrick Shepard .04 .02
❑ 396 Steve Walsh UER .10 .05
(Yards Passing 50.2; Percentage and yards data are switched)
❑ 397 Super Bowl MVP's .75 .35
(Jerry Rice and Joe Montana) HOR
❑ 398 Checklist Card UER .04 .02
(Card 103 not listed)
❑ 399 Checklist Card UER .04 .02
(Bengals misspelled)
❑ 400 Checklist Card .04 .02

1990 Fleer All-Pros

	MINT	NRMT
COMPLETE SET (25)	7.50	3.40
RANDOM INSERTS IN PACKS		

❑ 1 Joe Montana 1.50 .70
❑ 2 Jerry Rice UER 1.00 .45
(photo on front is actually John Taylor)
❑ 3 Keith Jackson .10 .05
❑ 4 Barry Sanders 3.00 1.35
❑ 5 Christian Okoye .05 .02
❑ 6 Tom Newberry .05 .02
❑ 7 Jim Covert .05 .02
❑ 8 Anthony Munoz .10 .05
❑ 9 Mike Munchak .05 .02
❑ 10 Jay Hilgenberg .05 .02
❑ 11 Chris Doleman .05 .02
❑ 12 Keith Millard .05 .02
❑ 13 Derrick Thomas .30 .14
❑ 14 Lawrence Taylor .30 .14
❑ 15 Karl Mecklenburg .05 .02
❑ 16 Reggie White .30 .14
❑ 17 Tim Harris .05 .02
❑ 18 David Fulcher .05 .02
❑ 19 Ronnie Lott .10 .05
❑ 20 Eric Allen .05 .02
❑ 21 Steve Atwater .05 .02
❑ 22 Rich Camarillo .05 .02
❑ 23 Morten Andersen .05 .02
❑ 24 Andre Reed .30 .14
❑ 25 Rod Woodson .30 .14

1990 Fleer Update

	MINT	NRMT
COMP.FACT.SET (120)	25.00	11.00
COMMON CARD (U1-U120)	.08	.04
SEMISTARS	.15	.07
UNLISTED STARS	.30	.14

❑ U1 Albert Bentley .08 .04
❑ U2 Dean Biasucci .08 .04
❑ U3 Ray Donaldson .08 .04
❑ U4 Jeff George 5.00 2.20
❑ U5 Ray Agnew RC .08 .04
❑ U6 Greg McMurtry RC .08 .04
❑ U7 Chris Singleton RC .08 .04
❑ U8 James Francis RC .08 .04
❑ U9 Harold Green RC .30 .14
❑ U10 John Elliott .08 .04
❑ U11 Rodney Hampton RC 1.00 .45
❑ U12 Gary Reasons .08 .04
❑ U13 Lewis Tillman .08 .04
❑ U14 Everson Walls .08 .04
❑ U15 David Alexander RC .08 .04
❑ U16 Jim McMahon .15 .07
❑ U17 Ben Smith RC .08 .04
❑ U18 Andre Waters .08 .04
❑ U19 Calvin Williams RC .15 .07
❑ U20 Earnest Byner .08 .04
❑ U21 Andre Collins RC .08 .04
❑ U22 Russ Grimm .08 .04
❑ U23 Stan Humphries RC .30 .14
❑ U24 Martin Mayhew RC .08 .04
❑ U25 Barry Foster RC .30 .14
❑ U26 Eric Green RC .15 .07
❑ U27 Tunch Ilkin .08 .04
❑ U28 Hardy Nickerson .15 .07
❑ U29 Jerrol Williams .08 .04
❑ U30 Mike Baab .08 .04
❑ U31 Leroy Hoard RC 1.00 .45
❑ U32 Eddie Johnson RC .08 .04
❑ U33 William Fuller .15 .07
❑ U34 Haywood Jeffires RC .30 .14
❑ U35 Don Maggs RC .08 .04
❑ U36 Allen Pinkett .08 .04
❑ U37 Robert Awalt .08 .04
❑ U38 Dennis McKinnon .08 .04
❑ U39 Ken Norton RC .15 .07
❑ U40 Emmitt Smith RC 25.00 11.00
❑ U41 Alexander Wright RC .08 .04
❑ U42 Eric Hill .08 .04
❑ U43 Johnny Johnson RC .15 .07
❑ U44 Timm Rosenbach .08 .04
❑ U45 Anthony Thompson RC .08 .04
❑ U46 Dexter Carter RC .08 .04
❑ U47 Eric Davis RC UER .15 .07
(Listed as WR on front, DB on back)
❑ U48 Keith DeLong .08 .04
❑ U49 Brent Jones RC .30 .14
❑ U50 Darryl Pollard RC .08 .04
❑ U51 Steve Wallace RC .30 .14
❑ U52 Bern Brostek RC .08 .04
❑ U53 Aaron Cox .08 .04
❑ U54 Cleveland Gary .08 .04
❑ U55 Fred Strickland RC .08 .04
❑ U56 Pat Terrell RC .08 .04
❑ U57 Steve Broussard RC .08 .04
❑ U58 Scott Case .08 .04
❑ U59 Brian Jordan RC .15 .07
❑ U60 Andre Rison .30 .14
❑ U61 Kevin Haverdink .08 .04
❑ U62 Rueben Mayes .08 .04
❑ U63 Steve Walsh .15 .07
❑ U64 Greg Bell .08 .04
❑ U65 Tim Brown .30 .14
❑ U66 Willie Gault .15 .07
❑ U67 Vance Mueller RC .08 .04
❑ U68 Bill Pickel .08 .04
❑ U69 Aaron Wallace RC .08 .04
❑ U70 Glenn Parker RC .08 .04
❑ U71 Frank Reich .30 .14
❑ U72 Leon Seals RC .08 .04
❑ U73 Darryl Talley .08 .04
❑ U74 Brad Baxter RC .08 .04
❑ U75 Jeff Criswell .08 .04
❑ U76 Jeff Lageman .08 .04
❑ U77 Rob Moore RC 4.00 1.80
❑ U78 Blair Thomas .15 .07
❑ U79 Louis Oliver .08 .04
❑ U80 Tony Paige .08 .04
❑ U81 Richmond Webb RC .08 .04
❑ U82 Robert Blackmon RC .08 .04
❑ U83 Derrick Fenner RC .08 .04
❑ U84 Andy Heck .08 .04
❑ U85 Cortez Kennedy RC .30 .14
❑ U86 Terry Wooden RC .08 .04
❑ U87 Jeff Donaldson .08 .04
❑ U88 Tim Grunhard RC .08 .04
❑ U89 Emile Harry RC .08 .04
❑ U90 Dan Saleaumua .08 .04
❑ U91 Percy Snow .08 .04
❑ U92 Andre Ware .30 .14
❑ U93 Darrell Fullington RC .08 .04
❑ U94 Mike Merriweather .08 .04
❑ U95 Henry Thomas .08 .04
❑ U96 Robert Brown .08 .04
❑ U97 LeRoy Butler RC .30 .14
❑ U98 Anthony Dilweg .08 .04
❑ U99 Darrell Thompson RC .08 .04
❑ U100 Keith Woodside .08 .04
❑ U101 Gary Plummer .08 .04
❑ U102 Junior Seau RC 4.00 1.80
❑ U103 Billy Joe Tolliver .08 .04
❑ U104 Mark Vlasic .08 .04
❑ U105 Gary Anderson RB .08 .04
❑ U106 Ian Beckles RC .08 .04
❑ U107 Reggie Cobb RC .08 .04
❑ U108 Keith McCants RC .08 .04
❑ U109 Mark Bortz RC .08 .04
❑ U110 Maury Buford .08 .04
❑ U111 Mark Carrier DB RC .30 .14
❑ U112 Dan Hampton .15 .07
❑ U113 William Perry .15 .07
❑ U114 Ron Rivera .08 .04
❑ U115 Lemuel Stinson .08 .04
❑ U116 Melvin Bratton RC .08 .04
❑ U117 Gary Kubiak RC .08 .04
❑ U118 Alton Montgomery RC .08 .04
❑ U119 Ricky Nattiel .08 .04
❑ U120 Checklist 1-132 .08 .04

1991 Fleer

	MINT	NRMT
COMPLETE SET (432)	8.00	3.60
COMMON CARD (1-432)	.04	.02
SEMISTARS	.10	.05
UNLISTED STARS	.25	.11

❑ 1 Shane Conlan .04 .02
❑ 2 John Davis RC .04 .02
❑ 3 Kent Hull .04 .02
❑ 4 James Lofton .10 .05
❑ 5 Keith McKeller .04 .02
❑ 6 Scott Norwood .04 .02
❑ 7 Nate Odomes .04 .02
❑ 8 Andre Reed .10 .05
❑ 9 Jim Ritcher .04 .02
❑ 10 Leon Seals .04 .02
❑ 11 Bruce Smith .25 .11
❑ 12 Leonard Smith .04 .02
❑ 13 Steve Tasker .10 .05
❑ 14 Thurman Thomas .25 .11
❑ 15 Lewis Billups .04 .02
❑ 16 James Brooks .10 .05
❑ 17 Eddie Brown .04 .02
❑ 18 Carl Carter .04 .02
❑ 19 Boomer Esiason .10 .05
❑ 20 James Francis .04 .02
❑ 21 David Fulcher .04 .02
❑ 22 Harold Green .10 .05
❑ 23 Rodney Holman .04 .02
❑ 24 Bruce Kozerski .04 .02
❑ 25 Tim McGee .04 .02
❑ 26 Anthony Munoz .10 .05
❑ 27 Bruce Reimers .04 .02
❑ 28 Ickey Woods .04 .02
❑ 29 Carl Zander .04 .02
❑ 30 Mike Baab .04 .02
❑ 31 Brian Brennan .04 .02
❑ 32 Rob Burnett RC .04 .02
❑ 33 Paul Farren .04 .02
❑ 34 Thane Gash .04 .02
❑ 35 David Grayson .04 .02
❑ 36 Mike Johnson .04 .02
❑ 37 Reggie Langhorne .04 .02
❑ 38 Kevin Mack .04 .02
❑ 39 Eric Metcalf .10 .05
❑ 40 Frank Minnifield .04 .02
❑ 41 Gregg Rakoczy .04 .02
❑ 42 Felix Wright .04 .02
❑ 43 Steve Atwater .04 .02
❑ 44 Michael Brooks .04 .02
❑ 45 John Elway 1.25 .55
❑ 46 Simon Fletcher .04 .02
❑ 47 Bobby Humphrey .04 .02
❑ 48 Mark Jackson .04 .02
❑ 49 Keith Kartz .04 .02
❑ 50 Clarence Kay .04 .02
❑ 51 Greg Kragen .04 .02
❑ 52 Karl Mecklenburg .04 .02
❑ 53 Warren Powers .04 .02
❑ 54 Dennis Smith .04 .02
❑ 55 Jim Szymanski .04 .02
❑ 56 David Treadwell .04 .02
❑ 57 Michael Young .04 .02
❑ 58 Ray Childress .04 .02
❑ 59 Curtis Duncan .04 .02
❑ 60 William Fuller .10 .05
❑ 61 Ernest Givins .10 .05
❑ 62 Drew Hill .04 .02
❑ 63 Haywood Jeffires .10 .05
❑ 64 Richard Johnson .04 .02
❑ 65 Sean Jones .10 .05
❑ 66 Don Maggs .04 .02
❑ 67 Bruce Matthews .10 .05
❑ 68 Johnny Meads .04 .02
❑ 69 Greg Montgomery .04 .02
❑ 70 Warren Moon .25 .11
❑ 71 Mike Munchak .04 .02
❑ 72 Allen Pinkett .04 .02
❑ 73 Lorenzo White .04 .02
❑ 74 Pat Beach .04 .02
❑ 75 Albert Bentley .04 .02
❑ 76 Dean Biasucci .04 .02
❑ 77 Duane Bickett .04 .02
❑ 78 Bill Brooks .04 .02
❑ 79 Sam Clancy .04 .02
❑ 80 Ray Donaldson .04 .02
❑ 81 Jeff George .25 .11
❑ 82 Alan Grant .04 .02
❑ 83 Jessie Hester .04 .02
❑ 84 Jeff Herrod .04 .02
❑ 85 Rohn Stark .04 .02
❑ 86 Jack Trudeau .04 .02
❑ 87 Clarence Verdin .04 .02
❑ 88 John Alt .04 .02
❑ 89 Steve DeBerg .04 .02
❑ 90 Tim Grunhard .04 .02
❑ 91 Dino Hackett .04 .02

❑ 92 Jonathan Hayes .04 .02
❑ 93 Albert Lewis .04 .02
❑ 94 Nick Lowery .04 .02
❑ 95 Bill Maas UER .04 .02
(Back photo actually David Szott)
❑ 96 Christian Okoye .04 .02
❑ 97 Stephone Paige .04 .02
❑ 98 Kevin Porter .04 .02
❑ 99 David Szott .04 .02
❑ 100 Derrick Thomas .25 .11
❑ 101 Barry Word .04 .02
❑ 102 Marcus Allen .25 .11
❑ 103 Thomas Benson .04 .02
❑ 104 Tim Brown .25 .11
❑ 105 Riki Ellison .04 .02
❑ 106 Mervyn Fernandez .04 .02
❑ 107 Willie Gault .10 .05
❑ 108 Bob Golic .04 .02
❑ 109 Ethan Horton .04 .02
❑ 110 Bo Jackson .10 .05
❑ 111 Howie Long .10 .05
❑ 112 Don Mosebar .04 .02
❑ 113 Jerry Robinson .04 .02
❑ 114 Jay Schroeder .04 .02
❑ 115 Steve Smith .04 .02
❑ 116 Greg Townsend .04 .02
❑ 117 Steve Wisniewski .04 .02
❑ 118 Mark Clayton .10 .05
❑ 119 Mark Duper .10 .05
❑ 120 Ferrell Edmunds .04 .02
❑ 121 Hugh Green .04 .02
❑ 122 David Griggs .04 .02
❑ 123 Jim C. Jensen .04 .02
❑ 124 Dan Marino 1.25 .55
❑ 125 Tim McKyer .04 .02
❑ 126 John Offerdahl .04 .02
❑ 127 Louis Oliver .04 .02
❑ 128 Tony Paige .04 .02
❑ 129 Reggie Roby .04 .02
❑ 130 Keith Sims .04 .02
❑ 131 Sammie Smith .04 .02
❑ 132 Pete Stoyanovich .04 .02
❑ 133 Richmond Webb .04 .02
❑ 134 Bruce Armstrong .04 .02
❑ 135 Vincent Brown .04 .02
❑ 136 Hart Lee Dykes .04 .02
❑ 137 Irving Fryar .10 .05
❑ 138 Tim Goad .04 .02
❑ 139 Tommy Hodson .04 .02
❑ 140 Maurice Hurst .04 .02
❑ 141 Ronnie Lippett .04 .02
❑ 142 Greg McMurtry .04 .02
❑ 143 Ed Reynolds .04 .02
❑ 144 John Stephens .04 .02
❑ 145 Andre Tippett .04 .02
❑ 146 Danny Villa .04 .02
(Old photo wearing retired number)
❑ 147 Brad Baxter .04 .02
❑ 148 Kyle Clifton .04 .02
❑ 149 Jeff Criswell .04 .02
❑ 150 James Hasty .04 .02
❑ 151 Jeff Lageman .04 .02
❑ 152 Pat Leahy .04 .02
❑ 153 Rob Moore .25 .11
❑ 154 Al Toon .10 .05
❑ 155 Gary Anderson K .04 .02
❑ 156 Bubby Brister .04 .02
❑ 157 Chris Calloway .04 .02
❑ 158 Donald Evans .04 .02
❑ 159 Eric Green .04 .02
❑ 160 Bryan Hinkle .04 .02
❑ 161 Merril Hoge .04 .02
❑ 162 Tunch Ilkin .04 .02
❑ 163 Louis Lipps .04 .02
❑ 164 David Little .04 .02
❑ 165 Mike Mularkey .04 .02
❑ 166 Gerald Williams .04 .02
❑ 167 Warren Williams .04 .02
❑ 168 Rod Woodson .25 .11
❑ 169 Tim Worley .04 .02
❑ 170 Martin Bayless .04 .02
❑ 171 Marion Butts .10 .05
❑ 172 Gill Byrd .04 .02
❑ 173 Frank Cornish .04 .02
❑ 174 Arthur Cox .04 .02
❑ 175 Burt Grossman .04 .02
❑ 176 Anthony Miller .10 .05
❑ 177 Leslie O'Neal .10 .05
❑ 178 Gary Plummer .04 .02
❑ 179 Junior Seau .25 .11
❑ 180 Billy Joe Tolliver .04 .02
❑ 181 Derrick Walker RC .04 .02
❑ 182 Lee Williams .04 .02
❑ 183 Robert Blackmon .04 .02
❑ 184 Brian Blades .10 .05
❑ 185 Grant Feasel .04 .02
❑ 186 Derrick Fenner .04 .02
❑ 187 Andy Heck .04 .02
❑ 188 Norm Johnson .04 .02
❑ 189 Tommy Kane .04 .02
❑ 190 Cortez Kennedy .25 .11
❑ 191 Dave Krieg .10 .05
❑ 192 Travis McNeal .04 .02
❑ 193 Eugene Robinson .04 .02
❑ 194 Chris Warren .25 .11
❑ 195 John L. Williams .04 .02
❑ 196 Steve Broussard .04 .02
❑ 197 Scott Case .04 .02
❑ 198 Shawn Collins .04 .02
❑ 199 Darion Conner UER .04 .02
(Player on back 8 is not Conner 56)
❑ 200 Tory Epps .04 .02
❑ 201 Bill Fralic .04 .02
❑ 202 Michael Haynes .25 .11
❑ 203 Chris Hinton .04 .02
❑ 204 Keith Jones .04 .02
❑ 205 Brian Jordan .10 .05
❑ 206 Mike Kenn .04 .02
❑ 207 Chris Miller .10 .05
❑ 208 Andre Rison .10 .05
❑ 209 Mike Rozier .04 .02
❑ 210 Deion Sanders .40 .18
❑ 211 Gary Wilkins .04 .02
❑ 212 Neal Anderson .10 .05
❑ 213 Trace Armstrong .04 .02
❑ 214 Mark Bortz .04 .02
❑ 215 Kevin Butler .04 .02
❑ 216 Mark Carrier DB .10 .05
❑ 217 Wendell Davis .04 .02
❑ 218 Richard Dent .10 .05
❑ 219 Dennis Gentry .04 .02
❑ 220 Jim Harbaugh .25 .11
❑ 221 Jay Hilgenberg .04 .02
❑ 222 Steve McMichael .10 .05
❑ 223 Ron Morris .04 .02
❑ 224 Brad Muster .04 .02
❑ 225 Mike Singletary .10 .05
❑ 226 James Thornton .04 .02
❑ 227 Tommie Agee .04 .02
❑ 228 Troy Aikman .75 .35
❑ 229 Jack Del Rio .04 .02
❑ 230 Issiac Holt .04 .02
❑ 231 Ray Horton .04 .02
❑ 232 Jim Jeffcoat .04 .02
❑ 233 Eugene Lockhart .04 .02
❑ 234 Kelvin Martin .04 .02
❑ 235 Nate Newton .10 .05
❑ 236 Mike Saxon .04 .02
❑ 237 Emmitt Smith 2.00 .90
❑ 238A Daniel Stubbs .10 .05
(Danny on back)
❑ 238B Danny Stubbs .10 .05
(Daniel on back)
❑ 239 Jim Arnold .04 .02
❑ 240 Jerry Ball .04 .02
❑ 241 Bennie Blades .04 .02
❑ 242 Lomas Brown .04 .02
❑ 243 Robert Clark .04 .02
❑ 244 Mike Cofer .04 .02
❑ 245 Mel Gray .10 .05
❑ 246 Rodney Peete .10 .05
❑ 247 Barry Sanders 1.50 .70
❑ 248 Andre Ware .10 .05
❑ 249 Matt Brock RC .04 .02
❑ 250 Robert Brown .04 .02
❑ 251 Anthony Dilweg .04 .02
❑ 252 Johnny Holland .04 .02
❑ 253 Tim Harris .04 .02
❑ 254 Chris Jacke .04 .02
❑ 255 Perry Kemp .04 .02
❑ 256 Don Majkowski UER .04 .02
(1990 attempts should be 264, not 265)
❑ 257 Tony Mandarich .04 .02
❑ 258 Mark Murphy .04 .02
❑ 259 Brian Noble .04 .02
❑ 260 Jeff Query .04 .02
❑ 261 Sterling Sharpe .25 .11
❑ 262 Ed West .04 .02
❑ 263 Keith Woodside .04 .02
❑ 264 Flipper Anderson .04 .02
❑ 265 Aaron Cox .04 .02
❑ 266 Henry Ellard .10 .05
❑ 267 Jim Everett .10 .05
❑ 268 Cleveland Gary .04 .02
❑ 269 Kevin Greene .25 .11
❑ 270 Pete Holohan .04 .02
❑ 271 Mike Lansford .04 .02
❑ 272 Duval Love RC .04 .02
❑ 273 Buford McGee .04 .02
❑ 274 Tom Newberry .04 .02
❑ 275 Jackie Slater .04 .02
❑ 276 Frank Stams .04 .02
❑ 277 Alfred Anderson .04 .02
❑ 278 Joey Browner .04 .02
❑ 279 Anthony Carter .10 .05
❑ 280 Chris Doleman .04 .02
❑ 281 Rick Fenney .04 .02
❑ 282 Rich Gannon .04 .02
❑ 283 Hassan Jones .04 .02
❑ 284 Steve Jordan .04 .02
❑ 285 Carl Lee .04 .02
❑ 286 Randall McDaniel .04 .02
❑ 287 Keith Millard .04 .02
❑ 288 Herschel Walker .10 .05
❑ 289 Wade Wilson .10 .05
❑ 290 Gary Zimmerman .04 .02
❑ 291 Morten Andersen .04 .02
❑ 292 Jim Dombrowski .04 .02
❑ 293 Gill Fenerty .04 .02
❑ 294 Craig Heyward .10 .05
❑ 295 Dalton Hilliard .04 .02
❑ 296 Rickey Jackson .04 .02
❑ 297 Vaughan Johnson .04 .02
❑ 298 Eric Martin .04 .02
❑ 299 Robert Massey .04 .02
❑ 300 Rueben Mayes .04 .02
❑ 301 Sam Mills .04 .02
❑ 302 Brett Perriman .25 .11
❑ 303 Pat Swilling .10 .05
❑ 304 Steve Walsh .04 .02
❑ 305 Ottis Anderson .10 .05
❑ 306 Matt Bahr .04 .02
❑ 307 Mark Bavaro .04 .02
❑ 308 Maurice Carthon .04 .02
❑ 309 Mark Collins .04 .02
❑ 310 John Elliott .04 .02
❑ 311 Rodney Hampton .25 .11
❑ 312 Jeff Hostetler .10 .05
❑ 313 Erik Howard .04 .02
❑ 314 Pepper Johnson .04 .02
❑ 315 Sean Landeta .04 .02
❑ 316 Dave Meggett .10 .05
❑ 317 Bart Oates .04 .02
❑ 318 Phil Simms .10 .05
❑ 319 Lawrence Taylor .25 .11
❑ 320 Reyna Thompson .04 .02
❑ 321 Everson Walls .04 .02
❑ 322 Eric Allen .04 .02
❑ 323 Fred Barnett .25 .11
❑ 324 Jerome Brown .04 .02
❑ 325 Keith Byars .04 .02
❑ 326 Randall Cunningham .25 .11
❑ 327 Byron Evans .04 .02
❑ 328 Ron Heller .04 .02
❑ 329 Keith Jackson .10 .05
❑ 330 Seth Joyner .10 .05
❑ 331 Heath Sherman .04 .02
❑ 332 Clyde Simmons .04 .02
❑ 333 Ben Smith .04 .02
❑ 334 Anthony Toney .04 .02
❑ 335 Andre Waters .04 .02
❑ 336 Reggie White .25 .11
❑ 337 Calvin Williams .10 .05
❑ 338 Anthony Bell .04 .02

❑ 339 Rich Camarillo .04 .02
❑ 340 Roy Green .04 .02
❑ 341 Tim Jorden RC .04 .02
❑ 342 Cedric Mack .04 .02
❑ 343 Dexter Manley .04 .02
❑ 344 Freddie Joe Nunn .04 .02
❑ 345 Ricky Proehl .04 .02
❑ 346 Tootie Robbins .04 .02
❑ 347 Timm Rosenbach .04 .02
❑ 348 Luis Sharpe .04 .02
❑ 349 Vai Sikahema .04 .02
❑ 350 Anthony Thompson .04 .02
❑ 351 Lonnie Young .04 .02
❑ 352 Dexter Carter .04 .02
❑ 353 Mike Cofer .04 .02
❑ 354 Kevin Fagan .04 .02
❑ 355 Don Griffin .04 .02
❑ 356 Charles Haley UER .10 .05
(Total fumbles should be 6, not 5)
❑ 357 Pierce Holt .04 .02
❑ 358 Brent Jones .25 .11
❑ 359 Guy McIntyre .04 .02
❑ 360 Joe Montana 1.25 .55
❑ 361 Darryl Pollard .04 .02
❑ 362 Tom Rathman .04 .02
❑ 363 Jerry Rice .75 .35
❑ 364 Bill Romanowski .04 .02
❑ 365 John Taylor .10 .05
❑ 366 Steve Wallace UER .10 .05
Listed as a DL on front of card
❑ 367 Steve Young .75 .35
❑ 368 Gary Anderson RB .04 .02
❑ 369 Ian Beckles .04 .02
❑ 370 Mark Carrier WR .25 .11
❑ 371 Reggie Cobb .04 .02
❑ 372 Reuben Davis .04 .02
❑ 373 Randy Grimes .04 .02
❑ 374 Wayne Haddix .04 .02
❑ 375 Ron Hall .04 .02
❑ 376 Harry Hamilton .04 .02
❑ 377 Bruce Hill .04 .02
❑ 378 Keith McCants .04 .02
❑ 379 Bruce Perkins .04 .02
❑ 380 Vinny Testaverde UER .10 .05
(Misspelled Vinnie on card front)
❑ 381 Broderick Thomas .04 .02
❑ 382 Jeff Bostic .04 .02
❑ 383 Earnest Byner .04 .02
❑ 384 Gary Clark .25 .11
❑ 385 Darryl Grant .04 .02
❑ 386 Darrell Green .04 .02
❑ 387 Stan Humphries .25 .11
❑ 388 Jim Lachey .04 .02
❑ 389 Charles Mann .04 .02
❑ 390 Wilber Marshall .04 .02
❑ 391 Art Monk .10 .05
❑ 392 Gerald Riggs .04 .02
❑ 393 Mark Rypien .10 .05
❑ 394 Ricky Sanders .04 .02
❑ 395 Don Warren .04 .02
❑ 396 Bruce Smith HIT .10 .05
❑ 397 Reggie White HIT .10 .05
❑ 398 Lawrence Taylor HIT .10 .05
❑ 399 David Fulcher HIT .04 .02
❑ 400 Derrick Thomas HIT .10 .05
❑ 401 Mark Carrier DB HIT .04 .02
❑ 402 Mike Singletary HIT .10 .05
❑ 403 Charles Haley HIT .04 .02
❑ 404 Jeff Cross HIT .04 .02
❑ 405 Leslie O'Neal HIT .10 .05
❑ 406 Tim Harris HIT .04 .02
❑ 407 Steve Atwater HIT .04 .02
❑ 408 Joe Montana LL UER .50 .23
(4th on yardage list, not 3rd)
❑ 409 Randall Cunningham LL .10 .05
❑ 410 Warren Moon LL .10 .05
❑ 411 Andre Rison LL UER .10 .05
(Card incorrectly numbered as 412 and Michigan State misspelled as Stage)
❑ 412 Haywood Jeffires LL .10 .05
(See number 411)
❑ 413 Stephone Paige LL .04 .02
❑ 414 Phil Simms LL .10 .05
❑ 415 Barry Sanders LL .60 .25
❑ 416 Bo Jackson LL .10 .05
❑ 417 Thurman Thomas LL .10 .05
❑ 418 Emmitt Smith LL 1.00 .45
❑ 419 John L. Williams LL .04 .02
❑ 420 Nick Bell RP RC .04 .02
❑ 421 Eric Bieniemy RP RC .04 .02
❑ 422 Mike Dumas RP RC UER .04 .02
(Returned interception vs. Purdue, not Michigan State)
❑ 423 Russell Maryland RP RC .25 .11
❑ 424 Derek Russell RP RC .04 .02
❑ 425 Chris Smith RP RC UER .04 .02
(Bengals misspelled as Bengels)
❑ 426 Mike Stonebreaker RP .04 .02
❑ 427 Pat Tyrance RP .04 .02
❑ 428 Kenny Walker RP RC .04 .02
(How Acquired has a different style)
❑ 429 Checklist 1-108 UER .04 .02
(David Grayson misspelled as Graysor)
❑ 430 Checklist 109-216 .04 .02
❑ 431 Checklist 217-324 .04 .02
❑ 432 Checklist 325-432 .04 .02

1991 Fleer All-Pros

	MINT	NRMT
COMPLETE SET (26)	5.00	2.20
RANDOM INSERTS IN PACKS		

❑ 1 Andre Reed UER .10 .05
(Caught 81 passes in '89, should say 88 passes)
❑ 2 Bobby Humphrey .05 .02
❑ 3 Kent Hull .05 .02
❑ 4 Mark Bortz .05 .02
❑ 5 Bruce Smith .25 .11
❑ 6 Greg Townsend .05 .02
❑ 7 Ray Childress .05 .02
❑ 8 Andre Rison .10 .05
❑ 9 Barry Sanders 1.50 .70
❑ 10 Bo Jackson .10 .05
❑ 11 Neal Anderson .10 .05
❑ 12 Keith Jackson .10 .05
❑ 13 Derrick Thomas .25 .11
❑ 14 John Offerdahl .05 .02
❑ 15 Lawrence Taylor .25 .11
❑ 16 Darrell Green .05 .02
❑ 17 Mark Carrier DB UER .10 .05
(No period in last sentence of bio)
❑ 18 David Fulcher UER .05 .02
(Bill Wyche, should be Sam)
❑ 19 Joe Montana 1.25 .55
❑ 20 Jerry Rice .75 .35
❑ 21 Charles Haley .10 .05
❑ 22 Mike Singletary .10 .05
❑ 23 Nick Lowery .05 .02
❑ 24 Jim Lachey UER .05 .02
(Acquired by trade in '87, not '88)
❑ 25 Anthony Munoz .10 .05
❑ 26 Thurman Thomas .25 .11

1991 Fleer Pro-Vision

	MINT	NRMT
COMPLETE SET (10)	5.00	2.20
RANDOM INSERTS IN PACKS		

❑ 1 Joe Montana 1.50 .70
❑ 2 Barry Sanders 2.00 .90
❑ 3 Lawrence Taylor .30 .14
❑ 4 Mike Singletary .10 .05
❑ 5 Dan Marino 1.50 .70
❑ 6 Bo Jackson .10 .05
❑ 7 Randall Cunningham .30 .14
❑ 8 Bruce Smith .30 .14
❑ 9 Derrick Thomas .30 .14
❑ 10 Howie Long .10 .05

1992 Fleer

	MINT	NRMT
COMPLETE SET (480)	10.00	4.50
COMMON CARD (1-480)	.04	.02
SEMISTARS	.10	.05
UNLISTED STARS	.25	.11
COMPLETE RYPIEN SET (12)	3.00	1.35
RYPIEN CERT.AUTOGRAPH	40.00	18.00
RYPIEN: RANDOM INSERTS IN PACKS		
COMMON RYP.SEND (13-15)	.50	.23

❑ 1 Steve Broussard .04 .02
❑ 2 Rick Bryan .04 .02
❑ 3 Scott Case .04 .02
❑ 4 Tory Epps .04 .02
❑ 5 Bill Fralic .04 .02
❑ 6 Moe Gardner .04 .02
❑ 7 Michael Haynes .10 .05
❑ 8 Chris Hinton .04 .02
❑ 9 Brian Jordan .10 .05
❑ 10 Mike Kenn .04 .02
❑ 11 Tim McKyer .04 .02
❑ 12 Chris Miller .10 .05
❑ 13 Erric Pegram .10 .05
❑ 14 Mike Pritchard .10 .05
❑ 15 Andre Rison .10 .05
❑ 16 Jessie Tuggle .04 .02
❑ 17 Carlton Bailey RC .10 .05
❑ 18 Howard Ballard .04 .02

❑ 19 Don Beebe .04 .02
❑ 20 Cornelius Bennett .10 .05
❑ 21 Shane Conlan .04 .02
❑ 22 Kent Hull .04 .02
❑ 23 Mark Kelso .04 .02
❑ 24 James Lofton .10 .05
❑ 25 Keith McKeller .04 .02
❑ 26 Scott Norwood .04 .02
❑ 27 Nate Odomes .04 .02
❑ 28 Frank Reich .10 .05
❑ 29 Jim Ritcher .04 .02
❑ 30 Leon Seals .04 .02
❑ 31 Darryl Talley .04 .02
❑ 32 Steve Tasker .10 .05
❑ 33 Thurman Thomas .25 .11
❑ 34 Will Wolford .04 .02
❑ 35 Neal Anderson .04 .02
❑ 36 Trace Armstrong .04 .02
❑ 37 Mark Carrier DB .04 .02
❑ 38 Richard Dent .10 .05
❑ 39 Shaun Gayle .04 .02
❑ 40 Jim Harbaugh .25 .11
❑ 41 Jay Hilgenberg .04 .02
❑ 42 Darren Lewis .04 .02
❑ 43 Steve McMichael .10 .05
❑ 44 Brad Muster .04 .02
❑ 45 William Perry .10 .05
❑ 46 John Roper .04 .02
❑ 47 Lemuel Stinson .04 .02
❑ 48 Stan Thomas .04 .02
❑ 49 Keith Van Horne .04 .02
❑ 50 Tom Waddle .04 .02
❑ 51 Donnell Woolford .04 .02
❑ 52 Chris Zorich .10 .05
❑ 53 Eddie Brown .04 .02
❑ 54 James Francis .04 .02
❑ 55 David Fulcher .04 .02
❑ 56 David Grant .04 .02
❑ 57 Harold Green .04 .02
❑ 58 Rodney Holman .04 .02
❑ 59 Lee Johnson .04 .02
❑ 60 Tim Krumrie .04 .02
❑ 61 Anthony Munoz .10 .05
❑ 62 Joe Walter RC .04 .02
❑ 63 Mike Baab .04 .02
❑ 64 Stephen Braggs .04 .02
❑ 65 Richard Brown RC .04 .02
❑ 66 Dan Fike .04 .02
❑ 67 Scott Galbraith RC .04 .02
❑ 68 Randy Hilliard RC .04 .02
❑ 69 Michael Jackson .10 .05
❑ 70 Tony Jones .04 .02
❑ 71 Ed King .04 .02
❑ 72 Kevin Mack .04 .02
❑ 73 Clay Matthews .10 .05
❑ 74 Eric Metcalf .10 .05
❑ 75 Vince Newsome .04 .02
❑ 76 John Rienstra .04 .02
❑ 77 Steve Beuerlein .04 .02
❑ 78 Larry Brown DB .04 .02
❑ 79 Tony Casillas .04 .02
❑ 80 Alvin Harper .10 .05
❑ 81 Issiac Holt .04 .02
❑ 82 Ray Horton .04 .02
❑ 83 Michael Irvin .25 .11
❑ 84 Daryl Johnston .25 .11
❑ 85 Kelvin Martin .04 .02
❑ 86 Nate Newton .10 .05
❑ 87 Ken Norton .25 .11
❑ 88 Jay Novacek .10 .05
❑ 89 Emmitt Smith 1.50 .70
❑ 90 Vinson Smith RC .04 .02
❑ 91 Mark Stepnoski .10 .05
❑ 92 Steve Atwater .04 .02
❑ 93 Mike Croel .04 .02
❑ 94 John Elway 1.25 .55
❑ 95 Simon Fletcher .04 .02
❑ 96 Gaston Green .04 .02
❑ 97 Mark Jackson .04 .02
❑ 98 Keith Kartz .04 .02
❑ 99 Greg Kragen .04 .02
❑ 100 Greg Lewis .04 .02
❑ 101 Karl Mecklenburg .04 .02
❑ 102 Derek Russell .04 .02
❑ 103 Steve Sewell .04 .02
❑ 104 Dennis Smith .04 .02
❑ 105 David Treadwell .04 .02
❑ 106 Kenny Walker .04 .02
❑ 107 Doug Widell .04 .02
❑ 108 Michael Young .04 .02
❑ 109 Jerry Ball .04 .02
❑ 110 Bennie Blades .04 .02
❑ 111 Lomas Brown .04 .02
❑ 112 Scott Conover RC .04 .02
❑ 113 Ray Crockett .04 .02
❑ 114 Mike Farr .04 .02
❑ 115 Mel Gray .10 .05
❑ 116 Willie Green .04 .02
❑ 117 Tracy Hayworth RC .04 .02
❑ 118 Erik Kramer .10 .05
❑ 119 Herman Moore .75 .35
❑ 120 Dan Owens .04 .02
❑ 121 Rodney Peete .10 .05
❑ 122 Brett Perriman .25 .11
❑ 123 Barry Sanders 1.50 .70
❑ 124 Chris Spielman .10 .05
❑ 125 Marc Spindler .04 .02
❑ 126 Tony Bennett .04 .02
❑ 127 Matt Brock .04 .02
❑ 128 LeRoy Butler .04 .02
❑ 129 Johnny Holland .04 .02
❑ 130 Perry Kemp .04 .02
❑ 131 Don Majkowski .04 .02
❑ 132 Mark Murphy .04 .02
❑ 133 Brian Noble .04 .02
❑ 134 Bryce Paup .25 .11
❑ 135 Sterling Sharpe .25 .11
❑ 136 Scott Stephen .04 .02
❑ 137 Darrell Thompson .04 .02
❑ 138 Mike Tomczak .04 .02
❑ 139 Esera Tuaolo .04 .02
❑ 140 Keith Woodside .04 .02
❑ 141 Ray Childress .04 .02
❑ 142 Cris Dishman .04 .02
❑ 143 Curtis Duncan .04 .02
❑ 144 John Flannery .04 .02
❑ 145 William Fuller .10 .05
❑ 146 Ernest Givins .10 .05
❑ 147 Haywood Jeffires .10 .05
❑ 148 Sean Jones .10 .05
❑ 149 Lamar Lathon .04 .02
❑ 150 Bruce Matthews .04 .02
❑ 151 Bubba McDowell .04 .02
❑ 152 Johnny Meads .04 .02
❑ 153 Warren Moon .25 .11
❑ 154 Mike Munchak .04 .02
❑ 155 Al Smith .04 .02
❑ 156 Doug Smith .04 .02
❑ 157 Lorenzo White .04 .02
❑ 158 Michael Ball .04 .02
❑ 159 Chip Banks .04 .02
❑ 160 Duane Bickett .04 .02
❑ 161 Bill Brooks .04 .02
❑ 162 Ken Clark .04 .02
❑ 163 Jon Hand .04 .02
❑ 164 Jeff Herrod .04 .02
❑ 165 Jessie Hester .04 .02
❑ 166 Scott Radecic .04 .02
❑ 167 Rohn Stark .04 .02
❑ 168 Clarence Verdin .04 .02
❑ 169 John Alt .04 .02
❑ 170 Tim Barnett .04 .02
❑ 171 Tim Grunhard .04 .02
❑ 172 Dino Hackett .04 .02
❑ 173 Jonathan Hayes .04 .02
❑ 174 Bill Maas .04 .02
❑ 175 Chris Martin .04 .02
❑ 176 Christian Okoye .04 .02
❑ 177 Stephone Paige .04 .02
❑ 178 Jayice Pearson RC .04 .02
❑ 179 Kevin Porter .04 .02
❑ 180 Kevin Ross .04 .02
❑ 181 Dan Saleaumua .04 .02
❑ 182 Tracy Simien RC .04 .02
❑ 183 Neil Smith .25 .11
❑ 184 Derrick Thomas .25 .11
❑ 185 Robb Thomas .04 .02
❑ 186 Mark Vlasic .04 .02
❑ 187 Barry Word .04 .02
❑ 188 Marcus Allen .25 .11
❑ 189 Eddie Anderson .04 .02
❑ 190 Nick Bell .04 .02
❑ 191 Tim Brown .25 .11
❑ 192 Scott Davis .04 .02
❑ 193 Riki Ellison .04 .02
❑ 194 Mervyn Fernandez .04 .02
❑ 195 Willie Gault .10 .05
❑ 196 Jeff Gossett .04 .02
❑ 197 Ethan Horton .04 .02
❑ 198 Jeff Jaeger .04 .02
❑ 199 Howie Long .10 .05
❑ 200 Ronnie Lott .10 .05
❑ 201 Todd Marinovich .04 .02
❑ 202 Don Mosebar .04 .02
❑ 203 Jay Schroeder .04 .02
❑ 204 Greg Townsend .04 .02
❑ 205 Lionel Washington .04 .02
❑ 206 Steve Wisniewski .04 .02
❑ 207 Flipper Anderson .04 .02
❑ 208 Bern Brostek .04 .02
❑ 209 Robert Delpino .04 .02
❑ 210 Henry Ellard .10 .05
❑ 211 Jim Everett .10 .05
❑ 212 Cleveland Gary .04 .02
❑ 213 Kevin Greene .25 .11
❑ 214 Darryl Henley .04 .02
❑ 215 Damone Johnson .04 .02
❑ 216 Larry Kelm .04 .02
❑ 217 Todd Lyght .04 .02
❑ 218 Jackie Slater .04 .02
❑ 219 Michael Stewart .04 .02
❑ 220 Pat Terrell UER .04 .02
(1991 stats have 74 tackles, text has 64)
❑ 221 Robert Young .04 .02
❑ 222 Mark Clayton .10 .05
❑ 223 Bryan Cox .10 .05
❑ 224 Aaron Craver .04 .02
❑ 225 Jeff Cross .04 .02
❑ 226 Mark Duper .04 .02
❑ 227 Harry Galbreath .04 .02
❑ 228 David Griggs .04 .02
❑ 229 Mark Higgs .04 .02
❑ 230 Vestee Jackson .04 .02
❑ 231 John Offerdahl .04 .02
❑ 232 Louis Oliver .04 .02
❑ 233 Tony Paige .04 .02
❑ 234 Reggie Roby .04 .02
❑ 235 Sammie Smith .04 .02
❑ 236 Pete Stoyanovich .04 .02
❑ 237 Richmond Webb .04 .02
❑ 238 Terry Allen .25 .11
❑ 239 Ray Berry .04 .02
❑ 240 Joey Browner .04 .02
❑ 241 Anthony Carter .10 .05
❑ 242 Cris Carter .50 .23
❑ 243 Chris Doleman .04 .02
❑ 244 Rich Gannon .04 .02
❑ 245 Tim Irwin .04 .02
❑ 246 Steve Jordan .04 .02
❑ 247 Carl Lee .04 .02
❑ 248 Randall McDaniel .04 .02
❑ 249 Mike Merriweather .04 .02
❑ 250 Harry Newsome .04 .02
❑ 251 John Randle .10 .05
❑ 252 Henry Thomas .04 .02
❑ 253 Herschel Walker .10 .05
❑ 254 Ray Agnew .04 .02
❑ 255 Bruce Armstrong .04 .02
❑ 256 Vincent Brown .04 .02
❑ 257 Marv Cook .04 .02
❑ 258 Irving Fryar .10 .05
❑ 259 Pat Harlow .04 .02
❑ 260 Tommy Hodson .04 .02
❑ 261 Maurice Hurst .04 .02
❑ 262 Ronnie Lippett .04 .02
❑ 263 Eugene Lockhart .04 .02
❑ 264 Greg McMurtry .04 .02
❑ 265 Hugh Millen .04 .02
❑ 266 Leonard Russell .10 .05
❑ 267 Andre Tippett .04 .02
❑ 268 Brent Williams .04 .02
❑ 269 Morten Andersen .04 .02
❑ 270 Gene Atkins .04 .02
❑ 271 Wesley Carroll .04 .02
❑ 272 Jim Dombrowski .04 .02
❑ 273 Quinn Early .10 .05
❑ 274 Gill Fenerty .04 .02

❑ 275 Bobby Hebert .04 .02
❑ 276 Joel Hilgenberg .04 .02
❑ 277 Rickey Jackson .04 .02
❑ 278 Vaughan Johnson .04 .02
❑ 279 Eric Martin .04 .02
❑ 280 Brett Maxie .04 .02
❑ 281 Fred McAfee RC .04 .02
❑ 282 Sam Mills .04 .02
❑ 283 Pat Swilling .10 .05
❑ 284 Floyd Turner .04 .02
❑ 285 Steve Walsh .04 .02
❑ 286 Frank Warren .04 .02
❑ 287 Stephen Baker .04 .02
❑ 288 Maurice Carthon .04 .02
❑ 289 Mark Collins .04 .02
❑ 290 John Elliott .04 .02
❑ 291 Myron Guyton .04 .02
❑ 292 Rodney Hampton .25 .11
❑ 293 Jeff Hostetler .10 .05
❑ 294 Mark Ingram .04 .02
❑ 295 Pepper Johnson .04 .02
❑ 296 Sean Landeta .04 .02
❑ 297 Leonard Marshall .04 .02
❑ 298 Dave Meggett .10 .05
❑ 299 Bart Oates .04 .02
❑ 300 Phil Simms .10 .05
❑ 301 Reyna Thompson .04 .02
❑ 302 Lewis Tillman .04 .02
❑ 303 Brad Baxter .04 .02
❑ 304 Kyle Clifton .04 .02
❑ 305 James Hasty .04 .02
❑ 306 Joe Kelly .04 .02
❑ 307 Jeff Lageman .04 .02
❑ 308 Mo Lewis .04 .02
❑ 309 Erik McMillan .04 .02
❑ 310 Rob Moore .10 .05
❑ 311 Tony Stargell .04 .02
❑ 312 Jim Sweeney .04 .02
❑ 313 Marvin Washington .04 .02
❑ 314 Lonnie Young .04 .02
❑ 315 Eric Allen .04 .02
❑ 316 Fred Barnett .25 .11
❑ 317 Jerome Brown .04 .02
❑ 318 Keith Byars .04 .02
❑ 319 Wes Hopkins .04 .02
❑ 320 Keith Jackson .10 .05
❑ 321 James Joseph .04 .02
❑ 322 Seth Joyner .10 .05
❑ 323 Jeff Kemp .04 .02
❑ 324 Roger Ruzek .04 .02
❑ 325 Clyde Simmons .04 .02
❑ 326 William Thomas .04 .02
❑ 327 Reggie White .25 .11
❑ 328 Calvin Williams .10 .05
❑ 329 Rich Camarillo .04 .02
❑ 330 Ken Harvey .04 .02
❑ 331 Eric Hill .04 .02
❑ 332 Johnny Johnson .04 .02
❑ 333 Ernie Jones .04 .02
❑ 334 Tim Jorden .04 .02
❑ 335 Tim McDonald .04 .02
❑ 336 Freddie Joe Nunn .04 .02
❑ 337 Luis Sharpe .04 .02
❑ 338 Eric Swann .10 .05
❑ 339 Aeneas Williams .10 .05
❑ 340 Gary Anderson K .04 .02
❑ 341 Bubby Brister .04 .02
❑ 342 Adrian Cooper .04 .02
❑ 343 Barry Foster .10 .05
❑ 344 Eric Green .04 .02
❑ 345 Bryan Hinkle .04 .02
❑ 346 Tunch Ilkin .04 .02
❑ 347 Carnell Lake .04 .02
❑ 348 Louis Lipps .04 .02
❑ 349 David Little .04 .02
❑ 350 Greg Lloyd .25 .11
❑ 351 Neil O'Donnell .25 .11
❑ 352 Dwight Stone .04 .02
❑ 353 Rod Woodson .25 .11
❑ 354 Rod Bernstine .04 .02
❑ 355 Eric Bieniemy .04 .02
❑ 356 Marion Butts .04 .02
❑ 357 Gill Byrd .04 .02
❑ 358 John Friesz .10 .05
❑ 359 Burt Grossman .04 .02
❑ 360 Courtney Hall .04 .02
❑ 361 Ronnie Harmon .04 .02
❑ 362 Shawn Jefferson .04 .02
❑ 363 Nate Lewis .04 .02
❑ 364 Craig McEwen RC .04 .02
❑ 365 Eric Moten .04 .02
❑ 366 Joe Phillips .04 .02
❑ 367 Gary Plummer .04 .02
❑ 368 Henry Rolling .04 .02
❑ 369 Broderick Thompson .04 .02
❑ 370 Harris Barton .04 .02
❑ 371 Steve Bono RC .25 .11
❑ 372 Todd Bowles .04 .02
❑ 373 Dexter Carter .04 .02
❑ 374 Michael Carter .04 .02
❑ 375 Mike Cofer .04 .02
❑ 376 Keith DeLong .04 .02
❑ 377 Charles Haley .10 .05
❑ 378 Merton Hanks .10 .05
❑ 379 Tim Harris .04 .02
❑ 380 Brent Jones .10 .05
❑ 381 Guy McIntyre .04 .02
❑ 382 Tom Rathman .04 .02
❑ 383 Bill Romanowski .04 .02
❑ 384 Jesse Sapolu .04 .02
❑ 385 John Taylor .10 .05
❑ 386 Steve Young .60 .25
❑ 387 Robert Blackmon .04 .02
❑ 388 Brian Blades .10 .05
❑ 389 Jacob Green .04 .02
❑ 390 Dwayne Harper .04 .02
❑ 391 Andy Heck .04 .02
❑ 392 Tommy Kane .04 .02
❑ 393 John Kasay .04 .02
❑ 394 Cortez Kennedy .10 .05
❑ 395 Bryan Millard .04 .02
❑ 396 Rufus Porter .04 .02
❑ 397 Eugene Robinson .04 .02
❑ 398 John L. Williams .04 .02
❑ 399 Terry Wooden .04 .02
❑ 400 Gary Anderson RB .04 .02
❑ 401 Ian Beckles .04 .02
❑ 402 Mark Carrier WR .10 .05
❑ 403 Reggie Cobb .04 .02
❑ 404 Lawrence Dawsey .10 .05
❑ 405 Ron Hall .04 .02
❑ 406 Keith McCants .04 .02
❑ 407 Charles McRae .04 .02
❑ 408 Tim Newton .04 .02
❑ 409 Jesse Solomon .04 .02
❑ 410 Vinny Testaverde .10 .05
❑ 411 Broderick Thomas .04 .02
❑ 412 Robert Wilson .04 .02
❑ 413 Jeff Bostic .04 .02
❑ 414 Earnest Byner .04 .02
❑ 415 Gary Clark .25 .11
❑ 416 Andre Collins .04 .02
❑ 417 Brad Edwards .04 .02
❑ 418 Kurt Gouveia .04 .02
❑ 419 Darrell Green .04 .02
❑ 420 Joe Jacoby .04 .02
❑ 421 Jim Lachey .04 .02
❑ 422 Chip Lohmiller .04 .02
❑ 423 Charles Mann .04 .02
❑ 424 Wilber Marshall .04 .02
❑ 425 Ron Middleton RC .04 .02
❑ 426 Brian Mitchell .10 .05
❑ 427 Art Monk UER .10 .05
(Born in 1967, should say 1957)
❑ 428 Mark Rypien .04 .02
❑ 429 Ricky Sanders .04 .02
❑ 430 Mark Schlereth RC .04 .02
❑ 431 Fred Stokes .04 .02
❑ 432 Edgar Bennett RC .25 .11
❑ 433 Brian Bollinger RC .04 .02
❑ 434 Joe Bowden RC .04 .02
❑ 435 Terrell Buckley RC .04 .02
❑ 436 Willie Clay RC .04 .02
❑ 437 Steve Gordon RC .04 .02
❑ 438 Keith Hamilton RC .04 .02
❑ 439 Carlos Huerta .04 .02
❑ 440 Matt LaBounty RC .04 .02
❑ 441 Amp Lee RC .04 .02
❑ 442 Ricardo McDonald RC .04 .02
❑ 443 Chris Mims RC .10 .05
❑ 444 Michael Mooney RC .04 .02
❑ 445 Patrick Rowe RC .04 .02
❑ 446 Leon Searcy RC .10 .05
❑ 447 Siran Stacy RC .04 .02
❑ 448 Kevin Turner RC .04 .02
❑ 449 Tommy Vardell RC .10 .05
❑ 450 Bob Whitfield RC .04 .02
❑ 451 Darryl Williams RC .04 .02
❑ 452 Thurman Thomas LL .10 .05
❑ 453 Emmitt Smith LL UER .75 .35
(Thr at start of second paragraph should be the)
❑ 454 Haywood Jeffires LL .04 .02
❑ 455 Michael Irvin LL .10 .05
❑ 456 Mark Clayton LL .04 .02
❑ 457 Barry Sanders LL .60 .25
❑ 458 Pete Stoyanovich LL .04 .02
❑ 459 Chip Lohmiller LL .04 .02
❑ 460 William Fuller LL .04 .02
❑ 461 Pat Swilling LL .04 .02
❑ 462 Ronnie Lott LL .04 .02
❑ 463 Ray Crockett LL .04 .02
❑ 464 Tim McKyer LL .04 .02
❑ 465 Aeneas Williams LL .04 .02
❑ 466 Rod Woodson LL .10 .05
❑ 467 Mel Gray LL .04 .02
❑ 468 Nate Lewis LL .04 .02
❑ 469 Steve Young LL .30 .14
❑ 470 Reggie Roby LL .04 .02
❑ 471 John Elway PV .60 .25
❑ 472 Ronnie Lott PV .04 .02
❑ 473 Art Monk PV UER .04 .02
(Born in 1967, should say 1957)
❑ 474 Warren Moon PV .10 .05
❑ 475 Emmitt Smith PV .75 .35
❑ 476 Thurman Thomas PV .10 .05
❑ 477 Checklist 1-120 .04 .02
❑ 478 Checklist 121-240 .04 .02
❑ 479 Checklist 241-360 .04 .02
❑ 480 Checklist 361-480 .04 .02

1992 Fleer All-Pros

	MINT	NRMT
COMPLETE SET (24)	5.00	2.20
RANDOM INSERTS IN WAX PACKS		

❑ 1 Marv Cook .10 .05
❑ 2 Mike Kenn .10 .05
❑ 3 Steve Wisniewski .10 .05
❑ 4 Jim Ritcher .10 .05
❑ 5 Jim Lachey .10 .05
❑ 6 Michael Irvin .75 .35
❑ 7 Andre Rison .30 .14
❑ 8 Thurman Thomas .75 .35
❑ 9 Barry Sanders 5.00 2.20
❑ 10 Bruce Matthews .10 .05
❑ 11 Mark Rypien .10 .05
❑ 12 Jeff Jaeger .10 .05
❑ 13 Reggie White .75 .35
❑ 14 Clyde Simmons .10 .05
❑ 15 Pat Swilling .30 .14
❑ 16 Sam Mills .10 .05
❑ 17 Ray Childress .10 .05
❑ 18 Jerry Ball .10 .05
❑ 19 Derrick Thomas .75 .35
❑ 20 Darrell Green .10 .05
❑ 21 Ronnie Lott .30 .14

❑ 22 Steve Atwater	.10	.05
❑ 23 Mark Carrier DB	.10	.05
❑ 24 Jeff Gossett	.10	.05

1992 Fleer Rookie Sensations

	MINT	NRMT
COMPLETE SET (20)	10.00	4.50
RANDOM INSERTS IN JUMBO PACKS		

❑ 1 Moe Gardner	.40	.18
❑ 2 Mike Pritchard	1.00	.45
❑ 3 Stan Thomas	.40	.18
❑ 4 Larry Brown DB	.40	.18
❑ 5 Todd Lyght	.40	.18
❑ 6 James Joseph	.40	.18
❑ 7 Aeneas Williams	1.00	.45
❑ 8 Michael Jackson	1.00	.45
❑ 9 Ed King	.40	.18
❑ 10 Mike Croel	.40	.18
❑ 11 Kenny Walker	.40	.18
❑ 12 Tim Barnett	.40	.18
❑ 13 Nick Bell	.40	.18
❑ 14 Todd Marinovich	.40	.18
❑ 15 Leonard Russell	1.00	.45
❑ 16 Pat Harlow	.40	.18
❑ 17 Mo Lewis	.40	.18
❑ 18 John Kasay	.40	.18
❑ 19 Lawrence Dawsey	1.00	.45
❑ 20 Charles McRae	.40	.18

1992 Fleer Team Leaders

	MINT	NRMT
COMPLETE SET (24)	40.00	18.00
COMMON CARD (1-24)	1.00	.45
SEMISTARS	2.50	1.10
UNLISTED STARS	4.00	1.80
ONE TL OR RYPIEN PER RACK PACK		

❑ 1 Chris Miller	2.50	1.10
❑ 2 Neal Anderson	2.50	1.10
❑ 3 Emmitt Smith	10.00	4.50
❑ 4 Chris Spielman	2.50	1.10
❑ 5 Brian Noble	1.00	.45
❑ 6 Jim Everett	2.50	1.10
❑ 7 Joey Browner	1.00	.45
❑ 8 Sam Mills	1.00	.45
❑ 9 Rodney Hampton	4.00	1.80
❑ 10 Reggie White	4.00	1.80
❑ 11 Tim McDonald	1.00	.45
❑ 12 Charles Haley	2.50	1.10
❑ 13 Mark Rypien	2.50	1.10
❑ 14 Cornelius Bennett	2.50	1.10
❑ 15 Clay Matthews	2.50	1.10
❑ 16 John Elway	10.00	4.50
❑ 17 Warren Moon	4.00	1.80
❑ 18 Derrick Thomas	4.00	1.80
❑ 19 Greg Townsend	1.00	.45
❑ 20 Bruce Armstrong	1.00	.45
❑ 21 Brad Baxter	1.00	.45
❑ 22 Rod Woodson	4.00	1.80
❑ 23 Marion Butts	2.50	1.10
❑ 24 Rufus Porter	1.00	.45

1993 Fleer

	MINT	NRMT
COMPLETE SET (500)	20.00	9.00
COMMON CARD (1-500)	.05	.02
SEMISTARS	.10	.05
UNLISTED STARS	.25	.11
COMPLETE S.YOUNG SET (10)	8.00	3.60
STATED ODDS 1:27		
CERT.YOUNG AUTOGRAPH	80.00	36.00
AUTO.STATED ODDS 1:5000		
YOUNG SEND-OFF 11-13	2.00	.90

❑ 1 Dan Saleaumua	.05	.02
❑ 2 Bryan Cox	.05	.02
❑ 3 Dermontti Dawson	.05	.02
❑ 4 Michael Jackson	.10	.05
❑ 5 Calvin Williams	.10	.05
❑ 6 Terry McDaniel	.05	.02
❑ 7 Jack Del Rio	.05	.02
❑ 8 Steve Atwater	.05	.02
❑ 9 Ernie Jones	.05	.02
❑ 10 Brad Muster (Signed with New Orleans Saints)	.05	.02
❑ 11 Harold Green	.05	.02
❑ 12 Eric Bieniemy	.05	.02
❑ 13 Eric Dorsey	.05	.02
❑ 14 Fred Barnett	.10	.05
❑ 15 Cleveland Gary	.05	.02
❑ 16 Darion Conner	.05	.02
❑ 17 Jerry Ball (Traded to Cleveland Browns)	.05	.02
❑ 18 Tony Casillas	.05	.02
❑ 19 Brian Blades	.10	.05
❑ 20 Tony Bennett	.05	.02
❑ 21 Reggie Cobb	.05	.02
❑ 22 Kurt Gouveia	.05	.02
❑ 23 Greg McMurtry	.05	.02
❑ 24 Kyle Clifton	.05	.02
❑ 25 Trace Armstrong	.05	.02
❑ 26 Terry Allen	.25	.11
❑ 27 Steve Bono	.25	.11
❑ 28 Barry Word	.05	.02
❑ 29 Mark Duper	.05	.02
❑ 30 Nate Newton	.10	.05
❑ 31 Will Wolford (Signed with Indianapolis Colts)	.05	.02
❑ 32 Curtis Duncan	.05	.02
❑ 33 Nick Bell	.05	.02
❑ 34 Don Beebe	.05	.02
❑ 35 Mike Croel	.05	.02
❑ 36 Rich Camarillo	.05	.02
❑ 37 Wade Wilson (Signed with New Orleans Saints)	.05	.02
❑ 38 John Taylor	.10	.05
❑ 39 Marion Butts	.05	.02
❑ 40 Rodney Hampton	.25	.11
❑ 41 Seth Joyner	.05	.02
❑ 42 Wilber Marshall	.05	.02
❑ 43 Bobby Hebert (Signed with Atlanta Falcons)	.05	.02
❑ 44 Bennie Blades	.05	.02
❑ 45 Thomas Everett	.05	.02
❑ 46 Ricky Sanders	.05	.02
❑ 47 Matt Brock	.05	.02
❑ 48 Lawrence Dawsey	.05	.02
❑ 49 Brad Edwards	.05	.02
❑ 50 Vincent Brown	.05	.02
❑ 51 Jeff Lageman	.05	.02
❑ 52 Mark Carrier DB	.05	.02
❑ 53 Cris Carter	.50	.23
❑ 54 Brent Jones	.10	.05
❑ 55 Barry Foster	.10	.05
❑ 56 Derrick Thomas	.25	.11
❑ 57 Scott Zolak	.05	.02
❑ 58 Mark Stepnoski	.05	.02
❑ 59 Eric Metcalf	.10	.05
❑ 60 Al Smith	.05	.02
❑ 61 Ronnie Harmon	.05	.02
❑ 62 Cornelius Bennett	.10	.05
❑ 63 Karl Mecklenburg	.05	.02
❑ 64 Chris Chandler	.10	.05
❑ 65 Toi Cook	.05	.02
❑ 66 Tim Krumrie	.05	.02
❑ 67 Gill Byrd	.05	.02
❑ 68 Mark Jackson (Signed with New York Giants)	.05	.02
❑ 69 Tim Harris (Signed with Philadelphia Eagles)	.05	.02
❑ 70 Shane Conlan (Signed with Los Angeles Rams)	.05	.02
❑ 71 Moe Gardner	.05	.02
❑ 72 Lomas Brown	.05	.02
❑ 73 Charles Haley	.10	.05
❑ 74 Mark Rypien	.05	.02
❑ 75 LeRoy Butler	.05	.02
❑ 76 Steve DeBerg	.05	.02
❑ 77 Darrell Green	.05	.02
❑ 78 Marv Cook	.05	.02
❑ 79 Chris Burkett	.05	.02
❑ 80 Richard Dent	.10	.05
❑ 81 Roger Craig	.10	.05
❑ 82 Amp Lee	.05	.02
❑ 83 Eric Green	.05	.02
❑ 84 Willie Davis	.25	.11
❑ 85 Mark Higgs	.05	.02
❑ 86 Carlton Haselrig	.05	.02
❑ 87 Tommy Vardell	.05	.02
❑ 88 Haywood Jeffires	.10	.05
❑ 89 Tim Brown	.25	.11
❑ 90 Randall McDaniel	.05	.02
❑ 91 John Elway	1.50	.70
❑ 92 Ken Harvey	.05	.02
❑ 93 Joel Hilgenberg	.05	.02
❑ 94 Steve Wallace	.05	.02
❑ 95 Stan Humphries	.25	.11
❑ 96 Greg Jackson	.05	.02
❑ 97 Clyde Simmons	.05	.02
❑ 98 Jim Everett	.10	.05
❑ 99 Michael Haynes	.10	.05
❑ 100 Mel Gray	.10	.05
❑ 101 Alvin Harper	.10	.05
❑ 102 Art Monk	.10	.05
❑ 103 Brett Favre	2.00	.90
❑ 104 Keith McCants	.05	.02
❑ 105 Charles Mann	.05	.02
❑ 106 Leonard Russell	.10	.05
❑ 107 Mo Lewis	.05	.02
❑ 108 Shaun Gayle	.05	.02

❑ 109 Chris Doleman .05 .02
❑ 110 Tim McDonald .05 .02
(Signed with
San Francisco 49ers)
❑ 111 Louis Oliver .05 .02
❑ 112 Greg Lloyd .25 .11
❑ 113 Chip Banks .05 .02
❑ 114 Sean Jones .05 .02
❑ 115 Ethan Horton .05 .02
❑ 116 Kenneth Davis .05 .02
❑ 117 Simon Fletcher .05 .02
❑ 118 Johnny Johnson .05 .02
(Traded to
New York Jets)
❑ 119 Vaughan Johnson .05 .02
❑ 120 Derrick Fenner .05 .02
❑ 121 Nate Lewis .05 .02
❑ 122 Pepper Johnson .05 .02
❑ 123 Heath Sherman .05 .02
❑ 124 Darryl Henley .05 .02
❑ 125 Pierce Holt .05 .02
(Signed with
Atlanta Falcons)
❑ 126 Herman Moore .50 .23
❑ 127 Michael Irvin .25 .11
❑ 128 Tommy Kane .05 .02
❑ 129 Jackie Harris .05 .02
❑ 130 Hardy Nickerson .10 .05
(Signed with
Tampa Bay Buccaneers)
❑ 131 Chip Lohmiller .05 .02
❑ 132 Andre Tippett .05 .02
❑ 133 Leonard Marshall .05 .02
(Signed with
New York Jets)
❑ 134 Craig Heyward .10 .05
(Signed with
Chicago Bears)
❑ 135 Anthony Carter .10 .05
❑ 136 Tom Rathman .05 .02
❑ 137 Lorenzo White .05 .02
❑ 138 Nick Lowery .05 .02
❑ 139 John Offerdahl .05 .02
❑ 140 Neil O'Donnell .25 .11
❑ 141 Clarence Verdin .05 .02
❑ 142 Ernest Givins .10 .05
❑ 143 Todd Marinovich .05 .02
❑ 144 Jeff Wright .05 .02
❑ 145 Michael Brooks .05 .02
❑ 146 Freddie Joe Nunn .05 .02
❑ 147 William Perry .10 .05
❑ 148 Daniel Stubbs .05 .02
❑ 149 Morten Andersen .05 .02
❑ 150 Dave Meggett .05 .02
❑ 151 Andre Waters .05 .02
❑ 152 Todd Lyght .05 .02
❑ 153 Chris Miller .10 .05
❑ 154 Rodney Peete .05 .02
❑ 155 Jim Jeffcoat .05 .02
❑ 156 Cortez Kennedy .10 .05
❑ 157 Johnny Holland .05 .02
❑ 158 Ricky Reynolds .05 .02
❑ 159 Kevin Greene .25 .11
(Signed with
Pittsburgh Steelers)
❑ 160 Jeff Herrod .05 .02
❑ 161 Bruce Matthews .05 .02
❑ 162 Anthony Smith .05 .02
❑ 163 Henry Jones .05 .02
❑ 164 Rob Burnett .05 .02
❑ 165 Eric Swann .10 .05
❑ 166 Tom Waddle .05 .02
❑ 167 Alfred Williams .05 .02
❑ 168 Darren Carrington RC .05 .02
❑ 169 Mike Sherrard .05 .02
(Signed with
New York Giants)
❑ 170 Frank Reich .10 .05
❑ 171 Anthony Newman RC .05 .02
❑ 172 Mike Pritchard .10 .05
❑ 173 Andre Ware .05 .02
❑ 174 Daryl Johnston .25 .11
❑ 175 Rufus Porter .05 .02
❑ 176 Reggie White .25 .11
(Signed with
Green Bay Packers)
❑ 177 Charles Mincy RC .05 .02
❑ 178 Pete Stoyanovich .05 .02
❑ 179 Rod Woodson .25 .11
❑ 180 Anthony Johnson .10 .05
❑ 181 Cody Carlson .05 .02
❑ 182 Gaston Green .05 .02
(Traded to
Los Angeles Raiders)
❑ 183 Audray McMillian .05 .02
❑ 184 Mike Johnson .05 .02
❑ 185 Aeneas Williams .05 .02
❑ 186 Jarrod Bunch .05 .02
❑ 187 Dennis Smith .05 .02
❑ 188 Quinn Early .10 .05
❑ 189 James Hasty .05 .02
❑ 190 Darryl Talley .05 .02
❑ 191 Jon Vaughn .05 .02
❑ 192 Andre Rison .10 .05
❑ 193 Kelvin Pritchett .05 .02
❑ 194 Ken Norton Jr. .10 .05
❑ 195 Chris Warren .10 .05
❑ 196 Sterling Sharpe .25 .11
❑ 197 Christian Okoye .05 .02
❑ 198 Richmond Webb .05 .02
❑ 199 James Francis .05 .02
❑ 200 Reggie Langhorne .05 .02
❑ 201 J.J. Birden .05 .02
❑ 202 Aaron Wallace .05 .02
❑ 203 Henry Thomas .05 .02
❑ 204 Clay Matthews .10 .05
❑ 205 Robert Massey .05 .02
❑ 206 Donnell Woolford .05 .02
❑ 207 Ricky Watters .25 .11
❑ 208 Wayne Martin .05 .02
❑ 209 Rob Moore .10 .05
❑ 210 Steve Tasker .10 .05
❑ 211 Jackie Slater .05 .02
❑ 212 Steve Young .75 .35
❑ 213 Barry Sanders 1.50 .70
❑ 214 Jay Novacek .10 .05
❑ 215 Eugene Robinson .05 .02
❑ 216 Duane Bickett .05 .02
❑ 217 Broderick Thomas .05 .02
❑ 218 David Fulcher .05 .02
❑ 219 Rohn Stark .05 .02
❑ 220 Warren Moon .25 .11
❑ 221 Steve Wisniewski .05 .02
❑ 222 Nate Odomes .05 .02
❑ 223 Shannon Sharpe .25 .11
❑ 224 Byron Evans .05 .02
❑ 225 Mark Collins .05 .02
❑ 226 Rod Bernstine .05 .02
(Signed with
Denver Broncos)
❑ 227 Sam Mills .05 .02
❑ 228 Marvin Washington .05 .02
❑ 229 Thurman Thomas .25 .11
❑ 230 Brent Williams .05 .02
❑ 231 Jessie Tuggle .05 .02
❑ 232 Chris Spielman .10 .05
❑ 233 Emmitt Smith 1.50 .70
❑ 234 John L. Williams .05 .02
❑ 235 Jeff Cross .05 .02
❑ 236 Chris Doleman AW .05 .02
❑ 237 John Elway AW .75 .35
❑ 238 Barry Foster AW .05 .02
❑ 239 Cortez Kennedy AW .05 .02
❑ 240 Steve Young AW .40 .18
❑ 241 Barry Foster LL .05 .02
❑ 242 Warren Moon LL .05 .02
❑ 243 Sterling Sharpe LL .05 .02
❑ 244 Emmitt Smith LL .75 .35
❑ 245 Thurman Thomas LL .10 .05
❑ 246 Michael Irvin PV .10 .05
❑ 247 Steve Young PV .40 .18
❑ 248 Barry Foster PV .05 .02
❑ 249 Checklist .05 .02
Teams Atlanta
through Detroit
❑ 250 Checklist .05 .02
Teams Detroit
through Miami
❑ 251 Checklist .05 .02
Teams Minnesota
through Pittsburgh
❑ 252 Checklist .05 .02
Teams Pittsburgh
through Washington
and Specials
❑ 253 Troy Aikman AW .40 .18
❑ 254 Jason Hanson AW .05 .02
❑ 255 Carl Pickens AW .25 .11
❑ 256 Santana Dotson AW .05 .02
❑ 257 Dale Carter AW .05 .02
❑ 258 Clyde Simmons LL .05 .02
❑ 259 Audray McMillian LL .05 .02
❑ 260 Henry Jones LL .05 .02
❑ 261 Deion Sanders LL .25 .11
❑ 262 Haywood Jeffires LL .05 .02
❑ 263 Deion Sanders PV .25 .11
❑ 264 Andre Reed PV .10 .05
❑ 265 Vince Workman .05 .02
(Signed with
Tampa Bay Buccaneers)
❑ 266 Robert Brown .05 .02
❑ 267 Ray Agnew .05 .02
❑ 268 Ronnie Lott .10 .05
(Signed with
New York Jets)
❑ 269 Wesley Carroll .05 .02
❑ 270 John Randle .05 .02
❑ 271 Rodney Culver .05 .02
❑ 272 David Alexander .05 .02
❑ 273 Troy Aikman .75 .35
❑ 274 Bernie Kosar .10 .05
❑ 275 Scott Case .05 .02
❑ 276 Dan McGwire .05 .02
❑ 277 John Alt .05 .02
❑ 278 Dan Marino 1.50 .70
❑ 279 Santana Dotson .10 .05
❑ 280 Johnny Mitchell .05 .02
❑ 281 Alonzo Spellman .05 .02
❑ 282 Adrian Cooper .05 .02
❑ 283 Gary Clark .10 .05
(Signed with
Phoenix Cardinals)
❑ 284 Vance Johnson .05 .02
❑ 285 Eric Martin .05 .02
❑ 286 Jesse Solomon .05 .02
❑ 287 Carl Banks .05 .02
❑ 288 Harris Barton .05 .02
❑ 289 Jim Harbaugh .25 .11
❑ 290 Bubba McDowell .05 .02
❑ 291 Anthony McDowell RC .05 .02
❑ 292 Terrell Buckley .05 .02
❑ 293 Bruce Armstrong .05 .02
❑ 294 Kurt Barber .05 .02
❑ 295 Reginald Jones .05 .02
❑ 296 Steve Jordan .05 .02
❑ 297 Kerry Cash .05 .02
❑ 298 Ray Crockett .05 .02
❑ 299 Keith Byars .05 .02
❑ 300 Russell Maryland .05 .02
❑ 301 Johnny Bailey .05 .02
❑ 302 Vinnie Clark .05 .02
(Traded to
Atlanta Falcons)
❑ 303 Terry Wooden .05 .02
❑ 304 Harvey Williams .10 .05
❑ 305 Marco Coleman .05 .02
❑ 306 Mark Wheeler .05 .02
❑ 307 Greg Townsend .05 .02
❑ 308 Tim McGee .05 .02
(Signed with
Washington Redskins)
❑ 309 Donald Evans .05 .02
❑ 310 Randal Hill .05 .02
❑ 311 Kenny Walker .05 .02
❑ 312 Dalton Hilliard .05 .02
❑ 313 Howard Ballard .05 .02
❑ 314 Phil Simms .10 .05
❑ 315 Jerry Rice 1.00 .45
❑ 316 Courtney Hall .05 .02
❑ 317 Darren Lewis .05 .02
❑ 318 Greg Montgomery .05 .02
❑ 319 Paul Gruber .05 .02
❑ 320 George Koonce RC .05 .02
❑ 321 Eugene Chung .05 .02
❑ 322 Mike Brim .05 .02
❑ 323 Patrick Hunter .05 .02
❑ 324 Todd Scott .05 .02
❑ 325 Steve Emtman .05 .02

❑ 326 Andy Harmon RC .10 .05
❑ 327 Larry Brown DB .05 .02
❑ 328 Chuck Cecil .05 .02
(Signed with
Phoenix Cardinals)
❑ 329 Tim McKyer .05 .02
❑ 330 Jeff Bryant .05 .02
❑ 331 Tim Barnett .05 .02
❑ 332 Irving Fryar .10 .05
(Traded to
Miami Dolphins)
❑ 333 Tyji Armstrong .05 .02
❑ 334 Brad Baxter .05 .02
❑ 335 Shane Collins .05 .02
❑ 336 Jeff Graham .10 .05
❑ 337 Ricky Proehl .05 .02
❑ 338 Tommy Maddox .05 .02
❑ 339 Jim Dombrowski .05 .02
❑ 340 Bill Brooks .05 .02
(Signed with
Buffalo Bills)
❑ 341 Dave Brown RC .25 .11
❑ 342 Eric Davis .05 .02
❑ 343 Leslie O'Neal .10 .05
❑ 344 Jim Morrissey .05 .02
❑ 345 Mike Munchak .05 .02
❑ 346 Ron Hall .05 .02
❑ 347 Brian Noble .05 .02
❑ 348 Chris Singleton .05 .02
❑ 349 Boomer Esiason UER .10 .05
(Signed with
New York Jets)
(Card front notes he was
signed instead of traded)
❑ 350 Ray Roberts .05 .02
❑ 351 Gary Zimmerman .05 .02
❑ 352 Quentin Coryatt .10 .05
❑ 353 Willie Green .05 .02
❑ 354 Randall Cunningham .25 .11
❑ 355 Kevin Smith .10 .05
❑ 356 Michael Dean Perry .10 .05
❑ 357 Tim Green .05 .02
❑ 358 Dwayne Harper .05 .02
❑ 359 Dale Carter .05 .02
❑ 360 Keith Jackson .10 .05
❑ 361 Martin Mayhew .05 .02
(Signed with
Tampa Bay Buccaneers)
❑ 362 Brian Washington .05 .02
❑ 363 Earnest Byner .05 .02
❑ 364 D.J. Johnson .05 .02
❑ 365 Timm Rosenbach .05 .02
❑ 366 Doug Widell .05 .02
❑ 367 Vaughn Dunbar .05 .02
❑ 368 Phil Hansen .05 .02
❑ 369 Mike Fox .05 .02
❑ 370 Dana Hall .05 .02
❑ 371 Junior Seau .25 .11
❑ 372 Steve McMichael .10 .05
❑ 373 Eddie Robinson .05 .02
❑ 374 Milton Mack RC .05 .02
❑ 375 Mike Prior .05 .02
(Signed with
Green Bay Packers)
❑ 376 Jerome Henderson .05 .02
❑ 377 Scott Mersereau .05 .02
❑ 378 Neal Anderson .05 .02
❑ 379 Harry Newsome .05 .02
❑ 380 John Baylor .05 .02
❑ 381 Bill Fralic .05 .02
(Signed with
Detroit Lions)
❑ 382 Mark Bavaro .05 .02
(Signed with
Philadelphia Eagles)
❑ 383 Robert Jones .05 .02
❑ 384 Tyronne Stowe .05 .02
❑ 385 Deion Sanders .50 .23
❑ 386 Robert Blackmon .05 .02
❑ 387 Neil Smith .25 .11
❑ 388 Mark Ingram .05 .02
(Signed with
Miami Dolphins)
❑ 389 Mark Carrier WR .10 .05
(Signed with
Cleveland Browns)
❑ 390 Browning Nagle .05 .02
❑ 391 Ricky Ervins .05 .02
❑ 392 Carnell Lake .05 .02
❑ 393 Luis Sharpe .05 .02
❑ 394 Greg Kragen .05 .02
❑ 395 Tommy Barnhardt .05 .02
❑ 396 Mark Kelso .05 .02
❑ 397 Kent Graham RC .25 .11
❑ 398 Bill Romanowski .05 .02
❑ 399 Anthony Miller .10 .05
❑ 400 John Roper .05 .02
❑ 401 Lamar Rogers .05 .02
❑ 402 Troy Auzenne .05 .02
❑ 403 Webster Slaughter .05 .02
❑ 404 David Brandon .05 .02
❑ 405 Chris Hinton .05 .02
❑ 406 Andy Heck .05 .02
❑ 407 Tracy Simien .05 .02
❑ 408 Troy Vincent .05 .02
❑ 409 Jason Hanson .05 .02
❑ 410 Rod Jones RC .05 .02
❑ 411 Al Noga .05 .02
(Signed with
Washington Redskins)
❑ 412 Ernie Mills .05 .02
❑ 413 Willie Gault .05 .02
❑ 414 Henry Ellard .10 .05
❑ 415 Rickey Jackson .05 .02
❑ 416 Bruce Smith .25 .11
❑ 417 Derek Brown TE .05 .02
❑ 418 Kevin Fagan .05 .02
❑ 419 Gary Plummer .05 .02
❑ 420 Wendell Davis .05 .02
❑ 421 Craig Thompson .05 .02
❑ 422 Wes Hopkins .05 .02
❑ 423 Ray Childress .05 .02
❑ 424 Pat Harlow .05 .02
❑ 425 Howie Long .10 .05
❑ 426 Shane Dronett .05 .02
❑ 427 Sean Salisbury .05 .02
❑ 428 Dwight Hollier RC .05 .02
❑ 429 Brett Perriman .25 .11
❑ 430 Donald Hollas RC .05 .02
❑ 431 Jim Lachey .05 .02
❑ 432 Darren Perry .05 .02
❑ 433 Lionel Washington .05 .02
❑ 434 Sean Gilbert .10 .05
❑ 435 Gene Atkins .05 .02
❑ 436 Jim Kelly .25 .11
❑ 437 Ed McCaffrey .10 .05
❑ 438 Don Griffin .05 .02
❑ 439 Jerrol Williams .05 .02
(Signed with
San Diego Chargers)
❑ 440 Bryce Paup .25 .11
❑ 441 Darryl Williams .05 .02
❑ 442 Vai Sikahema .05 .02
❑ 443 Cris Dishman .05 .02
❑ 444 Kevin Mack .05 .02
❑ 445 Winston Moss .05 .02
❑ 446 Tyrone Braxton .05 .02
❑ 447 Mike Merriweather .05 .02
❑ 448 Tony Paige .05 .02
❑ 449 Robert Porcher .05 .02
❑ 450 Ricardo McDonald .05 .02
❑ 451 Danny Copeland .05 .02
❑ 452 Tony Tolbert .05 .02
❑ 453 Eric Dickerson .10 .05
❑ 454 Flipper Anderson .05 .02
❑ 455 Dave Krieg .10 .05
❑ 456 Brad Lamb RC .05 .02
❑ 457 Bart Oates .05 .02
❑ 458 Guy McIntyre .05 .02
❑ 459 Stanley Richard .05 .02
❑ 460 Edgar Bennett .25 .11
❑ 461 Pat Carter .05 .02
❑ 462 Eric Allen .05 .02
❑ 463 William Fuller .05 .02
❑ 464 James Jones .05 .02
❑ 465 Chester McGlockton .10 .05
❑ 466 Charles Dimry .05 .02
❑ 467 Tim Grunhard .05 .02
❑ 468 Jarvis Williams .05 .02
❑ 469 Tracy Scroggins .05 .02
❑ 470 David Klingler .05 .02
❑ 471 Andre Collins .05 .02
❑ 472 Erik Williams .05 .02
❑ 473 Eddie Anderson .05 .02
❑ 474 Marc Boutte .05 .02
❑ 475 Joe Montana 1.50 .70
❑ 476 Andre Reed .10 .05
❑ 477 Lawrence Taylor .25 .11
❑ 478 Jeff George .25 .11
❑ 479 Chris Mims .05 .02
❑ 480 Ken Ruettgers .05 .02
❑ 481 Roman Phifer .05 .02
❑ 482 William Thomas .05 .02
❑ 483 Lamar Lathon .05 .02
❑ 484 Vinny Testaverde .10 .05
(Signed with
Cleveland Browns)
❑ 485 Mike Kenn .05 .02
❑ 486 Greg Lewis .05 .02
❑ 487 Chris Martin .05 .02
(Traded to
Los Angeles Rams)
❑ 488 Maurice Hurst .05 .02
❑ 489 Pat Swilling .05 .02
(Traded to
Detroit Lions)
❑ 490 Carl Pickens .25 .11
❑ 491 Tony Smith .05 .02
❑ 492 James Washington .05 .02
❑ 493 Jeff Hostetler .10 .05
(Signed with
Los Angeles Raiders)
❑ 494 Jeff Chadwick .05 .02
❑ 495 Kevin Ross .05 .02
❑ 496 Jim Ritcher .05 .02
❑ 497 Jessie Hester .05 .02
❑ 498 Burt Grossman .05 .02
❑ 499 Keith Van Horne .05 .02
❑ 500 Gerald Robinson .05 .02
❑ P1 Promo Panel 5.00 2.20
Steve Young
Kenny Walker
Chip Lohmiller
Kevin Greene
Craig Heyward
Ernie Jones
Emmitt Smith
Keith Byars

1993 Fleer All-Pros

	MINT	NRMT
COMPLETE SET (25)	30.00	13.50
RANDOM INSERTS IN PACKS		

❑ 1 Steve Atwater .40 .18
❑ 2 Rich Camarillo .40 .18
❑ 3 Ray Childress .40 .18
❑ 4 Chris Doleman .40 .18
❑ 5 Barry Foster .75 .35
❑ 6 Henry Jones .40 .18
❑ 7 Cortez Kennedy .75 .35
❑ 8 Nick Lowery .40 .18
❑ 9 Wilber Marshall .40 .18
❑ 10 Bruce Matthews .40 .18
❑ 11 Randall McDaniel .40 .18
❑ 12 Audray McMillian .40 .18
❑ 13 Sam Mills .40 .18
❑ 14 Jay Novacek .75 .35
❑ 15 Jerry Rice 8.00 3.60

❑ 16 Junior Seau	2.00	.90
❑ 17 Sterling Sharpe	2.00	.90
❑ 18 Clyde Simmons	.40	.18
❑ 19 Emmitt Smith	12.00	5.50
❑ 20 Derrick Thomas	2.00	.90
❑ 21 Steve Wallace	.40	.18
❑ 22 Richmond Webb	.40	.18
❑ 23 Steve Wisniewski	.40	.18
❑ 24 Rod Woodson	2.00	.90
❑ 25 Steve Young	6.00	2.70

1993 Fleer Prospects

	MINT	NRMT
COMPLETE SET (30)	40.00	18.00
COMMON CARD (1-30)	.75	.35
SEMISTARS	1.50	.70
UNLISTED STARS	3.00	1.35
RANDOM INSERTS IN PACKS		

❑ 1 Drew Bledsoe	12.00	5.50
❑ 2 Garrison Hearst	5.00	2.20
❑ 3 John Copeland	1.50	.70
❑ 4 Eric Curry	1.50	.70
❑ 5 Curtis Conway	3.00	1.35
❑ 6 Lincoln Kennedy	.75	.35
❑ 7 Jerome Bettis	5.00	2.20
❑ 8 Patrick Bates	.75	.35
❑ 9 Brad Hopkins	.75	.35
❑ 10 Tom Carter	1.50	.70
❑ 11 Irv Smith	1.50	.70
❑ 12 Robert Smith	5.00	2.20
❑ 13 Deon Figures	1.50	.70
❑ 14 Leonard Renfro	.75	.35
❑ 15 O.J. McDuffie	4.00	1.80
❑ 16 Dana Stubblefield	3.00	1.35
❑ 17 Todd Kelly	.75	.35
❑ 18 George Teague	1.50	.70
❑ 19 Demetrius DuBose	.75	.35
❑ 20 Coleman Rudolph	.75	.35
❑ 21 Carlton Gray	.75	.35
❑ 22 Troy Drayton	1.50	.70
❑ 23 Natrone Means UER (San Diego Chargers Receiver spelled Reveiver)	4.00	1.80
❑ 24 Qadry Ismail	3.00	1.35
❑ 25 Gino Torretta	1.50	.70
❑ 26 Carl Simpson	.75	.35
❑ 27 Glyn Milburn	1.50	.70
❑ 28 Chad Brown	1.50	.70
❑ 29 Reggie Brooks	1.50	.70
❑ 30 Billy Joe Hobert	1.50	.70

1993 Fleer Rookie Sensations

	MINT	NRMT
COMPLETE SET (20)	125.00	55.00
COMMON CARD (1-20)	6.00	2.70
SEMISTARS	8.00	3.60
RANDOM INSERTS IN JUMBO PACKS		

❑ 1 Dale Carter	8.00	3.60
❑ 2 Eugene Chung	6.00	2.70
❑ 3 Marco Coleman	8.00	3.60
❑ 4 Quentin Coryatt	8.00	3.60
❑ 5 Santana Dotson	6.00	2.70
❑ 6 Vaughn Dunbar	8.00	3.60
❑ 7 Steve Emtman	8.00	3.60
❑ 8 Sean Gilbert	8.00	3.60
❑ 9 Dana Hall	8.00	3.60
❑ 10 Jason Hanson	6.00	2.70
❑ 11 Robert Jones	6.00	2.70
❑ 12 David Klingler	8.00	3.60
❑ 13 Amp Lee	6.00	2.70
❑ 14 Troy Auzenne	6.00	2.70
❑ 15 Ricardo McDonald	6.00	2.70
❑ 16 Chris Mims	8.00	3.60
❑ 17 Johnny Mitchell	8.00	3.60
❑ 18 Carl Pickens	15.00	6.75
❑ 19 Darren Perry	6.00	2.70
❑ 20 Troy Vincent	8.00	3.60

1993 Fleer Team Leaders

	MINT	NRMT
COMPLETE SET (5)	30.00	13.50
RANDOM INSERTS IN PACKS		

❑ 1 Brett Favre	15.00	6.75
❑ 2 Derrick Thomas	2.00	.90
❑ 3 Steve Young	6.00	2.70
❑ 4 John Elway	12.00	5.50
❑ 5 Cortez Kennedy	.75	.35

1994 Fleer

	MINT	NRMT
COMPLETE SET (480)	20.00	9.00
COMMON CARD (1-480)	.05	.02
SEMISTARS	.10	.05
UNLISTED STARS	.25	.11
ONE INSERT PER PACK		
COMP.BETTIS SET (12)	8.00	3.60
BETTIS: RANDOM INS.IN PACKS		
BETTIS SEND-OFF 13-15	1.00	.45

❑ 1 Michael Bankston	.05	.02
❑ 2 Steve Beuerlein	.05	.02
❑ 3 John Booty	.05	.02
❑ 4 Rich Camarillo	.05	.02
❑ 5 Chuck Cecil	.05	.02
❑ 6 Larry Centers	.25	.11
❑ 7 Gary Clark	.10	.05
❑ 8 Garrison Hearst	.25	.11
❑ 9 Eric Hill	.05	.02
❑ 10 Randal Hill	.05	.02
❑ 11 Ronald Moore	.05	.02
❑ 12 Ricky Proehl	.05	.02
❑ 13 Luis Sharpe	.05	.02
❑ 14 Clyde Simmons	.05	.02
❑ 15 Tyronne Stowe	.05	.02
❑ 16 Eric Swann	.10	.05
❑ 17 Aeneas Williams	.05	.02
❑ 18 Darion Conner	.05	.02
❑ 19 Moe Gardner	.05	.02
❑ 20 Jumpy Geathers	.05	.02
❑ 21 Jeff George	.25	.11
❑ 22 Roger Harper	.05	.02
❑ 23 Bobby Hebert	.05	.02
❑ 24 Pierce Holt	.05	.02
❑ 25 D.J. Johnson	.05	.02
❑ 26 Mike Kenn	.05	.02
❑ 27 Lincoln Kennedy	.05	.02
❑ 28 Erric Pegram	.05	.02
❑ 29 Mike Pritchard	.05	.02
❑ 30 Andre Rison	.10	.05
❑ 31 Deion Sanders	.50	.23
❑ 32 Tony Smith	.05	.02
❑ 33 Jesse Solomon	.05	.02
❑ 34 Jessie Tuggle	.05	.02
❑ 35 Don Beebe	.05	.02
❑ 36 Cornelius Bennett	.10	.05
❑ 37 Bill Brooks	.05	.02
❑ 38 Kenneth Davis	.05	.02
❑ 39 John Fina	.05	.02
❑ 40 Phil Hansen	.05	.02
❑ 41 Kent Hull	.05	.02
❑ 42 Henry Jones	.05	.02
❑ 43 Jim Kelly	.25	.11
❑ 44 Pete Metzelaars	.05	.02
❑ 45 Marvcus Patton	.05	.02
❑ 46 Andre Reed	.10	.05
❑ 47 Frank Reich	.10	.05
❑ 48 Bruce Smith	.25	.11
❑ 49 Thomas Smith	.05	.02
❑ 50 Darryl Talley	.05	.02
❑ 51 Steve Tasker	.10	.05
❑ 52 Thurman Thomas	.25	.11
❑ 53 Jeff Wright	.05	.02
❑ 54 Neal Anderson	.05	.02
❑ 55 Trace Armstrong	.05	.02
❑ 56 Troy Auzenne	.05	.02
❑ 57 Joe Cain RC	.05	.02
❑ 58 Mark Carrier DB	.05	.02
❑ 59 Curtis Conway	.25	.11
❑ 60 Richard Dent	.10	.05
❑ 61 Shaun Gayle	.05	.02
❑ 62 Andy Heck	.05	.02
❑ 63 Dante Jones	.05	.02
❑ 64 Erik Kramer	.10	.05
❑ 65 Steve McMichael	.10	.05
❑ 66 Terry Obee	.05	.02
❑ 67 Vinson Smith	.05	.02
❑ 68 Alonzo Spellman	.05	.02
❑ 69 Tom Waddle	.05	.02
❑ 70 Donnell Woolford	.05	.02
❑ 71 Tim Worley	.05	.02
❑ 72 Chris Zorich	.05	.02
❑ 73 Mike Brim	.05	.02
❑ 74 John Copeland	.05	.02
❑ 75 Derrick Fenner	.05	.02
❑ 76 James Francis	.05	.02
❑ 77 Harold Green	.05	.02
❑ 78 Rod Jones	.05	.02
❑ 79 David Klingler	.05	.02

❑ 80 Bruce Kozerski .05 .02
❑ 81 Tim Krumrie .05 .02
❑ 82 Ricardo McDonald .05 .02
❑ 83 Tim McGee .05 .02
❑ 84 Tony McGee .05 .02
❑ 85 Louis Oliver .05 .02
❑ 86 Carl Pickens .25 .11
❑ 87 Jeff Query .05 .02
❑ 88 Daniel Stubbs .05 .02
❑ 89 Steve Tovar .05 .02
❑ 90 Alfred Williams .05 .02
❑ 91 Darryl Williams .05 .02
❑ 92 Rob Burnett .05 .02
❑ 93 Mark Carrier WR .10 .05
❑ 94 Leroy Hoard .05 .02
❑ 95 Michael Jackson .10 .05
❑ 96 Mike Johnson .05 .02
❑ 97 Pepper Johnson .05 .02
❑ 98 Tony Jones .05 .02
❑ 99 Clay Matthews .05 .02
❑ 100 Eric Metcalf .10 .05
❑ 101 Stevon Moore .05 .02
❑ 102 Michael Dean Perry .10 .05
❑ 103 Anthony Pleasant .05 .02
❑ 104 Vinny Testaverde .10 .05
❑ 105 Eric Turner .05 .02
❑ 106 Tommy Vardell .05 .02
❑ 107 Troy Aikman 1.00 .45
❑ 108 Larry Brown DB .05 .02
❑ 109 Dixon Edwards .05 .02
❑ 110 Charles Haley .10 .05
❑ 111 Alvin Harper .10 .05
❑ 112 Michael Irvin .25 .11
❑ 113 Jim Jeffcoat .05 .02
❑ 114 Daryl Johnston .10 .05
❑ 115 Leon Lett .05 .02
❑ 116 Russell Maryland .05 .02
❑ 117 Nate Newton .05 .02
❑ 118 Ken Norton Jr. .10 .05
❑ 119 Jay Novacek .10 .05
❑ 120 Darrin Smith .05 .02
❑ 121 Emmitt Smith 1.50 .70
❑ 122 Kevin Smith .05 .02
❑ 123 Mark Stepnoski .05 .02
❑ 124 Tony Tolbert .05 .02
❑ 125 Erik Williams .05 .02
❑ 126 Kevin Williams .10 .05
❑ 127 Darren Woodson .10 .05
❑ 128 Steve Atwater .05 .02
❑ 129 Rod Bernstine .05 .02
❑ 130 Ray Crockett .05 .02
❑ 131 Mike Croel .05 .02
❑ 132 Robert Delpino .05 .02
❑ 133 Shane Dronett .05 .02
❑ 134 Jason Elam .05 .02
❑ 135 John Elway 2.00 .90
❑ 136 Simon Fletcher .05 .02
❑ 137 Greg Kragen .05 .02
❑ 138 Karl Mecklenburg .05 .02
❑ 139 Glyn Milburn .10 .05
❑ 140 Anthony Miller .10 .05
❑ 141 Derek Russell .05 .02
❑ 142 Shannon Sharpe .10 .05
❑ 143 Dennis Smith .05 .02
❑ 144 Dan Williams .05 .02
❑ 145 Gary Zimmerman .05 .02
❑ 146 Bennie Blades .05 .02
❑ 147 Lomas Brown .05 .02
❑ 148 Bill Fralic .05 .02
❑ 149 Mel Gray .05 .02
❑ 150 Willie Green .05 .02
❑ 151 Jason Hanson .05 .02
❑ 152 Robert Massey .05 .02
❑ 153 Ryan McNeil .05 .02
❑ 154 Scott Mitchell .25 .11
❑ 155 Derrick Moore .05 .02
❑ 156 Herman Moore .25 .11
❑ 157 Brett Perriman .10 .05
❑ 158 Robert Porcher .05 .02
❑ 159 Kelvin Pritchett .05 .02
❑ 160 Barry Sanders 2.00 .90
❑ 161 Tracy Scroggins .05 .02
❑ 162 Chris Spielman .10 .05
❑ 163 Pat Swilling .05 .02
❑ 164 Edgar Bennett .25 .11
❑ 165 Robert Brooks .25 .11
❑ 166 Terrell Buckley .05 .02
❑ 167 LeRoy Butler .05 .02
❑ 168 Brett Favre 2.00 .90
❑ 169 Harry Galbreath .05 .02
❑ 170 Jackie Harris .05 .02
❑ 171 Johnny Holland .05 .02
❑ 172 Chris Jacke .05 .02
❑ 173 George Koonce .05 .02
❑ 174 Bryce Paup .25 .11
❑ 175 Ken Ruettgers .05 .02
❑ 176 Sterling Sharpe .10 .05
❑ 177 Wayne Simmons .05 .02
❑ 178 George Teague .05 .02
❑ 179 Darrell Thompson .05 .02
❑ 180 Reggie White .25 .11
❑ 181 Gary Brown .05 .02
❑ 182 Cody Carlson .05 .02
❑ 183 Ray Childress .05 .02
❑ 184 Cris Dishman .05 .02
❑ 185 Ernest Givins .10 .05
❑ 186 Haywood Jeffires .10 .05
❑ 187 Sean Jones .05 .02
❑ 188 Lamar Lathon .05 .02
❑ 189 Bruce Matthews .05 .02
❑ 190 Bubba McDowell .05 .02
❑ 191 Glenn Montgomery .05 .02
❑ 192 Greg Montgomery .05 .02
❑ 193 Warren Moon .25 .11
❑ 194 Bo Orlando .05 .02
❑ 195 Marcus Robertson .05 .02
❑ 196 Eddie Robinson .05 .02
❑ 197 Webster Slaughter .05 .02
❑ 198 Lorenzo White .05 .02
❑ 199 John Baylor .05 .02
❑ 200 Jason Belser .05 .02
❑ 201 Tony Bennett .05 .02
❑ 202 Dean Biasucci .05 .02
❑ 203 Ray Buchanan .05 .02
❑ 204 Kerry Cash .05 .02
❑ 205 Quentin Coryatt .05 .02
❑ 206 Eugene Daniel .05 .02
❑ 207 Steve Emtman .05 .02
❑ 208 Jon Hand .05 .02
❑ 209 Jim Harbaugh .25 .11
❑ 210 Jeff Herrod .05 .02
❑ 211 Anthony Johnson .10 .05
❑ 212 Roosevelt Potts .05 .02
❑ 213 Rohn Stark .05 .02
❑ 214 Will Wolford .05 .02
❑ 215 Marcus Allen .25 .11
❑ 216 John Alt .05 .02
❑ 217 Kimble Anders .10 .05
❑ 218 J.J. Birden .05 .02
❑ 219 Dale Carter .05 .02
❑ 220 Keith Cash .05 .02
❑ 221 Tony Casillas .05 .02
❑ 222 Willie Davis .10 .05
❑ 223 Tim Grunhard .05 .02
❑ 224 Nick Lowery .05 .02
❑ 225 Charles Mincy .05 .02
❑ 226 Joe Montana 2.00 .90
❑ 227 Dan Saleaumua .05 .02
❑ 228 Tracy Simien .05 .02
❑ 229 Neil Smith .25 .11
❑ 230 Derrick Thomas .25 .11
❑ 231 Eddie Anderson .05 .02
❑ 232 Tim Brown .25 .11
❑ 233 Nolan Harrison .05 .02
❑ 234 Jeff Hostetler .10 .05
❑ 235 Rocket Ismail .10 .05
❑ 236 Jeff Jaeger .05 .02
❑ 237 James Jett .05 .02
❑ 238 Joe Kelly .05 .02
❑ 239 Albert Lewis .05 .02
❑ 240 Terry McDaniel .05 .02
❑ 241 Chester McGlockton .05 .02
❑ 242 Winston Moss .05 .02
❑ 243 Gerald Perry .05 .02
❑ 244 Greg Robinson .05 .02
❑ 245 Anthony Smith .05 .02
❑ 246 Steve Smith .05 .02
❑ 247 Greg Townsend .05 .02
❑ 248 Lionel Washington .05 .02
❑ 249 Steve Wisniewski .05 .02
❑ 250 Alexander Wright .05 .02
❑ 251 Flipper Anderson .05 .02
❑ 252 Jerome Bettis .25 .11
❑ 253 Marc Boutte .05 .02
❑ 254 Shane Conlan .05 .02
❑ 255 Troy Drayton .05 .02
❑ 256 Henry Ellard .10 .05
❑ 257 Sean Gilbert .05 .02
❑ 258 Nate Lewis .05 .02
❑ 259 Todd Lyght .05 .02
❑ 260 Chris Miller .05 .02
❑ 261 Anthony Newman .05 .02
❑ 262 Roman Phifer .05 .02
❑ 263 Henry Rolling .05 .02
❑ 264 T.J. Rubley RC .05 .02
❑ 265 Jackie Slater .05 .02
❑ 266 Fred Stokes .05 .02
❑ 267 Robert Young .05 .02
❑ 268 Gene Atkins .05 .02
❑ 269 J.B. Brown .05 .02
❑ 270 Keith Byars .05 .02
❑ 271 Marco Coleman .05 .02
❑ 272 Bryan Cox .05 .02
❑ 273 Jeff Cross .05 .02
❑ 274 Irving Fryar .10 .05
❑ 275 Mark Higgs .05 .02
❑ 276 Dwight Hollier .05 .02
❑ 277 Mark Ingram .05 .02
❑ 278 Keith Jackson .05 .02
❑ 279 Terry Kirby .25 .11
❑ 280 Bernie Kosar .10 .05
❑ 281 Dan Marino 2.00 .90
❑ 282 O.J. McDuffie .25 .11
❑ 283 Keith Sims .05 .02
❑ 284 Pete Stoyanovich .05 .02
❑ 285 Troy Vincent .05 .02
❑ 286 Richmond Webb .05 .02
❑ 287 Terry Allen .10 .05
❑ 288 Anthony Carter .10 .05
❑ 289 Cris Carter .50 .23
❑ 290 Jack Del Rio .05 .02
❑ 291 Chris Doleman .05 .02
❑ 292 Vencie Glenn .05 .02
❑ 293 Scottie Graham RC .10 .05
❑ 294 Chris Hinton .05 .02
❑ 295 Qadry Ismail .25 .11
❑ 296 Carlos Jenkins .05 .02
❑ 297 Steve Jordan .05 .02
❑ 298 Carl Lee .05 .02
❑ 299 Randall McDaniel .05 .02
❑ 300 John Randle .05 .02
❑ 301 Todd Scott .05 .02
❑ 302 Robert Smith .25 .11
❑ 303 Fred Strickland .05 .02
❑ 304 Henry Thomas .05 .02
❑ 305 Bruce Armstrong .05 .02
❑ 306 Harlon Barnett .05 .02
❑ 307 Drew Bledsoe 1.25 .55
❑ 308 Vincent Brown .05 .02
❑ 309 Ben Coates .25 .11
❑ 310 Todd Collins .05 .02
❑ 311 Myron Guyton .05 .02
❑ 312 Pat Harlow .05 .02
❑ 313 Maurice Hurst .05 .02
❑ 314 Leonard Russell .05 .02
❑ 315 Chris Slade .05 .02
❑ 316 Michael Timpson .05 .02
❑ 317 Andre Tippett .05 .02
❑ 318 Morten Andersen .05 .02
❑ 319 Derek Brown RBK .05 .02
❑ 320 Vince Buck .05 .02
❑ 321 Toi Cook .05 .02
❑ 322 Quinn Early .10 .05
❑ 323 Jim Everett .10 .05
❑ 324 Michael Haynes .10 .05
❑ 325 Tyrone Hughes .10 .05
❑ 326 Rickey Jackson .05 .02
❑ 327 Vaughan Johnson .05 .02
❑ 328 Eric Martin .05 .02
❑ 329 Wayne Martin .05 .02
❑ 330 Sam Mills .05 .02
❑ 331 Willie Roaf .05 .02
❑ 332 Irv Smith .05 .02
❑ 333 Keith Taylor .05 .02
❑ 334 Renaldo Turnbull .05 .02
❑ 335 Carlton Bailey .05 .02
❑ 336 Michael Brooks .05 .02
❑ 337 Jarrod Bunch .05 .02

❑ 338 Chris Calloway	.05	.02
❑ 339 Mark Collins	.05	.02
❑ 340 Howard Cross	.05	.02
❑ 341 Stacey Dillard RC	.05	.02
❑ 342 John Elliott	.05	.02
❑ 343 Rodney Hampton	.25	.11
❑ 344 Greg Jackson	.05	.02
❑ 345 Mark Jackson	.05	.02
❑ 346 Dave Meggett	.05	.02
❑ 347 Corey Miller	.05	.02
❑ 348 Mike Sherrard	.05	.02
❑ 349 Phil Simms	.10	.05
❑ 350 Lewis Tillman	.05	.02
❑ 351 Brad Baxter	.05	.02
❑ 352 Kyle Clifton	.05	.02
❑ 353 Boomer Esiason	.10	.05
❑ 354 James Hasty	.05	.02
❑ 355 Bobby Houston	.05	.02
❑ 356 Johnny Johnson	.05	.02
❑ 357 Jeff Lageman	.05	.02
❑ 358 Mo Lewis	.05	.02
❑ 359 Ronnie Lott	.10	.05
❑ 360 Leonard Marshall	.05	.02
❑ 361 Johnny Mitchell	.05	.02
❑ 362 Rob Moore	.10	.05
❑ 363 Eric Thomas	.05	.02
❑ 364 Brian Washington	.05	.02
❑ 365 Marvin Washington	.05	.02
❑ 366 Eric Allen	.05	.02
❑ 367 Fred Barnett	.10	.05
❑ 368 Bubby Brister	.05	.02
❑ 369 Randall Cunningham	.25	.11
❑ 370 Byron Evans	.05	.02
❑ 371 William Fuller	.05	.02
❑ 372 Andy Harmon	.05	.02
❑ 373 Seth Joyner	.05	.02
❑ 374 William Perry	.10	.05
❑ 375 Leonard Renfro	.05	.02
❑ 376 Heath Sherman	.05	.02
❑ 377 Ben Smith	.05	.02
❑ 378 William Thomas	.05	.02
❑ 379 Herschel Walker	.10	.05
❑ 380 Calvin Williams	.10	.05
❑ 381 Chad Brown	.05	.02
❑ 382 Dermontti Dawson	.05	.02
❑ 383 Deon Figures	.05	.02
❑ 384 Barry Foster	.05	.02
❑ 385 Jeff Graham	.05	.02
❑ 386 Eric Green	.05	.02
❑ 387 Kevin Greene	.25	.11
❑ 388 Carlton Haselrig	.05	.02
❑ 389 Levon Kirkland	.05	.02
❑ 390 Carnell Lake	.05	.02
❑ 391 Greg Lloyd	.25	.11
❑ 392 Neil O'Donnell	.25	.11
❑ 393 Darren Perry	.05	.02
❑ 394 Dwight Stone	.05	.02
❑ 395 Leroy Thompson	.05	.02
❑ 396 Rod Woodson	.25	.11
❑ 397 Marion Butts	.05	.02
❑ 398 John Carney	.05	.02
❑ 399 Darren Carrington	.05	.02
❑ 400 Burt Grossman	.05	.02
❑ 401 Courtney Hall	.05	.02
❑ 402 Ronnie Harmon	.05	.02
❑ 403 Stan Humphries	.25	.11
❑ 404 Shawn Jefferson	.05	.02
❑ 405 Vance Johnson	.05	.02
❑ 406 Chris Mims	.05	.02
❑ 407 Leslie O'Neal	.05	.02
❑ 408 Stanley Richard	.05	.02
❑ 409 Junior Seau	.25	.11
❑ 410 Harris Barton	.05	.02
❑ 411 Dennis Brown	.05	.02
❑ 412 Eric Davis	.05	.02
❑ 413 Merton Hanks	.10	.05
❑ 414 John Johnson	.05	.02
❑ 415 Brent Jones	.10	.05
❑ 416 Marc Logan	.05	.02
❑ 417 Tim McDonald	.05	.02
❑ 418 Gary Plummer	.05	.02
❑ 419 Tom Rathman	.05	.02
❑ 420 Jerry Rice	1.00	.45
❑ 421 Bill Romanowski	.05	.02
❑ 422 Jesse Sapolu	.05	.02
❑ 423 Dana Stubblefield	.25	.11
❑ 424 John Taylor	.10	.05
❑ 425 Steve Wallace	.05	.02
❑ 426 Ted Washington	.05	.02
❑ 427 Ricky Watters	.25	.11
❑ 428 Troy Wilson RC	.05	.02
❑ 429 Steve Young	.75	.35
❑ 430 Howard Ballard	.05	.02
❑ 431 Michael Bates	.05	.02
❑ 432 Robert Blackmon	.05	.02
❑ 433 Brian Blades	.10	.05
❑ 434 Ferrell Edmunds	.05	.02
❑ 435 Carlton Gray	.05	.02
❑ 436 Patrick Hunter	.05	.02
❑ 437 Cortez Kennedy	.10	.05
❑ 438 Kelvin Martin	.05	.02
❑ 439 Rick Mirer	.25	.11
❑ 440 Nate Odomes	.05	.02
❑ 441 Ray Roberts	.05	.02
❑ 442 Eugene Robinson	.05	.02
❑ 443 Rod Stephens	.05	.02
❑ 444 Chris Warren	.10	.05
❑ 445 John L. Williams	.05	.02
❑ 446 Terry Wooden	.05	.02
❑ 447 Marty Carter	.05	.02
❑ 448 Reggie Cobb	.05	.02
❑ 449 Lawrence Dawsey	.05	.02
❑ 450 Santana Dotson	.10	.05
❑ 451 Craig Erickson	.05	.02
❑ 452 Thomas Everett	.05	.02
❑ 453 Paul Gruber	.05	.02
❑ 454 Courtney Hawkins	.05	.02
❑ 455 Martin Mayhew	.05	.02
❑ 456 Hardy Nickerson	.10	.05
❑ 457 Ricky Reynolds	.05	.02
❑ 458 Vince Workman	.05	.02
❑ 459 Reggie Brooks	.10	.05
❑ 460 Earnest Byner	.05	.02
❑ 461 Andre Collins	.05	.02
❑ 462 Brad Edwards	.05	.02
❑ 463 Kurt Gouveia	.05	.02
❑ 464 Darrell Green	.05	.02
❑ 465 Ken Harvey	.05	.02
❑ 466 Ethan Horton	.05	.02
❑ 467 A.J. Johnson	.05	.02
❑ 468 Tim Johnson	.05	.02
❑ 469 Jim Lachey	.05	.02
❑ 470 Chip Lohmiller	.05	.02
❑ 471 Art Monk	.10	.05
❑ 472 Sterling Palmer RC	.05	.02
❑ 473 Mark Rypien	.05	.02
❑ 474 Ricky Sanders	.05	.02
❑ 475 Checklist 1-106	.05	.02
❑ 476 Checklist 107-214	.05	.02
❑ 477 Checklist 215-317	.05	.02
❑ 478 Checklist 318-409	.05	.02
❑ 479 Checklist 410-480/Inserts	.05	.02
❑ 480 Inserts Checklist	.05	.02
❑ P244 Jerome Bettis Promo Numbered 244	1.00	.45

1994 Fleer All-Pros

	MINT	NRMT
COMPLETE SET (24)	20.00	9.00
RANDOM INSERTS IN PACKS....		
❑ 1 Troy Aikman	3.00	1.35
❑ 2 Eric Allen	.15	.07
❑ 3 Jerome Bettis	.75	.35
❑ 4 Barry Foster	.15	.07
❑ 5 Michael Irvin	.75	.35
❑ 6 Cortez Kennedy	.30	.14
❑ 7 Joe Montana	6.00	2.70
❑ 8 Hardy Nickerson	.30	.14
❑ 9 Jerry Rice	3.00	1.35
❑ 10 Andre Rison	.30	.14
❑ 11 Barry Sanders	6.00	2.70
❑ 12 Deion Sanders	1.50	.70
❑ 13 Junior Seau	.75	.35
❑ 14 Shannon Sharpe	.30	.14
❑ 15 Sterling Sharpe	.30	.14
❑ 16 Bruce Smith	.75	.35
❑ 17 Emmitt Smith	5.00	2.20
❑ 18 Neil Smith	.75	.35
❑ 19 Derrick Thomas	.75	.35
❑ 20 Thurman Thomas	.75	.35
❑ 21A Renaldo Turnbull ERR (Photo of Reggie White)	.15	.07
❑ 21B Renaldo Turnbull COR	.15	.07
❑ 22 Reggie White	.75	.35
❑ 23 Rod Woodson	.75	.35
❑ 24 Steve Young	2.50	1.10

1994 Fleer Award Winners

	MINT	NRMT
COMPLETE SET (5)	4.00	1.80
RANDOM INSERTS IN PACKS....		
❑ 1 Jerome Bettis	.50	.23
❑ 2 Rick Mirer	.30	.14
❑ 3 Deion Sanders	1.00	.45
❑ 4 Emmitt Smith	2.50	1.10
❑ 5 Dana Stubblefield	.30	.14

1994 Fleer League Leaders

	MINT	NRMT
COMPLETE SET (10)	10.00	4.50
RANDOM INSERTS IN PACKS....		
❑ 1 Marcus Allen	.50	.23
❑ 2 Tim Brown	.50	.23
❑ 3 John Elway	4.00	1.80
❑ 4 Tyrone Hughes	.20	.09
❑ 5 Jerry Rice	2.00	.90
❑ 6 Sterling Sharpe	.20	.09
❑ 7 Emmitt Smith	3.00	1.35

		MINT	NRMT
❑ 8	Neil Smith	.50	.23
❑ 9	Thurman Thomas	.50	.23
❑ 10	Steve Young	1.50	.70

1994 Fleer Living Legends

	MINT	NRMT
COMPLETE SET (6)	30.00	13.50

STATED ODDS 1:60 HOB/JUM....

		MINT	NRMT
❑ 1	Marcus Allen	2.00	.90
❑ 2	John Elway	15.00	6.75
❑ 3	Joe Montana	15.00	6.75
❑ 4	Jerry Rice	8.00	3.60
❑ 5	Emmitt Smith	12.00	5.50
❑ 6	Reggie White	2.00	.90

1994 Fleer Prospects

	MINT	NRMT
COMPLETE SET (25)	15.00	6.75
COMMON CARD (1-25)	.40	.18
SEMISTARS	.60	.25
UNLISTED STARS	1.00	.45

RANDOM INSERTS IN PACKS....

		MINT	NRMT
❑ 1	Sam Adams	.60	.25
❑ 2	Trev Alberts	.60	.25
❑ 3	Derrick Alexander WR	2.00	.90
❑ 4	Mario Bates	1.00	.45
❑ 5	Jeff Burris	.60	.25
❑ 6	Shante Carver	.40	.18
❑ 7	Marshall Faulk	6.00	2.70
❑ 8	William Floyd	1.00	.45
❑ 9	Rob Fredrickson	.60	.25
❑ 10	Wayne Gandy	.40	.18
❑ 11	Charlie Garner	4.00	1.80
❑ 12	Aaron Glenn	.60	.25
❑ 13	Charles Johnson	1.00	.45
❑ 14	Joe Johnson	.40	.18
❑ 15	Tre Johnson	.40	.18
❑ 16	Antonio Langham	.60	.25
❑ 17	Chuck Levy	.40	.18
❑ 18	Willie McGinest	1.00	.45
❑ 19	David Palmer	1.25	.55
❑ 20	Errict Rhett UER (Florida played in '94 Sugar Bowl, not Copper Bowl)	4.00	1.80
❑ 21	Jason Sehorn	.60	.25
❑ 22	Heath Shuler	1.00	.45
❑ 23	Charlie Ward Not Drafted	1.00	.45
❑ 24	Dewayne Washington	.60	.25
❑ 25	Bryant Young	1.00	.45

1994 Fleer Pro-Vision

	MINT	NRMT
COMPLETE SET (9)	6.00	2.70

RANDOM INSERTS IN PACKS....
*JUMBO CARDS: 1.2X to 3X BASIC CARDS
ONE JUMBO SET PER HOBBY CASE

		MINT	NRMT
❑ 1	Rodney Hampton	.40	.18
❑ 2	Ricky Watters	.40	.18
❑ 3	Rick Mirer	.40	.18
❑ 4	Brett Favre	3.00	1.35
❑ 5	Troy Aikman	1.50	.70
❑ 6	Jerome Bettis	.40	.18
❑ 7	Joe Montana	3.00	1.35
❑ 8	Cornelius Bennett	.15	.07
❑ 9	Rod Woodson	.40	.18

1994 Fleer Rookie Exchange

	MINT	NRMT
COMPLETE SET (12)	15.00	6.75
COMMON CARD (1-12)	.60	.25
SEMISTARS	1.00	.45
UNLISTED STARS	1.50	.70

TRADE CARD STATED ODDS 1:200 H/J PACKS
ONE SET PER TRADE CARD BY MAIL

		MINT	NRMT
❑ 1	Derrick Alexander WR	2.00	.90
❑ 2	Trent Dilfer	3.00	1.35
❑ 3	Marshall Faulk	8.00	3.60
❑ 4	Charlie Garner	3.00	1.35
❑ 5	Greg Hill	1.50	.70
❑ 6	Charles Johnson	1.50	.70
❑ 7	Antonio Langham	.60	.25
❑ 8	Willie McGinest	.60	.25
❑ 9	Heath Shuler	2.00	.90
❑ 10	Dewayne Washington	1.00	.45
❑ 11	Dan Wilkinson	1.00	.45
❑ 12	Bryant Young	1.50	.70
❑ NNO	Rookie Exch. Expired	.50	.23

1994 Fleer Rookie Sensations

	MINT	NRMT
COMPLETE SET (20)	100.00	45.00
COMMON CARD (1-20)	4.00	1.80
SEMISTARS	6.00	2.70
UNLISTED STARS	8.00	3.60

RANDOM INSERTS IN JUMBO PACKS

		MINT	NRMT
❑ 1	Jerome Bettis	12.00	5.50
❑ 2	Drew Bledsoe	25.00	11.00
❑ 3	Reggie Brooks	6.00	2.70
❑ 4	Tom Carter	4.00	1.80
❑ 5	John Copeland	4.00	1.80
❑ 6	Jason Elam	4.00	1.80
❑ 7	Garrison Hearst	12.00	5.50
❑ 8	Tyrone Hughes	4.00	1.80
❑ 9	James Jett	8.00	3.60
❑ 10	Lincoln Kennedy	4.00	1.80
❑ 11	Terry Kirby	8.00	3.60
❑ 12	Glyn Milburn	6.00	2.70
❑ 13	Rick Mirer	8.00	3.60
❑ 14	Ronald Moore	4.00	1.80
❑ 15	Willie Roaf	4.00	1.80
❑ 16	Wayne Simmons	4.00	1.80
❑ 17	Chris Slade	4.00	1.80
❑ 18	Darrin Smith	4.00	1.80
❑ 19	Dana Stubblefield	6.00	2.70
❑ 20	George Teague	4.00	1.80

1994 Fleer Scoring Machines

	MINT	NRMT
COMPLETE SET (20)	60.00	27.00

RANDOM INSERTS IN PACKS....

		MINT	NRMT
❑ 1	Marcus Allen	1.50	.70
❑ 2	Natrone Means	3.00	1.35
❑ 3	Jerome Bettis	1.50	.70
❑ 4	Tim Brown	1.50	.70
❑ 5	Barry Foster	.30	.14
❑ 6	Rodney Hampton	1.50	.70
❑ 7	Michael Irvin	1.50	.70
❑ 8	Nick Lowery	.30	.14
❑ 9	Dan Marino	12.00	5.50
❑ 10	Joe Montana	12.00	5.50
❑ 11	Warren Moon	1.50	.70
❑ 12	Andre Reed	.60	.25

		MINT	NRMT
❑ 13	Jerry Rice	6.00	2.70
❑ 14	Andre Rison	.60	.25
❑ 15	Barry Sanders	12.00	5.50
❑ 16	Shannon Sharpe	.60	.25
❑ 17	Sterling Sharpe	.60	.25
❑ 18	Emmitt Smith	10.00	4.50
❑ 19	Thurman Thomas	1.50	.70
❑ 20	Ricky Watters	1.50	.70

1995 Fleer

	MINT	NRMT
COMPLETE SET (400)	20.00	9.00
COMMON CARD (1-400)	.10	.05
SEMISTARS	.20	.09
UNLISTED STARS	.30	.14
TWO INSERTS PER PACK		
COMP.PRO-VISIONS SET (6)	3.00	1.35
PRO-VISIONS: STATED ODDS 1:6		

		MINT	NRMT
❑ 1	Michael Bankston	.10	.05
❑ 2	Larry Centers	.20	.09
❑ 3	Gary Clark	.10	.05
❑ 4	Eric Hill	.10	.05
❑ 5	Seth Joyner	.10	.05
❑ 6	Dave Krieg	.10	.05
❑ 7	Lorenzo Lynch	.10	.05
❑ 8	Jamir Miller	.10	.05
❑ 9	Ronald Moore	.10	.05
❑ 10	Ricky Proehl	.10	.05
❑ 11	Clyde Simmons	.10	.05
❑ 12	Eric Swann	.20	.09
❑ 13	Aeneas Williams	.10	.05
❑ 14	J.J. Birden	.10	.05
❑ 15	Chris Doleman	.10	.05
❑ 16	Bert Emanuel	.30	.14
❑ 17	Jumpy Geathers	.10	.05
❑ 18	Jeff George	.20	.09
❑ 19	Roger Harper	.10	.05
❑ 20	Craig Heyward	.20	.09
❑ 21	Pierce Holt	.10	.05
❑ 22	D.J. Johnson	.10	.05
❑ 23	Terance Mathis	.20	.09
❑ 24	Clay Matthews	.20	.09
❑ 25	Andre Rison	.20	.09
❑ 26	Chuck Smith	.10	.05
❑ 27	Jessie Tuggle	.10	.05
❑ 28	Cornelius Bennett	.20	.09
❑ 29	Bucky Brooks	.10	.05
❑ 30	Jeff Burris	.10	.05
❑ 31	Russell Copeland	.10	.05
❑ 32	Matt Darby	.10	.05
❑ 33	Phil Hansen	.10	.05
❑ 34	Henry Jones	.10	.05
❑ 35	Jim Kelly	.30	.14
❑ 36	Mark Maddox RC	.10	.05
❑ 37	Bryce Paup	.30	.14
❑ 38	Andre Reed	.20	.09
❑ 39	Bruce Smith	.30	.14
❑ 40	Darryl Talley	.10	.05
❑ 41	Dewell Brewer RC	.10	.05
❑ 42	Mike Fox	.10	.05
❑ 43	Eric Guliford	.10	.05
❑ 44	Lamar Lathon	.10	.05
❑ 45	Pete Metzelaars	.10	.05
❑ 46	Sam Mills	.20	.09
❑ 47	Frank Reich	.10	.05
❑ 48	Rod Smith DB	.20	.09
❑ 49	Jack Trudeau	.10	.05
❑ 50	Trace Armstrong	.10	.05
❑ 51	Joe Cain	.10	.05
❑ 52	Mark Carrier DB	.10	.05
❑ 53	Curtis Conway	.30	.14
❑ 54	Shaun Gayle	.10	.05
❑ 55	Jeff Graham	.10	.05
❑ 56	Raymont Harris	.10	.05
❑ 57	Erik Kramer	.10	.05
❑ 58	Lewis Tillman	.10	.05
❑ 59	Tom Waddle	.10	.05
❑ 60	Steve Walsh	.10	.05
❑ 61	Donnell Woolford	.10	.05
❑ 62	Chris Zorich	.10	.05
❑ 63	Jeff Blake RC	1.00	.45
❑ 64	Mike Brim	.10	.05
❑ 65	Steve Broussard	.10	.05
❑ 66	James Francis	.10	.05
❑ 67	Ricardo McDonald	.10	.05
❑ 68	Tony McGee	.10	.05
❑ 70	Darnay Scott	.30	.14
❑ 71	Steve Tovar	.10	.05
❑ 72	Dan Wilkinson	.20	.09
❑ 73	Alfred Williams	.10	.05
❑ 74	Darryl Williams	.10	.05
❑ 75	Derrick Alexander WR	.30	.14
❑ 76	Randy Baldwin	.10	.05
❑ 77	Carl Banks	.10	.05
❑ 78	Rob Burnett	.10	.05
❑ 79	Steve Everitt	.10	.05
❑ 80	Leroy Hoard	.10	.05
❑ 81	Michael Jackson	.20	.09
❑ 82	Pepper Johnson	.10	.05
❑ 83	Tony Jones	.10	.05
❑ 84	Antonio Langham	.10	.05
❑ 85	Eric Metcalf	.20	.09
❑ 86	Stevon Moore	.10	.05
❑ 87	Anthony Pleasant	.10	.05
❑ 88	Vinny Testaverde	.20	.09
❑ 89	Eric Turner	.10	.05
❑ 90	Troy Aikman	1.00	.45
❑ 91	Charles Haley	.20	.09
❑ 92	Michael Irvin	.30	.14
❑ 93	Daryl Johnston	.20	.09
❑ 94	Robert Jones	.10	.05
❑ 95	Leon Lett	.10	.05
❑ 96	Russell Maryland	.10	.05
❑ 97	Nate Newton	.20	.09
❑ 98	Jay Novacek	.20	.09
❑ 99	Darrin Smith	.10	.05
❑ 100	Emmitt Smith	1.50	.70
❑ 101	Kevin Smith	.10	.05
❑ 102	Erik Williams	.10	.05
❑ 103	Kevin Williams WR	.20	.09
❑ 104	Darren Woodson	.20	.09
❑ 105	Elijah Alexander	.10	.05
❑ 106	Steve Atwater	.10	.05
❑ 107	Ray Crockett	.10	.05
❑ 108	Shane Dronett	.10	.05
❑ 109	Jason Elam	.10	.05
❑ 110	John Elway	2.00	.90
❑ 111	Simon Fletcher	.10	.05
❑ 112	Glyn Milburn	.10	.05
❑ 113	Anthony Miller	.20	.09
❑ 114	Michael Dean Perry	.10	.05
❑ 115	Mike Pritchard	.10	.05
❑ 116	Derek Russell	.10	.05
❑ 117	Leonard Russell	.10	.05
❑ 118	Shannon Sharpe	.20	.09
❑ 119	Gary Zimmerman	.10	.05
❑ 120	Bennie Blades	.10	.05
❑ 121	Lomas Brown	.10	.05
❑ 122	Willie Clay	.10	.05
❑ 123	Mike Johnson	.10	.05
❑ 124	Robert Massey	.10	.05
❑ 125	Scott Mitchell	.20	.09
❑ 126	Herman Moore	.30	.14
❑ 127	Brett Perriman	.20	.09
❑ 128	Robert Porcher	.10	.05
❑ 129	Barry Sanders	2.00	.90
❑ 130	Chris Spielman	.20	.09
❑ 131	Henry Thomas	.10	.05
❑ 132	Edgar Bennett	.20	.09
❑ 134	LeRoy Butler	.10	.05
❑ 135	Brett Favre	2.00	.90
❑ 136	Sean Jones	.10	.05
❑ 137	John Jurkovic	.10	.05
❑ 138	George Koonce	.10	.05
❑ 139	Wayne Simmons	.10	.05
❑ 140	George Teague	.10	.05
❑ 141	Reggie White	.30	.14
❑ 142	Micheal Barrow	.10	.05
❑ 143	Gary Brown	.10	.05
❑ 144	Cody Carlson	.10	.05
❑ 145	Ray Childress	.10	.05
❑ 146	Cris Dishman	.10	.05
❑ 147	Ernest Givins	.10	.05
❑ 148	Mel Gray	.10	.05
❑ 149	Darryll Lewis	.10	.05
❑ 150	Bruce Matthews	.10	.05
❑ 151	Marcus Robertson	.10	.05
❑ 152	Webster Slaughter	.10	.05
❑ 153	Al Smith	.10	.05
❑ 154	Mark Stepnoski	.10	.05
❑ 155	Trev Alberts	.10	.05
❑ 156	Flipper Anderson	.10	.05
❑ 157	Jason Belser	.10	.05
❑ 158	Tony Bennett	.10	.05
❑ 159	Ray Buchanan	.10	.05
❑ 160	Quentin Coryatt	.20	.09
❑ 161	Sean Dawkins	.20	.09
❑ 162	Steve Emtman	.10	.05
❑ 163	Marshall Faulk	.50	.23
❑ 164	Stephen Grant RC	.10	.05
❑ 165	Jim Harbaugh	.20	.09
❑ 166	Jeff Herrod	.10	.05
❑ 167	Tony Siragusa	.10	.05
❑ 168	Steve Beuerlein	.10	.05
❑ 169	Darren Carrington	.10	.05
❑ 170	Reggie Cobb	.10	.05
❑ 171	Kelvin Martin	.10	.05
❑ 172	Kelvin Pritchett	.10	.05
❑ 173	Joel Smeenge	.10	.05
❑ 174	James Williams	.10	.05
❑ 175	Marcus Allen	.30	.14
❑ 176	Kimble Anders	.20	.09
❑ 177	Dale Carter	.20	.09
❑ 178	Mark Collins	.10	.05
❑ 179	Willie Davis	.20	.09
❑ 180	Lake Dawson	.20	.09
❑ 181	Greg Hill	.20	.09
❑ 182	Darren Mickell	.10	.05
❑ 183	Joe Montana	2.00	.90
❑ 184	Tracy Simien	.10	.05
❑ 185	Neil Smith	.20	.09
❑ 186	William White	.10	.05
❑ 187	Greg Biekert	.10	.05
❑ 188	Tim Brown	.30	.14
❑ 189	Rob Fredrickson	.10	.05
❑ 190	Andrew Glover RC	.10	.05
❑ 191	Nolan Harrison	.10	.05
❑ 192	Jeff Hostetler	.20	.09
❑ 193	Rocket Ismail	.20	.09
❑ 194	Terry McDaniel	.10	.05
❑ 195	Chester McGlockton	.20	.09
❑ 196	Winston Moss	.10	.05
❑ 197	Anthony Smith	.10	.05
❑ 198	Harvey Williams	.10	.05
❑ 199	Steve Wisniewski	.10	.05
❑ 200	Johnny Bailey	.10	.05
❑ 201	Jerome Bettis	.30	.14
❑ 202	Isaac Bruce	.50	.23
❑ 203	Shane Conlan	.10	.05
❑ 204	Troy Drayton	.10	.05
❑ 205	Sean Gilbert	.20	.09
❑ 206	Jessie Hester	.10	.05
❑ 207	Jimmie Jones	.10	.05
❑ 208	Todd Lyght	.10	.05
❑ 209	Chris Miller	.10	.05
❑ 210	Roman Phifer	.10	.05
❑ 211	Marquez Pope	.10	.05
❑ 212	Robert Young	.10	.05
❑ 213	Gene Atkins	.10	.05
❑ 214	Aubrey Beavers	.10	.05
❑ 215	Tim Bowens	.10	.05
❑ 216	Bryan Cox	.10	.05
❑ 217	Jeff Cross	.10	.05
❑ 218	Irving Fryar	.20	.09
❑ 219	Eric Green	.10	.05
❑ 220	Mark Ingram	.10	.05
❑ 221	Terry Kirby	.20	.09
❑ 222	Dan Marino	2.00	.90

❑ 223 O.J. McDuffie .30 .14
❑ 224 Bernie Parmalee .20 .09
❑ 225 Keith Sims .10 .05
❑ 226 Irving Spikes .20 .09
❑ 227 Michael Stewart .10 .05
❑ 228 Troy Vincent .10 .05
❑ 229 Richmond Webb .10 .05
❑ 230 Terry Allen .20 .09
❑ 231 Cris Carter .30 .14
❑ 232 Jack Del Rio .10 .05
❑ 233 Vencie Glenn .10 .05
❑ 234 Qadry Ismail .20 .09
❑ 235 Carlos Jenkins .10 .05
❑ 236 Ed McDaniel .10 .05
❑ 237 Randall McDaniel .10 .05
❑ 238 Warren Moon .20 .09
❑ 239 Anthony Parker .10 .05
❑ 240 John Randle .10 .05
❑ 241 Jake Reed .20 .09
❑ 242 Fuad Reveiz .10 .05
❑ 243 Broderick Thomas .10 .05
❑ 244 Dewayne Washington .20 .09
❑ 245 Bruce Armstrong .10 .05
❑ 246 Drew Bledsoe 1.00 .45
❑ 247 Vincent Brisby .10 .05
❑ 248 Vincent Brown .10 .05
❑ 249 Marion Butts .10 .05
❑ 250 Ben Coates .20 .09
❑ 251 Tim Goad .10 .05
❑ 252 Myron Guyton .10 .05
❑ 253 Maurice Hurst .10 .05
❑ 254 Mike Jones .10 .05
❑ 255 Willie McGinest .20 .09
❑ 256 Dave Meggett .10 .05
❑ 257 Ricky Reynolds .10 .05
❑ 258 Chris Slade .20 .09
❑ 259 Michael Timpson .10 .05
❑ 260 Mario Bates .30 .14
❑ 261 Derek Brown RBK .10 .05
❑ 262 Darion Conner .10 .05
❑ 263 Quinn Early .20 .09
❑ 264 Jim Everett .10 .05
❑ 265 Michael Haynes .20 .09
❑ 266 Tyrone Hughes .20 .09
❑ 267 Joe Johnson .10 .05
❑ 268 Wayne Martin .10 .05
❑ 269 Willie Roaf .10 .05
❑ 270 Irv Smith .10 .05
❑ 271 Jimmy Spencer .10 .05
❑ 272 Winfred Tubbs .10 .05
❑ 273 Renaldo Turnbull .10 .05
❑ 274 Michael Brooks .10 .05
❑ 275 Dave Brown .20 .09
❑ 276 Chris Calloway .10 .05
❑ 277 Jesse Campbell .10 .05
❑ 278 Howard Cross .10 .05
❑ 279 John Elliott .10 .05
❑ 280 Keith Hamilton .10 .05
❑ 281 Rodney Hampton .20 .09
❑ 282 Thomas Lewis .20 .09
❑ 283 Thomas Randolph .10 .05
❑ 284 Mike Sherrard .10 .05
❑ 285 Michael Strahan .10 .05
❑ 286 Brad Baxter .10 .05
❑ 287 Tony Casillas .10 .05
❑ 288 Kyle Clifton .10 .05
❑ 289 Boomer Esiason .20 .09
❑ 290 Aaron Glenn .10 .05
❑ 291 Bobby Houston .10 .05
❑ 292 Johnny Johnson .10 .05
❑ 293 Jeff Lageman .10 .05
❑ 294 Mo Lewis .10 .05
❑ 295 Johnny Mitchell .10 .05
❑ 296 Rob Moore .10 .05
❑ 297 Marcus Turner .10 .05
❑ 298 Marvin Washington .10 .05
❑ 299 Eric Allen .10 .05
❑ 300 Fred Barnett .20 .09
❑ 301 Randall Cunningham .30 .14
❑ 302 Byron Evans .10 .05
❑ 303 William Fuller .10 .05
❑ 304 Charlie Garner .20 .09
❑ 305 Andy Harmon .10 .05
❑ 306 Greg Jackson .10 .05
❑ 307 Bill Romanowski .10 .05
❑ 308 William Thomas .10 .05
❑ 309 Herschel Walker .20 .09
❑ 310 Calvin Williams .20 .09
❑ 311 Michael Zordich .10 .05
❑ 312 Chad Brown .20 .09
❑ 313 Dermontti Dawson .20 .09
❑ 314 Barry Foster .20 .09
❑ 315 Kevin Greene .20 .09
❑ 316 Charles Johnson .20 .09
❑ 317 Levon Kirkland .10 .05
❑ 318 Carnell Lake .10 .05
❑ 319 Greg Lloyd .20 .09
❑ 320 Byron Bam Morris .20 .09
❑ 321 Neil O'Donnell .20 .09
❑ 322 Darren Perry .10 .05
❑ 323 Ray Seals .10 .05
❑ 324 John L. Williams .10 .05
❑ 325 Rod Woodson .20 .09
❑ 326 John Carney .10 .05
❑ 327 Andre Coleman .10 .05
❑ 328 Courtney Hall .10 .05
❑ 329 Ronnie Harmon .10 .05
❑ 330 Dwayne Harper .10 .05
❑ 331 Stan Humphries .20 .09
❑ 332 Shawn Jefferson .10 .05
❑ 333 Tony Martin .20 .09
❑ 334 Natrone Means .30 .14
❑ 335 Chris Mims .10 .05
❑ 336 Leslie O'Neal .20 .09
❑ 337 Alfred Pupunu RC .10 .05
❑ 338 Junior Seau .30 .14
❑ 339 Mark Seay .20 .09
❑ 340 Eric Davis .10 .05
❑ 341 William Floyd .30 .14
❑ 342 Merton Hanks .10 .05
❑ 343 Rickey Jackson .10 .05
❑ 344 Brent Jones .10 .05
❑ 345 Tim McDonald .10 .05
❑ 346 Ken Norton Jr. .20 .09
❑ 347 Gary Plummer .10 .05
❑ 348 Jerry Rice 1.00 .45
❑ 349 Deion Sanders .40 .18
❑ 350 Jesse Sapolu .10 .05
❑ 351 Dana Stubblefield .30 .14
❑ 352 John Taylor .10 .05
❑ 353 Steve Wallace .10 .05
❑ 354 Ricky Watters .30 .14
❑ 355 Lee Woodall .10 .05
❑ 356 Bryant Young .20 .09
❑ 357 Steve Young .75 .35
❑ 358 Sam Adams .10 .05
❑ 359 Howard Ballard .10 .05
❑ 360 Robert Blackmon .10 .05
❑ 361 Brian Blades .20 .09
❑ 362 Carlton Gray .10 .05
❑ 363 Cortez Kennedy .20 .09
❑ 364 Rick Mirer .30 .14
❑ 365 Eugene Robinson .10 .05
❑ 366 Chris Warren .20 .09
❑ 367 Terry Wooden .10 .05
❑ 368 Brad Culpepper .10 .05
❑ 369 Lawrence Dawsey .10 .05
❑ 370 Trent Dilfer .30 .14
❑ 371 Santana Dotson .10 .05
❑ 372 Craig Erickson .10 .05
❑ 373 Thomas Everett .10 .05
❑ 374 Paul Gruber .10 .05
❑ 375 Alvin Harper .10 .05
❑ 376 Jackie Harris .10 .05
❑ 377 Courtney Hawkins .10 .05
❑ 378 Martin Mayhew .10 .05
❑ 379 Hardy Nickerson .10 .05
❑ 380 Errict Rhett .30 .14
❑ 381 Charles Wilson .10 .05
❑ 382 Reggie Brooks .20 .09
❑ 383 Tom Carter .10 .05
❑ 384 Andre Collins .10 .05
❑ 385 Henry Ellard .20 .09
❑ 386 Ricky Ervins .10 .05
❑ 387 Darrell Green .10 .05
❑ 388 Ken Harvey .10 .05
❑ 389 Brian Mitchell .10 .05
❑ 390 Stanley Richard .10 .05
❑ 391 Heath Shuler .30 .14
❑ 392 Rod Stephens .10 .05
❑ 393 Tyronne Stowe .10 .05
❑ 394 Tydus Winans .10 .05
❑ 395 Tony Woods .10 .05
❑ 396 Checklist (1-104) .10 .05
❑ 397 Checklist (105-212) .10 .05
❑ 398 Checklist (213-298) .10 .05
❑ 399 Checklist (299-400) .10 .05
❑ 400 Checklist (Inserts) .10 .05
❑ P1 Promo Panel 2.50 1.10
Reggie Brooks
Jerome Bettis
Rick Mirer

1995 Fleer Aerial Attack

	MINT	NRMT
COMPLETE SET (6)	35.00	16.00
STATED ODDS 1:37		
❑ 1 Tim Brown	2.50	1.10
❑ 2 Dan Marino	15.00	6.75
❑ 3 Joe Montana	15.00	6.75
❑ 4 Jerry Rice	8.00	3.60
❑ 5 Andre Rison	1.50	.70
❑ 6 Sterling Sharpe	1.50	.70

1995 Fleer Flair Preview

	MINT	NRMT
COMPLETE SET (30)	20.00	9.00
ONE PER PACK		
❑ 1 Aeneas Williams	.20	.09
❑ 2 Jeff George	.40	.18
❑ 3 Andre Reed	.40	.18
❑ 4 Kerry Collins	.40	.18
❑ 5 Mark Carrier DB	.20	.09
❑ 6 Jeff Blake	2.00	.90
❑ 7 Leroy Hoard	.20	.09
❑ 8 Emmitt Smith	3.00	1.35
❑ 9 Shannon Sharpe	.40	.18
❑ 10 Barry Sanders	4.00	1.80
❑ 11 Reggie White	.60	.25
❑ 12 Bruce Matthews	.20	.09
❑ 13 Marshall Faulk	1.00	.45
❑ 14 Tony Boselli	.20	.09
❑ 15 Joe Montana	4.00	1.80
❑ 16 Tim Brown	.60	.25
❑ 17 Jerome Bettis	.60	.25
❑ 18 Dan Marino	4.00	1.80
❑ 19 Cris Carter	.60	.25
❑ 20 Drew Bledsoe	2.00	.90
❑ 21 Willie Roaf	.20	.09
❑ 22 Rodney Hampton	.40	.18
❑ 23 Rob Moore	.20	.09
❑ 24 Fred Barnett	.40	.18
❑ 25 Rod Woodson	.40	.18
❑ 26 Natrone Means	.60	.25
❑ 27 Jerry Rice	2.00	.90
❑ 28 Chris Warren	.40	.18
❑ 29 Errict Rhett	.60	.25
❑ 30 Henry Ellard	.40	.18

1995 Fleer Gridiron Leaders

	MINT	NRMT
COMPLETE SET (10)	8.00	3.60
STATED ODDS 1:4		
❑ 1 Cris Carter	.40	.18
❑ 2 Ben Coates	.25	.11
❑ 3 Marshall Faulk	.60	.25
❑ 4 Jerry Rice	1.25	.55
❑ 5 Barry Sanders	2.50	1.10
❑ 6 Deion Sanders	.50	.23
❑ 7 Emmitt Smith	2.00	.90
❑ 8 Eric Turner	.10	.05
❑ 9 Chris Warren	.25	.11
❑ 10 Steve Young	1.00	.45

1995 Fleer Prospects

	MINT	NRMT
COMPLETE SET (20)	20.00	9.00
COMMON CARD (1-20)	.50	.23
SEMISTARS	.75	.35
UNLISTED STARS	1.50	.70
STATED ODDS 1:6		
❑ 1 Tony Boselli	.75	.35
❑ 2 Kyle Brady	.75	.35
❑ 3 Ruben Brown	.50	.23
❑ 4 Kevin Carter	1.50	.70
❑ 5 Ki-Jana Carter	1.50	.70
❑ 6 Kerry Collins	2.00	.90
❑ 7 Luther Elliss	.50	.23
❑ 8 Jimmy Hitchcock	.50	.23
❑ 9 Jack Jackson	.50	.23
❑ 10 Ellis Johnson	.50	.23
❑ 11 Rob Johnson	1.50	.70
❑ 12 Steve McNair	4.00	1.80
❑ 13 Rashaan Salaam	1.50	.70
❑ 14 Warren Sapp	.50	.23
❑ 15 J.J. Stokes	1.50	.70
❑ 16 Bobby Taylor	.75	.35
❑ 17 John Walsh	.50	.23
❑ 18 Michael Westbrook	3.00	1.35
❑ 19 Tyrone Wheatley	2.50	1.10
❑ 20 Sherman Williams	.75	.35

1995 Fleer Rookie Sensations

	MINT	NRMT
COMPLETE SET (20)	40.00	18.00
COMMON CARD (1-20)	1.25	.55
SEMISTARS	2.50	1.10
UNLISTED STARS	4.00	1.80
STATED ODDS 1:3 JUMBO		
❑ 1 Derrick Alexander WR	4.00	1.80
❑ 2 Mario Bates	1.25	.55
❑ 3 Tim Bowens	1.25	.55
❑ 4 Lake Dawson	2.50	1.10
❑ 5 Bert Emanuel	4.00	1.80
❑ 6 Marshall Faulk	6.00	2.70
❑ 7 William Floyd	2.50	1.10
❑ 8 Rob Fredrickson	1.25	.55
❑ 9 Greg Hill	2.50	1.10
❑ 10 Charles Johnson	2.50	1.10
❑ 11 Antonio Langham	1.25	.55
❑ 12 Willie McGinest	1.25	.55
❑ 13 Byron Bam Morris	2.50	1.10
❑ 14 Errict Rhett	4.00	1.80
❑ 15 Darnay Scott	6.00	2.70
❑ 16 Heath Shuler	4.00	1.80
❑ 17 Dewayne Washington	1.25	.55
❑ 18 Dan Wilkinson	1.25	.55
❑ 19 Lee Woodall	1.25	.55
❑ 20 Bryant Young	2.50	1.10

1995 Fleer TD Sensations

	MINT	NRMT
COMPLETE SET (10)	8.00	3.60
STATED ODDS 1:3 FOIL		
❑ 1 Marshall Faulk	.60	.25
❑ 2 Dan Marino	2.50	1.10
❑ 3 Natrone Means	.40	.18
❑ 4 Herman Moore	.40	.18
❑ 5 Jerry Rice	1.25	.55
❑ 6 Sterling Sharpe	.25	.11
❑ 7 Emmitt Smith	2.00	.90
❑ 8 Chris Warren	.25	.11
❑ 9 Ricky Watters	.40	.18
❑ 10 Steve Young	1.00	.45

1996 Fleer

	MINT	NRMT
COMPLETE SET (200)	20.00	9.00
COMMON CARD (1-200)	.10	.05
SEMISTARS	.20	.09
UNLISTED STARS	.30	.14
❑ 1 Garrison Hearst	.20	.09
❑ 2 Rob Moore	.20	.09
❑ 3 Frank Sanders	.20	.09
❑ 4 Eric Swann	.10	.05
❑ 5 Aeneas Williams	.10	.05
❑ 6 Jeff George	.20	.09
❑ 7 Craig Heyward	.10	.05
❑ 8 Terance Mathis	.10	.05
❑ 9 Eric Metcalf	.10	.05
❑ 10 Michael Jackson	.20	.09
❑ 11 Andre Rison	.20	.09
❑ 12 Vinny Testaverde	.20	.09
❑ 13 Eric Turner	.10	.05
❑ 14 Darick Holmes	.10	.05
❑ 15 Jim Kelly	.30	.14
❑ 16 Bryce Paup	.10	.05
❑ 17 Bruce Smith	.20	.09
❑ 18 Thurman Thomas	.30	.14
❑ 19 Kerry Collins	.30	.14
❑ 20 Lamar Lathon	.10	.05
❑ 21 Derrick Moore	.10	.05
❑ 22 Tyrone Poole	.10	.05
❑ 23 Curtis Conway	.30	.14
❑ 24 Bryan Cox	.10	.05
❑ 25 Erik Kramer	.10	.05
❑ 26 Rashaan Salaam	.30	.14
❑ 27 Jeff Blake	.30	.14
❑ 28 Ki-Jana Carter	.20	.09
❑ 29 Carl Pickens	.30	.14
❑ 30 Darnay Scott	.20	.09
❑ 31 Troy Aikman	.75	.35
❑ 32 Charles Haley	.20	.09
❑ 33 Michael Irvin	.30	.14
❑ 34 Daryl Johnston	.20	.09
❑ 35 Jay Novacek	.10	.05
❑ 36 Deion Sanders	.40	.18
❑ 37 Emmitt Smith	1.25	.55
❑ 38 Steve Atwater	.10	.05
❑ 39 Terrell Davis	2.00	.90
❑ 40 John Elway	1.50	.70
❑ 41 Anthony Miller	.20	.09
❑ 42 Shannon Sharpe	.20	.09
❑ 43 Scott Mitchell	.20	.09
❑ 44 Herman Moore	.30	.14
❑ 45 Johnnie Morton	.20	.09
❑ 46 Brett Perriman	.10	.05
❑ 47 Barry Sanders	1.50	.70
❑ 48 Edgar Bennett	.20	.09
❑ 49 Robert Brooks	.30	.14
❑ 50 Mark Chmura	.20	.09
❑ 51 Brett Favre	1.50	.70
❑ 52 Reggie White	.30	.14
❑ 53 Mel Gray	.10	.05
❑ 54 Steve McNair	.50	.23
❑ 55 Chris Sanders	.20	.09
❑ 56 Rodney Thomas	.10	.05
❑ 57 Quentin Coryatt	.10	.05
❑ 58 Sean Dawkins	.10	.05
❑ 59 Ken Dilger	.20	.09
❑ 60 Marshall Faulk	.30	.14

❑ 61 Jim Harbaugh .20 .09
❑ 62 Tony Boselli .10 .05
❑ 63 Mark Brunell .75 .35
❑ 64 Natrone Means .30 .14
❑ 65 James O.Stewart .20 .09
❑ 66 Marcus Allen .30 .14
❑ 67 Steve Bono .10 .05
❑ 68 Neil Smith .10 .05
❑ 69 Derrick Thomas .20 .09
❑ 70 Tamarick Vanover .20 .09
❑ 71 Fred Barnett .10 .05
❑ 72 Eric Green .10 .05
❑ 73 Dan Marino 1.50 .70
❑ 74 O.J. McDuffie .20 .09
❑ 75 Bernie Parmalee .10 .05
❑ 76 Cris Carter .30 .14
❑ 77 Qadry Ismail .10 .05
❑ 78 Warren Moon .20 .09
❑ 79 Jake Reed .20 .09
❑ 80 Robert Smith .20 .09
❑ 81 Drew Bledsoe .75 .35
❑ 82 Vincent Brisby .10 .05
❑ 83 Ben Coates .20 .09
❑ 84 Curtis Martin .50 .23
❑ 85 Dave Meggett .10 .05
❑ 86 Mario Bates .20 .09
❑ 87 Jim Everett .10 .05
❑ 88 Michael Haynes .10 .05
❑ 89 Renaldo Turnbull .10 .05
❑ 90 Dave Brown .10 .05
❑ 91 Rodney Hampton .20 .09
❑ 92 Thomas Lewis .10 .05
❑ 93 Tyrone Wheatley .20 .09
❑ 94 Kyle Brady .10 .05
❑ 95 Hugh Douglas .10 .05
❑ 96 Aaron Glenn .10 .05
❑ 97 Jeff Graham .10 .05
❑ 98 Adrian Murrell .30 .14
❑ 99 Neil O'Donnell .20 .09
❑ 100 Tim Brown .30 .14
❑ 101 Jeff Hostetler .10 .05
❑ 102 Napoleon Kaufman .40 .18
❑ 103 Chester McGlockton .10 .05
❑ 104 Harvey Williams .10 .05
❑ 105 William Fuller .10 .05
❑ 106 Charlie Garner .10 .05
❑ 107 Ricky Watters .20 .09
❑ 108 Calvin Williams .10 .05
❑ 109 Jerome Bettis .30 .14
❑ 110 Greg Lloyd .20 .09
❑ 111 Byron Bam Morris .20 .09
❑ 112 Kordell Stewart .50 .23
❑ 113 Yancey Thigpen .20 .09
❑ 114 Rod Woodson .20 .09
❑ 115 Isaac Bruce .30 .14
❑ 116 Troy Drayton .10 .05
❑ 117 Leslie O'Neal .10 .05
❑ 118 Steve Walsh .10 .05
❑ 119 Marco Coleman .10 .05
❑ 120 Aaron Hayden .10 .05
❑ 121 Stan Humphries .20 .09
❑ 122 Junior Seau .20 .09
❑ 123 William Floyd .20 .09
❑ 124 Brent Jones .10 .05
❑ 125 Ken Norton .10 .05
❑ 126 Jerry Rice .75 .35
❑ 127 J.J. Stokes .30 .14
❑ 128 Steve Young .60 .25
❑ 129 Brian Blades .10 .05
❑ 130 Joey Galloway .50 .23
❑ 131 Rick Mirer .20 .09
❑ 132 Chris Warren .20 .09
❑ 133 Trent Dilfer .30 .14
❑ 134 Alvin Harper .10 .05
❑ 135 Hardy Nickerson .10 .05
❑ 136 Errict Rhett .20 .09
❑ 137 Terry Allen .20 .09
❑ 138 Henry Ellard .10 .05
❑ 139 Heath Shuler .20 .09
❑ 140 Michael Westbrook .30 .14
❑ 141 Karim Abdul-Jabbar RC .50 .23
❑ 142 Mike Alstott RC 1.25 .55
❑ 143 Marco Battaglia RC .10 .05
❑ 144 Tim Biakabutuka RC .75 .35
❑ 145 Tony Brackens RC .20 .09
❑ 146 Duane Clemons RC .10 .05
❑ 147 Ernie Conwell RC .10 .05
❑ 148 Chris Darkins RC .10 .05
❑ 149 Stephen Davis RC 2.50 1.10
❑ 150 Brian Dawkins RC .10 .05
❑ 151 Rickey Dudley RC .30 .14
❑ 152 Jason Dunn RC .20 .09
❑ 153 Bobby Engram RC .30 .14
❑ 154 Daryl Gardener RC .10 .05
❑ 155 Eddie George RC 2.50 1.10
❑ 156 Terry Glenn RC 1.25 .55
❑ 157 Kevin Hardy RC .30 .14
❑ 158 Walt Harris RC .10 .05
❑ 159 Marvin Harrison RC 2.00 .90
❑ 160 Bobby Hoying RC .50 .23
❑ 161 Keyshawn Johnson RC 2.00 .90
❑ 162 Cedric Jones RC .10 .05
❑ 163 Marcus Jones RC .10 .05
❑ 164 Eddie Kennison RC .30 .14
❑ 165 Ray Lewis RC .10 .05
❑ 166 Derrick Mayes RC .60 .25
❑ 167 Leeland McElroy RC .30 .14
❑ 168 Johnny McWilliams RC .20 .09
❑ 169 John Mobley RC .10 .05
❑ 170 Alex Molden RC .10 .05
❑ 171 Eric Moulds RC 1.50 .70
❑ 172 Muhsin Muhammad RC .75 .35
❑ 173 Jonathan Ogden RC .10 .05
❑ 174 Lawrence Phillips RC .50 .23
❑ 175 Stanley Pritchett RC .20 .09
❑ 176 Simeon Rice RC .30 .14
❑ 177 Bryan Still RC .30 .14
❑ 178 Amani Toomer RC .30 .14
❑ 179 Regan Upshaw RC .10 .05
❑ 180 Alex Van Dyke RC .20 .09
❑ 181 Barry Sanders PFW .75 .35
❑ 182 Marcus Allen PFW .30 .14
❑ 183 Bryce Paup PFW .10 .05
❑ 184 Jerry Rice PFW .40 .18
❑ 185 Desmond Howard PFW .20 .09
Bob Christian
❑ 186 Leon Lett PFW .10 .05
❑ 187 Brett Favre PFW .75 .35
❑ 188 Greg Lloyd PFW .10 .05
Derrick Thomas
❑ 189 Jeff Blake PFW .20 .09
❑ 190 Emmitt Smith PFW .60 .25
❑ 191 John Elway PFW .40 .18
Jeff Hostetler
❑ 192 Chiefs PFW .10 .05
❑ 193 Marshall Faulk PFW .20 .09
❑ 194 Troy Aikman PFW .40 .18
Steve Young
❑ 195 Dan Marino PFW .75 .35
❑ 196 Donta Jones PFW .10 .05
❑ 197 Jim Kelly PFW .30 .14
❑ 198 Checklist .10 .05
❑ 199 Checklist .10 .05
❑ 200 Checklist .10 .05
❑ P1 Promo Sheet 4.00 1.80
William Floyd
Trent Dilfer
Brett Favre

1996 Fleer Breakthroughs

	MINT	NRMT
COMPLETE SET (24)	20.00	9.00

STATED ODDS 1:3

❑ 1 Tim Bowens .75 .35
❑ 2 Kyle Brady .75 .35
❑ 3 Devin Bush .75 .35
❑ 4 Kevin Carter .75 .35
❑ 5 Ki-Jana Carter .75 .35
❑ 6 Kerry Collins 1.25 .55
❑ 7 Trent Dilfer 1.50 .70
❑ 8 Ken Dilger .75 .35
❑ 9 Joey Galloway 2.00 .90
❑ 10 Aaron Hayden .75 .35
❑ 11 Napoleon Kaufman 2.00 .90
❑ 12 Craig Newsome .75 .35
❑ 13 Tyrone Poole .75 .35
❑ 14 Jake Reed 1.25 .55
❑ 15 Rashaan Salaam .75 .35
❑ 16 Chris Sanders 1.50 .70
❑ 17 Frank Sanders 1.25 .55
❑ 18 Kordell Stewart 4.00 1.80
❑ 19 J.J. Stokes 1.50 .70
❑ 20 Bobby Taylor .75 .35
❑ 21 Orlando Thomas .75 .35
❑ 22 Michael Timpson .75 .35
❑ 23 Tamarick Vanover 1.25 .55
❑ 24 Michael Westbrook 1.50 .70

1996 Fleer RAC Pack

	MINT	NRMT
COMPLETE SET (10)	20.00	9.00
COMMON CARD (1-10)	1.00	.45
SEMISTARS	2.00	.90
UNLISTED STARS	4.00	1.80

STATED ODDS 1:18

❑ 1 Robert Brooks 2.00 .90
❑ 2 Tim Brown 2.00 .90
❑ 3 Isaac Bruce 2.00 .90
❑ 4 Cris Carter 2.00 .90
❑ 5 Curtis Conway 1.00 .45
❑ 6 Michael Irvin 2.00 .90
❑ 7 Eric Metcalf 1.00 .45
❑ 8 Herman Moore 2.00 .90
❑ 9 Carl Pickens 2.00 .90
❑ 10 Jerry Rice 10.00 4.50

1996 Fleer Rookie Autographs

	MINT	NRMT
COMPLETE SET (3)	80.00	36.00
COMMON CARD (A1-A3)	12.00	5.50

STATED ODDS 1:288 HOBBY
BLUE SIGNATURES: 1.5X HI COLUMN

❑ A1 Tim Biakabutuka 20.00 9.00
❑ A2 Eddie George 50.00 22.00
❑ A3 Leeland McElroy 12.00 5.50

1996 Fleer Rookie Sensations

	MINT	NRMT
COMPLETE SET (11)	120.00	55.00
COMMON CARD (1-11)	5.00	2.20
SEMISTARS	8.00	3.60

STATED ODDS 1:72		
COMP.HOT PACK SET (11)	100.00	45.00
*HOT PACK: .35X TO .75X HI COL.		
HOT PACK SET STATED ODDS 1:960		
❑ 1 Karim Abdul-Jabbar	10.00	4.50
❑ 2 Tim Biakabutuka	12.00	5.50
❑ 3 Rickey Dudley	5.00	2.20
❑ 4 Eddie George	30.00	13.50
❑ 5 Terry Glenn	12.00	5.50
❑ 6 Kevin Hardy.....................	5.00	2.20
❑ 7 Marvin Harrison..............	25.00	11.00
❑ 8 Keyshawn Johnson	20.00	9.00
❑ 9 Jonathan Ogden	5.00	2.20
❑ 10 Lawrence Phillips	8.00	3.60
❑ 11 Simeon Rice	5.00	2.20

1996 Fleer Rookie Write-Ups

	MINT	NRMT
COMPLETE SET (10)	30.00	13.50
COMMON CARD (1-10)...........	1.25	.55
SEMISTARS............................	2.00	.90
UNLISTED STARS....................	2.50	1.10
STATED ODDS 1:12 HOBBY		
❑ 1 Tim Biakabutuka	3.00	1.35
❑ 2 Rickey Dudley	2.00	.90
❑ 3 Eddie George	6.00	2.70
❑ 4 Terry Glenn	2.50	1.10
❑ 5 Kevin Hardy.......................	1.25	.55
❑ 6 Marvin Harrison.................	5.00	2.20
❑ 7 Keyshawn Johnson	5.00	2.20
❑ 8 Leeland McElroy	2.00	.90
❑ 9 Lawrence Phillips	2.50	1.10
❑ 10 Simeon Rice	1.25	.55

1996 Fleer Statistically Speaking

	MINT	NRMT
COMPLETE SET (20)	80.00	36.00
STATED ODDS 1:37		
❑ 1 Troy Aikman	8.00	3.60
❑ 2 Larry Centers	1.00	.45
❑ 3 Ben Coates	1.00	.45
❑ 4 Brett Favre	15.00	6.75
❑ 5 Joey Galloway.....................	1.50	.70
❑ 6 Rodney Hampton	1.00	.45
❑ 7 Dan Marino	15.00	6.75
❑ 8 Curtis Martin	8.00	3.60
❑ 9 Anthony Miller	1.00	.45
❑ 10 Brian Mitchell..................	1.00	.45
❑ 11 Herman Moore	1.50	.70
❑ 12 Errict Rhett	1.00	.45
❑ 13 Rashaan Salaam............	1.00	.45
❑ 14 Barry Sanders	15.00	6.75
❑ 15 Deion Sanders	1.50	.70
❑ 16 Emmitt Smith................	12.00	5.50
❑ 17 Kordell Stewart	12.00	5.50
❑ 18 Chris Warren..................	1.00	.45
❑ 19 Ricky Watters	1.50	.70
❑ 20 Steve Young	6.00	2.70

1997 Fleer

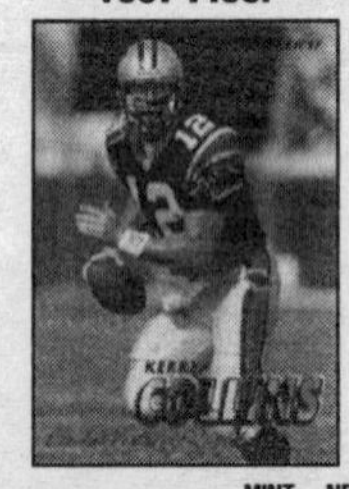

	MINT	NRMT
COMPLETE SET (450)	40.00	18.00
COMMON CARD (1-450)...........	.15	.07
SEMISTARS..............................	.30	.14
UNLISTED STARS....................	.50	.23
COMP.CRYST.SILVER (445)	150.00	70.00
CRYSTAL SILVER STARS: 1.5X TO 3X		
CRYSTAL SILVER ODDS 1:2		
COMP.TIFFANY BLUE (445)	1200.00	550.00
*TIFFANY BLUE STARS: 10X TO 25X		
TIFFANY BLUE ODDS 1:20..........		
COMP.MILL.DOL.INSERT (45)	4.00	1.80
COMP.MILL.DOL.PRIZE (50)	10.00	4.50
❑ 1 Mark Brunell	1.50	.70
❑ 2 Andre Reed........................	.30	.14
❑ 3 Darrell Green.....................	.30	.14
❑ 4 Mario Bates........................	.15	.07
❑ 5 Eddie George	1.50	.70
❑ 6 Cris Carter.........................	.50	.23
❑ 7 Terrell Owens	.50	.23
❑ 8 Bill Romanowski	.15	.07
❑ 9 Isaac Bruce	.50	.23
❑ 10 Eric Curry	.15	.07
❑ 11 Danny Kanell.....................	.30	.14
❑ 12 Ki-Jana Carter	.15	.07
❑ 13 Antonio Freeman...........	1.25	.55
❑ 14 Ricky Watters	.30	.14
❑ 15 Ty Law..............................	.15	.07
❑ 16 Alonzo Spellman	.15	.07
❑ 17 Kordell Stewart	.75	.35
❑ 18 Jerry Rice	1.50	.70
❑ 19 Derrick Alexander WR......	.30	.14
❑ 20 Barry Sanders	3.00	1.35
❑ 21 Keyshawn Johnson.........	.50	.23
❑ 22 Emmitt Smith.................	2.50	1.10
❑ 23 Ricky Proehl	.15	.07
❑ 24 Daryl Gardener	.15	.07
❑ 25 Dan Saleaumua	.15	.07
❑ 26 Kevin Greene	.30	.14
❑ 27 Junior Seau......................	.30	.14
❑ 28 Randall McDaniel	.15	.07
❑ 29 Marshall Faulk...................	.50	.23
❑ 30 Lorenzo Lynch..................	.15	.07
❑ 31 Terance Mathis	.30	.14
❑ 32 Warren Sapp.....................	.30	.14
❑ 33 Chris Sanders	.15	.07
❑ 34 Tom Carter	.15	.07
❑ 35 Aeneas Williams	.15	.07
❑ 36 Lawrence Phillips	.15	.07
❑ 37 John Elway	3.00	1.35
❑ 38 Stanley Richard................	.15	.07
❑ 39 Darryl Williams	.15	.07
❑ 40 Phillippi Sparks	.15	.07
❑ 41 Tedy Bruschi......................	.15	.07
❑ 42 Merton Hanks	.15	.07
❑ 43 Ray Lewis	.15	.07
❑ 44 Erik Williams......................	.15	.07
❑ 45 Jason Gildon	.15	.07
❑ 46 George Koonce	.15	.07
❑ 47 Louis Oliver	.15	.07
❑ 48 Muhsin Muhammad..........	.30	.14
❑ 49 Daryl Hobbs	.15	.07
❑ 50 Terry Glenn	.50	.23
❑ 51 Marvin Harrison...............	.50	.23
❑ 52 Brian Dawkins	.15	.07
❑ 53 Dale Carter	.15	.07
❑ 54 Alex Molden	.15	.07
❑ 55 Raymont Harris	.15	.07
❑ 56 Jeff Burris	.15	.07
❑ 57 Don Beebe	.15	.07
❑ 58 Jamir Miller	.15	.07
❑ 59 Carl Pickens	.50	.23
❑ 60 Antonio London...............	.15	.07
❑ 61 Courtney Hall	.15	.07
❑ 62 Derrick Brooks.................	.15	.07
❑ 63 Chris Boniol.......................	.15	.07
❑ 64 Jeff Lageman	.15	.07
❑ 65 Roy Barker	.15	.07
❑ 66 Devin Bush	.15	.07
❑ 67 Aaron Glenn	.15	.07
❑ 68 Wayne Simmons..............	.15	.07
❑ 69 Steve Atwater	.15	.07
❑ 70 Jimmie Jones	.15	.07
❑ 71 Mark Carrier WR	.15	.07
❑ 72 Chris Chandler	.30	.14
❑ 73 Andy Harmon	.15	.07
❑ 74 John Friesz	.15	.07
❑ 75 Karim Abdul-Jabbar	.50	.23
❑ 76 Levon Kirkland	.15	.07
❑ 77 Torrance Small	.15	.07
❑ 78 Harvey Williams	.15	.07
❑ 79 Chris Calloway	.15	.07
❑ 80 Vinny Testaverde	.30	.14
❑ 81 Bryant Young	.15	.07
❑ 82 Ray Buchanan..................	.15	.07
❑ 83 Robert Smith	.30	.14
❑ 84 Robert Brooks	.30	.14
❑ 85 Ray Crockett	.15	.07
❑ 86 Bennie Blades..................	.15	.07
❑ 87 Mark Carrier DB	.15	.07
❑ 88 Mike Tomczak..................	.15	.07
❑ 89 Darick Holmes..................	.15	.07
❑ 90 Drew Bledsoe	1.50	.70
❑ 91 Darren Woodson..............	.15	.07
❑ 92 Dan Wilkinson..................	.15	.07
❑ 93 Charles Way	.30	.14
❑ 94 Ray Farmer	.15	.07
❑ 95 Marcus Allen	.50	.23
❑ 96 Marco Coleman................	.15	.07
❑ 97 Zach Thomas	.30	.14
❑ 98 Wesley Walls....................	.30	.14
❑ 99 Frank Wycheck	.15	.07
❑ 100 Troy Aikman	1.50	.70
❑ 101 Clyde Simmons..............	.15	.07
❑ 102 Courtney Hawkins..........	.15	.07
❑ 103 Chuck Smith	.15	.07
❑ 104 Neil O'Donnell	.30	.14
❑ 105 Kevin Carter	.15	.07

❑ 106	Chris Slade	.15	.07
❑ 107	Jessie Armstead	.15	.07
❑ 108	Sean Dawkins	.15	.07
❑ 109	Robert Blackmon	.15	.07
❑ 110	Kevin Smith	.15	.07
❑ 111	Lonnie Johnson	.15	.07
❑ 112	Craig Newsome	.15	.07
❑ 113	Jonathan Ogden	.15	.07
❑ 114	Chris Zorich	.15	.07
❑ 115	Tim Brown	.50	.23
❑ 116	Fred Barnett	.15	.07
❑ 117	Michael Haynes	.15	.07
❑ 118	Eric Hill	.15	.07
❑ 119	Ronnie Harmon	.15	.07
❑ 120	Sean Gilbert	.15	.07
❑ 121	Derrick Alexander DE	.15	.07
❑ 122	Derrick Thomas	.30	.14
❑ 123	Tyrone Wheatley	.30	.14
❑ 124	Cortez Kennedy	.15	.07
❑ 125	Jeff George	.30	.14
❑ 126	Chad Cota	.15	.07
❑ 127	Gary Zimmerman	.15	.07
❑ 128	Johnnie Morton	.30	.14
❑ 129	Chad Brown	.15	.07
❑ 130	Marvcus Patton	.15	.07
❑ 131	James O.Stewart	.30	.14
❑ 132	Terry Kirby	.30	.14
❑ 133	Chris Mims	.15	.07
❑ 134	William Thomas	.15	.07
❑ 135	Steve Tasker	.15	.07
❑ 136	Jason Belser	.15	.07
❑ 137	Bryan Cox	.15	.07
❑ 138	Jessie Tuggle	.15	.07
❑ 139	Ashley Ambrose	.15	.07
❑ 140	Mark Chmura	.30	.14
❑ 141	Jeff Hostetler	.15	.07
❑ 142	Rich Owens	.15	.07
❑ 143	Willie Davis	.15	.07
❑ 144	Hardy Nickerson	.15	.07
❑ 145	Curtis Martin	.75	.35
❑ 146	Ken Norton	.15	.07
❑ 147	Victor Green	.15	.07
❑ 148	Anthony Miller	.15	.07
❑ 149	John Kasay	.15	.07
❑ 150	O.J. McDuffie	.30	.14
❑ 151	Darren Perry	.15	.07
❑ 152	Luther Elliss	.15	.07
❑ 153	Greg Hill	.15	.07
❑ 154	John Randle	.15	.07
❑ 155	Stephen Grant	.15	.07
❑ 156	Leon Lett	.15	.07
❑ 157	Darrien Gordon	.15	.07
❑ 158	Ray Zellars	.15	.07
❑ 159	Michael Jackson	.30	.14
❑ 160	Leslie O'Neal	.15	.07
❑ 161	Bruce Smith	.30	.14
❑ 162	Santana Dotson	.15	.07
❑ 163	Bobby Hebert	.15	.07
❑ 164	Keith Hamilton	.15	.07
❑ 165	Tony Boselli	.15	.07
❑ 166	Alfred Williams	.15	.07
❑ 167	Ty Detmer	.30	.14
❑ 168	Chester McGlockton	.15	.07
❑ 169	William Floyd	.30	.14
❑ 170	Bruce Matthews	.15	.07
❑ 171	Simeon Rice	.30	.14
❑ 172	Scott Mitchell	.30	.14
❑ 173	Ricardo McDonald	.15	.07
❑ 174	Tyrone Poole	.15	.07
❑ 175	Greg Lloyd	.15	.07
❑ 176	Bruce Armstrong	.15	.07
❑ 177	Erik Kramer	.15	.07
❑ 178	Kimble Anders	.30	.14
❑ 179	Lamar Smith	.15	.07
❑ 180	Tony Tolbert	.15	.07
❑ 181	Joe Aska	.15	.07
❑ 182	Eric Allen	.15	.07
❑ 183	Eric Turner	.15	.07
❑ 184	Brad Johnson	.75	.35
❑ 185	Tony Martin	.30	.14
❑ 186	Mike Mamula	.15	.07
❑ 187	Irving Spikes	.15	.07
❑ 188	Keith Jackson	.15	.07
❑ 189	Carlton Bailey	.15	.07
❑ 190	Tyrone Braxton	.15	.07
❑ 191	Chad Bratzke	.15	.07
❑ 192	Adrian Murrell	.30	.14
❑ 193	Roman Phifer	.15	.07
❑ 194	Todd Collins	.15	.07
❑ 195	Chris Warren	.30	.14
❑ 196	Kevin Hardy	.15	.07
❑ 197	Rick Mirer	.15	.07
❑ 198	Cornelius Bennett	.15	.07
❑ 199	Jimmy Hitchcock	.15	.07
❑ 200	Michael Irvin	.50	.23
❑ 201	Quentin Coryatt	.15	.07
❑ 202	Reggie White	.50	.23
❑ 203	Larry Centers	.30	.14
❑ 204	Rodney Thomas	.15	.07
❑ 205	Dana Stubblefield	.15	.07
❑ 206	Rod Woodson	.30	.14
❑ 207	Rhett Hall	.15	.07
❑ 208	Steve Tovar	.15	.07
❑ 209	Michael Westbrook	.30	.14
❑ 210	Steve Wisniewski	.15	.07
❑ 211	Carlester Crumpler	.15	.07
❑ 212	Elvis Grbac	.30	.14
❑ 213	Tim Bowens	.15	.07
❑ 214	Robert Porcher	.15	.07
❑ 215	John Carney	.15	.07
❑ 216	Anthony Newman	.15	.07
❑ 217	Earnest Byner	.15	.07
❑ 218	Dewayne Washington	.15	.07
❑ 219	Willie Green	.15	.07
❑ 220	Terry Allen	.50	.23
❑ 221	William Fuller	.15	.07
❑ 222	Al Del Greco	.15	.07
❑ 223	Trent Dilfer	.50	.23
❑ 224	Michael Dean Perry	.15	.07
❑ 225	Larry Allen	.15	.07
❑ 226	Mark Bruener	.15	.07
❑ 227	Clay Matthews	.15	.07
❑ 228	Reuben Brown	.15	.07
❑ 229	Edgar Bennett	.30	.14
❑ 230	Neil Smith	.30	.14
❑ 231	Ken Harvey	.15	.07
❑ 232	Kyle Brady	.15	.07
❑ 233	Corey Miller	.15	.07
❑ 234	Tony Siragusa	.15	.07
❑ 235	Todd Sauerbrun	.15	.07
❑ 236	Daniel Stubbs	.15	.07
❑ 237	Robb Thomas	.15	.07
❑ 238	Jimmy Smith	.30	.14
❑ 239	Marquez Pope	.15	.07
❑ 240	Tim Biakabutuka	.30	.14
❑ 241	Jamie Asher	.15	.07
❑ 242	Steve McNair	.75	.35
❑ 243	Harold Green	.15	.07
❑ 244	Frank Sanders	.30	.14
❑ 245	Joe Johnson	.15	.07
❑ 246	Eric Bieniemy	.15	.07
❑ 247	Kevin Turner	.15	.07
❑ 248	Rickey Dudley	.30	.14
❑ 249	Orlando Thomas	.15	.07
❑ 250	Dan Marino	3.00	1.35
❑ 251	Deion Sanders	.50	.23
❑ 252	Dan Williams	.15	.07
❑ 253	Sam Gash	.15	.07
❑ 254	Lonnie Marts	.15	.07
❑ 255	Mo Lewis	.15	.07
❑ 256	Charles Johnson	.30	.14
❑ 257	Chris Jacke	.15	.07
❑ 258	Keenan McCardell	.30	.14
❑ 259	Donnell Woolford	.15	.07
❑ 260	Terrance Shaw	.15	.07
❑ 261	Jason Dunn	.15	.07
❑ 262	Willie McGinest	.15	.07
❑ 263	Ken Dilger	.15	.07
❑ 264	Keith Lyle	.15	.07
❑ 265	Antonio Langham	.15	.07
❑ 266	Carlton Gray	.15	.07
❑ 267	LeShon Johnson	.15	.07
❑ 268	Thurman Thomas	.50	.23
❑ 269	Jesse Campbell	.15	.07
❑ 270	Carnell Lake	.15	.07
❑ 271	Cris Dishman	.15	.07
❑ 272	Kevin Williams	.15	.07
❑ 273	Troy Brown	.15	.07
❑ 274	William Roaf	.15	.07
❑ 275	Terrell Davis	2.50	1.10
❑ 276	Herman Moore	.50	.23
❑ 277	Walt Harris	.15	.07
❑ 278	Mark Collins	.15	.07
❑ 279	Bert Emanuel	.30	.14
❑ 280	Qadry Ismail	.30	.14
❑ 281	Phil Hansen	.15	.07
❑ 282	Steve Young	1.00	.45
❑ 283	Michael Sinclair	.15	.07
❑ 284	Jeff Graham	.15	.07
❑ 285	Sam Mills	.15	.07
❑ 286	Terry McDaniel	.15	.07
❑ 287	Eugene Robinson	.15	.07
❑ 288	Tony Bennett	.15	.07
❑ 289	Daryl Johnston	.30	.14
❑ 290	Eric Swann	.15	.07
❑ 291	Byron Bam Morris	.15	.07
❑ 292	Thomas Lewis	.15	.07
❑ 293	Terrell Fletcher	.15	.07
❑ 294	Gus Frerotte	.15	.07
❑ 295	Stanley Pritchett	.15	.07
❑ 296	Mike Alstott	.50	.23
❑ 297	Will Shields	.15	.07
❑ 298	Errict Rhett	.15	.07
❑ 299	Garrison Hearst	.30	.14
❑ 300	Kerry Collins	.30	.14
❑ 301	Darryll Lewis	.15	.07
❑ 302	Chris T. Jones	.15	.07
❑ 303	Yancey Thigpen	.30	.14
❑ 304	Jackie Harris	.15	.07
❑ 305	Steve Christie	.15	.07
❑ 306	Gilbert Brown	.15	.07
❑ 307	Terry Wooden	.15	.07
❑ 308	Pete Mitchell	.15	.07
❑ 309	Tim McDonald	.15	.07
❑ 310	Jake Reed	.30	.14
❑ 311	Ed McCaffrey	.30	.14
❑ 312	Chris Doleman	.15	.07
❑ 313	Eric Metcalf	.30	.14
❑ 314	Ricky Reynolds	.15	.07
❑ 315	David Sloan	.15	.07
❑ 316	Marvin Washington	.15	.07
❑ 317	Herschel Walker	.30	.14
❑ 318	Michael Timpson	.15	.07
❑ 319	Blaine Bishop	.15	.07
❑ 320	Irv Smith	.15	.07
❑ 321	Seth Joyner	.15	.07
❑ 322	Terrell Buckley	.15	.07
❑ 323	Michael Strahan	.15	.07
❑ 324	Sam Adams	.15	.07
❑ 325	Leslie Shepherd	.15	.07
❑ 326	James Jett	.30	.14
❑ 327	Anthony Pleasant	.15	.07
❑ 328	Lee Woodall	.15	.07
❑ 329	Shannon Sharpe	.30	.14
❑ 330	Jamal Anderson	1.00	.45
❑ 331	Andre Hastings	.15	.07
❑ 332	Troy Vincent	.15	.07
❑ 333	Sean LaChapelle	.15	.07
❑ 334	Winslow Oliver	.15	.07
❑ 335	Sean Jones	.15	.07
❑ 336	Darnay Scott	.30	.14
❑ 337	Todd Lyght	.15	.07
❑ 338	Leonard Russell	.15	.07
❑ 339	Nate Newton	.15	.07
❑ 340	Zack Crockett	.15	.07
❑ 341	Amp Lee	.15	.07
❑ 342	Bobby Engram	.30	.14
❑ 343	Mike Hollis	.15	.07
❑ 344	Rodney Hampton	.30	.14
❑ 345	Mel Gray	.15	.07
❑ 346	Van Malone	.15	.07
❑ 347	Aaron Craver	.15	.07
❑ 348	Jim Everett	.15	.07
❑ 349	Trace Armstrong	.15	.07
❑ 350	Pat Swilling	.15	.07
❑ 351	Brent Jones	.30	.14
❑ 352	Chris Spielman	.15	.07
❑ 353	Brett Perriman	.15	.07
❑ 354	Brian Kinchen	.15	.07
❑ 355	Joey Galloway	.75	.35
❑ 356	Henry Ellard	.15	.07
❑ 357	Ben Coates	.30	.14
❑ 358	Dorsey Levens	.50	.23
❑ 359	Charlie Garner	.15	.07
❑ 360	Erric Pegram	.15	.07
❑ 361	Anthony Johnson	.15	.07
❑ 362	Rashaan Salaam	.15	.07
❑ 363	Jeff Blake	.30	.14

	MINT	NRMT
❑ 364 Kent Graham	.15	.07
❑ 365 Broderick Thomas	.15	.07
❑ 366 Richmond Webb	.15	.07
❑ 367 Alfred Pupunu	.15	.07
❑ 368 Mark Stepnoski	.15	.07
❑ 369 David Dunn	.15	.07
❑ 370 Bobby Houston	.15	.07
❑ 371 Anthony Parker	.15	.07
❑ 372 Quinn Early	.15	.07
❑ 373 LeRoy Butler	.15	.07
❑ 374 Kurt Gouveia	.15	.07
❑ 375 Greg Biekert	.15	.07
❑ 376 Jim Harbaugh	.30	.14
❑ 377 Eric Bjornson	.15	.07
❑ 378 Craig Heyward	.15	.07
❑ 379 Steve Bono	.30	.14
❑ 380 Tony Banks	.30	.14
❑ 381 John Mobley	.15	.07
❑ 382 Irving Fryar	.30	.14
❑ 383 Dermontti Dawson	.15	.07
❑ 384 Eric Davis	.15	.07
❑ 385 Natrone Means	.50	.23
❑ 386 Jason Sehorn	.30	.14
❑ 387 Michael McCrary	.15	.07
❑ 388 Corwin Brown	.15	.07
❑ 389 Kevin Glover	.15	.07
❑ 390 Jerris McPhail	.15	.07
❑ 391 Bobby Taylor	.15	.07
❑ 392 Tony McGee	.15	.07
❑ 393 Curtis Conway	.30	.14
❑ 394 Napoleon Kaufman	.50	.23
❑ 395 Brian Blades	.15	.07
❑ 396 Richard Dent	.15	.07
❑ 397 Dave Brown	.15	.07
❑ 398 Stan Humphries	.30	.14
❑ 399 Stevon Moore	.15	.07
❑ 400 Brett Favre	3.00	1.35
❑ 401 Jerome Bettis	.50	.23
❑ 402 Darrin Smith	.15	.07
❑ 403 Chris Penn	.15	.07
❑ 404 Rob Moore	.30	.14
❑ 405 Micheal Barrow	.15	.07
❑ 406 Tony Brackens	.15	.07
❑ 407 Wayne Martin	.15	.07
❑ 408 Warren Moon	.50	.23
❑ 409 Jason Elam	.15	.07
❑ 410 J.J. Birden	.15	.07
❑ 411 Hugh Douglas	.15	.07
❑ 412 Lamar Lathon	.15	.07
❑ 413 John Kidd	.15	.07
❑ 414 Bryce Paup	.15	.07
❑ 415 Shawn Jefferson	.15	.07
❑ 416 Leeland McElroy SS	.15	.07
❑ 417 Elbert Shelley SS	.15	.07
❑ 418 Jermaine Lewis SS	.30	.14
❑ 419 Eric Moulds SS	.50	.23
❑ 420 Michael Bates SS	.15	.07
❑ 421 John Mangum SS	.15	.07
❑ 422 Corey Sawyer SS	.15	.07
❑ 423 Jim Schwantz SS RC	.15	.07
❑ 424 Rod Smith WR SS	.50	.23
❑ 425 Glyn Milburn SS	.15	.07
❑ 426 Desmond Howard SS	.30	.14
❑ 427 John Henry Mills SS RC	.15	.07
❑ 428 Cary Blanchard SS RC	.15	.07
❑ 429 Chris Hudson SS	.15	.07
❑ 430 Tamarick Vanover SS	.30	.14
❑ 431 Kirby Dar Dar SS	.15	.07
❑ 432 David Palmer SS	.15	.07
❑ 433 Dave Meggett SS	.15	.07
❑ 434 Tyrone Hughes SS	.15	.07
❑ 435 Amani Toomer SS	.30	.14
❑ 436 Wayne Chrebet SS	.30	.14
❑ 437 Carl Kidd SS RC	.15	.07
❑ 438 Derrick Witherspoon SS	.15	.07
❑ 439 Jahine Arnold SS	.15	.07
❑ 440 Andre Coleman SS	.15	.07
❑ 441 Jeff Wilkins SS	.15	.07
❑ 442 Jay Bellamy SS RC	.15	.07
❑ 443 Eddie Kennison SS	.30	.14
❑ 444 Nilo Silvan SS	.15	.07
❑ 445 Brian Mitchell SS	.15	.07
❑ 446 Garrison Hearst Checklist back	.30	.14
❑ 447 Napoleon Kaufman Checklist back	.50	.23
❑ 448 Brian Mitchell Checklist back	.15	.07
❑ 449 Rodney Hampton Checklist back	.15	.07
❑ 450 Edgar Bennett Checklist back	.15	.07
❑ S1 Mark Chmura Sample	1.00	.45
❑ AU1 Reggie White AUTO (numbered of 80)	125.00	55.00

1997 Fleer All-Pros

	MINT	NRMT
COMPLETE SET (24)	120.00	55.00
STATED ODDS 1:36 RETAIL		
❑ 1 Troy Aikman	12.00	5.50
❑ 2 Larry Allen	1.25	.55
❑ 3 Drew Bledsoe	12.00	5.50
❑ 4 Terrell Davis	20.00	9.00
❑ 5 Dermontti Dawson	1.25	.55
❑ 6 John Elway	25.00	11.00
❑ 7 Brett Favre	25.00	11.00
❑ 8 Herman Moore	4.00	1.80
❑ 9 Jerry Rice	12.00	5.50
❑ 10 Barry Sanders	25.00	11.00
❑ 11 Shannon Sharpe	2.50	1.10
❑ 12 Erik Williams	1.25	.55
❑ 13 Ashley Ambrose	1.25	.55
❑ 14 Chad Brown	1.25	.55
❑ 15 LeRoy Butler	1.25	.55
❑ 16 Kevin Greene	2.50	1.10
❑ 17 Sam Mills	1.25	.55
❑ 18 John Randle	1.25	.55
❑ 19 Deion Sanders	4.00	1.80
❑ 20 Junior Seau	2.50	1.10
❑ 21 Bruce Smith	2.50	1.10
❑ 22 Alfred Williams	1.25	.55
❑ 23 Darren Woodson	1.25	.55
❑ 24 Bryant Young	1.25	.55

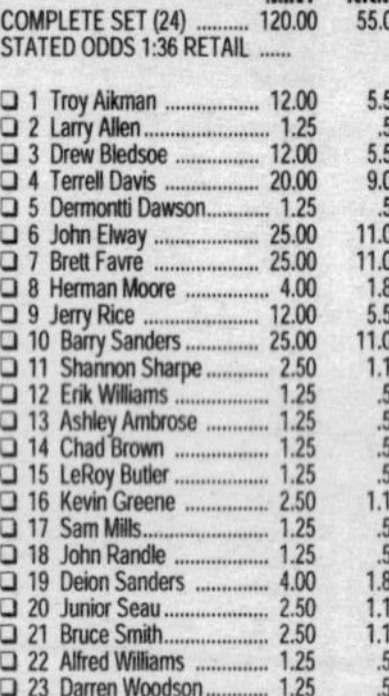

1997 Fleer Decade of Excellence

	MINT	NRMT
COMPLETE SET (12)	50.00	22.00
STATED ODDS 1:36 HOBBY		
❑ 1 Marcus Allen	2.50	1.10
❑ 2 Cris Carter	2.50	1.10
❑ 3 John Elway	15.00	6.75
❑ 4 Irving Fryar	1.50	.70
❑ 5 Darrell Green	1.50	.70
❑ 6 Dan Marino	15.00	6.75
❑ 7 Jerry Rice	8.00	3.60
❑ 8 Bruce Smith	1.50	.70
❑ 9 Herschel Walker	1.50	.70
❑ 10 Reggie White	2.50	1.10
❑ 11 Rod Woodson	1.50	.70
❑ 12 Steve Young	5.00	2.20

1997 Fleer Game Breakers

	MINT	NRMT
COMPLETE SET (20)	15.00	6.75
STATED ODDS 1:2 RETAIL		

*SUPREME CARDS: 2.5X TO 6X BASE CARD HI
SUPREME ODDS 1:18 HOB/RET

❑ 1 Troy Aikman	2.00	.90
❑ 2 Jerome Bettis	.60	.25
❑ 3 Drew Bledsoe	2.00	.90
❑ 4 Isaac Bruce	.60	.25
❑ 5 Mark Brunell	2.00	.90
❑ 6 Kerry Collins	.40	.18
❑ 7 Terrell Davis	3.00	1.35
❑ 8 Marshall Faulk	.60	.25
❑ 9 Antonio Freeman	1.50	.70
❑ 10 Joey Galloway	1.00	.45
❑ 11 Terry Glenn	.60	.25
❑ 12 Desmond Howard	.40	.18
❑ 13 Keyshawn Johnson	.60	.25
❑ 14 Eddie Kennison	.40	.18
❑ 15 Curtis Martin	1.00	.45
❑ 16 Herman Moore	.60	.25
❑ 17 Lawrence Phillips	.20	.09
❑ 18 Barry Sanders	4.00	1.80
❑ 19 Shannon Sharpe	.40	.18
❑ 20 Emmitt Smith	3.00	1.35

1997 Fleer Prospects

	MINT	NRMT
COMPLETE SET (10)	12.00	5.50
COMMON CARD (1-10)	1.00	.45
SEMISTARS	1.50	.70
STATED ODDS 1:6		
❑ 1 Peter Boulware	1.50	.70
❑ 2 Rae Carruth	1.50	.70
❑ 3 Jim Druckenmiller	1.50	.70
❑ 4 Warrick Dunn	2.50	1.10
❑ 5 Tony Gonzalez	2.50	1.10
❑ 6 Yatil Green	1.50	.70
❑ 7 Ike Hilliard	1.50	.70
❑ 8 Orlando Pace	1.00	.45
❑ 9 Darrell Russell	1.00	.45
❑ 10 Shawn Springs	1.50	.70

1997 Fleer Rookie Sensations

	MINT	NRMT
COMPLETE SET (20)	25.00	11.00
STATED ODDS 1:4		

❑ 1 Karim Abdul-Jabbar	2.00	.90
❑ 2 Mike Alstott	2.00	.90
❑ 3 Tony Banks	1.25	.55
❑ 4 Tony Brackens	.60	.25
❑ 5 Rickey Dudley	1.25	.55
❑ 6 Bobby Engram	1.25	.55
❑ 7 Eddie George	6.00	2.70
❑ 8 Terry Glenn	2.00	.90
❑ 9 Kevin Hardy	.60	.25
❑ 10 Marvin Harrison	2.00	.90
❑ 11 Keyshawn Johnson	2.00	.90
❑ 12 Eddie Kennison	1.25	.55
❑ 13 Jermaine Lewis	1.25	.55
❑ 14 Ray Lewis	.60	.25
❑ 15 John Mobley	.60	.25
❑ 16 Eric Moulds	2.00	.90
❑ 17 Jonathan Ogden	.60	.25
❑ 18 Lawrence Phillips	.60	.25
❑ 19 Simeon Rice	1.25	.55
❑ 20 Zach Thomas	1.25	.55

1997 Fleer Thrill Seekers

	MINT	NRMT
COMPLETE SET (12)	300.00	135.00
STATED ODDS 1:288		

❑ 1 Karim Abdul-Jabbar	8.00	3.60
❑ 2 Jerome Bettis	8.00	3.60
❑ 3 Terrell Davis	40.00	18.00
❑ 4 John Elway	50.00	22.00
❑ 5 Brett Favre	50.00	22.00
❑ 6 Eddie George	25.00	11.00
❑ 7 Terry Glenn	8.00	3.60
❑ 8 Keyshawn Johnson	8.00	3.60
❑ 9 Dan Marino	50.00	22.00
❑ 10 Curtis Martin	12.00	5.50
❑ 11 Deion Sanders	8.00	3.60
❑ 12 Emmitt Smith	40.00	18.00

1998 Fleer

	MINT	NRMT
COMPLETE SET (250)	40.00	18.00
COMMON CARD (1-250)	.10	.05
SEMISTARS	.20	.09
UNLISTED STARS	.40	.18
COMMON ROOKIE (223-247)	.50	.23
ROOKIE SEMISTARS	.75	.35
ROOKIE UNLISTED STARS	1.25	.55
COMMON HERITAGE	6.00	2.70

*HERITAGE STARS: 20X TO 50X HI COL.
*HERITAGE YOUNG STARS: 15X TO 40X
*HERITAGE RCs: 6X TO 15X
HERITAGE PRINT RUN 125 SERIAL #'d SETS

❑ 1 Brett Favre	2.00	.90
❑ 2 Barry Sanders	2.00	.90
❑ 3 John Elway	2.00	.90
❑ 4 Emmitt Smith	1.50	.70
❑ 5 Dan Marino	2.00	.90
❑ 6 Eddie George	.75	.35
❑ 7 Jerry Rice	1.00	.45
❑ 8 Jake Plummer	1.25	.55
❑ 9 Joey Galloway	.40	.18
❑ 10 Mike Alstott	.40	.18
❑ 11 Brian Mitchell	.10	.05
❑ 12 Keyshawn Johnson	.40	.18
❑ 13 Jerald Moore	.10	.05
❑ 14 Randal Hill	.10	.05
❑ 15 Byron Hanspard	.20	.09
❑ 16 Jeff George	.20	.09
❑ 17 Terry Glenn	.40	.18
❑ 18 Jerome Bettis	.40	.18
❑ 19 Curtis Conway	.20	.09
❑ 20 Fred Lane	.20	.09
❑ 21 Isaac Bruce	.40	.18
❑ 22 Tiki Barber	.20	.09
❑ 23 Bobby Hoying	.20	.09
❑ 24 Marcus Allen	.40	.18
❑ 25 Dana Stubblefield	.10	.05
❑ 26 Peter Boulware	.10	.05
❑ 27 John Randle	.20	.09
❑ 28 Jason Sehorn	.10	.05
❑ 29 Rod Smith	.20	.09
❑ 30 Michael Sinclair	.10	.05
❑ 31 Marshall Faulk	.40	.18
❑ 32 Karl Williams	.10	.05
❑ 33 Kordell Stewart	.40	.18
❑ 34 Corey Dillon	.60	.25
❑ 35 Bryant Young	.10	.05
❑ 36 Charlie Garner	.10	.05
❑ 37 Andre Reed	.20	.09
❑ 38 Ray Buchanan	.10	.05
❑ 39 Brett Perriman	.10	.05
❑ 40 Leon Lett	.10	.05
❑ 41 Keenan McCardell	.20	.09
❑ 42 Eric Swann	.10	.05
❑ 43 Leslie Shepherd	.10	.05
❑ 44 Curtis Martin	.40	.18
❑ 45 Andre Rison	.20	.09
❑ 46 Keith Lyle	.10	.05
❑ 47 Rae Carruth	.20	.09
❑ 48 William Henderson	.10	.05
❑ 49 Sean Dawkins	.10	.05
❑ 50 Terrell Davis	1.50	.70
❑ 51 Tim Brown	.40	.18
❑ 52 Willie McGinest	.10	.05
❑ 53 Jermaine Lewis	.20	.09
❑ 54 Ricky Watters	.20	.09
❑ 55 Freddie Jones	.10	.05
❑ 56 Robert Smith	.40	.18
❑ 57 Reidel Anthony	.20	.09
❑ 58 James Stewart	.20	.09
❑ 59 Earl Holmes RC	.50	.23
❑ 60 Dale Carter	.10	.05
❑ 61 Michael Irvin	.40	.18
❑ 62 Jason Taylor	.10	.05
❑ 63 Eric Metcalf	.10	.05
❑ 64 LeRoy Butler	.10	.05
❑ 65 Jamal Anderson	.40	.18
❑ 66 Jamie Asher	.10	.05
❑ 67 Chris Sanders	.10	.05
❑ 68 Warren Sapp	.20	.09
❑ 69 Ray Zellars	.10	.05
❑ 70 Carl Pickens	.40	.18
❑ 71 Garrison Hearst	.40	.18
❑ 72 Eddie Kennison	.20	.09
❑ 73 John Mobley	.10	.05
❑ 74 Rob Johnson	.20	.09
❑ 75 William Thomas	.10	.05
❑ 76 Drew Bledsoe	.75	.35
❑ 77 Micheal Barrow	.10	.05
❑ 78 Jim Harbaugh	.20	.09
❑ 79 Terry McDaniel	.10	.05
❑ 80 Johnnie Morton	.20	.09
❑ 81 Danny Kanell	.20	.09
❑ 82 Larry Centers	.10	.05
❑ 83 Courtney Hawkins	.10	.05
❑ 84 Tony Brackens	.10	.05
❑ 85 Tony Gonzalez	.10	.05
❑ 86 Aaron Glenn	.10	.05
❑ 87 Cris Carter	.40	.18
❑ 88 Chuck Smith	.10	.05
❑ 89 Tamarick Vanover	.10	.05
❑ 90 Karim Abdul-Jabbar	.40	.18
❑ 91 Bryant Westbrook	.10	.05
❑ 92 Mike Pritchard	.10	.05
❑ 93 Darren Woodson	.10	.05
❑ 94 Wesley Walls	.20	.09
❑ 95 Tony Banks	.20	.09
❑ 96 Michael Westbrook	.20	.09
❑ 97 Shannon Sharpe	.20	.09
❑ 98 Jeff Blake	.20	.09
❑ 99 Terrell Owens	.40	.18
❑ 100 Warrick Dunn	.60	.25
❑ 101 Levon Kirkland	.10	.05
❑ 102 Frank Wycheck	.10	.05
❑ 103 Gus Frerotte	.10	.05
❑ 104 Simeon Rice	.20	.09
❑ 105 Shawn Jefferson	.10	.05
❑ 106 Irving Fryar	.20	.09
❑ 107 Michael McCrary	.10	.05
❑ 108 Robert Brooks	.20	.09
❑ 109 Chris Chandler	.20	.09
❑ 110 Junior Seau	.20	.09
❑ 111 O.J. McDuffie	.20	.09
❑ 112 Glenn Foley	.20	.09
❑ 113 Darryl Williams	.10	.05
❑ 114 Elvis Grbac	.20	.09
❑ 115 Napoleon Kaufman	.40	.18
❑ 116 Anthony Miller	.10	.05
❑ 117 Troy Davis	.10	.05
❑ 118 Charles Way	.10	.05
❑ 119 Scott Mitchell	.20	.09
❑ 120 Ken Harvey	.10	.05
❑ 121 Tyrone Hughes	.10	.05
❑ 122 Mark Brunell	.75	.35
❑ 123 David Palmer	.10	.05
❑ 124 Rob Moore	.20	.09
❑ 125 Kerry Collins	.20	.09
❑ 126 Will Blackwell	.10	.05
❑ 127 Ray Crockett	.10	.05
❑ 128 Leslie O'Neal	.10	.05
❑ 129 Antowain Smith	.40	.18
❑ 130 Carlester Crumpler	.10	.05
❑ 131 Michael Jackson	.10	.05
❑ 132 Trent Dilfer	.40	.18
❑ 133 Dan Williams	.10	.05
❑ 134 Dorsey Levens	.40	.18
❑ 135 Ty Law	.10	.05
❑ 136 Rickey Dudley	.10	.05
❑ 137 Jessie Tuggle	.10	.05
❑ 138 Darrien Gordon	.10	.05
❑ 139 Kevin Turner	.10	.05
❑ 140 Willie Davis	.10	.05
❑ 141 Zach Thomas	.10	.05
❑ 142 Tony McGee	.10	.05
❑ 143 Dexter Coakley	.10	.05
❑ 144 Troy Brown	.10	.05
❑ 145 Leeland McElroy	.10	.05
❑ 146 Michael Strahan	.10	.05
❑ 147 Ken Dilger	.10	.05

		MINT	NRMT
❑ 148	Bryce Paup	.10	.05
❑ 149	Herman Moore	.40	.18
❑ 150	Reggie White	.40	.18
❑ 151	Dewayne Washington	.10	.05
❑ 152	Natrone Means	.40	.18
❑ 153	Ben Coates	.20	.09
❑ 154	Bert Emanuel	.20	.09
❑ 155	Steve Young	.60	.25
❑ 156	Jimmy Smith	.20	.09
❑ 157	Darrell Green	.20	.09
❑ 158	Troy Aikman	1.00	.45
❑ 159	Greg Hill	.10	.05
❑ 160	Raymont Harris	.10	.05
❑ 161	Troy Drayton	.10	.05
❑ 162	Stevon Moore	.10	.05
❑ 163	Warren Moon	.40	.18
❑ 164	Wayne Martin	.10	.05
❑ 165	Jason Gildon	.10	.05
❑ 166	Chris Calloway	.10	.05
❑ 167	Aeneas Williams	.10	.05
❑ 168	Michael Bates	.10	.05
❑ 169	Hugh Douglas	.10	.05
❑ 170	Brad Johnson	.40	.18
❑ 171	Bruce Smith	.20	.09
❑ 172	Neil Smith	.20	.09
❑ 173	James McKnight	.10	.05
❑ 174	Robert Porcher	.10	.05
❑ 175	Merton Hanks	.10	.05
❑ 176	Ki-Jana Carter	.10	.05
❑ 177	Mo Lewis	.10	.05
❑ 178	Chester McGlockton	.10	.05
❑ 179	Zack Crockett	.10	.05
❑ 180	Derrick Thomas	.20	.09
❑ 181	J.J. Stokes	.20	.09
❑ 182	Derrick Rodgers	.10	.05
❑ 183	Daryl Johnston	.20	.09
❑ 184	Chris Penn	.10	.05
❑ 185	Steve Atwater	.10	.05
❑ 186	Amp Lee	.10	.05
❑ 187	Frank Sanders	.20	.09
❑ 188	Chris Slade	.10	.05
❑ 189	Mark Chmura	.20	.09
❑ 190	Kimble Anders	.20	.09
❑ 191	Charles Johnson	.10	.05
❑ 192	William Floyd	.10	.05
❑ 193	Jay Graham	.10	.05
❑ 194	Hardy Nickerson	.10	.05
❑ 195	Terry Allen	.40	.18
❑ 196	James Jett	.20	.09
❑ 197	Jessie Armstead	.10	.05
❑ 198	Yancey Thigpen	.20	.09
❑ 199	Terance Mathis	.20	.09
❑ 200	Steve McNair	.40	.18
❑ 201	Wayne Chrebet	.40	.18
❑ 202	Jamir Miller	.10	.05
❑ 203	Duce Staley	.75	.35
❑ 204	Deion Sanders	.40	.18
❑ 205	Carnell Lake	.10	.05
❑ 206	Ed McCaffrey	.20	.09
❑ 207	Shawn Springs	.10	.05
❑ 208	Tony Martin	.20	.09
❑ 209	Jerris McPhail	.10	.05
❑ 210	Darnay Scott	.20	.09
❑ 211	Jake Reed	.20	.09
❑ 212	Adrian Murrell	.20	.09
❑ 213	Quinn Early	.10	.05
❑ 214	Marvin Harrison	.20	.09
❑ 215	Ryan McNeil	.10	.05
❑ 216	Derrick Alexander	.20	.09
❑ 217	Ray Lewis	.10	.05
❑ 218	Antonio Freeman	.40	.18
❑ 219	Dwayne Rudd	.10	.05
❑ 220	Muhsin Muhammad	.20	.09
❑ 221	Kevin Hardy	.10	.05
❑ 222	Andre Hastings	.10	.05
❑ 223	John Avery RC	1.25	.55
❑ 224	Keith Brooking RC	.75	.35
❑ 225	Kevin Dyson RC	2.00	.90
❑ 226	Robert Edwards RC	1.25	.55
❑ 227	Greg Ellis RC	.50	.23
❑ 228	Curtis Enis RC	2.50	1.10
❑ 229	Terry Fair RC	.75	.35
❑ 230	Ahman Green RC	2.00	.90
❑ 231	Jacquez Green RC	2.00	.90
❑ 232	Brian Griese RC	3.00	1.35
❑ 233	Skip Hicks RC	2.00	.90
❑ 234	Ryan Leaf RC	2.00	.90
❑ 235	Peyton Manning RC	10.00	4.50
❑ 236	R.W. McQuarters RC	.50	.23
❑ 237	Randy Moss RC	10.00	4.50
❑ 238	Marcus Nash RC	2.00	.90
❑ 239	Anthony Simmons RC	.50	.23
❑ 240	Brian Simmons RC	.50	.23
❑ 241	Takeo Spikes RC	.75	.35
❑ 242	Duane Starks RC	.50	.23
❑ 243	Fred Taylor RC	5.00	2.20
❑ 244	Andre Wadsworth RC	.75	.35
❑ 245	Shaun Williams RC	.50	.23
❑ 246	Grant Wistrom RC	.50	.23
❑ 247	Charles Woodson RC	2.50	1.10
❑ 248	Checklist	.10	.05
❑ 249	Checklist	.10	.05
❑ 250	Checklist	.10	.05

1998 Fleer Big Numbers

	MINT	NRMT
COMPLETE SET (99)	100.00	45.00
COMMON CARD (BN1A-BN9K)	.60	.25
STATED ODDS 1:4		
EACH PLAYER HAS 11-DIFF.CARD #'S		

		MINT	NRMT
❑ BN1A	Tim Brown	.60	.25
❑ BN2A	Cris Carter	.60	.25
❑ BN3A	Terrell Davis	2.50	1.10
❑ BN4A	John Elway	3.00	1.35
❑ BN5A	Brett Favre	3.00	1.35
❑ BN6A	Eddie George	1.25	.55
❑ BN7A	Dorsey Levens	.60	.25
❑ BN8A	Herman Moore	.60	.25
❑ BN9A	Steve Young	1.00	.45

1998 Fleer Playmakers Theatre

	MINT	NRMT
COMPLETE SET (15)	700.00	325.00
COMMON CARD (PT1-PT15)	30.00	13.50
STATED PRINT RUN 100 SERIAL #'d SETS		

		MINT	NRMT
❑ PT1	Terrell Davis	80.00	36.00
❑ PT2	Corey Dillon	30.00	13.50
❑ PT3	Warrick Dunn	50.00	22.00
❑ PT4	John Elway	120.00	55.00
❑ PT5	Brett Favre	120.00	55.00
❑ PT6	Antonio Freeman	40.00	18.00
❑ PT7	Joey Galloway	40.00	18.00
❑ PT8	Eddie George	60.00	27.00
❑ PT9	Terry Glenn	40.00	18.00
❑ PT10	Dan Marino	120.00	55.00
❑ PT11	Curtis Martin	40.00	18.00
❑ PT12	Jake Plummer	60.00	27.00
❑ PT13	Barry Sanders	120.00	55.00
❑ PT14	Deion Sanders	40.00	18.00
❑ PT15	Kordell Stewart	30.00	13.50

1998 Fleer Red Zone Rockers

	MINT	NRMT
COMPLETE SET (10)	60.00	27.00
COMMON CARD (RZ1-RZ10)	6.00	2.70
STATED ODDS 1:32		

		MINT	NRMT
❑ RZ1	Jerome Bettis	6.00	2.70
❑ RZ2	Drew Bledsoe	8.00	3.60
❑ RZ3	Mark Brunell	8.00	3.60
❑ RZ4	Corey Dillon	6.00	2.70
❑ RZ5	Joey Galloway	6.00	2.70
❑ RZ6	Keyshawn Johnson	6.00	2.70
❑ RZ7	Dorsey Levens	6.00	2.70
❑ RZ8	Dan Marino	20.00	9.00
❑ RZ9	Barry Sanders	20.00	9.00
❑ RZ10	Emmitt Smith	15.00	6.75

1998 Fleer Rookie Sensations

	MINT	NRMT
COMPLETE SET (15)	60.00	27.00
COMMON CARD (1RS-15RS)	2.00	.90
SEMISTARS	3.00	1.35
UNLISTED STARS	4.00	1.80
STATED ODDS 1:16		

		MINT	NRMT
❑ 1RS	John Avery	4.00	1.80
❑ 2RS	Keith Brooking	3.00	1.35
❑ 3RS	Kevin Dyson	4.00	1.80
❑ 4RS	Robert Edwards	4.00	1.80
❑ 5RS	Greg Ellis	2.00	.90
❑ 6RS	Curtis Enis	5.00	2.20
❑ 7RS	Terry Fair	3.00	1.35
❑ 8RS	Ryan Leaf	5.00	2.20
❑ 9RS	Peyton Manning	15.00	6.75
❑ 10RS	Randy Moss	15.00	6.75
❑ 11RS	Marcus Nash	4.00	1.80
❑ 12RS	Fred Taylor	10.00	4.50
❑ 13RS	Andre Wadsworth	3.00	1.35
❑ 14RS	Grant Wistrom	2.00	.90
❑ 15RS	Charles Woodson	5.00	2.20

1999 Fleer

	MINT	NRMT
COMPLETE SET (300)	40.00	18.00
COMMON CARD (1-250)	.10	.05
SEMISTARS	.20	.09
UNLISTED STARS	.40	.18
COMMON ROOKIE (251-300)	.40	.18
ROOKIE SEMISTARS	.75	.35
ROOKIE UNL.STARS	1.25	.55

COMP.BLITZ COLL.(300) 100.00 45.00
*BLITZ COLL.STARS: 1.2X TO 3X HI COL.
*BLITZ COLL.YOUNG STARS: 1X TO 2.5X
*BLITZ COLL.RCs: .5X TO 1.2X ..
ONE BLITZ COLLECTION PER RETAIL PACK

❑	1	Randy Moss	1.50	.70
❑	2	Peyton Manning	1.50	.70
❑	3	Barry Sanders	1.50	.70
❑	4	Terrell Davis	1.00	.45
❑	5	Brett Favre	1.50	.70
❑	6	Fred Taylor	1.00	.45
❑	7	Jake Plummer	.75	.35
❑	8	John Elway	1.50	.70
❑	9	Emmitt Smith	1.00	.45
❑	10	Kerry Collins	.20	.09
❑	11	Peter Boulware	.10	.05
❑	12	Jamal Anderson	.40	.18
❑	13	Doug Flutie	.50	.23
❑	14	Michael Bates	.10	.05
❑	15	Corey Dillon	.40	.18
❑	16	Curtis Conway	.20	.09
❑	17	Ty Detmer	.20	.09
❑	18	Robert Brooks	.20	.09
❑	19	Dale Carter	.10	.05
❑	20	Charlie Batch	.75	.35
❑	21	Ken Dilger	.10	.05
❑	22	Troy Aikman	1.00	.45
❑	23	Tavian Banks	.10	.05
❑	24	Cris Carter	.40	.18
❑	25	Derrick Alexander WR	.20	.09
❑	26	Chris Bordano RC	.10	.05
❑	27	Karim Abdul-Jabbar	.20	.09
❑	28	Jessie Armstead	.10	.05
❑	29	Drew Bledsoe	.60	.25
❑	30	Brian Dawkins	.10	.05
❑	31	Wayne Chrebet	.20	.09
❑	32	Garrison Hearst	.20	.09
❑	33	Eric Allen	.10	.05
❑	34	Tony Banks	.20	.09
❑	35	Jerome Bettis	.40	.18
❑	36	Stephen Alexander	.10	.05
❑	37	Rodney Harrison	.10	.05
❑	38	Mike Alstott	.40	.18
❑	39	Chad Brown	.10	.05
❑	40	Johnny McWilliams	.10	.05
❑	41	Kevin Dyson	.20	.09
❑	42	Keith Brooking	.10	.05
❑	43	Jim Harbaugh	.20	.09
❑	44	Bobby Engram	.20	.09
❑	45	John Holecek	.10	.05
❑	46	Steve Beuerlein	.10	.05
❑	47	Tony McGee	.10	.05
❑	48	Greg Ellis	.10	.05
❑	49	Corey Fuller	.10	.05
❑	50	Stephen Boyd	.10	.05
❑	51	Marshall Faulk	.40	.18
❑	52	Leroy Butler	.10	.05
❑	53	Reggie Barlow	.10	.05
❑	54	Randall Cunningham	.40	.18
❑	55	Aeneas Williams	.10	.05
❑	56	Kimble Anders	.20	.09
❑	57	Cam Cleeland	.10	.05
❑	58	John Avery	.20	.09
❑	59	Gary Brown	.10	.05
❑	60	Ben Coates	.20	.09
❑	61	Koy Detmer	.10	.05
❑	62	Bryan Cox	.10	.05
❑	63	Edgar Bennett	.10	.05
❑	64	Tim Brown	.40	.18
❑	65	Isaac Bruce	.40	.18
❑	66	Eddie George	.50	.23
❑	67	Reidel Anthony	.20	.09
❑	68	Charlie Jones	.10	.05
❑	69	Terry Allen	.20	.09
❑	70	Joey Galloway	.40	.18
❑	71	Jamir Miller	.10	.05
❑	72	Will Blackwell	.10	.05
❑	73	Ray Buchanan	.10	.05
❑	74	Priest Holmes	.40	.18
❑	75	Michael Irvin	.20	.09
❑	76	Jonathan Linton	.10	.05
❑	77	Curtis Enis	.40	.18
❑	78	Neil O'Donnell	.20	.09
❑	79	Tim Biakabutuka	.20	.09
❑	80	Terry Kirby	.10	.05
❑	81	Germane Crowell	.20	.09
❑	82	Jason Elam	.10	.05
❑	83	Mark Chmura	.10	.05
❑	84	Marvin Harrison	.40	.18
❑	85	Jimmy Hitchcock	.10	.05
❑	86	Tony Brackens	.10	.05
❑	87	Sean Dawkins	.10	.05
❑	88	Tony Gonzalez	.20	.09
❑	89	Kent Graham	.10	.05
❑	90	Oronde Gadsden	.10	.05
❑	91	Hugh Douglas	.10	.05
❑	92	Robert Edwards	.20	.09
❑	93	R.W. McQuarters	.10	.05
❑	94	Aaron Glenn	.10	.05
❑	95	Kevin Carter	.10	.05
❑	96	Rickey Dudley	.10	.05
❑	97	Derrick Brooks	.10	.05
❑	98	Mark Bruener	.10	.05
❑	99	Darrell Green	.10	.05
❑	100	Jessie Tuggle	.10	.05
❑	101	Freddie Jones	.10	.05
❑	102	Rob Moore	.20	.09
❑	103	Ahman Green	.20	.09
❑	104	Chris Chandler	.20	.09
❑	105	Steve McNair	.40	.18
❑	106	Kevin Greene	.10	.05
❑	107	Jermaine Lewis	.20	.09
❑	108	Erik Kramer	.10	.05
❑	109	Eric Moulds	.40	.18
❑	110	Terry Fair	.10	.05
❑	111	Carl Pickens	.20	.09
❑	112	La'Roi Glover	.10	.05
❑	113	Chris Spielman	.10	.05
❑	114	Leroy Hoard	.10	.05
❑	115	Mark Brunell	.60	.25
❑	116	Patrick Jeffers RC	3.00	1.35
❑	117	Elvis Grbac	.20	.09
❑	118	Ike Hilliard	.10	.05
❑	119	Sam Madison	.10	.05
❑	120	Terrell Owens	.40	.18
❑	121	Rich Gannon	.20	.09
❑	122	Skip Hicks	.40	.18
❑	123	Eric Green	.10	.05
❑	124	Trent Dilfer	.20	.09
❑	125	Terry Glenn	.40	.18
❑	126	Trent Green	.20	.09
❑	127	Charles Johnson	.10	.05
❑	128	Adrian Murrell	.20	.09
❑	129	Jason Gildon	.10	.05
❑	130	Tim Dwight	.40	.18
❑	131	Ryan Leaf	.40	.18
❑	132	Rocket Ismail	.20	.09
❑	133	Jon Kitna	.50	.23
❑	134	Alonzo Mayes	.10	.05
❑	135	Yancey Thigpen	.10	.05
❑	136	David LaFleur	.10	.05
❑	137	Ray Lewis	.10	.05
❑	138	Herman Moore	.40	.18
❑	139	Brian Griese	.75	.35
❑	140	Antonio Freeman	.40	.18
❑	141	Darnay Scott	.10	.05
❑	142	Ed McDaniel	.10	.05
❑	143	Andre Reed	.20	.09
❑	144	Andre Hastings	.10	.05
❑	145	Chris Warren	.10	.05
❑	146	Kevin Hardy	.10	.05
❑	147	Joe Jurevicius	.10	.05
❑	148	Jerome Pathon	.10	.05
❑	149	Duce Staley	.40	.18
❑	150	Dan Marino	1.50	.70
❑	151	Jerry Rice	1.00	.45
❑	152	Byron Bam Morris	.10	.05
❑	153	Az-Zahir Hakim	.10	.05
❑	154	Ty Law	.10	.05
❑	155	Warrick Dunn	.40	.18
❑	156	Keyshawn Johnson	.40	.18
❑	157	Brian Mitchell	.10	.05
❑	158	James Jett	.20	.09
❑	159	Fred Lane	.10	.05
❑	160	Courtney Hawkins	.10	.05
❑	161	Andre Wadsworth	.10	.05
❑	162	Natrone Means	.20	.09
❑	163	Andrew Glover	.10	.05
❑	164	Anthony Simmons	.10	.05
❑	165	Leon Lett	.10	.05
❑	166	Frank Wycheck	.10	.05
❑	167	Barry Minter	.10	.05
❑	168	Michael McCrary	.10	.05
❑	169	Johnnie Morton	.20	.09
❑	170	Jay Riemersma	.10	.05
❑	171	Vonnie Holliday	.10	.05
❑	172	Brian Simmons	.10	.05
❑	173	Joe Johnson	.10	.05
❑	174	Ed McCaffrey	.20	.09
❑	175	Jason Sehorn	.10	.05
❑	176	Keenan McCardell	.20	.09
❑	177	Bobby Taylor	.10	.05
❑	178	Andre Rison	.20	.09
❑	179	Greg Hill	.10	.05
❑	180	O.J. McDuffie	.20	.09
❑	181	Darren Woodson	.10	.05
❑	182	Willie McGinest	.10	.05
❑	183	J.J. Stokes	.20	.09
❑	184	Leon Johnson	.10	.05
❑	185	Bert Emanuel	.20	.09
❑	186	Napoleon Kaufman	.40	.18
❑	187	Leslie Shepherd	.10	.05
❑	188	Levon Kirkland	.10	.05
❑	189	Simeon Rice	.10	.05
❑	190	Mikhael Ricks	.10	.05
❑	191	Robert Smith	.40	.18
❑	192	Michael Sinclair	.10	.05
❑	193	Muhsin Muhammad	.20	.09
❑	194	Duane Starks	.10	.05
❑	195	Terance Mathis	.20	.09
❑	196	Antowain Smith	.40	.18
❑	197	Tony Parrish	.10	.05
❑	198	Takeo Spikes	.10	.05
❑	199	Ernie Mills	.10	.05
❑	200	John Mobley	.10	.05
❑	202	Pete Mitchell	.10	.05
❑	203	Darick Holmes	.10	.05
❑	204	Derrick Thomas	.20	.09
❑	205	David Palmer	.10	.05
❑	206	Jason Taylor	.10	.05
❑	207	Sammy Knight	.10	.05
❑	208	Dwayne Rudd	.10	.05
❑	209	Lawyer Milloy	.10	.05
❑	210	Michael Strahan	.10	.05
❑	211	Mo Lewis	.10	.05
❑	212	William Thomas	.10	.05
❑	213	Darrell Russell	.10	.05
❑	214	Brad Johnson	.40	.18
❑	215	Kordell Stewart	.40	.18
❑	216	Robert Holcombe	.20	.09
❑	217	Junior Seau	.20	.09
❑	218	Jacquez Green	.20	.09
❑	219	Shawn Springs	.10	.05
❑	220	Michael Westbrook	.20	.09
❑	221	Rod Woodson	.20	.09
❑	222	Frank Sanders	.20	.09
❑	223	Bruce Smith	.20	.09
❑	224	Eugene Robinson	.10	.05
❑	225	Bill Romanowski	.10	.05
❑	226	Wesley Walls	.20	.09
❑	227	Jimmy Smith	.20	.09
❑	228	Deion Sanders	.40	.18
❑	229	Lamar Thomas	.10	.05
❑	230	Dorsey Levens	.40	.18
❑	231	Tony Simmons	.10	.05
❑	232	John Randle	.20	.09
❑	233	Curtis Martin	.40	.18
❑	234	Bryant Young	.10	.05
❑	235	Charles Woodson	.40	.18

❑ 236 Charles Way	.10	.05
❑ 237 Zach Thomas	.20	.09
❑ 238 Ricky Proehl	.10	.05
❑ 239 Ricky Watters	.20	.09
❑ 240 Hardy Nickerson	.10	.05
❑ 241 Shannon Sharpe	.20	.09
❑ 242 O.J. Santiago	.10	.05
❑ 243 Vinny Testaverde	.20	.09
❑ 244 Roell Preston	.10	.05
❑ 245 James Stewart	.20	.09
❑ 246 Jake Reed	.20	.09
❑ 247 Steve Young	.60	.25
❑ 248 Shaun Williams	.10	.05
❑ 249 Rod Smith	.20	.09
❑ 250 Warren Sapp	.20	.09
❑ 251 Champ Bailey RC	1.50	.70
❑ 252 Karsten Bailey RC	.75	.35
❑ 253 D'Wayne Bates RC	1.25	.55
❑ 254 Michael Bishop RC	1.50	.70
❑ 255 David Boston RC	2.00	.90
❑ 256 Na Brown RC	1.25	.55
❑ 257 Fernando Bryant RC	.75	.35
❑ 258 Shawn Bryson RC	.40	.18
❑ 259 Darrin Chiaverini RC	.75	.35
❑ 260 Chris Claiborne RC	1.25	.55
❑ 261 Mike Cloud RC	1.25	.55
❑ 262 Cecil Collins RC	1.25	.55
❑ 263 Tim Couch RC	6.00	2.70
❑ 264 Scott Covington RC	1.25	.55
❑ 265 Daunte Culpepper RC	4.00	1.80
❑ 266 Antuan Edwards RC	.40	.18
❑ 267 Troy Edwards RC	2.00	.90
❑ 268 Ebenezer Ekuban RC	.75	.35
❑ 269 Kevin Faulk RC	1.50	.70
❑ 270 Jermaine Fazande RC	.75	.35
❑ 271 Joe Germaine RC	1.25	.55
❑ 272 Martin Gramatica RC	.40	.18
❑ 273 Torry Holt RC	3.00	1.35
❑ 274 Brock Huard RC	1.50	.70
❑ 275 Sedrick Irvin RC	1.25	.55
❑ 276 Sheldon Jackson RC	.75	.35
❑ 277 Edgerrin James RC	10.00	4.50
❑ 278 James Johnson RC	1.50	.70
❑ 279 Kevin Johnson RC	3.00	1.35
❑ 280 Malcolm Johnson RC	.75	.35
❑ 281 Andy Katzenmoyer RC	1.25	.55
❑ 282 Jevon Kearse RC	2.50	1.10
❑ 283 Patrick Kerney RC	.40	.18
❑ 284 Shaun King RC	4.00	1.80
❑ 285 Jim Kleinsasser RC	1.25	.55
❑ 286 Rob Konrad RC	1.25	.55
❑ 287 Chris McAlister RC	.75	.35
❑ 288 Donovan McNabb RC	4.00	1.80
❑ 289 Cade McNown RC	4.00	1.80
❑ 290 Dee Miller RC	.75	.35
❑ 291 Joe Montgomery RC	1.25	.55
❑ 292 De'Mond Parker RC	1.25	.55
❑ 293 Peerless Price RC	2.00	.90
❑ 294 Akili Smith RC	2.50	1.10
❑ 295 Justin Swift RC	.40	.18
❑ 296 Jerame Tuman RC	.75	.35
❑ 297 Ricky Williams RC	6.00	2.70
❑ 298 Antoine Winfield	.75	.35
❑ 299 Craig Yeast RC	.75	.35
❑ 300 Amos Zereoue RC	1.25	.55
❑ P6 Fred Taylor Promo	1.00	.45

1999 Fleer Trophy Collection

	MINT	NRMT
COMMON CARD (1-300)	20.00	9.00

*TC STARS: 80X TO 200X HI COLUMN
*TC UNLISTED STARS: 60X TO 150X HI COL.
*TROPHY COLL.RCs: 12X TO 30X
STATED PRINT RUN 20 SERIAL #'d SETS

1999 Fleer Aerial Assault

	MINT	NRMT
COMPLETE SET (15)	50.00	22.00
COMMON CARD (1-15)	2.00	.90
SEMISTARS	2.50	1.10

STATED ODDS 1:24

❑ 1 Troy Aikman	5.00	2.20
❑ 2 Jamal Anderson	3.00	1.35
❑ 3 Charlie Batch	2.50	1.10
❑ 4 Mark Brunell	3.00	1.35
❑ 5 Terrell Davis	5.00	2.20
❑ 6 John Elway	8.00	3.60
❑ 7 Brett Favre	8.00	3.60
❑ 8 Keyshawn Johnson	3.00	1.35
❑ 9 Jon Kitna	3.00	1.35
❑ 10 Peyton Manning	6.00	2.70
❑ 11 Dan Marino	8.00	3.60
❑ 12 Randy Moss	6.00	2.70
❑ 13 Eric Moulds	3.00	1.35
❑ 14 Jake Plummer	4.00	1.80
❑ 15 Jerry Rice	5.00	2.20

1999 Fleer Fresh Ink

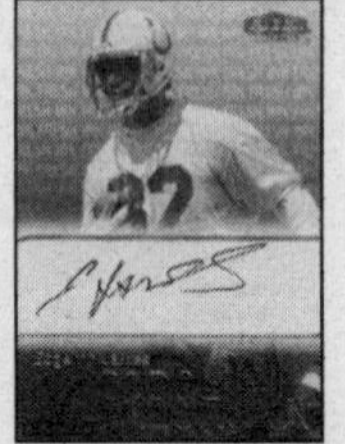

	MINT	NRMT
COMPLETE SET (14)	800.00	350.00
COMMON CARD (1-14)	30.00	13.50

STATED PRINT RUN 200 SERIAL #'d SETS

❑ 1 Champ Bailey	40.00	18.00
❑ 2 David Boston	50.00	22.00
❑ 3 Chris Claiborne	30.00	13.50
❑ 4 Torry Holt	60.00	27.00
❑ 5 Edgerrin James	200.00	90.00
❑ 6 James Johnson	40.00	18.00
❑ 7 Kevin Johnson	60.00	27.00
❑ 8 Jevon Kearse	50.00	22.00
❑ 9 Shaun King	100.00	45.00
❑ 10 Rob Konrad	30.00	13.50
❑ 11 Donovan McNabb	100.00	45.00
❑ 12 Cade McNown	100.00	45.00
❑ 13 Akili Smith	60.00	27.00
❑ 14 Ricky Williams	120.00	55.00

1999 Fleer Rookie Sensations

	MINT	NRMT
COMPLETE SET (20)	60.00	27.00
COMMON CARD (1-20)	2.00	.90
UNLISTED STARS	2.50	1.10

STATED ODDS 1:6

❑ 1 Champ Bailey	2.50	1.10
❑ 2 Michael Bishop	2.50	1.10
❑ 3 David Boston	3.00	1.35
❑ 4 Chris Claiborne	2.00	.90
❑ 5 Tim Couch	10.00	4.50
❑ 6 Daunte Culpepper	6.00	2.70
❑ 7 Troy Edwards	3.00	1.35
❑ 8 Kevin Faulk	2.50	1.10
❑ 9 Torry Holt	5.00	2.20
❑ 10 Brock Huard	2.50	1.10
❑ 11 Edgerrin James	15.00	6.75
❑ 12 Kevin Johnson	5.00	2.20
❑ 13 Shaun King	6.00	2.70
❑ 14 Rob Konrad	2.00	.90
❑ 15 Chris McAlister	2.00	.90
❑ 16 Donovan McNabb	6.00	2.70
❑ 17 Cade McNown	6.00	2.70
❑ 18 Peerless Price	3.00	1.35
❑ 19 Akili Smith	4.00	1.80
❑ 20 Ricky Williams	10.00	4.50

1999 Fleer Under Pressure

	MINT	NRMT
COMPLETE SET (15)	175.00	80.00
COMMON CARD (1-15)	8.00	3.60

STATED ODDS 1:96

❑ 1 Charlie Batch	8.00	3.60
❑ 2 Terrell Davis	15.00	6.75
❑ 3 Warrick Dunn	8.00	3.60
❑ 4 John Elway	25.00	11.00
❑ 5 Brett Favre	25.00	11.00
❑ 6 Keyshawn Johnson	8.00	3.60
❑ 7 Peyton Manning	20.00	9.00
❑ 8 Dan Marino	25.00	11.00
❑ 9 Curtis Martin	8.00	3.60
❑ 10 Randy Moss	20.00	9.00
❑ 11 Jake Plummer	12.00	5.50
❑ 12 Barry Sanders	25.00	11.00
❑ 13 Emmitt Smith	15.00	6.75
❑ 14 Fred Taylor	12.00	5.50
❑ 15 Charles Woodson	8.00	3.60

1999 Fleer Unsung Heroes

	MINT	NRMT
COMPLETE SET (30)	10.00	4.50
COMMON CARD (1UH-30UH)	.50	.23

SEMISTARS	.75	.35
STATED ODDS 1:3		

❑ 1UH Tommy Bennett	.50	.23
❑ 2UH Lester Archambeau	.50	.23
❑ 3UH James Jones DT	.50	.23
❑ 4UH Phil Hansen	.50	.23
❑ 5UH Anthony Johnson	.50	.23
❑ 6UH Bobby Engram	.75	.35
❑ 7UH Eric Bienemy	.50	.23
❑ 8UH Daryl Johnston	.75	.35
❑ 9UH Maa Tanuvasa	.50	.23
❑ 10UH Stephen Boyd	.50	.23
❑ 11UH Adam Timmerman	.50	.23
❑ 12UH Ken Dilger	.75	.35
❑ 13UH Bryan Barker	.50	.23
❑ 14UH Rich Gannon	.75	.35
❑ 15UH O.J. Brigance	.50	.23
❑ 16UH Jeff Christy	.50	.23
❑ 17UH Shawn Jefferson	.50	.23
❑ 18UH Aaron Craver	.50	.23
❑ 19UH Chris Calloway	.50	.23
❑ 20UH Pepper Johnson	.50	.23
❑ 21UH Greg Biekert	.50	.23
❑ 22UH Duce Staley	.75	.35
❑ 23UH Courtney Hawkins	.50	.23
❑ 24UH D'Marco Farr	.50	.23
❑ 25UH Rodney Harrison	.50	.23
❑ 26UH Ray Brown	.50	.23
❑ 27UH Jon Kitna	2.00	.90
❑ 28UH Brad Culpepper	.50	.23
❑ 29UH Steve Jackson	.50	.23
❑ 30UH Brian Mitchell	.50	.23

1998 Fleer Brilliants

	MINT	NRMT
COMPLETE SET (150)	175.00	80.00
COMMON CARD (1-150)	.25	.11
SEMISTARS	.50	.23
UNLISTED STARS	1.00	.45
COMMON ROOKIE	2.00	.90
ROOKIE SEMISTARS	3.00	1.35
ROOKIE UNLISTED STARS	4.00	1.80
ROOKIE SUBSET STATED ODDS 1:2		
COMP.BLUE SET (150)	400.00	180.00
*BLUE STARS: .75X TO 2X HI COL.		
*BLUE RCs: .5X TO 1.2X		
BLUE VETERAN STATED ODDS 1:3		
BLUE ROOKIE STATED ODDS 1:6		
COMMON GOLD	6.00	2.70
*GOLD STARS: 10X TO 25X HI COL.		
*GOLD YOUNG STARS: 7.5X TO 20X		
*GOLD RCs: 1.25X TO 3X		
GOLD PRINT RUN 99 SERIAL #'d SETS		

❑ 1 John Elway	5.00	2.20
❑ 2 Curtis Conway	.50	.23
❑ 3 Danny Wuerffel	.50	.23
❑ 4 Emmitt Smith	4.00	1.80
❑ 5 Marvin Harrison	.50	.23
❑ 6 Antowain Smith	1.00	.45
❑ 7 James Stewart	.50	.23
❑ 8 Junior Seau	.50	.23
❑ 9 Herman Moore	1.00	.45
❑ 10 Drew Bledsoe	2.00	.90
❑ 11 Rae Carruth	.50	.23
❑ 12 Trent Dilfer	1.00	.45
❑ 13 Derrick Alexander	.50	.23
❑ 14 Ike Hilliard	.50	.23
❑ 15 Bruce Smith	.50	.23
❑ 16 Warren Moon	1.00	.45
❑ 17 Jermaine Lewis	.50	.23
❑ 18 Mike Alstott	1.00	.45
❑ 19 Robert Brooks	.50	.23
❑ 20 Jerome Bettis	1.00	.45
❑ 21 Brett Favre	5.00	2.20
❑ 22 Garrison Hearst	1.00	.45
❑ 23 Neil O'Donnell	.50	.23
❑ 24 Joey Galloway	1.00	.45
❑ 25 Barry Sanders	5.00	2.20
❑ 26 Donnell Bennett	.25	.11
❑ 27 Jamal Anderson	1.00	.45
❑ 28 Isaac Bruce	1.00	.45
❑ 29 Chris Chandler	.50	.23
❑ 30 Kordell Stewart	1.00	.45
❑ 31 Corey Dillon	1.50	.70
❑ 32 Troy Aikman	2.50	1.10
❑ 33 Frank Sanders	.50	.23
❑ 34 Cris Carter	1.00	.45
❑ 35 Greg Hill	.25	.11
❑ 36 Tony Martin	.50	.23
❑ 37 Shannon Sharpe	.50	.23
❑ 38 Wayne Chrebet	1.00	.45
❑ 39 Trent Green	1.25	.55
❑ 40 Warrick Dunn	1.50	.70
❑ 41 Michael Irvin	1.00	.45
❑ 42 Eddie George	2.00	.90
❑ 43 Carl Pickens	1.00	.45
❑ 44 Wesley Walls	.50	.23
❑ 45 Steve McNair	1.00	.45
❑ 46 Bert Emanuel	.50	.23
❑ 47 Terry Glenn	1.00	.45
❑ 48 Elvis Grbac	.50	.23
❑ 49 Charles Way	.25	.11
❑ 50 Steve Young	1.50	.70
❑ 51 Deion Sanders	1.00	.45
❑ 52 Keyshawn Johnson	1.00	.45
❑ 53 Kerry Collins	.50	.23
❑ 54 O.J. McDuffie	.50	.23
❑ 55 Ricky Watters	.50	.23
❑ 56 Derrick Thomas	.50	.23
❑ 57 Antonio Freeman	1.00	.45
❑ 58 Jake Plummer	3.00	1.35
❑ 59 Andre Reed	.50	.23
❑ 60 Jerry Rice	2.50	1.10
❑ 61 Dorsey Levens	1.00	.45
❑ 62 Eddie Kennison	.50	.23
❑ 63 Marshall Faulk	1.00	.45
❑ 64 Michael Jackson	.25	.11
❑ 65 Karim Abdul-Jabbar	1.00	.45
❑ 66 Andre Rison	.50	.23
❑ 67 Glenn Foley	.50	.23
❑ 68 Jake Reed	.50	.23
❑ 69 Tony Banks	.50	.23
❑ 70 Dan Marino	5.00	2.20
❑ 71 Bryan Still	.25	.11
❑ 72 Tim Brown	1.00	.45
❑ 73 Charles Johnson	.25	.11
❑ 74 Jeff George	.50	.23
❑ 75 Jimmy Smith	.50	.23
❑ 76 Ben Coates	.50	.23
❑ 77 Rob Moore	.50	.23
❑ 78 Johnnie Morton	.50	.23
❑ 79 Peter Boulware	.25	.11
❑ 80 Curtis Martin	1.00	.45
❑ 81 James McKnight	.25	.11
❑ 82 Danny Kanell	.50	.23
❑ 83 Brad Johnson	1.00	.45
❑ 84 Amani Toomer	.50	.23
❑ 85 Terry Allen	1.00	.45
❑ 86 Rod Smith	.50	.23
❑ 87 Keenan McCardell	.50	.23
❑ 88 Leslie Shepherd	.25	.11
❑ 89 Irving Fryar	.50	.23
❑ 90 Terrell Davis	4.00	1.80
❑ 91 Robert Smith	1.00	.45
❑ 92 Duce Staley	1.50	.70
❑ 93 Rickey Dudley	.25	.11
❑ 94 Bobby Hoying	.50	.23
❑ 95 Terrell Owens	1.00	.45
❑ 96 Fred Lane	.50	.23
❑ 97 Natrone Means	1.00	.45
❑ 98 Yancey Thigpen	.25	.11
❑ 99 Reggie White	1.00	.45
❑ 100 Mark Brunell	2.00	.90
❑ 101 Ahman Green RC	.50	.23
❑ 102 Skip Hicks RC	6.00	2.70
❑ 103 Hines Ward RC	3.00	1.35
❑ 104 Marcus Nash RC	6.00	2.70
❑ 105 Terry Hardy RC	2.00	.90
❑ 106 Pat Johnson RC	3.00	1.35
❑ 107 Tremayne Stephens RC	2.00	.90
❑ 108 Joe Jurevicius RC	3.00	1.35
❑ 109 Moses Moreno RC	3.00	1.35
❑ 110 Charles Woodson RC	8.00	3.60
❑ 111 Kevin Dyson RC	6.00	2.70
❑ 112 Alvis Whitted RC	2.00	.90
❑ 113 Michael Pittman RC	3.00	1.35
❑ 114 Stephen Alexander RC	3.00	1.35
❑ 115 Tavian Banks RC	3.00	1.35
❑ 116 John Avery RC	4.00	1.80
❑ 117 Keith Brooking RC	3.00	1.35
❑ 118 Jerome Pathon RC	3.00	1.35
❑ 119 Terry Fair RC	3.00	1.35
❑ 120 Peyton Manning RC	30.00	13.50
❑ 121 R.W. McQuarters RC	2.00	.90
❑ 122 Charlie Batch RC	10.00	4.50
❑ 123 Jonathan Quinn RC	3.00	1.35
❑ 124 C.Fuamatu-Ma'afala RC	3.00	1.35
❑ 125 Jacquez Green RC	5.00	2.20
❑ 126 Germane Crowell RC	10.00	4.50
❑ 127 Oronde Gadsden RC	3.00	1.35
❑ 128 Koy Detmer	4.00	1.80
❑ 129 Robert Holcombe RC	4.00	1.80
❑ 130 Curtis Enis RC	8.00	3.60
❑ 131 Brian Griese RC	10.00	4.50
❑ 132 Tony Simmons RC	3.00	1.35
❑ 133 Vonnie Holliday RC	3.00	1.35
❑ 134 Alonzo Mayes RC	2.00	.90
❑ 135 Jon Ritchie RC	3.00	1.35
❑ 136 Robert Edwards RC	4.00	1.80
❑ 137 Mike Vanderjagt RC	2.00	.90
❑ 138 Jonathan Linton RC	4.00	1.80
❑ 139 Fred Taylor RC	15.00	6.75
❑ 140 Randy Moss RC	30.00	13.50
❑ 141 Rod Rutledge RC	2.00	.90
❑ 142 Andre Wadsworth RC	3.00	1.35
❑ 143 Rashaan Shehee RC	3.00	1.35
❑ 144 Shaun Williams RC	2.00	.90
❑ 145 Mikhael Ricks RC	3.00	1.35
❑ 146 Wade Richey RC	2.00	.90
❑ 147 Carlos King RC	2.00	.90
❑ 148 Tim Dwight RC	6.00	2.70
❑ 149 Scott Frost RC	3.00	1.35
❑ 150 Ryan Leaf RC	6.00	2.70

1998 Fleer Brilliants 24-Karat Gold

	MINT	NRMT
COMMON CARD (1-150)	30.00	13.50
*24K STARS: 50X TO 120X HI COL.		
*24K YOUNG STARS: 40X TO 100X		
*24K RCs: 5X TO 12X		
STATED PRINT RUN 24 SETS		

1998 Fleer Brilliants Illuminators

	MINT	NRMT
COMPLETE SET (15)	60.00	27.00
COMMON CARD (1-15)	3.00	1.35
STATED ODDS 1:10		

	MINT	NRMT
❑ 1 Robert Edwards	3.00	1.35
❑ 2 Fred Taylor	12.00	5.50
❑ 3 Kordell Stewart	3.00	1.35
❑ 4 Troy Aikman	8.00	3.60
❑ 5 Curtis Enis	6.00	2.70
❑ 6 Drew Bledsoe	6.00	2.70
❑ 7 Curtis Martin	3.00	1.35
❑ 8 Joey Galloway	3.00	1.35
❑ 9 Jerome Bettis	3.00	1.35
❑ 10 Glenn Foley	3.00	1.35
❑ 11 Karim Abdul-Jabbar	3.00	1.35
❑ 12 Jake Plummer	8.00	3.60
❑ 13 Jerry Rice	8.00	3.60
❑ 14 Charlie Batch	8.00	3.60
❑ 15 Jacquez Green	5.00	2.20

1998 Fleer Brilliants Shining Stars

	MINT	NRMT
COMPLETE SET (15)	120.00	55.00
COMMON CARD (1-15)	4.00	1.80
STATED ODDS 1:20		
*PULSAR STARS: 3X TO 8X HI COL.		
*PULSAR ROOKIES: 2X TO 5X HI COL.		
PULSARS STATED ODDS 1:400		

	MINT	NRMT
❑ 1 Terrell Davis	12.00	5.50
❑ 2 Emmitt Smith	12.00	5.50
❑ 3 Barry Sanders	15.00	6.75
❑ 4 Mark Brunell	6.00	2.70
❑ 5 Brett Favre	15.00	6.75
❑ 6 Ryan Leaf	5.00	2.20
❑ 7 Randy Moss	20.00	9.00
❑ 8 Warrick Dunn	6.00	2.70
❑ 9 Peyton Manning	20.00	9.00
❑ 10 Corey Dillon	5.00	2.20
❑ 11 Dan Marino	15.00	6.75
❑ 12 Keyshawn Johnson	5.00	2.20
❑ 13 John Elway	15.00	6.75
❑ 14 Eddie George	6.00	2.70
❑ 15 Antowain Smith	5.00	2.20

1999 Fleer Focus

	MINT	NRMT
COMPLETE SET (175)	400.00	180.00
COMP.SET w/o SP's (100)	40.00	18.00
COMMON CARD (1-100)	.20	.09
SEMISTARS	.40	.18
UNLISTED STARS	.75	.35
COMMON ROOKIE (101-110)	1.25	.55
ROOKIE SEMISTARS 101-110	2.00	.90
ROOKIE UNL.STARS 101-110	3.00	1.35
101-110 ROOKIE SUBSET STATED ODDS 1:4		
COMMON ROOKIE (111-135)	4.00	1.80
ROOKIE SEMISTARS 111-135	5.00	2.20
111-135 ROOKIE PRINT RUN 3850 SER.#'d SETS		
COMMON ROOKIE (136-160)	4.00	1.80
ROOKIE SEMISTARS 136-160	6.00	2.70
ROOKIE UNL.STARS 136-160	8.00	3.60
136-160 ROOKIE PRINT RUN 2500 SER.#'d SETS		
COMMON ROOKIE (161-175)	6.00	2.70
ROOKIE SEMISTARS 161-175	8.00	3.60
161-175 ROOKIE PRINT RUN 2250 SER.#'d SETS		
OVERALL ROOKIE SUBSET STATED ODDS 1:2		

	MINT	NRMT
❑ 1 Randy Moss	3.00	1.35
❑ 2 Andre Rison	.40	.18
❑ 3 Ed McCaffrey	.40	.18
❑ 4 Jerry Rice	2.00	.90
❑ 5 Tim Biakabutuka	.40	.18
❑ 6 Wayne Chrebet	.40	.18
❑ 7 Deion Sanders	.75	.35
❑ 8 Ricky Watters	.40	.18
❑ 9 Skip Hicks	.40	.18
❑ 10 Charlie Batch	1.50	.70
❑ 11 Joey Galloway	.75	.35
❑ 12 Stephen Alexander	.20	.09
❑ 13 Curtis Conway	.40	.18
❑ 14 Garrison Hearst	.40	.18
❑ 15 Kerry Collins	.40	.18
❑ 16 Cris Carter	.75	.35
❑ 17 Eddie George	1.00	.45
❑ 18 Eric Moulds	.75	.35
❑ 19 Vinny Testaverde	.40	.18
❑ 20 Curtis Enis	.75	.35
❑ 21 Gary Brown	.20	.09
❑ 22 Junior Seau	.40	.18
❑ 23 Kevin Dyson	.40	.18
❑ 24 Jeff Blake	.40	.18
❑ 25 Herman Moore	.75	.35
❑ 26 Natrone Means	.40	.18
❑ 27 Terry Glenn	.75	.35
❑ 28 Fred Taylor	2.00	.90
❑ 29 Ben Coates	.40	.18
❑ 30 Corey Dillon	.75	.35
❑ 31 Eddie Kennison	.40	.18
❑ 32 Byron Bam Morris	.20	.09
❑ 33 Doug Pederson	.20	.09
❑ 34 Jamal Anderson	.75	.35
❑ 35 Michael Westbrook	.40	.18
❑ 36 Peyton Manning	3.00	1.35
❑ 37 Carl Pickens	.40	.18
❑ 38 Drew Bledsoe	1.50	.70
❑ 39 Jim Harbaugh	.40	.18
❑ 40 Kurt Warner RC	15.00	6.75
❑ 41 Mark Chmura	.20	.09
❑ 42 Hines Ward	.20	.09
❑ 43 Terry Kirby	.20	.09
❑ 44 Brett Favre	3.00	1.35
❑ 45 Kordell Stewart	.75	.35
❑ 46 Leslie Shepherd	.20	.09
❑ 47 Marshall Faulk	.75	.35
❑ 48 Troy Aikman	2.00	.90
❑ 49 Isaac Bruce	.75	.35
❑ 50 Michael Irvin	.40	.18
❑ 51 Robert Smith	.40	.18
❑ 52 Dorsey Levens	.75	.35
❑ 53 Duce Staley	.75	.35
❑ 54 Jake Plummer	1.25	.55
❑ 55 Adrian Murrell	.40	.18
❑ 56 Antonio Freeman	.75	.35
❑ 57 Jerome Bettis	.40	.18
❑ 58 Elvis Grbac	.40	.18
❑ 59 Keyshawn Johnson	.75	.35
❑ 60 Steve Beuerlein	.20	.09
❑ 61 Yancey Thigpen	.20	.09
❑ 62 Doug Flutie	1.00	.45
❑ 63 Jacquez Green	.40	.18
❑ 64 Jimmy Smith	.40	.18
❑ 65 Tim Brown	.75	.35
❑ 66 Jason Sehorn	.20	.09
❑ 67 Muhsin Muhammad	.40	.18
❑ 68 Shannon Sharpe	.40	.18
❑ 69 Terrell Owens	.75	.35
❑ 70 Keenan McCardell	.40	.18
❑ 71 Rich Gannon	.40	.18
❑ 72 Scott Mitchell	.20	.09
❑ 73 Warrick Dunn	.75	.35
❑ 74 Brad Johnson	.40	.18
❑ 75 Charles Johnson	.20	.09
❑ 76 Chris Chandler	.40	.18
❑ 77 Marcus Pollard	.20	.09
❑ 78 Mike Alstott	.75	.35
❑ 79 Bubby Brister	.40	.18
❑ 80 Jon Kitna	1.00	.45
❑ 81 Randall Cunningham	.75	.35
❑ 82 Antowain Smith	.75	.35
❑ 83 Curtis Martin	.75	.35
❑ 84 Steve McNair	.75	.35
❑ 85 Tony Gonzalez	.40	.18
❑ 86 O.J. McDuffie	.40	.18
❑ 87 Steve Young	1.25	.55
❑ 88 Terrell Davis	2.00	.90
❑ 89 Mark Brunell	1.25	.55
❑ 90 Napoleon Kaufman	.75	.35
❑ 91 Priest Holmes	.75	.35
❑ 92 Trent Dilfer	.40	.18
❑ 93 Brian Griese	1.50	.70
❑ 94 J.J. Stokes	.40	.18
❑ 95 Karim Abdul-Jabbar	.40	.18
❑ 96 Barry Sanders	3.00	1.35
❑ 97 Dan Marino	3.00	1.35
❑ 98 Emmitt Smith	2.00	.90
❑ 99 Marvin Harrison	.75	.35
❑ 100 Rod Smith	.40	.18
❑ 101 Champ Bailey RC	4.00	1.80
❑ 102 Fernando Bryant RC	2.00	.90
❑ 103 Chris Claiborne RC	2.00	.90
❑ 104 Antuan Edwards RC	2.00	.90
❑ 105 Martin Gramatica RC	1.25	.55
❑ 106 Andy Katzenmoyer RC	3.00	1.35
❑ 107 Jevon Kearse RC	6.00	2.70
❑ 108 Chris McAlister RC	2.00	.90
❑ 109 Al Wilson RC	2.00	.90
❑ 110 Antoine Winfield RC	2.00	.90
❑ 111 Karsten Bailey RC	5.00	2.20
❑ 112 D'Wayne Bates RC	4.00	1.80
❑ 113 Marty Booker RC	5.00	2.20
❑ 114 David Boston RC	8.00	3.60
❑ 115 Na Brown RC	5.00	2.20
❑ 116 Desmond Clark RC	4.00	1.80
❑ 117 Dameane Douglas RC	4.00	1.80
❑ 118 Donald Driver RC	4.00	1.80
❑ 119 Troy Edwards RC	8.00	3.60
❑ 120 Torry Holt RC	12.00	5.50
❑ 121 Kevin Johnson RC	12.00	5.50
❑ 122 Reginald Kelly RC	4.00	1.80
❑ 123 Jimmy Kleinsasser RC	5.00	2.20
❑ 124 Jeremy McDaniel RC	4.00	1.80
❑ 125 Darnell McDonald RC	5.00	2.20
❑ 126 Travis McGriff RC	4.00	1.80
❑ 127 Billy Miller RC	4.00	1.80
❑ 128 Dee Miller RC	5.00	2.20

Card	MINT	NRMT
❑ 129 Peerless Price RC	8.00	3.60
❑ 130 Troy Smith RC	4.00	1.80
❑ 131 Brandon Stokley RC	4.00	1.80
❑ 132 Wane McGarity RC	4.00	1.80
❑ 133 Mark Campbell RC	4.00	1.80
❑ 134 Jerame Tuman RC	4.00	1.80
❑ 135 Craig Yeast RC	4.00	1.80
❑ 136 Jerry Azumah RC	6.00	2.70
❑ 137 Marlon Barnes RC	6.00	2.70
❑ 138 Michael Basnight RC	6.00	2.70
❑ 139 Shawn Bryson RC	6.00	2.70
❑ 140 Mike Cloud RC	8.00	3.60
❑ 141 Cecil Collins RC	5.00	2.20
❑ 142 Autry Denson RC	8.00	3.60
❑ 143 Kevin Faulk RC	10.00	4.50
❑ 144 Jermaine Fazande RC	6.00	2.70
❑ 145 James Finn RC	4.00	1.80
❑ 146 Madre Hill RC	6.00	2.70
❑ 147 Sedrick Irvin RC	8.00	3.60
❑ 148 Terry Jackson RC	6.00	2.70
❑ 149 Edgerrin James RC	80.00	36.00
❑ 150 James Johnson RC	10.00	4.50
❑ 151 Rob Konrad RC	8.00	3.60
❑ 152 Joel Makovicka RC	8.00	3.60
❑ 153 Cecil Martin RC	8.00	3.60
❑ 154 Joe Montgomery RC	8.00	3.60
❑ 155 De'Mond Parker RC	8.00	3.60
❑ 156 Sirr Parker RC	6.00	2.70
❑ 157 Jeff Paulk RC	6.00	2.70
❑ 158 Nick Williams RC	6.00	2.70
❑ 159 Ricky Williams RC	40.00	18.00
❑ 160 Amos Zereoue RC	8.00	3.60
❑ 161 Michael Bishop RC	10.00	4.50
❑ 162 Aaron Brooks RC	8.00	3.60
❑ 163 Tim Couch RC	50.00	22.00
❑ 164 Scott Covington RC	6.00	2.70
❑ 165 Daunte Culpepper RC	25.00	11.00
❑ 166 Kevin Daft RC	8.00	3.60
❑ 167 Joe Germaine RC	8.00	3.60
❑ 168 Chris Greisen RC	10.00	4.50
❑ 169 Brock Huard RC	10.00	4.50
❑ 170 Shaun King RC	25.00	11.00
❑ 171 Cory Sauter RC	6.00	2.70
❑ 172 Donovan McNabb RC	25.00	11.00
❑ 173 Cade McNown RC	25.00	11.00
❑ 174 Chad Plummer RC	6.00	2.70
❑ 175 Akili Smith RC	20.00	9.00
❑ P1 Promo Sheet	5.00	2.20

(SBXXXIV NFL Experience)
NFLX1 Kurt Warner
NFLX2 Jamal Anderson
NFLX3 Edgerrin James
NFLX4 Peyton Manning
NFLX5 Randy Moss
NFLX6 Dan Marino

1999 Fleer Focus Stealth

	MINT	NRMT
COMPLETE SET (175)	1000.00	450.00
COMMON CARD (1-100)	1.50	.70
*STARS: 3X TO 8X HI COL.		
*YOUNG STARS: 2.5X TO 6X		
COMMON ROOKIE (101-175)	2.50	1.10
*101-110 RCs: .8X TO 2X		
*111-135 RCs: .6X TO 1.5X		
*136-175 RCs: .5X TO 1.2X		

STATED PRINT RUN 300 SER.#'d SETS

Card	MINT	NRMT
❑ 40 Kurt Warner	100.00	45.00

1999 Fleer Focus Feel the Game

	MINT	NRMT
COMPLETE SET (10)	600.00	275.00
COMMON CARD (1FG-10FG)	40.00	18.00
SEMISTARS	50.00	22.00
STATED ODDS 1:192		
UNLESS NOTED ALL CARDS ARE JERSEYS		

Card	MINT	NRMT
❑ 1FG Vinny Testaverde	40.00	18.00
❑ 2FG Mark Brunell	60.00	27.00
❑ 3FG Brett Favre Shoe	120.00	55.00
❑ 4FG Fred Taylor	60.00	27.00
❑ 5FG Jeff Blake	40.00	18.00
❑ 6FG Emmitt Smith	100.00	45.00
❑ 7FG Joe Germaine	40.00	18.00
❑ 8FG Cecil Collins	40.00	18.00
❑ 9FG Charles Woodson	50.00	22.00
❑ 10FG Kurt Warner	175.00	80.00

1999 Fleer Focus Fresh Ink

	MINT	NRMT
COMPLETE SET (37)	1200.00	550.00
COMMON CARD (1-37)	12.00	5.50
SEMISTARS	20.00	9.00
UNLISTED STARS	25.00	11.00
STATED ODDS 1:48		

Card	MINT	NRMT
❑ 1 Reidel Anthony	20.00	9.00
❑ 2 Charlie Batch	40.00	18.00
❑ 3 Jeff Blake	20.00	9.00
❑ 4 Darrin Chiaverini	20.00	9.00
❑ 5 Wayne Chrebet	20.00	9.00
❑ 6 Daunte Culpepper	50.00	22.00
❑ 7 Terrell Davis	100.00	45.00
❑ 8 Koy Detmer	12.00	5.50
❑ 9 Corey Dillon	25.00	11.00
❑ 10 Troy Edwards	25.00	11.00
❑ 11 Doug Flutie	30.00	13.50
❑ 12 Eddie George	30.00	13.50
❑ 13 Trent Green	20.00	9.00
❑ 14 Marvin Harrison	25.00	11.00
❑ 15 Torry Holt	40.00	18.00
❑ 16 Sedrick Irvin	20.00	9.00
❑ 17 Edgerrin James	200.00	90.00
❑ 18 Brad Johnson	20.00	9.00
❑ 19 Charles Johnson	12.00	5.50
❑ 20 Jon Kitna	30.00	13.50
❑ 21 Jim Kleinsasser	25.00	11.00
❑ 22 Peyton Manning	100.00	45.00
❑ 23 O.J. McDuffie	20.00	9.00
❑ 24 Travis McGriff	12.00	5.50
❑ 25 Donovan McNabb	50.00	22.00
❑ 26 Cade McNown	60.00	27.00
❑ 27 Joe Montgomery	20.00	9.00
❑ 28 Randy Moss	100.00	45.00
❑ 29 Jake Plummer	40.00	18.00
❑ 30 Akili Smith	40.00	18.00
❑ 31 Antowain Smith	25.00	11.00
❑ 32 Duce Staley	20.00	9.00
❑ 33 Brandon Stokley	20.00	9.00
❑ 34 Fred Taylor	40.00	18.00
❑ 35 Vinny Testaverde	20.00	9.00
❑ 36 Ricky Williams	120.00	55.00
❑ 37 Steve Young	50.00	22.00

1999 Fleer Focus Glimmer Men

	MINT	NRMT
COMPLETE SET (10)	40.00	18.00
COMMON CARD (1R-10R)	4.00	1.80
STATED ODDS 1:20		

Card	MINT	NRMT
❑ 1R Tim Couch	8.00	3.60
❑ 2R Barry Sanders	8.00	3.60
❑ 3R Terrell Davis	5.00	2.20
❑ 4R Dan Marino	8.00	3.60
❑ 5R Troy Aikman	5.00	2.20
❑ 6R Brett Favre	8.00	3.60
❑ 7R Randy Moss	6.00	2.70
❑ 8R Emmitt Smith	5.00	2.20
❑ 9R Edgerrin James	12.00	5.50
❑ 10R Fred Taylor	4.00	1.80

1999 Fleer Focus Reflexions

	MINT	NRMT
COMPLETE SET (10)	300.00	135.00
COMMON CARD (1R-10R)	20.00	9.00
STATED PRINT RUN 100 SER.#'d SETS		

Card	MINT	NRMT
❑ 1R Tim Couch	50.00	22.00
❑ 2R Barry Sanders	40.00	18.00
❑ 3R Terrell Davis	25.00	11.00
❑ 4R Dan Marino	40.00	18.00
❑ 5R Troy Aikman	25.00	11.00
❑ 6R Brett Favre	40.00	18.00
❑ 7R Randy Moss	30.00	13.50
❑ 8R Emmitt Smith	25.00	11.00
❑ 9R Edgerrin James	80.00	36.00
❑ 10R Fred Taylor	20.00	9.00

1999 Fleer Focus Sparklers

	MINT	NRMT
COMPLETE SET (15)	30.00	13.50

COMMON CARD (1S-15S)	1.50	.70
STATED ODDS 1:10		

❑ 1S Tim Couch	6.00	2.70
❑ 2S Donovan McNabb	4.00	1.80
❑ 3S Akili Smith	2.50	1.10
❑ 4S Cade McNown	4.00	1.80
❑ 5S Daunte Culpepper	4.00	1.80
❑ 6S Ricky Williams	6.00	2.70
❑ 7S Edgerrin James	10.00	4.50
❑ 8S Kevin Faulk	1.50	.70
❑ 9S Torry Holt	3.00	1.35
❑ 10S David Boston	2.00	.90
❑ 11S Sedrick Irvin	1.50	.70
❑ 12S Peerless Price	2.00	.90
❑ 13S Troy Edwards	2.00	.90
❑ 14S Brock Huard	1.50	.70
❑ 15S Shaun King	4.00	1.80

1999 Fleer Focus Wondrous

	MINT	NRMT
COMPLETE SET	60.00	27.00
COMMON CARD (1W-20W)	2.00	.90
STATED ODDS 1:20		

❑ 1W Peyton Manning	6.00	2.70
❑ 2W Fred Taylor	4.00	1.80
❑ 3W Tim Couch	8.00	3.60
❑ 4W Charlie Batch	3.00	1.35
❑ 5W Jerry Rice	5.00	2.20
❑ 6W Randy Moss	6.00	2.70
❑ 7W Warrick Dunn	2.00	.90

❑ 8W Mark Brunell	3.00	1.35
❑ 9W Emmitt Smith	5.00	2.20
❑ 10W Eddie George	2.50	1.10
❑ 11W Brian Griese	3.00	1.35
❑ 12W Terrell Davis	5.00	2.20
❑ 13W Dan Marino	8.00	3.60
❑ 14W Ricky Williams	8.00	3.60
❑ 15W Brett Favre	8.00	3.60
❑ 16W Jake Plummer	3.00	1.35
❑ 17W Troy Aikman	5.00	2.20
❑ 18W Drew Bledsoe	3.00	1.35
❑ 19W Edgerrin James	12.00	5.50
❑ 20W Cade McNown	5.00	2.20

1999 Fleer Mystique

	MINT	NRMT
COMPLETE SET (160)	600.00	275.00
COMP.SHORT SET (100)	50.00	22.00
COMMON CARD (1-100)	.25	.11
SEMISTARS 1-100	.50	.23
UNL.STARS 1-100	1.00	.45
COMMON SP (1-100)	1.50	.70
COMMON ROOKIE (101-150)	4.00	1.80
ROOKIE SEMISTARS	6.00	2.70
ROOKIE UNL.STARS	8.00	3.60
ROOKIES PRINT RUN 2999 SER.#'d SETS		
COMMON CARD (151-160)	4.00	1.80
151-160 PRINT RUN 2500 SERIAL #'d SETS		
UNPRICED MASTERPIECES SERIAL #'d OF 1		

❑ 1 Terrell Davis SP	4.00	1.80
❑ 2 Jerome Bettis SP	1.50	.70
❑ 3 J.J. Stokes	.50	.23
❑ 4 Frank Wycheck	.25	.11
❑ 5 O.J. McDuffie	.50	.23
❑ 6 Johnnie Morton	.50	.23
❑ 7 Marshall Faulk SP	1.50	.70
❑ 8 Ryan Leaf	1.00	.45
❑ 9 Sean Dawkins	.25	.11
❑ 10 Brett Favre SP	6.00	2.70
❑ 11 Steve Young SP	2.50	1.10
❑ 12 Jimmy Smith	.50	.23
❑ 13 Isaac Bruce	1.00	.45
❑ 14 Trent Dilfer	.50	.23
❑ 15 Brian Mitchell	.25	.11
❑ 16 Kordell Stewart SP	1.50	.70
❑ 17 Herman Moore	1.00	.45
❑ 18 Troy Aikman SP	4.00	1.80
❑ 19 Cris Carter	1.00	.45
❑ 20 Barry Sanders SP	6.00	2.70
❑ 21 Tony Gonzalez	.50	.23
❑ 22 Skip Hicks	.50	.23
❑ 23 Steve McNair SP	1.50	.70
❑ 24 Brad Johnson	.50	.23
❑ 25 Mark Chmura	.25	.11
❑ 26 Randall Cunningham SP	1.50	.70
❑ 27 Jerry Rice SP	4.00	1.80
❑ 28 Jamie Asher	.25	.11
❑ 29 Brian Griese SP	3.00	1.35
❑ 30 Peyton Manning SP	6.00	2.70
❑ 31 Keith Poole	.25	.11
❑ 32 Wayne Chrebet	.50	.23
❑ 33 Rich Gannon	.50	.23
❑ 34 Michael Irvin	.50	.23
❑ 35 Yancey Thigpen	.25	.11
❑ 36 Corey Dillon	1.00	.45
❑ 37 Steve Beuerlein	.25	.11
❑ 38 Terry Kirby	.25	.11
❑ 39 Jacquez Green	.50	.23
❑ 40 Mark Brunell SP	2.50	1.10
❑ 41 Rickey Dudley	.25	.11
❑ 42 Shannon Sharpe	.50	.23
❑ 43 Andre Rison	.50	.23
❑ 44 Chris Chandler	.50	.23
❑ 45 Fred Taylor SP	4.00	1.80
❑ 46 Kerry Collins	.50	.23
❑ 47 Antowain Smith SP	1.50	.70
❑ 48 Wesley Walls	.25	.11
❑ 49 Rob Moore	.50	.23
❑ 50 Dan Marino SP	6.00	2.70
❑ 51 Robert Smith	1.00	.45
❑ 52 Keenan McCardell	.50	.23
❑ 53 Joey Galloway	1.00	.45
❑ 54 Fred Lane	.25	.11
❑ 55 Napoleon Kaufman	1.00	.45
❑ 56 Curtis Martin	1.00	.45
❑ 57 Rod Smith	.50	.23
❑ 58 Curtis Conway	.50	.23
❑ 59 Kevin Dyson	.50	.23
❑ 60 Warrick Dunn SP	1.50	.70
❑ 61 Ahman Green	.50	.23
❑ 62 Duce Staley	1.00	.45
❑ 63 Emmitt Smith SP	4.00	1.80
❑ 64 Adrian Murrell	.50	.23
❑ 65 Dorsey Levens	1.00	.45
❑ 66 Drew Bledsoe SP	2.50	1.10
❑ 67 Ed McCaffrey	.50	.23
❑ 68 Natrone Means	.50	.23
❑ 69 Deion Sanders	1.00	.45
❑ 70 Keyshawn Johnson SP	1.50	.70
❑ 71 Antonio Freeman	1.00	.45
❑ 72 James Stewart	.50	.23
❑ 73 Ben Coates	.50	.23
❑ 74 Priest Holmes	1.00	.45
❑ 75 Jake Reed	.50	.23
❑ 76 Mike Alstott	1.00	.45
❑ 77 Vinny Testaverde	.50	.23
❑ 78 Ricky Watters	.50	.23
❑ 79 Garrison Hearst	.50	.23
❑ 80 Junior Seau	.50	.23
❑ 81 Tim Brown	1.00	.45
❑ 82 Jamal Anderson	1.00	.45
❑ 83 Robert Brooks	.50	.23
❑ 84 Marc Edwards	.25	.11
❑ 85 Curtis Enis	1.00	.45
❑ 86 Doug Flutie	1.25	.55
❑ 87 Terry Glenn	.25	.11
❑ 88 Charlie Batch SP	3.00	1.35
❑ 89 Marvin Harrison	1.00	.45
❑ 90 Jake Plummer SP	3.00	1.35
❑ 91 Terrell Owens	1.00	.45
❑ 92 Scott Mitchell	.25	.11
❑ 93 Tim Dwight	.50	.23
❑ 94 Eddie George SP	2.00	.90
❑ 95 Ike Hilliard	.25	.11
❑ 96 Robert Holcombe	.25	.11
❑ 97 Charles Johnson	.25	.11
❑ 98 Eric Moulds	1.00	.45
❑ 99 Michael Westbrook	.50	.23
❑ 100 Randy Moss SP	6.00	2.70
❑ 101 Tim Couch RC	50.00	22.00
❑ 102 Donovan McNabb RC	25.00	11.00
❑ 103 Akili Smith RC	20.00	9.00
❑ 104 Cade McNown RC	25.00	11.00
❑ 105 Daunte Culpepper RC	25.00	11.00
❑ 106 Ricky Williams RC	50.00	22.00
❑ 107 Edgerrin James RC	80.00	36.00
❑ 108 Kevin Faulk RC	10.00	4.50
❑ 109 Torry Holt RC	20.00	9.00
❑ 110 David Boston RC	12.00	5.50
❑ 111 Chris Claiborne RC	6.00	2.70
❑ 112 Mike Cloud RC	8.00	3.60
❑ 113 Joe Germaine RC	8.00	3.60
❑ 114 Cecil Collins RC	8.00	3.60
❑ 115 Tim Alexander RC	4.00	1.80
❑ 116 Brandon Stokley RC	6.00	2.70
❑ 117 Lamarr Glenn RC	4.00	1.80
❑ 118 Shawn Bryson RC	6.00	2.70
❑ 119 Jeff Paulk RC	6.00	2.70
❑ 120 Kevin Johnson RC	20.00	9.00
❑ 121 Charlie Rogers RC	6.00	2.70
❑ 122 Joe Montgomery RC	8.00	3.60
❑ 123 Travis McGriff RC	6.00	2.70
❑ 124 Dee Miller RC	6.00	2.70
❑ 125 Rob Konrad RC	8.00	3.60
❑ 126 Peerless Price RC	12.00	5.50
❑ 127 D'Wayne Bates RC	6.00	2.70
❑ 128 Craig Yeast RC	6.00	2.70
❑ 129 Malcolm Johnson RC	6.00	2.70
❑ 130 Brock Huard RC	10.00	4.50
❑ 131 Sedrick Irvin RC	1.50	.70
❑ 132 Troy Smith RC	6.00	2.70
❑ 133 Troy Edwards RC	12.00	5.50
❑ 134 Al Wilson RC	6.00	2.70
❑ 135 Terry Jackson RC	6.00	2.70
❑ 136 Dameane Douglas RC	6.00	2.70
❑ 137 Amos Zereoue RC	8.00	3.60
❑ 138 Shaun King RC	25.00	11.00
❑ 139 James Johnson RC	10.00	4.50
❑ 140 Jermaine Fazande RC	6.00	2.70
❑ 141 Autry Denson RC	8.00	3.60
❑ 142 Darran Hall RC	6.00	2.70
❑ 143 Na Brown RC	8.00	3.60
❑ 144 Mike Lucky RC	4.00	1.80
❑ 145 Karsten Bailey RC	6.00	2.70
❑ 146 Kevin Daft RC	6.00	2.70
❑ 147 Sean Bennett RC	8.00	3.60
❑ 148 Madre Hill RC	4.00	1.80
❑ 149 Michael Bishop RC	10.00	4.50
❑ 150 Scott Covington RC	6.00	2.70
❑ 151 Randy Moss STAR	15.00	6.75
❑ 152 Fred Taylor STAR	10.00	4.50
❑ 153 Brett Favre STAR	15.00	6.75
❑ 154 Dan Marino STAR	15.00	6.75
❑ 155 Terrell Davis STAR	10.00	4.50

		MINT	NRMT
❑ 156	Barry Sanders STAR	15.00	6.75
❑ 157	Emmitt Smith STAR	10.00	4.50
❑ 158	Jake Plummer STAR	8.00	3.60
❑ 159	Warrick Dunn STAR	4.00	1.80
❑ 160	Troy Aikman STAR	10.00	4.50
❑ P86	Doug Flutie Promo	1.50	.70

1999 Fleer Mystique Gold

	MINT	NRMT
COMPLETE SET (100)	300.00	135.00

*GOLD STARS: 2X TO 5X HI COL.
*GOLD YOUNG STARS: 1.5X TO 4X
*GOLD SP STARS: 2.5X TO 6X HI COL.
*GOLD SP YOUNG STARS: 2X TO 5X
GOLDS RANDOM INSERTS IN PACKS

1999 Fleer Mystique Feel the Game

	MINT	NRMT
COMPLETE SET (10)	500.00	220.00
COMMON CARD (1-10)	30.00	13.50
SEMISTARS	40.00	18.00

RANDOM INSERTS IN PACKS

		MINT	NRMT
❑ 1	Terrell Davis/545	60.00	27.00
❑ 2	Charles Johnson/325	30.00	13.50
❑ 3	Jon Kitna/640	50.00	22.00
❑ 4	Dorsey Levens/515	40.00	18.00
❑ 5	Dan Marino/220	150.00	70.00
❑ 6	Curtis Martin/690	40.00	18.00
❑ 7	Johnnie Morton/580	30.00	13.50
❑ 8	Randy Moss/510	150.00	70.00
❑ 9	Brandon Stokley/85	40.00	18.00
❑ 10	Steve Young/580	60.00	27.00

1999 Fleer Mystique Fresh Ink

	MINT	NRMT
COMPLETE SET (30)	1800.00	800.00
COMMON CARD (1-30)	12.00	5.50
SEMISTARS	20.00	9.00
UNLISTED STARS	25.00	11.00

RANDOM INSERTS IN PACKS

		MINT	NRMT
❑ 1	Charlie Batch/250	50.00	22.00
❑ 2	Mark Brunell/45	150.00	70.00
❑ 3	Shawn Bryson/650	12.00	5.50
❑ 4	Cecil Collins/725	25.00	11.00
❑ 5	Daunte Culpepper/300	60.00	27.00
❑ 6	Randall Cunningham/200	40.00	18.00
❑ 7	Terrell Davis/50	200.00	90.00
❑ 8	Sean Dawkins/700	12.00	5.50
❑ 9	Corey Dillon/250	25.00	11.00
❑ 10	Dameane Douglas/750	12.00	5.50
❑ 11	Tim Dwight/725	25.00	11.00
❑ 12	Troy Edwards/200	50.00	22.00
❑ 13	Doug Flutie/250	40.00	18.00
❑ 14	Eddie George/250	30.00	13.50
❑ 15	Joe Germaine/575	20.00	9.00
❑ 16	Trent Green/350	20.00	9.00
❑ 17	Torry Holt/350	50.00	22.00
❑ 18	Brock Huard/700	25.00	11.00
❑ 19	Edgerrin James/150	300.00	135.00
❑ 20	Brad Johnson/300	25.00	11.00
❑ 21	Jon Kitna/350	40.00	18.00
❑ 22	Peyton Manning/250	150.00	70.00
❑ 23	Randy Moss/150	150.00	70.00
❑ 24	Doug Pederson/750	12.00	5.50
❑ 25	Jake Plummer/300	40.00	18.00
❑ 26	Peerless Price/675	25.00	11.00
❑ 27	Akili Smith/100	80.00	36.00
❑ 28	Emmitt Smith/125	150.00	70.00
❑ 29	Antowain Smith/150	40.00	18.00
❑ 30	Ricky Williams/150	150.00	70.00

1999 Fleer Mystique NFL 2000

	MINT	NRMT
COMPLETE SET (10)	40.00	18.00
COMMON CARD (1N-10N)	2.50	1.10
SEMISTARS	4.00	1.80

STATED PRINT RUN 999 SER.#'d SETS

		MINT	NRMT
❑ 1N	Peyton Manning	15.00	6.75
❑ 2N	Ryan Leaf	2.50	1.10
❑ 3N	Charlie Batch	8.00	3.60
❑ 4N	Fred Taylor	10.00	4.50
❑ 5N	Keyshawn Johnson	4.00	1.80
❑ 6N	J.J. Stokes	4.00	1.80
❑ 7N	Jake Plummer	8.00	3.60
❑ 8N	Brian Griese	8.00	3.60
❑ 9N	Antowain Smith	4.00	1.80
❑ 10N	Jamal Anderson	4.00	1.80

1999 Fleer Mystique Protential

	MINT	NRMT
COMPLETE SET (10)	60.00	27.00
COMMON CARD (1PT-10PT)	5.00	2.20

STATED PRINT RUN 1999 SER.#'d SETS

		MINT	NRMT
❑ 1PT	Tim Couch	15.00	6.75
❑ 2PT	Donovan McNabb	10.00	4.50
❑ 3PT	Akili Smith	6.00	2.70
❑ 4PT	Cade McNown	10.00	4.50
❑ 5PT	Daunte Culpepper	10.00	4.50
❑ 6PT	Ricky Williams	15.00	6.75
❑ 7PT	Edgerrin James	25.00	11.00
❑ 8PT	Kevin Faulk	5.00	2.20
❑ 9PT	Torry Holt	8.00	3.60
❑ 10PT	David Boston	5.00	2.20

1999 Fleer Mystique Star Power

	MINT	NRMT
COMPLETE SET (10)	300.00	135.00
COMMON CARD (1SP-10SP)	15.00	6.75

STATED PRINT RUN 100 SER.#'d SETS

		MINT	NRMT
❑ 1SP	Randy Moss	50.00	22.00
❑ 2SP	Warrick Dunn	15.00	6.75
❑ 3SP	Mark Brunell	25.00	11.00
❑ 4SP	Emmitt Smith	40.00	18.00
❑ 5SP	Eddie George	20.00	9.00
❑ 6SP	Barry Sanders	60.00	27.00
❑ 7SP	Terrell Davis	40.00	18.00
❑ 8SP	Dan Marino	60.00	27.00
❑ 9SP	Troy Aikman	40.00	18.00
❑ 10SP	Brett Favre	60.00	27.00

2000 Impact

	MINT	NRMT
COMPLETE SET (199)	25.00	11.00
COMMON CARD (1-200)	.10	.05
SEMISTARS	.20	.09
UNLISTED STARS	.40	.18
COMMON ROOKIE	.40	.18
ROOKIE SEMISTARS	.60	.25

FORMERLY KNOWN AS SKYBOX IMPACT
CARD #137 NOT RELEASED

		MINT	NRMT
❑ 1	Kurt Warner	2.00	.90
❑ 2	Dan Marino	1.50	.70
❑ 3	Sedrick Irvin	.10	.05
❑ 4	Chris Redman RC	1.00	.45
❑ 5	Robert Smith	.40	.18
❑ 6	Amani Toomer	.10	.05
❑ 7	Richard Huntley	.10	.05
❑ 8	Ahman Green	.20	.09
❑ 9	Fred Lane	.10	.05
❑ 10	Eddie George	.50	.23
❑ 11	Rocket Ismail	.20	.09
❑ 12	Shannon Sharpe	.20	.09
❑ 13	Shawn Jefferson	.10	.05
❑ 14	Michael Wiley RC	.75	.35
❑ 15	Jeff Graham	.10	.05
❑ 16	Steve Beuerlein	.20	.09
❑ 17	Tim Biakabutuka	.20	.09
❑ 18	Chris Watson	.10	.05
❑ 19	Kevin Faulk	.20	.09
❑ 20	Emmitt Smith	1.00	.45
❑ 21	Plaxico Burress RC	1.50	.70
❑ 22	Hines Ward	.10	.05
❑ 23	Jacquez Green	.20	.09
❑ 24	Doug Flutie	.50	.23
❑ 25	Leslie Shepherd	.10	.05
❑ 26	Johnnie Morton	.20	.09
❑ 27	Tom Brady RC	.60	.25
❑ 28	Jeff George	.20	.09
❑ 29	Derrick Mason	.10	.05
❑ 30	Marshall Faulk	.40	.18
❑ 31	Derrick Mayes	.20	.09
❑ 32	Jerome Bettis	.40	.18
❑ 33	Adrian Murrell	.20	.09
❑ 34	Curtis Enis	.40	.18
❑ 35	Kimble Anders	.10	.05
❑ 36	Travis Prentice RC	.75	.35
❑ 37	Curtis Martin	.40	.18
❑ 38	Ronnie Powell	.10	.05
❑ 39	Steve Christie	.10	.05
❑ 40	Brett Favre	1.50	.70
❑ 41	Michael Bates	.10	.05
❑ 42	Rondell Mealey RC	.40	.18
❑ 43	Randall Cunningham	.40	.18
❑ 44	Kerry Collins	.20	.09
❑ 45	William Thomas	.10	.05
❑ 46	Ricky Watters	.20	.09
❑ 47	Marvin Harrison	.40	.18
❑ 48	Corey Bradford	.20	.09
❑ 49	Terry Kirby	.10	.05
❑ 50	Troy Aikman	1.00	.45
❑ 51	Cris Carter	.40	.18

Card	MINT	NRMT
❑ 52 Jamal Lewis RC	2.00	.90
❑ 53 Duce Staley	.40	.18
❑ 54 Isaac Bruce	.40	.18
❑ 55 Yancey Thigpen	.10	.05
❑ 56 R. Jay Soward RC	.75	.35
❑ 57 Jermaine Lewis	.10	.05
❑ 58 Zach Thomas	.20	.09
❑ 59 Sylvester Morris RC	.75	.35
❑ 60 Steve McNair	.40	.18
❑ 61 Tiki Barber	.20	.09
❑ 62 Torrance Small	.10	.05
❑ 63 Champ Bailey	.20	.09
❑ 64 Tim Dwight	.40	.18
❑ 65 Willie Jackson	.10	.05
❑ 66 Edgerrin James	1.50	.70
❑ 67 Ron Dayne RC	3.00	1.35
❑ 68 Rich Gannon	.20	.09
❑ 69 Junior Seau	.20	.09
❑ 70 Warren Sapp	.20	.09
❑ 71 Rob Johnson	.20	.09
❑ 72 Antonio Freeman	.40	.18
❑ 73 O.J. McDuffie	.20	.09
❑ 74 Tamarick Vanover	.10	.05
❑ 75 Courtney Brown RC	1.25	.55
❑ 76 Donovan McNabb	.60	.25
❑ 77 Az-Zahir Hakim	.20	.09
❑ 78 Albert Connell	.10	.05
❑ 79 Qadry Ismail	.10	.05
❑ 80 Terrell Davis	1.00	.45
❑ 81 Dorsey Levens	.40	.18
❑ 82 Tony Martin	.20	.09
❑ 83 Laveranues Coles RC	.60	.25
❑ 84 Karim Abdul-Jabbar	.20	.09
❑ 85 Charles Johnson	.10	.05
❑ 86 Torry Holt	.40	.18
❑ 87 Stephen Davis	.40	.18
❑ 88 Tony Banks	.20	.09
❑ 89 Akili Smith	.50	.23
❑ 90 Tim Couch	1.00	.45
❑ 91 Bill Schroeder	.20	.09
❑ 92 Andre Hastings	.10	.05
❑ 93 Eddie Kennison	.10	.05
❑ 94 Randy Moss	1.25	.55
❑ 95 Tony Horne	.10	.05
❑ 96 Sherrod Gideon RC	.40	.18
❑ 97 Wesley Walls	.10	.05
❑ 98 Brian Griese	.50	.23
❑ 99 Jake Delhomme RC	1.50	.70
❑ 100 Peyton Manning	1.25	.55
❑ 101 Brad Johnson	.40	.18
❑ 102 Trung Canidate RC	.60	.25
❑ 103 Freddie Jones	.10	.05
❑ 104 Muhsin Muhammad	.20	.09
❑ 105 Eric Moulds	.40	.18
❑ 106 Ed McCaffrey	.20	.09
❑ 107 Joe Montgomery	.10	.05
❑ 108 Olandis Gary	.50	.23
❑ 109 J.J. Stokes	.10	.05
❑ 110 Ricky Williams	1.00	.45
❑ 111 Jim Harbaugh	.20	.09
❑ 112 Mike Alstott	.40	.18
❑ 113 Errict Rhett	.20	.09
❑ 114 Terance Mathis	.10	.05
❑ 115 Kevin Johnson	.40	.18
❑ 116 Tremain Mack	.10	.05
❑ 117 Peter Warrick RC	3.00	1.35
❑ 118 Lamont Warren	.10	.05
❑ 119 Damon Huard	.40	.18
❑ 120 Cade McNown	.60	.25
❑ 121 Natrone Means	.10	.05
❑ 122 Ken Oxendine	.10	.05
❑ 123 J.R. Redmond RC	1.00	.45
❑ 124 Ken Dilger	.10	.05
❑ 125 James Johnson	.20	.09
❑ 126 Napoleon Kaufman	.40	.18
❑ 127 Ryan Leaf	.40	.18
❑ 128 Michael Westbrook	.20	.09
❑ 129 Mario Bates	.10	.05
❑ 130 Jake Plummer	.40	.18
❑ 131 James Jett	.10	.05
❑ 132 Darnay Scott	.20	.09
❑ 133 Curtis Conway	.20	.09
❑ 134 Fred Taylor	.60	.25
❑ 135 Wayne Chrebet	.20	.09
❑ 136 Sean Dawkins	.10	.05
❑ 138 Keenan McCardell	.20	.09
❑ 139 Donnell Bennett	.10	.05
❑ 140 Jerry Rice	1.00	.45
❑ 141 Vinny Testaverde	.20	.09
❑ 142 Chad Pennington RC	2.50	1.10
❑ 143 Jonathan Linton	.10	.05
❑ 144 Herman Moore	.40	.18
❑ 145 David Patten	.10	.05
❑ 146 Troy Edwards	.40	.18
❑ 147 Jon Kitna	.40	.18
❑ 148 Jimmy Smith	.20	.09
❑ 149 Tee Martin RC	1.00	.45
❑ 150 Jevon Kearse	.40	.18
❑ 151 Frank Sanders	.10	.05
❑ 152 Marcus Robinson	.40	.18
❑ 153 Mike Hollis	.10	.05
❑ 154 Frank Wycheck	.10	.05
❑ 155 Tim Rattay RC	.75	.35
❑ 156 Dedric Ward	.10	.05
❑ 157 Terrell Owens	.40	.18
❑ 158 Chris Chandler	.20	.09
❑ 159 Damon Griffin	.10	.05
❑ 160 Mike Vanderjagt	.10	.05
❑ 161 Elvis Grbac	.10	.05
❑ 162 Rickey Dudley	.10	.05
❑ 163 Jeff Garcia	.40	.18
❑ 164 Thomas Jones RC	2.00	.90
❑ 165 Tyrone Wheatley	.20	.09
❑ 166 Rod Smith	.20	.09
❑ 167 Bubba Franks RC	.75	.35
❑ 168 Chris Warren	.10	.05
❑ 169 Anthony Lucas RC	.60	.25
❑ 170 Terry Glenn	.40	.18
❑ 171 John Carney	.10	.05
❑ 172 Warrick Dunn	.40	.18
❑ 173 Shaun Alexander RC	2.00	.90
❑ 174 David Boston	.40	.18
❑ 175 Bobby Engram	.10	.05
❑ 176 Travis Taylor RC	1.25	.55
❑ 177 Derrick Alexander	.20	.09
❑ 178 Keyshawn Johnson	.40	.18
❑ 179 Steve Young	.60	.25
❑ 180 Deion Sanders	.40	.18
❑ 181 Charlie Batch	.40	.18
❑ 182 Drew Bledsoe	.60	.25
❑ 183 Reuben Droughns RC	.75	.35
❑ 184 Ray Lucas	.40	.18
❑ 185 Shaun King	.60	.25
❑ 186 Jamal Anderson	.40	.18
❑ 187 Corey Dillon	.40	.18
❑ 188 Joe Hamilton RC	.60	.25
❑ 189 Terrence Wilkins	.40	.18
❑ 190 Mark Brunell	.60	.25
❑ 191 Tony Gonzalez	.20	.09
❑ 192 Tim Brown	.40	.18
❑ 193 Charlie Garner	.20	.09
❑ 194 Antowain Smith	.40	.18
❑ 195 David LaFleur	.10	.05
❑ 196 Germane Crowell	.20	.09
❑ 197 Terry Allen	.20	.09
❑ 198 Marc Bulger RC	.60	.25
❑ 199 Kevin Dyson	.20	.09
❑ 200 Kordell Stewart	.40	.18

2000 Impact Autographics

	MINT	NRMT
COMMON CARD	10.00	4.50
STATED ODDS 1:216		
❑ 1 Karim Abdul-Jabbar		
❑ 2 Troy Aikman	60.00	27.00
❑ 3 Kimble Anders	10.00	4.50
❑ 4 Corey Dillon	25.00	11.00
❑ 5 Olandis Gary	25.00	11.00
❑ 6 Sherrod Gideon	15.00	6.75
❑ 7 Marvin Harrison		
❑ 8 Torry Holt	20.00	9.00
❑ 9 Shane Matthews		
❑ 10 Cade McNown		
❑ 11 Jake Plummer		
❑ 12 Jake Reed	15.00	6.75
❑ 13 Marcus Robinson		
❑ 14 Bill Schroeder	20.00	9.00
❑ 15 Shannon Sharpe	20.00	9.00
❑ 16 R.Jay Soward		
❑ 17 Kordell Stewart	20.00	9.00
❑ 18 Dedric Ward	10.00	4.50
❑ 19 Chris Watson	10.00	4.50

2000 Impact Hats Off

	MINT	NRMT
COMMON CARD (1-21)	25.00	11.00
SEMISTARS	30.00	13.50
UNLISTED STARS	40.00	18.00
STATED ODDS 1:720H/1:1444R..		
❑ 1 Karim Abdul-Jabbar		
❑ 2 Jamal Anderson	40.00	18.00
❑ 3 David Boston	30.00	13.50
❑ 4 Isaac Bruce	40.00	18.00
❑ 5 Chris Chandler	30.00	13.50
❑ 6 Curtis Conway	30.00	13.50
❑ 7 Tim Couch	80.00	36.00
❑ 8 Tim Dwight	40.00	18.00
❑ 9 Curtis Enis	40.00	18.00
❑ 10 Marshall Faulk	50.00	22.00
❑ 11 Az-Zahir Hakim	30.00	13.50
❑ 12 Torry Holt	40.00	18.00
❑ 13 Kevin Johnson	40.00	18.00
❑ 14 Terry Kirby	25.00	11.00
❑ 15 Terance Mathis	30.00	13.50
❑ 16 Shane Matthews	25.00	11.00
❑ 17 Cade McNown	60.00	27.00
❑ 18 Rob Moore		
❑ 19 Jake Plummer	40.00	18.00
❑ 20 Marcus Robinson	40.00	18.00
❑ 21 Frank Sanders	30.00	13.50

2000 Impact Point of Impact

	MINT	NRMT
COMPLETE SET (10)	30.00	13.50
COMMON CARD (PI1-PI10)	2.00	.90
STATED ODDS 1:30		
❑ PI1 Peyton Manning	6.00	2.70
❑ PI2 Edgerrin James	6.00	2.70
❑ PI3 Brett Favre	8.00	3.60
❑ PI4 Marshall Faulk	2.00	.90
❑ PI5 Fred Taylor	3.00	1.35
❑ PI6 Tim Couch	4.00	1.80
❑ PI7 Emmitt Smith	5.00	2.20
❑ PI8 Eddie George	2.50	1.10
❑ PI9 Randy Moss	6.00	2.70
❑ PI10 Terrell Davis	5.00	2.20

2000 Impact Rewind '99

	MINT	NRMT
COMPLETE SET (40)	20.00	9.00
COMMON CARD (1-40)	.15	.07
SEMISTARS	.25	.11
UNLISTED STARS	.50	.23
ONE PER PACK		
❑ 1 Jake Plummer	.50	.23
❑ 2 Tim Dwight	.50	.23
❑ 3 Tony Banks	.25	.11
❑ 4 Doug Flutie	.60	.25
❑ 5 Tim Biakabutuka	.25	.11

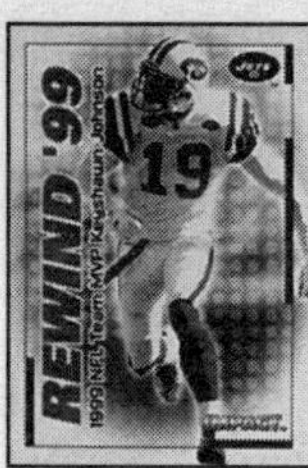

- ❑ 6 Marcus Robinson .50 .23
- ❑ 7 Corey Dillon .50 .23
- ❑ 8 Tim Couch 1.00 .45
- ❑ 9 Troy Aikman 1.25 .55
- ❑ 10 Olandis Gary .50 .23
- ❑ 11 Germane Crowell .25 .11
- ❑ 12 Brett Favre 2.00 .90
- ❑ 13 Peyton Manning 1.50 .70
- ❑ 14 Mark Brunell .75 .35
- ❑ 15 Tony Gonzalez .25 .11
- ❑ 16 Dan Marino 2.00 .90
- ❑ 17 Randy Moss 1.50 .70
- ❑ 18 Drew Bledsoe .75 .35
- ❑ 19 Ricky Williams 1.00 .45
- ❑ 20 Amani Toomer .25 .11
- ❑ 21 Keyshawn Johnson .50 .23
- ❑ 22 Rich Gannon .25 .11
- ❑ 23 Duce Staley .50 .23
- ❑ 24 Jerome Bettis .50 .23
- ❑ 25 Kenny Bynum .15 .07
- ❑ 26 Charlie Garner .25 .11
- ❑ 27 Jon Kitna .50 .23
- ❑ 28 Kurt Warner 2.00 .90
- ❑ 29 Mike Alstott .50 .23
- ❑ 30 Eddie George .60 .25
- ❑ 31 Stephen Davis .50 .23
- ❑ 32 Kurt Warner 2.00 .90
- ❑ 33 Edgerrin James 1.50 .70
- ❑ 34 Jevon Kearse .50 .23
- ❑ 35 Marshall Faulk .50 .23
- ❑ 36 Edgerrin James 1.50 .70
- ❑ 37 Marvin Harrison .50 .23
- ❑ 38 Jimmy Smith .25 .11
- ❑ 39 Steve Beuerlein .25 .11
- ❑ 40 Kurt Warner 2.00 .90

2000 Impact Team Tattoos

	MINT	NRMT
COMPLETE SET (31)	25.00	11.00
COMMON TATTOO	1.00	.45
STATED ODDS 1:4		

- ❑ 1 Bears 1.00 .45
- ❑ 2 Bengals 1.00 .45
- ❑ 3 Bills 1.00 .45
- ❑ 4 Broncos 1.00 .45
- ❑ 5 Browns 1.00 .45
- ❑ 6 Buccaneers 1.00 .45
- ❑ 7 Cardinals 1.00 .45
- ❑ 8 Chargers 1.00 .45
- ❑ 9 Chiefs 1.00 .45
- ❑ 10 Colts 1.00 .45
- ❑ 11 Cowboys 1.00 .45
- ❑ 12 Dolphins 1.00 .45
- ❑ 13 Eagles 1.00 .45
- ❑ 14 Falcons 1.00 .45
- ❑ 15 49ers 1.00 .45
- ❑ 16 Giants 1.00 .45
- ❑ 17 Jaguars 1.00 .45
- ❑ 18 Jets 1.00 .45
- ❑ 19 Lions 1.00 .45
- ❑ 20 Packers 1.00 .45
- ❑ 21 Panthers 1.00 .45
- ❑ 22 Patriots 1.00 .45
- ❑ 23 Raiders 1.00 .45
- ❑ 24 Rams 1.00 .45
- ❑ 25 Ravens 1.00 .45
- ❑ 26 Redskins 1.00 .45
- ❑ 27 Saints 1.00 .45
- ❑ 28 Seahawks 1.00 .45
- ❑ 29 Steelers 1.00 .45
- ❑ 30 Titans 1.00 .45
- ❑ 31 Vikings 1.00 .45

1996 Laser View

	MINT	NRMT
COMPLETE SET (40)	50.00	22.00
COMMON CARD (1-40)	.30	.14
SEMISTARS	.60	.25
UNLISTED STARS	1.25	.55
COMP.GOLD SET (40)	200.00	90.00
*GOLDS: 1X TO 2.5X HI COL.		
GOLD STATED ODDS 1:12		

- ❑ 1 Jim Kelly 1.25 .55
- ❑ 2 Troy Aikman 3.00 1.35
- ❑ 3 Michael Irvin 1.25 .55
- ❑ 4 Emmitt Smith 5.00 2.20
- ❑ 5 John Elway 6.00 2.70
- ❑ 6 Barry Sanders 6.00 2.70
- ❑ 7 Brett Favre 6.00 2.70
- ❑ 8 Jim Harbaugh .60 .25
- ❑ 9 Dan Marino 6.00 2.70
- ❑ 10 Warren Moon .60 .25
- ❑ 11 Drew Bledsoe 3.00 1.35
- ❑ 12 Jim Everett .30 .14
- ❑ 13 Jeff Hostetler .30 .14
- ❑ 14 Neil O'Donnell .60 .25
- ❑ 15 Junior Seau .60 .25
- ❑ 16 Jerry Rice 3.00 1.35
- ❑ 17 Steve Young 2.50 1.10
- ❑ 18 Rick Mirer .60 .25
- ❑ 19 Boomer Esiason .60 .25
- ❑ 20 Bernie Kosar .30 .14
- ❑ 21 Heath Shuler .60 .25
- ❑ 22 Dave Brown .30 .14
- ❑ 23 Jeff Blake 1.25 .55
- ❑ 24 Kerry Collins 1.25 .55
- ❑ 25 Kordell Stewart 2.00 .90
- ❑ 26 Scott Mitchell .60 .25
- ❑ 27 Kerry Collins PE 1.25 .55
- ❑ 28 Troy Aikman PE 2.00 .90
- ❑ 29 Kordell Stewart PE 1.25 .55
- ❑ 30 Michael Irvin PE .60 .25
- ❑ 31 Emmitt Smith PE 3.00 1.35
- ❑ 32 John Elway PE 4.00 1.80
- ❑ 33 Barry Sanders PE 4.00 1.80
- ❑ 34 Brett Favre PE 4.00 1.80
- ❑ 35 Dan Marino PE 4.00 1.80
- ❑ 36 Drew Bledsoe PE 2.00 .90
- ❑ 37 Neil O'Donnell PE .60 .25
- ❑ 38 Jerry Rice PE 2.00 .90
- ❑ 39 Steve Young PE 2.00 .90
- ❑ 40 Jeff Blake PE .60 .25
- ❑ P5 John Elway Promo 2.00 .90

1996 Laser View Eye on the Prize

	MINT	NRMT
COMPLETE SET (12)	100.00	45.00
STATED ODDS 1:24		

- ❑ 1 Troy Aikman 10.00 4.50
- ❑ 2 Emmitt Smith 15.00 6.75
- ❑ 3 Michael Irvin 4.00 1.80
- ❑ 4 Steve Young 8.00 3.60
- ❑ 5 Jerry Rice 10.00 4.50
- ❑ 6 Dan Marino 20.00 9.00
- ❑ 7 John Elway 20.00 9.00
- ❑ 8 Junior Seau 2.00 .90
- ❑ 9 Neil O'Donnell 2.00 .90
- ❑ 10 Jeff Hostetler 1.00 .45
- ❑ 11 Jim Kelly 4.00 1.80
- ❑ 12 Kordell Stewart 6.00 2.70

1996 Laser View Inscriptions

	MINT	NRMT
COMPLETE SET (25)	1000.00	450.00
COMMON CARD (1-25)	15.00	6.75
SEMISTARS	20.00	9.00
UNLISTED STARS	30.00	13.50
STATED ODDS 1:24		

- ❑ 1 Jeff Blake/3125 20.00 9.00
- ❑ 2 Drew Bledsoe/2775 40.00 18.00
- ❑ 3 Dave Brown/3100 15.00 6.75
- ❑ 4 Mark Brunell/3200 40.00 18.00
- ❑ 5 Kerry Collins/3000 20.00 9.00
- ❑ 6 John Elway/3100 80.00 36.00
- ❑ 7 Boomer Esiason/1500 150.00 70.00
- ❑ 8 Jim Everett/3100 15.00 6.75

❑ 9 Brett Favre/4850 .... 80.00 36.00
❑ 10 Jeff George/2900 .... 20.00 9.00
❑ 11 Jim Harbaugh/3500...... 20.00 9.00
❑ 12 Jeff Hostetler/3750 ...... 15.00 6.75
❑ 13 Michael Irvin/3050........ 30.00 13.50
❑ 14 Jim Kelly/3100.............. 30.00 13.50
❑ 15 Bernie Kosar/3200 ...... 15.00 6.75
❑ 16 Erik Kramer/3150 .... 15.00 6.75
❑ 17 Rick Mirer/3150............ 15.00 6.75
❑ 18 Scott Mitchell/4900 ...... 15.00 6.75
❑ 19 Warren Moon/2800 ...... 30.00 13.50
❑ 20 Neil O'Donnell/1600 .... 50.00 22.00
❑ 21 Jerry Rice/900............ 250.00 110.00
❑ 22 Barry Sanders/2900 .. 100.00 45.00
❑ 23 Junior Seau/3000 .... 20.00 9.00
❑ 24 Heath Shuler/3100 ...... 20.00 9.00
❑ 25 Steve Young/1950........ 60.00 27.00

1948 Leaf

	NRMT	VG-E
COMPLETE SET (98)	6000.00	2700.00
COMMON CARD (1-49)..........	25.00	11.00
SEMISTARS (1-49)	30.00	13.50
COMMON CARD (50-98)......	120.00	55.00

CARDS PRICED IN NM CONDITION !

❑ 1 Sid Luckman RC ! 350.00 90.00
❑ 2 Steve Suhey 25.00 11.00
❑ 3A Bulldog Turner RC 110.00 50.00
(Red background)
❑ 3B Bulldog Turner RC 110.00 50.00
(White background)
❑ 4 Doak Walker RC 175.00 80.00
❑ 5 Levi Jackson RC 30.00 13.50
❑ 6 Bobby Layne RC UER 325.00 145.00
(Name spelled Bobbie on front)
❑ 7 Bill Fischer..................... 25.00 11.00
❑ 8A Vince Banonis.............. 25.00 11.00
(White name on front)
❑ 8B Vince Banonis.............. 25.00 11.00
(Black name on front)
❑ 9 Tommy Thompson RC .. 30.00 13.50
❑ 10 Perry Moss 25.00 11.00
❑ 11 Terry Brennan RC 30.00 13.50
❑ 12A William Swiacki RC.... 25.00 11.00
(White name on front)
❑ 12B William Swiacki RC.... 25.00 11.00
(Black name on front)
❑ 13 Johnny Lujack RC...... 175.00 80.00
❑ 14A Mal Kutner RC 25.00 11.00
(White name on front)
❑ 14B Mal Kutner RC 25.00 11.00
(Black name on front)
❑ 15 Charlie Justice RC 90.00 40.00
❑ 16 Pete Pihos RC............ 100.00 45.00
❑ 17A Kenny Washington RC 55.00 25.00
(White name on front)
❑ 17B Kenny Washington RC 55.00 25.00
(Black name on front)
❑ 18 Harry Gilmer RC 40.00 18.00
❑ 19A George McAfee RC ERR 125.00 55.00
(Listed as Gorgeous George on front)
❑ 19B George McAfee COR RC 110.00 50.00
❑ 20 George Taliaferro RC .. 30.00 13.50
❑ 21 Paul Christman RC 50.00 22.00
❑ 22 Steve Van Buren RC.. 200.00 90.00
❑ 23 Ken Kavanaugh RC 30.00 13.50
❑ 24 Jim Martin RC 30.00 13.50
❑ 25 Elmer Bud Angsman RC 30.00 13.50
❑ 26 Bob Waterfield RC 225.00 100.00
❑ 27A Fred Davis 25.00 11.00
(Yellow background)
❑ 27B Fred Davis 25.00 11.00
(White background)
❑ 28 Whitey Wistert RC........ 30.00 13.50
❑ 29 Charley Trippi RC 110.00 50.00
❑ 30 Paul Governali RC 30.00 13.50
❑ 31 Tom McWilliams 25.00 11.00
❑ 32 Leroy Zimmerman........ 25.00 11.00
❑ 33 Pat Harder RC UER 55.00 25.00
(Misspelled Harber on front)
❑ 34 Sammy Baugh RC 500.00 220.00
❑ 35 Ted Fritsch Sr. RC 30.00 13.50
❑ 36 Bill Dudley RC 110.00 50.00
❑ 37 George Connor RC...... 80.00 36.00
❑ 38 Frank Dancewicz.......... 25.00 11.00
❑ 39 Billy Dewell 25.00 11.00
❑ 40 John Nolan 25.00 11.00
❑ 41A Harry Szulborski 25.00 11.00
Yellow jersey
❑ 41B Harry Szulborski 25.00 11.00
Orange jersey
❑ 42 Tex Coulter RC 30.00 13.50
❑ 43A Robert Nussbaumer .. 25.00 11.00
(Maroon Jersey)
❑ 43B Robert Nussbaumer .. 25.00 11.00
(Red Jersey)
❑ 44 Bob Mann 25.00 11.00
❑ 45 Jim White 25.00 11.00
❑ 46 Jack Jacobs 25.00 11.00
❑ 47 John Clement 25.00 11.00
❑ 48 Frank Reagan 25.00 11.00
❑ 49 Frank Tripucka RC 45.00 20.00
❑ 50 John Rauch RC.......... 120.00 55.00
❑ 51 Mike Dimitro 120.00 55.00
❑ 52 Leo Nomellini RC 350.00 160.00
❑ 53 Charley Conerly RC .. 350.00 160.00
❑ 54 Chuck Bednarik RC.... 425.00 190.00
❑ 55 Chick Jagade 120.00 55.00
❑ 56 Bob Folsom RC.......... 140.00 65.00
❑ 57 Gene Rossides RC 140.00 65.00
❑ 58 Art Weiner 120.00 55.00
❑ 59 Alex Sarkistian 120.00 55.00
❑ 60 Dick Harris................. 120.00 55.00
❑ 61 Len Younce 120.00 55.00
❑ 62 Gene Derricotte......... 120.00 55.00
❑ 63 Roy Rebel Steiner...... 120.00 55.00
❑ 64 Frank Seno 120.00 55.00
❑ 65 Bob Hendren RC........ 120.00 55.00
❑ 66 Jack Cloud 120.00 55.00
❑ 67 Harrell Collins 120.00 55.00
❑ 68 Clyde LeForce........... 120.00 55.00
❑ 69 Larry Joe 120.00 55.00
❑ 70 Phil O'Reilly............... 120.00 55.00
❑ 71 Paul Campbell........... 120.00 55.00
❑ 72 Ray Evans................. 120.00 55.00
❑ 73 Jackie Jensen RC UER 350.00 160.00
Spelled Jackey on card front
❑ 74 Russ Steger 120.00 55.00
❑ 75 Tony Minisi 120.00 55.00
❑ 76 Clayton Tonnemaker.. 120.00 55.00
❑ 77 George Savitsky 120.00 55.00
❑ 78 Clarence Self............ 120.00 55.00
❑ 79 Rod Franz 120.00 55.00
❑ 80 Jim Youle 120.00 55.00
❑ 81 Billy Bye 120.00 55.00
❑ 82 Fred Enke 120.00 55.00
❑ 83 Fred Folger 120.00 55.00
❑ 84 Jug Girard RC 140.00 65.00
❑ 85 Joe Scott 120.00 55.00
❑ 86 Bob Demoss 120.00 55.00
❑ 87 Dave Templeton 120.00 55.00
❑ 88 Herb Siegert 120.00 55.00
❑ 89 Bucky O'Conner 120.00 55.00
❑ 90 Joe Whisler 120.00 55.00
❑ 91 Leon Hart RC 200.00 90.00
❑ 92 Earl Banks................. 120.00 55.00
❑ 93 Frank Aschenbrenner 120.00 55.00
❑ 94 John Goldsberry 120.00 55.00
❑ 95 Porter Payne 120.00 55.00
❑ 96 Pete Perini................. 120.00 55.00
❑ 97 Jay Rhodemyre 120.00 55.00
❑ 98 Al DiMarco RC ! 250.00 60.00

1949 Leaf

	NRMT	VG-E
COMPLETE SET (49)	2200.00	1000.00
COMMON CARD (1-150)........	25.00	11.00
SEMISTARS........................	35.00	16.00

SET IS SKIP NUMBERED ....
CARDS PRICED IN NM CONDITION !

❑ 1 Bob Hendren................. 80.00 20.00
❑ 2 Joe Scott 25.00 11.00
❑ 3 Frank Reagan 25.00 11.00
❑ 4 John Rauch 25.00 11.00
❑ 7 Bill Fischer.................... 25.00 11.00
❑ 9 Elmer Bud Angsman 35.00 16.00
❑ 10 Billy Dewell 25.00 11.00
❑ 13 Tommy Thompson 35.00 16.00
❑ 15 Sid Luckman 125.00 55.00
❑ 16 Charley Trippi 55.00 25.00
❑ 17 Bob Mann 25.00 11.00
❑ 19 Paul Christman 35.00 16.00
❑ 22 Bill Dudley 55.00 25.00
❑ 23 Clyde LeForce............. 25.00 11.00
❑ 26 Sammy Baugh........... 300.00 135.00
❑ 28 Pete Pihos................... 55.00 25.00
❑ 31 Tex Coulter 35.00 16.00
❑ 32 Mal Kutner................... 35.00 16.00
❑ 35 Whitey Wistert 35.00 16.00
❑ 37 Ted Fritsch Sr.............. 35.00 16.00
❑ 38 Vince Banonis 25.00 11.00
❑ 39 Jim White 25.00 11.00
❑ 40 George Connor 55.00 25.00
❑ 41 George McAfee 55.00 25.00
❑ 43 Frank Tripucka 35.00 16.00
❑ 47 Fred Enke 25.00 11.00
❑ 49 Charley Conerly 100.00 45.00
❑ 51 Ken Kavanaugh........... 35.00 16.00
❑ 52 Bob Demoss 25.00 11.00
❑ 56 John Lujack 100.00 45.00
❑ 57 Jim Youle 25.00 11.00
❑ 62 Harry Gilmer 35.00 16.00
❑ 65 Robert Nussbaumer 25.00 11.00
❑ 67 Bobby Layne 175.00 80.00
❑ 70 Herb Siegert 25.00 11.00
❑ 74 Tony Minisi 25.00 11.00
❑ 79 Steve Van Buren....... 125.00 55.00
❑ 81 Perry Moss 25.00 11.00
❑ 89 Bob Waterfield.......... 100.00 45.00
❑ 90 Jack Jacobs 25.00 11.00
❑ 95 Kenny Washington 45.00 20.00
❑ 101 Pat Harder UER 35.00 16.00
(Misspelled Harber on front)
❑ 110 Bill Swiacki 35.00 16.00
❑ 118 Fred Davis.................. 25.00 11.00
❑ 126 Jay Rhodemyre........... 25.00 11.00
❑ 127 Frank Seno................. 25.00 11.00
❑ 134 Chuck Bednarik....... 150.00 70.00
❑ 144 George Savitsky 25.00 11.00
❑ 150 Bulldog Turner.......... 135.00 34.00

1996 Leaf

	MINT	NRMT
COMPLETE SET (190)	20.00	9.00
COMMON CARD (1-190)...........	.10	.05
SEMISTARS..............................	.20	.09
UNLISTED STARS.....................	.40	.18
COMP.PRESS PROOF (190)	400.00	180.00

*PP STARS: 4X TO 10X HI COL...
PRESS PROOF RCs: 2.5X TO 6X
PP STATED PRINT RUN 2000 SETS

COMP.COLL.EDITION SET (190) 20.00 9.00
COMP.COLL.ED.FACT.SET (191) 30.00 13.50
*COLLECTOR'S EDITIONS: SAME PRICE

❑ 1 Troy Aikman 1.00 .45
❑ 2 Ricky Watters .20 .09
❑ 3 Robert Brooks .40 .18
❑ 4 Ki-Jana Carter .20 .09
❑ 5 Drew Bledsoe 1.00 .45
❑ 6 Eric Swann .10 .05
❑ 7 Hardy Nickerson .10 .05
❑ 8 Tony Martin .20 .09
❑ 9 Garrison Hearst .20 .09
❑ 10 Bernie Parmalee .10 .05
❑ 11 Neil Smith .10 .05
❑ 12 Aaron Craver .10 .05
❑ 13 Rashaan Salaam .40 .18
❑ 14 Greg Hill .20 .09
❑ 15 Charlie Garner .10 .05
❑ 16 Kimble Anders .20 .09
❑ 17 Steve McNair .75 .35
❑ 18 Neil O'Donnell .20 .09
❑ 19 Greg Lloyd .20 .09
❑ 20 Warren Moon .20 .09
❑ 21 Bernie Kosar .10 .05
❑ 22 Derrick Thomas .20 .09
❑ 23 Andre Hastings .10 .05
❑ 24 Wayne Chrebet .20 .09
❑ 25 Mark Seay .10 .05
❑ 26 Eric Metcalf .10 .05
❑ 27 Shawn Jefferson .10 .05
❑ 28 Napoleon Kaufman .60 .25
❑ 29 Steve Walsh .10 .05
❑ 30 Derrick Alexander DE .10 .05
❑ 31 Rodney Peete .10 .05
❑ 32 Terance Mathis .10 .05
❑ 33 Michael Westbrook .40 .18
❑ 34 Kevin Carter .10 .05
❑ 35 Aaron Hayden RC .10 .05
❑ 36 J.J. Stokes .40 .18
❑ 37 Andre Reed .20 .09
❑ 38 Chris Warren .20 .09
❑ 39 Jerry Rice 1.00 .45
❑ 40 Ben Coates .20 .09
❑ 41 Reggie White .40 .18
❑ 42 Joey Galloway .75 .35
❑ 43 Sean Dawkins .10 .05
❑ 44 Brett Favre 2.00 .90
❑ 45 Jeff George .20 .09
❑ 46 Robert Smith .20 .09
❑ 47 Ken Dilger .20 .09
❑ 48 Larry Centers .20 .09
❑ 49 Jackie Harris .10 .05
❑ 50 Hugh Douglas .10 .05
❑ 51 Herschel Walker .20 .09
❑ 52 Kerry Collins .40 .18
❑ 53 Michael Irvin .40 .18
❑ 54 Willie McGinest .10 .05
❑ 55 Herman Moore .40 .18
❑ 56 Leroy Hoard .10 .05
❑ 57 Scott Mitchell .20 .09
❑ 58 Terrell Davis 2.50 1.10
❑ 59 Kevin Greene .20 .09
❑ 60 Yancey Thigpen .20 .09
❑ 61 Kevin Smith .10 .05
❑ 62 Trent Dilfer .40 .18
❑ 63 Cortez Kennedy .10 .05
❑ 64 Carnell Lake .10 .05
❑ 65 Quinn Early .10 .05
❑ 66 Kyle Brady .10 .05
❑ 67 Marshall Faulk .40 .18
❑ 68 Fred Barnett .10 .05
❑ 69 Quentin Coryatt .10 .05
❑ 70 Dan Marino 2.00 .90
❑ 71 Junior Seau .20 .09
❑ 72 Andre Coleman .10 .05
❑ 73 Terry Kirby .20 .09
❑ 74 Curtis Martin .75 .35
❑ 75 Isaac Bruce .40 .18
❑ 76 Mark Chmura .20 .09
❑ 77 Edgar Bennett .20 .09
❑ 78 Mario Bates .20 .09
❑ 79 Eric Zeier .10 .05
❑ 80 Adrian Murrell .40 .18
❑ 81 Mark Brunell 1.00 .45
❑ 82 Mark Rypien .10 .05
❑ 83 Erric Pegram .10 .05
❑ 84 Bryan Cox .10 .05
❑ 85 Heath Shuler .20 .09
❑ 86 Lake Dawson .10 .05
❑ 87 O.J. McDuffie .20 .09
❑ 88 Emmitt Smith 1.50 .70
❑ 89 Jim Harbaugh .20 .09
❑ 90 Aaron Bailey RC .10 .05
❑ 91 Jim Kelly .40 .18
❑ 92 Rodney Hampton .20 .09
❑ 93 Cris Carter .40 .18
❑ 94 Henry Ellard .10 .05
❑ 95 Darnay Scott .20 .09
❑ 96 Daryl Johnston .20 .09
❑ 97 Tamarick Vanover .20 .09
❑ 98 Jeff Blake .40 .18
❑ 99 Anthony Miller .20 .09
❑ 100 Darren Woodson .20 .09
❑ 101 Irving Fryar .20 .09
❑ 102 Craig Hayward .10 .05
❑ 103 Derek Loville .10 .05
❑ 104 Ernie Mills .10 .05
❑ 105 Brian Blades .10 .05
❑ 106 Gus Frerotte .40 .18
❑ 107 Alvin Harper .10 .05
❑ 108 Tyrone Wheatley .20 .09
❑ 109 John Elway 2.00 .90
❑ 110 Charles Haley .20 .09
❑ 111 Terrell Fletcher .10 .05
❑ 112 Vincent Brisby .10 .05
❑ 113 Jerome Bettis .40 .18
❑ 114 Barry Sanders 2.00 .90
❑ 115 Ken Norton Jr. .10 .05
❑ 116 Sherman Williams .10 .05
❑ 117 Antonio Freeman .75 .35
❑ 118 Bert Emanuel .20 .09
❑ 119 Marcus Allen .40 .18
❑ 120 Stan Humphries .20 .09
❑ 121 Chris Sanders .20 .09
❑ 122 Jeff Graham .10 .05
❑ 123 Jay Novacek .10 .05
❑ 124 Aeneas Williams .10 .05
❑ 125 Kordell Stewart .75 .35
❑ 126 Steve Young .75 .35
❑ 127 Jake Reed .20 .09
❑ 128 Rick Mirer .20 .09
❑ 129 Jeff Hostetler .10 .05
❑ 130 Tim Brown .40 .18
❑ 131 Shannon Sharpe .20 .09
❑ 132 Dave Brown .10 .05
❑ 133 Harvey Williams .10 .05
❑ 134 Rodney Thomas .10 .05
❑ 135 Frank Sanders .20 .09
❑ 136 Brett Perriman .10 .05
❑ 137 Steve Bono .10 .05
❑ 138 Steve Atwater .10 .05
❑ 139 Andre Rison .20 .09
❑ 140 Orlando Thomas .10 .05
❑ 141 Terry Allen .20 .09
❑ 142 Carl Pickens .40 .18
❑ 143 William Floyd .20 .09
❑ 144 Bryce Paup .10 .05
❑ 145 James O. Stewart .20 .09
❑ 146 Eric Bjornson .10 .05
❑ 147 Errict Rhett .20 .09
❑ 148 Darick Holmes .10 .05
❑ 149 Brian Mitchell .10 .05
❑ 150 Brent Jones .10 .05
❑ 151 Natrone Means .40 .18
❑ 152 Rod Woodson .20 .09
❑ 153 Bruce Smith .20 .09
❑ 154 Deion Sanders .60 .25
❑ 155 Kevin Williams .10 .05
❑ 156 Erik Kramer .10 .05
❑ 157 Jim Everett .10 .05
❑ 158 Vinny Testaverde .20 .09
❑ 159 Boomer Esiason .20 .09
❑ 160 Leslie O'Neal .10 .05
❑ 161 Curtis Conway .40 .18
❑ 162 Thurman Thomas .40 .18
❑ 163 Tony Brackens RC .20 .09
❑ 164 Stepfret Williams RC .20 .09
❑ 165 Alex Van Dyke RC .20 .09
❑ 166 Cedric Jones RC .10 .05
❑ 167 Stanley Pritchett RC .20 .09
❑ 168 Willie Anderson RC .10 .05
❑ 169 Regan Upshaw RC .10 .05
❑ 170 Daryl Gardener RC .10 .05
❑ 171 Alex Molden RC .10 .05
❑ 172 John Mobley RC .10 .05
❑ 173 Danny Kanell RC .40 .18
❑ 174 Marco Battaglia RC .10 .05
❑ 175 Simeon Rice RC .40 .18
❑ 176 Tony Banks RC 1.00 .45
❑ 177 Stephen Davis RC 2.50 1.10
❑ 178 Walt Harris RC .10 .05
❑ 179 Amani Toomer RC .40 .18
❑ 180 Derrick Mayes RC .75 .35
❑ 181 Jeff Lewis RC .60 .25
❑ 182 Chris Darkins RC .10 .05
❑ 183 Rickey Dudley RC .40 .18
❑ 184 Jonathan Ogden RC .10 .05
❑ 185 Mike Alstott RC 1.50 .70
❑ 186 Eric Moulds RC 2.00 .90
❑ 187 Karim Abdul-Jabbar RC .75 .35
❑ 188 Jerry Rice .40 .18
Checklist Card
❑ 189 Dan Marino .40 .18
Checklist Card
❑ 190 Emmitt Smith .40 .18
Checklist Card

1996 Leaf American All-Stars

	MINT	NRMT
COMPLETE SET (20)	150.00	70.00

STATED PRINT RUN 5000 SERIAL #'d SETS
*GOLD CARDS: .75X TO 2X SILVERS
GOLDS PRINT RUN 1000 SERIAL #'d SETS

❑ 1 Emmitt Smith 12.00 5.50
❑ 2 Drew Bledsoe 8.00 3.60
❑ 3 Jerry Rice 8.00 3.60
❑ 4 Kerry Collins 3.00 1.35
❑ 5 Eddie George 15.00 6.75
❑ 6 Keyshawn Johnson 10.00 4.50
❑ 7 Lawrence Phillips 3.00 1.35
❑ 8 Rashaan Salaam 3.00 1.35
❑ 9 Deion Sanders 5.00 2.20
❑ 10 Marshall Faulk 3.00 1.35
❑ 11 Steve Young 6.00 2.70
❑ 12 Ki-Jana Carter 1.50 .70
❑ 13 Curtis Martin 6.00 2.70
❑ 14 Joey Galloway 6.00 2.70
❑ 15 Troy Aikman 8.00 3.60

		MINT	NRMT
❑ 16	Barry Sanders	15.00	6.75
❑ 17	Dan Marino	15.00	6.75
❑ 18	John Elway	15.00	6.75
❑ 19	Steve McNair	6.00	2.70
❑ 20	Tim Biakabutuka	5.00	2.20

1996 Leaf Collector's Edition Autographs

	MINT	NRMT
COMPLETE SET (14)	200.00	90.00
COMMON CARD (1-14)	8.00	3.60
SEMISTARS	10.00	4.50
UNLISTED STARS	15.00	6.75

ONE PER COLL.EDITION FACT.SET
STATED PRINT RUN 2000 SETS
CARDS LISTED ALPHABETICALLY

		MINT	NRMT
❑ 1	Karim Abdul-Jabbar	15.00	6.75
❑ 2	Tony Banks	15.00	6.75
❑ 3	Tim Biakabutuka	20.00	9.00
❑ 4	Isaac Bruce	10.00	4.50
❑ 5	Terrell Davis	70.00	32.00
❑ 6	Bobby Engram	8.00	3.60
❑ 7	Joey Galloway	15.00	6.75
❑ 8	Eddie George	40.00	18.00
❑ 9	Marvin Harrison	30.00	13.50
❑ 10	Eddie Kennison	10.00	4.50
❑ 11	Leeland McElroy	8.00	3.60
❑ 12	Lawrence Phillips	15.00	6.75
❑ 13	Rashaan Salaam	10.00	4.50
❑ 14	Tamarick Vanover	10.00	4.50

1996 Leaf Gold Leaf Rookies

	MINT	NRMT
COMPLETE SET (10)	20.00	9.00
COMMON CARD (1-10)	1.50	.70
SEMISTARS	2.50	1.10

RANDOM INSERTS IN PACKS....

		MINT	NRMT
❑ 1	Leeland McElroy	1.50	.70
❑ 2	Marvin Harrison	5.00	2.20
❑ 3	Lawrence Phillips	2.50	1.10
❑ 4	Bobby Engram	1.50	.70
❑ 5	Kevin Hardy	1.50	.70
❑ 6	Keyshawn Johnson	5.00	2.20
❑ 7	Eddie Kennison	2.50	1.10
❑ 8	Tim Biakabutuka	3.00	1.35
❑ 9	Eddie George	6.00	2.70
❑ 10	Terry Glenn	2.50	1.10

1996 Leaf Gold Leaf Stars

	MINT	NRMT
COMPLETE SET (15)	200.00	90.00

RANDOM INSERTS IN RETAIL PACKS
STATED PRINT RUN 2500 SERIAL #'d SETS

		MINT	NRMT
❑ 1	Drew Bledsoe	15.00	6.75
❑ 2	Jerry Rice	15.00	6.75
❑ 3	Emmitt Smith	25.00	11.00
❑ 4	Dan Marino	30.00	13.50
❑ 5	Isaac Bruce	6.00	2.70

		MINT	NRMT
❑ 6	Kerry Collins	6.00	2.70
❑ 7	Barry Sanders	30.00	13.50
❑ 8	Keyshawn Johnson	15.00	6.75
❑ 9	Errict Rhett	3.00	1.35
❑ 10	Joey Galloway	12.00	5.50
❑ 11	Brett Favre	30.00	13.50
❑ 12	Curtis Martin	12.00	5.50
❑ 13	Steve Young	12.00	5.50
❑ 14	Troy Aikman	15.00	6.75
❑ 15	John Elway	30.00	13.50

1996 Leaf Grass Roots

	MINT	NRMT
COMPLETE SET (20)	80.00	36.00

STATED PRINT RUN 5000 SERIAL #'d SETS

		MINT	NRMT
❑ 1	Thurman Thomas	2.50	1.10
❑ 2	Eddie George	15.00	6.75
❑ 3	Rodney Hampton	1.25	.55
❑ 4	Rashaan Salaam	2.50	1.10
❑ 5	Natrone Means	2.50	1.10
❑ 6	Errict Rhett	1.25	.55
❑ 7	Leeland McElroy	.60	.25
❑ 8	Emmitt Smith	10.00	4.50
❑ 9	Marshall Faulk	2.50	1.10
❑ 10	Ricky Watters	1.25	.55
❑ 11	Chris Warren	1.25	.55
❑ 12	Tim Biakabutuka	5.00	2.20
❑ 13	Barry Sanders	12.00	5.50
❑ 14	Karim Abdul-Jabbar	4.00	1.80
❑ 15	Darick Holmes	.60	.25
❑ 16	Terrell Davis	15.00	6.75
❑ 17	Lawrence Phillips	3.00	1.35
❑ 18	Ki-Jana Carter	1.25	.55
❑ 19	Curtis Martin	5.00	2.20
❑ 20	Kordell Stewart	5.00	2.20

1996 Leaf Shirt Off My Back

	MINT	NRMT
COMPLETE SET (10)	150.00	70.00

RAND.INS.IN MAGAZINE PACKS
STATED PRINT RUN 2500 SETS

		MINT	NRMT
❑ 1	Steve Young	12.00	5.50
❑ 2	Jeff Blake	6.00	2.70
❑ 3	Drew Bledsoe	15.00	6.75
❑ 4	Kordell Stewart	12.00	5.50

		MINT	NRMT
❑ 5	Troy Aikman	15.00	6.75
❑ 6	Steve McNair	12.00	5.50
❑ 7	John Elway	30.00	13.50
❑ 8	Dan Marino	30.00	13.50
❑ 9	Kerry Collins	6.00	2.70
❑ 10	Brett Favre	30.00	13.50

1996 Leaf Statistical Standouts

	MINT	NRMT
COMPLETE SET (15)	200.00	90.00

RANDOM INSERTS IN HOBBY PACKS
STATED PRINT RUN 2500 SERIAL #'d SETS

		MINT	NRMT
❑ 1	John Elway	30.00	13.50
❑ 2	Jerry Rice	15.00	6.75
❑ 3	Reggie White	6.00	2.70
❑ 4	Drew Bledsoe	15.00	6.75
❑ 5	Chris Warren	3.00	1.35
❑ 6	Bruce Smith	3.00	1.35
❑ 7	Barry Sanders	30.00	13.50
❑ 8	Greg Lloyd	3.00	1.35
❑ 9	Emmitt Smith	25.00	11.00
❑ 10	Dan Marino	30.00	13.50
❑ 11	Steve Young	12.00	5.50
❑ 12	Steve Atwater	1.50	.70
❑ 13	Isaac Bruce	6.00	2.70
❑ 14	Deion Sanders	10.00	4.50
❑ 15	Brett Favre	30.00	13.50

1997 Leaf

	MINT	NRMT
COMPLETE SET (200)	25.00	11.00
COMMON CARD (1-200)	.10	.05
SEMISTARS	.25	.11
UNLISTED STARS	.50	.23
COMP.SIG.PROOF (200)	1200.00	550.00
*SIG.PROOF STARS: 10X TO 25X HI COL.		
*SIG.PROOF RCs: 5X TO 12X		
SIG.PROOF PRINT RUN 200 SERIAL #'d SETS		
SIG.PROOFS INSERTED IN LEAF SIGNATURE		

	MINT	NRMT
❑ 1 Steve Young	.75	.35
❑ 2 Brett Favre	2.50	1.10
❑ 3 Barry Sanders	2.50	1.10
❑ 4 Drew Bledsoe	1.25	.55
❑ 5 Troy Aikman	1.25	.55
❑ 6 Kerry Collins	.25	.11
❑ 7 Dan Marino	2.50	1.10
❑ 8 Jerry Rice	1.25	.55
❑ 9 John Elway	2.50	1.10
❑ 10 Emmitt Smith	2.00	.90
❑ 11 Tony Banks	.25	.11
❑ 12 Gus Frerotte	.10	.05
❑ 13 Elvis Grbac	.25	.11
❑ 14 Neil O'Donnell	.25	.11
❑ 15 Michael Irvin	.50	.23
❑ 16 Marshall Faulk	.50	.23
❑ 17 Todd Collins	.10	.05
❑ 18 Scott Mitchell	.25	.11
❑ 19 Trent Dilfer	.50	.23
❑ 20 Rick Mirer	.10	.05
❑ 21 Frank Sanders	.25	.11
❑ 22 Larry Centers	.25	.11
❑ 23 Brad Johnson	.60	.25
❑ 24 Garrison Hearst	.25	.11
❑ 25 Steve McNair	.75	.35
❑ 26 Dorsey Levens	.50	.23
❑ 27 Eric Metcalf	.25	.11
❑ 28 Jeff George	.25	.11
❑ 29 Rodney Hampton	.25	.11
❑ 30 Michael Westbrook	.25	.11
❑ 31 Cris Carter	.50	.23
❑ 32 Heath Shuler	.10	.05
❑ 33 Warren Moon	.50	.23
❑ 34 Rod Woodson	.25	.11
❑ 35 Ken Dilger	.10	.05
❑ 36 Ben Coates	.25	.11
❑ 37 Andre Reed	.25	.11
❑ 38 Terrell Owens	.50	.23
❑ 39 Jeff Blake	.25	.11
❑ 40 Vinny Testaverde	.25	.11
❑ 41 Robert Brooks	.25	.11
❑ 42 Shannon Sharpe	.25	.11
❑ 43 Terry Allen	.50	.23
❑ 44 Terance Mathis	.25	.11
❑ 45 Bobby Engram	.25	.11
❑ 46 Rickey Dudley	.25	.11
❑ 47 Alex Molden	.10	.05
❑ 48 Lawrence Phillips	.10	.05
❑ 49 Curtis Martin	.75	.35
❑ 50 Jim Harbaugh	.25	.11
❑ 51 Wayne Chrebet	.50	.23
❑ 52 Quentin Coryatt	.10	.05
❑ 53 Eddie George	1.00	.45
❑ 54 Michael Jackson	.25	.11
❑ 55 Greg Lloyd	.10	.05
❑ 56 Natrone Means	.50	.23
❑ 57 Marcus Allen	.50	.23
❑ 58 Desmond Howard	.25	.11
❑ 59 Stan Humphries	.25	.11
❑ 60 Reggie White	.50	.23
❑ 61 Brett Perriman	.10	.05
❑ 62 Warren Sapp	.25	.11
❑ 63 Adrian Murrell	.25	.11
❑ 64 Mark Brunell	1.25	.55
❑ 65 Carl Pickens	.50	.23
❑ 66 Kordell Stewart	.75	.35
❑ 67 Ricky Watters	.25	.11
❑ 68 Tyrone Wheatley	.25	.11
❑ 69 Stanley Pritchett	.10	.05
❑ 70 Kevin Greene	.25	.11
❑ 71 Karim Abdul-Jabbar	.50	.23
❑ 72 Ki-Jana Carter	.10	.05
❑ 73 Rashaan Salaam	.10	.05
❑ 74 Simeon Rice	.25	.11
❑ 75 Napoleon Kaufman	.50	.23
❑ 76 Muhsin Muhammad	.25	.11
❑ 77 Bruce Smith	.25	.11
❑ 78 Eric Moulds	.50	.23
❑ 79 O.J. McDuffie	.25	.11
❑ 80 Danny Kanell	.25	.11
❑ 81 Harvey Williams	.10	.05
❑ 82 Greg Hill	.10	.05
❑ 83 Terrell Davis	2.00	.90
❑ 84 Dan Wilkinson	.10	.05
❑ 85 Yancey Thigpen	.25	.11
❑ 86 Darrell Green	.25	.11
❑ 87 Tamarick Vanover	.25	.11
❑ 88 Mike Alstott	.50	.23
❑ 89 Johnnie Morton	.25	.11
❑ 90 Dale Carter	.10	.05
❑ 91 Jerome Bettis	.50	.23
❑ 92 James O.Stewart	.25	.11
❑ 93 Irving Fryar	.25	.11
❑ 94 Junior Seau	.25	.11
❑ 95 Sean Dawkins	.10	.05
❑ 96 J.J. Stokes	.25	.11
❑ 97 Tim Biakabutuka	.25	.11
❑ 98 Bert Emanuel	.25	.11
❑ 99 Eddie Kennison	.25	.11
❑ 100 Ray Zellars	.10	.05
❑ 101 Dave Brown	.10	.05
❑ 102 Leeland McElroy	.10	.05
❑ 103 Chris Warren	.25	.11
❑ 104 Byron Bam Morris	.10	.05
❑ 105 Thurman Thomas	.50	.23
❑ 106 Kyle Brady	.10	.05
❑ 107 Anthony Miller	.10	.05
❑ 108 Derrick Thomas	.25	.11
❑ 109 Mark Chmura	.25	.11
❑ 110 Deion Sanders	.50	.23
❑ 111 Eric Swann	.10	.05
❑ 112 Amani Toomer	.25	.11
❑ 113 Raymont Harris	.10	.05
❑ 114 Jake Reed	.25	.11
❑ 115 Bryant Young	.10	.05
❑ 116 Keenan McCardell	.25	.11
❑ 117 Herman Moore	.50	.23
❑ 118 Errict Rhett	.10	.05
❑ 119 Henry Ellard	.10	.05
❑ 120 Bobby Hoying	.25	.11
❑ 121 Robert Smith	.25	.11
❑ 122 Keyshawn Johnson	.50	.23
❑ 123 Zach Thomas	.25	.11
❑ 124 Charlie Garner	.10	.05
❑ 125 Terry Kirby	.25	.11
❑ 126 Darren Woodson	.10	.05
❑ 127 Darnay Scott	.25	.11
❑ 128 Chris Sanders	.10	.05
❑ 129 Charles Johnson	.25	.11
❑ 130 Joey Galloway	.75	.35
❑ 131 Curtis Conway	.25	.11
❑ 132 Isaac Bruce	.50	.23
❑ 133 Bobby Taylor	.10	.05
❑ 134 Jamal Anderson	.60	.25
❑ 135 Ken Norton	.10	.05
❑ 136 Darick Holmes	.10	.05
❑ 137 Tony Brackens	.10	.05
❑ 138 Tony Martin	.25	.11
❑ 139 Antonio Freeman	.75	.35
❑ 140 Neil Smith	.25	.11
❑ 141 Terry Glenn	.50	.23
❑ 142 Marvin Harrison	.50	.23
❑ 143 Daryl Johnston	.25	.11
❑ 144 Tim Brown	.50	.23
❑ 145 Kimble Anders	.25	.11
❑ 146 Derrick Alexander WR	.25	.11
❑ 147 LeShon Johnson	.10	.05
❑ 148 Anthony Johnson	.10	.05
❑ 149 Leslie Shepherd	.10	.05
❑ 150 Chris T. Jones	.10	.05
❑ 151 Edgar Bennett	.25	.11
❑ 152 Ty Detmer	.25	.11
❑ 153 Ike Hilliard RC	1.00	.45
❑ 154 Jim Druckenmiller RC	.75	.35
❑ 155 Warrick Dunn RC	1.50	.70
❑ 156 Yatil Green RC	.25	.11
❑ 157 Reidel Anthony RC	1.00	.45
❑ 158 Antowain Smith RC	1.25	.55
❑ 159 Rae Carruth RC	.50	.23
❑ 160 Tiki Barber RC	.75	.35
❑ 161 Byron Hanspard RC	1.00	.45
❑ 162 Jake Plummer RC	4.00	1.80
❑ 163 Joey Kent RC	.50	.23
❑ 164 Corey Dillon RC	2.00	.90
❑ 165 Kevin Lockett RC	.25	.11
❑ 166 Will Blackwell RC	.50	.23
❑ 167 Troy Davis RC	.50	.23
❑ 168 James Farrior RC	.10	.05
❑ 169 Danny Wuerffel RC	.75	.35
❑ 170 Pat Barnes RC	.50	.23
❑ 171 Darnell Autry RC	.25	.11
❑ 172 Tom Knight RC	.10	.05
❑ 173 David LaFleur RC	.25	.11
❑ 174 Tony Gonzalez RC	1.50	.70
❑ 175 Kenny Holmes RC	.10	.05
❑ 176 Reinard Wilson RC	.10	.05
❑ 177 Renaldo Wynn RC	.10	.05
❑ 178 Bryant Westbrook RC	.10	.05
❑ 179 Darrell Russell RC	.10	.05
❑ 180 Orlando Pace RC	.10	.05
❑ 181 Shawn Springs RC	.25	.11
❑ 182 Peter Boulware RC	.25	.11
❑ 183 Dan Marino L	1.25	.55
❑ 184 Brett Favre L	1.25	.55
❑ 185 Emmitt Smith L	1.00	.45
❑ 186 Eddie George L	.50	.23
❑ 187 Curtis Martin L	.25	.11
❑ 188 Tim Brown L	.25	.11
❑ 189 Mark Brunell L	.60	.25
❑ 190 Isaac Bruce L	.25	.11
❑ 191 Deion Sanders L	.25	.11
❑ 192 John Elway L	1.25	.55
❑ 193 Jerry Rice L	.60	.25
❑ 194 Barry Sanders L	1.25	.55
❑ 195 Herman Moore L	.25	.11
❑ 196 Carl Pickens L	.25	.11
❑ 197 Karim Abdul-Jabbar L	.25	.11
❑ 198 Drew Bledsoe CL	.50	.23
❑ 199 Troy Aikman CL	.50	.23
❑ 200 Terrell Davis CL	.50	.23

1997 Leaf Fractal Matrix

	MINT	NRMT
COMPLETE SET (200)	1000.00	450.00
COMMON BRONZE Y/Z	.75	.35
SEMISTARS BRONZE Y/Z	1.25	.55
STARS BRONZE Y/Z	2.50	1.10
COMMON BRONZE X	1.00	.45
SEMISTARS BRONZE X	1.50	.70
STARS BRONZE X	3.00	1.35
COMMON SILVER Y/Z	2.50	1.10
SEMISTARS SILVER Y/Z	4.00	1.80
STARS SILVER Y/Z	5.00	2.20
COMMON SILVER X	3.00	1.35
SEMISTARS SILVER X	5.00	2.20
STARS SILVER X	8.00	3.60
COMMON GOLD Z	4.00	1.80
SEMISTARS GOLD Z	6.00	2.70
STARS GOLD Z	10.00	4.50
COMMON GOLD Y	6.00	2.70
SEMISTARS GOLD Y	10.00	4.50
RANDOM INSERTS IN PACKS		

	MINT	NRMT
❑ 1 Steve Young GZ	15.00	6.75
❑ 2 Brett Favre GX	50.00	22.00
❑ 3 Barry Sanders GZ	40.00	18.00
❑ 4 Drew Bledsoe GZ	20.00	9.00
❑ 5 Troy Aikman GZ	20.00	9.00
❑ 7 Dan Marino GX	50.00	22.00
❑ 8 Jerry Rice GZ	20.00	9.00
❑ 9 John Elway GZ	40.00	18.00
❑ 10 Emmitt Smith GX	40.00	18.00
❑ 25 Steve McNair GZ	12.00	5.50
❑ 38 Terrell Owens SZ	5.00	2.20
❑ 49 Curtis Martin GZ	12.00	5.50
❑ 53 Eddie George GX	25.00	11.00
❑ 64 Mark Brunell GZ	20.00	9.00
❑ 66 Kordell Stewart GZ	12.00	5.50
❑ 75 Napoleon Kaufman SY	5.00	2.20
❑ 83 Terrell Davis GZ	30.00	13.50
❑ 130 Joey Galloway SZ	8.00	3.60
❑ 134 Jamal Anderson SY	6.00	2.70
❑ 141 Terry Glenn GZ	10.00	4.50
❑ 153 Ike Hilliard GX	10.00	4.50

❑ 154 Jim Druckenmiller SZ	5.00	2.20
❑ 155 Warrick Dunn GZ	12.00	5.50
❑ 158 Antowain Smith GZ	10.00	4.50
❑ 162 Jake Plummer SY	15.00	6.75
❑ 164 Corey Dillon SY	10.00	4.50
❑ 183 Dan Marino L BY	20.00	9.00
❑ 184 Brett Favre L BY	20.00	9.00
❑ 185 Emmitt Smith L BY	15.00	6.75
❑ 186 Eddie George L BY	10.00	4.50
❑ 187 Curtis Martin L BY	4.00	1.80
❑ 189 Mark Brunell L BY	10.00	4.50
❑ 192 John Elway L BY	20.00	9.00
❑ 193 Jerry Rice L BY	10.00	4.50
❑ 194 Barry Sanders L BY	20.00	9.00
❑ 198 Drew Bledsoe CL BY	6.00	2.70
❑ 199 Troy Aikman CL BY	6.00	2.70
❑ 200 Terrell Davis CL BY	8.00	3.60

1997 Leaf Fractal Matrix Die-Cuts

	MINT	NRMT
COMMON CARD BX	2.50	1.10
SEMISTARS BX	4.00	1.80
UNLISTED STARS BX	5.00	2.20
COMMON CARD BY/GX/SX	5.00	2.20
SEMISTARS BY/GX/SX	6.00	2.70
UNL.STARS BY/GX/SX	10.00	4.50
COMMON CARD BZ/GY/SY	8.00	3.60
SEMISTARS BZ/GY/SY	12.00	5.50
UNL.STARS BZ/GY/SY	20.00	9.00
COMMON CARD GZ/SZ	12.00	5.50
SEMISTARS GZ/SZ	20.00	9.00
UNLISTED STARS GZ/SZ	30.00	13.50
RANDOM INSERTS IN PACKS		

❑ 1 Steve Young GZ	50.00	22.00
❑ 2 Brett Favre GX	80.00	36.00
❑ 3 Barry Sanders GZ	120.00	55.00
❑ 4 Drew Bledsoe GZ	60.00	27.00
❑ 5 Troy Aikman GZ	60.00	27.00
❑ 7 Dan Marino GX	80.00	36.00
❑ 8 Jerry Rice GZ	60.00	27.00
❑ 9 John Elway GZ	120.00	55.00
❑ 10 Emmitt Smith GX	60.00	27.00
❑ 25 Steve McNair GZ	40.00	18.00
❑ 38 Terrell Owens SZ	30.00	13.50
❑ 49 Curtis Martin GZ	40.00	18.00
❑ 53 Eddie George GX	40.00	18.00
❑ 64 Mark Brunell GZ	60.00	27.00
❑ 66 Kordell Stewart GZ	40.00	18.00
❑ 75 Napoleon Kaufman SY	20.00	9.00
❑ 83 Terrell Davis GZ	120.00	55.00
❑ 130 Joey Galloway SZ	40.00	18.00
❑ 141 Terry Glenn GZ	30.00	13.50
❑ 154 Jim Druckenmiller SZ	30.00	13.50
❑ 155 Warrick Dunn GZ	50.00	22.00
❑ 158 Antowain Smith GZ	40.00	18.00
❑ 162 Jake Plummer SY	40.00	18.00
❑ 164 Corey Dillon SY	25.00	11.00
❑ 183 Dan Marino L BY	50.00	22.00
❑ 184 Brett Favre L BY	50.00	22.00
❑ 185 Emmitt Smith L BY	40.00	18.00
❑ 186 Eddie George L BY	25.00	11.00
❑ 187 Curtis Martin L BY	15.00	6.75
❑ 189 Mark Brunell L BY	25.00	11.00
❑ 192 John Elway L BY	50.00	22.00
❑ 193 Jerry Rice L BY	25.00	11.00
❑ 194 Barry Sanders L BY	50.00	22.00
❑ 198 Drew Bledsoe CL BY	15.00	6.75
❑ 199 Troy Aikman CL BY	15.00	6.75
❑ 200 Terrell Davis CL BY	20.00	9.00

1997 Leaf Hardwear

	MINT	NRMT
COMPLETE SET (20)	150.00	70.00
STATED PRINT RUN 3500 SERIAL #'d SETS		

❑ 1 Dan Marino	20.00	9.00
❑ 2 Brett Favre	20.00	9.00
❑ 3 Emmitt Smith	15.00	6.75
❑ 4 Jerry Rice	10.00	4.50
❑ 5 Barry Sanders	20.00	9.00
❑ 6 Deion Sanders	4.00	1.80

❑ 7 Reggie White	4.00	1.80
❑ 8 Tim Brown	4.00	1.80
❑ 9 Steve McNair	6.00	2.70
❑ 10 Steve Young	6.00	2.70
❑ 11 Mark Brunell	10.00	4.50
❑ 12 Ricky Watters	2.00	.90
❑ 13 Eddie Kennison	2.00	.90
❑ 14 Kordell Stewart	6.00	2.70
❑ 15 Kerry Collins	2.00	.90
❑ 16 Joey Galloway	6.00	2.70
❑ 17 Terrell Owens	4.00	1.80
❑ 18 Terry Glenn	4.00	1.80
❑ 19 Keyshawn Johnson	4.00	1.80
❑ 20 Eddie George	8.00	3.60

1997 Leaf Letterman

	MINT	NRMT
COMPLETE SET (15)	250.00	110.00
STATED PRINT RUN 1000 SERIAL #'d SETS		

❑ 1 Brett Favre	30.00	13.50
❑ 2 Emmitt Smith	25.00	11.00
❑ 3 Dan Marino	30.00	13.50
❑ 4 Jerry Rice	15.00	6.75
❑ 5 Mark Brunell	15.00	6.75
❑ 6 Barry Sanders	30.00	13.50
❑ 7 John Elway	30.00	13.50
❑ 8 Eddie George	12.00	5.50
❑ 9 Troy Aikman	15.00	6.75
❑ 10 Curtis Martin	10.00	4.50
❑ 11 Karim Abdul-Jabbar	6.00	2.70
❑ 12 Terrell Davis	25.00	11.00
❑ 13 Ike Hilliard	12.00	5.50
❑ 14 Terry Glenn	6.00	2.70
❑ 15 Drew Bledsoe	15.00	6.75

1997 Leaf Reproductions

	MINT	NRMT
COMPLETE SET (24)	250.00	110.00
STATED PRINT RUN 1948 SERIAL #'d SETS		

❑ 1 Emmitt Smith	25.00	11.00
❑ 2 Brett Favre	30.00	13.50
❑ 3 Dan Marino	30.00	13.50
❑ 4 Barry Sanders	30.00	13.50
❑ 5 Jerry Rice	15.00	6.75
❑ 6 Terrell Davis	25.00	11.00
❑ 7 Curtis Martin	10.00	4.50
❑ 8 Troy Aikman	15.00	6.75
❑ 9 Drew Bledsoe	15.00	6.75
❑ 10 Herman Moore	6.00	2.70
❑ 11 Isaac Bruce	6.00	2.70
❑ 12 Carl Pickens	6.00	2.70
❑ 13 Len Dawson	6.00	2.70
❑ 14 Dan Fouts	6.00	2.70
❑ 15 Jim Plunkett	6.00	2.70
❑ 16 Ken Stabler	6.00	2.70
❑ 17 Joe Theismann	6.00	2.70
❑ 18 Billy Kilmer	6.00	2.70
❑ 19 Danny White	6.00	2.70
❑ 20 Archie Manning	6.00	2.70
❑ 21 Ron Jaworski	3.00	1.35
❑ 22 Y.A. Tittle	6.00	2.70
❑ 23 Sid Luckman	6.00	2.70
❑ 24 Sammy Baugh	6.00	2.70

1997 Leaf Reproductions Autographs

	MINT	NRMT
COMPLETE SET (12)	400.00	180.00
COMMON CARD (13-24)	25.00	11.00
SEMISTARS	40.00	18.00
STATED PRINT RUN 500 SETS		

❑ 13 Len Dawson	40.00	18.00
❑ 14 Dan Fouts	40.00	18.00
❑ 15 Jim Plunkett	25.00	11.00
❑ 16 Ken Stabler	40.00	18.00
❑ 17 Joe Theismann	25.00	11.00
❑ 18 Billy Kilmer	25.00	11.00
❑ 18P Billy Kilmer	25.00	11.00
❑ 19 Danny White	25.00	11.00
❑ 20 Archie Manning	25.00	11.00
❑ 21 Ron Jaworski	25.00	11.00
❑ 22 Y.A. Tittle	40.00	18.00
❑ 23 Sid Luckman	100.00	45.00
❑ 24 Sammy Baugh	40.00	18.00
❑ 24P Sammy Baugh Gold Holofoil	25.00	11.00

1997 Leaf Run and Gun

	MINT	NRMT
COMPLETE SET (18)	200.00	90.00

COMMON CARD (1-18)	5.00	2.20
SEMISTARS	8.00	3.60
STATED PRINT RUN 3500 SERIAL #'d SETS		
❑ 1 Dan Marino Karim Abdul-Jabbar	25.00	11.00
❑ 2 Troy Aikman Emmitt Smith	25.00	11.00
❑ 3 John Elway Terrell Davis	30.00	13.50
❑ 4 Drew Bledsoe Curtis Martin	20.00	9.00
❑ 5 Kordell Stewart Jerome Bettis	15.00	6.75
❑ 6 Mark Brunell Natrone Means	15.00	6.75
❑ 7 Kerry Collins Tim Biakabutuka	8.00	3.60
❑ 8 Rick Mirer Rashaan Salaam	5.00	2.20
❑ 9 Scott Mitchell Barry Sanders	25.00	11.00
❑ 10 Steve McNair Eddie George	12.00	5.50
❑ 11 Trent Dilfer Warrick Dunn	10.00	4.50
❑ 12 Jeff Blake Ki-Jana Carter	8.00	3.60
❑ 13 Tony Banks Lawrence Phillips	8.00	3.60
❑ 14 Steve Young Garrison Hearst	12.00	5.50
❑ 15 Jim Harbaugh Marshall Faulk	8.00	3.60
❑ 16 Elvis Grbac Marcus Allen	8.00	3.60
❑ 17 Neil O'Donnell Adrian Murrell	5.00	2.20
❑ 18 Gus Frerotte Tery Allen	8.00	3.60

1999 Leaf Certified

	MINT	NRMT
COMPLETE SET (225)	400.00	180.00
COMP.SET w/o RCs 175)	60.00	27.00
COMMON CARD (1-100)	.20	.09
SEMISTARS 1-100	.40	.18
UNLISTED STARS 1-100	.75	.35
COMMON CARD (101-150)	.60	.25
SEMISTARS 101-150	1.25	.55
2-STAR 101-150 ODDS ONE PER PACK		
COMMON CARD (151-175)	1.00	.45
SEMISTARS 151-175	2.00	.90
3-STAR 151-175 ODDS 1:3		
COMMON ROOKIE (176-225)	6.00	2.70
ROOKIE SEMISTARS 176-225	10.00	4.50
ROOKIE UNL.STARS 176-225	12.00	5.50
4-STAR ROOKIE 176-225 ODDS 1:5		
❑ 1 Simeon Rice	.20	.09
❑ 2 Frank Sanders	.40	.18
❑ 3 Andre Wadsworth	.20	.09
❑ 4 Larry Centers	.20	.09
❑ 5 Byron Hanspard	.20	.09
❑ 6 Terance Mathis	.40	.18
❑ 7 O.J. Santiago	.20	.09
❑ 8 Chris Calloway	.20	.09
❑ 9 Michael Jackson	.20	.09
❑ 10 Rod Woodson	.40	.18
❑ 11 Pat Johnson	.20	.09
❑ 12 Rob Johnson	.40	.18
❑ 13 Andre Reed	.40	.18
❑ 14 Tim Biakabutuka	.40	.18
❑ 15 Rae Carruth	.40	.18
❑ 16 Fred Lane	.20	.09
❑ 17 Muhsin Muhammad	.40	.18
❑ 18 Wesley Walls	.40	.18
❑ 19 Edgar Bennett	.20	.09
❑ 20 Curtis Conway	.40	.18
❑ 21 Bobby Engram	.40	.18
❑ 22 Jeff Blake	.40	.18
❑ 23 Darnay Scott	.20	.09
❑ 24 Ty Detmer	.40	.18
❑ 25 Sedrick Shaw	.20	.09
❑ 26 Leslie Shepherd	.20	.09
❑ 27 Terry Kirby	.20	.09
❑ 28 Chris Warren	.20	.09
❑ 29 Rocket Ismail	.40	.18
❑ 30 Marcus Nash	.40	.18
❑ 31 Neil Smith	.40	.18
❑ 32 Bubby Brister	.20	.09
❑ 33 Brian Griese	2.00	.90
❑ 34 Germane Crowell	.40	.18
❑ 35 Johnnie Morton	.40	.18
❑ 36 Gus Frerotte	.20	.09
❑ 37 Robert Brooks	.40	.18
❑ 38 Mark Chmura	.20	.09
❑ 39 Derrick Mayes	.20	.09
❑ 40 Jerome Pathon	.20	.09
❑ 41 Jimmy Smith	.40	.18
❑ 42 James Stewart	.40	.18
❑ 43 Tavian Banks	.20	.09
❑ 44 Derrick Alexander WR	.40	.18
❑ 45 Kimble Anders	.40	.18
❑ 46 Elvis Grbac	.40	.18
❑ 47 Derrick Thomas	.40	.18
❑ 48 Byron Bam Morris	.20	.09
❑ 49 Tony Gonzalez	.40	.18
❑ 50 John Avery	.40	.18
❑ 51 Tyrone Wheatley	.40	.18
❑ 52 Zach Thomas	.40	.18
❑ 53 Lamar Thomas	.20	.09
❑ 54 Jeff George	.40	.18
❑ 55 John Randle	.40	.18
❑ 56 Jake Reed	.40	.18
❑ 57 Leroy Hoard	.20	.09
❑ 58 Robert Edwards	.40	.18
❑ 59 Ben Coates	.40	.18
❑ 60 Tony Simmons	.20	.09
❑ 61 Shawn Jefferson	.20	.09
❑ 62 Eddie Kennison	.40	.18
❑ 63 Lamar Smith	.20	.09
❑ 64 Tiki Barber	.20	.09
❑ 65 Kerry Collins	.40	.18
❑ 66 Ike Hilliard	.20	.09
❑ 67 Gary Brown	.20	.09
❑ 68 Joe Jurevicius	.20	.09
❑ 69 Kent Graham	.20	.09
❑ 70 Dedric Ward	.20	.09
❑ 71 Terry Allen	.40	.18
❑ 72 Neil O'Donnell	.40	.18
❑ 73 Desmond Howard	.40	.18
❑ 74 James Jett	.40	.18
❑ 75 Jon Ritchie	.20	.09
❑ 76 Rickey Dudley	.20	.09
❑ 77 Charles Johnson	.20	.09
❑ 78 Chris Fuamatu-Ma'afala	.20	.09
❑ 79 Hines Ward	.20	.09
❑ 80 Ryan Leaf	.75	.35
❑ 81 Jim Harbaugh	.40	.18
❑ 82 Junior Seau	.40	.18
❑ 83 Mikhael Ricks	.20	.09
❑ 84 J.J. Stokes	.40	.18
❑ 85 Ahman Green	.40	.18
❑ 86 Tony Banks	.40	.18
❑ 87 Robert Holcombe	.40	.18
❑ 88 Az-Zahir Hakim	.20	.09
❑ 89 Greg Hill	.20	.09
❑ 90 Trent Green	.40	.18
❑ 91 Eric Zeier	.20	.09
❑ 92 Reidel Anthony	.40	.18
❑ 93 Bert Emanuel	.40	.18
❑ 94 Warren Sapp	.20	.09
❑ 95 Kevin Dyson	.40	.18
❑ 96 Yancey Thigpen	.20	.09
❑ 97 Frank Wycheck	.20	.09
❑ 98 Michael Westbrook	.40	.18
❑ 99 Albert Connell	.20	.09
❑ 100 Darrell Green	.20	.09
❑ 101 Rob Moore	.40	.18
❑ 102 Adrian Murrell	.40	.18
❑ 103 Jake Plummer	2.50	1.10
❑ 104 Chris Chandler	.40	.18
❑ 105 Jamal Anderson	1.25	.55
❑ 106 Tim Dwight	1.25	.55
❑ 107 Jermaine Lewis	1.25	.55
❑ 108 Priest Holmes	1.25	.55
❑ 109 Bruce Smith	1.25	.55
❑ 110 Eric Moulds	1.25	.55
❑ 111 Antowain Smith	1.25	.55
❑ 112 Curtis Enis	1.25	.55
❑ 113 Corey Dillon	1.25	.55
❑ 114 Michael Irvin	1.25	.55
❑ 115 Ed McCaffrey	1.25	.55
❑ 116 Shannon Sharpe	1.25	.55
❑ 117 Terrell Davis	3.00	1.35
❑ 118 Charlie Batch	2.00	.90
❑ 119 Antonio Freeman	1.25	.55
❑ 120 Dorsey Levens	1.25	.55
❑ 121 Marvin Harrison	1.25	.55
❑ 122 Peyton Manning	5.00	2.20
❑ 123 Keenan McCardell	1.25	.55
❑ 124 Fred Taylor	3.00	1.35
❑ 125 Andre Rison	1.25	.55
❑ 126 O.J. McDuffie	1.25	.55
❑ 127 Karim Abdul-Jabbar	1.25	.55
❑ 128 Randy Moss	5.00	2.20
❑ 129 Terry Glenn	1.25	.55
❑ 130 Vinny Testaverde	1.25	.55
❑ 131 Keyshawn Johnson	1.25	.55
❑ 132 Curtis Martin	1.25	.55
❑ 133 Wayne Chrebet	1.25	.55
❑ 134 Napoleon Kaufman	1.25	.55
❑ 135 Charles Woodson	1.25	.55
❑ 136 Duce Staley	1.25	.55
❑ 137 Kordell Stewart	1.25	.55
❑ 138 Terrell Owens	1.25	.55
❑ 139 Ricky Watters	1.25	.55
❑ 140 Joey Galloway	1.25	.55
❑ 141 Jon Kitna	1.50	.70
❑ 142 Isaac Bruce	1.25	.55
❑ 143 Jacquez Green	1.25	.55
❑ 144 Warrick Dunn	1.25	.55
❑ 145 Mike Alstott	1.25	.55
❑ 146 Trent Dilfer	1.25	.55
❑ 147 Steve McNair	1.25	.55
❑ 148 Eddie George	1.50	.70
❑ 149 Skip Hicks	1.25	.55
❑ 150 Brad Johnson	1.25	.55
❑ 151 Doug Flutie	2.50	1.10
❑ 152 Thurman Thomas	1.25	.55
❑ 153 Carl Pickens	1.25	.55
❑ 154 Emmitt Smith	5.00	2.20
❑ 155 Troy Aikman	5.00	2.20
❑ 156 Deion Sanders	1.25	.55
❑ 157 John Elway	8.00	3.60
❑ 158 Rod Smith	1.25	.55
❑ 159 Barry Sanders	8.00	3.60
❑ 160 Herman Moore	2.00	.90
❑ 161 Brett Favre	8.00	3.60
❑ 162 Mark Brunell	3.00	1.35
❑ 163 Warren Moon	2.00	.90
❑ 164 Dan Marino	8.00	3.60
❑ 165 Randall Cunningham	2.00	.90
❑ 166 Robert Smith	2.00	.90
❑ 167 Cris Carter	2.00	.90
❑ 168 Drew Bledsoe	3.00	1.35
❑ 169 Tim Brown	2.00	.90
❑ 170 Jerome Bettis	2.00	.90
❑ 171 Natrone Means	1.25	.55
❑ 172 Jerry Rice	5.00	2.20
❑ 173 Steve Young	3.00	1.35
❑ 174 Garrison Hearst	2.00	.90
❑ 175 Marshall Faulk	2.00	.90
❑ 176 David Boston RC	20.00	9.00
❑ 177 Jeff Paulk RC	10.00	4.50
❑ 178 Reginald Kelly RC	6.00	2.70
❑ 179 Scott Covington RC	10.00	4.50
❑ 180 Chris McAlister RC	10.00	4.50

❑ 181 Shawn Bryson RC........ 6.00 2.70
❑ 182 Peerless Price RC...... 20.00 9.00
❑ 183 Cade McNown RC 30.00 13.50
❑ 184 Michael Bishop RC 15.00 6.75
❑ 185 D'Wayne Bates RC 10.00 4.50
❑ 186 Marty Booker RC........ 10.00 4.50
❑ 187 Akili Smith RC 25.00 11.00
❑ 188 Craig Yeast RC 10.00 4.50
❑ 189 Tim Couch RC........... 50.00 22.00
❑ 190 Kevin Johnson RC 25.00 11.00
❑ 191 Wane McGarity RC 10.00 4.50
❑ 192 Olandis Gary RC........ 30.00 13.50
❑ 193 Travis McGriff RC 12.00 5.50
❑ 194 Sedrick Irvin RC 12.00 5.50
❑ 195 Chris Claiborne RC 10.00 4.50
❑ 196 De'Mond Parker RC .. 12.00 5.50
❑ 197 Dee Miller RC 10.00 4.50
❑ 198 Edgerrin James RC.... 80.00 36.00
❑ 199 Mike Cloud RC 12.00 5.50
❑ 200 Larry Parker RC 10.00 4.50
❑ 201 Cecil Collins RC 6.00 2.70
❑ 202 James Johnson RC.... 15.00 6.75
❑ 203 Rob Konrad RC.......... 12.00 5.50
❑ 204 Daunte Culpepper RC 30.00 13.50
❑ 205 Jim Kleinsasser RC.... 12.00 5.50
❑ 206 Kevin Faulk RC 15.00 6.75
❑ 207 Andy Katzenmoyer RC 12.00 5.50
❑ 208 Ricky Williams RC...... 50.00 22.00
❑ 209 Joe Montgomery RC .. 12.00 5.50
❑ 210 Sean Bennett RC 12.00 5.50
❑ 211 Dameane Douglas RC 12.00 5.50
❑ 212 Donovan McNabb RC 30.00 13.50
❑ 213 Na Brown RC 12.00 5.50
❑ 214 Amos Zereoue RC 12.00 5.50
❑ 215 Troy Edwards RC 20.00 9.00
❑ 216 Jermaine Fazande RC 10.00 4.50
❑ 217 Tai Streets RC........... 10.00 4.50
❑ 218 Brock Huard RC 15.00 6.75
❑ 219 Charlie Rogers RC 10.00 4.50
❑ 220 Karsten Bailey RC...... 10.00 4.50
❑ 221 Joe Germaine RC 12.00 5.50
❑ 222 Torry Holt RC 25.00 11.00
❑ 223 Shaun King RC 30.00 13.50
❑ 224 Jevon Kearse RC 20.00 9.00
❑ 225 Champ Bailey RC 15.00 6.75

1999 Leaf Certified Mirror Gold

	MINT	NRMT
COMMON CARD (1-100)........	12.00	5.50
1-STAR 1-100: 25X TO 60X HI COL.		
1-STAR 1-100 PRINT RUN 45 SER.#'d SETS		
COMMON CARD 101-150	25.00	11.00
2-STAR 101-150: 15X TO 40X HI COL.		
2-STAR 101-150 PRINT RUN 35 SER.#'d SETS		
COMMON CARD 151-175	40.00	18.00
3-STAR 151-175: 15X TO 40X HI COL.		
3-STAR 151-175 PRINT RUN 25 SER.#'d SETS		
COMMON CARD 176-225	25.00	11.00
4-STAR 176-225: 1.5X TO 4X HI COL.		
4-STAR 176-225 PRINT RUN 30 SER.#'d SETS		

1999 Leaf Certified Mirror Red

	MINT	NRMT
COMMON CARD (1-100)..........	3.00	1.35
1-STAR 1-100: 6X TO 15X HI COL.		
1-STAR 1-100 STATED ODDS 1:17		
COMMON CARD (101-150)......	5.00	2.20
2-STAR 101-150: 3X TO 8X HI COL.		
2-STAR 101-150 STATED ODDS 1:53		
COMMON CARD (151-175)......	8.00	3.60
3-STAR 151-175: 3X TO 8X HI COL.		
3-STAR 151-175 STATED ODDS 1:125		
COMMON CARD (176-225)....	10.00	4.50
4-STAR 176-225: .6X TO 1.5X HI COL.		
4-STAR 176-225 STATED ODDS 1:89		

1999 Leaf Certified Skills

	MINT	NRMT
COMPLETE SET (20)	150.00	70.00
COMMON CARD (CS1-CS20)..	6.00	2.70
STATED ODDS 1:35		
*MIRROR BLACK: 3X TO 8X HI COL.		
MIRROR BLACK PRINT RUN 25 SER.#'d SETS		

❑ CS1 Deion Sanders 6.00 2.70
Champ Bailey
❑ CS2 John Elway............... 20.00 9.00
Cade McNown
❑ CS3 Cris Carter 6.00 2.70
Daivd Boston
❑ CS4 Marshall Faulk 25.00 11.00
Edgerrin James
❑ CS5 Jerry Rice 20.00 9.00
Randy Moss
❑ CS6 Antonio Freeman 6.00 2.70
Terrell Owens
❑ CS7 Terrell Davis............. 20.00 9.00
Ricky Williams
❑ CS8 Drew Bledsoe............. 8.00 3.60
Doug Flutie
❑ CS9 Eddie George............ 8.00 3.60
Jamal Anderson
❑ CS10 Troy Aikman........... 15.00 6.75
Peyton Manning
❑ CS11 Barry Sanders 20.00 9.00
Warrick Dunn
❑ CS12 Randall Cunningham 8.00 3.60
Daunte Culpepper
❑ CS13 Dan Marino.............. 25.00 11.00
Tim Couch
❑ CS14 Emmitt Smith 15.00 6.75
Fred Taylor
❑ CS15 Keyshawn Johnson .. 6.00 2.70
Eric Moulds
❑ CS16 Steve Young........... 10.00 4.50
Mark Brunell
❑ CS17 Donovan McNabb 8.00 3.60
Akili Smith
❑ CS18 Brett Favre 20.00 9.00
Jake Plummer
❑ CS19 Kordell Stewart.......... 6.00 2.70
Steve McNair
❑ CS20 Torry Holt 6.00 2.70
Troy Edwards

1999 Leaf Certified Fabric of the Game

	MINT	NRMT
COMPLETE SET (75)	1500.00	700.00
COMMON CARD/1000.............	6.00	2.70
SEMISTARS/1000	8.00	3.60
COMMON CARD/750...............	4.00	1.80
SEMISTARS/750	8.00	3.60
COMMON CARD/500...............	5.00	2.20
SEMISTARS/500	10.00	4.50
COMMON CARD/250.............	15.00	6.75
RANDOM INSERTS IN PACKS....		

❑ FG1 John Elway/100 .... 80.00 36.00
❑ FG2 Barry Sanders/100 .... 80.00 36.00
❑ FG3 Jerry Rice/100 .... 50.00 22.00
❑ FG4 Brett Favre/250 .... 60.00 27.00
❑ FG5 Steve Young/250 ...... 25.00 11.00
❑ FG6 Troy Aikman/250 ...... 40.00 18.00
❑ FG7 Deion Sanders/250 .. 15.00 6.75
❑ FG8 Terrell Davis/500 ...... 25.00 11.00
❑ FG9 Mark Brunell/500 ...... 15.00 6.75
❑ FG10 Drew Bledsoe/500 .. 15.00 6.75
❑ FG11 R.Cunningham/500 10.00 4.50
❑ FG12 Eddie George/500 .. 12.00 5.50
❑ FG13 Jamal Anderson/750 8.00 3.60
❑ FG14 Doug Flutie/750 ...... 10.00 4.50
❑ FG15 Robert Smith/750...... 8.00 3.60
❑ FG16 Garrison Hearst/750.. 8.00 3.60
❑ FG17 Keyshawn Johnson/750 8.00 3.60
❑ FG18 Randy Moss/750 .... 30.00 13.50
❑ FG19 Eric Moulds/1000...... 6.00 2.70
❑ FG20 Curtis Enis/1000........ 6.00 2.70
❑ FG21 Ricky Williams/1000 40.00 18.00
❑ FG22 Peyton Manning/1000 25.00 11.00
❑ FG23 Tim Couch/1000...... 40.00 18.00
❑ FG24 Cade McNown/1000 20.00 9.00
❑ FG25 Akili Smith/1000 ...... 12.00 5.50
❑ FG26 Dan Marino/100 ...... 80.00 36.00
❑ FG27 Jerry Rice/100 .... 50.00 22.00
❑ FG28 Emmitt Smith/100.... 60.00 27.00
❑ FG29 Cris Carter/250........ 15.00 6.75
❑ FG30 Steve Young/250 .... 25.00 11.00
❑ FG31 Herman Moore/250 15.00 6.75
❑ FG32 Tim Brown/250........ 15.00 6.75
❑ FG33 Jerome Bettis/500 .. 10.00 4.50
❑ FG34 Natrone Means/500 10.00 4.50
❑ FG35 Antonio Freeman/500 10.00 4.50
❑ FG36 Terrell Davis/500 .... 25.00 11.00

Card	Mint	NrMt
❑ FG37 Carl Pickens/500	5.00	2.20
❑ FG38 K.Abdul-Jabbar/750	8.00	3.60
❑ FG39 Mike Alstott/750	8.00	3.60
❑ FG40 Jake Plummer/750	15.00	6.75
❑ FG41 Steve McNair/750	8.00	3.60
❑ FG42 Terrell Owens/750	8.00	3.60
❑ FG43 Kordell Stewart/750	8.00	3.60
❑ FG44 Randy Moss/1000	25.00	11.00
❑ FG45 Fred Taylor/1000	15.00	6.75
❑ FG46 Peyton Manning/1000	25.00	11.00
❑ FG47 Tim Couch/1000	40.00	18.00
❑ FG48 Akili Smith/1000	12.00	5.50
❑ FG49 Torry Holt/1000	15.00	6.75
❑ FG50 Donovan McNabb/1000	20.00	9.00
❑ FG51 Barry Sanders/100	80.00	36.00
❑ FG52 Dan Marino/100	80.00	36.00
❑ FG53 Jerry Rice/100	50.00	22.00
❑ FG54 John Elway/250	60.00	27.00
❑ FG55 Brett Favre/250	60.00	27.00
❑ FG56 Emmitt Smith/250	40.00	18.00
❑ FG57 Mark Brunell/250	25.00	11.00
❑ FG58 Jake Plummer/500	20.00	9.00
❑ FG59 Ricky Watters/500	5.00	2.20
❑ FG60 Dorsey Levens/500	10.00	4.50
❑ FG61 Curtis Martin/500	10.00	4.50
❑ FG62 Marshall Faulk/500	10.00	4.50
❑ FG63 Eddie George/750	10.00	4.50
❑ FG64 Corey Dillon/750	8.00	3.60
❑ FG65 Warrick Dunn/750	8.00	3.60
❑ FG66 Antowain Smith/750	8.00	3.60
❑ FG67 Napoleon Kaufman/750	8.00	3.60
❑ FG68 Joey Galloway/750	8.00	3.60
❑ FG69 Fred Taylor/1000	15.00	6.75
❑ FG70 Charlie Batch/1000	12.00	5.50
❑ FG71 Ricky Williams/1000	40.00	18.00
❑ FG72 Edgerrin James/1000	60.00	27.00
❑ FG73 Jon Kitna/1000	10.00	4.50
❑ FG74 Daunte Culpepper/1000	20.00	9.00
❑ FG75 Skip Hicks/1000	6.00	2.70

1999 Leaf Certified Gold Future

	MINT	NRMT
COMPLETE SET (30)	200.00	90.00
COMMON CARD (1-30)	3.00	1.35
SEMISTARS	4.00	1.80
STATED ODDS 1:17		

*MIRROR BLACK: 4X TO 10X HI COL.
MIRROR BLACK PRINT RUN 25 SER.#'d SETS

Card	Mint	NrMt
❑ 1 Travis McGriff	4.00	1.80
❑ 2 Jermaine Fazande	4.00	1.80
❑ 3 Kevin Faulk	5.00	2.20
❑ 4 Edgerrin James	30.00	13.50
❑ 5 Ricky Williams	20.00	9.00
❑ 6 Tim Couch	20.00	9.00
❑ 7 Torry Holt	10.00	4.50
❑ 8 Kevin Johnson	10.00	4.50
❑ 9 Amos Zereoue	4.00	1.80
❑ 10 Joe Germaine	4.00	1.80
❑ 11 Shawn Bryson	4.00	1.80
❑ 12 D'Wayne Bates	4.00	1.80
❑ 13 Akili Smith	8.00	3.60
❑ 14 Shaun King	12.00	5.50
❑ 15 Joe Montgomery	4.00	1.80
❑ 16 Troy Edwards	6.00	2.70
❑ 17 Rob Konrad	4.00	1.80
❑ 18 David Boston	6.00	2.70
❑ 19 Reginald Kelly	3.00	1.35
❑ 20 Donovan McNabb	12.00	5.50
❑ 21 Champ Bailey	5.00	2.20
❑ 22 Craig Yeast	4.00	1.80
❑ 23 Daunte Culpepper	12.00	5.50
❑ 24 Peerless Price	6.00	2.70
❑ 25 Cecil Collins	4.00	1.80
❑ 26 Cade McNown	12.00	5.50
❑ 27 Karsten Bailey	4.00	1.80
❑ 28 James Johnson	5.00	2.20
❑ 29 Brock Huard	5.00	2.20
❑ 30 Mike Cloud	3.00	1.35

1999 Leaf Certified Gold Team

	MINT	NRMT
COMPLETE SET (30)	200.00	90.00
COMMON CARD (CGT1-CGT30)	5.00	2.20
STATED ODDS 1:17		

*MIRROR BLACK: 4X TO 10X HI COL.
MIRROR BLACK PRINT RUN 25 SER.#'d SETS

Card	Mint	NrMt
❑ CGT1 Randy Moss	15.00	6.75
❑ CGT2 Terrell Davis	12.00	5.50
❑ CGT3 Peyton Manning	15.00	6.75
❑ CGT4 Fred Taylor	10.00	4.50
❑ CGT5 Jake Plummer	10.00	4.50
❑ CGT6 Drew Bledsoe	8.00	3.60
❑ CGT7 John Elway	20.00	9.00
❑ CGT8 Mark Brunell	8.00	3.60
❑ CGT9 Joey Galloway	5.00	2.20
❑ CGT10 Troy Aikman	12.00	5.50
❑ CGT11 Jerome Bettis	5.00	2.20
❑ CGT12 Tim Brown	5.00	2.20
❑ CGT13 Dan Marino	20.00	9.00
❑ CGT14 Antonio Freeman	5.00	2.20
❑ CGT15 Steve Young	8.00	3.60
❑ CGT16 Jamal Anderson	5.00	2.20
❑ CGT17 Brett Favre	20.00	9.00
❑ CGT18 Jerry Rice	12.00	5.50
❑ CGT19 Corey Dillon	5.00	2.20
❑ CGT20 Barry Sanders	20.00	9.00
❑ CGT21 Doug Flutie	6.00	2.70
❑ CGT22 Emmitt Smith	12.00	5.50
❑ CGT23 Curtis Martin	5.00	2.20
❑ CGT24 Dorsey Levens	5.00	2.20
❑ CGT25 Kordell Stewart	5.00	2.20
❑ CGT26 Eddie George	6.00	2.70
❑ CGT27 Terrell Owens	5.00	2.20
❑ CGT28 Keyshawn Johnson	5.00	2.20
❑ CGT29 Steve McNair	5.00	2.20
❑ CGT30 Cris Carter	5.00	2.20

1999 Leaf Certified Gridiron Gear

	MINT	NRMT
COMPLETE SET (72)	4500.00	2000.00
COMMON CARD	30.00	13.50
SEMISTARS	40.00	18.00
UNLISTED STARS	50.00	22.00

*MULTI-COLORED SWATCHES: .6X TO 1.5X
STATED PRINT RUN 300 SER.#'d SETS

Card	Mint	NrMt
❑ AF86 Antonio Freeman	50.00	22.00
❑ BC87 Ben Coates	40.00	18.00
❑ BF4A Brett Favre White	120.00	55.00
❑ BF4H Brett Favre Green	120.00	55.00
❑ BS20 Barry Sanders	150.00	70.00
❑ CC80 Curtis Conway	40.00	18.00
❑ CM28 Curtis Martin	50.00	22.00
❑ CS81 Chris Sanders	30.00	13.50
❑ CW24 Charles Woodson	50.00	22.00
❑ DB11 Drew Bledsoe	80.00	36.00
❑ DF7A Doug Flutie White	60.00	27.00
❑ DF7H Doug Flutie Blue	60.00	27.00
❑ DG28 Darrell Green	40.00	18.00
❑ DH80 Desmond Howard	40.00	18.00
❑ DL25A Dorsey Levens White	50.00	22.00
❑ DL25H Dorsey Levens Green	50.00	22.00
❑ DM13A Dan Marino White	120.00	55.00
❑ DM13H Dan Marino Teal	120.00	55.00
❑ DS21 Deion Sanders	50.00	22.00
❑ DT58 Derrick Thomas	50.00	22.00
❑ EG27 Eddie George	80.00	36.00
❑ ES22 Emmitt Smith	150.00	70.00
❑ HM84 Herman Moore	50.00	22.00
❑ IB80 Isaac Bruce	40.00	18.00
❑ JA32 Jamal Anderson	50.00	22.00
❑ JB36 Jerome Bettis	50.00	22.00
❑ JE7H John Elway Blue	120.00	55.00
❑ JE7HC John Elway Orange	120.00	55.00
❑ JJ82 James Jett	40.00	18.00
❑ JK12 Jim Kelly	80.00	36.00
❑ JM19 Joe Montana	250.00	110.00
❑ JP16 Jake Plummer	60.00	27.00
❑ JR80A Jerry Rice White	100.00	45.00
❑ JR80H Jerry Rice Red	100.00	45.00
❑ JS33 James Stewart	40.00	18.00
❑ JS55 Junior Seau	40.00	18.00
❑ JS82 Jimmy Smith	40.00	18.00
❑ KA33 Karim Abdul-Jabbar	40.00	18.00
❑ KJ19 Keyshawn Johnson	50.00	22.00
❑ KM87 Keenan McCardell	40.00	18.00
❑ KS10 Kordell Stewart	50.00	22.00
❑ MB8A Mark Brunell White	60.00	27.00
❑ MB8H Mark Brunell Teal	60.00	27.00
❑ MC89 Mark Chmura	40.00	18.00
❑ MH88 Marvin Harrison	50.00	22.00
❑ MI88 Michael Irvin	40.00	18.00
❑ NK26A Nap.Kaufman White	50.00	22.00
❑ NK26H Nap.Kaufman Black	50.00	22.00
❑ NM20 Natrone Means	40.00	18.00
❑ NS90 Neil Smith	40.00	18.00
❑ OM81 O.J. McDuffie	40.00	18.00
❑ PM18 Peyton Manning	175.00	80.00
❑ PS12 Phil Simms	50.00	22.00
❑ RB87 Robert Brooks	40.00	18.00
❑ RC7 Randall Cunningham	50.00	22.00
❑ RL16 Ryan Leaf	30.00	13.50
❑ RM84A Randy Moss White	120.00	55.00
❑ RM84H Randy Moss Purple	120.00	55.00
❑ SM9 Steve McNair	50.00	22.00
❑ SY8 Steve Young	100.00	45.00
❑ TA8 Troy Aikman	100.00	45.00
❑ TB71 Tony Boselli	30.00	13.50
❑ TB81 Tim Brown	50.00	22.00
❑ TD12 Trent Dilfer	40.00	18.00
❑ TD30A Terrell Davis White	80.00	36.00
❑ TD30H Terrell Davis Blue	80.00	36.00
❑ TT34 Thurman Thomas	40.00	18.00
❑ VT12 Vinny Testaverde	40.00	18.00
❑ WD28 Warrick Dunn	50.00	22.00

❑ WM1 Warren Moon	40.00	18.00
❑ WS99 Warren Sapp	40.00	18.00
❑ ZT54 Zach Thomas	40.00	18.00

1998 Leaf Rookies and Stars

	MINT	NRMT
COMPLETE SET (300)	400.00	180.00
COMMON CARD (1-300)	.15	.07
SEMISTARS	.25	.11
UNLISTED STARS	.50	.23
COMMON ROOKIE (171-240)	2.50	1.10
ROOKIE SEMISTARS	5.00	2.20
ROOKIE UNLISTED STARS	8.00	3.60
COMMON POW.TOOLS (241-270)	2.50	1.10
RC/POWER TOOLS SUBSET ODDS 1:2		
COMMON LONGEVITY	12.00	5.50
*LONGEVITY STARS: 40X TO 100X HI COL.		
*LONGEVITY YOUNG STARS: 30X TO 80X		
*LONGEVITY RCs: 1.25X TO 3X..		
*LONGEVITY PT STARS: 12.5X TO 20X		
*LONGEVITY PT ROOKIES: 2X TO 5X		
LONGEVITY PRINT RUN 50 SERIAL #'d SETS		
COMP.TRUE BLUE (300)	800.00	350.00
*TRUE BLUE STARS: 4X TO 10X HI COL.		
*TRUE BLUE YOUNG STARS: 3X TO 8X		
*TRUE BLUE RCs: .3X TO .8X		
*TRUE BLUE POWER TOOLS: .75X TO 2X		
TRUE BLUE PRINT RUN 500 SETS		

❑ 1 Keyshawn Johnson	.50	.23
❑ 2 Marvin Harrison	.25	.11
❑ 3 Eddie Kennison	.25	.11
❑ 4 Bryant Young	.15	.07
❑ 5 Darren Woodson	.15	.07
❑ 6 Tyrone Wheatley	.25	.11
❑ 7 Michael Westbrook	.25	.11
❑ 8 Charles Way	.15	.07
❑ 9 Ricky Watters	.25	.11
❑ 10 Chris Warren	.25	.11
❑ 11 Wesley Walls	.25	.11
❑ 12 Tamarick Vanover	.15	.07
❑ 13 Zach Thomas	.15	.07
❑ 14 Derrick Thomas	.25	.11
❑ 15 Yancey Thigpen	.15	.07
❑ 16 Vinny Testaverde	.25	.11
❑ 17 Dana Stubblefield	.15	.07
❑ 18 J.J. Stokes	.25	.11
❑ 19 James Stewart	.25	.11
❑ 20 Jeff George	.25	.11
❑ 21 John Randle	.25	.11
❑ 22 Gary Brown	.15	.07
❑ 23 Ed McCaffrey	.25	.11
❑ 24 James Jett	.25	.11
❑ 25 Rob Johnson	.25	.11
❑ 26 Daryl Johnston	.25	.11
❑ 27 Jermaine Lewis	.25	.11
❑ 28 Tony Martin	.25	.11
❑ 29 Derrick Mayes	.25	.11
❑ 30 Keenan McCardell	.25	.11
❑ 31 O.J. McDuffie	.25	.11
❑ 32 Chris Chandler	.25	.11
❑ 33 Doug Flutie	.60	.25
❑ 34 Scott Mitchell	.25	.11
❑ 35 Warren Moon	.50	.23
❑ 36 Rob Moore	.25	.11
❑ 37 Johnnie Morton	.25	.11
❑ 38 Neil O'Donnell	.25	.11
❑ 39 Rich Gannon	.15	.07
❑ 40 Andre Reed	.25	.11
❑ 41 Jake Reed	.25	.11
❑ 42 Errict Rhett	.25	.11
❑ 43 Simeon Rice	.25	.11
❑ 44 Andre Rison	.25	.11
❑ 45 Eric Moulds	.50	.23
❑ 46 Frank Sanders	.25	.11
❑ 47 Darnay Scott	.25	.11
❑ 48 Junior Seau	.25	.11
❑ 49 Shannon Sharpe	.25	.11
❑ 50 Bruce Smith	.25	.11
❑ 51 Jimmy Smith	.25	.11
❑ 52 Robert Smith	.50	.23
❑ 53 Derrick Alexander	.25	.11
❑ 54 Kimble Anders	.25	.11
❑ 55 Jamal Anderson	.50	.23
❑ 56 Mario Bates	.25	.11
❑ 57 Edgar Bennett	.15	.07
❑ 58 Tim Biakabutuka	.25	.11
❑ 59 Ki-Jana Carter	.15	.07
❑ 60 Larry Centers	.15	.07
❑ 61 Mark Chmura	.25	.11
❑ 62 Wayne Chrebet	.50	.23
❑ 63 Ben Coates	.25	.11
❑ 64 Curtis Conway	.25	.11
❑ 65 Randall Cunningham	.50	.23
❑ 66 Rickey Dudley	.15	.07
❑ 67 Bert Emanuel	.25	.11
❑ 68 Bobby Engram	.25	.11
❑ 69 William Floyd	.15	.07
❑ 70 Irving Fryar	.25	.11
❑ 71 Elvis Grbac	.25	.11
❑ 72 Kevin Greene	.25	.11
❑ 73 Jim Harbaugh	.25	.11
❑ 74 Raymont Harris	.15	.07
❑ 75 Garrison Hearst	.50	.23
❑ 76 Greg Hill	.15	.07
❑ 77 Desmond Howard	.25	.11
❑ 78 Bobby Hoying	.25	.11
❑ 79 Michael Jackson	.15	.07
❑ 80 Terry Allen	.50	.23
❑ 81 Jerome Bettis	.50	.23
❑ 82 Jeff Blake	.25	.11
❑ 83 Robert Brooks	.25	.11
❑ 84 Tim Brown	.50	.23
❑ 85 Isaac Bruce	.50	.23
❑ 86 Cris Carter	.50	.23
❑ 87 Ty Detmer	.25	.11
❑ 88 Trent Dilfer	.50	.23
❑ 89 Marshall Faulk	.50	.23
❑ 90 Antonio Freeman	.50	.23
❑ 91 Gus Frerotte	.15	.07
❑ 92 Joey Galloway	.50	.23
❑ 93 Michael Irvin	.50	.23
❑ 94 Brad Johnson	.50	.23
❑ 95 Danny Kanell	.25	.11
❑ 96 Napoleon Kaufman	.50	.23
❑ 97 Dorsey Levens	.50	.23
❑ 98 Natrone Means	.50	.23
❑ 99 Herman Moore	.50	.23
❑ 100 Adrian Murrell	.25	.11
❑ 101 Carl Pickens	.50	.23
❑ 102 Rod Smith	.25	.11
❑ 103 Thurman Thomas	.50	.23
❑ 104 Reggie White	.50	.23
❑ 105 Jim Druckenmiller	.25	.11
❑ 106 Antowain Smith	.50	.23
❑ 107 Reidel Anthony	.25	.11
❑ 108 Ike Hilliard	.25	.11
❑ 109 Rae Carruth	.25	.11
❑ 110 Troy Davis	.15	.07
❑ 111 Terance Mathis	.25	.11
❑ 112 Brett Favre	2.50	1.10
❑ 113 Dan Marino	2.50	1.10
❑ 114 Emmitt Smith	2.00	.90
❑ 115 Barry Sanders	2.50	1.10
❑ 116 Eddie George	1.00	.45
❑ 117 Drew Bledsoe	1.00	.45
❑ 118 Troy Aikman	1.25	.55
❑ 119 Terrell Davis	2.00	.90
❑ 120 John Elway	2.50	1.10
❑ 121 Mark Brunell	1.00	.45
❑ 122 Jerry Rice	1.25	.55
❑ 123 Kordell Stewart	.50	.23
❑ 124 Steve McNair	.50	.23
❑ 125 Curtis Martin	.50	.23
❑ 126 Steve Young	.75	.35
❑ 127 Kerry Collins	.25	.11
❑ 128 Terry Glenn	.50	.23
❑ 129 Deion Sanders	.50	.23
❑ 130 Mike Alstott	.50	.23
❑ 131 Tony Banks	.25	.11
❑ 132 Karim Abdul-Jabbar	.50	.23
❑ 133 Terrell Owens	.50	.23
❑ 134 Yatil Green	.15	.07
❑ 135 Tony Gonzalez	.15	.07
❑ 136 Byron Hanspard	.25	.11
❑ 137 David LaFleur	.15	.07
❑ 138 Danny Wuerffel	.25	.11
❑ 139 Tiki Barber	.25	.11
❑ 140 Peter Boulware	.15	.07
❑ 141 Will Blackwell	.15	.07
❑ 142 Warrick Dunn	.75	.35
❑ 143 Corey Dillon	.75	.35
❑ 144 Jake Plummer	1.50	.70
❑ 145 Neil Smith	.25	.11
❑ 146 Charles Johnson	.15	.07
❑ 147 Fred Lane	.25	.11
❑ 148 Dan Wilkinson	.15	.07
❑ 149 Ken Norton	.15	.07
❑ 150 Stephen Davis	.15	.07
❑ 151 Gilbert Brown	.15	.07
❑ 152 Kenny Bynum RC	.15	.07
❑ 153 Derrick Cullors	.25	.11
❑ 154 Charlie Garner	.15	.07
❑ 155 Jeff Graham	.15	.07
❑ 156 Warren Sapp	.25	.11
❑ 157 Jerald Moore	.15	.07
❑ 158 Sean Dawkins	.15	.07
❑ 159 Charlie Jones	.15	.07
❑ 160 Kevin Lockett	.15	.07
❑ 161 James McKnight	.15	.07
❑ 162 Chris Penn	.15	.07
❑ 163 Leslie Shepherd	.15	.07
❑ 164 Karl Williams	.15	.07
❑ 165 Mark Bruener	.15	.07
❑ 166 Ernie Conwell	.15	.07
❑ 167 Ken Dilger	.15	.07
❑ 168 Troy Drayton	.15	.07
❑ 169 Freddie Jones	.15	.07
❑ 170 Dale Carter	.15	.07
❑ 171 Charles Woodson RC	15.00	6.75
❑ 172 Alonzo Mayes RC	2.50	1.10
❑ 173 Andre Wadsworth RC	5.00	2.20
❑ 174 Grant Wistrom RC	2.50	1.10
❑ 175 Greg Ellis RC	2.50	1.10
❑ 176 Chris Howard RC	5.00	2.20
❑ 177 Keith Brooking RC	5.00	2.20
❑ 178 Takeo Spikes RC	5.00	2.20
❑ 179 Anthony Simmons RC	2.50	1.10
❑ 180 Brian Simmons RC	2.50	1.10
❑ 181 Sam Cowart RC	2.50	1.10
❑ 182 Ken Oxendine RC	2.50	1.10
❑ 183 Vonnie Holliday RC	5.00	2.20
❑ 184 Terry Fair RC	5.00	2.20
❑ 185 Shaun Williams RC	2.50	1.10
❑ 186 Tremayne Stephens RC	2.50	1.10
❑ 187 Duane Starks RC	2.50	1.10
❑ 188 Jason Peter RC	2.50	1.10
❑ 189 Tebucky Jones RC	2.50	1.10
❑ 190 Donovin Darius RC	2.50	1.10
❑ 191 R.W. McQuarters RC	2.50	1.10
❑ 192 Corey Chavous RC	2.50	1.10
❑ 193 Cameron Cleeland RC	5.00	2.20
❑ 194 Stephen Alexander RC	5.00	2.20
❑ 195 Rod Rutledge RC	2.50	1.10
❑ 196 Scott Frost RC	5.00	2.20
❑ 197 Fred Beasley RC	2.50	1.10
❑ 198 Dorian Boose RC	2.50	1.10
❑ 199 Randy Moss RC	80.00	36.00
❑ 200 Jacquez Green RC	10.00	4.50
❑ 201 Marcus Nash RC	10.00	4.50
❑ 202 Hines Ward RC	5.00	2.20
❑ 203 Kevin Dyson RC	12.00	5.50
❑ 204 E.G. Green RC	5.00	2.20
❑ 205 Germane Crowell RC	15.00	6.75
❑ 206 Joe Jurevicius RC	5.00	2.20
❑ 207 Tony Simmons RC	5.00	2.20
❑ 208 Tim Dwight RC	12.00	5.50
❑ 209 Az-Zahir Hakim RC	10.00	4.50

❑ 210 Jerome Pathon RC	5.00	2.20
❑ 211 Pat Johnson RC	5.00	2.20
❑ 212 Mikhael Ricks RC	5.00	2.20
❑ 213 Donald Hayes RC	5.00	2.20
❑ 214 Jammi German RC	2.50	1.10
❑ 215 Larry Shannon RC	2.50	1.10
❑ 216 Brian Alford RC	5.00	2.20
❑ 217 Curtis Enis RC	15.00	6.75
❑ 218 Fred Taylor RC	30.00	13.50
❑ 219 Robert Edwards RC	8.00	3.60
❑ 220 Ahman Green RC	10.00	4.50
❑ 221 Tavian Banks RC	5.00	2.20
❑ 222 Skip Hicks RC	10.00	4.50
❑ 223 Robert Holcombe RC	8.00	3.60
❑ 224 John Avery RC	8.00	3.60
❑ 225 C.Fuamatu-Ma'afala RC	5.00	2.20
❑ 226 Michael Pittman RC	5.00	2.20
❑ 227 Rashaan Shehee RC	5.00	2.20
❑ 228 Jonathan Linton RC	10.00	4.50
❑ 229 Jon Ritchie RC	5.00	2.20
❑ 230 Chris Floyd RC	2.50	1.10
❑ 231 Wilmont Perry RC	2.50	1.10
❑ 232 Raymond Priester RC	2.50	1.10
❑ 233 Peyton Manning RC	80.00	36.00
❑ 234 Ryan Leaf RC	12.00	5.50
❑ 235 Brian Griese RC	20.00	9.00
❑ 236 Jeff Ogden RC	8.00	3.60
❑ 237 Charlie Batch RC	20.00	9.00
❑ 238 Moses Moreno RC	5.00	2.20
❑ 239 Jonathan Quinn RC UER back Jonathon	5.00	2.20
❑ 240 Flozell Adams RC	2.50	1.10
❑ 241 Brett Favre PT	12.00	5.50
❑ 242 Dan Marino PT	12.00	5.50
❑ 243 Emmitt Smith PT	10.00	4.50
❑ 244 Barry Sanders PT	12.00	5.50
❑ 245 Eddie George PT	5.00	2.20
❑ 246 Drew Bledsoe PT	5.00	2.20
❑ 247 Troy Aikman PT	6.00	2.70
❑ 248 Terrell Davis PT	10.00	4.50
❑ 249 John Elway PT	12.00	5.50
❑ 250 Carl Pickens PT	2.50	1.10
❑ 251 Jerry Rice PT	6.00	2.70
❑ 252 Kordell Stewart PT	2.50	1.10
❑ 253 Steve McNair PT	2.50	1.10
❑ 254 Curtis Martin PT	2.50	1.10
❑ 255 Steve Young PT	4.00	1.80
❑ 256 Herman Moore PT	2.50	1.10
❑ 257 Dorsey Levens PT	2.50	1.10
❑ 258 Deion Sanders PT	2.50	1.10
❑ 259 Napoleon Kaufman PT	2.50	1.10
❑ 260 Warrick Dunn PT	4.00	1.80
❑ 261 Corey Dillon PT	4.00	1.80
❑ 262 Jerome Bettis PT	2.50	1.10
❑ 263 Tim Brown PT	2.50	1.10
❑ 264 Cris Carter PT	2.50	1.10
❑ 265 Antonio Freeman PT	2.50	1.10
❑ 266 Randy Moss PT	20.00	9.00
❑ 267 Curtis Enis PT	6.00	2.70
❑ 268 Fred Taylor PT	10.00	4.50
❑ 269 Robert Edwards PT	20.00	9.00
❑ 270 Peyton Manning PT	25.00	11.00
❑ 271 Barry Sanders TL	1.25	.55
❑ 272 Eddie George TL	.50	.23
❑ 273 Troy Aikman TL	.60	.25
❑ 274 Mark Brunell TL	.50	.23
❑ 275 Kordell Stewart TL	.50	.23
❑ 276 Tim Biakabutuka TL	.15	.07
❑ 277 Terry Glenn TL	.15	.07
❑ 278 Mike Alstott TL	.15	.07
❑ 279 Tony Banks TL	.15	.07
❑ 280 Karim Abdul-Jabbar TL	.15	.07
❑ 281 Terrell Owens TL	.25	.11
❑ 282 Byron Hanspard TL	.15	.07
❑ 283 Jake Plummer TL	.75	.35
❑ 284 Terry Allen TL	.15	.07
❑ 285 Jeff Blake TL	.15	.07
❑ 286 Brad Johnson TL	.15	.07
❑ 287 Danny Kanell TL	.15	.07
❑ 288 Natrone Means TL	.15	.07
❑ 289 Rod Smith TL	.15	.07
❑ 290 Thurman Thomas TL	.15	.07
❑ 291 Reggie White TL	.15	.07
❑ 292 Troy Davis TL	.15	.07
❑ 293 Curtis Conway TL	.15	.07
❑ 294 Irving Fryar TL	.15	.07
❑ 295 Jim Harbaugh TL	.15	.07
❑ 296 Andre Rison TL	.15	.07
❑ 297 Ricky Watters TL	.15	.07
❑ 298 Keyshawn Johnson TL	.15	.07
❑ 299 Jeff George TL	.15	.07
❑ 300 Marshall Faulk TL	.25	.11

1998 Leaf Rookies and Stars Crosstraining

	MINT	NRMT
COMPLETE SET (10)	80.00	36.00
COMMON CARD (1-10)	5.00	2.20

STATED PRINT RUN 1000 SERIAL #'d SETS

❑ 1 Brett Favre	25.00	11.00
❑ 2 Mark Brunell	10.00	4.50
❑ 3 Barry Sanders	25.00	11.00
❑ 4 John Elway	25.00	11.00
❑ 5 Jerry Rice	12.00	5.50
❑ 6 Kordell Stewart	5.00	2.20
❑ 7 Steve McNair	6.00	2.70
❑ 8 Deion Sanders	6.00	2.70
❑ 9 Jake Plummer	12.00	5.50
❑ 10 Steve Young	8.00	3.60

1998 Leaf Rookies and Stars Crusade Green

	MINT	NRMT
COMPLETE SET (30)	500.00	220.00
COMMON CARD	10.00	4.50

GREEN PRINT RUN 250 SERIAL #'d SETS
*PURPLE CARDS: .6X TO 1.5X GREENS
PURPLE PRINT RUN 100 SERIAL #'d SETS
*RED STARS: 2.5X TO 6X GREENS
*RED ROOKIES: 2X TO 5X GREENS
RED PRINT RUN 25 SERIAL #'d SETS

❑ 1 Brett Favre	50.00	22.00
❑ 2 Dan Marino	50.00	22.00
❑ 3 Emmitt Smith	40.00	18.00
❑ 4 Barry Sanders	50.00	22.00
❑ 5 Eddie George	20.00	9.00
❑ 6 Drew Bledsoe	20.00	9.00
❑ 7 Troy Aikman	25.00	11.00
❑ 8 Terrell Davis	40.00	18.00
❑ 9 John Elway	50.00	22.00
❑ 10 Mark Brunell	20.00	9.00
❑ 11 Jerry Rice	25.00	11.00
❑ 12 Kordell Stewart	10.00	4.50
❑ 13 Steve McNair	12.00	5.50
❑ 14 Curtis Martin	12.00	5.50
❑ 16 Steve Young	15.00	6.75
❑ 18 Deion Sanders	12.00	5.50
❑ 22 Terrell Owens	12.00	5.50
❑ 23 Jamal Anderson	12.00	5.50
❑ 25 Jerome Bettis	12.00	5.50
❑ 30 Cris Carter	12.00	5.50
❑ 32 Marshall Faulk	12.00	5.50
❑ 33 Antonio Freeman	12.00	5.50
❑ 40 Dorsey Levens	12.00	5.50
❑ 49 Garrison Hearst	12.00	5.50
❑ 57 Warrick Dunn	12.00	5.50
❑ 59 Jake Plummer	25.00	11.00
❑ 66 Peyton Manning	80.00	36.00
❑ 69 Randy Moss	80.00	36.00
❑ 77 Fred Taylor	40.00	18.00
❑ 78 Robert Edwards	10.00	4.50

1998 Leaf Rookies and Stars Extreme Measures

	MINT	NRMT
COMPLETE SET (10)	120.00	55.00
COMMON CARD (1-10)	5.00	2.20

OVERALL PRINT RUN 1000 SER.#'d SETS

❑ 1 Barry Sanders/918	25.00	11.00
❑ 2 Warrick Dunn/941	8.00	3.60
❑ 3 Curtis Martin/930	5.00	2.20
❑ 4 Terrell Davis/419	25.00	11.00
❑ 5 Troy Aikman/929	12.00	5.50
❑ 6 Drew Bledsoe/972	10.00	4.50
❑ 7 Eddie George/191	30.00	13.50
❑ 8 Emmitt Smith/888	20.00	9.00
❑ 9 Dan Marino/615	30.00	13.50
❑ 10 Brett Favre/965	25.00	11.00

1998 Leaf Rookies and Stars Extreme Measures Die Cuts

	MINT	NRMT
COMPLETE SET (10)	700.00	325.00
COMMON CARD (1-10)	15.00	6.75

OVERALL PRINT RUN 1000 SER.#'d SETS

❑ 1 Barry Sanders/82	120.00	55.00
❑ 2 Warrick Dunn/59	25.00	11.00
❑ 3 Curtis Martin/70	25.00	11.00
❑ 4 Terrell Davis/581	25.00	11.00
❑ 5 Troy Aikman/71	60.00	27.00
❑ 6 Drew Bledsoe/28	150.00	70.00
❑ 7 Eddie George/809	15.00	6.75
❑ 8 Emmitt Smith/112	80.00	36.00
❑ 9 Dan Marino/385	50.00	22.00
❑ 10 Brett Favre/35	300.00	135.00

1998 Leaf Rookies and Stars Freshman Orientation

	MINT	NRMT
COMPLETE SET (20)	100.00	45.00
COMMON CARD (1-20)	4.00	1.80

STATED PRINT RUN 2500 SERIAL #'d SETS

❑ 1 Peyton Manning	25.00	11.00
❑ 2 Kevin Dyson	4.00	1.80
❑ 3 Joe Jurevicius	4.00	1.80
❑ 4 Tony Simmons	4.00	1.80
❑ 5 Marcus Nash	4.00	1.80
❑ 6 Ryan Leaf	5.00	2.20
❑ 7 Curtis Enis	6.00	2.70
❑ 8 Skip Hicks	4.00	1.80
❑ 9 Brian Griese	10.00	4.50
❑ 10 Jerome Pathon	4.00	1.80
❑ 11 John Avery	4.00	1.80
❑ 12 Fred Taylor	15.00	6.75
❑ 13 Robert Edwards	4.00	1.80
❑ 14 Robert Holcombe	4.00	1.80
❑ 15 Ahman Green	4.00	1.80
❑ 16 Hines Ward	4.00	1.80
❑ 17 Jacquez Green	4.00	1.80
❑ 18 Germane Crowell	6.00	2.70
❑ 19 Randy Moss	25.00	11.00
❑ 20 Charles Woodson	8.00	3.60

1998 Leaf Rookies and Stars Game Plan

	MINT	NRMT
COMPLETE SET (20)	40.00	18.00
COMMON CARD (1-20)	1.25	.55

STATED PRINT RUN 5000 SERIAL #'d SETS
*MASTERS: 1.25X TO 3X HI COL.
MASTERS PRINT RUN FIRST 500 SER.#'d SETS

❑ 1 Ryan Leaf	2.50	1.10

❑ 2 Peyton Manning	15.00	6.75
❑ 3 Brett Favre	6.00	2.70
❑ 4 Mark Brunell	2.50	1.10
❑ 5 Isaac Bruce	2.00	.90
❑ 6 Dan Marino	6.00	2.70
❑ 7 Jerry Rice	3.00	1.35
❑ 8 Cris Carter	2.00	.90
❑ 9 Emmitt Smith	5.00	2.20
❑ 10 Kordell Stewart	1.25	.55
❑ 11 Corey Dillon	1.50	.70
❑ 12 Barry Sanders	6.00	2.70
❑ 13 Curtis Martin	2.00	.90
❑ 14 Carl Pickens	2.00	.90
❑ 15 Eddie George	2.50	1.10
❑ 16 Warrick Dunn	2.00	.90
❑ 17 Jake Plummer	3.00	1.35
❑ 18 Curtis Enis	3.00	1.35
❑ 19 Drew Bledsoe	2.50	1.10
❑ 20 Terrell Davis	5.00	2.20

1998 Leaf Rookies and Stars Great American Heroes

	MINT	NRMT
COMPLETE SET (20)	80.00	36.00
COMMON CARD (1-20)	1.50	.70

STATED PRINT RUN 2500 SERIAL #'d SETS

❑ 1 Brett Favre	10.00	4.50
❑ 2 Dan Marino	10.00	4.50
❑ 3 Emmitt Smith	8.00	3.60
❑ 4 Barry Sanders	10.00	4.50
❑ 5 Eddie George	4.00	1.80
❑ 6 Drew Bledsoe	4.00	1.80
❑ 7 Troy Aikman	5.00	2.20
❑ 8 Terrell Davis	8.00	3.60
❑ 9 John Elway	10.00	4.50
❑ 10 Mark Brunell	4.00	1.80
❑ 11 Jerry Rice	5.00	2.20
❑ 12 Kordell Stewart	1.50	.70
❑ 13 Steve McNair	2.00	.90
❑ 14 Curtis Martin	2.00	.90
❑ 15 Steve Young	2.50	1.10
❑ 16 Dorsey Levens	2.00	.90
❑ 17 Herman Moore	2.00	.90
❑ 18 Deion Sanders	2.00	.90
❑ 19 Thurman Thomas	2.00	.90
❑ 20 Peyton Manning	20.00	9.00

1998 Leaf Rookies and Stars Greatest Hits

	MINT	NRMT
COMPLETE SET (20)	60.00	27.00
COMMON CARD (1-20)	1.50	.70

STATED PRINT RUN 2500 SERIAL #'d SETS

❑ 1 Brett Favre	10.00	4.50
❑ 2 Eddie George	4.00	1.80
❑ 3 John Elway	10.00	4.50
❑ 4 Steve Young	2.50	1.10
❑ 5 Napoleon Kaufman	2.00	.90
❑ 6 Dan Marino	10.00	4.50
❑ 7 Drew Bledsoe	4.00	1.80
❑ 8 Mark Brunell	4.00	1.80
❑ 9 Warrick Dunn	3.00	1.35
❑ 10 Dorsey Levens	2.00	.90
❑ 11 Emmitt Smith	8.00	3.60
❑ 12 Troy Aikman	5.00	2.20
❑ 13 Jerry Rice	5.00	2.20
❑ 14 Jake Plummer	5.00	2.20
❑ 15 Herman Moore	2.00	.90
❑ 16 Barry Sanders	10.00	4.50
❑ 17 Terrell Davis	8.00	3.60
❑ 18 Kordell Stewart	1.50	.70
❑ 19 Jerome Bettis	2.00	.90
❑ 20 Isaac Bruce	2.00	.90

1998 Leaf Rookies and Stars MVP Contenders

	MINT	NRMT
COMPLETE SET (20)	60.00	27.00
COMMON CARD (1-20)	1.50	.70

STATED PRINT RUN 2500 SERIAL #'d SETS

❑ 1 Tim Brown	2.00	.90
❑ 2 Herman Moore	2.00	.90
❑ 3 Jake Plummer	5.00	2.20
❑ 4 Warrick Dunn	3.00	1.35
❑ 5 Dorsey Levens	2.00	.90
❑ 6 Steve McNair	2.00	.90
❑ 7 John Elway	10.00	4.50
❑ 8 Troy Aikman	5.00	2.20
❑ 9 Steve Young	2.50	1.10
❑ 10 Curtis Martin	2.00	.90
❑ 11 Kordell Stewart	1.50	.70
❑ 12 Jerry Rice	5.00	2.20
❑ 13 Mark Brunell	4.00	1.80
❑ 14 Terrell Davis	8.00	3.60
❑ 15 Drew Bledsoe	4.00	1.80
❑ 16 Eddie George	4.00	1.80
❑ 17 Barry Sanders	10.00	4.50
❑ 18 Emmitt Smith	8.00	3.60
❑ 19 Dan Marino	10.00	4.50
❑ 20 Brett Favre	10.00	4.50

1998 Leaf Rookies and Stars Standing Ovation

	MINT	NRMT
COMPLETE SET (10)	30.00	13.50
COMMON CARD (1-10)	1.25	.55

STATED PRINT RUN 5000 SERIAL #'d SETS

❑ 1 Brett Favre	6.00	2.70
❑ 2 Dan Marino	6.00	2.70
❑ 3 Emmitt Smith	5.00	2.20
❑ 4 Barry Sanders	6.00	2.70
❑ 5 Terrell Davis	5.00	2.20
❑ 6 Jerry Rice	3.00	1.35
❑ 7 Steve Young	2.00	.90
❑ 8 Reggie White	1.25	.55
❑ 9 John Elway	6.00	2.70
❑ 10 Eddie George	2.50	1.10

1998 Leaf Rookies and Stars Ticket Masters

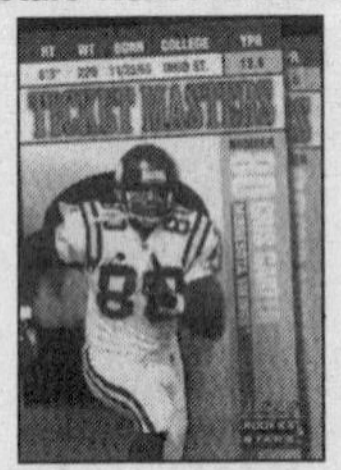

	MINT	NRMT
COMPLETE SET (20)	100.00	45.00
COMMON CARD (1-20)	2.50	1.10
SEMISTARS	4.00	1.80

STATED PRINT RUN 2500 SERIAL #'d SETS
*DIE CUTS: 1.25X TO 3X HI COL.
DIE CUT PRINT RUN FIRST 250 SER.#'d SETS

❑ 1 Brett Favre Dorsey Levens	12.00	5.50
❑ 2 Dan Marino Karim Abdul-Jabbar	12.00	5.50
❑ 3 Troy Aikman Deion Sanders	6.00	2.70
❑ 4 Barry Sanders Herman Moore	12.00	5.50
❑ 5 Steve McNair Eddie George	5.00	2.20
❑ 6 Drew Bledsoe Robert Edwards	5.00	2.20

☐ 7 Terrell Davis / John Elway	12.00	5.50
☐ 8 Jerry Rice / Steve Young	8.00	3.60
☐ 9 Kordell Stewart / Jerome Bettis	5.00	2.20
☐ 10 Curtis Martin / Keyshawn Johnson	2.50	1.10
☐ 11 Warrick Dunn / Trent Dilfer	5.00	2.20
☐ 12 Corey Dillon / Carl Pickens	4.00	1.80
☐ 13 Tim Brown / Napoleon Kaufman	2.50	1.10
☐ 14 Jake Plummer / Frank Sanders	6.00	2.70
☐ 15 Ryan Leaf / Natrone Means	5.00	2.20
☐ 16 Peyton Manning / Marshall Faulk	20.00	9.00
☐ 17 Mark Brunell / Fred Taylor	10.00	4.50
☐ 18 Curtis Enis / Curtis Conway	5.00	2.20
☐ 19 Cris Carter / Randy Moss	30.00	13.50
☐ 20 Isaac Bruce / Tony Banks	2.50	1.10

1998 Leaf Rookies and Stars Touchdown Club

	MINT	NRMT
COMPLETE SET (20)	50.00	22.00
COMMON CARD (1-20)	1.25	.55
STATED PRINT RUN 5000 SERIAL #'d SETS		
☐ 1 Brett Favre	6.00	2.70
☐ 2 Dan Marino	6.00	2.70
☐ 3 Emmitt Smith	5.00	2.20
☐ 4 Barry Sanders	6.00	2.70
☐ 5 Eddie George	2.50	1.10
☐ 6 Drew Bledsoe	2.50	1.10
☐ 7 Terrell Davis	5.00	2.20
☐ 8 Mark Brunell	2.50	1.10
☐ 9 Jerry Rice	3.00	1.35
☐ 10 Kordell Stewart	1.25	.55
☐ 11 Curtis Martin	1.50	.70
☐ 12 Karim Abdul-Jabbar	1.50	.70
☐ 13 Warrick Dunn	2.00	.90
☐ 14 Corey Dillon	1.50	.70
☐ 15 Jerome Bettis	1.50	.70
☐ 16 Antonio Freeman	1.50	.70
☐ 17 Keyshawn Johnson	1.50	.70
☐ 18 John Elway	6.00	2.70
☐ 19 Steve Young	2.00	.90
☐ 20 Jake Plummer	3.00	1.35

1999 Leaf Rookies and Stars

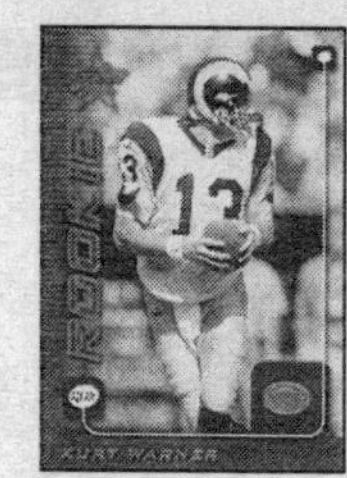

	MINT	NRMT
COMPLETE SET (300)	400.00	180.00
COMP.SET w/o SP's (200)	30.00	13.50
COMMON CARD (1-200)	.15	.07
SEMISTARS	.25	.11
UNLISTED STARS	.50	.23
COMMON ROOKIE (201-300)	2.00	.90
ROOKIE SEMISTARS	3.00	1.35
ROOKIE UNL.STARS	4.00	1.80
ROOKIE SUBSET STATED ODDS 1:2		
☐ 1 Frank Sanders	.25	.11
☐ 2 Adrian Murrell	.25	.11
☐ 3 Rob Moore	.25	.11
☐ 4 Simeon Rice	.15	.07
☐ 5 Michael Pittman	.15	.07
☐ 6 Jake Plummer	.75	.35
☐ 7 Chris Chandler	.25	.11
☐ 8 Tim Dwight	.25	.11
☐ 9 Chris Calloway	.15	.07
☐ 10 Terance Mathis	.25	.11
☐ 11 Jamal Anderson	.50	.23
☐ 12 Byron Hanspard	.25	.11
☐ 13 O.J. Santiago	.15	.07
☐ 14 Ken Oxendine	.15	.07
☐ 15 Priest Holmes	.15	.07
☐ 16 Scott Mitchell	.15	.07
☐ 17 Tony Banks	.25	.11
☐ 18 Patrick Johnson	.15	.07
☐ 19 Rod Woodson	.25	.11
☐ 20 Jermaine Lewis	.25	.11
☐ 21 Errict Rhett	.25	.11
☐ 22 Stoney Case	.15	.07
☐ 23 Andre Reed	.25	.11
☐ 24 Eric Moulds	.25	.11
☐ 25 Rob Johnson	.25	.11
☐ 26 Doug Flutie	.60	.25
☐ 27 Bruce Smith	.25	.11
☐ 28 Jay Riemersma	.15	.07
☐ 29 Antowain Smith	.15	.07
☐ 30 Thurman Thomas	.25	.11
☐ 31 Jonathan Linton	.15	.07
☐ 32 Muhsin Muhammad	.25	.11
☐ 33 Rae Carruth	.25	.11
☐ 34 Wesley Walls	.25	.11
☐ 35 Fred Lane	.25	.11
☐ 36 Kevin Greene	.15	.07
☐ 37 Tim Biakabutuka	.25	.11
☐ 38 Curtis Enis	.50	.23
☐ 39 Shane Matthews	.25	.11
☐ 40 Bobby Engram	.25	.11
☐ 41 Curtis Conway	.25	.11
☐ 42 Marcus Robinson	1.25	.55
☐ 43 Darnay Scott	.15	.07
☐ 44 Carl Pickens	.25	.11
☐ 45 Corey Dillon	.50	.23
☐ 46 Jeff Blake	.25	.11
☐ 47 Terry Kirby	.15	.07
☐ 48 Ty Detmer	.25	.11
☐ 49 Leslie Shepherd	.15	.07
☐ 50 Karim Abdul-Jabbar	.25	.11
☐ 51 Emmitt Smith	1.25	.55
☐ 52 Deion Sanders	.50	.23
☐ 53 Michael Irvin	.25	.11
☐ 54 Rocket Ismail	.25	.11
☐ 55 David LaFleur	.15	.07
☐ 56 Troy Aikman	1.25	.55
☐ 57 Ed McCaffrey	.25	.11
☐ 58 Rod Smith	.25	.11
☐ 59 Shannon Sharpe	.25	.11
☐ 60 Brian Griese	1.00	.45
☐ 61 John Elway	2.00	.90
☐ 62 Bubby Brister	.15	.07
☐ 63 Neil Smith	.25	.11
☐ 64 Terrell Davis	1.25	.55
☐ 65 John Avery	.25	.11
☐ 66 Derek Loville	.15	.07
☐ 67 Ron Rivers	.15	.07
☐ 68 Herman Moore	.50	.23
☐ 69 Johnnie Morton	.25	.11
☐ 70 Charlie Batch	1.00	.45
☐ 71 Barry Sanders	2.00	.90
☐ 72 Germane Crowell	.25	.11
☐ 73 Greg Hill	.15	.07
☐ 74 Gus Frerotte	.25	.11
☐ 75 Corey Bradford	.15	.07
☐ 76 Dorsey Levens	.50	.23
☐ 77 Antonio Freeman	.50	.23
☐ 78 Mark Chmura	.15	.07
☐ 79 Brett Favre	2.00	.90
☐ 80 Bill Schroeder	.25	.11
☐ 81 Matt Hasselbeck	.25	.11
☐ 82 E.G. Green	.15	.07
☐ 83 Ken Dilger	.15	.07
☐ 84 Jerome Pathon	.15	.07
☐ 85 Marvin Harrison	.50	.23
☐ 86 Peyton Manning	2.00	.90
☐ 87 Tavian Banks	.15	.07
☐ 88 Keenan McCardell	.25	.11
☐ 89 Mark Brunell	.75	.35
☐ 90 Fred Taylor	1.25	.55
☐ 91 Jimmy Smith	.25	.11
☐ 92 James Stewart	.25	.11
☐ 93 Kyle Brady	.15	.07
☐ 94 Derrick Thomas	.25	.11
☐ 95 Rashaan Shehee	.15	.07
☐ 96 Derrick Alexander WR	.25	.11
☐ 97 Byron Bam Morris	.15	.07
☐ 98 Andre Rison	.25	.11
☐ 99 Elvis Grbac	.25	.11
☐ 100 Tony Gonzalez	.25	.11
☐ 101 Donnell Bennett	.15	.07
☐ 102 Warren Moon	.50	.23
☐ 103 Zach Thomas	.25	.11
☐ 104 Oronde Gadsden	.15	.07
☐ 105 Dan Marino	2.00	.90
☐ 106 O.J. McDuffie	.25	.11
☐ 107 Tony Martin	.25	.11
☐ 108 Randy Moss	2.00	.90
☐ 109 Cris Carter	.50	.23
☐ 110 Robert Smith	.50	.23
☐ 111 Randall Cunningham	.50	.23
☐ 112 Jake Reed	.25	.11
☐ 113 John Randle	.25	.11
☐ 114 Leroy Hoard	.15	.07
☐ 115 Jeff George	.25	.11
☐ 116 Ty Law	.15	.07
☐ 117 Shawn Jefferson	.15	.07
☐ 118 Troy Brown	.15	.07
☐ 119 Robert Edwards	.15	.07
☐ 120 Tony Simmons	.15	.07
☐ 121 Terry Glenn	.50	.23
☐ 122 Ben Coates	.25	.11
☐ 123 Drew Bledsoe	.75	.35
☐ 124 Terry Allen	.25	.11
☐ 125 Cameron Cleeland	.15	.07
☐ 126 Eddie Kennison	.25	.11
☐ 127 Amani Toomer	.15	.07
☐ 128 Kerry Collins	.25	.11
☐ 129 Joe Jurevicius	.15	.07
☐ 130 Tiki Barber	.15	.07
☐ 131 Ike Hilliard	.15	.07
☐ 132 Michael Strahan	.15	.07
☐ 133 Gary Brown	.15	.07
☐ 134 Jason Sehorn	.15	.07
☐ 135 Curtis Martin	.50	.23
☐ 136 Vinny Testaverde	.25	.11
☐ 137 Dedric Ward	.15	.07
☐ 138 Keyshawn Johnson	.50	.23
☐ 139 Wayne Chrebet	.25	.11
☐ 140 Tyrone Wheatley	.25	.11
☐ 141 Napoleon Kaufman	.50	.23
☐ 142 Tim Brown	.50	.23
☐ 143 Rickey Dudley	.15	.07
☐ 144 Jon Ritchie	.15	.07
☐ 145 James Jett	.15	.07
☐ 146 Rich Gannon	.25	.11
☐ 147 Charles Woodson	.50	.23
☐ 148 Charles Johnson	.15	.07
☐ 149 Duce Staley	.50	.23
☐ 150 Will Blackwell	.15	.07
☐ 151 Kordell Stewart	.50	.23

Card	Mint	NrMt
☐ 152 Jerome Bettis	.50	.23
☐ 153 Hines Ward	.15	.07
☐ 154 Richard Huntley	.15	.07
☐ 155 Natrone Means	.25	.11
☐ 156 Mikhael Ricks	.15	.07
☐ 157 Junior Seau	.25	.11
☐ 158 Jim Harbaugh	.25	.11
☐ 159 Ryan Leaf	.50	.23
☐ 160 Erik Kramer	.15	.07
☐ 161 Terrell Owens	.50	.23
☐ 162 J.J. Stokes	.25	.11
☐ 163 Lawrence Phillips	.25	.11
☐ 164 Charlie Garner	.25	.11
☐ 165 Jerry Rice	1.25	.55
☐ 166 Garrison Hearst	.25	.11
☐ 167 Steve Young	.75	.35
☐ 168 Derrick Mayes	.25	.11
☐ 169 Ahman Green	.25	.11
☐ 170 Joey Galloway	.50	.23
☐ 171 Ricky Watters	.25	.11
☐ 172 Jon Kitna	.60	.25
☐ 173 Sean Dawkins	.15	.07
☐ 174 Az-Zahir Hakim	.15	.07
☐ 175 Robert Holcombe	.15	.07
☐ 176 Isaac Bruce	.50	.23
☐ 177 Amp Lee	.15	.07
☐ 178 Marshall Faulk	.50	.23
☐ 179 Trent Green	.25	.11
☐ 180 Eric Zeier	.25	.11
☐ 181 Bert Emanuel	.25	.11
☐ 182 Jacquez Green	.25	.11
☐ 183 Reidel Anthony	.25	.11
☐ 184 Warren Sapp	.15	.07
☐ 185 Mike Alstott	.50	.23
☐ 186 Warrick Dunn	.50	.23
☐ 187 Trent Dilfer	.50	.23
☐ 188 Neil O'Donnell	.25	.11
☐ 189 Eddie George	.60	.25
☐ 190 Yancey Thigpen	.15	.07
☐ 191 Steve McNair	.50	.23
☐ 192 Kevin Dyson	.25	.11
☐ 193 Frank Wycheck	.15	.07
☐ 194 Stephen Davis	.50	.23
☐ 195 Stephen Alexander	.15	.07
☐ 196 Darrell Green	.15	.07
☐ 197 Skip Hicks	.25	.11
☐ 198 Brad Johnson	.50	.23
☐ 199 Michael Westbrook	.25	.11
☐ 200 Albert Connell	.15	.07
☐ 201 David Boston RC	8.00	3.60
☐ 202 Joel Makovicka RC	4.00	1.80
☐ 203 Chris Greisen RC	6.00	2.70
☐ 204 Jeff Paulk RC	3.00	1.35
☐ 205 Reginald Kelly RC	3.00	1.35
☐ 206 Chris McAlister RC	3.00	1.35
☐ 207 Brandon Stokley RC	3.00	1.35
☐ 208 Antoine Winfield RC	3.00	1.35
☐ 209 Bobby Collins RC	4.00	1.80
☐ 210 Peerless Price RC	8.00	3.60
☐ 211 Shawn Bryson RC	3.00	1.35
☐ 212 Sheldon Jackson RC	3.00	1.35
☐ 213 Kamil Loud RC	3.00	1.35
☐ 214 D'Wayne Bates RC	3.00	1.35
☐ 215 Jerry Azumah RC	3.00	1.35
☐ 216 Marty Booker RC	4.00	1.80
☐ 217 Cade McNown RC	20.00	9.00
☐ 218 James Allen RC	3.00	1.35
☐ 219 Nick Williams RC	3.00	1.35
☐ 220 Akili Smith RC	15.00	6.75
☐ 221 Craig Yeast RC	3.00	1.35
☐ 222 Damon Griffen RC	4.00	1.80
☐ 223 Scott Covington RC	3.00	1.35
☐ 224 Michael Basnight RC	3.00	1.35
☐ 225 Ronnie Powell RC	3.00	1.35
☐ 226 Rahim Abdullah RC	3.00	1.35
☐ 227 Tim Couch RC	40.00	18.00
☐ 228 Kevin Johnson RC	15.00	6.75
☐ 229 Darrin Chiaverini RC	4.00	1.80
☐ 230 Mark Campbell RC	3.00	1.35
☐ 231 Mike Lucky RC	3.00	1.35
☐ 232 Robert Thomas RC	3.00	1.35
☐ 233 Ebenezer Ekuban RC	3.00	1.35
☐ 234 Dat Nguyen RC	4.00	1.80
☐ 235 Wane McGarity RC	3.00	1.35
☐ 236 Jason Tucker RC	15.00	6.75
☐ 237 Olandis Gary RC	20.00	9.00
☐ 238 Al Wilson RC	4.00	1.80
☐ 239 Travis McGriff RC	3.00	1.35
☐ 240 Desmond Clark RC	3.00	1.35
☐ 241 Andre Cooper RC	3.00	1.35
☐ 242 Chris Watson RC	2.00	.90
☐ 243 Sedrick Irvin RC	4.00	1.80
☐ 244 Chris Claiborne RC	3.00	1.35
☐ 245 Cory Sauter RC	3.00	1.35
☐ 246 Brock Olivo RC	3.00	1.35
☐ 247 De'Mond Parker RC	4.00	1.80
☐ 248 Aaron Brooks RC	4.00	1.80
☐ 249 Antuan Edwards RC	3.00	1.35
☐ 250 Basil Mitchell RC	3.00	1.35
☐ 251 Terrence Wilkins RC	12.00	5.50
☐ 252 Edgerrin James RC	60.00	27.00
☐ 253 Fernando Bryant RC	3.00	1.35
☐ 254 Mike Cloud RC	4.00	1.80
☐ 255 Larry Parker RC	3.00	1.35
☐ 256 Rob Konrad RC	4.00	1.80
☐ 257 Cecil Collins RC	4.00	1.80
☐ 258 James Johnson RC	6.00	2.70
☐ 259 Jim Kleinsasser RC	4.00	1.80
☐ 260 Daunte Culpepper RC	20.00	9.00
☐ 261 Michael Bishop RC	6.00	2.70
☐ 262 Andy Katzenmoyer RC	4.00	1.80
☐ 263 Kevin Faulk RC	6.00	2.70
☐ 264 Brett Bech RC	3.00	1.35
☐ 265 Ricky Williams RC	40.00	18.00
☐ 266 Sean Bennett RC	3.00	1.35
☐ 267 Joe Montgomery RC	4.00	1.80
☐ 268 Dan Campbell RC	2.00	.90
☐ 269 Ray Lucas RC	15.00	6.75
☐ 270 Scott Dreisbach RC	4.00	1.80
☐ 271 Jed Weaver RC	2.00	.90
☐ 272 Dameane Douglas RC	3.00	1.35
☐ 273 Cecil Martin RC	3.00	1.35
☐ 274 Donovan McNabb RC	20.00	9.00
☐ 275 Na Brown RC	4.00	1.80
☐ 276 Jerame Tuman RC	3.00	1.35
☐ 277 Amos Zereoue RC	4.00	1.80
☐ 278 Troy Edwards RC	8.00	3.60
☐ 279 Jermaine Fazande RC	3.00	1.35
☐ 280 Steve Heiden RC	2.00	.90
☐ 281 Jeff Garcia RC	12.00	5.50
☐ 282 Terry Jackson RC	3.00	1.35
☐ 283 Charlie Rogers RC	3.00	1.35
☐ 284 Brock Huard RC	6.00	2.70
☐ 285 Karsten Bailey RC	4.00	1.80
☐ 286 Lamar King RC	2.00	.90
☐ 287 Justin Watson RC	3.00	1.35
☐ 288 Kurt Warner RC	80.00	36.00
☐ 289 Torry Holt RC	15.00	6.75
☐ 290 Joe Germaine RC	4.00	1.80
☐ 291 Dre' Bly RC	3.00	1.35
☐ 292 Martin Gramatica RC	2.00	.90
☐ 293 Rabih Abdullah RC	3.00	1.35
☐ 294 Shaun King RC	20.00	9.00
☐ 295 Anthony McFarland RC	3.00	1.35
☐ 296 Darnell McDonald RC	3.00	1.35
☐ 297 Kevin Daft RC	4.00	1.80
☐ 298 Jevon Kearse RC	12.00	5.50
☐ 299 Mike Sellers	.15	.07
☐ 300 Champ Bailey RC	6.00	2.70

1999 Leaf Rookies and Stars Longevity

	MINT	NRMT
COMMON CARD (1-200)	8.00	3.60
*STARS: 25X TO 60X HI COL.		
*YOUNG STARS: 20X TO 50X		
1-200 STATED PRINT RUN 50 SER.#'d SETS		
COMMON ROOKIE (201-300)	10.00	4.50
*RCs: 2X TO 5X		
201-300 STATED PRINT RUN 30 SER.#'d SETS		

1999 Leaf Rookies and Stars Cross Training

	MINT	NRMT
COMPLETE SET (25)	120.00	55.00
COMMON CARD (CT1-CT25)	4.00	1.80
STATED PRINT RUN 1250 SER.#'d SETS		

Card	Mint	NrMt
☐ CT1 Champ Bailey	4.00	1.80
☐ CT2 Mark Brunell	6.00	2.70
☐ CT3 Daunte Culpepper	12.00	5.50
☐ CT4 Randall Cunningham	4.00	1.80
☐ CT5 Terrell Davis	10.00	4.50
☐ CT6 Charlie Batch	6.00	2.70
☐ CT7 Dorsey Levens	4.00	1.80
☐ CT8 John Elway	15.00	6.75
☐ CT9 Marshall Faulk	4.00	1.80
☐ CT10 Brett Favre	15.00	6.75
☐ CT11 Doug Flutie	5.00	2.20
☐ CT12 Edgerrin James	30.00	13.50
☐ CT13 Curtis Martin	4.00	1.80
☐ CT14 Donovan McNabb	12.00	5.50
☐ CT15 Steve McNair	4.00	1.80
☐ CT16 Cade McNown	12.00	5.50
☐ CT17 Randy Moss	12.00	5.50
☐ CT18 Jake Plummer	6.00	2.70
☐ CT19 Barry Sanders	15.00	6.75
☐ CT20 Deion Sanders	4.00	1.80
☐ CT21 Akili Smith	8.00	3.60
☐ CT22 Kordell Stewart	4.00	1.80
☐ CT23 Ricky Williams	20.00	9.00
☐ CT24 Charles Woodson	4.00	1.80
☐ CT25 Steve Young	6.00	2.70

1999 Leaf Rookies and Stars Dress for Success

	MINT	NRMT
COMPLETE SET (30)	3000.00	1350.00
COMMON CARD (1-30)	50.00	22.00
SINGLE JERSEY PRINT RUN 200 SER.#'d SETS		
DUAL JERSEYS PRINT RUN 100 SER.#'d SETS		
CARD NUMBERS HAVE DFS PREFIX		

Card	Mint	NrMt
☐ 1 Barry Sanders	150.00	70.00
☐ 2 Emmitt Smith	120.00	55.00
☐ 3 Barry Sanders Emmitt Smith	300.00	135.00
☐ 4 Eddie George	60.00	27.00
☐ 5 Terrell Davis	80.00	36.00
☐ 6 Eddie George Terrell Davis	200.00	90.00
☐ 7 Tim Couch	150.00	70.00
☐ 8 Dan Marino	150.00	70.00
☐ 9 Tim Couch Dan Marino	300.00	135.00
☐ 10 Brett Favre	150.00	70.00
☐ 11 Troy Aikman	100.00	45.00
☐ 12 Brett Favre Troy Aikman	300.00	135.00
☐ 13 Drew Bledsoe	60.00	27.00
☐ 14 Mark Brunell	60.00	27.00
☐ 15 Drew Bledsoe Mark Brunell	150.00	70.00
☐ 16 Randy Moss	150.00	70.00
☐ 17 Jerry Rice	120.00	55.00
☐ 18 Randy Moss Jerry Rice	250.00	110.00
☐ 19 Antonio Freeman	50.00	22.00
☐ 20 Terry Glenn	50.00	22.00
☐ 21 Antonio Freeman Terry Glenn	80.00	36.00
☐ 22 Steve Young	60.00	27.00
☐ 23 Kordell Stewart	50.00	22.00
☐ 24 Steve Young Kordell Stewart	120.00	55.00
☐ 25 Fred Taylor	80.00	36.00
☐ 26 Dorsey Levens	50.00	22.00
☐ 27 Fred Taylor Dorsey Levens	100.00	45.00
☐ 28 Keyshawn Johnson	50.00	22.00
☐ 29 Herman Moore	50.00	22.00
☐ 30 Keyshawn Johnson Herman Moore	80.00	36.00

1999 Leaf Rookies and Stars John Elway Collection

	MINT	NRMT
COMPLETE SET (5)	800.00	350.00
COMMON CARD (JEC1-JEC5)	100.00	45.00

HELMET/SHOES PRINT RUN 125 CARDS
JERSEY PRINT RUN 300 SERIAL #'d CARDS

❑ JEC1 John Elway Home Jer.	100.00	45.00
❑ JEC2 John Elway Away Jer.	100.00	45.00
❑ JEC3 John Elway Shoe ..	200.00	90.00
❑ JEC4 J.Elway Blue Helmet	250.00	110.00
❑ JEC5 J.Elway Orange Hel.	250.00	110.00

1999 Leaf Rookies and Stars Freshman Orientation

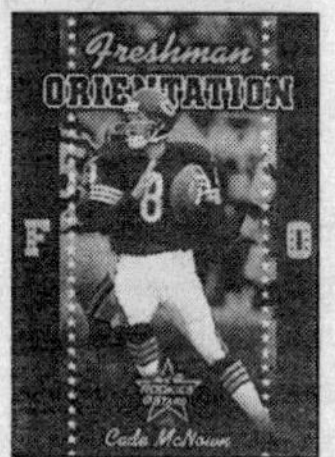

	MINT	NRMT
COMPLETE SET (25)	80.00	36.00
COMMON CARD (FO1-FO25)..	1.50	.70
SEMISTARS........................	2.00	.90

STATED PRINT RUN 2500 SER.#'d SETS

❑ FO1 Champ Bailey............	2.50	1.10
❑ FO2 D'Wayne Bates...........	1.50	.70
❑ FO3 David Boston	3.00	1.35
❑ FO4 Kurt Warner	30.00	13.50
❑ FO5 Cecil Collins	1.50	.70
❑ FO6 Tim Couch	12.00	5.50
❑ FO7 Daunte Culpepper	6.00	2.70
❑ FO8 Troy Edwards............	3.00	1.35
❑ FO9 Kevin Faulk	2.50	1.10
❑ FO10 Joe Germaine...........	2.00	.90
❑ FO11 Torry Holt	5.00	2.20
❑ FO12 Brock Huard.............	2.50	1.10
❑ FO13 Sedrick Irvin	1.50	.70
❑ FO14 Edgerrin James	20.00	9.00
❑ FO15 Kevin Johnson	5.00	2.20
❑ FO16 Shaun King...............	6.00	2.70
❑ FO17 Rob Konrad	2.00	.90
❑ FO18 Sean Bennett	1.50	.70
❑ FO19 Donovan McNabb	6.00	2.70
❑ FO20 Cade McNown	6.00	2.70
❑ FO21 Peerless Price	3.00	1.35
❑ FO22 Akili Smith	4.00	1.80
❑ FO23 Ricky Williams	12.00	5.50
❑ FO24 James Johnson	2.50	1.10
❑ FO25 Olandis Gary	6.00	2.70

1999 Leaf Rookies and Stars Game Plan

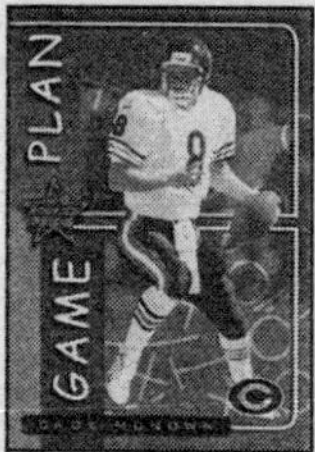

	MINT	NRMT
COMPLETE SET (25)	80.00	36.00
COMMON CARD (GP1-GP25)..	2.50	1.10

STATED PRINT RUN 2500 SER.#'d SETS
*MASTERS: 3X TO 8X HI COL. ....
MASTERS STATED PRINT RUN 50 SER.#'d SETS

❑ GP1 Jamal Anderson..........	2.50	1.10
❑ GP2 Jerome Bettis.............	2.50	1.10
❑ GP3 Drew Bledsoe.............	4.00	1.80
❑ GP4 Tim Brown	2.50	1.10
❑ GP5 Mark Brunell...............	4.00	1.80
❑ GP6 Tim Couch	12.00	5.50
❑ GP7 Terrell Davis...............	6.00	2.70
❑ GP8 Corey Dillon	2.50	1.10
❑ GP9 Warrick Dunn	2.50	1.10
❑ GP10 Brad Johnson............	2.50	1.10
❑ GP11 Brett Favre	10.00	4.50
❑ GP12 Doug Flutie..............	3.00	1.35
❑ GP13 Joey Galloway	2.50	1.10
❑ GP14 Eddie George............	3.00	1.35
❑ GP15 Keyshawn Johnson ..	2.50	1.10
❑ GP16 Peyton Manning........	8.00	3.60
❑ GP17 Dan Marino	10.00	4.50
❑ GP18 Donovan McNabb	6.00	2.70
❑ GP19 Cade McNown	6.00	2.70
❑ GP20 Randy Moss	8.00	3.60
❑ GP21 Jake Plummer	4.00	1.80
❑ GP22 Barry Sanders	10.00	4.50
❑ GP23 Emmitt Smith	6.00	2.70
❑ GP24 Ricky Williams	12.00	5.50
❑ GP25 Steve Young	4.00	1.80

1999 Leaf Rookies and Stars Great American Heroes

	MINT	NRMT
COMPLETE SET (25)	80.00	36.00
COMMON CARD (GAH1-GAH25)	2.50	1.10

STATED PRINT RUN 2500 SER.#'d SETS
CARD NUMBERS HAVE GAH PREFIX

❑ 1 Troy Aikman	6.00	2.70
❑ 2 Jamal Anderson	2.50	1.10
❑ 3 Drew Bledsoe	4.00	1.80
❑ 4 Mark Brunell	4.00	1.80
❑ 5 Cris Carter........................	2.50	1.10
❑ 6 Randall Cunningham........	2.50	1.10
❑ 7 Terrell Davis	6.00	2.70
❑ 8 John Elway	10.00	4.50
❑ 9 Brett Favre	10.00	4.50
❑ 10 Doug Flutie	3.00	1.35
❑ 11 Antonio Freeman..........	2.50	1.10
❑ 12 Eddie George	3.00	1.35
❑ 13 Peyton Manning	8.00	3.60
❑ 14 Dan Marino	10.00	4.50
❑ 15 Curtis Martin	2.50	1.10
❑ 16 Warren Moon	2.50	1.10
❑ 17 Randy Moss	8.00	3.60
❑ 18 Jake Plummer	4.00	1.80
❑ 19 Jerry Rice	6.00	2.70
❑ 20 Barry Sanders	10.00	4.50
❑ 21 Deion Sanders	2.50	1.10
❑ 22 Emmitt Smith..................	6.00	2.70
❑ 23 Fred Taylor	5.00	2.20
❑ 24 Ricky Williams	12.00	5.50
❑ 25 Steve Young	4.00	1.80

1999 Leaf Rookies and Stars Greatest Hits

	MINT	NRMT
COMPLETE SET (25)	60.00	27.00
COMMON CARD (GH1-GH25)	1.25	.55
SEMISTARS...........................	2.50	1.10

STATED PRINT RUN 2500 SER.#'d SETS

❑ GH1 Troy Aikman...............	6.00	2.70
❑ GH2 Terry Glenn	2.50	1.10
❑ GH3 Jamal Anderson..........	2.50	1.10
❑ GH4 Drew Bledsoe	4.00	1.80
❑ GH5 Cris Carter	2.50	1.10
❑ GH6 Terrell Davis...............	6.00	2.70
❑ GH7 John Elway	10.00	4.50
❑ GH8 Brett Favre	10.00	4.50
❑ GH9 Antonio Freeman	2.50	1.10
❑ GH10 Eddie George...........	3.00	1.35
❑ GH11 Priest Holmes	2.50	1.10
❑ GH12 Keyshawn Johnson ..	2.50	1.10
❑ GH13 Dorsey Levens..........	2.50	1.10
❑ GH14 Dan Marino	10.00	4.50
❑ GH15 Curtis Martin	2.50	1.10
❑ GH16 Randy Moss.............	8.00	3.60
❑ GH17 Eric Moulds	2.50	1.10
❑ GH18 Terrell Owens	2.50	1.10
❑ GH19 Carl Pickens.............	1.25	.55
❑ GH20 Jake Plummer	4.00	1.80
❑ GH21 Jerry Rice...............	6.00	2.70
❑ GH22 Barry Sanders	10.00	4.50
❑ GH23 Marvin Harrison	2.50	1.10
❑ GH24 Robert Smith	2.50	1.10
❑ GH25 Fred Taylor	5.00	2.20

1999 Leaf Rookies and Stars Prime Cuts

	MINT	NRMT
COMPLETE SET (15)	2000.00	900.00
COMMON CARD (PC1-PC15)	80.00	36.00

RANDOM INSERTS IN PACKS ....

❑ PC1 Tim Couch	250.00	110.00
❑ PC2 Fred Taylor.............	120.00	55.00
❑ PC3 Terry Glenn	80.00	36.00
❑ PC4 Drew Bledsoe..........	120.00	55.00
❑ PC5 Dan Marino.............	250.00	110.00
❑ PC6 Jerry Rice...............	150.00	70.00
❑ PC7 Barry Sanders	250.00	110.00
❑ PC8 Mark Brunell............	120.00	55.00
❑ PC9 Brett Favre	250.00	110.00
❑ PC10 Steve Young..........	120.00	55.00
❑ PC11 Keyshawn Johnson	80.00	36.00
❑ PC12 Antonio Freeman ..	100.00	45.00
❑ PC13 Randy Moss	250.00	110.00
❑ PC14 Troy Aikman..........	150.00	70.00
❑ PC15 Emmitt Smith	200.00	90.00

1999 Leaf Rookies and Stars Signature Series

	MINT	NRMT
COMMON CARD (SS1-SS30)	50.00	22.00

SINGLE SIGNED PRINT RUN 150 SER.#'d SETS
DUAL SIGNED PRINT RUN 50 SER.#'d SETS
TRADE CARD EXPIRATION 12/31/2000

❑ SS1 Terrell Davis.............	80.00	36.00
❑ SS2 Edgerrin James	300.00	135.00
❑ SS3 Terrell Davis Edgerrin James	350.00	160.00
❑ SS4 Eddie George Trade..	60.00	27.00
❑ SS5 Ricky Williams	175.00	80.00
❑ SS6 Eddie George	350.00	160.00
Ricky Williams		
❑ SS7 Jake Plummer	70.00	32.00
❑ SS8 Donovan McNabb....	120.00	55.00
❑ SS9 Jake Plummer	150.00	70.00
Donovan McNabb		
❑ SS10 Randall Cunningham	50.00	22.00
❑ SS11 Daunte Culpepper	100.00	45.00

		MINT	NRMT
❑ SS12	Randall Cunningham	150.00	70.00
	Daunte Culpepper		
❑ SS13	Fred Taylor	80.00	36.00
❑ SS14	Cecil Collins	50.00	22.00
❑ SS15	Fred Taylor	120.00	55.00
	Cecil Collins Trade		
❑ SS16	Randy Moss	150.00	70.00
❑ SS17	Torry Holt	100.00	45.00
❑ SS18	Randy Moss	300.00	135.00
	Torry Holt		
❑ SS19	Steve Young	60.00	27.00
❑ SS20	Cade McNown	100.00	45.00
❑ SS21	Steve Young	200.00	90.00
	Cade McNown		
❑ SS22	Jerry Rice	100.00	45.00
❑ SS23	David Boston	60.00	27.00
❑ SS24	Jerry Rice	150.00	70.00
	David Boston		
❑ SS25	Doug Flutie	60.00	27.00
❑ SS26	Akili Smith	80.00	36.00
❑ SS27	Doug Flutie	120.00	55.00
	Akili Smith		
❑ SS28	Dan Marino	150.00	70.00
❑ SS29	Tim Couch	150.00	70.00
❑ SS30	Dan Marino	300.00	135.00
	Tim Couch		

1999 Leaf Rookies and Stars Slide Show

	MINT	NRMT
COMP.RED SET (25)	500.00	220.00
COMMON RED (1-25)	12.00	5.50

RED STATED PRINT RUN 100 SER.#'d CARDS
*GREEN STARS: 1X TO 2.5X REDS
*GREEN ROOKIES: .6X TO 1.5X REDS
GREEN STATED PRINT RUN 50 SER.#'d CARDS
*BLUE STARS: 1.5X TO 4X REDS
*BLUE ROOKIES: 1X TO 2.5X REDS
BLUE STATED PRINT RUN 25 SER.#'d CARDS
UNPRICED STUDIOS SERIAL #'d OF 1 SET

		MINT	NRMT
❑ 1	Troy Aikman	30.00	13.50
❑ 2	Drew Bledsoe	20.00	9.00
❑ 3	Mark Brunell	20.00	9.00
❑ 4	Tim Couch	50.00	22.00
❑ 5	Terrell Davis	30.00	13.50
❑ 6	John Elway	50.00	22.00
❑ 7	Brett Favre	50.00	22.00
❑ 8	Antonio Freeman	12.00	5.50
❑ 9	Eddie George	15.00	6.75
❑ 10	Torry Holt	20.00	9.00
❑ 11	Edgerrin James	80.00	36.00
❑ 12	Keyshawn Johnson	12.00	5.50
❑ 13	Jon Kitna	15.00	6.75
❑ 14	Dorsey Levens	12.00	5.50
❑ 15	Peyton Manning	40.00	18.00
❑ 16	Dan Marino	50.00	22.00
❑ 17	Randy Moss	40.00	18.00
❑ 18	Jake Plummer	20.00	9.00
❑ 19	Jerry Rice	30.00	13.50
❑ 20	Barry Sanders	50.00	22.00
❑ 21	Marvin Harrison	12.00	5.50
❑ 22	Emmitt Smith	30.00	13.50
❑ 23	Fred Taylor	25.00	11.00
❑ 24	Ricky Williams	50.00	22.00
❑ 25	Steve Young	20.00	9.00

1999 Leaf Rookies and Stars Statistical Standouts

	MINT	NRMT
COMPLETE SET (25)	100.00	45.00
COMMON CARD (SS1-SS25)	2.00	.90
SEMISTARS	4.00	1.80

STATED PRINT RUN 1250 SER.#'d SETS

		MINT	NRMT
❑ SS1	Jamal Anderson	4.00	1.80
❑ SS2	Jerome Bettis	4.00	1.80
❑ SS3	Drew Bledsoe	6.00	2.70
❑ SS4	Cris Carter	4.00	1.80
❑ SS5	Randall Cunningham	4.00	1.80
❑ SS6	Terrell Davis	10.00	4.50
❑ SS7	John Elway	15.00	6.75
❑ SS8	Marshall Faulk	4.00	1.80
❑ SS9	Brett Favre	15.00	6.75
❑ SS10	Antonio Freeman	4.00	1.80
❑ SS11	Joey Galloway	4.00	1.80
❑ SS12	Eddie George	5.00	2.20
❑ SS13	Garrison Hearst	2.00	.90
❑ SS14	Keyshawn Johnson	4.00	1.80
❑ SS15	Peyton Manning	12.00	5.50
❑ SS16	Steve McNair	4.00	1.80
❑ SS17	Randy Moss	12.00	5.50
❑ SS18	Eric Moulds	4.00	1.80
❑ SS19	Terrell Owens	4.00	1.80
❑ SS20	Jake Plummer	6.00	2.70
❑ SS21	Barry Sanders	15.00	6.75
❑ SS22	Emmitt Smith	10.00	4.50
❑ SS23	Fred Taylor	8.00	3.60
❑ SS24	Vinny Testaverde	4.00	1.80
❑ SS25	Steve Young	6.00	2.70

1999 Leaf Rookies and Stars Statistical Standouts Die Cuts

	MINT	NRMT
COMPLETE SET (25)	1200.00	550.00
COMMON CARD (1-25)	20.00	9.00

RANDOM INSERTS IN PACKS

		MINT	NRMT
❑ 1	Jamal Anderson/12	60.00	27.00
❑ 2	Jerome Bettis/71	20.00	9.00
❑ 3	Drew Bledsoe/37	50.00	22.00
❑ 4	Cris Carter/12	60.00	27.00
❑ 5	Randall Cunningham/52	25.00	11.00
❑ 6	Terrell Davis/48	80.00	36.00
❑ 7	John Elway/47	120.00	55.00
❑ 8	Marshall Faulk/86	20.00	9.00
❑ 9	Brett Favre/63	100.00	45.00
❑ 10	Antonio Freeman/17	50.00	22.00
❑ 11	Joey Galloway/12	60.00	27.00
❑ 12	Eddie George/76	25.00	11.00
❑ 13	Garrison Hearst/51	25.00	11.00
❑ 14	Keyshawn Johnson/60	25.00	11.00
❑ 15	Peyton Manning/26	150.00	70.00
❑ 16	Steve McNair/71	20.00	9.00
❑ 17	Randy Moss/17	250.00	110.00
❑ 18	Eric Moulds/19	50.00	22.00
❑ 19	Terrell Owens/14	50.00	22.00
❑ 20	Jake Plummer/15	80.00	36.00
❑ 21	Barry Sanders/76	80.00	36.00
❑ 22	Emmitt Smith/25	100.00	45.00
❑ 23	Fred Taylor/77	40.00	18.00
❑ 24	Vinny Testaverde/29	20.00	9.00
❑ 25	Steve Young/34	50.00	22.00

1999 Leaf Rookies and Stars Ticket Masters

	MINT	NRMT
COMPLETE SET (25)	100.00	45.00
COMMON CARD (TM1-TM25)	3.00	1.35

STATED PRINT RUN 2500 SER.#'d SETS
*EXECUTIVES: 4X TO 10X HI COL.
EXEC.STATED PRINT RUN 50 SER.#'d SETS

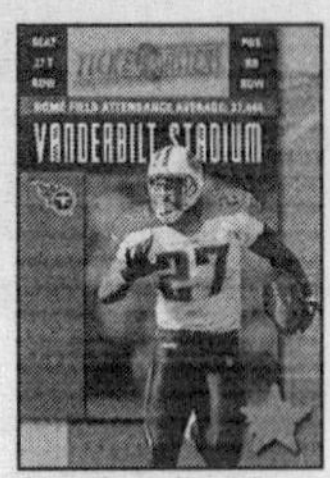

		MINT	NRMT
❑ TM1	Randy Moss	12.00	5.50
	Cris Carter		
❑ TM2	Brett Favre	12.00	5.50
	Antonio Freeman		
❑ TM3	Cecil Collins	12.00	5.50
	Dan Marino		
❑ TM4	Brian Griese	8.00	3.60
	Terrell Davis		
❑ TM5	Edgerrin James	25.00	11.00
	Peyton Manning		
❑ TM6	Emmitt Smith	8.00	3.60
	Troy Aikman		
❑ TM7	Jerry Rice	8.00	3.60
	Steve Young		
❑ TM8	Mark Brunell	6.00	2.70
	Fred Taylor		
❑ TM9	David Boston	5.00	2.20
	Jake Plummer		
❑ TM10	Terry Glenn	5.00	2.20
	Drew Bledsoe		
❑ TM11	Charlie Batch	5.00	2.20
	Herman Moore		
❑ TM12	Mike Alstott	3.00	1.35
	Warrick Dunn		
❑ TM13	Eddie George	4.00	1.80
	Steve McNair		
❑ TM14	Kordell Stewart	3.00	1.35
	Jerome Bettis		
❑ TM15	Chris Chandler	3.00	1.35
	Jamal Anderson		
❑ TM16	Akili Smith	3.00	1.35
	Corey Dillon		
❑ TM17	Curtis Enis	8.00	3.60
	Cade McNown		
❑ TM18	Isaac Bruce	3.00	1.35
	Marshall Faulk		
❑ TM19	Eric Moulds	4.00	1.80
	Doug Flutie		
❑ TM20	Joey Galloway	3.00	1.35
	Ricky Watters		
❑ TM21	Michael Westbrook	3.00	1.35
	Brad Johnson		
❑ TM22	Curtis Martin	3.00	1.35
	Keyshawn Johnson		
❑ TM23	Napoleon Kaufman	3.00	1.35
	Tim Brown		
❑ TM24	Kevin Johnson	15.00	6.75
	Tim Couch		
❑ TM25	Duce Staley	10.00	4.50
	Donovan McNabb		

1999 Leaf Rookies and Stars Touchdown Club

	MINT	NRMT
COMPLETE SET (20)	150.00	70.00
COMMON CARD (TC1-TC20)	5.00	2.20

STATED PRINT RUN 1000 SER.#'d SETS
*DIE CUTS: 2.5X TO 6X HI COL...
DIE CUT STATED PRINT RUN 60 SER.#'d SETS

		MINT	NRMT
❑ TC1	Randy Moss	15.00	6.75
❑ TC2	Brett Favre	20.00	9.00
❑ TC3	Dan Marino	20.00	9.00
❑ TC4	Barry Sanders	20.00	9.00
❑ TC5	John Elway	20.00	9.00
❑ TC6	Terrell Davis	12.00	5.50
❑ TC7	Peyton Manning	15.00	6.75
❑ TC8	Emmitt Smith	12.00	5.50

		MINT	NRMT
❑ TC9	Jerry Rice	12.00	5.50
❑ TC10	Fred Taylor	10.00	4.50
❑ TC11	Drew Bledsoe	8.00	3.60
❑ TC12	Steve Young	8.00	3.60
❑ TC13	Eddie George	6.00	2.70
❑ TC14	Cris Carter	5.00	2.20
❑ TC15	Antonio Freeman	5.00	2.20
❑ TC16	Marvin Harrison	5.00	2.20
❑ TC17	Kurt Warner	30.00	13.50
❑ TC18	Stephen Davis	5.00	2.20
❑ TC19	Terry Glenn	5.00	2.20
❑ TC20	Brad Johnson	5.00	2.20

1997 Leaf Signature

	MINT	NRMT
COMPLETE SET (1-116)	150.00	70.00
COMMON CARD (1-116)	.75	.35
SEMISTARS	1.25	.55
UNLISTED STARS	2.00	.90

8X10s ONE PER LEAF SIGNATURE PACK

		MINT	NRMT
❑ 1	Karim Abdul-Jabbar	2.00	.90
❑ 2	Troy Aikman	5.00	2.20
❑ 3	Derrick Alexander WR	1.25	.55
❑ 4	Terry Allen	2.00	.90
❑ 5	Mike Alstott	2.00	.90
❑ 6	Jamal Anderson	3.00	1.35
❑ 7	Reidel Anthony RC	2.50	1.10
❑ 8	Darnell Autry RC	1.25	.55
❑ 9	Tony Banks	1.25	.55
❑ 10	Tiki Barber RC	2.00	.90
❑ 11	Pat Barnes RC	2.00	.90
❑ 12	Jerome Bettis	2.00	.90
❑ 13	Tim Biakabutuka	1.25	.55
❑ 14	Will Blackwell RC	2.00	.90
❑ 15	Jeff Blake	1.25	.55
❑ 16	Drew Bledsoe	5.00	2.20
❑ 17	Peter Boulware RC	1.25	.55
❑ 18	Robert Brooks	1.25	.55
❑ 19	Tim Brown	2.00	.90
❑ 20	Isaac Bruce	2.00	.90
❑ 21	Mark Brunell	5.00	2.20
❑ 22	Rae Carruth RC	2.00	.90
❑ 23	Ki-Jana Carter	.75	.35
❑ 24	Cris Carter	2.00	.90
❑ 25	Larry Centers	1.25	.55
❑ 26	Ben Coates	1.25	.55
❑ 27	Kerry Collins	1.25	.55
❑ 28	Todd Collins	.75	.35
❑ 29	Albert Connell RC	4.00	1.80
❑ 30	Curtis Conway	1.25	.55
❑ 31	Terrell Davis	8.00	3.60
❑ 32	Troy Davis RC	2.00	.90
❑ 33	Corey Dillon RC	5.00	2.20
❑ 34	Jim Druckenmiller RC	2.00	.90
❑ 35	Warrick Dunn RC	4.00	1.80
❑ 36	John Elway	8.00	3.60
❑ 37	Bert Emanuel	1.25	.55
❑ 38	Bobby Engram	1.25	.55
❑ 39	Boomer Esiason	1.25	.55
❑ 40	Jim Everett	.75	.35
❑ 41	Marshall Faulk	2.00	.90
❑ 42	Brett Favre	8.00	3.60
❑ 43	Antonio Freeman	3.00	1.35
❑ 44	Gus Frerotte	.75	.35
❑ 45	Irving Fryar	1.25	.55
❑ 46	Joey Galloway	2.00	.90
❑ 47	Eddie George	5.00	2.20
❑ 48	Jeff George	1.25	.55
❑ 49	Tony Gonzalez RC	4.00	1.80
❑ 50	Jay Graham	2.00	.90
❑ 51	Elvis Grbac	1.25	.55
❑ 52	Darrell Green	1.25	.55
❑ 53	Yatil Green RC	1.25	.55
❑ 54	Rodney Hampton	1.25	.55
❑ 55	Byron Hanspard RC	2.50	1.10
❑ 56	Jim Harbaugh	1.25	.55
❑ 57	Marvin Harrison	2.00	.90
❑ 58	Garrison Hearst	1.25	.55
❑ 59	Greg Hill	.75	.35
❑ 60	Ike Hilliard RC	2.50	1.10
❑ 61	Jeff Hostetler	.75	.35
❑ 62	Brad Johnson	2.50	1.10
❑ 63	Keyshawn Johnson	2.00	.90
❑ 64	Daryl Johnston	1.25	.55
❑ 65	Napoleon Kaufman	2.00	.90
❑ 66	Jim Kelly	2.00	.90
❑ 67	Eddie Kennison	1.25	.55
❑ 68	Joey Kent	2.00	.90
❑ 69	Bernie Kosar	.75	.35
❑ 70	Erik Kramer	.75	.35
❑ 71	Dorsey Levens	2.00	.90
❑ 72	Kevin Lockett RC	1.25	.55
❑ 73	Dan Marino	8.00	3.60
❑ 74	Curtis Martin	3.00	1.35
❑ 75	Tony Martin	1.25	.55
❑ 76	Leeland McElroy	.75	.35
❑ 77	Steve McNair	3.00	1.35
❑ 78	Natrone Means	2.00	.90
❑ 79	Eric Metcalf	1.25	.55
❑ 80	Anthony Miller	.75	.35
❑ 81	Rick Mirer	.75	.35
❑ 82	Scott Mitchell	1.25	.55
❑ 83	Warren Moon	2.00	.90
❑ 84	Herman Moore	2.00	.90
❑ 85	Muhsin Muhammad	1.25	.55
❑ 86	Adrian Murrell	1.25	.55
❑ 87	Neil O'Donnell	1.25	.55
❑ 88	Terrell Owens	2.00	.90
❑ 89	Brett Perriman	.75	.35
❑ 90	Lawrence Phillips	.75	.35
❑ 91	Jake Plummer RC	10.00	4.50
❑ 92	Andre Reed	1.25	.55
❑ 93	Jerry Rice	5.00	2.20
❑ 94	Darrell Russell RC	.75	.35
❑ 95	Rashaan Salaam	.75	.35
❑ 96	Barry Sanders	8.00	3.60
❑ 97	Chris Sanders	.75	.35
❑ 98	Deion Sanders	2.00	.90
❑ 99	Frank Sanders	1.25	.55
❑ 100	Darnay Scott	1.25	.55
❑ 101	Junior Seau	1.25	.55
❑ 102	Shannon Sharpe	1.25	.55
❑ 103	Sedrick Shaw RC	2.00	.90
❑ 104	Heath Shuler	.75	.35
❑ 105	Antowain Smith RC	3.00	1.35
❑ 106	Bruce Smith	1.25	.55
❑ 107	Emmitt Smith	6.00	2.70
❑ 108	Kordell Stewart	3.00	1.35
❑ 109	J.J. Stokes	1.25	.55
❑ 110	Vinny Testaverde	1.25	.55
❑ 111	Thurman Thomas	2.00	.90
❑ 112	Tamarick Vanover	1.25	.55
❑ 113	Herschel Walker	1.25	.55
❑ 114	Michael Westbrook	1.25	.55
❑ 115	Danny Wuerffel RC	2.00	.90
❑ 116	Steve Young	4.00	1.80

1997 Leaf Signature Autographs

	MINT	NRMT
COMPLETE SET (107)	2500.00	1100.00
COMMON CARD (1-107)	8.00	3.60
SEMISTARS	10.00	4.50
UNLISTED STARS	15.00	6.75
COMMON QB CLUB/500	25.00	11.00
QB CLUB SEMISTARS	40.00	18.00

ONE AUTOGRAPH PER PACK....
REPORTED SIGNING #'s LISTED BELOW
*FIRST DOWN MARKERS: .75X TO 2X
F.D.SET REPORTED TO BE 87-CARDS

FIRST DOWN PRINT RUN 100 SETS

		MINT	NRMT
❑ 1	Karim Abdul-Jabbar/2500	10.00	4.50
❑ 2	Derrick Alexander WR/4000	10.00	4.50
❑ 3	Terry Allen/3000	15.00	6.75
❑ 4	Mike Alstott/4000	15.00	6.75
❑ 5	Jamal Anderson/4000	40.00	18.00
❑ 6	Reidel Anthony/2000	15.00	6.75
❑ 7	Darnell Autry/4000	10.00	4.50
❑ 8	Tony Banks/500	40.00	18.00
❑ 9	Tiki Barber/4000	15.00	6.75
❑ 10	Pat Barnes/4000	15.00	6.75
❑ 11	Jerome Bettis/500	60.00	27.00
❑ 12	Tim Biakabutuka/3000	8.00	3.60
❑ 13	Will Blackwell/2500	15.00	6.75
❑ 14	Jeff Blake/500	25.00	11.00
❑ 15	Drew Bledsoe/500	100.00	45.00
❑ 16	Peter Boulware/4000	10.00	4.50
❑ 17	Robert Brooks/1000	10.00	4.50
❑ 18	Dave Brown/500	25.00	11.00
❑ 19	Tim Brown/2500	15.00	6.75
❑ 20	Isaac Bruce/2500	15.00	6.75
❑ 21	Mark Brunell/500	100.00	45.00
❑ 22	Rae Carruth/5000	10.00	4.50
❑ 23	Cris Carter/2500	15.00	6.75
❑ 24	Larry Centers/4000	10.00	4.50
❑ 25	Ben Coates/4000	10.00	4.50
❑ 26	Todd Collins/4000	8.00	3.60
❑ 27	Albert Connell/4000	20.00	9.00
❑ 28	Curtis Conway/3000	10.00	4.50
❑ 29	Terrell Davis/2500	60.00	27.00
❑ 30	Troy Davis/4000	15.00	6.75
❑ 31	Trent Dilfer/500	40.00	18.00
❑ 32	Corey Dillon/4000	30.00	13.50
❑ 33	Jim Druckenmiller/5000	15.00	6.75
❑ 34	Warrick Dunn/2000	30.00	13.50
❑ 35	John Elway/500	175.00	80.00
❑ 36	Bert Emanuel/4000	10.00	4.50
❑ 37	Bobby Engram/3000	10.00	4.50
❑ 38	Boomer Esiason/500	40.00	18.00
❑ 39	Jim Everett/500	25.00	11.00
❑ 40	Marshall Faulk/3000	15.00	6.75
❑ 41	Antonio Freeman/2000	30.00	13.50
❑ 42	Gus Frerotte/500	25.00	11.00
❑ 43	Irving Fryar/3000	10.00	4.50
❑ 44	Joey Galloway/3000	15.00	6.75
❑ 45	Eddie George/300	100.00	45.00
❑ 46	Jeff George/500	25.00	11.00
❑ 47	Tony Gonzalez/4000	20.00	9.00
❑ 48	Jay Graham/1000	15.00	6.75
❑ 49	Elvis Grbac/500	25.00	11.00
❑ 50	Darrell Green/2500	10.00	4.50
❑ 51	Yatil Green/5000	15.00	6.75
❑ 52	Rodney Hampton/4000	10.00	4.50
❑ 53	Byron Hanspard/4000	15.00	6.75
❑ 54	Jim Harbaugh/500	40.00	18.00
❑ 55	Marvin Harrison/3000	30.00	13.50
❑ 56	Garrison Hearst/4000	10.00	4.50
❑ 57	Greg Hill/4000	8.00	3.60
❑ 58	Ike Hilliard/2000	15.00	6.75
❑ 59	Jeff Hostetler/500	25.00	11.00
❑ 60	Brad Johnson/2000	40.00	18.00
❑ 61	Keyshawn Johnson/1000	40.00	18.00
❑ 62	Daryl Johnston/3000	10.00	4.50
❑ 63	Jim Kelly/500	60.00	27.00
❑ 64	Eddie Kennison/3000	10.00	4.50
❑ 65	Joey Kent/4000	15.00	6.75
❑ 66	Bernie Kosar/500	25.00	11.00

		MINT	NRMT
❑ 67	Erik Kramer/500	25.00	11.00
❑ 68	Dorsey Levens/3000	15.00	6.75
❑ 69	Kevin Lockett/4000	10.00	4.50
❑ 70	Tony Martin/4000	10.00	4.50
❑ 71	Leeland McElroy/4000	8.00	3.60
❑ 72	Natrone Means/3000	15.00	6.75
❑ 73	Eric Metcalf/4000	10.00	4.50
❑ 74	Anthony Miller/3000	8.00	3.60
❑ 75	Rick Mirer/500	25.00	11.00
❑ 76	Scott Mitchell/500	40.00	18.00
❑ 77	Warren Moon/500	50.00	22.00
❑ 78	Herman Moore/2500	15.00	6.75
❑ 79	Muhsin Muhammad/3000	8.00	3.60
❑ 80	Adrian Murrell/3000	10.00	4.50
❑ 81	Neil O'Donnell/500	25.00	11.00
❑ 82	Terrell Owens/3000	30.00	13.50
❑ 83	Brett Perriman/1000	8.00	3.60
❑ 84	Lawrence Phillips/1000	8.00	3.60
❑ 85	Jake Plummer/5000	50.00	22.00
❑ 86	Andre Reed/3000	10.00	4.50
❑ 87	Darrell Russell/2000	8.00	3.60
❑ 88	Rashaan Salaam/3000	8.00	3.60
❑ 89	Barry Sanders/400	200.00	90.00
❑ 90	Chris Sanders/3000	8.00	3.60
❑ 91	Frank Sanders/3000	10.00	4.50
❑ 92	Darnay Scott/2000	10.00	4.50
❑ 93	Junior Seau/500	25.00	11.00
❑ 94	Shannon Sharpe/1000	10.00	4.50
❑ 95	Sedrick Shaw/4000	15.00	6.75
❑ 96	Heath Shuler/500	25.00	11.00
❑ 97	Antowain Smith/5000	10.00	4.50
❑ 98	Emmitt Smith/200	250.00	110.00
❑ 99	Kordell Stewart/500	60.00	27.00
❑ 100	J.J. Stokes/3000	10.00	4.50
❑ 101	Vinny Testaverde/200	60.00	27.00
❑ 102	Thurman Thomas/2500	15.00	6.75
❑ 103	Tamarick Vanover/4000	10.00	4.50
❑ 104	Herschel Walker/3000	10.00	4.50
❑ 105	Michael Westbrook/3000	8.00	3.60
❑ 106	Danny Wuerffel/4000	15.00	6.75
❑ 107	Steve Young/500	120.00	55.00

1997 Leaf Signature Old School Drafts Autographs

	MINT	NRMT
COMPLETE SET (11)	300.00	135.00
COMMON CARD (1-12)	20.00	9.00
SEMISTARS	25.00	11.00
CARD #10 NOT AVAILABLE		
STATED PRINT RUN 1000 SERIAL #'d SETS		

		MINT	NRMT
❑ 1	Joe Theismann	40.00	18.00
❑ 2	Archie Manning	40.00	18.00
❑ 3	Len Dawson	30.00	13.50
❑ 4	Sammy Baugh	60.00	27.00
❑ 5	Dan Fouts	40.00	18.00
❑ 6	Danny White	30.00	13.50
❑ 7	Ron Jaworski	20.00	9.00
❑ 8	Jim Plunkett	25.00	11.00
❑ 9	Y.A. Tittle	40.00	18.00
❑ 11	Ken Stabler	50.00	22.00
❑ 12	Billy Kilmer	25.00	11.00

1995 Metal

	MINT	NRMT
COMPLETE SET (200)	20.00	9.00
COMMON CARD (1-200)	.10	.05
SEMISTARS	.20	.09
UNLISTED STARS	.40	.18

		MINT	NRMT
❑ 1	Garrison Hearst	.40	.18
❑ 2	Seth Joyner	.10	.05
❑ 3	Dave Krieg	.10	.05
❑ 4	Lorenzo Lynch	.10	.05
❑ 5	Rob Moore	.10	.05
❑ 6	Eric Swann	.20	.09
❑ 7	Aeneas Williams	.10	.05
❑ 8	Chris Doleman	.10	.05
❑ 9	Bert Emanuel	.40	.18
❑ 10	Jeff George	.20	.09
❑ 11	Craig Heyward	.20	.09
❑ 12	Terance Mathis	.20	.09
❑ 13	Eric Metcalf	.20	.09
❑ 14	Cornelius Bennett	.20	.09
❑ 15	Bucky Brooks	.10	.05
❑ 16	Jeff Burris	.10	.05
❑ 17	Jim Kelly	.40	.18
❑ 18	Andre Reed	.20	.09
❑ 19	Bruce Smith	.40	.18
❑ 20	Don Beebe	.10	.05
❑ 21	Kerry Collins RC	1.00	.45
❑ 22	Barry Foster	.20	.09
❑ 23	Lamar Lathon	.10	.05
❑ 24	Sam Mills	.20	.09
❑ 25	Tyrone Poole RC	.20	.09
❑ 26	Frank Reich	.10	.05
❑ 27	Joe Cain	.10	.05
❑ 28	Curtis Conway	.40	.18
❑ 29	Jeff Graham	.10	.05
❑ 30	Erik Kramer	.10	.05
❑ 31	Rashaan Salaam RC	.40	.18
❑ 32	Lewis Tillman	.10	.05
❑ 33	Chris Zorich	.10	.05
❑ 34	Jeff Blake RC	1.00	.45
❑ 35	Ki-Jana Carter RC	.40	.18
❑ 36	Carl Pickens	.40	.18
❑ 37	Corey Sawyer	.10	.05
❑ 38	Darnay Scott	.40	.18
❑ 39	Dan Wilkinson	.20	.09
❑ 40	Darryl Williams	.10	.05
❑ 41	Derrick Alexander WR	.40	.18
❑ 42	Leroy Hoard	.10	.05
❑ 43	Michael Jackson	.20	.09
❑ 44	Antonio Langham	.10	.05
❑ 45	Andre Rison	.20	.09
❑ 46	Vinny Testaverde	.20	.09
❑ 47	Eric Turner	.10	.05
❑ 48	Troy Aikman	1.00	.45
❑ 49	Charles Haley	.20	.09
❑ 50	Michael Irvin	.40	.18
❑ 51	Daryl Johnston	.20	.09
❑ 52	Jay Novacek	.20	.09
❑ 53	Emmitt Smith	1.50	.70
❑ 54	Kevin Williams WR	.20	.09
❑ 55	Steve Atwater	.10	.05
❑ 56	Rod Bernstine	.10	.05
❑ 57	John Elway	2.00	.90
❑ 58	Glyn Milburn	.10	.05
❑ 59	Anthony Miller	.20	.09
❑ 60	Mike Pritchard	.10	.05
❑ 61	Shannon Sharpe	.20	.09
❑ 62	Mike Johnson	.10	.05
❑ 63	Scott Mitchell	.20	.09
❑ 64	Herman Moore	.40	.18
❑ 65	Brett Perriman	.20	.09
❑ 66	Barry Sanders	2.00	.90
❑ 67	Chris Spielman	.20	.09
❑ 68	Edgar Bennett	.20	.09
❑ 69	Robert Brooks	.40	.18
❑ 70	Brett Favre	2.00	.90
❑ 71	LeShon Johnson	.20	.09
❑ 72	George Koonce	.10	.05
❑ 73	Reggie White	.40	.18
❑ 74	Gary Brown	.10	.05
❑ 75	Cris Dishman	.10	.05
❑ 76	Mel Gray	.10	.05
❑ 77	Steve McNair RC	4.00	1.80
❑ 78	Webster Slaughter	.10	.05
❑ 79	Rodney Thomas RC	.40	.18
❑ 80	Trev Alberts	.10	.05
❑ 81	Quentin Coryatt	.20	.09
❑ 82	Sean Dawkins	.20	.09
❑ 83	Craig Erickson	.10	.05
❑ 84	Marshall Faulk	.60	.25
❑ 85	Stephen Grant RC	.10	.05
❑ 86	Steve Beuerlein	.10	.05
❑ 87	Tony Boselli RC	.20	.09
❑ 88	Desmond Howard	.20	.09
❑ 89	James O. Stewart RC	2.50	1.10
❑ 90	Marcus Allen	.40	.18
❑ 91	Kimble Anders	.20	.09
❑ 92	Steve Bono	.20	.09
❑ 93	Lake Dawson	.20	.09
❑ 94	Greg Hill	.20	.09
❑ 95	Neil Smith	.20	.09
❑ 96	William White	.10	.05
❑ 97	Tim Bowens	.10	.05
❑ 98	Bryan Cox	.10	.05
❑ 99	Irving Fryar	.20	.09
❑ 100	Eric Green	.10	.05
❑ 101	Dan Marino	2.00	.90
❑ 102	O.J. McDuffie	.40	.18
❑ 103	Bernie Parmalee	.20	.09
❑ 104	Cris Carter	.40	.18
❑ 105	Jack Del Rio	.10	.05
❑ 106	Rocket Ismail	.20	.09
❑ 107	Warren Moon	.20	.09
❑ 108	Jake Reed	.20	.09
❑ 109	Dewayne Washington	.20	.09
❑ 110	Bruce Armstrong	.10	.05
❑ 111	Drew Bledsoe	1.00	.45
❑ 112	Vincent Brisby	.10	.05
❑ 113	Ben Coates	.20	.09
❑ 114	Willie McGinest	.20	.09
❑ 115	Dave Meggett	.10	.05
❑ 116	Chris Slade	.20	.09
❑ 117	Mario Bates	.40	.18
❑ 118	Quinn Early	.20	.09
❑ 119	Jim Everett	.10	.05
❑ 120	Michael Haynes	.20	.09
❑ 121	Tyrone Hughes	.20	.09
❑ 122	Renaldo Turnbull	.10	.05
❑ 123	Ray Zellers RC	.20	.09
❑ 124	Dave Brown	.20	.09
❑ 125	Chris Calloway	.10	.05
❑ 126	Rodney Hampton	.20	.09
❑ 127	Thomas Lewis	.20	.09
❑ 128	Phillippi Sparks	.10	.05
❑ 129	Tyrone Wheatley RC	1.50	.70
❑ 130	Kyle Brady RC	.40	.18
❑ 131	Boomer Esiason	.20	.09
❑ 132	Aaron Glenn	.10	.05
❑ 133	Bobby Houston	.10	.05
❑ 134	Mo Lewis	.10	.05
❑ 135	Johnny Mitchell	.10	.05
❑ 136	Ronald Moore	.10	.05
❑ 137	Greg Biekert	.10	.05
❑ 138	Tim Brown	.40	.18
❑ 139	Jeff Hostetler	.20	.09
❑ 140	Rocket Ismail	.20	.09
❑ 141	Napoleon Kaufman RC	2.50	1.10
❑ 142	Chester McGlockton	.20	.09
❑ 143	Harvey Williams	.10	.05
❑ 144	Fred Barnett	.20	.09
❑ 145	Randall Cunningham	.40	.18
❑ 146	William Fuller	.10	.05
❑ 147	Charlie Garner	.20	.09
❑ 148	Andy Harmon	.10	.05
❑ 149	Ricky Watters	.40	.18
❑ 150	Calvin Williams	.20	.09

		MINT	NRMT
❑ 151	Kevin Greene	.20	.09
❑ 152	Charles Johnson	.20	.09
❑ 153	Greg Lloyd	.20	.09
❑ 154	Byron Bam Morris	.20	.09
❑ 155	Neil O'Donnell	.20	.09
❑ 156	Darren Perry	.10	.05
❑ 157	Rod Woodson	.20	.09
❑ 158	Jerome Bettis	.40	.18
❑ 159	Isaac Bruce	.60	.25
❑ 160	Troy Drayton	.10	.05
❑ 161	Sean Gilbert	.20	.09
❑ 162	Todd Lyght	.10	.05
❑ 163	Chris Miller	.10	.05
❑ 164	Andre Coleman	.10	.05
❑ 165	Stan Humphries	.20	.09
❑ 166	Shawn Jefferson	.10	.05
❑ 167	Natrone Means	.40	.18
❑ 168	Leslie O'Neal	.20	.09
❑ 169	Junior Seau	.40	.18
❑ 170	Mark Seay	.20	.09
❑ 171	William Floyd	.40	.18
❑ 172	Merton Hanks	.10	.05
❑ 173	Brent Jones	.10	.05
❑ 174	Jerry Rice	1.00	.45
❑ 175	Deion Sanders UER Card lists him as a linebacker	.60	.25
❑ 176	J.J. Stokes RC	1.25	.55
❑ 177	Lee Woodall	.10	.05
❑ 178	Bryant Young	.20	.09
❑ 179	Steve Young	.75	.35
❑ 180	Brian Blades	.20	.09
❑ 181	Joey Galloway RC	4.00	1.80
❑ 182	Cortez Kennedy	.20	.09
❑ 183	Kevin Mawae	.10	.05
❑ 184	Rick Mirer	.40	.18
❑ 185	Chris Warren	.20	.09
❑ 186	Lawrence Dawsey	.10	.05
❑ 187	Trent Dilfer	.40	.18
❑ 188	Paul Gruber	.10	.05
❑ 189	Hardy Nickerson	.10	.05
❑ 190	Errict Rhett	.40	.18
❑ 191	Warren Sapp RC	.60	.25
❑ 192	Tom Carter	.10	.05
❑ 193	Henry Ellard	.20	.09
❑ 194	Darrell Green	.10	.05
❑ 195	Brian Mitchell	.10	.05
❑ 196	Heath Shuler	.40	.18
❑ 197	Michael Westbrook RC	2.00	.90
❑ 198	Checklist 1-96	.10	.05
❑ 199	Checklist 97-200	.10	.05
❑ 200	Checklist Inserts	.10	.05
❑ S1	Trent Dilfer Sample	1.00	.45

1995 Metal Gold Blasters

	MINT	NRMT
COMPLETE SET (18)	30.00	13.50
STATED ODDS 1:6		

❑ 1	Troy Aikman	2.50	1.10
❑ 2	Jerome Bettis	1.00	.45
❑ 3	Tim Brown	1.00	.45
❑ 4	Ben Coates	.50	.23
❑ 5	John Elway	5.00	2.20
❑ 6	Brett Favre	5.00	2.20
❑ 7	William Floyd	1.00	.45
❑ 8	Joey Galloway	4.00	1.80
❑ 9	Rodney Hampton	.50	.23
❑ 10	Dan Marino	5.00	2.20
❑ 11	Steve McNair	4.00	1.80
❑ 12	Herman Moore	1.00	.45
❑ 13	Errict Rhett	1.00	.45
❑ 14	Rashaan Salaam	.40	.18
❑ 15	Chris Warren	.50	.23
❑ 16	Michael Westbrook	2.00	.90
❑ 17	Rod Woodson	.50	.23
❑ 18	Steve Young	2.00	.90

1995 Metal Platinum Portraits

	MINT	NRMT
COMPLETE SET (12)	25.00	11.00
STATED ODDS 1:9		

❑ 1	Drew Bledsoe	3.00	1.35
❑ 2	Ki-Jana Carter	1.25	.55
❑ 3	Marshall Faulk	2.00	.90
❑ 4	Natrone Means	1.25	.55
❑ 5	Byron Bam Morris	.60	.25
❑ 6	Jerry Rice	3.00	1.35
❑ 7	Andre Rison	.60	.25
❑ 8	Barry Sanders	6.00	2.70
❑ 9	Deion Sanders	2.00	.90
❑ 10	Emmitt Smith	5.00	2.20
❑ 11	J.J. Stokes	4.00	1.80
❑ 12	Ricky Watters	1.25	.55

1995 Metal Silver Flashers

	MINT	NRMT
COMPLETE SET (50)	50.00	22.00
STATED ODDS 1:2		

❑ 1	Troy Aikman	2.00	.90
❑ 2	Marcus Allen	.75	.35
❑ 3	Jerome Bettis	.75	.35
❑ 4	Drew Bledsoe	2.00	.90
❑ 5	Tim Brown	.75	.35
❑ 6	Cris Carter	.75	.35
❑ 7	Ki-Jana Carter	.40	.18
❑ 8	Ben Coates	.40	.18
❑ 9	Kerry Collins	1.00	.45
❑ 10	Randall Cunningham	.75	.35
❑ 11	Lake Dawson	.40	.18
❑ 12	Trent Dilfer	.75	.35
❑ 13	John Elway	4.00	1.80
❑ 14	Jim Everett	.20	.09
❑ 15	Marshall Faulk	1.25	.55
❑ 16	Brett Favre	4.00	1.80
❑ 17	William Floyd	.75	.35
❑ 18	Jeff George	.40	.18
❑ 19	Rodney Hampton	.40	.18
❑ 20	Jeff Hostetler	.40	.18
❑ 21	Stan Humphries	.40	.18
❑ 22	Michael Irvin	.75	.35
❑ 23	Cortez Kennedy	.40	.18
❑ 24	Dan Marino	4.00	1.80
❑ 25	Terance Mathis	.40	.18
❑ 26	Willie McGinest	.40	.18
❑ 27	Natrone Means	.75	.35
❑ 28	Rick Mirer	.75	.35
❑ 29	Warren Moon	.40	.18
❑ 30	Herman Moore	.75	.35
❑ 31	Byron Bam Morris	.40	.18
❑ 32	Carl Pickens	.75	.35
❑ 33	Errict Rhett	.75	.35
❑ 34	Jerry Rice	2.00	.90
❑ 35	Andre Rison	.40	.18
❑ 36	Rashaan Salaam	.40	.18
❑ 37	Barry Sanders	4.00	1.80
❑ 38	Deion Sanders	1.25	.55
❑ 39	Junior Seau	.75	.35
❑ 40	Shannon Sharpe	.40	.18
❑ 41	Heath Shuler	.75	.35
❑ 42	Emmitt Smith	3.00	1.35
❑ 43	J.J. Stokes	1.25	.55
❑ 44	Chris Warren	.40	.18
❑ 45	Ricky Watters	.75	.35
❑ 46	Michael Westbrook	2.00	.90
❑ 47	Tyrone Wheatley	1.50	.70
❑ 48	Reggie White	.75	.35
❑ 49	Rod Woodson	.40	.18
❑ 50	Steve Young	1.50	.70

1996 Metal

	MINT	NRMT
COMPLETE SET (150)	25.00	11.00
COMMON CARD (1-150)	.10	.05
SEMISTARS	.20	.09
UNLISTED STARS	.40	.18
COMP.PREC.METAL (148)	750.00	350.00

*PREC.METAL STARS: 10X TO 25X HI COL
*PREC.METAL RCs: 6X TO 15X ..
PREC.METAL: STATED ODDS ONE PER BOX

❑ 1	Garrison Hearst	.20	.09
❑ 2	Rob Moore	.20	.09
❑ 3	Frank Sanders	.20	.09
❑ 4	Eric Swann	.10	.05
❑ 5	Jeff George	.20	.09
❑ 6	Craig Heyward	.10	.05
❑ 7	Terance Mathis	.10	.05
❑ 8	Eric Metcalf	.10	.05
❑ 9	Derrick Alexander WR	.20	.09
❑ 10	Andre Rison	.20	.09
❑ 11	Vinny Testaverde	.20	.09
❑ 12	Eric Turner	.10	.05
❑ 13	Jim Kelly	.40	.18
❑ 14	Bryce Paup	.10	.05
❑ 15	Bruce Smith	.20	.09
❑ 16	Thurman Thomas	.40	.18
❑ 17	Bob Christian	.10	.05
❑ 18	Kerry Collins	.40	.18
❑ 19	Lamar Lathon	.10	.05
❑ 20	Tyrone Poole	.10	.05

❑ 21 Curtis Conway .40 .18
❑ 22 Bryan Cox .10 .05
❑ 23 Erik Kramer .10 .05
❑ 24 Rashaan Salaam .40 .18
❑ 25 Jeff Blake .40 .18
❑ 26 Ki-Jana Carter .20 .09
❑ 27 Carl Pickens .40 .18
❑ 28 Darnay Scott .20 .09
❑ 29 Troy Aikman 1.00 .45
❑ 30 Michael Irvin .40 .18
❑ 31 Daryl Johnston .20 .09
❑ 32 Deion Sanders .60 .25
❑ 33 Emmitt Smith 1.50 .70
❑ 34 Terrell Davis 3.00 1.35
❑ 35 John Elway 2.00 .90
❑ 36 Anthony Miller .20 .09
❑ 37 Shannon Sharpe .20 .09
❑ 38 Scott Mitchell .20 .09
❑ 39 Herman Moore .40 .18
❑ 40 Brett Perriman .10 .05
❑ 41 Barry Sanders 2.00 .90
❑ 42 Edgar Bennett .20 .09
❑ 43 Robert Brooks .40 .18
❑ 44 Mark Chmura .20 .09
❑ 45 Brett Favre 2.00 .90
❑ 46 Reggie White .40 .18
❑ 47 Mel Gray .10 .05
❑ 48 Steve McNair .75 .35
❑ 49 Chris Sanders .20 .09
❑ 50 Rodney Thomas .10 .05
❑ 51 Quentin Coryatt .10 .05
❑ 52 Sean Dawkins .10 .05
❑ 53 Ken Dilger .20 .09
❑ 54 Marshall Faulk .40 .18
❑ 55 Jim Harbaugh .20 .09
❑ 56 Tony Boselli .10 .05
❑ 57 Mark Brunell 1.00 .45
❑ 58 Natrone Means .40 .18
❑ 59 James O.Stewart .20 .09
❑ 60 Marcus Allen .40 .18
❑ 61 Steve Bono .10 .05
❑ 62 Neil Smith .10 .05
❑ 63 Tamarick Vanover .20 .09
❑ 64 Eric Green .10 .05
❑ 65 Terry Kirby .20 .09
❑ 66 Dan Marino 2.00 .90
❑ 67 O.J. McDuffie .20 .09
❑ 68 Cris Carter .40 .18
❑ 69 Qadry Ismail .10 .05
❑ 70 Warren Moon .20 .09
❑ 71 Jake Reed .20 .09
❑ 72 Drew Bledsoe 1.00 .45
❑ 73 Ben Coates .20 .09
❑ 74 Curtis Martin .75 .35
❑ 75 Dave Meggett .10 .05
❑ 76 Mario Bates .20 .09
❑ 77 Jim Everett .10 .05
❑ 78 Michael Haynes .10 .05
❑ 79 Tyrone Hughes .10 .05
❑ 80 Dave Brown .10 .05
❑ 81 Rodney Hampton .20 .09
❑ 82 Thomas Lewis .10 .05
❑ 83 Tyrone Wheatley .20 .09
❑ 84 Kyle Brady .10 .05
❑ 85 Hugh Douglas .10 .05
❑ 86 Adrian Murrell .40 .18
❑ 87 Neil O'Donnell .20 .09
❑ 88 Tim Brown .40 .18
❑ 89 Jeff Hostetler .10 .05
❑ 90 Napoleon Kaufman .60 .25
❑ 91 Harvey Williams .10 .05
❑ 92 Charlie Garner .10 .05
❑ 93 Rodney Peete .10 .05
❑ 94 Ricky Watters .20 .09
❑ 95 Calvin Williams .10 .05
❑ 96 Jerome Bettis .40 .18
❑ 97 Greg Lloyd .20 .09
❑ 98 Kordell Stewart .75 .35
❑ 99 Yancey Thigpen .20 .09
❑ 100 Rod Woodson .20 .09
❑ 101 Isaac Bruce .40 .18
❑ 102 Kevin Carter .10 .05
❑ 103 Steve Walsh .10 .05
❑ 104 Aaron Hayden .10 .05
❑ 105 Stan Humphries .20 .09
❑ 106 Junior Seau .20 .09
❑ 107 William Floyd .20 .09
❑ 108 Brent Jones .10 .05
❑ 109 Jerry Rice 1.00 .45
❑ 110 J.J. Stokes .40 .18
❑ 111 Steve Young .75 .35
❑ 112 Brian Blades .10 .05
❑ 113 Joey Galloway .75 .35
❑ 114 Rick Mirer .20 .09
❑ 115 Chris Warren .20 .09
❑ 116 Trent Dilfer .40 .18
❑ 117 Alvin Harper .10 .05
❑ 118 Hardy Nickerson .10 .05
❑ 119 Errict Rhett .20 .09
❑ 120 Terry Allen .20 .09
❑ 121 Brian Mitchell .10 .05
❑ 122 Heath Shuler .20 .09
❑ 123 Michael Westbrook .40 .18
❑ 124 Karim Abdul-Jabbar RC .75 .35
❑ 125 Tim Biakabutuka RC 1.00 .45
❑ 126 Duane Clemons RC .10 .05
❑ 127 Stephen Davis RC 4.00 1.80
❑ 128 Rickey Dudley RC .40 .18
❑ 129 Bobby Engram RC .40 .18
❑ 130 Daryl Gardener RC .10 .05
❑ 131 Eddie George RC 4.00 1.80
❑ 132 Terry Glenn RC 1.50 .70
❑ 133 Kevin Hardy RC .40 .18
❑ 134 Walt Harris RC .10 .05
❑ 135 Marvin Harrison RC 2.50 1.10
❑ 136 Keyshawn Johnson RC 2.50 1.10
❑ 137 Cedric Jones RC .10 .05
❑ 138 Eddie Kennison RC .40 .18
❑ 139 Sam Manuel RC .10 .05
Sean Manuel
❑ 140 Leeland McElroy RC .40 .18
❑ 141 Ray Mickens RC .10 .05
❑ 142 Jonathan Ogden RC .10 .05
❑ 143 Lawrence Phillips RC .50 .23
❑ 144 Kavika Pittman RC .10 .05
❑ 145 Simeon Rice RC .40 .18
❑ 146 Regan Upshaw RC .10 .05
❑ 147 Alex Van Dyke RC .20 .09
❑ 148 Stepfret Williams RC .20 .09
❑ 149 Checklist .10 .05
❑ 150 Checklist .10 .05
❑ P1 Promo Sheet 2.50 1.10
Brett Favre
Trent Dilfer
Dave Meggett

1996 Metal Freshly Forged

	MINT	NRMT
COMPLETE SET (10)	80.00	36.00
STATED ODDS 1:80 HOBBY		

❑ 1 Tim Biakabutuka 5.00 2.20
❑ 2 Jeff Blake 6.00 2.70
❑ 3 Ki-Jana Carter 3.00 1.35
❑ 4 Eddie George 20.00 9.00
❑ 5 Terry Glenn 8.00 3.60
❑ 6 Keyshawn Johnson 12.00 5.50
❑ 7 Curtis Martin 12.00 5.50
❑ 8 Leeland McElroy 2.00 .90
❑ 9 Lawrence Phillips 2.50 1.10
❑ 10 Kordell Stewart 12.00 5.50

1996 Metal Goldfingers

	MINT	NRMT
COMPLETE SET (12)	25.00	11.00
STATED ODDS 1:8		

❑ 1 Isaac Bruce 3.00 1.35
❑ 2 Joey Galloway 5.00 2.20
❑ 3 Michael Irvin 3.00 1.35
❑ 4 Herman Moore 3.00 1.35
❑ 5 Carl Pickens 3.00 1.35
❑ 6 Jerry Rice 8.00 3.60
❑ 7 Chris Sanders 1.50 .70
❑ 8 Frank Sanders 1.50 .70
❑ 9 J.J. Stokes 3.00 1.35
❑ 10 Yancey Thigpen 1.50 .70
❑ 11 Tamarick Vanover 1.50 .70
❑ 12 Michael Westbrook 3.00 1.35

1996 Metal Goldflingers

	MINT	NRMT
COMPLETE SET (12)	40.00	18.00
STATED ODDS 1:12 RETAIL		

❑ 1 Troy Aikman 6.00 2.70
❑ 2 Steve Bono .60 .25
❑ 3 Kerry Collins 2.50 1.10
❑ 4 Trent Dilfer 2.50 1.10
❑ 5 Brett Favre 12.00 5.50
❑ 6 Gus Frerotte 1.25 .55
❑ 7 Stan Humphries 1.25 .55
❑ 8 Dan Marino 12.00 5.50
❑ 9 Steve McNair 5.00 2.20
❑ 10 Scott Mitchell 1.25 .55
❑ 11 Steve Young 5.00 2.20
❑ 12 Eric Zeier 2.50 1.10

1996 Metal Molten Metal

	MINT	NRMT
COMPLETE SET (10)	100.00	45.00
STATED ODDS 1:120		

❑ 1 Troy Aikman 15.00 6.75
❑ 2 Ki-Jana Carter 3.00 1.35
❑ 3 Kerry Collins 6.00 2.70
❑ 4 Terrell Davis 50.00 22.00
❑ 5 Marshall Faulk 6.00 2.70

❑ 6 Brett Favre	30.00	13.50
❑ 7 Keyshawn Johnson	12.00	5.50
❑ 8 Curtis Martin	12.00	5.50
❑ 9 Deion Sanders	10.00	4.50
❑ 10 Emmitt Smith	25.00	11.00

1996 Metal Platinum Portraits

	MINT	NRMT
COMPLETE SET (10)	100.00	45.00
1-10: STATED ODDS 1:50		
11-12: AVAIL.VIA WRAPPER OFFER		
❑ 1 Isaac Bruce	6.00	2.70
❑ 2 Terrell Davis	25.00	11.00
❑ 3 John Elway	25.00	11.00
❑ 4 Joey Galloway	8.00	3.60
❑ 5 Steve McNair	12.00	5.50
❑ 6 Errict Rhett	4.00	1.80
❑ 7 Rashaan Salaam	4.00	1.80
❑ 8 Barry Sanders	30.00	13.50
❑ 9 Chris Warren	4.00	1.80
❑ 10 Steve Young	15.00	6.75
❑ 11 Eddie George	30.00	13.50
❑ 12 Simeon Rice	6.00	2.70

1997 Metal Universe

	MINT	NRMT
COMPLETE SET (200)	20.00	9.00
COMMON CARD (1-200)	.10	.05
SEMISTARS	.20	.09
UNLISTED STARS	.40	.18
COMP.PREC.METAL (200)	800.00	350.00
*PREC.METAL STARS: 15X TO 40X HI COL.		
*PREC.METAL RCs: 6X TO 15X		
STATED PRINT RUN 150 SERIAL #'D SETS		
*GREEN CARDS: 5X TO 10X GEMS		
FIRST 15 CARDS OF PRINT RUN WERE GREEN		
❑ 1 Terry Glenn	.40	.18
❑ 2 Terry Kirby	.20	.09
❑ 3 Thomas Lewis	.10	.05
❑ 4 Tim Biakabutuka	.20	.09
❑ 5 Tim Brown	.40	.18
❑ 6 Todd Collins	.10	.05
❑ 7 Tony Banks	.20	.09
❑ 8 Tony Brackens	.10	.05
❑ 9 Tony Martin	.20	.09
❑ 10 Trent Dilfer	.40	.18
❑ 11 Troy Aikman	1.00	.45
❑ 12 Ty Detmer	.20	.09
❑ 13 Tyrone Wheatley	.20	.09
❑ 14 Vinny Testaverde	.20	.09
❑ 15 Wayne Chrebet	.40	.18
❑ 16 Wesley Walls	.20	.09
❑ 17 William Floyd	.20	.09
❑ 18 Willie McGinest	.10	.05
❑ 19 Yancey Thigpen	.20	.09
❑ 20 Zach Thomas	.20	.09
❑ 21 Terry Allen	.40	.18
❑ 22 Terrell Owens	.40	.18
❑ 23 Terrell Davis	1.50	.70
❑ 24 Terance Mathis	.20	.09
❑ 25 Ted Johnson	.10	.05
❑ 26 Tamarick Vanover	.20	.09
❑ 27 Steve Young	.75	.35
❑ 28 Steve McNair	.75	.35
❑ 29 Stan Humphries	.20	.09
❑ 30 Simeon Rice	.20	.09
❑ 31 Shannon Sharpe	.20	.09
❑ 32 Sean Jones	.10	.05
❑ 33 Scott Mitchell	.20	.09
❑ 34 Sam Mills	.10	.05
❑ 35 Rodney Hampton	.20	.09
❑ 36 Rod Woodson	.20	.09
❑ 37 Robert Smith	.20	.09
❑ 38 Rob Moore	.20	.09
❑ 39 Ricky Watters	.20	.09
❑ 40 Rickey Dudley	.20	.09
❑ 41 Rick Mirer	.10	.05
❑ 42 Reggie White	.40	.18
❑ 43 Ray Zellars	.10	.05
❑ 44 Ray Lewis	.10	.05
❑ 45 Rashaan Salaam	.10	.05
❑ 46 Quentin Coryatt	.10	.05
❑ 47 Qadry Ismail	.20	.09
❑ 48 O.J. McDuffie	.20	.09
❑ 49 Nilo Silvan	.10	.05
❑ 50 Neil Smith	.20	.09
❑ 51 Neil O'Donnell	.20	.09
❑ 52 Natrone Means	.40	.18
❑ 53 Napoleon Kaufman	.40	.18
❑ 54 Mike Tomczak	.10	.05
❑ 55 Mike Alstott	.40	.18
❑ 56 Michael Westbrook	.20	.09
❑ 57 Michael Jackson	.20	.09
❑ 58 Michael Irvin	.40	.18
❑ 59 Michael Haynes	.10	.05
❑ 60 Michael Bates	.10	.05
❑ 61 Mel Gray	.10	.05
❑ 62 Marvin Harrison	.40	.18
❑ 63 Marshall Faulk	.40	.18
❑ 64 Mark Brunell	1.00	.45
❑ 65 Mario Bates	.10	.05
❑ 66 Marcus Allen	.40	.18
❑ 67 Lorenzo Neal	.10	.05
❑ 68 Levon Kirkland	.10	.05
❑ 69 Leonard Russell	.10	.05
❑ 70 Leeland McElroy	.10	.05
❑ 71 Lawyer Milloy	.10	.05
❑ 72 Lawrence Phillips	.10	.05
❑ 73 Larry Centers	.20	.09
❑ 74 Lamar Lathon	.10	.05
❑ 75 Kordell Stewart	.75	.35
❑ 76 Kimble Anders	.20	.09
❑ 77 Ki-Jana Carter	.10	.05
❑ 78 Keyshawn Johnson	.40	.18
❑ 79 Kevin Turner	.10	.05
❑ 80 Jermaine Lewis	.40	.18
❑ 81 Jerome Bettis	.40	.18
❑ 82 Jerris McPhail	.10	.05
❑ 83 Joey Galloway	.75	.35
❑ 84 Jerry Rice	1.00	.45
❑ 85 Jim Everett	.10	.05
❑ 86 Jimmy Smith	.20	.09
❑ 87 Jim Harbaugh	.20	.09
❑ 88 John Elway	2.00	.90
❑ 89 John Friesz	.10	.05
❑ 90 John Mobley	.10	.05
❑ 91 Johnnie Morton	.20	.09
❑ 92 Junior Seau	.20	.09
❑ 93 Karim Abdul-Jabbar	.40	.18
❑ 94 Keenan McCardell	.20	.09
❑ 95 Ken Dilger	.10	.05
❑ 96 Ken Norton	.10	.05
❑ 97 Kent Graham	.10	.05
❑ 98 Kerry Collins	.20	.09
❑ 99 Kevin Greene	.20	.09
❑ 100 Kevin Hardy	.10	.05
❑ 101 Jeff Lewis	.10	.05
❑ 102 Jeff George	.20	.09
❑ 103 Jeff Graham	.10	.05
❑ 104 Jeff Blake	.20	.09
❑ 105 Jason Sehorn	.20	.09
❑ 106 Jason Dunn	.10	.05
❑ 107 Jamie Asher	.10	.05
❑ 108 Jamal Anderson	.75	.35
❑ 109 Jake Reed	.20	.09
❑ 110 Isaac Bruce	.40	.18
❑ 111 Irving Fryar	.20	.09
❑ 112 Iheanyi Uwaezuoke	.20	.09
❑ 113 Hugh Douglas	.10	.05
❑ 114 Herman Moore	.40	.18
❑ 115 Harvey Williams	.10	.05
❑ 116 Hardy Nickerson	.10	.05
❑ 117 Gus Frerotte	.10	.05
❑ 118 Greg Hill	.10	.05
❑ 119 Glyn Milburn	.10	.05
❑ 120 Frank Wycheck	.10	.05
❑ 121 Frank Sanders	.20	.09
❑ 122 Errict Rhett	.10	.05
❑ 123 Erik Kramer	.10	.05
❑ 124 Eric Moulds	.40	.18
❑ 125 Eric Metcalf	.20	.09
❑ 126 Emmitt Smith	1.50	.70
❑ 127 Edgar Bennett	.20	.09
❑ 128 Eddie Kennison	.20	.09
❑ 129 Eddie George	1.00	.45
❑ 130 Drew Bledsoe	1.00	.45
❑ 131 Dorsey Levens	.40	.18
❑ 132 Desmond Howard	.20	.09
❑ 133 Derrick Thomas	.20	.09
❑ 134 Derrick Alexander WR	.20	.09
❑ 135 Deion Sanders	.40	.18
❑ 136 Dave Brown	.10	.05
❑ 137 Daryl Johnston	.20	.09
❑ 138 Darnay Scott	.20	.09
❑ 139 Darick Holmes	.10	.05
❑ 140 Dan Marino	2.00	.90
❑ 141 Curtis Martin	.75	.35
❑ 142 Curtis Conway	.20	.09
❑ 143 Cris Carter	.40	.18
❑ 144 Chris Warren	.20	.09
❑ 145 Chris T. Jones	.10	.05
❑ 146 Chris Slade	.10	.05
❑ 147 Chris Sanders	.10	.05
❑ 148 Chester McGlockton	.10	.05
❑ 149 Charlie Jones	.20	.09
❑ 150 Charles Way	.20	.09
❑ 151 Carl Pickens	.40	.18
❑ 152 Bryan Still	.10	.05
❑ 153 Bruce Smith	.20	.09
❑ 154 Brian Mitchell	.10	.05
❑ 155 Brett Perriman	.10	.05
❑ 156 Brett Favre	2.00	.90
❑ 157 Brad Johnson	.60	.25
❑ 158 Thurman Thomas	.40	.18
❑ 159 Bobby Engram	.20	.09
❑ 160 Bert Emanuel	.20	.09
❑ 161 Ben Coates	.20	.09
❑ 162 Barry Sanders	2.00	.90
❑ 163 Byron Bam Morris	.10	.05
❑ 164 Ashley Ambrose	.10	.05
❑ 165 Antonio Freeman	.75	.35
❑ 166 Anthony Miller	.10	.05
❑ 167 Anthony Johnson	.10	.05
❑ 168 Andre Rison	.20	.09
❑ 169 Andre Reed	.20	.09
❑ 170 Alex Molden	.10	.05
❑ 171 Aeneas Williams	.10	.05
❑ 172 Adrian Murrell	.20	.09
❑ 173 Aaron Hayden	.10	.05
❑ 174 Darnell Autry RC	.20	.09
❑ 175 Orlando Pace RC	.10	.05
❑ 176 Darrell Russell RC	.10	.05
❑ 177 Peter Boulware RC	.20	.09
❑ 178 Shawn Springs RC	.20	.09
❑ 179 Bryant Westbrook RC	.10	.05
❑ 180 Dwayne Rudd RC	.10	.05
❑ 181 Rae Carruth RC	.40	.18

	MINT	NRMT
❑ 182 Troy Davis RC	.40	.18
❑ 183 Antowain Smith RC	1.50	.70
❑ 184 James Farrior RC	.10	.05
❑ 185 Walter Jones RC	.10	.05
❑ 186 Sam Madison RC	.10	.05
❑ 187 Tom Knight RC	.10	.05
❑ 188 Reidel Anthony RC	1.25	.55
❑ 189 Warrick Dunn RC	2.00	.90
❑ 190 Reinard Wilson RC	.10	.05
❑ 191 Tyrus McCloud RC	.10	.05
❑ 192 Michael Booker RC	.10	.05
❑ 193 Tony Gonzalez RC	2.00	.90
❑ 194 Pat Barnes RC	.40	.18
❑ 195 Tiki Barber RC	.60	.25
❑ 196 Sedrick Shaw RC	.40	.18
❑ 197 Corey Dillon RC	2.50	1.10
❑ 198 Danny Wuerffel RC	1.00	.45
❑ 199 Checklist (1-152)	.10	.05
❑ 200 Checklist (153-200/inserts)	.10	.05
❑ S1 Terrell Davis Sample	3.00	1.35

1997 Metal Universe Body Shop

	MINT	NRMT
COMPLETE SET (15)	200.00	90.00
STATED ODDS 1:96		
❑ 1 Zach Thomas	6.00	2.70
❑ 2 Steve Young	25.00	11.00
❑ 3 Steve McNair	25.00	11.00
❑ 4 Simeon Rice	6.00	2.70
❑ 5 Shannon Sharpe	6.00	2.70
❑ 6 Napoleon Kaufman	12.00	5.50
❑ 7 Mike Alstott	12.00	5.50
❑ 8 Michael Westbrook	6.00	2.70
❑ 9 Kordell Stewart	25.00	11.00
❑ 10 Kevin Hardy	3.00	1.35
❑ 11 Kerry Collins	6.00	2.70
❑ 12 Junior Seau	6.00	2.70
❑ 13 Jamal Anderson	25.00	11.00
❑ 14 Drew Bledsoe	30.00	13.50
❑ 15 Deion Sanders	12.00	5.50

1997 Metal Universe Gold Universe

	MINT	NRMT
COMPLETE SET (10)	120.00	55.00
STATED ODDS 1:120 RETAIL		
❑ 1 Dan Marino	50.00	22.00
❑ 2 Deion Sanders	10.00	4.50
❑ 3 Drew Bledsoe	25.00	11.00
❑ 4 Isaac Bruce	10.00	4.50
❑ 5 Joey Galloway	20.00	9.00
❑ 6 Karim Abdul-Jabbar	10.00	4.50
❑ 7 Lawrence Phillips	2.50	1.10
❑ 8 Marshall Faulk	10.00	4.50
❑ 9 Marvin Harrison	10.00	4.50
❑ 10 Steve Young	20.00	9.00

1997 Metal Universe Iron Rookies

	MINT	NRMT
COMPLETE SET (15)	80.00	36.00
COMMON CARD (1-15)	1.50	.70
SEMISTARS	3.00	1.35
UNLISTED STARS	4.00	1.80
STATED ODDS 1:24		
❑ 1 Darnell Autry	3.00	1.35
❑ 2 Orlando Pace	1.50	.70
❑ 3 Peter Boulware	3.00	1.35
❑ 4 Shawn Springs	3.00	1.35
❑ 5 Bryant Westbrook	1.50	.70
❑ 6 Rae Carruth	4.00	1.80
❑ 7 Troy Davis	4.00	1.80
❑ 8 Antowain Smith	10.00	4.50
❑ 9 James Farrior	1.50	.70
❑ 10 Dwayne Rudd	1.50	.70
❑ 11 Darrell Russell	1.50	.70
❑ 12 Warrick Dunn	12.00	5.50
❑ 13 Sedrick Shaw	4.00	1.80
❑ 14 Danny Wuerffel	6.00	2.70
❑ 15 Sam Madison	1.50	.70

1997 Metal Universe Marvel Metal

	MINT	NRMT
COMPLETE SET (20)	50.00	22.00
STATED ODDS 1:6		
❑ 1 Barry Sanders	10.00	4.50
❑ 2 Bruce Smith	1.00	.45
❑ 3 Desmond Howard	1.00	.45
❑ 4 Eddie George	5.00	2.20
❑ 5 Eddie Kennison	1.00	.45
❑ 6 Jerry Rice	5.00	2.20
❑ 7 Joey Galloway	4.00	1.80
❑ 8 John Elway	10.00	4.50
❑ 9 Karim Abdul-Jabbar	2.00	.90
❑ 10 Kerry Collins	1.00	.45
❑ 11 Kevin Hardy	.50	.23
❑ 12 Kordell Stewart	4.00	1.80
❑ 13 Mark Brunell	5.00	2.20
❑ 14 Marshall Faulk	2.00	.90
❑ 15 Michael Westbrook	1.00	.45
❑ 16 Simeon Rice	1.00	.45
❑ 17 Steve McNair	4.00	1.80
❑ 18 Terry Glenn	2.00	.90
❑ 19 Tony Brackens	.50	.23
❑ 20 Tony Martin	1.00	.45

1997 Metal Universe Platinum Portraits

	MINT	NRMT
COMPLETE SET (10)	250.00	110.00
STATED ODDS 1:288		
❑ 1 Troy Aikman	20.00	9.00
❑ 2 Terrell Davis	30.00	13.50
❑ 3 Marvin Harrison	8.00	3.60
❑ 4 Keyshawn Johnson	8.00	3.60
❑ 5 Jerry Rice	20.00	9.00
❑ 6 Emmitt Smith	30.00	13.50
❑ 7 Dan Marino	40.00	18.00
❑ 8 Curtis Martin	15.00	6.75
❑ 9 Brett Favre	40.00	18.00
❑ 10 Barry Sanders	40.00	18.00

1997 Metal Universe Titanium

	MINT	NRMT
COMPLETE SET (20)	200.00	90.00
STATED ODDS 1:72 HOBBY		
❑ 1 Barry Sanders	25.00	11.00
❑ 2 Brett Favre	25.00	11.00
❑ 3 Curtis Martin	10.00	4.50
❑ 4 Eddie George	12.00	5.50
❑ 5 Eddie Kennison	2.50	1.10
❑ 6 Emmitt Smith	20.00	9.00
❑ 7 Herman Moore	5.00	2.20
❑ 8 Isaac Bruce	5.00	2.20
❑ 9 Jerry Rice	12.00	5.50
❑ 10 John Elway	25.00	11.00
❑ 11 Keyshawn Johnson	5.00	2.20
❑ 12 Lawrence Phillips	1.25	.55
❑ 13 Mark Brunell	12.00	5.50
❑ 14 Mike Alstott	5.00	2.20
❑ 15 Steve McNair	10.00	4.50
❑ 16 Steve Young	10.00	4.50
❑ 17 Terrell Davis	20.00	9.00
❑ 18 Terry Glenn	5.00	2.20
❑ 19 Tony Banks	2.50	1.10
❑ 20 Troy Aikman	12.00	5.50

1998 Metal Universe

	MINT	NRMT
COMPLETE SET (200)	40.00	18.00
COMMON CARD (1-200)	.10	.05
SEMISTARS	.20	.09
UNLISTED STARS	.40	.18
COMMON ROOKIE (173-197)	.75	.35
ROOKIE SEMISTARS	1.50	.70
COMMON PREC.METAL GEM	12.00	5.50

*PREC.METAL GEM STARS: 50X TO 120X HI
*PREC.MET.GEM YOUNG STARS: 35X TO 70X
*PREC.METAL GEM RCs: 10X TO 25X
PREC.METAL GEM PRINT RUN 50 SER.#'d SETS
UNPRICED GEM MASTERS SERIAL #'d TO 1

	MINT	NRMT
❑ 1 Jerry Rice	1.00	.45
❑ 2 Muhsin Muhammad	.20	.09
❑ 3 Ed McCaffrey	.20	.09
❑ 4 Brett Favre	2.00	.90
❑ 5 Troy Brown	.10	.05
❑ 6 Brad Johnson	.40	.18
❑ 7 John Elway	2.00	.90
❑ 8 Herman Moore	.40	.18
❑ 9 O.J. McDuffie	.20	.09
❑ 10 Tim Brown	.40	.18
❑ 11 Byron Hanspard	.20	.09
❑ 12 Rae Carruth	.20	.09
❑ 13 Rod Smith WR	.20	.09
❑ 14 John Randle	.20	.09
❑ 15 Karim Abdul-Jabbar	.40	.18
❑ 16 Bobby Hoying	.20	.09
❑ 17 Steve Young	.50	.23
❑ 18 Andre Hastings	.10	.05
❑ 19 Chidi Ahanotu	.10	.05
❑ 20 Barry Sanders	2.00	.90
❑ 21 Bruce Smith	.20	.09
❑ 22 Kimble Anders	.20	.09
❑ 23 Troy Davis	.10	.05
❑ 24 Jamal Anderson	.40	.18
❑ 25 Curtis Conway	.20	.09
❑ 26 Mark Chmura	.20	.09
❑ 27 Reggie White	.40	.18
❑ 28 Jake Reed	.20	.09
❑ 29 Willie McGinest	.10	.05
❑ 30 Terrell Davis	1.50	.70
❑ 31 Joey Galloway	.40	.18
❑ 32 Leslie Shepherd	.10	.05
❑ 33 Peter Boulware	.10	.05
❑ 34 Chad Lewis	.10	.05
❑ 35 Marcus Allen	.40	.18
❑ 36 Randal Hill	.10	.05
❑ 37 Jerome Bettis	.40	.18
❑ 38 William Floyd	.10	.05
❑ 39 Warren Moon	.40	.18
❑ 40 Mike Alstott	.40	.18
❑ 41 Jay Graham	.10	.05
❑ 42 Emmitt Smith	1.50	.70
❑ 43 James O. Stewart	.20	.09
❑ 44 Charlie Garner	.10	.05
❑ 45 Merton Hanks	.10	.05
❑ 46 Shawn Springs	.10	.05
❑ 47 Chris Calloway	.10	.05
❑ 48 Larry Centers	.10	.05
❑ 49 Michael Jackson	.10	.05
❑ 50 Deion Sanders	.40	.18
❑ 51 Jimmy Smith	.20	.09
❑ 52 Jason Sehorn	.10	.05
❑ 53 Charles Johnson	.10	.05
❑ 54 Garrison Hearst	.40	.18
❑ 55 Chris Warren	.20	.09
❑ 56 Warren Sapp	.20	.09

❑ 57 Corey Dillon	.50	.23
❑ 58 Marvin Harrison	.20	.09
❑ 59 Chris Sanders	.10	.05
❑ 60 Jamie Asher	.10	.05
❑ 61 Yancey Thigpen	.10	.05
❑ 62 Freddie Jones	.10	.05
❑ 63 Rob Moore	.20	.09
❑ 64 Jermaine Lewis	.20	.09
❑ 65 Michael Irvin	.40	.18
❑ 66 Natrone Means	.40	.18
❑ 67 Charles Way	.10	.05
❑ 68 Terry Kirby	.10	.05
❑ 69 Tony Banks	.20	.09
❑ 70 Steve McNair	.40	.18
❑ 71 Vinny Testaverde	.20	.09
❑ 72 Dexter Coakley	.10	.05
❑ 73 Keenan McCardell	.20	.09
❑ 74 Glenn Foley	.20	.09
❑ 75 Isaac Bruce	.40	.18
❑ 76 Terry Allen	.40	.18
❑ 77 Todd Collins	.10	.05
❑ 78 Troy Aikman	1.00	.45
❑ 79 Damon Jones	.10	.05
❑ 80 Leon Johnson	.10	.05
❑ 81 James Jett	.20	.09
❑ 82 Frank Wycheck	.10	.05
❑ 83 Andre Reed	.20	.09
❑ 84 Derrick Alexander WR	.20	.09
❑ 85 Jason Taylor	.10	.05
❑ 86 Wayne Chrebet	.40	.18
❑ 87 Napoleon Kaufman	.40	.18
❑ 88 Eddie George	.75	.35
❑ 89 Ernie Conwell	.10	.05
❑ 90 Antowain Smith	.40	.18
❑ 91 Johnnie Morton	.20	.09
❑ 92 Jerris McPhail	.10	.05
❑ 93 Cris Carter	.40	.18
❑ 94 Danny Kanell	.20	.09
❑ 95 Stan Humphries	.10	.05
❑ 96 Terrell Owens	.40	.18
❑ 97 Willie Davis	.10	.05
❑ 98 David Dunn	.10	.05
❑ 99 Tony Brackens	.10	.05
❑ 100 Kordell Stewart	.40	.18
❑ 101 Rodney Thomas	.10	.05
❑ 102 Keyshawn Johnson	.40	.18
❑ 103 Carl Pickens	.40	.18
❑ 104 Mark Brunell	.75	.35
❑ 105 Jeff George	.20	.09
❑ 106 Bert Emanuel	.20	.09
❑ 107 Wesley Walls	.20	.09
❑ 108 Bryant Westbrook	.10	.05
❑ 109 Dorsey Levens	.40	.18
❑ 110 Drew Bledsoe	.75	.35
❑ 111 Adrian Murrell	.20	.09
❑ 112 Aeneas Williams	.10	.05
❑ 113 Raymont Harris	.10	.05
❑ 114 Tony Gonzalez	.10	.05
❑ 115 Sean Dawkins	.10	.05
❑ 116 Billy Joe Hobert	.10	.05
❑ 117 James McKnight	.10	.05
❑ 118 Reidel Anthony	.20	.09
❑ 119 Terance Mathis	.20	.09
❑ 120 Darrien Gordon	.10	.05
❑ 121 Dale Carter	.10	.05
❑ 122 Duce Staley	.75	.35
❑ 123 Jerald Moore	.10	.05
❑ 124 Eric Swann	.10	.05
❑ 125 Antonio Freeman	.40	.18
❑ 126 Chris Penn	.10	.05
❑ 127 Ken Dilger	.10	.05
❑ 128 Robert Smith	.40	.18
❑ 129 Tiki Barber	.20	.09
❑ 130 Mark Bruener	.10	.05
❑ 131 Junior Seau	.20	.09
❑ 132 Trent Dilfer	.40	.18
❑ 133 Gus Frerotte	.10	.05
❑ 134 Jake Plummer	1.25	.55
❑ 135 Jeff Blake	.20	.09
❑ 136 Jim Harbaugh	.20	.09
❑ 137 Michael Strahan	.10	.05
❑ 138 Gary Brown	.10	.05
❑ 139 Tony Martin	.20	.09
❑ 140 Stephen Davis	.10	.05
❑ 141 Thurman Thomas	.40	.18
❑ 142 Scott Mitchell	.20	.09
❑ 143 Dan Marino	2.00	.90
❑ 144 David Palmer	.10	.05
❑ 145 J.J. Stokes	.20	.09
❑ 146 Chris Chandler	.20	.09
❑ 147 Darnell Autry	.10	.05
❑ 148 Robert Brooks	.20	.09
❑ 149 Derrick Mayes	.20	.09
❑ 150 Curtis Martin	.40	.18
❑ 151 Steve Broussard	.10	.05
❑ 152 Eddie Kennison UER ('97 stats incorrect)	.20	.09
❑ 153 Kerry Collins	.20	.09
❑ 154 Shannon Sharpe	.20	.09
❑ 155 Andre Rison	.20	.09
❑ 156 Dwayne Rudd	.10	.05
❑ 157 Orlando Pace	.10	.05
❑ 158 Terry Glenn	.40	.18
❑ 159 Frank Sanders	.20	.09
❑ 160 Ricky Proehl	.10	.05
❑ 161 Marshall Faulk	.40	.18
❑ 162 Irving Fryar	.20	.09
❑ 163 Courtney Hawkins	.10	.05
❑ 164 Eric Metcalf	.10	.05
❑ 165 Warrick Dunn	.50	.23
❑ 166 Cris Dishman	.10	.05
❑ 167 Fred Lane	.20	.09
❑ 168 John Mobley	.10	.05
❑ 169 Elvis Grbac	.20	.09
❑ 170 Ben Coates	.20	.09
❑ 171 Rickey Dudley	.10	.05
❑ 172 Ricky Watters	.20	.09
❑ 173 Alonzo Mayes RC	.75	.35
❑ 174 Andre Wadsworth RC	1.50	.70
❑ 175 Brian Simmons RC	.75	.35
❑ 176 Charles Woodson RC	2.50	1.10
❑ 177 Curtis Enis RC	2.50	1.10
❑ 178 Fred Taylor RC	5.00	2.20
❑ 179 Germane Crowell RC	2.50	1.10
❑ 180 Greg Ellis RC	.75	.35
❑ 181 Jacquez Green RC	2.00	.90
❑ 182 Jason Peter RC	.75	.35
❑ 183 John Dutton RC	.75	.35
❑ 184 Kevin Dyson RC	2.00	.90
❑ 185 Kivuusama Mays RC	.75	.35
❑ 186 Marcus Nash RC	2.00	.90
❑ 187 Michael Myers RC	.75	.35
❑ 188 Ahman Green RC	2.00	.90
❑ 189 Peyton Manning RC	10.00	4.50
❑ 190 Randy Moss RC	10.00	4.50
❑ 191 Robert Edwards RC	1.50	.70
❑ 192 Robert Holcombe RC	1.50	.70
❑ 193 Ryan Leaf RC	2.00	.90
❑ 194 Takeo Spikes RC	1.50	.70
❑ 195 Tavian Banks RC	1.50	.70
❑ 196 Tim Dwight RC	2.00	.90
❑ 197 Vonnie Holliday RC	1.50	.70
❑ 198 Dorsey Levens CL	.20	.09
❑ 199 Jerry Rice CL	.40	.18
❑ 200 Dan Marino CL	.75	.35

1998 Metal Universe Decided Edge

	MINT	NRMT
COMPLETE SET (10)	300.00	135.00
COMMON CARD (1-10)	15.00	6.75
STATED ODDS 1:288		
❑ 1 Terrell Davis	50.00	22.00
❑ 2 Brett Favre	60.00	27.00
❑ 3 John Elway	60.00	27.00
❑ 4 Barry Sanders	60.00	27.00
❑ 5 Eddie George	25.00	11.00
❑ 6 Jerry Rice	30.00	13.50
❑ 7 Emmitt Smith	50.00	22.00
❑ 8 Dan Marino	60.00	27.00
❑ 9 Troy Aikman	30.00	13.50
❑ 10 Marcus Allen	15.00	6.75

1998 Metal Universe E-X2001 Previews

	MINT	NRMT
COMPLETE SET (15)	300.00	135.00
COMMON CARD (1-15)	8.00	3.60
SEMISTARS	12.00	5.50
UNLISTED STARS	20.00	9.00
STATED ODDS 1:144		
❑ 1 Barry Sanders	60.00	27.00
❑ 2 Brett Favre	60.00	27.00
❑ 3 Corey Dillon	8.00	3.60
❑ 4 John Elway	60.00	27.00
❑ 5 Drew Bledsoe	25.00	11.00
❑ 6 Eddie George	25.00	11.00
❑ 7 Emmitt Smith	50.00	22.00
❑ 8 Joey Galloway	20.00	9.00
❑ 9 Karim Abdul-Jabbar	20.00	9.00
❑ 10 Kordell Stewart	20.00	9.00
❑ 11 Mark Brunell	25.00	11.00
❑ 12 Mike Alstott	20.00	9.00
❑ 13 Warrick Dunn	20.00	9.00
❑ 14 Antonio Freeman	20.00	9.00
❑ 15 Terrell Davis	40.00	18.00

1998 Metal Universe Planet Football

	MINT	NRMT
COMPLETE SET (15)	50.00	22.00
COMMON CARD (1-15)	2.00	.90
SEMISTARS	2.50	1.10
UNLISTED STARS	3.00	1.35
STATED ODDS 1:8		
❑ 1 Barry Sanders	10.00	4.50
❑ 2 Corey Dillon	2.00	.90
❑ 3 Warrick Dunn	3.00	1.35
❑ 4 Jake Plummer	5.00	2.20
❑ 5 John Elway	10.00	4.50
❑ 6 Kordell Stewart	3.00	1.35
❑ 7 Curtis Martin	3.00	1.35
❑ 8 Mark Brunell	4.00	1.80
❑ 9 Dorsey Levens	3.00	1.35
❑ 10 Troy Aikman	5.00	2.20
❑ 11 Terry Glenn	3.00	1.35
❑ 12 Eddie George	4.00	1.80
❑ 13 Keyshawn Johnson	3.00	1.35
❑ 14 Steve McNair	3.00	1.35
❑ 15 Jerry Rice	5.00	2.20

1998 Metal Universe Quasars

	MINT	NRMT
COMPLETE SET (15)	80.00	36.00
COMMON CARD (1-15)	2.50	1.10
SEMISTARS	4.00	1.80
STATED ODDS 1:20		
❑ 1 Peyton Manning	25.00	11.00
❑ 2 Ryan Leaf	5.00	2.20
❑ 3 Charles Woodson	6.00	2.70
❑ 4 Randy Moss	25.00	11.00
❑ 5 Curtis Enis	6.00	2.70
❑ 6 Tavian Banks	4.00	1.80
❑ 7 Germane Crowell	6.00	2.70
❑ 8 Kevin Dyson	5.00	2.20
❑ 9 Robert Edwards	4.00	1.80
❑ 10 Jacquez Green	5.00	2.20
❑ 11 Alonzo Mayes	2.50	1.10
❑ 12 Brian Simmons	2.50	1.10
❑ 13 Takeo Spikes	4.00	1.80
❑ 14 Andre Wadsworth	4.00	1.80
❑ 15 Ahman Green	4.00	1.80

1998 Metal Universe Titanium

	MINT	NRMT
COMPLETE SET (10)	100.00	45.00
COMMON CARD (1-10)	5.00	2.20
SEMISTARS	8.00	3.60
STATED ODDS 1:96		

	MINT	NRMT
❑ 1 Corey Dillon	5.00	2.20
❑ 2 Emmitt Smith	20.00	9.00
❑ 3 Terrell Davis	20.00	9.00
❑ 4 Brett Favre	25.00	11.00
❑ 5 Mark Brunell	10.00	4.50
❑ 6 Dan Marino	25.00	11.00
❑ 7 Curtis Martin	15.00	6.75
❑ 8 Kordell Stewart	8.00	3.60
❑ 9 Warrick Dunn	8.00	3.60
❑ 10 Steve McNair	15.00	6.75

1999 Metal Universe

	MINT	NRMT
COMPLETE SET (250)	40.00	18.00
COMMON CARD (1-250)	.10	.05
SEMISTARS	.20	.09
UNLISTED STARS	.40	.18
COMMON ROOKIE (207-247)	.40	.18
ROOKIE SEMISTARS	.75	.35
ROOKIE UNL.STARS	1.25	.55
COMMON PREC.METAL GEM	12.00	5.50

*PREC.METAL STARS: 60X TO 130X HI COL.
*PREC.METAL YOUNG STARS: 50X TO 120X
*PREC.METAL GEM RCs: 12X TO 30X
STATED PRINT RUN 50 SERIAL #'d SETS
PREC.METAL GEMS RAND.INSERTS IN HOBBY
UNPRICED GEM MASTERS SERIAL #'d TO 1

	MINT	NRMT
❑ 1 Eric Moulds	.40	.18
❑ 2 David Palmer	.10	.05
❑ 3 Ricky Watters	.20	.09
❑ 4 Antonio Freeman	.40	.18
❑ 5 Hugh Douglas	.10	.05
❑ 6 Johnnie Morton	.20	.09
❑ 7 Corey Fuller	.10	.05
❑ 8 J.J. Stokes	.20	.09
❑ 9 Keith Poole	.10	.05
❑ 10 Steve Beuerlein	.10	.05
❑ 11 Keenan McCardell	.20	.09
❑ 12 Carl Pickens	.20	.09
❑ 13 Mark Bruener	.10	.05
❑ 14 Warren Sapp	.20	.09
❑ 15 Rich Gannon	.20	.09
❑ 16 Bruce Smith	.20	.09
❑ 17 Mark Chmura	.10	.05
❑ 18 Drew Bledsoe	.60	.25
❑ 19 Charles Woodson	.40	.18
❑ 20 Ahman Green	.20	.09
❑ 21 Ricky Proehl	.10	.05
❑ 22 Corey Dillon	.40	.18
❑ 23 Terry Fair	.10	.05
❑ 24 Mark Brunell	.60	.25
❑ 25 Leroy Hoard	.10	.05
❑ 26 La'Roi Glover	.10	.05
❑ 27 Tim Brown	.40	.18
❑ 28 Kevin Turner	.10	.05
❑ 29 Terrell Owens	.40	.18
❑ 30 Mike Alstott	.40	.18
❑ 31 Rob Moore	.20	.09
❑ 32 Troy Aikman	1.00	.45
❑ 33 Derrick Alexander	.10	.05
❑ 34 Chris Calloway	.10	.05
❑ 35 Kordell Stewart	.40	.18
❑ 36 Reidel Anthony	.20	.09
❑ 37 Michael Westbrook	.20	.09
❑ 38 Ray Lewis	.10	.05
❑ 39 Alonzo Mayes	.10	.05
❑ 40 Rod Smith	.20	.09
❑ 41 Reggie Barlow	.10	.05
❑ 42 Sean Dawkins	.10	.05
❑ 43 Duce Staley	.40	.18
❑ 44 R.W. McQuarters	.10	.05
❑ 45 Robert Holcombe	.20	.09
❑ 46 Priest Holmes	.40	.18
❑ 47 Erik Kramer	.10	.05
❑ 48 Shannon Sharpe	.20	.09
❑ 49 Mike Vanderjagt	.10	.05
❑ 50 Cris Carter	.40	.18
❑ 51 Billy Joe Tolliver	.10	.05
❑ 52 Vinny Testaverde	.20	.09
❑ 53 Antonio Langham	.10	.05
❑ 54 Damon Gibson	.10	.05
❑ 55 Garrison Hearst	.20	.09
❑ 56 Brad Johnson	.40	.18
❑ 57 Randall Cunningham	.40	.18
❑ 58 Jim Harbaugh	.20	.09
❑ 59 Curtis Enis	.40	.18
❑ 60 Bill Romanowski	.10	.05
❑ 61 Marcus Pollard	.10	.05
❑ 62 Zach Thomas	.20	.09
❑ 63 Cameron Cleeland	.10	.05
❑ 64 Curtis Martin	.40	.18
❑ 65 Charlie Garner	.20	.09
❑ 66 Jerris McPhail	.10	.05
❑ 67 Jon Kitna	.50	.23
❑ 68 Chris Chandler	.20	.09
❑ 69 Emmitt Smith	1.00	.45
❑ 70 Andre Rison	.20	.09
❑ 71 Wayne Chrebet	.20	.09
❑ 72 Mikhael Ricks	.10	.05
❑ 73 Yancey Thigpen	.10	.05
❑ 74 Peter Boulware	.10	.05
❑ 75 Bobby Engram	.20	.09
❑ 76 John Mobley	.10	.05
❑ 77 Peyton Manning	1.50	.70
❑ 78 O.J. McDuffie	.20	.09
❑ 79 Tony Simmons	.10	.05
❑ 80 Mo Lewis	.10	.05
❑ 81 Bryan Still	.10	.05
❑ 82 Eugene Robinson	.10	.05
❑ 83 Curtis Conway	.20	.09
❑ 84 Ed McCaffrey	.20	.09
❑ 85 Marvin Harrison	.40	.18
❑ 86 Dan Marino	1.50	.70
❑ 87 Ty Law	.10	.05
❑ 88 Leon Johnson	.10	.05
❑ 89 Junior Seau	.20	.09
❑ 90 Terance Mathis	.20	.09
❑ 91 Wesley Walls	.20	.09
❑ 92 John Elway	1.50	.70
❑ 93 Marshall Faulk	.40	.18
❑ 94 Oronde Gadsden	.10	.05
❑ 95 Keyshawn Johnson	.40	.18
❑ 96 Muhsin Muhammad	.20	.09
❑ 97 Dorsey Levens	.40	.18
❑ 98 Shawn Jefferson	.10	.05
❑ 99 Rocket Ismail	.20	.09
❑ 100 Vonnie Holliday	.10	.05
❑ 101 Terry Glenn	.40	.18
❑ 102 Shawn Springs	.10	.05
❑ 103 Tim Dwight	.40	.18
❑ 104 Terrell Davis	1.00	.45
❑ 105 Karim Abdul-Jabbar	.20	.09
❑ 106 Bryan Cox	.10	.05
❑ 107 Steve McNair	.40	.18
❑ 108 Tony Martin	.20	.09
❑ 109 Jason Elam	.10	.05
❑ 110 John Avery	.20	.09
❑ 111 Aaron Glenn	.10	.05
❑ 112 Eddie George	.50	.23
❑ 113 Larry Centers	.10	.05
❑ 114 Darnay Scott	.10	.05
❑ 115 Jimmy Smith	.20	.09
❑ 116 Tiki Barber	.10	.05
❑ 117 Charles Johnson	.10	.05
❑ 118 Mike Archie RC	.20	.09
❑ 119 Adrian Murrell	.20	.09
❑ 120 Dexter Coakley	.10	.05
❑ 121 Dale Carter	.10	.05
❑ 122 Kent Graham	.10	.05
❑ 123 Hines Ward	.10	.05
❑ 124 Greg Hill	.10	.05
❑ 125 Skip Hicks	.20	.09
❑ 126 Doug Flutie	.50	.23
❑ 127 Leslie Shepherd	.10	.05
❑ 128 Neil O'Donnell	.20	.09
❑ 129 Herman Moore	.40	.18
❑ 130 Kevin Hardy	.10	.05
❑ 131 Randy Moss	1.50	.70
❑ 132 Andre Hastings	.10	.05
❑ 133 Rickey Dudley	.10	.05
❑ 134 Jerome Bettis	.40	.18
❑ 135 Jerry Rice	1.00	.45
❑ 136 Jake Plummer	.75	.35
❑ 137 Billy Davis	.10	.05
❑ 138 Tony Gonzalez	.20	.09
❑ 139 Ike Hilliard	.10	.05
❑ 140 Freddie Jones	.10	.05
❑ 141 Isaac Bruce	.40	.18
❑ 142 Darrell Green	.10	.05
❑ 143 Trent Green	.20	.09
❑ 144 Jamal Anderson	.40	.18
❑ 145 Deion Sanders	.40	.18
❑ 146 Byron Bam Morris	.10	.05
❑ 147 Charles Way	.10	.05
❑ 148 Natrone Means	.20	.09
❑ 149 Frank Wycheck	.10	.05
❑ 150 Brett Favre	1.50	.70
❑ 151 Michael Bates	.10	.05
❑ 152 Ben Coates	.20	.09
❑ 153 Koy Detmer	.10	.05
❑ 154 Eddie Kennison	.20	.09
❑ 155 Eric Metcalf	.10	.05
❑ 156 Takeo Spikes	.10	.05
❑ 157 Fred Taylor	1.00	.45
❑ 158 Gary Brown	.10	.05
❑ 159 Levon Kirkland	.10	.05
❑ 160 Trent Dilfer	.20	.09
❑ 161 Antowain Smith	.40	.18
❑ 162 Robert Brooks	.20	.09
❑ 163 Robert Smith	.40	.18
❑ 164 Napoleon Kaufman	.40	.18
❑ 165 Chad Brown	.10	.05
❑ 166 Warrick Dunn	.40	.18
❑ 167 Joey Galloway	.40	.18
❑ 168 Frank Sanders	.20	.09
❑ 169 Michael Irvin	.20	.09
❑ 170 Elvis Grbac	.20	.09
❑ 171 Michael Strahan	.10	.05
❑ 172 Ryan Leaf	.40	.18
❑ 173 Stephen Alexander	.10	.05
❑ 174 Andre Reed	.20	.09
❑ 175 Barry Sanders	1.50	.70
❑ 176 Jake Reed	.20	.09
❑ 177 James Jett	.20	.09
❑ 178 Steve Young	.60	.25
❑ 179 Jermaine Lewis	.20	.09
❑ 180 Charlie Batch	.75	.35
❑ 181 Jacquez Green	.20	.09
❑ 182 Kevin Dyson	.20	.09
❑ 183 Roell Preston PD	.10	.05
❑ 184 Randall Cunningham PD	.40	.18
❑ 185 Charlie Batch PD	.40	.18
❑ 186 Kordell Stewart PD	.40	.18
❑ 187 Bennie Thompson PD	.10	.05
❑ 188 Deion Sanders PD	.40	.18
❑ 189 Jake Plummer PD	.50	.23
❑ 190 Eric Moulds PD	.40	.18
❑ 191 Derrick Brooks PD	.10	.05
❑ 192 Steve McNair PD	.40	.18
❑ 193 Ryan Leaf PD	.20	.09
❑ 194 Keyshawn Johnson PD	.40	.18
❑ 195 Eddie George PD	.40	.18
❑ 196 Warrick Dunn PD	.40	.18
❑ 197 Jessie Tuggle PD	.10	.05
❑ 198 Rodney Harrison PD	.10	.05
❑ 199 Vinny Testaverde PD	.20	.09
❑ 200 Marshall Faulk PD	.40	.18
❑ 201 Ray Buchanan PD	.10	.05
❑ 202 Garrison Hearst PD	.20	.09

❑ 203 John Randle PD	.20	.09
❑ 204 Drew Bledsoe PD	.40	.18
❑ 205 Sam Gash PD	.10	.05
❑ 206 Troy Aikman PD	.50	.23
❑ 207 Michael McCrary	.10	.05
❑ 208 Chris Claiborne RC	.75	.35
❑ 209 Ricky Williams RC	6.00	2.70
❑ 210 Tim Couch RC	6.00	2.70
❑ 211 Champ Bailey RC	1.50	.70
❑ 212 Torry Holt RC	3.00	1.35
❑ 213 Donovan McNabb RC	4.00	1.80
❑ 214 David Boston RC	2.00	.90
❑ 215 Chris McAlister RC	.75	.35
❑ 216 Aaron Gibson RC	.10	.05
❑ 217 Daunte Culpepper RC	4.00	1.80
❑ 218 Matt Stinchcomb RC	.40	.18
❑ 219 Edgerrin James RC	12.00	5.50
❑ 220 Jevon Kearse RC	2.50	1.10
❑ 221 Ebenezer Ekuban RC	.75	.35
❑ 222 Kris Farris RC	.40	.18
❑ 223 Chris Terry RC	.40	.18
❑ 224 Cecil Collins RC	1.25	.55
❑ 225 Akili Smith RC	2.50	1.10
❑ 226 Shaun King RC	4.00	1.80
❑ 227 Rahim Abdullah RC	.75	.35
❑ 228 Peerless Price RC	2.00	.90
❑ 229 Antoine Winfield RC	.75	.35
❑ 230 Antuan Edwards RC	.40	.18
❑ 231 Rob Konrad RC	.75	.35
❑ 232 Troy Edwards RC	2.00	.90
❑ 233 John Thornton RC	.40	.18
❑ 234 Fred Vinson RC	.40	.18
❑ 235 Gary Stills RC	.40	.18
❑ 236 Desmond Clark RC	.75	.35
❑ 237 Lamar King RC	.40	.18
❑ 238 Jared DeVries RC	.75	.35
❑ 239 Martin Gramatica RC	.40	.18
❑ 240 Montae Reagor RC	.40	.18
❑ 241 Andy Katzenmoyer RC	1.25	.55
❑ 242 Rufus French RC	.40	.18
❑ 243 D'Wayne Bates RC	.75	.35
❑ 244 Amos Zereoue RC	1.25	.55
❑ 245 Dre' Bly RC	.75	.35
❑ 246 Kevin Johnson RC	3.00	1.35
❑ 247 Cade McNown RC	4.00	1.80
❑ 248 Kordell Stewart CL	.40	.18
❑ 249 Deion Sanders CL	.40	.18
❑ 250 Vinny Testaverde CL	.20	.09
❑ P1 Doug Flutie Promo	.40	.18

1999 Metal Universe Linchpins

	MINT	NRMT
COMPLETE SET (10)	250.00	110.00
COMMON CARD (LP1-LP10)	15.00	6.75
STATED ODDS 1:360 HOB, 1:480 RET		

❑ LP1 Emmitt Smith	30.00	13.50
❑ LP2 Charlie Batch	15.00	6.75
❑ LP3 Fred Taylor	25.00	11.00
❑ LP4 Jake Plummer	25.00	11.00
❑ LP5 Brett Favre	50.00	22.00
❑ LP6 Barry Sanders	50.00	22.00
❑ LP7 Mark Brunell	20.00	9.00
❑ LP8 Peyton Manning	40.00	18.00
❑ LP9 Randy Moss	40.00	18.00
❑ LP10 Terrell Davis	30.00	13.50

1999 Metal Universe Planet Metal

	MINT	NRMT
COMPLETE SET (15)	150.00	70.00
COMMON CARD (PM1-PM15)	5.00	2.20
STATED ODDS 1:36 HOB, 1:48 RET		

❑ PM1 Terrell Davis	12.00	5.50
❑ PM2 Troy Aikman	12.00	5.50
❑ PM3 Peyton Manning	15.00	6.75
❑ PM4 Mark Brunell	8.00	3.60
❑ PM5 John Elway	20.00	9.00
❑ PM6 Doug Flutie	6.00	2.70
❑ PM7 Dan Marino	20.00	9.00

❑ PM8 Brett Favre	20.00	9.00
❑ PM9 Barry Sanders	20.00	9.00
❑ PM10 Emmitt Smith	12.00	5.50
❑ PM11 Fred Taylor	10.00	4.50
❑ PM12 Jerry Rice	12.00	5.50
❑ PM13 Jamal Anderson	5.00	2.20
❑ PM14 Randall Cunningham	5.00	2.20
❑ PM15 Randy Moss	15.00	6.75

1999 Metal Universe Quasars

	MINT	NRMT
COMPLETE SET (15)	80.00	36.00
COMMON CARD (QS1-QS15)	2.50	1.10
SEMISTARS	3.00	1.35
STATED ODDS 1:18 HOB, 1:24 RET		
*PRISMS: .75X TO 2X HI COL.		
PRISMS PRINT RUN 99 SERIAL #'d SETS		

❑ QS1 Ricky Williams	12.00	5.50
❑ QS2 Tim Couch	12.00	5.50
❑ QS3 Shaun King	8.00	3.60
❑ QS4 Champ Bailey	3.00	1.35
❑ QS5 Torry Holt	6.00	2.70
❑ QS6 Donovan McNabb	8.00	3.60
❑ QS7 David Boston	4.00	1.80
❑ QS8 Andy Katzenmoyer	2.50	1.10
❑ QS9 Daunte Culpepper	8.00	3.60
❑ QS10 Edgerrin James	20.00	9.00
❑ QS11 Cade McNown	8.00	3.60
❑ QS12 Troy Edwards	4.00	1.80
❑ QS13 Akili Smith	5.00	2.20
❑ QS14 Peerless Price	4.00	1.80
❑ QS15 Amos Zereoue	3.00	1.35

1999 Metal Universe Starchild

	MINT	NRMT
COMPLETE SET (20)	25.00	11.00
COMMON CARD (1-20)	1.25	.55
SEMISTARS	2.50	1.10
STATED ODDS 1:6 HOB, 1:8 RET		

❑ SC1 Skip Hicks	2.50	1.10
❑ SC2 Mike Alstott	2.50	1.10
❑ SC3 Joey Galloway	2.50	1.10
❑ SC4 Tony Simmons	1.25	.55
❑ SC5 Jamal Anderson	2.50	1.10

❑ SC6 John Avery	2.50	1.10
❑ SC7 Charles Woodson	2.50	1.10
❑ SC8 Jon Kitna	3.00	1.35
❑ SC9 Marshall Faulk	2.50	1.10
❑ SC10 Eric Moulds	2.50	1.10
❑ SC11 Keyshawn Johnson	2.50	1.10
❑ SC12 Ryan Leaf	1.25	.55
❑ SC13 Curtis Enis	2.50	1.10
❑ SC14 Steve McNair	2.50	1.10
❑ SC15 Corey Dillon	2.50	1.10
❑ SC16 Tim Dwight	2.50	1.10
❑ SC17 Brian Griese	4.00	1.80
❑ SC18 Drew Bledsoe	4.00	1.80
❑ SC19 Eddie George	3.00	1.35
❑ SC20 Terrell Owens	2.50	1.10

1991 Pacific

	MINT	NRMT
COMPLETE SET (660)	15.00	6.75
COMP.SERIES 1 (550)	8.00	3.60
COMP.FACT.SER.1 (550)	10.00	4.50
COMP.SERIES 2 (110)	8.00	3.60
COMP.FACT.SER.2 (110)	12.00	5.50
COMMON CARD (1-660)	.05	.02
SEMISTARS	.10	.05
UNLISTED STARS	.25	.11
ERR/COR (170B/244B/318B)	.75	.35
ERR/COR (321B/353B/465B)	.75	.35
VAR (122A/128A/350B)	.50	.23
COMP.CHECKLIST SET (5)	15.00	6.75
CHECKLISTS: RANDOM INS.IN LATE PACKS		

❑ 1 Deion Sanders	.40	.18
❑ 2 Steve Broussard	.05	.02
❑ 3 Aundray Bruce	.05	.02
❑ 4 Rick Bryan	.05	.02
❑ 5 John Rade	.05	.02
❑ 6 Scott Case	.05	.02
❑ 7 Tony Casillas	.05	.02
❑ 8 Shawn Collins	.05	.02
❑ 9 Darion Conner	.05	.02
❑ 10 Tory Epps	.05	.02
❑ 11 Bill Fralic	.05	.02
❑ 12 Mike Gann	.05	.02
❑ 13 Tim Green UER (Listed as DT should say DE)	.05	.02
❑ 14 Chris Hinton	.05	.02
❑ 15 Houston Hoover UER (Deion misspelled as	.05	.02

Deon on card back)
❑ 16 Chris Miller .10 .05
❑ 17 Andre Rison .10 .05
❑ 18 Mike Rozier .05 .02
❑ 19 Jessie Tuggle .05 .02
❑ 20 Don Beebe .05 .02
❑ 21 Ray Bentley .05 .02
❑ 22 Shane Conlan .05 .02
❑ 23 Kent Hull .05 .02
❑ 24 Mark Kelso .05 .02
❑ 25 James Lofton UER .10 .05
(Photo on front
actually Flip Johnson)
❑ 26 Scott Norwood .05 .02
❑ 27 Andre Reed .10 .05
❑ 28 Leonard Smith .05 .02
❑ 29 Bruce Smith .25 .11
❑ 30 Leon Seals .05 .02
❑ 31 Darryl Talley .05 .02
❑ 32 Steve Tasker .10 .05
❑ 33 Thurman Thomas .25 .11
❑ 34 James Williams .05 .02
❑ 35 Will Wolford .05 .02
❑ 36 Frank Reich .10 .05
❑ 37 Jeff Wright RC .05 .02
❑ 38 Neal Anderson .10 .05
❑ 39 Trace Armstrong .05 .02
❑ 40 Johnny Bailey UER .05 .02
(Gained 5320 yards in
college, should be 6320)
❑ 41 Mark Bortz UER .05 .02
(Johnny Bailey misspelled
as Johnny on cardback)
❑ 42 Cap Boso RC .05 .02
❑ 43 Kevin Butler .05 .02
❑ 44 Mark Carrier DB .10 .05
❑ 45 Jim Covert .05 .02
❑ 46 Wendell Davis .05 .02
❑ 47 Richard Dent .10 .05
❑ 48 Shaun Gayle .05 .02
❑ 49 Jim Harbaugh .25 .11
❑ 50 Jay Hilgenberg .05 .02
❑ 51 Brad Muster .05 .02
❑ 52 William Perry .10 .05
❑ 53 Mike Singletary UER .10 .05
(No College listed
should say Baylor)
❑ 54 Peter Tom Willis .05 .02
❑ 55 Donnell Woolford .05 .02
❑ 56 Steve McMichael .10 .05
❑ 57 Eric Ball .05 .02
❑ 58 Lewis Billups .05 .02
❑ 59 Jim Breech .05 .02
❑ 60 James Brooks .10 .05
❑ 61 Eddie Brown .05 .02
❑ 62 Rickey Dixon .05 .02
❑ 63 Boomer Esiason .10 .05
❑ 64 James Francis .05 .02
❑ 65 David Fulcher .05 .02
❑ 66 David Grant .05 .02
❑ 67 Harold Green UER .05 .02
(Misplaced apostrophe
in Gamecocks)
❑ 68 Rodney Holman .05 .02
❑ 69 Stanford Jennings .05 .02
❑ 70A Tim Krumrie ERR .50 .23
(Misspelled Krumprie
on card front)
❑ 70B Tim Krumrie COR .30 .14
❑ 71 Tim McGee .05 .02
❑ 72 Anthony Munoz .10 .05
❑ 73 Mitchell Price RC .05 .02
❑ 74 Eric Thomas .05 .02
❑ 75 Ickey Woods .05 .02
❑ 76 Mike Baab .05 .02
❑ 77 Thane Gash .05 .02
❑ 78 David Grayson .05 .02
❑ 79 Mike Johnson .05 .02
❑ 80 Reggie Langhorne .05 .02
❑ 81 Kevin Mack .05 .02
❑ 82 Clay Matthews .10 .05
❑ 83A Eric Metcalf ERR .50 .23
("Terry is the son of Terry")
❑ 83B Eric Metcalf COR .30 .14
("Eric is the son of Terry")
❑ 84 Frank Minnifield .05 .02
❑ 85 Mike Oliphant .05 .02
❑ 86 Mike Pagel .05 .02
❑ 87 John Talley .05 .02
❑ 88 Lawyer Tillman .05 .02
❑ 89 Gregg Rakoczy UER .05 .02
(Misspelled Greg on
both sides of card)
❑ 90 Bryan Wagner .05 .02
❑ 91 Rob Burnett RC .05 .02
❑ 92 Tommie Agee .05 .02
❑ 93 Troy Aikman UER .75 .35
(4328 yards is career
total not season; text
has him breaking passing
record which is not true)
❑ 94A Bill Bates ERR .50 .23
(Black line on cardfront)
❑ 94B Bill Bates COR .30 .14
(No black line
on cardfront)
❑ 95 Jack Del Rio .05 .02
❑ 96 Issiac Holt UER .05 .02
(Photo on back
actually Timmy Newsome)
❑ 97 Michael Irvin .25 .11
❑ 98 Jim Jeffcoat UER .05 .02
(On back, red line
has Jeff not Jim)
❑ 99 Jimmie Jones .05 .02
❑ 100 Kelvin Martin .05 .02
❑ 101 Nate Newton .10 .05
❑ 102 Danny Noonan .05 .02
❑ 103 Ken Norton Jr. .25 .11
❑ 104 Jay Novacek .25 .11
❑ 105 Mike Saxon .05 .02
❑ 106 Derrick Shepard .05 .02
❑ 107 Emmitt Smith 2.00 .90
❑ 108 Daniel Stubbs .05 .02
❑ 109 Tony Tolbert .05 .02
❑ 110 Alexander Wright .05 .02
❑ 111 Steve Atwater .05 .02
❑ 112 Melvin Bratton .05 .02
❑ 113 Tyrone Braxton UER .05 .02
(Went to North Dakota
State, not South Dakota)
❑ 114 Alphonso Carreker .05 .02
❑ 115 John Elway 1.25 .55
❑ 116 Simon Fletcher .05 .02
❑ 117 Bobby Humphrey .05 .02
❑ 118 Mark Jackson .05 .02
❑ 119 Vance Johnson .05 .02
❑ 120 Greg Kragen UER .05 .02
(Recovered 20 fumbles
in '89, yet 11 in career)
❑ 121 Karl Mecklenburg UER .05 .02
(Misspelled Mecklenberg
on card front)
❑ 122A Orson Mobley ERR .50 .23
(Misspelled Orsen)
❑ 122B Orson Mobley COR .10 .05
❑ 123 Alton Montgomery .05 .02
❑ 124 Ricky Nattiel .05 .02
❑ 125 Steve Sewell .05 .02
❑ 126 Shannon Sharpe .50 .23
❑ 127 Dennis Smith .05 .02
❑ 128A Andre Townsend RC ERR .50 .23
(Misspelled Andie
on card front)
❑ 128B Andre Townsend COR RC .10 .05
❑ 129 Mike Horan .05 .02
❑ 130 Jerry Ball .05 .02
❑ 131 Bennie Blades .05 .02
❑ 132 Lomas Brown .05 .02
❑ 133 Jeff Campbell UER .05 .02
(No NFL totals line)
❑ 134 Robert Clark .05 .02
❑ 135 Michael Cofer .05 .02
❑ 136 Dennis Gibson .05 .02
❑ 137 Mel Gray .10 .05
❑ 138 LeRoy Irvin UER .05 .02
(Misspelled LEROY;
spent 10 years with
Rams, not 11)
❑ 139 George Jamison RC .05 .02
❑ 140 Richard Johnson .05 .02
❑ 141 Eddie Murray .05 .02
❑ 142 Dan Owens .05 .02
❑ 143 Rodney Peete .10 .05
❑ 144 Barry Sanders 1.50 .70
❑ 145 Chris Spielman .10 .05
❑ 146 Marc Spindler .05 .02
❑ 147 Andre Ware .10 .05
❑ 148 William White .05 .02
❑ 149 Tony Bennett .10 .05
❑ 150 Robert Brown .05 .02
❑ 151 LeRoy Butler .10 .05
❑ 152 Anthony Dilweg .05 .02
❑ 153 Michael Haddix .05 .02
❑ 154 Ron Hallstrom .05 .02
❑ 155 Tim Harris .05 .02
❑ 156 Johnny Holland .05 .02
❑ 157 Chris Jacke .05 .02
❑ 158 Perry Kemp .05 .02
❑ 159 Mark Lee .05 .02
❑ 160 Don Majkowski .05 .02
❑ 161 Tony Mandarich UER .05 .02
(United Stated on back)
❑ 162 Mark Murphy .05 .02
❑ 163 Brian Noble .05 .02
❑ 164 Shawn Patterson .05 .02
❑ 165 Jeff Query .05 .02
❑ 166 Sterling Sharpe .25 .11
❑ 167 Darrell Thompson .05 .02
❑ 168 Ed West .05 .02
❑ 169 Ray Childress UER .05 .02
(Front DE, back DT)
❑ 170A Cris Dishman RC ERR .10 .05
(Misspelled Chris
on both sides)
❑ 170B Cris Dishman RC COR/ERR .10 .05
(Misspelled Chris
on back only)
❑ 170C Cris Dishman RC COR .10 .05
❑ 171 Curtis Duncan .05 .02
❑ 172 William Fuller .10 .05
❑ 173 Ernest Givins UER .10 .05
(Missing a highlight
line on back)
❑ 174 Drew Hill .05 .02
❑ 175A Haywood Jeffires ERR .25 .11
(Misspelled Jeffries
on both sides of card)
❑ 175B Haywood Jeffires COR .25 .11
❑ 176 Sean Jones .10 .05
❑ 177 Lamar Lathon .05 .02
❑ 178 Bruce Matthews .10 .05
❑ 179 Bubba McDowell .05 .02
❑ 180 Johnny Meads .05 .02
❑ 181 Warren Moon UER .25 .11
(Birth listed as '65,
should be '56)
❑ 182 Mike Munchak .05 .02
❑ 183 Allen Pinkett .05 .02
❑ 184 Dean Steinkuhler UER .05 .02
(Oakland, should
be Outland)
❑ 185 Lorenzo White UER .05 .02
(Rout misspelled as
route on card back)
❑ 186A John Grimsley ERR .50 .23
(Misspelled Grimsby)
❑ 186B John Grimsley COR .10 .05
❑ 187 Pat Beach .05 .02
❑ 188 Albert Bentley .05 .02
❑ 189 Dean Biasucci .05 .02
❑ 190 Duane Bickett .05 .02
❑ 191 Bill Brooks .05 .02
❑ 192 Eugene Daniel .05 .02
❑ 193 Jeff George .25 .11
❑ 194 Jon Hand .05 .02
❑ 195 Jeff Herrod .05 .02
❑ 196A Jessie Hester ERR .30 .14
(Misspelled Jesse)
❑ 196B Jessie Hester ERR .10 .05
(Name corrected;
6-year player, not 7;
no NFL total line)
❑ 197 Mike Prior .05 .02
❑ 198 Stacey Simmons .05 .02

❑ 199 Rohn Stark	.05	.02
❑ 200 Pat Tomberlin	.05	.02
❑ 201 Clarence Verdin	.05	.02
❑ 202 Keith Taylor	.05	.02
❑ 203 Jack Trudeau	.05	.02
❑ 204 Chip Banks	.05	.02
❑ 205 John Alt	.05	.02
❑ 206 Deron Cherry	.05	.02
❑ 207 Steve DeBerg	.05	.02
❑ 208 Tim Grunhard	.05	.02
❑ 209 Albert Lewis	.05	.02
❑ 210 Nick Lowery UER (12 years NFL exp., should be 13)	.05	.02
❑ 211 Bill Maas	.05	.02
❑ 212 Chris Martin	.05	.02
❑ 213 Todd McNair	.05	.02
❑ 214 Christian Okoye	.05	.02
❑ 215 Stephone Paige	.05	.02
❑ 216 Steve Pelluer	.05	.02
❑ 217 Kevin Porter	.05	.02
❑ 218 Kevin Ross	.05	.02
❑ 219 Dan Saleaumua	.05	.02
❑ 220 Neil Smith	.25	.11
❑ 221 David Szott UER (Listed as Off. Guard)	.05	.02
❑ 222 Derrick Thomas	.25	.11
❑ 223 Barry Word	.05	.02
❑ 224 Percy Snow	.05	.02
❑ 225 Marcus Allen	.25	.11
❑ 226 Eddie Anderson UER (Began career with Seahawks, not Raiders)	.05	.02
❑ 227 Steve Beuerlein UER (Not injured during '90 season, but was inactive)	.10	.05
❑ 228A Tim Brown ERR (No position on card)	.25	.11
❑ 228B Tim Brown COR	.25	.11
❑ 229 Scott Davis	.05	.02
❑ 230 Mike Dyal	.05	.02
❑ 231 Mervyn Fernandez UER (Card says free agent in '87, but was drafted in '83)	.05	.02
❑ 232 Willie Gault UER (Text says 60 catches in '90, stats say 50)	.05	.02
❑ 233 Ethan Horton UER (No height and weight listings)	.05	.02
❑ 234 Bo Jackson UER (Drafted in '87, not '86)	.25	.11
❑ 235 Howie Long	.10	.05
❑ 236 Terry McDaniel	.05	.02
❑ 237 Max Montoya	.05	.02
❑ 238 Don Mosebar	.05	.02
❑ 239 Jay Schroeder	.05	.02
❑ 240 Steve Smith	.05	.02
❑ 241 Greg Townsend	.05	.02
❑ 242 Aaron Wallace	.05	.02
❑ 243 Lionel Washington	.05	.02
❑ 244A Steve Wisniewski ERR (Misspelled Winsniewski on both sides; Drafted, should say traded to)	.10	.05
❑ 244B Steve Wisniewski ERR (Misspelled Winsniewski on card back)	.75	.35
❑ 244C Steve Wisniewski COR	.10	.05
❑ 245 Flipper Anderson	.05	.02
❑ 246 Latin Berry RC	.05	.02
❑ 247 Robert Delpino	.05	.02
❑ 248 Marcus Dupree	.05	.02
❑ 249 Henry Ellard	.10	.05
❑ 250 Jim Everett	.10	.05
❑ 251 Cleveland Gary	.05	.02
❑ 252 Jerry Gray	.05	.02
❑ 253 Kevin Greene	.25	.11
❑ 254 Pete Holohan UER (Photo on back actually Kevin Greene)	.05	.02
❑ 255 Buford McGee	.05	.02
❑ 256 Tom Newberry	.05	.02
❑ 257A Irv Pankey ERR (Misspelled as Panky on both sides of card)	.50	.23
❑ 257B Irv Pankey COR	.10	.05
❑ 258 Jackie Slater	.05	.02
❑ 259 Doug Smith	.05	.02
❑ 260 Frank Stams	.05	.02
❑ 261 Michael Stewart	.05	.02
❑ 262 Fred Strickland	.05	.02
❑ 263 J.B. Brown UER (No periods after initials on card front)	.05	.02
❑ 264 Mark Clayton	.10	.05
❑ 265 Jeff Cross	.05	.02
❑ 266 Mark Dennis RC	.05	.02
❑ 267 Mark Duper	.10	.05
❑ 268 Ferrell Edmunds	.05	.02
❑ 269 Dan Marino	1.25	.55
❑ 270 John Offerdahl	.05	.02
❑ 271 Louis Oliver	.05	.02
❑ 272 Tony Paige	.05	.02
❑ 273 Reggie Roby	.05	.02
❑ 274 Sammie Smith (Picture is sideways on the card)	.05	.02
❑ 275 Keith Sims	.05	.02
❑ 276 Brian Sochia	.05	.02
❑ 277 Pete Stoyanovich	.05	.02
❑ 278 Richmond Webb	.05	.02
❑ 279 Jarvis Williams	.05	.02
❑ 280 Tim McKyer	.05	.02
❑ 281A Jim C. Jensen ERR (Misspelled Jenson on card back)	.50	.23
❑ 281B Jim C. Jensen COR (Plays a skill position, not skilled)	.10	.05
❑ 282 Scott Secules RC	.05	.02
❑ 283 Ray Berry	.05	.02
❑ 284 Joey Browner UER (Safetys, sic)	.05	.02
❑ 285 Anthony Carter	.10	.05
❑ 286A Cris Carter ERR (Misspelled Chris on both sides)	.50	.23
❑ 286B Cris Carter ERR/COR (Misspelled Chris on card back)	1.50	.70
❑ 286C Cris Carter COR	.50	.23
❑ 287 Chris Doleman	.05	.02
❑ 288 Mark Dusbabek UER (Front DT, back LB)	.05	.02
❑ 289 Hassan Jones	.05	.02
❑ 290 Steve Jordan	.05	.02
❑ 291 Carl Lee	.05	.02
❑ 292 Kirk Lowdermilk	.05	.02
❑ 293 Randall McDaniel	.05	.02
❑ 294 Mike Merriweather	.05	.02
❑ 295A Keith Millard UER (No position on card)	.20	.09
❑ 295B Keith Millard COR	10.00	4.50
❑ 296 Al Noga UER (Card says DT, should say DE)	.05	.02
❑ 297 Scott Studwell UER (83 career tackles, but bio says 156 tackles in '81 season)	.05	.02
❑ 298 Henry Thomas	.05	.02
❑ 299 Herschel Walker	.10	.05
❑ 300 Gary Zimmerman	.05	.02
❑ 301 Rick Gannon	.05	.02
❑ 302 Wade Wilson UER (Led AFC, should say led NFC)	.10	.05
❑ 303 Vincent Brown	.05	.02
❑ 304 Marv Cook	.05	.02
❑ 305 Hart Lee Dykes	.05	.02
❑ 306 Irving Fryar	.10	.05
❑ 307 Tommy Hodson UER (No NFL totals line)	.05	.02
❑ 308 Maurice Hurst	.05	.02
❑ 309 Ronnie Lippett UER (On back,reserves should be reserve)	.05	.02
❑ 310 Fred Marion	.05	.02
❑ 311 Greg McMurtry	.05	.02
❑ 312 Johnny Rembert	.05	.02
❑ 313 Chris Singleton	.05	.02
❑ 314 Ed Reynolds	.05	.02
❑ 315 Andre Tippett	.05	.02
❑ 316 Garin Veris	.05	.02
❑ 317 Brent Williams	.05	.02
❑ 318A John Stephens ERR (Misspelled Stevens on both sides of card)	.10	.05
❑ 318B John Stephens COR/ERR (Misspelled Stevens on card back)	.75	.35
❑ 318C John Stephens COR	.10	.05
❑ 319 Sammy Martin	.05	.02
❑ 320 Bruce Armstrong	.05	.02
❑ 321A Morten Andersen ERR (Misspelled Anderson on both sides of card)	.30	.14
❑ 321B Morten Andersen ERR/COR (Misspelled Anderson on card back)	.75	.35
❑ 321C Morten Andersen COR	.10	.05
❑ 322 Gene Atkins UER (No NFL Exp. line)	.05	.02
❑ 323 Vince Buck	.05	.02
❑ 324 John Fourcade	.05	.02
❑ 325 Kevin Haverdink	.05	.02
❑ 326 Bobby Hebert	.05	.02
❑ 327 Craig Heyward	.10	.05
❑ 328 Dalton Hilliard	.05	.02
❑ 329 Rickey Jackson	.05	.02
❑ 330A Vaughan Johnson ERR (Misspelled Vaughn)	.20	.09
❑ 330B Vaughan Johnson COR	10.00	4.50
❑ 331 Eric Martin	.05	.02
❑ 332 Wayne Martin	.05	.02
❑ 333 Rueben Mayes UER (Misspelled Reuben on card back)	.05	.02
❑ 334 Sam Mills	.05	.02
❑ 335 Brett Perriman	.25	.11
❑ 336 Pat Swilling	.10	.05
❑ 337 Renaldo Turnbull	.05	.02
❑ 338 Lonzell Hill	.05	.02
❑ 339 Steve Walsh UER (19 of 20 for 70.3, should be 95 percent)	.05	.02
❑ 340 Carl Banks UER (Led defensive in tackles should say defense)	.05	.02
❑ 341 Mark Bavaro UER (Weight on back 145, should say 245)	.05	.02
❑ 342 Maurice Carthon	.05	.02
❑ 343 Pat Harlow RC	.05	.02
❑ 344 Eric Dorsey	.05	.02
❑ 345 John Elliott	.05	.02
❑ 346 Rodney Hampton	.25	.11
❑ 347 Jeff Hostetler	.10	.05
❑ 348 Erik Howard UER (Listed as DT, should be NT)	.05	.02
❑ 349 Pepper Johnson	.05	.02
❑ 350A Sean Landeta ERR (Misspelled Landetta on both sides of card)	.10	.05
❑ 350B Sean Landeta COR	.50	.23
❑ 351 Leonard Marshall	.05	.02
❑ 352 Dave Meggett	.10	.05
❑ 353A Bart Oates ERR (Misspelled Oats on both sides; misspelled Megget in Did You Know)	.10	.05
❑ 353B Bart Oates COR/ERR (Misspelled Oats on card back; misspelled Megget in Did You Know)	.75	.35
❑ 353C Bart Oates COR (Dave Meggett still misspelled as Megget)	.10	.05
❑ 354 Gary Reasons	.05	.02
❑ 355 Phil Simms	.10	.05

❑ 356 Lawrence Taylor .25 .11
❑ 357 Reyna Thompson .05 .02
❑ 358 Brian Williams OL UER .05 .02
(Front C-G, back G)
❑ 359 Matt Bahr .05 .02
❑ 360 Mark Ingram .10 .05
❑ 361 Brad Baxter .05 .02
❑ 362 Mark Boyer .05 .02
❑ 363 Dennis Byrd .05 .02
❑ 364 Dave Cadigan UER .05 .02
(Terance misspelled as
Terrance on back)
❑ 365 Kyle Clifton .05 .02
❑ 366 James Hasty .05 .02
❑ 367 Joe Kelly UER .05 .02
(Front 50, back 58)
❑ 368 Jeff Lageman .05 .02
❑ 369 Pat Leahy UER .05 .02
(Career-best FG in
'65, should say '85)
❑ 370 Terance Mathis .10 .05
❑ 371 Erik McMillan .05 .02
❑ 372 Rob Moore .25 .11
❑ 373 Ken O'Brien .05 .02
❑ 374 Tony Stargell .05 .02
❑ 375 Jim Sweeney UER .05 .02
(Landetta, sic)
❑ 376 Al Toon .10 .05
❑ 377 Johnny Hector .05 .02
❑ 378 Jeff Criswell .05 .02
❑ 379 Mike Haight RC .05 .02
❑ 380 Troy Benson .05 .02
❑ 381 Eric Allen .05 .02
❑ 382 Fred Barnett .25 .11
❑ 383 Jerome Brown .05 .02
❑ 384 Keith Byars .05 .02
❑ 385 Randall Cunningham .25 .11
❑ 386 Byron Evans .05 .02
❑ 387 Wes Hopkins .05 .02
❑ 388 Keith Jackson .10 .05
❑ 389 Seth Joyner UER .10 .05
(Fumble recovery line
not aligned)
❑ 390 Bobby Wilson RC .05 .02
❑ 391 Heath Sherman .05 .02
❑ 392 Clyde Simmons UER .05 .02
(Listed as DT,
should say DE)
❑ 393 Ben Smith .05 .02
❑ 394 Andre Waters .05 .02
❑ 395 Reggie White UER .25 .11
(Derrick Thomas holds
NFL record with 7 sacks)
❑ 396 Calvin Williams .10 .05
❑ 397 Al Harris .05 .02
❑ 398 Anthony Toney .05 .02
❑ 399 Mike Quick .05 .02
❑ 400 Anthony Bell .05 .02
❑ 401 Rich Camarillo .05 .02
❑ 402 Roy Green .05 .02
❑ 403 Ken Harvey .10 .05
❑ 404 Eric Hill .05 .02
❑ 405 Garth Jax RC UER .05 .02
(Should have comma
before "the" and after
"Cowboys" on cardback)
❑ 406 Ernie Jones .05 .02
❑ 407A Cedric Mack ERR .20 .09
(Misspelled Cedrick
on card front)
❑ 407B Cedric Mack COR 10.00 4.50
(NFL Exp. line is
red instead of black)
❑ 408 Dexter Manley .05 .02
❑ 409 Tim McDonald .05 .02
❑ 410 Freddie Joe Nunn .05 .02
❑ 411 Ricky Proehl .05 .02
❑ 412 Moe Gardner RC .05 .02
❑ 413 Timm Rosenbach .05 .02
❑ 414 Luis Sharpe UER .05 .02
(Lomiller, sic)
❑ 415 Vai Sikahema UER .05 .02
(Front RB, back PR)
❑ 416 Anthony Thompson .05 .02
❑ 417 Ron Wolfley UER .05 .02
(Missing NFL fact line
under vital stats)
❑ 418 Lonnie Young .05 .02
❑ 419 Gary Anderson K .05 .02
❑ 420 Bubby Brister .05 .02
❑ 421 Thomas Everett .05 .02
❑ 422 Eric Green .05 .02
❑ 423 Delton Hall .05 .02
❑ 424 Bryan Hinkle .05 .02
❑ 425 Merril Hoge .05 .02
❑ 426 Carnell Lake .05 .02
❑ 427 Louis Lipps .05 .02
❑ 428 David Little .05 .02
❑ 429 Greg Lloyd .25 .11
❑ 430 Mike Mularkey .05 .02
❑ 431 Keith Willis UER .05 .02
(No period after C in
L.C. Greenwood on back)
❑ 432 Dwayne Woodruff .05 .02
❑ 433 Rod Woodson UER .25 .11
(No NFL experience
listed on card)
❑ 434 Tim Worley .05 .02
❑ 435 Warren Williams .05 .02
❑ 436 Terry Long UER .05 .02
(Not 5th NFL team,
tied for 7th)
❑ 437 Martin Bayless .05 .02
❑ 438 Jarrod Bunch RC .05 .02
❑ 439 Marion Butts .10 .05
❑ 440 Gill Byrd UER .05 .02
(Pickoffs misspelled
as two words)
❑ 441 Arthur Cox .05 .02
❑ 442 John Friesz .25 .11
❑ 443 Leo Goeas .05 .02
❑ 444 Burt Grossman .05 .02
❑ 445 Courtney Hall UER .05 .02
(In DYK section,
is should be in)
❑ 446 Ronnie Harmon .05 .02
❑ 447 Nate Lewis RC .05 .02
❑ 448 Anthony Miller .10 .05
❑ 449 Leslie O'Neal .10 .05
❑ 450 Gary Plummer .05 .02
❑ 451 Junior Seau .25 .11
❑ 452 Billy Ray Smith .05 .02
❑ 453 Billy Joe Tolliver .05 .02
❑ 454 Broderick Thompson .05 .02
❑ 455 Lee Williams .05 .02
❑ 456 Michael Carter .05 .02
❑ 457 Mike Cofer .05 .02
❑ 458 Kevin Fagan .05 .02
❑ 459 Charles Haley .10 .05
❑ 460 Pierce Holt .05 .02
❑ 461 Johnnie Jackson RC UER .05 .02
Johnny on front
❑ 462 Brent Jones .25 .11
❑ 463 Guy McIntyre .05 .02
❑ 464 Joe Montana 1.25 .55
❑ 465A Bubba Paris ERR .10 .05
(Misspelled Parris;
reversed negative)
❑ 465B Bubba Paris ERR/COR .50 .23
(Misspelled Parris;
photo corrected
❑ 465C Bubba Paris COR .10 .05
❑ 466 Tom Rathman UER .05 .02
(Born 10/7/62,
not 11/7/62)
❑ 467 Jerry Rice UER .75 .35
(4th to catch 100,
should say 2nd)
❑ 468 Mike Sherrard .05 .02
❑ 469 John Taylor UER .10 .05
(AL1-Time, sic)
❑ 470 Steve Young .75 .35
❑ 471 Dennis Brown .05 .02
❑ 472 Dexter Carter .05 .02
❑ 473 Bill Romanowski .05 .02
❑ 474 Dave Waymer .05 .02
❑ 475 Robert Blackmon .05 .02
❑ 476 Derrick Fenner .05 .02
❑ 477 Nesby Glasgow UER .05 .02
(Missing total line
for fumbles)
❑ 478 Jacob Green .05 .02
❑ 479 Andy Heck .05 .02
❑ 480 Norm Johnson UER .05 .02
(They own and operate
card store, not run)
❑ 481 Tommy Kane .05 .02
❑ 482 Cortez Kennedy .25 .11
❑ 483A Dave Krieg ERR .20 .09
(Misspelled Kreig
on both sides)
❑ 483B Dave Krieg COR 10.00 4.50
❑ 484 Bryan Millard .05 .02
❑ 485 Joe Nash .05 .02
❑ 486 Rufus Porter .05 .02
❑ 487 Eugene Robinson .05 .02
❑ 488 Mike Tice RC .05 .02
❑ 489 Chris Warren .25 .11
❑ 490 John L. Williams UER .05 .02
(No period after L
on card front)
❑ 491 Terry Wooden .05 .02
❑ 492 Tony Woods .05 .02
❑ 493 Brian Blades .10 .05
❑ 494 Paul Skansi .05 .02
❑ 495 Gary Anderson RB .05 .02
❑ 496 Mark Carrier WR .25 .11
❑ 497 Chris Chandler .25 .11
❑ 498 Steve Christie .05 .02
❑ 499 Reggie Cobb .05 .02
❑ 500 Reuben Davis .05 .02
❑ 501 Willie Drewrey UER .05 .02
(Misspelled Drewery on
both sides of card)
❑ 502 Randy Grimes .05 .02
❑ 503 Paul Gruber .05 .02
❑ 504 Wayne Haddix .05 .02
❑ 505 Ron Hall .05 .02
❑ 506 Harry Hamilton .05 .02
❑ 507 Bruce Hill .05 .02
❑ 508 Eugene Marve .05 .02
❑ 509 Keith McCants .05 .02
❑ 510 Winston Moss .05 .02
❑ 511 Kevin Murphy .05 .02
❑ 512 Mark Robinson .05 .02
❑ 513 Vinny Testaverde .10 .05
❑ 514 Broderick Thomas .05 .02
❑ 515A Jeff Bostic UER .08 .04
(Lomiller, sic;
on back, word "goal"
touches lower border)
❑ 515B Jeff Bostic UER .08 .04
(Lomiller, sic;
on back, word "goal"
is away from border)
❑ 516 Todd Bowles .05 .02
❑ 517 Earnest Byner .05 .02
❑ 518 Gary Clark .25 .11
❑ 519 Craig Erickson RC .25 .11
❑ 520 Darryl Grant .05 .02
❑ 521 Darrell Green .05 .02
❑ 522 Russ Grimm .05 .02
❑ 523 Stan Humphries .25 .11
❑ 524 Joe Jacoby UER .05 .02
(Lomiller, sic)
❑ 525 Jim Lachey .05 .02
❑ 526 Chip Lohmiller .05 .02
❑ 527 Charles Mann .05 .02
❑ 528 Wilber Marshall .05 .02
❑ 529A Art Monk .08 .04
(On back, "y" in history
touches copyright symbol)
❑ 529B Art Monk .08 .04
(On back, "y" in history
is away from symbol)
❑ 530 Tracy Rocker .05 .02
❑ 531 Mark Rypien .10 .05
❑ 532 Ricky Sanders UER .05 .02
(Stats say caught 56,
text says 57)
❑ 533 Alvin Walton UER .05 .02
(Listed as WR,
should be S)
❑ 534 Todd Marinovich RC UER .05 .02
(17 percent, should
be 71 percent)
❑ 535 Mike Dumas RC .05 .02
❑ 536A Russell Maryland RC ERR .25 .11

(No highlight line)
❑ 536B Russell Maryland RC COR .25 .11
(Highlight line added)
❑ 537 Eric Turner RC UER .10 .05
(Don Rogers misspelled as Rodgers)
❑ 538 Ernie Mills RC .10 .05
❑ 539 Ed King RC .05 .02
❑ 540 Mike Stonebreaker .05 .02
❑ 541 Chris Zorich RC .25 .11
❑ 542A Mike Croel RC UER .05 .02
(Missing highlight line under bio notes; front photo reversed negative; on back, "y" in weekly inside copyright)
❑ 542B Mike Croel RC UER .05 .02
(Missing highlight line under bio notes; front photo reversed negative; on back, "y" in weekly barely touches copyright)
❑ 543 Eric Moten RC .05 .02
❑ 544 Dan McGwire RC .05 .02
❑ 545 Keith Cash RC .05 .02
❑ 546 Kenny Walker RC UER .05 .02
(Drafted 8th round, not 7th)
❑ 547 Leroy Hoard UER .10 .05
(LeROY on card; not a draft pick)
❑ 548 Luis Cristobal UER .05 .02
(front LB, back G)
❑ 549 Stacy Danley .05 .02
❑ 550 Todd Lyght RC .05 .02
❑ 551 Brett Favre RC 5.00 2.20
❑ 552 Mike Pritchard RC .25 .11
❑ 553 Moe Gardner .05 .02
❑ 554 Tim McKyer .05 .02
❑ 555 Erric Pegram RC .25 .11
❑ 556 Norm Johnson .05 .02
❑ 557 Bruce Pickens RC .05 .02
❑ 558 Henry Jones RC .10 .05
❑ 559 Phil Hansen RC .05 .02
❑ 560 Cornelius Bennett .10 .05
❑ 561 Stan Thomas .05 .02
❑ 562 Chris Zorich .10 .05
❑ 563 Anthony Morgan RC .05 .02
❑ 564 Darren Lewis RC .05 .02
❑ 565 Mike Stonebreaker .05 .02
❑ 566 Alfred Williams RC .05 .02
❑ 567 Lamar Rogers RC .05 .02
❑ 568 Erik Wilhelm RC UER .05 .02
(No NFL Experience line on card back)
❑ 569 Ed King .05 .02
❑ 570 Michael Jackson RC .25 .11
❑ 571 James Jones RC .05 .02
❑ 572 Russell Maryland .25 .11
❑ 573 Dixon Edwards RC .05 .02
❑ 574 Darrick Brownlow RC .05 .02
❑ 575 Larry Brown DB RC .10 .05
❑ 576 Mike Croel .05 .02
❑ 577 Keith Traylor RC .05 .02
❑ 578 Kenny Walker .05 .02
❑ 579 Reggie Johnson RC .05 .02
❑ 580 Herman Moore RC 2.00 .90
❑ 581 Kelvin Pritchett RC .10 .05
❑ 582 Kevin Scott RC .05 .02
❑ 583 Vinnie Clark RC .05 .02
❑ 584 Esera Tuaolo RC .05 .02
❑ 585 Don Davey .05 .02
❑ 586 Blair Kiel RC .05 .02
❑ 587 Mike Dumas .05 .02
❑ 588 Darryll Lewis RC .10 .05
❑ 589 John Flannery RC .05 .02
❑ 590 Kevin Donnalley .05 .02
❑ 591 Shane Curry .05 .02
❑ 592 Mark Vander Poel RC .05 .02
❑ 593 Dave McCloughan .05 .02
❑ 594 Mel Agee RC .05 .02
❑ 595 Kerry Cash RC .05 .02
❑ 596 Harvey Williams RC .25 .11
❑ 597 Joe Valerio .05 .02
❑ 598 Tim Barnett RC UER .05 .02
(Harvey Williams pictured on front)
❑ 599 Todd Marinovich .10 .05
❑ 600 Nick Bell RC .05 .02
❑ 601 Roger Craig .10 .05
❑ 602 Ronnie Lott .10 .05
❑ 603 Mike Jones RC .05 .02
❑ 604 Todd Lyght .05 .02
❑ 605 Roman Phifer RC .05 .02
❑ 606 David Lang RC .05 .02
❑ 607 Aaron Craver RC .05 .02
❑ 608 Mark Higgs RC .05 .02
❑ 609 Chris Green .05 .02
❑ 610 Randy Baldwin RC .05 .02
❑ 611 Pat Harlow .05 .02
❑ 612 Leonard Russell RC .25 .11
❑ 613 Jerome Henderson RC .05 .02
❑ 614 Scott Zolak RC UER .05 .02
(Bio says drafted in 1984, should be 1991)
❑ 615 Jon Vaughn RC .05 .02
❑ 616 Harry Colon RC .05 .02
❑ 617 Wesley Carroll RC .05 .02
❑ 618 Quinn Early .10 .05
❑ 619 Reginald Jones RC .05 .02
❑ 620 Jarrod Bunch .05 .02
❑ 621 Kanavis McGhee RC .05 .02
❑ 622 Ed McCaffrey RC 2.00 .90
❑ 623 Browning Nagle RC .05 .02
❑ 624 Mo Lewis RC .10 .05
❑ 625 Blair Thomas .05 .02
❑ 626 Antone Davis RC .05 .02
❑ 627 Jim McMahon .10 .05
❑ 628 Scott Kowalkowski RC .05 .02
❑ 629 Brad Goebel RC .05 .02
❑ 630 William Thomas RC .05 .02
❑ 631 Eric Swann RC .25 .11
❑ 632 Mike Jones RC .05 .02
❑ 633 Aeneas Williams RC .25 .11
❑ 634 Dexter Davis RC .05 .02
❑ 635 Tom Tupa UER .05 .02
(Did play in 1990, but not as QB)
❑ 636 Johnny Johnson .05 .02
❑ 637 Randal Hill RC .10 .05
❑ 638 Jeff Graham RC .25 .11
❑ 639 Ernie Mills .05 .02
❑ 640 Adrian Cooper RC .05 .02
❑ 641 Stanley Richard RC .05 .02
❑ 642 Eric Bieniemy RC .05 .02
❑ 643 Eric Moten .05 .02
❑ 644 Shawn Jefferson RC .10 .05
❑ 645 Ted Washington RC .05 .02
❑ 646 John Johnson RC .05 .02
❑ 647 Dan McGwire .05 .02
❑ 648 Doug Thomas RC .05 .02
❑ 649 David Daniels RC .05 .02
❑ 650 John Kasay RC .10 .05
❑ 651 Jeff Kemp .05 .02
❑ 652 Charles McRae RC .05 .02
❑ 653 Lawrence Dawsey RC .10 .05
❑ 654 Robert Wilson RC .05 .02
❑ 655 Dexter Manley .05 .02
❑ 656 Chuck Weatherspoon .05 .02
❑ 657 Tim Ryan RC .05 .02
❑ 658 Bobby Wilson .05 .02
❑ 659 Ricky Ervins RC .10 .05
❑ 660 Matt Millen .10 .05

1991 Pacific Picks The Pros

	MINT	NRMT
COMPLETE SET (25)	50.00	22.00
*GOLD/SILVER: SAME PRICE		
RANDOM INSERTS IN PACKS		

❑ 1 Russell Maryland 2.50 1.10
❑ 2 Andre Reed 1.00 .45
❑ 3 Jerry Rice 8.00 3.60
❑ 4 Keith Jackson 1.00 .45
❑ 5 Jim Lachey .50 .23
❑ 6 Anthony Munoz 1.00 .45
❑ 7 Randall McDaniel .50 .23
❑ 8 Bruce Matthews 1.00 .45

❑ 9 Kent Hull .50 .23
❑ 10 Joe Montana 12.00 5.50
❑ 11 Barry Sanders 15.00 6.75
❑ 12 Thurman Thomas 2.50 1.10
❑ 13 Morten Andersen 3.00 1.35
❑ 14 Jerry Ball .50 .23
❑ 15 Jerome Brown .50 .23
❑ 16 Reggie White 2.50 1.10
❑ 17 Bruce Smith 2.50 1.10
❑ 18 Derrick Thomas 2.50 1.10
❑ 19 Lawrence Taylor 2.50 1.10
❑ 20 Charles Haley 1.00 .45
❑ 21 Albert Lewis .50 .23
❑ 22 Rod Woodson 2.50 1.10
❑ 23 David Fulcher .50 .23
❑ 24 Joey Browner .50 .23
❑ 25 Sean Landeta 1.00 .45

1992 Pacific

	MINT	NRMT
COMPLETE SET (660)	15.00	6.75
COMP.FACT.SET (690)	25.00	11.00
COMP.SERIES 1 (330)	8.00	3.60
COMP.SERIES 2 (330)	8.00	3.60
COMMON CARD (1-660)	.04	.02
SEMISTARS	.10	.05
UNLISTED STARS	.25	.11
COMP.CHECKLIST SET (5)	3.00	1.35
CHECKLISTS: RANDOM INS.IN PACKS		
COMP.GRIESE SET (9)	5.00	2.20
GRIESE AUTO/1000	50.00	22.00
COMP.LARGENT SET (9)	5.00	2.20
LARGENT AUTO/1000	80.00	36.00
RANDOM INSERTS IN PACKS		

❑ 1 Steve Broussard .04 .02
❑ 2 Darion Conner .04 .02
❑ 3 Tory Epps .04 .02
❑ 4 Michael Haynes .10 .05
❑ 5 Chris Hinton .04 .02
❑ 6 Mike Kenn .04 .02
❑ 7 Tim McKyer .04 .02
❑ 8 Chris Miller .10 .05
❑ 9 Erric Pegram .10 .05
❑ 10 Mike Pritchard .10 .05
❑ 11 Moe Gardner .04 .02
❑ 12 Tim Green .04 .02
❑ 13 Norm Johnson .04 .02
❑ 14 Don Beebe .04 .02
❑ 15 Cornelius Bennett .10 .05

❑ 16 Al Edwards .04 .02
❑ 17 Mark Kelso .04 .02
❑ 18 James Lofton .10 .05
❑ 19 Frank Reich .10 .05
❑ 20 Leon Seals .04 .02
❑ 21 Darryl Talley .04 .02
❑ 22 Thurman Thomas .25 .11
❑ 23 Kent Hull .04 .02
❑ 24 Jeff Wright .04 .02
❑ 25 Nate Odomes .04 .02
❑ 26 Carwell Gardner .04 .02
❑ 27 Neal Anderson .04 .02
❑ 28 Mark Carrier DB .04 .02
❑ 29 Johnny Bailey .04 .02
❑ 30 Jim Harbaugh .25 .11
❑ 31 Jay Hilgenberg .04 .02
❑ 32 William Perry .10 .05
❑ 33 Wendell Davis .04 .02
❑ 34 Donnell Woolford .04 .02
❑ 35 Keith Van Horne .04 .02
❑ 36 Shaun Gayle .04 .02
❑ 37 Tom Waddle .04 .02
❑ 38 Chris Zorich .10 .05
❑ 39 Tom Thayer .04 .02
❑ 40 Rickey Dixon .04 .02
❑ 41 James Francis .04 .02
❑ 42 David Fulcher .04 .02
❑ 43 Reggie Rembert .04 .02
❑ 44 Anthony Munoz .10 .05
❑ 45 Harold Green .04 .02
❑ 46 Mitchell Price .04 .02
❑ 47 Rodney Holman .04 .02
❑ 48 Bruce Kozerski .04 .02
❑ 49 Bruce Reimers .04 .02
❑ 50 Erik Wilhelm .04 .02
❑ 51 Harlon Barnett .04 .02
❑ 52 Mike Johnson .04 .02
❑ 53 Brian Brennan .04 .02
❑ 54 Ed King .04 .02
❑ 55 Reggie Langhorne .04 .02
❑ 56 James Jones .04 .02
❑ 57 Mike Baab .04 .02
❑ 58 Dan Fike .04 .02
❑ 59 Frank Minnifield .04 .02
❑ 60 Clay Matthews .10 .05
❑ 61 Kevin Mack .04 .02
❑ 62 Tony Casillas .04 .02
❑ 63 Jay Novacek .10 .05
❑ 64 Larry Brown DB .04 .02
❑ 65 Michael Irvin .25 .11
❑ 66 Jack Del Rio .04 .02
❑ 67 Ken Willis .04 .02
❑ 68 Emmitt Smith 1.50 .70
❑ 69 Alan Veingrad .04 .02
❑ 70 John Gesek .04 .02
❑ 71 Steve Beuerlein .04 .02
❑ 72 Vinson Smith RC .04 .02
❑ 73 Steve Atwater .04 .02
❑ 74 Mike Croel .04 .02
❑ 75 John Elway 1.25 .55
❑ 76 Gaston Green .04 .02
❑ 77 Mike Horan .04 .02
❑ 78 Vance Johnson .04 .02
❑ 79 Karl Mecklenburg .04 .02
❑ 80 Shannon Sharpe .25 .11
❑ 81 David Treadwell .04 .02
❑ 82 Kenny Walker .04 .02
❑ 83 Greg Lewis .04 .02
❑ 84 Shawn Moore .04 .02
❑ 85 Alton Montgomery .04 .02
❑ 86 Michael Young .04 .02
❑ 87 Jerry Ball .04 .02
❑ 88 Bennie Blades .04 .02
❑ 89 Mel Gray .10 .05
❑ 90 Herman Moore .75 .35
❑ 91 Erik Kramer .10 .05
❑ 92 Willie Green .04 .02
❑ 93 George Jamison .04 .02
❑ 94 Chris Spielman .10 .05
❑ 95 Kelvin Pritchett .04 .02
❑ 96 William White .04 .02
❑ 97 Mike Utley .10 .05
❑ 98 Tony Bennett .04 .02
❑ 99 LeRoy Butler .04 .02
❑ 100 Vinnie Clark .04 .02
❑ 101 Ron Hallstrom .04 .02
❑ 102 Chris Jacke .04 .02
❑ 103 Tony Mandarich .04 .02
❑ 104 Sterling Sharpe .25 .11
❑ 105 Don Majkowski .04 .02
❑ 106 Johnny Holland .04 .02
❑ 107 Esera Tuaolo .04 .02
❑ 108 Darrell Thompson .04 .02
❑ 109 Bubba McDowell .04 .02
❑ 110 Curtis Duncan .04 .02
❑ 111 Lamar Lathon .04 .02
❑ 112 Drew Hill .04 .02
❑ 113 Bruce Matthews .04 .02
❑ 114 Bo Orlando RC .04 .02
❑ 115 Don Maggs .04 .02
❑ 116 Lorenzo White .04 .02
❑ 117 Ernest Givins .10 .05
❑ 118 Tony Jones .04 .02
❑ 119 Dean Steinkuhler .04 .02
❑ 120 Dean Biasucci .04 .02
❑ 121 Duane Bickett .04 .02
❑ 122 Bill Brooks .04 .02
❑ 123 Ken Clark .04 .02
❑ 124 Jessie Hester .04 .02
❑ 125 Anthony Johnson .10 .05
❑ 126 Chip Banks .04 .02
❑ 127 Mike Prior .04 .02
❑ 128 Rohn Stark .04 .02
❑ 129 Jeff Herrod .04 .02
❑ 130 Clarence Verdin .04 .02
❑ 131 Tim Manoa .04 .02
❑ 132 Brian Baldinger RC .04 .02
❑ 133 Tim Barnett .04 .02
❑ 134 J.J. Birden .04 .02
❑ 135 Deron Cherry .04 .02
❑ 136 Steve DeBerg .04 .02
❑ 137 Nick Lowery .04 .02
❑ 138 Todd McNair .04 .02
❑ 139 Christian Okoye .04 .02
❑ 140 Mark Vlasic .04 .02
❑ 141 Dan Saleaumua .04 .02
❑ 142 Neil Smith .25 .11
❑ 143 Robb Thomas .04 .02
❑ 144 Eddie Anderson .04 .02
❑ 145 Nick Bell .04 .02
❑ 146 Tim Brown .25 .11
❑ 147 Roger Craig .10 .05
❑ 148 Jeff Gossett .04 .02
❑ 149 Ethan Horton .04 .02
❑ 150 Jamie Holland .04 .02
❑ 151 Jeff Jaeger .04 .02
❑ 152 Todd Marinovich .04 .02
❑ 153 Marcus Allen .25 .11
❑ 154 Steve Smith .04 .02
❑ 155 Flipper Anderson .04 .02
❑ 156 Robert Delpino .04 .02
❑ 157 Cleveland Gary .04 .02
❑ 158 Kevin Greene .25 .11
❑ 159 Dale Hatcher .04 .02
❑ 160 Duval Love .04 .02
❑ 161 Ron Brown .04 .02
❑ 162 Jackie Slater .04 .02
❑ 163 Doug Smith .04 .02
❑ 164 Aaron Cox .04 .02
❑ 165 Larry Kelm .04 .02
❑ 166 Mark Clayton .10 .05
❑ 167 Louis Oliver .04 .02
❑ 168 Mark Higgs .04 .02
❑ 169 Aaron Craver .04 .02
❑ 170 Sammie Smith .04 .02
❑ 171 Tony Paige .04 .02
❑ 172 Jeff Cross .04 .02
❑ 173 David Griggs .04 .02
❑ 174 Richmond Webb .04 .02
❑ 175 Vestee Jackson .04 .02
❑ 176 Jim C. Jensen .04 .02
❑ 177 Anthony Carter .10 .05
❑ 178 Cris Carter .50 .23
❑ 179 Chris Doleman .04 .02
❑ 180 Rich Gannon .04 .02
❑ 181 Al Noga .04 .02
❑ 182 Randall McDaniel .04 .02
❑ 183 Todd Scott .04 .02
❑ 184 Henry Thomas .04 .02
❑ 185 Felix Wright .04 .02
❑ 186 Gary Zimmerman .04 .02
❑ 187 Herschel Walker .10 .05
❑ 188 Vincent Brown .04 .02
❑ 189 Harry Colon .04 .02
❑ 190 Irving Fryar .10 .05
❑ 191 Marv Cook .04 .02
❑ 192 Leonard Russell .10 .05
❑ 193 Hugh Millen .04 .02
❑ 194 Pat Harlow .04 .02
❑ 195 Jon Vaughn .04 .02
❑ 196 Ben Coates RC 2.00 .90
❑ 197 Johnny Rembert .04 .02
❑ 198 Greg McMurtry .04 .02
❑ 199 Morten Andersen .04 .02
❑ 200 Tommy Barnhardt .04 .02
❑ 201 Bobby Hebert .04 .02
❑ 202 Dalton Hilliard .04 .02
❑ 203 Sam Mills .04 .02
❑ 204 Pat Swilling .10 .05
❑ 205 Rickey Jackson .04 .02
❑ 206 Stan Brock .04 .02
❑ 207 Reginald Jones .04 .02
❑ 208 Gill Fenerty .04 .02
❑ 209 Eric Martin .04 .02
❑ 210 Matt Bahr .04 .02
❑ 211 Rodney Hampton .25 .11
❑ 212 Jeff Hostetler .10 .05
❑ 213 Pepper Johnson .04 .02
❑ 214 Leonard Marshall .04 .02
❑ 215 Doug Riesenberg .04 .02
❑ 216 Stephen Baker .04 .02
❑ 217 Mike Fox .04 .02
❑ 218 Bart Oates .04 .02
❑ 219 Everson Walls .04 .02
❑ 220 Gary Reasons .04 .02
❑ 221 Jeff Lageman .04 .02
❑ 222 Joe Kelly .04 .02
❑ 223 Mo Lewis .04 .02
❑ 224 Tony Stargell .04 .02
❑ 225 Jim Sweeney .04 .02
❑ 226 Freeman McNeil .04 .02
❑ 227 Brian Washington .04 .02
❑ 228 Johnny Hector .04 .02
❑ 229 Terance Mathis .10 .05
❑ 230 Rob Moore .10 .05
❑ 231 Brad Baxter .04 .02
❑ 232 Eric Allen .04 .02
❑ 233 Fred Barnett .25 .11
❑ 234 Jerome Brown .04 .02
❑ 235 Keith Byars .04 .02
❑ 236 William Thomas .04 .02
❑ 237 Jessie Small .04 .02
❑ 238 Robert Drummond .04 .02
❑ 239 Reggie White .25 .11
❑ 240 James Joseph .04 .02
❑ 241 Brad Goebel .04 .02
❑ 242 Clyde Simmons .04 .02
❑ 243 Rich Camarillo .04 .02
❑ 244 Ken Harvey .04 .02
❑ 245 Garth Jax .04 .02
❑ 246 Johnny Johnson UER .04 .02
(Photo on back not him)
❑ 247 Mike Jones .04 .02
❑ 248 Ernie Jones .04 .02
❑ 249 Tom Tupa .04 .02
❑ 250 Ron Wolfley .04 .02
❑ 251 Luis Sharpe .04 .02
❑ 252 Eric Swann .10 .05
❑ 253 Anthony Thompson .04 .02
❑ 254 Gary Anderson K .04 .02
❑ 255 Dermontti Dawson .04 .02
❑ 256 Jeff Graham .25 .11
❑ 257 Eric Green .04 .02
❑ 258 Louis Lipps .04 .02
❑ 259 Neil O'Donnell .25 .11
❑ 260 Rod Woodson .25 .11
❑ 261 Dwight Stone .04 .02
❑ 262 Aaron Jones .04 .02
❑ 263 Keith Willis .04 .02
❑ 264 Ernie Mills .04 .02
❑ 265 Martin Bayless .04 .02
❑ 266 Rod Bernstine .04 .02
❑ 267 John Carney .04 .02
❑ 268 John Friesz .10 .05
❑ 269 Nate Lewis .04 .02
❑ 270 Shawn Jefferson .04 .02
❑ 271 Burt Grossman .04 .02
❑ 272 Eric Moten .04 .02

❑	273	Gary Plummer	.04	.02
❑	274	Henry Rolling	.04	.02
❑	275	Steve Hendrickson RC	.04	.02
❑	276	Michael Carter	.04	.02
❑	277	Steve Bono RC	.25	.11
❑	278	Dexter Carter	.04	.02
❑	279	Mike Cofer	.04	.02
❑	280	Charles Haley	.10	.05
❑	281	Tom Rathman	.04	.02
❑	282	Guy McIntyre	.04	.02
❑	283	John Taylor	.10	.05
❑	284	Dave Waymer	.04	.02
❑	285	Steve Wallace	.04	.02
❑	286	Jamie Williams	.04	.02
❑	287	Brian Blades	.10	.05
❑	288	Jeff Bryant	.04	.02
❑	289	Grant Feasel	.04	.02
❑	290	Jacob Green	.04	.02
❑	291	Andy Heck	.04	.02
❑	292	Kelly Stouffer	.04	.02
❑	293	John Kasay	.04	.02
❑	294	Cortez Kennedy	.10	.05
❑	295	Bryan Millard	.04	.02
❑	296	Eugene Robinson	.04	.02
❑	297	Tony Woods	.04	.02
❑	298	Jesse Anderson UER (Should have Tight End, not TIGHT END)	.04	.02
❑	299	Gary Anderson RB	.04	.02
❑	300	Mark Carrier WR	.10	.05
❑	301	Reggie Cobb	.04	.02
❑	302	Robert Wilson	.04	.02
❑	303	Jesse Solomon	.04	.02
❑	304	Broderick Thomas	.04	.02
❑	305	Lawrence Dawsey	.10	.05
❑	306	Charles McRae	.04	.02
❑	307	Paul Gruber	.04	.02
❑	308	Vinny Testaverde	.10	.05
❑	309	Brian Mitchell	.10	.05
❑	310	Darrell Green	.04	.02
❑	311	Art Monk	.10	.05
❑	312	Russ Grimm	.04	.02
❑	313	Mark Rypien	.04	.02
❑	314	Bobby Wilson	.04	.02
❑	315	Wilber Marshall	.04	.02
❑	316	Gerald Riggs	.04	.02
❑	317	Chip Lohmiller	.04	.02
❑	318	Joe Jacoby	.04	.02
❑	319	Martin Mayhew	.04	.02
❑	320	Amp Lee RC	.04	.02
❑	321	Terrell Buckley RC	.04	.02
❑	322	Tommy Vardell RC	.10	.05
❑	323	Ricardo McDonald RC	.04	.02
❑	324	Joe Bowden RC	.04	.02
❑	325	Darryl Williams RC	.04	.02
❑	326	Carlos Huerta	.04	.02
❑	327	Patrick Rowe RC	.04	.02
❑	328	Siran Stacy RC	.04	.02
❑	329	Dexter McNabb RC	.04	.02
❑	330	Willie Clay RC	.04	.02
❑	331	Oliver Barnett	.04	.02
❑	332	Aundray Bruce	.04	.02
❑	333	Ken Tippins RC	.04	.02
❑	334	Jessie Tuggle	.04	.02
❑	335	Brian Jordan	.10	.05
❑	336	Andre Rison	.10	.05
❑	337	Houston Hoover	.04	.02
❑	338	Bill Fralic	.04	.02
❑	339	Pat Chaffey RC	.04	.02
❑	340	Keith Jones	.04	.02
❑	341	Jamie Dukes RC	.04	.02
❑	342	Chris Mohr	.04	.02
❑	343	John Davis	.04	.02
❑	344	Ray Bentley	.04	.02
❑	345	Scott Norwood	.04	.02
❑	346	Shane Conlan	.04	.02
❑	347	Steve Tasker	.10	.05
❑	348	Will Wolford	.04	.02
❑	349	Gary Baldinger RC	.04	.02
❑	350	Kirby Jackson	.04	.02
❑	351	Jamie Mueller	.04	.02
❑	352	Pete Metzelaars	.04	.02
❑	353	Richard Dent	.10	.05
❑	354	Ron Rivera	.04	.02
❑	355	Jim Morrissey	.04	.02
❑	356	John Roper	.04	.02
❑	357	Steve McMichael	.10	.05
❑	358	Ron Morris	.04	.02
❑	359	Darren Lewis	.04	.02
❑	360	Anthony Morgan	.04	.02
❑	361	Stan Thomas	.04	.02
❑	362	James Thornton	.04	.02
❑	363	Brad Muster	.04	.02
❑	364	Tim Krumrie	.04	.02
❑	365	Lee Johnson	.04	.02
❑	366	Eric Ball	.04	.02
❑	367	Alonzo Mitz RC	.04	.02
❑	368	David Grant	.04	.02
❑	369	Lynn James	.04	.02
❑	370	Lewis Billups	.04	.02
❑	371	Jim Breech	.04	.02
❑	372	Alfred Williams	.04	.02
❑	373	Wayne Haddix	.04	.02
❑	374	Tim McGee	.04	.02
❑	375	Michael Jackson	.10	.05
❑	376	Leroy Hoard	.10	.05
❑	377	Tony Jones	.04	.02
❑	378	Vince Newsome	.04	.02
❑	379	Todd Philcox RC	.04	.02
❑	380	Eric Metcalf	.10	.05
❑	381	John Rienstra	.04	.02
❑	382	Matt Stover	.04	.02
❑	383	Brian Hansen	.04	.02
❑	384	Joe Morris	.04	.02
❑	385	Anthony Pleasant	.04	.02
❑	386	Mark Stepnoski	.10	.05
❑	387	Erik Williams	.04	.02
❑	388	Jimmie Jones	.04	.02
❑	389	Kevin Gogan	.04	.02
❑	390	Manny Hendrix RC	.04	.02
❑	391	Issiac Holt	.04	.02
❑	392	Ken Norton	.25	.11
❑	393	Tommie Agee	.04	.02
❑	394	Alvin Harper	.10	.05
❑	395	Alexander Wright	.04	.02
❑	396	Mike Saxon	.04	.02
❑	397	Michael Brooks	.04	.02
❑	398	Bobby Humphrey	.04	.02
❑	399	Ken Lanier	.04	.02
❑	400	Steve Sewell	.04	.02
❑	401	Robert Perryman	.04	.02
❑	402	Wymon Henderson	.04	.02
❑	403	Keith Kartz	.04	.02
❑	404	Clarence Kay	.04	.02
❑	405	Keith Traylor	.04	.02
❑	406	Doug Widell	.04	.02
❑	407	Dennis Smith	.04	.02
❑	408	Marc Spindler	.04	.02
❑	409	Lomas Brown	.04	.02
❑	410	Robert Clark	.04	.02
❑	411	Eric Andolsek	.04	.02
❑	412	Mike Farr	.04	.02
❑	413	Ray Crockett	.04	.02
❑	414	Jeff Campbell	.04	.02
❑	415	Dan Owens	.04	.02
❑	416	Jim Arnold	.04	.02
❑	417	Barry Sanders	1.50	.70
❑	418	Eddie Murray	.04	.02
❑	419	Vince Workman	.10	.05
❑	420	Ed West	.04	.02
❑	421	Charles Wilson	.04	.02
❑	422	Perry Kemp	.04	.02
❑	423	Chuck Cecil	.04	.02
❑	424	James Campen	.04	.02
❑	425	Robert Brown	.04	.02
❑	426	Brian Noble	.04	.02
❑	427	Rich Moran	.04	.02
❑	428	Vai Sikahema	.04	.02
❑	429	Allen Rice	.04	.02
❑	430	Haywood Jeffires	.10	.05
❑	431	Warren Moon	.25	.11
❑	432	Greg Montgomery	.04	.02
❑	433	Sean Jones	.10	.05
❑	434	Richard Johnson	.04	.02
❑	435	Al Smith	.04	.02
❑	436	Johnny Meads	.04	.02
❑	437	William Fuller	.10	.05
❑	438	Mike Munchak	.04	.02
❑	439	Ray Childress	.04	.02
❑	440	Cody Carlson	.04	.02
❑	441	Scott Radecic	.04	.02
❑	442	Quintus McDonald RC	.04	.02
❑	443	Eugene Daniel	.04	.02
❑	444	Mark Herrmann RC	.04	.02
❑	445	John Baylor RC	.04	.02
❑	446	Dave McCloughan	.04	.02
❑	447	Mark Vander Poel	.04	.02
❑	448	Randy Dixon	.04	.02
❑	449	Keith Taylor	.04	.02
❑	450	Alan Grant	.04	.02
❑	451	Tony Siragusa	.04	.02
❑	452	Rich Baldinger	.04	.02
❑	453	Derrick Thomas	.25	.11
❑	454	Bill Jones RC	.04	.02
❑	455	Troy Stradford	.04	.02
❑	456	Barry Word	.04	.02
❑	457	Tim Grunhard	.04	.02
❑	458	Chris Martin	.04	.02
❑	459	Jayice Pearson RC	.04	.02
❑	460	Dino Hackett	.04	.02
❑	461	David Lutz	.04	.02
❑	462	Albert Lewis	.04	.02
❑	463	Fred Jones RC	.04	.02
❑	464	Winston Moss	.04	.02
❑	465	Sam Graddy RC	.04	.02
❑	466	Steve Wisniewski	.04	.02
❑	467	Jay Schroeder	.04	.02
❑	468	Ronnie Lott	.10	.05
❑	469	Willie Gault	.10	.05
❑	470	Greg Townsend	.04	.02
❑	471	Max Montoya	.04	.02
❑	472	Howie Long	.10	.05
❑	473	Lionel Washington	.04	.02
❑	474	Riki Ellison	.04	.02
❑	475	Tom Newberry	.04	.02
❑	476	Damone Johnson	.04	.02
❑	477	Pat Terrell	.04	.02
❑	478	Marcus Dupree	.04	.02
❑	479	Todd Lyght	.04	.02
❑	480	Buford McGee	.04	.02
❑	481	Bern Brostek	.04	.02
❑	482	Jim Price	.04	.02
❑	483	Robert Young	.04	.02
❑	484	Tony Zendejas	.04	.02
❑	485	Robert Bailey RC	.04	.02
❑	486	Alvin Wright	.04	.02
❑	487	Pat Carter	.04	.02
❑	488	Pete Stoyanovich	.04	.02
❑	489	Reggie Roby	.04	.02
❑	490	Harry Galbreath	.04	.02
❑	491	Mike McGruder RC**/C	.04	.02
❑	492	J.B. Brown	.04	.02
❑	493	E.J. Junior	.04	.02
❑	494	Ferrell Edmunds	.04	.02
❑	495	Scott Secules	.04	.02
❑	496	Greg Baty RC	.04	.02
❑	497	Mike Iaquaniello	.04	.02
❑	498	Keith Sims	.04	.02
❑	499	John Randle	.10	.05
❑	500	Joey Browner	.04	.02
❑	501	Steve Jordan	.04	.02
❑	502	Darrin Nelson	.04	.02
❑	503	Audray McMillian	.04	.02
❑	504	Harry Newsome	.04	.02
❑	505	Hassan Jones	.04	.02
❑	506	Ray Berry	.04	.02
❑	507	Mike Merriweather	.04	.02
❑	508	Leo Lewis	.04	.02
❑	509	Tim Irwin	.04	.02
❑	510	Kirk Lowdermilk	.04	.02
❑	511	Alfred Anderson	.04	.02
❑	512	Michael Timpson RC	.10	.05
❑	513	Jerome Henderson	.04	.02
❑	514	Andre Tippett	.04	.02
❑	515	Chris Singleton	.04	.02
❑	516	John Stephens	.04	.02
❑	517	Ronnie Lippett	.04	.02
❑	518	Bruce Armstrong	.04	.02
❑	519	Marion Hobby RC	.04	.02
❑	520	Tim Goad	.04	.02
❑	521	Mickey Washington RC	.04	.02
❑	522	Fred Smerlas	.04	.02
❑	523	Wayne Martin	.04	.02
❑	524	Frank Warren	.04	.02
❑	525	Floyd Turner	.04	.02
❑	526	Wesley Carroll	.04	.02
❑	527	Gene Atkins	.04	.02
❑	528	Vaughan Johnson	.04	.02

❑ 529	Hoby Brenner	.04	.02
❑ 530	Renaldo Turnbull	.04	.02
❑ 531	Joel Hilgenberg	.04	.02
❑ 532	Craig Heyward	.10	.05
❑ 533	Vince Buck	.04	.02
❑ 534	Jim Dombrowski	.04	.02
❑ 535	Fred McAfee RC	.04	.02
❑ 536	Phil Simms	.10	.05
❑ 537	Lewis Tillman	.04	.02
❑ 538	John Elliott	.04	.02
❑ 539	Dave Meggett	.10	.05
❑ 540	Mark Collins	.04	.02
❑ 541	Ottis Anderson	.10	.05
❑ 542	Bobby Abrams RC	.04	.02
❑ 543	Sean Landeta	.04	.02
❑ 544	Brian Williams OL	.04	.02
❑ 545	Erik Howard	.04	.02
❑ 546	Mark Ingram	.04	.02
❑ 547	Kanavis McGhee	.04	.02
❑ 548	Kyle Clifton	.04	.02
❑ 549	Marvin Washington	.04	.02
❑ 550	Jeff Criswell	.04	.02
❑ 551	Dave Cadigan	.04	.02
❑ 552	Chris Burkett	.04	.02
❑ 553	Erik McMillan	.04	.02
❑ 554	James Hasty	.04	.02
❑ 555	Louie Aguiar RC	.04	.02
❑ 556	Troy Johnson RC	.04	.02
❑ 557	Troy Taylor RC	.04	.02
❑ 558	Pat Kelly RC	.04	.02
❑ 559	Heath Sherman	.04	.02
❑ 560	Roger Ruzek	.04	.02
❑ 561	Andre Waters	.04	.02
❑ 562	Izel Jenkins	.04	.02
❑ 563	Keith Jackson	.10	.05
❑ 564	Byron Evans	.04	.02
❑ 565	Wes Hopkins	.04	.02
❑ 566	Rich Miano	.04	.02
❑ 567	Seth Joyner	.10	.05
❑ 568	Thomas Sanders	.04	.02
❑ 569	David Alexander	.04	.02
❑ 570	Jeff Kemp	.04	.02
❑ 571	Jock Jones RC	.04	.02
❑ 572	Craig Patterson RC	.04	.02
❑ 573	Robert Massey	.04	.02
❑ 574	Bill Lewis	.04	.02
❑ 575	Freddie Joe Nunn	.04	.02
❑ 576	Aeneas Williams	.10	.05
❑ 577	John Jackson	.04	.02
❑ 578	Tim McDonald	.04	.02
❑ 579	Michael Zordich RC	.04	.02
❑ 580	Eric Hill	.04	.02
❑ 581	Lorenzo Lynch	.04	.02
❑ 582	Vernice Smith RC	.04	.02
❑ 583	Greg Lloyd	.25	.11
❑ 584	Carnell Lake	.04	.02
❑ 585	Hardy Nickerson	.10	.05
❑ 586	Delton Hall	.04	.02
❑ 587	Gerald Williams	.04	.02
❑ 588	Bryan Hinkle	.04	.02
❑ 589	Barry Foster	.10	.05
❑ 590	Bubby Brister	.04	.02
❑ 591	Rick Strom RC	.04	.02
❑ 592	David Little	.04	.02
❑ 593	Leroy Thompson RC	.04	.02
❑ 594	Eric Bieniemy	.04	.02
❑ 595	Courtney Hall	.04	.02
❑ 596	George Thornton	.04	.02
❑ 597	Donnie Elder	.04	.02
❑ 598	Billy Ray Smith	.04	.02
❑ 599	Gill Byrd	.04	.02
❑ 600	Marion Butts	.04	.02
❑ 601	Ronnie Harmon	.04	.02
❑ 602	Anthony Shelton	.04	.02
❑ 603	Mark May	.04	.02
❑ 604	Craig McEwen RC	.04	.02
❑ 605	Steve Young	.60	.25
❑ 606	Keith Henderson	.04	.02
❑ 607	Pierce Holt	.04	.02
❑ 608	Roy Foster	.04	.02
❑ 609	Don Griffin	.04	.02
❑ 610	Harry Sydney	.04	.02
❑ 611	Todd Bowles	.04	.02
❑ 612	Ted Washington	.04	.02
❑ 613	Johnnie Jackson	.04	.02
❑ 614	Jesse Sapolu	.04	.02
❑ 615	Brent Jones	.10	.05
❑ 616	Travis McNeal	.04	.02
❑ 617	Darrick Brilz RC	.04	.02
❑ 618	Terry Wooden	.04	.02
❑ 619	Tommy Kane	.04	.02
❑ 620	Nesby Glasgow	.04	.02
❑ 621	Dwayne Harper	.04	.02
❑ 622	Rick Tuten	.04	.02
❑ 623	Chris Warren	.25	.11
❑ 624	John L. Williams	.04	.02
❑ 625	Rufus Porter	.04	.02
❑ 626	David Daniels	.04	.02
❑ 627	Keith McCants	.04	.02
❑ 628	Reuben Davis	.04	.02
❑ 629	Mark Royals	.04	.02
❑ 630	Marty Carter RC	.04	.02
❑ 631	Ian Beckles	.04	.02
❑ 632	Ron Hall	.04	.02
❑ 633	Eugene Marve	.04	.02
❑ 634	Willie Drewrey	.04	.02
❑ 635	Tom McHale RC	.04	.02
❑ 636	Kevin Murphy	.04	.02
❑ 637	Robert Hardy RC	.04	.02
❑ 638	Ricky Sanders	.04	.02
❑ 639	Gary Clark	.25	.11
❑ 640	Andre Collins	.04	.02
❑ 641	Brad Edwards	.04	.02
❑ 642	Monte Coleman	.04	.02
❑ 643	Clarence Vaughn RC	.04	.02
❑ 644	Fred Stokes	.04	.02
❑ 645	Charles Mann	.04	.02
❑ 646	Earnest Byner	.04	.02
❑ 647	Jim Lachey	.04	.02
❑ 648	Jeff Bostic	.04	.02
❑ 649	Chris Mims RC	.10	.05
❑ 650	George Williams RC	.04	.02
❑ 651	Ed Cunningham RC	.04	.02
❑ 652	Tony Smith RC	.04	.02
❑ 653	Will Furrer RC	.04	.02
❑ 654	Matt Elliott RC	.04	.02
❑ 655	Mike Mooney RC	.04	.02
❑ 656	Eddie Blake RC	.04	.02
❑ 657	Leon Searcy RC	.10	.05
❑ 658	Kevin Turner RC	.04	.02
❑ 659	Keith Hamilton RC	.04	.02
❑ 660	Alan Haller RC	.04	.02

1992 Pacific Picks The Pros

		MINT	NRMT
COMPLETE SET (25)		20.00	9.00
*GOLD/SILVER: SAME PRICE			
RANDOM INSERTS IN PACKS			
❑ 1	Mark Rypien	.25	.11
❑ 2	Marv Cook	.25	.11
❑ 3	Jim Lachey	.25	.11
❑ 4	Darrell Green	.25	.11
❑ 5	Derrick Thomas	1.50	.70
❑ 6	Thurman Thomas	1.50	.70
❑ 7	Kent Hull	.25	.11
❑ 8	Tim McDonald	.25	.11
❑ 9	Mike Croel	.25	.11
❑ 10	Anthony Munoz	.60	.25
❑ 11	Jerome Brown	.25	.11
❑ 12	Reggie White	1.50	.70
❑ 13	Gill Byrd	.25	.11
❑ 14	Jessie Tuggle	.25	.11
❑ 15	Randall McDaniel	.25	.11
❑ 16	Sam Mills	.25	.11
❑ 17	Pat Swilling	.60	.25
❑ 18	Eugene Robinson	.25	.11
❑ 19	Michael Irvin	1.50	.70
❑ 20	Emmitt Smith	10.00	4.50
❑ 21	Jeff Gossett	.25	.11
❑ 22	Jeff Jaeger	.25	.11
❑ 23	William Fuller	.60	.25
❑ 24	Mike Munchak	.25	.11
❑ 25	Andre Rison	.60	.25

1992 Pacific Prism Inserts

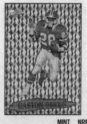

		MINT	NRMT
COMPLETE SET (10)		15.00	6.75
RANDOM INSERTS IN PACKS			
❑ 1	Thurman Thomas	1.00	.45
❑ 2	Gaston Green	.15	.07
❑ 3	Christian Okoye	.15	.07
❑ 4	Leonard Russell	.40	.18
❑ 5	Mark Higgs	.15	.07
❑ 6	Emmitt Smith	6.00	2.70
❑ 7	Barry Sanders	6.00	2.70
❑ 8	Rodney Hampton	1.00	.45
❑ 9	Earnest Byner	.15	.07
❑ 10	Herschel Walker	.40	.18

1992 Pacific Statistical Leaders

		MINT	NRMT
COMPLETE SET (30)		10.00	4.50
RANDOM INSERTS IN PACKS			
ONE SET PER FACTORY SET			
❑ 1	Chris Miller	.20	.09
❑ 2	Thurman Thomas	.50	.23
❑ 3	Jim Harbaugh	.50	.23
❑ 4	Jim Breech	.10	.05
❑ 5	Kevin Mack	.10	.05
❑ 6	Emmitt Smith	3.00	1.35
❑ 7	Gaston Green	.10	.05
❑ 8	Barry Sanders	3.00	1.35
❑ 9	Tony Bennett	.10	.05
❑ 10	Warren Moon	.50	.23
❑ 11	Bill Brooks	.10	.05

❑ 12 Christian Okoye .10 .05
❑ 13 Jay Schroeder .10 .05
❑ 14 Robert Delpino .10 .05
❑ 15 Mark Higgs .10 .05
❑ 16 John Randle .20 .09
❑ 17 Leonard Russell .20 .09
❑ 18 Pat Swilling .20 .09
❑ 19 Rodney Hampton .50 .23
❑ 20 Terance Mathis .20 .09
❑ 21 Fred Barnett .50 .23
❑ 22 Aeneas Williams .20 .09
❑ 23 Neil O'Donnell .50 .23
❑ 24 Marion Butts .10 .05
❑ 25 Steve Young 1.25 .55
❑ 26 John L. Williams .10 .05
❑ 27 Reggie Cobb .10 .05
❑ 28 Mark Rypien .10 .05
❑ 29 Thurman Thomas .50 .23
AFC Rushing Leaders
❑ 30 Emmitt Smith 3.00 1.35
NFC Rushing Leaders

1993 Pacific

	MINT	NRMT
COMPLETE SET (440)	20.00	9.00
COMMON CARD (1-440)	.05	.02
SEMISTARS	.10	.05
UNLISTED STARS	.25	.11
COMP.CHECKLIST SET (4)	4.00	1.80

CHECKLISTS: RANDOM INSERTS IN PACKS

❑ 1 Emmitt Smith 1.50 .70
❑ 2 Troy Aikman .75 .35
❑ 3 Larry Brown DB .05 .02
❑ 4 Tony Casillas .05 .02
❑ 5 Thomas Everett .05 .02
❑ 6 Alvin Harper .10 .05
❑ 7 Michael Irvin .25 .11
❑ 8 Charles Haley .10 .05
❑ 9 Leon Lett RC .10 .05
❑ 10 Kevin Smith .10 .05
❑ 11 Robert Jones .05 .02
❑ 12 Jimmy Smith .10 .05
❑ 13 Derrick Gainer RC .05 .02
❑ 14 Lin Elliott .05 .02
❑ 15 William Thomas .05 .02
❑ 16 Clyde Simmons .05 .02
❑ 17 Seth Joyner .05 .02
❑ 18 Randall Cunningham .25 .11
❑ 19 Byron Evans .05 .02
❑ 20 Fred Barnett .10 .05
❑ 21 Calvin Williams .10 .05
❑ 22 James Joseph .05 .02
❑ 23 Heath Sherman .05 .02
❑ 24 Siran Stacy .05 .02
❑ 25 Andy Harmon .10 .05
❑ 26 Eric Allen .05 .02
❑ 27 Herschel Walker .10 .05
❑ 28 Vai Sikahema .05 .02
❑ 29 Earnest Byner .05 .02
❑ 30 Jeff Bostic .05 .02
❑ 31 Monte Coleman .05 .02
❑ 32 Ricky Ervins .05 .02
❑ 33 Darrell Green .05 .02
❑ 34 Mark Schlereth .05 .02
❑ 35 Mark Rypien .05 .02
❑ 36 Art Monk .10 .05
❑ 37 Brian Mitchell .10 .05
❑ 38 Chip Lohmiller .05 .02
❑ 39 Charles Mann .05 .02
❑ 40 Shane Collins .05 .02
❑ 41 Jim Lachey .05 .02
❑ 42 Desmond Howard .10 .05
❑ 43 Rodney Hampton .25 .11
❑ 44 Dave Brown RC .25 .11
❑ 45 Mark Collins .05 .02
❑ 46 Jarrod Bunch .05 .02
❑ 47 William Roberts .05 .02
❑ 48 Sean Landeta .05 .02
❑ 49 Lawrence Taylor .25 .11
❑ 50 Ed McCaffrey .10 .05
❑ 51 Bart Oates .05 .02
❑ 52 Pepper Johnson .05 .02
❑ 53 Eric Dorsey .05 .02
❑ 54 Erik Howard .05 .02
❑ 55 Phil Simms .10 .05
❑ 56 Derek Brown TE .05 .02
❑ 57 Johnny Bailey .05 .02
❑ 58 Rich Camarillo .05 .02
❑ 59 Larry Centers RC .25 .11
❑ 60 Chris Chandler .10 .05
❑ 61 Randal Hill .05 .02
❑ 62 Ricky Proehl .05 .02
❑ 63 Freddie Joe Nunn .05 .02
❑ 64 Robert Massey .05 .02
❑ 65 Aeneas Williams .05 .02
❑ 66 Luis Sharpe .05 .02
❑ 67 Eric Swann .10 .05
❑ 68 Timm Rosenbach .05 .02
❑ 69 Anthony Edwards RC .05 .02
❑ 70 Greg Davis .05 .02
❑ 71 Terry Allen .25 .11
❑ 72 Anthony Carter .10 .05
❑ 73 Cris Carter .50 .23
❑ 74 Roger Craig .10 .05
❑ 75 Jack Del Rio .05 .02
❑ 76 Chris Doleman .05 .02
❑ 77 Rich Gannon .05 .02
❑ 78 Hassan Jones .05 .02
❑ 79 Steve Jordan .05 .02
❑ 80 Randall McDaniel .05 .02
❑ 81 Sean Salisbury .05 .02
❑ 82 Harry Newsome .05 .02
❑ 83 Carlos Jenkins .05 .02
❑ 84 Jake Reed .25 .11
❑ 85 Edgar Bennett .25 .11
❑ 86 Tony Bennett .05 .02
❑ 87 Terrell Buckley .05 .02
❑ 88 Ty Detmer .25 .11
❑ 89 Brett Favre 2.00 .90
❑ 90 Chris Jacke .05 .02
❑ 91 Sterling Sharpe .25 .11
❑ 92 James Campen .05 .02
❑ 93 Brian Noble .05 .02
❑ 94 Lester Archambeau RC .05 .02
❑ 95 Harry Sydney .05 .02
❑ 96 Corey Harris .05 .02
❑ 97 Don Majkowski .05 .02
❑ 98 Ken Ruettgers .05 .02
❑ 99 Lomas Brown .05 .02
❑ 100 Jason Hanson .05 .02
❑ 101 Robert Porcher .05 .02
❑ 102 Chris Spielman .10 .05
❑ 103 Erik Kramer .10 .05
❑ 104 Tracy Scroggins .05 .02
❑ 105 Rodney Peete .05 .02
❑ 106 Barry Sanders 1.50 .70
❑ 107 Herman Moore .50 .23
❑ 108 Brett Perriman .25 .11
❑ 109 Mel Gray .10 .05
❑ 110 Dennis Gibson .05 .02
❑ 111 Bennie Blades .05 .02
❑ 112 Andre Ware .05 .02
❑ 113 Gary Anderson RB .05 .02
❑ 114 Tyji Armstrong .05 .02
❑ 115 Reggie Cobb .05 .02
❑ 116 Marty Carter .05 .02
❑ 117 Lawrence Dawsey .05 .02
❑ 118 Steve DeBerg .05 .02
❑ 119 Ron Hall .05 .02
❑ 120 Courtney Hawkins .05 .02
❑ 121 Broderick Thomas .05 .02
❑ 122 Keith McCants .05 .02
❑ 123 Bruce Reimers .05 .02
❑ 124 Darrick Brownlow .05 .02
❑ 125 Mark Wheeler .05 .02
❑ 126 Ricky Reynolds .05 .02
❑ 127 Neal Anderson .05 .02
❑ 128 Trace Armstrong .05 .02
❑ 129 Mark Carrier DB .05 .02
❑ 130 Richard Dent .10 .05
❑ 131 Wendell Davis .05 .02
❑ 132 Darren Lewis .05 .02
❑ 133 Tom Waddle .05 .02
❑ 134 Jim Harbaugh .25 .11
❑ 135 Steve McMichael .10 .05
❑ 136 William Perry .10 .05
❑ 137 Alonzo Spellman .05 .02
❑ 138 John Roper .05 .02
❑ 139 Peter Tom Willis .05 .02
❑ 140 Dante Jones .05 .02
❑ 141 Harris Barton .05 .02
❑ 142 Michael Carter .05 .02
❑ 143 Eric Davis .05 .02
❑ 144 Dana Hall .05 .02
❑ 145 Amp Lee .05 .02
❑ 146 Don Griffin .05 .02
❑ 147 Jerry Rice 1.00 .45
❑ 148 Ricky Watters .25 .11
❑ 149 Steve Young .75 .35
❑ 150 Bill Romanowski .05 .02
❑ 151 Klaus Wilmsmeyer .05 .02
❑ 152 Steve Bono .25 .11
❑ 153 Tom Rathman .05 .02
❑ 154 Odessa Turner .05 .02
❑ 155 Morten Andersen .05 .02
❑ 156 Richard Cooper .05 .02
❑ 157 Toi Cook .05 .02
❑ 158 Quinn Early .10 .05
❑ 159 Vaughn Dunbar .05 .02
❑ 160 Rickey Jackson .05 .02
❑ 161 Wayne Martin .05 .02
❑ 162 Hoby Brenner .05 .02
❑ 163 Joel Hilgenberg .05 .02
❑ 164 Mike Buck .05 .02
❑ 165 Torrance Small .05 .02
❑ 166 Eric Martin .05 .02
❑ 167 Vaughan Johnson .05 .02
❑ 168 Sam Mills .05 .02
❑ 169 Steve Broussard .05 .02
❑ 170 Darion Conner .05 .02
❑ 171 Drew Hill .05 .02
❑ 172 Chris Hinton .05 .02
❑ 173 Chris Miller .10 .05
❑ 174 Tim McKyer .05 .02
❑ 175 Norm Johnson .05 .02
❑ 176 Mike Pritchard .10 .05
❑ 177 Andre Rison .10 .05
❑ 178 Deion Sanders .50 .23
❑ 179 Tony Smith .05 .02
❑ 180 Bruce Pickens .05 .02
❑ 181 Michael Haynes .10 .05
❑ 182 Jessie Tuggle .05 .02
❑ 183 Marc Boutte .05 .02
❑ 184 Don Bracken .05 .02
❑ 185 Bern Brostek .05 .02
❑ 186 Henry Ellard .10 .05
❑ 187 Jim Everett .10 .05
❑ 188 Sean Gilbert .10 .05
❑ 189 Cleveland Gary .05 .02
❑ 190 Todd Kinchen .05 .02
❑ 191 Pat Terrell .05 .02
❑ 192 Jackie Slater .05 .02
❑ 193 David Lang .05 .02
❑ 194 Flipper Anderson .05 .02
❑ 195 Tony Zendejas .05 .02
❑ 196 Roman Phifer .05 .02
❑ 197 Steve Christie .05 .02
❑ 198 Cornelius Bennett .10 .05
❑ 199 Phil Hansen .05 .02
❑ 200 Don Beebe .05 .02
❑ 201 Mark Kelso .05 .02
❑ 202 Bruce Smith .25 .11
❑ 203 Darryl Talley .05 .02
❑ 204 Andre Reed .10 .05
❑ 205 Mike Lodish .05 .02
❑ 206 Jim Kelly .25 .11
❑ 207 Thurman Thomas .25 .11

	No.	Player	Mint	NRMT
❑	208	Kenneth Davis	.05	.02
❑	209	Frank Reich	.10	.05
❑	210	Kent Hull	.05	.02
❑	211	Marco Coleman	.05	.02
❑	212	Bryan Cox	.05	.02
❑	213	Jeff Cross	.05	.02
❑	214	Mark Higgs	.05	.02
❑	215	Keith Jackson	.10	.05
❑	216	Scott Miller	.05	.02
❑	217	John Offerdahl	.05	.02
❑	218	Dan Marino	1.50	.70
❑	219	Keith Sims	.05	.02
❑	220	Chuck Klingbeil	.05	.02
❑	221	Troy Vincent	.05	.02
❑	222	Mike Williams RC	.05	.02
❑	223	Pete Stoyanovich	.05	.02
❑	224	J.B. Brown	.05	.02
❑	225	Ashley Ambrose	.05	.02
❑	226	Jason Belser RC	.05	.02
❑	227	Jeff George	.25	.11
❑	228	Quentin Coryatt	.10	.05
❑	229	Duane Bickett	.05	.02
❑	230	Steve Emtman	.05	.02
❑	231	Anthony Johnson	.10	.05
❑	232	Rohn Stark	.05	.02
❑	233	Jessie Hester	.05	.02
❑	234	Reggie Langhorne	.05	.02
❑	235	Clarence Verdin	.05	.02
❑	236	Dean Biasucci	.05	.02
❑	237	Jack Trudeau	.05	.02
❑	238	Tony Siragusa	.05	.02
❑	239	Chris Burkett	.05	.02
❑	240	Brad Baxter	.05	.02
❑	241	Rob Moore	.10	.05
❑	242	Browning Nagle	.05	.02
❑	243	Jim Sweeney	.05	.02
❑	244	Kurt Barber	.05	.02
❑	245	Siupeli Malamala RC	.05	.02
❑	246	Mike Brim	.05	.02
❑	247	Mo Lewis	.05	.02
❑	248	Johnny Mitchell	.05	.02
❑	249	Ken Whisenhunt RC	.05	.02
❑	250	James Hasty	.05	.02
❑	251	Kyle Clifton	.05	.02
❑	252	Terance Mathis	.10	.05
❑	253	Ray Agnew	.05	.02
❑	254	Eugene Chung	.05	.02
❑	255	Marv Cook	.05	.02
❑	256	Johnny Rembert	.05	.02
❑	257	Maurice Hurst	.05	.02
❑	258	Jon Vaughn	.05	.02
❑	259	Leonard Russell	.10	.05
❑	260	Pat Harlow	.05	.02
❑	261	Andre Tippett	.05	.02
❑	262	Michael Timpson	.05	.02
❑	263	Greg McMurtry	.05	.02
❑	264	Chris Singleton	.05	.02
❑	265	Reggie Redding RC	.05	.02
❑	266	Walter Stanley	.05	.02
❑	267	Gary Anderson K	.05	.02
❑	268	Merril Hoge	.05	.02
❑	269	Barry Foster	.10	.05
❑	270	Charles Davenport	.05	.02
❑	271	Jeff Graham	.10	.05
❑	272	Adrian Cooper	.05	.02
❑	273	David Little	.05	.02
❑	274	Neil O'Donnell	.25	.11
❑	275	Rod Woodson	.25	.11
❑	276	Ernie Mills	.05	.02
❑	277	Dwight Stone	.05	.02
❑	278	Darren Perry	.05	.02
❑	279	Dermontti Dawson	.05	.02
❑	280	Carlton Haselrig	.05	.02
❑	281	Pat Coleman	.05	.02
❑	282	Ernest Givins	.10	.05
❑	283	Warren Moon	.25	.11
❑	284	Haywood Jeffires	.10	.05
❑	285	Cody Carlson	.05	.02
❑	286	Ray Childress	.05	.02
❑	287	Bruce Matthews	.05	.02
❑	288	Webster Slaughter	.05	.02
❑	289	Bo Orlando	.05	.02
❑	290	Lorenzo White	.05	.02
❑	291	Eddie Robinson	.05	.02
❑	292	Bubba McDowell	.05	.02
❑	293	Bucky Richardson	.05	.02
❑	294	Sean Jones	.05	.02
❑	295	David Brandon	.05	.02
❑	296	Shawn Collins	.05	.02
❑	297	Lawyer Tillman	.05	.02
❑	298	Bob Dahl	.05	.02
❑	299	Kevin Mack	.05	.02
❑	300	Bernie Kosar	.10	.05
❑	301	Tommy Vardell	.05	.02
❑	302	Jay Hilgenberg	.05	.02
❑	303	Michael Dean Perry	.10	.05
❑	304	Michael Jackson	.10	.05
❑	305	Eric Metcalf	.10	.05
❑	306	Rico Smith RC	.05	.02
❑	307	Stevon Moore RC	.05	.02
❑	308	Leroy Hoard	.10	.05
❑	309	Eric Ball	.05	.02
❑	310	Derrick Fenner	.05	.02
❑	311	James Francis	.05	.02
❑	312	Ricardo McDonald	.05	.02
❑	313	Tim Krumrie	.05	.02
❑	314	Carl Pickens	.25	.11
❑	315	David Klingler	.05	.02
❑	316	Donald Hollas RC	.05	.02
❑	317	Harold Green	.05	.02
❑	318	Daniel Stubbs	.05	.02
❑	319	Alfred Williams	.05	.02
❑	320	Darryl Williams	.05	.02
❑	321	Mike Arthur RC	.05	.02
❑	322	Leonard Wheeler	.05	.02
❑	323	Gill Byrd	.05	.02
❑	324	Eric Bieniemy	.05	.02
❑	325	Marion Butts	.05	.02
❑	326	John Carney	.05	.02
❑	327	Stan Humphries	.25	.11
❑	328	Ronnie Harmon	.05	.02
❑	329	Junior Seau	.25	.11
❑	330	Nate Lewis	.05	.02
❑	331	Harry Swayne	.05	.02
❑	332	Leslie O'Neal	.10	.05
❑	333	Eric Moten	.05	.02
❑	334	Blaise Winter RC	.05	.02
❑	335	Anthony Miller	.10	.05
❑	336	Gary Plummer	.05	.02
❑	337	Willie Davis	.25	.11
❑	338	J.J. Birden	.05	.02
❑	339	Tim Barnett	.05	.02
❑	340	Dave Krieg	.10	.05
❑	341	Barry Word	.05	.02
❑	342	Tracy Simien	.05	.02
❑	343	Christian Okoye	.05	.02
❑	344	Todd McNair	.05	.02
❑	345	Dan Saleaumua	.05	.02
❑	346	Derrick Thomas	.25	.11
❑	347	Harvey Williams	.10	.05
❑	348	Kimble Anders RC	.25	.11
❑	349	Tim Grunhard	.05	.02
❑	350	Tony Hargain RC UER (Hargrain on front)	.05	.02
❑	351	Simon Fletcher	.05	.02
❑	352	John Elway	1.50	.70
❑	353	Mike Croel	.05	.02
❑	354	Steve Atwater	.05	.02
❑	355	Tommy Maddox	.05	.02
❑	356	Karl Mecklenburg	.05	.02
❑	357	Shane Dronett	.05	.02
❑	358	Kenny Walker	.05	.02
❑	359	Reggie Rivers RC	.05	.02
❑	360	Cedric Tillman RC	.05	.02
❑	361	Arthur Marshall RC	.05	.02
❑	362	Greg Lewis	.05	.02
❑	363	Shannon Sharpe	.25	.11
❑	364	Doug Widell	.05	.02
❑	365	Todd Marinovich	.05	.02
❑	366	Nick Bell	.05	.02
❑	367	Eric Dickerson	.10	.05
❑	368	Max Montoya	.05	.02
❑	369	Winston Moss	.05	.02
❑	370	Howie Long	.10	.05
❑	371	Willie Gault	.05	.02
❑	372	Tim Brown	.25	.11
❑	373	Steve Smith	.05	.02
❑	374	Steve Wisniewski	.05	.02
❑	375	Alexander Wright	.05	.02
❑	376	Ethan Horton	.05	.02
❑	377	Napoleon McCallum	.05	.02
❑	378	Terry McDaniel	.05	.02
❑	379	Patrick Hunter	.05	.02
❑	380	Robert Blackmon	.05	.02
❑	381	John Kasay	.05	.02
❑	382	Cortez Kennedy	.10	.05
❑	383	Andy Heck	.05	.02
❑	384	Bill Hitchcock RC	.05	.02
❑	385	Rick Mirer RC	.50	.23
❑	386	Jeff Bryant	.05	.02
❑	387	Eugene Robinson	.05	.02
❑	388	John L. Williams	.05	.02
❑	389	Chris Warren	.10	.05
❑	390	Rufus Porter	.05	.02
❑	391	Joe Tofflemire RC	.05	.02
❑	392	Dan McGwire	.05	.02
❑	393	Boomer Esiason	.10	.05
❑	394	Brad Muster	.05	.02
❑	395	James Lofton	.10	.05
❑	396	Tim McGee	.05	.02
❑	397	Steve Beuerlein	.05	.02
❑	398	Gaston Green	.05	.02
❑	399	Bill Brooks	.05	.02
❑	400	Ronnie Lott	.10	.05
❑	401	Jay Schroeder	.05	.02
❑	402	Marcus Allen	.25	.11
❑	403	Kevin Greene	.25	.11
❑	404	Kirk Lowdermilk	.05	.02
❑	405	Hugh Millen	.05	.02
❑	406	Pat Swilling	.05	.02
❑	407	Bobby Hebert	.05	.02
❑	408	Carl Banks	.05	.02
❑	409	Jeff Hostetler	.10	.05
❑	410	Leonard Marshall	.05	.02
❑	411	Ken O'Brien	.05	.02
❑	412	Joe Montana	1.50	.70
❑	413	Reggie White	.25	.11
❑	414	Gary Clark	.10	.05
❑	415	Johnny Johnson	.05	.02
❑	416	Tim McDonald	.05	.02
❑	417	Pierce Holt	.05	.02
❑	418	Gino Torretta RC	.10	.05
❑	419	Glyn Milburn RC	.25	.11
❑	420	O.J. McDuffie RC	.75	.35
❑	421	Coleman Rudolph RC	.05	.02
❑	422	Reggie Brooks RC	.10	.05
❑	423	Garrison Hearst RC	1.00	.45
❑	424	Leonard Renfro RC	.05	.02
❑	425	Kevin Williams RC	.25	.11
❑	426	Demetrius DuBose RC	.05	.02
❑	427	Elvis Grbac RC	.75	.35
❑	428	Lincoln Kennedy RC	.05	.02
❑	429	Carlton Gray RC	.05	.02
❑	430	Micheal Barrow	.05	.02
❑	431	George Teague RC	.10	.05
❑	432	Curtis Conway RC	.50	.23
❑	433	Natrone Means RC	.75	.35
❑	434	Jerome Bettis RC	1.00	.45
❑	435	Drew Bledsoe RC	3.00	1.35
❑	436	Robert Smith RC	1.00	.45
❑	437	Deon Figures RC	.10	.05
❑	438	Qadry Ismail RC	.25	.11
❑	439	Chris Slade RC	.10	.05
❑	440	Dana Stubblefield RC	.25	.11

1993 Pacific Picks the Pros Gold

	MINT	NRMT
COMPLETE SET (25)	40.00	18.00

RANDOM INSERTS IN PACKS ....

❑ 1 Jerry Rice	8.00	3.60
❑ 2 Sterling Sharpe	2.00	.90
❑ 3 Richmond Webb	.40	.18
❑ 4 Harris Barton	.40	.18
❑ 5 Randall McDaniel	.40	.18
❑ 6 Steve Wisniewski	.40	.18
❑ 7 Mark Stepnoski	.40	.18
❑ 8 Steve Young	6.00	2.70
❑ 9 Emmitt Smith	12.00	5.50
❑ 10 Barry Foster	.75	.35
❑ 11 Nick Lowery	.40	.18
❑ 12 Reggie White	2.00	.90
❑ 13 Leslie O'Neal	.75	.35
❑ 14 Cortez Kennedy	.75	.35
❑ 15 Ray Childress	.40	.18
❑ 16 Vaughan Johnson	.40	.18
❑ 17 Wilber Marshall	.40	.18
❑ 18 Junior Seau	2.00	.90
❑ 19 Sam Mills	.40	.18
❑ 20 Rod Woodson	2.00	.90
❑ 21 Ricky Reynolds	.40	.18
❑ 22 Steve Atwater	.40	.18
❑ 23 Chuck Cecil	.40	.18
❑ 24 Rich Camarillo	.40	.18
❑ 25 Dale Carter	.40	.18

1993 Pacific Silver Prism Inserts

	MINT	NRMT
COMPLETE SET (20)	60.00	27.00

TRI.BACKGRND:RAND.INS.IN REG.PACKS
*CIRCULAR STARS: 2.5X TO 6X BASE CARD HI
*CIRCULAR ROOKIES: 1.2X TO 3X BASE CARD HI....................................
CIRCULAR:ONE PER SPEC.RET.PACK

❑ 1 Troy Aikman	5.00	2.20
❑ 2 Jerome Bettis	3.00	1.35
❑ 3 Drew Bledsoe	10.00	4.50
❑ 4 Reggie Brooks	.30	.14
❑ 5 Brett Favre	12.00	5.50
❑ 6 Barry Foster	.60	.25
❑ 7 Garrison Hearst	3.00	1.35
❑ 8 Michael Irvin	1.50	.70
❑ 9 Cortez Kennedy	.60	.25
❑ 10 David Klingler	.30	.14
❑ 11 Dan Marino	10.00	4.50
❑ 12 Rick Mirer	1.50	.70
❑ 13 Joe Montana	10.00	4.50
❑ 14 Jay Novacek	.30	.14
❑ 15 Jerry Rice	6.00	2.70
❑ 16 Barry Sanders	10.00	4.50
❑ 17 Sterling Sharpe	1.50	.70
❑ 18 Emmitt Smith	10.00	4.50
❑ 19 Thurman Thomas	1.50	.70
❑ 20 Steve Young	5.00	2.20

1994 Pacific

	MINT	NRMT
COMPLETE SET (450)	30.00	13.50
COMMON CARD (1-450)	.05	.02
SEMISTARS	.10	.05
UNLISTED STARS	.25	.11

❑ 1 Troy Aikman	1.00	.45
❑ 2 Charles Haley	.10	.05
❑ 3 Alvin Harper	.10	.05
❑ 4 Michael Irvin	.25	.11
❑ 5 Jim Jeffcoat	.05	.02
❑ 6 Daryl Johnston	.10	.05
❑ 7 Robert Jones	.05	.02
❑ 8 Brock Marion RC	.05	.02
❑ 9 Russell Maryland	.05	.02
❑ 10 Ken Norton	.10	.05
❑ 11 Jay Novacek	.10	.05
❑ 12 Emmitt Smith	1.50	.70
❑ 13 Kevin Smith	.05	.02
❑ 14 Tony Tolbert	.05	.02
❑ 15 Kevin Williams WR	.10	.05
❑ 16 Don Beebe	.05	.02
❑ 17 Cornelius Bennett	.10	.05
❑ 18 Bill Brooks	.05	.02
❑ 19 Steve Christie	.05	.02
❑ 20 Russell Copeland	.05	.02
❑ 21 Kenneth Davis	.05	.02
❑ 22 Kent Hull	.05	.02
❑ 23 Jim Kelly	.25	.11
❑ 24 Pete Metzelaars	.05	.02
❑ 25 Andre Reed	.10	.05
❑ 26 Frank Reich	.10	.05
❑ 27 Bruce Smith	.25	.11
❑ 28 Darryl Talley	.05	.02
❑ 29 Steve Tasker	.10	.05
❑ 30 Thurman Thomas	.25	.11
❑ 31 Steve Bono	.10	.05
❑ 32 Dexter Carter	.05	.02
❑ 33 Kevin Fagan	.05	.02
❑ 34 Dana Hall	.05	.02
❑ 35 Brent Jones	.10	.05
❑ 36 Amp Lee	.05	.02
❑ 37 Marc Logan	.05	.02
❑ 38 Tim McDonald	.05	.02
❑ 39 Guy McIntyre	.05	.02
❑ 40 Tom Rathman	.05	.02
❑ 41 Jerry Rice	1.00	.45
❑ 42 Dana Stubblefield	.25	.11
❑ 43 Steve Wallace	.05	.02
❑ 44 Ricky Watters	.25	.11
❑ 45 Steve Young	.75	.35
❑ 46 Marcus Allen	.25	.11
❑ 47 Kimble Anders	.10	.05
❑ 48 Tim Barnett	.05	.02
❑ 49 J.J. Birden	.05	.02
❑ 50 Dale Carter	.05	.02
❑ 51 Jonathan Hayes	.05	.02
❑ 52 Dave Krieg	.10	.05
❑ 53 Albert Lewis	.05	.02
❑ 54 Nick Lowery	.05	.02
❑ 55 Joe Montana	2.00	.90
❑ 56 Neil Smith	.25	.11
❑ 57 John Stephens	.05	.02
❑ 58 Derrick Thomas	.25	.11
❑ 59 Harvey Williams	.10	.05
❑ 60 Micheal Barrow	.05	.02
❑ 61 Gary Brown	.05	.02
❑ 62 Cody Carlson	.05	.02
❑ 63 Ray Childress	.05	.02
❑ 64 Curtis Duncan	.05	.02
❑ 65 Ernest Givins	.10	.05
❑ 66 Haywood Jeffires	.10	.05
❑ 67 Wilber Marshall	.05	.02
❑ 68 Bubba McDowell	.05	.02
❑ 69 Warren Moon	.25	.11
❑ 70 Mike Munchak	.05	.02
❑ 71 Marcus Robertson	.05	.02
❑ 72 Webster Slaughter	.05	.02
❑ 73 Gary Wellman RC	.05	.02
❑ 74 Lorenzo White	.05	.02
❑ 75 Ray Crockett	.05	.02
❑ 76 Jason Hanson	.05	.02
❑ 77 Rodney Holman	.05	.02
❑ 78 George Jamison	.05	.02
❑ 79 Erik Kramer	.10	.05
❑ 80 Ryan McNeil	.05	.02
❑ 81 Derrick Moore	.05	.02
❑ 82 Herman Moore	.25	.11
❑ 83 Rodney Peete	.05	.02
❑ 84 Brett Perriman	.10	.05
❑ 85 Barry Sanders	2.00	.90
❑ 86 Chris Spielman	.10	.05
❑ 87 Pat Swilling	.05	.02
❑ 88 Vernon Turner	.05	.02
❑ 89 Andre Ware	.05	.02
❑ 90 Michael Brooks	.05	.02
❑ 91 Dave Brown	.10	.05
❑ 92 Derek Brown TE	.05	.02
❑ 93 Jarrod Bunch	.05	.02
❑ 94 Chris Calloway	.05	.02
❑ 95 Kent Graham	.10	.05
❑ 96 Rodney Hampton	.25	.11
❑ 97 Mark Jackson	.05	.02
❑ 98 Ed McCaffrey	.10	.05
❑ 99 Dave Meggett	.05	.02
❑ 100 Aaron Pierce	.05	.02
❑ 101 Mike Sherrard	.05	.02
❑ 102 Phil Simms	.10	.05
❑ 103 Lewis Tillman	.05	.02
❑ 104 Eddie Anderson	.05	.02
❑ 105 Patrick Bates	.05	.02
❑ 106 Nick Bell	.05	.02
❑ 107 Tim Brown	.25	.11
❑ 108 Willie Gault	.05	.02
❑ 109 Jeff Gossett	.05	.02
❑ 110 Ethan Horton	.05	.02
❑ 111 Jeff Hostetler	.10	.05
❑ 112 Rocket Ismail	.10	.05
❑ 113 Chester McGlockton	.05	.02
❑ 114 Anthony Smith	.05	.02
❑ 115 Steve Smith	.05	.02
❑ 116 Greg Townsend	.05	.02
❑ 117 Steve Wisniewski	.05	.02
❑ 118 Alexander Wright	.05	.02
❑ 119 Steve Atwater	.05	.02
❑ 120 Rod Bernstine	.05	.02
❑ 121 Mike Croel	.05	.02
❑ 122 Shane Dronett	.05	.02
❑ 123 Jason Elam	.05	.02
❑ 124 John Elway	2.00	.90
❑ 125 Brian Habib	.05	.02
❑ 126 Rondell Jones	.05	.02
❑ 127 Tommy Maddox	.05	.02
❑ 128 Karl Mecklenburg	.05	.02
❑ 129 Glyn Milburn	.10	.05
❑ 130 Derek Russell	.05	.02
❑ 131 Shannon Sharpe	.10	.05
❑ 132 Dennis Smith	.05	.02
❑ 133 Edgar Bennett	.25	.11
❑ 134 Tony Bennett	.05	.02
❑ 135 Robert Brooks	.25	.11
❑ 136 Terrell Buckley	.05	.02
❑ 137 LeRoy Butler	.05	.02
❑ 138 Mark Clayton	.05	.02
❑ 139 Ty Detmer	.10	.05
❑ 140 Brett Favre	2.00	.90
❑ 141 John Jurkovic RC	.10	.05
❑ 142 Bryce Paup	.25	.11
❑ 143 Sterling Sharpe	.10	.05
❑ 144 George Teague	.05	.02
❑ 145 Darrell Thompson	.05	.02
❑ 146 Ed West	.05	.02
❑ 147 Reggie White	.25	.11
❑ 148 Terry Allen	.10	.05
❑ 149 Anthony Carter	.10	.05
❑ 150 Cris Carter	.50	.23
❑ 151 Roger Craig	.10	.05
❑ 152 Jack Del Rio	.05	.02
❑ 153 Chris Doleman	.05	.02
❑ 154 Scottie Graham RC	.10	.05

❑	155 Eric Gulford RC	.05	.02
❑	156 Qadry Ismail	.25	.11
❑	157 Steve Jordan	.05	.02
❑	158 Randall McDaniel	.05	.02
❑	159 Jim McMahon	.05	.02
❑	160 Audray McMillian	.05	.02
❑	161 Sean Salisbury	.05	.02
❑	162 Robert Smith	.25	.11
❑	163 Henry Thomas	.05	.02
❑	164 Gary Anderson K	.05	.02
❑	165 Deon Figures	.05	.02
❑	166 Barry Foster	.05	.02
❑	167 Jeff Graham	.05	.02
❑	168 Kevin Greene	.25	.11
❑	169 Dave Hoffman	.05	.02
❑	170 Merril Hoge	.05	.02
❑	171 Gary Jones	.05	.02
❑	172 Greg Lloyd	.25	.11
❑	173 Ernie Mills	.05	.02
❑	174 Neil O'Donnell	.25	.11
❑	175 Darren Perry	.05	.02
❑	176 Leon Searcy	.05	.02
❑	177 Leroy Thompson	.05	.02
❑	178 Willie Williams	.05	.02
❑	179 Rod Woodson	.25	.11
❑	180 Keith Byars	.05	.02
❑	181 Marco Coleman	.05	.02
❑	182 Bryan Cox	.05	.02
❑	183 Irving Fryar	.10	.05
❑	184 John Grimsley	.05	.02
❑	185 Mark Higgs	.05	.02
❑	186 Mark Ingram	.05	.02
❑	187 Keith Jackson	.05	.02
❑	188 Terry Kirby	.25	.11
❑	189 Dan Marino	2.00	.90
❑	190 O.J. McDuffie	.25	.11
❑	191 Scott Mitchell	.25	.11
❑	192 Pete Stoyanovich	.05	.02
❑	193 Troy Vincent	.05	.02
❑	194 Richmond Webb	.05	.02
❑	195 Brad Baxter	.05	.02
❑	196 Chris Burkett	.05	.02
❑	197 Rob Carpenter	.05	.02
❑	198 Boomer Esiason	.10	.05
❑	199 Johnny Johnson	.05	.02
❑	200 Jeff Lageman	.05	.02
❑	201 Mo Lewis	.05	.02
❑	202 Ronnie Lott	.10	.05
❑	203 Leonard Marshall	.05	.02
❑	204 Terance Mathis	.10	.05
❑	205 Johnny Mitchell	.05	.02
❑	206 Rob Moore	.10	.05
❑	207 Anthony Prior	.05	.02
❑	208 Blair Thomas	.05	.02
❑	209 Brian Washington	.05	.02
❑	210 Eric Bieniemy	.05	.02
❑	211 Marion Butts	.05	.02
❑	212 Gill Byrd	.05	.02
❑	213 John Carney	.05	.02
❑	214 Darren Carrington	.05	.02
❑	215 John Friesz	.10	.05
❑	216 Ronnie Harmon	.05	.02
❑	217 Stan Humphries	.25	.11
❑	218 Nate Lewis	.05	.02
❑	219 Natrone Means	.25	.11
❑	220 Anthony Miller	.10	.05
❑	221 Chris Mims	.05	.02
❑	222 Eric Moten	.05	.02
❑	223 Leslie O'Neal	.05	.02
❑	224 Junior Seau	.25	.11
❑	225 Morten Andersen	.05	.02
❑	226 Gene Atkins	.05	.02
❑	227 Derek Brown RBK	.05	.02
❑	228 Toi Cook	.05	.02
❑	229 Vaughn Dunbar	.05	.02
❑	230 Quinn Early	.10	.05
❑	231 Reggie Freeman	.05	.02
❑	232 Tyrone Hughes	.10	.05
❑	233 Rickey Jackson	.05	.02
❑	234 Eric Martin	.05	.02
❑	235 Sam Mills	.05	.02
❑	236 Brad Muster	.05	.02
❑	237 Torrance Small	.05	.02
❑	238 Irv Smith	.05	.02
❑	239 Wade Wilson	.05	.02
❑	240 Eric Allen	.05	.02
❑	241 Victor Bailey	.05	.02
❑	242 Fred Barnett	.10	.05
❑	243 Mark Bavaro	.05	.02
❑	244 Bubby Brister	.05	.02
❑	245 Randall Cunningham	.25	.11
❑	246 Antone Davis	.05	.02
❑	247 Britt Hager RC	.05	.02
❑	248 Vaughn Hebron	.05	.02
❑	249 James Joseph	.05	.02
❑	250 Seth Joyner	.05	.02
❑	251 Rich Miano	.05	.02
❑	252 Heath Sherman	.05	.02
❑	253 Clyde Simmons	.05	.02
❑	254 Herschel Walker	.10	.05
❑	255 Calvin Williams	.10	.05
❑	256 Jerry Ball	.05	.02
❑	257 Mark Carrier WR	.10	.05
❑	258 Michael Jackson	.10	.05
❑	259 Mike Johnson	.05	.02
❑	260 James Jones	.05	.02
❑	261 Brian Kinchen	.10	.05
❑	262 Clay Matthews	.05	.02
❑	263 Eric Metcalf	.10	.05
❑	264 Stevon Moore	.05	.02
❑	265 Michael Dean Perry	.10	.05
❑	266 Todd Philcox	.05	.02
❑	267 Anthony Pleasant	.05	.02
❑	268 Vinny Testaverde	.10	.05
❑	269 Eric Turner	.05	.02
❑	270 Tommy Vardell	.05	.02
❑	271 Neal Anderson	.05	.02
❑	272 Trace Armstrong	.05	.02
❑	273 Mark Carrier DB	.05	.02
❑	274 Bob Christian	.05	.02
❑	275 Curtis Conway	.25	.11
❑	276 Richard Dent	.10	.05
❑	277 Robert Green	.05	.02
❑	278 Jim Harbaugh	.25	.11
❑	279 Craig Heyward	.10	.05
❑	280 Terry Obee	.05	.02
❑	281 Alonzo Spellman	.05	.02
❑	282 Tom Waddle	.05	.02
❑	283 Peter Tom Willis	.05	.02
❑	284 Donnell Woolford	.05	.02
❑	285 Tim Worley	.05	.02
❑	286 Chris Zorich	.05	.02
❑	287 Steve Broussard	.05	.02
❑	288 Darion Conner	.05	.02
❑	289 Jumpy Geathers	.05	.02
❑	290 Michael Haynes	.10	.05
❑	291 Bobby Hebert	.05	.02
❑	292 Lincoln Kennedy	.05	.02
❑	293 Chris Miller	.05	.02
❑	294 David Mims RC	.05	.02
❑	295 Erric Pegram	.05	.02
❑	296 Mike Pritchard	.05	.02
❑	297 Andre Rison	.10	.05
❑	298 Deion Sanders	.50	.23
❑	299 Chuck Smith	.05	.02
❑	300 Tony Smith	.05	.02
❑	301 Johnny Bailey	.05	.02
❑	302 Steve Beuerlein	.05	.02
❑	303 Chuck Cecil	.05	.02
❑	304 Chris Chandler	.10	.05
❑	305 Gary Clark	.10	.05
❑	306 Rick Cunningham RC	.05	.02
❑	307 Ken Harvey	.05	.02
❑	308 Garrison Hearst	.25	.11
❑	309 Randal Hill	.05	.02
❑	310 Robert Massey	.05	.02
❑	311 Ronald Moore	.05	.02
❑	312 Ricky Proehl	.05	.02
❑	313 Eric Swann	.10	.05
❑	314 Aeneas Williams	.05	.02
❑	315 Michael Bates	.05	.02
❑	316 Brian Blades	.10	.05
❑	317 Carlton Gray	.05	.02
❑	318 Paul Green RC	.05	.02
❑	319 Patrick Hunter	.05	.02
❑	320 John Kasay	.05	.02
❑	321 Cortez Kennedy	.10	.05
❑	322 Kelvin Martin	.05	.02
❑	323 Dan McGwire	.05	.02
❑	324 Rick Mirer	.25	.11
❑	325 Eugene Robinson	.05	.02
❑	326 Rick Tuten	.05	.02
❑	327 Chris Warren	.10	.05
❑	328 John L. Williams	.05	.02
❑	329 Reggie Cobb	.05	.02
❑	330 Horace Copeland	.05	.02
❑	331 Lawrence Dawsey	.05	.02
❑	332 Santana Dotson	.10	.05
❑	333 Craig Erickson	.05	.02
❑	334 Ron Hall	.05	.02
❑	335 Courtney Hawkins	.05	.02
❑	336 Keith McCants	.05	.02
❑	337 Hardy Nickerson	.10	.05
❑	338 Mazio Royster RC	.05	.02
❑	339 Broderick Thomas	.05	.02
❑	340 Casey Weldon RC	.25	.11
❑	341 Mark Wheeler	.05	.02
❑	342 Vince Workman	.05	.02
❑	343 Flipper Anderson	.05	.02
❑	344 Jerome Bettis	.25	.11
❑	345 Richard Buchanan	.05	.02
❑	346 Shane Conlan	.05	.02
❑	347 Troy Drayton	.05	.02
❑	348 Henry Ellard	.10	.05
❑	349 Jim Everett	.10	.05
❑	350 Cleveland Gary	.05	.02
❑	351 Sean Gilbert	.05	.02
❑	352 David Lang	.05	.02
❑	353 Todd Lyght	.05	.02
❑	354 T.J. Rubley	.05	.02
❑	355 Jackie Slater	.05	.02
❑	356 Russell White	.10	.05
❑	357 Bruce Armstrong	.05	.02
❑	358 Drew Bledsoe	1.25	.55
❑	359 Vincent Brisby	.25	.11
❑	360 Vincent Brown	.05	.02
❑	361 Ben Coates	.25	.11
❑	362 Marv Cook	.05	.02
❑	363 Ray Crittenden RC	.05	.02
❑	364 Corey Croom RC	.05	.02
❑	365 Pat Harlow	.05	.02
❑	366 Dion Lambert	.05	.02
❑	367 Greg McMurtry	.05	.02
❑	368 Leonard Russell	.05	.02
❑	369 Scott Secules	.05	.02
❑	370 Chris Slade	.05	.02
❑	371 Michael Timpson	.05	.02
❑	372 Kevin Turner	.05	.02
❑	373 Ashley Ambrose	.05	.02
❑	374 Dean Biasucci	.05	.02
❑	375 Duane Bickett	.05	.02
❑	376 Quentin Coryatt	.05	.02
❑	377 Rodney Culver	.05	.02
❑	378 Sean Dawkins RC	.25	.11
❑	379 Jeff George	.25	.11
❑	380 Jeff Herrod	.05	.02
❑	381 Jessie Hester	.05	.02
❑	382 Anthony Johnson	.10	.05
❑	383 Reggie Langhorne	.05	.02
❑	384 Roosevelt Potts	.05	.02
❑	385 William Schultz RC	.05	.02
❑	386 Rohn Stark	.05	.02
❑	387 Clarence Verdin	.05	.02
❑	388 Carl Banks	.05	.02
❑	389 Reggie Brooks	.10	.05
❑	390 Earnest Byner	.05	.02
❑	391 Tom Carter	.05	.02
❑	392 Cary Conklin	.05	.02
❑	393 Pat Eilers RC	.05	.02
❑	394 Ricky Ervins	.05	.02
❑	395 Rich Gannon	.05	.02
❑	396 Darrell Green	.05	.02
❑	397 Desmond Howard	.10	.05
❑	398 Chip Lohmiller	.05	.02
❑	399 Sterling Palmer RC	.05	.02
❑	400 Mark Rypien	.05	.02
❑	401 Ricky Sanders	.05	.02
❑	402 Johnny Thomas	.05	.02
❑	403 John Copeland	.05	.02
❑	404 Derrick Fenner	.05	.02
❑	405 Alex Gordon	.05	.02
❑	406 Harold Green	.05	.02
❑	407 Lance Gunn	.05	.02
❑	408 David Klingler	.05	.02
❑	409 Ricardo McDonald	.05	.02
❑	410 Tim McGee	.05	.02
❑	411 Reggie Rembert	.05	.02
❑	412 Patrick Robinson	.05	.02

		MINT	NRMT
❑ 413	Jay Schroeder	.05	.02
❑ 414	Erik Wilhelm	.05	.02
❑ 415	Alfred Williams	.05	.02
❑ 416	Darryl Williams	.05	.02
❑ 417	Sam Adams RC	.10	.05
❑ 418	Mario Bates RC	.25	.11
❑ 419	James Bostic RC	.25	.11
❑ 420	Bucky Brooks RC	.05	.02
❑ 421	Jeff Burris RC	.10	.05
❑ 422	Shante Carver RC	.05	.02
❑ 423	Jeff Cothran RC	.05	.02
❑ 424	Lake Dawson RC	.25	.11
❑ 425	Trent Dilfer RC	1.50	.70
❑ 426	Marshall Faulk RC	4.00	1.80
❑ 427	Cory Fleming RC	.05	.02
❑ 428	William Floyd RC	.25	.11
❑ 429	Glenn Foley RC	.25	.11
❑ 430	Rob Fredrickson RC	.10	.05
❑ 431	Charlie Garner RC	1.50	.70
❑ 432	Greg Hill RC	.50	.23
❑ 433	Charles Johnson RC	.25	.11
❑ 434	Calvin Jones RC	.05	.02
❑ 435	Jimmy Klingler RC	.10	.05
❑ 436	Antonio Langham RC	.10	.05
❑ 437	Kevin Lee RC	.05	.02
❑ 438	Chuck Levy RC	.05	.02
❑ 439	Willie McGinest RC	.25	.11
❑ 440	Jamir Miller RC	.05	.02
❑ 441	Johnnie Morton RC	.25	.11
❑ 442	David Palmer RC	.50	.23
❑ 443	Errict Rhett RC	1.50	.70
❑ 444	Cory Sawyer RC	.05	.02
❑ 445	Darnay Scott RC	.75	.35
❑ 446	Heath Shuler RC	.25	.11
❑ 447	Lamar Smith RC	.25	.11
❑ 448	Dan Wilkinson RC	.10	.05
❑ 449	Bernard Williams RC	.05	.02
❑ 450	Bryant Young RC	.25	.11
❑ P1	Sterling Sharpe Promo Numbered 000	.75	.35

1994 Pacific Crystalline

	MINT	NRMT
COMPLETE SET (20)	75.00	34.00

STATED ODDS 1:7

STATED PRINT RUN 7000 SETS

❑ 1	Emmitt Smith	25.00	11.00
❑ 2	Jerome Bettis	4.00	1.80
❑ 3	Thurman Thomas	4.00	1.80
❑ 4	Erric Pegram	.75	.35
❑ 5	Barry Sanders	30.00	13.50
❑ 6	Leonard Russell	.75	.35
❑ 7	Rodney Hampton	4.00	1.80
❑ 8	Chris Warren	1.50	.70
❑ 9	Reggie Brooks	1.50	.70
❑ 10	Ronald Moore	.75	.35
❑ 11	Gary Brown	.75	.35
❑ 12	Ricky Watters	4.00	1.80
❑ 13	Johnny Johnson	.75	.35
❑ 14	Rod Bernstine	.75	.35
❑ 15	Marcus Allen	4.00	1.80
❑ 16	Leroy Thompson	.75	.35
❑ 17	Marion Butts	.75	.35
❑ 18	Herschel Walker	1.50	.70
❑ 19	Barry Foster	.75	.35
❑ 20	Roosevelt Potts	.75	.35

1994 Pacific Gems of the Crown

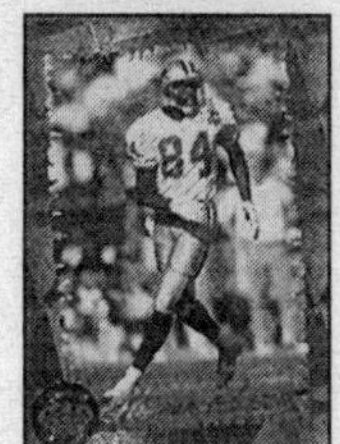

	MINT	NRMT
COMPLETE SET (36)	100.00	45.00

STATED ODDS 1:7

STATED PRINT RUN 7000 SETS

❑ 1	Troy Aikman	8.00	3.60
❑ 2	Marcus Allen	2.00	.90
❑ 3	Jerome Bettis	2.00	.90
❑ 4	Drew Bledsoe	10.00	4.50
❑ 5	Reggie Brooks	.75	.35
❑ 6	Gary Brown	.40	.18
❑ 7	Tim Brown	2.00	.90
❑ 8	Cody Carlson	.40	.18
❑ 9	John Elway	15.00	6.75
❑ 10	Boomer Esiason	.75	.35
❑ 11	Brett Favre	15.00	6.75
❑ 12	Rodney Hampton	2.00	.90
❑ 13	Alvin Harper	.75	.35
❑ 14	Jeff Hostetler	.75	.35
❑ 15	Jim Kelly	2.00	.90
❑ 16	Dan Marino	15.00	6.75
❑ 17	Eric Martin	.40	.18
❑ 18	O.J. McDuffie	2.00	.90
❑ 19	Natrone Means	2.00	.90
❑ 20	Rick Mirer	2.00	.90
❑ 21	Joe Montana	15.00	6.75
❑ 22	Herman Moore	2.00	.90
❑ 23	Ronald Moore	.40	.18
❑ 24	Neil O'Donnell	2.00	.90
❑ 25	Erric Pegram	.40	.18
❑ 26	Roosevelt Potts	.40	.18
❑ 27	Jerry Rice	8.00	3.60
❑ 28	Barry Sanders	15.00	6.75
❑ 29	Shannon Sharpe	.75	.35
❑ 30	Sterling Sharpe	.75	.35
❑ 31	Emmitt Smith	12.00	5.50
❑ 32	Thurman Thomas	2.00	.90
❑ 33	Herschel Walker	.75	.35
❑ 34	Chris Warren	.75	.35
❑ 35	Ricky Watters	2.00	.90
❑ 36	Steve Young	6.00	2.70

1994 Pacific Knights of the Gridiron

	MINT	NRMT
COMPLETE SET (20)	60.00	27.00

STATED ODDS 1:7

STATED PRINT RUN 7000 SETS

❑ 1	Mario Bates	.75	.35
❑ 2	Jerome Bettis	3.00	1.35
❑ 3	Drew Bledsoe	15.00	6.75
❑ 4	Vincent Brisby	3.00	1.35
❑ 5	Reggie Brooks	.30	.14
❑ 6	Derek Brown RBK	.60	.25
❑ 7	Jeff Burris	.30	.14
❑ 8	Trent Dilfer	5.00	2.20
❑ 9	Troy Drayton	.60	.25
❑ 10	Marshall Faulk	12.00	5.50
❑ 11	William Floyd	.75	.35
❑ 12	Rocket Ismail	1.25	.55
❑ 13	Terry Kirby	3.00	1.35
❑ 14	Thomas Lewis	.60	.25
❑ 15	Natrone Means	3.00	1.35
❑ 16	Rick Mirer	3.00	1.35
❑ 17	David Palmer	1.50	.70
❑ 18	Errict Rhett	5.00	2.20
❑ 19	Darnay Scott	2.50	1.10
❑ 20	Heath Shuler	.75	.35

1994 Pacific Marquee Prisms

	MINT	NRMT
COMPLETE SET (36)	25.00	11.00

ONE SILVER OR GOLD PER MARQUEE PACK

*GOLD STARS: 6X to 12X BASE CARD HI

*GOLD ROOKIES: 3X to 6X BASE CARD HI

GOLD STATED ODDS 1:18

❑ 1	Troy Aikman	2.00	.90
❑ 2	Marcus Allen	.50	.23
❑ 3	Jerome Bettis	.50	.23
❑ 4	Drew Bledsoe	2.50	1.10
❑ 5	Reggie Brooks	.20	.09
❑ 6	Dave Brown	.20	.09
❑ 7	Ben Coates	.50	.23
❑ 8	Reggie Cobb	.10	.05
❑ 9	Curtis Conway	.50	.23
❑ 10	John Elway	4.00	1.80
❑ 11	Marshall Faulk	4.00	1.80
❑ 12	Brett Favre	4.00	1.80
❑ 13	Barry Foster	.10	.05
❑ 14	Rodney Hampton	.50	.23
❑ 15	Michael Irvin	.50	.23
❑ 16	Terry Kirby	.50	.23
❑ 17	Dan Marino	4.00	1.80
❑ 18	Natrone Means	.50	.23
❑ 19	Rick Mirer	.50	.23
❑ 20	Joe Montana	4.00	1.80
❑ 21	Warren Moon	.50	.23
❑ 22	Ronald Moore	.10	.05
❑ 23	David Palmer	.50	.23
❑ 24	Errict Rhett	1.50	.70
❑ 25	Jerry Rice	2.00	.90
❑ 26	Bucky Richardson	.40	.18
❑ 27	Barry Sanders	4.00	1.80
❑ 28	Shannon Sharpe	.20	.09
❑ 29	Sterling Sharpe	.20	.09
❑ 30	Heath Shuler	.25	.11
❑ 31	Emmitt Smith	3.00	1.35
❑ 32	Irving Spikes	.40	.18
❑ 33	Thurman Thomas	.50	.23

Card	MINT	NRMT
❑ 34 Chris Warren	.20	.09
❑ 35 Ricky Watters	.50	.23
❑ 36 Steve Young	1.50	.70

1995 Pacific

	MINT	NRMT
COMPLETE SET (450)	30.00	13.50
COMMON CARD (1-450)	.10	.05
SEMISTARS	.20	.09
UNLISTED STARS	.30	.14
COMP.PLAT.SET (450)	225.00	100.00
*PLATINUM STARS: 3X TO 6X HI COLUMN		
*PLATINUM RCs: 1.5X TO 3X HI..		
PLAT: STATED ODDS 9:37 HOBBY		
COMP.BLUE SET (450)	250.00	110.00
*BLUE STARS: 3.5X TO 7X HI COLUMN		
*BLUE RCs: 2X TO 4X HI		
BLUES: STATED ODDS 9:37 RETAIL		

Card	MINT	NRMT
❑ 1 Randy Baldwin	.10	.05
❑ 2 Tommy Barnhardt	.10	.05
❑ 3 Tim McKyer	.10	.05
❑ 4 Sam Mills	.20	.09
❑ 5 Brian O'Neal	.10	.05
❑ 6 Frank Reich	.10	.05
❑ 7 Jack Trudeau	.10	.05
❑ 8 Vernon Turner	.10	.05
❑ 9 Kerry Collins RC	1.00	.45
❑ 10 Shawn King	.10	.05
❑ 11 Steve Beuerlein	.10	.05
❑ 12 Derek Brown	.10	.05
❑ 13 Reggie Clark	.10	.05
❑ 14 Reggie Cobb	.10	.05
❑ 15 Desmond Howard	.20	.09
❑ 16 Jeff Lageman	.10	.05
❑ 17 Kelvin Pritchett	.10	.05
❑ 18 Cedric Tillman	.10	.05
❑ 19 Tony Boselli RC	.20	.09
❑ 20 James O. Stewart RC	2.00	.90
❑ 21 Eric Davis	.10	.05
❑ 22 William Floyd	.30	.14
❑ 23 Elvis Grbac	.30	.14
❑ 24 Brent Jones	.10	.05
❑ 25 Ken Norton, Jr.	.20	.09
❑ 26 Bart Oates	.10	.05
❑ 27 Jerry Rice	1.00	.45
❑ 28 Deion Sanders	.40	.18
❑ 29 John Taylor	.10	.05
❑ 30 Adam Walker RC	.10	.05
❑ 31 Steve Wallace	.10	.05
❑ 32 Ricky Watters	.30	.14
❑ 33 Lee Woodall	.10	.05
❑ 34 Bryant Young	.20	.09
❑ 35 Steve Young	.75	.35
❑ 36 J.J. Stokes RC	.75	.35
❑ 37 Troy Aikman	1.00	.45
❑ 38 Larry Allen	.20	.09
❑ 39 Chris Boniol RC	.10	.05
❑ 40 Lincoln Coleman	.10	.05
❑ 41 Charles Haley	.20	.09
❑ 42 Alvin Harper	.10	.05
❑ 43 Chad Hennings	.20	.09
❑ 44 Michael Irvin	.30	.14
❑ 45 Daryl Johnston	.20	.09
❑ 46 Leon Lett	.10	.05
❑ 47 Nate Newton	.20	.09
❑ 48 Jay Novacek	.20	.09
❑ 49 Emmitt Smith	1.50	.70
❑ 50 James Washington	.10	.05
❑ 51 Kevin Williams	.20	.09
❑ 52 Sherman Williams RC	.10	.05
❑ 53 Barry Foster	.20	.09
❑ 54 Eric Green	.10	.05
❑ 55 Kevin Greene	.20	.09
❑ 56 Andre Hastings	.20	.09
❑ 57 Charles Johnson	.20	.09
❑ 58 Greg Lloyd	.20	.09
❑ 59 Ernie Mills	.10	.05
❑ 60 Byron Bam Morris	.20	.09
❑ 61 Neil O'Donnell	.20	.09
❑ 62 Darren Perry	.10	.05
❑ 63 Yancey Thigpen RC	.30	.14
❑ 64 Mike Tomczak	.10	.05
❑ 65 John L. Williams	.10	.05
❑ 66 Rod Woodson	.20	.09
❑ 67 Mark Bruener RC	.20	.09
❑ 68 Kordell Stewart RC	2.50	1.10
❑ 69 Jeff Brohm RC	.10	.05
❑ 70 Andre Coleman	.10	.05
❑ 71 Reuben Davis	.10	.05
❑ 72 Dennis Gibson	.10	.05
❑ 73 Darrien Gordon	.10	.05
❑ 74 Stan Humphries	.20	.09
❑ 75 Shawn Jefferson	.10	.05
❑ 76 Tony Martin	.20	.09
❑ 77 Natrone Means	.30	.14
❑ 78 Shannon Mitchell	.10	.05
❑ 79 Leslie O'Neal	.20	.09
❑ 80 Alfred Pupunu	.10	.05
❑ 81 Stanley Richard	.10	.05
❑ 82 Junior Seau	.30	.14
❑ 83 Mark Seay	.20	.09
❑ 84 Derrick Alexander WR	.30	.14
❑ 85 Carl Banks	.10	.05
❑ 86 Isaac Booth	.10	.05
❑ 87 Rob Burnett	.10	.05
❑ 88 Earnest Byner	.10	.05
❑ 89 Steve Everitt	.10	.05
❑ 90 Leroy Hoard	.10	.05
❑ 91 Pepper Johnson	.10	.05
❑ 92 Antonio Langham	.10	.05
❑ 93 Eric Metcalf	.20	.09
❑ 94 Anthony Pleasant	.10	.05
❑ 95 Frank Stams	.10	.05
❑ 96 Vinny Testaverde	.20	.09
❑ 97 Eric Turner	.10	.05
❑ 98 Mike Miller	.10	.05
❑ 99 Craig Powell	.10	.05
❑ 100 Gene Atkins	.10	.05
❑ 101 Aubrey Beavers	.10	.05
❑ 102 Tim Bowens	.10	.05
❑ 103 Keith Byars	.10	.05
❑ 104 Bryan Cox	.10	.05
❑ 105 Aaron Craver	.10	.05
❑ 106 Jeff Cross	.10	.05
❑ 107 Irving Fryar	.20	.09
❑ 108 Dan Marino	2.00	.90
❑ 109 O.J. McDuffie	.30	.14
❑ 110 Bernie Parmalee	.20	.09
❑ 111 James Saxon	.10	.05
❑ 112 Keith Sims	.10	.05
❑ 113 Irving Spikes	.20	.09
❑ 114 Pete Mitchell RC	.30	.14
❑ 115 Terry Allen	.20	.09
❑ 116 Cris Carter	.30	.14
❑ 117 Adrian Cooper	.10	.05
❑ 118 Bernard Dafney	.10	.05
❑ 119 Jack Del Rio	.10	.05
❑ 120 Vencie Glenn	.10	.05
❑ 121 Qadry Ismail	.20	.09
❑ 122 Carlos Jenkins	.10	.05
❑ 123 Andrew Jordan	.10	.05
❑ 124 Ed McDaniel	.10	.05
❑ 125 Warren Moon	.20	.09
❑ 126 David Palmer	.20	.09
❑ 127 John Randle	.10	.05
❑ 128 Jake Reed	.20	.09
❑ 129 Derrick Alexander DE RC	.10	.05
❑ 130 Chad May RC	.10	.05
❑ 131 Korey Stringer	.10	.05
❑ 132 Bruce Armstrong	.10	.05
❑ 133 Drew Bledsoe	1.00	.45
❑ 134 Vincent Brisby	.10	.05
❑ 135 Troy Brown	.20	.09
❑ 136 Vincent Brown	.10	.05
❑ 137 Marion Butts	.10	.05
❑ 138 Ben Coates	.20	.09
❑ 139 Ray Crittenden	.10	.05
❑ 140 Maurice Hurst	.10	.05
❑ 141 Aaron Jones	.10	.05
❑ 142 Willie McGinest	.20	.09
❑ 143 Marty Moore	.10	.05
❑ 144 Mike Pitts	.10	.05
❑ 145 Leroy Thompson	.10	.05
❑ 146 Michael Timpson	.10	.05
❑ 147 Bennie Blades	.10	.05
❑ 148 Jocelyn Borgella	.10	.05
❑ 149 Anthony Carter	.20	.09
❑ 150 Willie Clay	.10	.05
❑ 151 Mel Gray	.10	.05
❑ 152 Mike Johnson	.10	.05
❑ 153 Dave Krieg	.10	.05
❑ 154 Robert Massey	.10	.05
❑ 155 Scott Mitchell	.20	.09
❑ 156 Herman Moore	.30	.14
❑ 157 Johnnie Morton	.20	.09
❑ 158 Barry Sanders	2.00	.90
❑ 159 Chris Spielman	.20	.09
❑ 160 Broderick Thomas	.10	.05
❑ 161 Cory Schlesinger	.10	.05
❑ 162 Marcus Allen	.30	.14
❑ 163 Donnell Bennett	.20	.09
❑ 164 J.J. Birden	.10	.05
❑ 165 Matt Blundin RC	.10	.05
❑ 166 Steve Bono	.20	.09
❑ 167 Dale Carter	.20	.09
❑ 168 Lake Dawson	.20	.09
❑ 169 Ron Dickerson	.10	.05
❑ 170 Lin Elliott	.10	.05
❑ 171 Jaime Fields	.10	.05
❑ 172 Greg Hill	.20	.09
❑ 173 Danan Hughes	.10	.05
❑ 174 Neil Smith	.20	.09
❑ 175 Steve Stenstrom RC	.10	.05
❑ 176 Edgar Bennett	.20	.09
❑ 177 Robert Brooks	.30	.14
❑ 178 Mark Brunell	1.00	.45
❑ 179 Doug Evans	.10	.05
❑ 180 Brett Favre	2.00	.90
❑ 181 Corey Harris	.10	.05
❑ 182 LeShon Johnson	.20	.09
❑ 183 Sean Jones	.10	.05
❑ 184 Lenny McGill RC	.10	.05
❑ 185 Terry Mickens	.10	.05
❑ 186 Sterling Sharpe	.20	.09
❑ 187 Joe Sims	.10	.05
❑ 188 Darrell Thompson	.10	.05
❑ 189 Reggie White	.30	.14
❑ 190 Craig Newsome RC	.10	.05
❑ 191 Tim Brown	.30	.14
❑ 192 Vince Evans	.10	.05
❑ 193 Rob Fredrickson	.10	.05
❑ 194 Andrew Glover RC	.10	.05
❑ 195 Jeff Hostetler	.20	.09
❑ 196 Rocket Ismail	.20	.09
❑ 197 Jeff Jaeger	.10	.05
❑ 198 James Jett	.20	.09
❑ 199 Chester McGlockton	.20	.09
❑ 200 Don Mosebar	.10	.05
❑ 201 Tom Rathman	.10	.05
❑ 202 Harvey Williams	.10	.05
❑ 203 Steve Wisniewski	.10	.05
❑ 204 Alexander Wright	.10	.05
❑ 205 Napoleon Kaufman RC	2.00	.90
❑ 206 Trace Armstrong	.10	.05
❑ 207 Curtis Conway	.30	.14
❑ 208 Raymont Harris	.10	.05
❑ 209 Erik Kramer	.10	.05
❑ 210 Nate Lewis	.10	.05
❑ 211 Shane Matthews RC	2.00	.90
❑ 212 John Thierry	.10	.05
❑ 213 Lewis Tillman	.10	.05
❑ 214 Tom Waddle	.10	.05
❑ 215 Steve Walsh	.10	.05
❑ 216 James Williams T RC	.10	.05
❑ 217 Donnell Woolford	.10	.05
❑ 218 Chris Zorich	.10	.05
❑ 219 Rashaan Salaam RC	.30	.14
❑ 220 John Booty	.10	.05

❑ 221 Michael Brooks .10 .05
❑ 222 Dave Brown .20 .09
❑ 223 Chris Calloway .10 .05
❑ 224 Gary Downs .10 .05
❑ 225 Kent Graham .20 .09
❑ 226 Keith Hamilton .10 .05
❑ 227 Rodney Hampton .20 .09
❑ 228 Brian Kozlowski .10 .05
❑ 229 Thomas Lewis .20 .09
❑ 230 Dave Meggett .10 .05
❑ 231 Aaron Pierce .10 .05
❑ 232 Mike Sherrard .10 .05
❑ 233 Phillippi Sparks .10 .05
❑ 234 Tyrone Wheatley RC 1.25 .55
❑ 235 Trev Alberts .10 .05
❑ 236 Aaron Bailey .10 .05
❑ 237 Jason Belser .10 .05
❑ 238 Tony Bennett .10 .05
❑ 239 Kerry Cash .10 .05
❑ 240 Marshall Faulk .50 .23
❑ 241 Stephen Grant .10 .05
❑ 242 Jeff Herrod .10 .05
❑ 243 Ronald Humphrey .10 .05
❑ 244 Kirk Lowdermilk .10 .05
❑ 245 Don Majkowski .10 .05
❑ 246 Tony McCoy .10 .05
❑ 247 Floyd Turner .10 .05
❑ 248 Lamont Warren .10 .05
❑ 249 Zack Crockett RC .10 .05
❑ 250 Michael Bankston .10 .05
❑ 251 Larry Centers .20 .09
❑ 252 Gary Clark .10 .05
❑ 253 Ed Cunningham .10 .05
❑ 254 Garrison Hearst .30 .14
❑ 255 Eric Hill .10 .05
❑ 256 Terry Irving .10 .05
❑ 257 Lorenzo Lynch .10 .05
❑ 258 Jamir Miller .10 .05
❑ 259 Ronald Moore .10 .05
❑ 260 Terry Samuels .10 .05
❑ 261 Jay Schroeder .10 .05
❑ 262 Eric Swann .20 .09
❑ 263 Aeneas Williams .10 .05
❑ 264 Frank Sanders RC 1.00 .45
❑ 265 Morten Andersen .10 .05
❑ 266 Mario Bates .30 .14
❑ 267 Derek Brown RBK .10 .05
❑ 268 Darion Conner .10 .05
❑ 269 Quinn Early .20 .09
❑ 270 Jim Everett .10 .05
❑ 271 Michael Haynes .20 .09
❑ 272 Wayne Martin .10 .05
❑ 273 Derrell Mitchell .10 .05
❑ 274 Lorenzo Neal .10 .05
❑ 275 Jimmy Spencer .10 .05
❑ 276 Winfred Tubbs .10 .05
❑ 277 Renaldo Turnbull .10 .05
❑ 278 Jeff Uhlenhake .10 .05
❑ 279 Steve Atwater .10 .05
❑ 280 Keith Burns .10 .05
❑ 281 Butler By'Not'e .10 .05
❑ 282 Jeff Campbell .10 .05
❑ 283 Derrick Clark RC .10 .05
❑ 284 Shane Dronett .10 .05
❑ 285 Jason Elam .10 .05
❑ 286 John Elway 2.00 .90
❑ 287 Jerry Evans .10 .05
❑ 288 Karl Mecklenburg .10 .05
❑ 289 Glyn Milburn .10 .05
❑ 290 Anthony Miller .20 .09
❑ 291 Tom Rouen .10 .05
❑ 292 Leonard Russell .10 .05
❑ 293 Shannon Sharpe .20 .09
❑ 294 Steve Russ .10 .05
❑ 295 Mel Agee .10 .05
❑ 296 Lester Archambeau .10 .05
❑ 297 Bert Emanuel .30 .14
❑ 298 Jeff George .20 .09
❑ 299 Craig Heyward .20 .09
❑ 300 Bobby Hebert .10 .05
❑ 301 D.J. Johnson .10 .05
❑ 302 Mike Kenn .10 .05
❑ 303 Terance Mathis .20 .09
❑ 304 Clay Matthews .20 .09
❑ 305 Eric Pegram .20 .09
❑ 306 Andre Rison .20 .09
❑ 307 Chuck Smith .10 .05
❑ 308 Jessie Tuggle .10 .05
❑ 309 Lorenzo Styles RC .10 .05
❑ 310 Cornelius Bennett .20 .09
❑ 311 Bill Brooks .10 .05
❑ 312 Jeff Burris .10 .05
❑ 313 Carwell Gardner .10 .05
❑ 314 Kent Hull .10 .05
❑ 315 Yonel Jourdain .10 .05
❑ 316 Jim Kelly .30 .14
❑ 317 Vince Marrow .10 .05
❑ 318 Pete Metzelaars .10 .05
❑ 319 Andre Reed .20 .09
❑ 320 Kurt Schulz RC .10 .05
❑ 321 Bruce Smith .30 .14
❑ 322 Darryl Talley .10 .05
❑ 323 Matt Darby .10 .05
❑ 324 Justin Armour RC .10 .05
❑ 325 Todd Collins RC .30 .14
❑ 326 David Alexander DE .10 .05
❑ 327 Eric Allen .10 .05
❑ 328 Fred Barnett .20 .09
❑ 329 Randall Cunningham .30 .14
❑ 330 William Fuller .10 .05
❑ 331 Charlie Garner .20 .09
❑ 332 Vaughn Hebron .10 .05
❑ 333 James Joseph .10 .05
❑ 334 Bill Romanowski .10 .05
❑ 335 Ken Rose .10 .05
❑ 336 Jeff Snyder .10 .05
❑ 337 William Thomas .10 .05
❑ 338 Herschel Walker .20 .09
❑ 339 Calvin Williams .20 .09
❑ 340 Dave Barr RC .10 .05
❑ 341 Chidi Ahanotu .10 .05
❑ 342 Barney Bussey .10 .05
❑ 343 Horace Copeland .10 .05
❑ 344 Trent Dilfer .30 .14
❑ 345 Craig Erickson .10 .05
❑ 346 Paul Gruber .10 .05
❑ 347 Courtney Hawkins .10 .05
❑ 348 Lonnie Marts .10 .05
❑ 349 Martin Mayhew .10 .05
❑ 350 Hardy Nickerson .10 .05
❑ 351 Errict Rhett .30 .14
❑ 352 Lamar Thomas .10 .05
❑ 353 Charles Wilson .10 .05
❑ 354 Vince Workman .10 .05
❑ 355 Derrick Brooks .10 .05
❑ 356 Warren Sapp RC .60 .25
❑ 357 Sam Adams .10 .05
❑ 358 Michael Bates .10 .05
❑ 359 Brian Blades .20 .09
❑ 360 Carlton Gray .10 .05
❑ 361 Bill Hitchcock .10 .05
❑ 362 Cortez Kennedy .20 .09
❑ 363 Rick Mirer .30 .14
❑ 364 Eugene Robinson .10 .05
❑ 365 Michael Sinclair .10 .05
❑ 366 Steve Smith .10 .05
❑ 367 Bob Spitulski .10 .05
❑ 368 Rick Tuten .10 .05
❑ 369 Chris Warren .20 .09
❑ 370 Terrence Warren .10 .05
❑ 371 Christian Fauria RC .10 .05
❑ 372 Joey Galloway RC 2.50 1.10
❑ 373 Boomer Esiason .20 .09
❑ 374 Aaron Glenn .10 .05
❑ 375 Victor Green .10 .05
❑ 376 Johnny Johnson .10 .05
❑ 377 Mo Lewis .10 .05
❑ 378 Ronnie Lott .20 .09
❑ 379 Nick Lowery .10 .05
❑ 380 Johnny Mitchell .10 .05
❑ 381 Rob Moore .10 .05
❑ 382 Adrian Murrell .20 .09
❑ 383 Anthony Prior .10 .05
❑ 384 Brian Washington .10 .05
❑ 385 Matt Willig .10 .05
❑ 386 Kyle Brady RC .30 .14
❑ 387 Flipper Anderson .10 .05
❑ 388 Johnny Bailey .10 .05
❑ 389 Jerome Bettis .30 .14
❑ 390 Isaac Bruce .50 .23
❑ 391 Shane Conlan .10 .05
❑ 392 Troy Drayton .10 .05
❑ 393 D'Marco Farr .10 .05
❑ 394 Jessie Hester .10 .05
❑ 395 Todd Kinchen .10 .05
❑ 396 Ron Middleton .10 .05
❑ 397 Chris Miller .10 .05
❑ 398 Marquez Pope .10 .05
❑ 399 Robert Young .10 .05
❑ 400 Tony Zendejas .10 .05
❑ 401 Kevin Carter RC .30 .14
❑ 402 Reggie Brooks .20 .09
❑ 403 Tom Carter .10 .05
❑ 404 Andre Collins .10 .05
❑ 405 Pat Eilers .10 .05
❑ 406 Henry Ellard .20 .09
❑ 407 Ricky Ervins .10 .05
❑ 408 Gus Frerotte .30 .14
❑ 409 Ken Harvey .10 .05
❑ 410 Jim Lachey .10 .05
❑ 411 Brian Mitchell .10 .05
❑ 412 Reggie Roby .10 .05
❑ 413 Heath Shuler .30 .14
❑ 414 Tyronne Stowe .10 .05
❑ 415 Tydus Winans .10 .05
❑ 416 Cory Raymer .10 .05
❑ 417 Michael Westbrook RC 1.50 .70
❑ 418 Jeff Blake RC 1.00 .45
❑ 419 Steve Broussard .10 .05
❑ 420 Dave Cadigan .10 .05
❑ 421 Jeff Cothran .10 .05
❑ 422 Derrick Fenner .10 .05
❑ 423 James Francis .10 .05
❑ 424 Lee Johnson .10 .05
❑ 425 Louis Oliver .10 .05
❑ 426 Carl Pickens .30 .14
❑ 427 Jeff Query .10 .05
❑ 428 Corey Sawyer .10 .05
❑ 429 Darnay Scott .30 .14
❑ 430 Dan Wilkinson .20 .09
❑ 431 Alfred Williams .10 .05
❑ 432 Ki-Jana Carter RC .30 .14
❑ 433 David Dunn .10 .05
❑ 434 John Walsh RC .10 .05
❑ 435 Gary Brown .10 .05
❑ 436 Pat Carter .10 .05
❑ 437 Ray Childress .10 .05
❑ 438 Ernest Givins .10 .05
❑ 439 Haywood Jeffires .10 .05
❑ 440 Lamar Lathon .10 .05
❑ 441 Bruce Matthews .10 .05
❑ 442 Marcus Robertson .10 .05
❑ 443 Eddie Robinson .10 .05
❑ 444 Malcolm Seabron RC .10 .05
❑ 445 Webster Slaughter .10 .05
❑ 446 Al Smith .10 .05
❑ 447 Billy Joe Tolliver .10 .05
❑ 448 Lorenzo White .10 .05
❑ 449 Steve McNair RC 2.50 1.10
❑ 450 Rodney Thomas RC .30 .14
❑ P1 Natrone Means Promo 1.00 .45
❑ P1J Natrone Means Promo 1.00 .45
Jumbo card 7" by 9 3/4"

1995 Pacific Cramer's Choice

	MINT	NRMT
COMPLETE SET (6)	250.00	110.00
COMMON CARD (CC1-CC6)	25.00	11.00

STATED ODDS 1:720

	MINT	NRMT
❑ CC1 Ki-Jana Carter	25.00	11.00
❑ CC2 Emmitt Smith	80.00	36.00
❑ CC3 Marshall Faulk	25.00	11.00
❑ CC4 Jerry Rice	60.00	27.00
❑ CC5 Deion Sanders	30.00	13.50
❑ CC6 Steve Young	50.00	22.00

1995 Pacific Gems of the Crown

	MINT	NRMT
COMPLETE SET (36)	100.00	45.00
STATED ODDS 2:37		
❑ GC1 Jim Kelly	3.00	1.35
❑ GC2 Kerry Collins	4.00	1.80
❑ GC3 Darnay Scott	3.00	1.35
❑ GC4 Jeff Blake	4.00	1.80
❑ GC5 Terry Allen	2.00	.90
❑ GC6 Emmitt Smith	15.00	6.75
❑ GC7 Michael Irvin	3.00	1.35
❑ GC8 Troy Aikman	10.00	4.50
❑ GC9 John Elway	20.00	9.00
❑ GC10 Dave Krieg	1.00	.45
❑ GC11 Barry Sanders	20.00	9.00
❑ GC12 Brett Favre	20.00	9.00
❑ GC13 Marshall Faulk	5.00	2.20
❑ GC14 Marcus Allen	3.00	1.35
❑ GC15 Tim Brown	3.00	1.35
❑ GC16 Bernie Parmalee	2.00	.90
❑ GC17 Dan Marino	20.00	9.00
❑ GC18 Cris Carter	3.00	1.35
❑ GC19 Drew Bledsoe	10.00	4.50
❑ GC20 Mario Bates	3.00	1.35
❑ GC21 Rodney Hampton	2.00	.90
❑ GC22 Ben Coates	2.00	.90
❑ GC23 Charles Johnson	2.00	.90
❑ GC24 Byron Bam Morris	2.00	.90
❑ GC25 Stan Humphries	2.00	.90
❑ GC26 Deion Sanders	4.00	1.80
❑ GC27 Jerry Rice	10.00	4.50
❑ GC28 Ricky Watters	3.00	1.35
❑ GC29 Steve Young	8.00	3.60
❑ GC30 Natrone Means	3.00	1.35
❑ GC31 William Floyd	3.00	1.35
❑ GC32 Chris Warren	2.00	.90
❑ GC33 Rick Mirer	3.00	1.35
❑ GC34 Jerome Bettis	3.00	1.35
❑ GC35 Errict Rhett	3.00	1.35
❑ GC36 Heath Shuler	3.00	1.35

1995 Pacific G-Force

	MINT	NRMT
COMPLETE SET (10)	35.00	16.00
STATED ODDS 1:37		
❑ GF1 Marcus Allen	2.50	1.10
❑ GF2 Terry Allen	1.50	.70
❑ GF3 Emmitt Smith	12.00	5.50
❑ GF4 Barry Sanders	15.00	6.75
❑ GF5 Marshall Faulk	4.00	1.80
❑ GF6 Rodney Hampton	1.50	.70
❑ GF7 Natrone Means	2.50	1.10

❑ GF8 Chris Warren	1.50	.70
❑ GF9 Jerome Bettis	2.50	1.10
❑ GF10 Errict Rhett	2.50	1.10

1995 Pacific Gold Crown Die Cuts

	MINT	NRMT
COMP.HOLOFOIL SET (20)	100.00	45.00
*FLAT GOLDS: 7.5X TO 15X BASE CARD HI		
STATED ODDS 1:37		
❑ DC1 Ki-Jana Carter	3.00	1.35
❑ DC2 Michael Irvin	3.00	1.35
❑ DC3 Emmitt Smith	15.00	6.75
❑ DC4 Troy Aikman	10.00	4.50
❑ DC5 John Elway	20.00	9.00
❑ DC6 Barry Sanders	20.00	9.00
❑ DC7 Marshall Faulk	5.00	2.20
❑ DC8 Dan Marino	20.00	9.00
❑ DC9 Ben Coates	2.00	.90
❑ DC10 Drew Bledsoe	10.00	4.50
❑ DC11 Byron Bam Morris	2.00	.90
❑ DC12 Jerry Rice	10.00	4.50
❑ DC13 William Floyd	3.00	1.35
❑ DC14 Steve Young	8.00	3.60
❑ DC15 Natrone Means	3.00	1.35
❑ DC16 Deion Sanders	4.00	1.80
❑ DC17 Rick Mirer	3.00	1.35
❑ DC18 Chris Warren	2.00	.90
❑ DC19 Jerome Bettis	3.00	1.35
❑ DC20 Errict Rhett	3.00	1.35

1995 Pacific Hometown Heroes

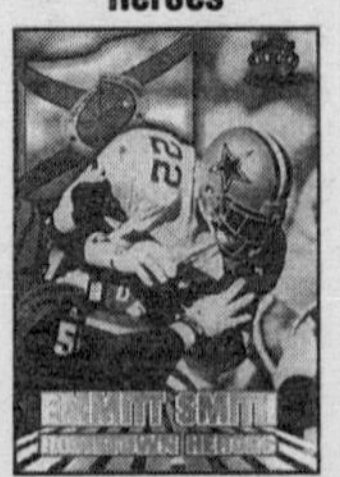

	MINT	NRMT
COMPLETE SET (10)	40.00	18.00
STATED ODDS 1:37		
❑ HH1 Emmitt Smith	8.00	3.60
❑ HH2 Troy Aikman	5.00	2.20
❑ HH3 Barry Sanders	10.00	4.50
❑ HH4 Marshall Faulk	2.50	1.10
❑ HH5 Dan Marino	10.00	4.50
❑ HH6 Drew Bledsoe	5.00	2.20
❑ HH7 Natrone Means	1.50	.70
❑ HH8 Steve Young	4.00	1.80
❑ HH9 Jerry Rice	5.00	2.20
❑ HH10 Errict Rhett	1.50	.70

1995 Pacific Rookies

	MINT	NRMT
COMPLETE SET (20)	40.00	18.00
STATED ODDS 2:37		
❑ 1 Dave Barr	.25	.11
❑ 2 Kyle Brady	.75	.35
❑ 3 Mark Bruener	.50	.23
❑ 4 Ki-Jana Carter	.75	.35
❑ 5 Kerry Collins	2.50	1.10
❑ 6 Todd Collins	.75	.35
❑ 7 Christian Fauria	.25	.11
❑ 8 Joey Galloway	6.00	2.70
❑ 9 Chris T. Jones	.25	.11
❑ 10 Napoleon Kaufman	5.00	2.20
❑ 11 Chad May	.25	.11
❑ 12 Steve McNair	6.00	2.70
❑ 13 Rashaan Salaam	.75	.35
❑ 14 Warren Sapp	1.50	.70
❑ 15 James O. Stewart	5.00	2.20
❑ 16 Kordell Stewart	6.00	2.70
❑ 17 J.J. Stokes	2.00	.90
❑ 18 Michael Westbrook	4.00	1.80
❑ 19 Tyrone Wheatley	3.00	1.35
❑ 20 Sherman Williams	.25	.11

1995 Pacific Young Warriors

	MINT	NRMT
COMPLETE SET (20)	30.00	13.50
STATED ODDS 2:37		
❑ 1 Bert Emanuel	3.00	1.35

❑ 2 Darnay Scott	3.00	1.35
❑ 3 Dan Wilkinson	2.00	.90
❑ 4 Derrick Alexander WR	3.00	1.35
❑ 5 Willie McGinest	2.00	.90
❑ 6 Marshall Faulk	5.00	2.20
❑ 7 Lake Dawson	2.00	.90
❑ 8 Greg Hill	2.00	.90
❑ 9 Tim Bowens	1.00	.45
❑ 10 David Palmer	2.00	.90
❑ 11 Aaron Glenn	1.00	.45
❑ 12 Mario Bates	3.00	1.35
❑ 13 Charles Johnson	2.00	.90
❑ 14 Byron Bam Morris	2.00	.90
❑ 15 William Floyd	3.00	1.35
❑ 16 Adam Walker	1.00	.45
❑ 17 Bryant Young	2.00	.90
❑ 18 Trent Dilfer	3.00	1.35
❑ 19 Errict Rhett	3.00	1.35
❑ 20 Heath Shuler	3.00	1.35

1996 Pacific

	MINT	NRMT
COMPLETE SET (450)	40.00	18.00
COMMON CARD (1-450)	.10	.05
SEMISTARS	.20	.09
UNLISTED STARS	.40	.18
COMP.BLUE SET (450)	300.00	135.00
*BLUE STARS: 3X TO 6X HI COLUMN		
*BLUE RCs: 1.5X TO 3X HI		
BLUE STATED ODDS 9:37 HOBBY		
COMP.RED SET (450)	400.00	180.00
*RED STARS: 4X TO 8X HI COLUMN		
*RED RCs: 2X TO 4X HI		
RED STATED ODDS 9:37 RETAIL		
COMP.SILVER SET (450)	300.00	135.00
*SILVER STARS: 3X TO 6X HI COLUMN		
*SILVER RCs: 1.5X TO 3X HI		
SILVERS:RAND.INS. IN SPEC.RETAIL PACKS		

❑ 1 Jeff Feagles	.10	.05
❑ 2 Rob Moore	.20	.09
❑ 3 Clyde Simmons	.10	.05
❑ 4 Mike Buck	.10	.05
❑ 5 Aeneas Williams	.10	.05
❑ 6 Simeon Rice RC	.40	.18
❑ 7 Garrison Hearst	.20	.09
❑ 8 Eric Swann	.10	.05
❑ 9 Dave Krieg	.10	.05
❑ 10 Leeland McElroy RC	.40	.18
❑ 11 Oscar McBride	.10	.05
❑ 12 Frank Sanders	.20	.09
❑ 13 Larry Centers	.20	.09
❑ 14 Seth Joyner	.10	.05
❑ 15 Stevie Anderson	.10	.05
❑ 16 Craig Heyward	.10	.05
❑ 17 Devin Bush	.10	.05
❑ 18 Eric Metcalf	.10	.05
❑ 19 Jeff George	.20	.09
❑ 20 Richard Huntley RC	.10	.05
❑ 21 Jamal Anderson RC	6.00	2.70
❑ 22 Bert Emanuel	.20	.09
❑ 23 Terance Mathis	.10	.05
❑ 24 Roman Fortin	.10	.05
❑ 25 Jessie Tuggle	.10	.05
❑ 26 Morten Andersen	.10	.05
❑ 27 Chris Doleman	.10	.05
❑ 28 D.J. Johnson	.10	.05
❑ 29 Kevin Ross	.10	.05
❑ 30 Michael Jackson	.20	.09
❑ 31 Eric Zeier	.10	.05
❑ 32 Jonathan Ogden RC	.10	.05
❑ 33 Eric Turner	.10	.05
❑ 34 Andre Rison	.20	.09
❑ 35 Lorenzo White	.10	.05
❑ 36 Earnest Byner	.10	.05
❑ 37 Derrick Alexander WR	.20	.09
❑ 38 Brian Kinchen	.10	.05
❑ 39 Anthony Pleasant	.10	.05
❑ 40 Vinny Testaverde	.20	.09
❑ 41 Pepper Johnson	.10	.05
❑ 42 Frank Hartley	.10	.05
❑ 43 Craig Powell	.10	.05
❑ 44 Leroy Hoard	.10	.05
❑ 45 Kent Hull	.10	.05
❑ 46 Bryce Paup	.10	.05
❑ 47 Andre Reed	.20	.09
❑ 48 Darick Holmes	.10	.05
❑ 49 Russell Copeland	.10	.05
❑ 50 Jerry Ostroski	.10	.05
❑ 51 Chris Green	.10	.05
❑ 52 Eric Moulds RC	1.50	.70
❑ 53 Justin Armour	.10	.05
❑ 54 Jim Kelly	.40	.18
❑ 55 Cornelius Bennett	.10	.05
❑ 56 Steve Tasker	.10	.05
❑ 57 Thurman Thomas	.40	.18
❑ 58 Bruce Smith	.20	.09
❑ 59 Todd Collins	.20	.09
❑ 60 Shawn King	.10	.05
❑ 61 Don Beebe	.10	.05
❑ 62 John Kasay	.10	.05
❑ 63 Tim McKyer	.10	.05
❑ 64 Darion Conner	.10	.05
❑ 65 Pete Metzelaars	.10	.05
❑ 66 Derrick Moore	.10	.05
❑ 67 Blake Brockermeyer	.10	.05
❑ 68 Tim Biakabutuka RC	1.00	.45
❑ 69 Sam Mills	.10	.05
❑ 70 Vince Workman	.10	.05
❑ 71 Kerry Collins	.40	.18
❑ 72 Carlton Bailey	.10	.05
❑ 73 Mark Carrier WR	.10	.05
❑ 74 Donnell Woolford	.10	.05
❑ 75 Walt Harris RC	.10	.05
❑ 76 John Thierry	.10	.05
❑ 77 Al Fontenot	.10	.05
❑ 78 Lewis Tillman	.10	.05
❑ 79 Curtis Conway	.40	.18
❑ 80 Chris Zorich	.10	.05
❑ 81 Mark Carrier DB	.10	.05
❑ 82 Bobby Engram RC	.40	.18
❑ 83 Alonzo Spellman	.10	.05
❑ 84 Rashaan Salaam	.40	.18
❑ 85 Michael Timpson	.10	.05
❑ 86 Nate Lewis	.10	.05
❑ 87 James Williams T	.10	.05
❑ 88 Jeff Graham	.10	.05
❑ 89 Erik Kramer	.10	.05
❑ 90 Willie Anderson	.10	.05
❑ 91 Tony McGee	.10	.05
❑ 92 Marco Battaglia	.10	.05
❑ 93 Dan Wilkinson	.10	.05
❑ 94 John Walsh	.10	.05
❑ 95 Eric Bieniemy	.10	.05
❑ 96 Ricardo McDonald	.10	.05
❑ 97 Carl Pickens	.40	.18
❑ 98 Kevin Sargent	.10	.05
❑ 99 David Dunn	.10	.05
❑ 100 Jeff Blake	.40	.18
❑ 101 Harold Green	.10	.05
❑ 102 James Francis	.10	.05
❑ 103 John Copeland	.10	.05
❑ 104 Darnay Scott	.20	.09
❑ 105 Darren Woodson	.20	.09
❑ 106 Jay Novacek	.10	.05
❑ 107 Charles Haley	.20	.09
❑ 108 Mark Tuinei	.10	.05
❑ 109 Michael Irvin	.40	.18
❑ 110 Troy Aikman	1.00	.45
❑ 111 Chris Boniol	.10	.05
❑ 112 Sherman Williams	.10	.05
❑ 113 Deion Sanders	.60	.25
❑ 114 Emmitt Smith	1.50	.70
❑ 115 Eric Bjornson	.10	.05
❑ 116 Nate Newton	.10	.05
❑ 117 Larry Allen	.10	.05
❑ 118 Kevin Williams	.10	.05
❑ 119 Leon Lett	.10	.05
❑ 120 John Mobley	.10	.05
❑ 121 Anthony Miller	.20	.09
❑ 122 Brian Habib	.10	.05
❑ 123 Aaron Craver	.10	.05
❑ 124 Glyn Milburn	.10	.05
❑ 125 Shannon Sharpe	.20	.09
❑ 126 Steve Atwater	.10	.05
❑ 127 Jason Elam	.10	.05
❑ 128 John Elway	2.00	.90
❑ 129 Reggie Rivers	.10	.05
❑ 130 Mike Pritchard	.10	.05
❑ 131 Vance Johnson	.10	.05
❑ 132 Terrell Davis	2.50	1.10
❑ 133 Tyrone Braxton	.10	.05
❑ 134 Ed McCaffrey	.20	.09
❑ 135 Brett Perriman	.10	.05
❑ 136 Chris Spielman	.10	.05
❑ 137 Luther Elliss	.10	.05
❑ 138 Johnnie Morton	.20	.09
❑ 139 Zefross Moss	.10	.05
❑ 140 Barry Sanders	2.00	.90
❑ 141 Lomas Brown	.10	.05
❑ 142 Cory Schlesinger	.10	.05
❑ 143 Jason Hanson	.10	.05
❑ 144 Kevin Glover	.10	.05
❑ 145 Ron Rivers RC	.75	.35
❑ 146 Aubrey Matthews	.10	.05
❑ 147 Reggie Brown LB RC	.10	.05
❑ 148 Herman Moore	.40	.18
❑ 149 Scott Mitchell	.20	.09
❑ 150 Brett Favre	2.00	.90
❑ 151 Sean Jones	.10	.05
❑ 152 LeRoy Butler	.10	.05
❑ 153 Mark Chmura	.20	.09
❑ 154 Derrick Mayes RC	.75	.35
❑ 155 Mark Ingram	.10	.05
❑ 156 Antonio Freeman	.75	.35
❑ 157 Chris Darkins RC	.10	.05
❑ 158 Robert Brooks	.40	.18
❑ 159 William Henderson	.10	.05
❑ 160 George Koonce	.10	.05
❑ 161 Craig Newsome	.10	.05
❑ 162 Darius Holland	.10	.05
❑ 163 George Teague	.10	.05
❑ 164 Edgar Bennett	.20	.09
❑ 165 Reggie White	.40	.18
❑ 166 Micheal Barrow	.10	.05
❑ 167 Mel Gray	.10	.05
❑ 168 Anthony Dorsett	.10	.05
❑ 169 Roderick Lewis	.10	.05
❑ 170 Henry Ford	.10	.05
❑ 171 Mark Stepnoski	.10	.05
❑ 172 Chris Sanders	.20	.09
❑ 173 Anthony Cook	.10	.05
❑ 174 Eddie Robinson	.10	.05
❑ 175 Steve McNair	.75	.35
❑ 176 Haywood Jeffires	.10	.05
❑ 177 Eddie George RC	3.00	1.35
❑ 178 Marion Butts	.10	.05
❑ 179 Malcolm Seabron	.10	.05
❑ 180 Rodney Thomas	.10	.05
❑ 181 Ken Dilger	.20	.09
❑ 182 Zack Crockett	.10	.05
❑ 183 Tony Bennett	.10	.05
❑ 184 Quentin Coryatt	.10	.05
❑ 185 Marshall Faulk	.40	.18
❑ 186 Sean Dawkins	.10	.05
❑ 187 Jim Harbaugh	.20	.09
❑ 188 Eugene Daniel	.10	.05
❑ 189 Roosevelt Potts	.10	.05
❑ 190 Lamont Warren	.10	.05
❑ 191 Will Wolford	.10	.05
❑ 192 Tony Siragusa	.10	.05
❑ 193 Aaron Bailey	.10	.05
❑ 194 Trev Alberts	.10	.05
❑ 195 Kevin Hardy	.20	.09
❑ 196 Greg Spann	.10	.05
❑ 197 Steve Beuerlein	.10	.05
❑ 198 Steve Taneyhill	.10	.05
❑ 199 Vaughn Dunbar	.10	.05

❑	200	Mark Brunell	1.00	.45
❑	201	Bernard Carter	.10	.05
❑	202	James O. Stewart	.20	.09
❑	203	Tony Boselli	.10	.05
❑	204	Chris Doering	.10	.05
❑	205	Willie Jackson	.10	.05
❑	206	Tony Brackens RC	.20	.09
❑	207	Ernest Givins	.10	.05
❑	208	Le'Shai Maston	.10	.05
❑	209	Pete Mitchell	.20	.09
❑	210	Desmond Howard	.20	.09
❑	211	Vinnie Clark	.10	.05
❑	212	Jeff Lageman	.10	.05
❑	213	Derrick Walker	.10	.05
❑	214	Dan Saleaumua	.10	.05
❑	215	Derrick Thomas	.20	.09
❑	216	Neil Smith	.10	.05
❑	217	Willie Davis	.10	.05
❑	218	Mark Collins	.10	.05
❑	219	Lake Dawson	.10	.05
❑	220	Greg Hill	.20	.09
❑	221	Anthony Davis	.10	.05
❑	222	Kimble Anders	.20	.09
❑	223	Webster Slaughter	.10	.05
❑	224	Tamarick Vanover	.20	.09
❑	225	Marcus Allen	.40	.18
❑	226	Steve Bono	.10	.05
❑	227	Will Shields	.10	.05
❑	228	Karim Abdul-Jabbar RC	.75	.35
❑	229	Tim Bowens	.10	.05
❑	230	Keith Sims	.10	.05
❑	231	Terry Kirby	.20	.09
❑	232	Gene Atkins	.10	.05
❑	233	Dan Marino	2.00	.90
❑	234	Richmond Webb	.10	.05
❑	235	Gary Clark	.10	.05
❑	236	O.J. McDuffie	.20	.09
❑	237	Marco Coleman	.10	.05
❑	238	Bernie Parmalee	.10	.05
❑	239	Randal Hill	.10	.05
❑	240	Bryan Cox	.10	.05
❑	241	Irving Fryar	.20	.09
❑	242	Derrick Alexander DE	.10	.05
❑	243	Qadry Ismail	.10	.05
❑	244	Warren Moon	.20	.09
❑	245	Cris Carter	.40	.18
❑	246	Chad May	.10	.05
❑	247	Robert Smith	.20	.09
❑	248	Fuad Reveiz	.10	.05
❑	249	Orlando Thomas	.10	.05
❑	250	Chris Hinton	.10	.05
❑	251	Jack Del Rio	.10	.05
❑	252	Moe Williams RC	.20	.09
❑	253	Roy Barker	.10	.05
❑	254	Jake Reed	.20	.09
❑	255	Adrian Cooper	.10	.05
❑	256	Curtis Martin	.75	.35
❑	257	Ben Coates	.20	.09
❑	258	Drew Bledsoe	1.00	.45
❑	259	Maurice Hurst	.10	.05
❑	260	Troy Brown	.10	.05
❑	261	Bruce Armstrong	.10	.05
❑	262	Myron Guyton	.10	.05
❑	263	Dave Meggett	.10	.05
❑	264	Terry Glenn RC	1.25	.55
❑	265	Chris Slade	.10	.05
❑	266	Vincent Brisby	.10	.05
❑	267	Willie McGinest	.10	.05
❑	268	Vincent Brown	.10	.05
❑	269	Will Moore	.10	.05
❑	270	Jay Barker RC	.10	.05
❑	271	Ray Zellars	.10	.05
❑	272	Derek Brown RBK	.10	.05
❑	273	William Roaf	.10	.05
❑	274	Quinn Early	.10	.05
❑	275	Michael Haynes	.10	.05
❑	276	Rufus Porter	.10	.05
❑	277	Renaldo Turnbull	.10	.05
❑	278	Wayne Martin	.10	.05
❑	279	Tyrone Hughes	.10	.05
❑	280	Irv Smith	.10	.05
❑	281	Eric Allen	.10	.05
❑	282	Mark Fields	.10	.05
❑	283	Mario Bates	.20	.09
❑	284	Jim Everett	.10	.05
❑	285	Vince Buck	.10	.05
❑	286	Alex Molden RC	.10	.05
❑	287	Tyrone Wheatley	.20	.09
❑	288	Chris Calloway	.10	.05
❑	289	Jessie Armstead	.10	.05
❑	290	Arthur Marshall	.10	.05
❑	291	Aaron Pierce	.10	.05
❑	292	Dave Brown	.10	.05
❑	293	Rodney Hampton	.20	.09
❑	294	Jumbo Elliott	.10	.05
❑	295	Mike Sherrard	.10	.05
❑	296	Howard Cross	.10	.05
❑	297	Michael Brooks	.10	.05
❑	298	Herschel Walker	.20	.09
❑	299	Danny Kanell RC	.40	.18
❑	300	Keith Elias	.10	.05
❑	301	Bobby Houston	.10	.05
❑	302	Dexter Carter	.10	.05
❑	303	Tony Casillas	.10	.05
❑	304	Kyle Brady	.10	.05
❑	305	Glenn Foley	.20	.09
❑	306	Ronald Moore	.10	.05
❑	307	Ryan Yarborough	.10	.05
❑	308	Aaron Glenn	.10	.05
❑	309	Adrian Murrell	.40	.18
❑	310	Boomer Esiason	.20	.09
❑	311	Kyle Clifton	.10	.05
❑	312	Wayne Chrebet	.20	.09
❑	313	Erik Howard	.10	.05
❑	314	Keyshawn Johnson RC	2.00	.90
❑	315	Marvin Washington	.10	.05
❑	316	Johnny Mitchell	.10	.05
❑	317	Alex Van Dyke RC	.20	.09
❑	318	Billy Joe Hobert	.20	.09
❑	319	Andrew Glover	.10	.05
❑	320	Vince Evans	.10	.05
❑	321	Chester McGlockton	.10	.05
❑	322	Pat Swilling	.10	.05
❑	323	Rocket Ismail	.10	.05
❑	324	Eddie Anderson	.10	.05
❑	325	Rickey Dudley RC	.40	.18
❑	326	Steve Wisniewski	.10	.05
❑	327	Harvey Williams	.10	.05
❑	328	Napoleon Kaufman	.50	.23
❑	329	Tim Brown	.40	.18
❑	330	Jeff Hostetler	.10	.05
❑	331	Anthony Smith	.10	.05
❑	332	Terry McDaniel	.10	.05
❑	333	Charlie Garner	.10	.05
❑	334	Ricky Watters	.20	.09
❑	335	Brian Dawkins	.10	.05
❑	336	Randall Cunningham	.40	.18
❑	337	Gary Anderson	.10	.05
❑	338	Calvin Williams	.10	.05
❑	339	Chris T. Jones	.20	.09
❑	340	Bobby Hoying RC	.60	.25
❑	341	William Fuller	.10	.05
❑	342	William Thomas	.10	.05
❑	343	Mike Mamula	.10	.05
❑	344	Fred Barnett	.10	.05
❑	345	Rodney Peete	.10	.05
❑	346	Mark McMillian	.10	.05
❑	347	Bobby Taylor	.10	.05
❑	348	Yancey Thigpen	.20	.09
❑	349	Neil O'Donnell	.20	.09
❑	350	Rod Woodson	.20	.09
❑	351	Kordell Stewart	.75	.35
❑	352	Dermontti Dawson	.10	.05
❑	353	Norm Johnson	.10	.05
❑	354	Ernie Mills	.10	.05
❑	355	Byron Bam Morris	.20	.09
❑	356	Mark Bruener	.10	.05
❑	357	Kevin Greene	.20	.09
❑	358	Greg Lloyd	.20	.09
❑	359	Andre Hastings	.10	.05
❑	360	Erric Pegram	.10	.05
❑	361	Carnell Lake	.10	.05
❑	362	Dwayne Harper	.10	.05
❑	363	Ronnie Harmon	.10	.05
❑	364	Leslie O'Neal	.10	.05
❑	365	John Carney	.10	.05
❑	366	Stan Humphries	.20	.09
❑	367	Brian Roche	.10	.05
❑	368	Terrell Fletcher	.10	.05
❑	369	Shaun Gayle	.10	.05
❑	370	Alfred Pupunu	.10	.05
❑	371	Shawn Jefferson	.10	.05
❑	372	Junior Seau	.20	.09
❑	373	Mark Seay	.10	.05
❑	374	Aaron Hayden	.10	.05
❑	375	Tony Martin	.20	.09
❑	376	Steve Young	.75	.35
❑	377	J.J. Stokes	.40	.18
❑	378	Jerry Rice	1.00	.45
❑	379	Derek Loville	.10	.05
❑	380	Lee Woodall	.10	.05
❑	381	Terrell Owens RC	2.00	.90
❑	382	Elvis Grbac	.20	.09
❑	383	Ricky Ervins	.10	.05
❑	384	Eric Davis	.10	.05
❑	385	Dana Stubblefield	.20	.09
❑	386	Gary Plummer	.10	.05
❑	387	Tim McDonald	.10	.05
❑	388	William Floyd	.20	.09
❑	389	Ken Norton Jr.	.10	.05
❑	390	Merton Hanks	.10	.05
❑	391	Bart Oates	.10	.05
❑	392	Brent Jones	.10	.05
❑	393	Steve Broussard	.10	.05
❑	394	Robert Blackmon	.10	.05
❑	395	Rick Tuten	.10	.05
❑	396	Pete Kendall	.10	.05
❑	397	John Friesz	.10	.05
❑	398	Terry Wooden	.10	.05
❑	399	Rick Mirer	.20	.09
❑	400	Chris Warren	.20	.09
❑	401	Joey Galloway	.75	.35
❑	402	Howard Ballard	.10	.05
❑	403	Jason Kyle	.10	.05
❑	404	Kevin Mawae	.10	.05
❑	405	Mack Strong	.10	.05
❑	406	Reggie Brown RB RC	.10	.05
❑	407	Cortez Kennedy	.10	.05
❑	408	Sean Gilbert	.10	.05
❑	409	J.T. Thomas	.10	.05
❑	410	Shane Conlan	.10	.05
❑	411	Johnny Bailey	.10	.05
❑	412	Mark Rypien	.10	.05
❑	413	Leonard Russell	.10	.05
❑	414	Troy Drayton	.10	.05
❑	415	Jerome Bettis	.40	.18
❑	416	Jessie Hester	.10	.05
❑	417	Isaac Bruce	.40	.18
❑	418	Roman Phifer	.10	.05
❑	419	Todd Kinchen	.10	.05
❑	420	Alexander Wright	.10	.05
❑	421	Marcus Jones RC	.10	.05
❑	422	Horace Copeland	.10	.05
❑	423	Eric Curry	.10	.05
❑	424	Courtney Hawkins	.10	.05
❑	425	Alvin Harper	.10	.05
❑	426	Derrick Brooks	.10	.05
❑	427	Errict Rhett	.20	.09
❑	428	Trent Dilfer	.40	.18
❑	429	Hardy Nickerson	.10	.05
❑	430	Brad Culpepper	.10	.05
❑	431	Warren Sapp	.10	.05
❑	432	Reggie Roby	.10	.05
❑	433	Santana Dotson	.10	.05
❑	434	Jerry Ellison	.10	.05
❑	435	Lawrence Dawsey	.10	.05
❑	436	Heath Shuler	.20	.09
❑	437	Stanley Richard	.20	.09
❑	438	Rod Stephens	.10	.05
❑	439	Stephen Davis RC	3.00	1.35
❑	440	Terry Allen	.20	.09
❑	441	Michael Westbrook	.40	.18
❑	442	Ken Harvey	.10	.05
❑	443	Coleman Bell	.10	.05
❑	444	Marvcus Patton	.10	.05
❑	445	Gus Frerotte	.40	.18
❑	446	Leslie Shepherd	.10	.05
❑	447	Tom Carter	.10	.05
❑	448	Brian Mitchell	.10	.05
❑	449	Darrell Green	.10	.05
❑	450A	Tony Woods (issued in packs)	.10	.05
❑	450B	Chris Warren Promo (issued as a promo)	.50	.23
❑	CW1	Chris Warren Promo (Gold Crown Die Cut style)	1.00	.45

1996 Pacific Bomb Squad

	MINT	NRMT
COMPLETE SET (10)	150.00	70.00
COMMON CARD (1-10)	8.00	3.60
SEMISTARS	12.00	5.50
STATED ODDS 1:73		

	MINT	NRMT
❑ 1 Jeff Blake Carl Pickens	8.00	3.60
❑ 2 John Elway Anthony Miller	40.00	18.00
❑ 3 Scott Mitchell Herman Moore	12.00	5.50
❑ 4 Troy Aikman Jay Novacek	15.00	6.75
❑ 5 Brett Favre Robert Brooks	40.00	18.00
❑ 6 Steve McNair Chris Sanders	12.00	5.50
❑ 7 Dan Marino Irving Fryar	40.00	18.00
❑ 8 Drew Bledsoe Terry Glenn	20.00	9.00
❑ 9 Kordell Stewart Kordell Stewart	12.00	5.50
❑ 10 Steve Young Jerry Rice	25.00	11.00

1996 Pacific Card Supials

	MINT	NRMT
COMPLETE SET (72)	550.00	250.00
COMP.LARGE SET (36)	350.00	160.00
COMP.SMALL SET (36)	200.00	90.00
LARGE CARDS PRICED BELOW		
*SMALL CARDS: 5X TO 10X BASE CARD HI		
STATED ODDS 1:37		

	MINT	NRMT
❑ 1 Garrison Hearst	3.00	1.35
❑ 2 Jeff George	3.00	1.35
❑ 3 Eric Zeier	1.50	.70
❑ 4 Jim Kelly	6.00	2.70
❑ 5 Kerry Collins	6.00	2.70
❑ 6 Rashaan Salaam	6.00	2.70
❑ 7 Jeff Blake	6.00	2.70
❑ 8 Troy Aikman	15.00	6.75
❑ 9 Emmitt Smith	25.00	11.00
❑ 10 Terrell Davis	40.00	18.00
❑ 11 John Elway	30.00	13.50
❑ 12 Deion Sanders	10.00	4.50
❑ 13 Barry Sanders	30.00	13.50
❑ 14 Brett Favre	30.00	13.50
❑ 15 Steve McNair	12.00	5.50
❑ 16 Marshall Faulk	6.00	2.70
❑ 17 Mark Brunell	15.00	6.75
❑ 18 Tamarick Vanover	3.00	1.35
❑ 19 Dan Marino	30.00	13.50
❑ 20 Cris Carter	6.00	2.70
❑ 21 Keyshawn Johnson	30.00	13.50
❑ 22 Rodney Hampton	3.00	1.35
❑ 23 Curtis Martin	12.00	5.50
❑ 24 Drew Bledsoe	15.00	6.75
❑ 25 Mario Bates	3.00	1.35
❑ 26 Napoleon Kaufman	8.00	3.60
❑ 27 Ricky Watters	3.00	1.35
❑ 28 Kordell Stewart	12.00	5.50
❑ 29 Junior Seau	3.00	1.35
❑ 30 Steve Young	12.00	5.50
❑ 31 Jerry Rice	15.00	6.75
❑ 32 Isaac Bruce	6.00	2.70
❑ 33 Joey Galloway	12.00	5.50
❑ 34 Chris Warren	3.00	1.35
❑ 35 Errict Rhett	3.00	1.35
❑ 36 Michael Westbrook	6.00	2.70

1996 Pacific Cramer's Choice

	MINT	NRMT
COMPLETE SET (10)	500.00	220.00
STATED ODDS 1:721		

	MINT	NRMT
❑ CC1 Emmitt Smith	60.00	27.00
❑ CC2 John Elway	80.00	36.00
❑ CC3 Barry Sanders	80.00	36.00
❑ CC4 Brett Favre	80.00	36.00
❑ CC5 Reggie White	15.00	6.75
❑ CC6 Dan Marino	80.00	36.00
❑ CC7 Curtis Martin	30.00	13.50
❑ CC8 Keyshawn Johnson	80.00	36.00
❑ CC9 Kordell Stewart	30.00	13.50
❑ CC10 Jerry Rice	40.00	18.00

1996 Pacific Gems of the Crown

	MINT	NRMT
COMPLETE SET (36)	250.00	110.00
COMMON CARD (GC1-GC36)	2.00	.90
1-18: STATED ODDS 2:37 DYNAGON		
19-36: STATED ODDS 1:37 PACIFIC		

	MINT	NRMT
❑ GC1 Kerry Collins	4.00	1.80
❑ GC2 Rashaan Salaam	4.00	1.80
❑ GC3 Steve Young	8.00	3.60
❑ GC4 Rodney Thomas	1.00	.45
❑ GC5 Michael Westbrook	4.00	1.80
❑ GC6 Cris Carter	4.00	1.80
❑ GC7 Jerry Rice	10.00	4.50
❑ GC8 Drew Bledsoe	10.00	4.50
❑ GC9 Steve McNair	8.00	3.60
❑ GC10 Terrell Davis	25.00	11.00
❑ GC11 Barry Sanders	20.00	9.00
❑ GC12 Robert Brooks	4.00	1.80
❑ GC13 Chris Warren	2.00	.90
❑ GC14 Marshall Faulk	4.00	1.80
❑ GC15 John Elway	20.00	9.00
❑ GC16 Isaac Bruce	4.00	1.80
❑ GC17 Emmitt Smith	15.00	6.75
❑ GC18 Thurman Thomas	4.00	1.80
❑ GC19 Garrison Hearst	2.00	.90
❑ GC20 Jeff Blake	4.00	1.80
❑ GC21 Troy Aikman	10.00	4.50
❑ GC22 Deion Sanders	6.00	2.70
❑ GC23 Brett Favre	20.00	9.00
❑ GC24 Robert Smith	2.00	.90
❑ GC25 Mario Bates	2.00	.90
❑ GC26 Napoleon Kaufman	5.00	2.20
❑ GC27 Kordell Stewart	8.00	3.60
❑ GC28 Jim Kelly	4.00	1.80
❑ GC29 Jim Harbaugh	2.00	.90
❑ GC30 Tamarick Vanover	2.00	.90
❑ GC31 Dan Marino	20.00	9.00
❑ GC32 Warren Moon	2.00	.90
❑ GC33 Curtis Martin	8.00	3.60
❑ GC34 Rodney Hampton	2.00	.90
❑ GC35 Ricky Watters	2.00	.90
❑ GC36 Joey Galloway	8.00	3.60

1996 Pacific Gold Crown Die Cuts

	MINT	NRMT
COMPLETE SET (20)	250.00	110.00
GOLD STATED ODDS 1:37		
*PLAT. STARS: 12X TO 30X BASE CARD HI		
*PLAT. ROOKIES: 5X TO 12X BASE CARD HI		
PLAT: INSERTS IN SPECIAL RETAIL PACKS		

	MINT	NRMT
❑ 1 Emmitt Smith	20.00	9.00
❑ 2 Troy Aikman	12.00	5.50
❑ 3 Barry Sanders	25.00	11.00
❑ 4 Kerry Collins	5.00	2.20
❑ 5 Jeff Blake	5.00	2.20
❑ 6 John Elway	25.00	11.00
❑ 7 Terrell Davis	30.00	13.50
❑ 8 Deion Sanders	8.00	3.60
❑ 9 Brett Favre	25.00	11.00
❑ 10 Dan Marino	25.00	11.00
❑ 11 Eddie George	15.00	6.75
❑ 12 Curtis Martin	10.00	4.50
❑ 13 Drew Bledsoe	12.00	5.50
❑ 14 Keyshawn Johnson	10.00	4.50
❑ 15 Napoleon Kaufman	6.00	2.70

❑ 16 Kordell Stewart	10.00	4.50
❑ 17 Steve Young	10.00	4.50
❑ 18 Jerry Rice	12.00	5.50
❑ 19 Joey Galloway	10.00	4.50
❑ 20 Chris Warren	2.50	1.10

1996 Pacific Power Corps

	MINT	NRMT
COMPLETE SET (20)	75.00	34.00
STATED ODDS 6:21 SPECIAL RETAIL		
FOIL PARAL(1/11/14/17-19):1.25X to 2.5X		
ONLY SIX FOIL CARDS MADE		

❑ PC1 Troy Aikman	5.00	2.20
❑ PC2 Jeff Blake	2.00	.90
❑ PC3 Drew Bledsoe	5.00	2.20
❑ PC4 Kerry Collins	2.00	.90
❑ PC5 Terrell Davis	12.00	5.50
❑ PC6 John Elway	10.00	4.50
❑ PC7 Marshall Faulk	2.00	.90
❑ PC8 Brett Favre	10.00	4.50
❑ PC9 Joey Galloway	4.00	1.80
❑ PC10 Garrison Hearst	1.00	.45
❑ PC11 Dan Marino	10.00	4.50
❑ PC12 Curtis Martin	4.00	1.80
❑ PC13 Steve McNair	4.00	1.80
❑ PC14 Jerry Rice	5.00	2.20
❑ PC15 Rashaan Salaam	2.00	.90
❑ PC16 Barry Sanders	10.00	4.50
❑ PC17 Emmitt Smith	8.00	3.60
❑ PC18 Kordell Stewart	4.00	1.80
❑ PC19 Chris Warren	1.00	.45
❑ PC20 Steve Young	4.00	1.80

1996 Pacific The Zone

	MINT	NRMT
COMPLETE SET (20)	300.00	135.00
STATED ODDS 1:145		

❑ 1 Jim Kelly	8.00	3.60
❑ 2 Rashaan Salaam	8.00	3.60
❑ 3 Carl Pickens	8.00	3.60
❑ 4 Jeff Blake	8.00	3.60
❑ 5 Kerry Collins	8.00	3.60
❑ 6 Emmitt Smith	30.00	13.50
❑ 7 Troy Aikman	20.00	9.00
❑ 8 John Elway	40.00	18.00
❑ 9 Barry Sanders	40.00	18.00
❑ 10 Herman Moore	8.00	3.60
❑ 11 Scott Mitchell	4.00	1.80
❑ 12 Brett Favre	40.00	18.00
❑ 13 Robert Brooks	8.00	3.60
❑ 14 Marshall Faulk	8.00	3.60
❑ 15 Dan Marino	40.00	18.00
❑ 16 Drew Bledsoe	20.00	9.00
❑ 17 Curtis Martin	15.00	6.75
❑ 18 Steve Young	15.00	6.75
❑ 19 Jerry Rice	20.00	9.00
❑ 20 Chris Warren	4.00	1.80

1997 Pacific

	MINT	NRMT
COMPLETE SET (450)	40.00	18.00
COMMON CARD (1-450)	.10	.05
SEMISTARS	.20	.09
UNLISTED STARS	.40	.18
COMP.COPPER SET (450)	300.00	135.00
*COPPER STARS: 3X TO 6X HI COL.		
*COPPER RCs: 1.5X TO 3X		
COPPERS ONE PER HOBBY PACK		
COMMON PLAT.BLUE	10.00	4.50
*PLAT.BLUE STARS: 30X TO 80X HI COL.		
*PLAT.BLUE RCs: 15X TO 40X		
PLATINUM BLUE STATED ODDS 1:73		
PLAT.BLUE STATED PRINT RUN 67 SETS		
COMP.RED SET (450)	500.00	220.00
*RED STARS: 5X TO 10X		
*RED RCs: 2.5X TO 5X		
REDS ONE PER SPECIAL RETAIL PACK		
COMP.SILVER SET (450)	400.00	180.00
*SILVER STARS: 4X TO 8X HI COL.		
*SILVER RCs: 2X TO 4X		
SILVERS ONE PER RETAIL PACK		
COMP.BRUNELL (8)	30.00	13.50
COMMON BRUNELL (1-8)	5.00	2.20
BRUNELL INSERTED IN VARIOUS PRODUCTS		

❑ 1 Lomas Brown	.10	.05
❑ 2 Pat Carter	.10	.05
❑ 3 Larry Centers	.20	.09
❑ 4 Matt Darby	.10	.05
❑ 5 Marcus Dowdell	.10	.05
❑ 6 Aaron Graham	.10	.05
❑ 7 Kent Graham	.10	.05
❑ 8 LeShon Johnson	.10	.05
❑ 9 Seth Joyner	.10	.05
❑ 10 Leeland McElroy	.10	.05
❑ 11 Rob Moore	.20	.09
❑ 12 Simeon Rice	.20	.09
❑ 13 Eric Swann	.10	.05
❑ 14 Aeneas Williams	.10	.05
❑ 15 Morten Andersen	.10	.05
❑ 16 Jamal Anderson	.60	.25
❑ 17 Lester Archambeau	.10	.05
❑ 18 Cornelius Bennett	.10	.05
❑ 19 J.J. Birden	.10	.05
❑ 20 Antone Davis	.10	.05
❑ 21 Bert Emanuel	.20	.09
❑ 22 Travis Hall	.10	.05
❑ 23 Bobby Hebert	.10	.05
❑ 24 Craig Heyward	.10	.05
❑ 25 Terance Mathis	.20	.09
❑ 26 Tim McKyer	.10	.05
❑ 27 Eric Metcalf	.20	.09
❑ 28 Jessie Tuggle	.10	.05
❑ 29 Derrick Alexander WR	.20	.09
❑ 30 Orlando Brown	.10	.05
❑ 31 Rob Burnett	.10	.05
❑ 32 Earnest Byner	.10	.05
❑ 33 Ray Ethridge	.10	.05
❑ 34 Steve Everitt	.10	.05
❑ 35 Carwell Gardner	.10	.05
❑ 36 Michael Jackson	.20	.09
❑ 37 Jermaine Lewis	.40	.18
❑ 38 Stevon Moore	.10	.05
❑ 39 Byron Bam Morris	.10	.05
❑ 40 Jonathan Ogden	.10	.05
❑ 41 Vinny Testaverde	.20	.09
❑ 42 Todd Collins	.10	.05
❑ 43 Russell Copeland	.10	.05
❑ 44 Quinn Early	.10	.05
❑ 45 John Fina	.10	.05
❑ 46 Phil Hansen	.10	.05
❑ 47 Eric Moulds	.40	.18
❑ 48 Bryce Paup	.10	.05
❑ 49 Andre Reed	.20	.09
❑ 50 Kurt Schulz	.10	.05
❑ 51 Bruce Smith	.20	.09
❑ 52 Chris Spielman	.10	.05
❑ 53 Steve Tasker	.10	.05
❑ 54 Thurman Thomas	.40	.18
❑ 55 Carlton Bailey	.10	.05
❑ 56 Michael Bates	.10	.05
❑ 57 Blake Brockermeyer	.10	.05
❑ 58 Mark Carrier WR	.10	.05
❑ 59 Kerry Collins	.20	.09
❑ 60 Eric Davis	.10	.05
❑ 61 Kevin Greene	.20	.09
❑ 62 Rocket Ismail	.20	.09
❑ 63 Anthony Johnson	.10	.05
❑ 64 Shawn King	.10	.05
❑ 65 Greg Kragen	.10	.05
❑ 66 Sam Mills	.10	.05
❑ 67 Tyrone Poole	.10	.05
❑ 68 Wesley Walls	.20	.09
❑ 69 Mark Carrier DB	.10	.05
❑ 70 Curtis Conway	.20	.09
❑ 71 Bobby Engram	.20	.09
❑ 72 Jim Flanigan	.10	.05
❑ 73 Al Fontenot	.10	.05
❑ 74 Raymont Harris	.10	.05
❑ 75 Walt Harris	.10	.05
❑ 76 Andy Heck	.10	.05
❑ 77 Dave Krieg	.10	.05
❑ 78 Rashaan Salaam	.10	.05
❑ 79 Vinson Smith	.10	.05
❑ 80 Alonzo Spellman	.10	.05
❑ 81 Michael Timpson	.10	.05
❑ 82 James Williams	.10	.05
❑ 83 Ashley Ambrose	.10	.05
❑ 84 Eric Bieniemy	.10	.05
❑ 85 Jeff Blake	.20	.09
❑ 86 Ki-Jana Carter	.10	.05
❑ 87 John Copeland	.10	.05
❑ 88 David Dunn	.10	.05
❑ 89 Jeff Hill	.10	.05
❑ 90 Ricardo McDonald	.10	.05
❑ 91 Tony McGee	.10	.05
❑ 92 Greg Myers	.10	.05
❑ 93 Carl Pickens	.40	.18
❑ 94 Corey Sawyer	.10	.05
❑ 95 Darnay Scott	.20	.09
❑ 96 Dan Wilkinson	.10	.05
❑ 97 Troy Aikman	1.00	.45
❑ 98 Larry Allen	.10	.05
❑ 99 Eric Bjornson	.10	.05
❑ 100 Ray Donaldson	.10	.05
❑ 101 Michael Irvin	.40	.18
❑ 102 Daryl Johnston	.20	.09
❑ 103 Nate Newton	.10	.05
❑ 104 Deion Sanders	.40	.18
❑ 105 Jim Schwantz RC	.10	.05
❑ 106 Emmitt Smith	1.50	.70
❑ 107 Broderick Thomas	.10	.05
❑ 108 Tony Tolbert	.10	.05
❑ 109 Erik Williams	.10	.05
❑ 110 Sherman Williams	.10	.05
❑ 111 Darren Woodson	.10	.05
❑ 112 Steve Atwater	.10	.05

113	Aaron Craver	.10	.05
114	Ray Crockett	.10	.05
115	Terrell Davis	1.50	.70
116	Jason Elam	.10	.05
117	John Elway	2.00	.90
118	Todd Kinchen	.10	.05
119	Ed McCaffrey	.20	.09
120	Anthony Miller	.10	.05
121	John Mobley	.10	.05
122	Michael Dean Perry	.10	.05
123	Reggie Rivers	.10	.05
124	Shannon Sharpe	.20	.09
125	Alfred Williams	.10	.05
126	Reggie Brown LB	.20	.09
127	Luther Elliss	.10	.05
128	Kevin Glover	.10	.05
129	Jason Hanson	.10	.05
130	Pepper Johnson	.10	.05
131	Glyn Milburn	.10	.05
132	Scott Mitchell	.20	.09
133	Herman Moore	.40	.18
134	Johnnie Morton	.20	.09
135	Brett Perriman	.10	.05
136	Robert Porcher	.10	.05
137	Ron Rivers	.10	.05
138	Barry Sanders	2.00	.90
139	Henry Thomas	.10	.05
140	Don Beebe	.10	.05
141	Edgar Bennett	.20	.09
142	Robert Brooks	.20	.09
143	LeRoy Butler	.10	.05
144	Mark Chmura	.20	.09
145	Brett Favre	2.00	.90
146	Antonio Freeman	.50	.23
147	Chris Jacke	.10	.05
148	Travis Jervey	.20	.09
149	Sean Jones	.10	.05
150	Dorsey Levens	.40	.18
151	John Michels	.10	.05
152	Craig Newsome	.10	.05
153	Eugene Robinson	.10	.05
154	Reggie White	.40	.18
155	Micheal Barrow	.10	.05
156	Blaine Bishop	.10	.05
157	Chris Chandler	.20	.09
158	Anthony Cook	.10	.05
159	Malcolm Floyd	.10	.05
160	Eddie George	1.00	.45
161	Roderick Lewis	.10	.05
162	Steve McNair	.50	.23
163	John Henry Mills RC	.10	.05
164	Derek Russell	.10	.05
165	Chris Sanders	.10	.05
166	Mark Stepnoski	.10	.05
167	Frank Wycheck	.10	.05
168	Robert Young	.10	.05
169	Trev Alberts	.10	.05
170	Aaron Bailey	.10	.05
171	Tony Bennett	.10	.05
172	Ray Buchanan	.10	.05
173	Quentin Coryatt	.10	.05
174	Eugene Daniel	.10	.05
175	Sean Dawkins	.10	.05
176	Ken Dilger	.10	.05
177	Marshall Faulk	.40	.18
178	Jim Harbaugh	.20	.09
179	Marvin Harrison	.40	.18
180	Paul Justin	.10	.05
181	Lamont Warren	.10	.05
182	Bernard Whittington	.10	.05
183	Tony Boselli	.10	.05
184	Tony Brackens	.10	.05
185	Mark Brunell	1.00	.45
186	Brian DeMarco	.10	.05
187	Rich Griffith	.10	.05
188	Kevin Hardy	.10	.05
189	Willie Jackson	.10	.05
190	Jeff Lageman	.10	.05
191	Keenan McCardell	.20	.09
192	Natrone Means	.40	.18
193	Pete Mitchell	.10	.05
194	Joel Smeenge	.10	.05
195	Jimmy Smith	.20	.09
196	James O.Stewart	.20	.09
197	Marcus Allen	.40	.18
198	John Alt	.10	.05
199	Kimble Anders	.20	.09
200	Steve Bono	.20	.09
201	Vaughn Booker	.10	.05
202	Dale Carter	.10	.05
203	Mark Collins	.10	.05
204	Greg Hill	.10	.05
205	Joe Horn	.10	.05
206	Dan Saleaumua	.10	.05
207	Will Shields	.10	.05
208	Neil Smith	.20	.09
209	Derrick Thomas	.20	.09
210	Tamarick Vanover	.20	.09
211	Karim Abdul-Jabbar	.40	.18
212	Fred Barnett	.10	.05
213	Tim Bowens	.10	.05
214	Kirby Dar Dar	.10	.05
215	Troy Drayton	.10	.05
216	Craig Erickson	.10	.05
217	Daryl Gardener	.10	.05
218	Randal Hill	.10	.05
219	Dan Marino	2.00	.90
220	O.J. McDuffie	.20	.09
221	Bernie Parmalee	.10	.05
222	Stanley Pritchett	.10	.05
223	Daniel Stubbs	.10	.05
224	Zach Thomas	.20	.09
225	Derrick Alexander DE	.10	.05
226	Cris Carter	.40	.18
227	Jeff Christy	.10	.05
228	Qadry Ismail	.20	.09
229	Brad Johnson	.50	.23
230	Andrew Jordan	.10	.05
231	Randall McDaniel	.10	.05
232	David Palmer	.10	.05
233	John Randle	.10	.05
234	Jake Reed	.20	.09
235	Scott Sisson	.10	.05
236	Korey Stringer	.10	.05
237	Darryl Talley	.10	.05
238	Orlando Thomas	.10	.05
239	Bruce Armstrong	.10	.05
240	Drew Bledsoe	1.00	.45
241	Willie Clay	.10	.05
242	Ben Coates	.20	.09
243	Ferric Collons RC	.10	.05
244	Terry Glenn	.40	.18
245	Jerome Henderson	.10	.05
246	Shawn Jefferson	.10	.05
247	Dietrich Jells	.10	.05
248	Ty Law	.10	.05
249	Curtis Martin	.50	.23
250	Willie McGinest	.10	.05
251	Dave Meggett	.10	.05
252	Lawyer Milloy	.10	.05
253	Chris Slade	.10	.05
254	Je'rod Cherry	.10	.05
255	Jim Everett	.10	.05
256	Mark Fields	.10	.05
257	Michael Haynes	.10	.05
258	Tyrone Hughes	.10	.05
259	Haywood Jeffires	.10	.05
260	Wayne Martin	.10	.05
261	Mark McMillian	.10	.05
262	Rufus Porter	.10	.05
263	William Roaf	.10	.05
264	Torrance Small	.10	.05
265	Renaldo Turnbull	.10	.05
266	Ray Zellars	.10	.05
267	Jessie Armstead	.10	.05
268	Chad Bratzke	.10	.05
269	Dave Brown	.10	.05
270	Chris Calloway	.10	.05
271	Howard Cross	.10	.05
272	Lawrence Dawsey	.10	.05
273	Rodney Hampton	.20	.09
274	Danny Kanell	.20	.09
275	Arthur Marshall	.10	.05
276	Aaron Pierce	.10	.05
277	Phillippi Sparks	.10	.05
278	Amani Toomer	.20	.09
279	Charles Way	.20	.09
280	Richie Anderson	.10	.05
281	Fred Baxter	.10	.05
282	Wayne Chrebet	.40	.18
283	Kyle Clifton	.10	.05
284	Jumbo Elliott	.10	.05
285	Aaron Glenn	.10	.05
286	Jeff Graham	.10	.05
287	Bobby Hamilton RC	.10	.05
288	Keyshawn Johnson	.40	.18
289	Adrian Murrell	.20	.09
290	Neil O'Donnell	.20	.09
291	Webster Slaughter	.10	.05
292	Alex Van Dyke	.10	.05
293	Marvin Washington	.10	.05
294	Joe Aska	.10	.05
295	Jerry Ball	.10	.05
296	Tim Brown	.40	.18
297	Rickey Dudley	.20	.09
298	Pat Harlow	.10	.05
299	Nolan Harrison	.10	.05
300	Billy Joe Hobert	.20	.09
301	James Jett	.20	.09
302	Napoleon Kaufman	.40	.18
303	Lincoln Kennedy	.10	.05
304	Albert Lewis	.10	.05
305	Chester McGlockton	.10	.05
306	Pat Swilling	.10	.05
307	Steve Wisniewski	.10	.05
308	Darion Conner	.10	.05
309	Ty Detmer	.20	.09
310	Jason Dunn	.10	.05
311	Irving Fryar	.20	.09
312	James Fuller	.10	.05
313	William Fuller	.10	.05
314	Charlie Garner	.10	.05
315	Bobby Hoying	.20	.09
316	Tom Hutton	.10	.05
317	Chris T. Jones	.10	.05
318	Mike Mamula	.10	.05
319	Mark Seay	.10	.05
320	Bobby Taylor	.10	.05
321	Ricky Watters	.20	.09
322	Jahine Arnold	.10	.05
323	Jerome Bettis	.40	.18
324	Chad Brown	.10	.05
325	Mark Bruener	.10	.05
326	Andre Hastings	.10	.05
327	Norm Johnson	.10	.05
328	Levon Kirkland	.10	.05
329	Carnell Lake	.10	.05
330	Greg Lloyd	.10	.05
331	Ernie Mills	.10	.05
332	Orpheus Roye	.10	.05
333	Kordell Stewart	.50	.23
334	Yancey Thigpen	.20	.09
335	Mike Tomczak	.10	.05
336	Rod Woodson	.20	.09
337	Tony Banks	.20	.09
338	Bern Brostek	.10	.05
339	Isaac Bruce	.40	.18
340	Ernie Conwell	.10	.05
341	Keith Crawford	.10	.05
342	Wayne Gandy	.10	.05
343	Harold Green	.10	.05
344	Carlos Jenkins	.10	.05
345	Jimmie Jones	.10	.05
346	Eddie Kennison	.20	.09
347	Todd Lyght	.10	.05
348	Leslie O'Neal	.10	.05
349	Lawrence Phillips	.10	.05
350	Greg Robinson	.10	.05
351	Darren Bennett	.10	.05
352	Lewis Bush	.10	.05
353	Eric Castle	.10	.05
354	Terrell Fletcher	.10	.05
355	Darrien Gordon	.10	.05
356	Kurt Gouveia	.10	.05
357	Aaron Hayden	.10	.05
358	Stan Humphries	.20	.09
359	Tony Martin	.20	.09
360	Vaughn Parker	.10	.05
361	Brian Roche	.10	.05
362	Leonard Russell	.10	.05
363	Junior Seau	.20	.09
364	Roy Barker	.10	.05
365	Harris Barton	.10	.05
366	Dexter Carter	.10	.05
367	Chris Doleman	.10	.05
368	Tyronne Drakeford	.10	.05
369	Elvis Grbac	.20	.09
370	Derek Loville	.10	.05

❑ 371	Tim McDonald	.10	.05
❑ 372	Ken Norton	.10	.05
❑ 373	Terrell Owens	.40	.18
❑ 374	Gary Plummer	.10	.05
❑ 375	Jerry Rice	1.00	.45
❑ 376	Dana Stubblefield	.10	.05
❑ 377	Lee Woodall	.10	.05
❑ 378	Steve Young	.60	.25
❑ 379	Robert Blackmon	.10	.05
❑ 380	Brian Blades	.10	.05
❑ 381	Carlester Crumpler	.10	.05
❑ 382	Christian Fauria	.10	.05
❑ 383	John Friesz	.10	.05
❑ 384	Joey Galloway	.50	.23
❑ 385	Derrick Graham	.10	.05
❑ 386	Cortez Kennedy	.10	.05
❑ 387	Warren Moon	.40	.18
❑ 388	Winston Moss	.10	.05
❑ 389	Mike Pritchard	.10	.05
❑ 390	Michael Sinclair	.10	.05
❑ 391	Lamar Smith	.10	.05
❑ 392	Chris Warren	.20	.09
❑ 393	Chidi Ahanotu	.10	.05
❑ 394	Mike Alstott	.40	.18
❑ 395	Reggie Brooks	.10	.05
❑ 396	Trent Dilfer	.40	.18
❑ 397	Jerry Ellison	.10	.05
❑ 398	Paul Gruber	.10	.05
❑ 399	Alvin Harper	.10	.05
❑ 400	Courtney Hawkins	.10	.05
❑ 401	Dave Moore	.10	.05
❑ 402	Errict Rhett	.10	.05
❑ 403	Warren Sapp	.20	.09
❑ 404	Nilo Silvan	.10	.05
❑ 405	Regan Upshaw	.10	.05
❑ 406	Casey Weldon	.10	.05
❑ 407	Terry Allen	.40	.18
❑ 408	Jamie Asher	.10	.05
❑ 409	Bill Brooks	.10	.05
❑ 410	Tom Carter	.10	.05
❑ 411	Henry Ellard	.10	.05
❑ 412	Gus Frerotte	.10	.05
❑ 413	Darrell Green	.20	.09
❑ 414	Ken Harvey	.10	.05
❑ 415	Tre Johnson	.10	.05
❑ 416	Brian Mitchell	.10	.05
❑ 417	Rich Owens	.10	.05
❑ 418	Heath Shuler	.10	.05
❑ 419	Michael Westbrook	.20	.09
❑ 420	Tony Woods RC	.10	.05
❑ 421	Reidel Anthony RC	.75	.35
❑ 422	Darnell Autry RC	.20	.09
❑ 423	Tiki Barber RC	.60	.25
❑ 424	Pat Barnes RC	.40	.18
❑ 425	Terry Battle RC	.10	.05
❑ 426	Will Blackwell RC	.40	.18
❑ 427	Peter Boulware RC	.20	.09
❑ 428	Rae Carruth RC	.40	.18
❑ 429	Troy Davis RC	.40	.18
❑ 430	Jim Druckenmiller RC	.60	.25
❑ 431	Warrick Dunn RC	1.25	.55
❑ 432	Marc Edwards RC	.10	.05
❑ 433	James Farrior RC	.10	.05
❑ 434	Yatil Green RC	.20	.09
❑ 435	Byron Hanspard RC	.75	.35
❑ 436	Ike Hilliard RC	.75	.35
❑ 437	David LaFleur RC	.20	.09
❑ 438	Kevin Lockett RC	.20	.09
❑ 439	Sam Madison RC	.10	.05
❑ 440	Brian Manning RC	.20	.09
❑ 441	Orlando Pace RC	.10	.05
❑ 442	Jake Plummer RC	3.00	1.35
❑ 443	Chad Scott RC	.10	.05
❑ 444	Sedrick Shaw RC	.40	.18
❑ 445	Antowain Smith RC	1.00	.45
❑ 446	Shawn Springs RC	.20	.09
❑ 447	Ross Verba RC	.10	.05
❑ 448	Bryant Westbrook RC	.10	.05
❑ 449	Renaldo Wynn RC	.10	.05
❑ 450	Jimmy Johnson CO	.20	.09
❑ S1	Mark Brunell Sample	1.00	.45

1997 Pacific Big Number Die Cuts

		MINT	NRMT
COMPLETE SET (20)		100.00	45.00
STATED ODDS 1:37			
❑ 1	Jamal Anderson	5.00	2.20
❑ 2	Kerry Collins	1.50	.70
❑ 3	Troy Aikman	8.00	3.60
❑ 4	Emmitt Smith	12.00	5.50
❑ 5	Terrell Davis	12.00	5.50
❑ 6	John Elway	15.00	6.75
❑ 7	Barry Sanders	15.00	6.75
❑ 8	Brett Favre	15.00	6.75
❑ 9	Eddie George	8.00	3.60
❑ 10	Mark Brunell	8.00	3.60
❑ 11	Marcus Allen	3.00	1.35
❑ 12	Karim Abdul-Jabbar	3.00	1.35
❑ 13	Dan Marino	15.00	6.75
❑ 14	Drew Bledsoe	8.00	3.60
❑ 15	Curtis Martin	4.00	1.80
❑ 16	Napoleon Kaufman	3.00	1.35
❑ 17	Jerome Bettis	3.00	1.35
❑ 18	Eddie Kennison	1.50	.70
❑ 19	Jerry Rice	8.00	3.60
❑ 20	Steve Young	5.00	2.20

1997 Pacific Card Supials

		MINT	NRMT
COMPLETE SET (72)		150.00	70.00
COMP.LARGE SET (36)		100.00	45.00
COMP.SMALL SET (36)		60.00	27.00
*SMALL CARDS: 3X TO 6X BASE CARD HI			
STATED ODDS 1:37			
❑ 1	Todd Collins	.75	.35
❑ 2	Kerry Collins	1.50	.70
❑ 3	Wesley Walls	1.50	.70
❑ 4	Jeff Blake	1.50	.70
❑ 5	Troy Aikman	8.00	3.60
❑ 6	Emmitt Smith	12.00	5.50
❑ 7	Terrell Davis	12.00	5.50
❑ 8	John Elway	15.00	6.75
❑ 9	Herman Moore	3.00	1.35
❑ 10	Barry Sanders	15.00	6.75
❑ 11	Brett Favre	15.00	6.75
❑ 12	Dorsey Levens	3.00	1.35
❑ 13	Eddie George	8.00	3.60
❑ 14	Steve McNair	4.00	1.80
❑ 15	Marshall Faulk	3.00	1.35
❑ 16	Mark Brunell	8.00	3.60
❑ 17	Natrone Means	3.00	1.35
❑ 18	Marcus Allen	3.00	1.35
❑ 19	Karim Abdul-Jabbar	3.00	1.35
❑ 20	Dan Marino	15.00	6.75
❑ 21	Brad Johnson	4.00	1.80
❑ 22	Drew Bledsoe	8.00	3.60
❑ 23	Terry Glenn	3.00	1.35
❑ 24	Curtis Martin	4.00	1.80
❑ 25	Napoleon Kaufman	3.00	1.35
❑ 26	Ricky Watters	1.50	.70
❑ 27	Jerome Bettis	3.00	1.35
❑ 28	Kordell Stewart	4.00	1.80
❑ 29	Tony Banks	1.50	.70
❑ 30	Isaac Bruce	3.00	1.35
❑ 31	Eddie Kennison	1.50	.70
❑ 32	Jerry Rice	8.00	3.60
❑ 33	Steve Young	5.00	2.20
❑ 34	Joey Galloway	4.00	1.80
❑ 35	Chris Warren	1.50	.70
❑ 36	Gus Frerotte	.75	.35

1997 Pacific Cramer's Choice

		MINT	NRMT
COMPLETE SET (10)		600.00	275.00
STATED ODDS 1:721			
❑ 1	Kevin Greene	10.00	4.50
❑ 2	Emmitt Smith	80.00	36.00
❑ 3	Terrell Davis	80.00	36.00
❑ 4	John Elway	100.00	45.00
❑ 5	Barry Sanders	100.00	45.00
❑ 6	Brett Favre	100.00	45.00
❑ 7	Eddie George	50.00	22.00
❑ 8	Mark Brunell	50.00	22.00
❑ 9	Terry Glenn	20.00	9.00
❑ 10	Jerry Rice	50.00	22.00

1997 Pacific Gold Crown Die Cuts

		MINT	NRMT
COMPLETE SET (36)		120.00	55.00
STATED ODDS 1:37			

Card	MINT	NRMT
❑ 1 Larry Centers	1.50	.70
❑ 2 Vinny Testaverde	1.50	.70
❑ 3 Kerry Collins	1.50	.70
❑ 4 Kevin Greene	1.50	.70
❑ 5 Anthony Johnson	.75	.35
❑ 6 Jeff Blake	1.50	.70
❑ 7 Troy Aikman	8.00	3.60
❑ 8 Emmitt Smith	12.00	5.50
❑ 9 Terrell Davis	12.00	5.50
❑ 10 John Elway	15.00	6.75
❑ 11 Barry Sanders	15.00	6.75
❑ 12 Brett Favre	15.00	6.75
❑ 13 Antonio Freeman	4.00	1.80
❑ 14 Eddie George	8.00	3.60
❑ 15 Marshall Faulk	3.00	1.35
❑ 16 Mark Brunell	8.00	3.60
❑ 17 Jimmy Smith	1.50	.70
❑ 18 Marcus Allen	3.00	1.35
❑ 19 Karim Abdul-Jabbar	3.00	1.35
❑ 20 Dan Marino	15.00	6.75
❑ 21 Brad Johnson	4.00	1.80
❑ 22 Drew Bledsoe	8.00	3.60
❑ 23 Terry Glenn	3.00	1.35
❑ 24 Curtis Martin	4.00	1.80
❑ 25 Adrian Murrell	1.50	.70
❑ 26 Tim Brown	3.00	1.35
❑ 27 Jerome Bettis	3.00	1.35
❑ 28 Kordell Stewart	4.00	1.80
❑ 29 Tony Banks	1.50	.70
❑ 30 Terrell Owens	3.00	1.35
❑ 31 Jerry Rice	8.00	3.60
❑ 32 Steve Young	5.00	2.20
❑ 33 Chris Warren	1.50	.70
❑ 34 Terry Allen	3.00	1.35
❑ 35 Gus Frerotte	.75	.35
❑ 36 Jim Druckenmiller	5.00	2.20

1997 Pacific Team Checklists

	MINT	NRMT
COMPLETE SET (30)	100.00	45.00
COMMON CARD (1-30)	1.50	.70
SEMISTARS	3.00	1.35
UNLISTED STARS	5.00	2.20
STATED ODDS 1:37		

Card	MINT	NRMT
❑ 1 Larry Centers	1.50	.70
Kent Graham		
LeShon Johnson		
❑ 2 Jamal Anderson	8.00	3.60
Bert Emanuel		
Morten Andersen		
❑ 3 Vinny Testaverde	3.00	1.35
Derrick Alexander WR		
Michael Jackson		
❑ 4 Todd Collins	1.50	.70
Steve Tasker		
Bruce Smith		
❑ 5 Kerry Collins	5.00	2.20
Wesley Walls		
Kevin Greene		
❑ 6 Rashaan Salaam	1.50	.70
Raymont Harris		
Curtis Conway		
❑ 7 Jeff Blake	1.50	.70
Carl Pickens		
Ki-Jana Carter		
❑ 8 Emmitt Smith	15.00	6.75
Troy Aikman		
Michael Irvin		
❑ 9 John Elway	12.00	5.50
Terrell Davis		
Steve Atwater		
❑ 10 Barry Sanders	12.00	5.50
Herman Moore		
Scott Mitchell		
❑ 11 Brett Favre	20.00	9.00
Reggie White		
Antonio Freeman		
❑ 12 Steve McNair	12.00	5.50
Eddie George		
Chris Sanders		
❑ 13 Marshall Faulk	3.00	1.35
Jim Harbaugh		
Marvin Harrison		
❑ 14 Mark Brunell	8.00	3.60
Keenan McCardell		
Natrone Means		
❑ 15 Marcus Allen	5.00	2.20
Dale Carter		
Derrick Thomas		
❑ 16 Dan Marino	20.00	9.00
Karim Abdul-Jabbar		
Zach Thomas		
❑ 17 Brad Johnson	5.00	2.20
Cris Carter		
Jake Reed		
❑ 18 Drew Bledsoe	12.00	5.50
Curtis Martin		
Terry Glenn		
❑ 19 Jim Everett	1.50	.70
Wayne Martin		
Ray Zellars		
❑ 20 Dave Brown	1.50	.70
Rodney Hampton		
Amani Toomer		
❑ 21 Keyshawn Johnson	5.00	2.20
Adrian Murrell		
Neil O'Donnell		
❑ 22 Napoleon Kaufman	5.00	2.20
Tim Brown		
Chester McGlockton		
❑ 23 Ricky Watters	3.00	1.35
Ty Detmer		
Irving Fryar		
❑ 24 Jerome Bettis	8.00	3.60
Kordell Stewart		
Will Blackwell		
❑ 25 Tony Banks	3.00	1.35
Eddie Kennison		
Isaac Bruce		
❑ 26 Tony Martin	1.50	.70
Stan Humphries		
Junior Seau		
❑ 27 Steve Young	12.00	5.50
Jerry Rice		
Terrell Owens		
❑ 28 Chris Warren	5.00	2.20
Joey Galloway		
Cortez Kennedy		
❑ 29 Trent Dilfer	3.00	1.35
Errict Rhett		
Mike Alstott		
❑ 30 Gus Frerotte	5.00	2.20
Terry Allen		
Michael Westbrook		

1997 Pacific The Zone

	MINT	NRMT
COMPLETE SET (20)	150.00	70.00
STATED ODDS 1:73		

Card	MINT	NRMT
❑ 1 Kerry Collins	2.00	.90
❑ 2 Jeff Blake	2.00	.90
❑ 3 Emmitt Smith	15.00	6.75
❑ 4 Terrell Davis	15.00	6.75
❑ 5 John Elway	20.00	9.00
❑ 6 Barry Sanders	20.00	9.00
❑ 7 Brett Favre	20.00	9.00
❑ 8 Mark Brunell	10.00	4.50
❑ 9 Karim Abdul-Jabbar	4.00	1.80
❑ 10 Dan Marino	20.00	9.00

Card	MINT	NRMT
❑ 11 Drew Bledsoe	10.00	4.50
❑ 12 Terry Glenn	4.00	1.80
❑ 13 Curtis Martin	5.00	2.20
❑ 14 Napoleon Kaufman	4.00	1.80
❑ 15 Jerome Bettis	4.00	1.80
❑ 16 Eddie Kennison	2.00	.90
❑ 17 Tony Martin	2.00	.90
❑ 18 Jerry Rice	10.00	4.50
❑ 19 Steve Young	6.00	2.70
❑ 20 Terry Allen	4.00	1.80

1998 Pacific

	MINT	NRMT
COMPLETE SET (450)	70.00	32.00
COMMON CARD (1-450)	.15	.07
SEMISTARS	.25	.11
UNLISTED STARS	.50	.23
COMMON ROOKIE	1.50	.70
COMP.RED SET (450)	150.00	70.00
*RED STARS: 1.25X TO 3X HI COL.		
*RED YOUNG STARS: .75X TO 2X		
*RED RCs: .5X TO 1X		
REDS ONE PER SPECIAL RETAIL		
COMMON PLAT.BLUE	10.00	4.50
*PLAT.BLUE STARS: 30X TO 80X HI COL.		
*PLAT.BLUE YOUNG STARS: 25X TO 60X		
*PLAT.BLUE RCs: 12.5X TO 25X		
PLAT.BLUE STATED ODDS 1:73		

Card	MINT	NRMT
❑ 1 Mario Bates	.25	.11
❑ 2 Lomas Brown	.15	.07
❑ 3 Larry Centers	.15	.07
❑ 4 Chris Gedney	.15	.07
❑ 5 Terry Irving	.15	.07
❑ 6 Tom Knight	.15	.07
❑ 7 Eric Metcalf	.15	.07
❑ 8 Jamir Miller	.15	.07
❑ 9 Rob Moore	.25	.11
❑ 10 Joe Nedney	.15	.07
❑ 11 Jake Plummer	1.25	.55
❑ 12 Simeon Rice	.25	.11
❑ 13 Frank Sanders	.25	.11
❑ 14 Eric Swann	.15	.07
❑ 15 Aeneas Williams	.15	.07
❑ 16 Morten Andersen	.15	.07
❑ 17 Jamal Anderson	.50	.23
❑ 18 Michael Booker	.15	.07
❑ 19 Keith Brooking RC	2.00	.90
❑ 20 Ray Buchanan	.15	.07
❑ 21 Devin Bush	.15	.07

❑ 22 Chris Chandler .25 .11
❑ 23 Tony Graziani .15 .07
❑ 24 Harold Green .15 .07
❑ 25 Byron Hanspard .25 .11
❑ 26 Todd Kinchen .15 .07
❑ 27 Tony Martin .25 .11
❑ 28 Terance Mathis .25 .11
❑ 29 Eugene Robinson .15 .07
❑ 30 O.J. Santiago .15 .07
❑ 31 Chuck Smith .15 .07
❑ 32 Jessie Tuggle .15 .07
❑ 33 Bob Whitfield .15 .07
❑ 34 Peter Boulware .15 .07
❑ 35 Jay Graham .15 .07
❑ 36 Eric Green .15 .07
❑ 37 Jim Harbaugh .25 .11
❑ 38 Michael Jackson .15 .07
❑ 39 Jermaine Lewis .25 .11
❑ 40 Ray Lewis .15 .07
❑ 41 Michael McCrary .15 .07
❑ 42 Stevon Moore .15 .07
❑ 43 Jonathan Ogden .15 .07
❑ 44 Errict Rhett .25 .11
❑ 45 Matt Stover .15 .07
❑ 46 Rod Woodson .25 .11
❑ 47 Eric Zeier .25 .11
❑ 48 Ruben Brown .15 .07
❑ 49 Steve Christie .15 .07
❑ 50 Quinn Early .15 .07
❑ 51 John Fina .15 .07
❑ 52 Doug Flutie .50 .23
❑ 53 Phil Hansen .15 .07
❑ 54 Lonnie Johnson .15 .07
❑ 55 Rob Johnson .25 .11
❑ 56 Henry Jones .15 .07
❑ 57 Eric Moulds .50 .23
❑ 58 Andre Reed .25 .11
❑ 59 Antowain Smith .50 .23
❑ 60 Bruce Smith .25 .11
❑ 61 Thurman Thomas .50 .23
❑ 62 Ted Washington .15 .07
❑ 63 Michael Bates .15 .07
❑ 64 Tim Biakabutuka .25 .11
❑ 65 Blake Brockermeyer .15 .07
❑ 66 Mark Carrier .15 .07
❑ 67 Rae Carruth .25 .11
❑ 68 Kerry Collins .25 .11
❑ 69 Doug Evans .15 .07
❑ 70 William Floyd .15 .07
❑ 71 Sean Gilbert .15 .07
❑ 72 Rocket Ismail .15 .07
❑ 73 John Kasay .15 .07
❑ 74 Fred Lane .25 .11
❑ 75 Lamar Lathon .15 .07
❑ 76 Muhsin Muhammad .25 .11
❑ 77 Wesley Walls .25 .11
❑ 78 Edgar Bennett .15 .07
❑ 79 Tom Carter .15 .07
❑ 80 Curtis Conway .25 .11
❑ 81 Bobby Engram .25 .11
❑ 82 Curtis Enis RC 2.50 1.10
❑ 83 Jim Flanigan .15 .07
❑ 84 Walt Harris .15 .07
❑ 85 Jeff Jaeger .15 .07
❑ 86 Erik Kramer .15 .07
❑ 87 John Mangum .15 .07
❑ 88 Glyn Milburn .15 .07
❑ 89 Barry Minter .15 .07
❑ 90 Chris Penn .15 .07
❑ 91 Todd Sauerbrun .15 .07
❑ 92 James Williams .15 .07
❑ 93 Ashley Ambrose .15 .07
❑ 94 Willie Anderson .15 .07
❑ 95 Eric Bieniemy .15 .07
❑ 96 Jeff Blake .25 .11
❑ 97 Ki-Jana Carter .15 .07
❑ 98 John Copeland .15 .07
❑ 99 Corey Dillon .75 .35
❑ 100 Tony McGee .15 .07
❑ 101 Neil O'Donnell .25 .11
❑ 102 Carl Pickens .50 .23
❑ 103 Kevin Sargent .15 .07
❑ 104 Darnay Scott .25 .11
❑ 105 Takeo Spikes .25 .11
❑ 106 Troy Aikman 1.25 .55
❑ 107 Larry Allen .15 .07
❑ 108 Eric Bjornson .15 .07
❑ 109 Billy Davis .15 .07
❑ 110 Jason Garrett .15 .07
❑ 111 Michael Irvin .50 .23
❑ 112 Daryl Johnston .25 .11
❑ 113 David LaFleur .15 .07
❑ 114 Everett McIver .15 .07
❑ 115 Ernie Mills .15 .07
❑ 116 Nate Newton .15 .07
❑ 117 Deion Sanders .50 .23
❑ 118 Emmitt Smith 2.00 .90
❑ 119 Kevin Smith .15 .07
❑ 120 Erik Williams .15 .07
❑ 121 Steve Atwater .15 .07
❑ 122 Tyrone Braxton .15 .07
❑ 123 Ray Crockett .15 .07
❑ 124 Terrell Davis 2.00 .90
❑ 125 Jason Elam .15 .07
❑ 126 John Elway 2.50 1.10
❑ 127 Willie Green .15 .07
❑ 128 Brian Griese RC 4.00 1.80
❑ 129 Tony Jones .15 .07
❑ 130 Ed McCaffrey .25 .11
❑ 131 John Mobley .15 .07
❑ 132 Tom Nalen .15 .07
❑ 133 Marcus Nash .50 .23
❑ 134 Bill Romanowski .15 .07
❑ 135 Shannon Sharpe .25 .11
❑ 136 Neil Smith .25 .11
❑ 137 Rod Smith .25 .11
❑ 138 Keith Traylor .15 .07
❑ 139 Stephen Boyd .15 .07
❑ 140 Mark Carrier DB .15 .07
❑ 141 Charlie Batch RC 4.00 1.80
❑ 142 Jason Hanson .15 .07
❑ 143 Scott Mitchell .25 .11
❑ 144 Herman Moore .50 .23
❑ 145 Johnnie Morton .25 .11
❑ 146 Robert Porcher .15 .07
❑ 147 Ron Rivers .15 .07
❑ 148 Barry Sanders 2.50 1.10
❑ 149 Tracy Scroggins .15 .07
❑ 150 David Sloan .15 .07
❑ 151 Tommy Vardell .15 .07
❑ 152 Kerwin Waldroup .15 .07
❑ 153 Bryant Westbrook .15 .07
❑ 154 Robert Brooks .25 .11
❑ 155 Gilbert Brown .15 .07
❑ 156 LeRoy Butler .15 .07
❑ 157 Mark Chmura .25 .11
❑ 158 Earl Dotson .15 .07
❑ 159 Santana Dotson .15 .07
❑ 160 Brett Favre 2.50 1.10
❑ 161 Antonio Freeman .50 .23
❑ 162 Raymont Harris .15 .07
❑ 163 William Henderson .15 .07
❑ 164 Vonnie Holliday RC .25 .11
❑ 165 George Koonce .15 .07
❑ 166 Dorsey Levens .50 .23
❑ 167 Derrick Mayes .25 .11
❑ 168 Craig Newsome .15 .07
❑ 169 Ross Verba .15 .07
❑ 170 Reggie White .50 .23
❑ 171 Elijah Alexander .15 .07
❑ 172 Aaron Bailey .15 .07
❑ 173 Jason Belser .15 .07
❑ 174 Robert Blackmon .15 .07
❑ 175 Zack Crockett .15 .07
❑ 176 Ken Dilger .15 .07
❑ 177 Marshall Faulk .50 .23
❑ 178 Tarik Glenn .15 .07
❑ 179 Marvin Harrison .25 .11
❑ 180 Tony Mandarich .15 .07
❑ 181 Peyton Manning RC 12.00 5.50
❑ 182 Marcus Pollard .15 .07
❑ 183 Lamont Warren .15 .07
❑ 184 Tavian Banks RC .25 .11
❑ 185 Reggie Barlow .15 .07
❑ 186 Tony Boselli .15 .07
❑ 187 Tony Brackens .15 .07
❑ 188 Mark Brunell 1.00 .45
❑ 189 Kevin Hardy .15 .07
❑ 190 Mike Hollis .15 .07
❑ 191 Jeff Lageman .15 .07
❑ 192 Keenan McCardell .25 .11
❑ 193 Pete Mitchell .15 .07
❑ 194 Bryce Paup .15 .07
❑ 195 Leon Searcy .15 .07
❑ 196 Jimmy Smith .25 .11
❑ 197 James Stewart .25 .11
❑ 198 Fred Taylor RC 6.00 2.70
❑ 199 Renaldo Wynn .15 .07
❑ 200 Derrick Alexander WR .25 .11
❑ 201 Kimble Anders .25 .11
❑ 202 Donnell Bennett .15 .07
❑ 203 Dale Carter .15 .07
❑ 204 Anthony Davis .15 .07
❑ 205 Rich Gannon .15 .07
❑ 206 Tony Gonzalez .15 .07
❑ 207 Elvis Grbac .25 .11
❑ 208 James Hasty .15 .07
❑ 209 Leslie O'Neal .15 .07
❑ 210 Andre Rison .25 .11
❑ 211 Rashaan Shehee RC 2.00 .90
❑ 212 Will Shields .15 .07
❑ 213 Pete Stoyanovich .15 .07
❑ 214 Derrick Thomas .25 .11
❑ 215 Tamarick Vanover .15 .07
❑ 216 Karim Abdul-Jabbar .50 .23
❑ 217 Trace Armstrong .15 .07
❑ 218 John Avery RC 1.50 .70
❑ 219 Tim Bowens .15 .07
❑ 220 Terrell Buckley .15 .07
❑ 221 Troy Drayton .15 .07
❑ 222 Daryl Gardener .15 .07
❑ 223 Damon Huard RC 12.00 5.50
❑ 224 Charles Jordan .15 .07
❑ 225 Dan Marino 2.50 1.10
❑ 226 O.J. McDuffie .25 .11
❑ 227 Bernie Parmalee .15 .07
❑ 228 Stanley Pritchett .15 .07
❑ 229 Derrick Rodgers .15 .07
❑ 230 Lamar Thomas .15 .07
❑ 231 Zach Thomas .15 .07
❑ 232 Richmond Webb .15 .07
❑ 233 Derrick Alexander DE .15 .07
❑ 234 Jerry Ball .15 .07
❑ 235 Cris Carter .50 .23
❑ 236 Randall Cunningham .50 .23
❑ 237 Charles Evans .15 .07
❑ 238 Corey Fuller .15 .07
❑ 239 Andrew Glover .15 .07
❑ 240 Leroy Hoard .15 .07
❑ 241 Brad Johnson .50 .23
❑ 242 Ed McDaniel .15 .07
❑ 243 Randall McDaniel .15 .07
❑ 244 Randy Moss RC 12.00 5.50
❑ 245 John Randle .25 .11
❑ 246 Jake Reed .25 .11
❑ 247 Dwayne Rudd .15 .07
❑ 248 Robert Smith .50 .23
❑ 249 Bruce Armstrong .15 .07
❑ 250 Drew Bledsoe 1.00 .45
❑ 251 Vincent Brisby .15 .07
❑ 252 Tedy Bruschi .15 .07
❑ 253 Ben Coates .25 .11
❑ 254 Derrick Cullors .25 .11
❑ 255 Terry Glenn .50 .23
❑ 256 Shawn Jefferson .15 .07
❑ 257 Ted Johnson .15 .07
❑ 258 Ty Law .15 .07
❑ 259 Willie McGinest .15 .07
❑ 260 Lawyer Milloy .15 .07
❑ 261 Sedrick Shaw .15 .07
❑ 262 Chris Slade .15 .07
❑ 263 Troy Davis .15 .07
❑ 264 Mark Fields .15 .07
❑ 265 Andre Hastings .15 .07
❑ 266 Billy Joe Hobert .15 .07
❑ 267 Qadry Ismail .15 .07
❑ 268 Tony Johnson .15 .07
❑ 269 Sammy Knight RC .15 .07
❑ 270 Wayne Martin .15 .07
❑ 271 Chris Naeole .15 .07
❑ 272 Keith Poole .15 .07
❑ 273 William Roaf .15 .07
❑ 274 Pio Sagapolutele .15 .07
❑ 275 Danny Wuerffel .25 .11
❑ 276 Ray Zellars .15 .07
❑ 277 Jessie Armstead .15 .07
❑ 278 Tiki Barber .25 .11
❑ 279 Chris Calloway .15 .07

Card	MINT	NRMT
❑ 280 Percy Ellsworth	.15	.07
❑ 281 Sam Garnes RC	.15	.07
❑ 282 Kent Graham	.15	.07
❑ 283 Ike Hilliard	.25	.11
❑ 284 Danny Kanell	.25	.11
❑ 285 Corey Miller	.15	.07
❑ 286 Phillippi Sparks	.15	.07
❑ 287 Michael Strahan	.15	.07
❑ 288 Amani Toomer	.25	.11
❑ 289 Charles Way	.15	.07
❑ 290 Tyrone Wheatley	.25	.11
❑ 291 Tito Wooten	.15	.07
❑ 292 Kyle Brady	.15	.07
❑ 293 Keith Byars	.15	.07
❑ 294 Wayne Chrebet	.50	.23
❑ 295 John Elliott	.15	.07
❑ 296 Glenn Foley	.25	.11
❑ 297 Aaron Glenn	.15	.07
❑ 298 Keyshawn Johnson	.50	.23
❑ 299 Curtis Martin	.50	.23
❑ 300 Otis Smith	.15	.07
❑ 301 Vinny Testaverde	.25	.11
❑ 302 Alex Van Dyke	.15	.07
❑ 303 Dedric Ward	.15	.07
❑ 304 Greg Biekert	.15	.07
❑ 305 Tim Brown	.50	.23
❑ 306 Rickey Dudley	.15	.07
❑ 307 Jeff George	.25	.11
❑ 308 Pat Harlow	.15	.07
❑ 309 Desmond Howard	.25	.11
❑ 310 James Jett	.25	.11
❑ 311 Napoleon Kaufman	.50	.23
❑ 312 Lincoln Kennedy	.15	.07
❑ 313 Russell Maryland	.15	.07
❑ 314 Darrell Russell	.15	.07
❑ 315 Eric Turner	.15	.07
❑ 316 Steve Wisniewski	.15	.07
❑ 317 Charles Woodson RC	2.50	1.10
❑ 318 James Darling RC	.15	.07
❑ 319 Jason Dunn	.15	.07
❑ 320 Irving Fryar	.25	.11
❑ 321 Charlie Garner	.15	.07
❑ 322 Jeff Graham	.15	.07
❑ 323 Bobby Hoying	.25	.11
❑ 324 Chad Lewis	.15	.07
❑ 325 Rodney Peete	.15	.07
❑ 326 Freddie Solomon	.15	.07
❑ 327 Duce Staley	1.00	.45
❑ 328 Bobby Taylor	.15	.07
❑ 329 William Thomas	.15	.07
❑ 330 Kevin Turner	.15	.07
❑ 331 Troy Vincent	.15	.07
❑ 332 Jerome Bettis	.50	.23
❑ 333 Will Blackwell	.15	.07
❑ 334 Mark Bruener	.15	.07
❑ 335 Andre Coleman	.15	.07
❑ 336 Dermontti Dawson	.15	.07
❑ 337 Jason Gildon	.15	.07
❑ 338 Courtney Hawkins	.15	.07
❑ 339 Charles Johnson	.15	.07
❑ 340 Levon Kirkland	.15	.07
❑ 341 Carnell Lake	.15	.07
❑ 342 Tim Lester	.15	.07
❑ 343 Joel Steed	.15	.07
❑ 344 Kordell Stewart	.50	.23
❑ 345 Will Wolford	.15	.07
❑ 346 Tony Banks	.25	.11
❑ 347 Isaac Bruce	.50	.23
❑ 348 Ernie Conwell	.15	.07
❑ 349 D'Marco Farr	.15	.07
❑ 350 Wayne Gandy	.15	.07
❑ 351 Jerome Pathon RC	2.00	.90
❑ 352 Eddie Kennison	.25	.11
❑ 353 Amp Lee	.15	.07
❑ 354 Keith Lyle	.15	.07
❑ 355 Ryan McNeil	.15	.07
❑ 356 Jerald Moore	.15	.07
❑ 357 Orlando Pace	.15	.07
❑ 358 Roman Phifer	.15	.07
❑ 359 David Thompson	.15	.07
❑ 360 Darren Bennett	.15	.07
❑ 361 John Carney	.15	.07
❑ 362 Marco Coleman	.15	.07
❑ 363 Terrell Fletcher	.15	.07
❑ 364 William Fuller	.15	.07
❑ 365 Charlie Jones	.15	.07
❑ 366 Freddie Jones	.15	.07
❑ 367 Ryan Leaf RC	2.00	.90
❑ 368 Natrone Means	.50	.23
❑ 369 Junior Seau	.25	.11
❑ 370 Terrance Shaw	.15	.07
❑ 371 Tremayne Stephens RC	.15	.07
❑ 372 Bryan Still	.15	.07
❑ 373 Aaron Taylor	.15	.07
❑ 374 Greg Clark	.15	.07
❑ 375 Ty Detmer	.25	.11
❑ 376 Jim Druckenmiller	.25	.11
❑ 377 Marc Edwards	.15	.07
❑ 378 Merton Hanks	.15	.07
❑ 379 Garrison Hearst	.50	.23
❑ 380 Chuck Levy	.15	.07
❑ 381 Ken Norton	.15	.07
❑ 382 Terrell Owens	.50	.23
❑ 383 Marquez Pope	.15	.07
❑ 384 Jerry Rice	1.25	.55
❑ 385 Irv Smith	.15	.07
❑ 386 J.J. Stokes	.25	.11
❑ 387 Iheanyi Uwaezuoke	.15	.07
❑ 388 Bryant Young	.15	.07
❑ 389 Steve Young	.75	.35
❑ 390 Sam Adams	.15	.07
❑ 391 Chad Brown	.15	.07
❑ 392 Christian Fauria	.15	.07
❑ 393 Joey Galloway	.50	.23
❑ 394 Ahman Green RC	2.00	.90
❑ 395 Walter Jones	.15	.07
❑ 396 Cortez Kennedy	.15	.07
❑ 397 Jon Kitna	1.50	.70
❑ 398 James McKnight	.15	.07
❑ 399 Warren Moon	.50	.23
❑ 400 Mike Pritchard	.15	.07
❑ 401 Michael Sinclair	.15	.07
❑ 402 Shawn Springs	.15	.07
❑ 403 Ricky Watters	.25	.11
❑ 404 Darryl Williams	.15	.07
❑ 405 Mike Alstott	.50	.23
❑ 406 Reidel Anthony	.25	.11
❑ 407 Derrick Brooks	.15	.07
❑ 408 Brad Culpepper	.15	.07
❑ 409 Trent Dilfer	.50	.23
❑ 410 Warrick Dunn	.75	.35
❑ 411 Bert Emanuel	.25	.11
❑ 412 Jacquez Green RC	2.00	.90
❑ 413 Paul Gruber	.15	.07
❑ 414 Patrick Hape RC	.15	.07
❑ 415 Dave Moore	.15	.07
❑ 416 Hardy Nickerson	.15	.07
❑ 417 Warren Sapp	.25	.11
❑ 418 Robb Thomas	.15	.07
❑ 419 Regan Upshaw	.15	.07
❑ 420 Karl Williams	.15	.07
❑ 421 Blaine Bishop	.15	.07
❑ 422 Anthony Cook	.15	.07
❑ 423 Willie Davis	.15	.07
❑ 424 Al Del Greco	.15	.07
❑ 425 Kevin Dyson	.50	.23
❑ 426 Henry Ford	.15	.07
❑ 427 Eddie George	1.00	.45
❑ 428 Jackie Harris	.15	.07
❑ 429 Steve McNair	.50	.23
❑ 430 Chris Sanders	.15	.07
❑ 431 Mark Stepnoski	.15	.07
❑ 432 Yancey Thigpen	.15	.07
❑ 433 Barron Wortham	.15	.07
❑ 434 Frank Wycheck	.15	.07
❑ 435 Stephen Alexander RC	2.00	.90
❑ 436 Terry Allen	.50	.23
❑ 437 Jamie Asher	.15	.07
❑ 438 Bob Dahl	.15	.07
❑ 439 Stephen Davis	.15	.07
❑ 440 Cris Dishman	.15	.07
❑ 441 Gus Frerotte	.15	.07
❑ 442 Darrell Green	.25	.11
❑ 443 Trent Green	.75	.35
❑ 444 Ken Harvey	.15	.07
❑ 445 Skip Hicks RC	2.00	.90
❑ 446 Jeff Hostetler	.15	.07
❑ 447 Brian Mitchell	.15	.07
❑ 448 Leslie Shepherd	.15	.07
❑ 449 Michael Westbrook	.25	.11
❑ 450 Dan Wilkinson	.15	.07
❑ S1 Warrick Dunn Sample	2.00	.90

1998 Pacific Cramer's Choice Awards

	MINT	NRMT
COMPLETE SET (10)	800.00	350.00
COMMON CARD (1-10)	50.00	22.00
STATED ODDS 1:721		
❑ 1 Terrell Davis	100.00	45.00
❑ 2 John Elway	150.00	70.00
❑ 3 Barry Sanders	150.00	70.00
❑ 4 Brett Favre	150.00	70.00
❑ 5 Peyton Manning	120.00	55.00
❑ 6 Mark Brunell	60.00	27.00
❑ 7 Dan Marino	150.00	70.00
❑ 8 Ryan Leaf	50.00	22.00
❑ 9 Jerry Rice	80.00	36.00
❑ 10 Warrick Dunn	50.00	22.00

1998 Pacific Dynagon Turf

	MINT	NRMT
COMPLETE SET (20)	100.00	45.00
COMMON CARD (1-20)	2.50	1.10
STATED ODDS 4:37		
*TITANIUMS: 5X TO 12X HI COL.		
TITANIUM STATED PRINT RUN 99 SETS		
❑ 1 Corey Dillon	2.50	1.10
❑ 2 Troy Aikman	6.00	2.70
❑ 3 Emmitt Smith	10.00	4.50
❑ 4 Terrell Davis	10.00	4.50
❑ 5 John Elway	12.00	5.50
❑ 6 Barry Sanders	12.00	5.50
❑ 7 Brett Favre	12.00	5.50
❑ 8 Peyton Manning	15.00	6.75
❑ 9 Mark Brunell	5.00	2.20
❑ 10 Dan Marino	12.00	5.50
❑ 11 Drew Bledsoe	5.00	2.20
❑ 12 Curtis Martin	2.50	1.10
❑ 13 Napoleon Kaufman	2.50	1.10
❑ 14 Jerome Bettis	2.50	1.10
❑ 15 Kordell Stewart	2.50	1.10
❑ 16 Ryan Leaf	3.00	1.35
❑ 17 Jerry Rice	6.00	2.70
❑ 18 Steve Young	4.00	1.80
❑ 19 Warrick Dunn	2.50	1.10
❑ 20 Eddie George	4.00	1.80

1998 Pacific Gold Crown Die Cuts

	MINT	NRMT
COMPLETE SET (36)	250.00	110.00
COMMON CARD (1-36)	4.00	1.80
SEMISTARS	6.00	2.70
STATED ODDS 1:37		
❑ 1 Jake Plummer	12.00	5.50
❑ 2 Antowain Smith	6.00	2.70
❑ 3 Curtis Enis	10.00	4.50
❑ 4 Corey Dillon	8.00	3.60
❑ 5 Troy Aikman	12.00	5.50
❑ 6 Deion Sanders	6.00	2.70
❑ 7 Emmitt Smith	20.00	9.00
❑ 8 Terrell Davis	20.00	9.00
❑ 9 John Elway	25.00	11.00
❑ 10 Barry Sanders	25.00	11.00
❑ 11 Brett Favre	25.00	11.00
❑ 12 Dorsey Levens	6.00	2.70
❑ 13 Marshall Faulk	6.00	2.70
❑ 14 Peyton Manning	30.00	13.50
❑ 15 Mark Brunell	10.00	4.50
❑ 16 Fred Taylor	15.00	6.75
❑ 17 Derrick Thomas	4.00	1.80
❑ 18 Dan Marino	25.00	11.00
❑ 19 Brad Johnson	6.00	2.70
❑ 20 Robert Smith	6.00	2.70
❑ 21 Drew Bledsoe	10.00	4.50
❑ 22 Glenn Foley	4.00	1.80
❑ 23 Curtis Martin	6.00	2.70
❑ 24 Napoleon Kaufman	6.00	2.70
❑ 25 Charles Woodson	10.00	4.50
❑ 26 Jerome Bettis	6.00	2.70
❑ 27 Kordell Stewart	6.00	2.70
❑ 28 Ryan Leaf	8.00	3.60
❑ 29 Garrison Hearst	6.00	2.70
❑ 30 Jerry Rice	12.00	5.50
❑ 31 J.J. Stokes	4.00	1.80
❑ 32 Steve Young	8.00	3.60
❑ 33 Joey Galloway	6.00	2.70
❑ 34 Ricky Watters	4.00	1.80
❑ 35 Warrick Dunn	10.00	4.50
❑ 36 Eddie George	10.00	4.50

1998 Pacific Team Checklists

	MINT	NRMT
COMPLETE SET (30)	150.00	70.00
COMMON CARD (1-30)	2.50	1.10
STATED ODDS 2:37		
❑ 1 Jake Plummer	10.00	4.50
❑ 2 Jamal Anderson	2.50	1.10
❑ 3 Eric Zeier	2.50	1.10
❑ 4 Rob Johnson	2.50	1.10
❑ 5 Fred Lane	2.50	1.10
❑ 6 Curtis Enis	8.00	3.60
❑ 7 Corey Dillon	4.00	1.80
❑ 8 Troy Aikman	10.00	4.50
❑ 9 John Elway	20.00	9.00
❑ 10 Barry Sanders	20.00	9.00
❑ 11 Brett Favre	20.00	9.00
❑ 12 Peyton Manning	25.00	11.00
❑ 13 Mark Brunell	8.00	3.60
❑ 14 Elvis Grbac	2.50	1.10
❑ 15 Dan Marino	20.00	9.00
❑ 16 Robert Smith	2.50	1.10
❑ 17 Drew Bledsoe	8.00	3.60
❑ 18 Danny Wuerffel	2.50	1.10
❑ 19 Tiki Barber	2.50	1.10
❑ 20 Curtis Martin	2.50	1.10
❑ 21 Napoleon Kaufman	2.50	1.10
❑ 22 Duce Staley	3.00	1.35
❑ 23 Kordell Stewart	3.00	1.35
❑ 24 Tony Banks	2.50	1.10
❑ 25 Ryan Leaf	5.00	2.20
❑ 26 Jerry Rice	10.00	4.50
❑ 27 Warren Moon	2.50	1.10
❑ 28 Warrick Dunn	4.00	1.80
❑ 29 Eddie George	8.00	3.60
❑ 30 Terry Allen	2.50	1.10

1998 Pacific Timelines

	MINT	NRMT
COMPLETE SET (20)	800.00	350.00
COMMON CARD (1-20)	12.00	5.50
STATED ODDS 1:181 HOBBY		
❑ 1 Troy Aikman	50.00	22.00
❑ 2 Deion Sanders	12.00	5.50
❑ 3 Emmitt Smith	80.00	36.00
❑ 4 Terrell Davis	80.00	36.00
❑ 5 John Elway	100.00	45.00
❑ 6 Barry Sanders	100.00	45.00
❑ 7 Brett Favre	100.00	45.00
❑ 8 Peyton Manning	100.00	45.00
❑ 9 Mark Brunell	40.00	18.00
❑ 10 Dan Marino	100.00	45.00
❑ 11 Drew Bledsoe	40.00	18.00
❑ 12 Curtis Martin	12.00	5.50
❑ 13 Jerome Bettis	12.00	5.50
❑ 14 Kordell Stewart	15.00	6.75
❑ 15 Ryan Leaf	25.00	11.00
❑ 16 Jerry Rice	50.00	22.00
❑ 17 Steve Young	30.00	13.50
❑ 18 Ricky Watters	12.00	5.50
❑ 19 Warrick Dunn	20.00	9.00
❑ 20 Eddie George	40.00	18.00

1999 Pacific

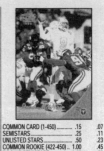

	MINT	NRMT
COMPLETE SET (450)	100.00	45.00
COMMON CARD (1-450)	.15	.07
SEMISTARS	.25	.11
UNLISTED STARS	.50	.23
COMMON ROOKIE (422-450)	1.00	.45
ROOKIE SEMISTARS	1.25	.55
ROOKIE UNL.STARS	1.50	.70
COMMON COPPER	8.00	3.60
*COPPER STARS: 20X TO 50X HI COL.		
*COPPER YOUNG STARS: 15X TO 40X		
*COPPER RCs: 4X TO 10X		
343 K.WARNER COPPER	250.00	110.00
COPPER PRINT RUN 99 SERIAL #'d SETS		
COPPERS INSERTED IN HOBBY PACKS		
COMP.GOLD SET (450)	1000.00	450.00
*GOLD STARS: 12X TO 30X HI COL.		
*GOLD YOUNG STARS: 10X TO 25X		
*GOLD RCs: 2.5X TO 6X		
343 K.WARNER GOLD	150.00	70.00
GOLD PRINT RUN 199 SERIAL #'d SETS		
GOLDS INSERTED IN HOBBY PACKS		
COMMON OPEN.DAY	15.00	6.75
*OPENING DAY STARS: 40X TO 100X HI COL.		
*OPENING DAY YOUNG STARS: 30X TO 80X		
*OPENING DAY RCs: 7X TO 20X		
343 K.WARNER OPEN.DAY	400.00	180.00
OPENING DAY PRINT RUN 45 SER.#'d SETS		
COMMON PLAT.BLUE	10.00	4.50
*PLAT.BLUE STARS: 30X TO 75X HI COL.		
*PLAT.BLUE YOUNG STARS: 25X TO 60X		
*PLATINUM BLUE RCs: 6X TO 15X		
343 K.WARNER PLAT.BLUE	400.00	180.00
PLAT.BLUE PRINT RUN 75 SER.#'d SETS		
COMP.RED SET (450)	1200.00	550.00
*RED STARS: 12X TO 30X HI COL.		
*RED YOUNG STARS: 10X TO 25X		
*RED RCs: 3X TO 8X		
343 K.WARNER RED	200.00	90.00
RED STATED ODDS 4:25 SPECIAL RETAIL		
❑ 1 Mario Bates	.15	.07
❑ 2 Larry Centers	.15	.07
❑ 3 Chris Gedney	.15	.07
❑ 4 Kwamie Lassiter RC	.15	.07
❑ 5 Johnny McWilliams	.15	.07
❑ 6 Eric Metcalf	.15	.07
❑ 7 Rob Moore	.25	.11
❑ 8 Adrian Murrell	.25	.11
❑ 9 Jake Plummer	1.00	.45
❑ 10 Simeon Rice	.15	.07
❑ 11 Frank Sanders	.25	.11
❑ 12 Andre Wadsworth	.15	.07
❑ 13 Aeneas Williams	.15	.07
❑ 14 Michael Pittman Ronnie Anderson RC	.15	.07
❑ 15 Morten Andersen	.15	.07
❑ 16 Jamal Anderson	.50	.23
❑ 17 Lester Archambeau	.15	.07
❑ 18 Chris Chandler	.25	.11
❑ 19 Bob Christian	.15	.07
❑ 20 Steve DeBerg	.15	.07
❑ 21 Tim Dwight	.50	.23
❑ 22 Tony Martin	.25	.11
❑ 23 Terance Mathis	.25	.11
❑ 24 Eugene Robinson	.15	.07

❑ 25 O.J. Santiago	.15	.07
❑ 26 Chuck Smith	.15	.07
❑ 27 Jessie Tuggle	.15	.07
❑ 28 Jammi German	.15	.07
Ken Oxendine RC		
❑ 29 Peter Boulware	.15	.07
❑ 30 Jay Graham	.15	.07
❑ 31 Jim Harbaugh	.25	.11
❑ 32 Priest Holmes	.50	.23
❑ 33 Michael Jackson	.15	.07
❑ 34 Jermaine Lewis	.25	.11
❑ 35 Ray Lewis	.15	.07
❑ 36 Michael McCrary	.15	.07
❑ 37 Jonathan Ogden	.15	.07
❑ 38 Errict Rhett	.15	.07
❑ 39 James Roe RC	.15	.07
❑ 40 Floyd Turner	.15	.07
❑ 41 Rod Woodson	.25	.11
❑ 42 Eric Zeier	.15	.07
❑ 43 Wally Richardson	.15	.07
Patrick Johnson		
❑ 44 Ruben Brown	.15	.07
❑ 45 Quinn Early	.15	.07
❑ 46 Doug Flutie	.60	.25
❑ 47 Sam Gash	.15	.07
❑ 48 Phil Hansen	.15	.07
❑ 49 Lonnie Johnson	.15	.07
❑ 50 Rob Johnson	.25	.11
❑ 51 Eric Moulds	.50	.23
❑ 52 Andre Reed	.25	.11
❑ 53 Jay Riemersma	.15	.07
❑ 54 Antowain Smith	.50	.23
❑ 55 Bruce Smith	.25	.11
❑ 56 Thurman Thomas	.25	.11
❑ 57 Ted Washington	.15	.07
❑ 58 Jonathan Linton	.15	.07
Kamil Loud RC		
❑ 59 Michael Bates	.15	.07
❑ 60 Steve Beuerlein	.15	.07
❑ 61 Tim Biakabutuka	.25	.11
❑ 62 Mark Carrier WR	.15	.07
❑ 63 Eric Davis	.15	.07
❑ 64 William Floyd	.15	.07
❑ 65 Sean Gilbert	.15	.07
❑ 66 Kevin Greene	.15	.07
❑ 67 Rocket Ismail	.25	.11
❑ 68 Anthony Johnson	.15	.07
❑ 69 Fred Lane	.15	.07
❑ 70 Muhsin Muhammad	.25	.11
❑ 71 Winslow Oliver	.15	.07
❑ 72 Wesley Walls	.25	.11
❑ 73 Dameyune Craig RC	1.50	.70
Shane Matthews		
❑ 74 Edgar Bennett	.15	.07
❑ 75 Curtis Conway	.25	.11
❑ 76 Bobby Engram	.25	.11
❑ 77 Curtis Enis	.50	.23
❑ 78 Ty Hallock RC	.15	.07
❑ 79 Walt Harris	.15	.07
❑ 80 Jeff Jaeger	.15	.07
❑ 81 Erik Kramer	.15	.07
❑ 82 Glyn Milburn	.15	.07
❑ 83 Chris Penn	.15	.07
❑ 84 Steve Stenstrom	.15	.07
❑ 85 Ryan Wetnight	.15	.07
❑ 86 Moses Moreno	.15	.07
James Allen RC		
❑ 87 Ashley Ambrose	.15	.07
❑ 88 Brandon Bennett RC	.15	.07
❑ 89 Eric Bieniemy	.15	.07
❑ 90 Jeff Blake	.25	.11
❑ 91 Corey Dillon	.50	.23
❑ 92 Paul Justin	.15	.07
❑ 93 Eric Kresser RC	.15	.07
❑ 94 Tremain Mack	.15	.07
❑ 95 Tony McGee	.15	.07
❑ 96 Neil O'Donnell	.25	.11
❑ 97 Carl Pickens	.25	.11
❑ 98 Darnay Scott	.15	.07
❑ 99 Takeo Spikes	.15	.07
❑ 100 Ty Detmer	.15	.07
❑ 101 Chris Gardocki	.15	.07
❑ 102 Damon Gibson	.15	.07
❑ 103 Antonio Langham	.15	.07
❑ 104 Jerris McPhail	.15	.07
❑ 105 Irv Smith	.15	.07
❑ 106 Freddie Solomon	.15	.07
❑ 107 Scott Milanovich	.15	.07
Fred Brock RC		
❑ 108 Troy Aikman	1.25	.55
❑ 109 Larry Allen	.15	.07
❑ 110 111	.15	.07
❑ 111 Billy Davis	.15	.07
❑ 112 Michael Irvin	.25	.11
❑ 113 David LaFleur	.15	.07
❑ 114 Ernie Mills	.15	.07
❑ 115 Nate Newton	.15	.07
❑ 116 Deion Sanders	.50	.23
❑ 117 Emmitt Smith	1.25	.55
❑ 118 Chris Warren	.15	.07
❑ 119 Bubby Brister	.25	.11
❑ 120 Terrell Davis	1.25	.55
❑ 121 Jason Elam	.15	.07
❑ 122 John Elway	2.00	.90
❑ 123 Willie Green	.15	.07
❑ 124 Howard Griffith	.15	.07
❑ 125 Vaughn Hebron	.15	.07
❑ 126 Ed McCaffrey	.25	.11
❑ 127 John Mobley	.15	.07
❑ 128 Bill Romanowski	.15	.07
❑ 129 Shannon Sharpe	.25	.11
❑ 130 Neil Smith	.25	.11
❑ 131 Rod Smith	.25	.11
❑ 132 Brian Griese	1.00	.45
Marcus Nash		
❑ 133 Charlie Batch	1.00	.45
❑ 134 Stephen Boyd	.15	.07
❑ 135 Mark Carrier DB	.15	.07
❑ 136 Germane Crowell	.25	.11
❑ 137 Terry Fair	.15	.07
❑ 138 Jason Hanson	.15	.07
❑ 139 Greg Jeffries RC	.15	.07
❑ 140 Herman Moore	.50	.23
❑ 141 Johnnie Morton	.25	.11
❑ 142 Robert Porcher	.15	.07
❑ 143 Ron Rivers	.15	.07
❑ 144 Barry Sanders	2.00	.90
❑ 145 Tommy Vardell	.15	.07
❑ 146 Bryant Westbrook	.15	.07
❑ 147 Robert Brooks	.25	.11
❑ 148 LeRoy Butler	.15	.07
❑ 149 Mark Chmura	.15	.07
❑ 150 Tyrone Davis	.15	.07
❑ 151 Brett Favre	2.00	.90
❑ 152 Antonio Freeman	.50	.23
❑ 153 Raymont Harris	.15	.07
❑ 154 Vonnie Holliday	.15	.07
❑ 155 Darick Holmes	.15	.07
❑ 156 Dorsey Levens	.50	.23
❑ 157 Brian Manning	.15	.07
❑ 158 Derrick Mayes	.15	.07
❑ 159 Roell Preston	.15	.07
❑ 160 Jeff Thomason	.15	.07
❑ 161 Tyrone Williams	.15	.07
❑ 162 Corey Bradford	.50	.23
Michael Blair RC		
❑ 163 Aaron Bailey	.15	.07
❑ 164 Ken Dilger	.15	.07
❑ 165 Marshall Faulk	.50	.23
❑ 166 E.G. Green	.15	.07
❑ 167 Marvin Harrison	.50	.23
❑ 168 Craig Heyward	.15	.07
❑ 169 Peyton Manning	2.00	.90
❑ 170 Jerome Pathon	.25	.11
❑ 171 Marcus Pollard	.15	.07
❑ 172 Torrance Small	.15	.07
❑ 173 Mike Vanderjagt	.15	.07
❑ 174 Lamont Warren	.15	.07
❑ 175 Tavian Banks	.25	.11
❑ 176 Reggie Barlow	.15	.07
❑ 177 Tony Boselli	.15	.07
❑ 178 Tony Brackens	.15	.07
❑ 179 Mark Brunell	.75	.35
❑ 180 Kevin Hardy	.15	.07
❑ 181 Damon Jones	.15	.07
❑ 182 Jamie Martin	.15	.07
❑ 183 Keenan McCardell	.25	.11
❑ 184 Pete Mitchell	.15	.07
❑ 185 Bryce Paup	.15	.07
❑ 186 Jimmy Smith	.25	.11
❑ 187 Fred Taylor	1.25	.55
❑ 188 Alvis Whitted	.15	.07
Chris Howard		
❑ 189 Derrick Alexander WR	.25	.11
❑ 190 Kimble Anders	.25	.11
❑ 191 Donnell Bennett	.15	.07
❑ 192 Dale Carter	.15	.07
❑ 193 Rich Gannon	.25	.11
❑ 194 Tony Gonzalez	.25	.11
❑ 195 Elvis Grbac	.25	.11
❑ 196 Joe Horn	.15	.07
❑ 197 Kevin Lockett	.15	.07
❑ 198 Byron Bam Morris	.15	.07
❑ 199 Andre Rison	.25	.11
❑ 200 Derrick Thomas	.25	.11
❑ 201 Tamarick Vanover	.15	.07
❑ 202 Gregory Favors	.15	.07
Rashaan Shehee		
❑ 203 Karim Abdul-Jabbar	.25	.11
❑ 204 Trace Armstrong	.15	.07
❑ 205 John Avery	.25	.11
❑ 206 Lorenzo Bromell RC	.15	.07
❑ 207 Terrell Buckley	.15	.07
❑ 208 Oronde Gadsden	.15	.07
❑ 209 Sam Madison	.15	.07
❑ 210 Dan Marino	2.00	.90
❑ 211 O.J. McDuffie	.25	.11
❑ 212 Ed Perry	.15	.07
❑ 213 Jason Taylor	.15	.07
❑ 214 Lamar Thomas	.15	.07
❑ 215 Zach Thomas	.25	.11
❑ 216 Henry Lusk	.15	.07
Nate Jacquet RC		
❑ 217 Damon Huard	4.00	1.80
Todd Doxzon RC		
❑ 218 Gary Anderson	.15	.07
❑ 219 Cris Carter	.50	.23
❑ 220 Randall Cunningham	.50	.23
❑ 221 Andrew Glover	.15	.07
❑ 222 Matthew Hatchette	.15	.07
❑ 223 Brad Johnson	.50	.23
❑ 224 Ed McDaniel	.15	.07
❑ 225 Randall McDaniel	.15	.07
❑ 226 Randy Moss	2.00	.90
❑ 227 David Palmer	.15	.07
❑ 228 John Randle	.25	.11
❑ 229 Jake Reed	.25	.11
❑ 230 Robert Smith	.50	.23
❑ 231 Todd Steussie	.15	.07
❑ 232 Stalin Colinet	.15	.07
Kivuusama Mays		
❑ 233 Jay Fiedler	5.00	2.20
Todd Bouman RC		
❑ 234 Drew Bledsoe	.75	.35
❑ 235 Troy Brown	.15	.07
❑ 236 Ben Coates	.25	.11
❑ 237 Derrick Cullors	.15	.07
❑ 238 Robert Edwards	.25	.11
❑ 239 Terry Glenn	.50	.23
❑ 240 Shawn Jefferson	.15	.07
❑ 241 Ty Law	.15	.07
❑ 242 Lawyer Milloy	.15	.07
❑ 243 Lovett Purnell RC	.15	.07
❑ 244 Sedrick Shaw	.15	.07
❑ 245 Tony Simmons	.15	.07
❑ 246 Chris Slade	.15	.07
❑ 247 Rod Rutledge	.15	.07
Anthony Ladd RC		
❑ 248 Chris Floyd	.15	.07
Harold Shaw		
❑ 249 Ink Aleaga	.15	.07
❑ 250 Cameron Cleeland	.25	.11
❑ 251 Kerry Collins	.25	.11
❑ 252 Troy Davis	.15	.07
❑ 253 Sean Dawkins	.15	.07
❑ 254 Mark Fields	.15	.07
❑ 255 Andre Hastings	.15	.07
❑ 256 Sammy Knight	.15	.07
❑ 257 Keith Poole	.15	.07
❑ 258 William Roaf	.15	.07
❑ 259 Lamar Smith	.15	.07
❑ 260 Danny Wuerffel	.15	.07
❑ 261 Josh Wilcox	.15	.07
Brett Bech RC		
❑ 262 Chris Bordano RC	.15	.07
Wilmont Perry		
❑ 263 Jessie Armstead	.15	.07
❑ 264 Tiki Barber	.15	.07

❑ 265	Chad Bratzke	.15	.07
❑ 266	Gary Brown	.15	.07
❑ 267	Chris Calloway	.15	.07
❑ 268	Howard Cross	.15	.07
❑ 269	Kent Graham	.15	.07
❑ 270	Ike Hilliard	.15	.07
❑ 271	Danny Kanell	.25	.11
❑ 272	Michael Strahan	.15	.07
❑ 273	Amani Toomer	.15	.07
❑ 274	Charles Way	.15	.07
❑ 275	Mike Cherry	.15	.07
	Greg Comella RC		
❑ 276	Kyle Brady	.15	.07
❑ 277	Keith Byars	.15	.07
❑ 278	Chad Cascadden	.15	.07
❑ 279	Wayne Chrebet	.25	.11
❑ 280	Bryan Cox	.15	.07
❑ 281	Glenn Foley	.25	.11
❑ 282	Aaron Glenn	.15	.07
❑ 283	Keyshawn Johnson	.50	.23
❑ 284	Leon Johnson	.15	.07
❑ 285	Mo Lewis	.15	.07
❑ 286	Curtis Martin	.50	.23
❑ 287	Otis Smith	.15	.07
❑ 288	Vinny Testaverde	.25	.11
❑ 289	Dedric Ward	.15	.07
❑ 290	Tim Brown	.50	.23
❑ 291	Rickey Dudley	.15	.07
❑ 292	Jeff George	.25	.11
❑ 293	Desmond Howard	.25	.11
❑ 294	James Jett	.25	.11
❑ 295	Lance Johnstone	.15	.07
❑ 296	Randy Jordan	.15	.07
❑ 297	Napoleon Kaufman	.50	.23
❑ 298	Lincoln Kennedy	.15	.07
❑ 299	Terry Mickens	.15	.07
❑ 300	Darrell Russell	.15	.07
❑ 301	Harvey Williams	.15	.07
❑ 302	Jon Ritchie	.50	.23
	Charles Woodson		
❑ 303	Rodney Williams	.15	.07
	Jermaine Williams		
❑ 304	Koy Detmer	.15	.07
❑ 305	Hugh Douglas	.15	.07
❑ 306	Jason Dunn	.15	.07
❑ 307	Irving Fryar	.25	.11
❑ 308	Charlie Garner	.25	.11
❑ 309	Jeff Graham	.15	.07
❑ 310	Bobby Hoying	.25	.11
❑ 311	Rodney Peete	.15	.07
❑ 312	Allen Rossum	.15	.07
❑ 313	Duce Staley	.50	.23
❑ 314	William Thomas	.15	.07
❑ 315	Kevin Turner	.15	.07
❑ 316	Kaseem Sinceno RC	.15	.07
	Corey Walker		
❑ 317	Jahine Arnold	.15	.07
❑ 318	Jerome Bettis	.50	.23
❑ 319	Will Blackwell	.15	.07
❑ 320	Mark Bruener	.15	.07
❑ 321	Dermontti Dawson	.15	.07
❑ 322	Chris Fuamatu-Ma'afala	.15	.07
❑ 323	Courtney Hawkins	.15	.07
❑ 324	Richard Huntley	.25	.11
❑ 325	Charles Johnson	.15	.07
❑ 326	Levon Kirkland	.15	.07
❑ 327	Kordell Stewart	.50	.23
❑ 328	Hines Ward	.25	.11
❑ 329	Dewayne Washington	.15	.07
❑ 330	Tony Banks	.25	.11
❑ 331	Steve Bono	.15	.07
❑ 332	Isaac Bruce	.50	.23
❑ 333	June Henley RC	.15	.07
❑ 334	Robert Holcombe	.25	.11
❑ 335	Mike Jones LB	.15	.07
❑ 336	Eddie Kennison	.25	.11
❑ 337	Amp Lee	.15	.07
❑ 338	Jerald Moore	.15	.07
❑ 339	Ricky Proehl	.15	.07
❑ 340	J.T. Thomas	.15	.07
❑ 341	Derrick Harris	.15	.07
	Az-Zahir Hakim		
❑ 342	Roland Williams	.15	.07
	Grant Wistrom		
❑ 343	Kurt Warner RC	50.00	22.00
	Tony Horne		
❑ 344	Terrell Fletcher	.15	.07
❑ 345	Greg Jackson	.15	.07
❑ 346	Charlie Jones	.15	.07
❑ 347	Freddie Jones	.15	.07
❑ 348	Ryan Leaf	.50	.23
❑ 349	Natrone Means	.25	.11
❑ 350	Mikhael Ricks	.15	.07
❑ 351	Junior Seau	.25	.11
❑ 352	Bryan Still	.15	.07
❑ 353	Tremayne Stephens	.15	.07
	Ryan Thelwell		
❑ 354	Greg Clark	.15	.07
❑ 355	Marc Edwards	.15	.07
❑ 356	Merton Hanks	.15	.07
❑ 357	Garrison Hearst	.25	.11
❑ 358	R.W. McQuarters	.15	.07
❑ 359	Ken Norton Jr.	.15	.07
❑ 360	Terrell Owens	.50	.23
❑ 361	Jerry Rice	1.25	.55
❑ 362	J.J. Stokes	.25	.11
❑ 363	Bryant Young	.15	.07
❑ 364	Steve Young	.75	.35
❑ 365	Chad Brown	.15	.07
❑ 366	Christian Fauria	.15	.07
❑ 367	Joey Galloway	.50	.23
❑ 368	Ahman Green	.25	.11
❑ 369	Cortez Kennedy	.15	.07
❑ 370	Jon Kitna	.60	.25
❑ 371	James McKnight	.15	.07
❑ 372	Mike Pritchard	.15	.07
❑ 373	Michael Sinclair	.15	.07
❑ 374	Shawn Springs	.15	.07
❑ 375	Ricky Watters	.25	.11
❑ 376	Darryl Williams	.15	.07
❑ 377	Robert Wilson RC	.15	.07
	Kerry Joseph		
❑ 378	Mike Alstott	.50	.23
❑ 379	Reidel Anthony	.25	.11
❑ 380	Derrick Brooks	.15	.07
❑ 381	Trent Dilfer	.50	.23
❑ 382	Warrick Dunn	.50	.23
❑ 383	Bert Emanuel	.25	.11
❑ 384	Jacquez Green	.25	.11
❑ 385	Patrick Hape	.15	.07
❑ 386	John Lynch	.15	.07
❑ 387	Dave Moore	.15	.07
❑ 388	Hardy Nickerson	.15	.07
❑ 389	Warren Sapp	.25	.11
❑ 390	Karl Williams	.15	.07
❑ 391	Blaine Bishop	.15	.07
❑ 392	Joe Bowden	.15	.07
❑ 393	Isaac Byrd	.15	.07
❑ 394	Willie Davis	.15	.07
❑ 395	Al Del Greco	.15	.07
❑ 396	Kevin Dyson	.25	.11
❑ 397	Eddie George	.60	.25
❑ 398	Jackie Harris	.15	.07
❑ 399	Dave Krieg	.15	.07
❑ 400	Steve McNair	.50	.23
❑ 401	Michael Roan	.15	.07
❑ 402	Yancey Thigpen	.15	.07
❑ 403	Frank Wycheck	.15	.07
❑ 404	Derrick Mason	.15	.07
	Steve Matthews		
❑ 405	Stephen Alexander	.15	.07
❑ 406	Terry Allen	.25	.11
❑ 407	Jamie Asher	.15	.07
❑ 408	Stephen Davis	.50	.23
❑ 409	Darrell Green	.15	.07
❑ 410	Trent Green	.25	.11
❑ 411	Skip Hicks	.50	.23
❑ 412	Brian Mitchell	.15	.07
❑ 413	Leslie Shepherd	.15	.07
❑ 414	Michael Westbrook	.25	.11
❑ 415	Terry Hardy RC	.15	.07
	Rabih Abdullah		
❑ 416	Corey Thomas RC	.15	.07
	Mike Quinn		
❑ 417	Jonathan Quinn	.15	.07
	Kelly Holcomb RC		
❑ 418	Brian Alford	.15	.07
	Blake Spence		
❑ 419	Andy Haase RC	.15	.07
	Carlos King		
❑ 420	Karl Hankton	.15	.07
	James Thrash RC		
❑ 421	Fred Beasley	.15	.07
	Itula Mili RC		
❑ 422	Champ Bailey RC	2.00	.90
❑ 423	D'Wayne Bates RC	1.25	.55
❑ 424	Michael Bishop RC	2.00	.90
❑ 425	David Boston RC	2.50	1.10
❑ 426	Shawn Bryson RC	1.00	.45
❑ 427	Tim Couch RC	8.00	3.60
❑ 428	Scott Covington RC	1.50	.70
❑ 429	Daunte Culpepper RC	5.00	2.20
❑ 430	Autry Denson RC	1.50	.70
❑ 431	Troy Edwards RC	2.50	1.10
❑ 432	Kevin Faulk RC	2.00	.90
❑ 433	Joe Germaine RC	1.50	.70
❑ 434	Torry Holt RC	4.00	1.80
❑ 435	Brock Huard RC	2.00	.90
❑ 436	Sedrick Irvin RC	1.50	.70
❑ 437	Edgerrin James RC	15.00	6.75
❑ 438	Andy Katzenmoyer RC	1.50	.70
❑ 439	Shaun King RC	5.00	2.20
❑ 440	Rob Konrad RC	1.25	.55
❑ 441	Donovan McNabb RC	5.00	2.20
❑ 442	Cade McNown RC	5.00	2.20
❑ 443	Billy Miller RC	1.25	.55
❑ 444	Dee Miller RC	1.25	.55
❑ 445	Sirr Parker RC	1.25	.55
❑ 446	Peerless Price RC	2.50	1.10
❑ 447	Akili Smith RC	3.00	1.35
❑ 448	Tai Streets RC	1.25	.55
❑ 449	Ricky Williams RC	8.00	3.60
❑ 450	Amos Zereoue RC	1.50	.70
❑ S1	Warrick Dunn Sample	.50	.23

1999 Pacific Cramer's Choice

		MINT	NRMT
COMPLETE SET (10)		400.00	180.00
COMMON CARD (1-10)		20.00	9.00

STATED PRINT RUN 299 SERIAL #'d SETS

❑ 1	Jamal Anderson	20.00	9.00
❑ 2	Terrell Davis	40.00	18.00
❑ 3	John Elway	60.00	27.00
❑ 4	Barry Sanders	60.00	27.00
❑ 5	Brett Favre	60.00	27.00
❑ 6	Peyton Manning	50.00	22.00
❑ 7	Fred Taylor	25.00	11.00
❑ 8	Dan Marino	60.00	27.00
❑ 9	Randall Cunningham	20.00	9.00
❑ 10	Randy Moss	50.00	22.00

1999 Pacific Dynagon Turf

		MINT	NRMT
COMPLETE SET (20)		80.00	36.00
COMMON CARD (1-20)		2.50	1.10

STATED ODDS 2:25
*TITANIUM CARDS: 4X TO 10X HI COL.
TITANIUM PRINT RUN 99 SERIAL #'d SETS

❑ 1	Jake Plummer	5.00	2.20
❑ 2	Jamal Anderson	2.50	1.10
❑ 3	Doug Flutie	3.00	1.35
❑ 4	Emmitt Smith	6.00	2.70
❑ 5	Terrell Davis	6.00	2.70

Card	MINT	NRMT
❑ 6 John Elway	10.00	4.50
❑ 7 Barry Sanders	10.00	4.50
❑ 8 Brett Favre	10.00	4.50
❑ 9 Peyton Manning	8.00	3.60
❑ 10 Mark Brunell	4.00	1.80
❑ 11 Fred Taylor	5.00	2.20
❑ 12 Dan Marino	10.00	4.50
❑ 13 Randall Cunningham	2.50	1.10
❑ 14 Randy Moss	8.00	3.60
❑ 15 Drew Bledsoe	4.00	1.80
❑ 16 Curtis Martin	2.50	1.10
❑ 17 Jerome Bettis	2.50	1.10
❑ 18 Jerry Rice	6.00	2.70
❑ 19 Jon Kitna	3.00	1.35
❑ 20 Eddie George	3.00	1.35

1999 Pacific Gold Crown Die Cuts

	MINT	NRMT
COMPLETE SET (36)	250.00	110.00
COMMON CARD (1-36)	5.00	2.20
STATED ODDS 1:25		

Card	MINT	NRMT
❑ 1 Jake Plummer	10.00	4.50
❑ 2 Jamal Anderson	5.00	2.20
❑ 3 Priest Holmes	5.00	2.20
❑ 4 Doug Flutie	6.00	2.70
❑ 5 Antowain Smith	5.00	2.20
❑ 6 Corey Dillon	5.00	2.20
❑ 7 Troy Aikman	12.00	5.50
❑ 8 Emmitt Smith	12.00	5.50
❑ 9 Terrell Davis	12.00	5.50
❑ 10 John Elway	20.00	9.00
❑ 11 Brian Griese	8.00	3.60
❑ 12 Charlie Batch	8.00	3.60
❑ 13 Barry Sanders	20.00	9.00
❑ 14 Brett Favre	20.00	9.00
❑ 15 Antonio Freeman	5.00	2.20
❑ 16 Marshall Faulk	5.00	2.20
❑ 17 Peyton Manning	15.00	6.75
❑ 18 Mark Brunell	8.00	3.60
❑ 19 Fred Taylor	10.00	4.50
❑ 20 Dan Marino	20.00	9.00
❑ 21 Randall Cunningham	5.00	2.20
❑ 22 Randy Moss	15.00	6.75
❑ 23 Drew Bledsoe	8.00	3.60
❑ 24 Keyshawn Johnson	5.00	2.20
❑ 25 Curtis Martin	5.00	2.20
❑ 26 Napoleon Kaufman	5.00	2.20
❑ 27 Jerome Bettis	5.00	2.20
❑ 28 Kordell Stewart	5.00	2.20
❑ 29 Terrell Owens	5.00	2.20
❑ 30 Jerry Rice	12.00	5.50
❑ 31 Steve Young	8.00	3.60
❑ 32 Joey Galloway	5.00	2.20
❑ 33 Jon Kitna	6.00	2.70
❑ 34 Trent Dilfer	5.00	2.20
❑ 35 Warrick Dunn	5.00	2.20
❑ 36 Eddie George	6.00	2.70

1999 Pacific Pro Bowl Die Cuts

	MINT	NRMT
COMPLETE SET (20)	150.00	70.00
COMMON CARD (1-20)	2.00	.90
SEMISTARS	4.00	1.80
UNLISTED STARS	6.00	2.70
STATED ODDS 1:49		

Card	MINT	NRMT
❑ 1 Jamal Anderson	6.00	2.70
❑ 2 Chris Chandler	4.00	1.80
❑ 3 Doug Flutie	8.00	3.60
❑ 4 Deion Sanders	6.00	2.70
❑ 5 Emmitt Smith	15.00	6.75
❑ 6 Terrell Davis	15.00	6.75
❑ 7 John Elway	25.00	11.00
❑ 8 Barry Sanders	25.00	11.00
❑ 9 Antonio Freeman	6.00	2.70
❑ 10 Marshall Faulk	6.00	2.70
❑ 11 Randall Cunningham	6.00	2.70
❑ 12 Randy Moss	25.00	11.00
❑ 13 Robert Smith	6.00	2.70
❑ 14 Ty Law	2.00	.90
❑ 15 Keyshawn Johnson	6.00	2.70
❑ 16 Curtis Martin	6.00	2.70
❑ 17 Jerry Rice	15.00	6.75
❑ 18 Steve Young	10.00	4.50
❑ 19 Mike Alstott	6.00	2.70
❑ 20 Eddie George	8.00	3.60

1999 Pacific Record Breakers

	MINT	NRMT
COMPLETE SET (20)	400.00	180.00
COMMON CARD (1-20)	12.00	5.50
STATED PRINT RUN 199 SERIAL #'d SETS		

Card	MINT	NRMT
❑ 1 Jake Plummer	20.00	9.00
❑ 2 Jamal Anderson	12.00	5.50
❑ 3 Doug Flutie	15.00	6.75
❑ 4 Troy Aikman	25.00	11.00
❑ 5 Emmitt Smith	25.00	11.00
❑ 6 Terrell Davis	25.00	11.00
❑ 7 John Elway	40.00	18.00
❑ 8 Barry Sanders	40.00	18.00
❑ 9 Brett Favre	40.00	18.00
❑ 10 Marshall Faulk	12.00	5.50
❑ 11 Peyton Manning	30.00	13.50
❑ 12 Mark Brunell	15.00	6.75
❑ 13 Fred Taylor	20.00	9.00
❑ 14 Dan Marino	40.00	18.00
❑ 15 Randall Cunningham	12.00	5.50
❑ 16 Randy Moss	30.00	13.50
❑ 17 Drew Bledsoe	15.00	6.75
❑ 18 Curtis Martin	12.00	5.50
❑ 19 Jerry Rice	25.00	11.00
❑ 20 Steve Young	15.00	6.75

1999 Pacific Team Checklists

	MINT	NRMT
COMPLETE SET (31)	80.00	36.00
COMMON CARD (1-31)	.75	.35
SEMISTARS	1.50	.70
UNLISTED STARS	2.50	1.10
STATED ODDS 2:25		

Card	MINT	NRMT
❑ 1 Jake Plummer	5.00	2.20
❑ 2 Jamal Anderson	2.50	1.10
❑ 3 Priest Holmes	2.50	1.10
❑ 4 Doug Flutie	3.00	1.35
❑ 5 Muhsin Muhammad	1.50	.70
❑ 6 Curtis Enis	2.50	1.10
❑ 7 Corey Dillon	2.50	1.10
❑ 8 Ty Detmer	1.50	.70
❑ 9 Emmitt Smith	6.00	2.70
❑ 10 John Elway	10.00	4.50
❑ 11 Barry Sanders	10.00	4.50
❑ 12 Brett Favre	10.00	4.50
❑ 13 Peyton Manning	8.00	3.60
❑ 14 Fred Taylor	5.00	2.20
❑ 15 Andre Rison	1.50	.70
❑ 16 Dan Marino	10.00	4.50
❑ 17 Randy Moss	8.00	3.60
❑ 18 Drew Bledsoe	4.00	1.80
❑ 19 Cameron Cleeland	.75	.35
❑ 20 Ike Hilliard	.75	.35
❑ 21 Curtis Martin	2.50	1.10
❑ 22 Napoleon Kaufman	2.50	1.10
❑ 23 Duce Staley	2.50	1.10
❑ 24 Jerome Bettis	2.50	1.10
❑ 25 Isaac Bruce	1.50	.70
❑ 26 Ryan Leaf	.75	.35
❑ 27 Steve Young	4.00	1.80
❑ 28 Joey Galloway	2.50	1.10
❑ 29 Warrick Dunn	2.50	1.10
❑ 30 Eddie George	3.00	1.35
❑ 31 Michael Westbrook	1.50	.70

2000 Pacific

	MINT	NRMT
COMPLETE SET (450)	70.00	32.00
COMMON CARD (1-400)	.15	.07

276 / 2000 Pacific

SEMISTARS .25 .11
UNLISTED STARS .50 .23
COMMON ROOKIES (401-450) .60 .25
ROOKIE SEMISTARS 1.00 .45
ROOKIE UNLISTED STARS 1.25 .55

❑ 1 Mario Bates .15 .07
❑ 2 David Boston .50 .23
❑ 3 Rob Fredrickson .15 .07
❑ 4 Terry Hardy .15 .07
❑ 5 Rob Moore .25 .11
❑ 6 Adrian Murrell .25 .11
❑ 7 Michael Pittman .15 .07
❑ 8 Jake Plummer .50 .23
❑ 9 Simeon Rice .15 .07
❑ 10 Frank Sanders .25 .11
❑ 11 Aeneas Williams .15 .07
❑ 12 Mac Cody .15 .07
Andy McCullough
❑ 13 Dennis McKinley RC .50 .23
Joel Makovicka
❑ 14 Jamal Anderson .50 .23
❑ 15 Chris Calloway .15 .07
❑ 16 Chris Chandler .25 .11
❑ 17 Bob Christian .15 .07
❑ 18 Tim Dwight .50 .23
❑ 19 Jammi German .15 .07
❑ 20 Ronnie Harris .15 .07
❑ 21 Terance Mathis .25 .11
❑ 22 Ken Oxendine .15 .07
❑ 23 O.J. Santiago .15 .07
❑ 24 Bob Whitfield .15 .07
❑ 25 Eugene Baker .15 .07
Reggie Kelly
❑ 26 Justin Armour .15 .07
❑ 27 Tony Banks .25 .11
❑ 28 Peter Boulware .15 .07
❑ 29 Stoney Case .15 .07
❑ 30 Priest Holmes .25 .11
❑ 31 Qadry Ismail .15 .07
❑ 32 Patrick Johnson .15 .07
❑ 33 Michael McCrary .15 .07
❑ 34 Jonathan Ogden .15 .07
❑ 35 Errict Rhett .25 .11
❑ 36 Duane Starks .15 .07
❑ 37 Doug Flutie .60 .25
❑ 38 Rob Johnson .25 .11
❑ 39 Jonathan Linton .15 .07
❑ 40 Eric Moulds .50 .23
❑ 41 Peerless Price .50 .23
❑ 42 Andre Reed .25 .11
❑ 43 Jay Riemersma .15 .07
❑ 44 Antowain Smith .50 .23
❑ 45 Bruce Smith .25 .11
❑ 46 Thurman Thomas .25 .11
❑ 47 Kevin Williams .15 .07
❑ 48 Bobby Collins .15 .07
Sheldon Jackson
❑ 49 Michael Bates .15 .07
❑ 50 Steve Beuerlein .25 .11
❑ 51 Tim Biakabutuka .25 .11
❑ 52 Antonio Edwards .15 .07
❑ 53 Donald Hayes .15 .07
❑ 54 Patrick Jeffers .50 .23
❑ 55 Anthony Johnson .15 .07
❑ 56 Jeff Lewis .15 .07
❑ 57 Eric Metcalf .15 .07
❑ 58 Muhsin Muhammad .25 .11
❑ 59 Jason Peter .15 .07
❑ 60 Wesley Walls .15 .07
❑ 61 John Allred .15 .07
❑ 62 Marty Booker .15 .07
❑ 63 Curtis Conway .25 .11
❑ 64 Bobby Engram .15 .07
❑ 65 Curtis Enis .50 .23
❑ 66 Shane Matthews .25 .11
❑ 67 Cade McNown .75 .35
❑ 68 Glyn Milburn .15 .07
❑ 69 Jim Miller .15 .07
❑ 70 Marcus Robinson .50 .23
❑ 71 Ryan Wetnight .15 .07
❑ 72 James Allen .15 .07
Macey Brooks
❑ 73 Jeff Blake .25 .11
❑ 74 Corey Dillon .50 .23
❑ 75 Rodney Heath RC .25 .11
❑ 76 Willie Jackson .15 .07
❑ 77 Tremain Mack .15 .07
❑ 78 Tony McGee .15 .07
❑ 79 Carl Pickens .25 .11
❑ 80 Darnay Scott .25 .11
❑ 81 Akili Smith .60 .25
❑ 82 Takeo Spikes .15 .07
❑ 83 Craig Yeast .15 .07
❑ 84 Michael Basnight .15 .07
Nick Williams
❑ 85 Karim Abdul-Jabbar .25 .11
❑ 86 Darrin Chiaverini .15 .07
❑ 87 Tim Couch 1.25 .55
❑ 88 Marc Edwards .15 .07
❑ 89 Kevin Johnson .50 .23
❑ 90 Terry Kirby .15 .07
❑ 91 Daylon McCutcheon .15 .07
❑ 92 Jamir Miller .15 .07
❑ 93 Leslie Shepherd .15 .07
❑ 94 Irv Smith .15 .07
❑ 95 Mark Campbell .15 .07
James Dearth
❑ 96 Zola Davis RC .15 .07
Damon Dunn
❑ 97 Madre Hill .15 .07
Tarek Saleh
❑ 98 Troy Aikman 1.25 .55
❑ 99 Eric Bjornson .15 .07
❑ 100 Dexter Coakley .15 .07
❑ 101 Greg Ellis .15 .07
❑ 102 Rocket Ismail .25 .11
❑ 103 David LaFleur .15 .07
❑ 104 Ernie Mills .15 .07
❑ 105 Jeff Ogden .25 .11
❑ 106 Ryan Neufeld RC .25 .11
Robert Thomas
❑ 107 Deion Sanders .50 .23
❑ 108 Emmitt Smith 1.25 .55
❑ 109 Chris Warren .15 .07
❑ 110 Mike Lucky .25 .11
Jason Tucker
❑ 111 Byron Chamberlain .15 .07
❑ 112 Terrell Davis 1.25 .55
❑ 113 Jason Elam .15 .07
❑ 114 Olandis Gary .60 .25
❑ 115 Brian Griese .60 .25
❑ 116 Ed McCaffrey .25 .11
❑ 117 Trevor Pryce .15 .07
❑ 118 Bill Romanowski .15 .07
❑ 119 Shannon Sharpe .25 .11
❑ 120 Rod Smith .25 .11
❑ 121 Al Wilson .15 .07
❑ 122 Andre Cooper .15 .07
Chris Watson
❑ 123 Charlie Batch .50 .23
❑ 124 Stephen Boyd .15 .07
❑ 125 Chris Claiborne .15 .07
❑ 126 Germane Crowell .25 .11
❑ 127 Terry Fair .15 .07
❑ 128 Gus Frerotte .15 .07
❑ 129 Jason Hanson .15 .07
❑ 130 Greg Hill .15 .07
❑ 131 Herman Moore .50 .23
❑ 132 Johnnie Morton .25 .11
❑ 133 Barry Sanders 2.00 .90
❑ 134 David Sloan .15 .07
❑ 135 Brock Olivo .15 .07
Cory Sauter
❑ 136 Corey Bradford .25 .11
❑ 137 Tyrone Davis .15 .07
❑ 138 Brett Favre 2.00 .90
❑ 139 Antonio Freeman .50 .23
❑ 140 Vonnie Holliday .15 .07
❑ 141 Dorsey Levens .50 .23
❑ 142 Keith McKenzie .15 .07
❑ 143 Mike McKenzie .15 .07
❑ 144 Bill Schroeder .25 .11
❑ 145 Jeff Thomason .15 .07
❑ 146 Frank Winters .15 .07
❑ 147 Cornelius Bennett .15 .07
❑ 148 Tony Blevins RC .25 .11
❑ 149 Chad Bratzke .15 .07
❑ 150 Ken Dilger .15 .07
❑ 151 Tarik Glenn .15 .07
❑ 152 E.G. Green .15 .07
❑ 153 Marvin Harrison .50 .23
❑ 154 Edgerrin James 2.00 .90
❑ 155 Peyton Manning 1.50 .70
❑ 156 Jerome Pathon .15 .07
❑ 157 Marcus Pollard .15 .07
❑ 158 Terrence Wilkins .50 .23
❑ 159 Isaac Jones RC .50 .23
Paul Shields
❑ 160 Reggie Barlow .15 .07
❑ 161 Aaron Beasley .15 .07
❑ 162 Tony Boselli .15 .07
❑ 163 Tony Brackens .15 .07
❑ 164 Kyle Brady .15 .07
❑ 165 Mark Brunell .75 .35
❑ 166 Jay Fiedler .50 .23
❑ 167 Kevin Hardy .15 .07
❑ 168 Carnell Lake .15 .07
❑ 169 Keenan McCardell .25 .11
❑ 170 Jonathan Quinn .15 .07
❑ 171 Jimmy Smith .25 .11
❑ 172 James Stewart .25 .11
❑ 173 Fred Taylor .75 .35
❑ 174 Lenzie Jackson RC .50 .23
Stacey Mack
❑ 175 Derrick Alexander .25 .11
❑ 176 Donnell Bennett .15 .07
❑ 177 Donnie Edwards .15 .07
❑ 178 Tony Gonzalez .25 .11
❑ 179 Elvis Grbac .25 .11
❑ 180 James Hasty .15 .07
❑ 181 Joe Horn .15 .07
❑ 182 Lonnie Johnson .15 .07
❑ 183 Kevin Lockett .15 .07
❑ 184 Larry Parker .15 .07
❑ 185 Tony Richardson .15 .07
❑ 186 Rashaan Shehee .15 .07
❑ 187 Tamarick Vanover .15 .07
❑ 188 Trace Armstrong .15 .07
❑ 189 Oronde Gadsden .15 .07
❑ 190 Damon Huard .50 .23
❑ 191 Nate Jacquet .15 .07
❑ 192 James Johnson .25 .11
❑ 193 Rob Konrad .15 .07
❑ 194 Sam Madison .15 .07
❑ 195 Dan Marino 2.00 .90
❑ 196 Tony Martin .25 .11
❑ 197 O.J. McDuffie .25 .11
❑ 198 Stanley Pritchett .15 .07
❑ 199 Tim Ruddy .15 .07
❑ 200 Patrick Surtain .15 .07
❑ 201 Zach Thomas .25 .11
❑ 202 Cris Carter .50 .23
❑ 203 Duane Clemons .15 .07
❑ 204 Carlester Crumpler .15 .07
❑ 205 Daunte Culpepper .75 .35
❑ 206 Jeff George .25 .11
❑ 207 Matthew Hatchette .25 .11
❑ 208 Leroy Hoard .15 .07
❑ 209 Randy Moss 1.50 .70
❑ 210 John Randle .25 .11
❑ 211 Jake Reed .25 .11
❑ 212 Robert Smith .50 .23
❑ 213 Robert Tate .15 .07
❑ 214 Terry Allen .25 .11
❑ 215 Bruce Armstrong .15 .07
❑ 216 Drew Bledsoe .75 .35
❑ 217 Ben Coates .15 .07
❑ 218 Kevin Faulk .25 .11
❑ 219 Terry Glenn .50 .23

❑ 220	Shawn Jefferson	.15	.07
❑ 221	Andy Katzenmoyer	.15	.07
❑ 222	Ty Law	.15	.07
❑ 223	Willie McGinest	.15	.07
❑ 224	Lawyer Milloy	.15	.07
❑ 225	Tony Simmons	.15	.07
❑ 226	Michael Bishop	.25	.11
	Sean Morey RC		
❑ 227	Cameron Cleeland	.15	.07
❑ 228	Troy Davis	.15	.07
❑ 229	Jake Delhomme RC	2.00	.90
❑ 230	Andre Hastings	.15	.07
❑ 231	Eddie Kennison	.25	.11
❑ 232	Wilmont Perry	.15	.07
❑ 233	Dino Philyaw	.15	.07
❑ 234	Keith Poole	.15	.07
❑ 235	William Roaf	.15	.07
❑ 236	Billy Joe Tolliver	.15	.07
❑ 237	Fred Weary	.15	.07
❑ 238	Ricky Williams	1.25	.55
❑ 239	P.J. Franklin RC	.50	.23
	Marvin Powell		
❑ 240	Jessie Armstead	.15	.07
❑ 241	Tiki Barber	.25	.11
❑ 242	Daniel Campbell	.15	.07
❑ 243	Kerry Collins	.25	.11
❑ 244	Percy Ellsworth	.15	.07
❑ 245	Kent Graham	.15	.07
❑ 246	Ike Hilliard	.25	.11
❑ 247	Cedric Jones	.15	.07
❑ 248	Bashir Livingston RC	.25	.11
❑ 249	Pete Mitchell	.15	.07
❑ 250	Michael Strahan	.15	.07
❑ 251	Amani Toomer	.15	.07
❑ 252	Charles Way	.15	.07
❑ 253	Andre Weathers RC	.25	.11
❑ 254	Richie Anderson	.15	.07
❑ 255	Wayne Chrebet	.25	.11
❑ 256	Marcus Coleman	.15	.07
❑ 257	Bryan Cox	.15	.07
❑ 258	Jason Fabini RC	.25	.11
❑ 259	Robert Farmer RC	.50	.23
❑ 260	Keyshawn Johnson	.50	.23
❑ 261	Ray Lucas	.50	.23
❑ 262	Curtis Martin	.50	.23
❑ 263	Kevin Mawae	.15	.07
❑ 264	Eric Ogbogu	.15	.07
❑ 265	Bernie Parmalee	.15	.07
❑ 266	Vinny Testaverde	.25	.11
❑ 267	Dedric Ward	.15	.07
❑ 268	Eric Barton RC	.25	.11
❑ 269	Tim Brown	.50	.23
❑ 270	Tony Bryant	.15	.07
❑ 271	Rickey Dudley	.15	.07
❑ 272	Rich Gannon	.25	.11
❑ 273	Bobby Hoying	.25	.11
❑ 274	James Jett	.15	.07
❑ 275	Napoleon Kaufman	.50	.23
❑ 276	Jon Ritchie	.15	.07
❑ 277	Darrell Russell	.15	.07
❑ 278	Kenny Shedd	.15	.07
❑ 279	Marquis Walker RC	.25	.11
❑ 280	Tyrone Wheatley	.25	.11
❑ 281	Charles Woodson	.25	.11
❑ 282	Luther Broughton RC	.25	.11
❑ 283	Al Harris	.15	.07
❑ 284	Greg Jefferson	.15	.07
❑ 285	Dietrich Jells	.15	.07
❑ 286	Charles Johnson	.15	.07
❑ 287	Chad Lewis	.15	.07
❑ 288	Mike Mamula	.15	.07
❑ 289	Donovan McNabb	.75	.35
❑ 290	Doug Pederson	.15	.07
❑ 291	Allen Rossum	.15	.07
❑ 292	Torrance Small	.15	.07
❑ 293	Duce Staley	.50	.23
❑ 294	Jerome Bettis	.50	.23
❑ 295	Kris Brown	.15	.07
❑ 296	Mark Bruener	.15	.07
❑ 297	Troy Edwards	.50	.23
❑ 298	Jason Gildon	.15	.07
❑ 299	Richard Huntley	.15	.07
❑ 300	Bobby Shaw	.15	.07
❑ 301	Scott Shields RC	.25	.11
❑ 302	Kordell Stewart	.50	.23
❑ 303	Hines Ward	.15	.07
❑ 304	Amos Zereoue	.15	.07
❑ 305	Matt Cushing RC	.25	.11
	Jerame Tuman		
❑ 306	Pete Gonzalez	.75	.35
	Anthony Wright RC		
❑ 307	Isaac Bruce	.50	.23
❑ 308	Kevin Carter	.15	.07
❑ 309	Marshall Faulk	.50	.23
❑ 310	London Fletcher RC	.25	.11
❑ 311	Joe Germaine	.15	.07
❑ 312	Az-Zahir Hakim	.25	.11
❑ 313	Torry Holt	.50	.23
❑ 314	Tony Horne	.15	.07
❑ 315	Mike Jones LB	.15	.07
❑ 316	Dexter McCleon RC	.25	.11
❑ 317	Orlando Pace	.15	.07
❑ 318	Ricky Proehl	.15	.07
❑ 319	Kurt Warner	2.50	1.10
❑ 320	Roland Williams	.15	.07
❑ 321	Grant Wistrom	.15	.07
❑ 322	James Hodgins RC	.25	.11
	Justin Watson		
❑ 323	Jermaine Fazande	.15	.07
❑ 324	Jeff Graham	.15	.07
❑ 325	Jim Harbaugh	.25	.11
❑ 326	Raylee Johnson	.15	.07
❑ 327	Charlie Jones	.15	.07
❑ 328	Freddie Jones	.15	.07
❑ 329	Natrone Means	.15	.07
❑ 330	Chris Penn	.15	.07
❑ 331	Mikhael Ricks	.15	.07
❑ 332	Junior Seau	.25	.11
❑ 333	Reginald Davis RC	.25	.11
	Robert Reed		
❑ 334	Fred Beasley	.15	.07
❑ 335	Brentson Buckner	.15	.07
❑ 336	Greg Clark	.15	.07
❑ 337	Dave Fiore RC	.15	.07
❑ 338	Charlie Garner	.25	.11
❑ 339	Mark Harris RC	.50	.23
❑ 340	Ramos McDonald RC	.25	.11
❑ 341	Terrell Owens	.50	.23
❑ 342	Jerry Rice	1.25	.55
❑ 343	Lance Schulters	.15	.07
❑ 344	J.J. Stokes	.25	.11
❑ 345	Bryant Young	.15	.07
❑ 346	Steve Young	.75	.35
❑ 347	Jeff Garcia	.50	.23
❑ 348	Fabien Bownes RC	.25	.11
❑ 349	Chad Brown	.15	.07
❑ 350	Reggie Brown	.15	.07
❑ 351	Sean Dawkins	.15	.07
❑ 352	Christian Fauria	.15	.07
❑ 353	Ahman Green	.25	.11
❑ 354	Walter Jones	.15	.07
❑ 355	Cortez Kennedy	.15	.07
❑ 356	Jon Kitna	.50	.23
❑ 357	Derrick Mayes	.25	.11
❑ 358	Charlie Rogers	.15	.07
❑ 359	Shawn Springs	.15	.07
❑ 360	Ricky Watters	.25	.11
❑ 361	Donne Abraham	.15	.07
❑ 362	Mike Alstott	.50	.23
❑ 363	Reidel Anthony	.15	.07
❑ 364	Ronde Barber	.15	.07
❑ 365	Derrick Brooks	.15	.07
❑ 366	Warrick Dunn	.50	.23
❑ 367	Jacquez Green	.25	.11
❑ 368	Marcus Jones	.15	.07
❑ 369	Shaun King	.75	.35
❑ 370	John Lynch	.15	.07
❑ 371	Warren Sapp	.25	.11
❑ 372	Steve White RC	.15	.07
❑ 373	Martin Gramatica	.25	.11
	Kevin McLeod RC		
❑ 374	Blaine Bishop	.15	.07
❑ 375	Al Del Greco	.15	.07
❑ 376	Kevin Dyson	.25	.11
❑ 377	Eddie George	.60	.25
❑ 378	Jevon Kearse	.50	.23
❑ 379	Derrick Mason	.15	.07
❑ 380	Bruce Matthews	.15	.07
❑ 381	Steve McNair	.50	.23
❑ 382	Neil O'Donnell	.15	.07
❑ 383	Yancey Thigpen	.15	.07
❑ 384	Frank Wycheck	.15	.07
❑ 385	Devin Daft	.15	.07
	Larry Brown		
❑ 386	Stephen Alexander	.15	.07
❑ 387	Champ Bailey	.25	.11
❑ 388	Larry Centers	.15	.07
❑ 389	Marco Coleman	.15	.07
❑ 390	Albert Connell	.15	.07
❑ 391	Stephen Davis	.50	.23
❑ 392	Irving Fryar	.15	.07
❑ 393	Skip Hicks	.25	.11
❑ 394	Brad Johnson	.50	.23
❑ 395	Michael Westbrook	.25	.11
❑ 396	Obafemi Ayanbadejo RC	.15	.07
	Lennox Gordon		
❑ 397	Donald Driver	.15	.07
	Ronnie Powell		
❑ 398	Todd Bouman	.50	.23
	Jeremy Brigham RC		
❑ 399	Brock Huard	.15	.07
	Sherdrick Bonner		
❑ 400	Mike Sellers	.25	.11
	Spencer George RC		
❑ 401	Shaun Alexander RC	4.00	1.80
❑ 402	LaVar Arrington RC	4.00	1.80
❑ 403	Tom Brady RC	1.25	.55
❑ 404	Demario Brown RC	1.25	.55
❑ 405	Plaxico Burress RC	3.00	1.35
❑ 406	Trung Canidate RC	1.25	.55
❑ 407	Giovanni Carmazzi RC	2.50	1.10
❑ 408	Kwame Cavil RC	1.00	.45
❑ 409	Chrys Chukwuma RC	1.00	.45
❑ 410	Ron Dayne RC	6.00	2.70
❑ 411	Reuben Droughns RC	1.50	.70
❑ 412	Ron Dugans RC	1.25	.55
❑ 413	Deon Dyer RC	1.00	.45
❑ 414	Danny Farmer RC	1.25	.55
❑ 415	Chafie Fields RC	1.00	.45
❑ 416	Trevor Gaylor RC	1.00	.45
❑ 417	Sherrod Gideon RC	1.00	.45
❑ 418	Joey Goodspeed RC	1.00	.45
❑ 419	Joe Hamilton RC	1.25	.55
❑ 420	Tony Hartley RC	1.00	.45
❑ 421	Todd Husak RC	1.25	.55
❑ 422	Trevor Insley RC	.60	.25
❑ 423	Thomas Jones RC	4.00	1.80
❑ 424	Marcus Knight RC	.60	.25
❑ 425	Jamal Lewis RC	4.00	1.80
❑ 426	Anthony Lucas RC	1.50	.70
❑ 427	Tee Martin RC	2.00	.90
❑ 428	Rondell Mealey RC	1.00	.45
❑ 429	Sylvester Morris RC	1.50	.70
❑ 430	Chad Morton RC	1.00	.45
❑ 431	Dennis Northcutt RC	1.50	.70
❑ 432	Chad Pennington RC	5.00	2.20
❑ 433	Rodnick Phillips RC	.60	.25
❑ 434	Mareno Philyaw RC	1.00	.45
❑ 435	Jerry Porter RC	1.50	.70
❑ 436	Travis Prentice RC	1.50	.70
❑ 437	Tim Rattay RC	1.50	.70
❑ 438	Chris Redman RC	2.00	.90
❑ 439	J.R. Redmond RC	2.00	.90
❑ 440	Gari Scott RC	1.25	.55
❑ 441	Keith Smith RC	1.25	.55
❑ 442	Terrelle Smith RC	1.00	.45
❑ 443	R.Jay Soward RC	1.50	.70
❑ 444	Q.Spotwood RC UER	1.00	.45
	yardage totals reads 3080		
❑ 445	Shyrone Stith RC	1.00	.45
❑ 446	Travis Taylor RC	2.50	1.10
❑ 447	Troy Walters RC	1.25	.55
❑ 448	Peter Warrick RC	6.00	2.70
❑ 449	Dez White RC	1.50	.70
❑ 450	Michael Wiley RC	1.50	.70

2000 Pacific Copper

	MINT	NRMT
COMMON CARD (1-400)	4.00	1.80
*COPPER STARS: 10X TO 25X HI COL.		
*COPPER YOUNG STARS: 8X TO 20X		
COMMON ROOKIE (401-450)	8.00	3.60
*COPPER ROOKIES: 5X TO 12X		
RANDOM INSERTS IN HOBBY PACKS		
STATED PRINT RUN 75 SERIAL #'d SETS		

2000 Pacific Gold

	MINT	NRMT
COMPLETE SET (450)	600.00	275.00
COMMON CARD (1-450)	2.00	.90
*GOLD STARS: 5X TO 12X HI COL.		
*GOLD YOUNG STARS: 4X TO 10X		
COMMON ROOKIE (401-450)	4.00	1.80
*GOLD ROOKIES: 2.5X TO 6X		
RANDOM INSERTS IN RETAIL PACKS		
STATED PRINT RUN 199 SERIAL #'d SETS		

2000 Pacific Platinum Blue Draft Picks

	MINT	NRMT
COMPLETE SET (50)	200.00	90.00
COMMON ROOKIE (401-450)	2.50	1.10
*PLAT.BLUE ROOKIES: 1.5X TO 4X HI COL.		
STATED PRINT RUN 399 SERIAL #'d SETS		

2000 Pacific Premiere Date

	MINT	NRMT
COMMON CARD (1-400)	4.00	1.80
*PREM.DATE STARS: 10X TO 25X HI COL.		
*PREM.DATE YOUNG STARS: 8X TO 20X		
COMMON ROOKIE (401-450)	8.00	3.60
*PREM.DATE ROOKIES: 5X TO 12X		
STATED PRINT RUN 78 SERIAL #'d SETS		

2000 Pacific Draft Picks 999

	MINT	NRMT
COMPLETE SET (50)	120.00	55.00
COMMON ROOKIE (401-450)	1.50	.70
*SERIAL NUMBERED: 1X TO 2.5X BASIC CARDS		
STATED PRINT RUN 999 SERIAL #'d SETS		

2000 Pacific AFC Leaders

	MINT	NRMT
COMPLETE SET (10)	20.00	9.00
COMMON CARD (1-10)	1.25	.55
SEMISTARS	2.00	.90
STATED ODDS 1:37		
❑ 1 Tim Couch	4.00	1.80
❑ 2 Olandis Gary	2.00	.90
❑ 3 Marvin Harrison	2.00	.90
❑ 4 Edgerrin James	6.00	2.70
❑ 5 Peyton Manning	6.00	2.70
❑ 6 Mark Brunell	3.00	1.35
❑ 7 Jimmy Smith	1.25	.55
❑ 8 Drew Bledsoe	3.00	1.35
❑ 9 Keyshawn Johnson	2.00	.90
❑ 10 Eddie George	2.50	1.10

2000 Pacific Autographs

	MINT	NRMT
COMMON CARD	10.00	4.50
SEMISTARS	15.00	6.75
UNLISTED STARS	20.00	9.00
RANDOM INSERTS IN PACKS		
STATED SIGNING NUMBERS LISTED BELOW		
REDEMPTION EXPIRATION: 3/31/2001		
❑ 51 Tim Biakabutuka/200	10.00	4.50
❑ 70 Marcus Robinson/200	40.00	18.00
❑ 87 Tim Couch/100	60.00	27.00
❑ 154 Edgerrin James/50	100.00	45.00
❑ 229 Jake Delhomme/500	20.00	9.00
❑ 307 Isaac Bruce/100	20.00	9.00
❑ 319 Kurt Warner/253 Trade	100.00	45.00
❑ 344 J.J. Stokes/100	15.00	6.75
❑ 362 Mike Alstott/100	20.00	9.00
❑ 377 Eddie George/60	50.00	22.00
❑ 391 Stephen Davis/100	25.00	11.00
❑ 401 Shaun Alexander/150	40.00	18.00
❑ 403 Tom Brady/200	15.00	6.75
❑ 404 Demario Brown/300	15.00	6.75
❑ 405 Plaxico Burress/300	30.00	13.50
❑ 406 Trung Canidate/300	15.00	6.75
❑ 407 Giovanni Carmazzi/200	25.00	11.00
❑ 408 Kwame Cavil/300	10.00	4.50
❑ 410 Ron Dayne/200	70.00	32.00
❑ 411 Reuben Droughns/200	20.00	9.00
❑ 412 Ron Dugans/400	15.00	6.75
❑ 414 Danny Farmer/250	15.00	6.75
❑ 415 Chafie Fields/400	10.00	4.50
❑ 417 Sherrod Gideon/200	10.00	4.50
❑ 419 Joe Hamilton/200	15.00	6.75
❑ 420 Tony Hartley/200	10.00	4.50
❑ 421 Todd Husak/300	15.00	6.75
❑ 423 Thomas Jones/300	40.00	18.00
❑ 424 Marcus Knight/200	10.00	4.50
❑ 425 Jamal Lewis/100	50.00	22.00
❑ 426 Anthony Lucas/200	15.00	6.75
❑ 427 Tee Martin/200	25.00	11.00
❑ 428 Rondell Mealey/200	10.00	4.50
❑ 429 Sylvester Morris/100	20.00	9.00
❑ 431 Dennis Northcutt/200	20.00	9.00
❑ 432 Chad Pennington/150	70.00	32.00
❑ 434 Mareno Philyaw/200	10.00	4.50
❑ 435 Jerry Porter/200	20.00	9.00
❑ 436 Travis Prentice/300	20.00	9.00
❑ 437 Tim Rattay/200	20.00	9.00
❑ 438 Chris Redman/150	30.00	13.50
❑ 439 J.R. Redmond/200	25.00	11.00
❑ 443 R.Jay Soward/400	20.00	9.00
❑ 445 Shyrone Stith/200	15.00	6.75
❑ 446 Travis Taylor/200	25.00	11.00
❑ 447 Troy Walters/300	15.00	6.75
❑ 448 Peter Warrick/288 Trade	70.00	32.00
❑ 449 Dez White/300	20.00	9.00
❑ 450 Michael Wiley/300	20.00	9.00

2000 Pacific Cramer's Choice

	MINT	NRMT
COMPLETE SET (10)	350.00	160.00
COMMON CARD (1-10)	20.00	9.00
STATED ODDS 1:721		
❑ 1 Tim Couch	50.00	22.00
❑ 2 Emmitt Smith	40.00	18.00
❑ 3 Brett Favre	60.00	27.00
❑ 4 Edgerrin James	60.00	27.00
❑ 5 Peyton Manning	50.00	22.00
❑ 6 Randy Moss	50.00	22.00
❑ 7 Marshall Faulk	20.00	9.00
❑ 8 Kurt Warner	80.00	36.00
❑ 9 Eddie George	20.00	9.00
❑ 10 Peter Warrick	50.00	22.00

2000 Pacific Finest Hour

	MINT	NRMT
COMPLETE SET (20)	100.00	45.00
COMMON CARD (1-20)	2.50	1.10
STATED ODDS 1:73		

❑ 1 Terrell Davis	6.00	2.70
❑ 2 Barry Sanders	8.00	3.60
❑ 3 Brett Favre	10.00	4.50
❑ 4 Edgerrin James	8.00	3.60
❑ 5 Drew Bledsoe	4.00	1.80
❑ 6 Damon Huard	2.50	1.10
❑ 7 Randy Moss	8.00	3.60
❑ 8 Kurt Warner	12.00	5.50
❑ 9 Jerry Rice	6.00	2.70
❑ 10 Stephen Davis	2.50	1.10
❑ 11 Shaun Alexander	10.00	4.50
❑ 12 Peter Warrick	15.00	6.75
❑ 13 Chris Redman	6.00	2.70
❑ 14 Chad Pennington	12.00	5.50
❑ 15 Tom Brady	4.00	1.80
❑ 16 Plaxico Burress	8.00	3.60
❑ 17 Todd Husak	4.00	1.80
❑ 18 Jamal Lewis	10.00	4.50
❑ 19 Thomas Jones	10.00	4.50
❑ 20 Ron Dayne	15.00	6.75

2000 Pacific Game Worn Jerseys

	MINT	NRMT
COMPLETE SET (9)	400.00	180.00
COMMON CARD (1-9)	20.00	9.00
STATED ODDS 1:5 BOXES		

❑ 1 Kurt Warner	120.00	55.00
❑ 2 Fred Taylor	50.00	22.00
❑ 3 Ricky Williams	60.00	27.00
❑ 4 Ike Hilliard	20.00	9.00
❑ 5 Tim Brown	30.00	13.50
❑ 6 Brett Favre	100.00	45.00
❑ 7 Jon Kitna	30.00	13.50
❑ 8 Kordell Stewart	30.00	13.50
❑ 9 Natrone Means	20.00	9.00

2000 Pacific Gold Crown Die Cuts

	MINT	NRMT
COMPLETE SET (36)	150.00	70.00
COMMON CARD (1-36)	3.00	1.35
STATED ODDS 1:37		

❑ 1 Jake Plummer	3.00	1.35
❑ 2 Cade McNown	4.00	1.80
❑ 3 Corey Dillon	3.00	1.35
❑ 4 Akili Smith	3.00	1.35
❑ 5 Tim Couch	6.00	2.70
❑ 6 Kevin Johnson	3.00	1.35
❑ 7 Olandis Gary	3.00	1.35
❑ 8 Brian Griese	4.00	1.80
❑ 9 Marvin Harrison	3.00	1.35
❑ 10 Edgerrin James	10.00	4.50
❑ 11 Mark Brunell	5.00	2.20
❑ 12 Fred Taylor	5.00	2.20
❑ 13 Damon Huard	3.00	1.35
❑ 14 Dan Marino	12.00	5.50
❑ 15 Randy Moss	10.00	4.50
❑ 16 Drew Bledsoe	5.00	2.20
❑ 17 Ricky Williams	6.00	2.70
❑ 18 Keyshawn Johnson	3.00	1.35
❑ 19 Donovan McNabb	4.00	1.80
❑ 20 Marshall Faulk	3.00	1.35
❑ 21 Kurt Warner	15.00	6.75
❑ 22 Jon Kitna	3.00	1.35
❑ 23 Jerry Rice	8.00	3.60
❑ 24 Shaun King	4.00	1.80
❑ 25 Eddie George	4.00	1.80
❑ 26 Steve McNair	3.00	1.35
❑ 27 Stephen Davis	3.00	1.35
❑ 28 Brad Johnson	3.00	1.35
❑ 29 Shaun Alexander	12.00	5.50
❑ 30 Plaxico Burress	10.00	4.50
❑ 31 Ron Dayne	20.00	9.00
❑ 32 Joe Hamilton	5.00	2.20
❑ 33 Thomas Jones	12.00	5.50
❑ 34 Chad Pennington	15.00	6.75
❑ 35 Chris Redman	8.00	3.60
❑ 36 Peter Warrick	20.00	9.00

2000 Pacific NFC Leaders

	MINT	NRMT
COMPLETE SET (10)	25.00	11.00
COMMON CARD (1-10)	2.00	.90
STATED ODDS 1:37		

❑ 1 Marcus Robinson	2.00	.90
❑ 2 Troy Aikman	5.00	2.20
❑ 3 Emmitt Smith	5.00	2.20
❑ 4 Cris Carter	2.00	.90
❑ 5 Randy Moss	6.00	2.70
❑ 6 Isaac Bruce	2.00	.90
❑ 7 Marshall Faulk	2.00	.90
❑ 8 Kurt Warner	10.00	4.50
❑ 9 Stephen Davis	2.00	.90
❑ 10 Brad Johnson	2.00	.90

2000 Pacific Pro Bowl Die Cuts

	MINT	NRMT
COMPLETE SET (20)	60.00	27.00
COMMON CARD (1-20)	2.00	.90
SEMISTARS	3.00	1.35
STATED ODDS 1:37		

❑ 1 Steve Beuerlein	2.00	.90
❑ 2 Corey Dillon	3.00	1.35
❑ 3 Emmitt Smith	8.00	3.60
❑ 4 Marvin Harrison	3.00	1.35
❑ 5 Edgerrin James	10.00	4.50
❑ 6 Peyton Manning	10.00	4.50
❑ 7 Mark Brunell	5.00	2.20
❑ 8 Jimmy Smith	2.00	.90
❑ 9 Tony Gonzalez	2.00	.90
❑ 10 Cris Carter	3.00	1.35
❑ 11 Randy Moss	10.00	4.50
❑ 12 Rich Gannon	2.00	.90
❑ 13 Keyshawn Johnson	3.00	1.35
❑ 14 Terry Glenn	3.00	1.35
❑ 15 Marshall Faulk	3.00	1.35
❑ 16 Kurt Warner	12.00	5.50
❑ 17 Mike Alstott	3.00	1.35
❑ 18 Eddie George	4.00	1.80
❑ 19 Stephen Davis	3.00	1.35
❑ 20 Brad Johnson	3.00	1.35

2000 Pacific Reflections

	MINT	NRMT
COMPLETE SET (20)	120.00	55.00
COMMON CARD (1-20)	4.00	1.80
STATED ODDS 1:145		

❑ 1 Cade McNown	5.00	2.20
❑ 2 Tim Couch	8.00	3.60
❑ 3 Troy Aikman	10.00	4.50
❑ 4 Emmitt Smith	10.00	4.50
❑ 5 Terrell Davis	10.00	4.50
❑ 6 Barry Sanders	12.00	5.50
❑ 7 Brett Favre	15.00	6.75
❑ 8 Marvin Harrison	4.00	1.80
❑ 9 Edgerrin James	12.00	5.50
❑ 10 Mark Brunell	6.00	2.70
❑ 11 Fred Taylor	6.00	2.70
❑ 12 Dan Marino	15.00	6.75
❑ 13 Randy Moss	12.00	5.50
❑ 14 Ricky Williams	8.00	3.60
❑ 15 Marshall Faulk	4.00	1.80
❑ 16 Kurt Warner	20.00	9.00
❑ 17 Jon Kitna	4.00	1.80
❑ 18 Shaun King	5.00	2.20
❑ 19 Eddie George	5.00	2.20
❑ 20 Stephen Davis	4.00	1.80

1996 Pacific Litho-Cel Game Time

	MINT	NRMT
COMPLETE SET (100)	20.00	9.00

COMMON CARD (GT1-GT96)	.10	.05
FOIL CARDS (GT97-GT100)	.30	.14
SEMISTARS	.20	.09
UNLISTED STARS	.40	.18

ONLY #GT97-GT100 PRINTED IN GOLD FOIL
ONE PER PACK

❑ GT1 Eddie George	2.00	.90
❑ GT2 Larry Bowie	.10	.05
❑ GT3 Jarius Hayes	.10	.05
❑ GT4 Jamal Anderson	2.00	.90
❑ GT5 Ernest Hunter	.10	.05
❑ GT6 Darick Holmes	.20	.09
❑ GT7 Kerry Collins	.40	.18
❑ GT8 Raymont Harris	.10	.05
❑ GT9 Jeff Blake	.40	.18
❑ GT10 Troy Aikman	1.00	.45
❑ GT11 Terrell Davis	2.50	1.10
❑ GT12 Kevin Glover	.10	.05
❑ GT13 Brett Favre	2.00	.90
❑ GT14 Al Del Greco	.10	.05
❑ GT15 Marshall Faulk	.40	.18
❑ GT16 Bryan Barker	.10	.05
❑ GT17 Rich Gannon	.10	.05
❑ GT18 Dwight Hollier	.10	.05
❑ GT19 Dixon Edwards	.10	.05
❑ GT20 Drew Bledsoe	1.00	.45
❑ GT21 Paul Green	.10	.05
❑ GT22 Lawrence Dawsey	.10	.05
❑ GT23 Ron Carpenter	.10	.05
❑ GT24 Joe Aska	.10	.05
❑ GT25 Joe Panos	.10	.05
❑ GT26 Norm Johnson	.10	.05
❑ GT27 Tony Banks	.40	.18
❑ GT28 Darren Bennett	.10	.05
❑ GT29 Steve Israel	.10	.05
❑ GT30 Michael Barber	.10	.05
❑ GT31 Dexter Nottage	.10	.05
❑ GT32 Kwamie Lassiter	.10	.05
❑ GT33 Travis Hall	.10	.05
❑ GT34 Greg Montgomery	.10	.05
❑ GT35 Jim Kelly	.40	.18
❑ GT36 Matt Elliott	.10	.05
❑ GT37 Jack Jackson	.10	.05
❑ GT38 Ki-Jana Carter	.20	.09
❑ GT39 Deion Sanders	.60	.25
❑ GT40 Jason Elam	.10	.05
❑ GT41 Johnnie Morton	.20	.09
❑ GT42 Darius Holland	.10	.05
❑ GT43 Sheddrick Wilson	.10	.05
❑ GT44 Derrick Frazier	.10	.05
❑ GT45 Travis Davis	.10	.05
❑ GT46 Pellom McDaniels	.10	.05
❑ GT47 Dan Marino	2.00	.90
❑ GT48 Ben Hanks	.10	.05
❑ GT49 Tedy Bruschi	.10	.05
❑ GT50 Tommy Hodson	.10	.05
❑ GT51 Amani Toomer	.40	.18
❑ GT52 Brian Hansen	.10	.05
❑ GT53 Paul Butcher	.10	.05
❑ GT54 Kevin Turner	.10	.05
❑ GT55 Darren Perry	.10	.05
❑ GT56 Mike Gruttadauria	.10	.05
❑ GT57 Charlie Jones	.10	.05
❑ GT58 Iheanyi Uwaezuoke	.10	.05
❑ GT59 Glenn Montgomery	.10	.05
❑ GT60 Mike Alstott	.40	.18
❑ GT61 Joe Patton	.10	.05
❑ GT62 Leeland McElroy	.40	.18
❑ GT63 Robbie Tobeck	.10	.05
❑ GT64 Vinny Testaverde	.20	.09
❑ GT65 Chris Spielman	.20	.09
❑ GT66 Anthony Johnson	.20	.09
❑ GT67 Todd Sauerbrun	.10	.05
❑ GT68 Jeff Hill	.10	.05
❑ GT69 Emmitt Smith	1.50	.70
❑ GT70 John Elway	2.00	.90
❑ GT71 Barry Sanders	2.00	.90
❑ GT72 Brian Williams LB	.10	.05
❑ GT73 Chris Gardocki	.10	.05
❑ GT74 Jimmy Smith	.20	.09
❑ GT75 Ricky Siglar	.10	.05
❑ GT76 Tim Ruddy	.10	.05
❑ GT77 Moe Williams	.10	.05
❑ GT78 Willie Clay	.10	.05
❑ GT79 Henry Lusk	.10	.05
❑ GT80 Brian Williams OL	.10	.05
❑ GT81 Ronald Moore	.10	.05
❑ GT82 Trey Junkin	.10	.05
❑ GT83 James Willis	.10	.05
❑ GT84 Joel Steed	.10	.05
❑ GT85 Jamie Martin	.20	.09
❑ GT86 Shawn Lee	.10	.05
❑ GT87 Steve Young	.75	.35
❑ GT88 Barrett Robbins	.10	.05
❑ GT89 Charles Dimry	.10	.05
❑ GT90 Darryl Pounds	.10	.05
❑ GT91 Herschel Walker	.20	.09
❑ GT92 Bill Romanowski	.10	.05
❑ GT93 David Tate	.10	.05
❑ GT94 Marrio Grier	.10	.05
❑ GT95 Rodney Young	.10	.05
❑ GT96 Lamar Smith	.10	.05
❑ GT97 Don Beebe	.30	.14
❑ GT98 Ty Detmer	.40	.18
❑ GT99 Ted Popson	.30	.14
❑ GT100 Natrone Means	.40	.18

1998 Pacific Omega

	MINT	NRMT
COMPLETE SET (250)	40.00	18.00
COMMON CARD (1-250)	.10	.05
SEMISTARS	.25	.11
UNLISTED STARS	.50	.23
COMMON ROOKIE	.50	.23
ROOKIE SEMISTARS	.75	.35
ROOKIE UNLISTED STARS	1.50	.70

❑ 1 Larry Centers	.10	.05
❑ 2 Rob Moore	.25	.11
❑ 3 Michael Pittman RC	.75	.35
❑ 4 Jake Plummer	1.50	.70
❑ 5 Simeon Rice	.25	.11
❑ 6 Frank Sanders	.25	.11
❑ 7 Eric Swann	.10	.05
❑ 8 Morten Andersen	.10	.05
❑ 9 Jamal Anderson	.50	.23
❑ 10 Chris Chandler	.25	.11
❑ 11 Harold Green	.10	.05
❑ 12 Byron Hanspard	.25	.11
❑ 13 Terance Mathis	.25	.11
❑ 14 O.J. Santiago	.10	.05
❑ 15 Peter Boulware	.10	.05
❑ 16 Jay Graham	.10	.05
❑ 17 Eric Green	.10	.05
❑ 18 Michael Jackson	.10	.05
❑ 19 Jermaine Lewis	.25	.11
❑ 20 Ray Lewis	.10	.05
❑ 21 Jonathan Ogden	.10	.05
❑ 22 Eric Zeier	.25	.11
❑ 23 Steve Christie	.10	.05
❑ 24 Todd Collins	.10	.05
❑ 25 Quinn Early	.10	.05
❑ 26 Eric Moulds	.50	.23
❑ 27 Andre Reed	.25	.11
❑ 28 Antowain Smith	.50	.23
❑ 29 Bruce Smith	.25	.11
❑ 30 Thurman Thomas	.50	.23
❑ 31 Ted Washington	.10	.05
❑ 32 Michael Bates	.10	.05
❑ 33 Tim Biakabutuka	.25	.11
❑ 34 Mark Carrier	.10	.05
❑ 35 Rae Carruth	.25	.11
❑ 36 Kerry Collins	.25	.11
❑ 37 Kevin Greene	.25	.11
❑ 38 Fred Lane	.25	.11
❑ 39 Muhsin Muhammad	.25	.11
❑ 40 Wesley Walls	.25	.11
❑ 41 Curtis Conway	.25	.11
❑ 42 Bobby Engram	.25	.11
❑ 43 Curtis Enis RC	2.50	1.10
❑ 44 Walt Harris	.10	.05
❑ 45 Erik Kramer	.10	.05
❑ 46 Chris Penn	.10	.05
❑ 47 Ryan Wetnight RC	.10	.05
❑ 48 Jeff Blake	.25	.11
❑ 49 Ki-Jana Carter	.10	.05
❑ 50 John Copeland	.10	.05
❑ 51 Corey Dillon	.75	.35
❑ 52 Tony McGee	.10	.05
❑ 53 Carl Pickens	.50	.23
❑ 54 Darnay Scott	.25	.11
❑ 55 Takeo Spikes RC	.75	.35
❑ 56 Troy Aikman	1.25	.55
❑ 57 Eric Bjornson	.10	.05
❑ 58 Greg Ellis RC	.50	.23
❑ 59 Michael Irvin	.50	.23
❑ 60 Daryl Johnston	.25	.11
❑ 61 David LaFleur	.10	.05
❑ 62 Deion Sanders	.50	.23
❑ 63 Emmitt Smith	2.00	.90
❑ 64 Herschel Walker	.25	.11
❑ 65 Nicky Sualua RC	.25	.11
❑ 66 Steve Atwater	.10	.05
❑ 67 Terrell Davis	2.00	.90
❑ 68 John Elway	2.50	1.10
❑ 69 Brian Griese RC	4.00	1.80
❑ 70 Ed McCaffrey	.25	.11
❑ 71 John Mobley	.10	.05
❑ 72 Marcus Nash RC	2.00	.90
❑ 73 Shannon Sharpe	.25	.11
❑ 74 Neil Smith	.25	.11
❑ 75 Rod Smith	.25	.11
❑ 76 Charlie Batch RC	4.00	1.80
❑ 77 Germane Crowell RC	2.50	1.10
❑ 78 Jason Hanson	.10	.05
❑ 79 Scott Mitchell	.25	.11
❑ 80 Herman Moore	.50	.23
❑ 81 Johnnie Morton	.25	.11
❑ 82 Barry Sanders	2.50	1.10
❑ 83 Tommy Vardell	.10	.05
❑ 84 Robert Brooks	.25	.11
❑ 85 Gilbert Brown	.10	.05
❑ 86 LeRoy Butler	.10	.05
❑ 87 Mark Chmura	.25	.11
❑ 88 Brett Favre	2.50	1.10
❑ 89 Antonio Freeman	.50	.23
❑ 90 William Henderson	.10	.05
❑ 91 Vonnie Holliday RC	.75	.35
❑ 92 Dorsey Levens	.50	.23
❑ 93 Reggie White	.50	.23
❑ 94 Aaron Bailey	.10	.05
❑ 95 Quentin Coryatt	.10	.05
❑ 96 Zack Crockett	.10	.05
❑ 97 Ken Dilger	.10	.05
❑ 98 Marshall Faulk	.50	.23
❑ 99 E.G. Green RC	.75	.35
❑ 100 Marvin Harrison	.25	.11
❑ 101 Peyton Manning RC	12.00	5.50
❑ 102 Jerome Pathon RC	1.50	.70
❑ 103 Tavian Banks RC	1.50	.70

❑ 104	Tony Boselli	.10	.05
❑ 105	Tony Brackens	.10	.05
❑ 106	Mark Brunell	1.00	.45
❑ 107	Kevin Hardy	.10	.05
❑ 108	Keenan McCardell	.25	.11
❑ 109	Pete Mitchell	.10	.05
❑ 110	Jimmy Smith	.25	.11
❑ 111	James Stewart	.25	.11
❑ 112	Fred Taylor RC	6.00	2.70
❑ 113	Kimble Anders	.25	.11
❑ 114	Dale Carter	.10	.05
❑ 115	Tony Gonzalez	.10	.05
❑ 116	Elvis Grbac	.25	.11
❑ 117	Donnell Bennett	.10	.05
❑ 118	Andre Rison	.25	.11
❑ 119	Rashaan Shehee RC	.75	.35
❑ 120	Derrick Thomas	.25	.11
❑ 121	Tamarick Vanover	.10	.05
❑ 122	Karim Abdul-Jabbar	.50	.23
❑ 123	John Avery RC	1.50	.70
❑ 124	Troy Drayton	.10	.05
❑ 125	John Dutton RC	.50	.23
❑ 126	Craig Erickson	.10	.05
❑ 127	Dan Marino	2.50	1.10
❑ 128	O.J. McDuffie	.25	.11
❑ 129	Jerris McPhail	.10	.05
❑ 130	Stanley Pritchett	.10	.05
❑ 131	Larry Shannon RC	.50	.23
❑ 132	Zach Thomas	.10	.05
❑ 133	Cris Carter	.50	.23
❑ 134	Randall Cunningham	.50	.23
❑ 135	Andrew Glover	.10	.05
❑ 136	Brad Johnson	.50	.23
❑ 137	Randall McDaniel	.10	.05
❑ 138	David Palmer	.10	.05
❑ 139	John Randle	.25	.11
❑ 140	Jake Reed	.25	.11
❑ 141	Robert Smith	.50	.23
❑ 142	Drew Bledsoe	1.00	.45
❑ 143	Ben Coates	.25	.11
❑ 144	Robert Edwards RC	1.50	.70
❑ 145	Terry Glenn	.50	.23
❑ 146	Shawn Jefferson	.10	.05
❑ 147	Willie McGinest	.10	.05
❑ 148	Tony Simmons RC	.75	.35
❑ 149	Chris Slade	.10	.05
❑ 150	Troy Davis	.10	.05
❑ 151	Mark Fields	.10	.05
❑ 152	Andre Hastings	.10	.05
❑ 153	Billy Joe Hobert	.10	.05
❑ 154	William Roaf	.10	.05
❑ 155	Heath Shuler	.10	.05
❑ 156	Danny Wuerffel	.25	.11
❑ 157	Ray Zellars	.10	.05
❑ 158	Jessie Armstead	.10	.05
❑ 159	Tiki Barber	.25	.11
❑ 160	Chris Calloway	.10	.05
❑ 161	Mike Cherry	.10	.05
❑ 162	Danny Kanell	.25	.11
❑ 163	Amani Toomer	.25	.11
❑ 164	Charles Way	.10	.05
❑ 165	Tyrone Wheatley	.25	.11
❑ 166	Kyle Brady	.10	.05
❑ 167	Wayne Chrebet	.50	.23
❑ 168	Glenn Foley	.25	.11
❑ 169	Scott Frost RC	.75	.35
❑ 170	Keyshawn Johnson	.50	.23
❑ 171	Leon Johnson	.10	.05
❑ 172	Alex Van Dyke	.10	.05
❑ 173	Dedric Ward	.10	.05
❑ 174	Tim Brown	.50	.23
❑ 175	Rickey Dudley	.10	.05
❑ 176	Jeff George	.25	.11
❑ 177	Desmond Howard	.25	.11
❑ 178	James Jett	.25	.11
❑ 179	Napoleon Kaufman	.50	.23
❑ 180	Darrell Russell	.10	.05
❑ 181	Charles Woodson RC	2.50	1.10
❑ 182	Jason Dunn	.10	.05
❑ 183	Irving Fryar	.25	.11
❑ 184	Charlie Garner	.10	.05
❑ 185	Bobby Hoying	.25	.11
❑ 186	Chris T. Jones	.10	.05
❑ 187	Michael Timpson	.10	.05
❑ 188	Kevin Turner	.10	.05
❑ 189	Jerome Bettis	.50	.23
❑ 190	Will Blackwell	.10	.05
❑ 191	Mark Bruener	.10	.05
❑ 192	Charles Johnson	.10	.05
❑ 193	George Jones	.10	.05
❑ 194	Levon Kirkland	.10	.05
❑ 195	Kordell Stewart	.50	.23
❑ 196	Hines Ward RC	1.50	.70
❑ 197	Tony Banks	.25	.11
❑ 198	Isaac Bruce	.50	.23
❑ 199	Ernie Conwell	.10	.05
❑ 200	Robert Holcombe RC	1.50	.70
❑ 201	Eddie Kennison	.25	.11
❑ 202	Amp Lee	.10	.05
❑ 203	Orlando Pace	.10	.05
❑ 204	Charlie Jones	.10	.05
❑ 205	Freddie Jones	.10	.05
❑ 206	Ryan Leaf RC	2.00	.90
❑ 207	Natrone Means	.50	.23
❑ 208	Junior Seau	.25	.11
❑ 209	Bryan Still	.10	.05
❑ 210	Greg Clark	.10	.05
❑ 211	Jim Druckenmiller	.25	.11
❑ 212	Marc Edwards	.10	.05
❑ 213	Garrison Hearst	.50	.23
❑ 214	Terrell Owens	.50	.23
❑ 215	Jerry Rice	1.25	.55
❑ 216	J.J. Stokes	.25	.11
❑ 217	Bryant Young	.10	.05
❑ 218	Steve Young	.75	.35
❑ 219	Chad Brown	.10	.05
❑ 220	Joey Galloway	.50	.23
❑ 221	Cortez Kennedy	.10	.05
❑ 222	Jon Kitna	1.50	.70
❑ 223	James McKnight	.10	.05
❑ 224	Warren Moon	.50	.23
❑ 225	Michael Sinclair	.10	.05
❑ 226	Ricky Watters	.25	.11
❑ 227	Mike Alstott	.50	.23
❑ 228	Reidel Anthony	.25	.11
❑ 229	Derrick Brooks	.10	.05
❑ 230	Trent Dilfer	.50	.23
❑ 231	Warrick Dunn	.75	.35
❑ 232	Dave Moore	.10	.05
❑ 233	Hardy Nickerson	.10	.05
❑ 234	Warren Sapp	.25	.11
❑ 235	Karl Williams	.10	.05
❑ 236	Willie Davis	.10	.05
❑ 237	Kevin Dyson RC	2.00	.90
❑ 238	Eddie George	1.00	.45
❑ 239	Derrick Mason	.10	.05
❑ 240	Steve McNair	.50	.23
❑ 241	Chris Sanders	.10	.05
❑ 242	Frank Wycheck	.10	.05
❑ 243	Terry Allen	.50	.23
❑ 244	Jamie Asher	.10	.05
❑ 245	Gus Frerotte	.10	.05
❑ 246	Darrell Green	.25	.11
❑ 247	Skip Hicks RC	2.00	.90
❑ 248	Brian Mitchell	.10	.05
❑ 249	Leslie Shepherd	.10	.05
❑ 250	Michael Westbrook	.25	.11

1998 Pacific Omega EO Portraits

	MINT	NRMT
COMPLETE SET (20)	300.00	135.00
COMMON CARD (1-20)	6.00	2.70
STATED ODDS 1:73		

❑ 1	Jake Plummer	15.00	6.75
❑ 2	Corey Dillon	8.00	3.60
❑ 3	Troy Aikman	15.00	6.75
❑ 4	Emmitt Smith	25.00	11.00
❑ 5	Terrell Davis	25.00	11.00
❑ 6	John Elway	30.00	13.50
❑ 7	Barry Sanders	30.00	13.50
❑ 8	Brett Favre	30.00	13.50
❑ 9	Dorsey Levens	6.00	2.70
❑ 10	Peyton Manning	40.00	18.00
❑ 11	Mark Brunell	12.00	5.50
❑ 12	Dan Marino	30.00	13.50
❑ 13	Drew Bledsoe	12.00	5.50
❑ 14	Jerome Bettis	6.00	2.70
❑ 15	Kordell Stewart	6.00	2.70
❑ 16	Ryan Leaf	6.00	2.70
❑ 17	Jerry Rice	15.00	6.75
❑ 18	Steve Young	10.00	4.50
❑ 19	Warrick Dunn	12.00	5.50
❑ 20	Eddie George	12.00	5.50

1998 Pacific Omega Face To Face

	MINT	NRMT
COMPLETE SET (10)	250.00	110.00
COMMON CARD (1-10)	12.00	5.50
STATED ODDS 1:145		

❑ 1	Peyton Manning Ryan Leaf	25.00	11.00
❑ 2	Barry Sanders Warrick Dunn	40.00	18.00
❑ 3	Dan Marino John Elway	40.00	18.00
❑ 4	Jerry Rice Antonio Freeman	20.00	9.00
❑ 5	Jake Plummer Drew Bledsoe	20.00	9.00
❑ 6	Corey Dillon Eddie George	15.00	6.75
❑ 7	Emmitt Smith Terrell Davis	30.00	13.50
❑ 8	Steve Young Mark Brunell	15.00	6.75
❑ 9	Kordell Stewart Steve McNair	12.00	5.50
❑ 10	Troy Aikman Brett Favre	40.00	18.00

1998 Pacific Omega Online

	MINT	NRMT
COMPLETE SET (36)	120.00	55.00
COMMON CARD (1-36)	2.00	.90
SEMISTARS	3.00	1.35
STATED ODDS 4:37		

❑ 1	Jake Plummer	6.00	2.70
❑ 2	Antowain Smith	3.00	1.35
❑ 3	Curtis Enis	5.00	2.20
❑ 4	Corey Dillon	4.00	1.80
❑ 5	Troy Aikman	6.00	2.70
❑ 6	Emmitt Smith	10.00	4.50
❑ 7	Terrell Davis	10.00	4.50
❑ 8	John Elway	12.00	5.50

❑ 9 Shannon Sharpe	3.00	1.35
❑ 10 Herman Moore	3.00	1.35
❑ 11 Barry Sanders	12.00	5.50
❑ 12 Brett Favre	12.00	5.50
❑ 13 Antonio Freeman	3.00	1.35
❑ 14 Dorsey Levens	3.00	1.35
❑ 15 Peyton Manning	15.00	6.75
❑ 16 Marshall Faulk	3.00	1.35
❑ 17 Mark Brunell	5.00	2.20
❑ 18 Fred Taylor	8.00	3.60
❑ 19 Dan Marino	12.00	5.50
❑ 20 Robert Smith	3.00	1.35
❑ 21 Drew Bledsoe	5.00	2.20
❑ 22 Tiki Barber	3.00	1.35
❑ 23 Danny Kanell	2.00	.90
❑ 24 Tim Brown	3.00	1.35
❑ 25 Napoleon Kaufman	3.00	1.35
❑ 26 Charles Woodson	5.00	2.20
❑ 27 Jerome Bettis	3.00	1.35
❑ 28 Kordell Stewart	3.00	1.35
❑ 29 Ryan Leaf	4.00	1.80
❑ 30 Jerry Rice	6.00	2.70
❑ 31 Steve Young	4.00	1.80
❑ 32 Joey Galloway	3.00	1.35
❑ 33 Trent Dilfer	3.00	1.35
❑ 34 Warrick Dunn	4.00	1.80
❑ 35 Eddie George	5.00	2.20
❑ 36 Steve McNair	3.00	1.35

1998 Pacific Omega Prisms

	MINT	NRMT
COMPLETE SET (20)	200.00	90.00
COMMON CARD (1-20)	4.00	1.80
STATED ODDS 1:37		

❑ 1 Jake Plummer	10.00	4.50
❑ 2 Corey Dillon	5.00	2.20
❑ 3 Troy Aikman	10.00	4.50
❑ 4 Emmitt Smith	15.00	6.75
❑ 5 Terrell Davis	15.00	6.75
❑ 6 John Elway	20.00	9.00
❑ 7 Barry Sanders	20.00	9.00
❑ 8 Brett Favre	20.00	9.00
❑ 9 Peyton Manning	25.00	11.00
❑ 10 Mark Brunell	8.00	3.60
❑ 11 Dan Marino	20.00	9.00
❑ 12 Drew Bledsoe	8.00	3.60
❑ 13 Napoleon Kaufman	4.00	1.80
❑ 14 Jerome Bettis	4.00	1.80
❑ 15 Kordell Stewart	4.00	1.80
❑ 16 Ryan Leaf	5.00	2.20
❑ 17 Jerry Rice	10.00	4.50
❑ 18 Steve Young	6.00	2.70
❑ 19 Warrick Dunn	5.00	2.20
❑ 20 Eddie George	8.00	3.60

1998 Pacific Omega Rising Stars

	MINT	NRMT
COMPLETE SET (30)	80.00	36.00
COMMON CARD (1-30)	1.25	.55
SEMISTARS	2.00	.90
UNLISTED STARS	3.00	1.35
STATED ODDS 4:37 HOBBY		

*BLUE CARDS: 4X TO 8X HI COL.
BLUE PRINT RUN 100 SERIAL #'d SETS
*GREEN CARDS: 5X TO 12X HI COL.
GREEN PRINT RUN 50 SERIAL #'d SETS
*PURPLE CARDS: 7.5X TO 20X HI COL.
PURPLE PRINT RUN 25 SERIAL #'d SETS
*RED CARDS: 4X TO 10X HI COL.
RED PRINT RUN 75 SERIAL #'d SETS
GOLD PRINT RUN 1 #'d SET

❑ 1 Michael Pittman	2.00	.90
❑ 2 Keith Brooking	2.00	.90
❑ 3 Duane Starks	1.25	.55
❑ 4 Curtis Enis	4.00	1.80
❑ 5 Marcus Nash	3.00	1.35
❑ 6 Brian Griese	6.00	2.70
❑ 7 Terry Fair	2.00	.90
❑ 8 Germane Crowell	4.00	1.80
❑ 9 Charlie Batch	6.00	2.70
❑ 10 E.G. Green	2.00	.90
❑ 11 Peyton Manning	15.00	6.75
❑ 12 Jerome Pathon	2.00	.90
❑ 13 Fred Taylor	10.00	4.50
❑ 14 Tavian Banks	2.00	.90
❑ 15 Rashaan Shehee	2.00	.90
❑ 16 John Avery	3.00	1.35
❑ 17 John Dutton	1.25	.55
❑ 18 Robert Edwards	3.00	1.35
❑ 19 Tony Simmons	2.00	.90
❑ 20 Joe Jurevicius	2.00	.90
❑ 21 Scott Frost	2.00	.90
❑ 22 Charles Woodson	4.00	1.80
❑ 23 Hines Ward	2.00	.90
❑ 24 Robert Holcombe	3.00	1.35
❑ 25 Az-Zahir Hakim	1.25	.55
❑ 26 Ryan Leaf	4.00	1.80
❑ 27 Ahman Green	2.00	.90
❑ 28 Kevin Dyson	3.00	1.35
❑ 29 Stephen Alexander	2.00	.90
❑ 30 Skip Hicks	2.00	.90

1999 Pacific Omega

	MINT	NRMT
COMPLETE SET (250)	40.00	18.00
COMMON CARD (1-250)	.15	.07
SEMISTARS	.25	.11
UNLISTED STARS	.50	.23
COMMON ROOKIE	.50	.23
ROOKIE SEMISTARS	1.00	.45
ROOKIE UNL.STARS	1.25	.55

❑ 1 Mario Bates	.15	.07
❑ 2 David Boston RC	2.00	.90
❑ 3 Rob Moore	.25	.11
❑ 4 Adrian Murrell	.25	.11
❑ 5 Jake Plummer	1.00	.45
❑ 6 Frank Sanders	.25	.11
❑ 7 Aeneas Williams	.15	.07
❑ 8 J.Makovicka/L.Shelton RC	1.25	.55
❑ 9 Jamal Anderson	.50	.23
❑ 10 Ray Buchanan	.15	.07
❑ 11 Chris Chandler	.25	.11
❑ 12 Tim Dwight	.50	.23
❑ 13 Byron Hanspard	.15	.07
❑ 14 Terance Mathis	.25	.11
❑ 15 O.J. Santiago	.15	.07
❑ 16 D.Kanell/C.Calloway	.15	.07
❑ 17 Peter Boulware	.15	.07
❑ 18 Priest Holmes	.25	.11
❑ 19 Patrick Johnson	.15	.07
❑ 20 Jermaine Lewis	.25	.11
❑ 21 Ray Lewis	.15	.07
❑ 22 Michael McCrary	.15	.07
❑ 23 Jonathan Ogden	.15	.07
❑ 24 Tony Banks	.15	.07
Scott Mitchell		
❑ 25 Doug Flutie	.60	.25
❑ 26 Rob Johnson	.25	.11
❑ 27 Eric Moulds	.50	.23
❑ 28 Andre Reed	.25	.11
❑ 29 Antowain Smith	.50	.23
❑ 30 Bruce Smith	.25	.11
❑ 31 Kevin Williams	.15	.07
❑ 32 Shawn Bryson	1.50	.70
Peerless Price RC		
❑ 33 Steve Beuerlein	.15	.07
❑ 34 Tim Biakabutuka	.25	.11
❑ 35 Rae Carruth	.25	.11
❑ 36 Dameyune Craig RC	2.00	.90
❑ 37 William Floyd	.15	.07
❑ 38 Kevin Greene	.15	.07
❑ 39 Muhsin Muhammad	.25	.11
❑ 40 Wesley Walls	.25	.11
❑ 41 Edgar Bennett	.15	.07
❑ 42 Robert Chancey RC	.50	.23
❑ 43 Curtis Conway	.25	.11
❑ 44 Bobby Engram	.25	.11
❑ 45 Curtis Enis	.50	.23
❑ 46 Cade McNown RC	4.00	1.80
❑ 47 Ryan Wetnight	.15	.07
❑ 48 Dwayne Bates	1.00	.45
Marty Booker RC		
❑ 49 Jeff Blake	.25	.11
❑ 50 Scott Covington RC	1.25	.55
❑ 51 Corey Dillon	.50	.23
❑ 52 James Hundon	.25	.11
❑ 53 Carl Pickens	.25	.11
❑ 54 Darnay Scott	.15	.07
❑ 55 Akili Smith RC	2.50	1.10
❑ 56 Craig Yeast RC	1.00	.45
❑ 57 Tim Couch RC	6.00	2.70
❑ 58 Ty Detmer	.25	.11
❑ 59 Marc Edwards	.15	.07
❑ 60 Kevin Johnson RC	3.00	1.35
❑ 61 Terry Kirby	.15	.07
❑ 62 Sedrick Shaw	.15	.07
❑ 63 Leslie Shepherd	.15	.07
❑ 64 Darrin Chiaverini	.50	.23
Daylon McCutcheon RC		
❑ 65 Troy Aikman	1.25	.55
❑ 66 Michael Irvin	.25	.11
❑ 67 David LaFleur	.15	.07
❑ 68 Wane McGarity RC	1.25	.55
❑ 69 Ernie Mills	.15	.07
❑ 70 Deion Sanders	.50	.23
❑ 71 Emmitt Smith	1.25	.55
❑ 72 Rocket Ismail	.15	.07
James McKnight		
❑ 73 Bubby Brister	.15	.07
❑ 74 Byron Chamberlain RC	1.00	.45
❑ 75 Terrell Davis	1.25	.55
❑ 76 Olandis Gary RC	4.00	1.80
❑ 77 Brian Griese	1.00	.45
❑ 78 Ed McCaffrey	.25	.11
❑ 79 Shannon Sharpe	.25	.11
❑ 80 Rod Smith	.25	.11

❑ 81 Travis McGriff 1.00 .45
Al Wilson RC
❑ 82 Charlie Batch 1.00 .45
❑ 83 Chris Claiborne RC 1.00 .45
❑ 84 Germane Crowell .25 .11
❑ 85 Terry Fair .15 .07
❑ 86 Sedrick Irvin RC 1.25 .55
❑ 87 Herman Moore .50 .23
❑ 88 Johnnie Morton .25 .11
❑ 89 Barry Sanders 2.00 .90
❑ 90 Mark Chmura .15 .07
❑ 91 Brett Favre 2.00 .90
❑ 92 Antonio Freeman .50 .23
❑ 93 Desmond Howard .25 .11
❑ 94 Dorsey Levens .50 .23
❑ 95 Derrick Mayes .15 .07
❑ 96 Bill Schroeder .50 .23
❑ 97 Aaron Brooks 1.25 .55
Dee Miller RC
❑ 98 E.G. Green .15 .07
❑ 99 Marvin Harrison .50 .23
❑ 100 Edgerrin James RC 10.00 4.50
❑ 101 Peyton Manning 2.00 .90
❑ 102 Jerome Pathon .15 .07
❑ 103 Marcus Pollard .15 .07
❑ 104 Ken Dilger .15 .07
❑ 105 Derrick Alexander WR .25 .11
❑ 106 Reggie Barlow .15 .07
❑ 107 Tony Boselli .15 .07
❑ 108 Mark Brunell .75 .35
❑ 109 George Jones .15 .07
❑ 110 Keenan McCardell .25 .11
❑ 111 Jimmy Smith .25 .11
❑ 112 James Stewart .25 .11
❑ 113 Fred Taylor 1.25 .55
❑ 114 Kimble Anders .25 .11
❑ 115 Mike Cloud RC 1.25 .55
❑ 116 Tony Gonzalez .25 .11
❑ 117 Elvis Grbac .25 .11
❑ 118 Byron Bam Morris .15 .07
❑ 119 Andre Rison .25 .11
❑ 120 Derrick Thomas .25 .11
❑ 121 Karim Abdul-Jabbar .25 .11
❑ 122 Oronde Gadsden .15 .07
❑ 123 James Johnson RC 1.50 .70
❑ 124 Rob Konrad RC 1.25 .55
❑ 125 Dan Marino 2.00 .90
❑ 126 O.J. McDuffie .25 .11
❑ 127 Lamar Thomas .15 .07
❑ 128 Zach Thomas .25 .11
❑ 129 Cris Carter .50 .23
❑ 130 Daunte Culpepper RC 4.00 1.80
❑ 131 Randall Cunningham .50 .23
❑ 132 Matthew Hatchette .15 .07
❑ 133 Leroy Hoard .15 .07
❑ 134 David Palmer .15 .07
❑ 135 John Randle .25 .11
❑ 136 Randy Moss 2.00 .90
❑ 137 Robert Smith .50 .23
❑ 138 Drew Bledsoe .75 .35
❑ 139 Ben Coates .25 .11
❑ 140 Kevin Faulk RC 1.50 .70
❑ 141 Terry Glenn .50 .23
❑ 142 Shawn Jefferson .15 .07
❑ 143 Ty Law .15 .07
❑ 144 Tony Simmons .15 .07
❑ 145 Michael Bishop 1.50 .70
Andy Katzenmoyer RC
❑ 146 Cameron Cleeland .15 .07
❑ 147 Andre Hastings .15 .07
❑ 148 Billy Joe Hobert .15 .07
❑ 149 Joe Johnson .15 .07
❑ 150 Keith Poole .15 .07
❑ 151 William Roaf .15 .07
❑ 152 Billy Joe Tolliver .15 .07
❑ 153 Ricky Williams RC 6.00 2.70
❑ 154 Tiki Barber .15 .07
❑ 155 Gary Brown .15 .07
❑ 156 Kent Graham .15 .07
❑ 157 Ike Hilliard .15 .07
❑ 158 David Patten .15 .07
❑ 159 Jason Sehorn .15 .07
❑ 160 Amani Toomer .15 .07
❑ 161 Joe Montgomery 1.25 .55
Luke Petitgout RC
❑ 162 Wayne Chrebet .25 .11
❑ 163 Bryan Cox .15 .07
❑ 164 Aaron Glenn .15 .07
❑ 165 Keyshawn Johnson .50 .23
❑ 166 Leon Johnson .15 .07
❑ 167 Curtis Martin .50 .23
❑ 168 Vinny Testaverde .25 .11
❑ 169 Dedric Ward .15 .07
❑ 170 Tim Brown .50 .23
❑ 171 Rickey Dudley .15 .07
❑ 172 James Jett .25 .11
❑ 173 Napoleon Kaufman .50 .23
❑ 174 Jon Ritchie .15 .07
❑ 175 Darrell Russell .15 .07
❑ 176 Charles Woodson .50 .23
❑ 177 Rich Gannon .15 .07
Heath Shuler
❑ 178 Hugh Douglas .15 .07
❑ 179 Donovan McNabb RC 4.00 1.80
❑ 180 Allen Rossum .15 .07
❑ 181 Duce Staley .25 .11
❑ 182 Kevin Turner .15 .07
❑ 183 Charles Johnson .15 .07
Doug Pederson
❑ 184 Barry Gardner 1.00 .45
Cecil Martin RC
❑ 185 Jerome Bettis .50 .23
❑ 186 Mark Bruener .15 .07
❑ 187 Troy Edwards RC 2.00 .90
❑ 188 Courtney Hawkins .15 .07
❑ 189 Levon Kirkland .15 .07
❑ 190 Kordell Stewart .50 .23
❑ 191 Hines Ward .15 .07
❑ 192 Malcolm Johnson 1.25 .55
Amos Zereoue RC
❑ 193 Greg Clark .15 .07
❑ 194 Terrell Fletcher .15 .07
❑ 195 Charlie Jones .15 .07
❑ 196 Cecil Collins RC 1.25 .55
❑ 197 Natrone Means .25 .11
❑ 198 Mikhael Ricks .15 .07
❑ 199 Junior Seau .25 .11
❑ 200 Bryan Still .15 .07
❑ 201 Ryan Thelwell .15 .07
❑ 202 Garrison Hearst .25 .11
❑ 203 Terry Jackson RC 1.00 .45
❑ 204 R.W. McQuarters .15 .07
❑ 205 Terrell Owens .50 .23
❑ 206 Jerry Rice 1.25 .55
❑ 207 J.J. Stokes .25 .11
❑ 208 Lawrence Phillips .15 .07
Tommy Vardell
❑ 209 Steve Young .75 .35
❑ 210 Karsten Bailey RC 1.00 .45
❑ 211 Chad Brown .15 .07
❑ 212 Christian Fauria .15 .07
❑ 213 Joey Galloway .50 .23
❑ 214 Ahman Green .25 .11
❑ 215 Brock Huard RC 1.50 .70
❑ 216 Cortez Kennedy .15 .07
❑ 217 Jon Kitna .50 .23
❑ 218 Ricky Watters .25 .11
❑ 219 Isaac Bruce .50 .23
❑ 220 Az-Zahir Hakim .15 .07
❑ 221 June Henley RC .15 .07
❑ 222 Greg Hill .15 .07
❑ 223 Torry Holt RC 3.00 1.35
❑ 224 Amp Lee .15 .07
❑ 225 Ricky Proehl .15 .07
❑ 226 Marshall Faulk .50 .23
Trent Green
❑ 227 Mike Alstott .50 .23
❑ 228 Reidel Anthony .25 .11
❑ 229 Trent Dilfer .25 .11
❑ 230 Warrick Dunn .50 .23
❑ 231 Bert Emanuel .25 .11
❑ 232 Jacquez Green .25 .11
❑ 233 Warren Sapp .15 .07
❑ 234 Shaun King 3.00 1.35
Anthony McFarland RC
❑ 235 Mike Archie RC .50 .23
❑ 236 Kevin Dyson .25 .11
❑ 237 Eddie George .60 .25
❑ 238 Derrick Mason .15 .07
❑ 239 Steve McNair .50 .23
❑ 240 Yancey Thigpen .15 .07
❑ 241 Frank Wycheck .15 .07
❑ 242 Darran Hall 2.00 .90
Jevon Kearse RC
❑ 243 Stephen Alexander .15 .07
❑ 244 Champ Bailey RC 1.50 .70
❑ 245 Stephen Davis .50 .23
❑ 246 Skip Hicks .25 .11
❑ 247 James Thrash RC .15 .07
❑ 248 Michael Westbrook .25 .11
❑ 249 Dan Wilkinson .15 .07
❑ 250 Brad Johnson .50 .23
Larry Centers

1999 Pacific Omega Copper

	MINT	NRMT
COMPLETE SET (250)	800.00	350.00
COMMON CARD (1-250)	4.00	1.80

*COPPER STARS: 10X TO 25X HI COL.
*COPPER YOUNG STARS: 8X TO 20X
*COPPER RCs: 3X TO 8X
COPPER STATED PRINT RUN 99 SER.#'d SETS
RANDOM INSERTS IN HOBBY PACKS

1999 Pacific Omega Gold

	MINT	NRMT
COMPLETE SET (250)	400.00	180.00
COMMON CARD (1-250)	2.00	.90

*GOLD STARS: 5X TO 12X HI COL.
*GOLD YOUNG STARS: 4X TO 10X
*GOLD RCs: 1.5X TO 4X
GOLD STATED PRINT RUN 299 SER.#'d SETS
RANDOM INSERTS IN RETAIL PACKS

1999 Pacific Omega Platinum Blue

	MINT	NRMT
COMPLETE SET (250)	1000.00	450.00
COMMON CARD (1-250)	5.00	2.20

*PLATINUM BLUE STARS: 12X TO 30X HI COL.
*PLATINUM BLUE YOUNG STARS: 10X TO 25X
*PLATINUM BLUE RCs: 4X TO 10X
PLATINUM BLUE PRINT RUN 75 SER.#'d SETS
RANDOM INSERTS IN HOBBY/RETAIL

1999 Pacific Omega Premiere Date

	MINT	NRMT
COMMON CARD (1-250)	6.00	2.70

*PREMIERE DATE STARS: 15X TO 40X HI COL.
*PREMIERE DATE YOUNG STARS: 12X TO 30X
*PREMIERE DATE RCs: 5X TO 12X
PREMIERE DATE PRINT RUN 60 SER.#'d SETS

1999 Pacific Omega 5-Star Attack

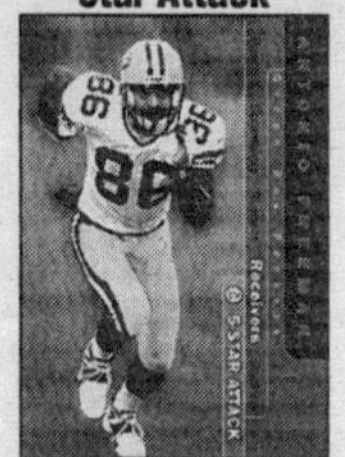

	MINT	NRMT
COMPLETE SET (30)	60.00	27.00
COMMON CARD (1-30)	1.50	.70

STATED ODDS 4:37
*BLUE FOILS: 2.5X TO 6X
BLUE STATED PRINT RUN 100 SER.#'d SETS
UNPRICED GOLDS SERIAL #'d OF 1
*GREEN FOILS: 4X TO 10X
GREEN STATED PRINT RUN 50 SER.#'d SETS
*PURPLE FOILS: 6X TO 15X
PURPLE STATED PRINT RUN 25 SER.#'d SETS
*RED FOILS: 3X TO 8X
RED STATED PRINT RUN 75 SER.#'d SETS

Card	MINT	NRMT
❑ 1 Chris Chandler	1.50	.70
❑ 2 Tim Couch	6.00	2.70
❑ 3 Peyton Manning	5.00	2.20
❑ 4 Dan Marino	6.00	2.70
❑ 5 Drew Bledsoe	2.50	1.10
❑ 6 Vinny Testaverde	1.50	.70
❑ 7 Randall Cunningham	2.50	1.10
❑ 8 Doug Flutie	2.00	.90
❑ 9 Charlie Batch	2.50	1.10
❑ 10 Mark Brunell	2.50	1.10
❑ 11 Steve Young	2.50	1.10
❑ 12 Jon Kitna	2.00	.90
❑ 13 Jamal Anderson	1.50	.70
❑ 14 Priest Holmes	1.50	.70
❑ 15 Emmitt Smith	4.00	1.80
❑ 16 Fred Taylor	3.00	1.35
❑ 17 Curtis Martin	2.50	1.10
❑ 18 Eddie George	2.00	.90
❑ 19 Ed McCaffrey	1.50	.70
❑ 20 Antonio Freeman	2.50	1.10
❑ 21 Randy Moss	5.00	2.20
❑ 22 Keyshawn Johnson	1.50	.70
❑ 23 Terrell Owens	1.50	.70
❑ 24 Joey Galloway	1.50	.70
❑ 25 Cade McNown	4.00	1.80
❑ 26 Akili Smith	2.50	1.10
❑ 27 Edgerrin James	10.00	4.50
❑ 28 Daunte Culpepper	4.00	1.80
❑ 29 Ricky Williams	6.00	2.70
❑ 30 Donovan McNabb	4.00	1.80

1999 Pacific Omega Draft Class

	MINT	NRMT
COMPLETE SET (10)	120.00	55.00
COMMON CARD (1-10)	8.00	3.60

STATED ODDS 1:145

Card	MINT	NRMT
❑ 1 Darrell Green Dan Marino	20.00	9.00
❑ 2 Jerry Rice Bruce Smith	12.00	5.50
❑ 3 Troy Aikman Barry Sanders	25.00	11.00
❑ 4 Shannon Sharpe Emmitt Smith	12.00	5.50
❑ 5 Brett Favre Herman Moore	20.00	9.00
❑ 6 Drew Bledsoe Mark Brunell	8.00	3.60
❑ 7 Terrell Davis Curtis Martin	12.00	5.50
❑ 8 Warrick Dunn Jake Plummer	8.00	3.60
❑ 9 Peyton Manning Randy Moss	20.00	9.00
❑ 10 Tim Couch Ricky Williams	20.00	9.00

1999 Pacific Omega EO Portraits

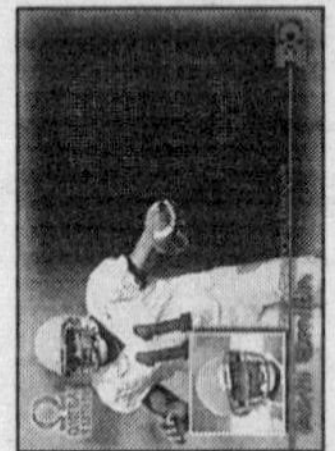

	MINT	NRMT
COMPLETE SET (20)	150.00	70.00
COMMON CARD (1-20)	4.00	1.80

STATED ODDS 1:73

Card	MINT	NRMT
❑ 1 Jake Plummer	8.00	3.60
❑ 2 Jamal Anderson	4.00	1.80
❑ 3 Akili Smith	6.00	2.70
❑ 4 Tim Couch	12.00	5.50
❑ 5 Troy Aikman	10.00	4.50
❑ 6 Emmitt Smith	10.00	4.50
❑ 7 Terrell Davis	10.00	4.50
❑ 8 Barry Sanders	15.00	6.75
❑ 9 Brett Favre	15.00	6.75
❑ 10 Peyton Manning	12.00	5.50
❑ 11 Mark Brunell	6.00	2.70
❑ 12 Fred Taylor	8.00	3.60
❑ 13 Dan Marino	15.00	6.75
❑ 14 Randy Moss	12.00	5.50
❑ 15 Ricky Williams	15.00	6.75
❑ 16 Curtis Martin	4.00	1.80
❑ 17 Jerry Rice	10.00	4.50
❑ 18 Jon Kitna	5.00	2.20
❑ 19 Warrick Dunn	4.00	1.80
❑ 20 Eddie George	5.00	2.20

1993 Pacific Prisms

	MINT	NRMT
COMPLETE SET (109)	50.00	22.00
COMMON CARD (1-108)	.40	.18
CL (NNO)	.40	.18
SEMISTARS	.75	.35
UNLISTED STARS	1.50	.70

STATED PRINT RUN 17,000 SETS

Card	MINT	NRMT
❑ 1 Chris Miller	.75	.35
❑ 2 Mike Pritchard	.75	.35
❑ 3 Andre Rison	.75	.35
❑ 4 Deion Sanders	2.50	1.10
❑ 5 Tony Smith	.40	.18
❑ 6 Jim Kelly	1.50	.70
❑ 7 Andre Reed	.75	.35
❑ 8 Thurman Thomas	1.50	.70
❑ 9 Neal Anderson	.40	.18
❑ 10 Jim Harbaugh	1.50	.70
❑ 11 Donnell Woolford	.40	.18
❑ 12 David Klingler	.40	.18
❑ 13 Carl Pickens	1.50	.70
❑ 14 Alfred Williams	.40	.18
❑ 15 Michael Jackson	.75	.35
❑ 16 Bernie Kosar	.75	.35
❑ 17 Tommy Vardell	.40	.18
❑ 18 Troy Aikman	4.00	1.80
❑ 19 Alvin Harper	.75	.35
❑ 20 Michael Irvin	1.50	.70
❑ 21 Russell Maryland	.40	.18
❑ 22 Emmitt Smith	8.00	3.60
❑ 23 John Elway	8.00	3.60
❑ 24 Tommy Maddox	.40	.18
❑ 25 Shannon Sharpe	1.50	.70
❑ 26 Herman Moore	3.00	1.35
❑ 27 Rodney Peete	.40	.18
❑ 28 Barry Sanders	8.00	3.60
❑ 29 Pat Swilling	.40	.18
❑ 30 Terrell Buckley	.40	.18
❑ 31 Brett Favre	10.00	4.50
❑ 32 Sterling Sharpe	1.50	.70
❑ 33 Reggie White	1.50	.70
❑ 34 Ernest Givins	.75	.35
❑ 35 Haywood Jeffires	.75	.35
❑ 36 Warren Moon	1.50	.70
❑ 37 Lorenzo White	.40	.18
❑ 38 Steve Emtman	.40	.18
❑ 39 Jeff George	1.50	.70
❑ 40 Reggie Langhorne	.40	.18
❑ 41 Dale Carter	.40	.18
❑ 42 Joe Montana	8.00	3.60
❑ 43 Derrick Thomas	1.50	.70
❑ 44 Barry Word	.40	.18
❑ 45 Nick Bell	.40	.18
❑ 46 Eric Dickerson	.75	.35
❑ 47 Jeff Jaeger	.40	.18
❑ 48 Jerome Bettis RC	4.00	1.80
❑ 49 Henry Ellard	.75	.35
❑ 50 Jim Everett	.75	.35
❑ 51 Cleveland Gary	.40	.18
❑ 52 Marco Coleman	.40	.18
❑ 53 Mark Higgs	.40	.18
❑ 54 Keith Jackson	.75	.35
❑ 55 Dan Marino	8.00	3.60
❑ 56 Troy Vincent	.40	.18
❑ 57 Terry Allen	1.50	.70
❑ 58 Jack Del Rio	.40	.18
❑ 59 Sean Salisbury	.40	.18
❑ 60 Robert Smith RC	4.00	1.80
❑ 61 Drew Bledsoe RC	12.00	5.50
❑ 62 Marv Cook	.40	.18
❑ 63 Irving Fryar	.75	.35
❑ 64 Leonard Russell	.75	.35
❑ 65 Andre Tippett	.40	.18
❑ 66 Morten Andersen	.40	.18
❑ 67 Vaughn Dunbar	.40	.18
❑ 68 Eric Martin	.40	.18
❑ 69 David Brown RC	1.50	.70
❑ 70 Rodney Hampton	1.50	.70

❑ 71 Phil Simms	.75	.35
❑ 72 Lawrence Taylor	1.50	.70
❑ 73 Ronnie Lott	.75	.35
❑ 74 Johnny Mitchell	.40	.18
❑ 75 Rob Moore	.75	.35
❑ 76 Browning Nagle	.40	.18
❑ 77 Fred Barnett	.75	.35
❑ 78 Randall Cunningham	1.50	.70
❑ 79 Herschel Walker	.75	.35
❑ 80 Gary Clark	.75	.35
❑ 81 Ken Harvey	.40	.18
❑ 82 Garrison Hearst RC	4.00	1.80
❑ 83 Ricky Proehl	.40	.18
❑ 84 Barry Foster	.75	.35
❑ 85 Ernie Mills	.40	.18
❑ 86 Neil O'Donnell	1.50	.70
❑ 87 Stan Humphries	1.50	.70
❑ 88 Leslie O'Neal	.75	.35
❑ 89 Junior Seau	1.50	.70
❑ 90 Amp Lee	.40	.18
❑ 91 Jerry Rice	5.00	2.20
❑ 92 Ricky Watters	1.50	.70
❑ 93 Steve Young	4.00	1.80
❑ 94 Cortez Kennedy	.75	.35
❑ 95 Rick Mirer RC	2.50	1.10
❑ 96 Eugene Robinson	.40	.18
❑ 97 Chris Warren	.75	.35
❑ 98 John L. Williams	.40	.18
❑ 99 Reggie Cobb	.40	.18
❑ 100 Lawrence Dawsey	.40	.18
❑ 101 Santana Dotson	.75	.35
❑ 102 Courtney Hawkins	.40	.18
❑ 103 Reggie Brooks RC	.75	.35
❑ 104 Ricky Ervins	.40	.18
❑ 105 Desmond Howard	.75	.35
❑ 106 Art Monk	.75	.35
❑ 107 Mark Rypien	.40	.18
❑ 108 Ricky Sanders	.40	.18
❑ P22 Emmitt Smith Promo	10.00	4.50
❑ P61 Drew Bledsoe Promo	15.00	6.75
❑ NNO Checklist Card	.40	.18

1994 Pacific Prisms

	MINT	NRMT
COMPLETE SET (128)	70.00	32.00
COMMON CARD (1-126)	.40	.18
CL (CL1-CL2)	.30	.14
SEMISTARS	.75	.35
UNLISTED STARS	1.25	.55
ONE SILVER OR GOLD PRISM PER PACK		
SILVER STATED PRINT RUN 16,000 SETS		
COMP.GOLD SET (128)	600.00	275.00
*GOLD STARS: 2X TO 4X HI COL.		
*GOLD RCs: 1.25X TO 2.5X		
GOLD STATED PRINT RUN 1138 SETS		
COMP.HELMET SET (30)	5.00	2.20
ONE HELMET PER PACK		

❑ 1 Troy Aikman UER (Text on back indicates he led Cowboys to victory in Super Bowl XXV. The Giants won SB XXV)	4.00	1.80
❑ 2 Marcus Allen	1.25	.55
❑ 3 Morten Andersen	.40	.18
❑ 4 Fred Barnett	.75	.35
❑ 5 Mario Bates RC	1.25	.55
❑ 6 Edgar Bennett	1.25	.55
❑ 7 Rod Bernstine	.40	.18
❑ 8 Jerome Bettis	1.25	.55
❑ 9 Steve Beuerlein	.40	.18
❑ 10 Brian Blades	.75	.35
❑ 11 Drew Bledsoe	4.00	1.80
❑ 12 Vincent Brisby	.75	.35
❑ 13 Reggie Brooks	.75	.35
❑ 14 Derek Brown RBK	.40	.18
❑ 15 Gary Brown	.40	.18
❑ 16 Tim Brown	.75	.35
❑ 17 Marion Butts	.40	.18
❑ 18 Keith Byars	.40	.18
❑ 19 Cody Carlson	.40	.18
❑ 20 Anthony Carter	.75	.35
❑ 21 Tom Carter	.40	.18
❑ 22 Gary Clark	.75	.35
❑ 23 Ben Coates	1.25	.55
❑ 24 Reggie Cobb	.40	.18
❑ 25 Curtis Conway	.75	.35
❑ 26 John Copeland	.40	.18
❑ 27 Randall Cunningham	1.25	.55
❑ 28 Willie Davis	.75	.35
❑ 29 Sean Dawkins RC	1.25	.55
❑ 30 Lawrence Dawsey	.40	.18
❑ 31 Richard Dent	.75	.35
❑ 32 Trent Dilfer RC	4.00	1.80
❑ 33 Troy Drayton	.40	.18
❑ 34 Vaughn Dunbar	.40	.18
❑ 35 Henry Ellard	.75	.35
❑ 36 John Elway	8.00	3.60
❑ 37 Craig Erickson	.40	.18
❑ 38 Boomer Esiason	.75	.35
❑ 39 Marshall Faulk RC	10.00	4.50
❑ 40 Brett Favre	8.00	3.60
❑ 41 William Floyd RC	1.25	.55
❑ 42 Glenn Foley RC	1.25	.55
❑ 43 Barry Foster	.40	.18
❑ 44 Irving Fryar	.75	.35
❑ 45 Jeff George	1.25	.55
❑ 46 Scottie Graham RC	.75	.35
❑ 47 Rodney Hampton	.75	.35
❑ 48 Jim Harbaugh	1.25	.55
❑ 49 Alvin Harper	.75	.35
❑ 50 Courtney Hawkins	.40	.18
❑ 51 Garrison Hearst	1.25	.55
❑ 52 Vaughn Hebron	.40	.18
❑ 53 Greg Hill RC	2.00	.90
❑ 54 Jeff Hostetler	.75	.35
❑ 55 Michael Irvin	1.25	.55
❑ 56 Qadry Ismail	.75	.35
❑ 57 Rocket Ismail	.75	.35
❑ 58 Anthony Johnson	.75	.35
❑ 59 Charles Johnson RC	1.25	.55
❑ 60 Johnny Johnson	.40	.18
❑ 61 Brent Jones	.75	.35
❑ 62 Kyle Clifton	.40	.18
❑ 63 Jim Kelly	.75	.35
❑ 64 Cortez Kennedy	.75	.35
❑ 65 Terry Kirby	1.25	.55
❑ 66 David Klingler	.40	.18
❑ 67 Erik Kramer	.75	.35
❑ 68 Reggie Langhorne	.40	.18
❑ 69 Chuck Levy RC	.40	.18
❑ 70 Dan Marino	8.00	3.60
❑ 71 O.J. McDuffie	1.25	.55
❑ 72 Natrone Means	1.25	.55
❑ 73 Eric Metcalf	.75	.35
❑ 74 Glyn Milburn	.75	.35
❑ 75 Anthony Miller	.75	.35
❑ 76 Rick Mirer	1.25	.55
❑ 77 Johnny Mitchell	.40	.18
❑ 78 Scott Mitchell	1.25	.55
❑ 79 Joe Montana	8.00	3.60
❑ 80 Warren Moon	.75	.35
❑ 81 Derrick Moore	.40	.18
❑ 82 Herman Moore	1.25	.55
❑ 83 Rob Moore	.75	.35
❑ 84 Ronald Moore	.40	.18
❑ 85 Johnnie Morton RC	4.00	1.80
❑ 86 Neil O'Donnell	.75	.35
❑ 87 David Palmer RC	2.00	.90
❑ 88 Erric Pegram	.40	.18
❑ 89 Carl Pickens	1.25	.55
❑ 90 Anthony Pleasant	.40	.18
❑ 91 Roosevelt Potts	.40	.18
❑ 92 Mike Pritchard	.40	.18
❑ 93 Andre Reed	.75	.35
❑ 94 Errict Rhett RC	4.00	1.80
❑ 95 Jerry Rice	4.00	1.80
❑ 96 Andre Rison	.75	.35
❑ 97 Greg Robinson	.40	.18
❑ 98 T.J. Rubley RC	.40	.18
❑ 99 Leonard Russell	.40	.18
❑ 100 Barry Sanders	8.00	3.60
❑ 101 Deion Sanders	2.50	1.10
❑ 102 Ricky Sanders	.40	.18
❑ 103 Junior Seau	.75	.35
❑ 104 Shannon Sharpe	.75	.35
❑ 105 Sterling Sharpe	.75	.35
❑ 106 Heath Shuler RC	1.25	.55
❑ 107 Phil Simms	.75	.35
❑ 108 Webster Slaughter	.40	.18
❑ 109 Bruce Smith	1.25	.55
❑ 110 Emmitt Smith	8.00	3.60
❑ 111 Irv Smith	.40	.18
❑ 112 Robert Smith	1.25	.55
❑ 113 Vinny Testaverde	.75	.35
❑ 114 Derrick Thomas	.75	.35
❑ 115 Thurman Thomas	.75	.35
❑ 116 Leroy Thompson	.40	.18
❑ 117 Lewis Tillman	.40	.18
❑ 118 Michael Timpson	.40	.18
❑ 119 Herschel Walker	.75	.35
❑ 120 Chris Warren	.75	.35
❑ 121 Ricky Watters	1.25	.55
❑ 122 Lorenzo White	.40	.18
❑ 123 Reggie White	1.25	.55
❑ 124 Dan Wilkinson RC	.75	.35
❑ 125 Kevin Williams	.75	.35
❑ 126 Steve Young	3.00	1.35
❑ CL1 Checklist 1	.30	.14
❑ CL2 Checklist 2	.30	.14
❑ S1 Sterling Sharpe Promo numbered S-1	1.00	.45

1995 Pacific Prisms

	MINT	NRMT
COMPLETE SET (216)	100.00	45.00
COMP.SERIES 1 (108)	50.00	22.00
COMP.SERIES 2 (108)	50.00	22.00
COMMON CARD (1-216)	.25	.11
SEMISTARS	.50	.23
UNLISTED STARS	1.00	.45
COMP.GOLD SET (216)	500.00	220.00
COMP.GOLD SER.1 (108)	250.00	110.00
COMP.GOLD SER.2 (108)	250.00	110.00
*GOLD STARS: 1.5X TO 3X HI COL.		
*GOLD RCs: 1X TO 2X HI		
GOLDS: STATED ODDS 2:37		

❑ 1 Chuck Levy	.25	.11
❑ 2 Ronald Moore	.25	.11
❑ 3 Jay Schroeder	.25	.11
❑ 4 Bert Emanuel	1.00	.45
❑ 5 Terance Mathis	.50	.23
❑ 6 Andre Rison	.50	.23
❑ 7 Bucky Brooks	.25	.11
❑ 8 Jeff Burris	.25	.11
❑ 9 Jim Kelly	1.00	.45
❑ 10 Lewis Tillman	.25	.11
❑ 11 Steve Walsh	.25	.11
❑ 12 Chris Zorich	.25	.11
❑ 13 Jeff Blake RC	3.00	1.35

❑ 14 Steve Broussard .25 .11
❑ 15 Jeff Cothran .25 .11
❑ 16 Earnset Byner .25 .11
❑ 17 Leroy Hoard .25 .11
❑ 18 Vinny Testaverde .50 .23
❑ 19 Troy Aikman 3.00 1.35
❑ 20 Alvin Harper .25 .11
❑ 21 Leon Lett .25 .11
❑ 22 Jay Novacek .50 .23
❑ 23 John Elway 6.00 2.70
❑ 24 Karl Mecklenburg .25 .11
❑ 25 Leonard Russell .25 .11
❑ 26 Mel Gray .25 .11
❑ 27 Dave Krieg .25 .11
❑ 28 Barry Sanders 6.00 2.70
❑ 29 Chris Spielman .50 .23
❑ 30 Robert Brooks 1.00 .45
❑ 31 LeShon Johnson .50 .23
❑ 32 Sterling Sharpe .50 .23
❑ 33 Ernest Givins .25 .11
❑ 34 Billy Joe Tolliver .25 .11
❑ 35 Lorenzo White .25 .11
❑ 36 Charles Arbuckle .25 .11
❑ 37 Sean Dawkins .50 .23
❑ 38 Marshall Faulk 1.50 .70
❑ 39 Marcus Allen 1.00 .45
❑ 40 Donnell Bennett .50 .23
❑ 41 Matt Blundin RC .25 .11
❑ 42 Greg Hill .50 .23
❑ 43 Tim Brown 1.00 .45
❑ 44 Billy Joe Hobert .50 .23
❑ 45 Rocket Ismail .50 .23
❑ 46 James Jett .50 .23
❑ 47 Tim Bowens .25 .11
❑ 48 Irving Fryar .50 .23
❑ 49 O.J. McDuffie 1.00 .45
❑ 50 Irving Spikes .50 .23
❑ 51 Terry Allen .50 .23
❑ 52 Cris Carter 1.00 .45
❑ 53 Amp Lee .25 .11
❑ 54 Drew Bledsoe 3.00 1.35
❑ 55 Willie McGinest .50 .23
❑ 56 Leroy Thompson .25 .11
❑ 57 Michael Timpson .25 .11
❑ 58 Michael Haynes .50 .23
❑ 59 Derrell Mitchell RC .25 .11
❑ 60 Dave Brown .50 .23
❑ 61 Thomas Lewis .50 .23
❑ 62 Dave Meggett .25 .11
❑ 63 Boomer Esiason .50 .23
❑ 64 Aaron Glenn .25 .11
❑ 65 Ronnie Lott .50 .23
❑ 66 Randall Cunningham 1.00 .45
❑ 67 Charlie Garner .50 .23
❑ 68 Herschel Walker .50 .23
❑ 69 Barry Foster .50 .23
❑ 70 Charles Johnson .50 .23
❑ 71 Jim Miller RC 2.00 .90
❑ 72 Rod Woodson .50 .23
❑ 73 Andre Coleman .25 .11
❑ 74 Natrone Means 1.00 .45
❑ 75 Shannon Mitchell RC .25 .11
❑ 76 Junior Seau 1.00 .45
❑ 77 Elvis Grbac 1.00 .45
❑ 78 Deion Sanders 2.00 .90
❑ 79 Adam Walker RC .25 .11
❑ 80 Ricky Watters 1.00 .45
❑ 81 Michael Bates .25 .11
❑ 82 Brian Blades .50 .23
❑ 83 Eugene Robinson .25 .11
❑ 84 Chris Warren .50 .23
❑ 85 Jerome Bettis 1.00 .45
❑ 86 Troy Drayton .25 .11
❑ 87 Chris Miller .25 .11
❑ 88 Trent Dilfer 1.00 .45
❑ 89 Hardy Nickerson .25 .11
❑ 90 Errict Rhett 1.00 .45
❑ 91 Henry Ellard .50 .23
❑ 92 Gus Frerotte 1.00 .45
❑ 93 Ricky Ervins .25 .11
❑ 94 Dave Barr RC .25 .11
❑ 95 Kyle Brady RC 1.00 .45
❑ 96 Mark Bruener RC .50 .23
❑ 97 Ki-Jana Carter RC 1.00 .45
❑ 98 Kerry Collins RC 3.00 1.35
❑ 99 Joey Galloway RC 10.00 4.50
❑ 100 Napoleon Kaufman RC 8.00 3.60
❑ 101 Steve McNair RC 10.00 4.50
❑ 102 Craig Newsome RC .25 .11
❑ 103 Rashaan Salaam RC 1.00 .45
❑ 104 Kordell Stewart RC 10.00 4.50
❑ 105 J.J. Stokes RC 2.50 1.10
❑ 106 Rodney Thomas RC 1.00 .45
❑ 107 Michael Westbrook RC 6.00 2.70
❑ 108 Tyrone Wheatley RC 5.00 2.20
❑ 109 Larry Centers .50 .23
❑ 110 Garrison Hearst 1.00 .45
❑ 111 Jamir Miller .25 .11
❑ 112 Jeff George .50 .23
❑ 113 Craig Heyward .50 .23
❑ 114 Cornelius Bennett .50 .23
❑ 115 Andre Reed .50 .23
❑ 116 Randy Baldwin .25 .11
❑ 117 Tommy Barnhardt .25 .11
❑ 118 Sam Mills .50 .23
❑ 119 Brian O'Neal .25 .11
❑ 120 Frank Reich .25 .11
❑ 121 Tony Smith .25 .11
❑ 122 Lawyer Tillman .25 .11
❑ 123 Jack Trudeau .25 .11
❑ 124 Vernon Turner .25 .11
❑ 125 Curtis Conway 1.00 .45
❑ 126 Erik Kramer .25 .11
❑ 127 Nate Lewis .25 .11
❑ 128 Carl Pickens 1.00 .45
❑ 129 Darnay Scott 1.00 .45
❑ 130 Dan Wilkinson .50 .23
❑ 131 Derrick Alexander WR 1.00 .45
❑ 132 Carl Banks .25 .11
❑ 133 Michael Irvin 1.00 .45
❑ 134 Emmitt Smith 5.00 2.20
❑ 135 Kevin Williams WR .50 .23
❑ 136 Glyn Milburn .25 .11
❑ 137 Anthony Miller .50 .23
❑ 138 Shannon Sharpe .50 .23
❑ 139 Scott Mitchell .50 .23
❑ 140 Herman Moore 1.00 .45
❑ 141 Edgar Bennett .50 .23
❑ 142 Brett Favre 6.00 2.70
❑ 143 Reggie White 1.00 .45
❑ 144 Gary Brown .25 .11
❑ 145 Haywood Jeffires .25 .11
❑ 146 Webster Slaughter .25 .11
❑ 147 Craig Erickson .25 .11
❑ 148 Paul Justin .25 .11
❑ 149 Lamont Warren .25 .11
❑ 150 Steve Beuerlein .25 .11
❑ 151 Derek Brown TE .25 .11
❑ 152 Mark Brunell 3.00 1.35
❑ 153 Reggie Cobb .25 .11
❑ 154 Desmond Howard .50 .23
❑ 155 Kelvin Pritchett .25 .11
❑ 156 James O. Stewart RC 8.00 3.60
❑ 157 Cedric Tillman .25 .11
❑ 158 Kimble Anders .50 .23
❑ 159 Lake Dawson .50 .23
❑ 160 Keith Byars .25 .11
❑ 161 Dan Marino 6.00 2.70
❑ 162 Bernie Parmalee .50 .23
❑ 163 Qadry Ismail .50 .23
❑ 164 Warren Moon .50 .23
❑ 165 Jake Reed .50 .23
❑ 166 Marion Butts .25 .11
❑ 167 Ben Coates .50 .23
❑ 168 Mario Bates 1.00 .45
❑ 169 Quinn Early .50 .23
❑ 170 Jim Everett .25 .11
❑ 171 Rodney Hampton .50 .23
❑ 172 Mike Horan .25 .11
❑ 173 Mike Sherrard .25 .11
❑ 174 Johnny Johnson .25 .11
❑ 175 Adrian Murrell 1.00 .45
❑ 176 Andrew Glover RC .25 .11
❑ 177 Jeff Hostetler .50 .23
❑ 178 Harvey Williams .25 .11
❑ 179 Fred Barnett .50 .23
❑ 180 Vaughn Hebron .25 .11
❑ 181 Jeff Sydner .25 .11
❑ 182 Kevin Greene .50 .23
❑ 183 Byron Bam Morris .50 .23
❑ 184 Neil O'Donnell .50 .23
❑ 185 Stan Humphries .50 .23
❑ 186 Tony Martin .50 .23
❑ 187 Mark Seay .50 .23
❑ 188 William Floyd 1.00 .45
❑ 189 Rickey Jackson .25 .11
❑ 190 Jerry Rice 3.00 1.35
❑ 191 Steve Young 2.50 1.10
❑ 192 Cortez Kennedy .50 .23
❑ 193 Rick Mirer 1.00 .45
❑ 194 Jessie Hester .25 .11
❑ 195 Curtis Martin RC 10.00 4.50
❑ 196 Horace Copeland .25 .11
❑ 197 Charles Wilson .25 .11
❑ 198 Reggie Brooks .50 .23
❑ 199 Brian Mitchell .25 .11
❑ 200 Heath Shuler 1.00 .45
❑ 201 Justin Armour RC .25 .11
❑ 202 Jay Barker RC .25 .11
❑ 203 Zack Crockett RC .25 .11
❑ 204 Christian Fauria RC .25 .11
❑ 205 Antonio Freeman RC 10.00 4.50
❑ 206 Chad May RC .25 .11
❑ 207 Frank Sanders RC 3.00 1.35
❑ 208 Steve Stenstrom RC .25 .11
❑ 209 Lorenzo Styles RC .25 .11
❑ 210 Sherman Williams RC .25 .11
❑ 211 Ray Zellars RC .50 .23
❑ 212 Eric Zeier RC 1.50 .70
❑ 213 Joey Galloway 4.00 1.80
❑ 214 Napoleon Kaufman 3.00 1.35
❑ 215 Rashaan Salaam 1.00 .45
❑ 216 J.J. Stokes 1.00 .45
❑ NNO Steve Beuerlein EE 2.00 .90
❑ NNO Barry Foster EE 2.00 .90
❑ AU9 John Elway AUTO 150.00 70.00
1994 Gems of the
Crown signed card
❑ P1 Natrone Means Promo 1.00 .45
Silver foil
❑ P2 Natrone Means Promo 1.00 .45
Gold foil

1995 Pacific Prisms Connections

	MINT	NRMT
COMPLETE GREEN SET (20)	120.00	55.00

1A-10A: STATED ODDS 1:73 SER.2 RET.
1B-10B: STATED ODDS 1:73 SER.2 HOB.
*BLUE HOLOFOILS: 5X TO 15X BASE CARD HI
BLUE HOLO:10% OF TOTAL PRINT RUN

❑ 1A Steve Young 10.00 4.50
❑ 1B Jerry Rice 12.00 5.50
❑ 2A Dan Marino 25.00 11.00
❑ 2B Irving Fryar 2.00 .90
❑ 3A Drew Bledsoe 12.00 5.50
❑ 3B Ben Coates 2.00 .90
❑ 4A John Elway 25.00 11.00
❑ 4B Shannon Sharpe 2.00 .90
❑ 5A Jeff Hostetler 2.00 .90
❑ 5B Tim Brown 4.00 1.80
❑ 6A Warren Moon 2.00 .90
❑ 6B Cris Carter 4.00 1.80
❑ 7A Neil O'Donnell 2.00 .90
❑ 7B Charles Johnson 2.00 .90
❑ 8A Troy Aikman 12.00 5.50
❑ 8B Michael Irvin 4.00 1.80
❑ 9A Stan Humphries 2.00 .90

		MINT	NRMT
❑ 9B	Shawn Jefferson	1.00	.45
❑ 10A	Jim Kelly	4.00	1.80
❑ 10B	Andre Reed	2.00	.90

1995 Pacific Prisms Kings of the NFL

	MINT	NRMT
COMPLETE SET (10)	250.00	110.00
SER.2 STATED ODDS 1:361		

		MINT	NRMT
❑ 1	Emmitt Smith	40.00	18.00
❑ 2	Steve Young	20.00	9.00
❑ 3	Jerry Rice	25.00	11.00
❑ 4	Deion Sanders	15.00	6.75
❑ 5	Emmitt Smith	40.00	18.00
❑ 6	Dan Marino	50.00	22.00
❑ 7	Drew Bledsoe	25.00	11.00
❑ 8	Barry Sanders	50.00	22.00
❑ 9	Marshall Faulk	12.00	5.50
❑ 10	Marshall Faulk Natrone Means	12.00	5.50

1995 Pacific Prisms Red Hot Rookies

	MINT	NRMT
COMPLETE SET (9)	100.00	45.00
STATED ODDS 1:73 SER.1 HOBBY		

		MINT	NRMT
❑ 1	Ki-Jana Carter	3.00	1.35
❑ 2	Joey Galloway	30.00	13.50
❑ 3	Steve McNair	30.00	13.50
❑ 4	Tyrone Wheatley	15.00	6.75
❑ 5	Kerry Collins	10.00	4.50
❑ 6	Rashaan Salaam	3.00	1.35
❑ 7	Michael Westbrook	20.00	9.00
❑ 8	J.J. Stokes	8.00	3.60
❑ 9	Napoleon Kaufman	25.00	11.00

1995 Pacific Prisms Red Hot Stars

	MINT	NRMT
COMPLETE SET (9)	120.00	55.00
STATED ODDS 1:73 SER.1 RETAIL		

		MINT	NRMT
❑ 1	Barry Sanders	30.00	13.50
❑ 2	Steve Young	12.00	5.50
❑ 3	Emmitt Smith	25.00	11.00

		MINT	NRMT
❑ 4	Drew Bledsoe	15.00	6.75
❑ 5	Natrone Means	5.00	2.20
❑ 6	Dan Marino	30.00	13.50
❑ 7	Marshall Faulk	8.00	3.60
❑ 8	Jerry Rice	15.00	6.75
❑ 9	Errict Rhett	5.00	2.20

1999 Pacific Prisms

	MINT	NRMT
COMPLETE SET (150)	80.00	36.00
COMMON CARD (1-150)	.20	.09
SEMISTARS	.40	.18
UNLISTED STARS	.75	.35
COMMON ROOKIE	1.50	.70
ROOKIE SEMISTARS	2.00	.90

		MINT	NRMT
❑ 1	David Boston RC	3.00	1.35
❑ 2	Rob Moore	.40	.18
❑ 3	Adrian Murrell	.40	.18
❑ 4	Jake Plummer	1.50	.70
❑ 5	Frank Sanders	.40	.18
❑ 6	Jamal Anderson	.75	.35
❑ 7	Chris Chandler	.40	.18
❑ 8	Tim Dwight	.40	.18
❑ 9	Terance Mathis	.40	.18
❑ 10	Peter Boulware	.20	.09
❑ 11	Priest Holmes	.75	.35
❑ 12	Pat Johnson	.20	.09
❑ 13	Jermaine Lewis	.40	.18
❑ 14	Doug Flutie	1.00	.45
❑ 15	Eric Moulds	.75	.35
❑ 16	Peerless Price RC	3.00	1.35
❑ 17	Antowain Smith	.75	.35
❑ 18	Bruce Smith	.40	.18
❑ 19	Steve Beuerlein	.20	.09
❑ 20	Tim Biakabutuka	.40	.18
❑ 21	Muhsin Muhammad	.40	.18
❑ 22	Wesley Walls	.40	.18
❑ 23	Edgar Bennett	.20	.09
❑ 24	Curtis Conway	.40	.18
❑ 25	Bobby Engram	.40	.18
❑ 26	Curtis Enis	.75	.35
❑ 27	Cade McNown RC	6.00	2.70
❑ 28	Jeff Blake	.40	.18
❑ 29	Scott Covington RC	2.00	.90
❑ 30	Corey Dillon	.75	.35
❑ 31	Carl Pickens	.75	.35
❑ 32	Akili Smith RC	4.00	1.80
❑ 33	Craig Yeast RC	1.50	.70
❑ 34	Tim Couch RC	10.00	4.50
❑ 35	Ty Detmer	.40	.18
❑ 36	Kevin Johnson RC	5.00	2.20
❑ 37	Terry Kirby	.20	.09
❑ 38	Leslie Shepherd	.20	.09
❑ 39	Troy Aikman	2.00	.90
❑ 40	Michael Irvin	.40	.18
❑ 41	Deion Sanders	.75	.35
❑ 42	Emmitt Smith	2.00	.90
❑ 43	Bubby Brister	.20	.09
❑ 44	Terrell Davis	2.00	.90
❑ 45	Brian Griese	1.50	.70
❑ 46	Ed McCaffrey	.40	.18
❑ 47	Shannon Sharpe	.40	.18
❑ 48	Rod Smith	.40	.18
❑ 49	Charlie Batch	1.50	.70
❑ 50	Germane Crowell	.40	.18
❑ 51	Sedrick Irvin RC	2.00	.90
❑ 52	Herman Moore	.75	.35
❑ 53	Johnnie Morton	.40	.18
❑ 54	Barry Sanders	3.00	1.35
❑ 55	Mark Chmura	.20	.09
❑ 56	Brett Favre	3.00	1.35
❑ 57	Antonio Freeman	.75	.35
❑ 58	Dorsey Levens	.75	.35
❑ 59	Ken Dilger	.20	.09
❑ 60	Marvin Harrison	.75	.35
❑ 61	Edgerrin James RC	15.00	6.75
❑ 62	Peyton Manning	3.00	1.35
❑ 63	Jerome Pathon	.20	.09
❑ 64	Mark Brunell	1.25	.55
❑ 65	Keenan McCardell	.40	.18
❑ 66	Jimmy Smith	.40	.18
❑ 67	Fred Taylor	2.00	.90
❑ 68	Derrick Alexander WR	.40	.18
❑ 69	Mike Cloud RC	2.00	.90
❑ 70	Tony Gonzalez	.40	.18
❑ 71	Elvis Grbac	.40	.18
❑ 72	Andre Rison	.40	.18
❑ 73	Cecil Collins RC	2.00	.90
❑ 74	Oronde Gadsden	.40	.18
❑ 75	James Johnson RC	2.50	1.10
❑ 76	Dan Marino	3.00	1.35
❑ 77	O.J. McDuffie	.40	.18
❑ 78	Lamar Thomas	.20	.09
❑ 79	Cris Carter	.75	.35
❑ 80	Daunte Culpepper RC	6.00	2.70
❑ 81	Randall Cunningham	.75	.35
❑ 82	Matthew Hatchette	.20	.09
❑ 83	Randy Moss	3.00	1.35
❑ 84	John Randle	.40	.18
❑ 85	Robert Smith	.75	.35
❑ 86	Drew Bledsoe	1.25	.55
❑ 87	Ben Coates	.40	.18
❑ 88	Kevin Faulk RC	2.50	1.10
❑ 89	Terry Glenn	.75	.35
❑ 90	Shawn Jefferson	.20	.09
❑ 91	Cam Cleeland	.20	.09
❑ 92	Billy Joe Hobert	.20	.09
❑ 93	Keith Poole	.20	.09
❑ 94	Ricky Williams RC	10.00	4.50
❑ 95	Gary Brown	.20	.09
❑ 96	Kent Graham	.20	.09
❑ 97	Ike Hilliard	.20	.09
❑ 98	Amani Toomer	.20	.09
❑ 99	Wayne Chrebet	.40	.18
❑ 100	Keyshawn Johnson	.75	.35
❑ 101	Curtis Martin	.75	.35
❑ 102	Vinny Testaverde	.40	.18
❑ 103	Tim Brown	.75	.35
❑ 104	James Jett	.40	.18
❑ 105	Napoleon Kaufman	.75	.35
❑ 106	Charles Woodson	.75	.35
❑ 107	Koy Detmer	.20	.09
❑ 108	Donovan McNabb RC	6.00	2.70
❑ 109	Duce Staley	.75	.35
❑ 110	Kevin Turner	.20	.09
❑ 111	Jerome Bettis	.75	.35
❑ 112	Mark Bruener	.20	.09
❑ 113	Troy Edwards RC	4.00	1.80
❑ 114	Levon Kirkland	.20	.09
❑ 115	Kordell Stewart	.75	.35
❑ 116	Amos Zereoue RC	2.00	.90
❑ 117	Isaac Bruce	.75	.35
❑ 118	Marshall Faulk	.75	.35
❑ 119	Joe Germaine RC	2.00	.90
❑ 120	Trent Green	.40	.18

Card	MINT	NRMT
❑ 121 Torry Holt RC	5.00	2.20
❑ 122 Ryan Leaf	.75	.35
❑ 123 Natrone Means	.40	.18
❑ 124 Mikhael Ricks	.20	.09
❑ 125 Junior Seau	.40	.18
❑ 126 Garrison Hearst	.40	.18
❑ 127 Terrell Owens	.75	.35
❑ 128 Jerry Rice	2.00	.90
❑ 129 J.J. Stokes	.40	.18
❑ 130 Steve Young	1.25	.55
❑ 131 Chad Brown	.20	.09
❑ 132 Joey Galloway	.75	.35
❑ 133 Brock Huard RC	2.50	1.10
❑ 134 Jon Kitna	1.00	.45
❑ 135 Ricky Watters	.40	.18
❑ 136 Mike Alstott	.75	.35
❑ 137 Reidel Anthony	.40	.18
❑ 138 Trent Dilfer	.40	.18
❑ 139 Warrick Dunn	.75	.35
❑ 140 Jacquez Green	.40	.18
❑ 141 Shaun King RC	6.00	2.70
❑ 142 Darnell McDonald RC	2.00	.90
❑ 143 Eddie George	1.00	.45
❑ 144 Steve McNair	.75	.35
❑ 145 Yancey Thigpen	.20	.09
❑ 146 Frank Wycheck	.20	.09
❑ 147 Champ Bailey RC	2.50	1.10
❑ 148 Albert Connell	.20	.09
❑ 149 Skip Hicks	.40	.18
❑ 150 Michael Westbrook	.20	.09

1999 Pacific Prisms Holographic Blue

	MINT	NRMT
COMPLETE SET (150)	1200.00	550.00
*STARS: 10X TO 25X HI COL.		
*YOUNG STARS: 8X TO 20X		
*RCs: 3X TO 8X		
STATED PRINT RUN 80 SER.#'d SETS		
RANDOM INSERTS IN HOBBY/RETAIL		

1999 Pacific Prisms Holographic Gold

	MINT	NRMT
COMPLETE SET (150)	300.00	135.00
*STARS: 2X TO 5X HI COL.		
*YOUNG STARS: 1.5X TO 4X		
*RCs: .8X TO 2X		
STATED PRINT RUN 480 SERIAL #'d SETS		
RANDOM INSERTS IN HOBBY/RETAIL		

1999 Pacific Prisms Holographic Mirror

	MINT	NRMT
COMPLETE SET (150)	800.00	350.00
*STARS: 6X TO 15X HI COL.		
*YOUNG STARS: 5X TO 12X		
*RCs: 2X TO 5X		
STATED PRINT RUN 160 SERIAL #'d SETS		
RANDOM INSERT IN HOBBY/RETAIL		

1999 Pacific Prisms Holographic Purple

	MINT	NRMT
COMPLETE SET (150)	500.00	220.00
*STARS: 3X TO 8X HI COL.		
*YOUNG STARS: 2.5X TO 6X		
*RCs: 1.2X TO 3X		
STATED ODDS 320 SERIAL #'d SETS		
RANDOM INSERTS IN HOBBY		

1999 Pacific Prisms Premiere Date

	MINT	NRMT
COMPLETE SET (150)	1200.00	550.00
*STARS: 10X TO 25X HI COL.		
*YOUNG STARS: 8X TO 20X		
*RCs: 3X TO 8X		
STATED PRINT RUN 61 SERIAL #'d SETS		
ONE PER HOBBY BOX		

1999 Pacific Prisms Dial-a-Stats

	MINT	NRMT
COMPLETE SET (10)	200.00	90.00
COMMON CARD (1-10)	10.00	4.50
STATED ODDS 1:193		
❑ 1 T Couch	40.00	18.00
❑ 2 Emm Smith	25.00	11.00
❑ 3 Ter Davis	25.00	11.00
❑ 4 Bar Sanders	40.00	18.00
❑ 5 Brett Favre	40.00	18.00
❑ 6 Mark Brunell	15.00	6.75
❑ 7 Dan Marino	40.00	18.00
❑ 8 Ricky Williams	40.00	18.00
❑ 9 Curtis Martin	10.00	4.50
❑ 10 Terrell Owens	10.00	4.50

1999 Pacific Prisms Ornaments

	MINT	NRMT
COMPLETE SET (20)	150.00	70.00
COMMON CARD (1-20)	5.00	2.20
STATED ODDS 1:25		
❑ 1 Jake Plummer	10.00	4.50
❑ 2 Jamal Anderson	5.00	2.20
❑ 3 Cade McNown	10.00	4.50
❑ 4 Tim Couch	15.00	6.75
❑ 5 Troy Aikman	12.00	5.50
❑ 6 Deion Sanders	5.00	2.20
❑ 7 Emmitt Smith	12.00	5.50
❑ 8 Terrell Davis	12.00	5.50
❑ 9 Barry Sanders	20.00	9.00
❑ 10 Brett Favre	20.00	9.00
❑ 11 Peyton Manning	15.00	6.75
❑ 12 Mark Brunell	8.00	3.60
❑ 13 Fred Taylor	10.00	4.50
❑ 14 Dan Marino	20.00	9.00
❑ 15 Randy Moss	15.00	6.75
❑ 16 Drew Bledsoe	8.00	3.60
❑ 17 Terrell Owens	5.00	2.20
❑ 18 Jerry Rice	12.00	5.50
❑ 19 Steve Young	8.00	3.60
❑ 20 Jon Kitna	6.00	2.70

1999 Pacific Prisms Prospects

	MINT	NRMT
COMPLETE SET (10)	80.00	36.00
COMMON CARD (1-10)	4.00	1.80
SEMISTARS	5.00	2.20
STATED ODDS 1:97 HOBBY		
❑ 1 David Boston	4.00	1.80
❑ 2 Cade McNown	10.00	4.50
❑ 3 Akili Smith	6.00	2.70
❑ 4 Tim Couch	15.00	6.75
❑ 5 Edgerrin James	25.00	11.00
❑ 6 Cecil Collins	4.00	1.80

Card	MINT	NRMT
❑ 7 Daunte Culpepper	10.00	4.50
❑ 8 Ricky Williams	15.00	6.75
❑ 9 Donovan McNabb	10.00	4.50
❑ 10 Torry Holt	8.00	3.60

1999 Pacific Prisms Sunday's Best

	MINT	NRMT
COMPLETE SET (20)	80.00	36.00
COMMON CARD (1-20)	2.50	1.10
STATED ODDS 2:25		
❑ 1 Jake Plummer	5.00	2.20
❑ 2 Akili Smith	4.00	1.80
❑ 3 Tim Couch	10.00	4.50
❑ 4 Emmitt Smith	6.00	2.70
❑ 5 Terrell Davis	6.00	2.70
❑ 6 Barry Sanders	10.00	4.50
❑ 7 Brett Favre	10.00	4.50
❑ 8 Peyton Manning	8.00	3.60
❑ 9 Mark Brunell	4.00	1.80
❑ 10 Fred Taylor	5.00	2.20
❑ 11 Dan Marino	10.00	4.50
❑ 12 Randy Moss	8.00	3.60
❑ 13 Drew Bledsoe	4.00	1.80
❑ 14 Ricky Williams	10.00	4.50
❑ 15 Curtis Martin	2.50	1.10
❑ 16 Terrell Owens	2.50	1.10
❑ 17 Jerry Rice	6.00	2.70
❑ 18 Steve Young	4.00	1.80
❑ 19 Jon Kitna	3.00	1.35
❑ 20 Eddie George	3.00	1.35

1998 Paramount

	MINT	NRMT
COMPLETE SET (250)	40.00	18.00
COMMON CARD (1-250)	.10	.05
SEMISTARS	.20	.09
UNLISTED STARS	.40	.18
COMP.COPPER SET (250)	80.00	36.00
*COPPER STARS: 1.5X TO 3X HI COL.		
*COPPER YOUNG STARS: 1.25X TO 2.5X		
*COPPER RCs: .6X TO 1.5X		
COPPERS ONE PER HOBBY PACK		
COMMON PLAT.BLUE (1-250)	15.00	6.75
*PLAT.BLUE STARS: 40X TO 80X HI COL.		
*PLAT.BLUE YOUNG STARS: 30X TO 60X		
*PLAT.BLUE RCs: 12.5X TO 25X		

PLAT.BLUE STATED ODDS 1:73
COMP.SILVER SET (250) 80.00 36.00
*SILVER STARS: 1.5X TO 3X HI COL.
*SILVER YOUNG STARS: 1.25X TO 2.5X
*SILVER RCs: .6X TO 1.5X ....
SILVERS ONE PER RETAIL PACK
COMP.RED SET (250)......... 120.00 55.00
*RED STARS: 1.5X TO 4X HI COL.
*RED YOUNG STARS: 1.25X TO 3X
*RED RCs: .75X TO 2X ....
REDS ONE PER SPECIAL RETAIL PACK

❑ 1	Larry Centers	.10	.05
❑ 2	Chris Gedney	.10	.05
❑ 3	Rob Moore	.20	.09
❑ 4	Jake Plummer	1.00	.45
❑ 5	Simeon Rice	.20	.09
❑ 6	Frank Sanders	.20	.09
❑ 7	Mark Smith DE	.10	.05
❑ 8	Eric Swann	.10	.05
❑ 9	Jamal Anderson	.40	.18
❑ 10	Chris Chandler	.20	.09
❑ 11	Bert Emanuel	.20	.09
❑ 12	Tony Graziani	.10	.05
❑ 13	Byron Hanspard	.20	.09
❑ 14	Terance Mathis	.20	.09
❑ 15	O.J. Santiago	.10	.05
❑ 16	Chuck Smith	.10	.05
❑ 17	Derrick Alexander WR	.20	.09
❑ 18	Peter Boulware	.10	.05
❑ 19	Jay Graham	.10	.05
❑ 20	Priest Holmes RC	6.00	2.70
❑ 21	Michael Jackson	.10	.05
❑ 22	Byron Bam Morris	.10	.05
❑ 23	Vinny Testaverde	.20	.09
❑ 24	Eric Zeier	.20	.09
❑ 25	Todd Collins	.10	.05
❑ 26	Quinn Early	.10	.05
❑ 27	Bryce Paup	.10	.05
❑ 28	Andre Reed	.20	.09
❑ 29	Jay Riemersma	.10	.05
❑ 30	Antowain Smith	.40	.18
❑ 31	Bruce Smith	.20	.09
❑ 32	Thurman Thomas	.40	.18
❑ 33	Michael Bates	.10	.05
❑ 34	Mark Carrier WR	.10	.05
❑ 35	Rae Carruth	.20	.09
❑ 36	Kerry Collins	.20	.09
❑ 37	Fred Lane	.20	.09
❑ 38	Lamar Lathon	.10	.05
❑ 39	Muhsin Muhammad	.20	.09
❑ 40	Wesley Walls	.20	.09
❑ 41	Darnell Autry	.10	.05
❑ 42	Curtis Conway	.20	.09
❑ 43	Raymont Harris	.10	.05
❑ 44	Tyrone Hughes	.10	.05
❑ 45	Chris Penn	.10	.05
❑ 46	Ricky Proehl	.10	.05
❑ 47	Steve Stenstrom	.10	.05
❑ 48	Ryan Wetnight RC	.10	.05
❑ 49	Jeff Blake	.20	.09
❑ 50	Ki-Jana Carter	.10	.05
❑ 51	Corey Dillon	.50	.23
❑ 52	David Dunn	.10	.05
❑ 53	Boomer Esiason	.10	.05
❑ 54	Brian Milne	.10	.05
❑ 55	Carl Pickens	.40	.18
❑ 56	Darnay Scott	.20	.09
❑ 57	Troy Aikman	1.00	.45
❑ 58	Eric Bjornson	.10	.05
❑ 59	Michael Irvin	.40	.18
❑ 60	Daryl Johnston	.20	.09
❑ 61	Anthony Miller	.10	.05
❑ 62	Deion Sanders	.40	.18
❑ 63	Emmitt Smith	1.50	.70
❑ 64	Omar Stoutmire RC	.10	.05
❑ 65	Sherman Williams	.10	.05
❑ 66	Terrell Davis	1.50	.70
❑ 67	John Elway	2.00	.90
❑ 68	Darrien Gordon	.10	.05
❑ 69	Ed McCaffrey	.20	.09
❑ 70	Bill Romanowski	.10	.05
❑ 71	Shannon Sharpe	.20	.09
❑ 72	Neil Smith	.20	.09
❑ 73	Rod Smith WR	.20	.09
❑ 74	Maa Tanuvasa	.10	.05
❑ 75	Tommie Boyd	.10	.05
❑ 76	Glyn Milburn	.10	.05
❑ 77	Scott Mitchell	.20	.09
❑ 78	Herman Moore	.40	.18
❑ 79	Johnnie Morton	.20	.09
❑ 80	Robert Porcher	.10	.05
❑ 81	Barry Sanders	2.00	.90
❑ 82	Bryant Westbrook	.10	.05
❑ 83	Robert Brooks	.20	.09
❑ 84	LeRoy Butler	.10	.05
❑ 85	Mark Chmura	.20	.09
❑ 86	Brett Favre	2.00	.90
❑ 87	Antonio Freeman	.40	.18
❑ 88	Dorsey Levens	.40	.18
❑ 89	Eugene Robinson	.10	.05
❑ 90	Bill Schroeder RC	6.00	2.70
❑ 91	Reggie White	.40	.18
❑ 92	Aaron Bailey	.10	.05
❑ 93	Quentin Coryatt	.10	.05
❑ 94	Zack Crockett	.10	.05
❑ 95	Sean Dawkins	.10	.05
❑ 96	Ken Dilger	.10	.05
❑ 97	Marshall Faulk	.40	.18
❑ 98	Jim Harbaugh	.20	.09
❑ 99	Marvin Harrison	.20	.09
❑ 100	Bryan Barker	.10	.05
❑ 101	Tony Boselli	.10	.05
❑ 102	Tony Brackens	.10	.05
❑ 103	Mark Brunell	.75	.35
❑ 104	Mike Hollis	.10	.05
❑ 105	Keenan McCardell	.20	.09
❑ 106	Natrone Means	.40	.18
❑ 107	Jimmy Smith	.20	.09
❑ 108	James Stewart	.20	.09
❑ 109	Marcus Allen	.40	.18
❑ 110	Kimble Anders	.20	.09
❑ 111	Dale Carter	.10	.05
❑ 112	Tony Gonzalez	.10	.05
❑ 113	Elvis Grbac	.20	.09
❑ 114	Greg Hill	.10	.05
❑ 115	Andre Rison	.20	.09
❑ 116	Will Shields	.10	.05
❑ 117	Derrick Thomas	.20	.09
❑ 118	Karim Abdul-Jabbar	.40	.18
❑ 119	Trace Armstrong	.10	.05
❑ 120	Damon Huard RC	12.00	5.50
❑ 121	Charles Jordan	.10	.05
❑ 122	Dan Marino	2.00	.90
❑ 123	O.J. McDuffie	.20	.09
❑ 124	Irving Spikes	.10	.05
❑ 125	Zach Thomas	.10	.05
❑ 126	Cris Carter	.40	.18
❑ 127	Charles Woodson RC	2.50	1.10
❑ 128	Brad Johnson	.40	.18
❑ 129	Randall McDaniel	.10	.05
❑ 130	John Randle	.20	.09
❑ 131	Jake Reed	.20	.09
❑ 132	Robert Smith	.40	.18
❑ 133	Todd Steussie	.10	.05
❑ 134	Bruce Armstrong	.10	.05
❑ 135	Drew Bledsoe	.75	.35
❑ 136	Ben Coates	.20	.09
❑ 137	Derrick Cullors RC	.20	.09
❑ 138	Terry Glenn	.40	.18
❑ 139	Shawn Jefferson	.10	.05
❑ 140	Curtis Martin	.40	.18
❑ 141	Chris Slade	.10	.05
❑ 142	Larry Whigham	.10	.05
❑ 143	Troy Davis	.10	.05
❑ 144	Andre Hastings	.10	.05
❑ 145	Randal Hill	.10	.05
❑ 146	Sammy Knight RC	.10	.05
❑ 147	William Roaf	.10	.05
❑ 148	Heath Shuler	.10	.05
❑ 149	Danny Wuerffel	.20	.09
❑ 150	Ray Zellars	.10	.05
❑ 151	Jessie Armstead	.10	.05
❑ 152	Tiki Barber	.20	.09
❑ 153	Chris Calloway	.10	.05
❑ 154	Danny Kanell	.20	.09
❑ 155	David Patten RC	.40	.18
❑ 156	Michael Strahan	.10	.05
❑ 157	Charles Way	.10	.05
❑ 158	Tyrone Wheatley	.20	.09
❑ 159	Kyle Brady	.10	.05
❑ 160	Wayne Chrebet	.40	.18
❑ 161	Glenn Foley	.20	.09
❑ 162	Aaron Glenn	.10	.05
❑ 163	Leon Johnson	.10	.05
❑ 164	Adrian Murrell	.20	.09
❑ 165	Neil O'Donnell	.20	.09
❑ 166	Dedric Ward	.10	.05
❑ 167	Tim Brown	.40	.18
❑ 168	Rickey Dudley	.10	.05
❑ 169	Jeff George	.20	.09
❑ 170	Desmond Howard	.20	.09
❑ 171	James Jett	.20	.09
❑ 172	Napoleon Kaufman	.40	.18
❑ 173	Chester McGlockton	.10	.05
❑ 174	Darrell Russell	.10	.05
❑ 175	Ty Detmer	.20	.09
❑ 176	Irving Fryar	.20	.09
❑ 177	Charlie Garner	.10	.05
❑ 178	Bobby Hoying	.20	.09
❑ 179	Chad Lewis	.10	.05
❑ 180	Duce Staley	.75	.35
❑ 181	Kevin Turner	.10	.05
❑ 182	Ricky Watters	.20	.09
❑ 183	Jerome Bettis	.40	.18
❑ 184	Will Blackwell	.10	.05
❑ 185	Charles Johnson	.10	.05
❑ 186	George Jones	.10	.05
❑ 187	Levon Kirkland	.10	.05
❑ 188	Carnell Lake	.10	.05
❑ 189	Kordell Stewart	.40	.18
❑ 190	Yancey Thigpen	.10	.05
❑ 191	Tony Banks	.20	.09
❑ 192	Isaac Bruce	.40	.18
❑ 193	Ernie Conwell	.10	.05
❑ 194	Craig Heyward	.10	.05
❑ 195	Eddie Kennison	.20	.09
❑ 196	Amp Lee	.10	.05
❑ 197	Orlando Pace	.10	.05
❑ 198	Torrance Small	.10	.05
❑ 199	Gary Brown	.10	.05
❑ 200	Kenny Bynum RC	.10	.05
❑ 201	Freddie Jones	.10	.05
❑ 202	Tony Martin	.20	.09
❑ 203	Eric Metcalf	.10	.05
❑ 204	Junior Seau	.20	.09
❑ 205	Craig Whelihan RC	.10	.05
❑ 206	William Floyd	.10	.05
❑ 207	Merton Hanks	.10	.05
❑ 208	Garrison Hearst	.40	.18
❑ 209	Brent Jones	.10	.05
❑ 210	Terrell Owens	.40	.18
❑ 211	Jerry Rice	1.00	.45
❑ 212	J.J. Stokes	.20	.09
❑ 213	Rod Woodson	.20	.09
❑ 214	Steve Young	.50	.23
❑ 215	Steve Broussard	.10	.05
❑ 216	Joey Galloway	.40	.18
❑ 217	Cortez Kennedy	.10	.05
❑ 218	Jon Kitna	1.25	.55
❑ 219	James McKnight	.10	.05
❑ 220	Warren Moon	.40	.18
❑ 221	Michael Sinclair	.10	.05
❑ 222	Ryan Leaf RC	2.00	.90
❑ 223	Darryl Williams	.10	.05
❑ 224	Mike Alstott	.40	.18
❑ 225	Reidel Anthony	.20	.09
❑ 226	Derrick Brooks	.10	.05
❑ 227	Horace Copeland	.10	.05
❑ 228	Trent Dilfer	.40	.18

❑ 229 Warrick Dunn	.50	.23
❑ 230 Hardy Nickerson	.10	.05
❑ 231 Warren Sapp	.20	.09
❑ 232 Karl Williams	.10	.05
❑ 233 Blaine Bishop	.10	.05
❑ 234 Willie Davis	.10	.05
❑ 235 Eddie George	.75	.35
❑ 236 Derrick Mason	.10	.05
❑ 237 Bruce Matthews	.10	.05
❑ 238 Steve McNair	.40	.18
❑ 239 Chris Sanders	.10	.05
❑ 240 Rodney Thomas	.10	.05
❑ 241 Frank Wycheck	.10	.05
❑ 242 Terry Allen	.40	.18
❑ 243 Jamie Asher	.10	.05
❑ 244 Larry Bowie	.10	.05
❑ 245 Albert Connell	.10	.05
❑ 246 Stephen Davis	.10	.05
❑ 247 Gus Frerotte	.10	.05
❑ 248 Ken Harvey	.10	.05
❑ 249 Leslie Shepherd	.10	.05
❑ 250 Michael Westbrook	.20	.09
❑ S1 Mark Brunell Sample	1.00	.45

1998 Paramount Kings of the NFL

	MINT	NRMT
COMPLETE SET (20)	250.00	110.00
COMMON CARD (1-20)	8.00	3.60
STATED ODDS 1:73		

*PROOF CARDS: 7.5X TO 20X HI COL.
PROOFS STATED PRINT RUN 20 SETS

❑ 1 Antowain Smith	8.00	3.60
❑ 2 Corey Dillon	12.00	5.50
❑ 3 Troy Aikman	15.00	6.75
❑ 4 Emmitt Smith	25.00	11.00
❑ 5 Terrell Davis	25.00	11.00
❑ 6 John Elway	30.00	13.50
❑ 7 Barry Sanders	30.00	13.50
❑ 8 Brett Favre	30.00	13.50
❑ 9 Dorsey Levens	8.00	3.60
❑ 10 Reggie White	8.00	3.60
❑ 11 Mark Brunell	12.00	5.50
❑ 12 Dan Marino	30.00	13.50
❑ 13 Curtis Martin	8.00	3.60
❑ 14 Drew Bledsoe	12.00	5.50
❑ 15 Jerome Bettis	8.00	3.60
❑ 16 Kordell Stewart	8.00	3.60
❑ 17 Jerry Rice	15.00	6.75
❑ 18 Steve Young	10.00	4.50
❑ 19 Warrick Dunn	12.00	5.50
❑ 20 Eddie George	12.00	5.50

1998 Paramount Personal Bests

	MINT	NRMT
COMPLETE SET (36)	100.00	45.00
COMMON CARD (1-36)	2.00	.90
SEMISTARS	3.00	1.35
STATED ODDS 4:37		

❑ 1 Jake Plummer	6.00	2.70
❑ 2 Antowain Smith	3.00	1.35
❑ 3 Kerry Collins	3.00	1.35
❑ 4 Raymont Harris	2.00	.90
❑ 5 Corey Dillon	6.00	2.70
❑ 6 Troy Aikman	6.00	2.70
❑ 7 Deion Sanders	3.00	1.35
❑ 8 Emmitt Smith	10.00	4.50
❑ 9 Terrell Davis	10.00	4.50
❑ 10 John Elway	12.00	5.50
❑ 11 Shannon Sharpe	3.00	1.35
❑ 12 Herman Moore	3.00	1.35
❑ 13 Barry Sanders	12.00	5.50
❑ 14 Brett Favre	12.00	5.50
❑ 15 Antonio Freeman	3.00	1.35
❑ 16 Dorsey Levens	3.00	1.35
❑ 17 Marshall Faulk	3.00	1.35
❑ 18 Mark Brunell	5.00	2.20
❑ 19 Dan Marino	12.00	5.50
❑ 20 Robert Smith	3.00	1.35
❑ 21 Curtis Martin	3.00	1.35
❑ 22 Drew Bledsoe	5.00	2.20
❑ 23 Danny Kanell	3.00	1.35
❑ 24 Adrian Murrell	3.00	1.35
❑ 25 Napoleon Kaufman	3.00	1.35
❑ 26 Jerome Bettis	3.00	1.35
❑ 27 Kordell Stewart	3.00	1.35
❑ 28 Terrell Owens	3.00	1.35
❑ 29 Jerry Rice	6.00	2.70
❑ 30 Steve Young	4.00	1.80
❑ 31 Warren Moon	3.00	1.35
❑ 32 Mike Alstott	3.00	1.35
❑ 33 Trent Dilfer	3.00	1.35
❑ 34 Warrick Dunn	6.00	2.70
❑ 35 Eddie George	5.00	2.20
❑ 36 Steve McNair	3.00	1.35

1998 Paramount Pro Bowl Die Cuts

	MINT	NRMT
COMPLETE SET (20)	150.00	70.00
COMMON CARD (1-20)	4.00	1.80
SEMISTARS	6.00	2.70
STATED ODDS 1:37		

❑ 1 Terrell Davis	15.00	6.75
❑ 2 John Elway	25.00	11.00
❑ 3 Shannon Sharpe	6.00	2.70
❑ 4 Herman Moore	7.00	3.10
❑ 5 Barry Sanders	25.00	11.00
❑ 6 Mark Chmura	6.00	2.70
❑ 7 Brett Favre	25.00	11.00
❑ 8 Dorsey Levens	7.00	3.10
❑ 9 Mark Brunell	10.00	4.50
❑ 10 Andre Rison	4.00	1.80
❑ 11 Cris Carter	7.00	3.10
❑ 12 Drew Bledsoe	10.00	4.50
❑ 13 Ben Coates	6.00	2.70
❑ 14 Jerome Bettis	7.00	3.10
❑ 15 Steve Young	8.00	3.60
❑ 16 Warren Moon	7.00	3.10
❑ 17 Mike Alstott	7.00	3.10
❑ 18 Trent Dilfer	7.00	3.10
❑ 19 Warrick Dunn	10.00	4.50
❑ 20 Eddie George	10.00	4.50

1998 Paramount Super Bowl XXXII

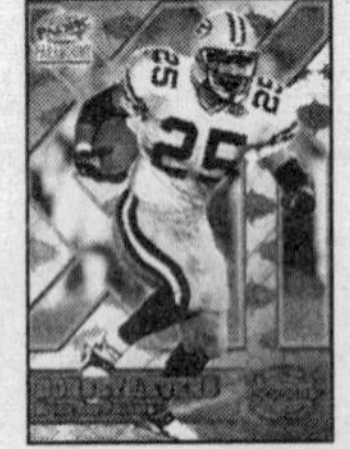

	MINT	NRMT
COMPLETE SET (10)	60.00	27.00
COMMON CARD (1-10)	3.00	1.35
SEMISTARS	5.00	2.20
STATED ODDS 2:37		

❑ 1 Terrell Davis	12.00	5.50
❑ 2 John Elway	15.00	6.75
❑ 3 John Elway	15.00	6.75
❑ 4 Brett Favre	20.00	9.00
❑ 5 Antonio Freeman	8.00	3.60
❑ 6 Dorsey Levens	8.00	3.60
❑ 7 Ed McCaffrey	5.00	2.20
❑ 8 Eugene Robinson	3.00	1.35
❑ 9 Bill Romanowski	3.00	1.35
❑ 10 Darren Sharper	3.00	1.35

1999 Paramount

	MINT	NRMT
COMPLETE SET (250)	50.00	22.00
COMMON CARD (1-250)	.10	.05
SEMISTARS	.20	.09
UNLISTED STARS	.40	.18
COMMON ROOKIE	.40	.18
ROOKIE SEMISTARS	.75	.35
ROOKIE UNL.STARS	1.25	.55
COMP.COPPER SET (250)	120.00	55.00

*COPPER STARS: 1.25X TO 3X HI COL.
*COPPER YOUNG STARS: 1X TO 2.5X
*COPPER RC's: .5X TO 1.2X
COPPERS ONE PER HOBBY PACK

COMP.GOLD SET (250)	120.00	55.00

*GOLD STARS: 1.25X TO 3X HI COL.

*GOLD YOUNG STARS: 1X TO 2.5X
*GOLD RC's .5X TO 1.2X
GOLDS ONE PER RETAIL PACK

❑	1	David Boston RC	2.00	.90
❑	2	Larry Centers	.10	.05
❑	3	Joel Makovicka RC	1.25	.55
❑	4	Eric Metcalf	.10	.05
❑	5	Rob Moore	.20	.09
❑	6	Adrian Murrell	.20	.09
❑	7	Jake Plummer	.75	.35
❑	8	Frank Sanders	.20	.09
❑	9	Aeneas Williams	.10	.05
❑	10	Morten Andersen	.10	.05
❑	11	Jamal Anderson	.40	.18
❑	12	Chris Chandler	.20	.09
❑	13	Tim Dwight	.40	.18
❑	14	Terance Mathis	.20	.09
❑	15	Jeff Paulk RC	1.25	.55
❑	16	O.J. Santiago	.10	.05
❑	17	Chuck Smith	.10	.05
❑	18	Peter Boulware	.10	.05
❑	19	Priest Holmes	.40	.18
❑	20	Michael Jackson	.10	.05
❑	21	Jermaine Lewis	.20	.09
❑	22	Ray Lewis	.10	.05
❑	23	Michael McCrary	.10	.05
❑	24	Bennie Thompson	.10	.05
❑	25	Rod Woodson	.20	.09
❑	26	Shawn Bryson RC	.40	.18
❑	27	Doug Flutie	.50	.23
❑	28	Eric Moulds	.40	.18
❑	29	Peerless Price RC	2.00	.90
❑	30	Andre Reed	.20	.09
❑	31	Jay Riemersma	.10	.05
❑	32	Antowain Smith	.40	.18
❑	33	Bruce Smith	.20	.09
❑	34	Michael Bates	.10	.05
❑	35	Steve Beuerlein	.10	.05
❑	36	Tim Biakabutuka	.20	.09
❑	37	Kevin Greene	.10	.05
❑	38	Anthony Johnson	.10	.05
❑	39	Fred Lane	.10	.05
❑	40	Muhsin Muhammad	.20	.09
❑	41	Wesley Walls	.20	.09
❑	42	D'Wayne Bates RC	.75	.35
❑	43	Edgar Bennett	.10	.05
❑	44	Marty Booker RC	.75	.35
❑	45	Curtis Conway	.20	.09
❑	46	Bobby Engram	.20	.09
❑	47	Curtis Enis	.40	.18
❑	48	Erik Kramer	.10	.05
❑	49	Cade McNown RC	4.00	1.80
❑	50	Jeff Blake	.20	.09
❑	51	Scott Covington RC	1.25	.55
❑	52	Corey Dillon	.40	.18
❑	53	Quincy Jackson RC	.75	.35
❑	54	Carl Pickens	.20	.09
❑	55	Darnay Scott	.10	.05
❑	56	Akili Smith RC	2.50	1.10
❑	57	Craig Yeast RC	.75	.35
❑	58	Jerry Ball	.10	.05
❑	59	Darrin Chiaverini RC	.75	.35
❑	60	Tim Couch RC	6.00	2.70
❑	61	Ty Detmer	.20	.09
❑	62	Kevin Johnson RC	3.00	1.35
❑	63	Terry Kirby	.10	.05
❑	64	Daylon McCutcheon RC	.40	.18
❑	65	Irv Smith	.10	.05
❑	66	Troy Aikman	1.00	.45
❑	67	Ebenezer Ekuban RC	.75	.35
❑	68	Michael Irvin	.20	.09
❑	69	Daryl Johnston	.10	.05
❑	70	Wane McGarity RC	.75	.35
❑	71	Dat Nguyen RC	1.25	.55
❑	72	Deion Sanders	.40	.18
❑	73	Emmitt Smith	1.00	.45
❑	74	Bubby Brister	.10	.05
❑	75	Terrell Davis	1.00	.45
❑	76	Jason Elam	.10	.05
❑	77	Olandis Gary RC	4.00	1.80
❑	78	Brian Griese	.75	.35
❑	79	Ed McCaffrey	.20	.09
❑	80	Travis McGriff RC	1.25	.55
❑	81	Shannon Sharpe	.20	.09
❑	82	Rod Smith	.20	.09
❑	83	Charlie Batch	.75	.35
❑	84	Chris Claiborne RC	.75	.35
❑	85	Germane Crowell	.20	.09
❑	86	Sedrick Irvin RC	1.25	.55
❑	87	Herman Moore	.40	.18
❑	88	Johnnie Morton	.20	.09
❑	89	Barry Sanders	1.50	.70
❑	90	Robert Brooks	.20	.09
❑	91	Aaron Brooks RC	1.25	.55
❑	92	Mark Chmura	.10	.05
❑	93	Brett Favre	1.50	.70
❑	94	Antonio Freeman	.40	.18
❑	95	Vonnie Holliday	.10	.05
❑	96	Dorsey Levens	.40	.18
❑	97	De'Mond Parker RC	1.25	.55
❑	98	Ken Dilger	.10	.05
❑	99	Marvin Harrison	.40	.18
❑	100	Edgerrin James RC	10.00	4.50
❑	101	Peyton Manning	1.50	.70
❑	102	Jerome Pathon	.10	.05
❑	103	Mike Peterson RC	.75	.35
❑	104	Marcus Pollard	.10	.05
❑	105	Tavian Banks	.10	.05
❑	106	Reggie Barlow	.10	.05
❑	107	Tony Boselli	.10	.05
❑	108	Mark Brunell	.60	.25
❑	109	Keenan McCardell	.20	.09
❑	110	Bryce Paup	.10	.05
❑	111	Jimmy Smith	.20	.09
❑	112	Fred Taylor	1.00	.45
❑	113	Dave Thomas RC	.10	.05
❑	114	Kimble Anders	.20	.09
❑	115	Donnell Bennett	.10	.05
❑	116	Mike Cloud RC	1.25	.55
❑	117	Tony Gonzalez	.20	.09
❑	118	Elvis Grbac	.20	.09
❑	119	Larry Parker RC	.75	.35
❑	120	Andre Rison	.20	.09
❑	121	Brian Shay RC	.75	.35
❑	122	Karim Abdul-Jabbar	.20	.09
❑	123	Oronde Gadsden	.10	.05
❑	124	James Johnson RC	1.50	.70
❑	125	Rob Konrad RC	.75	.35
❑	126	Dan Marino	1.50	.70
❑	127	O.J. McDuffie	.20	.09
❑	128	Zach Thomas	.20	.09
❑	129	Cris Carter	.40	.18
❑	130	Daunte Culpepper RC	4.00	1.80
❑	131	Randall Cunningham	.40	.18
❑	132	Matthew Hatchette	.10	.05
❑	133	Leroy Hoard	.10	.05
❑	134	Randy Moss	1.50	.70
❑	135	John Randle	.20	.09
❑	136	Jake Reed	.20	.09
❑	137	Robert Smith	.40	.18
❑	138	Michael Bishop RC	1.50	.70
❑	139	Drew Bledsoe	.60	.25
❑	140	Ben Coates	.20	.09
❑	141	Kevin Faulk RC	1.50	.70
❑	142	Terry Glenn	.40	.18
❑	143	Shawn Jefferson	.10	.05
❑	144	Andy Katzenmoyer RC	1.25	.55
❑	145	Tony Simmons	.10	.05
❑	146	Cuncho Brown RC	.75	.35
❑	147	Cam Cleeland	.10	.05
❑	148	Mark Fields	.10	.05
❑	149	La'Roi Glover	.10	.05
❑	150	Andre Hastings	.10	.05
❑	151	Billy Joe Hobert	.10	.05
❑	152	William Roaf	.10	.05
❑	153	Billy Joe Tolliver	.10	.05
❑	154	Ricky Williams RC	6.00	2.70
❑	155	Jessie Armstead	.10	.05
❑	156	Tiki Barber	.10	.05
❑	157	Gary Brown	.10	.05
❑	158	Kent Graham	.10	.05
❑	159	Ike Hilliard	.10	.05
❑	160	Joe Montgomery RC	1.25	.55
❑	161	Amani Toomer	.10	.05
❑	162	Charles Way	.10	.05
❑	163	Wayne Chrebet	.20	.09
❑	164	Bryan Cox	.10	.05
❑	165	Aaron Glenn	.10	.05
❑	166	Keyshawn Johnson	.40	.18
❑	167	Leon Johnson	.10	.05
❑	168	Curtis Martin	.40	.18
❑	169	Vinny Testaverde	.20	.09
❑	170	Dedric Ward	.10	.05
❑	171	Tim Brown	.40	.18
❑	172	Dameane Douglas RC	1.25	.55
❑	173	Rickey Dudley	.10	.05
❑	174	James Jett	.20	.09
❑	175	Napoleon Kaufman	.40	.18
❑	176	Darrell Russell	.10	.05
❑	177	Harvey Williams	.10	.05
❑	178	Charles Woodson	.40	.18
❑	179	Na Brown RC	1.25	.55
❑	180	Hugh Douglas	.10	.05
❑	181	Cecil Martin RC	.75	.35
❑	182	Donovan McNabb RC	4.00	1.80
❑	183	Duce Staley	.40	.18
❑	184	Kevin Turner	.10	.05
❑	185	Jerome Bettis	.40	.18
❑	186	Troy Edwards RC	2.00	.90
❑	187	Jason Gildon	.10	.05
❑	188	Courtney Hawkins	.10	.05
❑	189	Malcolm Johnson RC	.75	.35
❑	190	Kordell Stewart	.40	.18
❑	191	Jerame Tuman RC	.75	.35
❑	192	Amos Zereoue RC	1.25	.55
❑	193	Isaac Bruce	.40	.18
❑	194	Kevin Carter	.10	.05
❑	195	Jeremaine Copeland RC	.75	.35
❑	196	Joe Germaine RC	1.25	.55
❑	197	Az-Zahir Hakim	.10	.05
❑	198	Torry Holt RC	3.00	1.35
❑	199	Amp Lee	.10	.05
❑	200	Ricky Proehl	.10	.05
❑	201	Charlie Jones	.10	.05
❑	202	Freddie Jones	.10	.05
❑	203	Ryan Leaf	.40	.18
❑	204	Natrone Means	.20	.09
❑	205	Mikhael Ricks	.10	.05
❑	206	Junior Seau	.20	.09
❑	207	Bryan Still	.10	.05
❑	208	Garrison Hearst	.20	.09
❑	209	Terry Jackson RC	.75	.35
❑	210	R.W. McQuarters	.10	.05
❑	211	Ken Norton Jr.	.10	.05
❑	212	Terrell Owens	.40	.18
❑	213	Jerry Rice	1.00	.45
❑	214	J.J. Stokes	.20	.09
❑	215	Tai Streets RC	.75	.35
❑	216	Steve Young	.60	.25
❑	217	Karsten Bailey RC	.75	.35
❑	218	Chad Brown	.10	.05
❑	219	Joey Galloway	.40	.18
❑	220	Ahman Green	.20	.09
❑	221	Brock Huard RC	1.50	.70
❑	222	Cortez Kennedy	.10	.05
❑	223	Jon Kitna	.50	.23
❑	224	Shawn Springs	.10	.05
❑	225	Ricky Watters	.20	.09
❑	226	Mike Alstott	.40	.18
❑	227	Reidel Anthony	.20	.09
❑	228	Trent Dilfer	.20	.09
❑	229	Warrick Dunn	.40	.18
❑	230	Bert Emanuel	.20	.09
❑	231	Martin Gramatica RC	.40	.18
❑	232	Jacquez Green	.20	.09
❑	233	Shaun King RC	4.00	1.80
❑	234	Anthony McFarland RC	1.25	.55
❑	235	Warren Sapp	.20	.09
❑	236	Willie Davis	.10	.05
❑	237	Kevin Dyson	.20	.09
❑	238	Eddie George	.50	.23
❑	239	Darran Hall RC	.75	.35
❑	240	Jackie Harris	.10	.05
❑	241	Steve McNair	.40	.18
❑	242	Yancey Thigpen	.10	.05
❑	243	Frank Wycheck	.10	.05
❑	244	Stephen Alexander	.10	.05
❑	245	Champ Bailey RC	1.50	.70
❑	246	Stephen Davis	.40	.18
❑	247	Darrell Green	.10	.05
❑	248	Skip Hicks	.40	.18
❑	249	Brian Mitchell	.10	.05
❑	250	Michael Westbrook	.20	.09

1999 Paramount Premiere Date

	MINT	NRMT
COMMON PREMIERE DATE	10.00	4.50

*PREMIERE DATE STARS: 25X TO 60X HI COL.
*PREMIERE DATE YOUNG STARS: 20X TO 50X
*PREMIERE DATE DAY RCs: 6X TO 15X
PREM.DATE STATED ODDS 1:37 HOB
PREMIERE DATE PRINT RUN 62 SER.#'d SETS

1999 Paramount HoloGold

	MINT	NRMT
COMMON HOLO.GOLD (1-250)	3.00	1.35

*HOLO.GOLD STARS: 12X TO 30X HI COL.
*HOLO.GOLD YOUNG STARS: 10X TO 25X
*HOLO.GOLD RCs: 2.5X TO 6X ..
HOLO.GOLD PRINT RUN 199 SERIAL #'d SETS
HOLO.GOLDS INSERTED IN RETAIL PACKS

1999 Paramount HoloSilver

	MINT	NRMT
COMMON HOLO.SILVER (1-250)	6.00	2.70

*HOLO.SILVER STARS: 20X TO 50X HI COL.
*HOLO.SILVER YOUNG STARS: 15X TO 40X
*HOLO.SILVER RCs: 5X TO 12X
HOLO.SILVER PRINT RUN 99 SERIAL #'d SETS
HOLO.SILVER INSERTED IN HOBBY PACKS

1999 Paramount Platinum Blue

	MINT	NRMT
COMMON PLAT.BLUE	6.00	2.70

*PLATINUM BLUE STARS: 25X TO 60X HI COL.
*PLATINUM BLUE YOUNG STARS: 20X TO 50X
*PLATINUM BLUE RCs: 5X TO 12X
PLATINUM BLUE STATED ODDS 1:73

1999 Paramount Canton Bound

	MINT	NRMT
COMPLETE SET (10)	250.00	110.00
COMMON CARD (1-10)	20.00	9.00

STATED ODDS 1:361
*PROOFS: 1.2X TO 3X HI COL. ..
PROOFS STATED PRINT RUN 20 SER.#'d SETS

	MINT	NRMT
❑ 1 Troy Aikman	30.00	13.50
❑ 2 Emmitt Smith	30.00	13.50
❑ 3 Terrell Davis	30.00	13.50
❑ 4 Barry Sanders	50.00	22.00
❑ 5 Brett Favre	50.00	22.00
❑ 6 Dan Marino	50.00	22.00
❑ 7 Randy Moss	40.00	18.00
❑ 8 Drew Bledsoe	20.00	9.00
❑ 9 Jerry Rice	30.00	13.50
❑ 10 Steve Young	20.00	9.00

1999 Paramount End Zone Net-Fusions

	MINT	NRMT
COMPLETE SET (20)	300.00	135.00
COMMON CARD (1-20)	8.00	3.60

STATED ODDS 1:73

	MINT	NRMT
❑ 1 Jake Plummer	15.00	6.75
❑ 2 Jamal Anderson	10.00	4.50
❑ 3 Doug Flutie	10.00	4.50
❑ 4 Tim Couch	30.00	13.50
❑ 5 Troy Aikman	20.00	9.00
❑ 6 Emmitt Smith	20.00	9.00
❑ 7 Terrell Davis	20.00	9.00
❑ 8 Barry Sanders	30.00	13.50
❑ 9 Brett Favre	30.00	13.50
❑ 10 Peyton Manning	25.00	11.00
❑ 11 Mark Brunell	12.00	5.50
❑ 12 Fred Taylor	15.00	6.75
❑ 13 Dan Marino	30.00	13.50
❑ 14 Randy Moss	25.00	11.00
❑ 15 Drew Bledsoe	12.00	5.50
❑ 16 Ricky Williams	30.00	13.50
❑ 17 Jerry Rice	20.00	9.00
❑ 18 Steve Young	12.00	5.50
❑ 19 Jon Kitna	10.00	4.50
❑ 20 Eddie George	10.00	4.50

1999 Paramount Personal Bests

	MINT	NRMT
COMPLETE SET (36)	250.00	110.00
COMMON CARD (1-36)	5.00	2.20

STATED ODDS 1:37

	MINT	NRMT
❑ 1 Jake Plummer	10.00	4.50
❑ 2 Jamal Anderson	5.00	2.20
❑ 3 Priest Holmes	5.00	2.20
❑ 4 Doug Flutie	6.00	2.70
❑ 5 Antowain Smith	5.00	2.20
❑ 6 Corey Dillon	5.00	2.20
❑ 7 Akili Smith	6.00	2.70
❑ 8 Tim Couch	15.00	6.75
❑ 9 Troy Aikman	12.00	5.50
❑ 10 Emmitt Smith	12.00	5.50
❑ 11 Terrell Davis	12.00	5.50
❑ 12 Barry Sanders	20.00	9.00
❑ 13 Brett Favre	20.00	9.00
❑ 14 Antonio Freeman	5.00	2.20
❑ 15 Edgerrin James	25.00	11.00
❑ 16 Peyton Manning	15.00	6.75
❑ 17 Mark Brunell	8.00	3.60
❑ 18 Fred Taylor	10.00	4.50
❑ 19 Dan Marino	20.00	9.00
❑ 20 Randall Cunningham	5.00	2.20
❑ 21 Randy Moss	15.00	6.75
❑ 22 Drew Bledsoe	8.00	3.60
❑ 23 Kevin Faulk	5.00	2.20
❑ 24 Ricky Williams	15.00	6.75
❑ 25 Curtis Martin	5.00	2.20
❑ 26 Napoleon Kaufman	5.00	2.20
❑ 27 Donovan McNabb	10.00	4.50
❑ 28 Jerome Bettis	5.00	2.20
❑ 29 Kordell Stewart	5.00	2.20
❑ 30 Terrell Owens	5.00	2.20
❑ 31 Jerry Rice	12.00	5.50
❑ 32 Steve Young	8.00	3.60
❑ 33 Jon Kitna	6.00	2.70
❑ 34 Warrick Dunn	5.00	2.20
❑ 35 Eddie George	6.00	2.70
❑ 36 Steve McNair	5.00	2.20

1999 Paramount Team Checklists

	MINT	NRMT
COMPLETE SET (31)	120.00	55.00

COMMON CARD (1-31)	1.50	.70
SEMISTARS	3.00	1.35
STATED ODDS 2:37		
❑ 1 Jake Plummer	6.00	2.70
❑ 2 Jamal Anderson	3.00	1.35
❑ 3 Priest Holmes	3.00	1.35
❑ 4 Doug Flutie	4.00	1.80
❑ 5 Muhsin Muhammad	3.00	1.35
❑ 6 Cade McNown	6.00	2.70
❑ 7 Corey Dillon	3.00	1.35
❑ 8 Tim Couch	10.00	4.50
❑ 9 Troy Aikman	8.00	3.60
❑ 10 Terrell Davis	8.00	3.60
❑ 11 Barry Sanders	12.00	5.50
❑ 12 Brett Favre	12.00	5.50
❑ 13 Peyton Manning	10.00	4.50
❑ 14 Fred Taylor	6.00	2.70
❑ 15 Elvis Grbac	3.00	1.35
❑ 16 Dan Marino	12.00	5.50
❑ 17 Randy Moss	10.00	4.50
❑ 18 Drew Bledsoe	5.00	2.20
❑ 19 Ricky Williams	10.00	4.50
❑ 20 Ike Hilliard	1.50	.70
❑ 21 Curtis Martin	3.00	1.35
❑ 22 Napoleon Kaufman	3.00	1.35
❑ 23 Donovan McNabb	6.00	2.70
❑ 24 Jerome Bettis	3.00	1.35
❑ 25 Torry Holt	5.00	2.20
❑ 26 Natrone Means	3.00	1.35
❑ 27 Jerry Rice	8.00	3.60
❑ 28 Jon Kitna	4.00	1.80
❑ 29 Warrick Dunn	3.00	1.35
❑ 30 Eddie George	4.00	1.80
❑ 31 Skip Hicks	3.00	1.35

1964 Philadelphia

	NRMT	VG-E
COMPLETE SET (198)	900.00	400.00
COMMON CARD (1-198)	2.50	1.10
SEMISTARS	3.00	1.35
UNLISTED STARS	4.00	1.80
TEAM CARDS	3.00	1.35
CARDS PRICED IN NM CONDITION		
❑ 1 Raymond Berry	20.00	9.00
❑ 2 Tom Gilburg	2.50	1.10
❑ 3 John Mackey RC	30.00	13.50
❑ 4 Gino Marchetti	5.00	2.20
❑ 5 Jim Martin	2.50	1.10
❑ 6 Tom Matte RC	6.00	2.70
❑ 7 Jimmy Orr	2.50	1.10
❑ 8 Jim Parker	4.00	1.80
❑ 9 Bill Pellington	2.50	1.10
❑ 10 Alex Sandusky	2.50	1.10
❑ 11 Dick Szymanski	2.50	1.10
❑ 12 John Unitas	45.00	20.00
❑ 13 Baltimore Colts Team Card	3.00	1.35
❑ 14 Baltimore Colts Play Card (Don Shula)	35.00	16.00
❑ 15 Doug Atkins	5.00	2.20
❑ 16 Ron Bull	2.50	1.10
❑ 17 Mike Ditka	40.00	18.00
❑ 18 Joe Fortunato	2.50	1.10
❑ 19 Willie Galimore	3.00	1.35
❑ 20 Joe Marconi	2.50	1.10
❑ 21 Bennie McRae RC	2.50	1.10
❑ 22 Johnny Morris	2.50	1.10
❑ 23 Richie Petitbon	2.50	1.10
❑ 24 Mike Pyle	2.50	1.10
❑ 25 Roosevelt Taylor RC	4.00	1.80
❑ 26 Bill Wade	3.00	1.35
❑ 27 Chicago Bears Team Card	3.00	1.35
❑ 28 Chicago Bears Play Card (George Halas)	12.00	5.50
❑ 29 Johnny Brewer	2.50	1.10
❑ 30 Jim Brown	80.00	36.00
❑ 31 Gary Collins RC	8.00	3.60
❑ 32 Vince Costello	2.50	1.10
❑ 33 Galen Fiss	2.50	1.10
❑ 34 Bill Glass	2.50	1.10
❑ 35 Ernie Green RC	3.00	1.35
❑ 36 Rich Kreitling	2.50	1.10
❑ 37 John Morrow	2.50	1.10
❑ 38 Frank Ryan	3.00	1.35
❑ 39 Charlie Scales RC	2.50	1.10
❑ 40 Dick Schafrath RC	2.50	1.10
❑ 41 Cleveland Browns Team Card	3.00	1.35
❑ 42 Cleveland Browns Play Card (Blanton Collier)	2.50	1.10
❑ 43 Don Bishop	2.50	1.10
❑ 44 Frank Clarke RC	3.00	1.35
❑ 45 Mike Connelly	2.50	1.10
❑ 46 Lee Folkins	2.50	1.10
❑ 47 Cornell Green RC	8.00	3.60
❑ 48 Bob Lilly	40.00	18.00
❑ 49 Amos Marsh	2.50	1.10
❑ 50 Tommy McDonald	4.00	1.80
❑ 51 Don Meredith	30.00	13.50
❑ 52 Pettis Norman RC	3.00	1.35
❑ 53 Don Perkins	3.00	1.35
❑ 54 Guy Reese	2.50	1.10
❑ 55 Dallas Cowboys Team Card	3.00	1.35
❑ 56 Dallas Cowboys Play Card (Tom Landry)	15.00	6.75
❑ 57 Terry Barr	2.50	1.10
❑ 58 Roger Brown	3.00	1.35
❑ 59 Gail Cogdill	2.50	1.10
❑ 60 John Gordy	2.50	1.10
❑ 61 Dick Lane	4.00	1.80
❑ 62 Yale Lary	4.00	1.80
❑ 63 Dan Lewis	2.50	1.10
❑ 64 Darris McCord	2.50	1.10
❑ 65 Earl Morrall	3.00	1.35
❑ 66 Joe Schmidt	5.00	2.20
❑ 67 Pat Studstill RC	3.00	1.35
❑ 68 Wayne Walker RC	3.00	1.35
❑ 69 Detroit Lions Team Card	3.00	1.35
❑ 70 Detroit Lions Play Card (George Wilson CO)	2.50	1.10
❑ 71 Herb Adderley RC	35.00	16.00
❑ 72 Willie Davis RC	30.00	13.50
❑ 73 Forrest Gregg	5.00	2.20
❑ 74 Paul Hornung	35.00	16.00
❑ 75 Hank Jordan	5.00	2.20
❑ 76 Jerry Kramer	6.00	2.70
❑ 77 Tom Moore	3.00	1.35
❑ 78 Jim Ringo UER (Green Bay on front, Philadelphia on back)	5.00	2.20
❑ 79 Bart Starr	40.00	18.00
❑ 80 Jim Taylor	25.00	11.00
❑ 81 Jesse Whittenton RC	3.00	1.35
❑ 82 Willie Wood	8.00	3.60
❑ 83 Green Bay Packers Team Card	6.00	2.70
❑ 84 Green Bay Packers Play Card (Vince Lombardi)	35.00	16.00
❑ 85 Jon Arnett	2.50	1.10
❑ 86 Pervis Atkins RC	2.50	1.10
❑ 87 Dick Bass	3.00	1.35
❑ 88 Carroll Dale	4.00	1.80
❑ 89 Roman Gabriel	6.00	2.70
❑ 90 Ed Meador	2.50	1.10
❑ 91 Merlin Olsen RC	50.00	22.00
❑ 92 Jack Pardee RC	4.00	1.80
❑ 93 Jim Phillips	2.50	1.10
❑ 94 Carver Shannon	2.50	1.10
❑ 95 Frank Varrichione	2.50	1.10
❑ 96 Danny Villanueva	2.50	1.10
❑ 97 Los Angeles Rams Team Card	3.00	1.35
❑ 98 Los Angeles Rams Play Card (Harland Svare)	2.50	1.10
❑ 99 Grady Alderman RC	3.00	1.35
❑ 100 Larry Bowie	2.50	1.10
❑ 101 Bill Brown RC	6.00	2.70
❑ 102 Paul Flatley RC	2.50	1.10
❑ 103 Rip Hawkins	2.50	1.10
❑ 104 Jim Marshall	8.00	3.60
❑ 105 Tommy Mason	3.00	1.35
❑ 106 Jim Prestel	2.50	1.10
❑ 107 Jerry Reichow	2.50	1.10
❑ 108 Ed Sharockman	2.50	1.10
❑ 109 Fran Tarkenton	35.00	16.00
❑ 110 Mick Tingelhoff RC	6.00	2.70
❑ 111 Minnesota Vikings Team Card	3.00	1.35
❑ 112 Minnesota Vikings Play Card (Norm Van Brocklin)	4.00	1.80
❑ 113 Erich Barnes	2.50	1.10
❑ 114 Roosevelt Brown	4.00	1.80
❑ 115 Don Chandler	2.50	1.10
❑ 116 Darrell Dess	2.50	1.10
❑ 117 Frank Gifford	30.00	13.50
❑ 118 Dick James	2.50	1.10
❑ 119 Jim Katcavage	2.50	1.10
❑ 120 John Lovetere	2.50	1.10
❑ 121 Dick Lynch RC	3.00	1.35
❑ 122 Jim Patton	2.50	1.10
❑ 123 Del Shofner	2.50	1.10
❑ 124 Y.A. Tittle	20.00	9.00
❑ 125 New York Giants Team Card	3.00	1.35
❑ 126 New York Giants Play Card (Allie Sherman)	2.50	1.10
❑ 127 Sam Baker	2.50	1.10
❑ 128 Maxie Baughan	2.50	1.10
❑ 129 Timmy Brown	3.00	1.35
❑ 130 Mike Clark	2.50	1.10
❑ 131 Irv Cross RC	3.00	1.35
❑ 132 Ted Dean	2.50	1.10
❑ 133 Ron Goodwin	2.50	1.10
❑ 134 King Hill	2.50	1.10
❑ 135 Clarence Peaks	2.50	1.10
❑ 136 Pete Retzlaff	3.00	1.35
❑ 137 Jim Schrader	2.50	1.10
❑ 138 Norm Snead	3.00	1.35
❑ 139 Philadelphia Eagles Team Card	3.00	1.35
❑ 140 Philadelphia Eagles Play Card (Nick Skorich)	2.50	1.10
❑ 141 Gary Ballman RC	2.50	1.10
❑ 142 Charley Bradshaw	2.50	1.10
❑ 143 Ed Brown	3.00	1.35
❑ 144 John Henry Johnson	4.00	1.80
❑ 145 Joe Krupa	2.50	1.10
❑ 146 Bill Mack	2.50	1.10
❑ 147 Lou Michaels	2.50	1.10
❑ 148 Buzz Nutter	2.50	1.10
❑ 149 Myron Pottios	2.50	1.10
❑ 150 John Reger	2.50	1.10
❑ 151 Mike Sandusky	2.50	1.10
❑ 152 Clendon Thomas	2.50	1.10
❑ 153 Pittsburgh Steelers Team Card	3.00	1.35
❑ 154 Pittsburgh Steelers Play Card (Buddy Parker)	2.50	1.10
❑ 155 Kermit Alexander RC	3.00	1.35
❑ 156 Bernie Casey	3.00	1.35
❑ 157 Dan Colchico	2.50	1.10
❑ 158 Clyde Conner	2.50	1.10
❑ 159 Tommy Davis	2.50	1.10
❑ 160 Matt Hazeltine	2.50	1.10
❑ 161 Jim Johnson RC	15.00	6.75

❑ 162 Don Lisbon RC 2.50 1.10
❑ 163 Lamar McHan 2.50 1.10
❑ 164 Bob St. Clair 4.00 1.80
❑ 165 J.D. Smith 2.50 1.10
❑ 166 Abe Woodson 2.50 1.10
❑ 167 San Francisco 49ers 3.00 1.35
Team Card
❑ 168 San Francisco 49ers 2.50 1.10
Play Card
(Red Hickey)
❑ 169 Garland Boyette UER .. 2.50 1.10
(Photo on front
is not Boyette)
❑ 170 Bobby Joe Conrad 3.00 1.35
❑ 171 Bob DeMarco RC 2.50 1.10
❑ 172 Ken Gray RC............... 2.50 1.10
❑ 173 Jimmy Hill 2.50 1.10
❑ 174 Charlie Johnson UER .. 3.00 1.35
(Misspelled Charley
on both sides)
❑ 175 Ernie McMillan............. 2.50 1.10
❑ 176 Dale Meinert 2.50 1.10
❑ 177 Luke Owens 2.50 1.10
❑ 178 Sonny Randle 2.50 1.10
❑ 179 Joe Robb...................... 2.50 1.10
❑ 180 Bill Stacy 2.50 1.10
❑ 181 St. Louis Cardinals 3.00 1.35
Team Card
❑ 182 St. Louis Cardinals 2.50 1.10
Play Card
(Wally Lemm)
❑ 183 Bill Barnes 2.50 1.10
❑ 184 Don Bosseler............... 2.50 1.10
❑ 185 Sam Huff 6.00 2.70
❑ 186 Sonny Jurgensen 20.00 9.00
❑ 187 Bob Khayat 2.50 1.10
❑ 188 Riley Mattson 2.50 1.10
❑ 189 Bobby Mitchell............. 6.00 2.70
❑ 190 John Nisby 2.50 1.10
❑ 191 Vince Promuto............. 2.50 1.10
❑ 192 Joe Rutgens 2.50 1.10
❑ 193 Lonnie Sanders........... 2.50 1.10
❑ 194 Jim Steffen 2.50 1.10
❑ 195 Washington Redskins .. 3.00 1.35
Team Card
❑ 196 Washington Redskins .. 2.50 1.10
Play Card
(Bill McPeak)
❑ 197 Checklist 1 UER 30.00 13.50
(Dated 1963)
❑ 198 Checklist 2 UER 55.00 25.00
(Dated 1963,
174 Charley Johnson
should be Charlie)

1965 Philadelphia

	NRMT	VG-E
COMPLETE SET (198)	800.00	350.00
COMMON CARD (1-198)	2.00	.90
SEMISTARS	3.00	1.35
UNLISTED STARS	4.00	1.80
TEAM CARDS	3.00	1.35

CARDS PRICED IN NM CONDITION

❑ 1 Baltimore Colts 15.00 6.75
Team Card
❑ 2 Raymond Berry 8.00 3.60
❑ 3 Bob Boyd......................... 2.00 .90
❑ 4 Wendell Harris.................. 2.00 .90
❑ 5 Jerry Logan .... 2.00 .90
❑ 6 Tony Lorick .... 2.00 .90
❑ 7 Lou Michaels.................... 2.00 .90
❑ 8 Lenny Moore 8.00 3.60
❑ 9 Jimmy Orr 3.00 1.35
❑ 10 Jim Parker....................... 4.00 1.80
❑ 11 Dick Szymanski.............. 2.00 .90
❑ 12 John Unitas 35.00 16.00
❑ 13 Bob Vogel RC .... 2.00 .90
❑ 14 Baltimore Colts 20.00 9.00
Play Card
(Don Shula)
❑ 15 Chicago Bears................ 3.00 1.35
Team Card
❑ 16 Jon Arnett .... 2.00 .90
❑ 17 Doug Atkins.................... 5.00 2.20
❑ 18 Rudy Bukich RC 3.00 1.35
❑ 19 Mike Ditka 30.00 13.50
❑ 20 Dick Evey .... 2.00 .90
❑ 21 Joe Fortunato .... 2.00 .90
❑ 22 Bobby Joe Green RC .... 2.00 .90
❑ 23 Johnny Morris .... 2.00 .90
❑ 24 Mike Pyle........................ 2.00 .90
❑ 25 Roosevelt Taylor 3.00 1.35
❑ 26 Bill Wade 3.00 1.35
❑ 27 Bob Wetoska .... 2.00 .90
❑ 28 Chicago Bears................ 8.00 3.60
Play Card
(George Halas)
❑ 29 Cleveland Browns 3.00 1.35
Team Card
❑ 30 Walter Beach.................. 2.00 .90
❑ 31 Jim Brown 70.00 32.00
❑ 32 Gary Collins.................... 3.00 1.35
❑ 33 Bill Glass .... 2.00 .90
❑ 34 Ernie Green.................... 2.00 .90
❑ 35 Jim Houston RC .... 2.00 .90
❑ 36 Dick Modzelewski .... 2.00 .90
❑ 37 Bernie Parrish .... 2.00 .90
❑ 38 Walter Roberts .... 2.00 .90
❑ 39 Frank Ryan 3.00 1.35
❑ 40 Dick Schafrath................ 2.00 .90
❑ 41 Paul Warfield RC.......... 75.00 34.00
❑ 42 Cleveland Browns .... 2.00 .90
Play Card
(Blanton Collier)
❑ 43 Dallas Cowboys 3.00 1.35
Team Card UER
(Cowboys Dallas on back)
❑ 44 Frank Clarke 3.00 1.35
❑ 45 Mike Connelly .... 2.00 .90
❑ 46 Buddy Dial...................... 2.00 .90
❑ 47 Bob Lilly..................... 30.00 13.50
❑ 48 Tony Liscio RC .... 2.00 .90
❑ 49 Tommy McDonald 4.00 1.80
❑ 50 Don Meredith............... 25.00 11.00
❑ 51 Pettis Norman .... 2.00 .90
❑ 52 Don Perkins.................... 3.00 1.35
❑ 53 Mel Renfro RC 40.00 18.00
❑ 54 Jim Ridlon .... 2.00 .90
❑ 55 Jerry Tubbs .... 2.00 .90
❑ 56 Dallas Cowboys 12.00 5.50
Play Card
(Tom Landry)
❑ 57 Detroit Lions 3.00 1.35
Team Card
❑ 58 Terry Barr .... 2.00 .90
❑ 59 Roger Brown .... 2.00 .90
❑ 60 Gail Cogdill .... 2.00 .90
❑ 61 Jim Gibbons .... 2.00 .90
❑ 62 John Gordy .... 2.00 .90
❑ 63 Yale Lary........................ 4.00 1.80
❑ 64 Dick LeBeau RC 3.00 1.35
❑ 65 Earl Morrall 3.00 1.35
❑ 66 Nick Pietrosante .... 2.00 .90
❑ 67 Pat Studstill .... 2.00 .90
❑ 68 Wayne Walker................ 3.00 1.35
❑ 69 Tom Watkins .... 2.00 .90
❑ 70 Detroit Lions .... 2.00 .90
Play Card
(George Wilson CO)
❑ 71 Green Bay Packers 6.00 2.70
Team Card
❑ 72 Herb Adderley 8.00 3.60
❑ 73 Willie Davis 8.00 3.60
❑ 74 Boyd Dowler 4.00 1.80
❑ 75 Forrest Gregg 5.00 2.20
❑ 76 Paul Hornung 30.00 13.50
❑ 77 Hank Jordan 5.00 2.20
❑ 78 Tom Moore 3.00 1.35
❑ 79 Ray Nitschke 20.00 9.00
❑ 80 Elijah Pitts RC 8.00 3.60
❑ 81 Bart Starr.................... 40.00 18.00
❑ 82 Jim Taylor 20.00 9.00
❑ 83 Willie Wood 6.00 2.70
❑ 84 Green Bay Packers 20.00 9.00
Play Card
(Vince Lombardi)
❑ 85 Los Angeles Rams 3.00 1.35
Team Card
❑ 86 Dick Bass 3.00 1.35
❑ 87 Roman Gabriel 5.00 2.20
❑ 88 Roosevelt Grier 4.00 1.80
❑ 89 Deacon Jones 10.00 4.50
❑ 90 Lamar Lundy RC 4.00 1.80
❑ 91 Marlin McKeever .... 2.00 .90
❑ 92 Ed Meador..................... 2.00 .90
❑ 93 Bill Munson RC 4.00 1.80
❑ 94 Merlin Olsen 15.00 6.75
❑ 95 Bobby Smith .... 2.00 .90
❑ 96 Frank Varrichione .... 2.00 .90
❑ 97 Ben Wilson .... 2.00 .90
❑ 98 Los Angeles Rams .... 2.00 .90
Play Card
(Harland Svare)
❑ 99 Minnesota Vikings 3.00 1.35
Team Card
❑ 100 Grady Alderman .... 2.00 .90
❑ 101 Hal Bedsole RC............ 2.00 .90
❑ 102 Bill Brown 3.00 1.35
❑ 103 Bill Butler...................... 2.00 .90
❑ 104 Fred Cox RC 3.00 1.35
❑ 105 Carl Eller RC 25.00 11.00
❑ 106 Paul Flatley .... 2.00 .90
❑ 107 Jim Marshall 6.00 2.70
❑ 108 Tommy Mason .... 2.00 .90
❑ 109 George Rose................ 2.00 .90
❑ 110 Fran Tarkenton 20.00 9.00
❑ 111 Mick Tingelhoff 3.00 1.35
❑ 112 Minnesota Vikings 4.00 1.80
Play Card
(Norm Van Brocklin)
❑ 113 New York Giants 3.00 1.35
Team Card
❑ 114 Erich Barnes .... 2.00 .90
❑ 115 Roosevelt Brown.......... 4.00 1.80
❑ 116 Clarence Childs............ 2.00 .90
❑ 117 Jerry Hillebrand .... 2.00 .90
❑ 118 Greg Larson RC .... 2.00 .90
❑ 119 Dick Lynch.................... 2.00 .90
❑ 120 Joe Morrison RC 4.00 1.80
❑ 121 Lou Slaby .... 2.00 .90
❑ 122 Aaron Thomas RC .... 2.00 .90
❑ 123 Steve Thurlow .... 2.00 .90
❑ 124 Ernie Wheelwright........ 2.00 .90
❑ 125 Gary Wood RC .... 2.00 .90
❑ 126 New York Giants .... 2.00 .90
Play Card
(Allie Sherman)
❑ 127 Philadelphia Eagles...... 3.00 1.35
Team Card
❑ 128 Sam Baker .... 2.00 .90
❑ 129 Maxie Baughan .... 2.00 .90
❑ 130 Timmy Brown 3.00 1.35
❑ 131 Jack Concannon RC .... 2.00 .90
❑ 132 Irv Cross 3.00 1.35
❑ 133 Earl Gros .... 2.00 .90
❑ 134 Dave Lloyd .... 2.00 .90
❑ 135 Floyd Peters RC .... 2.00 .90
❑ 136 Nate Ramsey .... 2.00 .90
❑ 137 Pete Retzlaff 3.00 1.35
❑ 138 Jim Ringo 4.00 1.80
❑ 139 Norm Snead 4.00 1.80
❑ 140 Philadelphia Eagles...... 2.00 .90
Play Card
(Joe Kuharich)
❑ 141 Pittsburgh Steelers 3.00 1.35
Team Card
❑ 142 John Baker .... 2.00 .90
❑ 143 Gary Ballman .... 2.00 .90

	NRMT	VG-E
❑ 144 Charley Bradshaw	2.00	.90
❑ 145 Ed Brown	2.00	.90
❑ 146 Dick Haley	2.00	.90
❑ 147 John Henry Johnson	4.00	1.80
❑ 148 Brady Keys	2.00	.90
❑ 149 Ray Lemek	2.00	.90
❑ 150 Ben McGee	2.00	.90
❑ 151 Clarence Peaks	2.00	.90
❑ 152 Myron Pottios	2.00	.90
❑ 153 Clendon Thomas	2.00	.90
❑ 154 Pittsburgh Steelers Play Card (Buddy Parker)	2.00	.90
❑ 155 St. Louis Cardinals Team Card	3.00	1.35
❑ 156 Jim Bakken RC	3.00	1.35
❑ 157 Joe Childress	2.00	.90
❑ 158 Bobby Joe Conrad	3.00	1.35
❑ 159 Bob DeMarco	2.00	.90
❑ 160 Pat Fischer RC	4.00	1.80
❑ 161 Irv Goode	2.00	.90
❑ 162 Ken Gray	2.00	.90
❑ 163 Charlie Johnson UER (Misspelled Charley on both sides)	3.00	1.35
❑ 164 Bill Koman	2.00	.90
❑ 165 Dale Meinert	2.00	.90
❑ 166 Jerry Stovall RC	3.00	1.35
❑ 167 Abe Woodson	2.00	.90
❑ 168 St. Louis Cardinals Play Card (Wally Lemm)	2.00	.90
❑ 169 San Francisco 49ers Team Card	3.00	1.35
❑ 170 Kermit Alexander	2.00	.90
❑ 171 John Brodie	10.00	4.50
❑ 172 Bernie Casey	3.00	1.35
❑ 173 John David Crow	3.00	1.35
❑ 174 Tommy Davis	2.00	.90
❑ 175 Matt Hazeltine	2.00	.90
❑ 176 Jim Johnson	4.00	1.80
❑ 177 Charlie Krueger RC	2.00	.90
❑ 178 Roland Lakes	2.00	.90
❑ 179 George Mira RC	3.00	1.35
❑ 180 Dave Parks RC	3.00	1.35
❑ 181 John Thomas	2.00	.90
❑ 182 San Francisco 49ers Play Card (Jack Christiansen)	2.00	.90
❑ 183 Washington Redskins Team Card	3.00	1.35
❑ 184 Pervis Atkins	2.00	.90
❑ 185 Preston Carpenter	2.00	.90
❑ 186 Angelo Coia	2.00	.90
❑ 187 Sam Huff	6.00	2.70
❑ 188 Sonny Jurgensen	15.00	6.75
❑ 189 Paul Krause RC	20.00	9.00
❑ 190 Jim Martin	2.00	.90
❑ 191 Bobby Mitchell	5.00	2.20
❑ 192 John Nisby	2.00	.90
❑ 193 John Paluck	2.00	.90
❑ 194 Vince Promuto	2.00	.90
❑ 195 Charley Taylor RC	50.00	22.00
❑ 196 Washington Redskins Play Card (Bill McPeak)	2.00	.90
❑ 197 Checklist 1	30.00	13.50
❑ 198 Checklist 2 UER (163 Charley Johnson should be Charlie)	50.00	22.00

1966 Philadelphia

	NRMT	VG-E
COMPLETE SET (198)	900.00	400.00
COMMON CARD (1-198)	2.00	.90
SEMISTARS	3.00	1.35
UNLISTED STARS	4.00	1.80
TEAM CARDS	3.00	1.35

CARDS PRICED IN NM CONDITION

	NRMT	VG-E
❑ 1 Atlanta Falcons Insignia	12.00	5.50
❑ 2 Larry Benz	2.00	.90
❑ 3 Dennis Claridge	2.00	.90
❑ 4 Perry Lee Dunn	2.00	.90
❑ 5 Dan Grimm	2.00	.90
❑ 6 Alex Hawkins	2.00	.90
❑ 7 Ralph Heck	2.00	.90
❑ 8 Frank Lasky	2.00	.90
❑ 9 Guy Reese	2.00	.90
❑ 10 Bob Richards	2.00	.90
❑ 11 Ron Smith RC	2.00	.90
❑ 12 Ernie Wheelwright	2.00	.90
❑ 13 Atlanta Falcons Roster	3.00	1.35
❑ 14 Baltimore Colts Team Card	3.00	1.35
❑ 15 Raymond Berry	8.00	3.60
❑ 16 Bob Boyd	2.00	.90
❑ 17 Jerry Logan	2.00	.90
❑ 18 John Mackey	6.00	2.70
❑ 19 Tom Matte	4.00	1.80
❑ 20 Lou Michaels	2.00	.90
❑ 21 Lenny Moore	8.00	3.60
❑ 22 Jimmy Orr	2.00	.90
❑ 23 Jim Parker	4.00	1.80
❑ 24 John Unitas	35.00	16.00
❑ 25 Bob Vogel	2.00	.90
❑ 26 Baltimore Colts Play Card (Lenny Moore Jim Parker)	4.00	1.80
❑ 27 Chicago Bears Team Card	3.00	1.35
❑ 28 Doug Atkins	4.00	1.80
❑ 29 Rudy Bukich	2.00	.90
❑ 30 Ron Bull	2.00	.90
❑ 31 Dick Butkus RC !	225.00	100.00
❑ 32 Mike Ditka	35.00	16.00
❑ 33 Joe Fortunato	2.00	.90
❑ 34 Bobby Joe Green	2.00	.90
❑ 35 Roger LeClerc	2.00	.90
❑ 36 Johnny Morris	2.00	.90
❑ 37 Mike Pyle	2.00	.90
❑ 38 Gale Sayers RC !	200.00	90.00
❑ 39 Chicago Bears Play Card (Gale Sayers)	35.00	16.00
❑ 40 Cleveland Browns Team Card	3.00	1.35
❑ 41 Jim Brown	70.00	32.00
❑ 42 Gary Collins	3.00	1.35
❑ 43 Ross Fichtner	2.00	.90
❑ 44 Ernie Green	2.00	.90
❑ 45 Gene Hickerson RC	3.00	1.35
❑ 46 Jim Houston	2.00	.90
❑ 47 John Morrow	2.00	.90
❑ 48 Walter Roberts	2.00	.90
❑ 49 Frank Ryan	3.00	1.35
❑ 50 Dick Schafrath	2.00	.90
❑ 51 Paul Wiggin RC	2.00	.90
❑ 52 Cleveland Browns Play Card (Ernie Green sweep)	2.00	.90
❑ 53 Dallas Cowboys Team Card	3.00	1.35
❑ 54 George Andrie RC UER (Text says startling, should be starting)	2.00	.90
❑ 55 Frank Clarke	3.00	1.35
❑ 56 Mike Connelly	2.00	.90
❑ 57 Cornell Green	4.00	1.80
❑ 58 Bob Hayes RC	45.00	20.00
❑ 59 Chuck Howley RC	18.00	8.00
❑ 60 Bob Lilly	20.00	9.00
❑ 61 Don Meredith	25.00	11.00
❑ 62 Don Perkins	3.00	1.35
❑ 63 Mel Renfro	15.00	6.75
❑ 64 Danny Villanueva	2.00	.90
❑ 65 Dallas Cowboys Play Card (Danny Villanueva)	2.00	.90
❑ 66 Detroit Lions Team Card	3.00	1.35
❑ 67 Roger Brown	2.00	.90
❑ 68 John Gordy	2.00	.90
❑ 69 Alex Karras	10.00	4.50
❑ 70 Dick LeBeau	2.00	.90
❑ 71 Amos Marsh	2.00	.90
❑ 72 Milt Plum	3.00	1.35
❑ 73 Bobby Smith	2.00	.90
❑ 74 Wayne Rasmussen	2.00	.90
❑ 75 Pat Studstill	2.00	.90
❑ 76 Wayne Walker	2.00	.90
❑ 77 Tom Watkins	2.00	.90
❑ 78 Detroit Lions Play Card (George Izo pass)	2.00	.90
❑ 79 Green Bay Packers Team Card	6.00	2.70
❑ 80 Herb Adderley UER (Adderly on back)	6.00	2.70
❑ 81 Lee Roy Caffey RC	4.00	1.80
❑ 82 Don Chandler	3.00	1.35
❑ 83 Willie Davis	6.00	2.70
❑ 84 Boyd Dowler	4.00	1.80
❑ 85 Forrest Gregg	4.00	1.80
❑ 86 Tom Moore	3.00	1.35
❑ 87 Ray Nitschke	15.00	6.75
❑ 88 Bart Starr	40.00	18.00
❑ 89 Jim Taylor	20.00	9.00
❑ 90 Willie Wood	5.00	2.20
❑ 91 Green Bay Packers Play Card (Don Chandler FG)	2.00	.90
❑ 92 Los Angeles Rams Team Card	3.00	1.35
❑ 93 Willie Brown WR	2.00	.90
❑ 94 Dick Bass and Roman Gabriel	4.00	1.80
❑ 95 Bruce Gossett RC (Tom Landry small photo on back)	3.00	1.35
❑ 96 Deacon Jones	6.00	2.70
❑ 97 Tommy McDonald	4.00	1.80
❑ 98 Marlin McKeever	2.00	.90
❑ 99 Aaron Martin	2.00	.90
❑ 100 Ed Meador	2.00	.90
❑ 101 Bill Munson	3.00	1.35
❑ 102 Merlin Olsen	8.00	3.60
❑ 103 Jim Stiger	2.00	.90
❑ 104 Los Angeles Rams Play Card (Willie Brown run)	3.00	1.35
❑ 105 Minnesota Vikings Team Card	3.00	1.35
❑ 106 Grady Alderman	2.00	.90
❑ 107 Bill Brown	3.00	1.35
❑ 108 Fred Cox	2.00	.90
❑ 109 Paul Flatley	2.00	.90
❑ 110 Rip Hawkins	2.00	.90
❑ 111 Tommy Mason	2.00	.90
❑ 112 Ed Sharockman	2.00	.90
❑ 113 Gordon Smith	2.00	.90
❑ 114 Fran Tarkenton	25.00	11.00
❑ 115 Mick Tingelhoff	3.00	1.35
❑ 116 Bobby Walden RC**/C	2.00	.90
❑ 117 Minnesota Vikings Play Card (Bill Brown run)	2.00	.90
❑ 118 New York Giants Team Card	3.00	1.35
❑ 119 Roosevelt Brown	4.00	1.80
❑ 120 Henry Carr RC	3.00	1.35
❑ 121 Clarence Childs	2.00	.90
❑ 122 Tucker Frederickson RC	3.00	1.35
❑ 123 Jerry Hillebrand	2.00	.90
❑ 124 Greg Larson	2.00	.90
❑ 125 Spider Lockhart RC	3.00	1.35

❑ 126 Dick Lynch 2.00 .90
❑ 127 Earl Morrall and Bob Scholtz 3.00 1.35
❑ 128 Joe Morrison 2.00 .90
❑ 129 Steve Thurlow 2.00 .90
❑ 130 New York Giants Play Card (Chuck Mercein over) 2.00 .90
❑ 131 Philadelphia Eagles Team Card 3.00 1.35
❑ 132 Sam Baker 2.00 .90
❑ 133 Maxie Baughan 2.00 .90
❑ 134 Bob Brown OT RC 6.00 2.70
❑ 135 Timmy Brown (Lou Groza small photo on back) 3.00 1.35
❑ 136 Irv Cross 3.00 1.35
❑ 137 Earl Gros 2.00 .90
❑ 138 Ray Poage 2.00 .90
❑ 139 Nate Ramsey 2.00 .90
❑ 140 Pete Retzlaff 3.00 1.35
❑ 141 Jim Ringo (Joe Schmidt small photo on back) 4.00 1.80
❑ 142 Norm Snead (Norm Van Brocklin small photo on back) 4.00 1.80
❑ 143 Philadelphia Eagles Play Card (Earl Gros tackled) 2.00 .90
❑ 144 Pittsburgh Steelers Team Card (Lee Roy Jordan small photo on back) 3.00 1.35
❑ 145 Gary Ballman 2.00 .90
❑ 146 Charley Bradshaw 2.00 .90
❑ 147 Jim Butler 2.00 .90
❑ 148 Mike Clark 2.00 .90
❑ 149 Dick Hoak RC 2.00 .90
❑ 150 Roy Jefferson RC 3.00 1.35
❑ 151 Frank Lambert 2.00 .90
❑ 152 Mike Lind 2.00 .90
❑ 153 Bill Nelsen RC 4.00 1.80
❑ 154 Clarence Peaks 2.00 .90
❑ 155 Clendon Thomas 2.00 .90
❑ 156 Pittsburgh Steelers Play Card (Gary Ballman scores) 2.00 .90
❑ 157 St. Louis Cardinals Team Card 3.00 1.35
❑ 158 Jim Bakken 2.00 .90
❑ 159 Bobby Joe Conrad 3.00 1.35
❑ 160 Willis Crenshaw RC 2.00 .90
❑ 161 Bob DeMarco 2.00 .90
❑ 162 Pat Fischer 3.00 1.35
❑ 163 Charlie Johnson UER (Misspelled Charley on both sides) 3.00 1.35
❑ 164 Dale Meinert 2.00 .90
❑ 165 Sonny Randle 2.00 .90
❑ 166 Sam Silas RC 2.00 .90
❑ 167 Bill Triplett 2.00 .90
❑ 168 Larry Wilson 4.00 1.80
❑ 169 St. Louis Cardinals Play Card (Bill Triplett tackled by Roosevelt Davis and Roger LaLonde) 2.00 .90
❑ 170 San Francisco 49ers Team Card (Vince Lombardi small photo on back) 3.00 1.35
❑ 171 Kermit Alexander 2.00 .90
❑ 172 Bruce Bosley 2.00 .90
❑ 173 John Brodie 6.00 2.70
❑ 174 Bernie Casey 3.00 1.35
❑ 175 John David Crow (Don Shula small photo on back) 4.00 1.80
❑ 176 Tommy Davis 2.00 .90
❑ 177 Jim Johnson 4.00 1.80
❑ 178 Gary Lewis 2.00 .90
❑ 179 Dave Parks 2.00 .90
❑ 180 Walter Rock (Paul Hornung small photo on back) 3.00 1.35
❑ 181 Ken Willard RC (George Halas small photo on back) 4.00 1.80
❑ 182 San Francisco 49ers Play Card (Tommy Davis FG) 2.00 .90
❑ 183 Washington Redskins Team Card 3.00 1.35
❑ 184 Rickie Harris 2.00 .90
❑ 185 Sonny Jurgensen 8.00 3.60
❑ 186 Paul Krause 6.00 2.70
❑ 187 Bobby Mitchell 5.00 2.20
❑ 188 Vince Promuto 2.00 .90
❑ 189 Pat Richter RC (Craig Morton small photo on back) 2.00 .90
❑ 190 Joe Rutgens 2.00 .90
❑ 191 Johnny Sample 2.00 .90
❑ 192 Lonnie Sanders 2.00 .90
❑ 193 Jim Steffen 2.00 .90
❑ 194 Charley Taylor UER (Called Charley and Charlie on card back 15.00 6.75
❑ 195 Washington Redskins Play Card (Dan Lewis tackled by Roger LaLonde) 2.00 .90
❑ 196 Referee Signals 3.00 1.35
❑ 197 Checklist 1 25.00 11.00
❑ 198 Checklist 2 UER (163 Charley Johnson should be Charlie) 50.00 22.00

1967 Philadelphia

	NRMT	VG-E
COMPLETE SET (198)	650.00	300.00
COMMON CARD (1-198)	2.00	.90
SEMISTARS	3.00	1.35
UNLISTED STARS	4.00	1.80
TEAM CARDS	3.00	1.35

CARDS PRICED IN NM CONDITION

❑ 1 Atlanta Falcons Team Card 10.00 4.50
❑ 2 Junior Coffey RC 3.00 1.35
❑ 3 Alex Hawkins 2.00 .90
❑ 4 Randy Johnson RC 3.00 1.35
❑ 5 Lou Kirouac 2.00 .90
❑ 6 Billy Martin E 2.00 .90
❑ 7 Tommy Nobis RC 20.00 9.00
❑ 8 Jerry Richardson RC 4.00 1.80
❑ 9 Marion Rushing 2.00 .90
❑ 10 Ron Smith 2.00 .90
❑ 11 Ernie Wheelwright UER (Misspelled Wheelright on both sides) 2.00 .90
❑ 12 Atlanta Falcons Insignia 2.00 .90
❑ 13 Baltimore Colts Team Card 3.00 1.35
❑ 14 Raymond Berry UER (Photo actually Bob Boyd 7.00 3.10
❑ 15 Bob Boyd 2.00 .90
❑ 16 Ordell Braase 2.00 .90
❑ 17 Alvin Haymond 2.00 .90
❑ 18 Tony Lorick 2.00 .90
❑ 19 Lenny Lyles 2.00 .90
❑ 20 John Mackey 5.00 2.20
❑ 21 Tom Matte 3.00 1.35
❑ 22 Lou Michaels 2.00 .90
❑ 23 John Unitas 30.00 13.50
❑ 24 Baltimore Colts Insignia 2.00 .90
❑ 25 Chicago Bears Team Card 3.00 1.35
❑ 26 Rudy Bukich UER (Misspelled Buckich on card back) 2.00 .90
❑ 27 Ron Bull 2.00 .90
❑ 28 Dick Butkus 75.00 34.00
❑ 29 Mike Ditka 25.00 11.00
❑ 30 Dick Gordon RC 3.00 1.35
❑ 31 Roger LeClerc 2.00 .90
❑ 32 Bennie McRae 2.00 .90
❑ 33 Richie Petitbon 2.00 .90
❑ 34 Mike Pyle 2.00 .90
❑ 35 Gale Sayers 75.00 34.00
❑ 36 Chicago Bears Insignia 2.00 .90
❑ 37 Cleveland Browns Team Card 3.00 1.35
❑ 38 Johnny Brewer 2.00 .90
❑ 39 Gary Collins 3.00 1.35
❑ 40 Ross Fichtner 2.00 .90
❑ 41 Ernie Green 2.00 .90
❑ 42 Gene Hickerson 2.00 .90
❑ 43 Leroy Kelly RC 35.00 16.00
❑ 44 Frank Ryan 3.00 1.35
❑ 45 Dick Schafrath 2.00 .90
❑ 46 Paul Warfield 18.00 8.00
❑ 47 John Wooten 2.00 .90
❑ 48 Cleveland Browns Insignia 2.00 .90
❑ 49 Dallas Cowboys Team Card 3.00 1.35
❑ 50 George Andrie 2.00 .90
❑ 51 Cornell Green 3.00 1.35
❑ 52 Bob Hayes 15.00 6.75
❑ 53 Chuck Howley 4.00 1.80
❑ 54 Lee Roy Jordan RC 20.00 9.00
❑ 55 Bob Lilly 15.00 6.75
❑ 56 Dave Manders RC 2.00 .90
❑ 57 Don Meredith 25.00 11.00
❑ 58 Dan Reeves RC 25.00 11.00
❑ 59 Mel Renfro 6.00 2.70
❑ 60 Dallas Cowboys Insignia 3.00 1.35
❑ 61 Detroit Lions Team Card 3.00 1.35
❑ 62 Roger Brown 3.00 1.35
❑ 63 Gail Cogdill 2.00 .90
❑ 64 John Gordy 2.00 .90
❑ 65 Ron Kramer 2.00 .90
❑ 66 Dick LeBeau 2.00 .90
❑ 67 Mike Lucci RC 4.00 1.80
❑ 68 Amos Marsh 2.00 .90
❑ 69 Tom Nowatzke 2.00 .90
❑ 70 Pat Studstill 2.00 .90
❑ 71 Karl Sweetan 2.00 .90
❑ 72 Detroit Lions Insignia 2.00 .90
❑ 73 Green Bay Packers Team Card 5.00 2.20
❑ 74 Herb Adderley UER (Adderly on back) 5.00 2.20
❑ 75 Lee Roy Caffey 3.00 1.35
❑ 76 Willie Davis 5.00 2.20
❑ 77 Forrest Gregg 4.00 1.80
❑ 78 Hank Jordan 4.00 1.80
❑ 79 Ray Nitschke 12.00 5.50
❑ 80 Dave Robinson RC 6.00 2.70
❑ 81 Bob Skoronski 3.00 1.35
❑ 82 Bart Starr 30.00 13.50
❑ 83 Willie Wood 5.00 2.20
❑ 84 Green Bay Packers Insignia 3.00 1.35
❑ 85 Los Angeles Rams Team Card 3.00 1.35
❑ 86 Dick Bass 3.00 1.35
❑ 87 Maxie Baughan 2.00 .90
❑ 88 Roman Gabriel 4.00 1.80
❑ 89 Bruce Gossett 2.00 .90
❑ 90 Deacon Jones 5.00 2.20

❑ 91 Tommy McDonald 4.00 1.80
❑ 92 Marlin McKeever 2.00 .90
❑ 93 Tom Moore 2.00 .90
❑ 94 Merlin Olsen 6.00 2.70
❑ 95 Clancy Williams 2.00 .90
❑ 96 Los Angeles Rams 2.00 .90
Insignia
❑ 97 Minnesota Vikings 3.00 1.35
Team Card
❑ 98 Grady Alderman 2.00 .90
❑ 99 Bill Brown 3.00 1.35
❑ 100 Fred Cox 2.00 .90
❑ 101 Paul Flatley 2.00 .90
❑ 102 Dale Hackbart RC 2.00 .90
❑ 103 Jim Marshall 4.00 1.80
❑ 104 Tommy Mason 2.00 .90
❑ 105 Milt Sunde RC 2.00 .90
❑ 106 Fran Tarkenton 18.00 8.00
❑ 107 Mick Tingelhoff 3.00 1.35
❑ 108 Minnesota Vikings 2.00 .90
Insignia
❑ 109 New York Giants 3.00 1.35
Team Card
❑ 110 Henry Carr 2.00 .90
❑ 111 Clarence Childs 2.00 .90
❑ 112 Allen Jacobs 2.00 .90
❑ 113 Homer Jones RC 3.00 1.35
❑ 114 Tom Kennedy 2.00 .90
❑ 115 Spider Lockhart 2.00 .90
❑ 116 Joe Morrison 2.00 .90
❑ 117 Francis Peay 2.00 .90
❑ 118 Jeff Smith 2.00 .90
❑ 119 Aaron Thomas 2.00 .90
❑ 120 New York Giants 2.00 .90
Insignia
❑ 121 New Orleans Saints 3.00 1.35
Insignia
(See also card 132)
❑ 122 Charley Bradshaw 2.00 .90
❑ 123 Paul Hornung 20.00 9.00
❑ 124 Elbert Kimbrough 2.00 .90
❑ 125 Earl Leggett RC 2.00 .90
❑ 126 Obert Logan 2.00 .90
❑ 127 Riley Mattson 2.00 .90
❑ 128 John Morrow 2.00 .90
❑ 129 Bob Scholtz 2.00 .90
❑ 130 Dave Whitsell RC 2.00 .90
❑ 131 Gary Wood 2.00 .90
❑ 132 New Orleans Saints 3.00 1.35
Roster UER
(121 on back)
❑ 133 Philadelphia Eagles 3.00 1.35
Team Card
❑ 134 Sam Baker 2.00 .90
❑ 135 Bob Brown OT 3.00 1.35
❑ 136 Timmy Brown 3.00 1.35
❑ 137 Earl Gros 2.00 .90
❑ 138 Dave Lloyd 2.00 .90
❑ 139 Floyd Peters 2.00 .90
❑ 140 Pete Retzlaff 3.00 1.35
❑ 141 Joe Scarpati 2.00 .90
❑ 142 Norm Snead 3.00 1.35
❑ 143 Jim Skaggs 2.00 .90
❑ 144 Philadelphia Eagles 2.00 .90
Insignia
❑ 145 Pittsburgh Steelers 3.00 1.35
Team Card
❑ 146 Bill Asbury 2.00 .90
❑ 147 John Baker 2.00 .90
❑ 148 Gary Ballman 2.00 .90
❑ 149 Mike Clark 2.00 .90
❑ 150 Riley Gunnels 2.00 .90
❑ 151 John Hilton 2.00 .90
❑ 152 Roy Jefferson 3.00 1.35
❑ 153 Brady Keys 2.00 .90
❑ 154 Ben McGee 2.00 .90
❑ 155 Bill Nelsen 3.00 1.35
❑ 156 Pittsburgh Steelers 2.00 .90
Insignia
❑ 157 St. Louis Cardinals 3.00 1.35
Team Card
❑ 158 Jim Bakken 2.00 .90
❑ 159 Bobby Joe Conrad 3.00 1.35
❑ 160 Ken Gray 2.00 .90
❑ 161 Charlie Johnson UER 3.00 1.35
(Misspelled Charley
on both sides)
❑ 162 Joe Robb 2.00 .90
❑ 163 Johnny Roland RC 3.00 1.35
❑ 164 Roy Shivers 2.00 .90
❑ 165 Jackie Smith RC 15.00 6.75
❑ 166 Jerry Stovall 2.00 .90
❑ 167 Larry Wilson 4.00 1.80
❑ 168 St. Louis Cardinals 2.00 .90
Insignia
❑ 169 San Francisco 49ers 3.00 1.35
Team Card
❑ 170 Kermit Alexander 2.00 .90
❑ 171 Bruce Bosley 2.00 .90
❑ 172 John Brodie 6.00 2.70
❑ 173 Bernie Casey 3.00 1.35
❑ 174 Tommy Davis 2.00 .90
❑ 175 Howard Mudd 2.00 .90
❑ 176 Dave Parks 2.00 .90
❑ 177 John Thomas 2.00 .90
❑ 178 Dave Wilcox RC 5.00 2.20
❑ 179 Ken Willard 3.00 1.35
❑ 180 San Francisco 49ers 2.00 .90
Insignia
❑ 181 Washington Redskins 3.00 1.35
Team Card
❑ 182 Charlie Gogolak RC 2.00 .90
❑ 183 Chris Hanburger RC 5.00 2.20
❑ 184 Len Hauss RC 3.00 1.35
❑ 185 Sonny Jurgensen 7.00 3.10
❑ 186 Bobby Mitchell 5.00 2.20
❑ 187 Brig Owens 2.00 .90
❑ 188 Jim Shorter 2.00 .90
❑ 189 Jerry Smith RC 3.00 1.35
❑ 190 Charley Taylor 8.00 3.60
❑ 191 A.D. Whitfield 2.00 .90
❑ 192 Washington Redskins 2.00 .90
Insignia
❑ 193 Cleveland Browns 6.00 2.70
Play Card
(Leroy Kelly)
❑ 194 New York Giants 2.00 .90
Play Card
(Joe Morrison)
❑ 195 Atlanta Falcons 2.00 .90
Play Card
(Ernie Wheelright)
❑ 196 Referee Signals 3.00 1.35
❑ 197 Checklist 1 20.00 9.00
❑ 198 Checklist 2 UER 40.00 18.00
(161 Charley Johnson
should be Charlie)

1991 Pinnacle

	MINT	NRMT
COMPLETE SET (415)	20.00	9.00
COMMON CARD (1-415)	.10	.05
SEMISTARS	.20	.09
UNLISTED STARS	.40	.18

❑ 1 Warren Moon .40 .18
❑ 2 Morten Andersen .10 .05
❑ 3 Rohn Stark .10 .05
❑ 4 Mark Bortz .10 .05
❑ 5 Mark Higgs RC .10 .05
❑ 6 Troy Aikman 2.50 1.10
❑ 7 John Elway 4.00 1.80
❑ 8 Neal Anderson .20 .09
❑ 9 Chris Doleman .10 .05
❑ 10 Jay Schroeder .10 .05
❑ 11 Sterling Sharpe .40 .18
❑ 12 Steve DeBerg .10 .05
❑ 13 Ronnie Lott .20 .09
❑ 14 Sean Landeta .10 .05
❑ 15 Jim Everett .20 .09
❑ 16 Jim Breech .10 .05
❑ 17 Barry Foster .20 .09
❑ 18 Mike Merriweather .10 .05
❑ 19 Eric Metcalf .20 .09
❑ 20 Mark Carrier DB .20 .09
❑ 21 James Brooks .20 .09
❑ 22 Nate Odomes .10 .05
❑ 23 Rodney Hampton .40 .18
❑ 24 Chris Miller .20 .09
❑ 25 Roger Craig .20 .09
❑ 26 Louis Oliver .10 .05
❑ 27 Allen Pinkett .10 .05
❑ 28 Bubby Brister .10 .05
❑ 29 Reyna Thompson .10 .05
❑ 30 Issiac Holt .10 .05
❑ 31 Steve Broussard .10 .05
❑ 32 Christian Okoye .10 .05
❑ 33 Dave Meggett .20 .09
❑ 34 Andre Reed .20 .09
❑ 35 Shane Conlan .10 .05
❑ 36 Eric Ball .10 .05
❑ 37 Johnny Bailey .10 .05
❑ 38 Don Majkowski .10 .05
❑ 39 Gerald Williams .10 .05
❑ 40 Kevin Mack .10 .05
❑ 41 Jeff Herrod .10 .05
❑ 42 Emmitt Smith 6.00 2.70
❑ 43 Wendell Davis .10 .05
❑ 44 Lorenzo White .10 .05
❑ 45 Andre Rison .20 .09
❑ 46 Jerry Gray .10 .05
❑ 47 Dennis Smith .10 .05
❑ 48 Gaston Green .10 .05
❑ 49 Dermontti Dawson .10 .05
❑ 50 Jeff Hostetler .20 .09
❑ 51 Nick Lowery .10 .05
❑ 52 Merril Hoge .10 .05
❑ 53 Bobby Hebert .10 .05
❑ 54 Scott Case .10 .05
❑ 55 Jack Del Rio .10 .05
❑ 56 Cornelius Bennett .20 .09
❑ 57 Tony Mandarich .10 .05
❑ 58 Bill Brooks .10 .05
❑ 59 Jessie Tuggle .10 .05
❑ 60 Hugh Millen RC .10 .05
❑ 61 Tony Bennett .20 .09
❑ 62 Cris Dishman RC .10 .05
❑ 63 Darryl Henley RC .10 .05
❑ 64 Duane Bickett .10 .05
❑ 65 Jay Hilgenberg .10 .05
❑ 66 Joe Montana 4.00 1.80
❑ 67 Bill Fralic .10 .05
❑ 68 Sam Mills .10 .05
❑ 69 Bruce Armstrong .10 .05
❑ 70 Dan Marino 4.00 1.80
❑ 71 Jim Lachey .10 .05
❑ 72 Rod Woodson .40 .18
❑ 73 Simon Fletcher .10 .05
❑ 74 Bruce Matthews .20 .09
❑ 75 Howie Long .20 .09
❑ 76 John Friesz .40 .18
❑ 77 Karl Mecklenburg .10 .05
❑ 78 John L. Williams UER .10 .05
(Two photos show
42 Chris Warren)
❑ 79 Rob Burnett RC .10 .05
❑ 80 Anthony Carter .20 .09
❑ 81 Henry Ellard .20 .09
❑ 82 Don Beebe .10 .05
❑ 83 Louis Lipps .10 .05
❑ 84 Greg McMurtry .10 .05
❑ 85 Will Wolford .10 .05
❑ 86 Eric Green .10 .05
❑ 87 Irving Fryar .20 .09
❑ 88 John Offerdahl .10 .05
❑ 89 John Alt .10 .05
❑ 90 Tom Tupa .10 .05
❑ 91 Don Mosebar .10 .05
❑ 92 Jeff George .75 .35

❑ 93	Vinny Testaverde	.20	.09
❑ 94	Greg Townsend	.10	.05
❑ 95	Derrick Fenner	.10	.05
❑ 96	Brian Mitchell	.20	.09
❑ 97	Herschel Walker	.20	.09
❑ 98	Ricky Proehl	.10	.05
❑ 99	Mark Clayton	.20	.09
❑ 100	Derrick Thomas	.40	.18
❑ 101	Jim Harbaugh	.40	.18
❑ 102	Barry Word	.10	.05
❑ 103	Jerry Rice	2.50	1.10
❑ 104	Keith Byars	.10	.05
❑ 105	Marion Butts	.20	.09
❑ 106	Rich Moran	.10	.05
❑ 107	Thurman Thomas	.40	.18
❑ 108	Stephone Paige	.10	.05
❑ 109	D.J. Johnson	.10	.05
❑ 110	William Perry	.20	.09
❑ 111	Haywood Jeffires	.20	.09
❑ 112	Rodney Peete	.20	.09
❑ 113	Andy Heck	.10	.05
❑ 114	Kevin Ross	.10	.05
❑ 115	Michael Carter	.10	.05
❑ 116	Tim McKyer	.10	.05
❑ 117	Kenneth Davis	.10	.05
❑ 118	Richmond Webb	.10	.05
❑ 119	Rich Camarillo	.10	.05
❑ 120	James Francis	.10	.05
❑ 121	Craig Heyward	.20	.09
❑ 122	Hardy Nickerson	.20	.09
❑ 123	Michael Brooks	.10	.05
❑ 124	Fred Barnett	.40	.18
❑ 125	Cris Carter	1.25	.55
❑ 126	Brian Jordan	.20	.09
❑ 127	Pat Leahy	.10	.05
❑ 128	Kevin Greene	.40	.18
❑ 129	Trace Armstrong	.10	.05
❑ 130	Eugene Lockhart	.10	.05
❑ 131	Albert Lewis	.10	.05
❑ 132	Ernie Jones	.10	.05
❑ 133	Eric Martin	.10	.05
❑ 134	Anthony Thompson	.10	.05
❑ 135	Tim Krumrie	.10	.05
❑ 136	James Lofton	.20	.09
❑ 137	John Taylor	.20	.09
❑ 138	Jeff Cross	.10	.05
❑ 139	Tommy Kane	.10	.05
❑ 140	Robb Thomas	.10	.05
❑ 141	Gary Anderson K	.10	.05
❑ 142	Mark Murphy	.10	.05
❑ 143	Rickey Jackson	.10	.05
❑ 144	Ken O'Brien	.10	.05
❑ 145	Ernest Givins	.20	.09
❑ 146	Jessie Hester	.10	.05
❑ 147	Deion Sanders	1.00	.45
❑ 148	Keith Henderson RC	.10	.05
❑ 149	Chris Singleton	.10	.05
❑ 150	Rod Bernstine	.10	.05
❑ 151	Quinn Early	.20	.09
❑ 152	Boomer Esiason	.20	.09
❑ 153	Mike Gann	.10	.05
❑ 154	Dino Hackett	.10	.05
❑ 155	Perry Kemp	.10	.05
❑ 156	Mark Ingram	.20	.09
❑ 157	Daryl Johnston	1.00	.45
❑ 158	Eugene Daniel	.10	.05
❑ 159	Dalton Hilliard	.10	.05
❑ 160	Rufus Porter	.10	.05
❑ 161	Tunch Ilkin	.10	.05
❑ 162	James Hasty	.10	.05
❑ 163	Keith McKeller	.10	.05
❑ 164	Heath Sherman	.10	.05
❑ 165	Vai Sikahema	.10	.05
❑ 166	Pat Terrell	.10	.05
❑ 167	Anthony Munoz	.20	.09
❑ 168	Brad Edwards RC	.10	.05
❑ 169	Tom Rathman	.10	.05
❑ 170	Steve McMichael	.20	.09
❑ 171	Vaughan Johnson	.10	.05
❑ 172	Nate Lewis RC	.10	.05
❑ 173	Mark Rypien	.20	.09
❑ 174	Rob Moore	.75	.35
❑ 175	Tim Green	.10	.05
❑ 176	Tony Casillas	.10	.05
❑ 177	Jon Hand	.10	.05
❑ 178	Todd McNair	.10	.05
❑ 179	Toi Cook RC	.10	.05
❑ 180	Eddie Brown	.10	.05
❑ 181	Mark Jackson	.10	.05
❑ 182	Pete Stoyanovich	.10	.05
❑ 183	Bryce Paup RC	.40	.18
❑ 184	Anthony Miller	.20	.09
❑ 185	Dan Saleaumua	.10	.05
❑ 186	Guy McIntyre	.10	.05
❑ 187	Broderick Thomas	.10	.05
❑ 188	Frank Warren	.10	.05
❑ 189	Drew Hill	.10	.05
❑ 190	Reggie White	.40	.18
❑ 191	Chris Hinton	.10	.05
❑ 192	David Little	.10	.05
❑ 193	David Fulcher	.10	.05
❑ 194	Clarence Verdin	.10	.05
❑ 195	Junior Seau	.75	.35
❑ 196	Blair Thomas	.10	.05
❑ 197	Stan Brock	.10	.05
❑ 198	Gary Clark	.40	.18
❑ 199	Michael Irvin	.40	.18
❑ 200	Ronnie Harmon	.10	.05
❑ 201	Steve Young	2.50	1.10
❑ 202	Brian Noble	.10	.05
❑ 203	Dan Stryzinski	.10	.05
❑ 204	Darryl Talley	.10	.05
❑ 205	David Alexander	.10	.05
❑ 206	Pat Swilling	.20	.09
❑ 207	Gary Plummer	.10	.05
❑ 208	Robert Delpino	.10	.05
❑ 209	Norm Johnson	.10	.05
❑ 210	Mike Singletary	.20	.09
❑ 211	Anthony Johnson	.40	.18
❑ 212	Eric Allen	.10	.05
❑ 213	Gill Fenerty	.10	.05
❑ 214	Neil Smith	.40	.18
❑ 215	Joe Phillips	.10	.05
❑ 216	Ottis Anderson	.20	.09
❑ 217	LeRoy Butler	.20	.09
❑ 218	Ray Childress	.10	.05
❑ 219	Rodney Holman	.10	.05
❑ 220	Kevin Fagan	.10	.05
❑ 221	Bruce Smith	.40	.18
❑ 222	Brad Muster	.10	.05
❑ 223	Mike Horan	.10	.05
❑ 224	Steve Atwater	.10	.05
❑ 225	Rich Gannon	.10	.05
❑ 226	Anthony Pleasant	.10	.05
❑ 227	Steve Jordan	.10	.05
❑ 228	Lomas Brown	.10	.05
❑ 229	Jackie Slater	.10	.05
❑ 230	Brad Baxter	.10	.05
❑ 231	Joe Morris	.10	.05
❑ 232	Marcus Allen	.40	.18
❑ 233	Chris Warren	.40	.18
❑ 234	Johnny Johnson	.10	.05
❑ 235	Phil Simms	.20	.09
❑ 236	Dave Krieg	.20	.09
❑ 237	Jim McMahon	.20	.09
❑ 238	Richard Dent	.20	.09
❑ 239	John Washington RC	.10	.05
❑ 240	Sammie Smith	.10	.05
❑ 241	Brian Brennan	.10	.05
❑ 242	Cortez Kennedy	.40	.18
❑ 243	Tim McDonald	.10	.05
❑ 244	Charles Haley	.20	.09
❑ 245	Joey Browner	.10	.05
❑ 246	Eddie Murray	.10	.05
❑ 247	Bob Golic	.10	.05
❑ 248	Myron Guyton	.10	.05
❑ 249	Dennis Byrd	.10	.05
❑ 250	Barry Sanders	5.00	2.20
❑ 251	Clay Matthews	.20	.09
❑ 252	Pepper Johnson	.10	.05
❑ 253	Eric Swann RC	.40	.18
❑ 254	Lamar Lathon	.10	.05
❑ 255	Andre Tippett	.10	.05
❑ 256	Tom Newberry	.10	.05
❑ 257	Kyle Clifton	.10	.05
❑ 258	Leslie O'Neal	.20	.09
❑ 259	Bubba McDowell	.10	.05
❑ 260	Scott Davis	.10	.05
❑ 261	Wilber Marshall	.10	.05
❑ 262	Marv Cook	.10	.05
❑ 263	Jeff Lageman	.10	.05
❑ 264	Michael Young	.10	.05
❑ 265	Gary Zimmerman	.10	.05
❑ 266	Mike Munchak	.10	.05
❑ 267	David Treadwell	.10	.05
❑ 268	Steve Wisniewski	.10	.05
❑ 269	Mark Duper	.20	.09
❑ 270	Chris Spielman	.20	.09
❑ 271	Brett Perriman	.40	.18
❑ 272	Lionel Washington	.10	.05
❑ 273	Lawrence Taylor	.40	.18
❑ 274	Mark Collins	.10	.05
❑ 275	Mark Carrier WR	.40	.18
❑ 276	Paul Gruber	.10	.05
❑ 277	Earnest Byner	.10	.05
❑ 278	Andre Collins	.10	.05
❑ 279	Reggie Cobb	.10	.05
❑ 280	Art Monk	.20	.09
❑ 281	Henry Jones RC	.20	.09
❑ 282	Mike Pritchard RC	.40	.18
❑ 283	Moe Gardner RC	.10	.05
❑ 284	Chris Zorich RC	.40	.18
❑ 285	Keith Traylor RC	.10	.05
❑ 286	Mike Dumas RC	.10	.05
❑ 287	Ed King RC	.10	.05
❑ 288	Russell Maryland RC	.40	.18
❑ 289	Alfred Williams RC	.10	.05
❑ 290	Derek Russell RC	.10	.05
❑ 291	Vinnie Clark RC	.10	.05
❑ 292	Mike Croel RC	.10	.05
❑ 293	Todd Marinovich RC	.10	.05
❑ 294	Phil Hansen RC	.10	.05
❑ 295	Aaron Craver RC	.10	.05
❑ 296	Nick Bell RC	.10	.05
❑ 297	Kenny Walker RC	.10	.05
❑ 298	Roman Phifer RC	.10	.05
❑ 299	Kanavis McGhee RC	.10	.05
❑ 300	Ricky Ervins RC	.20	.09
❑ 301	Jim Price RC	.10	.05
❑ 302	John Johnson RC	.10	.05
❑ 303	George Thornton RC	.10	.05
❑ 304	Huey Richardson RC	.10	.05
❑ 305	Harry Colon RC	.10	.05
❑ 306	Antone Davis RC	.10	.05
❑ 307	Todd Lyght RC	.10	.05
❑ 308	Bryan Cox RC	.40	.18
❑ 309	Brad Goebel RC	.10	.05
❑ 310	Eric Moten RC	.10	.05
❑ 311	John Kasay RC	.20	.09
❑ 312	Esera Tuaolo RC	.10	.05
❑ 313	Bobby Wilson RC	.10	.05
❑ 314	Mo Lewis RC	.20	.09
❑ 315	Harvey Williams RC	.40	.18
❑ 316	Mike Stonebreaker	.10	.05
❑ 317	Charles McRae RC	.10	.05
❑ 318	John Flannery RC	.10	.05
❑ 319	Ted Washington RC	.10	.05
❑ 320	Stanley Richard RC	.10	.05
❑ 321	Browning Nagle RC	.10	.05
❑ 322	Ed McCaffery RC	5.00	2.20
❑ 323	Jeff Graham RC	.40	.18
❑ 324	Stan Thomas	.10	.05
❑ 325	Lawrence Dawsey RC	.20	.09
❑ 326	Eric Bieniemy RC	.10	.05
❑ 327	Tim Barnett RC	.10	.05
❑ 328	Erric Pegram RC	.40	.18
❑ 329	Lamar Rogers RC	.10	.05
❑ 330	Ernie Mills RC	.20	.09
❑ 331	Pat Harlow RC	.10	.05
❑ 332	Greg Lewis RC	.10	.05
❑ 333	Jarrod Bunch RC	.10	.05
❑ 334	Dan McGwire RC	.10	.05
❑ 335	Randal Hill RC	.20	.09
❑ 336	Leonard Russell RC	.40	.18
❑ 337	Carnell Lake	.10	.05
❑ 338	Brian Blades	.20	.09
❑ 339	Darrell Green	.10	.05
❑ 340	Bobby Humphrey	.10	.05
❑ 341	Mervyn Fernandez	.10	.05
❑ 342	Ricky Sanders	.10	.05
❑ 343	Keith Jackson	.20	.09
❑ 344	Carl Banks	.10	.05
❑ 345	Gill Byrd	.10	.05
❑ 346	Al Toon	.20	.09
❑ 347	Stephen Baker	.10	.05
❑ 348	Randall Cunningham	.40	.18
❑ 349	Flipper Anderson	.10	.05
❑ 350	Jay Novacek	.40	.18

Card	Mint	Nrmt
❑ 351 Steve Young HH vs. Bruce Smith	.40	.18
❑ 352 Barry Sanders HH vs. Joey Browner	1.00	.45
❑ 353 Joe Montana HH vs. Mark Carrier	.50	.23
❑ 354 Thurman Thomas HH vs. Lawrence Taylor	.20	.09
❑ 355 Jerry Rice HH vs. Darrell Green	.60	.25
❑ 356 Warren Moon TECH	.20	.09
❑ 357 Anthony Munoz TECH	.10	.05
❑ 358 Barry Sanders TECH	2.50	1.10
❑ 359 Jerry Rice TECH	1.25	.55
❑ 360 Joey Browner TECH	.10	.05
❑ 361 Morten Andersen TECH	.10	.05
❑ 362 Sean Landeta TECH	.10	.05
❑ 363 Thurman Thomas GW	.40	.18
❑ 364 Emmitt Smith GW	3.00	1.35
❑ 365 Gaston Green GW	.10	.05
❑ 366 Barry Sanders GW	2.50	1.10
❑ 367 Christian Okoye GW	.10	.05
❑ 368 Earnest Byner GW	.10	.05
❑ 369 Neal Anderson GW	.10	.05
❑ 370 Herschel Walker GW	.20	.09
❑ 371 Rodney Hampton GW	.40	.18
❑ 372 Darryl Talley IDOL Ted Hendricks	.10	.05
❑ 373 Mark Carrier IDOL Ronnie Lott	.10	.05
❑ 374 Jim Breech IDOL Jan Stenerud	.10	.05
❑ 375 Rodney Hampton IDOL Ottis Anderson	.10	.05
❑ 376 Kevin Mack IDOL Earnest Byner	.10	.05
❑ 377 Steve Jordan IDOL Oscar Robertson	.10	.05
❑ 378 Boomer Esiason IDOL Bert Jones	.10	.05
❑ 379 Steve DeBerg IDOL Roman Gabriel	.20	.09
❑ 380 Al Toon IDOL Wesley Walker	.10	.05
❑ 381 Ronnie Lott IDOL Charley Taylor	.20	.09
❑ 382 Henry Ellard IDOL Bob Hayes	.10	.05
❑ 383 Troy Aikman IDOL Roger Staubach	1.25	.55
❑ 384 Thurman Thomas IDOL Earl Campbell	.40	.18
❑ 385 Dan Marino IDOL Terry Bradshaw	1.50	.70
❑ 386 Howie Long IDOL Joe Greene	.20	.09
❑ 387 Franco Harris Immaculate Reception	.20	.09
❑ 388 Esera Tuaolo	.10	.05
❑ 389 Super Bowl XXVI (Super Bowl Records)	.10	.05
❑ 390 Charles Mann	.10	.05
❑ 391 Kenny Walker	.10	.05
❑ 392 Reggie Roby	.10	.05
❑ 393 Bruce Pickens RC	.10	.05
❑ 394 Ray Childress SIDE	.10	.05
❑ 395 Karl Mecklenburg SIDE	.10	.05
❑ 396 Dean Biasucci SIDE	.10	.05
❑ 397 John Alt SIDE	.10	.05
❑ 398 Marcus Allen SIDE	.20	.09
❑ 399 John Offerdahl SIDE	.10	.05
❑ 400 Richard Tardits SIDE RC	.10	.05
❑ 401 Al Toon SIDE	.10	.05
❑ 402 Joey Browner SIDE	.10	.05
❑ 403 Spencer Tillman SIDE RC	.10	.05
❑ 404 Jay Novacek SIDE	.20	.09
❑ 405 Stephen Braggs SIDE	.10	.05
❑ 406 Mike Tice SIDE RC	.10	.05
❑ 407 Kevin Greene SIDE	.20	.09
❑ 408 Reggie White SIDE	.20	.09
❑ 409 Brian Noble SIDE	.10	.05
❑ 410 Bart Oates SIDE	.10	.05
❑ 411 Art Monk SIDE	.20	.09
❑ 412 Ron Wolfley SIDE	.10	.05
❑ 413 Louis Lipps SIDE	.10	.05
❑ 414 Dante Jones SIDE RC	.20	.09
❑ 415 Kenneth Davis SIDE	.10	.05
❑ P1 Emmitt Smith Promo numbered 42 Mentions holdout on back	25.00	11.00

1992 Pinnacle

	MINT	NRMT
COMPLETE SET (360)	25.00	11.00
COMMON CARD (1-360)	.15	.07
SEMISTARS	.30	.14
UNLISTED STARS	.50	.23

Card	Mint	Nrmt
❑ 1 Reggie White	.50	.23
❑ 2 Eric Green	.15	.07
❑ 3 Craig Heyward	.30	.14
❑ 4 Phil Simms	.30	.14
❑ 5 Pepper Johnson	.15	.07
❑ 6 Sean Landeta	.15	.07
❑ 7 Dino Hackett	.15	.07
❑ 8 Andre Ware	.15	.07
❑ 9 Ricky Nattiel	.15	.07
❑ 10 Jim Price	.15	.07
❑ 11 Jim Ritcher	.15	.07
❑ 12 Kelly Stouffer	.15	.07
❑ 13 Ray Crockett	.15	.07
❑ 14 Steve Tasker	.30	.14
❑ 15 Barry Sanders	4.00	1.80
❑ 16 Pat Swilling	.30	.14
❑ 17 Moe Gardner	.15	.07
❑ 18 Steve Young	2.00	.90
❑ 19 Chris Spielman	.30	.14
❑ 20 Richard Dent	.30	.14
❑ 21 Anthony Munoz	.30	.14
❑ 22 Thurman Thomas	.50	.23
❑ 23 Ricky Sanders	.15	.07
❑ 24 Steve Atwater	.15	.07
❑ 25 Tony Tolbert	.15	.07
❑ 26 Haywood Jeffires	.30	.14
❑ 27 Duane Bickett	.15	.07
❑ 28 Tim McDonald	.15	.07
❑ 29 Cris Carter	.75	.35
❑ 30 Derrick Thomas	.50	.23
❑ 31 Hugh Millen	.15	.07
❑ 32 Bart Oates	.15	.07
❑ 33 Darryl Talley	.15	.07
❑ 34 Marion Butts	.15	.07
❑ 35 Pete Stoyanovich	.15	.07
❑ 36 Ronnie Lott	.30	.14
❑ 37 Simon Fletcher	.15	.07
❑ 38 Morten Andersen	.15	.07
❑ 39 Clyde Simmons	.15	.07
❑ 40 Mark Rypien	.15	.07
❑ 41 Henry Ellard	.30	.14
❑ 42 Michael Irvin	.50	.23
❑ 43 Louis Lipps	.15	.07
❑ 44 John L. Williams	.15	.07
❑ 45 Broderick Thomas	.15	.07
❑ 46 Don Majkowski	.15	.07
❑ 47 William Perry	.30	.14
❑ 48 David Fulcher	.15	.07
❑ 49 Tony Bennett	.15	.07
❑ 50 Clay Matthews	.30	.14
❑ 51 Warren Moon	.50	.23
❑ 52 Bruce Armstrong	.15	.07
❑ 53 Bill Brooks	.15	.07
❑ 54 Greg Townsend	.15	.07
❑ 55 Steve Broussard	.15	.07
❑ 56 Mel Gray	.30	.14
❑ 57 Kevin Mack	.15	.07
❑ 58 Emmitt Smith	4.00	1.80
❑ 59 Mike Croel	.15	.07
❑ 60 Brian Mitchell	.30	.14
❑ 61 Bennie Blades	.15	.07
❑ 62 Carnell Lake	.15	.07
❑ 63 Cornelius Bennett	.30	.14
❑ 64 Darrell Thompson	.15	.07
❑ 65 Jessie Hester	.15	.07
❑ 66 Marv Cook	.15	.07
❑ 67 Tim Brown	.50	.23
❑ 68 Mark Duper	.15	.07
❑ 69 Robert Delpino	.15	.07
❑ 70 Eric Martin	.15	.07
❑ 71 Wendell Davis	.15	.07
❑ 72 Vaughan Johnson	.15	.07
❑ 73 Brian Blades	.30	.14
❑ 74 Ed King	.15	.07
❑ 75 Gaston Green	.15	.07
❑ 76 Christian Okoye	.15	.07
❑ 77 Rohn Stark	.15	.07
❑ 78 Kevin Greene	.50	.23
❑ 79 Jay Novacek	.30	.14
❑ 80 Chip Lohmiller	.15	.07
❑ 81 Cris Dishman	.15	.07
❑ 82 Ethan Horton	.15	.07
❑ 83 Pat Harlow	.15	.07
❑ 84 Mark Ingram	.15	.07
❑ 85 Mark Carrier DB	.15	.07
❑ 86 Sam Mills	.15	.07
❑ 87 Mark Higgs	.15	.07
❑ 88 Keith Jackson	.30	.14
❑ 89 Gary Anderson K	.15	.07
❑ 90 Ken Harvey	.15	.07
❑ 91 Anthony Carter	.30	.14
❑ 92 Randall McDaniel	.15	.07
❑ 93 Johnny Johnson	.15	.07
❑ 94 Shane Conlan	.15	.07
❑ 95 Sterling Sharpe	.50	.23
❑ 96 Guy McIntyre	.15	.07
❑ 97 Albert Lewis	.15	.07
❑ 98 Chris Doleman	.15	.07
❑ 99 Andre Rison	.30	.14
❑ 100 Bobby Hebert	.15	.07
❑ 101 Dan Owens	.15	.07
❑ 102 Rodney Hampton	.50	.23
❑ 103 Ernie Jones	.15	.07
❑ 104 Reggie Cobb	.15	.07
❑ 105 Wilber Marshall	.15	.07
❑ 106 Mike Munchak	.15	.07
❑ 107 Cortez Kennedy	.30	.14
❑ 108 Todd Lyght	.15	.07
❑ 109 Burt Grossman	.15	.07
❑ 110 Ferrell Edmunds	.15	.07
❑ 111 Jim Everett	.30	.14
❑ 112 Hardy Nickerson	.30	.14
❑ 113 Andre Tippett	.15	.07
❑ 114 Ronnie Harmon	.15	.07
❑ 115 Andre Waters	.15	.07
❑ 116 Ernest Givins	.30	.14
❑ 117 Eric Hill	.15	.07
❑ 118 Erric Pegram	.30	.14
❑ 119 Jarrod Bunch	.15	.07
❑ 120 Marcus Allen	.50	.23
❑ 121 Barry Foster	.30	.14
❑ 122 Kent Hull	.15	.07
❑ 123 Neal Anderson	.15	.07
❑ 124 Stephen Braggs	.15	.07
❑ 125 Nick Lowery	.15	.07
❑ 126 Jeff Hostetler	.30	.14
❑ 127 Michael Carter	.15	.07
❑ 128 Don Warren	.15	.07
❑ 129 Brad Baxter	.15	.07
❑ 130 John Taylor	.30	.14
❑ 131 Harold Green	.15	.07
❑ 132 Mike Merriweather	.15	.07
❑ 133 Gary Clark	.50	.23
❑ 134 Vince Buck	.15	.07
❑ 135 Dan Saleaumua	.15	.07
❑ 136 Gary Zimmerman	.15	.07
❑ 137 Richmond Webb	.15	.07
❑ 138 Art Monk	.30	.14
❑ 139 Mervyn Fernandez	.15	.07
❑ 140 Mark Jackson	.15	.07
❑ 141 Freddie Joe Nunn	.15	.07
❑ 142 Jeff Lageman	.15	.07

- ❑ 143 Kenny Walker .15 .07
- ❑ 144 Mark Carrier WR .30 .14
- ❑ 145 Jon Vaughn .15 .07
- ❑ 146 Greg Davis .15 .07
- ❑ 147 Bubby Brister .15 .07
- ❑ 148 Mo Lewis .15 .07
- ❑ 149 Howie Long .30 .14
- ❑ 150 Rod Bernstine .15 .07
- ❑ 151 Nick Bell .15 .07
- ❑ 152 Terry Allen .50 .23
- ❑ 153 William Fuller .30 .14
- ❑ 154 Dexter Carter .15 .07
- ❑ 155 Gene Atkins .15 .07
- ❑ 156 Don Beebe .15 .07
- ❑ 157 Mark Collins .15 .07
- ❑ 158 Jerry Ball .15 .07
- ❑ 159 Fred Barnett .50 .23
- ❑ 160 Rodney Holman .15 .07
- ❑ 161 Stephen Baker .15 .07
- ❑ 162 Jeff Graham .50 .23
- ❑ 163 Leonard Russell .30 .14
- ❑ 164 Jeff Gossett .15 .07
- ❑ 165 Vinny Testaverde .30 .14
- ❑ 166 Maurice Hurst .15 .07
- ❑ 167 Louis Oliver .15 .07
- ❑ 168 Jim Morrissey .15 .07
- ❑ 169 Greg Kragen .15 .07
- ❑ 170 Andre Collins .15 .07
- ❑ 171 Dave Meggett .30 .14
- ❑ 172 Keith Henderson .15 .07
- ❑ 173 Vince Newsome .15 .07
- ❑ 174 Chris Hinton .15 .07
- ❑ 175 James Hasty .15 .07
- ❑ 176 John Offerdahl .15 .07
- ❑ 177 Lomas Brown .15 .07
- ❑ 178 Neil O'Donnell .50 .23
- ❑ 179 Leonard Marshall .15 .07
- ❑ 180 Bubba McDowell .15 .07
- ❑ 181 Herman Moore 2.00 .90
- ❑ 182 Rob Moore .30 .14
- ❑ 183 Earnest Byner .15 .07
- ❑ 184 Keith McCants .15 .07
- ❑ 185 Floyd Turner .15 .07
- ❑ 186 Steve Jordan .15 .07
- ❑ 187 Nate Odomes .15 .07
- ❑ 188 Jeff Herrod .15 .07
- ❑ 189 Jim Harbaugh .50 .23
- ❑ 190 Jessie Tuggle .15 .07
- ❑ 191 Al Smith .15 .07
- ❑ 192 Lawrence Dawsey .30 .14
- ❑ 193 Steve Bono RC .50 .23
- ❑ 194 Greg Lloyd .50 .23
- ❑ 195 Steve Wisniewski .15 .07
- ❑ 196 Larry Kelm .15 .07
- ❑ 197 Tommy Kane .15 .07
- ❑ 198 Mark Schlereth RC .15 .07
- ❑ 199 Ray Childress .15 .07
- ❑ 200 Vincent Brown .15 .07
- ❑ 201 Rodney Peete .30 .14
- ❑ 202 Dennis Smith .15 .07
- ❑ 203 Bruce Matthews .15 .07
- ❑ 204 Rickey Jackson .15 .07
- ❑ 205 Eric Allen .15 .07
- ❑ 206 Rich Camarillo .15 .07
- ❑ 207 Jim Lachey .15 .07
- ❑ 208 Kevin Ross .15 .07
- ❑ 209 Irving Fryar .30 .14
- ❑ 210 Mark Clayton .30 .14
- ❑ 211 Keith Byars .15 .07
- ❑ 212 John Elway 3.00 1.35
- ❑ 213 Harris Barton .15 .07
- ❑ 214 Aeneas Williams .30 .14
- ❑ 215 Rich Gannon .15 .07
- ❑ 216 Toi Cook .15 .07
- ❑ 217 Rod Woodson .50 .23
- ❑ 218 Gary Anderson RB .15 .07
- ❑ 219 Reggie Roby .15 .07
- ❑ 220 Karl Mecklenburg .15 .07
- ❑ 221 Rufus Porter .15 .07
- ❑ 222 Jon Hand .15 .07
- ❑ 223 Tim Barnett .15 .07
- ❑ 224 Eric Swann .30 .14
- ❑ 225 Eugene Robinson .15 .07
- ❑ 226 Michael Young .15 .07
- ❑ 227 Frank Warren .15 .07
- ❑ 228 Mike Kenn .15 .07
- ❑ 229 Tim Green .15 .07
- ❑ 230 Barry Word .15 .07
- ❑ 231 Mike Pritchard .30 .14
- ❑ 232 John Kasay .15 .07
- ❑ 233 Derek Russell .15 .07
- ❑ 234 Jim Breech .15 .07
- ❑ 235 Pierce Holt .15 .07
- ❑ 236 Tim Krumrie .15 .07
- ❑ 237 William Roberts .15 .07
- ❑ 238 Erik Kramer .30 .14
- ❑ 239 Brett Perriman .50 .23
- ❑ 240 Reyna Thompson .15 .07
- ❑ 241 Chris Miller .30 .14
- ❑ 242 Drew Hill .15 .07
- ❑ 243 Curtis Duncan .15 .07
- ❑ 244 Seth Joyner .30 .14
- ❑ 245 Ken Norton Jr. .50 .23
- ❑ 246 Calvin Williams .30 .14
- ❑ 247 James Joseph .15 .07
- ❑ 248 Bennie Thompson RC .15 .07
- ❑ 249 Tunch Ilkin .15 .07
- ❑ 250 Brad Edwards .15 .07
- ❑ 251 Jeff Jaeger .15 .07
- ❑ 252 Gill Byrd .15 .07
- ❑ 253 Jeff Feagles .15 .07
- ❑ 254 Jamie Dukes RC .15 .07
- ❑ 255 Greg McMurtry .15 .07
- ❑ 256 Anthony Johnson .30 .14
- ❑ 257 Lamar Lathon .15 .07
- ❑ 258 John Roper .15 .07
- ❑ 259 Lorenzo White .15 .07
- ❑ 260 Brian Noble .15 .07
- ❑ 261 Chris Singleton .15 .07
- ❑ 262 Todd Marinovich .15 .07
- ❑ 263 Jay Hilgenberg .15 .07
- ❑ 264 Kyle Clifton .15 .07
- ❑ 265 Tony Casillas .15 .07
- ❑ 266 James Francis .15 .07
- ❑ 267 Eddie Anderson .15 .07
- ❑ 268 Tim Harris .15 .07
- ❑ 269 James Lofton .30 .14
- ❑ 270 Jay Schroeder .15 .07
- ❑ 271 Ed West .15 .07
- ❑ 272 Don Mosebar .15 .07
- ❑ 273 Jackie Slater .15 .07
- ❑ 274 Fred McAfee RC .15 .07
- ❑ 275 Steve Sewell .15 .07
- ❑ 276 Charles Mann .15 .07
- ❑ 277 Ron Hall .15 .07
- ❑ 278 Darrell Green .15 .07
- ❑ 279 Jeff Cross .15 .07
- ❑ 280 Jeff Wright .15 .07
- ❑ 281 Issiac Holt .15 .07
- ❑ 282 Dermontti Dawson .15 .07
- ❑ 283 Michael Haynes .30 .14
- ❑ 284 Tony Mandarich .15 .07
- ❑ 285 Leroy Hoard .30 .14
- ❑ 286 Darryl Henley .15 .07
- ❑ 287 Tim McGee .15 .07
- ❑ 288 Willie Gault .30 .14
- ❑ 289 Dalton Hilliard .15 .07
- ❑ 290 Tim McKyer .15 .07
- ❑ 291 Tom Waddle .15 .07
- ❑ 292 Eric Thomas .15 .07
- ❑ 293 Herschel Walker .30 .14
- ❑ 294 Donnell Woolford .15 .07
- ❑ 295 James Brooks .30 .14
- ❑ 296 Brad Muster .15 .07
- ❑ 297 Brent Jones .30 .14
- ❑ 298 Erik Howard .15 .07
- ❑ 299 Alvin Harper UER .30 .14
(Born in Frostproof,
not Frostfree)
- ❑ 300 Joey Browner .15 .07
- ❑ 301 Jack Del Rio .15 .07
- ❑ 302 Cleveland Gary .15 .07
- ❑ 303 Brett Favre 6.00 2.70
- ❑ 304 Freeman McNeil .15 .07
- ❑ 305 Willie Green .15 .07
- ❑ 306 Percy Snow .15 .07
- ❑ 307 Neil Smith .50 .23
- ❑ 308 Eric Bieniemy .15 .07
- ❑ 309 Keith Traylor .15 .07
- ❑ 310 Ernie Mills .15 .07
- ❑ 311 Will Wolford .15 .07
- ❑ 312 Robert Young .15 .07
- ❑ 313 Anthony Smith .15 .07
- ❑ 314 Robert Porcher RC .30 .14
- ❑ 315 Leon Searcy RC .30 .14
- ❑ 316 Amp Lee RC .15 .07
- ❑ 317 Siran Stacy RC .15 .07
- ❑ 318 Patrick Rowe RC .15 .07
- ❑ 319 Chris Mims RC .30 .14
- ❑ 320 Matt Elliott RC .15 .07
- ❑ 321 Ricardo McDonald RC .15 .07
- ❑ 322 Keith Hamilton RC .15 .07
- ❑ 323 Edgar Bennett RC .75 .35
- ❑ 324 Chris Hakel RC .15 .07
- ❑ 325 Dexter McNabb RC .15 .07
- ❑ 326 Rod Milstead RC .15 .07
- ❑ 327 Joe Bowden RC .15 .07
- ❑ 328 Brian Bollinger RC .15 .07
- ❑ 329 Darryl Williams RC .15 .07
- ❑ 330 Tommy Vardell RC .30 .14
- ❑ 331 Glenn Parker SIDE .15 .07
Mitch Frerotte
- ❑ 332 Herschel Walker SIDE .15 .07
- ❑ 333 Mike Cofer SIDE .15 .07
- ❑ 334 Mark Rypien SIDE .15 .07
- ❑ 335 Andre Rison GW .30 .14
- ❑ 336 Henry Ellard GW .15 .07
- ❑ 337 Rob Moore GW .15 .07
- ❑ 338 Fred Barnett GW .15 .07
- ❑ 339 Mark Clayton GW .15 .07
- ❑ 340 Eric Martin GW .15 .07
- ❑ 341 Irving Fryar GW .15 .07
- ❑ 342 Tim Brown GW .30 .14
- ❑ 343 Sterling Sharpe GW .30 .14
- ❑ 344 Gary Clark GW .15 .07
- ❑ 345 John Mackey HOF .15 .07
- ❑ 346 Lem Barney HOF .15 .07
- ❑ 347 John Riggins HOF .30 .14
- ❑ 348 Marion Butts IDOL .15 .07
William Andrews
- ❑ 349 Jeff Lageman IDOL .15 .07
Jack Lambert
- ❑ 350 Eric Green IDOL .15 .07
Sam Rutigliano
- ❑ 351 Reggie White IDOL .30 .14
Bobby Jones
- ❑ 352 Marv Cook IDOL .15 .07
Dan Gable
- ❑ 353 John Elway IDOL 1.25 .55
Roger Staubach
- ❑ 354 Steve Tasker IDOL .15 .07
Ed Podolak
- ❑ 355 Nick Lowery IDOL .15 .07
Jan Stenerud
- ❑ 356 Mark Clayton IDOL .15 .07
Paul Warfield
- ❑ 357 Warren Moon IDOL .30 .14
Roman Gabriel
- ❑ 358 Eric Metcalf .30 .14
- ❑ 359 Charles Haley .30 .14
- ❑ 360 Terrell Buckley RC .15 .07
- ❑ P1 Promo Panel 5.00 2.20
Super Bowl XXVII promo
John Elway
Sterling Sharpe
Warren Moon
Tommy Vardell
Derrick Thomas
Pat Swilling
Neil Smith
Cortez Kennedy

1992 Pinnacle Team Pinnacle

	MINT	NRMT
COMPLETE SET (13)	60.00	27.00
COMMON PAIR (1-13)	4.00	1.80
SEMISTARS	6.00	2.70
UNLISTED STARS	8.00	3.60

RANDOM INSERTS IN FOIL PACKS

- ❑ 1 Mark Rypien 6.00 2.70
Ronnie Lott
- ❑ 2 Barry Sanders 15.00 6.75
Derrick Thomas
- ❑ 3 Thurman Thomas 8.00 3.60

Card	Mint	Nrmt
Pat Swilling		
❑ 4 Eric Green	6.00	2.70
Steve Atwater		
❑ 5 Haywood Jeffires	6.00	2.70
Darrell Green		
❑ 6 Michael Irvin	8.00	3.60
Eric Allen		
❑ 7 Bruce Matthews	4.00	1.80
Jerry Ball		
❑ 8 Steve Wisniewski	4.00	1.80
Pepper Johnson		
❑ 9 William Roberts	4.00	1.80
Karl Mecklenburg		
❑ 10 Jim Lachey	4.00	1.80
William Fuller		
❑ 11 Anthony Munoz	8.00	3.60
Reggie White		
❑ 12 Mel Gray	6.00	2.70
Steve Tasker		
❑ 13 Jeff Jaeger	4.00	1.80
Jeff Gossett		

1992 Pinnacle Team 2000

	MINT	NRMT
COMPLETE SET (30)	15.00	6.75
TWO PER JUMBO PACK		

Card	Mint	Nrmt
❑ 1 Todd Marinovich	.10	.05
❑ 2 Rodney Hampton	.40	.18
❑ 3 Mike Croel	.10	.05
❑ 4 Leonard Russell	.25	.11
❑ 5 Herman Moore	1.50	.70
❑ 6 Rob Moore	.25	.11
❑ 7 Jon Vaughn	.10	.05
❑ 8 Lamar Lathon	.10	.05
❑ 9 Ed King	.10	.05
❑ 10 Moe Gardner	.10	.05
❑ 11 Barry Foster	.25	.11
❑ 12 Eric Green	.10	.05
❑ 13 Kenny Walker	.10	.05
❑ 14 Tim Barnett	.10	.05
❑ 15 Derrick Thomas	.40	.18
❑ 16 Steve Atwater	.10	.05
❑ 17 Nick Bell	.10	.05
❑ 18 John Friesz	.10	.05
❑ 19 Emmitt Smith	3.00	1.35
❑ 20 Eric Swann	.25	.11
❑ 21 Barry Sanders	3.00	1.35
❑ 22 Mark Carrier DB	.10	.05
❑ 23 Brett Favre	5.00	2.20
❑ 24 James Francis	.10	.05
❑ 25 Lawrence Dawsey	.25	.11
❑ 26 Keith McCants	.10	.05
❑ 27 Broderick Thomas	.10	.05
❑ 28 Mike Pritchard	.25	.11
❑ 29 Bruce Pickens	.10	.05
❑ 30 Todd Lyght	.10	.05

1993 Pinnacle

	MINT	NRMT
COMPLETE SET (360)	25.00	11.00
COMMON CARD (1-360)	.10	.05
SEMISTARS	.20	.09
UNLISTED STARS	.40	.18

Card	Mint	Nrmt
❑ 1 Brett Favre	4.00	1.80
❑ 2 Tommy Vardell	.10	.05
❑ 3 Jarrod Bunch	.10	.05
❑ 4 Mike Croel	.10	.05
❑ 5 Morten Andersen	.10	.05
❑ 6 Barry Foster	.20	.09
❑ 7 Chris Spielman	.20	.09
❑ 8 Jim Jeffcoat	.10	.05
❑ 9 Ken Ruettgers	.10	.05
❑ 10 Cris Dishman	.10	.05
❑ 11 Ricky Watters	.40	.18
❑ 12 Alfred Williams	.10	.05
❑ 13 Mark Kelso	.10	.05
❑ 14 Moe Gardner	.10	.05
❑ 15 Terry Allen	.40	.18
❑ 16 Willie Gault	.10	.05
❑ 17 Bubba McDowell	.10	.05
❑ 18 Brian Mitchell	.20	.09
❑ 19 Karl Mecklenburg	.10	.05
❑ 20 Jim Everett	.20	.09
❑ 21 Bobby Humphrey	.10	.05
❑ 22 Tim Krumrie	.10	.05
❑ 23 Ken Norton Jr.	.20	.09
❑ 24 Wendell Davis	.10	.05
❑ 25 Brad Baxter	.10	.05
❑ 26 Mel Gray	.20	.09
❑ 27 Jon Vaughn	.10	.05
❑ 28 James Hasty	.10	.05
❑ 29 Chris Warren	.20	.09
❑ 30 Tim Harris	.10	.05
❑ 31 Eric Metcalf	.20	.09
❑ 32 Rob Moore	.20	.09
❑ 33 Charles Haley	.20	.09
❑ 34 Leonard Marshall	.10	.05
❑ 35 Jeff Graham	.20	.09
❑ 36 Eugene Robinson	.10	.05
❑ 37 Darryl Talley	.10	.05
❑ 38 Brent Jones	.20	.09
❑ 39 Reggie Roby	.10	.05
❑ 40 Bruce Armstrong	.10	.05
❑ 41 Audray McMillian	.10	.05
❑ 42 Bern Brostek	.10	.05
❑ 43 Tony Bennett	.10	.05
❑ 44 Albert Lewis	.10	.05
❑ 45 Derrick Thomas	.40	.18
❑ 46 Cris Carter	.75	.35
❑ 47 Richmond Webb	.10	.05
❑ 48 Sean Landeta	.10	.05
❑ 49 Cleveland Gary	.10	.05
❑ 50 Mark Carrier DB	.10	.05
❑ 51 Lawrence Dawsey	.10	.05
❑ 52 Lamar Lathon	.10	.05
❑ 53 Nick Bell	.10	.05
❑ 54 Curtis Duncan	.10	.05
❑ 55 Irving Fryar	.20	.09
❑ 56 Seth Joyner	.10	.05
❑ 57 Jay Novacek	.20	.09
❑ 58 John L. Williams	.10	.05
❑ 59 Amp Lee	.10	.05
❑ 60 Marion Butts	.10	.05
❑ 61 Clyde Simmons	.10	.05
❑ 62 Rich Gannon	.10	.05
❑ 63 Anthony Johnson	.20	.09
❑ 64 Dave Meggett	.10	.05
❑ 65 James Francis	.10	.05
❑ 66 Trace Armstrong	.10	.05
❑ 67 Mo Lewis	.10	.05
❑ 68 Cornelius Bennett	.20	.09
❑ 69 Mark Duper	.10	.05
❑ 70 Frank Reich	.20	.09
❑ 71 Eric Green	.10	.05
❑ 72 Bruce Matthews	.10	.05
❑ 73 Steve Broussard	.10	.05
❑ 74 Anthony Carter	.20	.09
❑ 75 Sterling Sharpe	.40	.18
❑ 76 Mike Kenn	.10	.05
❑ 77 Andre Rison	.20	.09
❑ 78 Todd Marinovich	.10	.05
❑ 79 Vincent Brown	.10	.05
❑ 80 Harold Green	.10	.05
❑ 81 Art Monk	.20	.09
❑ 82 Reggie Cobb	.10	.05
❑ 83 Johnny Johnson	.10	.05
❑ 84 Tommy Kane	.10	.05
❑ 85 Rohn Stark	.10	.05
❑ 86 Steve Tasker	.20	.09
❑ 87 Ronnie Harmon	.10	.05
❑ 88 Pepper Johnson	.10	.05
❑ 89 Hardy Nickerson	.20	.09
❑ 90 Alvin Harper	.20	.09
❑ 91 Louis Oliver	.10	.05
❑ 92 Rod Woodson	.40	.18
❑ 93 Sam Mills	.10	.05
❑ 94 Randall McDaniel	.10	.05
❑ 95 Johnny Holland	.10	.05
❑ 96 Jackie Slater	.10	.05
❑ 97 Don Mosebar	.10	.05
❑ 98 Andre Ware	.10	.05
❑ 99 Kelvin Martin	.10	.05
❑ 100 Emmitt Smith	3.00	1.35
❑ 101 Michael Brooks	.10	.05
❑ 102 Dan Saleaumua	.10	.05
❑ 103 John Elway	3.00	1.35
❑ 104 Henry Jones	.10	.05
❑ 105 William Perry	.20	.09
❑ 106 James Lofton	.20	.09
❑ 107 Carnell Lake	.10	.05
❑ 108 Chip Lohmiller	.10	.05
❑ 109 Andre Tippett	.10	.05
❑ 110 Barry Word	.10	.05
❑ 111 Haywood Jeffires	.20	.09
❑ 112 Kenny Walker	.10	.05
❑ 113 John Randle	.10	.05
❑ 114 Donnell Woolford	.10	.05
❑ 115 Johnny Bailey	.10	.05
❑ 116 Marcus Allen	.40	.18
❑ 117 Mark Jackson	.10	.05
❑ 118 Ray Agnew	.10	.05
❑ 119 Gill Byrd	.10	.05
❑ 120 Kyle Clifton	.10	.05
❑ 121 Marv Cook	.10	.05
❑ 122 Jerry Ball	.10	.05
❑ 123 Steve Jordan	.10	.05
❑ 124 Shannon Sharpe	.40	.18
❑ 125 Brian Blades	.20	.09
❑ 126 Rodney Hampton	.40	.18
❑ 127 Bobby Hebert	.10	.05
❑ 128 Jessie Tuggle	.10	.05
❑ 129 Tom Newberry	.10	.05
❑ 130 Keith McCants	.10	.05
❑ 131 Richard Dent	.20	.09
❑ 132 Herman Moore	1.00	.45
❑ 133 Michael Irvin	.40	.18
❑ 134 Ernest Givins	.20	.09
❑ 135 Mark Rypien	.10	.05
❑ 136 Leonard Russell	.20	.09

❑ 137 Reggie White .40 .18
❑ 138 Thurman Thomas .40 .18
❑ 139 Nick Lowery .10 .05
❑ 140 Al Smith .10 .05
❑ 141 Jackie Harris .10 .05
❑ 142 Duane Bickett .10 .05
❑ 143 Lawyer Tillman .10 .05
❑ 144 Steve Wisniewski .10 .05
❑ 145 Derrick Fenner .10 .05
❑ 146 Harris Barton .10 .05
❑ 147 Rich Camarillo .10 .05
❑ 148 John Offerdahl .10 .05
❑ 149 Mike Johnson .10 .05
❑ 150 Ricky Reynolds .10 .05
❑ 151 Fred Barnett .20 .09
❑ 152 Nate Newton .20 .09
❑ 153 Chris Doleman .10 .05
❑ 154 Todd Scott .10 .05
❑ 155 Tim McKyer .10 .05
❑ 156 Ken Harvey .10 .05
❑ 157 Jeff Feagles .10 .05
❑ 158 Vince Workman .10 .05
❑ 159 Bart Oates .10 .05
❑ 160 Chris Miller .20 .09
❑ 161 Pete Stoyanovich .10 .05
❑ 162 Steve Wallace .10 .05
❑ 163 Dermontti Dawson .10 .05
❑ 164 Kenneth Davis .10 .05
❑ 165 Mike Munchak .10 .05
❑ 166 George Jamison .10 .05
❑ 167 Christian Okoye .10 .05
❑ 168 Chris Hinton .10 .05
❑ 169 Vaughan Johnson .10 .05
❑ 170 Gaston Green .10 .05
❑ 171 Kevin Greene .40 .18
❑ 172 Rob Burnett .10 .05
❑ 173 Norm Johnson .10 .05
❑ 174 Eric Hill .10 .05
❑ 175 Lomas Brown .10 .05
❑ 176 Chip Banks .10 .05
❑ 177 Greg Townsend .10 .05
❑ 178 David Fulcher .10 .05
❑ 179 Gary Anderson RB .10 .05
❑ 180 Brian Washington .10 .05
❑ 181 Brett Perriman .40 .18
❑ 182 Chris Chandler .20 .09
❑ 183 Phil Hansen .10 .05
❑ 184 Mark Clayton .10 .05
❑ 185 Frank Warren .10 .05
❑ 186 Tim Brown .40 .18
❑ 187 Mark Stepnoski .10 .05
❑ 188 Bryan Cox .10 .05
❑ 189 Gary Zimmerman .10 .05
❑ 190 Neil O'Donnell .40 .18
❑ 191 Anthony Smith .10 .05
❑ 192 Craig Heyward .20 .09
❑ 193 Keith Byars .10 .05
❑ 194 Sean Salisbury .10 .05
❑ 195 Todd Lyght .10 .05
❑ 196 Jessie Hester .10 .05
❑ 197 Rufus Porter .10 .05
❑ 198 Steve Christie .10 .05
❑ 199 Nate Lewis .10 .05
❑ 200 Barry Sanders 3.00 1.35
❑ 201 Michael Haynes .20 .09
❑ 202 John Taylor .20 .09
❑ 203 John Friesz .20 .09
❑ 204 William Fuller .10 .05
❑ 205 Dennis Smith .10 .05
❑ 206 Adrian Cooper .10 .05
❑ 207 Henry Thomas .10 .05
❑ 208 Gerald Williams .10 .05
❑ 209 Chris Burkett .10 .05
❑ 210 Broderick Thomas .10 .05
❑ 211 Marvin Washington .10 .05
❑ 212 Bennie Blades .10 .05
❑ 213 Tony Casillas .10 .05
❑ 214 Bubby Brister .10 .05
❑ 215 Don Griffin .10 .05
❑ 216 Jeff Cross .10 .05
❑ 217 Derrick Walker .10 .05
❑ 218 Lorenzo White .10 .05
❑ 219 Ricky Sanders .10 .05
❑ 220 Rickey Jackson .10 .05
❑ 221 Simon Fletcher .10 .05
❑ 222 Troy Vincent .10 .05
❑ 223 Gary Clark .20 .09
❑ 224 Stanley Richard .10 .05
❑ 225 Dave Krieg .20 .09
❑ 226 Warren Moon .40 .18
❑ 227 Reggie Langhorne .10 .05
❑ 228 Kent Hull .10 .05
❑ 229 Ferrell Edmunds .10 .05
❑ 230 Cortez Kennedy .20 .09
❑ 231 Hugh Millen .10 .05
❑ 232 Eugene Chung .10 .05
❑ 233 Rodney Peete .10 .05
❑ 234 Tom Waddle .10 .05
❑ 235 David Klingler .10 .05
❑ 236 Mark Carrier WR .20 .09
❑ 237 Jay Schroeder .10 .05
❑ 238 James Jones .10 .05
❑ 239 Phil Simms .20 .09
❑ 240 Steve Atwater .10 .05
❑ 241 Jeff Herrod .10 .05
❑ 242 Dale Carter .10 .05
❑ 243 Glenn Cadrez RC .10 .05
❑ 244 Wayne Martin .10 .05
❑ 245 Willie Davis .40 .18
❑ 246 Lawrence Taylor .40 .18
❑ 247 Stan Humphries .40 .18
❑ 248 Byron Evans .10 .05
❑ 249 Wilber Marshall .10 .05
❑ 250 Michael Bankston RC .10 .05
❑ 251 Steve McMichael .20 .09
❑ 252 Brad Edwards .10 .05
❑ 253 Will Wolford .10 .05
❑ 254 Paul Gruber .10 .05
❑ 255 Steve Young 1.50 .70
❑ 256 Chuck Cecil .10 .05
❑ 257 Pierce Holt .10 .05
❑ 258 Anthony Miller .20 .09
❑ 259 Carl Banks .10 .05
❑ 260 Brad Muster .10 .05
❑ 261 Clay Matthews .20 .09
❑ 262 Rod Bernstine .10 .05
❑ 263 Tim Barnett .10 .05
❑ 264 Greg Lloyd .40 .18
❑ 265 Sean Jones .10 .05
❑ 266 J.J. Birden .10 .05
❑ 267 Tim McDonald .10 .05
❑ 268 Charles Mann .10 .05
❑ 269 Bruce Smith .40 .18
❑ 270 Sean Gilbert .20 .09
❑ 271 Ricardo McDonald .10 .05
❑ 272 Jeff Hostetler .20 .09
❑ 273 Russell Maryland .10 .05
❑ 274 Dave Brown RC .40 .18
❑ 275 Ronnie Lott .20 .09
❑ 276 Jim Kelly .40 .18
❑ 277 Joe Montana 3.00 1.35
❑ 278 Eric Allen .10 .05
❑ 279 Browning Nagle .10 .05
❑ 280 Neal Anderson .10 .05
❑ 281 Troy Aikman 1.50 .70
❑ 282 Ed McCaffrey .20 .09
❑ 283 Robert Jones .10 .05
❑ 284 Dalton Hilliard .10 .05
❑ 285 Johnny Mitchell .10 .05
❑ 286 Jay Hilgenberg .10 .05
❑ 287 Eric Martin .10 .05
❑ 288 Steve Emtman .10 .05
❑ 289 Vaughn Dunbar .10 .05
❑ 290 Mark Wheeler .10 .05
❑ 291 Leslie O'Neal .20 .09
❑ 292 Jerry Rice 2.00 .90
❑ 293 Neil Smith .40 .18
❑ 294 Kerry Cash .10 .05
❑ 295 Dan McGwire .10 .05
❑ 296 Carl Pickens .40 .18
❑ 297 Terrell Buckley .10 .05
❑ 298 Randall Cunningham .40 .18
❑ 299 Santana Dotson .20 .09
❑ 300 Keith Jackson .20 .09
❑ 301 Jim Lachey .10 .05
❑ 302 Dan Marino 3.00 1.35
❑ 303 Lee Williams .10 .05
❑ 304 Burt Grossman .10 .05
❑ 305 Kevin Mack .10 .05
❑ 306 Pat Swilling .10 .05
❑ 307 Arthur Marshall RC .10 .05
❑ 308 Jim Harbaugh .40 .18
❑ 309 Kurt Barber .10 .05
❑ 310 Harvey Williams .20 .09
❑ 311 Ricky Ervins .10 .05
❑ 312 Flipper Anderson .10 .05
❑ 313 Bernie Kosar .20 .09
❑ 314 Boomer Esiason .20 .09
❑ 315 Deion Sanders 1.00 .45
❑ 316 Ray Childress .10 .05
❑ 317 Howie Long .20 .09
❑ 318 Henry Ellard .20 .09
❑ 319 Marco Coleman .10 .05
❑ 320 Chris Mims .10 .05
❑ 321 Quentin Coryatt .20 .09
❑ 322 Jason Hanson .10 .05
❑ 323 Ricky Proehl .10 .05
❑ 324 Randal Hill .10 .05
❑ 325 Vinny Testaverde .20 .09
❑ 326 Jeff George .40 .18
❑ 327 Junior Seau .40 .18
❑ 328 Earnest Byner .10 .05
❑ 329 Andre Reed .20 .09
❑ 330 Phillippi Sparks .10 .05
❑ 331 Kevin Ross .10 .05
❑ 332 Clarence Verdin .10 .05
❑ 333 Darryl Henley .10 .05
❑ 334 Dana Hall .10 .05
❑ 335 Greg McMurtry .10 .05
❑ 336 Ron Hall .10 .05
❑ 337 Darrell Green .10 .05
❑ 338 Carlton Bailey .10 .05
❑ 339 Irv Eatman .10 .05
❑ 340 Greg Kragen .10 .05
❑ 341 Wade Wilson .10 .05
❑ 342 Klaus Wilmsmeyer .10 .05
❑ 343 Derek Brown TE .10 .05
❑ 344 Erik Williams .10 .05
❑ 345 Jim McMahon .10 .05
❑ 346 Mike Sherrard .10 .05
❑ 347 Mark Bavaro .10 .05
❑ 348 Anthony Munoz .20 .09
❑ 349 Eric Dickerson .20 .09
❑ 350 Steve Beuerlein .10 .05
❑ 351 Tim McGee .10 .05
❑ 352 Terry McDaniel .10 .05
❑ 353 Dan Fouts HOF .10 .05
❑ 354 Chuck Noll HOF .20 .09
❑ 355 Bill Walsh HOF RC .20 .09
❑ 356 Larry Little HOF .10 .05
❑ 357 Todd Marinovich HH .10 .05
❑ 358 Jeff George HH .40 .18
❑ 359 Bernie Kosar HH .20 .09
❑ 360 Rob Moore HH .20 .09
❑ NNO Franco Harris AU/3000 30.00 13.50

1993 Pinnacle Men of Autumn

	MINT	NRMT
COMPLETE SET (55)	10.00	4.50

ONE PER SCORE FOIL AND JUMBO PACK

❑ 1 Andre Rison .15 .07
❑ 2 Thurman Thomas .30 .14
❑ 3 Wendell Davis .10 .05
❑ 4 Harold Green .10 .05
❑ 5 Eric Metcalf .15 .07
❑ 6 Michael Irvin .30 .14
❑ 7 John Elway 2.50 1.10
❑ 8 Barry Sanders 2.50 1.10
❑ 9 Sterling Sharpe .30 .14
❑ 10 Warren Moon .30 .14
❑ 11 Rohn Stark .10 .05
❑ 12 Derrick Thomas .30 .14
❑ 13 Terry McDaniel .10 .05
❑ 14 Cleveland Gary .10 .05
❑ 15 Dan Marino 2.50 1.10
❑ 16 Terry Allen .30 .14
❑ 17 Marv Cook .10 .05
❑ 18 Bobby Hebert .10 .05
❑ 19 Rodney Hampton .30 .14
❑ 20 Brad Baxter .10 .05
❑ 21 Reggie White .30 .14
❑ 22 Ricky Proehl .10 .05
❑ 23 Barry Foster .15 .07
❑ 24 Junior Seau .30 .14
❑ 25 Steve Young 1.25 .55

	MINT	NRMT
❑ 26 Cortez Kennedy	.15	.07
❑ 27 Reggie Cobb	.10	.05
❑ 28 Mark Rypien	.10	.05
❑ 29 Deion Sanders	.75	.35
❑ 30 Bruce Smith	.30	.14
❑ 31 Richard Dent	.15	.07
❑ 32 Alfred Williams	.10	.05
❑ 33 Clay Matthews	.15	.07
❑ 34 Emmitt Smith	2.50	1.10
❑ 35 Simon Fletcher	.10	.05
❑ 36 Chris Spielman	.15	.07
❑ 37 Brett Favre	3.00	1.35
❑ 38 Bruce Matthews	.10	.05
❑ 39 Jeff Herrod	.10	.05
❑ 40 Nick Lowery	.10	.05
❑ 41 Steve Wisniewski	.10	.05
❑ 42 Jim Everett	.15	.07
❑ 43 Keith Jackson	.15	.07
❑ 44 Chris Doleman	.10	.05
❑ 45 Irving Fryar	.15	.07
❑ 46 Rickey Jackson	.10	.05
❑ 47 Pepper Johnson	.10	.05
❑ 48 Randall Cunningham	.30	.14
❑ 49 Rich Camarillo	.10	.05
❑ 50 Rod Woodson	.30	.14
❑ 51 Ronnie Harmon	.10	.05
❑ 52 Ricky Watters	.30	.14
❑ 53 Chris Warren	.15	.07
❑ 54 Lawrence Dawsey	.10	.05
❑ 55 Wilber Marshall	.10	.05

1993 Pinnacle Rookies

	MINT	NRMT
COMPLETE SET (25)	300.00	135.00
COMMON CARD (1-25)	6.00	2.70
SEMISTARS	8.00	3.60
UNLISTED STARS	10.00	4.50
STATED ODDS 1:36 HOB/RET		

	MINT	NRMT
❑ 1 Drew Bledsoe UER Card has drafted in 92 He was 1st pick of 93 draft	150.00	70.00
❑ 2 Garrison Hearst	30.00	13.50
❑ 3 John Copeland	6.00	2.70
❑ 4 Eric Curry	8.00	3.60
❑ 5 Curtis Conway	15.00	6.75
❑ 6 Lincoln Kennedy	6.00	2.70
❑ 7 Jerome Bettis	30.00	13.50
❑ 8 Dan Williams	6.00	2.70
❑ 9 Patrick Bates	6.00	2.70
❑ 10 Brad Hopkins	6.00	2.70
❑ 11 Wayne Simmons	6.00	2.70
❑ 12 Rick Mirer	15.00	6.75
❑ 13 Tom Carter	6.00	2.70
❑ 14 Irv Smith	8.00	3.60
❑ 15 Marvin Jones	6.00	2.70
❑ 16 Deon Figures	6.00	2.70
❑ 17 Leonard Renfro	6.00	2.70
❑ 18 O.J.McDuffie	20.00	9.00
❑ 19 Dana Stubblefield	10.00	4.50
❑ 20 Carlton Gray	6.00	2.70
❑ 21 Demetrius DuBose	6.00	2.70
❑ 22 Troy Drayton	6.00	2.70
❑ 23 Natrone Means	20.00	9.00
❑ 24 Reggie Brooks	8.00	3.60
❑ 25 Glyn Milburn	10.00	4.50

1993 Pinnacle Super Bowl XXVII

	MINT	NRMT
COMPLETE SET (10)	110.00	50.00
COMMON CARD (1-10)	8.00	3.60
SEMISTARS	10.00	4.50
ONE PER SEALED HOBBY FOIL BOX		

	MINT	NRMT
❑ 1 Rose Bowl	8.00	3.60
❑ 2 Thomas Everett	8.00	3.60
❑ 3 Emmitt Smith	35.00	16.00
❑ 4 Ken Norton Jr.	10.00	4.50
❑ 5 Michael Irvin	15.00	6.75
❑ 6 Jay Novacek	10.00	4.50
❑ 7 Charles Haley	10.00	4.50
❑ 8 Leon Lett	10.00	4.50
❑ 9 Alvin Harper	10.00	4.50
❑ 10 Tony Casillas	8.00	3.60

1993 Pinnacle Team Pinnacle

	MINT	NRMT
COMPLETE SET (13)	175.00	80.00
COMMON PAIR (1-13)	8.00	3.60
SEMISTARS	12.00	5.50
STATED ODDS 1:90 HOB/RET		

	MINT	NRMT
❑ 1 Troy Aikman Joe Montana	80.00	36.00
❑ 2 Thurman Thomas Emmitt Smith	40.00	18.00
❑ 3 Rodney Hampton Barry Foster	12.00	5.50
❑ 4 Sterling Sharpe Anthony Miller	12.00	5.50
❑ 5 Haywood Jeffires Michael Irvin	15.00	6.75
❑ 6 Jay Novacek Keith Jackson	12.00	5.50
❑ 7 Richmond Webb Steve Wallace	8.00	3.60
❑ 8 Reggie White Leslie O'Neal	15.00	6.75
❑ 9 Cortez Kennedy Sean Gilbert	8.00	3.60
❑ 10 Derrick Thomas Wilber Marshall	12.00	5.50
❑ 11 Sam Mills Junior Seau	15.00	6.75
❑ 12 Rod Woodson Deion Sanders	20.00	9.00
❑ 13 Steve Atwater Tim McDonald	8.00	3.60

1993 Pinnacle Team 2001

	MINT	NRMT
COMPLETE SET (30)	15.00	6.75
ONE PER JUMBO PACK		

	MINT	NRMT
❑ 1 Junior Seau	.75	.35
❑ 2 Cortez Kennedy	.40	.18
❑ 3 Carl Pickens	.75	.35
❑ 4 David Klingler	.20	.09
❑ 5 Santana Dotson	.40	.18
❑ 6 Sean Gilbert	.40	.18
❑ 7 Brett Favre	8.00	3.60
❑ 8 Steve Emtman	.20	.09
❑ 9 Rodney Hampton	.75	.35
❑ 10 Browning Nagle	.20	.09
❑ 11 Amp Lee	.20	.09
❑ 12 Vaughn Dunbar	.20	.09
❑ 13 Quentin Coryatt	.40	.18
❑ 14 Marco Coleman	.20	.09
❑ 15 Johnny Mitchell	.20	.09
❑ 16 Arthur Marshall	.20	.09
❑ 17 Dale Carter	.20	.09
❑ 18 Henry Jones	.20	.09
❑ 19 Terrell Buckley	.20	.09
❑ 20 Tommy Vardell	.20	.09
❑ 21 Tommy Maddox	.20	.09
❑ 22 Barry Foster	.40	.18
❑ 23 Herman Moore	2.00	.90
❑ 24 Ricky Watters	.75	.35
❑ 25 Mike Croel	.20	.09
❑ 26 Russell Maryland	.20	.09
❑ 27 Terry Allen	.75	.35
❑ 28 Jon Vaughn	.20	.09
❑ 29 Todd Marinovich	.20	.09
❑ 30 Jeff Graham	.40	.18

1994 Pinnacle

	MINT	NRMT
COMPLETE SET (270)	20.00	9.00
COMMON CARD (1-270)	.10	.05
SEMISTARS	.20	.09

UNLISTED STARS .... .40 .18
271 RICE ISSUED IN JUMBO PACKS ONLY
BLEDSOE PASSER ODDS 1:360
COMP.TROPHY COLL.(270) 200.00 90.00
*TC STARS: 3X TO 8X HI COL.....
*TC RCs: 2X to 5X HI ....
STATED ODDS 1:4 HOB/JUM......

❑	1	Deion Sanders	.50	.23
❑	2	Eric Metcalf	.20	.09
❑	3	Barry Sanders	2.50	1.10
❑	4	Ernest Givins	.20	.09
❑	5	Phil Simms	.20	.09
❑	6	Rod Woodson	.40	.18
❑	7	Michael Irvin	.40	.18
❑	8	Cortez Kennedy	.20	.09
❑	9	Eric Martin	.10	.05
❑	10	Jeff Hostetler	.20	.09
❑	11	Sterling Sharpe	.20	.09
❑	12	John Elway	2.50	1.10
❑	13	Neal Anderson	.10	.05
❑	14	Terry Kirby	.40	.18
❑	15	Jim Everett	.20	.09
❑	16	Lawrence Dawsey	.10	.05
❑	17	Kelvin Martin	.10	.05
❑	18	Tim McGee	.10	.05
❑	19	Cris Carter	.50	.23
❑	20	Ronnie Harmon	.10	.05
❑	21	Jim Kelly	.40	.18
❑	22	Steve Young	1.00	.45
❑	23	Johnny Johnson	.10	.05
❑	24	Sean Gilbert	.10	.05
❑	25	Brian Mitchell	.10	.05
❑	26	Carl Pickens	.40	.18
❑	27	Tim Brown	.40	.18
❑	28	Reggie Langhorne	.10	.05
❑	29	Webster Slaughter	.10	.05
❑	30	Alvin Harper	.20	.09
❑	31	Andre Rison	.20	.09
❑	32	Derrick Thomas	.40	.18
❑	33	Irving Fryar	.20	.09
❑	34	Vinny Testaverde	.20	.09
❑	35	Steve Beuerlein	.10	.05
❑	36	Brett Favre	2.50	1.10
❑	37	Barry Foster	.10	.05
❑	38	Vaughan Johnson	.10	.05
❑	39	Carlton Bailey	.10	.05
❑	40	Steve Emtman	.10	.05
❑	41	Anthony Miller	.20	.09
❑	42	Jeff Cross	.10	.05
❑	43	Trace Armstrong	.10	.05
❑	44	Derek Russell	.10	.05
❑	45	Vincent Brisby	.40	.18
❑	46	Mark Jackson	.10	.05
❑	47	Eugene Robinson	.10	.05
❑	48	John Friesz	.20	.09
❑	49	Scott Mitchell	.40	.18
❑	50	Steve Atwater	.10	.05
❑	51	Ken Norton	.20	.09
❑	52	Vincent Brown	.10	.05
❑	53	Morten Andersen	.10	.05
❑	54	Gary Anderson K	.10	.05
❑	55	Eric Curry	.10	.05
❑	56	Henry Jones	.10	.05
❑	57	Flipper Anderson	.10	.05
❑	58	Pat Swilling	.10	.05
❑	59	Erric Pegram	.10	.05
❑	60	Bruce Matthews	.10	.05
❑	61	Willie Davis	.20	.09
❑	62	O.J. McDuffie	.40	.18
❑	63	Qadry Ismail	.40	.18
❑	64	Anthony Smith	.10	.05
❑	65	Eric Allen	.10	.05
❑	66	Marion Butts	.10	.05
❑	67	Chris Miller	.10	.05
❑	68	Terrell Buckley	.10	.05
❑	69	Thurman Thomas	.40	.18
❑	70	Roosevelt Potts	.10	.05
❑	71	Tony McGee	.10	.05
❑	72	Jason Hanson	.10	.05
❑	73	Victor Bailey	.10	.05
❑	74	Albert Lewis	.10	.05
❑	75	Nate Odomes	.10	.05
❑	76	Ben Coates	.40	.18
❑	77	Warren Moon	.40	.18
❑	78	Derek Brown RBK	.10	.05
❑	79	David Klingler	.10	.05
❑	80	Cleveland Gary	.10	.05
❑	81	Emmitt Smith	2.00	.90
❑	82	Jay Novacek	.20	.09
❑	83	Dana Stubblefield	.40	.18
❑	84	Michael Brooks	.10	.05
❑	85	James Jett	.10	.05
❑	86	J.J. Birden	.10	.05
❑	87	William Fuller	.10	.05
❑	88	Glyn Milburn	.20	.09
❑	89	Tim Worley	.10	.05
❑	90	Brett Perriman	.20	.09
❑	91	Randall Cunningham	.40	.18
❑	92	Drew Bledsoe	1.25	.55
❑	93	Jerome Bettis	.40	.18
❑	94	Boomer Esiason	.20	.09
❑	95	Garrison Hearst	.40	.18
❑	96	Bruce Smith	.40	.18
❑	97	Jackie Harris	.10	.05
❑	98	Jeff George	.40	.18
❑	99	Tom Waddle	.10	.05
❑	100	John Copeland	.10	.05
❑	101	Bobby Hebert	.10	.05
❑	102	Joe Montana	2.50	1.10
❑	103	Herman Moore	.40	.18
❑	104	Rick Mirer	.40	.18
❑	105	Ricky Watters	.40	.18
❑	106	Neil O'Donnell	.40	.18
❑	107	Herschel Walker	.20	.09
❑	108	Rob Moore	.20	.09
❑	109	Reggie Brooks	.20	.09
❑	110	Tommy Vardell	.10	.05
❑	111	Eric Green	.10	.05
❑	112	Stan Humphries	.40	.18
❑	113	Greg Robinson	.10	.05
❑	114	Eric Swann	.20	.09
❑	115	Courtney Hawkins	.10	.05
❑	116	Andre Reed	.20	.09
❑	117	Steve McMichael	.20	.09
❑	118	Gary Brown	.10	.05
❑	119	Terry Allen	.20	.09
❑	120	Dan Marino	2.50	1.10
❑	121	Gary Clark	.20	.09
❑	122	Chris Warren	.20	.09
❑	123	Pierce Holt	.10	.05
❑	124	Anthony Carter	.20	.09
❑	125	Quentin Coryatt	.10	.05
❑	126	Harold Green	.10	.05
❑	127	Leonard Russell	.10	.05
❑	128	Tim McDonald	.10	.05
❑	129	Chris Spielman	.20	.09
❑	130	Cody Carlson	.10	.05
❑	131	Ronald Moore	.10	.05
❑	132	Renaldo Turnbull	.10	.05
❑	133	Ronnie Lott	.20	.09
❑	134	Natrone Means	.40	.18
❑	135	Keith Byars	.10	.05
❑	136	Henry Ellard	.20	.09
❑	137	Steve Jordan	.10	.05
❑	138	Calvin Williams	.20	.09
❑	139	Brian Blades	.20	.09
❑	140	Michael Jackson	.20	.09
❑	141	Charles Haley	.20	.09
❑	142	Curtis Conway	.40	.18
❑	143	Nick Lowery	.10	.05
❑	144	Bill Brooks	.10	.05
❑	145	Michael Haynes	.20	.09
❑	146	Willie Green	.10	.05
❑	147	Duane Bickett	.10	.05
❑	148	Shannon Sharpe	.20	.09
❑	149	Ricky Proehl	.10	.05
❑	150	Troy Aikman	1.25	.55
❑	151	Mike Sherrard	.10	.05
❑	152	Reggie Cobb	.10	.05
❑	153	Norm Johnson	.10	.05
❑	154	Neil Smith	.40	.18
❑	155	James Francis	.10	.05
❑	156	Greg McMurtry	.10	.05
❑	157	Greg Townsend	.10	.05
❑	158	Mel Gray	.10	.05
❑	159	Rocket Ismail	.20	.09
❑	160	Leslie O'Neal	.10	.05
❑	161	Johnny Mitchell	.10	.05
❑	162	Brent Jones	.20	.09
❑	163	Chris Doleman	.10	.05
❑	164	Seth Joyner	.10	.05
❑	165	Marco Coleman	.10	.05
❑	166	Mark Higgs	.10	.05
❑	167	John L. Williams	.10	.05
❑	168	Darrell Green	.10	.05
❑	169	Mark Carrier WR	.20	.09
❑	170	Reggie White	.40	.18
❑	171	Darryl Talley	.10	.05
❑	172	Russell Maryland	.10	.05
❑	173	Mark Collins	.10	.05
❑	174	Chris Jacke	.10	.05
❑	175	Richard Dent	.20	.09
❑	176	John Taylor	.20	.09
❑	177	Rodney Hampton	.40	.18
❑	178	Dwight Stone	.10	.05
❑	179	Cornelius Bennett	.20	.09
❑	180	Cris Dishman	.10	.05
❑	181	Jerry Rice	1.25	.55
❑	182	Rod Bernstine	.10	.05
❑	183	Keith Hamilton	.10	.05
❑	184	Keith Jackson	.10	.05
❑	185	Craig Erickson	.10	.05
❑	186	Marcus Allen	.40	.18
❑	187	Marcus Robertson	.10	.05
❑	188	Junior Seau	.40	.18
❑	189	LeShon Johnson RC	.20	.09
❑	190	Perry Klein RC	.10	.05
❑	191	Bryant Young RC	.40	.18
❑	192	Byron Bam Morris RC	.40	.18
❑	193	Jeff Cothran RC	.10	.05
❑	194	Lamar Smith RC	.40	.18
❑	195	Calvin Jones RC	.10	.05
❑	196	James Bostic RC	.40	.18
❑	197	Dan Wilkinson RC	.20	.09
❑	198	Marshall Faulk RC	5.00	2.20
❑	199	Heath Shuler RC	.40	.18
❑	200	Willie McGinest RC	.40	.18
❑	201	Trev Alberts RC	.20	.09
❑	202	Trent Dilfer RC	2.00	.90
❑	203	Sam Adams RC	.20	.09
❑	204	Charles Johnson RC	.40	.18
❑	205	Johnnie Morton RC	1.25	.55
❑	206	Thomas Lewis RC	.20	.09
❑	207	Greg Hill RC	1.00	.45
❑	208	William Floyd RC	.40	.18
❑	209	Derrick Alexander WR RC	1.00	.45
❑	210	Darnay Scott RC	1.25	.55
❑	211	Lake Dawson RC	.40	.18
❑	212	Errict Rhett RC	2.00	.90
❑	213	Kevin Lee RC	.10	.05
❑	214	Chuck Levy RC	.10	.05
❑	215	David Palmer RC	1.00	.45
❑	216	Ryan Yarborough RC	.10	.05
❑	217	Charlie Garner RC	2.00	.90
❑	218	Mario Bates RC	.40	.18
❑	219	Jamir Miller RC	.10	.05
❑	220	Bucky Brooks RC	.10	.05
❑	221	Donnell Bennett RC	.40	.18
❑	222	Kevin Greene	.40	.18
❑	223	LeRoy Butler	.10	.05
❑	224	Anthony Pleasant	.10	.05
❑	225	Steve Christie	.10	.05
❑	226	Bill Romanowski	.10	.05
❑	227	Darren Carrington	.10	.05
❑	228	Chester McGlockton	.10	.05
❑	229	Jack Del Rio	.10	.05
❑	230	Kevin Smith	.10	.05
❑	231	Chris Zorich	.10	.05
❑	232	Donnell Woolford	.10	.05
❑	233	Tony Casillas	.10	.05
❑	234	Terry McDaniel	.10	.05
❑	235	Ray Childress	.10	.05
❑	236	John Randle	.10	.05
❑	237	Clyde Simmons	.10	.05
❑	238	Dante Jones	.10	.05
❑	239	Karl Mecklenburg	.10	.05
❑	240	Daryl Johnston	.20	.09
❑	241	Hardy Nickerson	.20	.09
❑	242	Jeff Lageman	.10	.05
❑	243	Lewis Tillman	.10	.05
❑	244	Jim McMahon	.10	.05
❑	245	Mike Pritchard	.10	.05
❑	246	Harvey Williams	.20	.09
❑	247	Sean Jones	.10	.05
❑	248	Stevon Moore	.10	.05
❑	249	Pete Metzelaars	.10	.05
❑	250	Mike Johnson	.10	.05

		MINT	NRMT
❑ 251	Chris Slade	.10	.05
❑ 252	Jessie Hester	.10	.05
❑ 253	Louis Oliver	.10	.05
❑ 254	Ken Harvey	.10	.05
❑ 255	Bryan Cox	.10	.05
❑ 256	Erik Kramer	.20	.09
❑ 257	Andy Harmon	.10	.05
❑ 258	Rickey Jackson	.10	.05
❑ 259	Mark Carrier DB	.10	.05
❑ 260	Greg Lloyd	.40	.18
❑ 261	Robert Brooks	.40	.18
❑ 262	Dave Brown	.20	.09
❑ 263	Dennis Smith	.10	.05
❑ 264	Michael Dean Perry	.20	.09
❑ 265	Dan Saleaumua	.10	.05
❑ 266	Mo Lewis	.10	.05
❑ 267	AFC Checklist	.10	.05
❑ 268	AFC Checklist	.10	.05
❑ 269	NFC Checklist	.10	.05
❑ 270	NFC Checklist	.10	.05
❑ 271SP	Jerry Rice TD King	8.00	3.60
❑ NNO	Drew Bledsoe Pinnacle Passer	40.00	18.00

1994 Pinnacle Draft Pinnacle

	MINT	NRMT
COMPLETE SET (10)	30.00	13.50
STATED ODDS 1:24 HOBBY		
*DUFEX CARDS: SAME PRICE		
DUFEX: PRIZES FOR PICK PINN.WINNERS		

		MINT	NRMT
❑ DP1	Dan Wilkinson	1.00	.45
❑ DP2	Marshall Faulk	25.00	11.00
❑ DP3	Heath Shuler	2.00	.90
❑ DP4	Trent Dilfer	10.00	4.50
❑ DP5	Charles Johnson	2.00	.90
❑ DP6	Johnnie Morton	6.00	2.70
❑ DP7	Darnay Scott	6.00	2.70
❑ DP8	William Floyd	2.00	.90
❑ DP9	Errict Rhett	10.00	4.50
❑ DP10	Chuck Levy	.50	.23

1994 Pinnacle Performers

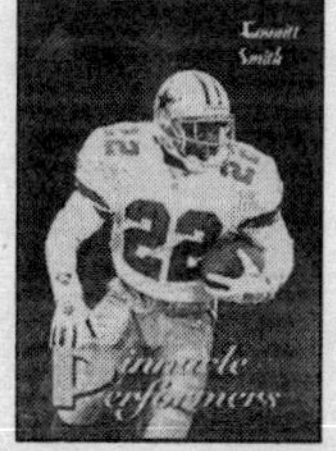

	MINT	NRMT
COMPLETE SET (18)	25.00	11.00
STATED ODDS 1:4 JUMBO		

		MINT	NRMT
❑ PP1	Troy Aikman	3.00	1.35
❑ PP2	Emmitt Smith	5.00	2.20
❑ PP3	Sterling Sharpe	.50	.23
❑ PP4	Barry Sanders	6.00	2.70
❑ PP5	Jerry Rice	3.00	1.35
❑ PP6	Steve Young	2.50	1.10
❑ PP7	John Elway	6.00	2.70
❑ PP8	Michael Irvin	1.00	.45
❑ PP9	Jerome Bettis	1.00	.45
❑ PP10	Tim Brown	1.00	.45
❑ PP11	Joe Montana	6.00	2.70
❑ PP12	Reggie Brooks	.50	.23
❑ PP13	Brett Favre	6.00	2.70
❑ PP14	Drew Bledsoe	3.00	1.35
❑ PP15	Ricky Watters	1.00	.45
❑ PP16	Garrison Hearst	1.00	.45
❑ PP17	Rodney Hampton	1.00	.45
❑ PP18	Dan Marino	6.00	2.70

1994 Pinnacle Team Pinnacle

	MINT	NRMT
COMPLETE SET (10)	60.00	27.00
COMMON CARD (TP1-TP10)	2.00	.90
SEMISTARS	3.00	1.35
UNLISTED STARS	5.00	2.20
ONE SIDE OF CARD IS DUFEX		
BOTH DUFEX VERSIONS SAME PRICE		
STATED ODDS 1:90		

		MINT	NRMT
❑ TP1	Troy Aikman Joe Montana	15.00	6.75
❑ TP2	Brett Favre Rick Mirer	12.00	5.50
❑ TP3	Emmitt Smith Thurman Thomas	10.00	4.50
❑ TP4	Barry Sanders Barry Foster	12.00	5.50
❑ TP5	Jerome Bettis Natrone Means	5.00	2.20
❑ TP6	Sterling Sharpe Tim Brown	3.00	1.35
❑ TP7	Jerry Rice Anthony Miller	8.00	3.60
❑ TP8	Michael Irvin James Jett	5.00	2.20
❑ TP9	Reggie White Bruce Smith	5.00	2.20
❑ TP10	Sean Gilbert Cortez Kennedy	2.00	.90

1995 Pinnacle

	MINT	NRMT
COMPLETE SET (250)	20.00	9.00
COMMON CARD (1-250)	.10	.05
SEMISTARS	.20	.09
UNLISTED STARS	.40	.18
251SP D.SANDERS ISSUED IN JUMBO PACKS		
COMP.TROPHY COLL. (250)	250.00	110.00
JOE MONTANA TC 193	50.00	22.00
*TC STARS: 2X TO 5X HI COLUMN		
*TC RCs: 1.25X TO 3X HI		
TC: STATED ODDS 1:4 H, 1:3 JUM, 1:2 R		
COMP.ART.PROOF (250)	1200.00	550.00
*AP STARS: 7.5X TO 20X HI COL.		

*AP RCs: 4X TO 10X HI

APs: STATED ODDS 1:48 HOB, 1:20 RET

		MINT	NRMT
❑ 1	Reggie White	.40	.18
❑ 2	Troy Aikman	1.00	.45
❑ 3	Willie Davis	.20	.09
❑ 4	Jerry Rice	1.00	.45
❑ 5	Bruce Smith	.40	.18
❑ 6	Keith Byars	.10	.05
❑ 7	Chris Warren	.20	.09
❑ 8	Erik Kramer	.10	.05
❑ 9	Leon Lett	.10	.05
❑ 10	Greg Lloyd	.20	.09
❑ 11	Jackie Harris	.10	.05
❑ 12	Irving Fryar	.20	.09
❑ 13	Rodney Hampton	.20	.09
❑ 14	Michael Irvin	.40	.18
❑ 15	Michael Haynes	.20	.09
❑ 16	Irving Spikes	.20	.09
❑ 17	Calvin Williams	.20	.09
❑ 18	Ken Norton Jr.	.20	.09
❑ 19	Herman Moore	.40	.18
❑ 20	Lewis Tillman	.10	.05
❑ 21	Cortez Kennedy	.20	.09
❑ 22	Dan Marino	2.00	.90
❑ 23	Eric Pegram	.20	.09
❑ 24	Tim Brown	.40	.18
❑ 25	Jeff Blake RC	1.00	.45
❑ 26	Brett Favre	2.00	.90
❑ 27	Garrison Hearst	.40	.18
❑ 28	Ronnie Harmon	.10	.05
❑ 29	Qadry Ismail	.20	.09
❑ 30	Ben Coates	.20	.09
❑ 31	Deion Sanders	.60	.25
❑ 32	John Elway	2.00	.90
❑ 33	Natrone Means	.40	.18
❑ 34	Derrick Alexander WR	.40	.18
❑ 35	Craig Heyward	.20	.09
❑ 36	Jake Reed	.20	.09
❑ 37	Steve Walsh	.10	.05
❑ 38	John Randle	.10	.05
❑ 39	Barry Sanders	2.00	.90
❑ 40	Tydus Winans	.10	.05
❑ 41	Thomas Lewis	.20	.09
❑ 42	Jim Kelly	.40	.18
❑ 43	Gus Frerotte	.40	.18
❑ 44	Cris Carter	.40	.18
❑ 45	Kevin Williams WR	.20	.09
❑ 46	Dave Meggett	.10	.05
❑ 47	Pat Swilling	.10	.05
❑ 48	Neil O'Donnell	.20	.09
❑ 49	Terance Mathis	.20	.09
❑ 50	Desmond Howard	.20	.09
❑ 51	Bryant Young	.20	.09
❑ 52	Stan Humphries	.20	.09
❑ 53	Alvin Harper	.10	.05
❑ 54	Henry Ellard	.20	.09
❑ 55	Jessie Hester	.10	.05
❑ 56	Lorenzo White	.10	.05
❑ 57	John Friesz	.20	.09
❑ 58	Anthony Smith	.10	.05
❑ 59	Bert Emanuel	.40	.18
❑ 60	Gary Clark	.10	.05
❑ 61	Bill Brooks	.10	.05
❑ 62	Steve Young	.75	.35
❑ 63	Jerome Bettis	.40	.18
❑ 64	John Taylor	.10	.05
❑ 65	Ricky Proehl	.10	.05

❑ 66 Junior Seau	.40	.18
❑ 67 Bubby Brister	.10	.05
❑ 68 Neil Smith	.20	.09
❑ 69 Dan McGwire	.10	.05
❑ 70 Brett Perriman	.20	.09
❑ 71 Chris Spielman	.20	.09
❑ 72 Jeff George	.20	.09
❑ 73 Emmitt Smith	1.00	.45
❑ 74 Chris Penn	.10	.05
❑ 75 Derrick Fenner	.10	.05
❑ 76 Reggie Brooks	.20	.09
❑ 77 Chris Chandler	.20	.09
❑ 78 Rod Woodson	.20	.09
❑ 79 Isaac Bruce	.60	.25
❑ 80 Reggie Cobb	.10	.05
❑ 81 Bryce Paup	.40	.18
❑ 82 Warren Moon	.20	.09
❑ 83 Bryan Reeves	.10	.05
❑ 84 Lake Dawson	.20	.09
❑ 85 Larry Centers	.20	.09
❑ 86 Marshall Faulk	.60	.25
❑ 87 Jim Harbaugh	.20	.09
❑ 88 Ray Childress	.10	.05
❑ 89 Eric Metcalf	.20	.09
❑ 90 Ernie Mills	.10	.05
❑ 91 Lamar Lathon	.10	.05
❑ 92 Erric Rhett	.40	.18
❑ 93 David Klingler	.20	.09
❑ 94 Vincent Brown	.10	.05
❑ 95 Andre Rison	.20	.09
❑ 96 Brian Mitchell	.10	.05
❑ 97 Mark Rypien	.10	.05
❑ 98 Eugene Robinson	.10	.05
❑ 99 Eric Green	.10	.05
❑ 100 Rocket Ismail	.20	.09
❑ 101 Flipper Anderson	.10	.05
❑ 102 Randall Cunningham	.40	.18
❑ 103 Ricky Watters	.40	.18
❑ 104 Amp Lee	.10	.05
❑ 105 Ernest Givins	.10	.05
❑ 106 Daryl Johnston	.20	.09
❑ 107 Dave Krieg	.10	.05
❑ 108 Dana Stubblefield	.40	.18
❑ 109 Torrance Small	.10	.05
❑ 110 Yancey Thigpen RC	.40	.18
❑ 111 Chester McGlockton	.20	.09
❑ 112 Craig Erickson	.10	.05
❑ 113 Herschel Walker	.20	.09
❑ 114 Mike Sherrard	.10	.05
❑ 115 Tony McGee	.10	.05
❑ 116 Adrian Murrell	.20	.09
❑ 117 Frank Reich	.10	.05
❑ 118 Hardy Nickerson	.10	.05
❑ 119 Andre Reed	.20	.09
❑ 120 Leonard Russell	.10	.05
❑ 121 Eric Allen	.10	.05
❑ 122 Jeff Hostetler	.20	.09
❑ 123 Barry Foster	.20	.09
❑ 124 Anthony Miller	.20	.09
❑ 125 Shawn Jefferson	.10	.05
❑ 126 Richie Anderson RC	.10	.05
❑ 127 Steve Bono	.20	.09
❑ 128 Seth Joyner	.10	.05
❑ 129 Darnay Scott	.40	.18
❑ 130 Johnny Mitchell	.10	.05
❑ 131 Eric Swann	.20	.09
❑ 132 Drew Bledsoe	1.00	.45
❑ 133 Marcus Allen	.40	.18
❑ 134 Carl Pickens	.40	.18
❑ 135 Michael Brooks	.10	.05
❑ 136 John L. Williams	.10	.05
❑ 137 Steve Beuerlein	.10	.05
❑ 138 Robert Smith	.40	.18
❑ 139 O.J. McDuffie	.40	.18
❑ 140 Haywood Jeffires	.10	.05
❑ 141 Aeneas Williams	.10	.05
❑ 142 Rick Mirer	.40	.18
❑ 143 William Floyd	.40	.18
❑ 144 Fred Barnett	.20	.09
❑ 145 Leroy Hoard	.10	.05
❑ 146 Terry Kirby	.20	.09
❑ 147 Boomer Esiason	.20	.09
❑ 148 Ken Harvey	.10	.05
❑ 149 Cleveland Gary	.10	.05
❑ 150 Brian Blades	.20	.09
❑ 151 Eric Turner	.10	.05
❑ 152 Vinny Testaverde	.20	.09
❑ 153 Ronald Moore UER card pictures Rob Moore	.10	.05
❑ 154 Curtis Conway	.40	.18
❑ 155 Johnnie Morton	.20	.09
❑ 156 Kenneth Davis	.10	.05
❑ 157 Scott Mitchell	.20	.09
❑ 158 Sean Gilbert	.20	.09
❑ 159 Shannon Sharpe	.20	.09
❑ 160 Mark Seay	.20	.09
❑ 161 Cornelius Bennett	.20	.09
❑ 162 Heath Shuler	.40	.18
❑ 163 Byron Bam Morris	.20	.09
❑ 164 Robert Brooks	.40	.18
❑ 165 Glyn Milburn	.10	.05
❑ 166 Gary Brown	.10	.05
❑ 167 Jim Everett	.10	.05
❑ 168 Steve Atwater	.10	.05
❑ 169 Darren Woodson	.20	.09
❑ 170 Mark Ingram	.10	.05
❑ 171 Donnell Woolford	.10	.05
❑ 172 Trent Dilfer	.40	.18
❑ 173 Charlie Garner	.20	.09
❑ 174 Charles Johnson	.20	.09
❑ 175 Mike Pritchard	.10	.05
❑ 176 Derek Brown RBK	.10	.05
❑ 177 Chris Miller	.10	.05
❑ 178 Charles Haley	.20	.09
❑ 179 J.J. Birden	.10	.05
❑ 180 Jeff Graham	.10	.05
❑ 181 Bernie Parmalee	.20	.09
❑ 182 Mark Brunell	1.00	.45
❑ 183 Greg Hill	.20	.09
❑ 184 Michael Timpson	.10	.05
❑ 185 Terry Allen	.20	.09
❑ 186 Ricky Ervins	.10	.05
❑ 187 Dave Brown	.20	.09
❑ 188 Dan Wilkinson	.20	.09
❑ 189 Jay Novacek	.20	.09
❑ 190 Harvey Williams	.10	.05
❑ 191 Mario Bates	.40	.18
❑ 192 Steve Young	.50	.23
❑ 193 Joe Montana	2.00	.90
❑ 194 Steve Young PP	.50	.23
❑ 195 Troy Aikman PP	.60	.25
❑ 196 Drew Bledsoe PP	.60	.25
❑ 197 Dan Marino PP	1.00	.45
❑ 198 John Elway PP	1.00	.45
❑ 199 Brett Favre PP	1.00	.45
❑ 200 Heath Shuler PP	.40	.18
❑ 201 Warren Moon PP	.10	.05
❑ 202 Jim Kelly PP	.40	.18
❑ 203 Jeff Hostetler PP	.20	.09
❑ 204 Rick Mirer PP	.20	.09
❑ 205 Dave Brown PP	.20	.09
❑ 206 Randall Cunningham PP	.20	.09
❑ 207 Neil O'Donnell PP	.20	.09
❑ 208 Jim Everett PP	.10	.05
❑ 209 Ki-Jana Carter RC	.40	.18
❑ 210 Steve McNair RC	2.50	1.10
❑ 211 Michael Westbrook RC	1.50	.70
❑ 212 Kerry Collins RC	1.00	.45
❑ 213 Joey Galloway RC	2.50	1.10
❑ 214 Kyle Brady RC	.40	.18
❑ 215 J.J. Stokes RC	1.25	.55
❑ 216 Tyrone Wheatley RC	1.25	.55
❑ 217 Rashaan Salaam RC	.40	.18
❑ 218 Napoleon Kaufman RC	2.00	.90
❑ 219 Frank Sanders RC	1.00	.45
❑ 220 Stoney Case RC	.60	.25
❑ 221 Todd Collins RC	.40	.18
❑ 222 Warren Sapp RC	.60	.25
❑ 223 Sherman Williams RC	.10	.05
❑ 224 Rob Johnson RC	1.50	.70
❑ 225 Mark Bruener RC	.20	.09
❑ 226 Derrick Brooks RC	.10	.05
❑ 227 Chad May RC	.10	.05
❑ 228 James A.Stewart RC	.10	.05
❑ 229 Ray Zellars RC	.20	.09
❑ 230 Dave Barr RC	.10	.05
❑ 231 Kordell Stewart RC	2.50	1.10
❑ 232 Jimmy Oliver RC	.10	.05
❑ 233 Tony Boselli RC	.20	.09
❑ 234 James O. Stewart RC	2.00	.90
❑ 235 Derrick Alexander DE RC	.10	.05
❑ 236 Lovell Pinkney RC	.10	.05
❑ 237 John Walsh RC	.10	.05
❑ 238 Tyrone Davis RC	.10	.05
❑ 239 Joe Aska RC	.20	.09
❑ 240 Korey Stringer RC	.10	.05
❑ 241 Hugh Douglas RC	.20	.09
❑ 242 Christian Fauria RC	.10	.05
❑ 243 Terrell Fletcher RC	.10	.05
❑ 244 Dan Marino	.60	.25
❑ 245 Drew Bledsoe	.40	.18
❑ 246 John Elway	.40	.18
❑ 247 Emmitt Smith	.50	.23
❑ 248 Steve Young	.40	.18
❑ 249 Barry Sanders	.60	.25
❑ 250 Jerry Rice CL Junior Seau CL	.40	.18
❑ 251SP Deion Sanders SP	4.00	1.80

1995 Pinnacle Black 'N Blue

	MINT	NRMT
COMPLETE SET (30)	60.00	27.00
STATED ODDS 1:18 JUMBO		
❑ 1 Junior Seau	2.50	1.10
❑ 2 Byron Bam Morris	1.25	.55
❑ 3 Craig Heyward	1.25	.55
❑ 4 Drew Bledsoe	6.00	2.70
❑ 5 Barry Sanders	12.00	5.50
❑ 6 Jerome Bettis	2.50	1.10
❑ 7 William Floyd	2.50	1.10
❑ 8 Greg Lloyd	1.25	.55
❑ 9 John Elway	12.00	5.50
❑ 10 Jerry Rice	6.00	2.70
❑ 11 Kevin Greene	.60	.25
❑ 12 Errict Rhett	2.50	1.10
❑ 13 Steve Young	5.00	2.20
❑ 14 Bruce Smith	2.50	1.10
❑ 15 Steve Atwater	.60	.25
❑ 16 Natrone Means	2.50	1.10
❑ 17 Ben Coates	1.25	.55
❑ 18 Reggie White	2.50	1.10
❑ 19 Ken Harvey	.60	.25
❑ 20 Dan Marino	12.00	5.50
❑ 21 Marshall Faulk	4.00	1.80
❑ 22 Seth Joyner	.60	.25
❑ 23 Rod Woodson	1.25	.55
❑ 24 Hardy Nickerson	.60	.25
❑ 25 Brett Favre	12.00	5.50
❑ 26 Bryan Cox	.60	.25
❑ 27 Rodney Hampton	1.25	.55
❑ 28 Jeff Hostetler	1.25	.55
❑ 29 Brent Jones	.60	.25
❑ 30 Emmitt Smith	6.00	2.70

1995 Pinnacle Clear Shots

	MINT	NRMT
COMPLETE SET (10)	60.00	27.00
STATED ODDS 1:60 HOB, 1:33 RETAIL		
❑ 1 Jerry Rice	6.00	2.70
❑ 2 Dan Marino	12.00	5.50
❑ 3 Steve Young	5.00	2.20
❑ 4 Drew Bledsoe	6.00	2.70
❑ 5 Emmitt Smith	6.00	2.70

	MINT	NRMT
❑ 6 Barry Sanders	12.00	5.50
❑ 7 Marshall Faulk	4.00	1.80
❑ 8 Troy Aikman	6.00	2.70
❑ 9 Ki-Jana Carter	1.25	.55
❑ 10 Steve McNair	8.00	3.60

1995 Pinnacle Gamebreakers

	MINT	NRMT
COMPLETE SET (15)	50.00	22.00
STATED ODDS 1:24 HOBBY		

❑ 1 Marshall Faulk	2.50	1.10
❑ 2 Emmitt Smith	4.00	1.80
❑ 3 Steve Young	3.00	1.35
❑ 4 Ki-Jana Carter	.75	.35
❑ 5 Drew Bledsoe	4.00	1.80
❑ 6 Troy Aikman	4.00	1.80
❑ 7 Rashaan Salaam	.75	.35
❑ 8 Tyrone Wheatley	2.50	1.10
❑ 9 Dan Marino	8.00	3.60
❑ 10 Natrone Means	1.50	.70
❑ 11 Barry Sanders	8.00	3.60
❑ 12 Jerry Rice	4.00	1.80
❑ 13 Byron Bam Morris	.75	.35
❑ 14 Steve McNair	5.00	2.20
❑ 15 Kerry Collins	2.00	.90

1995 Pinnacle Showcase

	MINT	NRMT
COMPLETE SET (21)	30.00	13.50
STATED ODDS 1:18 HOB,1:14 JUM,1:10 RET		

❑ 1 Drew Bledsoe	2.50	1.10
❑ 2 Joey Galloway	2.50	1.10
❑ 3 Steve Young	2.00	.90
❑ 4 Joe Aska	.20	.09
❑ 5 Barry Sanders	5.00	2.20
❑ 6 Troy Aikman	2.50	1.10
❑ 7 Dan Marino	5.00	2.20
❑ 8 Randall Cunningham	1.00	.45
❑ 9 John Elway	5.00	2.20
❑ 10 Brett Favre	5.00	2.20
❑ 11 Jim Kelly	1.00	.45
❑ 12 Warren Moon	.50	.23
❑ 13 Dave Brown	.50	.23
❑ 14 Jeff Hostetler	.50	.23
❑ 15 Rick Mirer	1.00	.45
❑ 16 Ki-Jana Carter	.40	.18
❑ 17 Kerry Collins	1.00	.45
❑ 18 J.J. Stokes	1.25	.55
❑ 19 Kordell Stewart	6.00	2.70
❑ 20 Michael Westbrook	1.50	.70
❑ 21 Todd Collins	.40	.18

1995 Pinnacle Team Pinnacle

	MINT	NRMT
COMPLETE SET (10)	80.00	36.00
COMMON CARD (1-10)	5.00	2.20
STATED ODDS 1:90 HOBBY, 1:49 RETAIL		

❑ 1 Steve Young / Drew Bledsoe	10.00	4.50
❑ 2 Emmitt Smith / Marshall Faulk	12.00	5.50
❑ 3 Barry Sanders / Natrone Means	12.00	5.50
❑ 4 Dan Marino / Troy Aikman	12.00	5.50
❑ 5 Jerry Rice / Tim Brown	10.00	4.50
❑ 6 Errict Rhett / Byron Bam Morris	5.00	2.20
❑ 7 Brett Favre / John Elway	15.00	6.75
❑ 8 Rashaan Salaam / Ki-Jana Carter	5.00	2.20
❑ 9 Kery Collins / Steve McNair	6.00	2.70
❑ 10 Joey Galloway / Michael Westbrook	6.00	2.70

1996 Pinnacle

	MINT	NRMT
COMPLETE SET (200)	20.00	9.00
COMMON CARD (1-200)	.10	.05
SEMISTARS	.20	.09
UNLISTED STARS	.40	.18
COMP.ARTIST PROOF (200)	600.00	275.00
*AP STARS: 8X TO 20X HI COL.		
*AP RCs: 4X TO 10X HI		
AP STAT.ODDS 1:48 HOB, 1:12 PS, 1:67 JUM		
COMP.TROPHY COLL. (200)	250.00	110.00

*TC STARS: 3X TO 8X HI COL.		
*TC RCs: 1.5X TO 4X HI		
TC STAT.ODDS 1:5 HOB, 1:2 PS, 1:7 JUM		
COMP.PREM.STOCK (200)	30.00	13.50
*PREMIUM STOCK SILVERS: .6X TO 1.5X HI		
SILVERS INSERTS IN HOBBY PREM.STOCK		
COMP.FOIL SET (200)	20.00	9.00
*FOILS: SAME PRICE		
FOILS AVAILABLE IN RETAIL JUMBOS		

❑ 1 Emmitt Smith	1.50	.70
❑ 2 Robert Brooks	.40	.18
❑ 3 Joey Galloway	.75	.35
❑ 4 Dan Marino	2.00	.90
❑ 5 Frank Sanders	.20	.09
❑ 6 Cris Carter	.40	.18
❑ 7 Jeff Blake	.40	.18
❑ 8 Steve McNair	.75	.35
❑ 9 Tamarick Vanover	.20	.09
❑ 10 Andre Reed	.20	.09
❑ 11 Junior Seau	.20	.09
❑ 12 Alvin Harper	.10	.05
❑ 13 Trent Dilfer	.40	.18
❑ 14 Kordell Stewart	.75	.35
❑ 15 Kyle Brady	.10	.05
❑ 16 Charles Haley	.20	.09
❑ 17 Greg Lloyd	.20	.09
❑ 18 Mario Bates	.20	.09
❑ 19 Shannon Sharpe	.20	.09
❑ 20 Scott Mitchell	.20	.09
❑ 21 Craig Heyward	.10	.05
❑ 22 Marcus Allen	.40	.18
❑ 23 Curtis Martin	.75	.35
❑ 24 Drew Bledsoe	1.00	.45
❑ 25 Jerry Rice	1.00	.45
❑ 26 Charlie Garner	.10	.05
❑ 27 Michael Irvin	.40	.18
❑ 28 Curtis Conway	.40	.18
❑ 29 Terrell Davis	2.50	1.10
❑ 30 Jeff Hostetler	.10	.05
❑ 31 Neil O'Donnell	.20	.09
❑ 32 Errict Rhett	.20	.09
❑ 33 Stan Humphries	.20	.09
❑ 34 Jeff Graham	.10	.05
❑ 35 Floyd Turner	.10	.05
❑ 36 Vincent Brisby	.10	.05
❑ 37 Steve Young	.75	.35
❑ 38 Carl Pickens	.40	.18
❑ 39 Terance Mathis	.10	.05
❑ 40 Brett Favre	2.00	.90
❑ 41 Ki-Jana Carter	.20	.09
❑ 42 Jim Everett	.10	.05
❑ 43 Marshall Faulk	.40	.18
❑ 44 William Floyd	.20	.09
❑ 45 Deion Sanders	.60	.25
❑ 46 Garrison Hearst	.20	.09
❑ 47 Chris Sanders	.20	.09
❑ 48 Isaac Bruce	.40	.18
❑ 49 Natrone Means	.40	.18
❑ 50 Troy Aikman	1.00	.45
❑ 51 Ben Coates	.20	.09
❑ 52 Tony Martin	.20	.09
❑ 53 Rod Woodson	.20	.09
❑ 54 Edgar Bennett	.20	.09
❑ 55 Eric Zeier	.10	.05
❑ 56 Steve Bono	.10	.05
❑ 57 Tim Brown	.40	.18
❑ 58 Kevin Williams	.10	.05
❑ 59 Erik Kramer	.10	.05

		Mint	NrMt
❑ 60	Jim Kelly	.40	.18
❑ 61	Larry Centers	.20	.09
❑ 62	Terrell Fletcher	.10	.05
❑ 63	Michael Westbrook	.40	.18
❑ 64	Kerry Collins	.40	.18
❑ 65	Jay Novacek	.10	.05
❑ 66	J.J. Stokes	.40	.18
❑ 67	John Elway	2.00	.90
❑ 68	Jim Harbaugh	.20	.09
❑ 69	Aeneas Williams	.10	.05
❑ 70	Tyrone Wheatley	.20	.09
❑ 71	Chris Warren	.20	.09
❑ 72	Rodney Thomas	.10	.05
❑ 73	Jeff George	.20	.09
❑ 74	Rick Mirer	.20	.09
❑ 75	Yancey Thigpen	.20	.09
❑ 76	Herman Moore	.40	.18
❑ 77	Gus Frerotte	.40	.18
❑ 78	Anthony Miller	.20	.09
❑ 79	Ricky Watters	.20	.09
❑ 80	Sherman Williams	.10	.05
❑ 81	Hardy Nickerson	.10	.05
❑ 82	Henry Ellard	.10	.05
❑ 83	Aaron Craver	.10	.05
❑ 84	Rodney Peete	.10	.05
❑ 85	Eric Metcalf	.10	.05
❑ 86	Brian Blades	.10	.05
❑ 87	Rob Moore	.20	.09
❑ 88	Kimble Anders	.20	.09
❑ 89	Harvey Williams	.10	.05
❑ 90	Thurman Thomas	.40	.18
❑ 91	Dave Brown	.10	.05
❑ 92	Terry Allen	.20	.09
❑ 93	Ken Norton Jr.	.10	.05
❑ 94	Reggie White	.40	.18
❑ 95	Mark Chmura	.20	.09
❑ 96	Bert Emanuel	.20	.09
❑ 97	Brett Perriman	.10	.05
❑ 98	Antonio Freeman	.75	.35
❑ 99	Brian Mitchell	.10	.05
❑ 100	Orlando Thomas	.10	.05
❑ 101	Aaron Hayden	.10	.05
❑ 102	Quinn Early	.10	.05
❑ 103	Lovell Pinkney	.10	.05
❑ 104	Napoleon Kaufman	.50	.23
❑ 105	Daryl Johnston	.20	.09
❑ 106	Steve Tasker	.10	.05
❑ 107	Brent Jones	.10	.05
❑ 108	Mark Brunell	1.00	.45
❑ 109	Leslie O'Neal	.10	.05
❑ 110	Irving Fryar	.20	.09
❑ 111	Jim Miller	.10	.05
❑ 112	Sean Dawkins	.10	.05
❑ 113	Boomer Esiason	.20	.09
❑ 114	Heath Shuler	.20	.09
❑ 115	Bruce Smith	.20	.09
❑ 116	Russell Maryland	.10	.05
❑ 117	Jake Reed	.20	.09
❑ 118	O.J. McDuffie	.20	.09
❑ 119	Erik Williams	.10	.05
❑ 120	Willie McGinest	.10	.05
❑ 121	Terry Kirby	.20	.09
❑ 122	Fred Barnett	.10	.05
❑ 123	Andre Hastings	.10	.05
❑ 124	Dale Hellestrae	.10	.05
❑ 125	Darren Woodson	.20	.09
❑ 126	Steve Atwater	.10	.05
❑ 127	Quentin Coryatt	.10	.05
❑ 128	Derrick Thomas	.20	.09
❑ 129	Nate Newton	.10	.05
❑ 130	Kevin Greene	.20	.09
❑ 131	Barry Sanders	2.00	.90
❑ 132	Warren Moon	.20	.09
❑ 133	Rashaan Salaam	.40	.18
❑ 134	Rodney Hampton	.20	.09
❑ 135	James O.Stewart	.20	.09
❑ 136	Erric Pegram	.10	.05
❑ 137	Bryan Cox	.10	.05
❑ 138	Adrian Murrell	.40	.18
❑ 139	Robert Smith	.20	.09
❑ 140	Bernie Parmalee	.10	.05
❑ 141	Bryce Paup	.10	.05
❑ 142	Darick Holmes	.10	.05
❑ 143	Hugh Douglas	.10	.05
❑ 144	Ken Dilger	.20	.09
❑ 145	Derek Loville	.10	.05
❑ 146	Horace Copeland	.10	.05
❑ 147	Wayne Chrebet	.20	.09
❑ 148	Andre Coleman	.10	.05
❑ 149	Greg Hill	.20	.09
❑ 150	Eric Swann	.10	.05
❑ 151	Tyrone Hughes	.10	.05
❑ 152	Ernie Mills	.10	.05
❑ 153	Terry Glenn RC	1.50	.70
❑ 154	Cedric Jones RC	.10	.05
❑ 155	Leeland McElroy RC	.40	.18
❑ 156	Bobby Engram RC	.40	.18
❑ 157	Willie Anderson RC	.10	.05
❑ 158	Mike Alstott RC	1.50	.70
❑ 159	Alex Van Dyke RC	.20	.09
❑ 160	Jeff Lewis RC	.50	.23
❑ 161	Keyshawn Johnson RC	2.50	1.10
❑ 162	Regan Upshaw RC	.10	.05
❑ 163	Eric Moulds RC	2.00	.90
❑ 164	Tim Biakabutuka RC	1.00	.45
❑ 165	Kevin Hardy RC	.40	.18
❑ 166	Marvin Harrison RC	2.50	1.10
❑ 167	Karim Abdul-Jabbar RC	.75	.35
❑ 168	Tony Brackens RC	.20	.09
❑ 169	Stepfret Williams RC	.20	.09
❑ 170	Eddie George RC	4.00	1.80
❑ 171	Lawrence Phillips RC	.50	.23
❑ 172	Danny Kanell RC	.40	.18
❑ 173	Derrick Mayes RC	.75	.35
❑ 174	Daryl Gardener RC	.10	.05
❑ 175	Jonathan Ogden RC	.10	.05
❑ 176	Alex Molden RC	.10	.05
❑ 177	Chris Darkins RC	.10	.05
❑ 178	Stephen Davis RC	4.00	1.80
❑ 179	Rickey Dudley RC	.40	.18
❑ 180	Eddie Kennison RC	.40	.18
❑ 181	Simeon Rice RC	.40	.18
❑ 182	Bobby Hoying RC	.50	.23
❑ 183	Troy Aikman BF6	.50	.23
❑ 184	Emmitt Smith BF6	1.00	.45
❑ 185	Michael Irvin BF6	.20	.09
❑ 186	Deion Sanders BF6	.40	.18
❑ 187	Daryl Johnston BF6	.20	.09
❑ 188	Jay Novacek BF6	.10	.05
❑ 189	Steve Young BF6	.40	.18
❑ 190	Jerry Rice BF6	.50	.23
❑ 191	J.J. Stokes BF6	.40	.18
❑ 192	Ken Norton BF6	.10	.05
❑ 193	William Floyd BF6	.20	.09
❑ 194	Brent Jones BF6	.10	.05
❑ 195	Dan Marino CL	.40	.18
❑ 196	Brett Favre CL	.40	.18
❑ 197	Emmitt Smith CL	.40	.18
❑ 198	Barry Sanders CL	.40	.18
❑ 199	Dan Marino CL Emmitt Smith CL Brett Favre CL Barry Sanders CL	.40	.18
❑ 200	Brett Favre Packer Backer	2.00	.90

1996 Pinnacle Black 'N Blue

	MINT	NRMT
COMPLETE SET (25)	200.00	90.00
STATED ODDS 1:33 JUMBO		

		Mint	NrMt
❑ 1	Steve Young	12.00	5.50
❑ 2	Troy Aikman	15.00	6.75
❑ 3	Dan Marino	30.00	13.50
❑ 4	Michael Irvin	6.00	2.70
❑ 5	Jerry Rice	15.00	6.75
❑ 6	Emmitt Smith	25.00	11.00
❑ 7	Brett Favre	30.00	13.50
❑ 8	Drew Bledsoe	15.00	6.75
❑ 9	John Elway	30.00	13.50
❑ 10	Barry Sanders	30.00	13.50
❑ 11	Cris Carter	6.00	2.70
❑ 12	Jeff Blake	6.00	2.70
❑ 13	Chris Warren	3.00	1.35
❑ 14	Kerry Collins	6.00	2.70
❑ 15	Natrone Means	6.00	2.70
❑ 16	Herman Moore	6.00	2.70
❑ 17	Steve McNair	12.00	5.50
❑ 18	Ricky Watters	3.00	1.35
❑ 19	Tamarick Vanover	3.00	1.35
❑ 20	Deion Sanders	10.00	4.50
❑ 21	Terrell Davis	40.00	18.00
❑ 22	Rodney Thomas	1.50	.70
❑ 23	Rashaan Salaam	6.00	2.70
❑ 24	Darick Holmes	1.50	.70
❑ 25	Eric Zeier	1.50	.70

1996 Pinnacle Die Cut Jerseys

	MINT	NRMT
COMPLETE SET (20)	150.00	70.00
STATED ODDS 1:24 HOBBY		
*HOLO STARS: 10X TO 20X BASE CARD HI		
*HOLO ROOKIES: 3X TO 8X BASE CARD HI		
HOLOFOIL STATED ODDS 1:6 PREM.STOCK		

		Mint	NrMt
❑ 1	Errict Rhett	2.50	1.10
❑ 2	Marshall Faulk	5.00	2.20
❑ 3	Isaac Bruce	5.00	2.20
❑ 4	William Floyd	2.50	1.10
❑ 5	Heath Shuler	2.50	1.10
❑ 6	Kerry Collins	5.00	2.20
❑ 7	Kordell Stewart	10.00	4.50
❑ 8	Rashaan Salaam	5.00	2.20
❑ 9	Terrell Davis	30.00	13.50
❑ 10	Rodney Thomas	1.25	.55
❑ 11	Curtis Martin	10.00	4.50
❑ 12	Steve McNair	10.00	4.50
❑ 13	J.J. Stokes	5.00	2.20
❑ 14	Joey Galloway	10.00	4.50
❑ 15	Michael Westbrook	5.00	2.20
❑ 16	Keyshawn Johnson	12.00	5.50
❑ 17	Lawrence Phillips	2.50	1.10
❑ 18	Terry Glenn	8.00	3.60
❑ 19	Tim Biakabutuka	5.00	2.20
❑ 20	Eddie George	20.00	9.00

1996 Pinnacle Double Disguise

	MINT	NRMT
COMPLETE SET (20)	100.00	45.00
COMMON CARD (1-20)	4.00	1.80
SEMISTARS	6.00	2.70
UNLISTED STARS	8.00	3.60
STATED ODDS 1:18 HOB, 1:5 PS, 1:25 JUM		
PRICES ARE FOR PEELED CARDS		
CONDITION SENSITIVE SET !		

❑ 1 Emmitt Smith / Emmitt Smith	8.00	3.60
❑ 2 Emmitt Smith / Dan Marino	10.00	4.50
❑ 3 Emmitt Smith / Brett Favre	10.00	4.50
❑ 4 Emmitt Smith / Steve Young	8.00	3.60
❑ 5 Dan Marino / Dan Marino	10.00	4.50
❑ 6 Dan Marino / Emmitt Smith	10.00	4.50
❑ 7 Dan Marino / Kerry Collins	8.00	3.60
❑ 8 Dan Marino / Steve Young	8.00	3.60
❑ 9 Kerry Collins / Kerry Collins	6.00	2.70
❑ 10 Kerry Collins / Dan Marino	8.00	3.60
❑ 11 Kerry Collins / Brett Favre	8.00	3.60
❑ 12 Kerry Collins / Steve Young	6.00	2.70
❑ 13 Brett Favre / Brett Favre	10.00	4.50
❑ 14 Brett Favre / Kerry Collins	8.00	3.60
❑ 15 Brett Favre / Dan Marino	10.00	4.50
❑ 16 Brett Favre / Emmitt Smith	10.00	4.50
❑ 17 Steve Young / Steve Young	4.00	1.80
❑ 18 Steve Young / Brett Favre	8.00	3.60
❑ 19 Steve Young / Emmitt Smith	8.00	3.60
❑ 20 Steve Young / Kerry Collins	6.00	2.70

1996 Pinnacle On The Line

	MINT	NRMT
COMPLETE SET (15)	100.00	45.00
STATED ODDS 1:23 RETAIL		
❑ 1 Michael Irvin	10.00	4.50
❑ 2 Robert Brooks	10.00	4.50
❑ 3 Herman Moore	10.00	4.50
❑ 4 Cris Carter	10.00	4.50
❑ 5 Chris Sanders	5.00	2.20
❑ 6 Jerry Rice	25.00	11.00
❑ 7 Michael Westbrook	10.00	4.50
❑ 8 Carl Pickens	10.00	4.50
❑ 9 Bobby Engram	2.00	.90
❑ 10 Alex Van Dyke	1.00	.45
❑ 11 Keyshawn Johnson	12.00	5.50
❑ 12 Terry Glenn	8.00	3.60
❑ 13 Eric Moulds	10.00	4.50
❑ 14 Marvin Harrison	12.00	5.50
❑ 15 Eddie Kennison	2.00	.90

1996 Pinnacle Team Pinnacle

	MINT	NRMT
COMPLETE SET (10)	100.00	45.00
COMMON CARD (1-10)	8.00	3.60
STATED ODDS 1:90 H/R,1:20 PREM.STOCK		
❑ 1 Troy Aikman / Drew Bledsoe	12.00	5.50
❑ 2 Steve Young / Jeff Blake	10.00	4.50
❑ 3 Brett Favre / John Elway	25.00	11.00
❑ 4 Kerry Collins / Dan Marino	15.00	6.75
❑ 5 Emmitt Smith / Curtis Martin	15.00	6.75
❑ 6 Barry Sanders / Chris Warren	15.00	6.75
❑ 7 Errict Rhett / Marshall Faulk	8.00	3.60
❑ 8 Jerry Rice / Carl Pickens	12.00	5.50
❑ 9 Michael Irvin / Joey Galloway	10.00	4.50
❑ 10 Isaac Bruce / Kordell Stewart	10.00	4.50

1997 Pinnacle

	MINT	NRMT
COMPLETE SET (200)	20.00	9.00
COMMON CARD (1-200)	.10	.05
SEMISTARS	.20	.09
UNLISTED STARS	.30	.14
COMP.ARTIST PROOF (100)	500.00	220.00
*AP STARS: 8X TO 20X HI COL...		
*AP RCs: 4X TO 10X HI COL.		
ART.PROOF STATED ODDS 1:39		
COMP.TROPHY COLL (100)	250.00	110.00
*TROPHY STARS: 3X TO 8X HI COL.		
*TROPHY RCs: 1.5X TO 4X		
TROPHY COLL.STATED ODDS 1:9		
PARALLEL CARDS ARE RE-NUMBERED!		
❑ 1 Brett Favre	2.00	.90
❑ 2 Dan Marino	2.00	.90
❑ 3 Emmitt Smith	1.50	.70
❑ 4 Steve Young	.60	.25
❑ 5 Drew Bledsoe	1.00	.45
❑ 6 Eddie George	1.00	.45
❑ 7 Barry Sanders	2.00	.90
❑ 8 Jerry Rice	1.00	.45
❑ 9 John Elway	2.00	.90
❑ 10 Troy Aikman	1.00	.45
❑ 11 Kerry Collins	.20	.09
❑ 12 Rick Mirer	.10	.05
❑ 13 Jim Harbaugh	.20	.09
❑ 14 Elvis Grbac	.20	.09
❑ 15 Gus Frerotte	.10	.05
❑ 16 Neil O'Donnell	.20	.09
❑ 17 Jeff George	.20	.09
❑ 18 Kordell Stewart	.50	.23
❑ 19 Junior Seau	.20	.09
❑ 20 Vinny Testaverde	.20	.09
❑ 21 Terry Glenn	.30	.14
❑ 22 Anthony Johnson	.10	.05
❑ 23 Boomer Esiason	.20	.09
❑ 24 Terrell Owens	.30	.14
❑ 25 Natrone Means	.30	.14
❑ 26 Marcus Allen	.30	.14
❑ 27 James Jett	.20	.09
❑ 28 Chris T. Jones	.10	.05
❑ 29 Stan Humphries	.20	.09
❑ 30 Keith Byars	.10	.05
❑ 31 John Friesz	.10	.05
❑ 32 Mike Alstott	.30	.14
❑ 33 Eddie Kennison	.20	.09
❑ 34 Eric Moulds	.30	.14
❑ 35 Frank Sanders	.20	.09
❑ 36 Daryl Johnston	.20	.09
❑ 37 Cris Carter	.30	.14
❑ 38 Errict Rhett	.10	.05
❑ 39 Ben Coates	.20	.09
❑ 40 Shannon Sharpe	.20	.09
❑ 41 Jamal Anderson	.60	.25
❑ 42 Tim Biakabutuka	.20	.09
❑ 43 Jeff Blake	.20	.09
❑ 44 Michael Irvin	.30	.14
❑ 45 Terrell Davis	1.50	.70
❑ 46 Byron Bam Morris	.10	.05
❑ 47 Rashaan Salaam	.10	.05
❑ 48 Adrian Murrell	.20	.09
❑ 49 Ty Detmer	.20	.09
❑ 50 Terry Allen	.30	.14
❑ 51 Mark Brunell	1.00	.45
❑ 52 O.J. McDuffie	.20	.09
❑ 53 Willie McGinest	.10	.05
❑ 54 Chris Warren	.20	.09
❑ 55 Trent Dilfer	.30	.14
❑ 56 Jerome Bettis	.30	.14
❑ 57 Tamarick Vanover	.20	.09
❑ 58 Ki-Jana Carter	.10	.05
❑ 59 Ray Zellars	.10	.05
❑ 60 J.J. Stokes	.20	.09
❑ 61 Cornelius Bennett	.10	.05
❑ 62 Scott Mitchell	.20	.09
❑ 63 Tyrone Wheatley	.20	.09
❑ 64 Steve McNair	.50	.23
❑ 65 Tony Banks	.20	.09
❑ 66 James O.Stewart	.20	.09
❑ 67 Robert Smith	.20	.09
❑ 68 Thurman Thomas	.30	.14
❑ 69 Mark Chmura	.20	.09
❑ 70 Napoleon Kaufman	.30	.14
❑ 71 Ken Norton	.10	.05
❑ 72 Herschel Walker	.20	.09
❑ 73 Joey Galloway	.50	.23
❑ 74 Neil Smith	.20	.09
❑ 75 Simeon Rice	.20	.09
❑ 76 Michael Jackson	.20	.09

	Card		
❑	77 Muhsin Muhammad	.20	.09
❑	78 Kevin Hardy	.10	.05
❑	79 Irving Fryar	.20	.09
❑	80 Jeff Hostetler	.10	.05
❑	81 Eric Swann	.10	.05
❑	82 Jim Everett	.10	.05
❑	83 Karim Abdul-Jabbar	.30	.14
❑	84 Garrison Hearst	.20	.09
❑	85 Lawrence Phillips	.10	.05
❑	86 Bryan Cox	.10	.05
❑	87 Larry Centers	.20	.09
❑	88 Wesley Walls	.20	.09
❑	89 Curtis Conway	.20	.09
❑	90 Darnay Scott	.20	.09
❑	91 Anthony Miller	.10	.05
❑	92 Edgar Bennett	.20	.09
❑	93 Willie Green	.10	.05
❑	94 Kent Graham	.10	.05
❑	95 Dave Brown	.10	.05
❑	96 Wayne Chrebet	.30	.14
❑	97 Ricky Watters	.20	.09
❑	98 Tony Martin	.20	.09
❑	99 Warren Moon	.30	.14
❑	100 Curtis Martin	.50	.23
❑	101 Dorsey Levens	.30	.14
❑	102 Jim Pyne	.10	.05
❑	103 Antonio Freeman	.50	.23
❑	104 Leeland McElroy	.10	.05
❑	105 Isaac Bruce	.30	.14
❑	106 Chris Sanders	.10	.05
❑	107 Tim Brown	.30	.14
❑	108 Greg Lloyd	.10	.05
❑	109 Terrell Buckley	.10	.05
❑	110 Deion Sanders	.30	.14
❑	111 Carl Pickens	.30	.14
❑	112 Bobby Engram	.20	.09
❑	113 Andre Reed	.20	.09
❑	114 Terance Mathis	.20	.09
❑	115 Herman Moore	.30	.14
❑	116 Robert Brooks	.20	.09
❑	117 Ken Dilger	.10	.05
❑	118 Keenan McCardell	.20	.09
❑	119 Andre Hastings	.10	.05
❑	120 Willie Davis	.10	.05
❑	121 Bruce Smith	.20	.09
❑	122 Rob Moore	.20	.09
❑	123 Johnnie Morton	.20	.09
❑	124 Sean Dawkins	.10	.05
❑	125 Mario Bates	.10	.05
❑	126 Henry Ellard	.10	.05
❑	127 Derrick Alexander WR	.20	.09
❑	128 Kevin Greene	.20	.09
❑	129 Derrick Thomas	.20	.09
❑	130 Rod Woodson	.20	.09
❑	131 Rodney Hampton	.20	.09
❑	132 Marshall Faulk	.30	.14
❑	133 Michael Westbrook	.20	.09
❑	134 Erik Kramer	.10	.05
❑	135 Todd Collins	.10	.05
❑	136 Bill Romanowski	.10	.05
❑	137 Jake Reed	.20	.09
❑	138 Heath Shuler	.10	.05
❑	139 Keyshawn Johnson	.30	.14
❑	140 Marvin Harrison	.30	.14
❑	141 Andre Rison	.20	.09
❑	142 Zach Thomas	.20	.09
❑	143 Eric Metcalf	.20	.09
❑	144 Amani Toomer	.20	.09
❑	145 Desmond Howard	.20	.09
❑	146 Jimmy Smith	.20	.09
❑	147 Brad Johnson	.50	.23
❑	148 Troy Vincent	.10	.05
❑	149 Bryce Paup	.10	.05
❑	150 Reggie White	.30	.14
❑	151 Jake Plummer RC	3.00	1.35
❑	152 Darnell Autry RC	.20	.09
❑	153 Tiki Barber RC	.50	.23
❑	154 Pat Barnes RC	.30	.14
❑	155 Orlando Pace RC	.10	.05
❑	156 Peter Boulware RC	.20	.09
❑	157 Shawn Springs RC	.20	.09
❑	158 Troy Davis RC	.30	.14
❑	159 Ike Hilliard RC	.75	.35
❑	160 Jim Druckenmiller RC	.50	.23
❑	161 Warrick Dunn RC	1.25	.55
❑	162 James Farrior RC	.10	.05
❑	163 Tony Gonzalez RC	1.25	.55
❑	164 Darrell Russell RC	.10	.05
❑	165 Byron Hanspard RC	.75	.35
❑	166 Corey Dillon RC	1.50	.70
❑	167 Kenny Holmes RC	.10	.05
❑	168 Walter Jones RC	.10	.05
❑	169 Danny Wuerffel RC	.60	.25
❑	170 Tom Knight RC	.10	.05
❑	171 David LaFleur RC	.20	.09
❑	172 Kevin Lockett RC	.20	.09
❑	173 Will Blackwell RC	.30	.14
❑	174 Reidel Anthony RC	.75	.35
❑	175 Dwayne Rudd RC	.10	.05
❑	176 Yatil Green RC	.20	.09
❑	177 Antowain Smith RC	1.00	.45
❑	178 Rae Carruth RC	.30	.14
❑	179 Bryant Westbrook RC	.10	.05
❑	180 Reinard Wilson RC	.10	.05
❑	181 Joey Kent RC	.30	.14
❑	182 Renaldo Wynn RC	.10	.05
❑	183 Brett Favre I	1.00	.45
❑	184 Emmitt Smith I	.75	.35
❑	185 Dan Marino I	1.00	.45
❑	186 Troy Aikman I	.50	.23
❑	187 Jerry Rice I	.50	.23
❑	188 Drew Bledsoe I	.50	.23
❑	189 Eddie George I	.50	.23
❑	190 Terry Glenn I	.20	.09
❑	191 John Elway I	1.00	.45
❑	192 Steve Young I	.30	.14
❑	193 Mark Brunell I	.50	.23
❑	194 Barry Sanders I	1.00	.45
❑	195 Kerry Collins I	.20	.09
❑	196 Curtis Martin I	.30	.14
❑	197 Terrell Davis I	.75	.35
❑	198 Drew Bledsoe Kerry Collins Dan Marino Checklist back	.30	.14
❑	199 Steve Young Jeff George Mark Brunell Checklist back	.10	.05
❑	200 Troy Aikman John Elway Rick Mirer CL	.10	.05

1997 Pinnacle Scoring Core

		MINT	NRMT
	COMPLETE SET (24)	400.00	180.00
	STATED ODDS 1:89 HOBBY		
❑	1 Emmitt Smith	50.00	22.00
❑	2 Troy Aikman	30.00	13.50
❑	3 Michael Irvin	10.00	4.50
❑	4 Robert Brooks	6.00	2.70
❑	5 Brett Favre	60.00	27.00
❑	6 Antonio Freeman	15.00	6.75
❑	7 Curtis Martin	15.00	6.75
❑	8 Drew Bledsoe	30.00	13.50
❑	9 Terry Glenn	10.00	4.50
❑	10 Tim Biakabutuka	6.00	2.70
❑	11 Kerry Collins	6.00	2.70
❑	12 Muhsin Muhammad	6.00	2.70
❑	13 Karim Abdul-Jabbar	10.00	4.50
❑	14 Dan Marino	60.00	27.00
❑	15 O.J. McDuffie	6.00	2.70
❑	16 Terrell Davis	50.00	22.00
❑	17 John Elway	60.00	27.00
❑	18 Shannon Sharpe	6.00	2.70
❑	19 Garrison Hearst	6.00	2.70
❑	20 Steve Young	20.00	9.00
❑	21 Jerry Rice	30.00	13.50
❑	22 Natrone Means	10.00	4.50
❑	23 Mark Brunell	30.00	13.50
❑	24 Keenan McCardell	6.00	2.70
❑	P1 Emmitt Smith Promo	3.00	1.35
❑	P2 Troy Aikman Promo	2.00	.90
❑	P3 Michael Irvin Promo	1.00	.45

1997 Pinnacle Team Pinnacle

		MINT	NRMT
	COMPLETE SET (10)	200.00	90.00
	COMMON CARD (1-10)	10.00	4.50
	STATED ODDS 1:240 HOBBY		
	*MIRRORS: .75X TO 2X HI COL.		
	MIRRORS RANDOM INSERTS IN PACKS		
❑	1 Dan Marino Troy Aikman	30.00	13.50
❑	2 Drew Bledsoe Brett Favre	30.00	13.50
❑	3 Mark Brunell Kerry Collins	15.00	6.75
❑	4 John Elway Steve Young	30.00	13.50
❑	5 Terrell Davis Emmitt Smith	30.00	13.50
❑	6 Curtis Martin Barry Sanders	30.00	13.50
❑	7 Eddie George Tim Biakabutuka	20.00	9.00
❑	8 Karim Abdul-Jabbar Lawrence Phillips	10.00	4.50
❑	9 Terry Glenn Jerry Rice	20.00	9.00
❑	10 Joey Galloway Michael Irvin	12.00	5.50

1997 Pinnacle Epix

		MINT	NRMT
	COMP.ORANGE SET (24)	200.00	90.00
	COMMON GAME (E1-E8)	3.00	1.35
	COMMON MOMENT (E9-E16)	6.00	2.70
	COMMON SEASON (E17-E24)	5.00	2.20
	OVERALL STATED ODDS 1:19 HOBBY		
	*PURPLE CARDS: .75X TO 1.5X ORANGE		
	*EMERALD CARDS: 1.5X TO 3X ORANGE		
	ONLY ORANGE CARDS PRICED BELOW		
❑	E1 Emmitt Smith GAME	15.00	6.75
❑	E2 Troy Aikman GAME	10.00	4.50
❑	E3 Terrell Davis GAME	15.00	6.75
❑	E4 Drew Bledsoe GAME	10.00	4.50
❑	E5 Jeff George GAME	3.00	1.35
❑	E6 Kerry Collins GAME	3.00	1.35
❑	E7 Antonio Freeman GAME	6.00	2.70
❑	E8 Herman Moore GAME	3.00	1.35
❑	E9 Barry Sanders MOMENT	25.00	11.00
❑	E10 Brett Favre MOMENT	25.00	11.00
❑	E11 Michael Irvin MOMENT	6.00	2.70
❑	E12 Steve Young MOMENT	12.00	5.50
❑	E13 Mark Brunell MOMENT	12.00	5.50
❑	E14 Jerome Bettis MOMENT	6.00	2.70
❑	E15 Deion Sanders MOMENT	10.00	4.50
❑	E16 Jeff Blake MOMENT	6.00	2.70
❑	E17 Dan Marino SEASON	20.00	9.00
❑	E18 Eddie George SEASON	10.00	4.50
❑	E19 Jerry Rice SEASON	12.00	5.50
❑	E20 John Elway SEASON	20.00	9.00
❑	E21 Curtis Martin SEASON	10.00	4.50
❑	E22 Kordell Stewart SEASON	10.00	4.50
❑	E23 Junior Seau SEASON	5.00	2.20
❑	E24 Reggie White SEASON	5.00	2.20

1997 Pinnacle Certified

	MINT	NRMT
COMPLETE SET (150)	40.00	18.00
COMMON CARD (1-150)	.20	.09
SEMISTARS	.40	.18
UNLISTED STARS	.75	.35
COMP.CERT.RED (150)	300.00	135.00
*CERT.RED STARS: 1.5X TO 4X HI COL.		
*CERT.RED RCs: 1X TO 2X		
CERTIFIED RED STATED ODDS 1:5		
COMP.MIRROR RED (150)	2000.00	900.00
*MIRROR RED STARS: 10X TO 25X HI COL.		
*MIRROR RED RCs: 5X TO 12X		
MIRROR RED STATED ODDS 1:99		

	MINT	NRMT
❑ 1 Emmitt Smith	3.00	1.35
❑ 2 Dan Marino	4.00	1.80
❑ 3 Brett Favre	4.00	1.80
❑ 4 Steve Young	1.25	.55
❑ 5 Kerry Collins	.40	.18
❑ 6 Troy Aikman	2.00	.90
❑ 7 Drew Bledsoe	2.00	.90
❑ 8 Eddie George	2.50	1.10
❑ 9 Jerry Rice	2.00	.90
❑ 10 John Elway	4.00	1.80
❑ 11 Barry Sanders	4.00	1.80
❑ 12 Mark Brunell	2.00	.90
❑ 13 Elvis Grbac	.40	.18
❑ 14 Tony Banks	.40	.18
❑ 15 Vinny Testaverde	.40	.18
❑ 16 Rick Mirer	.20	.09
❑ 17 Carl Pickens	.75	.35
❑ 18 Deion Sanders	.75	.35
❑ 19 Terry Glenn	.75	.35
❑ 20 Heath Shuler	.20	.09
❑ 21 Dave Brown	.20	.09
❑ 22 Keyshawn Johnson	.75	.35
❑ 23 Jeff George	.40	.18
❑ 24 Ricky Watters	.40	.18
❑ 25 Kordell Stewart	1.00	.45
❑ 26 Junior Seau	.40	.18
❑ 27 Terrell Owens	.75	.35
❑ 28 Warren Moon	.75	.35
❑ 29 Isaac Bruce	.75	.35
❑ 30 Steve McNair	1.00	.45
❑ 31 Gus Frerotte	.20	.09
❑ 32 Trent Dilfer	.75	.35
❑ 33 Shannon Sharpe	.40	.18
❑ 34 Scott Mitchell	.40	.18
❑ 35 Antonio Freeman	1.00	.45
❑ 36 Jim Harbaugh	.40	.18
❑ 37 Natrone Means	.75	.35
❑ 38 Marcus Allen	.75	.35
❑ 39 Karim Abdul-Jabbar	.75	.35
❑ 40 Tim Biakabutuka	.40	.18
❑ 41 Jeff Blake	.40	.18
❑ 42 Michael Irvin	.75	.35
❑ 43 Herschel Walker	.40	.18
❑ 44 Curtis Martin	1.00	.45
❑ 45 Eddie Kennison	.40	.18
❑ 46 Napoleon Kaufman	.75	.35
❑ 47 Larry Centers	.40	.18
❑ 48 Jamal Anderson	1.25	.55
❑ 49 Derrick Alexander WR	.40	.18
❑ 50 Bruce Smith	.40	.18
❑ 51 Wesley Walls	.40	.18
❑ 52 Rod Smith WR	.75	.35
❑ 53 Keenan McCardell	.40	.18
❑ 54 Robert Brooks	.40	.18
❑ 55 Willie Green	.20	.09
❑ 56 Jake Reed	.40	.18
❑ 57 Joey Galloway	1.00	.45
❑ 58 Eric Metcalf	.40	.18
❑ 59 Chris Sanders	.20	.09
❑ 60 Jeff Hostetler	.20	.09
❑ 61 Kevin Greene	.40	.18
❑ 62 Frank Sanders	.40	.18
❑ 63 Dorsey Levens	.75	.35
❑ 64 Sean Dawkins	.20	.09
❑ 65 Cris Carter	.75	.35
❑ 66 Andre Hastings	.20	.09
❑ 67 Amani Toomer	.40	.18
❑ 68 Adrian Murrell	.40	.18
❑ 69 Ty Detmer	.40	.18
❑ 70 Yancey Thigpen	.40	.18
❑ 71 Jim Everett	.20	.09
❑ 72 Todd Collins	.20	.09
❑ 73 Curtis Conway	.40	.18
❑ 74 Herman Moore	.75	.35
❑ 75 Neil O'Donnell	.40	.18
❑ 76 Rod Woodson	.40	.18
❑ 77 Tony Martin	.40	.18
❑ 78 Kent Graham	.20	.09
❑ 79 Andre Reed	.40	.18
❑ 80 Reggie White	.75	.35
❑ 81 Thurman Thomas	.75	.35
❑ 82 Garrison Hearst	.40	.18
❑ 83 Chris Warren	.40	.18
❑ 84 Wayne Chrebet	.75	.35
❑ 85 Chris T. Jones	.20	.09
❑ 86 Anthony Miller	.20	.09
❑ 87 Chris Chandler	.40	.18
❑ 88 Terrell Davis	4.00	1.80
❑ 89 Mike Alstott	.75	.35
❑ 90 Terry Allen	.75	.35
❑ 91 Jerome Bettis	.75	.35
❑ 92 Stan Humphries	.40	.18
❑ 93 Andre Rison	.40	.18
❑ 94 Marshall Faulk	.75	.35
❑ 95 Erik Kramer	.20	.09
❑ 96 O.J. McDuffie	.40	.18
❑ 97 Robert Smith	.40	.18
❑ 98 Keith Byars	.20	.09
❑ 99 Rodney Hampton	.40	.18
❑ 100 Desmond Howard	.40	.18
❑ 101 Lawrence Phillips	.20	.09
❑ 102 Michael Westbrook	.40	.18
❑ 103 Johnnie Morton	.40	.18
❑ 104 Ben Coates	.40	.18
❑ 105 J.J. Stokes	.40	.18
❑ 106 Terance Mathis	.40	.18
❑ 107 Errict Rhett	.20	.09
❑ 108 Tim Brown	.75	.35
❑ 109 Marvin Harrison	.75	.35
❑ 110 Muhsin Muhammad	.40	.18
❑ 111 Byron Bam Morris	.20	.09
❑ 112 Mario Bates	.20	.09
❑ 113 Jimmy Smith	.40	.18
❑ 114 Irving Fryar	.40	.18
❑ 115 Tamarick Vanover	.40	.18
❑ 116 Brad Johnson	1.00	.45
❑ 117 Rashaan Salaam	.20	.09
❑ 118 Ki-Jana Carter	.20	.09
❑ 119 Tyrone Wheatley	.40	.18
❑ 120 John Friesz	.20	.09
❑ 121 Orlando Pace RC	.20	.09
❑ 122 Jim Druckenmiller RC	1.50	.70
❑ 123 Byron Hanspard RC	3.00	1.35
❑ 124 David LaFleur RC	.75	.35
❑ 125 Reidel Anthony RC	3.00	1.35
❑ 126 Antowain Smith RC	4.00	1.80
❑ 127 Bryant Westbrook RC	.20	.09
❑ 128 Fred Lane RC	1.50	.70
❑ 129 Tiki Barber RC	1.50	.70
❑ 130 Shawn Springs RC	.40	.18
❑ 131 Ike Hilliard RC	3.00	1.35
❑ 132 James Farrior RC	.20	.09
❑ 133 Darrell Russell RC	.20	.09
❑ 134 Walter Jones RC	.20	.09
❑ 135 Tom Knight RC	.20	.09
❑ 136 Yatil Green RC	.40	.18
❑ 137 Joey Kent RC	.75	.35
❑ 138 Kevin Lockett RC	.40	.18
❑ 139 Troy Davis RC	.75	.35
❑ 140 Darnell Autry RC	.40	.18
❑ 141 Pat Barnes RC	1.50	.70
❑ 142 Rae Carruth RC	.75	.35
❑ 143 Will Blackwell RC	.75	.35
❑ 144 Warrick Dunn RC	5.00	2.20
❑ 145 Corey Dillon RC	6.00	2.70
❑ 146 Dwayne Rudd RC	.20	.09
❑ 147 Reinard Wilson RC	.20	.09
❑ 148 Peter Boulware RC	.40	.18
❑ 149 Tony Gonzalez RC	5.00	2.20
❑ 150 Danny Wuerffel RC	.75	.35

1997 Pinnacle Certified Mirror Blue

	MINT	NRMT
COMPLETE SET (150)	3000.00	1350.00
COMMON CARD (1-150)	12.00	5.50
*MIRROR BLUE STARS: 12X TO 30X HI COL.		
*MIRROR BLUE RCs: 6X TO 15X		
STATED ODDS 1:199		

1997 Pinnacle Certified Mirror Gold

	MINT	NRMT
COMMON CARD (1-150)	15.00	6.75
*MIR.GOLD STARS: 20X TO 50X HI COL.		
*MIR.GOLD RCs: 10X TO 25X		
STATED ODDS 1:299		

1997 Pinnacle Certified Certified Team

	MINT	NRMT
COMPLETE SET (20)	100.00	45.00
SILVER STATED ODDS 1:19		
*GOLD CARDS: 5X TO 12X BASE CARD HI		
GOLD STATED ODDS 1:119		
*MIRROR GOLDS: 50X TO 100X BASE CARD HI		
MIRROR GOLD STATED PRINT RUN 25 SETS		

	MINT	NRMT
❑ 1 Brett Favre	10.00	4.50
❑ 2 Dan Marino	10.00	4.50
❑ 3 Emmitt Smith	8.00	3.60
❑ 4 Eddie George	6.00	2.70

Card	Mint	Nrmt
❑ 5 Jerry Rice	5.00	2.20
❑ 6 Troy Aikman	5.00	2.20
❑ 7 Barry Sanders	10.00	4.50
❑ 8 Terrell Davis	10.00	4.50
❑ 9 Drew Bledsoe	5.00	2.20
❑ 10 Curtis Martin	2.50	1.10
❑ 11 Terry Glenn	2.00	.90
❑ 12 Kerry Collins	1.00	.45
❑ 13 John Elway	10.00	4.50
❑ 14 Kordell Stewart	2.50	1.10
❑ 15 Karim Abdul-Jabbar	2.00	.90
❑ 16 Steve Young	3.00	1.35
❑ 17 Steve McNair	2.50	1.10
❑ 18 Terrell Owens	2.00	.90
❑ 19 Keyshawn Johnson	2.00	.90
❑ 20 Mark Brunell	5.00	2.20

1997 Pinnacle Certified Epix

	MINT	NRMT
COMP.ORANGE SET (24)	300.00	135.00
COMMON MOMENT (E1-E8)	6.00	2.70
COMMON SEASON (E9-E16)	5.00	2.20
COMMON GAME (E17-E24)	4.00	1.80

OVERALL STATED ODDS 1:15
*PURPLE CARDS: .75X TO 1.5X ORANGE
*EMERALD CARDS: 1.5X TO 3X ORANGE
ONLY ORANGE CARDS PRICED BELOW

Card	Mint	Nrmt
❑ E1 Emmitt Smith MOMENT	30.00	13.50
❑ E2 Troy Aikman MOMENT	20.00	9.00
❑ E3 Terrell Davis MOMENT	30.00	13.50
❑ E4 Drew Bledsoe MOMENT	20.00	9.00
❑ E5 Jeff George MOMENT	6.00	2.70
❑ E6 Kerry Collins MOMENT	6.00	2.70
❑ E7 A.Freeman MOMENT	10.00	4.50
❑ E8 Herman Moore MOMENT	6.00	2.70
❑ E9 Barry Sanders SEASON	25.00	11.00
❑ E10 Brett Favre SEASON	25.00	11.00
❑ E11 Michael Irvin SEASON	5.00	2.20
❑ E12 Steve Young SEASON	12.00	5.50
❑ E13 Mark Brunell SEASON	12.00	5.50
❑ E14 Jerome Bettis SEASON	5.00	2.20
❑ E15 Deion Sanders SEASON	10.00	4.50
❑ E16 Jeff Blake SEASON	5.00	2.20
❑ E17 Dan Marino GAME	20.00	9.00
❑ E18 Eddie George GAME	10.00	4.50
❑ E19 Jerry Rice GAME	12.00	5.50
❑ E20 John Elway GAME	20.00	9.00
❑ E21 Curtis Martin GAME	8.00	3.60
❑ E22 Kordell Stewart GAME	8.00	3.60
❑ E23 Junior Seau GAME	4.00	1.80
❑ E24 Reggie White GAME	4.00	1.80

1997 Pinnacle Totally Certified Platinum Red

	MINT	NRMT
COMPLETE SET (150)	200.00	90.00
COMMON CARD (1-150)	.75	.35
SEMISTARS	1.50	.70
UNLISTED STARS	3.00	1.35

RED PRINT RUN 4999 SERIAL #'d SETS

	MINT	NRMT
COMP.PLAT.BLUE (150)	400.00	180.00

*PLATINUM BLUE CARDS: .75X TO 2X HI
PLATINUM BLUES ONE PER PACK
BLUE PRINT RUN 2499 SERIAL #'d SETS

	MINT	NRMT
COMMON PLAT.GOLD	30.00	13.50

*PLATINUM GOLD STARS: 12X TO 30X HI
*PLATINUM GOLD RCs: 5X TO 12X
GOLD PRINT RUN 30 SERIAL #'d SETS
GOLD STATED ODDS 1:79

Card	Mint	Nrmt
❑ 1 Emmitt Smith	12.00	5.50
❑ 2 Dan Marino	15.00	6.75
❑ 3 Brett Favre	15.00	6.75
❑ 4 Steve Young	6.00	2.70
❑ 5 Kerry Collins	1.50	.70
❑ 6 Troy Aikman	8.00	3.60
❑ 7 Drew Bledsoe	8.00	3.60
❑ 8 Eddie George	8.00	3.60
❑ 9 Jerry Rice	8.00	3.60
❑ 10 John Elway	15.00	6.75
❑ 11 Barry Sanders	15.00	6.75
❑ 12 Mark Brunell	8.00	3.60
❑ 13 Elvis Grbac	1.50	.70
❑ 14 Tony Banks	1.50	.70
❑ 15 Vinny Testaverde	1.50	.70
❑ 16 Rick Mirer	.75	.35
❑ 17 Carl Pickens	3.00	1.35
❑ 18 Deion Sanders	3.00	1.35
❑ 19 Terry Glenn	3.00	1.35
❑ 20 Heath Shuler	.75	.35
❑ 21 Dave Brown	.75	.35
❑ 22 Keyshawn Johnson	3.00	1.35
❑ 23 Jeff George	1.50	.70
❑ 24 Ricky Watters	1.50	.70
❑ 25 Kordell Stewart	4.00	1.80
❑ 26 Junior Seau	1.50	.70
❑ 27 Terrell Owens	3.00	1.35
❑ 28 Warren Moon	3.00	1.35
❑ 29 Isaac Bruce	3.00	1.35
❑ 30 Steve McNair	4.00	1.80
❑ 31 Gus Frerotte	.75	.35
❑ 32 Trent Dilfer	3.00	1.35
❑ 33 Shannon Sharpe	1.50	.70
❑ 34 Scott Mitchell	1.50	.70
❑ 35 Antonio Freeman	4.00	1.80
❑ 36 Jim Harbaugh	1.50	.70
❑ 37 Natrone Means	3.00	1.35
❑ 38 Marcus Allen	3.00	1.35
❑ 39 Karim Abdul-Jabbar	3.00	1.35
❑ 40 Tim Biakabutuka	1.50	.70
❑ 41 Jeff Blake	1.50	.70
❑ 42 Michael Irvin	3.00	1.35
❑ 43 Herschel Walker	1.50	.70
❑ 44 Curtis Martin	4.00	1.80
❑ 45 Eddie Kennison	1.50	.70
❑ 46 Napoleon Kaufman	3.00	1.35
❑ 47 Larry Centers	1.50	.70
❑ 48 Jamal Anderson	5.00	2.20
❑ 49 Derrick Alexander WR	1.50	.70
❑ 50 Bruce Smith	1.50	.70
❑ 51 Wesley Walls	1.50	.70
❑ 52 Rod Smith WR	3.00	1.35
❑ 53 Keenan McCardell	1.50	.70
❑ 54 Robert Brooks	1.50	.70
❑ 55 Willie Green	.75	.35
❑ 56 Jake Reed	1.50	.70
❑ 57 Joey Galloway	4.00	1.80
❑ 58 Eric Metcalf	1.50	.70
❑ 59 Chris Sanders	.75	.35
❑ 60 Jeff Hostetler	.75	.35
❑ 61 Kevin Greene	1.50	.70
❑ 62 Frank Sanders	1.50	.70
❑ 63 Dorsey Levens	3.00	1.35
❑ 64 Sean Dawkins	.75	.35
❑ 65 Cris Carter	3.00	1.35
❑ 66 Andre Hastings	.75	.35
❑ 67 Amani Toomer	1.50	.70
❑ 68 Adrian Murrell	1.50	.70
❑ 69 Ty Detmer	1.50	.70
❑ 70 Yancey Thigpen	.75	.35
❑ 71 Jim Everett	.75	.35
❑ 72 Todd Collins	.75	.35
❑ 73 Curtis Conway	1.50	.70
❑ 74 Herman Moore	3.00	1.35
❑ 75 Neil O'Donnell	1.50	.70
❑ 76 Rod Woodson	1.50	.70
❑ 77 Tony Martin	1.50	.70
❑ 78 Kent Graham	.75	.35
❑ 79 Andre Reed	1.50	.70
❑ 80 Reggie White	3.00	1.35
❑ 81 Thurman Thomas	3.00	1.35
❑ 82 Garrison Hearst	1.50	.70
❑ 83 Chris Warren	1.50	.70
❑ 84 Wayne Chrebet	3.00	1.35
❑ 85 Chris T. Jones	.75	.35
❑ 86 Anthony Miller	.75	.35
❑ 87 Chris Chandler	1.50	.70
❑ 88 Terrell Davis	12.00	5.50
❑ 89 Mike Alstott	3.00	1.35
❑ 90 Terry Allen	3.00	1.35
❑ 91 Jerome Bettis	3.00	1.35
❑ 92 Stan Humphries	1.50	.70
❑ 93 Andre Rison	1.50	.70
❑ 94 Marshall Faulk	3.00	1.35
❑ 95 Erik Kramer	.75	.35
❑ 96 O.J. McDuffie	1.50	.70
❑ 97 Robert Smith	1.50	.70
❑ 98 Keith Byars	.75	.35
❑ 99 Rodney Hampton	1.50	.70
❑ 100 Desmond Howard	1.50	.70
❑ 101 Lawrence Phillips	.75	.35
❑ 102 Michael Westbrook	1.50	.70
❑ 103 Johnnie Morton	1.50	.70
❑ 104 Ben Coates	1.50	.70
❑ 105 J.J. Stokes	1.50	.70
❑ 106 Terance Mathis	1.50	.70
❑ 107 Errict Rhett	.75	.35
❑ 108 Tim Brown	3.00	1.35
❑ 109 Marvin Harrison	3.00	1.35
❑ 110 Muhsin Muhammad	1.50	.70
❑ 111 Byron Bam Morris	.75	.35
❑ 112 Mario Bates	.75	.35
❑ 113 Jimmy Smith	1.50	.70
❑ 114 Irving Fryar	1.50	.70
❑ 115 Tamarick Vanover	1.50	.70
❑ 116 Brad Johnson	4.00	1.80
❑ 117 Rashaan Salaam	.75	.35
❑ 118 Ki-Jana Carter	.75	.35
❑ 119 Tyrone Wheatley	1.50	.70
❑ 120 John Friesz	.75	.35
❑ 121 Orlando Pace RC	.75	.35
❑ 122 Jim Druckenmiller RC	4.00	1.80
❑ 123 Byron Hanspard RC	6.00	2.70
❑ 124 David LaFleur RC	3.00	1.35
❑ 125 Reidel Anthony RC	6.00	2.70
❑ 126 Antowain Smith RC	8.00	3.60
❑ 127 Bryant Westbrook RC	.75	.35
❑ 128 Fred Lane RC	4.00	1.80
❑ 129 Tiki Barber RC	4.00	1.80
❑ 130 Shawn Springs RC	1.50	.70
❑ 131 Ike Hilliard RC	6.00	2.70

❑ 132 James Farrior RC .75 .35
❑ 133 Darrell Russell RC .75 .35
❑ 134 Walter Jones RC .75 .35
❑ 135 Tom Knight RC .75 .35
❑ 136 Yatil Green RC 1.50 .70
❑ 137 Joey Kent RC 3.00 1.35
❑ 138 Kevin Lockett RC 3.00 1.35
❑ 139 Troy Davis RC 3.00 1.35
❑ 140 Darnell Autry RC 1.50 .70
❑ 141 Pat Barnes RC 4.00 1.80
❑ 142 Rae Carruth RC 3.00 1.35
❑ 143 Will Blackwell RC 3.00 1.35
❑ 144 Warrick Dunn RC 10.00 4.50
❑ 145 Corey Dillon RC 12.00 5.50
❑ 146 Dwayne Rudd RC .75 .35
❑ 147 Reinard Wilson RC .75 .35
❑ 148 Peter Boulware RC 1.50 .70
❑ 149 Tony Gonzalez RC 10.00 4.50
❑ 150 Danny Wuerffel RC 3.00 1.35

1992 Playoff

	MINT	NRMT
COMPLETE SET (150)	40.00	18.00
COMMON CARD (1-150)	.25	.11
SEMISTARS	.40	.18
UNLISTED STARS	.75	.35

❑ 1 Emmitt Smith 8.00 3.60
❑ 2 Steve Young 3.00 1.35
❑ 3 Jack Del Rio .25 .11
❑ 4 Bobby Hebert .25 .11
❑ 5 Shannon Sharpe .75 .35
❑ 6 Gary Clark .75 .35
❑ 7 Christian Okoye .25 .11
❑ 8 Ernest Givins .40 .18
❑ 9 Mike Horan .25 .11
❑ 10 Dennis Gentry .25 .11
❑ 11 Michael Irvin .75 .35
❑ 12 Eric Floyd .25 .11
❑ 13 Brent Jones .40 .18
❑ 14 Anthony Carter .40 .18
❑ 15 Tony Martin .75 .35
❑ 16 Greg Lewis UER .25 .11
("Returning" should be "returned" on back)
❑ 17 Todd McNair .25 .11
❑ 18 Earnest Byner .25 .11
❑ 19 Steve Beuerlein .25 .11
❑ 20 Roger Craig .40 .18
❑ 21 Mark Higgs .25 .11
❑ 22 Guy McIntyre .25 .11
❑ 23 Don Warren .25 .11
❑ 24 Alvin Harper .40 .18
❑ 25 Mark Jackson .25 .11
❑ 26 Chris Doleman .25 .11
❑ 27 Jesse Sapolu .25 .11
❑ 28 Tony Tolbert .25 .11
❑ 29 Wendell Davis .25 .11
❑ 30 Dan Saleaumua .25 .11
❑ 31 Jeff Bostic .25 .11
❑ 32 Jay Novacek .40 .18
❑ 33 Cris Carter 1.00 .45
❑ 34 Tony Paige .25 .11
❑ 35 Greg Kragen .25 .11
❑ 36 Jeff Dellenbach .25 .11
❑ 37 Keith DeLong .25 .11
❑ 38 Todd Scott .25 .11
❑ 39 Jeff Feagles .25 .11
❑ 40 Mike Saxon .25 .11
❑ 41 Martin Mayhew .25 .11
❑ 42 Steve Bono RC .75 .35
❑ 43 Willie Davis RC 1.00 .45
❑ 44 Mark Stepnoski .40 .18
❑ 45 Harry Newsome .25 .11
❑ 46 Thane Gash .25 .11
❑ 47 Gaston Green .25 .11
❑ 48 James Washington .25 .11
❑ 49 Kenny Walker .25 .11
❑ 50 Jeff Davidson RC .25 .11
❑ 51 Shane Conlan .25 .11
❑ 52 Richard Dent .40 .18
❑ 53 Haywood Jeffires .40 .18
❑ 54 Harry Galbreath .25 .11
❑ 55 Terry Allen .75 .35
❑ 56 Tommy Barnhardt .25 .11
❑ 57 Mike Golic .25 .11
❑ 58 Dalton Hilliard .25 .11
❑ 59 Danny Copeland .25 .11
❑ 60 Jerry Fontenot RC .25 .11
❑ 61 Kelvin Martin .25 .11
❑ 62 Mark Kelso .25 .11
❑ 63 Wymon Henderson .25 .11
❑ 64 Mark Rypien .25 .11
❑ 65 Bobby Humphrey .25 .11
❑ 66 Rich Gannon UER .25 .11
(Tarkington misspelled; Minneapolis instead of Minnesota on back)
❑ 67 Darren Lewis .25 .11
❑ 68 Barry Foster .40 .18
❑ 69 Ken Norton Jr. .75 .35
❑ 70 James Lofton .40 .18
❑ 71 Trace Armstrong .25 .11
❑ 72 Vestee Jackson .25 .11
❑ 73 Clyde Simmons .25 .11
❑ 74 Brad Muster .25 .11
❑ 75 Cornelius Bennett .40 .18
❑ 76 Mike Merriweather .25 .11
❑ 77 John Elway 4.00 1.80
❑ 78 Herschel Walker .40 .18
❑ 79 Hassan Jones UER .25 .11
(Minneapolis instead of Minnesota on back)
❑ 80 Jim Harbaugh .75 .35
❑ 81 Issiac Holt .25 .11
❑ 82 David Alexander .25 .11
❑ 83 Brian Mitchell .40 .18
❑ 84 Mark Tuinei .25 .11
❑ 85 Tom Rathman .25 .11
❑ 86 Reggie White .75 .35
❑ 87 William Perry .40 .18
❑ 88 Jeff Wright .25 .11
❑ 89 Keith Kartz .25 .11
❑ 90 Andre Waters .25 .11
❑ 91 Darryl Talley .25 .11
❑ 92 Morten Andersen .25 .11
❑ 93 Tom Waddle .25 .11
❑ 94 Felix Wright UER .25 .11
(Minneapolis instead of Minnesota on back)
❑ 95 Keith Jackson .40 .18
❑ 96 Art Monk .40 .18
❑ 97 Seth Joyner .40 .18
❑ 98 Steve McMichael .40 .18
❑ 99 Thurman Thomas .75 .35
❑ 100 Warren Moon .75 .35
❑ 101 Tony Casillas .25 .11
❑ 102 Vance Johnson .25 .11
❑ 103 Doug Dawson RC .25 .11
❑ 104 Bill Maas .25 .11
❑ 105 Mark Clayton .40 .18
❑ 106 Hoby Brenner .25 .11
❑ 107 Gary Anderson K .25 .11
❑ 108 Marc Logan .25 .11
❑ 109 Ricky Sanders .25 .11
❑ 110 Vai Sikahema .25 .11
❑ 111 Neil Smith .75 .35
❑ 112 Cody Carlson .25 .11
❑ 113 Jimmie Jones .25 .11
❑ 114 Pat Swilling .40 .18
❑ 115 Neil O'Donnell .75 .35
❑ 116 Chip Lohmiller .25 .11
❑ 117 Mike Croel .25 .11
❑ 118 Pete Metzelaars .25 .11
❑ 119 Ray Childress .25 .11
❑ 120 Fred Banks .25 .11
❑ 121 Derek Kennard .25 .11
❑ 122 Daryl Johnston .75 .35
❑ 123 Lorenzo White UER .25 .11
(Minneapolis instead of Minnesota on back)
❑ 124 Hardy Nickerson .40 .18
❑ 125 Derrick Thomas .75 .35
❑ 126 Steve Walsh .25 .11
❑ 127 Doug Widell .25 .11
❑ 128 Calvin Williams .40 .18
❑ 129 Tim Harris .25 .11
❑ 130 Rod Woodson .75 .35
❑ 131 Craig Heyward .40 .18
❑ 132 Barry Word .25 .11
❑ 133 Mark Duper .25 .11
❑ 134 Tim Johnson .25 .11
❑ 135 John Gesek .25 .11
❑ 136 Steve Jackson .25 .11
❑ 137 Dave Krieg .40 .18
❑ 138 Barry Sanders UER 5.00 2.20
(Won Heisman in 1988, not 1986)
❑ 139 Michael Haynes .40 .18
❑ 140 Eric Metcalf .40 .18
❑ 141 Stan Humphries .75 .35
❑ 142 Sterling Sharpe .75 .35
❑ 143 Todd Marinovich .25 .11
❑ 144 Rodney Hampton .75 .35
❑ 145 Rodney Peete .40 .18
❑ 146 Darryl Williams RC .25 .11
❑ 147 Darren Perry RC .25 .11
❑ 148 Terrell Buckley RC .25 .11
❑ 149 Amp Lee RC .25 .11
❑ 150 Ricky Watters .75 .35

1993 Playoff

	MINT	NRMT
COMPLETE SET (315)	25.00	11.00
COMMON CARD (1-315)	.10	.05
SEMISTARS	.20	.09
UNLISTED STARS	.40	.18
COMPLETE CL SET (8)	6.00	2.70

CHECKLISTS: RANDOM INSERTS IN PACKS

COMP.BRETT FAVRE SET (5)	80.00	36.00

FAVRE: RANDOM INS.IN HOBBY PACKS

COMP.R.WATTERS SET (5)	20.00	9.00

WATTERS: RANDOM INS.IN RETAIL PACKS

❑ 1 Troy Aikman 1.50 .70
❑ 2 Jerry Rice 2.00 .90
❑ 3 Keith Jackson .20 .09
❑ 4 Sean Gilbert .20 .09
❑ 5 Jim Kelly .40 .18
❑ 6 Junior Seau .40 .18
❑ 7 Deion Sanders 1.00 .45
❑ 8 Joe Montana 3.00 1.35
❑ 9 Terrell Buckley .10 .05
❑ 10 Emmitt Smith 3.00 1.35
❑ 11 Pete Stoyanovich .10 .05
❑ 12 Randall Cunningham .40 .18
❑ 13 Boomer Esiason .20 .09
❑ 14 Mike Saxon .10 .05
❑ 15 Chuck Cecil .10 .05
❑ 16 Vinny Testaverde .20 .09

❑ 17 Jeff Hostetler .20 .09
❑ 18 Mark Clayton .10 .05
❑ 19 Nick Bell .10 .05
❑ 20 Frank Reich .20 .09
❑ 21 Henry Ellard .20 .09
❑ 22 Andre Reed .20 .09
❑ 23 Mark Ingram .10 .05
❑ 24 Mike Brim .10 .05
❑ 25A Bernie Kosar UER .20 .09
(Name spelled Kozar on both sides)
❑ 25B Bernie Kosar COR .20 .09
❑ 26 Jeff George .40 .18
❑ 27 Tommy Maddox .10 .05
❑ 28 Kent Graham RC .40 .18
❑ 29 David Klingler .10 .05
❑ 30 Robert Delpino .10 .05
❑ 31 Kevin Fagan .10 .05
❑ 32 Mark Bavaro .10 .05
❑ 33 Harold Green .10 .05
❑ 34 Shawn McCarthy .10 .05
❑ 35 Ricky Proehl .10 .05
❑ 36 Eugene Robinson .10 .05
❑ 37 Phil Simms .20 .09
❑ 38 David Lang .10 .05
❑ 39 Santana Dotson .20 .09
❑ 40 Brett Perriman .40 .18
❑ 41 Jim Harbaugh .40 .18
❑ 42 Keith Byars .10 .05
❑ 43 Quentin Coryatt .20 .09
❑ 44 Louis Oliver .10 .05
❑ 45 Howie Long .20 .09
❑ 46 Mike Sherrard .10 .05
❑ 47 Earnest Byner .10 .05
❑ 48 Neil Smith .40 .18
❑ 49 Audray McMillian .10 .05
❑ 50 Vaughn Dunbar .10 .05
❑ 51 Ronnie Lott .20 .09
❑ 52 Clyde Simmons .10 .05
❑ 53 Kevin Scott .10 .05
❑ 54 Bubby Brister .10 .05
❑ 55 Randal Hill .10 .05
❑ 56 Pat Swilling .10 .05
❑ 57 Steve Beuerlein .10 .05
❑ 58 Gary Clark .20 .09
❑ 59 Brian Noble .10 .05
❑ 60 Leslie O'Neal .20 .09
❑ 61 Vincent Brown .10 .05
❑ 62 Edgar Bennett .40 .18
❑ 63 Anthony Carter .20 .09
❑ 64 Glenn Cadrez RC UER .10 .05
(Name misspelled Cadez on front)
❑ 65 Dalton Hilliard .10 .05
❑ 66 James Lofton .20 .09
❑ 67 Walter Stanley .10 .05
❑ 68 Tim Harris .10 .05
❑ 69 Carl Banks .10 .05
❑ 70 Andre Ware .10 .05
❑ 71 Karl Mecklenburg .10 .05
❑ 72 Russell Maryland .10 .05
❑ 73 Leroy Thompson .10 .05
❑ 74 Tommy Kane .10 .05
❑ 75 Dan Marino 3.00 1.35
❑ 76 Darrell Fullington .10 .05
❑ 77 Jessie Tuggle .10 .05
❑ 78 Bruce Smith .40 .18
❑ 79 Neal Anderson .10 .05
❑ 80 Kevin Mack .10 .05
❑ 81 Shane Dronett .10 .05
❑ 82 Nick Lowery .10 .05
❑ 83 Sheldon White .10 .05
❑ 84 Flipper Anderson .10 .05
❑ 85 Jeff Herrod .10 .05
❑ 86 Dwight Stone .10 .05
❑ 87 Dave Krieg .20 .09
❑ 88 Bryan Cox .10 .05
❑ 89 Greg McMurtry .10 .05
❑ 90 Rickey Jackson .10 .05
❑ 91 Ernie Mills .10 .05
❑ 92 Browning Nagle .10 .05
❑ 93 John Taylor .20 .09
❑ 94 Eric Dickerson .20 .09
❑ 95 Johnny Holland .10 .05
❑ 96 Anthony Miller .20 .09
❑ 97 Fred Barnett .20 .09
❑ 98 Ricky Ervins UER .10 .05
(Name misspelled Rickey on back)
❑ 99 Leonard Russell .20 .09
❑ 100 Lawrence Taylor .40 .18
❑ 101 Tony Casillas .10 .05
❑ 102 John Elway 3.00 1.35
❑ 103 Bennie Blades .10 .05
❑ 104 Harry Sydney .10 .05
❑ 105 Bubba McDowell .10 .05
❑ 106 Todd McNair .10 .05
❑ 107 Steve Smith .10 .05
❑ 108 Jim Everett .20 .09
❑ 109 Bobby Humphrey .10 .05
❑ 110 Rich Gannon .10 .05
❑ 111 Marv Cook .10 .05
❑ 112 Wayne Martin .10 .05
❑ 113 Sean Landeta .10 .05
❑ 114 Brad Baxter UER .10 .05
(Reversed negative on front)
❑ 115 Reggie White .40 .18
❑ 116 Johnny Johnson .10 .05
❑ 117 Jeff Graham .20 .09
❑ 118 Darren Carrington RC .10 .05
❑ 119 Ricky Watters .40 .18
❑ 120 Art Monk UER .20 .09
(Reversed negative on back)
❑ 121 Cornelius Bennett .20 .09
❑ 122 Wade Wilson .10 .05
❑ 123 Daniel Stubbs .10 .05
❑ 124 Brad Muster .10 .05
❑ 125 Mike Tomczak .10 .05
❑ 126 Jay Novacek .20 .09
❑ 127 Shannon Sharpe .40 .18
❑ 128 Rodney Peete .10 .05
❑ 129 Daryl Johnston .40 .18
❑ 130 Warren Moon .40 .18
❑ 131 Willie Gault .10 .05
❑ 132 Tony Martin .40 .18
❑ 133 Terry Allen .40 .18
❑ 134 Hugh Millen .10 .05
❑ 135 Rob Moore .20 .09
❑ 136 Andy Harmon RC .20 .09
❑ 137 Kelvin Martin .10 .05
❑ 138 Rod Woodson .40 .18
❑ 139 Nate Lewis .10 .05
❑ 140 Darryl Talley .10 .05
❑ 141 Guy McIntyre .10 .05
❑ 142 John L. Williams .10 .05
❑ 143 Brad Edwards .10 .05
❑ 144 Trace Armstrong .10 .05
❑ 145 Kenneth Davis .10 .05
❑ 146 Clay Matthews .20 .09
❑ 147 Gaston Green .10 .05
❑ 148 Chris Spielman .20 .09
❑ 149 Cody Carlson .10 .05
❑ 150 Derrick Thomas .40 .18
❑ 151 Terry McDaniel .10 .05
❑ 152 Kevin Greene .40 .18
❑ 153 Roger Craig .20 .09
❑ 154 Craig Heyward .20 .09
❑ 155 Rodney Hampton .40 .18
❑ 156 Heath Sherman .10 .05
❑ 157 Mark Stepnoski .10 .05
❑ 158 Chris Chandler .20 .09
❑ 159 Rod Bernstine .10 .05
❑ 160 Pierce Holt .10 .05
❑ 161 Wilber Marshall .10 .05
❑ 162 Reggie Cobb .10 .05
❑ 163 Tom Rathman .10 .05
❑ 164 Michael Haynes .20 .09
❑ 165 Nate Odomes .10 .05
❑ 166 Tom Waddle .10 .05
❑ 167 Eric Ball .10 .05
❑ 168 Brett Favre UER 4.00 1.80
(Photo of Don Majkowski on back)
❑ 169 Michael Jackson .20 .09
❑ 170 Lorenzo White .10 .05
❑ 171 Cleveland Gary .10 .05
❑ 172 Jay Schroeder .10 .05
❑ 173 Tony Paige .10 .05
❑ 174 Jack Del Rio .10 .05
❑ 175 Jon Vaughn .10 .05
❑ 176 Morten Andersen UER .10 .05
(Misspelled Morton)
❑ 177 Chris Burkett .10 .05
❑ 178 Vai Sikahema .10 .05
❑ 179 Ronnie Harmon .10 .05
❑ 180 Amp Lee .10 .05
❑ 181 Chip Lohmiller .10 .05
❑ 182 Steve Broussard .10 .05
❑ 183 Don Beebe .10 .05
❑ 184 Tommy Vardell .10 .05
❑ 185 Keith Jennings .10 .05
❑ 186 Simon Fletcher .10 .05
❑ 187 Mel Gray .20 .09
❑ 188 Vince Workman .10 .05
❑ 189 Haywood Jeffires .20 .09
❑ 190 Barry Word .10 .05
❑ 191 Ethan Horton .10 .05
❑ 192 Mark Higgs .10 .05
❑ 193 Irving Fryar .20 .09
❑ 194 Charles Haley .20 .09
❑ 195 Steve Bono .40 .18
❑ 196 Mike Golic .10 .05
❑ 197 Gary Anderson K .10 .05
❑ 198 Sterling Sharpe .40 .18
❑ 199 Andre Tippett .10 .05
❑ 200 Thurman Thomas .40 .18
❑ 201 Chris Miller .20 .09
❑ 202 Henry Jones .10 .05
❑ 203 Mo Lewis .10 .05
❑ 204 Marion Butts .10 .05
❑ 205 Mike Johnson .10 .05
❑ 206 Alvin Harper .20 .09
❑ 207 Ray Childress .10 .05
❑ 208 Anthony Johnson .20 .09
❑ 209 Tony Bennett .10 .05
❑ 210 Anthony Newman RC .10 .05
❑ 211 Christian Okoye .10 .05
❑ 212 Marcus Allen .40 .18
❑ 213 Jackie Harris .10 .05
❑ 214 Mark Duper .10 .05
❑ 215 Cris Carter 1.00 .45
❑ 216 John Stephens .10 .05
❑ 217 Barry Sanders 3.00 1.35
❑ 218A Herman Moore ERR 1.25 .55
(First name misspelled Sherman)
❑ 218B Herman Moore COR 2.50 1.10
name spelled correctly
❑ 219 Marvin Washington .10 .05
❑ 220 Calvin Williams .20 .09
❑ 221 John Randle .10 .05
❑ 222 Marco Coleman .10 .05
❑ 223 Eric Martin .10 .05
❑ 224 Dave Meggett .10 .05
❑ 225 Brian Washington .10 .05
❑ 226 Barry Foster .20 .09
❑ 227 Michael Zordich .10 .05
❑ 228 Stan Humphries .40 .18
❑ 229 Mike Cofer .10 .05
❑ 230 Chris Warren .20 .09
❑ 231 Keith McCants .10 .05
❑ 232 Mark Rypien .10 .05
❑ 233 James Francis .10 .05
❑ 234 Andre Rison .20 .09
❑ 235 William Perry .20 .09
❑ 236 Chip Banks .10 .05
❑ 237 Willie Davis .40 .18
❑ 238 Chris Doleman .10 .05
❑ 239 Tim Brown .40 .18
❑ 240 Darren Perry .10 .05
❑ 241 Johnny Bailey .10 .05
❑ 242 Ernest Givins UER .20 .09
(Spelled Givens on back)
❑ 243 John Carney .10 .05
❑ 244 Cortez Kennedy .20 .09
❑ 245 Lawrence Dawsey .10 .05
❑ 246 Martin Mayhew .10 .05
❑ 247 Shane Conlan .10 .05
❑ 248 J.J. Birden .10 .05
❑ 249 Quinn Early .20 .09
❑ 250 Michael Irvin .40 .18
❑ 251 Neil O'Donnell .40 .18
❑ 252 Stan Gelbaugh .10 .05
❑ 253 Drew Hill .10 .05
❑ 254 Wendell Davis .10 .05
❑ 255 Tim Johnson .10 .05
❑ 256 Seth Joyner .10 .05
❑ 257 Derrick Fenner .10 .05
❑ 258 Steve Young 1.50 .70
❑ 259 Jackie Slater .10 .05
❑ 260 Eric Metcalf .20 .09

	MINT	NRMT
❑ 261 Rufus Porter	.10	.05
❑ 262 Ken Norton Jr.	.20	.09
❑ 263 Tim McDonald	.10	.05
❑ 264 Mark Jackson	.10	.05
❑ 265 Hardy Nickerson	.20	.09
❑ 266 Anthony Munoz	.20	.09
❑ 267 Mark Carrier WR	.20	.09
❑ 268 Mike Pritchard	.20	.09
❑ 269 Steve Emtman	.10	.05
❑ 270 Ricky Sanders	.10	.05
❑ 271 Robert Massey	.10	.05
❑ 272 Pete Metzelaars	.10	.05
❑ 273 Reggie Langhorne	.10	.05
❑ 274 Tim McGee	.10	.05
❑ 275 Reggie Rivers RC	.10	.05
❑ 276 Jimmie Jones	.10	.05
❑ 277 Lorenzo White TB	.10	.05
❑ 278 Emmitt Smith TB	2.00	.90
❑ 279 Thurman Thomas TB	.40	.18
❑ 280 Barry Sanders TB UER Ten TD's in '92; should be nine)	2.00	.90
❑ 281 Rodney Hampton TB	.20	.09
❑ 282 Barry Foster TB	.20	.09
❑ 283 Troy Aikman PC	1.00	.45
❑ 284 Michael Irvin PC	.20	.09
❑ 285 Brett Favre PC	2.50	1.10
❑ 286 Sterling Sharpe PC	.20	.09
❑ 287 Steve Young PC	1.00	.45
❑ 288 Jerry Rice PC	1.25	.55
❑ 289 Stan Humphries PC	.20	.09
❑ 290 Anthony Miller PC	.20	.09
❑ 291 Dan Marino PC	2.00	.90
❑ 292 Keith Jackson PC	.10	.05
❑ 293 Patrick Bates PC	.10	.05
❑ 294 Jerome Bettis RC	3.00	1.35
❑ 295 Drew Bledsoe RC	8.00	3.60
❑ 296 Tom Carter RC	.20	.09
❑ 297 Curtis Conway RC	2.00	.90
❑ 298 John Copeland RC	.20	.09
❑ 299 Eric Curry RC	.10	.05
❑ 300 Reggie Brooks RC	.20	.09
❑ 301 Steve Everitt RC	.10	.05
❑ 302 Deon Figures RC	.20	.09
❑ 303 Garrison Hearst RC	3.00	1.35
❑ 304 Qadry Ismail RC UER (Misspelled Quadry on both sides)	.40	.18
❑ 305 Marvin Jones RC	.10	.05
❑ 306 Lincoln Kennedy RC	.10	.05
❑ 307 O.J. McDuffie RC	2.50	1.10
❑ 308 Rick Mirer RC	.75	.35
❑ 309 Wayne Simmons RC	.10	.05
❑ 310 Irv Smith RC	.10	.05
❑ 311 Robert Smith RC	3.00	1.35
❑ 312 Dana Stubblefield RC	.40	.18
❑ 313 George Teague RC	.20	.09
❑ 314 Dan Williams RC	.10	.05
❑ 315 Kevin Williams RC	.40	.18
❑ NNO Santa Claus	2.00	.90

1993 Playoff Club

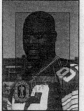

	MINT	NRMT
COMPLETE SET (7)	15.00	6.75
RANDOM INSERTS IN PACKS		
❑ PC1 Joe Montana	12.00	5.50
❑ PC2 Art Monk	.75	.35
❑ PC3 Lawrence Taylor	1.50	.70
❑ PC4 Ronnie Lott	.75	.35
❑ PC5 Reggie White	1.50	.70
❑ PC6 Anthony Munoz	.75	.35
❑ PC7 Jackie Slater	.40	.18

1993 Playoff Headliners Redemption

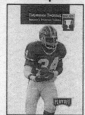

	MINT	NRMT
COMPLETE SET (6)	15.00	6.75
ONE SET PER REDEMPTION CARD BY MAIL		
❑ H1 Brett Favre	6.00	2.70
❑ H2 Sterling Sharpe	.60	.25
❑ H3 Emmitt Smith	5.00	2.20
❑ H4 Jerry Rice	3.00	1.35
❑ H5 Thurman Thomas	.60	.25
❑ H6 David Klingler	.15	.07
❑ NNO Headliner Redemption	1.25	.55

1993 Playoff Rookie Roundup Redemption

	MINT	NRMT
COMPLETE SET (10)	30.00	13.50
ONE SET PER REDEMPTION CARD BY MAIL		
❑ R1 Jerome Bettis	6.00	2.70
❑ R2 Drew Bledsoe	15.00	6.75
❑ R3 Reggie Brooks	.40	.18
❑ R4 Derek Brown RBK	.20	.09
❑ R5 Garrison Hearst	6.00	2.70
❑ R6 Terry Kirby	.20	.09
❑ R7 Glyn Milburn	.20	.09
❑ R8 Rick Mirer	1.50	.70
❑ R9 Roosevelt Potts	.20	.09
❑ R10 Dana Stubblefield	.75	.35
❑ NNO Rookie Roundup Redemption Card	.50	.23

1994 Playoff

	MINT	NRMT
COMPLETE SET (336)	30.00	13.50
COMMON CARD (1-336)	.15	.07
EXPANSION TEAMS (261-262)	.40	.18
SEMISTARS	.30	.14
UNLISTED STARS	.50	.23
SAYERS STATED ODDS 1:102		
SAYERS AUTO.STATED ODDS 1:12,096		

COMP.CHECKLIST SET (10)	5.00	2.20
RANDOM INSERTS IN PACKS		
COMP. J.BETTIS SET (5)	60.00	27.00
BETTIS STATED ODDS 1:102 HOBBY		
COMP. J.RICE SET (5)	60.00	27.00
RICE STATED ODDS 1:102 RETAIL		
COMP.B.SANDERS SET (5)	100.00	45.00
SANDERS ODDS 1:102 FOUR STAR		
❑ 1 Joe Montana	4.00	1.80
❑ 2 Derrick Thomas	.50	.23
❑ 3 Dan Marino	4.00	1.80
❑ 4 Cris Carter	.75	.35
❑ 5 Boomer Esiason	.30	.14
❑ 6 Bruce Smith	.50	.23
❑ 7 Andre Rison	.30	.14
❑ 8 Curtis Conway	.50	.23
❑ 9 Michael Irvin	.50	.23
❑ 10 Shannon Sharpe	.30	.14
❑ 11 Pat Swilling	.15	.07
❑ 12 John Parrella	.15	.07
❑ 13 Mel Gray	.15	.07
❑ 14 Ray Childress	.15	.07
❑ 15 Willie Davis	.30	.14
❑ 16 Rocket Ismail	.30	.14
❑ 17 Jim Everett	.30	.14
❑ 18 Mark Higgs	.15	.07
❑ 19 Trace Armstrong	.15	.07
❑ 20 Jim Kelly	.50	.23
❑ 21 Rob Burnett	.15	.07
❑ 22 Jay Novacek	.30	.14
❑ 23 Robert Delpino	.15	.07
❑ 24 Brett Perriman	.30	.14
❑ 25 Troy Aikman	2.00	.90
❑ 26 Reggie White	.50	.23
❑ 27 Lorenzo White	.15	.07
❑ 28 Bubba McDowell	.15	.07
❑ 29 Steve Emtman	.15	.07
❑ 30 Brett Favre	4.00	1.80
❑ 31 Derek Russell	.15	.07
❑ 32 Jeff Hostetler	.30	.14
❑ 33 Henry Ellard	.30	.14
❑ 34 Jack Del Rio	.15	.07
❑ 35 Mike Saxon	.15	.07
❑ 36 Rickey Jackson	.15	.07
❑ 37 Phil Simms	.30	.14
❑ 38 Quinn Early	.30	.14
❑ 39 Russell Copeland	.15	.07
❑ 40 Carl Pickens	.50	.23
❑ 41 Lance Gunn	.15	.07
❑ 42 Bernie Kosar	.30	.14
❑ 43 John Elway	4.00	1.80
❑ 44 George Teague	.15	.07
❑ 45 Nick Lowery	.15	.07
❑ 46 Haywood Jeffires	.30	.14
❑ 47 Will Shields	.15	.07
❑ 48 Daryl Johnston	.30	.14
❑ 49 Pete Metzelaars	.15	.07
❑ 50 Warren Moon	.50	.23
❑ 51 Cornelius Bennett	.30	.14
❑ 52 Vinny Testaverde	.30	.14
❑ 53 John Mangum RC	.15	.07
❑ 54 Tommy Vardell	.15	.07
❑ 55 Lincoln Coleman RC	.15	.07
❑ 56 Karl Mecklenburg	.15	.07
❑ 57 Jackie Harris	.15	.07
❑ 58 Curtis Duncan	.15	.07
❑ 59 Quentin Coryatt	.15	.07
❑ 60 Tim Brown	.50	.23

61	Irving Fryar	.30	.14
62	Sean Gilbert	.15	.07
63	Qadry Ismail	.50	.23
64	Irv Smith	.15	.07
65	Mark Jackson	.15	.07
66	Ronnie Lott	.30	.14
67	Henry Jones	.15	.07
68	Horace Copeland	.15	.07
69	John Copeland	.15	.07
70	Mark Carrier WR	.30	.14
71	Michael Jackson	.30	.14
72	Jason Elam	.15	.07
73	Rod Bernstine	.15	.07
74	Wayne Simmons	.15	.07
75	Cody Carlson	.15	.07
76	Alexander Wright	.15	.07
77	Shane Conlan	.15	.07
78	Keith Jackson	.15	.07
79	Sean Salisbury	.15	.07
80	Vaughan Johnson	.15	.07
81	Rob Moore	.30	.14
82	Andre Reed	.30	.14
83	David Klinger	.15	.07
84	Jim Harbaugh	.50	.23
85	John Jett RC	.15	.07
86	Sterling Sharpe	.30	.14
87	Webster Slaughter	.15	.07
88	J.J. Birden	.15	.07
89	O.J. McDuffie	.50	.23
90	Andre Tippett	.15	.07
91	Don Beebe	.15	.07
92	Mark Stepnoski	.15	.07
93	Neil Smith	.50	.23
94	Terry Kirby	.50	.23
95	Wade Wilson	.15	.07
96	Darryl Talley	.15	.07
97	Anthony Smith	.15	.07
98	Willie Roaf	.15	.07
99	Mo Lewis	.15	.07
100	James Washington	.15	.07
101	Nate Odomes	.15	.07
102	Chris Gedney	.15	.07
103	Joe Walter	.15	.07
104	Alvin Harper	.30	.14
105	Simon Fletcher	.15	.07
106	Rodney Peete	.15	.07
107	Terrell Buckley	.15	.07
108	Jeff George	.50	.23
109	James Jett	.15	.07
110	Tony Casillas	.15	.07
111	Marco Coleman	.15	.07
112	Anthony Carter	.30	.14
113	Lincoln Kennedy	.15	.07
114	Chris Calloway	.15	.07
115	Randall Cunningham	.50	.23
116	Steve Beuerlein	.15	.07
117	Neil O'Donnell	.50	.23
118	Stan Humphries	.50	.23
119	John Taylor	.30	.14
120	Cortez Kennedy	.30	.14
121	Santana Dotson	.30	.14
122	Thomas Smith	.15	.07
123	Kevin Williams	.30	.14
124	Andre Ware	.15	.07
125	Ethan Horton	.15	.07
126	Mike Sherrard	.15	.07
127	Fred Barnett	.30	.14
128	Ricky Proehl	.15	.07
129	Kevin Greene	.50	.23
130	John Carney	.15	.07
131	Tim McDonald	.15	.07
132	Rick Mirer	.50	.23
133	Blair Thomas	.15	.07
134	Hardy Nickerson	.30	.14
135	Heath Sherman	.15	.07
136	Andre Hastings	.30	.14
137	Randal Hill	.15	.07
138	Mike Cofer	.15	.07
139	Brian Blades	.30	.14
140	Earnest Byner	.15	.07
141	Bill Bates	.30	.14
142	Junior Seau	.50	.23
143	Johnny Bailey	.15	.07
144	Dwight Stone	.15	.07
145	Todd Kelly	.15	.07
146	Tyrone Montgomery	.15	.07
147	Herschel Walker	.30	.14
148	Gary Clark	.30	.14
149	Eric Green	.15	.07
150	Steve Young	1.50	.70
151	Anthony Miller	.30	.14
152	Dana Stubblefield	.50	.23
153	Dean Wells RC	.15	.07
154	Vincent Brisby	.50	.23
155	Chris Chandler	.30	.14
156	Clyde Simmons	.15	.07
157	Rod Woodson	.50	.23
158	Nate Lewis	.15	.07
159	Martin Harrison	.15	.07
160	Kelvin Martin	.15	.07
161	Craig Erickson	.15	.07
162	Johnny Mitchell	.15	.07
163	Calvin Williams	.30	.14
164	Deon Figures	.15	.07
165	Tom Rathman	.15	.07
166	Rick Hamilton	.15	.07
167	John L. Williams	.15	.07
168	Demetrius DuBose	.15	.07
169	Michael Brooks	.15	.07
170	Marion Butts	.15	.07
171	Brent Jones	.30	.14
172	Bobby Hebert	.15	.07
173	Brad Edwards	.15	.07
174	David Wyman	.15	.07
175	Herman Moore	.50	.23
176	LeRoy Butler	.15	.07
177	Reggie Langhorne	.15	.07
178	Dave Krieg	.30	.14
179	Patrick Bates	.15	.07
180	Erik Kramer	.30	.14
181	Troy Drayton	.15	.07
182	Dave Meggett	.15	.07
183	Eric Allen	.15	.07
184	Mark Bavaro	.15	.07
185	Leslie O'Neal	.15	.07
186	Jerry Rice	2.00	.90
187	Desmond Howard	.30	.14
188	Deion Sanders	.75	.35
189	Bill Maas	.15	.07
190	Frank Wycheck RC	1.00	.45
191	Ernest Givins	.30	.14
192	Terry McDaniel	.15	.07
193	Bryan Cox	.15	.07
194	Guy McIntyre	.15	.07
195	Pierce Holt	.15	.07
196	Fred Stokes	.15	.07
197	Mike Pritchard	.15	.07
198	Terry Obee	.15	.07
199	Mark Collins	.15	.07
200	Drew Bledsoe	2.00	.90
201	Barry Word	.15	.07
202	Derrick Lassic	.15	.07
203	Chris Spielman	.30	.14
204	John Jurkovic RC	.30	.14
205	Ken Norton Jr.	.30	.14
206	Dale Carter	.15	.07
207	Chris Doleman	.15	.07
208	Keith Hamilton	.15	.07
209	Andy Harmon	.15	.07
210	John Friesz	.30	.14
211	Steve Bono	.30	.14
212	Mark Rypien	.15	.07
213	Ricky Sanders	.15	.07
214	Michael Haynes	.30	.14
215	Todd McNair	.15	.07
216	Leon Lett	.15	.07
217	Scott Mitchell	.50	.23
218	Mike Morris RC	.15	.07
219	Darrin Smith	.15	.07
220	Jim McMahon	.15	.07
221	Garrison Hearst	.50	.23
222	Leroy Thompson	.15	.07
223	Darren Carrington	.15	.07
224	Pete Stoyanovich	.15	.07
225	Chris Miller	.15	.07
226	Bruce Smith SP	.30	.14
227	Simon Fletcher SP	.15	.07
228	Reggie White SP	.50	.23
229	Neil Smith SP	.50	.23
230	Chris Doleman SP	.15	.07
231	Keith Hamilton SP	.15	.07
232	Dana Stubblefield SP	.15	.07
233	Erric Pegram GA	.15	.07
234	Thurman Thomas GA	.50	.23
235	Lewis Tillman GA	.15	.07
236	Harold Green GA	.15	.07
237	Eric Metcalf GA	.30	.14
238	Emmitt Smith GA	3.00	1.35
239	Glyn Milburn GA	.30	.14
240	Barry Sanders GA	4.00	1.80
241	Edgar Bennett GA	.30	.14
242	Gary Brown GA	.15	.07
243	Roosevelt Potts GA	.15	.07
244	Marcus Allen GA	.50	.23
245	Greg Robinson GA	.15	.07
246	Jerome Bettis GA	.50	.23
247	Keith Byars GA	.15	.07
248	Robert Smith GA	.50	.23
249	Leonard Russell GA	.15	.07
250	Derek Brown RBK GA	.15	.07
251	Rodney Hampton GA	.30	.14
252	Johnny Johnson GA	.15	.07
253	Vaughn Hebron GA	.15	.07
254	Ronald Moore GA	.15	.07
255	Barry Foster GA	.15	.07
256	Natrone Means GA	.50	.23
257	Ricky Watters GA	.50	.23
258	Chris Warren GA	.50	.23
259	Vince Workman GA	.15	.07
260	Reggie Brooks GA	.15	.07
261	Carolina Panthers Logo	.40	.18
262	Jacksonville Jaguars Logo	.40	.18
263	Troy Aikman SB	1.00	.45
264	Barry Sanders SB	2.00	.90
265	Emmitt Smith SB	1.50	.70
266	Michael Irvin SB	.50	.23
267	Jerry Rice SB	1.00	.45
268	Shannon Sharpe SB	.30	.14
269	Bob Kratch SB	.15	.07
270	Howard Ballard SB	.15	.07
271	Erik Williams SB	.15	.07
272	Guy McIntyre SB	.15	.07
273	Kelvin Williams SB	.30	.14
274	Mel Gray SB	.15	.07
275	Eddie Murray SB	.15	.07
276	Mark Stepnoski SB	.15	.07
277	Tommy Barnhardt SB	.15	.07
278	Derrick Thomas SB	.30	.14
279	Ken Norton Jr. SB	.30	.14
280	Chris Spielman SB	.15	.07
281	Deion Sanders SB	.50	.23
282	Mark Collins SB	.15	.07
283	Bruce Smith SB	.30	.14
284	Reggie White SB	.50	.23
285	Sean Gilbert SB	.15	.07
286	Cortez Kennedy SB	.30	.14
287	Steve Atwater SB	.15	.07
288	Tim McDonald SB	.15	.07
289	Jerome Bettis SB	.30	.14
290	Dana Stubblefield SB	.30	.14
291	Bert Emanuel RC	1.50	.70
292	Jeff Burris RC	.30	.14
293	Bucky Brooks RC	.15	.07
294	Dan Wilkinson RC	.30	.14
295	Darnay Scott RC	1.50	.70
296	Derrick Alexander WR RC	1.25	.55
297	Antonio Langham RC	.30	.14
298	Shante Carver RC	.15	.07
299	Shelby Hill RC	.15	.07
300	Larry Allen RC	.30	.14
301	Johnnie Morton RC	1.50	.70
302	Van Malone RC	.15	.07
303	Aaron Taylor RC	.15	.07
304	Marshall Faulk RC	5.00	2.20
305	Eric Mahlum RC	.15	.07
306	Trev Alberts RC	.30	.14
307	Greg Hill RC	1.25	.55
308	Donnell Bennett RC	.50	.23
309	Rob Fredrickson RC	.30	.14
310	James Folston RC	.15	.07
311	Isaac Bruce RC	5.00	2.20
312	Tim Ruddy RC	.15	.07
313	Aubrey Beavers RC	.15	.07
314	David Palmer RC	1.25	.55
315	Dewayne Washington RC	.30	.14
316	Willie McGinest RC	.50	.23
317	Mario Bates RC	.50	.23
318	Kevin Lee RC	.15	.07

❑ 319 Jason Sehorn RC	.15	.07
❑ 320 Thomas Randolph RC	.15	.07
❑ 321 Ryan Yarborough RC	.15	.07
❑ 322 Bernard Williams RC	.15	.07
❑ 323 Chuck Levy RC	.15	.07
❑ 324 Jamir Miller RC	.15	.07
❑ 325 Charles Johnson RC	.50	.23
❑ 326 Bryant Young RC	.50	.23
❑ 327 William Floyd RC	.50	.23
❑ 328 Kevin Mitchell RC	.15	.07
❑ 329 Sam Adams RC	.30	.14
❑ 330 Kevin Mawae RC	.15	.07
❑ 331 Errict Rhett RC	2.00	.90
❑ 332 Trent Dilfer RC	2.00	.90
❑ 333 Heath Shuler RC	.50	.23
❑ 334 Aaron Glenn RC	.30	.14
❑ 335 Todd Steussie RC	.30	.14
❑ 336 Toby Wright RC	.15	.07
❑ NNO Gale Sayers Player's Club	8.00	3.60
❑ NNO Gale Sayers AUTO signed Player's Club	80.00	36.00

1994 Playoff Club

	MINT	NRMT
COMPLETE SET (6)	20.00	9.00
STATED ODDS 1:20		

❑ PC8 Jerry Rice	12.00	5.50
❑ PC9 Marcus Allen	3.00	1.35
❑ PC10 Howie Long	3.00	1.35
❑ PC11 Clay Matthews	1.00	.45
❑ PC12 Richard Dent	2.00	.90
❑ PC13 Morten Andersen	1.00	.45

1994 Playoff Headliners Redemption

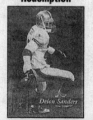

	MINT	NRMT
COMPLETE SET (6)	6.00	2.70
TRADE CARD STATED ODDS 1:102		
ONE SET PER TRADE CARD BY MAIL		

❑ 1 Tim Brown	1.50	.70
❑ 2 Bernie Parmalee	.50	.23
❑ 3 Sterling Sharpe	1.00	.45
❑ 4 Natrone Means	1.50	.70
❑ 5 Alvin Harper	1.00	.45
❑ 6 Deion Sanders	2.50	1.10
❑ NNO Headliners Redemption	.50	.23

1994 Playoff Rookie Roundup Redemption

	MINT	NRMT
COMPLETE SET (9)	30.00	13.50
COMMON CARD (1-9)	2.00	.90
SEMISTARS	3.00	1.35
TRADE CARD STATED ODDS 1:102		
ONE SET PER TRADE CARD BY MAIL		

❑ 1 Heath Shuler	3.00	1.35
❑ 2 David Palmer	3.00	1.35
❑ 3 Dan Wilkinson	2.00	.90
❑ 4 Marshall Faulk	12.00	5.50
❑ 5 Charlie Garner	5.00	2.20
❑ 6 Errict Rhett	5.00	2.20
❑ 7 Trent Dilfer	5.00	2.20
❑ 8 Antonio Langham	2.00	.90
❑ 9 Gus Frerotte	3.00	1.35
❑ NNO Redemption Card	.50	.23

1994 Playoff Super Bowl Redemption

	MINT	NRMT
COMPLETE SET (6)	20.00	9.00
TRADE CARD STATED ODDS 1:102		
ONE SET PER TRADE CARD BY MAIL		

❑ 1 Troy Aikman	8.00	3.60
❑ 2 Emmitt Smith	12.00	5.50
❑ 3 Leon Lett	.60	.25
❑ 4 Michael Irvin	2.00	.90
❑ 5 James Washington	.60	.25
❑ 6 Darrin Smith	.60	.25
❑ NNO0 Super Bowl Redemp.	.50	.23

1995 Playoff Absolute

	MINT	NRMT
COMPLETE SET (200)	20.00	9.00
COMMON CARD (1-200)	.10	.05
SEMISTARS	.20	.09
UNLISTED STARS	.40	.18
DRAFT INSERTS ODDS 1:288		

❑ 1 John Elway	2.00	.90
❑ 2 Reggie White	.40	.18
❑ 3 Errict Rhett	.40	.18
❑ 4 Deion Sanders	.50	.23
❑ 5 Rocket Ismail	.20	.09
❑ 6 Jerome Bettis	.40	.18
❑ 7 Randall Cunningham	.40	.18
❑ 8 Mario Bates	.40	.18
❑ 9 Dave Brown	.20	.09
❑ 10 Stan Humphries	.20	.09
❑ 11 Drew Bledsoe	1.00	.45
❑ 12 Neil O'Donnell	.20	.09
❑ 13 Dan Marino	2.00	.90
❑ 14 Larry Centers	.20	.09
❑ 15 Craig Heyward	.20	.09
❑ 16 Bruce Smith	.40	.18
❑ 17 Erik Kramer	.10	.05
❑ 18 Jeff Blake RC	1.25	.55
❑ 19 Vinny Testaverde	.20	.09
❑ 20 Barry Sanders	2.00	.90
❑ 21 Boomer Esiason	.20	.09
❑ 22 Emmitt Smith	1.50	.70
❑ 23 Warren Moon	.20	.09
❑ 24 Junior Seau	.40	.18
❑ 25 Heath Shuler	.40	.18
❑ 26 Jackie Harris	.10	.05
❑ 27 Terance Mathis	.20	.09
❑ 28 Raymont Harris	.10	.05
❑ 29 Jim Kelly	.40	.18
❑ 30 Dan Wilkinson	.20	.09
❑ 31 Herman Moore	.40	.18
❑ 32 Shannon Sharpe	.20	.09
❑ 33 Antonio Langham	.10	.05
❑ 34 Charles Haley	.20	.09
❑ 35 Brett Favre	2.00	.90
❑ 36 Marshall Faulk	.75	.35
❑ 37 Neil Smith	.20	.09
❑ 38 Harvey Williams	.10	.05
❑ 39 Johnny Bailey	.10	.05
❑ 40 O.J. McDuffie	.40	.18
❑ 41 David Palmer	.20	.09
❑ 42 Willie McGinest	.20	.09
❑ 43 Quinn Early	.20	.09
❑ 44 Johnny Johnson	.10	.05
❑ 45 Derek Brown TE	.10	.05
❑ 46 Charlie Garner	.20	.09
❑ 47 Byron Bam Morris	.20	.09
❑ 48 Natrone Means	.40	.18
❑ 49 Ken Norton Jr.	.20	.09
❑ 50 Troy Aikman	1.00	.45
❑ 51 Reggie Brooks	.20	.09
❑ 52 Trent Dilfer	.40	.18
❑ 53 Cortez Kennedy	.20	.09
❑ 54 Chuck Levy	.10	.05
❑ 55 Jeff George	.20	.09
❑ 56 Steve Young	.75	.35
❑ 57 Lewis Tillman	.10	.05
❑ 58 Carl Pickens	.40	.18
❑ 59 Brett Perriman	.20	.09
❑ 60 Jay Novacek	.20	.09
❑ 61 Greg Hill	.20	.09
❑ 62 James Jett	.20	.09
❑ 63 Terry Kirby	.20	.09
❑ 64 Qadry Ismail	.20	.09
❑ 65 Ben Coates	.20	.09
❑ 66 Kevin Greene	.20	.09
❑ 67 Bryant Young	.20	.09
❑ 68 Brian Mitchell	.10	.05
❑ 69 Steve Walsh	.10	.05
❑ 70 Darnay Scott	.40	.18
❑ 71 Daryl Johnston	.20	.09
❑ 72 Glyn Milburn	.10	.05

Card	Mint	Nrmt
❑ 73 Tim Brown	.40	.18
❑ 74 Isaac Bruce	.75	.35
❑ 75 Bernie Parmalee	.20	.09
❑ 76 Terry Allen	.20	.09
❑ 77 Jim Everett	.10	.05
❑ 78 Thomas Lewis	.20	.09
❑ 79 Vaughn Hebron	.10	.05
❑ 80 Rod Woodson	.20	.09
❑ 81 Rick Mirer	.40	.18
❑ 82 Dana Stubblefield	.40	.18
❑ 83 Bert Emanuel	.40	.18
❑ 84 Andre Reed	.20	.09
❑ 85 Jeff Graham	.10	.05
❑ 86 Johnnie Morton	.20	.09
❑ 87 LeShon Johnson	.20	.09
❑ 88 Michael Irvin	.40	.18
❑ 89 Derrick Alexander WR	.40	.18
❑ 90 Lake Dawson	.20	.09
❑ 91 Cody Carlson	.10	.05
❑ 92 Chris Warren	.20	.09
❑ 93 William Floyd	.40	.18
❑ 94 Charles Johnson	.20	.09
❑ 95 Roosevelt Potts	.10	.05
❑ 96 Cris Carter	.40	.18
❑ 97 Aaron Glenn	.10	.05
❑ 98 Curtis Conway	.40	.18
❑ 99 Kevin Williams WR	.20	.09
❑ 100 Jerry Rice	1.00	.45
❑ 101 Frank Reich	.10	.05
❑ 102 Harold Green	.10	.05
❑ 103 Russell Copeland	.10	.05
❑ 104 Rob Moore	.10	.05
❑ 105 Edgar Bennett	.20	.09
❑ 106 Darren Carrington	.10	.05
❑ 107 Tommy Maddox	.10	.05
❑ 108 Dave Meggett	.10	.05
❑ 109 Fred Barnett	.20	.09
❑ 110 Mark Seay	.20	.09
❑ 111 Gus Frerotte	.40	.18
❑ 112 Brent Jones	.10	.05
❑ 113 Chris Miller	.10	.05
❑ 114 Cedric Tillman	.10	.05
❑ 115 Mark Ingram	.10	.05
❑ 116 Eric Turner	.10	.05
❑ 117 Mark Carrier WR	.20	.09
❑ 118 Garrison Hearst	.40	.18
❑ 119 Craig Erickson	.10	.05
❑ 120 Derek Russell	.10	.05
❑ 121 Mike Sherrard	.10	.05
❑ 122 Horace Copeland	.10	.05
❑ 123 Jack Trudeau	.10	.05
❑ 124 Leroy Hoard	.10	.05
❑ 125 Gary Brown	.10	.05
❑ 126 Mel Gray	.10	.05
❑ 127 Steve Beuerlein	.10	.05
❑ 128 Marcus Allen	.40	.18
❑ 129 Irving Fryar	.20	.09
❑ 130 Marion Butts	.10	.05
❑ 131 Ricky Watters	.40	.18
❑ 132 Tony Martin	.20	.09
❑ 133 Lawrence Dawsey	.10	.05
❑ 134 Ronnie Harmon	.10	.05
❑ 135 Herschel Walker	.20	.09
❑ 136 Michael Haynes	.20	.09
❑ 137 Eric Green	.10	.05
❑ 138 Steve Bono	.20	.09
❑ 139 Jamir Miller	.10	.05
❑ 140 Rod Smith DB	.20	.09
❑ 141 Andre Rison	.20	.09
❑ 142 Eric Metcalf	.20	.09
❑ 143 Michael Timpson	.10	.05
❑ 144 Cornelius Bennett	.20	.09
❑ 145 Sean Dawkins	.20	.09
❑ 146 Scott Mitchell	.20	.09
❑ 147 Ray Childress	.10	.05
❑ 148 Jim Harbaugh	.20	.09
❑ 149 Reggie Cobb	.10	.05
❑ 150 Willie Roaf	.10	.05
❑ 151 Stevie Anderson	.10	.05
❑ 152 Barry Foster	.20	.09
❑ 153 Joe Montana	2.00	.90
❑ 154 David Klingler	.20	.09
❑ 155 Chris Chandler	.20	.09
❑ 156 Carnell Lake	.10	.05
❑ 157 Calvin Williams	.20	.09
❑ 158 Kenneth Davis	.10	.05
❑ 159 Tydus Winans	.10	.05
❑ 160 Sam Adams	.10	.05
❑ 161 Ronald Moore	.10	.05
❑ 162 Vincent Brisby	.10	.05
❑ 163 Alvin Harper	.10	.05
❑ 164 Jake Reed	.20	.09
❑ 165 Jeff Hostetler	.20	.09
❑ 166 Mark Brunell	1.00	.45
❑ 167 Leonard Russell	.10	.05
❑ 168 Greg Truitt	.10	.05
❑ 169 Pete Metzelaars	.10	.05
❑ 170 Dave Krieg	.10	.05
❑ 171 Lorenzo White	.10	.05
❑ 172 Robert Brooks	.40	.18
❑ 173 Willie Davis	.20	.09
❑ 174 Irving Spikes	.20	.09
❑ 175 Rodney Hampton	.20	.09
❑ 176 Erric Pegram	.20	.09
❑ 177 Brian Blades	.20	.09
❑ 178 Shawn Jefferson	.10	.05
❑ 179 Tyrone Poole RC	.20	.09
❑ 180 Rob Johnson RC	3.00	1.35
❑ 181 Ki-Jana Carter RC	.40	.18
❑ 182 Steve McNair RC	5.00	2.20
❑ 183 Michael Westbrook RC	3.00	1.35
❑ 184 Kerry Collins RC	1.25	.55
❑ 185 Kevin Carter RC	.40	.18
❑ 186 Tony Boselli RC	.20	.09
❑ 187 Joey Galloway RC	5.00	2.20
❑ 188 Kyle Brady RC	.40	.18
❑ 189 J.J. Stokes RC	1.00	.45
❑ 190 Warren Sapp RC	.60	.25
❑ 191 Tyrone Wheatley RC	2.50	1.10
❑ 192 Napolean Kaufman RC	4.00	1.80
❑ 193 James O. Stewart RC	4.00	1.80
❑ 194 Rashaan Salaam RC	.40	.18
❑ 195 Ray Zellars RC	.20	.09
❑ 196 Todd Collins RC	.40	.18
❑ 197 Sherman Williams RC	.10	.05
❑ 198 Frank Sanders RC	1.25	.55
❑ 199 Terrell Fletcher RC	.10	.05
❑ 200 Chad May RC	.10	.05
❑ DP1G T.Boselli Draft Gold	3.00	1.35
❑ DP1S T.Boselli Draft Silver	2.00	.90
❑ DP2G K.Collins Draft Gold	6.00	2.70
❑ DP2S K.Collins Draft Silver	5.00	2.20

1995 Playoff Prime

	MINT	NRMT
COMPLETE SET (200)	12.00	5.50
*PRIME CARDS: .3X TO .8X ABSOLUTE		

1995 Playoff Absolute Die Cut Helmets

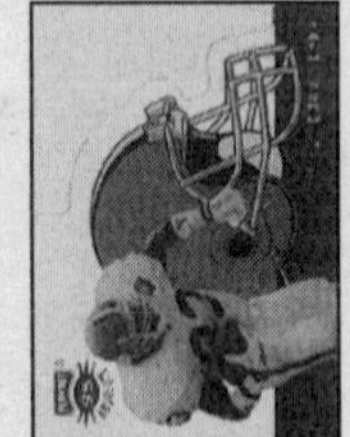

	MINT	NRMT
COMPLETE SET (30)	200.00	90.00
STATED ODDS 1:25 ABSOLUTE		

Card	Mint	Nrmt
❑ 1 Garrison Hearst	5.00	2.20
❑ 2 Jim Kelly	5.00	2.20
❑ 3 Jeff Blake	15.00	6.75
❑ 4 Emmitt Smith	20.00	9.00
❑ 5 John Elway	25.00	11.00
❑ 6 Brett Favre	25.00	11.00
❑ 7 Marshall Faulk	10.00	4.50
❑ 8 Marcus Allen	5.00	2.20
❑ 9 Jerome Bettis	5.00	2.20
❑ 10 Dan Marino	25.00	11.00
❑ 11 Cris Carter	5.00	2.20
❑ 12 Drew Bledsoe	12.00	5.50
❑ 13 Jim Everett	1.25	.55
❑ 14 Rodney Hampton	2.50	1.10
❑ 15 Natrone Means	5.00	2.20
❑ 16 Steve Young	10.00	4.50
❑ 17 Rick Mirer	5.00	2.20
❑ 18 Errict Rhett	5.00	2.20
❑ 19 Heath Shuler	5.00	2.20
❑ 20 Lewis Tillman	1.25	.55
❑ 21 Barry Sanders	25.00	11.00
❑ 22 Leroy Hoard	1.25	.55
❑ 23 Rod Woodson	2.50	1.10
❑ 24 Gary Brown	1.25	.55
❑ 25 Terance Mathis	2.50	1.10
❑ 26 Frank Reich	1.25	.55
❑ 27 Steve Beuerlein	1.25	.55
❑ 28 Rocket Ismail	2.50	1.10
❑ 29 Johnny Johnson	1.25	.55
❑ 30 Charlie Garner	2.50	1.10

1995 Playoff Prime Fantasy Team

	MINT	NRMT
COMPLETE SET (20)	80.00	36.00
STATED ODDS 1:25 PRIME		

Card	Mint	Nrmt
❑ FT1 Jerome Bettis	3.00	1.35
❑ FT2 Shannon Sharpe	1.50	.70
❑ FT3 Fuad Reveiz	.75	.35
❑ FT4 John Carney	.75	.35
❑ FT5 Steve Young	6.00	2.70
❑ FT6 Brett Favre	15.00	6.75
❑ FT7 Tim Brown	3.00	1.35
❑ FT8 Ben Coates	1.50	.70
❑ FT9 Marshall Faulk	6.00	2.70
❑ FT10 Stan Humphries	1.50	.70
❑ FT11 Dan Marino	15.00	6.75
❑ FT12 Jerry Rice	8.00	3.60
❑ FT13 Errict Rhett	3.00	1.35
❑ FT14 Chris Warren	1.50	.70
❑ FT15 Barry Sanders	15.00	6.75
❑ FT16 Cris Carter	3.00	1.35
❑ FT17 Michael Irvin	3.00	1.35
❑ FT18 Emmitt Smith	12.00	5.50
❑ FT19 Terance Mathis	1.50	.70
❑ FT20 Herman Moore	3.00	1.35

1995 Playoff Prime Minis

	MINT	NRMT
COMPLETE SET (200)	250.00	110.00

*STARS: 5X TO 12X BASE ABSOLUTES
*ROOKIES: 1.5X TO 4X BASE ABSOLUTES
STATED ODDS 1:7 PRIME

1995 Playoff Absolute/Prime Pigskin Previews

	MINT	NRMT
COMPLETE SET (12)	250.00	110.00
COMP.SERIES 1 (6)	150.00	70.00
COMP.SERIES 2 (6)	100.00	45.00

1-6 STATED ODDS 1:145 ABSOLUTE
7-12 STATED ODDS 1:145 PRIME

❑ 1 Emmitt Smith	40.00	18.00
❑ 2 Steve Young	20.00	9.00
❑ 3 Barry Sanders	50.00	22.00
❑ 4 Deion Sanders	12.00	5.50
❑ 5 Cris Carter	10.00	4.50
❑ 6 Errict Rhett	10.00	4.50
❑ 7 Dan Marino	50.00	22.00
❑ 8 Marshall Faulk	20.00	9.00
❑ 9 Natrone Means	10.00	4.50
❑ 10 Tim Brown	10.00	4.50
❑ 11 Drew Bledsoe	25.00	11.00
❑ 12 Marcus Allen	10.00	4.50

1995 Playoff Absolute Quad Series

	MINT	NRMT
COMPLETE SET (50)	800.00	350.00
COMMON QUAD (Q1-Q50)	6.00	2.70
SEMISTARS	10.00	4.50
UNLISTED STARS	15.00	6.75

STATED ODDS 1:25 ABSOLUTE

❑ Q1 Joe Montana	100.00	45.00
Dan Marino		
Steve Young		
John Elway		
❑ Q2 Troy Aikman	80.00	36.00
Brett Favre		
Drew Bledsoe		
Rick Mirer		
❑ Q3 Trent Dilfer	40.00	18.00
Heath Shuler		
Mark Brunell		
Jeff Blake		
❑ Q4 Randall Cunningham	6.00	2.70
Warren Moon		
Jim Kelly		
Boomer Esiason		
❑ Q5 Jeff George	10.00	4.50
Dave Brown		
Stan Humphries		
Jim Everett		
❑ Q6 Barry Sanders	60.00	27.00
Emmitt Smith		
Marshall Faulk		
Errict Rhett		
❑ Q7 Marcus Allen	15.00	6.75
Ricky Watters		
William Floyd		
Natrone Means		
❑ Q8 Garrison Hearst	10.00	4.50
Jerome Bettis		
Lewis Tillman		
Gary Brown		
❑ Q9 Michael Irvin	40.00	18.00
Jerry Rice		
Tim Brown		
Cris Carter		
❑ Q10 Pete Metzelaars	10.00	4.50
Byron Bam Morris		
Ben Coates		
Andre Rison		
❑ Q11 Reggie White	30.00	13.50
Bruce Smith		
Deion Sanders		
Junior Seau		
❑ Q12 Rob Moore	10.00	4.50
Larry Centers		
Jamir Miller		
Chuck Levy		
❑ Q13 Craig Heyward UER	10.00	4.50
Terance Mathis		
Bert Emanuel		
Eric Metcalf		
❑ Q14 Kenneth Davis	10.00	4.50
Andre Reed		
Russell Copeland		
Cornelius Bennett		
❑ Q15 Frank Reich	10.00	4.50
Jack Trudeau		
Mark Carrier WR		
Tyrone Poole		
❑ Q16 Jeff Graham	10.00	4.50
Curtis Conway		
Erik Kramer		
Steve Walsh		
❑ Q17 Carl Pickens	10.00	4.50
Darnay Scott		
Harold Green		
David Klingler		
❑ Q18 Vinny Testaverde	6.00	2.70
Derrick Alexander WR		
Leroy Hoard		
Lorenzo White		
❑ Q19 Charles Haley	10.00	4.50
Kevin Williams WR		
Daryl Johnston		
Jay Novacek		
❑ Q20 Glyn Milburn	6.00	2.70
Leonard Russell		
Derek Russell		
Shannon Sharpe		
❑ Q21 Scott Mitchell	15.00	6.75
Brett Perriman		
Herman Moore		
Johnnie Morton		
❑ Q22 Edgar Bennett	10.00	4.50
LeShon Johnson		
Robert Brooks		
Mark Ingram		
❑ Q23 Cody Carlson	6.00	2.70
Mel Gray		
Chris Chandler		
Ray Childress		
❑ Q24 Craig Erickson	10.00	4.50
Jim Harbaugh		
Roosevelt Potts		
Sean Dawkins		
❑ Q25 Steve Beuerlein	20.00	9.00
Rob Johnson		
Cedric Tillman		
Reggie Cobb		
❑ Q26 Greg Hill	10.00	4.50
Willie Davis		
Lake Dawson		
Steve Bono		
❑ Q27 Harvey Williams	6.00	2.70
Jeff Hostetler		
James Jett		
Rocket Ismail		
❑ Q28 Bernie Parmalee	6.00	2.70
Irving Spikes		
Terry Kirby		
Irving Fryar		
❑ Q29 Terry Allen	6.00	2.70
David Palmer		
Qadry Ismail		
Jake Reed		
❑ Q30 Marion Butts	6.00	2.70
Vincent Brisby		
Dave Meggett		
Willie McGinest		
❑ Q31 Willie Roaf	6.00	2.70
Mario Bates		
Quinn Early		
Michael Haynes		
❑ Q32 Herschel Walker	6.00	2.70
Mike Sherrard		
Derek Brown TE		
Thomas Lewis		
❑ Q33 Stevie Anderson	6.00	2.70
Aaron Glenn		
Johnny Johnson		
Ron Moore		
❑ Q34 Calvin Williams	10.00	4.50
Fred Barnett		
Vaughn Hebron		
Charlie Garner		
❑ Q35 Charles Johnson	10.00	4.50
Neil O'Donnell		
Rod Woodson		
Erric Pegram		
❑ Q36 Ronnie Harmon	6.00	2.70
Shawn Jefferson		
Tony Martin		
Mark Seay		
❑ Q37 Brent Jones	10.00	4.50
Dana Stubblefield		
Bryant Young		
Ken Norton		
❑ Q38 Chris Warren	10.00	4.50
Cortez Kennedy		
Sam Adams		
Brian Blades		
❑ Q39 Tommy Maddox	15.00	6.75
Chris Miller		
Johnny Bailey		
Isaac Bruce		
❑ Q40 Lawrence Dawsey	6.00	2.70
Alvin Harper		
Jackie Harris		

Horace Copeland
❑ Q41 Gus Frerotte 15.00 6.75
Brian Mitchell
Reggie Brooks
Tydus Winans
❑ Q42 Steve McNair 25.00 11.00
Kerry Collins
Todd Collins
Chad May
❑ Q43 Ki-Jana Carter 20.00 9.00
Tyrone Wheatley
Napoleon Kaufman
Rashaan Salaam
❑ Q44 Terrell Fletcher 20.00 9.00
Sherman Williams
Ray Zellars
James O.Stewart
❑ Q45 Michael Westbrook 25.00 11.00
Joey Galloway
J.J. Stokes
Frank Sanders
❑ Q46 Kevin Carter 10.00 4.50
Tony Boselli
Warren Sapp
Kyle Brady
❑ Q47 Greg Truitt 6.00 2.70
Dan Wilkinson
Eric Turner
Antonio Langham
❑ Q48 Carnell Lake 10.00 4.50
Neil Smith
Rod Smith DB
Kevin Greene
❑ Q49 O.J. McDuffie 10.00 4.50
Darren Carrington
Michael Timpson
Raymont Harris
❑ Q50 Rodney Hampton 6.00 2.70
Dave Krieg
Barry Foster
Eric Green

1995 Playoff Absolute Unsung Heroes

	MINT	NRMT
COMPLETE SET (28)	20.00	9.00
COMMON CARD (1-28)	.50	.23
SEMISTARS	.75	.35
UNLISTED STARS	1.50	.70
*GOLD/SILVER: SAME VALUE		
GOLD ODDS 1:13 ABSOLUTE		
SILVER ODDS 1:13 PRIME		

❑ 1 Garth Jax .50 .23
❑ 2 Craig Heyward .75 .35
❑ 3 Steve Tasker .75 .35
❑ 4 Raymont Harris .50 .23
❑ 5 Jeff Blake 1.50 .70
❑ 6 Bob Dahl .50 .23
❑ 7 Jason Garrett .50 .23
❑ 8 Gary Zimmerman .50 .23
❑ 9 Tom Beer .50 .23
❑ 10 John Jurkovic .50 .23
❑ 11 Spencer Tillman .50 .23
❑ 12 Devon McDonald .50 .23
❑ 13 John Alt .50 .23
❑ 14 Steve Wisniewski .50 .23
❑ 15 Tim Bowens .50 .23
❑ 16 Amp Lee .50 .23
❑ 17 Todd Rucci .50 .23
❑ 18 Tyrone Hughes .75 .35
❑ 19 Michael Strahan .50 .23
❑ 20 Brad Baxter .50 .23
❑ 21 Mark Bavaro .50 .23
❑ 22 Yancey Thigpen 1.50 .70
❑ 23 Courtney Hall .50 .23
❑ 24 Eric Davis .50 .23
❑ 25 Rufus Porter .50 .23
❑ 26 Jackie Slater .75 .35
❑ 27 Courtney Hawkins .75 .35
❑ 28 Gus Frerotte .75 .35

1996 Playoff Absolute

	MINT	NRMT
COMPLETE SET (200)	100.00	45.00
COMP.RED SET (100)	15.00	6.75
COMMON RED CARD (1-100)	.15	.07
SEMISTARS RED	.30	.14
UNLISTED STARS RED	.60	.25
COMMON WHITE (101-150)	.50	.23
SEMISTARS WHITE	1.00	.45
UNLISTED STARS WHITE	2.00	.90
STATED WHITE PACK ODDS 16:24		
COMMON BLUE (151-200)	.75	.35
SEMISTARS BLUE	1.50	.70
UNLISTED STARS BLUE	3.00	1.35
STATED BLUE PACK ODDS 8:24		

❑ 1 Jim Kelly .60 .25
❑ 2 Michael Irvin .60 .25
❑ 3 Jim Harbaugh .30 .14
❑ 4 Warren Moon .30 .14
❑ 5 Rick Mirer .30 .14
❑ 6 Drew Bledsoe 1.50 .70
❑ 7 Steve Young 1.25 .55
❑ 8 Junior Seau .30 .14
❑ 9 Sherman Williams .15 .07
❑ 10 Jay Novacek .15 .07
❑ 11 Bill Brooks .15 .07
❑ 12 Steve Bono .15 .07
❑ 13 Leroy Hoard .15 .07
❑ 14 Willie Jackson .15 .07
❑ 15 Irving Fryar .30 .14
❑ 16 Tony McGee .15 .07
❑ 17 Neil O'Donnell .30 .14
❑ 18 Fred Barnett .15 .07
❑ 19 Erric Pegram .15 .07
❑ 20 Derrick Moore .15 .07
❑ 21 Johnnie Morton .30 .14
❑ 22 James Jett .30 .14
❑ 23 Tim Brown .60 .25
❑ 24 Kevin Miniefield .15 .07
❑ 25 Jim McMahon .15 .07
❑ 26 Brian Blades .15 .07
❑ 27 Henry Ellard .15 .07
❑ 28 Calvin Williams .15 .07
❑ 29 Chris Chandler .30 .14
❑ 30 Rod Woodson .30 .14
❑ 31 Ronnie Harmon .15 .07
❑ 32 Brent Jones .15 .07
❑ 33 Qadry Ismail .15 .07
❑ 34 Steve Tasker .15 .07
❑ 35 Eric Green .15 .07
❑ 36 Brian Mitchell .15 .07
❑ 37 Herschel Walker .30 .14
❑ 38 Sean Dawkins .15 .07
❑ 39 Bryce Paup .15 .07
❑ 40 Dorsey Levens 1.00 .45
❑ 41 Andre Rison .30 .14
❑ 42 Lamont Warren .15 .07
❑ 43 Earnest Byner .15 .07
❑ 44 Bobby Engram RC .60 .25
❑ 45 Simeon Rice RC .60 .25
❑ 46 Michael Jackson .30 .14
❑ 47 Marvin Harrison RC 3.00 1.35
❑ 48 Thurman Thomas .60 .25
❑ 49 Charles Haley .30 .14
❑ 50 Rob Moore .30 .14
❑ 51 Bryan Cox .15 .07
❑ 52 Horace Copeland .15 .07
❑ 53 Rodney Peete .15 .07
❑ 54 Jeff Graham .15 .07
❑ 55 Charles Johnson .15 .07
❑ 56 Natrone Means .60 .25
❑ 57 Terrell Fletcher .15 .07
❑ 58 Eric Bieniemy .15 .07
❑ 59 Karim Abdul-Jabbar RC .75 .35
❑ 60 Quinn Early .15 .07
❑ 61 Mark Bruener .15 .07
❑ 62 Shawn Jefferson .15 .07
❑ 63 Vinny Testaverde .30 .14
❑ 64 Derrick Mayes RC 1.00 .45
❑ 65 Mario Bates .30 .14
❑ 66 J.J. Birden .15 .07
❑ 67 Eddie Kennison RC .60 .25
❑ 68 Steve Walsh .15 .07
❑ 69 Mark Chmura .30 .14
❑ 70 Mike Sherrard .15 .07
❑ 71 Boomer Esiason .30 .14
❑ 72 Alex Van Dyke RC .30 .14
❑ 73 Jake Reed .30 .14
❑ 74 Jackie Harris .15 .07
❑ 75 Mark Rypien .15 .07
❑ 76 Chris Calloway .15 .07
❑ 77 Amani Toomer RC .60 .25
❑ 78 Terrell Davis 8.00 3.60
❑ 79 Rocket Ismail .15 .07
❑ 80 Derek Loville .15 .07
❑ 81 Ben Coates .30 .14
❑ 82 Kyle Brady .15 .07
❑ 83 Willie Green .15 .07
❑ 84 Randall Cunningham .60 .25
❑ 85 Amp Lee .15 .07
❑ 86 Bert Emanuel .30 .14
❑ 87 Jason Dunn RC .30 .14
❑ 88 Michael Haynes .15 .07
❑ 89 Robert Green .15 .07
❑ 90 Willie Davis .15 .07
❑ 91 O.J. McDuffie .30 .14
❑ 92 Harold Green .15 .07
❑ 93 Ken Dilger .30 .14
❑ 94 Brett Perriman .15 .07
❑ 95 Eric Zeier .15 .07
❑ 96 Jerome Bettis .60 .25
❑ 97 Rickey Dudley RC .60 .25
❑ 98 Darnay Scott .30 .14
❑ 99 Mark Brunell 1.50 .70
❑ 100 Christian Fauria .15 .07
❑ 101 Jeff Blake 2.00 .90
❑ 102 Troy Aikman 5.00 2.20
❑ 103 John Elway 10.00 4.50
❑ 104 Barry Sanders 10.00 4.50
❑ 105 Curtis Conway 2.00 .90
❑ 106 Wayne Chrebet 1.00 .45
❑ 107 Lake Dawson 1.00 .45
❑ 108 Jerry Rice 5.00 2.20
❑ 109 Kevin Williams .50 .23
❑ 110 Zack Crockett .50 .23
❑ 111 Vincent Brisby .50 .23
❑ 112 Rodney Thomas .50 .23
❑ 113 Rodney Hampton 1.00 .45
❑ 114 Adrian Murrell .60 .25
❑ 115 Bruce Smith 2.00 .90
❑ 116 Napoleon Kaufman 2.50 1.10
❑ 117 Byron Bam Morris 1.00 .45
❑ 118 Anthony Miller 1.00 .45
❑ 119 Aaron Hayden RC 1.00 .45
❑ 120 Joey Galloway 3.00 1.35
❑ 121 Trent Dilfer 1.00 .45
❑ 122 Stoney Case .50 .23
❑ 123 Tamarick Vanover .30 .14
❑ 124 Eric Metcalf 1.00 .45

Card	Mint	NRMT
☐ 125 Marcus Allen	2.00	.90
☐ 126 James O. Stewart	2.00	.90
☐ 127 Charlie Garner	.50	.23
☐ 128 Yancey Thigpen	1.00	.45
☐ 129 William Floyd	1.00	.45
☐ 130 Terry Allen	1.00	.45
☐ 131 Robert Smith	1.00	.45
☐ 132 Todd Kinchen	.50	.23
☐ 133 Gus Frerotte	2.00	.90
☐ 134 Frank Sanders	1.00	.45
☐ 135 Scott Mitchell	1.00	.45
☐ 136 Greg Hill	1.00	.45
☐ 137 Edgar Bennett	1.00	.45
☐ 138 Alvin Harper	.50	.23
☐ 139 Reggie White	2.00	.90
☐ 140 Craig Heyward	.50	.23
☐ 141 Todd Collins	1.00	.45
☐ 142 Ernie Mills	.50	.23
☐ 143 Keyshawn Johnson RC	6.00	2.70
☐ 144 Mark Carrier WR	.50	.23
☐ 145 Robert Brooks	2.00	.90
☐ 146 Bernie Parmalee	.50	.23
☐ 147 Carl Pickens	2.00	.90
☐ 148 Kevin Hardy RC	2.00	.90
☐ 149 Jonathan Ogden RC	.50	.23
☐ 150 Lawrence Phillips RC	2.50	1.10
☐ 151 Emmitt Smith	15.00	6.75
☐ 152 Brett Favre	20.00	9.00
☐ 153 Dan Marino	20.00	9.00
☐ 154 Jim Everett	.75	.35
☐ 155 Dave Brown	1.50	.70
☐ 156 Jeff Hostetler	1.50	.70
☐ 157 Heath Shuler	3.00	1.35
☐ 158 Daryl Johnston	1.50	.70
☐ 159 Terance Mathis	.75	.35
☐ 160 Curtis Martin	8.00	3.60
☐ 161 Ray Zellars	.75	.35
☐ 162 Ricky Watters	1.50	.70
☐ 163 Chris Warren	1.50	.70
☐ 164 Larry Centers	1.50	.70
☐ 165 Steve McNair	8.00	3.60
☐ 166 Terry Kirby	1.50	.70
☐ 167 Rob Johnson	3.00	1.35
☐ 168 Dave Meggett	.75	.35
☐ 169 Antonio Freeman	8.00	3.60
☐ 170 Marshall Faulk	3.00	1.35
☐ 171 Andre Hastings	.15	.07
☐ 172 Stan Humphries	1.50	.70
☐ 173 Errict Rhett	1.50	.70
☐ 174 Michael Westbrook	3.00	1.35
☐ 175 Deion Sanders	6.00	2.70
☐ 176 Jeff George	1.50	.70
☐ 177 Cris Carter	3.00	1.35
☐ 178 Chris Sanders	1.50	.70
☐ 179 Ki-Jana Carter	1.50	.70
☐ 180 Kordell Stewart	8.00	3.60
☐ 181 Isaac Bruce	3.00	1.35
☐ 182 Terry Glenn RC	6.00	2.70
☐ 183 Garrison Hearst	1.50	.70
☐ 184 Erik Kramer	.75	.35
☐ 185 Leeland McElroy RC	3.00	1.35
☐ 186 Rashaan Salaam	3.00	1.35
☐ 187 Kimble Anders	.75	.35
☐ 188 Chad May	.75	.35
☐ 189 Tony Martin	1.50	.70
☐ 190 J.J. Stokes	3.00	1.35
☐ 191 Darick Holmes	1.50	.70
☐ 192 Eric Moulds RC	8.00	3.60
☐ 193 Shannon Sharpe	1.50	.70
☐ 194 Tim Biakabutuka RC	5.00	2.20
☐ 195 Eddie George RC	15.00	6.75
☐ 196 Mike Alstott RC	6.00	2.70
☐ 197 Kerry Collins	3.00	1.35
☐ 198 Harvey Williams	.75	.35
☐ 199 Herman Moore	3.00	1.35
☐ 200 Tyrone Wheatley	1.50	.70

1996 Playoff Absolute Metal XL

	MINT	NRMT
COMPLETE SET (36)	500.00	220.00
COMP.SERIES 1 SET (18)	250.00	110.00
COMP.SERIES 2 SET (18)	150.00	70.00
COMMON CARD (1-36)	4.00	1.80

SEMISTARS	6.00	2.70
UNLISTED STARS	10.00	4.50

1-18: STATED ODDS 1:96 ABSOLUTE PACKS
19-36: STATED ODDS 1:80 PRIME PACKS

Card	Mint	NRMT
☐ 1 Troy Aikman	20.00	9.00
☐ 2 Emmitt Smith	30.00	13.50
☐ 3 Barry Sanders	40.00	18.00
☐ 4 Brett Favre	40.00	18.00
☐ 5 Dan Marino	40.00	18.00
☐ 6 Jerry Rice	20.00	9.00
☐ 7 Marshall Faulk	10.00	4.50
☐ 8 Curtis Martin	12.00	5.50
☐ 9 Rashaan Salaam	10.00	4.50
☐ 10 Harvey Williams	4.00	1.80
☐ 11 Ricky Watters	6.00	2.70
☐ 12 Yancey Thigpen	4.00	1.80
☐ 13 Chris Warren	6.00	2.70
☐ 14 Errict Rhett	6.00	2.70
☐ 15 Terry Allen	6.00	2.70
☐ 16 Robert Brooks	10.00	4.50
☐ 17 Anthony Miller	4.00	1.80
☐ 18 Erik Kramer	4.00	1.80
☐ 19 Michael Irvin	10.00	4.50
☐ 20 John Elway	40.00	18.00
☐ 21 Jim Harbaugh	6.00	2.70
☐ 22 Steve Young	15.00	6.75
☐ 23 Deion Sanders	12.00	5.50
☐ 24 Terrell Davis	50.00	22.00
☐ 25 Reggie White	10.00	4.50
☐ 26 Herman Moore	10.00	4.50
☐ 27 Rodney Hampton	6.00	2.70
☐ 28 Cris Carter	6.00	2.70
☐ 29 Isaac Bruce	10.00	4.50
☐ 30 Kordell Stewart	12.00	5.50
☐ 31 Brett Perriman	4.00	1.80
☐ 32 Joey Galloway	10.00	4.50
☐ 33 Drew Bledsoe	20.00	9.00
☐ 34 J.J. Stokes	10.00	4.50
☐ 35 Napoleon Kaufman	10.00	4.50
☐ 36 Tim Brown	6.00	2.70

1996 Playoff Absolute Quad Series

	MINT	NRMT
COMPLETE SET (35)	400.00	180.00
COMMON CARD (1-35)	6.00	2.70
SEMISTARS	10.00	4.50
UNLISTED STARS	15.00	6.75

STATED ODDS 1:24

Card	Mint	NRMT
☐ 1 Stoney Case	10.00	4.50
Garrison Hearst		
Rob Moore		
Frank Sanders		
☐ 2 J.J.Birden	6.00	2.70
Bert Emanuel		
Jeff George		
Craig Heyward		
☐ 3 Todd Collins	15.00	6.75
Bill Brooks		
Jim Kelly		
Bryce Paup		
☐ 4 Mark Carrier WR	15.00	6.75
Kerry Collins		
Willie Green		
Derrick Moore		
☐ 5 Curtis Conway	10.00	4.50
Robert Green		
Erik Kramer		
Kevin Miniefield		
☐ 6 Eric Bieniemy	15.00	6.75
Jeff Blake		
Harold Green		
Tony McGee		
☐ 7 Earnest Byner	6.00	2.70
Michael Jackson		
Andre Rison		
Eric Zeier		
☐ 8 Michael Irvin	20.00	9.00
Jay Novacek		
Deion Sanders		
Kevin Williams		
☐ 9 Terrell Davis	50.00	22.00
John Elway		
Anthony Miller		
Shannon Sharpe		
☐ 10 Scott Mitchell	15.00	6.75
Herman Moore		
Johnnie Morton		
Brett Perriman		
☐ 11 Edgar Bennett	25.00	11.00
Mark Chmura		
Antonio Freeman		
Reggie White		
☐ 12 Chris Chandler	15.00	6.75
Steve McNair		
Chris Sanders		
Rodney Thomas		
☐ 13 Zack Crockett	10.00	4.50
Sean Dawkins		
Ken Dilger		
Jim Harbaugh		
☐ 14 Mark Brunell	25.00	11.00
Willie Jackson		
Rob Johnson		
James O.Stewart		
☐ 15 Marcus Allen	15.00	6.75
Kimble Anders		
Lake Dawson		
Tamarick Vanover		
☐ 16 Eric Green	10.00	4.50
Terry Kirby		
O.J. McDuffie		
Bernie Parmalee		
☐ 17 Cris Carter	10.00	4.50
Warren Moon		
Robert Smith		
Chad May		
☐ 18 Drew Bledsoe	30.00	13.50
Vincent Brisby		
Ben Coates		
Dave Meggett		
☐ 19 Mario Bates	6.00	2.70
Jim Everett		
Michael Haynes		
Ray Zellars		
☐ 20 Dave Brown	10.00	4.50
Chris Calloway		
Rodney Hampton		
Tyrone Wheatley		
☐ 21 Kyle Brady	10.00	4.50
Wayne Chrebet		
Adrian Murrell		
Neil O'Donnell		
☐ 22 Tim Brown	10.00	4.50

Jeff Hostetler
Rocket Ismail
Napoleon Kaufman
❑ 23 Charlie Garner 10.00 4.50
Rodney Peete
Ricky Watters
Calvin Williams
❑ 24 Andre Hastings 30.00 13.50
Ernie Mills
Kordell Stewart
Rod Woodson
❑ 25 Terrell Fletcher 15.00 6.75
Ronnie Harmon
Aaron Hayden
Junior Seau
❑ 26 William Floyd 30.00 13.50
Derek Loville
J.J.Stokes
Steve Young
❑ 27 Brian Blades 15.00 6.75
Christian Fauria
Joey Galloway
Rick Mirer
❑ 28 Mark Rypien 15.00 6.75
Isaac Bruce
Todd Kinchen
Steve Walsh
❑ 29 Horace Copeland 10.00 4.50
Trent Dilfer
Alvin Harper
James Harris
❑ 30 Henry Ellard 15.00 6.75
Gus Frerotte
Heath Shuler
Michael Westbrook
❑ 31 Keyshawn Johnson 25.00 11.00
Kevin Hardy
Simeon Rice
Jonathan Ogden
❑ 32 Lawrence Phillips 20.00 9.00
Tim Biakabutuka
Terry Glenn
Rickey Dudley
❑ 33 Eddie George 40.00 18.00
Marvin Harrison
Eric Moulds
Eddie Kennison
❑ 34 Derrick Mayes 15.00 6.75
Karim Abdul-Jabbar
Alex Van Dyke
Bobby Engram
❑ 35 Leeland McElroy 20.00 9.00
Jason Dunn
Mike Alstott
Amani Toomer

1996 Playoff Absolute Unsung Heroes

	MINT	NRMT
COMPLETE SET (30)	30.00	13.50
COMP.SERIES 1 SET (15)	12.00	5.50
COMP.SERIES 2 SET (15)	18.00	8.00
COMMON CARD (1-30)	.75	.35
SEMISTARS	1.25	.55

1-15: STATED ODDS 1:24 ABSOLUTE PACKS
16-30: STATED ODDS 1:24 PRIME PACKS

❑ 1 Bill Bates .... 1.25 .55
❑ 2 Jeff Brady .... .75 .35
❑ 3 Ray Brown.......................... .75 .35
❑ 4 Isaac Bruce .... 1.50 .70
❑ 5 Larry Centers .... 1.25 .55
❑ 6 Mark Chmura .... 1.50 .70
❑ 7 Keith Elias .... .75 .35
❑ 8 Robert Green .... .75 .35
❑ 9 Andy Harmon .... .75 .35
❑ 10 Rodney Holman .... .75 .35
❑ 11 Derek Loville .... 1.25 .55
❑ 12 J.J. McCleskey .... .75 .35
❑ 13 Sam Mills.......................... 1.25 .55
❑ 14 Hardy Nickerson .... 1.25 .55
❑ 15 Jessie Tuggle .... .75 .35
❑ 16 Eric Bieniemy .... .75 .35
❑ 17 Blaine Bishop .... .75 .35
❑ 18 Mark Brunell 6.00 2.70
❑ 19 Wayne Chrebet .... 1.25 .55
❑ 20 Vince Evans .... .75 .35
❑ 21 Sam Gash .... .75 .35
❑ 22 Tim Grunhard .... .75 .35
❑ 23 Jim Harbaugh .... 1.25 .55
❑ 24 Dwayne Harper .... .75 .35
❑ 25 Bernie Parmalee .... 1.25 .55
❑ 26 Reggie Rivers .... .75 .35
❑ 27 Eugene Robinson .... .75 .35
❑ 28 Kordell Stewart 5.00 2.20
❑ 29 Steve Tasker .... .75 .35
❑ 30 Bennie Thompson .... .75 .35

1996 Playoff Absolute Xtreme Team

	MINT	NRMT
COMPLETE SET (30)	300.00	135.00
COMMON CARD (1-30)	5.00	2.20
SEMISTARS	8.00	3.60

STATED ODDS 1:24 ....

❑ 1 Troy Aikman 20.00 9.00
❑ 2 Emmitt Smith 30.00 13.50
❑ 3 Jerry Rice 20.00 9.00
❑ 4 Dan Marino 35.00 16.00
❑ 5 Brett Favre 35.00 16.00
❑ 6 Barry Sanders 35.00 16.00
❑ 7 Michael Irvin 10.00 4.50
❑ 8 John Elway 35.00 16.00
❑ 9 Joey Galloway 10.00 4.50
❑ 10 Steve Young 15.00 6.75
❑ 11 Deion Sanders 12.00 5.50
❑ 12 Terrell Davis 40.00 18.00
❑ 13 Herman Moore 10.00 4.50
❑ 14 Reggie White 10.00 4.50
❑ 15 Cris Carter 8.00 3.60
❑ 16 Rodney Hampton 5.00 2.20
❑ 17 Isaac Bruce 10.00 4.50
❑ 18 Brett Perriman 5.00 2.20
❑ 19 Curtis Conway 8.00 3.60
❑ 20 Scott Mitchell 5.00 2.20
❑ 21 Rashaan Salaam 10.00 4.50
❑ 22 Robert Brooks 10.00 4.50
❑ 23 Marshall Faulk 10.00 4.50
❑ 24 Curtis Martin 12.00 5.50
❑ 25 Harvey Williams 5.00 2.20
❑ 26 Yancey Thigpen 8.00 3.60
❑ 27 Chris Warren 8.00 3.60
❑ 28 Ernict Rhett 8.00 3.60
❑ 29 Terry Allen 8.00 3.60
❑ 30 Carl Pickens 8.00 3.60

1997 Playoff Absolute

	MINT	NRMT
COMPLETE SET (200)	150.00	70.00
COMP.GREEN SET (100)	25.00	11.00
COMMON GREEN (1-100)	.15	.07
SEMISTARS GREEN	.25	.11
UNLISTED STARS GREEN	.50	.23
COMMON BLUE (101-150)	.50	.23
SEMISTARS BLUE	.75	.35
UNLISTED STARS BLUE	1.25	.55
BLUES ONE PER PACK		
COMMON RED (151-200)	.75	.35
SEMISTARS RED	1.25	.55
UNLISTED STARS RED	2.00	.90
RED ODDS 1:2		

❑ 1 Marcus Allen .... .50 .23
❑ 2 Eric Bieniemy .... .15 .07
❑ 3 Jason Dunn .... .15 .07
❑ 4 Jim Harbaugh .... .25 .11
❑ 5 Michael Westbrook .... .25 .11
❑ 6 Tiki Barber RC .... .75 .35
❑ 7 Frank Reich .... .15 .07
❑ 8 Irving Fryar .... .25 .11
❑ 9 Courtney Hawkins .... .15 .07
❑ 10 Eric Zeier .... .25 .11
❑ 11 Kent Graham .... .15 .07
❑ 12 Trent Dilfer .... .50 .23
❑ 13 Neil O'Donnell .... .25 .11
❑ 14 Reidel Anthony RC .... 1.25 .55
❑ 15 Jeff Hostetler .... .15 .07
❑ 16 Lawrence Phillips .... .15 .07
❑ 17 Dave Brown .... .15 .07
❑ 18 Mike Tomczak .... .15 .07
❑ 19 Jake Reed .... .25 .11
❑ 20 Anthony Miller .... .15 .07
❑ 21 Eric Metcalf .... .25 .11
❑ 22 Sedrick Shaw RC .... .50 .23
❑ 23 Anthony Johnson .... .15 .07
❑ 24 Mario Bates .... .15 .07
❑ 25 Dorsey Levens .... .50 .23
❑ 26 Stan Humphries .... .25 .11
❑ 27 Ben Coates .... .25 .11
❑ 28 Tyrone Wheatley .... .25 .11
❑ 29 Adrian Murrell .... .25 .11
❑ 30 William Henderson .... .15 .07
❑ 31 Warrick Dunn RC .... 2.00 .90
❑ 32 LeShon Johnson .... .15 .07
❑ 33 James O.Stewart .... .25 .11
❑ 34 Edgar Bennett .... .25 .11
❑ 35 Raymont Harris .... .15 .07
❑ 36 LeRoy Butler .... .15 .07
❑ 37 Darren Woodson .... .15 .07
❑ 38 Darnell Autry RC .... .25 .11
❑ 39 Johnnie Morton .... .25 .11
❑ 40 William Floyd .... .25 .11
❑ 41 Terrell Fletcher .... .15 .07
❑ 42 Leonard Russell .... .15 .07
❑ 43 Henry Ellard .... .15 .07
❑ 44 Terrell Owens .... .50 .23
❑ 45 John Friesz .... .15 .07
❑ 46 Antowain Smith RC ...... 1.50 .70
❑ 47 Charles Johnson .... .25 .11
❑ 48 Rickey Dudley .... .25 .11
❑ 49 Lake Dawson .... .15 .07

❑ 50 Bert Emanuel .25 .11
❑ 51 Zach Thomas .25 .11
❑ 52 Earnest Byner .15 .07
❑ 53 Yatil Green RC .25 .11
❑ 54 Chris Spielman .15 .07
❑ 55 Muhsin Muhammad .25 .11
❑ 56 Bobby Engram .25 .11
❑ 57 Eric Bjornson .15 .07
❑ 58 Willie Green .15 .07
❑ 59 Derrick Mayes .25 .11
❑ 60 Chris Sanders .15 .07
❑ 61 Jimmy Smith .25 .11
❑ 62 Tony Gonzalez RC 2.00 .90
❑ 63 Rich Gannon .15 .07
❑ 64 Stanley Pritchett .15 .07
❑ 65 Brad Johnson .75 .35
❑ 66 Rodney Peete .15 .07
❑ 67 Sam Gash .15 .07
❑ 68 Chris Calloway .15 .07
❑ 69 Chris T. Jones .15 .07
❑ 70 Will Blackwell RC .50 .23
❑ 71 Mark Bruener .15 .07
❑ 72 Terry Kirby .25 .11
❑ 73 Brian Blades .15 .07
❑ 74 Craig Heyward .15 .07
❑ 75 Jamie Asher .15 .07
❑ 76 Terance Mathis .25 .11
❑ 77 Troy Davis RC .50 .23
❑ 78 Bruce Smith .25 .11
❑ 79 Simeon Rice .25 .11
❑ 80 Fred Barnett .15 .07
❑ 81 Tim Brown .50 .23
❑ 82 James Jett .25 .11
❑ 83 Mark Carrier WR .15 .07
❑ 84 Shawn Jefferson .15 .07
❑ 85 Ken Dilger .15 .07
❑ 86 Rae Carruth RC .50 .23
❑ 87 Keenan McCardell .25 .11
❑ 88 Michael Irvin .50 .23
❑ 89 Mark Chmura .25 .11
❑ 90 Derrick Alexander WR .25 .11
❑ 91 Andre Reed .25 .11
❑ 92 Ed McCaffrey .25 .11
❑ 93 Erik Kramer .15 .07
❑ 94 Albert Connell RC 2.50 1.10
❑ 95 Frank Wycheck .15 .07
❑ 96 Zack Crockett .15 .07
❑ 97 Jim Everett .15 .07
❑ 98 Michael Haynes .15 .07
❑ 99 Jeff Graham .15 .07
❑ 100 Brent Jones .25 .11
❑ 101 Troy Aikman 4.00 1.80
❑ 102 Byron Hanspard RC 2.50 1.10
❑ 103 Robert Brooks 1.25 .55
❑ 104 Karim Abdul-Jabbar 1.25 .55
❑ 105 Drew Bledsoe 4.00 1.80
❑ 106 Napoleon Kaufman 1.25 .55
❑ 107 Steve Young 3.00 1.35
❑ 108 Leeland McElroy .15 .07
❑ 109 Jamal Anderson 2.00 .90
❑ 110 David LaFleur RC 1.25 .55
❑ 111 Vinny Testaverde .75 .35
❑ 112 Eric Moulds 1.25 .55
❑ 113 Tim Biakabutuka 1.25 .55
❑ 114 Rick Mirer .75 .35
❑ 115 Jeff Blake 1.25 .55
❑ 116 Jim Schwantz RC .50 .23
❑ 117 Herman Moore 1.25 .55
❑ 118 Ike Hilliard RC 2.50 1.10
❑ 119 Reggie White 1.25 .55
❑ 120 Steve McNair 2.00 .90
❑ 121 Marshall Faulk 1.25 .55
❑ 122 Natrone Means 1.25 .55
❑ 123 Greg Hill .75 .35
❑ 124 O.J. McDuffie .75 .35
❑ 125 Robert Smith .75 .35
❑ 126 Bryant Westbrook RC 1.25 .55
❑ 127 Ray Zellars .50 .23
❑ 128 Rodney Hampton .75 .35
❑ 129 Wayne Chrebet .50 .23
❑ 130 Desmond Howard .75 .35
❑ 131 Ty Detmer .75 .35
❑ 132 Erric Pegram .50 .23
❑ 133 Yancey Thigpen .75 .35
❑ 134 Danny Wuerffel RC .75 .35
❑ 135 Charlie Jones .50 .23
❑ 136 Chris Warren .75 .35
❑ 137 Isaac Bruce 1.25 .55
❑ 138 Errict Rhett .75 .35
❑ 139 Gus Frerotte 1.25 .55
❑ 140 Frank Sanders .75 .35
❑ 141 Todd Collins .75 .35
❑ 142 Jake Plummer RC UER 12.00 5.50
(height listed at 6'-24")
❑ 143 Darnay Scott .75 .35
❑ 144 Rashaan Salaam 1.25 .55
❑ 145 Terrell Davis 8.00 3.60
❑ 146 Scott Mitchell .75 .35
❑ 147 Junior Seau 1.25 .55
❑ 148 Warren Moon .75 .35
❑ 149 Wesley Walls .50 .23
❑ 150 Daryl Johnston .75 .35
❑ 151 Brett Favre 15.00 6.75
❑ 152 Emmitt Smith 12.00 5.50
❑ 153 Dan Marino 15.00 6.75
❑ 154 Larry Centers 1.25 .55
❑ 155 Michael Jackson 1.25 .55
❑ 156 Kerry Collins .25 .11
❑ 157 Curtis Conway 1.25 .55
❑ 158 Peter Boulware RC 1.25 .55
❑ 159 Carl Pickens 2.00 .90
❑ 160 Shannon Sharpe 1.25 .55
❑ 161 Brett Perriman .75 .35
❑ 162 Eddie George 8.00 3.60
❑ 163 Mark Brunell 8.00 3.60
❑ 164 Tamarick Vanover 1.25 .55
❑ 165 Cris Carter 2.00 .90
❑ 166 Corey Dillon RC 10.00 4.50
❑ 167 Curtis Martin 4.00 1.80
❑ 168 Amani Toomer 1.25 .55
❑ 169 Jeff George 1.25 .55
❑ 170 Kordell Stewart 4.00 1.80
❑ 171 Garrison Hearst 1.25 .55
❑ 172 Tony Banks 1.25 .55
❑ 173 Mike Alstott 2.00 .90
❑ 174 Jim Druckenmiller RC 3.00 1.35
❑ 175 Chris Chandler 1.25 .55
❑ 176 Byron Bam Morris .75 .35
❑ 177 Billy Joe Hobert 1.25 .55
❑ 178 Ernie Mills .75 .35
❑ 179 Ki-Jana Carter .75 .35
❑ 180 Deion Sanders 2.00 .90
❑ 181 Ricky Watters 1.25 .55
❑ 182 Shawn Springs RC 2.00 .90
❑ 183 Barry Sanders 15.00 6.75
❑ 184 Antonio Freeman 4.00 1.80
❑ 185 Marvin Harrison 2.00 .90
❑ 186 Elvis Grbac 1.25 .55
❑ 187 Terry Glenn 2.00 .90
❑ 188 Willie Roaf .75 .35
❑ 189 Keyshawn Johnson 2.00 .90
❑ 190 Orlando Pace RC .75 .35
❑ 191 Jerome Bettis 2.00 .90
❑ 192 Tony Martin 1.25 .55
❑ 193 Jerry Rice 8.00 3.60
❑ 194 Joey Galloway 4.00 1.80
❑ 195 Terry Allen 2.00 .90
❑ 196 Eddie Kennison 1.25 .55
❑ 197 Thurman Thomas 2.00 .90
❑ 198 Darrell Russell RC .75 .35
❑ 199 Rob Moore 1.25 .55
❑ 200 John Elway 15.00 6.75

1997 Playoff Absolute Bronze Redemption

	MINT	NRMT
COMP.BRONZE SET (200)	200.00	90.00
*BRONZE 1-100: .75X TO 1.5X HI COL.		
*BRONZE 101-150: .75X TO 1.5X HI COL.		
*BRONZE 151-200: .5X TO 1X HI COL.		
BRONZE REDEMPTION SET ODDS 1:1440		
COMP.GOLD SET (200)	500.00	220.00
*GOLD 1-100: 1.5X TO 4X BASE CARD HI		
*GOLD 101-150: 1.5X TO 4X BASE CARD HI		
*GOLD 151-200: 1X TO 2.5X BASE CARD HI		
GOLD REDEMPTION SET ODDS 1:2880		
COMP.SILVER SET (200)	300.00	135.00
*SILVER 1-100: 1X TO 2.5X BASE CARD HI		
*SILVER 101-150: 1X TO 2.5X BASE CARD HI		
*SILVER 151-200: .75X TO 1.5X BASE CARD HI		

SILVER REDEMPTION SET ODDS 1:1920
FOIL SET AVAILABLE VIA MAIL-REDEMPTION

1997 Playoff Absolute Chip Shots

	MINT	NRMT
COMPLETE SET (200)	250.00	110.00
COMMON CHIP (1-200)	.40	.18
SEMISTARS	.75	.35
UNLISTED STARS	1.50	.70
EACH PRINTED IN BLUE, BLACK, AND RED		
WITH SILVER STRIPES ON COIN'S EDGE		
ONE PER PACK		

❑ 1 Marcus Allen 1.50 .70
❑ 2 Eric Bieniemy .40 .18
❑ 3 Jason Dunn .40 .18
❑ 4 Jim Harbaugh .75 .35
❑ 5 Michael Westbrook .75 .35
❑ 6 Tiki Barber 1.50 .70
❑ 7 Frank Reich .40 .18
❑ 8 Irving Fryar .75 .35
❑ 9 Courtney Hawkins .40 .18
❑ 10 Eric Zeier .75 .35
❑ 11 Kent Graham .40 .18
❑ 12 Trent Dilfer 1.50 .70
❑ 13 Neil O'Donnell .75 .35
❑ 14 Reidel Anthony 1.50 .70
❑ 15 Jeff Hostetler .40 .18
❑ 16 Lawrence Phillips .40 .18
❑ 17 Dave Brown .40 .18
❑ 18 Mike Tomczak .40 .18
❑ 19 Jake Reed .75 .35
❑ 20 Anthony Miller .40 .18
❑ 21 Eric Metcalf .75 .35
❑ 22 Sedrick Shaw .75 .35
❑ 23 Anthony Johnson .40 .18
❑ 24 Mario Bates .40 .18
❑ 25 Dorsey Levens 1.50 .70
❑ 26 Stan Humphries .75 .35
❑ 27 Ben Coates .75 .35
❑ 28 Tyrone Wheatley .75 .35
❑ 29 Adrian Murrell .75 .35
❑ 30 William Henderson .40 .18
❑ 31 Warrick Dunn 2.00 .90
❑ 32 LeShon Johnson .40 .18
❑ 33 James O.Stewart 1.50 .70
❑ 34 Edgar Bennett .75 .35
❑ 35 Raymont Harris .40 .18
❑ 36 LeRoy Butler .40 .18
❑ 37 Darren Woodson .40 .18
❑ 38 Darnell Autry .40 .18
❑ 39 Johnnie Morton .75 .35

Card	MINT	NRMT
❑ 40 William Floyd	.40	.18
❑ 41 Terrell Fletcher	.40	.18
❑ 42 Leonard Russell	.40	.18
❑ 43 Henry Ellard	.40	.18
❑ 44 Terrell Owens	1.50	.70
❑ 45 John Friesz	.40	.18
❑ 46 Antowain Smith	2.00	.90
❑ 47 Charles Johnson	.75	.35
❑ 48 Rickey Dudley	.75	.35
❑ 49 Lake Dawson	.40	.18
❑ 50 Bert Emanuel	.75	.35
❑ 51 Zach Thomas	1.50	.70
❑ 52 Earnest Byner	.40	.18
❑ 53 Yatil Green	.75	.35
❑ 54 Chris Spielman	.40	.18
❑ 55 Muhsin Muhammad	.75	.35
❑ 56 Bobby Engram	.75	.35
❑ 57 Eric Bjornson	.40	.18
❑ 58 Willie Green	.40	.18
❑ 59 Derrick Mayes	.75	.35
❑ 60 Chris Sanders	.40	.18
❑ 61 Jimmy Smith	.75	.35
❑ 62 Tony Gonzalez	2.00	.90
❑ 63 Rich Gannon	.40	.18
❑ 64 Stanley Pritchett	.40	.18
❑ 65 Brad Johnson	1.50	.70
❑ 66 Rodney Peete	.40	.18
❑ 67 Sam Gash	.40	.18
❑ 68 Chris Calloway	.40	.18
❑ 69 Chris T. Jones	.40	.18
❑ 70 Will Blackwell	.75	.35
❑ 71 Mark Bruener	.40	.18
❑ 72 Terry Kirby	.75	.35
❑ 73 Brian Blades	.40	.18
❑ 74 Craig Heyward	.40	.18
❑ 75 Jamie Asher	.40	.18
❑ 76 Terance Mathis	.75	.35
❑ 77 Troy Davis	.75	.35
❑ 78 Bruce Smith	.75	.35
❑ 79 Simeon Rice	.75	.35
❑ 80 Fred Barnett	.40	.18
❑ 81 Tim Brown	1.50	.70
❑ 82 James Jett	.75	.35
❑ 83 Mark Carrier	.40	.18
❑ 84 Shawn Jefferson	.40	.18
❑ 85 Ken Dilger	.40	.18
❑ 86 Rae Carruth	.75	.35
❑ 87 Keenan McCardell	.75	.35
❑ 88 Michael Irvin	1.50	.70
❑ 89 Mark Chmura	.75	.35
❑ 90 Derrick Alexander	.75	.35
❑ 91 Andre Reed	.75	.35
❑ 92 Ed McCaffrey	.75	.35
❑ 93 Erik Kramer	.40	.18
❑ 94 Albert Connell	.40	.18
❑ 95 Frank Wycheck	.40	.18
❑ 96 Zack Crockett	.40	.18
❑ 97 Jim Everett	.40	.18
❑ 98 Michael Haynes	.40	.18
❑ 99 Jeff Graham	.40	.18
❑ 100 Brent Jones	.40	.18
❑ 101 Troy Aikman	5.00	2.20
❑ 102 Byron Hanspard	1.50	.70
❑ 103 Robert Brooks	.75	.35
❑ 104 Karim Abdul-Jabbar	1.50	.70
❑ 105 Drew Bledsoe	5.00	2.20
❑ 106 Napoleon Kaufman	1.50	.70
❑ 107 Steve Young	4.00	1.80
❑ 108 Leeland McElroy	.40	.18
❑ 109 Jamal Anderson	3.00	1.35
❑ 110 David LaFleur	1.50	.70
❑ 111 Vinny Testaverde	.75	.35
❑ 112 Eric Moulds	1.50	.70
❑ 113 Tim Biakabutuka	.75	.35
❑ 114 Rick Mirer	.40	.18
❑ 115 Jeff Blake	.75	.35
❑ 116 Jim Schwantz	.40	.18
❑ 117 Herman Moore	1.50	.70
❑ 118 Ike Hilliard	1.50	.70
❑ 119 Reggie White	1.50	.70
❑ 120 Steve McNair	2.00	.90
❑ 121 Marshall Faulk	1.50	.70
❑ 122 Natrone Means	1.50	.70
❑ 123 Greg Hill	.40	.18
❑ 124 O.J. McDuffie	.75	.35
❑ 125 Robert Smith	.75	.35
❑ 126 Bryant Westbrook	.40	.18
❑ 127 Ray Zellars	.40	.18
❑ 128 Rodney Hampton	.75	.35
❑ 129 Wayne Chrebet	1.50	.70
❑ 130 Desmond Howard	.75	.35
❑ 131 Ty Detmer	.75	.35
❑ 132 Erric Pegram	.40	.18
❑ 133 Yancey Thigpen	.75	.35
❑ 134 Danny Wuerffel	.75	.35
❑ 135 Charlie Jones	.75	.35
❑ 136 Chris Warren	.75	.35
❑ 137 Isaac Bruce	1.50	.70
❑ 138 Errict Rhett	.40	.18
❑ 139 Gus Frerotte	.40	.18
❑ 140 Frank Sanders	.40	.18
❑ 141 Todd Collins	.40	.18
❑ 142 Jake Plummer	6.00	2.70
❑ 143 Darnay Scott	.75	.35
❑ 144 Rashaan Salaam	.40	.18
❑ 145 Terrell Davis	10.00	4.50
❑ 146 Scott Mitchell	.75	.35
❑ 147 Junior Seau	.75	.35
❑ 148 Warren Moon	1.50	.70
❑ 149 Wesley Walls	.75	.35
❑ 150 Daryl Johnston	.75	.35
❑ 151 Brett Favre	10.00	4.50
❑ 152 Emmitt Smith	8.00	3.60
❑ 153 Dan Marino	10.00	4.50
❑ 154 Larry Centers	.75	.35
❑ 155 Michael Jackson	.75	.35
❑ 156 Kerry Collins	.75	.35
❑ 157 Curtis Conway	.75	.35
❑ 158 Peter Boulware	.75	.35
❑ 159 Carl Pickens	1.50	.70
❑ 160 Shannon Sharpe	.75	.35
❑ 161 Brett Perriman	.40	.18
❑ 162 Eddie George	5.00	2.20
❑ 163 Mark Brunell	5.00	2.20
❑ 164 Tamarick Vanover	.75	.35
❑ 165 Cris Carter	1.50	.70
❑ 166 Corey Dillon	3.00	1.35
❑ 167 Curtis Martin	2.00	.90
❑ 168 Amani Toomer	.75	.35
❑ 169 Jeff George	.75	.35
❑ 170 Kordell Stewart	2.00	.90
❑ 171 Garrison Hearst	.75	.35
❑ 172 Tony Banks	1.50	.70
❑ 173 Mike Alstott	1.50	.70
❑ 174 Jim Druckenmiller	1.50	.70
❑ 175 Chris Chandler	.75	.35
❑ 176 Byron Bam Morris	.40	.18
❑ 177 Billy Joe Hobert	.75	.35
❑ 178 Ernie Mills	.40	.18
❑ 179 Ki-Jana Carter	.40	.18
❑ 180 Deion Sanders	1.50	.70
❑ 181 Ricky Watters	.75	.35
❑ 182 Shawn Springs	.40	.18
❑ 183 Barry Sanders	10.00	4.50
❑ 184 Antonio Freeman	2.00	.90
❑ 185 Marvin Harrison	4.00	1.80
❑ 186 Elvis Grbac	.75	.35
❑ 187 Terry Glenn	1.50	.70
❑ 188 Willie Roaf	.40	.18
❑ 189 Keyshawn Johnson	1.50	.70
❑ 190 Orlando Pace	.40	.18
❑ 191 Jerome Bettis	1.50	.70
❑ 192 Tony Martin	.75	.35
❑ 193 Jerry Rice	5.00	2.20
❑ 194 Joey Galloway	2.00	.90
❑ 195 Terry Allen	1.50	.70
❑ 196 Eddie Kennison	.75	.35
❑ 197 Thurman Thomas	1.50	.70
❑ 198 Darrell Russell	.40	.18
❑ 199 Rob Moore	.40	.18
❑ 200 John Elway	10.00	4.50
❑ S162 Eddie George Sample (marked "Sample" on back)	2.00	.90

1997 Playoff Absolute Honors

	MINT	NRMT
COMPLETE SET (3)	350.00	160.00
COMMON CARD (PH7-PH9)	50.00	22.00
STATED ODDS 1:7200		
❑ PH7 Jerry Rice	120.00	55.00
❑ PH8 Reggie White	50.00	22.00
❑ PH9 John Elway	200.00	90.00

1997 Playoff Absolute Leather Quads

	MINT	NRMT
COMPLETE SET (18)	500.00	220.00
COMMON CARD (1-18)	10.00	4.50
SEMISTARS	15.00	6.75
STATED ODDS 1:144		
*GOLD CARDS: 1.2X TO 3X HI COL.		
GOLD REDEMPTION SET ODDS 1:28,800		
❑ 1 Emmitt Smith, Dan Marino, Jerry Rice, Brett Favre	120.00	55.00
❑ 2 Eddie George, Curtis Martin, Barry Sanders, Terrell Davis	80.00	36.00
❑ 3 Herman Moore, Kordell Stewart, Elvis Grbac, Chris Warren	25.00	11.00
❑ 4 Leeland McElroy, Troy Aikman, Zach Thomas, Cris Carter	40.00	18.00
❑ 5 Jim Harbaugh, Michael Jackson, Drew Bledsoe, Jamal Anderson	30.00	13.50
❑ 6 John Elway, Reggie White, Warren Moon, Terrell Owens	60.00	27.00
❑ 7 Rashaan Salaam, Kerry Collins, Shannon Sharpe, Ricky Watters	15.00	6.75
❑ 8 Larry Centers, Mario Bates, Eric Moulds, Mark Brunell	30.00	13.50
❑ 9 Jerome Bettis, Carl Pickens, Robert Brooks	15.00	6.75

	MINT	NRMT
Karim Abdul-Jabbar		
❑ 10 Jeff George	25.00	11.00
Tony Martin		
Steve Young		
Tim Biakabutuka		
❑ 11 Terry Glenn	25.00	11.00
Jeff Blake		
Mike Alstott		
Curtis Conway		
❑ 12 Rick Mirer	20.00	9.00
Anthony Johnson		
Antonio Freemn		
Joey Galloway		
❑ 13 Steve McNair	20.00	9.00
Marshall Faulk		
Jimmy Smith		
Isaac Bruce		
❑ 14 Vinny Testaverde	15.00	6.75
Rodney Hampton		
Deion Sanders		
Tony Banks		
❑ 15 Chris Chandler	10.00	4.50
Thurman Thomas		
Marvin Harrison		
Lawrence Phillips		
❑ 16 Greg Hill	20.00	9.00
Gus Frerotte		
Napoleon Kaufman		
Keyshawn Johnson		
❑ 17 Terry Allen	15.00	6.75
Eddie Kennison		
Errict Rhett		
Scott Mitchell		
❑ 18 Warrick Dunn	25.00	11.00
Jim Druckenmiller		
Orlando Pace		
Darrell Russell		

1997 Playoff Absolute Pennants

	MINT	NRMT
COMPLETE SET (192)	600.00	275.00
COMMON CARD (1-192)	4.00	1.80
SEMISTARS	6.00	2.70
UNLISTED STARS	10.00	4.50
ONE PER BOX		
*GOLD REDEMPTION CARDS: .3X TO .8X		
GOLD REDEMPTION SET ODDS 1:14,400		
❑ 14 Reidel Anthony	10.00	4.50
❑ 22 Sedrick Shaw	6.00	2.70
❑ 31 Warrick Dunn	15.00	6.75
❑ 38 Darnell Autry	4.00	1.80
❑ 44 Terrell Owens	10.00	4.50
❑ 46 Antowain Smith	12.00	5.50
❑ 53 Yatil Green	6.00	2.70
❑ 62 Tony Gonzalez	15.00	6.75
❑ 77 Troy Davis	6.00	2.70
❑ 81 Jerry Rice	30.00	13.50
❑ 86 Rae Carruth	6.00	2.70
❑ 101 Troy Aikman	30.00	13.50
❑ 102 Byron Hanspard	10.00	4.50
❑ 105 Drew Bledsoe	30.00	13.50
❑ 106 Eddie Kennison	6.00	2.70
❑ 107 Steve Young	25.00	11.00
❑ 110 David LaFleur	10.00	4.50
❑ 118 Ike Hilliard	10.00	4.50
❑ 120 Steve McNair	15.00	6.75
❑ 134 Danny Wuerffel	6.00	2.70
❑ 142 Jake Plummer	40.00	18.00
❑ 145 Terrell Davis	60.00	27.00
❑ 151 Brett Favre	60.00	27.00
❑ 152 Emmitt Smith	50.00	22.00
❑ 153 Dan Marino	60.00	27.00
❑ 156 Kerry Collins	6.00	2.70
❑ 163 Mark Brunell	30.00	13.50
❑ 166 Corey Dillon	20.00	9.00
❑ 167 Curtis Martin	15.00	6.75
❑ 174 Jim Druckenmiller	10.00	4.50
❑ 180 Deion Sanders	10.00	4.50
❑ 182 Shawn Springs	6.00	2.70
❑ 183 Barry Sanders	60.00	27.00
❑ 185 Marvin Harrison	12.00	5.50
❑ 187 John Elway	60.00	27.00
❑ 189 Keyshawn Johnson	10.00	4.50

1997 Playoff Absolute Pennant Autographs

	MINT	NRMT
COMPLETE SET (8)	400.00	180.00
COMMON CARD (A1-A8)	40.00	18.00
RANDOMLY INSERTED BOX TOPPER		
❑ A1 Kordell Stewart	60.00	27.00
❑ A2 Eddie George	100.00	45.00
❑ A3 Karim Abdul-Jabbar	40.00	18.00
❑ A4 Mike Alstott	50.00	22.00
❑ A5 Terry Glenn	50.00	22.00
❑ A6 Napoleon Kaufman	40.00	18.00
❑ A7 Terry Allen	40.00	18.00
❑ A8 Tim Brown	40.00	18.00

1997 Playoff Absolute Reflex

	MINT	NRMT
COMMON CARD (1-200)	12.00	5.50
SEMISTARS	25.00	11.00
UNLISTED STARS	40.00	18.00
STATED ODDS 1:288		
❑ 1 Brett Favre	200.00	90.00
❑ 3 Antonio Freeman	60.00	27.00
❑ 7 Drew Bledsoe	100.00	45.00
❑ 8 Curtis Martin	60.00	27.00
❑ 16 Mark Brunell	100.00	45.00
❑ 19 John Elway	200.00	90.00
❑ 20 Terrell Davis	200.00	90.00
❑ 23 Steve Young	80.00	36.00
❑ 25 Jerry Rice	100.00	45.00
❑ 26 Troy Aikman	100.00	45.00
❑ 28 Emmitt Smith	150.00	70.00
❑ 30 Kordell Stewart	60.00	27.00
❑ 57 Dan Marino	200.00	90.00
❑ 61 Steve McNair	60.00	27.00
❑ 62 Eddie George	120.00	55.00
❑ 78 Joey Galloway	60.00	27.00
❑ 88 Barry Sanders	200.00	90.00
❑ 95 Jamal Anderson	60.00	27.00
❑ 149 Corey Dillon	60.00	27.00
❑ 163 Jake Plummer	100.00	45.00
❑ 177 Warrick Dunn	50.00	22.00

1997 Playoff Absolute Unsung Heroes

	MINT	NRMT
COMPLETE SET (30)	25.00	11.00
COMMON CARD (1-30)	1.00	.45
SEMISTARS	1.50	.70
UNLISTED STARS	2.00	.90
STATED ODDS 1:12		
❑ 1 Larry Centers	1.50	.70
❑ 2 Jessie Tuggle	1.00	.45
❑ 3 Stevon Moore	1.00	.45
❑ 4 Mark Pike	1.00	.45
❑ 5 Anthony Johnson	1.50	.70
❑ 6 Anthony Carter RB	1.00	.45
❑ 7 Eric Bieniemy	1.00	.45
❑ 8 Jim Schwantz	1.00	.45
❑ 9 Tyrone Braxton	1.00	.45
❑ 10 Bennie Blades	1.00	.45
❑ 11 Don Beebe	1.00	.45
❑ 12 Barron Wortham	1.00	.45
❑ 13 Jason Belser	1.00	.45
❑ 14 Mickey Washington	1.00	.45
❑ 15 Dave Szott	1.00	.45
❑ 16 Zach Thomas	2.00	.90
❑ 17 Chris Walsh	1.00	.45
❑ 18 Sam Gash	1.00	.45
❑ 19 Willie Roaf	1.00	.45
❑ 20 Charles Way	1.50	.70
❑ 21 Wayne Chrebet	2.00	.90
❑ 22 Russell Maryland	1.00	.45
❑ 23 Michael Zordich	1.00	.45
❑ 24 Tim Lester	1.00	.45
❑ 25 Harold Green	1.00	.45
❑ 26 Rodney Harrison	1.00	.45
❑ 27 Gary Plummer	1.00	.45
❑ 28 Winston Moss	1.00	.45
❑ 29, Robb Thomas	1.00	.45
❑ 30 Darrick Brownlow	1.00	.45

1998 Playoff Absolute Hobby

MINT		NRMT
COMPLETE SET (200)	250.00	110.00
COMMON CARD (1-200)	.60	.25
SEMISTARS	1.25	.55
UNLISTED STARS	2.50	1.10
CONDITION SENSITIVE SET !		
COMMON ROOKIE	2.00	.90

ROOKIE SEMISTARS 3.00 1.35
ROOKIE UNLISTED STARS 5.00 2.20
COMP.SILVER HOBBY (200) 1000.00 450.00
*SILVER HOBBY STARS: 1.25X TO 2.5X HI COL.
*SILVER HOBBY YOUNG STARS: 1X TO 2X
*SILVER HOBBY RCs: .75X TO 1.5X
SILVER HOBBY STATED ODDS 1:3 HOB
COMP.RETAIL SET (200) 150.00 70.00
*RETAIL CARDS: .25X TO .5X HOBBY SSD
COMP.RETAIL RED (200) 500.00 220.00
*RED RETAIL STARS: 1.5X TO 3X BASIC RETAIL.
*RED RETAIL YOUNG STARS: 1.25X TO 2.5X
*RED RETAIL RCs: 1X TO 2X ......
RED RETAIL STATED ODDS 1:3 RETAIL

❑ 1 John Elway 12.00 5.50
❑ 2 Marcus Nash RC 8.00 3.60
❑ 3 Brian Griese RC 10.00 4.50
❑ 4 Terrell Davis 10.00 4.50
❑ 5 Rod Smith WR .... 1.25 .55
❑ 6 Shannon Sharpe .... 1.25 .55
❑ 7 Ed McCaffrey .... 1.25 .55
❑ 8 Brett Favre 12.00 5.50
❑ 9 Dorsey Levens 2.50 1.10
❑ 10 Derrick Mayes .... 1.25 .55
❑ 11 Antonio Freeman 2.50 1.10
❑ 12 Robert Brooks .... 1.25 .55
❑ 13 Mark Chmura .... 1.25 .55
❑ 14 Reggie White 2.50 1.10
❑ 15 Kordell Stewart 2.50 1.10
❑ 16 Hines Ward RC 3.00 1.35
❑ 17 Jerome Bettis 2.50 1.10
❑ 18 Charles Johnson .... .60 .25
❑ 19 Courtney Hawkins .... .60 .25
❑ 20 Will Blackwell .... .60 .25
❑ 21 Mark Bruener .... .60 .25
❑ 22 Steve Young 4.00 1.80
❑ 23 Jim Druckenmiller .... 1.25 .55
❑ 24 Garrison Hearst 2.50 1.10
❑ 25 R.W. McQuarters RC .... 2.00 .90
❑ 26 Marc Edwards .... .60 .25
❑ 27 Irv Smith .... .60 .25
❑ 28 Jerry Rice 6.00 2.70
❑ 29 Terrell Owens 2.50 1.10
❑ 30 J.J. Stokes .... 1.25 .55
❑ 31 Elvis Grbac .... 1.25 .55
❑ 32 Rashaan Shehee RC 3.00 1.35
❑ 33 Donnell Bennett .... .60 .25
❑ 34 Kimble Anders .... 1.25 .55
❑ 35 Ted Popson .... .60 .25
❑ 36 Derrick Alexander WR.... 1.25 .55
❑ 37 Tony Gonzalez .... .60 .25
❑ 38 Andre Rison .... 1.25 .55
❑ 39 Brad Johnson 2.50 1.10
❑ 40 Randy Moss RC 25.00 11.00
❑ 41 Robert Smith 2.50 1.10
❑ 42 Leroy Hoard .... .60 .25
❑ 43 Cris Carter 2.50 1.10
❑ 44 Jake Reed .... 1.25 .55
❑ 45 Drew Bledsoe 5.00 2.20
❑ 46 Tony Simmons RC 3.00 1.35
❑ 47 Chris Floyd RC .... 2.00 .90
❑ 48 Robert Edwards RC 5.00 2.20
❑ 49 Shawn Jefferson .... .60 .25
❑ 50 Ben Coates .... 1.25 .55
❑ 51 Terry Glenn 2.50 1.10
❑ 52 Trent Dilfer 2.50 1.10
❑ 53 Jacquez Green RC 6.00 2.70
❑ 54 Warrick Dunn 4.00 1.80
❑ 55 Mike Alstott 2.50 1.10
❑ 56 Reidel Anthony .... 1.25 .55
❑ 57 Bert Emanuel .... 1.25 .55
❑ 58 Warren Sapp .... 1.25 .55
❑ 59 Charlie Batch RC 10.00 4.50
❑ 60 Germane Crowell RC .. 10.00 4.50
❑ 61 Scott Mitchell .... 1.25 .55
❑ 62 Barry Sanders 12.00 5.50
❑ 63 Tommy Vardell .... .60 .25
❑ 64 Herman Moore 2.50 1.10
❑ 65 Johnnie Morton .... 1.25 .55
❑ 66 Mark Brunell 5.00 2.20
❑ 67 Jonathon Quinn RC 3.00 1.35
❑ 68 Fred Taylor RC 15.00 6.75
❑ 69 James Stewart .... 1.25 .55
❑ 70 Jimmy Smith .... 1.25 .55
❑ 71 Damon Jones .... .60 .25
❑ 72 Keenan McCardell .... 1.25 .55
❑ 73 Dan Marino 12.00 5.50
❑ 74 Larry Shannon RC .... 2.00 .90
❑ 75 John Avery RC 5.00 2.20
❑ 76 Troy Drayton .... .60 .25
❑ 77 Stanley Pritchett .... .60 .25
❑ 78 Karim Abdul-Jabbar 2.50 1.10
❑ 79 O.J. McDuffie .... 1.25 .55
❑ 80 Yatil Green .... .60 .25
❑ 81 Danny Kanell .... 1.25 .55
❑ 82 Tiki Barber .... 1.25 .55
❑ 83 Tyrone Wheatley .... 1.25 .55
❑ 84 Charles Way .... .60 .25
❑ 85 Gary Brown .... .60 .25
❑ 86 Brian Alford RC 3.00 1.35
❑ 87 Joe Jurevicius RC 3.00 1.35
❑ 88 Ike Hilliard .... 1.25 .55
❑ 89 Troy Aikman 6.00 2.70
❑ 90 Deion Sanders 2.50 1.10
❑ 91 Emmitt Smith 10.00 4.50
❑ 92 Chris Warren .... 1.25 .55
❑ 93 Daryl Johnston .... 1.25 .55
❑ 94 Michael Irvin 2.50 1.10
❑ 95 David LaFleur .... .60 .25
❑ 96 Kevin Dyson RC 6.00 2.70
❑ 97 Steve McNair 2.50 1.10
❑ 98 Eddie George 5.00 2.20
❑ 99 Yancey Thigpen .... .60 .25
❑ 100 Frank Wycheck .... .60 .25
❑ 101 Glenn Foley .... 1.25 .55
❑ 102 Vinny Testaverde .... 1.25 .55
❑ 103 Keyshawn Johnson 2.50 1.10
❑ 104 Curtis Martin 2.50 1.10
❑ 105 Keith Byars .... .60 .25
❑ 106 Scott Frost RC 3.00 1.35
❑ 107 Wayne Chrebet 2.50 1.10
❑ 108 Warren Moon 2.50 1.10
❑ 109 Ahman Green RC .... 1.25 .55
❑ 110 Steve Broussard .... .60 .25
❑ 111 Ricky Watters .... 1.25 .55
❑ 112 Joey Galloway 2.50 1.10
❑ 113 Mike Pritchard .... .60 .25
❑ 114 Brian Blades .... .60 .25
❑ 115 Gus Frerotte .... .60 .25
❑ 116 Skip Hicks RC 8.00 3.60
❑ 117 Terry Allen 2.50 1.10
❑ 118 Michael Westbrook .... 1.25 .55
❑ 119 Jamie Asher .... .60 .25
❑ 120 Leslie Shepherd .... .60 .25
❑ 121 Jeff Blake .... 1.25 .55
❑ 122 Corey Dillon 4.00 1.80
❑ 123 Carl Pickens 2.50 1.10
❑ 124 Tony McGee .... .60 .25
❑ 125 Darnay Scott .... 1.25 .55
❑ 126 Kerry Collins .... 1.25 .55
❑ 127 Fred Lane .... 1.25 .55
❑ 128 William Floyd .... .60 .25
❑ 129 Rae Carruth .... 1.25 .55
❑ 130 Wesley Walls .... 1.25 .55
❑ 131 Muhsin Muhammad .... 1.25 .55
❑ 132 Jake Plummer 8.00 3.60
❑ 133 Adrian Murrell .... 1.25 .55
❑ 134 Michael Pittman RC 3.00 1.35
❑ 135 Larry Centers .... .60 .25
❑ 136 Frank Sanders .... 1.25 .55
❑ 137 Rob Moore .... 1.25 .55
❑ 138 Andre Wadsworth RC .. 3.00 1.35
❑ 139 Mario Bates .... 1.25 .55
❑ 140 Chris Chandler .... 1.25 .55
❑ 141 Byron Hanspard .... 1.25 .55
❑ 142 Jamal Anderson 2.50 1.10
❑ 143 Terance Mathis .... 1.25 .55
❑ 144 O.J. Santiago .... .60 .25
❑ 145 Tony Martin .... 1.25 .55
❑ 146 Jammi German RC ...... 2.00 .90
❑ 147 Jim Harbaugh .... 1.25 .55
❑ 148 Errict Rhett .... 1.25 .55
❑ 149 Michael Jackson .... .60 .25
❑ 150 Pat Johnson RC 3.00 1.35
❑ 151 Eric Green .... .60 .25
❑ 152 Doug Flutie 3.00 1.35
❑ 153 Rob Johnson .... 1.25 .55
❑ 154 Antowain Smith 2.50 1.10
❑ 155 Bruce Smith .... 1.25 .55
❑ 156 Eric Moulds 2.50 1.10
❑ 157 Andre Reed .... 1.25 .55
❑ 158 Erik Kramer .... .60 .25
❑ 159 Darnell Autry .... .60 .25
❑ 160 Edgar Bennett .... .60 .25
❑ 161 Curtis Enis RC 8.00 3.60
❑ 162 Curtis Conway .... 1.25 .55
❑ 163 E.G. Green RC 3.00 1.35
❑ 164 Jerome Pathon RC 3.00 1.35
❑ 165 Peyton Manning RC .. 25.00 11.00
❑ 166 Marshall Faulk 2.50 1.10
❑ 167 Zack Crockett .... .60 .25
❑ 168 Ken Dilger .... .60 .25
❑ 169 Marvin Harrison .... 1.25 .55
❑ 170 Danny Wuerffel .... 1.25 .55
❑ 171 Lamar Smith .... .60 .25
❑ 172 Ray Zellars .... .60 .25
❑ 173 Qadry Ismail .... .60 .25
❑ 174 Sean Dawkins .... .60 .25
❑ 175 Andre Hastings .... .60 .25
❑ 176 Jeff George .... 1.25 .55
❑ 177 Charles Woodson RC .. 8.00 3.60
❑ 178 Napoleon Kaufman 2.50 1.10
❑ 179 Jon Ritchie RC 3.00 1.35
❑ 180 Desmond Howard .... 1.25 .55
❑ 181 Tim Brown 2.50 1.10
❑ 182 James Jett .... 1.25 .55
❑ 183 Rickey Dudley .... .60 .25
❑ 184 Bobby Hoying .... 1.25 .55
❑ 185 Rodney Peete .... .60 .25
❑ 186 Charlie Garner .... .60 .25
❑ 187 Irving Fryar .... 1.25 .55
❑ 188 Chris T. Jones .... .60 .25
❑ 189 Jason Dunn .... .60 .25
❑ 190 Tony Banks .... 1.25 .55
❑ 191 Robert Holcombe RC .. 5.00 2.20
❑ 192 Craig Heyward .... .60 .25
❑ 193 Isaac Bruce 2.50 1.10
❑ 194 Az-Zahir Hakim RC 8.00 3.60
❑ 195 Eddie Kennison .... 1.25 .55
❑ 196 Mikhael Ricks RC 3.00 1.35
❑ 197 Ryan Leaf RC 8.00 3.60
❑ 198 Natrone Means 2.50 1.10
❑ 199 Junior Seau .... 1.25 .55
❑ 200 Freddie Jones .... .60 .25

1998 Playoff Absolute Hobby Gold

	MINT	NRMT
COMMON CARD (1-200)........	25.00	11.00

*GOLD STARS: 15X TO 30X HI COL.
*GOLD YOUNG STARS: 12.5X TO 25X
*GOLD RCs: 5X TO 10X ....
STATED PRINT RUN 25 SERIAL #'d SETS

1998 Playoff Absolute Checklists

	MINT	NRMT
COMPLETE SET (30)	250.00	110.00
COMMON CARD (1-30)...........	4.00	1.80
SEMISTARS........................	6.00	2.70

STATED ODDS 1:19 ....
*DIE CUT SILVERS: .3X TO .6X HI COL.
DIE CUT SILVER STATED ODDS 1:25 RETAIL

❑ 1 Jake Plummer	15.00	6.75
❑ 2 Jamal Anderson	6.00	2.70
❑ 3 Jim Harbaugh	6.00	2.70
❑ 4 Rob Johnson	6.00	2.70
❑ 5 Fred Lane	6.00	2.70
❑ 6 Curtis Enis	10.00	4.50
❑ 7 Corey Dillon	8.00	3.60
❑ 8 Troy Aikman	15.00	6.75
❑ 9 Terrell Davis	25.00	11.00
❑ 10 Barry Sanders	30.00	13.50
❑ 11 Brett Favre	30.00	13.50
❑ 12 Peyton Manning	40.00	18.00
❑ 13 Mark Brunell	12.00	5.50
❑ 14 Elvis Grbac	6.00	2.70
❑ 15 Dan Marino	30.00	13.50
❑ 16 Cris Carter	6.00	2.70
❑ 17 Drew Bledsoe	12.00	5.50
❑ 18 Ray Zellars	4.00	1.80
❑ 19 Charles Way	4.00	1.80
❑ 20 Curtis Martin	6.00	2.70
❑ 21 Napoleon Kaufman	6.00	2.70
❑ 22 Irving Fryar	6.00	2.70
❑ 23 Kordell Stewart	6.00	2.70
❑ 24 Tony Banks	6.00	2.70
❑ 25 Ryan Leaf	8.00	3.60
❑ 26 Jerry Rice	15.00	6.75
❑ 27 Warren Moon	6.00	2.70
❑ 28 Warrick Dunn	8.00	3.60
❑ 29 Eddie George	12.00	5.50
❑ 30 Terry Allen	6.00	2.70

1998 Playoff Absolute Draft Picks

	MINT	NRMT
COMPLETE SET (36)	150.00	70.00
COMMON CARD (1-36)	1.50	.70
SEMISTARS	2.50	1.10
UNLISTED STARS	4.00	1.80

STATED ODDS 1:10
*BRONZE BONUS: SAME PRICE
BRONZE BONUS PACKS 1:4 BOXES
*DIE CUT SILVERS: .3X TO .6X GOLDS
DIE CUT SILVER ODDS 1:13 RETAIL
*BLUE CARDS: SAME PRICE
BLUES INSERTED IN SPECIAL RETAIL

❑ 1 Peyton Manning	30.00	13.50
❑ 2 Ryan Leaf	5.00	2.20
❑ 3 Andre Wadsworth	2.50	1.10
❑ 4 Charles Woodson	6.00	2.70
❑ 5 Curtis Enis	6.00	2.70
❑ 6 Fred Taylor	15.00	6.75
❑ 7 Kevin Dyson	5.00	2.20
❑ 8 Robert Edwards	4.00	1.80
❑ 9 Randy Moss	30.00	13.50
❑ 10 R.W. McQuarters	1.50	.70
❑ 11 John Avery	4.00	1.80
❑ 12 Marcus Nash	10.00	4.50
❑ 13 Jerome Pathon	4.00	1.80
❑ 14 Jacquez Green	6.00	2.70
❑ 15 Robert Holcombe	4.00	1.80
❑ 16 Pat Johnson	2.50	1.10
❑ 17 Germane Crowell	6.00	2.70
❑ 18 Tony Simmons	2.50	1.10
❑ 19 Joe Jurevicius	2.50	1.10
❑ 20 Mikhael Ricks	2.50	1.10
❑ 21 Charlie Batch	10.00	4.50
❑ 22 Jon Ritchie	2.50	1.10
❑ 23 Scott Frost	2.50	1.10
❑ 24 Skip Hicks	4.00	1.80
❑ 25 Brian Alford	2.50	1.10
❑ 26 E.G. Green	2.50	1.10
❑ 27 Jammi German	1.50	.70
❑ 28 Ahman Green	10.00	4.50
❑ 29 Chris Floyd	1.50	.70
❑ 30 Larry Shannon	1.50	.70
❑ 31 Jonathan Quinn	2.50	1.10
❑ 32 Rashaan Shehee	2.50	1.10
❑ 33 Brian Griese	10.00	4.50
❑ 34 Hines Ward	2.50	1.10
❑ 35 Michael Pittman	2.50	1.10
❑ 36 Az-Zahir Hakim	6.00	2.70

1998 Playoff Absolute Honors

	MINT	NRMT
COMPLETE SET (3)	400.00	180.00
COMMON CARD (PH13-PH15)	80.00	36.00

STATED ODDS 1:3970

❑ PH13 John Elway	250.00	110.00
❑ PH14 Jerome Bettis	80.00	36.00
❑ PH15 Steve Young	100.00	45.00

1998 Playoff Absolute Dan Marino Milestones

	MINT	NRMT
COMPLETE SET (15)	1800.00	800.00
COMMON CARD (1-15)	100.00	45.00

1-5: STATED ODDS 1:321 PRESTIGE
6-10: STATED ODDS 1:397 ABSOLUTE
11-15: STATED ODDS 1:385 MOMENTUM

❑ 1 Dan Marino	100.00	45.00
❑ 2 Dan Marino	100.00	45.00
❑ 3 Dan Marino	100.00	45.00
❑ 4 Dan Marino	100.00	45.00
❑ 5 Dan Marino	100.00	45.00
❑ 6 Dan Marino	100.00	45.00
❑ 7 Dan Marino	100.00	45.00
❑ 8 Dan Marino	100.00	45.00
❑ 9 Dan Marino	100.00	45.00
❑ 10 Dan Marino	100.00	45.00
❑ 11 Dan Marino	100.00	45.00
❑ 12 Dan Marino	100.00	45.00
❑ 13 Dan Marino	100.00	45.00
❑ 14 Dan Marino	100.00	45.00
❑ 15 Dan Marino	100.00	45.00

1998 Playoff Absolute Platinum Quads

	MINT	NRMT
COMPLETE SET (18)	800.00	350.00
COMMON CARD (1-18)	25.00	11.00

STATED ODDS 1:73

❑ 1 Brett Favre	120.00	55.00
John Elway		
Barry Sanders		
Warrick Dunn		
❑ 2 Dan Marino	100.00	45.00
Terrell Davis		
Napoleon Kaufman		
Jerome Bettis		
❑ 3 Jerry Rice	50.00	22.00
Brad Johnson		
Marshall Faulk		
Jimmy Smith		
❑ 4 Troy Aikman	50.00	22.00
Herman Moore		
Mark Chmura		
Gus Frerotte		
❑ 5 Steve Young	30.00	13.50
Mike Alstott		
Tiki Barber		
Keyshawn Johnson		
❑ 6 Kordell Stewart	40.00	18.00
Robert Brooks		
Karim Abdul-Jabbar		
Shannon Sharpe		
❑ 7 Mark Brunell	40.00	18.00
Dorsey Levens		
Carl Pickens		
Rob Moore		
❑ 8 Drew Bledsoe	40.00	18.00
Joey Galloway		
Tim Brown		
Fred Lane		
❑ 9 Eddie George	40.00	18.00
Rob Johnson		
Irving Fryar		
Andre Rison		
❑ 10 Jake Plummer	40.00	18.00
Antonio Freeman		
Steve McNair		
Warren Moon		
❑ 11 Emmitt Smith	80.00	36.00
Cris Carter		
Junior Seau		
Danny Kanell		
❑ 12 Corey Dillon	25.00	11.00
Jake Reed		
Curtis Martin		
Bobby Hoying		
❑ 13 Deion Sanders	25.00	11.00
Jim Druckenmiller		
Reidel Anthony		
Terry Allen		
❑ 14 Antowain Smith	25.00	11.00
Wesley Walls		
Isaac Bruce		
Terry Glenn		
❑ 15 Charlie Batch	50.00	22.00
Scott Frost		
Jonathan Quinn		
Brian Griese		
❑ 16 Kevin Dyson	80.00	36.00
Randy Moss		
Marcus Nash		
Jerome Pathon		
❑ 17 Curtis Enis	60.00	27.00
Fred Taylor		
Robert Edwards		
John Avery		
❑ 18 Peyton Manning	80.00	36.00
Ryan Leaf		
Andre Wadsworth		
Charles Woodson		

1998 Playoff Absolute Red Zone

	MINT	NRMT
COMPLETE SET (26)	200.00	90.00
COMMON CARD (1-26)	3.00	1.35

STATED ODDS 1:19
*DIE CUT RETAIL: .3X TO .6X HOBBY
DIE CUT RETAIL ODDS 1:25 RETAIL

❑ 1 Terrell Davis	20.00	9.00
❑ 2 Jerome Bettis	3.00	1.35
❑ 3 Mike Alstott	3.00	1.35
❑ 4 Brett Favre	25.00	11.00
❑ 5 Mark Brunell	10.00	4.50
❑ 6 Jeff George	3.00	1.35

❑ 7 John Elway	25.00	11.00
❑ 8 Troy Aikman	12.00	5.50
❑ 9 Steve Young	8.00	3.60
❑ 10 Kordell Stewart	4.00	1.80
❑ 11 Drew Bledsoe	10.00	4.50
❑ 12 James Jett	3.00	1.35
❑ 13 Dan Marino	25.00	11.00
❑ 14 Brad Johnson	3.00	1.35
❑ 15 Jake Plummer	12.00	5.50
❑ 16 Karim Abdul-Jabbar	3.00	1.35
❑ 17 Eddie George	10.00	4.50
❑ 18 Warrick Dunn	6.00	2.70
❑ 19 Cris Carter	3.00	1.35
❑ 20 Barry Sanders	25.00	11.00
❑ 21 Corey Dillon	6.00	2.70
❑ 22 Steve McNair	3.00	1.35
❑ 23 Herman Moore	3.00	1.35
❑ 24 Antonio Freeman	3.00	1.35
❑ 25 Dorsey Levens	3.00	1.35
❑ 26 James Stewart	3.00	1.35

1998 Playoff Absolute Shields

	MINT	NRMT
COMP.HOBBY SET (20)	250.00	110.00
COMMON CARD (1-20)	8.00	3.60
STATED ODDS 1:37		
*RETAIL DIE CUT CORNER: .3X TO .6X HOBBY		
RETAIL DIE CUT CORNER ODDS 1:49 RETAIL		

❑ 1 Terrell Davis	30.00	13.50
❑ 2 Corey Dillon	10.00	4.50
❑ 3 Dorsey Levens	8.00	3.60
❑ 4 Brett Favre	40.00	18.00
❑ 5 Warrick Dunn	10.00	4.50
❑ 6 Jerome Bettis	8.00	3.60
❑ 7 John Elway	40.00	18.00
❑ 8 Troy Aikman	20.00	9.00
❑ 9 Mark Brunell	15.00	6.75
❑ 10 Kordell Stewart	8.00	3.60
❑ 11 Eddie George	15.00	6.75
❑ 12 Jerry Rice	20.00	9.00
❑ 13 Dan Marino	40.00	18.00
❑ 14 Emmitt Smith	30.00	13.50
❑ 15 Napoleon Kaufman	8.00	3.60
❑ 16 Ryan Leaf	10.00	4.50
❑ 17 Curtis Martin	8.00	3.60
❑ 18 Peyton Manning	50.00	22.00
❑ 19 Cris Carter	8.00	3.60
❑ 20 Barry Sanders	40.00	18.00

1998 Playoff Absolute Statistically Speaking

	MINT	NRMT
COMPLETE SET (18)	200.00	90.00
COMMON CARD (1-18)	4.00	1.80
STATED ODDS 1:55		
*DIE CUT RETAIL: .3X TO .6X HOBBY		
DIE CUT RETAIL ODDS 1:73		

❑ 1 Jerry Rice	15.00	6.75
❑ 2 Barry Sanders	30.00	13.50
❑ 3 Deion Sanders	4.00	1.80
❑ 4 Brett Favre	30.00	13.50
❑ 5 Curtis Martin	4.00	1.80
❑ 6 Warrick Dunn	6.00	2.70
❑ 7 John Elway	30.00	13.50
❑ 8 Steve Young	10.00	4.50
❑ 9 Cris Carter	4.00	1.80
❑ 10 Kordell Stewart	5.00	2.20
❑ 11 Terrell Davis	25.00	11.00
❑ 12 Irving Fryar	5.00	2.20
❑ 13 Dan Marino	30.00	13.50
❑ 14 Tim Brown	4.00	1.80
❑ 15 Jerome Bettis	4.00	1.80
❑ 16 Troy Aikman	15.00	6.75
❑ 17 Napoleon Kaufman	4.00	1.80
❑ 18 Emmitt Smith	25.00	11.00

1998 Playoff Absolute Tandems

	MINT	NRMT
COMPLETE SET (6)	250.00	110.00
COMMON CARD (1-6)	15.00	6.75
ONLY ONE SIDE OF CARD IS MICRO-ETCHED		
EACH PLAYER HAS BOTH VERSIONS		
STATED ODDS 1:97 RETAIL		

❑ 1 Terrell Davis Curtis Enis	40.00	18.00
❑ 2 John Elway Ryan Leaf	50.00	22.00
❑ 3 Brett Favre Peyton Manning	60.00	27.00
❑ 4 Randy Moss Jerry Rice	60.00	27.00
❑ 5 Barry Sanders Fred Taylor	50.00	22.00
❑ 6 Deion Sanders Charles Woodson	15.00	6.75

1999 Playoff Absolute EXP

	MINT	NRMT
COMPLETE SET (200)	50.00	22.00
COMMON CARD (1-200)	.15	.07
SEMISTARS	.30	.14
UNLISTED STARS	.60	.25
COMMON ROOKIE (1-40)	.50	.23
ROOKIE SEMISTARS	.75	.35
ROOKIE UNL.STARS	1.25	.55

❑ 1 Tim Couch RC	6.00	2.70
❑ 2 Donovan McNabb RC	4.00	1.80
❑ 3 Akili Smith RC	2.50	1.10
❑ 4 Edgerrin James RC	10.00	4.50
❑ 5 Ricky Williams RC	6.00	2.70
❑ 6 Torry Holt RC	3.00	1.35
❑ 7 Champ Bailey RC	1.50	.70
❑ 8 David Boston RC	2.00	.90
❑ 9 Chris Claiborne RC	.75	.35
❑ 10 Chris McAlister RC	.75	.35
❑ 11 Daunte Culpepper RC	4.00	1.80
❑ 12 Cade McNown RC	4.00	1.80
❑ 13 Troy Edwards RC	2.00	.90
❑ 14 Kevin Johnson RC	3.00	1.35
❑ 15 James Johnson RC	1.50	.70
❑ 16 Rob Konrad RC	1.25	.55
❑ 17 Jim Kleinsasser RC	1.25	.55
❑ 18 Kevin Faulk RC	1.50	.70
❑ 19 Joe Montgomery RC	1.25	.55
❑ 20 Shaun King RC	4.00	1.80
❑ 21 Peerless Price RC	2.00	.90
❑ 22 Mike Cloud RC	1.25	.55
❑ 23 Jermaine Fazande RC	.75	.35
❑ 24 D'Wayne Bates RC	1.25	.55
❑ 25 Brock Huard RC	1.50	.70
❑ 26 Marty Booker RC	.75	.35
❑ 27 Karsten Bailey RC	.75	.35
❑ 28 Shawn Bryson RC	.50	.23
❑ 29 Jeff Paulk RC	1.25	.55
❑ 30 Sedrick Irvin RC	1.25	.55
❑ 31 Craig Yeast RC	.75	.35
❑ 32 Joe Germaine RC	1.25	.55
❑ 33 Demeane Douglas RC	1.25	.55
❑ 34 Brandon Stokley RC	.75	.35
❑ 35 Larry Parker RC	.75	.35
❑ 36 Wane McGarity RC	1.25	.55
❑ 37 Na Brown RC	1.25	.55
❑ 38 Cecil Collins RC	1.25	.55
❑ 39 Darrin Chiaverini RC	.75	.35
❑ 40 Madre Hill RC	.50	.23
❑ 41 Adrian Murrell	.30	.14
❑ 42 Jake Plummer	1.25	.55
❑ 43 Frank Sanders	.30	.14
❑ 44 Rob Moore	.30	.14
❑ 45 Andre Wadsworth	.15	.07
❑ 46 Simeon Rice	.15	.07
❑ 47 Eric Swann	.15	.07
❑ 48 Terance Mathis	.30	.14
❑ 49 Tim Dwight	.60	.25
❑ 50 Jamal Anderson	.60	.25
❑ 51 Chris Chandler	.30	.14
❑ 52 Chris Calloway	.15	.07
❑ 53 O.J. Santiago	.15	.07

No.	Player	MINT	NRMT
❑ 54	Jermaine Lewis	.30	.14
❑ 55	Priest Holmes	.60	.25
❑ 56	Scott Mitchell	.15	.07
❑ 57	Tony Banks	.30	.14
❑ 58	Rod Woodson	.30	.14
❑ 59	Andre Reed	.30	.14
❑ 60	Thurman Thomas	.30	.14
❑ 61	Bruce Smith	.30	.14
❑ 62	Rob Johnson	.30	.14
❑ 63	Eric Moulds	.60	.25
❑ 64	Doug Flutie	.75	.35
❑ 65	Antowain Smith	.60	.25
❑ 66	Tim Biakabutuka	.30	.14
❑ 67	Muhsin Muhammad	.30	.14
❑ 68	Steve Beuerlein	.15	.07
❑ 69	Bobby Engram	.30	.14
❑ 70	Curtis Conway	.30	.14
❑ 71	Curtis Enis	.60	.25
❑ 72	Edgar Bennett	.15	.07
❑ 73	Jeff Blake	.30	.14
❑ 74	Darnay Scott	.15	.07
❑ 75	Carl Pickens	.30	.14
❑ 76	Corey Dillon	.60	.25
❑ 77	Ty Detmer	.30	.14
❑ 78	Leslie Shepherd	.15	.07
❑ 79	Sedrick Shaw	.15	.07
❑ 80	Rocket Ismail	.30	.14
❑ 81	Emmitt Smith	1.50	.70
❑ 82	Michael Irvin	.30	.14
❑ 83	Troy Aikman	1.50	.70
❑ 84	Deion Sanders	.60	.25
❑ 85	Darren Woodson	.15	.07
❑ 86	Chris Warren	.15	.07
❑ 87	John Elway	2.50	1.10
❑ 88	Brian Griese	1.25	.55
❑ 89	Shannon Sharpe	.30	.14
❑ 90	Terrell Davis	1.50	.70
❑ 91	Bubby Brister	.15	.07
❑ 92	Ed McCaffrey	.30	.14
❑ 93	Rod Smith	.30	.14
❑ 94	Germane Crowell	.30	.14
❑ 95	Johnnie Morton	.30	.14
❑ 96	Barry Sanders	2.50	1.10
❑ 97	Herman Moore	.60	.25
❑ 98	Charlie Batch	1.25	.55
❑ 99	Mark Chmura	.15	.07
❑ 100	Derrick Mayes	.15	.07
❑ 101	Dorsey Levens	.60	.25
❑ 102	Brett Favre	2.50	1.10
❑ 103	Antonio Freeman	.60	.25
❑ 104	Robert Brooks	.30	.14
❑ 105	Desmond Howard	.30	.14
❑ 106	Jerome Pathon	.15	.07
❑ 107	Marvin Harrison	.60	.25
❑ 108	Peyton Manning	2.50	1.10
❑ 109	E.G. Green	.15	.07
❑ 110	Tavian Banks	.15	.07
❑ 111	Keenan McCardell	.30	.14
❑ 112	Jimmy Smith	.30	.14
❑ 113	Mark Brunell	1.00	.45
❑ 114	Fred Taylor	1.50	.70
❑ 115	Byron Bam Morris	.15	.07
❑ 116	Andre Rison	.30	.14
❑ 117	Elvis Grbac	.30	.14
❑ 118	Warren Moon	.60	.25
❑ 119	Tony Gonzalez	.30	.14
❑ 120	Derrick Alexander WR	.30	.14
❑ 121	Rashaan Shehee	.15	.07
❑ 122	Zach Thomas	.30	.14
❑ 123	Oronde Gadsden	.15	.07
❑ 124	Dan Marino	2.50	1.10
❑ 125	Karim Abdul-Jabbar	.30	.14
❑ 126	O.J. McDuffie	.30	.14
❑ 127	Jake Reed	.30	.14
❑ 128	John Randle	.30	.14
❑ 129	Randy Moss	2.50	1.10
❑ 130	Cris Carter	.60	.25
❑ 131	Randall Cunningham	.60	.25
❑ 132	Robert Smith	.60	.25
❑ 133	Terry Glenn	.60	.25
❑ 134	Ben Coates	.30	.14
❑ 135	Drew Bledsoe	1.00	.45
❑ 136	Ty Law	.15	.07
❑ 137	Tony Simmons	.15	.07
❑ 138	Eddie Kennison	.30	.14
❑ 139	Cam Cleeland	.15	.07
❑ 140	Ike Hilliard	.15	.07
❑ 141	Joe Jurevicius	.15	.07
❑ 142	Gary Brown	.15	.07
❑ 143	Kerry Collins	.30	.14
❑ 144	Tiki Barber	.15	.07
❑ 145	Jason Sehorn	.15	.07
❑ 146	Dedric Ward	.15	.07
❑ 147	Vinny Testaverde	.30	.14
❑ 148	Wayne Chrebet	.30	.14
❑ 149	Curtis Martin	.60	.25
❑ 150	Keyshawn Johnson	.60	.25
❑ 151	James Jett	.30	.14
❑ 152	Napoleon Kaufman	.60	.25
❑ 153	Tim Brown	.60	.25
❑ 154	Charles Woodson	.60	.25
❑ 155	Rickey Dudley	.15	.07
❑ 156	Charles Johnson	.15	.07
❑ 157	Duce Staley	.60	.25
❑ 158	Chris Fuamatu-Ma'afala	.15	.07
❑ 159	Jerome Bettis	.60	.25
❑ 160	Kordell Stewart	.60	.25
❑ 161	Levon Kirkland	.15	.07
❑ 162	Hines Ward	.15	.07
❑ 163	Mikhael Ricks	.15	.07
❑ 164	Natrone Means	.30	.14
❑ 165	Ryan Leaf	.60	.25
❑ 166	Jim Harbaugh	.30	.14
❑ 167	Junior Seau	.30	.14
❑ 168	Steve Young	1.00	.45
❑ 169	J.J. Stokes	.30	.14
❑ 170	Terrell Owens	.60	.25
❑ 171	Jerry Rice	1.50	.70
❑ 172	Garrison Hearst	.30	.14
❑ 173	Ricky Watters	.30	.14
❑ 174	Jon Kitna	.75	.35
❑ 175	Joey Galloway	.60	.25
❑ 176	Ahman Green	.30	.14
❑ 177	Isaac Bruce	.60	.25
❑ 178	Marshall Faulk	.60	.25
❑ 179	Trent Green	.30	.14
❑ 180	Amp Lee	.15	.07
❑ 181	Greg Hill	.15	.07
❑ 182	Warren Sapp	.15	.07
❑ 183	Hardy Nickerson	.15	.07
❑ 184	Trent Dilfer	.30	.14
❑ 185	Reidel Anthony	.30	.14
❑ 186	Jacquez Green	.30	.14
❑ 187	Warrick Dunn	.60	.25
❑ 188	Mike Alstott	.60	.25
❑ 189	Kevin Dyson	.30	.14
❑ 190	Eddie George	.75	.35
❑ 191	Yancey Thigpen	.15	.07
❑ 192	Steve McNair	.60	.25
❑ 193	Chris Sanders	.15	.07
❑ 194	Frank Wycheck	.15	.07
❑ 195	Darrell Green	.15	.07
❑ 196	Stephen Alexander	.15	.07
❑ 197	Albert Connell	.15	.07
❑ 198	Michael Westbrook	.30	.14
❑ 199	Brad Johnson	.60	.25
❑ 200	Skip Hicks	.60	.25

1999 Playoff Absolute EXP Tools of the Trade

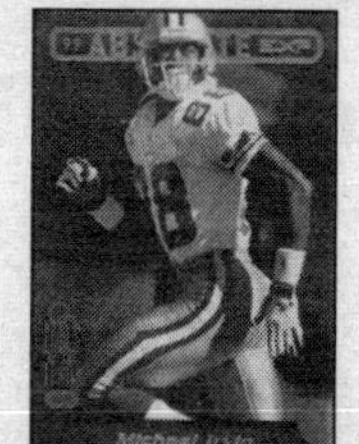

	MINT	NRMT
COMPLETE SET (200)	600.00	275.00
COMMON DEFENSE	.60	.25
*DEFENSIVE STARS: 1.5X TO 4X HI COL.		
*DEFENSIVE RCs: .6X TO 1.5X HI COL.		
DEFENSIVE PLAYERS SER.#'d OF 1000		
COMMON RECEIVER	.75	.35
*RECEIVER STARS: 2X TO 5X HI COL.		
*RECEIVER RCs: .8X TO 2X HI COL.		
RECEIVERS SERIAL #'d OF 750		
COMMON RUN.BACK	1.25	.55
*RUNNING BACK STARS: 3X TO 8X HI COL.		
*RUNNING BACK RCs: 1.2X TO 3X HI COL.		
RUNNING BACKS SERIAL #'d OF 500		
COMMON QUARTERBACK	2.00	.90
*QUARTERBACK STARS: 5X TO 12X HI COL.		
*QUARTERBACK RCs: 2X TO 5X HI COL.		
QUARTERBACKS SERIAL #'d OF 250		

1999 Playoff Absolute EXP Terrell Davis Salute

	MINT	NRMT
COMPLETE SET (5)	40.00	18.00
COMMON CARD (TD6-TD10)	10.00	4.50
STATED ODDS 1:289		
COMMON AUTO	60.00	27.00
AUTOS PRINT RUN 150 SER.#'d SETS		

No.	Player	MINT	NRMT
❑ TD6	Terrell Davis	10.00	4.50
❑ TD7	Terrell Davis	10.00	4.50
❑ TD8	Terrell Davis	10.00	4.50
❑ TD9	Terrell Davis	10.00	4.50
❑ TD10	Terrell Davis	10.00	4.50

1999 Playoff Absolute EXP Extreme Team

	MINT	NRMT
COMPLETE SET (36)	150.00	70.00
COMMON CARD (ET1-ET36)	3.00	1.35
STATED ODDS 1:25		

No.	Player	MINT	NRMT
❑ ET1	Steve Young	5.00	2.20
❑ ET2	Fred Taylor	6.00	2.70
❑ ET3	Kordell Stewart	3.00	1.35
❑ ET4	Emmitt Smith	8.00	3.60
❑ ET5	Barry Sanders	12.00	5.50
❑ ET6	Jerry Rice	8.00	3.60
❑ ET7	Jake Plummer	6.00	2.70
❑ ET8	Eric Moulds	3.00	1.35
❑ ET9	Randy Moss	10.00	4.50
❑ ET10	Steve McNair	3.00	1.35
❑ ET11	Curtis Martin	3.00	1.35
❑ ET12	Dan Marino	12.00	5.50
❑ ET13	Peyton Manning	10.00	4.50
❑ ET14	Jon Kitna	4.00	1.80
❑ ET15	Napoleon Kaufman	3.00	1.35
❑ ET16	Eddie George	4.00	1.80
❑ ET17	Brett Favre	12.00	5.50
❑ ET18	Marshall Faulk	3.00	1.35
❑ ET19	John Elway	12.00	5.50
❑ ET20	Corey Dillon	3.00	1.35
❑ ET21	Terrell Davis	8.00	3.60
❑ ET22	Randal Cunningham	3.00	1.35
❑ ET23	Mark Brunell	5.00	2.20
❑ ET24	Tim Brown	3.00	1.35
❑ ET25	Drew Bledsoe	5.00	2.20
❑ ET26	Jerome Bettis	3.00	1.35
❑ ET27	Charlie Batch	5.00	2.20

❑ ET28 Jamal Anderson	3.00	1.35
❑ ET29 Mike Alstott	3.00	1.35
❑ ET30 Troy Aikman	8.00	3.60
❑ ET31 Dorsey Levens	3.00	1.35
❑ ET32 Joey Galloway	3.00	1.35
❑ ET33 Skip Hicks	3.00	1.35
❑ ET34 Terrell Owens	3.00	1.35
❑ ET35 Keyshawn Johnson	3.00	1.35
❑ ET36 Doug Flutie	4.00	1.80

1999 Playoff Absolute EXP Heroes

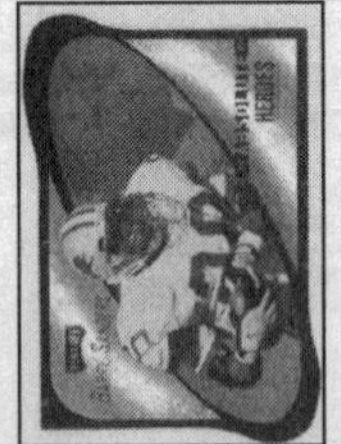

	MINT	NRMT
COMPLETE SET (24)	60.00	27.00
COMMON CARD (HE1-HE24)	2.00	.90
STATED ODDS 1:25		
EXP RETAIL CARDS HAVE SILVER BORDER		
❑ HE1 Terrell Owens	2.50	1.10
❑ HE2 Troy Aikman	5.00	2.20
❑ HE3 Cris Carter	2.50	1.10
❑ HE4 Brett Favre	8.00	3.60
❑ HE5 Jamal Anderson	2.50	1.10
❑ HE6 Doug Flutie	2.50	1.10
❑ HE7 John Elway	8.00	3.60
❑ HE8 Steve Young	3.00	1.35
❑ HE9 Jerome Bettis	2.50	1.10
❑ HE10 Emmitt Smith	5.00	2.20
❑ HE11 Drew Bledsoe	3.00	1.35
❑ HE12 Fred Taylor	4.00	1.80
❑ HE13 Dan Marino	8.00	3.60
❑ HE14 Antonio Freeman	2.50	1.10
❑ HE15 Mark Brunell	3.00	1.35
❑ HE16 Jake Plummer	4.00	1.80
❑ HE17 Warrick Dunn	2.50	1.10
❑ HE18 Peyton Manning	6.00	2.70
❑ HE19 Randy Moss	6.00	2.70
❑ HE20 Barry Sanders	8.00	3.60
❑ HE21 Keyshawn Johnson	2.50	1.10
❑ HE22 Eddie George	2.50	1.10
❑ HE23 Terrell Davis	5.00	2.20
❑ HE24 Jerry Rice	5.00	2.20

1999 Playoff Absolute EXP Rookie Reflex

	MINT	NRMT
COMPLETE SET (18)	100.00	45.00
COMMON CARD (RR1-RR18)	3.00	1.35
STATED ODDS 1:49		
❑ RR1 Peerless Price	5.00	2.20
❑ RR2 Daunte Culpepper	10.00	4.50
❑ RR3 Joe Montgomery	4.00	1.80
❑ RR4 David Boston	5.00	2.20
❑ RR5 Shaun King	10.00	4.50
❑ RR6 Champ Bailey	4.00	1.80
❑ RR7 Rob Konrad	4.00	1.80
❑ RR8 Torry Holt	8.00	3.60
❑ RR9 Kevin Faulk	4.00	1.80
❑ RR10 Ricky Williams	15.00	6.75
❑ RR11 James Johnson	4.00	1.80
❑ RR12 Edgerrin James	25.00	11.00
❑ RR13 Kevin Johnson	8.00	3.60
❑ RR14 Akili Smith	6.00	2.70
❑ RR15 Troy Edwards	5.00	2.20
❑ RR16 Donovan McNabb	10.00	4.50
❑ RR17 Cade McNown	10.00	4.50
❑ RR18 Tim Couch	15.00	6.75

1999 Playoff Absolute EXP Rookies Inserts

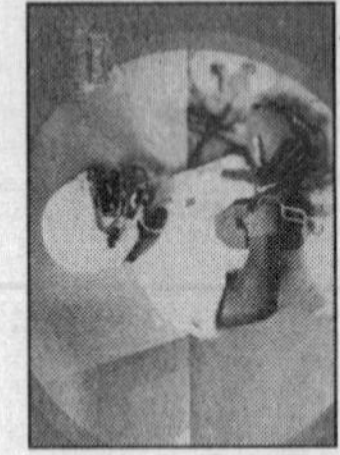

	MINT	NRMT
COMPLETE SET (36)	60.00	27.00
COMMON CARD (AR1-AR36)	.50	.23
SEMISTARS	.75	.35
UNLISTED STARS	1.25	.55
STATED ODDS 1:13		
EXP RETAIL CARDS HAVE GREEN BORDER		
❑ AR1 Champ Bailey	1.50	.70
❑ AR2 Karsten Bailey	.75	.35
❑ AR3 D'Wayne Bates	.75	.35
❑ AR4 Marty Booker	.50	.23
❑ AR5 David Boston	2.00	.90
❑ AR6 Shawn Bryson	.75	.35
❑ AR7 Chris Claiborne	.75	.35
❑ AR8 Mike Cloud	1.25	.55
❑ AR9 Cecil Collins	1.25	.55
❑ AR10 Tim Couch	6.00	2.70
❑ AR11 Daunte Culpepper	4.00	1.80
❑ AR12 Demeane Douglas	.75	.35
❑ AR13 Troy Edwards	2.00	.90
❑ AR14 Kevin Faulk	1.50	.70
❑ AR15 Jermaine Fazande	.75	.35
❑ AR16 Joe Germaine	1.25	.55
❑ AR17 Torry Holt	3.00	1.35
❑ AR18 Brock Huard	1.50	.70
❑ AR19 Edgerrin James	10.00	4.50
❑ AR20 James Johnson	1.50	.70
❑ AR21 Kevin Johnson	3.00	1.35
❑ AR22 Shaun King	4.00	1.80
❑ AR23 Jim Kleinsasser	1.25	.55
❑ AR24 Rob Konrad	1.25	.55
❑ AR25 Chris McAlister	.75	.35
❑ AR26 Travis McGriff	1.25	.55
❑ AR27 Donovan McNabb	4.00	1.80
❑ AR28 Cade McNown	4.00	1.80
❑ AR29 Joe Montgomery	1.25	.55
❑ AR30 Larry Parker	.75	.35
❑ AR31 Jeff Paulk	1.25	.55
❑ AR32 Peerless Price	2.00	.90
❑ AR33 Akili Smith	2.50	1.10
❑ AR34 Brandon Stokley	.75	.35
❑ AR35 Ricky Williams	6.00	2.70
❑ AR36 Craig Yeast	.75	.35

1999 Playoff Absolute EXP Barry Sanders Commemorative

	MINT	NRMT
COMPLETE SET (5)	70.00	32.00
COMMON CARD (RR2-RR6)	15.00	6.75
STATED ODDS 1:289		
❑ RR2 Barry Sanders	15.00	6.75
❑ RR3 Barry Sanders	15.00	6.75
❑ RR4 Barry Sanders	15.00	6.75
❑ RR5 Barry Sanders	15.00	6.75
❑ RR6 Barry Sanders	15.00	6.75

1999 Playoff Absolute EXP Team Jersey Tandems

	MINT	NRMT
COMPLETE SET (31)	1000.00	450.00
COMMON CARD (TJ1-TJ31)	15.00	6.75
SEMISTARS	25.00	11.00
UNLISTED STARS	30.00	13.50
STATED ODDS 1:97		
❑ TJ1 Jake Plummer / D.Boston	40.00	18.00
❑ TJ2 Troy Aikman / Emmitt Smith	60.00	27.00
❑ TJ3 Skip Hicks / Brad Johnson	30.00	13.50
❑ TJ4 Joe Montgomery / Ike Hilliard	15.00	6.75
❑ TJ5 Charles Johnson / Donovan McNabb	40.00	18.00
❑ TJ6 Randy Moss / Cris Carter	80.00	36.00
❑ TJ7 Warrick Dunn / Mike Alstott	25.00	11.00
❑ TJ8 Barry Sanders / Charlie Batch	80.00	36.00
❑ TJ9 Antonio Freeman / Brett Favre	80.00	36.00
❑ TJ10 Curtis Enis / Cade McNown	40.00	18.00
❑ TJ11 Tim Biakabutuka / Muhsin Muhammad	15.00	6.75
❑ TJ12 Eddie Kennison / Rusty Williams	60.00	27.00
❑ TJ13 Steve Young / Jerry Rice	60.00	27.00
❑ TJ14 Marshall Faulk / Torry Holt	25.00	11.00
❑ TJ15 Jamal Anderson / Chris Chandler	25.00	11.00
❑ TJ16 Dan Marino / O.J. McDuffie	80.00	36.00
❑ TJ17 Drew Bledsoe / Terry Glenn	40.00	18.00
❑ TJ18 Eric Moulds / Doug Flutie	40.00	18.00
❑ TJ19 Peyton Manning / Edgerrin James	100.00	45.00
❑ TJ20 Keyshawn Johnson / Wayne Chrebet	30.00	13.50
❑ TJ21 Kordell Stewart / Jerome Bettis	30.00	13.50
❑ TJ22 Mark Brunell / Fred Taylor	40.00	18.00
❑ TJ23 Tim Couch / Kevin Johnson	60.00	27.00
❑ TJ24 Carl Pickens / Akili Smith	15.00	6.75
❑ TJ25 Jermiane Lewis / Tony Banks	15.00	6.75
❑ TJ26 Eddie George / Steve McNair	40.00	18.00
❑ TJ27 Napoleon Kaufman / Tim Brown	40.00	18.00
❑ TJ28 John Elway / Terrell Davis	80.00	36.00
❑ TJ29 Jon Kitna	30.00	13.50

Joey Galloway
❑ TJ30 Andre Rison 25.00 11.00
Elvis Grbac
❑ TJ31 Natrone Means 15.00 6.75
Mikhael Ricks

1999 Playoff Absolute SSD

	MINT	NRMT
COMPLETE SET (200)	250.00	110.00
COMP.SET w/o SPs (110)	30.00	13.50
COMMON CARD (1-200)	.40	.18
SEMISTARS	.75	.35
UNLISTED STARS	1.50	.70
COMMON CA (111-129)	5.00	2.20
CANTON ABSOLUTE STATED ODDS 1:17		
COMMON CL (130-160)	3.00	1.35
CL SEMISTARS	4.00	1.80
CL UNLISTED STARS	8.00	3.60
TEAM CHECKLIST STATED ODDS 1:9		
COMMON ROOKIE (161-200)	1.00	.45
ROOKIE SEMISTARS	1.50	.70
ROOKIE UNL.STARS	2.50	1.10
*PURPLE CARDS: .6X TO 1.5X HI COL.		
*GREEN/BLUE/RED CARDS SAME PRICE		
COMMON ORANGE	3.00	1.35
*ORANGE STARS: 3X TO 8X HI COL.		
*ORANGE YOUNG STARS: 2.5X TO 6X		
*ORANGE RCs: 1.2X TO 3X HI COL.		

❑ 1 Rob Moore .75 .35
❑ 2 Frank Sanders .75 .35
❑ 3 Jake Plummer 3.00 1.35
❑ 4 Adrian Murrell .75 .35
❑ 5 Chris Chandler .75 .35
❑ 6 Jamal Anderson 1.50 .70
❑ 7 Tim Dwight 1.50 .70
❑ 8 Terance Mathis .75 .35
❑ 9 Priest Holmes 1.50 .70
❑ 10 Jermaine Lewis .75 .35
❑ 11 Antowain Smith 1.50 .70
❑ 12 Doug Flutie 2.00 .90
❑ 13 Eric Moulds 1.50 .70
❑ 14 Muhsin Muhammad .75 .35
❑ 15 Tim Biakabutuka .75 .35
❑ 16 Curtis Enis 1.50 .70
❑ 17 Curtis Conway .75 .35
❑ 18 Bobby Engram .75 .35
❑ 19 Corey Dillon 1.50 .70
❑ 20 Carl Pickens .75 .35
❑ 21 Darnay Scott .40 .18
❑ 22 Sedrick Shaw .40 .18
❑ 23 Leslie Shepherd .40 .18
❑ 24 Ty Detmer .75 .35
❑ 25 Deion Sanders 1.50 .70
❑ 26 Troy Aikman 4.00 1.80
❑ 27 Michael Irvin .75 .35
❑ 28 Emmitt Smith 4.00 1.80
❑ 29 Rocket Ismail .75 .35
❑ 30 Rod Smith WR .75 .35
❑ 31 Ed McCaffrey .75 .35
❑ 32 Bubby Brister .40 .18
❑ 33 Terrell Davis 4.00 1.80
❑ 34 Shannon Sharpe .75 .35
❑ 35 Brian Griese 3.00 1.35
❑ 36 John Elway 6.00 2.70
❑ 37 Charlie Batch 3.00 1.35
❑ 38 Herman Moore 1.50 .70
❑ 39 Barry Sanders 6.00 2.70
❑ 40 Johnnie Morton .75 .35
❑ 41 Antonio Freeman 1.50 .70
❑ 42 Brett Favre 6.00 2.70
❑ 43 Dorsey Levens 1.50 .70
❑ 44 Derrick Mayes .75 .35
❑ 45 Mark Chmura .40 .18
❑ 46 Peyton Manning 6.00 2.70
❑ 47 Marvin Harrison 1.50 .70
❑ 48 Jerome Pathon .40 .18
❑ 49 Fred Taylor 4.00 1.80
❑ 50 Mark Brunell 2.50 1.10
❑ 51 Jimmy Smith .75 .35
❑ 52 Keenan McCardell .75 .35
❑ 53 Elvis Grbac .75 .35
❑ 54 Andre Rison .75 .35
❑ 55 Byron Bam Morris .40 .18
❑ 56 O.J. McDuffie .75 .35
❑ 57 Karim Abdul-Jabbar .75 .35
❑ 58 Dan Marino 6.00 2.70
❑ 59 Oronde Gadsden .40 .18
❑ 60 Robert Smith 1.50 .70
❑ 61 Randall Cunningham 1.50 .70
❑ 62 Cris Carter 1.50 .70
❑ 63 Randy Moss 6.00 2.70
❑ 64 Drew Bledsoe 2.50 1.10
❑ 65 Ben Coates .75 .35
❑ 66 Terry Glenn 1.50 .70
❑ 67 Cam Cleeland .40 .18
❑ 68 Eddie Kennison .75 .35
❑ 69 Kerry Collins .75 .35
❑ 70 Gary Brown .40 .18
❑ 71 Joe Jurevicius .40 .18
❑ 72 Ike Hilliard .40 .18
❑ 73 Keyshawn Johnson 1.50 .70
❑ 74 Curtis Martin 1.50 .70
❑ 75 Wayne Chrebet .75 .35
❑ 76 Tim Brown 1.50 .70
❑ 77 Napoleon Kaufman 1.50 .70
❑ 78 James Jett .75 .35
❑ 79 Duce Staley 1.50 .70
❑ 80 Charles Johnson .40 .18
❑ 81 Kordell Stewart 1.50 .70
❑ 82 Jerome Bettis 1.50 .70
❑ 83 Chris Fuamatu-Ma'afala .40 .18
❑ 84 Jim Harbaugh .75 .35
❑ 85 Ryan Leaf 1.50 .70
❑ 86 Natrone Means .75 .35
❑ 87 Mikhael Ricks .40 .18
❑ 88 Garrison Hearst .75 .35
❑ 89 Jerry Rice 4.00 1.80
❑ 90 Terrell Owens 1.50 .70
❑ 91 J.J. Stokes .75 .35
❑ 92 Steve Young 2.50 1.10
❑ 93 Joey Galloway 1.50 .70
❑ 94 Jon Kitna 2.00 .90
❑ 95 Ricky Watters .75 .35
❑ 96 Trent Green .75 .35
❑ 97 Marshall Faulk 1.50 .70
❑ 98 Isaac Bruce 1.50 .70
❑ 99 Mike Alstott 1.50 .70
❑ 100 Warrick Dunn 1.50 .70
❑ 101 Jacquez Green .75 .35
❑ 102 Reidel Anthony .75 .35
❑ 103 Trent Dilfer .75 .35
❑ 104 Steve McNair 1.50 .70
❑ 105 Yancey Thigpen .40 .18
❑ 106 Eddie George 2.00 .90
❑ 107 Kevin Dyson .75 .35
❑ 108 Skip Hicks 1.50 .70
❑ 109 Brad Johnson 1.50 .70
❑ 110 Michael Westbrook .75 .35
❑ 111 Thurman Thomas CA .75 .35
❑ 112 Andre Reed CA .75 .35
❑ 113 Emmitt Smith CA 10.00 4.50
❑ 114 Troy Aikman CA 10.00 4.50
❑ 115 Deion Sanders CA 1.50 .70
❑ 116 John Elway CA 15.00 6.75
❑ 117 Terrell Davis CA 10.00 4.50
❑ 118 Barry Sanders CA 15.00 6.75
❑ 119 Brett Favre CA 15.00 6.75
❑ 120 Warren Moon CA 1.50 .70
❑ 121 Dan Marino CA 15.00 6.75
❑ 122 Cris Carter CA 1.50 .70
❑ 124 Tim Brown CA 1.50 .70
❑ 125 Jerome Bettis CA 1.50 .70
❑ 126 Junior Seau CA .75 .35
❑ 127 Jerry Rice CA 10.00 4.50
❑ 127 Vinny Testaverde CA .75 .35
❑ 128 Steve Young CA 6.00 2.70
❑ 129 Eddie George CA .40 .18
❑ 130 Cardinals CL .40 .18
Rob Moore
Jake Plummer
Adrian Murrell
Frank Sanders
David Boston
❑ 131 Falcons CL .40 .18
Jamal Anderson
Chris Chandler
Terance Mathis
Tim Dwight
Jeff Paulk
❑ 132 Ravens CL .40 .18
Priest Holmes
Chris McAllister
Jermaine Lewis
Brandon Stokely
❑ 133 Bills CL .40 .18
Antowain Smith
Thurman Thomas
Shawn Bryson
Doug Flutie
Andre Reed
Eric Moulds
Peerless Price
❑ 134 Panthers CL .40 .18
Tim Biakabutuka
Muhsin Muhammad
❑ 135 Bears CL .40 .18
❑ 136 Bengals CL .40 .18
Corey Dillon
Carl Pickens
Akili Smith
Darnay Scott
Craig Yeast
❑ 137 Browns CL .40 .18
Sedrick Shaw
Tim Couch
Madre Hill
Leslie Shepard
Kevin Johnson
Ty Detmer
Darrin Chiaverini
❑ 138 Cowboys CL .40 .18
Emmitt Smith
Michael Irvin
Deion Sanders
Wane McGarity
Rocket Ismail
Troy Aikman
❑ 139 Broncos CL .40 .18
John Elway
Terrell Davis
Bubby Brister
Ed McCaffrey
Rod Smith
Brian Griese
Shannon Sharpe
❑ 140 Lions CL .40 .18
Barry Sanders
Charlie Batch
Herman Moore
Chris Claiborne
Sedrick Irvin
❑ 141 Packers CL .40 .18
Brett Favre
Dorsey Levens
Derrick Mayes
Mark Chmura
Antonio Freeman
❑ 142 Colts CL .40 .18
Peyton Manning
Jerome Pathon
Marvin Harrison
Edgerrin James
❑ 143 Jaguars CL .40 .18
Mark Brunell
Fred Taylor
Jimmy Smith
Keenan McCardell

❑ 144 Chiefs CL .... .40 .18
Andre Rison
Elvis Grbac
Warren Moon
Michael Cloud
Byron Bam Morris
Larry Parker
❑ 145 Dolphins CL.......... .40 .18
Dan Marino
Rob Konrad
Cecil Collins
James Johnson
❑ 146 Vikings CL.......... .40 .18
Randy Moss
Robert Smith
Jim Kleinsasser
Randall Cunningham
Cris Carter
Daunte Culpepper
❑ 147 Patriots CL .... .40 .18
Drew Bledsoe
Terry Glenn
Ben Coates
Kevin Faulk
❑ 148 Saints CL.......... .40 .18
Ricky Williams
Eddie Kennison
Cam Cleeland
❑ 149 Giants CL .... .40 .18
❑ 150 Jets CL .... .40 .18
Keyshawn Johnson
Wayne Chrebet
Curtis Martin
Vinny Testaverde
❑ 151 Raiders CL .... .40 .18
Tim Brown
Napoleon Kaufman
James Jett
Dameane Douglas
❑ 152 EaglesCL.......... .40 .18
Duce Staley
Donovan McNabb
Na Brown
Charles Johnson
❑ 153 Steelers CL .... .40 .18
❑ 154 Chargers CL .... .40 .18
Jim Harbough
Michael Ricks
Ryan Leaf
Junior Seau
Natrone Means
Jermaine Fazande
❑ 155 49ers CL .... .40 .18
Steve Young
Jerry Rice
Terrell Owens
J.J. Stokes
❑ 156 Seahawks CL .... .40 .18
Joey Galloway
Jon Kitna
Ricky Watters
Brock Huard
Karsten Bailey
❑ 157 Rams CL .... .40 .18
Trent Green
Torry Holt
Marshall Faulk
Isaac Bruce
Joe Germaine
❑ 158 Buccaneers CL .... .40 .18
❑ 159 Titans CL.......... .40 .18
Eddie George
Yancy Thigpen
Kevin Dyson
Steve McNair
❑ 160 Redskins CL .... .40 .18
Brad Johnson
Champ Bailey
Skip Hicks
Michael Westbrook
❑ 161 Tim Couch RC.......... 12.00 5.50
❑ 162 Donovan McNabb RC .. 8.00 3.60
❑ 163 Akili Smith RC 5.00 2.20
❑ 164 Edgerrin James RC.... 20.00 9.00
❑ 165 Ricky Williams RC...... 12.00 5.50
❑ 166 Torry Holt RC 6.00 2.70
❑ 167 Champ Bailey RC 3.00 1.35
❑ 168 David Boston RC.......... 4.00 1.80
❑ 169 Chris Claiborne RC 2.50 1.10
❑ 170 Chris McAlister RC ...... 1.50 .70
❑ 171 Daunte Culpepper RC.. 8.00 3.60
❑ 172 Cade McNown RC 8.00 3.60
❑ 173 Troy Edwards RC 4.00 1.80
❑ 174 Kevin Johnson RC 6.00 2.70
❑ 175 James Johnson RC...... 3.00 1.35
❑ 176 Rob Konrad RC.......... 2.50 1.10
❑ 177 Jim Kleinsasser RC...... 2.50 1.10
❑ 178 Kevin Faulk RC 3.00 1.35
❑ 179 Joe Montgomery RC 2.50 1.10
❑ 180 Shaun King RC 8.00 3.60
❑ 181 Peerless Price RC........ 4.00 1.80
❑ 182 Mike Cloud RC 2.50 1.10
❑ 183 Jermaine Fazande RC 1.50 .70
❑ 184 D'Wayne Bates RC 2.50 1.10
❑ 185 Brock Huard RC 3.00 1.35
❑ 186 Marty Booker RC.......... 1.50 .70
❑ 187 Karsten Bailey RC........ 1.50 .70
❑ 188 Shawn Bryson RC........ 1.00 .45
❑ 189 Jeff Paulk RC 2.50 1.10
❑ 190 Sedrick Irvin RC 2.50 1.10
❑ 191 Craig Yeast RC.......... 1.50 .70
❑ 192 Joe Germaine RC 2.50 1.10
❑ 193 Dameane Douglas RC 2.50 1.10
❑ 194 Brandon Stokley RC .... 1.50 .70
❑ 195 Larry Parker RC .... 1.50 .70
❑ 196 Wane McGarity RC ...... 1.50 .70
❑ 197 Na Brown RC 2.50 1.10
❑ 198 Cecil Collins RC 2.50 1.10
❑ 199 Darrin Chiaverini RC .... 1.50 .70
❑ 200 Madre Hill RC .... 1.00 .45

1999 Playoff Absolute SSD Coaches Collection Gold

	MINT	NRMT
COMMON CARD (1-200)........	12.00	5.50

*GOLD STARS: 12X TO 30X HI COL.
*GOLD YOUNG STARS: 10X TO 25X
*GOLD CANTON ABSOLUTE: 4X TO 10X
*GOLD CHECKLISTS: 3X TO 8X..
*GOLD RCs: 4X TO 10X ....
GOLD PRINT RUN 25 SER. #'d SETS

1999 Playoff Absolute SSD Coaches Collection Silver

	MINT	NRMT
COMPLETE SET (200)	400.00	180.00
COMMON CARD (1-200)..........	1.50	.70

*SILVER STARS: 1.5X TO 4X HI COL.
*SILVER YOUNG STARS: 1.2X TO 3X
*SILVER CANTON ABSOLUTE: .6X TO 1.5X
*SILVER CHECKLISTS: .75X TO 2X
*SILVER RCs: .6X TO 1.5X ....
SILVER PRINT RUN 500 SER.#'d SETS

1999 Playoff Absolute SSD Honors Red

	MINT	NRMT
COMPLETE SET (150)	600.00	275.00
COMMON RED (1-200)	3.00	1.35

*RED STARS: 3X TO 8X HI COL.
*RED YOUNG STARS: 2.5X TO 6X
*RED RCs: .8X TO 2X ....
RED PRINT RUN 200 SERIAL #'d SETS

COMMON GOLD	15.00	6.75

*GOLD CARDS: 1.5X TO 4X REDS
GOLD PRINT RUN 25 SERIAL #'d SETS

COMMON SILVER..........	5.00	2.20

*SILVER CARDS: .6X TO 1.5X REDS
SILVER PRINT RUN 100 SERIAL #'d SETS

1999 Playoff Absolute SSD Boss Hogs Autographs

	MINT	NRMT
COMPLETE SET (10)	600.00	275.00
COMMON CARD (BH1-BH10)	30.00	13.50

STATED PRINT RUN 400 SER.#'d SETS

❑ BH1 Ricky Williams 120.00 55.00
❑ BH2 Terrell Davis.......... 60.00 27.00
❑ BH3 Mike Alstott.......... 30.00 13.50
❑ BH4 Jake Plummer 50.00 22.00
❑ BH5 Vinny Testaverde 30.00 13.50
❑ BH6 Cris Carter 40.00 18.00
❑ BH7 Peyton Manning...... 120.00 55.00
❑ BH8 Natrone Means.......... 30.00 13.50
❑ BH9 Eddie George.......... 50.00 22.00
❑ BH10 Barry Sanders 150.00 70.00

1999 Playoff Absolute SSD Force

	MINT	NRMT
COMPLETE SET (36)	150.00	70.00
COMMON CARD (AF1-AF36) ..	4.00	1.80

STATED ODDS 1:19 ....

❑ AF1 Steve Young.......... 6.00 2.70
❑ AF2 Fred Taylor.......... 8.00 3.60
❑ AF3 Kordell Stewart 5.00 2.20

Card	MINT	NRMT
❑ AF4 Emmitt Smith	10.00	4.50
❑ AF5 Barry Sanders	15.00	6.75
❑ AF6 Jerry Rice	10.00	4.50
❑ AF7 Jake Plummer	8.00	3.60
❑ AF8 Eric Moulds	5.00	2.20
❑ AF9 Randy Moss	12.00	5.50
❑ AF10 Steve McNair	5.00	2.20
❑ AF11 Curtis Martin	5.00	2.20
❑ AF12 Dan Marino	15.00	6.75
❑ AF13 Peyton Manning	12.00	5.50
❑ AF14 Jon Kitna	5.00	2.20
❑ AF15 Napoleon Kaufman	5.00	2.20
❑ AF16 Keyshawn Johnson	5.00	2.20
❑ AF17 Eddie George	5.00	2.20
❑ AF18 Antonio Freeman	5.00	2.20
❑ AF19 Doug Flutie	5.00	2.20
❑ AF20 Brett Favre	15.00	6.75
❑ AF21 Marshall Faulk	5.00	2.20
❑ AF22 John Elway	15.00	6.75
❑ AF23 Warrick Dunn	5.00	2.20
❑ AF24 Corey Dillon	5.00	2.20
❑ AF25 Terrell Davis	10.00	4.50
❑ AF26 Randall Cunningham	5.00	2.20
❑ AF27 Cris Carter	5.00	2.20
❑ AF28 Mark Brunell	6.00	2.70
❑ AF29 Tim Brown	5.00	2.20
❑ AF30 Drew Bledsoe	6.00	2.70
❑ AF31 Jerome Bettis	5.00	2.20
❑ AF32 Charlie Batch	6.00	2.70
❑ AF33 Jamal Anderson	5.00	2.20
❑ AF34 Mike Alstott	5.00	2.20
❑ AF35 Troy Aikman	10.00	4.50
❑ AF36 Terrell Owens	5.00	2.20

1999 Playoff Absolute SSD Heroes

	MINT	NRMT
COMPLETE SET (24)	120.00	55.00
COMMON CARD (HE1-HE24)	3.00	1.35
STATED ODDS 1:19		
SSD HOBBY CARDS HAVE GOLD BORDER		
*JUMBOS: .3X TO .8X HI COL.		
JUMBOS ONE PER HOBBY BOX		
*REDS: 3X TO 8X HI COL.		
REDS STATED PRINT RUN 100 SETS		

Card	MINT	NRMT
❑ HE1 Terrell Owens	4.00	1.80
❑ HE2 Troy Aikman	8.00	3.60
❑ HE3 Cris Carter	4.00	1.80
❑ HE4 Brett Favre	12.00	5.50
❑ HE5 Jamal Anderson	4.00	1.80
❑ HE6 Doug Flutie	4.00	1.80
❑ HE7 John Elway	12.00	5.50
❑ HE8 Steve Young	5.00	2.20
❑ HE9 Jerome Bettis	4.00	1.80
❑ HE10 Emmitt Smith	8.00	3.60
❑ HE11 Drew Bledsoe	5.00	2.20
❑ HE12 Fred Taylor	6.00	2.70
❑ HE13 Dan Marino	12.00	5.50
❑ HE14 Antonio Freeman	4.00	1.80
❑ HE15 Mark Brunell	5.00	2.20
❑ HE16 Jake Plummer	6.00	2.70
❑ HE17 Warrick Dunn	4.00	1.80
❑ HE18 Peyton Manning	10.00	4.50
❑ HE19 Randy Moss	10.00	4.50
❑ HE20 Barry Sanders	12.00	5.50
❑ HE21 Keyshawn Johnson	4.00	1.80
❑ HE22 Eddie George	4.00	1.80
❑ HE23 Terrell Davis	8.00	3.60
❑ HE24 Jerry Rice	8.00	3.60

1999 Playoff Absolute SSD Rookie Roundup

	MINT	NRMT
COMPLETE SET (18)	100.00	45.00
COMMON CARD (RR1-RR18)	3.00	1.35
SEMISTARS	4.00	1.80
1ST ROUNDER STATED ODDS 1:46		
2ND ROUNDER STATED ODDS 1:69		

Card	MINT	NRMT
❑ RR1 Peerless Price 2	8.00	3.60
❑ RR2 Daunte Culpepper	10.00	4.50
❑ RR3 Joe Montgomery 2	3.00	1.35
❑ RR4 David Boston	5.00	2.20
❑ RR5 Shaun King 2	15.00	6.75
❑ RR6 Champ Bailey	3.00	1.35
❑ RR7 Rob Konrad 2	3.00	1.35
❑ RR8 Torry Holt	8.00	3.60
❑ RR9 Kevin Faulk 2	6.00	2.70
❑ RR10 Ricky Williams	15.00	6.75
❑ RR11 James Johnson 2	4.00	1.80
❑ RR12 Edgerrin James	25.00	11.00
❑ RR13 Kevin Johnson 2	12.00	5.50
❑ RR14 Akili Smith	6.00	2.70
❑ RR15 Troy Edwards	5.00	2.20
❑ RR16 Donovan McNabb	10.00	4.50
❑ RR17 Cade McNown	10.00	4.50
❑ RR18 Tim Couch	15.00	6.75

1999 Playoff Absolute SSD Rookies Inserts

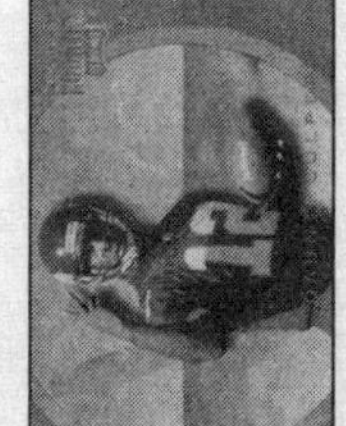

	MINT	NRMT
COMPLETE SET (36)	80.00	36.00
COMMON CARD (AR1-AR36)	.75	.35
SEMISTARS	1.25	.55
UNLISTED STARS	2.00	.90
STATED ODDS 1:10		
BASE SSD HOBBY CARDS HAVE BLUE BORDER		
*REDS: 3X TO 8X HI COL.		
RED STATED PRINT RUN 100 SER.#'d SETS		

Card	MINT	NRMT
❑ AR1 Champ Bailey	2.50	1.10
❑ AR2 Karsten Bailey	1.25	.55
❑ AR3 D'Wayne Bates	1.25	.55
❑ AR4 Marty Booker	1.25	.55
❑ AR5 David Boston	3.00	1.35
❑ AR6 Shawn Bryson	.75	.35
❑ AR7 Chris Claiborne	1.25	.55
❑ AR8 Mike Cloud	2.00	.90
❑ AR9 Cecil Collins	2.00	.90
❑ AR10 Tim Couch	10.00	4.50
❑ AR11 Daunte Culpepper	6.00	2.70
❑ AR12 Demeane Douglas	2.00	.90
❑ AR13 Troy Edwards	3.00	1.35
❑ AR14 Kevin Faulk	2.50	1.10
❑ AR15 Jermaine Fazande	1.25	.55
❑ AR16 Joe Germaine	2.00	.90
❑ AR17 Torry Holt	5.00	2.20
❑ AR18 Brock Huard	2.50	1.10
❑ AR19 Edgerrin James	15.00	6.75
❑ AR20 James Johnson	2.50	1.10
❑ AR21 Kevin Johnson	5.00	2.20
❑ AR22 Shaun King	6.00	2.70
❑ AR23 Jim Kleinsasser	2.00	.90
❑ AR24 Rob Konrad	2.00	.90
❑ AR25 Chris McAlister	1.25	.55
❑ AR26 Travis McGriff	2.00	.90
❑ AR27 Donovan McNabb	6.00	2.70
❑ AR28 Cade McNown	6.00	2.70
❑ AR29 Joe Montgomery	2.00	.90
❑ AR30 Larry Parker	1.25	.55
❑ AR31 Jeff Paulk	2.00	.90
❑ AR32 Peerless Price	3.00	1.35
❑ AR33 Akili Smith	4.00	1.80
❑ AR34 Brandon Stokley	.75	.35
❑ AR35 Ricky Williams	10.00	4.50
❑ AR36 Craig Yeast	1.25	.55

1999 Playoff Absolute SSD Team Jersey Quad

	MINT	NRMT
COMPLETE SET (31)	1500.00	700.00
COMMON CARD (TQ1-TQ31)	30.00	13.50
SEMISTARS	40.00	18.00
SOME CARDS ISSUED VIA MAIL REDEMPTION		
STATED ODDS 1:73		

Card	MINT	NRMT
❑ TQ1 David Boston Adrian Murrell Jake Plummer Frank Sanders	50.00	22.00
❑ TQ2 Troy Aikman Michael Irvin Deion Sanders Emmitt Smith	80.00	36.00
❑ TQ3 Champ Bailey Skip Hicks Brad Johnson Michael Westbrook	40.00	18.00
❑ TQ4 Gary Brown Kerry Collins Ike Hilliard Joe Montgomery	30.00	13.50
❑ TQ5 Na Brown Charles Johnson Donovan McNabb Duce Staley	50.00	22.00
❑ TQ6 Cris Carter Randall Cunningham Randy Moss Robert Smith	100.00	45.00
❑ TQ7 Mike Alstott Anthony Reidel Trent Dilfer Warrick Dunn	30.00	13.50
❑ TQ8 Charlie Batch Herman Moore Johnnie Morton Barry Sanders	100.00	45.00
❑ TQ9 Mark Chmura Brett Favre Antonio Freeman Dorsey Levens	100.00	45.00
❑ TQ10 Curtis Conway Bobby Engram Curtis Enis Cade McNown	50.00	22.00
❑ TQ11 Steve Beuerlein Tim Biakabutuka Muhsin Muhammad	30.00	13.50

Wesley Walls
❑ TQ12 Cam Cleeland 60.00 27.00
Eddie Kennison
Willie Roaf
Ricky Williams
❑ TQ13 Garrison Hearst 80.00 36.00
Terrell Owens
Jerry Rice
Steve Young
❑ TQ14 Bruce Isaac 40.00 18.00
Marshall Faulk
Trent Green
Torry Holt
❑ TQ15 Jamal Anderson 30.00 13.50
Chris Chandler
Tim Dwight
Terrance Mathis
❑ TQ16 Karim Abdul-Jabbar 80.00 36.00
Cecil Collins
Dan Marino
O.J. McDuffie
❑ TQ17 Drew Bledsoe.......... 50.00 22.00
Ben Coates
Kevin Faulk
Terry Glenn
❑ TQ18 Doug Flutie............. 50.00 22.00
Eric Moulds
Peerless Price
Antowain Smith
❑ TQ19 Marvin Harrison 100.00 45.00
Edgerrin James
Peyton Manning
Jerome Pathon
❑ TQ20 Wayne Chrebet 40.00 18.00
Keyshawn Johnson
Curtis Martin
Vinny Testaverde
❑ TQ21 Jerome Bettis 40.00 18.00
Troy Edwards
Kordell Stewart
Hines Ward
❑ TQ22 Mark Brunell............ 50.00 22.00
Keenan McCardell
Jimmy Smith
Fred Taylor
❑ TQ23 Tim Couch 80.00 36.00
Kevin Johnson
Sedrick Shaw
Leslie Shepherd
❑ TQ24 Corey Dillon 30.00 13.50
Carl Pickens
Darnay Scott
Akili Smith
❑ TQ25 Tony Banks 30.00 13.50
Priest Holmes
Jermaine Lewis
Chris McAlister
❑ TQ26 Kevin Dyson........... 50.00 22.00
Eddie George
Steve McNair
Yancey Thigpen
❑ TQ27 Tim Brown 50.00 22.00
James Jett
Napoleon Kaufman
Charles Woodson
❑ TQ28 Terrell Davis............ 60.00 27.00
John Elway
Ed McCaffrey
Rod Smith
❑ TQ29 Joey Galloway 40.00 18.00
Ahman Green
Jon Kitna
Ricky Watters
❑ TQ30 Mike Cloud 30.00 13.50
Elvis Grbac
Byron Bam Morris
Andre Rison
❑ TQ31 Ryan Leaf................ 30.00 13.50
Natrone Means
Mikhael Ricks
Junior Seau

1993 Playoff Contenders

	MINT	NRMT
COMPLETE SET (150)	25.00	11.00
COMMON CARD (1-150)...........	.10	.05
SEMISTARS..............................	.20	.09
UNLISTED STARS......................	.40	.18
COMP.RICK MIRER SET (5) ..	40.00	18.00
MIRER STATED ODDS 1:80		

❑ 1 Brett Favre 3.00 1.35
❑ 2 Thurman Thomas .... .40 .18
❑ 3 Barry Word .... .10 .05
❑ 4 Herman Moore .... .75 .35
❑ 5 Reggie Langhorne............. .10 .05
❑ 6 Wilber Marshall .... .10 .05
❑ 7 Ricky Watters .... .40 .18
❑ 8 Marcus Allen .... .40 .18
❑ 9 Jeff Hostetler .... .20 .09
❑ 10 Steve Young .... 1.00 .45
❑ 11 Bobby Hebert .... .10 .05
❑ 12 David Klingler .... .10 .05
❑ 13 Craig Heyward .... .20 .09
❑ 14 Andre Reed....................... .20 .09
❑ 15 Tommy Vardell .... .10 .05
❑ 16 Anthony Carter .... .20 .09
❑ 17 Mel Gray .... .20 .09
❑ 18 Dan Marino 2.50 1.10
❑ 19 Haywood Jeffires.............. .20 .09
❑ 20 Joe Montana 2.50 1.10
❑ 21 Tim Brown .... .40 .18
❑ 22 Jim McMahon .... .10 .05
❑ 23 Scott Mitchell.................... .40 .18
❑ 24 Rickey Jackson .... .10 .05
❑ 25 Troy Aikman .... 1.50 .70
❑ 26 Rodney Hampton .... .40 .18
❑ 27 Fred Barnett .... .20 .09
❑ 28 Gary Clark......................... .20 .09
❑ 29 Barry Foster .... .20 .09
❑ 30 Brian Blades .... .20 .09
❑ 31 Tim McDonald................... .10 .05
❑ 32 Kelvin Martin .... .10 .05
❑ 33 Henry Jones .... .10 .05
❑ 34 Eric Pegram .... .20 .09
❑ 35 Don Beebe .... .10 .05
❑ 36 Eric Metcalf .... .20 .09
❑ 37 Charles Haley .... .20 .09
❑ 38 Robert Delpino .... .10 .05
❑ 39 Leonard Russell UER ...... .20 .09
(Detroit Lions logo on back)
❑ 40 Jackie Harris .... .10 .05
❑ 41 Ernest Givins..................... .20 .09
❑ 42 Willie Davis .... .40 .18
❑ 43 Alexander Wright............. .10 .05
❑ 44 Keith Byars .... .10 .05
❑ 45 Dave Meggett .... .10 .05
❑ 46 Johnny Johnson .... .10 .05
❑ 47 Mark Bavaro .... .10 .05
❑ 48 Seth Joyner....................... .10 .05
❑ 49 Junior Seau .... .40 .18
❑ 50 Emmitt Smith................. 2.50 1.10
❑ 51 Shannon Sharpe .... .40 .18
❑ 52 Rodney Peete .... .10 .05
❑ 53 Andre Rison .... .20 .09
❑ 54 Cornelius Bennett .... .20 .09
❑ 55 Mark Carrier WR .... .20 .09
❑ 56 Mark Clayton.................... .10 .05
❑ 57 Warren Moon .... .40 .18
❑ 58 J.J. Birden........................ .10 .05
❑ 59 Howie Long...................... .20 .09
❑ 60 Irving Fryar .... .20 .09
❑ 61 Mark Jackson .... .10 .05
❑ 62 Eric Martin........................ .10 .05
❑ 63 Herschel Walker .... .20 .09
❑ 64 Cortez Kennedy .... .20 .09
❑ 65 Steve Beuerlein................ .10 .05
❑ 66 Jim Kelly .... .40 .18
❑ 67 Bernie Kosar .... .20 .09
❑ 68 Pat Swilling .... .10 .05
❑ 69 Michael Irvin .... .40 .18
❑ 70 Harvey Williams .... .20 .09
❑ 71 Steve Smith...................... .10 .05
❑ 72 Wade Wilson.................... .10 .05
❑ 73 Phil Simms .... .20 .09
❑ 74 Vinny Testaverde .... .20 .09
❑ 75 Barry Sanders 2.50 1.10
❑ 76 Ken Norton Jr. .... .20 .09
❑ 77 Rod Woodson .... .40 .18
❑ 78 Webster Slaughter .... .10 .05
❑ 79 Derrick Thomas................ .40 .18
❑ 80 Mike Sherrard .... .10 .05
❑ 81 Calvin Williams .... .20 .09
❑ 82 Jay Novacek .... .20 .09
❑ 83 Michael Brooks .... .10 .05
❑ 84 Randall Cunningham........ .40 .18
❑ 85 Chris Warren.................... .20 .09
❑ 86 Johnny Mitchell .... .10 .05
❑ 87 Jim Harbaugh .... .40 .18
❑ 88 Rod Bernstine .... .10 .05
❑ 89 John Elway 2.50 1.10
❑ 90 Jerry Rice .... 1.50 .70
❑ 91 Brent Jones...................... .20 .09
❑ 92 Cris Carter........................ .75 .35
❑ 93 Alvin Harper .... .20 .09
❑ 94 Horace Copeland RC ...... .20 .09
❑ 95 Raghib Ismail .... .20 .09
❑ 96 Darrin Smith RC .... .20 .09
❑ 97 Reggie Brooks RC .... .20 .09
❑ 98 Demetrius DuBose RC .... .10 .05
❑ 99 Eric Curry RC .... .10 .05
❑ 100 Rick Mirer RC .... .75 .35
❑ 101 Carlton Gray RC UER .... .10 .05
(Name spelled Grey on front)
❑ 102 Dana Stubblefield RC .... .40 .18
❑ 103 Todd Kelly RC .... .10 .05
❑ 104 Natrone Means RC ...... 1.50 .70
❑ 105 Darrien Gordon RC .... .10 .05
❑ 106 Deon Figures RC .... .20 .09
❑ 107 Garrison Hearst RC...... 2.00 .90
❑ 108 Ronald Moore RC .... .20 .09
❑ 109 Leonard Renfro RC .... .10 .05
❑ 110 Lester Holmes............... .10 .05
❑ 111 Vaughn Hebron RC........ .10 .05
❑ 112 Marvin Jones RC........... .10 .05
❑ 113 Irv Smith RC .... .10 .05
❑ 114 Willie Roaf RC .... .20 .09
❑ 115 Derek Brown RBK RC.... .20 .09
❑ 116 Vincent Brisby RC......... .40 .18
❑ 117 Drew Bledsoe RC 5.00 2.20
❑ 118 Gino Torretta RC............ .20 .09
❑ 119 Robert Smith RC .... 2.00 .90
❑ 120 Qadry Ismail RC .... .40 .18
❑ 121 O.J. McDuffie RC .... 1.50 .70
❑ 122 Terry Kirby RC .... .40 .18
❑ 123 Troy Drayton RC .... .20 .09
❑ 124 Jerome Bettis RC .... 2.00 .90
❑ 125 Patrick Bates RC........... .10 .05
❑ 126 Roosevelt Potts RC........ .10 .05
❑ 127 Tom Carter RC .... .20 .09
❑ 128 Patrick Robinson RC...... .10 .05
❑ 129 Brad Hopkins RC .... .10 .05
❑ 130 George Teague RC........ .20 .09
❑ 131 Wayne Simmons RC...... .10 .05
❑ 132 Mark Brunell RC 5.00 2.20
❑ 133 Ryan McNeil RC .... .10 .05
❑ 134 Dan Williams RC........... .10 .05
❑ 135 Glyn Milburn RC .... .40 .18
❑ 136 Kevin Williams RC......... .40 .18
❑ 137 Derrick Lassic RC .... .10 .05
❑ 138 Steve Everitt RC .... .10 .05
❑ 139 Lance Gunn RC .... .10 .05
❑ 140 John Copeland RC .... .20 .09
❑ 141 Curtis Conway RC........ 1.00 .45

❑ 142 Thomas Smith RC	.20	.09
❑ 143 Russell Copeland RC	.20	.09
❑ 144 Lincoln Kennedy RC	.10	.05
❑ 145 Boomer Esiason CL	.10	.05
❑ 146 Neil Smith CL	.10	.05
❑ 147 Jack Del Rio CL	.10	.05
❑ 148 Morten Andersen CL	.10	.05
❑ 149 Sterling Sharpe CL	.20	.09
❑ 150 Reggie White CL	.20	.09

1993 Playoff Contenders Rookie Contenders

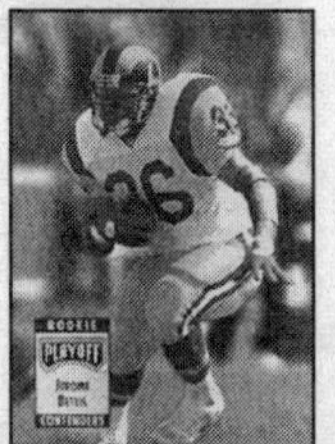

	MINT	NRMT
COMPLETE SET (10)	60.00	27.00
STATED ODDS 1:40		

❑ 1 Jerome Bettis	12.00	5.50
❑ 2 Drew Bledsoe UER (Text states he played for Washington; he played for Washington St.)	30.00	13.50
❑ 3 Reggie Brooks	1.25	.55
❑ 4 Derek Brown RBK	1.25	.55
❑ 5 Garrison Hearst	12.00	5.50
❑ 6 Vaughn Hebron	.60	.25
❑ 7 Qadry Ismail	2.50	1.10
❑ 8 Derrick Lassic	.60	.25
❑ 9 Glyn Milburn	2.50	1.10
❑ 10 Dana Stubblefield	2.50	1.10

1994 Playoff Contenders

	MINT	NRMT
COMPLETE SET (120)	20.00	9.00
COMMON CARD (1-120)	.10	.05
SEMISTARS	.20	.09
UNLISTED STARS	.40	.18

❑ 1 Drew Bledsoe	1.50	.70
❑ 2 Barry Sanders	3.00	1.35
❑ 3 Jerry Rice	1.50	.70
❑ 4 Rod Woodson	.40	.18
❑ 5 Irving Fryar	.20	.09
❑ 6 Charles Haley	.20	.09
❑ 7 Chris Warren	.20	.09
❑ 8 Craig Erickson	.10	.05
❑ 9 Eric Metcalf	.20	.09
❑ 10 Marcus Allen	.40	.18
❑ 11 Chris Miller	.10	.05
❑ 12 Andre Rison	.20	.09
❑ 13 Art Monk	.20	.09
❑ 14 Calvin Williams	.20	.09
❑ 15 Shannon Sharpe	.20	.09
❑ 16 Rodney Hampton	.40	.18
❑ 17 Marion Butts	.10	.05
❑ 18 John Jurkovic RC	.20	.09
❑ 19 Jim Kelly	.40	.18
❑ 20 Emmitt Smith	2.50	1.10
❑ 21 Jeff Hostetler	.20	.09
❑ 22 Barry Foster	.10	.05
❑ 23 Boomer Esiason	.20	.09
❑ 24 Jim Harbaugh	.40	.18
❑ 25 Joe Montana	3.00	1.35
❑ 26 Jeff George	.40	.18
❑ 27 Warren Moon	.40	.18
❑ 28 Steve Young	1.25	.55
❑ 29 Randall Cunningham	.40	.18
❑ 30 Shawn Jefferson	.10	.05
❑ 31 Cortez Kennedy	.20	.09
❑ 32 Reggie Brooks	.20	.09
❑ 33 Alvin Harper	.20	.09
❑ 34 Brent Jones	.20	.09
❑ 35 O.J. McDuffie	.40	.18
❑ 36 Jerome Bettis	.40	.18
❑ 37 Daryl Johnston	.20	.09
❑ 38 Herman Moore	.40	.18
❑ 39 Dave Meggett	.10	.05
❑ 40 Reggie White	.40	.18
❑ 41 Junior Seau	.40	.18
❑ 42 Dan Marino	3.00	1.35
❑ 43 Scott Mitchell	.40	.18
❑ 44 John Elway	3.00	1.35
❑ 45 Troy Aikman	1.50	.70
❑ 46 Terry Allen	.20	.09
❑ 47 David Klingler	.10	.05
❑ 48 Stan Humphries	.40	.18
❑ 49 Rick Mirer	.40	.18
❑ 50 Neil O'Donnell	.40	.18
❑ 51 Keith Jackson	.10	.05
❑ 52 Ricky Watters	.40	.18
❑ 53 Dave Brown	.20	.09
❑ 54 Neil Smith	.40	.18
❑ 55 Johnny Mitchell	.10	.05
❑ 56 Jackie Harris	.10	.05
❑ 57 Terry Kirby	.40	.18
❑ 58 Willie Davis	.20	.09
❑ 59 Rob Moore	.20	.09
❑ 60 Nate Newton	.10	.05
❑ 61 Deion Sanders	.75	.35
❑ 62 John Taylor	.20	.09
❑ 63 Sterling Sharpe	.20	.09
❑ 64 Natrone Means	.40	.18
❑ 65 Steve Beuerlein	.10	.05
❑ 66 Erik Kramer	.20	.09
❑ 67 Qadry Ismail	.40	.18
❑ 68 Johnny Johnson	.10	.05
❑ 69 Herschel Walker	.20	.09
❑ 70 Mark Stepnoski	.10	.05
❑ 71 Brett Favre	3.00	1.35
❑ 72 Dana Stubblefield	.40	.18
❑ 73 Bruce Smith	.40	.18
❑ 74 Leroy Hoard	.10	.05
❑ 75 Steve Walsh	.10	.05
❑ 76 Jay Novacek	.20	.09
❑ 77 Derrick Thomas	.40	.18
❑ 78 Keith Byars	.10	.05
❑ 79 Ben Coates	.40	.18
❑ 80 Lorenzo Neal	.10	.05
❑ 81 Ronnie Lott	.20	.09
❑ 82 Tim Brown	.40	.18
❑ 83 Michael Irvin	.40	.18
❑ 84 Ronald Moore	.10	.05
❑ 85 Andre Reed	.20	.09
❑ 86 James Jett	.10	.05
❑ 87 Curtis Conway	.40	.18
❑ 88 Bernie Parmalee RC	.40	.18
❑ 89 Keith Cash	.10	.05
❑ 90 Russell Copeland	.10	.05
❑ 91 Kevin Williams	.20	.09
❑ 92 Gary Brown	.10	.05
❑ 93 Thurman Thomas	.40	.18
❑ 94 Jamir Miller RC	.10	.05
❑ 95 Bert Emanuel RC	1.25	.55
❑ 96 Bucky Brooks RC	.10	.05
❑ 97 Jeff Burris RC	.20	.09
❑ 98 Antonio Langham RC	.20	.09
❑ 99 Derrick Alexander WR RC	1.25	.55
❑ 100 Dan Wilkinson RC	.20	.09
❑ 101 Shante Carver RC	.10	.05
❑ 102 Johnnie Morton RC	1.50	.70
❑ 103 LeShon Johnson RC	.20	.09
❑ 104 Marshall Faulk RC	5.00	2.20
❑ 105 Greg Hill RC	1.25	.55
❑ 106 Lake Dawson RC	.40	.18
❑ 107 Irving Spikes RC	.20	.09
❑ 108 David Palmer RC	1.25	.55
❑ 109 Willie McGinest RC	.40	.18
❑ 110 Joe Johnson RC	.10	.05
❑ 111 Aaron Glenn RC	.20	.09
❑ 112 Charlie Garner RC	2.00	.90
❑ 113 Charles Johnson RC	.40	.18
❑ 114 Byron Bam Morris RC	.40	.18
❑ 115 Bryant Young RC	.40	.18
❑ 116 William Floyd RC	.40	.18
❑ 117 Trent Dilfer RC	2.00	.90
❑ 118 Errict Rhett RC	2.00	.90
❑ 119 Heath Shuler RC	.40	.18
❑ 120 Gus Frerotte RC	1.25	.55

1994 Playoff Contenders Back-to-Back

	MINT	NRMT
COMPLETE SET (60)	800.00	350.00
COMMON PAIR (1-60)	8.00	3.60
SEMISTARS	10.00	4.50
UNLISTED STARS	15.00	6.75
STATED ODDS 1:24		

❑ 1 Joe Montana / Dan Marino	120.00	55.00
❑ 2 Drew Bledsoe / John Elway	80.00	36.00
❑ 3 Jerry Rice / Sterling Sharpe	40.00	18.00
❑ 4 Barry Sanders / Emmitt Smith	100.00	45.00
❑ 5 Troy Aikman / Steve Young	60.00	27.00
❑ 6 Erik Kramer / Steve Walsh	8.00	3.60
❑ 7 Nate Newton / Bruce Smith	10.00	4.50
❑ 8 Johnny Mitchell / Aaron Glenn	8.00	3.60
❑ 9 Neil O'Donnell / Jay Novacek	8.00	3.60
❑ 10 Herman Moore / Calvin Williams	15.00	6.75
❑ 11 Alvin Harper / Michael Irvin	15.00	6.75
❑ 12 Jim Harbaugh / Curtis Conway	15.00	6.75
❑ 13 Brett Favre / LeShon Johnson	60.00	27.00
❑ 14 Eric Metcalf / Marshall Faulk	20.00	9.00
❑ 15 Qadry Ismail	10.00	4.50

Card	MINT	NRMT
David Palmer		
❑ 16 Deion Sanders	20.00	9.00
Andre Rison		
❑ 17 Jackie Harris	15.00	6.75
Errict Rhett		
❑ 18 Keith Jackson	8.00	3.60
Irving Spikes		
❑ 19 Dave Meggett	8.00	3.60
Jeff Burris		
❑ 20 Dana Stubblefield	10.00	4.50
William Floyd		
❑ 21 Randall Cunningham	15.00	6.75
Reggie White		
❑ 22 Shannon Sharpe	8.00	3.60
Keith Cash		
❑ 23 Marcus Allen	15.00	6.75
Derrick Thomas		
❑ 24 Irving Fryar	8.00	3.60
Russell Copeland		
❑ 25 Johnny Johnson	8.00	3.60
Ben Coates		
❑ 26 John Taylor	10.00	4.50
Brent Jones		
❑ 27 Terry Kirby	10.00	4.50
Bernie Parmalee		
❑ 28 Ricky Watters	15.00	6.75
Ronnie Lott		
❑ 29 Scott Mitchell	8.00	3.60
James Jett		
❑ 30 O.J. McDuffie	15.00	6.75
Keith Byars		
❑ 31 Shawn Jefferson	10.00	4.50
Andre Reed		
❑ 32 Rodney Hampton	10.00	4.50
Lorenzo Neal		
❑ 33 Chris Miller	8.00	3.60
Ronald Moore		
❑ 34 Charles Haley	15.00	6.75
Thurman Thomas		
❑ 35 Herschel Walker	8.00	3.60
Leroy Hoard		
❑ 36 Natrone Means	15.00	6.75
Stan Humphries		
❑ 37 Willie Davis	10.00	4.50
Kevin Williams WR		
❑ 38 Dave Brown	8.00	3.60
Gary Brown		
❑ 39 Jerome Bettis	15.00	6.75
Terry Allen		
❑ 40 Cortez Kennedy	10.00	4.50
Junior Seau		
❑ 41 David Klingler	10.00	4.50
Derrick Alexander		
❑ 42 Chris Warren	10.00	4.50
Bucky Brooks		
❑ 43 Mark Stepnoski	10.00	4.50
Greg Hill		
❑ 44 Steve Beuerlein	10.00	4.50
Johnnie Morton		
❑ 45 Rob Moore	8.00	3.60
James Jett		
❑ 46 Neil Smith	10.00	4.50
Lake Dawson		
❑ 47 Rick Mirer	15.00	6.75
Bryant Young		
❑ 48 Daryl Johnston	15.00	6.75
Charlie Garner		
❑ 49 Reggie Brooks	15.00	6.75
Gus Frerotte		
❑ 50 Barry Foster	10.00	4.50
Byron Bam Morris		
❑ 51 Art Monk	15.00	6.75
Heath Shuler		
❑ 52 Craig Erickson	15.00	6.75
Trent Dilfer		
❑ 53 Jeff George	10.00	4.50
Bert Emanuel		
❑ 54 Rod Woodson	10.00	4.50
Antonio Langham		
❑ 55 Marion Butts	8.00	3.60
Willie McGinest		
❑ 56 John Jurkovic	8.00	3.60
Dan Wilkinson		
❑ 57 Jim Kelly	15.00	6.75
Shante Carver		
❑ 58 Jeff Hostetler	8.00	3.60
Charles Johnson		
❑ 59 Boomer Esiason	8.00	3.60
Jamir Miller		
❑ 60 Warren Moon	10.00	4.50
Joe Johnson		

1994 Playoff Contenders Rookie Contenders

	MINT	NRMT
COMPLETE SET (6)	40.00	18.00
COMMON CARD (1-6)	2.50	1.10
SEMISTARS	4.00	1.80
STATED ODDS 1:48		
❑ 1 Heath Shuler	4.00	1.80
❑ 2 Trent Dilfer	8.00	3.60
❑ 3 David Palmer	2.50	1.10
❑ 4 Marshall Faulk	25.00	11.00
❑ 5 Charlie Garner	8.00	3.60
❑ 6 Dan Wilkinson	2.50	1.10

1994 Playoff Contenders Sophomore Contenders

	MINT	NRMT
COMPLETE SET (6)	60.00	27.00
STATED ODDS 1:48		
❑ 1 Drew Bledsoe	25.00	11.00
❑ 2 Jerome Bettis	6.00	2.70
❑ 3 Reggie Brooks	3.00	1.35
❑ 4 Rick Mirer	6.00	2.70
❑ 5 Natrone Means	6.00	2.70
❑ 6 O.J.McDuffie	6.00	2.70

1994 Playoff Contenders Throwbacks

	MINT	NRMT
COMPLETE SET (30)	120.00	55.00
STATED ODDS 1:12		
❑ 1 Larry Centers	1.00	.45
❑ 2 Andre Rison	1.00	.45
❑ 3 Jim Kelly	2.00	.90

	MINT	NRMT
❑ 4 Curtis Conway	2.00	.90
❑ 5 David Klingler	.50	.23
❑ 6 Vinny Testaverde	2.00	.90
❑ 7 Troy Aikman	8.00	3.60
❑ 8 Emmitt Smith	12.00	5.50
❑ 9 John Elway	15.00	6.75
❑ 10 Barry Sanders	15.00	6.75
❑ 11 Sterling Sharpe	1.00	.45
❑ 12 Gary Brown	.50	.23
❑ 13 Jim Harbaugh	2.00	.90
❑ 14 Joe Montana	15.00	6.75
❑ 15 Tim Brown	2.00	.90
❑ 16 Chris Miller	.50	.23
❑ 17 Dan Marino	15.00	6.75
❑ 18 Terry Allen	1.00	.45
❑ 19 Marion Butts	.50	.23
❑ 20 Jim Everett	.50	.23
❑ 21 Dave Brown	1.00	.45
❑ 22 Johnny Johnson	.50	.23
❑ 23 Randall Cunningham	2.00	.90
❑ 24 Barry Foster	.50	.23
❑ 25 Stan Humphries	2.00	.90
❑ 26 Jerry Rice	8.00	3.60
❑ 27 Steve Young	6.00	2.70
❑ 28 Chris Warren	1.00	.45
❑ 29 Errict Rhett	10.00	4.50
❑ 30 John Friesz	.50	.23

1995 Playoff Contenders

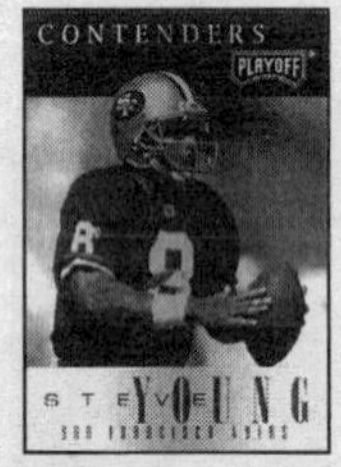

	MINT	NRMT
COMPLETE SET (150)	25.00	11.00
COMMON CARD (1-150)	.10	.05
SEMISTARS	.20	.09
UNLISTED STARS	.40	.18
❑ 1 Steve Young	1.00	.45
❑ 2 Jeff Blake RC	1.00	.45
❑ 3 Rick Mirer	.40	.18
❑ 4 Brett Favre	2.50	1.10
❑ 5 Heath Shuler	.40	.18
❑ 6 Steve Bono	.20	.09
❑ 7 John Elway	2.50	1.10
❑ 8 Troy Aikman	1.25	.55
❑ 9 Rodney Peete	.10	.05
❑ 10 Gus Frerotte	.40	.18
❑ 11 Drew Bledsoe	1.25	.55
❑ 12 Jim Kelly	.40	.18
❑ 13 Dan Marino	2.50	1.10
❑ 14 Errict Rhett	.40	.18

❑ 15 Jeff Hostetler .20 .09
❑ 16 Erik Kramer .10 .05
❑ 17 Jim Everett .10 .05
❑ 18 Elvis Grbac .40 .18
❑ 19 Scott Mitchell .20 .09
❑ 20 Barry Sanders 2.50 1.10
❑ 21 Deion Sanders .75 .35
❑ 22 Emmitt Smith 2.00 .90
❑ 23 Garrison Hearst .40 .18
❑ 24 Mario Bates .40 .18
❑ 25 Mark Brunell 1.25 .55
❑ 26 Robert Smith .40 .18
❑ 27 Rodney Hampton .20 .09
❑ 28 Marshall Faulk .75 .35
❑ 29 Greg Hill .20 .09
❑ 30 Bernie Parmalee .20 .09
❑ 31 Natrone Means .40 .18
❑ 32 Marcus Allen .40 .18
❑ 33 Byron Bam Morris .20 .09
❑ 34 Edgar Bennett .20 .09
❑ 35 Vincent Brisby .10 .05
❑ 36 Jerome Bettis .40 .18
❑ 37 Craig Heyward .20 .09
❑ 38 Anthony Miller .20 .09
❑ 39 Curtis Conway .40 .18
❑ 40 William Floyd .40 .18
❑ 41 Chris Warren .20 .09
❑ 42 Terry Kirby .20 .09
❑ 43 Herschel Walker .20 .09
❑ 44 Eric Metcalf .20 .09
❑ 45 Darnay Scott .40 .18
❑ 46 Jackie Harris .10 .05
❑ 47 Dana Stubblefield .40 .18
❑ 48 Daryl Johnston .20 .09
❑ 49 Dave Meggett .10 .05
❑ 50 Ricky Watters .40 .18
❑ 51 Ken Norton .20 .09
❑ 52 Boomer Esiason .20 .09
❑ 53 Lake Dawson .20 .09
❑ 54 Eric Green .10 .05
❑ 55 Junior Seau .40 .18
❑ 56 Yancey Thigpen RC .40 .18
❑ 57 James Jett .20 .09
❑ 58 Leonard Russell .10 .05
❑ 59 Brent Jones .10 .05
❑ 60 Trent Dilfer .40 .18
❑ 61 Terance Mathis .20 .09
❑ 62 Jeff George .20 .09
❑ 63 Alvin Harper .10 .05
❑ 64 Terry Allen .20 .09
❑ 65 Stan Humphries .20 .09
❑ 66 Robert Green .10 .05
❑ 67 Bryce Paup .40 .18
❑ 68 Tamarick Vanover RC .40 .18
❑ 69 Desmond Howard .20 .09
❑ 70 Derek Loville .10 .05
❑ 71 Dave Brown .20 .09
❑ 72 Carl Pickens .40 .18
❑ 73 Gary Clark .10 .05
❑ 74 Gary Brown .10 .05
❑ 75 Brett Perriman .20 .09
❑ 76 Charlie Garner .20 .09
❑ 77 Ben Coates .20 .09
❑ 78 Bruce Smith .40 .18
❑ 79 Erric Pegram .20 .09
❑ 80 Jerry Rice 1.25 .55
❑ 81 Tim Brown .40 .18
❑ 82 John Taylor .10 .05
❑ 83 Will Moore .10 .05
❑ 84 Jay Novacek .20 .09
❑ 85 Kevin Williams .20 .09
❑ 86 Rocket Ismail .20 .09
❑ 87 Robert Brooks .40 .18
❑ 88 Michael Irvin .40 .18
❑ 89 Mark Chmura .40 .18
❑ 90 Shannon Sharpe .20 .09
❑ 91 Henry Ellard .20 .09
❑ 92 Reggie White .40 .18
❑ 93 Isaac Bruce .75 .35
❑ 94 Charles Haley .20 .09
❑ 95 Jake Reed .20 .09
❑ 96 Pete Metzelaars .10 .05
❑ 97 Dave Krieg .10 .05
❑ 98 Tony Martin .20 .09
❑ 99 Charles Jordan .10 .05
❑ 100 Bert Emanuel .40 .18
❑ 101 Andre Rison .20 .09
❑ 102 Jeff Graham .10 .05
❑ 103 O.J. McDuffie .40 .18
❑ 104 Randall Cunningham .40 .18
❑ 105 Harvey Williams .10 .05
❑ 106 Cris Carter .40 .18
❑ 107 Irving Fryar .20 .09
❑ 108 Jim Harbaugh .20 .09
❑ 109 Bernie Kosar .10 .05
❑ 110 Charles Johnson .20 .09
❑ 111 Warren Moon .20 .09
❑ 112 Neil O'Donnell .20 .09
❑ 113 Fred Barnett .20 .09
❑ 114 Herman Moore .40 .18
❑ 115 Chris Miller .10 .05
❑ 116 Vinny Testaverde .20 .09
❑ 117 Craig Erickson .10 .05
❑ 118 Qadry Ismail .20 .09
❑ 119 Willie Davis .20 .09
❑ 120 Michael Jackson .20 .09
❑ 121 Stoney Case RC .50 .23
❑ 122 Frank Sanders RC 1.00 .45
❑ 123 Todd Collins RC .40 .18
❑ 124 Kerry Collins RC 1.00 .45
❑ 125 Sherman Williams RC .10 .05
❑ 126 Terrell Davis RC 12.00 5.50
❑ 127 Luther Elliss RC .10 .05
❑ 128 Steve McNair RC 3.00 1.35
❑ 129 Chris Sanders RC .40 .18
❑ 130 Ki-Jana Carter RC .40 .18
❑ 131 Rodney Thomas RC .40 .18
❑ 132 Tony Boselli RC .20 .09
❑ 133 Rob Johnson RC 1.50 .70
❑ 134 James O. Stewart RC 2.00 .90
❑ 135 Chad May RC .10 .05
❑ 136 Eric Bjornson RC .20 .09
❑ 137 Tyrone Wheatley RC 1.25 .55
❑ 138 Kyle Brady RC .40 .18
❑ 139 Curtis Martin RC 3.00 1.35
❑ 140 Eric Zeier RC .50 .23
❑ 141 Ray Zellars RC .20 .09
❑ 142 Napoleon Kaufman RC 2.00 .90
❑ 143 Mike Mamula RC .20 .09
❑ 144 Mark Bruener RC .20 .09
❑ 145 Kordell Stewart RC 3.00 1.35
❑ 146 J.J. Stokes RC .75 .35
❑ 147 Joey Galloway RC 3.00 1.35
❑ 148 Warren Sapp RC .50 .23
❑ 149 Michael Westbrook RC 1.50 .70
❑ 150 Rashaan Salaam RC .40 .18

1995 Playoff Contenders Back-to-Back

	MINT	NRMT
COMPLETE SET (75)	600.00	275.00
COMMON CARD (1-75)	3.00	1.35
SEMISTARS	5.00	2.20
UNLISTED STARS	8.00	3.60
STATED ODDS 1:19		

❑ 1 Dan Marino 25.00 11.00
Troy Aikman
❑ 2 Marshall Faulk 25.00 11.00
Emmitt Smith
❑ 3 John Elway 40.00 18.00
Brett Favre
❑ 4 Drew Bledsoe 15.00 6.75
Steve Young
❑ 5 Errict Rhett 30.00 13.50
Barry Sanders
❑ 6 Jerry Rice 15.00 6.75
Deion Sanders
❑ 7 Rick Mirer 8.00 3.60
Jeff Blake
❑ 8 Tim Brown 8.00 3.60
Michael Irvin
❑ 9 Ricky Watters 5.00 2.20
Chris Warren
❑ 10 Vincent Brisby 8.00 3.60
Herman Moore
❑ 11 Eric Metcalf 5.00 2.20
James Jett
❑ 12 Terance Mathis 5.00 2.20
Henry Ellard
❑ 13 Isaac Bruce 12.00 5.50
Curtis Conway
❑ 14 Jeff Hostetler 5.00 2.20
Steve Bono
❑ 15 Harvey Williams 5.00 2.20
Greg Hill
❑ 16 Jerome Bettis 10.00 4.50
Garrison Hearst
❑ 17 Brent Jones 5.00 2.20
Jay Novacek
❑ 18 Bruce Smith 8.00 3.60
Reggie White
❑ 19 Shannon Sharpe 5.00 2.20
Eric Green
❑ 20 Jeff George 5.00 2.20
Gus Frerotte
❑ 21 Scott Mitchell 3.00 1.35
Erik Kramer
❑ 22 Jim Kelly 8.00 3.60
Warren Moon
❑ 23 Ben Coates 5.00 2.20
Mark Chmura
❑ 24 Heath Shuler 8.00 3.60
Trent Dilfer
❑ 25 Edgar Bennett 5.00 2.20
Craig Heyward
❑ 26 Dave Brown 3.00 1.35
Jim Everett
❑ 27 Ande Rison 3.00 1.35
Bert Emanuel
❑ 28 Alvin Harper 3.00 1.35
Robert Brooks
❑ 29 Tony Martin 5.00 2.20
Desmond Howard
❑ 30 Fred Barnett 3.00 1.35
Rodney Peete
❑ 31 William Floyd 5.00 2.20
Natrone Means
❑ 32 Rocket Ismail 3.00 1.35
Brett Perriman
❑ 33 Irving Fryar 5.00 2.20
Cris Carter
❑ 34 Darnay Scott 8.00 3.60
Tamarick Vanover
❑ 35 Dana Stubblefield 5.00 2.20
Charles Haley
❑ 36 Ken Norton 3.00 1.35
Bryce Paup
❑ 37 Herschel Walker 8.00 3.60
Marcus Allen
❑ 38 Terry Allen 3.00 1.35
Leonard Russell
❑ 39 Derek Loville 5.00 2.20
Junior Seau
❑ 40 Charles Johnson 5.00 2.20
Lake Dawson
❑ 41 Charles Jordan 3.00 1.35
Kevin Williams
❑ 42 Carl Pickens 5.00 2.20
Jeff Graham
❑ 43 O.J.McDuffie 5.00 2.20
Anthony Miller
❑ 44 Jim Harbaugh 5.00 2.20
Elvis Grbac
❑ 45 Terry Kirby 5.00 2.20
Dave Meggett
❑ 46 Stan Humphries 3.00 1.35

Dave Krieg
❑ 47 Boomer Esiason 12.00 5.50
Mark Brunell
❑ 48 Vinny Testaverde 3.00 1.35
Craig Erickson
❑ 49 Bernie Kosar 3.00 1.35
Randall Cunningham
❑ 50 Charlie Garner................ 3.00 1.35
Erric Pegram
❑ 51 Gary Clark...................... 3.00 1.35
Will Moore
❑ 52 Willie Davis 5.00 2.20
Qadry Ismail
❑ 53 Chris Miller 3.00 1.35
Neil O'Donnell
❑ 54 Robert Smith.................. 5.00 2.20
Mario Bates
❑ 55 Bernie Parmalee 5.00 2.20
Rodney Hampton
❑ 56 Daryl Johnston 5.00 2.20
Byron Bam Morris
❑ 57 Jake Reed...................... 3.00 1.35
Jack Harris
❑ 58 Pete Metzelaars 3.00 1.35
John Taylor
❑ 59 Michael Jackson 8.00 3.60
Yancey Thigpen
❑ 60 Robert Green 3.00 1.35
Gary Brown
❑ 61 N.Kaufman 10.00 4.50
Rashaan Salaam
❑ 62 Kyle Brady...................... 3.00 1.35
Mark Bruener
❑ 63 Rodney Thomas 8.00 3.60
Ki-Jana Carter
❑ 64 Steve McNair................ 10.00 4.50
Chad May
❑ 65 J.J.Stokes 10.00 4.50
Frank Sanders
❑ 66 Warren Sapp.................. 3.00 1.35
Mike Mamula
❑ 67 Stoney Case 15.00 6.75
Kordell Stewart
❑ 68 Curtis Martin 30.00 13.50
Terrell Davis
❑ 69 Chris Sanders 8.00 3.60
Sherman Williams
❑ 70 Eric Bjornson................ 10.00 4.50
James O. Stewart
❑ 71 Ray Zellars 10.00 4.50
Tyrone Wheatley
❑ 72 Luther Elliss.................... 5.00 2.20
Tony Boselli
❑ 73 Todd Collins 10.00 4.50
Rob Johnson
❑ 74 Eric Zeier........................ 8.00 3.60
Kerry Collins
❑ 75 Michael Westbrook 12.00 5.50
Joey Galloway

1995 Playoff Contenders Hog Heaven

	MINT	NRMT
COMPLETE SET (30)	300.00	135.00
STATED ODDS 1:48		

❑ HH1 Troy Aikman.............. 25.00 11.00
❑ HH2 Marcus Allen 8.00 3.60
❑ HH3 Jeff Blake 20.00 9.00
❑ HH4 Drew Bledsoe............ 25.00 11.00
❑ HH5 Steve Bono 4.00 1.80
❑ HH6 Isaac Bruce 15.00 6.75
❑ HH7 Trent Dilfer 8.00 3.60
❑ HH8 John Elway................ 50.00 22.00
❑ HH9 Marshall Faulk 15.00 6.75
❑ HH10 Brett Favre 50.00 22.00
❑ HH11 Gus Frerotte................ 8.00 3.60
❑ HH12 Irving Fryar................ 4.00 1.80
❑ HH13 Jeff George 4.00 1.80
❑ HH14 Rodney Hampton...... 4.00 1.80
❑ HH15 Garrison Hearst 8.00 3.60
❑ HH16 Michael Irvin.............. 8.00 3.60
❑ HH17 Erik Kramer .... 2.00 .90
❑ HH18 Dan Marino 50.00 22.00
❑ HH19 Natrone Means 8.00 3.60
❑ HH20 Errict Rhett................ 8.00 3.60
❑ HH21 Jerry Rice................ 25.00 11.00
❑ HH22 Barry Sanders 50.00 22.00
❑ HH23 Deion Sanders........ 15.00 6.75
❑ HH24 Shannon Sharpe 4.00 1.80
❑ HH25 Emmitt Smith 40.00 18.00
❑ HH26 Robert Smith 8.00 3.60
❑ HH27 Chris Warren 4.00 1.80
❑ HH28 Reggie White 8.00 3.60
❑ HH29 Harvey Williams........ 2.00 .90
❑ HH30 Steve Young 20.00 9.00

1995 Playoff Contenders Rookie Kickoff

	MINT	NRMT
COMPLETE SET (30)	200.00	90.00
STATED ODDS 1:24		

❑ RKO1 Eric Bjornson............ 1.00 .45
❑ RKO2 Tony Boselli.............. 1.00 .45
❑ RKO3 Kyle Brady................ 2.00 .90
❑ RKO4 Mark Bruener............ 1.00 .45
❑ RKO5 Ki-Jana Carter .... 2.00 .90
❑ RKO6 Stoney Case 2.50 1.10
❑ RKO7 Kerry Collins 5.00 2.20
❑ RKO8 Todd Collins .... 2.00 .90
❑ RKO9 Terrell Davis 60.00 27.00
❑ RKO10 Luther Elliss.............. .50 .23
❑ RKO11 Joey Galloway...... 15.00 6.75
❑ RKO12 Rob Johnson.......... 8.00 3.60
❑ RKO13 Napoleon Kaufman 10.00 4.50
❑ RKO14 Mike Mamula.......... 1.00 .45
❑ RKO15 Curtis Martin 15.00 6.75
❑ RKO16 Chad May .... .50 .23
❑ RKO17 Steve McNair........ 15.00 6.75
❑ RKO18 Rashaan Salaam.... 2.00 .90
❑ RKO19 Chris Sanders .... 2.00 .90
❑ RKO20 Frank Sanders........ 5.00 2.20
❑ RKO21 Warren Sapp.......... 2.50 1.10
❑ RKO22 James O. Stewart 10.00 4.50
❑ RKO23 Kordell Stewart 15.00 6.75
❑ RKO24 J.J. Stokes.............. 4.00 1.80
❑ RKO25 Rodney Thomas .... 2.00 .90
❑ RKO26 Michael Westbrook 8.00 3.60
❑ RKO27 Tyrone Wheatley.... 6.00 2.70
❑ RKO28 Sherman Williams .... .50 .23
❑ RKO29 Eric Zeier............... 2.50 1.10
❑ RKO30 Ray Zellars .... 1.00 .45

1996 Playoff Contenders Leather

	MINT	NRMT
COMPLETE SET (100)	400.00	180.00
COMMON GREEN....................	1.00	.45
SEMISTARS GREEN................	2.00	.90
UNLISTED STARS GREEN......	3.00	1.35
COMMON PURPLE	1.50	.70
SEMISTARS PURPLE	3.00	1.35
UNLISTED STARS PURPLE	5.00	2.20
PURPLE STATED ODDS 1:11......		
COMMON RED	2.50	1.10
SEMISTARS RED	4.00	1.80
UNLISTED STARS RED	8.00	3.60
RED STATED ODDS 1:22		

❑ 1 Brett Favre R.................. 40.00 18.00
❑ 2 Steve Young P 12.00 5.50
❑ 3 Herman Moore P............ 5.00 2.20
❑ 4 Jim Harbaugh P 3.00 1.35
❑ 5 Curtis Martin R 15.00 6.75
❑ 6 Junior Seau G................ 2.00 .90
❑ 7 John Elway R 40.00 18.00
❑ 8 Troy Aikman R 20.00 9.00
❑ 9 Terry Allen G.................. 2.00 .90
❑ 10 Kordell Stewart R 15.00 6.75
❑ 11 Drew Bledsoe R 20.00 9.00
❑ 12 Jim Kelly R 8.00 3.60
❑ 13 Dan Marino R 40.00 18.00
❑ 14 Andre Rison G.............. 2.00 .90
❑ 15 Jeff Hostetler G .... 1.00 .45
❑ 16 Scott Mitchell G............ 2.00 .90
❑ 17 Carl Pickens G 3.00 1.35
❑ 18 Larry Centers R............ 4.00 1.80
❑ 19 Craig Heyward G.......... 1.00 .45
❑ 20 Barry Sanders R 40.00 18.00
❑ 21 Deion Sanders P.......... 10.00 4.50
❑ 22 Emmitt Smith R 30.00 13.50
❑ 23 Rashaan Salaam P 5.00 2.20
❑ 24 Mario Bates G .... 2.00 .90
❑ 25 Lawrence Phillips R........ 8.00 3.60
❑ 26 Napoleon Kaufman P 8.00 3.60
❑ 27 Rodney Hampton G ...... 2.00 .90
❑ 28 Marshall Faulk R 8.00 3.60
❑ 29 Trent Dilfer G.................. 3.00 1.35
❑ 30 Leeland McElroy G 3.00 1.35
❑ 31 Marcus Allen G 3.00 1.35
❑ 32 Ricky Watters R 4.00 1.80
❑ 33 Karim Abdul-Jabbar R.... 8.00 3.60
❑ 34 Herschel Walker G .... 2.00 .90
❑ 35 Thurman Thomas G 3.00 1.35
❑ 36 Jerome Bettis G 3.00 1.35
❑ 37 Gus Frerotte P................ 5.00 2.20
❑ 38 Neil O'Donnell P 3.00 1.35
❑ 39 Rick Mirer G .... 2.00 .90
❑ 40 Mike Alstott P 10.00 4.50
❑ 41 Vinny Testaverde P........ 3.00 1.35
❑ 42 Derek Loville G .... 1.00 .45
❑ 43 Ben Coates G .... 2.00 .90
❑ 44 Steve McNair G.............. 5.00 2.20
❑ 45 Bobby Engram G............ 3.00 1.35
❑ 46 Yancey Thigpen G .... 2.00 .90
❑ 47 Lake Dawson G.............. 1.00 .45
❑ 48 Terrell Davis G 12.00 5.50
❑ 49 Kerry Collins P 5.00 2.20
❑ 50 Eric Metcalf G .... 1.00 .45
❑ 51 Stanley Pritchett P.......... 3.00 1.35

❑ 52 Robert Brooks G	3.00	1.35
❑ 53 Isaac Bruce R	8.00	3.60
❑ 54 Tim Brown G	3.00	1.35
❑ 55 Edgar Bennett G	2.00	.90
❑ 56 Warren Moon G	2.00	.90
❑ 57 Jerry Rice R	20.00	9.00
❑ 58 Michael Westbrook G	3.00	1.35
❑ 59 Keyshawn Johnson R	15.00	6.75
❑ 60 Steve Bono G	1.00	.45
❑ 61 Derrick Mayes G	2.00	.90
❑ 62 Erik Kramer G	1.00	.45
❑ 63 Rodney Peete G	1.00	.45
❑ 64 Eddie Kennison P	5.00	2.20
❑ 65 Derrick Thomas G	2.00	.90
❑ 66 Joey Galloway P	10.00	4.50
❑ 67 Amani Toomer G	3.00	1.35
❑ 68 Reggie White P	5.00	2.20
❑ 69 Heath Shuler R	8.00	3.60
❑ 70 Dave Brown R	4.00	1.80
❑ 71 Tony Banks G	3.00	1.35
❑ 72 Chris Warren R	4.00	1.80
❑ 73 J.J. Stokes R	8.00	3.60
❑ 74 Rickey Dudley G	3.00	1.35
❑ 75 Stan Humphries G	2.00	.90
❑ 76 Jason Dunn G	1.00	.45
❑ 77 Tyrone Wheatley P	3.00	1.35
❑ 78 Jim Everett R	2.50	1.10
❑ 79 Cris Carter P	5.00	2.20
❑ 80 Alex Van Dyke G	2.00	.90
❑ 81 O.J. McDuffie G	2.00	.90
❑ 82 Mark Chmura G	2.00	.90
❑ 83 Terry Glenn G	5.00	2.20
❑ 84 Boomer Esiason G	2.00	.90
❑ 85 Bruce Smith G	2.00	.90
❑ 86 Curtis Conway P	5.00	2.20
❑ 87 Ki-Jana Carter G	2.00	.90
❑ 88 Tamarick Vanover G	2.00	.90
❑ 89 Michael Jackson G	2.00	.90
❑ 90 Mark Brunell P	15.00	6.75
❑ 91 Tim Biakabutuka P	8.00	3.60
❑ 92 Anthony Miller P	3.00	1.35
❑ 93 Marvin Harrison P	12.00	5.50
❑ 94 Jeff George R	4.00	1.80
❑ 95 Jeff Blake P	5.00	2.20
❑ 96 Eddie George R	20.00	9.00
❑ 97 Eric Moulds G	3.00	1.35
❑ 98 Mike Tomczak P	1.50	.70
❑ 99 Chris Sanders P	3.00	1.35
❑ 100 Chris Chandler G	2.00	.90

1996 Playoff Contenders Leather Accents

	MINT	NRMT
COMPLETE SET (100)	1500.00	700.00
COMMON CARD (1-100)	8.00	3.60
SEMISTARS	15.00	6.75
UNLISTED STARS	25.00	11.00
STATED ODDS 1:216		
❑ 1 Brett Favre	120.00	55.00
❑ 2 Steve Young	50.00	22.00
❑ 5 Curtis Martin	40.00	18.00
❑ 7 John Elway	120.00	55.00
❑ 8 Troy Aikman	60.00	27.00
❑ 10 Kordell Stewart	40.00	18.00
❑ 11 Drew Bledsoe	60.00	27.00
❑ 13 Dan Marino	120.00	55.00
❑ 20 Barry Sanders	120.00	55.00
❑ 21 Deion Sanders	40.00	18.00
❑ 22 Emmitt Smith	100.00	45.00
❑ 26 Napoleon Kaufman	30.00	13.50
❑ 44 Steve McNair	40.00	18.00
❑ 48 Terrell Davis	120.00	55.00
❑ 57 Jerry Rice	60.00	27.00
❑ 59 Keyshawn Johnson	40.00	18.00
❑ 66 Joey Galloway	40.00	18.00
❑ 83 Terry Glenn	25.00	11.00
❑ 90 Mark Brunell	60.00	27.00
❑ 93 Marvin Harrison	40.00	18.00
❑ 96 Eddie George	50.00	22.00

1996 Playoff Contenders Open Field Foil

	MINT	NRMT
COMPLETE SET (100)	150.00	70.00
COMMON GREEN	.75	.35
SEMISTARS GREEN	1.25	.55
UNLISTED STARS GREEN	2.00	.90
COMMON PURPLE	1.00	.45
SEMISTARS PURPLE	1.50	.70
UNLISTED STARS PURPLE	2.50	1.10
PURPLE STATED ODDS 1:5		
COMMON RED	1.50	.70
SEMISTARS RED	3.00	1.35
UNLISTED STARS RED	5.00	2.20
RED STATED ODDS 1:9		
❑ 1 Brett Favre P	12.00	5.50
❑ 2 Steve Young R	10.00	4.50
❑ 3 Herman Moore P	2.50	1.10
❑ 4 Jim Harbaugh G	1.25	.55
❑ 5 Curtis Martin P	6.00	2.70
❑ 6 Junior Seau P	2.50	1.10
❑ 7 John Elway P	12.00	5.50
❑ 8 Troy Aikman R	12.00	5.50
❑ 9 Terry Allen G	1.25	.55
❑ 10 Kordell Stewart P	6.00	2.70
❑ 11 Drew Bledsoe G	5.00	2.20
❑ 12 Jim Kelly G	2.00	.90
❑ 13 Dan Marino R	25.00	11.00
❑ 14 Andre Rison P	1.50	.70
❑ 15 Jeff Hostetler G	.75	.35
❑ 16 Scott Mitchell R	3.00	1.35
❑ 17 Carl Pickens G	2.00	.90
❑ 18 Larry Centers G	1.25	.55
❑ 19 Craig Heyward R	1.50	.70
❑ 20 Barry Sanders R	25.00	11.00
❑ 21 Deion Sanders P	4.00	1.80
❑ 22 Emmitt Smith P	10.00	4.50
❑ 23 Rashaan Salaam R	5.00	2.20
❑ 24 Mario Bates P	1.00	.45
❑ 25 Lawrence Phillips P	2.50	1.10
❑ 26 Napoleon Kaufman G	3.00	1.35
❑ 27 Rodney Hampton G	1.25	.55
❑ 28 Marshall Faulk R	5.00	2.20
❑ 29 Trent Dilfer G	2.00	.90
❑ 30 Leeland McElroy R	5.00	2.20
❑ 31 Marcus Allen G	2.00	.90
❑ 32 Ricky Watters P	1.50	.70
❑ 33 Karim Abdul-Jabbar P	3.00	1.35
❑ 34 Herschel Walker R	3.00	1.35
❑ 35 Thurman Thomas G	2.00	.90
❑ 36 Jerome Bettis G	2.00	.90
❑ 37 Gus Frerotte R	5.00	2.20
❑ 38 Neil O'Donnell G	1.25	.55
❑ 39 Rick Mirer G	1.25	.55
❑ 40 Mike Alstott G	3.00	1.35
❑ 41 Vinny Testaverde G	1.25	.55
❑ 42 Derek Loville G	.75	.35
❑ 43 Ben Coates G	1.25	.55
❑ 44 Steve McNair G	4.00	1.80
❑ 45 Bobby Engram R	5.00	2.20
❑ 46 Yancey Thigpen G	1.25	.55
❑ 47 Lake Dawson P	1.50	.70
❑ 48 Terrell Davis G	8.00	3.60
❑ 49 Kerry Collins P	2.50	1.10
❑ 50 Eric Metcalf G	.75	.35
❑ 51 Stanley Pritchett G	.75	.35
❑ 52 Robert Brooks P	2.50	1.10
❑ 53 Isaac Bruce P	2.50	1.10
❑ 54 Tim Brown P	1.50	.70
❑ 55 Edgar Bennett G	1.25	.55
❑ 56 Warren Moon P	1.50	.70
❑ 57 Jerry Rice P	6.00	2.70
❑ 58 Michael Westbrook G	2.00	.90
❑ 59 Keyshawn Johnson P	6.00	2.70
❑ 60 Steve Bono G	.75	.35
❑ 61 Derrick Mayes R	5.00	2.20
❑ 62 Erik Kramer G	.75	.35
❑ 63 Rodney Peete G	.75	.35
❑ 64 Eddie Kennison G	2.00	.90
❑ 65 Derrick Thomas G	1.25	.55
❑ 66 Joey Galloway R	8.00	3.60
❑ 67 Amani Toomer R	5.00	2.20
❑ 68 Reggie White R	5.00	2.20
❑ 69 Heath Shuler P	2.50	1.10
❑ 70 Dave Brown G	.75	.35
❑ 71 Tony Banks R	5.00	2.20
❑ 72 Chris Warren G	1.25	.55
❑ 73 J.J. Stokes G	2.00	.90
❑ 74 Rickey Dudley R	5.00	2.20
❑ 75 Stan Humphries G	1.25	.55
❑ 76 Jason Dunn R	3.00	1.35
❑ 77 Tyrone Wheatley G	1.25	.55
❑ 78 Jim Everett G	.75	.35
❑ 79 Cris Carter G	2.00	.90
❑ 80 Alex Van Dyke R	3.00	1.35
❑ 81 O.J. McDuffie P	1.50	.70
❑ 82 Mark Chmura G	1.25	.55
❑ 83 Terry Glenn R	6.00	2.70
❑ 84 Boomer Esiason G	1.25	.55
❑ 85 Bruce Smith G	1.25	.55
❑ 86 Curtis Conway G	1.25	.55
❑ 87 Ki-Jana Carter R	3.00	1.35
❑ 88 Tamarick Vanover P	2.50	1.10
❑ 89 Michael Jackson R	3.00	1.35
❑ 90 Mark Brunell G	5.00	2.20
❑ 91 Tim Biakabutuka G	2.50	1.10
❑ 92 Anthony Miller G	1.25	.55
❑ 93 Marvin Harrison G	4.00	1.80
❑ 94 Jeff George G	1.25	.55
❑ 95 Jeff Blake G	2.00	.90
❑ 96 Eddie George P	8.00	3.60
❑ 97 Eric Moulds R	8.00	3.60
❑ 98 Mike Tomczak R	1.50	.70
❑ 99 Chris Sanders G	1.25	.55
❑ 100 Chris Chandler G	1.25	.55

1996 Playoff Contenders Pennants

	MINT	NRMT
COMPLETE SET (100)	250.00	110.00
COMMON GREEN	1.00	.45
SEMISTARS GREEN	2.00	.90
UNLISTED STARS GREEN	3.00	1.35
COMMON PURPLE	1.25	.55
SEMISTARS PURPLE	2.50	1.10
UNLISTED STARS PURPLE	4.00	1.80
PURPLE STATED ODDS 1:8		
COMMON RED	2.50	1.10
SEMISTARS RED	5.00	2.20
UNLISTED STARS RED	8.00	3.60
RED STATED ODDS 1:16		

❑ 1 Brett Favre R	40.00	18.00
❑ 2 Steve Young R	15.00	6.75
❑ 3 Herman Moore R	8.00	3.60
❑ 4 Jim Harbaugh R	5.00	2.20
❑ 5 Curtis Martin R	15.00	6.75
❑ 6 Junior Seau G	2.00	.90
❑ 7 John Elway R	40.00	18.00
❑ 8 Troy Aikman P	10.00	4.50
❑ 9 Terry Allen G	2.00	.90
❑ 10 Kordell Stewart R	15.00	6.75
❑ 11 Drew Bledsoe G	10.00	4.50
❑ 12 Jim Kelly P	4.00	1.80
❑ 13 Dan Marino P	20.00	9.00
❑ 14 Andre Rison G	2.00	.90
❑ 15 Jeff Hostetler G	1.00	.45
❑ 16 Scott Mitchell G	2.00	.90
❑ 17 Carl Pickens R	8.00	3.60
❑ 18 Larry Centers P	2.50	1.10
❑ 19 Craig Heyward G	1.00	.45
❑ 20 Barry Sanders P	20.00	9.00
❑ 21 Deion Sanders R	12.00	5.50
❑ 22 Emmitt Smith R	30.00	13.50
❑ 23 Rashaan Salaam R	8.00	3.60
❑ 24 Mario Bates G	2.00	.90
❑ 25 Lawrence Phillips G	3.00	1.35
❑ 26 Napoleon Kaufman G	5.00	2.20
❑ 27 Rodney Hampton G	2.00	.90
❑ 28 Marshall Faulk P	4.00	1.80
❑ 29 Trent Dilfer G	3.00	1.35
❑ 30 Leeland McElroy P	4.00	1.80
❑ 31 Marcus Allen P	4.00	1.80
❑ 32 Ricky Watters G	2.00	.90
❑ 33 Karim Abdul-Jabbar G	4.00	1.80
❑ 34 Herschel Walker P	2.50	1.10
❑ 35 Thurman Thomas R	8.00	3.60
❑ 36 Jerome Bettis P	4.00	1.80
❑ 37 Gus Frerotte G	3.00	1.35
❑ 38 Neil O'Donnell G	2.00	.90
❑ 39 Rick Mirer G	2.00	.90
❑ 40 Mike Alstott R	10.00	4.50
❑ 41 Vinny Testaverde R	2.50	1.10
❑ 42 Derek Loville G	1.00	.45
❑ 43 Ben Coates G	2.00	.90
❑ 44 Steve McNair R	15.00	6.75
❑ 45 Bobby Engram P	4.00	1.80
❑ 46 Yancey Thigpen G	2.00	.90
❑ 47 Lake Dawson G	1.00	.45
❑ 48 Terrell Davis P	25.00	11.00
❑ 49 Kerry Collins R	8.00	3.60
❑ 50 Eric Metcalf G	1.00	.45
❑ 51 Stanley Pritchett R	2.50	1.10
❑ 52 Robert Brooks R	8.00	3.60
❑ 53 Isaac Bruce G	3.00	1.35
❑ 54 Tim Brown G	3.00	1.35
❑ 55 Edgar Bennett P	2.50	1.10
❑ 56 Warren Moon G	2.00	.90
❑ 57 Jerry Rice R	20.00	9.00
❑ 58 Michael Westbrook G	3.00	1.35
❑ 59 Keyshawn Johnson G	6.00	2.70
❑ 60 Steve Bono R	1.00	.45
❑ 61 Derrick Mayes P	4.00	1.80
❑ 62 Erik Kramer P	1.25	.55
❑ 63 Rodney Peete G	1.00	.45
❑ 64 Eddie Kennison G	3.00	1.35
❑ 65 Derrick Thomas G	2.00	.90
❑ 66 Joey Galloway R	15.00	6.75
❑ 67 Amani Toomer P	4.00	1.80
❑ 68 Reggie White G	3.00	1.35
❑ 69 Heath Shuler G	2.00	.90
❑ 70 Dave Brown G	1.00	.45
❑ 71 Tony Banks P	4.00	1.80
❑ 72 Chris Warren G	2.00	.90
❑ 73 J.J. Stokes G	3.00	1.35
❑ 74 Rickey Dudley P	4.00	1.80
❑ 75 Stan Humphries G	2.00	.90
❑ 76 Jason Dunn P	2.50	1.10
❑ 77 Tyrone Wheatley G	2.00	.90
❑ 78 Jim Everett G	1.00	.45
❑ 79 Cris Carter P	4.00	1.80
❑ 80 Alex Van Dyke P	2.50	1.10
❑ 81 O.J. McDuffie G	2.00	.90
❑ 82 Mark Chmura P	2.50	1.10
❑ 83 Terry Glenn P	5.00	2.20
❑ 84 Boomer Esiason R	5.00	2.20
❑ 85 Bruce Smith G	2.00	.90
❑ 86 Curtis Conway G	2.00	.90
❑ 87 Ki-Jana Carter G	2.00	.90
❑ 88 Tamarick Vanover G	2.00	.90
❑ 89 Michael Jackson G	2.00	.90
❑ 90 Mark Brunell G	10.00	4.50
❑ 91 Tim Biakabutuka R	8.00	3.60
❑ 92 Anthony Miller G	2.00	.90
❑ 93 Marvin Harrison R	12.00	5.50
❑ 94 Jeff George P	2.50	1.10
❑ 95 Jeff Blake R	8.00	3.60
❑ 96 Eddie George G	10.00	4.50
❑ 97 Eric Moulds P	6.00	2.70
❑ 98 Mike Tomczak G	1.00	.45
❑ 99 Chris Sanders G	2.00	.90
❑ 100 Chris Chandler G	2.00	.90

1996 Playoff Contenders Air Command

	MINT	NRMT
COMPLETE SET (8)	120.00	55.00
COMMON CARD (AC1-AC8)	10.00	4.50
STATED ODDS 1:96		
❑ AC1 Dan Marino	30.00	13.50
❑ AC2 Brett Favre	30.00	13.50
❑ AC3 Troy Aikman	20.00	9.00
❑ AC4 Mike Tomczak	10.00	4.50
❑ AC5 John Elway	30.00	13.50
❑ AC6 Jeff George	20.00	9.00
❑ AC7 Chris Chandler	20.00	9.00
❑ AC8 Steve Bono	10.00	4.50

1996 Playoff Contenders Ground Hogs

	MINT	NRMT
COMPLETE SET (8)	150.00	70.00
COMMON CARD (GH1-GH8)	15.00	6.75
SEMISTARS	20.00	9.00
STATED ODDS 1:144		
❑ GH1 Emmitt Smith	30.00	13.50
❑ GH2 Barry Sanders	40.00	18.00
❑ GH3 Marshall Faulk	20.00	9.00
❑ GH4 Curtis Martin	20.00	9.00
❑ GH5 Chris Warren	15.00	6.75
❑ GH6 Ricky Watters	15.00	6.75
❑ GH7 Thurman Thomas	20.00	9.00
❑ GH8 Terrell Davis	30.00	13.50

1996 Playoff Contenders Honors

	MINT	NRMT
COMPLETE SET (3)	300.00	135.00
COMMON CARD (PH4-PH6)	50.00	22.00
STATED ODDS 1:7200		
❑ PH4 Dan Marino	200.00	90.00
❑ PH5 Deion Sanders	60.00	27.00
❑ PH6 Marcus Allen	50.00	22.00

1996 Playoff Contenders Pennant Flyers

	MINT	NRMT
COMPLETE SET (8)	120.00	55.00
COMMON CARD (PF1-PF8)	10.00	4.50
SEMISTARS	15.00	6.75
STATED ODDS 1:48		
❑ PF1 Jerry Rice	40.00	18.00
❑ PF2 Joey Galloway	15.00	6.75
❑ PF3 Isaac Bruce	15.00	6.75
❑ PF4 Herman Moore	15.00	6.75
❑ PF5 Carl Pickens	10.00	4.50
❑ PF6 Yancey Thigpen	10.00	4.50
❑ PF7 Deion Sanders	20.00	9.00
❑ PF8 Robert Brooks	15.00	6.75

1997 Playoff Contenders

	MINT	NRMT
COMPLETE SET (150)	80.00	36.00
COMMON CARD (1-150)	.40	.18
SEMISTARS	.75	.35
UNLISTED STARS	1.50	.70
COMP.BLUE SET (150)	300.00	135.00
*BLUE STARS: 1.5X TO 4X HI COL.		
*BLUE RCs: .75X TO 2X HI		
BLUE STATED ODDS 1:4		
COMMON RED	15.00	6.75
*RED STARS: 15X TO 40X HI COL.		
*RED RCs: 8X TO 20X		
STATED PRINT RUN 25 SERIAL #'d SETS		

		MINT	NRMT
❑ 1	Kent Graham	.40	.18
❑ 2	Leeland McElroy	.40	.18
❑ 3	Rob Moore	.75	.35
❑ 4	Frank Sanders	.75	.35
❑ 5	Jake Plummer RC	12.00	5.50
❑ 6	Chris Chandler	.75	.35
❑ 7	Bert Emanuel	.75	.35
❑ 8	O.J. Santiago RC	2.00	.90
❑ 9	Byron Hanspard RC	2.50	1.10
❑ 10	Vinny Testaverde	.75	.35
❑ 11	Michael Jackson	.75	.35
❑ 12	Earnest Byner	.40	.18
❑ 13	Jermaine Lewis	1.50	.70
❑ 14	Derrick Alexander WR	.75	.35
❑ 15	Jay Graham RC	1.50	.70
❑ 16	Todd Collins	.40	.18
❑ 17	Thurman Thomas	1.50	.70
❑ 18	Bruce Smith	.75	.35
❑ 19	Andre Reed	.75	.35
❑ 20	Quinn Early	.40	.18
❑ 21	Antowain Smith RC	3.00	1.35
❑ 22	Kerry Collins	.75	.35
❑ 23	Tim Biakabutuka	.75	.35
❑ 24	Anthony Johnson	.40	.18
❑ 25	Wesley Walls	.75	.35
❑ 26	Fred Lane RC	2.00	.90
❑ 27	Rae Carruth RC	1.50	.70
❑ 28	Raymont Harris	.40	.18
❑ 29	Rick Mirer	.40	.18
❑ 30	Darnell Autry RC	.75	.35
❑ 31	Jeff Blake	.75	.35
❑ 32	Ki-Jana Carter	.40	.18
❑ 33	Carl Pickens	1.50	.70
❑ 34	Darnay Scott	.75	.35
❑ 35	Corey Dillon RC	6.00	2.70
❑ 36	Troy Aikman	4.00	1.80
❑ 37	Emmitt Smith	6.00	2.70
❑ 38	Michael Irvin	1.50	.70
❑ 39	Deion Sanders	1.50	.70
❑ 40	Anthony Miller	.40	.18
❑ 41	Eric Bjornson	.40	.18
❑ 42	David LaFleur RC	2.00	.90
❑ 43	John Elway	8.00	3.60
❑ 44	Terrell Davis	6.00	2.70
❑ 45	Shannon Sharpe	.75	.35
❑ 46	Ed McCaffrey	.75	.35
❑ 47	Rod Smith WR	1.50	.70
❑ 48	Scott Mitchell	.75	.35
❑ 49	Barry Sanders	8.00	3.60
❑ 50	Herman Moore	1.50	.70
❑ 51	Brett Favre	8.00	3.60
❑ 52	Dorsey Levens	1.50	.70
❑ 53	William Henderson	.40	.18
❑ 54	Derrick Mayes	.75	.35
❑ 55	Antonio Freeman	2.00	.90
❑ 56	Robert Brooks	.75	.35
❑ 57	Mark Chmura	.75	.35
❑ 58	Reggie White	1.50	.70
❑ 59	Darren Sharper RC	.40	.18
❑ 60	Jim Harbaugh	.75	.35
❑ 61	Marshall Faulk	1.50	.70
❑ 62	Marvin Harrison	1.50	.70
❑ 63	Mark Brunell	4.00	1.80
❑ 64	Natrone Means	1.50	.70
❑ 65	Jimmy Smith	.75	.35
❑ 66	Keenan McCardell	.75	.35
❑ 67	Elvis Grbac	.75	.35
❑ 68	Greg Hill	.40	.18
❑ 69	Marcus Allen	1.50	.70
❑ 70	Andre Rison	.75	.35
❑ 71	Kimble Anders	.75	.35
❑ 72	Tony Gonzalez RC	5.00	2.20
❑ 73	Pat Barnes RC	1.50	.70
❑ 74	Dan Marino	8.00	3.60
❑ 75	Karim Abdul-Jabbar	1.50	.70
❑ 76	Zach Thomas	.75	.35
❑ 77	O.J. McDuffie	.75	.35
❑ 78	Brian Manning RC	.40	.18
❑ 79	Brad Johnson	2.00	.90
❑ 80	Cris Carter	1.50	.70
❑ 81	Jake Reed	.75	.35
❑ 82	Robert Smith	.75	.35
❑ 83	Drew Bledsoe	4.00	1.80
❑ 84	Curtis Martin	2.00	.90
❑ 85	Ben Coates	.75	.35
❑ 86	Terry Glenn	1.50	.70
❑ 87	Shawn Jefferson	.40	.18
❑ 88	Heath Shuler	.40	.18
❑ 89	Mario Bates	.40	.18
❑ 90	Andre Hastings	.40	.18
❑ 91	Troy Davis RC	1.50	.70
❑ 92	Danny Wuerffel RC	2.00	.90
❑ 93	Dave Brown	.40	.18
❑ 94	Chris Calloway	.40	.18
❑ 95	Tiki Barber RC	2.00	.90
❑ 96	Mike Cherry RC	.40	.18
❑ 97	Neil O'Donnell	.75	.35
❑ 98	Keyshawn Johnson	1.50	.70
❑ 99	Adrian Murrell	.75	.35
❑ 100	Wayne Chrebet	1.50	.70
❑ 101	Dedric Ward RC	2.50	1.10
❑ 102	Leon Johnson RC	.40	.18
❑ 103	Jeff George	.75	.35
❑ 104	Napoleon Kaufman	1.50	.70
❑ 105	Tim Brown	1.50	.70
❑ 106	James Jett	.75	.35
❑ 107	Ty Detmer	.75	.35
❑ 108	Ricky Watters	.75	.35
❑ 109	Irving Fryar	.75	.35
❑ 110	Michael Timpson	.40	.18
❑ 111	Chad Lewis RC	.40	.18
❑ 112	Kordell Stewart	2.00	.90
❑ 113	Jerome Bettis	1.50	.70
❑ 114	Charles Johnson	.75	.35
❑ 115	George Jones RC	.75	.35
❑ 116	Will Blackwell RC	1.50	.70
❑ 117	Stan Humphries	.75	.35
❑ 118	Junior Seau	.75	.35
❑ 119	Freddie Jones RC	.75	.35
❑ 120	Steve Young	2.50	1.10
❑ 121	Jerry Rice	4.00	1.80
❑ 122	Garrison Hearst	.75	.35
❑ 123	William Floyd	.75	.35
❑ 124	Terrell Owens	1.50	.70
❑ 125	J.J. Stokes	.75	.35
❑ 126	Marc Edwards RC	.40	.18
❑ 127	Jim Druckenmiller RC	2.00	.90
❑ 128	Warren Moon	1.50	.70
❑ 129	Chris Warren	.75	.35
❑ 130	Joey Galloway	2.00	.90
❑ 131	Shawn Springs RC	.75	.35
❑ 132	Tony Banks	.75	.35
❑ 133	Lawrence Phillips	.40	.18
❑ 134	Isaac Bruce	1.50	.70
❑ 135	Eddie Kennison	.75	.35
❑ 136	Orlando Pace RC	.40	.18
❑ 137	Trent Dilfer	1.50	.70
❑ 138	Mike Alstott	1.50	.70
❑ 139	Horace Copeland	.40	.18
❑ 140	Jackie Harris	.40	.18
❑ 141	Warrick Dunn RC	5.00	2.20
❑ 142	Reidel Anthony RC	2.50	1.10
❑ 143	Steve McNair	2.00	.90
❑ 144	Eddie George	4.00	1.80
❑ 145	Chris Sanders	.40	.18
❑ 146	Gus Frerotte	.40	.18
❑ 147	Terry Allen	1.50	.70
❑ 148	Henry Ellard	.40	.18
❑ 149	Leslie Shepherd	.40	.18
❑ 150	Michael Westbrook	.75	.35
❑ S1	Terrell Davis Sample	3.00	1.35

1997 Playoff Contenders Clash

	MINT	NRMT
COMPLETE SET (12)	400.00	180.00
COMMON CARD (1-12)	15.00	6.75
SILVER STATED ODDS 1:48		
*BLUE CARDS: .75X TO 2X HI COL.		
BLUE STATED ODDS 1:192		

❑ 1	Brett Favre Troy Aikman	60.00	27.00
❑ 2	Barry Sanders Brad Johnson	60.00	27.00
❑ 3	Curtis Martin Warrick Dunn	20.00	9.00
❑ 4	Steve Young John Elway	60.00	27.00
❑ 5	Jerry Rice Marcus Allen	30.00	13.50
❑ 6	Dan Marino Drew Bledsoe	60.00	27.00
❑ 7	Terrell Davis Napoleon Kaufman	50.00	22.00
❑ 8	Eddie George Emmitt Smith	50.00	22.00
❑ 9	Mark Brunell Tim Brown	25.00	11.00
❑ 10	Kerry Collins Reggie White	15.00	6.75
❑ 11	Deion Sanders Carl Pickens	15.00	6.75
❑ 12	Mike Alstott Keyshawn Johnson	20.00	9.00

1997 Playoff Contenders Leather Helmet Die Cuts

	MINT	NRMT
COMPLETE SET (18)	400.00	180.00
SILVER STATED ODDS 1:24		
*BLUE STARS: 8X TO 20X BASE CARD HI		
*BLUE ROOKIES: 3X TO 8X BASE CARD HI		
BLUE STATED ODDS 1:216		
*RED STARS: 25X TO 60X BASE CARD HI		
*RED ROOKIES: 10X TO 25X BASE CARD HI		
RED STATED PRINT RUN 25 SERIAL #'d SETS		

❑ 1	Dan Marino	50.00	22.00
❑ 2	Troy Aikman	25.00	11.00
❑ 3	Brett Favre	50.00	22.00
❑ 4	Barry Sanders	50.00	22.00
❑ 5	Drew Bledsoe	25.00	11.00
❑ 6	Deion Sanders	10.00	4.50
❑ 7	Curtis Martin	12.00	5.50
❑ 8	Warrick Dunn	12.00	5.50
❑ 9	Napoleon Kaufman	10.00	4.50
❑ 10	Eddie George	25.00	11.00
❑ 11	Antowain Smith	8.00	3.60
❑ 12	Emmitt Smith	40.00	18.00
❑ 13	John Elway	50.00	22.00
❑ 14	Steve Young	15.00	6.75
❑ 15	Mark Brunell	25.00	11.00
❑ 16	Terrell Davis	40.00	18.00
❑ 17	Terry Glenn	10.00	4.50
❑ 18	Terrell Owens	10.00	4.50

1997 Playoff Contenders Pennants

	MINT	NRMT
COMPLETE SET (36)	500.00	220.00
SILVER STATED ODDS 1:12		
*BLUE STARS: 4X TO 10X BASE CARD HI		
*BLUE ROOKIES: 1.5X TO 4X BASE CARD HI		
BLUE STATED ODDS 1:72		

Card	MINT	NRMT
❑ 1 Dan Marino	40.00	18.00
❑ 2 Kordell Stewart	10.00	4.50
❑ 3 Drew Bledsoe	20.00	9.00
❑ 4 Kerry Collins	4.00	1.80
❑ 5 John Elway	40.00	18.00
❑ 6 Trent Dilfer	8.00	3.60
❑ 7 Jerry Rice	20.00	9.00
❑ 8 Emmitt Smith	30.00	13.50
❑ 9 Jeff George	4.00	1.80
❑ 10 Eddie George	20.00	9.00
❑ 11 Terrell Davis	30.00	13.50
❑ 12 Mike Alstott	8.00	3.60
❑ 13 Jim Druckenmiller	4.00	1.80
❑ 14 Antowain Smith	6.00	2.70
❑ 15 Marcus Allen	8.00	3.60
❑ 16 Jerome Bettis	8.00	3.60
❑ 17 Terrell Owens	8.00	3.60
❑ 18 Gus Frerotte	2.00	.90
❑ 19 Troy Aikman	20.00	9.00
❑ 20 Andre Rison	4.00	1.80
❑ 21 Mark Brunell	20.00	9.00
❑ 22 Antonio Freeman	10.00	4.50
❑ 23 Brett Favre	40.00	18.00
❑ 24 Steve McNair	10.00	4.50
❑ 25 Barry Sanders	40.00	18.00
❑ 26 Steve Young	12.00	5.50
❑ 27 Curtis Martin	10.00	4.50
❑ 28 Napoleon Kaufman	8.00	3.60
❑ 29 Deion Sanders	8.00	3.60
❑ 30 Terry Glenn	8.00	3.60
❑ 31 Warrick Dunn	10.00	4.50
❑ 32 Danny Wuerffel	4.00	1.80
❑ 33 Elvis Grbac	4.00	1.80
❑ 34 Cris Carter	8.00	3.60
❑ 35 Joey Galloway	10.00	4.50
❑ 36 Corey Dillon	12.00	5.50

1997 Playoff Contenders Performer Plaques

	MINT	NRMT
COMPLETE SET (45)	500.00	220.00
SILVER STATED ODDS 1:12		
*BLUE STARS: 5X TO 10X BASE CARD HI		
BLUE STATED ODDS 1:36		

Card	MINT	NRMT
❑ 1 Jim Druckenmiller	4.00	1.80
❑ 2 Danny Wuerffel	4.00	1.80
❑ 3 Antowain Smith	6.00	2.70
❑ 4 Warrick Dunn	10.00	4.50
❑ 5 Terrell Owens	8.00	3.60
❑ 6 Elvis Grbac	4.00	1.80
❑ 7 Andre Rison	4.00	1.80
❑ 8 Tim Brown	8.00	3.60
❑ 9 Trent Dilfer	8.00	3.60
❑ 10 Brad Johnson	10.00	4.50
❑ 11 Deion Sanders	8.00	3.60
❑ 12 Dan Marino	40.00	18.00
❑ 13 Kerry Collins	4.00	1.80
❑ 14 Steve McNair	10.00	4.50
❑ 15 Eddie George	20.00	9.00
❑ 16 Ricky Watters	4.00	1.80
❑ 17 Jerome Bettis	8.00	3.60
❑ 18 Robert Brooks	4.00	1.80
❑ 19 Keyshawn Johnson	8.00	3.60
❑ 20 Antonio Freeman	10.00	4.50
❑ 21 Eddie Kennison	4.00	1.80
❑ 22 Mike Alstott	8.00	3.60
❑ 23 Brett Favre	40.00	18.00
❑ 24 Troy Aikman	20.00	9.00
❑ 25 Emmitt Smith	30.00	13.50
❑ 26 Terrell Davis	30.00	13.50
❑ 27 John Elway	40.00	18.00
❑ 28 Barry Sanders	40.00	18.00
❑ 29 Steve Young	12.00	5.50
❑ 30 Curtis Martin	10.00	4.50
❑ 31 Cris Carter	8.00	3.60
❑ 32 Drew Bledsoe	20.00	9.00
❑ 33 Mark Brunell	20.00	9.00
❑ 34 Kordell Stewart	10.00	4.50
❑ 35 Tony Banks	4.00	1.80
❑ 36 Napoleon Kaufman	8.00	3.60
❑ 37 Marcus Allen	8.00	3.60
❑ 38 Terry Glenn	8.00	3.60
❑ 39 Herman Moore	8.00	3.60
❑ 40 Michael Irvin	8.00	3.60
❑ 41 Joey Galloway	10.00	4.50
❑ 42 Karim Abdul-Jabbar	8.00	3.60
❑ 43 Reggie White	8.00	3.60
❑ 44 Jerry Rice	20.00	9.00
❑ 45 Gus Frerotte	2.00	.90

1997 Playoff Contenders Rookie Wave Pennants

	MINT	NRMT
COMPLETE SET (27)	175.00	80.00
COMMON CARD (1-27)	2.00	.90
SEMISTARS	4.00	1.80
UNLISTED STARS	6.00	2.70
STATED ODDS 1:6		

Card	MINT	NRMT
❑ 1 Jim Druckenmiller	6.00	2.70
❑ 2 Antowain Smith	8.00	3.60
❑ 3 Will Blackwell	6.00	2.70
❑ 4 Tiki Barber	6.00	2.70
❑ 5 Rae Carruth	4.00	1.80
❑ 6 Jay Graham	6.00	2.70
❑ 7 Darnell Autry	4.00	1.80
❑ 8 David LaFleur	4.00	1.80
❑ 9 Tony Gonzalez	10.00	4.50
❑ 10 Chad Lewis	2.00	.90
❑ 11 Freddie Jones	4.00	1.80
❑ 12 Shawn Springs	4.00	1.80
❑ 13 Danny Wuerffel	4.00	1.80
❑ 14 Warrick Dunn	10.00	4.50
❑ 15 Troy Davis	6.00	2.70
❑ 16 Reidel Anthony	6.00	2.70
❑ 17 Jake Plummer	25.00	11.00
❑ 18 Byron Hanspard	6.00	2.70
❑ 19 Fred Lane	6.00	2.70
❑ 20 Corey Dillon	12.00	5.50
❑ 21 Darren Sharper	2.00	.90
❑ 22 Pat Barnes	6.00	2.70
❑ 23 Mike Cherry	2.00	.90
❑ 24 Leon Johnson	2.00	.90
❑ 25 George Jones	4.00	1.80
❑ 26 Marc Edwards	2.00	.90
❑ 27 Orlando Pace	2.00	.90

1998 Playoff Contenders Leather

	MINT	NRMT
COMPLETE SET (100)	200.00	90.00
COMMON CARD (1-100)	.50	.23
SEMISTARS	1.00	.45
UNLISTED STARS	2.00	.90
ONE LEATHER CARD PER PACK		
COMMON ROOKIE	.75	.35
ROOKIE SEMISTARS	1.50	.70
ROOKIE UNLISTED STARS	2.50	1.10
COMP.RED SET (100)	400.00	180.00
*RED STARS: 1X TO 2.5X HI COL.		
*RED ROOKIES: .6X TO 1.5X HI COL.		
RED LEATHER STATED ODDS 1:9 HOB		

Card	MINT	NRMT
❑ 1 Adrian Murrell	1.00	.45
❑ 2 Michael Pittman	1.50	.70
❑ 3 Jake Plummer	6.00	2.70
❑ 4 Andre Wadsworth	1.50	.70
❑ 5 Jamal Anderson	2.00	.90
❑ 6 Chris Chandler	1.00	.45
❑ 7 Tim Dwight	4.00	1.80
❑ 8 Pat Johnson	1.50	.70
❑ 9 Jermaine Lewis	1.00	.45
❑ 10 Doug Flutie	2.50	1.10
❑ 11 Antowain Smith	2.00	.90
❑ 12 Muhsin Muhammad	1.00	.45
❑ 13 Bobby Engram	1.00	.45
❑ 14 Curtis Enis	5.00	2.20
❑ 15 Alonzo Mayes	.75	.35
❑ 16 Corey Dillon	3.00	1.35
❑ 17 Carl Pickens	2.00	.90
❑ 18 Troy Aikman	5.00	2.20
❑ 19 Michael Irvin	2.00	.90
❑ 20 Deion Sanders	2.00	.90
❑ 21 Emmitt Smith	8.00	3.60
❑ 22 Terrell Davis	8.00	3.60
❑ 23 John Elway	10.00	4.50
❑ 24 Brian Griese	8.00	3.60
❑ 25 Rod Smith WR	1.00	.45
❑ 26 Charlie Batch	8.00	3.60

Card	MINT	NRMT
❑ 27 Germane Crowell	5.00	2.20
❑ 28 Terry Fair	1.50	.70
❑ 29 Herman Moore	2.00	.90
❑ 30 Barry Sanders	10.00	4.50
❑ 31 Brett Favre	10.00	4.50
❑ 32 Antonio Freeman	2.00	.90
❑ 33 Vonnie Holliday UER front and back Holiday	1.50	.70
❑ 34 Reggie White	2.00	.90
❑ 35 Marshall Faulk	2.00	.90
❑ 36 Marvin Harrison	1.00	.45
❑ 37 Peyton Manning	20.00	9.00
❑ 38 Jerome Pathon	1.50	.70
❑ 39 Tavian Banks	1.50	.70
❑ 40 Mark Brunell	4.00	1.80
❑ 41 Keenan McCardell	1.00	.45
❑ 42 Fred Taylor	12.00	5.50
❑ 43 Elvis Grbac	1.00	.45
❑ 44 Andre Rison	1.00	.45
❑ 45 Rashaan Shehee	1.50	.70
❑ 46 Karim Abdul-Jabbar	2.00	.90
❑ 47 John Avery	2.50	1.10
❑ 48 Dan Marino	10.00	4.50
❑ 49 O.J. McDuffie	1.00	.45
❑ 50 Cris Carter	2.00	.90
❑ 51 Brad Johnson	2.00	.90
❑ 52 Randy Moss	20.00	9.00
❑ 53 Robert Smith	2.00	.90
❑ 54 Drew Bledsoe	4.00	1.80
❑ 55 Ben Coates	1.00	.45
❑ 56 Robert Edwards	2.00	.90
❑ 57 Chris Floyd	.75	.35
❑ 58 Terry Glenn	2.00	.90
❑ 59 Cameron Cleeland	1.50	.70
❑ 60 Kerry Collins	1.00	.45
❑ 61 Danny Kanell	1.00	.45
❑ 62 Charles Way	.50	.23
❑ 63 Glenn Foley	1.00	.45
❑ 64 Keyshawn Johnson	2.00	.90
❑ 65 Curtis Martin	2.00	.90
❑ 66 Tim Brown	2.00	.90
❑ 67 Jeff George	1.00	.45
❑ 68 Napoleon Kaufman	2.00	.90
❑ 69 Charles Woodson	5.00	2.20
❑ 70 Irving Fryar	1.00	.45
❑ 71 Bobby Hoying	1.00	.45
❑ 72 Jerome Bettis	2.00	.90
❑ 73 Kordell Stewart	2.00	.90
❑ 74 Hines Ward	1.50	.70
❑ 75 Ryan Leaf	4.00	1.80
❑ 76 Natrone Means	2.00	.90
❑ 77 Mikhael Ricks	1.50	.70
❑ 78 Junior Seau	1.00	.45
❑ 79 Garrison Hearst	2.00	.90
❑ 80 Terrell Owens	2.00	.90
❑ 81 Jerry Rice	5.00	2.20
❑ 82 Steve Young	3.00	1.35
❑ 83 Joey Galloway	2.00	.90
❑ 84 Ahman Green	2.50	1.10
❑ 85 Warren Moon	2.00	.90
❑ 86 Ricky Watters	1.00	.45
❑ 87 Tony Banks	1.00	.45
❑ 88 Isaac Bruce	2.00	.90
❑ 89 Robert Holcombe	2.50	1.10
❑ 90 Mike Alstott	2.00	.90
❑ 91 Trent Dilfer	2.00	.90
❑ 92 Warrick Dunn	3.00	1.35
❑ 93 Jacquez Green	3.00	1.35
❑ 94 Kevin Dyson	4.00	1.80
❑ 95 Eddie George	4.00	1.80
❑ 96 Steve McNair	2.00	.90
❑ 97 Yancey Thigpen	.50	.23
❑ 98 Terry Allen	2.00	.90
❑ 99 Skip Hicks	2.50	1.10
❑ 100 Michael Westbrook	1.00	.45

1998 Playoff Contenders Leather Gold

	MINT	NRMT
COMMON CARD (1-100)	10.00	4.50
SEMISTARS	15.00	6.75
UNLISTED STARS	20.00	9.00

CARDS SERIAL #'d TO FEATURED STAT

Card	MINT	NRMT
❑ 1 Adrian Murrell/27	40.00	18.00
❑ 2 Michael Pittman/32	40.00	18.00
❑ 3 Jake Plummer/53	100.00	45.00
❑ 4 Andre Wadsworth/29	50.00	22.00
❑ 5 Jamal Anderson/29	80.00	36.00
❑ 6 Chris Chandler/94	15.00	6.75
❑ 7 Tim Dwight/39	60.00	27.00
❑ 8 Pat Johnson/55	20.00	9.00
❑ 9 Jermaine Lewis/42	25.00	11.00
❑ 10 Doug Flutie/48	50.00	22.00
❑ 11 Antowain Smith/28	80.00	36.00
❑ 12 Muhsin Muhammad/52	20.00	9.00
❑ 13 Bobby Engram/78	15.00	6.75
❑ 14 Curtis Enis/36	80.00	36.00
❑ 15 Alonzo Mayes/92	10.00	4.50
❑ 16 Corey Dillon/27	100.00	45.00
❑ 17 Carl Pickens/52	30.00	13.50
❑ 18 Troy Aikman/62	100.00	45.00
❑ 19 Michael Irvin/61	40.00	18.00
❑ 20 Deion Sanders/36	50.00	22.00
❑ 21 Emmitt Smith/40	175.00	80.00
❑ 22 Terrell Davis/35	250.00	110.00
❑ 23 John Elway/27	300.00	135.00
❑ 24 Brian Griese/33	120.00	55.00
❑ 25 Rod Smith/70	15.00	6.75
❑ 26 Charlie Batch/23	120.00	55.00
❑ 27 Germane Crowell/53	40.00	18.00
❑ 28 Terry Fair/42	30.00	13.50
❑ 29 Herman Moore/52	40.00	18.00
❑ 30 Barry Sanders/33	300.00	135.00
❑ 31 Brett Favre/35	300.00	135.00
❑ 32 Antonio Freeman/58	40.00	18.00
❑ 33 Vonnie Holliday/64	25.00	11.00
❑ 34 Reggie White/36	60.00	27.00
❑ 35 Marshall Faulk/47	50.00	22.00
❑ 36 Marvin Harrison/73	15.00	6.75
❑ 37 Peyton Manning/36	250.00	110.00
❑ 38 Jerome Pathon/69	25.00	11.00
❑ 39 Tavian Banks/33	40.00	18.00
❑ 40 Mark Brunell/52	80.00	36.00
❑ 41 Keenan McCardell/85	15.00	6.75
❑ 42 Fred Taylor/31	150.00	70.00
❑ 43 Elvis Grbac/29	40.00	18.00
❑ 44 Andre Rison/72	10.00	4.50
❑ 45 Rashaan Shehee/44	25.00	11.00
❑ 46 Karim Abdul-Jabbar/26	80.00	36.00
❑ 47 John Avery/35	40.00	18.00
❑ 48 Dan Marino/16	500.00	220.00
❑ 49 O.J. McDuffie/55	20.00	9.00
❑ 50 Cris Carter/89	20.00	9.00
❑ 51 Brad Johnson/37	50.00	22.00
❑ 52 Randy Moss/25	400.00	180.00
❑ 53 Robert Smith/90	20.00	9.00
❑ 54 Drew Bledsoe/28	150.00	70.00
❑ 55 Ben Coates/42	30.00	13.50
❑ 56 Robert Edwards/27	50.00	22.00
❑ 57 Chris Floyd/63	10.00	4.50
❑ 58 Terry Glenn/50	40.00	18.00
❑ 59 Cameron Cleeland/50	25.00	11.00
❑ 60 Kerry Collins/39	30.00	13.50
❑ 61 Danny Kanell/53	15.00	6.75
❑ 62 Charles Way/76	10.00	4.50
❑ 63 Glenn Foley/56	20.00	9.00
❑ 64 Keyshawn Johnson/70	25.00	11.00
❑ 65 Curtis Martin/41	50.00	22.00
❑ 66 Tim Brown/60	40.00	18.00
❑ 67 Jeff George/29	40.00	18.00
❑ 68 Napoleon Kaufman/40	50.00	22.00
❑ 69 Charles Woodson/27	80.00	36.00
❑ 70 Irving Fryar/75	10.00	4.50
❑ 71 Bobby Hoying/53	15.00	6.75
❑ 72 Jerome Bettis/38	60.00	27.00
❑ 73 Kordell Stewart/22	100.00	45.00
❑ 74 Hines Ward/55	25.00	11.00
❑ 75 Ryan Leaf/33	60.00	27.00
❑ 76 Natrone Means/78	25.00	11.00
❑ 77 Mikhael Ricks/47	30.00	13.50
❑ 78 Junior Seau/33	40.00	18.00
❑ 79 Garrison Hearst/74	25.00	11.00
❑ 80 Terrell Owens/60	30.00	13.50
❑ 81 Jerry Rice/16	300.00	135.00
❑ 82 Steve Young/19	150.00	70.00
❑ 83 Joey Galloway/72	25.00	11.00
❑ 84 Ahman Green/42	25.00	11.00
❑ 85 Warren Moon/25	80.00	36.00
❑ 86 Ricky Watters/56	20.00	9.00
❑ 87 Tony Banks/51	15.00	6.75
❑ 88 Isaac Bruce/56	40.00	18.00
❑ 89 Robert Holcombe/35	40.00	18.00
❑ 90 Mike Alstott/88	20.00	9.00
❑ 91 Trent Dilfer/38	60.00	27.00
❑ 92 Warrick Dunn/39	50.00	22.00
❑ 93 Jacquez Green/61	30.00	13.50
❑ 94 Kevin Dyson/60	30.00	13.50
❑ 95 Eddie George/30	150.00	70.00
❑ 96 Steve McNair/52	40.00	18.00
❑ 97 Yancey Thigpen/79	10.00	4.50
❑ 98 Terry Allen/58	40.00	18.00
❑ 99 Skip Hicks/48	40.00	18.00
❑ 100 Michael Westbrook/45	25.00	11.00

1998 Playoff Contenders Pennants

	MINT	NRMT
COMPLETE SET (100)	200.00	90.00
COMMON CARD (1-100)	.50	.23
SEMISTARS	1.00	.45
UNLISTED STARS	2.00	.90
ONE PENNANT PER PACK		
EACH BASE CARD ISSUED IN 6-COLORS		
COMMON ROOKIE	.75	.35
ROOKIE SEMISTARS	1.50	.70
ROOKIE UNLISTED STARS	2.00	.90
COMP.RED SET (100)	400.00	180.00
*RED STARS: 1X TO 2.5X HI COL.		
*RED ROOKIES: .6X TO 1.5X HI COL.		
RED PENNANT STATED ODDS 1:9		
COMP.GOLD SET (100)	2000.00	900.00
*GOLD CARDS: 4X TO 10X HI COL.		
*GOLD ROOKIES: 3X TO 7X HI COL.		
GOLD PENNANT PRINT RUN 98 SETS		

Card	MINT	NRMT
❑ 1 Jake Plummer	6.00	2.70
❑ 2 Frank Sanders	1.00	.45
❑ 3 Jamal Anderson	2.00	.90
❑ 4 Tim Dwight	4.00	1.80
❑ 5 Jammi German	.75	.35
❑ 6 Tony Martin	1.00	.45
❑ 7 Jim Harbaugh	1.00	.45
❑ 8 Rod Woodson	1.00	.45
❑ 9 Rob Johnson	1.00	.45
❑ 10 Eric Moulds	2.00	.90
❑ 11 Antowain Smith	2.00	.90
❑ 12 Steve Beuerlein	.50	.23
❑ 13 Fred Lane	1.00	.45
❑ 14 Curtis Enis	5.00	2.20
❑ 15 Corey Dillon	3.00	1.35
❑ 16 Neil O'Donnell	1.00	.45
❑ 17 Carl Pickens	2.00	.90
❑ 18 Darnay Scott	1.00	.45
❑ 19 Takeo Spikes	1.50	.70
❑ 20 Troy Aikman	5.00	2.20
❑ 21 Michael Irvin	2.00	.90
❑ 22 Deion Sanders	2.00	.90
❑ 23 Emmitt Smith	8.00	3.60
❑ 24 Chris Warren	1.00	.45
❑ 25 Terrell Davis	8.00	3.60
❑ 26 John Elway	10.00	4.50
❑ 27 Brian Griese	8.00	3.60
❑ 28 Ed McCaffrey	1.00	.45
❑ 29 Marcus Nash	3.00	1.35

❑ 30 Shannon Sharpe 1.00 .45
❑ 31 Rod Smith WR 1.00 .45
❑ 32 Charlie Batch 8.00 3.60
❑ 33 Germane Crowell 5.00 2.20
❑ 34 Herman Moore 2.00 .90
❑ 35 Barry Sanders 10.00 4.50
❑ 36 Mark Chmura 1.00 .45
❑ 37 Brett Favre 10.00 4.50
❑ 38 Antonio Freeman 2.00 .90
❑ 39 Reggie White 2.00 .90
❑ 40 Marshall Faulk 2.00 .90
❑ 41 E.G. Green 1.50 .70
❑ 42 Peyton Manning 20.00 9.00
❑ 43 Jerome Pathon 1.50 .70
❑ 44 Mark Brunell 4.00 1.80
❑ 45 Jonathan Quinn 1.50 .70
❑ 46 Fred Taylor 12.00 5.50
❑ 47 Tony Gonzalez .50 .23
❑ 48 Andre Rison 1.00 .45
❑ 49 Karim Abdul-Jabbar 2.00 .90
❑ 50 John Avery 2.00 .90
❑ 51 Dan Marino 10.00 4.50
❑ 52 Cris Carter 2.00 .90
❑ 53 Randall Cunningham 2.00 .90
❑ 54 Brad Johnson 2.00 .90
❑ 55 Randy Moss 20.00 9.00
❑ 56 Robert Smith 2.00 .90
❑ 57 Drew Bledsoe 4.00 1.80
❑ 58 Robert Edwards 2.00 .90
❑ 59 Terry Glenn 2.00 .90
❑ 60 Tony Simmons 1.50 .70
❑ 61 Tiki Barber 1.00 .45
❑ 62 Joe Jurevicius 1.50 .70
❑ 63 Danny Kanell 1.00 .45
❑ 64 Keyshawn Johnson 2.00 .90
❑ 65 Curtis Martin 2.00 .90
❑ 66 Vinny Testaverde 1.00 .45
❑ 67 Tim Brown 2.00 .90
❑ 68 Jeff George 1.00 .45
❑ 69 Napoleon Kaufman 2.00 .90
❑ 70 Jon Ritchie 1.50 .70
❑ 71 Charles Woodson 5.00 2.20
❑ 72 Irving Fryar 1.00 .45
❑ 73 Duce Staley 3.00 1.35
❑ 74 Jerome Bettis 2.00 .90
❑ 75 Chris Fuamatu-Ma'afala 1.50 .70
❑ 76 Kordell Stewart 2.00 .90
❑ 77 Hines Ward 1.50 .70
❑ 78 Ryan Leaf 4.00 1.80
❑ 79 Natrone Means 2.00 .90
❑ 80 Mikhael Ricks 1.50 .70
❑ 81 Garrison Hearst 2.00 .90
❑ 82 R.W. McQuarters .75 .35
❑ 83 Jerry Rice 5.00 2.20
❑ 84 J.J. Stokes 1.00 .45
❑ 85 Steve Young 3.00 1.35
❑ 86 Joey Galloway 2.00 .90
❑ 87 Ahman Green 1.00 .45
❑ 88 Warren Moon 2.00 .90
❑ 89 Ricky Watters 1.00 .45
❑ 90 Isaac Bruce 2.00 .90
❑ 91 Robert Holcombe 2.00 .90
❑ 92 Mike Alstott 2.00 .90
❑ 93 Trent Dilfer 2.00 .90
❑ 94 Warrick Dunn 3.00 1.35
❑ 95 Jacquez Green 3.00 1.35
❑ 96 Kevin Dyson 4.00 1.80
❑ 97 Eddie George 4.00 1.80
❑ 98 Steve McNair 2.00 .90
❑ 99 Terry Allen 2.00 .90
❑ 100 Skip Hicks 3.00 1.35

1998 Playoff Contenders Ticket

	MINT	NRMT
COMPLETE SET (99)	1000.00	450.00
COMMON CARD (1-103)	.40	.18
SEMISTARS	.75	.35
UNLISTED STARS	1.50	.70
ONE TICKET CARD PER PACK		
COMMON ROOKIE AUTO	20.00	9.00
ROOKIE AUTOS ARE SKIP NUMBERED		
ROOKIES PRINT RUN 500 SIGNED CARDS		

❑ 1 Rob Moore .75 .35
❑ 2 Jake Plummer 5.00 2.20
❑ 3 Jamal Anderson 1.50 .70
❑ 4 Terance Mathis .75 .35
❑ 5 Priest Holmes 12.00 5.50
❑ 6 Michael Jackson .40 .18
❑ 7 Eric Zeier .75 .35
❑ 8 Andre Reed .75 .35
❑ 9 Antowain Smith 1.50 .70
❑ 10 Bruce Smith .75 .35
❑ 11 Thurman Thomas 1.50 .70
❑ 12 Rocket Ismail .40 .18
❑ 13 Wesley Walls .75 .35
❑ 14 Curtis Conway .75 .35
❑ 15 Jeff Blake .75 .35
❑ 16 Corey Dillon 2.00 .90
❑ 17 Carl Pickens 1.50 .70
❑ 18 Troy Aikman 4.00 1.80
❑ 19 Michael Irvin 1.50 .70
❑ 20 Ernie Mills .40 .18
❑ 21 Deion Sanders 1.50 .70
❑ 22 Emmitt Smith 6.00 2.70
❑ 23 Terrell Davis 6.00 2.70
❑ 24 John Elway 8.00 3.60
❑ 25 Neil Smith .75 .35
❑ 26 Rod Smith WR .75 .35
❑ 27 Herman Moore 1.50 .70
❑ 28 Johnnie Morton .75 .35
❑ 29 Barry Sanders 8.00 3.60
❑ 30 Robert Brooks .75 .35
❑ 31 Brett Favre 8.00 3.60
❑ 32 Antonio Freeman 1.50 .70
❑ 33 Dorsey Levens 1.50 .70
❑ 34 Reggie White 1.50 .70
❑ 35 Marshall Faulk 1.50 .70
❑ 36 Mark Brunell 3.00 1.35
❑ 37 Jimmy Smith .75 .35
❑ 38 James Stewart .75 .35
❑ 39 Donnell Bennett .40 .18
❑ 40 Andre Rison .75 .35
❑ 41 Derrick Thomas .75 .35
❑ 42 Karim Abdul-Jabbar 1.50 .70
❑ 43 Dan Marino 8.00 3.60
❑ 44 Cris Carter 1.50 .70
❑ 45 Brad Johnson 1.50 .70
❑ 46 Robert Smith 1.50 .70
❑ 47 Drew Bledsoe 3.00 1.35
❑ 48 Terry Glenn 1.50 .70
❑ 49 Lamar Smith .40 .18
❑ 50 Ike Hilliard .75 .35
❑ 51 Danny Kanell .75 .35
❑ 52 Wayne Chrebet 1.50 .70
❑ 53 Keyshawn Johnson 1.50 .70
❑ 54 Curtis Martin 1.50 .70
❑ 55 Tim Brown 1.50 .70
❑ 56 Rickey Dudley .40 .18
❑ 57 Jeff George .75 .35
❑ 58 Napoleon Kaufman 1.50 .70
❑ 59 Irving Fryar .75 .35
❑ 60 Jerome Bettis 1.50 .70
❑ 61 Charles Johnson .40 .18
❑ 62 Kordell Stewart 1.50 .70
❑ 63 Natrone Means 1.50 .70
❑ 64 Bryan Still .40 .18
❑ 65 Garrison Hearst 1.50 .70
❑ 66 Jerry Rice 4.00 1.80
❑ 67 Steve Young 2.00 .90
❑ 68 Joey Galloway 1.50 .70
❑ 69 Warren Moon 1.50 .70
❑ 70 Ricky Watters .75 .35
❑ 71 Isaac Bruce 1.50 .70
❑ 72 Mike Alstott 1.50 .70
❑ 73 Reidel Anthony .75 .35
❑ 74 Trent Dilfer 1.50 .70
❑ 75 Warrick Dunn 2.00 .90
❑ 76 Warren Sapp .75 .35
❑ 77 Eddie George 3.00 1.35
❑ 78 Steve McNair 1.50 .70
❑ 79 Terry Allen 1.50 .70
❑ 80 Gus Frerotte .40 .18
❑ 81 Andre Wadsworth AUTO 20.00 9.00
❑ 82 Tim Dwight AUTO 40.00 18.00
❑ 83 Curtis Enis AUTO/400 60.00 27.00
❑ 85 Charlie Batch AUTO 60.00 27.00
❑ 86 Germane Crowell AUTO 50.00 22.00
❑ 87 P.Manning AUTO/200 400.00 180.00
❑ 88 Jerome Pathon AUTO 25.00 11.00
❑ 89 Fred Taylor AUTO 175.00 80.00
❑ 90 Tavian Banks AUTO 20.00 9.00
❑ 92 Randy Moss AUTO/300 300.00 135.00
❑ 93 Robert Edwards AUTO 20.00 9.00
❑ 94 Hines Ward AUTO 20.00 9.00
❑ 95 Ryan Leaf AUTO/200 50.00 22.00
❑ 96 Mikhael Ricks AUTO 20.00 9.00
❑ 97 Ahman Green AUTO 25.00 11.00
❑ 98 Jacquez Green AUTO 30.00 13.50
❑ 99 Kevin Dyson AUTO 40.00 18.00
❑ 100 Skip Hicks AUTO 25.00 11.00
❑ 103 Chris Fuamatu-Ma'afala AU 20.00 9.00

1998 Playoff Contenders Ticket Red

	MINT	NRMT
COMP.RED SET (99)	400.00	180.00
COMMON RED (1-103)	1.00	.45
*RED STARS: 1X TO 2.5X HI COL.		
COMMON ROOKIE RED	5.00	2.20
RED TICKET STATED ODDS 1:9 HOB		
COMMON GOLD CARD	20.00	9.00
*GOLD STARS: 8X TO 20X REDS		
*GOLD YOUNG STARS: 6X TO 15X REDS		
*GOLD ROOKIES: 4X TO 10X REDS		
GOLD PRINT RUN 25 SER.#'d SETS		

❑ 82 Tim Dwight 8.00 3.60
❑ 83 Curtis Enis 10.00 4.50

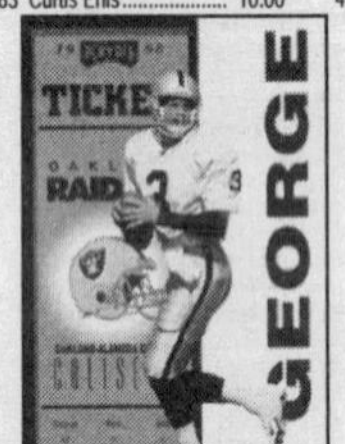

❑ 85 Charlie Batch 15.00 6.75
❑ 86 Germane Crowell 10.00 4.50
❑ 87 Peyton Manning 40.00 18.00
❑ 89 Fred Taylor 25.00 11.00
❑ 92 Randy Moss 40.00 18.00
❑ 95 Ryan Leaf 8.00 3.60
❑ 97 Ahman Green 5.00 2.20
❑ 98 Jacquez Green 6.00 2.70
❑ 99 Kevin Dyson 8.00 3.60
❑ 100 Skip Hicks 5.00 2.20

1998 Playoff Contenders Checklist Jumbos

	MINT	NRMT
COMPLETE SET (30)	150.00	70.00
COMMON CARD (1-30)	2.00	.90
SEMISTARS	4.00	1.80
ONE PER HOBBY BOX		

❑ 1 Jake Plummer	10.00	4.50
❑ 2 Jamal Anderson	5.00	2.20
❑ 3 Jermaine Lewis	4.00	1.80
❑ 4 Antowain Smith	5.00	2.20
❑ 5 Muhsin Muhammad	4.00	1.80
❑ 6 Curtis Enis	5.00	2.20
❑ 7 Corey Dillon	6.00	2.70
❑ 8 Deion Sanders	5.00	2.20
❑ 9 Terrell Davis	15.00	6.75
❑ 10 Barry Sanders	20.00	9.00
❑ 11 Brett Favre	20.00	9.00
❑ 12 Peyton Manning	15.00	6.75
❑ 13 Mark Brunell	8.00	3.60
❑ 14 Andre Rison	4.00	1.80
❑ 15 Dan Marino	20.00	9.00
❑ 16 Randy Moss	15.00	6.75
❑ 17 Drew Bledsoe	8.00	3.60
❑ 18 Kerry Collins	2.00	.90
❑ 19 Danny Kanell	4.00	1.80
❑ 20 Curtis Martin	5.00	2.20
❑ 21 Tim Brown	5.00	2.20
❑ 22 Irving Fryar	4.00	1.80
❑ 23 Kordell Stewart	4.00	1.80
❑ 24 Natrone Means	5.00	2.20
❑ 25 Steve Young	6.00	2.70
❑ 26 Isaac Bruce	5.00	2.20
❑ 27 Warren Moon	5.00	2.20
❑ 28 Warrick Dunn	6.00	2.70
❑ 29 Eddie George	8.00	3.60
❑ 30 Terry Allen	5.00	2.20

1998 Playoff Contenders Honors

	MINT	NRMT
COMPLETE SET (3)	300.00	135.00
COMMON CARD (19-21)	80.00	36.00
STATED ODDS 1:3241 HOBBY		

❑ 19 Dan Marino	150.00	70.00
❑ 20 Jerry Rice	100.00	45.00
❑ 21 Mark Brunell	80.00	36.00

1998 Playoff Contenders MVP Contenders

	MINT	NRMT
COMPLETE SET (36)	150.00	70.00
COMMON CARD (1-36)	4.00	1.80
STATED ODDS 1:19 HOBBY		

❑ 1 Terrell Davis	15.00	6.75
❑ 2 Jerry Rice	10.00	4.50
❑ 3 Jerome Bettis	4.00	1.80
❑ 4 Brett Favre	20.00	9.00
❑ 5 Natrone Means	4.00	1.80
❑ 6 Steve Young	6.00	2.70
❑ 7 John Elway	20.00	9.00
❑ 8 Troy Aikman	10.00	4.50
❑ 9 Steve McNair	4.00	1.80
❑ 10 Kordell Stewart	4.00	1.80
❑ 11 Drew Bledsoe	8.00	3.60
❑ 12 Tim Brown	4.00	1.80
❑ 13 Dan Marino	20.00	9.00
❑ 14 Mark Brunell	8.00	3.60
❑ 15 Marshall Faulk	4.00	1.80
❑ 16 Jake Plummer	10.00	4.50
❑ 17 Corey Dillon	6.00	2.70
❑ 18 Carl Pickens	4.00	1.80
❑ 19 Keyshawn Johnson	4.00	1.80
❑ 20 Barry Sanders	20.00	9.00
❑ 21 Deion Sanders	4.00	1.80
❑ 22 Emmitt Smith	15.00	6.75
❑ 23 Antowain Smith	4.00	1.80
❑ 24 Curtis Martin	4.00	1.80
❑ 25 Cris Carter	4.00	1.80
❑ 26 Napoleon Kaufman	4.00	1.80
❑ 27 Eddie George	8.00	3.60
❑ 28 Warrick Dunn	6.00	2.70
❑ 29 Antonio Freeman	4.00	1.80
❑ 30 Joey Galloway	4.00	1.80
❑ 31 Herman Moore	4.00	1.80
❑ 32 Jamal Anderson	4.00	1.80
❑ 33 Terry Glenn	4.00	1.80
❑ 34 Garrison Hearst	4.00	1.80
❑ 35 Robert Smith	4.00	1.80
❑ 36 Mike Alstott	4.00	1.80

1998 Playoff Contenders Rookie of the Year

	MINT	NRMT
COMPLETE SET (12)	150.00	70.00
COMMON CARD (1-12)	6.00	2.70
STATED ODDS 1:55 HOBBY		

❑ 1 Tim Dwight	8.00	3.60
❑ 2 Curtis Enis	10.00	4.50
❑ 3 Charlie Batch	15.00	6.75
❑ 4 Peyton Manning	40.00	18.00
❑ 5 Fred Taylor	25.00	11.00
❑ 6 John Avery	6.00	2.70
❑ 7 Randy Moss	40.00	18.00
❑ 8 Robert Edwards	6.00	2.70
❑ 9 Charles Woodson	10.00	4.50
❑ 10 Ryan Leaf	8.00	3.60
❑ 11 Jacquez Green	6.00	2.70
❑ 12 Kevin Dyson	6.00	2.70

1998 Playoff Contenders Rookie Stallions

	MINT	NRMT
COMPLETE SET (18)	100.00	45.00
COMMON CARD (1-18)	5.00	2.20
STATED ODDS 1:19 HOBBY		

❑ 1 Tim Dwight	5.00	2.20
❑ 2 Curtis Enis	6.00	2.70
❑ 3 Brian Griese	10.00	4.50
❑ 4 Charlie Batch	10.00	4.50
❑ 5 Germane Crowell	6.00	2.70
❑ 6 Peyton Manning	25.00	11.00
❑ 7 Tavian Banks	5.00	2.20
❑ 8 Fred Taylor	15.00	6.75
❑ 9 Rashaan Shehee	5.00	2.20
❑ 10 John Avery	5.00	2.20
❑ 11 Randy Moss	25.00	11.00
❑ 12 Robert Edwards	5.00	2.20
❑ 13 Charles Woodson	6.00	2.70
❑ 14 Ryan Leaf	5.00	2.20
❑ 15 Ahman Green	5.00	2.20
❑ 16 Jacquez Green	5.00	2.20
❑ 17 Kevin Dyson	5.00	2.20
❑ 18 Skip Hicks	5.00	2.20

1998 Playoff Contenders Super Bowl Leather

	MINT	NRMT
COMPLETE SET (6)	1000.00	450.00
COMMON CARD (1-6)	80.00	36.00
STATED ODDS 1:2401 HOBBY		

❑ 1 Brett Favre	300.00	135.00
❑ 2 John Elway	300.00	135.00
❑ 3 Robert Brooks	80.00	36.00
❑ 4 Rod Smith	80.00	36.00
❑ 5 Antonio Freeman	100.00	45.00
❑ 6 Terrell Davis	250.00	110.00

1998 Playoff Contenders Touchdown Tandems

	MINT	NRMT
COMPLETE SET (24)	150.00	70.00
COMMON CARD (1-24)	4.00	1.80
SEMISTARS	5.00	2.20
STATED ODDS 1:19 HOBBY		

❑ 1 Brett Favre	20.00	9.00
Antonio Freeman		
❑ 2 Dan Marino	20.00	9.00
Karim Abdul-Jabbar		
❑ 3 Emmitt Smith	15.00	6.75
Troy Aikman		
❑ 4 Barry Sanders	20.00	9.00

Card		MINT	NRMT
	Herman Moore		
❑ 5	Eddie George / Steve McNair	8.00	3.60
❑ 6	Robert Edwards / Drew Bledsoe	6.00	2.70
❑ 7	Terrell Davis / Rod Smith	15.00	6.75
❑ 8	Mark Brunell / Fred Taylor	12.00	5.50
❑ 9	Jerry Rice / Steve Young	10.00	4.50
❑ 10	Jerome Bettis / Kordell Stewart	5.00	2.20
❑ 11	Curtis Martin / Keyshawn Johnson	4.00	1.80
❑ 12	Mike Alstott / Warrick Dunn	4.00	1.80
❑ 13	Isaac Bruce / Tony Banks	4.00	1.80
❑ 14	Adrian Murrell / Jake Plummer	10.00	4.50
❑ 15	Tim Brown / Napoleon Kaufman	4.00	1.80
❑ 16	Cris Carter / Randy Moss	20.00	9.00
❑ 17	Joey Galloway / Ricky Watters	4.00	1.80
❑ 18	Peyton Manning / Marshall Faulk	20.00	9.00
❑ 19	Ryan Leaf / Natrone Means	6.00	2.70
❑ 20	Carl Pickens / Corey Dillon	4.00	1.80
❑ 21	Dooug Flutie / Antowain Smith	5.00	2.20
❑ 22	Randall Cunningham / Robert Smith	4.00	1.80
❑ 23	Chris Chandler / Jamal Anderson	5.00	2.20
❑ 24	John Elway / Ed McCaffrey	20.00	9.00

1999 Playoff Contenders SSD

	MINT	NRMT
COMPLETE SET (200)	1800.00	800.00
COMP.SET w/o RC/PT's (141)	60.00	27.00
COMMON CARD (1-145)	.40	.18
SEMISTARS	.75	.35
UNLISTED STARS	1.50	.70
COMMON ROOKIE AUTO	15.00	6.75
ROOKIE SEMISTARS	20.00	9.00
ROOKIE UNL.STARS	25.00	11.00

MOST RC AUTOS MAIL REDEMPTIONS
TRADE CARD EXPIRATION: 12/31/2000
REPORTED RC AUTO.PRINT RUNS 325-1825

	MINT	NRMT
COMMON PT (186-200)	2.50	1.10

PT STATED ODDS 1:7

Card		MINT	NRMT
❑ 1	Randy Moss	6.00	2.70
❑ 2	Randall Cunningham	1.50	.70
❑ 3	Cris Carter	1.50	.70
❑ 4	Robert Smith	1.50	.70
❑ 5	Jake Reed	.75	.35
❑ 6	Albert Connell	.40	.18
❑ 7	Jeff George	.75	.35
❑ 8	Brett Favre	6.00	2.70
❑ 9	Antonio Freeman	1.50	.70
❑ 10	Dorsey Levens	1.50	.70
❑ 11	Mark Chmura	.75	.35
❑ 12	Mike Alstott	1.50	.70
❑ 13	Warrick Dunn	1.50	.70
❑ 14	Trent Dilfer	.75	.35
❑ 15	Jacquez Green	.40	.18
❑ 16	Reidel Anthony	.40	.18
❑ 17	Warren Sapp	.75	.35
❑ 18	Amani Toomer	.40	.18
❑ 19	Curtis Enis	1.50	.70
❑ 20	Curtis Conway	.75	.35
❑ 21	Bobby Engram	.75	.35
❑ 22	Barry Sanders	6.00	2.70
❑ 23	Charlie Batch	3.00	1.35
❑ 24	Herman Moore	1.50	.70
❑ 25	Johnnie Morton	.75	.35
❑ 26	Greg Hill	.40	.18
❑ 27	Germane Crowell	.75	.35
❑ 28	Kerry Collins	.75	.35
❑ 29	Ike Hilliard	.40	.18
❑ 30	Joe Jurevicius	.40	.18
❑ 31	Stephen Davis	1.50	.70
❑ 32	Brad Johnson	1.50	.70
❑ 33	Skip Hicks	.75	.35
❑ 34	Michael Westbrook	.75	.35
❑ 35	Jake Plummer	2.50	1.10
❑ 36	Adrian Murrell	.40	.18
❑ 37	Frank Sanders	.75	.35
❑ 38	Rob Moore	.75	.35
❑ 39	Gary Brown	.40	.18
❑ 40	Duce Staley	1.50	.70
❑ 41	Charles Johnson	.75	.35
❑ 42	Emmitt Smith	4.00	1.80
❑ 43	Troy Aikman	4.00	1.80
❑ 44	Michael Irvin	.75	.35
❑ 45	Deion Sanders	1.50	.70
❑ 46	Rocket Ismail	.75	.35
❑ 47	Jerry Rice	4.00	1.80
❑ 48	Terrell Owens	1.50	.70
❑ 49	Steve Young	2.50	1.10
❑ 50	Garrison Hearst	.75	.35
❑ 51	J.J. Stokes	.75	.35
❑ 52	Lawrence Phillips	.75	.35
❑ 53	Jamal Anderson	1.50	.70
❑ 54	Chris Chandler	.75	.35
❑ 55	Terance Mathis	.75	.35
❑ 56	Tim Dwight	1.50	.70
❑ 57	Charlie Garner	.75	.35
❑ 58	Chris Calloway	.75	.35
❑ 59	Eddie Kennison	.75	.35
❑ 60	Billy Joe Hobert	.40	.18
❑ 61	Tim Biakabutuka	.75	.35
❑ 62	Muhsin Muhammad	.75	.35
❑ 63	Olandis Gary RC	60.00	27.00
❑ 64	Wesley Walls	.75	.35
❑ 65	Isaac Bruce	1.50	.70
❑ 66	Marshall Faulk	1.50	.70
❑ 67	Kordell Stewart	1.50	.70
❑ 68	Jerome Bettis	1.50	.70
❑ 69	Hines Ward	.40	.18
❑ 70	Corey Dillon	1.50	.70
❑ 71	Carl Pickens	.75	.35
❑ 72	Darnay Scott	.75	.35
❑ 73	Steve McNair	1.50	.70
❑ 74	Eddie George	2.00	.90
❑ 75	Yancey Thigpen	.40	.18
❑ 76	Kevin Dyson	.75	.35
❑ 77	Fred Taylor	4.00	1.80
❑ 78	Mark Brunell	2.50	1.10
❑ 79	Jimmy Smith	.75	.35
❑ 80	Keenan McCardell	.75	.35
❑ 81	James Stewart	.75	.35
❑ 82	Jermaine Lewis	.75	.35
❑ 83	Priest Holmes	1.50	.70
❑ 84	Stoney Case	.40	.18
❑ 85	Errict Rhett	.75	.35
❑ 86	Bill Schroeder	1.50	.70
❑ 87	Terry Kirby	.40	.18
❑ 88	Leslie Shepherd	.40	.18
❑ 89	Terrence Wilkins RC SP	80.00	36.00
❑ 90	Dan Marino	6.00	2.70
❑ 91	O.J. McDuffie	.75	.35
❑ 92	Karim Abdul-Jabbar	.75	.35
❑ 93	Zach Thomas	.75	.35
❑ 94	Terry Allen	.75	.35
❑ 95	Tony Martin	.75	.35
❑ 96	Drew Bledsoe	2.50	1.10
❑ 97	Terry Glenn	1.50	.70
❑ 98	Ben Coates	.75	.35
❑ 99	Tony Simmons	.40	.18
❑ 100	Curtis Martin	1.50	.70
❑ 101	Keyshawn Johnson	1.50	.70
❑ 102	Vinny Testaverde	.75	.35
❑ 103	Wayne Chrebet	1.50	.70
❑ 104	Peyton Manning	6.00	2.70
❑ 105	Marvin Harrison	1.50	.70
❑ 106	E.G. Green	.40	.18
❑ 107	Doug Flutie	2.00	.90
❑ 108	Thurman Thomas	.75	.35
❑ 109	Andre Reed	.75	.35
❑ 110	Eric Moulds	1.50	.70
❑ 111	Antowain Smith	1.50	.70
❑ 112	Bruce Smith	.75	.35
❑ 113	Terrell Davis	4.00	1.80
❑ 114	John Elway	6.00	2.70
❑ 115	Ed McCaffrey	.75	.35
❑ 116	Rod Smith	.75	.35
❑ 117	Shannon Sharpe	.75	.35
❑ 118	Jeff Garcia RC	300.00	135.00
❑ 119	Brian Griese	3.00	1.35
❑ 120	Justin Watson RC SP	150.00	70.00
❑ 121	Bubby Brister	.75	.35
❑ 122	Ryan Leaf	1.50	.70
❑ 123	Natrone Means	.75	.35
❑ 124	Mikhael Ricks	.40	.18
❑ 125	Junior Seau	.75	.35
❑ 126	Jim Harbaugh	.75	.35
❑ 127	Andre Rison	.75	.35
❑ 128	Elvis Grbac	.75	.35
❑ 129	Bam Morris	.40	.18
❑ 130	Rashaan Shehee	.40	.18
❑ 131	Warren Moon	1.50	.70
❑ 132	Tony Gonzalez	.75	.35
❑ 133	Derrick Alexander	.75	.35
❑ 134	Jon Kitna	2.00	.90
❑ 135	Ricky Watters	.75	.35
❑ 136	Joey Galloway	1.50	.70
❑ 137	Ahman Green	.40	.18
❑ 138	Derrick Mayes	.75	.35
❑ 139	Tyrone Wheatley	.75	.35
❑ 140	Napoleon Kaufman	1.50	.70
❑ 141	Tim Brown	1.50	.70
❑ 142	Charles Woodson	1.50	.70
❑ 143	Rich Gannon	.75	.35
❑ 144	Rickey Dudley	.40	.18
❑ 145	Az-Zahir Hakim	.40	.18
❑ 146	Kurt Warner RC	200.00	90.00
❑ 147	Sean Bennett RC	15.00	6.75
❑ 148	Brandon Stokley RC	15.00	6.75
❑ 149	Amos Zereoue RC	25.00	11.00
❑ 150	Brock Huard RC	25.00	11.00
❑ 151	Tim Couch RC	120.00	55.00
❑ 152	Ricky Williams RC	120.00	55.00
❑ 153	D. McNabb SP Trade RC	200.00	90.00
❑ 154	Edgerrin James RC SP	250.00	110.00
❑ 155	Torry Holt RC	50.00	22.00
❑ 156	Daunte Culpepper RC	100.00	45.00
❑ 157	Akili Smith RC	80.00	36.00
❑ 158	Champ Bailey RC	25.00	11.00
❑ 159	Chris Claiborne RC	20.00	9.00
❑ 160	Chris McAlister Trade RC	15.00	6.75
❑ 161	Troy Edwards RC	35.00	16.00
❑ 162	Jevon Kearse RC SP	125.00	55.00

❑ 163 Darnell McDonald RC	25.00	11.00
❑ 164 David Boston RC	30.00	13.50
❑ 165 Peerless Price RC	30.00	13.50
❑ 166 Cecil Collins RC	25.00	11.00
❑ 167 Rob Konrad RC	20.00	9.00
❑ 168 Cade McNown RC	100.00	45.00
❑ 169 Shawn Bryson RC	15.00	6.75
❑ 170 Kevin Faulk RC	25.00	11.00
❑ 171 Corby Jones	15.00	6.75
❑ 172 J. Johnson Trade RC	25.00	11.00
❑ 173 Autry Denson RC	20.00	9.00
❑ 174 Sedrick Irvin RC	25.00	11.00
❑ 175 Michael Bishop RC	25.00	11.00
❑ 176 Joe Germaine RC	25.00	11.00
❑ 177 De'Mond Parker RC	25.00	11.00
❑ 178 Shaun King Trade RC	60.00	27.00
❑ 179 D'Wayne Bates RC	20.00	9.00
❑ 180 Tai Streets RC	20.00	9.00
❑ 181 Na Brown RC	20.00	9.00
❑ 182 Desmond Clark RC	15.00	6.75
❑ 183 Jim Kleinsasser RC	20.00	9.00
❑ 184 Kevin Johnson RC	50.00	22.00
❑ 185 Joe Montgomery RC	20.00	9.00
❑ 186 John Elway PT	10.00	4.50
❑ 187 Dan Marino PT	10.00	4.50
❑ 188 Jerry Rice PT	6.00	2.70
❑ 189 Barry Sanders PT	10.00	4.50
❑ 190 Steve Young PT	4.00	1.80
❑ 191 Doug Flutie PT	3.00	1.35
❑ 192 Troy Aikman PT	6.00	2.70
❑ 193 Drew Bledsoe PT	4.00	1.80
❑ 194 Brett Favre PT	10.00	4.50
❑ 195 Randall Cunningham PT	2.50	1.10
❑ 196 Terrell Davis PT	6.00	2.70
❑ 197 Kordell Stewart PT	2.50	1.10
❑ 198 Keyshawn Johnson PT	2.50	1.10
❑ 199 Jake Plummer PT	4.00	1.80
❑ 200 Peyton Manning PT	10.00	4.50

1999 Playoff Contenders SSD Finesse Gold

	MINT	NRMT
COMMON CARD (1-145)	15.00	6.75
*STARS: 15X TO 30X HI COL.		
*YOUNG STARS: 12X TO 25X		
COMMON ROOKIE AUTO	40.00	18.00
ROOKIE SEMISTARS AUTO	50.00	22.00
ROOKIE UNL.STARS AUTO	60.00	27.00

MOST ROOKIE AUTOS MAIL REDEMPTIONS
*PT STARS: 8X TO 20X
*PT YOUNG STARS: 6X TO 15X
STATED PRINT RUN 25 SERIAL #'d SETS

❑ 63 Olandis Gary	120.00	55.00
❑ 89 Terrence Wilkins	100.00	45.00
❑ 118 Jeff Garcia	400.00	180.00
❑ 120 Justin Watson	250.00	110.00
❑ 146 Kurt Warner	600.00	275.00
❑ 151 Tim Couch	250.00	110.00
❑ 152 Ricky Williams	250.00	110.00
❑ 153 Donovan McNabb	250.00	110.00
❑ 154 Edgerrin James	500.00	220.00
❑ 155 Torry Holt	120.00	55.00
❑ 156 Daunte Culpepper	150.00	70.00
❑ 157 Akili Smith	100.00	45.00
❑ 161 Troy Edwards	80.00	36.00
❑ 162 Jevon Kearse	200.00	90.00
❑ 164 David Boston	80.00	36.00
❑ 165 Peerless Price	80.00	36.00
❑ 168 Cade McNown	150.00	70.00
❑ 178 Shaun King	150.00	70.00
❑ 184 Kevin Johnson	120.00	55.00

1999 Playoff Contenders SSD Power Blue

	MINT	NRMT
COMMON CARD (1-145)	6.00	2.70
*STARS: 6X TO 15X HI COL.		
*YOUNG STARS: 5X TO 12X		
COMMON ROOKIE AUTO	25.00	11.00
ROOKIE SEMISTARS AUTO	30.00	13.50
ROOKIE UNL.STARS AUTO	40.00	18.00

MOST ROOKIE AUTOS MAIL REDEMPTIONS
*PT STARS: 4X TO 10X
*PT YOUNG STARS: 3X TO 8X
STATED PRINT RUN 50 SERIAL #'d SETS

❑ 63 Olandis Gary	80.00	36.00
❑ 89 Terrence Wilkins	80.00	36.00
❑ 118 Jeff Garcia	350.00	160.00
❑ 120 Justin Watson	200.00	90.00
❑ 146 Kurt Warner	400.00	180.00
❑ 151 Tim Couch	150.00	70.00
❑ 152 Ricky Williams	150.00	70.00
❑ 153 Donovan McNabb	250.00	110.00
❑ 154 Edgerrin James	350.00	160.00
❑ 155 Torry Holt	80.00	36.00
❑ 156 Daunte Culpepper	100.00	45.00
❑ 157 Akili Smith	60.00	27.00
❑ 161 Troy Edwards	50.00	22.00
❑ 162 Jevon Kearse	150.00	70.00
❑ 164 David Boston	50.00	22.00
❑ 165 Peerless Price	50.00	22.00
❑ 168 Cade McNown	100.00	45.00
❑ 178 Shaun King	100.00	45.00
❑ 184 Kevin Johnson	80.00	36.00

1999 Playoff Contenders SSD Speed Red

	MINT	NRMT
COMPLETE SET (200)	2000.00	900.00
COMMON CARD (1-145)	3.00	1.35
*STARS: 3X TO 8X HI COL.		
*YOUNG STARS: 2.5X TO 6X		
COMMON ROOKIE AUTO	20.00	9.00
ROOKIE SEMISTARS AUTO	25.00	11.00
ROOKIE UNL.STARS AUTO	30.00	13.50

MOST ROOKIE AUTOS MAIL REDEMPTIONS
*PT STARS: 2X TO 5X
*PT YOUNG STARS: 1.5X TO 4X
STATED PRINT RUN 100 SERIAL #'d SETS

❑ 63 Olandis Gary	60.00	27.00
❑ 89 Terrence Wilkins	60.00	27.00
❑ 118 Jeff Garcia	300.00	135.00
❑ 120 Justin Watson	150.00	70.00
❑ 146 Kurt Warner	300.00	135.00
❑ 151 Tim Couch	120.00	55.00
❑ 152 Ricky Williams	120.00	55.00
❑ 153 Donovan McNabb	200.00	90.00
❑ 154 Edgerrin James	300.00	135.00
❑ 155 Torry Holt	60.00	27.00
❑ 156 Daunte Culpepper	80.00	36.00
❑ 157 Akili Smith	50.00	22.00
❑ 161 Troy Edwards	40.00	18.00
❑ 162 Jevon Kearse	120.00	55.00
❑ 164 David Boston	40.00	18.00
❑ 165 Peerless Price	40.00	18.00
❑ 168 Cade McNown	80.00	36.00
❑ 178 Shaun King	80.00	36.00
❑ 184 Kevin Johnson	60.00	27.00

1999 Playoff Contenders SSD Game Day Souvenirs

	MINT	NRMT
COMPLETE SET (15)	1200.00	550.00
COMMON CARD (GS1-GS15)	50.00	22.00
STATED ODDS 1:308		
❑ GS1 Terrell Owens	50.00	22.00
❑ GS2 Jerry Rice	100.00	45.00
❑ GS3 Steve Young	80.00	36.00
❑ GS4 Akili Smith	50.00	22.00
❑ GS5 Tim Couch	120.00	55.00
❑ GS6 Mark Brunell	60.00	27.00
❑ GS7 Eddie George	60.00	27.00
❑ GS8 Dorsey Levens	50.00	22.00
❑ GS9 Brett Favre	120.00	55.00
❑ GS10 Antonio Freeman	50.00	22.00
❑ GS11 Ricky Williams	120.00	55.00
❑ GS12 Steve McNair	50.00	22.00
❑ GS13 Kurt Warner	250.00	110.00
❑ GS14 John Elway	120.00	55.00
❑ GS15 Terrell Davis	100.00	45.00

1999 Playoff Contenders SSD MVP Contenders

	MINT	NRMT
COMPLETE SET (20)	150.00	70.00
COMMON CARD (MC1-MC20)	6.00	2.70
STATED ODDS 1:43		
❑ MC1 Jamal Anderson	6.00	2.70
❑ MC2 Eddie George	8.00	3.60
❑ MC3 Emmitt Smith	15.00	6.75
❑ MC4 Jerry Rice	15.00	6.75
❑ MC5 Barry Sanders	25.00	11.00
❑ MC6 Keyshawn Johnson	6.00	2.70
❑ MC7 Brett Favre	25.00	11.00
❑ MC8 Randy Moss	20.00	9.00
❑ MC9 Mark Brunell	10.00	4.50
❑ MC10 Fred Taylor	12.00	5.50
❑ MC11 Dan Marino	25.00	11.00
❑ MC12 Peyton Manning	20.00	9.00
❑ MC13 Drew Bledsoe	10.00	4.50
❑ MC14 Antonio Freeman	6.00	2.70
❑ MC15 Steve Young	10.00	4.50
❑ MC16 Terrell Davis	15.00	6.75
❑ MC17 Terrell Owens	6.00	2.70
❑ MC18 Troy Aikman	15.00	6.75
❑ MC19 Steve McNair	6.00	2.70
❑ MC20 Jake Plummer	10.00	4.50

1999 Playoff Contenders SSD Quads

	MINT	NRMT
COMPLETE SET (12)	200.00	90.00
COMMON CARD (CQ1-CQ12)	12.00	5.50
STATED ODDS 1:57		
❑ CQ1 Jake Plummer David Boston Emmitt Smith Troy Aikman	20.00	9.00
❑ CQ2 Jerry Rice Steve Young Jamal Anderson Chris Chandler	20.00	9.00
❑ CQ3 Randy Moss Cris Carter Brett Favre Antonio Freeman	30.00	13.50
❑ CQ4 Warrick Dunn Mike Alstott Stephen Davis Brad Johnson	12.00	5.50
❑ CQ5 Cade McNown Curtis Enis Barry Sanders Charlie Batch	30.00	13.50

		MINT	NRMT
❑ CQ6	Ricky Williams Eddie Kennison Marshall Faulk Torry Holt	25.00	11.00
❑ CQ7	Kordell Stewart Jerome Bettis Eddie George Steve McNair	12.00	5.50
❑ CQ8	Doug Flutie Eric Moulds Drew Bledsoe Terry Glenn	12.00	5.50
❑ CQ9	Dan Marino Cecil Collins Keyshawn Johnson Curtis Martin	30.00	13.50
❑ CQ10	Terrell Davis Brian Griese Mark Brunell Fred Taylor	15.00	6.75
❑ CQ11	Jon Kitna Joey Galloway Napolean Kaufman Tim Brown	12.00	5.50
❑ CQ12	Peyton Manning Edgerrin James Tim Couch Kevin Johnson	50.00	22.00

1999 Playoff Contenders SSD Round Numbers Autographs

	MINT	NRMT
COMPLETE SET (10)	600.00	275.00
COMMON CARD (RN1-RN10)	25.00	11.00

STATED ODDS 1:109
SOME CARDS ISSUED VIA MAIL REDEMPTION
TRADE CARD EXPIRATION: 12/31/2000

		MINT	NRMT
❑ RN1	Kevin Johnson Peerless Price	60.00	27.00
❑ RN2	Ricky Williams Edgerrin James	250.00	110.00
❑ RN3	Donovan McNabb Akili Smith	80.00	36.00
❑ RN4	Sean Bennett Brandon Stokley	25.00	11.00
❑ RN5	Tim Couch Cade McNown	150.00	70.00
❑ RN6	David Boston Troy Edwards	40.00	18.00
❑ RN7	Daunte Culpepper Torry Holt	80.00	36.00
❑ RN8	Kevin Faulk Trade James Johnson Trade	30.00	13.50
❑ RN9	Joe Montgomery Rob Konrad	25.00	11.00
❑ RN10	Cecil Collins De'Mond Parker	30.00	13.50

1999 Playoff Contenders SSD ROY Contenders

	MINT	NRMT
COMPLETE SET (12)	100.00	45.00
COMMON CARD (1-12)	5.00	2.20

CARD NUMBERS HAVE ROYC PREFIX
STATED ODDS 1:29

		MINT	NRMT
❑ 1	Tim Couch	15.00	6.75
❑ 2	Donovan McNabb	12.00	5.50
❑ 3	Akili Smith	8.00	3.60
❑ 4	Daunte Culpepper	12.00	5.50
❑ 5	Cade McNown	12.00	5.50
❑ 6	Edgerrin James	25.00	11.00
❑ 7	Ricky Williams	15.00	6.75
❑ 8	Cecil Collins	5.00	2.20
❑ 9	Torry Holt	10.00	4.50
❑ 10	David Boston	8.00	3.60
❑ 11	Troy Edwards	8.00	3.60
❑ 12	Champ Bailey	6.00	2.70

1999 Playoff Contenders SSD ROY Contenders Autographs

	MINT	NRMT
COMPLETE SET (12)	1000.00	450.00
COMMON CARD (1-12)	25.00	11.00

CARD NUMBERS HAVE ROYC PREFIX
STATED PRINT RUN 100 SER.#'d SETS
TRADE CARD EXPIRATION: 12/31/2000

		MINT	NRMT
❑ 1	Tim Couch	175.00	80.00
❑ 2	Donovan McNabb	100.00	45.00
❑ 3	Akili Smith	60.00	27.00
❑ 4	Daunte Culpepper	100.00	45.00
❑ 5	Cade McNown	100.00	45.00
❑ 6	Edgerrin James	250.00	110.00
❑ 7	Ricky Williams	175.00	80.00
❑ 8	Cecil Collins	25.00	11.00
❑ 9	Torry Holt	70.00	32.00
❑ 10	David Boston	40.00	18.00
❑ 11	Troy Edwards	40.00	18.00
❑ 12	Champ Bailey	30.00	13.50

1999 Playoff Contenders SSD Touchdown Tandems

	MINT	NRMT
COMPLETE SET (24)	100.00	45.00
COMMON CARD (T1-T24)	3.00	1.35
SEMISTARS	4.00	1.80

STATED ODDS 1:15

		MINT	NRMT
❑ T1	Keyshawn Johnson Curtis Martin	3.00	1.35
❑ T2	Dan Marino Tony Martin	12.00	5.50
❑ T3	Drew Bledsoe Terry Glenn	5.00	2.20
❑ T4	Peyton Manning Marvin Harrison	10.00	4.50
❑ T5	Doug Flutie Thurman Thomas	4.00	1.80
❑ T6	Steve McNair Eddie George	5.00	2.20
❑ T7	Kordell Stewart Jerome Bettis	3.00	1.35
❑ T8	Akili Smith Carl Pickens	4.00	1.80
❑ T9	Mark Brunell Jimmy Smith	5.00	2.20
❑ T10	Jon Kitna Joey Galloway	4.00	1.80
❑ T11	John Elway Terrell Davis	12.00	5.50
❑ T12	Napoleon Kaufman Tim Brown	3.00	1.35
❑ T13	Troy Aikman Emmitt Smith	8.00	3.60
❑ T14	Jake Plummer Rob Moore	5.00	2.20
❑ T15	Donovan McNabb Charles Johnson	6.00	2.70
❑ T16	Brad Johnson Michael Westbrook	3.00	1.35
❑ T17	Brett Favre Antonio Freeman	10.00	4.50
❑ T18	Randall Cunningham Randy Moss	10.00	4.50
❑ T19	Mike Alstott Warrick Dunn	3.00	1.35
❑ T20	Cade McNown Curtis Enis	6.00	2.70
❑ T21	Barry Sanders Herman Moore	10.00	4.50
❑ T22	Steve Young Jerry Rice	8.00	3.60
❑ T23	Chris Chandler Jamal Anderson	3.00	1.35
❑ T24	Marshall Faulk Isaac Bruce	4.00	1.80

1999 Playoff Contenders SSD Touchdown Tandems Die Cuts

	MINT	NRMT
COMMON CARD (T1A-T24B)	15.00	6.75

RANDOM INSERTS IN PACKS

		MINT	NRMT
❑ T1	Keyshawn Johnson Curtis Martin	40.00	18.00
❑ T2	Dan Marino	100.00	45.00

Tony Martin
❑ T3 Drew Bledsoe 50.00 22.00
Terry Glenn
❑ T4 Peyton Manning 100.00 45.00
Marvin Harrison
❑ T5 Doug Flutie 40.00 18.00
Thurman Thomas
❑ T6 Steve McNair 40.00 18.00
Eddie George
❑ T7 Kordell Stewart 50.00 22.00
Jerome Bettis
❑ T8 Akili Smith 20.00 9.00
Carl Pickens
❑ T9 Mark Brunell 50.00 22.00
Jimmy Smith
❑ T10 Jon Kitna 60.00 27.00
Joey Galloway
❑ T11 John Elway 60.00 27.00
Terrell Davis
❑ T12 Napoleon Kaufman 60.00 27.00
Tim Brown
❑ T13 Troy Aikman 80.00 36.00
Emmitt Smith
❑ T14 Jake Plummer 50.00 22.00
Rob Moore
❑ T15 Donovan McNabb 30.00 13.50
Charles Johnson
❑ T16 Brad Johnson 60.00 27.00
Michael Westbrook
❑ T17 Brett Favre 50.00 22.00
Antonio Freeman
❑ T18 Randall Cunningham 40.00 18.00
Randy Moss
❑ T19 Mike Alstott 60.00 27.00
Warrick Dunn
❑ T20 Cade McNown 60.00 27.00
Curtis Enis
❑ T21 Barry Sanders 250.00 110.00
Herman Moore
❑ T22 Steve Young 30.00 13.50
Jerry Rice
❑ T23 Chris Chandler 15.00 6.75
Jamal Anderson
❑ T24 Marshall Faulk 80.00 36.00
Isaac Bruce

1999 Playoff Contenders SSD Triple Threat

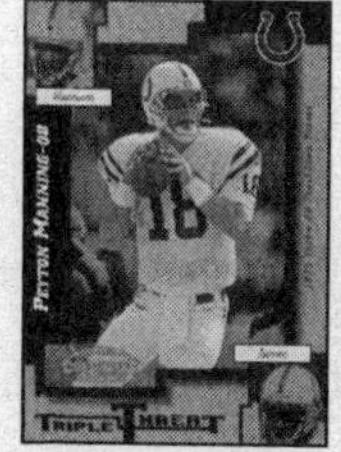

	MINT	NRMT
COMPLETE SET (20)	60.00	27.00
COMMON CARD (TT1-TT20) ..	2.50	1.10
STATED ODDS 1:15		

❑ TT1 Jake Plummer 4.00 1.80
David Boston
Frank Sanders
❑ TT2 Deion Sanders 6.00 2.70
Troy Aikman
Emmitt Smith
❑ TT3 Terrell Owens 5.00 2.20
Jerry Rice
Steve Young
❑ TT4 Dan Marino 8.00 3.60
O.J. McDuffie
Cecil Collins
❑ TT5 Keyshawn Johnson...... 2.50 1.10
Wayne Chrebet
Curtis Martin
❑ TT6 Jamal Anderson 2.50 1.10
Chris Chandler
Terance Mathis
❑ TT7 Brian Griese 5.00 2.20
Terrell Davis
Shannon Sharpe
❑ TT8 Fred Taylor 4.00 1.80
Mark Brunell
Keenan McCardell
❑ TT9 Randy Moss 8.00 3.60
Cris Carter
Randall Cunningham
❑ TT10 Antonio Freeman 8.00 3.60
Brett Favre
Dorsey Levens
❑ TT11 Brad Johnson 3.00 1.35
Skip Hicks
Champ Bailey
❑ TT12 Barry Sanders........... 8.00 3.60
Herman Moore
Charlie Batch
❑ TT13 Eddie George 4.00 1.80
Steve McNair
Yancey Thigpen
❑ TT14 Kordell Stewart 3.00 1.35
Jerome Bettis
Troy Edwards
❑ TT15 Antowain Smith.......... 3.00 1.35
Eric Moulds
Doug Flutie
❑ TT16 Terry Glenn................ 4.00 1.80
Kevin Faulk
Drew Bledsoe
❑ TT17 Mike Alstott 6.00 2.70
Warrick Dunn
Shaun King
❑ TT18 Peyton Manning 15.00 6.75
Marvin Harrison
Edgerrin James
❑ TT19 Corey Dillon 2.50 1.10
Akili Smith
Carl Pickens
❑ TT20 Isaac Bruce............... 5.00 2.20
Torry Holt
Marshall Faulk

1999 Playoff Contenders SSD Triple Threat Parallel

	MINT	NRMT
COMMON CARD (TT1-TT60) ..	6.00	2.70
RANDOM INSERTS IN PACKS....		
CARDS SER.#'d UNDER 12 NOT PRICED		

❑ TT1 Jake Plummer/17 ...... 80.00 36.00
❑ TT2 Deion Sanders/16...... 50.00 22.00
❑ TT3 Terrell Owens/14 ...... 50.00 22.00
❑ TT4 Dan Marino/23 .... 200.00 90.00
❑ TT5 Keyshawn Johnson/10 ....
❑ TT6 Jamal Anderson/14.... 50.00 22.00
❑ TT7 Brian Griese/33.......... 60.00 27.00
❑ TT8 Fred Taylor/14 .... 100.00 45.00
❑ TT9 Randy Moss/17........ 250.00 110.00
❑ TT10 Antonio Freeman/14 50.00 22.00
❑ TT11 Brad Johnson/48....... 20.00 9.00
❑ TT12 Barry Sanders/73 .... 60.00 27.00
❑ TT13 Eddie George/37...... 40.00 18.00
❑ TT14 Kordell Stewart/11 ....
❑ TT15 Antowain Smith/8 ....
❑ TT16 Terry Glenn/86 .... 12.00 5.50
❑ TT17 Mike Alstott/8 ....
❑ TT18 Peyton Manning/26 200.00 90.00
❑ TT19 Corey Dillon/66 .... 15.00 6.75
❑ TT20 Isaac Bruce/80 .... 12.00 5.50
❑ TT21 David Boston/13 .... 100.00 45.00
❑ TT22 Troy Aikman/12....... 150.00 70.00
❑ TT23 Jerry Rice/75............ 40.00 18.00
❑ TT24 O.J. McDuffie/90 .... 6.00 2.70
❑ TT25 Wayne Chrebet/63 .. 15.00 6.75
❑ TT26 Chris Chandler/25.... 40.00 18.00
❑ TT27 Terrell Davis/21 .... 80.00 36.00
❑ TT28 Mark Brunell/20........ 80.00 36.00
❑ TT29 Cris Carter/12 .... 60.00 27.00
❑ TT30 Brett Favre/31 .... 150.00 70.00
❑ TT31 Skip Hicks/8 ....
❑ TT32 Herman Moore/82 .... 12.00 5.50
❑ TT33 Steve McNair/15 ..... 60.00 27.00
❑ TT34 Jerome Bettis/4.............
❑ TT35 Eric Moulds/84 .... 12.00 5.50
❑ TT36 Kevin Faulk/12 .... 80.00 36.00
❑ TT37 Warrick Dunn/50 ...... 20.00 9.00
❑ TT38 Marvin Harrison/61 .. 15.00 6.75
❑ TT39 Akili Smith/32 .... 60.00 27.00
❑ TT40 Torry Holt/11 ....
❑ TT41 Frank Sanders/89 ...... 6.00 2.70
❑ TT42 Emmitt Smith/13 .... 150.00 70.00
❑ TT43 Steve Young/36 ...... 80.00 36.00
❑ TT44 Cecil Collins/28 .... 40.00 18.00
❑ TT45 Curtis Martin/60 ...... 15.00 6.75
❑ TT46 Terance Mathis/11 ....
❑ TT47 Shannon Sharpe/10 ......
❑ TT48 Keenan McCardell/67 8.00 3.60
❑ TT49 Randall Cunningham/34 30.00 13.50
❑ TT50 Dorsey Levens/50.... 20.00 9.00
❑ TT51 Champ Bailey/22 .... 50.00 22.00
❑ TT52 Charlie Batch/98 ...... 20.00 9.00
❑ TT53 Yancey Thigpen/13.. 25.00 11.00
❑ TT54 Troy Edwards/27...... 60.00 27.00
❑ TT55 Doug Flutie/20 .... 80.00 36.00
❑ TT56 Drew Bledsoe/20 .... 80.00 36.00
❑ TT57 Shaun King/36 ...... 100.00 45.00
❑ TT58 Edgerrin James/17 500.00 220.00
❑ TT59 Carl Pickens/67.......... 8.00 3.60
❑ TT60 Marshall Faulk/78 .... 15.00 6.75

1998 Playoff Momentum Hobby

	MINT	NRMT
COMPLETE SET (250)	400.00	180.00
COMMON CARD (1-250)...........	.60	.25
SEMISTARS............................	1.25	.55
UNLISTED STARS....................	2.00	.90
COMMON ROOKIE	5.00	2.20
ROOKIE SEMISTARS	8.00	3.60
ROOKIE UNLISTED STARS ..	10.00	4.50
ROOKIE SUBSET STATED ODDS 1:6		
COMMON GOLD (1-250)........	25.00	11.00
*GOLD STARS: 20X TO 40X HI COL.		
*GOLD YOUNG STARS: 15X TO 30X		
*GOLD RCs: 2.5X TO 5X..............		
STATED PRINT RUN 25 SERIAL #'d SETS		
COMP.RED SET (250)..........	800.00	350.00
*RED STARS: 1.2X TO 3X HI COL.		
*RED YOUNG STARS: 1X TO 2.5X		
*RED RCs: .6X TO 1.2X................		
RED STATED ODDS 1:4 HOBBY		

❑ 1 Jake Plummer 6.00 2.70
❑ 2 Eric Metcalf .... .60 .25
❑ 3 Adrian Murrell .... 1.25 .55
❑ 4 Larry Centers .... .60 .25
❑ 5 Frank Sanders.................. 1.25 .55
❑ 6 Rob Moore .... 1.25 .55
❑ 7 Andre Wadsworth RC 8.00 3.60
❑ 8 Chris Chandler .... 1.25 .55
❑ 9 Jamal Anderson .... 2.00 .90
❑ 10 Tony Martin.................... 1.25 .55

❑ 11 Terance Mathis .... 1.25 .55
❑ 12 Tim Dwight RC 15.00 6.75
❑ 13 Jammi German RC 5.00 2.20
❑ 14 O.J. Santiago .... .60 .25
❑ 15 Jim Harbaugh .... 1.25 .55
❑ 16 Eric Zeier........................ 1.25 .55
❑ 17 Duane Starks RC 5.00 2.20
❑ 18 Rod Woodson .... 1.25 .55
❑ 19 Errict Rhett .... 1.25 .55
❑ 20 Jay Graham...................... .60 .25
❑ 21 Ray Lewis .... .60 .25
❑ 22 Michael Jackson .... .60 .25
❑ 23 Jermaine Lewis .... 1.25 .55
❑ 24 Pat Johnson RC 8.00 3.60
❑ 25 Eric Green......................... .60 .25
❑ 26 Doug Flutie .... 2.00 .90
❑ 27 Rob Johnson.................. 1.25 .55
❑ 28 Antowain Smith .... 2.00 .90
❑ 29 Thurman Thomas .... 2.00 .90
❑ 30 Jonathan Linton RC 12.00 5.50
❑ 31 Bruce Smith.................... 1.25 .55
❑ 32 Eric Moulds .... 2.00 .90
❑ 33 Kevin Williams.................. .60 .25
❑ 34 Andre Reed..................... 1.25 .55
❑ 35 Steve Beuerlein................ .60 .25
❑ 36 Kerry Collins .... 1.25 .55
❑ 37 Anthony Johnson .... .60 .25
❑ 38 Fred Lane .... 1.25 .55
❑ 39 William Floyd.................... .60 .25
❑ 40 Rocket Ismail.................... .60 .25
❑ 41 Wesley Walls.................. 1.25 .55
❑ 42 Muhsin Muhammad........ 1.25 .55
❑ 43 Rae Carruth..................... 1.25 .55
❑ 44 Kevin Greene .... 1.25 .55
❑ 45 Greg Lloyd......................... .60 .25
❑ 46 Moses Moreno RC 8.00 3.60
❑ 47 Erik Kramer .... .60 .25
❑ 48 Edgar Bennett .... .60 .25
❑ 49 Curtis Enis RC............. 15.00 6.75
❑ 50 Curtis Conway................ 1.25 .55
❑ 51 Bobby Engram .... 1.25 .55
❑ 52 Alonzo Mayes RC 5.00 2.20
❑ 53 Jeff Blake .... 1.25 .55
❑ 54 Neil O'Donnell .... 1.25 .55
❑ 55 Corey Dillon..................... 3.00 1.35
❑ 56 Takeo Spikes RC 8.00 3.60
❑ 57 Carl Pickens .... 2.00 .90
❑ 58 Tony McGee .... .60 .25
❑ 59 Darnay Scott .... 1.25 .55
❑ 60 Troy Aikman 5.00 2.20
❑ 61 Deion Sanders .... 2.00 .90
❑ 62 Emmitt Smith................... 8.00 3.60
❑ 63 Darren Woodson............... .60 .25
❑ 64 Chris Warren................... 1.25 .55
❑ 65 Daryl Johnston .... 1.25 .55
❑ 66 Ernie Mills .... .60 .25
❑ 67 Billy Davis .... .60 .25
❑ 68 Michael Irvin .... 2.00 .90
❑ 69 David LaFleur .... .60 .25
❑ 70 John Elway 10.00 4.50
❑ 71 Brian Griese RC 20.00 9.00
❑ 72 Steve Atwater .... .60 .25
❑ 73 Terrell Davis 8.00 3.60
❑ 74 Rod Smith .... 1.25 .55
❑ 75 Marcus Nash RC.......... 12.00 5.50
❑ 76 Shannon Sharpe............ 1.25 .55
❑ 77 Ed McCaffrey .... 1.25 .55
❑ 78 Neil Smith .... 1.25 .55
❑ 79 Charlie Batch RC 20.00 9.00
❑ 80 Germane Crowell RC .. 20.00 9.00
❑ 81 Scott Mitchell.................. 1.25 .55
❑ 82 Barry Sanders 10.00 4.50
❑ 83 Terry Fair RC 8.00 3.60
❑ 84 Herman Moore .... 2.00 .90
❑ 85 Johnnie Morton .... 1.25 .55
❑ 86 Brett Favre 10.00 4.50
❑ 87 Rick Mirer .... .60 .25
❑ 88 Dorsey Levens .... 2.00 .90
❑ 89 William Henderson .... .60 .25
❑ 90 Derrick Mayes .... 1.25 .55
❑ 91 Antonio Freeman............ 2.00 .90
❑ 92 Robert Brooks .... 1.25 .55
❑ 93 Mark Chmura .... 1.25 .55
❑ 94 Vonnie Holliday RC........ 8.00 3.60
❑ 95 Reggie White.................. 2.00 .90
❑ 96 E.G. Green RC 8.00 3.60
❑ 97 Jerome Pathon RC 8.00 3.60
❑ 98 Peyton Manning RC 60.00 27.00
❑ 99 Marshall Faulk................ 2.00 .90
❑ 100 Zack Crockett .... .60 .25
❑ 101 Ken Dilger .... .60 .25
❑ 102 Marvin Harrison........... 1.25 .55
❑ 103 Mark Brunell 4.00 1.80
❑ 104 Jonathan Quinn RC...... 8.00 3.60
❑ 105 Tavian Banks RC 8.00 3.60
❑ 106 Fred Taylor RC 30.00 13.50
❑ 107 James Stewart .... 1.25 .55
❑ 108 Jimmy Smith .... 1.25 .55
❑ 109 Keenan McCardell....... 1.25 .55
❑ 110 Elvis Grbac .... 1.25 .55
❑ 111 Rich Gannon .... .60 .25
❑ 112 Rashaan Shehee RC .. 8.00 3.60
❑ 113 Donnell Bennett.............. .60 .25
❑ 114 Kimble Anders............ 1.25 .55
❑ 115 Derrick Thomas........... 1.25 .55
❑ 116 Kevin Lockett.................. .60 .25
❑ 117 Derrick Alexander WR.. 1.25 .55
❑ 118 Tony Gonzalez .... .60 .25
❑ 119 Andre Rison .... 1.25 .55
❑ 120 Craig Erickson................ .60 .25
❑ 121 Dan Marino 10.00 4.50
❑ 122 John Avery RC 10.00 4.50
❑ 123 Karim Abdul-Jabbar .... 2.00 .90
❑ 124 Zach Thomas .... .60 .25
❑ 125 O.J. McDuffie .... 1.25 .55
❑ 126 Troy Drayton .... .60 .25
❑ 127 Randall Cunningham.... 2.00 .90
❑ 128 Brad Johnson .... 2.00 .90
❑ 129 Robert Smith .... 2.00 .90
❑ 130 Cris Carter.................. 2.00 .90
❑ 131 Randy Moss RC 60.00 27.00
❑ 132 Jake Reed................... 1.25 .55
❑ 133 John Randle .... 1.25 .55
❑ 134 Drew Bledsoe 4.00 1.80
❑ 135 Tony Simmons RC 8.00 3.60
❑ 136 Sedrick Shaw .... .60 .25
❑ 137 Chris Floyd RC 5.00 2.20
❑ 138 Robert Edwards RC .. 10.00 4.50
❑ 139 Rod Rutledge RC 5.00 2.20
❑ 140 Shawn Jefferson .... .60 .25
❑ 141 Ben Coates .... 1.25 .55
❑ 142 Terry Glenn .... 2.00 .90
❑ 143 Heath Shuler .... .60 .25
❑ 144 Danny Wuerffel .... 1.25 .55
❑ 145 Troy Davis...................... .60 .25
❑ 146 Qadry Ismail .... .60 .25
❑ 147 Ray Zellars .... .60 .25
❑ 148 Lamar Smith .... .60 .25
❑ 149 Cameron Cleeland RC 8.00 3.60
❑ 150 Sean Dawkins................. .60 .25
❑ 151 Andre Hastings .... .60 .25
❑ 152 Danny Kanell............... 1.25 .55
❑ 153 Tiki Barber................... 1.25 .55
❑ 154 Tyrone Wheatley......... 1.25 .55
❑ 155 Charles Way .... .60 .25
❑ 156 Gary Brown .... .60 .25
❑ 157 Shaun Williams RC 5.00 2.20
❑ 158 Chris Calloway .... .60 .25
❑ 159 Amani Toomer............. 1.25 .55
❑ 160 Brian Alford RC 8.00 3.60
❑ 161 Joe Jurevicius RC 8.00 3.60
❑ 162 Ike Hilliard .... 1.25 .55
❑ 163 Michael Strahan .... .60 .25
❑ 164 Glenn Foley................. 1.25 .55
❑ 165 Vinny Testaverde .... 1.25 .55
❑ 166 Keyshawn Johnson...... 2.00 .90
❑ 167 Curtis Martin .... 2.00 .90
❑ 168 Leon Johnson .... .60 .25
❑ 169 Keith Byars .... .60 .25
❑ 170 Wayne Chrebet .... 2.00 .90
❑ 171 Kyle Brady...................... .60 .25
❑ 172 Dedric Ward .... .60 .25
❑ 173 Jeff George .... 1.25 .55
❑ 174 Charles Woodson RC 15.00 6.75
❑ 175 Napoleon Kaufman ...... 2.00 .90
❑ 176 Jon Ritchie RC 8.00 3.60
❑ 177 Tim Brown................... 2.00 .90
❑ 178 James Jett................... 1.25 .55
❑ 179 Rickey Dudley .... .60 .25
❑ 180 Bobby Hoying .... 1.25 .55
❑ 181 Duce Staley................. 3.00 1.35
❑ 182 Charlie Garner................ .60 .25
❑ 183 Irving Fryar .... 1.25 .55
❑ 184 Jeff Graham .... .60 .25
❑ 185 Jason Dunn.................... .60 .25
❑ 186 Kordell Stewart .... 2.00 .90
❑ 187 Jerome Bettis .... 2.00 .90
❑ 188 Andre Coleman .... .60 .25
❑ 189 Chris Fuamatu-Ma'afala RC 8.00 3.60
❑ 190 Charles Johnson .... .60 .25
❑ 191 Hines Ward RC 8.00 3.60
❑ 192 Mark Bruener .... .60 .25
❑ 193 Courtney Hawkins.......... .60 .25
❑ 194 Will Blackwell .... .60 .25
❑ 195 Levon Kirkland .... .60 .25
❑ 196 Mikhael Ricks RC 8.00 3.60
❑ 197 Ryan Leaf RC 12.00 5.50
❑ 198 Natrone Means .... 2.00 .90
❑ 199 Junior Seau................ 1.25 .55
❑ 200 Bryan Still .... .60 .25
❑ 201 Freddie Jones .... .60 .25
❑ 202 Steve Young 3.00 1.35
❑ 203 Jim Druckenmiller .... 1.25 .55
❑ 204 Garrison Hearst........... 2.00 .90
❑ 205 R.W. McQuarters RC .. 5.00 2.20
❑ 206 Merton Hanks .... .60 .25
❑ 207 Marc Edwards .... .60 .25
❑ 208 Jerry Rice 5.00 2.20
❑ 209 Terrell Owens .... 2.00 .90
❑ 210 J.J. Stokes................. 1.25 .55
❑ 211 Tony Banks .... 1.25 .55
❑ 212 Robert Holcombe RC 10.00 4.50
❑ 213 Greg Hill .... .60 .25
❑ 214 Amp Lee .... .60 .25
❑ 215 Jerald Moore .... .60 .25
❑ 216 Isaac Bruce .... 2.00 .90
❑ 217 Az-Zahir Hakim RC 15.00 6.75
❑ 218 Eddie Kennison........... 1.25 .55
❑ 219 Grant Wistrom RC....... 5.00 2.20
❑ 220 Warren Moon .... 2.00 .90
❑ 221 Ahman Green RC 15.00 6.75
❑ 222 Steve Broussard .... .60 .25
❑ 223 Ricky Watters .... 1.25 .55
❑ 224 James McKnight .... .60 .25
❑ 225 Joey Galloway............. 2.00 .90
❑ 226 Mike Pritchard .... .60 .25
❑ 227 Trent Dilfer .... 2.00 .90
❑ 228 Warrick Dunn 3.00 1.35
❑ 229 Mike Alstott .... 2.00 .90
❑ 230 John Lynch .... .60 .25
❑ 231 Jacquez Green RC 15.00 6.75
❑ 232 Reidel Anthony .... 1.25 .55
❑ 233 Bert Emanuel .... 1.25 .55
❑ 234 Warren Sapp............... 1.25 .55
❑ 235 Steve McNair.............. 2.00 .90
❑ 236 Eddie George 4.00 1.80
❑ 237 Chris Sanders .... .60 .25
❑ 238 Yancey Thigpen .... .60 .25
❑ 239 Willie Davis .... .60 .25
❑ 240 Kevin Dyson RC 15.00 6.75
❑ 241 Frank Wycheck .... .60 .25
❑ 242 Trent Green................. 2.50 1.10
❑ 243 Gus Frerotte .... .60 .25
❑ 244 Skip Hicks RC 15.00 6.75
❑ 245 Terry Allen.................. 2.00 .90
❑ 246 Stephen Davis................ .60 .25
❑ 247 Stephen Alexander RC 8.00 3.60
❑ 248 Michael Westbrook ...... 1.25 .55
❑ 249 Dana Stubblefield SP .. 2.00 .90
❑ 250 Dan Wilkinson SP .... 2.00 .90

1998 Playoff Momentum Retail

	MINT	NRMT
COMPLETE SET (250)	150.00	70.00
COMMON CARD (1-250)...........	.15	.07
SEMISTARS..............................	.30	.14
UNLISTED STARS......................	.60	.25
COMMON ROOKIE	1.25	.55
ROOKIE SEMISTARS	2.00	.90
ROOKIE UNLISTED STARS	3.00	1.35
ROOKIE SUBSET ODDS 1:3 RETAIL		
COMP.RED SET (250).........	250.00	110.00
*RED STARS: 1.5X TO 3X HI COL.		
*RED YOUNG STARS: 1.25X TO 2.5X		
*RED RCs: .6X TO 1.2X................		

RED STATED ODDS 1:4 RETAIL

❑ 1 Karim Abdul-Jabbar	.60	.25
❑ 2 Troy Aikman	1.50	.70
❑ 3 Derrick Alexander	.30	.14
❑ 4 Stephen Alexander	.15	.07
❑ 5 Brian Alford RC	2.00	.90
❑ 6 Terry Allen	.60	.25
❑ 7 Mike Alstott	.60	.25
❑ 8 Kimble Anders	.30	.14
❑ 9 Jamal Anderson	.60	.25
❑ 10 Reidel Anthony	.30	.14
❑ 11 Steve Atwater	.15	.07
❑ 12 John Avery RC	3.00	1.35
❑ 13 Tavian Banks RC	2.00	.90
❑ 14 Tony Banks	.30	.14
❑ 15 Tiki Barber	.30	.14
❑ 16 Charlie Batch RC	10.00	4.50
❑ 17 Donnell Bennett	.15	.07
❑ 18 Edgar Bennett	.15	.07
❑ 19 Jerome Bettis	.60	.25
❑ 20 Steve Beuerlein	.15	.07
❑ 21 Will Blackwell	.15	.07
❑ 22 Jeff Blake	.30	.14
❑ 23 Drew Bledsoe	1.25	.55
❑ 24 Kyle Brady	.15	.07
❑ 25 Robert Brooks	.30	.14
❑ 26 Steve Broussard	.15	.07
❑ 27 Gary Brown	.15	.07
❑ 28 Tim Brown	.60	.25
❑ 29 Isaac Bruce	.60	.25
❑ 30 Mark Bruener	.15	.07
❑ 31 Mark Brunell	1.25	.55
❑ 32 Keith Byars	.15	.07
❑ 33 Chris Calloway	.15	.07
❑ 34 Rae Carruth	.30	.14
❑ 35 Cris Carter	.60	.25
❑ 36 Larry Centers	.15	.07
❑ 37 Chris Chandler	.30	.14
❑ 38 Mark Chmura	.30	.14
❑ 39 Wayne Chrebet	.60	.25
❑ 40 Cameron Cleeland RC	2.00	.90
❑ 41 Ben Coates	.30	.14
❑ 42 Kerry Collins	.30	.14
❑ 43 Andre Coleman	.15	.07
❑ 44 Curtis Conway	.30	.14
❑ 45 Zack Crockett	.15	.07
❑ 46 Germane Crowell RC	6.00	2.70
❑ 47 Randall Cunningham	.60	.25
❑ 48 Billy Davis	.15	.07
❑ 49 Stephen Davis	.15	.07
❑ 50 Terrell Davis	2.50	1.10
❑ 51 Troy Davis	.15	.07
❑ 52 Willie Davis	.15	.07
❑ 53 Sean Dawkins	.15	.07
❑ 54 Trent Dilfer	.60	.25
❑ 55 Ken Dilger	.15	.07
❑ 56 Corey Dillon	1.00	.45
❑ 57 Troy Drayton	.15	.07
❑ 58 Jim Druckenmiller	.30	.14
❑ 59 Rickey Dudley	.15	.07
❑ 60 Jason Dunn	.15	.07
❑ 61 Warrick Dunn	1.00	.45
❑ 62 Tim Dwight RC	5.00	2.20
❑ 63 Kevin Dyson RC	5.00	2.20
❑ 64 Marc Edwards	.15	.07
❑ 65 Robert Edwards RC	3.00	1.35
❑ 66 John Elway	3.00	1.35
❑ 67 Bert Emanuel	.30	.14
❑ 68 Bobby Engram	.30	.14
❑ 69 Curtis Enis RC	6.00	2.70
❑ 70 Craig Erickson	.15	.07
❑ 71 Terry Fair RC	2.00	.90
❑ 72 Marshall Faulk	.60	.25
❑ 73 Brett Favre	3.00	1.35
❑ 74 Chris Floyd	.15	.07
❑ 75 William Floyd	.15	.07
❑ 76 Doug Flutie	.60	.25
❑ 77 Glenn Foley	.30	.14
❑ 78 Antonio Freeman	.60	.25
❑ 79 Gus Frerotte	.15	.07
❑ 80 Irving Fryar	.30	.14
❑ 81 Chris Fuamatu-Ma'afala RC	2.00	.90
❑ 82 Joey Galloway	.60	.25
❑ 83 Rich Gannon	.15	.07
❑ 84 Charlie Garner	.15	.07
❑ 85 Eddie George	1.25	.55
❑ 86 Jeff George	.30	.14
❑ 87 Jammi German RC	1.25	.55
❑ 88 Terry Glenn	.60	.25
❑ 89 Tony Gonzalez	.15	.07
❑ 90 Jay Graham	.15	.07
❑ 91 Jeff Graham	.15	.07
❑ 92 Elvis Grbac	.30	.14
❑ 93 Ahman Green RC	2.00	.90
❑ 94 E.G. Green RC	2.00	.90
❑ 95 Eric Green	.15	.07
❑ 96 Jacquez Green RC	4.00	1.80
❑ 97 Trent Green	.15	.07
❑ 98 Kevin Greene	.30	.14
❑ 99 Brian Griese RC	10.00	4.50
❑ 100 Az-Zahir Hakim RC	4.00	1.80
❑ 101 Merton Hanks	.15	.07
❑ 102 Jim Harbaugh	.30	.14
❑ 103 Marvin Harrison	.30	.14
❑ 104 Andre Hastings	.15	.07
❑ 105 Courtney Hawkins	.15	.07
❑ 106 Garrison Hearst	.60	.25
❑ 107 William Henderson	.15	.07
❑ 108 Skip Hicks RC	3.00	1.35
❑ 109 Greg Hill	.15	.07
❑ 110 Ike Hilliard	.30	.14
❑ 111 Robert Holcombe RC	3.00	1.35
❑ 112 Vonnie Holliday RC	2.00	.90
❑ 113 Bobby Hoying	.30	.14
❑ 114 Michael Irvin	.60	.25
❑ 115 Qadry Ismail	.15	.07
❑ 116 Rocket Ismail	.15	.07
❑ 117 Michael Jackson	.15	.07
❑ 118 Shawn Jefferson	.15	.07
❑ 119 James Jett	.30	.14
❑ 120 Anthony Johnson	.15	.07
❑ 121 Brad Johnson	.60	.25
❑ 122 Charles Johnson	.15	.07
❑ 123 Keyshawn Johnson	.60	.25
❑ 124 Leon Johnson	.15	.07
❑ 125 Pat Johnson RC	2.00	.90
❑ 126 Rob Johnson	.30	.14
❑ 127 Daryl Johnston	.30	.14
❑ 128 Freddie Jones	.15	.07
❑ 129 Joe Jurevicius RC	2.00	.90
❑ 130 Danny Kanell	.30	.14
❑ 131 Napoleon Kaufman	.60	.25
❑ 132 Eddie Kennison	.30	.14
❑ 133 Levon Kirkland	.15	.07
❑ 134 Erik Kramer	.15	.07
❑ 135 David LaFleur	.15	.07
❑ 136 Fred Lane	.30	.14
❑ 137 Ryan Leaf RC	5.00	2.20
❑ 138 Amp Lee	.15	.07
❑ 139 Dorsey Levens	.60	.25
❑ 140 Jermaine Lewis	.30	.14
❑ 141 Ray Lewis	.15	.07
❑ 142 Jonathan Linton RC	4.00	1.80
❑ 143 Greg Lloyd	.15	.07
❑ 144 Kevin Lockett	.15	.07
❑ 145 John Lynch	.15	.07
❑ 146 Peyton Manning RC	25.00	11.00
❑ 147 Dan Marino	3.00	1.35
❑ 148 Curtis Martin	.60	.25
❑ 149 Tony Martin	.30	.14
❑ 150 Terance Mathis	.30	.14
❑ 151 Alonzo Mayes RC	1.25	.55
❑ 152 Derrick Mayes	.30	.14
❑ 153 Ed McCaffrey	.30	.14
❑ 154 Keenan McCardell	.30	.14
❑ 155 O.J. McDuffie	.30	.14
❑ 156 Tony McGee	.15	.07
❑ 157 James McKnight	.15	.07
❑ 158 Steve McNair	.60	.25
❑ 159 R.W. McQuarters RC	1.25	.55
❑ 160 Natrone Means	.60	.25
❑ 161 Eric Metcalf	.15	.07
❑ 162 Ernie Mills	.15	.07
❑ 163 Rick Mirer	.15	.07
❑ 164 Scott Mitchell	.30	.14
❑ 165 Warren Moon	.60	.25
❑ 166 Herman Moore	.60	.25
❑ 167 Jerald Moore	.15	.07
❑ 168 Rob Moore	.30	.14
❑ 169 Moses Moreno RC	2.00	.90
❑ 170 Johnnie Morton	.30	.14
❑ 171 Randy Moss RC	25.00	11.00
❑ 172 Eric Moulds	.60	.25
❑ 173 Muhsin Muhammad	.30	.14
❑ 174 Adrian Murrell	.30	.14
❑ 175 Marcus Nash RC	4.00	1.80
❑ 176 Neil O'Donnell	.30	.14
❑ 177 Terrell Owens	.60	.25
❑ 178 Jerome Pathon RC	2.00	.90
❑ 179 Carl Pickens	.60	.25
❑ 180 Jake Plummer	1.50	.70
❑ 181 Mike Pritchard	.15	.07
❑ 182 Jonathan Quinn RC	2.00	.90
❑ 183 John Randle	.30	.14
❑ 184 Andre Reed	.30	.14
❑ 185 Jake Reed	.30	.14
❑ 186 Errict Rhett	.30	.14
❑ 187 Jerry Rice	1.50	.70
❑ 188 Mikhael Ricks RC	2.00	.90
❑ 189 Andre Rison	.30	.14
❑ 190 Jon Ritchie RC	2.00	.90
❑ 191 Rod Rutledge	.15	.07
❑ 192 Barry Sanders	3.00	1.35
❑ 193 Chris Sanders	.15	.07
❑ 194 Deion Sanders	.60	.25
❑ 195 Frank Sanders	.30	.14
❑ 196 O.J. Santiago	.15	.07
❑ 197 Warren Sapp	.30	.14
❑ 198 Darnay Scott	.30	.14
❑ 199 Junior Seau	.30	.14
❑ 200 Shannon Sharpe	.30	.14
❑ 201 Sedrick Shaw	.15	.07
❑ 202 Rashaan Shehee RC	2.00	.90
❑ 203 Heath Shuler	.15	.07
❑ 204 Tony Simmons RC	2.00	.90
❑ 205 Antowain Smith	.60	.25
❑ 206 Bruce Smith	.30	.14
❑ 207 Emmitt Smith	2.50	1.10
❑ 208 Jimmy Smith	.30	.14
❑ 209 Lamar Smith	.15	.07
❑ 210 Neil Smith	.30	.14
❑ 211 Robert Smith	.60	.25
❑ 212 Rod Smith	.30	.14
❑ 213 Takeo Spikes RC	2.00	.90
❑ 214 Duce Staley	1.00	.45
❑ 215 Duane Starks RC	1.25	.55
❑ 216 James Stewart	.30	.14
❑ 217 Kordell Stewart	.60	.25
❑ 218 Bryan Still	.15	.07
❑ 219 J.J. Stokes	.30	.14
❑ 220 Michael Strahan	.15	.07
❑ 221 Dana Stubblefield	.15	.07
❑ 222 Fred Taylor RC	15.00	6.75
❑ 223 Vinny Testaverde	.30	.14
❑ 224 Yancey Thigpen	.15	.07
❑ 225 Derrick Thomas	.30	.14
❑ 226 Thurman Thomas	.60	.25
❑ 227 Zach Thomas	.15	.07
❑ 228 Amani Toomer	.30	.14
❑ 229 Andre Wadsworth RC	2.00	.90
❑ 230 Wesley Walls	.30	.14
❑ 231 Dedric Ward	.15	.07
❑ 232 Hines Ward RC	2.00	.90
❑ 233 Chris Warren	.30	.14
❑ 234 Ricky Watters	.30	.14
❑ 235 Charles Way	.15	.07
❑ 236 Michael Westbrook	.30	.14
❑ 237 Tyrone Wheatley	.30	.14
❑ 238 Reggie White	.60	.25
❑ 239 Dan Wilkinson	.15	.07

		MINT	NRMT
❑ 240	Kevin Williams	.15	.07
❑ 241	Shaun Williams RC	1.25	.55
❑ 242	Grant Wistrom RC	1.25	.55
❑ 243	Charles Woodson RC	6.00	2.70
❑ 244	Darren Woodson	.15	.07
❑ 245	Rod Woodson	.30	.14
❑ 246	Danny Wuerffel	.30	.14
❑ 247	Frank Wycheck	.15	.07
❑ 248	Steve Young	1.00	.45
❑ 249	Eric Zeier	.30	.14
❑ 250	Ray Zellars	.15	.07

1998 Playoff Momentum Class Reunion Quads

	MINT	NRMT
COMPLETE SET (16)	400.00	180.00
COMMON CARD (1-16)	10.00	4.50
SEMISTARS	15.00	6.75

STATED ODDS 1:81 HOBBY
*JUMBOS: .1X TO .25X HI COL.
JUMBOS: ONE PER HOBBY BOX

		MINT	NRMT
❑ 1	Dan Marino	50.00	22.00
	John Elway		
	Bruce Matthews		
	Darrell Green		
❑ 2	Steve Young	20.00	9.00
	Irving Fryar		
	Reggie White		
	Jeff Hostetler		
❑ 3	Jerry Rice	25.00	11.00
	Bruce Smith		
	Andre Reed		
	Doug Flutie		
❑ 4	Keith Byars	10.00	4.50
	Leslie O'Neal		
	Seth Joyner		
	Ray Brown		
❑ 5	Cris Carter	15.00	6.75
	Vinny Testaverde		
	Jim Harbaugh		
	Rod Woodson		
❑ 6	Tim Brown	15.00	6.75
	Chris Chandler		
	Michael Irvin		
	Neil Smith		
❑ 7	Troy Aikman	50.00	22.00
	Barry Sanders		
	Deion Sanders		
	Andre Rison		
❑ 8	Emmitt Smith	30.00	13.50
	Jeff George		
	Neil O'Donnell		
	Shannon Sharpe		
❑ 9	Brett Favre	40.00	18.00
	Herman Moore		
	Yancey Thigpen		
	Ricky Watters		
❑ 10	Mark Chmura	15.00	6.75
	Brad Johnson		
	Carl Pickens		
	Robert Brooks		
❑ 11	Drew Bledsoe	30.00	13.50
	Jerome Bettis		
	Mark Brunell		
	Garrison Hearst		
❑ 12	Trent Dilfer	20.00	9.00
	Dorsey Levens		
	Marshall Faulk		
	Isaac Bruce		
❑ 13	Terrell Davis	40.00	18.00
	Kordell Stewart		
	Napoleon Kaufman		
	Curtis Martin		
❑ 14	Eddie George	20.00	9.00
	Keyshawn Johnson		
	Karim Abdul-Jabbar		
	Terry Glenn		
❑ 15	Warrick Dunn	20.00	9.00
	Corey Dillon		
	Jake Plummer		
	Antowain Smith		
❑ 16	Peyton Manning	30.00	13.50
	Ryan Leaf		
	Curtis Enis		
	Randy Moss		

1998 Playoff Momentum Class Reunion Tandems

	MINT	NRMT
COMPLETE SET (16)	500.00	220.00
COMMON CARD (1-16)	15.00	6.75
SEMISTARS	25.00	11.00

STATED ODDS 1:121 RETAIL

		MINT	NRMT
❑ 1	Dan Marino	80.00	36.00
	John Elway		
❑ 2	Steve Young	30.00	13.50
	Reggie White		
❑ 3	Jerry Rice	40.00	18.00
	Bruce Smith		
❑ 4	Keith Byars	15.00	6.75
	Leslie O'Neil		
❑ 5	Cris Carter	25.00	11.00
	Vinny Testaverde		
❑ 6	Tim Brown	25.00	11.00
	Michael Irvin		
❑ 7	Troy Aikman	80.00	36.00
	Barry Sanders		
❑ 8	Emmitt Smith	50.00	22.00
	Jeff George		
❑ 9	Brett Favre	60.00	27.00
	Herman Moore		
❑ 10	Brad Johnson	25.00	11.00
	Carl Pickens		
❑ 11	Drew Bledsoe	50.00	22.00
	Mark Brunell		
❑ 12	Dorsey Levens	30.00	13.50
	Isaac Bruce		
❑ 13	Terrell Davis	60.00	27.00
	Kordell Stewart		
❑ 14	Eddie George	30.00	13.50
	Keyshawn Johnson		
❑ 15	Warrick Dunn	30.00	13.50
	Jake Plummer		
❑ 16	Peyton Manning	40.00	18.00
	Ryan Leaf		

1998 Playoff Momentum Endzone X-press

	MINT	NRMT
COMP.DIE CUT SET (29)	120.00	55.00
COMMON DIE CUT (1-29)	1.50	.70
SEMISTARS	3.00	1.35
UNLISTED STARS	5.00	2.20

DIE CUT STATED ODDS 1:9 HOBBY
*NON-DIE CUTS: .4X TO .8X DIE CUTS
NON-DIE CUT STATED ODDS 1:13 RETAIL

		MINT	NRMT
❑ 1	Jake Plummer	8.00	3.60
❑ 2	Herman Moore	5.00	2.20
❑ 3	Terrell Davis	12.00	5.50
❑ 4	Antowain Smith	5.00	2.20
❑ 5	Curtis Enis	5.00	2.20
❑ 6	Corey Dillon	5.00	2.20
❑ 7	Troy Aikman	8.00	3.60
❑ 8	John Elway	15.00	6.75
❑ 9	Barry Sanders	15.00	6.75
❑ 10	Brett Favre	15.00	6.75
❑ 11	Peyton Manning	20.00	9.00
❑ 12	Mark Brunell	6.00	2.70
❑ 13	Andre Rison	1.50	.70
❑ 14	Dan Marino	15.00	6.75
❑ 15	Randy Moss	20.00	9.00
❑ 16	Drew Bledsoe	6.00	2.70
❑ 17	Jerome Bettis	5.00	2.20
❑ 18	Tim Brown	5.00	2.20
❑ 19	Antonio Freeman	5.00	2.20
❑ 20	Napoleon Kaufman	5.00	2.20
❑ 21	Emmitt Smith	12.00	5.50
❑ 22	Kordell Stewart	5.00	2.20
❑ 23	Curtis Martin	5.00	2.20
❑ 24	Ryan Leaf	5.00	2.20
❑ 25	Jerry Rice	8.00	3.60
❑ 26	Joey Galloway	5.00	2.20
❑ 27	Warrick Dunn	5.00	2.20
❑ 28	Eddie George	6.00	2.70
❑ 29	Steve McNair	5.00	2.20

1998 Playoff Momentum Headliners

	MINT	NRMT
COMPLETE SET (23)	200.00	90.00
COMMON CARD (1-23)	6.00	2.70

BLUE STATED ODDS 1:49 HOBBY
*RED CARDS: .4X TO .8X BLUES

RED STATED ODDS 1:73 RETAIL

❑ 1 Brett Favre	25.00	11.00
❑ 2 Jerry Rice	12.00	5.50
❑ 3 Barry Sanders	25.00	11.00
❑ 4 Troy Aikman	12.00	5.50
❑ 5 Warrick Dunn	12.00	5.50
❑ 6 Dan Marino	25.00	11.00
❑ 7 John Elway	25.00	11.00
❑ 8 Drew Bledsoe	10.00	4.50
❑ 9 Kordell Stewart	6.00	2.70
❑ 10 Mark Brunell	10.00	4.50
❑ 11 Eddie George	10.00	4.50
❑ 12 Terrell Davis	20.00	9.00
❑ 13 Emmitt Smith	20.00	9.00
❑ 14 Steve McNair	8.00	3.60
❑ 15 Mike Alstott	8.00	3.60
❑ 16 Peyton Manning	25.00	11.00
❑ 17 Antonio Freeman	8.00	3.60
❑ 18 Curtis Martin	8.00	3.60
❑ 19 Terry Glenn	8.00	3.60
❑ 20 Brad Johnson	8.00	3.60
❑ 21 Karim Abdul-Jabbar	8.00	3.60
❑ 22 Ryan Leaf	8.00	3.60
❑ 23 Jerome Bettis	8.00	3.60

1998 Playoff Momentum Headliners Gold

	MINT	NRMT
COMMON CARD (1-23)	25.00	11.00

RANDOM INSERTS IN HOBBY PACKS
CARDS SERIAL #'d BY FEATURED STAT
CARDS NUMBERED UNDER 12 NOT PRICED

❑ 1 Brett Favre/3		
❑ 2 Jerry Rice/166	50.00	22.00
❑ 3 Barry Sanders/13	800.00	350.00
❑ 4 Troy Aikman/8		
❑ 5 Warrick Dunn/49	50.00	22.00
❑ 6 Dan Marino/24	500.00	220.00
❑ 7 John Elway/138	100.00	45.00
❑ 8 Drew Bledsoe/44	100.00	45.00
❑ 9 Kordell Stewart/11		
❑ 10 Mark Brunell/6		
❑ 11 Eddie George/32	150.00	70.00
❑ 12 Terrell Davis/3		
❑ 13 Emmitt Smith/112	60.00	27.00
❑ 14 Steve McNair/19	100.00	45.00
❑ 15 Mike Alstott/65	50.00	22.00
❑ 16 Peyton Manning/33	250.00	110.00
❑ 17 Antonio Freeman/13	150.00	70.00
❑ 18 Curtis Martin/8		
❑ 19 Terry Glenn/90	25.00	11.00
❑ 20 Brad Johnson/3		
❑ 21 Karim Abdul-Jabbar/16	100.00	45.00
❑ 22 Ryan Leaf/33	100.00	45.00
❑ 23 Jerome Bettis/10		

1998 Playoff Momentum Honors

	MINT	NRMT
COMPLETE SET (3)	400.00	180.00
COMMON CARD (PH16-PH18)	100.00	45.00

STATED ODDS 1:3841 HOBBY

❑ PH16 Brett Favre	200.00	90.00
❑ PH17 Kordell Stewart	100.00	45.00
❑ PH18 Troy Aikman	120.00	55.00

1998 Playoff Momentum NFL Rivals

	MINT	NRMT
COMP.HOBBY SET (22)	200.00	90.00
COMMON HOBBY (1-22)	5.00	2.20
SEMISTARS	8.00	3.60

STATED ODDS 1:49 HOBBY
*RETAIL CARDS: .4X TO .8X HOBBY
STATED ODDS 1:73 RETAIL
RETAIL CARDS NUMBERED WITH R PREFIX

❑ 1 Mark Brunell John Elway	20.00	9.00
❑ 2 Jerome Bettis Eddie George	12.00	5.50
❑ 3 Barry Sanders Emmitt Smith	25.00	11.00
❑ 4 Dan Marino Drew Bledsoe	20.00	9.00
❑ 5 Troy Aikman Jake Plummer	12.00	5.50
❑ 6 Terrell Davis Napoleon Kaufman	20.00	9.00
❑ 7 Cris Carter Herman Moore	5.00	2.20
❑ 8 Warrick Dunn Dorsey Levens	8.00	3.60
❑ 9 Kordell Stewart Steve McNair	8.00	3.60
❑ 10 Curtis Martin Antowain Smith	8.00	3.60
❑ 11 Jerry Rice Michael Irvin	12.00	5.50
❑ 12 Steve Young Brett Favre	25.00	11.00
❑ 13 Corey Dillon Fred Taylor	15.00	6.75
❑ 14 Tim Brown Andre Rison	8.00	3.60
❑ 15 Mike Alstott Robert Smith	5.00	2.20
❑ 16 Brad Johnson Scott Mitchell	5.00	2.20
❑ 17 Robert Edwards John Avery	8.00	3.60
❑ 18 Deion Sanders Rob Moore	5.00	2.20
❑ 19 Antonio Freeman Randy Moss	30.00	13.50
❑ 20 Peyton Manning Ryan Leaf	30.00	13.50
❑ 21 Curtis Enis Jacquez Green	10.00	4.50
❑ 22 Keyshawn Johnson Terry Glenn	5.00	2.20

1998 Playoff Momentum Rookie Double Feature Hobby

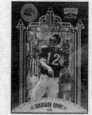

	MINT	NRMT
COMPLETE SET (20)	120.00	55.00
COMMON CARD (1-20)	4.00	1.80
SEMISTARS	5.00	2.20
UNLISTED STARS	6.00	2.70

STATED ODDS 1:17 HOBBY

❑ 1 Peyton Manning Brian Griese	30.00	13.50
❑ 2 Ryan Leaf Charlie Batch	15.00	6.75
❑ 3 Charles Woodson Terry Fair	8.00	3.60
❑ 4 Curtis Enis Tavian Banks	8.00	3.60
❑ 5 Fred Taylor John Avery	15.00	6.75
❑ 6 Kevin Dyson E.G. Green	6.00	2.70
❑ 7 Robert Edwards Chris Fuamatu-Ma'afala	6.00	2.70
❑ 8 Randy Moss Tim Dwight	30.00	13.50
❑ 9 Marcus Nash Joe Jurevicius	6.00	2.70
❑ 10 Jerome Pathon Az Hakim	8.00	3.60
❑ 11 Jacquez Green Tony Simmons	6.00	2.70
❑ 12 Robert Holcombe Jon Ritchie	6.00	2.70
❑ 13 Cameron Cleeland Alonzo Mayes	4.00	1.80
❑ 14 Patrick Johnson Mikhael Ricks	5.00	2.20
❑ 15 Germaine Crowell Hines Ward	8.00	3.60
❑ 16 Skip Hicks Chris Floyd	6.00	2.70
❑ 17 Brian Alford Jammi German	5.00	2.20
❑ 18 Ahman Green Rashan Shehee	6.00	2.70
❑ 19 Jonathan Quinn Moses Moreno	4.00	1.80
❑ 20 R.W. McQuarters Duane Starks	4.00	1.80

1998 Playoff Momentum Rookie Double Feature Retail

	MINT	NRMT
COMPLETE SET (40)	150.00	70.00
COMMON CARD (R1-R40)	1.25	.55
SEMISTARS	2.00	.90
UNLISTED STARS	3.00	1.35

STATED ODDS 1:25 RETAIL

❑ R1 Peyton Manning	25.00	11.00
❑ R2 Ryan Leaf	5.00	2.20
❑ R3 Charles Woodson	6.00	2.70
❑ R4 Curtis Enis	6.00	2.70
❑ R5 Fred Taylor	15.00	6.75
❑ R6 Kevin Dyson	5.00	2.20
❑ R7 Robert Edwards	3.00	1.35
❑ R8 Randy Moss	25.00	11.00

Card	MINT	NRMT
❑ R9 Marcus Nash	3.00	1.35
❑ R10 Jerome Pathon	2.00	.90
❑ R11 Jacquez Green	4.00	1.80
❑ R12 Robert Holcombe	3.00	1.35
❑ R13 Cameron Cleeland	2.00	.90
❑ R14 Pat Johnson	2.00	.90
❑ R15 Germane Crowell	6.00	2.70
❑ R16 Skip Hicks	2.00	.90
❑ R17 Brian Alford	2.00	.90
❑ R18 Ahman Green	2.00	.90
❑ R19 Jonathan Quinn	2.00	.90
❑ R20 R.W. McQuarters	1.25	.55
❑ R21 Brian Griese	10.00	4.50
❑ R22 Charlie Batch	10.00	4.50
❑ R23 Terry Fair	2.00	.90
❑ R24 Tavian Banks	2.00	.90
❑ R25 John Avery	3.00	1.35
❑ R26 E.G. Green	2.00	.90
❑ R27 Chris Fuamatu-Ma'afala	2.00	.90
❑ R28 Tim Dwight	5.00	2.20
❑ R29 Joe Jurevicius	2.00	.90
❑ R30 Az-Zahir Hakim	4.00	1.80
❑ R31 Tony Simmons	2.00	.90
❑ R32 Jon Ritchie	2.00	.90
❑ R33 Alonzo Mayes	1.25	.55
❑ R34 Mikhael Ricks	2.00	.90
❑ R35 Hines Ward	2.00	.90
❑ R36 Chris Floyd	1.25	.55
❑ R37 Jammi German	1.25	.55
❑ R38 Rashaan Shehee	2.00	.90
❑ R39 Moses Moreno	2.00	.90
❑ R40 Duane Starks	1.25	.55

1998 Playoff Momentum Team Threads Home

	MINT	NRMT
COMP.HOBBY SET (20)	400.00	180.00
COMMON HOBBY (1-20)	15.00	6.75

HOME STATED ODDS 1:33 HOBBY
HOME JERSEYS COLORED EXCEPT COWBOYS
*AWAY CARDS: .6X TO 1.5X
AWAY CARD STATED ODDS 1:65 HOBBY
ALL AWAY JERSEYS WHITE EXCEPT COWBOYS
*RETAIL HOME: .4X TO .8X HOBBY HOME
RETAIL HOME STATED ODDS 1:49
*RETAIL AWAY: .4X TO .8X HOBBY AWAY
RETAIL AWAY STATED ODDS 1:97

Card	MINT	NRMT
❑ 1 Jerry Rice	35.00	16.00
❑ 2 Terrell Davis	50.00	22.00
❑ 3 Warrick Dunn	20.00	9.00
❑ 4 Brett Favre	60.00	27.00
❑ 5 Napoleon Kaufman	15.00	6.75
❑ 6 Corey Dillon	15.00	6.75
❑ 7 John Elway	60.00	27.00
❑ 8 Troy Aikman	35.00	16.00
❑ 9 Mark Brunell	30.00	13.50
❑ 10 Kordell Stewart	15.00	6.75
❑ 11 Drew Bledsoe	30.00	13.50
❑ 12 Curtis Martin	15.00	6.75
❑ 13 Dan Marino	60.00	27.00
❑ 14 Jerome Bettis	15.00	6.75
❑ 15 Eddie George	25.00	11.00
❑ 16 Ryan Leaf	20.00	9.00
❑ 17 Jake Plummer	35.00	16.00
❑ 18 Peyton Manning	60.00	27.00
❑ 19 Steve Young	25.00	11.00
❑ 20 Barry Sanders	60.00	27.00

1999 Playoff Momentum SSD

	MINT	NRMT
COMPLETE SET (200)	400.00	180.00
COMP.SHORT SET (150)	100.00	45.00
COMMON CARD (1-100)	.15	.07
SEMISTARS 1-100	.30	.14
UNL.STARS 1-100	.60	.25
COMMON CARD (101-150)	.25	.11
SEMISTARS 101-150	.50	.23
UNL.STARS 101-150	1.00	.45
101-150 STATED ODDS 1:1		
COMMON ROOKIE (151-200)	3.00	1.35
ROOKIE SEMISTARS	5.00	2.20
ROOKIE UNL.STARS	6.00	2.70
151-200 STATED ODDS 1:5		

Card	MINT	NRMT
❑ 1 Rob Moore	.30	.14
❑ 2 Adrian Murrell	.30	.14
❑ 3 Frank Sanders	.30	.14
❑ 4 Andre Wadsworth	.15	.07
❑ 5 Tim Dwight	.60	.25
❑ 6 Terance Mathis	.30	.14
❑ 7 Priest Holmes	.60	.25
❑ 8 Jermaine Lewis	.30	.14
❑ 9 Scott Mitchell	.15	.07
❑ 10 Patrick Johnson	.15	.07
❑ 11 Tony Banks	.30	.14
❑ 12 Thurman Thomas	.30	.14
❑ 13 Andre Reed	.30	.14
❑ 14 Bruce Smith	.30	.14
❑ 15 Tim Biakabutuka	.30	.14
❑ 16 Muhsin Muhammad	.30	.14
❑ 17 Wesley Walls	.30	.14
❑ 18 Rae Carruth	.30	.14
❑ 19 Curtis Conway	.30	.14
❑ 20 Bobby Engram	.30	.14
❑ 21 Jeff Blake	.30	.14
❑ 22 Darnay Scott	.15	.07
❑ 23 Ty Detmer	.30	.14
❑ 24 Leslie Shepherd	.15	.07
❑ 25 Sedrick Shaw	.15	.07
❑ 26 Michael Irvin	.30	.14
❑ 27 Rocket Ismail	.30	.14
❑ 28 Ed McCaffrey	.30	.14
❑ 29 Marcus Nash	.30	.14
❑ 30 Shannon Sharpe	.30	.14
❑ 31 Neil Smith	.30	.14
❑ 32 Rod Smith	.30	.14
❑ 33 Bubby Brister	.15	.07
❑ 34 Germane Crowell	.30	.14
❑ 35 Johnnie Morton	.30	.14
❑ 36 Bill Schroeder	.60	.25
❑ 37 Mark Chmura	.15	.07
❑ 38 Marvin Harrison	.60	.25
❑ 39 E.G. Green	.15	.07
❑ 40 Jerome Pathon	.15	.07
❑ 41 Keenan McCardell	.30	.14
❑ 42 Jimmy Smith	.30	.14
❑ 43 Kyle Brady	.15	.07
❑ 44 Tavian Banks	.15	.07
❑ 45 Warren Moon	.60	.25
❑ 46 Derrick Alexander WR	.30	.14
❑ 47 Elvis Grbac	.30	.14
❑ 48 Andre Rison	.30	.14
❑ 49 Byron Bam Morris	.15	.07
❑ 50 Rashaan Shehee	.15	.07
❑ 51 Karim Abdul-Jabbar	.30	.14
❑ 52 John Avery	.30	.14
❑ 53 Tony Martin	.30	.14
❑ 54 O.J. McDuffie	.30	.14
❑ 55 Oronde Gadsden	.15	.07
❑ 56 Robert Smith	.60	.25
❑ 57 Jeff George	.30	.14
❑ 58 Jake Reed	.30	.14
❑ 59 Leroy Hoard	.15	.07
❑ 60 Terry Allen	.30	.14
❑ 61 Terry Glenn	.60	.25
❑ 62 Ben Coates	.30	.14
❑ 63 Tony Simmons	.15	.07
❑ 64 Cameron Cleeland	.15	.07
❑ 65 Eddie Kennison	.30	.14
❑ 66 Billy Joe Hobert	.15	.07
❑ 67 Amani Toomer	.15	.07
❑ 68 Kerry Collins	.30	.14
❑ 69 Ike Hilliard	.15	.07
❑ 70 Gary Brown	.15	.07
❑ 71 Joe Jurevicius	.15	.07
❑ 72 Wayne Chrebet	.30	.14
❑ 73 Vinny Testaverde	.30	.14
❑ 74 Charles Woodson	.60	.25
❑ 75 James Jett	.30	.14
❑ 76 Charles Johnson	.15	.07
❑ 77 Duce Staley	.60	.25
❑ 78 Hines Ward	.15	.07
❑ 79 Jim Harbaugh	.30	.14
❑ 80 Ryan Leaf	.60	.25
❑ 81 Junior Seau	.30	.14
❑ 82 Mikhael Ricks	.15	.07
❑ 83 Garrison Hearst	.30	.14
❑ 84 J.J. Stokes	.30	.14
❑ 85 Lawrence Phillips	.30	.14
❑ 86 Derrick Mayes	.15	.07
❑ 87 Mike Pritchard	.15	.07
❑ 88 Ahman Green	.30	.14
❑ 89 Ricky Watters	.30	.14
❑ 90 Robert Holcombe	.30	.14
❑ 91 Isaac Bruce	.60	.25
❑ 92 Trent Dilfer	.30	.14
❑ 93 Reidel Anthony	.15	.07
❑ 94 Jacquez Green	.30	.14
❑ 95 Warren Sapp	.15	.07
❑ 96 Kevin Dyson	.30	.14
❑ 97 Yancey Thigpen	.15	.07
❑ 98 Stephen Davis	.60	.25
❑ 99 Irving Fryar	.30	.14
❑ 100 Michael Westbrook	.30	.14
❑ 101 Jake Plummer	2.00	.90
❑ 102 Jamal Anderson	1.00	.45
❑ 103 Chris Chandler	.50	.23
❑ 104 Doug Flutie	1.25	.55
❑ 105 Eric Moulds	1.00	.45
❑ 106 Antowain Smith	1.00	.45
❑ 107 Jonathan Linton	.25	.11
❑ 108 Curtis Enis	1.00	.45
❑ 109 Corey Dillon	1.00	.45
❑ 110 Carl Pickens	.50	.23
❑ 111 Emmitt Smith	2.50	1.10
❑ 112 Troy Aikman	2.50	1.10
❑ 113 Deion Sanders	1.00	.45
❑ 114 John Elway	4.00	1.80
❑ 115 Terrell Davis	2.50	1.10
❑ 116 Brian Griese	2.00	.90
❑ 117 Barry Sanders	4.00	1.80
❑ 118 Charlie Batch	2.00	.90
❑ 119 Herman Moore	1.00	.45
❑ 120 Brett Favre	4.00	1.80
❑ 121 Antonio Freeman	1.00	.45
❑ 122 Dorsey Levens	1.00	.45
❑ 123 Peyton Manning	4.00	1.80
❑ 124 Fred Taylor	2.50	1.10
❑ 125 Mark Brunell	1.50	.70
❑ 126 Dan Marino	4.00	1.80
❑ 127 Randy Moss	4.00	1.80
❑ 128 Cris Carter	1.00	.45
❑ 129 Randall Cunningham	1.00	.45
❑ 130 Drew Bledsoe	1.50	.70
❑ 131 Keyshawn Johnson	1.00	.45
❑ 132 Curtis Martin	1.00	.45
❑ 133 Tim Brown	1.00	.45
❑ 134 Napoleon Kaufman	1.00	.45
❑ 135 Kordell Stewart	1.00	.45
❑ 136 Jerome Bettis	1.00	.45

	MINT	NRMT
☐ 137 Natrone Means	.50	.23
☐ 138 Jerry Rice	2.50	1.10
☐ 139 Steve Young	1.50	.70
☐ 140 Terrell Owens	1.00	.45
☐ 141 Joey Galloway	1.00	.45
☐ 142 Jon Kitna	1.25	.55
☐ 143 Marshall Faulk	1.00	.45
☐ 144 Kurt Warner RC	25.00	11.00
☐ 145 Warrick Dunn	1.00	.45
☐ 146 Mike Alstott	1.00	.45
☐ 147 Eddie George	1.25	.55
☐ 148 Steve McNair	1.00	.45
☐ 149 Brad Johnson	1.00	.45
☐ 150 Skip Hicks	1.00	.45
☐ 151 Tim Couch RC	30.00	13.50
☐ 152 Donovan McNabb RC	20.00	9.00
☐ 153 Akili Smith RC	12.00	5.50
☐ 154 Edgerrin James RC	50.00	22.00
☐ 155 Ricky Williams RC	30.00	13.50
☐ 156 Torry Holt RC	15.00	6.75
☐ 157 Champ Bailey RC	8.00	3.60
☐ 158 David Boston RC	10.00	4.50
☐ 159 Chris Claiborne RC	5.00	2.20
☐ 160 Chris McAlister RC	5.00	2.20
☐ 161 Daunte Culpepper RC	20.00	9.00
☐ 162 Cade McNown RC	20.00	9.00
☐ 163 Troy Edwards RC	10.00	4.50
☐ 164 Jevon Kearse RC	12.00	5.50
☐ 165 Kevin Johnson RC	15.00	6.75
☐ 166 James Johnson RC	8.00	3.60
☐ 167 Reginald Kelly RC	3.00	1.35
☐ 168 Rob Konrad RC	6.00	2.70
☐ 169 Jim Kleinsasser RC	6.00	2.70
☐ 170 Kevin Faulk RC	8.00	3.60
☐ 171 Joe Montgomery RC	6.00	2.70
☐ 172 Shaun King RC	20.00	9.00
☐ 173 Peerless Price RC	10.00	4.50
☐ 174 Mike Cloud RC	6.00	2.70
☐ 175 Jermaine Fazande RC	5.00	2.20
☐ 176 D'Wayne Bates RC	5.00	2.20
☐ 177 Brock Huard RC	8.00	3.60
☐ 178 Marty Booker RC	6.00	2.70
☐ 179 Karsten Bailey RC	5.00	2.20
☐ 180 Shawn Bryson RC	5.00	2.20
☐ 181 Jeff Paulk RC	5.00	2.20
☐ 182 Travis McGriff RC	5.00	2.20
☐ 183 Amos Zereoue RC	6.00	2.70
☐ 184 Craig Yeast RC	5.00	2.20
☐ 185 Joe Germaine RC	6.00	2.70
☐ 186 Dameane Douglas RC	5.00	2.20
☐ 187 Sedrick Irvin RC	6.00	2.70
☐ 188 Brandon Stokley RC	5.00	2.20
☐ 189 Larry Parker RC	5.00	2.20
☐ 190 Sean Bennett RC	6.00	2.70
☐ 191 Wane McGarity RC	5.00	2.20
☐ 192 Olandis Gary RC	20.00	9.00
☐ 193 Na Brown RC	6.00	2.70
☐ 194 Aaron Brooks RC	6.00	2.70
☐ 195 Cecil Collins RC	6.00	2.70
☐ 196 Darrin Chiaverini RC	5.00	2.20
☐ 197 Kevin Daft RC	5.00	2.20
☐ 198 Darnell McDonald RC	6.00	2.70
☐ 199 Joel Makovicka RC	6.00	2.70
☐ 200 Michael Bishop RC	8.00	3.60

1999 Playoff Momentum SSD O's

	MINT	NRMT
COMMON CARD (1-200)	15.00	6.75

*1-100 STARS: 30X TO 80X HI COL.
*1-100 YOUNG STARS: 25X TO 60X
*101-150 STARS: 20X TO 50X HI COL.
*101-150 YOUNG STARS: 15X TO 40X
*144/151-200 RCs: 2X TO 5X
STATED PRINT RUN 25 SERIAL #'d SETS

1999 Playoff Momentum SSD X's

	MINT	NRMT
COMPLETE SET (200)	1200.00	550.00

*1-100 STARS: 4X TO 10X HI COL.
*1-100 YOUNG STARS: 3X TO 8X

*101-150 STARS: 2.5X TO 6X HI COL.
*101-150 YOUNG STARS: 2X TO 5X
*144/151-200 RCs: .6X TO 1.5X
STATED PRINT RUN 300 SERIAL #'d SETS

1999 Playoff Momentum SSD Chart Toppers

	MINT	NRMT
COMPLETE SET (24)	150.00	70.00
COMMON CARD (CT1-CT24)	4.00	1.80
STATED ODDS 1:33		

	MINT	NRMT
☐ CT1 Donovan McNabb	8.00	3.60
☐ CT2 Randy Moss	12.00	5.50
☐ CT3 Cade McNown	8.00	3.60
☐ CT4 Brett Favre	15.00	6.75
☐ CT5 Edgerrin James	20.00	9.00
☐ CT6 Dan Marino	15.00	6.75
☐ CT7 Jamal Anderson	4.00	1.80
☐ CT8 Barry Sanders	15.00	6.75
☐ CT9 Kordell Stewart	4.00	1.80
☐ CT10 John Elway	15.00	6.75
☐ CT11 Eddie George	5.00	2.20
☐ CT12 Terrell Davis	10.00	4.50
☐ CT13 Ricky Williams	12.00	5.50
☐ CT14 Peyton Manning	12.00	5.50
☐ CT15 Tim Couch	12.00	5.50
☐ CT16 Emmitt Smith	10.00	4.50
☐ CT17 Doug Flutie	5.00	2.20
☐ CT18 Troy Aikman	10.00	4.50
☐ CT19 Steve Young	6.00	2.70
☐ CT20 Jerry Rice	10.00	4.50
☐ CT21 Mark Brunell	6.00	2.70
☐ CT22 Fred Taylor	8.00	3.60
☐ CT23 Jake Plummer	8.00	3.60
☐ CT24 Drew Bledsoe	6.00	2.70

1999 Playoff Momentum SSD Terrell Davis Salute

	MINT	NRMT
COMPLETE SET (5)	50.00	22.00
COMMON CARD (TD11-TD15)	10.00	4.50
STATED ODDS 1:255		
COMMON AUTO (1-5)	60.00	27.00
AUTOS PRINT RUN 150 SER.#'d SETS		

	MINT	NRMT
☐ TD11 Terrell Davis	10.00	4.50
☐ TD12 Terrell Davis	10.00	4.50
☐ TD13 Terrell Davis	10.00	4.50
☐ TD14 Terrell Davis	10.00	4.50
☐ TD15 Terrell Davis	10.00	4.50

1999 Playoff Momentum SSD Gridiron Force

	MINT	NRMT
COMPLETE SET (24)	80.00	36.00
COMMON CARD (GF1-GF24)	2.50	1.10
STATED ODDS 1:17		

	MINT	NRMT
☐ GF1 Cris Carter	2.50	1.10
☐ GF2 Brett Favre	10.00	4.50
☐ GF3 Jamal Anderson	2.50	1.10
☐ GF4 Dan Marino	10.00	4.50
☐ GF5 Deion Sanders	2.50	1.10
☐ GF6 Barry Sanders	10.00	4.50
☐ GF7 Jerome Bettis	2.50	1.10
☐ GF8 John Elway	10.00	4.50
☐ GF9 Eddie George	3.00	1.35
☐ GF10 Peyton Manning	8.00	3.60
☐ GF11 Warrick Dunn	2.50	1.10
☐ GF12 Troy Aikman	6.00	2.70
☐ GF13 Keyshawn Johnson	2.50	1.10
☐ GF14 Jerry Rice	6.00	2.70
☐ GF15 Terrell Owens	2.50	1.10
☐ GF16 Randy Moss	8.00	3.60
☐ GF17 Fred Taylor	4.00	1.80
☐ GF18 Mark Brunell	4.00	1.80
☐ GF19 Steve Young	4.00	1.80
☐ GF20 Drew Bledsoe	4.00	1.80
☐ GF21 Kordell Stewart	2.50	1.10
☐ GF22 Emmitt Smith	6.00	2.70
☐ GF23 Terrell Davis	6.00	2.70
☐ GF24 Jake Plummer	5.00	2.20

1999 Playoff Momentum SSD Hog Heaven

	MINT	NRMT
COMPLETE SET (12)	200.00	90.00
COMMON CARD (HH1-HH12)	15.00	6.75
STATED ODDS 1:81		

	MINT	NRMT
☐ HH1 Ricky Williams	30.00	13.50
☐ HH2 Terrell Davis	20.00	9.00
☐ HH3 Emmitt Smith	20.00	9.00
☐ HH4 Brett Favre	30.00	13.50
☐ HH5 Fred Taylor	15.00	6.75

❑ HH6 Tim Couch	30.00	13.50
❑ HH7 John Elway	30.00	13.50
❑ HH8 Dan Marino	30.00	13.50
❑ HH9 Randy Moss	25.00	11.00
❑ HH10 Barry Sanders	30.00	13.50
❑ HH11 Jerry Rice	20.00	9.00
❑ HH12 Jake Plummer	15.00	6.75

1999 Playoff Momentum SSD Rookie Quads

	MINT	NRMT
COMPLETE SET (12)	250.00	110.00
COMMON CARD (1-12)	12.00	5.50
STATED ODDS 1:97		
*GOLDS: 1X TO 2.5X HI COL.		
GOLDS STATED PRINT RUN 50 SER.#'d SETS		

❑ 1 Tim Couch Aaron Brooks Shaun King Michael Bishop	40.00	18.00
❑ 2 Edgerrin James Mike Cloud Jeff Paulk Joel Makovicka	50.00	22.00
❑ 3 Torry Holt Reggie Kelly Marty Booker Dameane Douglas	20.00	9.00
❑ 4 Champ Bailey Chris Claiborne Chris McAlister Anthony McFarland	12.00	5.50
❑ 5 David Boston Jim Kleinsasser Karsten Bailey Brandon Stokley	15.00	6.75
❑ 6 Ricky Williams Amos Zereoue Cecil Collins Olandis Gary	50.00	22.00
❑ 7 Donovan McNabb Brock Huard Daunte Culpepper Scott Covington	25.00	11.00
❑ 8 James Johnson Jerame Fazande Sedrick Irvin Sean Bennett	15.00	6.75
❑ 9 Troy Edwards Peerless Price Travis McGriff Larry Parker	25.00	11.00
❑ 10 Rob Konrad Kevin Faulk Joe Montgomery Shawn Bryson	12.00	5.50
❑ 11 Cade McNown Joe Germaine Akili Smith Chris Greisen	25.00	11.00
❑ 12 Kevin Johnson D'Wayne Bates Craig Yeast Wane McGarity	25.00	11.00

1999 Playoff Momentum SSD Rookie Recall

	MINT	NRMT
COMPLETE SET (30)	200.00	90.00
COMMON CARD (1-30)	5.00	2.20
STATED ODDS 1:49		

❑ 1 Jerome Bettis	5.00	2.20
❑ 2 Tim Brown	5.00	2.20
❑ 3 Cris Carter	5.00	2.20
❑ 4 Marshall Faulk	5.00	2.20
❑ 5 Doug Flutie	6.00	2.70
❑ 6 Randall Cunningham	5.00	2.20
❑ 7 Brett Favre	20.00	9.00
❑ 8 Dan Marino	20.00	9.00
❑ 9 Barry Sanders	20.00	9.00
❑ 10 John Elway	20.00	9.00
❑ 11 Emmitt Smith	12.00	5.50
❑ 12 Troy Aikman	12.00	5.50
❑ 13 Jerry Rice	12.00	5.50
❑ 14 Steve Young	8.00	3.60
❑ 15 Randy Moss	15.00	6.75
❑ 16 Peyton Manning	15.00	6.75
❑ 17 Fred Taylor	10.00	4.50
❑ 18 Jake Plummer	10.00	4.50
❑ 19 Drew Bledsoe	8.00	3.60
❑ 20 Mark Brunell	8.00	3.60
❑ 21 Charlie Batch	8.00	3.60
❑ 22 Antonio Freeman	5.00	2.20
❑ 23 Curtis Martin	5.00	2.20
❑ 24 Eddie George	6.00	2.70
❑ 25 Kordell Stewart	5.00	2.20
❑ 26 Jamal Anderson	5.00	2.20
❑ 27 Curtis Enis	5.00	2.20
❑ 28 Terrell Davis	12.00	5.50
❑ 29 Eric Moulds	5.00	2.20
❑ 30 Terrell Owens	5.00	2.20

1999 Playoff Momentum SSD Barry Sanders Commemorative

	MINT	NRMT
COMPLETE SET (5)	70.00	32.00
COMMON CARD (RR7-RR11)	15.00	6.75
STATED ODDS 1:275		

❑ RR7 Barry Sanders	15.00	6.75
❑ RR8 Barry Sanders	15.00	6.75
❑ RR9 Barry Sanders	15.00	6.75
❑ RR10 Barry Sanders	15.00	6.75
❑ RR11 Barry Sanders	15.00	6.75
❑ RR1GJ B.Sanders Game Jer.	100.00	45.00

1999 Playoff Momentum SSD Star Gazing

	MINT	NRMT
COMPLETE SET (45)	500.00	220.00
COMMON RED AUTO (SG1-SG8)		30.00
13.50		
RED AUTOGRAPH STATED ODDS 1:185		
COMMON BLUE (SG9-SG30)	1.50	.70
SEMISTARS BLUE	2.50	1.10
BLUE STATED ODDS 1:17		
COMMON GREEN (SG31-SG45)	5.00	2.20
GREEN STATED ODDS 1:65		
TRADE CARD EXPIRATION: 10/31/2000		

❑ SG1 Terrell Davis	60.00	27.00
❑ SG2 Dan Marino	100.00	45.00
❑ SG3 Joey Galloway	30.00	13.50
❑ SG4 Steve McNair	30.00	13.50
❑ SG5 Doug Flutie	40.00	18.00
❑ SG6 Kordell Stewart	30.00	13.50
❑ SG7 Fred Taylor	40.00	18.00
❑ SG8 Jamal Anderson	30.00	13.50
❑ SG9 Karim Abdul-Jabbar	1.50	.70
❑ SG10 Mike Alstott	2.50	1.10
❑ SG11 Jerome Bettis	2.50	1.10
❑ SG12 Carl Pickens	1.50	.70
❑ SG13 Cris Carter	2.50	1.10
❑ SG14 Randall Cunningham	2.50	1.10
❑ SG15 Corey Dillon	2.50	1.10
❑ SG16 Tim Dwight	2.50	1.10
❑ SG17 Cade McNown	6.00	2.70
❑ SG18 Marshall Faulk	2.50	1.10
❑ SG19 Napoleon Kaufman	2.50	1.10
❑ SG20 Antonio Freeman	2.50	1.10
❑ SG21 Edgerrin James	15.00	6.75
❑ SG22 Terrell Owens	2.50	1.10
❑ SG23 Garrison Hearst	1.50	.70
❑ SG24 Keyshawn Johnson	2.50	1.10
❑ SG25 Akili Smith	4.00	1.80
❑ SG26 Curtis Martin	2.50	1.10
❑ SG27 Dorsey Levens	2.50	1.10
❑ SG28 Deion Sanders	2.50	1.10
❑ SG29 Herman Moore	2.50	1.10
❑ SG30 Eric Moulds	2.50	1.10
❑ SG31 Randy Moss	12.00	5.50
❑ SG32 Eddie George	5.00	2.20
❑ SG33 Barry Sanders	15.00	6.75
❑ SG34 John Elway	15.00	6.75
❑ SG35 Peyton Manning	12.00	5.50
❑ SG36 Emmitt Smith	10.00	4.50
❑ SG37 Troy Aikman	10.00	4.50
❑ SG38 Jerry Rice	10.00	4.50
❑ SG39 Mark Brunell	6.00	2.70
❑ SG40 Steve Young	6.00	2.70
❑ SG41 Tim Couch	15.00	6.75
❑ SG42 Ricky Williams	15.00	6.75
❑ SG43 Donovan McNabb	10.00	4.50
❑ SG44 Drew Bledsoe	6.00	2.70
❑ SG45 Brett Favre	15.00	6.75

1999 Playoff Momentum SSD Star Gazing Gold

	MINT	NRMT
COMPLETE SET (45)	1000.00	450.00
COMMON CARD (SG1-SG8)	20.00	9.00
*SG9-SG30 STARS: 3X TO 8X BASIC INSERTS		
*SG9-SG30 ROOKIES: 1.5X TO 4X BASIC INS.		
*SG31-SG45 STARS: 2X TO 5X BASIC INSERTS		
*SG31-SG45 ROOKIES: 1.2X TO 3X BASIC INS.		
GOLD STATED PRINT RUN 50 SER.#'d SETS		

❑ SG1 Terrell Davis	50.00	22.00
❑ SG2 Dan Marino	80.00	36.00
❑ SG5 Doug Flutie	25.00	11.00
❑ SG7 Fred Taylor	40.00	18.00
❑ SG32 Eddie George	25.00	11.00

1999 Playoff Momentum SSD Team Thread Checklists

	MINT	NRMT
COMPLETE SET (31)	400.00	180.00
COMMON CARD (TTC1-TTC31)	6.00	2.70
SEMISTARS	10.00	4.50
STATED ODDS 1:17		

❑ TTC1 Dan Marino	30.00	13.50
❑ TTC2 Drew Bledsoe	15.00	6.75
❑ TTC3 Keyshawn Johnson	10.00	4.50
❑ TTC4 Eric Moulds	10.00	4.50
❑ TTC5 Peyton Manning	30.00	13.50
❑ TTC6 Natrone Means	10.00	4.50
❑ TTC7 Jon Kitna	12.00	5.50

❑ TTC8 Byron Bam Morris 6.00 2.70
❑ TTC9 Tim Brown 10.00 4.50
❑ TTC10 Terrell Davis 20.00 9.00
❑ TTC11 Kordell Stewart...... 10.00 4.50
❑ TTC12 Fred Taylor 20.00 9.00
❑ TTC13 Tim Couch 30.00 13.50
❑ TTC14 Eddie George 12.00 5.50
❑ TTC15 Priest Holmes........ 10.00 4.50
❑ TTC16 Akili Smith 12.00 5.50
❑ TTC17 Emmitt Smith 25.00 11.00
❑ TTC18 Skip Hicks 10.00 4.50
❑ TTC19 Jake Plummer 15.00 6.75
❑ TTC20 Donovan McNabb 20.00 9.00
❑ TTC21 Ike Hilliard 6.00 2.70
❑ TTC22 Barry Sanders 30.00 13.50
❑ TTC23 Cade McNown 20.00 9.00
❑ TTC24 Randy Moss 30.00 13.50
❑ TTC25 Brett Favre 30.00 13.50
❑ TTC26 Mike Alstott............ 10.00 4.50
❑ TTC27 Marshall Faulk 20.00 9.00
❑ TTC28 Ricky Williams 30.00 13.50
❑ TTC29 Jamal Anderson 10.00 4.50
❑ TTC30 Jerry Rice 20.00 9.00
❑ TTC31 Tim Biakabutuka .. 10.00 4.50

1998 Playoff Prestige Hobby

	MINT	NRMT
COMP.HOBBY SET (200)	150.00	70.00
COMMON CARD (1-164)	.40	.18
SEMISTARS.....................................	.75	.35
UNLISTED STARS....................	1.50	.70
COMMON ROOKIE (165-200) ..	2.00	.90
ROOKIE SEMISTARS	3.00	1.35
ROOKIE UNLISTED STARS	4.00	1.80

SSD HOBBY PACK CARDS ARE PRICED BELOW
COMP.RED HOBBY (200) 600.00 275.00
*RED HOBBY STARS: 1.5X TO 3X HI COL.
*RED HOB.YOUNG STARS: 1.25X TO 2.5X
*RED HOBBY RCs: .75X TO 2X ..
RED HOBBY STATED ODDS 1:3 HOBBY
COMP.RETAIL SET (200) 80.00 36.00
*RETAIL CARDS: .25X TO .5X HOBBY
COMP.RETAIL RED (200) 300.00 135.00
*RED RET.STARS: 1.5X TO 3X BASIC RETAIL
*RED RET.YOUNG STARS: 1.25X TO 2.5X
*RED RETAIL RCs: .75X TO 2X BASIC RETAIL
RED RETAIL STATED ODDS 1:3 RETAIL
COMP.RETAIL GREEN (200) 300.00 135.00
*GREEN RET.STARS: 1.5X TO 3X BASIC RETAIL.......................................
*GREEN RET.YOUNG STARS: 1.25X TO 2.5X
*GREEN RET.RCs: .75X TO 2X ..
GREEN RETAIL ONE PER SPEC.RET.PACK

❑ 1 John Elway 8.00 3.60
❑ 2 Steve Atwater .... .40 .18
❑ 3 Terrell Davis 6.00 2.70
❑ 4 Bill Romanowski .... .40 .18
❑ 5 Rod Smith .... .75 .35
❑ 6 Shannon Sharpe .... .75 .35
❑ 7 Ed McCaffrey .... .75 .35
❑ 8 Neil Smith .... .75 .35
❑ 9 Brett Favre 8.00 3.60
❑ 10 Dorsey Levens .... 1.50 .70
❑ 11 LeRoy Butler .... .40 .18
❑ 12 Antonio Freeman............ 1.50 .70
❑ 13 Robert Brooks .... .75 .35
❑ 14 Mark Chmura .... .75 .35
❑ 15 Gilbert Brown .... .40 .18
❑ 16 Kordell Stewart .... 1.50 .70
❑ 17 Jerome Bettis .... 1.50 .70
❑ 18 Carnell Lake .... .40 .18
❑ 19 Dermontti Dawson........... .40 .18
❑ 20 Charles Johnson .... .40 .18
❑ 21 Greg Lloyd........................ .40 .18
❑ 22 Levon Kirkland .... .40 .18
❑ 23 Steve Young 2.50 1.10
❑ 24 Jim Druckenmiller .... .75 .35
❑ 25 Garrison Hearst.............. 1.50 .70
❑ 26 Merton Hanks .... .40 .18
❑ 27 Ken Norton .... .40 .18
❑ 28 Jerry Rice 4.00 1.80
❑ 29 Terrell Owens .... 1.50 .70
❑ 30 J.J. Stokes......................... .75 .35
❑ 31 Trent Dilfer .... 1.50 .70
❑ 32 Warrick Dunn 2.50 1.10
❑ 33 Mike Alstott .... 1.50 .70
❑ 34 Reidel Anthony .... .75 .35
❑ 35 Warren Sapp .... .75 .35
❑ 36 Elvis Grbac .... .75 .35
❑ 37 Kimble Anders.................. .75 .35
❑ 38 Ted Popson....................... .40 .18
❑ 39 Derrick Thomas................ .75 .35
❑ 40 Tony Gonzalez .... .40 .18
❑ 41 Andre Rison .... .75 .35
❑ 42 Derrick Alexander .... .75 .35
❑ 43 Brad Johnson .... 1.50 .70
❑ 44 Robert Smith .... 1.50 .70
❑ 45 Randall McDaniel .... .40 .18
❑ 46 Cris Carter...................... 1.50 .70
❑ 47 Jake Reed .... .75 .35
❑ 48 John Randle .... .75 .35
❑ 49 Drew Bledsoe 3.00 1.35
❑ 50 Willie Clay .... .40 .18
❑ 51 Chris Slade .... .40 .18
❑ 52 Willie McGinest .... .40 .18
❑ 53 Shawn Jefferson .... .40 .18
❑ 54 Ben Coates .... .75 .35
❑ 55 Terry Glenn .... 1.50 .70
❑ 56 Jason Hanson .... .40 .18
❑ 57 Scott Mitchell.................... .75 .35
❑ 58 Barry Sanders 8.00 3.60
❑ 59 Herman Moore .... 1.50 .70
❑ 60 Johnnie Morton .... .75 .35
❑ 61 Mark Brunell 3.00 1.35
❑ 62 James Stewart .... .75 .35
❑ 63 Tony Boselli...................... .40 .18
❑ 64 Jimmy Smith .... .75 .35
❑ 65 Keenan McCardell............ .75 .35
❑ 66 Dan Marino 8.00 3.60
❑ 67 Troy Drayton .... .40 .18
❑ 68 Bernie Parmalee .... .40 .18
❑ 69 Karim Abdul-Jabbar ...... 1.50 .70
❑ 70 Zach Thomas .... .40 .18
❑ 71 O.J. McDuffie .... .75 .35
❑ 72 Tim Bowens .... .40 .18
❑ 73 Danny Kanell.................... .75 .35
❑ 74 Tiki Barber........................ .75 .35
❑ 75 Tyrone Wheatley .... .75 .35
❑ 76 Charles Way .... .40 .18
❑ 77 Jason Sehorn .... .40 .18
❑ 78 Ike Hilliard .... .75 .35
❑ 79 Michael Strahan .... .40 .18
❑ 80 Troy Aikman 4.00 1.80
❑ 81 Deion Sanders .... 1.50 .70
❑ 82 Emmitt Smith.................. 6.00 2.70
❑ 83 Darren Woodson............... .40 .18
❑ 84 Daryl Johnston .... .75 .35
❑ 85 Michael Irvin .... 1.50 .70
❑ 86 David LaFleur .... .40 .18
❑ 87 Glenn Foley...................... .75 .35
❑ 88 Neil O'Donnell .... .75 .35
❑ 89 Keyshawn Johnson........ 1.50 .70
❑ 90 Aaron Glenn .... .40 .18
❑ 91 Wayne Chrebet .... 1.50 .70
❑ 92 Curtis Martin .... 1.50 .70
❑ 93 Steve McNair.................. 1.50 .70
❑ 94 Eddie George 3.00 1.35
❑ 95 Bruce Matthews .... .40 .18
❑ 96 Frank Wycheck .... .40 .18
❑ 97 Yancey Thigpen .... .40 .18
UER back Yancy
❑ 98 Gus Frerotte .... .40 .18
❑ 99 Terry Allen...................... 1.50 .70
❑ 100 Michael Westbrook .... .75 .35
❑ 101 Jamie Asher .... .40 .18
❑ 102 Marshall Faulk............. 1.50 .70
❑ 103 Zack Crockett .... .40 .18
❑ 104 Ken Dilger .... .40 .18
❑ 105 Marvin Harrison............. .75 .35
❑ 106 Chris Chandler .... .75 .35
❑ 107 Byron Hanspard .... .75 .35
❑ 108 Jamal Anderson .... 1.50 .70
❑ 109 Terance Mathis .... .75 .35
❑ 110 Peter Boulware .... .40 .18
❑ 111 Michael Jackson .... .40 .18
❑ 112 Jim Harbaugh .... .75 .35
❑ 113 Errict Rhett .... .75 .35
❑ 114 Antowain Smith .... 1.50 .70
❑ 115 Thurman Thomas .... 1.50 .70
❑ 116 Bruce Smith.................... .75 .35
❑ 117 Doug Flutie .... 2.00 .90
❑ 118 Rob Johnson .... .75 .35
❑ 119 Kerry Collins .... .75 .35
❑ 120 Fred Lane .... .75 .35
❑ 121 Wesley Walls.................. .75 .35
❑ 122 William Floyd................. .40 .18
❑ 123 Kevin Greene .... .75 .35
❑ 124 Erik Kramer .... .40 .18
❑ 125 Darnell Autry .... .40 .18
❑ 126 Curtis Conway............... .75 .35
❑ 127 Edgar Bennett .... .40 .18
❑ 128 Jeff Blake .... .75 .35
❑ 129 Corey Dillon................. 2.50 1.10
❑ 130 Carl Pickens .... 1.50 .70
❑ 131 Darnay Scott .... .75 .35
❑ 132 Jake Plummer 5.00 2.20
❑ 133 Larry Centers .... .40 .18
❑ 134 Frank Sanders............... .75 .35
❑ 135 Rob Moore .... .75 .35
❑ 136 Adrian Murrell .... .75 .35
❑ 137 Troy Davis...................... .40 .18
❑ 138 Ray Zellars .... .40 .18
❑ 139 Willie Roaf...................... .40 .18
❑ 140 Andre Hastings .... .40 .18
❑ 141 Jeff George .... .75 .35
❑ 142 Napoleon Kaufman ...... 1.50 .70
❑ 143 Desmond Howard .... .75 .35
❑ 144 Tim Brown.................... 1.50 .70
❑ 145 James Jett...................... .75 .35
❑ 146 Rickey Dudley .... .40 .18
❑ 147 Bobby Hoying .... .75 .35
❑ 148 Duce Staley................. 2.50 1.10
❑ 149 Charlie Garner............... .40 .18
❑ 150 Irving Fryar .... .75 .35
❑ 151 Chris T. Jones .... .40 .18
❑ 152 Tony Banks .... .75 .35
❑ 153 Craig Heyward .... .40 .18
❑ 154 Isaac Bruce .... 1.50 .70
❑ 155 Eddie Kennison.............. .75 .35
❑ 156 Junior Seau .... .75 .35
❑ 157 Tony Martin .... .75 .35
❑ 158 Freddie Jones .... .40 .18
❑ 159 Natrone Means .... 1.50 .70
❑ 160 Warren Moon .... 1.50 .70
❑ 161 Steve Broussard .... .40 .18
❑ 162 Joey Galloway............. 1.50 .70
❑ 163 Brian Blades .... .40 .18
❑ 164 Ricky Watters .... .75 .35
❑ 165 Peyton Manning RC .. 25.00 11.00
❑ 166 Ryan Leaf RC 6.00 2.70
❑ 167 Andre Wadsworth RC .. 3.00 1.35
❑ 168 Charles Woodson RC .. 8.00 3.60
❑ 169 Curtis Enis RC.............. 8.00 3.60
❑ 170 Fred Taylor RC 15.00 6.75
❑ 171 Kevin Dyson RC 6.00 2.70
❑ 172 Robert Edwards RC 4.00 1.80
❑ 173 Randy Moss RC 25.00 11.00
❑ 174 R.W. McQuarters RC .. 2.00 .90
❑ 175 John Avery RC 4.00 1.80
❑ 176 Marcus Nash RC.......... 6.00 2.70
❑ 177 Jerome Pathon RC 3.00 1.35
❑ 178 Jacquez Green RC 6.00 2.70
❑ 179 Robert Holcombe RC .. 4.00 1.80
❑ 180 Pat Johnson RC 3.00 1.35
❑ 181 Germane Crowell RC .. 8.00 3.60
❑ 182 Tony Simmons RC 3.00 1.35
❑ 183 Joe Jurevicius RC 3.00 1.35
❑ 184 Mikhael Ricks RC 3.00 1.35
❑ 185 Charlie Batch RC 10.00 4.50
❑ 186 Jon Ritchie RC 3.00 1.35
❑ 187 Scott Frost RC............. 3.00 1.35
❑ 188 Skip Hicks RC 6.00 2.70
❑ 189 Brian Alford RC 3.00 1.35
❑ 190 E.G. Green RC 3.00 1.35
❑ 191 Jammi German RC ...... 2.00 .90
❑ 192 Ahman Green RC 6.00 2.70
❑ 193 Chris Floyd RC .... 2.00 .90
❑ 194 Larry Shannon RC ...... 2.00 .90
❑ 195 Jonathan Quinn RC...... 3.00 1.35
❑ 196 Rashaan Shehee RC .. 3.00 1.35
❑ 197 Brian Griese RC 10.00 4.50
❑ 198 Hines Ward RC 3.00 1.35
❑ 199 Michael Pittman RC 3.00 1.35
❑ 200 Az-Zahir Hakim RC 6.00 2.70

1998 Playoff Prestige Hobby Gold

	MINT	NRMT
COMMON GOLD (1-200)	25.00	11.00
*GOLD STARS: 25X TO 50X HI COL.		
*GOLD YOUNG STARS: 20X TO 40X		
*GOLD RCs: 7.5X TO 15X		
GOLDS PRINT RUN 25 SERIAL #'d SETS		

1998 Playoff Prestige Alma Maters

	MINT	NRMT
COMP.SILVER SET (28)	350.00	160.00
COMMON SILVER (1-28)	8.00	3.60
SEMISTARS	10.00	4.50
SILVER STATED ODDS 1:17 HOBBY		
*BLUE CARDS: .3X TO .6X SILVERS		
BLUE STATED ODDS 1:25 RETAIL		

Card	MINT	NRMT
❑ 1 Brett Favre Michael Jackson Pat Carter	40.00	18.00
❑ 2 Michael Irvin Russell Maryland Vinny Testaverde	8.00	3.60
❑ 3 Warrick Dunn Andre Wadsworth Peter Boulware	12.00	5.50
❑ 4 Deion Sanders Edgar Bennett Brad Johnson	10.00	4.50
❑ 5 Emmitt Smith Fred Taylor Reidel Anthony	25.00	11.00
❑ 6 Antowain Smith Kimble Anders Lamar Lathon	10.00	4.50
❑ 7 Barry Sanders Thurman Thomas R.W. McQuarters	40.00	18.00
❑ 8 Ryan Leaf Drew Bledsoe Brian Hansen	20.00	9.00
❑ 9 Mark Brunell Warren Moon Rashaan Shehee	15.00	6.75
❑ 10 Napoleon Kaufman Corey Dillon Jerome Pathon	12.00	5.50
❑ 11 Peyton Manning Carl Pickens Reggie White	35.00	16.00
❑ 12 Kordell Stewart Rae Carruth Michael Westbrook	12.00	5.50
❑ 13 Curtis Enis Kerry Collins O.J. McDuffie	15.00	6.75
❑ 14 Eddie George Bobby Hoying Ricky Dudley	15.00	6.75
❑ 15 Cris Carter Terry Glenn Joey Galloway	8.00	3.60
❑ 16 Elvis Grbac Jim Harbaugh Charles Woodson	8.00	3.60
❑ 17 John Elway Ed McCaffrey Glyn Milburn	40.00	18.00
❑ 18 Terrell Davis Garrison Hearst Robert Edwards	30.00	13.50
❑ 19 Herschel Walker Andre Hastings Hines Ward	8.00	3.60
❑ 20 Dan Marino Curtis Martin Craig Heyward	40.00	18.00
❑ 21 Troy Aikman J.J. Stokes Skip Hicks	20.00	9.00
❑ 22 Junior Seau Keyshawn Johnson Johnnie Morton	8.00	3.60
❑ 23 Jerome Bettis Tim Brown Ricky Watters	8.00	3.60
❑ 24 Marshall Faulk Darnay Scott Az-Zahir Hakim	12.00	5.50
❑ 25 Bruce Smith Jim Druckenmiller Antonio Freeman	10.00	4.50
❑ 26 Jake Plummer Rod Woodson Mario Bates	15.00	6.75
❑ 27 Herman Moore Tiki Barber Charles Way	8.00	3.60
❑ 28 John Avery Wesley Walls Tim Bowens	8.00	3.60

1998 Playoff Prestige Award Winning Performers

	MINT	NRMT
COMP.SILVER SET (22)	800.00	350.00
COMMON SILVER (1-22)	25.00	11.00
SILVER STATED ODDS 1:65 HOBBY		
*BLUE CARDS: .3X TO .6X SILVERS		
BLUE STATED ODDS 1:97 RETAIL		

Card	MINT	NRMT
❑ 1 Terrell Davis	80.00	36.00
❑ 2 Troy Aikman	50.00	22.00
❑ 3 Brett Favre	100.00	45.00
❑ 4 Barry Sanders	100.00	45.00
❑ 5 Warrick Dunn	30.00	13.50
❑ 6 John Elway	100.00	45.00
❑ 7 Jerome Bettis	25.00	11.00
❑ 8 Jake Plummer	50.00	22.00
❑ 9 Corey Dillon	30.00	13.50
❑ 10 Jerry Rice	50.00	22.00
❑ 11 Steve Young	30.00	13.50
❑ 12 Mark Brunell	40.00	18.00
❑ 13 Drew Bledsoe	40.00	18.00
❑ 14 Dan Marino	100.00	45.00
❑ 15 Kordell Stewart	25.00	11.00
❑ 16 Emmitt Smith	80.00	36.00
❑ 17 Deion Sanders	25.00	11.00
❑ 18 Mike Alstott	25.00	11.00
❑ 19 Herman Moore	25.00	11.00
❑ 20 Cris Carter	25.00	11.00
❑ 21 Eddie George	40.00	18.00
❑ 22 Dorsey Levens	25.00	11.00

1998 Playoff Prestige Best of the NFL

	MINT	NRMT
COMP.DIE CUT SET (24)	250.00	110.00
COMMON DIE CUT (1-24)	8.00	3.60
DIE CUT STATED ODDS 1:33 HOBBY		
*NON-DIE CUTS: .3X TO .6X DIE CUTS		
NON-DIE CUT STATED ODDS 1:49 HOBBY		

Card	MINT	NRMT
❑ 1 Terrell Davis	25.00	11.00
❑ 2 Troy Aikman	15.00	6.75
❑ 3 Brett Favre	30.00	13.50
❑ 4 Barry Sanders	30.00	13.50
❑ 5 Warrick Dunn	12.00	5.50
❑ 6 John Elway	30.00	13.50
❑ 7 Jerome Bettis	10.00	4.50
❑ 8 Jake Plummer	15.00	6.75
❑ 9 Corey Dillon	10.00	4.50
❑ 10 Jerry Rice	15.00	6.75
❑ 11 Steve Young	10.00	4.50
❑ 12 Mark Brunell	12.00	5.50
❑ 13 Drew Bledsoe	12.00	5.50
❑ 14 Dan Marino	30.00	13.50
❑ 15 Kordell Stewart	8.00	3.60
❑ 16 Emmitt Smith	25.00	11.00
❑ 17 Deion Sanders	10.00	4.50
❑ 18 Mike Alstott	10.00	4.50
❑ 19 Herman Moore	10.00	4.50
❑ 20 Cris Carter	10.00	4.50
❑ 21 Eddie George	12.00	5.50
❑ 22 Dorsey Levens	10.00	4.50
❑ 23 Peyton Manning	40.00	18.00
❑ 24 Ryan Leaf	10.00	4.50

1998 Playoff Prestige Checklists

	MINT	NRMT
COMP.SILVER SET (30)	250.00	110.00
COMMON SILVER (1-30)	5.00	2.20
SEMISTARS	6.00	2.70
SILVER STATED ODDS 1:17 HOBBY		
*GOLD CARDS: .25X TO .5X SILVERS		
GOLD STATED ODDS 1:17 RETAIL		

UNNUMBERED CARDS LISTED ALHABETI-CALLY ....

Card	Mint	NrMt
❑ 1 Troy Aikman	15.00	6.75
❑ 2 Drew Bledsoe	12.00	5.50
❑ 3 Isaac Bruce	10.00	4.50
❑ 4 Mark Brunell	12.00	5.50
❑ 5 Cris Carter	10.00	4.50
❑ 6 Troy Davis	5.00	2.20
❑ 7 Corey Dillon	8.00	3.60
❑ 8 Warrick Dunn	10.00	4.50
❑ 9 John Elway	25.00	11.00
❑ 10 Brett Favre	25.00	11.00
❑ 11 Glenn Foley	6.00	2.70
❑ 12 Gus Frerotte	5.00	2.20
❑ 13 Joey Galloway	10.00	4.50
❑ 14 Eddie George	12.00	5.50
❑ 15 Byron Hanspard	6.00	2.70
❑ 16 Bobby Hoying	6.00	2.70
❑ 17 Michael Jackson	5.00	2.20
❑ 18 Danny Kanell	6.00	2.70
❑ 19 Napoleon Kaufman	10.00	4.50
❑ 20 Erik Kramer	5.00	2.20
❑ 21 Ryan Leaf	8.00	3.60
❑ 22 Peyton Manning	30.00	13.50
❑ 23 Dan Marino	25.00	11.00
❑ 24 Jake Plummer	15.00	6.75
❑ 25 Jerry Rice	15.00	6.75
❑ 26 Andre Rison	6.00	2.70
❑ 27 Barry Sanders	25.00	11.00
❑ 28 Antowain Smith	10.00	4.50
❑ 29 Kordell Stewart	6.00	2.70
❑ 30 Wesley Walls	6.00	2.70

1998 Playoff Prestige Draft Picks

	MINT	NRMT
COMP.SILVER SET (33)	150.00	70.00
COMMON SILVER (1-33)	1.50	.70
SEMISTARS	2.50	1.10
UNLISTED STARS	4.00	1.80

SILVER STATED ODDS 1:9 HOBBY
*SILVER JUMBOS: .5X TO 1.2X HI COL.
SILVER JUMBOS ONE PER HOBBY BOX
*BRONZE CARDS: .25X TO .5X SILVERS
BRONZE STATED ODDS 1:9 RETAIL
*BRONZE JUMBOS: 2.5X TO 5X SILVERS
BRONZE JUMBOS PRINT RUN 50 SER.#'d SETS
*GREEN CARDS: .4X TO .8X SILVERS
GREEN ODDS 1 PER SPECIAL RETAIL BOX
*GREEN JUMBOS SAME PRICE AS BASE GREEN
GREEN JUMBOS ONE PER SPECIAL RET.BOX ....
*GREEN NUMBERED: 4X TO 10X SILVERS
GREEN NUMBER.PRINT RUN 25 SER.#'d SETS

Card	Mint	NrMt
❑ 1 Peyton Manning	30.00	13.50
❑ 2 Ryan Leaf	5.00	2.20
❑ 3 Andre Wadsworth	2.50	1.10
❑ 4 Charles Woodson	6.00	2.70
❑ 5 Curtis Enis	6.00	2.70
❑ 6 Fred Taylor	15.00	6.75
❑ 7 Kevin Dyson	5.00	2.20
❑ 8 Robert Edwards	4.00	1.80
❑ 9 Randy Moss	30.00	13.50
❑ 10 R.W. McQuarters	1.50	.70
❑ 11 John Avery	4.00	1.80
❑ 12 Marcus Nash	10.00	4.50
❑ 13 Jerome Pathon	2.50	1.10
❑ 14 Jacquez Green	5.00	2.20
❑ 15 Robert Holcombe	4.00	1.80
❑ 16 Pat Johnson	2.50	1.10
❑ 17 Germane Crowell	6.00	2.70
❑ 18 Tony Simmons	2.50	1.10
❑ 19 Joe Jurevicius	2.50	1.10
❑ 20 Mikhael Ricks	2.50	1.10
❑ 21 Charlie Batch	10.00	4.50
❑ 22 Jon Ritchie	2.50	1.10
❑ 23 Scott Frost	2.50	1.10
❑ 24 Skip Hicks	4.00	1.80
❑ 25 Brian Alford	2.50	1.10
❑ 26 E.G. Green	2.50	1.10
❑ 27 Jammi German	1.50	.70
❑ 28 Ahman Green	2.50	1.10
❑ 29 Chris Floyd	1.50	.70
❑ 30 Larry Shannon	1.50	.70
❑ 31 Jonathan Quinn	2.50	1.10
❑ 32 Rashaan Shehee	2.50	1.10
❑ 33 Brian Griese	10.00	4.50

1998 Playoff Prestige Honors

	MINT	NRMT
COMPLETE SET (3)	350.00	160.00
COMMON CARD (1-3)	80.00	36.00

UNNUMBERED CARDS LISTED ALPHABET.
STATED ODDS 1:3200 HOBBY ..

Card	Mint	NrMt
❑ 1 Terrell Davis	120.00	55.00
❑ 2 Warrick Dunn	100.00	45.00
❑ 3 Barry Sanders	200.00	90.00

1998 Playoff Prestige Inside the Numbers

	MINT	NRMT
COMP.DIE CUT (18)	300.00	135.00
COMMON DIE CUT (1-18)	10.00	4.50

DIE CUT STATED ODDS 1:49 HOBBY
*NON-DIE CUTS: .3X TO .6X DIE CUTS
NON-DIE CUT STATED ODDS 1:72 RETAIL

Card	Mint	NrMt
❑ 1 Barry Sanders	50.00	22.00
❑ 2 Terrell Davis	40.00	18.00
❑ 3 Jerry Rice	25.00	11.00
❑ 4 Kordell Stewart	10.00	4.50
❑ 5 Dan Marino	50.00	22.00
❑ 6 Warrick Dunn	25.00	11.00
❑ 7 Corey Dillon UER (Dillion on front)	10.00	4.50
❑ 8 Drew Bledsoe	20.00	9.00
❑ 9 Herman Moore	20.00	9.00
❑ 10 Troy Aikman	25.00	11.00
❑ 11 Brett Favre	50.00	22.00
❑ 12 Mark Brunell	20.00	9.00
❑ 13 Tim Brown	20.00	9.00
❑ 14 Jerome Bettis	20.00	9.00
❑ 15 Eddie George	20.00	9.00
❑ 16 Dorsey Levens	20.00	9.00
❑ 17 Napoleon Kaufman	20.00	9.00
❑ 18 John Elway	50.00	22.00

1999 Playoff Prestige EXP

	MINT	NRMT
COMPLETE SET (200)	50.00	22.00
COMMON CARD (1-200)	.20	.09
SEMISTARS	.40	.18
UNLISTED STARS	.75	.35
COMMON ROOKIE (1-40)	.75	.35
ROOKIE SEMISTARS	1.00	.45
ROOKIE UNL.STARS	1.50	.70

BARRY SANDERS RFR STATED ODDS 1:289

Card	Mint	NrMt
❑ 1 Anthony McFarland RC	1.50	.70
❑ 2 Al Wilson RC	1.00	.45
❑ 3 Jevon Kearse RC	3.00	1.35
❑ 4 Aaron Brooks RC	1.50	.70
❑ 5 Travis McGriff RC	1.50	.70
❑ 6 Jeff Paulk RC	1.50	.70
❑ 7 Shawn Bryson RC	.75	.35
❑ 8 Karsten Bailey RC	1.00	.45
❑ 9 Mike Cloud RC	1.50	.70
❑ 10 James Johnson RC	2.00	.90
❑ 11 Tai Streets RC	1.00	.45
❑ 12 Jermaine Fazande RC	1.00	.45
❑ 13 Ebenezer Ekuban RC	1.00	.45
❑ 14 Joe Montgomery RC	1.50	.70
❑ 15 Craig Yeast RC	1.00	.45
❑ 16 Joe Germaine RC	1.50	.70
❑ 17 Andy Katzenmoyer RC	1.50	.70
❑ 18 Kevin Faulk RC	2.00	.90
❑ 19 Chris McAlister RC	1.00	.45
❑ 20 Sedrick Irvin RC	1.50	.70
❑ 21 Brock Huard RC	2.00	.90
❑ 22 Cade McNown RC	5.00	2.20
❑ 23 Shaun King RC	5.00	2.20
❑ 24 Amos Zereoue RC	1.50	.70
❑ 25 Dameane Douglas RC	1.00	.45
❑ 26 D'Wayne Bates RC	1.50	.70
❑ 27 Kevin Johnson RC	4.00	1.80
❑ 28 Rob Konrad RC	1.50	.70
❑ 29 Troy Edwards RC	2.50	1.10
❑ 30 Peerless Price RC	2.50	1.10
❑ 31 Daunte Culpepper RC	5.00	2.20
❑ 32 Akili Smith RC	3.00	1.35
❑ 33 David Boston RC	2.50	1.10
❑ 34 Chris Claiborne RC	1.50	.70
❑ 35 Torry Holt RC	4.00	1.80
❑ 36 Champ Bailey RC	2.00	.90
❑ 37 Edgerrin James RC	12.00	5.50
❑ 38 Donovan McNabb RC	5.00	2.20
❑ 39 Ricky Williams RC	8.00	3.60

Card	MINT	NRMT
❑ 40 Tim Couch RC	8.00	3.60
❑ 41 Charles Woodson RP	.75	.35
❑ 42 Skip Hicks RP	.75	.35
❑ 43 Brian Griese RP	.75	.35
❑ 44 Tim Dwight RP	.75	.35
❑ 45 Ryan Leaf RP	.40	.18
❑ 46 Curtis Enis RP	.75	.35
❑ 47 Charlie Batch RP	.75	.35
❑ 48 Fred Taylor RP	1.00	.45
❑ 49 Peyton Manning RP	1.50	.70
❑ 50 Randy Moss RP	1.50	.70
❑ 51 Jim Harbaugh	.40	.18
❑ 52 Warren Moon	.75	.35
❑ 53 Jeff George	.40	.18
❑ 54 Rich Gannon	.40	.18
❑ 55 Scott Mitchell	.20	.09
❑ 56 Kerry Collins	.40	.18
❑ 57 Brad Johnson	.75	.35
❑ 58 Charles Johnson	.20	.09
❑ 59 Chris Calloway	.20	.09
❑ 60 Tyrone Wheatley	.40	.18
❑ 61 Michael Westbrook	.40	.18
❑ 62 Skip Hicks	.75	.35
❑ 63 Terry Allen	.40	.18
❑ 64 Albert Connell	.20	.09
❑ 65 Kevin Dyson	.40	.18
❑ 66 Frank Wycheck	.20	.09
❑ 67 Yancey Thigpen	.20	.09
❑ 68 Steve McNair	.75	.35
❑ 69 Eddie George	1.00	.45
❑ 70 Eric Zeier	.20	.09
❑ 71 Jacquez Green	.40	.18
❑ 72 Reidel Anthony	.40	.18
❑ 73 Warren Sapp	.40	.18
❑ 74 Mike Alstott	.75	.35
❑ 75 Warrick Dunn	.75	.35
❑ 76 Trent Dilfer	.40	.18
❑ 77 Ahman Green	.40	.18
❑ 78 Joey Galloway	.75	.35
❑ 79 Ricky Watters	.40	.18
❑ 80 Jon Kitna	1.00	.45
❑ 81 Amp Lee	.20	.09
❑ 82 Isaac Bruce	.75	.35
❑ 83 Robert Holcombe	.40	.18
❑ 84 Greg Hill	.20	.09
❑ 85 Marshall Faulk	.75	.35
❑ 86 Trent Green	.40	.18
❑ 87 J.J. Stokes	.40	.18
❑ 88 Terrell Owens	.75	.35
❑ 89 Jerry Rice	2.00	.90
❑ 90 Garrison Hearst	.40	.18
❑ 91 Steve Young	1.25	.55
❑ 92 Junior Seau	.40	.18
❑ 93 Mikhael Ricks	.20	.09
❑ 94 Natrone Means	.40	.18
❑ 95 Ryan Leaf	.75	.35
❑ 96 Courtney Hawkins	.20	.09
❑ 97 Chris Fuamatu-Ma'afala UER	.20	.09
❑ 98 Jerome Bettis	.75	.35
❑ 99 Kordell Stewart	.75	.35
❑ 100 Bobby Hoying	.40	.18
❑ 101 Charlie Garner	.40	.18
❑ 102 Duce Staley	.75	.35
❑ 103 Charles Woodson	.75	.35
❑ 104 James Jett	.40	.18
❑ 105 Rickey Dudley	.20	.09
❑ 106 Tim Brown	.75	.35
❑ 107 Napoleon Kaufman	.75	.35
❑ 108 Wayne Chrebet	.40	.18
❑ 109 Keyshawn Johnson	.75	.35
❑ 110 Vinny Testaverde	.40	.18
❑ 111 Curtis Martin	.75	.35
❑ 112 Joe Jurevicius	.20	.09
❑ 113 Tiki Barber	.20	.09
❑ 114 Ike Hilliard	.20	.09
❑ 115 Kent Graham	.20	.09
❑ 116 Gary Brown	.20	.09
❑ 117 Lamar Smith	.20	.09
❑ 118 Eddie Kennison	.40	.18
❑ 119 Cam Cleeland	.20	.09
❑ 120 Tony Simmons	.20	.09
❑ 121 Ben Coates	.40	.18
❑ 122 Darick Holmes	.20	.09
❑ 123 Terry Glenn	.75	.35
❑ 124 Drew Bledsoe	1.25	.55
❑ 125 Leroy Hoard	.20	.09
❑ 126 Jake Reed	.40	.18
❑ 127 Randy Moss	3.00	1.35
❑ 128 Cris Carter	.75	.35
❑ 129 Robert Smith	.75	.35
❑ 130 Randall Cunningham	.75	.35
❑ 131 Lamar Thomas	.20	.09
❑ 132 John Avery	.40	.18
❑ 133 O.J. McDuffie	.40	.18
❑ 134 Dan Marino	3.00	1.35
❑ 135 Karim Abdul-Jabbar	.40	.18
❑ 136 Rashaan Shehee	.20	.09
❑ 137 Derrick Alexander WR	.40	.18
❑ 138 Byron Bam Morris	.20	.09
❑ 139 Andre Rison	.40	.18
❑ 140 Elvis Grbac	.40	.18
❑ 141 Tavian Banks	.20	.09
❑ 142 Keenan McCardell	.40	.18
❑ 143 Jimmy Smith	.40	.18
❑ 144 Fred Taylor	2.00	.90
❑ 145 Mark Brunell	1.25	.55
❑ 146 Jerome Pathon	.20	.09
❑ 147 Marvin Harrison	.75	.35
❑ 148 Peyton Manning	3.00	1.35
❑ 149 Robert Brooks	.40	.18
❑ 150 Mark Chmura	.20	.09
❑ 151 Antonio Freeman	.75	.35
❑ 152 Dorsey Levens	.75	.35
❑ 153 Brett Favre	3.00	1.35
❑ 154 Johnnie Morton	.40	.18
❑ 155 Germane Crowell	.40	.18
❑ 156 Barry Sanders	3.00	1.35
❑ 157 Herman Moore	.75	.35
❑ 158 Charlie Batch	1.50	.70
❑ 159 Marcus Nash	.40	.18
❑ 160 Shannon Sharpe	.40	.18
❑ 161 Rod Smith	.40	.18
❑ 162 Ed McCaffrey	.40	.18
❑ 163 Terrell Davis	2.00	.90
❑ 164 John Elway	3.00	1.35
❑ 165 Ernie Mills	.20	.09
❑ 166 Michael Irvin	.40	.18
❑ 167 Deion Sanders	.75	.35
❑ 168 Emmitt Smith	2.00	.90
❑ 169 Troy Aikman	2.00	.90
❑ 170 Chris Spielman	.20	.09
❑ 171 Terry Kirby	.20	.09
❑ 172 Ty Detmer	.40	.18
❑ 173 Leslie Shepherd	.20	.09
❑ 174 Darnay Scott	.20	.09
❑ 175 Jeff Blake	.40	.18
❑ 176 Carl Pickens	.40	.18
❑ 177 Corey Dillon	.75	.35
❑ 178 Bobby Engram	.40	.18
❑ 179 Curtis Conway	.40	.18
❑ 180 Curtis Enis	.75	.35
❑ 181 Muhsin Muhammad	.40	.18
❑ 182 Steve Beuerlein	.20	.09
❑ 183 Tim Biakabutuka	.40	.18
❑ 184 Bruce Smith	.40	.18
❑ 185 Andre Reed	.40	.18
❑ 186 Thurman Thomas	.40	.18
❑ 187 Eric Moulds	.75	.35
❑ 188 Antowain Smith	.75	.35
❑ 189 Doug Flutie	1.00	.45
❑ 190 Jermaine Lewis	.40	.18
❑ 191 Priest Holmes	.75	.35
❑ 192 O.J. Santiago	.20	.09
❑ 193 Tim Dwight	.75	.35
❑ 194 Terance Mathis	.40	.18
❑ 195 Chris Chandler	.40	.18
❑ 196 Jamal Anderson	.75	.35
❑ 197 Rob Moore	.40	.18
❑ 198 Frank Sanders	.40	.18
❑ 199 Adrian Murrell	.40	.18
❑ 200 Jake Plummer	1.50	.70
❑ RR1 Barry Sanders (Run For the Record Insert)	20.00	9.00

1999 Playoff Prestige EXP Reflections Gold

	MINT	NRMT
COMPLETE SET (200)	250.00	110.00
COMMON CARD (1-200)	1.00	.45

*GOLD STARS: 2X TO 5X HI COL.

*GOLD YOUNG STARS: 1.5X TO 4X
*GOLD RCs: 1.25X TO 3X
GOLD STATED PRINT RUN 1000 SER.#'d SETS

1999 Playoff Prestige EXP Reflections Silver

	MINT	NRMT
COMPLETE SET (200)	120.00	55.00
COMMON CARD (1-200)	.50	.23

*SILVER STARS: 1X TO 2.5X HI COL.
*SILVER YOUNG STARS: .75X TO 2X
*SILVER RCs: .6X TO 1.5X
SILVER PRINT RUN 3250 SERIAL #'d SETS

1999 Playoff Prestige EXP Alma Maters

	MINT	NRMT
COMPLETE SET (30)	100.00	45.00
COMMON CARD (AM1-AM30)	2.50	1.10
SEMISTARS	3.00	1.35
STATED ODDS 1:25		
❑ AM1 Priest Holmes / Ricky Williams	8.00	3.60
❑ AM2 Tim Couch / Dermontti Dawson	8.00	3.60
❑ AM3 Terrell Davis / Garrison Hearst	8.00	3.60
❑ AM4 Troy Brown	8.00	3.60

Randy Moss
- ❑ AM5 Barry Sanders 10.00 4.50
  Thurman Thomas
- ❑ AM6 Emmitt Smith 8.00 3.60
  Fred Taylor
- ❑ AM7 Doug Flutie 4.00 1.80
  Bill Romanowski
- ❑ AM8 Brett Favre 10.00 4.50
  Michael Jackson
- ❑ AM9 Charlie Batch 5.00 2.20
  Ron Rice
- ❑ AM10 Mark Brunell.............. 4.00 1.80
  Chris Chandler
- ❑ AM11 Warrick Dunn............ 3.00 1.35
  Deion Sanders
- ❑ AM12 Cris Carter 4.00 1.80
  Eddie George
- ❑ AM13 Drew Bledsoe 4.00 1.80
  Ryan Leaf
- ❑ AM14 Corey Dillon 2.50 1.10
  Napoleon Kaufman
- ❑ AM15 Jerome Bettis............ 2.50 1.10
  Tim Brown
- ❑ AM16 Marshall Faulk 2.50 1.10
  Darnay Scott
- ❑ AM17 Tiki Barber 2.50 1.10
  Herman Moore
- ❑ AM18 Jamal Anderson........ 2.50 1.10
  Chris Fuamatu-Maafala
- ❑ AM19 Troy Aikman.............. 6.00 2.70
  Cade McNown
- ❑ AM20 Brian Griese.............. 5.00 2.20
  Charles Woodson
- ❑ AM21 Charles Johnson 2.50 1.10
  Kordell Stewart
- ❑ AM22 Kevin Faulk 3.00 1.35
  Eddie Kennison
- ❑ AM23 Donovan McNabb 4.00 1.80
  Rob Moore
- ❑ AM24 Steve McNair 2.50 1.10
  John Thierry
- ❑ AM25 Michael Irvin.............. 2.50 1.10
  Vinny Testaverde
- ❑ AM26 Randall Cunningham 2.50 1.10
  Keenan McCardell
- ❑ AM27 Keyshawn Johnson .. 2.50 1.10
  Junior Seau
- ❑ AM28 Karim Abdul-Jabbar .. 2.50 1.10
  Skip Hicks
- ❑ AM29 Curtis Enis 2.50 1.10
  O.J. McDuffie
- ❑ AM30 Joey Galloway 2.50 1.10
  Robert Smith

1999 Playoff Prestige EXP Checklists

	MINT	NRMT
COMPLETE SET (31)	100.00	45.00
COMMON CARD (CL1-CL31) ..	1.25	.55
SEMISTARS..........................	2.50	1.10
STATED ODDS 1:25		

- ❑ CL1 Jake Plummer.............. 5.00 2.20
- ❑ CL2 Chris Chandler 2.50 1.10
- ❑ CL3 Priest Holmes.............. 2.50 1.10
- ❑ CL4 Doug Flutie 3.00 1.35
- ❑ CL5 Wesley Walls .... 1.25 .55
- ❑ CL6 Curtis Enis 2.50 1.10
- ❑ CL7 Corey Dillon 2.50 1.10
- ❑ CL8 Kevin Johnson 4.00 1.80
- ❑ CL9 Troy Aikman 6.00 2.70
- ❑ CL10 Terrell Davis 6.00 2.70
- ❑ CL11 Barry Sanders.......... 10.00 4.50
- ❑ CL12 Antonio Freeman 2.50 1.10
- ❑ CL13 Peyton Manning 8.00 3.60
- ❑ CL14 Fred Taylor 5.00 2.20
- ❑ CL15 Andre Rison 2.50 1.10
- ❑ CL16 Dan Marino.............. 10.00 4.50
- ❑ CL17 Randy Moss 8.00 3.60
- ❑ CL18 Kevin Faulk................ 3.00 1.35
- ❑ CL19 Ricky Williams 10.00 4.50
- ❑ CL20 Joe Montgomery........ 1.25 .55
- ❑ CL21 Vinny Testaverde 2.50 1.10
- ❑ CL22 Tim Brown 2.50 1.10
- ❑ CL23 Duce Staley 2.50 1.10
- ❑ CL24 Jerome Bettis 2.50 1.10
- ❑ CL25 Natrone Means.......... 2.50 1.10
- ❑ CL26 Terrell Owens............ 2.50 1.10
- ❑ CL27 Joey Galloway 2.50 1.10
- ❑ CL28 Isaac Bruce................ 2.50 1.10
- ❑ CL29 Mike Alstott................ 2.50 1.10
- ❑ CL30 Eddie George 3.00 1.35
- ❑ CL31 Skip Hicks.................. 2.50 1.10

1999 Playoff Prestige EXP Crowd Pleasers

	MINT	NRMT
COMPLETE SET (30)	200.00	90.00
COMMON CARD (CP1-CP30) ..	2.00	.90
SEMISTARS..........................	4.00	1.80
STATED ODDS 1:49		

- ❑ CP1 Terrell Davis.............. 10.00 4.50
- ❑ CP2 Fred Taylor.................. 8.00 3.60
- ❑ CP3 Corey Dillon 4.00 1.80
- ❑ CP4 Eddie George.............. 5.00 2.20
- ❑ CP5 Napoleon Kaufman 4.00 1.80
- ❑ CP6 Jamal Anderson.......... 4.00 1.80
- ❑ CP7 Tim Couch 12.00 5.50
- ❑ CP8 Emmitt Smith 10.00 4.50
- ❑ CP9 Deion Sanders 4.00 1.80
- ❑ CP10 Garrison Hearst .... 2.00 .90
- ❑ CP11 Peyton Manning...... 12.00 5.50
- ❑ CP12 Ricky Williams 12.00 5.50
- ❑ CP13 Barry Sanders 15.00 6.75
- ❑ CP14 Jerry Rice.............. 10.00 4.50
- ❑ CP15 Jake Plummer 8.00 3.60
- ❑ CP16 Tim Brown 4.00 1.80
- ❑ CP17 Terrell Owens............ 4.00 1.80
- ❑ CP18 Dan Marino.............. 15.00 6.75
- ❑ CP19 Chris Chandler 4.00 1.80
- ❑ CP20 Drew Bledsoe............ 6.00 2.70
- ❑ CP21 Charlie Batch 6.00 2.70
- ❑ CP22 Mark Brunell.............. 6.00 2.70
- ❑ CP23 Troy Aikman............ 10.00 4.50
- ❑ CP24 John Elway.............. 15.00 6.75
- ❑ CP25 Jon Kitna 5.00 2.20
- ❑ CP26 Jerome Bettis 4.00 1.80
- ❑ CP27 Brett Favre 15.00 6.75
- ❑ CP28 Steve Young.............. 6.00 2.70
- ❑ CP29 Randy Moss 12.00 5.50
- ❑ CP30 Antonio Freeman 4.00 1.80

1999 Playoff Prestige EXP Draft Picks

	MINT	NRMT
COMPLETE SET (30)	70.00	32.00
COMMON CARD (DP1-DP30)..	1.50	.70
SEMISTARS............................	2.00	.90
STATED ODDS 1:13		

- ❑ DP1 Tim Couch 8.00 3.60
- ❑ DP2 Ricky Williams 8.00 3.60
- ❑ DP3 Donovan McNabb 5.00 2.20
- ❑ DP4 Edgerrin James 12.00 5.50
- ❑ DP5 Champ Bailey.............. 2.50 1.10
- ❑ DP6 Torry Holt 4.00 1.80
- ❑ DP7 Chris Claiborne .... 2.00 .90
- ❑ DP8 David Boston 3.00 1.35
- ❑ DP9 Akili Smith 3.00 1.35
- ❑ DP10 Daunte Culpepper 5.00 2.20
- ❑ DP11 Peerless Price 3.00 1.35
- ❑ DP12 Troy Edwards............ 3.00 1.35
- ❑ DP13 Rob Konrad .... 2.00 .90
- ❑ DP14 Kevin Johnson 4.00 1.80
- ❑ DP15 D'Wayne Bates.......... 2.00 .90
- ❑ DP16 Cecil Collins .... 2.00 .90
- ❑ DP17 Amos Zereoue .... 2.00 .90
- ❑ DP18 Shaun King................ 5.00 2.20
- ❑ DP19 Cade McNown 5.00 2.20
- ❑ DP20 Brock Huard 2.50 1.10
- ❑ DP21 Sedrick Irvin .... 2.00 .90
- ❑ DP22 Chris McAlister.......... 2.00 .90
- ❑ DP23 Kevin Faulk 2.50 1.10
- ❑ DP24 Jevon Kearse 3.00 1.35
- ❑ DP25 Joe Germaine............ 2.00 .90
- ❑ DP26 Andy Katzenmoyer.... 2.00 .90
- ❑ DP27 Joe Montgomery ...... 2.00 .90
- ❑ DP28 Al Wilson .... 2.00 .90
- ❑ DP29 Jermaine Fazande .... 1.50 .70
- ❑ DP30 Ebenezer Ekuban...... 1.50 .70

1999 Playoff Prestige EXP Performers

	MINT	NRMT
COMPLETE SET (24)	200.00	90.00
COMMON CARD (PP1-PP24) ..	3.00	1.35
SEMISTARS............................	6.00	2.70
STATED ODDS 1:97		

- ❑ PP1 Marshall Faulk 6.00 2.70
- ❑ PP2 Jake Plummer 12.00 5.50
- ❑ PP3 Antonio Freeman 6.00 2.70
- ❑ PP4 Brett Favre 25.00 11.00
- ❑ PP5 Troy Aikman 15.00 6.75
- ❑ PP6 Randy Moss 20.00 9.00
- ❑ PP7 John Elway................ 25.00 11.00
- ❑ PP8 Mark Brunell 10.00 4.50
- ❑ PP9 Jamal Anderson 6.00 2.70
- ❑ PP10 Doug Flutie................ 8.00 3.60
- ❑ PP11 Drew Bledsoe 10.00 4.50
- ❑ PP12 Barry Sanders 25.00 11.00
- ❑ PP13 Dan Marino.............. 25.00 11.00
- ❑ PP14 Randall Cunningham 6.00 2.70
- ❑ PP15 Steve Young............ 10.00 4.50
- ❑ PP16 Carl Pickens 6.00 2.70
- ❑ PP17 Peyton Manning 20.00 9.00
- ❑ PP18 Herman Moore 6.00 2.70
- ❑ PP19 Eddie George 8.00 3.60

❑ PP20	Fred Taylor	12.00	5.50
❑ PP21	Garrison Hearst	3.00	1.35
❑ PP22	Emmitt Smith	15.00	6.75
❑ PP23	Jerry Rice	15.00	6.75
❑ PP24	Terrell Davis	15.00	6.75

1999 Playoff Prestige EXP Stars of the NFL

	MINT	NRMT
COMPLETE SET (20)	150.00	70.00
COMMON CARD (ST1-ST20)	5.00	2.20
STATED ODDS 1:73		

❑ ST1	Jerry Rice	12.00	5.50
❑ ST2	Steve Young	8.00	3.60
❑ ST3	Drew Bledsoe	8.00	3.60
❑ ST4	Jamal Anderson	5.00	2.20
❑ ST5	Eddie George	6.00	2.70
❑ ST6	Keyshawn Johnson	5.00	2.20
❑ ST7	Kordell Stewart	5.00	2.20
❑ ST8	Barry Sanders	20.00	9.00
❑ ST9	Tim Brown	5.00	2.20
❑ ST10	Mark Brunell	8.00	3.60
❑ ST11	Fred Taylor	10.00	4.50
❑ ST12	Randy Moss	15.00	6.75
❑ ST13	Peyton Manning	15.00	6.75
❑ ST14	Emmitt Smith	12.00	5.50
❑ ST15	Deion Sanders	5.00	2.20
❑ ST16	Troy Aikman	12.00	5.50
❑ ST17	Brett Favre	20.00	9.00
❑ ST18	Dan Marino	20.00	9.00
❑ ST19	Terrell Davis	12.00	5.50
❑ ST20	John Elway	20.00	9.00

1999 Playoff Prestige EXP Terrell Davis Salute

	MINT	NRMT
COMPLETE SET (5)	40.00	18.00
COMMON CARD (TD1-TD5)	10.00	4.50
STATED ODDS 1:289		
COMMON AUTOGRAPH	60.00	27.00
FIRST 150-CARDS WERE AUTOGRAPHED		
AUTO.REDEMPTION EXPIRATION: MAY 2000		

❑ TD1	Terrell Davis	10.00	4.50
❑ TD2	Terrell Davis	10.00	4.50
❑ TD3	Terrell Davis	10.00	4.50
❑ TD4	Terrell Davis	10.00	4.50
❑ TD5	Terrell Davis	10.00	4.50

1999 Playoff Prestige SSD

	MINT	NRMT
COMPLETE SET (200)	150.00	70.00
COMP.SET w/o SP's (150)	50.00	22.00
COMMON CARD (1-200)	.25	.11
SEMISTARS	.50	.23
UNLISTED STARS	1.00	.45
COMMON RP (151-160)	1.50	.70
COMMON ROOKIE (161-200)	2.00	.90
ROOKIE SEMISTARS	3.00	1.35
ROOKIE UNL.STARS	4.00	1.80
ROOKIE/RP SUBSETS STATED ODDS 1:2		
COMP.SPECT.BLUE (200)	400.00	180.00
*SPECTRUM BLUE STARS: 1.25X TO 3X HI COL.		
*SPECTRUM BLUE YOUNG STARS: 1X TO 2.5X		
*SPECTRUM BLUE RCs: .6X TO 1.5X		
SPECT.BLUE PRINT RUN 500 SER.#'d SETS		
*SPECTRUM GOLDS: SAME PRICE AS BLUES		
SPECT.GOLD PRINT RUN 500 SER.#'d SETS		
*SPECTRUM GREENS: SAME PRICE AS BLUES		
SPECT.GREEN PRINT RUN 500 SER.#'d SETS		
*SPECTRUM PURPLES:SAME PRICE AS BLUES		
SPECT.PURPLE PRINT RUN 500 SER.#'d SETS		
*SPECTRUM REDS: SAME PRICE AS BLUES		
SPECT.RED PRINT RUN 500 SER.#'d SETS		

❑ 1	Jake Plummer	2.50	1.10
❑ 2	Adrian Murrell	.50	.23
❑ 3	Frank Sanders	.50	.23
❑ 4	Rob Moore	.50	.23
❑ 5	Jamal Anderson	1.00	.45
❑ 6	Chris Chandler	.50	.23
❑ 7	Terance Mathis	.50	.23
❑ 8	Tim Dwight	1.00	.45
❑ 9	O.J. Santiago	.25	.11
❑ 10	Priest Holmes	1.00	.45
❑ 11	Jermaine Lewis	.50	.23
❑ 12	Doug Flutie	1.25	.55
❑ 13	Antowain Smith	1.00	.45
❑ 14	Eric Moulds	1.00	.45
❑ 15	Thurman Thomas	.50	.23
❑ 16	Andre Reed	.50	.23
❑ 17	Bruce Smith	.50	.23
❑ 18	Tim Biakabutuka	.50	.23
❑ 19	Steve Beuerlein	.25	.11
❑ 20	Muhsin Muhammad	.50	.23
❑ 21	Curtis Enis	1.00	.45
❑ 22	Curtis Conway	.50	.23
❑ 23	Bobby Engram	.50	.23
❑ 24	Corey Dillon	1.00	.45
❑ 25	Carl Pickens	.50	.23
❑ 26	Jeff Blake	.50	.23
❑ 27	Darnay Scott	.25	.11
❑ 28	Leslie Shepherd	.25	.11
❑ 29	Ty Detmer	.50	.23
❑ 30	Terry Kirby	.25	.11
❑ 31	Chris Spielman	.25	.11
❑ 32	Troy Aikman	3.00	1.35
❑ 33	Emmitt Smith	3.00	1.35
❑ 34	Deion Sanders	1.00	.45
❑ 35	Michael Irvin	.50	.23
❑ 36	Ernie Mills	.25	.11
❑ 37	John Elway	5.00	2.20
❑ 38	Terrell Davis	3.00	1.35
❑ 39	Ed McCaffrey	.50	.23
❑ 40	Rod Smith	.50	.23
❑ 41	Shannon Sharpe	.50	.23
❑ 42	Marcus Nash	.50	.23
❑ 43	Charlie Batch	2.50	1.10
❑ 44	Herman Moore	1.00	.45
❑ 45	Barry Sanders	5.00	2.20
❑ 46	Germane Crowell	.50	.23
❑ 47	Johnnie Morton	.50	.23
❑ 48	Brett Favre	5.00	2.20
❑ 49	Dorsey Levens	1.00	.45
❑ 50	Antonio Freeman	1.00	.45
❑ 51	Mark Chmura	.25	.11
❑ 52	Robert Brooks	.50	.23
❑ 53	Peyton Manning	5.00	2.20
❑ 54	Marvin Harrison	1.00	.45
❑ 55	Jerome Pathon	.25	.11
❑ 56	Mark Brunell	2.00	.90
❑ 57	Fred Taylor	3.00	1.35
❑ 58	Jimmy Smith	.50	.23
❑ 59	Keenan McCardell	.50	.23
❑ 60	Tavian Banks	.25	.11
❑ 61	Elvis Grbac	.50	.23
❑ 62	Andre Rison	.50	.23
❑ 63	Byron Bam Morris	.25	.11
❑ 64	Derrick Alexander WR	.50	.23
❑ 65	Rashaan Shehee	.25	.11
❑ 66	Karim Abdul-Jabbar	.50	.23
❑ 67	Dan Marino	5.00	2.20
❑ 68	O.J. McDuffie	.50	.23
❑ 69	John Avery	.50	.23
❑ 70	Lamar Thomas	.25	.11
❑ 71	Randall Cunningham	1.00	.45
❑ 72	Robert Smith	1.00	.45
❑ 73	Cris Carter	1.00	.45
❑ 74	Randy Moss	5.00	2.20
❑ 75	Jake Reed	.50	.23
❑ 76	Leroy Hoard	.25	.11
❑ 77	Drew Bledsoe	2.00	.90
❑ 78	Terry Glenn	1.00	.45
❑ 79	Darick Holmes	.25	.11
❑ 80	Ben Coates	.50	.23
❑ 81	Tony Simmons	.25	.11
❑ 82	Cam Cleeland	.25	.11
❑ 83	Eddie Kennison	.50	.23
❑ 84	Lamar Smith	.25	.11
❑ 85	Gary Brown	.25	.11
❑ 86	Kent Graham	.25	.11
❑ 87	Ike Hilliard	.25	.11
❑ 88	Tiki Barber	.25	.11
❑ 89	Joe Jurevicius	.25	.11
❑ 90	Curtis Martin	1.00	.45
❑ 91	Vinny Testaverde	.50	.23
❑ 92	Keyshawn Johnson	1.00	.45
❑ 93	Wayne Chrebet	.50	.23
❑ 94	Napoleon Kaufman	1.00	.45
❑ 95	Tim Brown	1.00	.45
❑ 96	Rickey Dudley	.25	.11
❑ 97	James Jett	.50	.23
❑ 98	Charles Woodson	1.00	.45
❑ 99	Duce Staley	1.00	.45
❑ 100	Charlie Garner	.50	.23
❑ 101	Bobby Hoying	.50	.23
❑ 102	Kordell Stewart	1.00	.45
❑ 103	Jerome Bettis	1.00	.45
❑ 104	Chris Fuamatu-Ma'afala	.25	.11
❑ 105	Courtney Hawkins	.25	.11
❑ 106	Ryan Leaf	1.00	.45
❑ 107	Natrone Means	.50	.23
❑ 108	Mikhael Ricks	.25	.11
❑ 109	Junior Seau	.50	.23
❑ 110	Steve Young	2.00	.90
❑ 111	Garrison Hearst	.50	.23
❑ 112	Jerry Rice	3.00	1.35
❑ 113	Terrell Owens	1.00	.45
❑ 114	J.J. Stokes	.50	.23
❑ 115	Trent Green	.50	.23
❑ 116	Marshall Faulk	1.00	.45
❑ 117	Greg Hill	.25	.11
❑ 118	Robert Holcombe	.50	.23
❑ 119	Isaac Bruce	1.00	.45
❑ 120	Amp Lee	.25	.11
❑ 121	Jon Kitna	1.50	.70
❑ 122	Ricky Watters	.50	.23
❑ 123	Joey Galloway	1.00	.45
❑ 124	Ahman Green	.50	.23
❑ 125	Trent Dilfer	.50	.23
❑ 126	Warrick Dunn	1.00	.45

#	Player	MINT	NRMT
❑ 127	Mike Alstott	1.00	.45
❑ 128	Warren Sapp	.50	.23
❑ 129	Reidel Anthony	.50	.23
❑ 130	Jacquez Green	.50	.23
❑ 131	Eric Zeier	.25	.11
❑ 132	Eddie George	1.00	.45
❑ 133	Steve McNair	1.00	.45
❑ 134	Yancey Thigpen	.25	.11
❑ 135	Frank Wycheck	.25	.11
❑ 136	Kevin Dyson	.50	.23
❑ 137	Albert Connell	.25	.11
❑ 138	Terry Allen	.50	.23
❑ 139	Skip Hicks	1.00	.45
❑ 140	Michael Westbrook	.50	.23
❑ 141	Tyrone Wheatley	.50	.23
❑ 142	Chris Calloway	.25	.11
❑ 143	Charles Johnson	.25	.11
❑ 144	Brad Johnson	1.00	.45
❑ 145	Kerry Collins	.50	.23
❑ 146	Scott Mitchell	.25	.11
❑ 147	Rich Gannon	.50	.23
❑ 148	Jeff George	.50	.23
❑ 149	Warren Moon	1.00	.45
❑ 150	Jim Harbaugh	.50	.23
❑ 151	Randy Moss RP	8.00	3.60
❑ 152	Peyton Manning RP	8.00	3.60
❑ 153	Fred Taylor RP	5.00	2.20
❑ 154	Charlie Batch RP	4.00	1.80
❑ 155	Curtis Enis RP	1.50	.70
❑ 156	Ryan Leaf RP	1.50	.70
❑ 157	Tim Dwight RP	1.50	.70
❑ 158	Brian Griese RP	4.00	1.80
❑ 159	Skip Hicks RP	1.50	.70
❑ 160	Charles Woodson RP	1.50	.70
❑ 161	Tim Couch RC	20.00	9.00
❑ 162	Ricky Williams RC	20.00	9.00
❑ 163	Donovan McNabb RC	12.00	5.50
❑ 164	Edgerrin James RC	30.00	13.50
❑ 165	Champ Bailey RC	5.00	2.20
❑ 166	Torry Holt RC	10.00	4.50
❑ 167	Chris Claiborne RC	3.00	1.35
❑ 168	David Boston RC	6.00	2.70
❑ 169	Akili Smith RC	8.00	3.60
❑ 170	Daunte Culpepper RC	12.00	5.50
❑ 171	Peerless Price RC	6.00	2.70
❑ 172	Troy Edwards RC	6.00	2.70
❑ 173	Rob Konrad RC	4.00	1.80
❑ 174	Kevin Johnson RC	10.00	4.50
❑ 175	D'Wayne Bates RC	3.00	1.35
❑ 176	Dameane Douglas RC	3.00	1.35
❑ 177	Amos Zereoue RC	4.00	1.80
❑ 178	Shaun King RC	12.00	5.50
❑ 179	Cade McNown RC	12.00	5.50
❑ 180	Brock Huard RC	5.00	2.20
❑ 181	Sedrick Irvin RC	4.00	1.80
❑ 182	Chris McAlister RC	3.00	1.35
❑ 183	Kevin Faulk RC	5.00	2.20
❑ 184	Andy Katzenmoyer RC	4.00	1.80
❑ 185	Joe Germaine RC	4.00	1.80
❑ 186	Craig Yeast RC	3.00	1.35
❑ 187	Joe Montgomery RC	4.00	1.80
❑ 188	Ebenezer Ekuban RC	3.00	1.35
❑ 189	Jermaine Fazande RC	3.00	1.35
❑ 190	Tai Streets RC	3.00	1.35
❑ 191	James Johnson RC	5.00	2.20
❑ 192	Mike Cloud RC	4.00	1.80
❑ 193	Karsten Bailey RC	4.00	1.80
❑ 194	Shawn Bryson RC	2.00	.90
❑ 195	Jeff Paulk RC	4.00	1.80
❑ 196	Travis McGriff RC	4.00	1.80
❑ 197	Aaron Brooks RC	4.00	1.80
❑ 198	Jevon Kearse RC	8.00	3.60
❑ 199	Al Wilson RC	3.00	1.35
❑ 200	Anthony McFarland RC	4.00	1.80

1999 Playoff Prestige SSD Alma Maters

	MINT	NRMT
COMPLETE SET (30)	200.00	90.00
COMMON CARD (AM1-AM30)	5.00	2.20
SEMISTARS	6.00	2.70

STATED ODDS 1:17
*JUMBOS: .3X TO .8X HI COL.
JUMBOS ONE PER SSD HOBBY BOX

#	Players	MINT	NRMT
❑ AM1	Ricky Williams	15.00	6.75
	Priest Holmes		
❑ AM2	Tim Couch	15.00	6.75
	Dermontti Dawson		
❑ AM3	Terrell Davis	15.00	6.75
	Garrison Hearst		
❑ AM4	Randy Moss	15.00	6.75
	Troy Brown		
❑ AM5	Barry Sanders	20.00	9.00
	Thurman Thomas		
❑ AM6	Fred Taylor	15.00	6.75
	Emmitt Smith		
❑ AM7	Doug Flutie	8.00	3.60
	Bill Romanowski		
❑ AM8	Brett Favre	20.00	9.00
	Michael Jackson		
❑ AM9	Charlie Batch	10.00	4.50
	Ron Rice		
❑ AM10	Mark Brunell	8.00	3.60
	Chris Chandler		
❑ AM11	Warrick Dunn	6.00	2.70
	Deion Sanders		
❑ AM12	Eddie George	8.00	3.60
	Cris Carter		
❑ AM13	Drew Bledsoe	8.00	3.60
	Ryan Leaf		
❑ AM14	Corey Dillon	5.00	2.20
	Napoloen Kaufman		
❑ AM15	Jerome Bettis	5.00	2.20
	Tim Brown		
❑ AM16	Marshall Faulk	5.00	2.20
	Darnay Scott		
❑ AM17	Herman Moore	5.00	2.20
	Tiki Barber		
❑ AM18	Jamal Anderson	5.00	2.20
	Chris Fuamatu-Ma'afala		
❑ AM19	Troy Aikman	12.00	5.50
	Cade McNown		
❑ AM20	Brian Griese	10.00	4.50
	Charles Woodson		
❑ AM21	Kordell Stewart	5.00	2.20
	Charles Johnson		
❑ AM22	Kevin Faulk	6.00	2.70
	Eddie Kennison		
❑ AM23	Donovan McNabb	8.00	3.60
	Rob Moore		
❑ AM24	Steve McNair	5.00	2.20
	John Thierry		
❑ AM25	Vinny Testaverde	5.00	2.20
	Michael Irvin		
❑ AM26	Randall Cunningham	5.00	2.20
	Keenan McCardell		
❑ AM27	Keyshawn Johnson	5.00	2.20
	Junior Seau		
❑ AM28	Skip Hicks	5.00	2.20
	Karim Abdul-Jabbar		
❑ AM29	Curtis Enis	5.00	2.20
	O.J. McDuffie		
❑ AM30	Joey Galloway	5.00	2.20
	Robert Smith		

1999 Playoff Prestige SSD Checklists

	MINT	NRMT
COMPLETE SET (31)	200.00	90.00
COMMON CARD (CL1-CL31)	2.50	1.10
SEMISTARS	5.00	2.20

STATED ODDS 1:17

#	Player	MINT	NRMT
❑ CL1	Jake Plummer	10.00	4.50
❑ CL2	Chris Chandler	5.00	2.20
❑ CL3	Priest Holmes	5.00	2.20
❑ CL4	Doug Flutie	6.00	2.70
❑ CL5	Wesley Walls	5.00	2.20
❑ CL6	Curtis Enis	5.00	2.20
❑ CL7	Corey Dillon	5.00	2.20
❑ CL8	Kevin Johnson	8.00	3.60
❑ CL9	Troy Aikman	12.00	5.50
❑ CL10	Terrell Davis	12.00	5.50
❑ CL11	Barry Sanders	20.00	9.00
❑ CL12	Antonio Freeman	5.00	2.20
❑ CL13	Peyton Manning	15.00	6.75
❑ CL14	Fred Taylor	10.00	4.50
❑ CL15	Byron Bam Morris	2.50	1.10
❑ CL16	Dan Marino	20.00	9.00
❑ CL17	Randy Moss	15.00	6.75
❑ CL18	Kevin Faulk	5.00	2.20
❑ CL19	Ricky Williams	15.00	6.75
❑ CL20	Joe Montgomery	2.50	1.10
❑ CL21	Vinny Testaverde	5.00	2.20
❑ CL22	Tim Brown	5.00	2.20
❑ CL23	Duce Staley	5.00	2.20
❑ CL24	Jerome Bettis	5.00	2.20
❑ CL25	Natrone Means	5.00	2.20
❑ CL26	Terrell Owens	5.00	2.20
❑ CL27	Joey Galloway	5.00	2.20
❑ CL28	Isaac Bruce	5.00	2.20
❑ CL29	Mike Alstott	5.00	2.20
❑ CL30	Eddie George	6.00	2.70
❑ CL31	Skip Hicks	5.00	2.20

1999 Playoff Prestige SSD Checklists Autographs

	MINT	NRMT
COMPLETE SET (31)	1500.00	700.00
COMMON CARD (CL1-CL31)	20.00	9.00
SEMISTARS	30.00	13.50
UNLISTED STARS	40.00	18.00

STATED PRINT RUN 250 SERIAL #'d SETS
REDEMPTION EXPIRATION: 5/1/2000

#	Player	MINT	NRMT
❑ CL1	Jake Plummer	60.00	27.00
❑ CL2	Chris Chandler	30.00	13.50
❑ CL3	Priest Holmes	40.00	18.00
❑ CL4	Doug Flutie	50.00	22.00

❑ CL5 Wesley Walls	30.00	13.50
❑ CL6 Curtis Enis	40.00	18.00
❑ CL7 Corey Dillon	40.00	18.00
❑ CL8 Kevin Johnson	50.00	22.00
❑ CL9 Troy Aikman	80.00	36.00
❑ CL10 Terrell Davis	80.00	36.00
❑ CL11 Barry Sanders	120.00	55.00
❑ CL12 Antonio Freeman	40.00	18.00
❑ CL13 Peyton Manning	150.00	70.00
❑ CL14 Fred Taylor	60.00	27.00
❑ CL15 Byron Bam Morris SP	20.00	9.00
❑ CL16 Dan Marino	120.00	55.00
❑ CL17 Randy Moss	150.00	70.00
❑ CL18 Kevin Faulk	40.00	18.00
❑ CL19 Ricky Williams	120.00	55.00
❑ CL20 Joe Montgomery	20.00	9.00
❑ CL21 Vinny Testaverde	30.00	13.50
❑ CL22 Tim Brown	20.00	9.00
❑ CL23 Duce Staley	40.00	18.00
❑ CL24 Jerome Bettis	40.00	18.00
❑ CL25 Natrone Means	30.00	13.50
❑ CL26 Terrell Owens	50.00	22.00
❑ CL27 Joey Galloway	40.00	18.00
❑ CL28 Isaac Bruce	40.00	18.00
❑ CL29 Mike Alstott	40.00	18.00
❑ CL30 Eddie George	50.00	22.00
❑ CL31 Skip Hicks	40.00	18.00

1999 Playoff Prestige SSD Draft Picks

	MINT	NRMT
COMPLETE SET (30)	150.00	70.00
COMMON CARD (DP1-DP30)	3.00	1.35
SEMISTARS	4.00	1.80
STATED ODDS 1:9		

❑ DP1 Tim Couch	15.00	6.75
❑ DP2 Ricky Williams	15.00	6.75
❑ DP3 Donovan McNabb	10.00	4.50
❑ DP4 Edgerrin James	25.00	11.00
❑ DP5 Champ Bailey	5.00	2.20
❑ DP6 Torry Holt	8.00	3.60
❑ DP7 Chris Claiborne	4.00	1.80
❑ DP8 David Boston	6.00	2.70
❑ DP9 Akili Smith	6.00	2.70
❑ DP10 Daunte Culpepper	10.00	4.50
❑ DP11 Peerless Price	6.00	2.70
❑ DP12 Troy Edwards	6.00	2.70
❑ DP13 Rob Konrad	4.00	1.80
❑ DP14 Kevin Johnson	8.00	3.60
❑ DP15 D'Wayne Bates	3.00	1.35
❑ DP16 Cecil Collins	4.00	1.80
❑ DP17 Amos Zereoue	4.00	1.80
❑ DP18 Shaun King	10.00	4.50
❑ DP19 Cade McNown	10.00	4.50
❑ DP20 Brock Huard	5.00	2.20
❑ DP21 Sedrick Irvin	4.00	1.80
❑ DP22 Chris McAlister	4.00	1.80
❑ DP23 Kevin Faulk	5.00	2.20
❑ DP24 Jevon Kearse	6.00	2.70
❑ DP25 Joe Germaine	4.00	1.80
❑ DP26 Andy Katzenmoyer	4.00	1.80
❑ DP27 Joe Montgomery	4.00	1.80
❑ DP28 Al Wilson	4.00	1.80
❑ DP29 Jermaine Fazande	3.00	1.35
❑ DP30 Ebenezer Ekuban	3.00	1.35

1999 Playoff Prestige SSD For the Record

	MINT	NRMT
COMPLETE SET (30)	700.00	325.00
COMMON CARD (FR1-FR30)	15.00	6.75
SEMISTARS	20.00	9.00
STATED ODDS 1:161		

❑ FR1 Mark Brunell	25.00	11.00
❑ FR2 Jerry Rice	40.00	18.00
❑ FR3 Peyton Manning	50.00	22.00
❑ FR4 Barry Sanders	60.00	27.00
❑ FR5 Deion Sanders	20.00	9.00
❑ FR6 Eddie George	25.00	11.00
❑ FR7 Corey Dillon	20.00	9.00
❑ FR8 Jerome Bettis	20.00	9.00
❑ FR9 Curtis Martin	20.00	9.00
❑ FR10 Ricky Williams	50.00	22.00
❑ FR11 Jake Plummer	30.00	13.50
❑ FR12 Emmitt Smith	40.00	18.00
❑ FR13 Dan Marino	60.00	27.00
❑ FR14 Terrell Davis	40.00	18.00
❑ FR15 Fred Taylor	30.00	13.50
❑ FR16 Warrick Dunn	20.00	9.00
❑ FR17 Steve McNair	20.00	9.00
❑ FR18 Cris Carter	20.00	9.00
❑ FR19 Mike Alstott	20.00	9.00
❑ FR20 Steve Young	25.00	11.00
❑ FR21 Charlie Batch	15.00	6.75
❑ FR22 Tim Couch	50.00	22.00
❑ FR23 Jamal Anderson	20.00	9.00
❑ FR24 Randy Moss	50.00	22.00
❑ FR25 Brett Favre	60.00	27.00
❑ FR26 Drew Bledsoe	25.00	11.00
❑ FR27 Troy Aikman	40.00	18.00
❑ FR28 John Elway	60.00	27.00
❑ FR29 Kordell Stewart	20.00	9.00
❑ FR30 Keyshawn Johnson	20.00	9.00

1999 Playoff Prestige SSD Gridiron Heritage

	MINT	NRMT
COMPLETE SET (24)	350.00	160.00
COMMON CARD (GH1-GH24)	8.00	3.60
SEMISTARS	10.00	4.50
STATED ODDS 1:33		

❑ GH1 Randy Moss	25.00	11.00
❑ GH2 Terrell Davis	20.00	9.00
❑ GH3 Brett Favre	30.00	13.50
❑ GH4 Barry Sanders	30.00	13.50
❑ GH5 Peyton Manning	25.00	11.00
❑ GH6 John Elway	30.00	13.50
❑ GH7 Fred Taylor	15.00	6.75
❑ GH8 Cris Carter	10.00	4.50
❑ GH9 Jamal Anderson	10.00	4.50
❑ GH10 Jake Plummer	15.00	6.75
❑ GH11 Steve Young	12.00	5.50
❑ GH12 Mark Brunell	12.00	5.50
❑ GH13 Dan Marino	30.00	13.50
❑ GH14 Emmitt Smith	20.00	9.00
❑ GH15 Deion Sanders	10.00	4.50
❑ GH16 Troy Aikman	20.00	9.00
❑ GH17 Drew Bledsoe	12.00	5.50
❑ GH18 Jerry Rice	20.00	9.00
❑ GH19 Ricky Williams	30.00	13.50
❑ GH20 Tim Couch	30.00	13.50
❑ GH21 Jerome Bettis	8.00	3.60
❑ GH22 Eddie George	12.00	5.50
❑ GH23 Marshall Faulk	10.00	4.50
❑ GH24 Terrell Owens	10.00	4.50

1999 Playoff Prestige SSD Inside the Numbers

	MINT	NRMT
COMPLETE SET (20)	300.00	135.00
COMMON CARD (IN1-IN20)	8.00	3.60
SEMISTARS	10.00	4.50
OVERALL STATED ODDS 1:49		

❑ IN1 Tim Brown/1012	8.00	3.60
❑ IN2 Charlie Batch/2178	10.00	4.50
❑ IN3 Deion Sanders/226	12.00	5.50
❑ IN4 Eddie George/1294	12.00	5.50
❑ IN5 Keyshawn Johnson/1131	12.00	5.50
❑ IN6 Jamal Anderson/1846	12.00	5.50
❑ IN7 Steve Young/4170	12.00	5.50
❑ IN8 Tim Couch/4275	20.00	9.00
❑ IN9 Ricky Williams/6279	15.00	6.75
❑ IN10 Jerry Rice/1157	25.00	11.00
❑ IN11 Randy Moss/1313	30.00	13.50
❑ IN12 Edgerrin James/1416	40.00	18.00
❑ IN13 Peyton Manning/3739	20.00	9.00
❑ IN14 John Elway/2803	30.00	13.50
❑ IN15 Terrell Davis/2008	20.00	9.00
❑ IN16 Fred Taylor/1213	20.00	9.00
❑ IN17 Brett Favre/4212	25.00	11.00
❑ IN18 Jake Plummer/3737	12.00	5.50
❑ IN19 Mark Brunell/2601	12.00	5.50
❑ IN20 Barry Sanders/1491	40.00	18.00

1999 Playoff Prestige SSD Barry Sanders

	MINT	NRMT
COMPLETE SET (10)	700.00	325.00
COMMON CARD (1-10)	80.00	36.00
OVERALL STATED ODDS 1:161		
CARD NUMBERS HAVE RFTR PREFIX		

❑ 1 Barry Sanders/89	80.00	36.00
❑ 2 Barry Sanders/90	80.00	36.00
❑ 3 Barry Sanders/91	80.00	36.00
❑ 4 Barry Sanders/92	80.00	36.00
❑ 5 Barry Sanders/93	80.00	36.00
❑ 6 Barry Sanders/94	80.00	36.00
❑ 7 Barry Sanders/95	80.00	36.00
❑ 8 Barry Sanders/96	80.00	36.00
❑ 9 Barry Sanders/97	80.00	36.00
❑ 10 Barry Sanders/98	80.00	36.00

1996 Playoff Prime

	MINT	NRMT
COMPLETE SET (200)	100.00	45.00
COMP. BRONZE SET (100)	15.00	6.75
COMMON BRONZE (1-100)	.10	.05
SEMISTARS BRONZE	.25	.11
UNLISTED STARS BRONZE	.50	.23
COMMON SILVER (101-150)	.50	.23
SEMISTARS SILVER	1.00	.45
UNLISTED STARS SILVER	2.00	.90

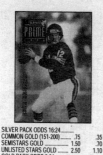

SILVER PACK ODDS 16:24
COMMON GOLD (151-200) .75 .35
SEMISTARS GOLD 1.50 .70
UNLISTED STARS GOLD 2.50 1.10
GOLD PACK ODDS 8:24

❑ 1 Brett Favre 3.00 1.35
❑ 2 Jerry Rice 1.50 .70
❑ 3 Troy Aikman 1.50 .70
❑ 4 Bruce Smith .25 .11
❑ 5 Marshall Faulk .50 .23
❑ 6 Erik Kramer .10 .05
❑ 7 Carl Pickens .50 .23
❑ 8 Anthony Miller .25 .11
❑ 9 Cris Carter .50 .23
❑ 10 Todd Kinchen .10 .05
❑ 11 Stoney Case .10 .05
❑ 12 Chris Calloway .10 .05
❑ 13 Andre Rison .25 .11
❑ 14 Bill Brooks .10 .05
❑ 15 Shawn Jefferson .10 .05
❑ 16 Eric Zeier .10 .05
❑ 17 Yancey Thigpen .25 .11
❑ 18 Edgar Bennett .25 .11
❑ 19 Garrison Hearst .25 .11
❑ 20 Daryl Johnston .25 .11
❑ 21 Tyrone Wheatley .25 .11
❑ 22 Darick Holmes .10 .05
❑ 23 Dave Brown .10 .05
❑ 24 Leeland McElroy RC .50 .23
❑ 25 Craig Heyward .10 .05
❑ 26 Kevin Hardy RC .50 .23
❑ 27 Scott Mitchell .25 .11
❑ 28 Willie Green .10 .05
❑ 29 Vincent Brisby .10 .05
❑ 30 Mike Tomczak .10 .05
❑ 31 Luther Elliss .10 .05
❑ 32 Mike Pritchard .10 .05
❑ 33 Robert Green .10 .05
❑ 34 Jeff Graham .10 .05
❑ 35 Tamarick Vanover .25 .11
❑ 36 William Floyd .25 .11
❑ 37 Alvin Harper .10 .05
❑ 38 Stan Humphries .25 .11
❑ 39 Herman Moore .50 .23
❑ 40 Tony Martin .25 .11
❑ 41 Jonathan Ogden RC .10 .05
❑ 42 Randall Cunningham .50 .23
❑ 43 Chris Warren .25 .11
❑ 44 Bobby Hebert .10 .05
❑ 45 Jerome Bettis .50 .23
❑ 46 Joey Galloway 1.00 .45
❑ 47 Ernie Mills .10 .05
❑ 48 Steve McNair 1.00 .45
❑ 49 Karim Abdul-Jabbar RC 1.00 .45
❑ 50 Chad May .10 .05
❑ 51 Jim Everett .10 .05
❑ 52 Robert Smith .25 .11
❑ 53 Tony Boselli .10 .05
❑ 54 William Henderson .10 .05
❑ 55 Terry Glenn RC UER 2.00 .90
(Joey Galloway biography on back of card)
❑ 56 Neil O'Donnell .25 .11
❑ 57 Chris Chandler .25 .11
❑ 58 Michael Jackson .25 .11
❑ 59 Jason Dunn RC .25 .11
❑ 60 James O. Stewart .25 .11
❑ 61 Greg Hill .25 .11
❑ 62 Mark Carrier WR .10 .05
❑ 63 Bernie Parmalee .10 .05
❑ 64 Chris Sanders .25 .11
❑ 65 Jeff Hostetler .10 .05
❑ 66 Eric Moulds RC .40 .18
❑ 67 James Jett .25 .11
❑ 68 Henry Ellard .10 .05
❑ 69 Mario Bates .25 .11
❑ 70 Natrone Means .50 .23
❑ 71 Bobby Engram RC .50 .23
❑ 72 Christian Fauria .10 .05
❑ 73 Gus Frerotte .50 .23
❑ 74 Aaron Hayden .10 .05
❑ 75 Reggie White .50 .23
❑ 76 Dave Meggett .10 .05
❑ 77 Harvey Williams .10 .05
❑ 78 Terance Mathis .10 .05
❑ 79 Byron Bam Morris .25 .11
❑ 80 Trent Dilfer .50 .23
❑ 81 Irving Fryar .25 .11
❑ 82 Quinn Early .10 .05
❑ 83 Lake Dawson .10 .05
❑ 84 Todd Collins .25 .11
❑ 85 Eric Metcalf .10 .05
❑ 86 Tim Biakabutuka RC 1.25 .55
❑ 87 Rob Johnson .50 .23
❑ 88 Charlie Garner .10 .05
❑ 89 Mike Mamula .10 .05
❑ 90 Steve Walsh .10 .05
❑ 91 Charles Haley .25 .11
❑ 92 Mike Alstott RC 2.00 .90
❑ 93 Wayne Chrebet .25 .11
❑ 94 Vinny Testaverde .25 .11
❑ 95 Fred Barnett .10 .05
❑ 96 Boomer Esiason .25 .11
❑ 97 Zack Crockett .10 .05
❑ 98 Kevin Williams .10 .05
❑ 99 Eric Bieniemy .10 .05
❑ 100 Bryan Cox .10 .05
❑ 101 Larry Centers 1.00 .45
❑ 102 Jeff George 1.00 .45
❑ 103 Bryce Paup 1.00 .45
❑ 104 Kerry Collins 2.00 .90
❑ 105 Derrick Moore .50 .23
❑ 106 Adrian Murrell 1.00 .45
❑ 107 Harold Green .50 .23
❑ 108 Ki-Jana Carter 1.00 .45
❑ 109 Sherman Williams .50 .23
❑ 110 Deion Sanders 4.00 1.80
❑ 111 Emmitt Smith 8.00 3.60
❑ 112 Shannon Sharpe 1.00 .45
❑ 113 Johnnie Morton 1.00 .45
❑ 114 Eddie Kennison RC 2.00 .90
❑ 115 Marvin Harrison RC 8.00 3.60
❑ 116 Amani Toomer RC 2.00 .90
❑ 117 Rickey Dudley RC 2.00 .90
❑ 118 Alex Van Dyke RC 1.00 .45
❑ 119 Dorsey Levens 3.00 1.35
❑ 120 Antonio Freeman 4.00 1.80
❑ 121 Willie Davis 1.00 .45
❑ 122 Lamont Warren .50 .23
❑ 123 Sean Dawkins .50 .23
❑ 124 Willie Jackson 1.00 .45
❑ 125 Kimble Anders .50 .23
❑ 126 Dan Marino 10.00 4.50
❑ 127 Terry Kirby 1.00 .45
❑ 128 Amp Lee .50 .23
❑ 129 Jake Reed 1.00 .45
❑ 130 Curtis Martin 4.00 1.80
❑ 131 Ray Zellars .50 .23
❑ 132 Herschel Walker 1.00 .45
❑ 133 Mike Sherrard .50 .23
❑ 134 Kyle Brady 1.00 .45
❑ 135 Rocket Ismail 1.00 .45
❑ 136 Ricky Watters 1.00 .45
❑ 137 Kordell Stewart 4.00 1.80
❑ 138 Andre Hastings .10 .05
❑ 139 Ronnie Harmon .50 .23
❑ 140 Terrell Fletcher .50 .23
❑ 141 J.J. Stokes 2.00 .90
❑ 142 Brent Jones .50 .23
❑ 143 Tony McGee .50 .23
❑ 144 Brian Blades 1.00 .45
❑ 145 Isaac Bruce 2.00 .90
❑ 146 Errict Rhett 1.00 .45
❑ 147 Warren Sapp .50 .23
❑ 148 Horace Copeland .50 .23
❑ 149 Heath Shuler 2.00 .90
❑ 150 Michael Westbrook 2.00 .90
❑ 151 Frank Sanders 1.50 .70
❑ 152 Rob Moore .75 .35
❑ 153 Bert Emanuel 1.50 .70
❑ 154 J.J. Birden .75 .35
❑ 155 Thurman Thomas 2.50 1.10
❑ 156 Jim Kelly 2.50 1.10
❑ 157 Curtis Conway 2.50 1.10
❑ 158 Darnay Scott 1.50 .70
❑ 159 Jeff Blake 2.50 1.10
❑ 160 Jay Novacek 1.50 .70
❑ 161 Michael Irvin 2.50 1.10
❑ 162 John Elway 15.00 6.75
❑ 163 Terrell Davis 15.00 6.75
❑ 164 Barry Sanders 12.00 5.50
❑ 165 Brett Perriman 1.50 .70
❑ 166 Keyshawn Johnson RC 8.00 3.60
❑ 167 Eddie George RC 12.00 5.50
❑ 168 Derrick Mayes RC 3.00 1.35
❑ 169 Simeon Rice RC 2.50 1.10
❑ 170 Lawrence Phillips RC 2.50 1.10
❑ 171 Robert Brooks 2.50 1.10
❑ 172 Mark Chmura 1.50 .70
❑ 173 Rodney Thomas .75 .35
❑ 174 Jim Harbaugh 1.50 .70
❑ 175 Ken Dilger 1.50 .70
❑ 176 Mark Brunell 10.00 4.50
❑ 177 Steve Bono 1.50 .70
❑ 178 Marcus Allen 2.50 1.10
❑ 179 O.J. McDuffie 1.50 .70
❑ 180 Eric Green .75 .35
❑ 181 Warren Moon 1.50 .70
❑ 182 Drew Bledsoe 10.00 4.50
❑ 183 Ben Coates 1.50 .70
❑ 184 Michael Haynes 1.50 .70
❑ 185 Rodney Hampton 1.50 .70
❑ 186 Rashaan Salaam 2.50 1.10
❑ 187 Napoleon Kaufman 4.00 1.80
❑ 188 Tim Brown 1.50 .70
❑ 189 Rodney Peete .75 .35
❑ 190 Calvin Williams .75 .35
❑ 191 Erric Pegram 1.50 .70
❑ 192 Mark Bruener .75 .35
❑ 193 Junior Seau 2.50 1.10
❑ 194 Steve Young 8.00 3.60
❑ 195 Derek Loville .75 .35
❑ 196 Rick Mirer 1.50 .70
❑ 197 Mark Rypien .75 .35
❑ 198 Jackie Harris .75 .35
❑ 199 Terry Allen 1.50 .70
❑ 200 Brian Mitchell .75 .35

1996 Playoff Prime Boss Hogs

	MINT	NRMT
COMPLETE SET (18)	150.00	70.00
COMMON CARD (1-18)	4.00	1.80
SEMISTARS	6.00	2.70
STATED ODDS 1:96		

❑ 1 Curtis Martin 8.00 3.60
❑ 2 Chris Warren 4.00 1.80
❑ 3 Emmitt Smith 20.00 9.00
❑ 4 Barry Sanders 25.00 11.00
❑ 5 Rashaan Salaam 6.00 2.70

❑ 6 Marshall Faulk	6.00	2.70
❑ 7 Errict Rhett	4.00	1.80
❑ 8 Thurman Thomas	6.00	2.70
❑ 9 Kerry Collins	6.00	2.70
❑ 10 Dan Marino	25.00	11.00
❑ 11 Jerry Rice	12.00	5.50
❑ 12 Troy Aikman	12.00	5.50
❑ 13 Jeff George	4.00	1.80
❑ 14 Brett Favre	25.00	11.00
❑ 15 Robert Brooks	6.00	2.70
❑ 16 John Elway	25.00	11.00
❑ 17 Deion Sanders	8.00	3.60
❑ 18 Kordell Stewart	8.00	3.60

1996 Playoff Prime Honors

	MINT	NRMT
COMPLETE SET (3)	300.00	135.00
COMMON CARD (1-3)	60.00	27.00
STATED ODDS 1:7200		
❑ PH1 Emmitt Smith	100.00	45.00
❑ PH2 Curtis Martin	60.00	27.00
❑ PH3 Brett Favre	150.00	70.00

1996 Playoff Prime Surprise

	MINT	NRMT
COMPLETE SET (14)	250.00	110.00
COMMON CARD (1-14)	8.00	3.60
SEMISTARS	10.00	4.50
STATED ODDS 1:288		
❑ 1 Dan Marino	40.00	18.00
❑ 2 Brett Favre	40.00	18.00
❑ 3 Emmitt Smith	30.00	13.50
❑ 4 Kordell Stewart	15.00	6.75
❑ 5 Jerry Rice	25.00	11.00
❑ 6 Troy Aikman	25.00	11.00
❑ 7 Barry Sanders	40.00	18.00
❑ 8 Curtis Martin	15.00	6.75
❑ 9 Marshall Faulk	10.00	4.50
❑ 10 Joey Galloway	10.00	4.50
❑ 11 Robert Brooks	8.00	3.60
❑ 12 Deion Sanders	15.00	6.75
❑ 13 Reggie White	10.00	4.50
❑ 14 Marcus Allen	10.00	4.50

1996 Playoff Prime X's and O's

	MINT	NRMT
COMPLETE SET (200)	500.00	220.00

*1-100 STARS: 5X TO 12X BASE CARD HI
*1-100 ROOKIES: 2X TO 5X BASE CARD HI
*101-150 STARS: 1.5X TO 4X BASE CARD HI
*101-150 ROOKIES: .8X TO 2X BASE CARD HI
*151-200 STARS: 1X TO 2.5X BASE CARD HI
*151-200 ROOKIES: .6X TO 1.5X BASE CARD HI
STATED ODDS 1:7.2

1993 Power Update Prospects

	MINT	NRMT
COMPLETE SET (60)	12.00	5.50
COMMON CARD (1-60)	.05	.02
SEMISTARS	.10	.05
UNLISTED STARS	.25	.11
COMP.GOLD SET (60)	25.00	11.00

*GOLD CARDS: 1X to 2X
ONE GOLD PER UPDATE PACK
TWO GOLDS PER UPDATE JUMBO PACK

❑ 1 Drew Bledsoe RC	3.00	1.35
❑ 2 Rick Mirer RC	.50	.23
❑ 3 Trent Green RC	6.00	2.70
❑ 4 Mark Brunell RC	3.00	1.35
❑ 5 Billy Joe Hobert RC UER	.25	.11
Name spelled Hebert on back		
❑ 6 Ronald Moore RC	.10	.05
❑ 7 Elvis Grbac RC UER	.75	.35
(Spelled Grback on both sides)		
❑ 8 Garrison Hearst RC	1.00	.45
❑ 9 Jerome Bettis RC	1.00	.45
❑ 10 Reggie Brooks RC	.10	.05
❑ 11 Robert Smith RC	1.00	.45
❑ 12 Vaughn Hebron RC	.05	.02
❑ 13 Derek Brown RBK RC	.10	.05
❑ 14 Roosevelt Potts RC	.10	.05
❑ 15 Terry Kirby RC UER	.10	.05
(Card says wide receiver; he is a running back)		
❑ 16 Glyn Milburn RC	.10	.05
❑ 17 Greg Robinson RC	.05	.02
❑ 18 Natrone Means RC	.75	.35
❑ 19 Curtis Conway RC	1.00	.45
❑ 20 James Jett RC	.50	.23
❑ 21 O.J. McDuffie RC	.75	.35
❑ 22 Rocket Ismail	.10	.05
❑ 23 Qadry Ismail RC	.25	.11
❑ 24 Kevin Williams RC	.10	.05
❑ 25 Victor Bailey RC UER	.05	.02
(Name spelled Baily on front)		
❑ 26 Vincent Brisby RC	.10	.05
❑ 27 Irv Smith RC	.05	.02
❑ 28 Troy Drayton RC	.05	.02
❑ 29 Wayne Simmons RC	.05	.02
❑ 30 Marvin Jones RC	.05	.02
❑ 31 Demetrius DuBose RC	.05	.02
❑ 32 Chad Brown RC	.10	.05
❑ 33 Micheal Barrow	.05	.02
❑ 34 Darrin Smith RC	.05	.02
❑ 35 Deon Figures RC	.05	.02
❑ 36 Darrien Gordon RC	.05	.02
❑ 37 Patrick Bates RC	.05	.02
❑ 38 George Teague RC	.05	.02
❑ 39 Lance Gunn RC	.05	.02
❑ 40 Tom Carter RC	.05	.02
❑ 41 Carlton Gray RC	.05	.02
❑ 42 John Copeland RC	.05	.02
❑ 43 Eric Curry RC	.05	.02
❑ 44 Dana Stubblefield RC	.10	.05
❑ 45 Leonard Renfro RC	.05	.02
❑ 46 Dan Williams RC	.05	.02
❑ 47 Todd Kelly RC	.05	.02
❑ 48 Chris Slade RC	.05	.02
❑ 49 Carl Simpson RC UER	.05	.02
(Defensive Back spelled Dfensive on back)		
❑ 50 Coleman Rudolph RC	.05	.02
❑ 51 Michael Strahan RC	.05	.02
❑ 52 Dan Footman RC	.05	.02
❑ 53 Steve Everitt RC	.05	.02
❑ 54 Will Shields RC	.05	.02
❑ 55 Ben Coleman RC	.05	.02
❑ 56 William Roaf RC	.05	.02
❑ 57 Lincoln Kennedy RC	.05	.02
❑ 58 Brad Hopkins RC	.05	.02
❑ 59 Ernest Dye RC	.05	.02
❑ 60 Jason Elam RC	.10	.05

1991 Pro Line Portraits Autographs

	MINT	NRMT
COMPLETE SET (301)	5500.00	2500.00
COMMON CARD (1-300)	8.00	3.60
SEMISTARS	10.00	4.50
UNLISTED STARS	15.00	6.75
RANDOM INSERTS IN PACKS		
❑ 1 Ray Agnew	8.00	3.60
❑ 2 Troy Aikman	100.00	45.00
❑ 3 Eric Allen	8.00	3.60
❑ 4 Morten Andersen	10.00	4.50
❑ 5 Flipper Anderson	10.00	4.50
❑ 6 Gary Anderson K	8.00	3.60
❑ 7 Gary Anderson RB	10.00	4.50
❑ 8 Neal Anderson	10.00	4.50
❑ 9 Ottis Anderson	10.00	4.50
❑ 10 Bruce Armstrong	8.00	3.60
❑ 11 Steve Atwater	10.00	4.50
❑ 12 Robert Awalt	8.00	3.60
❑ 13 Carl Banks	8.00	3.60

14	Reggie Barrett	8.00	3.60
15	Harris Barton	8.00	3.60
16	Martin Bayless	8.00	3.60
17	Bill Belichick CO	8.00	3.60
18	Nick Bell	8.00	3.60
19	Cornelius Bennett	15.00	6.75
20	Albert Bentley	8.00	3.60
21	Rod Bernstine	8.00	3.60
22	Dean Biasucci	8.00	3.60
23	Duane Bickett	8.00	3.60
24	Bennie Blades	8.00	3.60
25	Brian Blades	10.00	4.50
26	Mel Blount RET	20.00	9.00
27	Mark Bortz	8.00	3.60
28	Bubby Brister	8.00	3.60
	(Signed Bubby 6)		
29	James Brooks	10.00	4.50
30	Steve Broussard	8.00	3.60
31	Lomas Brown	8.00	3.60
32	Maury Buford	8.00	3.60
33	Joe Bugel CO	8.00	3.60
34	Jarrod Bunch	8.00	3.60
35	Jerry Burns CO	8.00	3.60
36	Kevin Butler	8.00	3.60
37	Marion Butts	10.00	4.50
38	Keith Byars	10.00	4.50
39	Earnest Byner	10.00	4.50
40	Mark Carrier DB	100.00	45.00
41	Mark Carrier WR	10.00	4.50
42	Anthony Carter	25.00	11.00
	(Signatures usually miscut)		
43	Dexter Carter	8.00	3.60
44	Deron Cherry	8.00	3.60
45	Ray Childress	10.00	4.50
46	Vinnie Clark	8.00	3.60
47	Mark Clayton	10.00	4.50
48	Michael Cofer	8.00	3.60
49	Monte Coleman	8.00	3.60
50	Andre Collins	8.00	3.60
51	Shane Conlan	8.00	3.60
52	Darion Conner	8.00	3.60
53	Bruce Coslet CO	8.00	3.60
54	Jim Covert	8.00	3.60
55	Roger Craig	15.00	6.75
56	Randall Cunningham	25.00	11.00
57	Steve DeBerg	10.00	4.50
58	Eric Dickerson	40.00	18.00
59	Mike Ditka CO	30.00	13.50
60	Ray Donaldson	8.00	3.60
61	Eric Dorsey	8.00	3.60
62	Mike Dumas	8.00	3.60
63	Marcus Dupree	8.00	3.60
64	Hart Lee Dykes	8.00	3.60
65	Ferrell Edmunds	8.00	3.60
66	Henry Ellard	10.00	4.50
67	Jumbo Elliott	8.00	3.60
68	John Elway	100.00	45.00
69	Boomer Esiason	15.00	6.75
70	Jim Everett	10.00	4.50
71	Thomas Everett	8.00	3.60
72	Kevin Fagan	8.00	3.60
73	Paul Farren	8.00	3.60
74	Wayne Fontes CO	8.00	3.60
75	John Fourcade	8.00	3.60
76	Bill Fralic	8.00	3.60
77	James Francis	300.00	135.00
78	Irving Fryar	15.00	6.75
79	David Fulcher	8.00	3.60
80	Cleveland Gary	8.00	3.60
81	Shaun Gayle	8.00	3.60
82	Jeff George	20.00	9.00
83	Joe Gibbs CO	20.00	9.00
84	Ernest Givins	10.00	4.50
85	Jerry Glanville CO	8.00	3.60
86	Bob Golic	8.00	3.60
87	Mel Gray	10.00	4.50
88	Jacob Green	8.00	3.60
89	Kevin Greene	15.00	6.75
90	Burt Grossman	8.00	3.60
91	Tim Grunhard	8.00	3.60
	(Two different signatures known for this card)		
92	Myron Guyton	8.00	3.60
93	Ray Handley CO	8.00	3.60
94	Jim Harbaugh	20.00	9.00
95	Franco Harris RET	40.00	18.00
	Most signatures are cut off		
96	Andy Heck	8.00	3.60
97	Dan Henning CO	8.00	3.60
98	Alonzo Highsmith	60.00	27.00
99	Jay Hilgenberg	8.00	3.60
100	Bruce Hill	8.00	3.60
101	Derek Hill	8.00	3.60
102	Randal Hill	10.00	4.50
103	Dalton Hilliard	25.00	11.00
	(Signatures usually miscut)		
104	Bryan Hinkle	8.00	3.60
105	Chris Hinton	8.00	3.60
106	Leroy Hoard	15.00	6.75
107	Merril Hoge	8.00	3.60
108	Rodney Holman	250.00	110.00
109	Issiac Holt	8.00	3.60
110	Pierce Holt	8.00	3.60
111	Jeff Hostetler	10.00	4.50
112	Erik Howard	8.00	3.60
113	Bobby Humphrey	8.00	3.60
114	Lindy Infante CO	8.00	3.60
115	Michael Irvin	30.00	13.50
116	Mark Jackson	8.00	3.60
117	Rickey Jackson	10.00	4.50
118	Haywood Jeffires	10.00	4.50
119	D.J. Johnson	8.00	3.60
120	Jimmy Johnson CO	40.00	18.00
121	Pepper Johnson	8.00	3.60
122	Tracy Johnson	8.00	3.60
123	Vaughan Johnson	8.00	3.60
124	Brent Jones	10.00	4.50
125	Henry Jones	8.00	3.60
126	Keith Jones	8.00	3.60
127A	Jim Kelly	15.00	6.75
	(Autopenned)		
127B	Jim Kelly	250.00	110.00
	(Real signature)		
128	Jack Kemp RET	25.00	11.00
	(Autopenned)		
129	Cortez Kennedy	10.00	4.50
130	Chuck Knox CO	10.00	4.50
131	Bernie Kosar	20.00	9.00
132	Rich Kotite CO	8.00	3.60
133	Greg Kragen	8.00	3.60
134	Dave Krieg	10.00	4.50
135	Jim Lachey	8.00	3.60
136	Carnell Lake	10.00	4.50
137	Sean Landeta	8.00	3.60
138	Reggie Langhorne	50.00	22.00
139	Steve Largent RET	30.00	13.50
140	Albert Lewis	50.00	22.00
	Most signatures are cut off		
141	Louis Lipps	10.00	4.50
142	David Little	8.00	3.60
143	Eugene Lockhart	8.00	3.60
144	James Lofton	20.00	9.00
145	Chip Lohmiller	8.00	3.60
146	Howie Long	30.00	13.50
147	Ronnie Lott	15.00	6.75
148	Nick Lowery	8.00	3.60
	(May be autopenned)		
149	Dick MacPherson CO	8.00	3.60
150	Ed McCaffrey	20.00	9.00
151	Keith McCants	8.00	3.60
152	Vann McElroy	8.00	3.60
153	Tim McGee	8.00	3.60
154	Kanavis McGhee	8.00	3.60
155	Dan McGwire	8.00	3.60
156	Guy McIntyre	80.00	36.00
157	Jim McMahon	300.00	135.00
158	Steve McMichael	10.00	4.50
159	Erik McMillan	8.00	3.60
160	Bill Maas	8.00	3.60
161	Tony Mandarich	8.00	3.60
162	Charles Mann	8.00	3.60
163	Dan Marino	200.00	90.00
164	Leonard Marshall	8.00	3.60
	(Frequently miscut)		
165	Eric Martin	8.00	3.60
166	Russell Maryland	10.00	4.50
167	Ron Meyer CO	8.00	3.60
168	Matt Millen	10.00	4.50
169	Anthony Miller	10.00	4.50
170	Chris Miller	10.00	4.50
171	Sam Mills	10.00	4.50
172	Warren Moon	30.00	13.50
173	Herman Moore	60.00	27.00
174	Rob Moore	20.00	9.00
175	Jim Mora CO	8.00	3.60
176	Jim Morrissey	8.00	3.60
177	Anthony Munoz	15.00	6.75
178	Mark Murphy	8.00	3.60
179	Browning Nagle	8.00	3.60
180	Tom Newberry	8.00	3.60
181	Brian Noble	8.00	3.60
182	Chuck Noll CO	30.00	13.50
183	Danny Noonan	8.00	3.60
184	Ken O'Brien	10.00	4.50
185	Leslie O'Neal	10.00	4.50
186	Bart Oates	8.00	3.60
187	Christian Okoye	8.00	3.60
188	Louis Oliver	8.00	3.60
189	Stephone Paige	8.00	3.60
190	Irv Pankey	8.00	3.60
191	Jack Pardee CO	8.00	3.60
192	Walter Payton RET	150.00	70.00
193	Drew Pearson RET	15.00	6.75
194	Danny Peebles	8.00	3.60
195	Rodney Peete	10.00	4.50
196	Michael Dean Perry	10.00	4.50
197	William Perry	20.00	9.00
198	Roman Phifer	8.00	3.60
199	Bill Pickel	8.00	3.60
200	Gary Plummer	8.00	3.60
201	Kevin Porter	8.00	3.60
202	Rufus Porter	8.00	3.60
203	Mike Pritchard	8.00	3.60
204	Ricky Proehl	8.00	3.60
205	Ahmad Rashad RET	175.00	80.00
206	Tom Rathman	8.00	3.60
207	Andre Reed	20.00	9.00
208	Dan Reeves CO	15.00	6.75
209	Johnny Rembert	8.00	3.60
210	Jerry Rice	150.00	70.00
211	Doug Riesenberg	8.00	3.60
212	John Riggins RET	50.00	22.00
213A	Andre Rison	12.00	5.50
	(Ball-point pen)		
213B	Andre Rison	30.00	13.50
	(Signed in Sharpie)		
214	William Roberts	8.00	3.60
215	Eugene Robinson	10.00	4.50
216	John Robinson CO	8.00	3.60
217	Reggie Roby	8.00	3.60
218	John Roper	8.00	3.60
219	Timm Rosenbach	8.00	3.60
220	Kevin Ross	8.00	3.60
221	Ricky Sanders	8.00	3.60
222	Dan Saleaumua	8.00	3.60
223	Gale Sayers RET	30.00	13.50
224	Mike Schad	8.00	3.60
225	Marty Schottenheimer CO	10.00	4.50
226	Jay Schroeder	8.00	3.60
227	Junior Seau	20.00	9.00
228	George Seifert CO	10.00	4.50
229	Art Shell CO	15.00	6.75
230	Mike Sherrard	8.00	3.60
231	Don Shula CO	40.00	18.00
232	O.J. Simpson RET	275.00	125.00
233	Phil Simms	30.00	13.50
234	Keith Sims	8.00	3.60
235	Mike Singletary	35.00	16.00
236	Jackie Slater	8.00	3.60
237	Webster Slaughter	10.00	4.50
238	Al Smith	8.00	3.60
239	Billy Ray Smith	8.00	3.60
240	Bruce Smith	15.00	6.75
241	Dennis Smith	8.00	3.60
242	J.T. Smith	8.00	3.60
243	Neil Smith	60.00	27.00
	(Most signatures are cut off)		
244	Steve Smith	8.00	3.60
245	Ernest Spears	8.00	3.60
246	Chris Spielman	10.00	4.50
247	Rohn Stark	8.00	3.60
248	Roger Staubach RET	135.00	60.00
249	Eric Swann	10.00	4.50
250	Pat Swilling	10.00	4.50
251	Darryl Talley	8.00	3.60
252	Steve Tasker	10.00	4.50
253	John Taylor	10.00	4.50
254	Lawrence Taylor	35.00	16.00

❑ 255 Vinny Testaverde 10.00 4.50
❑ 256 Tom Thayer 8.00 3.60
❑ 257 Joe Theismann RET 30.00 13.50
❑ 258 Blair Thomas 8.00 3.60
❑ 259 Broderick Thomas 8.00 3.60
❑ 260 Derrick Thomas 45.00 20.00
❑ 261 Eric Thomas 8.00 3.60
❑ 262 Thurman Thomas 30.00 13.50
❑ 263 Anthony Thompson 8.00 3.60
❑ 264 Andre Tippett 10.00 4.50
❑ 265 Billy Joe Tolliver 8.00 3.60
❑ 266 Al Toon 10.00 4.50
❑ 267 Greg Townsend 125.00 55.00
❑ 268 David Treadwell 8.00 3.60
❑ 269 Jack Trudeau 8.00 3.60
❑ 270 Renaldo Turnbull 10.00 4.50
❑ 271 Eric Turner 15.00 6.75
❑ 272 Clarence Verdin 8.00 3.60
❑ 273 Everson Walls 8.00 3.60
❑ 274 Steve Walsh 8.00 3.60
❑ 275 Alvin Walton 8.00 3.60
❑ 276 Andre Ware 10.00 4.50
❑ 277 Paul Warfield RET 20.00 9.00
❑ 278 Don Warren 8.00 3.60
❑ 279 Lionel Washington 125.00 55.00
Most signatures are cut off
❑ 280 Ted Washington 8.00 3.60
❑ 281 Andre Waters 8.00 3.60
❑ 282 Lorenzo White 8.00 3.60
❑ 283 David Whitmore 8.00 3.60
❑ 284 Alfred Williams 8.00 3.60
❑ 285 Lee Williams 8.00 3.60
❑ 286 Richard Williamson CO 8.00 3.60
❑ 287 Wade Wilson 8.00 3.60
❑ 288 Ickey Woods 8.00 3.60
❑ 289 Tony Woods 8.00 3.60
❑ 290 Rod Woodson 15.00 6.75
❑ 291 Donnell Woolford 8.00 3.60
❑ 292 Barry Word 8.00 3.60
❑ 293 Tim Worley 8.00 3.60
❑ 294 Sam Wyche CO 10.00 4.50
❑ 295 David Wyman 8.00 3.60
❑ 296 Lonnie Young 8.00 3.60
❑ 297 Steve Young 100.00 45.00
❑ 298 Gary Zimmerman 8.00 3.60
❑ 299 Chris Zorich 10.00 4.50
❑ PLC2 Payne Stewart 125.00 55.00
Golfer
❑ NNO Santa Claus Sendaway 30.00 13.50
(Signed, not numbered)
❑ NNO Santa Claus Sendaway 50.00 22.00
(Signed and numbered)

1992 Pro Line Portraits Autographs

	MINT	NRMT
COMPLETE SET (161)	1200.00	550.00
COMMON CARD (1-161)	5.00	2.20
SEMISTARS	8.00	3.60
UNLISTED STARS	12.00	5.50
RANDOM INSERTS IN PACKS		

❑ 1 Kurt Barber 5.00 2.20
❑ 2 Fred Barnett 8.00 3.60
❑ 3 Lem Barney RET 8.00 3.60
❑ 4 Brad Baxter 5.00 2.20
❑ 5 Edgar Bennett 12.00 5.50
❑ 6 Fred Biletnikoff RET 175.00 80.00
❑ 7 Lewis Billups 5.00 2.20
❑ 8 Brian Brennan 5.00 2.20
❑ 9 Bill Brooks 8.00 3.60
❑ 10 Derek Brown TE 5.00 2.20
❑ 11 Terrell Buckley 5.00 2.20
❑ 12 Rob Burnett 5.00 2.20
❑ 13 Dick Butkus RET 20.00 9.00
❑ 14 LeRoy Butler 8.00 3.60
❑ 15 Jeff Carlson 5.00 2.20
❑ 16 Cris Carter 25.00 11.00
❑ 17 Dale Carter 8.00 3.60
❑ 18 Toby Caston 8.00 3.60
❑ 19 Eugene Chung 5.00 2.20
❑ 20 Gary Clark 8.00 3.60
❑ 21 Greg Clark 5.00 2.20
❑ 22 Marco Coleman 8.00 3.60
❑ 23 Cary Conklin 5.00 2.20
❑ 24 Marv Cook 5.00 2.20
❑ 25 Quentin Coryatt 8.00 3.60
❑ 26 Bill Cowher CO 15.00 6.75
❑ 27 Aaron Cox 5.00 2.20
❑ 28 Ray Crockett 5.00 2.20
❑ 29 Jeff Cross 5.00 2.20
❑ 30 Joe DeLamielleure RET 5.00 2.20
❑ 31 Keith DeLong 5.00 2.20
❑ 32 Steve DeOssie 5.00 2.20
❑ 33 Al Davis OWN 350.00 160.00
❑ 34 Antone Davis 5.00 2.20
❑ 35 Wendell Davis 5.00 2.20
❑ 36 Robert Delpino 5.00 2.20
❑ 37 Chris Doleman 8.00 3.60
❑ 38 Tony Dorsett RET 25.00 11.00
❑ 39 Vaughn Dunbar 5.00 2.20
❑ 40 Al Edwards 5.00 2.20
❑ 41 Steve Emtman 5.00 2.20
❑ 42 Ricky Ervins 8.00 3.60
❑ 43 Gill Fenerty 5.00 2.20
❑ 44 Derrick Fenner 5.00 2.20
❑ 45 John Fina 5.00 2.20
❑ 46 Tom Flores CO 8.00 3.60
❑ 47 Dan Fouts RET 15.00 6.75
❑ 48 Mike Fox 5.00 2.20
❑ 49 Mitch Frerotte 5.00 2.20
❑ 50 John Friesz 5.00 2.20
❑ 51 William Fuller 8.00 3.60
❑ 52 Willie Gault 8.00 3.60
❑ 53 John Gesek 5.00 2.20
❑ 54 Sean Gilbert 8.00 3.60
❑ 55 Otto Graham RET 20.00 9.00
❑ 56 Eric Green 5.00 2.20
❑ 57 Harold Green 5.00 2.20
❑ 58 Paul Gruber 5.00 2.20
❑ 59 Dino Hackett 5.00 2.20
❑ 60 Charles Haley 8.00 3.60
❑ 61 Jason Hanson 8.00 3.60
❑ 62 Alvin Harper 8.00 3.60
❑ 63 Michael Haynes 8.00 3.60
❑ 64 Keith Henderson 5.00 2.20
❑ 65 Jeff Herrod 5.00 2.20
❑ 66 Jessie Hester 5.00 2.20
(Signed in ball-point pen)
❑ 67 Craig Heyward 8.00 3.60
❑ 68 Mark Higgs 5.00 2.20
❑ 69 Tommy Hodson 5.00 2.20
❑ 70 Mike Holmgren CO 25.00 11.00
❑ 71 Ethan Horton 5.00 2.20
❑ 72 Patrick Hunter 5.00 2.20
❑ 73 Steve Israel 5.00 2.20
❑ 74 Keith Jackson 8.00 3.60
❑ 75 Joe Jacoby 5.00 2.20
❑ 76 Jim C. Jensen 5.00 2.20
❑ 77 Vance Johnson 5.00 2.20
❑ 78 Ernie Jones 5.00 2.20
❑ 79 Robert Jones 5.00 2.20
❑ 80 Sean Jones 8.00 3.60
❑ 81 Brian Jordan 12.00 5.50
❑ 82 Sonny Jurgensen RET 20.00 9.00
❑ 83 David Klingler 8.00 3.60
❑ 84 Chuck Knox CO 5.00 2.20
❑ 85 Tim Krumrie 5.00 2.20
❑ 86 Eddie LeBaron RET 12.00 5.50
❑ 87 Darren Lewis 5.00 2.20
❑ 88 Nate Lewis 5.00 2.20
❑ 89 Greg Lloyd 12.00 5.50
❑ 90 Bubba McDowell 5.00 2.20
❑ 91 Chester McGlockton 8.00 3.60
❑ 92 Tommy Maddox 5.00 2.20
❑ 93 Ted Marchibroda CO 12.00 5.50
❑ 94 Chris Martin 5.00 2.20
❑ 95 Mike Merriweather 5.00 2.20
❑ 96 Eric Metcalf 8.00 3.60
❑ 97 Chris Mims 8.00 3.60
❑ 98 Hugh Millen 5.00 2.20
❑ 99 Brian Mitchell 8.00 3.60
❑ 100 Johnny Mitchell 5.00 2.20
❑ 101 Joe Montana 125.00 55.00
❑ 102 Eric Moore 5.00 2.20
❑ 103 Brad Muster 5.00 2.20
❑ 104 Ken Norton Jr. 8.00 3.60
❑ 105 Jay Novacek 8.00 3.60
❑ 106 Neil O'Donnell 12.00 5.50
❑ 107 Marquez Pope 5.00 2.20
❑ 108 Robert Porcher 5.00 2.20
❑ 109 Mike Prior 5.00 2.20
❑ 110 Ervin Randle 5.00 2.20
❑ 111 Walter Reeves 5.00 2.20
❑ 112 Ricky Reynolds 5.00 2.20
❑ 113 Bobby Ross CO 5.00 2.20
❑ 114 Deion Sanders 35.00 16.00
(Deion also signed and numbered 200 cards from his personal stock; these are worth double)
❑ 115 Tracy Scroggins 5.00 2.20
❑ 116 Leon Searcy 5.00 2.20
❑ 117 Sterling Sharpe 20.00 9.00
❑ 118 David Shula CO 5.00 2.20
❑ 119 Chris Singleton 5.00 2.20
❑ 120 Greg Skrepenak 5.00 2.20
❑ 121 Chuck Smith 5.00 2.20
❑ 122 Doug Smith 5.00 2.20
❑ 123 Emmitt Smith 80.00 36.00
❑ 124 Kevin Smith 8.00 3.60
❑ 125 Lance Smith 5.00 2.20
❑ 126 Sammie Smith 5.00 2.20
❑ 127 Phillippi Sparks 5.00 2.20
❑ 128 Alonzo Spellman 5.00 2.20
❑ 129 Ken Stabler RET 30.00 13.50
❑ 130 Kelly Stouffer 5.00 2.20
❑ 131 Lynn Swann RET 70.00 32.00
❑ 132 Jim Sweeney 5.00 2.20
❑ 133 Harry Sydney 5.00 2.20
❑ 134 Charley Taylor RET 12.00 5.50
❑ 135 Pat Terrell 5.00 2.20
❑ 136 Henry Thomas 5.00 2.20
❑ 137 Stan Thomas 5.00 2.20
❑ 138 Y.A. Tittle RET 20.00 9.00
❑ 139 Mike Tomczak 5.00 2.20
❑ 140 Jessie Tuggle 5.00 2.20
❑ 141 Floyd Turner 5.00 2.20
❑ 142 Tommy Vardell 8.00 3.60
❑ 143 Jon Vaughn 5.00 2.20
❑ 144 Troy Vincent 8.00 3.60
❑ 145 Tom Waddle 5.00 2.20
❑ 146 Van Waiters 5.00 2.20
❑ 147 Aaron Wallace 5.00 2.20
❑ 148 Brian Washington 5.00 2.20
❑ 149 William White 5.00 2.20
❑ 150 Dave Widell 8.00 3.60
Doug Widell
❑ 151 Calvin Williams 8.00 3.60
❑ 152 Darryl Williams 5.00 2.20
❑ 153 Harvey Williams 8.00 3.60
❑ 154 John L. Williams 8.00 3.60
❑ 155 Warren Williams 5.00 2.20
❑ 156 Ken Willis 5.00 2.20
❑ 157 Kellen Winslow RET 12.00 5.50
❑ 158 Darren Woodson 8.00 3.60
❑ 159 Sam Wyche CO 8.00 3.60
❑ 160 Michael Young 5.00 2.20
❑ 161 Tony Zendejas 5.00 2.20
❑ NNO Santa Claus 12.00 5.50
❑ NNO Mrs. Santa Claus 12.00 5.50

1992 Pro Line Profiles Autographs

	MINT	NRMT
COMPLETE SET (473)	4000.00	1800.00
COMMON CARD (1-503)	5.00	2.20

SEMISTARS 8.00 3.60
UNLISTED STARS 12.00 5.50
TROY AIKMAN (181-189) 40.00 18.00
R.CUNNINGHAM (469-477).... 20.00 9.00
MIKE DITKA (487-495).......... 20.00 9.00
JOHN ELWAY (226-234) 70.00 32.00
MICHAEL IRVIN (289-297) 25.00 11.00
JIM KELLY (424-432).......... 25.00 11.00
JACK KEMP (154-162).......... 30.00 13.50
STEVE LARGENT (298-306) .. 25.00 11.00
HOWIE LONG (388-396) 20.00 9.00
ART MONK (496-504) 40.00 18.00
JERRY RICE (46-54) 50.00 22.00
DEION SANDERS (451-459) .. 35.00 16.00
DON SHULA (118-126) 20.00 9.00
PHIL SIMMS (343-351) 20.00 9.00
MIKE SINGLETARY (397-405) 15.00 6.75
ROGER STAUBACH (37-45) .. 30.00 13.50
LAW.TAYLOR (460-468) 20.00 9.00
DERRICK THOMAS (361-369) 40.00 18.00
THURMAN THOMAS (28-36).. 15.00 6.75
SOME CARDS WERE NEVER SIGNED
RANDOM INSERTS IN PACKS....

❑ 1 Ronnie Lott 10.00 4.50
(Tackling opponent)
❑ 2 Ronnie Lott 10.00 4.50
(As youth, in baseball uniform: signed by wife Karen)
❑ 3 Ronnie Lott 10.00 4.50
(Playing for USC)
❑ 4 Ronnie Lott 10.00 4.50
(Arms raised in triumph)
❑ 5 Ronnie Lott 10.00 4.50
(Portrait by Chris Hopkins)
❑ 6 Ronnie Lott 10.00 4.50
(At the Sports City Cafe)
❑ 7 Ronnie Lott 10.00 4.50
(With family)
❑ 8 Ronnie Lott 10.00 4.50
(Catching)
❑ 9 Ronnie Lott 10.00 4.50
(In tuxedo)
❑ 10 Rodney Peete 6.00 2.70
(Right arm raised)
❑ 11 Rodney Peete 6.00 2.70
(As youth, in football uniform)
❑ 12 Rodney Peete 6.00 2.70
(Playing baseball)
❑ 13 Rodney Peete 6.00 2.70
(In sweats with ball)
❑ 14 Rodney Peete 6.00 2.70
(Portrait by Merv Corning)
❑ 15 Rodney Peete 6.00 2.70
(Looking for receiver)
❑ 16 Rodney Peete 6.00 2.70
(Playing pool)
❑ 17 Rodney Peete 6.00 2.70
(Passing)
❑ 18 Rodney Peete 6.00 2.70
(Injured)
❑ 19 Carl Banks 6.00 2.70
(In action on field)
❑ 20 Carl Banks 6.00 2.70
(Playing basketball at Beecher High School)
❑ 21 Carl Banks 6.00 2.70
(In Michigan State uniform)
❑ 22 Carl Banks 6.00 2.70
(With family)
❑ 23 Carl Banks 6.00 2.70
(Portrait by Merv Corning)
❑ 24 Carl Banks 6.00 2.70
(Talking, wearing suit)
❑ 25 Carl Banks 6.00 2.70
(Tackling opponent)
❑ 26 Carl Banks 6.00 2.70
(On the air)
❑ 27 Carl Banks 6.00 2.70
(Close-up)
❑ 28 Thurman Thomas 15.00 6.75
(Running with ball, blue jersey)
❑ 29 Thurman Thomas 15.00 6.75
(With mother, Terlisha Cockrell)
❑ 30 Thurman Thomas 15.00 6.75
(At Oklahoma State)
❑ 31 Thurman Thomas 15.00 6.75
(With family)
❑ 32 Thurman Thomas 15.00 6.75
(Portrait by Gary Kelley)
❑ 33 Thurman Thomas 15.00 6.75
(Running with ball, white jersey)
❑ 34 Thurman Thomas 15.00 6.75
(Fishing)
❑ 35 Thurman Thomas 15.00 6.75
(Stretching)
❑ 36 Thurman Thomas 15.00 6.75
(Close-up)
❑ 37 Roger Staubach RET .. 30.00 13.50
(With Heisman Trophy)
❑ 38 Roger Staubach RET .. 30.00 13.50
(At Naval Academy)
❑ 39 Roger Staubach RET .. 30.00 13.50
(In Navy dress whites)
❑ 40 Roger Staubach RET .. 30.00 13.50
(Front view, running with ball)
❑ 41 Roger Staubach RET .. 30.00 13.50
(Portrait by John Collier)
❑ 42 Roger Staubach RET .. 30.00 13.50
(Passing, side view)
❑ 43 Roger Staubach RET .. 30.00 13.50
(With family)
❑ 44 Roger Staubach RET .. 30.00 13.50
(With young person at Daytop, substance abuse recovery facility)
❑ 45 Roger Staubach RET .. 30.00 13.50
(Calling the play)
❑ 50 Jerry Rice 50.00 22.00
(Portrait by Gary Kelley)
❑ 51 Jerry Rice 50.00 22.00
(With March of Dimes Ambassador, Ashley Johnson)
❑ 52 Jerry Rice 50.00 22.00
(Playing tennis)
❑ 53 Jerry Rice 50.00 22.00
(Arms raised in triumph)
❑ 54 Jerry Rice 50.00 22.00
(Close-up)
❑ 55 Vinny Testaverde 6.00 2.70
(Posed with Heisman)
❑ 57 Vinny Testaverde 6.00 2.70
(Playing for the University of Miami)
❑ 59 Vinny Testaverde 6.00 2.70
(Portrait by Merv Corning)
❑ 60 Vinny Testaverde 6.00 2.70
(Running with ball)
❑ 61 Vinny Testaverde 6.00 2.70
(With family)
❑ 62 Vinny Testaverde 6.00 2.70
(View from hips up, fist raised in triumph)
❑ 63 Vinny Testaverde 6.00 2.70
(With Vince Hanley)
❑ 64 Anthony Carter 6.00 2.70
(Maneuvering around opponent, with ball)
❑ 65 Anthony Carter 6.00 2.70
(In high school football game, black-and-white)
❑ 66 Anthony Carter 6.00 2.70
(At Michigan, running with ball)
❑ 67 Anthony Carter 6.00 2.70
(Fishing)
❑ 68 Anthony Carter 6.00 2.70
(Portrait by John Collier)
❑ 69 Anthony Carter 6.00 2.70
(Running, looking over shoulder)
❑ 70 Anthony Carter 6.00 2.70
(With family)
❑ 71 Anthony Carter 6.00 2.70
(Catching pass)
❑ 72 Anthony Carter 6.00 2.70
(Close-up)
❑ 73 Sterling Sharpe 20.00 9.00
(Catching)
❑ 74 Sterling Sharpe 20.00 9.00
(Passing, in high school)
❑ 75 Sterling Sharpe 20.00 9.00
(Walking on field at South Carolina)
❑ 76 Sterling Sharpe 20.00 9.00
(With books on SC campus)
❑ 77 Sterling Sharpe 20.00 9.00
(Portrait by Chris Hopkins)
❑ 78 Sterling Sharpe 20.00 9.00
(Running with ball against Rams)
❑ 79 Sterling Sharpe 20.00 9.00
(At the piano)
❑ 80 Sterling Sharpe 20.00 9.00
(Running with ball against Lions)
❑ 81 Sterling Sharpe 20.00 9.00
(In brick arch with football)
❑ 82 Anthony Munoz 8.00 3.60
(With NFL Man of the Year award)
❑ 83 Anthony Munoz 8.00 3.60
(As youth, batting)
❑ 84 Anthony Munoz 8.00 3.60
(Playing for USC)
❑ 85 Anthony Munoz 8.00 3.60
(With child at Children's Hospital)
❑ 86 Anthony Munoz 8.00 3.60
(Portrait by Merv Corning)
❑ 87 Anthony Munoz 8.00 3.60
(Blocking opponent)
❑ 88 Anthony Munoz 8.00 3.60
(Holding baby, with fellow players and children)
❑ 89 Anthony Munoz 8.00 3.60
(In action for Bengals)
❑ 90 Anthony Munoz 8.00 3.60
(Close-up)
❑ 91 Bubby Brister 6.00 2.70
(Passing, white

jersey)
❑ 92 Bubby Brister 6.00 2.70
(NLU uniform)
❑ 93 Bubby Brister 6.00 2.70
(Baseball uniform)
❑ 94 Bubby Brister 6.00 2.70
(With kids at Ronald McDonald House)
❑ 95 Bubby Brister 6.00 2.70
(Portrait by Greg Spalenka)
❑ 96 Bubby Brister 6.00 2.70
(Wearing western attire)
❑ 97 Bubby Brister 6.00 2.70
(Running with ball, white jersey)
❑ 98 Bubby Brister 6.00 2.70
(Passing, black jersey)
❑ 99 Bubby Brister 6.00 2.70
(Close-up)
❑ 100 Bernie Kosar 10.00 4.50
(Passing, white jersey)
❑ 101 Bernie Kosar 10.00 4.50
(In high school)
❑ 102 Bernie Kosar 10.00 4.50
(Playing for Miami)
❑ 103 Bernie Kosar 10.00 4.50
(Being tackled)
❑ 104 Bernie Kosar 10.00 4.50
(Portrait by Greg Spalenka)
❑ 105 Bernie Kosar 10.00 4.50
(With family)
❑ 106 Bernie Kosar 10.00 4.50
(Playing golf)
❑ 107 Bernie Kosar 10.00 4.50
(Looking for receiver)
❑ 108 Bernie Kosar 10.00 4.50
(Close-up)
❑ 109 Art Shell CO 10.00 4.50
(On sidelines)
❑ 110 Art Shell CO 10.00 4.50
(At Maryland State)
❑ 111 Art Shell CO 10.00 4.50
(Playing for Raiders)
❑ 112 Art Shell CO 10.00 4.50
(Playing basketball with sons)
❑ 113 Art Shell CO 10.00 4.50
(Portrait by Chris Hopkins)
❑ 114 Art Shell CO 10.00 4.50
(Talking to player on sidelines)
❑ 115 Art Shell CO 10.00 4.50
(In front of big screen TV)
❑ 116 Art Shell CO 10.00 4.50
(In line of scrimmage)
❑ 117 Art Shell CO 10.00 4.50
(With teddy bear)
❑ 118 Don Shula CO 20.00 9.00
(With players)
❑ 119 Don Shula CO 20.00 9.00
(At John Carroll University)
❑ 120 Don Shula CO 20.00 9.00
(Coaching Baltimore Colts)
❑ 121 Don Shula CO 20.00 9.00
(With son, Mike)
❑ 122 Don Shula CO 20.00 9.00
(Portrait by Merv Corning)
❑ 123 Don Shula CO 20.00 9.00
(With daughters)
❑ 124 Don Shula CO 20.00 9.00
(With Dan Marino)
❑ 125 Don Shula CO 20.00 9.00
(With doctor at The Don Shula Foundation)
❑ 126 Don Shula CO 20.00 9.00
(With Super Bowl Trophies)
❑ 127 Joe Gibbs CO 8.00 3.60
(Writing out play)
❑ 128 Joe Gibbs CO 8.00 3.60
(Playing for San Diego State)
❑ 129 Joe Gibbs CO 8.00 3.60
(Coaching on sidelines)
❑ 130 Joe Gibbs CO 8.00 3.60
(With sons)
❑ 131 Joe Gibbs CO 8.00 3.60
(Portrait by John Collier)
❑ 132 Joe Gibbs CO 8.00 3.60
(Reading in office)
❑ 133 Joe Gibbs CO 8.00 3.60
(With Youth For Tomorrow group)
❑ 134 Joe Gibbs CO 8.00 3.60
(In front of race car)
❑ 135 Joe Gibbs CO 8.00 3.60
(In front of Church)
❑ 136 Junior Seau 8.00 3.60
(Holding ball)
❑ 137 Junior Seau 8.00 3.60
(As youth, in football uniform)
❑ 138 Junior Seau 8.00 3.60
(At USC)
❑ 139 Junior Seau 8.00 3.60
(Finger pointing up)
❑ 140 Junior Seau 8.00 3.60
(Portrait by Merv Corning)
❑ 141 Junior Seau 8.00 3.60
(With wife, Gina)
❑ 142 Junior Seau 8.00 3.60
(Running on beach)
❑ 143 Junior Seau 8.00 3.60
(Lifting weights)
❑ 144 Junior Seau 8.00 3.60
(In swim trunks with seaweed)
❑ 145 Al Toon 6.00 2.70
(Running with ball, white jersey)
❑ 146 Al Toon 6.00 2.70
(During Pee-Wee football days)
❑ 147 Al Toon 6.00 2.70
(On the field at Wisconsin)
❑ 148 Al Toon 6.00 2.70
(With family)
❑ 149 Al Toon 6.00 2.70
(Portrait by Gary Kelley)
❑ 150 Al Toon 6.00 2.70
(Catching)
❑ 151 Al Toon 6.00 2.70
(Working out)
❑ 152 Al Toon 6.00 2.70
(Running with ball, green jersey)
❑ 153 Al Toon 6.00 2.70
(Close-up)
❑ 154 Jack Kemp RET 30.00 13.50
(In office)
❑ 155 Jack Kemp RET 30.00 13.50
(Portrait from Occidental College)
❑ 156 Jack Kemp RET 30.00 13.50
(Playing for Chargers)
❑ 157 Jack Kemp RET 30.00 13.50
(With family)
❑ 158 Jack Kemp RET 30.00 13.50
(Portrait by Merv Corning)
❑ 159 Jack Kemp RET 30.00 13.50
(Playing for Buffalo)
❑ 160 Jack Kemp RET 30.00 13.50
(Passing)
❑ 161 Jack Kemp RET 30.00 13.50
(With son, Jeff)
❑ 162 Jack Kemp RET 30.00 13.50
(In Washington)
❑ 163 Jim Harbaugh 8.00 3.60
(Passing, blue jersey)
❑ 164 Jim Harbaugh 8.00 3.60
(Playing in high school)
❑ 165 Jim Harbaugh 8.00 3.60
(Playing for Michigan)
❑ 166 Jim Harbaugh 8.00 3.60
(Passing, white jersey)
❑ 167 Jim Harbaugh 8.00 3.60
(Portrait by Gary Kelley)
❑ 168 Jim Harbaugh 8.00 3.60
(With children in children's home)
❑ 169 Jim Harbaugh 8.00 3.60
(Working out)
❑ 170 Jim Harbaugh 8.00 3.60
(Calling play)
❑ 171 Jim Harbaugh 8.00 3.60
(Close-up)
❑ 172 Dan McGwire 4.00 1.80
(From waist up)
❑ 173 Dan McGwire 4.00 1.80
(At Purdue)
❑ 174 Dan McGwire 4.00 1.80
(At San Diego)
❑ 175 Dan McGwire 4.00 1.80
(From waist down)
❑ 176 Dan McGwire 4.00 1.80
(Portrait by Chris Hopkins)
❑ 177 Dan McGwire 4.00 1.80
(Passing, blue jersey)
❑ 178 Dan McGwire 4.00 1.80
(Passing, white jersey)
❑ 179 Dan McGwire 4.00 1.80
(Working out)
❑ 180 Dan McGwire 4.00 1.80
(With wife, Dana)
❑ 181 Troy Aikman 40.00 18.00
(Passing, wearing blue jersey)
❑ 182 Troy Aikman 40.00 18.00
(As youth)
❑ 183 Troy Aikman 40.00 18.00
(Passing, at UCLA)
❑ 184 Troy Aikman 40.00 18.00
(Preparing to pass, with Cowboys)
❑ 185 Troy Aikman 40.00 18.00
(Portrait by Greg Spalenka)
❑ 186 Troy Aikman 40.00 18.00
(Golfing)
❑ 187 Troy Aikman 40.00 18.00
(Looking for opening, front view)
❑ 188 Troy Aikman 40.00 18.00
(In sweats, passing)
❑ 189 Troy Aikman 40.00 18.00
(In cowboy hat)
❑ 190 Keith Byars 6.00 2.70
(With little brother)
❑ 191 Keith Byars 6.00 2.70
(Childhood picture)
❑ 192 Keith Byars 6.00 2.70
(High School football photo)
❑ 193 Keith Byars 6.00 2.70
(Ohio State photo, red jersey)
❑ 194 Keith Byars 6.00 2.70
(Portrait by Chris Hopkins)
❑ 195 Keith Byars 6.00 2.70
(Working out)
❑ 196 Keith Byars 6.00 2.70
(Running, green

jersey)
❑ 197 Keith Byars 6.00 2.70
(Running, white jersey)
❑ 198 Keith Byars 6.00 2.70
(Close-up)
❑ 199 Timm Rosenbach 10.00 4.50
(Running with ball, red jersey)
❑ 200 Timm Rosenbach 10.00 4.50
(In high school football uniform)
❑ 201 Timm Rosenbach 10.00 4.50
(At Washington State)
❑ 202 Timm Rosenbach 10.00 4.50
(With wife, Kerry)
❑ 203 Timm Rosenbach 10.00 4.50
(Portrait by John Collier)
❑ 204 Timm Rosenbach 10.00 4.50
(Passing, white jersey)
❑ 205 Timm Rosenbach 10.00 4.50
(Roping a calf)
❑ 206 Timm Rosenbach 10.00 4.50
(Working out)
❑ 207 Timm Rosenbach 10.00 4.50
(Seated on hay, in western attire)
❑ 208 Gary Clark 4.00 1.80
(In the end zone)
❑ 209 Gary Clark 4.00 1.80
(Playing for James Madison Univ.)
❑ 210 Gary Clark 4.00 1.80
(Catching ball in end zone)
❑ 211 Gary Clark 4.00 1.80
(With daughter)
❑ 212 Gary Clark 4.00 1.80
(Portrait by John Collier)
❑ 213 Gary Clark 4.00 1.80
(Running, slouched position)
❑ 214 Gary Clark 4.00 1.80
(Playing basketball)
❑ 215 Gary Clark 4.00 1.80
(Lifted by teammates)
❑ 216 Gary Clark 4.00 1.80
(Close-up)
❑ 217 Chris Doleman 6.00 2.70
(Playing for Vikings, white jersey)
❑ 218 Chris Doleman 6.00 2.70
(In Pittsburgh uniform)
❑ 219 Chris Doleman 6.00 2.70
(With wife, Toni, and dog)
❑ 220 Chris Doleman 6.00 2.70
(Playing for Vikings, blue jersey)
❑ 221 Chris Doleman 6.00 2.70
(Portrait by John Collier)
❑ 222 Chris Doleman 6.00 2.70
(Working out)
❑ 223 Chris Doleman 6.00 2.70
(Leaping over opponent)
❑ 224 Chris Doleman 6.00 2.70
(Playing golf)
❑ 225 Chris Doleman 6.00 2.70
(Close-up)
❑ 226 John Elway 70.00 32.00
(Passing, orange jersey)
❑ 227 John Elway 70.00 32.00
(Playing for Stanford)
❑ 228 John Elway 70.00 32.00
(Passing, white jersey)
❑ 229 John Elway 70.00 32.00
(With family)
❑ 230 John Elway 70.00 32.00
(Portrait by Greg Spalenka)
❑ 231 John Elway 70.00 32.00
(Working out)
❑ 232 John Elway 70.00 32.00
(Sitting on car)
❑ 233 John Elway 70.00 32.00
(Running with ball)
❑ 234 John Elway 70.00 32.00
(Close-up)
❑ 235 Boomer Esiason 10.00 4.50
(Calling play)
❑ 236 Boomer Esiason 10.00 4.50
(In high school)
❑ 237 Boomer Esiason 10.00 4.50
(In Terps uniform)
❑ 238 Boomer Esiason 10.00 4.50
(Passing)
❑ 239 Boomer Esiason 10.00 4.50
(Portrait by Greg Spalenka)
❑ 240 Boomer Esiason 10.00 4.50
(With dogs)
❑ 241 Boomer Esiason 10.00 4.50
(With Kinny McQuade)
❑ 242 Boomer Esiason 10.00 4.50
(Looking for pass receiver)
❑ 243 Boomer Esiason 10.00 4.50
(Close-up)
❑ 244 Jim Everett 30.00 13.50
(Passing, white jersey)
❑ 245 Jim Everett 30.00 13.50
(In high school uniform)
❑ 246 Jim Everett 30.00 13.50
(Playing for Purdue)
❑ 247 Jim Everett 30.00 13.50
(With family)
❑ 248 Jim Everett 30.00 13.50
(Portrait by Greg Spalenka)
❑ 249 Jim Everett 30.00 13.50
(Running with ball, blue jersey)
❑ 250 Jim Everett 30.00 13.50
(Fishing)
❑ 251 Jim Everett 30.00 13.50
(Handing off ball)
❑ 252 Jim Everett 30.00 13.50
(Close-up)
❑ 253 Eric Green 8.00 3.60
(Running with ball)
❑ 254 Eric Green 8.00 3.60
(With coach Sam Rutigliano)
❑ 255 Eric Green 8.00 3.60
(Being blocked by opponent)
❑ 256 Eric Green 8.00 3.60
(Playing basketball)
❑ 257 Eric Green 8.00 3.60
(Portrait by Merv Corning)
❑ 258 Eric Green 8.00 3.60
(In locker room)
❑ 259 Eric Green 8.00 3.60
(Blocking opponent)
❑ 260 Eric Green 8.00 3.60
(Catching)
❑ 261 Eric Green 8.00 3.60
(Close-up)
❑ 262 Jerry Glanville CO 6.00 2.70
(On motorcycle)
❑ 263 Jerry Glanville CO 6.00 2.70
(With Lions coaching staff)
❑ 264 Jerry Glanville CO 6.00 2.70
(Coaching, clapping)
❑ 265 Jerry Glanville CO 6.00 2.70
(With family)
❑ 266 Jerry Glanville CO 6.00 2.70
(Portrait by Gary Kelley)
❑ 267 Jerry Glanville CO 6.00 2.70
(Coaching, with players)
❑ 268 Jerry Glanville CO 6.00 2.70
(In race car)
❑ 269 Jerry Glanville CO 6.00 2.70
(With country music stars)
❑ 270 Jerry Glanville CO 6.00 2.70
(In black western attire)
❑ 271 Jeff Hostetler 8.00 3.60
(Passing, blue jersey)
❑ 272 Jeff Hostetler 8.00 3.60
(Playing for West Virginia)
❑ 273 Jeff Hostetler 8.00 3.60
(Lifting weights)
❑ 274 Jeff Hostetler 8.00 3.60
(With family)
❑ 275 Jeff Hostetler 8.00 3.60
(Portrait by John Collier)
❑ 276 Jeff Hostetler 8.00 3.60
(Passing, white jersey)
❑ 277 Jeff Hostetler 8.00 3.60
(At Ronald McDonald house)
❑ 278 Jeff Hostetler 8.00 3.60
(With father-in-law)
❑ 279 Jeff Hostetler 8.00 3.60
(Close-up)
❑ 280 Haywood Jeffires 10.00 4.50
(Catching, Houston uniform)
❑ 281 Haywood Jeffires 10.00 4.50
(Playing for North Carolina)
❑ 282 Haywood Jeffires 10.00 4.50
(With wife, Robin)
❑ 283 Haywood Jeffires 10.00 4.50
(Pushing past opponent)
❑ 284 Haywood Jeffires 10.00 4.50
(Portrait by John Collier)
❑ 285 Haywood Jeffires 10.00 4.50
(With car)
❑ 286 Haywood Jeffires 10.00 4.50
(With Boy and Girls Club members)
❑ 287 Haywood Jeffires 10.00 4.50
(Being tackled)
❑ 288 Haywood Jeffires 10.00 4.50
(Close-up)
❑ 289 Michael Irvin 25.00 11.00
(Running with ball)
❑ 290 Michael Irvin 25.00 11.00
(Playing basketball)
❑ 291 Michael Irvin 25.00 11.00
(In Miami uniform)
❑ 292 Michael Irvin 25.00 11.00
(With wife, Sandy)
❑ 293 Michael Irvin 25.00 11.00
(Portrait by Gary Kelley)
❑ 294 Michael Irvin 25.00 11.00
(Catching)
❑ 295 Michael Irvin 25.00 11.00
(With student, Nyna Sherte)
❑ 296 Michael Irvin 25.00 11.00
(Playing in Pro Bowl)
❑ 297 Michael Irvin 25.00 11.00
(Close-up)
❑ 298 Steve Largent RET 25.00 11.00
(Catching, blue jersey)
❑ 299 Steve Largent RET 25.00 11.00
(Playing for Tulsa)
❑ 300 Steve Largent RET 25.00 11.00
(With family)
❑ 301 Steve Largent RET 25.00 11.00
(At school for disabled children)
❑ 302 Steve Largent RET 25.00 11.00

(Portrait by Chris Hopkins)

❑ 303 Steve Largent RET .... 25.00 11.00 (Catching, white jersey)

❑ 304 Steve Largent RET .... 25.00 11.00 (In dress attire)

❑ 305 Steve Largent RET .... 25.00 11.00 (Running, white jersey)

❑ 306 Steve Largent RET .... 25.00 11.00 (Close-up)

❑ 307 Ken O'Brien .... 6.00 2.70 (Passing, side view)

❑ 308 Ken O'Brien .... 6.00 2.70 (With University of California-Davis)

❑ 309 Ken O'Brien .... 6.00 2.70 (With family)

❑ 310 Ken O'Brien .... 6.00 2.70 (Passing, front view)

❑ 311 Ken O'Brien .... 6.00 2.70 (Portrait by Chris Hopkins)

❑ 312 Ken O'Brien .... 6.00 2.70 (Shaking hands with Tony Eason)

❑ 313 Ken O'Brien .... 6.00 2.70 (Playing golf)

❑ 314 Ken O'Brien .... 6.00 2.70 (Handing off the ball)

❑ 315 Ken O'Brien .... 6.00 2.70 (Close-up)

❑ 316 Christian Okoye .... 6.00 2.70 (Running with ball, red jersey)

❑ 317 Christian Okoye .... 6.00 2.70 (Close-up at Asuza Pacific Univ.)

❑ 318 Christian Okoye .... 6.00 2.70 (Cooking)

❑ 319 Christian Okoye .... 6.00 2.70 (Running with ball, white jersey)

❑ 320 Christian Okoye .... 6.00 2.70 (Portrait by Chris Hopkins)

❑ 321 Christian Okoye .... 6.00 2.70 (In Nigerian attire)

❑ 322 Christian Okoye .... 6.00 2.70 (With daughter, Christiana)

❑ 323 Christian Okoye .... 6.00 2.70 (Withstanding an opponent)

❑ 324 Christian Okoye .... 6.00 2.70 (In casual attire)

❑ 325 Michael Dean Perry ...... 4.00 1.80 (Blocking opponent, white jersey)

❑ 326 Michael Dean Perry ...... 4.00 1.80 (Playing for Clemson)

❑ 327 Michael Dean Perry ...... 4.00 1.80 (Blocking opponent, brown jersey)

❑ 328 Michael Dean Perry ...... 4.00 1.80 (With family)

❑ 329 Michael Dean Perry ...... 4.00 1.80 (Portrait by Merv Corning)

❑ 330 Michael Dean Perry ...... 4.00 1.80 (At Children's Hospital)

❑ 331 Michael Dean Perry ...... 4.00 1.80 (Playing basketball)

❑ 332 Michael Dean Perry ...... 4.00 1.80 (Blocking opponent, horizontal shot)

❑ 333 Michael Dean Perry ...... 4.00 1.80 (With AFC Player of the Year trophy)

❑ 343 Phil Simms .... 20.00 9.00 (Passing, blue jersey)

❑ 344 Phil Simms .... 20.00 9.00 (Calling the play)

❑ 345 Phil Simms .... 20.00 9.00 (With family)

❑ 346 Phil Simms .... 20.00 9.00 (Playing pool)

❑ 347 Phil Simms .... 20.00 9.00 (Portrait by Greg Spalenka)

❑ 348 Phil Simms .... 20.00 9.00 (Running with ball)

❑ 349 Phil Simms .... 20.00 9.00 (With young man from the Eastern Christian School for handicapped children)

❑ 350 Phil Simms .... 20.00 9.00 (Passing, white jersey)

❑ 351 Phil Simms .... 20.00 9.00 (Close-up)

❑ 352 Bruce Smith .... 12.00 5.50 (Tackling opponent, white jersey)

❑ 353 Bruce Smith .... 12.00 5.50 (At Virginia Tech)

❑ 354 Bruce Smith .... 12.00 5.50 (Close-up in game)

❑ 355 Bruce Smith .... 12.00 5.50 (With wife, Carmen)

❑ 357 Bruce Smith .... 12.00 5.50 (In Pro Bowl)

❑ 358 Bruce Smith .... 12.00 5.50 (Working out)

❑ 359 Bruce Smith .... 12.00 5.50 (Blocking, blue jersey)

❑ 360 Bruce Smith .... 12.00 5.50 (Close-up)

❑ 361 Derrick Thomas .... 40.00 18.00 (Running, red jersey)

❑ 362 Derrick Thomas .... 40.00 18.00 (At the University of Alabama)

❑ 363 Derrick Thomas .... 40.00 18.00 (With his father's Air Force momentos)

❑ 364 Derrick Thomas .... 40.00 18.00 (Seated on helmet)

❑ 365 Derrick Thomas .... 40.00 18.00 (Portrait by Merv Corning)

❑ 366 Derrick Thomas .... 40.00 18.00 (With motivational program participants)

❑ 367 Derrick Thomas .... 40.00 18.00 (Posed with Limo)

❑ 368 Derrick Thomas .... 40.00 18.00 (In Pro Bowl)

❑ 369 Derrick Thomas .... 40.00 18.00 (Close-up)

❑ 370 Pat Swilling .... 8.00 3.60 (Relaxed against tree)

❑ 371 Pat Swilling .... 8.00 3.60 (At Georgia Tech)

❑ 372 Pat Swilling .... 8.00 3.60 (With family)

❑ 373 Pat Swilling .... 8.00 3.60 (Running on field)

❑ 374 Pat Swilling .... 8.00 3.60 (Portrait by John Collier)

❑ 375 Pat Swilling .... 8.00 3.60 (Working out)

❑ 377 Pat Swilling .... 8.00 3.60 (With underprivileged children)

❑ 378 Pat Swilling .... 8.00 3.60 (Relaxed at home)

❑ 379 Eric Dickerson .... 20.00 9.00 (Close-up in Rams football gear)

❑ 380 Eric Dickerson .... 20.00 9.00 (Playing for SMU)

❑ 381 Eric Dickerson .... 20.00 9.00 (With great aunt Viola)

❑ 382 Eric Dickerson .... 20.00 9.00 (Running with ball, Rams uniform)

❑ 384 Eric Dickerson .... 20.00 9.00 (Running with ball, Colts uniform)

❑ 385 Eric Dickerson .... 20.00 9.00 (Working out)

❑ 386 Eric Dickerson .... 20.00 9.00 (Leaping over other players, Colts uniform)

❑ 387 Eric Dickerson .... 20.00 9.00 (Close-up)

❑ 388 Howie Long .... 20.00 9.00 (Being blocked by opponent)

❑ 389 Howie Long .... 20.00 9.00 (At Villanova)

❑ 390 Howie Long .... 20.00 9.00 (Rushing Quarterback)

❑ 391 Howie Long .... 20.00 9.00 (With family)

❑ 392 Howie Long .... 20.00 9.00 (Portrait by Chris Hopkins)

❑ 393 Howie Long .... 20.00 9.00 (On sidelines)

❑ 394 Howie Long .... 20.00 9.00 (Boxing)

❑ 395 Howie Long .... 20.00 9.00 (Blocking pass)

❑ 396 Howie Long .... 20.00 9.00 (Close-up)

❑ 397 Mike Singletary .... 15.00 6.75 (Crouched, ready for play)

❑ 398 Mike Singletary .... 15.00 6.75 (At Baylor)

❑ 399 Mike Singletary .... 15.00 6.75 (With children)

❑ 400 Mike Singletary .... 15.00 6.75 (In the gym)

❑ 401 Mike Singletary .... 15.00 6.75 (Portrait by Gary Kelley)

❑ 402 Mike Singletary .... 15.00 6.75 (Rushing, white jersey)

❑ 403 Mike Singletary .... 15.00 6.75 (With Man of the Year Award)

❑ 404 Mike Singletary .... 15.00 6.75 (Tackling, blue jersey)

❑ 405 Mike Singletary .... 15.00 6.75 (In sweatshirt)

❑ 406 John Taylor .... 4.00 1.80 (Celebrating on the field)

❑ 407 John Taylor .... 4.00 1.80 (In high school)

❑ 408 John Taylor .... 4.00 1.80 (Playing for Delaware State)

❑ 409 John Taylor .... 4.00 1.80 (Posed with bowling ball and pins)

❑ 410 John Taylor .... 4.00 1.80 (Portrait by John Collier)

❑ 411 John Taylor .... 4.00 1.80 (With family)

❑ 412 John Taylor .... 4.00 1.80 (With kids from Northern Light School)

❑ 413 John Taylor .... 4.00 1.80 (Catching)

❑ 414 John Taylor .... 4.00 1.80 (Close-up)

❑ 415 Andre Tippett .... 6.00 2.70 (Blocking opponent, arms outspred)

❑ 416 Andre Tippett .... 6.00 2.70 (At Iowa State)

❑ 417	Andre Tippett (With daughter, Janea Lynn)	6.00	2.70
❑ 418	Andre Tippett (In Okinawa with karate masters)	6.00	2.70
❑ 419	Andre Tippett (Portrait by Gary Kelley)	6.00	2.70
❑ 420	Andre Tippett (Running on the field)	6.00	2.70
❑ 421	Andre Tippett (Performing karate move)	6.00	2.70
❑ 422	Andre Tippett (In action, from knees up)	6.00	2.70
❑ 423	Andre Tippett (Close-up)	6.00	2.70
❑ 424	Jim Kelly (Passing, white jersey)	25.00	11.00
❑ 425	Jim Kelly (With Punt, Pass, and Kick trophy)	25.00	11.00
❑ 426	Jim Kelly (Passing for Miami)	25.00	11.00
❑ 427	Jim Kelly (With family)	25.00	11.00
❑ 428	Jim Kelly (Portrait by Greg Spalenka)	25.00	11.00
❑ 429	Jim Kelly (With sports jersey collection)	25.00	11.00
❑ 430	Jim Kelly (With young cancer patients)	25.00	11.00
❑ 431	Jim Kelly (Calling play)	25.00	11.00
❑ 432	Jim Kelly (Close-up)	25.00	11.00
❑ 442	Warren Moon (Passing, white jersey)	20.00	9.00
❑ 443	Warren Moon (As youth, in football uniform)	20.00	9.00
❑ 444	Warren Moon (Playing for Washington)	20.00	9.00
❑ 445	Warren Moon (With Edmonton Eskimos)	20.00	9.00
❑ 446	Warren Moon (Portrait by Greg Spalenka)	20.00	9.00
❑ 447	Warren Moon (With family)	20.00	9.00
❑ 448	Warren Moon (Calling the play)	20.00	9.00
❑ 449	Warren Moon (In his office)	20.00	9.00
❑ 450	Warren Moon (Posed with football and helmet)	20.00	9.00
❑ 451	Deion Sanders (In position for a play)	35.00	16.00
❑ 452	Deion Sanders (As youth, in football uniform)	35.00	16.00
❑ 453	Deion Sanders (With Florida State)	35.00	16.00
❑ 454	Deion Sanders (Playing baseball)	35.00	16.00
❑ 455	Deion Sanders (Portrait by Gary Kelley)	35.00	16.00
❑ 456	Deion Sanders (Running with ball)	35.00	16.00
❑ 460	Lawrence Taylor (Facing opponent, blue jersey)	20.00	9.00
❑ 461	Lawrence Taylor (At North Carolina State)	20.00	9.00
❑ 462	Lawrence Taylor (Side view, white jersey)	20.00	9.00
❑ 463	Lawrence Taylor (Playing golf on football field)	20.00	9.00
❑ 464	Lawrence Taylor (Portrait by Chris Hopkins)	20.00	9.00
❑ 465	Lawrence Taylor (In Honolulu)	20.00	9.00
❑ 466	Lawrence Taylor (In front of his restaurant)	20.00	9.00
❑ 467	Lawrence Taylor (Stepping over Jets player)	20.00	9.00
❑ 468	Lawrence Taylor (Close-up)	20.00	9.00
❑ 469	Randall Cunningham (Looking for receiver)	20.00	9.00
❑ 470	Randall Cunningham (In Pop Warner team uniform)	20.00	9.00
❑ 471	Randall Cunningham (Playing for UNLV)	20.00	9.00
❑ 472	Randall Cunningham (Running with ball)	20.00	9.00
❑ 473	Randall Cunningham (Portrait by Greg Spalenka)	20.00	9.00
❑ 474	Randall Cunningham (Playing golf)	20.00	9.00
❑ 475	Randall Cunningham (Passing)	20.00	9.00
❑ 476	Randall Cunningham (Working out)	20.00	9.00
❑ 477	Randall Cunningham (In dress attire)	20.00	9.00
❑ 478	Earnest Byner (Redskins uniform, running, side view)	6.00	2.70
❑ 479	Earnest Byner (At East Carolina, black and white)	6.00	2.70
❑ 480	Earnest Byner (Browns, brown jersey)	6.00	2.70
❑ 481	Earnest Byner (With family)	6.00	2.70
❑ 482	Earnest Byner (Portrait by Chris Hopkins)	6.00	2.70
❑ 483	Earnest Byner (Browns, white jersey)	6.00	2.70
❑ 484	Earnest Byner (Fishing)	6.00	2.70
❑ 485	Earnest Byner (Redskins uniform, running, front view)	6.00	2.70
❑ 486	Earnest Byner (In workout attire)	6.00	2.70
❑ 487	Mike Ditka CO (On sideline, in shirt and tie)	20.00	9.00
❑ 488	Mike Ditka CO (Playing for Bears)	20.00	9.00
❑ 489	Mike Ditka CO (With family)	20.00	9.00
❑ 490	Mike Ditka CO (Playing for Cowboys)	20.00	9.00
❑ 491	Mike Ditka CO (Portrait by Garry Kelley)	20.00	9.00
❑ 492	Mike Ditka CO (With antique car)	20.00	9.00
❑ 493	Mike Ditka CO (Playing golf)	20.00	9.00
❑ 494	Mike Ditka CO (Eating)	20.00	9.00
❑ 495	Mike Ditka CO (Close-up)	20.00	9.00
❑ 496	Art Monk (Catching, close-up)	40.00	18.00
❑ 497	Art Monk (Running hurdles in high school)	40.00	18.00
❑ 498	Art Monk (Running with ball, front view)	40.00	18.00
❑ 499	Art Monk (With family)	40.00	18.00
❑ 500	Art Monk (Portrait by Gary Kelley)	40.00	18.00
❑ 501	Art Monk (With youth at his football camp)	40.00	18.00
❑ 502	Art Monk (Running with ball, side view)	40.00	18.00
❑ 503	Art Monk (Working out)	40.00	18.00

1993 Pro Line Live

	MINT	NRMT
COMPLETE SET (285)	15.00	6.75
COMMON CARD (1-285)	.05	.02
SEMISTARS	.10	.05
UNLISTED STARS	.25	.11

❑ 1	Michael Haynes	.10	.05
❑ 2	Chris Hinton	.05	.02
❑ 3	Pierce Holt	.05	.02
❑ 4	Chris Miller	.10	.05
❑ 5	Mike Pritchard	.10	.05
❑ 6	Andre Rison	.10	.05
❑ 7	Deion Sanders	.50	.23
❑ 8	Jessie Tuggle	.05	.02
❑ 9	Lincoln Kennedy RC	.05	.02
❑ 10	Roger Harper RC	.05	.02
❑ 11	Cornelius Bennett	.10	.05
❑ 12	Henry Jones	.05	.02
❑ 13	Jim Kelly	.25	.11
❑ 14	Bill Brooks	.05	.02
❑ 15	Nate Odomes	.05	.02
❑ 16	Andre Reed	.10	.05
❑ 17	Frank Reich	.10	.05
❑ 18	Bruce Smith	.25	.11
❑ 19	Steve Tasker	.10	.05
❑ 20	Thurman Thomas	.25	.11
❑ 21	Thomas Smith RC	.10	.05
❑ 22	John Parrella RC	.05	.02
❑ 23	Neal Anderson	.05	.02
❑ 24	Mark Carrier DB	.05	.02
❑ 25	Jim Harbaugh	.25	.11
❑ 26	Darren Lewis	.05	.02
❑ 27	Steve McMichael	.10	.05
❑ 28	Alonzo Spellman	.05	.02
❑ 29	Tom Waddle	.05	.02
❑ 30	Curtis Conway RC	.50	.23
❑ 31	Carl Simpson RC	.05	.02
❑ 32	David Fulcher	.05	.02
❑ 33	Harold Green	.05	.02
❑ 34	David Klingler	.05	.02
❑ 35	Tim Krumrie	.05	.02
❑ 36	Carl Pickens	.25	.11
❑ 37	Alfred Williams	.05	.02
❑ 38	Darryl Williams	.05	.02

❑ 39 John Copeland RC .10 .05
❑ 40 Tony McGee RC .10 .05
❑ 41 Bernie Kosar .10 .05
❑ 42 Kevin Mack .05 .02
❑ 43 Clay Matthews .10 .05
❑ 44 Eric Metcalf .10 .05
❑ 45 Michael Dean Perry .10 .05
❑ 46 Vinny Testaverde .10 .05
❑ 47 Jerry Ball .05 .02
❑ 48 Tommy Vardell .05 .02
❑ 49 Steve Everitt RC .05 .02
❑ 50 Dan Footman RC .05 .02
❑ 51 Troy Aikman .75 .35
❑ 52 Daryl Johnston .25 .11
❑ 53 Tony Casillas .05 .02
❑ 54 Charles Haley .10 .05
❑ 55 Alvin Harper .10 .05
❑ 56 Michael Irvin .25 .11
❑ 57 Robert Jones .05 .02
❑ 58 Russell Maryland .05 .02
❑ 59 Nate Newton .10 .05
❑ 60 Ken Norton Jr. .10 .05
❑ 61 Jay Novacek .10 .05
❑ 62 Emmitt Smith 1.50 .70
❑ 63 Kevin Smith .10 .05
❑ 64 Kevin Williams RC .05 .02
❑ 65 Darrin Smith RC .10 .05
❑ 66 Steve Atwater .05 .02
❑ 67 Rod Bernstine .05 .02
❑ 68 Mike Croel .05 .02
❑ 69 John Elway 1.50 .70
❑ 70 Tommy Maddox .05 .02
❑ 71 Karl Mecklenburg .05 .02
❑ 72 Shannon Sharpe .25 .11
❑ 73 Dennis Smith .05 .02
❑ 74 Dan Williams RC .05 .02
❑ 75 Glyn Milburn RC .25 .11
❑ 76 Pat Swilling .05 .02
❑ 77 Bennie Blades .05 .02
❑ 78 Herman Moore .50 .23
❑ 79 Rodney Peete .05 .02
❑ 80 Brett Perriman .25 .11
❑ 81 Barry Sanders 1.50 .70
❑ 82 Chris Spielman .10 .05
❑ 83 Andre Ware .05 .02
❑ 84 Ryan McNeil RC .05 .02
❑ 85 Antonio London RC .05 .02
❑ 86 Tony Bennett .05 .02
❑ 87 Terrell Buckley .05 .02
❑ 88 Brett Favre 2.00 .90
❑ 89 Brian Noble .05 .02
❑ 90 Ken O'Brien .05 .02
❑ 91 Sterling Sharpe .25 .11
❑ 92 Reggie White .25 .11
❑ 93 John Stephens .05 .02
❑ 94 Wayne Simmons RC .05 .02
❑ 95 George Teague RC .10 .05
❑ 96 Ray Childress .05 .02
❑ 97 Curtis Duncan .05 .02
❑ 98 Ernest Givins .10 .05
❑ 99 Haywood Jeffires .10 .05
❑ 100 Bubba McDowell .05 .02
❑ 101 Warren Moon .25 .11
❑ 102 Al Smith .05 .02
❑ 103 Lorenzo White .05 .02
❑ 104 Brad Hopkins RC .05 .02
❑ 105 Micheal Barrow RC UER .05 .02
(Name misspelled Michael)
❑ 106 Duane Bickett .05 .02
❑ 107 Quentin Coryatt .10 .05
❑ 108 Steve Emtman .05 .02
❑ 109 Jeff George .25 .11
❑ 110 Anthony Johnson .10 .05
❑ 111 Reggie Langhorne .05 .02
❑ 112 Jack Trudeau .05 .02
❑ 113 Clarence Verdin .05 .02
❑ 114 Jessie Hester .05 .02
❑ 115 Roosevelt Potts RC .05 .02
❑ 116 Dale Carter .05 .02
❑ 117 Dave Krieg .10 .05
❑ 118 Nick Lowery .05 .02
❑ 119 Christian Okoye .05 .02
❑ 120 Neil Smith .25 .11
❑ 121 Derrick Thomas .25 .11
❑ 122 Harvey Williams .10 .05
❑ 123 Barry Word .05 .02
❑ 124 Joe Montana 1.50 .70
❑ 125 Marcus Allen .25 .11
❑ 126 James Lofton .10 .05
❑ 127 Nick Bell .05 .02
❑ 128 Tim Brown .25 .11
❑ 129 Eric Dickerson .10 .05
❑ 130 Jeff Hostetler .10 .05
❑ 131 Howie Long .10 .05
❑ 132 Todd Marinovich .05 .02
❑ 133 Greg Townsend .05 .02
❑ 134 Patrick Bates RC .05 .02
❑ 135 Billy Joe Hobert RC .25 .11
❑ 136 Flipper Anderson .05 .02
❑ 137 Shane Conlan .05 .02
❑ 138 Henry Ellard .10 .05
❑ 139 Jim Everett .10 .05
❑ 140 Cleveland Gary .05 .02
❑ 141 Sean Gilbert .10 .05
❑ 142 Todd Lyght .05 .02
❑ 143 Jerome Bettis RC 1.00 .45
❑ 144 Troy Drayton RC .10 .05
❑ 145 Louis Oliver .05 .02
❑ 146 Marco Coleman .05 .02
❑ 147 Bryan Cox .05 .02
❑ 148 Mark Duper .05 .02
❑ 149 Irving Fryar .10 .05
❑ 150 Mark Higgs .05 .02
❑ 151 Keith Jackson .10 .05
❑ 152 Dan Marino 1.50 .70
❑ 153 Troy Vincent .05 .02
❑ 154 Richmond Webb .05 .02
❑ 155 O.J. McDuffie RC .75 .35
❑ 156 Terry Kirby RC .25 .11
❑ 157 Terry Allen .25 .11
❑ 158 Anthony Carter .10 .05
❑ 159 Cris Carter .50 .23
❑ 160 Chris Doleman .05 .02
❑ 161 Randall McDaniel .05 .02
❑ 162 Audray McMillian .05 .02
❑ 163 Henry Thomas .05 .02
❑ 164 Gary Zimmerman .05 .02
❑ 165 Robert Smith RC 1.00 .45
❑ 166 Qadry Ismail RC .25 .11
❑ 167 Vincent Brown .05 .02
❑ 168 Marv Cook .05 .02
❑ 169 Greg McMurtry .05 .02
❑ 170 Jon Vaughn .05 .02
❑ 171 Leonard Russell .10 .05
❑ 172 Andre Tippett .05 .02
❑ 173 Scott Zolak .05 .02
❑ 174 Drew Bledsoe RC 3.00 1.35
❑ 175 Chris Slade RC .10 .05
❑ 176 Morten Andersen .05 .02
❑ 177 Vaughn Dunbar .05 .02
❑ 178 Rickey Jackson .05 .02
❑ 179 Vaughan Johnson .05 .02
❑ 180 Eric Martin .05 .02
❑ 181 Sam Mills .05 .02
❑ 182 Brad Muster .05 .02
❑ 183 Willie Roaf RC .10 .05
❑ 184 Irv Smith RC UER .05 .02
(Birthdate is 7/31/61; should be 9/13/71)
❑ 185 Reggie Freeman RC .05 .02
❑ 186 Michael Brooks .05 .02
❑ 187 Dave Brown RC .25 .11
❑ 188 Rodney Hampton .25 .11
❑ 189 Pepper Johnson .05 .02
❑ 190 Ed McCaffrey .10 .05
❑ 191 Dave Meggett .05 .02
❑ 192 Bart Oates .05 .02
❑ 193 Phil Simms .10 .05
❑ 194 Lawrence Taylor .25 .11
❑ 195 Michael Strahan RC .05 .02
❑ 196 Brad Baxter .05 .02
❑ 197 Johnny Johnson .05 .02
❑ 198 Boomer Esiason .10 .05
❑ 199 Ronnie Lott .10 .05
❑ 200 Johnny Mitchell .05 .02
❑ 201 Rob Moore .10 .05
❑ 202 Browning Nagle .05 .02
❑ 203 Blair Thomas .05 .02
❑ 204 Marvin Jones RC .05 .02
❑ 205 Coleman Rudolph RC .05 .02
❑ 206 Eric Allen .05 .02
❑ 207 Fred Barnett .10 .05
❑ 208 Tim Harris .05 .02
❑ 209 Randall Cunningham .25 .11
❑ 210 Seth Joyner .05 .02
❑ 211 Clyde Simmons .05 .02
❑ 212 Herschel Walker .10 .05
❑ 213 Calvin Williams .10 .05
❑ 214 Lester Holmes RC .05 .02
❑ 215 Leonard Renfro RC .05 .02
❑ 216 Chris Chandler .10 .05
❑ 217 Gary Clark .10 .05
❑ 218 Ken Harvey .05 .02
❑ 219 Randal Hill .05 .02
❑ 220 Steve Beuerlein .05 .02
❑ 221 Ricky Proehl .05 .02
❑ 222 Timm Rosenbach .05 .02
❑ 223 Garrison Hearst RC 1.00 .45
❑ 224 Ernest Dye RC UER .05 .02
(Birthdate 7/31/61: should be 7/15/71)
❑ 225 Bubby Brister .05 .02
❑ 226 Dermontti Dawson .05 .02
❑ 227 Barry Foster .10 .05
❑ 228 Kevin Greene .25 .11
❑ 229 Merril Hoge .05 .02
❑ 230 Greg Lloyd .25 .11
❑ 231 Neil O'Donnell .25 .11
❑ 232 Rod Woodson .25 .11
❑ 233 Deon Figures RC .10 .05
❑ 234 Chad Brown RC .10 .05
❑ 235 Marion Butts .05 .02
❑ 236 Gill Byrd .05 .02
❑ 237 Ronnie Harmon .05 .02
❑ 238 Stan Humphries .25 .11
❑ 239 Anthony Miller .10 .05
❑ 240 Leslie O'Neal .10 .05
❑ 241 Stanley Richard .05 .02
❑ 242 Junior Seau .25 .11
❑ 243 Darrien Gordon RC .05 .02
❑ 244 Natrone Means RC .75 .35
❑ 245 Dana Hall .05 .02
❑ 246 Brent Jones .10 .05
❑ 247 Tim McDonald .05 .02
❑ 248 Steve Bono .25 .11
❑ 249 Jerry Rice 1.00 .45
❑ 250 John Taylor .10 .05
❑ 251 Ricky Watters .25 .11
❑ 252 Steve Young .75 .35
❑ 253 Dana Stubblefield RC .25 .11
❑ 254 Todd Kelly RC .05 .02
❑ 255 Brian Blades .10 .05
❑ 256 Ferrell Edmunds .05 .02
❑ 257 Stan Gelbaugh .05 .02
❑ 258 Cortez Kennedy .10 .05
❑ 259 Dan McGwire .05 .02
❑ 260 Chris Warren .10 .05
❑ 261 John L. Williams .05 .02
❑ 262 David Wyman .05 .02
❑ 263 Rick Mirer RC .50 .23
❑ 264 Carlton Gray RC .05 .02
❑ 265 Marty Carter .05 .02
❑ 266 Reggie Cobb .05 .02
❑ 267 Lawrence Dawsey .05 .02
❑ 268 Santana Dotson .10 .05
❑ 269 Craig Erickson .10 .05
❑ 270 Paul Gruber .05 .02
❑ 271 Keith McCants .05 .02
❑ 272 Broderick Thomas .05 .02
❑ 273 Eric Curry RC .05 .02
❑ 274 Demetrius DuBose RC .05 .02
❑ 275 Earnest Byner .05 .02
❑ 276 Ricky Ervins .05 .02
❑ 277 Brad Edwards .05 .02
❑ 278 Jim Lachey .05 .02
❑ 279 Charles Mann .05 .02
❑ 280 Carl Banks .05 .02
❑ 281 Art Monk .10 .05
❑ 282 Mark Rypien .05 .02
❑ 283 Ricky Sanders .05 .02
❑ 284 Tom Carter RC .10 .05
❑ 285 Reggie Brooks RC .10 .05
❑ P1 Troy Aikman Promo 1.50 .70
Numbered 51
❑ P2 Troy Aikman Promo 1.00 .45
Tri-Star Prod. Back

1993 Pro Line Live Autographs

	MINT	NRMT
COMPLETE SET (38)	1250.00	550.00
COMMON 900 OR MORE	12.00	5.50
COMMON 750 OR 800	16.00	7.25
SEMISTARS	20.00	9.00
UNLISTED STARS	25.00	11.00

LISTED BY CORRESPONDING REGULAR CARD
RANDOM INSERTS IN PACKS
AIKMAN CARD MAY BE AUTOPENNED

	MINT	NRMT
❑ 1 Troy Aikman (700)	75.00	34.00
❑ 2 Neal Anderson (1050)	20.00	9.00
❑ 3 Rod Bernstine (1000)	12.00	5.50
❑ 4 Terrell Buckley (1050)	12.00	5.50
❑ 5 Earnest Byner (750)	16.00	7.25
❑ 6 Anthony Carter (950)	20.00	9.00
❑ 7 Ray Childress (950)	12.00	5.50
❑ 8 Gary Clark (1050)	20.00	9.00
❑ 9 Marco Coleman (1000)	12.00	5.50
❑ 10 Quentin Coryatt (900)	20.00	9.00
❑ 11 Eric Dickerson (900)	20.00	9.00
❑ 12 Chris Doleman (1000)	12.00	5.50
❑ 13 Steve Emtman (800)	16.00	7.25
❑ 14 Brett Favre (650)	150.00	70.00
❑ 15 Barry Foster (750)	20.00	9.00
❑ 16 Jeff George (1050)	20.00	9.00
❑ 17 Rodney Hampton (650)	25.00	11.00
❑ 18 Keith Jackson (650)	16.00	7.25
❑ 19 Haywood Jeffires (950)	20.00	9.00
❑ 20 David Klingler (1200)	12.00	5.50
❑ 21 Howie Long (950)	30.00	13.50
❑ 22 Ronnie Lott (1050)	20.00	9.00
❑ 23 Tommy Maddox (1050)	12.00	5.50
❑ 24 Art Monk (750)	30.00	13.50
❑ 25 Joe Montana (600)	150.00	70.00
❑ 26 Rob Moore (950)	20.00	9.00
❑ 27 Neil O'Donnell (1050)	20.00	9.00
❑ 28 Christian Okoye (900)	12.00	5.50
❑ 29 Rodney Peete (1000)	20.00	9.00
❑ 30 Andre Reed (1050)	25.00	11.00
❑ 31 Deion Sanders (900)	50.00	22.00
❑ 32 Junior Seau (900)	25.00	11.00
❑ 33 Sterling Sharpe (1050)	25.00	11.00
❑ 34 Neil Smith (1050)	25.00	11.00
❑ 35 Pat Swilling (950)	20.00	9.00
❑ 36 Vinny Testaverde (900)	20.00	9.00
❑ 37 Derrick Thomas (550)	60.00	27.00
❑ 38 Herschel Walker (400)	20.00	9.00

1993 Pro Line Portraits Autographs

	MINT	NRMT
COMPLETE SET (26)	800.00	350.00
COMMON CARD (468-511)	20.00	9.00
SEMISTARS	25.00	11.00

RANDOM INSERTS IN PACKS

	MINT	NRMT
❑ 1 Patrick Bates	20.00	9.00
❑ 2 Jerome Bettis	50.00	22.00
❑ 3 Steve Beuerlein	25.00	11.00
❑ 4 Tony Casillas	20.00	9.00
❑ 5 Chuck Cecil	20.00	9.00
❑ 6 Reggie Cobb	20.00	9.00
❑ 7 John Copeland	20.00	9.00
❑ 8 Eric Curry	20.00	9.00
❑ 9 Brett Favre	225.00	100.00
❑ 10 Gaston Green	20.00	9.00
❑ 11 Rodney Hampton	25.00	11.00
❑ 12 Pat Harlow	20.00	9.00
❑ 13 Bert Jones TB	25.00	11.00
❑ 14 Marvin Jones	20.00	9.00
❑ 15 Lincoln Kennedy	20.00	9.00
❑ 16 Billy Kilmer TB	25.00	11.00
❑ 17 Jeff Lageman	20.00	9.00
❑ 18 Archie Manning TB	30.00	13.50
❑ 19 Harvey Martin TB	25.00	11.00
❑ 20 Terry McDaniel	20.00	9.00
❑ 21 Mike Munchak	20.00	9.00
❑ 22 Frank Reich	20.00	9.00
❑ 23 Willie Roaf	20.00	9.00
❑ 24 Shannon Sharpe	40.00	18.00
❑ 25 Tony Smith	20.00	9.00
❑ 26 Gino Torretta	20.00	9.00

1993 Pro Line Profiles Autographs

	MINT	NRMT
COMMON CARD (1-62)	8.00	3.60
SEMISTARS	12.00	5.50
UNLISTED STARS	25.00	11.00
J.JOHNSON (532/534/536/537)	50.00	22.00

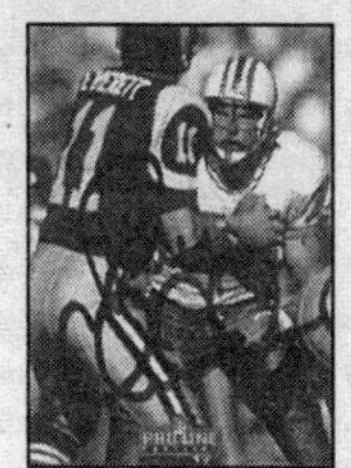

	MINT	NRMT
GALE SAYERS (577-585)	40.00	18.00

SOME CARDS WERE NEVER SIGNED
RANDOM INSERTS IN PACKS

	MINT	NRMT
❑ 1 Ray Childress (Versus Steelers)	8.00	3.60
❑ 2 Ray Childress (Childhood Photo)	8.00	3.60
❑ 3 Ray Childress (With Aggie trophies)	8.00	3.60
❑ 4 Ray Childress (Versus Rams)	8.00	3.60
❑ 5 Ray Childress (Portrait)	8.00	3.60
❑ 6 Ray Childress (With family)	8.00	3.60
❑ 7 Ray Childress (Lifting Weights)	8.00	3.60
❑ 8 Ray Childress (During Pro Bowl)	8.00	3.60
❑ 9 Ray Childress (Holding calf)	8.00	3.60
❑ 10 Jeff George	25.00	11.00
❑ 11 Jeff George (Childhood Photo)	25.00	11.00
❑ 12 Jeff George (Playing billiards)	25.00	11.00
❑ 13 Jeff George (In varsity jacket)	25.00	11.00
❑ 14 Jeff George (Portrait)	25.00	11.00
❑ 15 Jeff George	25.00	11.00
❑ 16 Jeff George (With handicapped boy)	25.00	11.00
❑ 17 Jeff George (Versus Buccaneers)	25.00	11.00
❑ 18 Jeff George (Studio with football)	25.00	11.00
❑ 19 Franco Harris	25.00	11.00
❑ 20 Franco Harris	25.00	11.00
❑ 21 Franco Harris	25.00	11.00
❑ 22 Franco Harris	25.00	11.00
❑ 23 Franco Harris	25.00	11.00
❑ 24 Franco Harris	25.00	11.00
❑ 25 Franco Harris	25.00	11.00
❑ 26 Franco Harris	25.00	11.00
❑ 27 Keith Jackson (Carrying football)	8.00	3.60
❑ 28 Keith Jackson (With family)	8.00	3.60
❑ 29 Keith Jackson (On Sooner sideline)	8.00	3.60
❑ 30 Keith Jackson (In recording studio)	8.00	3.60
❑ 31 Keith Jackson (Portrait)	8.00	3.60
❑ 32 Keith Jackson (with Eagles)	8.00	3.60
❑ 33 Keith Jackson (Dunking Basketball)	8.00	3.60
❑ 34 Keith Jackson (Running with Ball)	8.00	3.60
❑ 35 Keith Jackson (Studio Closeup)	8.00	3.60
❑ 36 Jimmy Johnson (With SB XXVII trophy)	50.00	22.00
❑ 37 Jimmy Johnson (In Arkansas uniform)	12.00	5.50
❑ 38 Jimmy Johnson	50.00	22.00

(Smiling)
❑ 39 Jimmy Johnson CO...... 12.00 5.50
(With sons)
❑ 40 Jimmy Johnson........... 50.00 22.00
(Portrait)
❑ 41 Jimmy Johnson........... 50.00 22.00
(On telephone)
❑ 42 Jimmy Johnson........... 12.00 5.50
(Lifting Weights)
❑ 43 Jimmy Johnson........... 12.00 5.50
(Scuba Diving with Shark)
❑ 44 Jimmy Johnson........... 12.00 5.50
(with Jerry Jones)
❑ 45 Jay Novacek............... 12.00 5.50
(Running with Ball)
❑ 46 Jay Novacek............... 12.00 5.50
(Young Jay with pooch)
❑ 47 Jay Novacek............... 12.00 5.50
(Hurling javelin)
❑ 48 Jay Novacek............... 12.00 5.50
(In Cardinal uniform)
❑ 49 Jay Novacek............... 12.00 5.50
(Portrait)
❑ 50 Jay Novacek............... 12.00 5.50
(With wife)
❑ 51 Jay Novacek............... 12.00 5.50
(Rodeo)
❑ 52 Jay Novacek............... 12.00 5.50
(Doing pushups)
❑ 53 Jay Novacek............... 12.00 5.50
(Riding horse)
❑ 54 Gale Sayers............... 40.00 18.00
(Bust)
❑ 55 Gale Sayers............... 40.00 18.00
(In Kansas jersey)
❑ 56 Gale Sayers............... 40.00 18.00
(Versus Lions)
❑ 57 Gale Sayers............... 40.00 18.00
(Carrying ball)
❑ 58 Gale Sayers............... 40.00 18.00
(Portrait)
❑ 59 Gale Sayers............... 40.00 18.00
(Versus Redskins)
❑ 60 Gale Sayers............... 40.00 18.00
(With wife)
❑ 61 Gale Sayers............... 40.00 18.00
(With disabled kids)
❑ 62 Gale Sayers............... 40.00 18.00
(Dressed in Suit)

1994 Pro Line Live

	MINT	NRMT
COMPLETE SET (405)	20.00	9.00
COMMON CARD (1-405)	.05	.02
EXPANSION TEAMS (395-396)	.15	.07
SEMISTARS	.10	.05
UNLISTED STARS	.25	.11

E.SMITH MVP STATED ODDS 1:360
BETTIS ROY STATED ODDS 1:270

❑ 1 Emmitt Smith.................. 1.25 .55
❑ 2 Andre Rison..................... .10 .05
❑ 3 Deion Sanders.................. .40 .18
❑ 4 Jeff George....................... .25 .11
❑ 5 Cornelius Bennett.............. .10 .05
❑ 6 Jim Kelly............................ .25 .11
❑ 7 Andre Reed........................ .10 .05
❑ 8 Bruce Smith....................... .25 .11
❑ 9 Thurman Thomas.............. .25 .11
❑ 10 Mark Carrier DB.............. .05 .02
❑ 11 Curtis Conway.................. .25 .11
❑ 12 Donnell Woolford.............. .05 .02
❑ 13 Chris Zorich...................... .05 .02
❑ 14 Erik Kramer...................... .10 .05
❑ 15 John Copeland.................. .05 .02
❑ 16 Harold Green..................... .05 .02
❑ 17 David Klingler................... .05 .02
❑ 18 Tony McGee...................... .05 .02
❑ 19 Carl Pickens...................... .25 .11
❑ 20 Michael Jackson............... .10 .05
❑ 21 Eric Metcalf...................... .10 .05
❑ 22 Michael Dean Perry......... .10 .05
❑ 23 Vinny Testaverde............. .10 .05
❑ 24 Eric Turner........................ .05 .02
❑ 25 Tommy Vardell................. .05 .02
❑ 26 Troy Aikman..................... .75 .35
❑ 27 Charles Haley................... .10 .05
❑ 28 Michael Irvin..................... .25 .11
❑ 29 Pierce Holt........................ .05 .02
❑ 30 Russell Maryland.............. .05 .02
❑ 31 Erik Williams..................... .05 .02
❑ 32 Thomas Everett................ .05 .02
❑ 33 Steve Atwater................... .05 .02
❑ 34 John Elway..................... 1.50 .70
❑ 35 Glyn Milburn..................... .10 .05
❑ 36 Shannon Sharpe............... .10 .05
❑ 37 Anthony Miller.................. .10 .05
❑ 38 Barry Sanders................ 1.50 .70
❑ 39 Chris Spielman.................. .10 .05
❑ 40 Pat Swilling....................... .05 .02
❑ 41 Brett Perriman.................. .10 .05
❑ 42 Herman Moore.................. .25 .11
❑ 43 Scott Mitchell.................... .25 .11
❑ 44 Edgar Bennett................... .25 .11
❑ 45 Terrell Buckley.................. .05 .02
❑ 46 LeRoy Butler..................... .05 .02
❑ 47 Brett Favre..................... 1.50 .70
❑ 48 Jackie Harris..................... .05 .02
❑ 49 Sterling Sharpe................. .10 .05
❑ 50 Reggie White.................... .25 .11
❑ 51 Gary Brown....................... .05 .02
❑ 52 Cody Carlson..................... .05 .02
❑ 53 Ray Childress.................... .05 .02
❑ 54 Ernest Givins..................... .10 .05
❑ 55 Bruce Matthews................. .05 .02
❑ 56 Quentin Coryatt................. .05 .02
❑ 57 Steve Emtman................... .05 .02
❑ 58 Roosevelt Potts.................. .05 .02
❑ 59 Tony Bennett..................... .05 .02
❑ 60 Marcus Allen..................... .25 .11
❑ 61 Joe Montana.................. 1.50 .70
❑ 62 Neil Smith.......................... .25 .11
❑ 63 Derrick Thomas................. .25 .11
❑ 64 Dale Carter........................ .05 .02
❑ 65 Tim Brown......................... .25 .11
❑ 66 Jeff Hostetler..................... .10 .05
❑ 67 Terry McDaniel.................. .05 .02
❑ 68 Chester McGlockton.......... .05 .02
❑ 69 Anthony Smith................... .05 .02
❑ 70 Albert Lewis....................... .05 .02
❑ 71 Jerome Bettis..................... .25 .11
❑ 72 Shane Conlan..................... .05 .02
❑ 73 Troy Drayton...................... .05 .02
❑ 74 Sean Gilbert....................... .05 .02
❑ 75 Chris Miller........................ .05 .02
❑ 76 Bryan Cox.......................... .05 .02
❑ 77 Irving Fryar........................ .10 .05
❑ 78 Keith Jackson.................... .05 .02
❑ 79 Terry Kirby......................... .25 .11
❑ 80 Dan Marino.................... 1.50 .70
❑ 81 O.J. McDuffie..................... .25 .11
❑ 82 Terry Allen......................... .10 .05
❑ 83 Cris Carter.......................... .40 .18
❑ 84 Chris Doleman................... .05 .02
❑ 85 Randall McDaniel............... .05 .02
❑ 86 John Randle........................ .05 .02
❑ 87 Robert Smith...................... .25 .11
❑ 88 Jason Belser....................... .05 .02
❑ 89 Jack Del Rio........................ .05 .02
❑ 90 Vincent Brown.................... .05 .02
❑ 91 Ben Coates......................... .25 .11
❑ 92 Chris Slade......................... .05 .02
❑ 93 Derek Brown RBK.............. .05 .02
❑ 94 Morten Andersen................ .05 .02
❑ 95 Willie Roaf........................... .05 .02
❑ 96 Irv Smith.............................. .05 .02
❑ 97 Tyrone Hughes.................... .10 .05
❑ 98 Michael Haynes................... .10 .05
❑ 99 Jim Everett........................... .10 .05
❑ 100 Michael Brooks.................. .05 .02
❑ 101 Leroy Thompson................ .05 .02
❑ 102 Rodney Hampton............... .25 .11
❑ 103 Dave Meggett.................... .05 .02
❑ 104 Phil Simms......................... .10 .05
❑ 105 Boomer Esiason................ .10 .05
❑ 106 Johnny Johnson................ .05 .02
❑ 107 Gary Anderson K............... .05 .02
❑ 108 Mo Lewis............................ .05 .02
❑ 109 Ronnie Lott......................... .10 .05
❑ 110 Johnny Mitchell.................. .05 .02
❑ 111 Howard Cross..................... .05 .02
❑ 112 Victor Bailey........................ .05 .02
❑ 113 Fred Barnett........................ .10 .05
❑ 114 Randall Cunningham.......... .25 .11
❑ 115 Calvin Williams................... .10 .05
❑ 116 Steve Beuerlein.................. .05 .02
❑ 117 Gary Clark........................... .10 .05
❑ 118 Ronald Moore...................... .05 .02
❑ 119 Ricky Proehl........................ .05 .02
❑ 120 Eric Swann.......................... .10 .05
❑ 121 Barry Foster......................... .05 .02
❑ 122 Kevin Greene....................... .25 .11
❑ 123 Greg Lloyd............................ .25 .11
❑ 124 Neil O'Donnell...................... .25 .11
❑ 125 Rod Woodson....................... .25 .11
❑ 126 Ronnie Harmon..................... .05 .02
❑ 127 Mark Higgs............................ .05 .02
❑ 128 Stan Humphries.................... .25 .11
❑ 129 Leslie O'Neal......................... .05 .02
❑ 130 Chris Mims............................ .05 .02
❑ 131 Stanley Richard..................... .05 .02
❑ 132 Junior Seau............................ .25 .11
❑ 133 Brent Jones............................ .10 .05
❑ 134 Tim McDonald........................ .05 .02
❑ 135 Jerry Rice................................ .75 .35
❑ 136 Dana Stubblefield.................. .25 .11
❑ 137 Ricky Watters......................... .25 .11
❑ 138 Steve Young........................... .60 .25
❑ 139 Cortez Kennedy..................... .10 .05
❑ 140 Rick Mirer................................ .25 .11
❑ 141 Eugene Robinson................... .05 .02
❑ 142 Chris Warren........................... .10 .05
❑ 143 Nate Odomes.......................... .05 .02
❑ 144 Howard Ballard....................... .05 .02
❑ 145 Flipper Anderson.................... .05 .02
❑ 146 Chris Jacke.............................. .05 .02
❑ 147 Santana Dotson....................... .10 .05
❑ 148 Craig Erickson.......................... .05 .02
❑ 149 Hardy Nickerson....................... .10 .05
❑ 150 Lawrence Dawsey.................... .05 .02
❑ 151 Terry Wooden........................... .05 .02
❑ 152 Ethan Horton............................ .05 .02
❑ 153 John Kasay................................ .05 .02
❑ 154 Desmond Howard..................... .10 .05
❑ 155 Ken Harvey................................ .05 .02
❑ 156 William Fuller............................ .05 .02
❑ 157 Clyde Simmons......................... .05 .02
❑ 158 Randal Hill.................................. .05 .02
❑ 159 Garrison Hearst.......................... .25 .11
❑ 160 Mike Pritchard............................ .05 .02
❑ 161 Jessie Tuggle.............................. .05 .02
❑ 162 Erric Pegram................................ .05 .02
❑ 163 Kevin Ross.................................. .05 .02
❑ 164 Bill Brooks.................................. .05 .02
❑ 165 Darryl Talley................................ .05 .02
❑ 166 Steve Tasker................................ .10 .05
❑ 167 Pete Stoyanovich......................... .05 .02
❑ 168 Dante Jones.................................. .05 .02
❑ 169 Vencie Glenn................................ .05 .02
❑ 170 Tom Waddle.................................. .05 .02
❑ 171 Harlon Barnett............................... .05 .02
❑ 172 Trace Armstrong............................ .05 .02
❑ 173 Tim Worley...................................... .05 .02
❑ 174 Alfred Williams................................ .05 .02
❑ 175 Louis Oliver..................................... .05 .02
❑ 176 Darryl Williams................................ .05 .02
❑ 177 Clay Matthews................................. .05 .02
❑ 178 Kyle Clifton...................................... .05 .02
❑ 179 Alvin Harper..................................... .10 .05
❑ 180 Jay Novacek..................................... .10 .05

181	Ken Norton Jr.	.10	.05
182	Kevin Williams	.10	.05
183	Daryl Johnston	.10	.05
184	Rod Bernstine	.05	.02
185	Karl Mecklenburg	.05	.02
186	Dennis Smith	.05	.02
187	Robert Delpino	.05	.02
188	Bennie Blades	.05	.02
189	Jason Hanson	.05	.02
190	Derrick Moore	.05	.02
191	Mark Clayton	.05	.02
192	Webster Slaughter	.05	.02
193	Haywood Jeffires	.10	.05
194	Bubba McDowell	.05	.02
195	Warren Moon	.25	.11
196	Al Smith	.05	.02
197	Bill Romanowski	.05	.02
198	John Carney	.05	.02
199	Kerry Cash	.05	.02
200	Darren Carrington	.05	.02
201	Jeff Lageman	.05	.02
202	Tracy Simien	.05	.02
203	Willie Davis	.10	.05
204	Dan Saleaumua	.05	.02
205	Rocket Ismail	.10	.05
206	James Jett	.05	.02
207	Todd Lyght	.05	.02
208	Roman Phifer	.05	.02
209	Jimmie Jones	.05	.02
210	Jeff Cross	.05	.02
211	Eric Davis	.05	.02
212	Keith Byars	.05	.02
213	Richmond Webb	.05	.02
214	Anthony Carter	.10	.05
215	Henry Thomas	.05	.02
216	Andre Tippett	.05	.02
217	Rickey Jackson	.05	.02
218	Vaughan Johnson	.05	.02
219	Eric Martin	.05	.02
220	Sam Mills	.05	.02
221	Renaldo Turnbull	.05	.02
222	Mark Collins	.05	.02
223	Mike Johnson	.05	.02
224	Rob Moore	.10	.05
225	Seth Joyner	.05	.02
226	Herschel Walker	.10	.05
227	Eric Green	.05	.02
228	Marion Butts	.05	.02
229	John Friesz	.10	.05
230	John Taylor	.10	.05
231	Dexter Carter	.05	.02
232	Brian Blades	.10	.05
233	Reggie Cobb	.05	.02
234	Paul Gruber	.05	.02
235	Ricky Reynolds	.05	.02
236	Vince Workman	.05	.02
237	Darrell Green	.05	.02
238	Jim Lachey	.05	.02
239	James Hasty	.05	.02
240	Howie Long	.10	.05
241	Aeneas Williams	.05	.02
242	Mike Kenn	.05	.02
243	Henry Jones	.05	.02
244	Kenneth Davis	.05	.02
245	Tim Krumrie	.05	.02
246	Derrick Fenner	.05	.02
247	Mark Carrier WR	.10	.05
248	Robert Porcher	.05	.02
249	Darren Woodson	.10	.05
250	Kevin Smith	.05	.02
251	Mark Stepnoski	.05	.02
252	Simon Fletcher	.05	.02
253	Derek Russell	.05	.02
254	Mike Croel	.05	.02
255	Johnny Holland	.05	.02
256	Bryce Paup	.25	.11
257	Cris Dishman	.05	.02
258	Sean Jones	.05	.02
259	Marcus Robertson	.05	.02
260	Steve Jackson	.05	.02
261	Jeff Herrod	.05	.02
262	John Alt	.05	.02
263	Nick Lowery	.05	.02
264	Greg Robinson	.05	.02
265	Alexander Wright	.05	.02
266	Steve Wisniewski	.05	.02
267	Henry Ellard	.10	.05
268	Tracy Scroggins	.05	.02
269	Jackie Slater	.05	.02
270	Troy Vincent	.05	.02
271	Qadry Ismail	.25	.11
272	Steve Jordan	.05	.02
273	Leonard Russell	.05	.02
274	Maurice Hurst	.05	.02
275	Scottie Graham RC	.10	.05
276	Carlton Bailey	.05	.02
277	John Elliott	.05	.02
278	Corey Miller	.05	.02
279	Brad Baxter	.05	.02
280	Brian Washington	.05	.02
281	Tim Harris	.05	.02
282	Byron Evans	.05	.02
283	Dermontti Dawson	.05	.02
284	Carnell Lake	.05	.02
285	Jeff Graham	.05	.02
286	Merton Hanks	.10	.05
287	Harris Barton	.05	.02
288	Guy McIntyre	.05	.02
289	Kelvin Martin	.05	.02
290	John L. Williams	.05	.02
291	Courtney Hawkins	.05	.02
292	Vaughn Hebron	.05	.02
293	Brian Mitchell	.05	.02
294	Andre Collins	.05	.02
295	Art Monk	.10	.05
296	Mark Rypien	.05	.02
297	Ricky Sanders	.05	.02
298	Eric Hill	.05	.02
299	Larry Centers	.25	.11
300	Norm Johnson	.05	.02
301	Pete Metzelaars	.05	.02
302	Ricardo McDonald	.05	.02
303	Stevon Moore	.05	.02
304	Mike Sherrard	.05	.02
305	Andy Harmon	.05	.02
306	Anthony Johnson	.10	.05
307	J.J. Birden	.05	.02
308	Neal Anderson	.05	.02
309	Lewis Tillman	.05	.02
310	Richard Dent	.10	.05
311	Nate Newton	.05	.02
312	Sean Dawkins RC	.25	.11
313	Lawrence Taylor	.25	.11
314	Wilber Marshall	.05	.02
315	Tom Carter	.05	.02
316	Reggie Brooks	.10	.05
317	Eric Curry	.05	.02
318	Horace Copeland	.05	.02
319	Natrone Means	.25	.11
320	Eric Allen	.05	.02
321	Marvin Jones	.05	.02
322	Keith Hamilton	.05	.02
323	Vincent Brisby	.25	.11
324	Drew Bledsoe	1.00	.45
325	Tom Rathman	.05	.02
326	Ed McCaffrey	.10	.05
327	Steve Israel	.05	.02
328	Dan Wilkinson RC	.10	.05
329	Marshall Faulk RC	4.00	1.80
330	Heath Shuler RC	.25	.11
331	Willie McGinest RC	.25	.11
332	Trev Alberts RC	.10	.05
333	Trent Dilfer RC	1.50	.70
334	Bryant Young RC	.25	.11
335	Sam Adams RC	.10	.05
336	Antonio Langham RC	.10	.05
337	Jamir Miller RC	.05	.02
338	John Thierry RC	.05	.02
339	Aaron Glenn RC	.10	.05
340	Joe Johnson RC	.05	.02
341	Bernard Williams RC	.05	.02
342	Wayne Gandy RC	.05	.02
343	Aaron Taylor RC	.05	.02
344	Charles Johnson RC	.25	.11
345	Dewayne Washington RC	.10	.05
346	Todd Steussie RC	.10	.05
347	Tim Bowens RC	.10	.05
348	Johnnie Morton RC	.25	.11
349	Rob Fredrickson RC	.10	.05
350	Shante Carver RC	.05	.02
351	Thomas Lewis RC	.10	.05
352	Greg Hill RC	.50	.23
353	Henry Ford RC	.05	.02
354	Jeff Burris RC	.10	.05
355	William Floyd RC	.25	.11
356	Derrick Alexander WR RC	.50	.23
357	Darnay Scott RC	.75	.35
358	Isaac Bruce RC	4.00	1.80
359	Errict Rhett RC	1.50	.70
360	Kevin Lee RC	.05	.02
361	Chuck Levy RC	.05	.02
362	David Palmer RC	.50	.23
363	Ryan Yarborough RC	.05	.02
364	Charlie Garner RC	1.50	.70
365	Isaac Davis RC	.05	.02
366	Mario Bates RC	.25	.11
367	Bert Emanuel RC	.50	.23
368	Thomas Randolph RC	.05	.02
369	Bucky Brooks RC	.05	.02
370	Allen Aldridge RC	.05	.02
371	Charlie Ward RC 1993 Heisman Trophy Winner	.25	.11
372	Aubrey Beavers RC	.05	.02
373	Donnell Bennett RC	.25	.11
374	Jason Sehorn RC	.05	.02
375	Lonnie Johnson RC	.05	.02
376	Tyronne Drakeford RC	.05	.02
377	Andre Coleman RC	.05	.02
378	Lamar Smith RC	.25	.11
379	Calvin Jones RC	.05	.02
380	LeShon Johnson RC	.10	.05
381	Byron Bam Morris RC	.25	.11
382	Lake Dawson RC	.25	.11
383	Corey Sawyer RC	.05	.02
384	Willie Jackson RC	.25	.11
385	Perry Klein RC	.05	.02
386	Ronnie Woolfork RC	.05	.02
387	Doug Nussmeier RC	.05	.02
388	Rob Waldrop RC	.05	.02
389	Glenn Foley RC	.25	.11
390	Troy Aikman CC Michael Irvin	.40	.18
391	Steve Young CC Jerry Rice	.40	.18
392	Brett Favre CC Sterling Sharpe	.75	.35
393	Jim Kelly CC Andre Reed	.25	.11
394	John Elway CC Shannon Sharpe	.75	.35
395	Carolina Panthers	.15	.07
396	Jacksonville Jaguars	.15	.07
397	Checklist 1	.05	.02
398	Checklist 2	.05	.02
399	Checklist 3	.05	.02
400	Checklist 4	.05	.02
401	Sterling Sharpe ILL	.10	.05
402	Derrick Thomas ILL	.10	.05
403	Joe Montana ILL	.60	.25
404	Emmitt Smith ILL	.50	.23
405	Barry Sanders ILL	1.00	.45
ES1	Emmitt Smith/15000 Super Bowl MVP	20.00	9.00
JB1	Jerome Bettis ROY	15.00	6.75
P1	Troy Aikman Promo International Sportscard Expo back	1.25	.55
PR1	Emmitt Smith Promo numbered PR1	2.00	.90

1994 Pro Line Live Autographs

	MINT	NRMT
COMPLETE SET (134)	2500.00	1100.00
COMMON AUTO	10.00	4.50
SEMISTARS	15.00	6.75
UNLISTED STARS	25.00	11.00
STATED ODDS 1:36		

1	Troy Aikman/340	100.00	45.00
2	Derrick Alexander WR/950	30.00	13.50
3	Eric Allen/1980	10.00	4.50
4	Steve Atwater/1040	10.00	4.50
5	Victor Bailey/450	15.00	6.75
6	Harris Barton/2120	10.00	4.50
7	Mario Bates/1145	15.00	6.75

❑ 8 Brad Baxter/1070 10.00 4.50
❑ 9 Aubrey Beavers/1150 10.00 4.50
❑ 10 Donnell Bennett/1130 25.00 11.00
❑ 11 Rod Bernstine/1010 10.00 4.50
❑ 12 Steve Beuerlein/970 15.00 6.75
❑ 13 Drew Bledsoe/1150 50.00 22.00
❑ 14 Bill Brooks/1030 10.00 4.50
❑ 15 Bucky Brooks/1090 10.00 4.50
❑ 16 Reggie Brooks/460 15.00 6.75
❑ 17 Derek Brown RBK/449 15.00 6.75
❑ 18 Gary Brown/950 10.00 4.50
❑ 19 Tim Brown/1920 25.00 11.00
❑ 20 Jeff Burris/1140 10.00 4.50
❑ 21 Marion Butts/2040 10.00 4.50
❑ 22 Keith Byars/1020 10.00 4.50
❑ 23 Anthony Carter/1020 15.00 6.75
❑ 24 Dale Carter/1031 15.00 6.75
❑ 25 Tom Carter/460 15.00 6.75
❑ 26 Shante Carver/1160 10.00 4.50
❑ 27 Ray Childress/2240 10.00 4.50
❑ 28 Andre Coleman/1000 10.00 4.50
❑ 29 Andre Collins/1100 10.00 4.50
❑ 30 Shane Conlan/1110 10.00 4.50
❑ 31 Horace Copeland/450 15.00 6.75
❑ 32 Quentin Coryatt/970 15.00 6.75
❑ 33 Isaac Davis/1150 10.00 4.50
❑ 34 Kenneth Davis/1170 10.00 4.50
❑ 35 Lake Dawson/1100 25.00 11.00
❑ 36 Robert Delpino/1030 10.00 4.50
❑ 37 Trent Dilfer/2680 25.00 11.00
❑ 38 Troy Drayton/450 15.00 6.75
❑ 39 John Elliott/2150 10.00 4.50
❑ 40 John Elway/1000 100.00 45.00
❑ 41 Steve Emtman/1900 10.00 4.50
❑ 42 Boomer Esiason/920 15.00 6.75
❑ 43 Jim Everett/1265 15.00 6.75
❑ 44 Marshall Faulk/2230 50.00 22.00
❑ 45 Brett Favre/1130 100.00 45.00
❑ 46 William Floyd/950 25.00 11.00
❑ 47 Glenn Foley/890 15.00 6.75
❑ 48 Henry Ford/1110 10.00 4.50
❑ 49 Barry Foster/1080 15.00 6.75
❑ 50 Rob Fredrickson/1160 10.00 4.50
❑ 51 John Friesz/2150 10.00 4.50
❑ 52 Irving Fryar/1040 15.00 6.75
❑ 53 Wayne Gandy/1040 10.00 4.50
❑ 54 Charlie Garner/1130 30.00 13.50
❑ 55 Jeff George/2140 15.00 6.75
❑ 56 Aaron Glenn/1140 15.00 6.75
❑ 58 Rodney Hampton/1090 25.00 11.00
❑ 59 Garrison Hearst/1435 25.00 11.00
❑ 60 Mark Higgs/980 10.00 4.50
❑ 61 Greg Hill/1145 25.00 11.00
❑ 62 Pierce Holt/2020 10.00 4.50
❑ 63 Jeff Hostetler/955 15.00 6.75
❑ 64 Tyrone Hughes/470 15.00 6.75
❑ 65 Michael Irvin/450 30.00 13.50
❑ 66 Qadry Ismail/450 25.00 11.00
❑ 67 Steve Israel/2020 10.00 4.50
❑ 68 Keith Jackson/1020 10.00 4.50
❑ 69 Michael Jackson/1490 15.00 6.75
❑ 70 Willie Jackson/1140 10.00 4.50
❑ 71 Charles Johnson/950 25.00 11.00
❑ 72 Brent Jones/1880 15.00 6.75
❑ 73 Calvin Jones/960 10.00 4.50
❑ 74 Perry Klein/1000 10.00 4.50
❑ 75 David Klingler/2140 10.00 4.50
❑ 76 Erik Kramer/1020 15.00 6.75
❑ 77 Jim Lachey/1850 10.00 4.50
❑ 78 Carnell Lake/1985 10.00 4.50
❑ 79 Antonio Langham/1240 15.00 6.75
❑ 80 Kevin Lee/1190 10.00 4.50
❑ 81 Chuck Levy/950 15.00 6.75
❑ 82 Thomas Lewis/1140 15.00 6.75
❑ 83 Ronnie Lott/910 15.00 6.75
❑ 84 Ed McCaffrey/2030 15.00 6.75
❑ 85 Terry McDaniel/1980 10.00 4.50
❑ 86 Tim McDonald/2040 10.00 4.50
❑ 87 Willie McGinest/3520 10.00 4.50
❑ 88 Russell Maryland/1945 10.00 4.50
❑ 89 Clay Matthews/2000 10.00 4.50
❑ 90 Natrone Means/445 35.00 16.00
❑ 91 Glyn Milburn/440 25.00 11.00
❑ 92 Anthony Miller/2070 15.00 6.75
❑ 93 Sam Mills/1115 15.00 6.75
❑ 94 Joe Montana/920 120.00 55.00
❑ 95 Rob Moore/1025 15.00 6.75
❑ 96 Byron Bam Morris/1130 25.00 11.00
❑ 97 Johnnie Morton/2945 15.00 6.75
❑ 98 Hardy Nickerson/1175 10.00 4.50
❑ 99 Doug Nussmeier/1150 10.00 4.50
❑ 100 Leslie O'Neal/2050 10.00 4.50
❑ 101 David Palmer/950 15.00 6.75
❑ 102 Erric Pegram/1020 15.00 6.75
❑ 103 Roman Phifer/2140 10.00 4.50
❑ 104 Ricky Proehl/1020 10.00 4.50
❑ 105 Thomas Randolph/1100 10.00 4.50
❑ 106 Tom Rathman/2230 10.00 4.50
❑ 107 Errict Rhett/1120 30.00 13.50
❑ 108 Darnay Scott/1400 25.00 11.00
❑ 109 Jason Sehorn/950 10.00 4.50
❑ 110 Shannon Sharpe/1020 25.00 11.00
❑ 111 Sterling Sharpe/450 40.00 18.00
❑ 112 Heath Shuler/2020 25.00 11.00
❑ 113 Jackie Slater/1110 10.00 4.50
❑ 114 Emmitt Smith/925 100.00 45.00
❑ 115 Irv Smith/470 15.00 6.75
❑ 116 Lamar Smith/1130 10.00 4.50
❑ 117 Neil Smith/1000 25.00 11.00
❑ 118 Todd Steussie/2100 15.00 6.75
❑ 119 Aaron Taylor/950 10.00 4.50
❑ 120 John Taylor/1030 10.00 4.50
❑ 121 John Thierry/1150 10.00 4.50
❑ 122 Derrick Thomas/1087 50.00 22.00
❑ 123 Andre Tippett/1090 10.00 4.50
❑ 124 Renaldo Turnbull/945 10.00 4.50
❑ 125 Eric Turner/1030 25.00 11.00
❑ 126 Tommy Vardell/1000 15.00 6.75
❑ 127 D.Washington/1040 15.00 6.75
❑ 128 Richmond Webb/1020 10.00 4.50
❑ 129 Dan Wilkinson/1960 15.00 6.75
❑ 130 Steve Wisniewski/2150 10.00 4.50
❑ 131 Donnell Woolford/1000 10.00 4.50
❑ 132 Steve Young/925 60.00 27.00
❑ 132 Ronnie Woolfork/360 10.00 4.50
❑ 133 Troy Aikman Combo/345 200.00 90.00
Michael Irvin
❑ 134 Steve Young Combo/450 250.00 110.00
Jerry Rice

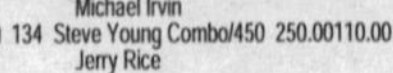

1995 Pro Line

	MINT	NRMT
COMPLETE SET (400)	18.00	8.00
COMMON CARD (1-400)	.05	.02
SEMISTARS	.10	.05
UNLISTED STARS	.25	.11
COMP.SILVER SET (400)	40.00	18.00
*SILVER STARS: 1X to 2X HI COL.		
*SILVER RCs: .75X to 1.5X HI		
ONE SILVER PER PACK		
COMP.PRINT.PROOF (400)	300.00	135.00
*PP STARS: 4X TO 10X HI COL.		
*PP RCs: 2X TO 5X HI		
PPs: STATED ODDS 1:18 HOBBY		
COMP.PP SILVER (400)	500.00	220.00
*PRINTER'S PROOF SILVERS: 1.5X PPs		
PP SILVERS: STATED ODDS 1:36 HOBBY		
COMP.NATL.SILVER (400)	250.00	110.00
*NATL.SILVER STARS: 5X TO 10X HI COL.		
*NATIONAL SILVER RCs: 3X TO 6X HI		
NATIONAL SILVER: ONE PER NATL.PACK		

❑ 1 Garrison Hearst .25 .11
❑ 2 Anthony Miller .10 .05

❑ 3 Brett Favre 1.50 .70
❑ 4 Jessie Hester .05 .02
❑ 5 Mike Fox .05 .02
❑ 6 Jeff Blake RC .75 .35
❑ 7 J.J. Birden .05 .02
❑ 8 Greg Jackson .05 .02
❑ 9 Leon Lett .05 .02
❑ 10 Bruce Matthews .05 .02
❑ 11 Andre Reed .10 .05
❑ 12 Joe Montana 1.50 .70
❑ 13 Craig Heyward .10 .05
❑ 14 Henry Ellard UER .10 .05
❑ 15 Chris Spielman .10 .05
❑ 16 Tony Woods .05 .02
❑ 17 Carl Banks .05 .02
❑ 18 Eric Zeier RC .50 .23
❑ 19 Michael Brooks .05 .02
❑ 20 Kevin Ross .05 .02
❑ 21 Qadry Ismail .10 .05
❑ 22 Mel Gray .05 .02
❑ 23 Ty Law RC .10 .05
❑ 24 Mark Collins .05 .02
❑ 25 Neil O'Donnell .10 .05
❑ 26 Ellis Johnson RC .05 .02
❑ 27 Rick Mirer .25 .11
❑ 28 Fred Barnett .10 .05
❑ 29 Mike Mamula RC .10 .05
❑ 30 Jim Jeffcoat .05 .02
❑ 31 Reggie Cobb .05 .02
❑ 32 Mark Carrier WR UER .10 .05
Mark Carrier of the Bears
is on front of card
❑ 33 Darnay Scott .25 .11
❑ 34 Michael Jackson .10 .05
❑ 35 Terrell Buckley .05 .02
❑ 36 Nolan Harrison .05 .02
❑ 37 Thurman Thomas .25 .11
❑ 38 Anthony Smith .05 .02
❑ 39 Phillippi Sparks .05 .02
❑ 40 Cornelius Bennett .10 .05
❑ 41 Robert Young .05 .02
❑ 42 Pierce Holt .05 .02
❑ 43 Greg Lloyd .10 .05
❑ 44 Chad May RC .05 .02
❑ 45 Darrien Gordon .05 .02
❑ 46 Bryan Cox .05 .02
❑ 47 Junior Seau .25 .11
❑ 48 Al Smith .05 .02
❑ 49 Chris Slade .10 .05
❑ 50 Hardy Nickerson .05 .02
❑ 51 Brad Baxter .05 .02
❑ 52 Darryll Lewis .05 .02
❑ 53 Bryant Young .10 .05
❑ 54 Chris Warren .10 .05
❑ 55 Darion Conner .05 .02
❑ 56 Thomas Everett .05 .02
❑ 57 Charles Haley .10 .05
❑ 58 Chris Mims .05 .02
❑ 59 Sean Jones .05 .02
❑ 60 Tamarick Vanover RC .25 .11
❑ 61 Daryl Johnston .10 .05
❑ 62 Rashaan Salaam RC .25 .11
❑ 63 James Hasty .05 .02
❑ 64 Dante Jones .05 .02
❑ 65 Darren Perry UER .05 .02
Card is numbered as 367
❑ 66 Troy Drayton .05 .02
❑ 67 Mark Fields RC .05 .02
❑ 68 Brian Williams LB RC .05 .02

❑ 69	Steve Bono UER	.10	.05
	Name spelled Bond on card		
❑ 70	Eric Allen	.05	.02
❑ 71	Chris Zorich	.05	.02
❑ 72	Dave Brown	.10	.05
❑ 73	Ken Norton Jr.	.10	.05
❑ 74	Wayne Martin	.05	.02
❑ 75	Mo Lewis	.05	.02
❑ 76	Johnny Mitchell	.05	.02
❑ 77	Todd Lyght	.05	.02
❑ 78	Erric Pegram	.10	.05
❑ 79	Kevin Greene	.10	.05
❑ 80	Randal Hill	.05	.02
❑ 81	Brett Perriman	.10	.05
❑ 82	Mike Sherrard	.05	.02
❑ 83	Curtis Conway	.25	.11
❑ 84	Mark Tuinei	.05	.02
❑ 85	Mark Seay	.10	.05
❑ 86	Randy Baldwin	.05	.02
❑ 87	Ricky Ervins	.05	.02
❑ 88	Chester McGlockton	.10	.05
❑ 89	Tyrone Wheatley RC	1.00	.45
❑ 90	Micheal Barrow UER	.05	.02
❑ 91	Kenneth Davis	.05	.02
❑ 92	Napoleon Kaufman RC	1.50	.70
❑ 93	Webster Slaughter	.05	.02
❑ 94	Darren Woodson	.10	.05
❑ 95	Pete Stoyanovich	.05	.02
❑ 96	Jimmie Jones	.05	.02
❑ 97	Craig Erickson	.05	.02
❑ 98	Michael Westbrook RC	1.25	.55
❑ 99	Steve McNair RC	2.50	1.10
❑ 100	Errict Rhett	.25	.11
❑ 101	Devin Bush RC	.05	.02
❑ 102	Dewayne Washington	.10	.05
❑ 103	Bart Oates	.05	.02
❑ 104	Aaron Pierce	.05	.02
❑ 105	Warren Sapp RC	.50	.23
❑ 106	Eric Green	.05	.02
❑ 107	Glyn Milburn	.05	.02
❑ 108	Johnny Johnson	.05	.02
❑ 109	Marshall Faulk	.40	.18
❑ 110	William Thomas	.05	.02
❑ 111	George Koonce	.05	.02
❑ 112	Dana Stubblefield	.25	.11
❑ 113	Steve Tovar	.05	.02
❑ 114	Steve Israel	.05	.02
❑ 115	Brent Williams	.05	.02
❑ 116	Shane Conlan	.05	.02
❑ 117	Winston Moss	.05	.02
❑ 118	Nate Newton	.10	.05
❑ 119	Michael Irvin	.25	.11
❑ 120	Jeff Lageman	.05	.02
❑ 121	Ki-Jana Carter RC	.25	.11
❑ 122	Dan Marino	1.50	.70
❑ 123	Tony Casillas	.05	.02
❑ 124	Kevin Carter RC	.25	.11
❑ 125	Warren Moon	.10	.05
❑ 126	Byron Bam Morris	.10	.05
❑ 127	Ben Coates	.10	.05
❑ 128	Michael Bankston	.05	.02
❑ 129	Anthony Parker	.05	.02
❑ 130	LeRoy Butler	.05	.02
❑ 131	Tony Bennett	.05	.02
❑ 132	Alvin Harper	.05	.02
❑ 133	Tim Brown	.25	.11
❑ 134	Tom Carter	.05	.02
❑ 135	Lorenzo White	.05	.02
❑ 136	Shane Dronett	.05	.02
❑ 137	John Elliott UER	.05	.02
❑ 138	Korey Stringer	.05	.02
❑ 139	Jerry Rice	.75	.35
❑ 140	Sherman Williams RC	.05	.02
❑ 141	Kevin Turner	.05	.02
❑ 142	Randall Cunningham	.25	.11
❑ 143	Vinny Testaverde	.10	.05
❑ 144	Tim Bowens	.05	.02
❑ 145	Russell Maryland	.05	.02
❑ 146	Chris Miller	.05	.02
❑ 147	Vince Buck	.05	.02
❑ 148	Willie Clay	.05	.02
❑ 149	Jeff Graham	.05	.02
❑ 150	Shannon Sharpe	.10	.05
❑ 151	Carnell Lake	.05	.02
❑ 152	Mark Bruener RC	.10	.05
❑ 153	James Washington	.05	.02
❑ 154	Pepper Johnson	.05	.02
❑ 155	Bert Emanuel	.25	.11
❑ 156	Mark Stepnoski	.05	.02
❑ 157	Robert Jones	.05	.02
❑ 158	Cris Dishman	.05	.02
❑ 159	Henry Jones	.05	.02
❑ 160	Henry Thomas	.05	.02
❑ 161	John L. Williams	.05	.02
❑ 162	Joe Cain	.05	.02
❑ 163	Mike Johnson	.05	.02
❑ 164	Merton Hanks	.05	.02
❑ 165	Deion Sanders	.40	.18
❑ 166	William Floyd	.25	.11
❑ 167	Leroy Thompson	.05	.02
❑ 168	Ray Childress	.05	.02
❑ 169	Donnell Woolford	.05	.02
❑ 170	Tony Siragusa	.05	.02
❑ 171	Chad Brown	.10	.05
❑ 172	Stanley Richard	.05	.02
❑ 173	Rob Johnson RC	1.25	.55
❑ 174	Derrick Brooks RC	.05	.02
❑ 175	Drew Bledsoe	.75	.35
❑ 176	Maurice Hurst	.05	.02
❑ 177	Ricky Watters	.25	.11
❑ 178	Myron Guyton	.05	.02
❑ 179	Ricky Proehl	.05	.02
❑ 180	Haywood Jeffires	.05	.02
❑ 181	Michael Strahan	.05	.02
❑ 182	Charles Wilson	.05	.02
❑ 183	Mark Carrier DB	.05	.02
❑ 184	James O. Stewart RC	1.50	.70
❑ 185	Andy Harmon	.05	.02
❑ 186	Ronnie Lott	.10	.05
❑ 187	Clay Matthews	.10	.05
❑ 188	John Carney	.05	.02
❑ 189	Andre Rison	.10	.05
❑ 190	Aeneas Williams	.05	.02
❑ 191	Alexander Wright	.05	.02
❑ 192	Desmond Howard	.10	.05
❑ 193	Herman Moore	.25	.11
❑ 194	Alfred Williams	.05	.02
❑ 195	Tyrone Poole RC	.10	.05
❑ 196	Darren Mickell	.05	.02
❑ 197	Steve Young	.60	.25
❑ 198	Roman Phifer	.05	.02
❑ 199	Darrell Green	.05	.02
❑ 200	Terry Wooden	.05	.02
❑ 201	Chris Calloway	.05	.02
❑ 202	Lewis Tillman	.05	.02
❑ 203	Cris Carter	.25	.11
❑ 204	Jim Everett	.05	.02
❑ 205	Adrian Murrell	.10	.05
❑ 206	Barry Sanders	1.50	.70
❑ 207	Mario Bates	.25	.11
❑ 208	Shawn Lee	.05	.02
❑ 209	Charles Mincy	.05	.02
❑ 210	Kerry Collins RC	.75	.35
❑ 211	Steve Walsh	.05	.02
❑ 212	Chris Chandler	.10	.05
❑ 213	Bennie Blades	.05	.02
❑ 214	Kevin Williams WR	.10	.05
❑ 215	Jim Kelly	.25	.11
❑ 216	Marion Butts	.05	.02
❑ 217	Jay Novacek	.10	.05
❑ 218	Shawn Jefferson	.05	.02
❑ 219	O.J. McDuffie	.25	.11
❑ 220	Ray Seals	.05	.02
❑ 221	Arthur Marshall	.05	.02
❑ 222	Karl Mecklenburg	.05	.02
❑ 223	Terance Mathis	.10	.05
❑ 224	David Klingler	.10	.05
❑ 225	Rod Woodson	.10	.05
❑ 226	Quentin Coryatt	.10	.05
❑ 227	Leroy Hoard	.05	.02
❑ 228	Brian Blades	.10	.05
❑ 229	Rob Moore	.05	.02
❑ 230	Boomer Esiason	.10	.05
❑ 231	Dave Krieg	.05	.02
❑ 232	Sterling Sharpe	.10	.05
❑ 233	Marcus Allen	.25	.11
❑ 234	John Randle	.05	.02
❑ 235	Craig Powell	.05	.02
❑ 236	John Elway	1.50	.70
❑ 237	Mark Ingram	.05	.02
❑ 238	Cortez Kennedy	.10	.05
❑ 239	Brent Jones	.05	.02
❑ 240	Ken Harvey	.05	.02
❑ 241	Keenan McCardell	.25	.11
❑ 242	Dan Wilkinson	.10	.05
❑ 243	Don Beebe	.05	.02
❑ 244	Jack Del Rio	.05	.02
❑ 245	Byron Evans	.05	.02
❑ 246	Ronald Moore	.05	.02
❑ 247	Edgar Bennett	.10	.05
❑ 248	William Fuller	.05	.02
❑ 249	James Williams	.05	.02
❑ 250	Neil Smith	.10	.05
❑ 251	Sam Mills	.10	.05
❑ 252	Willie McGinest	.10	.05
❑ 253	Howard Cross	.05	.02
❑ 254	Troy Aikman	.75	.35
❑ 255	Herschel Walker	.10	.05
❑ 256	Dale Carter	.10	.05
❑ 257	Sean Dawkins	.10	.05
❑ 258	Greg Hill	.10	.05
❑ 259	Stan Humphries	.10	.05
❑ 260	Erik Kramer	.05	.02
❑ 261	Leslie O'Neal	.10	.05
❑ 262	Trezelle Jenkins RC	.05	.02
❑ 263	Antonio Langham	.05	.02
❑ 264	Bryce Paup	.25	.11
❑ 265	Jake Reed	.10	.05
❑ 266	Richmond Webb	.05	.02
❑ 267	Eric Davis	.05	.02
❑ 268	Mark McMillian	.05	.02
❑ 269	John Walsh RC	.05	.02
❑ 270	Irving Fryar	.10	.05
❑ 271	Rocket Ismail	.10	.05
❑ 272	Phil Hansen	.05	.02
❑ 273	J.J. Stokes RC	.60	.25
❑ 274	Craig Newsome RC	.05	.02
❑ 275	Leonard Russell	.05	.02
❑ 276	Derrick Deese	.05	.02
❑ 277	Broderick Thomas	.05	.02
❑ 278	Bobby Houston	.05	.02
❑ 279	Lamar Lathon	.05	.02
❑ 280	Eugene Robinson	.05	.02
❑ 281	Dan Saleaumua	.05	.02
❑ 282	Kyle Brady RC	.25	.11
❑ 283	John Taylor UER	.05	.02
	Card lists him as a Tight End		
❑ 284	Tony Boselli RC	.10	.05
❑ 285	Seth Joyner	.05	.02
❑ 286	Steve Beuerlein	.05	.02
❑ 287	Sam Adams	.05	.02
❑ 288	Frank Reich	.05	.02
❑ 289	Patrick Hunter	.05	.02
❑ 290	Sean Gilbert	.10	.05
❑ 291	Dermontti Dawson UER	.10	.05
❑ 292	Shaun Gayle	.05	.02
❑ 293	Vincent Brown	.05	.02
❑ 294	Terry Kirby	.10	.05
❑ 295	Courtney Hawkins	.05	.02
❑ 296	Carl Pickens	.25	.11
❑ 297	Luther Elliss RC	.05	.02
❑ 298	Steve Atwater	.05	.02
❑ 299	James Francis	.05	.02
❑ 300	Rob Burnett	.05	.02
❑ 301	Keith Hamilton	.05	.02
❑ 302	Rob Fredrickson	.05	.02
❑ 303	Jerome Bettis	.25	.11
❑ 304	Emmitt Smith	1.25	.55
❑ 305	Clyde Simmons	.05	.02
❑ 306	Reggie White	.25	.11
❑ 307	Rodney Hampton	.10	.05
❑ 308	Steve Emtman	.05	.02
❑ 309	Hugh Douglas RC	.10	.05
❑ 310	Bernie Parmalee	.10	.05
❑ 311	Trent Dilfer	.25	.11
❑ 312	Flipper Anderson	.05	.02
❑ 313	Heath Shuler	.25	.11
❑ 314	Rod Smith DB	.10	.05
❑ 315	Ray Zellars RC	.10	.05
❑ 316	Robert Brooks	.25	.11
❑ 317	Lee Woodall	.05	.02
❑ 318	Robert Porcher	.05	.02
❑ 319	Todd Collins RC	.25	.11
❑ 320	Willie Roaf	.05	.02
❑ 321	Erik Williams	.05	.02
❑ 322	Steve Wisniewski	.05	.02
❑ 323	Derrick Alexander DE RC	.05	.02
❑ 324	Frank Warren	.05	.02

		MINT	NRMT
❑ 325	Kelvin Pritchett	.05	.02
❑ 326	Dennis Gibson	.05	.02
❑ 327	Jason Belser	.05	.02
❑ 328	Vincent Brisby	.05	.02
❑ 329	Calvin Williams	.10	.05
❑ 330	Derek Brown RBK	.05	.02
❑ 331	Blake Brockermeyer	.05	.02
❑ 332	Jeff Herrod	.05	.02
❑ 333	Darryl Williams	.05	.02
❑ 334	Aaron Glenn	.05	.02
❑ 335	Eric Metcalf	.10	.05
❑ 336	Billy Milner	.05	.02
❑ 337	Terry McDaniel	.05	.02
❑ 338	Trace Armstrong	.05	.02
❑ 339	Yancey Thigpen RC	.25	.11
❑ 340	Jackie Harris	.05	.02
❑ 341	Jeff George	.10	.05
❑ 342	Darryl Talley	.05	.02
❑ 343	Marcus Robertson	.05	.02
❑ 344	Robert Massey	.05	.02
❑ 345	Jessie Tuggle	.05	.02
❑ 346	Scott Mitchell	.10	.05
❑ 347	Harvey Williams	.05	.02
❑ 348	Jack Jackson RC	.05	.02
❑ 349	Brian Mitchell	.05	.02
❑ 350	Lawrence Dawsey	.05	.02
❑ 351	Erik Howard	.05	.02
❑ 352	Quinn Early	.10	.05
❑ 353	Terry Allen	.10	.05
❑ 354	Simon Fletcher	.05	.02
❑ 355	Eric Turner	.05	.02
❑ 356	Natrone Means	.25	.11
❑ 357	Frank Sanders RC	.75	.35
❑ 358	Michael Timpson	.05	.02
❑ 359	Michael Haynes	.10	.05
❑ 360	Ruben Brown RC	.05	.02
❑ 361	Troy Vincent UER Name spelled Vicent on back	.05	.02
❑ 362	Floyd Turner	.05	.02
❑ 363	Larry Centers	.10	.05
❑ 364	Eric Swann	.10	.05
❑ 365	Albert Lewis	.05	.02
❑ 366	Barry Foster	.10	.05
❑ 367	Michael Dean Perry	.05	.02
❑ 368	Jumpy Geathers UER Name spelled Jummpy on front	.05	.02
❑ 369	Kordell Stewart RC	2.50	1.10
❑ 370	Chuck Smith	.05	.02
❑ 371	Lake Dawson	.10	.05
❑ 372	Terry Hoage	.05	.02
❑ 373	Jeff Cross	.05	.02
❑ 374	Tony McGee	.05	.02
❑ 375	Eric Curry	.05	.02
❑ 376	Harold Green	.05	.02
❑ 377	Eric Hill	.05	.02
❑ 378	Ray Buchanan	.05	.02
❑ 379	Willie Davis	.10	.05
❑ 380	Chris T. Jones RC	.25	.11
❑ 381	Martin Mayhew	.05	.02
❑ 382	Anthony Pleasant	.05	.02
❑ 383	Joey Galloway RC	2.50	1.10
❑ 384	Anthony Morgan	.05	.02
❑ 385	Harlon Barnett	.05	.02
❑ 386	Bruce Smith	.25	.11
❑ 387	Jeff Hostetler	.10	.05
❑ 388	Randall McDaniel	.05	.02
❑ 389	Dave Meggett	.05	.02
❑ 390	Bill Romanowski	.05	.02
❑ 391	Gary Brown	.05	.02
❑ 392	Charles Johnson	.10	.05
❑ 393	Chris Doleman	.05	.02
❑ 394	Tony Martin	.10	.05
❑ 395	Raymont Harris	.05	.02
❑ 396	John Copeland	.05	.02
❑ 397	Emmitt Smith CL UER Several wrong names	.25	.11
❑ 398	Steve Young CL UER Many wrong names	.10	.05
❑ 399	Marshall Faulk CL UER Many wrong names	.10	.05
❑ 400	Ki-Jana Carter CL UER Many wrong names	.10	.05
❑ P1	Marshall Faulk Promo GameBreakers card 1995 National Convention back	1.00	.45

1995 Pro Line Autographs

	MINT	NRMT
COMPLETE SET (128)	2400.00	1100.00
COMMON AUTO	6.00	2.70
SEMISTARS	12.00	5.50
UNLISTED STARS	15.00	6.75

SET PRICE INCLUDES ONE CARD OF EACH PLAYER MINUS ELWAY ..
STATED ODDS 1:36H,1:24J,1:90R SER.1

		MINT	NRMT
❑ 1	Troy Aikman/500	80.00	36.00
❑ 2A	Eric Allen/1225	6.00	2.70
❑ 2B	Eric Allen/2398AP	6.00	2.70
❑ 2C	Eric Allen/745AP	6.00	2.70
❑ 3	Flipper Anderson/1140	6.00	2.70
❑ 4A	Randy Baldwin/1435	6.00	2.70
❑ 4B	Randy Baldwin/2405AP	6.00	2.70
❑ 4C	Randy Baldwin/760AP	6.00	2.70
❑ 5	Mario Bates/1480	12.00	5.50
❑ 6A	Don Beebe/1200	12.00	5.50
❑ 6B	Don Beebe/275AP	12.00	5.50
❑ 7A	Cornelius Bennett/1200	12.00	5.50
❑ 7B	Cornelius Bennett/255AP	12.00	5.50
❑ 8	Edgar Bennett/1475	15.00	6.75
❑ 9	Tony Bennett/1475	6.00	2.70
❑ 10	Steve Beuerlein/1465	12.00	5.50
❑ 11	J.J. Birden/775	12.00	5.50
❑ 12	Brian Blades/1465	12.00	5.50
❑ 13	Jeff Blake/1200	15.00	6.75
❑ 14	Drew Bledsoe/515	60.00	27.00
❑ 15A	B.Brockermeyer/1445	6.00	2.70
❑ 15B	Blake Brockermeyer/ 2315AP	6.00	2.70
❑ 16	Derrick Brooks/1470	6.00	2.70
❑ 17	Tim Brown/2410	15.00	6.75
❑ 18	Dale Carter/1400	12.00	5.50
❑ 19A	Ray Childress/1200	6.00	2.70
❑ 19B	Ray Childress/235AP	6.00	2.70
❑ 20	Ben Coates/1175	15.00	6.75
❑ 21	Mark Collins/1430	6.00	2.70
❑ 22	Kerry Collins/3300	20.00	9.00
❑ 23	Curtis Conway/1200	12.00	5.50
❑ 24	Quentin Coryatt/1400	12.00	5.50
❑ 25	R. Cunningham/470	30.00	13.50
❑ 26A	Jack Del Rio/1480	6.00	2.70
❑ 26B	Jack Del Rio/930AP	6.00	2.70
❑ 27	Willie Davis/1500	12.00	5.50
❑ 28A	Derrick Deese/1200	6.00	2.70
❑ 28B	Derrick Deese/2375AP	6.00	2.70
❑ 28C	Derrick Deese/735AP	6.00	2.70
❑ 29A	Trent Dilfer/2010	20.00	9.00
❑ 29B	Trent Dilfer/306AP	20.00	9.00
❑ 30	Troy Drayton/1375	6.00	2.70
❑ 31	Quinn Early/1200	12.00	5.50
❑ 32	Henry Ellard/1440	12.00	5.50
❑ 33	John Elliott/2380	6.00	2.70
❑ 34	Luther Elliss/1470	6.00	2.70
❑ 36	Bert Emanuel/1445	12.00	5.50
❑ 37	Steve Emtman/2365	6.00	2.70
❑ 38A	Craig Erickson/630	12.00	5.50
❑ 38B	Craig Erickson/890AP	6.00	2.70
❑ 39	Boomer Esiason/1700	12.00	5.50
❑ 40	Marshall Faulk/1030	40.00	18.00
❑ 41	Barry Foster/1455	12.00	5.50
❑ 42	Mike Fox/1445	6.00	2.70
❑ 43	Irving Fryar/1500	12.00	5.50
❑ 44	Joey Galloway/1445	30.00	13.50
❑ 45A	Shaun Gayle/1200	6.00	2.70
❑ 45B	Shaun Gayle/265AP	12.00	5.50
❑ 46	Jeff George/1295	12.00	5.50
❑ 47	Darrien Gordon/2400	6.00	2.70
❑ 48	Jeff Graham/1465	12.00	5.50
❑ 49	Eric Green/1460	6.00	2.70
❑ 50	Charles Haley/1420	12.00	5.50
❑ 51	Rodney Hampton/1120	12.00	5.50
❑ 52	Andy Harmon/1200	6.00	2.70
❑ 53	Courtney Hawkins/1445	6.00	2.70
❑ 54	Michael Haynes/1180	12.00	5.50
❑ 55	Garrison Hearst/1460	20.00	9.00
❑ 56A	Craig Heyward/1200	6.00	2.70
❑ 56B	Craig Heyward/265AP	12.00	5.50
❑ 57	Greg Hill/1455	12.00	5.50
❑ 58	Pierce Holt/1440	6.00	2.70
❑ 59	Patrick Hunter/2375	6.00	2.70
❑ 60	Michael Irvin/1490	15.00	6.75
❑ 61	Sean Jones/2385	6.00	2.70
❑ 62	Qadry Ismail/1170	12.00	5.50
❑ 63A	Steve Israel/1200	6.00	2.70
❑ 63B	Steve Israel/2413AP	6.00	2.70
❑ 63C	Steve Israel/750AP	6.00	2.70
❑ 64	Jack Jackson/1475	6.00	2.70
❑ 65	Michael Jackson/1200	12.00	5.50
❑ 66A	Shawn Jefferson/1200	6.00	2.70
❑ 66B	Shawn Jefferson/240AP	12.00	5.50
❑ 67	Haywood Jeffires/1470	12.00	5.50
❑ 68	Trezelle Jenkins/1470	6.00	2.70
❑ 69A	Rob Johnson/2815	15.00	6.75
❑ 69B	Rob Johnson/500	15.00	6.75
❑ 70	Seth Joyner/1480	6.00	2.70
❑ 71	Jim Kelly/470	40.00	18.00
❑ 72	Cortez Kennedy/1380	12.00	5.50
❑ 73	Terry Kirby/1450	12.00	5.50
❑ 74	Dave Krieg/1470	12.00	5.50
❑ 75A	Antonio Langham/1200	6.00	2.70
❑ 75B	Antonio Langham/260AP	6.00	2.70
❑ 76	Ty Law/1460	12.00	5.50
❑ 77	Leon Lett/1550	6.00	2.70
❑ 78	Ronnie Lott/1900	15.00	6.75
❑ 79A	K.McCardell/1235	12.00	5.50
❑ 79B	Keenan McCardell/ 2403AP	12.00	5.50
❑ 80	Terry McDaniel/2340	6.00	2.70
❑ 81	Tony McGee/1385	12.00	5.50
❑ 82A	Willie McGinest/1160	12.00	5.50
❑ 82B	Willie McGinest/2407AP	12.00	5.50
❑ 82C	Willie McGinest/754AP	12.00	5.50
❑ 83	Chester McGlockton/1280	12.00	5.50
❑ 84A	Mark McMillian/1175	6.00	2.70
❑ 84B	Mark McMillian/2400AP	6.00	2.70
❑ 84C	Mark McMillian/825AP	6.00	2.70
❑ 85	Steve McNair/3490	25.00	11.00
❑ 86	Mike Mamula/1250	6.00	2.70
❑ 87A	Arthur Marshall/1165	6.00	2.70
❑ 87B	Arthur Marshall/2400AP	6.00	2.70
❑ 87C	Arthur Marshall/870AP	6.00	2.70
❑ 88	Russell Maryland/1250	12.00	5.50
❑ 89	Clay Matthews/2385	12.00	5.50
❑ 90A	Chad May/1180	6.00	2.70
❑ 90B	Chad May/2410AP	6.00	2.70
❑ 91	Natrone Means/1058	15.00	6.75
❑ 92	Anthony Miller/2385	12.00	5.50
❑ 93	Sam Mills/1470	12.00	5.50
❑ 94	Herman Moore/2070	15.00	6.75
❑ 95	Byron Bam Morris/1430	12.00	5.50
❑ 96	Jay Novacek/1195	12.00	5.50
❑ 97A	Brett Perriman/1380	12.00	5.50
❑ 97B	Brett Perriman/935	12.00	5.50
❑ 98A	Michael D. Perry/1200	12.00	5.50
❑ 98B	Michael D.Perry/295AP	12.00	5.50
❑ 99	Roman Phifer/2395	6.00	2.70
❑ 100	Ricky Proehl/1475	6.00	2.70
❑ 101A	John Randle/1170	6.00	2.70
❑ 101B	John Randle/2400AP	6.00	2.70
❑ 101C	John Randle/757AP	6.00	2.70
❑ 102	Andre Reed/1440	12.00	5.50
❑ 103	Jake Reed/1470	12.00	5.50
❑ 104	Errict Rhett/1400	15.00	6.75
❑ 105A	Willie Roaf/1200	12.00	5.50
❑ 105B	Willie Roaf/245AP	12.00	5.50
❑ 106	Bill Romanowski/1450	6.00	2.70
❑ 107	Rashaan Salaam/1320	15.00	6.75
❑ 108	Mike Sherrard/1450	6.00	2.70

	MINT	NRMT
❑ 109A Heath Shuler/2000	15.00	6.75
❑ 109B Heath Shuler/366AP	15.00	6.75
❑ 110 Clyde Simmons/735	12.00	5.50
❑ 111A Chris Slade/1100	6.00	2.70
❑ 111B Chris Slade/2417AP	6.00	2.70
❑ 112 Al Smith/1360	6.00	2.70
❑ 113 Emmitt Smith/500	150.00	70.00
❑ 114 Neil Smith/1465	12.00	5.50
❑ 115 Mark Stepnoski/1500	6.00	2.70
❑ 116 J.J. Stokes/1435	20.00	9.00
❑ 117 Vinny Testaverde/1020	12.00	5.50
❑ 118 Henry Thomas/1420	6.00	2.70
❑ 119 Lewis Tillman/1170	6.00	2.70
❑ 120A Jessie Tuggle/1200	6.00	2.70
❑ 120B Jessie Tuggle/195AP	12.00	5.50
❑ 121 Tamarick Vanover/1155	15.00	6.75
❑ 122 Troy Vincent/1490	6.00	2.70
❑ 123 John Walsh/3340	6.00	2.70
❑ 124A Steve Walsh/1185	12.00	5.50
❑ 124B Steve Walsh/1015AP	12.00	5.50
❑ 125A Brian Williams LB/1175	6.00	2.70
❑ 125B Brian Williams LB/2670AP	6.00	2.70
❑ 125C Brian Williams LB/865AP	6.00	2.70
❑ 126 Calvin Williams/1200	12.00	5.50
❑ 127 Sherman Williams/1460	6.00	2.70
❑ 128 Steve Young/500	70.00	32.00
❑ 129 Eric Zeier/500	25.00	11.00

1995 Pro Line Autograph Printer's Proofs

	MINT	NRMT
COMPLETE SET (8)	1500.00	700.00
COMMON CARD (230/311)	80.00	36.00

RANDOM INSERTS IN PACKS....
STATED PRINT RUN 50 NUMBERED SETS

	MINT	NRMT
❑ 99 Steve McNair	200.00	90.00
❑ 175 Drew Bledsoe	200.00	90.00
❑ 197 Steve Young	200.00	90.00
❑ 210 Kerry Collins	100.00	45.00
❑ 230 Boomer Esiason	80.00	36.00
❑ 254 Troy Aikman	250.00	110.00
❑ 304 Emmitt Smith	400.00	180.00
❑ 311 Trent Dilfer	80.00	36.00

1995 Pro Line Series 2

	MINT	NRMT
COMPLETE SET (75)	15.00	6.75
COMMON CARD (1-75)	.05	.02
SEMISTARS	.10	.05
UNLISTED STARS	.25	.11
CONDITION SENSITIVE SET!......		
COMPLETE PP SET (75)	200.00	90.00
*PP STARS: 6X TO 12X HI COLUMN		
*PP RCs: 3X TO 6X HI		
PP STATED ODDS 1:18 SER.2....		

	MINT	NRMT
❑ 1 Jim Kelly	.25	.11
❑ 2 Steve Walsh	.05	.02
❑ 3 Jeff Blake	.25	.11
❑ 4 Vinny Testaverde	.10	.05
❑ 5 Jeff Hostetler	.10	.05
❑ 6 Dan Marino	2.00	.90
❑ 7 Cris Carter	.25	.11
❑ 8 Drew Bledsoe	1.00	.45
❑ 9 Jim Everett	.05	.02
❑ 10 Neil O'Donnell	.10	.05
❑ 11 Rodney Hampton	.10	.05
❑ 12 Troy Aikman	1.00	.45
❑ 13 John Elway	2.00	.90
❑ 14 Barry Sanders	2.00	.90
❑ 15 Reggie White	.25	.11
❑ 16 Marshall Faulk	.40	.18
❑ 17 Marcus Allen	.25	.11
❑ 18 James O. Stewart	1.00	.45
❑ 19 Randall Cunningham	.25	.11
❑ 20 Natrone Means	.25	.11
❑ 21 Rick Mirer	.25	.11
❑ 22 Jerry Rice	1.00	.45
❑ 23 Errict Rhett	.25	.11
❑ 24 Heath Shuler	.25	.11
❑ 25 Jerome Bettis	.25	.11
❑ 26 Garrison Hearst	.25	.11
❑ 27 Jeff George	.10	.05
❑ 28 Andre Reed	.10	.05
❑ 29 Warren Moon	.10	.05
❑ 30 Ben Coates	.10	.05
❑ 31 Mario Bates	.25	.11
❑ 32 Byron Bam Morris	.10	.05
❑ 33 Dave Brown	.10	.05
❑ 34 Emmitt Smith	1.50	.70
❑ 35 Anthony Miller	.10	.05
❑ 36 Herman Moore	.25	.11
❑ 37 Brett Favre	2.00	.90
❑ 38 Steve Bono	.10	.05
❑ 39 Stan Humphries	.10	.05
❑ 40 Steve Young	.75	.35
❑ 41 Trent Dilfer	.25	.11
❑ 42 Chris Miller	.05	.02
❑ 43 Herschel Walker	.10	.05
❑ 44 Michael Irvin	.25	.11
❑ 45 Junior Seau	.25	.11
❑ 46 Deion Sanders	.60	.25
❑ 47 William Floyd	.25	.11
❑ 48 Ki-Jana Carter	.25	.11
❑ 49 Kerry Collins	.50	.23
❑ 50 Steve McNair	1.25	.55
❑ 51 Tony Boselli	.10	.05
❑ 52 Kyle Brady	.25	.11
❑ 53 Mike Mamula	.10	.05
❑ 54 Warren Sapp	.10	.05
❑ 55 J.J. Stokes	.50	.23
❑ 56 Joey Galloway	1.25	.55
❑ 57 Hugh Douglas	.10	.05
❑ 58 Michael Westbrook	.75	.35
❑ 59 Napoleon Kaufman	1.00	.45
❑ 60 Rashaan Salaam	.25	.11
❑ 61 Tyrone Wheatley	.60	.25
❑ 62 Terrell Fletcher RC	.05	.02
❑ 63 Eric Metcalf	.10	.05
❑ 64 Kevin Carter	.25	.11
❑ 65 Andre Rison	.10	.05
❑ 66 Eric Green	.05	.02
❑ 67 Dave Meggett	.05	.02
❑ 68 Ricky Watters	.25	.11
❑ 69 Steve Beuerlein	.05	.02
❑ 70 Craig Erickson	.05	.02
❑ 71 Michael Dean Perry	.05	.02
❑ 72 Alvin Harper	.05	.02
❑ 73 Rob Moore	.05	.02
❑ 74 Frank Reich	.05	.02
❑ 75 Checklist	.10	.05

1996 Pro Line

	MINT	NRMT
COMPLETE SET (350)	25.00	11.00
COMMON CARD (1-350)	.10	.05
SEMISTARS	.20	.09
UNLISTED STARS	.40	.18
COMP.PRINT.PROOF (350)	500.00	220.00
*PP STARS: 5X TO 12X HI COL...		
*PP RCs: 2.5X TO 6X HI		
PP STATED ODDS 1:10 RETAIL..		
COMP.HEADLINERS SET (350)	300.00	135.00
*HEADLINERS STARS: 3X TO 8X HI COL		
*HEADLINERS RCs: 1.5X TO 4X HI		
HEADLINERS:ONE PER JUMBO PACK		
COMP.NATIONAL SET (350)	300.00	135.00
*NATIONAL STARS: 3X TO 8X HI COL		
*NATIONAL RCs: 1.5 TO 4X HI....		
NATIONALS:ONE PER NATIONAL PACK		

	MINT	NRMT
❑ 1 Troy Aikman	1.00	.45
❑ 2 Steve Young	.75	.35
❑ 3 John Elway	2.00	.90
❑ 4 Jim Kelly	.40	.18
❑ 5 Dan Marino	2.00	.90
❑ 6 Brett Favre	2.00	.90
❑ 7 Kerry Collins	.40	.18
❑ 8 Jeff Blake	.40	.18
❑ 9 Stan Humphries	.20	.09
❑ 10 Steve Bono	.10	.05
❑ 11 Jeff George	.20	.09
❑ 12 Mark Brunell	1.00	.45
❑ 13 Scott Mitchell	.20	.09
❑ 14 Steve McNair	.75	.35
❑ 15 Jeff Hostetler	.10	.05
❑ 16 Jim Everett	.10	.05
❑ 17 Rick Mirer	.20	.09
❑ 18 Boomer Esiason	.20	.09
❑ 19 Neil O'Donnell	.20	.09
❑ 20 Dave Brown	.10	.05
❑ 21 Erik Kramer	.10	.05
❑ 22 Trent Dilfer	.40	.18
❑ 23 Jim Harbaugh	.20	.09
❑ 24 Vinny Testaverde	.20	.09
❑ 25 Thurman Thomas	.40	.18
❑ 26 Rodney Peete	.10	.05
❑ 27 Gus Frerotte	.40	.18
❑ 28 Warren Moon	.20	.09
❑ 29 Eric Zeier	.10	.05
❑ 30 Randall Cunningham	.40	.18
❑ 31 Heath Shuler	.20	.09
❑ 32 John Friesz	.10	.05
❑ 33 Tommy Maddox	.10	.05
❑ 34 Glenn Foley	.20	.09
❑ 35 Drew Bledsoe	1.00	.45
❑ 36 Kordell Stewart	.75	.35
❑ 37 Natrone Means	.40	.18
❑ 38 Errict Rhett	.20	.09
❑ 39 Rashaan Salaam	.40	.18
❑ 40 Emmitt Smith	1.50	.70
❑ 41 Larry Centers	.20	.09
❑ 42 Terrell Davis	2.50	1.10
❑ 43 Marshall Faulk	.40	.18
❑ 44 Rodney Hampton	.20	.09
❑ 45 Byron Bam Morris	.20	.09
❑ 46 Chris Warren	.20	.09

❑ 47 Curtis Martin .75 .35
❑ 48 Ricky Watters .20 .09
❑ 49 Marcus Allen .40 .18
❑ 50 Barry Sanders 2.00 .90
❑ 51 Edgar Bennett .20 .09
❑ 52 Adrian Murrell .40 .18
❑ 53 James O. Stewart .20 .09
❑ 54 Leroy Hoard .10 .05
❑ 55 Jerome Bettis .40 .18
❑ 56 Craig Heyward .10 .05
❑ 57 Harvey Williams .10 .05
❑ 58 Bernie Parmalee .10 .05
❑ 59 Garrison Hearst .20 .09
❑ 60 Terry Allen .20 .09
❑ 61 Charlie Garner .10 .05
❑ 62 Dorsey Levens .50 .23
❑ 63 Derek Loville .10 .05
❑ 64 Greg Hill .20 .09
❑ 65 Derrick Moore .10 .05
❑ 66 Rodney Thomas .10 .05
❑ 67 Daryl Johnston .20 .09
❑ 68 Mario Bates .20 .09
❑ 69 Aaron Hayden RC .10 .05
❑ 70 Napoleon Kaufman .50 .23
❑ 71 Terry Kirby .20 .09
❑ 72 Glyn Milburn .10 .05
❑ 73 Robert Smith .20 .09
❑ 74 Ki-Jana Carter .20 .09
❑ 75 Tyrone Wheatley .20 .09
❑ 76 Erric Pegram .10 .05
❑ 77 Brian Mitchell .10 .05
❑ 78 Vaughn Dunbar .10 .05
❑ 79 Dave Meggett .10 .05
❑ 80 Scottie Graham .10 .05
❑ 81 Darick Holmes .10 .05
❑ 82 Marion Butts .10 .05
❑ 83 Harold Green .10 .05
❑ 84 Zack Crockett .10 .05
❑ 85 Amp Lee .10 .05
❑ 86 Lamont Warren .10 .05
❑ 87 Mark Chmura .20 .09
❑ 88 Irving Fryar .20 .09
❑ 89 Tim Brown .40 .18
❑ 90 Michael Irvin .40 .18
❑ 91 Tony Martin .20 .09
❑ 92 Alvin Harper .10 .05
❑ 93 Darnay Scott .20 .09
❑ 94 Eric Metcalf .10 .05
❑ 95 Michael Timpson .10 .05
❑ 96 Sean Dawkins .10 .05
❑ 97 Qadry Ismail .10 .05
❑ 98 Yancey Thigpen .20 .09
❑ 99 Joey Galloway .75 .35
❑ 100 Herman Moore .40 .18
❑ 101 J.J. Stokes .40 .18
❑ 102 Wayne Chrebet .20 .09
❑ 103 Ernest Givins .10 .05
❑ 104 Michael Jackson .20 .09
❑ 105 Henry Ellard .10 .05
❑ 106 Thomas Lewis .10 .05
❑ 107 Anthony Miller .20 .09
❑ 108 Terance Mathis .10 .05
❑ 109 Horace Copeland .10 .05
❑ 110 Rocket Ismail .10 .05
❑ 111 Quinn Early .10 .05
❑ 112 Haywood Jeffires .10 .05
❑ 113 Mark Carrier WR .10 .05
❑ 114 Brent Jones .10 .05
❑ 115 Ben Coates .20 .09
❑ 116 Ken Dilger .20 .09
❑ 117 Irv Smith .10 .05
❑ 118 Jay Novacek .10 .05
❑ 119 Tony McGee .10 .05
❑ 120 Troy Drayton .10 .05
❑ 121 Johnny Mitchell .10 .05
❑ 122 Rob Moore .20 .09
❑ 123 Kevin Williams WR .10 .05
❑ 124 O.J. McDuffie .20 .09
❑ 125 Carl Pickens .40 .18
❑ 126 Curtis Conway .40 .18
❑ 127 Ed McCaffrey .20 .09
❑ 128 Arthur Marshall .10 .05
❑ 129 Ernie Mills .10 .05
❑ 130 Cris Carter .40 .18
❑ 131 Isaac Bruce .40 .18
❑ 132 Brian Blades .10 .05
❑ 133 Michael Westbrook .40 .18
❑ 134 Andre Reed .20 .09
❑ 135 Andre Rison .20 .09
❑ 136 Brett Perriman .10 .05
❑ 137 Willie Jackson .10 .05
❑ 138 Ryan Yarborough .10 .05
❑ 139 Chris T. Jones .20 .09
❑ 140 Jerry Rice 1.00 .45
❑ 141 Lake Dawson .10 .05
❑ 142 Robert Brooks .40 .18
❑ 143 Vincent Brisby .10 .05
❑ 144 Desmond Howard .20 .09
❑ 145 Johnnie Morton .20 .09
❑ 146 Steve Tasker .10 .05
❑ 147 Ty Detmer .20 .09
❑ 148 Todd Kinchen .10 .05
❑ 149 Mike Sherrard .10 .05
❑ 150 Eric Green .10 .05
❑ 151 Mark Bruener .10 .05
❑ 152 Kyle Brady .10 .05
❑ 153 Frank Sanders .20 .09
❑ 154 Willie Green .10 .05
❑ 155 Jeff Graham .10 .05
❑ 156 Bert Emanuel .20 .09
❑ 157 Courtney Hawkins .10 .05
❑ 158 Mark Seay .10 .05
❑ 159 Chris Calloway .10 .05
❑ 160 John Taylor .10 .05
❑ 161 Fred Barnett .10 .05
❑ 162 Tamarick Vanover .20 .09
❑ 163 Keenan McCardell .40 .18
❑ 164 Bill Brooks .10 .05
❑ 165 Alexander Wright .10 .05
❑ 166 Jake Reed .20 .09
❑ 167 Floyd Turner .10 .05
❑ 168 Mike Pritchard .10 .05
❑ 169 Lawrence Dawsey .10 .05
❑ 170 Shawn Jefferson .10 .05
❑ 171 Michael Haynes .10 .05
❑ 172 Shannon Sharpe .20 .09
❑ 173 Jackie Harris .10 .05
❑ 174 Daryl Hobbs .10 .05
❑ 175 Chris Sanders .20 .09
❑ 176 Willie Davis .10 .05
❑ 177 Marco Coleman .10 .05
❑ 178 Pat Swilling .10 .05
❑ 179 Alonzo Spellman .10 .05
❑ 180 Simon Fletcher .10 .05
❑ 181 Sean Gilbert .10 .05
❑ 182 Tracy Scroggins .10 .05
❑ 183 Hugh Douglas .10 .05
❑ 184 Eric Swann .10 .05
❑ 185 Russell Maryland .10 .05
❑ 186 Warren Sapp .10 .05
❑ 187 Jim Flanigan .10 .05
❑ 188 Cortez Kennedy .10 .05
❑ 189 Andy Harmon .10 .05
❑ 190 Dan Saleaumua .10 .05
❑ 191 Kelvin Pritchett .10 .05
❑ 192 John Randle .10 .05
❑ 193 Dan Wilkinson .10 .05
❑ 194 Chester McGlockton .10 .05
❑ 195 Leon Lett .10 .05
❑ 196 Neil Smith .10 .05
❑ 197 Mike Mamula .10 .05
❑ 198 Mike Jones .10 .05
❑ 199 Reggie White .40 .18
❑ 200 Anthony Pleasant .10 .05
❑ 201 Phil Hansen .10 .05
❑ 202 Ray Seals .10 .05
❑ 203 Tony Bennett .10 .05
❑ 204 Leslie O'Neal .10 .05
❑ 205 Jeff Cross .10 .05
❑ 206 Anthony Cook .10 .05
❑ 207 Clyde Simmons .10 .05
❑ 208 Renaldo Turnbull .10 .05
❑ 209 Charles Haley .20 .09
❑ 210 John Copeland .10 .05
❑ 211 John Thierry .10 .05
❑ 212 Michael Strahan .10 .05
❑ 213 Jeff Lageman .10 .05
❑ 214 William Fuller .10 .05
❑ 215 Rickey Jackson .10 .05
❑ 216 Wayne Martin .10 .05
❑ 217 Steve Emtman .10 .05
❑ 218 Shawn Lee .10 .05
❑ 219 Chris Zorich .10 .05
❑ 220 Henry Thomas .10 .05
❑ 221 Dana Stubblefield .20 .09
❑ 222 D'Marco Farr .10 .05
❑ 223 Pierce Holt .10 .05
❑ 224 Sean Jones .10 .05
❑ 225 Robert Porcher .10 .05
❑ 226 Kevin Carter .10 .05
❑ 227 Chris Doleman .10 .05
❑ 228 Tony Tolbert .10 .05
❑ 229 Bruce Smith .20 .09
❑ 230 Marvin Washington .10 .05
❑ 231 Blaine Bishop .10 .05
❑ 232 Bryant Young .20 .09
❑ 233 Rob Burnett .10 .05
❑ 234 Lawrence Phillips RC .50 .23
❑ 235 Trev Alberts .10 .05
❑ 236 Eric Curry .10 .05
❑ 237 Anthony Smith .10 .05
❑ 238 Sam Mills .10 .05
❑ 239 Seth Joyner .10 .05
❑ 240 Quentin Coryatt .10 .05
❑ 241 Levon Kirkland .10 .05
❑ 242 Cornelius Bennett .10 .05
❑ 243 Chris Spielman .10 .05
❑ 244 Mo Lewis .10 .05
❑ 245 Lee Woodall .10 .05
❑ 246 Derrick Thomas .20 .09
❑ 247 Willie McGinest .10 .05
❑ 248 Terry Wooden .10 .05
❑ 249 Greg Lloyd .20 .09
❑ 250 Jack Del Rio .10 .05
❑ 251 Hardy Nickerson .10 .05
❑ 252 Micheal Barrow .10 .05
❑ 253 Lamar Lathon .10 .05
❑ 254 Bryan Cox .10 .05
❑ 255 Randy Kirk .10 .05
❑ 256 Jessie Tuggle .10 .05
❑ 257 Roman Phifer .10 .05
❑ 258 Ken Harvey .10 .05
❑ 259 Junior Seau .20 .09
❑ 260 Pepper Johnson .10 .05
❑ 261 Chris Slade .10 .05
❑ 262 Gary Plummer .10 .05
❑ 263 Wayne Simmons .10 .05
❑ 264 Bryce Paup .10 .05
❑ 265 William Thomas .10 .05
❑ 266 Kevin Greene .20 .09
❑ 267 Bobby Engram RC .40 .18
❑ 268 Ken Norton .10 .05
❑ 269 Eric Hill .10 .05
❑ 270 Darion Conner .10 .05
❑ 271 Tyrone Poole .10 .05
❑ 272 Cris Dishman .10 .05
❑ 273 Marcus Jones RC .10 .05
❑ 274 Rod Woodson .20 .09
❑ 275 Mark McMillian .10 .05
❑ 276 Dale Carter .10 .05
❑ 277 Darrell Green .10 .05
❑ 278 Donnell Woolford .10 .05
❑ 279 Troy Vincent .10 .05
❑ 280 Larry Brown .10 .05
❑ 281 Aeneas Williams .10 .05
❑ 282 Eric Allen .10 .05
❑ 283 Ray Buchanan .10 .05
❑ 284 Ty Law .10 .05
❑ 285 Eric Davis .10 .05
❑ 286 Todd Lyght .10 .05
❑ 287 Terry McDaniel .10 .05
❑ 288 Darryll Lewis .10 .05
❑ 289 Deion Sanders .60 .25
❑ 290 Phillippi Sparks .10 .05
❑ 291 Bobby Taylor .10 .05
❑ 292 Mark Collins .10 .05
❑ 293 Steve Atwater .10 .05
❑ 294 Stanley Richard .20 .09
❑ 295 Stevon Moore .10 .05
❑ 296 Bennie Blades .10 .05
❑ 297 Tim McDonald .10 .05
❑ 298 Shaun Gayle .10 .05
❑ 299 Darren Woodson .20 .09
❑ 300 Mark Carrier DB .10 .05
❑ 301 Carnell Lake .10 .05
❑ 302 James Washington .10 .05
❑ 303 LeRoy Butler .10 .05
❑ 304 Henry Jones .10 .05

Card	Mint	NrMt
❑ 305 Darryl Williams	.10	.05
❑ 306 Darren Perry	.10	.05
❑ 307 Merton Hanks	.10	.05
❑ 308 Orlando Thomas	.10	.05
❑ 309 Eric Turner	.10	.05
❑ 310 Nate Newton	.10	.05
❑ 311 Steve Wisniewski	.10	.05
❑ 312 Derrick Deese	.10	.05
❑ 313 Larry Allen	.10	.05
❑ 314 Aaron Taylor	.10	.05
❑ 315 Blake Brockermeyer	.10	.05
❑ 316 William Roaf	.10	.05
❑ 317 Jumbo Elliott	.10	.05
❑ 318 Keyshawn Johnson RC	2.00	.90
❑ 319 Karim Abdul-Jabbar RC	.75	.35
❑ 320 Kevin Hardy RC	.40	.18
❑ 321 Duane Clemons RC	.10	.05
❑ 322 Jevon Langford RC	.10	.05
❑ 323 Mike Alstott RC	1.25	.55
❑ 324 Scott Greene RC	.10	.05
❑ 325 Derrick Mayes RC	.75	.35
❑ 326 Chris Doering RC	.10	.05
❑ 327 Amani Toomer RC	.40	.18
❑ 328 Eric Moulds RC	1.50	.70
❑ 329 Alex Molden RC	.10	.05
❑ 330 Lawyer Milloy RC	.20	.09
❑ 331 Daryl Gardener RC	.10	.05
❑ 332 Randall Godfrey RC	.10	.05
❑ 333 Willie Anderson RC	.10	.05
❑ 334 Tony Banks RC	.75	.35
❑ 335 Jeff Lewis RC	.50	.23
❑ 336 Roman Oben RC	.10	.05
❑ 337 Andre Johnson RC	.10	.05
❑ 338 Brian Roche RC	.10	.05
❑ 339 Johnny McWilliams RC	.20	.09
❑ 340 Alex Van Dyke RC	.20	.09
❑ 341 Ray Mickens RC	.10	.05
❑ 342 Marvin Harrison RC	2.00	.90
❑ 343 Terry Glenn RC	1.25	.55
❑ 344 Tim Biakabutuka RC	.75	.35
❑ 345 Simeon Rice RC	.40	.18
❑ 346 Cedric Jones RC	.10	.05
❑ 347 Eddie George RC	2.50	1.10
❑ 348 Drew Bledsoe Checklist	.40	.18
❑ 349 Emmitt Smith Checklist	.30	.14
❑ 350 Keyshawn Johnson Checklist	.40	.18

1996 Pro Line Autographs

	MINT	NRMT
COMP.GOLD SET (73)	2800.00	1250.00
COMMON GOLD FOIL	12.00	5.50
SEMISTARS GOLD FOIL	20.00	9.00
STARS GOLD FOIL	30.00	13.50

GOLD CARDS PRICED BELOW..
FIVE CARDS EXIST W/GOLD FOIL ONLY
GOLD STAT.ODDS 1:170 HOB/RET, 1:200 JUM

COMP.BLUE SET (68)	650.00	300.00
COMMON BLUE FOIL	6.00	2.70
SEMISTARS BLUE FOIL	10.00	4.50

*BLUE FOIL CARDS: .3X TO .6X GOLDS
BLUE STAT.ODDS 1:25 HOB/RET, 1:90 JUM
UNNUMBERED CARDS LISTED ALPHA.

Card	Mint	NrMt
❑ 1 Troy Aikman Emmitt Smith Gold Only	500.00	220.00
❑ 2 Eric Allen	12.00	5.50
❑ 3 Mike Alstott	30.00	13.50
❑ 4 Tony Banks	30.00	13.50
❑ 5 Blaine Bishop	12.00	5.50
❑ 6 Drew Bledsoe	80.00	36.00
❑ 7 Tim Brown	20.00	9.00
❑ 8 Marion Butts	12.00	5.50
❑ 9 Sedric Clark	12.00	5.50
❑ 10 Duane Clemons	12.00	5.50
❑ 11 Marco Coleman	12.00	5.50
❑ 12 Eric Davis	12.00	5.50
❑ 13 Derrick Deese	12.00	5.50
❑ 14 Jack Del Rio	12.00	5.50
❑ 15 Ty Detmer	20.00	9.00
❑ 16 Chris Doering	12.00	5.50
❑ 17 Jumbo Elliott	12.00	5.50
❑ 18 Marshall Faulk	40.00	18.00
❑ 19 Glenn Foley	12.00	5.50
❑ 20 John Friesz	12.00	5.50
❑ 21 Daryl Gardener	20.00	9.00
❑ 22 Randall Godfrey	12.00	5.50
❑ 23 Scott Greene	12.00	5.50
❑ 24 Rhett Hall	12.00	5.50
❑ 25 Merton Hanks	12.00	5.50
❑ 26 Kevin Hardy	12.00	5.50
❑ 27 Richard Huntley	12.00	5.50
❑ 28 Michael Jackson	12.00	5.50
❑ 29 Ron Jaworski	20.00	9.00
❑ 30 Andre Johnson	12.00	5.50
❑ 31 Keyshawn Johnson	60.00	27.00
❑ 32 Keyshawn Johnson Neil O'Donnell Gold Only	175.00	80.00
❑ 33 Mike Jones	12.00	5.50
❑ 34 Jim Kiick	30.00	13.50
❑ 35 Jeff Lewis	20.00	9.00
❑ 36 Tommy Maddox	12.00	5.50
❑ 37 Arthur Marshall	12.00	5.50
❑ 38 Russell Maryland	12.00	5.50
❑ 39 Derrick Mayes	30.00	13.50
❑ 40 Ed McCaffrey	20.00	9.00
❑ 41 Keenan McCardell	20.00	9.00
❑ 42 Terry McDaniel	12.00	5.50
❑ 43 Tim McDonald	12.00	5.50
❑ 44 Willie McGinest	12.00	5.50
❑ 45 Mark McMillian	12.00	5.50
❑ 46 Johnny McWilliams	12.00	5.50
❑ 47 Ray Mickens	12.00	5.50
❑ 48 Anthony Miller	12.00	5.50
❑ 49 Rick Mirer	30.00	13.50
❑ 50 Alex Molden	12.00	5.50
❑ 51 Johnnie Morton	20.00	9.00
❑ 52 Eric Moulds	30.00	13.50
❑ 53 Roman Oben	12.00	5.50
❑ 54 Neil O'Donnell Gold Only	60.00	27.00
❑ 55 Leslie O'Neal	12.00	5.50
❑ 56 Roman Phifer	12.00	5.50
❑ 57 Gary Plummer	12.00	5.50
❑ 58 Jim Plunkett	30.00	13.50
❑ 59 Stanley Pritchett	20.00	9.00
❑ 60 John Randle	12.00	5.50
❑ 61 Brian Roche	12.00	5.50
❑ 62 Orpheus Roye	12.00	5.50
❑ 63 Mark Seay	12.00	5.50
❑ 64 Mike Sherrard	12.00	5.50
❑ 65 Chris Slade	12.00	5.50
❑ 66 Scott Slutzker	12.00	5.50
❑ 67 Emmitt Smith Gold Only	300.00	135.00
❑ 68 Steve Taneyhill	12.00	5.50
❑ 69 Robb Thomas	12.00	5.50
❑ 70 William Thomas	12.00	5.50
❑ 71 Alex Van Dyke	30.00	13.50
❑ 72 Randy White	30.00	13.50
❑ 73 Steve Young Gold Only	120.00	55.00

1997 Pro Line

	MINT	NRMT
COMPLETE SET (300)	25.00	11.00
COMMON CARD (1-300)	.10	.05
SEMISTARS	.20	.09
UNLISTED STARS	.40	.18
COMP.FAVRE SET (9)	70.00	32.00
COMMON FAVRE (BF1-BF9)	8.00	3.60
BRETT FAVRE (BF10)	120.00	55.00

1-9 STATED ODDS 1:28
10 STATED ODDS 1:3024

Card	Mint	NrMt
❑ 1 Larry Centers	.20	.09
❑ 2 Kent Graham	.10	.05
❑ 3 LeShon Johnson	.10	.05
❑ 4 Leeland McElroy	.10	.05
❑ 5 Rob Moore	.20	.09
❑ 6 Simeon Rice	.20	.09
❑ 7 Frank Sanders	.20	.09
❑ 8 Eric Swann	.10	.05
❑ 9 Aeneas Williams	.10	.05
❑ 10 Jamal Anderson	.60	.25
❑ 11 Cornelius Bennett	.10	.05
❑ 12 Ray Buchanan	.10	.05
❑ 13 Bert Emanuel	.20	.09
❑ 14 Terance Mathis	.20	.09
❑ 15 Eric Metcalf	.20	.09
❑ 16 Jessie Tuggle	.10	.05
❑ 17 Derrick Alexander WR	.20	.09
❑ 18 Earnest Byner	.10	.05
❑ 19 Michael Jackson	.20	.09
❑ 20 Antonio Langham	.10	.05
❑ 21 Ray Lewis	.10	.05
❑ 22 Byron Bam Morris	.10	.05
❑ 23 Jonathan Ogden	.10	.05
❑ 24 Vinny Testaverde	.20	.09
❑ 25 Eric Moulds	.40	.18
❑ 26 Todd Collins	.10	.05
❑ 27 Quinn Early	.10	.05
❑ 28 Phil Hansen	.10	.05
❑ 29 Darick Holmes	.10	.05
❑ 30 Bryce Paup	.10	.05
❑ 31 Andre Reed	.20	.09
❑ 32 Bruce Smith	.20	.09
❑ 33 Chris Spielman	.10	.05
❑ 34 Matt Stevens	.10	.05
❑ 35 Steve Tasker	.10	.05
❑ 36 Thurman Thomas	.40	.18
❑ 37 Mark Carrier WR	.10	.05
❑ 38 Kerry Collins	.20	.09
❑ 39 Tim Biakabutuka	.20	.09
❑ 40 Eric Davis	.10	.05
❑ 41 Kevin Greene	.20	.09
❑ 42 Anthony Johnson	.10	.05
❑ 43 Lamar Lathon	.10	.05
❑ 44 Sam Mills	.10	.05
❑ 45 Wesley Walls	.20	.09
❑ 46 Muhsin Muhammad	.20	.09
❑ 47 Mark Carrier DB	.10	.05
❑ 48 Curtis Conway	.20	.09
❑ 49 Bryan Cox	.10	.05
❑ 50 Bobby Engram	.20	.09
❑ 51 Raymont Harris	.10	.05
❑ 52 Walt Harris	.10	.05
❑ 53 Rick Mirer	.10	.05
❑ 54 Rashaan Salaam	.10	.05
❑ 55 Alonzo Spellman	.10	.05
❑ 56 Ashley Ambrose	.10	.05
❑ 57 Jeff Blake	.20	.09
❑ 58 Ki-Jana Carter	.10	.05
❑ 59 John Copeland	.10	.05
❑ 60 James Francis	.10	.05
❑ 61 Tony McGee	.10	.05
❑ 62 Carl Pickens	.40	.18
❑ 63 Darnay Scott	.20	.09
❑ 64 Steve Tovar	.10	.05
❑ 65 Dan Wilkinson	.10	.05
❑ 66 Troy Aikman	1.00	.45
❑ 67 Eric Bjornson	.10	.05
❑ 68 Michael Irvin	.40	.18
❑ 69 Daryl Johnston	.20	.09
❑ 70 Nate Newton	.10	.05
❑ 71 Deion Sanders	.40	.18
❑ 72 Emmitt Smith	1.50	.70
❑ 73 Kevin Smith	.10	.05
❑ 74 Kevin Williams	.10	.05
❑ 75 Darren Woodson	.10	.05
❑ 76 Mark Tuinei	.10	.05
❑ 77 Steve Atwater	.10	.05
❑ 78 Terrell Davis	1.50	.70

❑ 79 John Elway 2.00 .90
❑ 80 Ed McCaffrey .20 .09
❑ 81 Anthony Miller .10 .05
❑ 82 John Mobley .10 .05
❑ 83 Michael Dean Perry .10 .05
❑ 84 Shannon Sharpe .20 .09
❑ 85 Alfred Williams .10 .05
❑ 86 Reggie Brown LB .20 .09
❑ 87 Luther Elliss .10 .05
❑ 88 Scott Mitchell .20 .09
❑ 89 Herman Moore .40 .18
❑ 90 Johnnie Morton .20 .09
❑ 91 Brett Perriman .10 .05
❑ 92 Robert Porcher .10 .05
❑ 93 Barry Sanders 2.00 .90
❑ 94 Henry Thomas .10 .05
❑ 95 Edgar Bennett .20 .09
❑ 96 Robert Brooks .20 .09
❑ 97 Gilbert Brown .10 .05
❑ 98 LeRoy Butler .10 .05
❑ 99 Mark Chmura .20 .09
❑ 100 Brett Favre 2.00 .90
❑ 101 Santana Dotson .10 .05
❑ 102 Antonio Freeman .50 .23
❑ 103 Dorsey Levens .40 .18
❑ 104 Wayne Simmons .10 .05
❑ 105 Reggie White .40 .18
❑ 106 Willie Davis .10 .05
❑ 107 Eddie George 1.00 .45
❑ 108 Darryll Lewis .10 .05
❑ 109 Steve McNair .50 .23
❑ 110 Marcus Robertson .10 .05
❑ 111 Chris Sanders .10 .05
❑ 112 Al Smith .10 .05
❑ 113 Tony Bennett .10 .05
❑ 114 Quentin Coryatt .10 .05
❑ 115 Ken Dilger .10 .05
❑ 116 Sean Dawkins .10 .05
❑ 117 Marshall Faulk .40 .18
❑ 118 Jim Harbaugh .20 .09
❑ 119 Marvin Harrison .40 .18
❑ 120 Jeff Herrod .10 .05
❑ 121 Tony Boselli .10 .05
❑ 122 Tony Brackens .10 .05
❑ 123 Mark Brunell 1.00 .45
❑ 124 Kevin Hardy .10 .05
❑ 125 Jeff Lageman .10 .05
❑ 126 Keenan McCardell .20 .09
❑ 127 Natrone Means .40 .18
❑ 128 Eddie Robinson .10 .05
❑ 129 Jimmy Smith .20 .09
❑ 130 James O.Stewart .20 .09
❑ 131 Marcus Allen .40 .18
❑ 132 Dale Carter .10 .05
❑ 133 Mark Collins .10 .05
❑ 134 Lake Dawson .10 .05
❑ 135 Greg Hill .10 .05
❑ 136 Sean LaChapelle .10 .05
❑ 137 Chris Penn .10 .05
❑ 138 Derrick Thomas .20 .09
❑ 139 Tamarick Vanover .20 .09
❑ 140 Elvis Grbac .20 .09
❑ 141 Karim Abdul-Jabbar .40 .18
❑ 142 Fred Barnett .10 .05
❑ 143 Terrell Buckley .10 .05
❑ 144 Daryl Gardener .10 .05
❑ 145 Randal Hill .10 .05
❑ 146 Dan Marino 2.00 .90
❑ 147 O.J. McDuffie .20 .09
❑ 148 Jerris McPhail .10 .05
❑ 149 Zach Thomas .20 .09
❑ 150 Cris Carter .40 .18
❑ 151 Dixon Edwards .10 .05
❑ 152 Leroy Hoard .10 .05
❑ 153 Qadry Ismail .20 .09
❑ 154 Brad Johnson .50 .23
❑ 155 John Randle .10 .05
❑ 156 Jake Reed .20 .09
❑ 157 Robert Smith .20 .09
❑ 158 Orlando Thomas .10 .05
❑ 159 Dewayne Washington .10 .05
❑ 160 Drew Bledsoe 1.00 .45
❑ 161 Tedy Bruschi .10 .05
❑ 162 Willie Clay .10 .05
❑ 163 Ben Coates .20 .09
❑ 164 Terry Glenn .40 .18
❑ 165 Shawn Jefferson .10 .05
❑ 166 Ty Law .10 .05
❑ 167 Curtis Martin .50 .23
❑ 168 Willie McGinest .10 .05
❑ 169 Chris Slade .10 .05
❑ 170 Eric Allen .10 .05
❑ 171 Mario Bates .10 .05
❑ 172 Heath Shuler .10 .05
❑ 173 Michael Haynes .10 .05
❑ 174 Wayne Martin .10 .05
❑ 175 Torrance Small .10 .05
❑ 176 Dave Brown .10 .05
❑ 177 Chris Calloway .10 .05
❑ 178 Rodney Hampton .20 .09
❑ 179 Danny Kanell .20 .09
❑ 180 Thomas Lewis .10 .05
❑ 181 Jason Sehorn .20 .09
❑ 182 Amani Toomer .20 .09
❑ 183 Charles Way .20 .09
❑ 184 Tyrone Wheatley .20 .09
❑ 185 Wayne Chrebet .40 .18
❑ 186 Hugh Douglas .10 .05
❑ 187 Aaron Glenn .10 .05
❑ 188 Jeff Graham .10 .05
❑ 189 Keyshawn Johnson .40 .18
❑ 190 Mo Lewis .10 .05
❑ 191 Adrian Murrell .20 .09
❑ 192 Neil O'Donnell .20 .09
❑ 193 Tim Brown .40 .18
❑ 194 Rickey Dudley .20 .09
❑ 195 Jeff George .20 .09
❑ 196 Napoleon Kaufman .40 .18
❑ 197 Russell Maryland .10 .05
❑ 198 Terry McDaniel .10 .05
❑ 199 Chester McGlockton .10 .05
❑ 200 Desmond Howard .20 .09
❑ 201 Pat Swilling .10 .05
❑ 202 Ty Detmer .20 .09
❑ 203 Jason Dunn .10 .05
❑ 204 Ray Farmer .10 .05
❑ 205 Irving Fryar .20 .09
❑ 206 Chris T. Jones .10 .05
❑ 207 Bobby Taylor .10 .05
❑ 208 William Thomas .10 .05
❑ 209 Hollis Thomas .10 .05
❑ 210 Kevin Turner .10 .05
❑ 211 Ricky Watters .20 .09
❑ 212 Jerome Bettis .40 .18
❑ 213 Andre Hastings .10 .05
❑ 214 Charles Johnson .20 .09
❑ 215 Levon Kirkland .10 .05
❑ 216 Carnell Lake .10 .05
❑ 217 Greg Lloyd .10 .05
❑ 218 Darren Perry .10 .05
❑ 219 Kordell Stewart .50 .23
❑ 220 Rod Woodson .20 .09
❑ 221 Andre Coleman .10 .05
❑ 222 Marco Coleman .10 .05
❑ 223 Leonard Russell .10 .05
❑ 224 Stan Humphries .20 .09
❑ 225 Shawn Lee .10 .05
❑ 226 Tony Martin .20 .09
❑ 227 Chris Mims .10 .05
❑ 228 Junior Seau .20 .09
❑ 229 Chris Doleman .10 .05
❑ 230 William Floyd .20 .09
❑ 231 Merton Hanks .10 .05
❑ 232 Brent Jones .20 .09
❑ 233 Terry Kirby .20 .09
❑ 234 Ken Norton .10 .05
❑ 235 Terrell Owens .40 .18
❑ 236 Jerry Rice 1.00 .45
❑ 237 Bryant Young .10 .05
❑ 238 Steve Young .60 .25
❑ 239 Garrison Hearst .20 .09
❑ 240 Brian Blades .10 .05
❑ 241 Chad Brown .10 .05
❑ 242 John Friesz .10 .05
❑ 243 Joey Galloway .50 .23
❑ 244 Cortez Kennedy .10 .05
❑ 245 Chris Warren .20 .09
❑ 246 Darryl Williams .10 .05
❑ 247 Tony Banks .20 .09
❑ 248 Isaac Bruce .40 .18
❑ 249 Kevin Carter .10 .05
❑ 250 Eddie Kennison .20 .09
❑ 251 Todd Lyght .10 .05
❑ 252 Leslie O'Neal .10 .05
❑ 253 Anthony Parker .10 .05
❑ 254 Roman Phifer .10 .05
❑ 255 Lawrence Phillips .10 .05
❑ 256 Mike Alstott .40 .18
❑ 257 Derrick Brooks .10 .05
❑ 258 Trent Dilfer .40 .18
❑ 259 Jackie Harris .10 .05
❑ 260 Hardy Nickerson .10 .05
❑ 261 Errict Rhett .10 .05
❑ 262 Warren Sapp .20 .09
❑ 263 Terry Allen .40 .18
❑ 264 Jamie Asher .10 .05
❑ 265 Henry Ellard .10 .05
❑ 266 Gus Frerotte .10 .05
❑ 267 Sean Gilbert .10 .05
❑ 268 Darrell Green .20 .09
❑ 269 Ken Harvey .10 .05
❑ 270 Brian Mitchell .10 .05
❑ 271 Michael Westbrook .20 .09
❑ 272 Koy Detmer RC .50 .23
❑ 273 Yatil Green RC .20 .09
❑ 274 Troy Davis RC .40 .18
❑ 275 Darrell Russell RC .10 .05
❑ 276 Warrick Dunn RC 1.25 .55
❑ 277 David LaFleur RC .20 .09
❑ 278 Tony Gonzalez RC 1.25 .55
❑ 279 Jake Plummer RC 3.00 1.35
❑ 280 Antowain Smith RC 1.00 .45
❑ 281 Peter Boulware RC .20 .09
❑ 282 Shawn Springs RC .20 .09
❑ 283 Bryant Westbrook RC .10 .05
❑ 284 Rae Carruth RC .40 .18
❑ 285 Corey Dillon RC 1.50 .70
❑ 286 Byron Hanspard RC .75 .35
❑ 287 Greg Jones RC .10 .05
❑ 288 Trevor Pryce RC .10 .05
❑ 289 Michael Booker RC .10 .05
❑ 290 Orlando Pace RC .10 .05
❑ 291 James Farrior RC .10 .05
❑ 292 Walter Jones RC .10 .05
❑ 293 Reinard Wilson RC .10 .05
❑ 294 Ike Hilliard RC .75 .35
❑ 295 Kenard Lang RC .10 .05
❑ 296 Reidel Anthony RC .75 .35
❑ 297 Brett Favre .40 .18
Checklist back
❑ 298 Kerry Collins .20 .09
Checklist back
❑ 299 Drew Bledsoe .20 .09
Checklist back
❑ 300 Terrell Davis .40 .18
Checklist back

1997 Pro Line Autographs

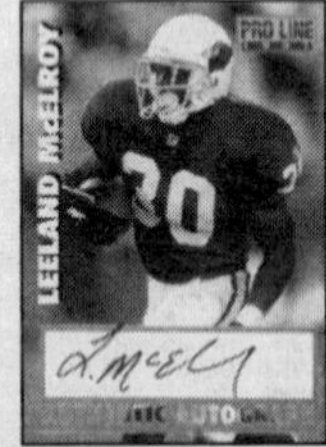

	MINT	NRMT
COMPLETE SET (55)	1000.00	450.00
COMMON CARD	10.00	4.50
SEMISTARS	15.00	6.75
UNLISTED STARS	20.00	9.00
STATED ODDS 1:28		

❑ 1 Karim Abdul-Jabbar 20.00 9.00
❑ 2 Troy Aikman 120.00 55.00
❑ 3 Eric Allen 10.00 4.50

Card	MINT	NRMT
❑ 4 Mike Alstott	30.00	13.50
❑ 5 Marco Battaglia	10.00	4.50
❑ 6 Eric Bjornson	10.00	4.50
❑ 7 Peter Boulware	15.00	6.75
❑ 8 Ray Buchanon	10.00	4.50
❑ 9 Rae Carruth	15.00	6.75
❑ 10 Kerry Collins	15.00	6.75
❑ 11 Stephen Davis	40.00	18.00
❑ 12 Terrell Davis	100.00	45.00
❑ 13 Derrick Deese	10.00	4.50
❑ 14 Koy Detmer	10.00	4.50
❑ 15 Ken Dilger	10.00	4.50
❑ 16 Corey Dillon	30.00	13.50
❑ 17 Hugh Douglas	10.00	4.50
❑ 18 Jason Dunn	10.00	4.50
❑ 19 Warrick Dunn	25.00	11.00
❑ 20 Ray Farmer	10.00	4.50
❑ 21 Brett Favre	150.00	70.00
❑ 22 Joey Galloway	20.00	9.00
❑ 23 Norberto Garrido	10.00	4.50
❑ 24 Terry Glenn	30.00	13.50
❑ 25 Tony Gonzalez	25.00	11.00
❑ 26 Byron Hanspard	20.00	9.00
❑ 27 Kevin Hardy	10.00	4.50
❑ 28 Steve Israel	10.00	4.50
❑ 29 Brad Johnson	30.00	13.50
❑ 30 Keyshawn Johnson	50.00	22.00
❑ 31 Lance Johnstone	10.00	4.50
❑ 32 Greg Jones	10.00	4.50
❑ 33 Mike Jones	10.00	4.50
❑ 34 Danny Kanell	15.00	6.75
❑ 35 David LaFleur	15.00	6.75
❑ 36 Keenan McCardell	15.00	6.75
❑ 37 Leeland McElroy	10.00	4.50
❑ 38 Willie McGinest	10.00	4.50
❑ 39 Mark McMillian	10.00	4.50
❑ 40 Nate Newton	10.00	4.50
❑ 41 Jake Plummer	50.00	22.00
❑ 42 Trevor Pryce	10.00	4.50
❑ 43 John Randle	10.00	4.50
❑ 44 Simeon Rice	15.00	6.75
❑ 45 Jon Runyan	10.00	4.50
❑ 46 Chris Slade	10.00	4.50
❑ 47 Antowain Smith	20.00	9.00
❑ 48 Emmitt Smith	150.00	70.00
❑ 49 Jimmy Smith	15.00	6.75
❑ 50 Matt Stevens	10.00	4.50
❑ 51 Kordell Stewart	50.00	22.00
❑ 52 Mark Tuinei	10.00	4.50
❑ 53 Bryant Westbrook	10.00	4.50
❑ 54 Brian Williams LB	10.00	4.50
❑ 55 Dusty Zeigler	10.00	4.50

1997 Pro Line Autographs Emerald

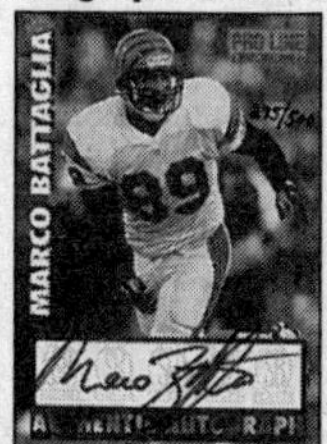

	MINT	NRMT
COMPLETE SET (43)	2000.00	900.00
COMMON CARD	20.00	9.00
SEMISTARS	25.00	11.00
UNLISTED STARS	40.00	18.00

RANDOM INSERTS IN PACKS
SET REPORTED TO BE 43-CARDS

Card	MINT	NRMT
❑ 1 Karim Abdul-Jabbar/190	40.00	18.00
❑ 2 Troy Aikman/40	400.00	180.00
❑ 3 Eric Allen/250	20.00	9.00
❑ 4 Marco Battaglia/500	20.00	9.00
❑ 5 Eric Bjornson/390	20.00	9.00
❑ 6 Peter Boulware/430	25.00	11.00
❑ 7 Ray Buchanon/390	20.00	9.00
❑ 8 Rae Carruth/525	40.00	18.00
❑ 9 Kerry Collins/170	40.00	18.00
❑ 10 Stephen Davis/530	60.00	27.00
❑ 11 Terrell Davis/100	200.00	90.00
❑ 14 Ken Dilger/525	20.00	9.00
❑ 15 Corey Dillon/470	50.00	22.00
❑ 16 Hugh Douglas/400	20.00	9.00
❑ 17 Jason Dunn/525	20.00	9.00
❑ 18 Warrick Dunn/430	40.00	18.00
❑ 19 Ray Farmer/340	20.00	9.00
❑ 20 Brett Favre/100	300.00	135.00
❑ 21 Joey Galloway/300	50.00	22.00
❑ 23 Terry Glenn/380	50.00	22.00
❑ 24 Byron Hanspard/500	40.00	18.00
❑ 25 Kevin Hardy/500	20.00	9.00
❑ 27 Brad Johnson/410	50.00	22.00
❑ 28 Keyshawn Johnson/100	100.00	45.00
❑ 29 Greg Jones/470	20.00	9.00
❑ 31 Danny Kanell/450	25.00	11.00
❑ 32 David LaFleur/500	20.00	9.00
❑ 33 Keenan McCardell/220	25.00	11.00
❑ 34 Leeland McElroy/440	20.00	9.00
❑ 35 Willie McGinest/210	20.00	9.00
❑ 37 Nate Newton/340	20.00	9.00
❑ 38 Jake Plummer/440	100.00	45.00
❑ 39 John Randle/400	20.00	9.00
❑ 40 Simeon Rice/375	25.00	11.00
❑ 41 Jon Runyan/500	20.00	9.00
❑ 42 Chris Slade/260	20.00	9.00
❑ 44 Emmitt Smith/200	150.00	70.00
❑ 45 Jimmy Smith/280	25.00	11.00
❑ 46 Matt Stevens/450	20.00	9.00
❑ 47 Kordell Stewart/130	80.00	36.00
❑ 48 Mark Tuinei/400	20.00	9.00
❑ 49 Bryant Westbrook/525	25.00	11.00
❑ 51 Dusty Zeigler/480	20.00	9.00

1997 Pro Line DC3 Autographs

	MINT	NRMT
COMPLETE SET (6)	500.00	220.00
COMMON CARD (1-6)	25.00	11.00

STATED ODDS 1:240
STATED PRINT RUN 300 SER.#'d SETS

Card	MINT	NRMT
❑ 1 Kordell Stewart	80.00	36.00
❑ 2 Kerry Collins	25.00	11.00
❑ 3 Terrell Davis	200.00	90.00
❑ 4 Eddie George	120.00	55.00
❑ 5 Karim Abdul-Jabbar	30.00	13.50
❑ 6 Keyshawn Johnson	100.00	45.00

1997 Pro Line Gems

	MINT	NRMT
COMPLETE SET (100)	20.00	9.00
COMMON CARD (1-100)	.10	.05
SEMISTARS	.20	.09
UNLISTED STARS	.30	.14

FAVRE CR1 STATED ODDS 1:240

Card	MINT	NRMT
❑ 1 Brett Favre	2.00	.90
❑ 2 Robert Brooks	.20	.09
❑ 3 Reggie White	.30	.14
❑ 4 Drew Bledsoe	1.00	.45
❑ 5 Curtis Martin	.50	.23
❑ 6 Terry Glenn	.30	.14
❑ 7 Kerry Collins	.20	.09
❑ 8 Kevin Greene	.20	.09
❑ 9 Troy Aikman	1.00	.45
❑ 10 Emmitt Smith	1.50	.70
❑ 11 Deion Sanders	.30	.14
❑ 12 John Elway	2.00	.90
❑ 13 Terrell Davis	1.50	.70
❑ 14 Kordell Stewart	.50	.23
❑ 15 Jerome Bettis	.30	.14
❑ 16 Steve Young	.60	.25
❑ 17 Jerry Rice	1.00	.45
❑ 18 Bruce Smith	.20	.09
❑ 19 Thurman Thomas	.30	.14
❑ 20 Jim Harbaugh	.20	.09
❑ 21 Marshall Faulk	.30	.14
❑ 22 Marvin Harrison	.30	.14
❑ 23 Ricky Watters	.20	.09
❑ 24 Seth Joyner	.10	.05
❑ 25 Mark Brunell	1.00	.45
❑ 26 Natrone Means	.30	.14
❑ 27 Dan Marino	2.00	.90
❑ 28 Zach Thomas	.20	.09
❑ 29 Karim Abdul-Jabbar	.30	.14
❑ 30 Isaac Bruce	.30	.14
❑ 31 Eddie Kennison	.20	.09
❑ 32 Tony Banks	.20	.09
❑ 33 Tony Martin	.20	.09
❑ 34 Junior Seau	.20	.09
❑ 35 Barry Sanders	2.00	.90
❑ 36 Herman Moore	.30	.14
❑ 37 Leeland McElroy	.10	.05
❑ 38 Jamal Anderson	.30	.14
❑ 39 Rick Mirer	.10	.05
❑ 40 Rashaan Salaam	.10	.05
❑ 41 Vinny Testaverde	.20	.09
❑ 42 Elvis Grbac	.20	.09
❑ 43 Cris Carter	.30	.14
❑ 44 Brad Johnson	.50	.23
❑ 45 Keyshawn Johnson	.30	.14
❑ 46 Adrian Murrell	.20	.09
❑ 47 Joey Galloway	.30	.14
❑ 48 Trent Dilfer	.30	.14
❑ 49 Gus Frerotte	.10	.05
❑ 50 Terry Allen	.30	.14
❑ 51 Tim Brown	.30	.14
❑ 52 Desmond Howard	.20	.09
❑ 53 Jeff George	.20	.09
❑ 54 Heath Shuler	.10	.05
❑ 55 Steve McNair	.50	.23
❑ 56 Eddie George	1.00	.45
❑ 57 Jeff Blake	.20	.09
❑ 58 Carl Pickens	.30	.14
❑ 59 Dave Brown	.10	.05
❑ 60 Brett Favre CL	.40	.18
❑ 61 Antowain Smith	.30	.14
❑ 62 Emmitt Smith PL	.75	.35
❑ 63 Terry Glenn PL	.20	.09
❑ 64 Herman Moore PL	.20	.09
❑ 65 Barry Sanders PL	1.00	.45
❑ 66 Derrick Thomas PL	.20	.09
❑ 67 Brett Favre PL	1.00	.45
❑ 68 Warrick Dunn	.50	.23
❑ 69 Emmitt Smith PL	.75	.35
❑ 70 Brett Favre CL	.40	.18
❑ 71 Orlando Pace RC	.10	.05
❑ 72 Darrell Russell RC	.10	.05
❑ 73 Shawn Springs RC	.20	.09
❑ 74 Warrick Dunn RC	1.25	.55
❑ 75 Tiki Barber RC	.50	.23
❑ 76 Tom Knight RC	.10	.05
❑ 77 Peter Boulware RC	.20	.09
❑ 78 David LaFleur RC	.20	.09
❑ 79 Tony Gonzalez RC	1.25	.55
❑ 80 Yatil Green RC	.20	.09
❑ 81 Ike Hilliard RC	.75	.35
❑ 82 James Farrior RC	.10	.05
❑ 83 Jim Druckenmiller RC	.50	.23
❑ 84 Jon Harris RC	.10	.05
❑ 85 Walter Jones RC	.10	.05
❑ 86 Reidel Anthony RC	.75	.35
❑ 87 Jake Plummer RC	3.00	1.35
❑ 88 Reinard Wilson RC	.10	.05
❑ 89 Kevin Lockett RC	.20	.09

	MINT	NRMT
❑ 90 Rae Carruth RC	.30	.14
❑ 91 Byron Hanspard RC	.75	.35
❑ 92 Renaldo Wynn RC	.10	.05
❑ 93 Troy Davis RC	.30	.14
❑ 94 Duce Staley RC	5.00	2.20
❑ 95 Kenard Lang RC	.10	.05
❑ 96 Freddie Jones RC	.20	.09
❑ 97 Corey Dillon RC	1.50	.70
❑ 98 Antowain Smith RC	1.00	.45
❑ 99 Dwayne Rudd RC	.10	.05
❑ 100 Warrick Dunn CL	.30	.14
❑ CR1 Brett Favre Ring (1997 cards produced)	60.00	27.00

1996 Pro Line Memorabilia Rookie Autographs

	MINT	NRMT
COMPLETE SET (15)	500.00	220.00
COMMON CARD	15.00	6.75
SEMISTARS	20.00	9.00
STATED ODDS 1:12		
❑ 1 Tim Biakabutuka/210	80.00	36.00
❑ 2 Tim Biakabutuka/600 Eddie George	100.00	45.00
❑ 3 Duane Clemons/1255	15.00	6.75
❑ 4 Daryl Gardener/1390	15.00	6.75
❑ 5 Eddie George/395	100.00	45.00
❑ 6 Terry Glenn/600 Keyshawn Johnson	100.00	45.00
❑ 7 Kevin Hardy/940	20.00	9.00
❑ 8 Jeff Hartings/1370	15.00	6.75
❑ 9 Andre Johnson/1370	15.00	6.75
❑ 10 Keyshawn Johnson/195	100.00	45.00
❑ 11 Pete Kendall/1495	15.00	6.75
❑ 12 Alex Molden/1320	15.00	6.75
❑ 13 Eric Moulds/1010	30.00	13.50
❑ 14 Jamain Stephens/795	15.00	6.75
❑ 15 Jerome Woods/1375	15.00	6.75

1997 Pro Line Memorabilia Rookie Autographs

	MINT	NRMT
COMPLETE SET (26)	250.00	110.00
COMMON CARD (1-26)	6.00	2.70
SEMISTARS	10.00	4.50
UNLISTED STARS	15.00	6.75
STATED ODDS 1:10		
❑ 1 John Allred	6.00	2.70
❑ 2 Darnell Autry	6.00	2.70
❑ 3 Pat Barnes	6.00	2.70
❑ 4 Michael Booker	6.00	2.70
❑ 5 Peter Boulware	10.00	4.50
❑ 6 Rae Carruth	15.00	6.75
❑ 7 Troy Davis	10.00	4.50
❑ 8 Jim Druckenmiller	15.00	6.75
❑ 9 Warrick Dunn	25.00	11.00
❑ 10 James Farrior	6.00	2.70
❑ 11 Tony Gonzalez	25.00	11.00
❑ 12 Yatil Green	15.00	6.75
❑ 13 Byron Hanspard	15.00	6.75
❑ 14 Ike Hilliard	10.00	4.50
❑ 15 David LaFleur	10.00	4.50
❑ 16 Kevin Lockett	10.00	4.50
❑ 17 Jake Plummer	60.00	27.00
❑ 18 Trevor Pryce	6.00	2.70
❑ 19 Derrick Rodgers	6.00	2.70
❑ 20 Dwayne Rudd	6.00	2.70
❑ 21 Darrell Russell	6.00	2.70
❑ 22 Matt Russell	6.00	2.70
❑ 23 Sedrick Shaw	10.00	4.50
❑ 24 Antowain Smith	20.00	9.00
❑ 25 Reinard Wilson	6.00	2.70
❑ 26 Bryant Westbrook	10.00	4.50

1989 Pro Set

	MINT	NRMT
COMPLETE SET (561)	25.00	11.00
COMP.SERIES 1 (440)	6.00	2.70
COMP.SERIES 2 (100)	20.00	9.00
COMP.FINAL FACT.SET (21)	2.00	.90
COMMON CARD (1-561)	.04	.02
SEMISTARS	.10	.05
UNLISTED STARS	.25	.11
VAR (193B/214A/266A)	.50	.23
VAR (478C/480C/483C)	40.00	18.00
COMP.ANNOUNCER SET (30)	3.00	1.35
ONE ANNOUNCER PER SER.2 PACK		
❑ 1 Stacey Bailey	.04	.02
❑ 2 Aundray Bruce RC	.04	.02
❑ 3 Rick Bryan	.04	.02
❑ 4 Bobby Butler	.04	.02
❑ 5 Scott Case RC	.04	.02
❑ 6 Tony Casillas	.04	.02
❑ 7 Floyd Dixon	.04	.02
❑ 8 Rick Donnelly	.04	.02
❑ 9 Bill Fralic	.04	.02
❑ 10 Mike Gann	.04	.02
❑ 11 Mike Kenn	.04	.02
❑ 12 Chris Miller RC	.25	.11
❑ 13 John Rade	.04	.02
❑ 14 Gerald Riggs UER (Uniform number is 42 but 43 on back)	.10	.05
❑ 15 John Settle RC	.04	.02
❑ 16 Marion Campbell CO	.04	.02
❑ 17 Cornelius Bennett	.10	.05
❑ 18 Derrick Burroughs	.04	.02
❑ 19 Shane Conlan	.04	.02
❑ 20 Ronnie Harmon	.10	.05
❑ 21 Kent Hull RC	.04	.02
❑ 22 Jim Kelly	.50	.23
❑ 23 Mark Kelso	.04	.02
❑ 24 Pete Metzelaars	.04	.02
❑ 25 Scott Norwood RC**	.04	.02
❑ 26 Andre Reed	.25	.11
❑ 27 Fred Smerlas	.04	.02
❑ 28 Bruce Smith	.25	.11
❑ 29 Leonard Smith	.04	.02
❑ 30 Art Still	.04	.02
❑ 31 Darryl Talley	.10	.05
❑ 32 Thurman Thomas RC	1.00	.45
❑ 33 Will Wolford RC	.04	.02
❑ 34 Marv Levy CO	.04	.02
❑ 35 Neal Anderson	.10	.05
❑ 36 Kevin Butler	.04	.02
❑ 37 Jim Covert	.04	.02
❑ 38 Richard Dent	.10	.05
❑ 39 Dave Duerson	.04	.02
❑ 40 Dennis Gentry	.04	.02
❑ 41 Dan Hampton	.10	.05
❑ 42 Jay Hilgenberg	.04	.02
❑ 43 Dennis McKinnon UER (Caught 20 or 21 passes as a rookie)	.04	.02
❑ 44 Jim McMahon	.10	.05
❑ 45 Steve McMichael	.10	.05
❑ 46 Brad Muster RC	.04	.02
❑ 47A William Perry SP	5.00	2.20
❑ 47B Ron Morris RC	.04	.02
❑ 48 Ron Rivera	.04	.02
❑ 49 Vestee Jackson RC	.04	.02
❑ 50 Mike Singletary	.10	.05
❑ 51 Mike Tomczak	.10	.05
❑ 52 Keith Van Horne RC	.04	.02
❑ 53A Mike Ditka CO (No HOF mention on card front)	.25	.11
❑ 53B Mike Ditka CO (HOF banner on front)	.25	.11
❑ 54 Lewis Billups	.04	.02
❑ 55 James Brooks	.10	.05
❑ 56 Eddie Brown	.04	.02
❑ 57 Jason Buck RC	.04	.02
❑ 58 Boomer Esiason	.10	.05
❑ 59 David Fulcher	.10	.05
❑ 60A Rodney Holman RC (BENGALS on front)	.10	.05
❑ 60B Rodney Holman RC (Bengals on front)	.25	.11
❑ 61 Reggie Williams	.04	.02
❑ 62 Joe Kelly RC	.04	.02
❑ 63 Tim Krumrie	.04	.02
❑ 64 Tim McGee	.04	.02
❑ 65 Max Montoya	.04	.02
❑ 66 Anthony Munoz	.10	.05
❑ 67 Jim Skow	.04	.02
❑ 68 Eric Thomas RC	.04	.02
❑ 69 Leon White	.04	.02
❑ 70 Ickey Woods RC	.10	.05
❑ 71 Carl Zander	.04	.02
❑ 72 Sam Wyche CO	.04	.02
❑ 73 Brian Brennan	.04	.02
❑ 74 Earnest Byner	.04	.02
❑ 75 Hanford Dixon	.04	.02
❑ 76 Mike Pagel	.04	.02
❑ 77 Bernie Kosar	.10	.05
❑ 78 Reggie Langhorne RC	.04	.02
❑ 79 Kevin Mack	.04	.02
❑ 80 Clay Matthews	.10	.05
❑ 81 Gerald McNeil	.04	.02
❑ 82 Frank Minnifield	.04	.02
❑ 83 Cody Risien	.04	.02
❑ 84 Webster Slaughter	.10	.05
❑ 85 Felix Wright	.04	.02
❑ 86 Bud Carson CO UER (NFLPA logo on back)	.04	.02
❑ 87 Bill Bates	.10	.05
❑ 88 Kevin Brooks	.04	.02
❑ 89 Michael Irvin RC	1.25	.55
❑ 90 Jim Jeffcoat	.04	.02
❑ 91 Ed Too Tall Jones	.10	.05
❑ 92 Eugene Lockhart RC	.04	.02
❑ 93 Nate Newton RC	.10	.05
❑ 94 Danny Noonan	.04	.02
❑ 95 Steve Pelluer	.04	.02
❑ 96 Herschel Walker	.10	.05
❑ 97 Everson Walls	.04	.02
❑ 98 Jimmy Johnson CO RC	.10	.05
❑ 99 Keith Bishop	.04	.02
❑ 100A John Elway ERR (Drafted 1st Round)	6.00	2.70
❑ 100B John Elway COR (Acquired Trade)	2.00	.90
❑ 101 Simon Fletcher RC	.04	.02
❑ 102 Mike Harden	.04	.02
❑ 103 Mike Horan	.04	.02
❑ 104 Mark Jackson	.04	.02
❑ 105 Vance Johnson	.10	.05
❑ 106 Rulon Jones	.04	.02
❑ 107 Clarence Kay	.04	.02
❑ 108 Karl Mecklenburg	.04	.02
❑ 109 Ricky Nattiel	.04	.02
❑ 110 Steve Sewell RC	.04	.02

❑ 111 Dennis Smith .10 .05
❑ 112 Gerald Willhite .04 .02
❑ 113 Sammy Winder .04 .02
❑ 114 Dan Reeves CO .04 .02
❑ 115 Jim Arnold .04 .02
❑ 116 Jerry Ball RC .04 .02
❑ 117 Bennie Blades RC .04 .02
❑ 118 Lomas Brown .04 .02
❑ 119 Mike Cofer .04 .02
❑ 120 Garry James .04 .02
❑ 121 James Jones .04 .02
❑ 122 Chuck Long .04 .02
❑ 123 Pete Mandley .04 .02
❑ 124 Eddie Murray .04 .02
❑ 125 Chris Spielman RC .25 .11
❑ 126 Dennis Gibson .04 .02
❑ 127 Wayne Fontes CO .04 .02
❑ 128 John Anderson .04 .02
❑ 129 Brent Fullwood RC .04 .02
❑ 130 Mark Cannon .04 .02
❑ 131 Tim Harris .04 .02
❑ 132 Mark Lee .04 .02
❑ 133 Don Majkowski RC .10 .05
❑ 134 Mark Murphy .04 .02
❑ 135 Brian Noble .04 .02
❑ 136 Ken Ruettgers RC .04 .02
❑ 137 Johnny Holland .04 .02
❑ 138 Randy Wright .04 .02
❑ 139 Lindy Infante CO .04 .02
❑ 140 Steve Brown .04 .02
❑ 141 Ray Childress .04 .02
(Sacking Joe Montana)
❑ 142 Jeff Donaldson .04 .02
❑ 143 Ernest Givins .10 .05
❑ 144 John Grimsley .04 .02
❑ 145 Alonzo Highsmith .04 .02
❑ 146 Drew Hill .04 .02
❑ 147 Robert Lyles .04 .02
❑ 148 Bruce Matthews RC .25 .11
❑ 149 Warren Moon .25 .11
❑ 150 Mike Munchak .04 .02
❑ 151 Allen Pinkett RC .04 .02
❑ 152 Mike Rozier .04 .02
❑ 153 Tony Zendejas .04 .02
❑ 154 Jerry Glanville CO .04 .02
❑ 155 Albert Bentley .04 .02
❑ 156 Dean Biasucci .04 .02
❑ 157 Duane Bickett .04 .02
❑ 158 Bill Brooks .10 .05
❑ 159 Chris Chandler RC .75 .35
❑ 160 Pat Beach .04 .02
❑ 161 Ray Donaldson .04 .02
❑ 162 Jon Hand .04 .02
❑ 163 Chris Hinton .04 .02
❑ 164 Rohn Stark .04 .02
❑ 165 Fredd Young .04 .02
❑ 166 Ron Meyer CO .04 .02
❑ 167 Lloyd Burruss .04 .02
❑ 168 Carlos Carson .04 .02
❑ 169 Deron Cherry .10 .05
❑ 170 Irv Eatman .04 .02
❑ 171 Dino Hackett .04 .02
❑ 172 Steve DeBerg .04 .02
❑ 173 Albert Lewis .04 .02
❑ 174 Nick Lowery .04 .02
❑ 175 Bill Maas .04 .02
❑ 176 Christian Okoye .04 .02
❑ 177 Stephone Paige .04 .02
❑ 178 Mark Adickes .04 .02
(Out of alphabetical sequence for his team)
❑ 179 Kevin Ross RC .10 .05
❑ 180 Neil Smith RC .50 .23
❑ 181 M. Schottenheimer CO .04 .02
❑ 182 Marcus Allen .25 .11
❑ 183 Tim Brown RC 1.50 .70
❑ 184 Willie Gault .10 .05
❑ 185 Bo Jackson .25 .11
❑ 186 Howie Long .10 .05
❑ 187 Vann McElroy .04 .02
❑ 188 Matt Millen .10 .05
❑ 189 Don Mosebar RC .04 .02
❑ 190 Bill Pickel .04 .02
❑ 191 Jerry Robinson UER .04 .02
(Stats show 1 TD, but text says 2 TD's)
❑ 192 Jay Schroeder .04 .02
❑ 193A Stacey Toran .04 .02
(No mention of death on card front)
❑ 193B Stacey Toran .50 .23
(1961-1989 banner on card front)
❑ 194 Mike Shanahan CO .04 .02
❑ 195 Greg Bell .04 .02
❑ 196 Ron Brown .04 .02
❑ 197 Aaron Cox RC .04 .02
❑ 198 Henry Ellard .25 .11
❑ 199 Jim Everett .10 .05
❑ 200 Jerry Gray .04 .02
❑ 201 Kevin Greene .25 .11
❑ 202 Pete Holohan .04 .02
❑ 203 LeRoy Irvin .04 .02
❑ 204 Mike Lansford .04 .02
❑ 205 Tom Newberry RC .04 .02
❑ 206 Mel Owens .04 .02
❑ 207 Jackie Slater .04 .02
❑ 208 Doug Smith .04 .02
❑ 209 Mike Wilcher .04 .02
❑ 210 John Robinson CO .04 .02
❑ 211 John Bosa .04 .02
❑ 212 Mark Brown .04 .02
❑ 213 Mark Clayton .10 .05
❑ 214A Ferrell Edmunds RC ERR .50
.23
(Misspelled Edmonds on front and back)
❑ 214B Ferrell Edmunds COR RC .04
.02
❑ 215 Roy Foster .04 .02
❑ 216 Lorenzo Hampton .04 .02
❑ 217 Jim C. Jensen RC UER .04 .02
(Born Albington, should be Abington)
❑ 218 William Judson .04 .02
❑ 219 Eric Kumerow RC .04 .02
❑ 220 Dan Marino 2.00 .90
❑ 221 John Offerdahl .04 .02
❑ 222 Fuad Reveiz .04 .02
❑ 223 Reggie Roby .04 .02
❑ 224 Brian Sochia .04 .02
❑ 225 Don Shula CO RC .25 .11
❑ 226 Alfred Anderson .04 .02
❑ 227 Joey Browner .04 .02
❑ 228 Anthony Carter .10 .05
❑ 229 Chris Doleman .10 .05
❑ 230 Hassan Jones RC .04 .02
❑ 231 Steve Jordan .04 .02
❑ 232 Tommy Kramer .04 .02
❑ 233 Carl Lee RC .04 .02
❑ 234 Kirk Lowdermilk RC .04 .02
❑ 235 Randall McDaniel RC .10 .05
❑ 236 Doug Martin .04 .02
❑ 237 Keith Millard .04 .02
❑ 238 Darrin Nelson .04 .02
❑ 239 Jesse Solomon .04 .02
❑ 240 Scott Studwell .04 .02
❑ 241 Wade Wilson .10 .05
❑ 242 Gary Zimmerman .04 .02
❑ 243 Jerry Burns CO .04 .02
❑ 244 Bruce Armstrong RC .04 .02
❑ 245 Raymond Clayborn .04 .02
❑ 246 Reggie Dupard .04 .02
❑ 247 Tony Eason .04 .02
❑ 248 Sean Farrell .04 .02
❑ 249 Doug Flutie .75 .35
❑ 250 Brent Williams RC .04 .02
❑ 251 Roland James .04 .02
❑ 252 Ronnie Lippett .04 .02
❑ 253 Fred Marion .04 .02
❑ 254 Larry McGrew .04 .02
❑ 255 Stanley Morgan .04 .02
❑ 256 Johnny Rembert RC .04 .02
❑ 257 John Stephens RC .04 .02
❑ 258 Andre Tippett .04 .02
❑ 259 Garin Veris .04 .02
❑ 260A Raymond Berry CO .04 .02
(No HOF mention on card front)
❑ 260B Raymond Berry CO .04 .02
(HOF banner on card front)
❑ 261 Morten Andersen .04 .02
❑ 262 Hoby Brenner .04 .02
❑ 263 Stan Brock .04 .02
❑ 264 Brad Edelman .04 .02
❑ 265 Jumpy Geathers .04 .02
❑ 266A Bobby Hebert ERR .50 .23
("passers" in 42-0)
❑ 266B Bobby Hebert COR .04 .02
("passes" in 42-0)
❑ 267 Craig Heyward RC .25 .11
❑ 268 Lonzell Hill .04 .02
❑ 269 Dalton Hilliard .04 .02
❑ 270 Rickey Jackson .10 .05
❑ 271 Steve Korte .04 .02
❑ 272 Eric Martin .04 .02
❑ 273 Rueben Mayes .04 .02
❑ 274 Sam Mills .10 .05
❑ 275 Brett Perriman RC .25 .11
❑ 276 Pat Swilling .10 .05
❑ 277 John Tice .04 .02
❑ 278 Jim Mora CO .04 .02
❑ 279 Eric Moore .04 .02
❑ 280 Carl Banks .04 .02
❑ 281 Mark Bavaro .10 .05
❑ 282 Maurice Carthon .04 .02
❑ 283 Mark Collins RC .04 .02
❑ 284 Erik Howard .04 .02
❑ 285 Terry Kinard .04 .02
❑ 286 Sean Landeta .04 .02
❑ 287 Lionel Manuel .04 .02
❑ 288 Leonard Marshall .04 .02
❑ 289 Joe Morris .04 .02
❑ 290 Bart Oates .04 .02
❑ 291 Phil Simms .10 .05
❑ 292 Lawrence Taylor .25 .11
❑ 293 Bill Parcells CO RC .10 .05
❑ 294 Dave Cadigan .04 .02
❑ 295 Kyle Clifton RC .04 .02
❑ 296 Alex Gordon .04 .02
❑ 297 James Hasty RC .04 .02
❑ 298 Johnny Hector .04 .02
❑ 299 Bobby Humphery .04 .02
❑ 300 Pat Leahy .04 .02
❑ 301 Marty Lyons .04 .02
❑ 302 Reggie McElroy RC .04 .02
❑ 303 Erik McMillan RC .04 .02
❑ 304 Freeman McNeil .04 .02
❑ 305 Ken O'Brien .04 .02
❑ 306 Pat Ryan .04 .02
❑ 307 Mickey Shuler .04 .02
❑ 308 Al Toon .10 .05
❑ 309 Jo Jo Townsell .04 .02
❑ 310 Roger Vick .04 .02
❑ 311 Joe Walton CO .04 .02
❑ 312 Jerome Brown .10 .05
❑ 313 Keith Byars .10 .05
❑ 314 Cris Carter RC 2.50 1.10
❑ 315 Randall Cunningham .40 .18
❑ 316 Terry Hoage .04 .02
❑ 317 Wes Hopkins .04 .02
❑ 318 Keith Jackson RC .25 .11
❑ 319 Mike Quick .04 .02
❑ 320 Mike Reichenbach .04 .02
❑ 321 Dave Rimington .04 .02
❑ 322 John Teltschik .04 .02
❑ 323 Anthony Toney .04 .02
❑ 324 Andre Waters .04 .02
❑ 325 Reggie White .25 .11
❑ 326 Luis Zendejas .04 .02
❑ 327 Buddy Ryan CO .04 .02
❑ 328 Robert Awalt .04 .02
❑ 329 Tim McDonald RC .10 .05
❑ 330 Roy Green .10 .05
❑ 331 Neil Lomax .04 .02
❑ 332 Cedric Mack .04 .02
❑ 333 Stump Mitchell .04 .02
❑ 334 Niko Noga RC .04 .02
❑ 335 Jay Novacek RC .25 .11
❑ 336 Freddie Joe Nunn .04 .02
❑ 337 Luis Sharpe .04 .02
❑ 338 Vai Sikahema .04 .02
❑ 339 J.T. Smith .04 .02
❑ 340 Ron Wolfley .04 .02
❑ 341 Gene Stallings CO RC .10 .05
❑ 342 Gary Anderson K .04 .02
❑ 343 Bubby Brister RC .50 .23

❑ 344 Dermontti Dawson RC .. .10 .05
❑ 345 Thomas Everett RC........ .04 .02
❑ 346 Delton Hall RC .... .04 .02
❑ 347 Bryan Hinkle RC .... .04 .02
❑ 348 Merril Hoge RC .... .04 .02
❑ 349 Tunch Ilkin RC............... .04 .02
❑ 350 Aaron Jones RC .... .04 .02
❑ 351 Louis Lipps .... .10 .05
❑ 352 David Little .... .04 .02
❑ 353 Hardy Nickerson RC .... .25 .11
❑ 354 Rod Woodson RC .... .50 .23
❑ 355A Chuck Noll RC CO ERR .10 .05
("one of only three")
❑ 355B Chuck Noll RC CO COR .10 .05
("one of only two")
❑ 356 Gary Anderson RB .... .04 .02
❑ 357 Rod Bernstine RC .... .04 .02
❑ 358 Gill Byrd.......................... .04 .02
❑ 359 Vencie Glenn.................. .04 .02
❑ 360 Dennis McKnight............ .04 .02
❑ 361 Lionel James.................. .04 .02
❑ 362 Mark Malone .... .04 .02
❑ 363A Anthony Miller RC ERR .25 .11
(TD total 14.8)
❑ 363B Anthony Miller RC COR .25 .11
(TD total 3)
❑ 364 Ralf Mojsiejenko .... .04 .02
❑ 365 Leslie O'Neal.................. .10 .05
❑ 366 Jamie Holland RC .... .04 .02
❑ 367 Lee Williams .... .04 .02
❑ 368 Dan Henning CO............ .04 .02
❑ 369 Harris Barton RC............ .04 .02
❑ 370 Michael Carter................ .04 .02
❑ 371 Mike Cofer RC................ .04 .02
(Joe Montana holding)
❑ 372 Roger Craig..................... .25 .11
❑ 373 Riki Ellison RC .... .04 .02
❑ 374 Jim Fahnhorst .... .04 .02
❑ 375 John Frank .... .04 .02
❑ 376 Jeff Fuller .... .04 .02
❑ 377 Don Griffin...................... .04 .02
❑ 378 Charles Haley .... .25 .11
❑ 379 Ronnie Lott .... .10 .05
❑ 380 Tim McKyer.................... .04 .02
❑ 381 Joe Montana .... 2.00 .90
❑ 382 Tom Rathman .... .04 .02
❑ 383 Jerry Rice .... 1.50 .70
❑ 384 John Taylor RC .... .25 .11
❑ 385 Keena Turner .... .04 .02
❑ 386 Michael Walter .... .04 .02
❑ 387 Bubba Paris.................... .04 .02
❑ 388 Steve Young .... 1.00 .45
❑ 389 George Seifert CO RC UER .10
.05
(NFLPA logo on back)
❑ 390 Brian Blades RC .... .25 .11
❑ 391A Brian Bosworth ERR..... .30 .14
(Seattle on front)
❑ 391B Brian Bosworth COR .. .10 .05
(Listed by team nick-
name on front)
❑ 392 Jeff Bryant....................... .04 .02
❑ 393 Jacob Green .... .04 .02
❑ 394 Norm Johnson............... .04 .02
❑ 395 Dave Krieg .... .10 .05
❑ 396 Steve Largent .... .25 .11
❑ 397 Bryan Millard RC............ .04 .02
❑ 398 Paul Moyer .... .04 .02
❑ 399 Joe Nash......................... .04 .02
❑ 400 Rufus Porter RC .... .04 .02
❑ 401 Eugene Robinson RC .... .04 .02
❑ 402 Bruce Scholtz .... .04 .02
❑ 403 Kelly Stouffer RC............ .04 .02
❑ 404A Curt Warner ERR ...... 1.25 .55
("yards 1455")
❑ 404B Curt Warner COR .... .10 .05
("yards 6074")
❑ 405 John L. Williams .... .04 .02
❑ 406 Tony Woods RC .... .04 .02
❑ 407 David Wyman .... .04 .02
❑ 408 Chuck Knox CO .... .04 .02
❑ 409 Mark Carrier WR RC...... .25 .11
❑ 410 Randy Grimes............... .04 .02
❑ 411 Paul Gruber RC.............. .04 .02
❑ 412 Harry Hamilton .... .04 .02
❑ 413 Ron Holmes .... .04 .02
❑ 414 Donald Igwebuike .... .04 .02
❑ 415 Dan Turk .... .04 .02
❑ 416 Ricky Reynolds .... .04 .02
❑ 417 Bruce Hill RC.................. .04 .02
❑ 418 Lars Tate .... .04 .02
❑ 419 Vinny Testaverde .... .30 .14
❑ 420 James Wilder .... .04 .02
❑ 421 Ray Perkins CO .... .04 .02
❑ 422 Jeff Bostic .... .04 .02
❑ 423 Kelvin Bryant.................. .04 .02
❑ 424 Gary Clark...................... .25 .11
❑ 425 Monte Coleman............. .04 .02
❑ 426 Darrell Green.................. .10 .05
❑ 427 Joe Jacoby .... .04 .02
❑ 428 Jim Lachey .... .04 .02
❑ 429 Charles Mann .... .04 .02
❑ 430 Dexter Manley................ .04 .02
❑ 431 Darryl Grant.................... .04 .02
❑ 432 Mark May RC .... .04 .02
❑ 433 Art Monk .... .10 .05
❑ 434 Mark Rypien RC .... .25 .11
❑ 435 Ricky Sanders................ .04 .02
❑ 436 Alvin Walton RC .... .04 .02
❑ 437 Don Warren.................... .04 .02
❑ 438 Jamie Morris .... .04 .02
❑ 439 Doug Williams .... .10 .05
❑ 440 Joe Gibbs CO RC .... .10 .05
❑ 441 Marcus Cotton............... .04 .02
❑ 442 Joel Williams .... .04 .02
❑ 443 Joe Devlin .... .04 .02
❑ 444 Robb Riddick.................. .04 .02
❑ 445 William Perry................. .10 .05
❑ 446 Thomas Sanders RC...... .04 .02
❑ 447 Brian Blados .... .04 .02
❑ 448 Cris Collinsworth .... .10 .05
❑ 449 Stanford Jennings .... .04 .02
❑ 450 Barry Krauss UER.......... .04 .02
(Listed as playing for
Indianapolis 1979-88)
❑ 451 Ozzie Newsome .... .10 .05
❑ 452 Mike Oliphant RC .... .04 .02
❑ 453 Tony Dorsett .... .25 .11
❑ 454 Bruce McNorton .... .04 .02
❑ 455 Eric Dickerson................ .10 .05
❑ 456 Keith Bostic .... .04 .02
❑ 457 Sam Clancy RC.............. .04 .02
❑ 458 Jack Del Rio RC .... .10 .05
❑ 459 Mike Webster .... .10 .05
❑ 460 Bob Golic........................ .04 .02
❑ 461 Otis Wilson .... .04 .02
❑ 462 Mike Haynes .... .10 .05
❑ 463 Greg Townsend............. .04 .02
❑ 464 Mark Duper .... .10 .05
❑ 465 E.J. Junior .... .04 .02
❑ 466 Troy Stradford .... .04 .02
❑ 467 Mike Merriweather.......... .04 .02
❑ 468 Irving Fryar .... .25 .11
❑ 469 Vaughan Johnson RC** .04 .02
❑ 470 Pepper Johnson .... .04 .02
❑ 471 Gary Reasons RC.......... .04 .02
❑ 472 Perry Williams RC.......... .04 .02
❑ 473 Wesley Walker .... .04 .02
❑ 474 Anthony Bell RC .... .04 .02
❑ 475 Earl Ferrell...................... .04 .02
❑ 476 Craig Wolfley.................. .04 .02
❑ 477 Billy Ray Smith .... .04 .02
❑ 478A Jim McMahon .... .10 .05
(No mention of trade
on card front)
❑ 478B Jim McMahon .... .10 .05
(Traded banner
on card front)
❑ 478C Jim McMahon 40.00 18.00
(Traded banner
on card front but no
line on back saying
also see card 44)
❑ 479 Eric Wright...................... .04 .02
❑ 480A Earnest Byner............. .04 .02
(No mention of trade
on card front)
❑ 480B Earnest Byner............. .30 .14
(Traded banner
on card front)
❑ 480C Earnest Byner.......... 40.00 18.00
(Traded banner
on card front but no
line on back saying
also see card 74)
❑ 481 Russ Grimm .... .04 .02
❑ 482 Wilber Marshall .... .04 .02
❑ 483A Gerald Riggs................ .10 .05
(No mention of trade
on card front)
❑ 483B Gerald Riggs................ .30 .14
(Traded banner
on card front)
❑ 483C Gerald Riggs........... 40.00 18.00
(Traded banner
on card front but no
line on back saying
also see card 14)
❑ 484 Brian Davis RC .... .04 .02
❑ 485 Shawn Collins RC.......... .04 .02
❑ 486 Deion Sanders RC ...... 2.00 .90
❑ 487 Trace Armstrong RC ...... .04 .02
❑ 488 Donnell Woolford RC .... .10 .05
❑ 489 Eric Metcalf RC .... .25 .11
❑ 490 Troy Aikman RC 6.00 2.70
❑ 491 Steve Walsh RC .... .10 .05
❑ 492 Steve Atwater RC .... .25 .11
❑ 493 Bobby Humphrey RC UER .04
.02
(Jersey 41 on back,
should be 26)
❑ 494 Barry Sanders RC...... 12.00 5.50
❑ 495 Tony Mandarich RC ...... .04 .02
❑ 496 David Williams RC .... .04 .02
❑ 497 Andre Rison RC UER .. 1.00 .45
(Jersey number not
listed on back)
❑ 498 Derrick Thomas RC...... 1.50 .70
❑ 499 Cleveland Gary RC .... .04 .02
❑ 500 Bill Hawkins RC.............. .04 .02
❑ 501 Louis Oliver RC............. .10 .05
❑ 502 Sammie Smith RC.......... .04 .02
❑ 503 Hart Lee Dykes RC .... .04 .02
❑ 504 Wayne Martin RC .... .04 .02
❑ 505 Brian Williams OL .... .04 .02
❑ 506 Jeff Lageman RC .... .10 .05
❑ 507 Eric Hill RC .... .04 .02
❑ 508 Joe Wolf RC .... .04 .02
❑ 509 Timm Rosenbach RC .... .04 .02
❑ 510 Tom Ricketts.................. .04 .02
❑ 511 Tim Worley RC .... .04 .02
❑ 512 Burt Grossman RC .... .04 .02
❑ 513 Keith DeLong RC .... .04 .02
❑ 514 Andy Heck RC................ .04 .02
❑ 515 Broderick Thomas RC.... .25 .11
❑ 516 Don Beebe RC .... .25 .11
❑ 517 James Thornton RC ...... .04 .02
❑ 518 Eric Kattus...................... .04 .02
❑ 519 Bruce Kozerski RC .... .04 .02
❑ 520 Brian Washington RC .... .04 .02
❑ 521 Rodney Peete RC UER.. .25 .11
(Jersey 19 on back,
should be 9)
❑ 522 Erik Affholter RC .... .04 .02
❑ 523 Anthony Dilweg RC........ .04 .02
❑ 524 O'Brien Alston .... .04 .02
❑ 525 Mike Elkins .... .04 .02
❑ 526 Jonathan Hayes RC ...... .04 .02
❑ 527 Terry McDaniel RC .... .04 .02
❑ 528 Frank Stams RC .... .04 .02
❑ 529 Darryl Ingram RC .... .04 .02
❑ 530 Henry Thomas............... .04 .02
❑ 531 Eric Coleman DB............ .04 .02
❑ 532 Sheldon White RC.......... .04 .02
❑ 533 Eric Allen RC.................. .25 .11
❑ 534 Robert Drummond.......... .04 .02
❑ 535A Gizmo Williams RC** 10.00 4.50
(Without Scouting Photo
on front and "Footbal"
misspelled on back)
❑ 535B Gizmo Williams RC** .. .25 .11
(Without Scouting Photo
on front but "Canadian
Football" on back)
❑ 535C Gizmo Williams RC** .. .04 .02
(With Scouting Photo
on card front)
❑ 536 Billy Joe Tolliver RC ...... .04 .02

- ❑ 537 Daniel Stubbs RC .... .04 .02
- ❑ 538 Wesley Walls RC .... .40 .18
- ❑ 539A James Jefferson RC* ERR .30 .14
  (No Prospect banner on card front)
- ❑ 539B James Jefferson RC* COR .04 .02
  (Prospect banner on card front)
- ❑ 540 Tracy Rocker.................. .04 .02
- ❑ 541 Art Shell CO .... .10 .05
- ❑ 542 Lemuel Stinson RC........ .04 .02
- ❑ 543 Tyrone Braxton RC UER .04 .02
  (back photo actually Ken Bell)
- ❑ 544 David Treadwell RC ...... .04 .02
- ❑ 545 Flipper Anderson RC...... .25 .11
- ❑ 546 Dave Meggett RC .... .25 .11
- ❑ 547 Lewis Tillman RC .... .04 .02
- ❑ 548 Carnell Lake RC .... .10 .05
- ❑ 549 Marion Butts RC .... .10 .05
- ❑ 550 Sterling Sharpe RC ...... 1.00 .45
- ❑ 551 Ezra Johnson .... .04 .02
- ❑ 552 Clarence Verdin RC** .... .04 .02
- ❑ 553 Mervyn Fernandez RC**/C .04 .02
- ❑ 554 Ottis Anderson .... .10 .05
- ❑ 555 Gary Hogeboom .... .04 .02
- ❑ 556 Paul Palmer TR.............. .04 .02
- ❑ 557 Jesse Solomon TR .... .04 .02
- ❑ 558 Chip Banks TR .... .04 .02
- ❑ 559 Steve Pelluer TR........... .04 .02
- ❑ 560 Darrin Nelson TR .... .04 .02
- ❑ 561 Herschel Walker TR ...... .10 .05
- ❑ CC1 Pete Rozelle SP............ .50 .23
  (Commissioner)

1990 Pro Set

	MINT	NRMT
COMPLETE SET (801)	15.00	6.75
COMP.SERIES 1 (377)	6.00	2.70
COMP.SERIES 2 (392)	6.00	2.70
COMP.FINAL SERIES (32)	3.00	1.35
COMP.FINAL FACT. (32)..........	3.00	1.35
COMMON CARD (1-800/SC4)....	.04	.02
SEMISTARS............................	.10	.05
UNLISTED STARS....................	.25	.11
COMPLETE SB ART SET (24)	3.00	1.35
ONE SB ART PER SER.1 PACK..		
COMPLETE SB MVPS SET (24)	4.00	1.80
ONE SB MVP PER SER.2 PACK..		

- ❑ 1A Barry Sanders ROY .. 100.00 45.00
  (Distributed to dealers at the Hawaii trade show in February 1990; distinguished from the regular card by profile head shot photo without ROY trophy on on card back)
- ❑ 1B Barry Sanders UER ...... 1.00 .45
  Rookie of the Year (TD total says 14, but adds up to 11)
- ❑ 2A Joe Montana ERR .... .50 .23
  Player of the Year (Jim Kelly's stats in text)
- ❑ 2B Joe Montana COR .... .50 .23
  Player of the Year (Corrected from 3521 yards to 3130)
- ❑ 3 Lindy Infante UER............. .04 .02
  Coach of the Year (missing Coach next to Packers)
- ❑ 4 Warren Moon UER .... .25 .11
  Man of the Year (missing R symbol)
- ❑ 5 Keith Millard .... .04 .02
  Defensive Player of the Year
- ❑ 6 Derrick Thomas UER .... .25 .11
  Defensive Rookie of the Year (no 1989 on front banner of card)
- ❑ 7 Ottis Anderson .... .10 .05
  Comeback Player of the Year
- ❑ 8 Joe Montana .... .50 .23
  Passing Leader
- ❑ 9 Christian Okoye................. .04 .02
  Rushing Leader
- ❑ 10 Thurman Thomas .... .25 .11
  Total Yardage Leader
- ❑ 11 Mike Cofer........................ .04 .02
  Kick Scoring Leader
- ❑ 12 Dalton Hilliard UER.......... .04 .02
  TD Scoring Leader (O.J. Simpson not listed in stats, but is mentioned in text)
- ❑ 13 Sterling Sharpe .... .25 .11
  Receiving Leader
- ❑ 14 Rich Camarillo................. .04 .02
  Punting Leader
- ❑ 15A Walter Stanley ERR ...... .50 .23
  Punt Return Leader (jersey on front reads 87, back says 8 or 86)
- ❑ 15B Walter Stanley COR ...... .04 .02
  Punt Return Leader
- ❑ 16 Rod Woodson .... .25 .11
  Kickoff Return Leader
- ❑ 17 Felix Wright..................... .04 .02
  Interception Leader
- ❑ 18A Chris Doleman ERR ...... .50 .23
  Sack Leader (Townsent, Jeffcoact)
- ❑ 18B Chris Doleman COR...... .50 .23
  Sack Leader (Townsend, Jeffcoat)
- ❑ 19A Andre Ware RC .... .10 .05
  Heisman Trophy (No drafted stripe on card front)
- ❑ 19B Andre Ware RC .... .10 .05
  Heisman Trophy (Drafted stripe on card front)
- ❑ 20A Mo Elewonibi .... .04 .02
  Outland Trophy (No drafted stripe on card front)
- ❑ 20B Mo Elewonibi .... .04 .02
  Outland Trophy (Drafted stripe on card front)
- ❑ 21A Percy Snow.................... .50 .23
  Lombardi Award (No drafted stripe on card front)
- ❑ 21B Percy Snow.................... .04 .02
  Lombardi Award (Drafted stripe on card front)
- ❑ 22A Anthony Thompson RC .04 .02
  Maxwell Award (No drafted stripe on card front)
- ❑ 22B Anthony Thompson RC .04 .02
  Maxwell Award (Drafted stripe on card front)
- ❑ 23 Buck Buchanan................ .04 .02
  (Sacking Bart Starr) 1990 HOF Selection
- ❑ 24 Bob Griese .... .10 .05
  1990 HOF Selection
- ❑ 25A Franco Harris ERR .... .50 .23
  1990 HOF Selection (Born 2/7/50)
- ❑ 25B Franco Harris COR........ .10 .05
  1990 HOF Selection (Born 3/7/50)
- ❑ 26 Ted Hendricks.................. .04 .02
  1990 HOF Selection
- ❑ 27A Jack Lambert ERR .... .50 .23
  1990 HOF Selection (Born 7/2/52)
- ❑ 27B Jack Lambert COR........ .50 .23
  1990 HOF Selection (Born 7/8/52)
- ❑ 28 Tom Landry...................... .10 .05
  1990 HOF Selection
- ❑ 29 Bob St.Clair..................... .04 .02
  1990 HOF Selection
- ❑ 30 Aundray Bruce UER .... .04 .02
  (Stats say Falcons)
- ❑ 31 Tony Casillas UER .... .04 .02
  (Stats say Falcons)
- ❑ 32 Shawn Collins .... .04 .02
- ❑ 33 Marcus Cotton.................. .04 .02
- ❑ 34 Bill Fralic .... .04 .02
- ❑ 35 Chris Miller .... .10 .05
- ❑ 36 Deion Sanders UER .... .50 .23
  (Stats say Falcons)
- ❑ 37 John Settle .... .04 .02
- ❑ 38 Jerry Glanville CO............ .04 .02
- ❑ 39 Cornelius Bennett .... .10 .05
- ❑ 40 Jim Kelly .... .25 .11
- ❑ 41 Mark Kelso UER .... .04 .02
  (No fumble rec. in '88; mentioned in '89)
- ❑ 42 Scott Norwood.................. .04 .02
- ❑ 43 Nate Odomes RC .... .10 .05
- ❑ 44 Scott Radecic .... .04 .02
- ❑ 45 Jim Ritcher RC .... .04 .02
- ❑ 46 Leonard Smith.................. .04 .02
- ❑ 47 Darryl Talley .... .04 .02
- ❑ 48 Marv Levy CO .... .04 .02
- ❑ 49 Neal Anderson .... .10 .05
- ❑ 50 Kevin Butler...................... .04 .02
- ❑ 51 Jim Covert......................... .04 .02
- ❑ 52 Richard Dent..................... .10 .05
- ❑ 53 Jay Hilgenberg .... .04 .02
- ❑ 54 Steve McMichael............... .10 .05
- ❑ 55 Ron Morris.......................... .04 .02
- ❑ 56 John Roper .... .04 .02
- ❑ 57 Mike Singletary .... .10 .05
- ❑ 58 Keith Van Horne .... .04 .02
- ❑ 59 Mike Ditka CO .... .25 .11
- ❑ 60 Lewis Billups .... .04 .02
- ❑ 61 Eddie Brown .... .04 .02
- ❑ 62 Jason Buck .... .04 .02
- ❑ 63A Rickey Dixon RC ERR .. .50 .23
  (Info missing under bio notes)
- ❑ 63B Rickey Dixon RC COR .. .50 .23
- ❑ 64 Tim McGee .... .04 .02
- ❑ 65 Eric Thomas .... .04 .02
- ❑ 66 Ickey Woods .... .04 .02
- ❑ 67 Carl Zander .... .04 .02
- ❑ 68A Sam Wyche CO ERR .... .50 .23
  (Info missing under bio notes)
- ❑ 68B Sam Wyche CO COR .... .50 .23
- ❑ 69 Paul Farren .... .04 .02
- ❑ 70 Thane Gash RC .... .04 .02
- ❑ 71 David Grayson .... .04 .02
- ❑ 72 Bernie Kosar .... .10 .05
- ❑ 73 Reggie Langhorne............ .04 .02
- ❑ 74 Eric Metcalf .... .25 .11
- ❑ 75A Ozzie Newsome ERR .... .50 .23
  (Born Muscle Shoals)
- ❑ 75B Ozzie Newsome COR.... .50 .23
  (Born Little Rock)

❑ 75C Cody Risien SP .50 .23 (withdrawn)
❑ 76 Felix Wright .04 .02
❑ 77 Bud Carson CO .04 .02
❑ 78 Troy Aikman .75 .35
❑ 79 Michael Irvin .25 .11
❑ 80 Jim Jeffcoat .04 .02
❑ 81 Crawford Ker .04 .02
❑ 82 Eugene Lockhart .04 .02
❑ 83 Kelvin Martin RC .04 .02
❑ 84 Ken Norton RC .25 .11
❑ 85 Jimmy Johnson CO .10 .05
❑ 86 Steve Atwater .04 .02
❑ 87 Tyrone Braxton .04 .02
❑ 88 John Elway 1.25 .55
❑ 89 Simon Fletcher .04 .02
❑ 90 Ron Holmes .04 .02
❑ 91 Bobby Humphrey .04 .02
❑ 92 Vance Johnson .04 .02
❑ 93 Ricky Nattiel .04 .02
❑ 94 Dan Reeves CO .04 .02
❑ 95 Jim Arnold .04 .02
❑ 96 Jerry Ball .04 .02
❑ 97 Bennie Blades .04 .02
❑ 98 Lomas Brown .04 .02
❑ 99 Michael Cofer .04 .02
❑ 100 Richard Johnson .04 .02
❑ 101 Eddie Murray .04 .02
❑ 102 Barry Sanders 2.50 1.10
❑ 103 Chris Spielman .25 .11
❑ 104 William White RC .04 .02
❑ 105 Eric Williams RC .04 .02
❑ 106 Wayne Fontes CO UER .04 .02 (Says born in MO, actually born in MA)
❑ 107 Brent Fullwood .04 .02
❑ 108 Ron Hallstrom RC .04 .02
❑ 109 Tim Harris .04 .02
❑ 110A Johnny Holland ERR .50 .23 (No name or position at top of reverse)
❑ 110B Johnny Holland COR .50 .23
❑ 111A Perry Kemp ERR .50 .23 (Photo on back is actually Ken Stiles, wearing gray shirt)
❑ 111B Perry Kemp COR .50 .23 (Wearing green shirt)
❑ 112 Don Majkowski .04 .02
❑ 113 Mark Murphy .04 .02
❑ 114A Sterling Sharpe ERR .25 .11 (Born Glenville, Ga.)
❑ 114B Sterling Sharpe COR .50 .23 (Born Chicago)
❑ 115 Ed West RC .04 .02
❑ 116 Lindy Infante CO .04 .02
❑ 117 Steve Brown .04 .02
❑ 118 Ray Childress .04 .02
❑ 119 Ernest Givins .10 .05
❑ 120 John Grimsley .04 .02
❑ 121 Alonzo Highsmith .04 .02
❑ 122 Drew Hill .04 .02
❑ 123 Bubba McDowell .04 .02
❑ 124 Dean Steinkuhler .04 .02
❑ 125 Lorenzo White .10 .05
❑ 126 Tony Zendejas .04 .02
❑ 127 Jack Pardee CO .04 .02
❑ 128 Albert Bentley .04 .02
❑ 129 Dean Biasucci .04 .02
❑ 130 Duane Bickett .04 .02
❑ 131 Bill Brooks .04 .02
❑ 132 Jon Hand .04 .02
❑ 133 Mike Prior .04 .02
❑ 134A Andre Rison .25 .11 (No mention of trade on card front)
❑ 134B Andre Rison .25 .11 (Traded banner on card front; also reissued with Final Update)
❑ 134C Andre Rison .25 .11 (Traded banner on card front; message from Lud Denny on back)
❑ 135 Rohn Stark .04 .02
❑ 136 Donnell Thompson .04 .02
❑ 137 Clarence Verdin .04 .02
❑ 138 Fredd Young .04 .02
❑ 139 Ron Meyer CO .04 .02
❑ 140 John Alt RC .04 .02
❑ 141 Steve DeBerg .04 .02
❑ 142 Irv Eatman .04 .02
❑ 143 Dino Hackett .04 .02
❑ 144 Nick Lowery .04 .02
❑ 145 Bill Maas .04 .02
❑ 146 Stephone Paige .04 .02
❑ 147 Neil Smith .25 .11
❑ 148 Marty Schottenheimer CO .04 .02
❑ 149 Steve Beuerlein .10 .05
❑ 150 Tim Brown .25 .11
❑ 151 Mike Dyal .04 .02
❑ 152A Mervyn Fernandez ERR .75 .35 (Acquired: Free Agent '87)
❑ 152B Mervyn Fernandez COR .75 .35 (Acquired: Drafted 10th Round, 1983)
❑ 153 Willie Gault .10 .05
❑ 154 Bob Golic .04 .02
❑ 155 Bo Jackson .25 .11
❑ 156 Don Mosebar .04 .02
❑ 157 Steve Smith .04 .02
❑ 158 Greg Townsend .04 .02
❑ 159 Bruce Wilkerson RC .04 .02
❑ 160 Steve Wisniewski .10 .05 (Blocking for Bo Jackson)
❑ 161A Art Shell CO ERR .50 .23 (Born 11/25/46)
❑ 161B Art Shell CO COR .50 .23 (Born 11/26/46; large HOF print on front)
❑ 161C Art Shell CO COR .50 .23 (Born 11/26/46; small HOF print on front)
❑ 162 Flipper Anderson .04 .02
❑ 163 Greg Bell UER .04 .02 (Stats have 5 catches, should be 9)
❑ 164 Henry Ellard .10 .05
❑ 165 Jim Everett .10 .05
❑ 166 Jerry Gray .04 .02
❑ 167 Kevin Greene .25 .11
❑ 168 Pete Holohan .04 .02
❑ 169 Larry Kelm RC .04 .02
❑ 170 Tom Newberry .04 .02
❑ 171 Vince Newsome RC .04 .02
❑ 172 Irv Pankey .04 .02
❑ 173 Jackie Slater .04 .02
❑ 174 Fred Strickland RC .04 .02
❑ 175 Mike Wilcher UER .04 .02 (Fumble rec. number different from 1989 Pro Set card)
❑ 176 John Robinson CO UER .04 .02 (Stats say Rams, should say L.A. Rams)
❑ 177 Mark Clayton .10 .05
❑ 178 Roy Foster .04 .02
❑ 179 Harry Galbreath RC .04 .02
❑ 180 Jim C. Jensen .04 .02
❑ 181 Dan Marino 1.25 .55
❑ 182 Louis Oliver .04 .02
❑ 183 Sammie Smith .04 .02
❑ 184 Brian Sochia .04 .02
❑ 185 Don Shula CO .10 .05
❑ 186 Joey Browner .04 .02
❑ 187 Anthony Carter .10 .05
❑ 188 Chris Doleman .04 .02
❑ 189 Steve Jordan .04 .02
❑ 190 Carl Lee .04 .02
❑ 191 Randall McDaniel .04 .02
❑ 192 Mike Merriweather .04 .02
❑ 193 Keith Millard .04 .02
❑ 194 Al Noga .04 .02
❑ 195 Scott Studwell .04 .02
❑ 196 Henry Thomas .04 .02
❑ 197 Herschel Walker .10 .05
❑ 198 Wade Wilson .10 .05
❑ 199 Gary Zimmerman .04 .02
❑ 200 Jerry Burns CO .04 .02
❑ 201 Vincent Brown RC .04 .02
❑ 202 Hart Lee Dykes .04 .02
❑ 203 Sean Farrell .04 .02
❑ 204A Fred Marion .04 .02 (Belt visible on John Taylor)
❑ 204B Fred Marion .04 .02 (Belt not visible)
❑ 205 Stanley Morgan UER .04 .02 (Text says he reached 10,000 yards fastest; 3 players did it in 10 seasons)
❑ 206 Eric Sievers RC .04 .02
❑ 207 John Stephens .04 .02
❑ 208 Andre Tippett .04 .02
❑ 209 Rod Rust CO .04 .02
❑ 210A Morten Andersen ERR .50 .23 (Card number and name on back in white)
❑ 210B Morten Andersen COR .50 .23 (Card number and name on back in black)
❑ 211 Brad Edelman .04 .02
❑ 212 John Fourcade .04 .02
❑ 213 Dalton Hilliard .04 .02
❑ 214 Rickey Jackson .10 .05 (Forcing Jim Kelly fumble)
❑ 215 Vaughan Johnson .04 .02
❑ 216A Eric Martin ERR .50 .23 (Card number and name on back in white)
❑ 216B Eric Martin COR .50 .23 (Card number and name on back in black)
❑ 217 Sam Mills .10 .05
❑ 218 Pat Swilling UER .10 .05 (Total fumble recoveries listed as 4, should be 5)
❑ 219 Frank Warren RC .04 .02
❑ 220 Jim Wilks .04 .02
❑ 221A Jim Mora CO ERR .50 .23 (Card number and name on back in white)
❑ 221B Jim Mora CO COR .50 .23 (Card number and name on back in black)
❑ 222 Raul Allegre .04 .02
❑ 223 Carl Banks .04 .02
❑ 224 John Elliott .04 .02
❑ 225 Erik Howard .04 .02
❑ 226 Pepper Johnson .04 .02
❑ 227 Leonard Marshall UER .04 .02 (In Super Bowl XXI, George Martin had the safety)
❑ 228 Dave Meggett .10 .05
❑ 229 Bart Oates .04 .02
❑ 230 Phil Simms .10 .05
❑ 231 Lawrence Taylor .25 .11
❑ 232 Bill Parcells CO .10 .05
❑ 233 Troy Benson .04 .02
❑ 234 Kyle Clifton UER .04 .02 (Born: Onley, should be Olney)
❑ 235 Johnny Hector .04 .02
❑ 236 Jeff Lageman .04 .02
❑ 237 Pat Leahy .04 .02
❑ 238 Freeman McNeil .04 .02
❑ 239 Ken O'Brien .04 .02
❑ 240 Al Toon .10 .05
❑ 241 Jo Jo Townsell .04 .02
❑ 242 Bruce Coslet CO .04 .02
❑ 243 Eric Allen .04 .02
❑ 244 Jerome Brown .04 .02
❑ 245 Keith Byars .04 .02
❑ 246 Cris Carter .50 .23
❑ 247 Randall Cunningham .25 .11
❑ 248 Keith Jackson .10 .05
❑ 249 Mike Quick .04 .02 (Darrell Green also in photo)
❑ 250 Clyde Simmons .04 .02
❑ 251 Andre Waters .04 .02
❑ 252 Reggie White .25 .11
❑ 253 Buddy Ryan CO .04 .02
❑ 254 Rich Camarillo .04 .02
❑ 255 Earl Ferrell .04 .02

(No mention of retirement on card front)
❑ 256 Roy Green .10 .05
❑ 257 Ken Harvey RC .25 .11
❑ 258 Ernie Jones RC .04 .02
❑ 259 Tim McDonald .04 .02
❑ 260 Timm Rosenbach UER .. .04 .02
(Born '67, should be '66)
❑ 261 Luis Sharpe .04 .02
❑ 262 Vai Sikahema .04 .02
❑ 263 J.T. Smith .04 .02
❑ 264 Ron Wolfley UER .04 .02
(Born Blaisdel, should be Blasdel)
❑ 265 Joe Bugel CO .04 .02
❑ 266 Gary Anderson K .04 .02
❑ 267 Bubby Brister .04 .02
❑ 268 Merril Hoge .04 .02
❑ 269 Carnell Lake .04 .02
❑ 270 Louis Lipps .10 .05
❑ 271 David Little .04 .02
❑ 272 Greg Lloyd .25 .11
❑ 273 Keith Willis .04 .02
❑ 274 Tim Worley .04 .02
❑ 275 Chuck Noll CO .10 .05
❑ 276 Marion Butts .10 .05
❑ 277 Gill Byrd .04 .02
❑ 278 Vencie Glenn UER .04 .02
(Sack total should be 2, not 2.5)
❑ 279 Burt Grossman .04 .02
❑ 280 Gary Plummer .04 .02
❑ 281 Billy Ray Smith .04 .02
❑ 282 Billy Joe Tolliver .04 .02
❑ 283 Dan Henning CO .04 .02
❑ 284 Harris Barton .04 .02
❑ 285 Michael Carter .04 .02
❑ 286 Mike Cofer .04 .02
❑ 287 Roger Craig .10 .05
❑ 288 Don Griffin .04 .02
❑ 289A Charles Haley ERR.. 30.00 13.50
(Fumble recoveries 1 in '86 and 4 total)
❑ 289B Charles Haley COR .... .75 .35
(Fumble recoveries 2 in '86 and 5 total)
❑ 290 Pierce Holt RC .04 .02
❑ 291 Ronnie Lott .10 .05
❑ 292 Guy McIntyre .04 .02
❑ 293 Joe Montana 1.25 .55
❑ 294 Tom Rathman .04 .02
❑ 295 Jerry Rice .75 .35
❑ 296 Jesse Sapolu RC .04 .02
❑ 297 John Taylor .10 .05
❑ 298 Michael Walter .04 .02
❑ 299 George Seifert CO .10 .05
❑ 300 Jeff Bryant .04 .02
❑ 301 Jacob Green .04 .02
❑ 302 Norm Johnson UER .04 .02
(Card shop not in Garden Grove, should say Fullerton)
❑ 303 Bryan Millard .04 .02
❑ 304 Joe Nash .04 .02
❑ 305 Eugene Robinson .04 .02
❑ 306 John L. Williams .04 .02
❑ 307 David Wyman .04 .02
(NFL EXP is in caps, inconsistent with rest of the set)
❑ 308 Chuck Knox CO .04 .02
❑ 309 Mark Carrier WR .25 .11
❑ 310 Paul Gruber .04 .02
❑ 311 Harry Hamilton .04 .02
❑ 312 Bruce Hill .04 .02
❑ 313 Donald Igwebuike .04 .02
❑ 314 Kevin Murphy .04 .02
❑ 315 Ervin Randle .04 .02
❑ 316 Mark Robinson .04 .02
❑ 317 Lars Tate .04 .02
❑ 318 Vinny Testaverde .10 .05
❑ 319A Ray Perkins CO ERR .. .75 .35
(No name or title at top of reverse)
❑ 319B Ray Perkins CO COR .. .04 .02
❑ 320 Earnest Byner .04 .02
❑ 321 Gary Clark .25 .11
❑ 322 Darryl Grant .04 .02
❑ 323 Darrell Green .10 .05
❑ 324 Jim Lachey .04 .02
❑ 325 Charles Mann .04 .02
❑ 326 Wilber Marshall .04 .02
❑ 327 Ralf Mojsiejenko .04 .02
❑ 328 Art Monk .10 .05
❑ 329 Gerald Riggs .10 .05
❑ 330 Mark Rypien .10 .05
❑ 331 Ricky Sanders .04 .02
❑ 332 Alvin Walton .04 .02
❑ 333 Joe Gibbs CO .10 .05
❑ 334 Aloha Stadium .04 .02
Site of Pro Bowl
❑ 335 Brian Blades PB .04 .02
❑ 336 James Brooks PB .04 .02
❑ 337 Shane Conlan PB .04 .02
❑ 338 Eric Dickerson PB SP .. 2.50 1.10
(Card withdrawn)
❑ 339 Ray Donaldson PB .04 .02
❑ 340 Ferrell Edmunds PB .04 .02
❑ 341 Boomer Esiason PB .04 .02
❑ 342 David Fulcher PB .04 .02
❑ 343A Chris Hinton PB .50 .23
(No mention of trade on card front)
❑ 343B Chris Hinton PB .04 .02
(Traded banner on card front)
❑ 344 Rodney Holman PB .04 .02
❑ 345 Kent Hull PB .04 .02
❑ 346 Tunch Ilkin PB .04 .02
❑ 347 Mike Johnson PB .04 .02
❑ 348 Greg Kragen PB .04 .02
❑ 349 Dave Krieg PB .10 .05
❑ 350 Albert Lewis PB .04 .02
❑ 351 Howie Long PB .10 .05
❑ 352 Bruce Matthews PB .04 .02
❑ 353 Clay Matthews PB .04 .02
❑ 354 Erik McMillan PB .04 .02
❑ 355 Karl Mecklenburg PB .... .04 .02
❑ 356 Anthony Miller PB .04 .02
❑ 357 Frank Minnifield PB .04 .02
❑ 358 Max Montoya PB .04 .02
❑ 359 Warren Moon PB .25 .11
❑ 360 Mike Munchak PB .04 .02
❑ 361 Anthony Munoz PB .04 .02
❑ 362 John Offerdahl PB .04 .02
❑ 363 Christian Okoye PB .04 .02
❑ 364 Leslie O'Neal PB .04 .02
❑ 365 Rufus Porter PB UER .... .04 .02
(TM logo missing)
❑ 366 Andre Reed PB .10 .05
❑ 367 Johnny Rembert PB .04 .02
❑ 368 Reggie Roby PB .04 .02
❑ 369 Kevin Ross PB .04 .02
❑ 370 Webster Slaughter PB.... .04 .02
❑ 371 Bruce Smith PB .10 .05
❑ 372 Dennis Smith PB .04 .02
❑ 373 Derrick Thomas PB .10 .05
❑ 374 Thurman Thomas PB .... .25 .11
❑ 375 David Treadwell PB .04 .02
❑ 376 Lee Williams PB .04 .02
❑ 377 Rod Woodson PB .10 .05
❑ 378 Bud Carson CO PB .04 .02
❑ 379 Eric Allen PB .04 .02
❑ 380 Neal Anderson PB .10 .05
❑ 381 Jerry Ball PB .04 .02
❑ 382 Joey Browner PB .04 .02
❑ 383 Rich Camarillo PB .04 .02
❑ 384 Mark Carrier WR PB .04 .02
❑ 385 Roger Craig PB .10 .05
❑ 386A Randall Cunningham PB .50 .23
(Small print on front)
❑ 386B Randall Cunningham PB .50 .23
(Large print on front)
❑ 387 Chris Doleman PB .04 .02
❑ 388 Henry Ellard PB .04 .02
❑ 389 Bill Fralic PB .04 .02
❑ 390 Brent Fullwood PB .04 .02
❑ 391 Jerry Gray PB .04 .02
❑ 392 Kevin Greene PB .10 .05
❑ 393 Tim Harris PB .04 .02
❑ 394 Jay Hilgenberg PB .04 .02
❑ 395 Dalton Hilliard PB .04 .02
❑ 396 Keith Jackson PB .10 .05
❑ 397 Vaughan Johnson PB .... .04 .02
❑ 398 Steve Jordan PB .04 .02
❑ 399 Carl Lee PB .04 .02
❑ 400 Ronnie Lott PB .10 .05
❑ 401 Don Majkowski PB .04 .02
❑ 402 Charles Mann PB .04 .02
❑ 403 Randall McDaniel PB .... .04 .02
❑ 404 Tim McDonald PB .04 .02
❑ 405 Guy McIntyre PB .04 .02
❑ 406 Dave Meggett PB .04 .02
❑ 407 Keith Millard PB .04 .02
❑ 408 Joe Montana PB .50 .23
(not pictured in Pro Bowl uniform)
❑ 409 Eddie Murray PB .04 .02
❑ 410 Tom Newberry PB .04 .02
❑ 411 Jerry Rice PB .50 .23
❑ 412 Mark Rypien PB .04 .02
❑ 413 Barry Sanders PB 1.00 .45
❑ 414 Luis Sharpe PB .04 .02
❑ 415 Sterling Sharpe PB .04 .02
❑ 416 Mike Singletary PB .10 .05
❑ 417 Jackie Slater PB .04 .02
❑ 418 Doug Smith PB .04 .02
❑ 419 Chris Spielman PB .04 .02
❑ 420 Pat Swilling PB .04 .02
❑ 421 John Taylor PB .04 .02
❑ 422 Lawrence Taylor PB .10 .05
❑ 423 Reggie White PB .10 .05
❑ 424 Ron Wolfley PB .04 .02
❑ 425 Gary Zimmerman PB .... .04 .02
❑ 426 John Robinson CO PB .. .04 .02
❑ 427 Scott Case UER .04 .02
(front CB, back S)
❑ 428 Mike Kenn .04 .02
❑ 429 Mike Gann .04 .02
❑ 430 Tim Green RC .04 .02
❑ 431 Michael Haynes RC .25 .11
❑ 432 Jessie Tuggle RC UER .. .04 .02
(Front Jesse, back Jessie)
❑ 433 John Rade .04 .02
❑ 434 Andre Rison .25 .11
❑ 435 Don Beebe .10 .05
❑ 436 Ray Bentley .04 .02
❑ 437 Shane Conlan .04 .02
❑ 438 Kent Hull .04 .02
❑ 439 Pete Metzelaars .04 .02
❑ 440 Andre Reed UER .25 .11
(Vance Johnson also had more catches in '85)
❑ 441 Frank Reich .25 .11
❑ 442 Leon Seals RC .04 .02
❑ 443 Bruce Smith .25 .11
❑ 444 Thurman Thomas .25 .11
❑ 445 Will Wolford .04 .02
❑ 446 Trace Armstrong .04 .02
❑ 447 Mark Bortz RC .04 .02
❑ 448 Tom Thayer RC .04 .02
❑ 449A Dan Hampton ERR .50 .23
(Card back says DE)
❑ 449B Dan Hampton COR.. 30.00 13.50
(Card back says DT)
❑ 450 Shaun Gayle RC .04 .02
❑ 451 Dennis Gentry .04 .02
❑ 452 Jim Harbaugh .25 .11
❑ 453 Vestee Jackson .04 .02
❑ 454 Brad Muster .04 .02
❑ 455 William Perry .10 .05
❑ 456 Ron Rivera .04 .02
❑ 457 James Thornton .04 .02
❑ 458 Mike Tomczak .10 .05
❑ 459 Donnell Woolford .04 .02
❑ 460 Eric Ball .04 .02
❑ 461 James Brooks .10 .05
❑ 462 David Fulcher .04 .02
❑ 463 Boomer Esiason .10 .05
❑ 464 Rodney Holman .04 .02
❑ 465 Bruce Kozerski .04 .02
❑ 466 Tim Krumrie .04 .02
❑ 467 Anthony Munoz .10 .05
(Type on front smaller compared to other cards)

❑ 468 Brian Blados .04 .02
❑ 469 Mike Baab .04 .02
❑ 470 Brian Brennan .04 .02
❑ 471 Raymond Clayborn .04 .02
❑ 472 Mike Johnson .04 .02
❑ 473 Kevin Mack .04 .02
❑ 474 Clay Matthews .10 .05
❑ 475 Frank Minnifield .04 .02
❑ 476 Gregg Rakoczy RC .04 .02
❑ 477 Webster Slaughter .10 .05
❑ 478 James Dixon .04 .02
❑ 479 Robert Awalt UER .04 .02
(front 89, back 46)
❑ 480 Dennis McKinnon UER .04 .02
(front 81, back 85)
❑ 481 Danny Noonan .04 .02
❑ 482 Jesse Solomon .04 .02
❑ 483 Daniel Stubbs UER .04 .02
(front 66, back 96)
❑ 484 Steve Walsh .10 .05
❑ 485 Michael Brooks RC .04 .02
❑ 486 Mark Jackson .04 .02
❑ 487 Greg Kragen .04 .02
❑ 488 Ken Lanier RC .04 .02
❑ 489 Karl Mecklenburg .04 .02
❑ 490 Steve Sewell .04 .02
❑ 491 Dennis Smith .04 .02
❑ 492 David Treadwell .04 .02
❑ 493 Michael Young RC .04 .02
❑ 494 Robert Clark RC .04 .02
❑ 495 Dennis Gibson .04 .02
❑ 496A Kevin Glover RC ERR .20 .09
(Card back says C/G)
❑ 496B Kevin Glover RC COR .04 .02
(Card back says C)
❑ 497 Mel Gray .10 .05
❑ 498 Rodney Peete .10 .05
❑ 499 Dave Brown DB .04 .02
❑ 500 Jerry Holmes .04 .02
❑ 501 Chris Jacke .04 .02
❑ 502 Alan Veingrad .04 .02
❑ 503 Mark Lee .04 .02
❑ 504 Tony Mandarich .04 .02
❑ 505 Brian Noble .04 .02
❑ 506 Jeff Query .04 .02
❑ 507 Ken Ruettgers .04 .02
❑ 508 Patrick Allen .04 .02
❑ 509 Curtis Duncan .04 .02
❑ 510 William Fuller .10 .05
❑ 511 Haywood Jeffires RC .25 .11
❑ 512 Sean Jones .10 .05
❑ 513 Terry Kinard .04 .02
❑ 514 Bruce Matthews .10 .05
❑ 515 Gerald McNeil .04 .02
❑ 516 Greg Montgomery RC .04 .02
❑ 517 Warren Moon .25 .11
❑ 518 Mike Munchak .04 .02
❑ 519 Allen Pinkett .04 .02
❑ 520 Pat Beach .04 .02
❑ 521 Eugene Daniel .04 .02
❑ 522 Kevin Call .04 .02
❑ 523 Ray Donaldson .04 .02
❑ 524 Jeff Herrod RC .04 .02
❑ 525 Keith Taylor .04 .02
❑ 526 Jack Trudeau .04 .02
❑ 527 Deron Cherry .04 .02
❑ 528 Jeff Donaldson .04 .02
❑ 529 Albert Lewis .04 .02
❑ 530 Pete Mandley .04 .02
❑ 531 Chris Martin RC .04 .02
❑ 532 Christian Okoye .04 .02
❑ 533 Steve Pelluer .04 .02
❑ 534 Kevin Ross .04 .02
❑ 535 Dan Saleaumua .04 .02
❑ 536 Derrick Thomas .25 .11
❑ 537 Mike Webster .10 .05
❑ 538 Marcus Allen .25 .11
❑ 539 Greg Bell .04 .02
❑ 540 Thomas Benson .04 .02
❑ 541 Ron Brown .04 .02
❑ 542 Scott Davis .04 .02
❑ 543 Riki Ellison .04 .02
❑ 544 Jamie Holland .04 .02
❑ 545 Howie Long .10 .05
❑ 546 Terry McDaniel .04 .02
❑ 547 Max Montoya .04 .02
❑ 548 Jay Schroeder .04 .02
❑ 549 Lionel Washington .04 .02
❑ 550 Robert Delpino .04 .02
❑ 551 Bobby Humphery .04 .02
❑ 552 Mike Lansford .04 .02
❑ 553 Michael Stewart RC .04 .02
❑ 554 Doug Smith .04 .02
❑ 555 Curt Warner .04 .02
❑ 556 Alvin Wright RC .04 .02
❑ 557 Jeff Cross .04 .02
❑ 558 Jeff Dellenbach RC .04 .02
❑ 559 Mark Duper .10 .05
❑ 560 Ferrell Edmunds .04 .02
❑ 561 Tim McKyer .04 .02
❑ 562 John Offerdahl .04 .02
❑ 563 Reggie Roby .04 .02
❑ 564 Pete Stoyanovich .04 .02
❑ 565 Alfred Anderson .04 .02
❑ 566 Ray Berry .04 .02
❑ 567 Rick Fenney .04 .02
❑ 568 Rich Gannon RC .75 .35
❑ 569 Tim Irwin .04 .02
❑ 570 Hassan Jones .04 .02
❑ 571 Cris Carter .50 .23
❑ 572 Kirk Lowdermilk .04 .02
❑ 573 Reggie Rutland RC .04 .02
❑ 574 Ken Stills .04 .02
❑ 575 Bruce Armstrong .04 .02
❑ 576 Irving Fryar .10 .05
❑ 577 Roland James .04 .02
❑ 578 Robert Perryman .04 .02
❑ 579 Cedric Jones .04 .02
❑ 580 Steve Grogan .10 .05
❑ 581 Johnny Rembert .04 .02
❑ 582 Ed Reynolds .04 .02
❑ 583 Brent Williams .04 .02
❑ 584 Marc Wilson .04 .02
❑ 585 Hoby Brenner .04 .02
❑ 586 Stan Brock .04 .02
❑ 587 Jim Dombrowski RC .04 .02
❑ 588 Joel Hilgenberg RC .04 .02
❑ 589 Robert Massey .04 .02
❑ 590 Floyd Turner .04 .02
❑ 591 Ottis Anderson .10 .05
❑ 592 Mark Bavaro .04 .02
❑ 593 Maurice Carthon .04 .02
❑ 594 Eric Dorsey RC .04 .02
❑ 595 Myron Guyton .04 .02
❑ 596 Jeff Hostetler RC .25 .11
❑ 597 Sean Landeta .04 .02
❑ 598 Lionel Manuel .04 .02
❑ 599 Odessa Turner RC .04 .02
❑ 600 Perry Williams .04 .02
❑ 601 James Hasty .04 .02
❑ 602 Erik McMillan .04 .02
❑ 603 Alex Gordon UER .04 .02
(reversed photo on back)
❑ 604 Ron Stallworth .04 .02
❑ 605 Byron Evans RC .04 .02
❑ 606 Ron Heller RC .04 .02
❑ 607 Wes Hopkins .04 .02
(Hitting Ottis Anderson)
❑ 608 Mickey Shuler UER .04 .02
(Reversed photo on back)
❑ 609 Seth Joyner .10 .05
❑ 610 Jim McMahon .10 .05
❑ 611 Mike Pitts .04 .02
❑ 612 Izel Jenkins RC .04 .02
❑ 613 Anthony Bell .04 .02
❑ 614 David Galloway .04 .02
❑ 615 Eric Hill .04 .02
❑ 616 Cedric Mack .04 .02
❑ 617 Freddie Joe Nunn .04 .02
❑ 618 Tootie Robbins .04 .02
❑ 619 Tom Tupa RC .04 .02
❑ 620 Joe Wolf .04 .02
❑ 621 Dermontti Dawson .10 .05
❑ 622 Thomas Everett .04 .02
❑ 623 Tunch Ilkin .04 .02
❑ 624 Hardy Nickerson .10 .05
❑ 625 Gerald Williams RC .04 .02
❑ 626 Rod Woodson .25 .11
❑ 627A Rod Bernstine TE ERR .20 .09
❑ 627B Rod Bernstine RB COR .04 .02
❑ 628 Courtney Hall .04 .02
❑ 629 Ronnie Harmon .10 .05
❑ 630A Anthony Miller ERR .25 .11
(Back says WR)
❑ 630B Anthony Miller COR .10 .05
(Back says WR-KR)
❑ 631 Joe Phillips .04 .02
❑ 632A Leslie O'Neal ERR .50 .23
(Listed as LB-DE on front and back)
❑ 632B Leslie O'Neal ERR .12 .05
(Listed as LB-DE on front and LB on back)
❑ 632C Leslie O'Neal COR .10 .05
(Listed as LB on front and back)
❑ 633A David Richards RC ERR .12 .05
(Back says G-T)
❑ 633B David Richards RC COR .12 .05
(Back says G)
❑ 634 Mark Vlasic .04 .02
❑ 635 Lee Williams .04 .02
❑ 636 Chet Brooks .04 .02
❑ 637 Keena Turner .04 .02
❑ 638 Kevin Fagan RC .04 .02
❑ 639 Brent Jones RC .25 .11
❑ 640 Matt Millen .10 .05
❑ 641 Bubba Paris .04 .02
❑ 642 Bill Romanowski RC .30 .14
❑ 643 Fred Smerlas UER .04 .02
(Front 67, back 76)
❑ 644 Dave Waymer .04 .02
❑ 645 Steve Young .50 .23
❑ 646 Brian Blades .10 .05
❑ 647 Andy Heck .04 .02
❑ 648 Dave Krieg .10 .05
❑ 649 Rufus Porter .04 .02
❑ 650 Kelly Stouffer .04 .02
❑ 651 Tony Woods .04 .02
❑ 652 Gary Anderson RB .04 .02
❑ 653 Reuben Davis .04 .02
❑ 654 Randy Grimes .04 .02
❑ 655 Ron Hall .04 .02
❑ 656 Eugene Marve .04 .02
❑ 657A Curt Jarvis ERR .50 .23
(No "Official NFL Card" on front)
❑ 657B Curt Jarvis COR 30.00 13.50
❑ 658 Ricky Reynolds .04 .02
❑ 659 Broderick Thomas .04 .02
❑ 660 Jeff Bostic .04 .02
❑ 661 Todd Bowles RC .04 .02
❑ 662 Ravin Caldwell .04 .02
❑ 663 Russ Grimm UER .04 .02
(Back photo is actually Jeff Bostic)
❑ 664 Joe Jacoby .04 .02
❑ 665 Mark May .04 .02
(Front G, back G/T)
❑ 666 Walter Stanley .04 .02
❑ 667 Don Warren .04 .02
❑ 668 Stan Humphries RC .25 .11
❑ 669A Jeff George SP 1.00 .45
(Illinois uniform; issued in first series)
❑ 669B Jeff George RC 1.00 .45
(Colts uniform; issued in second series)
❑ 670 Blair Thomas RC .10 .05
(No color stripe along line with AFC symbol and Jets logo)
❑ 671 Cortez Kennedy RC UER .25 .11
(No scouting photo line on back)
❑ 672 Keith McCants RC .04 .02
❑ 673 Junior Seau RC 1.00 .45
❑ 674 Mark Carrier DB RC .25 .11
❑ 675 Andre Ware .10 .05
❑ 676 Chris Singleton RC UER .04 .02
(Parsippany High, should be Parsippany Hills High)
❑ 677 Richmond Webb RC .04 .02
❑ 678 Ray Agnew RC .04 .02
❑ 679 Anthony Smith RC .04 .02
❑ 680 James Francis RC .04 .02

❑ 681 Percy Snow .04 .02
❑ 682 Renaldo Turnbull RC .04 .02
❑ 683 Lamar Lathon RC .10 .05
❑ 684 James Williams RC .04 .02
❑ 685 Emmitt Smith RC 4.00 1.80
❑ 686 Tony Bennett RC .25 .11
❑ 687 Darrell Thompson RC .04 .02
❑ 688 Steve Broussard RC .04 .02
❑ 689 Eric Green RC .10 .05
❑ 690 Ben Smith RC .04 .02
❑ 691 Bern Brostek RC UER .04 .02
(Listed as Center but is playing Guard)
❑ 692 Rodney Hampton RC .40 .18
❑ 693 Dexter Carter RC .04 .02
❑ 694 Rob Moore RC 1.25 .55
❑ 695 Alexander Wright RC .04 .02
❑ 696 Darion Conner RC .10 .05
❑ 697 Reggie Rembert RC UER .04 .02
(Missing Scouting Line credit on the front)
❑ 698A Terry Wooden RC ERR .20 .09
(Number on back is 51)
❑ 698B Terry Wooden RC COR .04 .02
(Number on back is 90)
❑ 699 Reggie Cobb RC .04 .02
❑ 700 Anthony Thompson .04 .02
❑ 701 Fred Washington .04 .02
(Final Update version mentions his death; this card does not)
❑ 702 Ron Cox RC .04 .02
❑ 703 Robert Blackmon RC .04 .02
❑ 704 Dan Owens RC .04 .02
❑ 705 Anthony Johnson RC .25 .11
❑ 706 Aaron Wallace RC .04 .02
❑ 707 Harold Green RC .25 .11
❑ 708 Keith Sims RC .04 .02
❑ 709 Tim Grunhard RC .04 .02
❑ 710 Jeff Alm RC .04 .02
❑ 711 Carwell Gardner RC .04 .02
❑ 712 Kenny Davidson RC .04 .02
❑ 713 Vince Buck RC .04 .02
❑ 714 Leroy Hoard RC .40 .18
❑ 715 Andre Collins RC .04 .02
❑ 716 Dennis Brown RC .04 .02
❑ 717 LeRoy Butler RC .25 .11
❑ 718A Pat Terrell 41 ERR RC .20 .09
❑ 718B Pat Terrell 37 COR RC .04 .02
❑ 719 Mike Bellamy .04 .02
❑ 720 Mike Fox RC .04 .02
❑ 721 Alton Montgomery RC .04 .02
❑ 722 Eric Davis RC .10 .05
❑ 723A Oliver Barnett RC ERR .50 .23
(Front says DT)
❑ 723B Oliver Barnett RC COR .04 .02
(Front says NT)
❑ 724 Houston Hoover RC .04 .02
❑ 725 Howard Ballard RC .04 .02
❑ 726 Keith McKeller RC .04 .02
❑ 727 Wendell Davis RC .04 .02
(Pro Set Prospect in white, not black)
❑ 728 Peter Tom Willis RC .04 .02
❑ 729 Bernard Clark .04 .02
❑ 730 Doug Widell RC .04 .02
❑ 731 Eric Andolsek .04 .02
❑ 732 Jeff Campbell RC .04 .02
❑ 733 Marc Spindler RC .04 .02
❑ 734 Keith Woodside .04 .02
❑ 735 Willis Peguese RC .04 .02
❑ 736 Frank Stams .04 .02
❑ 737 Jeff Uhlenhake .04 .02
❑ 738 Todd Kalis .04 .02
❑ 739 Tommy Hodson RC UER .04 .02
(Born Matthews, should be Mathews)
❑ 740 Greg McMurtry RC .04 .02
❑ 741 Mike Buck RC .04 .02
❑ 742 Kevin Haverdink UER .04 .02
(Jersey says 70, back says 74)
❑ 743A Johnny Bailey RC .10 .05
(Back says 46)
❑ 743B Johnny Bailey RC .10 .05
(Back says 22)
❑ 744A Eric Moore .12 .05
(No Pro Set Prospect on front of card)
❑ 744B Eric Moore 30.00 13.50
(Pro Set Prospect on front of card)
❑ 745 Tony Stargell RC .04 .02
❑ 746 Fred Barnett RC .25 .11
❑ 747 Walter Reeves .04 .02
❑ 748 Derek Hill .04 .02
❑ 749 Quinn Early .25 .11
❑ 750 Ronald Lewis .04 .02
❑ 751 Ken Clark RC .04 .02
❑ 752 Garry Lewis .04 .02
❑ 753 James Lofton .10 .05
❑ 754 Steve Tasker UER .04 .02
(Back says photo is against Raiders, but front shows a Steeler)
❑ 755 Jim Shofner CO .04 .02
❑ 756 Jimmie Jones RC .04 .02
❑ 757 Jay Novacek .25 .11
❑ 758 Jessie Hester RC .04 .02
❑ 759 Barry Word RC .04 .02
❑ 760 Eddie Anderson RC .04 .02
❑ 761 Cleveland Gary .04 .02
❑ 762 Marcus Dupree RC** .04 .02
❑ 763 David Griggs RC .04 .02
❑ 764 Rueben Mayes .04 .02
❑ 765 Stephen Baker .04 .02
❑ 766 Reyna Thompson RC UER .04 .02
(Front CB, back ST-CB)
❑ 767 Everson Walls .04 .02
❑ 768 Brad Baxter RC .04 .02
❑ 769 Steve Walsh .10 .05
❑ 770 Heath Sherman RC .04 .02
❑ 771 Johnny Johnson RC .10 .05
❑ 772A Dexter Manley 30.00 13.50
(Back mentions substance abuse violation)
❑ 772B Dexter Manley .04 .02
(Bio on back changed; doesn't mention substance abuse violation)
❑ 773 Ricky Proehl RC .10 .05
❑ 774 Frank Cornish .04 .02
❑ 775 Tommy Kane RC .04 .02
❑ 776 Derrick Fenner RC .04 .02
❑ 777 Steve Christie RC .04 .02
❑ 778 Wayne Haddix RC .04 .02
❑ 779 Richard Williamson UER .04 .02
(Experience is misspelled as esperience)
❑ 780 Brian Mitchell RC .25 .11
❑ 781 American Bowl/London .04 .02
Raiders vs. Saints
❑ 782 American Bowl/Berlin .04 .02
Rams vs. Chiefs
❑ 783 American Bowl/Tokyo .04 .02
Broncos vs. Seahawks
❑ 784 American Bowl/Montreal .04 .02
Steelers vs. Patriots
❑ 785A Berlin Wall .75 .35
Paul Tagliabue
("Peered through the Berlin Wall")
❑ 785B Berlin Wall .75 .35
Paul Tagliabue
("Posed at the Berlin Wall")
❑ 786 Raiders Stay in LA .04 .02
(Al Davis RC)
❑ 787 Falcons Back in Black .04 .02
(Jerry Glanville)
❑ 788 NFL Goes International .04 .02
World League Spring Debut
(Number on back is black, Newsreel cards are otherwise white; only Newsreel card with silver borders)
❑ 789 Overseas Appeal .04 .02
(Cheerleaders)
❑ 790 Photo Contest .04 .02
(Mike Mularkey awash)
❑ 791 Photo Contest .04 .02
(Gary Reasons hitting Bobby Humphrey)
❑ 792 Photo Contest .04 .02
(Maurice Hurst covering Drew Hill)
❑ 793 Photo Contest .04 .02
(Ronnie Lott celebrating)
❑ 794 Photo Contest .75 .35
(Felix Wright grabbing Barry Sanders' jersey)
❑ 795 Photo Contest .04 .02
(George Seifert in Gatorade Shower)
❑ 796 Photo Contest .04 .02
(Doug Smith praying)
❑ 797 Photo Contest .04 .02
(Doug Widell keeping cool)
❑ 798 Photo Contest .04 .02
(Todd Bowles covering Cris Carter)
❑ 799 Ronnie Lott .10 .05
(Stay in School)
❑ 800D Mark Carrier (Defensive ROY) .10 .05
❑ 800O Emmitt Smith 1.25 .55
(Offensive ROY)
❑ 1990 Santa Claus SP .50 .23
(Second series only; No quote mark after Andre Ware)
❑ CC2 Paul Tagliabue SP .40 .18
NFL Commissioner
(First series only)
❑ CC3 Joe Robbie Mem SP .50 .23
(Second series only)
❑ SC Super Pro SP .50 .23
(Second series only)
❑ SC4 Fred Washington UER .04 .02
(Memorial to his death; word patches repeated in fourth line of text)
❑ SP1 Payne Stewart SP 1.00 .45
(First series only)
❑ NNO Lombardi Trophy SP 80.00 36.00
(Hologram: numbered out of 10,000)
❑ NNO Super Bowl XXIV Logo .04 .02

1991 Pro Set

	MINT	NRMT
COMPLETE SET (850)	15.00	6.75
COMP.SERIES 1 (405)	7.00	3.10
COMP.SERIES 2 (407)	7.00	3.10
COMP.FINAL FACT. (38)	2.00	.90
COMMON CARD (1-850)	.05	.02
SEMISTARS	.10	.05
UNLISTED STARS	.25	.11
VAR NO TEXT (523A/529A)	.50	.23
PIONEER CARDS (SC3-SC5)	.75	.35
COMP.WLAF PLAYER SET (32)	4.00	1.80
COMP.WLAF HELMET SET (10)	2.00	.90

WLAF: RANDOM INSERTS IN SER.1 PACKS

❑ 1D Mark Carrier DB .10 .05
Defensive ROY
❑ 1O Emmitt Smith 1.00 .45
Offensive ROY
❑ 2 Does Not Exist
❑ 3 Joe Montana .50 .23

NFL Player of the Year
❑ 4 Art Shell .10 .05
NFL Coach of the Year
❑ 5 Mike Singletary .10 .05
NFL Man of the Year
❑ 6 Bruce Smith .10 .05
NFL Defensive
Player of the Year
❑ 7 Barry Word .05 .02
NFL Comeback Player
of the Year
❑ 8A Jim Kelly .25 .11
NFL Passing Leader
(NFLPA logo on back)
❑ 8B Jim Kelly .25 .11
NFL Passing Leader
(No NFLPA logo on back)
❑ 8C Jim Kelly 6.00 2.70
NFL Passing Leader
(No NFLPA logo on back
but the registered
symbol remains)
❑ 9 Warren Moon .10 .05
NFL Passing Yardage
and TD Leader
❑ 10 Barry Sanders .60 .25
NFL Rushing and
TD Leader
❑ 11 Jerry Rice .40 .18
NFL Receiving and
Receiving Yardage
Leader
❑ 12 Jay Novacek .10 .05
Tight End Leader
❑ 13 Thurman Thomas .10 .05
NFL Total Yardage
Leader
❑ 14 Nick Lowery .05 .02
NFL Scoring Leader,
Kickers
❑ 15 Mike Horan .05 .02
NFL Punting Leader
❑ 16 Clarence Verdin .05 .02
NFL Punt Return Leader
❑ 17 Kevin Clark RC .05 .02
NFL Kickoff Return
Leader
❑ 18 Mark Carrier DB .10 .05
NFL Interception
Leader
❑ 19A Derrick Thomas ERR 10.00 4.50
NFL Sack Leader
(Bills helmet on front)
❑ 19B Derrick Thomas COR .10 .05
NFL Sack Leader
(Chiefs helmet on front)
❑ 20 Ottis Anderson ML .10 .05
10000 Career
Rushing Yards
❑ 21 Roger Craig ML .10 .05
Most Career
Receptions by RB
❑ 22 Art Monk ML .10 .05
700 Career Receptions
❑ 23 Chuck Noll ML .10 .05
200 Victories
❑ 24 Randall Cunningham ML .10 .05
Leads team in rushing,
fourth straight year
UER (586 rushes, should
be 486; average 5.9,
should be 7.1)
❑ 25 Dan Marino ML .50 .23
7th Straight 3000
yard season
❑ 26 49ers Road Record ML .05 .02
18 victories in row,
still alive
❑ 27 Earl Campbell HOF .05 .02
❑ 28 John Hannah HOF .05 .02
❑ 29 Stan Jones HOF .05 .02
❑ 30 Tex Schramm HOF .05 .02
❑ 31 Jan Stenerud HOF .05 .02
❑ 32 Russell Maryland RC .10 .05
Outland Winner
❑ 33 Chris Zorich RC .10 .05
Lombardi Winner
❑ 34 Darryll Lewis RC UER .10 .05
Thorpe Winner
(Name misspelled
Darryl on card)
❑ 35 Alfred Williams RC .05 .02
Butkus Winner
❑ 36 Raghib(Rocket) Ismail RC 1.00 .45
Walter Camp POY
❑ 37 Ty Detmer HH RC .40 .18
❑ 38 Andre Ware HH .10 .05
❑ 39 Barry Sanders HH .60 .25
❑ 40 Tim Brown HH UER .10 .05
(No %%Official Photo
and Stat Card of the
NFL~ on card back)
❑ 41 Vinny Testaverde HH .10 .05
❑ 42 Bo Jackson HH .10 .05
❑ 43 Mike Rozier HH .05 .02
❑ 44 Herschel Walker HH .10 .05
❑ 45 Marcus Allen HH .10 .05
❑ 46A James Lofton SB .10 .05
(NFLPA logo on back)
❑ 46B James Lofton SB .10 .05
(No NFLPA logo on back)
❑ 47A Bruce Smith SB .10 .05
(Official NFL Card
in black letters)
❑ 47B Bruce Smith SB .10 .05
(Official NFL Card
in white letters)
❑ 48 Myron Guyton SB .05 .02
❑ 49 Stephen Baker SB .05 .02
❑ 50 Mark Ingram SB UER .05 .02
(First repeated twice
on back title)
❑ 51 Ottis Anderson SB .10 .05
❑ 52 Thurman Thomas SB .25 .11
❑ 53 Matt Bahr SB .05 .02
❑ 54 Scott Norwood SB .05 .02
❑ 55 Stephen Baker .05 .02
❑ 56 Carl Banks .05 .02
❑ 57 Mark Collins .05 .02
❑ 58 Steve DeOssie .05 .02
❑ 59 Eric Dorsey .05 .02
❑ 60 John Elliott .05 .02
❑ 61 Myron Guyton .05 .02
❑ 62 Rodney Hampton .25 .11
❑ 63 Jeff Hostetler .10 .05
❑ 64 Erik Howard .05 .02
❑ 65 Mark Ingram .10 .05
❑ 66 Greg Jackson RC .05 .02
❑ 67 Leonard Marshall .05 .02
❑ 68 David Meggett .10 .05
❑ 69 Eric Moore .05 .02
❑ 70 Bart Oates .05 .02
❑ 71 Gary Reasons .05 .02
❑ 72 Bill Parcells CO .10 .05
❑ 73 Howard Ballard .05 .02
❑ 74A Cornelius Bennett .25 .11
(NFLPA logo on back)
❑ 74B Cornelius Bennett .05 .02
(No NFLPA logo on back)
❑ 75 Shane Conlan .05 .02
❑ 76 Kent Hull .05 .02
❑ 77 Kirby Jackson RC .05 .02
❑ 78A Jim Kelly .60 .25
(NFLPA logo on back)
❑ 78B Jim Kelly .25 .11
(No NFLPA logo on back)
❑ 79 Mark Kelso .05 .02
❑ 80 Nate Odomes .05 .02
❑ 81 Andre Reed .10 .05
❑ 82 Jim Ritcher .05 .02
❑ 83 Bruce Smith .25 .11
❑ 84 Darryl Talley .05 .02
❑ 85 Steve Tasker .10 .05
❑ 86 Thurman Thomas .25 .11
❑ 87 James Williams .05 .02
❑ 88 Will Wolford .05 .02
❑ 89 Jeff Wright RC UER .05 .02
(Went to Central
Missouri State, not
Central Missouri)
❑ 90 Marv Levy CO .05 .02
❑ 91 Steve Broussard .05 .02
❑ 92A Darion Conner ERR 10.00 4.50
(Drafted 1st round, '99)
❑ 92B Darion Conner COR .15 .07
(Drafted 2nd round, '90)
❑ 93 Bill Fralic .05 .02
❑ 94 Tim Green .05 .02
❑ 95 Michael Haynes .25 .11
❑ 96 Chris Hinton .05 .02
❑ 97 Chris Miller UER .10 .05
(Two commas after city
in his birth info)
❑ 98 Deion Sanders UER .40 .18
(Career TD's 3, but
only 2 in yearly stats)
❑ 99 Jerry Glanville CO .05 .02
❑ 100 Kevin Butler .05 .02
❑ 101 Mark Carrier DB .10 .05
❑ 102 Jim Covert .05 .02
❑ 103 Richard Dent .10 .05
❑ 104 Jim Harbaugh .25 .11
❑ 105 Brad Muster .05 .02
❑ 106 Lemuel Stinson .05 .02
❑ 107 Keith Van Horne .05 .02
❑ 108 Mike Ditka CO UER .25 .11
(Winning percent in '87
was .733, not .753)
❑ 109 Lewis Billups .05 .02
❑ 110 James Brooks .10 .05
❑ 111 Boomer Esiason .10 .05
❑ 112 James Francis .05 .02
❑ 113 David Fulcher .05 .02
❑ 114 Rodney Holman .05 .02
❑ 115 Tim McGee .05 .02
❑ 116 Anthony Munoz .10 .05
❑ 117 Sam Wyche CO .05 .02
❑ 118 Paul Farren .05 .02
❑ 119 Thane Gash .05 .02
❑ 120 Mike Johnson .05 .02
❑ 121A Bernie Kosar .10 .05
(NFLPA logo on back)
❑ 121B Bernie Kosar .10 .05
(No NFLPA logo on back)
❑ 122 Clay Matthews .10 .05
❑ 123 Eric Metcalf .10 .05
❑ 124 Frank Minnifield .05 .02
❑ 125A Webster Slaughter .10 .05
(NFLPA logo on back)
❑ 125B Webster Slaughter .20 .09
(No NFLPA logo on back)
❑ 126 Bill Belichick CO .05 .02
❑ 127 Tommie Agee .05 .02
❑ 128 Troy Aikman .75 .35
❑ 129 Jack Del Rio .05 .02
❑ 130 John Gesek RC .05 .02
❑ 131 Issiac Holt .05 .02
❑ 132 Michael Irvin .25 .11
❑ 133 Ken Norton .25 .11
❑ 134 Daniel Stubbs .05 .02
❑ 135 Jimmy Johnson CO .10 .05
❑ 136 Steve Atwater .05 .02
❑ 137 Michael Brooks .05 .02
❑ 138 John Elway 1.25 .55
❑ 139 Wymon Henderson .05 .02
❑ 140 Bobby Humphrey .05 .02
❑ 141 Mark Jackson .05 .02
❑ 142 Karl Mecklenburg .05 .02
❑ 143 Doug Widell .05 .02
❑ 144 Dan Reeves CO .05 .02
❑ 145 Eric Andolsek .05 .02
❑ 146 Jerry Ball .05 .02
❑ 147 Bennie Blades .05 .02
❑ 148 Lomas Brown .05 .02
❑ 149 Robert Clark .05 .02
❑ 150 Michael Cofer .05 .02
❑ 151 Dan Owens .05 .02
❑ 152 Rodney Peete .10 .05
❑ 153 Wayne Fontes CO .05 .02
❑ 154 Tim Harris .05 .02
❑ 155 Johnny Holland .05 .02
❑ 156 Don Majkowski .05 .02
❑ 157 Tony Mandarich .05 .02
❑ 158 Mark Murphy .05 .02
❑ 159 Brian Noble .05 .02
❑ 160 Jeff Query .05 .02
❑ 161 Sterling Sharpe .25 .11
❑ 162 Lindy Infante CO .05 .02

❑ 163 Ray Childress .... .05 .02
❑ 164 Ernest Givins .... .10 .05
❑ 165 Richard Johnson .... .05 .02
❑ 166 Bruce Matthews .... .10 .05
❑ 167 Warren Moon .... .25 .11
❑ 168 Mike Munchak .... .05 .02
❑ 169 Al Smith .... .05 .02
❑ 170 Lorenzo White .... .05 .02
❑ 171 Jack Pardee CO .... .05 .02
❑ 172 Albert Bentley .... .05 .02
❑ 173 Duane Bickett .... .05 .02
❑ 174 Bill Brooks .... .05 .02
❑ 175A Eric Dickerson .... .40 .18
(NFLPA logo on back)
❑ 175B Eric Dickerson .... 1.25 .55
(No NFLPA logo on back
and 667 yards rushing
for 1990 in text)
❑ 175C Eric Dickerson .... .25 .11
(No NFLPA logo on back
and 677 yards rushing
for 1990 in text)
❑ 176 Ray Donaldson .... .05 .02
❑ 177 Jeff George .... .25 .11
❑ 178 Jeff Herrod .... .05 .02
❑ 179 Clarence Verdin .... .05 .02
❑ 180 Ron Meyer CO .... .05 .02
❑ 181 John Alt .... .05 .02
❑ 182 Steve DeBerg .... .05 .02
❑ 183 Albert Lewis .... .05 .02
❑ 184 Nick Lowery UER .... .05 .02
(In his 13th year,
not 12th)
❑ 185 Christian Okoye .... .05 .02
❑ 186 Stephone Paige .... .05 .02
❑ 187 Kevin Porter .... .05 .02
❑ 188 Derrick Thomas .... .25 .11
❑ 189 Marty Schottenheimer .... .05 .02
CO
❑ 190 Willie Gault .... .10 .05
❑ 191 Howie Long .... .10 .05
❑ 192 Terry McDaniel .... .05 .02
❑ 193 Jay Schroeder UER .... .05 .02
(Passing total yards
13863, should be 13683)
❑ 194 Steve Smith .... .05 .02
❑ 195 Greg Townsend .... .05 .02
❑ 196 Lionel Washington .... .05 .02
❑ 197 Steve Wisniewski UER .. .05 .02
(Back says drafted,
should say traded to)
❑ 198 Art Shell CO .... .10 .05
❑ 199 Henry Ellard .... .10 .05
❑ 200 Jim Everett .... .10 .05
❑ 201 Jerry Gray .... .05 .02
❑ 202 Kevin Greene .... .25 .11
❑ 203 Buford McGee .... .05 .02
❑ 204 Tom Newberry .... .05 .02
❑ 205 Frank Stams .... .05 .02
❑ 206 Alvin Wright .... .05 .02
❑ 207 John Robinson CO .... .05 .02
❑ 208 Jeff Cross .... .05 .02
❑ 209 Mark Duper .... .10 .05
❑ 210 Dan Marino .... 1.25 .55
❑ 211A Tim McKyer .... .25 .11
(No Traded box on front)
❑ 211B Tim McKyer .... .15 .07
(Traded box on front)
❑ 212 John Offerdahl .... .05 .02
❑ 213 Sammie Smith .... .05 .02
❑ 214 Richmond Webb .... .05 .02
❑ 215 Jarvis Williams .... .05 .02
❑ 216 Don Shula CO .... .10 .05
❑ 217A Darrell Fullington .... .08 .04
ERR (No registered
symbol on card back)
❑ 217B Darrell Fullington .... .08 .04
COR (Registered
symbol on card back)
❑ 218 Tim Irwin .... .05 .02
❑ 219 Mike Merriweather .... .05 .02
❑ 220 Keith Millard .... .05 .02
❑ 221 Al Noga .... .05 .02
❑ 222 Henry Thomas .... .05 .02
❑ 223 Wade Wilson .... .10 .05
❑ 224 Gary Zimmerman .... .05 .02
❑ 225 Jerry Burns CO .... .05 .02
❑ 226 Bruce Armstrong .... .05 .02
❑ 227 Marv Cook .... .05 .02
❑ 228 Hart Lee Dykes .... .05 .02
❑ 229 Tommy Hodson .... .05 .02
❑ 230 Ronnie Lippett .... .05 .02
❑ 231 Ed Reynolds .... .05 .02
❑ 232 Chris Singleton .... .05 .02
❑ 233 John Stephens .... .05 .02
❑ 234 Dick MacPherson CO .... .05 .02
❑ 235 Stan Brock .... .05 .02
❑ 236 Craig Heyward .... .10 .05
❑ 237 Vaughan Johnson .... .05 .02
❑ 238 Robert Massey .... .05 .02
❑ 239 Brett Maxie .... .05 .02
❑ 240 Rueben Mayes .... .05 .02
❑ 241 Pat Swilling .... .10 .05
❑ 242 Renaldo Turnbull .... .05 .02
❑ 243 Jim Mora CO .... .05 .02
❑ 244 Kyle Clifton .... .05 .02
❑ 245 Jeff Criswell .... .05 .02
❑ 246 James Hasty .... .05 .02
❑ 247 Erik McMillan .... .05 .02
❑ 248 Scott Mersereau RC .... .05 .02
❑ 249 Ken O'Brien .... .05 .02
❑ 250A Blair Thomas .... .25 .11
(NFLPA logo on back)
❑ 250B Blair Thomas .... .10 .05
(No NFLPA logo on back)
❑ 251 Al Toon .... .10 .05
❑ 252 Bruce Coslet CO .... .05 .02
❑ 253 Eric Allen .... .05 .02
❑ 254 Fred Barnett .... .25 .11
❑ 255 Keith Byars .... .05 .02
❑ 256 Randall Cunningham .... .25 .11
❑ 257 Seth Joyner .... .10 .05
❑ 258 Clyde Simmons .... .05 .02
❑ 259 Jessie Small .... .05 .02
❑ 260 Andre Waters .... .05 .02
❑ 261 Rich Kotite CO .... .05 .02
❑ 262 Roy Green .... .05 .02
❑ 263 Ernie Jones .... .05 .02
❑ 264 Tim McDonald .... .05 .02
❑ 265 Timm Rosenbach .... .05 .02
❑ 266 Rod Saddler .... .05 .02
❑ 267 Luis Sharpe .... .05 .02
❑ 268 Anthony Thompson UER .05 .02
(Terra Haute should
be Terre Haute)
❑ 269 Marcus Turner RC .... .05 .02
❑ 270 Joe Bugel CO .... .05 .02
❑ 271 Gary Anderson K .... .05 .02
❑ 272 Dermontti Dawson .... .05 .02
❑ 273 Eric Green .... .05 .02
❑ 274 Merril Hoge .... .05 .02
❑ 275 Tunch Ilkin .... .05 .02
❑ 276 D.J. Johnson .... .05 .02
❑ 277 Louis Lipps .... .05 .02
❑ 278 Rod Woodson .... .25 .11
❑ 279 Chuck Noll CO .... .10 .05
❑ 280 Martin Bayless .... .05 .02
❑ 281 Marion Butts UER .... .10 .05
(2 years exp.,
should be 3)
❑ 282 Gill Byrd .... .05 .02
❑ 283 Burt Grossman .... .05 .02
❑ 284 Courtney Hall .... .05 .02
❑ 285 Anthony Miller .... .10 .05
❑ 286 Leslie O'Neal .... .10 .05
❑ 287 Billy Joe Tolliver .... .05 .02
❑ 288 Dan Henning CO .... .05 .02
❑ 289 Dexter Carter .... .05 .02
❑ 290 Michael Carter .... .05 .02
❑ 291 Kevin Fagan .... .05 .02
❑ 292 Pierce Holt .... .05 .02
❑ 293 Guy McIntyre .... .05 .02
(Joe Montana also in photo)
❑ 294 Tom Rathman .... .05 .02
❑ 295 John Taylor .... .10 .05
❑ 296 Steve Young .... .75 .35
❑ 297 George Seifert CO .... .10 .05
❑ 298 Brian Blades .... .10 .05
❑ 299 Jeff Bryant .... .05 .02
❑ 300 Norm Johnson .... .05 .02
❑ 301 Tommy Kane .... .05 .02
❑ 302 Cortez Kennedy UER .... .25 .11
(Played for Seattle
in '90, not Miami)
❑ 303 Bryan Millard .... .05 .02
❑ 304 John L. Williams .... .05 .02
❑ 305 David Wyman .... .05 .02
❑ 306A Chuck Knox CO ERR .. .05 .02
(Has NFLPA logo,
but should not)
❑ 306B Chuck Knox CO COR .. .50 .23
(No NFLPA logo on back)
❑ 307 Gary Anderson RB .... .05 .02
❑ 308 Reggie Cobb .... .05 .02
❑ 309 Randy Grimes .... .05 .02
❑ 310 Harry Hamilton .... .05 .02
❑ 311 Bruce Hill .... .05 .02
❑ 312 Eugene Marve .... .05 .02
❑ 313 Ervin Randle .... .05 .02
❑ 314 Vinny Testaverde .... .10 .05
❑ 315 Richard Williamson CO .. .05 .02
UER (Coach: 1st year,
should be 2nd year)
❑ 316 Earnest Byner .... .05 .02
❑ 317 Gary Clark .... .25 .11
❑ 318A Andre Collins .... .10 .05
(NFLPA logo on back)
❑ 318B Andre Collins .... .20 .09
(No NFLPA logo on back)
❑ 319 Darryl Grant .... .05 .02
❑ 320 Chip Lohmiller .... .05 .02
❑ 321 Martin Mayhew .... .05 .02
❑ 322 Mark Rypien .... .10 .05
❑ 323 Alvin Walton .... .05 .02
❑ 324 Joe Gibbs CO UER .... .10 .05
(Has registered
symbol but should not)
❑ 325 Jerry Glanville REP .... .05 .02
❑ 326A John Elway REP 4.00 1.80
(NFLPA logo on back)
❑ 326B John Elway REP .... 2.00 .90
(No NFLPA logo on back)
❑ 327 Boomer Esiason REP .... .05 .02
❑ 328A Steve Tasker REP 4.00 1.80
(NFLPA logo on back)
❑ 328B Steve Tasker REP .... 2.00 .90
(No NFLPA logo on back)
❑ 329 Jerry Rice REP .... .40 .18
❑ 330 Jeff Rutledge REP .... .05 .02
❑ 331 K.C. Defense REP .... .05 .02
❑ 332 49ers Streak REP .... .05 .02
(Cleveland Gary)
❑ 333 Monday Meeting REP .... .05 .02
(John Taylor)
❑ 334A Randall Cunningham .. .05 .02
REP
(NFLPA logo on back)
❑ 334B Randall Cunningham .. .05 .02
REP
(No NFLPA logo on back)
❑ 335A Bo Jackson and .... .50 .23
Barry Sanders REP
(NFLPA logo on back)
❑ 335B Bo Jackson and .... .50 .23
Barry Sanders REP
(No NFLPA logo on back)
❑ 336 Lawrence Taylor REP .... .25 .11
❑ 337 Warren Moon REP .... .25 .11
❑ 338 Alan Grant REP .... .05 .02
❑ 339 Todd McNair REP .... .05 .02
❑ 340A Miami Dolphins REP .... .05 .02
(Mark Clayton;
TM symbol on Chiefs
player's shoulder)
❑ 340B Miami Dolphins REP .... .05 .02
(Mark Clayton;
TM symbol off Chiefs
player's shoulder)
❑ 341A Highest Scoring REP 4.00 1.80
Jim Kelly Passing
(NFLPA logo on back)
❑ 341B Highest Scoring REP 2.00 .90
Jim Kelly Passing
(No NFLPA logo on back)
❑ 342 Matt Bahr REP .... .05 .02
❑ 343 Robert Tisch NEW .... .05 .02
(With Wellington Mara)
❑ 344 Sam Jankovich NEW .... .05 .02

❑ 345	In-the-Grasp NEW (John Elway)	.05	.02
❑ 346	Bo Jackson NEW (Career in Jeopardy)	.10	.05
❑ 347	NFL Teacher of the Year Jack Williams with Paul Tagliabue	.05	.02
❑ 348	Ronnie Lott NEW (Plan B Free Agent)	.10	.05
❑ 349	Super Bowl XXV Teleclinic NEW (Greg Gumbel with Warren Moon, Derrick Thomas, and Wade Wilson)	.05	.02
❑ 350	Whitney Houston NEW RC	.05	.02
❑ 351	U.S. Troops in Saudia Arabia NEW (Troops watching TV with gas masks)	.05	.02
❑ 352	Art McNally OFF	.05	.02
❑ 353	Dick Jorgensen OFF	.05	.02
❑ 354	Jerry Seeman OFF	.05	.02
❑ 355	Jim Tunney OFF	.05	.02
❑ 356	Gerry Austin OFF	.05	.02
❑ 357	Gene Barth OFF	.05	.02
❑ 358	Red Cashion OFF	.05	.02
❑ 359	Tom Dooley OFF	.05	.02
❑ 360	Johnny Grier OFF	.05	.02
❑ 361	Pat Haggerty OFF	.05	.02
❑ 362	Dale Hamer OFF	.05	.02
❑ 363	Dick Hantak OFF	.05	.02
❑ 364	Jerry Markbreit OFF	.05	.02
❑ 365	Gordon McCarter OFF	.05	.02
❑ 366	Bob McElwee OFF	.05	.02
❑ 367	Howard Roe OFF (Illustrations on back smaller than other officials' cards)	.05	.02
❑ 368	Tom White OFF	.05	.02
❑ 369	Norm Schachter OFF	.05	.02
❑ 370A	Warren Moon Crack Kills (Small type on back)	.25	.11
❑ 370B	Warren Moon Crack Kills (Large type on back)	.25	.11
❑ 371A	Boomer Esiason Don't Drink (Small type on back)	.50	.23
❑ 371B	Boomer Esiason Don't Drink (Large type on back)	.10	.05
❑ 372A	Troy Aikman Play It Straight (Small type on back)	.40	.18
❑ 372B	Troy Aikman Play It Straight (Large type on back)	.40	.18
❑ 373A	Carl Banks Read (Small type on back)	.50	.23
❑ 373B	Carl Banks Read (Large type on back)	.05	.02
❑ 374A	Jim Everett Study (Small type on back)	.50	.23
❑ 374B	Jim Everett Study (Large type on back)	.10	.05
❑ 375A	Anthony Munoz Quadante en la Escuela (Dificul; small type)	.10	.05
❑ 375B	Anthony Munoz Quadante en la Escuela (Dificil; small type)	.10	.05
❑ 375C	Anthony Munoz Quadante en la Escuela (Dificil; large type)	.10	.05
❑ 375D	Anthony Munoz Quedate en la Escuela (Large type)	.10	.05
❑ 376A	Ray Childress Don't Pollute (Small type on back)	1.25	.55
❑ 376B	Ray Childress Don't Pollute (Large type on back)	.05	.02
❑ 377A	Charles Mann Steroids Destroy (Small type on back)	1.25	.55
❑ 377B	Charles Mann Steroids Destroy (Large type on back)	.05	.02
❑ 378A	Jackie Slater Keep the Peace (Small type on back)	1.25	.55
❑ 378B	Jackie Slater Keep the Peace (Large type on back)	.05	.02
❑ 379	Jerry Rice NFC	.40	.18
❑ 380	Andre Rison NFC	.10	.05
❑ 381	Jim Lachey NFC	.05	.02
❑ 382	Jackie Slater NFC	.05	.02
❑ 383	Randall McDaniel NFC	.05	.02
❑ 384	Mark Bortz NFC	.05	.02
❑ 385	Jay Hilgenberg NFC	.05	.02
❑ 386	Keith Jackson NFC	.05	.02
❑ 387	Joe Montana NFC	.50	.23
❑ 388	Barry Sanders NFC	.60	.25
❑ 389	Neal Anderson NFC	.05	.02
❑ 390	Reggie White NFC	.25	.11
❑ 391	Chris Doleman NFC	.05	.02
❑ 392	Jerome Brown NFC	.05	.02
❑ 393	Charles Haley NFC	.05	.02
❑ 394	Lawrence Taylor NFC	.25	.11
❑ 395	Pepper Johnson NFC	.05	.02
❑ 396	Mike Singletary NFC	.10	.05
❑ 397	Darrell Green NFC	.05	.02
❑ 398	Carl Lee NFC	.05	.02
❑ 399	Joey Browner NFC	.05	.02
❑ 400	Ronnie Lott NFC	.10	.05
❑ 401	Sean Landeta NFC	.05	.02
❑ 402	Morten Andersen NFC	.05	.02
❑ 403	Mel Gray NFC	.05	.02
❑ 404	Reyna Thompson NFC	.05	.02
❑ 405	Jimmy Johnson CO NFC	.10	.05
❑ 406	Andre Reed AFC	.10	.05
❑ 407	Anthony Miller AFC	.10	.05
❑ 408	Anthony Munoz AFC	.10	.05
❑ 409	Bruce Armstrong AFC	.05	.02
❑ 410	Bruce Matthews AFC	.05	.02
❑ 411	Mike Munchak AFC	.05	.02
❑ 412	Kent Hull AFC	.05	.02
❑ 413	Rodney Holman AFC	.05	.02
❑ 414	Warren Moon AFC	.25	.11
❑ 415	Thurman Thomas AFC	.25	.11
❑ 416	Marion Butts AFC	.10	.05
❑ 417	Bruce Smith AFC	.10	.05
❑ 418	Greg Townsend AFC	.05	.02
❑ 419	Ray Childress AFC	.05	.02
❑ 420	Derrick Thomas AFC	.25	.11
❑ 421	Leslie O'Neal AFC	.10	.05
❑ 422	John Offerdahl AFC	.05	.02
❑ 423	Shane Conlan AFC	.05	.02
❑ 424	Rod Woodson AFC	.25	.11
❑ 425	Albert Lewis AFC	.05	.02
❑ 426	Steve Atwater AFC	.05	.02
❑ 427	David Fulcher AFC	.05	.02
❑ 428	Rohn Stark AFC	.05	.02
❑ 429	Nick Lowery AFC	.05	.02
❑ 430	Clarence Verdin AFC	.05	.02
❑ 431	Steve Tasker AFC	.05	.02
❑ 432	Art Shell CO AFC	.10	.05
❑ 433	Scott Case	.05	.02
❑ 434	Tory Epps UER (No TM next to Pro Set on card back)	.05	.02
❑ 435	Mike Gann UER (Text has 2 fumble recoveries, stats say 3)	.05	.02
❑ 436	Brian Jordan UER (No TM next to Pro Set on card back)	.10	.05
❑ 437	Mike Kenn	.05	.02
❑ 438	John Rade	.05	.02
❑ 439	Andre Rison	.10	.05
❑ 440	Mike Rozier	.05	.02
❑ 441	Jessie Tuggle	.05	.02
❑ 442	Don Beebe	.05	.02
❑ 443	John Davis RC	.05	.02
❑ 444	James Lofton	.10	.05
❑ 445	Keith McKeller	.05	.02
❑ 446	Jamie Mueller	.05	.02
❑ 447	Scott Norwood	.05	.02
❑ 448	Frank Reich	.10	.05
❑ 449	Leon Seals	.05	.02
❑ 450	Leonard Smith	.05	.02
❑ 451	Neal Anderson	.10	.05
❑ 452	Trace Armstrong	.05	.02
❑ 453	Mark Bortz	.05	.02
❑ 454	Wendell Davis	.05	.02
❑ 455	Shaun Gayle	.05	.02
❑ 456	Jay Hilgenberg	.05	.02
❑ 457	Steve McMichael	.10	.05
❑ 458	Mike Singletary	.10	.05
❑ 459	Donnell Woolford	.05	.02
❑ 460	Jim Breech	.05	.02
❑ 461	Eddie Brown	.05	.02
❑ 462	Barney Bussey RC	.05	.02
❑ 463	Bruce Kozerski	.05	.02
❑ 464	Tim Krumrie	.05	.02
❑ 465	Bruce Reimers	.05	.02
❑ 466	Kevin Walker RC	.05	.02
❑ 467	Ickey Woods	.05	.02
❑ 468	Carl Zander UER (DOB: 4/12/63, should be 3/23/63)	.05	.02
❑ 469	Mike Baab	.05	.02
❑ 470	Brian Brennan	.05	.02
❑ 471	Rob Burnett RC	.05	.02
❑ 472	Raymond Clayborn	.05	.02
❑ 473	Reggie Langhorne	.05	.02
❑ 474	Kevin Mack	.05	.02
❑ 475	Anthony Pleasant	.05	.02
❑ 476	Joe Morris	.05	.02
❑ 477	Dan Fike	.05	.02
❑ 478	Ray Horton	.05	.02
❑ 479	Jim Jeffcoat	.05	.02
❑ 480	Jimmie Jones	.05	.02
❑ 481	Kelvin Martin	.05	.02
❑ 482	Nate Newton	.10	.05
❑ 483	Danny Noonan	.05	.02
❑ 484	Jay Novacek	.25	.11
❑ 485	Emmitt Smith	2.00	.90
❑ 486	James Washington RC	.05	.02
❑ 487	Simon Fletcher	.05	.02
❑ 488	Ron Holmes	.05	.02
❑ 489	Mike Horan	.05	.02
❑ 490	Vance Johnson	.05	.02
❑ 491	Keith Kartz	.05	.02
❑ 492	Greg Kragen	.05	.02
❑ 493	Ken Lanier	.05	.02
❑ 494	Warren Powers	.05	.02
❑ 495	Dennis Smith	.05	.02
❑ 496	Jeff Campbell	.05	.02
❑ 497	Ken Dallafior	.05	.02
❑ 498	Dennis Gibson	.05	.02
❑ 499	Kevin Glover	.05	.02
❑ 500	Mel Gray	.10	.05
❑ 501	Eddie Murray	.05	.02
❑ 502	Barry Sanders	1.50	.70
❑ 503	Chris Spielman	.10	.05
❑ 504	William White	.05	.02
❑ 505	Matt Brock RC	.05	.02
❑ 506	Robert Brown	.05	.02
❑ 507	LeRoy Butler	.10	.05
❑ 508	James Campen RC	.05	.02
❑ 509	Jerry Holmes	.05	.02
❑ 510	Perry Kemp	.05	.02
❑ 511	Ken Ruettgers	.05	.02
❑ 512	Scott Stephen RC	.05	.02
❑ 513	Ed West	.05	.02
❑ 514	Cris Dishman RC	.05	.02
❑ 515	Curtis Duncan	.05	.02
❑ 516	Drew Hill UER (Text says 390 catches and 6368 yards, stats say 450 and 7715)	.05	.02
❑ 517	Haywood Jeffires	.10	.05
❑ 518	Sean Jones	.10	.05
❑ 519	Lamar Lathon	.05	.02
❑ 520	Don Maggs	.05	.02
❑ 521	Bubba McDowell	.05	.02
❑ 522	Johnny Meads	.05	.02
❑ 523A	Chip Banks ERR	.50	.23

(No text)
❑ 523B Chip Banks COR .... .08 .04
❑ 524 Pat Beach .... .05 .02
❑ 525 Sam Clancy .... .05 .02
❑ 526 Eugene Daniel .... .05 .02
❑ 527 Jon Hand .... .05 .02
❑ 528 Jessie Hester .... .05 .02
❑ 529A Mike Prior ERR .... .50 .23
(No textual information)
❑ 529B Mike Prior COR .... .08 .04
❑ 530 Keith Taylor .... .05 .02
❑ 531 Donnell Thompson .... .05 .02
❑ 532 Dino Hackett .... .05 .02
❑ 533 David Lutz RC .... .05 .02
❑ 534 Chris Martin .... .05 .02
❑ 535 Kevin Ross .... .05 .02
❑ 536 Dan Saleaumua .... .05 .02
❑ 537 Neil Smith .... .25 .11
❑ 538 Percy Snow .... .05 .02
❑ 539 Robb Thomas .... .05 .02
❑ 540 Barry Word .... .05 .02
❑ 541 Marcus Allen .... .25 .11
❑ 542 Eddie Anderson .... .05 .02
❑ 543 Scott Davis .... .05 .02
❑ 544 Mervyn Fernandez .... .05 .02
❑ 545 Ethan Horton .... .05 .02
❑ 546 Ronnie Lott .... .10 .05
❑ 547 Don Mosebar .... .05 .02
❑ 548 Jerry Robinson .... .05 .02
❑ 549 Aaron Wallace .... .05 .02
❑ 550 Flipper Anderson .... .05 .02
❑ 551 Cleveland Gary .... .05 .02
❑ 552 Damone Johnson RC .... .05 .02
❑ 553 Duval Love RC .... .05 .02
❑ 554 Irv Pankey .... .05 .02
❑ 555 Mike Piel .... .05 .02
❑ 556 Jackie Slater .... .05 .02
❑ 557 Michael Stewart .... .05 .02
❑ 558 Pat Terrell .... .05 .02
❑ 559 J.B. Brown .... .05 .02
❑ 560 Mark Clayton .... .10 .05
❑ 561 Ferrell Edmunds .... .05 .02
❑ 562 Harry Galbreath .... .05 .02
❑ 563 David Griggs .... .05 .02
❑ 564 Jim C. Jensen .... .05 .02
❑ 565 Louis Oliver .... .05 .02
❑ 566 Tony Paige .... .05 .02
❑ 567 Keith Sims .... .05 .02
❑ 568 Joey Browner .... .05 .02
❑ 569 Anthony Carter .... .10 .05
❑ 570 Chris Doleman .... .05 .02
❑ 571 Rich Gannon UER .... .05 .02
(Acquired in '87, not '88 as in text)
❑ 572 Hassan Jones .... .05 .02
❑ 573 Steve Jordan .... .05 .02
❑ 574 Carl Lee .... .05 .02
❑ 575 Randall McDaniel .... .05 .02
❑ 576 Herschel Walker .... .10 .05
❑ 577 Ray Agnew .... .05 .02
❑ 578 Vincent Brown .... .05 .02
❑ 579 Irving Fryar .... .10 .05
❑ 580 Tim Goad .... .05 .02
❑ 581 Maurice Hurst .... .05 .02
❑ 582 Fred Marion .... .05 .02
❑ 583 Johnny Rembert .... .05 .02
❑ 584 Andre Tippett .... .05 .02
❑ 585 Brent Williams .... .05 .02
❑ 586 Morten Andersen .... .05 .02
❑ 587 Toi Cook RC .... .05 .02
❑ 588 Jim Dombrowski .... .05 .02
❑ 589 Dalton Hilliard .... .05 .02
❑ 590 Rickey Jackson .... .05 .02
❑ 591 Eric Martin .... .05 .02
❑ 592 Sam Mills .... .05 .02
❑ 593 Bobby Hebert .... .05 .02
❑ 594 Steve Walsh .... .05 .02
❑ 595 Ottis Anderson .... .10 .05
❑ 596 Pepper Johnson .... .05 .02
❑ 597 Bob Kratch RC .... .05 .02
❑ 598 Sean Landeta .... .05 .02
❑ 599 Doug Riesenberg .... .05 .02
❑ 600 William Roberts .... .05 .02
❑ 601 Phil Simms .... .10 .05
❑ 602 Lawrence Taylor .... .25 .11
❑ 603 Everson Walls .... .05 .02
❑ 604 Brad Baxter .... .05 .02
❑ 605 Dennis Byrd .... .05 .02
❑ 606 Jeff Lageman .... .05 .02
❑ 607 Pat Leahy .... .05 .02
❑ 608 Rob Moore .... .25 .11
❑ 609 Joe Mott .... .05 .02
❑ 610 Tony Stargell .... .05 .02
❑ 611 Brian Washington .... .05 .02
❑ 612 Marvin Washington RC .... .05 .02
❑ 613 David Alexander .... .05 .02
❑ 614 Jerome Brown .... .05 .02
❑ 615 Byron Evans .... .05 .02
❑ 616 Ron Heller .... .05 .02
❑ 617 Wes Hopkins .... .05 .02
❑ 618 Keith Jackson .... .10 .05
❑ 619 Heath Sherman .... .05 .02
❑ 620 Reggie White .... .25 .11
❑ 621 Calvin Williams .... .10 .05
❑ 622 Ken Harvey .... .10 .05
❑ 623 Eric Hill .... .05 .02
❑ 624 Johnny Johnson .... .05 .02
❑ 625 Freddie Joe Nunn .... .05 .02
❑ 626 Ricky Proehl .... .05 .02
❑ 627 Tootie Robbins .... .05 .02
❑ 628 Jay Taylor .... .05 .02
❑ 629 Tom Tupa .... .05 .02
❑ 630 Jim Wahler RC .... .05 .02
❑ 631 Bubby Brister .... .05 .02
❑ 632 Thomas Everett .... .05 .02
❑ 633 Bryan Hinkle .... .05 .02
❑ 634 Carnell Lake .... .05 .02
❑ 635 David Little .... .05 .02
❑ 636 Hardy Nickerson .... .10 .05
❑ 637 Gerald Williams .... .05 .02
❑ 638 Keith Willis .... .05 .02
❑ 639 Tim Worley .... .05 .02
❑ 640 Rod Bernstine .... .05 .02
❑ 641 Frank Cornish .... .05 .02
❑ 642 Gary Plummer .... .05 .02
❑ 643 Henry Rolling RC .... .05 .02
❑ 644 Sam Seale .... .05 .02
❑ 645 Junior Seau .... .25 .11
❑ 646 Billy Ray Smith .... .05 .02
❑ 647 Broderick Thompson .... .05 .02
❑ 648 Derrick Walker RC .... .05 .02
❑ 649 Todd Bowles .... .05 .02
❑ 650 Don Griffin .... .05 .02
❑ 651 Charles Haley .... .10 .05
❑ 652 Brent Jones UER .... .10 .05
(Born in Santa Clara, not San Jose)
❑ 653 Joe Montana .... 1.25 .55
❑ 654 Jerry Rice .... .75 .35
❑ 655 Bill Romanowski .... .05 .02
❑ 656 Michael Walter .... .05 .02
❑ 657 Dave Waymer .... .05 .02
❑ 658 Jeff Chadwick .... .05 .02
❑ 659 Derrick Fenner .... .05 .02
❑ 660 Nesby Glasgow .... .05 .02
❑ 661 Jacob Green .... .05 .02
❑ 662 Dwayne Harper RC .... .05 .02
❑ 663 Andy Heck .... .05 .02
❑ 664 Dave Krieg .... .10 .05
❑ 665 Rufus Porter .... .05 .02
❑ 666 Eugene Robinson .... .05 .02
❑ 667 Mark Carrier WR .... .25 .11
❑ 668 Steve Christie .... .05 .02
❑ 669 Reuben Davis .... .05 .02
❑ 670 Paul Gruber .... .05 .02
❑ 671 Wayne Haddix .... .05 .02
❑ 672 Ron Hall .... .05 .02
❑ 673 Keith McCants UER .... .05 .02
(Senior All-American, sic, left school after junior year)
❑ 674 Ricky Reynolds .... .05 .02
❑ 675 Mark Robinson .... .05 .02
❑ 676 Jeff Bostic .... .05 .02
❑ 677 Darrell Green .... .05 .02
❑ 678 Markus Koch .... .05 .02
❑ 679 Jim Lachey .... .05 .02
❑ 680 Charles Mann .... .05 .02
❑ 681 Wilber Marshall .... .05 .02
❑ 682 Art Monk .... .10 .05
❑ 683 Gerald Riggs .... .05 .02
❑ 684 Ricky Sanders .... .05 .02
❑ 685 Ray Handley NEW .... .05 .02
(Replaces Bill Parcells as Giants head coach)
❑ 686 NFL announces NEW .... .05 .02
expansion
❑ 687 Miami gets NEW .... .05 .02
Super Bowl XXIX
❑ 688 Giants' George Young NEW .05 .02
is named NFL Executive of the Year by The Sporting News
❑ 689 Five-millionth fan NEW .... .05 .02
visits Pro Football Hall of Fame
❑ 690 Sports Illustrated NEW .... .05 .02
poll finds pro football is America's Number 1 spectator sport
❑ 691 American Bowl NEW .... .05 .02
London Theme Art
❑ 692 American Bowl NEW .... .05 .02
Berlin Theme Art
❑ 693 American Bowl NEW .... .05 .02
Tokyo Theme Art
❑ 694A Russell Maryland .... .25 .11
(Says he runs a 4.91 40, card 32 has 4.8)
❑ 694B Joe Ferguson LEG .... .05 .02
❑ 695 Carl Hairston LEG .... .10 .05
❑ 696 Dan Hampton LEG .... .10 .05
❑ 697 Mike Haynes LEG .... .05 .02
❑ 698 Marty Lyons LEG .... .05 .02
❑ 699 Ozzie Newsome LEG .... .10 .05
❑ 700 Scott Studwell LEG .... .05 .02
❑ 701 Mike Webster LEG .... .05 .02
❑ 702 Dwayne Woodruff LEG .... .05 .02
❑ 703 Larry Kennan CO .... .05 .02
London Monarchs
❑ 704 Stan Gelbaugh RC LL .... .10 .05
London Monarchs
❑ 705 John Brantley LL .... .05 .02
Birmingham Fire
❑ 706 Danny Lockett LL .... .05 .02
London Monarchs
❑ 707 Anthony Parker RC LL .... .10 .05
NY/NJ Knights
❑ 708 Dan Crossman LL .... .05 .02
London Monarchs
❑ 709 Eric Wilkerson LL .... .05 .02
NY/NJ Knights
❑ 710 Judd Garrett RC LL .... .05 .02
London Monarchs
❑ 711 Tony Baker LL .... .05 .02
Frankfurt Galaxy
❑ 712 1st Place BW PHOTO .... .05 .02
Randall Cunningham
❑ 713 2nd Place BW PHOTO .... .05 .02
Mark Ingram
❑ 714 3rd Place BW PHOTO .... .05 .02
Pete Holohan
Barney Bussey
Carl Carter
❑ 715 1st Place Color PHOTO .05 .02
Action
Sterling Sharpe
❑ 716 2nd Place Color PHOTO .05 .02
Action
Jim Harbaugh
❑ 717 3rd Place Color PHOTO .05 .02
Action
Anthony Miller
David Fulcher
❑ 718 1st Place Color PHOTO .05 .02
Feature
Bill Parcells CO
Lawrence Taylor
❑ 719 2nd Place Color PHOTO .05 .02
Feature
Patriotic Crowd
❑ 720 3rd Place Color PHOTO .05 .02
Feature
Alfredo Roberts
❑ 721 Ray Bentley .... .05 .02
Read And Study
❑ 722 Earnest Byner .... .05 .02

Never Give Up
❑ 723 Bill Fralic .05 .02
Steroids Destroy
❑ 724 Joe Jacoby .05 .02
Don't Pollute
❑ 725 Howie Long .10 .05
Aids Kills
❑ 726 Dan Marino .50 .23
School's The Ticket
❑ 727 Ron Rivera .05 .02
Leer Y Estudiar
❑ 728 Mike Singletary .10 .05
Be The Best
❑ 729 Cornelius Bennett .10 .05
Chill
❑ 730 Russell Maryland .25 .11
❑ 731 Eric Turner RC .10 .05
❑ 732 Bruce Pickens RC UER .05 .02
(Wearing 38, but card back lists 39)
❑ 733 Mike Croel RC .05 .02
❑ 734 Todd Lyght RC .05 .02
❑ 735 Eric Swann RC .25 .11
❑ 736 Charles McRae RC .05 .02
❑ 737 Antone Davis RC .05 .02
❑ 738 Stanley Richard RC .05 .02
❑ 739 Herman Moore RC 2.00 .90
❑ 740 Pat Harlow RC .05 .02
❑ 741 Alvin Harper RC .25 .11
❑ 742 Mike Pritchard RC .25 .11
❑ 743 Leonard Russell RC .25 .11
❑ 744 Huey Richardson RC .05 .02
❑ 745 Dan McGwire RC .05 .02
❑ 746 Bobby Wilson RC .05 .02
❑ 747 Alfred Williams .05 .02
❑ 748 Vinnie Clark RC .05 .02
❑ 749 Kelvin Pritchett RC .10 .05
❑ 750 Harvey Williams RC .25 .11
❑ 751 Stan Thomas .05 .02
❑ 752 Randal Hill RC .10 .05
❑ 753 Todd Marinovich RC .05 .02
❑ 754 Ted Washington RC .05 .02
❑ 755 Henry Jones RC .10 .05
❑ 756 Jarrod Bunch RC .05 .02
❑ 757 Mike Dumas RC .05 .02
❑ 758 Ed King RC .05 .02
❑ 759 Reggie Johnson RC .05 .02
❑ 760 Roman Phifer RC .05 .02
❑ 761 Mike Jones RC .05 .02
❑ 762 Brett Favre RC 5.00 2.20
❑ 763 Browning Nagle RC .05 .02
❑ 764 Esera Tuaolo RC .05 .02
❑ 765 George Thornton RC .05 .02
❑ 766 Dixon Edwards RC .05 .02
❑ 767 Darryll Lewis .10 .05
❑ 768 Eric Bieniemy RC .05 .02
❑ 769 Shane Curry .05 .02
❑ 770 Jerome Henderson RC .05 .02
❑ 771 Wesley Carroll RC .05 .02
❑ 772 Nick Bell RC .05 .02
❑ 773 John Flannery RC .05 .02
❑ 774 Ricky Watters RC 1.50 .70
❑ 775 Jeff Graham RC .25 .11
❑ 776 Eric Moten RC .05 .02
❑ 777 Jesse Campbell RC .05 .02
❑ 778 Chris Zorich .10 .05
❑ 779 Joe Valerio .05 .02
❑ 780 Doug Thomas RC .05 .02
❑ 781 Lamar Rogers RC UER .05 .02
(No %%Official Card of NFL– and TM on card front)
❑ 782 John Johnson RC .05 .02
❑ 783 Phil Hansen RC .05 .02
❑ 784 Kanavis McGhee RC .05 .02
❑ 785 Calvin Stephens RC UER .05 .02
(Card says New England, others say New England Patriots)
❑ 786 James Jones RC .05 .02
❑ 787 Reggie Barrett .05 .02
❑ 788 Aeneas Williams RC .25 .11
❑ 789 Aaron Craver RC .05 .02
❑ 790 Keith Traylor RC .05 .02
❑ 791 Godfrey Myles RC .05 .02
❑ 792 Mo Lewis RC .10 .05
❑ 793 James Richards RC .05 .02
❑ 794 Carlos Jenkins RC .05 .02
❑ 795 Lawrence Dawsey RC .10 .05
❑ 796 Don Davey .05 .02
❑ 797 Jake Reed RC .75 .35
❑ 798 Dave McCloughan .05 .02
❑ 799 Erik Williams RC .10 .05
❑ 800 Steve Jackson RC .05 .02
❑ 801 Bob Dahl .05 .02
❑ 802 Ernie Mills RC .10 .05
❑ 803 David Daniels RC .05 .02
❑ 804 Rob Selby RC .05 .02
❑ 805 Ricky Ervins RC .10 .05
❑ 806 Tim Barnett RC .05 .02
❑ 807 Chris Gardocki .05 .02
❑ 808 Kevin Donnalley .05 .02
❑ 809 Robert Wilson RC .05 .02
❑ 810 Chuck Webb RC .05 .02
❑ 811 Darryl Wren RC .05 .02
❑ 812 Ed McCaffrey RC 2.00 .90
❑ 813 Shula's 300th Victory .05 .02
NEWS
❑ 814 Raiders-49ers sell .05 .02
out Coliseum NEWS
❑ 815 NFL International NEWS .05 .02
❑ 816 Moe Gardner RC .05 .02
❑ 817 Tim McKyer .05 .02
❑ 818 Tom Waddle RC .05 .02
❑ 819 Michael Jackson RC .25 .11
❑ 820 Tony Casillas .05 .02
❑ 821 Gaston Green .05 .02
❑ 822 Kenny Walker RC .05 .02
❑ 823 Willie Green RC .05 .02
❑ 824 Erik Kramer RC .40 .18
❑ 825 William Fuller .10 .05
❑ 826 Allen Pinkett .05 .02
❑ 827 Rick Venturi CO .05 .02
❑ 828 Bill Maas .05 .02
❑ 829 Jeff Jaeger .05 .02
❑ 830 Robert Delpino .05 .02
❑ 831 Mark Higgs RC .05 .02
❑ 832 Reggie Roby .05 .02
❑ 833 Terry Allen RC 1.25 .55
❑ 834 Cris Carter .50 .23
(No indication when acquired on waivers)
❑ 835 John Randle RC .60 .25
❑ 836 Hugh Millen RC .05 .02
❑ 837 Jon Vaughn RC .05 .02
❑ 838 Gill Fenerty .05 .02
❑ 839 Floyd Turner .05 .02
❑ 840 Irv Eatman .05 .02
❑ 841 Lonnie Young .05 .02
❑ 842 Jim McMahon .10 .05
❑ 843 Randal Hill UER .05 .02
(Traded to Phoenix, not drafted)
❑ 844 Barry Foster .10 .05
❑ 845 Neil O'Donnell RC 1.00 .45
❑ 846 John Friesz UER .25 .11
(Wears 17, not 7)
❑ 847 Broderick Thomas .05 .02
❑ 848 Brian Mitchell .10 .05
❑ 849 Mike Utley RC .10 .05
❑ 850 Mike Croel ROY .05 .02
❑ SC1 Super Bowl XXVI .25 .11
Theme Art UER
(Card says SB 26, should be 25)
❑ SC3 Jim Thorpe .75 .35
Pioneers of the Game
❑ SC4 Otto Graham .75 .35
Pioneers of the Game
❑ SC5 Paul Brown .75 .35
Pioneers of the Game
❑ PSS1 Walter Payton .50 .23
and Team 34
❑ PSS2 Red Grange .50 .23
❑ MVPC25 Ottis Anderson .25 .11
MVP Super Bowl XXV
❑ AU336 Lawrence Taylor.. 175.00 80.00
REP (autographed/500)
❑ AU394 Lawrence Taylor.. 175.00 80.00
PB (autographed/500)
❑ AU699 Ozzie Newsome 50.00 22.00
(Certified autograph)
❑ AU824 Erik Kramer 50.00 22.00
(Certified autograph)
❑ NNO Mini Pro Set Gazette .25 .11
❑ NNO Pro Set Gazette .25 .11
❑ NNO Santa Claus .50 .23
❑ NNO Super Bowl XXV Art .25 .11
❑ NNO Super Bowl XXV Logo .25 .11

1991 Pro Set Platinum

	MINT	NRMT
COMPLETE SET (315)	10.00	4.50
COMP.SERIES 1 (150)	4.00	1.80
COMP.SERIES 2 (165)	6.00	2.70
COMMON CARD (1-315)	.05	.02
SEMISTARS	.10	.05
UNLISTED STARS	.25	.11

❑ 1 Chris Miller .10 .05
❑ 2 Andre Rison .25 .11
❑ 3 Tim Green .05 .02
❑ 4 Jessie Tuggle .05 .02
❑ 5 Thurman Thomas .25 .11
❑ 6 Darryl Talley .05 .02
❑ 7 Kent Hull .05 .02
❑ 8 Bruce Smith .25 .11
❑ 9 Shane Conlan .05 .02
❑ 10 Jim Harbaugh .25 .11
❑ 11 Neal Anderson .10 .05
❑ 12 Mark Bortz .05 .02
❑ 13 Richard Dent .10 .05
❑ 14 Steve McMichael .05 .02
❑ 15 James Brooks .05 .02
❑ 16 Boomer Esiason .10 .05
❑ 17 Tim Krumrie .05 .02
❑ 18 James Francis .05 .02
❑ 19 Lewis Billups .05 .02
❑ 20 Eric Metcalf .25 .11
❑ 21 Kevin Mack .05 .02
❑ 22 Clay Matthews .10 .05
❑ 23 Mike Johnson .05 .02
❑ 24 Troy Aikman .75 .35
❑ 25 Emmitt Smith 2.00 .90
❑ 26 Daniel Stubbs .05 .02
❑ 27 Ken Norton .25 .11
❑ 28 John Elway 1.25 .55
❑ 29 Bobby Humphrey .05 .02
❑ 30 Simon Fletcher .05 .02
❑ 31 Karl Mecklenburg .05 .02
❑ 32 Rodney Peete .10 .05
❑ 33 Barry Sanders 1.50 .70
❑ 34 Michael Cofer .05 .02
❑ 35 Jerry Ball .05 .02
❑ 36 Sterling Sharpe .25 .11
❑ 37 Tony Mandarich .05 .02
❑ 38 Brian Noble .05 .02
❑ 39 Tim Harris .05 .02
❑ 40 Warren Moon .10 .05
❑ 41 Ernest Givins UER .10 .05
(Misspelled Givens on card back)
❑ 42 Mike Munchak .05 .02
❑ 43 Sean Jones .10 .05
❑ 44 Ray Childress .10 .05
❑ 45 Jeff George .25 .11
❑ 46 Albert Bentley .05 .02
❑ 47 Duane Bickett .05 .02
❑ 48 Steve DeBerg .10 .05
❑ 49 Christian Okoye .10 .05

❑ 50 Neil Smith .25 .11
❑ 51 Derrick Thomas .25 .11
❑ 52 Willie Gault .10 .05
❑ 53 Don Mosebar .05 .02
❑ 54 Howie Long .10 .05
❑ 55 Greg Townsend .05 .02
❑ 56 Terry McDaniel .10 .05
❑ 57 Jackie Slater .05 .02
❑ 58 Jim Everett .10 .05
❑ 59 Cleveland Gary .05 .02
❑ 60 Mike Piel .05 .02
❑ 61 Jerry Gray .05 .02
❑ 62 Dan Marino 1.25 .55
❑ 63 Sammie Smith .05 .02
❑ 64 Richmond Webb .05 .02
❑ 65 Louis Oliver .05 .02
❑ 66 Ferrell Edmunds .05 .02
❑ 67 Jeff Cross .05 .02
❑ 68 Wade Wilson .05 .02
❑ 69 Chris Doleman .10 .05
❑ 70 Joey Browner .05 .02
❑ 71 Keith Millard .05 .02
❑ 72 John Stephens .05 .02
❑ 73 Andre Tippett .05 .02
❑ 74 Brent Williams .05 .02
❑ 75 Craig Heyward .10 .05
❑ 76 Eric Martin .05 .02
❑ 77 Pat Swilling .10 .05
❑ 78 Sam Mills .10 .05
❑ 79 Jeff Hostetler .10 .05
❑ 80 Ottis Anderson .10 .05
❑ 81 Lawrence Taylor .25 .11
❑ 82 Pepper Johnson .05 .02
❑ 83 Blair Thomas .05 .02
❑ 84 Al Toon .10 .05
❑ 85 Ken O'Brien .05 .02
❑ 86 Erik McMillan .05 .02
❑ 87 Dennis Byrd .10 .05
❑ 88 Randall Cunningham .25 .11
❑ 89 Fred Barnett .25 .11
❑ 90 Seth Joyner .10 .05
❑ 91 Reggie White .25 .11
❑ 92 Timm Rosenbach .05 .02
❑ 93 Johnny Johnson .05 .02
❑ 94 Tim McDonald .05 .02
❑ 95 Freddie Joe Nunn .05 .02
❑ 96 Bubby Brister .10 .05
❑ 97 Gary Anderson K UER .05 .02
(Listed as RB)
❑ 98 Merril Hoge .05 .02
❑ 99 Keith Willis .05 .02
❑ 100 Rod Woodson .25 .11
❑ 101 Billy Joe Tolliver .05 .02
❑ 102 Marion Butts .10 .05
❑ 103 Rod Bernstine .05 .02
❑ 104 Lee Williams .05 .02
❑ 105 Burt Grossman UER .05 .02
(Photo on back
is reversed)
❑ 106 Tom Rathman .05 .02
❑ 107 John Taylor .10 .05
❑ 108 Michael Carter .05 .02
❑ 109 Guy McIntyre .05 .02
❑ 110 Pierce Holt .05 .02
❑ 111 John L. Williams .05 .02
❑ 112 Dave Krieg .10 .05
❑ 113 Bryan Millard .05 .02
❑ 114 Cortez Kennedy .25 .11
❑ 115 Derrick Fenner .05 .02
❑ 116 Vinny Testaverde .10 .05
❑ 117 Reggie Cobb .05 .02
❑ 118 Gary Anderson RB .05 .02
❑ 119 Bruce Hill .05 .02
❑ 120 Wayne Haddix .05 .02
❑ 121 Broderick Thomas .05 .02
❑ 122 Keith McCants .05 .02
❑ 123 Andre Collins .10 .05
❑ 124 Earnest Byner .05 .02
❑ 125 Jim Lachey .05 .02
❑ 126 Mark Rypien .10 .05
❑ 127 Charles Mann .05 .02
❑ 128 Nick Lowery .05 .02
❑ 129 Chip Lohmiller .05 .02
❑ 130 Mike Horan .05 .02
❑ 131 Rohn Stark .05 .02
❑ 132 Sean Landeta .05 .02
❑ 133 Clarence Verdin .05 .02
❑ 134 Johnny Bailey .05 .02
❑ 135 Herschel Walker .10 .05
❑ 136 Bo Jackson PP .25 .11
❑ 137 Dexter Carter PP .05 .02
❑ 138 Warren Moon PP .10 .05
❑ 139 Joe Montana PP 1.25 .55
❑ 140 Jerry Rice PP .75 .35
❑ 141 Deion Sanders PP .40 .18
❑ 142 Ronnie Lippett PP .05 .02
❑ 143 Terance Mathis PP .25 .11
❑ 144 Gaston Green PP .05 .02
❑ 145 Dean Biasucci PP .05 .02
❑ 146 Charles Haley PP .10 .05
❑ 147 Derrick Thomas PP .25 .11
❑ 148 Lawrence Taylor PP .10 .05
❑ 149 Art Shell CO PP .10 .05
❑ 150 Bill Parcells CO PP .10 .05
❑ 151 Steve Broussard .05 .02
❑ 152 Darion Conner .05 .02
❑ 153 Bill Fralic .05 .02
❑ 154 Mike Gann .05 .02
❑ 155 Tim McKyer .05 .02
❑ 156 Don Beebe UER .05 .02
(4 TD's against
Dolphins, should be
against Steelers)
❑ 157 Cornelius Bennett .10 .05
❑ 158 Andre Reed .25 .11
❑ 159 Leonard Smith .05 .02
❑ 160 Will Wolford .05 .02
❑ 161 Mark Carrier DB .10 .05
❑ 162 Wendell Davis .05 .02
❑ 163 Jay Hilgenberg .05 .02
❑ 164 Brad Muster .05 .02
❑ 165 Mike Singletary .10 .05
❑ 166 Eddie Brown .05 .02
❑ 167 David Fulcher .05 .02
❑ 168 Rodney Holman .05 .02
❑ 169 Anthony Munoz .10 .05
❑ 170 Craig Taylor RC .05 .02
❑ 171 Mike Baab .05 .02
❑ 172 David Grayson .05 .02
❑ 173 Reggie Langhorne .05 .02
❑ 174 Joe Morris .05 .02
❑ 175 Kevin Gogan RC .05 .02
❑ 176 Jack Del Rio .05 .02
❑ 177 Issiac Holt .05 .02
❑ 178 Michael Irvin .25 .11
❑ 179 Jay Novacek .25 .11
❑ 180 Steve Atwater .05 .02
❑ 181 Mark Jackson .05 .02
❑ 182 Ricky Nattiel .05 .02
❑ 183 Warren Powers .05 .02
❑ 184 Dennis Smith .05 .02
❑ 185 Bennie Blades .05 .02
❑ 186 Lomas Brown UER .05 .02
(Spent 6 seasons with
Detroit, not 7)
❑ 187 Robert Clark UER .05 .02
(Plan B acquisition
in '89, not '90)
❑ 188 Mel Gray .10 .05
❑ 189 Chris Spielman .10 .05
❑ 190 Johnny Holland .05 .02
❑ 191 Don Majkowski .05 .02
❑ 192 Bryce Paup RC .25 .11
❑ 193 Darrell Thompson .05 .02
❑ 194 Ed West UER .05 .02
(Photo on back
is reversed)
❑ 195 Cris Dishman RC .10 .05
❑ 196 Drew Hill .10 .05
❑ 197 Bruce Matthews .10 .05
❑ 198 Bubba McDowell .05 .02
❑ 199 Allen Pinkett .05 .02
❑ 200 Bill Brooks .10 .05
❑ 201 Jeff Herrod .05 .02
❑ 202 Anthony Johnson .10 .05
❑ 203 Mike Prior .05 .02
❑ 204 John Alt .05 .02
❑ 205 Stephone Paige .05 .02
❑ 206 Kevin Ross .05 .02
❑ 207 Dan Saleaumua .05 .02
❑ 208 Barry Word .05 .02
❑ 209 Marcus Allen .25 .11
❑ 210 Roger Craig .10 .05
❑ 211 Ronnie Lott .10 .05
❑ 212 Winston Moss .05 .02
❑ 213 Jay Schroeder .05 .02
❑ 214 Robert Delpino .05 .02
❑ 215 Henry Ellard .10 .05
❑ 216 Kevin Greene .25 .11
❑ 217 Tom Newberry .05 .02
❑ 218 Michael Stewart .05 .02
❑ 219 Mark Duper .10 .05
❑ 220 Mark Higgs RC .05 .02
❑ 221 John Offerdahl UER .05 .02
(2nd round pick in
'86, not 6th)
❑ 222 Keith Sims .05 .02
❑ 223 Anthony Carter .10 .05
❑ 224 Cris Carter .50 .23
❑ 225 Steve Jordan .05 .02
❑ 226 Randall McDaniel .05 .02
❑ 227 Al Noga .05 .02
❑ 228 Ray Agnew .05 .02
❑ 229 Bruce Armstrong .05 .02
❑ 230 Irving Fryar .10 .05
❑ 231 Greg McMurtry .05 .02
❑ 232 Chris Singleton .05 .02
❑ 233 Morten Andersen .05 .02
❑ 234 Vince Buck .05 .02
❑ 235 Gill Fenerty .05 .02
❑ 236 Rickey Jackson .10 .05
❑ 237 Vaughan Johnson .05 .02
❑ 238 Carl Banks .05 .02
❑ 239 Mark Collins .05 .02
❑ 240 Rodney Hampton .25 .11
❑ 241 David Meggett .10 .05
❑ 242 Bart Oates .05 .02
❑ 243 Kyle Clifton .05 .02
❑ 244 Jeff Lageman .10 .05
❑ 245 Freeman McNeil UER .10 .05
(Drafted in '81,
not '80)
❑ 246 Rob Moore .25 .11
❑ 247 Eric Allen .05 .02
❑ 248 Keith Byars .10 .05
❑ 249 Keith Jackson .10 .05
❑ 250 Jim McMahon .10 .05
❑ 251 Andre Waters .05 .02
❑ 252 Ken Harvey .10 .05
❑ 253 Ernie Jones .05 .02
❑ 254 Luis Sharpe .05 .02
❑ 255 Anthony Thompson .05 .02
❑ 256 Tom Tupa .05 .02
❑ 257 Eric Green .10 .05
❑ 258 Barry Foster .10 .05
❑ 259 Bryan Hinkle .05 .02
❑ 260 Tunch Ilkin .05 .02
❑ 261 Louis Lipps .05 .02
❑ 262 Gill Byrd .05 .02
❑ 263 John Friesz .10 .05
❑ 264 Anthony Miller .10 .05
❑ 265 Junior Seau .25 .11
❑ 266 Ronnie Harmon .10 .05
❑ 267 Harris Barton .05 .02
❑ 268 Todd Bowles .05 .02
❑ 269 Don Griffin .05 .02
❑ 270 Bill Romanowski .05 .02
❑ 271 Steve Young .75 .35
❑ 272 Brian Blades .10 .05
❑ 273 Jacob Green .05 .02
❑ 274 Rufus Porter .05 .02
❑ 275 Eugene Robinson .05 .02
❑ 276 Mark Carrier WR .10 .05
❑ 277 Reuben Davis .05 .02
❑ 278 Paul Gruber .05 .02
❑ 279 Gary Clark .25 .11
❑ 280 Darrell Green .10 .05
❑ 281 Wilber Marshall .05 .02
❑ 282 Matt Millen .10 .05
❑ 283 Alvin Walton .05 .02
❑ 284 Joe Gibbs CO UER .10 .05
(NFLPA logo on back)
❑ 285 Don Shula CO UER .10 .05
(NFLPA logo on back)
❑ 286 Larry Brown DB RC .10 .05
❑ 287 Mike Croel RC .05 .02
❑ 288 Antone Davis RC .05 .02
❑ 289 Ricky Ervins RC UER .10 .05

(2nd round choice, should say 3rd)
- ❑ 290 Brett Favre RC 5.00 2.20
- ❑ 291 Pat Harlow RC .... .05 .02
- ❑ 292 Michael Jackson RC ...... .25 .11
- ❑ 293 Henry Jones RC .... .10 .05
- ❑ 294 Aaron Craver RC........... .05 .02
- ❑ 295 Nick Bell RC .... .05 .02
- ❑ 296 Todd Lyght RC .... .10 .05
- ❑ 297 Todd Marinovich RC ...... .05 .02
- ❑ 298 Russell Maryland RC .... .10 .05
- ❑ 299 Kanavis McGhee RC...... .05 .02
- ❑ 300 Dan McGwire RC .... .10 .05
- ❑ 301 Charles McRae RC .... .05 .02
- ❑ 302 Eric Moten RC............... .05 .02
- ❑ 303 Jerome Henderson RC .. .05 .02
- ❑ 304 Browning Nagle RC........ .05 .02
- ❑ 305 Mike Pritchard RC.......... .25 .11
- ❑ 306 Stanley Richard RC........ .10 .05
- ❑ 307 Randal Hill RC............... .10 .05
- ❑ 308 Leonard Russell RC ...... .10 .05
- ❑ 309 Eric Swann RC .... .10 .05
- ❑ 310 Phil Hansen RC............. .05 .02
- ❑ 311 Moe Gardner RC........... .05 .02
- ❑ 312 Jon Vaughn RC............. .05 .02
- ❑ 313 Aeneas Williams RC UER .25 .11 (Misspelled Aaneas on card back)
- ❑ 314 Alfred Williams RC .... .05 .02
- ❑ 315 Harvey Williams RC ...... .25 .11
- ❑ PM1 Emmitt Smith .... 250.00 110.00 Platinum metal card
- ❑ PM2 Paul Brown .... 80.00 36.00 Platinum metal card

1992 Pro Set

	MINT	NRMT
COMPLETE SET (700)	15.00	6.75
COMP.SERIES 1 (400)	8.00	3.60
COMP.SERIES 2 (300)	8.00	3.60
COMMON CARD (1-700)	.04	.02
SEMISTARS.............................	.10	.05
UNLISTED STARS....................	.25	.11
COMPLETE HOF INDUCT.SET (4)	1.50	.70

HOF: RANDOM INSERTS IN SER.1 PACKS

- ❑ 1 Mike Croel LL .... .04 .02 Rookie of the Year
- ❑ 2 Thurman Thomas LL.......... .25 .11 Player of the Year
- ❑ 3 Wayne Fontes CO LL .... .04 .02 Coach of the Year
- ❑ 4 Anthony Munoz LL .... .10 .05 Man of the Year
- ❑ 5 Steve Young LL................ .30 .14 Passing Leader
- ❑ 6 Warren Moon LL .... .10 .05 Passing Yardage Leader
- ❑ 7 Emmitt Smith LL .... .60 .25 Rushing Leader
- ❑ 8 Haywood Jeffires LL .... .04 .02 Receiving Leader
- ❑ 9 Marv Cook LL .... .04 .02 Receiving Leader/TE
- ❑ 10 Michael Irvin LL............... .25 .11 Receiving Yardage Leader
- ❑ 11 Thurman Thomas LL UER .25 .11 Total Yardage Leader (Total combined yards should be 2,038)
- ❑ 12 Chip Lohmiller LL UER .... .04 .02 Scoring Leader (FG Attempt Totals are off by one)
- ❑ 13 Barry Sanders LL .... .60 .25 Scoring Leader TD's
- ❑ 14 Reggie Roby LL .... .04 .02 Punting Leader
- ❑ 15 Mel Gray LL..................... .04 .02 Kickoff/Punt Return Leader
- ❑ 16 Ronnie Lott LL................. .10 .05 Interception Leader
- ❑ 17 Pat Swilling LL................. .04 .02 Sack Leader
- ❑ 18 Reggie White LL .... .10 .05 Defensive MVP
- ❑ 19 Haywood Jeffires MILE .... .04 .02 100 Receptions
- ❑ 20 Pat Leahy MILE............... .04 .02 300 Field Goals
- ❑ 21 James Lofton MILE .... .10 .05 13,000 Yards
- ❑ 22 Art Monk MILE .... .10 .05 800 Receptions
- ❑ 23 Don Shula MILE .... .10 .05 300 Wins
- ❑ 24A Nick Lowery MILE ERR .04 .02 9th 100-Point Season (Says he wears 9)
- ❑ 24B Nick Lowery MILE COR .04 .02 9th 100-Point Season (Says he wears 8)
- ❑ 25 John Elway MILE .... .50 .23 2,000 Completed Passes
- ❑ 26 Chicago Bears MILE .... .04 .02 8 Straight Opening Wins
- ❑ 27 Marcus Allen MILE .... .10 .05 2,000 Rushing Attempts
- ❑ 28 Terrell Buckley DD RC .... .04 .02
- ❑ 29 Amp Lee DD RC .... .04 .02
- ❑ 30 Chris Mims DD RC......... .10 .05
- ❑ 31 Leon Searcy DD RC........ .10 .05
- ❑ 32 Jimmy Smith DD RC 2.50 1.10
- ❑ 33 Siran Stacy DD RC .... .04 .02
- ❑ 34 Pete Gogolak INN .... .04 .02
- ❑ 35 Cheerleaders INN .... .04 .02
- ❑ 36 Houston Astrodome INN .. .04 .02
- ❑ 37 Week 1 REPLAY............. .04 .02 Chiefs 14, Falcons 3 (Christian Okoye)
- ❑ 38 Week 2 REPLAY............. .04 .02 Bills 52, Steelers 34 (Don Beebe)
- ❑ 39 Week 3 REPLAY............. .04 .02 Bears 20, Giants 17 (Wendell Davis)
- ❑ 40 Week 4 REPLAY............. .04 .02 Dolphins 16, Packers 13 (Don Shula CO)
- ❑ 41 Week 5 REPLAY............. .04 .02 Raiders 12 49ers 6 (Ronnie Lott)
- ❑ 42 Week 6 REPLAY............. .04 .02 Redskins 20, Bears 7 (Art Monk)
- ❑ 43 Week 7 REPLAY............. .10 .05 Bills 42, Colts 6 (Thurman Thomas)
- ❑ 44 Week 8 REPLAY............. .04 .02 Patriots 26 Vikings 23 (John Stephens)
- ❑ 45 Week 9 REPLAY UER .... .04 .02 Vikings 28, Cardinals 0 (Herschel Walker; misspelled Hershel on card back)
- ❑ 46 Week 10 REPLAY........... .04 .02 Jets 19 Packers 16 (Chris Burkett)
- ❑ 47 Week 11 REPLAY........... .04 .02 Colts 28 Jets 27 (Line play)
- ❑ 48 Week 12 REPLAY........... .04 .02 Falcons 43 Buccaneers 7 (Andre Rison)
- ❑ 49 Week 13 REPLAY........... .04 .02 Cowboys 24 Redskins 21 (Steve Beuerlein and Michael Irvin)
- ❑ 50 Week 14 REPLAY........... .04 .02 Broncos 20 Patriots 3 (Irving Fryar)
- ❑ 51 Week 15 REPLAY........... .04 .02 Bills 30 Raiders 27 (Bills' Defense)
- ❑ 52 Week 16 REPLAY........... .04 .02 Cowboys 25 Eagles 13 (Kelvin Martin)
- ❑ 53 Week 17 REPLAY........... .04 .02 Jets 23 Dolphins 20 (Bruce Coslet CO)
- ❑ 54 AFC Wild Card REPLAY.. .04 .02 Chiefs 10 Raiders 6 (Fred Jones)
- ❑ 55 AFC Wild Card REPLAY.. .04 .02 Oilers 17 Jets 10 (Oilers' Run-and-Shoot)
- ❑ 56 NFC Wild Card REPLAY.. .04 .02 Cowboys 17 Bears 13 (Bill Bates)
- ❑ 57 NFC Wild Card REPLAY.. .04 .02 Falcons 27 Saints 20 (Michael Haynes)
- ❑ 58 AFC Playoff REPLAY ...... .04 .02 Broncos 26 Oilers 24 (Bronco interception)
- ❑ 59 AFC Playoff REPLAY ...... .10 .05 Bills 37 Chiefs 14 (Thurman Thomas)
- ❑ 60 NFC Playoff REPLAY ...... .04 .02 Lions 38 Cowboys 6 (Eric Kramer)
- ❑ 61 NFC Playoff REPLAY ...... .04 .02 Redskins 24 Falcons 7 (Darrell Green)
- ❑ 62 AFC Champ. REPLAY .... .04 .02 Bills 10 Broncos 7 (Carlton Bailey)
- ❑ 63 NFC Champ. REPLAY .... .04 .02 Redskins 41 Lions 10 (Mark Rypien)
- ❑ 64 Super Bowl XXVI REPLAY .04 .02 TD Reversed, FG Botched
- ❑ 65 Super Bowl XXVI REPLAY .04 .02 (Brad) Edwards Picks Off First of Two
- ❑ 66 Super Bowl XXVI REPLAY .04 .02 Rypien to Byner, 10-0
- ❑ 67 Super Bowl XXVI REPLAY .04 .02 Riggs Puts Redskins Up 17-10
- ❑ 68 Super Bowl XXVI REPLAY .04 .02 Gouveia Interception Buries Bills
- ❑ 69 Super Bowl XXVI REPLAY .10 .05 Thomas Scores Bills' First TD
- ❑ 70 Super Bowl XXVI REPLAY .04 .02 Clark Catches Rypien's Second TD
- ❑ 71 Super Bowl XXVI REPLAY .04 .02 Bills Convert Late Break
- ❑ 72 Super Bowl XXVI REPLAY .04 .02 Redskins Run Out the Clock
- ❑ 73 Jeff Bostic .... .04 .02
- ❑ 74 Earnest Byner .... .04 .02
- ❑ 75 Gary Clark........................ .25 .11
- ❑ 76 Andre Collins.................... .04 .02
- ❑ 77 Darrell Green.................... .04 .02
- ❑ 78 Joe Jacoby .... .04 .02
- ❑ 79 Jim Lachey .... .04 .02
- ❑ 80 Chip Lohmiller .... .04 .02
- ❑ 81 Charles Mann .... .04 .02
- ❑ 82 Martin Mayhew .... .04 .02
- ❑ 83 Matt Millen....................... .10 .05
- ❑ 84 Brian Mitchell................... .10 .05
- ❑ 85 Art Monk .... .10 .05
- ❑ 86 Gerald Riggs.................... .04 .02
- ❑ 87 Mark Rypien .... .04 .02
- ❑ 88 Fred Stokes...................... .04 .02
- ❑ 89 Bobby Wilson .... .04 .02
- ❑ 90 Joe Gibbs CO .... .10 .05

❑ 91	Howard Ballard	.04	.02
❑ 92	Cornelius Bennett UER (Interception total reads 0; he had 4)	.10	.05
❑ 93	Kenneth Davis	.04	.02
❑ 94	Al Edwards	.04	.02
❑ 95	Kent Hull	.04	.02
❑ 96	Kirby Jackson	.04	.02
❑ 97	Mark Kelso	.04	.02
❑ 98	James Lofton UER (Says he played in '75 Pro Bowl, but he wasn't in NFL until 1978)	.10	.05
❑ 99	Keith McKeller	.04	.02
❑ 100	Nate Odomes	.04	.02
❑ 101	Jim Ritcher	.04	.02
❑ 102	Leon Seals	.04	.02
❑ 103	Steve Tasker	.10	.05
❑ 104	Darryl Talley	.04	.02
❑ 105	Thurman Thomas	.25	.11
❑ 106	Will Wolford	.04	.02
❑ 107	Jeff Wright	.04	.02
❑ 108	Marv Levy CO	.04	.02
❑ 109	Darion Conner	.04	.02
❑ 110	Bill Fralic	.04	.02
❑ 111	Moe Gardner	.04	.02
❑ 112	Michael Haynes	.10	.05
❑ 113	Chris Miller	.10	.05
❑ 114	Erric Pegram	.10	.05
❑ 115	Bruce Pickens	.04	.02
❑ 116	Andre Rison	.10	.05
❑ 117	Jerry Glanville CO	.04	.02
❑ 118	Neal Anderson	.04	.02
❑ 119	Trace Armstrong	.04	.02
❑ 120	Wendell Davis	.04	.02
❑ 121	Richard Dent	.10	.05
❑ 122	Jay Hilgenberg	.04	.02
❑ 123	Lemuel Stinson	.04	.02
❑ 124	Stan Thomas	.04	.02
❑ 125	Tom Waddle	.04	.02
❑ 126	Mike Ditka CO	.25	.11
❑ 127	James Brooks	.10	.05
❑ 128	Eddie Brown	.04	.02
❑ 129	David Fulcher	.04	.02
❑ 130	Harold Green	.04	.02
❑ 131	Tim Krumrie UER (Misspelled Krumerie on card front)	.04	.02
❑ 132	Anthony Munoz	.10	.05
❑ 133	Craig Taylor	.04	.02
❑ 134	Eric Thomas	.04	.02
❑ 135	David Shula CO RC	.04	.02
❑ 136	Mike Baab	.04	.02
❑ 137	Brian Brennan	.04	.02
❑ 138	Michael Jackson	.10	.05
❑ 139	James Jones UER (DL on front, DT on back)	.04	.02
❑ 140	Ed King	.04	.02
❑ 141	Clay Matthews	.10	.05
❑ 142	Eric Metcalf	.10	.05
❑ 143	Joe Morris	.04	.02
❑ 144A	Bill Belichick CO ERR (No HC next to name on back)	.10	.05
❑ 144B	Bill Belichick CO COR (HC next to name on back)	.10	.05
❑ 145	Steve Beuerlein	.04	.02
❑ 146	Larry Brown DB	.04	.02
❑ 147	Ray Horton	.04	.02
❑ 148	Ken Norton	.25	.11
❑ 149	Mike Saxon	.04	.02
❑ 150	Emmitt Smith	1.50	.70
❑ 151	Mark Stepnoski	.10	.05
❑ 152	Alexander Wright	.04	.02
❑ 153	Jimmy Johnson CO	.10	.05
❑ 154	Mike Croel	.04	.02
❑ 155	John Elway	1.25	.55
❑ 156	Gaston Green UER (Lists 1991 team as Rams, but was Broncos)	.04	.02
❑ 157	Wymon Henderson	.04	.02
❑ 158	Karl Mecklenburg UER (Card back repeats Super Bowl XXI)	.04	.02
❑ 159	Warren Powers	.04	.02
❑ 160	Steve Sewell UER (Card back repeats Super Bowl XXI)	.04	.02
❑ 161	Doug Widell	.04	.02
❑ 162	Dan Reeves CO	.04	.02
❑ 163	Eric Andolsek	.04	.02
❑ 164	Jerry Ball	.04	.02
❑ 165	Bennie Blades	.04	.02
❑ 166	Ray Crockett	.04	.02
❑ 167	Willie Green UER (Card back repeats and in last sentence)	.04	.02
❑ 168	Erik Kramer	.10	.05
❑ 169	Barry Sanders	1.50	.70
❑ 170	Chris Spielman UER (Card says named to Pro Bowl 1989-90, should say 1989-91)	.04	.02
❑ 171	Wayne Fontes CO	.04	.02
❑ 172	Vinnie Clark	.04	.02
❑ 173	Tony Mandarich	.04	.02
❑ 174	Brian Noble	.04	.02
❑ 175	Bryce Paup	.25	.11
❑ 176	Sterling Sharpe	.25	.11
❑ 177	Darrell Thompson	.04	.02
❑ 178	Esera Tuaolo UER (Text has 1 TD via interception, stats do not)	.04	.02
❑ 179	Ed West	.04	.02
❑ 180	Mike Holmgren CO RC	.10	.05
❑ 181	Ray Childress	.04	.02
❑ 182	Cris Dishman	.04	.02
❑ 183	Curtis Duncan	.04	.02
❑ 184	William Fuller	.10	.05
❑ 185	Lamar Lathon	.04	.02
❑ 186	Warren Moon	.25	.11
❑ 187	Bo Orlando RC	.04	.02
❑ 188	Lorenzo White	.04	.02
❑ 189	Jack Pardee CO	.04	.02
❑ 190	Chip Banks	.04	.02
❑ 191	Dean Biasucci UER (PK on front, K on back)	.04	.02
❑ 192	Bill Brooks	.04	.02
❑ 193	Ray Donaldson	.04	.02
❑ 194	Jeff Herrod	.04	.02
❑ 195	Mike Prior	.04	.02
❑ 196	Mark Vander Poel	.04	.02
❑ 197	Clarence Verdin	.04	.02
❑ 198	Ted Marchibroda CO	.04	.02
❑ 199	John Alt	.04	.02
❑ 200	Deron Cherry	.04	.02
❑ 201	Steve DeBerg	.04	.02
❑ 202	Nick Lowery	.04	.02
❑ 203	Neil Smith	.25	.11
❑ 204	Derrick Thomas	.25	.11
❑ 205	Joe Valerio	.04	.02
❑ 206	Barry Word	.04	.02
❑ 207	Marty Schottenheimer CO	.04	.02
❑ 208	Marcus Allen	.25	.11
❑ 209	Nick Bell	.04	.02
❑ 210	Tim Brown	.25	.11
❑ 211	Howie Long	.10	.05
❑ 212	Ronnie Lott	.10	.05
❑ 213	Todd Marinovich	.04	.02
❑ 214	Greg Townsend	.04	.02
❑ 215	Steve Wright	.04	.02
❑ 216	Art Shell CO	.10	.05
❑ 217	Flipper Anderson	.04	.02
❑ 218	Robert Delpino	.04	.02
❑ 219	Henry Ellard	.10	.05
❑ 220	Kevin Greene	.25	.11
❑ 221	Todd Lyght	.04	.02
❑ 222	Tom Newberry	.04	.02
❑ 223	Roman Phifer	.04	.02
❑ 224	Michael Stewart	.04	.02
❑ 225	Chuck Knox CO	.04	.02
❑ 226	Aaron Craver	.04	.02
❑ 227	Jeff Cross	.04	.02
❑ 228	Mark Duper	.04	.02
❑ 229	Ferrell Edmunds	.04	.02
❑ 230	Jim C. Jensen	.04	.02
❑ 231	Louis Oliver UER (Card has 215 tackles, but he only had 88)	.04	.02
❑ 232	Reggie Roby	.04	.02
❑ 233	Sammie Smith	.04	.02
❑ 234	Don Shula CO	.10	.05
❑ 235	Joey Browner	.04	.02
❑ 236	Anthony Carter	.10	.05
❑ 237	Chris Doleman	.04	.02
❑ 238	Steve Jordan	.04	.02
❑ 239	Kirk Lowdermilk	.04	.02
❑ 240	Henry Thomas	.04	.02
❑ 241	Herschel Walker	.10	.05
❑ 242	Felix Wright	.04	.02
❑ 243	Dennis Green CO RC	.04	.02
❑ 244	Ray Agnew	.04	.02
❑ 245	Marv Cook	.04	.02
❑ 246	Irving Fryar UER (WR/KR on front, WR on back)	.10	.05
❑ 247	Pat Harlow	.04	.02
❑ 248	Hugh Millen	.04	.02
❑ 249	Leonard Russell	.10	.05
❑ 250	Andre Tippett	.04	.02
❑ 251	Jon Vaughn	.04	.02
❑ 252	Dick MacPherson CO	.04	.02
❑ 253	Morten Andersen	.04	.02
❑ 254	Bobby Hebert	.04	.02
❑ 255	Joel Hilgenberg	.04	.02
❑ 256	Vaughan Johnson	.04	.02
❑ 257	Sam Mills	.04	.02
❑ 258	Pat Swilling	.10	.05
❑ 259	Floyd Turner	.04	.02
❑ 260	Steve Walsh	.04	.02
❑ 261	Jim Mora CO UER (No TM by Pro Set logo)	.04	.02
❑ 262	Stephen Baker	.04	.02
❑ 263	Mark Collins	.04	.02
❑ 264	Rodney Hampton	.25	.11
❑ 265	Jeff Hostetler	.10	.05
❑ 266	Erik Howard	.04	.02
❑ 267	Sean Landeta	.04	.02
❑ 268	Gary Reasons UER (Fumble recovery noted on card, but not in stats)	.04	.02
❑ 269	Everson Walls	.04	.02
❑ 270	Ray Handley CO	.04	.02
❑ 271	Louis Aguiar RC	.04	.02
❑ 272	Brad Baxter	.04	.02
❑ 273	Chris Burkett	.04	.02
❑ 274	Irv Eatman	.04	.02
❑ 275	Jeff Lageman	.04	.02
❑ 276	Freeman McNeil	.04	.02
❑ 277	Rob Moore	.10	.05
❑ 278	Lonnie Young	.04	.02
❑ 279	Bruce Coslet CO	.04	.02
❑ 280	Jerome Brown	.04	.02
❑ 281	Keith Byars	.04	.02
❑ 282	Bruce Collie UER (No stats on back)	.04	.02
❑ 283	Keith Jackson	.10	.05
❑ 284	James Joseph	.04	.02
❑ 285	Seth Joyner	.10	.05
❑ 286	Andre Waters	.04	.02
❑ 287	Reggie White	.25	.11
❑ 288	Rich Kotite CO	.04	.02
❑ 289	Rich Camarillo	.04	.02
❑ 290	Garth Jax	.04	.02
❑ 291	Ernie Jones	.04	.02
❑ 292	Tim McDonald	.04	.02
❑ 293	Rod Saddler	.04	.02
❑ 294	Anthony Thompson UER (NO TD stats for 1991 receiving)	.04	.02
❑ 295	Tom Tupa UER (QB/P on front, QB on back)	.04	.02
❑ 296	Ron Wolfley	.04	.02
❑ 297	Joe Bugel CO	.04	.02
❑ 298	Gary Anderson K	.04	.02
❑ 299	Jeff Graham	.25	.11
❑ 300	Eric Green	.04	.02
❑ 301	Bryan Hinkle	.04	.02
❑ 302	Tunch Ilkin	.04	.02
❑ 303	Louis Lipps	.04	.02
❑ 304	Neil O'Donnell	.25	.11
❑ 305	Rod Woodson	.25	.11
❑ 306	Bill Cowher CO RC	.10	.05
❑ 307	Eric Bieniemy	.04	.02
❑ 308	Marion Butts	.04	.02
❑ 309	John Friesz	.10	.05

❑ 310 Courtney Hall .04 .02
❑ 311 Ronnie Harmon .04 .02
❑ 312 Henry Rolling .04 .02
❑ 313 Billy Ray Smith .04 .02
❑ 314 George Thornton .04 .02
❑ 315 Bobby Ross CO RC .04 .02
❑ 316 Todd Bowles .04 .02
❑ 317 Michael Carter .04 .02
❑ 318 Don Griffin .04 .02
❑ 319 Charles Haley .10 .05
❑ 320 Brent Jones .10 .05
❑ 321 John Taylor .10 .05
❑ 322 Ted Washington .04 .02
❑ 323 Steve Young .60 .25
❑ 324 George Seifert CO .10 .05
❑ 325 Brian Blades .10 .05
❑ 326 Jacob Green .04 .02
❑ 327 Patrick Hunter .04 .02
❑ 328 Tommy Kane .04 .02
❑ 329 Cortez Kennedy .10 .05
❑ 330 Dave Krieg .10 .05
❑ 331 Rufus Porter .04 .02
❑ 332 John L. Williams .04 .02
❑ 333 Tom Flores CO .04 .02
❑ 334 Gary Anderson RB .04 .02
❑ 335 Mark Carrier WR .10 .05
❑ 336 Reuben Davis .04 .02
❑ 337 Lawrence Dawsey .10 .05
❑ 338 Keith McCants UER .04 .02
(LB on front, DE on back)
❑ 339 Vinny Testaverde .10 .05
❑ 340 Broderick Thomas .04 .02
❑ 341 Robert Wilson .04 .02
❑ 342 Sam Wyche CO .04 .02
❑ 343 1991 Teacher of .04 .02
the Year NEWS
❑ 344 Owners Reject Instant .04 .02
Replay NEWS
❑ 345 NFL Experience .04 .02
Unveiled NEWS
❑ 346 Chuck Noll Retires .10 .05
Tosses Coin NEWS
❑ 347 Isaac Curtis .04 .02
and Tim McGee MN UER
(Birthdates switched)
❑ 348 Drew Pearson .10 .05
Michael Irvin MN
❑ 349 Billy Sims .50 .23
Barry Sanders MN
❑ 350 Ken Stabler .04 .02
Todd Marinovich MN
❑ 351 Craig James .10 .05
Leonard Russell MN
❑ 352 Bob Golic .04 .02
Graffiti
It's a Sign of
Ignorance
❑ 353 Pat Harlow .04 .02
Vote, Let
Your Choice Be Heard
❑ 354 Esera Tuaolo .04 .02
Stand Tall, Be Proud
of Your Heritage
❑ 355 Mark Schlereth RC .04 .02
Save The Environment
Be a Team Player
❑ 356 Trace Armstrong .04 .02
Drug Abuse
Stay in Control
❑ 357 Eric Bieniemy .04 .02
Save a Life
Buckle Up
❑ 358 Bill Romanowski .04 .02
Education
Stay In School
❑ 359 Irv Eatman .04 .02
Exercise
Be Active
❑ 360 Jonathan Hayes .04 .02
Diabetes
Be Your Best
❑ 361 Atlanta Falcons .04 .02
Spirit of the Game
(Helmet)
❑ 362 Chicago Bears .04 .02
Spirit of the Game
(Vintage game photo)
❑ 363 Dallas Cowboys .04 .02
Spirit of the Game
(Mascot)
❑ 364 Detroit Lions .04 .02
Spirit of the Game
(Overhead game photo)
❑ 365 Green Bay Packers .04 .02
Spirit of the Game
(60's huddle)
❑ 366 Los Angeles Rams .04 .02
Spirit of the Game
(Fans)
❑ 367 Minnesota Vikings .04 .02
Spirit of the Game
(Vintage game photo)
❑ 368 New Orleans Saints UER .04 .02
Spirit of the Game
(Fans; Post-season record
was 0-3, not 0-2)
❑ 369 New York Giants .04 .02
Spirit of the Game
(Fan's banner)
❑ 370 Philadelphia Eagles .04 .02
Spirit of the Game
(Eric Allen)
❑ 371 Phoenix Cardinals .04 .02
Spirit of the Game
(Fan)
❑ 372 San Francisco 49ers .04 .02
Spirit of the Game
(Tom Rathman)
❑ 373 Tampa Bay Buccaneers .04 .02
Spirit of the Game
(Mascot)
❑ 374 Washington Redskins .04 .02
Spirit of the Game
(Fans)
❑ 375 Steve Atwater PB UER .04 .02
(Photo shows regular
game instead of Pro Bowl)
❑ 376 Cornelius Bennett PB .10 .05
❑ 377 Tim Brown PB .10 .05
❑ 378 Marion Butts PB .04 .02
❑ 379 Ray Childress PB .04 .02
(Photo shows regular
game instead of Pro Bowl)
❑ 380 Mark Clayton PB .04 .02
❑ 381 Marv Cook PB .04 .02
❑ 382 Cris Dishman PB .04 .02
❑ 383 William Fuller PB .04 .02
❑ 384 Gaston Green PB .04 .02
❑ 385 Jeff Jaeger PB .04 .02
❑ 386 Haywood Jeffires PB .10 .05
❑ 387 James Lofton PB .10 .05
❑ 388 Ronnie Lott PB .10 .05
❑ 389 K.Mecklenburg PB UER .04 .02
(Back and front read ...berg)
❑ 390 Warren Moon PB .10 .05
❑ 391 Anthony Munoz PB .04 .02
❑ 392 Dennis Smith PB .04 .02
❑ 393 Neil Smith PB .10 .05
❑ 394 Darryl Talley PB .04 .02
❑ 395 Derrick Thomas PB .10 .05
❑ 396 Thurman Thomas PB .10 .05
❑ 397 Greg Townsend PB .04 .02
❑ 398 Richmond Webb PB .04 .02
❑ 399 Rod Woodson PB .10 .05
❑ 400 Dan Reeves CO PB .04 .02
❑ 401 Troy Aikman PB .40 .18
❑ 402 Eric Allen PB .04 .02
❑ 403 Bennie Blades PB .04 .02
❑ 404 Lomas Brown PB .04 .02
❑ 405 Mark Carrier DB PB .04 .02
❑ 406 Gary Clark PB .10 .05
❑ 407 Mel Gray PB .04 .02
❑ 408 Darrell Green PB .04 .02
❑ 409 Michael Irvin PB .25 .11
❑ 410 Vaughan Johnson PB .04 .02
❑ 411 Seth Joyner PB .04 .02
❑ 412 Jim Lachey PB .04 .02
❑ 413 Chip Lohmiller PB .04 .02
❑ 414 Charles Mann PB .04 .02
❑ 415 Chris Miller PB .10 .05
❑ 416 Sam Mills PB .04 .02
❑ 417 Bart Oates PB .04 .02
❑ 418 Jerry Rice PB .40 .18
❑ 419 Andre Rison PB .10 .05
❑ 420 Mark Rypien PB .04 .02
❑ 421 Barry Sanders PB .60 .25
❑ 422 Deion Sanders PB .25 .11
❑ 423 Mark Schlereth PB .04 .02
❑ 424 Mike Singletary PB .04 .02
❑ 425 Emmitt Smith PB .60 .25
❑ 426 Pat Swilling PB .04 .02
❑ 427 Reggie White PB .10 .05
❑ 428 Rick Bryan .04 .02
❑ 429 Tim Green .04 .02
❑ 430 Drew Hill .04 .02
❑ 431 Norm Johnson .04 .02
❑ 432 Keith Jones .04 .02
❑ 433 Mike Pritchard .10 .05
❑ 434 Deion Sanders .50 .23
❑ 435 Tony Smith RC .04 .02
❑ 436 Jessie Tuggle .04 .02
❑ 437 Steve Christie .04 .02
❑ 438 Shane Conlan .04 .02
❑ 439 Matt Darby RC .04 .02
❑ 440 John Fina RC .04 .02
❑ 441 Henry Jones .04 .02
❑ 442 Jim Kelly .25 .11
❑ 443 Pete Metzelaars .04 .02
❑ 444 Andre Reed .10 .05
❑ 445 Bruce Smith .25 .11
❑ 446 Troy Auzenne RC .04 .02
❑ 447 Mark Carrier DB .04 .02
❑ 448 Will Furrer RC .04 .02
❑ 449 Jim Harbaugh .25 .11
❑ 450 Brad Muster .04 .02
❑ 451 Darren Lewis .04 .02
❑ 452 Mike Singletary .10 .05
❑ 453 Alonzo Spellman RC .10 .05
❑ 454 Chris Zorich .10 .05
❑ 455 Jim Breech .04 .02
❑ 456 Boomer Esiason .10 .05
❑ 457 Derrick Fenner .04 .02
❑ 458 James Francis .04 .02
❑ 459 David Klingler RC .10 .05
❑ 460 Tim McGee .04 .02
❑ 461 Carl Pickens RC .60 .25
❑ 462 Alfred Williams .04 .02
❑ 463 Darryl Williams RC .04 .02
❑ 464 Mark Bavaro .04 .02
❑ 465 Jay Hilgenberg .04 .02
❑ 466 Leroy Hoard .10 .05
❑ 467 Bernie Kosar .10 .05
❑ 468 Michael Dean Perry .10 .05
❑ 469 Todd Philcox RC .04 .02
❑ 470 Patrick Rowe RC .04 .02
❑ 471 Tommy Vardell RC .10 .05
❑ 472 Everson Walls .04 .02
❑ 473 Troy Aikman .75 .35
❑ 474 Kenneth Gant RC .04 .02
❑ 475 Charles Haley .10 .05
❑ 476 Michael Irvin .25 .11
❑ 477 Robert Jones RC .04 .02
❑ 478 Russell Maryland .10 .05
❑ 479 Jay Novacek .10 .05
❑ 480 Kevin Smith RC .25 .11
❑ 481 Tony Tolbert .04 .02
❑ 482 Steve Atwater .04 .02
❑ 483 Shane Dronett RC .04 .02
❑ 484 Simon Fletcher .04 .02
❑ 485 Greg Lewis .04 .02
❑ 486 Tommy Maddox RC .04 .02
❑ 487 Shannon Sharpe .25 .11
❑ 488 Dennis Smith .04 .02
❑ 489 Sammie Smith .04 .02
❑ 490 Kenny Walker .04 .02
❑ 491 Lomas Brown .04 .02
❑ 492 Mike Farr .04 .02
❑ 493 Mel Gray .10 .05
❑ 494 Jason Hanson RC .10 .05
❑ 495 Herman Moore .75 .35
❑ 496 Rodney Peete .10 .05
❑ 497 Robert Porcher RC .10 .05
❑ 498 Kelvin Pritchett .04 .02
❑ 499 Andre Ware .04 .02
❑ 500 Sanjay Beach RC .04 .02
❑ 501 Edgar Bennett RC .25 .11
❑ 502 Lewis Billups .04 .02
❑ 503 Terrell Buckley .04 .02

Card	Player	Price	Price
❑ 504	Ty Detmer	.25	.11
❑ 505	Brett Favre	2.50	1.10
❑ 506	Johnny Holland	.04	.02
❑ 507	Dexter McNabb RC	.04	.02
❑ 508	Vince Workman	.10	.05
❑ 509	Cody Carlson	.04	.02
❑ 510	Ernest Givins	.10	.05
❑ 511	Jerry Gray	.04	.02
❑ 512	Haywood Jeffires	.10	.05
❑ 513	Bruce Matthews	.04	.02
❑ 514	Bubba McDowell	.04	.02
❑ 515	Bucky Richardson RC	.04	.02
❑ 516	Webster Slaughter	.04	.02
❑ 517	Al Smith	.04	.02
❑ 518	Mel Agee	.04	.02
❑ 519	Ashley Ambrose RC	.10	.05
❑ 520	Kevin Call	.04	.02
❑ 521	Ken Clark	.04	.02
❑ 522	Quentin Coryatt RC	.25	.11
❑ 523	Steve Emtman RC	.04	.02
❑ 524	Jeff George	.25	.11
❑ 525	Jessie Hester	.04	.02
❑ 526	Anthony Johnson	.10	.05
❑ 527	Tim Barnett	.04	.02
❑ 528	Martin Bayless	.04	.02
❑ 529	J.J. Birden	.04	.02
❑ 530	Dale Carter RC	.25	.11
❑ 531	Dave Krieg	.10	.05
❑ 532	Albert Lewis	.04	.02
❑ 533	Nick Lowery	.04	.02
❑ 534	Christian Okoye	.04	.02
❑ 535	Harvey Williams	.25	.11
❑ 536	Aundray Bruce	.04	.02
❑ 537	Eric Dickerson	.10	.05
❑ 538	Willie Gault	.10	.05
❑ 539	Ethan Horton	.04	.02
❑ 540	Jeff Jaeger	.04	.02
❑ 541	Napoleon McCallum	.04	.02
❑ 542	Chester McGlockton RC	.25	.11
❑ 543	Steve Smith	.04	.02
❑ 544	Steve Wisniewski	.04	.02
❑ 545	Marc Boutte RC	.04	.02
❑ 546	Pat Carter	.04	.02
❑ 547	Jim Everett	.10	.05
❑ 548	Cleveland Gary	.04	.02
❑ 549	Sean Gilbert RC	.25	.11
❑ 550	Steve Israel RC	.04	.02
❑ 551	Todd Kinchen RC	.04	.02
❑ 552	Jackie Slater	.04	.02
❑ 553	Tony Zendejas	.04	.02
❑ 554	Robert Clark	.04	.02
❑ 555	Mark Clayton	.10	.05
❑ 556	Marco Coleman RC	.10	.05
❑ 557	Bryan Cox	.10	.05
❑ 558	Keith Jackson UER (Card says drafted in '88, but acquired as free agent in '92)	.10	.05
❑ 559	Dan Marino	1.25	.55
❑ 560	John Offerdahl	.04	.02
❑ 561	Troy Vincent RC	.10	.05
❑ 562	Richmond Webb	.04	.02
❑ 563	Terry Allen	.25	.11
❑ 564	Cris Carter	.50	.23
❑ 565	Roger Craig	.10	.05
❑ 566	Rich Gannon	.04	.02
❑ 567	Hassan Jones	.04	.02
❑ 568	Randall McDaniel	.04	.02
❑ 569	Al Noga	.04	.02
❑ 570	Todd Scott	.04	.02
❑ 571	Van Waiters RC	.04	.02
❑ 572	Bruce Armstrong	.04	.02
❑ 573	Gene Chilton RC	.04	.02
❑ 574	Eugene Chung RC	.04	.02
❑ 575	Todd Collins RC	.04	.02
❑ 576	Hart Lee Dykes	.04	.02
❑ 577	David Howard RC	.04	.02
❑ 578	Eugene Lockhart	.04	.02
❑ 579	Greg McMurtry	.04	.02
❑ 580	Rod Smith DB RC	.04	.02
❑ 581	Gene Atkins	.04	.02
❑ 582	Vince Buck	.04	.02
❑ 583	Wesley Carroll	.04	.02
❑ 584	Jim Dombrowski	.04	.02
❑ 585	Vaughn Dunbar RC	.04	.02
❑ 586	Craig Heyward	.10	.05
❑ 587	Dalton Hilliard	.04	.02
❑ 588	Wayne Martin	.04	.02
❑ 589	Renaldo Turnbull	.04	.02
❑ 590	Carl Banks	.04	.02
❑ 591	Derek Brown TE RC	.04	.02
❑ 592	Jarrod Bunch	.04	.02
❑ 593	Mark Ingram	.04	.02
❑ 594	Ed McCaffrey	.30	.14
❑ 595	Phil Simms	.10	.05
❑ 596	Phillippi Sparks RC	.04	.02
❑ 597	Lawrence Taylor	.25	.11
❑ 598	Lewis Tillman	.04	.02
❑ 599	Kyle Clifton	.04	.02
❑ 600	Mo Lewis	.04	.02
❑ 601	Terance Mathis	.10	.05
❑ 602	Scott Mersereau	.04	.02
❑ 603	Johnny Mitchell RC	.04	.02
❑ 604	Browning Nagle	.04	.02
❑ 605	Ken O'Brien	.04	.02
❑ 606	Al Toon	.10	.05
❑ 607	Marvin Washington	.04	.02
❑ 608	Eric Allen	.04	.02
❑ 609	Fred Barnett	.25	.11
❑ 610	John Booty	.04	.02
❑ 611	Randall Cunningham	.25	.11
❑ 612	Rich Miano	.04	.02
❑ 613	Clyde Simmons	.04	.02
❑ 614	Siran Stacy	.04	.02
❑ 615	Herschel Walker	.10	.05
❑ 616	Calvin Williams	.10	.05
❑ 617	Chris Chandler	.25	.11
❑ 618	Randal Hill	.04	.02
❑ 619	Johnny Johnson	.04	.02
❑ 620	Lorenzo Lynch	.04	.02
❑ 621	Robert Massey	.04	.02
❑ 622	Ricky Proehl	.04	.02
❑ 623	Timm Rosenbach	.04	.02
❑ 624	Tony Sacca RC	.04	.02
❑ 625	Aeneas Williams UER (Name misspelled Aaneas)	.10	.05
❑ 626	Bubby Brister	.04	.02
❑ 627	Barry Foster	.10	.05
❑ 628	Merril Hoge	.04	.02
❑ 629	D.J. Johnson	.04	.02
❑ 630	David Little	.04	.02
❑ 631	Greg Lloyd	.25	.11
❑ 632	Ernie Mills	.04	.02
❑ 633	Leon Searcy RC	.10	.05
❑ 634	Dwight Stone	.04	.02
❑ 635	Sam Anno RC	.04	.02
❑ 636	Burt Grossman	.04	.02
❑ 637	Stan Humphries	.25	.11
❑ 638	Nate Lewis	.04	.02
❑ 639	Anthony Miller	.10	.05
❑ 640	Chris Mims	.25	.11
❑ 641	Marquez Pope RC	.04	.02
❑ 642	Stanley Richard	.04	.02
❑ 643	Junior Seau	.25	.11
❑ 644	Brian Bollinger RC	.04	.02
❑ 645	Steve Bono RC	.25	.11
❑ 646	Dexter Carter	.04	.02
❑ 647	Dana Hall RC	.10	.05
❑ 648	Amp Lee	.04	.02
❑ 649	Joe Montana	1.25	.55
❑ 650	Tom Rathman	.04	.02
❑ 651	Jerry Rice	.75	.35
❑ 652	Ricky Watters	.25	.11
❑ 653	Robert Blackmon	.04	.02
❑ 654	John Kasay	.04	.02
❑ 655	Ronnie Lee RC	.04	.02
❑ 656	Dan McGwire	.04	.02
❑ 657	Ray Roberts RC	.04	.02
❑ 658	Kelly Stouffer	.04	.02
❑ 659	Chris Warren	.25	.11
❑ 660	Tony Woods	.04	.02
❑ 661	David Wyman	.04	.02
❑ 662	Reggie Cobb	.04	.02
❑ 663A	Steve DeBerg ERR (Career yardage 1455; found in foil packs)	.10	.05
❑ 663B	Steve DeBerg COR (Career yardage 31,455; found in jumbo packs)	.10	.05
❑ 664	Santana Dotson RC	.25	.11
❑ 665	Willie Drewery	.04	.02
❑ 666	Paul Gruber	.04	.02
❑ 667	Ron Hall	.04	.02
❑ 668	Courtney Hawkins RC	.10	.05
❑ 669	Charles McRae	.04	.02
❑ 670	Ricky Reynolds	.04	.02
❑ 671	Monte Coleman	.04	.02
❑ 672	Brad Edwards	.04	.02
❑ 673	Jumpy Geathers UER (Card says played in New Orleans in '89; should say Washington)	.04	.02
❑ 674	Kelly Goodburn	.04	.02
❑ 675	Kurt Gouveia	.04	.02
❑ 676	Chris Hakel RC	.04	.02
❑ 677	Wilber Marshall	.04	.02
❑ 678	Ricky Sanders	.04	.02
❑ 679	Mark Schlereth	.04	.02
❑ 680	Buffalo Bills Spirit of the Game Rich Stadium	.04	.02
❑ 681	Cincinnati Bengals Spirit of the Game Boomer Esiason (with tiger cub)	.04	.02
❑ 682	Cleveland Browns Spirit of the Game The Dog Pound	.04	.02
❑ 683	Denver Broncos Spirit of the Game Bronco Statue	.04	.02
❑ 684	Houston Oilers Spirit of the Game "Luv Ya Blue"	.04	.02
❑ 685	Indianapolis Colts Spirit of the Game Hoosier Dome	.04	.02
❑ 686	Kansas City Chiefs Spirit of the Game Mack Lee Hill Award Mack Lee Hill Tracy Simien	.04	.02
❑ 687	Los Angeles Raiders Spirit of the Game The Team of the Decades	.04	.02
❑ 688	Miami Dolphins Spirit of the Game Dolphins' helmet	.04	.02
❑ 689	New England Patriots Spirit of the Game Francis J. Kilroy VP	.04	.02
❑ 690	New York Jets Spirit of the Game Team mascot	.04	.02
❑ 691	Pittsburgh Steelers Spirit of the Game Steelers' helmet	.04	.02
❑ 692	San Diego Chargers Spirit of the Game Charger in parachute	.04	.02
❑ 693	Seattle Seahawks Spirit of the Game Kingdome	.04	.02
❑ 694	Play Smart Stephen Baker	.04	.02
❑ 695	Hank Williams Jr. NEWS RC	.04	.02
❑ 696	3 Brothers in NFL NEWS Brian Baldinger Gary Baldinger Rich Baldinger	.04	.02
❑ 697	Japan Bowl NEWS August 2, 1992	.04	.02
❑ 698	Georgia Dome NEWS	.04	.02
❑ 699	Theme Art NEWS Super Bowl XXVII	.04	.02
❑ 700	Mark Rypien NEWS Super Bowl XXVI MVP	.04	.02
❑ AU150	Emmitt Smith AU (Certified autograph)	200.00	90.00
❑ AU168	Erik Kramer AU (Certified autograph)	50.00	22.00
❑ NNO	Emmitt Smith Power Preview Card	.75	.35
❑ NNO	Santa Claus Spirit of the Season	.50	.23
❑ SC5	Super Bowl XXVI Logo card	.30	.14

❑ P1 Cover Card Promo	1.00	.45
Hologram, numbered of 2000		

1992 Pro Set Emmitt Smith Holograms

	MINT	NRMT
COMPLETE SET (4)	60.00	27.00
COMMON SMITH (ES1-ES4)	6.00	2.70
RANDOM INSERTS IN SER.1 PACKS		

❑ ES1 Emmitt Smith	6.00	2.70
Stats 1990-1999		
❑ ES2 Emmitt Smith	10.00	4.50
Drafted by Cowboys		
❑ ES3 Emmitt Smith	20.00	9.00
'90 Pro Set Offensive Rookie of the Year		
❑ ES4 Emmitt Smith	25.00	11.00
'91 NFL Rushing Leader		

1992 Pro Set Gold MVPs

	MINT	NRMT
COMPLETE SET (30)	15.00	6.75
ONE PER JUMBO PACK		

❑ MVP1 Thurman Thomas	.50	.23
❑ MVP2 Anthony Munoz	.20	.09
❑ MVP3 Clay Matthews	.20	.09
❑ MVP4 John Elway	2.50	1.10
❑ MVP5 Warren Moon	.50	.23
❑ MVP6 Bill Brooks	.10	.05
❑ MVP7 Derrick Thomas	.50	.23
❑ MVP8 Todd Marinovich	.10	.05
❑ MVP9 Mark Higgs	.10	.05
❑ MVP10 Leonard Russell	.20	.09
❑ MVP11 Rob Moore	.20	.09
❑ MVP12 Rod Woodson	.50	.23
❑ MVP13 Marion Butts	.10	.05
❑ MVP14 Brian Blades	.20	.09
❑ MVP15 Don Shula CO	.20	.09
❑ MVP16 Deion Sanders	1.00	.45
❑ MVP17 Neal Anderson	.10	.05
❑ MVP18 Emmitt Smith	3.00	1.35
❑ MVP19 Barry Sanders	3.00	1.35
❑ MVP20 Brett Favre	5.00	2.20
❑ MVP21 Kevin Greene	.50	.23
❑ MVP22 Terry Allen	.50	.23
❑ MVP23 Pat Swilling	.20	.09
❑ MVP24 Rodney Hampton	.50	.23
❑ MVP25 Randall Cunningham	.50	.23
❑ MVP26 Randal Hill	.10	.05
❑ MVP27 Jerry Rice	1.50	.70
❑ MVP28 Vinny Testaverde	.20	.09
❑ MVP29 Mark Rypien	.10	.05
❑ MVP30 Jimmy Johnson CO	.20	.09

1992 Pro Set Ground Force

	MINT	NRMT
COMPLETE SET (6)	25.00	11.00
COMMON (86/118/206/249)	2.50	1.10
RANDOM INSERTS IN SER.1 PACKS		

❑ 86 Gerald Riggs	2.50	1.10
❑ 105 Thurman Thomas	4.00	1.80
❑ 118 Neal Anderson	2.50	1.10
❑ 150 Emmitt Smith	15.00	6.75
❑ 206 Barry Word	2.50	1.10
❑ 249 Leonard Russell	2.50	1.10

1992 Pro Set HOF 2000

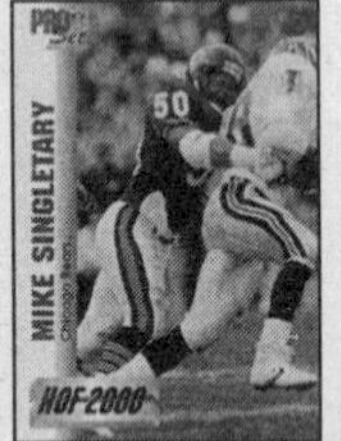

	MINT	NRMT
COMPLETE SET (10)	20.00	9.00
RANDOM INSERTS IN SER.2 FOIL PACKS		

❑ 1 Marcus Allen	2.00	.90
❑ 2 Richard Dent	.75	.35
❑ 3 Eric Dickerson	.75	.35
❑ 4 Ronnie Lott	.75	.35
❑ 5 Art Monk	.75	.35
❑ 6 Joe Montana	10.00	4.50
❑ 7 Warren Moon	2.00	.90
❑ 8 Anthony Munoz	.75	.35
❑ 9 Mike Singletary	.75	.35
❑ 10 Lawrence Taylor	2.00	.90

1993 Pro Set

	MINT	NRMT
COMPLETE SET (449)	12.00	5.50
COMMON CARD (1-449)	.05	.02
SEMISTARS	.10	.05
UNLISTED STARS	.25	.11

❑ 1 Marco Coleman	.05	.02
Rookie of the Year		
❑ 2 Steve Young	.30	.14
Player of the Year		
❑ 3 Mike Holmgren	.10	.05
Coach of the Year		
❑ 4 John Elway	.75	.35
Man of the Year		
❑ 5 Steve Young	.30	.14
Passing Leader		
❑ 6 Dan Marino	.75	.35
Passing Yardage		
❑ 7 Emmitt Smith	.75	.35
Rushing Leader		
❑ 8 Sterling Sharpe	.10	.05
Receiving Leader		
❑ 9 Jay Novacek	.10	.05
Receiving TE		
❑ 10 Sterling Sharpe	.10	.05
Receiving Yardage		
❑ 11 Thurman Thomas	.10	.05
Total Yardage		
❑ 12 Pete Stoyanovich	.05	.02
Scoring Leader		
❑ 13 Greg Montgomery	.05	.02
Punting Leader		
❑ 14 Johnny Bailey	.05	.02
Punt Return		
❑ 15 Jon Vaughn	.05	.02
Kickoff Return		
❑ 16 Audray McMillian	.05	.02
Henry Jones UER Interception (Name spelled McMillan on back)		
❑ 17 Clyde Simmons	.05	.02
Sack Leader		
❑ 18 Cortez Kennedy	.05	.02
Defensive MVP		
❑ 19 AFC Wildcard	.05	.02
(Stan Humphries)		
❑ 20 AFC Wildcard	.05	.02
(Don Beebe)		
❑ 21 NFC Wildcard	.05	.02
(Eric Allen)		
❑ 22 NFC Wildcard	.05	.02
(Brian Mitchell)		
❑ 23 AFC Divisional	.05	.02
(Frank Reich)		
❑ 24 AFC Divisional	.75	.35
(Dan Marino)		
❑ 25 NFC Divisional	.50	.23
(Troy Aikman)		
❑ 26 NFC Divisional	.10	.05
(Ricky Watters)		
❑ 27 AFC Championship	.05	.02
(Bruce Smith sacking Dan Marino)		
❑ 28 NFC Championship	.05	.02
(Tony Casillas sacking Steve Young)		
❑ 29 Super Bowl XXVIII Logo	.05	.02
❑ 30 Troy Aikman	.75	.35
❑ 31 Thomas Everett	.05	.02
❑ 32 Charles Haley	.10	.05
❑ 33 Alvin Harper	.10	.05
❑ 34 Michael Irvin	.25	.11
❑ 35 Robert Jones	.05	.02
❑ 36 Russell Maryland	.05	.02
❑ 37 Ken Norton	.10	.05
❑ 38 Jay Novacek	.10	.05
❑ 39 Emmitt Smith	1.50	.70
❑ 40 Darrin Smith RC	.10	.05

❑ 41 Mark Stepnoski .05 .02
❑ 42 Kevin Williams RC .25 .11
❑ 43 Daryl Johnston .25 .11
❑ 44 Derrick Lassic RC .05 .02
❑ 45 Don Beebe .05 .02
❑ 46 Cornelius Bennett .10 .05
❑ 47 Bill Brooks .05 .02
❑ 48 Kenneth Davis .05 .02
❑ 49 Jim Kelly .25 .11
❑ 50 Andre Reed .10 .05
❑ 51 Bruce Smith .25 .11
❑ 52 Thomas Smith RC .10 .05
❑ 53 Darryl Talley .05 .02
❑ 54 Thurman Thomas .25 .11
❑ 55 Russell Copeland RC .10 .05
❑ 56 Steve Christie .05 .02
❑ 57 Pete Metzelaars .05 .02
❑ 58 Frank Reich .10 .05
❑ 59 Henry Jones .05 .02
❑ 60 Vinnie Clark .05 .02
❑ 61 Eric Dickerson .10 .05
❑ 62 Jumpy Geathers .05 .02
❑ 63 Roger Harper RC .05 .02
❑ 64 Michael Haynes .10 .05
❑ 65 Bobby Hebert .05 .02
❑ 66 Lincoln Kennedy RC .05 .02
❑ 67 Chris Miller .10 .05
❑ 68 Andre Rison .10 .05
❑ 69 Deion Sanders .50 .23
❑ 70 Jessie Tuggle .05 .02
❑ 71 Ron George .05 .02
❑ 72 Erric Pegram .10 .05
❑ 73 Melvin Jenkins .05 .02
❑ 74 Pierce Holt .05 .02
❑ 75 Neal Anderson .05 .02
❑ 76 Mark Carrier DB .05 .02
❑ 77 Curtis Conway RC .50 .23
❑ 78 Richard Dent .10 .05
❑ 79 Jim Harbaugh .25 .11
❑ 80 Craig Heyward .10 .05
❑ 81 Darren Lewis .05 .02
❑ 82 Alonzo Spellman .05 .02
❑ 83 Tom Waddle .05 .02
❑ 84 Wendell Davis .05 .02
❑ 85 Chris Zorich .05 .02
❑ 86 Carl Simpson RC .05 .02
❑ 87 Chris Gedney RC .05 .02
❑ 88 Trace Armstrong .05 .02
❑ 89 Peter Tom Willis .05 .02
❑ 90 John Copeland RC .10 .05
❑ 91 Derrick Fenner .05 .02
❑ 92 James Francis .05 .02
❑ 93 Harold Green .05 .02
❑ 94 David Klingler .05 .02
❑ 95 Tim Krumrie .05 .02
❑ 96 Tony McGee RC .10 .05
❑ 97 Carl Pickens .25 .11
❑ 98 Alfred Williams .05 .02
❑ 99 Doug Pelfrey RC .05 .02
❑ 100 Lance Gunn RC .05 .02
❑ 101 Jay Schroeder .05 .02
❑ 102 Steve Tovar RC .05 .02
❑ 103 Jeff Query .05 .02
❑ 104 Ty Parten RC .05 .02
❑ 105 Jerry Ball .05 .02
❑ 106 Mark Carrier WR .10 .05
❑ 107 Rob Burnett .05 .02
❑ 108 Michael Jackson .10 .05
❑ 109 Mike Johnson .05 .02
❑ 110 Bernie Kosar .10 .05
❑ 111 Clay Matthews .10 .05
❑ 112 Eric Metcalf .10 .05
❑ 113 Michael Dean Perry .10 .05
❑ 114 Vinny Testaverde .10 .05
❑ 115 Eric Turner .05 .02
❑ 116 Tommy Vardell .05 .02
❑ 117 Leroy Hoard .10 .05
❑ 118 Steve Everitt RC .05 .02
❑ 119 Everson Walls .05 .02
❑ 120 Steve Atwater .05 .02
❑ 121 Rod Bernstine .05 .02
❑ 122 Mike Croel .05 .02
❑ 123 John Elway 1.50 .70
❑ 124 Simon Fletcher .05 .02
❑ 125 Glyn Milburn RC .25 .11
❑ 126 Reggie Rivers RC .05 .02
❑ 127 Shannon Sharpe .25 .11
❑ 128 Dennis Smith .05 .02
❑ 129 Dan Williams RC .05 .02
❑ 130 Rondell Jones RC .05 .02
❑ 131 Jason Elam RC .10 .05
❑ 132 Arthur Marshall RC .05 .02
❑ 133 Gary Zimmerman .05 .02
❑ 134 Karl Mecklenburg .05 .02
❑ 135 Bennie Blades .05 .02
❑ 136 Lomas Brown .05 .02
❑ 137 Bill Fralic .05 .02
❑ 138 Mel Gray .10 .05
❑ 139 Willie Green .05 .02
❑ 140 Ryan McNeil RC .05 .02
❑ 141 Rodney Peete .05 .02
❑ 142 Barry Sanders 1.50 .70
❑ 143 Chris Spielman .10 .05
❑ 144 Pat Swilling .05 .02
❑ 145 Andre Ware .05 .02
❑ 146 Herman Moore .50 .23
❑ 147 Tim McKyer .05 .02
❑ 148 Brett Perriman .25 .11
❑ 149 Antonio London RC .05 .02
❑ 150 Edgar Bennett .25 .11
❑ 151 Terrell Buckley .05 .02
❑ 152 Brett Favre 2.00 .90
❑ 153 Jackie Harris .05 .02
❑ 154 Johnny Holland .05 .02
❑ 155 Sterling Sharpe .25 .11
❑ 156 Tim Hauck .05 .02
❑ 157 George Teague RC .10 .05
❑ 158 Reggie White .25 .11
❑ 159 Mark Clayton .05 .02
❑ 160 Ty Detmer .25 .11
❑ 161 Wayne Simmons RC .05 .02
❑ 162 Mark Brunell RC 3.00 1.35
❑ 163 Tony Bennett .05 .02
❑ 164 Brian Noble .05 .02
❑ 165 Cody Carlson .05 .02
❑ 166 Ray Childress .05 .02
❑ 167 Cris Dishman .05 .02
❑ 168 Curtis Duncan .05 .02
❑ 169 Brad Hopkins RC .05 .02
❑ 170 Haywood Jeffires .10 .05
❑ 171 Wilber Marshall .05 .02
❑ 172 Micheal Barrow UER .05 .02
(Name spelled Michael on both sided)
❑ 173 Bubba McDowell .05 .02
❑ 174 Warren Moon .25 .11
❑ 175 Webster Slaughter .05 .02
❑ 176 Travis Hannah RC .05 .02
❑ 177 Lorenzo White .05 .02
❑ 178 Ernest Givins UER .10 .05
(Name spelled Givens on front)
❑ 179 Keith McCants .05 .02
❑ 180 Kerry Cash .05 .02
❑ 181 Quentin Coryatt .10 .05
❑ 182 Kirk Lowdermilk .05 .02
❑ 183 Rodney Culver .05 .02
❑ 184 Rohn Stark .05 .02
❑ 185 Steve Emtman .05 .02
❑ 186 Jeff George .25 .11
❑ 187 Jeff Herrod .05 .02
❑ 188 Reggie Langhorne .05 .02
❑ 189 Roosevelt Potts RC .05 .02
❑ 190 Jack Trudeau .05 .02
❑ 191 Will Wolford .05 .02
❑ 192 Jessie Hester .05 .02
❑ 193 Anthony Johnson .10 .05
❑ 194 Ray Buchanan RC .05 .02
❑ 195 Dale Carter .05 .02
❑ 196 Willie Davis .25 .11
❑ 197 John Alt .05 .02
❑ 198 Joe Montana 1.50 .70
❑ 199 Will Shields RC .05 .02
❑ 200 Neil Smith .25 .11
❑ 201 Derrick Thomas .25 .11
❑ 202 Harvey Williams .10 .05
❑ 203 Marcus Allen .25 .11
❑ 204 J.J. Birden .05 .02
❑ 205 Tim Barnett .05 .02
❑ 206 Albert Lewis .05 .02
❑ 207 Nick Lowery .05 .02
❑ 208 Dave Krieg .10 .05
❑ 209 Keith Cash .05 .02
❑ 210 Patrick Bates RC .05 .02
❑ 211 Nick Bell .05 .02
❑ 212 Tim Brown .25 .11
❑ 213 Willie Gault .05 .02
❑ 214 Ethan Horton .05 .02
❑ 215 Jeff Hostetler .10 .05
❑ 216 Howie Long .10 .05
❑ 217 Greg Townsend .05 .02
❑ 218 Raghib Ismail .10 .05
❑ 219 Alexander Wright .05 .02
❑ 220 Greg Robinson RC .05 .02
❑ 221 Billy Joe Hobert RC .25 .11
❑ 222 Steve Wisniewski .05 .02
❑ 223 Steve Smith .05 .02
❑ 224 Vince Evans .05 .02
❑ 225 Flipper Anderson .05 .02
❑ 226 Jerome Bettis RC 1.00 .45
❑ 227 Troy Drayton RC .10 .05
❑ 228 Henry Ellard .10 .05
❑ 229 Jim Everett .10 .05
❑ 230 Tony Zendejas .05 .02
❑ 231 Todd Lyght .05 .02
❑ 232 Todd Kinchen .05 .02
❑ 233 Jackie Slater .05 .02
❑ 234 Fred Stokes .05 .02
❑ 235 Russell White RC .10 .05
❑ 236 Cleveland Gary .05 .02
❑ 237 Sean LaChapelle RC .05 .02
❑ 238 Steve Israel .05 .02
❑ 239 Shane Conlan .05 .02
❑ 240 Keith Byars .05 .02
❑ 241 Marco Coleman .05 .02
❑ 242 Bryan Cox .05 .02
❑ 243 Irving Fryar .10 .05
❑ 244 Richmond Webb .05 .02
❑ 245 Mark Higgs .05 .02
❑ 246 Terry Kirby RC .25 .11
❑ 247 Mark Ingram .05 .02
❑ 248 John Offerdahl .05 .02
❑ 249 Keith Jackson .10 .05
❑ 250 Dan Marino 1.50 .70
❑ 251 O.J. McDuffie RC .75 .35
❑ 252 Louis Oliver .05 .02
❑ 253 Pete Stoyanovich .05 .02
❑ 254 Troy Vincent .05 .02
❑ 255 Anthony Carter .10 .05
❑ 256 Cris Carter .50 .23
❑ 257 Roger Craig .10 .05
❑ 258 Jack Del Rio .05 .02
❑ 259 Chris Doleman .05 .02
❑ 260 Barry Word .05 .02
❑ 261 Qadry Ismail RC .25 .11
❑ 262 Jim McMahon .05 .02
❑ 263 Robert Smith RC 1.00 .45
❑ 264 Fred Strickland .05 .02
❑ 265 Randall McDaniel .05 .02
❑ 266 Carl Lee .05 .02
❑ 267 Olanda Truitt RC UER .05 .02
(Name spelled Olanda on front)
❑ 268 Terry Allen .25 .11
❑ 269 Audray McMillian .05 .02
❑ 270 Drew Bledsoe RC 3.00 1.35
❑ 271 Eugene Chung .05 .02
❑ 272 Marv Cook .05 .02
❑ 273 Pat Harlow .05 .02
❑ 274 Greg McMurtry .05 .02
❑ 275 Leonard Russell .10 .05
❑ 276 Chris Slade RC .10 .05
❑ 277 Andre Tippett .05 .02
❑ 278 Vincent Brisby RC .25 .11
❑ 279 Ben Coates .50 .23
❑ 280 Sam Gash RC .05 .02
❑ 281 Bruce Armstrong .05 .02
❑ 282 Rod Smith DB .05 .02
❑ 283 Michael Timpson .05 .02
❑ 284 Scott Sisson RC .05 .02
❑ 285 Morten Andersen .05 .02
❑ 286 Reggie Freeman RC .05 .02
❑ 287 Dalton Hilliard .05 .02
❑ 288 Rickey Jackson .05 .02
❑ 289 Vaughan Johnson .05 .02
❑ 290 Eric Martin .05 .02
❑ 291 Sam Mills .05 .02
❑ 292 Brad Muster .05 .02
❑ 293 William Roaf RC .10 .05
❑ 294 Irv Smith RC .05 .02

Card	MINT	NRMT
❑ 295 Wade Wilson	.05	.02
❑ 296 Derek Brown RBK RC	.10	.05
❑ 297 Quinn Early	.10	.05
❑ 298 Steve Walsh	.05	.02
❑ 299 Renaldo Turnbull	.05	.02
❑ 300 Jessie Armstead RC	.05	.02
❑ 301 Carlton Bailey	.05	.02
❑ 302 Michael Brooks	.05	.02
❑ 303 Rodney Hampton	.25	.11
❑ 304 Ed McCaffrey	.10	.05
❑ 305 Dave Meggett	.05	.02
❑ 306 Bart Oates	.05	.02
❑ 307 Mike Sherrard	.05	.02
❑ 308 Phil Simms	.10	.05
❑ 309 Lawrence Taylor	.25	.11
❑ 310 Mark Jackson	.05	.02
❑ 311 Jarrod Bunch	.05	.02
❑ 312 Howard Cross	.05	.02
❑ 313 Michael Strahan RC	.05	.02
❑ 314 Marcus Buckley RC	.05	.02
❑ 315 Brad Baxter	.05	.02
❑ 316 Adrian Murrell RC	.75	.35
❑ 317 Boomer Esiason	.10	.05
❑ 318 Johnny Johnson	.05	.02
❑ 319 Marvin Jones RC	.05	.02
❑ 320 Jeff Lageman	.05	.02
❑ 321 Ronnie Lott	.10	.05
❑ 322 Leonard Marshall	.05	.02
❑ 323 Johnny Mitchell	.05	.02
❑ 324 Rob Moore	.10	.05
❑ 325 Browning Nagle	.05	.02
❑ 326 Blair Thomas	.05	.02
❑ 327 Brian Washington	.05	.02
❑ 328 Terance Mathis	.10	.05
❑ 329 Kyle Clifton	.05	.02
❑ 330 Eric Allen	.05	.02
❑ 331 Victor Bailey RC	.05	.02
❑ 332 Fred Barnett	.10	.05
❑ 333 Mark Bavaro	.05	.02
❑ 334 Randall Cunningham	.25	.11
❑ 335 Ken O'Brien	.05	.02
❑ 336 Seth Joyner	.05	.02
❑ 337 Leonard Renfro RC	.05	.02
❑ 338 Heath Sherman	.05	.02
❑ 339 Clyde Simmons	.05	.02
❑ 340 Herschel Walker	.10	.05
❑ 341 Calvin Williams	.10	.05
❑ 342 Bubby Brister	.05	.02
❑ 343 Vaughn Hebron RC	.05	.02
❑ 344 Keith Millard	.05	.02
❑ 345 Johnny Bailey	.05	.02
❑ 346 Steve Beuerlein	.05	.02
❑ 347 Chuck Cecil	.05	.02
❑ 348 Larry Centers RC	.25	.11
❑ 349 Chris Chandler	.10	.05
❑ 350 Ernest Dye RC	.05	.02
❑ 351 Garrison Hearst RC	1.00	.45
❑ 352 Randal Hill	.05	.02
❑ 353 John Booty	.05	.02
❑ 354 Gary Clark	.10	.05
❑ 355 Ronald Moore RC	.10	.05
❑ 356 Ricky Proehl	.05	.02
❑ 357 Eric Swann	.10	.05
❑ 358 Ken Harvey	.05	.02
❑ 359 Ben Coleman RC	.05	.02
❑ 360 Deon Figures RC	.10	.05
❑ 361 Barry Foster	.10	.05
❑ 362 Jeff Graham	.10	.05
❑ 363 Eric Green	.05	.02
❑ 364 Kevin Greene	.25	.11
❑ 365 Andre Hastings RC	.25	.11
❑ 366 Greg Lloyd	.25	.11
❑ 367 Neil O'Donnell	.25	.11
❑ 368 Dwight Stone	.05	.02
❑ 369 Mike Tomczak	.05	.02
❑ 370 Rod Woodson	.25	.11
❑ 371 Chad Brown RC	.10	.05
❑ 372 Ernie Mills	.05	.02
❑ 373 Darren Perry	.05	.02
❑ 374 Leon Searcy	.05	.02
❑ 375 Marion Butts	.05	.02
❑ 376 John Carney	.05	.02
❑ 377 Ronnie Harmon	.05	.02
❑ 378 Stan Humphries	.25	.11
❑ 379 Nate Lewis	.05	.02
❑ 380 Natrone Means RC	.75	.35
❑ 381 Anthony Miller	.10	.05
❑ 382 Chris Mims	.05	.02
❑ 383 Leslie O'Neal	.10	.05
❑ 384 Joe Cocozzo RC	.05	.02
❑ 385 Junior Seau	.25	.11
❑ 386 Jerrol Williams	.05	.02
❑ 387 John Friesz	.10	.05
❑ 388 Darrien Gordon RC	.05	.02
❑ 389 Derrick Walker	.05	.02
❑ 390 Dana Hall	.05	.02
❑ 391 Brent Jones	.10	.05
❑ 392 Todd Kelly RC	.05	.02
❑ 393 Amp Lee	.05	.02
❑ 394 Tim McDonald	.05	.02
❑ 395 Jerry Rice	1.00	.45
❑ 396 Dana Stubblefield RC	.25	.11
❑ 397 John Taylor	.10	.05
❑ 398 Ricky Watters	.25	.11
❑ 399 Steve Young	.75	.35
❑ 400 Steve Bono	.25	.11
❑ 401 Adrian Hardy	.05	.02
❑ 402 Tom Rathman	.05	.02
❑ 403 Elvis Grbac RC UER	.75	.35
(Name spelled Grabac on front)		
❑ 404 Bill Romanowski	.05	.02
❑ 405 Brian Blades	.10	.05
❑ 406 Ferrell Edmunds	.05	.02
❑ 407 Carlton Gray RC	.05	.02
❑ 408 Cortez Kennedy	.10	.05
❑ 409 Kelvin Martin	.05	.02
❑ 410 Dan McGwire	.05	.02
❑ 411 Rick Mirer RC	.50	.23
❑ 412 Rufus Porter	.05	.02
❑ 413 Chris Warren	.10	.05
❑ 414 Jon Vaughn	.05	.02
❑ 415 John L. Williams	.05	.02
❑ 416 Eugene Robinson	.05	.02
❑ 417 Michael McCrary RC	.05	.02
❑ 418 Michael Bates RC	.05	.02
❑ 419 Stan Gelbaugh	.05	.02
❑ 420 Reggie Cobb	.05	.02
❑ 421 Eric Curry RC	.05	.02
❑ 422 Lawrence Dawsey	.05	.02
❑ 423 Santana Dotson	.10	.05
❑ 424 Craig Erickson	.10	.05
❑ 425 Ron Hall	.05	.02
❑ 426 Courtney Hawkins	.05	.02
❑ 427 Broderick Thomas	.05	.02
❑ 428 Vince Workman	.05	.02
❑ 429 Demetrius DuBose RC	.05	.02
❑ 430 Lamar Thomas RC	.05	.02
❑ 431 John Lynch RC	.05	.02
❑ 432 Hardy Nickerson	.10	.05
❑ 433 Horace Copeland RC	.10	.05
❑ 434 Steve DeBerg	.05	.02
❑ 435 Joe Jacoby	.05	.02
❑ 436 Tom Carter RC	.10	.05
❑ 437 Andre Collins	.05	.02
❑ 438 Darrell Green	.05	.02
❑ 439 Desmond Howard	.10	.05
❑ 440 Chip Lohmiller	.05	.02
❑ 441 Charles Mann	.05	.02
❑ 442 Tim McGee	.05	.02
❑ 443 Art Monk	.10	.05
❑ 444 Mark Rypien	.05	.02
❑ 445 Ricky Sanders	.05	.02
❑ 446 Brian Mitchell	.10	.05
❑ 447 Reggie Brooks RC	.10	.05
❑ 448 Carl Banks	.05	.02
❑ 449 Cary Conklin	.05	.02
❑ NNO Santa Card	1.50	.70

1993 Pro Set All-Rookies

	MINT	NRMT
COMPLETE SET (27)	8.00	3.60
RANDOM INSERTS IN FOIL PACKS		
❑ 1 Rick Mirer	.75	.35
❑ 2 Garrison Hearst	1.50	.70
❑ 3 Jerome Bettis	1.50	.70
❑ 4 Vincent Brisby	.40	.18
❑ 5 O.J. McDuffie	1.25	.55
❑ 6 Curtis Conway	.75	.35
❑ 7 Rocket Ismail	.15	.07

Card	MINT	NRMT
❑ 8 Steve Everitt	.10	.05
❑ 9 Ernest Dye	.10	.05
❑ 10 Todd Rucci	.10	.05
❑ 11 Willie Roaf	.15	.07
❑ 12 Lincoln Kennedy	.10	.05
❑ 13 Irv Smith	.10	.05
❑ 14 Jason Elam	.15	.07
❑ 15 Harold Alexander	.10	.05
❑ 16 John Copeland	.15	.07
❑ 17 Eric Curry	.10	.05
❑ 18 Dana Stubblefield	.40	.18
❑ 19 Leonard Renfro	.10	.05
❑ 20 Marvin Jones	.10	.05
❑ 21 Demetrius DuBose	.10	.05
❑ 22 Chris Slade	.15	.07
❑ 23 Darrin Smith	.15	.07
❑ 24 Deon Figures	.15	.07
❑ 25 Darrien Gordon	.10	.05
❑ 26 Patrick Bates	.10	.05
❑ 27 George Teague	.15	.07

1993 Pro Set College Connections

	MINT	NRMT
COMPLETE SET (10)	30.00	13.50
COMMON PAIR (CC1-CC10)	1.00	.45
SEMISTARS	1.25	.55
RANDOM INSERTS IN JUMBO PACKS		
❑ CC1 Barry Sanders / Thurman Thomas	6.00	2.70
❑ CC2 Jerome Bettis / Reggie Brooks	1.25	.55
❑ CC3 Neal Anderson / Cedric Smith	6.00	2.70
❑ CC4 Rocket Ismail / Tim Brown	1.25	.55
❑ CC5 Rodney Hampton / Garrison Hearst UER (Hearst listed with Lions instead of Cardinals)	1.50	.70
❑ CC6 Derrick Thomas / Cornelius Bennett	1.00	.45
❑ CC7 Jim McMahon / Steve Young	3.00	1.35
❑ CC8 Rick Mirer / Joe Montana	5.00	2.20
❑ CC9 Terrell Buckley / Deion Sanders	3.00	1.35

❑ CC10 Mark Rypien / Drew Bledsoe	5.00	2.20

1993 Pro Set Rookie Quarterbacks

	MINT	NRMT
COMPLETE SET (6)	8.00	3.60
COMMON CARD (RQ1-RQ6)	.25	.11

RANDOM INSERTS IN JUMBO PACKS

❑ RQ1 Drew Bledsoe	3.00	1.35
❑ RQ2 Rick Mirer	.75	.35
❑ RQ3 Mark Brunell	3.00	1.35
❑ RQ4 Billy Joe Hobert	.25	.11
❑ RQ5 Trent Green	3.00	1.35
❑ RQ6 Elvis Grbac	.25	.11

1993 Pro Set Rookie Running Backs

	MINT	NRMT
COMPLETE SET (14)	6.00	2.70

RANDOM INSERTS IN FOIL PACKS

❑ 1 Derrick Lassic	.10	.05
❑ 2 Reggie Brooks	.15	.07
❑ 3 Garrison Hearst	1.50	.70
❑ 4 Ronald Moore	.15	.07
❑ 5 Robert Smith	1.50	.70
❑ 6 Jerome Bettis	1.50	.70
❑ 7 Russell White	.15	.07
❑ 8 Derek Brown RBK	.15	.07
❑ 9 Roosevelt Potts	.10	.05
❑ 10 Terry Kirby	.40	.18
❑ 11 Glyn Milburn	.40	.18
❑ 12 Greg Robinson	.10	.05
❑ 13 Natrone Means	1.25	.55
❑ 14 Vaughn Hebron	.10	.05

2000 Quantum Leaf

	MINT	NRMT
COMPLETE SET (350)	175.00	80.00
COMMON CARD (1-300)	.25	.11
SEMISTARS	.50	.23
UNLISTED STARS	1.00	.45
COMMON ROOKIE (301-350)	2.00	.90
ROOKIE SEMISTARS	2.50	1.10

ROOKIE SUBSET ODDS 1:2

KURT WARNER MVP 1000 SERIAL #'d CARDS
FIRST 100 SERIAL #'d CARDS SIGNED

❑ 1 Frank Sanders	.50	.23
❑ 2 Adrian Murrell	.50	.23
❑ 3 Rob Moore	.50	.23
❑ 4 Simeon Rice	.25	.11
❑ 5 Michael Pittman	.25	.11
❑ 6 Jake Plummer	1.00	.45
❑ 7 David Boston	1.00	.45
❑ 8 Mario Bates	.25	.11
❑ 9 Chris Chandler	.50	.23
❑ 10 Tim Dwight	1.00	.45
❑ 11 Chris Calloway	.25	.11
❑ 12 Terance Mathis	.50	.23
❑ 13 Jamal Anderson	1.00	.45
❑ 14 Byron Hanspard	.50	.23
❑ 15 Ken Oxendine	.25	.11
❑ 16 Tony Graziani	.25	.11
❑ 17 Bob Christian	.25	.11
❑ 18 Priest Holmes	.50	.23
❑ 19 Tony Banks	.50	.23
❑ 20 Patrick Johnson	.25	.11
❑ 21 Rod Woodson	.25	.11
❑ 22 Jermaine Lewis	.25	.11
❑ 23 Errict Rhett	.50	.23
❑ 24 Stoney Case	.25	.11
❑ 25 Peter Boulware	.25	.11
❑ 26 Qadry Ismail	.25	.11
❑ 27 Brandon Stokley	.25	.11
❑ 28 Andre Reed	.50	.23
❑ 29 Eric Moulds	1.00	.45
❑ 30 Doug Flutie	1.25	.55
❑ 31 Bruce Smith	.50	.23
❑ 32 Jay Riemersma	.25	.11
❑ 33 Antowain Smith	1.00	.45
❑ 34 Thurman Thomas	.50	.23
❑ 35 Jonathan Linton	.25	.11
❑ 36 Peerless Price	1.00	.45
❑ 37 Rob Johnson	.50	.23
❑ 38 Sam Gash	.25	.11
❑ 39 Muhsin Muhammad	.50	.23
❑ 40 Wesley Walls	.25	.11
❑ 41 Fred Lane	.25	.11
❑ 42 Kevin Greene	.25	.11
❑ 43 Tim Biakabutuka	.50	.23
❑ 44 Steve Beuerlein	.50	.23
❑ 45 Donald Hayes	.25	.11
❑ 46 Patrick Jeffers	1.00	.45
❑ 47 Curtis Enis	1.00	.45
❑ 48 Bobby Engram	.25	.11
❑ 49 Curtis Conway	.50	.23
❑ 50 Marcus Robinson	1.00	.45
❑ 51 Marty Booker	.25	.11
❑ 52 Cade McNown	1.50	.70
❑ 53 Shane Matthews	.50	.23
❑ 54 Jim Miller	.25	.11
❑ 55 Darnay Scott	.50	.23
❑ 56 Carl Pickens	.50	.23
❑ 57 Corey Dillon	1.00	.45
❑ 58 Jeff Blake	.50	.23
❑ 59 Akili Smith	1.25	.55
❑ 60 Michael Basnight	.25	.11
❑ 61 Karim Abdul-Jabbar	.50	.23
❑ 62 Tim Couch	2.50	1.10
❑ 63 Kevin Johnson	1.00	.45
❑ 64 Terry Kirby	.25	.11
❑ 65 Ty Detmer	.50	.23
❑ 66 Leslie Shepherd	.25	.11
❑ 67 Darrin Chiaverini	.25	.11
❑ 68 Emmitt Smith	2.50	1.10
❑ 69 Deion Sanders	1.00	.45
❑ 70 Michael Irvin	.50	.23
❑ 71 Rocket Ismail	.50	.23
❑ 72 Troy Aikman	2.50	1.10
❑ 73 Daryl Johnston	.50	.23
❑ 74 Chris Warren	.25	.11
❑ 75 Jason Garrett	.50	.23
❑ 76 Jason Tucker	.50	.23
❑ 77 Lawyer Milloy	.25	.11
❑ 78 Dexter Coakley	.25	.11
❑ 79 Greg Ellis	.25	.11
❑ 80 David LaFleur	.25	.11
❑ 81 Todd Lyght	.25	.11
❑ 82 Ernie Mills	.25	.11
❑ 83 Wane McGarity	.25	.11
❑ 84 Chris Brazzell RC	.25	.11
❑ 85 Ed McCaffrey	.50	.23
❑ 86 Rod Smith	.50	.23
❑ 87 Shannon Sharpe	.50	.23
❑ 88 Brian Griese	1.25	.55
❑ 89 John Elway	4.00	1.80
❑ 90 Neil Smith	.50	.23
❑ 91 Terrell Davis	2.50	1.10
❑ 92 Olandis Gary	1.25	.55
❑ 93 Derek Loville	.25	.11
❑ 94 John Avery	.25	.11
❑ 95 Bubby Brister	.25	.11
❑ 96 Byron Chamberlain	.25	.11
❑ 97 Dale Carter	.25	.11
❑ 98 Johnnie Morton	.50	.23
❑ 99 Charlie Batch	1.00	.45
❑ 100 Barry Sanders	3.00	1.35
❑ 101 Germane Crowell	.50	.23
❑ 102 Gus Frerotte	.25	.11
❑ 103 Desmond Howard	.25	.11
❑ 104 Terry Fair	.25	.11
❑ 105 Ron Rivers	.25	.11
❑ 106 Greg Hill	.25	.11
❑ 107 Sedrick Irvin	.25	.11
❑ 108 David Sloan	.25	.11
❑ 109 Herman Moore	1.00	.45
❑ 110 Robert Porcher	.25	.11
❑ 111 Corey Bradford	.50	.23
❑ 112 Dorsey Levens	1.00	.45
❑ 113 Antonio Freeman	1.00	.45
❑ 114 Brett Favre	4.00	1.80
❑ 115 De'Mond Parker	.50	.23
❑ 116 Bill Schroeder	.50	.23
❑ 117 Matt Hasselbeck	.25	.11
❑ 118 Donald Driver	.25	.11
❑ 119 Basil Mitchell	.25	.11
❑ 120 E.G. Green	.25	.11
❑ 121 Ken Dilger	.25	.11
❑ 122 Marvin Harrison	1.00	.45
❑ 123 Peyton Manning	3.00	1.35
❑ 124 Terrence Wilkins	1.00	.45
❑ 125 Edgerrin James	4.00	1.80
❑ 126 Jerome Pathon	.25	.11
❑ 127 Marcus Pollard	.25	.11
❑ 128 Keenan McCardell	.50	.23
❑ 129 Mark Brunell	1.50	.70
❑ 130 Fred Taylor	1.50	.70
❑ 131 Jimmy Smith	.50	.23
❑ 132 James Stewart	.50	.23
❑ 133 Kyle Brady	.25	.11
❑ 134 Tony Brackens	.25	.11
❑ 135 Derrick Thomas	.50	.23
❑ 136 Rashaan Shehee	.25	.11
❑ 137 Derrick Alexander	.50	.23
❑ 138 Bam Morris	.25	.11
❑ 139 Andre Rison	.50	.23
❑ 140 Elvis Grbac	.50	.23
❑ 141 Tony Gonzalez	.50	.23
❑ 142 Donnell Bennett	.25	.11
❑ 143 Warren Moon	1.00	.45
❑ 144 Tamarick Vanover	.25	.11
❑ 145 Kimble Anders	.25	.11
❑ 146 Tony Richardson	.25	.11
❑ 147 Zach Thomas	.50	.23
❑ 148 Oronde Gadsden	.25	.11
❑ 149 Dan Marino	4.00	1.80
❑ 150 O.J. McDuffie	.50	.23
❑ 151 Tony Martin	.50	.23
❑ 152 Cecil Collins	.25	.11

- ❑ 153 James Johnson .50 .23
- ❑ 154 Rob Konrad .25 .11
- ❑ 155 Yatil Green .25 .11
- ❑ 156 Damon Huard 1.00 .45
- ❑ 157 Nate Jacquet .25 .11
- ❑ 158 Stanley Pritchett .25 .11
- ❑ 159 Sam Madison .25 .11
- ❑ 160 Randy Moss 3.00 1.35
- ❑ 161 Cris Carter 1.00 .45
- ❑ 162 Robert Smith 1.00 .45
- ❑ 163 Randall Cunningham 1.00 .45
- ❑ 164 Jake Reed .50 .23
- ❑ 165 John Randle .50 .23
- ❑ 166 Leroy Hoard .25 .11
- ❑ 167 Jeff George .50 .23
- ❑ 168 Daunte Culpepper 1.50 .70
- ❑ 169 Matthew Hatchette .50 .23
- ❑ 170 Robert Tate .25 .11
- ❑ 171 Ty Law .25 .11
- ❑ 172 Troy Brown .25 .11
- ❑ 173 Tony Simmons .25 .11
- ❑ 174 Terry Glenn 1.00 .45
- ❑ 175 Ben Coates .25 .11
- ❑ 176 Drew Bledsoe 1.50 .70
- ❑ 177 Terry Allen .50 .23
- ❑ 178 Kevin Faulk .50 .23
- ❑ 179 Shawn Jefferson .25 .11
- ❑ 180 Andy Katzenmoyer .25 .11
- ❑ 181 Willie McGinest .25 .11
- ❑ 182 Cameron Cleeland .25 .11
- ❑ 183 Eddie Kennison .50 .23
- ❑ 184 Ricky Williams 2.50 1.10
- ❑ 185 Danny Wuerffel .50 .23
- ❑ 186 Brett Bech .25 .11
- ❑ 187 Billy Joe Hobert .25 .11
- ❑ 188 Jake Delhomme RC 4.00 1.80
- ❑ 189 Wilmont Perry .25 .11
- ❑ 190 Keith Poole .25 .11
- ❑ 191 Ashley Ambrose .25 .11
- ❑ 192 Amani Toomer .25 .11
- ❑ 193 Kerry Collins .50 .23
- ❑ 194 Tiki Barber .50 .23
- ❑ 195 Ike Hilliard .50 .23
- ❑ 196 Jason Sehorn .25 .11
- ❑ 197 Joe Montgomery .25 .11
- ❑ 198 Joe Jurevicius .25 .11
- ❑ 199 Michael Strahan .25 .11
- ❑ 200 Sean Bennett .25 .11
- ❑ 201 Jessie Armstead .25 .11
- ❑ 202 Pete Mitchell .25 .11
- ❑ 203 Curtis Martin 1.00 .45
- ❑ 204 Vinny Testaverde .50 .23
- ❑ 205 Keyshawn Johnson 1.00 .45
- ❑ 206 Wayne Chrebet .50 .23
- ❑ 207 Ray Lucas 1.00 .45
- ❑ 208 Tyrone Wheatley .50 .23
- ❑ 209 Napoleon Kaufman 1.00 .45
- ❑ 210 Tim Brown 1.00 .45
- ❑ 211 Rickey Dudley .25 .11
- ❑ 212 James Jett .25 .11
- ❑ 213 Rich Gannon .50 .23
- ❑ 214 Charles Woodson .50 .23
- ❑ 215 Zack Crockett .25 .11
- ❑ 216 Darrell Russell .25 .11
- ❑ 217 Duce Staley 1.00 .45
- ❑ 218 Donovan McNabb 1.50 .70
- ❑ 219 Charles Johnson .25 .11
- ❑ 220 Dameane Douglas .25 .11
- ❑ 221 Doug Pederson .25 .11
- ❑ 222 Torrance Small .25 .11
- ❑ 223 Troy Vincent .25 .11
- ❑ 224 Na Brown .25 .11
- ❑ 225 Kordell Stewart 1.00 .45
- ❑ 226 Jerome Bettis 1.00 .45
- ❑ 227 Hines Ward .25 .11
- ❑ 228 Troy Edwards 1.00 .45
- ❑ 229 Richard Huntley .25 .11
- ❑ 230 Mark Bruener .25 .11
- ❑ 231 Pete Gonzalez .25 .11
- ❑ 232 Levon Kirkland .25 .11
- ❑ 233 Bobby Shaw .25 .11
- ❑ 234 Amos Zereoue .25 .11
- ❑ 235 Natrone Means .25 .11
- ❑ 236 Junior Seau .50 .23
- ❑ 237 Jim Harbaugh .50 .23
- ❑ 238 Ryan Leaf 1.00 .45
- ❑ 239 Mikhael Ricks .25 .11
- ❑ 240 Jermaine Fazande .25 .11
- ❑ 241 Jeff Graham .25 .11
- ❑ 242 Tremayne Stephens .25 .11
- ❑ 243 Terrell Owens 1.00 .45
- ❑ 244 J.J. Stokes .50 .23
- ❑ 245 Charlie Garner .50 .23
- ❑ 246 Jerry Rice 2.50 1.10
- ❑ 247 Garrison Hearst .50 .23
- ❑ 248 Steve Young 1.50 .70
- ❑ 249 Jeff Garcia 1.00 .45
- ❑ 250 Fred Beasley .25 .11
- ❑ 251 Bryant Young .25 .11
- ❑ 252 Derrick Mayes .50 .23
- ❑ 253 Ahman Green .50 .23
- ❑ 254 Joey Galloway 1.00 .45
- ❑ 255 Ricky Watters .50 .23
- ❑ 256 Jon Kitna 1.00 .45
- ❑ 257 Sean Dawkins .25 .11
- ❑ 258 Sam Adams .25 .11
- ❑ 259 Christian Fauria .25 .11
- ❑ 260 Shawn Springs .25 .11
- ❑ 261 Az-Zahir Hakim .50 .23
- ❑ 262 Isaac Bruce 1.00 .45
- ❑ 263 Marshall Faulk 1.00 .45
- ❑ 264 Trent Green .50 .23
- ❑ 265 Kurt Warner 5.00 2.20
- ❑ 266 Torry Holt 1.00 .45
- ❑ 267 Robert Holcombe .25 .11
- ❑ 268 Kevin Carter .25 .11
- ❑ 269 Amp Lee .25 .11
- ❑ 270 Roland Williams .25 .11
- ❑ 271 Jacquez Green .50 .23
- ❑ 272 Reidel Anthony .25 .11
- ❑ 273 Warren Sapp .50 .23
- ❑ 274 Mike Alstott 1.00 .45
- ❑ 275 Warrick Dunn 1.00 .45
- ❑ 276 Trent Dilfer .50 .23
- ❑ 277 Shaun King 1.50 .70
- ❑ 278 Bert Emanuel .25 .11
- ❑ 279 Eric Zeier .25 .11
- ❑ 280 Neil O'Donnell .25 .11
- ❑ 281 Eddie George 1.25 .55
- ❑ 282 Yancey Thigpen .25 .11
- ❑ 283 Steve McNair 1.00 .45
- ❑ 284 Kevin Dyson .50 .23
- ❑ 285 Frank Wycheck .25 .11
- ❑ 286 Jevon Kearse 1.00 .45
- ❑ 287 Bruce Matthews .25 .11
- ❑ 288 Lorenzo Neal .25 .11
- ❑ 289 Stephen Davis 1.00 .45
- ❑ 290 Stephen Alexander .25 .11
- ❑ 291 Darrell Green .25 .11
- ❑ 292 Skip Hicks .50 .23
- ❑ 293 Brad Johnson 1.00 .45
- ❑ 294 Michael Westbrook .50 .23
- ❑ 295 Albert Connell .25 .11
- ❑ 296 Irving Fryar .25 .11
- ❑ 297 Champ Bailey .50 .23
- ❑ 298 Larry Centers .25 .11
- ❑ 299 Brian Mitchell .25 .11
- ❑ 300 James Thrash .25 .11
- ❑ 301 LaVar Arrington RC 8.00 3.60
- ❑ 302 Peter Warrick RC 12.00 5.50
- ❑ 303 Courtney Brown RC 5.00 2.20
- ❑ 304 Plaxico Burress RC 6.00 2.70
- ❑ 305 Corey Simon RC 2.50 1.10
- ❑ 306 Thomas Jones RC 8.00 3.60
- ❑ 307 Travis Taylor RC 5.00 2.20
- ❑ 308 Shaun Alexander RC 8.00 3.60
- ❑ 309 Chris Redman RC 4.00 1.80
- ❑ 310 Chad Pennington RC 10.00 4.50
- ❑ 311 Jamal Lewis RC 8.00 3.60
- ❑ 312 Brian Urlacher RC 3.00 1.35
- ❑ 313 Keith Bullock RC 2.50 1.10
- ❑ 314 Bubba Franks RC 3.00 1.35
- ❑ 315 Dez White RC 3.00 1.35
- ❑ 316 Ahmed Plummer RC 2.00 .90
- ❑ 317 Ron Dayne RC 12.00 5.50
- ❑ 318 Shaun Ellis RC 2.00 .90
- ❑ 319 Sylvester Morris RC 3.00 1.35
- ❑ 320 Deltha O'Neal RC 2.00 .90
- ❑ 321 R.Jay Soward RC 3.00 1.35
- ❑ 322 Sherrod Gideon RC 2.00 .90
- ❑ 323 John Abraham RC 2.00 .90
- ❑ 324 Travis Prentice RC 3.00 1.35
- ❑ 325 Darrell Jackson RC 2.50 1.10
- ❑ 326 Giovanni Carmazzi RC 5.00 2.20
- ❑ 327 Anthony Lucas RC 2.50 1.10
- ❑ 328 Danny Farmer RC 2.50 1.10
- ❑ 329 Dennis Northcutt RC 3.00 1.35
- ❑ 330 Troy Walters RC 2.50 1.10
- ❑ 331 Laveranues Coles RC 2.50 1.10
- ❑ 332 Tee Martin RC 4.00 1.80
- ❑ 333 J.R. Redmond RC 4.00 1.80
- ❑ 334 Jerry Porter RC 3.00 1.35
- ❑ 335 Sebastian Janikowski RC 2.00 .90
- ❑ 336 Michael Wiley RC 2.50 1.10
- ❑ 337 Reuben Droughns RC 3.00 1.35
- ❑ 338 Trung Canidate RC 2.50 1.10
- ❑ 339 Shyrone Stith RC 2.00 .90
- ❑ 340 Trevor Gaylor RC 2.00 .90
- ❑ 341 Rob Morris RC 2.00 .90
- ❑ 342 Marc Bulger RC 2.50 1.10
- ❑ 343 Tom Brady RC 2.50 1.10
- ❑ 344 Todd Husak RC 2.50 1.10
- ❑ 345 Gari Scott RC 2.50 1.10
- ❑ 346 Erron Kinney RC 2.00 .90
- ❑ 347 Julian Peterson RC 2.50 1.10
- ❑ 348 Doug Chapman RC 3.00 1.35
- ❑ 349 Ron Dugans RC 2.50 1.10
- ❑ 350 Todd Pinkston RC 2.50 1.10
- ❑ SB1 Kurt Warner MVP
- ❑ SB1A K.Warner MVP Auto/100
- ❑ NFL1 Kurt Warner MVP 12.00 5.50
- ❑ NFL1A K.Warner MVP Auto/100 120.00 55.00

2000 Quantum Leaf All-Millennium Team

	MINT	NRMT
COMPLETE SET (28)	120.00	55.00
COMMON CARD	3.00	1.35
SEMISTARS	4.00	1.80

STATED PRINT RUN 1000 SERIAL #'d SETS
CARD NUMBERS CARRY "AMT" PREFIX

- ❑ BS Barry Sanders 10.00 4.50
- ❑ CC Cris Carter 4.00 1.80
- ❑ DM Dan Marino 12.00 5.50
- ❑ EC Earl Campbell 6.00 2.70
- ❑ ED Eric Dickerson 3.00 1.35
- ❑ ES Emmitt Smith 8.00 3.60
- ❑ FB Fred Biletnikoff 4.00 1.80
- ❑ GS Gale Sayers 8.00 3.60
- ❑ JB Jim Brown 12.00 5.50
- ❑ JE John Elway 12.00 5.50
- ❑ JL James Lofton 3.00 1.35
- ❑ JM Joe Montana 25.00 11.00
- ❑ JR Jerry Rice 8.00 3.60
- ❑ JU Johnny Unitas 12.00 5.50
- ❑ KW Kellen Winslow 3.00 1.35
- ❑ LA Lance Alworth 4.00 1.80
- ❑ MA Marcus Allen 4.00 1.80
- ❑ PH Paul Hornung 4.00 1.80
- ❑ PW Paul Warfield 4.00 1.80
- ❑ RB Raymond Berry 3.00 1.35
- ❑ RM Randy Moss 10.00 4.50
- ❑ RS Roger Staubach 10.00 4.50
- ❑ SB Sammy Baugh 6.00 2.70
- ❑ SL Steve Largent 6.00 2.70
- ❑ TB Terry Bradshaw 10.00 4.50
- ❑ TD Terrell Davis 8.00 3.60

		MINT	NRMT
❑ BST	Bart Starr	12.00	5.50
❑ TDO	Tony Dorsett	8.00	3.60

2000 Quantum Leaf All-Millennium Team Autographs

	MINT	NRMT
COMPLETE SET (28)	3000.00	1350.00
COMMON CARD	40.00	18.00
SEMISTARS	60.00	27.00

FIRST 100 SERIAL #'d CARDS SIGNED
CARD NUMBERS CARRY AMT PREFIX

		MINT	NRMT
❑ BS	Barry Sanders	250.00	110.00
❑ CC	Cris Carter	60.00	27.00
❑ DM	Dan Marino	250.00	110.00
❑ EC	Earl Campbell	60.00	27.00
❑ ED	Eric Dickerson	60.00	27.00
❑ ES	Emmitt Smith	200.00	90.00
❑ FB	Fred Biletnikoff	60.00	27.00
❑ GS	Gale Sayers	60.00	27.00
❑ JB	Jim Brown	200.00	90.00
❑ JE	John Elway	250.00	110.00
❑ JL	James Lofton	40.00	18.00
❑ JM	Joe Montana	300.00	135.00
❑ JR	Jerry Rice	150.00	70.00
❑ JU	Johnny Unitas	200.00	90.00
❑ KW	Kellen Winslow	40.00	18.00
❑ LA	Lance Alworth	40.00	18.00
❑ MA	Marcus Allen	60.00	27.00
❑ PH	Paul Hornung	60.00	27.00
❑ PW	Paul Warfield	60.00	27.00
❑ RB	Raymond Berry	40.00	18.00
❑ RM	Randy Moss	150.00	70.00
❑ RS	Roger Staubach	175.00	80.00
❑ SB	Sammy Baugh	120.00	55.00
❑ SL	Steve Largent	60.00	27.00
❑ TB	Terry Bradshaw	175.00	80.00
❑ TD	Terrell Davis	100.00	45.00
❑ BST	Bart Starr	200.00	90.00
❑ TDO	Tony Dorsett	100.00	45.00

2000 Quantum Leaf Banner Season

	MINT	NRMT
COMPLETE SET (40)	100.00	45.00
COMMON CARD (BS1-BS40)	2.00	.90
SEMISTARS	3.00	1.35

CARDS SERIAL #'d TO 1999 SEASON STAT

		MINT	NRMT
❑ BS1	Brett Favre/4091	6.00	2.70
❑ BS2	Marvin Harrison/1663	3.00	1.35
❑ BS3	Tim Brown/1344	3.00	1.35
❑ BS4	Randy Moss/1413	10.00	4.50
❑ BS5	Edgerrin James/2139	8.00	3.60
❑ BS6	Kurt Warner/4353	8.00	3.60
❑ BS7	Marshall Faulk/2429	2.00	.90
❑ BS8	Dan Marino/2448	8.00	3.60
❑ BS9	Tim Couch/2447	6.00	2.70
❑ BS10	Ricky Williams/884	8.00	3.60
❑ BS11	Eddie George/1304	4.00	1.80
❑ BS12	Jerry Rice/830	8.00	3.60
❑ BS13	Troy Aikman/2964	5.00	2.20
❑ BS14	Emmitt Smith/1397	8.00	3.60
❑ BS15	Antonio Freeman/1074	3.00	1.35
❑ BS16	Jimmy Smith/1636	2.00	.90
❑ BS17	Charlie Batch/4857	2.00	.90
❑ BS18	Jake Plummer/2111	2.00	.90
❑ BS19	Drew Bledsoe/3985	2.50	1.10
❑ BS20	Germane Crowell/1338	3.00	1.35
❑ BS21	Cris Carter/1241	3.00	1.35
❑ BS22	Deion Sanders/334	4.00	1.80
❑ BS23	Donovan McNabb/948	5.00	2.20
❑ BS24	Mark Brunell/3060	3.00	1.35
❑ BS25	Fred Taylor/732	5.00	2.20
❑ BS26	Stephen Davis/1405	3.00	1.35
❑ BS27	Brad Johnson/4005	2.00	.90
❑ BS28	Jon Kitna/3346	2.00	.90
❑ BS29	Curtis Martin/1464	3.00	1.35
❑ BS30	Keyshawn Johnson/1170	3.00	1.35
❑ BS31	Shaun King/875	5.00	2.20
❑ BS32	Isaac Bruce/1165	3.00	1.35
❑ BS33	Kevin Johnson/986	3.00	1.35
❑ BS34	Steve McNair/2179	2.00	.90
❑ BS35	Eric Moulds/994	3.00	1.35
❑ BS36	Peyton Manning/4136	5.00	2.20
❑ BS37	Dorsey Levens/1607	3.00	1.35
❑ BS38	Olandis Gary/1159	3.00	1.35
❑ BS39	James Stewart/931	2.00	.90
❑ BS40	Terry Glenn/1147	3.00	1.35

2000 Quantum Leaf Banner Season Century

	MINT	NRMT
COMPLETE SET (40)	500.00	220.00
COMMON CARD (BS1-BS40)	8.00	3.60
SEMISTARS	12.00	5.50

STATED PRINT RUN 99 SERIAL #'d SETS

		MINT	NRMT
❑ BS1	Brett Favre	50.00	22.00
❑ BS2	Marvin Harrison	12.00	5.50
❑ BS3	Tim Brown	12.00	5.50
❑ BS4	Randy Moss	40.00	18.00
❑ BS5	Edgerrin James	40.00	18.00
❑ BS6	Kurt Warner	60.00	27.00
❑ BS7	Marshall Faulk	12.00	5.50
❑ BS8	Dan Marino	50.00	22.00
❑ BS9	Tim Couch	25.00	11.00
❑ BS10	Ricky Williams	25.00	11.00
❑ BS11	Eddie George	15.00	6.75
❑ BS12	Jerry Rice	30.00	13.50
❑ BS13	Troy Aikman	30.00	13.50
❑ BS14	Emmitt Smith	30.00	13.50
❑ BS15	Antonio Freeman	12.00	5.50
❑ BS16	Jimmy Smith	8.00	3.60
❑ BS17	Charlie Batch	12.00	5.50
❑ BS18	Jake Plummer	12.00	5.50
❑ BS19	Drew Bledsoe	20.00	9.00
❑ BS20	Germane Crowell	8.00	3.60
❑ BS21	Cris Carter	12.00	5.50
❑ BS22	Deion Sanders	12.00	5.50
❑ BS23	Donovan McNabb	15.00	6.75
❑ BS24	Mark Brunell	20.00	9.00
❑ BS25	Fred Taylor	20.00	9.00
❑ BS26	Stephen Davis	12.00	5.50
❑ BS27	Brad Johnson	12.00	5.50
❑ BS28	Jon Kitna	12.00	5.50
❑ BS29	Curtis Martin	12.00	5.50
❑ BS30	Keyshawn Johnson	12.00	5.50
❑ BS31	Shaun King	15.00	6.75
❑ BS32	Isaac Bruce	12.00	5.50
❑ BS33	Kevin Johnson	12.00	5.50
❑ BS34	Steve McNair	12.00	5.50
❑ BS35	Eric Moulds	12.00	5.50
❑ BS36	Peyton Manning	40.00	18.00
❑ BS37	Dorsey Levens	12.00	5.50
❑ BS38	Olandis Gary	12.00	5.50
❑ BS39	James Stewart	8.00	3.60
❑ BS40	Terry Glenn	12.00	5.50

2000 Quantum Leaf Double Team

	MINT	NRMT
COMPLETE SET (30)	60.00	27.00
COMMON CARD (DT1-DT30)	1.25	.55
SEMISTARS	2.00	.90

STATED PRINT RUN 1500 SERIAL #'d SETS

		MINT	NRMT
❑ DT1	J.J. Johnson Dan Marino	8.00	3.60
❑ DT2	Edgerrin James Peyton Manning	8.00	3.60
❑ DT3	Kevin Faulk Drew Bledsoe	3.00	1.35
❑ DT4	Antowain Smith Doug Flutie	2.50	1.10
❑ DT5	Curtis Martin Vinny Testaverde	2.00	.90
❑ DT6	Jerome Bettis Kordell Stewart	2.00	.90
❑ DT7	Eddie George Steve McNair	2.50	1.10
❑ DT8	Fred Taylor Mark Brunell	3.00	1.35
❑ DT9	Errict Rhett Tony Banks	1.25	.55
❑ DT10	Karim Abdul-Jabbar Tim Couch	5.00	2.20
❑ DT11	Corey Dillon Akili Smith	2.00	.90
❑ DT12	Terrell Davis Brian Griese	5.00	2.20
❑ DT13	Donnell Bennett Elvis Grbac	1.25	.55
❑ DT14	Ricky Watters Jon Kitna	2.00	.90
❑ DT15	Tyrone Wheatley Rich Gannon	1.25	.55
❑ DT16	Natrone Means Jim Harbaugh	1.25	.55
❑ DT17	Emmitt Smith Troy Aikman	6.00	2.70
❑ DT18	Stephen Davis Brad Johnson	2.00	.90
❑ DT19	Duce Staley Donovan McNabb	3.00	1.35
❑ DT20	Michael Pittman Jake Plummer	2.00	.90
❑ DT21	Dorsey Levens Brett Favre	8.00	3.60
❑ DT22	Robert Smith Jeff George	2.00	.90
❑ DT23	Mike Alstott Shaun King	3.00	1.35
❑ DT24	Curtis Enis Cade McNown	3.00	1.35
❑ DT25	Barry Sanders Charlie Batch	5.00	2.20
❑ DT26	Marshall Faulk Kurt Warner	10.00	4.50
❑ DT27	Ricky Williams Jeff Blake	4.00	1.80
❑ DT28	Charlie Garner Steve Young	2.50	1.10
❑ DT29	Tim Biakabutuka Steve Beuerlein	1.25	.55
❑ DT30	Jamal Anderson Chris Chandler	2.00	.90

2000 Quantum Leaf Gamers

	MINT	NRMT
COMPLETE SET (20)	3500.00	1600.00
COMMON CARD (G1-G20)	100.00	45.00

RANDOM INSERTS IN HOBBY PACKS

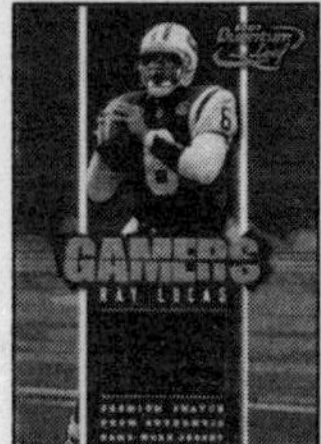

STATED PRINT RUN 25 SERIAL #'d SETS

- ❑ G1 Brett Favre 400.00 180.00
- ❑ G2 Dan Marino............... 400.00 180.00
- ❑ G3 Barry Sanders 350.00 160.00
- ❑ G4 John Elway............... 350.00 160.00
- ❑ G5 Peyton Manning 350.00 160.00
- ❑ G6 Terrell Davis 200.00 90.00
- ❑ G7 Fred Taylor 200.00 90.00
- ❑ G8 Drew Bledsoe 175.00 80.00
- ❑ G9 Mark Brunell 175.00 80.00
- ❑ G10 Eddie George 175.00 80.00
- ❑ G11 Isaac Bruce 100.00 45.00
- ❑ G12 Jerry Rice 250.00 110.00
- ❑ G13 Ray Lucas 100.00 45.00
- ❑ G14 Olandis Gary 120.00 55.00
- ❑ G15 Emmitt Smith 250.00 110.00
- ❑ G16 Shaun King............. 175.00 80.00
- ❑ G17 Edgerrin James 300.00 135.00
- ❑ G18 Cris Carter 120.00 55.00
- ❑ G19 Jimmy Smith........... 100.00 45.00
- ❑ G20 Brian Griese 120.00 55.00

2000 Quantum Leaf Hardwear

	MINT	NRMT
COMPLETE SET (15)	800.00	350.00
COMMON CARD (HW1-HW15)	30.00	13.50
SEMISTARS............................	40.00	18.00

RANDOM INSERTS IN HOBBY PACKS
STATED PRINT RUN 125 SERIAL #'d SETS

- ❑ HW1 Brett Favre 120.00 55.00
- ❑ HW2 Dan Marino 120.00 55.00
- ❑ HW3 Barry Sanders 100.00 45.00
- ❑ HW4 John Elway 120.00 55.00
- ❑ HW5 Terrell Davis 80.00 36.00
- ❑ HW6 Troy Aikman 80.00 36.00
- ❑ HW7 Steve Young 70.00 32.00
- ❑ HW8 Eddie George 60.00 27.00
- ❑ HW9 Brad Johnson 40.00 18.00
- ❑ HW10 Herman Moore 30.00 13.50
- ❑ HW11 Antowain Smith...... 30.00 13.50
- ❑ HW12 Kordell Stewart 50.00 22.00
- ❑ HW13 Dorsey Levens 40.00 18.00
- ❑ HW14 Peyton Manning .. 100.00 45.00
- ❑ HW15 Jerry Rice 80.00 36.00

2000 Quantum Leaf Infinity Green

	MINT	NRMT
COMMON CARD (1-100)..........	4.00	1.80

*STARS: 6X TO 15X HI COL. ......
*YOUNG STARS: 5X TO 12X HI COL.
1-100: PRINT RUN 100 SERIAL #'d SETS
COMMON CARD (101-200) 10.00 4.50
*STARS: 15X TO 40X HI COL. ....
*YOUNG STARS: 12X TO 30X HI COL.
101-200 PRINT RUN 25 SERIAL #'d SETS
COMMON CARD (201-300)...... 6.00 2.70
*STARS: 10X TO 25X HI COL. ....
*YOUNG STARS: 8X TO 20X HI COL.
201-300 PRINT RUN 50 SERIAL #'d SETS
COMMON CARD (301-350) 12.00 5.50
*ROOKIES: 2.5X TO 6X HI COL...

301-350 PRINT RUN 75 SERIAL #'d SETS

2000 Quantum Leaf Infinity Purple

	MINT	NRMT
COMMON CARD (1-100)........	10.00	4.50

*STARS: 15X TO 40X HI COL. ....
*YOUNG STARS: 12X TO 30X HI COL.
1-100 PRINT RUN 25 SERIAL #'d SETS
COMMON CARD (101-200)...... 6.00 2.70
*STARS: 10X TO 25X HI COL. ....
*YOUNG STARS: 8X TO 20X HI COL.
101-200 PRINT RUN 50 SERIAL #'d SETS
COMMON CARD (201-300)...... 4.00 1.80
*STARS: 6X TO 15X HI COL. ......
*YOUNG STARS: 5X TO 12X HI COL.
201-300 PRINT RUN 100 SERIAL #'d SETS
COMMON CARD (301-350) 40.00 18.00
*ROOKIES: 8X TO 20X HI COL. ..
301-350 PRINT RUN 15 SERIAL #'d SETS

2000 Quantum Leaf Infinity Red

	MINT	NRMT
COMMON CARD (1-100)..........	6.00	2.70

*STARS: 10X TO 25X HI COL. ....
*YOUNG STARS: 8X TO 20X HI COL.
1-100 PRINT RUN 50 SERIAL #'d SETS
COMMON CARD (101-200)...... 4.00 1.80
*STARS: 6X TO 15X HI COL. ......
*YOUNG STARS: 5X TO 12X HI COL.
101-200 PRINT RUN 100 SERIAL #'d SETS
COMMON CARD (201-300).... 10.00 4.50
*STARS: 15X TO 40X HI COL. ....
*YOUNG STARS: 12X TO 30X HI COL.
201-300 PRINT RUN 25 SERIAL #'d SETS
COMMON CARD (301-350) 20.00 9.00
*ROOKIES: 4X TO 10X HI COL. ..
301-350 PRINT RUN 35 SERIAL #'d SETS

2000 Quantum Leaf Millennium Moments

	MINT	NRMT
COMPLETE SET (20)	80.00	36.00
COMMON CARD (MM1-MM20)	2.50	1.10

STATED PRINT RUN 1000 SERIAL #'d SETS

- ❑ MM1 Drew Bledsoe 4.00 1.80
- ❑ MM2 Emmitt Smith............. 6.00 2.70
- ❑ MM3 Mark Brunell 4.00 1.80
- ❑ MM4 Brett Favre 10.00 4.50
- ❑ MM5 Randy Moss 8.00 3.60
- ❑ MM6 Kurt Warner............. 12.00 5.50
- ❑ MM7 John Elway 10.00 4.50
- ❑ MM8 Steve Young 4.00 1.80
- ❑ MM9 Eddie George 3.00 1.35
- ❑ MM10 Marshall Faulk.......... 2.50 1.10
- ❑ MM11 Edgerrin James 8.00 3.60
- ❑ MM12 Antonio Freeman...... 2.50 1.10
- ❑ MM13 Dan Marino 10.00 4.50
- ❑ MM14 Terrell Davis 6.00 2.70
- ❑ MM15 Doug Flutie 3.00 1.35
- ❑ MM16 Jerry Rice 6.00 2.70
- ❑ MM17 Fred Taylor 4.00 1.80
- ❑ MM18 Peyton Manning 8.00 3.60
- ❑ MM19 Troy Aikman 6.00 2.70
- ❑ MM20 Barry Sanders 8.00 3.60

2000 Quantum Leaf Rookie Revolution

	MINT	NRMT
COMPLETE SET (20)	50.00	22.00
COMMON CARD (RR1-RR20)..	1.50	.70
SEMISTARS............................	2.00	.90

STATED PRINT RUN 5000 SERIAL #'d SETS
*FIRST STRIKE: 4X TO 10X BASIC INSERTS
FIRST STRIKE PRINT RUN 50 SER.#'d SETS
RANDOM INSERTS IN RETAIL PACKS

		MINT	NRMT
❑ RR1	Peter Warrick	10.00	4.50
❑ RR2	J.R. Redmond	3.00	1.35
❑ RR3	Chris Redman	3.00	1.35
❑ RR4	R.Jay Soward	2.50	1.10
❑ RR5	Ron Dayne	10.00	4.50
❑ RR6	Chad Pennington	8.00	3.60
❑ RR7	Anthony Lucas	2.00	.90
❑ RR8	Tim Rattay	2.50	1.10
❑ RR9	Shaun Alexander	6.00	2.70
❑ RR10	Dez White	2.50	1.10
❑ RR11	Tee Martin	3.00	1.35
❑ RR12	Travis Taylor	4.00	1.80
❑ RR13	Travis Prentice	2.50	1.10
❑ RR14	Sylvester Morris	2.50	1.10
❑ RR15	Jamal Lewis	6.00	2.70
❑ RR16	Plaxico Burress	5.00	2.20
❑ RR17	Sherrod Gideon	1.50	.70
❑ RR18	Shyrone Stith	1.50	.70
❑ RR19	Thomas Jones	6.00	2.70
❑ RR20	Kwame Cavil	1.50	.70

2000 Quantum Leaf Shirt Off My Back

	MINT	NRMT
COMPLETE SET (20)	1500.00	700.00
COMMON CARD (SB1-SB20)	50.00	22.00

STATED PRINT RUN 100 SERIAL #'d SETS

		MINT	NRMT
❑ SB1	Brett Favre	150.00	70.00
❑ SB2	Dan Marino	150.00	70.00
❑ SB3	Barry Sanders	120.00	55.00
❑ SB4	John Elway	150.00	70.00
❑ SB5	Peyton Manning	175.00	80.00
❑ SB6	Terrell Davis	80.00	36.00
❑ SB7	Fred Taylor	80.00	36.00
❑ SB8	Drew Bledsoe	60.00	27.00
❑ SB9	Mark Brunell	60.00	27.00
❑ SB10	Eddie George	60.00	27.00
❑ SB11	Isaac Bruce	50.00	22.00
❑ SB12	Jerry Rice	100.00	45.00
❑ SB13	Ray Lucas	50.00	22.00
❑ SB14	Olandis Gary	50.00	22.00
❑ SB15	Emmitt Smith	120.00	55.00
❑ SB16	Shaun King	80.00	36.00
❑ SB17	Edgerrin James	150.00	70.00
❑ SB18	Cris Carter	60.00	27.00
❑ SB19	Jimmy Smith	50.00	22.00
❑ SB20	Brian Griese	60.00	27.00

2000 Quantum Leaf Star Factor

	MINT	NRMT
COMPLETE SET (40)	80.00	36.00
COMMON CARD (SF1-SF40)	1.50	.70

STATED PRINT RUN 2500 SERIAL #'d SETS
*QUASARS: 5X TO 12X BASIC INSERTS
QUASAR STATED PRINT RUN 50 SER.#'d SETS
RANDOM INSERTS IN RETAIL PACKS

		MINT	NRMT
❑ SF1	Edgerrin James	5.00	2.20
❑ SF2	Cris Carter	1.50	.70
❑ SF3	Terrell Owens	1.50	.70
❑ SF4	Brett Favre	6.00	2.70
❑ SF5	Tim Couch	3.00	1.35
❑ SF6	Terry Glenn	1.50	.70

		MINT	NRMT
❑ SF7	John Elway	6.00	2.70
❑ SF8	Troy Aikman	4.00	1.80
❑ SF9	Charlie Batch	1.50	.70
❑ SF10	Steve McNair	1.50	.70
❑ SF11	Drew Bledsoe	2.50	1.10
❑ SF12	Joey Galloway	1.50	.70
❑ SF13	Dan Marino	6.00	2.70
❑ SF14	Marshall Faulk	1.50	.70
❑ SF15	Jamal Anderson	1.50	.70
❑ SF16	Jake Plummer	1.50	.70
❑ SF17	Curtis Martin	1.50	.70
❑ SF18	Peyton Manning	5.00	2.20
❑ SF19	Keyshawn Johnson	1.50	.70
❑ SF20	Barry Sanders	5.00	2.20
❑ SF21	Jerry Rice	4.00	1.80
❑ SF22	Emmitt Smith	4.00	1.80
❑ SF23	Daunte Culpepper	2.00	.90
❑ SF24	Brad Johnson	1.50	.70
❑ SF25	Kurt Warner	8.00	3.60
❑ SF26	Steve Young	2.50	1.10
❑ SF27	Eddie George	2.00	.90
❑ SF28	Fred Taylor	2.50	1.10
❑ SF29	Randy Moss	5.00	2.20
❑ SF30	Terrell Davis	4.00	1.80
❑ SF31	Eric Moulds	1.50	.70
❑ SF32	Antonio Freeman	1.50	.70
❑ SF33	Isaac Bruce	1.50	.70
❑ SF34	Ricky Williams	3.00	1.35
❑ SF35	Donovan McNabb	2.00	.90
❑ SF36	Stephen Davis	1.50	.70
❑ SF37	Jon Kitna	1.50	.70
❑ SF38	Marvin Harrison	1.50	.70
❑ SF39	Doug Flutie	2.00	.90
❑ SF40	Mark Brunell	2.50	1.10

1997 Revolution

	MINT	NRMT
COMPLETE SET (150)	100.00	45.00
COMMON CARD (1-150)	.50	.23
SEMISTARS	.75	.35
UNLISTED STARS	1.50	.70
COMP.COPPER SET (150)	1200.00	550.00
*COPPER STARS: 3X TO 8X HI COL.		
*COPPER RCs: 1.5X TO 4X		
COPPER STATED ODDS 2:25 HOBBY		
COMP.PLAT.BLUE SET (150)	2500.00	1100.00
*PLAT.BLUE STARS: 8X TO 20X HI COL.		
*PLAT.BLUE RCs: 4X TO 10X		
PLAT.BLUE STATED ODDS 1:49		
COMP.RED SET (150)	1500.00	700.00
*RED STARS: 4X TO 10X HI COL.		
*RED RCs: 2.5X TO 6X		
RED STATED ODDS 2:25 SPECIAL RETAIL		
COMP.SILVER SET (150)	1500.00	700.00
*SILVER STARS: 4X TO 10X HI COL.		
*SILVER RCs: 2X TO 5X		
SILVER STATED ODDS 2:25 RETAIL		

		MINT	NRMT
❑ 1	Larry Centers	.75	.35
❑ 2	Kent Graham	.50	.23
❑ 3	Leeland McElroy	.50	.23
❑ 4	Rob Moore	.75	.35
❑ 5	Jake Plummer RC	12.00	5.50
❑ 6	Jamal Anderson	2.50	1.10
❑ 7	Bert Emanuel	.75	.35
❑ 8	Byron Hanspard RC	3.00	1.35
❑ 9	Terance Mathis	.75	.35
❑ 10	O.J. Santiago RC	2.00	.90
❑ 11	Derrick Alexander WR	.75	.35
❑ 12	Peter Boulware RC	.75	.35
❑ 13	Jay Graham RC	1.50	.70
❑ 14	Michael Jackson	.75	.35
❑ 15	Vinny Testaverde	.75	.35
❑ 16	Todd Collins	.50	.23
❑ 17	Andre Reed	.75	.35
❑ 18	Jay Riemersma	.50	.23
❑ 19	Antowain Smith RC	4.00	1.80
❑ 20	Bruce Smith	.75	.35
❑ 21	Thurman Thomas	1.50	.70
❑ 22	Rae Carruth RC	1.50	.70
❑ 23	Kerry Collins	.75	.35
❑ 24	Anthony Johnson	.50	.23
❑ 25	Muhsin Muhammad	.75	.35
❑ 26	Wesley Walls	.75	.35
❑ 27	Curtis Conway	.75	.35
❑ 28	Bobby Engram	.75	.35
❑ 29	Raymont Harris	.50	.23
❑ 30	Rick Mirer	.50	.23
❑ 31	Rashaan Salaam	.50	.23
❑ 32	Jeff Blake	.75	.35
❑ 33	Corey Dillon RC	6.00	2.70
❑ 34	Carl Pickens	1.50	.70
❑ 35	Darnay Scott	.75	.35
❑ 36	Troy Aikman	4.00	1.80
❑ 37	Michael Irvin	1.50	.70
❑ 38	Daryl Johnston	.75	.35
❑ 39	Deion Sanders	1.50	.70
❑ 40	Emmitt Smith	6.00	2.70
❑ 41	Terrell Davis	6.00	2.70
❑ 42	John Elway	8.00	3.60
❑ 43	Ed McCaffrey	.75	.35
❑ 44	Shannon Sharpe	.75	.35
❑ 45	Neil Smith	.75	.35
❑ 46	Scott Mitchell	.75	.35
❑ 47	Herman Moore	1.50	.70
❑ 48	Johnnie Morton	.75	.35
❑ 49	Barry Sanders	8.00	3.60
❑ 50	Robert Brooks	.75	.35
❑ 51	LeRoy Butler	.50	.23
❑ 52	Brett Favre	8.00	3.60
❑ 53	Antonio Freeman	2.00	.90
❑ 54	Dorsey Levens	1.50	.70
❑ 55	Reggie White	1.50	.70
❑ 56	Sean Dawkins	.50	.23
❑ 57	Ken Dilger	.50	.23
❑ 58	Marshall Faulk	1.50	.70
❑ 59	Jim Harbaugh	.75	.35
❑ 60	Marvin Harrison	1.50	.70
❑ 61	Mark Brunell	4.00	1.80
❑ 62	Keenan McCardell	.75	.35
❑ 63	Natrone Means	1.50	.70
❑ 64	Jimmy Smith	.75	.35
❑ 65	James O.Stewart	.75	.35
❑ 66	Marcus Allen	1.50	.70
❑ 67	Tony Gonzalez RC	5.00	2.20
❑ 68	Elvis Grbac	.75	.35
❑ 69	Greg Hill	.50	.23
❑ 70	Andre Rison	.75	.35
❑ 71	Karim Abdul-Jabbar	1.50	.70
❑ 72	Fred Barnett	.50	.23
❑ 73	Dan Marino	8.00	3.60
❑ 74	O.J. McDuffie	.75	.35
❑ 75	Irving Spikes	.50	.23
❑ 76	Cris Carter	1.50	.70
❑ 77	Matthew Hatchette RC	5.00	2.20
❑ 78	Brad Johnson	2.00	.90

Card	MINT	NRMT
❑ 79 Jake Reed	.75	.35
❑ 80 Robert Smith	.75	.35
❑ 81 Drew Bledsoe	4.00	1.80
❑ 82 Ben Coates	.75	.35
❑ 83 Terry Glenn	1.50	.70
❑ 84 Curtis Martin	2.00	.90
❑ 85 Dave Meggett	.50	.23
❑ 86 Troy Davis RC	1.50	.70
❑ 87 Andre Hastings	.50	.23
❑ 88 Heath Shuler	.50	.23
❑ 89 Irv Smith	.50	.23
❑ 90 Danny Wuerffel RC	1.50	.70
❑ 91 Ray Zellars	.50	.23
❑ 92 Tiki Barber RC	2.00	.90
❑ 93 Dave Brown	.50	.23
❑ 94 Chris Calloway	.50	.23
❑ 95 Rodney Hampton	.75	.35
❑ 96 Amani Toomer	.75	.35
❑ 97 Wayne Chrebet	1.50	.70
❑ 98 Keyshawn Johnson	1.50	.70
❑ 99 Adrian Murrell	.75	.35
❑ 100 Neil O'Donnell	.75	.35
❑ 101 Dedric Ward RC	2.50	1.10
❑ 102 Tim Brown	1.50	.70
❑ 103 Rickey Dudley	.75	.35
❑ 104 Jeff George	.75	.35
❑ 105 Desmond Howard	.75	.35
❑ 106 Napoleon Kaufman	1.50	.70
❑ 107 Ty Detmer	.75	.35
❑ 108 Jason Dunn	.50	.23
❑ 109 Irving Fryar	.75	.35
❑ 110 Rodney Peete	.50	.23
❑ 111 Ricky Watters	.75	.35
❑ 112 Jerome Bettis	1.50	.70
❑ 113 Will Blackwell RC	1.50	.70
❑ 114 Charles Johnson	.75	.35
❑ 115 Kordell Stewart	2.00	.90
❑ 116 Tony Banks	.75	.35
❑ 117 Isaac Bruce	1.50	.70
❑ 118 Ernie Conwell	.50	.23
❑ 119 Eddie Kennison	.75	.35
❑ 120 Lawrence Phillips	.50	.23
❑ 121 Stan Humphries	.75	.35
❑ 122 Tony Martin	.75	.35
❑ 123 Eric Metcalf	.75	.35
❑ 124 Junior Seau	.75	.35
❑ 125 Jim Druckenmiller RC	2.00	.90
❑ 126 Kevin Greene	.75	.35
❑ 127 Garrison Hearst	.75	.35
❑ 128 Terrell Owens	1.50	.70
❑ 129 Jerry Rice	4.00	1.80
❑ 130 J.J. Stokes	.75	.35
❑ 131 Rod Woodson	.75	.35
❑ 132 Steve Young	2.50	1.10
❑ 133 Joey Galloway	2.00	.90
❑ 134 Cortez Kennedy	.50	.23
❑ 135 Jon Kitna RC	30.00	13.50
❑ 136 Warren Moon	1.50	.70
❑ 137 Chris Warren	.75	.35
❑ 138 Mike Alstott	1.50	.70
❑ 139 Reidel Anthony RC	3.00	1.35
❑ 140 Trent Dilfer	1.50	.70
❑ 141 Warrick Dunn RC	5.00	2.20
❑ 142 Willie Davis	.50	.23
❑ 143 Eddie George	4.00	1.80
❑ 144 Steve McNair	2.00	.90
❑ 145 Chris Sanders	.50	.23
❑ 146 Terry Allen	1.50	.70
❑ 147 Jamie Asher	.50	.23
❑ 148 Henry Ellard	.50	.23
❑ 149 Gus Frerotte	.50	.23
❑ 150 Leslie Shepherd	.50	.23
❑ S1 Mark Brunell Sample	1.00	.45

1997 Revolution Air Mail Die Cuts

	MINT	NRMT
COMPLETE SET (36)	500.00	220.00
STATED ODDS 1:25		
❑ 1 Vinny Testaverde	4.00	1.80
❑ 2 Andre Reed	4.00	1.80
❑ 3 Kerry Collins	4.00	1.80
❑ 4 Jeff Blake	4.00	1.80
❑ 5 Troy Aikman	20.00	9.00

Card	MINT	NRMT
❑ 6 Deion Sanders	8.00	3.60
❑ 7 Emmitt Smith	30.00	13.50
❑ 8 Michael Irvin	8.00	3.60
❑ 9 Terrell Davis	30.00	13.50
❑ 10 John Elway	40.00	18.00
❑ 11 Barry Sanders	40.00	18.00
❑ 12 Brett Favre	40.00	18.00
❑ 13 Antonio Freeman	10.00	4.50
❑ 14 Mark Brunell	20.00	9.00
❑ 15 Marcus Allen	8.00	3.60
❑ 16 Elvis Grbac	4.00	1.80
❑ 17 Dan Marino	40.00	18.00
❑ 18 Brad Johnson	10.00	4.50
❑ 19 Drew Bledsoe	20.00	9.00
❑ 20 Terry Glenn	8.00	3.60
❑ 21 Curtis Martin	10.00	4.50
❑ 22 Danny Wuerffel	5.00	2.20
❑ 23 Jeff George	4.00	1.80
❑ 24 Napoleon Kaufman	8.00	3.60
❑ 25 Kordell Stewart	10.00	4.50
❑ 26 Tony Banks	4.00	1.80
❑ 27 Isaac Bruce	8.00	3.60
❑ 28 Jim Druckenmiller	6.00	2.70
❑ 29 Jerry Rice	20.00	9.00
❑ 30 Steve Young	12.00	5.50
❑ 31 Warren Moon	8.00	3.60
❑ 32 Trent Dilfer	8.00	3.60
❑ 33 Warrick Dunn	15.00	6.75
❑ 34 Eddie George	20.00	9.00
❑ 35 Steve McNair	10.00	4.50
❑ 36 Gus Frerotte	2.50	1.10

1997 Revolution Proteges

	MINT	NRMT
COMPLETE SET (20)	150.00	70.00
COMMON CARD (1-20)	1.50	.70
SEMISTARS	2.50	1.10
UNLISTED STARS	4.00	1.80
GOLD STATED ODDS 2:25		
*SILVER CARDS: .25X TO .5X GOLDS		
SILVERS ONE PER SPECIAL RETAIL BOX		
❑ 1 Kent Graham Jake Plummer	10.00	4.50
❑ 2 Jamal Anderson Byron Hanspard	5.00	2.20
❑ 3 Thurman Thomas Antowain Smith	5.00	2.20
❑ 4 Troy Aikman Jason Garrett	10.00	4.50
❑ 5 Emmitt Smith Sherman Williams	15.00	6.75
❑ 6 John Elway Jeff Lewis	20.00	9.00
❑ 7 Barry Sanders Ron Rivers	20.00	9.00
❑ 8 Brett Favre Doug Pederson	20.00	9.00
❑ 9 Mark Brunell Rob Johnson	10.00	4.50
❑ 10 Marcus Allen Greg Hill	4.00	1.80
❑ 11 Dan Marino Damon Huard	40.00	18.00
❑ 12 Curtis Martin Marrio Grier	6.00	2.70
❑ 13 Heath Shuler Danny Wuerffel	1.50	.70
❑ 14 Rodney Hampton Tiki Barber	4.00	1.80
❑ 15 Jerome Bettis George Jones	4.00	1.80
❑ 16 Jerry Rice Terrell Owens	15.00	6.75
❑ 17 Steve Young Jim Druckenmiller	8.00	3.60
❑ 18 Warren Moon Jon Kitna	15.00	6.75
❑ 19 Errict Rhett Warrick Dunn	5.00	2.20
❑ 20 Terry Allen Stephen Davis	10.00	4.50

1997 Revolution Ring Bearers

	MINT	NRMT
COMPLETE SET (12)	400.00	180.00
STATED ODDS 1:121		
❑ 1 Emmitt Smith	50.00	22.00
❑ 2 John Elway	60.00	27.00
❑ 3 Barry Sanders	60.00	27.00
❑ 4 Brett Favre	60.00	27.00
❑ 5 Mark Brunell	30.00	13.50
❑ 6 Dan Marino	60.00	27.00
❑ 7 Drew Bledsoe	30.00	13.50

Card	MINT	NRMT
❑ 8 Steve Young	20.00	9.00
❑ 9 Warrick Dunn	20.00	9.00
❑ 10 Eddie George	30.00	13.50
❑ 11 Troy Aikman	30.00	13.50
❑ 12 Jerry Rice	30.00	13.50

1997 Revolution Silks

	MINT	NRMT
COMPLETE SET (18)	350.00	160.00
STATED ODDS 1:49		
❑ 1 Kerry Collins	4.00	1.80
❑ 2 Troy Aikman	20.00	9.00
❑ 3 Deion Sanders	8.00	3.60
❑ 4 Emmitt Smith	30.00	13.50
❑ 5 Terrell Davis	30.00	13.50
❑ 6 John Elway	40.00	18.00
❑ 7 Barry Sanders	40.00	18.00
❑ 8 Brett Favre	40.00	18.00

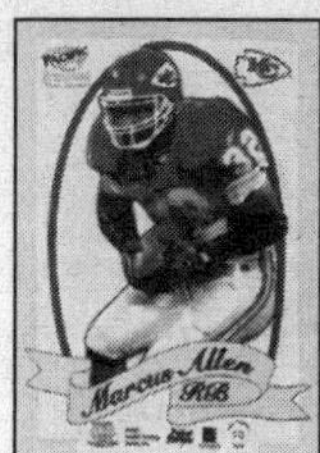

❑ 9 Mark Brunell	20.00	9.00
❑ 10 Marcus Allen	8.00	3.60
❑ 11 Dan Marino	40.00	18.00
❑ 12 Drew Bledsoe	20.00	9.00
❑ 13 Curtis Martin	10.00	4.50
❑ 14 Jerome Bettis	8.00	3.60
❑ 15 Jim Druckenmiller	5.00	2.20
❑ 16 Jerry Rice	20.00	9.00
❑ 17 Warrick Dunn	12.00	5.50
❑ 18 Eddie George	20.00	9.00
❑ P1 Mark Brunell Promo	10.00	4.50

1998 Revolution

	MINT	NRMT
COMPLETE SET (150)	135.00	60.00
COMMON CARD (1-150)	.40	.18
SEMISTARS	.75	.35
UNLISTED STARS	1.50	.70
COMMON ROOKIE	3.00	1.35
COMMON SHADOW	12.00	5.50

*SHADOW STARS: 7.5X TO 20X HI COL.
*SHADOW YOUNG STARS: 6X TO 15X
*SHADOW RCs: 3X TO 8X
SHADOW PRINT RUN 99 SERIAL #'d SETS

Card	MINT	NRMT
❑ 1 Larry Centers	.40	.18
❑ 2 Leeland McElroy	.40	.18
❑ 3 Rob Moore	.75	.35
❑ 4 Jake Plummer	5.00	2.20
❑ 5 Frank Sanders	.75	.35
❑ 6 Jamal Anderson	1.50	.70
❑ 7 Chris Chandler	.75	.35
❑ 8 Byron Hanspard	.75	.35
❑ 9 Jay Graham	.40	.18
❑ 10 Michael Jackson	.40	.18
❑ 11 Vinny Testaverde	.75	.35
❑ 12 Eric Zeier	.75	.35
❑ 13 Todd Collins	.40	.18
❑ 14 Quinn Early	.40	.18
❑ 15 Andre Reed	.75	.35
❑ 16 Antowain Smith	1.50	.70
❑ 17 Bruce Smith	.75	.35
❑ 18 Thurman Thomas	1.50	.70
❑ 19 Rae Carruth	.75	.35
❑ 20 Kerry Collins	.75	.35
❑ 21 Wesley Walls	.75	.35
❑ 22 Darnell Autry	.40	.18
❑ 23 Curtis Conway	.75	.35
❑ 24 Bobby Engram	.75	.35
❑ 25 Curtis Enis RC	5.00	2.20
❑ 26 Raymont Harris	.40	.18
❑ 27 Jeff Blake	.75	.35
❑ 28 Corey Dillon	2.50	1.10
❑ 29 Carl Pickens	1.50	.70
❑ 30 Darnay Scott	.75	.35
❑ 31 Troy Aikman	4.00	1.80
❑ 32 Michael Irvin	1.50	.70
❑ 33 Deion Sanders	1.50	.70
❑ 34 Emmitt Smith	6.00	2.70
❑ 35 Steve Atwater	.40	.18
❑ 36 Terrell Davis	6.00	2.70
❑ 37 John Elway	8.00	3.60
❑ 38 Brian Griese RC	6.00	2.70
❑ 39 Ed McCaffrey	.75	.35
❑ 40 Marcus Nash RC	4.00	1.80
❑ 41 Shannon Sharpe	.75	.35
❑ 42 Neil Smith	.75	.35
❑ 43 Rod Smith	.75	.35
❑ 44 Charlie Batch RC	6.00	2.70
❑ 45 Germane Crowell RC	5.00	2.20
❑ 46 Scott Mitchell	.75	.35
❑ 47 Herman Moore	1.50	.70
❑ 48 Barry Sanders	8.00	3.60
❑ 49 Robert Brooks	.75	.35
❑ 50 Mark Chmura	.75	.35
❑ 51 Brett Favre	8.00	3.60
❑ 52 Antonio Freeman	1.50	.70
❑ 53 Dorsey Levens	1.50	.70
❑ 54 Aaron Bailey	.40	.18
❑ 55 Ken Dilger	.40	.18
❑ 56 Marshall Faulk	1.50	.70
❑ 57 Marvin Harrison	.75	.35
❑ 58 Peyton Manning RC	20.00	9.00
❑ 59 Tavian Banks RC	.75	.35
❑ 60 Tony Brackens	.40	.18
❑ 61 Mark Brunell	3.00	1.35
❑ 62 Keenan McCardell	.75	.35
❑ 63 Natrone Means	1.50	.70
❑ 64 Jimmy Smith	.75	.35
❑ 65 James Stewart	.75	.35
❑ 66 Fred Taylor RC	10.00	4.50
❑ 67 Tony Gonzalez	.40	.18
❑ 68 Elvis Grbac	.75	.35
❑ 69 Greg Hill	.40	.18
❑ 70 Andre Rison	.75	.35
❑ 71 Derrick Thomas	.75	.35
❑ 72 Karim Abdul-Jabbar	1.50	.70
❑ 73 John Avery RC	3.00	1.35
❑ 74 Troy Drayton	.40	.18
❑ 75 Dan Marino	8.00	3.60
❑ 76 O.J. McDuffie	.75	.35
❑ 77 Cris Carter	1.50	.70
❑ 78 Brad Johnson	1.50	.70
❑ 79 John Randle	.75	.35
❑ 80 Jake Reed	.75	.35
❑ 81 Robert Smith	1.50	.70
❑ 82 Drew Bledsoe	3.00	1.35
❑ 83 Ben Coates	.75	.35
❑ 84 Robert Edwards RC	3.00	1.35
❑ 85 Terry Glenn	1.50	.70
❑ 86 Tony Simmons RC	3.00	1.35
❑ 87 Troy Davis	.40	.18
❑ 88 Heath Shuler	.40	.18
❑ 89 Danny Wuerffel	.75	.35
❑ 90 Ray Zellars	.40	.18
❑ 91 Tiki Barber	.75	.35
❑ 92 Joe Jurevicius RC	3.00	1.35
❑ 93 Danny Kanell	.75	.35
❑ 94 Charles Way	.40	.18
❑ 95 Tyrone Wheatley	.75	.35
❑ 96 Wayne Chrebet	1.50	.70
❑ 97 Glenn Foley	.75	.35
❑ 98 Keyshawn Johnson	1.50	.70
❑ 99 Curtis Martin	1.50	.70
❑ 100 Tim Brown	1.50	.70
❑ 101 Rickey Dudley	.40	.18
❑ 102 Jeff George	.75	.35
❑ 103 Desmond Howard	.75	.35
❑ 104 Napoleon Kaufman	1.50	.70
❑ 105 Charles Woodson RC	5.00	2.20
❑ 106 Jason Dunn	.40	.18
❑ 107 Irving Fryar	.75	.35
❑ 108 Charlie Garner	.40	.18
❑ 109 Bobby Hoying	.75	.35
❑ 110 Jerome Bettis	1.50	.70
❑ 111 Mark Bruener	.40	.18
❑ 112 Charles Johnson	.40	.18
❑ 113 Levon Kirkland	.40	.18
❑ 114 Kordell Stewart	1.50	.70
❑ 115 Hines Ward RC	3.00	1.35
❑ 116 Tony Banks	.75	.35
❑ 117 Isaac Bruce	1.50	.70
❑ 118 Robert Holcombe RC	3.00	1.35
❑ 119 Eddie Kennison	.75	.35
❑ 120 Freddie Jones	.40	.18
❑ 121 Ryan Leaf RC	4.00	1.80
❑ 122 Tony Martin	.75	.35
❑ 123 Junior Seau	.75	.35
❑ 124 Jim Druckenmiller	.75	.35
❑ 125 Garrison Hearst	1.50	.70
❑ 126 Terrell Owens	1.50	.70
❑ 127 Jerry Rice	4.00	1.80
❑ 128 J.J. Stokes	.75	.35
❑ 129 Steve Young	2.50	1.10
❑ 130 Joey Galloway	1.50	.70
❑ 131 Ahman Green RC	.75	.35
❑ 132 Cortez Kennedy	.40	.18
❑ 133 Jon Kitna	4.00	1.80
❑ 134 James McKnight	.40	.18
❑ 135 Warren Moon	1.50	.70
❑ 136 Mike Alstott	1.50	.70
❑ 137 Reidel Anthony	.75	.35
❑ 138 Trent Dilfer	1.50	.70
❑ 139 Warrick Dunn	2.50	1.10
❑ 140 Warren Sapp	.75	.35
❑ 141 Kevin Dyson RC	4.00	1.80
❑ 142 Eddie George	3.00	1.35
❑ 143 Steve McNair	1.50	.70
❑ 144 Chris Sanders	.40	.18
❑ 145 Frank Wycheck	.40	.18
❑ 146 Stephen Alexander RC	3.00	1.35
❑ 147 Terry Allen	1.50	.70
❑ 148 Gus Frerotte	.40	.18
❑ 149 Skip Hicks RC	4.00	1.80
❑ 150 Michael Westbrook	.75	.35
❑ S1 Warrick Dunn Sample	1.50	.70

1998 Revolution Icons

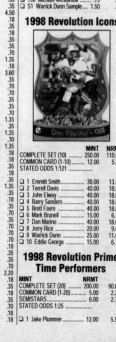

	MINT	NRMT
COMPLETE SET (10)	250.00	110.00
COMMON CARD (1-10)	12.00	5.50

STATED ODDS 1:121

Card	MINT	NRMT
❑ 1 Emmitt Smith	30.00	13.50
❑ 2 Terrell Davis	40.00	18.00
❑ 3 John Elway	40.00	18.00
❑ 4 Barry Sanders	40.00	18.00
❑ 5 Brett Favre	40.00	18.00
❑ 6 Mark Brunell	15.00	6.75
❑ 7 Dan Marino	40.00	18.00
❑ 8 Jerry Rice	20.00	9.00
❑ 9 Warrick Dunn	25.00	11.00
❑ 10 Eddie George	15.00	6.75

1998 Revolution Prime Time Performers

	MINT	NRMT
COMPLETE SET (20)	200.00	90.00
COMMON CARD (1-20)	5.00	2.20
SEMISTARS	6.00	2.70

STATED ODDS 1:25

Card	MINT	NRMT
❑ 1 Jake Plummer	12.00	5.50

	MINT	NRMT
❑ 2 Corey Dillon	5.00	2.20
❑ 3 Troy Aikman	12.00	5.50
❑ 4 Deion Sanders	8.00	3.60
❑ 5 Emmitt Smith	20.00	9.00
❑ 6 Terrell Davis	20.00	9.00
❑ 7 John Elway	25.00	11.00
❑ 8 Barry Sanders	25.00	11.00
❑ 9 Brett Favre	25.00	11.00
❑ 10 Peyton Manning	30.00	13.50
❑ 11 Mark Brunell	10.00	4.50
❑ 12 Dan Marino	25.00	11.00
❑ 13 Drew Bledsoe	10.00	4.50
❑ 14 Jerome Bettis	8.00	3.60
❑ 15 Kordell Stewart	6.00	2.70
❑ 16 Jerry Rice	12.00	5.50
❑ 17 Steve Young	8.00	3.60
❑ 18 Warrick Dunn	10.00	4.50
❑ 19 Eddie George	10.00	4.50
❑ 20 Steve McNair	8.00	3.60

1998 Revolution Rookies and Stars

	MINT	NRMT
COMPLETE SET (30)	150.00	70.00
COMMON CARD (1-30)	2.00	.90
SEMISTARS	3.00	1.35
UNLISTED STARS	4.00	1.80
STATED ODDS 4:25		
*GOLDS: 7.5X TO 15X HI COL.		
GOLD PRINT RUN 50 SERIAL #'d SETS		

❑ 1 Michael Pittman	3.00	1.35
❑ 2 Curtis Enis	5.00	2.20
❑ 3 Takeo Spikes	3.00	1.35
❑ 4 Greg Ellis	2.00	.90
❑ 5 Emmitt Smith	12.00	5.50
❑ 6 Terrell Davis	12.00	5.50
❑ 7 John Elway	15.00	6.75
❑ 8 Brian Griese	8.00	3.60
❑ 9 Marcus Nash	4.00	1.80
❑ 10 Charlie Batch	8.00	3.60
❑ 11 Barry Sanders	15.00	6.75
❑ 12 Brett Favre	15.00	6.75
❑ 13 Vonnie Holliday	3.00	1.35
❑ 14 E.G. Green	3.00	1.35
❑ 15 Peyton Manning	20.00	9.00
❑ 16 Fred Taylor	12.00	5.50
❑ 17 John Avery	4.00	1.80
❑ 18 Dan Marino	15.00	6.75
❑ 19 Drew Bledsoe	6.00	2.70
❑ 20 Robert Edwards	4.00	1.80
❑ 21 Joe Jurevicius	3.00	1.35
❑ 22 Charles Woodson	5.00	2.20
❑ 23 Kordell Stewart	4.00	1.80
❑ 24 Robert Holcombe	4.00	1.80
❑ 25 Ryan Leaf	4.00	1.80
❑ 26 Warrick Dunn	5.00	2.20
❑ 27 Jacquez Green	4.00	1.80
❑ 28 Kevin Dyson	4.00	1.80
❑ 29 Eddie George	6.00	2.70
❑ 30 Stephen Alexander	2.00	.90

1998 Revolution Showstoppers

	MINT	NRMT
COMPLETE SET (36)	200.00	90.00
COMMON CARD (1-36)	3.00	1.35
SEMISTARS	5.00	2.20
STATED ODDS 2:25		
*RED CARDS: SAME PRICE AS SILVERS		

❑ 1 Jake Plummer	10.00	4.50
❑ 2 Antowain Smith	5.00	2.20
❑ 3 Kerry Collins	5.00	2.20
❑ 4 Corey Dillon	3.00	1.35
❑ 5 Troy Aikman	10.00	4.50
❑ 6 Deion Sanders	5.00	2.20
❑ 7 Emmitt Smith	15.00	6.75
❑ 8 Terrell Davis	15.00	6.75
❑ 9 John Elway	20.00	9.00
❑ 10 Shannon Sharpe	5.00	2.20
❑ 11 Herman Moore	5.00	2.20
❑ 12 Barry Sanders	20.00	9.00
❑ 13 Brett Favre	20.00	9.00
❑ 14 Antonio Freeman	5.00	2.20
❑ 15 Dorsey Levens	5.00	2.20
❑ 16 Peyton Manning	25.00	11.00
❑ 17 Mark Brunell	8.00	3.60
❑ 18 Dan Marino	20.00	9.00
❑ 19 Robert Smith	5.00	2.20
❑ 20 Drew Bledsoe	8.00	3.60
❑ 21 Danny Kanell	5.00	2.20
❑ 22 Curtis Martin	5.00	2.20
❑ 23 Tim Brown	5.00	2.20
❑ 24 Napoleon Kaufman	5.00	2.20
❑ 25 Jerome Bettis	5.00	2.20
❑ 26 Kordell Stewart	5.00	2.20
❑ 27 Ryan Leaf	6.00	2.70
❑ 28 Terrell Owens	5.00	2.20
❑ 29 Jerry Rice	10.00	4.50
❑ 30 Steve Young	6.00	2.70
❑ 31 Ricky Watters	5.00	2.20
❑ 32 Mike Alstott	5.00	2.20
❑ 33 Trent Dilfer	5.00	2.20
❑ 34 Warrick Dunn	5.00	2.20
❑ 35 Eddie George	8.00	3.60
❑ 36 Steve McNair	5.00	2.20

1998 Revolution Touchdown

	MINT	NRMT
COMPLETE SET (20)	200.00	90.00
COMMON CARD (1-20)	6.00	2.70
STATED ODDS 1:49		

❑ 1 Jake Plummer	12.00	5.50
❑ 2 Corey Dillon	6.00	2.70
❑ 3 Troy Aikman	12.00	5.50
❑ 4 Emmitt Smith	20.00	9.00
❑ 5 Terrell Davis	20.00	9.00
❑ 6 John Elway	25.00	11.00
❑ 7 Barry Sanders	25.00	11.00
❑ 8 Brett Favre	25.00	11.00
❑ 9 Dorsey Levens	6.00	2.70
❑ 10 Peyton Manning	30.00	13.50
❑ 11 Mark Brunell	10.00	4.50
❑ 12 Marcus Allen	6.00	2.70
❑ 13 Dan Marino	25.00	11.00
❑ 14 Drew Bledsoe	10.00	4.50
❑ 15 Jerome Bettis	6.00	2.70
❑ 16 Kordell Stewart	6.00	2.70
❑ 17 Jerry Rice	12.00	5.50
❑ 18 Steve Young	8.00	3.60
❑ 19 Warrick Dunn	6.00	2.70
❑ 20 Eddie George	10.00	4.50

1999 Revolution

	MINT	NRMT
COMPLETE SET (175)	100.00	45.00
COMMON CARD (1-175)	.25	.11
SEMISTARS	.50	.23
UNLISTED STARS	1.00	.45
COMMON ROOKIE	1.25	.55
ROOKIE SEMISTARS	2.00	.90
ROOKIE UNL.STARS	2.50	1.10
COMMON ROOKIE SP (45)	1.50	.70
SP SEMISTARS (28/39/49/71)	2.50	1.10
SP SEMISTARS (76/85/87/97)	2.50	1.10
SP SEMISTARS (114/128/129)	2.50	1.10
SP SEMISTARS (136/138/150)	2.50	1.10
SP UNL.STARS (2/11/50/57)	3.00	1.35
SP UNL.STARS (66/71/106/123)	3.00	1.35
SP ROOKIES STATED ODDS 1:4		
COMMON SHADOW	6.00	2.70
*SHADOW STARS: 10X TO 25X HI COL.		
*SHADOW YOUNG: 8X TO 20X		
*SHADOW RCs: 2X TO 5X		
SHADOW PRINT RUN 99 SERIAL #'d SETS		
COMMON OPEN.DAY	8.00	3.60
*OPEN.DAY STARS: 12X TO 30X HI COL.		
*OPEN.DAY YOUNG STARS: 10X TO 25X		
*OPEN.DAY RCs: 2.5X TO 6X		
OPEN.DAY PRINT RUN 68 SERIAL #'d SETS		
COMP.RED SET (175)	300.00	135.00

*RED STARS: 2X TO 5X HI COL.
*RED YOUNG STARS: 1.5X TO 4X
*RED RCs: .8X TO 2X
RED STATED PRINT RUN 299 SER.#'d SETS

❑ 1 David Boston SP RC 4.00 1.80
❑ 2 Joel Makovicka RC SP 3.00 1.35
❑ 3 Rob Moore .... .50 .23
❑ 4 Adrian Murrell .... .50 .23
❑ 5 Jake Plummer .... 2.00 .90
❑ 6 Frank Sanders .... .50 .23
❑ 7 Jamal Anderson .... 1.00 .45
❑ 8 Chris Chandler .... .50 .23
❑ 9 Tim Dwight .... 1.00 .45
❑ 10 Terance Mathis .... .50 .23
❑ 11 Jeff Paulk RC SP 3.00 1.35
❑ 12 O.J. Santiago .... .25 .11
❑ 13 Peter Boulware .... .25 .11
❑ 14 Priest Holmes .... 1.00 .45
❑ 15 Michael Jackson .... .25 .11
❑ 16 Jermaine Lewis .... .50 .23
❑ 17 Doug Flutie .... 1.25 .55
❑ 18 Eric Moulds .... 1.00 .45
❑ 19 Peerless Price RC SP 5.00 2.20
❑ 20 Andre Reed .... .50 .23
❑ 21 Antowain Smith .... 1.00 .45
❑ 22 Bruce Smith .... .50 .23
❑ 23 Steve Beuerlein .... .25 .11
❑ 24 Kevin Greene .... .50 .23
❑ 25 Fred Lane .... .25 .11
❑ 26 Muhsin Muhammad .... .50 .23
❑ 27 Wesley Walls .... .50 .23
❑ 28 Marty Booker RC SP 2.50 1.10
❑ 29 Curtis Conway .... .50 .23
❑ 30 Bobby Engram .... .50 .23
❑ 31 Curtis Enis .... 1.00 .45
❑ 32 Erik Kramer .... .25 .11
❑ 33 Cade McNown SP RC.... 8.00 3.60
❑ 34 Scott Covington RC........ 2.50 1.10
❑ 35 Corey Dillon .... 1.00 .45
❑ 36 Carl Pickens .... .50 .23
❑ 37 Darnay Scott .... .25 .11
❑ 38 Akili Smith RC 5.00 2.20
❑ 39 Craig Yeast RC SP 2.50 1.10
❑ 40 Darrin Chiaverini RC SP 2.50 1.10
❑ 41 Tim Couch SP RC........ 12.00 5.50
❑ 42 Ty Detmer .... .50 .23
❑ 43 Kevin Johnson SP RC.... 6.00 2.70
❑ 44 Terry Kirby .... .25 .11
❑ 45 Daylon McCutcheon RC SP 1.50 .70
❑ 46 Irv Smith .... .25 .11
❑ 47 Troy Aikman 2.50 1.10
❑ 48 Michael Irvin .... .50 .23
❑ 49 Wane McGarity RC SP .. 2.50 1.10
❑ 50 Dat Nguyen RC SP 3.00 1.35
❑ 51 Deion Sanders .... 1.00 .45
❑ 52 Emmitt Smith 2.50 1.10
❑ 53 Terrell Davis 2.50 1.10
❑ 54 John Elway 4.00 1.80
❑ 55 Brian Griese .... 2.00 .90
❑ 56 Ed McCaffrey .... .50 .23
❑ 57 Travis McGriff RC SP 3.00 1.35
❑ 58 Shannon Sharpe .... .50 .23
❑ 59 Rod Smith WR .... .50 .23
❑ 60 Charlie Batch .... 2.00 .90
❑ 61 Chris Claiborne RC 2.50 1.10
❑ 62 Sedrick Irvin RC 2.50 1.10
❑ 63 Herman Moore .... 1.00 .45
❑ 64 Johnnie Morton .... .50 .23
❑ 65 Barry Sanders 4.00 1.80
❑ 66 Aaron Brooks RC SP 3.00 1.35
❑ 67 Mark Chmura .... .25 .11
❑ 68 Brett Favre 4.00 1.80
❑ 69 Antonio Freeman .... 1.00 .45
❑ 70 Dorsey Levens .... 1.00 .45
❑ 71 De'Mond Parker RC SP 3.00 1.35
❑ 72 Marvin Harrison .... 1.00 .45
❑ 73 Edgerrin James SP RC 20.00 9.00
❑ 74 Peyton Manning 4.00 1.80
❑ 75 Jerome Pathon .... .25 .11
❑ 76 Mike Peterson RC SP 2.50 1.10
❑ 77 Reggie Barlow .... .25 .11
❑ 78 Mark Brunell .... 1.50 .70
❑ 79 Keenan McCardell .... .50 .23
❑ 80 Jimmy Smith .... .50 .23
❑ 81 Fred Taylor 2.50 1.10
❑ 82 Mike Cloud RC 2.50 1.10
❑ 83 Tony Gonzalez .... .50 .23
❑ 84 Elvis Grbac .... .50 .23
❑ 85 Larry Parker RC SP 2.50 1.10
❑ 86 Andre Rison .... .50 .23
❑ 87 Brian Shay RC SP 2.50 1.10
❑ 88 Karim Abdul-Jabbar .... .50 .23
❑ 89 Oronde Gadsden .... .25 .11
❑ 90 James Johnson SP RC .. 3.00 1.35
❑ 91 Rob Konrad RC .... 2.00 .90
❑ 92 Dan Marino 4.00 1.80
❑ 93 O.J. McDuffie .... .50 .23
❑ 94 Cris Carter .... 1.00 .45
❑ 95 Daunte Culpepper SP RC 8.00 3.60
❑ 96 Randall Cunningham...... 1.00 .45
❑ 97 Jim Kleinsasser RC SP .. 2.50 1.10
❑ 98 Randy Moss 4.00 1.80
❑ 99 Jake Reed .... .50 .23
❑ 100 Robert Smith .... 1.00 .45
❑ 101 Drew Bledsoe .... 1.50 .70
❑ 102 Ben Coates .... .50 .23
❑ 103 Kevin Faulk SP RC 3.00 1.35
❑ 104 Terry Glenn .... 1.00 .45
❑ 105 Shawn Jefferson .... .25 .11
❑ 106 Andy Katzenmoyer RC SP 3.00 1.35
❑ 107 Cameron Cleeland .... .25 .11
❑ 108 Andre Hastings .... .25 .11
❑ 109 Billy Joe Tolliver .... .25 .11
❑ 110 Ricky Williams RC...... 12.00 5.50
❑ 111 Gary Brown .... .25 .11
❑ 112 Kent Graham .... .25 .11
❑ 113 Ike Hilliard .... .25 .11
❑ 114 Joe Montgomery RC SP 2.50 1.10
❑ 115 Amani Toomer .... .25 .11
❑ 116 Wayne Chrebet .... .50 .23
❑ 117 Keyshawn Johnson ...... 1.00 .45
❑ 118 Leon Johnson .... .25 .11
❑ 119 Curtis Martin .... 1.00 .45
❑ 120 Vinny Testaverde .... .50 .23
❑ 121 Dedric Ward .... .25 .11
❑ 122 Tim Brown .... 1.00 .45
❑ 123 Dameane Douglas RC SP 3.00 1.35
❑ 124 Rickey Dudley .... .25 .11
❑ 125 James Jett .... .50 .23
❑ 126 Napoleon Kaufman ...... 1.00 .45
❑ 127 Charles Woodson .... 1.00 .45
❑ 128 Na Brown RC SP 3.00 1.35
❑ 129 Cecil Martin RC SP 2.50 1.10
❑ 130 Donovan McNabb SP RC 8.00 3.60
❑ 131 Duce Staley .... 1.00 .45
❑ 132 Kevin Turner .... .25 .11
❑ 133 Jerome Bettis .... 1.00 .45
❑ 134 Troy Edwards SP RC .. 4.00 1.80
❑ 135 Courtney Hawkins .... .25 .11
❑ 136 Malcolm Johnson RC SP 2.50 1.10
❑ 137 Kordell Stewart .... 1.00 .45
❑ 138 Jerame Tuman RC SP 2.50 1.10
❑ 139 Amos Zereoue RC 2.50 1.10
❑ 140 Isaac Bruce .... 1.00 .45
❑ 141 Joe Germaine RC 2.50 1.10
❑ 142 Torry Holt RC SP 8.00 3.60
❑ 143 Amp Lee .... .25 .11
❑ 144 Ricky Proehl .... .25 .11
❑ 145 Freddie Jones .... .25 .11
❑ 146 Ryan Leaf .... 1.00 .45
❑ 147 Natrone Means .... .50 .23
❑ 148 Mikhael Ricks .... .25 .11
❑ 149 Garrison Hearst .... .50 .23
❑ 150 Terry Jackson RC SP .. 2.50 1.10
❑ 151 Terrell Owens .... 1.00 .45
❑ 152 Jerry Rice 2.50 1.10
❑ 153 J.J. Stokes .... .50 .23
❑ 154 Steve Young .... 1.50 .70
❑ 155 Karsten Bailey RC........ 2.50 1.10
❑ 156 Joey Galloway .... 1.00 .45
❑ 157 Ahman Green .... .50 .23
❑ 158 Brock Huard SP RC 3.00 1.35
❑ 159 Jon Kitna .... 1.25 .55
❑ 160 Ricky Watters .... .50 .23
❑ 161 Mike Alstott .... 1.00 .45
❑ 162 Reidel Anthony .... .50 .23
❑ 163 Trent Dilfer .... .50 .23
❑ 164 Warrick Dunn .... 1.00 .45
❑ 165 Shaun King SP RC 8.00 3.60
❑ 166 Anthony McFarland RC 2.50 1.10
❑ 167 Kevin Dyson .... .50 .23
❑ 168 Eddie George .... 1.25 .55
❑ 169 Darran Hall RC .... 2.00 .90
❑ 170 Steve McNair.......... 1.00 .45
❑ 171 Frank Wycheck .... .25 .11
❑ 172 Stephen Alexander .... .25 .11
❑ 173 Champ Bailey .... .25 .11
❑ 174 Skip Hicks .... 1.00 .45
❑ 175 Michael Westbrook .... .50 .23

1999 Revolution Chalk Talk

	MINT	NRMT
COMPLETE SET (20)	200.00	90.00
COMMON CARD (1-20)..........	5.00	2.20
STATED ODDS 1:49		

❑ 1 Jake Plummer 10.00 4.50
❑ 2 Jamal Anderson 6.00 2.70
❑ 3 Doug Flutie 6.00 2.70
❑ 4 Tim Couch 20.00 9.00
❑ 5 Troy Aikman 12.00 5.50
❑ 6 Emmitt Smith 12.00 5.50
❑ 7 Terrell Davis 12.00 5.50
❑ 8 John Elway 20.00 9.00
❑ 9 Barry Sanders 20.00 9.00
❑ 10 Brett Favre 20.00 9.00
❑ 11 Peyton Manning 15.00 6.75
❑ 12 Mark Brunell 8.00 3.60
❑ 13 Fred Taylor 10.00 4.50
❑ 14 Dan Marino 20.00 9.00
❑ 15 Randy Moss 15.00 6.75
❑ 16 Drew Bledsoe 8.00 3.60
❑ 17 Ricky Williams 20.00 9.00
❑ 18 Jerry Rice 12.00 5.50
❑ 19 Jon Kitna 6.00 2.70
❑ 20 Eddie George 6.00 2.70

1999 Revolution Icons

	MINT	NRMT
COMPLETE SET (10)	150.00	70.00
COMMON CARD (1-10)..........	10.00	4.50
STATED ODDS 1:121		

❑ 1 Emmitt Smith 15.00 6.75
❑ 2 Terrell Davis 15.00 6.75
❑ 3 John Elway 25.00 11.00

Card	MINT	NRMT
❑ 4 Barry Sanders	25.00	11.00
❑ 5 Brett Favre	25.00	11.00
❑ 6 Peyton Manning	20.00	9.00
❑ 7 Dan Marino	25.00	11.00
❑ 8 Randy Moss	20.00	9.00
❑ 9 Jerry Rice	15.00	6.75
❑ 10 Jon Kitna	12.00	5.50

1999 Revolution Showstoppers

	MINT	NRMT
COMPLETE SET (36)	150.00	70.00
COMMON CARD (1-36)	3.00	1.35
STATED ODDS 2:25		

Card	MINT	NRMT
❑ 1 Jake Plummer	6.00	2.70
❑ 2 Jamal Anderson	3.00	1.35
❑ 3 Priest Holmes	3.00	1.35
❑ 4 Doug Flutie	4.00	1.80
❑ 5 Antowain Smith	3.00	1.35
❑ 6 Cade McNown	6.00	2.70
❑ 7 Tim Couch	12.00	5.50
❑ 8 Corey Dillon	3.00	1.35
❑ 9 Akili Smith	4.00	1.80
❑ 10 Troy Aikman	8.00	3.60
❑ 11 Emmitt Smith	8.00	3.60
❑ 12 Terrell Davis	8.00	3.60
❑ 13 John Elway	12.00	5.50
❑ 14 Charlie Batch	5.00	2.20
❑ 15 Barry Sanders	12.00	5.50
❑ 16 Brett Favre	12.00	5.50
❑ 17 Antonio Freeman	3.00	1.35
❑ 18 Edgerrin James	20.00	9.00
❑ 19 Peyton Manning	10.00	4.50
❑ 20 Mark Brunell	5.00	2.20
❑ 21 Fred Taylor	6.00	2.70
❑ 22 Dan Marino	12.00	5.50
❑ 23 Randall Cunningham	3.00	1.35
❑ 24 Randy Moss	10.00	4.50
❑ 25 Drew Bledsoe	5.00	2.20
❑ 26 Ricky Williams	12.00	5.50
❑ 27 Curtis Martin	3.00	1.35
❑ 28 Napoleon Kaufman	3.00	1.35
❑ 29 Donovan McNabb	6.00	2.70
❑ 30 Kordell Stewart	3.00	1.35
❑ 31 Terrell Owens	3.00	1.35
❑ 32 Jerry Rice	8.00	3.60
❑ 33 Steve Young	5.00	2.20
❑ 34 Jon Kitna	4.00	1.80
❑ 35 Warrick Dunn	3.00	1.35
❑ 36 Eddie George	4.00	1.80

1999 Revolution Thorn in the Side

	MINT	NRMT
COMPLETE SET (20)	120.00	55.00
COMMON CARD (1-20)	3.00	1.35
STATED ODDS 1:25		

Card	MINT	NRMT
❑ 1 Jake Plummer	6.00	2.70
❑ 2 Jamal Anderson	4.00	1.80
❑ 3 Doug Flutie	4.00	1.80
❑ 4 Tim Couch	10.00	4.50
❑ 5 Troy Aikman	8.00	3.60
❑ 6 Emmitt Smith	8.00	3.60
❑ 7 Terrell Davis	8.00	3.60

Card	MINT	NRMT
❑ 8 John Elway	12.00	5.50
❑ 9 Barry Sanders	12.00	5.50
❑ 10 Brett Favre	12.00	5.50
❑ 11 Peyton Manning	10.00	4.50
❑ 12 Fred Taylor	6.00	2.70
❑ 13 Dan Marino	12.00	5.50
❑ 14 Randy Moss	10.00	4.50
❑ 15 Drew Bledsoe	5.00	2.20
❑ 16 Ricky Williams	10.00	4.50
❑ 17 Curtis Martin	4.00	1.80
❑ 18 Jerome Bettis	4.00	1.80
❑ 19 Jerry Rice	8.00	3.60
❑ 20 Jon Kitna	4.00	1.80

1999 Revolution Three-Deep Zone

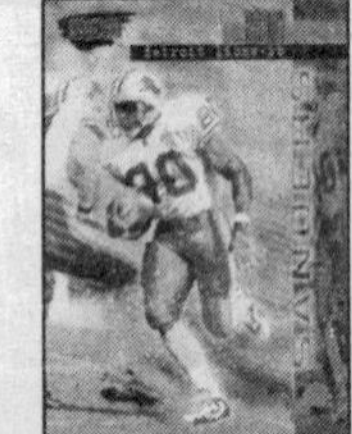

	MINT	NRMT
COMPLETE SET (30)	70.00	32.00
COMMON CARD (1-30)	1.25	.55
GOLD STATED ODDS 4:25		

*SILVERS 1-10: 5X TO 12X GOLDS
SILVER 1-10 PRINT RUN 99 SER.#'d SETS
*SILVERS 11-20: 1.25X TO 3X GOLDS
SILVER 11-20 PRINT RUN 199 SER.#'d SETS
*SILVERS 21-30: .6X TO 1.5X GOLDS
SILVER 21-30 PRINT RUN 299 SER.#'d SETS

Card	MINT	NRMT
❑ 1 Troy Aikman	3.00	1.35
❑ 2 Emmitt Smith	3.00	1.35
❑ 3 Terrell Davis	3.00	1.35
❑ 4 John Elway	5.00	2.20
❑ 5 Barry Sanders	5.00	2.20
❑ 6 Brett Favre	5.00	2.20
❑ 7 Peyton Manning	4.00	1.80
❑ 8 Dan Marino	5.00	2.20
❑ 9 Randy Moss	4.00	1.80
❑ 10 Drew Bledsoe	2.00	.90
❑ 11 Jake Plummer	2.50	1.10
❑ 12 Jamal Anderson	1.25	.55
❑ 13 Doug Flutie	1.50	.70
❑ 14 Mark Brunell	2.00	.90
❑ 15 Fred Taylor	2.50	1.10
❑ 16 Randall Cunningham	1.25	.55
❑ 17 Terrell Owens	1.25	.55
❑ 18 Jerry Rice	3.00	1.35
❑ 19 Steve Young	2.00	.90
❑ 20 Jon Kitna	1.50	.70
❑ 21 Antowain Smith	1.25	.55
❑ 22 Antonio Freeman	1.25	.55
❑ 23 Curtis Martin	1.25	.55
❑ 24 Eddie George	1.50	.70
❑ 25 Cade McNown	4.00	1.80
❑ 26 Tim Couch	6.00	2.70
❑ 27 Akili Smith	2.50	1.10
❑ 28 Edgerrin James	10.00	4.50
❑ 29 Ricky Williams	6.00	2.70
❑ 30 Donovan McNabb	4.00	1.80

1989 Score

	MINT	NRMT
COMPLETE SET (330)	225.00	100.00
COMP.FACT.SET (330)	225.00	100.00
COMMON CARD (1-330)	.10	.05
SEMISTARS	.20	.09
UNLISTED STARS	.50	.23

BEWARE SANDERS/AIKMAN COUNTERFEIT

Card	MINT	NRMT
❑ 1 Joe Montana	4.00	1.80
❑ 2 Bo Jackson	.50	.23
❑ 3 Boomer Esiason	.20	.09
❑ 4 Roger Craig	.50	.23
❑ 5 Ed Too Tall Jones	.20	.09
❑ 6 Phil Simms	.20	.09
❑ 7 Dan Hampton	.20	.09
❑ 8 John Settle RC	.10	.05
❑ 9 Bernie Kosar	.20	.09
❑ 10 Al Toon	.20	.09
❑ 11 Bubby Brister RC	4.00	1.80
❑ 12 Mark Clayton	.20	.09
❑ 13 Dan Marino	4.00	1.80
❑ 14 Joe Morris	.10	.05
❑ 15 Warren Moon	.50	.23
❑ 16 Chuck Long	.10	.05
❑ 17 Mark Jackson	.10	.05
❑ 18 Michael Irvin RC	8.00	3.60
❑ 19 Bruce Smith	.50	.23
❑ 20 Anthony Carter	.20	.09
❑ 21 Charles Haley	.50	.23
❑ 22 Dave Duerson	.10	.05
❑ 23 Troy Stradford	.10	.05
❑ 24 Freeman McNeil	.10	.05
❑ 25 Jerry Gray	.10	.05
❑ 26 Bill Maas	.10	.05
❑ 27 Chris Chandler RC	5.00	2.20
❑ 28 Tom Newberry RC	.10	.05
❑ 29 Albert Lewis	.10	.05
❑ 30 Jay Schroeder	.10	.05
❑ 31 Dalton Hilliard	.10	.05
❑ 32 Tony Eason	.10	.05
❑ 33 Rick Donnelly UER (229.11 yards per punt)	.10	.05
❑ 34 Herschel Walker	.20	.09
❑ 35 Wesley Walker	.10	.05
❑ 36 Chris Doleman	.20	.09
❑ 37 Pat Swilling	.20	.09
❑ 38 Joey Browner	.10	.05
❑ 39 Shane Conlan	.10	.05
❑ 40 Mike Tomczak	.20	.09
❑ 41 Webster Slaughter	.20	.09
❑ 42 Ray Donaldson	.10	.05
❑ 43 Christian Okoye	.10	.05
❑ 44 John Bosa	.10	.05
❑ 45 Aaron Cox RC	.10	.05
❑ 46 Bobby Hebert	.20	.09
❑ 47 Carl Banks	.10	.05
❑ 48 Jeff Fuller	.10	.05
❑ 49 Gerald Willhite	.10	.05
❑ 50 Mike Singletary	.20	.09

❑ 51 Stanley Morgan .10 .05
❑ 52 Mark Bavaro .20 .09
❑ 53 Mickey Shuler .10 .05
❑ 54 Keith Millard .10 .05
❑ 55 Andre Tippett .10 .05
❑ 56 Vance Johnson .20 .09
❑ 57 Bennie Blades RC .10 .05
❑ 58 Tim Harris .10 .05
❑ 59 Hanford Dixon .10 .05
❑ 60 Chris Miller RC 1.50 .70
❑ 61 Cornelius Bennett .50 .23
❑ 62 Neal Anderson .20 .09
❑ 63 Ickey Woods RC UER .20 .09
(Jersey is 31 but listed as 30 on card back)
❑ 64 Gary Anderson RB .10 .05
❑ 65 Vaughan Johnson RC** .10 .05
❑ 66 Ronnie Lippett .10 .05
❑ 67 Mike Quick .10 .05
❑ 68 Roy Green .20 .09
❑ 69 Tim Krumrie .10 .05
❑ 70 Mark Malone .10 .05
❑ 71 James Jones .10 .05
❑ 72 Cris Carter RC 20.00 9.00
❑ 73 Ricky Nattiel .10 .05
❑ 74 Jim Arnold UER .10 .05
(238.83 yards per punt)
❑ 75 Randall Cunningham 1.00 .45
❑ 76 John L. Williams .10 .05
❑ 77 Paul Gruber RC .10 .05
❑ 78 Rod Woodson RC 3.00 1.35
❑ 79 Ray Childress .10 .05
❑ 80 Doug Williams .20 .09
❑ 81 Deron Cherry .20 .09
❑ 82 John Offerdahl .10 .05
❑ 83 Louis Lipps .20 .09
❑ 84 Neil Lomax .10 .05
❑ 85 Wade Wilson .20 .09
❑ 86 Tim Brown RC 10.00 4.50
❑ 87 Chris Hinton .10 .05
❑ 88 Stump Mitchell .10 .05
❑ 89 Tunch Ilkin RC .10 .05
❑ 90 Steve Pelluer .10 .05
❑ 91 Brian Noble .10 .05
❑ 92 Reggie White .50 .23
❑ 93 Aundray Bruce RC .10 .05
❑ 94 Garry James .10 .05
❑ 95 Drew Hill .10 .05
❑ 96 Anthony Munoz .20 .09
❑ 97 James Wilder .10 .05
❑ 98 Dexter Manley .10 .05
❑ 99 Lee Williams .10 .05
❑ 100 Dave Krieg .20 .09
❑ 101A Keith Jackson RC ERR .50 .23
(Listed as 84 on card back)
❑ 101B Keith Jackson RC COR .50 .23
(Listed as 88 on card back)
❑ 102 Luis Sharpe .10 .05
❑ 103 Kevin Greene .50 .23
❑ 104 Duane Bickett .10 .05
❑ 105 Mark Rypien RC .50 .23
❑ 106 Curt Warner .10 .05
❑ 107 Jacob Green .10 .05
❑ 108 Gary Clark .50 .23
❑ 109 Bruce Matthews RC .50 .23
❑ 110 Bill Fralic .10 .05
❑ 111 Bill Bates .20 .09
❑ 112 Jeff Bryant .10 .05
❑ 113 Charles Mann .10 .05
❑ 114 Richard Dent .20 .09
❑ 115 Bruce Hill RC .10 .05
❑ 116 Mark May RC .10 .05
❑ 117 Mark Collins RC .10 .05
❑ 118 Ron Holmes .10 .05
❑ 119 Scott Case RC .10 .05
❑ 120 Tom Rathman .10 .05
❑ 121 Dennis McKinnon .10 .05
❑ 122A Ricky Sanders ERR .25 .11
(Listed as 46 on card back)
❑ 122B Ricky Sanders COR .50 .23
(Listed as 83 on card back)

❑ 123 Michael Carter .10 .05
❑ 124 Ozzie Newsome .20 .09
❑ 125 Irving Fryar UER .20 .09
("wide reveiver")
❑ 126A Ron Hall RC ERR .25 .11
(wrong photos on card)
❑ 126B Ron Hall RC COR .50 .23
(correct photos used)
❑ 127 Clay Matthews .20 .09
❑ 128 Leonard Marshall .10 .05
❑ 129 Kevin Mack .10 .05
❑ 130 Art Monk .20 .09
❑ 131 Garin Veris .10 .05
❑ 132 Steve Jordan .10 .05
❑ 133 Frank Minnifield .10 .05
❑ 134 Eddie Brown .10 .05
❑ 135 Stacey Bailey .10 .05
❑ 136 Rickey Jackson .20 .09
❑ 137 Henry Ellard .20 .09
❑ 138 Jim Burt .10 .05
❑ 139 Jerome Brown .20 .09
❑ 140 Rodney Holman RC .10 .05
❑ 141 Sammy Winder .10 .05
❑ 142 Marcus Cotton .10 .05
❑ 143 Jim Jeffcoat .10 .05
❑ 144 Rueben Mayes .10 .05
❑ 145 Jim McMahon .20 .09
❑ 146 Reggie Williams .10 .05
❑ 147 John Anderson .10 .05
❑ 148 Harris Barton RC .10 .05
❑ 149 Phillip Epps .10 .05
❑ 150 Jay Hilgenberg .10 .05
❑ 151 Earl Ferrell .10 .05
❑ 152 Andre Reed .50 .23
❑ 153 Dennis Gentry .10 .05
❑ 154 Max Montoya .10 .05
❑ 155 Darrin Nelson .10 .05
❑ 156 Jeff Chadwick .10 .05
❑ 157 James Brooks .20 .09
❑ 158 Keith Bishop .10 .05
❑ 159 Robert Awalt .10 .05
❑ 160 Marty Lyons .10 .05
❑ 161 Johnny Hector .10 .05
❑ 162 Tony Casillas .10 .05
❑ 163 Kyle Clifton RC .10 .05
❑ 164 Cody Risien .10 .05
❑ 165 Jamie Holland RC .10 .05
❑ 166 Merril Hoge RC .10 .05
❑ 167 Chris Spielman RC 1.00 .45
❑ 168 Carlos Carson .10 .05
❑ 169 Jerry Ball RC .10 .05
❑ 170 Don Majkowski RC .20 .09
❑ 171 Everson Walls .10 .05
❑ 172 Mike Rozier .10 .05
❑ 173 Matt Millen .20 .09
❑ 174 Karl Mecklenburg .10 .05
❑ 175 Paul Palmer .10 .05
❑ 176 Brian Blades RC UER .50 .23
(Photo on back is reversed negative)
❑ 177 Brent Fullwood RC .10 .05
❑ 178 Anthony Miller RC .50 .23
❑ 179 Brian Sochia .10 .05
❑ 180 Stephen Baker RC .20 .09
❑ 181 Jesse Solomon .10 .05
❑ 182 John Grimsley .10 .05
❑ 183 Timmy Newsome .10 .05
❑ 184 Steve Sewell RC .10 .05
❑ 185 Dean Biasucci .10 .05
❑ 186 Alonzo Highsmith .10 .05
❑ 187 Randy Grimes .10 .05
❑ 188A Mark Carrier RC WR ERR 1.00 .45
(Photo on back is actually Bruce Hill)
❑ 188B Mark Carrier RC WR COR 1.00 .45
(Wearing helmet in photo on back)
❑ 189 Vann McElroy .10 .05
❑ 190 Greg Bell .10 .05
❑ 191 Quinn Early RC 1.50 .70
❑ 192 Lawrence Taylor .50 .23
❑ 193 Albert Bentley .10 .05
❑ 194 Ernest Givins .20 .09
❑ 195 Jackie Slater .10 .05
❑ 196 Jim Sweeney .10 .05
❑ 197 Freddie Joe Nunn .10 .05

❑ 198 Keith Byars .20 .09
❑ 199 Hardy Nickerson RC .50 .23
❑ 200 Steve Beuerlein RC 5.00 2.20
❑ 201 Bruce Armstrong RC .10 .05
❑ 202 Lionel Manuel .10 .05
❑ 203 J.T. Smith .10 .05
❑ 204 Mark Ingram RC .50 .23
❑ 205 Fred Smerlas .10 .05
❑ 206 Bryan Hinkle RC .10 .05
❑ 207 Steve McMichael .20 .09
❑ 208 Nick Lowery .10 .05
❑ 209 Jack Trudeau .10 .05
❑ 210 Lorenzo Hampton .10 .05
❑ 211 Thurman Thomas RC 6.00 2.70
❑ 212 Steve Young 1.50 .70
❑ 213 James Lofton .50 .23
❑ 214 Jim Covert .10 .05
❑ 215 Ronnie Lott .20 .09
❑ 216 Stephone Paige .10 .05
❑ 217 Mark Duper .20 .09
❑ 218A Willie Gault ERR .25 .11
(Front photo actually 93 Greg Townsend)
❑ 218B Willie Gault COR .50 .23
(83 clearly visible)
❑ 219 Ken Ruettgers RC .10 .05
❑ 220 Kevin Ross RC .20 .09
❑ 221 Jerry Rice 3.00 1.35
❑ 222 Billy Ray Smith .10 .05
❑ 223 Jim Kelly 1.00 .45
❑ 224 Vinny Testaverde 1.00 .45
❑ 225 Steve Largent .50 .23
❑ 226 Warren Williams RC .10 .05
❑ 227 Morten Andersen .10 .05
❑ 228 Bill Brooks .20 .09
❑ 229 Reggie Langhorne RC .10 .05
❑ 230 Pepper Johnson .10 .05
❑ 231 Pat Leahy .10 .05
❑ 232 Fred Marion .10 .05
❑ 233 Gary Zimmerman .10 .05
❑ 234 Marcus Allen .50 .23
❑ 235 Gaston Green RC .10 .05
❑ 236 John Stephens RC .10 .05
❑ 237 Terry Kinard .10 .05
❑ 238 John Taylor RC .50 .23
❑ 239 Brian Bosworth .20 .09
❑ 240 Anthony Toney .10 .05
❑ 241 Ken O'Brien .10 .05
❑ 242 Howie Long .20 .09
❑ 243 Doug Flutie 2.50 1.10
❑ 244 Jim Everett .50 .23
❑ 245 Broderick Thomas RC .50 .23
❑ 246 Deion Sanders RC 20.00 9.00
❑ 247 Donnell Woolford RC .20 .09
❑ 248 Wayne Martin RC .10 .05
❑ 249 David Williams RC .10 .05
❑ 250 Bill Hawkins RC .10 .05
❑ 251 Eric Hill RC .10 .05
❑ 252 Burt Grossman RC .10 .05
❑ 253 Tracy Rocker .10 .05
❑ 254 Steve Wisniewski RC .20 .09
❑ 255 Jessie Small RC .10 .05
❑ 256 David Braxton .10 .05
❑ 257 Barry Sanders RC 125.00 55.00
❑ 258 Derrick Thomas RC 10.00 4.50
❑ 259 Eric Metcalf RC 1.00 .45
❑ 260 Keith DeLong RC .10 .05
❑ 261 Hart Lee Dykes RC .10 .05
❑ 262 Sammie Smith RC .10 .05
❑ 263 Steve Atwater RC .50 .23
❑ 264 Eric Ball RC .10 .05
❑ 265 Don Beebe RC .50 .23
❑ 266 Brian Williams OL .10 .05
❑ 267 Jeff Lageman RC .20 .09
❑ 268 Tim Worley RC .10 .05
❑ 269 Tony Mandarich RC .10 .05
❑ 270 Troy Aikman RC 50.00 22.00
❑ 271 Andy Heck RC .10 .05
❑ 272 Andre Rison RC 5.00 2.20
❑ 273 AFC Championship .10 .05
Bengals over Bills (Ickey Woods and Boomer Esiason)
❑ 274 NFC Championship 1.00 .45
49ers over Bears

Card	Mint	NRMT
(Joe Montana)		
❑ 275 Super Bowl XXIII	2.00	.90
49ers over Bengals		
(Joe Montana and		
Jerry Rice)		
❑ 276 Rodney Carter	.10	.05
❑ 277 Mark Jackson,	.10	.05
Vance Johnson,		
and Ricky Nattiel		
❑ 278 John L. Williams	.10	.05
and Curt Warner		
❑ 279 Joe Montana and	2.00	.90
Jerry Rice		
❑ 280 Roy Green and	.10	.05
Neil Lomax		
❑ 281 Randall Cunningham	.10	.05
and Keith Jackson		
❑ 282 Chris Doleman and	.10	.05
Keith Millard		
❑ 283 Mark Duper and	.10	.05
Mark Clayton		
❑ 284 Marcus Allen and	.50	.23
Bo Jackson		
❑ 285 Frank Minnifield AP	.10	.05
❑ 286 Bruce Matthews AP	.20	.09
❑ 287 Joey Browner AP	.10	.05
❑ 288 Jay Hilgenberg AP	.10	.05
❑ 289 Carl Lee AP RC	.10	.05
❑ 290 Scott Norwood AP RC	.10	.05
❑ 291 John Taylor AP	.50	.23
❑ 292 Jerry Rice AP	1.50	.70
❑ 293A Keith Jackson AP ERR	.50	.23
(Listed as 84		
on card back)		
❑ 293B Keith Jackson AP COR	.50	.23
(Listed as 88		
on card back)		
❑ 294 Gary Zimmerman AP	.10	.05
❑ 295 Lawrence Taylor AP	.50	.23
❑ 296 Reggie White AP	.50	.23
❑ 297 Roger Craig AP	.20	.09
❑ 298 Boomer Esiason AP	.20	.09
❑ 299 Cornelius Bennett AP	.20	.09
❑ 300 Mike Horan AP	.10	.05
❑ 301 Deron Cherry AP	.10	.05
❑ 302 Tom Newberry AP	.10	.05
❑ 303 Mike Singletary AP	.20	.09
❑ 304 Shane Conlan AP	.10	.05
❑ 305A Tim Brown ERR AP	2.00	.90
(Photo on front act-		
ually 80 James Lofton)		
❑ 305B Tim Brown COR AP	2.00	.90
(Dark jersey 81)		
❑ 306 Henry Ellard AP	.20	.09
❑ 307 Bruce Smith AP	.20	.09
❑ 308 Tim Krumrie AP	.10	.05
❑ 309 Anthony Munoz AP	.20	.09
❑ 310 Darrell Green SPEED	.10	.05
❑ 311 Anthony Miller SPEED	.50	.23
❑ 312 Wesley Walker SPEED	.10	.05
❑ 313 Ron Brown SPEED	.10	.05
❑ 314 Bo Jackson SPEED	.50	.23
❑ 315 Phillip Epps SPEED	.10	.05
❑ 316A Eric Thomas RC ERR SPEED	.25	.11
(Listed as 31		
on card back)		
❑ 316B Eric Thomas RC COR SPEED	.50	.23
(Listed as 22		
on card back)		
❑ 317 Herschel Walker SPEED	.20	.09
❑ 318 Jacob Green PRED	.10	.05
❑ 319 Andre Tippett PRED	.10	.05
❑ 320 Freddie Joe Nunn PRED	.10	.05
❑ 321 Reggie White PRED	.50	.23
❑ 322 Lawrence Taylor PRED	.50	.23
❑ 323 Greg Townsend PRED	.10	.05
❑ 324 Tim Harris PRED	.10	.05
❑ 325 Bruce Smith PRED	.20	.09
❑ 326 Tony Dorsett RB	.50	.23
❑ 327 Steve Largent RB	.50	.23
❑ 328 Tim Brown RB	2.00	.90
❑ 329 Joe Montana RB	1.50	.70
❑ 330 Tom Landry Tribute	1.00	.45

1989 Score Supplemental

	MINT	NRMT
COMP.FACT.SET (110)	10.00	4.50
COMMON CARD (331S-440S)	.10	.05
SEMISTARS	.20	.09
UNLISTED STARS	.40	.18
❑ 331S Herschel Walker	.40	.18
❑ 332S Allen Pinkett RC	.10	.05
❑ 333S Sterling Sharpe RC	3.00	1.35
❑ 334S Alvin Walton RC	.10	.05
❑ 335S Frank Reich RC	.40	.18
❑ 336S Jim Thornton RC	.10	.05
❑ 337S David Fulcher	.20	.09
❑ 338S Raul Allegre	.10	.05
❑ 339S John Elway	4.00	1.80
❑ 340S Michael Cofer	.10	.05
❑ 341S Jim Skow	.10	.05
❑ 342S Steve DeBerg	.10	.05
❑ 343S Mervyn Fernandez RC**/C	.10	.05
❑ 344S Mike Lansford	.10	.05
❑ 345S Reggie Roby	.10	.05
❑ 346S Raymond Clayborn	.10	.05
❑ 347S Lonzell Hill	.10	.05
❑ 348S Ottis Anderson	.20	.09
❑ 349S Erik McMillan RC	.10	.05
❑ 350S Al Harris	.10	.05
❑ 351S Jack Del Rio RC	.20	.09
❑ 352S Gary Anderson K	.10	.05
❑ 353S Jim McMahon	.20	.09
❑ 354S Keena Turner	.10	.05
❑ 355S Tony Woods RC	.10	.05
❑ 356S Donald Igwebuike	.10	.05
❑ 357S Gerald Riggs	.20	.09
❑ 358S Eddie Murray	.10	.05
❑ 359S Dino Hackett	.10	.05
❑ 360S Brad Muster RC	.10	.05
❑ 361S Paul Palmer	.10	.05
❑ 362S Jerry Robinson	.10	.05
❑ 363S Simon Fletcher RC	.20	.09
❑ 364S Tommy Kramer	.10	.05
❑ 365S Jim C. Jensen RC	.10	.05
❑ 366S Lorenzo White RC	.40	.18
❑ 367S Fredd Young	.10	.05
❑ 368S Ron Jaworski	.10	.05
❑ 369S Mel Owens	.10	.05
❑ 370S Dave Waymer	.10	.05
❑ 371S Sean Landeta	.10	.05
❑ 372S Sam Mills	.20	.09
❑ 373S Todd Blackledge	.10	.05
❑ 374S Jo Jo Townsell	.10	.05
❑ 375S Ron Wolfley	.10	.05
❑ 376S Ralf Mojsiejenko	.10	.05
❑ 377S Eric Wright	.10	.05
❑ 378S Nesby Glasgow	.10	.05
❑ 379S Darryl Talley	.20	.09
❑ 380S Eric Allen RC	.40	.18
❑ 381S Dennis Smith	.20	.09
❑ 382S John Tice	.10	.05
❑ 383S Jesse Solomon	.10	.05
❑ 384S Bo Jackson	1.00	.45
(FB/BB Pose)		
❑ 385S Mike Merriweather	.10	.05
❑ 386S Maurice Carthon	.10	.05
❑ 387S David Grayson	.10	.05
❑ 388S Wilber Marshall	.10	.05
❑ 389S David Wyman	.10	.05
❑ 390S Thomas Everett RC	.10	.05
❑ 391S Alex Gordon	.10	.05
❑ 392S D.J. Dozier	.10	.05
❑ 393S Scott Radecic RC	.10	.05
❑ 394S Eric Thomas	.10	.05
❑ 395S Mike Gann	.10	.05
❑ 396S William Perry	.20	.09
❑ 397S Carl Hairston	.10	.05
❑ 398S Billy Ard	.10	.05
❑ 399S Donnell Thompson	.10	.05
❑ 400S Mike Webster	.20	.09
❑ 401S Scott Davis RC	.10	.05
❑ 402S Sean Farrell	.10	.05
❑ 403S Mike Golic RC	.10	.05
❑ 404S Mike Kenn	.10	.05
❑ 405S Keith Van Horne RC	.10	.05
❑ 406S Bob Golic	.10	.05
❑ 407S Neil Smith RC	2.00	.90
❑ 408S Dermontti Dawson RC	.20	.09
❑ 409S Leslie O'Neal	.20	.09
❑ 410S Matt Bahr	.10	.05
❑ 411S Guy McIntyre RC	.10	.05
❑ 412S Bryan Millard	.10	.05
❑ 413S Joe Jacoby	.10	.05
❑ 414S Rob Taylor RC	.10	.05
❑ 415S Tony Zendejas	.10	.05
❑ 416S Vai Sikahema	.10	.05
❑ 417S Gary Reasons RC	.10	.05
❑ 418S Shawn Collins RC	.10	.05
❑ 419S Mark Green RC	.10	.05
❑ 420S Courtney Hall RC	.10	.05
❑ 421S Bobby Humphrey RC	.10	.05
❑ 422S Myron Guyton RC	.10	.05
❑ 423S Darryl Ingram RC	.10	.05
❑ 424S Chris Jacke RC	.10	.05
❑ 425S Keith Jones RC	.10	.05
❑ 426S Robert Massey RC	.10	.05
❑ 427S Bubba McDowell RC	.40	.18
❑ 428S Dave Meggett RC	.40	.18
❑ 429S Louis Oliver RC	.20	.09
❑ 430S Danny Peebles	.10	.05
❑ 431S Rodney Peete RC	.40	.18
❑ 432S Jeff Query RC	.10	.05
❑ 433S Timm Rosenbach RC UER	.10	.05
(Photo actually		
Gary Hogeboom)		
❑ 434S Frank Stams RC	.10	.05
❑ 435S Lawyer Tillman RC	.10	.05
❑ 436S Billy Joe Tolliver RC	.10	.05
❑ 437S Floyd Turner RC	.20	.09
❑ 438S Steve Walsh RC	.20	.09
❑ 439S Joe Wolf RC	.10	.05
❑ 440S Trace Armstrong RC	.10	.05

1990 Score

	MINT	NRMT
COMPLETE SET (660)	7.50	3.40
COMP.FACT.SET (665)	8.00	3.60
COMMON CARD (1-660/B1-B5)	.04	.02
SEMISTARS	.10	.05
UNLISTED STARS	.25	.11
❑ 1 Joe Montana	1.25	.55
❑ 2 Christian Okoye	.04	.02
❑ 3 Mike Singletary UER	.10	.05
(Text says 146 tackles		
in '89, should be 151)		

❑ 4 Jim Everett UER .10 .05
(Text says 415 yards against Saints, should be 454)
❑ 5 Phil Simms .10 .05
❑ 6 Brent Fullwood .04 .02
❑ 7 Bill Fralic .04 .02
❑ 8 Leslie O'Neal .10 .05
❑ 9 John Taylor .25 .11
❑ 10 Bo Jackson .25 .11
❑ 11 John Stephens .04 .02
❑ 12 Art Monk .10 .05
❑ 13 Dan Marino 1.25 .55
❑ 14 John Settle .04 .02
❑ 15 Don Majkowski .04 .02
❑ 16 Bruce Smith .25 .11
❑ 17 Brad Muster .04 .02
❑ 18 Jason Buck .04 .02
❑ 19 James Brooks .10 .05
❑ 20 Barry Sanders 2.50 1.10
❑ 21 Troy Aikman .75 .35
❑ 22 Allen Pinkett .04 .02
❑ 23 Duane Bickett .04 .02
❑ 24 Kevin Ross .04 .02
❑ 25 John Elway 1.25 .55
❑ 26 Jeff Query .04 .02
❑ 27 Eddie Murray .04 .02
❑ 28 Richard Dent .10 .05
❑ 29 Lorenzo White .04 .02
❑ 30 Eric Metcalf .25 .11
❑ 31 Jeff Dellenbach RC .04 .02
❑ 32 Leon White .04 .02
❑ 33 Jim Jeffcoat .04 .02
❑ 34 Herschel Walker .10 .05
❑ 35 Mike Johnson UER .04 .02
(Front photo actually 51 Eddie Johnson)
❑ 36 Joe Phillips .04 .02
❑ 37 Willie Gault .10 .05
❑ 38 Keith Millard .04 .02
❑ 39 Fred Marion .04 .02
❑ 40 Boomer Esiason .10 .05
❑ 41 Dermontti Dawson .10 .05
❑ 42 Dino Hackett .04 .02
❑ 43 Reggie Roby .04 .02
❑ 44 Roger Vick .04 .02
❑ 45 Bobby Hebert .04 .02
❑ 46 Don Beebe .10 .05
❑ 47 Neal Anderson .10 .05
❑ 48 Johnny Holland .04 .02
❑ 49 Bobby Humphery .04 .02
❑ 50 Lawrence Taylor .25 .11
❑ 51 Billy Ray Smith .04 .02
❑ 52 Robert Perryman .04 .02
❑ 53 Gary Anderson K .04 .02
❑ 54 Raul Allegre .04 .02
❑ 55 Pat Swilling .10 .05
❑ 56 Chris Doleman .04 .02
❑ 57 Andre Reed .25 .11
❑ 58 Seth Joyner .10 .05
❑ 59 Bart Oates .04 .02
❑ 60 Bernie Kosar .10 .05
❑ 61 Dave Krieg .10 .05
❑ 62 Lars Tate .04 .02
❑ 63 Scott Norwood .04 .02
❑ 64 Kyle Clifton .04 .02
❑ 65 Alan Veingrad .04 .02
❑ 66 Gerald Riggs UER .10 .05
(Text begins Depite, should be Despite)
❑ 67 Tim Worley .04 .02
❑ 68 Rodney Holman .04 .02
❑ 69 Tony Zendejas .04 .02
❑ 70 Chris Miller .25 .11
❑ 71 Wilber Marshall .04 .02
❑ 72 Skip McClendon RC .04 .02
❑ 73 Jim Covert .04 .02
❑ 74 Sam Mills .10 .05
❑ 75 Chris Hinton .04 .02
❑ 76 Irv Eatman .04 .02
❑ 77 Bubba Paris UER .04 .02
(No draft team mentioned)
❑ 78 John Elliott UER .04 .02
(No draft team mentioned; missing Team/FA status)
❑ 79 Thomas Everett .04 .02
❑ 80 Steve Smith .04 .02
❑ 81 Jackie Slater .04 .02
❑ 82 Kelvin Martin RC .04 .02
❑ 83 Jo Jo Townsell .04 .02
❑ 84 Jim C. Jensen .04 .02
❑ 85 Bobby Humphrey .04 .02
❑ 86 Mike Dyal .04 .02
❑ 87 Andre Rison UER .25 .11
(Front 87, back 85)
❑ 88 Brian Sochia .04 .02
❑ 89 Greg Bell .04 .02
❑ 90 Dalton Hilliard .04 .02
❑ 91 Carl Banks .04 .02
❑ 92 Dennis Smith .04 .02
❑ 93 Bruce Matthews .10 .05
❑ 94 Charles Haley .10 .05
❑ 95 Deion Sanders UER .50 .23
(Reversed photo on back)
❑ 96 Stephone Paige .04 .02
❑ 97 Marion Butts .10 .05
❑ 98 Howie Long .10 .05
❑ 99 Donald Igwebuike .04 .02
❑ 100 Roger Craig UER .10 .05
(Text says 2 TD's in SB XXIV, should be 1; everything misspelled)
❑ 101 Charles Mann .04 .02
❑ 102 Fredd Young .04 .02
❑ 103 Chris Jacke .04 .02
❑ 104 Scott Case .04 .02
❑ 105 Warren Moon .25 .11
❑ 106 Clyde Simmons .04 .02
❑ 107 Steve Atwater .04 .02
❑ 108 Morten Andersen .04 .02
❑ 109 Eugene Marve .04 .02
❑ 110 Thurman Thomas .25 .11
❑ 111 Carnell Lake .04 .02
❑ 112 Jim Kelly .25 .11
❑ 113 Stanford Jennings .04 .02
❑ 114 Jacob Green .04 .02
❑ 115 Karl Mecklenburg .04 .02
❑ 116 Ray Childress .04 .02
❑ 117 Erik McMillan .04 .02
❑ 118 Harry Newsome .04 .02
❑ 119 James Dixon .04 .02
❑ 120 Hassan Jones .04 .02
❑ 121 Eric Allen .04 .02
❑ 122 Felix Wright .04 .02
❑ 123 Merril Hoge .04 .02
❑ 124 Eric Ball .04 .02
❑ 125 Flipper Anderson .04 .02
❑ 126 James Jefferson .04 .02
❑ 127 Tim McDonald .04 .02
❑ 128 Larry Kinnebrew .04 .02
❑ 129 Mark Collins .04 .02
❑ 130 Ickey Woods .04 .02
❑ 131 Jeff Donaldson UER .04 .02
(Stats say 0 int. and 0 fumble rec., text says 4 and 1)
❑ 132 Rich Camarillo .04 .02
❑ 133 Melvin Bratton RC .04 .02
❑ 134A Kevin Butler .35 .16
(Photo on back has helmet on)
❑ 134B Kevin Butler .50 .23
(Photo on back has no helmet on)
❑ 135 Albert Bentley .04 .02
❑ 136A Vai Sikahema .35 .16
(Photo on back has helmet on)
❑ 136B Vai Sikahema .50 .23
(Photo on back has no helmet on)
❑ 137 Todd McNair RC .04 .02
❑ 138 Alonzo Highsmith .04 .02
❑ 139 Brian Blades .10 .05
❑ 140 Jeff Lageman .04 .02
❑ 141 Eric Thomas .04 .02
❑ 142 Derek Hill .04 .02
❑ 143 Rick Fenney .04 .02
❑ 144 Herman Heard .04 .02
❑ 145 Steve Young .50 .23
❑ 146 Kent Hull .04 .02
❑ 147A Joey Browner .35 .16
(Photo on back looking to side)
❑ 147B Joey Browner .50 .23
(Photo on back looking up)
❑ 148 Frank Minnifield .04 .02
❑ 149 Robert Massey .04 .02
❑ 150 Dave Meggett .10 .05
❑ 151 Bubba McDowell .04 .02
❑ 152 Rickey Dixon RC .04 .02
❑ 153 Ray Donaldson .04 .02
❑ 154 Alvin Walton .04 .02
❑ 155 Mike Cofer .04 .02
❑ 156 Darryl Talley .04 .02
❑ 157 A.J. Johnson .04 .02
❑ 158 Jerry Gray .04 .02
❑ 159 Keith Byars .04 .02
❑ 160 Andy Heck .04 .02
❑ 161 Mike Munchak .04 .02
❑ 162 Dennis Gentry .04 .02
❑ 163 Timm Rosenbach UER .04 .02
(Born 1967 in Everett, Wa., should be 1966 in Missoula, Mont.)
❑ 164 Randall McDaniel .04 .02
❑ 165 Pat Leahy .04 .02
❑ 166 Bubby Brister .04 .02
❑ 167 Aundray Bruce .04 .02
❑ 168 Bill Brooks .04 .02
❑ 169 Eddie Anderson RC .04 .02
❑ 170 Ronnie Lott .10 .05
❑ 171 Jay Hilgenberg .04 .02
❑ 172 Joe Nash .04 .02
❑ 173 Simon Fletcher .04 .02
❑ 174 Shane Conlan .04 .02
❑ 175 Sean Landeta .04 .02
❑ 176 John Alt RC .04 .02
❑ 177 Clay Matthews .10 .05
❑ 178 Anthony Munoz .10 .05
❑ 179 Pete Holohan .04 .02
❑ 180 Robert Awalt .04 .02
❑ 181 Rohn Stark .04 .02
❑ 182 Vance Johnson .04 .02
❑ 183 David Fulcher .04 .02
❑ 184 Robert Delpino .04 .02
❑ 185 Drew Hill .04 .02
❑ 186 Reggie Langhorne UER .04 .02
(Stats read 1988, not 1989)
❑ 187 Lonzell Hill .04 .02
❑ 188 Tom Rathman UER .04 .02
(On back, blocker misspelled)
❑ 189 Greg Montgomery RC .04 .02
❑ 190 Leonard Smith .04 .02
❑ 191 Chris Spielman .25 .11
❑ 192 Tom Newberry .04 .02
❑ 193 Cris Carter .50 .23
❑ 194 Kevin Porter RC .04 .02
❑ 195 Donnell Thompson .04 .02
❑ 196 Vaughan Johnson .04 .02
❑ 197 Steve McMichael .10 .05
❑ 198 Jim Sweeney .04 .02
❑ 199 Rich Karlis UER .04 .02
(No comma between day and year in birth data)
❑ 200 Jerry Rice .75 .35
❑ 201 Dan Hampton UER .10 .05
(Card says he's a DE, should be DT)
❑ 202 Jim Lachey .04 .02
❑ 203 Reggie White .25 .11
❑ 204 Jerry Ball .04 .02
❑ 205 Russ Grimm .04 .02
❑ 206 Tim Green RC .04 .02
❑ 207 Shawn Collins .04 .02
❑ 208A Ralf Mojsiejenko ERR .15 .07
(Chargers stats)
❑ 208B Ralf Mojsiejenko COR .50 .23
(Redskins stats)
❑ 209 Trace Armstrong .04 .02
❑ 210 Keith Jackson .10 .05
❑ 211 Jamie Holland .04 .02
❑ 212 Mark Clayton .10 .05
❑ 213 Jeff Cross .04 .02
❑ 214 Bob Gagliano .04 .02

❑ 215 Louis Oliver UER .04 .02
(Text says played at Miami, should be Florida as in bio)
❑ 216 Jim Arnold .04 .02
❑ 217 Robert Clark RC .04 .02
❑ 218 Gill Byrd .04 .02
❑ 219 Rodney Peete .10 .05
❑ 220 Anthony Miller .25 .11
❑ 221 Steve Grogan .10 .05
❑ 222 Vince Newsome RC .04 .02
❑ 223 Thomas Benson .04 .02
❑ 224 Kevin Murphy .04 .02
❑ 225 Henry Ellard .10 .05
❑ 226 Richard Johnson .04 .02
❑ 227 Jim Skow .04 .02
❑ 228 Keith Jones .04 .02
❑ 229 Dave Brown DB .04 .02
❑ 230 Marcus Allen .25 .11
❑ 231 Steve Walsh .10 .05
❑ 232 Jim Harbaugh .25 .11
❑ 233 Mel Gray .10 .05
❑ 234 David Treadwell .04 .02
❑ 235 John Offerdahl .04 .02
❑ 236 Gary Reasons .04 .02
❑ 237 Tim Krumrie .04 .02
❑ 238 Dave Duerson .04 .02
❑ 239 Gary Clark UER .25 .11
(Stats read 1988, not 1989)
❑ 240 Mark Jackson .04 .02
❑ 241 Mark Murphy .04 .02
❑ 242 Jerry Holmes .04 .02
❑ 243 Tim McGee .04 .02
❑ 244 Mike Tomczak .10 .05
❑ 245 Sterling Sharpe UER .25 .11
(Broke 47-yard-old record, should be year)
❑ 246 Bennie Blades .04 .02
❑ 247 Ken Harvey RC UER .25 .11
(Sacks and fumble recovery listings are switched; dis-appointing misspelled)
❑ 248 Ron Heller .04 .02
❑ 249 Louis Lipps .10 .05
❑ 250 Wade Wilson .10 .05
❑ 251 Freddie Joe Nunn .04 .02
❑ 252 Jerome Brown UER .04 .02
('89 stats show 2 fum-ble rec., should be 1)
❑ 253 Myron Guyton .04 .02
❑ 254 Nate Odomes RC .10 .05
❑ 255 Rod Woodson .25 .11
❑ 256 Cornelius Bennett .10 .05
❑ 257 Keith Woodside .04 .02
❑ 258 Jeff Uhlenhake UER .04 .02
(Text calls him Ron)
❑ 259 Harry Hamilton .04 .02
❑ 260 Mark Bavaro .04 .02
❑ 261 Vinny Testaverde .10 .05
❑ 262 Steve DeBerg .04 .02
❑ 263 Steve Wisniewski UER .10 .05
(Drafted by Dallas, not the Raiders)
❑ 264 Pete Mandley .04 .02
❑ 265 Tim Harris .04 .02
❑ 266 Jack Trudeau .04 .02
❑ 267 Mark Kelso .04 .02
❑ 268 Brian Noble .04 .02
❑ 269 Jessie Tuggle RC .04 .02
❑ 270 Ken O'Brien .04 .02
❑ 271 David Little .04 .02
❑ 272 Pete Stoyanovich .04 .02
❑ 273 Odessa Turner RC .04 .02
❑ 274 Anthony Toney .04 .02
❑ 275 Tunch Ilkin .04 .02
❑ 276 Carl Lee .04 .02
❑ 277 Hart Lee Dykes .04 .02
❑ 278 Al Noga .04 .02
❑ 279 Greg Lloyd .25 .11
❑ 280 Billy Joe Tolliver .04 .02
❑ 281 Kirk Lowdermilk .04 .02
❑ 282 Earl Ferrell .04 .02
❑ 283 Eric Sievers RC .04 .02
❑ 284 Steve Jordan .04 .02
❑ 285 Burt Grossman .04 .02
❑ 286 Johnny Rembert .04 .02
❑ 287 Jeff Jaeger RC .04 .02
❑ 288 James Hasty .04 .02
❑ 289 Tony Mandarich DRAFT .04 .02
❑ 290 Chris Singleton DRAFT RC DRAFT .04 .02
❑ 291 Lynn James DRAFT .04 .02
❑ 292 Andre Ware DRAFT RC DRAFT .25 .11
❑ 293 Ray Agnew DRAFT RC DRAFT .04 .02
❑ 294 Joel Smeenge DRAFT RC DRAFT .04 .02
❑ 295 Marc Spindler DRAFT RC DRAFT .04 .02
❑ 296 Renaldo Turnbull DRAFT RC DRAFT .04 .02
❑ 297 Reggie Rembert DRAFT RC DRAFT .04 .02
❑ 298 Jeff Alm DRAFT RC DRAFT .04 .02
❑ 299 Cortez Kennedy DRAFT RC DRAFT .25 .11
❑ 300 Blair Thomas DRAFT RC DRAFT .10 .05
❑ 301 Pat Terrell DRAFT RC DRAFT .04 .02
❑ 302 Junior Seau DRAFT RC DRAFT 1.00 .45
❑ 303 Mo Elewonibi DRAFT .04 .02
❑ 304 Tony Bennett DRAFT RC DRAFT .25 .11
❑ 305 Percy Snow DRAFT RC DRAFT .04 .02
❑ 306 Richmond Webb DRAFT RC DRAFT .04 .02
❑ 307 Rodney Hampton DRAFT RC DRAFT .40 .18
❑ 308 Barry Foster DRAFT RC DRAFT .25 .11
❑ 309 John Friesz DRAFT RC DRAFT .25 .11
❑ 310 Ben Smith DRAFT RC DRAFT .04 .02
❑ 311 Joe Montana HG .50 .23
❑ 312 Jim Everett HG .10 .05
❑ 313 Mark Rypien HG .10 .05
❑ 314 Phil Simms HG UER .10 .05
(Lists him as playing in the AFC)
❑ 315 Don Majkowski HG .04 .02
❑ 316 Boomer Esiason HG .04 .02
❑ 317 Warren Moon HG .25 .11
(Moon on card)
❑ 318 Jim Kelly HG .25 .11
❑ 319 Bernie Kosar HG UER .10 .05
(Word just is mis-spelled as justs)
❑ 320 Dan Marino HG UER .50 .23
(Text says 378 com-pletions in 1984, should be 1986)
❑ 321 Christian Okoye GF .04 .02
❑ 322 Thurman Thomas GF .25 .11
❑ 323 James Brooks GF .10 .05
❑ 324 Bobby Humphrey GF .04 .02
❑ 325 Barry Sanders GF 1.00 .45
❑ 326 Neal Anderson GF .04 .02
❑ 327 Dalton Hilliard GF .04 .02
❑ 328 Greg Bell GF .04 .02
❑ 329 Roger Craig GF UER .10 .05
(Text says 2 TD's in SB XXIV, should be 1)
❑ 330 Bo Jackson GF .25 .11
❑ 331 Don Warren .04 .02
❑ 332 Rufus Porter .04 .02
❑ 333 Sammie Smith .04 .02
❑ 334 Lewis Tillman UER .04 .02
(Born 4/16/67, should be 1966)
❑ 335 Michael Walter .04 .02
❑ 336 Marc Logan .04 .02
❑ 337 Ron Hallstrom RC .04 .02
❑ 338 Stanley Morgan .04 .02
❑ 339 Mark Robinson .04 .02
❑ 340 Frank Reich .25 .11
❑ 341 Chip Lohmiller .04 .02
❑ 342 Steve Beuerlein .10 .05
❑ 343 John L. Williams .04 .02
❑ 344 Irving Fryar .25 .11
❑ 345 Anthony Carter .10 .05
❑ 346 Al Toon .10 .05
❑ 347 J.T. Smith .04 .02
❑ 348 Pierce Holt RC .04 .02
❑ 349 Ferrell Edmunds .04 .02
❑ 350 Mark Rypien .10 .05
❑ 351 Paul Gruber .04 .02
❑ 352 Ernest Givins .10 .05
❑ 353 Ervin Randle .04 .02
❑ 354 Guy McIntyre .04 .02
❑ 355 Webster Slaughter .10 .05
❑ 356 Reuben Davis .04 .02
❑ 357 Rickey Jackson .10 .05
❑ 358 Earnest Byner .04 .02
❑ 359 Eddie Brown .04 .02
❑ 360 Troy Stradford .04 .02
❑ 361 Pepper Johnson .04 .02
❑ 362 Ravin Caldwell .04 .02
❑ 363 Chris Mohr RC .04 .02
❑ 364 Jeff Bryant .04 .02
❑ 365 Bruce Collie .04 .02
❑ 366 Courtney Hall .04 .02
❑ 367 Jerry Olsavsky .04 .02
❑ 368 David Galloway .04 .02
❑ 369 Wes Hopkins .04 .02
❑ 370 Johnny Hector .04 .02
❑ 371 Clarence Verdin .04 .02
❑ 372 Nick Lowery .04 .02
❑ 373 Tim Brown .25 .11
❑ 374 Kevin Greene .25 .11
❑ 375 Leonard Marshall .04 .02
❑ 376 Roland James .04 .02
❑ 377 Scott Studwell .04 .02
❑ 378 Jarvis Williams .04 .02
❑ 379 Mike Saxon .04 .02
❑ 380 Kevin Mack .04 .02
❑ 381 Joe Kelly .04 .02
❑ 382 Tom Thayer RC .04 .02
❑ 383 Roy Green .10 .05
❑ 384 Michael Brooks RC .04 .02
❑ 385 Michael Cofer .04 .02
❑ 386 Ken Ruettgers .04 .02
❑ 387 Dean Steinkuhler .04 .02
❑ 388 Maurice Carthon .04 .02
❑ 389 Ricky Sanders .04 .02
❑ 390 Winston Moss RC .04 .02
❑ 391 Tony Woods .04 .02
❑ 392 Keith DeLong .04 .02
❑ 393 David Wyman .04 .02
❑ 394 Vencie Glenn .04 .02
❑ 395 Harris Barton .04 .02
❑ 396 Bryan Hinkle .04 .02
❑ 397 Derek Kennard .04 .02
❑ 398 Heath Sherman RC .04 .02
❑ 399 Troy Benson .04 .02
❑ 400 Gary Zimmerman .04 .02
❑ 401 Mark Duper .10 .05
❑ 402 Eugene Lockhart .04 .02
❑ 403 Tim Manoa .04 .02
❑ 404 Reggie Williams .04 .02
❑ 405 Mark Bortz RC .04 .02
❑ 406 Mike Kenn .04 .02
❑ 407 John Grimsley .04 .02
❑ 408 Bill Romanowski RC .30 .14
❑ 409 Perry Kemp .04 .02
❑ 410 Norm Johnson .04 .02
❑ 411 Broderick Thomas .04 .02
❑ 412 Joe Wolf .04 .02
❑ 413 Andre Waters .04 .02
❑ 414 Jason Staurovsky .04 .02
❑ 415 Eric Martin .04 .02
❑ 416 Joe Prokop .04 .02
❑ 417 Steve Sewell .04 .02
❑ 418 Cedric Jones .04 .02
❑ 419 Alphonso Carreker .04 .02
❑ 420 Keith Willis .04 .02
❑ 421 Bobby Butler .04 .02
❑ 422 John Roper .04 .02
❑ 423 Tim Spencer .04 .02
❑ 424 Jesse Sapolu RC .04 .02
❑ 425 Ron Wolfley .04 .02
❑ 426 Doug Smith .04 .02
❑ 427 William Howard .04 .02
❑ 428 Keith Van Horne .04 .02
❑ 429 Tony Jordan .04 .02
❑ 430 Mervyn Fernandez .04 .02
❑ 431 Shaun Gayle RC .04 .02
❑ 432 Ricky Nattiel .04 .02
❑ 433 Albert Lewis .04 .02
❑ 434 Fred Banks RC .04 .02
❑ 435 Henry Thomas .04 .02
❑ 436 Chet Brooks .04 .02
❑ 437 Mark Ingram .10 .05
❑ 438 Jeff Gossett .04 .02
❑ 439 Mike Wilcher .04 .02
❑ 440 Deron Cherry UER .04 .02
(Text says 7 cons. Pro Bowls, but he didn't play in 1989 Pro Bowl)
❑ 441 Mike Rozier .04 .02

❑ 442 Jon Hand .04 .02
❑ 443 Ozzie Newsome .10 .05
❑ 444 Sammy Martin .04 .02
❑ 445 Luis Sharpe .04 .02
❑ 446 Lee Williams .04 .02
❑ 447 Chris Martin RC .04 .02
❑ 448 Kevin Fagan RC .04 .02
❑ 449 Gene Lang .04 .02
❑ 450 Greg Townsend .04 .02
❑ 451 Robert Lyles .04 .02
❑ 452 Eric Hill .04 .02
❑ 453 John Teltschik .04 .02
❑ 454 Vestee Jackson .04 .02
❑ 455 Bruce Reimers .04 .02
❑ 456 Butch Rolle RC .04 .02
❑ 457 Lawyer Tillman .04 .02
❑ 458 Andre Tippett .04 .02
❑ 459 James Thornton .04 .02
❑ 460 Randy Grimes .04 .02
❑ 461 Larry Roberts .04 .02
❑ 462 Ron Holmes .04 .02
❑ 463 Mike Wise .04 .02
❑ 464 Danny Copeland RC .04 .02
❑ 465 Bruce Wilkerson RC .04 .02
❑ 466 Mike Quick .04 .02
❑ 467 Mickey Shuler .04 .02
❑ 468 Mike Prior .04 .02
❑ 469 Ron Rivera .04 .02
❑ 470 Dean Biasucci .04 .02
❑ 471 Perry Williams .04 .02
❑ 472 Darren Comeaux UER .04 .02
(Front 53, back 52)
❑ 473 Freeman McNeil .04 .02
❑ 474 Tyrone Braxton .04 .02
❑ 475 Jay Schroeder .04 .02
❑ 476 Naz Worthen .04 .02
❑ 477 Lionel Washington .04 .02
❑ 478 Carl Zander .04 .02
❑ 479 Al(Bubba) Baker .10 .05
❑ 480 Mike Merriweather .04 .02
❑ 481 Mike Gann .04 .02
❑ 482 Brent Williams .04 .02
❑ 483 Eugene Robinson .04 .02
❑ 484 Ray Horton .04 .02
❑ 485 Bruce Armstrong .04 .02
❑ 486 John Fourcade .04 .02
❑ 487 Lewis Billups .04 .02
❑ 488 Scott Davis .04 .02
❑ 489 Kenneth Sims .04 .02
❑ 490 Chris Chandler .25 .11
❑ 491 Mark Lee .04 .02
❑ 492 Johnny Meads .04 .02
❑ 493 Tim Irwin .04 .02
❑ 494 E.J. Junior .04 .02
❑ 495 Hardy Nickerson .10 .05
❑ 496 Rob McGovern .04 .02
❑ 497 Fred Strickland RC .04 .02
❑ 498 Reggie Rutland RC .04 .02
❑ 499 Mel Owens .04 .02
❑ 500 Derrick Thomas .25 .11
❑ 501 Jerrol Williams .04 .02
❑ 502 Maurice Hurst RC .04 .02
❑ 503 Larry Kelm RC .04 .02
❑ 504 Herman Fontenot .04 .02
❑ 505 Pat Beach .04 .02
❑ 506 Haywood Jeffires RC .25 .11
❑ 507 Neil Smith .25 .11
❑ 508 Cleveland Gary .04 .02
❑ 509 William Perry .10 .05
❑ 510 Michael Carter .04 .02
❑ 511 Walker Lee Ashley .04 .02
❑ 512 Bob Golic .04 .02
❑ 513 Danny Villa RC .04 .02
❑ 514 Matt Millen .10 .05
❑ 515 Don Griffin .04 .02
❑ 516 Jonathan Hayes .04 .02
❑ 517 Gerald Williams RC .04 .02
❑ 518 Scott Fulhage .04 .02
❑ 519 Irv Pankey .04 .02
❑ 520 Randy Dixon RC .04 .02
❑ 521 Terry McDaniel .04 .02
❑ 522 Dan Saleaumua .04 .02
❑ 523 Darrin Nelson .04 .02
❑ 524 Leonard Griffin .04 .02
❑ 525 Michael Ball RC .04 .02
❑ 526 Ernie Jones RC .04 .02
❑ 527 Tony Eason UER .04 .02
(Drafted in 1963, should be 1983)
❑ 528 Ed Reynolds .04 .02
❑ 529 Gary Hogeboom .04 .02
❑ 530 Don Mosebar .04 .02
❑ 531 Ottis Anderson .10 .05
❑ 532 Bucky Scribner .04 .02
❑ 533 Aaron Cox .04 .02
❑ 534 Sean Jones .10 .05
❑ 535 Doug Flutie .50 .23
❑ 536 Leo Lewis .04 .02
❑ 537 Art Still .04 .02
❑ 538 Matt Bahr .04 .02
❑ 539 Keena Turner .04 .02
❑ 540 Sammy Winder .04 .02
❑ 541 Mike Webster .10 .05
❑ 542 Doug Riesenberg RC .04 .02
❑ 543 Dan Fike .04 .02
❑ 544 Clarence Kay .04 .02
❑ 545 Jim Burt .04 .02
❑ 546 Mike Horan .04 .02
❑ 547 Al Harris .04 .02
❑ 548 Maury Buford .04 .02
❑ 549 Jerry Robinson .04 .02
❑ 550 Tracy Rocker .04 .02
❑ 551 Karl Mecklenburg CC .04 .02
❑ 552 Lawrence Taylor CC .25 .11
❑ 553 Derrick Thomas CC .25 .11
❑ 554 Mike Singletary CC .10 .05
❑ 555 Tim Harris CC .04 .02
❑ 556 Jerry Rice RM .50 .23
❑ 557 Art Monk RM .10 .05
❑ 558 Mark Carrier WR RM .10 .05
❑ 559 Andre Reed RM .10 .05
❑ 560 Sterling Sharpe RM .25 .11
❑ 561 Herschel Walker GF .10 .05
❑ 562 Ottis Anderson GF .10 .05
❑ 563 Randall Cunningham HG .10 .05
❑ 564 John Elway HG .50 .23
❑ 565 David Fulcher AP .04 .02
❑ 566 Ronnie Lott AP .10 .05
❑ 567 Jerry Gray AP .04 .02
❑ 568 Albert Lewis AP .04 .02
❑ 569 Karl Mecklenburg AP .04 .02
❑ 570 Mike Singletary AP .10 .05
❑ 571 Lawrence Taylor AP .25 .11
❑ 572 Tim Harris AP .04 .02
❑ 573 Keith Millard AP .04 .02
❑ 574 Reggie White AP .25 .11
❑ 575 Chris Doleman AP .04 .02
❑ 576 Dave Meggett AP .10 .05
❑ 577 Rod Woodson AP .25 .11
❑ 578 Sean Landeta AP .04 .02
❑ 579 Eddie Murray AP .04 .02
❑ 580 Barry Sanders AP 1.00 .45
❑ 581 Christian Okoye AP .04 .02
❑ 582 Joe Montana AP .50 .23
❑ 583 Jay Hilgenberg AP .04 .02
❑ 584 Bruce Matthews AP .10 .05
❑ 585 Tom Newberry AP .04 .02
❑ 586 Gary Zimmerman AP .04 .02
❑ 587 Anthony Munoz AP .10 .05
❑ 588 Keith Jackson AP .10 .05
❑ 589 Sterling Sharpe AP .25 .11
❑ 590 Jerry Rice AP .50 .23
❑ 591 Bo Jackson RB .25 .11
❑ 592 Steve Largent RB .25 .11
❑ 593 Flipper Anderson RB .04 .02
❑ 594 Joe Montana RB .50 .23
❑ 595 Franco Harris HOF .10 .05
❑ 596 Bob St. Clair HOF .04 .02
❑ 597 Tom Landry HOF .10 .05
❑ 598 Jack Lambert HOF .10 .05
❑ 599 Ted Hendricks HOF UER .04 .02
(Int. avg. says 12.8, should be 8.9)
❑ 600A Buck Buchanan HOF UER .10 .05
(Drafted in 1983)
❑ 600B Buck Buchanan HOF COR .10 .05
(Drafted in 1963)
❑ 601 Bob Griese HOF .10 .05
❑ 602 Super Bowl Wrap .04 .02
❑ 603A Vince Lombardi UER .20 .09
Lombardi Legend (Disciplinarian misspelled; no logo for Curtis Mgt. at bottom)
❑ 603B Vince Lombardi UER .20 .09
Lombardi Legend (Disciplinarian misspelled; logo for Curtis Mgt. at bottom)
❑ 604 Mark Carrier UER .10 .05
(Front 88, back 89)
❑ 605 Randall Cunningham .25 .11
❑ 606 Percy Snow C90 .04 .02
❑ 607 Andre Ware C90 .25 .11
❑ 608 Blair Thomas C90 .10 .05
❑ 609 Eric Green C90 .04 .02
❑ 610 Reggie Rembert C90 .04 .02
❑ 611 Richmond Webb C90 .04 .02
❑ 612 Bern Brostek C90 .04 .02
❑ 613 James Williams C90 .04 .02
❑ 614 Mark Carrier DB C90 .10 .05
❑ 615 Renaldo Turnbull C90 .04 .02
❑ 616 Cortez Kennedy C90 .10 .05
❑ 617 Keith McCants C90 .04 .02
❑ 618 An.Thompson DRAFT RC DRAFT .04 .02
❑ 619 LeRoy Butler DRAFT RC DRAFT .25 .11
❑ 620 Aaron Wallace DRAFT RC DRAFT .04 .02
❑ 621 Alexander Wright DRAFT RC DRAFT .04 .02
❑ 622 Keith McCants DRAFT RC DRAFT .04 .02
❑ 623 Jim.Jones RC UER DRAFT .04 .02
January misspelled
❑ 624 Anthony Johnson DRAFT RC DRAFT .25 .11
❑ 625 Fred Washington DRAFT .04 .02
❑ 626 Mike Bellamy DRAFT .04 .02
❑ 627 Mark Carrier DB DRAFT RC .25 .11
❑ 628 Harold Green DRAFT RC DRAFT .25 .11
❑ 629 Eric Green DRAFT RC DRAFT .10 .05
❑ 630 Andre Collins DRAFT RC DRAFT .04 .02
❑ 631 Lamar Lathon DRAFT RC DRAFT .10 .05
❑ 632 Terry Wooden DRAFT RC DRAFT .04 .02
❑ 633 Jesse Anderson DRAFT .04 .02
❑ 634 Jeff George DRAFT RC DRAFT 1.00 .45
❑ 635 Carwell Gardner DRAFT RC DRAFT .04 .02
❑ 636 Darrell Thompson DRAFT RC DRAFT .04 .02
❑ 637 Vince Buck DRAFT RC DRAFT .04 .02
❑ 638 Mike Jones DRAFT RC DRAFT .04 .02
❑ 639 Charles Arbuckle DRAFT RC DRAFT .04 .02
❑ 640 Dennis Brown DRAFT RC DRAFT .04 .02
❑ 641 James Williams DRAFT RC .04 .02
❑ 642 Bern Brostek DRAFT RC DRAFT .04 .02
❑ 643 Darion Conner DRAFT RC DRAFT .10 .05
❑ 644 Mike Fox DRAFT RC DRAFT .04 .02
❑ 645 Cary Conklin DRAFT RC DRAFT .04 .02
❑ 646 Tim Grunhard DRAFT RC DRAFT .04 .02
❑ 647 Ron Cox DRAFT RC DRAFT .04 .02
❑ 648 Keith Sims DRAFT RC DRAFT .04 .02
❑ 649 Alton Montgomery DRAFT RC DRAFT .04 .02
❑ 650 Greg McMurtry DRAFT RC DRAFT .04 .02
❑ 651 Scott Mitchell DRAFT RC DRAFT .25 .11
❑ 652 Tim Ryan DRAFT RC DRAFT .04 .02
❑ 653 Jeff Mills DRAFT .04 .02
❑ 654 Ricky Proehl DRAFT RC DRAFT .10 .05
❑ 655 Steve Broussard DRAFT RC DRAFT .04 .02
❑ 656 Peter Tom Willis DRAFT RC DRAFT .04 .02
❑ 657 Dexter Carter DRAFT RC DRAFT .04 .02
❑ 658 Tony Casillas .04 .02
❑ 659 Joe Morris .04 .02
❑ 660 Greg Kragen .04 .02
❑ B1 Matt Stover .10 .05
❑ B2 Demetrius Davis .04 .02
❑ B3 Ken McMichel .04 .02
❑ B4 Judd Garrett .04 .02
❑ B5 Elliott Searcy .04 .02

1990 Score Hot Cards

	MINT	NRMT
COMPLETE SET (10)	25.00	11.00
ONE PER BLISTER PACK		

❑ 1 Joe Montana 6.00 2.70
❑ 2 Bo Jackson 1.25 .55
❑ 3 Barry Sanders 12.00 5.50
❑ 4 Jerry Rice 4.00 1.80
❑ 5 Eric Metcalf 1.25 .55

	MINT	NRMT
❑ 6 Don Majkowski	.20	.09
❑ 7 Christian Okoye	.20	.09
❑ 8 Bobby Humphrey	.20	.09
❑ 9 Dan Marino	6.00	2.70
❑ 10 Sterling Sharpe	1.25	.55

1990 Score Supplemental

	MINT	NRMT
COMP.FACT.SET (110)	100.00	45.00
COMMON CARD (1T-110T)	.15	.07
SEMISTARS	.30	.14
UNLISTED STARS	.60	.25
❑ 1T Marcus Dupree RC**	.15	.07
❑ 2T Jerry Kauric	.15	.07
❑ 3T Everson Walls	.15	.07
❑ 4T Elliott Smith	.15	.07
❑ 5T Donald Evans RC UER (Misspelled Pittsburg on card back)	.30	.14
❑ 6T Jerry Holmes	.15	.07
❑ 7T Dan Stryzinski RC	.15	.07
❑ 8T Gerald McNeil	.15	.07
❑ 9T Rick Tuten RC	.15	.07
❑ 10T Mickey Shuler	.15	.07
❑ 11T Jay Novacek	.60	.25
❑ 12T Eric Williams RC	.15	.07
❑ 13T Stanley Morgan	.15	.07
❑ 14T Wayne Haddix RC	.15	.07
❑ 15T Gary Anderson RB	.15	.07
❑ 16T Stan Humphries RC	1.00	.45
❑ 17T Raymond Clayborn	.15	.07
❑ 18T Mark Boyer RC	.15	.07
❑ 19T Dave Waymer	.15	.07
❑ 20T Andre Rison	.60	.25
❑ 21T Daniel Stubbs	.15	.07
❑ 22T Mike Rozier	.15	.07
❑ 23T Damian Johnson	.15	.07
❑ 24T Don Smith	.15	.07
❑ 25T Max Montoya	.15	.07
❑ 26T Terry Kinard	.15	.07
❑ 27T Herb Welch	.15	.07
❑ 28T Cliff Odom	.15	.07
❑ 29T John Kidd	.15	.07
❑ 30T Barry Word RC	.15	.07
❑ 31T Rich Karlis	.15	.07
❑ 32T Mike Baab	.15	.07
❑ 33T Ronnie Harmon	.30	.14
❑ 34T Jeff Donaldson	.15	.07
❑ 35T Riki Ellison	.15	.07
❑ 36T Steve Walsh	.30	.14
❑ 37T Bill Lewis RC	.15	.07
❑ 38T Tim McKyer	.15	.07
❑ 39T James Wilder	.15	.07
❑ 40T Tony Paige	.15	.07
❑ 41T Derrick Fenner RC	.15	.07
❑ 42T Thane Gash RC	.15	.07
❑ 43T Dave Duerson	.15	.07
❑ 44T Clarence Weathers	.15	.07
❑ 45T Matt Bahr	.15	.07
❑ 46T Alonzo Highsmith	.15	.07
❑ 47T Joe Kelly	.15	.07
❑ 48T Chris Hinton	.15	.07
❑ 49T Bobby Humphery	.15	.07
❑ 50T Greg Bell	.15	.07
❑ 51T Fred Smerlas	.15	.07
❑ 52T Walter Stanley	.15	.07
❑ 53T Jim Skow	.15	.07
❑ 54T Renaldo Turnbull	.15	.07
❑ 55T Bern Brostek	.15	.07
❑ 56T Charles Wilson RC	.15	.07
❑ 57T Keith McCants	.15	.07
❑ 58T Alexander Wright	.30	.14
❑ 59T Ian Beckles RC	.15	.07
❑ 60T Eric Davis RC	.30	.14
❑ 61T Chris Singleton	.15	.07
❑ 62T Rob Moore RC	10.00	4.50
❑ 63T Darion Conner	.30	.14
❑ 64T Tim Grunhard	.15	.07
❑ 65T Junior Seau	5.00	2.20
❑ 66T Tony Stargell RC	.15	.07
❑ 67T Anthony Thompson	.15	.07
❑ 68T Cortez Kennedy	.60	.25
❑ 69T Darrell Thompson	.15	.07
❑ 70T Calvin Williams RC	.60	.25
❑ 71T Rodney Hampton	1.00	.45
❑ 72T Terry Wooden	.15	.07
❑ 73T Leo Goeas RC	.15	.07
❑ 74T Ken Willis	.15	.07
❑ 75T Ricky Proehl	.30	.14
❑ 76T Steve Christie RC	.15	.07
❑ 77T Andre Ware	.60	.25
❑ 78T Jeff George	12.00	5.50
❑ 79T Walter Wilson	.15	.07
❑ 80T Johnny Bailey RC	.15	.07
❑ 81T Harold Green	.30	.14
❑ 82T Mark Carrier	.60	.25
❑ 83T Frank Cornish	.15	.07
❑ 84T James Williams	.15	.07
❑ 85T James Francis RC	.15	.07
❑ 86T Percy Snow	.15	.07
❑ 87T Anthony Johnson	.60	.25
❑ 88T Tim Ryan	.15	.07
❑ 89T Dan Owens RC	.15	.07
❑ 90T Aaron Wallace RC	.15	.07
❑ 91T Steve Broussard	.15	.07
❑ 92T Eric Green	.15	.07
❑ 93T Blair Thomas	.30	.14
❑ 94T Robert Blackmon RC	.15	.07
❑ 95T Alan Grant RC	.15	.07
❑ 96T Andre Collins	.15	.07
❑ 97T Dexter Carter	.15	.07
❑ 98T Reggie Cobb RC	.15	.07
❑ 99T Dennis Brown	.15	.07
❑ 100T Kenny Davidson RC	.15	.07
❑ 101T Emmitt Smith RC	100.00	45.00
❑ 102T Jeff Alm	.15	.07
❑ 103T Alton Montgomery	.15	.07
❑ 104T Tony Bennett	.60	.25
❑ 105T Johnny Johnson RC	.30	.14
❑ 106T Leroy Hoard RC	2.00	.90
❑ 107T Ray Agnew	.15	.07
❑ 108T Richmond Webb	.15	.07
❑ 109T Keith Sims	.15	.07
❑ 110T Barry Foster	.60	.25

1991 Score

	MINT	NRMT
COMPLETE SET (686)	8.00	3.60
COMP.FACT.SET (690)	10.00	4.50
COMMON CARD (1-686/B1-B4)	.04	.02
SEMISTARS	.10	.05
UNLISTED STARS	.25	.11
COMP.HOT ROOKIES (10)	12.00	5.50

ONE PER BLISTER PACK

	MINT	NRMT
❑ 1 Joe Montana	1.25	.55
❑ 2 Eric Allen	.04	.02
❑ 3 Rohn Stark	.04	.02
❑ 4 Frank Reich	.10	.05
❑ 5 Derrick Thomas	.25	.11
❑ 6 Mike Singletary	.10	.05
❑ 7 Boomer Esiason	.10	.05
❑ 8 Matt Millen	.10	.05
❑ 9 Chris Spielman	.10	.05
❑ 10 Gerald McNeil	.04	.02
❑ 11 Nick Lowery	.04	.02
❑ 12 Randall Cunningham	.25	.11
❑ 13 Marion Butts	.10	.05
❑ 14 Tim Brown	.25	.11
❑ 15 Emmitt Smith	2.00	.90
❑ 16 Rich Camarillo	.04	.02
❑ 17 Mike Merriweather	.04	.02
❑ 18 Derrick Fenner	.04	.02
❑ 19 Clay Matthews	.10	.05
❑ 20 Barry Sanders	1.50	.70
❑ 21 James Brooks	.10	.05
❑ 22 Alton Montgomery	.04	.02
❑ 23 Steve Atwater	.04	.02
❑ 24 Ron Morris	.04	.02
❑ 25 Brad Muster	.04	.02
❑ 26 Andre Rison	.10	.05
❑ 27 Brian Brennan	.04	.02
❑ 28 Leonard Smith	.04	.02
❑ 29 Kevin Butler	.04	.02
❑ 30 Tim Harris	.04	.02
❑ 31 Jay Novacek	.25	.11
❑ 32 Eddie Murray	.04	.02
❑ 33 Keith Woodside	.04	.02
❑ 34 Ray Crockett RC	.04	.02
❑ 35 Eugene Lockhart	.04	.02
❑ 36 Bill Romanowski	.04	.02
❑ 37 Eddie Brown	.04	.02
❑ 38 Eugene Daniel	.04	.02
❑ 39 Scott Fulhage	.04	.02
❑ 40 Harold Green	.10	.05
❑ 41 Mark Jackson	.04	.02
❑ 42 Sterling Sharpe	.25	.11
❑ 43 Mel Gray	.10	.05
❑ 44 Jerry Holmes	.04	.02
❑ 45 Allen Pinkett	.04	.02
❑ 46 Warren Powers	.04	.02
❑ 47 Rodney Peete	.10	.05
❑ 48 Lorenzo White	.04	.02
❑ 49 Dan Owens	.04	.02
❑ 50 James Francis	.04	.02
❑ 51 Ken Norton	.25	.11
❑ 52 Ed West	.04	.02
❑ 53 Andre Reed	.10	.05
❑ 54 John Grimsley	.04	.02
❑ 55 Michael Cofer	.04	.02
❑ 56 Chris Doleman	.04	.02
❑ 57 Pat Swilling	.10	.05
❑ 58 Jessie Tuggle	.04	.02
❑ 59 Mike Johnson	.04	.02
❑ 60 Steve Walsh	.04	.02
❑ 61 Sam Mills	.04	.02
❑ 62 Don Mosebar	.04	.02
❑ 63 Jay Hilgenberg	.04	.02
❑ 64 Cleveland Gary	.04	.02
❑ 65 Andre Tippett	.04	.02
❑ 66 Tom Newberry	.04	.02
❑ 67 Maurice Hurst	.04	.02

68	Louis Oliver	.04	.02
69	Fred Marion	.04	.02
70	Christian Okoye	.04	.02
71	Marv Cook	.04	.02
72	Darryl Talley	.04	.02
73	Rick Fenney	.04	.02
74	Kelvin Martin	.04	.02
75	Howie Long	.10	.05
76	Steve Wisniewski	.04	.02
77	Karl Mecklenburg	.04	.02
78	Dan Saleaumua	.04	.02
79	Ray Childress	.04	.02
80	Henry Ellard	.10	.05
81	Ernest Givins UER (3rd on Oilers in receiving, not 4th)	.10	.05
82	Ferrell Edmunds	.04	.02
83	Steve Jordan	.04	.02
84	Tony Mandarich	.04	.02
85	Eric Martin	.04	.02
86	Rich Gannon	.04	.02
87	Irving Fryar	.10	.05
88	Tom Rathman	.04	.02
89	Dan Hampton	.10	.05
90	Barry Word	.04	.02
91	Kevin Greene	.25	.11
92	Sean Landeta	.04	.02
93	Trace Armstrong	.04	.02
94	Dennis Byrd	.04	.02
95	Timm Rosenbach	.04	.02
96	Anthony Toney	.04	.02
97	Tim Krumrie	.04	.02
98	Jerry Ball	.04	.02
99	Tim Green	.04	.02
100	Bo Jackson	.10	.05
101	Myron Guyton	.04	.02
102	Mike Mularkey	.04	.02
103	Jerry Gray	.04	.02
104	Scott Stephen RC	.04	.02
105	Anthony Bell	.04	.02
106	Lomas Brown	.04	.02
107	David Little	.04	.02
108	Brad Baxter	.04	.02
109	Freddie Joe Nunn	.04	.02
110	Dave Meggett	.10	.05
111	Mark Rypien	.10	.05
112	Warren Williams	.04	.02
113	Ron Rivera	.04	.02
114	Terance Mathis	.10	.05
115	Anthony Munoz	.10	.05
116	Jeff Bryant	.04	.02
117	Issiac Holt	.04	.02
118	Steve Sewell	.04	.02
119	Tim Newton	.04	.02
120	Emile Harry	.04	.02
121	Gary Anderson K	.04	.02
122	Mark Lee	.04	.02
123	Alfred Anderson	.04	.02
124	Anthony Blaylock	.04	.02
125	Earnest Byner	.04	.02
126	Bill Maas	.04	.02
127	Keith Taylor	.04	.02
128	Cliff Odom	.04	.02
129	Bob Golic	.04	.02
130	Bart Oates	.04	.02
131	Jim Arnold	.04	.02
132	Jeff Herrod	.04	.02
133	Bruce Armstrong	.04	.02
134	Craig Heyward	.10	.05
135	Joey Browner	.04	.02
136	Darren Comeaux	.04	.02
137	Pat Beach	.04	.02
138	Dalton Hilliard	.04	.02
139	David Treadwell	.04	.02
140	Gary Anderson RB	.04	.02
141	Eugene Robinson	.04	.02
142	Scott Case	.04	.02
143	Paul Farren	.04	.02
144	Gill Fenerty	.04	.02
145	Tim Irwin	.04	.02
146	Norm Johnson	.04	.02
147	Willie Gault	.10	.05
148	Clarence Verdin	.04	.02
149	Jeff Uhlenhake	.04	.02
150	Erik McMillan	.04	.02
151	Kevin Ross	.04	.02
152	Pepper Johnson	.04	.02
153	Bryan Hinkle	.04	.02
154	Gary Clark	.25	.11
155	Robert Delpino	.04	.02
156	Doug Smith	.04	.02
157	Chris Martin	.04	.02
158	Ray Berry	.04	.02
159	Steve Christie	.04	.02
160	Don Smith	.04	.02
161	Greg McMurtry	.04	.02
162	Jack Del Rio	.04	.02
163	Floyd Dixon	.04	.02
164	Buford McGee	.04	.02
165	Brett Maxie	.04	.02
166	Morten Andersen	.04	.02
167	Kent Hull	.04	.02
168	Skip McClendon	.04	.02
169	Keith Sims	.04	.02
170	Leonard Marshall	.04	.02
171	Tony Woods	.04	.02
172	Byron Evans	.04	.02
173	Rob Burnett RC	.04	.02
174	Tory Epps	.04	.02
175	Toi Cook RC	.04	.02
176	John Elliott	.04	.02
177	Tommie Agee	.04	.02
178	Keith Van Horne	.04	.02
179	Dennis Smith	.04	.02
180	James Lofton	.10	.05
181	Art Monk	.10	.05
182	Anthony Carter	.10	.05
183	Louis Lipps	.04	.02
184	Bruce Hill	.04	.02
185	Michael Young	.04	.02
186	Eric Green	.04	.02
187	Barney Bussey RC	.04	.02
188	Curtis Duncan	.04	.02
189	Robert Awalt	.04	.02
190	Johnny Johnson	.04	.02
191	Jeff Cross	.04	.02
192	Keith McKeller	.04	.02
193	Robert Brown	.04	.02
194	Vincent Brown	.04	.02
195	Calvin Williams	.10	.05
196	Sean Jones	.10	.05
197	Willie Drewrey	.04	.02
198	Bubba McDowell	.04	.02
199	Al Noga	.04	.02
200	Ronnie Lott	.10	.05
201	Warren Moon	.25	.11
202	Chris Hinton	.04	.02
203	Jim Sweeney	.04	.02
204	Wayne Haddix	.04	.02
205	Tim Jorden RC	.04	.02
206	Marvin Allen	.04	.02
207	Jim Morrissey RC	.04	.02
208	Ben Smith	.04	.02
209	William White	.04	.02
210	Jim C. Jensen	.04	.02
211	Doug Reed	.04	.02
212	Ethan Horton	.04	.02
213	Chris Jacke	.04	.02
214	Johnny Hector	.04	.02
215	Drew Hill UER (Tied for the NFC lead, should say AFC)	.04	.02
216	Roy Green	.04	.02
217	Dean Steinkuhler	.04	.02
218	Cedric Mack	.04	.02
219	Chris Miller	.10	.05
220	Keith Byars	.04	.02
221	Lewis Billups	.04	.02
222	Roger Craig	.10	.05
223	Shaun Gayle	.04	.02
224	Mike Rozier	.04	.02
225	Troy Aikman	.75	.35
226	Bobby Humphrey	.04	.02
227	Eugene Marve	.04	.02
228	Michael Carter	.04	.02
229	Richard Johnson RC	.04	.02
230	Billy Joe Tolliver	.04	.02
231	Mark Murphy	.04	.02
232	John L. Williams	.04	.02
233	Ronnie Harmon	.04	.02
234	Thurman Thomas	.25	.11
235	Martin Mayhew	.04	.02
236	Richmond Webb	.04	.02
237	Gerald Riggs UER (Earnest Byner misspelled as Ernest)	.10	.05
238	Mike Prior	.04	.02
239	Mike Gann	.04	.02
240	Alvin Walton	.04	.02
241	Tim McGee	.04	.02
242	Bruce Matthews	.10	.05
243	Johnny Holland	.04	.02
244	Martin Bayless	.04	.02
245	Eric Metcalf	.10	.05
246	John Alt	.04	.02
247	Max Montoya	.04	.02
248	Rod Bernstine	.04	.02
249	Paul Gruber	.04	.02
250	Charles Haley	.10	.05
251	Scott Norwood	.04	.02
252	Michael Haddix	.04	.02
253	Ricky Sanders	.04	.02
254	Ervin Randle	.04	.02
255	Duane Bickett	.04	.02
256	Mike Munchak	.04	.02
257	Keith Jones	.04	.02
258	Riki Ellison	.04	.02
259	Vince Newsome	.04	.02
260	Lee Williams	.04	.02
261	Steve Smith	.04	.02
262	Sam Clancy	.04	.02
263	Pierce Holt	.04	.02
264	Jim Harbaugh	.25	.11
265	Dino Hackett	.04	.02
266	Andy Heck	.04	.02
267	Leo Goeas	.04	.02
268	Russ Grimm	.04	.02
269	Gill Byrd	.04	.02
270	Neal Anderson	.10	.05
271	Jackie Slater	.04	.02
272	Joe Nash	.04	.02
273	Todd Bowles	.04	.02
274	D.J. Dozier	.04	.02
275	Kevin Fagan	.04	.02
276	Don Warren	.04	.02
277	Jim Jeffcoat	.04	.02
278	Bruce Smith	.25	.11
279	Cortez Kennedy	.25	.11
280	Thane Gash	.04	.02
281	Perry Kemp	.04	.02
282	John Taylor	.10	.05
283	Stephone Paige	.04	.02
284	Paul Skansi	.04	.02
285	Shawn Collins	.04	.02
286	Mervyn Fernandez	.04	.02
287	Daniel Stubbs	.04	.02
288	Chip Lohmiller	.04	.02
289	Brian Blades	.10	.05
290	Mark Carrier WR	.25	.11
291	Carl Zander	.04	.02
292	David Wyman	.04	.02
293	Jeff Bostic	.04	.02
294	Irv Pankey	.04	.02
295	Keith Millard	.04	.02
296	Jamie Mueller	.04	.02
297	Bill Fralic	.04	.02
298	Wendell Davis	.04	.02
299	Ken Clarke	.04	.02
300	Wymon Henderson	.04	.02
301	Jeff Campbell	.04	.02
302	Cody Carlson RC	.04	.02
303	Matt Brock RC	.04	.02
304	Maurice Carthon	.04	.02
305	Scott Mersereau RC	.04	.02
306	Steve Wright RC	.04	.02
307	J.B. Brown	.04	.02
308	Ricky Reynolds	.04	.02
309	Darryl Pollard	.04	.02
310	Donald Evans	.04	.02
311	Nick Bell RC	.04	.02
312	Pat Harlow RC	.04	.02
313	Dan McGwire RC	.04	.02
314	Mike Dumas RC	.04	.02
315	Mike Croel RC	.04	.02
316	Chris Smith RC	.04	.02
317	Kenny Walker RC	.04	.02
318	Todd Lyght RC	.04	.02
319	Mike Stonebreaker	.04	.02

No.	Player	Mint	Ex
❑ 320	Randall Cunningham 90	.10	.05
❑ 321	Terance Mathis 90	.25	.11
❑ 322	Gaston Green 90	.04	.02
❑ 323	Johnny Bailey 90	.04	.02
❑ 324	Donnie Elder 90	.04	.02
❑ 325	Dwight Stone 90 UER (No '91 copyright on card back)	.04	.02
❑ 326	J.J. Birden 90 RC	.10	.05
❑ 327	Alexander Wright 90	.04	.02
❑ 328	Eric Metcalf 90	.10	.05
❑ 329	Andre Rison TL	.10	.05
❑ 330	Warren Moon TL UER (Not Blanda's record, should be Van Brocklin)	.10	.05
❑ 331	Steve Tasker DT	.04	.02
❑ 332	Mel Gray DT	.10	.05
❑ 333	Nick Lowery DT	.04	.02
❑ 334	Sean Landeta DT	.04	.02
❑ 335	David Fulcher DT	.04	.02
❑ 336	Joey Browner DT	.04	.02
❑ 337	Albert Lewis DT	.04	.02
❑ 338	Rod Woodson DT	.10	.05
❑ 339	Shane Conlan DT	.04	.02
❑ 340	Pepper Johnson DT	.04	.02
❑ 341	Chris Spielman DT	.04	.02
❑ 342	Derrick Thomas DT	.10	.05
❑ 343	Ray Childress DT	.04	.02
❑ 344	Reggie White DT	.10	.05
❑ 345	Bruce Smith DT	.10	.05
❑ 346	Darrell Green	.04	.02
❑ 347	Ray Bentley	.04	.02
❑ 348	Herschel Walker	.10	.05
❑ 349	Rodney Holman	.04	.02
❑ 350	Al Toon	.10	.05
❑ 351	Harry Hamilton	.04	.02
❑ 352	Albert Lewis	.04	.02
❑ 353	Renaldo Turnbull	.04	.02
❑ 354	Junior Seau	.25	.11
❑ 355	Merril Hoge	.04	.02
❑ 356	Shane Conlan	.04	.02
❑ 357	Jay Schroeder	.04	.02
❑ 358	Steve Broussard	.04	.02
❑ 359	Mark Bavaro	.04	.02
❑ 360	Jim Lachey	.04	.02
❑ 361	Greg Townsend	.04	.02
❑ 362	Dave Krieg	.10	.05
❑ 363	Jessie Hester	.04	.02
❑ 364	Steve Tasker	.10	.05
❑ 365	Ron Hall	.04	.02
❑ 366	Pat Leahy	.04	.02
❑ 367	Jim Everett	.10	.05
❑ 368	Felix Wright	.04	.02
❑ 369	Ricky Proehl	.04	.02
❑ 370	Anthony Miller	.10	.05
❑ 371	Keith Jackson	.10	.05
❑ 372	Pete Stoyanovich	.04	.02
❑ 373	Tommy Kane	.04	.02
❑ 374	Richard Johnson	.04	.02
❑ 375	Randall McDaniel	.04	.02
❑ 376	John Stephens	.04	.02
❑ 377	Haywood Jeffires	.10	.05
❑ 378	Rodney Hampton	.25	.11
❑ 379	Tim Grunhard	.04	.02
❑ 380	Jerry Rice	.75	.35
❑ 381	Ken Harvey	.10	.05
❑ 382	Vaughan Johnson	.04	.02
❑ 383	J.T. Smith	.04	.02
❑ 384	Carnell Lake	.04	.02
❑ 385	Dan Marino	1.25	.55
❑ 386	Kyle Clifton	.04	.02
❑ 387	Wilber Marshall	.04	.02
❑ 388	Pete Holohan	.04	.02
❑ 389	Gary Plummer	.04	.02
❑ 390	William Perry	.10	.05
❑ 391	Mark Robinson	.04	.02
❑ 392	Nate Odomes	.04	.02
❑ 393	Ickey Woods	.04	.02
❑ 394	Reyna Thompson	.04	.02
❑ 395	Deion Sanders	.40	.18
❑ 396	Harris Barton	.04	.02
❑ 397	Sammie Smith	.04	.02
❑ 398	Vinny Testaverde	.10	.05
❑ 399	Ray Donaldson	.04	.02
❑ 400	Tim McKyer	.04	.02
❑ 401	Nesby Glasgow	.04	.02
❑ 402	Brent Williams	.04	.02
❑ 403	Rob Moore	.25	.11
❑ 404	Bubby Brister	.04	.02
❑ 405	David Fulcher	.04	.02
❑ 406	Reggie Cobb	.04	.02
❑ 407	Jerome Brown	.04	.02
❑ 408	Erik Howard	.04	.02
❑ 409	Tony Paige	.04	.02
❑ 410	John Elway	1.25	.55
❑ 411	Charles Mann	.04	.02
❑ 412	Luis Sharpe	.04	.02
❑ 413	Hassan Jones	.04	.02
❑ 414	Frank Minnifield	.04	.02
❑ 415	Steve DeBerg	.04	.02
❑ 416	Mark Carrier DB	.10	.05
❑ 417	Brian Jordan	.10	.05
❑ 418	Reggie Langhorne	.04	.02
❑ 419	Don Majkowski	.04	.02
❑ 420	Marcus Allen	.25	.11
❑ 421	Michael Brooks	.04	.02
❑ 422	Vai Sikahema	.04	.02
❑ 423	Dermontti Dawson	.04	.02
❑ 424	Jacob Green	.04	.02
❑ 425	Flipper Anderson	.04	.02
❑ 426	Bill Brooks	.04	.02
❑ 427	Keith McCants	.04	.02
❑ 428	Ken O'Brien	.04	.02
❑ 429	Fred Barnett	.25	.11
❑ 430	Mark Duper	.10	.05
❑ 431	Mark Kelso	.04	.02
❑ 432	Leslie O'Neal	.10	.05
❑ 433	Ottis Anderson	.10	.05
❑ 434	Jesse Sapolu	.04	.02
❑ 435	Gary Zimmerman	.04	.02
❑ 436	Kevin Porter	.04	.02
❑ 437	Anthony Thompson	.04	.02
❑ 438	Robert Clark	.04	.02
❑ 439	Chris Warren	.25	.11
❑ 440	Gerald Williams	.04	.02
❑ 441	Jim Skow	.04	.02
❑ 442	Rick Donnelly	.04	.02
❑ 443	Guy McIntyre	.04	.02
❑ 444	Jeff Lageman	.04	.02
❑ 445	John Offerdahl	.04	.02
❑ 446	Clyde Simmons	.04	.02
❑ 447	John Kidd	.04	.02
❑ 448	Chip Banks	.04	.02
❑ 449	Johnny Meads	.04	.02
❑ 450	Rickey Jackson	.04	.02
❑ 451	Lee Johnson	.04	.02
❑ 452	Michael Irvin	.25	.11
❑ 453	Leon Seals	.04	.02
❑ 454	Darrell Thompson	.04	.02
❑ 455	Everson Walls	.04	.02
❑ 456	LeRoy Butler	.10	.05
❑ 457	Marcus Dupree	.04	.02
❑ 458	Kirk Lowdermilk	.04	.02
❑ 459	Chris Singleton	.04	.02
❑ 460	Seth Joyner	.10	.05
❑ 461	Rueben Mayes UER (Hayes in bio should be Heyward)	.04	.02
❑ 462	Ernie Jones	.04	.02
❑ 463	Greg Kragen	.04	.02
❑ 464	Bennie Blades	.04	.02
❑ 465	Mark Bortz	.04	.02
❑ 466	Tony Stargell	.04	.02
❑ 467	Mike Cofer	.04	.02
❑ 468	Randy Grimes	.04	.02
❑ 469	Tim Worley	.04	.02
❑ 470	Kevin Mack	.04	.02
❑ 471	Wes Hopkins	.04	.02
❑ 472	Will Wolford	.04	.02
❑ 473	Sam Seale	.04	.02
❑ 474	Jim Ritcher	.04	.02
❑ 475	Jeff Hostetler	.25	.11
❑ 476	Mitchell Price RC	.04	.02
❑ 477	Ken Lanier	.04	.02
❑ 478	Naz Worthen	.04	.02
❑ 479	Ed Reynolds	.04	.02
❑ 480	Mark Clayton	.10	.05
❑ 481	Matt Bahr	.04	.02
❑ 482	Gary Reasons	.04	.02
❑ 483	David Szott	.04	.02
❑ 484	Barry Foster	.10	.05
❑ 485	Bruce Reimers	.04	.02
❑ 486	Dean Biasucci	.04	.02
❑ 487	Cris Carter	.50	.23
❑ 488	Albert Bentley	.04	.02
❑ 489	Robert Massey	.04	.02
❑ 490	Al Smith	.04	.02
❑ 491	Greg Lloyd	.25	.11
❑ 492	Steve McMichael UER (Photo on back actually Dan Hampton)	.10	.05
❑ 493	Jeff Wright RC	.04	.02
❑ 494	Scott Davis	.04	.02
❑ 495	Freeman McNeil	.04	.02
❑ 496	Simon Fletcher	.04	.02
❑ 497	Terry McDaniel	.04	.02
❑ 498	Heath Sherman	.04	.02
❑ 499	Jeff Jaeger	.04	.02
❑ 500	Mark Collins	.04	.02
❑ 501	Tim Goad	.04	.02
❑ 502	Jeff George	.25	.11
❑ 503	Jimmie Jones	.04	.02
❑ 504	Henry Thomas	.04	.02
❑ 505	Steve Young	.75	.35
❑ 506	William Roberts	.04	.02
❑ 507	Neil Smith	.25	.11
❑ 508	Mike Saxon	.04	.02
❑ 509	Johnny Bailey	.04	.02
❑ 510	Broderick Thomas	.04	.02
❑ 511	Wade Wilson	.10	.05
❑ 512	Hart Lee Dykes	.04	.02
❑ 513	Hardy Nickerson	.10	.05
❑ 514	Tim McDonald	.04	.02
❑ 515	Frank Cornish	.04	.02
❑ 516	Jarvis Williams	.04	.02
❑ 517	Carl Lee	.04	.02
❑ 518	Carl Banks	.04	.02
❑ 519	Mike Golic	.04	.02
❑ 520	Brian Noble	.04	.02
❑ 521	James Hasty	.04	.02
❑ 522	Bubba Paris	.04	.02
❑ 523	Kevin Walker RC	.04	.02
❑ 524	William Fuller	.10	.05
❑ 525	Eddie Anderson	.04	.02
❑ 526	Roger Ruzek	.04	.02
❑ 527	Robert Blackmon	.04	.02
❑ 528	Vince Buck	.04	.02
❑ 529	Lawrence Taylor	.25	.11
❑ 530	Reggie Roby	.04	.02
❑ 531	Doug Riesenberg	.04	.02
❑ 532	Joe Jacoby	.04	.02
❑ 533	Kirby Jackson RC	.04	.02
❑ 534	Robb Thomas	.04	.02
❑ 535	Don Griffin	.04	.02
❑ 536	Andre Waters	.04	.02
❑ 537	Marc Logan	.04	.02
❑ 538	James Thornton	.04	.02
❑ 539	Ray Agnew	.04	.02
❑ 540	Frank Stams	.04	.02
❑ 541	Brett Perriman	.25	.11
❑ 542	Andre Ware	.10	.05
❑ 543	Kevin Haverdink	.04	.02
❑ 544	Greg Jackson RC	.04	.02
❑ 545	Tunch Ilkin	.04	.02
❑ 546	Dexter Carter	.04	.02
❑ 547	Rod Woodson	.25	.11
❑ 548	Donnell Woolford	.04	.02
❑ 549	Mark Boyer	.04	.02
❑ 550	Jeff Query	.04	.02
❑ 551	Burt Grossman	.04	.02
❑ 552	Mike Kenn	.04	.02
❑ 553	Richard Dent	.10	.05
❑ 554	Gaston Green	.04	.02
❑ 555	Phil Simms	.10	.05
❑ 556	Brent Jones	.25	.11
❑ 557	Ronnie Lippett	.04	.02
❑ 558	Mike Horan	.04	.02
❑ 559	Danny Noonan	.04	.02
❑ 560	Reggie White	.25	.11
❑ 561	Rufus Porter	.04	.02
❑ 562	Aaron Wallace	.04	.02
❑ 563	Vance Johnson	.04	.02
❑ 564A	Aaron Craver RC ERR (No copyright line on back)	.04	.02
❑ 564B	Aaron Craver COR RC	.04	.02
❑ 565A	Russell Maryland RC ERR (No copyright line	.25	.11

No.	Player	MINT	NRMT
	on back)		
❑ 565B	Russell Maryland COR RC	.25	.11
❑ 566	Paul Justin RC	.04	.02
❑ 567	Walter Dean	.04	.02
❑ 568	Herman Moore RC	2.00	.90
❑ 569	Bill Musgrave RC	.04	.02
❑ 570	Rob Carpenter RC	.04	.02
❑ 571	Greg Lewis RC	.04	.02
❑ 572	Ed King RC	.04	.02
❑ 573	Ernie Mills RC	.10	.05
❑ 574	Jake Reed RC	.75	.35
❑ 575	Ricky Watters RC	1.50	.70
❑ 576	Derek Russell RC	.04	.02
❑ 577	Shawn Moore RC	.04	.02
❑ 578	Eric Bieniemy RC	.04	.02
❑ 579	Chris Zorich RC	.25	.11
❑ 580	Scott Miller	.04	.02
❑ 581	Jarrod Bunch RC	.04	.02
❑ 582	Ricky Ervins RC	.10	.05
❑ 583	Browning Nagle RC	.04	.02
❑ 584	Eric Turner RC	.10	.05
❑ 585	William Thomas RC	.04	.02
❑ 586	Stanley Richard RC	.04	.02
❑ 587	Adrian Cooper RC	.04	.02
❑ 588	Harvey Williams RC	.25	.11
❑ 589	Alvin Harper RC	.25	.11
❑ 590	John Carney	.04	.02
❑ 591	Mark Vander Poel RC	.04	.02
❑ 592	Mike Pritchard RC	.25	.11
❑ 593	Eric Moten RC	.04	.02
❑ 594	Moe Gardner RC	.04	.02
❑ 595	Wesley Carroll RC	.04	.02
❑ 596	Eric Swann RC	.25	.11
❑ 597	Joe Kelly	.04	.02
❑ 598	Steve Jackson RC	.04	.02
❑ 599	Kelvin Pritchett RC	.10	.05
❑ 600	Jesse Campbell RC	.04	.02
❑ 601	Darryll Lewis RC UER (Name misspelled Darryl)	.10	.05
❑ 602	Howard Griffith	.04	.02
❑ 603	Blaise Bryant	.04	.02
❑ 604	Vinnie Clark RC	.04	.02
❑ 605	Mel Agee RC	.04	.02
❑ 606	Bobby Wilson RC	.04	.02
❑ 607	Kevin Donnalley	.04	.02
❑ 608	Randal Hill RC	.10	.05
❑ 609	Stan Thomas	.04	.02
❑ 610	Mike Heldt	.04	.02
❑ 611	Brett Favre RC	5.00	2.20
❑ 612	L. Dawsey RC UER (Went to Florida State, not Florida)	.10	.05
❑ 613	Dennis Gibson	.04	.02
❑ 614	Dean Dingman	.04	.02
❑ 615	Bruce Pickens RC	.04	.02
❑ 616	Todd Marinovich RC	.04	.02
❑ 617	Gene Atkins	.04	.02
❑ 618	Marcus Dupree (Comeback Player)	.04	.02
❑ 619	Warren Moon (Man of the Year)	.10	.05
❑ 620	Joe Montana MVP	.50	.23
❑ 621	Neal Anderson MVP	.04	.02
❑ 622	James Brooks MVP	.10	.05
❑ 623	Thurman Thomas MVP	.10	.05
❑ 624	Bobby Humphrey MVP	.04	.02
❑ 625	Kevin Mack MVP	.04	.02
❑ 626	Mark Carrier WR MVP	.04	.02
❑ 627	Johnny Johnson MVP	.04	.02
❑ 628	Marion Butts MVP	.10	.05
❑ 629	Steve DeBerg MVP	.04	.02
❑ 630	Jeff George MVP	.10	.05
❑ 631	Troy Aikman MVP	.40	.18
❑ 632	Dan Marino MVP	.50	.23
❑ 633	Randall Cunningham MVP	.10	.05
❑ 634	Andre Rison MVP	.10	.05
❑ 635	Pepper Johnson MVP	.04	.02
❑ 636	Pat Leahy MVP	.04	.02
❑ 637	Barry Sanders MVP	.60	.25
❑ 638	Warren Moon MVP	.10	.05
❑ 639	Sterling Sharpe MVP	.04	.02
❑ 640	Bruce Armstrong MVP	.04	.02
❑ 641	Bo Jackson MVP	.10	.05
❑ 642	Henry Ellard MVP	.10	.05
❑ 643	Earnest Byner MVP	.04	.02
❑ 644	Pat Swilling MVP	.04	.02
❑ 645	John L. Williams MVP	.04	.02
❑ 646	Rod Woodson MVP	.10	.05
❑ 647	Chris Doleman MVP	.04	.02
❑ 648	Joey Browner CC	.04	.02
❑ 649	Erik McMillan CC	.04	.02
❑ 650	David Fulcher CC	.04	.02
❑ 651A	Ronnie Lott CC ERR (Front 47, back 42)	.10	.05
❑ 651B	Ronnie Lott CC COR (Front 47, back 42 is now blacked out)	.10	.05
❑ 652	Louis Oliver CC	.04	.02
❑ 653	Mark Robinson CC	.04	.02
❑ 654	Dennis Smith CC	.04	.02
❑ 655	Reggie White SA	.10	.05
❑ 656	Charles Haley SA	.04	.02
❑ 657	Leslie O'Neal SA	.10	.05
❑ 658	Kevin Greene SA	.10	.05
❑ 659	Dennis Byrd SA	.04	.02
❑ 660	Bruce Smith SA	.10	.05
❑ 661	Derrick Thomas SA	.10	.05
❑ 662	Steve DeBerg TL	.04	.02
❑ 663	Barry Sanders TL	.60	.25
❑ 664	Thurman Thomas TL	.10	.05
❑ 665	Jerry Rice TL	.40	.18
❑ 666	Derrick Thomas TL	.10	.05
❑ 667	Bruce Smith TL	.10	.05
❑ 668	Mark Carrier DB TL	.04	.02
❑ 669	Richard Johnson TL	.04	.02
❑ 670	Jan Stenerud HOF	.04	.02
❑ 671	Stan Jones HOF	.04	.02
❑ 672	John Hannah HOF	.04	.02
❑ 673	Tex Schramm HOF	.04	.02
❑ 674	Earl Campbell HOF	.25	.11
❑ 675	Mark Carrier and Emmitt Smith (Rookies of the Year)	.50	.23
❑ 676	Warren Moon DT	.10	.05
❑ 677	Barry Sanders DT	.60	.25
❑ 678	Thurman Thomas DT	.25	.11
❑ 679	Andre Reed DT	.10	.05
❑ 680	Andre Rison DT	.10	.05
❑ 681	Keith Jackson DT	.04	.02
❑ 682	Bruce Armstrong DT	.04	.02
❑ 683	Jim Lachey DT	.04	.02
❑ 684	Bruce Matthews DT	.04	.02
❑ 685	Mike Munchak DT	.04	.02
❑ 686	Don Mosebar DT	.04	.02
❑ B1	Jeff Hostetler SB	.25	.11
❑ B2	Matt Bahr SB	.04	.02
❑ B3	Ottis Anderson SB	.10	.05
❑ B4	Ottis Anderson SB	.10	.05

1991 Score Dream Team Autographs

	MINT	NRMT
COMPLETE SET (11)	800.00	350.00
COMMON CARD (676-686)	40.00	18.00
SEMISTARS	75.00	34.00
UNLISTED STARS	100.00	45.00

No.	Player	MINT	NRMT
❑ 676	Warren Moon	100.00	45.00
❑ 677	Barry Sanders	400.00	180.00
❑ 678	Thurman Thomas	100.00	45.00
❑ 679	Andre Reed	100.00	45.00
❑ 680	Andre Rison	75.00	34.00
❑ 681	Keith Jackson	40.00	18.00
❑ 682	Bruce Armstrong	40.00	18.00
❑ 683	Jim Lachey	40.00	18.00
❑ 684	Bruce Matthews	40.00	18.00
❑ 685	Mike Munchak	40.00	18.00
❑ 686	Don Mosebar	40.00	18.00

1991 Score Hot Rookies

	MINT	NRMT
COMPLETE SET (10)	4.00	1.80
ONE PER BLISTER PACK		

No.	Player	MINT	NRMT
❑ 1	Dan McGwire	.40	.18
❑ 2	Todd Lyght	.40	.18
❑ 3	Mike Dumas	.40	.18
❑ 4	Pat Harlow	.40	.18
❑ 5	Nick Bell	.40	.18
❑ 6	Chris Smith	.40	.18
❑ 7	Mike Stonebreaker	.40	.18
❑ 8	Mike Croel	.40	.18
❑ 9	Kenny Walker	.40	.18
❑ 10	Rob Carpenter	.40	.18

1991 Score Supplemental

	MINT	NRMT
COMPLETE FACT.SET (110)	3.00	1.35
COMMON CARD (1T-110T)	.04	.02
SEMISTARS	.10	.05
UNLISTED STARS	.25	.11

No.	Player	MINT	NRMT
❑ 1T	Ronnie Lott	.10	.05
❑ 2T	Matt Millen	.10	.05
❑ 3T	Tim McKyer	.04	.02
❑ 4T	Vince Newsome	.04	.02
❑ 5T	Gaston Green	.04	.02
❑ 6T	Brett Perriman	.25	.11
❑ 7T	Roger Craig	.10	.05
❑ 8T	Pete Holohan	.04	.02
❑ 9T	Tony Zendejas	.04	.02
❑ 10T	Lee Williams	.04	.02
❑ 11T	Mike Stonebreaker	.04	.02
❑ 12T	Felix Wright	.04	.02
❑ 13T	Lonnie Young	.04	.02
❑ 14T	Hugh Millen RC	.04	.02
❑ 15T	Roy Green	.04	.02
❑ 16T	Greg Davis RC	.04	.02
❑ 17T	Dexter Manley	.04	.02

- ❑ 18T Ted Washington RC .04 .02
- ❑ 19T Norm Johnson .04 .02
- ❑ 20T Joe Morris .04 .02
- ❑ 21T Robert Perryman .04 .02
- ❑ 22T Mike Iaquaniello RC UER .04 .02 (Free agent in '91, not '87)
- ❑ 23T Gerald Perry RC UER .04 .02 (School should be Southern University A and M)
- ❑ 24T Zeke Mowatt .04 .02
- ❑ 25T Rich Miano RC .04 .02
- ❑ 26T Nick Bell .04 .02
- ❑ 27T Terry Orr RC .04 .02
- ❑ 28T Matt Stover RC .10 .05
- ❑ 29T Bubba Paris .04 .02
- ❑ 30T Ron Brown .04 .02
- ❑ 31T Don Davey .04 .02
- ❑ 32T Lee Rouson .04 .02
- ❑ 33T Terry Hoage UER .04 .02 (Eaqgles, sic)
- ❑ 34T Tony Covington .04 .02
- ❑ 35T John Rienstra .04 .02
- ❑ 36T Charles Dimry RC .04 .02
- ❑ 37T Todd Marinovich .04 .02
- ❑ 38T Winston Moss .04 .02
- ❑ 39T Vestee Jackson .04 .02
- ❑ 40T Brian Hansen .04 .02
- ❑ 41T Irv Eatman .04 .02
- ❑ 42T Jarrod Bunch .04 .02
- ❑ 43T Kanavis McGhee RC .04 .02
- ❑ 44T Vai Sikahema .04 .02
- ❑ 45T Charles McRae RC .04 .02
- ❑ 46T Quinn Early .10 .05
- ❑ 47T Jeff Faulkner RC .04 .02
- ❑ 48T William Frizzell RC .04 .02
- ❑ 49T John Booty .04 .02
- ❑ 50T Tim Harris .04 .02
- ❑ 51T Derek Russell .04 .02
- ❑ 52T John Flannery RC .04 .02
- ❑ 53T Tim Barnett RC .04 .02
- ❑ 54T Alfred Williams RC .04 .02
- ❑ 55T Dan McGwire .04 .02
- ❑ 56T Ernie Mills .04 .02
- ❑ 57T Stanley Richard .04 .02
- ❑ 58T Huey Richardson RC .04 .02
- ❑ 59T Jerome Henderson RC .04 .02
- ❑ 60T Bryan Cox RC .25 .11
- ❑ 61T Russell Maryland .10 .05
- ❑ 62T Reginald Jones RC .04 .02
- ❑ 63T Mo Lewis RC .10 .05
- ❑ 64T Moe Gardner .04 .02
- ❑ 65T Wesley Carroll .04 .02
- ❑ 66T Michael Jackson RC .25 .11
- ❑ 67T Shawn Jefferson RC .10 .05
- ❑ 68T Chris Zorich .10 .05
- ❑ 69T Kenny Walker .04 .02
- ❑ 70T Eric Pegram RC .25 .11
- ❑ 71T Alvin Harper .25 .11
- ❑ 72T Harry Colon RC .04 .02
- ❑ 73T Scott Miller .04 .02
- ❑ 74T Lawrence Dawsey .10 .05
- ❑ 75T Phil Hansen RC .04 .02
- ❑ 76T Roman Phifer RC .04 .02
- ❑ 77T Greg Lewis .04 .02
- ❑ 78T Merton Hanks RC .25 .11
- ❑ 79T James Jones RC .04 .02
- ❑ 80T Vinnie Clark .04 .02
- ❑ 81T R.J. Kors .04 .02
- ❑ 82T Mike Pritchard .25 .11
- ❑ 83T Stan Thomas .04 .02
- ❑ 84T Lamar Rogers RC .04 .02
- ❑ 85T Erik Williams RC .10 .05
- ❑ 86T Keith Traylor RC .04 .02
- ❑ 87T Mike Dumas .04 .02
- ❑ 88T Mel Agee .04 .02
- ❑ 89T Harvey Williams .25 .11
- ❑ 90T Todd Lyght .04 .02
- ❑ 91T Jake Reed .40 .18
- ❑ 92T Pat Harlow .04 .02
- ❑ 93T Antone Davis RC .04 .02
- ❑ 94T Aeneas Williams RC .25 .11
- ❑ 95T Eric Bieniemy .04 .02
- ❑ 96T John Kasay RC .10 .05
- ❑ 97T Robert Wilson RC .04 .02
- ❑ 98T Ricky Ervins .10 .05
- ❑ 99T Mike Croel .04 .02
- ❑ 100T David Lang RC .04 .02
- ❑ 101T Esera Tuaolo RC .04 .02
- ❑ 102T Randal Hill .10 .05
- ❑ 103T Jon Vaughn RC .04 .02
- ❑ 104T Dave McCloughan .04 .02
- ❑ 105T David Daniels RC .04 .02
- ❑ 106T Eric Moten .04 .02
- ❑ 107T Anthony Morgan RC .04 .02
- ❑ 108T Ed King .04 .02
- ❑ 109T Leonard Russell RC .10 .05
- ❑ 110T Aaron Craver .04 .02

1992 Score

	MINT	NRMT
COMPLETE SET (550)	25.00	11.00
COMMON CARD (1-550)	.05	.02
SEMISTARS	.10	.05
UNLISTED STARS	.25	.11

- ❑ 1 Barry Sanders 2.50 1.10
- ❑ 2 Pat Swilling .10 .05
- ❑ 3 Moe Gardner .05 .02
- ❑ 4 Steve Young 1.00 .45
- ❑ 5 Chris Spielman .10 .05
- ❑ 6 Richard Dent .10 .05
- ❑ 7 Anthony Munoz .10 .05
- ❑ 8 Martin Mayhew .05 .02
- ❑ 9 Terry McDaniel .05 .02
- ❑ 10 Thurman Thomas .25 .11
- ❑ 11 Ricky Sanders .05 .02
- ❑ 12 Steve Atwater .05 .02
- ❑ 13 Tony Tolbert .05 .02
- ❑ 14 Vince Workman .10 .05
- ❑ 15 Haywood Jeffires .10 .05
- ❑ 16 Duane Bickett .05 .02
- ❑ 17 Jeff Uhlenhake .05 .02
- ❑ 18 Tim McDonald .05 .02
- ❑ 19 Cris Carter .50 .23
- ❑ 20 Derrick Thomas .25 .11
- ❑ 21 Hugh Millen .05 .02
- ❑ 22 Bart Oates .05 .02
- ❑ 23 Eugene Robinson .05 .02
- ❑ 24 Jerrol Williams .05 .02
- ❑ 25 Reggie White .25 .11
- ❑ 26 Marion Butts .05 .02
- ❑ 27 Jim Sweeney .05 .02
- ❑ 28 Tom Newberry .05 .02
- ❑ 29 Pete Stoyanovich .05 .02
- ❑ 30 Ronnie Lott .10 .05
- ❑ 31 Simon Fletcher .05 .02
- ❑ 32 Dino Hackett .05 .02
- ❑ 33 Morten Andersen .05 .02
- ❑ 34 Clyde Simmons .05 .02
- ❑ 35 Mark Rypien .05 .02
- ❑ 36 Greg Montgomery .05 .02
- ❑ 37 Nate Lewis .05 .02
- ❑ 38 Henry Ellard .10 .05
- ❑ 39 Luis Sharpe .05 .02
- ❑ 40 Michael Irvin .25 .11
- ❑ 41 Louis Lipps .05 .02
- ❑ 42 John L. Williams .05 .02
- ❑ 43 Broderick Thomas .05 .02
- ❑ 44 Michael Haynes .10 .05
- ❑ 45 Don Majkowski .05 .02
- ❑ 46 William Perry .10 .05
- ❑ 47 David Fulcher .05 .02
- ❑ 48 Tony Bennett .05 .02
- ❑ 49 Clay Matthews .10 .05
- ❑ 50 Warren Moon .25 .11
- ❑ 51 Bruce Armstrong .05 .02
- ❑ 52 Harry Newsome .05 .02
- ❑ 53 Bill Brooks .05 .02
- ❑ 54 Greg Townsend .05 .02
- ❑ 55 Tom Rathman .05 .02
- ❑ 56 Sean Landeta .05 .02
- ❑ 57 Kyle Clifton .05 .02
- ❑ 58 Steve Broussard .05 .02
- ❑ 59 Mark Carrier WR .10 .05
- ❑ 60 Mel Gray .10 .05
- ❑ 61 Tim Krumrie .05 .02
- ❑ 62 Rufus Porter .05 .02
- ❑ 63 Kevin Mack .05 .02
- ❑ 64 Todd Bowles .05 .02
- ❑ 65 Emmitt Smith 2.50 1.10
- ❑ 66 Mike Croel .05 .02
- ❑ 67 Brian Mitchell .10 .05
- ❑ 68 Bennie Blades .05 .02
- ❑ 69 Carnell Lake .05 .02
- ❑ 70 Cornelius Bennett .10 .05
- ❑ 71 Darrell Thompson .05 .02
- ❑ 72 Wes Hopkins .05 .02
- ❑ 73 Jessie Hester .05 .02
- ❑ 74 Irv Eatman .05 .02
- ❑ 75 Marv Cook .05 .02
- ❑ 76 Tim Brown .25 .11
- ❑ 77 Pepper Johnson .05 .02
- ❑ 78 Mark Duper .05 .02
- ❑ 79 Robert Delpino .05 .02
- ❑ 80 Charles Mann .05 .02
- ❑ 81 Brian Jordan .10 .05
- ❑ 82 Wendell Davis .05 .02
- ❑ 83 Lee Johnson .05 .02
- ❑ 84 Ricky Reynolds .05 .02
- ❑ 85 Vaughan Johnson .05 .02
- ❑ 86 Brian Blades .10 .05
- ❑ 87 Sam Seale .05 .02
- ❑ 88 Ed King .05 .02
- ❑ 89 Gaston Green .05 .02
- ❑ 90 Christian Okoye .05 .02
- ❑ 91 Chris Jacke .05 .02
- ❑ 92 Rohn Stark .05 .02
- ❑ 93 Kevin Greene .25 .11
- ❑ 94 Jay Novacek .10 .05
- ❑ 95 Chip Lohmiller .05 .02
- ❑ 96 Cris Dishman .05 .02
- ❑ 97 Ethan Horton .05 .02
- ❑ 98 Pat Harlow .05 .02
- ❑ 99 Mark Ingram .05 .02
- ❑ 100 Mark Carrier DB .05 .02
- ❑ 101 Deron Cherry .05 .02
- ❑ 102 Sam Mills .05 .02
- ❑ 103 Mark Higgs .05 .02
- ❑ 104 Keith Jackson .10 .05
- ❑ 105 Steve Tasker .10 .05
- ❑ 106 Ken Harvey .05 .02
- ❑ 107 Bryan Hinkle .05 .02
- ❑ 108 Anthony Carter .10 .05
- ❑ 109 Johnny Hector .05 .02
- ❑ 110 Randall McDaniel .05 .02
- ❑ 111 Johnny Johnson .05 .02
- ❑ 112 Shane Conlan .05 .02
- ❑ 113 Ray Horton .05 .02
- ❑ 114 Sterling Sharpe .25 .11
- ❑ 115 Guy McIntyre .05 .02
- ❑ 116 Tom Waddle .05 .02
- ❑ 117 Albert Lewis .05 .02
- ❑ 118 Riki Ellison .05 .02
- ❑ 119 Chris Doleman .05 .02
- ❑ 120 Andre Rison .10 .05
- ❑ 121 Bobby Hebert .05 .02
- ❑ 122 Dan Owens .05 .02
- ❑ 123 Rodney Hampton .25 .11
- ❑ 124 Ron Holmes .05 .02
- ❑ 125 Ernie Jones .05 .02
- ❑ 126 Michael Carter .05 .02
- ❑ 127 Reggie Cobb .05 .02
- ❑ 128 Esera Tuaolo .05 .02
- ❑ 129 Wilber Marshall .05 .02
- ❑ 130 Mike Munchak .05 .02
- ❑ 131 Cortez Kennedy .10 .05
- ❑ 132 Lamar Lathon .05 .02
- ❑ 133 Todd Lyght .05 .02

- ❑ 134 Jeff Feagles .05 .02
- ❑ 135 Burt Grossman .05 .02
- ❑ 136 Mike Cofer .05 .02
- ❑ 137 Frank Warren .05 .02
- ❑ 138 Jarvis Williams .05 .02
- ❑ 139 Eddie Brown .05 .02
- ❑ 140 John Elliott .05 .02
- ❑ 141 Jim Everett .10 .05
- ❑ 142 Hardy Nickerson .10 .05
- ❑ 143 Eddie Murray .05 .02
- ❑ 144 Andre Tippett .05 .02
- ❑ 145 Heath Sherman .05 .02
- ❑ 146 Ronnie Harmon .05 .02
- ❑ 147 Eric Metcalf .10 .05
- ❑ 148 Tony Martin .25 .11
- ❑ 149 Chris Burkett .05 .02
- ❑ 150 Andre Waters .05 .02
- ❑ 151 Ray Donaldson .05 .02
- ❑ 152 Paul Gruber .05 .02
- ❑ 153 Chris Singleton .05 .02
- ❑ 154 Clarence Kay .05 .02
- ❑ 155 Ernest Givins .10 .05
- ❑ 156 Eric Hill .05 .02
- ❑ 157 Jesse Sapolu .05 .02
- ❑ 158 Jack Del Rio .05 .02
- ❑ 159 Erric Pegram .10 .05
- ❑ 160 Joey Browner .05 .02
- ❑ 161 Marcus Allen .25 .11
- ❑ 162 Eric Moten .05 .02
- ❑ 163 Donnell Thompson .05 .02
- ❑ 164 Chuck Cecil .05 .02
- ❑ 165 Matt Millen .10 .05
- ❑ 166 Barry Foster .10 .05
- ❑ 167 Kent Hull .05 .02
- ❑ 168 Tony Jones .05 .02
- ❑ 169 Mike Prior .05 .02
- ❑ 170 Neal Anderson .05 .02
- ❑ 171 Roger Craig .10 .05
- ❑ 172 Felix Wright .05 .02
- ❑ 173 James Francis .05 .02
- ❑ 174 Eugene Lockhart .05 .02
- ❑ 175 Dalton Hilliard .05 .02
- ❑ 176 Nick Lowery .05 .02
- ❑ 177 Tim McKyer .05 .02
- ❑ 178 Lorenzo White .05 .02
- ❑ 179 Jeff Hostetler .10 .05
- ❑ 180 Jackie Harris RC .10 .05
- ❑ 181 Ken Norton .25 .11
- ❑ 182 Flipper Anderson .05 .02
- ❑ 183 Don Warren .05 .02
- ❑ 184 Brad Baxter .05 .02
- ❑ 185 John Taylor .10 .05
- ❑ 186 Harold Green .05 .02
- ❑ 187 James Washington .05 .02
- ❑ 188 Aaron Craver .05 .02
- ❑ 189 Mike Merriweather .05 .02
- ❑ 190 Gary Clark .25 .11
- ❑ 191 Vince Buck .05 .02
- ❑ 192 Cleveland Gary .05 .02
- ❑ 193 Dan Saleaumua .05 .02
- ❑ 194 Gary Zimmerman .05 .02
- ❑ 195 Richmond Webb .05 .02
- ❑ 196 Gary Plummer .05 .02
- ❑ 197 Willie Green .05 .02
- ❑ 198 Chris Warren .25 .11
- ❑ 199 Mike Pritchard .10 .05
- ❑ 200 Art Monk .10 .05
- ❑ 201 Matt Stover .05 .02
- ❑ 202 Tim Grunhard .05 .02
- ❑ 203 Mervyn Fernandez .05 .02
- ❑ 204 Mark Jackson .05 .02
- ❑ 205 Freddie Joe Nunn .05 .02
- ❑ 206 Stan Thomas .05 .02
- ❑ 207 Keith McKeller .05 .02
- ❑ 208 Jeff Lageman .05 .02
- ❑ 209 Kenny Walker .05 .02
- ❑ 210 Dave Krieg .10 .05
- ❑ 211 Dean Biasucci .05 .02
- ❑ 212 Herman Moore 1.25 .55
- ❑ 213 Jon Vaughn .05 .02
- ❑ 214 Howard Cross .05 .02
- ❑ 215 Greg Davis .05 .02
- ❑ 216 Bubby Brister .05 .02
- ❑ 217 John Kasay .05 .02
- ❑ 218 Ron Hall .05 .02
- ❑ 219 Mo Lewis .05 .02
- ❑ 220 Eric Green .05 .02
- ❑ 221 Scott Case .05 .02
- ❑ 222 Sean Jones .10 .05
- ❑ 223 Winston Moss .05 .02
- ❑ 224 Reggie Langhorne .05 .02
- ❑ 225 Greg Lewis .05 .02
- ❑ 226 Todd McNair .05 .02
- ❑ 227 Rod Bernstine .05 .02
- ❑ 228 Joe Jacoby .05 .02
- ❑ 229 Brad Muster .05 .02
- ❑ 230 Nick Bell .05 .02
- ❑ 231 Terry Allen .25 .11
- ❑ 232 Cliff Odom .05 .02
- ❑ 233 Brian Hansen .05 .02
- ❑ 234 William Fuller .10 .05
- ❑ 235 Issiac Holt .05 .02
- ❑ 236 Dexter Carter .05 .02
- ❑ 237 Gene Atkins .05 .02
- ❑ 238 Pat Beach .05 .02
- ❑ 239 Tim McGee .05 .02
- ❑ 240 Dermontti Dawson .05 .02
- ❑ 241 Dan Fike .05 .02
- ❑ 242 Don Beebe .05 .02
- ❑ 243 Jeff Bostic .05 .02
- ❑ 244 Mark Collins .05 .02
- ❑ 245 Steve Sewell .05 .02
- ❑ 246 Steve Walsh .05 .02
- ❑ 247 Erik Kramer .10 .05
- ❑ 248 Scott Norwood .05 .02
- ❑ 249 Jesse Solomon .05 .02
- ❑ 250 Jerry Ball .05 .02
- ❑ 251 Eugene Daniel .05 .02
- ❑ 252 Michael Stewart .05 .02
- ❑ 253 Fred Barnett .25 .11
- ❑ 254 Rodney Holman .05 .02
- ❑ 255 Stephen Baker .05 .02
- ❑ 256 Don Griffin .05 .02
- ❑ 257 Will Wolford .05 .02
- ❑ 258 Perry Kemp .05 .02
- ❑ 259 Leonard Russell .10 .05
- ❑ 260 Jeff Gossett .05 .02
- ❑ 261 Dwayne Harper .05 .02
- ❑ 262 Vinny Testaverde .10 .05
- ❑ 263 Maurice Hurst .05 .02
- ❑ 264 Tony Casillas .05 .02
- ❑ 265 Louis Oliver .05 .02
- ❑ 266 Jim Morrissey .05 .02
- ❑ 267 Kenneth Davis .05 .02
- ❑ 268 John Alt .05 .02
- ❑ 269 Michael Zordich RC .05 .02
- ❑ 270 Brian Brennan .05 .02
- ❑ 271 Greg Kragen .05 .02
- ❑ 272 Andre Collins .05 .02
- ❑ 273 Dave Meggett .10 .05
- ❑ 274 Scott Fulhage .05 .02
- ❑ 275 Tony Zendejas .05 .02
- ❑ 276 Herschel Walker .10 .05
- ❑ 277 Keith Henderson .05 .02
- ❑ 278 Johnny Bailey .05 .02
- ❑ 279 Vince Newsome .05 .02
- ❑ 280 Chris Hinton .05 .02
- ❑ 281 Robert Blackmon .05 .02
- ❑ 282 James Hasty .05 .02
- ❑ 283 John Offerdahl .05 .02
- ❑ 284 Wesley Carroll .05 .02
- ❑ 285 Lomas Brown .05 .02
- ❑ 286 Neil O'Donnell .25 .11
- ❑ 287 Kevin Porter .05 .02
- ❑ 288 Lionel Washington .05 .02
- ❑ 289 Carlton Bailey RC .10 .05
- ❑ 290 Leonard Marshall .05 .02
- ❑ 291 John Carney .05 .02
- ❑ 292 Bubba McDowell .05 .02
- ❑ 293 Nate Newton .10 .05
- ❑ 294 Dave Waymer .05 .02
- ❑ 295 Rob Moore .10 .05
- ❑ 296 Earnest Byner .05 .02
- ❑ 297 Jason Staurovsky .05 .02
- ❑ 298 Keith McCants .05 .02
- ❑ 299 Floyd Turner .05 .02
- ❑ 300 Steve Jordan .05 .02
- ❑ 301 Nate Odomes .05 .02
- ❑ 302 Gerald Riggs .05 .02
- ❑ 303 Marvin Washington .05 .02
- ❑ 304 Anthony Thompson .05 .02
- ❑ 305 Steve DeBerg .05 .02
- ❑ 306 Jim Harbaugh .25 .11
- ❑ 307 Larry Brown DB .05 .02
- ❑ 308 Roger Ruzek .05 .02
- ❑ 309 Jessie Tuggle .05 .02
- ❑ 310 Al Smith .05 .02
- ❑ 311 Mark Kelso .05 .02
- ❑ 312 Lawrence Dawsey .10 .05
- ❑ 313 Steve Bono RC .25 .11
- ❑ 314 Greg Lloyd .25 .11
- ❑ 315 Steve Wisniewski .05 .02
- ❑ 316 Gill Fenerty .05 .02
- ❑ 317 Mark Stepnoski .10 .05
- ❑ 318 Derek Russell .05 .02
- ❑ 319 Chris Martin .05 .02
- ❑ 320 Shaun Gayle .05 .02
- ❑ 321 Bob Golic .05 .02
- ❑ 322 Larry Kelm .05 .02
- ❑ 323 Mike Brim RC .05 .02
- ❑ 324 Tommy Kane .05 .02
- ❑ 325 Mark Schlereth RC .05 .02
- ❑ 326 Ray Childress .05 .02
- ❑ 327 Richard Brown RC .05 .02
- ❑ 328 Vincent Brown .05 .02
- ❑ 329 Mike Farr UER .05 .02
  (Back of card refers to him as Mel)
- ❑ 330 Eric Swann .10 .05
- ❑ 331 Bill Fralic .05 .02
- ❑ 332 Rodney Peete .10 .05
- ❑ 333 Jerry Gray .05 .02
- ❑ 334 Ray Berry .05 .02
- ❑ 335 Dennis Smith .05 .02
- ❑ 336 Jeff Herrod .05 .02
- ❑ 337 Tony Mandarich .05 .02
- ❑ 338 Matt Bahr .05 .02
- ❑ 339 Mike Saxon .05 .02
- ❑ 340 Bruce Matthews .05 .02
- ❑ 341 Rickey Jackson .05 .02
- ❑ 342 Eric Allen .05 .02
- ❑ 343 Lonnie Young .05 .02
- ❑ 344 Steve McMichael .10 .05
- ❑ 345 Willie Gault .10 .05
- ❑ 346 Barry Word .05 .02
- ❑ 347 Rich Camarillo .05 .02
- ❑ 348 Bill Romanowski .05 .02
- ❑ 349 Jim Lachey .05 .02
- ❑ 350 Jim Ritcher .05 .02
- ❑ 351 Irving Fryar .10 .05
- ❑ 352 Gary Anderson K .05 .02
- ❑ 353 Henry Rolling .05 .02
- ❑ 354 Mark Bortz .05 .02
- ❑ 355 Mark Clayton .10 .05
- ❑ 356 Keith Woodside .05 .02
- ❑ 357 Jonathan Hayes .05 .02
- ❑ 358 Derrick Fenner .05 .02
- ❑ 359 Keith Byars .05 .02
- ❑ 360 Drew Hill .05 .02
- ❑ 361 Harris Barton .05 .02
- ❑ 362 John Kidd .05 .02
- ❑ 363 Aeneas Williams .10 .05
- ❑ 364 Brian Washington .05 .02
- ❑ 365 John Stephens .05 .02
- ❑ 366 Norm Johnson .05 .02
- ❑ 367 Darryl Henley .05 .02
- ❑ 368 William White .05 .02
- ❑ 369 Mark Murphy .05 .02
- ❑ 370 Myron Guyton .05 .02
- ❑ 371 Leon Seals .05 .02
- ❑ 372 Rich Gannon .05 .02
- ❑ 373 Toi Cook .05 .02
- ❑ 374 Anthony Johnson .10 .05
- ❑ 375 Rod Woodson .25 .11
- ❑ 376 Alexander Wright .05 .02
- ❑ 377 Kevin Butler .05 .02
- ❑ 378 Neil Smith .25 .11
- ❑ 379 Gary Anderson RB .05 .02
- ❑ 380 Reggie Roby .05 .02
- ❑ 381 Jeff Bryant .05 .02
- ❑ 382 Ray Crockett .05 .02
- ❑ 383 Richard Johnson .05 .02
- ❑ 384 Hassan Jones .05 .02
- ❑ 385 Karl Mecklenburg .05 .02
- ❑ 386 Jeff Jaeger .05 .02
- ❑ 387 Keith Willis .05 .02
- ❑ 388 Phil Simms .10 .05
- ❑ 389 Kevin Ross .05 .02

	Mint	Nrmt
❑ 390 Chris Miller	.10	.05
❑ 391 Brian Noble	.05	.02
❑ 392 Jamie Dukes RC	.05	.02
❑ 393 George Jamison	.05	.02
❑ 394 Rickey Dixon	.05	.02
❑ 395 Carl Lee	.05	.02
❑ 396 Jon Hand	.05	.02
❑ 397 Kirby Jackson	.05	.02
❑ 398 Pat Terrell	.05	.02
❑ 399 Howie Long	.10	.05
❑ 400 Michael Young	.05	.02
❑ 401 Keith Sims	.05	.02
❑ 402 Tommy Barnhardt	.05	.02
❑ 403 Greg McMurtry	.05	.02
❑ 404 Keith Van Horne	.05	.02
❑ 405 Seth Joyner	.10	.05
❑ 406 Jim Jeffcoat	.05	.02
❑ 407 Courtney Hall	.05	.02
❑ 408 Tony Covington	.05	.02
❑ 409 Jacob Green	.05	.02
❑ 410 Charles Haley	.10	.05
❑ 411 Darryl Talley	.05	.02
❑ 412 Jeff Cross	.05	.02
❑ 413 John Elway	2.00	.90
❑ 414 Donald Evans	.05	.02
❑ 415 Jackie Slater	.05	.02
❑ 416 John Friesz	.10	.05
❑ 417 Anthony Smith	.05	.02
❑ 418 Gill Byrd	.05	.02
❑ 419 Willie Drewrey	.05	.02
❑ 420 Jay Hilgenberg	.05	.02
❑ 421 David Treadwell	.05	.02
❑ 422 Curtis Duncan	.05	.02
❑ 423 Sammie Smith	.05	.02
❑ 424 Henry Thomas	.05	.02
❑ 425 James Lofton	.10	.05
❑ 426 Fred Marion	.05	.02
❑ 427 Bryce Paup	.25	.11
❑ 428 Michael Timpson RC	.10	.05
❑ 429 Reyna Thompson	.05	.02
❑ 430 Mike Kenn	.05	.02
❑ 431 Bill Maas	.05	.02
❑ 432 Quinn Early	.10	.05
❑ 433 Everson Walls	.05	.02
❑ 434 Jimmie Jones	.05	.02
❑ 435 Dwight Stone	.05	.02
❑ 436 Harry Colon	.05	.02
❑ 437 Don Mosebar	.05	.02
❑ 438 Calvin Williams	.10	.05
❑ 439 Tom Tupa	.05	.02
❑ 440 Darrell Green	.05	.02
❑ 441 Eric Thomas	.05	.02
❑ 442 Terry Wooden	.05	.02
❑ 443 Brett Perriman	.25	.11
❑ 444 Todd Marinovich	.05	.02
❑ 445 Jim Breech	.05	.02
❑ 446 Eddie Anderson	.05	.02
❑ 447 Jay Schroeder	.05	.02
❑ 448 William Roberts	.05	.02
❑ 449 Brad Edwards	.05	.02
❑ 450 Tunch Ilkin	.05	.02
❑ 451 Ivy Joe Hunter RC	.05	.02
❑ 452 Robert Clark	.05	.02
❑ 453 Tim Barnett	.05	.02
❑ 454 Jarrod Bunch	.05	.02
❑ 455 Tim Harris	.05	.02
❑ 456 James Brooks	.10	.05
❑ 457 Trace Armstrong	.05	.02
❑ 458 Michael Brooks	.05	.02
❑ 459 Andy Heck	.05	.02
❑ 460 Greg Jackson	.05	.02
❑ 461 Vance Johnson	.05	.02
❑ 462 Kirk Lowdermilk	.05	.02
❑ 463 Erik McMillan	.05	.02
❑ 464 Scott Mersereau	.05	.02
❑ 465 Jeff Wright	.05	.02
❑ 466 Mike Tomczak	.05	.02
❑ 467 David Alexander	.05	.02
❑ 468 Bryan Millard	.05	.02
❑ 469 John Randle	.10	.05
❑ 470 Joel Hilgenberg	.05	.02
❑ 471 Bennie Thompson RC	.05	.02
❑ 472 Freeman McNeil	.05	.02
❑ 473 Terry Orr RC	.05	.02
❑ 474 Mike Horan	.05	.02
❑ 475 Leroy Hoard	.10	.05
❑ 476 Patrick Rowe DRAFT RC DRAFT	.05	.02
❑ 477 Siran Stacy DRAFT RC DRAFT	.05	.02
❑ 478 Amp Lee DRAFT RC DRAFT	.05	.02
❑ 479 Eddie Blake DRAFT RC DRAFT	.05	.02
❑ 480 Joe Bowden DRAFT RC DRAFT	.05	.02
❑ 481 Rod Milstead DRAFT RC DRAFT	.05	.02
❑ 482 Keith Hamilton DRAFT RC DRAFT	.05	.02
❑ 483 Darryl Williams DRAFT RC DRAFT	.05	.02
❑ 484 Robert Porcher DRAFT RC DRAFT	.10	.05
❑ 485 Ed Cunningham DRAFT RC DRAFT	.05	.02
❑ 486 Chris Mims DRAFT RC DRAFT	.10	.05
❑ 487 Chris Hakel DRAFT RC DRAFT	.05	.02
❑ 488 Jimmy Smith DRAFT RC DRAFT	3.00	1.35
❑ 489 Todd Harrison DRAFT RC DRAFT	.05	.02
❑ 490 Edgar Bennett DRAFT RC DRAFT	.50	.23
❑ 491 Dexter McNabb DRAFT RC DRAFT	.05	.02
❑ 492 Leon Searcy DRAFT RC DRAFT	.10	.05
❑ 493 Tommy Vardell DRAFT RC DRAFT	.10	.05
❑ 494 Terrell Buckley DRAFT RC DRAFT	.05	.02
❑ 495 Kevin Turner DRAFT RC DRAFT	.05	.02
❑ 496 Russ Campbell DRAFT RC DRAFT	.05	.02
❑ 497 Torrance Small DRAFT RC DRAFT	.10	.05
❑ 498 Nate Turner DRAFT RC DRAFT	.05	.02
❑ 499 Cornelius Benton DRAFT RC DRAFT	.10	.05
❑ 500 Matt Elliott DRAFT RC DRAFT	.05	.02
❑ 501 Robert Stewart DRAFT RC DRAFT	.05	.02
❑ 502 M.Shamsid-Deen RC DRAFT	.05	.02
❑ 503 George Williams DRAFT RC DRAFT	.05	.02
❑ 504 Pumpy Tudors DRAFT RC DRAFT	.05	.02
❑ 505 Matt LaBounty DRAFT RC DRAFT	.05	.02
❑ 506 Darryl Hardy DRAFT RC DRAFT	.05	.02
❑ 507 Derrick Moore DRAFT RC DRAFT	.10	.05
❑ 508 Willie Clay DRAFT RC DRAFT	.05	.02
❑ 509 Bob Whitfield DRAFT RC DRAFT	.05	.02
❑ 510 Ricardo McDonald DRAFT RC DRAFT	.05	.02
❑ 511 Carlos Huerta DRAFT	.05	.02
❑ 512 Selwyn Jones DRAFT RC DRAFT	.05	.02
❑ 513 Steve Gordon DRAFT RC DRAFT	.05	.02
❑ 514 Bob Meeks DRAFT RC DRAFT	.05	.02
❑ 515 Bennie Blades CC	.05	.02
❑ 516 Andre Waters CC	.05	.02
❑ 517 Bubba McDowell CC	.05	.02
❑ 518 Kevin Porter CC	.05	.02
❑ 519 Carnell Lake CC	.05	.02
❑ 520 Leonard Russell ROY	.10	.05
❑ 521 Mike Croel ROY	.05	.02
❑ 522 Lawrence Dawsey ROY	.05	.02
❑ 523 Moe Gardner ROY	.05	.02
❑ 524 Steve Broussard LBM	.05	.02
❑ 525 Dave Meggett LBM	.05	.02
❑ 526 Darrell Green LBM	.05	.02
❑ 527 Tony Jones LBM	.05	.02
❑ 528 Barry Sanders LBM	1.25	.55
❑ 529 Pat Swilling SA	.05	.02
❑ 530 Reggie White SA	.10	.05
❑ 531 William Fuller SA	.05	.02
❑ 532 Simon Fletcher SA	.05	.02
❑ 533 Derrick Thomas SA	.10	.05
❑ 534 Mark Rypien MOY	.05	.02
❑ 535 John Mackey HOF	.05	.02
❑ 536 John Riggins HOF	.10	.05
❑ 537 Lem Barney HOF	.05	.02
❑ 538 Shawn McCarthy 90 RC	.05	.02
❑ 539 Al Edwards 90	.05	.02
❑ 540 Alexander Wright 90	.05	.02
❑ 541 Ray Crockett 90	.05	.02
❑ 542 Steve Young 90 and John Taylor 90	.25	.11
❑ 543 Nate Lewis 90	.05	.02
❑ 544 Dexter Carter 90	.05	.02
❑ 545 Reggie Rutland 90	.05	.02
❑ 546 Jon Vaughn 90	.05	.02
❑ 547 Chris Martin 90	.05	.02
❑ 548 Warren Moon HL	.10	.05
❑ 549 Super Bowl Highlights	.05	.02
❑ 550 Robb Thomas	.05	.02
❑ NNO Dick Butkus Promo	10.00	4.50

1992 Score Dream Team

	MINT	NRMT
COMPLETE SET (25)	60.00	27.00
COMMON CARD (1-25)	1.50	.70
SEMISTARS	2.50	1.10
UNLISTED STARS	4.00	1.80

RANDOM INSERTS IN FOIL PACKS

	Mint	Nrmt
❑ 1 Michael Irvin	4.00	1.80
❑ 2 Haywood Jeffires	2.50	1.10
❑ 3 Emmitt Smith	15.00	6.75
❑ 4 Barry Sanders	15.00	6.75
❑ 5 Marv Cook	1.50	.70
❑ 6 Bart Oates	1.50	.70
❑ 7 Steve Wisniewski	1.50	.70
❑ 8 Randall McDaniel	1.50	.70
❑ 9 Jim Lachey	1.50	.70
❑ 10 Lomas Brown	1.50	.70
❑ 11 Reggie White	4.00	1.80
❑ 12 Clyde Simmons	1.50	.70
❑ 13 Jerome Brown	1.50	.70
❑ 14 Seth Joyner	2.50	1.10
❑ 15 Darryl Talley	1.50	.70
❑ 16 Karl Mecklenburg	1.50	.70
❑ 17 Sam Mills	2.50	1.10
❑ 18 Darrell Green	2.50	1.10
❑ 19 Steve Atwater	1.50	.70
❑ 20 Mark Carrier DB	2.50	1.10
❑ 21 Jeff Gossett UER (Card says Rams, should say Raiders)	1.50	.70
❑ 22 Chip Lohmiller	1.50	.70
❑ 23 Mel Gray	2.50	1.10
❑ 24 Steve Tasker	1.50	.70
❑ 25 Mark Rypien	1.50	.70

1992 Score Gridiron Stars

	MINT	NRMT
COMPLETE SET (45)	8.00	3.60
THREE PER JUMBO PACK		
❑ 1 Barry Sanders	2.50	1.10
❑ 2 Mike Croel	.05	.02
❑ 3 Thurman Thomas	.25	.11
❑ 4 Lawrence Dawsey	.10	.05
❑ 5 Brad Baxter	.05	.02
❑ 6 Moe Gardner	.05	.02
❑ 7 Emmitt Smith	2.50	1.10
❑ 8 Sammie Smith	.05	.02
❑ 9 Rodney Hampton	.25	.11
❑ 10 Mark Carrier DB	.05	.02
❑ 11 Mo Lewis	.05	.02
❑ 12 Andre Rison	.10	.05
❑ 13 Eric Green	.05	.02
❑ 14 Richmond Webb	.05	.02

❑ 15 Johnny Bailey .05 .02
❑ 16 Mike Pritchard .10 .05
❑ 17 John Friesz .10 .05
❑ 18 Leonard Russell .10 .05
❑ 19 Derrick Thomas .25 .11
❑ 20 Ken Harvey .05 .02
❑ 21 Fred Barnett .25 .11
❑ 22 Aeneas Williams .10 .05
❑ 23 Marion Butts .05 .02
❑ 24 Harold Green .05 .02
❑ 25 Michael Irvin .25 .11
❑ 26 Dan Owens .05 .02
❑ 27 Curtis Duncan .05 .02
❑ 28 Rodney Peete .10 .05
❑ 29 Brian Blades .10 .05
❑ 30 Marv Cook .05 .02
❑ 31 Burt Grossman .05 .02
❑ 32 Michael Haynes .10 .05
❑ 33 Bennie Blades .05 .02
❑ 34 Cornelius Bennett .10 .05
❑ 35 Louis Oliver .05 .02
❑ 36 Rod Woodson .25 .11
❑ 37 Steve Wisniewski .05 .02
❑ 38 Neil Smith .25 .11
❑ 39 Gaston Green .05 .02
❑ 40 Jeff Lageman .05 .02
❑ 41 Chip Lohmiller .05 .02
❑ 42 Tim McDonald .05 .02
❑ 43 John Elliott .05 .02
❑ 44 Steve Atwater .05 .02
❑ 45 Flipper Anderson .05 .02

1993 Score

	MINT	NRMT
COMPLETE SET (440)	16.00	7.25
COMMON CARD (1-440)	.05	.02
SEMISTARS	.10	.05
UNLISTED STARS	.25	.11

ONE BUTKUS AUTO PER HOBBY CASE

❑ 1 Barry Sanders 1.50 .70
❑ 2 Moe Gardner .05 .02
❑ 3 Ricky Watters .25 .11
❑ 4 Todd Lyght .05 .02
❑ 5 Rodney Hampton .25 .11
❑ 6 Curtis Duncan .05 .02
❑ 7 Barry Word .05 .02
❑ 8 Reggie Cobb .05 .02
❑ 9 Mike Kenn .05 .02
❑ 10 Michael Irvin .25 .11
❑ 11 Bryan Cox .05 .02
❑ 12 Chris Doleman .05 .02
❑ 13 Rod Woodson .25 .11
❑ 14 Emmitt Smith 1.50 .70
❑ 15 Pete Stoyanovich .05 .02
❑ 16 Steve Young .75 .35
❑ 17 Randall McDaniel .05 .02
❑ 18 Cortez Kennedy .10 .05
❑ 19 Mel Gray .10 .05
❑ 20 Barry Foster .10 .05
❑ 21 Tim Brown .25 .11
❑ 22 Todd McNair .05 .02
❑ 23 Anthony Johnson .10 .05
❑ 24 Nate Odomes .05 .02
❑ 25 Brett Favre 2.00 .90
❑ 26 Jack Del Rio .05 .02
❑ 27 Terry McDaniel .05 .02
❑ 28 Haywood Jeffires .10 .05
❑ 29 Jay Novacek .10 .05
❑ 30 Wilber Marshall .05 .02
❑ 31 Richmond Webb .05 .02
❑ 32 Steve Atwater .05 .02
❑ 33 James Lofton .10 .05
❑ 34 Harold Green .05 .02
❑ 35 Eric Metcalf .10 .05
❑ 36 Bruce Matthews .05 .02
❑ 37 Albert Lewis .05 .02
❑ 38 Jeff Herrod .05 .02
❑ 39 Vince Workman .05 .02
❑ 40 John Elway 1.50 .70
❑ 41 Brett Perriman .25 .11
❑ 42 Jon Vaughn .05 .02
❑ 43 Terry Allen .25 .11
❑ 44 Clyde Simmons .05 .02
❑ 45 Bennie Thompson .05 .02
❑ 46 Wendell Davis .05 .02
❑ 47 Bobby Hebert .05 .02
❑ 48 John Offerdahl .05 .02
❑ 49 Jeff Graham .10 .05
❑ 50 Steve Wisniewski .05 .02
❑ 51 Louis Oliver .05 .02
❑ 52 Rohn Stark .05 .02
❑ 53 Cleveland Gary .05 .02
❑ 54 John Randle .05 .02
❑ 55 Jim Everett .10 .05
❑ 56 Donnell Woolford .05 .02
❑ 57 Pepper Johnson .05 .02
❑ 58 Irving Fryar .10 .05
❑ 59 Greg Townsend .05 .02
❑ 60 Chris Burkett .05 .02
❑ 61 Johnny Johnson .05 .02
❑ 62 Ronnie Harmon .05 .02
❑ 63 Don Griffin .05 .02
❑ 64 Wayne Martin .05 .02
❑ 65 John L. Williams .05 .02
❑ 66 Brad Edwards .05 .02
❑ 67 Toi Cook .05 .02
❑ 68 Lawrence Dawsey .05 .02
❑ 69 Johnny Bailey .05 .02
❑ 70 Mike Brim .05 .02
❑ 71 Andre Rison .10 .05
❑ 72 Cornelius Bennett .10 .05
❑ 73 Brad Muster .05 .02
❑ 74 Broderick Thomas .05 .02
❑ 75 Tom Waddle .05 .02
❑ 76 Paul Gruber .05 .02
❑ 77 Jackie Harris .05 .02
❑ 78 Kenneth Davis .05 .02
❑ 79 Norm Johnson .05 .02
❑ 80 Jim Jeffcoat .05 .02
❑ 81 Chris Warren .10 .05
❑ 82 Greg Kragen .05 .02
❑ 83 Ricky Reynolds .05 .02
❑ 84 Hardy Nickerson .10 .05
❑ 85 Brian Mitchell .10 .05
❑ 86 Rufus Porter .05 .02
❑ 87 Greg Jackson .05 .02
❑ 88 Seth Joyner .05 .02
❑ 89 Tim Grunhard .05 .02
❑ 90 Tim Harris .05 .02
❑ 91 Sterling Sharpe .25 .11
❑ 92 Daniel Stubbs .05 .02
❑ 93 Rob Burnett .05 .02
❑ 94 Rich Camarillo .05 .02
❑ 95 Al Smith .05 .02
❑ 96 Thurman Thomas .25 .11
❑ 97 Morten Andersen .05 .02
❑ 98 Reggie White .25 .11
❑ 99 Gill Byrd .05 .02
❑ 100 Pierce Holt .05 .02
❑ 101 Tim McGee .05 .02
❑ 102 Rickey Jackson .05 .02
❑ 103 Vince Newsome .05 .02
❑ 104 Chris Spielman .10 .05
❑ 105 Tim McDonald .05 .02
❑ 106 James Francis .05 .02
❑ 107 Andre Tippett .05 .02
❑ 108 Sam Mills .05 .02
❑ 109 Hugh Millen .05 .02
❑ 110 Brad Baxter .05 .02
❑ 111 Ricky Sanders .05 .02
❑ 112 Marion Butts .05 .02
❑ 113 Fred Barnett .10 .05
❑ 114 Wade Wilson .05 .02
❑ 115 Dave Meggett .05 .02
❑ 116 Kevin Greene .25 .11
❑ 117 Reggie Langhorne .05 .02
❑ 118 Simon Fletcher .05 .02
❑ 119 Tommy Vardell .05 .02
❑ 120 Darion Conner .05 .02
❑ 121 Darren Lewis .05 .02
❑ 122 Charles Mann .05 .02
❑ 123 David Fulcher .05 .02
❑ 124 Tommy Kane .05 .02
❑ 125 Richard Brown .05 .02
❑ 126 Nate Lewis .05 .02
❑ 127 Tony Tolbert .05 .02
❑ 128 Greg Lloyd .25 .11
❑ 129 Herman Moore .50 .23
❑ 130 Robert Massey .05 .02
❑ 131 Chris Jacke .05 .02
❑ 132 Keith Byars .05 .02
❑ 133 William Fuller .05 .02
❑ 134 Rob Moore .10 .05
❑ 135 Duane Bickett .05 .02
❑ 136 Jarrod Bunch .05 .02
❑ 137 Ethan Horton .05 .02
❑ 138 Leonard Russell .10 .05
❑ 139 Darryl Henley .05 .02
❑ 140 Tony Bennett .05 .02
❑ 141 Harry Newsome .05 .02
❑ 142 Kelvin Martin .05 .02
❑ 143 Audray McMillian .05 .02
❑ 144 Chip Lohmiller .05 .02
❑ 145 Henry Jones .05 .02
❑ 146 Rod Bernstine .05 .02
❑ 147 Darryl Talley .05 .02
❑ 148 Clarence Verdin .05 .02
❑ 149 Derrick Thomas .25 .11
❑ 150 Raleigh McKenzie .05 .02
❑ 151 Phil Hansen .05 .02
❑ 152 Lin Elliott RC .05 .02
❑ 153 Chip Banks .05 .02
❑ 154 Shannon Sharpe .25 .11
❑ 155 David Williams .05 .02
❑ 156 Gaston Green .05 .02
❑ 157 Trace Armstrong .05 .02
❑ 158 Todd Scott .05 .02
❑ 159 Stan Humphries .25 .11
❑ 160 Christian Okoye .05 .02
❑ 161 Dennis Smith .05 .02
❑ 162 Derek Kennard .05 .02
❑ 163 Melvin Jenkins .05 .02
❑ 164 Tommy Barnhardt .05 .02
❑ 165 Eugene Robinson .05 .02
❑ 166 Tom Rathman .05 .02
❑ 167 Chris Chandler .10 .05
❑ 168 Steve Broussard .05 .02
❑ 169 Wymon Henderson .05 .02
❑ 170 Bryce Paup .25 .11
❑ 171 Kent Hull .05 .02
❑ 172 Willie Davis .25 .11
❑ 173 Richard Dent .10 .05
❑ 174 Rodney Peete .05 .02
❑ 175 Clay Matthews .10 .05
❑ 176 Erik Williams .05 .02
❑ 177 Mike Cofer .05 .02
❑ 178 Mark Kelso .05 .02
❑ 179 Kurt Gouveia .05 .02
❑ 180 Keith McCants .05 .02
❑ 181 Jim Arnold .05 .02
❑ 182 Sean Jones .05 .02
❑ 183 Chuck Cecil .05 .02
❑ 184 Mark Rypien .05 .02
❑ 185 William Perry .10 .05
❑ 186 Mark Jackson .05 .02
❑ 187 Jim Dombrowski .05 .02
❑ 188 Heath Sherman .05 .02
❑ 189 Bubba McDowell .05 .02
❑ 190 Fuad Reveiz .05 .02
❑ 191 Darren Perry .05 .02
❑ 192 Karl Mecklenburg .05 .02
❑ 193 Frank Reich .10 .05
❑ 194 Tony Casillas .05 .02
❑ 195 Jerry Ball .05 .02
❑ 196 Jessie Hester .05 .02
❑ 197 David Lang .05 .02
❑ 198 Sean Landeta .05 .02
❑ 199 Jerry Gray .05 .02
❑ 200 Mark Higgs .05 .02

	No.	Player	Mint	NrMt
❑	201	Bruce Armstrong	.05	.02
❑	202	Vaughan Johnson	.05	.02
❑	203	Calvin Williams	.10	.05
❑	204	Leonard Marshall	.05	.02
❑	205	Mike Munchak	.05	.02
❑	206	Kevin Ross	.05	.02
❑	207	Daryl Johnston	.25	.11
❑	208	Jay Schroeder	.05	.02
❑	209	Mo Lewis	.05	.02
❑	210	Carlton Haselrig	.05	.02
❑	211	Cris Carter	.50	.23
❑	212	Marv Cook	.05	.02
❑	213	Mark Duper	.05	.02
❑	214	Jackie Slater	.05	.02
❑	215	Mike Prior	.05	.02
❑	216	Warren Moon	.25	.11
❑	217	Mike Saxon	.05	.02
❑	218	Derrick Fenner	.05	.02
❑	219	Brian Washington	.05	.02
❑	220	Jessie Tuggle	.05	.02
❑	221	Jeff Hostetler	.10	.05
❑	222	Deion Sanders	.50	.23
❑	223	Neal Anderson	.05	.02
❑	224	Kevin Mack	.05	.02
❑	225	Tommy Maddox	.05	.02
❑	226	Neil Smith	.25	.11
❑	227	Ronnie Lott	.10	.05
❑	228	Flipper Anderson	.05	.02
❑	229	Keith Jackson	.10	.05
❑	230	Pat Swilling	.05	.02
❑	231	Carl Banks	.05	.02
❑	232	Eric Allen	.05	.02
❑	233	Randal Hill	.05	.02
❑	234	Burt Grossman	.05	.02
❑	235	Jerry Rice	1.00	.45
❑	236	Santana Dotson	.10	.05
❑	237	Andre Reed	.10	.05
❑	238	Troy Aikman	.75	.35
❑	239	Ray Childress	.05	.02
❑	240	Phil Simms	.10	.05
❑	241	Steve McMichael	.10	.05
❑	242	Browning Nagle	.05	.02
❑	243	Anthony Miller	.10	.05
❑	244	Earnest Byner	.05	.02
❑	245	Jay Hilgenberg	.05	.02
❑	246	Jeff George	.25	.11
❑	247	Marco Coleman	.05	.02
❑	248	Mark Carrier DB	.05	.02
❑	249	Howie Long	.10	.05
❑	250	Ed McCaffrey	.10	.05
❑	251	Jim Kelly	.25	.11
❑	252	Henry Ellard	.10	.05
❑	253	Joe Montana	1.50	.70
❑	254	Dale Carter	.05	.02
❑	255	Boomer Esiason	.10	.05
❑	256	Gary Clark	.10	.05
❑	257	Carl Pickens	.25	.11
❑	258	Dave Krieg	.10	.05
❑	259	Russell Maryland	.05	.02
❑	260	Randall Cunningham	.25	.11
❑	261	Leslie O'Neal	.10	.05
❑	262	Vinny Testaverde	.10	.05
❑	263	Ricky Ervins	.05	.02
❑	264	Chris Mims	.05	.02
❑	265	Dan Marino	1.50	.70
❑	266	Eric Martin	.05	.02
❑	267	Bruce Smith	.25	.11
❑	268	Jim Harbaugh	.25	.11
❑	269	Steve Emtman	.05	.02
❑	270	Ricky Proehl	.05	.02
❑	271	Vaughn Dunbar	.05	.02
❑	272	Junior Seau	.25	.11
❑	273	Sean Gilbert	.10	.05
❑	274	Jim Lachey	.05	.02
❑	275	Dalton Hilliard	.05	.02
❑	276	David Klingler	.05	.02
❑	277	Robert Jones	.05	.02
❑	278	David Treadwell	.05	.02
❑	279	Tracy Scroggins	.05	.02
❑	280	Terrell Buckley	.05	.02
❑	281	Quentin Coryatt	.10	.05
❑	282	Jason Hanson	.05	.02
❑	283	Shane Conlan	.05	.02
❑	284	Guy McIntyre	.05	.02
❑	285	Gary Zimmerman	.05	.02
❑	286	Marty Carter	.05	.02
❑	287	Jim Sweeney	.05	.02
❑	288	Arthur Marshall RC	.05	.02
❑	289	Eugene Chung	.05	.02
❑	290	Mike Pritchard	.10	.05
❑	291	Jim Ritcher	.05	.02
❑	292	Todd Marinovich	.05	.02
❑	293	Courtney Hall	.05	.02
❑	294	Mark Collins	.05	.02
❑	295	Troy Auzenne	.05	.02
❑	296	Aeneas Williams	.05	.02
❑	297	Andy Heck	.05	.02
❑	298	Shaun Gayle	.05	.02
❑	299	Kevin Fagan	.05	.02
❑	300	Carnell Lake	.05	.02
❑	301	Bernie Kosar	.10	.05
❑	302	Maurice Hurst	.05	.02
❑	303	Mike Merriweather	.05	.02
❑	304	Reggie Roby	.05	.02
❑	305	Darryl Williams	.05	.02
❑	306	Jerome Bettis RC	1.00	.45
❑	307	Curtis Conway RC	.50	.23
❑	308	Drew Bledsoe RC	3.00	1.35
❑	309	John Copeland RC	.10	.05
❑	310	Eric Curry RC	.05	.02
❑	311	Lincoln Kennedy RC	.05	.02
❑	312	Dan Williams RC	.05	.02
❑	313	Patrick Bates RC	.05	.02
❑	314	Tom Carter RC	.10	.05
❑	315	Garrison Hearst RC	1.00	.45
❑	316	Joel Hilgenberg	.05	.02
❑	317	Harris Barton	.05	.02
❑	318	Jeff Lageman	.05	.02
❑	319	Charles Mincy RC	.05	.02
❑	320	Ricardo McDonald	.05	.02
❑	321	Lorenzo White	.05	.02
❑	322	Troy Vincent	.05	.02
❑	323	Bennie Blades	.05	.02
❑	324	Dana Hall	.05	.02
❑	325	Ken Norton Jr.	.10	.05
❑	326	Will Wolford	.05	.02
❑	327	Neil O'Donnell	.25	.11
❑	328	Tracy Simien	.05	.02
❑	329	Darrell Green	.05	.02
❑	330	Kyle Clifton	.05	.02
❑	331	Elbert Shelley RC	.05	.02
❑	332	Jeff Wright	.05	.02
❑	333	Mike Johnson	.05	.02
❑	334	John Gesek	.05	.02
❑	335	Michael Brooks	.05	.02
❑	336	George Jamison	.05	.02
❑	337	Johnny Holland	.05	.02
❑	338	Lamar Lathon	.05	.02
❑	339	Bern Brostek	.05	.02
❑	340	Steve Jordan	.05	.02
❑	341	Gene Atkins	.05	.02
❑	342	Aaron Wallace	.05	.02
❑	343	Adrian Cooper	.05	.02
❑	344	Amp Lee	.05	.02
❑	345	Vincent Brown	.05	.02
❑	346	James Hasty	.05	.02
❑	347	Ron Hall	.05	.02
❑	348	Matt Elliott	.05	.02
❑	349	Tim Krumrie	.05	.02
❑	350	Mark Stepnoski	.05	.02
❑	351	Matt Stover	.05	.02
❑	352	James Washington	.05	.02
❑	353	Marc Spindler	.05	.02
❑	354	Frank Warren	.05	.02
❑	355	Vai Sikahema	.05	.02
❑	356	Dan Saleaumua	.05	.02
❑	357	Mark Clayton	.05	.02
❑	358	Brent Jones	.10	.05
❑	359	Andy Harmon RC	.10	.05
❑	360	Anthony Parker	.05	.02
❑	361	Chris Hinton	.05	.02
❑	362	Greg Montgomery	.05	.02
❑	363	Greg McMurtry	.05	.02
❑	364	Craig Heyward	.10	.05
❑	365	D.J. Johnson	.05	.02
❑	366	Bill Romanowski	.05	.02
❑	367	Steve Christie	.05	.02
❑	368	Art Monk	.10	.05
❑	369	Howard Ballard	.05	.02
❑	370	Andre Collins	.05	.02
❑	371	Alvin Harper	.10	.05
❑	372	Blaise Winter RC	.05	.02
❑	373	Al Del Greco	.05	.02
❑	374	Eric Green	.05	.02
❑	375	Chris Mohr	.05	.02
❑	376	Tom Newberry	.05	.02
❑	377	Cris Dishman	.05	.02
❑	378	Jumpy Geathers	.05	.02
❑	379	Don Mosebar	.05	.02
❑	380	Andre Ware	.05	.02
❑	381	Marvin Washington	.05	.02
❑	382	Bobby Humphrey	.05	.02
❑	383	Marc Logan	.05	.02
❑	384	Lomas Brown	.05	.02
❑	385	Steve Tasker	.10	.05
❑	386	Chris Miller	.10	.05
❑	387	Tony Paige	.05	.02
❑	388	Charles Haley	.10	.05
❑	389	Rich Moran	.05	.02
❑	390	Mike Sherrard	.05	.02
❑	391	Nick Lowery	.05	.02
❑	392	Henry Thomas	.05	.02
❑	393	Keith Sims	.05	.02
❑	394	Thomas Everett	.05	.02
❑	395	Steve Wallace	.05	.02
❑	396	John Carney	.05	.02
❑	397	Tim Johnson	.05	.02
❑	398	Jeff Gossett	.05	.02
❑	399	Anthony Smith	.05	.02
❑	400	Kelvin Pritchett	.05	.02
❑	401	Dermontti Dawson	.05	.02
❑	402	Alfred Williams	.05	.02
❑	403	Michael Haynes	.10	.05
❑	404	Bart Oates	.05	.02
❑	405	Ken Lanier	.05	.02
❑	406	Vencie Glenn	.05	.02
❑	407	John Taylor	.10	.05
❑	408	Nate Newton	.10	.05
❑	409	Mark Carrier WR	.10	.05
❑	410	Ken Harvey	.05	.02
❑	411	Troy Aikman SB	.40	.18
❑	412	Charles Haley SB	.05	.02
❑	413	Warren Moon DT Haywood Jeffires	.10	.05
❑	414	Henry Jones DT Mark Kelso	.05	.02
❑	415	Rickey Jackson DT Sam Mills	.05	.02
❑	416	Clyde Simmons DT Reggie White	.05	.02
❑	417	Dale Carter ROY	.05	.02
❑	418	Carl Pickens ROY	.25	.11
❑	419	Vaughn Dunbar ROY	.05	.02
❑	420	Santana Dotson ROY	.05	.02
❑	421	Steve Emtman 90	.05	.02
❑	422	Louis Oliver 90	.05	.02
❑	423	Carl Pickens 90	.25	.11
❑	424	Eddie Anderson 90	.05	.02
❑	425	Deion Sanders 90	.25	.11
❑	426	Jon Vaughn 90	.05	.02
❑	427	Darren Lewis 90	.05	.02
❑	428	Kevin Ross 90	.05	.02
❑	429	David Brandon 90	.05	.02
❑	430	Dave Meggett 90	.05	.02
❑	431	Jerry Rice HL	.50	.23
❑	432	Sterling Sharpe HL	.10	.05
❑	433	Art Monk HL	.05	.02
❑	434	James Lofton HL	.05	.02
❑	435	Lawrence Taylor	.10	.05
❑	436	Bill Walsh HOF RC	.10	.05
❑	437	Chuck Noll HOF	.10	.05
❑	438	Dan Fouts HOF	.05	.02
❑	439	Larry Little HOF	.05	.02
❑	440	Steve Young MOY	.40	.18
❑	NNO	Dick Butkus AUTO/3000	40.00	18.00

1993 Score Dream Team

	MINT	NRMT
COMPLETE SET (26)	25.00	11.00
ONE PER SUPER PACK		

			MINT	NRMT
❑	1	Steve Young	5.00	2.20
❑	2	Emmitt Smith	10.00	4.50
❑	3	Barry Foster	.60	.25
❑	4	Sterling Sharpe	1.50	.70
❑	5	Jerry Rice	6.00	2.70
❑	6	Keith Jackson	.60	.25

	MINT	NRMT
❑ 7 Steve Wallace	.30	.14
❑ 8 Richmond Webb	.30	.14
❑ 9 Guy McIntyre	.30	.14
❑ 10 Carlton Haselrig	.30	.14
❑ 11 Bruce Matthews	.30	.14
❑ 12 Morten Andersen	.30	.14
❑ 13 Rich Camarillo	.30	.14
❑ 14 Deion Sanders	3.00	1.35
❑ 15 Steve Tasker	.60	.25
❑ 16 Clyde Simmons	.30	.14
❑ 17 Reggie White	1.50	.70
❑ 18 Cortez Kennedy	.60	.25
❑ 19 Rod Woodson	1.50	.70
❑ 20 Terry McDaniel	.30	.14
❑ 21 Chuck Cecil	.30	.14
❑ 22 Steve Atwater	.30	.14
❑ 23 Bryan Cox	.30	.14
❑ 24 Derrick Thomas	1.50	.70
❑ 25 Wilber Marshall	.30	.14
❑ 26 Sam Mills	.30	.14

1993 Score Franchise

	MINT	NRMT
COMPLETE SET (28)	100.00	45.00
STATED ODDS 1:24		
❑ 1 Andre Rison	1.25	.55
❑ 2 Thurman Thomas	3.00	1.35
❑ 3 Richard Dent	1.25	.55
❑ 4 Harold Green	.60	.25
❑ 5 Eric Metcalf	1.25	.55
❑ 6 Emmitt Smith	20.00	9.00
❑ 7 John Elway	20.00	9.00
❑ 8 Barry Sanders	20.00	9.00
❑ 9 Sterling Sharpe	3.00	1.35
❑ 10 Warren Moon	3.00	1.35
❑ 11 Jeff Herrod	.60	.25
❑ 12 Derrick Thomas	3.00	1.35
❑ 13 Steve Wisniewski	.60	.25
❑ 14 Cleveland Gary	.60	.25
❑ 15 Dan Marino	20.00	9.00
❑ 16 Chris Doleman	.60	.25
❑ 17 Marv Cook	.60	.25
❑ 18 Rickey Jackson	.60	.25
❑ 19 Rodney Hampton	3.00	1.35
❑ 20 Jeff Lageman	.60	.25
❑ 21 Clyde Simmons	.60	.25
❑ 22 Rich Camarillo	.60	.25
❑ 23 Rod Woodson	3.00	1.35
❑ 24 Ronnie Harmon	.60	.25
❑ 25 Steve Young	10.00	4.50
❑ 26 Cortez Kennedy	1.25	.55
❑ 27 Reggie Cobb	.60	.25
❑ 28 Mark Rypien	.60	.25

1994 Score

	MINT	NRMT
COMPLETE SET (330)	15.00	6.75
COMMON CARD (1-330)	.05	.02
SEMISTARS	.10	.05
UNLISTED STARS	.25	.11
COMP.GOLD SET (330)	100.00	45.00
*GOLD STARS: 3X to 6X HI COLUMN		
*GOLD RCs: 1.5X to 3X HI		
ONE PER PACK		
❑ 1 Barry Sanders	1.50	.70
❑ 2 Troy Aikman	.75	.35
❑ 3 Sterling Sharpe	.10	.05
❑ 4 Deion Sanders	.50	.23
❑ 5 Bruce Smith	.25	.11
❑ 6 Eric Metcalf	.10	.05
❑ 7 John Elway	1.50	.70
❑ 8 Bruce Matthews	.05	.02
❑ 9 Rickey Jackson	.05	.02
❑ 10 Cortez Kennedy	.10	.05
❑ 11 Jerry Rice	.75	.35
❑ 12 Stanley Richard	.05	.02
❑ 13 Rod Woodson	.10	.05
❑ 14 Eric Swann	.10	.05
❑ 15 Eric Allen	.05	.02
❑ 16 Richard Dent	.10	.05
❑ 17 Carl Pickens	.25	.11
❑ 18 Rohn Stark	.05	.02
❑ 19 Marcus Allen	.25	.11
❑ 20 Steve Wisniewski	.05	.02
❑ 21 Jerome Bettis	.25	.11
❑ 22 Darrell Green	.05	.02
❑ 23 Lawrence Dawsey	.05	.02
❑ 24 Larry Centers	.25	.11
❑ 25 Steve Jordan	.05	.02
❑ 26 Johnny Johnson	.05	.02
❑ 27 Phil Simms	.10	.05
❑ 28 Bruce Armstrong	.05	.02
❑ 29 Willie Roaf	.05	.02
❑ 30 Andre Rison	.10	.05
❑ 31 Henry Jones	.05	.02
❑ 32 Warren Moon	.25	.11
❑ 33 Sean Gilbert	.05	.02
❑ 34 Ben Coates	.25	.11
❑ 35 Seth Joyner	.05	.02
❑ 36 Ronnie Harmon	.05	.02
❑ 37 Quentin Coryatt	.05	.02
❑ 38 Ricky Sanders	.05	.02
❑ 39 Gerald Williams	.05	.02
❑ 40 Emmitt Smith	1.00	.45
❑ 41 Jason Hanson	.05	.02
❑ 42 Kevin Smith	.05	.02
❑ 43 Irving Fryar	.10	.05
❑ 44 Boomer Esiason	.10	.05
❑ 45 Darryl Talley	.05	.02
❑ 46 Paul Gruber	.05	.02
❑ 47 Anthony Smith	.05	.02
❑ 48 John Copeland	.05	.02
❑ 49 Michael Jackson	.10	.05
❑ 50 Shannon Sharpe	.10	.05
❑ 51 Reggie White	.25	.11
❑ 52 Andre Collins	.05	.02
❑ 53 Jack Del Rio	.05	.02
❑ 54 John Elliott	.05	.02
❑ 55 Kevin Greene	.25	.11
❑ 56 Steve Young	.60	.25
❑ 57 Erric Pegram	.05	.02
❑ 58 Donnell Woolford	.05	.02
❑ 59 Darryl Williams	.05	.02
❑ 60 Michael Irvin	.25	.11
❑ 61 Mel Gray	.05	.02
❑ 62 Greg Montgomery	.05	.02
❑ 63 Neil Smith	.10	.05
❑ 64 Andy Harmon	.05	.02
❑ 65 Dan Marino	1.50	.70
❑ 66 Leonard Russell	.05	.02
❑ 67 Joe Montana	1.50	.70
❑ 68 John Taylor	.10	.05
❑ 69 Cris Dishman	.05	.02
❑ 70 Cornelius Bennett	.10	.05
❑ 71 Harold Green	.05	.02
❑ 72 Anthony Pleasant	.05	.02
❑ 73 Dennis Smith	.05	.02
❑ 74 Bryce Paup	.25	.11
❑ 75 Jeff George	.25	.11
❑ 76 Henry Ellard	.10	.05
❑ 77 Randall McDaniel	.05	.02
❑ 78 Derek Brown RBK	.05	.02
❑ 79 Johnny Mitchell	.05	.02
❑ 80 Leroy Thompson	.05	.02
❑ 81 Junior Seau	.10	.05
❑ 82 Kelvin Martin	.05	.02
❑ 83 Guy McIntyre	.05	.02
❑ 84 Elbert Shelley	.05	.02
❑ 85 Louis Oliver	.05	.02
❑ 86 Tommy Vardell	.05	.02
❑ 87 Jeff Herrod	.05	.02
❑ 88 Edgar Bennett	.25	.11
❑ 89 Reggie Langhorne	.05	.02
❑ 90 Terry Kirby	.25	.11
❑ 91 Marcus Robertson	.05	.02
❑ 92 Mark Collins	.05	.02
❑ 93 Calvin Williams	.10	.05
❑ 94 Barry Foster	.05	.02
❑ 95 Brent Jones	.10	.05
❑ 96 Reggie Cobb	.05	.02
❑ 97 Ray Childress	.05	.02
❑ 98 Chris Miller	.05	.02
❑ 99 John Carney	.05	.02
❑ 100 Ricky Proehl	.05	.02
❑ 101 Renaldo Turnbull	.05	.02
❑ 102 John Randle	.05	.02
❑ 103 Flipper Anderson	.05	.02
❑ 104 Scottie Graham RC	.10	.05
❑ 105 Webster Slaughter	.05	.02
❑ 106 Tyrone Hughes	.10	.05
❑ 107 Ken Norton Jr.	.10	.05
❑ 108 Jim Kelly	.25	.11
❑ 109 Michael Haynes	.10	.05
❑ 110 Mark Carrier DB	.05	.02
❑ 111 Eddie Murray	.05	.02
❑ 112 Glyn Milburn	.10	.05
❑ 113 Jackie Harris	.05	.02
❑ 114 Dean Biasucci	.05	.02
❑ 115 Tim Brown	.25	.11
❑ 116 Mark Higgs	.05	.02
❑ 117 Steve Emtman	.05	.02
❑ 118 Clay Matthews	.05	.02
❑ 119 Clyde Simmons	.05	.02
❑ 120 Howard Ballard	.05	.02
❑ 121 Ricky Watters	.25	.11
❑ 122 William Fuller	.05	.02
❑ 123 Robert Brooks	.25	.11
❑ 124 Brian Blades	.10	.05
❑ 125 Leslie O'Neal	.05	.02
❑ 126 Gary Clark	.10	.05
❑ 127 Jim Sweeney	.05	.02
❑ 128 Vaughan Johnson	.05	.02
❑ 129 Gary Brown	.05	.02
❑ 130 Todd Lyght	.05	.02
❑ 131 Nick Lowery	.05	.02
❑ 132 Ernest Givins	.10	.05
❑ 133 Lomas Brown	.05	.02
❑ 134 Craig Erickson	.05	.02
❑ 135 James Francis	.05	.02
❑ 136 Andre Reed	.10	.05
❑ 137 Jim Everett	.10	.05
❑ 138 Nate Odomes	.05	.02
❑ 139 Tom Waddle	.05	.02

❑ 140 Stevon Moore .05 .02
❑ 141 Rod Bernstine .05 .02
❑ 142 Brett Favre 1.50 .70
❑ 143 Roosevelt Potts .05 .02
❑ 144 Chester McGlockton .05 .02
❑ 145 LeRoy Butler .05 .02
❑ 146 Charles Haley .10 .05
❑ 147 Rodney Hampton .25 .11
❑ 148 George Teague .05 .02
❑ 149 Gary Anderson K .05 .02
❑ 150 Mark Stepnoski .05 .02
❑ 151 Courtney Hawkins .05 .02
❑ 152 Tim Grunhard .05 .02
❑ 153 David Klingler .05 .02
❑ 154 Erik Williams .05 .02
❑ 155 Herman Moore .25 .11
❑ 156 Daryl Johnston .10 .05
❑ 157 Chris Zorich .05 .02
❑ 158 Shane Conlan .05 .02
❑ 159 Santana Dotson .10 .05
❑ 160 Sam Mills .05 .02
❑ 161 Ronnie Lott .10 .05
❑ 162 Jesse Sapolu .05 .02
❑ 163 Marion Butts .05 .02
❑ 164 Eugene Robinson .05 .02
❑ 165 Mark Schlereth .05 .02
❑ 166 John L. Williams .05 .02
❑ 167 Anthony Miller .10 .05
❑ 168 Rich Camarillo .05 .02
❑ 169 Jeff Lageman .05 .02
❑ 170 Michael Brooks .05 .02
❑ 171 Scott Mitchell .25 .11
❑ 172 Duane Bickett .05 .02
❑ 173 Willie Davis .10 .05
❑ 174 Maurice Hurst .05 .02
❑ 175 Brett Perriman .10 .05
❑ 176 Jay Novacek .10 .05
❑ 177 Terry Allen .10 .05
❑ 178 Pete Metzelaars .05 .02
❑ 179 Erik Kramer .10 .05
❑ 180 Neal Anderson .05 .02
❑ 181 Ethan Horton .05 .02
❑ 182 Tony Bennett .05 .02
❑ 183 Gary Zimmerman .05 .02
❑ 184 Jeff Hostetler .10 .05
❑ 185 Jeff Cross .05 .02
❑ 186 Vincent Brown .05 .02
❑ 187 Herschel Walker .10 .05
❑ 188 Courtney Hall .05 .02
❑ 189 Norm Johnson .05 .02
❑ 190 Hardy Nickerson .10 .05
❑ 191 Greg Townsend .05 .02
❑ 192 Mike Munchak .05 .02
❑ 193 Dante Jones .05 .02
❑ 194 Vinny Testaverde .10 .05
❑ 195 Vance Johnson .05 .02
❑ 196 Chris Jacke .05 .02
❑ 197 Will Wolford .05 .02
❑ 198 Terry McDaniel .05 .02
❑ 199 Bryan Cox .05 .02
❑ 200 Nate Newton .05 .02
❑ 201 Keith Byars .05 .02
❑ 202 Neil O'Donnell .25 .11
❑ 203 Harris Barton .05 .02
❑ 204 Thurman Thomas .25 .11
❑ 205 Jeff Query .05 .02
❑ 206 Russell Maryland .05 .02
❑ 207 Pat Swilling .05 .02
❑ 208 Haywood Jeffires .10 .05
❑ 209 John Alt .05 .02
❑ 210 O.J. McDuffie .25 .11
❑ 211 Keith Sims .05 .02
❑ 212 Eric Martin .05 .02
❑ 213 Kyle Clifton .05 .02
❑ 214 Luis Sharpe .05 .02
❑ 215 Thomas Everett .05 .02
❑ 216 Chris Warren .10 .05
❑ 217 Chris Doleman .05 .02
❑ 218 Tony Jones .05 .02
❑ 219 Karl Mecklenburg .05 .02
❑ 220 Rob Moore .10 .05
❑ 221 Jessie Hester .05 .02
❑ 222 Jeff Jaeger .05 .02
❑ 223 Keith Jackson .05 .02
❑ 224 Mo Lewis .05 .02
❑ 225 Mike Horan .05 .02
❑ 226 Eric Green .05 .02
❑ 227 Jim Ritcher .05 .02
❑ 228 Eric Curry .05 .02
❑ 229 Stan Humphries .25 .11
❑ 230 Mike Johnson .05 .02
❑ 231 Alvin Harper .10 .05
❑ 232 Bennie Blades .05 .02
❑ 233 Cris Carter .50 .23
❑ 234 Morten Andersen .05 .02
❑ 235 Brian Washington .05 .02
❑ 236 Eric Hill .05 .02
❑ 237 Natrone Means .25 .11
❑ 238 Carlton Bailey .05 .02
❑ 239 Anthony Carter .10 .05
❑ 240 Jessie Tuggle .05 .02
❑ 241 Tim Irwin .05 .02
❑ 242 Mark Carrier WR .10 .05
❑ 243 Steve Atwater .05 .02
❑ 244 Sean Jones .05 .02
❑ 245 Bernie Kosar .10 .05
❑ 246 Richmond Webb .05 .02
❑ 247 Dave Meggett .05 .02
❑ 248 Vincent Brisby .25 .11
❑ 249 Fred Barnett .10 .05
❑ 250 Greg Lloyd .25 .11
❑ 251 Tim McDonald .05 .02
❑ 252 Mike Pritchard .05 .02
❑ 253 Greg Robinson .05 .02
❑ 254 Tony McGee .05 .02
❑ 255 Chris Spielman .10 .05
❑ 256 Keith Loneker RC .05 .02
❑ 257 Derrick Thomas .25 .11
❑ 258 Wayne Martin .05 .02
❑ 259 Art Monk .10 .05
❑ 260 Andy Heck .05 .02
❑ 261 Chip Lohmiller .05 .02
❑ 262 Simon Fletcher .05 .02
❑ 263 Ricky Reynolds .05 .02
❑ 264 Chris Hinton .05 .02
❑ 265 Ronald Moore .05 .02
❑ 266 Rocket Ismail .10 .05
❑ 267 Pete Stoyanovich .05 .02
❑ 268 Mark Jackson .05 .02
❑ 269 Randall Cunningham .25 .11
❑ 270 Dermontti Dawson .05 .02
❑ 271 Bill Romanowski .05 .02
❑ 272 Tim Johnson .05 .02
❑ 273 Steve Tasker .05 .02
❑ 274 Keith Hamilton .05 .02
❑ 275 Pierce Holt .05 .02
❑ 276 Heath Shuler RC .25 .11
❑ 277 Marshall Faulk RC 4.00 1.80
❑ 278 Charles Johnson RC .25 .11
❑ 279 Sam Adams RC .10 .05
❑ 280 Trev Alberts RC .10 .05
❑ 281 Derrick Alexander WR RC .50 .23
❑ 282 Bryant Young RC .25 .11
❑ 283 Greg Hill RC .50 .23
❑ 284 Darnay Scott RC .75 .35
❑ 285 Willie McGinest RC .25 .11
❑ 286 Thomas Randolph RC .05 .02
❑ 287 Errict Rhett RC 1.50 .70
❑ 288 Lamar Smith RC .25 .11
❑ 289 William Floyd RC .25 .11
❑ 290 Johnnie Morton RC .25 .11
❑ 291 Jamir Miller RC .05 .02
❑ 292 David Palmer RC .50 .23
❑ 293 Dan Wilkinson RC .10 .05
❑ 294 Trent Dilfer RC 1.50 .70
❑ 295 Antonio Langham RC .10 .05
❑ 296 Chuck Levy RC .05 .02
❑ 297 John Thierry RC .05 .02
❑ 298 Kevin Lee RC .05 .02
❑ 299 Aaron Glenn RC .10 .05
❑ 300 Charlie Garner RC 1.50 .70
❑ 301 Lonnie Johnson RC .05 .02
❑ 302 LeShon Johnson RC .10 .05
❑ 303 Thomas Lewis RC .10 .05
❑ 304 Ryan Yarborough RC .05 .02
❑ 305 Mario Bates RC .25 .11
❑ 306 Buffalo Bills TC .05 .02
❑ 307 Cincinnati Bengals TC .05 .02
❑ 308 Cleveland Browns TC .05 .02
❑ 309 Denver Broncos TC .05 .02
❑ 310 Houston Oilers TC .05 .02
❑ 311 Indianapolis Colts TC .05 .02
❑ 312 Kansas City Chiefs TC .05 .02
❑ 313 Los Angeles Raiders TC .05 .02
❑ 314 Miami Dolphins TC .05 .02
❑ 315 New England Patriots TC .05 .02
❑ 316 New York Jets TC .05 .02
❑ 317 Pittsburgh Steelers TC .05 .02
❑ 318 San Diego Charges TC .05 .02
❑ 319 Seattle Seahawks TC .05 .02
❑ 320 Garrison Hearst FF .25 .11
❑ 321 Drew Bledsoe FF 1.00 .45
❑ 322 Tyrone Hughes FF .10 .05
❑ 323 James Jett FF .05 .02
❑ 324 Tom Carter FF .05 .02
❑ 325 Reggie Brooks FF .05 .02
❑ 326 Dana Stubblefield FF .25 .11
❑ 327 Jerome Bettis FF .10 .05
❑ 328 Chris Slade FF .05 .02
❑ 329 Rick Mirer FF .25 .11
❑ 330 Emmitt Smith NFL MVP .50 .23

1994 Score Dream Team

	MINT	NRMT
COMPLETE SET (18)	100.00	45.00
STATED ODDS 1:72		

❑ DT1 Troy Aikman 15.00 6.75
❑ DT2 Steve Atwater 1.00 .45
❑ DT3 Cornelius Bennett 2.00 .90
❑ DT4 Tim Brown 5.00 2.20
❑ DT5 Michael Irvin 5.00 2.20
❑ DT6 Bruce Matthews 1.00 .45
❑ DT7 Eric Metcalf 2.00 .90
❑ DT8 Anthony Miller 2.00 .90
❑ DT9 Jerry Rice 15.00 6.75
❑ DT10 Andre Rison 2.00 .90
❑ DT11 Barry Sanders 30.00 13.50
❑ DT12 Deion Sanders 10.00 4.50
❑ DT13 Sterling Sharpe 2.00 .90
❑ DT14 Neil Smith 2.00 .90
❑ DT15 Derrick Thomas 5.00 2.20
❑ DT16 Thurman Thomas 5.00 2.20
❑ DT17 Rod Woodson 2.00 .90
❑ DT18 Steve Young 12.00 5.50

1994 Score Rookie Redemption

	MINT	NRMT
COMPLETE SET (10)	140.00	65.00
EXPIRED ROOK.RED.CARDS	.50	.23

TRADE CARD STATED ODDS 1:72

Card		
❑ 1 Heath Shuler	3.00	1.35
❑ 2 Trent Dilfer	20.00	9.00
❑ 3 Marshall Faulk	50.00	22.00
❑ 4 Charlie Garner	20.00	9.00
❑ 5 LeShon Johnson	1.25	.55
❑ 6 Charles Johnson	3.00	1.35
❑ 7 Errict Rhett	20.00	9.00
❑ 8 Lake Dawson	.60	.25
❑ 9 Bert Emanuel	1.25	.55
❑ 10 Greg Hill	6.00	2.70

1994 Score Sophomore Showcase

	MINT	NRMT
COMPLETE SET (18)	60.00	27.00

RANDOM INSERTS IN JUMBO PACKS

❑ SS1 Jerome Bettis	5.00	2.20
❑ SS2 Rick Mirer	5.00	2.20
❑ SS3 Reggie Brooks	1.00	.45
❑ SS4 Drew Bledsoe	20.00	9.00
❑ SS5 Ronald Moore	1.00	.45
❑ SS6 Derek Brown RBK	1.00	.45
❑ SS7 Roosevelt Potts	1.00	.45
❑ SS8 Terry Kirby	5.00	2.20
❑ SS9 James Jett	1.00	.45
❑ SS10 Vincent Brisby	5.00	2.20
❑ SS11 Tyrone Hughes	2.00	.90
❑ SS12 Rocket Ismail	2.00	.90
❑ SS13 Tony McGee	1.00	.45
❑ SS14 Garrison Hearst	5.00	2.20
❑ SS15 Eric Curry	1.00	.45
❑ SS16 Dana Stubblefield	5.00	2.20
❑ SS17 Tom Carter	1.00	.45
❑ SS18 Chris Slade	1.00	.45

1995 Score

	MINT	NRMT
COMPLETE SET (275)	15.00	6.75
COMMON CARD (1-275)	.05	.02
SEMISTARS	.10	.05
UNLISTED STARS	.25	.11
COMP.RED SIEGE (275)	150.00	70.00

*RED SIEGE STARS: 4X to 8X HI COL.
*RED SIEGE RCS: 2X to 4X HI ....
STATED ODDS 1:3 HOB,1:2 JUM,1:3 RET

COMP. RS ART.PROOF (275)	900.00	400.00

*RS ART.PROOF STARS: 25X to 50X HI COL.
*RS ART.PROOF RCS: 12X to 25X HI
RS AP: STATED ODDS 1:36 HOB/RET

❑ 1 Steve Young	.60	.25
❑ 2 Barry Sanders	1.50	.70
❑ 3 Jerry Rice	.75	.35
❑ 4 Marshall Faulk	.40	.18
❑ 5 Terance Mathis	.10	.05
❑ 6 Rod Woodson	.10	.05
❑ 7 Seth Joyner	.05	.02
❑ 8 Michael Timpson	.05	.02
❑ 9 Deion Sanders	.50	.23
❑ 10 Emmitt Smith	1.25	.55
❑ 11 Cris Carter	.25	.11
❑ 12 Jake Reed	.10	.05
❑ 13 Reggie White	.25	.11
❑ 14 Shannon Sharpe	.10	.05
❑ 15 Troy Aikman	.75	.35
❑ 16 Andre Reed	.10	.05
❑ 17 Tyrone Hughes	.10	.05
❑ 18 Sterling Sharpe	.10	.05
❑ 19 Jerome Bettis	.25	.11
❑ 20 Irving Fryar	.10	.05
❑ 21 Warren Moon	.10	.05
❑ 22 Ben Coates	.10	.05
❑ 23 Frank Reich	.05	.02
❑ 24 Henry Ellard	.10	.05
❑ 25 Steve Atwater	.05	.02
❑ 26 Willie Davis	.10	.05
❑ 27 Michael Irvin	.25	.11
❑ 28 Harvey Williams	.05	.02
❑ 29 Aeneas Williams	.05	.02
❑ 30 Errict Rhett	.25	.11
❑ 31 Lorenzo White	.05	.02
❑ 32 John Elway	1.50	.70
❑ 33 Rodney Hampton	.10	.05
❑ 34 Webster Slaughter	.05	.02
❑ 35 Eric Turner	.05	.02
❑ 36 Dan Marino	1.50	.70
❑ 37 Daryl Johnston	.10	.05
❑ 38 Bruce Smith	.25	.11
❑ 39 Ronald Moore	.05	.02
❑ 40 Larry Centers	.10	.05
❑ 41 Curtis Conway	.25	.11
❑ 42 Drew Bledsoe	.75	.35
❑ 43 Quinn Early	.10	.05
❑ 44 Marcus Allen	.25	.11
❑ 45 Andre Rison	.10	.05
❑ 46 Jeff Blake RC	.60	.25
❑ 47 Barry Foster	.10	.05
❑ 48 Antonio Langham	.05	.02
❑ 49 Herman Moore	.25	.11
❑ 50 Flipper Anderson	.05	.02
❑ 51 Rick Mirer	.25	.11
❑ 52 Jay Novacek	.10	.05
❑ 53 Tim Bowens	.05	.02
❑ 54 Carl Pickens	.25	.11
❑ 55 Lewis Tillman	.05	.02
❑ 56 Lawrence Dawsey	.05	.02
❑ 57 Leroy Hoard	.05	.02
❑ 58 Steve Broussard	.05	.02
❑ 59 Dave Krieg	.05	.02
❑ 60 John Taylor	.05	.02
❑ 61 Johnny Mitchell	.05	.02
❑ 62 Jessie Hester	.05	.02
❑ 63 Johnny Bailey	.05	.02
❑ 64 Brett Favre	1.50	.70
❑ 65 Bryce Paup	.25	.11
❑ 66 J.J. Birden	.05	.02
❑ 67 Steve Tasker	.10	.05
❑ 68 Edgar Bennett	.10	.05
❑ 69 Ray Buchanan	.05	.02
❑ 70 Brent Jones	.05	.02
❑ 71 Dave Meggett	.05	.02
❑ 72 Jeff Graham	.05	.02
❑ 73 Michael Brooks	.05	.02
❑ 74 Ricky Ervins	.05	.02
❑ 75 Chris Warren	.10	.05
❑ 76 Natrone Means	.25	.11
❑ 77 Tim Brown	.25	.11
❑ 78 Jim Everett	.05	.02
❑ 79 Chris Calloway	.05	.02
❑ 80 John L. Williams	.05	.02
❑ 81 Chris Chandler	.10	.05
❑ 82 Tim McDonald	.05	.02
❑ 83 Calvin Williams	.10	.05
❑ 84 Tony McGee	.05	.02
❑ 85 Erik Kramer	.05	.02
❑ 86 Eric Green	.05	.02
❑ 87 Nate Newton	.10	.05
❑ 88 Leonard Russell	.05	.02
❑ 89 Jeff George	.10	.05
❑ 90 Raymont Harris	.05	.02
❑ 91 Darnay Scott	.25	.11
❑ 92 Brian Mitchell	.05	.02
❑ 93 Craig Erickson	.05	.02
❑ 94 Cortez Kennedy	.10	.05
❑ 95 Derrick Alexander WR	.25	.11
❑ 96 Charles Haley	.10	.05
❑ 97 Randall Cunningham	.25	.11
❑ 98 Haywood Jeffires	.05	.02
❑ 99 Ronnie Harmon	.05	.02
❑ 100 Dale Carter	.10	.05
❑ 101 Dave Brown	.10	.05
❑ 102 Michael Haynes	.10	.05
❑ 103 Johnny Johnson	.05	.02
❑ 104 William Floyd	.25	.11
❑ 105 Jeff Hostetler	.10	.05
❑ 106 Bernie Parmalee	.10	.05
❑ 107 Mo Lewis	.05	.02
❑ 108 Byron Bam Morris	.10	.05
❑ 109 Vincent Brisby	.05	.02
❑ 110 John Randle	.05	.02
❑ 111 Steve Walsh	.05	.02
❑ 112 Terry Allen	.10	.05
❑ 113 Greg Lloyd	.10	.05
❑ 114 Merton Hanks	.05	.02
❑ 115 Mel Gray	.05	.02
❑ 116 Jim Kelly	.25	.11
❑ 117 Don Beebe	.05	.02
❑ 118 Floyd Turner	.05	.02
❑ 119 Neil Smith	.10	.05
❑ 120 Keith Byars	.05	.02
❑ 121 Rocket Ismail	.10	.05
❑ 122 Leslie O'Neal	.10	.05
❑ 123 Mike Sherrard	.05	.02
❑ 124 Marion Butts	.05	.02
❑ 125 Andre Coleman	.05	.02
❑ 126 Charles Johnson	.10	.05
❑ 127 Derrick Fenner	.05	.02
❑ 128 Vinny Testaverde	.10	.05
❑ 129 Chris Spielman	.10	.05
❑ 130 Bert Emanuel	.25	.11
❑ 131 Craig Heyward	.10	.05
❑ 132 Anthony Miller	.10	.05
❑ 133 Rob Moore	.05	.02
❑ 134 Gary Brown	.05	.02
❑ 135 David Klingler UER Photo on back is Erik Wilhelm	.10	.05
❑ 136 Sean Dawkins	.10	.05
❑ 137 Terry McDaniel	.05	.02
❑ 138 Fred Barnett	.10	.05
❑ 139 Bryan Cox	.05	.02
❑ 140 Andrew Jordan	.05	.02
❑ 141 Leroy Thompson	.05	.02
❑ 142 Richmond Webb	.05	.02
❑ 143 Kimble Anders	.10	.05
❑ 144 Mario Bates	.25	.11
❑ 145 Irv Smith	.05	.02
❑ 146 Carnell Lake	.05	.02
❑ 147 Mark Seay	.10	.05
❑ 148 Dana Stubblefield	.25	.11
❑ 149 Kelvin Martin	.05	.02
❑ 150 Pete Metzelaars	.05	.02
❑ 151 Roosevelt Potts	.05	.02
❑ 152 Bubby Brister	.05	.02
❑ 153 Trent Dilfer	.25	.11
❑ 154 Ricky Proehl	.05	.02
❑ 155 Aaron Glenn	.05	.02
❑ 156 Eric Metcalf	.10	.05
❑ 157 Kevin Williams WR	.10	.05
❑ 158 Charlie Garner	.10	.05
❑ 159 Glyn Milburn	.05	.02
❑ 160 Fuad Reveiz	.05	.02
❑ 161 Brett Perriman	.10	.05
❑ 162 Neil O'Donnell	.10	.05
❑ 163 Tony Martin	.10	.05
❑ 164 Sam Adams	.05	.02
❑ 165 John Friesz	.10	.05
❑ 166 Bryant Young	.10	.05

Card	Mint	Nrmt
❑ 167 Junior Seau	.25	.11
❑ 168 Ken Harvey	.05	.02
❑ 169 Bill Brooks	.05	.02
❑ 170 Eugene Robinson	.05	.02
❑ 171 Ricky Sanders	.10	.05
❑ 172 Rodney Peete	.05	.02
❑ 173 Boomer Esiason	.10	.05
❑ 174 Reggie Roby	.05	.02
❑ 175 Michael Jackson	.10	.05
❑ 176 Gus Frerotte	.25	.11
❑ 177 Terry Kirby	.10	.05
❑ 178 Jessie Tuggle	.05	.02
❑ 179 Courtney Hawkins	.05	.02
❑ 180 Heath Shuler	.25	.11
❑ 181 Jack Del Rio	.05	.02
❑ 182 O.J. McDuffie	.25	.11
❑ 183 Ricky Watters	.25	.11
❑ 184 Willie Roaf	.05	.02
❑ 185 Glenn Foley	.05	.02
❑ 186 Blair Thomas	.05	.02
❑ 187 Darren Woodson	.10	.05
❑ 188 Kevin Greene	.10	.05
❑ 189 Jeff Burris	.05	.02
❑ 190 Jay Schroeder	.05	.02
❑ 191 Stan Humphries	.10	.05
❑ 192 Irving Spikes	.10	.05
❑ 193 Jim Harbaugh	.10	.05
❑ 194 Robert Brooks	.25	.11
❑ 195 Greg Hill	.10	.05
❑ 196 Herschel Walker	.10	.05
❑ 197 Brian Blades	.10	.05
❑ 198 Mark Ingram	.05	.02
❑ 199 Kevin Turner	.05	.02
❑ 200 Lake Dawson	.10	.05
❑ 201 Alvin Harper	.05	.02
❑ 202 Derek Brown RBK	.05	.02
❑ 203 Qadry Ismail	.10	.05
❑ 204 Reggie Brooks	.10	.05
❑ 205 Steve Young SS	.30	.14
❑ 206 Emmitt Smith SS	.60	.25
❑ 207 Stan Humphries SS	.05	.02
❑ 208 Barry Sanders SS	.75	.35
❑ 209 Marshall Faulk SS	.25	.11
❑ 210 Drew Bledsoe SS	.40	.18
❑ 211 Jerry Rice SS	.40	.18
❑ 212 Tim Brown SS	.10	.05
❑ 213 Cris Carter SS	.25	.11
❑ 214 Dan Marino SS	.75	.35
❑ 215 Troy Aikman SS	.40	.18
❑ 216 Jerome Bettis SS	.10	.05
❑ 217 Deion Sanders SS	.25	.11
❑ 218 Junior Seau SS	.10	.05
❑ 219 John Elway SS	.75	.35
❑ 220 Warren Moon SS	.05	.02
❑ 221 Sterling Sharpe SS	.10	.05
❑ 222 Marcus Allen SS	.25	.11
❑ 223 Michael Irvin SS	.10	.05
❑ 224 Brett Favre SS	.75	.35
❑ 225 Rodney Hampton SS	.05	.02
❑ 226 Dave Brown SS	.10	.05
❑ 227 Ben Coates SS	.10	.05
❑ 228 Jim Kelly SS	.25	.11
❑ 229 Heath Shuler SS	.25	.11
❑ 230 Herman Moore SS	.25	.11
❑ 231 Jeff Hostetler SS	.10	.05
❑ 232 Rick Mirer SS	.10	.05
❑ 233 Byron Bam Morris SS	.10	.05
❑ 234 Terance Mathis SS	.05	.02
❑ 235 John Elway CL Barry Sanders CL	.40	.18
❑ 236 Troy Aikman CL	.25	.11
❑ 237 Jerry Rice CL	.25	.11
❑ 238 Emmitt Smith CL	.25	.11
❑ 239 Steve Young CL	.25	.11
❑ 240 Drew Bledsoe CL	.25	.11
❑ 241 Marshall Faulk CL	.25	.11
❑ 242 Dan Marino CL	.40	.18
❑ 243 Junior Seau CL	.10	.05
❑ 244 Ray Zellars RC	.10	.05
❑ 245 Rob Johnson RC	1.25	.55
❑ 246 Tony Boselli RC	.10	.05
❑ 247 Kevin Carter RC	.25	.11
❑ 248 Steve McNair RC	2.50	1.10
❑ 249 Tyrone Wheatley RC	1.00	.45
❑ 250 Steve Stenstrom RC	.05	.02
❑ 251 Stoney Case RC	.40	.18
❑ 252 Rodney Thomas RC	.25	.11
❑ 253 Michael Westbrook RC	1.25	.55
❑ 254 Derrick Alexander DE RC	.05	.02
❑ 255 Kyle Brady RC	.25	.11
❑ 256 Kerry Collins RC	.60	.25
❑ 257 Rashaan Salaam RC	.25	.11
❑ 258 Frank Sanders RC	.60	.25
❑ 259 John Walsh RC	.05	.02
❑ 260 Sherman Williams RC	.05	.02
❑ 261 Ki-Jana Carter RC	.25	.11
❑ 262 Jack Jackson RC	.05	.02
❑ 263 J.J. Stokes RC	.75	.35
❑ 264 Kordell Stewart RC	2.50	1.10
❑ 265 Dave Barr RC	.05	.02
❑ 266 Eddie Goines RC	.05	.02
❑ 267 Warren Sapp RC	.40	.18
❑ 268 James O. Stewart RC	1.50	.70
❑ 269 Joey Galloway RC	2.50	1.10
❑ 270 Tyrone Davis RC	.05	.02
❑ 271 Napoleon Kaufman RC	1.50	.70
❑ 272 Mark Bruener RC	.10	.05
❑ 273 Todd Collins RC	.25	.11
❑ 274 Billy Williams RC	.05	.02
❑ 275 James A.Stewart RC	.05	.02
❑ AD3 Steve Young Ad Contest Redemption	3.00	1.35

1995 Score Dream Team

	MINT	NRMT
COMPLETE SET (10)	40.00	18.00
STATED ODDS 1:72 HOB/RET		
❑ DT1 Steve Young	4.00	1.80
❑ DT2 Troy Aikman	5.00	2.20
❑ DT3 Dan Marino	10.00	4.50
❑ DT4 Drew Bledsoe	5.00	2.20
❑ DT5 Emmitt Smith	8.00	3.60
❑ DT6 Barry Sanders	10.00	4.50
❑ DT7 Jerry Rice	5.00	2.20
❑ DT8 Marshall Faulk	2.50	1.10
❑ DT9 Deion Sanders	3.00	1.35
❑ DT10 John Elway	10.00	4.50

1995 Score Offense Inc.

	MINT	NRMT
COMPLETE SET (30)	80.00	36.00
STATED ODDS 1:16 HOB, 1:8 JUM, 1:16 RET		
❑ 1 Steve Young	4.00	1.80
❑ 2 Emmitt Smith	8.00	3.60
❑ 3 Dan Marino	10.00	4.50
❑ 4 Barry Sanders	10.00	4.50
❑ 5 Jeff Blake	2.00	.90
❑ 6 Jerry Rice	5.00	2.20
❑ 7 Troy Aikman	5.00	2.20
❑ 8 Brett Favre	10.00	4.50
❑ 9 Marshall Faulk	3.00	1.35
❑ 10 Drew Bledsoe	5.00	2.20
❑ 11 Natrone Means	2.00	.90
❑ 12 John Elway	10.00	4.50
❑ 13 Chris Warren	.75	.35
❑ 14 Michael Irvin	2.00	.90
❑ 15 Mario Bates	2.00	.90
❑ 16 Warren Moon	.75	.35
❑ 17 Jerome Bettis	2.00	.90
❑ 18 Herman Moore	2.00	.90
❑ 19 Barry Foster	.75	.35
❑ 20 Jeff George	.75	.35
❑ 21 Cris Carter	2.00	.90
❑ 22 Sterling Sharpe	.75	.35
❑ 23 Jim Kelly	2.00	.90
❑ 24 Heath Shuler	2.00	.90
❑ 25 Marcus Allen	2.00	.90
❑ 26 Dave Brown	.75	.35
❑ 27 Rick Mirer	2.00	.90
❑ 28 Rodney Hampton	.75	.35
❑ 29 Errict Rhett	2.00	.90
❑ 30 Ben Coates	.75	.35

1995 Score Pass Time

	MINT	NRMT
COMPLETE SET (18)	150.00	70.00
COMMON CARD (PT1-PT18)	1.00	.45
STATED ODDS 1:18 JUMBO		
❑ PT1 Steve Young	12.00	5.50
❑ PT2 Dan Marino	30.00	13.50
❑ PT3 Drew Bledsoe	15.00	6.75
❑ PT4 Troy Aikman	15.00	6.75
❑ PT5 Glenn Foley	1.00	.45
❑ PT6 John Elway	30.00	13.50
❑ PT7 Brett Favre	30.00	13.50
❑ PT8 Heath Shuler	5.00	2.20
❑ PT9 Warren Moon	2.00	.90
❑ PT10 Rick Mirer	5.00	2.20
❑ PT11 Stan Humphries	2.00	.90
❑ PT12 Jeff Hostetler	2.00	.90
❑ PT13 Jim Kelly	5.00	2.20
❑ PT14 Randall Cunningham	5.00	2.20
❑ PT15 Jeff Blake	5.00	2.20
❑ PT16 Trent Dilfer	5.00	2.20
❑ PT17 Jeff George	2.00	.90
❑ PT18 Dave Brown	2.00	.90

1995 Score Reflextions

	MINT	NRMT
COMPLETE SET (10)	60.00	27.00
COMMON CARD (RF1-RF10)	2.50	1.10
SEMISTARS	4.00	1.80
STATED ODDS 1:36 HOBBY		
❑ RF1 Drew Bledsoe Dan Marino	15.00	6.75
❑ RF2 Charlie Garner Barry Sanders	15.00	6.75
❑ RF3 Rick Mirer Warren Moon	4.00	1.80

❑ RF4 Heath Shuler Steve Young	6.00	2.70
❑ RF5 Marshall Faulk Emmitt Smith	12.00	5.50
❑ RF6 Derrick Alexander WR Jerry Rice	8.00	3.60
❑ RF7 Barry Foster Byron Bam Morris	2.50	1.10
❑ RF8 Natrone Means Chris Warren	4.00	1.80
❑ RF9 Tim Brown Lake Dawson	4.00	1.80
❑ RF10 Mario Bates Rodney Hampton	2.50	1.10

1996 Score

	MINT	NRMT
COMPLETE SET (275)	15.00	6.75
COMMON CARD (1-275)	.10	.05
SEMISTARS	.20	.09
UNLISTED STARS	.40	.18
COMP.FIELD FORCE (275)	200.00	90.00
*FF STARS: 2.5X TO 6X HI COL.		
*FF RCs: 1.2X TO 3X HI		
FF STATED ODDS 1:6 HOB/RET, 1:3 JUM		
COMP.ART.PROOF (275)	500.00	220.00
*AP STARS: 6X TO 15X HI COL...		
*AP RCs: 3X TO 8X		
AP STATED ODDS 1:36 HOB/RET, 1:18 JUM		

❑ 1 Emmitt Smith	1.25	.55
❑ 2 Flipper Anderson	.10	.05
❑ 3 Kordell Stewart	.50	.23
❑ 4 Bruce Smith	.20	.09
❑ 5 Marshall Faulk	.40	.18
❑ 6 William Floyd	.20	.09
❑ 7 Darren Woodson	.20	.09
❑ 8 Lake Dawson	.10	.05
❑ 9 Terry Allen	.20	.09
❑ 10 Ki-Jana Carter	.20	.09
❑ 11 Tony Boselli	.10	.05
❑ 12 Christian Fauria	.10	.05
❑ 13 Jeff George	.20	.09
❑ 14 Dan Marino	1.50	.70
❑ 15 Rodney Thomas	.10	.05
❑ 16 Anthony Miller	.20	.09
❑ 17 Chris Sanders	.20	.09
❑ 18 Natrone Means	.40	.18
❑ 19 Curtis Conway	.40	.18
❑ 20 Ben Coates	.20	.09
❑ 21 Alvin Harper	.10	.05
❑ 22 Frank Sanders	.20	.09
❑ 23 Boomer Esiason	.20	.09
❑ 24 Lovell Pinkney	.10	.05
❑ 25 Troy Aikman	.75	.35
❑ 26 Quinn Early	.10	.05
❑ 27 Adrian Murrell	.40	.18
❑ 28 Chris Spielman	.10	.05
❑ 29 Tyrone Wheatley	.20	.09
❑ 30 Tim Brown	.40	.18
❑ 31 Erik Kramer	.10	.05
❑ 32 Warren Moon	.20	.09
❑ 33 Jimmy Oliver	.10	.05
❑ 34 Herman Moore	.40	.18
❑ 35 Quentin Coryatt	.10	.05
❑ 36 Heath Shuler	.20	.09
❑ 37 Jim Kelly	.40	.18
❑ 38 Mike Morris	.10	.05
❑ 39 Harvey Williams	.10	.05
❑ 40 Vinny Testaverde	.20	.09
❑ 41 Steve McNair	.50	.23
❑ 42 Jerry Rice	.75	.35
❑ 43 Darick Holmes	.10	.05
❑ 44 Kyle Brady	.10	.05
❑ 45 Greg Lloyd	.20	.09
❑ 46 Kerry Collins	.40	.18
❑ 47 Willie McGinest	.10	.05
❑ 48 Isaac Bruce	.40	.18
❑ 49 Carnell Lake	.10	.05
❑ 50 Charles Haley	.20	.09
❑ 51 Troy Vincent	.10	.05
❑ 52 Randall Cunningham	.40	.18
❑ 53 Rashaan Salaam	.40	.18
❑ 54 Willie Jackson	.10	.05
❑ 55 Chris Warren	.20	.09
❑ 56 Michael Irvin	.40	.18
❑ 57 Mario Bates	.20	.09
❑ 58 Warren Sapp	.10	.05
❑ 59 John Elway	1.50	.70
❑ 60 Shannon Sharpe	.20	.09
❑ 61 Cornelius Bennett	.10	.05
❑ 62 Robert Brooks	.40	.18
❑ 63 Rodney Hampton	.20	.09
❑ 64 Ken Norton Jr.	.10	.05
❑ 65 Bryce Paup	.10	.05
❑ 66 Eric Swann	.10	.05
❑ 67 Rodney Peete	.10	.05
❑ 68 Larry Centers	.20	.09
❑ 69 Lamont Warren	.10	.05
❑ 70 Jay Novacek	.10	.05
❑ 71 Cris Carter	.40	.18
❑ 72 Terrell Fletcher	.10	.05
❑ 73 Andre Rison	.20	.09
❑ 74 Ricky Watters	.20	.09
❑ 75 Napoleon Kaufman	.40	.18
❑ 76 Reggie White	.40	.18
❑ 77 Yancey Thigpen	.20	.09
❑ 78 Terry Kirby	.20	.09
❑ 79 Deion Sanders	.40	.18
❑ 80 Irving Fryar	.20	.09
❑ 81 Marcus Allen	.40	.18
❑ 82 Carl Pickens	.40	.18
❑ 83 Drew Bledsoe	.75	.35
❑ 84 Eric Metcalf	.10	.05
❑ 85 Robert Smith	.20	.09
❑ 86 Tamarick Vanover	.20	.09
❑ 87 Henry Ellard	.10	.05
❑ 88 Kevin Greene	.20	.09
❑ 89 Mark Brunell	.75	.35
❑ 90 Terrell Davis	2.00	.90
❑ 91 Brian Mitchell	.10	.05
❑ 92 Aaron Bailey	.10	.05
❑ 93 Rocket Ismail	.10	.05
❑ 94 Dave Brown	.10	.05
❑ 95 Rod Woodson	.20	.09
❑ 96 Sean Gilbert	.10	.05
❑ 97 Mark Seay	.10	.05
❑ 98 Zack Crockett	.10	.05
❑ 99 Scott Mitchell	.20	.09
❑ 100 Erric Pegram	.10	.05
❑ 101 David Palmer	.10	.05
❑ 102 Vincent Brisby	.10	.05
❑ 103 Brett Perriman	.10	.05
❑ 104 Jim Everett	.10	.05
❑ 105 Tony Martin	.20	.09
❑ 106 Desmond Howard	.20	.09
❑ 107 Stan Humphries	.20	.09
❑ 108 Bill Brooks	.10	.05
❑ 109 Neil Smith	.10	.05
❑ 110 Michael Westbrook	.40	.18
❑ 111 Herschel Walker	.20	.09
❑ 112 Andre Coleman	.10	.05
❑ 113 Derrick Alexander WR	.20	.09
❑ 114 Jeff Blake	.40	.18
❑ 115 Sherman Williams	.10	.05
❑ 116 James O.Stewart	.20	.09
❑ 117 Hardy Nickerson	.10	.05
❑ 118 Elvis Grbac	.20	.09
❑ 119 Brett Favre	1.50	.70
❑ 120 Mike Sherrard	.10	.05
❑ 121 Edgar Bennett	.20	.09
❑ 122 Calvin Williams	.10	.05
❑ 123 Brian Blades	.10	.05
❑ 124 Jeff Graham	.10	.05
❑ 125 Gary Brown	.10	.05
❑ 126 Bernie Parmalee	.10	.05
❑ 127 Kimble Anders	.20	.09
❑ 128 Hugh Douglas	.10	.05
❑ 129 James A.Stewart	.10	.05
❑ 130 Eric Bjornson	.10	.05
❑ 131 Ken Dilger	.20	.09
❑ 132 Jerome Bettis	.40	.18
❑ 133 Cortez Kennedy	.10	.05
❑ 134 Bryan Cox	.10	.05
❑ 135 Darnay Scott	.20	.09
❑ 136 Bert Emanuel	.20	.09
❑ 137 Steve Bono	.10	.05
❑ 138 Charles Johnson	.10	.05
❑ 139 Glyn Milburn	.10	.05
❑ 140 Derrick Alexander DE	.10	.05
❑ 141 Dave Meggett	.10	.05
❑ 142 Trent Dilfer	.40	.18
❑ 143 Eric Zeier	.10	.05
❑ 144 Jim Harbaugh	.20	.09
❑ 145 Antonio Freeman	.50	.23
❑ 146 Orlando Thomas	.10	.05
❑ 147 Russell Maryland	.10	.05
❑ 148 Chad May	.10	.05
❑ 149 Craig Heyward	.10	.05
❑ 150 Aeneas Williams	.10	.05
❑ 151 Kevin Williams WR	.10	.05
❑ 152 Charlie Garner	.10	.05
❑ 153 J.J. Stokes	.40	.18
❑ 154 Stoney Case	.10	.05
❑ 155 Mark Chmura	.20	.09
❑ 156 Mark Bruener	.10	.05
❑ 157 Derek Loville	.10	.05
❑ 158 Justin Armour	.10	.05
❑ 159 Brent Jones	.10	.05
❑ 160 Aaron Craver	.10	.05
❑ 161 Terance Mathis	.10	.05
❑ 162 Chris Zorich	.10	.05
❑ 163 Glenn Foley	.20	.09
❑ 164 Johnny Mitchell	.10	.05
❑ 165 Junior Seau	.20	.09
❑ 166 Willie Davis	.10	.05
❑ 167 Rick Mirer	.20	.09
❑ 168 Mike Jones	.10	.05
❑ 169 Greg Hill	.20	.09
❑ 170 Steve Tasker	.10	.05
❑ 171 Tony Bennett	.10	.05
❑ 172 Jeff Hostetler	.10	.05
❑ 173 Dave Krieg	.10	.05
❑ 174 Mark Carrier WR	.10	.05
❑ 175 Michael Haynes	.10	.05
❑ 176 Chris Chandler	.20	.09
❑ 177 Ernie Mills	.10	.05
❑ 178 Jake Reed	.20	.09
❑ 179 Errict Rhett	.20	.09
❑ 180 Garrison Hearst	.20	.09
❑ 181 Derrick Thomas	.20	.09
❑ 182 Aaron Hayden RC	.10	.05
❑ 183 Jackie Harris	.10	.05
❑ 184 Curtis Martin	.50	.23
❑ 185 Neil O'Donnell	.20	.09
❑ 186 Derrick Moore	.10	.05
❑ 187 Steve Young	.60	.25
❑ 188 Pat Swilling	.10	.05
❑ 189 Amp Lee	.10	.05
❑ 190 Rob Johnson	.40	.18
❑ 191 Todd Collins	.20	.09

- ❑ 192 J.J. Birden .... .10 .05
- ❑ 193 O.J. McDuffie .... .20 .09
- ❑ 194 Shawn Jefferson .... .10 .05
- ❑ 195 Sean Dawkins .... .10 .05
- ❑ 196 Fred Barnett .... .10 .05
- ❑ 197 Roosevelt Potts .... .10 .05
- ❑ 198 Rob Moore .... .20 .09
- ❑ 199 Kevin Miniefield .... .10 .05
- ❑ 200 Barry Sanders .... 1.50 .70
- ❑ 201 Floyd Turner .... .10 .05
- ❑ 202 Wayne Chrebet .... .20 .09
- ❑ 203 Andre Reed .... .20 .09
- ❑ 204 Tyrone Hughes .... .10 .05
- ❑ 205 Keenan McCardell .... .40 .18
- ❑ 206 Gus Frerotte .... .40 .18
- ❑ 207 Daryl Johnston .... .20 .09
- ❑ 208 Steve Broussard .... .10 .05
- ❑ 209 Steve Atwater .... .10 .05
- ❑ 210 Thurman Thomas .... .40 .18
- ❑ 211 Andre Hastings .... .10 .05
- ❑ 212 Joey Galloway .... .50 .23
- ❑ 213 Kevin Carter .... .10 .05
- ❑ 214 Keyshawn Johnson RC 2.00 .90
- ❑ 215 Tony Brackens RC .... .20 .09
- ❑ 216 Stepfret Williams RC .... .20 .09
- ❑ 217 Mike Alstott RC .... 1.25 .55
- ❑ 218 Terry Glenn RC .... 1.25 .55
- ❑ 219 Tim Biakabutuka RC .... .75 .35
- ❑ 220 Eric Moulds RC .... 1.50 .70
- ❑ 221 Jeff Lewis RC .... .50 .23
- ❑ 222 Bobby Engram RC .... .40 .18
- ❑ 223 Cedric Jones RC .... .10 .05
- ❑ 224 Stanley Pritchett RC .... .20 .09
- ❑ 225 Kevin Hardy RC .... .40 .18
- ❑ 226 Alex Van Dyke RC .... .20 .09
- ❑ 227 Willie Anderson RC .... .10 .05
- ❑ 228 Regan Upshaw RC .... .10 .05
- ❑ 229 Leeland McElroy RC .... .40 .18
- ❑ 230 Marvin Harrison RC.......... 2.00 .90
- ❑ 231 Eddie George RC 2.50 1.10
- ❑ 232 Lawrence Phillips RC .... .50 .23
- ❑ 233 Daryl Gardener RC .... .10 .05
- ❑ 234 Alex Molden RC .... .10 .05
- ❑ 235 Derrick Mayes RC .... .60 .25
- ❑ 236 John Mobley RC .... .10 .05
- ❑ 237 Israel Ifeanyi RC .... .10 .05
- ❑ 238 Pete Kendall RC .... .10 .05
- ❑ 239 Danny Kanell RC .... .40 .18
- ❑ 240 Jonathan Ogden RC .... .10 .05
- ❑ 241 Reggie Brown LB RC .... .10 .05
- ❑ 242 Marcus Jones RC .... .10 .05
- ❑ 243 Jon Stark RC .... .10 .05
- ❑ 244 Barry Sanders SE .... .75 .35
- ❑ 245 Brett Favre SE .... .75 .35
- ❑ 246 John Elway SE .... .75 .35
- ❑ 247 Dan Marino SE .... .75 .35
- ❑ 248 Drew Bledsoe SE .... .40 .18
- ❑ 249 Michael Irvin SE .... .20 .09
- ❑ 250 Troy Aikman SE .... .40 .18
- ❑ 251 Emmitt Smith SE .... .50 .23
- ❑ 252 Steve Young SE .... .40 .18
- ❑ 253 Jerry Rice SE .... .40 .18
- ❑ 254 Jeff Blake SE .... .20 .09
- ❑ 255 Tim Brown SE .... .20 .09
- ❑ 256 Eric Metcalf SE .... .10 .05
- ❑ 257 Rodney Hampton SE .... .10 .05
- ❑ 258 Scott Mitchell SE .... .10 .05
- ❑ 259 Garrison Hearst SE .... .20 .09
- ❑ 260 Larry Centers SE .... .20 .09
- ❑ 261 Neil O'Donnell SE .... .20 .09
- ❑ 262 Orlando Thomas SE .... .10 .05
- ❑ 263 Hugh Douglas SE .... .10 .05
- ❑ 264 Bill Brooks SE .... .10 .05
- ❑ 265 Harvey Williams SE .... .10 .05
- ❑ 266 Charles Haley SE .... .20 .09
- ❑ 267 Greg Lloyd SE .... .20 .09
- ❑ 268 Daryl Johnston SE .... .20 .09
- ❑ 269 Dan Marino CL .... .30 .14
- ❑ 270 Jeff Blake CL .... .20 .09
- ❑ 271 John Elway CL .... .40 .18
- ❑ 272 Emmitt Smith CL .... .40 .18
- ❑ 273 Brett Favre CL .... .30 .14
- ❑ 274 Jerry Rice CL .... .40 .18
- ❑ 275 Dan Marino .... .40 .18
  Jeff Blake
  John Elway
  Emmitt Smith
  Brett Favre
  Jerry Rice
  Checklist
- ❑ P1 Barry Sanders Promo .... 2.00 .90
  Dream Team card

1996 Score Dream Team

	MINT	NRMT
COMPLETE SET (10)	80.00	36.00
STATED ODDS 1:72		

- ❑ 1 Troy Aikman 8.00 3.60
- ❑ 2 Michael Irvin 4.00 1.80
- ❑ 3 Emmitt Smith 12.00 5.50
- ❑ 4 John Elway 15.00 6.75
- ❑ 5 Barry Sanders 15.00 6.75
- ❑ 6 Brett Favre 15.00 6.75
- ❑ 7 Dan Marino 15.00 6.75
- ❑ 8 Drew Bledsoe 8.00 3.60
- ❑ 9 Jerry Rice 8.00 3.60
- ❑ 10 Steve Young 6.00 2.70

1996 Score Footsteps

	MINT	NRMT
COMPLETE SET (15)	120.00	55.00
COMMON CARD (1-15)	2.50	1.10
SEMISTARS	4.00	1.80
STATED ODDS 1:35 HOBBY		

- ❑ 1 Darick Holmes 4.00 1.80
  Errict Rhett
- ❑ 2 Rashaan Salaam 5.00 2.20
  Natrone Means
- ❑ 3 Ki-Jana Carter 20.00 9.00
  Barry Sanders
- ❑ 4 Terrell Davis 25.00 11.00
  Marshall Faulk
- ❑ 5 Rodney Thomas 2.50 1.10
  Chris Warren
- ❑ 6 Curtis Martin 20.00 9.00
  Emmitt Smith
- ❑ 7 Kerry Collins 15.00 6.75
  Troy Aikman
- ❑ 8 Eric Zeier 12.00 5.50
  Drew Bledsoe
- ❑ 9 Steve McNair 20.00 9.00
  Brett Favre
- ❑ 10 Steve Young 12.00 5.50
  Kordell Stewart
- ❑ 11 J.J.Stokes 12.00 5.50
  Jerry Rice
- ❑ 12 Joey Galloway 5.00 2.20
  Michael Irvin
- ❑ 13 Michael Westbrook 5.00 2.20
  Cris Carter
- ❑ 14 Tamarick Vanover 4.00 1.80
  Isaac Bruce
- ❑ 15 Orlando Thomas 6.00 2.70
  Deion Sanders

1996 Score In The Zone

	MINT	NRMT
COMPLETE SET (20)	175.00	80.00
STATED ODDS 1:33 RETAIL		

- ❑ 1 Brett Favre 30.00 13.50
- ❑ 2 Warren Moon 4.00 1.80
- ❑ 3 Erik Kramer .... 2.00 .90
- ❑ 4 Scott Mitchell 4.00 1.80
- ❑ 5 Jeff Blake 8.00 3.60
- ❑ 6 Steve Bono .... 2.00 .90
- ❑ 7 Dan Marino 30.00 13.50
- ❑ 8 Troy Aikman 15.00 6.75
- ❑ 9 Emmitt Smith 25.00 11.00
- ❑ 10 Curtis Martin 10.00 4.50
- ❑ 11 Errict Rhett 4.00 1.80
- ❑ 12 Terrell Davis 40.00 18.00
- ❑ 13 Derek Loville .... 2.00 .90
- ❑ 14 Rodney Hampton 4.00 1.80
- ❑ 15 Cris Carter 8.00 3.60
- ❑ 16 Herman Moore 8.00 3.60
- ❑ 17 Jerry Rice 15.00 6.75
- ❑ 18 Ben Coates 4.00 1.80
- ❑ 19 Michael Irvin 8.00 3.60
- ❑ 20 Carl Pickens 8.00 3.60

1996 Score Numbers Game

	MINT	NRMT
COMPLETE SET (25)	80.00	36.00
STATED ODDS 1:17 HOB/RET, 1:9 JUM		

- ❑ 1 Barry Sanders 10.00 4.50
- ❑ 2 Drew Bledsoe 5.00 2.20
- ❑ 3 Brett Favre 10.00 4.50
- ❑ 4 John Elway 10.00 4.50
- ❑ 5 Dan Marino 10.00 4.50

Card	MINT	NRMT
❑ 6 Michael Irvin	3.00	1.35
❑ 7 Troy Aikman	5.00	2.20
❑ 8 Emmitt Smith	8.00	3.60
❑ 9 Steve Young	4.00	1.80
❑ 10 Jerry Rice	5.00	2.20
❑ 11 Chris Sanders	1.50	.70
❑ 12 Herman Moore	3.00	1.35
❑ 13 Frank Sanders	1.50	.70
❑ 14 Kordell Stewart	4.00	1.80
❑ 15 Jeff Blake	3.00	1.35
❑ 16 Robert Brooks	3.00	1.35
❑ 17 Marshall Faulk	3.00	1.35
❑ 18 Carl Pickens	3.00	1.35
❑ 19 Greg Lloyd	1.50	.70
❑ 20 Curtis Conway	3.00	1.35
❑ 21 Chris Warren	1.50	.70
❑ 22 Natrone Means	3.00	1.35
❑ 23 Deion Sanders	3.00	1.35
❑ 24 Neil O'Donnell	1.50	.70
❑ 25 Ricky Watters	1.50	.70

1996 Score Settle the Score

	MINT	NRMT
COMPLETE SET (30)	500.00	220.00
COMMON CARD (1-30)	4.00	1.80
SEMISTARS	6.00	2.70
UNLISTED STARS	10.00	4.50

STATED ODDS 1:36 JUM, 1:72 SPEC.RETAIL

Card	MINT	NRMT
❑ 1 Frank Sanders Charlie Garner	6.00	2.70
❑ 2 Drew Bledsoe Neil O'Donnell	15.00	6.75
❑ 3 Jerry Rice Craig Heyward	15.00	6.75
❑ 4 Emmitt Smith Rod Woodson	25.00	11.00
❑ 5 Derrick Holmes Dan Marino	30.00	13.50
❑ 6 Kerry Collins Steve Young	12.00	5.50
❑ 7 Rashaan Salaam Brett Favre	30.00	13.50
❑ 8 Curtis Conway Barry Sanders	30.00	13.50
❑ 9 Troy Aikman Dan Marino	30.00	13.50
❑ 10 Dan Marino Neil O'Donnell	30.00	13.50
❑ 11 Eric Zeier Steve McNair	10.00	4.50
❑ 12 Jeff Blake Kordell Stewart	12.00	5.50
❑ 13 Troy Aikman Heath Shuler	15.00	6.75
❑ 14 Michael Irvin Jerry Rice	15.00	6.75
❑ 15 Emmitt Smith Ricky Watters	25.00	11.00
❑ 16 John Elway Steve Bono	30.00	13.50
❑ 17 John Elway Rick Mirer	30.00	13.50
❑ 18 John Elway Tim Brown	30.00	13.50
❑ 19 Barry Sanders Brett Favre	40.00	18.00
❑ 20 Barry Sanders Warren Moon	30.00	13.50
❑ 21 Trent Dilfer Brett Favre	30.00	13.50
❑ 22 Rodney Thomas James O.Stewart	4.00	1.80
❑ 23 Jim Harbaugh Drew Bledsoe	15.00	6.75
❑ 24 Marcus Allen Harvey Williams	6.00	2.70
❑ 25 Tamarick Vanover Joey Galloway	10.00	4.50
❑ 26 Dan Marino Drew Bledsoe	30.00	13.50
❑ 27 Mario Bates Jerry Rice	15.00	6.75
❑ 28 Tyrone Wheatley Michael Westbrook	6.00	2.70
❑ 29 Napoleon Kaufman Junior Seau	10.00	4.50
❑ 30 J.J.Stokes Isaac Bruce	6.00	2.70

1997 Score

	MINT	NRMT
COMPLETE SET (330)	20.00	9.00
COMMON CARD (1-330)	.10	.05
SEMISTARS	.20	.09
UNLISTED STARS	.40	.18
COMP.HOBBY RESER.(330)	30.00	13.50

*HOBBY RESERVE CARDS: .75X TO 1.5X

COMP.RES.COLLECT.(330)	400.00	180.00

*RESERVE COLL.STARS: 6X TO 15X HI
*RESERVE COLL.RCs: 3X TO 8X
RESERVE COLL.ODDS 1:11 HOBBY RESERVE

COMP.SHOWCASE SET (330)	150.00	70.00

*SHOWCASE STARS: 2.5X TO 6X HI COL.
*SHOWCASE RCs: 1.2X TO 3X ..
SHOWCASE STATED ODDS 1:4H,1:7R,1:5H.R.

COMP.SHOW.ART.PROOF..	600.00	275.00

*SHOWCASE AP STARS: 8X TO 20X
*SHOWCASE AP RCs: 4X TO 10X
SHOWCASE ART.PROOF ODDS 1:17H,1:35R,1:23H.R.

Card	MINT	NRMT
❑ 1 John Elway	2.00	.90
❑ 2 Drew Bledsoe	1.00	.45
❑ 3 Brett Favre	2.00	.90
❑ 4 Emmitt Smith	1.50	.70
❑ 5 Kerry Collins	.20	.09
❑ 6 Jerry Rice	1.00	.45
❑ 7 Kordell Stewart	.50	.23
❑ 8 Barry Sanders	2.00	.90
❑ 9 Dan Marino	2.00	.90
❑ 10 Steve Young	.60	.25
❑ 11 Erik Kramer	.10	.05
❑ 12 Warren Moon	.40	.18
❑ 13 Chris Calloway	.10	.05
❑ 14 Doug Evans	.10	.05
❑ 15 Darren Woodson	.10	.05
❑ 16 Alonzo Spellman	.10	.05
❑ 17 Greg Hill	.10	.05
❑ 18 Aaron Craver	.10	.05
❑ 19 Jeff Hostetler	.10	.05
❑ 20 William Thomas	.10	.05
❑ 21 Marco Coleman	.10	.05
❑ 22 Wayne Simmons	.10	.05
❑ 23 Donnell Woolford	.10	.05
❑ 24 Vinny Testaverde	.20	.09
❑ 25 Ed McCaffrey	.20	.09
❑ 26 Jim Everett	.10	.05
❑ 27 Gilbert Brown	.10	.05
❑ 28 Jason Dunn	.10	.05
❑ 29 Stanley Pritchett	.10	.05
❑ 30 Joey Galloway	.50	.23
❑ 31 Amani Toomer	.20	.09
❑ 32 Chris Penn	.10	.05
❑ 33 Aeneas Williams	.10	.05
❑ 34 Bobby Taylor	.10	.05
❑ 35 Bryan Still	.10	.05
❑ 36 Ty Law	.10	.05
❑ 37 Shannon Sharpe	.20	.09
❑ 38 Marty Carter	.10	.05
❑ 39 Sam Mills	.10	.05
❑ 40 William Floyd	.20	.09
❑ 41 Brad Johnson	.50	.23
❑ 42 Sean Dawkins	.10	.05
❑ 43 Michael Irvin	.40	.18
❑ 44 Jeff George	.20	.09
❑ 45 Brent Jones	.20	.09
❑ 46 Mark Brunell	1.00	.45
❑ 47 Rob Moore	.20	.09
❑ 48 Hardy Nickerson	.10	.05
❑ 49 Chris Chandler	.20	.09
❑ 50 Willie Anderson	.10	.05
❑ 51 Isaac Bruce	.40	.18
❑ 52 Natrone Means	.40	.18
❑ 53 Tony Banks	.20	.09
❑ 54 Marshall Faulk	.40	.18
❑ 55 Michael Westbrook	.20	.09
❑ 56 Bruce Smith	.20	.09
❑ 57 Jamal Anderson	.60	.25
❑ 58 Jackie Harris	.10	.05
❑ 59 Sean Gilbert	.10	.05
❑ 60 Ki-Jana Carter	.10	.05
❑ 61 Eric Moulds	.40	.18
❑ 62 James O.Stewart	.20	.09
❑ 63 Jeff Blake	.20	.09
❑ 64 O.J. McDuffie	.20	.09
❑ 65 Neil Smith	.20	.09
❑ 66 Kevin Smith	.10	.05
❑ 67 Terry Allen	.40	.18
❑ 68 Sean LaChapelle	.10	.05
❑ 69 Rashaan Salaam	.10	.05
❑ 70 Jeff Graham	.10	.05
❑ 71 Mark Carrier WR	.10	.05
❑ 72 Allen Aldridge	.10	.05
❑ 73 Keenan McCardell	.20	.09
❑ 74 Willie McGinest	.10	.05
❑ 75 Napoleon Kaufman	.40	.18
❑ 76 Jerris McPhail	.10	.05
❑ 77 Eric Swann	.10	.05
❑ 78 Kimble Anders	.20	.09
❑ 79 Charles Johnson	.20	.09
❑ 80 Bryan Cox	.10	.05
❑ 81 Johnnie Morton	.20	.09
❑ 82 Andre Rison	.20	.09
❑ 83 Corey Miller	.10	.05
❑ 84 Troy Drayton	.10	.05
❑ 85 Jim Harbaugh	.20	.09
❑ 86 Wesley Walls	.20	.09
❑ 87 Bryce Paup	.10	.05
❑ 88 Curtis Martin	.50	.23
❑ 89 Michael Sinclair	.10	.05
❑ 90 Chris T. Jones	.10	.05
❑ 91 Jake Reed	.20	.09
❑ 92 LeRoy Butler	.10	.05
❑ 93 Reggie Tongue	.10	.05
❑ 94 Bert Emanuel	.20	.09
❑ 95 Stan Humphries	.20	.09
❑ 96 Neil O'Donnell	.20	.09
❑ 97 Troy Vincent	.10	.05
❑ 98 Mike Alstott	.40	.18
❑ 99 Chad Cota	.10	.05
❑ 100 Marvin Harrison	.40	.18
❑ 101 Terrell Owens	.40	.18
❑ 102 Dave Brown	.10	.05
❑ 103 Harvey Williams	.10	.05
❑ 104 Desmond Howard	.20	.09
❑ 105 Carl Pickens	.40	.18
❑ 106 Kent Graham	.10	.05
❑ 107 Michael Bates	.10	.05

❑ 108 Terrell Davis 1.50 .70
❑ 109 Marcus Allen .40 .18
❑ 110 Ray Zellars .10 .05
❑ 111 Chris Warren .20 .09
❑ 112 Phillippi Sparks .10 .05
❑ 113 Craig Erickson .10 .05
❑ 114 Eddie George 1.00 .45
❑ 115 Daryl Johnston .20 .09
❑ 116 Ricky Watters .20 .09
❑ 117 Tedy Bruschi .10 .05
❑ 118 Mike Mamula .10 .05
❑ 119 Ken Harvey .10 .05
❑ 120 John Randle .10 .05
❑ 121 Mark Chmura .20 .09
❑ 122 Sam Gash .10 .05
❑ 123 John Kasay .10 .05
❑ 124 Barry Minter .10 .05
❑ 125 Raymont Harris .10 .05
❑ 126 Derrick Thomas .20 .09
❑ 127 Trent Dilfer .40 .18
❑ 128 Carnell Lake .10 .05
❑ 129 Brian Dawkins .10 .05
❑ 130 Tyronne Drakeford .10 .05
❑ 131 Daryl Gardener .10 .05
❑ 132 Fred Strickland .10 .05
❑ 133 Kevin Hardy .10 .05
❑ 134 Winslow Oliver .10 .05
❑ 135 Herman Moore .40 .18
❑ 136 Keith Byars .10 .05
❑ 137 Harold Green .10 .05
❑ 138 Ty Detmer .20 .09
❑ 139 Lamar Thomas .10 .05
❑ 140 Elvis Grbac .20 .09
❑ 141 Edgar Bennett .20 .09
❑ 142 Cornelius Bennett .10 .05
❑ 143 Tony Tolbert .10 .05
❑ 144 James Hasty .10 .05
❑ 145 Ben Coates .20 .09
❑ 146 Errict Rhett .10 .05
❑ 147 Jason Sehorn .20 .09
❑ 148 Michael Jackson .20 .09
❑ 149 John Mobley .10 .05
❑ 150 Walt Harris .10 .05
❑ 151 Terry Kirby .20 .09
❑ 152 Devin Wyman .10 .05
❑ 153 Ray Crockett .10 .05
❑ 154 Quinn Early .10 .05
❑ 155 Rodney Thomas .10 .05
❑ 156 Mark Seay .10 .05
❑ 157 Derrick Alexander WR .20 .09
❑ 158 Lamar Lathon .10 .05
❑ 159 Anthony Miller .10 .05
❑ 160 Shawn Wooden .10 .05
❑ 161 Antonio Freeman .50 .23
❑ 162 Cortez Kennedy .10 .05
❑ 163 Rickey Dudley .20 .09
❑ 164 Tony Carter .10 .05
❑ 165 Kevin Williams .10 .05
❑ 166 Reggie White .40 .18
❑ 167 Tim Bowens .10 .05
❑ 168 Roy Barker .10 .05
❑ 169 Adrian Murrell .20 .09
❑ 170 Anthony Johnson .10 .05
❑ 171 Terry Glenn .40 .18
❑ 172 Jeff Lewis .10 .05
❑ 173 Dorsey Levens .40 .18
❑ 174 Willie Jackson .10 .05
❑ 175 Willie Clay .10 .05
❑ 176 Richmond Webb .10 .05
❑ 177 Shawn Lee .10 .05
❑ 178 Joe Aska .10 .05
❑ 179 Rod Woodson .20 .09
❑ 180 Jim Schwantz RC .10 .05
❑ 181 Alfred Williams .10 .05
❑ 182 Ferric Collons .10 .05
❑ 183 Ken Norton Jr. .10 .05
❑ 184 Rick Mirer .10 .05
❑ 185 Leeland McElroy .10 .05
❑ 186 Rodney Hampton .20 .09
❑ 187 Ted Popson .10 .05
❑ 188 Fred Barnett .10 .05
❑ 189 Junior Seau .20 .09
❑ 190 Micheal Barrow .10 .05
❑ 191 Corey Widmer .10 .05
❑ 192 Rodney Peete .10 .05
❑ 193 Rod Smith WR .40 .18
❑ 194 Muhsin Muhammad .20 .09
❑ 195 Keith Jackson .10 .05
❑ 196 Jimmy Smith .20 .09
❑ 197 Dave Meggett .10 .05
❑ 198 Lawrence Phillips .10 .05
❑ 199 Chad Brown .10 .05
❑ 200 Darrin Smith .10 .05
❑ 201 Larry Centers .20 .09
❑ 202 Kevin Greene .20 .09
❑ 203 Sherman Williams .10 .05
❑ 204 Chris Sanders .10 .05
❑ 205 Shawn Jefferson .10 .05
❑ 206 Thurman Thomas .40 .18
❑ 207 Keyshawn Johnson .40 .18
❑ 208 Bryant Young .10 .05
❑ 209 Tim Biakabutuka .20 .09
❑ 210 Troy Aikman 1.00 .45
❑ 211 Quentin Coryatt .10 .05
❑ 212 Karim Abdul-Jabbar .40 .18
❑ 213 Brian Blades .10 .05
❑ 214 Ray Farmer .10 .05
❑ 215 Simeon Rice .20 .09
❑ 216 Tyrone Braxton .10 .05
❑ 217 Jerome Woods .10 .05
❑ 218 Charles Way .20 .09
❑ 219 Garrison Hearst .20 .09
❑ 220 Bobby Engram .20 .09
❑ 221 Billy Davis RC .10 .05
❑ 222 Ken Dilger .10 .05
❑ 223 Robert Smith .20 .09
❑ 224 John Friesz .10 .05
❑ 225 Charlie Garner .10 .05
❑ 226 Jerome Bettis .40 .18
❑ 227 Darnay Scott .20 .09
❑ 228 Terance Mathis .20 .09
❑ 229 Brian Williams LB .10 .05
❑ 230 Cris Carter .40 .18
❑ 231 Michael Haynes .10 .05
❑ 232 Cedric Jones .10 .05
❑ 233 Danny Kanell .20 .09
❑ 234 Deion Sanders .40 .18
❑ 235 Steve Atwater .10 .05
❑ 236 Jonathan Ogden .10 .05
❑ 237 Lake Dawson .10 .05
❑ 238 Eric Allen .10 .05
❑ 239 Eddie Kennison .20 .09
❑ 240 Irving Fryar .20 .09
❑ 241 Michael Strahan .10 .05
❑ 242 Steve McNair .50 .23
❑ 243 Terrell Buckley .10 .05
❑ 244 Merton Hanks .10 .05
❑ 245 Jessie Armstead .10 .05
❑ 246 Dana Stubblefield .10 .05
❑ 247 Brett Perriman .10 .05
❑ 248 Mark Collins .10 .05
❑ 249 Willie Roaf .10 .05
❑ 250 Gus Frerotte .10 .05
❑ 251 William Fuller .10 .05
❑ 252 Tamarick Vanover .20 .09
❑ 253 Scott Mitchell .20 .09
❑ 254 Eric Metcalf .20 .09
❑ 255 Herschel Walker .20 .09
❑ 256 Robert Brooks .20 .09
❑ 257 Zach Thomas .20 .09
❑ 258 Alvin Harper .10 .05
❑ 259 Wayne Chrebet .40 .18
❑ 260 Bill Romanowski .10 .05
❑ 261 Willie Green .10 .05
❑ 262 Dale Carter .10 .05
❑ 263 Chris Slade .10 .05
❑ 264 J.J. Stokes .20 .09
❑ 265 Tim Brown .40 .18
❑ 266 Eric Davis .10 .05
❑ 267 Mark Carrier DB .10 .05
❑ 268 Tony Martin .20 .09
❑ 269 Tyrone Wheatley .20 .09
❑ 270 Eugene Robinson .10 .05
❑ 271 Curtis Conway .20 .09
❑ 272 Michael Timpson .10 .05
❑ 273 Orlando Pace RC .10 .05
❑ 274 Tiki Barber RC .60 .25
❑ 275 Byron Hanspard RC .75 .35
❑ 276 Warrick Dunn RC 1.25 .55
❑ 277 Rae Carruth RC .40 .18
❑ 278 Bryant Westbrook RC .10 .05
❑ 279 Antowain Smith RC 1.00 .45
❑ 280 Peter Boulware RC .20 .09
❑ 281 Reidel Anthony RC .75 .35
❑ 282 Troy Davis RC .40 .18
❑ 283 Jake Plummer RC 3.00 1.35
❑ 284 Chris Canty RC .10 .05
❑ 285 Dwayne Rudd RC .10 .05
❑ 286 Ike Hilliard RC .75 .35
❑ 287 Reinard Wilson RC .10 .05
❑ 288 Corey Dillon RC 1.50 .70
❑ 289 Tony Gonzalez RC 1.25 .55
❑ 290 Darnell Autry RC .20 .09
❑ 291 Kevin Lockett RC .20 .09
❑ 292 Darrell Russell RC .10 .05
❑ 293 Jim Druckenmiller RC .60 .25
❑ 294 Simon Mitchell RC .10 .05
❑ 295 Joey Kent RC .40 .18
❑ 296 Shawn Springs RC .20 .09
❑ 297 James Farrior RC .10 .05
❑ 298 Sedrick Shaw RC .40 .18
❑ 299 Marcus Harris RC .10 .05
❑ 300 Danny Wuerffel RC .60 .25
❑ 301 Marc Edwards RC .10 .05
❑ 302 Michael Booker RC .10 .05
❑ 303 David LaFleur RC .20 .09
❑ 304 Mike Adams WR RC .10 .05
❑ 305 Pat Barnes RC .40 .18
❑ 306 George Jones RC .20 .09
❑ 307 Yatil Green RC .20 .09
❑ 308 Drew Bledsoe TBP .50 .23
❑ 309 Troy Aikman TBP .50 .23
❑ 310 Terrell Davis TBP .75 .35
❑ 311 Jim Everett TBP .10 .05
❑ 312 John Elway TBP 1.00 .45
❑ 313 Barry Sanders TBP 1.00 .45
❑ 314 Jim Harbaugh TBP .20 .09
❑ 315 Steve Young TBP .40 .18
❑ 316 Dan Marino TBP 1.00 .45
❑ 317 Michael Irvin TBP .40 .18
❑ 318 Emmitt Smith TBP .75 .35
❑ 319 Jeff Hostetler TBP .10 .05
❑ 320 Mark Brunell TBP .50 .23
❑ 321 Jeff Blake TBP .40 .18
❑ 322 Scott Mitchell TBP .10 .05
❑ 323 Boomer Esiason TBP .20 .09
❑ 324 Jerome Bettis TBP .40 .18
❑ 325 Warren Moon TBP .20 .09
❑ 326 Neil O'Donnell TBP .20 .09
❑ 327 Jim Kelly TBP .40 .18
❑ 328 Dan Marino CL .40 .18
❑ 329 John Elway CL
❑ 330 Drew Bledsoe CL .20 .09
❑ P1 Troy Aikman 1.00 .45
(Ad Back Promo)
❑ P2 Brett Favre 2.00 .90
(Ad Back Promo)
❑ P3 Dan Marino 2.00 .90
(Ad Back Promo)
❑ P4 Barry Sanders 1.50 .70
(Ad Back Promo)

1997 Score Franchise

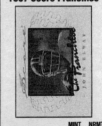

	MINT	NRMT
COMPLETE SET (16)	150.00	70.00

STATED ODDS 1:30 RETAIL
*HOLO.ENHANCED: 8X TO 20X BASE CARD HI
HOLO.ENHANCED STATED ODDS 1:125

❑ 1 Emmitt Smith 20.00 9.00

Card	MINT	NRMT
❑ 2 Barry Sanders	25.00	11.00
❑ 3 Brett Favre	25.00	11.00
❑ 4 Drew Bledsoe	12.00	5.50
❑ 5 Jerry Rice	12.00	5.50
❑ 6 Troy Aikman	12.00	5.50
❑ 7 Dan Marino	25.00	11.00
❑ 8 John Elway	25.00	11.00
❑ 9 Steve Young	8.00	3.60
❑ 10 Eddie George	12.00	5.50
❑ 11 Keyshawn Johnson	5.00	2.20
❑ 12 Terrell Davis	20.00	9.00
❑ 13 Marshall Faulk	5.00	2.20
❑ 14 Kerry Collins	2.50	1.10
❑ 15 Deion Sanders	5.00	2.20
❑ 16 Joey Galloway	6.00	2.70

1997 Score New Breed

	MINT	NRMT
COMPLETE SET (18)	70.00	32.00
COMP.SERIES 1 SET (9)	30.00	13.50
COMP.SERIES 2 SET (9)	40.00	18.00

1-9: STATED ODDS 1:12 RETAIL
10-18: STATED ODDS 1:15 HOBBY RESERVE

Card	MINT	NRMT
❑ 1 Eddie George	8.00	3.60
❑ 2 Terrell Davis	12.00	5.50
❑ 3 Curtis Martin	4.00	1.80
❑ 4 Tony Banks	1.50	.70
❑ 5 Lawrence Phillips	.75	.35
❑ 6 Terry Glenn	3.00	1.35
❑ 7 Jerome Bettis	3.00	1.35
❑ 8 Karim Abdul-Jabbar	3.00	1.35
❑ 9 Napoleon Kaufman	3.00	1.35
❑ 10 Isaac Bruce	3.00	1.35
❑ 11 Keyshawn Johnson	3.00	1.35
❑ 12 Rickey Dudley	1.50	.70
❑ 13 Eddie Kennison	1.50	.70
❑ 14 Marvin Harrison	3.00	1.35
❑ 15 Emmitt Smith	12.00	5.50
❑ 16 Barry Sanders	15.00	6.75
❑ 17 Kerry Collins	1.50	.70
❑ 18 Brett Favre	15.00	6.75

1997 Score Specialists

	MINT	NRMT
COMPLETE SET (18)	100.00	45.00

STATED ODDS 1:15 HOBBY RESERVE

Card	MINT	NRMT
❑ 1 Brett Favre	15.00	6.75
❑ 2 Drew Bledsoe	8.00	3.60
❑ 3 Mark Brunell	8.00	3.60
❑ 4 Kerry Collins	1.50	.70
❑ 5 John Elway	15.00	6.75
❑ 6 Barry Sanders	15.00	6.75
❑ 7 Troy Aikman	8.00	3.60
❑ 8 Jerry Rice	8.00	3.60
❑ 9 Dan Marino	15.00	6.75
❑ 10 Neil O'Donnell	1.50	.70
❑ 11 Scott Mitchell	1.50	.70
❑ 12 Jim Harbaugh	1.50	.70
❑ 13 Emmitt Smith	12.00	5.50
❑ 14 Steve Young	5.00	2.20
❑ 15 Dave Brown	.75	.35
❑ 16 Jeff Blake	1.50	.70
❑ 17 Jim Everett	.75	.35
❑ 18 Kordell Stewart	4.00	1.80

1998 Score

	MINT	NRMT
COMPLETE SET (270)	40.00	18.00
COMMON CARD (1-270)	.10	.05
SEMISTARS	.20	.09
UNLISTED STARS	.40	.18
COMMON ROOKIE (233-252)	.75	.35
COMP.SHOWCASE (110)	150.00	70.00

*SHOWCASE STARS: 2.5X TO 6X HI COL.
*SHOWCASE YOUNG STARS: 2X TO 5X
*SHOWCASE RCs: .6X TO 1.5X ..
SHOWCASE STATED ODDS 1:7

	MINT	NRMT
COMP.SHOW.ART.PROOF (50)	300.00	135.00

*SHOWCASE AP STARS: 4X TO 10X HI COL.
*SHOWCASE AP YOUNG STARS: 3X TO 8X
*SHOWCASE AP RCs: 1.25X TO 3X
SHOWCASE AP STATED ODDS 1:35
LEAF AU/TRADE EXPIRATION: 12/31/99

Card	MINT	NRMT
❑ 1 John Elway	2.00	.90
❑ 2 Kordell Stewart	.40	.18
❑ 3 Warrick Dunn	.50	.23
❑ 4 Brad Johnson	.40	.18
❑ 5 Kerry Collins	.20	.09
❑ 6 Danny Kanell	.20	.09
❑ 7 Emmitt Smith	1.50	.70
❑ 8 Jamal Anderson	.40	.18
❑ 9 Jim Harbaugh	.20	.09
❑ 10 Tony Martin	.20	.09
❑ 11 Rod Smith	.20	.09
❑ 12 Dorsey Levens	.40	.18
❑ 13 Steve McNair	.40	.18
❑ 14 Derrick Thomas	.20	.09
❑ 15 Rob Moore	.20	.09
❑ 16 Peter Boulware	.10	.05
❑ 17 Terry Allen	.40	.18
❑ 18 Joey Galloway	.40	.18
❑ 19 Jerome Bettis	.40	.18
❑ 20 Carl Pickens	.40	.18
❑ 21 Napoleon Kaufman	.40	.18
❑ 22 Troy Aikman	1.00	.45
❑ 23 Curtis Conway	.20	.09
❑ 24 Adrian Murrell	.20	.09
❑ 25 Elvis Grbac	.20	.09
❑ 26 Garrison Hearst	.40	.18
❑ 27 Chris Sanders	.10	.05
❑ 28 Scott Mitchell	.20	.09
❑ 29 Junior Seau	.20	.09
❑ 30 Chris Chandler	.20	.09
❑ 31 Kevin Hardy	.10	.05
❑ 32 Terrell Davis	1.50	.70
❑ 33 Keyshawn Johnson	.40	.18
❑ 34 Natrone Means	.40	.18
❑ 35 Antowain Smith	.40	.18
❑ 36 Jake Plummer	1.00	.45
❑ 37 Isaac Bruce	.40	.18
❑ 38 Tony Banks	.20	.09
❑ 39 Reidel Anthony	.20	.09
❑ 40 Darren Woodson	.10	.05
❑ 41 Corey Dillon	.50	.23
❑ 42 Antonio Freeman	.40	.18
❑ 43 Eddie George	.75	.35
❑ 44 Yancey Thigpen	.10	.05
❑ 45 Tim Brown	.40	.18
❑ 46 Wayne Chrebet	.40	.18
❑ 47 Andre Rison	.20	.09
❑ 48 Michael Strahan	.10	.05
❑ 49 Deion Sanders	.40	.18
❑ 50 Eric Moulds	.40	.18
❑ 51 Mark Brunell	.75	.35
❑ 52 Rae Carruth	.20	.09
❑ 53 Warren Sapp	.20	.09
❑ 54 Mark Chmura	.20	.09
❑ 55 Darrell Green	.20	.09
❑ 56 Quinn Early	.10	.05
❑ 57 Barry Sanders	2.00	.90
❑ 58 Neil O'Donnell	.20	.09
❑ 59 Tony Brackens	.10	.05
❑ 60 Willie Davis	.10	.05
❑ 61 Shannon Sharpe	.20	.09
❑ 62 Shawn Springs	.10	.05
❑ 63 Tony Gonzalez	.10	.05
❑ 64 Rodney Thomas	.10	.05
❑ 65 Terance Mathis	.20	.09
❑ 66 Brett Favre	2.00	.90
❑ 67 Eric Swann	.10	.05
❑ 68 Kevin Turner	.10	.05
❑ 69 Tyrone Wheatley	.20	.09
❑ 70 Trent Dilfer	.40	.18
❑ 71 Bryan Cox	.10	.05
❑ 72 Lake Dawson	.10	.05
❑ 73 Will Blackwell	.10	.05
❑ 74 Fred Lane	.20	.09
❑ 75 Ty Detmer	.20	.09
❑ 76 Eddie Kennison	.20	.09
❑ 77 Jimmy Smith	.20	.09
❑ 78 Chris Calloway	.10	.05
❑ 79 Shawn Jefferson	.10	.05
❑ 80 Dan Marino	2.00	.90
❑ 81 LeRoy Butler	.10	.05
❑ 82 William Roaf	.10	.05
❑ 83 Rick Mirer	.10	.05
❑ 84 Dermontti Dawson	.10	.05
❑ 85 Errict Rhett	.20	.09
❑ 86 Lamar Thomas	.10	.05
❑ 87 Lamar Lathon	.10	.05
❑ 88 John Randle	.20	.09
❑ 89 Darryl Williams	.10	.05
❑ 90 Keenan McCardell	.20	.09
❑ 91 Erik Kramer	.10	.05
❑ 92 Ken Dilger	.10	.05
❑ 93 Dave Meggett	.10	.05
❑ 94 Jeff Blake	.20	.09
❑ 95 Ed McCaffrey	.20	.09
❑ 96 Charles Johnson	.10	.05
❑ 97 Irving Spikes	.10	.05
❑ 98 Mike Alstott	.40	.18
❑ 99 Vincent Brisby	.10	.05
❑ 100 Michael Westbrook	.20	.09
❑ 101 Rickey Dudley	.10	.05
❑ 102 Bert Emanuel	.20	.09
❑ 103 Daryl Johnston	.20	.09
❑ 104 Lawrence Phillips	.10	.05
❑ 105 Eric Bieniemy	.10	.05
❑ 106 Bryant Westbrook	.10	.05
❑ 107 Rob Johnson	.20	.09
❑ 108 Ray Zellars	.10	.05
❑ 109 Anthony Johnson	.10	.05
❑ 110 Reggie White	.40	.18
❑ 111 Wesley Walls	.20	.09
❑ 112 Amani Toomer	.20	.09
❑ 113 Gary Brown	.10	.05
❑ 114 Brian Blades	.10	.05
❑ 115 Alex Van Dyke	.10	.05
❑ 116 Michael Haynes	.10	.05
❑ 117 Jessie Armstead	.10	.05
❑ 118 James Jett	.20	.09

❑	119 Troy Drayton	.10	.05
❑	120 Craig Heyward	.10	.05
❑	121 Steve Atwater	.10	.05
❑	122 Tiki Barber	.20	.09
❑	123 Karim Abdul-Jabbar	.40	.18
❑	124 Kimble Anders	.20	.09
❑	125 Frank Sanders	.20	.09
❑	126 David Sloan	.10	.05
❑	127 Andre Hastings	.10	.05
❑	128 Vinny Testaverde	.20	.09
❑	129 Robert Smith	.40	.18
❑	130 Horace Copeland	.10	.05
❑	131 Larry Centers	.10	.05
❑	132 J.J. Stokes	.20	.09
❑	133 Ike Hilliard	.20	.09
❑	134 Muhsin Muhammad	.20	.09
❑	135 Sean Dawkins	.10	.05
❑	136 Raymont Harris	.10	.05
❑	137 Lamar Smith	.10	.05
❑	138 David Palmer	.10	.05
❑	139 Steve Young	.50	.23
❑	140 Bryan Still	.10	.05
❑	141 Keith Byars	.10	.05
❑	142 Cris Carter	.40	.18
❑	143 Charlie Garner	.10	.05
❑	144 Drew Bledsoe	.75	.35
❑	145 Simeon Rice	.20	.09
❑	146 Merton Hanks	.10	.05
❑	147 Aeneas Williams	.10	.05
❑	148 Rodney Hampton	.20	.09
❑	149 Zach Thomas	.10	.05
❑	150 Mark Bruener	.10	.05
❑	151 Jason Dunn	.10	.05
❑	152 Danny Wuerffel	.20	.09
❑	153 Jim Druckenmiller	.20	.09
❑	154 Greg Hill	.10	.05
❑	155 Earnest Byner	.10	.05
❑	156 Greg Lloyd	.10	.05
❑	157 John Mobley	.10	.05
❑	158 Tim Biakabutuka	.20	.09
❑	159 Terrell Owens	.40	.18
❑	160 O.J. McDuffie	.20	.09
❑	161 Glenn Foley	.20	.09
❑	162 Derrick Brooks	.10	.05
❑	163 Dave Brown	.10	.05
❑	164 Ki-Jana Carter	.10	.05
❑	165 Bobby Hoying	.20	.09
❑	166 Randal Hill	.10	.05
❑	167 Michael Irvin	.40	.18
❑	168 Bruce Smith	.20	.09
❑	169 Troy Davis	.10	.05
❑	170 Derrick Mayes	.20	.09
❑	171 Henry Ellard	.20	.09
❑	172 Dana Stubblefield	.10	.05
❑	173 Willie McGinest	.10	.05
❑	174 Leeland McElroy	.10	.05
❑	175 Edgar Bennett	.10	.05
❑	176 Robert Porcher	.10	.05
❑	177 Randall Cunningham	.40	.18
❑	178 Jim Everett	.10	.05
❑	179 Jake Reed	.20	.09
❑	180 Quentin Coryatt	.10	.05
❑	181 William Floyd	.10	.05
❑	182 Jason Sehorn	.10	.05
❑	183 Carnell Lake	.10	.05
❑	184 Dexter Coakley	.10	.05
❑	185 Derrick Alexander WR	.20	.09
❑	186 Johnnie Morton	.20	.09
❑	187 Irving Fryar	.20	.09
❑	188 Warren Moon	.40	.18
❑	189 Todd Collins	.10	.05
❑	190 Ken Norton	.10	.05
❑	191 Terry Glenn	.40	.18
❑	192 Rashaan Salaam	.10	.05
❑	193 Jerry Rice	1.00	.45
❑	194 James O.Stewart	.20	.09
❑	195 David LaFleur	.10	.05
❑	196 Eric Green	.10	.05
❑	197 Gus Frerotte	.10	.05
❑	198 Willie Green	.10	.05
❑	199 Marshall Faulk	.40	.18
❑	200 Brett Perriman	.10	.05
❑	201 Darnay Scott	.20	.09
❑	202 Marvin Harrison	.20	.09
❑	203 Joe Aska	.10	.05
❑	204 Darrien Gordon	.10	.05
❑	205 Herman Moore	.40	.18
❑	206 Curtis Martin	.40	.18
❑	207 Derek Loville	.10	.05
❑	208 Dale Carter	.10	.05
❑	209 Heath Shuler	.10	.05
❑	210 Jonathan Ogden	.10	.05
❑	211 Leslie Shepherd	.10	.05
❑	212 Tony Boselli	.10	.05
❑	213 Eric Metcalf	.10	.05
❑	214 Neil Smith	.20	.09
❑	215 Anthony Miller	.10	.05
❑	216 Jeff George	.20	.09
❑	217 Charles Way	.10	.05
❑	218 Mario Bates	.20	.09
❑	219 Ben Coates	.20	.09
❑	220 Michael Jackson	.10	.05
❑	221 Thurman Thomas	.40	.18
❑	222 Kyle Brady	.10	.05
❑	223 Marcus Allen	.40	.18
❑	224 Robert Brooks	.20	.09
❑	225 Yatil Green	.10	.05
❑	226 Byron Hanspard	.20	.09
❑	227 Andre Reed	.20	.09
❑	228 Chris Warren	.20	.09
❑	229 Jackie Harris	.10	.05
❑	230 Ricky Watters	.20	.09
❑	231 Bobby Engram	.20	.09
❑	232 Tamarick Vanover	.10	.05
❑	233 Peyton Manning RC	10.00	4.50
❑	234 Curtis Enis RC	2.50	1.10
❑	235 Randy Moss RC	10.00	4.50
❑	236 Charles Woodson RC	2.50	1.10
❑	237 Robert Edwards RC	1.00	.45
❑	238 Jacquez Green RC	1.50	.70
❑	239 Keith Brooking RC	.75	.35
❑	240 Jerome Pathon RC	.75	.35
❑	241 Kevin Dyson RC	2.00	.90
❑	242 Fred Taylor RC	5.00	2.20
❑	243 Tavian Banks RC	.75	.35
❑	244 Marcus Nash RC	1.50	.70
❑	245 Brian Griese RC	3.00	1.35
❑	246 Andre Wadsworth RC	.75	.35
❑	247 Ahman Green RC	1.50	.70
❑	248 Joe Jurevicius RC	.75	.35
❑	249 Germane Crowell RC	2.50	1.10
❑	250 Skip Hicks RC	1.50	.70
❑	251 Ryan Leaf RC	2.00	.90
❑	252 Hines Ward RC	.75	.35
❑	253 John Elway OS	1.00	.45
❑	254 Mark Brunell OS	.40	.18
❑	255 Brett Favre OS	1.00	.45
❑	256 Troy Aikman OS	.50	.23
❑	257 Warrick Dunn OS	.20	.09
❑	258 Barry Sanders OS	1.00	.45
❑	259 Eddie George OS	.40	.18
❑	260 Kordell Stewart OS	.40	.18
❑	261 Emmitt Smith OS	.75	.35
❑	262 Steve Young OS	.40	.18
❑	263 Terrell Davis OS	.75	.35
❑	264 Dorsey Levens OS	.20	.09
❑	265 Dan Marino OS	1.00	.45
❑	266 Jerry Rice OS	.50	.23
❑	267 Drew Bledsoe OS	.40	.18
❑	268 Brett Favre CL	.60	.25
❑	269 Barry Sanders CL	.60	.25
❑	270 Terrell Davis CL	.40	.18
❑	251AU Ryan Leaf AUTO	80.00	36.00

1998 Score Complete Players

		MINT	NRMT
	COMPLETE SET (30)	80.00	36.00
	COMMON CARD (1A-10C)	1.50	.70

EACH PLAYER HAS THREE CARDS
ALL THREE PRICED THE SAME
STATED ODDS 1:11

❑	1A Brett Favre	5.00	2.20
❑	1B Brett Favre	8.00	3.60
❑	1C Brett Favre	8.00	3.60
❑	2A John Elway	5.00	2.20
❑	2B John Elway	5.00	2.20
❑	2C John Elway	5.00	2.20
❑	3A Emmitt Smith	4.00	1.80
❑	3B Emmitt Smith	6.00	2.70

❑	3C Emmitt Smith	6.00	2.70
❑	4A Kordell Stewart	1.50	.70
❑	4B Kordell Stewart	1.50	.70
❑	4C Kordell Stewart	1.50	.70
❑	5A Dan Marino	5.00	2.20
❑	5B Dan Marino	8.00	3.60
❑	5C Dan Marino	8.00	3.60
❑	6A Mark Brunell	2.00	.90
❑	6B Mark Brunell	3.00	1.35
❑	6C Mark Brunell	3.00	1.35
❑	7A Terrell Davis	5.00	2.20
❑	7B Terrell Davis	5.00	2.20
❑	7C Terrell Davis	5.00	2.20
❑	8A Barry Sanders	5.00	2.20
❑	8B Barry Sanders	8.00	3.60
❑	8C Barry Sanders	8.00	3.60
❑	9A Warrick Dunn	1.50	.70
❑	9B Warrick Dunn	1.50	.70
❑	9C Warrick Dunn	1.50	.70
❑	10A Jerry Rice	2.50	1.10
❑	10B Jerry Rice	4.00	1.80
❑	10C Jerry Rice	4.00	1.80

1998 Score Epix

		MINT	NRMT
	COMP.ORANGE SET (24)	250.00	110.00
	COMMON SEASON (E1-E8)	5.00	2.20
	COMMON GAME (E9-E16)	4.00	1.80
	COMMON MOMENT (E17-E24)	6.00	2.70

OVERALL STATED ODDS 1:61 HOBBY
*PURPLE CARDS: .75X TO 2X ORANGE
*EMERALD CARDS: 2X TO 4X ORANGE
ONLY ORANGE CARDS PRICED BELOW

❑	E1 Emmitt Smith SEASON	25.00	11.00
❑	E2 Troy Aikman SEASON	15.00	6.75
❑	E3 Terrell Davis SEASON	25.00	11.00
❑	E4 Drew Bledsoe SEASON	12.00	5.50
❑	E5 Jeff George SEASON	5.00	2.20
❑	E6 Kerry Collins SEASON	5.00	2.20
❑	E7 A.Freeman SEASON	6.00	2.70
❑	E8 Herman Moore SEASON	6.00	2.70
❑	E9 Barry Sanders GAME	20.00	9.00
❑	E10 Brett Favre GAME	20.00	9.00
❑	E11 Michael Irvin GAME	4.00	1.80
❑	E12 Steve Young GAME	6.00	2.70
❑	E13 Mark Brunell GAME	8.00	3.60
❑	E14 Jerome Bettis GAME	4.00	1.80
❑	E15 Deion Sanders GAME	4.00	1.80
❑	E16 Jeff Blake GAME	4.00	1.80
❑	E17 Dan Marino MOMENT	30.00	13.50

		MINT	NRMT
❑ E18	Eddie George MOMENT	12.00	5.50
❑ E19	Jerry Rice MOMENT..	15.00	6.75
❑ E20	John Elway MOMENT	30.00	13.50
❑ E21	Curtis Martin MOMENT	8.00	3.60
❑ E22	K.Stewart MOMENT	8.00	3.60
❑ E23	Junior Seau MOMENT	6.00	2.70
❑ E24	Reggie White MOMENT	6.00	2.70

1998 Score Epix Hobby

	MINT	NRMT
COMPLETE SET (24)	120.00	55.00
COMMON IMAGE (I1-I6)	3.00	1.35
RED IMAGE PRINT RUN 1500 SETS		
COMMON MILESTONE (M7-M12)	5.00	2.20
RED MILESTONE PRINT RUN 500 SETS		
COMMON JOURNEY (J13-J18)	1.50	.70
RED JOURNEY PRINT RUN 3500 SETS		
COMMON SHOW.(S19-S24)	2.00	.90
RED SHOWDOWN PRINT RUN 2500 SETS		
*PURPLE CARDS: .6X TO 1.5X REDS		
PURPLE IMAGE PRINT RUN 750 SETS		
PURPLE MILESTONE PRINT RUN 200 SETS		
PURPLE JOURNEY PRINT RUN 1750 SETS		
PURPLE SHOWDOWN PRINT RUN 1250 SETS		
*EMERALD 1-6/13-24: 1.5X TO 4X REDS		
EMERALD IMAGE PRINT RUN 250 SETS		
EMERALD JOURNEY PRINT RUN 500 SETS		
EMERALD SHOWDOWN PRINT RUN 350 SETS		
*EMERALD M7-M12: 4X TO 10X REDS		
EMERALD MILESTONE PRINT RUN 30 SETS		
OVERALL STATED ODDS 1:61 ..		

		MINT	NRMT
❑ I1	Barry Sanders Image	15.00	6.75
❑ I2	Curtis Martin Image	3.00	1.35
❑ I3	John Elway Image	15.00	6.75
❑ I4	Jerome Bettis Image	3.00	1.35
❑ I5	Deion Sanders Image	3.00	1.35
❑ I6	Corey Dillon Image..........	3.00	1.35
❑ M7	Terrell Davis Milestone	30.00	13.50
❑ M8	Jerry Rice Milestone....	20.00	9.00
❑ M9	Eddie George Milestone	15.00	6.75
❑ M10	Mark Brunell Milestone	15.00	6.75
❑ M11	Dorsey Levens Milestone	8.00	3.60
❑ M12	Kerry Collins Milestone	5.00	2.20
❑ J13	Brett Favre Journey......	8.00	3.60
❑ J14	Kordell Stewart Journey	2.00	.90
❑ J15	Steve Young Journey ..	2.50	1.10
❑ J16	Steve McNair Journey..	1.50	.70
❑ J17	Emmitt Smith Journey..	6.00	2.70
❑ J18	Terry Glenn Journey	1.50	.70
❑ S19	Warrick Dunn Showdown	3.00	1.35
❑ S20	Dan Marino Showdown	10.00	4.50
❑ S21	Drew Bledsoe Showdown	4.00	1.80
❑ S22	Troy Aikman Showdown	5.00	2.20
❑ S23	Antonio Freeman Showdown	2.00	.90
❑ S24	Nap. Kaufman Showdown	2.00	.90

1998 Score Rookie Autographs

	MINT	NRMT
COMPLETE SET (34)	1200.00	550.00
COMMON CARD (1-34)..........	20.00	9.00
SEMISTARS..........................	30.00	13.50
UNLISTED STARS.................	40.00	18.00

		MINT	NRMT
❑ 1	Stephen Alexander	30.00	13.50
❑ 2	Tavian Banks	30.00	13.50
❑ 3	Charlie Batch.................	60.00	27.00
❑ 4	Keith Brooking..............	30.00	13.50
❑ 5	Thad Busby....................	20.00	9.00
❑ 6	John Dutton....................	20.00	9.00
❑ 7	Tim Dwight	60.00	27.00
❑ 8	Kevin Dyson	40.00	18.00
❑ 9	Robert Edwards	40.00	18.00
❑ 10	Greg Ellis......................	20.00	9.00
❑ 11	Robert Ellis	20.00	9.00
❑ 12A	Curtis Enis Black Ink..	60.00	27.00
❑ 12B	Curtis Enis Blue Ink ..	60.00	27.00
❑ 13	Chris Fuamatu-Ma'afala	30.00	13.50
❑ 14	Ahman Green	30.00	13.50
❑ 15	Jacquez Green	40.00	18.00
❑ 16	Brian Griese	60.00	27.00
❑ 17	Skip Hicks	30.00	13.50
❑ 18	Robert Holcombe	40.00	18.00
❑ 19	Tebucky Jones	20.00	9.00
❑ 20	Joe Jurevicius	30.00	13.50
❑ 21	Ryan Leaf	50.00	22.00
❑ 22	Leonard Little	20.00	9.00
❑ 23	Alonzo Mayes	20.00	9.00
❑ 24	Randy Moss	200.00	90.00
❑ 25	Michael Myers..............	20.00	9.00
❑ 26	Marcus Nash................	40.00	18.00
❑ 27	Jerome Pathon	30.00	13.50
❑ 28	Jason Peter..................	20.00	9.00
❑ 29	Anthony Simmons........	20.00	9.00
❑ 30	Tony Simmons	30.00	13.50
❑ 31	Takeo Spikes	30.00	13.50
❑ 32	Duane Starks	20.00	9.00
❑ 33	Fred Taylor	80.00	36.00
❑ 34	Hines Ward	30.00	13.50

1998 Score Star Salute

	MINT	NRMT
COMPLETE SET (20)	150.00	70.00
COMMON CARD (1-20)...........	5.00	2.20
STATED ODDS 1:35		

		MINT	NRMT
❑ 1	Terrell Davis	10.00	4.50
❑ 2	Barry Sanders..............	20.00	9.00
❑ 3	Steve Young	6.00	2.70
❑ 4	Drew Bledsoe	8.00	3.60
❑ 5	Kordell Stewart	5.00	2.20
❑ 6	Emmitt Smith................	15.00	6.75
❑ 7	Dorsey Levens	5.00	2.20
❑ 8	Corey Dillon..................	6.00	2.70
❑ 9	Jerome Bettis	5.00	2.20
❑ 10	Herman Moore	5.00	2.20
❑ 11	Brett Favre	20.00	9.00
❑ 12	Antonio Freeman...........	5.00	2.20
❑ 13	Mark Brunell	8.00	3.60
❑ 14	John Elway	20.00	9.00
❑ 15	Terry Glenn	5.00	2.20
❑ 16	Warrick Dunn	5.00	2.20
❑ 17	Eddie George	8.00	3.60
❑ 18	Troy Aikman	10.00	4.50
❑ 19	Deion Sanders	5.00	2.20
❑ 20	Jerry Rice	10.00	4.50

1999 Score

	MINT	NRMT
COMPLETE SET (275)	135.00	60.00
COMP.SET w/o SP's (220)......	15.00	6.75
COMMON CARD (1-275)............	.15	.07
SEMISTARS..............................	.25	.11
UNLISTED STARS.....................	.50	.23
COMMON ROOKIE (221-260) ..	1.25	.55
ROOKIE SEMISTARS	2.00	.90
ROOKIE UNL.STARS	3.00	1.35
COMMON ALL-PROS (261-270)	1.50	.70
SP ROOKIES AND SUBSET ODDS 1:3 H,1:9 R		
COMP.SHOWCASE (275)	400.00	180.00
*SHOWCASE STARS: 2.5X TO 6X HI COL.		
*SHOWCASE YOUNG STARS: 2X TO 5X		
*SHOWCASE RCs: .6X TO 1.5X ..		
*SHOWCASE AP/GC: .75X TO 2X		
SHOWCASE PRINT RUN 1989 SERIAL #'d SETS		
*ART.PROOF STARS: 80X TO 200X HI COL.		
*ART.PROOF YOUNG STARS: 60X TO 150X		
*ART.PROOF RCs: 8X TO 20X		
ART.PROOFS PRINT RUN 10 SER.#'d SETS		
ART.PROOFS INSERTED IN HOBBY PACKS ONLY		

		MINT	NRMT
❑ 1	Randy Moss	2.00	.90
❑ 2	Randall Cunningham..........	.50	.23
❑ 3	Cris Carter........................	.50	.23
❑ 4	Robert Smith.....................	.50	.23
❑ 5	Jake Reed.........................	.25	.11
❑ 6	Leroy Hoard	.15	.07
❑ 7	John Randle	.25	.11
❑ 8	Brett Favre	2.00	.90
❑ 9	Antonio Freeman...............	.50	.23
❑ 10	Dorsey Levens	.50	.23
❑ 11	Robert Brooks	.25	.11
❑ 12	Derrick Mayes	.25	.11
❑ 13	Mark Chmura	.25	.11
❑ 14	Darick Holmes.................	.15	.07
❑ 15	Vonnie Holliday	.15	.07
❑ 16	Mike Alstott	.50	.23
❑ 17	Warrick Dunn	.50	.23
❑ 18	Trent Dilfer	.25	.11
❑ 19	Jacquez Green	.25	.11
❑ 20	Reidel Anthony	.25	.11
❑ 21	Warren Sapp..................	.25	.11
❑ 22	Bert Emanuel	.25	.11
❑ 23	Curtis Enis......................	.50	.23
❑ 24	Curtis Conway................	.25	.11
❑ 25	Bobby Engram	.25	.11
❑ 26	Erik Kramer	.25	.11

❑ 27 Moses Moreno .15 .07
❑ 28 Edgar Bennett .15 .07
❑ 29 Barry Sanders 2.00 .90
❑ 30 Charlie Batch .75 .35
❑ 31 Herman Moore .50 .23
❑ 32 Johnnie Morton .25 .11
❑ 33 Germane Crowell .25 .11
❑ 34 Terry Fair .15 .07
❑ 35 Gary Brown .15 .07
❑ 36 Kent Graham .15 .07
❑ 37 Kerry Collins .25 .11
❑ 38 Charles Way .15 .07
❑ 39 Tiki Barber .15 .07
❑ 40 Ike Hilliard .15 .07
❑ 41 Joe Jurevicius .15 .07
❑ 42 Michael Strahan .15 .07
❑ 43 Jason Sehorn .15 .07
❑ 44 Brad Johnson .50 .23
❑ 45 Terry Allen .25 .11
❑ 46 Skip Hicks .50 .23
❑ 47 Michael Westbrook .25 .11
❑ 48 Leslie Shepherd .15 .07
❑ 49 Stephen Alexander .15 .07
❑ 50 Albert Connell .15 .07
❑ 51 Darrell Green .25 .11
❑ 52 Jake Plummer 1.00 .45
❑ 53 Adrian Murrell .25 .11
❑ 54 Frank Sanders .25 .11
❑ 55 Rob Moore .25 .11
❑ 56 Larry Centers .15 .07
❑ 57 Simeon Rice .25 .11
❑ 58 Andre Wadsworth .15 .07
❑ 59 Duce Staley .50 .23
❑ 60 Charles Johnson .15 .07
❑ 61 Charlie Garner .25 .11
❑ 62 Bobby Hoying .25 .11
❑ 63 Daryl Johnston .25 .11
❑ 64 Emmitt Smith 1.25 .55
❑ 65 Troy Aikman 1.25 .55
❑ 66 Michael Irvin .25 .11
❑ 67 Deion Sanders .50 .23
❑ 68 Chris Warren .15 .07
❑ 69 Darren Woodson .15 .07
❑ 70 Rod Woodson .25 .11
❑ 71 Travis Jervey .15 .07
❑ 72 Jerry Rice 1.25 .55
❑ 73 Terrell Owens .50 .23
❑ 74 Steve Young .75 .35
❑ 75 Garrison Hearst .25 .11
❑ 76 J.J. Stokes .25 .11
❑ 77 Ken Norton .15 .07
❑ 78 R.W. McQuarters .15 .07
❑ 79 Bryant Young .15 .07
❑ 80 Jamal Anderson .50 .23
❑ 81 Chris Chandler .25 .11
❑ 82 Terance Mathis .25 .11
❑ 83 Tim Dwight .50 .23
❑ 84 O.J. Santiago .15 .07
❑ 85 Chris Calloway .15 .07
❑ 86 Keith Brooking .15 .07
❑ 87 Eddie Kennison .25 .11
❑ 88 Willie Roaf .15 .07
❑ 89 Cam Cleeland .15 .07
❑ 90 Lamar Smith .15 .07
❑ 91 Sean Dawkins .15 .07
❑ 92 Tim Biakabutuka .25 .11
❑ 93 Muhsin Muhammad .25 .11
❑ 94 Steve Beuerlein .15 .07
❑ 95 Rae Carruth .25 .11
❑ 96 Wesley Walls .25 .11
❑ 97 Kevin Greene .25 .11
❑ 98 Trent Green .25 .11
❑ 99 Tony Banks .25 .11
❑ 100 Greg Hill .15 .07
❑ 101 Robert Holcombe .25 .11
❑ 102 Isaac Bruce .50 .23
❑ 103 Amp Lee .15 .07
❑ 104 Az-Zahir Hakim .15 .07
❑ 105 Warren Moon .50 .23
❑ 106 Jeff George .25 .11
❑ 107 Rocket Ismail .25 .11
❑ 108 Kordell Stewart .50 .23
❑ 109 Jerome Bettis .50 .23
❑ 110 Courtney Hawkins .15 .07
❑ 111 Chris Fuamatu-Ma'afala .15 .07
❑ 112 Levon Kirkland .15 .07
❑ 113 Hines Ward .15 .07
❑ 114 Will Blackwell .15 .07
❑ 115 Corey Dillon .50 .23
❑ 116 Carl Pickens .25 .11
❑ 117 Neil O'Donnell .25 .11
❑ 118 Jeff Blake .25 .11
❑ 119 Darnay Scott .15 .07
❑ 120 Takeo Spikes .15 .07
❑ 121 Steve McNair .50 .23
❑ 122 Frank Wycheck .15 .07
❑ 123 Eddie George .60 .25
❑ 124 Chris Sanders .15 .07
❑ 125 Yancey Thigpen .15 .07
❑ 126 Kevin Dyson .25 .11
❑ 127 Blaine Bishop .15 .07
❑ 128 Fred Taylor 1.00 .45
❑ 129 Mark Brunell .75 .35
❑ 130 Jimmy Smith .25 .11
❑ 131 Keenan McCardell .25 .11
❑ 132 Kyle Brady .15 .07
❑ 133 Tavian Banks .15 .07
❑ 134 James Stewart .25 .11
❑ 135 Kevin Hardy .15 .07
❑ 136 Jonathan Quinn .15 .07
❑ 137 Jermaine Lewis .25 .11
❑ 138 Priest Holmes .50 .23
❑ 139 Scott Mitchell .25 .11
❑ 140 Eric Zeier .25 .11
❑ 141 Patrick Johnson .15 .07
❑ 142 Ray Lewis .15 .07
❑ 143 Terry Kirby .15 .07
❑ 144 Ty Detmer .15 .07
❑ 145 Irv Smith .15 .07
❑ 146 Chris Spielman .15 .07
❑ 147 Antonio Langham .15 .07
❑ 148 Dan Marino 2.00 .90
❑ 149 O.J. McDuffie .25 .11
❑ 150 Oronde Gadsden .15 .07
❑ 151 Karim Abdul-Jabbar .25 .11
❑ 152 Yatil Green .15 .07
❑ 153 Zach Thomas .25 .11
❑ 154 John Avery .25 .11
❑ 155 Lamar Thomas .15 .07
❑ 156 Drew Bledsoe .75 .35
❑ 157 Terry Glenn .50 .23
❑ 158 Ben Coates .25 .11
❑ 159 Shawn Jefferson .15 .07
❑ 160 Sedrick Shaw .15 .07
❑ 161 Tony Simmons .15 .07
❑ 162 Ty Law .15 .07
❑ 163 Robert Edwards .25 .11
❑ 164 Curtis Martin .50 .23
❑ 165 Keyshawn Johnson .50 .23
❑ 166 Vinny Testaverde .25 .11
❑ 167 Aaron Glenn .15 .07
❑ 168 Wayne Chrebet .25 .11
❑ 169 Dedric Ward .15 .07
❑ 170 Peyton Manning 2.00 .90
❑ 171 Marshall Faulk .50 .23
❑ 172 Marvin Harrison .50 .23
❑ 173 Jerome Pathon .15 .07
❑ 174 Ken Dilger .15 .07
❑ 175 E.G. Green .15 .07
❑ 176 Doug Flutie .60 .25
❑ 177 Thurman Thomas .25 .11
❑ 178 Andre Reed .25 .11
❑ 179 Eric Moulds .50 .23
❑ 180 Antowain Smith .50 .23
❑ 181 Bruce Smith .25 .11
❑ 182 Rob Johnson .25 .11
❑ 183 Terrell Davis 1.25 .55
❑ 184 John Elway 2.00 .90
❑ 185 Ed McCaffrey .25 .11
❑ 186 Rod Smith .25 .11
❑ 187 Shannon Sharpe .25 .11
❑ 188 Marcus Nash .25 .11
❑ 189 Brian Griese .75 .35
❑ 190 Neil Smith .25 .11
❑ 191 Bubby Brister .15 .07
❑ 192 Ryan Leaf .50 .23
❑ 193 Natrone Means .25 .11
❑ 194 Mikhael Ricks .15 .07
❑ 195 Junior Seau .25 .11
❑ 196 Jim Harbaugh .25 .11
❑ 197 Bryan Still .15 .07
❑ 198 Freddie Jones .15 .07
❑ 199 Andre Rison .25 .11
❑ 200 Elvis Grbac .25 .11
❑ 201 Byron Bam Morris .15 .07
❑ 202 Rashaan Shehee .15 .07
❑ 203 Kimble Anders .25 .11
❑ 204 Donnell Bennett .15 .07
❑ 205 Tony Gonzalez .25 .11
❑ 206 Derrick Alexander WR .25 .11
❑ 207 Jon Kitna .60 .25
❑ 208 Ricky Watters .25 .11
❑ 209 Joey Galloway .50 .23
❑ 210 Ahman Green .25 .11
❑ 211 Shawn Springs .15 .07
❑ 212 Michael Sinclair .15 .07
❑ 213 Napoleon Kaufman .50 .23
❑ 214 Tim Brown .50 .23
❑ 215 Charles Woodson .50 .23
❑ 216 Harvey Williams .15 .07
❑ 217 Jon Ritchie .15 .07
❑ 218 Rich Gannon .25 .11
❑ 219 Rickey Dudley .15 .07
❑ 220 James Jett .25 .11
❑ 221 Tim Couch RC 15.00 6.75
❑ 222 Ricky Williams RC 15.00 6.75
❑ 223 Donovan McNabb RC 10.00 4.50
❑ 224 Edgerrin James RC 25.00 11.00
❑ 225 Torry Holt RC 8.00 3.60
❑ 226 Daunte Culpepper RC 10.00 4.50
❑ 227 Akili Smith RC 6.00 2.70
❑ 228 Champ Bailey RC 4.00 1.80
❑ 229 Chris Claiborne RC 2.00 .90
❑ 230 Chris McAlister RC 2.00 .90
❑ 231 Troy Edwards RC 5.00 2.20
❑ 232 Jevon Kearse RC 6.00 2.70
❑ 233 Shaun King RC 10.00 4.50
❑ 234 David Boston RC 5.00 2.20
❑ 235 Peerless Price RC 5.00 2.20
❑ 236 Cecil Collins RC 3.00 1.35
❑ 237 Rob Konrad RC 2.00 .90
❑ 238 Cade McNown RC UER 10.00 4.50
(college listed as UNLV)
❑ 239 Shawn Bryson RC 2.00 .90
❑ 240 Kevin Faulk RC 4.00 1.80
❑ 241 Scott Covington RC 3.00 1.35
❑ 242 James Johnson RC 4.00 1.80
❑ 243 Mike Cloud RC 3.00 1.35
❑ 244 Aaron Brooks RC 3.00 1.35
❑ 245 Sedrick Irvin RC 3.00 1.35
❑ 246 Amos Zereoue RC 3.00 1.35
❑ 247 Jermaine Fazande RC 2.00 .90
❑ 248 Joe Germaine RC 3.00 1.35
❑ 249 Brock Huard RC 4.00 1.80
❑ 250 Craig Yeast RC 2.00 .90
❑ 251 Travis McGriff RC 3.00 1.35
❑ 252 D'Wayne Bates RC 2.00 .90
❑ 253 Na Brown RC 3.00 1.35
❑ 254 Tai Streets RC 2.00 .90
❑ 255 Andy Katzenmoyer RC 3.00 1.35
❑ 256 Kevin Johnson RC 8.00 3.60
❑ 257 Joe Montgomery RC 2.00 .90
❑ 258 Karsten Bailey RC 3.00 1.35
❑ 259 De'Mond Parker RC 3.00 1.35
❑ 260 Reginald Kelly RC 1.25 .55
❑ 261 Eddie George AP 1.25 .55
❑ 262 Jamal Anderson AP 1.25 .55
❑ 263 Barry Sanders AP 6.00 2.70
❑ 264 Fred Taylor AP 3.00 1.35
❑ 265 Keyshawn Johnson AP 1.25 .55
❑ 266 Jerry Rice AP 4.00 1.80
❑ 267 Doug Flutie AP 2.00 .90
❑ 268 Deion Sanders AP 1.25 .55
❑ 269 Randall Cunningham AP 1.25 .55
❑ 270 Steve Young AP 2.50 1.10
❑ 271 John Elway GC 6.00 2.70
Terrell Davis GC
❑ 272 Peyton Manning GC 5.00 2.20
Marshall Faulk GC
❑ 273 Brett Favre GC 6.00 2.70
Antonio Freeman GC
❑ 274 Troy Aikman GC 4.00 1.80
Emmitt Smith GC
❑ 275 Cris Carter GC 5.00 2.20
Randy Moss GC

1999 Score 10th Anniversary Reprints

	MINT	NRMT
COMPLETE SET (20)	60.00	27.00
COMMON CARD (1-20)	2.50	1.10
SEMISTARS	4.00	1.80

STATED PRINT RUN 1989 SERIAL #'d SETS
FIRST 150-CARDS WERE SIGNED

		MINT	NRMT
❑ 1	Barry Sanders	20.00	9.00
❑ 2	Troy Aikman	12.00	5.50
❑ 3	John Elway	12.00	5.50
❑ 4	Cris Carter	4.00	1.80
❑ 5	Tim Brown	4.00	1.80
❑ 6	Doug Flutie	5.00	2.20
❑ 7	Chris Chandler	2.50	1.10
❑ 8	Thurman Thomas	4.00	1.80
❑ 9	Steve Young	5.00	2.20
❑ 10	Dan Marino	12.00	5.50
❑ 11	Derrick Thomas	2.50	1.10
❑ 12	Bubby Brister	2.50	1.10
❑ 13	Jerry Rice	8.00	3.60
❑ 14	Andre Rison	2.50	1.10
❑ 15	Randall Cunningham	4.00	1.80
❑ 16	Vinny Testaverde	2.50	1.10
❑ 17	Michael Irvin	2.50	1.10
❑ 18	Rod Woodson	2.50	1.10
❑ 19	Neil Smith	2.50	1.10
❑ 20	Deion Sanders	4.00	1.80

1999 Score 10th Anniversary Reprints Autographs

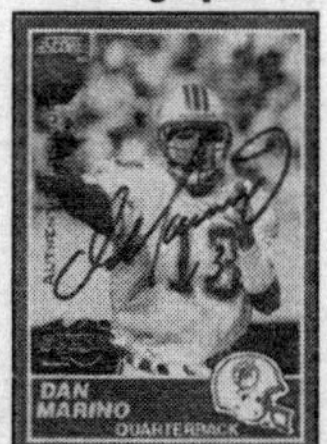

	MINT	NRMT
COMPLETE SET (20)	1500.00	700.00
COMMON CARD (1-20)	40.00	18.00
SEMISTARS	60.00	27.00

STATED PRINT RUN 150 SERIAL #'d SETS
SOME CARDS ISSUED VIA MAIL REDEMPTION
REDEMPTION EXPIRATION: 5/1/2000

		MINT	NRMT
❑ 1	Barry Sanders	300.00	135.00
❑ 2	Troy Aikman	175.00	80.00
❑ 3	John Elway	250.00	110.00
❑ 4	Cris Carter	60.00	27.00
❑ 5	Tim Brown	60.00	27.00
❑ 6	Doug Flutie	100.00	45.00
❑ 7	Chris Chandler	40.00	18.00
❑ 8	Thurman Thomas	40.00	18.00
❑ 9	Steve Young	100.00	45.00
❑ 10	Dan Marino	250.00	110.00
❑ 11	Derrick Thomas	125.00	55.00
❑ 12	Bubby Brister	40.00	18.00
❑ 13	Jerry Rice	175.00	80.00
❑ 14	Andre Rison	40.00	18.00
❑ 15	Randall Cunningham	60.00	27.00
❑ 16	Vinny Testaverde	40.00	18.00
❑ 17	Michael Irvin	40.00	18.00
❑ 18	Rod Woodson	40.00	18.00
❑ 19	Neil Smith	40.00	18.00
❑ 20	Deion Sanders	100.00	45.00

1999 Score Complete Players

	MINT	NRMT
COMPLETE SET (30)	70.00	32.00
COMMON CARD (1-30)	1.50	.70

STATED ODDS 1:17 HOB, 1:35 RET

		MINT	NRMT
❑ 1	Antonio Freeman	2.00	.90
❑ 2	Troy Aikman	4.00	1.80
❑ 3	Jerry Rice	4.00	1.80
❑ 4	Brett Favre	6.00	2.70
❑ 5	Cris Carter	2.00	.90
❑ 6	Jamal Anderson	2.00	.90
❑ 7	John Elway	6.00	2.70
❑ 8	Mark Brunell	2.50	1.10
❑ 9	Steve McNair	2.00	.90
❑ 10	Kordell Stewart	2.00	.90
❑ 11	Drew Bledsoe	2.50	1.10
❑ 12	Tim Couch	8.00	3.60
❑ 13	Dan Marino	6.00	2.70
❑ 14	Akili Smith	2.50	1.10
❑ 15	Peyton Manning	5.00	2.20
❑ 16	Jake Plummer	3.00	1.35
❑ 17	Jerome Bettis	2.00	.90
❑ 18	Randy Moss	5.00	2.20
❑ 19	Keyshawn Johnson	2.00	.90
❑ 20	Barry Sanders	6.00	2.70
❑ 21	Ricky Williams	8.00	3.60
❑ 22	Emmitt Smith	4.00	1.80
❑ 23	Corey Dillon	2.00	.90
❑ 24	Dorsey Levens	2.00	.90
❑ 25	Donovan McNabb	4.00	1.80
❑ 26	Curtis Martin	2.00	.90
❑ 27	Eddie George	2.00	.90
❑ 28	Fred Taylor	2.50	1.10
❑ 29	Steve Young	2.50	1.10
❑ 30	Terrell Davis	4.00	1.80

1999 Score Franchise

	MINT	NRMT
COMPLETE SET (31)	120.00	55.00
COMMON CARD (1-31)	2.50	1.10
SEMISTARS	4.00	1.80

STATED ODDS 1:35

		MINT	NRMT
❑ 1	Brett Favre	15.00	6.75
❑ 2	Randy Moss	12.00	5.50
❑ 3	Mike Alstott	4.00	1.80
❑ 4	Barry Sanders	15.00	6.75
❑ 5	Curtis Enis	4.00	1.80
❑ 6	Ike Hilliard	2.50	1.10
❑ 7	Emmitt Smith	10.00	4.50
❑ 8	Jake Plummer	8.00	3.60
❑ 9	Brad Johnson	4.00	1.80
❑ 10	Duce Staley	4.00	1.80
❑ 11	Jamal Anderson	4.00	1.80
❑ 12	Steve Young	6.00	2.70
❑ 13	Eddie Kennison	2.50	1.10
❑ 14	Isaac Bruce	4.00	1.80
❑ 15	Muhsin Muhammad	2.50	1.10
❑ 16	Dan Marino	15.00	6.75
❑ 17	Drew Bledsoe	6.00	2.70
❑ 18	Curtis Martin	4.00	1.80
❑ 19	Doug Flutie	5.00	2.20
❑ 20	Peyton Manning	12.00	5.50
❑ 21	Kordell Stewart	4.00	1.80
❑ 22	Ty Detmer	2.50	1.10
❑ 23	Corey Dillon	4.00	1.80
❑ 24	Mark Brunell	6.00	2.70
❑ 25	Priest Holmes	4.00	1.80
❑ 26	Eddie George	5.00	2.20
❑ 27	John Elway	15.00	6.75
❑ 28	Natrone Means	2.50	1.10
❑ 29	Tim Brown	4.00	1.80
❑ 30	Andre Rison	2.50	1.10
❑ 31	Joey Galloway	4.00	1.80

1999 Score Future Franchise

	MINT	NRMT
COMPLETE SET (31)	150.00	70.00
COMMON CARD (1-31)	3.00	1.35
SEMISTARS	4.00	1.80

STATED ODDS 1:35 HOBBY

		MINT	NRMT
❑ 1	Aaron Brooks Brett Favre	12.00	5.50
❑ 2	Daunte Culpepper Randy Moss	15.00	6.75
❑ 3	Shaun King Mike Alstott	10.00	4.50
❑ 4	Sedrick Irvin Barry Sanders	12.00	5.50
❑ 5	Cade McNown Curtis Enis	10.00	4.50
❑ 6	Joe Montgomery Ike Hilliard	3.00	1.35
❑ 7	Wane McGarity Emmitt Smith	8.00	3.60
❑ 8	David Boston Jake Plummer	5.00	2.20
❑ 9	Champ Bailey	4.00	1.80

Brad Johnson		
❑ 10 Donovan McNabb	10.00	4.50
Duce Staley		
❑ 11 Reginald Kelly	4.00	1.80
Jamal Anderson		
❑ 12 Tai Streets	5.00	2.20
Steve Young		
❑ 13 Ricky Williams	15.00	6.75
Eddie Kennison		
❑ 14 Torry Holt	6.00	2.70
Isaac Bruce		
❑ 15 Mike Rucker	3.00	1.35
Mushin Muhammad		
❑ 16 James Johnson	12.00	5.50
Dan Marino		
❑ 17 Kevin Faulk	5.00	2.20
Drew Bledsoe		
❑ 18 Randy Thomas	3.00	1.35
Curtis Martin		
❑ 19 Peerless Price	5.00	2.20
Doug Flutie		
❑ 20 Edgerrin James	25.00	11.00
Peyton Manning		
❑ 21 Troy Edwards	4.00	1.80
Kordell Stewart		
❑ 22 Tim Couch	15.00	6.75
Ty Detmer		
❑ 23 Akili Smith	6.00	2.70
Corey Dillon		
❑ 24 Fernando Bryant	5.00	2.20
Mark Brunell		
❑ 25 Chris McAlister	4.00	1.80
Priest Holmes		
❑ 26 Jevon Kearse	6.00	2.70
Eddie George		
❑ 27 Travis McGriff	12.00	5.50
John Elway		
❑ 28 Jermaine Fazande	3.00	1.35
Natrone Means		
❑ 29 Dameane Douglas	4.00	1.80
Tim Brown		
❑ 30 Mike Cloud	3.00	1.35
Andre Rison		
❑ 31 Brock Huard	4.00	1.80
Joey Galloway		

1999 Score Millenium Men

	MINT	NRMT
COMPLETE SET (3)	60.00	27.00
COMMON CARD (1-3)	25.00	11.00

STATED PRINT RUN 1000 SERIAL #'d SETS
FIRST 100-CARDS WERE SIGNED
REDEMPTION EXPIRATION: 5/1/2000
INSERTED IN RETAIL PACKS ONLY

❑ 1 Barry Sanders	25.00	11.00
❑ 2 Ricky Williams	20.00	9.00
❑ 3 Barry Sanders	25.00	11.00
Ricky Williams		
❑ 1AU Barry Sanders AUTO	300.00	135.00
❑ 2AU Ricky Williams AUTO	250.00	110.00
❑ 3AU Barry Sanders AUTO	400.00	180.00
Ricky Williams AUTO		

1999 Score Numbers Game

	MINT	NRMT
COMPLETE SET (30)	70.00	32.00
COMMON CARD (1-7)	1.50	.70
COMMON CARD (8-14)	2.00	.90
COMMON CARD (15-30)	1.50	.70
SEMISTARS 15-30	2.50	1.10

RANDOM INSERTS IN HOBBY PACKS

❑ 1 Brett Favre/4212	6.00	2.70
❑ 2 Steve Young/4170	2.50	1.10
❑ 3 Jake Plummer/3737	3.00	1.35
❑ 4 Drew Bledsoe/3633	2.50	1.10
❑ 5 Dan Marino/3497	6.00	2.70
❑ 6 Peyton Manning/3739	5.00	2.20
❑ 7 Randall Cunningham/3704	1.50	.70
❑ 8 John Elway/2806	8.00	3.60
❑ 9 Doug Flutie/2711	2.50	1.10
❑ 10 Mark Brunell/2601	3.00	1.35
❑ 11 Troy Aikman/2330	5.00	2.20
❑ 12 Terrell Davis/2008	5.00	2.20
❑ 13 Jamal Anderson/1846	2.00	.90
❑ 14 Garrison Hearst/1570	2.00	.90
❑ 15 Barry Sanders/1491	10.00	4.50
❑ 16 Emmitt Smith/1332	6.00	2.70
❑ 17 Marshall Faulk/1319	2.50	1.10
❑ 18 Eddie George/1294	3.00	1.35
❑ 19 Curtis Martin/1287	2.50	1.10
❑ 20 Fred Taylor/1223	5.00	2.20
❑ 21 Corey Dillon/1130	2.50	1.10
❑ 22 Antonio Freeman/1424	2.50	1.10
❑ 23 Eric Moulds/1368	2.50	1.10
❑ 24 Randy Moss/1313	8.00	3.60
❑ 25 Rod Smith/1222	1.50	.70
❑ 26 Jerry Rice/1157	6.00	2.70
❑ 27 Keyshawn Johnson/1131	2.50	1.10
❑ 28 Terrell Owens/1097	2.50	1.10
❑ 29 Tim Brown/1012	2.50	1.10
❑ 30 Cris Carter/1011	2.50	1.10

1999 Score Rookie Preview Autographs

	MINT	NRMT
COMPLETE SET (35)	800.00	350.00
COMMON CARD (1-35)	12.00	5.50
SEMISTARS	15.00	6.75
UNLISTED STARS	20.00	9.00

STATED PRINT RUN 600 SIGNED SETS
RANDOM INSERTS IN HOBBY PACKS
SOME CARDS ISSUED VIA MAIL REDEMPTION
REDEMPTION EXPIRATION: 5/1/2000

❑ 1 Champ Bailey	25.00	11.00
❑ 2 D'Wayne Bates	15.00	6.75
❑ 3 Michael Bishop	25.00	11.00
❑ 4 David Boston	30.00	13.50
❑ 5 Na Brown	15.00	6.75
❑ 6 Shawn Bryson	12.00	5.50
❑ 7 Chris Claiborne	20.00	9.00
❑ 8 Mike Cloud	15.00	6.75
❑ 9 Cecil Collins	12.00	5.50
❑ 10 Daunte Culpepper	50.00	22.00
❑ 11 Autry Denson	20.00	9.00
❑ 12 Troy Edwards	30.00	13.50
❑ 13 Kevin Faulk	25.00	11.00
❑ 14 Joe Germaine	20.00	9.00
❑ 15 Torry Holt	40.00	18.00
❑ 16 Brock Huard	25.00	11.00
❑ 17 Sedrick Irvin	20.00	9.00
❑ 18 Edgerrin James	120.00	55.00
❑ 19 James Johnson	25.00	11.00
❑ 20 Kevin Johnson	40.00	18.00
❑ 21 Corby Jones	12.00	5.50
❑ 22 Jevon Kearse	40.00	18.00
❑ 23 Shaun King Trade	50.00	22.00
❑ 24 Jim Kleinsasser	20.00	9.00
❑ 25 Rob Konrad	15.00	6.75
❑ 26 Chris McAlister	15.00	6.75
❑ 27 Darnell McDonald	20.00	9.00
❑ 28 Travis McGriff	20.00	9.00
❑ 29 Donovan McNabb	50.00	22.00
❑ 30 Cade McNown	50.00	22.00
❑ 31 De'Mond Parker	20.00	9.00
❑ 32 Peerless Price	30.00	13.50
❑ 33 Akili Smith	40.00	18.00
❑ 34 Tai Streets	20.00	9.00
❑ 35 Ricky Williams	100.00	45.00

1999 Score Scoring Core

	MINT	NRMT
COMPLETE SET (30)	70.00	32.00
COMMON CARD (1-30)	1.25	.55
SEMISTARS	1.50	.70

STATED ODDS 1:17 HOB, 1:35 RET

❑ 1 Antonio Freeman	2.00	.90
❑ 2 Troy Aikman	4.00	1.80
❑ 3 Jerry Rice	4.00	1.80
❑ 4 Brett Favre	6.00	2.70
❑ 5 Cris Carter	2.00	.90
❑ 6 Jamal Anderson	2.00	.90
❑ 7 John Elway	6.00	2.70
❑ 8 Tim Brown	2.00	.90
❑ 9 Mark Brunell	2.50	1.10
❑ 10 Terrell Owens	2.00	.90
❑ 11 Drew Bledsoe	2.50	1.10
❑ 12 Tim Couch	8.00	3.60
❑ 13 Dan Marino	6.00	2.70
❑ 14 Marshall Faulk	2.00	.90
❑ 15 Peyton Manning	5.00	2.20
❑ 16 Jake Plummer	3.00	1.35
❑ 17 Jerome Bettis	2.00	.90
❑ 18 Randy Moss	5.00	2.20
❑ 19 Charlie Batch	2.50	1.10
❑ 20 Barry Sanders	6.00	2.70
❑ 21 Ricky Williams	8.00	3.60
❑ 22 Emmitt Smith	4.00	1.80
❑ 23 Joey Galloway	2.00	.90
❑ 24 Herman Moore	2.00	.90
❑ 25 Natrone Means	1.25	.55
❑ 26 Mike Alstott	2.00	.90
❑ 27 Eddie George	2.00	.90
❑ 28 Fred Taylor	3.00	1.35
❑ 29 Steve Young	2.50	1.10
❑ 30 Terrell Davis	4.00	1.80

1999 Score Settle the Score

	MINT	NRMT
COMPLETE SET (30)	60.00	27.00
COMMON CARD (1-30)	1.50	.70
SEMISTARS	2.00	.90

STATED ODDS 1:17 RETAIL ......

Card	MINT	NRMT
❑ 1 Brett Favre / Randall Cunningham	6.00	2.70
❑ 2 Dan Marino / Doug Flutie	6.00	2.70
❑ 3 Emmitt Smith / Terry Allen	4.00	1.80
❑ 4 Barry Sanders / Warrick Dunn	6.00	2.70
❑ 5 Eddie George / Corey Dillon	2.50	1.10
❑ 6 Drew Bledsoe / Vinny Testaverde	2.50	1.10
❑ 7 Troy Aikman / Jake Plummer	4.00	1.80
❑ 8 Terrell Davis / Jamaal Anderson	4.00	1.80
❑ 9 John Elway / Chris Chandler	6.00	2.70
❑ 10 Mark Brunell / Steve Young	2.50	1.10
❑ 11 Cris Carter / Herman Moore	2.00	.90
❑ 12 Kordell Stewart / Steve McNair	2.00	.90
❑ 13 Natrone Means / Napoleon Kaufman	2.00	.90
❑ 14 Curtis Martin / Marshall Faulk	2.00	.90
❑ 15 Antonio Freeman / Terrell Owens	2.00	.90
❑ 16 Terry Glenn / Wayne Chrebet	1.50	.70
❑ 17 Garrison Hearst / Dorsey Levens	1.50	.70
❑ 18 Ryan Leaf / Jon Kitna	2.00	.90
❑ 19 Robert Smith / Mike Alstott	1.50	.70
❑ 20 Jerry Rice / Randy Moss	5.00	2.20
❑ 21 Peyton Manning / Charlie Batch	5.00	2.20
❑ 22 Fred Taylor / Jerome Bettis	2.50	1.10
❑ 23 Keyshawn Johnson / Eric Moulds	2.00	.90
❑ 24 Tim Couch / Ricky Williams	20.00	9.00
❑ 25 Carl Pickens / Isaac Bruce	1.50	.70
❑ 26 Deion Sanders / Charles Woodson	2.00	.90
❑ 27 Tim Brown / Rod Smith	2.00	.90
❑ 28 Daunte Culpepper / Donovan McNabb	8.00	3.60
❑ 29 Joey Galloway / Ed McCaffrey	2.00	.90
❑ 30 Karim Abdul-Jabbar / Antowain Smith	1.50	.70

1999 Score Supplemental

	MINT	NRMT
COMPLETE SET (110)	35.00	16.00
COMP.FACT.SET (110)	40.00	18.00
COMMON CARD (1-110)	.10	.05
SEMISTARS	.20	.09
UNLISTED STARS	.40	.18
COMMON ROOKIE	.75	.35
ROOKIE SEMISTARS	1.25	.55
ROOKIE UNL.STARS	2.00	.90

Card	MINT	NRMT
❑ 1 Chris Greisen RC	2.50	1.10
❑ 2 Sherdrick Bonner RC	1.25	.55
❑ 3 Joel Makovicka RC	2.00	.90
❑ 4 Andy McCullough RC	1.25	.55
❑ 5 Jeff Paulk RC	1.25	.55
❑ 6 Brandon Stokley RC	1.25	.55
❑ 7 Sheldon Jackson RC	1.25	.55
❑ 8 Bobby Collins RC	2.00	.90
❑ 9 Kamil Loud RC	1.25	.55
❑ 10 Antoine Winfield RC	1.25	.55
❑ 11 Jerry Azumah RC	1.25	.55
❑ 12 James Allen RC	.75	.35
❑ 13 Nick Williams RC	1.25	.55
❑ 14 Michael Basnight RC	1.25	.55
❑ 15 Damon Griffin RC	1.25	.55
❑ 16 Ronnie Powell RC	1.25	.55
❑ 17 Darrin Chiaverini RC	2.00	.90
❑ 18 Mark Campbell RC	1.25	.55
❑ 19 Mike Lucky RC	1.25	.55
❑ 20 Wane McGarity RC	1.25	.55
❑ 21 Jason Tucker RC	5.00	2.20
❑ 22 Ebenezer Ekuban RC	1.25	.55
❑ 23 Robert Thomas RC	1.25	.55
❑ 24 Dat Nguyen RC	1.25	.55
❑ 25 Olandis Gary RC	6.00	2.70
❑ 26 Desmond Clark RC	1.25	.55
❑ 27 Andre Cooper RC	1.25	.55
❑ 28 Chris Watson RC	.75	.35
❑ 29 Al Wilson RC	2.00	.90
❑ 30 Cory Sauter RC	1.25	.55
❑ 31 Brock Olivo RC	1.25	.55
❑ 32 Basil Mitchell RC	1.25	.55
❑ 33 Matt Snider RC	.75	.35
❑ 34 Antuan Edwards RC	1.25	.55
❑ 35 Mike McKenzie RC	1.25	.55
❑ 36 Terrence Wilkins RC	5.00	2.20
❑ 37 Fernando Bryant RC	1.25	.55
❑ 38 Larry Parker RC	1.25	.55
❑ 39 Autry Denson RC	2.00	.90
❑ 40 Jim Kleinsasser RC	2.00	.90
❑ 41 Michael Bishop RC	2.50	1.10
❑ 42 Andy Katzenmoyer	.20	.09
❑ 43 Brett Bech RC	1.25	.55
❑ 44 Sean Bennett RC	2.00	.90
❑ 45 Dan Campbell RC	.75	.35
❑ 46 Ray Lucas RC	5.00	2.20
❑ 47 Scott Dreisbach RC	2.00	.90
❑ 48 Cecil Martin RC	1.25	.55
❑ 49 Dameane Douglas RC	1.25	.55
❑ 50 Jed Weaver RC	1.25	.55
❑ 51 Jerame Tuman RC	1.25	.55
❑ 52 Steve Heiden RC	.75	.35
❑ 53 Jeff Garcia RC	4.00	1.80
❑ 54 Terry Jackson RC	1.25	.55
❑ 55 Charlie Rogers RC	1.25	.55
❑ 56 Lamar King RC	1.25	.55
❑ 57 Kurt Warner RC	20.00	9.00
❑ 58 Dre' Bly RC	1.25	.55
❑ 59 Justin Watson RC	.75	.35
❑ 60 Rabih Abdullah RC	1.25	.55
❑ 61 Martin Gramatica RC	.75	.35
❑ 62 Darnell McDonald RC	1.25	.55
❑ 63 Anthony McFarland RC	1.25	.55
❑ 64 Larry Brown TE RC	.75	.35
❑ 65 Kevin Daft RC	1.25	.55
❑ 66 Mike Sellers	.10	.05
❑ 67 Ken Oxendine	.10	.05
❑ 68 Errict Rhett	.20	.09
❑ 69 Stoney Case	.10	.05
❑ 70 Jonathan Linton	.10	.05
❑ 71 Marcus Robinson	1.25	.55
❑ 72 Shane Matthews	.20	.09
❑ 73 Cade McNown	3.00	1.35
❑ 74 Akili Smith	2.00	.90
❑ 75 Karim Abdul-Jabbar	.20	.09
❑ 76 Tim Couch	5.00	2.20
❑ 77 Kevin Johnson	2.50	1.10
❑ 78 Ron Rivers	.10	.05
❑ 79 Bill Schroeder	.40	.18
❑ 80 Edgerrin James	8.00	3.60
❑ 81 Cecil Collins	1.00	.45
❑ 82 Matthew Hatchette	.10	.05
❑ 83 Daunte Culpepper	3.00	1.35
❑ 84 Ricky Williams	5.00	2.20
❑ 85 Tyrone Wheatley	.40	.18
❑ 86 Donovan McNabb	3.00	1.35
❑ 87 Marshall Faulk	.40	.18
❑ 88 Torry Holt	2.50	1.10
❑ 89 Stephen Davis	.40	.18
❑ 90 Brad Johnson	.40	.18
❑ 91 Jake Plummer SS	.60	.25
❑ 92 Emmitt Smith SS	1.00	.45
❑ 93 Troy Aikman SS	1.00	.45
❑ 94 John Elway SS	1.50	.70
❑ 95 Terrell Davis SS	1.00	.45
❑ 96 Barry Sanders SS	1.50	.70
❑ 97 Brett Favre SS	1.50	.70
❑ 98 Antonio Freeman SS	.40	.18
❑ 99 Peyton Manning SS	1.50	.70
❑ 100 Fred Taylor SS	1.00	.45
❑ 101 Mark Brunell SS	.60	.25
❑ 102 Dan Marino SS	1.50	.70
❑ 103 Randy Moss SS	1.50	.70
❑ 104 Cris Carter SS	.40	.18
❑ 105 Drew Bledsoe SS	.60	.25
❑ 106 Terry Glenn SS	.40	.18
❑ 107 Keyshawn Johnson SS	.40	.18
❑ 108 Jerry Rice SS	1.00	.45
❑ 109 Steve Young SS	.60	.25
❑ 110 Eddie George SS	.50	.23

1999 Score Supplemental Behind the Numbers

	MINT	NRMT
COMPLETE SET (30)	200.00	90.00
COMMON CARD (BN1-BN30)	5.00	2.20

STATED PRINT RUN 1000 SER.#'d SETS

Card	MINT	NRMT
❑ BN1 Kurt Warner	35.00	16.00
❑ BN2 Tim Couch	20.00	9.00
❑ BN3 Randy Moss	15.00	6.75
❑ BN4 Brett Favre	20.00	9.00
❑ BN5 Marvin Harrison	5.00	2.20
❑ BN6 Terry Glenn	5.00	2.20
❑ BN7 John Elway	20.00	9.00
❑ BN8 Troy Aikman	12.00	5.50

	MINT	NRMT
❑ BN9 Steve McNair	5.00	2.20
❑ BN10 Kordell Stewart	5.00	2.20
❑ BN11 Drew Bledsoe	8.00	3.60
❑ BN12 Jon Kitna	6.00	2.70
❑ BN13 Dan Marino	20.00	9.00
❑ BN14 Jerry Rice	12.00	5.50
❑ BN15 Edgerrin James	30.00	13.50
❑ BN16 Jake Plummer	8.00	3.60
❑ BN17 Antonio Freeman	5.00	2.20
❑ BN18 Peyton Manning	15.00	6.75
❑ BN19 Keyshawn Johnson	5.00	2.20
❑ BN20 Barry Sanders	20.00	9.00
❑ BN21 Cris Carter	5.00	2.20
❑ BN22 Emmitt Smith	12.00	5.50
❑ BN23 Steve Young	8.00	3.60
❑ BN24 Ricky Williams	20.00	9.00
❑ BN25 Doug Flutie	6.00	2.70
❑ BN26 Mark Brunell	8.00	3.60
❑ BN27 Eddie George	6.00	2.70
❑ BN28 Fred Taylor	10.00	4.50
❑ BN29 Donovan McNabb	12.00	5.50
❑ BN30 Terrell Davis	12.00	5.50

1999 Score Supplemental Behind the Numbers Gold

	MINT	NRMT
COMMON CARD (BN1-BN30)	15.00	6.75
GOLDS SERIAL #'d TO PLAYER'S JERSEY		
CARDS SERIAL #'d UNDER 13 NOT PRICED		
❑ BN1 Kurt Warner/13	500.00	220.00
❑ BN2 Tim Couch/2		
❑ BN3 Randy Moss/84	60.00	27.00
❑ BN4 Brett Favre/4		
❑ BN5 Marvin Harrison/88	15.00	6.75
❑ BN6 Terry Glenn/88	15.00	6.75
❑ BN7 John Elway/7		
❑ BN8 Troy Aikman/8		
❑ BN9 Steve McNair/9		
❑ BN10 Kordell Stewart/10		
❑ BN11 Drew Bledsoe/11		
❑ BN12 Jon Kitna/7		
❑ BN13 Dan Marino/13	400.00	180.00
❑ BN14 Jerry Rice/80	40.00	18.00
❑ BN15 Edgerrin James/32	300.00	135.00
❑ BN16 Jake Plummer/16	150.00	70.00
❑ BN17 Antonio Freeman/86	15.00	6.75
❑ BN18 Peyton Manning/18	200.00	90.00
❑ BN19 Keyshawn Johnson/19	60.00	27.00
❑ BN20 Barry Sanders/20	250.00	110.00
❑ BN21 Cris Carter/80	15.00	6.75
❑ BN22 Emmitt Smith/22	150.00	70.00
❑ BN23 Steve Young/8		
❑ BN24 Ricky Williams/34	150.00	70.00
❑ BN25 Doug Flutie/7		
❑ BN26 Mark Brunell/8		
❑ BN27 Eddie George/27	70.00	32.00
❑ BN28 Fred Taylor/28	100.00	45.00
❑ BN29 Donovan McNabb/5		
❑ BN30 Terrell Davis/30	120.00	55.00

1999 Score Supplemental Inscriptions

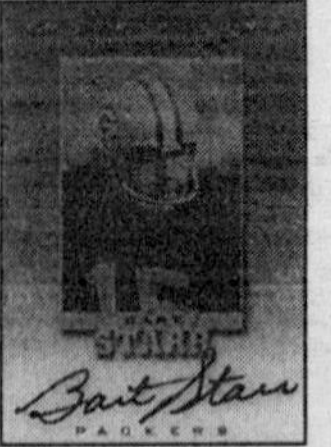

	MINT	NRMT
COMPLETE SET (30)	1000.00	450.00
COMMON CARD	15.00	6.75
SEMISTARS	25.00	11.00
RANDOM INSERTS IN PACKS		
SOME CARDS ISSUED VIA MAIL REDEMPTION		
TRADE CARD EXPIRATION: 5/31/2005		
❑ BG14 Brian Griese	50.00	22.00
❑ BJ14 Brad Johnson	25.00	11.00
❑ BS15 Bart Starr	100.00	45.00
❑ CC12 Chris Chandler	15.00	6.75
❑ CD28 Corey Dillon	25.00	11.00
❑ DL25 Dorsey Levens	25.00	11.00
❑ DS22 Duce Staley	25.00	11.00
❑ EC34 Earl Campbell	40.00	18.00
❑ EM79 Eric Moss	15.00	6.75
❑ EM80 Eric Moulds	25.00	11.00
❑ IB80 Isaac Bruce	30.00	13.50
❑ JB32 Jim Brown	120.00	55.00
❑ JG84 Joey Galloway	25.00	11.00
❑ JK7 Jon Kitna	25.00	11.00
❑ JU19 Johnny Unitas	100.00	45.00
❑ KS10 Kordell Stewart	25.00	11.00
❑ KW13 Kurt Warner	175.00	80.00
❑ MH88 Marvin Harrison	40.00	18.00
❑ NM20 Natrone Means	15.00	6.75
❑ PH33 Priest Holmes	25.00	11.00
❑ RW34 Ricky Williams	120.00	55.00
❑ SD48 Stephen Davis	25.00	11.00
❑ SH20 Skip Hicks	15.00	6.75
❑ SM9 Steve McNair	30.00	13.50
❑ TB21 Tim Biakabutuka	15.00	6.75
❑ TB81 Tim Brown	25.00	11.00
❑ TO81 Terrell Owens	25.00	11.00
❑ TT34 Thurman Thomas	25.00	11.00
❑ VT16 Vinny Testaverde	15.00	6.75
❑ WW85 Wesley Walls	15.00	6.75

1999 Score Supplemental Quantum Leaf Previews

	MINT	NRMT
COMPLETE SET (18)	150.00	70.00
COMMON CARD (1-18)	4.00	1.80
RANDOM INSERTS IN PACKS		
❑ 1 Barry Sanders	15.00	6.75
❑ 2 Ricky Williams	12.00	5.50
❑ 3 Terrell Davis	10.00	4.50
❑ 4 John Elway	15.00	6.75
❑ 5 Edgerrin James	20.00	9.00
❑ 6 Tim Couch	12.00	5.50
❑ 7 Peyton Manning	12.00	5.50
❑ 8 Kurt Warner	30.00	13.50
❑ 9 Randy Moss	12.00	5.50
❑ 10 Dan Marino	15.00	6.75
❑ 11 Brett Favre	15.00	6.75
❑ 12 Eddie George	5.00	2.20
❑ 13 Marvin Harrison	4.00	1.80
❑ 14 Jerry Rice	10.00	4.50
❑ 15 Emmitt Smith	10.00	4.50
❑ 16 Keyshawn Johnson	4.00	1.80
❑ 17 Drew Bledsoe	6.00	2.70
❑ 18 Marshall Faulk	4.00	1.80

1999 Score Supplemental Zenith Z-Team

	MINT	NRMT
COMPLETE SET (20)	500.00	220.00
COMMON CARD (1-20)	12.00	5.50
STATED PRINT RUN 100 SER.#'d SETS		
❑ 1 Steve Young	20.00	9.00
❑ 2 Barry Sanders	50.00	22.00
❑ 3 Fred Taylor	25.00	11.00
❑ 4 Marshall Faulk	12.00	5.50
❑ 5 Emmitt Smith	30.00	13.50
❑ 6 Brett Favre	50.00	22.00
❑ 7 Troy Aikman	30.00	13.50
❑ 8 Terrell Davis	30.00	13.50
❑ 9 Edgerrin James	80.00	36.00
❑ 10 Drew Bledsoe	20.00	9.00
❑ 11 Dan Marino	50.00	22.00
❑ 12 Randy Moss	40.00	18.00
❑ 13 Ricky Williams	50.00	22.00
❑ 14 Mark Brunell	20.00	9.00
❑ 15 Jake Plummer	20.00	9.00
❑ 16 Jerry Rice	30.00	13.50
❑ 17 Peyton Manning	40.00	18.00
❑ 18 Tim Couch	50.00	22.00
❑ 19 Eddie George	15.00	6.75
❑ 20 John Elway	50.00	22.00

2000 Score

	MINT	NRMT
COMPLETE SET (329)	150.00	70.00
COMP.SET w/o SP's (220)	20.00	9.00
COMMON CARD (1-220)	.15	.07
SEMISTARS	.25	.11
UNLISTED STARS	.50	.23
COMMON CARD (221-275)	.20	.09
SEMISTARS 221-275	.30	.14
UNL.STARS 221-275	.60	.25
SUBSET 221-275 STATED ODDS 1:2		
COMMON ROOKIE (276-330)	1.50	.70
ROOKIE SEMISTARS	2.00	.90
ROOKIE STATED ODDS 1:4HOB, 1:6RET		
CARD 118 NOT RELEASED		
❑ 1 Michael Pittman	.15	.07
❑ 2 Jake Plummer	.50	.23
❑ 3 Rob Moore	.25	.11
❑ 4 David Boston	.50	.23
❑ 5 Frank Sanders	.25	.11
❑ 6 Jamal Anderson	.50	.23
❑ 7 Chris Chandler	.25	.11
❑ 8 Tim Dwight	.50	.23
❑ 9 Terance Mathis	.25	.11
❑ 10 Shawn Jefferson	.15	.07
❑ 11 Ashley Ambrose	.15	.07
❑ 12 Peter Boulware	.15	.07
❑ 13 Priest Holmes	.25	.11
❑ 14 Tony Banks	.25	.11
❑ 15 Qadry Ismail	.15	.07
❑ 16 Shannon Sharpe	.25	.11
❑ 17 Rod Woodson	.15	.07
❑ 18 Matt Stover	.15	.07
❑ 19 Michael McCrary	.15	.07
❑ 20 Doug Flutie	.60	.25
❑ 21 Rob Johnson	.25	.11

❑ 22 Eric Moulds .50 .23
❑ 23 Peerless Price .50 .23
❑ 24 Jonathan Linton .15 .07
❑ 25 Antowain Smith .50 .23
❑ 26 Jay Riemersma .15 .07
❑ 27 Muhsin Muhammad .25 .11
❑ 28 Tim Biakabutuka .25 .11
❑ 29 Patrick Jeffers .50 .23
❑ 30 Wesley Walls .15 .07
❑ 31 Steve Beuerlein .25 .11
❑ 32 John Kasay .15 .07
❑ 33 Curtis Enis .50 .23
❑ 34 Cade McNown .75 .35
❑ 35 Marcus Robinson .50 .23
❑ 36 Bobby Engram .15 .07
❑ 37 Eddie Kennison .15 .07
❑ 38 Akili Smith .60 .25
❑ 39 Carl Pickens .25 .11
❑ 40 Corey Dillon .50 .23
❑ 41 Darnay Scott .25 .11
❑ 42 Errict Rhett .25 .11
❑ 43 Karim Abdul-Jabbar .25 .11
❑ 44 Tim Couch 1.25 .55
❑ 45 Kevin Johnson .50 .23
❑ 46 Darrin Chiaverini .15 .07
❑ 47 Terry Kirby .15 .07
❑ 48 Jason Tucker .25 .11
❑ 49 Rocket Ismail .25 .11
❑ 50 Joey Galloway .50 .23
❑ 51 Michael Irvin .25 .11
❑ 52 Troy Aikman 1.25 .55
❑ 53 Emmitt Smith 1.25 .55
❑ 54 David LaFleur .15 .07
❑ 55 Trevor Pryce .15 .07
❑ 56 Brian Griese .60 .25
❑ 57 Olandis Gary .60 .25
❑ 58 Terrell Davis 1.25 .55
❑ 59 Rod Smith .25 .11
❑ 60 Ed McCaffrey .25 .11
❑ 61 Gus Frerotte .15 .07
❑ 62 Jason Elam .15 .07
❑ 63 Kavika Pittman .15 .07
❑ 64 James Stewart .25 .11
❑ 65 Charlie Batch .50 .23
❑ 66 Johnnie Morton .25 .11
❑ 67 Herman Moore .50 .23
❑ 68 Germane Crowell .25 .11
❑ 69 Barry Sanders 1.50 .70
❑ 70 Chris Claiborne .15 .07
❑ 71 Brett Favre 2.00 .90
❑ 72 Antonio Freeman .50 .23
❑ 73 Dorsey Levens .50 .23
❑ 74 De'Mond Parker .15 .07
❑ 75 Corey Bradford .25 .11
❑ 76 Basil Mitchell .15 .07
❑ 77 Bill Schroeder .25 .11
❑ 78 Peyton Manning 1.50 .70
❑ 79 Marvin Harrison .50 .23
❑ 80 Terrence Wilkins .50 .23
❑ 81 Edgerrin James 2.00 .90
❑ 82 E.G. Green .15 .07
❑ 83 Chad Bratzke .15 .07
❑ 84 Mark Brunell .75 .35
❑ 85 Fred Taylor .75 .35
❑ 86 Jimmy Smith .25 .11
❑ 87 Keenan McCardell .25 .11
❑ 88 Kevin Hardy .15 .07
❑ 89 Aaron Beasley .15 .07
❑ 90 Elvis Grbac .25 .11
❑ 91 Derrick Alexander .25 .11
❑ 92 Tony Gonzalez .25 .11
❑ 93 Donnell Bennett .15 .07
❑ 94 Warren Moon .50 .23
❑ 95 Andre Rison .25 .11
❑ 96 James Hasty .15 .07
❑ 97 Dan Marino 2.00 .90
❑ 98 Thurman Thomas .25 .11
❑ 99 James Johnson .25 .11
❑ 100 O.J. McDuffie .25 .11
❑ 101 Tony Martin .25 .11
❑ 102 Oronde Gadsden .15 .07
❑ 103 Zach Thomas .25 .11
❑ 104 Sam Madison .15 .07
❑ 105 Jay Fiedler .50 .23
❑ 106 Damon Huard .50 .23
❑ 107 Robert Smith .50 .23
❑ 108 Leroy Hoard .15 .07
❑ 109 Randy Moss 1.50 .70
❑ 110 Cris Carter .50 .23
❑ 111 Daunte Culpepper .75 .35
❑ 112 John Randle .25 .11
❑ 113 Randall Cunningham .50 .23
❑ 114 Gary Anderson .15 .07
❑ 115 Drew Bledsoe .75 .35
❑ 116 Terry Glenn .50 .23
❑ 117 Kevin Faulk .25 .11
❑ 119 Adam Vinatieri .15 .07
❑ 120 Ty Law .15 .07
❑ 121 Lawyer Milloy .15 .07
❑ 122 Troy Brown .15 .07
❑ 123 Ben Coates .15 .07
❑ 124 Cam Cleeland .15 .07
❑ 125 Jeff Blake .25 .11
❑ 126 Ricky Williams 1.25 .55
❑ 127 Jake Reed .25 .11
❑ 128 Jake Delhomme RC 2.00 .90
❑ 129 Andrew Glover .15 .07
❑ 130 Keith Poole .15 .07
❑ 131 Joe Horn .15 .07
❑ 132 Kerry Collins .25 .11
❑ 133 Joe Montgomery .15 .07
❑ 134 Sean Bennett .15 .07
❑ 135 Amani Toomer .15 .07
❑ 136 Ike Hilliard .25 .11
❑ 137 Joe Jurevicius .15 .07
❑ 138 Tiki Barber .25 .11
❑ 139 Victor Green .15 .07
❑ 140 Ray Lucas .50 .23
❑ 141 Vinny Testaverde .25 .11
❑ 142 Curtis Martin .50 .23
❑ 143 Wayne Chrebet .25 .11
❑ 144 Tyrone Wheatley .25 .11
❑ 145 Rich Gannon .25 .11
❑ 146 Napoleon Kaufman .50 .23
❑ 147 Tim Brown .15 .07
❑ 148 Rickey Dudley .15 .07
❑ 149 Charles Woodson .50 .23
❑ 150 James Jett .15 .07
❑ 151 Duce Staley .50 .23
❑ 152 Charles Johnson .15 .07
❑ 153 Donovan McNabb .75 .35
❑ 154 Troy Vincent .15 .07
❑ 155 Troy Edwards .50 .23
❑ 156 Jerome Bettis .50 .23
❑ 157 Kordell Stewart .50 .23
❑ 158 Richard Huntley .15 .07
❑ 159 Hines Ward .15 .07
❑ 160 Levon Kirkland .15 .07
❑ 161 Ryan Leaf .50 .23
❑ 162 Jim Harbaugh .25 .11
❑ 163 Jermaine Fazande .15 .07
❑ 164 Natrone Means .15 .07
❑ 165 Junior Seau .25 .11
❑ 166 Curtis Conway .25 .11
❑ 167 Freddie Jones .15 .07
❑ 168 Jeff Graham .15 .07
❑ 169 Terrell Owens .50 .23
❑ 170 Jeff Garcia .50 .23
❑ 171 Jerry Rice 1.25 .55
❑ 172 Steve Young .75 .35
❑ 173 Garrison Hearst .25 .11
❑ 174 Charlie Garner .25 .11
❑ 175 Fred Beasley .15 .07
❑ 176 Bryant Young .15 .07
❑ 177 Derrick Mayes .25 .11
❑ 178 Sean Dawkins .15 .07
❑ 179 Jon Kitna .50 .23
❑ 180 Ricky Watters .25 .11
❑ 181 Charlie Rogers .15 .07
❑ 182 Kurt Warner 2.50 1.10
❑ 183 Marshall Faulk .50 .23
❑ 184 Isaac Bruce .50 .23
❑ 185 Az-Zahir Hakim .25 .11
❑ 186 Trent Green .25 .11
❑ 187 Jeff Wilkins .15 .07
❑ 188 Torry Holt .50 .23
❑ 189 London Fletcher RC .25 .11
❑ 190 Robert Holcombe .15 .07
❑ 191 Todd Lyght .15 .07
❑ 192 Keyshawn Johnson .50 .23
❑ 193 Derrick Brooks .15 .07
❑ 194 Warren Sapp .25 .11
❑ 195 Shaun King .75 .35
❑ 196 Warrick Dunn .50 .23
❑ 197 Mike Alstott .50 .23
❑ 198 Jacquez Green .25 .11
❑ 199 Reidel Anthony .15 .07
❑ 200 Martin Gramatica .15 .07
❑ 201 Donnie Abraham .15 .07
❑ 202 Steve McNair .50 .23
❑ 203 Eddie George .60 .25
❑ 204 Jevon Kearse .50 .23
❑ 205 Frank Wycheck .15 .07
❑ 206 Kevin Dyson .25 .11
❑ 207 Yancey Thigpen .15 .07
❑ 208 Al Del Greco .15 .07
❑ 209 Jeff George .25 .11
❑ 210 Adrian Murrell .25 .11
❑ 211 Brad Johnson .50 .23
❑ 212 Stephen Davis .50 .23
❑ 213 Stephen Alexander .15 .07
❑ 214 Michael Westbrook .25 .11
❑ 215 Darrell Green .15 .07
❑ 216 Champ Bailey .50 .23
❑ 217 Albert Connell .15 .07
❑ 218 Larry Centers .15 .07
❑ 219 Bruce Smith .25 .11
❑ 220 Deion Sanders .50 .23
❑ 221 Ricky Williams SS 1.25 .55
❑ 222 Edgerrin James SS 2.00 .90
❑ 223 Tim Couch SS 1.25 .55
❑ 224 Cade McNown SS .75 .35
❑ 225 Olandis Gary SS .60 .25
❑ 226 Torry Holt SS .60 .25
❑ 227 Donovan McNabb SS .75 .35
❑ 228 Shaun King SS .75 .35
❑ 229 Kevin Johnson SS .60 .25
❑ 230 Kurt Warner SS 3.00 1.35
❑ 231 Tony Gonzalez AP .30 .14
❑ 232 Frank Wycheck AP .20 .09
❑ 233 Eddie George AP .75 .35
❑ 234 Mark Brunell AP 1.00 .45
❑ 235 Corey Dillon AP .60 .25
❑ 236 Peyton Manning AP 2.00 .90
❑ 237 Keyshawn Johnson AP .60 .25
❑ 238 Rich Gannon AP .30 .14
❑ 239 Terry Glenn AP .60 .25
❑ 240 Tony Brackens AP .20 .09
❑ 241 Edgerrin James AP 2.00 .90
❑ 242 Tim Brown AP .60 .25
❑ 243 Michael Strahan AP .20 .09
❑ 244 Kurt Warner AP 3.00 1.35
❑ 245 Brad Johnson AP .60 .25
❑ 246 Aeneas Williams AP .20 .09
❑ 247 Marshall Faulk AP .60 .25
❑ 248 Dexter Coakley AP .20 .09
❑ 249 Warren Sapp AP .30 .14
❑ 250 Mike Alstott AP .60 .25
❑ 251 David Sloan AP .20 .09
❑ 252 Cris Carter AP .60 .25
❑ 253 Muhsin Muhammad AP .20 .09
❑ 254 Isaac Bruce AP .60 .25
❑ 255 Wesley Walls AP .20 .09
❑ 256 Steve Beuerlein LL .30 .14
❑ 257 Kurt Warner LL 3.00 1.35
❑ 258 Peyton Manning LL 2.00 .90
❑ 259 Brad Johnson LL .60 .25
❑ 260 Edgerrin James LL 2.00 .90
❑ 261 Curtis Martin LL .60 .25
❑ 262 Stephen Davis LL .60 .25
❑ 263 Emmitt Smith LL 1.50 .70
❑ 264 Marvin Harrison LL .60 .25
❑ 265 Jimmy Smith LL .30 .14
❑ 266 Randy Moss LL 2.00 .90
❑ 267 Marcus Robinson LL .60 .25
❑ 268 Kevin Carter LL .20 .09
❑ 269 Simeon Rice LL .20 .09
❑ 270 Robert Porcher LL .20 .09
❑ 271 Jevon Kearse LL .60 .25
❑ 272 Mike Vanderjagt LL .20 .09
❑ 273 Olindo Mare LL .20 .09
❑ 274 Todd Peterson LL .20 .09
❑ 275 Mike Hollis LL .20 .09
❑ 276 Rookie Redemption 12.00 5.50
❑ 277 Peter Warrick RC 10.00 4.50
❑ 278 Courtney Brown RC 4.00 1.80
❑ 279 Plaxico Burress RC 5.00 2.20
❑ 280 Corey Simon RC 2.00 .90

❑ 281 Thomas Jones RC	6.00	2.70
❑ 282 Travis Taylor RC	4.00	1.80
❑ 283 Shaun Alexander RC	6.00	2.70
❑ 284 Rookie Redemption	5.00	2.20
❑ 285 Chris Redman RC	3.00	1.35
❑ 286 Chad Pennington RC	8.00	3.60
❑ 287 Jamal Lewis RC	6.00	2.70
❑ 288 Brian Urlacher RC	2.50	1.10
❑ 289 Bubba Franks RC	2.50	1.10
❑ 290 Dez White RC	2.50	1.10
❑ 291 Frank Moreau RC	5.00	2.20
❑ 292 Ron Dayne RC	10.00	4.50
❑ 293 Sylvester Morris RC	2.50	1.10
❑ 294 R.Jay Soward RC	2.50	1.10
❑ 295 Curtis Keaton RC	1.50	.70
❑ 296 Rookie Redemption	5.00	2.20
❑ 297 Rondell Mealey RC	1.50	.70
❑ 298 Travis Prentice RC	2.50	1.10
❑ 299 Darrell Jackson RC	2.00	.90
❑ 300 Giovanni Carmazzi RC	4.00	1.80
❑ 301 Anthony Lucas RC	2.00	.90
❑ 302 Danny Farmer RC	2.00	.90
❑ 303 Dennis Northcutt RC	2.50	1.10
❑ 304 Troy Walters RC	2.00	.90
❑ 305 Laveranues Coles RC	2.00	.90
❑ 306 Kwame Cavil RC	1.50	.70
❑ 307 Tee Martin RC	3.00	1.35
❑ 308 J.R. Redmond RC	3.00	1.35
❑ 309 Tim Rattay RC	2.50	1.10
❑ 310 Jerry Porter RC	2.50	1.10
❑ 311 Michael Wiley RC	2.50	1.10
❑ 312 Reuben Droughns RC	2.50	1.10
❑ 313 Trung Canidate RC	2.00	.90
❑ 314 Shyrone Stith RC	1.50	.70
❑ 315 Marc Bulger RC	2.00	.90
❑ 316 Tom Brady RC	2.00	.90
❑ 317 Doug Johnson RC	2.50	1.10
❑ 318 Todd Husak RC	2.00	.90
❑ 319 Gari Scott RC	2.00	.90
❑ 320 Rookie Redemption	5.00	2.20
❑ 321 Chris Cole RC	1.50	.70
❑ 322 Sammy Morris RC	2.00	.90
❑ 323 Trevor Gaylor RC	1.50	.70
❑ 324 Jarious Jackson RC	2.00	.90
❑ 325 Doug Chapman RC Trade	6.00	2.70
❑ 326 Ron Dugans RC	2.00	.90
❑ 327 Ron Dixon RC Trade	5.00	2.20
❑ 328 Joe Hamilton RC	2.00	.90
❑ 329 Todd Pinkston RC	2.00	.90
❑ 330 Chad Morton RC	1.50	.70

2000 Score Final Score

	MINT	NRMT
COMMON CARD/25-35	8.00	3.60
*STARS/25-35: 20X TO 50X HI COL.		
*YOUNG STARS/25-35: 15X TO 40X		
*SUBSETS/25-35: 8X TO 20X		
*RCs/25-35: 5X TO 12X		
COMMON CARD/40-54	6.00	2.70
*STARS/40-54: 15X TO 40X HI COL.		
*YOUNG STARS/40-54: 12X TO 30X		
*SUBSETS/40-54: 6X TO 15X		
*RCs/40-54: 4X TO 10X		
COMMON CARD/66	5.00	2.20
*STARS/66: 12X TO 30X HI COL.		
*YOUNG STARS/66: 10X TO 25X		
*SUBSETS/66: 5X TO 12X		
*RCs/66: 3X TO 8X		

CARDS SERIAL #'d TO A 1999 SEASON STAT
CARD 118 NOT RELEASED

2000 Score Scorecard

	MINT	NRMT
COMPLETE SET (329)	400.00	180.00

*SCORECARD STARS: 2X TO 5X HI COL.
*SCORECARD YOUNG STARS: 1.5X TO 4X
*SCORECARD SUBSETS: .8X TO 2X
*SCORECARD RCs: .8X TO 2X
STATED PRINT RUN 2000 SERIAL #'d SETS
CARD 118 NOT RELEASED

2000 Score Air Mail

	MINT	NRMT
COMPLETE SET (30)	120.00	55.00
COMMON CARD (AM1-AM30)	2.00	.90
SEMISTARS	3.00	1.35

STATED ODDS 1:70 HOB/RET
*FIRST CLASS: 1.5X TO 4X HI COL.
FIRST CLASS PRINT RUN 50 SER.#'d SETS

❑ AM1 Isaac Bruce	3.00	1.35
❑ AM2 Cris Carter	3.00	1.35
❑ AM3 Tim Dwight	3.00	1.35
❑ AM4 Joey Galloway	3.00	1.35
❑ AM5 Marvin Harrison	3.00	1.35
❑ AM6 Keyshawn Johnson	3.00	1.35
❑ AM7 Jon Kitna	3.00	1.35
❑ AM8 Steve McNair	3.00	1.35
❑ AM9 Eric Moulds	3.00	1.35
❑ AM10 Drew Bledsoe	5.00	2.20
❑ AM11 John Elway	12.00	5.50
❑ AM12 Brett Favre	12.00	5.50
❑ AM13 Antonio Freeman	3.00	1.35
❑ AM14 Peyton Manning	10.00	4.50
❑ AM15 Randy Moss	10.00	4.50
❑ AM16 Jake Plummer	5.00	2.20
❑ AM17 Steve Young	3.00	1.35
❑ AM18 Troy Aikman	8.00	3.60
❑ AM19 Mark Brunell	5.00	2.20
❑ AM20 Tim Couch	8.00	3.60
❑ AM21 Dan Marino	12.00	5.50
❑ AM22 Jerry Rice	8.00	3.60
❑ AM23 Kevin Johnson	2.00	.90
❑ AM24 Michael Westbrook	2.00	.90
❑ AM25 Kurt Warner	12.00	5.50
❑ AM26 Doug Flutie	4.00	1.80
❑ AM27 Jimmy Smith	2.00	.90
❑ AM28 Germane Crowell	2.00	.90
❑ AM29 Cade McNown	4.00	1.80
❑ AM30 Muhsin Muhammad	2.00	.90

2000 Score Building Blocks

	MINT	NRMT
COMPLETE SET (30)	30.00	13.50
COMMON CARD (BB1-BB30)	.75	.35
SEMISTARS	1.25	.55

STATED ODDS 1:17 HOB, 1:35 RET

❑ BB1 Cade McNown	1.50	.70
❑ BB2 Peerless Price	.75	.35
❑ BB3 Akili Smith	1.25	.55
❑ BB4 Randy Moss	4.00	1.80
❑ BB5 Edgerrin James	4.00	1.80
❑ BB6 Kurt Warner	5.00	2.20
❑ BB7 Ray Lucas	.75	.35
❑ BB8 Jevon Kearse	.75	.35
❑ BB9 Torry Holt	.75	.35
❑ BB10 Ricky Williams	2.50	1.10
❑ BB11 Daunte Culpepper	1.50	.70
❑ BB12 Fred Taylor	2.00	.90
❑ BB13 Brian Griese	1.25	.55
❑ BB14 Marcus Robinson	1.25	.55
❑ BB15 David Boston	.75	.35
❑ BB16 James Johnson	.75	.35
❑ BB17 Charlie Batch	1.25	.55
❑ BB18 Jake Plummer	1.25	.55
❑ BB19 Duce Staley	1.25	.55
❑ BB20 Germane Crowell	.75	.35
❑ BB21 Curtis Enis	.75	.35
❑ BB22 Donovan McNabb	1.50	.70
❑ BB23 Tim Couch	2.50	1.10
❑ BB24 Stephen Davis	1.25	.55
❑ BB25 Jon Kitna	.75	.35
❑ BB26 Shaun King	1.50	.70
❑ BB27 Kevin Johnson	1.25	.55
❑ BB28 Peyton Manning	4.00	1.80
❑ BB29 Olandis Gary	1.25	.55
❑ BB30 Muhsin Muhammad	.75	.35

2000 Score Complete Players

	MINT	NRMT
COMPLETE SET (40)	60.00	27.00
COMMON CARD (CP1-CP40)	.75	.35

		MINT	NRMT
SEMISTARS		1.25	.55

STATED ODDS 1:17 HOB, 1:35 RET
*BLUE: 3X TO 8X HI COL
BLUE STATED ODDS 1:359 HOB, 1:718 RET
*GREEN: 5X TO 12X HI COL
GREEN STATED ODDS 1:718HOB,1:1435RET

Card	Player	MINT	NRMT
❑ CP1	Eric Moulds	1.25	.55
❑ CP2	Tim Couch	2.50	1.10
❑ CP3	Marvin Harrison	1.25	.55
❑ CP4	Brett Favre	5.00	2.20
❑ CP5	Steve Young	2.00	.90
❑ CP6	Brad Johnson	1.25	.55
❑ CP7	Randy Moss	4.00	1.80
❑ CP8	Mark Brunell	2.00	.90
❑ CP9	Steve McNair	1.25	.55
❑ CP10	Donovan McNabb	1.50	.70
❑ CP11	Drew Bledsoe	2.00	.90
❑ CP12	Kurt Warner	5.00	2.20
❑ CP13	Dan Marino	5.00	2.20
❑ CP14	Muhsin Muhammad	.75	.35
❑ CP15	Jimmy Smith	.75	.35
❑ CP16	Fred Taylor	2.00	.90
❑ CP17	Corey Dillon	1.25	.55
❑ CP18	Peyton Manning	4.00	1.80
❑ CP19	Keyshawn Johnson	1.25	.55
❑ CP20	Barry Sanders	4.00	1.80
❑ CP21	Brian Griese	1.25	.55
❑ CP22	Emmitt Smith	3.00	1.35
❑ CP23	Jerry Rice	3.00	1.35
❑ CP24	Joey Galloway	1.25	.55
❑ CP25	Cris Carter	1.25	.55
❑ CP26	Robert Smith	1.25	.55
❑ CP27	Eddie George	1.50	.70
❑ CP28	Marshall Faulk	1.25	.55
❑ CP29	Tim Brown	1.25	.55
❑ CP30	Terrell Davis	3.00	1.35
❑ CP31	Jamal Anderson	1.25	.55
❑ CP32	Edgerrin James	4.00	1.80
❑ CP33	Antowain Smith	1.25	.55
❑ CP34	Antonio Freeman	1.25	.55
❑ CP35	Isaac Bruce	1.25	.55
❑ CP36	Stephen Davis	1.25	.55
❑ CP37	Troy Aikman	3.00	1.35
❑ CP38	Kevin Johnson	1.25	.55
❑ CP39	Ricky Watters	.75	.35
❑ CP40	Mike Alstott	1.25	.55

2000 Score Franchise

	MINT	NRMT
COMPLETE SET (31)	60.00	27.00
COMMON CARD (1-31)	1.25	.55
SEMISTARS	2.00	.90

STATED ODDS 1:35 RETAIL

Card	Player	MINT	NRMT
❑ F1	Emmitt Smith	5.00	2.20
❑ F2	Amani Toomer	1.25	.55
❑ F3	Jake Plummer	2.00	.90
❑ F4	Brad Johnson	2.00	.90
❑ F5	Donovan McNabb	2.50	1.10
❑ F6	Jerry Rice	5.00	2.20
❑ F7	Jamal Anderson	2.00	.90
❑ F8	Marshall Faulk	2.00	.90
❑ F9	Steve Beuerlein	1.25	.55
❑ F10	Ricky Williams	4.00	1.80
❑ F11	Brett Favre	8.00	3.60
❑ F12	Barry Sanders	6.00	2.70
❑ F13	Randy Moss	6.00	2.70
❑ F14	Shaun King	2.50	1.10
❑ F15	Cade McNown	2.50	1.10
❑ F16	Dan Marino	8.00	3.60
❑ F17	Drew Bledsoe	3.00	1.35
❑ F18	Curtis Martin	2.00	.90
❑ F19	Peyton Manning	6.00	2.70
❑ F20	Eric Moulds	2.00	.90
❑ F21	Mark Brunell	3.00	1.35
❑ F22	Akili Smith	2.00	.90
❑ F23	Tim Couch	4.00	1.80
❑ F24	Jerome Bettis	2.00	.90
❑ F25	Qadry Ismail	1.25	.55
❑ F26	Eddie George	2.50	1.10
❑ F27	Jim Harbaugh	1.25	.55
❑ F28	Terrell Davis	5.00	2.20
❑ F29	Elvis Grbac	1.25	.55
❑ F30	Tim Brown	2.00	.90
❑ F31	Jon Kitna	2.00	.90

2000 Score Future Franchise

	MINT	NRMT
COMPLETE SET (30)	100.00	45.00
COMMON CARD (FF1-FF31)	1.50	.70
SEMISTARS	2.00	.90

STATED ODDS 1:35 HOBBY

Card	Player	MINT	NRMT
❑ FF1	Michael Wiley	5.00	2.20
	Emmitt Smith		
❑ FF2	Ron Dayne	10.00	4.50
	Amani Toomer		
❑ FF3	Thomas Jones	6.00	2.70
	Jake Plummer		
❑ FF4	LaVar Arrington		
	Brad Johnson		
❑ FF5	Todd Pinkston	2.50	1.10
	Donovan McNabb		
❑ FF6	Giovanni Carmazzi	5.00	2.20
	Jerry Rice		
❑ FF7	Mareno Philyaw	2.00	.90
	Jamal Anderson		
❑ FF8	Trung Canidate	2.00	.90
	Marshall Faulk		
❑ FF9	Deon Grant	1.50	.70
	Steve Beuerlein		
❑ FF10	Marc Bulger	4.00	1.80
	Ricky Williams		
❑ FF11	Bubba Franks	8.00	3.60
	Brett Favre		
❑ FF12	Reuben Droughns	6.00	2.70
	Barry Sanders		
❑ FF13	Randy Moss	6.00	2.70
	Doug Chapman		
❑ FF14	Joe Hamilton	2.50	1.10
	Shaun King		
❑ FF15	Dez White	2.50	1.10
	Cade McNown		
❑ FF16	Ben Kelly	8.00	3.60
	Dan Marino		
❑ FF17	J.R. Redmond	3.00	1.35
	Drew Bledsoe		
❑ FF18	Chad Pennington	8.00	3.60
	Curtis Martin		
❑ FF19	Rob Morris	6.00	2.70
	Peyton Manning		
❑ FF20	Sammy Morris		
	Eric Moulds	2.00	.90
❑ FF21	R.Jay Soward	3.00	1.35
	Mark Brunell		
❑ FF22	Peter Warrick	10.00	4.50
	Akili Smith		
❑ FF23	Courtney Brown	5.00	2.20
	Tim Couch		
❑ FF24	Plaxico Burress	5.00	2.20
	Jerome Bettis		
❑ FF25	Jamal Lewis	6.00	2.70
	Qadry Ismail		
❑ FF26	Keith Bulluck	2.00	.90
	Eddie George		
❑ FF27	Trevor Gaylor	1.50	.70
	Jim Harbaugh		
❑ FF28	Chris Cole	5.00	2.20
	Terrell Davis		
❑ FF29	Sylvester Morris	2.50	1.10
	Elvis Grbac		
❑ FF30	Jerry Porter	2.50	1.10
	Tim Brown		
❑ FF31	Shaun Alexander	6.00	2.70
	Jon Kitna		

2000 Score Millennium Men

	MINT	NRMT
COMPLETE SET (6)	80.00	36.00
COMMON CARD (MM4-MM9)	12.00	5.50

STATED PRINT RUN 1000 SERIAL #'d SETS
FIRST 200-CARDS WERE SIGNED
RANDOM INSERTS IN RETAIL PACKS

Card	Player	MINT	NRMT
❑ MM4	Randy Moss	20.00	9.00
❑ MM5	Chad Pennington	25.00	11.00
❑ MM6	Randy Moss	25.00	11.00
	Chad Pennington		
❑ MM7	Tee Martin	12.00	5.50
❑ MM8	Peyton Manning	20.00	9.00
❑ MM9	Tee Martin	20.00	9.00
	Peyton Manning		

2000 Score Millennium Men Autographs

	MINT	NRMT
COMPLETE SET (6)		
COMMON CARD (MM4-MM9)		
SEMISTARS		

FIRST 200-CARDS OF PRINT RUN
RANDOM INSERTS IN RETAIL PACKS

Card	Player	MINT	NRMT
❑ MM4	Randy Moss		
❑ MM5	Chad Pennington		
❑ MM6	Randy Moss		
	Chad Pennington		
❑ MM7	Tee Martin		
❑ MM8	Peyton Manning		
❑ MM9	Tee Martin		
	Peyton Manning		

2000 Score Numbers Game

	MINT	NRMT
COMPLETE SET (50)	120.00	55.00
COMMON CARD (NG1A-NG25B)	.75	.35
SEMISTARS	1.25	.55
UNLISTED STARS	1.50	.70

CARDS SERIAL #'d TO A 1999 SEASON STAT

Card	Player	MINT	NRMT
❑ 1A	Kurt Warner/4353	5.00	2.20
❑ 1B	Kurt Warner/325	12.00	5.50
❑ 2A	Steve Beuerlein/4436	.75	.35
❑ 2B	Steve Beuerlein/343	2.00	.90
❑ 3A	Peyton Manning/4135	4.00	1.80
❑ 3B	Peyton Manning/331	10.00	4.50
❑ 4A	Brad Johnson/4005	1.25	.55
❑ 4B	Brad Johnson/316	3.00	1.35
❑ 5A	Steve McNair/2179	1.50	.70
❑ 5B	Steve McNair/187	6.00	2.70
❑ 6A	Mark Brunell/3060	2.00	.90
❑ 6B	Mark Brunell/259	5.00	2.20
❑ 7A	Marvin Harrison/1663	1.50	.70
❑ 7B	Marvin Harrison/115	4.00	1.80
❑ 8A	Isaac Bruce/1165	1.50	.70

Card	Mint	NRMT
❑ 8B Isaac Bruce/77	5.00	2.20
❑ 9A Cris Carter/1241	1.50	.70
❑ 9B Cris Carter/90	5.00	2.20
❑ 10A Randy Moss/1413	5.00	2.20
❑ 10B Randy Moss/80	15.00	6.75
❑ 11A Marcus Robinson/1444	1.50	.70
❑ 11B Marcus Robinson/88	5.00	2.20
❑ 12A Terry Glenn/1147	1.50	.70
❑ 12B Terry Glenn/69	5.00	2.20
❑ 13A Edgerrin James/1553	5.00	2.20
❑ 13B Edgerrin James/369	10.00	4.50
❑ 14A Curtis Martin/1464	1.50	.70
❑ 14B Curtis Martin/367	3.00	1.35
❑ 15A Stephen Davis/1405	1.50	.70
❑ 15B Stephen Davis/290	3.00	1.35
❑ 16A Emmitt Smith/1397	4.00	1.80
❑ 16B Emmitt Smith/329	8.00	3.60
❑ 17A Marshall Faulk/1381	1.50	.70
❑ 17B Marshall Faulk/253	3.00	1.35
❑ 18A Eddie George/1304	2.00	.90
❑ 18B Eddie George/320	4.00	1.80
❑ 19A Olandis Gary/1159	1.50	.70
❑ 19B Olandis Gary/276	3.00	1.35
❑ 20A Dorsey Levens/1034	1.50	.70
❑ 20B Dorsey Levens/279	3.00	1.35
❑ 21A Robert Smith/1015	1.50	.70
❑ 21B Robert Smith/221	3.00	1.35
❑ 22A Jerome Bettis/1091	1.50	.70
❑ 22B Jerome Bettis/299	3.00	1.35
❑ 23A Corey Dillon/1200	1.50	.70
❑ 23B Corey Dillon/263	3.00	1.35
❑ 24A Drew Bledsoe/3985	2.00	.90
❑ 24B Drew Bledsoe/305	5.00	2.20
❑ 25A Fred Taylor/732	3.00	1.35
❑ 25B Fred Taylor/159	6.00	2.70

2000 Score Rookie Preview Autographs

	MINT	NRMT
COMPLETE SET (45)	800.00	350.00
COMMON CARD	12.00	5.50
SEMISTARS	15.00	6.75

STATED ODDS 1:70H
300-700 OF EACH CARD WERE SIGNED
*ROLL CALL: .8X TO 2X HI COL..
ROLL CALL PRINT RUN 50 SER.#'d SETS
REDEMPTION EXPIRATION: 7/01/2001

Card	Mint	NRMT
❑ SR1 Ahmed Plummer Trade	12.00	5.50
❑ SR2 Peter Warrick Trade	80.00	36.00
❑ SR4 Plaxico Burress	40.00	18.00
❑ SR5 Corey Simon Trade	15.00	6.75
❑ SR6 Thomas Jones Trade	50.00	22.00
❑ SR7 Travis Taylor Trade	30.00	13.50
❑ SR8 Shaun Alexander	50.00	22.00
❑ SR9 Deon Grant	12.00	5.50
❑ SR10 Chris Redman	30.00	13.50
❑ SR11 Chad Pennington	80.00	36.00
❑ SR12 Jamal Lewis Trade	50.00	22.00
❑ SR15 Dez White	20.00	9.00
❑ SR17 Ron Dayne	80.00	36.00
❑ SR18 Sylvester Morris	20.00	9.00
❑ SR19 R.Jay Soward	20.00	9.00
❑ SR20 Sherrod Gideon	12.00	5.50
❑ SR23 Travis Prentice Trade	20.00	9.00
❑ SR24 Darrell Jackson	15.00	6.75
❑ SR25 Giovanni Carmazzi	30.00	13.50
❑ SR26 Anthony Lucas	15.00	6.75
❑ SR27 Danny Farmer	15.00	6.75
❑ SR28 Dennis Northcutt	20.00	9.00
❑ SR29 Troy Walters	15.00	6.75
❑ SR30 Laveranues Coles	15.00	6.75
❑ SR31 Kwame Cavil	12.00	5.50
❑ SR32 Tee Martin Trade	25.00	11.00
❑ SR33 J.R. Redmond	25.00	11.00
❑ SR34 Tim Rattay	20.00	9.00
❑ SR35 Jerry Porter	20.00	9.00
❑ SR36 Michael Wiley	20.00	9.00
❑ SR37 Reuben Droughns	20.00	9.00
❑ SR38 Trung Canidate	15.00	6.75
❑ SR39 Shyrone Stith	12.00	5.50
❑ SR40 Marc Bulger	15.00	6.75
❑ SR41 Tom Brady	15.00	6.75
❑ SR42 Doug Johnson Trade	20.00	9.00
❑ SR43 Todd Husak	15.00	6.75
❑ SR44 Gari Scott Trade	15.00	6.75
❑ SR45 Chafie Fields	12.00	5.50
❑ SR47 Sammy Morris	15.00	6.75
❑ SR50 Trevor Gaylor	12.00	5.50
❑ SR51 Ron Dugans Trade	15.00	6.75
❑ SR52 Chris Daniels	12.00	5.50
❑ SR53 Joe Hamilton Trade	15.00	6.75
❑ SR54 Todd Pinkston	15.00	6.75

2000 Score Team 2000

	MINT	NRMT
COMPLETE SET (20)	50.00	22.00
COMMON CARD (TM1-TM20)	1.00	.45
SEMISTARS	1.50	.70

BLUE PRINT RUN 1500 SERIAL #'d SETS
BLUES INSERTED AS HOBBY BOX TOPPER
*GOLDS: .4X TO 1X BASIC INSERTS
GOLDS SER.#'d TO PLAYER'S ROOKIE YEAR
GOLDS RANDOM INSERTS IN RETAIL
*GREEN: 1X TO 2.5X HI COL
GREEN PRINT RUN 500 SERIAL #'d SETS
*RED: .6X TO 1.5X HI COL
RED PRINT RUN 200 SERIAL #'d SETS

Card	Mint	NRMT
❑ TM1 Barry Sanders	5.00	2.20
❑ TM2 Troy Aikman	4.00	1.80
❑ TM3 Cris Carter	1.50	.70
❑ TM4 Emmitt Smith	4.00	1.80
❑ TM5 Brett Favre	6.00	2.70
❑ TM6 Jimmy Smith	1.00	.45
❑ TM7 Drew Bledsoe	2.50	1.10
❑ TM8 Marshall Faulk	1.50	.70
❑ TM9 Steve McNair	1.50	.70
❑ TM10 Marvin Harrison	1.50	.70
❑ TM11 Eddie George	2.00	.90
❑ TM12 Eric Moulds	1.50	.70
❑ TM13 Jake Plummer	1.50	.70
❑ TM14 Antowain Smith	1.50	.70
❑ TM15 Fred Taylor	2.50	1.10
❑ TM16 Randy Moss	5.00	2.20
❑ TM17 Peyton Manning	5.00	2.20
❑ TM18 Ricky Williams	3.00	1.35
❑ TM19 Edgerrin James	5.00	2.20
❑ TM20 Kurt Warner	6.00	2.70

2000 Score Team 2000 Autographs

	MINT	NRMT
COMMON CARD (TM1-TM20)	40.00	18.00
SEMISTARS	60.00	27.00

RANDOM INSERTS IN HOBBY PACKS
AUTO PRINT RUN 50 SERIAL #'d SETS
REDEMPTION EXPIRATION: 7/01/2001

Card	Mint	NRMT
❑ TM1 Barry Sanders Trade	200.00	90.00
❑ TM2 Troy Aikman	150.00	70.00
❑ TM3 Cris Carter	60.00	27.00
❑ TM4 Emmitt Smith Trade		
❑ TM5 Brett Favre Trade	250.00	110.00
❑ TM6 Jimmy Smith	40.00	18.00
❑ TM7 Drew Bledsoe Trade	100.00	45.00
❑ TM8 Marshall Faulk Trade	60.00	27.00
❑ TM9 Steve McNair Trade	60.00	27.00
❑ TM10 Marvin Harrison	60.00	27.00
❑ TM11 Eddie George	80.00	36.00
❑ TM12 Eric Moulds	40.00	18.00
❑ TM13 Jake Plummer	60.00	27.00
❑ TM14 Antowain Smith	40.00	18.00
❑ TM15 Fred Taylor	80.00	36.00
❑ TM16 Randy Moss	150.00	70.00
❑ TM17 Peyton Manning Trade	150.00	70.00
❑ TM18 Ricky Williams Trade		
❑ TM19 Edgerrin James	200.00	90.00
❑ TM20 Kurt Warner	250.00	110.00

1995 Select Certified

	MINT	NRMT
COMPLETE SET (135)	135.00	60.00
COMMON CARD (1-135)	.25	.11
SEMISTARS	.50	.23
UNLISTED STARS	1.00	.45

Card	Mint	NRMT
❑ 1 Marshall Faulk	2.00	.90
❑ 2 Heath Shuler	1.00	.45
❑ 3 Garrison Hearst	1.00	.45
❑ 4 Errict Rhett	1.00	.45
❑ 5 Jeff George	.50	.23
❑ 6 Jerome Bettis	1.00	.45
❑ 7 Jim Kelly	1.00	.45
❑ 8 Rick Mirer	1.00	.45
❑ 9 Willie Davis	.50	.23
❑ 10 Steve Young	2.50	1.10
❑ 11 Erik Kramer	.25	.11
❑ 12 Natrone Means	1.00	.45
❑ 13 Jeff Blake RC	5.00	2.20
❑ 14 Neil O'Donnell	.50	.23
❑ 15 Andre Rison	.50	.23
❑ 16 Randall Cunningham	1.00	.45
❑ 17 Emmitt Smith	5.00	2.20
❑ 18 Tim Brown	1.00	.45
❑ 19 Shannon Sharpe	.50	.23
❑ 20 Boomer Esiason	.50	.23
❑ 21 Barry Sanders	6.00	2.70
❑ 22 Rodney Hampton	.50	.23
❑ 23 Robert Brooks	1.00	.45
❑ 24 Jim Everett	.25	.11
❑ 25 Gary Brown	.25	.11
❑ 26 Drew Bledsoe	3.00	1.35
❑ 27 Desmond Howard	.50	.23
❑ 28 Cris Carter	1.00	.45
❑ 29 Marcus Allen	1.00	.45
❑ 30 Dan Marino	6.00	2.70
❑ 31 Warren Moon	.50	.23
❑ 32 Dave Krieg	.25	.11
❑ 33 Ben Coates	.50	.23

Card	Mint	Nrmt
❑ 34 Terance Mathis	.50	.23
❑ 35 Mario Bates	1.00	.45
❑ 36 Andre Reed	.50	.23
❑ 37 Dave Brown	.50	.23
❑ 38 Jeff Graham	.25	.11
❑ 39 Johnny Mitchell	.25	.11
❑ 40 Carl Pickens	1.00	.45
❑ 41 Jeff Hostetler	.50	.23
❑ 42 Vinny Testaverde	.50	.23
❑ 43 Ricky Watters	1.00	.45
❑ 44 Troy Aikman	3.00	1.35
❑ 45 Byron Bam Morris	.50	.23
❑ 46 John Elway	6.00	2.70
❑ 47 Junior Seau	1.00	.45
❑ 48 Scott Mitchell	.50	.23
❑ 49 Jerry Rice	3.00	1.35
❑ 50 Brett Favre	6.00	2.70
❑ 51 Chris Warren	.50	.23
❑ 52 Chris Chandler	.50	.23
❑ 53 Lorenzo White	.25	.11
❑ 54 Craig Erickson	.25	.11
❑ 55 Alvin Harper	.25	.11
❑ 56 Steve Beuerlein	.25	.11
❑ 57 Edgar Bennett	.50	.23
❑ 58 Steve Bono	.50	.23
❑ 59 Eric Green	.25	.11
❑ 60 Jake Reed	.50	.23
❑ 61 Terry Kirby	.50	.23
❑ 62 Vincent Brisby	.25	.11
❑ 63 Lake Dawson	.50	.23
❑ 64 Torrance Small	.25	.11
❑ 65 Mark Brunell	3.00	1.35
❑ 66 Haywood Jeffires	.25	.11
❑ 67 Flipper Anderson	.25	.11
❑ 68 Ronald Moore	.25	.11
❑ 69 LeShon Johnson	.50	.23
❑ 70 Rocket Ismail	.50	.23
❑ 71 Herman Moore	1.00	.45
❑ 72 Charlie Garner	.50	.23
❑ 73 Anthony Miller	.50	.23
❑ 74 Greg Lloyd	.50	.23
❑ 75 Michael Irvin	1.00	.45
❑ 76 Stan Humphries	.50	.23
❑ 77 Leroy Hoard	.25	.11
❑ 78 Deion Sanders Card mailed to dealers	3.00	1.35
❑ 79 Darnay Scott	1.00	.45
❑ 80 Chris Miller	.25	.11
❑ 81 Curtis Conway	1.00	.45
❑ 82 Trent Dilfer	1.00	.45
❑ 83 Bruce Smith	1.00	.45
❑ 84 Reggie Brooks	.50	.23
❑ 85 Frank Reich	.25	.11
❑ 86 Henry Ellard	.50	.23
❑ 87 Eric Metcalf	.50	.23
❑ 88 Sean Gilbert	.50	.23
❑ 89 Larry Centers	.50	.23
❑ 90 Ricky Ervins	.25	.11
❑ 91 Craig Heyward	.50	.23
❑ 92 Rod Woodson	.50	.23
❑ 93 Steve Walsh	.25	.11
❑ 94 Fred Barnett	.50	.23
❑ 95 William Floyd	1.00	.45
❑ 96 Harvey Williams	.25	.11
❑ 97 Greg Hill	.50	.23
❑ 98 Irving Fryar	.50	.23
❑ 99 Kevin Williams	.50	.23
❑ 100 Herschel Walker	.50	.23
❑ 101 Sean Dawkins	.50	.23
❑ 102 Michael Haynes	.50	.23
❑ 103 Reggie White	1.00	.45
❑ 104 Robert Smith	1.00	.45
❑ 105 Todd Collins RC	1.00	.45
❑ 106 Michael Westbrook RC	10.00	4.50
❑ 107 Frank Sanders RC	6.00	2.70
❑ 108 Christian Fauria RC	.25	.11
❑ 109 Stoney Case RC	2.00	.90
❑ 110 Jimmy Oliver RC	.25	.11
❑ 111 Mark Bruener RC	.50	.23
❑ 112 Rodney Thomas RC	1.00	.45
❑ 113 Chris T.Jones RC	1.00	.45
❑ 114 James A.Stewart RC	.25	.11
❑ 115 Kevin Carter RC	1.00	.45
❑ 116 Eric Zeier RC	2.00	.90
❑ 117 Curtis Martin RC	15.00	6.75
❑ 118 James O. Stewart RC	12.00	5.50
❑ 119 Joe Aska RC	.50	.23
❑ 120 Ken Dilger RC	.50	.23
❑ 121 Tyrone Wheatley RC	8.00	3.60
❑ 122 Ray Zellars RC	.50	.23
❑ 123 Kyle Brady RC	1.00	.45
❑ 124 Chad May RC	.25	.11
❑ 125 Napoleon Kaufman RC	12.00	5.50
❑ 126 Terrell Davis RC	80.00	36.00
❑ 127 Warren Sapp RC	2.50	1.10
❑ 128 Sherman Williams RC	.25	.11
❑ 129 Kordell Stewart RC	15.00	6.75
❑ 130 Ki-Jana Carter RC	1.00	.45
❑ 131 Terrell Fletcher RC	.25	.11
❑ 132 Rashaan Salaam RC	1.00	.45
❑ 133 J.J. Stokes RC	4.00	1.80
❑ 134 Kerry Collins RC	6.00	2.70
❑ 135 Joey Galloway RC	15.00	6.75
❑ P7 Dan Marino Promo Gold Team Card	5.00	2.20
❑ P10 Steve Young Promo	2.00	.90
❑ P44 Troy Aikman Promo	2.50	1.10

1995 Select Certified Mirror Gold

	MINT	NRMT
COMPLETE SET (135)	1200.00	550.00
COMMON CARD (1-135)	2.00	.90

*MIRROR GOLD STARS: 3X TO 8X HI COL.
*MIRROR GOLD RCs: 1.5X TO 3X
MIRROR GOLDS: STATED ODDS 1:5

1995 Select Certified Future

	MINT	NRMT
COMPLETE SET (10)	50.00	22.00
COMMON CARD (1-10)	2.00	.90
SEMISTARS	3.00	1.35
STATED ODDS 1:19		

Card	Mint	Nrmt
❑ 1 Ki-Jana Carter	2.00	.90
❑ 2 Steve McNair	15.00	6.75
❑ 3 Kerry Collins	5.00	2.20
❑ 4 Michael Westbrook	8.00	3.60
❑ 5 Joey Galloway	15.00	6.75
❑ 6 J.J. Stokes	4.00	1.80
❑ 7 Rashaan Salaam	2.00	.90
❑ 8 Tyrone Wheatley	6.00	2.70
❑ 9 Todd Collins	3.00	1.35
❑ 10 Curtis Martin	15.00	6.75

1995 Select Certified Gold Team

	MINT	NRMT
COMPLETE SET (10)	150.00	70.00
STATED ODDS 1:41		

Card	Mint	Nrmt
❑ 1 Jerry Rice	15.00	6.75
❑ 2 Emmitt Smith	25.00	11.00
❑ 3 Drew Bledsoe	15.00	6.75
❑ 4 Marshall Faulk	10.00	4.50
❑ 5 Troy Aikman	15.00	6.75
❑ 6 Barry Sanders	30.00	13.50
❑ 7 Dan Marino	30.00	13.50
❑ 8 Errict Rhett	5.00	2.20
❑ 9 Brett Favre	30.00	13.50
❑ 10 Steve McNair	20.00	9.00

1995 Select Certified Select Few

	MINT	NRMT
COMPLETE SET (20)	250.00	110.00
STATED ODDS 1:32		

PRICED CARDS ARE NUMBERED OF 2250
*1028 STARS: 2.5X TO 6X BASE CARD HI
*1028 ROOKIES: 1.25X TO 3X BASE CARD HI
CARDS ARE NUMBERED OF 1028

Card	Mint	Nrmt
❑ 1 Dan Marino	25.00	11.00
❑ 2 Emmitt Smith	20.00	9.00
❑ 3 Marshall Faulk	8.00	3.60
❑ 4 Barry Sanders	25.00	11.00
❑ 5 Drew Bledsoe	12.00	5.50
❑ 6 Brett Favre	25.00	11.00
❑ 7 Troy Aikman	12.00	5.50
❑ 8 Jerry Rice	12.00	5.50
❑ 9 Steve Young	10.00	4.50
❑ 10 Natrone Means	4.00	1.80
❑ 11 Byron Bam Morris	2.00	.90
❑ 12 Errict Rhett	4.00	1.80
❑ 13 John Elway	25.00	11.00
❑ 14 Heath Shuler	4.00	1.80
❑ 15 Ki-Jana Carter	2.00	.90
❑ 16 Kerry Collins	12.00	5.50
❑ 17 Steve McNair	30.00	13.50
❑ 18 Rashaan Salaam	2.00	.90
❑ 19 Tyrone Wheatley	15.00	6.75
❑ 20 J.J. Stokes	8.00	3.60

1996 Select Certified

	MINT	NRMT
COMPLETE SET (125)	60.00	27.00
COMMON CARD (1-125)	.25	.11
SEMISTARS	.50	.23
UNLISTED STARS	.75	.35
COMP.ART.PROOF SET (125)	600.00	275.00

*AP STARS: 3X TO 8X HI COL....
*AP RC'S: 1.5X TO 4X HI............
AP STATED PRINT RUN 560 SETS
AP STATED ODDS 1:18 ....

COMP.CERT.BLUE SET (125)	1200.00	550.00

*CERT.BLUE STARS: 6X TO 15X HI COL.
*CERT.BLUE RC's: 3X TO 8X HI..
CERT.BLUE STATED PRINT RUN 200 SETS
CERT.BLUE STATED ODDS 1:50

COMP.CERT.RED SET (125)	300.00	135.00

*CERT.RED STARS: 2X TO 5X HI COL.
*CERT.RED RC's: 1X TO 2.5X HI
CERT.RED STATED PRINT RUN 2000 SETS
CERT.RED STATED ODDS 1:5....

COMP.PREM.STOCK SET (125)	100.00	45.00

*PREM.STOCK STARS: .75X TO 2X HI COL
*PREM.STOCK RCs: .6X TO 1.5X HI
STATED PRINT RUN LESS THAN 7000 SETS

❑ 1 Isaac Bruce	.75	.35
❑ 2 Rick Mirer	.50	.23
❑ 3 Jake Reed	.50	.23
❑ 4 Reggie White	.75	.35
❑ 5 Harvey Williams	.25	.11
❑ 6 Jim Everett	.25	.11
❑ 7 Tony Martin	.50	.23
❑ 8 Craig Heyward	.25	.11
❑ 9 Tamarick Vanover	.50	.23
❑ 10 Hugh Douglas	.25	.11
❑ 11 Erik Kramer	.25	.11
❑ 12 Charlie Garner	.25	.11
❑ 13 Errict Pegram	.25	.11
❑ 14 Scott Mitchell	.50	.23
❑ 15 Michael Westbrook	.75	.35
❑ 16 Robert Smith	.50	.23
❑ 17 Kerry Collins	.75	.35
❑ 18 Derek Loville	.25	.11
❑ 19 Jeff Blake	.75	.35
❑ 20 Terry Kirby	.50	.23
❑ 21 Bruce Smith	.50	.23
❑ 22 Stan Humphries	.50	.23
❑ 23 Rodney Thomas	.25	.11
❑ 24 Wayne Chrebet	1.00	.45
❑ 25 Napoleon Kaufman	1.25	.55
❑ 26 Marshall Faulk	.75	.35
❑ 27 Emmitt Smith	3.00	1.35
❑ 28 Natrone Means	.75	.35
❑ 29 Neil O'Donnell	.50	.23
❑ 30 Warren Moon	.50	.23
❑ 31 Junior Seau	.50	.23
❑ 32 Chris Sanders	.50	.23
❑ 33 Barry Sanders	4.00	1.80
❑ 34 Jeff Graham	.25	.11
❑ 35 Kordell Stewart	1.50	.70
❑ 36 Jim Harbaugh	.50	.23
❑ 37 Chris Warren	.50	.23
❑ 38 Cris Carter	.75	.35
❑ 39 J.J. Stokes	.75	.35
❑ 40 Tyrone Wheatley	.50	.23
❑ 41 Terrell Davis	5.00	2.20
❑ 42 Mark Brunell	2.00	.90
❑ 43 Steve Young	1.50	.70
❑ 44 Rodney Hampton	.50	.23
❑ 45 Drew Bledsoe	2.00	.90
❑ 46 Larry Centers	.50	.23
❑ 47 Ken Norton Jr.	.25	.11
❑ 48 Deion Sanders	1.25	.55
❑ 49 Alvin Harper	.25	.11
❑ 50 Trent Dilfer	.75	.35
❑ 51 Steve McNair	1.50	.70
❑ 52 Robert Brooks	.75	.35
❑ 53 Edgar Bennett	.50	.23
❑ 54 Troy Aikman	2.00	.90
❑ 55 Dan Marino	4.00	1.80
❑ 56 Steve Bono	.25	.11
❑ 57 Marcus Allen	.75	.35
❑ 58 Rodney Peete	.25	.11
❑ 59 Ben Coates	.50	.23
❑ 60 Yancey Thigpen	.50	.23
❑ 61 Tim Brown	.75	.35
❑ 62 Jerry Rice	2.00	.90
❑ 63 Quinn Early	.25	.11
❑ 64 Ricky Watters	.50	.23
❑ 65 Thurman Thomas	.75	.35
❑ 66 Greg Lloyd	.50	.23
❑ 67 Eric Metcalf	.25	.11
❑ 68 Jeff George	.50	.23
❑ 69 John Elway	4.00	1.80
❑ 70 Frank Sanders	.50	.23
❑ 71 Curtis Conway	.75	.35
❑ 72 Greg Hill	.50	.23
❑ 73 Darick Holmes	.25	.11
❑ 74 Herman Moore	.75	.35
❑ 75 Carl Pickens	.75	.35
❑ 76 Eric Zeier	.25	.11
❑ 77 Curtis Martin	1.50	.70
❑ 78 Rashaan Salaam	.75	.35
❑ 79 Joey Galloway	1.50	.70
❑ 80 Jeff Hostetler	.25	.11
❑ 81 Jim Kelly	.75	.35
❑ 82 Dave Brown	.25	.11
❑ 83 Sean Dawkins	.25	.11
❑ 84 Michael Irvin	.75	.35
❑ 85 Brett Favre	4.00	1.80
❑ 86 Cedric Jones RC	.25	.11
❑ 87 Jeff Lewis RC	2.00	.90
❑ 88 Alex Van Dyke RC	.50	.23
❑ 89 Regan Upshaw RC	.25	.11
❑ 90 Karim Abdul-Jabbar RC	2.50	1.10
❑ 91 Marvin Harrison RC	10.00	4.50
❑ 92 Stephen Davis RC	15.00	6.75
❑ 93 Terry Glenn RC	5.00	2.20
❑ 94 Kevin Hardy RC	.75	.35
❑ 95 Stanley Pritchett RC	.50	.23
❑ 96 Willie Anderson RC	.25	.11
❑ 97 Lawrence Phillips RC	1.50	.70
❑ 98 Bobby Hoying RC	2.00	.90
❑ 99 Amani Toomer RC	.75	.35
❑ 100 Eddie George RC	15.00	6.75
❑ 101 Stepfret Williams RC	.50	.23
❑ 102 Eric Moulds RC	6.00	2.70
❑ 103 Simeon Rice RC	.75	.35
❑ 104 John Mobley RC	.25	.11
❑ 105 Keyshawn Johnson RC	8.00	3.60
❑ 106 Daryl Gardener RC	.25	.11
❑ 107 Tony Banks RC	4.00	1.80
❑ 108 Bobby Engram RC	.75	.35
❑ 109 Jonathan Ogden RC	.25	.11
❑ 110 Eddie Kennison RC	.75	.35
❑ 111 Danny Kanell RC	.75	.35
❑ 112 Tony Brackens RC	.50	.23
❑ 113 Tim Biakabutuka RC	3.00	1.35
❑ 114 Leeland McElroy RC	1.00	.45
❑ 115 Rickey Dudley RC	.75	.35
❑ 116 Troy Aikman SS	1.00	.45
❑ 117 Brett Favre SS	2.00	.90
❑ 118 Drew Bledsoe SS	1.00	.45
❑ 119 Steve Young SS	.75	.35
❑ 120 Kerry Collins SS	.75	.35
❑ 121 John Elway SS	2.00	.90
❑ 122 Dan Marino SS	2.00	.90
❑ 123 Kordell Stewart SS	.75	.35
❑ 124 Jeff Blake SS	.50	.23
❑ 125 Jim Harbaugh SS	.50	.23

1996 Select Certified Gold Team

	MINT	NRMT
COMPLETE SET (18)	150.00	70.00
STATED ODDS 1:38		
❑ 1 Emmitt Smith	15.00	6.75
❑ 2 Barry Sanders	20.00	9.00
❑ 3 Dan Marino	20.00	9.00
❑ 4 Steve Young	8.00	3.60
❑ 5 Troy Aikman	10.00	4.50
❑ 6 Jerry Rice	10.00	4.50
❑ 7 Rashaan Salaam	4.00	1.80
❑ 8 Marshall Faulk	4.00	1.80
❑ 9 Drew Bledsoe	10.00	4.50
❑ 10 Steve McNair	8.00	3.60
❑ 11 Brett Favre	20.00	9.00
❑ 12 Terrell Davis	25.00	11.00
❑ 13 Kordell Stewart	8.00	3.60
❑ 14 Keyshawn Johnson	15.00	6.75
❑ 15 Kerry Collins	4.00	1.80
❑ 16 Curtis Martin	8.00	3.60
❑ 17 Isaac Bruce	4.00	1.80
❑ 18 Terry Glenn	10.00	4.50

1996 Select Certified Mirror Blue

	MINT	NRMT
COMMON CARD (1-125)	15.00	6.75

*MIR.BLUE STARS: 20X TO 50X HI COL
*MIR.BLUE RC'S: 8X TO 20X HI ..
STATED ODDS 1:200 ....
STATED PRINT RUN 50 SETS ....

1996 Select Certified Mirror Gold

	MINT	NRMT
COMMON CARD (1-125)	25.00	11.00

*MIR.GOLD STARS: 30X TO 60X HI COL
*MIR.GOLD RC'S: 12X TO 25X HI
STATED ODDS 1:300 ....
STATED PRINT RUN 35 SETS ....

1996 Select Certified Mirror Red

	MINT	NRMT
COMPLETE SET (125)	2000.00	900.00

*MIR.RED STARS: 12X TO 30X HI COL
*MIR.RED RC'S: 5X TO 12X HI ....
MIRROR RED STATED ODDS 1:100
MIRROR RED STATED PRINT RUN 90 SETS

1996 Select Certified Mirror Red Premium Stock

	MINT	NRMT
COMMON CARD (1-125)	40.00	18.00

*MIRROR RED PS STARS: 60X TO 120X
*MIRROR RED PS RC'S: 25X TO 50X
PRE.STOCK STATED PRINT RUN 20 SETS

1996 Select Certified Thumbs Up

	MINT	NRMT
COMPLETE SET (24)	250.00	110.00
STATED ODDS 1:41		
❑ 1 Steve Young	12.00	5.50
❑ 2 Jeff Blake	6.00	2.70
❑ 3 Dan Marino	30.00	13.50
❑ 4 Kerry Collins	6.00	2.70
❑ 5 John Elway	30.00	13.50
❑ 6 Neil O'Donnell	4.00	1.80
❑ 7 Brett Favre	30.00	13.50
❑ 8 Scott Mitchell	4.00	1.80

❑ 9 Troy Aikman	15.00	6.75
❑ 10 Jim Harbaugh	4.00	1.80
❑ 11 Drew Bledsoe	15.00	6.75
❑ 12 Jeff Hostetler	2.00	.90
❑ 13 Marvin Harrison	20.00	9.00
❑ 14 Tim Biakabutuka	6.00	2.70
❑ 15 Eddie George	30.00	13.50
❑ 16 Tony Brackens	1.00	.45
❑ 17 Karim Abdul-Jabbar	5.00	2.20
❑ 18 Daryl Gardener	.50	.23
❑ 19 Alex Van Dyke	1.00	.45
❑ 20 Terry Glenn	10.00	4.50
❑ 21 Eric Moulds	12.00	5.50
❑ 22 Eddie Kennison	1.50	.70
❑ 23 Regan Upshaw	.50	.23
❑ 24 Mike Alstott	10.00	4.50

1999 SkyBox Dominion

	MINT	NRMT
COMPLETE SET (250)	40.00	18.00
COMMON CARD (1-200)	.10	.05
SEMISTARS	.20	.09
UNLISTED STARS	.40	.18
COMMON ROOKIE (201-250)	.50	.23
ROOKIE SEMISTARS	.75	.35
ROOKIE UNL.STARS	1.00	.45

❑ 1 Randy Moss	1.50	.70
❑ 2 James Jett	.20	.09
❑ 3 Lawyer Milloy	.10	.05
❑ 4 Mike Alstott	.40	.18
❑ 5 Courtney Hawkins	.10	.05
❑ 6 Carl Pickens	.20	.09
❑ 7 Marvin Harrison	.40	.18
❑ 8 Robert Smith	.40	.18
❑ 9 Fred Taylor	1.00	.45
❑ 10 Barry Sanders	1.50	.70
❑ 11 Tony Gonzalez	.20	.09
❑ 12 Leroy Hoard	.10	.05
❑ 13 Drew Bledsoe	.60	.25
❑ 14 Cam Cleeland	.10	.05
❑ 15 Steve Atwater	.10	.05
❑ 16 Eric Moulds	.40	.18
❑ 17 Herman Moore	.40	.18
❑ 18 Rickey Dudley	.10	.05
❑ 19 Jeff Blake	.20	.09
❑ 20 Eddie George	.50	.23
❑ 21 Antonio Freeman	.40	.18
❑ 22 Stephen Alexander	.10	.05
❑ 23 Larry Centers	.10	.05
❑ 24 Chris Chandler	.20	.09
❑ 25 James Stewart	.20	.09
❑ 26 Randall Cunningham	.40	.18
❑ 27 Mark Brunell	.60	.25
❑ 28 David Palmer	.10	.05
❑ 29 Eric Green	.10	.05
❑ 30 Terry Glenn	.40	.18
❑ 31 Jerry Rice	1.00	.45
❑ 32 Ricky Proehl	.10	.05
❑ 33 Tony Banks	.20	.09
❑ 34 John Elway	1.50	.70
❑ 35 Johnnie Morton	.20	.09
❑ 36 Tony Simmons	.10	.05
❑ 37 Jon Kitna	.50	.23
❑ 38 Trent Green	.20	.09
❑ 39 Peyton Manning	1.50	.70
❑ 40 Emmitt Smith	1.00	.45
❑ 41 Warrick Dunn	.40	.18
❑ 42 Jerome Bettis	.40	.18
❑ 43 Ricky Watters	.20	.09
❑ 44 Rocket Ismail	.20	.09
❑ 45 Ryan Leaf	.40	.18
❑ 46 Jackie Harris	.10	.05
❑ 47 Robert Holcombe	.20	.09
❑ 48 Dorsey Levens	.40	.18
❑ 49 Duce Staley	.40	.18
❑ 50 Brett Favre	1.50	.70
❑ 51 Andre Rison	.20	.09
❑ 52 Curtis Conway	.20	.09
❑ 53 Mark Chmura	.10	.05
❑ 54 Doug Flutie	.50	.23
❑ 55 Ernie Mills	.10	.05
❑ 56 Jeff George	.20	.09
❑ 57 Chris Warren	.10	.05
❑ 58 Alonzo Mayes	.10	.05
❑ 59 Freddie Jones	.10	.05
❑ 60 Shannon Sharpe	.20	.09
❑ 61 O.J. Santiago	.10	.05
❑ 62 Shawn Springs	.10	.05
❑ 63 Kent Graham	.10	.05
❑ 64 Muhsin Muhammad	.20	.09
❑ 65 Keith Poole	.10	.05
❑ 66 Chris Spielman	.10	.05
❑ 67 Curtis Enis	.40	.18
❑ 68 Lamar Smith	.10	.05
❑ 69 Charles Johnson	.10	.05
❑ 70 Kerry Collins	.20	.09
❑ 71 Charlie Batch	.75	.35
❑ 72 Keenan McCardell	.20	.09
❑ 73 Ty Detmer	.20	.09
❑ 74 Mark Bruener	.10	.05
❑ 75 Lamar Thomas	.10	.05
❑ 76 Kwamie Lassiter	.10	.05
❑ 77 Byron Bam Morris	.10	.05
❑ 78 Michael Sinclair	.10	.05
❑ 79 Darnay Scott	.10	.05
❑ 80 Napoleon Kaufman	.40	.18
❑ 81 Ed McCaffrey	.20	.09
❑ 82 Reidel Anthony	.20	.09
❑ 83 Kevin Greene	.10	.05
❑ 84 Michael Irvin	.20	.09
❑ 85 Charles Way	.10	.05
❑ 86 Tim Brown	.40	.18
❑ 87 Johnny McWilliams	.10	.05
❑ 88 Brad Johnson	.40	.18
❑ 89 Antonio Langham	.10	.05
❑ 90 Bruce Smith	.20	.09
❑ 91 Reggie Barlow	.10	.05
❑ 92 Ty Law	.10	.05
❑ 93 Bobby Engram	.20	.09
❑ 94 Kimble Anders	.20	.09
❑ 95 Dale Carter	.10	.05
❑ 96 Jimmy Smith	.20	.09
❑ 97 Marc Edwards	.10	.05
❑ 98 Ken Dilger	.10	.05
❑ 99 Adrian Murrell	.20	.09
❑ 100 Terance Mathis	.20	.09
❑ 101 Gary Anderson	.10	.05
❑ 102 Garrison Hearst	.20	.09
❑ 103 Ahman Green	.20	.09
❑ 104 Daryl Johnston	.10	.05
❑ 105 O.J. McDuffie	.20	.09
❑ 106 Matthew Hatchette	.10	.05
❑ 107 Chris Doleman	.10	.05
❑ 108 Steve McNair	.40	.18
❑ 109 Leon Johnson	.10	.05
❑ 110 Terrell Davis	1.00	.45
❑ 111 Rob Moore	.20	.09
❑ 112 Troy Aikman	1.00	.45
❑ 113 John Avery	.20	.09
❑ 114 Frank Wycheck	.10	.05
❑ 115 Curtis Martin	.40	.18
❑ 116 Jim Harbaugh	.20	.09
❑ 117 Sean Dawkins	.10	.05
❑ 118 Glenn Foley	.20	.09
❑ 119 Warren Sapp	.10	.05
❑ 120 R.W. McQuarters	.10	.05
❑ 121 Yancey Thigpen	.10	.05
❑ 122 Frank Sanders	.20	.09
❑ 123 Tim Dwight	.40	.18
❑ 124 Pete Mitchell	.10	.05
❑ 125 Steve Beuerlein	.10	.05
❑ 126 Tyrone Davis	.10	.05
❑ 127 Jamie Asher	.10	.05
❑ 128 Corey Dillon	.40	.18
❑ 129 Doug Pederson	.10	.05
❑ 130 Deion Sanders	.40	.18
❑ 131 J.J. Stokes	.20	.09
❑ 132 Jermaine Lewis	.20	.09
❑ 133 Gary Brown	.10	.05
❑ 134 Derrick Alexander	.10	.05
❑ 135 Tony McGee	.10	.05
❑ 136 Kyle Brady	.10	.05
❑ 137 Mikhael Ricks	.10	.05
❑ 138 Germane Crowell	.20	.09
❑ 139 Skip Hicks	.40	.18
❑ 140 Ben Coates	.20	.09
❑ 141 Will Blackwell	.10	.05
❑ 142 Al Del Greco	.10	.05
❑ 143 Jake Plummer	.75	.35
❑ 144 Marshall Faulk	.40	.18
❑ 145 Antowain Smith	.40	.18
❑ 146 Corey Fuller	.10	.05
❑ 147 Keyshawn Johnson	.40	.18
❑ 148 John Randle	.20	.09
❑ 149 Terrell Buckley	.10	.05
❑ 150 Terry Kirby	.10	.05
❑ 151 Robert Brooks	.20	.09
❑ 152 Karim Abdul-Jabbar	.20	.09
❑ 153 Jason Sehorn	.10	.05
❑ 154 Elvis Grbac	.20	.09
❑ 155 Andre Reed	.20	.09
❑ 156 Ike Hilliard	.10	.05
❑ 157 Jamal Anderson	.40	.18
❑ 158 Jake Reed	.20	.09
❑ 159 Rich Gannon	.20	.09
❑ 160 Michael Jackson	.10	.05
❑ 161 Bert Emanuel	.20	.09
❑ 162 Charles Woodson	.40	.18
❑ 163 Ray Lewis	.10	.05
❑ 164 Trent Dilfer	.20	.09
❑ 165 Oronde Gadsden	.10	.05
❑ 166 Wesley Walls	.20	.09
❑ 167 Joey Galloway	.40	.18
❑ 168 Mo Lewis	.10	.05
❑ 169 Darren Woodson	.10	.05
❑ 170 Cris Carter	.40	.18
❑ 171 Brian Mitchell	.10	.05
❑ 172 Tim Biakabutuka	.20	.09
❑ 173 Michael Westbrook	.20	.09
❑ 174 Dan Marino	1.50	.70
❑ 175 Greg Hill	.10	.05
❑ 176 Priest Holmes	.40	.18
❑ 177 Fred Lane	.10	.05
❑ 178 Isaac Bruce	.40	.18
❑ 179 Erik Kramer	.10	.05
❑ 180 Steve Young	.60	.25
❑ 181 Terry Fair	.10	.05
❑ 182 Brian Griese	.75	.35
❑ 183 Leslie Shepherd	.10	.05
❑ 184 Kordell Stewart	.40	.18
❑ 185 Charlie Jones	.10	.05
❑ 186 Chris Calloway	.10	.05
❑ 187 Wayne Chrebet	.20	.09
❑ 188 Natrone Means	.20	.09
❑ 189 David LaFleur	.10	.05
❑ 190 Rod Smith WR	.20	.09
❑ 191 Kevin Dyson	.20	.09
❑ 192 Scott Mitchell	.10	.05
❑ 193 Andre Wadsworth	.10	.05
❑ 194 Vinny Testaverde	.20	.09
❑ 195 Az-Zahir Hakim	.10	.05

❑ 196 Joe Jurevicius	.10	.05
❑ 197 Junior Seau	.20	.09
❑ 198 Jason Elam	.10	.05
❑ 199 Terrell Owens	.40	.18
❑ 200 Jacquez Green	.20	.09
❑ 201 Tim Couch RC	6.00	2.70
❑ 202 Donovan McNabb RC	3.00	1.35
❑ 203 Cade McNown RC	3.00	1.35
❑ 204 Akili Smith RC	2.00	.90
❑ 205 Kevin Faulk RC	1.25	.55
❑ 206 Sedrick Irvin RC	1.00	.45
❑ 207 Edgerrin James RC	10.00	4.50
❑ 208 Ricky Williams RC	6.00	2.70
❑ 209 D'Wayne Bates RC	.75	.35
❑ 210 David Boston RC	1.50	.70
❑ 211 Torry Holt RC	2.50	1.10
❑ 212 Peerless Price RC	1.50	.70
❑ 213 Daunte Culpepper RC	3.00	1.35
❑ 214 Troy Edwards RC	1.50	.70
❑ 215 Rob Konrad RC	1.00	.45
❑ 216 Joe Germaine RC	1.00	.45
❑ 217 James Johnson RC	1.25	.55
❑ 218 Brock Huard RC	1.25	.55
❑ 219 Cecil Collins RC	1.00	.45
❑ 220 Jeff Paulk	.75	.35
Eugene Baker RC		
❑ 221 Marty Booker	.50	.23
James Finn RC		
❑ 222 Scott Covington	.75	.35
Nick Williams RC		
❑ 223 Kevin Johnson	2.00	.90
Darrin Chiaverini RC		
❑ 224 Ebenezer Ekuban	.75	.35
Dat Nguyen RC		
❑ 225 Al Wilson	.50	.23
Chad Plummer RC		
❑ 226 Chris Claiborn	.50	.23
Aaron Gibson RC		
❑ 227 Aaron Brooks	1.00	.45
De'Mond Parker RC		
❑ 228 John Tait	.75	.35
Mike Cloud RC		
❑ 229 Andy Katzenmoyer	1.00	.45
Michael Bishop RC		
❑ 230 Joe Montgomery	.75	.35
Dan Campbell RC		
❑ 231 Na Brown	.75	.35
Cecil Martin RC		
❑ 232 Amos Zereoue	.75	.35
Jerame Tuman RC		
❑ 233 Jermaine Fazande	.50	.23
Steve Heiden RC		
❑ 234 Karsten Bailey	.50	.23
Charlie Rogers RC		
❑ 235 Shaun King	2.00	.90
Martin Gramatica RC		
❑ 236 Jevon Kearse	1.50	.70
Kevin Daft RC		
❑ 237 Champ Bailey	1.00	.45
Tim Alexander RC		
❑ 238 Karsten Bailey	1.00	.45
Darnell McDonald RC		
❑ 239 Lamarr Glenn	.50	.23
Terry Jackson RC		
❑ 240 Troy Smith	.50	.23
Malcolm Johnson RC		
❑ 241 Rondel Menendez	.50	.23
Craig Yeast RC		
❑ 242 Jed Weaver	.50	.23
James Dearth RC		
❑ 243 Joel Makovicka	.75	.35
Shawn Bryson RC		
❑ 244 Desmond Clark	.75	.35
Jim Kleinsasser RC		
❑ 245 Sean Bennett	.75	.35
Autry Denson RC		
❑ 246 Billy Miller	.75	.35
Wane McGarity RC		
❑ 247 Mike Lucky	.50	.23
Justin Swift RC		
❑ 248 Travis McGriff	.75	.35
MarTay Jenkins RC		
❑ 249 Donald Driver RC	.50	.23
Larry Parker		
❑ 250 Antoine Winfield	.50	.23
Dre' Bly RC		

1999 SkyBox Dominion Atlantattitude

	MINT	NRMT
COMPLETE SET (15)	80.00	36.00
COMMON CARD (1-15)	3.00	1.35
STATED ODDS 1:24		
*PLUS CARDS: 1.2X TO 3X HI COL.		
PLUS STATED ODDS 1:240		
❑ 1 Charlie Batch	5.00	2.20
❑ 2 Mark Brunell	5.00	2.20
❑ 3 Tim Couch	12.00	5.50
❑ 4 Terrell Davis	8.00	3.60
❑ 5 Warrick Dunn	4.00	1.80
❑ 6 Brett Favre	12.00	5.50
❑ 7 Peyton Manning	10.00	4.50
❑ 8 Dan Marino	12.00	5.50
❑ 9 Randy Moss	10.00	4.50
❑ 10 Jake Plummer	6.00	2.70
❑ 11 Barry Sanders	12.00	5.50
❑ 12 Akili Smith	4.00	1.80
❑ 13 Emmitt Smith	8.00	3.60
❑ 14 Fred Taylor	6.00	2.70
❑ 15 Ricky Williams	12.00	5.50

1999 SkyBox Dominion Atlantattitude Warp Tek

	MINT	NRMT
COMMON CARD (1-15)	60.00	27.00
RANDOM INSERTS IN PACKS		
WARP TEKS #'d TO PLAYER'S JERSEY		
CARDS SERIAL #'d UNDER 10 NOT PRICED		
❑ 1 Charlie Batch/10	120.00	55.00
❑ 2 Mark Brunell/8		
❑ 3 Tim Couch/2		
❑ 4 Terrell Davis/30	120.00	55.00
❑ 5 Warrick Dunn/28	60.00	27.00
❑ 6 Brett Favre/4		
❑ 7 Peyton Manning/18	200.00	90.00
❑ 8 Dan Marino/13	300.00	135.00
❑ 9 Randy Moss/84	80.00	36.00
❑ 10 Jake Plummer/16	120.00	55.00
❑ 11 Barry Sanders/20	250.00	110.00
❑ 12 Akili Smith/11	120.00	55.00
❑ 13 Emmitt Smith/22	150.00	70.00
❑ 14 Fred Taylor/28	100.00	45.00
❑ 15 Ricky Williams/34	200.00	90.00

1999 SkyBox Dominion Gen Next

	MINT	NRMT
COMPLETE SET (20)	25.00	11.00
COMMON CARD (1-20)	.75	.35
SEMISTARS	1.00	.45
STATED ODDS 1:3		
*PLUS CARDS: 1X TO 2.5X HI COL.		
PLUS STATED ODDS 1:30		
*WARP TEK CARDS: 3X TO 8X HI COL.		
WARP TEK STATED ODDS 1:300		
❑ 1 D'Wayne Bates	.75	.35
❑ 2 David Boston	1.25	.55
❑ 3 Cecil Collins	1.00	.45
❑ 4 Tim Couch	4.00	1.80
❑ 5 Daunte Culpepper	2.50	1.10
❑ 6 Troy Edwards	1.25	.55
❑ 7 Kevin Faulk	1.00	.45
❑ 8 Joe Germaine	1.00	.45
❑ 9 Torry Holt	2.00	.90
❑ 10 Brock Huard	1.00	.45
❑ 11 Sedrick Irvin	1.00	.45
❑ 12 Edgerrin James	6.00	2.70
❑ 13 James Johnson	1.00	.45
❑ 14 Kevin Johnson	2.00	.90
❑ 15 Shaun King	2.50	1.10
❑ 16 Donovan McNabb	2.50	1.10
❑ 17 Cade McNown	2.50	1.10
❑ 18 Akili Smith	1.50	.70
❑ 19 Ricky Williams	4.00	1.80
❑ 20 Amos Zereoue	1.00	.45

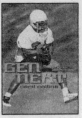

1999 SkyBox Dominion Goal 2 Go

	MINT	NRMT
COMPLETE SET (10)	25.00	11.00
COMMON CARD (1-10)	2.00	.90
STATED ODDS 1:9		
*PLUS CARDS: 1.25X TO 3X HI COL.		
PLUS STATED ODDS 1:90		
*WARP TEK CARDS: 3X TO 8X HI COL.		
WARP TEK STATED ODDS 1:900		
❑ 1 Joe Montana	3.00	1.35
Jamal Anderson		
❑ 2 Brett Favre	5.00	2.20
Jake Plummer		
❑ 3 Randy Moss	4.00	1.80
Jerry Rice		
❑ 4 Warrick Dunn	4.00	1.80
Barry Sanders		
❑ 5 Eddie George	2.50	1.10
Fred Taylor		
❑ 6 Emmitt Smith	3.00	1.35
Marshall Faulk		
❑ 7 Keyshawn Johnson	2.00	.90
Terrell Owens		
❑ 8 Peyton Manning	4.00	1.80
Ryan Leaf		
❑ 9 Dan Marino	5.00	2.20
John Elway		
❑ 10 Cade McNown	4.00	1.80
Charlie Batch		

1999 SkyBox Dominion Hats Off

	MINT	NRMT
COMPLETE SET (6)	750.00	350.00
COMMON CARD (1-6)	100.00	45.00
RANDOM INSERTS IN PACKS		
❑ 1 Tim Couch/135	200.00	90.00
❑ 2 Donovan McNabb/130	100.00	45.00
❑ 3 Akili Smith/85	120.00	55.00
❑ 4 Ricky Williams/130	200.00	90.00
❑ 5 Daunte Culpepper/100	100.00	45.00
❑ 6 Cade McNown/120	100.00	45.00

1999 SkyBox Dominion Hats Off Autographs

	MINT	NRMT
COMPLETE SET (5)	2200.00	1000.00
COMMON CARD (2-6)	350.00	160.00
RANDOM INSERTS IN PACKS		
STATED PRINT RUN 20 SER.#'d SETS		
COUCH DID NOT SIGN FOR THE SET		
❑ 2 Donovan McNabb	400.00	180.00
❑ 3 Akili Smith	350.00	160.00
❑ 4 Ricky Williams	600.00	275.00
❑ 5 Daunte Culpepper	400.00	180.00
❑ 6 Cade McNown	400.00	180.00

1992 SkyBox Impact

	MINT	NRMT
COMPLETE SET (350)	12.00	5.50
COMMON CARD (1-350)	.05	.02
SEMISTARS	.10	.05
UNLISTED STARS	.25	.11
❑ 1 Jim Kelly	.25	.11
❑ 2 Andre Rison	.10	.05
❑ 3 Michael Dean Perry	.10	.05
❑ 4 Herman Moore	.75	.35
❑ 5 Fred McAfee RC	.05	.02
❑ 6 Ricky Proehl	.05	.02
❑ 7 Jim Everett	.10	.05
❑ 8 Mark Carrier DB	.05	.02
❑ 9 Eric Martin	.05	.02
❑ 10 John Elway	1.25	.55
❑ 11 Michael Irvin	.25	.11
❑ 12 Keith McCants	.05	.02
❑ 13 Greg Lloyd	.25	.11
❑ 14 Lawrence Taylor	.25	.11
❑ 15 Mike Tomczak	.05	.02
❑ 16 Cortez Kennedy	.10	.05
❑ 17 William Fuller	.10	.05
❑ 18 James Lofton	.10	.05
❑ 19 Kevin Fagan	.05	.02
❑ 20 Bill Brooks	.05	.02
❑ 21 Roger Craig UER (Text is about Vikings, but Raiders logo still on card)	.10	.05
❑ 22 Jay Novacek	.10	.05
❑ 23 Steve Sewell	.05	.02
❑ 24 William Perry UER (Card has him injured for 1988, but he did play)	.10	.05
❑ 25 Jerry Rice	.75	.35
❑ 26 James Joseph	.05	.02
❑ 27 Timm Rosenbach	.05	.02
❑ 28 Pat Terrell	.05	.02
❑ 29 Jon Vaughn	.05	.02
❑ 30 Steve Walsh	.05	.02
❑ 31 James Hasty	.05	.02
❑ 32 Dwight Stone	.05	.02
❑ 33 Derrick Fenner UER (Text mentions Bengals, but Seahawks logo still on front)	.05	.02
❑ 34 Mark Bortz	.05	.02
❑ 35 Dan Saleaumua	.05	.02
❑ 36 Sammie Smith UER (Text mentions Broncos, but Dolphins logo still on front)	.05	.02
❑ 37 Antone Davis	.05	.02
❑ 38 Steve Young	.60	.25
❑ 39 Mike Baab	.05	.02
❑ 40 Rick Fenney	.05	.02
❑ 41 Chris Hinton	.05	.02
❑ 42 Bart Oates	.05	.02
❑ 43 Bryan Hinkle	.05	.02
❑ 44 James Francis	.05	.02
❑ 45 Ray Crockett	.05	.02
❑ 46 Eric Dickerson UER (Text mentions Raiders, but Colts logo still on front)	.10	.05
❑ 47 Hart Lee Dykes	.05	.02
❑ 48 Percy Snow	.05	.02
❑ 49 Ron Hall	.05	.02
❑ 50 Warren Moon	.25	.11
❑ 51 Ed West	.05	.02
❑ 52 Clarence Verdin	.05	.02
❑ 53 Eugene Lockhart	.05	.02
❑ 54 Andre Reed	.10	.05
❑ 55 Kevin Ross	.05	.02
❑ 56 Al Noga	.05	.02
❑ 57 Wes Hopkins	.05	.02
❑ 58 Rufus Porter	.05	.02
❑ 59 Brian Mitchell	.10	.05
❑ 60 Reggie Roby	.05	.02
❑ 61 Rodney Peete	.10	.05
❑ 62 Jeff Herrod	.05	.02
❑ 63 Anthony Smith	.05	.02
❑ 64 Brad Muster	.05	.02
❑ 65 Jessie Tuggle	.05	.02
❑ 66 Al Smith	.05	.02
❑ 67 Jeff Hostetler	.10	.05
❑ 68 John L. Williams	.05	.02
❑ 69 Paul Gruber	.05	.02
❑ 70 Cornelius Bennett	.10	.05
❑ 71 William White	.05	.02
❑ 72 Tom Rathman	.05	.02
❑ 73 Boomer Esiason	.10	.05
❑ 74 Neil Smith	.25	.11
❑ 75 Sterling Sharpe	.25	.11
❑ 76 James Jones	.05	.02
❑ 77 David Treadwell	.05	.02
❑ 78 Flipper Anderson	.05	.02
❑ 79 Eric Allen	.05	.02
❑ 80 Joe Jacoby	.05	.02
❑ 81 Keith Sims	.05	.02
❑ 82 Bubba McDowell	.05	.02
❑ 83 Ronnie Lippett	.05	.02
❑ 84 Cris Carter	.50	.23
❑ 85 Chris Burkett	.05	.02
❑ 86 Issiac Holt	.05	.02
❑ 87 Duane Bickett	.05	.02
❑ 88 Leslie O'Neal	.10	.05
❑ 89 Gill Fenerty	.05	.02
❑ 90 Pierce Holt	.05	.02
❑ 91 Willie Drewrey	.05	.02
❑ 92 Brian Blades	.10	.05
❑ 93 Tony Martin	.25	.11
❑ 94 Jessie Hester	.05	.02
❑ 95 John Stephens	.05	.02
❑ 96 Keith Willis UER (Text mentions Redskins, but Steelers logo still on front)	.05	.02
❑ 97 Vai Sikahema UER (Text mentions Eagles, but Cardinals logo still on front)	.05	.02
❑ 98 Mark Higgs	.05	.02
❑ 99 Steve McMichael	.10	.05
❑ 100 Deion Sanders	.50	.23
❑ 101 Marvin Washington	.05	.02
❑ 102 Ken Norton	.25	.11
❑ 103 Barry Word	.05	.02
❑ 104 Sean Jones	.10	.05
❑ 105 Ronnie Harmon	.05	.02
❑ 106 Donnell Woolford	.05	.02
❑ 107 Ray Agnew	.05	.02
❑ 108 Lemuel Stinson	.05	.02
❑ 109 Dennis Smith	.05	.02
❑ 110 Lorenzo White	.05	.02
❑ 111 Craig Heyward	.10	.05
❑ 112 Jeff Query UER (Text mentions Oilers, but Packers logo still on front)	.05	.02
❑ 113 Gary Plummer	.05	.02
❑ 114 John Taylor	.10	.05
❑ 115 Rohn Stark	.05	.02
❑ 116 Tom Waddle	.05	.02
❑ 117 Jeff Cross	.05	.02
❑ 118 Tim Green	.05	.02
❑ 119 Anthony Munoz	.10	.05
❑ 120 Mel Gray	.10	.05
❑ 121 Ray Donaldson	.05	.02
❑ 122 Dennis Byrd	.05	.02
❑ 123 Carnell Lake	.05	.02
❑ 124 Broderick Thomas	.05	.02
❑ 125 Charles Mann	.05	.02
❑ 126 Darion Conner	.05	.02
❑ 127 John Roper	.05	.02
❑ 128 Jack Del Rio UER (Text mentions Vikings, but Cowboys logo still on front)	.05	.02
❑ 129 Rickey Dixon	.05	.02
❑ 130 Eddie Anderson	.05	.02
❑ 131 Steve Broussard	.05	.02
❑ 132 Michael Young	.05	.02
❑ 133 Lamar Lathon	.05	.02
❑ 134 Rickey Jackson	.05	.02
❑ 135 Billy Ray Smith	.05	.02
❑ 136 Tony Casillas	.05	.02
❑ 137 Ickey Woods	.05	.02
❑ 138 Ray Childress	.05	.02
❑ 139 Vance Johnson	.05	.02
❑ 140 Brett Perriman	.25	.11
❑ 141 Calvin Williams	.10	.05
❑ 142 Dino Hackett	.05	.02
❑ 143 Jacob Green	.05	.02
❑ 144 Robert Delpino	.05	.02
❑ 145 Marv Cook	.05	.02
❑ 146 Dwayne Harper	.05	.02
❑ 147 Ricky Ervins	.05	.02
❑ 148 Kelvin Martin	.05	.02
❑ 149 Leroy Hoard	.10	.05
❑ 150 Dan Marino	1.25	.55
❑ 151 Richard Johnson UER (He and Carrier had 2 interceptions, only given credit for 1 on card)	.05	.02
❑ 152 Henry Ellard	.10	.05
❑ 153 Al Toon	.10	.05
❑ 154 Dermontti Dawson	.05	.02

❑	155	Robert Blackmon	.05	.02
❑	156	Howie Long	.10	.05
❑	157	David Fulcher	.05	.02
❑	158	Mike Merriweather	.05	.02
❑	159	Gary Anderson K	.05	.02
❑	160	John Friesz	.10	.05
❑	161	Eugene Robinson	.05	.02
❑	162	Brad Baxter	.05	.02
❑	163	Bennie Blades	.05	.02
❑	164	Harold Green	.05	.02
❑	165	Ernest Givins	.10	.05
❑	166	Deron Cherry	.05	.02
❑	167	Carl Banks	.05	.02
❑	168	Keith Jackson	.10	.05
❑	169	Pat Leahy	.05	.02
❑	170	Alvin Harper	.10	.05
❑	171	David Little	.05	.02
❑	172	Anthony Carter	.10	.05
❑	173	Willie Gault	.10	.05
❑	174	Bruce Armstrong	.05	.02
❑	175	Junior Seau	.25	.11
❑	176	Eric Metcalf	.10	.05
❑	177	Tony Mandarich	.05	.02
❑	178	Ernie Jones	.05	.02
❑	179	Albert Bentley	.05	.02
❑	180	Mike Pritchard	.10	.05
❑	181	Bubby Brister	.05	.02
❑	182	Vaughan Johnson	.05	.02
❑	183	Robert Clark UER (Text mentions Dolphins, but Seahawks logo on front)	.05	.02
❑	184	Lawrence Dawsey	.10	.05
❑	185	Eric Green	.05	.02
❑	186	Jay Schroeder	.05	.02
❑	187	Andre Tippett	.05	.02
❑	188	Vinny Testaverde	.10	.05
❑	189	Wendell Davis	.05	.02
❑	190	Russell Maryland	.10	.05
❑	191	Chris Singleton	.05	.02
❑	192	Ken O'Brien	.05	.02
❑	193	Merril Hoge	.05	.02
❑	194	Steve Bono RC	.25	.11
❑	195	Earnest Byner	.05	.02
❑	196	Mike Singletary	.10	.05
❑	197	Gaston Green	.05	.02
❑	198	Mark Carrier WR	.10	.05
❑	199	Harvey Williams	.25	.11
❑	200	Randall Cunningham	.25	.11
❑	201	Cris Dishman	.05	.02
❑	202	Greg Townsend	.05	.02
❑	203	Christian Okoye	.05	.02
❑	204	Sam Mills	.05	.02
❑	205	Kyle Clifton	.05	.02
❑	206	Jim Harbaugh	.25	.11
❑	207	Anthony Thompson	.05	.02
❑	208	Rob Moore	.10	.05
❑	209	Irving Fryar	.10	.05
❑	210	Derrick Thomas	.25	.11
❑	211	Chris Miller	.10	.05
❑	212	Doug Smith	.05	.02
❑	213	Michael Haynes	.10	.05
❑	214	Phil Simms	.10	.05
❑	215	Charles Haley	.10	.05
❑	216	Burt Grossman	.05	.02
❑	217	Rod Bernstine	.05	.02
❑	218	Louis Lipps	.05	.02
❑	219	Dan McGwire UER (Actually drafted in 1991, not 1990)	.05	.02
❑	220	Ethan Horton	.05	.02
❑	221	Michael Carter	.05	.02
❑	222	Neil O'Donnell	.25	.11
❑	223	Anthony Miller	.10	.05
❑	224	Eric Swann	.10	.05
❑	225	Thurman Thomas	.25	.11
❑	226	Jeff George	.25	.11
❑	227	Joe Montana	1.25	.55
❑	228	Leonard Marshall	.05	.02
❑	229	Haywood Jeffires	.10	.05
❑	230	Mark Clayton	.10	.05
❑	231	Chris Doleman	.05	.02
❑	232	Troy Aikman	.75	.35
❑	233	Gary Anderson RB	.05	.02
❑	234	Pat Swilling	.10	.05
❑	235	Ronnie Lott	.10	.05
❑	236	Brian Jordan	.10	.05
❑	237	Bruce Smith	.25	.11
❑	238	Tony Jones UER (Text mentions Falcons, but Oilers logo still on front)	.05	.02
❑	239	Tim McKyer	.05	.02
❑	240	Gary Clark	.25	.11
❑	241	Mitchell Price	.05	.02
❑	242	John Kasay	.05	.02
❑	243	Stephone Paige	.05	.02
❑	244	Jeff Wright	.05	.02
❑	245	Shannon Sharpe	.25	.11
❑	246	Keith Byars	.05	.02
❑	247	Charles Dimry	.05	.02
❑	248	Steve Smith	.05	.02
❑	249	Eric Pegram	.10	.05
❑	250	Bernie Kosar	.10	.05
❑	251	Peter Tom Willis	.05	.02
❑	252	Mark Ingram	.05	.02
❑	253	Keith McKeller	.05	.02
❑	254	Lewis Billups UER (Text mentions Packers, but Bengals logo still on front)	.05	.02
❑	255	Alton Montgomery	.05	.02
❑	256	Jimmie Jones	.05	.02
❑	257	Brent Williams	.05	.02
❑	258	Gene Atkins	.05	.02
❑	259	Reggie Rutland	.05	.02
❑	260	Sam Seale UER (Text mentions Raiders, but Chargers logo still on back)	.05	.02
❑	261	Andre Ware	.05	.02
❑	262	Fred Barnett	.25	.11
❑	263	Randal Hill	.05	.02
❑	264	Patrick Hunter	.05	.02
❑	265	Johnny Rembert UER (Card says DNP in 1991, but he played 12 games)	.05	.02
❑	266	Monte Coleman	.05	.02
❑	267	Aaron Wallace	.05	.02
❑	268	Ferrell Edmunds	.05	.02
❑	269	Stan Thomas	.05	.02
❑	270	Robb Thomas	.05	.02
❑	271	Martin Bayless UER (Text mentions Chiefs, but Chargers logo still on front)	.05	.02
❑	272	Dean Biasucci	.05	.02
❑	273	Keith Henderson	.05	.02
❑	274	Vinnie Clark	.05	.02
❑	275	Emmitt Smith	1.50	.70
❑	276	Mark Rypien	.05	.02
❑	277	Atlanta Falcons CL Wing and a Prayer (Michael Haynes)	.05	.02
❑	278	Buffalo Bills CL Machine Gun (Jim Kelly)	.10	.05
❑	279	Chicago Bears CL Grizzly (Tom Waddle)	.05	.02
❑	280	Cincinnati Bengals CL Price is Right (Mitchell Price)	.05	.02
❑	281	Cleveland Browns CL Coasting (Bernie Kosar)	.05	.02
❑	282	Dallas Cowboys CL Gunned Down (Michael Irvin)	.10	.05
❑	283	Denver Broncos CL The Drive II (John Elway)	.50	.23
❑	284	Detroit Lions CL Lions Roar (Mel Gray)	.05	.02
❑	285	Green Bay Packers CL Razor Sharpe (Sterling Sharpe)	.10	.05
❑	286	Houston Oilers CL Oil's Well (Warren Moon)	.10	.05
❑	287	Indianapolis Colts CL Whew (Jeff George)	.10	.05
❑	288	Kansas City Chiefs CL Ambush (Derrick Thomas)	.10	.05
❑	289	Los Angeles Raiders CL Lott of Defense (Ronnie Lott)	.05	.02
❑	290	Los Angeles Rams CL Ram It (Robert Delpino)	.05	.02
❑	291	Miami Dolphins CL Miami Ice (Dan Marino)	.50	.23
❑	292	Minnesota Vikings CL Purple Blaze (Cris Carter)	.25	.11
❑	293	New England Patriots CL Surprise Attack (Irving Fryar)	.05	.02
❑	294	New Orleans Saints CL Marching In (Gene Atkins)	.05	.02
❑	295	New York Giants CL Almost Perfect (Phil Simms)	.05	.02
❑	296	New York Jets CL Playoff Bound (Ken O'Brien)	.05	.02
❑	297	Philadelphia Eagles CL Flying High (Keith Jackson)	.05	.02
❑	298	Phoenix Cardinals CL Airborne (Ricky Proehl)	.05	.02
❑	299	Pittsburgh Steelers CL Steel Curtain (Bryan Hinkle)	.05	.02
❑	300	San Diego Chargers CL Lightning (John Friesz)	.05	.02
❑	301	San Francisco 49ers CL Instant Rice (Jerry Rice)	.50	.23
❑	302	Seattle Seahawks CL Defense Never Rests (Eugene Robinson)	.05	.02
❑	303	Tampa Bay Buccaneers CL Stunned (Broderick Thomas)	.05	.02
❑	304	Washington Redskins CL Super (Mark Rypien)	.05	.02
❑	305	Jim Kelly LL	.10	.05
❑	306	Steve Young LL	.30	.14
❑	307	Thurman Thomas LL	.10	.05
❑	308	Emmitt Smith LL	.75	.35
❑	309	Haywood Jeffires LL	.05	.02
❑	310	Michael Irvin LL	.10	.05
❑	311	William Fuller LL	.05	.02
❑	312	Pat Swilling LL	.05	.02
❑	313	Ronnie Lott LL	.05	.02
❑	314	Deion Sanders LL	.25	.11
❑	315	Cornelius Bennett HH	.05	.02
❑	316	David Fulcher HH	.05	.02
❑	317	Ronnie Lott HH	.05	.02
❑	318	Pat Swilling HH	.05	.02
❑	319	Lawrence Taylor HH	.10	.05
❑	320	Derrick Thomas HH	.10	.05
❑	321	Steve Emtman RC	.05	.02
❑	322	Carl Pickens RC	.60	.25
❑	323	David Klingler RC	.10	.05
❑	324	Dale Carter RC	.25	.11
❑	325	Mike Gaddis RC	.05	.02
❑	326	Quentin Coryatt RC	.25	.11
❑	327	Darryl Williams RC	.05	.02
❑	328	Jeremy Lincoln RC	.05	.02
❑	329	Robert Jones RC	.05	.02
❑	330	Bucky Richardson RC	.05	.02
❑	331	Tony Brooks RC	.05	.02
❑	332	Alonzo Spellman RC	.10	.05
❑	333	Robert Brooks RC	1.00	.45
❑	334	Marco Coleman RC	.10	.05
❑	335	Siran Stacy RC UER (Misspelled Stacey)	.05	.02
❑	336	Tommy Maddox RC	.05	.02
❑	337	Steve Israel RC	.05	.02

❑ 338 Vaughn Dunbar RC	.05	.02
❑ 339 Shane Collins RC	.05	.02
❑ 340 Kevin Smith RC	.25	.11
❑ 341 Chris Mims RC	.10	.05
❑ 342 Chester McGlockton RC UER (Misspelled McGlokton on both sides)	.25	.11
❑ 343 Tracy Scroggins RC	.05	.02
❑ 344 Howard Dinkins RC	.05	.02
❑ 345 Levon Kirkland RC	.05	.02
❑ 346 Terrell Buckley RC	.05	.02
❑ 347 Marquez Pope RC	.05	.02
❑ 348 Phillippi Sparks RC	.05	.02
❑ 349 Joe Bowden RC	.05	.02
❑ 350 Edgar Bennett RC	.25	.11
❑ SP1 Jim Kelly	8.00	3.60
❑ SP1AU Jim Kelly AUTO	50.00	22.00
❑ SP2AU Kelly/Magic AUTO	400.00	180.00

1992 SkyBox Impact Holograms

	MINT	NRMT
COMPLETE SET (6)	20.00	9.00

H1-H2 RANDOM INSERTS IN PACKS
*H1-H2 SINGLES: 4X TO 10X BASIC CARDS
*H3-H6 SINGLES: 40X TO 80X BASIC CARDS
H3-H6 AVAILABLE VIA MAIL REDEMPT.

❑ H1 Jim Kelly	2.50	1.10
❑ H2 Lawrence Taylor	2.50	1.10
❑ H3 Christian Okoye	4.00	1.80
❑ H4 Mark Rypien	4.00	1.80
❑ H5 Pat Swilling	8.00	3.60
❑ H6 Ricky Ervins	4.00	1.80

1992 SkyBox Impact Major Impact

	MINT	NRMT
COMPLETE SET (20)	16.00	7.25

RANDOM INSERTS IN JUMBO PACKS

❑ M1 Cornelius Bennett	.25	.11
❑ M2 David Fulcher	.15	.07
❑ M3 Haywood Jeffires	.25	.11
❑ M4 Ronnie Lott	.25	.11
❑ M5 Dan Marino	3.00	1.35
❑ M6 Warren Moon	.60	.25
❑ M7 Christian Okoye	.15	.07
❑ M8 Andre Reed	.25	.11
❑ M9 Derrick Thomas	.60	.25
❑ M10 Thurman Thomas	.60	.25
❑ M11 Troy Aikman	2.00	.90
❑ M12 Randall Cunningham	.60	.25
❑ M13 Michael Irvin	.60	.25
❑ M14 Jerry Rice	2.00	.90
❑ M15 Joe Montana	3.00	1.35
❑ M16 Mark Rypien	.15	.07
❑ M17 Deion Sanders	1.25	.55
❑ M18 Emmitt Smith	4.00	1.80
❑ M19 Pat Swilling	.25	.11
❑ M20 Lawrence Taylor	.60	.25

1993 SkyBox Impact

	MINT	NRMT
COMPLETE SET (400)	15.00	6.75
COMMON CARD (1-400)	.05	.02
SEMISTARS	.10	.05
UNLISTED STARS	.25	.11
COMP.COLORS SET (392)	80.00	36.00

*COLOR STARS: 2X TO 4X HI COLUMN
*COLOR RCs: 1.25X TO 2.5X HI..
ONE PER FOIL PACK

❑ 1 Steve Broussard	.05	.02
❑ 2 Michael Haynes	.10	.05
❑ 3 Tony Smith	.05	.02
❑ 4 Tory Epps	.05	.02
❑ 5 Chris Hinton	.05	.02
❑ 6 Bobby Hebert	.05	.02
❑ 7 Tim McKyer	.05	.02
❑ 8 Chris Miller	.10	.05
❑ 9 Bruce Pickens	.05	.02
❑ 10 Mike Pritchard	.10	.05
❑ 11 Andre Rison	.10	.05
❑ 12 Deion Sanders	.50	.23
❑ 13 Pierce Holt	.05	.02
❑ 14 Jessie Tuggle	.05	.02
❑ 15 Don Beebe	.05	.02
❑ 16 Cornelius Bennett	.10	.05
❑ 17 Kenneth Davis	.05	.02
❑ 18 Kent Hull	.05	.02
❑ 19 Jim Kelly	.25	.11
❑ 20 Mark Kelso	.05	.02
❑ 21 Keith McKeller UER (Name misspelled McKellar on front)	.05	.02
❑ 22 Andre Reed	.10	.05
❑ 23 Jim Ritcher	.05	.02
❑ 24 Bruce Smith	.25	.11
❑ 25 Thurman Thomas	.25	.11
❑ 26 Steve Christie	.05	.02
❑ 27 Darryl Talley UER (Name misspelled Darrell on front)	.05	.02
❑ 28 Pete Metzelaars	.05	.02
❑ 29 Steve Tasker	.10	.05
❑ 30 Henry Jones	.05	.02
❑ 31 Neal Anderson	.05	.02
❑ 32 Trace Armstrong	.05	.02
❑ 33 Mark Bortz	.05	.02
❑ 34 Mark Carrier DB	.05	.02
❑ 35 Wendell Davis	.05	.02
❑ 36 Richard Dent	.10	.05
❑ 37 Jim Harbaugh	.25	.11
❑ 38 Steve McMichael	.10	.05
❑ 39 Craig Heyward	.10	.05
❑ 40 William Perry	.10	.05
❑ 41 Donnell Woolford	.05	.02
❑ 42 Tom Waddle	.05	.02
❑ 43 Anthony Morgan	.05	.02
❑ 44 Jim Breech	.05	.02
❑ 45 David Klingler	.05	.02
❑ 46 Derrick Fenner	.05	.02
❑ 47 David Fulcher	.05	.02
❑ 48 James Francis	.05	.02
❑ 49 Harold Green	.05	.02
❑ 50 Carl Pickens	.25	.11
❑ 51 Jay Schroeder	.05	.02
❑ 52 Alex Gordon	.05	.02
❑ 53 Eric Ball	.05	.02
❑ 54 Eddie Brown	.05	.02
❑ 55 Jay Hilgenberg UER (Name misspelled Hilgenburg on front)	.05	.02
❑ 56 Michael Jackson	.10	.05
❑ 57 Bernie Kosar	.10	.05
❑ 58 Kevin Mack	.05	.02
❑ 59 Eric Metcalf	.10	.05
❑ 60 Michael Dean Perry	.10	.05
❑ 61 Tommy Vardell	.05	.02
❑ 62 Leroy Hoard	.10	.05
❑ 63 Clay Matthews	.10	.05
❑ 64 Vinny Testaverde	.10	.05
❑ 65 Mark Carrier WR	.10	.05
❑ 66 Troy Aikman	.75	.35
❑ 67 Lin Elliott RC UER (Name misspelled Elliot on front)	.05	.02
❑ 68 Thomas Everett	.05	.02
❑ 69 Alvin Harper	.10	.05
❑ 70 Ray Horton	.05	.02
❑ 71 Michael Irvin	.25	.11
❑ 72 Russell Maryland	.05	.02
❑ 73 Jay Novacek	.10	.05
❑ 74 Emmitt Smith	1.50	.70
❑ 75 Tony Casillas	.05	.02
❑ 76 Robert Jones	.05	.02
❑ 77 Ken Norton Jr.	.10	.05
❑ 78 Daryl Johnston	.25	.11
❑ 79 Charles Haley	.10	.05
❑ 80 Leon Lett RC	.10	.05
❑ 81 Steve Atwater	.05	.02
❑ 82 Mike Croel	.05	.02
❑ 83 John Elway	1.50	.70
❑ 84 Simon Fletcher	.05	.02
❑ 85 Vance Johnson	.05	.02
❑ 86 Shannon Sharpe	.25	.11
❑ 87 Rod Bernstine	.05	.02
❑ 88 Robert Delpino	.05	.02
❑ 89 Karl Mecklenburg	.05	.02
❑ 90 Steve Sewell	.05	.02
❑ 91 Tommy Maddox UER (Name misspelled Maddux on front and back)	.05	.02
❑ 92 Arthur Marshall RC	.05	.02
❑ 93 Dennis Smith	.05	.02
❑ 94 Derek Russell	.05	.02
❑ 95 Bennie Blades	.05	.02
❑ 96 Michael Cofer	.05	.02
❑ 97 Willie Green	.05	.02
❑ 98 Herman Moore	.50	.23
❑ 99 Rodney Peete	.05	.02
❑ 100 Andre Ware	.05	.02
❑ 101 Barry Sanders UER (Brett Perriman is pictured on front)	1.50	.70
❑ 102 Chris Spielman	.10	.05
❑ 103 Jason Hanson	.05	.02
❑ 104 Mel Gray	.10	.05
❑ 105 Pat Swilling	.05	.02
❑ 106 Bill Fralic	.05	.02
❑ 107 Rodney Holman	.05	.02
❑ 108 Brett Favre	2.00	.90
❑ 109 Sterling Sharpe	.25	.11
❑ 110 Reggie White	.25	.11
❑ 111 Terrell Buckley	.05	.02
❑ 112 Sanjay Beach	.05	.02
❑ 113 Tony Bennett	.05	.02
❑ 114 Jackie Harris	.05	.02
❑ 115 Bryce Paup	.25	.11

❑ 116 Shawn Patterson .05 .02
❑ 117 John Stephens .05 .02
❑ 118 Cris Dishman .05 .02
❑ 119 Ernest Givins .10 .05
❑ 120 Haywood Jeffires .10 .05
❑ 121 Lamar Lathon .05 .02
❑ 122 Warren Moon .25 .11
❑ 123 Lorenzo White .05 .02
❑ 124 Curtis Duncan .05 .02
❑ 125 Webster Slaughter .05 .02
❑ 126 Cody Carlson .05 .02
❑ 127 Leonard Harris .05 .02
❑ 128 Bruce Matthews .05 .02
❑ 129 Ray Childress .05 .02
❑ 130 Al Smith .05 .02
❑ 131 Jeff George .25 .11
❑ 132 Anthony Johnson .10 .05
❑ 133 Steve Emtman .05 .02
❑ 134 Quentin Coryatt .10 .05
❑ 135 Rodney Culver .05 .02
❑ 136 Jessie Hester .05 .02
❑ 137 Aaron Cox .05 .02
❑ 138 Clarence Verdin .05 .02
❑ 139 Joe Montana 1.50 .70
❑ 140 Dave Krieg .10 .05
❑ 141 Harvey Williams .10 .05
❑ 142 Derrick Thomas .25 .11
❑ 143 Barry Word .05 .02
❑ 144 Christian Okoye .05 .02
❑ 145 Nick Lowery .05 .02
❑ 146 Dale Carter .05 .02
❑ 147 Willie Davis .25 .11
❑ 148 Tim Barnett .05 .02
❑ 149 Neil Smith UER .25 .11
(Name misspelled Neal on front)
❑ 150 Marcus Allen .25 .11
❑ 151 Nick Bell .05 .02
❑ 152 Tim Brown .25 .11
❑ 153 Eric Dickerson .10 .05
❑ 154 Willie Gault .05 .02
❑ 155 Howie Long .10 .05
❑ 156 Gaston Green .05 .02
❑ 157 Chester McGlockton .10 .05
❑ 158 Eddie Anderson .05 .02
❑ 159 Ethan Horton .05 .02
❑ 160 James Lofton .10 .05
❑ 161 Jeff Hostetler .10 .05
❑ 162 Terry McDaniel .05 .02
❑ 163 Flipper Anderson .05 .02
❑ 164 Shane Conlan .05 .02
❑ 165 Jim Everett .10 .05
❑ 166 Henry Ellard .10 .05
❑ 167 Cleveland Gary .05 .02
❑ 168 Todd Lyght .05 .02
❑ 169 Sean Gilbert .10 .05
❑ 170 Jim Price .05 .02
❑ 171 Bill Hawkins .05 .02
❑ 172 Mark Clayton .05 .02
❑ 173 Mark Higgs .05 .02
❑ 174 Dan Marino 1.50 .70
❑ 175 Louis Oliver .05 .02
❑ 176 Reggie Roby .05 .02
❑ 177 Bobby Humphrey .05 .02
❑ 178 Troy Vincent .05 .02
❑ 179 Marco Coleman .05 .02
❑ 180 Aaron Craver .05 .02
❑ 181 Keith Jackson .10 .05
❑ 182 Mark Duper .05 .02
❑ 183 Pete Stoyanovich .05 .02
❑ 184 Irving Fryar .10 .05
❑ 185 Bryan Cox UER .05 .02
(Name misspelled Brian on front and back)
❑ 186 Terry Allen .25 .11
❑ 187 Anthony Carter .10 .05
❑ 188 Cris Carter .50 .23
❑ 189 Chris Doleman .05 .02
❑ 190 Rich Gannon .05 .02
❑ 191 Sean Salisbury .05 .02
❑ 192 Hassan Jones .05 .02
❑ 193 Steve Jordan .05 .02
❑ 194 Roger Craig .10 .05
❑ 195 Todd Scott .05 .02
❑ 196 Esera Tuaolo .05 .02
❑ 197 Ray Agnew .05 .02
❑ 198 Marv Cook .05 .02
❑ 199 Tommy Hodson .05 .02
❑ 200 Chris Singleton .05 .02
❑ 201 Michael Timpson .05 .02
❑ 202 Jon Vaughn ERR .05 .02
(Photo on back is Keith Byars)
❑ 203 Leonard Russell .10 .05
❑ 204 Scott Zolak .05 .02
❑ 205 Reyna Thompson .05 .02
❑ 206 Andre Tippett .05 .02
❑ 207 Morten Andersen UER .05 .02
(Name misspelled Morton Anderson on front)
❑ 208 Wesley Carroll .05 .02
❑ 209 Vince Buck .05 .02
❑ 210 Rickey Jackson .05 .02
❑ 211 Vaughan Johnson UER .05 .02
(Name misspelled Vaughn on front)
❑ 212 Eric Martin .05 .02
❑ 213 Sam Mills .05 .02
❑ 214 Steve Walsh .05 .02
❑ 215 Wade Wilson .05 .02
❑ 216 Vaughn Dunbar .05 .02
❑ 217 Brad Muster .05 .02
❑ 218 Dalton Hilliard .05 .02
❑ 219 Floyd Turner .05 .02
❑ 220 Stephen Baker .05 .02
❑ 221 Mark Jackson .05 .02
❑ 222 Jarrod Bunch .05 .02
❑ 223 Mark Collins .05 .02
❑ 224 Rodney Hampton .25 .11
❑ 225 Phil Simms .10 .05
❑ 226 Pepper Johnson .05 .02
❑ 227 Dave Meggett .05 .02
❑ 228 Derek Brown TE .05 .02
❑ 229 Mike Sherrard .05 .02
❑ 230 Lawrence Taylor .25 .11
❑ 231 Leonard Marshall .05 .02
❑ 232 Brad Baxter .05 .02
❑ 233 Dennis Byrd .05 .02
❑ 234 Ronnie Lott .10 .05
❑ 235 Boomer Esiason .10 .05
❑ 236 Browning Nagle .05 .02
❑ 237 Rob Moore .10 .05
❑ 238 Jeff Lageman .05 .02
❑ 239 Johnny Mitchell .05 .02
❑ 240 Chris Burkett .05 .02
❑ 241 Eric Thomas .05 .02
❑ 242 Johnny Johnson .05 .02
❑ 243 Eric Allen .05 .02
❑ 244 Fred Barnett .10 .05
❑ 245 Keith Byars .05 .02
❑ 246 Randall Cunningham .25 .11
❑ 247 Heath Sherman .05 .02
❑ 248 Calvin Williams .10 .05
❑ 249 Erik McMillan .05 .02
❑ 250 Byron Evans .05 .02
❑ 251 Seth Joyner .05 .02
❑ 252 Vai Sikahema .05 .02
❑ 253 Andre Waters .05 .02
❑ 254 Tim Harris .05 .02
❑ 255 Mark Bavaro .05 .02
❑ 256 Clyde Simmons .05 .02
❑ 257 Steve Beuerlein .05 .02
❑ 258 Randal Hill UER .05 .02
(Name misspelled Randall on front)
❑ 259 Ernie Jones .05 .02
❑ 260 Robert Massey .05 .02
❑ 261 Ricky Proehl UER .05 .02
(Name misspelled Rickey on front)
❑ 262 Aeneas Williams .05 .02
❑ 263 Johnny Bailey .05 .02
❑ 264 Chris Chandler UER .10 .05
(Name misspelled Cris on front)
❑ 265 Anthony Thompson .05 .02
❑ 266 Gary Clark .10 .05
❑ 267 Chuck Cecil .05 .02
❑ 268 Rich Camarillo .05 .02
❑ 269 Neil O'Donnell .25 .11
❑ 270 Gerald Williams .05 .02
❑ 271 Greg Lloyd .25 .11
❑ 272 Eric Green .05 .02
❑ 273 Merril Hoge .05 .02
❑ 274 Ernie Mills .05 .02
❑ 275 Rod Woodson .25 .11
❑ 276 Gary Anderson K .05 .02
❑ 277 Barry Foster .10 .05
❑ 278 Jeff Graham .10 .05
❑ 279 Dwight Stone .05 .02
❑ 280 Kevin Greene .25 .11
❑ 281 Eric Bieniemy .05 .02
❑ 282 Marion Butts .05 .02
❑ 283 Gill Byrd .05 .02
❑ 284 Stan Humphries .25 .11
❑ 285 Anthony Miller .10 .05
❑ 286 Leslie O'Neal .10 .05
❑ 287 Junior Seau .25 .11
❑ 288 Ronnie Harmon .05 .02
❑ 289 Nate Lewis .05 .02
❑ 290 John Kidd .05 .02
❑ 291 Steve Young .75 .35
❑ 292 John Taylor .10 .05
❑ 293 Jerry Rice 1.00 .45
❑ 294 Tim McDonald .05 .02
❑ 295 Brent Jones .10 .05
❑ 296 Tom Rathman .05 .02
❑ 297 Dexter Carter .05 .02
❑ 298 Mike Cofer .05 .02
❑ 299 Ricky Watters .25 .11
❑ 300 Mervyn Fernandez .05 .02
❑ 301 Amp Lee .05 .02
❑ 302 Kevin Fagan .05 .02
❑ 303 Roy Foster .05 .02
❑ 304 Bill Romanowski .05 .02
❑ 305 Brian Blades .10 .05
❑ 306 John L. Williams .05 .02
❑ 307 Tommy Kane .05 .02
❑ 308 John Kasay .05 .02
❑ 309 Chris Warren .10 .05
❑ 310 Rufus Porter .05 .02
❑ 311 Cortez Kennedy .10 .05
❑ 312 Dan McGwire UER .05 .02
(Name misspelled McGuire on front)
❑ 313 Stan Gelbaugh .05 .02
❑ 314 Kelvin Martin .05 .02
❑ 315 Ferrell Edmunds .05 .02
❑ 316 Eugene Robinson .05 .02
❑ 317 Gary Anderson RB .05 .02
❑ 318 Reggie Cobb .05 .02
❑ 319 Lawrence Dawsey .05 .02
❑ 320 Courtney Hawkins .05 .02
❑ 321 Santana Dotson .10 .05
❑ 322 Ron Hall .05 .02
❑ 323 Keith McCants .05 .02
❑ 324 Martin Mayhew .05 .02
❑ 325 Anthony Munoz .10 .05
❑ 326 Steve DeBerg .05 .02
❑ 327 Vince Workman .05 .02
❑ 328 Earnest Byner .05 .02
❑ 329 Ricky Ervins .05 .02
❑ 330 Jim Lachey .05 .02
❑ 331 Chip Lohmiller .05 .02
❑ 332 Ricky Sanders UER .05 .02
(Name misspelled Rickey on front)
❑ 333 Brad Edwards .05 .02
❑ 334 Tim McGee .05 .02
❑ 335 Darrell Green .05 .02
❑ 336 Charles Mann .05 .02
❑ 337 Wilber Marshall .05 .02
❑ 338 Brian Mitchell .10 .05
❑ 339 Art Monk .10 .05
❑ 340 Mark Rypien .05 .02
❑ 341 John Elway C83 .75 .35
❑ 342 Jim Kelly C83 .10 .05
❑ 343 Dan Marino C83 .75 .35
❑ 344 Eric Dickerson C83 .10 .05
❑ 345 Willie Gault C83 .05 .02
❑ 346 Ken O'Brien C83 .05 .02
❑ 347 Darrell Green C83 .05 .02
❑ 348 Richard Dent C83 .05 .02
❑ 349 Karl Mecklenburg C83 .05 .02
❑ 350 Henry Ellard C83 .05 .02
❑ 351 Roger Craig C83 .05 .02
❑ 352 Charles Mann C83 .05 .02

❑ 353 Checklist A UER .05 .02
(Misspellings)
❑ 354 Checklist B UER .05 .02
(Misspellings)
❑ 355 Checklist C UER .05 .02
(Numbering out of order)
❑ 356 Checklist D UER .05 .02
(Misspellings and numbering out of order)
❑ 357 Checklist E UER .05 .02
(Misspelling and numbering out of order)
❑ 358 Checklist F UER .05 .02
(Misspelling and numbering out of order)
❑ 359 Checklist G UER .05 .02
(Misspellings and numbering out of order)
❑ 360 Rookies Checklist UER .05 .02
(Misspelling on 391)
❑ 361 Drew Bledsoe IR RC UER 3.00 1.35
(Text indicates drafted in '92; should be '93)
❑ 362 Rick Mirer IR RC .50 .23
❑ 363 Garrison Hearst IR RC 1.00 .45
❑ 364 Marvin Jones IR RC .05 .02
❑ 365 John Copeland IR RC .10 .05
❑ 366 Eric Curry IR RC .05 .02
❑ 367 Curtis Conway IR RC .50 .23
❑ 368 Willie Roaf IR RC .10 .05
❑ 369 Lincoln Kennedy IR RC .05 .02
❑ 370 Jerome Bettis IR RC 1.00 .45
❑ 371 Dan Williams IR RC .05 .02
❑ 372 Patrick Bates IR RC .05 .02
❑ 373 Brad Hopkins IR RC .05 .02
❑ 374 Steve Everitt IR RC .05 .02
❑ 375 Wayne Simmons IR RC .05 .02
❑ 376 Tom Carter IR RC .10 .05
❑ 377 Ernest Dye IR RC .05 .02
❑ 378 Lester Holmes IR RC .05 .02
❑ 379 Irv Smith IR RC .05 .02
❑ 380 Robert Smith IR RC 1.00 .45
❑ 381 Darrien Gordon IR RC .05 .02
❑ 382 Deon Figures IR RC .10 .05
❑ 383 O.J. McDuffie IR RC .75 .35
❑ 384 Dana Stubblefield IR RC .25 .11
❑ 385 Todd Kelly IR RC .05 .02
❑ 386 Thomas Smith IR RC .10 .05
❑ 387 George Teague IR RC .10 .05
❑ 388 Carlton Gray IR RC .05 .02
❑ 389 Chris Slade IR RC .10 .05
❑ 390 Ben Coleman IR RC .05 .02
❑ 391 Ryan McNeil IR RC UER .05 .02
(Name misspelled McNeill on front)
❑ 392 Demetrius DuBose IR RC .05 .02
❑ 393 Carl Simpson IR RC .05 .02
❑ 394 Coleman Rudolph IR RC .05 .02
❑ 395 Tony McGee IR RC .10 .05
❑ 396 Roger Harper IR RC .05 .02
❑ 397 Troy Drayton IR RC .10 .05
❑ 398 Michael Strahan IR RC .05 .02
❑ 399 Natrone Means IR RC .75 .35
❑ 400 Glyn Milburn IR RC .25 .11

1993 SkyBox Impact Kelly/Magic

	MINT	NRMT
COMPLETE SET (12)	18.00	8.00
COMMON PAIR (1-12)	1.00	.45
SEMISTARS	2.00	.90
STATED ODDS 1:12		
AUTO.STATED ODDS 1:2071		

❑ 1 Jim Kelly 2.00 .90
Magic Johnson Header
❑ 2 Dan Marino 5.00 2.20
Jim Kelly
❑ 3 Jay Novacek 1.00 .45
Keith Jackson
❑ 4 Thurman Thomas 5.00 2.20
Barry Sanders
❑ 5 Barry Sanders 6.00 2.70
Emmitt Smith

❑ 6 Jerry Rice 3.00 1.35
Sterling Sharpe
❑ 7 Andre Reed 3.00 1.35
Jerry Rice
❑ 8 Derrick Thomas 2.00 .90
Pat Swilling
❑ 9 Darryl Talley 2.00 .90
Lawrence Taylor
❑ 10 Rod Woodson 2.00 .90
Darrell Green
❑ 11 Steve Tasker 1.00 .45
Elvis Patterson
❑ 12 Chip Lohmiller 1.00 .45
Morten Andersen
❑ AU1 Kelly/Magic Header AU 40.00 18.00
2500 signed by Jim Kelly

1993 SkyBox Impact Update

	MINT	NRMT
COMPLETE SET (20)	10.00	4.50
SET AVAILABLE VIA MAIL OFFER		

❑ U1 Pierce Holt .25 .11
❑ U2 Vinny Testaverde .50 .23
❑ U3 Rod Bernstine .25 .11
❑ U4 Reggie White 1.25 .55
❑ U5 Mark Clayton .25 .11
❑ U6 Joe Montana 8.00 3.60
❑ U7 Marcus Allen 1.25 .55
❑ U8 Jeff Hostetler .50 .23
❑ U9 Shane Conlan .25 .11
❑ U10 Brad Muster .25 .11
❑ U11 Mike Sherrard .25 .11
❑ U12 Ronnie Lott .50 .23
❑ U13 Steve Beuerlein .25 .11
❑ U14 Gary Clark .50 .23
❑ U15 Kevin Greene 1.25 .55
❑ U16 Tim McDonald .25 .11
❑ U17 Wilber Marshall .25 .11
❑ U18 Keith Byars .25 .11
❑ U19 Pat Swilling .25 .11
❑ U20 Boomer Esiason .50 .23

1993 SkyBox Impact Rookie Redemption

	MINT	NRMT
COMPLETE SET (29)	15.00	6.75

TRADE CARD STATED ODDS 1:180 PACKS
ONE SET PER REDEMPTION CARD BY MAIL

❑ R1 Drew Bledsoe 2.50 1.10
Title Card Checklist
❑ R2 Drew Bledsoe 5.00 2.20
❑ R3 Rick Mirer .75 .35
❑ R4 Garrison Hearst 1.50 .70
❑ R5 Marvin Jones .10 .05
❑ R6 John Copeland .15 .07
❑ R7 Eric Curry UER .10 .05
(Card front states he was selected in sixth round instead of sixth pick)
❑ R8 Curtis Conway .75 .35
❑ R9 Willie Roaf .15 .07
❑ R10 Lincoln Kennedy .10 .05
❑ R11 Jerome Bettis 1.50 .70
❑ R12 Dan Williams .10 .05
❑ R13 Patrick Bates .10 .05
❑ R14 Brad Hopkins .10 .05
❑ R15 Steve Everitt .10 .05
❑ R16 Wayne Simmons .10 .05
❑ R17 Tom Carter .15 .07
❑ R18 Ernest Dye .10 .05
❑ R19 Lester Holmes .10 .05
❑ R20 Irv Smith .10 .05
❑ R21 Robert Smith 1.50 .70
❑ R22 Darrien Gordon .10 .05
❑ R23 Deon Figures .15 .07
❑ R24 Leonard Renfro .10 .05
❑ R25 O.J. McDuffie 1.25 .55
❑ R26 Dana Stubblefield .40 .18
❑ R27 Todd Kelly .10 .05
❑ R28 Thomas Smith .15 .07
❑ R29 George Teague .15 .07
❑ NNO Rookie Redemption .50 .23
Card Expired

1994 SkyBox Impact

	MINT	NRMT
COMPLETE SET (300)	15.00	6.75
COMMON CARD (1-300)	.05	.02
EXPANSION TEAMS (271-272)	.15	.07
SEMISTARS	.10	.05
UNLISTED STARS	.25	.11
PANTHERS HOLO.STATED ODDS 1:350		
COMP.QB UPDATE SET (11)	4.00	1.80
QB UPDATE:ONE PER SPEC.RETAIL BOX		

❑ 1 Johnny Bailey .05 .02

- ❑ 2 Steve Beuerlein .05 .02
- ❑ 3 Gary Clark .10 .05
- ❑ 4 Garrison Hearst .25 .11
- ❑ 5 Ronald Moore .05 .02
- ❑ 6 Ricky Proehl .05 .02
- ❑ 7 Eric Swann .10 .05
- ❑ 8 Aeneas Williams .05 .02
- ❑ 9 Robert Massey .05 .02
- ❑ 10 Chuck Cecil .05 .02
- ❑ 11 Ken Harvey .05 .02
- ❑ 12 Michael Haynes .10 .05
- ❑ 13 Tony Smith .05 .02
- ❑ 14 Bobby Hebert .05 .02
- ❑ 15 Mike Pritchard .05 .02
- ❑ 16 Andre Rison .10 .05
- ❑ 17 Deion Sanders .40 .18
- ❑ 18 Pierce Holt .05 .02
- ❑ 19 Erric Pegram .05 .02
- ❑ 20 Jessie Tuggle .05 .02
- ❑ 21 Steve Broussard .05 .02
- ❑ 22 Don Beebe .05 .02
- ❑ 23 Cornelius Bennett .10 .05
- ❑ 24 Kenneth Davis .05 .02
- ❑ 25 Bill Brooks .05 .02
- ❑ 26 Jim Kelly .25 .11
- ❑ 27 Andre Reed .10 .05
- ❑ 28 Bruce Smith .25 .11
- ❑ 29 Darryl Talley .05 .02
- ❑ 30 Thurman Thomas .25 .11
- ❑ 31 Steve Tasker .10 .05
- ❑ 32 Neal Anderson .05 .02
- ❑ 33 Mark Carrier DB .05 .02
- ❑ 34 Richard Dent .10 .05
- ❑ 35 Jim Harbaugh .25 .11
- ❑ 36 Chris Gedney .05 .02
- ❑ 37 Tom Waddle .05 .02
- ❑ 38 Curtis Conway .25 .11
- ❑ 39 Dante Jones .05 .02
- ❑ 40 Donnell Woolford .05 .02
- ❑ 41 Tim Worley .05 .02
- ❑ 42 John Copeland .05 .02
- ❑ 43 David Klingler .05 .02
- ❑ 44 Derrick Fenner .05 .02
- ❑ 45 Harold Green .05 .02
- ❑ 46 Carl Pickens .25 .11
- ❑ 47 Tony McGee .05 .02
- ❑ 48 Darryl Williams .05 .02
- ❑ 49 Steve Everitt .05 .02
- ❑ 50 Michael Jackson .10 .05
- ❑ 51 Eric Metcalf .10 .05
- ❑ 52 Tommy Vardell .05 .02
- ❑ 53 Vinny Testaverde .10 .05
- ❑ 54 Mark Carrier WR .10 .05
- ❑ 55 Michael Dean Perry .10 .05
- ❑ 56 Eric Turner .05 .02
- ❑ 57 Troy Aikman .75 .35
- ❑ 58 Alvin Harper .10 .05
- ❑ 59 Michael Irvin .25 .11
- ❑ 60 Leon Lett .05 .02
- ❑ 61 Russell Maryland .05 .02
- ❑ 62 Jay Novacek .10 .05
- ❑ 63 Emmitt Smith 1.25 .55
- ❑ 64 Ken Norton .10 .05
- ❑ 65 Charles Haley .10 .05
- ❑ 66 Daryl Johnston .10 .05
- ❑ 67 Kevin Smith .05 .02
- ❑ 68 James Washington .05 .02
- ❑ 69 Kevin Williams .10 .05
- ❑ 70 Bernie Kosar .10 .05
- ❑ 71 Mike Croel .05 .02
- ❑ 72 John Elway 1.50 .70
- ❑ 73 Shannon Sharpe .10 .05
- ❑ 74 Rod Bernstine .05 .02
- ❑ 75 Simon Fletcher .05 .02
- ❑ 76 Arthur Marshall .05 .02
- ❑ 77 Glyn Milburn .10 .05
- ❑ 78 Dennis Smith .05 .02
- ❑ 79 Herman Moore .25 .11
- ❑ 80 Rodney Peete .05 .02
- ❑ 81 Barry Sanders 1.50 .70
- ❑ 82 Mel Gray .05 .02
- ❑ 83 Erik Kramer .10 .05
- ❑ 84 Pat Swilling .05 .02
- ❑ 85 Willie Green .05 .02
- ❑ 86 Chris Spielman .10 .05
- ❑ 87 Robert Porcher .05 .02
- ❑ 88 Derrick Moore .05 .02
- ❑ 89 Edgar Bennett .25 .11
- ❑ 90 Tony Bennett .05 .02
- ❑ 91 LeRoy Butler .05 .02
- ❑ 92 Brett Favre 1.50 .70
- ❑ 93 Jackie Harris .05 .02
- ❑ 94 Sterling Sharpe .10 .05
- ❑ 95 Darrell Thompson .05 .02
- ❑ 96 Reggie White .25 .11
- ❑ 97 Terrell Buckley .05 .02
- ❑ 98 Cris Dishman .05 .02
- ❑ 99 Ernest Givins .10 .05
- ❑ 100 Haywood Jeffires .10 .05
- ❑ 101 Warren Moon .25 .11
- ❑ 102 Lorenzo White .05 .02
- ❑ 103 Webster Slaughter .05 .02
- ❑ 104 Ray Childress .05 .02
- ❑ 105 Wilber Marshall .05 .02
- ❑ 106 Gary Brown .05 .02
- ❑ 107 Marcus Robertson .05 .02
- ❑ 108 Sean Jones .05 .02
- ❑ 109 Jeff George .25 .11
- ❑ 110 Steve Emtman .05 .02
- ❑ 111 Quentin Coryatt .05 .02
- ❑ 112 Sean Dawkins RC .25 .11
- ❑ 113 Jeff Herrod .05 .02
- ❑ 114 Roosevelt Potts .05 .02
- ❑ 115 Marcus Allen .25 .11
- ❑ 116 Kimble Anders .10 .05
- ❑ 117 Tim Barnett .05 .02
- ❑ 118 J.J. Birden .05 .02
- ❑ 119 Dale Carter .05 .02
- ❑ 120 Willie Davis .10 .05
- ❑ 121 Nick Lowery .05 .02
- ❑ 122 Joe Montana 1.50 .70
- ❑ 123 Kevin Ross .05 .02
- ❑ 124 Neil Smith .25 .11
- ❑ 125 Derrick Thomas .25 .11
- ❑ 126 Keith Cash .05 .02
- ❑ 127 Tim Brown .25 .11
- ❑ 128 Rocket Ismail .10 .05
- ❑ 129 Ethan Horton .05 .02
- ❑ 130 Jeff Hostetler .10 .05
- ❑ 131 Patrick Bates .05 .02
- ❑ 132 Terry McDaniel .05 .02
- ❑ 133 Anthony Smith .05 .02
- ❑ 134 Greg Robinson .05 .02
- ❑ 135 James Jett .05 .02
- ❑ 136 Alexander Wright .05 .02
- ❑ 137 Flipper Anderson .05 .02
- ❑ 138 Shane Conlan .05 .02
- ❑ 139 Jim Everett .10 .05
- ❑ 140 Henry Ellard .10 .05
- ❑ 141 Jerome Bettis .25 .11
- ❑ 142 Troy Drayton .05 .02
- ❑ 143 Sean Gilbert .05 .02
- ❑ 144 Chris Miller .05 .02
- ❑ 145 Keith Byars .05 .02
- ❑ 146 Marco Coleman .05 .02
- ❑ 147 Bryan Cox .05 .02
- ❑ 148 Irving Fryar .10 .05
- ❑ 149 Mark Ingram .05 .02
- ❑ 150 Keith Jackson .05 .02
- ❑ 151 Terry Kirby .25 .11
- ❑ 152 Dan Marino 1.50 .70
- ❑ 153 O.J. McDuffie .25 .11
- ❑ 154 Scott Mitchell .25 .11
- ❑ 155 Anthony Carter .10 .05
- ❑ 156 Cris Carter .40 .18
- ❑ 157 Chris Doleman .05 .02
- ❑ 158 Steve Jordan .05 .02
- ❑ 159 Qadry Ismail .25 .11
- ❑ 160 Randall McDaniel .05 .02
- ❑ 161 John Randle .05 .02
- ❑ 162 Robert Smith .25 .11
- ❑ 163 Henry Thomas .05 .02
- ❑ 164 Terry Allen .10 .05
- ❑ 165 Scottie Graham RC .10 .05
- ❑ 166 Drew Bledsoe 1.00 .45
- ❑ 167 Vincent Brown .05 .02
- ❑ 168 Ben Coates .25 .11
- ❑ 169 Leonard Russell .05 .02
- ❑ 170 Andre Tippett .05 .02
- ❑ 171 Vincent Brisby .25 .11
- ❑ 172 Michael Timpson .05 .02
- ❑ 173 Bruce Armstrong .05 .02
- ❑ 174 Morten Andersen UER .05 .02 (Morton on front)
- ❑ 175 Derek Brown RBK .05 .02
- ❑ 176 Quinn Early .10 .05
- ❑ 177 Rickey Jackson .05 .02
- ❑ 178 Vaughan Johnson .05 .02
- ❑ 179 Lorenzo Neal .05 .02
- ❑ 180 Sam Mills .05 .02
- ❑ 181 Irv Smith .05 .02
- ❑ 182 Renaldo Turnbull .05 .02
- ❑ 183 Wade Wilson .05 .02
- ❑ 184 Willie Roaf .05 .02
- ❑ 185 Michael Brooks .05 .02
- ❑ 186 Mark Jackson .05 .02
- ❑ 187 Rodney Hampton .25 .11
- ❑ 188 Phil Simms .10 .05
- ❑ 189 Dave Meggett .05 .02
- ❑ 190 Mike Sherrard .05 .02
- ❑ 191 Chris Calloway .05 .02
- ❑ 192 Brad Baxter .05 .02
- ❑ 193 Ronnie Lott .10 .05
- ❑ 194 Boomer Esiason .10 .05
- ❑ 195 Rob Moore .10 .05
- ❑ 196 Johnny Johnson .05 .02
- ❑ 197 Marvin Jones .05 .02
- ❑ 198 Mo Lewis .05 .02
- ❑ 199 Johnny Mitchell .05 .02
- ❑ 200 Brian Washington .05 .02
- ❑ 201 Eric Allen .05 .02
- ❑ 202 Fred Barnett .10 .05
- ❑ 203 Mark Bavaro .05 .02
- ❑ 204 Randall Cunningham .25 .11
- ❑ 205 Vaughn Hebron .05 .02
- ❑ 206 Seth Joyner .05 .02
- ❑ 207 Clyde Simmons .05 .02
- ❑ 208 Herschel Walker .10 .05
- ❑ 209 Calvin Williams .10 .05
- ❑ 210 Neil O'Donnell .25 .11
- ❑ 211 Eric Green .05 .02
- ❑ 212 Leroy Thompson .05 .02
- ❑ 213 Rod Woodson .25 .11
- ❑ 214 Barry Foster .05 .02
- ❑ 215 Jeff Graham .05 .02
- ❑ 216 Kevin Greene .25 .11
- ❑ 217 Deon Figures .05 .02
- ❑ 218 Greg Lloyd .25 .11
- ❑ 219 Marion Butts .05 .02
- ❑ 220 Chris Mims .05 .02
- ❑ 221 Eric Curry .05 .02
- ❑ 222 Ronnie Harmon .05 .02
- ❑ 223 Stan Humphries .25 .11
- ❑ 224 Nate Lewis .05 .02
- ❑ 225 Natrone Means .25 .11
- ❑ 226 Anthony Miller .10 .05
- ❑ 227 Leslie O'Neal .05 .02
- ❑ 228 Junior Seau .25 .11
- ❑ 229 Brent Jones .10 .05
- ❑ 230 Tim McDonald .05 .02
- ❑ 231 Tom Rathman .05 .02
- ❑ 232 Jerry Rice .75 .35
- ❑ 233 Dana Stubblefield .25 .11
- ❑ 234 John Taylor .10 .05
- ❑ 235 Ricky Watters .25 .11
- ❑ 236 Steve Young .60 .25
- ❑ 237 Amp Lee .05 .02
- ❑ 238 Robert Blackmon .05 .02
- ❑ 239 Brian Blades .10 .05
- ❑ 240 Cortez Kennedy .10 .05
- ❑ 241 Kelvin Martin .05 .02
- ❑ 242 Rick Mirer .25 .11
- ❑ 243 Eugene Robinson .05 .02
- ❑ 244 Chris Warren .10 .05
- ❑ 245 John L. Williams .05 .02
- ❑ 246 Jon Vaughn .05 .02
- ❑ 247 Reggie Cobb .05 .02
- ❑ 248 Horace Copeland .05 .02
- ❑ 249 Derrick Alexander WR RC .50 .23
- ❑ 250 Santana Dotson .10 .05
- ❑ 251 Craig Erickson .05 .02
- ❑ 252 Courtney Hawkins .05 .02
- ❑ 253 Hardy Nickerson .10 .05
- ❑ 254 Vince Workman .05 .02
- ❑ 255 Paul Gruber .05 .02
- ❑ 256 Reggie Brooks .10 .05
- ❑ 257 Tom Carter .05 .02
- ❑ 258 Andre Collins .05 .02

	MINT	NRMT
❑ 259 Darrell Green	.05	.02
❑ 260 Desmond Howard	.10	.05
❑ 261 Tim McGee	.05	.02
❑ 262 Brian Mitchell	.05	.02
❑ 263 Art Monk	.10	.05
❑ 264 John Friesz	.10	.05
❑ 265 Ricky Sanders	.05	.02
❑ 266 Checklist	.05	.02
❑ 267 Checklist	.05	.02
❑ 268 Checklist	.05	.02
❑ 269 Checklist	.05	.02
❑ 270 Checklist	.05	.02
❑ 271 Carolina Panthers Logo Card	.15	.07
❑ 272 Jacksonville Jaguars Logo Card	.15	.07
❑ 273 Dan Wilkinson RC	.10	.05
❑ 274 Marshall Faulk RC	4.00	1.80
❑ 275 Heath Shuler RC	.25	.11
❑ 276 Willie McGinest RC	.25	.11
❑ 277 Trev Alberts RC	.10	.05
❑ 278 Trent Dilfer RC	1.50	.70
❑ 279 Bryant Young RC	.25	.11
❑ 280 Sam Adams RC	.10	.05
❑ 281 Antonio Langham RC	.10	.05
❑ 282 Jamir Miller RC	.05	.02
❑ 283 John Thierry RC	.05	.02
❑ 284 Aaron Glenn RC	.10	.05
❑ 285 Joe Johnson RC	.05	.02
❑ 286 Bernard Williams RC	.05	.02
❑ 287 Wayne Gandy RC	.05	.02
❑ 288 Aaron Taylor RC	.05	.02
❑ 289 Charles Johnson RC	.25	.11
❑ 290 Dewayne Washington RC	.10	.05
❑ 291 Todd Steussie RC	.10	.05
❑ 292 Tim Bowens RC	.10	.05
❑ 293 Johnnie Morton RC	.25	.11
❑ 294 Rob Frederickson RC	.10	.05
❑ 295 Shante Carver RC	.05	.02
❑ 296 Thomas Lewis RC	.10	.05
❑ 297 Greg Hill RC	.50	.23
❑ 298 Henry Ford RC	.05	.02
❑ 299 Jeff Burris RC	.10	.05
❑ 300 William Floyd RC	.25	.11
❑ P1 Jim Kelly Promo	.75	.35
❑ NNO Carolina Panthers HOLO	20.00	9.00

1994 SkyBox Impact Instant Impact

	MINT	NRMT
COMPLETE SET (12)	30.00	13.50
STATED ODDS 1:30		
❑ R1 Rick Mirer	2.50	1.10
❑ R2 Jerome Bettis	2.50	1.10
❑ R3 Reggie Brooks	1.00	.45
❑ R4 Terry Kirby	2.50	1.10
❑ R5 Vincent Brisby	2.50	1.10
❑ R6 James Jett	.50	.23
❑ R7 Drew Bledsoe	10.00	4.50
❑ R8 Dana Stubblefield	2.50	1.10
❑ R9 Natrone Means	2.50	1.10
❑ R10 Curtis Conway	2.50	1.10
❑ R11 O.J. McDuffie	2.50	1.10
❑ R12 Garrison Hearst	2.50	1.10

1994 SkyBox Impact Rookie Redemption

	MINT	NRMT
COMPLETE SET (30)	15.00	6.75
TRADE CARD STATED ODDS 1:350		
SET AVAILABLE VIA MAIL REDEMPTION		
❑ 1 Dan Wilkinson	.20	.09
❑ 2 Marshall Faulk	8.00	3.60
❑ 3 Heath Shuler	.50	.23
❑ 4 Willie McGinest	.50	.23
❑ 5 Trev Alberts	.20	.09
❑ 6 Trent Dilfer	3.00	1.35
❑ 7 Bryant Young	.50	.23
❑ 8 Sam Adams	.20	.09
❑ 9 Antonio Langham	.20	.09
❑ 10 Jamir Miller	.10	.05
❑ 11 John Thierry	.10	.05
❑ 12 Aaron Glenn	.20	.09
❑ 13 Joe Johnson	.10	.05
❑ 14 Bernard Williams	.10	.05
❑ 15 Wayne Gandy	.10	.05
❑ 16 Aaron Taylor	.10	.05
❑ 17 Charles Johnson	.50	.23
❑ 18 Dewayne Washington	.20	.09
❑ 19 Todd Steussie	.20	.09
❑ 20 Tim Bowens	.20	.09
❑ 21 Johnnie Morton	.50	.23
❑ 22 Rob Fredrickson	.20	.09
❑ 23 Shante Carver	.10	.05
❑ 24 Thomas Lewis	.20	.09
❑ 25 Greg Hill	1.00	.45
❑ 26 Henry Ford	.10	.05
❑ 27 Jeff Burris	.20	.09
❑ 28 William Floyd	.50	.23
❑ 29 Derrick Alexander WR	1.00	.45
❑ 30 Title/Checklist Card	.10	.05
❑ NNO Redemption Card Expired 1/31/1995	.60	.25

1994 SkyBox Impact Ultimate Impact

	MINT	NRMT
COMPLETE SET (15)	60.00	27.00
STATED ODDS 1:15		
❑ U1 Troy Aikman	6.00	2.70
❑ U2 Emmitt Smith UER	10.00	4.50
❑ U3 Michael Irvin	2.00	.90
❑ U4 Joe Montana	12.00	5.50
❑ U5 Jerry Rice	6.00	2.70
❑ U6 Sterling Sharpe	.75	.35
❑ U7 Steve Young	5.00	2.20
❑ U8 Ricky Watters	2.00	.90
❑ U9 Barry Sanders	12.00	5.50
❑ U10 John Elway	12.00	5.50
❑ U11 Reggie White	2.00	.90
❑ U12 Jim Kelly	2.00	.90
❑ U13 Thurman Thomas	2.00	.90
❑ U14 Dan Marino	12.00	5.50
❑ U15 Brett Favre	12.00	5.50

1995 SkyBox Impact

	MINT	NRMT
COMPLETE SET (200)	15.00	6.75
COMMON CARD (1-200)	.05	.02
SEMISTARS	.10	.05
UNLISTED STARS	.25	.11
COMP.ROOKIE RB SET (9)	8.00	3.60
ONE SET PER SPECIAL RETAIL BOX		
M1 STATED ODDS 1:360		
❑ 1 Garrison Hearst	.25	.11
❑ 2 Ronald Moore	.05	.02
❑ 3 Eric Swann	.10	.05
❑ 4 Aeneas Williams	.05	.02
❑ 5 Jeff George	.10	.05
❑ 6 Craig Heyward	.10	.05
❑ 7 Terance Mathis	.10	.05
❑ 8 Andre Rison	.10	.05
❑ 9 Cornelius Bennett	.10	.05
❑ 10 Jim Kelly	.25	.11
❑ 11 Andre Reed	.10	.05
❑ 12 Bruce Smith	.25	.11
❑ 13 Thurman Thomas	.25	.11
❑ 14 Frank Reich	.05	.02
❑ 15 Lamar Lathon	.05	.02
❑ 16 Darion Conner	.05	.02
❑ 17 Randy Baldwin	.05	.02
❑ 18 Don Beebe	.05	.02
❑ 19 Mark Carrier DB	.05	.02
❑ 20 Jeff Graham	.05	.02
❑ 21 Raymont Harris	.05	.02
❑ 22 Alonzo Spellman	.05	.02
❑ 23 Lewis Tillman	.05	.02
❑ 24 Steve Walsh	.05	.02
❑ 25 Jeff Blake RC	.75	.35
❑ 26 Carl Pickens	.25	.11
❑ 27 Darnay Scott	.25	.11
❑ 28 Dan Wilkinson	.10	.05
❑ 29 Derrick Alexander WR	.25	.11
❑ 30 Leroy Hoard	.05	.02
❑ 31 Antonio Langham	.05	.02
❑ 32 Vinny Testaverde	.10	.05
❑ 33 Eric Turner	.05	.02
❑ 34 Troy Aikman	.75	.35
❑ 35 Charles Haley	.10	.05
❑ 36 Alvin Harper	.05	.02
❑ 37 Michael Irvin	.25	.11
❑ 38 Daryl Johnston	.10	.05
❑ 39 Jay Novacek	.10	.05
❑ 40 Leon Lett	.05	.02
❑ 41 Emmitt Smith	1.25	.55
❑ 42 John Elway	1.50	.70
❑ 43 Glyn Milburn	.05	.02
❑ 44 Anthony Miller	.10	.05
❑ 45 Leonard Russell	.05	.02
❑ 46 Shannon Sharpe	.10	.05
❑ 47 Scott Mitchell	.10	.05
❑ 48 Herman Moore	.25	.11
❑ 49 Barry Sanders	1.50	.70
❑ 50 Chris Spielman	.10	.05
❑ 51 Edgar Bennett	.10	.05
❑ 52 Robert Brooks	.25	.11
❑ 53 Brett Favre	1.50	.70
❑ 54 Bryce Paup	.25	.11
❑ 55 Sterling Sharpe	.10	.05
❑ 56 Reggie White	.25	.11
❑ 57 Ray Childress	.05	.02
❑ 58 Haywood Jeffires	.05	.02

❑ 59 Webster Slaughter	.05	.02
❑ 60 Lorenzo White	.05	.02
❑ 61 Trev Alberts	.05	.02
❑ 62 Quentin Coryatt	.10	.05
❑ 63 Sean Dawkins	.10	.05
❑ 64 Marshall Faulk	.40	.18
❑ 65 Jeff Lageman	.05	.02
❑ 66 Steve Beuerlein	.05	.02
❑ 67 Desmond Howard	.10	.05
❑ 68 Kelvin Martin	.05	.02
❑ 69 Reggie Cobb	.05	.02
❑ 70 Marcus Allen	.25	.11
❑ 71 Greg Hill	.10	.05
❑ 72 Joe Montana	1.50	.70
❑ 73 Neil Smith	.10	.05
❑ 74 Derrick Thomas	.10	.05
❑ 75 Tim Brown	.25	.11
❑ 76 Rocket Ismail	.10	.05
❑ 77 Jeff Hostetler	.10	.05
❑ 78 Chester McGlockton	.10	.05
❑ 79 Harvey Williams	.05	.02
❑ 80 Tim Bowens	.05	.02
❑ 81 Irving Fryar	.10	.05
❑ 82 Keith Jackson	.05	.02
❑ 83 Terry Kirby	.10	.05
❑ 84 Dan Marino	1.50	.70
❑ 85 O.J. McDuffie	.25	.11
❑ 86 Bernie Parmalee	.10	.05
❑ 87 Terry Allen	.10	.05
❑ 88 Cris Carter	.25	.11
❑ 89 Qadry Ismail	.10	.05
❑ 90 Warren Moon	.10	.05
❑ 91 Jake Reed	.10	.05
❑ 92 Drew Bledsoe	.75	.35
❑ 93 Vincent Brisby	.05	.02
❑ 94 Ben Coates	.10	.05
❑ 95 Michael Timpson	.05	.02
❑ 96 Jim Everett	.05	.02
❑ 97 Michael Haynes	.10	.05
❑ 98 Willie Roaf	.05	.02
❑ 99 Michael Brooks	.05	.02
❑ 100 Dave Brown	.10	.05
❑ 101 Rodney Hampton	.10	.05
❑ 102 Thomas Lewis	.10	.05
❑ 103 Dave Meggett	.05	.02
❑ 104 Boomer Esiason	.10	.05
❑ 105 Johnny Johnson	.05	.02
❑ 106 Johnny Mitchell	.05	.02
❑ 107 Rob Moore	.05	.02
❑ 108 Fred Barnett	.10	.05
❑ 109 Randall Cunningham	.25	.11
❑ 110 Charlie Garner	.10	.05
❑ 111 Herschel Walker	.10	.05
❑ 112 Barry Foster	.10	.05
❑ 113 Eric Green	.05	.02
❑ 114 Charles Johnson	.10	.05
❑ 115 Greg Lloyd	.10	.05
❑ 116 Byron Bam Morris	.10	.05
❑ 117 Neil O'Donnell	.10	.05
❑ 118 Rod Woodson	.10	.05
❑ 119 Flipper Anderson	.05	.02
❑ 120 Jerome Bettis	.25	.11
❑ 121 Troy Drayton	.05	.02
❑ 122 Sean Gilbert	.10	.05
❑ 123 Ronnie Harmon	.05	.02
❑ 124 Stan Humphries	.10	.05
❑ 125 Shawn Jefferson	.05	.02
❑ 126 Natrone Means	.25	.11
❑ 127 Leslie O'Neal	.10	.05
❑ 128 Junior Seau	.25	.11
❑ 129 William Floyd	.25	.11
❑ 130 Brent Jones	.05	.02
❑ 131 Jerry Rice	.75	.35
❑ 132 Deion Sanders	.50	.23
❑ 133 Dana Stubblefield	.25	.11
❑ 134 Ricky Watters	.25	.11
❑ 135 Bryant Young	.10	.05
❑ 136 Steve Young	.60	.25
❑ 137 Brian Blades	.10	.05
❑ 138 Cortez Kennedy	.10	.05
❑ 139 Rick Mirer	.25	.11
❑ 140 Chris Warren	.10	.05
❑ 141 Horace Copeland	.05	.02
❑ 142 Trent Dilfer	.25	.11
❑ 143 Hardy Nickerson	.05	.02
❑ 144 Errict Rhett	.25	.11
❑ 145 Henry Ellard	.10	.05
❑ 146 Brian Mitchell	.05	.02
❑ 147 Heath Shuler	.25	.11
❑ 148 Tydus Winans	.05	.02
❑ 149 Steve Tasker	.10	.05
❑ 150 Jeff Burris	.05	.02
❑ 151 Tyrone Hughes	.10	.05
❑ 152 Mel Gray	.05	.02
❑ 153 Kevin Williams WR	.10	.05
❑ 154 Andre Coleman	.05	.02
❑ 155 Corey Sawyer	.05	.02
❑ 156 Darrien Gordon	.05	.02
❑ 157 Aaron Glenn	.05	.02
❑ 158 Eric Metcalf	.10	.05
❑ 159 Errict Rhett SS	.25	.11
❑ 160 Marshall Faulk SS	.25	.11
❑ 161 Darnay Scott SS	.25	.11
❑ 162 William Floyd SS	.05	.02
❑ 163 Charlie Garner SS	.10	.05
❑ 164 Heath Shuler SS	.25	.11
❑ 165 Trent Dilfer SS	.25	.11
❑ 166 Willie McGinest SS	.10	.05
❑ 167 Byron Bam Morris SS	.10	.05
❑ 168 Mario Bates SS	.25	.11
❑ 169 Ki-Jana Carter RC	.25	.11
❑ 170 Tony Boselli RC	.10	.05
❑ 171 Steve McNair RC	2.50	1.10
❑ 172 Michael Westbrook RC	1.25	.55
❑ 173 Kerry Collins RC	.75	.35
❑ 174 Kevin Carter RC	.25	.11
❑ 175 Mike Mamula RC	.10	.05
❑ 176 Joey Galloway RC	2.50	1.10
❑ 177 Kyle Brady RC	.25	.11
❑ 178 J.J. Stokes RC	.60	.25
❑ 179 Warren Sapp RC	.40	.18
❑ 180 Rob Johnson RC	1.25	.55
❑ 181 Tyrone Wheatley RC	1.00	.45
❑ 182 Napoleon Kaufman RC	1.50	.70
❑ 183 James O. Stewart RC	1.50	.70
❑ 184 Dino Philyaw RC	.05	.02
❑ 185 Rashaan Salaam RC	.25	.11
❑ 186 Tyrone Poole RC	.10	.05
❑ 187 Ty Law RC	.10	.05
❑ 188 Joe Aska RC	.10	.05
❑ 189 Mark Bruener RC	.10	.05
❑ 190 Derrick Brooks RC	.05	.02
❑ 191 Jack Jackson RC	.05	.02
❑ 192 Ray Zellars RC	.10	.05
❑ 193 Eddie Goines RC	.05	.02
❑ 194 Chris Sanders RC	.25	.11
❑ 195 Charlie Simmons RC	.05	.02
❑ 196 Lee DeRamus RC	.05	.02
❑ 197 Frank Sanders RC	.75	.35
❑ 198 Rodney Thomas RC	.25	.11
❑ 199 Checklist A 1-128	.05	.02
❑ 200 Checklist B 129-200	.05	.02
❑ M1 Brett Favre SkyMotion	35.00	16.00
❑ M2 Brett Favre SkyMotion	35.00	16.00
❑ P1 Promo Sheet	3.00	1.35

Chris Spielman
Ronald Moore
Bernie Parmalee
Tyrone Hughes
Brett Favre Countdown
Bryan Cox Impact Power

1995 SkyBox Impact Countdown

	MINT	NRMT
COMPLETE SET (10)	60.00	27.00

STATED ODDS 1:20 H/R, 1:60 SPEC.RET

❑ C1 Barry Sanders	12.00	5.50
❑ C2 Jerry Rice	6.00	2.70
❑ C3 Steve Young	5.00	2.20
❑ C4 Troy Aikman	6.00	2.70
❑ C5 Dan Marino	12.00	5.50
❑ C6 Emmitt Smith	10.00	4.50
❑ C7 Junior Seau	2.00	.90
❑ C8 Drew Bledsoe	6.00	2.70
❑ C9 Brett Favre	12.00	5.50
❑ C10 Deion Sanders	4.00	1.80

1995 SkyBox Impact Future Hall of Famers

	MINT	NRMT
COMP.SHORT SET (7)	100.00	45.00

HF2 ISSUED EARLY ONLY AND PULLED
STATED ODDS 1:60 HOBBY

❑ HF1 Jerry Rice	12.00	5.50
❑ HF2 Joe Montana SP	800.00	350.00
❑ HF3 Steve Young	10.00	4.50
❑ HF4 John Elway	25.00	11.00
❑ HF5 Dan Marino	25.00	11.00
❑ HF6 Emmitt Smith	20.00	9.00
❑ HF7 Barry Sanders	25.00	11.00
❑ HF8 Troy Aikman	12.00	5.50

1995 SkyBox Impact More Attitude

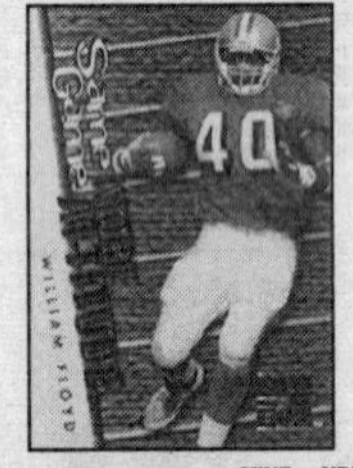

	MINT	NRMT
COMPLETE SET (15)	30.00	13.50

STATED ODDS 1:9 H/R, 1:27 SPEC.RET

❑ F1 Ki-Jana Carter	.60	.25
❑ F2 Steve McNair	6.00	2.70
❑ F3 Michael Westbrook	3.00	1.35
❑ F4 Kerry Collins	2.00	.90
❑ F5 Joey Galloway	6.00	2.70
❑ F6 J.J. Stokes	1.50	.70
❑ F7 James O. Stewart	4.00	1.80
❑ F8 Rashaan Salaam	.60	.25
❑ F9 Trent Dilfer	2.00	.90
❑ F10 William Floyd	2.00	.90
❑ F11 Marshall Faulk	3.00	1.35
❑ F12 Errict Rhett	2.00	.90
❑ F13 Heath Shuler	2.00	.90
❑ F14 Drew Bledsoe	6.00	2.70
❑ F15 Ben Coates	.75	.35

1995 SkyBox Impact Power

	MINT	NRMT
COMP.SHORT SET (29)	30.00	13.50

IP25 ISSUED EARLY ONLY AND PULLED
STATED ODDS 1:3 H/R, 1:9 SPEC.RET

❑ IP1 Junior Seau	1.00	.45
❑ IP2 Reggie White	1.00	.45

Card	Mint	NRMT
❑ IP3 Eric Swann	.40	.18
❑ IP4 Bruce Smith	1.00	.45
❑ IP5 Rod Woodson	.40	.18
❑ IP6 Derrick Thomas	.40	.18
❑ IP7 Chester McGlockton	.40	.18
❑ IP8 Cortez Kennedy	.40	.18
❑ IP9 Deion Sanders	2.00	.90
❑ IP10 Bryan Cox	.20	.09
❑ IP11 Jerry Rice	3.00	1.35
❑ IP12 Sterling Sharpe	.40	.18
❑ IP13 Tim Brown	1.00	.45
❑ IP14 Marshall Faulk	1.50	.70
❑ IP15 Brett Favre	6.00	2.70
❑ IP16 Chris Warren	.40	.18
❑ IP17 Herman Moore	1.00	.45
❑ IP18 Steve Young	2.50	1.10
❑ IP19 Andre Rison	.40	.18
❑ IP20 Thurman Thomas	1.00	.45
❑ IP21 Marcus Allen	1.00	.45
❑ IP22 Michael Irvin	1.00	.45
❑ IP23 Emmitt Smith	5.00	2.20
❑ IP24 John Elway	6.00	2.70
❑ IP25 Joe Montana SP	800.00	350.00
❑ IP26 Barry Sanders	6.00	2.70
❑ IP27 Troy Aikman	3.00	1.35
❑ IP28 Natrone Means	1.00	.45
❑ IP29 Ben Coates	.40	.18
❑ IP30 Errict Rhett	1.00	.45

1996 SkyBox Impact

	MINT	NRMT
COMPLETE SET (200)	15.00	6.75
COMMON CARD (1-200)	.10	.05
FAVRE HIGHLIGHTS (194-198)	.30	.14
SEMISTARS	.20	.09
UNLISTED STARS	.30	.14
FAVRE EXCH.EXPIRED (BF1-BF2)	.50	.23

Card	Mint	NRMT
❑ 1 Garrison Hearst	.20	.09
❑ 2 Rob Moore	.20	.09
❑ 3 Frank Sanders	.20	.09
❑ 4 Eric Swann	.10	.05
❑ 5 Aeneas Williams	.10	.05
❑ 6 Bert Emanuel	.20	.09
❑ 7 Jeff George	.20	.09
❑ 8 Craig Heyward	.10	.05
❑ 9 Terance Mathis	.10	.05
❑ 10 Eric Metcalf	.10	.05
❑ 11 Leroy Hoard	.10	.05
❑ 12 Michael Jackson	.20	.09
❑ 13 Andre Rison	.20	.09
❑ 14 Vinny Testaverde	.20	.09
❑ 15 Eric Turner	.10	.05
❑ 16 Darick Holmes	.10	.05
❑ 17 Jim Kelly	.30	.14
❑ 18 Bryce Paup	.10	.05
❑ 19 Bruce Smith	.20	.09
❑ 20 Thurman Thomas	.30	.14
❑ 21 Mark Carrier WR	.10	.05
❑ 22 Kerry Collins	.30	.14
❑ 23 Derrick Moore	.10	.05
❑ 24 Tyrone Poole	.10	.05
❑ 25 Curtis Conway	.30	.14
❑ 26 Jeff Graham	.10	.05
❑ 27 Erik Kramer	.10	.05
❑ 28 Rashaan Salaam	.30	.14
❑ 29 Jeff Blake	.30	.14
❑ 30 Ki-Jana Carter	.20	.09
❑ 31 Carl Pickens	.30	.14
❑ 32 Darnay Scott	.20	.09
❑ 33 Troy Aikman	.75	.35
❑ 34 Charles Haley	.20	.09
❑ 35 Michael Irvin	.30	.14
❑ 36 Daryl Johnston	.20	.09
❑ 37 Jay Novacek	.10	.05
❑ 38 Deion Sanders	.40	.18
❑ 39 Emmitt Smith	1.25	.55
❑ 40 Steve Atwater	.10	.05
❑ 41 Terrell Davis	2.00	.90
❑ 42 John Elway	1.50	.70
❑ 43 Anthony Miller	.20	.09
❑ 44 Shannon Sharpe	.20	.09
❑ 45 Scott Mitchell	.20	.09
❑ 46 Herman Moore	.30	.14
❑ 47 Brett Perriman	.10	.05
❑ 48 Barry Sanders	1.50	.70
❑ 49 Edgar Bennett	.20	.09
❑ 50 Robert Brooks	.30	.14
❑ 51 Mark Chmura	.20	.09
❑ 52 Brett Favre	1.50	.70
❑ 53 Reggie White	.30	.14
❑ 54 Mel Gray	.10	.05
❑ 55 Steve McNair	.50	.23
❑ 56 Chris Sanders	.20	.09
❑ 57 Rodney Thomas	.10	.05
❑ 58 Quentin Coryatt	.10	.05
❑ 59 Sean Dawkins	.10	.05
❑ 60 Ken Dilger	.20	.09
❑ 61 Marshall Faulk	.30	.14
❑ 62 Jim Harbaugh	.20	.09
❑ 63 Tony Boselli	.10	.05
❑ 64 Mark Brunell	.75	.35
❑ 65 Keenan McCardell	.30	.14
❑ 66 James O.Stewart	.20	.09
❑ 67 Marcus Allen	.30	.14
❑ 68 Steve Bono	.10	.05
❑ 69 Neil Smith	.10	.05
❑ 70 Derrick Thomas	.20	.09
❑ 71 Tamarick Vanover	.20	.09
❑ 72 Bryan Cox	.10	.05
❑ 73 Irving Fryar	.20	.09
❑ 74 Eric Green	.10	.05
❑ 75 Dan Marino	1.50	.70
❑ 76 O.J. McDuffie	.20	.09
❑ 77 Bernie Parmalee	.10	.05
❑ 78 Cris Carter	.30	.14
❑ 79 Qadry Ismail	.10	.05
❑ 80 Warren Moon	.20	.09
❑ 81 Jake Reed	.20	.09
❑ 82 Robert Smith	.20	.09
❑ 83 Drew Bledsoe	.75	.35
❑ 84 Ben Coates	.20	.09
❑ 85 Curtis Martin	.50	.23
❑ 86 Willie McGinest	.10	.05
❑ 87 Dave Meggett	.10	.05
❑ 88 Mario Bates	.20	.09
❑ 89 Quinn Early	.10	.05
❑ 90 Jim Everett	.10	.05
❑ 91 Michael Haynes	.10	.05
❑ 92 Renaldo Turnbull	.10	.05
❑ 93 Dave Brown	.10	.05
❑ 94 Rodney Hampton	.20	.09
❑ 95 Thomas Lewis	.10	.05
❑ 96 Phillippi Sparks	.10	.05
❑ 97 Tyrone Wheatley	.20	.09
❑ 98 Kyle Brady	.10	.05
❑ 99 Hugh Douglas	.10	.05
❑ 100 Mo Lewis	.10	.05
❑ 101 Adrian Murrell	.30	.14
❑ 102 Tim Brown	.30	.14
❑ 103 Jeff Hostetler	.10	.05
❑ 104 Rocket Ismail	.10	.05
❑ 105 Chester McGlockton	.10	.05
❑ 106 Harvey Williams	.10	.05
❑ 107 Fred Barnett	.10	.05
❑ 108 William Fuller	.10	.05
❑ 109 Charlie Garner	.10	.05
❑ 110 Rodney Peete	.10	.05
❑ 111 Ricky Watters	.20	.09
❑ 112 Calvin Williams	.10	.05
❑ 113 Byron Bam Morris	.20	.09
❑ 114 Neil O'Donnell	.20	.09
❑ 115 Erric Pegram	.10	.05
❑ 116 Kordell Stewart	.50	.23
❑ 117 Yancey Thigpen	.20	.09
❑ 118 Rod Woodson	.20	.09
❑ 119 Jerome Bettis	.30	.14
❑ 120 Isaac Bruce	.30	.14
❑ 121 Troy Drayton	.10	.05
❑ 122 Leslie O'Neal	.10	.05
❑ 123 Aaron Hayden RC	.10	.05
❑ 124 Stan Humphries	.20	.09
❑ 125 Natrone Means	.30	.14
❑ 126 Junior Seau	.20	.09
❑ 127 William Floyd	.20	.09
❑ 128 Brent Jones	.10	.05
❑ 129 Derek Loville	.10	.05
❑ 130 Ken Norton	.10	.05
❑ 131 Jerry Rice	.75	.35
❑ 132 J.J. Stokes	.30	.14
❑ 133 Steve Young	.60	.25
❑ 134 Brian Blades	.10	.05
❑ 135 Joey Galloway	.50	.23
❑ 136 Cortez Kennedy	.10	.05
❑ 137 Rick Mirer	.20	.09
❑ 138 Chris Warren	.20	.09
❑ 139 Trent Dilfer	.30	.14
❑ 140 Alvin Harper	.10	.05
❑ 141 Jackie Harris	.10	.05
❑ 142 Hardy Nickerson	.10	.05
❑ 143 Errict Rhett	.20	.09
❑ 144 Terry Allen	.20	.09
❑ 145 Henry Ellard	.10	.05
❑ 146 Brian Mitchell	.10	.05
❑ 147 Heath Shuler	.20	.09
❑ 148 Michael Westbrook	.30	.14
❑ 149 Karim Abdul-Jabbar RC	.60	.25
❑ 150 Mike Alstott RC	1.25	.55
❑ 151 Marco Battaglia RC	.10	.05
❑ 152 Tim Biakabutuka RC	.75	.35
❑ 153 Sean Boyd RC	.20	.09
❑ 154 Tony Brackens RC	.20	.09
❑ 155 Duane Clemons RC	.10	.05
❑ 156 Marcus Coleman RC	.10	.05
❑ 157 Chris Darkins RC	.10	.05
❑ 158 Rickey Dudley RC	.30	.14
❑ 159 Jason Dunn RC	.20	.09
❑ 160 Bobby Engram RC	.30	.14
❑ 161 Daryl Gardener RC	.10	.05
❑ 162 Eddie George RC	2.50	1.10
❑ 163 Terry Glenn RC	1.25	.55
❑ 164 Kevin Hardy RC	.30	.14
❑ 165 Marvin Harrison RC	2.00	.90
❑ 166 Dietrich Jells RC	.10	.05
❑ 167 DeRon Jenkins RC	.20	.09
❑ 168 Darrius Johnson RC	.10	.05
❑ 169 Keyshawn Johnson RC	2.00	.90
❑ 170 Lance Johnstone RC	.20	.09
❑ 171 Cedric Jones RC	.10	.05
❑ 172 Marcus Jones RC	.10	.05
❑ 173 Danny Kanell RC	.30	.14
❑ 174 Eddie Kennison RC	.30	.14
❑ 175 Jevon Langford RC	.10	.05
❑ 176 Markco Maddox RC	.20	.09
❑ 177 Derrick Mayes RC	.60	.25
❑ 178 Leeland McElroy RC	.30	.14
❑ 179 Dell McGee RC	.10	.05
❑ 180 Johnny McWilliams RC	.20	.09
❑ 181 Alex Molden RC	.10	.05
❑ 182 Eric Moulds RC	1.50	.70
❑ 183 Jonathan Ogden RC	.10	.05
❑ 184 Lawrence Phillips RC	.50	.23
❑ 185 Simeon Rice RC	.30	.14

❑ 186 Amani Toomer RC .... .30 .14
❑ 187 Regan Upshaw RC .... .10 .05
❑ 188 Jerome Woods RC .... .10 .05
❑ 189 Darrell Green I................ .10 .05
❑ 190 Daryl Johnston I .... .20 .09
❑ 191 Sam Mills I.......................... .10 .05
❑ 192 Earnest Byner I .... .10 .05
❑ 193 Herschel Walker I .... .20 .09
❑ 194 Brett Favre HL................ .30 .14
❑ 195 Brett Favre HL................ .30 .14
Card says Pack beat 49ers in Jan 1995
Right year is 1996 for that victory
❑ 196 Brett Favre HL................ .30 .14
❑ 197 Brett Favre HL................ .30 .14
❑ 198 Brett Favre HL................ .30 .14
❑ 199 Checklist .... .10 .05
❑ 200 Checklist .... .10 .05
❑ BF1 Brett Favre .... .50 .23
Expired SkyMotion
Exchange Card
❑ BF2 Brett Favre .... .50 .23
Expired SkyMint
Exchange Card
❑ P1 Promo Sheet................. 2.00 .90
Brett Favre
William Floyd Excelerators
Daryl Johnston Inspirations

1996 SkyBox Impact Excelerators

	MINT	NRMT
COMPLETE SET (15)	30.00	13.50
STATED ODDS 1:12		

❑ 1 Robert Brooks .... 2.00 .90
❑ 2 Isaac Bruce .... 2.00 .90
❑ 3 William Floyd.................... 1.25 .55
❑ 4 Joey Galloway.................. 3.00 1.35
❑ 5 Michael Irvin .... 2.00 .90
❑ 6 Napoleon Kaufman .... 2.00 .90
❑ 7 Anthony Miller .... 1.25 .55
❑ 8 Herman Moore .... 2.00 .90
❑ 9 Barry Sanders 10.00 4.50
❑ 10 Chris Sanders .... 1.25 .55
❑ 11 Kordell Stewart 3.00 1.35
❑ 12 Rodney Thomas .... .60 .25
❑ 13 Tamarick Vanover......... 1.25 .55
❑ 14 Ricky Watters .... 1.25 .55
❑ 15 Michael Westbrook .... 2.00 .90

1996 SkyBox Impact Intimidators

	MINT	NRMT
COMPLETE SET (10)	50.00	22.00
STATED ODDS 1:20		

❑ 1 Terrell Davis 20.00 9.00
❑ 2 Hugh Douglas .... 1.00 .45
❑ 3 Dan Marino 15.00 6.75
❑ 4 Curtis Martin 5.00 2.20
❑ 5 Carl Pickens 3.00 1.35
❑ 6 Errict Rhett .... 2.00 .90
❑ 7 Jerry Rice 8.00 3.60
❑ 8 Emmitt Smith.................. 12.00 5.50
❑ 9 Eric Swann .... 1.00 .45

❑ 10 Chris Warren.................. 2.00 .90

1996 SkyBox Impact More Attitude

	MINT	NRMT
COMPLETE SET (20)	25.00	11.00
STATED ODDS 1:3		

❑ 1 Karim Abdul-Jabbar .... 1.25 .55
❑ 2 Tim Biakabutuka .... 1.25 .55
❑ 3 Bobby Engram .... 1.25 .55
❑ 4 Daryl Gardener .... .75 .35
❑ 5 Eddie George 6.00 2.70
❑ 6 Terry Glenn 4.00 1.80
❑ 7 Kevin Hardy...................... 1.25 .55
❑ 8 Marvin Harrison............... 2.00 .90
❑ 9 DeRon Jenkins .... .75 .35
❑ 10 Keyshawn Johnson........ 2.50 1.10
❑ 11 Cedric Jones .... .75 .35
❑ 12 Eddie Kennison.............. 2.00 .90
❑ 13 Jevon Langford .... .75 .35
❑ 14 Leeland McElroy .... 1.25 .55
❑ 15 Johnny McWilliams .... .75 .35
❑ 16 Eric Moulds .... 2.00 .90
❑ 17 Lawrence Phillips .... .75 .35
❑ 18 Jonathan Ogden .... .75 .35
❑ 19 Simeon Rice .... 1.25 .55
❑ 20 Amani Toomer............... 1.25 .55

1996 SkyBox Impact No Surrender

	MINT	NRMT
COMPLETE SET (20)	100.00	45.00
STATED ODDS 1:40 HOBBY		

❑ 1 Marcus Allen 5.00 2.20
❑ 2 Jeff Blake 5.00 2.20
❑ 3 Drew Bledsoe 12.00 5.50
❑ 4 Ben Coates 3.00 1.35
❑ 5 Brett Favre 25.00 11.00
❑ 6 Terry Glenn..................... 12.00 5.50
❑ 7 Jim Harbaugh 3.00 1.35
❑ 8 Kevin Hardy....................... 3.00 1.35
❑ 9 Keyshawn Johnson........ 20.00 9.00
❑ 10 Dan Marino 25.00 11.00
❑ 11 Leeland McElroy 3.00 1.35
❑ 12 Steve McNair.................. 8.00 3.60
❑ 13 Herman Moore 5.00 2.20

❑ 14 Lawrence Phillips 5.00 2.20
❑ 15 Errict Rhett 3.00 1.35
❑ 16 Jerry Rice 12.00 5.50
❑ 17 Simeon Rice 3.00 1.35
❑ 18 Barry Sanders 25.00 11.00
❑ 19 Rodney Thomas .... 1.50 .70
❑ 20 Tyrone Wheatley........... 3.00 1.35

1996 SkyBox Impact VersaTeam

	MINT	NRMT
COMPLETE SET (10)	120.00	55.00
STATED ODDS 1:120		

❑ 1 Tim Brown........................ 6.00 2.70
❑ 2 Terrell Davis 40.00 18.00
❑ 3 John Elway 30.00 13.50
❑ 4 Marshall Faulk.................. 6.00 2.70
❑ 5 Joey Galloway................ 10.00 4.50
❑ 6 Curtis Martin 10.00 4.50
❑ 7 Deion Sanders 8.00 3.60
❑ 8 Kordell Stewart 10.00 4.50
❑ 9 Chris Warren.................... 4.00 1.80
❑ 10 Steve Young 12.00 5.50

1996 SkyBox Impact Rookies

	MINT	NRMT
COMPLETE SET (150)	12.00	5.50
COMMON CARD (1-150)............	.05	.02
SEMISTARS................................	.10	.05

UNLISTED STARS .20 .09

❑ 1 Leeland McElroy RC .20 .09
❑ 2 Johnny McWilliams .05 .02
❑ 3 Simeon Rice RC .20 .09
❑ 4 DeRon Jenkins .05 .02
❑ 5 Jermaine Lewis RC .50 .23
❑ 6 Ray Lewis .05 .02
❑ 7 Jonathan Ogden .05 .02
❑ 8 Eric Moulds RC UER 1.25 .55
card misnumbered 123
❑ 9 Tim Biakabutuka RC .60 .25
❑ 10 Muhsin Muhammad RC .60 .25
❑ 11 Winslow Oliver .05 .02
❑ 12 Bobby Engram RC .20 .09
❑ 13 Walt Harris .05 .02
❑ 14 Willie Anderson .05 .02
❑ 15 Marco Battaglia .05 .02
❑ 16 Jevon Langford .05 .02
❑ 17 Kavika Pittman .05 .02
❑ 18 Stepfret Williams .05 .02
❑ 19 Tory James .05 .02
❑ 20 Jeff Lewis RC .40 .18
❑ 21 John Mobley .05 .02
❑ 22 Detron Smith .05 .02
❑ 23 Derrick Mayes RC .60 .25
❑ 24 Eddie George RC 2.50 1.10
❑ 25 Marvin Harrison RC 1.50 .70
❑ 26 Dedric Mathis .05 .02
❑ 27 Tony Brackens RC .10 .05
❑ 28 Kevin Hardy RC .20 .09
❑ 29 Jerome Woods .05 .02
❑ 30 Karim Abdul-Jabbar RC .60 .25
❑ 31 Daryl Gardener .05 .02
❑ 32 Jerris McPhail .05 .02
❑ 33 Stanley Pritchett .05 .02
❑ 34 Zach Thomas RC .50 .23
❑ 35 Duane Clemons .05 .02
❑ 36 Moe Williams RC .10 .05
❑ 37 Tedy Bruschi .05 .02
❑ 38 Terry Glenn RC 1.00 .45
❑ 39 Alex Molden .05 .02
❑ 40 Ricky Whittle .05 .02
❑ 41 Cedric Jones .05 .02
❑ 42 Danny Kanell RC .20 .09
❑ 43 Amani Toomer RC .20 .09
❑ 44 Marcus Coleman .05 .02
❑ 45 Keyshawn Johnson RC 1.50 .70
❑ 46 Ray Mickens .05 .02
❑ 47 Alex Van Dyke RC .10 .05
❑ 48 Rickey Dudley .20 .09
❑ 49 Lance Johnstone .05 .02
❑ 50 Brian Dawkins .05 .02
❑ 51 Jason Dunn .05 .02
❑ 52 Ray Farmer .05 .02
❑ 53 Bobby Hoying RC .40 .18
❑ 54 Jermane Mayberry .05 .02
❑ 55 Bryan Still RC .20 .09
❑ 56 Tony Banks RC .75 .35
❑ 57 Ernie Conwell .05 .02
❑ 58 Eddie Kennison RC .20 .09
❑ 59 Jerald Moore RC .20 .09
❑ 60 Lawrence Phillips RC .40 .18
❑ 61 Israel Ifeanyi .05 .02
❑ 62 Terrell Owens RC 1.50 .70
❑ 63 Iheanyi Uwaezuoke RC .20 .09
❑ 64 Mike Alstott RC 1.00 .45
❑ 65 Marcus Jones .05 .02
❑ 66 Nilo Silvan .05 .02
❑ 67 Regan Upshaw .05 .02
❑ 68 Stephen Davis RC 2.50 1.10
❑ 69 Troy Aikman AIR .50 .23
❑ 70 Terry Allen AIR .10 .05
❑ 71 Edgar Bennett AIR .10 .05
❑ 72 Jerome Bettis AIR .10 .05
❑ 73 Drew Bledsoe AIR .50 .23
❑ 74 Tim Brown AIR .10 .05
❑ 75 Mark Brunell AIR .50 .23
❑ 76 Cris Carter AIR .20 .09
❑ 77 Kerry Collins AIR .20 .09
❑ 78 Terrell Davis AIR 1.25 .55
❑ 79 John Elway AIR 1.00 .45
❑ 80 Marshall Faulk AIR .20 .09
❑ 81 Brett Favre AIR 1.00 .45
❑ 82 Joey Galloway AIR .40 .18
❑ 83 Rodney Hampton AIR .05 .02
❑ 84 Jim Harbaugh AIR .10 .05
❑ 85 Michael Irvin AIR .10 .05
❑ 86 Chris T. Jones AIR .20 .09
❑ 87 Napoleon Kaufman AIR .30 .14
❑ 88 Jim Kelly AIR .20 .09
❑ 89 Dan Marino AIR 1.00 .45
❑ 90 Curtis Martin AIR .40 .18
❑ 91 Terance Mathis AIR .05 .02
❑ 92 Steve McNair AIR .40 .18
❑ 93 Anthony Miller AIR .10 .05
❑ 94 Scott Mitchell AIR .05 .02
❑ 95 Herman Moore AIR .20 .09
❑ 96 Brett Perriman AIR .05 .02
❑ 97 Carl Pickens AIR .20 .09
❑ 98 Jerry Rice AIR .50 .23
❑ 99 Andre Rison AIR .10 .05
❑ 100 Rashaan Salaam AIR .10 .05
❑ 101 Barry Sanders AIR 1.00 .45
❑ 102 Chris Sanders AIR .10 .05
❑ 103 Deion Sanders AIR .20 .09
❑ 104 Frank Sanders AIR .10 .05
❑ 105 Bruce Smith AIR .10 .05
❑ 106 Emmitt Smith AIR .75 .35
❑ 107 Robert Smith AIR .10 .05
❑ 108 Kordell Stewart AIR .40 .18
❑ 109 J.J. Stokes AIR .20 .09
❑ 110 Yancey Thigpen AIR .10 .05
❑ 111 Thurman Thomas AIR .10 .05
❑ 112 Eric Turner AIR .05 .02
❑ 113 Tamarick Vanover AIR .10 .05
❑ 114 Chris Warren AIR .10 .05
❑ 115 Ricky Watters AIR .10 .05
❑ 116 Michael Westbrook AIR .20 .09
❑ 117 Reggie White AIR .20 .09
❑ 118 Steve Young AIR .40 .18
❑ 119 Jeff Blake AIR .10 .05
❑ 120 Robert Brooks AIR .10 .05
❑ 121 Isaac Bruce RS .20 .09
❑ 122 Mark Chmura RS .10 .05
❑ 123 Wayne Chrebet RS .20 .09
see card #8
❑ 124 Ben Coates RS .10 .05
❑ 125 Ken Dilger RS .10 .05
❑ 126 Bert Emanuel RS .10 .05
❑ 127 Gus Frerotte RS .20 .09
❑ 128 Kevin Greene RS .10 .05
❑ 129 Erik Kramer RS .05 .02
❑ 130 Greg Lloyd RS .10 .05
❑ 131 Tony Martin RS .05 .02
❑ 132 Brian Mitchell RS .05 .02
❑ 133 Bryce Paup RS .05 .02
❑ 134 Jake Reed RS .10 .05
❑ 135 Errict Rhett RS .10 .05
❑ 136 Yancey Thigpen RS .10 .05
❑ 137 Tamarick Vanover RS .10 .05
❑ 138 Chris Warren RS .10 .05
❑ 139 Marcus Allen RS .20 .09
❑ 140 Jerome Bettis RS .20 .09
❑ 141 Tim Brown RRH .10 .05
❑ 142 Mark Carrier RRH .05 .02
❑ 143 Marshall Faulk RRH .10 .05
❑ 144 Tyrone Hughes RRH .05 .02
❑ 145 Dan Marino RRH 1.00 .45
❑ 146 Curtis Martin RRH .40 .18
❑ 147 Barry Sanders RRH 1.00 .45
❑ 148 Orlando Thomas RRH .05 .02
❑ 149 Checklist (1-107) UER .05 .02
card #24 missing from list
❑ 150 Checklist (108-150/inserts) .05 .02
❑ NNO Draft Exchange Card 1.00 .45
Expired 7/22/97

1996 SkyBox Impact Rookies All-Rookie Team

	MINT	NRMT
COMPLETE SET (10)	20.00	9.00
STATED ODDS 1:6		

❑ 1 Karim Abdul-Jabbar 3.00 1.35
❑ 2 Tim Biakabutuka 1.25 .55
❑ 3 Eddie George 6.00 2.70
❑ 4 Marvin Harrison 3.00 1.35
❑ 5 Keyshawn Johnson 2.50 1.10

❑ 6 Eddie Kennison 3.00 1.35
❑ 7 Lawrence Phillips 1.25 .55
❑ 8 Zach Thomas 2.50 1.10
❑ 9 Amani Toomer 1.25 .55
❑ 10 Simeon Rice 1.25 .55

1996 SkyBox Impact Rookies Draft Board

	MINT	NRMT
COMPLETE SET (20)	100.00	45.00
COMMON CARD (1-20)	3.00	1.35
SEMISTARS	5.00	2.20
STATED ODDS 1:48		

❑ 1 Terry Glenn 8.00 3.60
Rickey Dudley
Bobby Hoying
❑ 2 Simeon Rice 3.00 1.35
Kevin Hardy
❑ 3 Emmitt Smith 15.00 6.75
Errict Rhett
❑ 4 Deion Sanders 6.00 2.70
Corey Sawyer
Derrick Brooks
❑ 5 Terry Allen 5.00 2.20
Marcus Allen
❑ 6 John Mobley 3.00 1.35
Andre Reed
❑ 7 Drew Bledsoe 10.00 4.50
Rick Mirer
Mark Brunell
❑ 8 John Elway 15.00 6.75
Jim Kelly
Dan Marino
❑ 9 Carl Pickens 3.00 1.35
Anthony Miller
❑ 10 Antonio Freeman 5.00 2.20
Robert Brooks
Cedric Jones
❑ 11 Jerome Bettis 5.00 2.20
Ricky Watters
Tim Brown
❑ 12 Jerry Rice 10.00 4.50
Herman Moore
Michael Irvin
❑ 13 Terrell Davis 20.00 9.00
Rodney Hampton
Garrison Hearst
❑ 14 Kerry Collins 5.00 2.20

Ki-Jana Carter Kyle Brady		
❑ 15 Barry Sanders Thurman Thomas	15.00	6.75
❑ 16 Jermaine Lewis Jeff Lewis Ray Lewis	3.00	1.35
❑ 17 Steve Young Troy Aikman	10.00	4.50
❑ 18 Curtis Martin Chris Warren Jamal Anderson	10.00	4.50
❑ 19 Kordell Stewart Rashaan Salaam Michael Westbrook	8.00	3.60
❑ 20 Tony Banks Muhsin Muhammad	5.00	2.20

1996 SkyBox Impact Rookies 1996 Rookies

	MINT	NRMT
COMPLETE SET (10)	150.00	70.00
COMMON CARD (1-10)	6.00	2.70
STATED ODDS 1:144		
❑ 1 Karim Abdul-Jabbar	12.00	5.50
❑ 2 Tim Biakabutuka	6.00	2.70
❑ 3 Rickey Dudley	6.00	2.70
❑ 4 Eddie George	50.00	22.00
❑ 5 Terry Glenn	20.00	9.00
❑ 6 Marvin Harrison	25.00	11.00
❑ 7 Keyshawn Johnson	25.00	11.00
❑ 8 Eddie Kennison	12.00	5.50
❑ 9 Lawrence Phillips	12.00	5.50
❑ 10 Amani Toomer	6.00	2.70

1996 SkyBox Impact Rookies 1996 Rookies Autographs

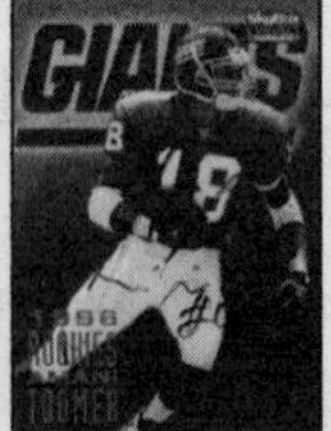

	MINT	NRMT
COMPLETE SET (6)	150.00	70.00
COMMON CARD (A1-A6)	20.00	9.00
SEMISTARS	25.00	11.00
CASE TOPPER REDEMPTION INSERT		
❑ A1 Karim Abdul-Jabbar	25.00	11.00
❑ A2 Rickey Dudley	25.00	11.00
❑ A3 Marvin Harrison	50.00	22.00
❑ A4 Eddie Kennison	25.00	11.00
❑ A5 Lawrence Phillips	25.00	11.00
❑ A6 Amani Toomer	20.00	9.00

1996 SkyBox Impact Rookies Rookie Rewind

	MINT	NRMT
COMPLETE SET (10)	30.00	13.50
COMMON CARD (1-10)	1.50	.70
SEMISTARS	2.50	1.10
STATED ODDS 1:36 HOBBY		
❑ 1 Jamal Anderson	10.00	4.50
❑ 2 Jeff Blake	2.50	1.10
❑ 3 Robert Brooks	2.50	1.10
❑ 4 Mark Brunell	6.00	2.70

❑ 5 Brett Favre	12.00	5.50
❑ 6 Aaron Hayden	1.50	.70
❑ 7 Derek Loville	1.50	.70
❑ 8 Emmitt Smith	10.00	4.50
❑ 9 Robert Smith	1.50	.70
❑ 10 Tamarick Vanover	2.50	1.10

1997 SkyBox Impact

	MINT	NRMT
COMPLETE SET (250)	15.00	6.75
COMMON CARD (1-250)	.10	.05
SEMISTARS	.20	.09
UNLISTED STARS	.40	.18
COMP.RAVE SET (250)	800.00	350.00
*RAVE STARS: 12X TO 30X HI COL.		
*RAVE RCs: 8X TO 20X		
RAVE STATED ODDS 1:36 HOBBY		
STATED PRINT RUN 150 SERIAL #'d SETS		
❑ 1 Carl Pickens	.40	.18
❑ 2 Ray Lewis	.10	.05
❑ 3 Darrell Green	.20	.09
❑ 4 Brett Favre	2.00	.90
❑ 5 Todd Collins	.10	.05
❑ 6 Errict Rhett	.10	.05
❑ 7 John Elway	2.00	.90
❑ 8 Troy Aikman	1.00	.45
❑ 9 Steve McNair	.50	.23
❑ 10 Kordell Stewart	.50	.23
❑ 11 Drew Bledsoe	1.00	.45
❑ 12 Kerry Collins	.20	.09
❑ 13 Dan Marino	2.00	.90
❑ 14 Ricky Watters	.20	.09
❑ 15 Marvin Harrison	.40	.18
❑ 16 Simeon Rice	.20	.09
❑ 17 Qadry Ismail	.20	.09
❑ 18 Andre Coleman	.10	.05
❑ 19 Keyshawn Johnson	.40	.18
❑ 20 Barry Sanders	2.00	.90
❑ 21 Rickey Dudley	.20	.09
❑ 22 Emmitt Smith	1.50	.70
❑ 23 Erik Kramer	.10	.05
❑ 24 Tony Boselli	.10	.05
❑ 25 Steve Young	.60	.25
❑ 26 Rod Woodson	.20	.09
❑ 27 Eddie George	1.00	.45
❑ 28 Curtis Martin	.50	.23
❑ 29 Amani Toomer	.20	.09
❑ 30 Terrell Davis	1.50	.70
❑ 31 Jim Everett	.10	.05
❑ 32 Marcus Allen	.40	.18
❑ 33 Karim Abdul-Jabbar	.40	.18
❑ 34 Thurman Thomas	.40	.18
❑ 35 Cortez Kennedy	.10	.05
❑ 36 Jerome Bettis	.40	.18
❑ 37 Kevin Carter	.10	.05
❑ 38 Gilbert Brown	.10	.05
❑ 39 Bert Emanuel	.20	.09
❑ 40 Kyle Brady	.10	.05
❑ 41 Trent Dilfer	.40	.18
❑ 42 Garrison Hearst	.20	.09
❑ 43 Kevin Greene	.20	.09
❑ 44 Bryan Cox	.10	.05
❑ 45 Desmond Howard	.20	.09
❑ 46 Larry Centers	.20	.09
❑ 47 Quentin Coryatt	.10	.05
❑ 48 Michael Jackson	.20	.09
❑ 49 John Randle	.10	.05
❑ 50 Mark Brunell	1.00	.45
❑ 51 William Thomas	.10	.05
❑ 52 Glyn Milburn	.10	.05
❑ 53 Mike Alstott	.40	.18
❑ 54 Chris Spielman	.10	.05
❑ 55 Junior Seau	.20	.09
❑ 56 Brian Blades	.10	.05
❑ 57 Lamar Lathon	.10	.05
❑ 58 Derrick Thomas	.20	.09
❑ 59 Dave Brown	.10	.05
❑ 60 Frank Wycheck	.10	.05
❑ 61 Chris Slade	.10	.05
❑ 62 Neil Smith	.20	.09
❑ 63 Ashley Ambrose	.10	.05
❑ 64 Alex Molden	.10	.05
❑ 65 Edgar Bennett	.20	.09
❑ 66 Alvin Harper	.10	.05
❑ 67 Jamal Anderson	.60	.25
❑ 68 Eddie Kennison	.20	.09
❑ 69 Ken Norton	.10	.05
❑ 70 Zach Thomas	.20	.09
❑ 71 Leeland McElroy	.10	.05
❑ 72 Terry Allen	.40	.18
❑ 73 Raymont Harris	.10	.05
❑ 74 Ken Dilger	.10	.05
❑ 75 Jason Dunn	.10	.05
❑ 76 Robert Smith	.20	.09
❑ 77 William Roaf	.10	.05
❑ 78 Bruce Smith	.20	.09
❑ 79 Vinny Testaverde	.20	.09
❑ 80 Jerry Rice	1.00	.45
❑ 81 Tim Brown	.40	.18
❑ 82 James O.Stewart	.20	.09
❑ 83 Andre Reed	.20	.09
❑ 84 Herman Moore	.40	.18
❑ 85 Stan Humphries	.20	.09
❑ 86 Chris Warren	.20	.09
❑ 87 Tyrone Wheatley	.20	.09
❑ 88 Michael Irvin	.40	.18
❑ 89 Dan Wilkinson	.10	.05
❑ 90 Tony Banks	.20	.09
❑ 91 Chester McGlockton	.10	.05
❑ 92 Reggie White	.40	.18
❑ 93 Elvis Grbac	.20	.09
❑ 94 Willie Davis	.10	.05
❑ 95 Greg Lloyd	.10	.05
❑ 96 Ben Coates	.20	.09
❑ 97 Rashaan Salaam	.10	.05
❑ 98 Eric Swann	.10	.05
❑ 99 Hugh Douglas	.10	.05
❑ 100 Henry Ellard	.10	.05
❑ 101 Rod Smith WR	.40	.18
❑ 102 Tim Biakabutuka	.20	.09
❑ 103 Chad Brown	.10	.05
❑ 104 Kevin Hardy	.10	.05
❑ 105 Chris T. Jones	.10	.05
❑ 106 Antonio Freeman	.50	.23
❑ 107 Lamont Warren	.10	.05
❑ 108 Derrick Alexander DE	.10	.05
❑ 109 Brett Perriman	.10	.05
❑ 110 Antonio Langham	.10	.05
❑ 111 Eric Moulds	.40	.18
❑ 112 O.J. McDuffie	.20	.09
❑ 113 Eric Metcalf	.20	.09
❑ 114 Ray Zellars	.10	.05
❑ 115 Marco Coleman	.10	.05
❑ 116 Terry Kirby	.20	.09
❑ 117 Darren Woodson	.10	.05
❑ 118 Charles Johnson	.20	.09

❑ 119 Sam Mills .10 .05
❑ 120 Rodney Hampton .20 .09
❑ 121 Rick Mirer .10 .05
❑ 122 Derrick Brooks .10 .05
❑ 123 Greg Hill .10 .05
❑ 124 John Mobley .10 .05
❑ 125 Chris Sanders .10 .05
❑ 126 Kent Graham .10 .05
❑ 127 Michael Westbrook .20 .09
❑ 128 Harvey Williams .10 .05
❑ 129 Keenan McCardell .20 .09
❑ 130 Neil O'Donnell .20 .09
❑ 131 LeRoy Butler .10 .05
❑ 132 Willie McGinest .10 .05
❑ 133 Ki-Jana Carter .10 .05
❑ 134 Robert Jones .10 .05
❑ 135 Jim Harbaugh .20 .09
❑ 136 Wesley Walls .20 .09
❑ 137 Jackie Harris .10 .05
❑ 138 Jermaine Lewis .40 .18
❑ 139 Jake Reed .20 .09
❑ 140 John Friesz .10 .05
❑ 141 Jerris McPhail .10 .05
❑ 142 Charlie Garner .10 .05
❑ 143 Bryce Paup .10 .05
❑ 144 Tony Martin .20 .09
❑ 145 Shannon Sharpe .20 .09
❑ 146 Terrell Owens .40 .18
❑ 147 Curtis Conway .20 .09
❑ 148 Jamie Asher .10 .05
❑ 149 Lawrence Phillips .10 .05
❑ 150 Deion Sanders .40 .18
❑ 151 Frank Sanders .20 .09
❑ 152 Joey Galloway .50 .23
❑ 153 Mel Gray .10 .05
❑ 154 Robert Brooks .20 .09
❑ 155 Jeff George .20 .09
❑ 156 Michael Haynes .10 .05
❑ 157 Chris Chandler .20 .09
❑ 158 Adrian Murrell .20 .09
❑ 159 Tamarick Vanover .20 .09
❑ 160 Marshall Faulk .40 .18
❑ 161 Thomas Lewis .10 .05
❑ 162 Ty Detmer .20 .09
❑ 163 Darnay Scott .20 .09
❑ 164 Byron Bam Morris .10 .05
❑ 165 Scott Mitchell .20 .09
❑ 166 Brad Johnson .50 .23
❑ 167 Dave Meggett .10 .05
❑ 168 Bobby Engram .20 .09
❑ 169 Natrone Means .40 .18
❑ 170 Eric Pegram .10 .05
❑ 171 Leonard Russell .10 .05
❑ 172 Muhsin Muhammad .20 .09
❑ 173 Aeneas Williams .10 .05
❑ 174 Fred Barnett .10 .05
❑ 175 William Floyd .20 .09
❑ 176 Kimble Anders .20 .09
❑ 177 Darick Holmes .10 .05
❑ 178 Willie Green .10 .05
❑ 179 Rodney Thomas .10 .05
❑ 180 Derrick Alexander WR .20 .09
❑ 181 Sean Dawkins .10 .05
❑ 182 Dorsey Levens .40 .18
❑ 183 Napoleon Kaufman .40 .18
❑ 184 Mario Bates .10 .05
❑ 185 Yancey Thigpen .20 .09
❑ 186 Johnnie Morton .20 .09
❑ 187 Gus Frerotte .10 .05
❑ 188 Terance Mathis .20 .09
❑ 189 Tyrone Hughes .10 .05
❑ 190 Wayne Chrebet .40 .18
❑ 191 Tony Brackens .10 .05
❑ 192 Hardy Nickerson .10 .05
❑ 193 Daryl Johnston .20 .09
❑ 194 Irving Fryar .20 .09
❑ 195 Jeff Blake .20 .09
❑ 196 Charles Way .20 .09
❑ 197 Brian Mitchell .10 .05
❑ 198 Brent Jones .20 .09
❑ 199 Mark Chmura .20 .09
❑ 200 Terry Glenn .40 .18
❑ 201 Cris Carter .40 .18
❑ 202 Steve Atwater .10 .05
❑ 203 Rob Moore .20 .09
❑ 204 Anthony Johnson .10 .05
❑ 205 Warren Moon .40 .18
❑ 206 Darrien Gordon .10 .05
❑ 207 Isaac Bruce .40 .18
❑ 208 Reidel Anthony RC .75 .35
❑ 209 Darnell Autry RC .20 .09
❑ 210 Tiki Barber RC .60 .25
❑ 211 Pat Barnes RC .40 .18
❑ 212 Terry Battle RC .10 .05
❑ 213 Michael Booker RC .10 .05
❑ 214 Peter Boulware RC .20 .09
❑ 215 Chris Canty RC .10 .05
❑ 216 Rae Carruth RC .40 .18
❑ 217 Troy Davis RC .40 .18
❑ 218 Corey Dillon RC 1.50 .70
❑ 219 Jim Druckenmiller RC .60 .25
❑ 220 Warrick Dunn RC 1.25 .55
❑ 221 James Farrior RC .10 .05
❑ 222 Tarik Glenn RC .10 .05
❑ 223 Tony Gonzalez RC 1.25 .55
❑ 224 Yatil Green RC .20 .09
❑ 225 Byron Hanspard RC .75 .35
❑ 226 Ike Hilliard RC .75 .35
❑ 227 Kenny Holmes RC .10 .05
❑ 228 Walter Jones RC .10 .05
❑ 229 Tom Knight RC .10 .05
❑ 230 David LaFleur RC .20 .09
❑ 231 Kenard Lang RC .10 .05
❑ 232 Kevin Lockett RC .20 .09
❑ 233 Tremain Mack RC .10 .05
❑ 234 Sam Madison RC .10 .05
❑ 235 Chris Naeole RC .10 .05
❑ 236 Orlando Pace RC .10 .05
❑ 237 Jake Plummer RC 3.00 1.35
❑ 238 Dwayne Rudd RC .10 .05
❑ 239 Darrell Russell RC .10 .05
❑ 240 Jamie Sharper RC .10 .05
❑ 241 Sedrick Shaw RC .40 .18
❑ 242 Antowain Smith RC 1.00 .45
❑ 243 Shawn Springs RC .20 .09
❑ 244 Bryant Westbrook RC .10 .05
❑ 245 Reinard Wilson RC .10 .05
❑ 246 Danny Wuerffel RC .60 .25
❑ 247 Renaldo Wynn RC .10 .05
❑ 248 Checklist .10 .05
❑ 249 Checklist .10 .05
❑ 250 Checklist .10 .05
❑ S1 Karim Abdul-Jabbar Sample Card .40 .18
❑ S1AU K.Abdul-Jabbar AUTO 50.00 22.00 (Sample Card Signed; Numbered of 500)

1997 SkyBox Impact Boss

	MINT	NRMT
COMPLETE SET (20)	40.00	18.00
STATED ODDS 1:6		

*SUPER BOSS STARS: 1.5X TO 3X BASE INS.
*SUPER BOSS ROOKIES: 1X TO 2X BASE INS.
SUPER BOSS STATED ODDS 1:36

❑ 1 Karim Abdul-Jabbar 1.25 .55
❑ 2 Troy Aikman 3.00 1.35
❑ 3 Tim Biakabutuka .60 .25
❑ 4 Mark Brunell 3.00 1.35
❑ 5 Rae Carruth .75 .35
❑ 6 Kerry Collins .60 .25
❑ 7 Corey Dillon 3.00 1.35
❑ 8 Jim Druckenmiller 1.25 .55
❑ 9 Warrick Dunn 2.50 1.10
❑ 10 Brett Favre 6.00 2.70
❑ 11 Eddie George 3.00 1.35
❑ 12 Marvin Harrison 1.25 .55
❑ 13 Keyshawn Johnson 1.25 .55
❑ 14 Eddie Kennison .60 .25
❑ 15 Dan Marino 6.00 2.70
❑ 16 Curtis Martin 1.50 .70
❑ 17 Steve McNair 1.50 .70
❑ 18 Orlando Pace .20 .09
❑ 19 Barry Sanders 6.00 2.70
❑ 20 Steve Young 2.00 .90

1997 SkyBox Impact Excelerators

	MINT	NRMT
COMPLETE SET (12)	60.00	27.00
STATED ODDS 1:48		

❑ 1 Mark Brunell 12.00 5.50
❑ 2 Rae Carruth 5.00 2.20
❑ 3 Terrell Davis 20.00 9.00
❑ 4 Joey Galloway 6.00 2.70
❑ 5 Marvin Harrison 5.00 2.20
❑ 6 Keyshawn Johnson 5.00 2.20
❑ 7 Eddie Kennison 2.50 1.10
❑ 8 Steve McNair 6.00 2.70
❑ 9 Jerry Rice 12.00 5.50
❑ 10 Emmitt Smith 20.00 9.00
❑ 11 Shawn Springs 2.50 1.10
❑ 12 Kordell Stewart 6.00 2.70

1997 SkyBox Impact Instant Impact

	MINT	NRMT
COMPLETE SET (15)	40.00	18.00
STATED ODDS 1:24		

❑ 1 Reidel Anthony 6.00 2.70
❑ 2 Darnell Autry 1.50 .70
❑ 3 Tiki Barber 5.00 2.20
❑ 4 Peter Boulware 1.50 .70
❑ 5 Troy Davis 3.00 1.35
❑ 6 Jim Druckenmiller 5.00 2.20
❑ 7 Warrick Dunn 10.00 4.50
❑ 8 Yatil Green 1.50 .70

		MINT	NRMT
❑ 9	Ike Hilliard	6.00	2.70
❑ 10	Orlando Pace	.75	.35
❑ 11	Darrell Russell	.75	.35
❑ 12	Sedrick Shaw	3.00	1.35
❑ 13	Shawn Springs	1.50	.70
❑ 14	Bryant Westbrook	.75	.35
❑ 15	Danny Wuerffel	5.00	2.20

1997 SkyBox Impact Rave Reviews

	MINT	NRMT
COMPLETE SET (12)	250.00	110.00
STATED ODDS 1:288		

		MINT	NRMT
❑ 1	Terrell Davis	30.00	13.50
❑ 2	John Elway	40.00	18.00
❑ 3	Brett Favre	40.00	18.00
❑ 4	Joey Galloway	10.00	4.50
❑ 5	Eddie George	20.00	9.00
❑ 6	Terry Glenn	8.00	3.60
❑ 7	Dan Marino	40.00	18.00
❑ 8	Curtis Martin	10.00	4.50
❑ 9	Jerry Rice	20.00	9.00
❑ 10	Barry Sanders	40.00	18.00
❑ 11	Deion Sanders	8.00	3.60
❑ 12	Emmitt Smith	30.00	13.50

1997 SkyBox Impact Total Impact

	MINT	NRMT
COMPLETE SET (10)	70.00	32.00
STATED ODDS 1:36 RETAIL		

		MINT	NRMT
❑ 1	Karim Abdul-Jabbar	5.00	2.20
❑ 2	Troy Aikman	12.00	5.50
❑ 3	Drew Bledsoe	12.00	5.50
❑ 4	Isaac Bruce	5.00	2.20
❑ 5	Kerry Collins	2.50	1.10
❑ 6	John Elway	25.00	11.00
❑ 7	Terry Glenn	5.00	2.20
❑ 8	Lawrence Phillips	1.25	.55
❑ 9	Deion Sanders	5.00	2.20
❑ 10	Kordell Stewart	6.00	2.70

1999 SkyBox Molten Metal

	MINT	NRMT
COMPLETE SET (151)	100.00	45.00
COMP.SET w/o SP's (125)	30.00	13.50
COMMON CARD (1-125)	.30	.14
SEMISTARS	.60	.25
UNLISTED STARS	1.25	.55
COMMON ROOKIE (126-151)	2.00	.90
ROOKIE SEMISTARS	2.50	1.10
ROOKIE SUBSET STATED ODDS 1:5		
COMP.MILLENNIUM SILV.(125)	30.00	13.50
*MILLENNIUM SILVERS: SAME PRICE		

		MINT	NRMT
❑ 1	Terrell Davis	3.00	1.35
❑ 2	Chris Chandler	.60	.25
❑ 3	Terry Glenn	1.25	.55
❑ 4	Jon Kitna	1.50	.70
❑ 5	Bubby Brister	.60	.25
❑ 6	Jermaine Lewis	.60	.25
❑ 7	Doug Flutie	1.50	.70
❑ 8	Napoleon Kaufman	1.25	.55
❑ 9	Yancey Thigpen	.30	.14
❑ 10	Bobby Engram	.60	.25
❑ 11	Barry Sanders	5.00	2.20
❑ 12	Ben Coates	.30	.14
❑ 13	Joey Galloway	1.25	.55
❑ 14	Charlie Batch	2.50	1.10
❑ 15	Jerome Bettis	1.25	.55
❑ 16	Brad Johnson	1.25	.55
❑ 17	Brian Griese	2.50	1.10
❑ 18	Jeff Lewis	.30	.14
❑ 19	Jake Plummer	2.00	.90
❑ 20	Mark Brunell	2.00	.90
❑ 21	Robert Smith	1.25	.55
❑ 22	Steve Young	2.00	.90
❑ 23	Derrick Mayes	.60	.25
❑ 24	Wayne Chrebet	1.25	.55
❑ 25	Rich Gannon	.60	.25
❑ 26	Steve McNair	1.25	.55
❑ 27	Charles Johnson	.60	.25
❑ 28	Stephen Alexander	.30	.14
❑ 29	Jeff Blake	.60	.25
❑ 30	Tony Gonzalez	.60	.25
❑ 31	Eddie Kennison	.60	.25
❑ 32	Hines Ward	.30	.14
❑ 33	Isaac Bruce	1.25	.55
❑ 34	Peyton Manning	5.00	2.20
❑ 35	Doug Pederson	.60	.25
❑ 36	Stephen Davis	1.25	.55
❑ 37	Terance Mathis	.60	.25
❑ 38	Herman Moore	1.25	.55
❑ 39	Fred Taylor	3.00	1.35
❑ 40	Courtney Hawkins	.30	.14
❑ 41	Michael Westbrook	.60	.25
❑ 42	Vinny Testaverde	.60	.25
❑ 43	Jacquez Green	.30	.14
❑ 44	Rocket Ismail	.60	.25
❑ 45	Curtis Martin	1.25	.55
❑ 46	Tim Brown	1.25	.55
❑ 47	Kevin Dyson	.60	.25
❑ 48	Steve Beuerlein	.60	.25
❑ 49	Adrian Murrell	.60	.25
❑ 50	Randall Cunningham	1.25	.55
❑ 51	Jerry Rice	3.00	1.35
❑ 52	Tim Biakabutuka	.60	.25
❑ 53	Muhsin Muhammad	.60	.25
❑ 54	Antonio Freeman	1.25	.55
❑ 55	Cris Carter	1.25	.55
❑ 56	Lawrence Phillips	.60	.25
❑ 57	Michael Irvin	.60	.25
❑ 58	Terrell Owens	1.25	.55
❑ 59	Warrick Dunn	1.25	.55
❑ 60	Leslie Shepherd	.30	.14
❑ 61	O.J. McDuffie	.60	.25
❑ 62	Byron Hanspard	.60	.25
❑ 63	Trent Dilfer	.60	.25
❑ 64	Eric Moulds	1.25	.55
❑ 65	Scott Mitchell	.60	.25
❑ 66	Marc Edwards	.30	.14
❑ 67	Dorsey Levens	1.25	.55
❑ 68	Dan Marino	5.00	2.20
❑ 69	Jason Sehorn	.30	.14
❑ 70	Junior Seau	.60	.25
❑ 71	Reidel Anthony	.30	.14
❑ 72	Rob Moore	.60	.25
❑ 73	Deion Sanders	1.25	.55
❑ 74	Rickey Dudley	.30	.14
❑ 75	Keyshawn Johnson	1.25	.55
❑ 76	Eddie George	1.50	.70
❑ 77	E.G. Green	.30	.14
❑ 78	Terry Kirby	.60	.25
❑ 79	John Avery	.60	.25
❑ 80	Pete Mitchell	.30	.14
❑ 81	Natrone Means	.60	.25
❑ 82	Mike Alstott	1.25	.55
❑ 83	Carl Pickens	.60	.25
❑ 84	Karim Abdul-Jabbar	.60	.25
❑ 85	Kerry Collins	.60	.25
❑ 86	Erik Kramer	.30	.14
❑ 87	Robert Holcombe	.30	.14
❑ 88	Willie Jackson	.30	.14
❑ 89	Marcus Pollard	.30	.14
❑ 90	Bam Morris	.30	.14
❑ 91	Gary Brown	.30	.14
❑ 92	Freddie Jones	.30	.14
❑ 93	Kurt Warner RC	20.00	9.00
❑ 94	Priest Holmes	1.25	.55
❑ 95	Duce Staley	1.25	.55
❑ 96	Skip Hicks	.60	.25
❑ 97	Frank Sanders	.60	.25
❑ 98	Corey Dillon	1.25	.55
❑ 99	Shannon Sharpe	.60	.25
❑ 100	Randy Moss	5.00	2.20
❑ 101	Sean Dawkins	.30	.14
❑ 102	Marshall Faulk	1.25	.55
❑ 103	Mark Chmura	.30	.14
❑ 104	Keenan McCardell	.60	.25
❑ 105	Jimmy Smith	.60	.25
❑ 106	Jim Harbaugh	.60	.25
❑ 107	Jamal Anderson	1.25	.55
❑ 108	Elvis Grbac	.60	.25
❑ 109	Ed McCaffrey	.60	.25
❑ 110	Drew Bledsoe	2.00	.90
❑ 111	Curtis Conway	.60	.25
❑ 112	Billy Joe Tolliver	.30	.14
❑ 113	J.J. Stokes	.60	.25
❑ 114	Curtis Enis	1.25	.55
❑ 115	Antowain Smith	1.25	.55
❑ 116	Troy Aikman	3.00	1.35
❑ 117	Ricky Watters	.60	.25
❑ 118	Kordell Stewart	1.25	.55
❑ 119	Derrick Alexander	.60	.25
❑ 120	Emmitt Smith	3.00	1.35
❑ 121	Billy Joe Hobert	.30	.14
❑ 122	Johnnie Morton	.60	.25
❑ 123	Rod Smith	.60	.25
❑ 124	Marvin Harrison	1.25	.55
❑ 125	Brett Favre	5.00	2.20
❑ 126	Craig Yeast RC	2.00	.90
❑ 127	Ricky Williams RC	15.00	6.75
❑ 128	Brandon Stokley RC	2.00	.90
❑ 129	Akili Smith RC	5.00	2.20
❑ 130	Peerless Price RC	4.00	1.80
❑ 131	Joe Montgomery RC	2.50	1.10
❑ 132	Cade McNown RC	8.00	3.60
❑ 133	Donovan McNabb RC	8.00	3.60
❑ 134	Shaun King RC	8.00	3.60
❑ 135	J.J. Johnson RC	3.00	1.35
❑ 136	Kevin Johnson RC	6.00	2.70
❑ 137	Edgerrin James RC	25.00	11.00
❑ 138	Terry Jackson RC	2.00	.90
❑ 139	Sedrick Irvin RC	2.50	1.10
❑ 140	Brock Huard RC	3.00	1.35
❑ 141	Torry Holt RC	6.00	2.70
❑ 142	Amos Zereoue RC	2.50	1.10
❑ 143	Kevin Faulk RC	3.00	1.35
❑ 144	Troy Edwards RC	4.00	1.80
❑ 145	Donald Driver RC	2.00	.90
❑ 146	Daunte Culpepper RC	8.00	3.60
❑ 147	Tim Couch RC	15.00	6.75
❑ 148	Cecil Collins RC	2.50	1.10
❑ 149	David Boston RC	4.00	1.80
❑ 150	Champ Bailey RC	3.00	1.35
❑ 151	Olandis Gary RC	8.00	3.60
❑ P133	Donovan McNabb Promo	3.00	1.35

1999 SkyBox Molten Metal Gridiron Gods

	MINT	NRMT
COMPLETE SET (20)	50.00	22.00
COMMON CARD (GG1-GG20)	2.00	.90

STATED ODDS 1:6 ....
*BLUE CARDS: 2.5X TO 6X BRONZE
BLUE STATED PRINT RUN 99 SER.#'d SETS
*GOLD CARDS: 1.5X TO 4X BRONZE
GOLD STATED ODDS 1:72..........
*SILVER CARDS: .8X TO 2X BRONZE
SILVER STATED ODDS 1:24 ......

Card	MINT	NRMT
❑ GG1 Randy Moss	6.00	2.70
❑ GG2 Keyshawn Johnson	2.00	.90
❑ GG3 Mike Alstott	2.00	.90
❑ GG4 Brian Griese	3.00	1.35
❑ GG5 Tim Couch	8.00	3.60
❑ GG6 Troy Aikman	5.00	2.20
❑ GG7 Warrick Dunn	2.00	.90
❑ GG8 Mark Brunell	3.00	1.35
❑ GG9 Jerry Rice	5.00	2.20
❑ GG10 Dorsey Levens	2.00	.90
❑ GG11 Fred Taylor	4.00	1.80
❑ GG12 Emmitt Smith	5.00	2.20
❑ GG13 Edgerrin James	12.00	5.50
❑ GG14 Eddie George	2.50	1.10
❑ GG15 Drew Bledsoe	3.00	1.35
❑ GG16 Deion Sanders	2.00	.90
❑ GG17 Charlie Batch	3.00	1.35
❑ GG18 Kordell Stewart	2.00	.90
❑ GG19 Brad Johnson	2.00	.90
❑ GG20 Akili Smith	3.00	1.35

1999 SkyBox Molten Metal Patchworks

	MINT	NRMT
COMPLETE SET (16)	1600.00	700.00
COMP.PACK SET (9)	1000.00	450.00
COMMON CARD (1-16)	60.00	27.00

STATED ODDS 1:360 HOBBY ....
FS CARDS IN FACTORY SETS ONLY

Card	MINT	NRMT
❑ 1 Drew Bledsoe	100.00	45.00
❑ 2 Randall Cunningham FS	80.00	36.00
❑ 3 Terrell Davis	100.00	45.00
❑ 4 Marshall Faulk FS	100.00	45.00
❑ 5 Brett Favre	200.00	90.00
❑ 6 Antonio Freeman FS	80.00	36.00
❑ 7 Dorsey Levens FS	80.00	36.00
❑ 8 Peyton Manning	200.00	90.00
❑ 9 Dan Marino	200.00	90.00
❑ 10 Keenan McCardell FS	60.00	27.00
❑ 11 Herman Moore	60.00	27.00
❑ 12 Randy Moss	250.00	110.00
❑ 13 Jake Plummer FS	100.00	45.00
❑ 14 Jerry Rice	150.00	70.00
❑ 15 Fred Taylor FS	100.00	45.00
❑ 16 Steve Young	100.00	45.00

1999 SkyBox Molten Metal Perfect Fit

	MINT	NRMT
COMPLETE SET (10)	60.00	27.00
COMMON CARD (PF1-PF10)	6.00	2.70

STATED ODDS 1:24 ....
*GOLD CARDS: 1.2X TO 3X BRONZE
GOLD STATED ODDS 1:216..........
*RED CARDS: 6X TO 12X BRONZE
RED STATED PRINT RUN 25 SER.#'d SETS
*SILVER CARDS: .6X TO 1.5X BRONZE
SILVER STATED ODDS 1:72 ......

Card	MINT	NRMT
❑ PF1 Barry Sanders	12.00	5.50
❑ PF2 Brett Favre	12.00	5.50
❑ PF3 Dan Marino	12.00	5.50
❑ PF4 Edgerrin James	20.00	9.00
❑ PF5 Emmitt Smith	8.00	3.60
❑ PF6 Fred Taylor	6.00	2.70
❑ PF7 Randy Moss	10.00	4.50
❑ PF8 Terrell Davis	8.00	3.60
❑ PF9 Tim Couch	12.00	5.50
❑ PF10 Peyton Manning	10.00	4.50

1999 SkyBox Molten Metal Top Notch

	MINT	NRMT
COMPLETE SET (15)	50.00	22.00
COMMON CARD (TN1-TN15)	2.50	1.10

STATED ODDS 1:12 ....
*GOLD CARDS: 1.2X TO 3X BRONZE
GOLD STATED ODDS 1:108........
*GREEN CARDS: 3X TO 8X BRONZE
GREEN STATED PRINT RUN 75 SER.#'d SETS
*SILVER CARDS: .6X TO 1.5X BRONZE
SILVER STATED ODDS 1:36 ......

Card	MINT	NRMT
❑ TN1 Jake Plummer	4.00	1.80
❑ TN2 Cade McNown	6.00	2.70
❑ TN3 Tim Couch	10.00	4.50
❑ TN4 Emmitt Smith	6.00	2.70
❑ TN5 Charlie Batch	4.00	1.80
❑ TN6 Donovan McNabb	6.00	2.70
❑ TN7 Steve Young	4.00	1.80
❑ TN8 Brian Griese	4.00	1.80
❑ TN9 Doug Flutie	3.00	1.35
❑ TN10 Edgerrin James	15.00	6.75
❑ TN11 Fred Taylor	5.00	2.20
❑ TN12 Keyshawn Johnson	2.50	1.10
❑ TN13 Mark Brunell	4.00	1.80
❑ TN14 Randy Moss	8.00	3.60
❑ TN15 Ricky Williams	10.00	4.50

1993 SkyBox Premium

	MINT	NRMT
COMPLETE SET (270)	30.00	13.50
COMMON CARD (1-270)	.10	.05
SEMISTARS	.20	.09
UNLISTED STARS	.40	.18
COMP.POSTER CARDS (10)	5.00	2.20

POSTER CARDS:RANDOM INSERTS IN PACKS ....

Card	MINT	NRMT
❑ 1 Eric Martin	.10	.05
❑ 2 Earnest Byner	.10	.05
❑ 3 Ricky Proehl	.10	.05
❑ 4 Mark Carrier WR	.20	.09
❑ 5 Shannon Sharpe	.40	.18
❑ 6 Anthony Thompson	.10	.05
❑ 7 Drew Bledsoe RC	6.00	2.70
❑ 8 Tom Carter RC	.20	.09
❑ 9 Ryan McNeil RC	.10	.05
❑ 10 Troy Aikman	1.50	.70
❑ 11 Robert Jones	.10	.05
❑ 12 Rodney Peete	.10	.05
❑ 13 Wendell Davis	.10	.05
❑ 14 Thurman Thomas	.40	.18
❑ 15 John Stephens	.10	.05
❑ 16 Rodney Hampton	.40	.18
❑ 17 Eric Bieniemy	.10	.05
❑ 18 Santana Dotson	.20	.09
❑ 19 Jeff George	.40	.18
❑ 20 John L. Williams	.10	.05
❑ 21 Barry Word	.10	.05
❑ 22 Chris Miller	.20	.09
❑ 23 Jeff Hostetler	.20	.09
❑ 24 Dwight Stone	.10	.05
❑ 25 Brad Baxter	.10	.05
❑ 26 Randall Cunningham	.40	.18
❑ 27 Mark Higgs	.10	.05
❑ 28 Vaughn Dunbar	.10	.05
❑ 29 Ricky Ervins	.10	.05
❑ 30 Johnny Bailey	.10	.05
❑ 31 Michael Jackson	.20	.09
❑ 32 Mike Croel	.10	.05
❑ 33 Steve Young	1.50	.70
❑ 34 Deon Figures RC	.20	.09
❑ 35 Robert Smith RC	2.00	.90
❑ 36 Irv Smith RC	.10	.05
❑ 37 Charles Haley	.20	.09
❑ 38 Cris Dishman	.10	.05
❑ 39 Barry Sanders	3.00	1.35
❑ 40 Jim Harbaugh	.40	.18
❑ 41 Darryl Talley	.10	.05
❑ 42 Jackie Harris	.10	.05
❑ 43 Phil Simms	.20	.09
❑ 44 Marion Butts	.10	.05
❑ 45 Anthony Munoz	.20	.09
❑ 46 Steve Emtman	.10	.05
❑ 47 Kelvin Martin	.10	.05
❑ 48 Joe Montana	3.00	1.35

❑ 49 Andre Rison .20 .09
❑ 50 Ethan Horton .10 .05
❑ 51 Kevin Greene .40 .18
❑ 52 Browning Nagle .10 .05
❑ 53 Tim Harris .10 .05
❑ 54 Keith Byars .10 .05
❑ 55 Terry Allen .40 .18
❑ 56 Chip Lohmiller .10 .05
❑ 57 Robert Massey .10 .05
❑ 58 Michael Dean Perry .20 .09
❑ 59 Tommy Maddox .10 .05
❑ 60 Jerry Rice 2.00 .90
❑ 61 Lincoln Kennedy RC .10 .05
❑ 62 Jerome Bettis RC 2.00 .90
❑ 63 Coleman Rudolph RC .10 .05
❑ 64 Emmitt Smith 3.00 1.35
❑ 65 Curtis Duncan .10 .05
❑ 66 Andre Ware .10 .05
❑ 67 Neal Anderson .10 .05
❑ 68 Jim Kelly .40 .18
❑ 69 Reggie White .40 .18
❑ 70 Dave Meggett .10 .05
❑ 71 Junior Seau .40 .18
❑ 72 Courtney Hawkins .10 .05
❑ 73 Clarence Verdin .10 .05
❑ 74 Tommy Kane .10 .05
❑ 75 Dale Carter .10 .05
❑ 76 Michael Haynes .20 .09
❑ 77 Willie Gault .10 .05
❑ 78 Eric Green .10 .05
❑ 79 Ronnie Lott .20 .09
❑ 80 Vai Sikahema .10 .05
❑ 81 Mark Ingram .10 .05
❑ 82 Anthony Carter .20 .09
❑ 83 Mark Rypien .10 .05
❑ 84 Gary Clark .20 .09
❑ 85 Bernie Kosar .20 .09
❑ 86 Cleveland Gary .10 .05
❑ 87 Tom Rathman .10 .05
❑ 88 Tony McGee RC .20 .09
❑ 89 Rick Mirer RC .75 .35
❑ 90 John Copeland RC .20 .09
❑ 91 Michael Irvin .40 .18
❑ 92 Wilber Marshall .10 .05
❑ 93 Mel Gray .20 .09
❑ 94 Craig Heyward .20 .09
❑ 95 Don Beebe .10 .05
❑ 96 Andre Tippett .10 .05
❑ 97 Derek Brown TE .10 .05
❑ 98 Ronnie Harmon .10 .05
❑ 99 Derrick Fenner .10 .05
❑ 100 Rodney Culver .10 .05
❑ 101 Cortez Kennedy .20 .09
❑ 102 Marcus Allen .40 .18
❑ 103 Steve Broussard .10 .05
❑ 104 Tim Brown .40 .18
❑ 105 Merril Hoge .10 .05
❑ 106 Chris Burkett .10 .05
❑ 107 Fred Barnett .20 .09
❑ 108 Dan Marino 3.00 1.35
❑ 109 Chris Doleman .10 .05
❑ 110 Art Monk .20 .09
❑ 111 Ernie Jones .10 .05
❑ 112 Jay Hilgenberg .10 .05
❑ 113 Jim Everett .20 .09
❑ 114 John Taylor .20 .09
❑ 115 Steve Everitt RC .10 .05
❑ 116 Carlton Gray RC .10 .05
❑ 117 Eric Curry RC .10 .05
❑ 118 Ken Norton Jr. .20 .09
❑ 119 Lorenzo White .10 .05
❑ 120 Pat Swilling .10 .05
❑ 121 William Perry .20 .09
❑ 122 Brett Favre 4.00 1.80
❑ 123 Jon Vaughn .10 .05
❑ 124 Mark Jackson .10 .05
❑ 125 Stan Humphries .40 .18
❑ 126 Harold Green .10 .05
❑ 127 Anthony Johnson .20 .09
❑ 128 Brian Blades .20 .09
❑ 129 Willie Davis .40 .18
❑ 130 Bobby Hebert .10 .05
❑ 131 Terry McDaniel .10 .05
❑ 132 Jeff Graham .20 .09
❑ 133 Jeff Lageman .10 .05
❑ 134 Andre Waters .10 .05
❑ 135 Steve Walsh .10 .05
❑ 136 Cris Carter .75 .35
❑ 137 Tim McGee .10 .05
❑ 138 Chuck Cecil .10 .05
❑ 139 John Elway 3.00 1.35
❑ 140 Todd Lyght .10 .05
❑ 141 Brent Jones .20 .09
❑ 142 Patrick Bates RC .10 .05
❑ 143 Darrien Gordon RC .10 .05
❑ 144 Michael Strahan RC .10 .05
❑ 145 Jay Novacek .20 .09
❑ 146 Warren Moon .40 .18
❑ 147 Rodney Holman .10 .05
❑ 148 Anthony Morgan .10 .05
❑ 149 Sterling Sharpe .40 .18
❑ 150 Leonard Russell .20 .09
❑ 151 Lawrence Taylor .40 .18
❑ 152 Leslie O'Neal .20 .09
❑ 153 Carl Pickens .40 .18
❑ 154 Aaron Cox .10 .05
❑ 155 Ferrell Edmunds .10 .05
❑ 156 Neil O'Donnell .40 .18
❑ 157 Tony Smith .10 .05
❑ 158 James Lofton .20 .09
❑ 159 George Teague RC .20 .09
❑ 160 Boomer Esiason .20 .09
❑ 161 Eric Allen .10 .05
❑ 162 Floyd Turner .10 .05
❑ 163 Esera Tuaolo .10 .05
❑ 164 Darrell Green .10 .05
❑ 165 Steve Beuerlein .10 .05
❑ 166 Vance Johnson .10 .05
❑ 167 Flipper Anderson .10 .05
❑ 168 Ricky Watters .40 .18
❑ 169 Marvin Jones RC .10 .05
❑ 170 Dana Stubblefield RC .40 .18
❑ 171 Willie Roaf RC .20 .09
❑ 172 Russell Maryland .10 .05
❑ 173 Ernest Givins .20 .09
❑ 174 Willie Green .10 .05
❑ 175 Bruce Smith .40 .18
❑ 176 Terrell Buckley .10 .05
❑ 177 Scott Zolak .10 .05
❑ 178 Mike Sherrard .10 .05
❑ 179 Lawrence Dawsey .10 .05
❑ 180 Jay Schroeder .10 .05
❑ 181 Quentin Coryatt .20 .09
❑ 182 Harvey Williams .20 .09
❑ 183 Natrone Means RC 1.50 .70
❑ 184 Eric Dickerson .20 .09
❑ 185 Gaston Green .10 .05
❑ 186 Thomas Smith RC .20 .09
❑ 187 Johnny Johnson .10 .05
❑ 188 Marco Coleman .10 .05
❑ 189 Wade Wilson .10 .05
❑ 190 Rich Gannon .10 .05
❑ 191 Brian Mitchell .20 .09
❑ 192 Eric Metcalf .20 .09
❑ 193 Robert Delpino .10 .05
❑ 194 Shane Conlan .10 .05
❑ 195 Dexter Carter .10 .05
❑ 196 Garrison Hearst RC 2.00 .90
❑ 197 Chris Slade RC .20 .09
❑ 198 Troy Drayton RC .20 .09
❑ 199 Lin Elliott .10 .05
❑ 200 Haywood Jeffires .20 .09
❑ 201 Herman Moore 1.00 .45
❑ 202 Cornelius Bennett .20 .09
❑ 203 Mark Clayton .10 .05
❑ 204 Marv Cook .10 .05
❑ 205 Stephen Baker .10 .05
❑ 206 Gary Anderson RB .10 .05
❑ 207 Eddie Brown .10 .05
❑ 208 Will Wolford .10 .05
❑ 209 Derrick Thomas .40 .18
❑ 210 Seth Joyner .10 .05
❑ 211 Mike Pritchard .20 .09
❑ 212 Rod Woodson .40 .18
❑ 213 Todd Kelly RC .10 .05
❑ 214 Rob Moore .20 .09
❑ 215 Keith Jackson .20 .09
❑ 216 Wesley Carroll .10 .05
❑ 217 Steve Jordan .10 .05
❑ 218 Ricky Sanders .10 .05
❑ 219 Tommy Vardell .10 .05
❑ 220 Rod Bernstine .10 .05
❑ 221 Henry Ellard .20 .09
❑ 222 Amp Lee .10 .05
❑ 223 O.J. McDuffie RC 1.50 .70
❑ 224 Carl Simpson RC .10 .05
❑ 225 Dan Williams RC .10 .05
❑ 226 Thomas Everett .10 .05
❑ 227 Webster Slaughter .10 .05
❑ 228 Trace Armstrong .10 .05
❑ 229 Kenneth Davis .10 .05
❑ 230 Tony Bennett .10 .05
❑ 231 Reyna Thompson .10 .05
❑ 232 Anthony Miller .20 .09
❑ 233 Reggie Cobb .10 .05
❑ 234 Mark Duper .10 .05
❑ 235 Chris Warren .20 .09
❑ 236 Christian Okoye .10 .05
❑ 237 Irving Fryar .20 .09
❑ 238 Deion Sanders .75 .35
❑ 239 Barry Foster .20 .09
❑ 240 Ernest Dye RC .10 .05
❑ 241 Calvin Williams .20 .09
❑ 242 Louis Oliver .10 .05
❑ 243 Dalton Hilliard .10 .05
❑ 244 Roger Craig .20 .09
❑ 245 Randal Hill .10 .05
❑ 246 Vinny Testaverde .20 .09
❑ 247 Steve Atwater .10 .05
❑ 248 Jim Price .10 .05
❑ 249 Martin Harrison RC .10 .05
❑ 250 Curtis Conway RC 1.00 .45
❑ 251 Demetrius DuBose RC .10 .05
❑ 252 Leonard Renfro RC .10 .05
❑ 253 Alvin Harper .20 .09
❑ 254 Leonard Harris .10 .05
❑ 255 Tom Waddle .10 .05
❑ 256 Andre Reed .20 .09
❑ 257 Sanjay Beach .10 .05
❑ 258 Michael Timpson .10 .05
❑ 259 Nate Lewis .10 .05
❑ 260 Steve DeBerg .10 .05
❑ 261 David Klingler .10 .05
❑ 262 Dan McGwire .10 .05
❑ 263 Dave Krieg .20 .09
❑ 264 Brad Muster .10 .05
❑ 265 Nick Bell .10 .05
❑ 266 Checklist 1 .10 .05
❑ 267 Checklist 2 .10 .05
❑ 268 Checklist 3 .10 .05
❑ 269 Checklist 4 .10 .05
❑ 270 Checklist 5 .10 .05
❑ P1 Promo Panel 2.00 .90
Jim Kelly
Derrick Thomas
Lawrence Taylor
Neal Anderson
Marco Coleman
Chris Doleman
❑ P2 Promo Panel 2.00 .90
Lawrence Taylor
Chris Doleman
Jim Kelly
Michael Irvin
Neal Anderson
Derrick Thomas

1993 SkyBox Premium Prime Time Rookies

	MINT	NRMT
COMPLETE SET (10)	50.00	22.00
COMMON CARD (PR1-PR10)	2.00	.90
SEMISTARS	3.00	1.35
RANDOM INSERTS IN PACKS		
❑ 1 Patrick Bates	2.00	.90
❑ 2 Drew Bledsoe	20.00	9.00
❑ 3 Darrien Gordon	2.00	.90
❑ 4 Garrison Hearst	8.00	3.60
❑ 5 Marvin Jones	2.00	.90
❑ 6 Terry Kirby	3.00	1.35
❑ 7 Natrone Means	6.00	2.70
❑ 8 Rick Mirer	4.00	1.80
❑ 9 Willie Roaf	3.00	1.35
❑ 10 Dan Williams	2.00	.90

1993 SkyBox Premium Thunder and Lightning

	MINT	NRMT
COMPLETE SET (9)	20.00	9.00
COMMON PAIR (TL1-TL9)	1.50	.70
SEMISTARS	2.50	1.10
UNLISTED STARS	4.00	1.80
RANDOM INSERTS IN PACKS		
❑ 1 Jim Kelly Thurman Thomas	4.00	1.80
❑ 2 Randall Cunningham Fred Barnett	4.00	1.80
❑ 3 Dan Marino Keith Jackson	8.00	3.60
❑ 4 Sam Mills Vaughan Johnson	1.50	.70
❑ 5 Warren Moon Haywood Jeffires	2.50	1.10
❑ 6 Troy Aikman Michael Irvin	5.00	2.20
❑ 7 Brett Favre Sterling Sharpe	8.00	3.60
❑ 8 Steve Young Jerry Rice	6.00	2.70
❑ 9 Dennis Smith Steve Atwater	1.50	.70

1994 SkyBox Premium

	MINT	NRMT
COMPLETE SET (200)	25.00	11.00
COMMON CARD (1-200)	.10	.05
SEMISTARS	.20	.09
UNLISTED STARS	.40	.18
COMP. QB AUTO SET (3)	200.00	90.00
QB AUTO.STATED ODDS 1:9000		
❑ 1 Steve Beuerlein	.10	.05
❑ 2 Gary Clark	.20	.09
❑ 3 Garrison Hearst	.40	.18
❑ 4 Ronald Moore	.10	.05
❑ 5 Eric Swann	.20	.09
❑ 6 Chuck Cecil	.10	.05
❑ 7 Seth Joyner	.10	.05
❑ 8 Clyde Simmons	.10	.05
❑ 9 Andre Rison	.20	.09
❑ 10 Deion Sanders	.50	.23
❑ 11 Erric Pegram	.10	.05
❑ 12 Steve Broussard	.10	.05
❑ 13 Chris Doleman	.10	.05
❑ 14 Jeff George	.40	.18
❑ 15 Cornelius Bennett	.20	.09
❑ 16 Jim Kelly	.40	.18
❑ 17 Andre Reed	.20	.09
❑ 18 Bruce Smith	.40	.18
❑ 19 Darryl Talley	.10	.05
❑ 20 Thurman Thomas	.40	.18
❑ 21 Mark Carrier DB	.10	.05
❑ 22 Dante Jones	.10	.05
❑ 23 Curtis Conway	.40	.18
❑ 24 Tim Worley	.10	.05
❑ 25 Erik Kramer	.20	.09
❑ 26 John Copeland	.10	.05
❑ 27 David Klingler	.10	.05
❑ 28 Derrick Fenner	.10	.05
❑ 29 Harold Green	.10	.05
❑ 30 Carl Pickens	.40	.18
❑ 31 Tony McGee	.10	.05
❑ 32 Steve Everitt	.10	.05
❑ 33 Michael Jackson	.20	.09
❑ 34 Eric Metcalf	.20	.09
❑ 35 Vinny Testaverde	.20	.09
❑ 36 Michael Dean Perry	.20	.09
❑ 37 Troy Aikman	1.50	.70
❑ 38 Alvin Harper	.20	.09
❑ 39 Michael Irvin	.40	.18
❑ 40 Jay Novacek	.20	.09
❑ 41 Emmitt Smith	2.50	1.10
❑ 42 Charles Haley	.20	.09
❑ 43 Daryl Johnston	.20	.09
❑ 44 Kevin Williams	.20	.09
❑ 45 Rodney Peete	.10	.05
❑ 46 John Elway	3.00	1.35
❑ 47 Shannon Sharpe	.20	.09
❑ 48 Rod Bernstine	.10	.05
❑ 49 Glyn Milburn	.20	.09
❑ 50 Mike Pritchard	.10	.05
❑ 51 Anthony Miller	.20	.09
❑ 52 Herman Moore	.40	.18
❑ 53 Barry Sanders	3.00	1.35
❑ 54 Scott Mitchell	.40	.18
❑ 55 Pat Swilling	.10	.05
❑ 56 Willie Green	.10	.05
❑ 57 Edgar Bennett	.40	.18
❑ 58 Brett Favre	3.00	1.35
❑ 59 Sterling Sharpe	.20	.09
❑ 60 Reggie White	.40	.18
❑ 61 Sean Jones	.10	.05
❑ 62 Reggie Cobb	.10	.05
❑ 63 Haywood Jeffires	.20	.09
❑ 64 Lorenzo White	.10	.05
❑ 65 Webster Slaughter	.10	.05
❑ 66 Gary Brown	.10	.05
❑ 67 Steve Emtman	.10	.05
❑ 68 Quentin Coryatt	.10	.05
❑ 69 Sean Dawkins RC	.40	.18
❑ 70 Jim Harbaugh	.40	.18
❑ 71 Tony Bennett	.10	.05
❑ 72 Marcus Allen	.40	.18
❑ 73 Steve Bono	.20	.09
❑ 74 Dale Carter	.10	.05
❑ 75 Joe Montana	3.00	1.35
❑ 76 Neil Smith	.40	.18
❑ 77 Derrick Thomas	.40	.18
❑ 78 Keith Cash	.10	.05
❑ 79 Tim Brown	.40	.18
❑ 80 Rocket Ismail	.20	.09
❑ 81 Jeff Hostetler	.20	.09
❑ 82 Patrick Bates	.10	.05
❑ 83 James Jett	.10	.05
❑ 84 Jerome Bettis	.40	.18
❑ 85 Chris Miller	.10	.05
❑ 86 Marc Boutte	.10	.05
❑ 87 Sean Gilbert	.10	.05
❑ 88 Keith Jackson	.10	.05
❑ 89 Terry Kirby	.40	.18
❑ 90 Dan Marino	3.00	1.35
❑ 91 Bryan Cox	.10	.05
❑ 92 Bernie Kosar	.20	.09
❑ 93 Qadry Ismail	.40	.18
❑ 94 Robert Smith	.40	.18
❑ 95 Terry Allen	.20	.09
❑ 96 Scottie Graham RC	.20	.09
❑ 97 Warren Moon	.40	.18
❑ 98 Drew Bledsoe	2.00	.90
❑ 99 Ben Coates	.40	.18
❑ 100 Leonard Russell	.10	.05
❑ 101 Vincent Brisby	.40	.18
❑ 102 Marion Butts	.10	.05
❑ 103 Morten Andersen	.10	.05
❑ 104 Derek Brown RBK	.10	.05
❑ 105 Michael Haynes	.20	.09
❑ 106 Sam Mills	.10	.05
❑ 107 Lorenzo Neal	.10	.05
❑ 108 Willie Roaf	.10	.05
❑ 109 Jim Everett	.20	.09
❑ 110 Michael Brooks	.10	.05
❑ 111 Rodney Hampton	.40	.18
❑ 112 Dave Brown	.20	.09
❑ 113 Dave Meggett	.10	.05
❑ 114 Ronnie Lott	.20	.09
❑ 115 Boomer Esiason	.20	.09
❑ 116 Rob Moore	.20	.09
❑ 117 Johnny Johnson	.10	.05
❑ 118 Marvin Jones	.10	.05
❑ 119 Johnny Mitchell	.10	.05
❑ 120 Fred Barnett	.20	.09
❑ 121 Randall Cunningham	.40	.18
❑ 122 Herschel Walker	.20	.09
❑ 123 Calvin Williams	.20	.09
❑ 124 Neil O'Donnell	.40	.18
❑ 125 Eric Green	.10	.05
❑ 126 Leroy Thompson	.10	.05
❑ 127 Rod Woodson	.40	.18
❑ 128 Barry Foster	.10	.05
❑ 129 Deon Figures	.10	.05
❑ 130 John L. Williams	.10	.05
❑ 131 Chris Mims	.10	.05
❑ 132 Darrien Gordon	.10	.05
❑ 133 Stan Humphries	.40	.18
❑ 134 Natrone Means	.40	.18
❑ 135 Junior Seau	.40	.18
❑ 136 Brent Jones	.20	.09
❑ 137 Jerry Rice	1.50	.70
❑ 138 Dana Stubblefield	.40	.18
❑ 139 John Taylor	.20	.09
❑ 140 Ricky Watters	.40	.18
❑ 141 Steve Young	1.25	.55
❑ 142 Ken Norton Jr.	.20	.09
❑ 143 Brian Blades	.20	.09
❑ 144 Cortez Kennedy	.20	.09
❑ 145 Kelvin Martin	.10	.05
❑ 146 Rick Mirer	.40	.18
❑ 147 Chris Warren	.20	.09
❑ 148 Eric Curry	.10	.05
❑ 149 Santana Dotson	.20	.09
❑ 150 Craig Erickson	.10	.05
❑ 151 Hardy Nickerson	.20	.09
❑ 152 Paul Gruber	.10	.05
❑ 153 Reggie Brooks	.20	.09
❑ 154 Tom Carter	.10	.05
❑ 155 Desmond Howard	.20	.09
❑ 156 Ken Harvey	.10	.05
❑ 157 Dan Wilkinson RC	.20	.09
❑ 158 Marshall Faulk RC	5.00	2.20
❑ 159 Heath Shuler RC	.40	.18
❑ 160 Willie McGinest RC	.40	.18
❑ 161 Trev Alberts RC	.20	.09
❑ 162 Trent Dilfer RC	2.00	.90
❑ 163 Bryant Young RC	.40	.18
❑ 164 Sam Adams RC	.20	.09
❑ 165 Antonio Langham RC	.20	.09
❑ 166 Jamir Miller RC	.10	.05
❑ 167 John Thierry RC	.10	.05

❑ 168 Aaron Glenn RC	.20	.09
❑ 169 Joe Johnson RC	.10	.05
❑ 170 Bernard Williams RC	.10	.05
❑ 171 Wayne Gandy RC	.10	.05
❑ 172 Aaron Taylor RC	.10	.05
❑ 173 Charles Johnson RC	.40	.18
❑ 174 Dewayne Washington RC	.20	.09
❑ 175 Todd Steussie RC	.20	.09
❑ 176 Tim Bowens RC	.20	.09
❑ 177 Johnnie Morton RC	1.25	.55
❑ 178 Rob Fredrickson	.20	.09
❑ 179 Shante Carver RC	.10	.05
❑ 180 Thomas Lewis RC	.20	.09
❑ 181 Greg Hill RC	1.00	.45
❑ 182 Henry Ford RC	.10	.05
❑ 183 Jeff Burris RC	.20	.09
❑ 184 William Floyd RC	.40	.18
❑ 185 Derrick Alexander WR RC	1.00	.45
❑ 186 Glenn Foley RC	.40	.18
❑ 187 Charlie Garner RC	2.00	.90
❑ 188 Errict Rhett RC	2.00	.90
❑ 189 Chuck Levy RC	.10	.05
❑ 190 Byron Bam Morris RC	.40	.18
❑ 191 Donnell Bennett RC	.40	.18
❑ 192 LeShon Johnson RC	.20	.09
❑ 193 Mario Bates RC	.40	.18
❑ 194 David Palmer RC	1.00	.45
❑ 195 Darnay Scott RC	1.25	.55
❑ 196 Lake Dawson RC	.40	.18
❑ 197 Checklist	.10	.05
❑ 198 Checklist	.10	.05
❑ 199 Checklist	.10	.05
❑ 200 Checklist for Inserts	.10	.05
❑ NNO NFL Anniversary Commemorative	.30	.14

1994 SkyBox Premium Inside the Numbers

	MINT	NRMT
COMPLETE SET (20)	15.00	6.75
ONE PER SPECIAL RETAIL PACK		
❑ 1 Jim Kelly	.75	.35
❑ 2 Ronnie Lott	.40	.18
❑ 3 Morten Andersen	.20	.09
❑ 4 Reggie White	.75	.35
❑ 5 Terry Kirby	.75	.35
❑ 6 Marcus Allen	.75	.35
❑ 7 Thurman Thomas	.75	.35
❑ 8 Joe Montana	6.00	2.70
❑ 9 Tom Carter	.20	.09
❑ 10 Jerome Bettis	.75	.35
❑ 11 Sterling Sharpe	.40	.18
❑ 12 Andre Rison	.40	.18
❑ 13 Reggie Brooks	.40	.18
❑ 14 Hardy Nickerson	.40	.18
❑ 15 Ricky Watters	.75	.35
❑ 16 Gary Brown	.20	.09
❑ 17 Natrone Means	.75	.35
❑ 18 LeShon Johnson	.25	.11
❑ 19 Errict Rhett	2.50	1.10
❑ 20 Trent Dilfer	2.50	1.10

1994 SkyBox Premium Revolution

	MINT	NRMT
COMPLETE SET (15)	30.00	13.50
STATED ODDS 1:20		
❑ R1 Jim Kelly	1.25	.55
❑ R2 Thurman Thomas	1.25	.55
❑ R3 Troy Aikman	5.00	2.20
❑ R4 Michael Irvin	1.25	.55
❑ R5 Emmitt Smith	8.00	3.60
❑ R6 John Elway	10.00	4.50
❑ R7 Barry Sanders	10.00	4.50
❑ R8 Sterling Sharpe	.60	.25
❑ R9 Joe Montana	10.00	4.50
❑ R10 Jerome Bettis	1.25	.55
❑ R11 Dan Marino	10.00	4.50
❑ R12 Drew Bledsoe	6.00	2.70
❑ R13 Jerry Rice	5.00	2.20
❑ R14 Steve Young	4.00	1.80
❑ R15 Rick Mirer	1.25	.55

1994 SkyBox Premium Prime Time Rookies

	MINT	NRMT
COMPLETE SET (10)	60.00	27.00
STATED ODDS 1:96		
❑ PT1 Trent Dilfer	12.00	5.50
❑ PT2 Heath Shuler	2.50	1.10
❑ PT3 Marshall Faulk	30.00	13.50
❑ PT4 Charlie Garner	12.00	5.50
❑ PT5 Errict Rhett	12.00	5.50
❑ PT6 Greg Hill	6.00	2.70
❑ PT7 William Floyd	2.50	1.10
❑ PT8 Charles Johnson	2.50	1.10
❑ PT9 Derrick Alexander WR	6.00	2.70
❑ PT10 David Palmer	6.00	2.70

1994 SkyBox Premium SkyTech Stars

	MINT	NRMT
COMPLETE SET (30)	30.00	13.50
STATED ODDS 1:6		
❑ ST1 Troy Aikman	4.00	1.80
❑ ST2 Emmitt Smith	6.00	2.70
❑ ST3 Michael Irvin	1.00	.45
❑ ST4 John Elway	8.00	3.60
❑ ST5 Sterling Sharpe	.50	.23
❑ ST6 Joe Montana	8.00	3.60
❑ ST7 Drew Bledsoe	5.00	2.20
❑ ST8 Rick Mirer	1.00	.45
❑ ST9 Junior Seau	1.00	.45
❑ ST10 Jerome Bettis	1.00	.45
❑ ST11 Rod Woodson	1.00	.45
❑ ST12 Tim Brown	1.00	.45
❑ ST13 Jeff George	1.00	.45
❑ ST14 Brett Favre	8.00	3.60
❑ ST15 Reggie White	1.00	.45
❑ ST16 Cortez Kennedy	.50	.23
❑ ST17 Ricky Watters	1.00	.45
❑ ST18 Shannon Sharpe	.50	.23
❑ ST19 Reggie Brooks	.50	.23
❑ ST20 Heath Shuler	.50	.23
❑ ST21 Marshall Faulk	6.00	2.70
❑ ST22 Thurman Thomas	1.00	.45
❑ ST23 Barry Foster	.25	.11
❑ ST24 Sean Gilbert	.25	.11
❑ ST25 Jerry Rice	4.00	1.80
❑ ST26 Andre Rison	.50	.23
❑ ST27 Barry Sanders	8.00	3.60
❑ ST28 Jim Kelly	1.00	.45
❑ ST29 Steve Young	3.00	1.35
❑ ST30 Dan Marino	8.00	3.60

1995 SkyBox Premium

	MINT	NRMT
COMPLETE SET (200)	20.00	9.00
COMMON CARD (1-200)	.10	.05
SEMISTARS	.20	.09
UNLISTED STARS	.40	.18
COMP.ROOKIE REC.SET (8)	6.00	2.70
ONE SET PER SPECIAL RETAIL BOX		
❑ 1 Garrison Hearst	.40	.18
❑ 2 Dave Krieg	.10	.05
❑ 3 Rob Moore	.10	.05
❑ 4 Eric Swann	.20	.09
❑ 5 Larry Centers	.20	.09
❑ 6 Jeff George	.20	.09
❑ 7 Craig Heyward	.20	.09
❑ 8 Terance Mathis	.20	.09
❑ 9 Eric Metcalf	.20	.09
❑ 10 Jim Kelly	.40	.18
❑ 11 Andre Reed	.20	.09
❑ 12 Bruce Smith	.40	.18
❑ 13 Cornelius Bennett	.20	.09
❑ 14 Randy Baldwin	.10	.05
❑ 15 Don Beebe	.10	.05
❑ 16 Barry Foster	.20	.09
❑ 17 Lamar Lathon	.10	.05

		MINT	NRMT
18	Frank Reich	.10	.05
19	Jeff Graham	.10	.05
20	Raymont Harris	.10	.05
21	Lewis Tillman	.10	.05
22	Michael Timpson	.10	.05
23	Jeff Blake RC	1.25	.55
24	Carl Pickens	.40	.18
25	Darnay Scott	.40	.18
26	Dan Wilkinson	.20	.09
27	Derrick Alexander WR	.40	.18
28	Leroy Hoard	.10	.05
29	Antonio Langham	.10	.05
30	Andre Rison	.20	.09
31	Eric Turner	.10	.05
32	Troy Aikman	1.25	.55
33	Michael Irvin	.40	.18
34	Daryl Johnston	.20	.09
35	Emmitt Smith	2.00	.90
36	John Elway	2.50	1.10
37	Glyn Milburn	.10	.05
38	Anthony Miller	.20	.09
39	Shannon Sharpe	.20	.09
40	Scott Mitchell	.20	.09
41	Herman Moore	.40	.18
42	Barry Sanders	2.50	1.10
43	Chris Spielman	.20	.09
44	Edgar Bennett	.20	.09
45	Robert Brooks	.40	.18
46	Brett Favre	2.50	1.10
47	Reggie White	.40	.18
48	Mel Gray	.10	.05
49	Haywood Jeffires	.10	.05
50	Gary Brown	.10	.05
51	Craig Erickson	.10	.05
52	Quentin Coryatt	.20	.09
53	Sean Dawkins	.20	.09
54	Marshall Faulk	.60	.25
55	Steve Beuerlein	.10	.05
56	Reggie Cobb	.10	.05
57	Desmond Howard	.20	.09
58	Ernest Givins	.10	.05
59	Jeff Lageman	.10	.05
60	Marcus Allen	.40	.18
61	Steve Bono	.20	.09
62	Greg Hill	.20	.09
63	Willie Davis	.20	.09
64	Tim Brown	.40	.18
65	Rocket Ismail	.20	.09
66	Jeff Hostetler	.20	.09
67	Chester McGlockton	.20	.09
68	Tim Bowens	.10	.05
69	Irving Fryar	.20	.09
70	Eric Green	.10	.05
71	Terry Kirby	.20	.09
72	Dan Marino	2.50	1.10
73	O.J. McDuffie	.40	.18
74	Bernie Parmalee	.20	.09
75	Dewayne Washington	.20	.09
76	Cris Carter	.40	.18
77	Qadry Ismail	.20	.09
78	Warren Moon	.20	.09
79	Jake Reed	.20	.09
80	Drew Bledsoe	1.25	.55
81	Vincent Brisby	.10	.05
82	Ben Coates	.20	.09
83	Dave Meggett	.10	.05
84	Mario Bates	.40	.18
85	Jim Everett	.10	.05
86	Michael Haynes	.20	.09
87	Tyrone Hughes	.20	.09
88	Dave Brown	.20	.09
89	Rodney Hampton	.20	.09
90	Thomas Lewis	.20	.09
91	Herschel Walker	.20	.09
92	Mike Sherrard	.10	.05
93	Boomer Esiason	.20	.09
94	Aaron Glenn	.10	.05
95	Johnny Johnson	.10	.05
96	Johnny Mitchell	.10	.05
97	Ronald Moore	.10	.05
98	Fred Barnett	.20	.09
99	Randall Cunningham	.40	.18
100	Charlie Garner	.20	.09
101	Ricky Watters	.40	.18
102	Calvin Williams	.40	.18
103	Charles Johnson	.20	.09
104	Byron Bam Morris	.20	.09
105	Neil O'Donnell	.20	.09
106	Rod Woodson	.20	.09
107	Jerome Bettis	.40	.18
108	Troy Drayton	.10	.05
109	Sean Gilbert	.20	.09
110	Chris Miller	.10	.05
111	Leonard Russell	.10	.05
112	Ronnie Harmon	.10	.05
113	Stan Humphries	.20	.09
114	Shawn Jefferson	.10	.05
115	Natrone Means	.40	.18
116	Junior Seau	.40	.18
117	William Floyd	.40	.18
118	Brent Jones	.10	.05
119	Jerry Rice	1.25	.55
120	Deion Sanders	.75	.35
121	Dana Stubblefield	.40	.18
122	Bryant Young	.20	.09
123	Steve Young	1.00	.45
124	Brian Blades	.20	.09
125	Cortez Kennedy	.20	.09
126	Rick Mirer	.40	.18
127	Ricky Proehl	.10	.05
128	Chris Warren	.20	.09
129	Horace Copeland	.10	.05
130	Trent Dilfer	.40	.18
131	Alvin Harper	.10	.05
132	Jackie Harris	.10	.05
133	Hardy Nickerson	.10	.05
134	Errict Rhett	.40	.18
135	Henry Ellard	.20	.09
136	Brian Mitchell	.10	.05
137	Heath Shuler	.40	.18
138	Tydus Winans	.10	.05
139	Brett Favre Drew Bledsoe	1.00	.45
140	Marshall Faulk William Floyd	.40	.18
141	Brett Favre Trent Dilfer	.75	.35
142	Dan Marino Brett Favre	1.00	.45
143	Trent Dilfer Errict Rhett	.40	.18
144	Jerry Rice Eric Turner	.50	.23
145	Andre Rison Eric Turner	.20	.09
146	Barry Sanders Dave Meggett	.75	.35
147	Emmitt Smith Daryl Johnston	.60	.25
148	Steve Young Brett Favre	1.00	.45
149	Emmitt Smith Errict Rhett	.60	.25
150	Marshall Faulk Barry Sanders	.75	.35
151	Jerry Rice Darnay Scott	.50	.23
152	William Floyd Daryl Johnston	.40	.18
153	Dan Marino Trent Dilfer	.75	.35
154	John Elway Heath Shuler	.75	.35
155	Byron Bam Morris Natrone Means	.20	.09
156	Dan Wilkinson Reggie White	.20	.09
157	Mario Bates Rodney Hampton	.20	.09
158	Junior Seau Marvin Jones	.40	.18
159	Ki-Jana Carter RC	.40	.18
160	Tony Boselli RC	.20	.09
161	Steve McNair RC	4.00	1.80
162	Michael Westbrook RC	2.50	1.10
163	Kerry Collins RC	1.25	.55
164	Kevin Carter RC	.40	.18
165	Mike Mamula RC	.20	.09
166	Joey Galloway RC	4.00	1.80
167	Kyle Brady RC	.40	.18
168	J.J. Stokes RC	1.00	.45
169	Warren Sapp RC	.60	.25
170	Rob Johnson RC	2.50	1.10
171	Tyrone Wheatley RC	2.00	.90
172	Napoleon Kaufman RC	3.00	1.35
173	James O. Stewart RC	3.00	1.35
174	Joe Aska RC	.20	.09
175	Rashaan Salaam RC	.40	.18
176	Tyrone Poole RC	.20	.09
177	Ty Law RC	.20	.09
178	Dino Philyaw RC	.10	.05
179	Mark Bruener RC	.20	.09
180	Derrick Brooks RC	.10	.05
181	Jack Jackson RC	.10	.05
182	Ray Zellars RC	.20	.09
183	Eddie Goines RC	.10	.05
184	Chris Sanders RC	.40	.18
185	Charlie Simmons RC	.10	.05
186	Lee DeRamus RC	.10	.05
187	Frank Sanders RC	1.50	.70
188	Rodney Thomas RC	.40	.18
189	Steve Stenstrom RC	.10	.05
190	Stoney Case RC	.60	.25
191	Tyrone Davis RC	.10	.05
192	Kordell Stewart RC	4.00	1.80
193	Christian Fauria RC	.10	.05
194	Todd Collins RC	.40	.18
195	Sherman Williams RC	.10	.05
196	Lovell Pinkney RC	.10	.05
197	Eric Zeier RC	.60	.25
198	Zack Crockett RC	.10	.05
199	Checklist A	.10	.05
200	Checklist B	.10	.05
P1	Promo Sheet Trent Dilfer Promise Eric Turner Quickstrike William Floyd Dave Meggett Daryl Johnston Brett Favre	2.00	.90
AU36	John Elway AUTO	150.00	70.00

1995 SkyBox Premium Inside the Numbers

	MINT	NRMT
COMPLETE SET (20)	20.00	9.00

ONE PER SPECIAL RETAIL PACK

		MINT	NRMT
1	William Floyd	.60	.25
2	Marshall Faulk	1.00	.45
3	Warren Moon	.30	.14
4	Cris Carter	.60	.25
5	Deion Sanders	1.25	.55
6	Drew Bledsoe	2.00	.90
7	Natrone Means	.60	.25
8	Herschel Walker	.30	.14
9	Ben Coates	.30	.14
10	Mel Gray	.15	.07
11	Barry Sanders	4.00	1.80
12	Steve Young	1.50	.70
13	Rashaan Salaam	.30	.14
14	Andre Reed	.30	.14
15	Tyrone Hughes	.30	.14
16	Eric Turner	.15	.07
17	Ki-Jana Carter	.30	.14
18	Dan Marino	4.00	1.80
19	Errict Rhett	.60	.25
20	Jerry Rice	2.00	.90

1995 SkyBox Premium Paydirt

	MINT	NRMT
COMPLETE GOLD SET (30)	50.00	22.00

STATED ODDS 1:4
*COLOR STARS: 6X TO 15X BASE CARD HI
*COLOR ROOKIES: 2.5X TO 6X BASE CARD HI
COLORS STATED PRINT RUN 5% OF TOTAL

		MINT	NRMT
PD1	Troy Aikman	3.00	1.35
PD2	J.J. Stokes	1.00	.45
PD3	Ki-Jana Carter	.40	.18
PD4	Steve McNair	4.00	1.80
PD5	Jerome Bettis	1.00	.45
PD6	Tim Brown	1.00	.45
PD7	Cris Carter	1.00	.45

❑ PD8 John Elway	6.00	2.70
❑ PD9 Marshall Faulk	1.50	.70
❑ PD10 Brett Favre	6.00	2.70
❑ PD11 Michael Westbrook	2.50	1.10
❑ PD12 Rodney Hampton	.50	.23
❑ PD13 Michael Irvin	1.00	.45
❑ PD14 Dan Marino	6.00	2.70
❑ PD15 Natrone Means	1.00	.45
❑ PD16 Dave Meggett	.25	.11
❑ PD17 Joey Galloway	4.00	1.80
❑ PD18 Herman Moore	1.00	.45
❑ PD19 Byron Bam Morris	.50	.23
❑ PD20 Carl Pickens	1.00	.45
❑ PD21 Errict Rhett	1.00	.45
❑ PD22 Kerry Collins	1.25	.55
❑ PD23 Barry Sanders	6.00	2.70
❑ PD24 Deion Sanders	2.00	.90
❑ PD25 Emmitt Smith	5.00	2.20
❑ PD26 Drew Bledsoe	3.00	1.35
❑ PD27 Ricky Watters	1.00	.45
❑ PD28 Rod Woodson	.50	.23
❑ PD29 Chris Warren	.50	.23
❑ PD30 Steve Young	2.50	1.10

1995 SkyBox Premium Promise

	MINT	NRMT
COMPLETE SET (14)	25.00	11.00
COMMON CARD (P1-P14)	2.00	.90
SEMISTARS	4.00	1.80
STATED ODDS 1:24		
❑ P1 Derrick Alexander WR	4.00	1.80
❑ P2 Mario Bates	2.00	.90
❑ P3 Trent Dilfer	5.00	2.20
❑ P4 Marshall Faulk	6.00	2.70
❑ P5 William Floyd	2.00	.90
❑ P6 Aaron Glenn	2.00	.90
❑ P7 Raymont Harris	2.00	.90
❑ P8 Greg Hill	2.00	.90
❑ P9 Charles Johnson	4.00	1.80
❑ P10 Byron Bam Morris	2.00	.90
❑ P11 Errict Rhett	4.00	1.80
❑ P12 Darnay Scott	5.00	2.20
❑ P13 Heath Shuler	4.00	1.80
❑ P14 Dan Wilkinson	2.00	.90

1995 SkyBox Premium Quickstrike

	MINT	NRMT
COMPLETE SET (10)	20.00	9.00
STATED ODDS 1:15		
❑ Q1 Chris Warren	.60	.25
❑ Q2 Marshall Faulk	2.00	.90
❑ Q3 William Floyd	1.25	.55
❑ Q4 Jerry Rice	4.00	1.80
❑ Q5 Eric Turner	.30	.14
❑ Q6 Tim Brown	1.25	.55
❑ Q7 Deion Sanders	2.50	1.10
❑ Q8 Emmitt Smith	6.00	2.70
❑ Q9 Rod Woodson	.60	.25
❑ Q10 Steve Young	3.00	1.35

1995 SkyBox Premium Prime Time Rookies

	MINT	NRMT
COMPLETE SET (10)	100.00	45.00
STATED ODDS 1:96		
❑ PT1 Ki-Jana Carter	2.50	1.10
❑ PT2 Kerry Collins	8.00	3.60
❑ PT3 Joey Galloway	25.00	11.00
❑ PT4 Steve McNair	25.00	11.00
❑ PT5 Rashaan Salaam	2.50	1.10
❑ PT6 James O. Stewart	20.00	9.00
❑ PT7 J.J. Stokes	6.00	2.70
❑ PT8 Rodney Thomas	2.50	1.10
❑ PT9 Michael Westbrook	15.00	6.75
❑ PT10 Tyrone Wheatley	12.00	5.50

1996 SkyBox Premium

	MINT	NRMT
COMPLETE SET (250)	20.00	9.00
COMMON CARD (1-250)	.10	.05
SEMISTARS	.25	.11
UNLISTED STARS	.50	.23
COMP.RUBY SET (248)	800.00	350.00
*RUBY STARS: 10X TO 25X		
*RUBY RCs: 5X TO 12X		
RUBIES: ONE PER HOBBY BOX		
❑ 1 Larry Centers	.25	.11
❑ 2 Boomer Esiason	.25	.11
❑ 3 Garrison Hearst	.25	.11
❑ 4 Rob Moore	.25	.11
❑ 5 Frank Sanders	.25	.11
❑ 6 Eric Swann	.10	.05
❑ 7 Bert Emanuel	.25	.11
❑ 8 Jeff George	.25	.11
❑ 9 Craig Heyward	.10	.05
❑ 10 Terance Mathis	.10	.05
❑ 11 Eric Metcalf	.10	.05
❑ 12 Derrick Alexander WR	.25	.11
❑ 13 Leroy Hoard	.10	.05
❑ 14 Michael Jackson	.25	.11
❑ 15 Vinny Testaverde	.25	.11
❑ 16 Eric Turner	.10	.05
❑ 17 Darick Holmes	.10	.05
❑ 18 Jim Kelly	.50	.23
❑ 19 Bryce Paup	.10	.05
❑ 20 Andre Reed	.25	.11
❑ 21 Bruce Smith	.25	.11
❑ 22 Thurman Thomas	.50	.23
❑ 23 Tim Tindale RC	.10	.05
❑ 24 Mark Carrier WR	.10	.05
❑ 25 Kerry Collins	.50	.23
❑ 26 Willie Green	.10	.05
❑ 27 Kevin Greene	.25	.11
❑ 28 Tyrone Poole	.10	.05
❑ 29 Curtis Conway	.50	.23
❑ 30 Bryan Cox	.10	.05
❑ 31 Erik Kramer	.10	.05
❑ 32 Nate Lewis	.10	.05
❑ 33 Rashaan Salaam	.50	.23
❑ 34 Alonzo Spellman	.10	.05
❑ 35 Michael Timpson	.10	.05
❑ 36 Jeff Blake	.50	.23
❑ 37 Ki-Jana Carter	.25	.11
❑ 38 David Dunn	.10	.05
❑ 39 Carl Pickens	.50	.23
❑ 40 Darnay Scott	.25	.11
❑ 41 Troy Aikman	1.25	.55
❑ 42 Charles Haley	.25	.11
❑ 43 Michael Irvin	.50	.23
❑ 44 Daryl Johnston	.25	.11
❑ 45 Jay Novacek	.10	.05
❑ 46 Deion Sanders	.75	.35
❑ 47 Emmitt Smith	2.00	.90
❑ 48 Kevin Williams	.10	.05
❑ 49 Steve Atwater	.10	.05
❑ 50 Terrell Davis	3.00	1.35
❑ 51 John Elway	2.50	1.10
❑ 52 Anthony Miller	.25	.11
❑ 53 Shannon Sharpe	.25	.11
❑ 54 Mike Sherrard	.10	.05
❑ 55 Scott Mitchell	.25	.11
❑ 56 Herman Moore	.50	.23
❑ 57 Johnnie Morton	.25	.11
❑ 58 Brett Perriman	.10	.05
❑ 59 Barry Sanders	2.50	1.10
❑ 60 Edgar Bennett	.25	.11
❑ 61 Robert Brooks	.50	.23
❑ 62 Mark Chmura	.25	.11
❑ 63 Brett Favre	2.50	1.10
❑ 64 Antonio Freeman	1.00	.45
❑ 65 Keith Jackson	.10	.05
❑ 66 Reggie White	.50	.23
❑ 67 Chris Chandler	.25	.11
❑ 68 Mel Gray	.10	.05
❑ 69 Steve McNair	1.00	.45
❑ 70 Chris Sanders	.25	.11
❑ 71 Rodney Thomas	.10	.05
❑ 72 Quentin Coryatt	.10	.05
❑ 73 Sean Dawkins	.10	.05
❑ 74 Ken Dilger	.25	.11
❑ 75 Marshall Faulk	.50	.23
❑ 76 Jim Harbaugh	.25	.11
❑ 77 Lamont Warren	.10	.05
❑ 78 Tony Boselli	.10	.05
❑ 79 Mark Brunell	1.25	.55
❑ 80 Willie Jackson	.10	.05
❑ 81 Natrone Means	.50	.23
❑ 82 James O.Stewart	.25	.11
❑ 83 Marcus Allen	.50	.23
❑ 84 Kimble Anders	.25	.11
❑ 85 Steve Bono	.10	.05
❑ 86 Lake Dawson	.10	.05
❑ 87 Neil Smith	.10	.05
❑ 88 Derrick Thomas	.25	.11

No.	Player	Mint	NrMt
❑ 89	Tamarick Vanover	.25	.11
❑ 90	Fred Barnett	.10	.05
❑ 91	Terry Kirby	.25	.11
❑ 92	Dan Marino	2.50	1.10
❑ 93	O.J. McDuffie	.25	.11
❑ 94	Bernie Parmalee	.10	.05
❑ 95	Richmond Webb	.10	.05
❑ 96	Cris Carter	.50	.23
❑ 97	Scottie Graham	.10	.05
❑ 98	Qadry Ismail	.10	.05
❑ 99	Warren Moon	.25	.11
❑ 100	Jake Reed	.25	.11
❑ 101	Robert Smith	.25	.11
❑ 102	Drew Bledsoe	1.25	.55
❑ 103	Vincent Brisby	.10	.05
❑ 104	Ben Coates	.25	.11
❑ 105	Curtis Martin	1.00	.45
❑ 106	Dave Meggett	.10	.05
❑ 107	Chris Slade	.10	.05
❑ 108	Mario Bates	.25	.11
❑ 109	Jim Everett	.10	.05
❑ 110	Michael Haynes	.10	.05
❑ 111	Tyrone Hughes	.10	.05
❑ 112	Renaldo Turnbull	.10	.05
❑ 113	Dave Brown	.10	.05
❑ 114	Chris Calloway	.10	.05
❑ 115	Rodney Hampton	.25	.11
❑ 116	Thomas Lewis	.10	.05
❑ 117	Tyrone Wheatley	.25	.11
❑ 118	Kyle Brady	.10	.05
❑ 119	Hugh Douglas	.10	.05
❑ 120	Aaron Glenn	.10	.05
❑ 121	Jeff Graham	.10	.05
❑ 122	Adrian Murrell	.50	.23
❑ 123	Neil O'Donnell	.25	.11
❑ 124	Tim Brown	.50	.23
❑ 125	Nolan Harrison	.10	.05
❑ 126	Billy Joe Hobert	.25	.11
❑ 127	Jeff Hostetler	.10	.05
❑ 128	Napoleon Kaufman	.75	.35
❑ 129	Chester McGlockton	.10	.05
❑ 130	Harvey Williams	.10	.05
❑ 131	Charlie Garner	.10	.05
❑ 132	Andy Harmon	.10	.05
❑ 133	Chris T. Jones	.25	.11
❑ 134	Mike Mamula	.10	.05
❑ 135	Rodney Peete	.10	.05
❑ 136	Bobby Taylor	.10	.05
❑ 137	Ricky Watters	.25	.11
❑ 138	Jerome Bettis	.50	.23
❑ 139	Greg Lloyd	.25	.11
❑ 140	Jim Miller	.10	.05
❑ 141	Ernie Mills	.10	.05
❑ 142	Kordell Stewart	1.00	.45
❑ 143	Yancey Thigpen	.25	.11
❑ 144	Rod Woodson	.25	.11
❑ 145	Andre Coleman	.10	.05
❑ 146	Terrell Fletcher	.10	.05
❑ 147	Aaron Hayden RC	.10	.05
❑ 148	Stan Humphries	.25	.11
❑ 149	Junior Seau	.25	.11
❑ 150	Isaac Bruce	.50	.23
❑ 151	Kevin Carter	.10	.05
❑ 152	Todd Kinchen	.10	.05
❑ 153	Leslie O'Neal	.10	.05
❑ 154	Steve Walsh	.10	.05
❑ 155	William Floyd	.25	.11
❑ 156	Merton Hanks	.10	.05
❑ 157	Brent Jones	.10	.05
❑ 158	Derek Loville	.10	.05
❑ 159	Ken Norton	.10	.05
❑ 160	Jerry Rice	1.25	.55
❑ 161	J.J. Stokes	.50	.23
❑ 162	Steve Young	1.00	.45
❑ 163	Brian Blades	.10	.05
❑ 164	Christian Fauria	.10	.05
❑ 165	Joey Galloway	1.00	.45
❑ 166	Rick Mirer	.25	.11
❑ 167	Chris Warren	.25	.11
❑ 168	Trent Dilfer	.50	.23
❑ 169	Alvin Harper	.10	.05
❑ 170	Jackie Harris	.10	.05
❑ 171	Hardy Nickerson	.10	.05
❑ 172	Errict Rhett	.25	.11
❑ 173	Terry Allen	.25	.11
❑ 174	Henry Ellard	.10	.05
❑ 175	Gus Frerotte	.50	.23
❑ 176	Brian Mitchell	.10	.05
❑ 177	Heath Shuler	.25	.11
❑ 178	Michael Westbrook	.50	.23
❑ 179	Karim Abdul-Jabbar RC	.75	.35
❑ 180	Mike Alstott RC	1.50	.70
❑ 181	Willie Anderson RC	.10	.05
❑ 182	Marco Battaglia RC	.10	.05
❑ 183	Tim Biakabutuka RC	1.00	.45
❑ 184	Tony Brackens RC	.25	.11
❑ 185	Duane Clemons RC	.10	.05
❑ 186	Marcus Coleman RC	.10	.05
❑ 187	Ernie Conwell RC	.10	.05
❑ 188	Chris Darkins RC	.10	.05
❑ 189	Stephen Davis RC	4.00	1.80
❑ 190	Brian Dawkins RC	.10	.05
❑ 191	Rickey Dudley RC	.50	.23
❑ 192	Jason Dunn RC	.25	.11
❑ 193	Bobby Engram RC	.50	.23
❑ 194	Daryl Gardener RC	.10	.05
❑ 195	Eddie George RC	4.00	1.80
❑ 196	Terry Glenn RC	1.50	.70
❑ 197	Kevin Hardy RC	.50	.23
❑ 198	Walt Harris RC	.10	.05
❑ 199	Marvin Harrison RC	2.50	1.10
❑ 200	Bobby Hoying RC	.60	.25
❑ 201	Israel Ifeanyi RC	.10	.05
❑ 202	DeRon Jenkins RC	.10	.05
❑ 203	Keyshawn Johnson RC	2.50	1.10
❑ 204	Lance Johnstone RC	.10	.05
❑ 205	Cedric Jones RC	.10	.05
❑ 206	Marcus Jones RC	.10	.05
❑ 207	Eddie Kennison RC	.50	.23
❑ 208	Jevon Langford RC	.10	.05
❑ 209	Dedric Mathis RC	.10	.05
❑ 210	Jermane Mayberry RC	.10	.05
❑ 211	Leeland McElroy RC	.50	.23
❑ 212	Johnny McWilliams RC	.25	.11
❑ 213	Ray Mickens RC	.10	.05
❑ 214	John Mobley RC	.10	.05
❑ 215	Jerald Moore RC	.50	.23
❑ 216	Eric Moulds RC	2.00	.90
❑ 217	Muhsin Muhammad RC (photo actually Tim Biakabutuka)	1.00	.45
❑ 218	Jonathan Ogden RC	.10	.05
❑ 219	Lawrence Phillips RC	.60	.25
❑ 220	Kavika Pittman RC	.10	.05
❑ 221	Stanley Pritchett RC	.25	.11
❑ 222	Simeon Rice RC	.50	.23
❑ 223	Detron Smith RC	.10	.05
❑ 224	Bryan Still RC	.50	.23
❑ 225	Amani Toomer RC	.50	.23
❑ 226	Regan Upshaw RC	.10	.05
❑ 227	Alex Van Dyke RC	.25	.11
❑ 228	Stepfret Williams RC	.25	.11
❑ 229	Retrospective Quentin Coryatt Chester McGlockton Carl Pickens Robert Brooks	.25	.11
❑ 230	Retrospective Dale Carter Edgar Bennett Drew Bledsoe Garrison Hearst	.50	.23
❑ 231	Retrospective Natrone Means Rick Mirer Jerome Bettis Robert Smith	.25	.11
❑ 232	Retrospective O.J.McDuffie Curtis Conway Marshall Faulk Greg Hill	.25	.11
❑ 233	Retrospective Heath Shuler Trent Dilfer William Floyd Charles Johnson	.25	.11
❑ 234	Retrospective Errict Rhett Sean Dawkins Mario Bates Ki-Jana Carter	.25	.11
❑ 235	Retrospective Kerry Collins Steve McNair Joey Galloway Rashaan Salaam	.50	.23
❑ 236	Retrospective J.J.Stokes Michael Westbrook Kyle Brady Kordell Stewart	.50	.23
❑ 237	Retrospective Keyshawn Johnson Eddie George Leeland McElroy Lawrence Phillips	.25	.11
❑ 238	Retrospective Bobby Engram Rickey Dudley Eric Moulds Tim Biakabutuka	.25	.11
❑ 239	Panorama Jan.14, 1996 Kordell Stewart Quentin Coryatt	.50	.23
❑ 240	Panorama Nov.26, 1995 Robert Brooks	.25	.11
❑ 241	Panorama Nov.12, 1995 Henry Jones Terance Mathis	.10	.05
❑ 242	Panorama Dec.9, 1995 Mark Seay Alfred Pupunu	.10	.05
❑ 243	Panorama Sept.17, 1995 Robert Brooks Willie Beamon	.25	.11
❑ 244	Panorama Oct.29, 1995 49ers Halloween	.10	.05
❑ 245	Panorama Oct.15, 1995	.10	.05
❑ 246	Panorama Dec.31, 1995 Zack Crockett Junior Seau	.25	.11
❑ 247	Panorama Jan.14, 1996 Kevin Williams Doug Evans	.10	.05
❑ 248	Panorama Nov.19, 1995 Tim Jacobs Antonio Freeman	.25	.11
❑ 249	Checklist Card 1	.10	.05
❑ 250	Checklist Card 2	.10	.05
❑ P1	Promo Sheet Brett Favre Leeland McElroy Kordell Stewart and Quentin Coryatt Panorama	2.50	1.10

1996 SkyBox Premium Close-ups

	MINT	NRMT
COMPLETE SET (10)	120.00	55.00
RANDOM INS.IN RETAIL PACKS		
❑ 1 Troy Aikman	15.00	6.75
❑ 2 Drew Bledsoe	15.00	6.75
❑ 3 Isaac Bruce	6.00	2.70
❑ 4 Terrell Davis	40.00	18.00
❑ 5 John Elway	30.00	13.50
❑ 6 Barry Sanders	30.00	13.50
❑ 7 Emmitt Smith	25.00	11.00
❑ 8 Kordell Stewart	12.00	5.50

❑ 9 Tamarick Vanover	3.00	1.35
❑ 10 Ricky Watters	3.00	1.35

1996 SkyBox Premium Brett Favre MVP

	MINT	NRMT
COMPLETE SET (7)	100.00	45.00
COMMON CARD (1-2/4-5)	12.00	5.50
LENTICULAR EXCH.(3A/3B)	.30	.14

1-3A: RANDOM INSERTS IN IMPACT PACKS
3B-5: RANDOM INSERTS IN SKYBOX PACKS

❑ 1 Brett Favre Foil	12.00	5.50
❑ 2 Brett Favre Acrylic	12.00	5.50
❑ 3A Brett Favre Lent.Exch.A	.30	.14
❑ 3B Brett Favre Lent.Exch.B	.30	.14
❑ 3C Brett Favre Lent.Prize	40.00	18.00
❑ 4 Brett Favre Die Cut	15.00	6.75
❑ 5 Brett Favre Leather	15.00	6.75

1996 SkyBox Premium Next Big Thing

	MINT	NRMT
COMPLETE SET (15)	80.00	36.00
COMMON CARD (1-15)	2.00	.90
STATED ODDS 1:40		

❑ 1 Mark Brunell	12.00	5.50
❑ 2 Rickey Dudley	2.00	.90
❑ 3 Bobby Engram	2.00	.90
❑ 4 Antonio Freeman	10.00	4.50
❑ 5 Eddie George	6.00	2.70
❑ 6 Terry Glenn	6.00	2.70
❑ 7 Marvin Harrison	10.00	4.50
❑ 8 Keyshawn Johnson	6.00	2.70
❑ 9 Napoleon Kaufman	8.00	3.60
❑ 10 Steve McNair	10.00	4.50
❑ 11 Alex Molden	2.00	.90
❑ 12 Frank Sanders	2.50	1.10
❑ 13 Kordell Stewart	10.00	4.50
❑ 14 Amani Toomer	2.00	.90
❑ 15 Alex Van Dyke	2.00	.90

1996 SkyBox Premium Prime Time Rookies

	MINT	NRMT
COMPLETE SET (10)	150.00	70.00
COMMON CARD (1-10)	5.00	2.20
STATED ODDS 1:96 HOBBY		

❑ 1 Tim Biakabutuka	10.00	4.50
❑ 2 Rickey Dudley	5.00	2.20
❑ 3 Bobby Engram	5.00	2.20
❑ 4 Eddie George	40.00	18.00
❑ 5 Terry Glenn	15.00	6.75
❑ 6 Marvin Harrison	25.00	11.00
❑ 7 Keyshawn Johnson	25.00	11.00
❑ 8 Leeland McElroy	5.00	2.20
❑ 9 Eric Moulds	20.00	9.00
❑ 10 Lawrence Phillips	6.00	2.70

1996 SkyBox Premium Autographs

	MINT	NRMT
COMPLETE SET (6)	300.00	135.00
COMMON CARD (1-6)	20.00	9.00
SEMISTARS	40.00	18.00
STATED ODDS 1:900		

❑ 1 Trent Dilfer	40.00	18.00
❑ 2 Brett Favre	150.00	70.00
❑ 3 William Floyd	20.00	9.00
❑ 4 Daryl Johnston	40.00	18.00
❑ 5 Dave Meggett	20.00	9.00
❑ 6 Eric Turner	40.00	18.00

1996 SkyBox Premium Thunder and Lightning

	MINT	NRMT
COMPLETE SET (10)	150.00	70.00
COMMON CARD (1-10)	10.00	4.50
SEMISTARS	15.00	6.75
STATED ODDS 1:72		

❑ 1 Emmitt Smith	20.00	9.00
Troy Aikman		
❑ 2 Barry Sanders	25.00	11.00
Scott Mitchell		
❑ 3 Marshall Faulk	15.00	6.75
Jim Harbaugh		
❑ 4 Dan Marino	25.00	11.00
O.J.McDuffie		
❑ 5 Jerry Rice	25.00	11.00
Steve Young		
❑ 6 Jeff Blake	15.00	6.75
Carl Pickens		
❑ 7 Brett Favre	25.00	11.00
Robert Brooks		
❑ 8 Curtis Martin	25.00	11.00
Drew Bledsoe		
❑ 9 Errict Rhett	10.00	4.50
Trent Dilfer		
❑ 10 Rick Mirer	10.00	4.50
Chris Warren		

1996 SkyBox Premium V

	MINT	NRMT
COMPLETE SET (10)	30.00	13.50
STATED ODDS 1:18		

❑ 1 Ki-Jana Carter	2.50	1.10
❑ 2 Kerry Collins	5.00	2.20
❑ 3 Trent Dilfer	5.00	2.20
❑ 4 Joey Galloway	10.00	4.50
❑ 5 Herman Moore	5.00	2.20
❑ 6 Errict Rhett	2.50	1.10
❑ 7 Rashaan Salaam	5.00	2.20
❑ 8 Deion Sanders	8.00	3.60
❑ 9 Thurman Thomas	5.00	2.20
❑ 10 Reggie White	5.00	2.20

1997 SkyBox Premium

	MINT	NRMT
COMPLETE SET (250)	35.00	16.00
COMMON CARD (1-250)	.15	.07
SEMISTARS	.25	.11
UNLISTED STARS	.50	.23
COMMON RUBY	10.00	4.50

*RUBY STARS: 40X TO 100X HI COL.
*RUBY RCs: 15X TO 40X
RUBY PRINT RUN 50 SERIAL #'D SETS

❑ 1 Brett Favre	2.50	1.10
❑ 2 Michael Bates	.15	.07
❑ 3 Jeff Graham	.15	.07
❑ 4 Terry Glenn	.50	.23
❑ 5 Stephen Davis	.60	.25
❑ 6 Wesley Walls	.25	.11
❑ 7 Barry Sanders	2.50	1.10
❑ 8 Chris Sanders	.15	.07
❑ 9 O.J. McDuffie	.25	.11
❑ 10 Ken Dilger	.15	.07
❑ 11 Kimble Anders	.25	.11

	No.	Player	Mint	NrMt
❑	12	Keenan McCardell	.25	.11
❑	13	Ki-Jana Carter	.15	.07
❑	14	Gary Brown	.15	.07
❑	15	Andre Rison	.25	.11
❑	16	Edgar Bennett	.25	.11
❑	17	Jerome Bettis	.50	.23
❑	18	Ted Johnson	.15	.07
❑	19	John Friesz	.15	.07
❑	20	Tony Brackens	.15	.07
❑	21	Bryan Cox	.15	.07
❑	22	Eric Moulds	.50	.23
❑	23	Johnnie Morton	.25	.11
❑	24	Brad Johnson	.60	.25
❑	25	Byron Bam Morris	.15	.07
❑	26	Anthony Johnson	.15	.07
❑	27	Jim Harbaugh	.25	.11
❑	28	Keyshawn Johnson	.50	.23
❑	29	Cary Blanchard	.15	.07
❑	30	Curtis Conway	.25	.11
❑	31	Herschel Walker	.25	.11
❑	32	Thurman Thomas	.50	.23
❑	33	Frank Sanders	.25	.11
❑	34	Lawrence Phillips	.15	.07
❑	35	Scottie Graham	.15	.07
❑	36	Jim Everett	.15	.07
❑	37	Dale Carter	.15	.07
❑	38	Ashley Ambrose	.15	.07
❑	39	Mark Chmura	.25	.11
❑	40	James O.Stewart	.25	.11
❑	41	John Mobley	.15	.07
❑	42	Terrell Davis	2.00	.90
❑	43	Ben Coates	.25	.11
❑	44	Jeff George	.25	.11
❑	45	Ty Detmer	.25	.11
❑	46	Isaac Bruce	.50	.23
❑	47	Chris Warren	.25	.11
❑	48	Steve Walsh	.15	.07
❑	49	Bruce Smith	.25	.11
❑	50	Cris Carter	.50	.23
❑	51	Jamal Anderson	.75	.35
❑	52	Tim Biakabutuka	.25	.11
❑	53	Steve Young	.75	.35
❑	54	Eric Turner	.15	.07
❑	55	Jessie Tuggle	.15	.07
❑	56	Chris T. Jones	.15	.07
❑	57	Daryl Johnston	.25	.11
❑	58	Randall Cunningham	.50	.23
❑	59	Trent Dilfer	.50	.23
❑	60	Mark Brunell	1.25	.55
❑	61	Warren Moon	.50	.23
❑	62	Terry Kirby	.25	.11
❑	63	Eddie George	1.25	.55
❑	64	Neil Smith	.25	.11
❑	65	Gilbert Brown	.15	.07
❑	66	Emmitt Smith	2.00	.90
❑	67	Chad Brown	.15	.07
❑	68	Jamie Asher	.15	.07
❑	69	Willie McGinest	.15	.07
❑	70	Tim Brown	.50	.23
❑	71	Quentin Coryatt	.15	.07
❑	72	Mario Bates	.15	.07
❑	73	Fred Barnett	.15	.07
❑	74	Hugh Douglas	.15	.07
❑	75	Eric Swann	.15	.07
❑	76	Chris Chandler	.25	.11
❑	77	Larry Centers	.25	.11
❑	78	Vinny Testaverde	.25	.11
❑	79	Jermaine Lewis	.50	.23
❑	80	Junior Seau	.25	.11
❑	81	Kevin Greene	.25	.11
❑	82	Ricky Watters	.25	.11
❑	83	Billy Davis RC	.15	.07
❑	84	Michael Westbrook	.25	.11
❑	85	Charles Way	.25	.11
❑	86	Andre Reed	.25	.11
❑	87	Darrell Green	.25	.11
❑	88	Troy Aikman	1.25	.55
❑	89	Jim Pyne	.15	.07
❑	90	Dan Marino	2.50	1.10
❑	91	Elvis Grbac	.25	.11
❑	92	Mel Gray	.15	.07
❑	93	Marcus Allen	.50	.23
❑	94	Terry Allen	.50	.23
❑	95	Karim Abdul-Jabbar	.50	.23
❑	96	Rick Mirer	.15	.07
❑	97	Bert Emanuel	.25	.11
❑	98	John Elway	2.50	1.10
❑	99	Tony Martin	.25	.11
❑	100	Zach Thomas	.25	.11
❑	101	Harvey Williams	.15	.07
❑	102	Jason Sehorn	.25	.11
❑	103	Lawyer Milloy	.15	.07
❑	104	Thomas Lewis	.15	.07
❑	105	Michael Irvin	.50	.23
❑	106	James Hundon RC	.15	.07
❑	107	Willie Green	.15	.07
❑	108	Bobby Engram	.25	.11
❑	109	Mike Alstott	.50	.23
❑	110	Greg Lloyd	.15	.07
❑	111	Shannon Sharpe	.25	.11
❑	112	Desmond Howard	.25	.11
❑	113	Jason Elam	.15	.07
❑	114	Qadry Ismail	.25	.11
❑	115	William Thomas	.15	.07
❑	116	Marshall Faulk	.50	.23
❑	117	Tyrone Wheatley	.25	.11
❑	118	Tommy Vardell	.15	.07
❑	119	Rashaan Salaam	.15	.07
❑	120	Brian Mitchell	.15	.07
❑	121	Terance Mathis	.25	.11
❑	122	Dorsey Levens	.50	.23
❑	123	Todd Collins	.15	.07
❑	124	Derrick Alexander WR	.25	.11
❑	125	Stan Humphries	.25	.11
❑	126	Kordell Stewart	.60	.25
❑	127	Kent Graham	.15	.07
❑	128	Yancey Thigpen	.25	.11
❑	129	Bryan Still	.15	.07
❑	130	Carl Pickens	.50	.23
❑	131	Ray Lewis	.15	.07
❑	132	Curtis Martin	.60	.25
❑	133	Kerry Collins	.25	.11
❑	134	Ed McCaffrey	.25	.11
❑	135	Darick Holmes	.15	.07
❑	136	Glyn Milburn	.15	.07
❑	137	Rickey Dudley	.25	.11
❑	138	Terrell Owens	.50	.23
❑	139	Kevin Williams	.15	.07
❑	140	Reggie White	.50	.23
❑	141	Darnay Scott	.25	.11
❑	142	Brett Perriman	.15	.07
❑	143	Neil O'Donnell	.25	.11
❑	144	Natrone Means	.50	.23
❑	145	Jerris McPhail	.15	.07
❑	146	Lamar Lathon	.15	.07
❑	147	Michael Jackson	.25	.11
❑	148	Simeon Rice	.25	.11
❑	149	Greg Hill	.15	.07
❑	150	Erik Kramer	.15	.07
❑	151	Quinn Early	.15	.07
❑	152	Tamarick Vanover	.25	.11
❑	153	Derrick Thomas	.25	.11
❑	154	Nilo Silvan	.15	.07
❑	155	Deion Sanders	.50	.23
❑	156	Lorenzo Neal	.15	.07
❑	157	Steve McNair	.60	.25
❑	158	Levon Kirkland	.15	.07
❑	159	Bobby Hebert	.15	.07
❑	160	William Floyd	.25	.11
❑	161	Leeland McElroy	.15	.07
❑	162	Chester McGlockton	.15	.07
❑	163	Michael Haynes	.15	.07
❑	164	Aeneas Williams	.15	.07
❑	165	Hardy Nickerson	.15	.07
❑	166	Ray Zellars	.15	.07
❑	167	Iheanyi Uwaezuoke	.25	.11
❑	168	Chris Slade	.15	.07
❑	169	Herman Moore	.50	.23
❑	170	Rob Moore	.25	.11
❑	171	Andre Hastings	.15	.07
❑	172	Antonio Freeman	.60	.25
❑	173	Tony Boselli	.15	.07
❑	174	Drew Bledsoe	1.25	.55
❑	175	Sam Mills	.15	.07
❑	176	Robert Smith	.25	.11
❑	177	Jimmy Smith	.25	.11
❑	178	Alex Molden	.15	.07
❑	179	Joey Galloway	.60	.25
❑	180	Irving Fryar	.25	.11
❑	181	Wayne Chrebet	.50	.23
❑	182	Dave Brown	.15	.07
❑	183	Robert Brooks	.25	.11
❑	184	Tony Banks	.25	.11
❑	185	Eric Metcalf	.25	.11
❑	186	Napoleon Kaufman	.50	.23
❑	187	Frank Wycheck	.15	.07
❑	188	Donnell Woolford	.15	.07
❑	189	Kevin Turner	.15	.07
❑	190	Eddie Kennison	.25	.11
❑	191	Cortez Kennedy	.15	.07
❑	192	Raymont Harris	.15	.07
❑	193	Ronnie Harmon	.15	.07
❑	194	Kevin Hardy	.15	.07
❑	195	Gus Frerotte	.15	.07
❑	196	Marvin Harrison	.50	.23
❑	197	Jeff Blake	.25	.11
❑	198	Mike Tomczak	.15	.07
❑	199	William Roaf	.15	.07
❑	200	Jerry Rice	1.25	.55
❑	201	Jake Reed	.25	.11
❑	202	Ken Norton	.15	.07
❑	203	Errict Rhett	.15	.07
❑	204	Adrian Murrell	.25	.11
❑	205	Rodney Hampton	.25	.11
❑	206	Scott Mitchell	.25	.11
❑	207	Jason Dunn	.15	.07
❑	208	Mike Adams RC	.15	.07
❑	209	John Allred RC	.15	.07
❑	210	Reidel Anthony RC	1.00	.45
❑	211	Darnell Autry RC	.25	.11
❑	212	Tiki Barber RC	.75	.35
❑	213	Will Blackwell RC	.50	.23
❑	214	Peter Boulware RC	.25	.11
❑	215	Macey Brooks RC	.15	.07
❑	216	Rae Carruth RC	.50	.23
❑	217	Troy Davis RC	.50	.23
❑	218	Corey Dillon RC	2.50	1.10
❑	219	Jim Druckenmiller RC	.75	.35
❑	220	Warrick Dunn RC	2.00	.90
❑	221	Marc Edwards RC	.15	.07
❑	222	James Farrior RC	.15	.07
❑	223	Tony Gonzalez RC	2.00	.90
❑	224	Jay Graham RC	.50	.23
❑	225	Yatil Green RC	.25	.11
❑	226	Byron Hanspard RC	1.00	.45
❑	227	Ike Hilliard RC	1.00	.45
❑	228	Leon Johnson RC	.15	.07
❑	229	Damon Jones RC	.15	.07
❑	230	Freddie Jones RC	.25	.11
❑	231	Joey Kent RC	.50	.23
❑	232	David LaFleur RC	.25	.11
❑	233	Kevin Lockett RC	.25	.11
❑	234	Sam Madison RC	.15	.07
❑	235	Brian Manning RC	.15	.07
❑	236	Ronnie McAda RC	.15	.07
❑	237	Orlando Pace RC	.15	.07
❑	238	Jake Plummer RC	5.00	2.20
❑	239	Keith Poole RC	.50	.23
❑	240	Darrell Russell RC	.15	.07
❑	241	Sedrick Shaw RC	.50	.23
❑	242	Antowain Smith RC	1.25	.55
❑	243	Shawn Springs RC	.25	.11
❑	244	Duce Staley RC	8.00	3.60
❑	245	Dedric Ward RC	1.25	.55
❑	246	Bryant Westbrook RC	.15	.07
❑	247	Danny Wuerffel RC	.75	.35
❑	248	Checklist	.15	.07
❑	249	Checklist	.15	.07
❑	250	Checklist	.15	.07
❑	S1	Terrell Davis Sample	2.00	.90

1997 SkyBox Premium Autographics

	MINT	NRMT
COMPLETE SET (70)	2500.00	1100.00
COMMON CARD	10.00	4.50
SEMISTARS	15.00	6.75
UNLISTED STARS	25.00	11.00

ODDS: 1:120 IMPACT/1:500 METAL UNI./
1:72 SKYBOX/1:60 E-X2000 ....
5-CARDS/SKYBOX HOT PACK 1:288 ODDS
*CENTURY MARKS: .5X TO 1.2X HI COL
CENT.MARK PRINT RUN 100 SERIAL #'d SETS
FAVRE/R.WHITE SIGNED CENT.MARKS ONLY

	No.	Player	Mint	NrMt
❑	1	Karim Abdul-Jabbar (EX/IM/MU/S)	25.00	11.00

❑ 2 Larry Allen IM/S 10.00 4.50
❑ 3 Terry Allen IM/S 25.00 11.00
❑ 4 Mike Alstott IM/MU/S...... 40.00 18.00
❑ 5 Darnell Autry EX/IM/MU/S 10.00 4.50
❑ 6 Tony Banks IM 15.00 6.75
❑ 7 Pat Barnes EX/S 10.00 4.50
❑ 8 Jeff Blake S.................. 25.00 11.00
❑ 9 Michael Booker IM/S...... 10.00 4.50
❑ 10 Rueben Brown EX/S 10.00 4.50
❑ 11 Rae Carruth EX/IM/MU/S 15.00 6.75
❑ 12 Cris Carter EX/IM/S...... 25.00 11.00
❑ 13 Ben Coates EX/IM/S 15.00 6.75
❑ 14 Ernie Conwell EX/IM/S 10.00 4.50
❑ 15 Terrell Davis EX/IM/S .. 80.00 36.00
❑ 16 Ty Detmer EX/IM/MU/S 15.00 6.75
❑ 17 Ken Dilger EX/IM/S 10.00 4.50
❑ 18 Corey Dillon IM/S 40.00 18.00
❑ 19 Jim Druckenmiller EX/S 25.00 11.00
❑ 20 Rickey Dudley EX/IM/S 15.00 6.75
❑ 21 Brett Favre CENT.EX 400.00 180.00
❑ 22 Antonio Freeman EX/IM/S 30.00 13.50
❑ 23 Daryl Gardener EX/IM/S 10.00 4.50
❑ 24 Chris Gedney IM/S 10.00 4.50
❑ 25 Eddie George S........... 80.00 36.00
❑ 26 Hunter Goodwin EX/IM/S 10.00 4.50
❑ 27 Marvin Harrison EX/S .. 25.00 11.00
❑ 28 Garrison Hearst EX/S .. 15.00 6.75
❑ 29 W.Henderson EX/IM/S 10.00 4.50
❑ 30 Michael Jackson EX/IM/S 15.00 6.75
❑ 31 Tory James EX/IM/S 10.00 4.50
❑ 32 Rob Johnson EX/IM/S.. 25.00 11.00
❑ 33 Chris T. Jones IM/S...... 10.00 4.50
❑ 34 Pete Kendall EX/S........ 10.00 4.50
❑ 35 Eddie Kennison EX/MU/S 15.00 6.75
❑ 36 David LaFleur EX/IM/S 15.00 6.75
❑ 37 Jeff Lewis EX/IM/S 10.00 4.50
❑ 38 Thomas Lewis IM/S...... 10.00 4.50
❑ 39 Kevin Lockett EX/IM/S 10.00 4.50
❑ 40 Brian Manning IM/MU/S 10.00 4.50
❑ 41 Dan Marino S 400.00 180.00
❑ 42 Ed McCaffrey EX/IM/MU/S 15.00 6.75
❑ 43 Keenan McCardell EX/S 15.00 6.75
❑ 44 Glyn Milburn EX/IM/S .. 10.00 4.50
❑ 45 Alex Molden EX/IM/S .. 10.00 4.50
❑ 46 Johnnie Morton IM/S.... 15.00 6.75
❑ 47 Winslow Oliver EX/S 10.00 4.50
❑ 48 Jerry Rice MU 300.00 135.00
❑ 49 Rashaan Salaam EX/S 10.00 4.50
❑ 50 Frank Sanders EX/IM/S 25.00 11.00
❑ 51 Sh.Sharpe EX/IM/MU/S 15.00 6.75
❑ 52 Sedrick Shaw EX/IM/S 15.00 6.75
❑ 53 Alex Smith EX/IM/S...... 10.00 4.50
❑ 54 Antowain Smith EX/S .. 25.00 11.00
❑ 55 Emmitt Smith EX 120.00 55.00
❑ 56 Jimmy Smith IM/S 15.00 6.75
❑ 57 Shawn Springs S......... 15.00 6.75
❑ 58 James O.Stewart EX/IM/S 15.00 6.75
❑ 59 Kordell Stewart IM........ 50.00 22.00
❑ 60 Rodney Thomas EX/S.. 10.00 4.50
❑ 61 Amani Toomer EX/IM/S 10.00 4.50
❑ 62 Floyd Turner EX/IM/S .. 10.00 4.50
❑ 63 Alex Van Dyke EX/IM/S 10.00 4.50
❑ 64 Mike Vrabel IM/MU/S .. 10.00 4.50
❑ 65 Charles Way EX/S 10.00 4.50
❑ 66 Chris Warren EX/MU/S 10.00 4.50
❑ 67 Reggie White CENT. EX/S 80.00 36.00
❑ 68 Ricky Whittle EX/IM/S .. 10.00 4.50
❑ 69 Sherman Williams EX/IM/S 10.00 4.50
❑ 70 Jon Witman EX/IM/S 10.00 4.50

1997 SkyBox Premium Close-ups

	MINT	NRMT
COMPLETE SET (10)	60.00	27.00
STATED ODDS 1:18		
❑ 1 Terrell Davis	20.00	9.00
❑ 2 Troy Aikman	12.00	5.50
❑ 3 Drew Bledsoe	12.00	5.50
❑ 4 Steve McNair...................	6.00	2.70
❑ 5 Jerry Rice	12.00	5.50
❑ 6 Kordell Stewart	6.00	2.70
❑ 7 Kerry Collins	2.50	1.10
❑ 8 John Elway	25.00	11.00
❑ 9 Deion Sanders	5.00	2.20
❑ 10 Joey Galloway................	6.00	2.70

1997 SkyBox Premium Larger Than Life

	MINT	NRMT
COMPLETE SET (10)	250.00	110.00
STATED ODDS 1:360		
❑ 1 Emmitt Smith.................	40.00	18.00
❑ 2 Barry Sanders	50.00	22.00
❑ 3 Curtis Martin	12.00	5.50
❑ 4 Dan Marino	50.00	22.00
❑ 5 Keyshawn Johnson........	10.00	4.50
❑ 6 Marvin Harrison..............	10.00	4.50
❑ 7 Terry Glenn	10.00	4.50
❑ 8 Eddie George	25.00	11.00
❑ 9 Brett Favre	50.00	22.00
❑ 10 Karim Abdul-Jabbar	10.00	4.50

1997 SkyBox Premium Players

	MINT	NRMT
COMPLETE SET (15)	300.00	135.00
STATED ODDS 1:192		
❑ 1 Eddie George	20.00	9.00
❑ 2 Terry Glenn....................	8.00	3.60
❑ 3 Karim Abdul-Jabbar	8.00	3.60
❑ 4 Emmitt Smith...................	30.00	13.50
❑ 5 Dan Marino	40.00	18.00
❑ 6 Brett Favre	40.00	18.00
❑ 7 Keyshawn Johnson..........	8.00	3.60

❑ 8 Curtis Martin	10.00	4.50
❑ 9 Marvin Harrison................	8.00	3.60
❑ 10 Barry Sanders	40.00	18.00
❑ 11 Jerry Rice	20.00	9.00
❑ 12 Terrell Davis	30.00	13.50
❑ 13 Troy Aikman	20.00	9.00
❑ 14 Drew Bledsoe	20.00	9.00
❑ 15 John Elway	40.00	18.00

1997 SkyBox Premium Prime Time Rookies

	MINT	NRMT
COMPLETE SET (10)	100.00	45.00
STATED ODDS 1:96		
❑ 1 Jim Druckenmiller	12.00	5.50
❑ 2 Antowain Smith..............	20.00	9.00
❑ 3 Rae Carruth.....................	8.00	3.60
❑ 4 Yatil Green	4.00	1.80
❑ 5 Ike Hilliard	15.00	6.75
❑ 6 Reidel Anthony	15.00	6.75
❑ 7 Orlando Pace	2.50	1.10
❑ 8 Peter Boulware	4.00	1.80
❑ 9 Warrick Dunn	30.00	13.50
❑ 10 Troy Davis......................	8.00	3.60

1997 SkyBox Premium Reebok

	MINT	NRMT
COMP.BRONZE SET (15)	4.00	1.80
COMMON BRONZE...................	.20	.09
SEMISTARS BRONZE...............	.30	.14
UNLISTED STARS BRONZE......	.40	.18

*REEBOK GREENS: 25X TO 50X BRONZES
*REEBOK GOLDS: 2X TO 5X BRONZES
*REEBOK REDS: 12.5X TO 25X BRONZES
*REEBOK SILVERS: .75X TO 2X BRONZES
OVERALL REEBOK ODDS ONE PER PACK

❑ 12 Keenan McCardell............	.30	.14
❑ 37 Dale Carter	.20	.09
❑ 38 Ashley Ambrose	.20	.09
❑ 43 Ben Coates	.30	.14
❑ 66 Emmitt Smith..................	1.00	.45
❑ 95 Karim Abdul-Jabbar	.40	.18
❑ 98 John Elway	1.25	.55
❑ 110 Greg Lloyd.....................	.20	.09
❑ 123 Todd Collins	.20	.09
❑ 161 Leeland McElroy	.20	.09
❑ 169 Herman Moore	.40	.18
❑ 175 Sam Mills.......................	.20	.09
❑ 180 Irving Fryar	.30	.14
❑ 202 Ken Norton	.20	.09
❑ 205 Rodney Hampton	.30	.14

1997 SkyBox Premium Rookie Preview

	MINT	NRMT
COMPLETE SET (15)	25.00	11.00
STATED ODDS 1:6		
❑ 1 Reidel Anthony	2.00	.90
❑ 2 Tiki Barber........................	2.00	.90
❑ 3 Peter Boulware	1.25	.55

❑ 4 Rae Carruth	1.25	.55
❑ 5 Jim Druckenmiller	2.00	.90
❑ 6 Warrick Dunn	5.00	2.20
❑ 7 James Farrior	.75	.35
❑ 8 Yatil Green	1.25	.55
❑ 9 Byron Hanspard	2.00	.90
❑ 10 Ike Hilliard	2.00	.90
❑ 11 Orlando Pace	.75	.35
❑ 12 Darrell Russell	.75	.35
❑ 13 Antowain Smith	4.00	1.80
❑ 14 Shawn Springs	1.25	.55
❑ 15 Bryant Westbrook	.75	.35

1998 SkyBox Premium

	MINT	NRMT
COMPLETE SET (250)	200.00	90.00
COMMON CARD (1-210)	.15	.07
SEMISTARS	.25	.11
UNLISTED STARS	.50	.23
COMMON ROOKIE (211-250)	2.00	.90
ROOKIE SEMISTARS	2.50	1.10
ROOKIE UNLISTED STARS	4.00	1.80
ROOKIE SUBSET ODDS 1:4		
COMMON RUBIES	12.00	5.50
*RUBY STARS: 40X TO 100X HI COL.		
*RUBY YOUNG STARS: 30X TO 80X		
RUBY VETS PRINT RUN 50 SER.#'d SETS		
COMMON RUBY ROOKIE	25.00	11.00
*RUBY RCs: 4X TO 10X		
RUBY ROOKIES PRINT RUN 35 SER.#'d SETS		

Card	MINT	NRMT
❑ 1 John Elway	2.50	1.10
❑ 2 Drew Bledsoe	1.00	.45
❑ 3 Antonio Freeman	.50	.23
❑ 4 Merton Hanks	.15	.07
❑ 5 James Jett	.25	.11
❑ 6 Ricky Proehl	.15	.07
❑ 7 Deion Sanders	.50	.23
❑ 8 Frank Sanders	.25	.11
❑ 9 Bruce Smith	.25	.11
❑ 10 Tiki Barber	.25	.11
❑ 11 Isaac Bruce	.50	.23
❑ 12 Mark Brunell	1.00	.45
❑ 13 Quinn Early	.15	.07
❑ 14 Terry Glenn	.50	.23
❑ 15 Damien Gordon	.15	.07
❑ 16 Keith Byars	.15	.07
❑ 17 Terrell Davis	2.00	.90
❑ 18 Charlie Garner	.15	.07
❑ 19 Eddie Kennison	.25	.11
❑ 20 Keenan McCardell	.25	.11
❑ 21 Eric Moulds	.50	.23
❑ 22 Jimmy Smith	.25	.11
❑ 23 Reidel Anthony	.25	.11
❑ 24 Rae Carruth	.25	.11
❑ 25 Michael Irvin	.50	.23
❑ 26 Dorsey Levens	.50	.23
❑ 27 Derrick Mayes	.25	.11
❑ 28 Adrian Murrell	.25	.11
❑ 29 Dwayne Rudd	.15	.07
❑ 30 Leslie Shepherd	.15	.07
❑ 31 Jamal Anderson	.50	.23
❑ 32 Robert Brooks	.25	.11
❑ 33 Sean Dawkins	.15	.07
❑ 34 Cris Dishman	.15	.07
❑ 35 Rickey Dudley	.15	.07
❑ 36 Bobby Engram	.25	.11
❑ 37 Chester McGlockton	.15	.07
❑ 38 Terrell Owens	.50	.23
❑ 39 Wayne Chrebet	.50	.23
❑ 40 Dexter Coakley	.15	.07
❑ 41 Kerry Collins	.25	.11
❑ 42 Trent Dilfer	.50	.23
❑ 43 Bobby Hoying	.25	.11
❑ 44 Glyn Milburn	.15	.07
❑ 45 Rob Moore	.25	.11
❑ 46 Jake Reed	.25	.11
❑ 47 Dana Stubblefield	.15	.07
❑ 48 Reggie White	.50	.23
❑ 49 Natrone Means	.50	.23
❑ 50 Troy Aikman	1.25	.55
❑ 51 Aaron Bailey	.15	.07
❑ 52 William Floyd	.15	.07
❑ 53 Eric Metcalf	.15	.07
❑ 54 Warrick Dunn	.75	.35
❑ 55 Chad Lewis	.15	.07
❑ 56 Curtis Martin	.50	.23
❑ 57 Tony Martin	.25	.11
❑ 58 John Randle	.25	.11
❑ 59 Jeff Burris	.15	.07
❑ 60 Larry Centers	.15	.07
❑ 61 Bert Emanuel	.25	.11
❑ 62 Sean Gilbert	.15	.07
❑ 63 David Palmer	.15	.07
❑ 64 Eric Bieniemy	.15	.07
❑ 65 Peter Boulware	.15	.07
❑ 66 Charles Johnson	.15	.07
❑ 67 Jerris McPhail	.15	.07
❑ 68 Scott Mitchell	.25	.11
❑ 69 Chris Sanders	.15	.07
❑ 70 Ken Dilger	.15	.07
❑ 71 Brad Johnson	.50	.23
❑ 72 Danny Kanell	.25	.11
❑ 73 Fred Lane	.25	.11
❑ 74 Warren Sapp	.25	.11
❑ 75 Carl Pickens	.50	.23
❑ 76 Cris Carter	.50	.23
❑ 77 Marshall Faulk	.50	.23
❑ 78 Keyshawn Johnson	.50	.23
❑ 79 Tony McGee	.15	.07
❑ 80 Muhsin Muhammad	.25	.11
❑ 81 Kordell Stewart	.50	.23
❑ 82 Karl Williams	.15	.07
❑ 83 Willie Davis	.15	.07
❑ 84 David Dunn	.15	.07
❑ 85 Marvin Harrison	.25	.11
❑ 86 Michael Jackson	.15	.07
❑ 87 John Mobley	.15	.07
❑ 88 Shawn Springs	.15	.07
❑ 89 Wesley Walls	.25	.11
❑ 90 Jermaine Lewis	.25	.11
❑ 91 Ed McCaffrey	.25	.11
❑ 92 Chris Calloway	.15	.07
❑ 93 Lamont Warren	.15	.07
❑ 94 Ricky Watters	.25	.11
❑ 95 Tony Banks	.25	.11
❑ 96 Tony Brackens	.15	.07
❑ 97 Gary Brown	.15	.07
❑ 98 Howard Griffith	.15	.07
❑ 99 Ray Lewis	.15	.07
❑ 100 Jeff Blake	.25	.11
❑ 101 Charlie Jones	.15	.07
❑ 102 Glenn Foley	.25	.11
❑ 103 Jay Graham	.15	.07
❑ 104 James McKnight	.15	.07
❑ 105 Steve McNair	.50	.23
❑ 106 Chad Scott	.15	.07
❑ 107 Rod Smith WR	.25	.11
❑ 108 Jason Taylor	.15	.07
❑ 109 Corey Dillon	.75	.35
❑ 110 Eddie George	1.00	.45
❑ 111 Jim Harbaugh	.25	.11
❑ 112 Warren Moon	.50	.23
❑ 113 Shannon Sharpe	.25	.11
❑ 114 Darnell Autry	.15	.07
❑ 115 Brett Favre	2.50	1.10
❑ 116 Jeff George	.25	.11
❑ 117 Tony Gonzalez	.15	.07
❑ 118 Garrison Hearst	.50	.23
❑ 119 Randal Hill	.15	.07
❑ 120 Eric Swann	.15	.07
❑ 121 Jamie Asher	.15	.07
❑ 122 Tim Brown	.50	.23
❑ 123 Stephen Davis	.15	.07
❑ 124 Chris Chandler	.25	.11
❑ 125 Jerry Rice	1.25	.55
❑ 126 Troy Davis	.15	.07
❑ 127 Ronnie Harmon	.15	.07
❑ 128 Andre Rison	.25	.11
❑ 129 Duce Staley	1.00	.45
❑ 130 Charles Way	.15	.07
❑ 131 Bryant Westbrook	.15	.07
❑ 132 Mike Alstott	.50	.23
❑ 133 Gus Frerotte	.15	.07
❑ 134 Travis Jervey	.25	.11
❑ 135 Daryl Johnston	.25	.11
❑ 136 Jake Plummer	1.50	.70
❑ 137 Junior Seau	.25	.11
❑ 138 Robert Smith	.50	.23
❑ 139 Thurman Thomas	.50	.23
❑ 140 Karim Abdul-Jabbar	.50	.23
❑ 141 Jerome Bettis	.50	.23
❑ 142 Byron Hanspard	.25	.11
❑ 143 Raymont Harris	.15	.07
❑ 144 Willie McGinest	.15	.07
❑ 145 Barry Sanders	2.50	1.10
❑ 146 Irv Smith	.15	.07
❑ 147 Michael Strahan	.15	.07
❑ 148 Frank Wycheck	.15	.07
❑ 149 Steve Broussard	.15	.07
❑ 150 Joey Galloway	.50	.23
❑ 151 Courtney Hawkins	.15	.07
❑ 152 O.J. McDuffie	.25	.11
❑ 153 Herman Moore	.50	.23
❑ 154 Chris Penn	.15	.07
❑ 155 O.J. Santiago	.15	.07
❑ 156 Yancey Thigpen	.15	.07
❑ 157 Jason Sehorn	.15	.07
❑ 158 Ben Coates	.25	.11
❑ 159 Ernie Conwell	.15	.07
❑ 160 Dale Carter	.15	.07
❑ 161 Jeff Graham	.15	.07
❑ 162 Rob Johnson	.25	.11
❑ 163 Damon Jones	.15	.07
❑ 164 Mark Chmura	.25	.11
❑ 165 Curtis Conway	.25	.11
❑ 166 Elvis Grbac	.25	.11
❑ 167 Andre Hastings	.15	.07
❑ 168 Terry Kirby	.15	.07
❑ 169 Aeneas Williams	.15	.07
❑ 170 Derrick Alexander WR	.25	.11
❑ 171 Troy Brown	.15	.07
❑ 172 Irving Fryar	.25	.11
❑ 173 Jerald Moore	.15	.07
❑ 174 Andre Reed	.25	.11
❑ 175 James Stewart	.25	.11
❑ 176 Chris Warren	.25	.11
❑ 177 Will Blackwell	.15	.07
❑ 178 Erik Kramer	.15	.07
❑ 179 Dan Marino	2.50	1.10
❑ 180 Terance Mathis	.25	.11
❑ 181 Johnnie Morton	.25	.11
❑ 182 J.J. Stokes	.25	.11
❑ 183 Rodney Thomas	.15	.07
❑ 184 Steve Young	.75	.35
❑ 185 Kimble Anders	.25	.11
❑ 186 Napoleon Kaufman	.50	.23
❑ 187 Orlando Pace	.15	.07
❑ 188 Antowain Smith	.50	.23
❑ 189 Emmitt Smith	2.00	.90
❑ 190 Terry Allen	.50	.23
❑ 191 Mark Bruener	.15	.07

❑ 192 Rodney Harrison .... .25 .11
❑ 193 Billy Joe Hobert .... .15 .07
❑ 194 Leon Johnson .... .15 .07
❑ 195 Freddie Jones .... .15 .07
❑ 196 John Elway OFA .... 1.00 .45
❑ 197 Brett Favre OFA .... .75 .35
Steve Atwater OFA
❑ 198 Brett Favre OFA .... .75 .35
Steve Atwater OFA
❑ 199 Dorsey Levens OFA ...... .25 .11
Keith Traylor OFA
❑ 200 Packers Offense OFA .... .50 .23
Broncos Defense OFA
❑ 201 Mark Chmura OFA .... .15 .07
Tyrone Braxton OFA
❑ 202 Dorsey Levens OFA ...... .25 .11
Steve Atwater OFA
Bill Romanowski OFA
❑ 203 Robert Brooks OFA........ .25 .11
Ray Crockett OFA
❑ 204 Tim McKyer OFA............ .15 .07
❑ 205 Allen Aldridge OFA .... .15 .07
❑ 206 Terrell Davis OFA .... .75 .35
Rod Smith WR OFA
❑ 207 Bill Romanowski OFA .... .15 .07
❑ 208 John Elway OFA .... 1.00 .45
Rod Smith WR OFA
Ed McCaffrey OFA
❑ 209 Ray Crockett OFA .... .15 .07
❑ 210 John Elway OFA .... 1.00 .45
❑ 211 Robert Edwards RC 4.00 1.80
❑ 212 Roland Williams RC .... 2.00 .90
❑ 213 Joe Jurevicius RC 2.50 1.10
❑ 214 Wilmont Perry RC .... 2.00 .90
❑ 215 Robert Holcombe RC .. 4.00 1.80
❑ 216 Larry Shannon RC ...... 2.00 .90
❑ 217 Skip Hicks RC 8.00 3.60
❑ 218 Pat Johnson RC 2.50 1.10
❑ 219 Pat Palmer RC .... 2.00 .90
❑ 220 John Dutton RC............ 2.00 .90
❑ 221 Az-Zahir Hakim RC 8.00 3.60
❑ 222 Mikhael Ricks RC 2.50 1.10
❑ 223 Rashaan Shehee RC .. 2.50 1.10
❑ 224 Ryan Leaf RC 8.00 3.60
❑ 225 Alvis Whitted RC .... 2.00 .90
❑ 226 Marcus Nash RC.......... 8.00 3.60
❑ 227 Fred Taylor RC 20.00 9.00
❑ 228 Hines Ward RC 2.50 1.10
❑ 229 Chris Fuamatu-Ma'afala RC 2.50 1.10
❑ 230 Jerome Pathon RC 2.50 1.10
❑ 231 Peyton Manning RC .. 40.00 18.00
❑ 232 Charles Woodson RC 10.00 4.50
❑ 233 Jon Ritchie RC 2.50 1.10
❑ 234 Scott Frost R RC 2.50 1.10
❑ 235 John Avery RC 4.00 1.80
❑ 236 Jonathan Linton RC 5.00 2.20
❑ 237 Jacquez Green RC 6.00 2.70
❑ 238 Andre Wadsworth RC .. 2.50 1.10
❑ 239 Cam Quayle RC .... 2.00 .90
❑ 240 Randy Moss RC 40.00 18.00
❑ 241 Raymond Priester RC .. 2.00 .90
❑ 242 Donald Hayes RC 2.50 1.10
❑ 243 Brian Griese RC 15.00 6.75
❑ 244 Brian Alford RC 2.50 1.10
❑ 245 Kevin Dyson RC 8.00 3.60
❑ 246 Jammi German RC ...... 2.00 .90
❑ 247 Cameron Cleeland RC 2.50 1.10
❑ 248 Curtis Enis RC............ 10.00 4.50
❑ 249 Terry Hardy RC............ 2.00 .90
❑ 250 Tony Simmons RC 2.50 1.10
❑ P136 Jake Plummer Promo 1.50 .70
❑ NNO Checklist Card.............. .15 .07

1998 SkyBox Premium Autographics

	MINT	NRMT
COMPLETE SET (73)	1200.00	550.00
COMMON CARD (1-73)	10.00	4.50
SEMISTARS..........................	15.00	6.75
UNLISTED STARS..................	25.00	11.00

ODDS: 1:48 E-X2001/1:68 METAL UNIVERSE
1:68 SKYBOX PREMIUM/1:112 SKY.THUNDER
ALL BUT PLUMMER INSERTED INTO E-X2001
23-ALSO ISSUED AS RET.REDEMPTIONS(*)

RETAIL REDEMPTION EXPIRATION 4/30/99
*BLUE SIGNATURES: .8X TO 2X
BLUE SIGNATURES PRINT RUN 50 SETS

❑ 1 Kevin Abrams S/ST........ 25.00 11.00
❑ 2 Mike Alstott MU/S 25.00 11.00
❑ 3 Jamie Asher MU/S/ST* .. 10.00 4.50
❑ 4 John Avery S................. 15.00 6.75
❑ 5 Tavian Banks MU/S/ST* 15.00 6.75
❑ 6 Pat Barnes MU/ST 10.00 4.50
❑ 7 Jerome Bettis MU/S*...... 25.00 11.00
❑ 8 Eric Bjornson MU/S* 10.00 4.50
❑ 9 Peter Boulware MU/ST* 10.00 4.50
❑ 10 Troy Brown MU/S/ST .. 10.00 4.50
❑ 11 Mark Bruener MU/S*.... 10.00 4.50
❑ 12 Mark Brunell MU/ST* .. 80.00 36.00
❑ 13 Rae Carruth MU/S/ST .. 15.00 6.75
❑ 14 Ray Crockett S/ST*...... 10.00 4.50
❑ 15 Germane Crowell S/ST 40.00 18.00
❑ 16 Stephen Davis MU/S* .. 10.00 4.50
❑ 17 Troy Davis MU/ST........ 10.00 4.50
❑ 18 Sean Dawkins MU/ST .. 10.00 4.50
❑ 19 Trent Dilfer S/ST 25.00 11.00
❑ 20 Corey Dillon MU/S........ 50.00 22.00
❑ 21 Jim Druckenmiller S/ST 15.00 6.75
❑ 22 Kevin Dyson MU/S/ST 15.00 6.75
❑ 23 Marc Edwards S/ST 10.00 4.50
❑ 24 Robert Edwards S/ST .. 25.00 11.00
❑ 25 Bobby Engram MU/S/ST 15.00 6.75
❑ 26 Curtis Enis S/ST 50.00 22.00
❑ 27 William Floyd MU/ST.... 15.00 6.75
❑ 28 Glenn Foley MU/ST...... 15.00 6.75
❑ 29 C.Fuamatu-Ma'afala 15.00 6.75
MU/S/ST*
❑ 30 Joey Galloway MU/S/ST* 25.00 11.00
❑ 31 Jeff George MU/ST 15.00 6.75
❑ 32 Ahman Green S/ST 15.00 6.75
❑ 33 Jacquez Green S/ST 15.00 6.75
❑ 34 Yatil Green MU/S/ST 10.00 4.50
❑ 35 Byron Hanspard MU/S* 15.00 6.75
❑ 36 Marvin Harrison MU/S* 15.00 6.75
❑ 37 Skip Hicks S/ST 15.00 6.75
❑ 38 Robert Holcombe MU/S 25.00 11.00
❑ 39 Bobby Hoying MU/S 15.00 6.75
❑ 40 Travis Jervey MU/S/ST 15.00 6.75
❑ 41 Rob Johnson MU/S...... 15.00 6.75
❑ 42 Freddie Jones MU/S/ST 10.00 4.50
❑ 43 Eddie Kennison S/ST .. 15.00 6.75
❑ 44 Fred Lane MU/S 25.00 11.00
❑ 45 Ryan Leaf EX 50.00 22.00
❑ 46 Dorsey Levens MU/ST 25.00 11.00
❑ 47 Jeff Lewis S.................. 10.00 4.50
❑ 48 Jermaine Lewis MU/ST 15.00 6.75
❑ 49 Dan Marino S 250.00 110.00
❑ 50 Curtis Martin MU/S/ST* 40.00 18.00
❑ 51 Steve Matthews MU/ST 10.00 4.50
❑ 52 Alonzo Mayes S/ST...... 10.00 4.50
❑ 53 Keenan McCardell MU/ST* 15.00 6.75
❑ 54 Willie McGinest S/ST* .. 10.00 4.50
❑ 55 James McKnight S 10.00 4.50
❑ 56 Glyn Milburn MU/ST* .. 10.00 4.50
❑ 57 Randy Moss MU/ST .. 200.00 90.00
❑ 58 Marcus Nash MU/S/ST 15.00 6.75
❑ 59 Terrell Owens S/ST* 25.00 11.00
❑ 60 Jason Peter S/ST 10.00 4.50
❑ 61 Jake Plummer MU........ 70.00 32.00
❑ 62 John Randle MU/ST 15.00 6.75
❑ 63 Shannon Sharpe MU/S* 15.00 6.75
❑ 64 Jimmy Smith MU/ST 15.00 6.75
❑ 65 Robert Smith MU/ST 25.00 11.00
❑ 66 Duce Staley MU/S........ 30.00 13.50
❑ 67 Kordell Stewart S* 60.00 27.00
❑ 68 Fred Taylor MU/S/ST 100.00 45.00
❑ 69 Rodney Thomas 10.00 4.50
MU/S/ST*
❑ 70 Kevin Turner MU/S/ST 10.00 4.50
❑ 71 Hines Ward MU/S/ST* 15.00 6.75
❑ 72 Charles Way MU/S* 10.00 4.50
❑ 73 Frank Wycheck MU/ST 10.00 4.50
❑ NNO E-X2001 Checklist Card .10 .05
❑ NNO Premium Checklist Card .10 .05
❑ NNO Premium Retail Checklist .10 .05

1998 SkyBox Premium D'stroyers

	MINT	NRMT
COMPLETE SET (15)	40.00	18.00
COMMON CARD (1D-15D)	2.00	.90
SEMISTARS............................	3.00	1.35
STATED ODDS 1:6		

❑ 1D Antowain Smith............. 3.00 1.35
❑ 2D Corey Dillon .... 2.00 .90
❑ 3D Charles Woodson.......... 3.00 1.35
❑ 4D Randy Moss 10.00 4.50
❑ 5D Deion Sanders 3.00 1.35
❑ 6D Robert Edwards 3.00 1.35
❑ 7D Herman Moore 3.00 1.35
❑ 8D Mark Brunell 4.00 1.80
❑ 9D Dorsey Levens 3.00 1.35
❑ 10D Curtis Enis 3.00 1.35
❑ 11D Drew Bledsoe 4.00 1.80
❑ 12D Steve McNair 3.00 1.35
❑ 13D Keyshawn Johnson 3.00 1.35
❑ 14D Bobby Hoying 3.00 1.35
❑ 15D Trent Dilfer 3.00 1.35

1998 SkyBox Premium Intimidation Nation

	MINT	NRMT
COMPLETE SET (15)	400.00	180.00
COMMON CARD (1IN-15IN) ..	15.00	6.75
STATED ODDS 1:360		

❑ 1IN Terrell Davis 50.00 22.00
❑ 2IN Emmitt Smith.............. 50.00 22.00
❑ 3IN Barry Sanders 60.00 27.00
❑ 4IN Brett Favre................. 60.00 27.00

❑ 5IN Eddie George	25.00	11.00
❑ 6IN Jerry Rice	30.00	13.50
❑ 7IN John Elway	60.00	27.00
❑ 8IN Mark Brunell	25.00	11.00
❑ 9IN Troy Aikman	30.00	13.50
❑ 10IN Peyton Manning	60.00	27.00
❑ 11IN Ryan Leaf	20.00	9.00
❑ 12IN Curtis Martin	40.00	18.00
❑ 13IN Dan Marino	60.00	27.00
❑ 14IN Warrick Dunn	30.00	13.50
❑ 15IN Jake Plummer	30.00	13.50

1998 SkyBox Premium Prime Time Rookies

	MINT	NRMT
COMPLETE SET (10)	150.00	70.00
COMMON CARD (1PT-10PT)	5.00	2.20
SEMISTARS	8.00	3.60
UNLISTED STARS	10.00	4.50
STATED ODDS 1:96		
❑ 1PT Curtis Enis	15.00	6.75
❑ 2PT Robert Edwards	10.00	4.50
❑ 3PT Fred Taylor	25.00	11.00
❑ 4PT Robert Holcombe	10.00	4.50
❑ 5PT Ryan Leaf	12.00	5.50
❑ 6PT Peyton Manning	40.00	18.00
❑ 7PT Randy Moss	40.00	18.00
❑ 8PT Charles Woodson	15.00	6.75
❑ 9PT Andre Wadsworth	5.00	2.20
❑ 10PT Kevin Dyson	10.00	4.50

1998 SkyBox Premium Rap Show

	MINT	NRMT
COMPLETE SET (15)	60.00	27.00
COMMON CARD (1-15)	2.00	.90
SEMISTARS	2.50	1.10
STATED ODDS 1:36		
❑ 1 John Elway	12.00	5.50
❑ 2 Drew Bledsoe	5.00	2.20
❑ 3 Corey Dillon	3.00	1.35
❑ 4 Brett Favre	12.00	5.50
❑ 5 Barry Sanders	12.00	5.50
❑ 6 Eddie George	5.00	2.20
❑ 7 Emmitt Smith	10.00	4.50
❑ 8 Jake Plummer	6.00	2.70
❑ 9 Joey Galloway	2.50	1.10
❑ 10 Ricky Watters	2.00	.90
❑ 11 Mike Alstott	2.50	1.10
❑ 12 Kordell Stewart	2.50	1.10
❑ 13 Antonio Freeman	2.50	1.10
❑ 14 Terrell Davis	10.00	4.50
❑ 15 Warrick Dunn	3.00	1.35

1998 SkyBox Premium Soul of the Game

	MINT	NRMT
COMPLETE SET (15)	30.00	13.50
COMMON CARD (1-15)	2.00	.90
STATED ODDS 1:18		
❑ 1 Troy Aikman	5.00	2.20
❑ 2 Dorsey Levens	3.00	1.35
❑ 3 Deion Sanders	3.00	1.35
❑ 4 Antonio Freeman	3.00	1.35
❑ 5 Dan Marino	10.00	4.50
❑ 6 Keyshawn Johnson	3.00	1.35
❑ 7 Terry Glenn	3.00	1.35
❑ 8 Tim Brown	3.00	1.35
❑ 9 Curtis Martin	3.00	1.35
❑ 10 Bobby Hoying	3.00	1.35
❑ 11 Kordell Stewart	2.00	.90
❑ 12 Jerry Rice	5.00	2.20
❑ 13 Steve McNair	3.00	1.35
❑ 14 Joey Galloway	3.00	1.35
❑ 15 Steve Young	3.00	1.35

1999 SkyBox Premium

	MINT	NRMT
COMPLETE SET (290)	350.00	160.00
COMP.SET w/o SPs (250)	50.00	22.00
COMMON CARD (1-210)	.15	.07
SEMISTARS	.25	.11
UNLISTED STARS	.50	.23
COMMON ROOKIE (211-250)	.50	.23
ROOKIE SEMISTARS	.75	.35
ROOKIE UNL.STARS	1.25	.55
COMMON SP (211-250)	2.00	.90
SP SEMISTARS	3.00	1.35
SP UNLISTED STARS	5.00	2.20
SP DRAFT PICKS FEATURE ACTION PHOTOS		
SP DRAFT PICK STATED ODDS 1:8		
❑ 1 Randy Moss	2.00	.90
❑ 2 Jamie Asher	.15	.07
❑ 3 Joey Galloway	.50	.23
❑ 4 Kent Graham	.15	.07
❑ 5 Leslie Shepherd	.15	.07
❑ 6 Levon Kirkland	.15	.07
❑ 7 Marcus Pollard	.15	.07
❑ 8 O.J. McDuffie	.25	.11
❑ 9 Bill Romanowski	.15	.07
❑ 10 Priest Holmes	.50	.23
❑ 11 Tim Biakabutuka	.25	.11
❑ 12 Duce Staley	.50	.23
❑ 13 Isaac Bruce	.50	.23
❑ 14 Jay Riemersma	.15	.07
❑ 15 Karim Abdul-Jabbar	.25	.11
❑ 16 Kevin Dyson	.25	.11
❑ 17 Rickey Dudley	.15	.07
❑ 18 Rocket Ismail	.25	.11
❑ 19 Billy Davis	.15	.07
❑ 20 James Jett	.25	.11
❑ 21 Jerome Bettis	.50	.23
❑ 22 Michael McCrary	.15	.07
❑ 23 Michael Westbrook	.25	.11
❑ 24 Oronde Gadsden	.15	.07
❑ 25 Brad Johnson	.50	.23
❑ 26 Shawn Springs	.15	.07
❑ 27 Cris Carter	.50	.23
❑ 28 Ed McCaffrey	.25	.11
❑ 29 Gary Brown	.15	.07
❑ 30 Hines Ward	.15	.07
❑ 31 Hugh Douglas	.15	.07
❑ 32 Jamir Miller	.15	.07
❑ 33 Michael Bates	.15	.07
❑ 34 Peyton Manning	2.00	.90
❑ 35 Tony Banks	.25	.11
❑ 36 Charles Way	.15	.07
❑ 37 Charlie Batch	1.00	.45
❑ 38 Jake Reed	.25	.11
❑ 39 Mark Brunell	.75	.35
❑ 40 Skip Hicks	.50	.23
❑ 41 Steve Young	.75	.35
❑ 42 Wesley Walls	.25	.11
❑ 43 Antonio Langham	.15	.07
❑ 44 Antowain Smith	.50	.23
❑ 45 Brian Griese	1.00	.45
❑ 46 Jessie Armstead	.15	.07
❑ 47 Thurman Thomas	.25	.11
❑ 48 Jeff George	.25	.11
❑ 49 Jessie Tuggle	.15	.07
❑ 50 Jim Harbaugh	.25	.11
❑ 51 Marvin Harrison	.50	.23
❑ 52 Randall Cunningham	.50	.23
❑ 53 Stephen Alexander	.15	.07
❑ 54 Tiki Barber	.15	.07
❑ 55 Billy Joe Tolliver	.15	.07
❑ 56 Bruce Smith	.25	.11
❑ 57 Eddie George	.60	.25
❑ 58 Eugene Robinson	.15	.07
❑ 59 John Elway	2.00	.90
❑ 60 Kent Dilger	.15	.07
❑ 61 Rodney Harrison	.15	.07
❑ 62 Ty Detmer	.25	.11
❑ 63 Andre Reed	.25	.11
❑ 64 Dorsey Levens	.50	.23
❑ 65 Eddie Kennison	.25	.11
❑ 66 Freddie Jones	.15	.07
❑ 67 Jacquez Green	.25	.11
❑ 68 Jason Elam	.15	.07
❑ 69 Marc Edwards	.15	.07
❑ 70 Terance Mathis	.25	.11
❑ 71 Alonzo Mayes	.15	.07
❑ 72 Andre Wadsworth	.15	.07
❑ 73 Barry Sanders	2.00	.90
❑ 74 Derrick Alexander	.15	.07
❑ 75 Garrison Hearst	.25	.11
❑ 76 Leon Johnson	.15	.07
❑ 77 Mike Alstott	.50	.23
❑ 78 Shawn Jefferson	.15	.07
❑ 79 Andre Hastings	.15	.07
❑ 80 Eric Moulds	.50	.23
❑ 81 Ryan Leaf	.50	.23
❑ 82 Takeo Spikes	.15	.07
❑ 83 Terrell Davis	1.25	.55
❑ 84 Tim Dwight	.50	.23
❑ 85 Trent Dilfer	.25	.11
❑ 86 Vonnie Holliday	.15	.07
❑ 87 Antonio Freeman	.50	.23
❑ 88 Carl Pickens	.25	.11
❑ 89 Chris Chandler	.25	.11

❑ 90 Dale Carter	.15	.07
❑ 91 La'Roi Glover	.15	.07
❑ 92 Natrone Means	.25	.11
❑ 93 Reidel Anthony	.25	.11
❑ 94 Brett Favre	2.00	.90
❑ 95 Bubby Brister	.15	.07
❑ 96 Cameron Cleeland	.15	.07
❑ 97 Chris Calloway	.15	.07
❑ 98 Corey Dillon	.50	.23
❑ 99 Greg Hill	.15	.07
❑ 100 Vinny Testaverde	.25	.11
❑ 101 Trent Green	.25	.11
❑ 102 Sam Gash	.15	.07
❑ 103 Mikhael Ricks	.15	.07
❑ 104 Emmitt Smith	1.25	.55
❑ 105 Doug Flutie	.60	.25
❑ 106 Deion Sanders	.50	.23
❑ 107 Charles Johnson	.15	.07
❑ 108 Byron Bam Morris	.15	.07
❑ 109 Andre Rison	.25	.11
❑ 110 Doug Pederson	.15	.07
❑ 111 Marshall Faulk	.50	.23
❑ 112 Tim Brown	.50	.23
❑ 113 Warren Sapp	.15	.07
❑ 114 Bryan Still	.15	.07
❑ 115 Chris Penn	.15	.07
❑ 116 Jamal Anderson	.50	.23
❑ 117 Keyshawn Johnson	.50	.23
❑ 118 Ricky Proehl	.15	.07
❑ 119 Robert Brooks	.25	.11
❑ 120 Tony Gonzalez	.25	.11
❑ 121 Ty Law	.15	.07
❑ 122 Elvis Grbac	.25	.11
❑ 123 Jeff Blake	.25	.11
❑ 124 Mark Chmura	.15	.07
❑ 125 Junior Seau	.25	.11
❑ 126 Mo Lewis	.15	.07
❑ 127 Ray Buchanan	.15	.07
❑ 128 Robert Holcombe	.25	.11
❑ 129 Tony Simmons	.15	.07
❑ 130 David Palmer	.15	.07
❑ 131 Ike Hilliard	.15	.07
❑ 132 Mike Vanderjagt	.15	.07
❑ 133 Rae Carruth	.25	.11
❑ 134 Sean Dawkins	.15	.07
❑ 135 Shannon Sharpe	.25	.11
❑ 136 Curtis Conway	.25	.11
❑ 137 Darrell Green	.15	.07
❑ 138 Germane Crowell	.25	.11
❑ 139 J.J. Stokes	.25	.11
❑ 140 Kevin Hardy	.15	.07
❑ 141 Rob Moore	.25	.11
❑ 142 Robert Smith	.50	.23
❑ 143 Wayne Chrebet	.25	.11
❑ 144 Yancey Thigpen	.15	.07
❑ 145 Jerome Pathon	.15	.07
❑ 146 John Mobley	.15	.07
❑ 147 Kerry Collins	.25	.11
❑ 148 Peter Boulware	.15	.07
❑ 149 Matthew Hatchette	.15	.07
❑ 150 Kordell Stewart	.50	.23
❑ 151 Koy Detmer	.15	.07
❑ 152 Sedrick Shaw	.15	.07
❑ 153 Steve Beuerlein	.15	.07
❑ 154 Zach Thomas	.25	.11
❑ 155 Adrian Murrell	.25	.11
❑ 156 Bobby Engram	.25	.11
❑ 157 Bryan Cox	.15	.07
❑ 158 Drew Bledsoe	.75	.35
❑ 159 Jerry Rice	1.25	.55
❑ 160 Keenan McCardell	.25	.11
❑ 161 Steve McNair	.50	.23
❑ 162 Terry Fair	.15	.07
❑ 163 Derrick Brooks	.15	.07
❑ 164 Eric Green	.15	.07
❑ 165 Erik Kramer	.15	.07
❑ 166 Frank Sanders	.25	.11
❑ 167 Fred Taylor	1.25	.55
❑ 168 Johnnie Morton	.25	.11
❑ 169 R.W. McQuarters	.15	.07
❑ 170 Terry Glenn	.50	.23
❑ 171 Frank Wycheck	.15	.07
❑ 172 John Avery	.25	.11
❑ 173 Kevin Turner	.15	.07
❑ 174 Larry Centers	.15	.07
❑ 175 Michael Irvin	.25	.11
❑ 176 Rich Gannon	.25	.11
❑ 177 Ricky Watters	.25	.11
❑ 178 Rodney Thomas	.15	.07
❑ 179 Scott Mitchell	.15	.07
❑ 180 Chad Brown	.15	.07
❑ 181 John Randle	.25	.11
❑ 182 Michael Strahan	.15	.07
❑ 183 Muhsin Muhammad	.25	.11
❑ 184 Reggie Barlow	.15	.07
❑ 185 Rod Smith	.25	.11
❑ 186 Dan Marino	2.00	.90
❑ 187 Dexter Coakley	.15	.07
❑ 188 Jermaine Lewis	.25	.11
❑ 189 Jon Kitna	.60	.25
❑ 190 Napoleon Kaufman	.50	.23
❑ 191 Will Blackwell	.15	.07
❑ 192 Aaron Glenn	.15	.07
❑ 193 Ben Coates	.25	.11
❑ 194 Curtis Enis	.50	.23
❑ 195 Herman Moore	.50	.23
❑ 196 Jake Plummer	1.00	.45
❑ 197 Jimmy Smith	.25	.11
❑ 198 Terrell Owens	.50	.23
❑ 199 Warrick Dunn	.50	.23
❑ 200 Charles Woodson	.50	.23
❑ 201 Ahman Green	.25	.11
❑ 202 Mark Bruener	.15	.07
❑ 203 Ray Lewis	.15	.07
❑ 204 Tony Martin	.25	.11
❑ 205 Troy Aikman	1.25	.55
❑ 206 Curtis Martin	.50	.23
❑ 207 Darnay Scott	.15	.07
❑ 208 Derrick Mayes	.15	.07
❑ 209 Keith Poole	.15	.07
❑ 210 Warren Moon	.50	.23
❑ 211 Chris Claiborne RC	.75	.35
❑ 211S Chris Claiborne SP	3.00	1.35
❑ 212 Ricky Williams RC	6.00	2.70
❑ 212S Ricky Williams SP	25.00	11.00
❑ 213 Tim Couch RC	6.00	2.70
❑ 213S Tim Couch SP	25.00	11.00
❑ 214 Champ Bailey RC	1.50	.70
❑ 214S Champ Bailey SP	6.00	2.70
❑ 215 Torry Holt RC	3.00	1.35
❑ 215S Torry Holt SP	12.00	5.50
❑ 216 Donovan McNabb RC	4.00	1.80
❑ 216S Donovan McNabb SP	15.00	6.75
❑ 217 David Boston RC	2.00	.90
❑ 217S David Boston SP	8.00	3.60
❑ 218 Chris McAlister RC	.75	.35
❑ 218S Chris McAlister SP	3.00	1.35
❑ 219 Michael Bishop RC	1.50	.70
❑ 219S Michael Bishop SP	6.00	2.70
❑ 220 Daunte Culpepper RC	4.00	1.80
❑ 220S Daunte Culpepper SP	15.00	6.75
❑ 221 Joe Germaine RC	1.25	.55
❑ 221S Joe Germaine SP	5.00	2.20
❑ 222 Edgerrin James RC	10.00	4.50
❑ 222S Edgerrin James SP	40.00	18.00
❑ 223 Jevon Kearse RC	2.50	1.10
❑ 223S Jevon Kearse SP	10.00	4.50
❑ 224 Ebenezer Ekuban RC	.75	.35
❑ 224S Ebenezer Ekuban SP	3.00	1.35
❑ 225 Scott Covington RC	1.25	.55
❑ 225S Scott Covington SP	5.00	2.20
❑ 226 Aaron Brooks RC	1.25	.55
❑ 226S Aaron Brooks SP	5.00	2.20
❑ 227 Cecil Collins RC	1.25	.55
❑ 227S Cecil Collins SP	5.00	2.20
❑ 228 Akili Smith RC	2.50	1.10
❑ 228S Akili Smith SP	10.00	4.50
❑ 229 Shaun King RC	4.00	1.80
❑ 229S Shaun King SP	15.00	6.75
❑ 230 Chad Plummer RC	.50	.23
❑ 230S Chad Plummer SP	2.00	.90
❑ 231 Peerless Price RC	2.00	.90
❑ 231S Peerless Price SP	8.00	3.60
❑ 232 Antoine Winfield RC	.75	.35
❑ 232S Antoine Winfield SP	3.00	1.35
❑ 233 Antuan Edwards RC	.50	.23
❑ 233S Antuan Edwards SP	2.00	.90
❑ 234 Rob Konrad RC	1.25	.55
❑ 234S Rob Konrad SP	5.00	2.20
❑ 235 Troy Edwards RC	2.00	.90
❑ 235S Troy Edwards SP	8.00	3.60
❑ 236 Terry Jackson RC	.75	.35
❑ 236S Terry Jackson SP	3.00	1.35
❑ 237 Jim Kleinsasser RC	1.25	.55
❑ 237S Jim Kleinsasser SP	5.00	2.20
❑ 238 Joe Montgomery RC	1.25	.55
❑ 238S Joe Montgomery SP	5.00	2.20
❑ 239 Desmond Clark RC	.75	.35
❑ 239S Desmond Clark SP	3.00	1.35
❑ 240 Lamar King RC	.50	.23
❑ 240S Lamar King SP	2.00	.90
❑ 241 Dameane Douglas RC	.75	.35
❑ 241S Dameane Douglas SP	3.00	1.35
❑ 242 Martin Gramatica RC	.50	.23
❑ 242S Martin Gramatica SP	2.00	.90
❑ 243 James Finn RC	.50	.23
❑ 243S James Finn SP	2.00	.90
❑ 244 Andy Katzenmoyer RC	1.25	.55
❑ 244S Andy Katzenmoyer SP	5.00	2.20
❑ 245 Dee Miller RC	.75	.35
❑ 245S Dee Miller SP	3.00	1.35
❑ 246 D'Wayne Bates RC	1.25	.55
❑ 246S D'Wayne Bates SP	5.00	2.20
❑ 247 Amos Zereoue RC	1.25	.55
❑ 247S Amos Zereoue SP	5.00	2.20
❑ 248 Karsten Bailey RC	.75	.35
❑ 248S Karsten Bailey SP	3.00	1.35
❑ 249 Kevin Johnson RC	3.00	1.35
❑ 249S Kevin Johnson SP	12.00	5.50
❑ 250 Cade McNown RC	4.00	1.80
❑ 250S Cade McNown SP	15.00	6.75

1999 SkyBox Premium Shining Star Rubies

	MINT	NRMT
COMMON CARD (1-210)	15.00	6.75
*RUBY STARS: 40X TO 100X HI COL.		
*RUBY YOUNG STARS: 30X TO 80X		
COMMON ROOKIE (211-250)	15.00	6.75
*RUBY RCs: 12X TO 30X		
STAR RUBIES PRINT RUN 30 SER.#'d SETS		
COMMON SP (211-250)	25.00	11.00
*RUBY SPs: 6X TO 12X		
RUBY SPs FEATURE ACTION PHOTOS		
STAR RUBIES SP PRINT RUN 15 SER.#'d SETS		

1999 SkyBox Premium 2000 Men

	MINT	NRMT
COMPLETE SET (15)	600.00	275.00
COMMON CARD (1TM-15TM)	20.00	9.00
STATED PRINT RUN 100 SER.#'d SETS		
❑ 1TM Warrick Dunn	20.00	9.00
❑ 2TM Tim Couch	60.00	27.00
❑ 3TM Fred Taylor	40.00	18.00
❑ 4TM Jake Plummer	40.00	18.00
❑ 5TM Jerry Rice	50.00	22.00
❑ 6TM Edgerrin James	100.00	45.00
❑ 7TM Mark Brunell	30.00	13.50
❑ 8TM Peyton Manning	60.00	27.00
❑ 9TM Randy Moss	60.00	27.00
❑ 10TM Terrell Davis	50.00	22.00
❑ 11TM Charlie Batch	30.00	13.50

❑ 12TM Dan Marino 80.00 36.00
❑ 13TM Emmitt Smith 50.00 22.00
❑ 14TM Brett Favre 80.00 36.00
❑ 15TM Barry Sanders 80.00 36.00

1999 SkyBox Premium Autographics

	MINT	NRMT
COMPLETE SET (82)	2500.00	1100.00
COMMON CARD	12.00	5.50
SEMISTARS..........................	20.00	9.00
UNLISTED STARS.................	25.00	11.00
STATED ODDS 1:68H, 1:90R		
COMMON CHECKLIST	.25	.11

*RED FOIL STARS: 1X TO 2.5X BASIC AUTOS
*RED FOIL ROOKIES: .8X TO 2X BASIC AUTOS ....
RED FOIL STATED PRINT RUN 50 SER.#'d SETS

❑ 1 Stephen Alexander 12.00 5.50
EX/MM/MU/S
❑ 2 Mike Alstott D/EX/S........ 25.00 11.00
❑ 3 Champ Bailey D/EX/MM/MU/S 20.00 9.00
❑ 4 Karsten Bailey EX/MM/MU/S .. 20.00 9.00
❑ 5 Charlie Batch EX/MM/MU/S 50.00 22.00
❑ 6 D'Wayne Bates D/EX/MM/MU/S 12.00 5.50
❑ 7 Michael Bishop D/EX/MM/S 25.00 11.00
❑ 8 Dre' Bly D/EX/MM/MU/S 12.00 5.50
❑ 9 David Boston D/EX/MM/S 30.00 13.50
❑ 10 Gary Brown D/EX/MM/S 12.00 5.50
❑ 11 Na Brown D/EX/MM/S.. 12.00 5.50
❑ 12 Tim Brown D/EX/MM/S 25.00 11.00
❑ 13 Troy Brown EX/MM/MU/S 12.00 5.50
❑ 14 Mark Bruener D/EX/MM/MU/S 12.00 5.50
❑ 15 Mark Brunell D/EX/MM/S 60.00 27.00
❑ 16 Shawn Bryson EX 12.00 5.50
❑ 17 Wayne Chrebet EX/MM/MU/S 25.00 11.00
❑ 18 Chris Claiborne D/EX/MM/S .. 12.00 5.50
❑ 19 Cam Cleeland D/EX/MM/MU/S 12.00 5.50
❑ 20 Cecil Collins D/EX/MM/S 25.00 11.00
❑ 21 Daunte Culpepper D/EX/MM.. 50.00 22.00
❑ 22 Randall Cunningham.... 25.00 11.00
D/EX/MM
❑ 23 Terrell Davis EX/MU/S 80.00 36.00
❑ 24 Ty Detmer D/EX/MM/S 12.00 5.50
❑ 25 Jared DeVries D/EX/MM/MU/S 12.00
5.50
❑ 26 Troy Edwards D/EX/MM/S 30.00 13.50
❑ 27 Kevin Faulk D/EX/MM/S 25.00 11.00
❑ 28 Marshall Faulk D/EX/MM/S 25.00 11.00
❑ 29 Doug Flutie EX/MM/MU/S 40.00 18.00
❑ 30 Oronde Gadsden MU/S 12.00 5.50
❑ 31 Joey Galloway D/EX/MM/S 25.00 11.00
❑ 32 Eddie George D/MM/S 40.00 18.00
❑ 33 Martin Gramatica.......... 12.00 5.50
EX/MM/MU/S
❑ 34 Anthony Gray MM/MU/S 12.00 5.50
❑ 35 Ahman Green D/EX/MM/S 20.00 9.00
❑ 36 Brian Griese D/EX/MM/S 60.00 27.00
❑ 37 Howard Griffith EX/MM/MU/S 12.00 5.50
❑ 38 Marvin Harrison MM/MU/S 25.00 11.00
❑ 39 Courtney Hawkins........ 12.00 5.50
D/MM/MU/S
❑ 40 Vonnie Holliday 12.00 5.50
D/EX/MM/MU/S
❑ 41 Priest Holmes MM........ 25.00 11.00
❑ 42 Torry Holt D/EX/MM 50.00 22.00
❑ 43 Sedrick Irvin D/S 20.00 9.00
❑ 44 Edgerrin James.......... 175.00 80.00
D/EX/MM/MU
❑ 45 Patrick Jeffers D/MU/S 30.00 13.50
❑ 46 James Johnson D/MM/S 20.00 9.00
❑ 47 Kevin Johnson D/EX/MM/S 40.00 18.00
❑ 48 Freddie Jones D/EX/MM/S 12.00 5.50
❑ 49 Jevon Kearse D/EX/MM/S 40.00 18.00
❑ 50 Shaun King D/EX/MM/S 50.00 22.00
❑ 51 Jon Kitna EX/MM/MU/S 25.00 11.00
❑ 52 Rob Konrad D/EX/MM/S 20.00 9.00
❑ 53 Dorsey Levens MU/S .. 25.00 11.00
❑ 54 Peyton Manning D/EX/MM 120.00 55.00
❑ 55 Darnell McDonald 20.00 9.00
D/EX/MM/MU/S
❑ 56 Donovan McNabb 50.00 22.00
D/EX/MM/S
❑ 57 Cade McNown D/EX/MM/S 60.00 27.00
❑ 58 Eric Moss D/MM/S 12.00 5.50
❑ 59 Randy Moss EX/MM/S 120.00 55.00
❑ 60 Eric Moulds EX/MM/S .. 20.00 9.00
❑ 61 Marcus Nash EX/MM/MU/S .. 20.00 9.00
❑ 62 Terrell Owens D/EX/MM 25.00 11.00
❑ 63 Jerome Pathon EX/MM/MU/S 20.00 9.00
❑ 64 Jake Plummer D/EX/MM 50.00 22.00
❑ 65 Peerless Price EX/MM 30.00 13.50
❑ 66 Mikhael Ricks D/EX/MM/MU/S 12.00 5.50
❑ 67 Frank Sanders EX/MM/MU/S 20.00 9.00
❑ 68 Tony Simmons 12.00 5.50
D/EX/MM/MU/S
❑ 69 Akili Smith D/S 50.00 22.00
❑ 70 Antowain Smith........... 25.00 11.00
EX/MM/MU/S
❑ 71 L.C. Stevens D/EX/MM/S 12.00 5.50
❑ 72 Michael Strahan EX/MM/MU/S 12.00 5.50
❑ 73 Tai Streets D/EX/MM/MU/S .. 12.00 5.50
❑ 74 Fred Taylor MM........... 50.00 22.00
❑ 75 Lamar Thomas EX/MM 12.00 5.50
❑ 76 Jerame Tuman D/EX/MM/S .. 12.00 5.50
❑ 77 Kevin Turner D/EX/MM/MU/S 12.00 5.50
❑ 78 Kurt Warner MM 175.00 80.00
❑ 79 Tyrone Wheatley 20.00 9.00
D/EX/MM/MU/S
❑ 80 Ricky Williams D/EX/MM/S 120.00 55.00
❑ 81 Frank Wycheck 12.00 5.50
D/EX/MM/MU/S
❑ 82 Amos Zereoue EX/MM/MU/S 25.00 11.00
❑ CL1 Dominion CL................. .25 .11
❑ CL2 E-X Century CL .... .25 .11
❑ CL3 Metal Universe CL .... .25 .11
❑ CL4 Premium CL .... .25 .11

1999 SkyBox Premium Box Tops

	MINT	NRMT
COMPLETE SET (15)	40.00	18.00
COMMON CARD (1BT-15BT) ..	1.50	.70
STATED ODDS 1:12		

❑ 1BT Terrell Davis 4.00 1.80
❑ 2BT Troy Aikman 4.00 1.80
❑ 3BT Peyton Manning 5.00 2.20
❑ 4BT Mark Brunell 2.50 1.10
❑ 5BT Eddie George .... 2.00 .90
❑ 6BT Corey Dillon 3.00 1.35
❑ 7BT Dan Marino.................... 6.00 2.70
❑ 8BT Brett Favre 6.00 2.70
❑ 9BT Barry Sanders.............. 6.00 2.70
❑ 10BT Emmitt Smith 4.00 1.80
❑ 11BT Fred Taylor 3.00 1.35
❑ 12BT Jerry Rice 4.00 1.80
❑ 13BT Jamal Anderson 3.00 1.35
❑ 14BT Joey Galloway 3.00 1.35
❑ 15BT Randy Moss 5.00 2.20

1999 SkyBox Premium DejaVu

	MINT	NRMT
COMPLETE SET (15)	50.00	22.00
COMMON CARD (1DV-15DV)..	1.50	.70
SEMISTARS.............................	2.00	.90
STATED ODDS 1:36		

*DIE CUTS: 2X TO 5X HI COL. ....
DIE CUTS PRINT RUN 99 SER.#'d SETS

❑ 1DV Akili Smith 8.00 3.60
Barry Sanders
❑ 2DV Cade McNown 5.00 2.20
Warrick Dunn
❑ 3DV Cecil Collins .... 2.00 .90
Jerris McPhail
❑ 4DV Champ Bailey.............. 1.50 .70
Curtis Conway
❑ 5DV Daunte Culpepper 5.00 2.20
Michael Irvin
❑ 6DV David Boston 2.50 1.10
Tim Biakabutuka
❑ 7DV Donovan McNabb 5.00 2.20
Marshall Faulk
❑ 8DV Edgerrin James 12.00 5.50
Michael Westbrook
❑ 9DV Kevin Faulk .... 2.00 .90
Joey Kent
❑ 10DV Kevin Johnson 4.00 1.80
Jerome Pathon
❑ 11DV Ricky Williams 8.00 3.60
Deion Sanders
❑ 12DV Shaun King............... 5.00 2.20
Germane Crowell
❑ 13DV Tim Couch 10.00 4.50
Troy Aikman
❑ 14DV Torry Holt 4.00 1.80
Tim Brown
❑ 15DV Troy Edwards............ 2.50 1.10
Eric Metcalf

1999 SkyBox Premium Genuine Coverage

	MINT	NRMT
COMPLETE SET (6)	500.00	220.00
COMMON CARD (1GC-6GC)	40.00	18.00
RANDOM INSERTS IN PACKS		

*MULTI-COLORED SWATCHES: .6X TO 1.5X

❑ 1GC Mark Brunell/420 ...... 60.00 27.00
❑ 2GC Randy Moss/265 .... 150.00 70.00
❑ 3GC Herman Moore/400 .. 40.00 18.00
❑ 4GC Brett Favre/410 ...... 120.00 55.00
❑ 5GC Randall Cunningham/425 50.00
22.00
❑ 6GC Drew Bledsoe/440 .... 60.00 27.00

1999 SkyBox Premium Prime Time Rookies

	MINT	NRMT
COMPLETE SET (15)	150.00	70.00
COMMON CARD (1PR-15PR)..	6.00	2.70
STATED ODDS 1:96		

❑ 1PR Ricky Williams 25.00 11.00
❑ 2PR Tim Couch 25.00 11.00
❑ 3PR Edgerrin James 40.00 18.00
❑ 4PR Daunte Culpepper 15.00 6.75
❑ 5PR David Boston 8.00 3.60
❑ 6PR Akili Smith 10.00 4.50
❑ 7PR Cecil Collins 6.00 2.70
❑ 8PR Cade McNown 15.00 6.75
❑ 9PR Torry Holt 12.00 5.50
❑ 10PR Donovan McNabb .. 15.00 6.75

Card	MINT	NRMT
❑ 11PR Kevin Johnson	12.00	5.50
❑ 12PR Shaun King	15.00	6.75
❑ 13PR Champ Bailey	6.00	2.70
❑ 14PR Troy Edwards	8.00	3.60
❑ 15PR Kevin Faulk	8.00	3.60

1999 SkyBox Premium Prime Time Rookies Autographs

	MINT	NRMT
COMMON CARD (1PR-15PR)	100.00	45.00
STATED PRINT RUN 25 SERIAL #'d SETS		

Card	MINT	NRMT
❑ 1PR Ricky Williams	400.00	180.00
❑ 3PR Edgerrin James	500.00	220.00
❑ 4PR Daunte Culpepper		
❑ 5PR David Boston	150.00	70.00
❑ 6PR Akili Smith	200.00	90.00
❑ 7PR Cecil Collins	100.00	45.00
❑ 8PR Cade McNown	200.00	90.00
❑ 9PR Torry Holt	200.00	90.00
❑ 10PR Donovan McNabb	200.00	90.00
❑ 11PR Kevin Johnson	175.00	80.00
❑ 12PR Shaun King	200.00	90.00
❑ 13PR Champ Bailey		
❑ 14PR Troy Edwards	150.00	70.00
❑ 15PR Kevin Faulk		

1999 SkyBox Premium Year 2

	MINT	NRMT
COMPLETE SET (15)	15.00	6.75
COMMON CARD (1Y2-15Y2)	1.00	.45
SEMISTARS	1.50	.70
STATED ODDS 1:6		

Card	MINT	NRMT
❑ 1Y2 Ahman Green	1.50	.70
❑ 2Y2 Terry Fair	1.00	.45
❑ 3Y2 Charlie Batch	2.50	1.10
❑ 4Y2 Ryan Leaf	1.00	.45
❑ 5Y2 Skip Hicks	2.50	1.10
❑ 6Y2 John Avery	1.50	.70
❑ 7Y2 Charles Woodson	2.50	1.10
❑ 8Y2 Jacquez Green	1.50	.70
❑ 9Y2 Kevin Dyson	1.50	.70
❑ 10Y2 Marcus Nash	1.50	.70
❑ 11Y2 Robert Holcombe	1.50	.70
❑ 12Y2 Germane Crowell	1.50	.70
❑ 13Y2 Curtis Enis	2.50	1.10
❑ 14Y2 Tim Dwight	1.50	.70
❑ 15Y2 Brian Griese	2.50	1.10

1992 SkyBox Prime Time

	MINT	NRMT
COMPLETE SET (360)	25.00	11.00
COMMON CARD (1-360)	.10	.05
SEMISTARS	.20	.09
UNLISTED STARS	.40	.18

Card	MINT	NRMT
❑ 1 Deion Sanders	1.00	.45
❑ 2 Shane Collins RC UER (Photo actually Terry Smith; see also number 216)	.10	.05
❑ 3 James Patton RC	.10	.05
❑ 4 Reggie Roby	.10	.05
❑ 5 Merril Hoge	.10	.05
❑ 6 Vinny Testaverde	.20	.09
❑ 7 Boomer Esiason	.20	.09
❑ 8 Troy Aikman	2.00	.90
❑ 9 Tommy Jeter RC	.10	.05
❑ 10 Brent Williams	.10	.05
❑ 11 Mark Rypien	.10	.05
❑ 12 Jim Kelly	.40	.18
❑ 13 Dan Marino	3.00	1.35
❑ 14 Bill Cowher CO RC	.20	.09
❑ 15 Leslie O'Neal	.20	.09
❑ 16 Joe Montana	3.00	1.35
❑ 17 William Fuller	.20	.09
❑ 18 Paul Gruber	.10	.05
❑ 19 Bernie Kosar	.20	.09
❑ 20 Rickey Jackson	.10	.05
❑ 21 Earnest Byner	.10	.05
❑ 22 Emmitt Smith	4.00	1.80
❑ 23 Neal Anderson PC	.10	.05
❑ 24 Greg Lloyd	.40	.18
❑ 25 Ronnie Harmon	.10	.05
❑ 26 Ray Donaldson	.10	.05
❑ 27 Kevin Ross	.10	.05
❑ 28 Irving Fryar	.20	.09
❑ 29 John L. Williams	.10	.05
❑ 30 Chris Hinton	.10	.05
❑ 31 Tracy Scroggins RC	.10	.05
❑ 32 Rohn Stark	.10	.05
❑ 33 David Fulcher	.10	.05
❑ 34 Thurman Thomas	.40	.18
❑ 35 Christian Okoye	.10	.05
❑ 36 Vaughn Dunbar RC	.10	.05
❑ 37 Joel Steed RC	.10	.05
❑ 38 James Francis UER (card number on back is actually 354)	.10	.05
❑ 39 Dermontti Dawson	.10	.05
❑ 40 Mark Higgs	.10	.05
❑ 41 Flipper Anderson UER 5,301 receiving yards in 1991	.10	.05
❑ 42 Ronnie Lott	.20	.09
❑ 43 Jim Everett	.20	.09
❑ 44 Burt Grossman	.10	.05
❑ 45 Charles Haley	.20	.09
❑ 46 Ricky Proehl	.10	.05
❑ 47 Marquez Pope RC	.10	.05
❑ 48 David Treadwell	.10	.05
❑ 49 William White	.10	.05
❑ 50 John Elway	3.00	1.35
❑ 51 Mark Carrier WR	.20	.09
❑ 52 Brian Blades	.20	.09
❑ 53 Keith McKeller	.10	.05
❑ 54 Art Monk	.20	.09
❑ 55 Lamar Lathon	.10	.05
❑ 56 Pat Swilling	.20	.09
❑ 57 Steve Broussard	.10	.05
❑ 58 Derrick Thomas	.40	.18
❑ 59 Keith Jackson	.20	.09
❑ 60 Leonard Marshall	.10	.05
❑ 61 Eric Metcalf UER (card number on back is actually 350)	.40	.18
❑ 62 Andy Heck	.10	.05
❑ 63 Mark Carrier DB	.10	.05
❑ 64 Neil O'Donnell	.40	.18
❑ 65 Broderick Thomas MVP	.10	.05
❑ 66 Eric Kramer	.20	.09
❑ 67 Joe Montana PC	1.50	.70
❑ 68 Robert Delpino MVP	.10	.05
❑ 69 Steve Israel RC	.10	.05
❑ 70 Herman Moore	1.50	.70
❑ 71 Jacob Green	.10	.05
❑ 72 Lorenzo White	.10	.05
❑ 73 Nick Lowery	.10	.05
❑ 74 Eugene Robinson	.10	.05
❑ 75 Carl Banks	.10	.05
❑ 76 Bruce Smith	.40	.18
❑ 77 Mark Rypien MVP	.10	.05
❑ 78 Anthony Munoz	.20	.09
❑ 79 Clayton Holmes RC	.10	.05
❑ 80 Jerry Rice	2.00	.90
❑ 81 Henry Ellard	.20	.09
❑ 82 Tim McGee	.10	.05
❑ 83 Al Toon	.20	.09
❑ 84 Haywood Jeffires	.20	.09
❑ 85 Mike Singletary	.20	.09
❑ 86 Thurman Thomas PC	.20	.09
❑ 87 Jessie Hester	.10	.05
❑ 88 Michael Irvin	.40	.18
❑ 89 Jack Del Rio	.10	.05
❑ 90 Eagles MVP Seth Joyner listed	.10	.05
❑ 91 Jeff Herrod	.10	.05
❑ 92 Michael Dean Perry	.20	.09
❑ 93 Louis Oliver	.10	.05
❑ 94 Dan McGwire	.10	.05
❑ 95 Cris Carter MVP	.20	.09
❑ 96 Dale Carter RC	.40	.18
❑ 97 Cornelius Bennett	.20	.09
❑ 98 Edgar Bennett RC	.50	.23
❑ 99 Steve Young	1.50	.70
❑ 100 Warren Moon	.40	.18
❑ 101 Deion Sanders MVP	.60	.25
❑ 102 Mel Gray	.20	.09
❑ 103 Mark Murphy	.10	.05
❑ 104 Jeff George	.40	.18
❑ 105 Anthony Miller	.20	.09
❑ 106 Tom Rathman	.10	.05
❑ 107 Fred McAfee RC	.10	.05
❑ 108 Paul Siever RC	.10	.05
❑ 109 Lemuel Stinson	.10	.05
❑ 110 Vance Johnson	.10	.05
❑ 111 Jay Schroeder	.10	.05
❑ 112 Calvin Williams	.20	.09
❑ 113 Cortez Kennedy	.20	.09
❑ 114 Quentin Coryatt RC	.40	.18
❑ 115 Ronnie Lippett	.10	.05
❑ 116 Brad Baxter	.10	.05
❑ 117 Bubba McDowell	.10	.05
❑ 118 Cris Carter	1.00	.45
❑ 119 John Stephens	.10	.05
❑ 120 James Hasty	.10	.05
❑ 121 Bubby Brister	.10	.05
❑ 122 Robert Jones RC	.10	.05
❑ 123 Sterling Sharpe	.40	.18
❑ 124 Jason Hanson RC	.20	.09
❑ 125 Sam Mills	.10	.05
❑ 126 Ernie Jones	.10	.05
❑ 127 Chester McGlockton RC	.40	.18
❑ 128 Troy Vincent RC	.20	.09
❑ 129 Chuck Smith RC	.10	.05
❑ 130 Tim McKyer	.10	.05
❑ 131 Tom Newberry	.10	.05
❑ 132 Leonard Wheeler RC	.10	.05

❑ 133 Patrick Rowe RC .10 .05
❑ 134 Eric Swann .20 .09
❑ 135 Jeremy Lincoln RC .10 .05
❑ 136 Brian Noble .10 .05
❑ 137 Allen Pinkett .10 .05
❑ 138 Carl Pickens RC UER .. 1.25 .55
(card number on back is actually 358)
❑ 139 Eric Green .10 .05
❑ 140 Louis Lipps .10 .05
❑ 141 Chris Singleton .10 .05
❑ 142 Gary Clark .40 .18
❑ 143 Tim Green .10 .05
❑ 144 Dennis Green CO RC .10 .05
❑ 145 Gary Anderson K .10 .05
❑ 146 Mark Clayton .20 .09
❑ 147 Kelvin Martin .10 .05
❑ 148 Mike Holmgren CO RC .. .20 .09
❑ 149 Gaston Green .10 .05
❑ 150 Terrell Buckley RC .10 .05
❑ 151 Robert Brooks RC 2.00 .90
❑ 152 Anthony Smith .10 .05
❑ 153 Jay Novacek .20 .09
❑ 154 Webster Slaughter .10 .05
❑ 155 John Roper .10 .05
❑ 156 Steve Emtman RC .10 .05
❑ 157 Tony Sacca RC .10 .05
❑ 158 Ray Crockett .10 .05
❑ 159 Jerry Rice MVP 1.00 .45
❑ 160 Alonzo Spellman RC .20 .09
❑ 161 Deion Sanders PC .60 .25
❑ 162 Robert Clark .10 .05
❑ 163 Mark Ingram .10 .05
❑ 164 Ricardo McDonald RC .. .10 .05
❑ 165 Emmitt Smith PC 2.00 .90
❑ 166 Tommy Maddox RC .10 .05
❑ 167 Tom Myslinski RC .10 .05
❑ 168 Packers MVP .10 .05
Tony Bennett listed
❑ 169 Ernest Givins .20 .09
❑ 170 Eugene Robinson MVP .. .10 .05
❑ 171 Roger Craig .20 .09
❑ 172 Irving Fryar MVP .10 .05
❑ 173 Jeff Herrod MVP .10 .05
❑ 174 Chris Mims RC .20 .09
❑ 175 Bart Oates .10 .05
❑ 176 Michael Irvin MVP .40 .18
❑ 177 Lawrence Dawsey .20 .09
❑ 178 Warren Moon MVP .20 .09
❑ 179 Timm Rosenbach .10 .05
❑ 180 Bobby Ross CO RC .10 .05
❑ 181 Chris Burkett MVP .10 .05
❑ 182 Tony Brooks RC .10 .05
❑ 183 Clarence Verdin .10 .05
❑ 184 Bernie Kosar PC .10 .05
❑ 185 Eric Martin .10 .05
❑ 186 Jeff Bryant .10 .05
❑ 187 Carnell Lake .10 .05
❑ 188 Darren Woodson RC .40 .18
❑ 189 Dwayne Harper .10 .05
❑ 190 Bernie Kosar MVP .10 .05
❑ 191 Keith Sims .10 .05
❑ 192 Rich Gannon .10 .05
❑ 193 Broderick Thomas .10 .05
❑ 194 Michael Young .10 .05
❑ 195 Cris Dishman .10 .05
❑ 196 Wes Hopkins .10 .05
❑ 197 Christian Okoye PC .10 .05
❑ 198 David Little .10 .05
❑ 199 Chris Crooms RC .10 .05
❑ 200 Lawrence Taylor .40 .18
❑ 201 Marc Boutte RC .10 .05
❑ 202 Mark Carrier DB PC .10 .05
❑ 203 Keith McCants .10 .05
❑ 204 Dwayne Sabb RC .10 .05
❑ 205 Brian Mitchell .20 .09
❑ 206 Keith Byars .10 .05
❑ 207 Jeff Hostetler .20 .09
❑ 208 Percy Snow .10 .05
❑ 209 Lawrence Taylor MVP .... .20 .09
❑ 210 Troy Auzenne RC .10 .05
❑ 211 Warren Moon PC .20 .09
❑ 212 Mike Pritchard .20 .09
❑ 213 Eric Dickerson .20 .09
❑ 214 Harvey Williams .40 .18
❑ 215 Phil Simms UER .20 .09
(Misspelled Sims on card front)
❑ 216 Sean Lumpkin RC UER .10 .05
(Card number on back is actually 002)
❑ 217 Marco Coleman RC .20 .09
❑ 218 Phillippi Sparks RC .10 .05
❑ 219 Gerald Dixon RC .10 .05
❑ 220 Steve Walsh .10 .05
❑ 221 Russell Maryland .20 .09
❑ 222 Eddie Anderson .10 .05
❑ 223 Shane Dronett RC .10 .05
❑ 224 Todd Collins RC .10 .05
❑ 225 Leon Searcy RC .20 .09
❑ 226 Andre Rison .20 .09
❑ 227 James Lofton .20 .09
❑ 228 Ken O'Brien .10 .05
❑ 229 Mike Tomczak .10 .05
❑ 230 Nick Bell .10 .05
❑ 231 Ben Smith .10 .05
❑ 232 Wendell Davis MVP .10 .05
❑ 233 Craig Thompson RC .10 .05
❑ 234 Dana Hall RC .20 .09
❑ 235 Larry Webster RC .10 .05
❑ 236 Jerry Rice PC 1.00 .45
❑ 237 Rod Bernstine .10 .05
❑ 238 David Klingler RC .20 .09
❑ 239 Greg Skrepenak RC .10 .05
❑ 240 Mark Wheeler RC .10 .05
❑ 241 Kevin Smith RC .40 .18
❑ 242 Charles Mann .10 .05
❑ 243 Lions MVP .10 .05
Barry Sanders listed
❑ 244 Curtis Whitley RC .10 .05
❑ 245 Ronnie Harmon MVP .... .10 .05
❑ 246 Brent Jones .20 .09
❑ 247 Robert Harris RC .10 .05
❑ 248 Ted Marchibroda CO .10 .05
❑ 249 Willie Gault .20 .09
❑ 250 Siran Stacy RC .10 .05
❑ 251 Dennis Byrd .10 .05
❑ 252 Corey Harris RC .10 .05
❑ 253 Al Noga .10 .05
❑ 254 David Shula CO RC .10 .05
❑ 255 Rob Moore .20 .09
❑ 256 Marv Cook .10 .05
❑ 257 John Elway MVP 1.50 .70
❑ 258 Harold Green .10 .05
❑ 259 Tom Flores CO .10 .05
❑ 260 Andre Reed .20 .09
❑ 261 Anthony Thompson .10 .05
❑ 262 Issiac Holt .10 .05
❑ 263 Mike Evans RC .10 .05
❑ 264 Jimmy Smith RC 4.00 1.80
❑ 265 Anthony Carter .20 .09
❑ 266 Ashley Ambrose RC .20 .09
❑ 267 John Fina RC .10 .05
(card number on back is actually 357)
❑ 268 Sean Gilbert RC .40 .18
❑ 269 Ken Norton Jr. .40 .18
❑ 270 Barry Word .10 .05
❑ 271 Pat Swilling MVP .10 .05
❑ 272 Dan Marino PC 1.50 .70
❑ 273 David Fulcher MVP .10 .05
❑ 274 William Perry .20 .09
❑ 275 Ed West .10 .05
❑ 276 Gene Atkins .10 .05
❑ 277 Neal Anderson .10 .05
❑ 278 Dino Hackett .10 .05
❑ 279 Greg Townsend .10 .05
❑ 280 Andre Tippett .10 .05
❑ 281 Darryl Williams RC .10 .05
❑ 282 Kurt Barber RC .10 .05
❑ 283 Pat Terrell .10 .05
❑ 284 Derrick Thomas PC .20 .09
❑ 285 Eddie Robinson RC .10 .05
❑ 286 Howie Long .20 .09
❑ 287 Cardinals MVP .10 .05
Tim McDonald listed
❑ 288 Thurman Thomas MVP .. .20 .09
❑ 289 Wendell Davis .10 .05
❑ 290 Jeff Cross .10 .05
❑ 291 Duane Bickett .10 .05
❑ 292 Tony Smith RC .10 .05
❑ 293 Jerry Ball .10 .05
❑ 294 Jessie Tuggle .10 .05
❑ 295 Chris Burkett .10 .05
❑ 296 Eugene Chung RC .10 .05
❑ 297 Chris Miller .20 .09
❑ 298 Albert Bentley .10 .05
❑ 299 Richard Johnson .10 .05
❑ 300 Randall Cunningham .40 .18
❑ 301 Courtney Hawkins RC .20 .09
❑ 302 Ray Childress .10 .05
❑ 303 Rodney Peete .20 .09
❑ 304 Kevin Fagan .10 .05
❑ 305 Ronnie Lott MVP .10 .05
❑ 306 Michael Carter .10 .05
❑ 307 Derrick Thomas MVP .... .20 .09
❑ 308 Jarvis Williams .10 .05
❑ 309 Greg Lloyd MVP .20 .09
❑ 310 Ethan Horton .10 .05
❑ 311 Ricky Ervins .10 .05
❑ 312 Bennie Blades .10 .05
❑ 313 Troy Aikman PC 1.00 .45
❑ 314 Bruce Armstrong .10 .05
❑ 315 Leroy Hoard .20 .09
❑ 316 Gary Anderson RB .10 .05
❑ 317 Steve McMichael .20 .09
❑ 318 Junior Seau .40 .18
❑ 319 Mark Thomas RC .10 .05
❑ 320 Fred Barnett .40 .18
❑ 321 Mike Merriweather .10 .05
❑ 322 Keith Willis .10 .05
❑ 323 Brett Perriman .40 .18
❑ 324 Michael Haynes .20 .09
❑ 325 Jim Harbaugh .40 .18
❑ 326 Sammie Smith .10 .05
❑ 327 Robert Delpino .10 .05
❑ 328 Tony Mandarich .10 .05
❑ 329 Mark Bortz .10 .05
❑ 330 Ray Etheridge RC UER .. .10 .05
(Name misspelled Ethridge)
❑ 331 Jarvis Williams PC .10 .05
Louis Oliver
❑ 332 Dan Marino MVP 1.50 .70
❑ 333 Dwight Stone .10 .05
❑ 334 Billy Ray Smith .10 .05
❑ 335 Darion Conner .10 .05
❑ 336 Howard Dinkins RC .10 .05
❑ 337 Robert Porcher RC .20 .09
❑ 338 Chris Doleman .10 .05
❑ 339 Alvin Harper .20 .09
❑ 340 John Taylor .20 .09
❑ 341 Ray Agnew .10 .05
❑ 342 Jon Vaughn .10 .05
❑ 343 James Brown RC .10 .05
❑ 344 Michael Irvin PC .40 .18
❑ 345 Neil Smith .20 .09
❑ 346 Vaughan Johnson .10 .05
❑ 347 Checklist .10 .05
❑ 348 Checklist .10 .05
❑ 349 Checklist .10 .05
❑ 350 Checklist .10 .05
(See also number 61)
❑ 351 Checklist .10 .05
❑ 352 Checklist .10 .05
❑ 353 Checklist .10 .05
❑ 354 Checklist .10 .05
(See also number 38)
❑ 355 Checklist .10 .05
❑ 356 Checklist .10 .05
❑ 357 Checklist .10 .05
(See also number 267)
❑ 358 Checklist .10 .05
(See also number 138)
❑ 359 Checklist .10 .05
❑ 360 Checklist .10 .05
❑ H1 Jim Kelly 2.50 1.10
(Flip Hologram)
❑ S1 Steve Emtman .75 .35
Spectra-Etch ("Horse Power"))

1992 SkyBox Prime Time Poster Cards

	MINT	NRMT
COMPLETE SET (16)	30.00	13.50
RANDOM INSERTS IN FOIL PACKS		

❑ M1 Bernie Kosar .40 .18
Air Raid 19
❑ M2 Mark Carrier DB .20 .09
Monster of the Midway
❑ M3 Neal Anderson .20 .09
The Bear Necessity
❑ M4 Thurman Thomas .75 .35
Thurmanator
❑ M5 Deion Sanders 2.00 .90
PrimeTime
❑ M6 Joe Montana 6.00 2.70
Sweet Sixteen
❑ M7 Jerry Rice 4.00 1.80
Speed of Light
❑ M8 Jarvis Williams .20 .09
Louis Oliver
B2 Bombers
❑ M9 Dan Marino 6.00 2.70
Armed and Dangerous
❑ M10 Derrick Thomas .75 .35
Sacred Ground
❑ M11 Christian Okoye .20 .09
Nigerian Nightmare
❑ M12 Warren Moon .75 .35
Moonlighting
❑ M13 Michael Irvin .75 .35
Playmaker
❑ M14 Troy Aikman 4.00 1.80
Strong Arm of the Law
❑ M15 Emmitt Smith 8.00 3.60
Catch 22
❑ M16 Checklist .20 .09

1998 SkyBox Thunder

	MINT	NRMT
COMPLETE SET (250)	50.00	22.00
COMMON CARD (1-200)	.10	.05
SEMISTARS	.20	.09
UNLISTED STARS	.40	.18
COMMON CARD (201-225)	.60	.25
COMMON ROOKIE (226-250)	.40	.18
ROOKIE SEMISTARS	.60	.25
ROOKIE UNLISTED STARS	1.25	.55
201-250: ONE PER PACK		
COMMON RAVE	10.00	4.50

*1-200 RAVE STARS: 30X TO 60X HI COL.
*1-200 RAVE YOUNG STARS: 20X TO 40X
*201-225 RAVE STARS: 20X TO 40X HI COL.
*201-225 RAVE YOUNG STARS: 12.5X TO 25X
*226-250 RAVE RCs: 5X TO 10X.
RAVE PRINT RUN 125 SERIAL #'d SETS
COMMON SUPER RAVE 30.00 13.50
*1-200 SUPER RAVE STARS: 100X TO 200X
*1-200 SR YOUNG STARS: 80X TO 160X
*201-225 SUPER RAVE STARS: 80X TO 160X
*201-225 SR YOUNG STARS: 70X TO 140X
*226-250 SUPER RAVE RCs: 12X TO 30X
SUPER RAVE PRINT RUN 25 SER. #'d SETS

❑ 1 Reggie White .40 .18
❑ 2 Elvis Grbac .20 .09
❑ 3 Ed McCaffrey .20 .09
❑ 4 O.J. McDuffie .20 .09
❑ 5 Scott Mitchell .20 .09
❑ 6 Byron Hanspard .20 .09
❑ 7 John Randle .20 .09
❑ 8 Shawn Jefferson .10 .05
❑ 9 Peter Boulware .10 .05
❑ 10 Karl Williams .10 .05
❑ 11 Napoleon Kaufman .40 .18
UER front Napolean
❑ 12 Barry Minter .10 .05
❑ 13 Cris Dishman .10 .05
❑ 14 James Stewart .20 .09
❑ 15 Marcus Robertson .10 .05
❑ 16 Rodney Harrison .20 .09
❑ 17 Michael Barrow .10 .05
UER front Micheal
❑ 18 Michael Sinclair .10 .05
❑ 19 Dewayne Washington .10 .05
❑ 20 Phillippi Sparks .10 .05
❑ 21 Ernie Conwell .10 .05
❑ 22 Ken Dilger .10 .05
❑ 23 Johnnie Morton .20 .09
❑ 24 Eric Swann .10 .05
❑ 25 Curtis Conway .20 .09
❑ 26 Duce Staley .75 .35
❑ 27 Darrell Green .20 .09
❑ 28 Quinn Early .10 .05
❑ 29 LeRoy Butler .10 .05
❑ 30 Winfred Tubbs .10 .05
❑ 31 Darren Woodson .10 .05
❑ 32 Marcus Allen .40 .18
❑ 33 Glenn Foley .20 .09
❑ 34 Tom Knight .10 .05
❑ 35 Sam Shade .10 .05
❑ 36 James McKnight .10 .05
❑ 37 Leeland McElroy .10 .05
❑ 38 Earl Holmes RC .60 .25
❑ 39 Ryan McNeil .10 .05
❑ 40 Cris Carter .40 .18
❑ 41 Jessie Armstead .10 .05
❑ 42 Bryce Paup .10 .05
❑ 43 Chris Slade .10 .05
❑ 44 Eric Metcalf .10 .05
❑ 45 Jim Harbaugh .20 .09
❑ 46 Terry Kirby .10 .05
❑ 47 Donnie Edwards .10 .05
❑ 48 Darryl Williams .10 .05
❑ 49 Neil Smith .20 .09
❑ 50 Warren Sapp .20 .09
❑ 51 Jason Taylor .10 .05
❑ 52 Irving Fryar .20 .09
❑ 53 Jeff George .20 .09
❑ 54 Yancey Thigpen .10 .05
❑ 55 Ricky Proehl .10 .05
❑ 56 Kevin Greene .20 .09
❑ 57 Joel Steed .10 .05
❑ 58 Larry Allen .10 .05
❑ 59 Thurman Thomas .40 .18
❑ 60 Aaron Glenn .10 .05
❑ 61 Natrone Means .40 .18
❑ 62 Chris Calloway .10 .05
❑ 63 Chuck Smith .10 .05
❑ 64 Chidi Ahanotu .10 .05
❑ 65 Mario Bates .20 .09
❑ 66 Jonathan Ogden .10 .05
❑ 67 Drew Bledsoe CL .40 .18
❑ 68 John Mobley CL .10 .05
❑ 69 Antowain Smith CL .20 .09
❑ 70 Aeneas Williams .10 .05
❑ 71 Brian Williams .10 .05
❑ 72 Derrick Thomas .20 .09
❑ 73 Ted Johnson .10 .05
❑ 74 Troy Drayton .10 .05
❑ 75 Mike Pritchard .10 .05
❑ 76 Darnay Scott .20 .09
❑ 77 James Jett .20 .09
❑ 78 Dwayne Rudd .10 .05
❑ 79 Marvin Harrison .20 .09
❑ 80 Dermontti Dawson .10 .05
❑ 81 Keith Lyle .10 .05
❑ 82 Steve Atwater .10 .05
❑ 83 Tyrone Wheatley .20 .09
❑ 84 Tony Brackens .10 .05
❑ 85 Dale Carter .10 .05
❑ 86 Robert Porcher .10 .05
❑ 87 Merton Hanks .10 .05
❑ 88 Leon Johnson .10 .05
❑ 89 Simeon Rice .20 .09
❑ 90 Robert Brooks .20 .09
❑ 91 William Thomas .10 .05
❑ 92 Wesley Walls .20 .09
❑ 93 Chester McGlockton .10 .05
❑ 94 Chris Chandler .20 .09
❑ 95 Michael Strahan .10 .05
❑ 96 Ray Zellars .10 .05
❑ 97 Dexter Coakley .10 .05
❑ 98 Rob Johnson .20 .09
❑ 99 Eric Green .10 .05
❑ 100 Darrien Gordon .10 .05
❑ 101 Gary Brown .10 .05
❑ 102 Reidel Anthony .20 .09
❑ 103 Keenan McCardell .20 .09
❑ 104 Leslie O'Neal .10 .05
❑ 105 Bryant Westbrook .10 .05
❑ 106 Derrick Alexander .20 .09
❑ 107 Jeff Blake .20 .09
❑ 108 Ben Coates .20 .09
❑ 109 Shawn Springs .10 .05
❑ 110 Robert Smith .40 .18
❑ 111 Karim Abdul-Jabbar .40 .18
❑ 112 Willie Davis .10 .05
❑ 113 Mark Chmura .20 .09
❑ 114 Terry Allen .40 .18
❑ 115 Will Blackwell .10 .05
❑ 116 Jamal Anderson .40 .18
❑ 117 Dana Stubblefield .10 .05
❑ 118 Trent Dilfer .40 .18
❑ 119 Jermaine Lewis .20 .09
❑ 120 Chad Brown .10 .05
❑ 121 Tamarick Vanover .10 .05
❑ 122 Tony Martin .20 .09
❑ 123 Larry Centers .10 .05
❑ 124 J.J. Stokes .20 .09
❑ 125 Danny Kanell .20 .09
❑ 126 Wayne Chrebet .40 .18
❑ 127 Kerry Collins .20 .09
❑ 128 Tony Banks .20 .09
❑ 129 Randal Hill .10 .05
❑ 130 Jimmy Smith .20 .09
❑ 131 Tim Brown .40 .18
❑ 132 Zach Thomas .10 .05
❑ 133 Rod Smith .20 .09
❑ 134 Frank Wycheck .10 .05
❑ 135 Garrison Hearst .40 .18
❑ 136 Bruce Smith .20 .09
❑ 137 Hardy Nickerson .10 .05
❑ 138 Sean Dawkins .10 .05
❑ 139 Willie McGinest .10 .05
❑ 140 Kimble Anders .20 .09
❑ 141 Michael Westbrook .20 .09
❑ 142 Chris Doleman .10 .05
❑ 143 Ricky Watters .20 .09
❑ 144 Levon Kirkland .10 .05
❑ 145 Rob Moore .20 .09
❑ 146 Eddie Kennison .20 .09
❑ 147 Rickey Dudley .10 .05
❑ 148 Jay Graham .10 .05
❑ 149 Brad Johnson .40 .18
❑ 150 Bobby Hoying .20 .09
❑ 151 Sherman Williams .10 .05
❑ 152 Charles Way .10 .05
❑ 153 Adrian Murrell .20 .09
❑ 154 Chris Sanders .10 .05
❑ 155 Greg Hill .10 .05
❑ 156 Rae Carruth .20 .09
❑ 157 Mike Alstott .40 .18
❑ 158 Terance Mathis .20 .09
❑ 159 Antonio Freeman .40 .18
❑ 160 Junior Seau .20 .09
❑ 161 Chris Warren .20 .09

❑ 162 Shannon Sharpe	.20	.09
❑ 163 Derrick Rodgers	.10	.05
❑ 164 Charles Johnson	.10	.05
❑ 165 Marshall Faulk	.40	.18
❑ 166 Jamie Asher	.10	.05
❑ 167 Michael Jackson	.10	.05
❑ 168 Terrell Owens	.40	.18
❑ 169 Jason Sehorn	.10	.05
❑ 170 Raymont Harris	.10	.05
❑ 171 Jake Reed	.20	.09
❑ 172 Kevin Hardy	.10	.05
❑ 173 Jerald Moore	.10	.05
❑ 174 Michael Irvin	.40	.18
❑ 175 Freddie Jones	.10	.05
❑ 176 Steve McNair	.40	.18
❑ 177 Carnell Lake	.10	.05
❑ 178 Troy Brown	.10	.05
❑ 179 Hugh Douglas	.10	.05
❑ 180 Andre Rison	.20	.09
❑ 181 Leslie Shepherd	.10	.05
❑ 182 Andre Hastings	.10	.05
❑ 183 Fred Lane	.20	.09
❑ 184 Andre Reed	.20	.09
❑ 185 Darrell Russell	.10	.05
❑ 186 Frank Sanders	.20	.09
❑ 187 Derrick Brooks	.10	.05
❑ 188 Charlie Garner	.10	.05
❑ 189 Bert Emanuel	.20	.09
❑ 190 Terrell Buckley	.10	.05
❑ 191 Carl Pickens	.40	.18
❑ 192 Tiki Barber	.20	.09
❑ 193 Pete Mitchell	.10	.05
❑ 194 Gilbert Brown	.10	.05
❑ 195 Isaac Bruce	.40	.18
❑ 196 Ray Lewis	.10	.05
❑ 197 Warren Moon	.40	.18
❑ 198 Tony Gonzalez	.10	.05
❑ 199 John Mobley	.10	.05
❑ 200 Gus Frerotte	.10	.05
❑ 201 Brett Favre	3.00	1.35
❑ 202 Terrell Davis	2.50	1.10
❑ 203 Dan Marino	3.00	1.35
❑ 204 Barry Sanders	3.00	1.35
❑ 205 Steve Young	.75	.35
❑ 206 Deion Sanders	.60	.25
❑ 207 Kordell Stewart	.60	.25
❑ 208 Eddie George	1.25	.55
❑ 209 Jake Plummer	2.00	.90
❑ 210 Warrick Dunn	.75	.35
❑ 211 John Elway	3.00	1.35
❑ 212 Terry Glenn	.60	.25
❑ 213 Mark Brunell	1.25	.55
❑ 214 Corey Dillon	.75	.35
❑ 215 Joey Galloway	.60	.25
❑ 216 Dorsey Levens	.60	.25
❑ 217 Troy Aikman	1.50	.70
❑ 218 Keyshawn Johnson	.60	.25
❑ 219 Jerome Bettis	.60	.25
❑ 220 Curtis Martin	.60	.25
❑ 221 Herman Moore	.60	.25
❑ 222 Emmitt Smith	2.50	1.10
❑ 223 Jerry Rice	1.50	.70
❑ 224 Drew Bledsoe	1.25	.55
❑ 225 Antowain Smith	.60	.25
❑ 226 Stephen Alexander RC	.60	.25
❑ 227 John Avery RC	.60	.25
❑ 228 Kevin Dyson RC	2.50	1.10
❑ 229 Robert Edwards RC	.60	.25
❑ 230 Greg Ellis RC	.40	.18
❑ 231 Curtis Enis RC	3.00	1.35
❑ 232 Chris Fuamatu-Ma'afala RC	.60	.25
❑ 233 Ahman Green RC	2.00	.90
❑ 234 Jacquez Green RC	2.00	.90
❑ 235 Az-Zahir Hakim RC	2.00	.90
❑ 236 Skip Hicks RC	2.00	.90
❑ 237 Joe Jurevicius RC	.60	.25
❑ 238 Ryan Leaf RC	3.00	1.35
❑ 239 Peyton Manning RC	20.00	9.00
❑ 240 Alonzo Mayes RC	.40	.18
❑ 241 R.W. McQuarters RC	.40	.18
❑ 242 Randy Moss RC	20.00	9.00
❑ 243 Marcus Nash RC	2.00	.90
❑ 244 Jerome Pathon RC	.60	.25
❑ 245 Jason Peter RC	.40	.18
❑ 246 Brian Simmons RC	.40	.18
❑ 247 Takeo Spikes RC	.60	.25
❑ 248 Fred Taylor RC	8.00	3.60
❑ 249 Andre Wadsworth RC	.60	.25
❑ 250 Charles Woodson RC	3.00	1.35
❑ P162 Shannon Sharpe Promo	1.00	.45

1998 SkyBox Thunder Boss

	MINT	NRMT
COMPLETE SET (20)	30.00	13.50
COMMON CARD (1B-20B)	1.00	.45
SEMISTARS	1.50	.70
UNLISTED STARS	2.50	1.10
STATED ODDS 1:8		
❑ 1B Troy Aikman	6.00	2.70
❑ 2B Drew Bledsoe	5.00	2.20
❑ 3B Tim Brown	2.50	1.10
❑ 4B Antonio Freeman	2.50	1.10
❑ 5B Joey Galloway	2.50	1.10
❑ 6B Terry Glenn	2.50	1.10
❑ 7B Bobby Hoying	1.50	.70
❑ 8B Michael Irvin	2.50	1.10
❑ 9B Keyshawn Johnson	2.50	1.10
❑ 10B Dorsey Levens	2.50	1.10
❑ 11B Curtis Martin	2.50	1.10
❑ 12B John Mobley	1.00	.45
❑ 13B Jake Plummer	6.00	2.70
❑ 14B John Randle	1.50	.70
❑ 15B Deion Sanders	2.50	1.10
❑ 16B Junior Seau	1.50	.70
❑ 17B Shannon Sharpe	1.50	.70
❑ 18B Bruce Smith	1.50	.70
❑ 19B Robert Smith	2.50	1.10
❑ 20B Dana Stubblefield	1.00	.45

1998 SkyBox Thunder Destination Endzone

	MINT	NRMT
COMPLETE SET (15)	250.00	110.00
COMMON CARD (1DE-15DE)	8.00	3.60
STATED ODDS 1:96		
❑ 1DE Jerome Bettis	10.00	4.50
❑ 2DE Mark Brunell	15.00	6.75
❑ 3DE Terrell Davis	30.00	13.50
❑ 4DE Corey Dillon	10.00	4.50
❑ 5DE Warrick Dunn	12.00	5.50
❑ 6DE John Elway	40.00	18.00
❑ 7DE Brett Favre	40.00	18.00
❑ 8DE Eddie George	15.00	6.75
❑ 9DE Dorsey Levens	10.00	4.50
❑ 10DE Curtis Martin	8.00	3.60
❑ 11DE Herman Moore	10.00	4.50
❑ 12DE Barry Sanders	40.00	18.00
❑ 13DE Emmitt Smith	30.00	13.50
❑ 14DE Kordell Stewart	10.00	4.50
❑ 15DE Steve Young	12.00	5.50

1998 SkyBox Thunder Number Crushers

	MINT	NRMT
COMPLETE SET (10)	35.00	16.00
COMMON CARD (1NC-10NC)	2.00	.90
STATED ODDS 1:16		
❑ 1NC Troy Aikman	6.00	2.70
❑ 2NC Jerome Bettis	3.00	1.35
❑ 3NC Tim Brown	3.00	1.35
❑ 4NC Mark Brunell	5.00	2.20
❑ 5NC Dan Marino	12.00	5.50
❑ 6NC Herman Moore	3.00	1.35
❑ 7NC Rob Moore	2.00	.90
❑ 8NC Jerry Rice	6.00	2.70
❑ 9NC Shannon Sharpe	2.00	.90
❑ 10NC Emmitt Smith	10.00	4.50

1998 SkyBox Thunder Quick Strike

	MINT	NRMT
COMPLETE SET (12)	250.00	110.00
COMMON CARD (1QS-12QS)	12.00	5.50
STATED ODDS 1:300		
❑ 1QS Terrell Davis	40.00	18.00
❑ 2QS John Elway	50.00	22.00
❑ 3QS Brett Favre	50.00	22.00
❑ 4QS Joey Galloway	20.00	9.00
❑ 5QS Eddie George	20.00	9.00
❑ 6QS Keyshawn Johnson	20.00	9.00
❑ 7QS Dan Marino	50.00	22.00
❑ 8QS Jerry Rice	25.00	11.00
❑ 9QS Barry Sanders	50.00	22.00
❑ 10QS Deion Sanders	20.00	9.00
❑ 11QS Kordell Stewart	12.00	5.50
❑ 12QS Steve Young	15.00	6.75

1998 SkyBox Thunder StarBurst

	MINT	NRMT
COMPLETE SET (10)	80.00	36.00
COMMON CARD (1SB-10SB)	4.00	1.80
STATED ODDS 1:32		
❑ 1SB Tiki Barber	5.00	2.20
❑ 2SB Corey Dillon	5.00	2.20
❑ 3SB Warrick Dunn	5.00	2.20
❑ 4SB Curtis Enis	5.00	2.20
❑ 5SB Ryan Leaf	5.00	2.20
❑ 6SB Peyton Manning	20.00	9.00
❑ 7SB Randy Moss	20.00	9.00
❑ 8SB Jake Plummer	10.00	4.50
❑ 9SB Antowain Smith	5.00	2.20

❑ 10SB Charles Woodson	5.00	2.20

1993 SP

	MINT	NRMT
COMPLETE SET (270)	150.00	70.00
COMMON CARD (1-270)	.30	.14
SEMISTARS	.50	.23
UNLISTED STARS	1.00	.45
FOILS CONDITION SENSITIVE !		
FOIL PROSPECTS (1-18)	.75	.35
FOIL SEMISTARS	1.50	.70
❑ 1 Curtis Conway FOIL RC	5.00	2.20
❑ 2 John Copeland FOIL RC	.75	.35
❑ 3 Kevin Williams FOIL RC	1.50	.70
❑ 4 Dan Williams FOIL RC	.75	.35
❑ 5 Patrick Bates FOIL RC	.75	.35
❑ 6 Jerome Bettis FOIL RC	12.00	5.50
❑ 7 O.J. McDuffie FOIL RC	8.00	3.60
❑ 8 Robert Smith FOIL RC	12.00	5.50
❑ 9 Drew Bledsoe FOIL RC	60.00	27.00
❑ 10 Irv Smith FOIL RC	.75	.35
❑ 11 Marvin Jones FOIL RC	.75	.35
❑ 12 Victor Bailey FOIL RC	.75	.35
❑ 13 Garrison Hearst FOIL RC	12.00	5.50
❑ 14 Natrone Means FOIL RC	8.00	3.60
❑ 15 Todd Kelly FOIL RC	.75	.35
❑ 16 Rick Mirer FOIL RC	5.00	2.20
❑ 17 Eric Curry FOIL RC	.75	.35
❑ 18 Reggie Brooks FOIL RC	1.50	.70
❑ 19 Eric Dickerson	.50	.23
❑ 20 Roger Harper RC	.30	.14
❑ 21 Michael Haynes	.50	.23
❑ 22 Bobby Hebert	.30	.14
❑ 23 Lincoln Kennedy RC	.30	.14
❑ 24 Chris Miller	.50	.23
❑ 25 Mike Pritchard	.50	.23
❑ 26 Andre Rison	.50	.23
❑ 27 Deion Sanders	1.50	.70
❑ 28 Cornelius Bennett	.50	.23
❑ 29 Kenneth Davis	.30	.14
❑ 30 Henry Jones	.30	.14
❑ 31 Jim Kelly	1.00	.45
❑ 32 John Parrella RC	.30	.14
❑ 33 Andre Reed	.50	.23
❑ 34 Bruce Smith	1.00	.45
❑ 35 Thomas Smith RC	.50	.23
❑ 36 Thurman Thomas	1.00	.45
❑ 37 Neal Anderson	.30	.14
❑ 38 Myron Baker RC	.30	.14
❑ 39 Mark Carrier DB	.30	.14
❑ 40 Richard Dent	.50	.23
❑ 41 Chris Gedney RC	.30	.14
❑ 42 Jim Harbaugh	1.00	.45
❑ 43 Craig Heyward	.50	.23
❑ 44 Carl Simpson RC	.30	.14
❑ 45 Alonzo Spellman	.30	.14
❑ 46 Derrick Fenner	.30	.14
❑ 47 Harold Green	.30	.14
❑ 48 David Klingler	.30	.14
❑ 49 Ricardo McDonald	.30	.14
❑ 50 Tony McGee RC	.50	.23
❑ 51 Carl Pickens	1.00	.45
❑ 52 Steve Tovar RC	.30	.14
❑ 53 Alfred Williams	.30	.14
❑ 54 Darryl Williams	.30	.14
❑ 55 Jerry Ball	.30	.14
❑ 56 Mike Caldwell RC	.30	.14
❑ 57 Mark Carrier WR	.50	.23
❑ 58 Steve Everitt RC	.30	.14
❑ 59 Dan Footman RC	.30	.14
❑ 60 Pepper Johnson	.30	.14
❑ 61 Bernie Kosar	.50	.23
❑ 62 Eric Metcalf	.50	.23
❑ 63 Michael Dean Perry	.50	.23
❑ 64 Troy Aikman	2.50	1.10
❑ 65 Charles Haley	.50	.23
❑ 66 Michael Irvin	1.00	.45
❑ 67 Robert Jones	.30	.14
❑ 68 Derrick Lassic RC	.30	.14
❑ 69 Russell Maryland	.30	.14
❑ 70 Ken Norton Jr.	.50	.23
❑ 71 Darrin Smith RC	.50	.23
❑ 72 Emmitt Smith	5.00	2.20
❑ 73 Steve Atwater	.30	.14
❑ 74 Rod Bernstine	.30	.14
❑ 75 Jason Elam RC	1.00	.45
❑ 76 John Elway	5.00	2.20
❑ 77 Simon Fletcher	.30	.14
❑ 78 Tommy Maddox	.30	.14
❑ 79 Glyn Milburn RC	1.00	.45
❑ 80 Derek Russell	.30	.14
❑ 81 Shannon Sharpe	1.00	.45
❑ 82 Bennie Blades	.30	.14
❑ 83 Willie Green	.30	.14
❑ 84 Antonio London RC	.30	.14
❑ 85 Ryan McNeil RC	.30	.14
❑ 86 Herman Moore	1.50	.70
❑ 87 Rodney Peete	.30	.14
❑ 88 Barry Sanders	5.00	2.20
❑ 89 Chris Spielman	.50	.23
❑ 90 Pat Swilling	.30	.14
❑ 91 Mark Brunell RC	40.00	18.00
❑ 92 Terrell Buckley	.30	.14
❑ 93 Brett Favre	6.00	2.70
❑ 94 Jackie Harris	.30	.14
❑ 95 Sterling Sharpe	1.00	.45
❑ 96 John Stephens	.30	.14
❑ 97 Wayne Simmons RC	.30	.14
❑ 98 George Teague RC	.50	.23
❑ 99 Reggie White	1.00	.45
❑ 100 Micheal Barrow	.30	.14
❑ 101 Cody Carlson	.30	.14
❑ 102 Ray Childress	.30	.14
❑ 103 Brad Hopkins RC	.30	.14
❑ 104 Haywood Jeffires	.50	.23
❑ 105 Wilber Marshall	.30	.14
❑ 106 Warren Moon	1.00	.45
❑ 107 Webster Slaughter	.30	.14
❑ 108 Lorenzo White	.30	.14
❑ 109 John Baylor	.30	.14
❑ 110 Duane Bickett	.30	.14
❑ 111 Quentin Coryatt	.50	.23
❑ 112 Steve Emtman	.30	.14
❑ 113 Jeff George	1.00	.45
❑ 114 Jessie Hester	.30	.14
❑ 115 Anthony Johnson	.50	.23
❑ 116 Reggie Langhorne	.30	.14
❑ 117 Roosevelt Potts RC	.30	.14
❑ 118 Marcus Allen	1.00	.45
❑ 119 J.J. Birden	.30	.14
❑ 120 Willie Davis	1.00	.45
❑ 121 Jaime Fields RC	.30	.14
❑ 122 Joe Montana	5.00	2.20
❑ 123 Will Shields RC	.30	.14
❑ 124 Neil Smith	1.00	.45
❑ 125 Derrick Thomas	1.00	.45
❑ 126 Harvey Williams	.50	.23
❑ 127 Tim Brown	1.00	.45
❑ 128 Billy Joe Hobert RC	1.50	.70
❑ 129 Jeff Hostetler	.50	.23
❑ 130 Ethan Horton	.30	.14
❑ 131 Raghib Ismail	.50	.23
❑ 132 Howie Long	.50	.23
❑ 133 Terry McDaniel	.30	.14
❑ 134 Greg Robinson RC	.30	.14
❑ 135 Anthony Smith	.30	.14
❑ 136 Flipper Anderson	.30	.14
❑ 137 Marc Boutte	.30	.14
❑ 138 Shane Conlan	.30	.14
❑ 139 Troy Drayton RC	.50	.23
❑ 140 Henry Ellard	.50	.23
❑ 141 Jim Everett	.50	.23
❑ 142 Cleveland Gary	.30	.14
❑ 143 Sean Gilbert	.50	.23
❑ 144 Robert Young	.30	.14
❑ 145 Marco Coleman	.30	.14
❑ 146 Bryan Cox	.30	.14
❑ 147 Irving Fryar	.50	.23
❑ 148 Keith Jackson	.50	.23
❑ 149 Terry Kirby RC	1.00	.45
❑ 150 Dan Marino	5.00	2.20
❑ 151 Scott Mitchell	1.00	.45
❑ 152 Louis Oliver	.30	.14
❑ 153 Troy Vincent	.30	.14
❑ 154 Anthony Carter	.50	.23
❑ 155 Cris Carter	1.50	.70
❑ 156 Roger Craig	.50	.23
❑ 157 Chris Doleman	.30	.14
❑ 158 Qadry Ismail RC	2.50	1.10
❑ 159 Steve Jordan	.30	.14
❑ 160 Randall McDaniel	.30	.14
❑ 161 Audray McMillian	.30	.14
❑ 162 Barry Word	.30	.14
❑ 163 Vincent Brown	.30	.14
❑ 164 Marv Cook	.30	.14
❑ 165 Sam Gash RC	.30	.14
❑ 166 Pat Harlow	.30	.14
❑ 167 Greg McMurtry	.30	.14
❑ 168 Todd Rucci RC	.30	.14
❑ 169 Leonard Russell	.50	.23
❑ 170 Scott Sisson RC	.30	.14
❑ 171 Chris Slade RC	.50	.23
❑ 172 Morten Andersen	.30	.14
❑ 173 Derek Brown RBK RC	.50	.23
❑ 174 Reggie Freeman RC	.30	.14
❑ 175 Rickey Jackson	.30	.14
❑ 176 Eric Martin	.30	.14
❑ 177 Wayne Martin	.30	.14
❑ 178 Brad Muster	.30	.14
❑ 179 Willie Roaf RC	.50	.23
❑ 180 Renaldo Turnbull	.30	.14
❑ 181 Derek Brown TE	.30	.14
❑ 182 Marcus Buckley RC	.30	.14
❑ 183 Jarrod Bunch	.30	.14
❑ 184 Rodney Hampton	1.00	.45
❑ 185 Ed McCaffrey	.50	.23
❑ 186 Kanavis McGhee	.30	.14
❑ 187 Mike Sherrard	.30	.14
❑ 188 Phil Simms	.50	.23
❑ 189 Lawrence Taylor	1.00	.45
❑ 190 Kurt Barber	.30	.14
❑ 191 Boomer Esiason	.50	.23
❑ 192 Johnny Johnson	.30	.14
❑ 193 Ronnie Lott	.50	.23
❑ 194 Johnny Mitchell	.30	.14
❑ 195 Rob Moore	.50	.23
❑ 196 Adrian Murrell RC	8.00	3.60
❑ 197 Browning Nagle	.30	.14
❑ 198 Marvin Washington	.30	.14
❑ 199 Eric Allen	.30	.14
❑ 200 Fred Barnett	.50	.23
❑ 201 Randall Cunningham	1.00	.45
❑ 202 Byron Evans	.30	.14
❑ 203 Tim Harris	.30	.14
❑ 204 Seth Joyner	.30	.14
❑ 205 Leonard Renfro RC	.30	.14
❑ 206 Heath Sherman	.30	.14
❑ 207 Clyde Simmons	.30	.14
❑ 208 Johnny Bailey	.30	.14
❑ 209 Steve Beuerlein	.30	.14
❑ 210 Chuck Cecil	.30	.14
❑ 211 Larry Centers RC	1.50	.70

	MINT	NRMT
❑ 212 Gary Clark	.50	.23
❑ 213 Ernest Dye RC	.30	.14
❑ 214 Ken Harvey	.30	.14
❑ 215 Randal Hill	.30	.14
❑ 216 Ricky Proehl	.30	.14
❑ 217 Deon Figures RC	.50	.23
❑ 218 Barry Foster	.50	.23
❑ 219 Eric Green	.30	.14
❑ 220 Kevin Greene	1.00	.45
❑ 221 Carlton Haselrig	.30	.14
❑ 222 Andre Hastings RC	1.00	.45
❑ 223 Greg Lloyd	1.00	.45
❑ 224 Neil O'Donnell	1.00	.45
❑ 225 Rod Woodson	1.00	.45
❑ 226 Marion Butts	.30	.14
❑ 227 Darren Carrington RC	.30	.14
❑ 228 Darrien Gordon RC	.30	.14
❑ 229 Ronnie Harmon	.30	.14
❑ 230 Stan Humphries	1.00	.45
❑ 231 Anthony Miller	.50	.23
❑ 232 Chris Mims	.30	.14
❑ 233 Leslie O'Neal	.50	.23
❑ 234 Junior Seau	1.00	.45
❑ 235 Dana Hall	.30	.14
❑ 236 Adrian Hardy	.30	.14
❑ 237 Brent Jones	.50	.23
❑ 238 Tim McDonald	.30	.14
❑ 239 Tom Rathman	.30	.14
❑ 240 Jerry Rice	3.00	1.35
❑ 241 Dana Stubblefield RC	1.00	.45
❑ 242 Ricky Watters	1.00	.45
❑ 243 Steve Young	2.50	1.10
❑ 244 Brian Blades	.50	.23
❑ 245 Ferrell Edmunds	.30	.14
❑ 246 Carlton Gray RC	.30	.14
❑ 247 Cortez Kennedy	.50	.23
❑ 248 Kelvin Martin	.30	.14
❑ 249 Dan McGwire	.30	.14
❑ 250 Jon Vaughn	.30	.14
❑ 251 Chris Warren	.50	.23
❑ 252 John L. Williams	.30	.14
❑ 253 Reggie Cobb	.30	.14
❑ 254 Horace Copeland RC	.50	.23
❑ 255 Lawrence Dawsey	.30	.14
❑ 256 Demetrius DuBose RC	.30	.14
❑ 257 Craig Erickson	.50	.23
❑ 258 Courtney Hawkins	.30	.14
❑ 259 John Lynch RC	.30	.14
❑ 260 Hardy Nickerson	.50	.23
❑ 261 Lamar Thomas RC	.30	.14
❑ 262 Carl Banks	.30	.14
❑ 263 Tom Carter RC	.50	.23
❑ 264 Brad Edwards	.30	.14
❑ 265 Kurt Gouveia	.30	.14
❑ 266 Desmond Howard	.50	.23
❑ 267 Charles Mann	.30	.14
❑ 268 Art Monk	.50	.23
❑ 269 Mark Rypien	.30	.14
❑ 270 Ricky Sanders	.30	.14
❑ P1 Joe Montana Promo numbered 19	5.00	2.20

1993 SP All-Pros

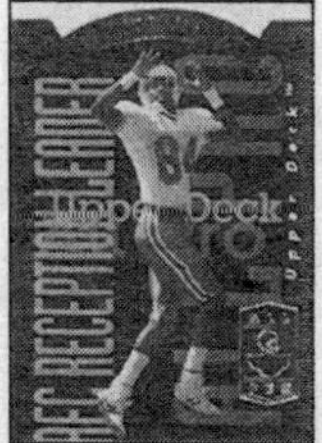

	MINT	NRMT
COMPLETE SET (15)	120.00	55.00
STATED ODDS 1:15		
❑ AP1 Steve Young	12.00	5.50
❑ AP2 Warren Moon	5.00	2.20
❑ AP3 Troy Aikman	12.00	5.50
❑ AP4 Dan Marino	25.00	11.00
❑ AP5 Barry Sanders	25.00	11.00
❑ AP6 Barry Foster	2.50	1.10
❑ AP7 Emmitt Smith	25.00	11.00
❑ AP8 Thurman Thomas	5.00	2.20
❑ AP9 Jerry Rice	15.00	6.75
❑ AP10 Sterling Sharpe	5.00	2.20
❑ AP11 Anthony Miller	2.50	1.10
❑ AP12 Haywood Jeffires	2.50	1.10
❑ AP13 Junior Seau	5.00	2.20
❑ AP14 Reggie White	5.00	2.20
❑ AP15 Derrick Thomas	5.00	2.20

1994 SP

	MINT	NRMT
COMPLETE SET (200)	50.00	22.00
COMMON CARD (1-200)	.15	.07
SEMISTARS	.30	.14
UNLISTED STARS	.50	.23
FOIL PROSPECTS (1-20)	.40	.18
FOIL SEMISTARS	.75	.35
COMP.DIE CUT SET (200)	80.00	36.00
*DIE CUT STARS: .8X to 2X HI COL.		
*DIE CUT RCs: .5X to 1.2X HI		
DIE CUTS: ONE PER PACK		
❑ 1 Dan Wilkinson RC	.75	.35
❑ 2 Heath Shuler RC	.75	.35
❑ 3 Marshall Faulk RC	40.00	18.00
❑ 4 Willie McGinest RC	.40	.18
❑ 5 Trent Dilfer RC	5.00	2.20
❑ 6 Bryant Young RC	.75	.35
❑ 7 Antonio Langham RC	.40	.18
❑ 8 John Thierry RC	.40	.18
❑ 9 Aaron Glenn RC	.40	.18
❑ 10 Charles Johnson RC	.75	.35
❑ 11 Dewayne Washington RC	.40	.18
❑ 12 Johnnie Morton RC	2.00	.90
❑ 13 Greg Hill RC	1.50	.70
❑ 14 William Floyd RC	.75	.35
❑ 15 Derrick Alexander WR RC	1.50	.70
❑ 16 Darnay Scott RC	2.00	.90
❑ 17 Errict Rhett RC	6.00	2.70
❑ 18 Charlie Garner RC	5.00	2.20
❑ 19 Thomas Lewis RC	.40	.18
❑ 20 David Palmer RC	1.50	.70
❑ 21 Andre Reed	.30	.14
❑ 22 Thurman Thomas	.50	.23
❑ 23 Bruce Smith	.50	.23
❑ 24 Jim Kelly	.50	.23
❑ 25 Cornelius Bennett	.30	.14
❑ 26 Bucky Brooks RC	.15	.07
❑ 27 Jeff Burris RC	.30	.14
❑ 28 Jim Harbaugh	.50	.23
❑ 29 Tony Bennett	.15	.07
❑ 30 Quentin Coryatt	.15	.07
❑ 31 Floyd Turner	.15	.07
❑ 32 Roosevelt Potts	.15	.07
❑ 33 Jeff Herrod	.15	.07
❑ 34 Irving Fryar	.30	.14
❑ 35 Bryan Cox	.15	.07
❑ 36 Dan Marino	4.00	1.80
❑ 37 Terry Kirby	.50	.23
❑ 38 Michael Stewart	.15	.07
❑ 39 Bernie Kosar	.30	.14
❑ 40 Aubrey Beavers RC	.15	.07
❑ 41 Vincent Brisby	.50	.23
❑ 42 Ben Coates	.50	.23
❑ 43 Drew Bledsoe	2.50	1.10
❑ 44 Marion Butts	.15	.07
❑ 45 Chris Slade	.15	.07
❑ 46 Michael Timpson	.15	.07
❑ 47 Ray Crittenden RC	.15	.07
❑ 48 Rob Moore	.30	.14
❑ 49 Johnny Mitchell	.15	.07
❑ 50 Art Monk	.30	.14
❑ 51 Boomer Esiason	.30	.14
❑ 52 Ronnie Lott	.30	.14
❑ 53 Ryan Yarborough RC	.15	.07
❑ 54 Carl Pickens	.50	.23
❑ 55 David Klingler	.15	.07
❑ 56 Harold Green	.15	.07
❑ 57 John Copeland	.15	.07
❑ 58 Louis Oliver	.15	.07
❑ 59 Corey Sawyer	.15	.07
❑ 60 Michael Jackson	.30	.14
❑ 61 Mark Rypien	.15	.07
❑ 62 Vinny Testaverde	.30	.14
❑ 63 Eric Metcalf	.30	.14
❑ 64 Eric Turner	.15	.07
❑ 65 Haywood Jeffires	.30	.14
❑ 66 Micheal Barrow	.15	.07
❑ 67 Cody Carlson	.15	.07
❑ 68 Gary Brown	.15	.07
❑ 69 Bucky Richardson	.15	.07
❑ 70 Al Smith	.15	.07
❑ 71 Eric Green	.15	.07
❑ 72 Neil O'Donnell	.50	.23
❑ 73 Barry Foster	.15	.07
❑ 74 Greg Lloyd	.50	.23
❑ 75 Rod Woodson	.50	.23
❑ 76 Byron Bam Morris RC	.50	.23
❑ 77 John L. Williams	.15	.07
❑ 78 Anthony Miller	.30	.14
❑ 79 Mike Pritchard	.15	.07
❑ 80 John Elway	4.00	1.80
❑ 81 Shannon Sharpe	.30	.14
❑ 82 Steve Atwater	.15	.07
❑ 83 Simon Fletcher	.15	.07
❑ 84 Glyn Milburn	.30	.14
❑ 85 Mark Collins	.15	.07
❑ 86 Keith Cash	.15	.07
❑ 87 Willie Davis	.30	.14
❑ 88 Joe Montana	4.00	1.80
❑ 89 Marcus Allen	.50	.23
❑ 90 Neil Smith	.50	.23
❑ 91 Derrick Thomas	.50	.23
❑ 92 Tim Brown	.50	.23
❑ 93 Jeff Hostetler	.30	.14
❑ 94 Terry McDaniel	.15	.07
❑ 95 Rocket Ismail	.30	.14
❑ 96 Rob Fredrickson RC	.30	.14
❑ 97 Harvey Williams	.30	.14
❑ 98 Steve Wisniewski	.15	.07
❑ 99 Stan Humphries	.50	.23
❑ 100 Natrone Means	.50	.23
❑ 101 Leslie O'Neal	.15	.07
❑ 102 Junior Seau	.50	.23
❑ 103 Ronnie Harmon	.15	.07
❑ 104 Shawn Jefferson	.15	.07
❑ 105 Howard Ballard	.15	.07
❑ 106 Rick Mirer	.50	.23
❑ 107 Cortez Kennedy	.30	.14
❑ 108 Chris Warren	.30	.14
❑ 109 Brian Blades	.30	.14
❑ 110 Sam Adams RC	.30	.14
❑ 111 Gary Clark	.30	.14
❑ 112 Steve Beuerlein	.15	.07
❑ 113 Ronald Moore	.15	.07
❑ 114 Eric Swann	.30	.14
❑ 115 Clyde Simmons	.15	.07
❑ 116 Seth Joyner	.15	.07
❑ 117 Troy Aikman	2.00	.90
❑ 118 Charles Haley	.30	.14
❑ 119 Alvin Harper	.30	.14
❑ 120 Michael Irvin	.50	.23
❑ 121 Daryl Johnston	.30	.14
❑ 122 Emmitt Smith	3.00	1.35
❑ 123 Shante Carver RC	.15	.07
❑ 124 Dave Brown	.30	.14
❑ 125 Rodney Hampton	.50	.23

Card	MINT	NRMT
❑ 126 Dave Meggett	.15	.07
❑ 127 Chris Calloway	.15	.07
❑ 128 Mike Sherrard	.15	.07
❑ 129 Carlton Bailey	.15	.07
❑ 130 Randall Cunningham	.50	.23
❑ 131 William Fuller	.15	.07
❑ 132 Eric Allen	.15	.07
❑ 133 Calvin Williams	.30	.14
❑ 134 Herschel Walker	.30	.14
❑ 135 Bernard Williams RC	.15	.07
❑ 136 Henry Ellard	.30	.14
❑ 137 Ethan Horton	.15	.07
❑ 138 Desmond Howard	.30	.14
❑ 139 Reggie Brooks	.30	.14
❑ 140 John Friesz	.30	.14
❑ 141 Tom Carter	.15	.07
❑ 142 Terry Allen	.30	.14
❑ 143 Adrian Cooper	.15	.07
❑ 144 Qadry Ismail	.50	.23
❑ 145 Warren Moon	.50	.23
❑ 146 Henry Thomas	.15	.07
❑ 147 Todd Steussie RC	.30	.14
❑ 148 Cris Carter	.75	.35
❑ 149 Andy Heck	.15	.07
❑ 150 Curtis Conway	.50	.23
❑ 151 Erik Kramer	.30	.14
❑ 152 Lewis Tillman	.15	.07
❑ 153 Dante Jones	.15	.07
❑ 154 Alonzo Spellman	.15	.07
❑ 155 Herman Moore	.50	.23
❑ 156 Broderick Thomas	.15	.07
❑ 157 Scott Mitchell	.50	.23
❑ 158 Barry Sanders	4.00	1.80
❑ 159 Chris Spielman	.30	.14
❑ 160 Pat Swilling	.15	.07
❑ 161 Bennie Blades	.15	.07
❑ 162 Sterling Sharpe	.30	.14
❑ 163 Brett Favre	4.00	1.80
❑ 164 Reggie Cobb	.15	.07
❑ 165 Reggie White	.50	.23
❑ 166 Sean Jones	.15	.07
❑ 167 George Teague	.15	.07
❑ 168 LeShon Johnson RC	.30	.14
❑ 169 Courtney Hawkins	.15	.07
❑ 170 Jackie Harris	.15	.07
❑ 171 Craig Erickson	.15	.07
❑ 172 Santana Dotson	.30	.14
❑ 173 Eric Curry	.15	.07
❑ 174 Hardy Nickerson	.30	.14
❑ 175 Derek Brown RBK	.15	.07
❑ 176 Jim Everett	.30	.14
❑ 177 Michael Haynes	.30	.14
❑ 178 Tyrone Hughes	.30	.14
❑ 179 Wayne Martin	.15	.07
❑ 180 Willie Roaf	.15	.07
❑ 181 Irv Smith	.15	.07
❑ 182 Jeff George	.50	.23
❑ 183 Andre Rison	.30	.14
❑ 184 Erric Pegram	.15	.07
❑ 185 Bret Emanuel RC	1.50	.70
❑ 186 Chris Doleman	.15	.07
❑ 187 Ron George	.15	.07
❑ 188 Chris Miller	.15	.07
❑ 189 Troy Drayton	.15	.07
❑ 190 Chris Chandler	.30	.14
❑ 191 Jerome Bettis	.75	.35
❑ 192 Jimmie Jones	.15	.07
❑ 193 Sean Gilbert	.15	.07
❑ 194 Jerry Rice	2.00	.90
❑ 195 Brent Jones	.30	.14
❑ 196 Deion Sanders	1.00	.45
❑ 197 Steve Young	1.50	.70
❑ 198 Ricky Watters	.50	.23
❑ 199 Dana Stubblefield	.50	.23
❑ 200 Ken Norton Jr.	.30	.14
❑ RB1 Dan Marino 300 TDs	30.00	13.50
❑ RB2 Jerry Rice 127 TDs	25.00	11.00
❑ P16 Joe Montana Promo	4.00	1.80

1994 SP Holoviews

	MINT	NRMT
COMPLETE SET (40)	50.00	22.00
STATED ODDS 1:5		
*DIE CUT STARS: 5X to 12X BASE CARD HI		
*DIE CUT ROOKIES: 2X to 5X BASE CARD HI		

DIE CUT STATED ODDS 1:75......

Card	MINT	NRMT
❑ PB1 Jamir Miller	.40	.18
❑ PB2 Andre Rison	.75	.35
❑ PB3 Bucky Brooks	.15	.07
❑ PB4 Thurman Thomas	1.25	.55
❑ PB5 John Thierry	.40	.18
❑ PB6 Dan Wilkinson	.75	.35
❑ PB7 Darnay Scott	2.00	.90
❑ PB8 Antonio Langham	.40	.18
❑ PB9 Troy Aikman	5.00	2.20
❑ PB10 Emmitt Smith	8.00	3.60
❑ PB11 John Elway	10.00	4.50
❑ PB12 Barry Sanders	10.00	4.50
❑ PB13 Johnnie Morton	2.00	.90
❑ PB14 Reggie White	1.25	.55
❑ PB15 Brett Favre	10.00	4.50
❑ PB16 LeShon Johnson	.30	.14
❑ PB17 Joe Montana	10.00	4.50
❑ PB18 Greg Hill	1.50	.70
❑ PB19 Calvin Jones	.40	.18
❑ PB20 Tim Brown	1.25	.55
❑ PB21 Isaac Bruce	6.00	2.70
❑ PB22 Jerome Bettis	2.00	.90
❑ PB23 Dan Marino	10.00	4.50
❑ PB24 O.J.McDuffie	3.00	1.35
❑ PB25 Willie McGinest	.40	.18
❑ PB26 Mario Bates	.40	.18
❑ PB27 Rodney Hampton	1.25	.55
❑ PB28 Thomas Lewis	.40	.18
❑ PB29 Aaron Glenn	.40	.18
❑ PB30 Barry Foster	.40	.18
❑ PB31 Charles Johnson	.75	.35
❑ PB32 Steve Young	4.00	1.80
❑ PB33 Jerry Rice	5.00	2.20
❑ PB34 Bryant Young	.75	.35
❑ PB35 William Floyd	.75	.35
❑ PB36 Sam Adams	.30	.14
❑ PB37 Rick Mirer	1.25	.55
❑ PB38 Errict Rhett	6.00	2.70
❑ PB39 Reggie Brooks	.75	.35
❑ PB40 Heath Shuler	.75	.35

1995 SP

	MINT	NRMT
COMPLETE SET (200)	80.00	36.00
COMMON CARD (1-200)	.20	.09
SEMISTARS	.40	.18
UNLISTED STARS	.75	.35
FOIL PROSPECTS (1-20)	.50	.23
FOIL SEMISTARS	1.00	.45
FOIL UNLISTED STARS	2.00	.90
FOILS CONDITION SENSITIVE!		
NNO's: STATED ODDS 1:380		

Card	MINT	NRMT
❑ 1 Ki-Jana Carter PP RC	1.25	.55
❑ 2 Eric Zeier PP RC UER Height listed at 6'11"	2.50	1.10
❑ 3 Steve McNair PP RC	10.00	4.50
❑ 4 Michael Westbrook PP RC	5.00	2.20
❑ 5 Kerry Collins PP RC	3.00	1.35
❑ 6 Joey Galloway PP RC	8.00	3.60
❑ 7 Kevin Carter PP RC	2.00	.90
❑ 8 Mike Mamula PP RC	.50	.23
❑ 9 Kyle Brady PP RC	1.00	.45
❑ 10 J.J. Stokes PP RC	2.50	1.10
❑ 11 Tyrone Poole PP RC	1.00	.45
❑ 12 Rashaan Salaam PP RC	2.00	.90
❑ 13 Sherman Williams PP RC	.50	.23
❑ 14 Luther Elliss PP RC	.50	.23
❑ 15 James O. Stewart PP RC	6.00	2.70
❑ 16 Tamarick Vanover PP RC	2.00	.90
❑ 17 Napoleon Kaufman PP RC	6.00	2.70
❑ 18 Curtis Martin PP RC	8.00	3.60
❑ 19 Tyrone Wheatley PP RC	4.00	1.80
❑ 20 Frank Sanders PP RC	3.00	1.35
❑ 21 Devin Bush	.20	.09
❑ 22 Terance Mathis	.40	.18
❑ 23 Bert Emanuel	.75	.35
❑ 24 Eric Metcalf	.40	.18
❑ 25 Craig Heyward	.40	.18
❑ 26 Jeff George	.40	.18
❑ 27 Mark Carrier WR	.40	.18
❑ 28 Pete Metzelaars	.20	.09
❑ 29 Frank Reich	.20	.09
❑ 30 Sam Mills	.40	.18
❑ 31 John Kasay	.20	.09
❑ 32 Willie Green	.40	.18
❑ 33 Jeff Graham	.20	.09
❑ 34 Curtis Conway	.75	.35
❑ 35 Steve Walsh	.20	.09
❑ 36 Erik Kramer	.20	.09
❑ 37 Michael Timpson	.20	.09
❑ 38 Mark Carrier	.20	.09
❑ 39 Troy Aikman	2.00	.90
❑ 40 Michael Irvin	.75	.35
❑ 41 Charles Haley	.40	.18
❑ 42 Deion Sanders	1.25	.55
❑ 43 Jay Novacek	.40	.18
❑ 44 Emmitt Smith	3.00	1.35
❑ 45 Herman Moore	.75	.35
❑ 46 Scott Mitchell UER front reads Mitcehill	.40	.18
❑ 47 Bennie Blades	.20	.09
❑ 48 Johnnie Morton	.40	.18
❑ 49 Chris Spielman	.40	.18
❑ 50 Barry Sanders	4.00	1.80
❑ 51 Edgar Bennett	.40	.18
❑ 52 Reggie White	.75	.35
❑ 53 Sean Jones	.20	.09
❑ 54 Mark Ingram	.20	.09
❑ 55 Robert Brooks	.75	.35
❑ 56 Brett Favre	4.00	1.80
❑ 57 Lovell Pinkney RC	.20	.09
❑ 58 Chris Miller	.20	.09
❑ 59 Isaac Bruce	1.25	.55
❑ 60 Roman Phifer	.20	.09
❑ 61 Sean Gilbert	.40	.18
❑ 62 Jerome Bettis	.75	.35
❑ 63 Derrick Alexander DE RC	.20	.09
❑ 64 Cris Carter	.75	.35
❑ 65 Jake Reed	.40	.18
❑ 66 Robert Smith	.75	.35
❑ 67 David Palmer	.40	.18
❑ 68 Warren Moon	.40	.18
❑ 69 Ray Zellars RC	.40	.18
❑ 70 Jim Everett	.20	.09
❑ 71 Michael Haynes	.40	.18
❑ 72 Quinn Early	.40	.18
❑ 73 Willie Roaf	.20	.09
❑ 74 Mario Bates	.75	.35
❑ 75 Mike Sherrard	.20	.09
❑ 76 Chris Calloway	.20	.09
❑ 77 Dave Brown	.40	.18
❑ 78 Thomas Lewis	.40	.18
❑ 79 Herschel Walker	.40	.18

❑ 80	Rodney Hampton	.40	.18
❑ 81	Fred Barnett	.40	.18
❑ 82	Calvin Williams	.40	.18
❑ 83	Randall Cunningham	.75	.35
❑ 84	Charlie Garner	.40	.18
❑ 85	Bobby Taylor RC	.40	.18
❑ 86	Ricky Watters	.75	.35
❑ 87	Dave Krieg	.20	.09
❑ 88	Rob Moore	.20	.09
❑ 89	Eric Swann	.40	.18
❑ 90	Clyde Simmons	.20	.09
❑ 91	Seth Joyner	.20	.09
❑ 92	Garrison Hearst	.75	.35
❑ 93	Jerry Rice	2.00	.90
❑ 94	Bryant Young	.40	.18
❑ 95	Brent Jones	.20	.09
❑ 96	Ken Norton	.40	.18
❑ 97	William Floyd	.75	.35
❑ 98	Steve Young	1.50	.70
❑ 99	Warren Sapp RC	2.50	1.10
❑ 100	Trent Dilfer	.75	.35
❑ 101	Alvin Harper	.20	.09
❑ 102	Hardy Nickerson	.20	.09
❑ 103	Derrick Brooks	.20	.09
❑ 104	Errict Rhett	.75	.35
❑ 105	Henry Ellard	.40	.18
❑ 106	Ken Harvey	.20	.09
❑ 107	Gus Frerotte	.75	.35
❑ 108	Brian Mitchell	.20	.09
❑ 109	Terry Allen	.40	.18
❑ 110	Heath Shuler	.75	.35
❑ 111	Jim Kelly	.75	.35
❑ 112	Andre Reed	.40	.18
❑ 113	Bruce Smith	.75	.35
❑ 114	Darick Holmes RC	.40	.18
❑ 115	Bryce Paup	.75	.35
❑ 116	Cornelius Bennett	.40	.18
❑ 117	Carl Pickens	.75	.35
❑ 118	Darnay Scott	.75	.35
❑ 119	Jeff Blake RC	3.00	1.35
❑ 120	Steve Tovar	.20	.09
❑ 121	Tony McGee	.20	.09
❑ 122	Dan Wilkinson	.40	.18
❑ 123	Craig Powell	.20	.09
❑ 124	Vinny Testaverde	.40	.18
❑ 125	Eric Turner	.20	.09
❑ 126	Leroy Hoard	.20	.09
❑ 127	Lorenzo White	.20	.09
❑ 128	Andre Rison	.40	.18
❑ 129	Shannon Sharpe	.40	.18
❑ 130	Terrell Davis RC	35.00	16.00
❑ 131	Anthony Miller	.40	.18
❑ 132	Mike Pritchard	.20	.09
❑ 133	Steve Atwater	.20	.09
❑ 134	John Elway	4.00	1.80
❑ 135	Haywood Jeffires	.20	.09
❑ 136	Gary Brown	.20	.09
❑ 137	Al Smith	.20	.09
❑ 138	Rodney Thomas RC	.75	.35
❑ 139	Chris Chandler	.40	.18
❑ 140	Mel Gray	.20	.09
❑ 141	Craig Erickson	.20	.09
❑ 142	Sean Dawkins	.40	.18
❑ 143	Ken Dilger RC	.40	.18
❑ 144	Ellis Johnson RC UER	.20	.09
	front reads Elliss		
❑ 145	Quentin Coryatt	.40	.18
❑ 146	Marshall Faulk	1.25	.55
❑ 147	Tony Boselli RC	.40	.18
❑ 148	Rob Johnson RC	5.00	2.20
❑ 149	Desmond Howard	.40	.18
❑ 150	Steve Beuerlein	.20	.09
❑ 151	Reggie Cobb	.20	.09
❑ 152	Jeff Lageman	.20	.09
❑ 153	Willie Davis	.40	.18
❑ 154	Marcus Allen	.75	.35
❑ 155	Neil Smith	.40	.18
❑ 156	Greg Hill	.40	.18
❑ 157	Steve Bono	.40	.18
❑ 158	Derrick Thomas	.40	.18
❑ 159	Jeff Hostetler	.40	.18
❑ 160	Harvey Williams	.20	.09
❑ 161	Rocket Ismail	.40	.18
❑ 162	Chester McGlockton	.40	.18
❑ 163	Terry McDaniel	.20	.09
❑ 164	Tim Brown	.75	.35
❑ 165	Terry Kirby	.40	.18
❑ 166	Irving Fryar	.40	.18
❑ 167	O.J. McDuffie	.75	.35
❑ 168	Bryan Cox	.20	.09
❑ 169	Eric Green	.20	.09
❑ 170	Dan Marino	4.00	1.80
❑ 171	Ben Coates	.40	.18
❑ 172	Vincent Brisby	.20	.09
❑ 173	Chris Slade	.40	.18
❑ 174	Ty Law	.40	.18
❑ 175	Vincent Brown	.20	.09
❑ 176	Drew Bledsoe	2.00	.90
❑ 177	Johnny Mitchell	.20	.09
❑ 178	Boomer Esiason	.40	.18
❑ 179	Wayne Chrebet RC	8.00	3.60
❑ 180	Mo Lewis	.20	.09
❑ 181	Ronald Moore	.20	.09
❑ 182	Aaron Glenn	.20	.09
❑ 183	Mark Bruener RC	.40	.18
❑ 184	Neil O'Donnell	.40	.18
❑ 185	Charles Johnson	.40	.18
❑ 186	Greg Lloyd	.40	.18
❑ 187	Rod Woodson	.40	.18
❑ 188	Byron Bam Morris	.40	.18
❑ 189	Terrell Fletcher RC	.20	.09
❑ 190	Terrance Shaw RC UER	.20	.09
	front reads Terrence		
❑ 191	Stan Humphries	.40	.18
❑ 192	Junior Seau	.75	.35
❑ 193	Leslie O'Neal	.40	.18
❑ 194	Natrone Means	.75	.35
❑ 195	Christian Fauria RC	.20	.09
❑ 196	Rick Mirer	.75	.35
❑ 197	Sam Adams	.20	.09
❑ 198	Cortez Kennedy	.40	.18
❑ 199	Eugene Robinson	.20	.09
❑ 200	Chris Warren	.40	.18
❑ P113	Dan Marino Promo	3.00	1.35
❑ DM1	Dan Marino Tribute	25.00	11.00
❑ JM1	Joe Montana Salute	25.00	11.00
❑ NNO	Dan Marino TRI Jumbo	25.00	11.00
	Card measures 3 1/2" by 5" Issued by Upper Deck Authenticated Numbered of 10,000		
❑ NNO	Joe Montana SAL Jumbo	25.00	11.00
	Card meaures 3 1/2" by 5" Issued by Upper Deck Authenticated Numbered of 10,000		
❑ P1	Joe Montana Promo	4.00	1.80
	All-Pro Silver card		

1995 SP All-Pros

	MINT	NRMT
COMPLETE SET (20)	40.00	18.00
STATED ODDS 1:5		

*GOLD STARS: 2.5X TO 6X BASE CARD HI
*GOLD ROOKIES: .6X TO 1.5X BASE CARD HI
GOLD STATED ODDS 1:62

❑ 1	Marshall Faulk	2.50	1.10
❑ 2	Natrone Means	1.50	.70
❑ 3	Emmitt Smith	6.00	2.70
❑ 4	Brett Favre	8.00	3.60
❑ 5	Michael Westbrook	2.50	1.10
❑ 6	Jerry Rice	4.00	1.80
❑ 7	John Elway	8.00	3.60
❑ 8	Troy Aikman	4.00	1.80
❑ 9	Rashaan Salaam	1.00	.45
❑ 10	Jerome Bettis	1.50	.70
❑ 11	Drew Bledsoe	4.00	1.80
❑ 12	Kerry Collins	1.50	.70
❑ 13	Dan Marino	8.00	3.60
❑ 14	Tyrone Wheatley	2.00	.90
❑ 15	Steve McNair	5.00	2.20
❑ 16	Steve Young	3.00	1.35
❑ 17	Eric Zeier	1.25	.55
❑ 18	Errict Rhett	1.50	.70
❑ 19	Michael Irvin	1.50	.70
❑ 20	Barry Sanders	8.00	3.60

1995 SP Holoviews

	MINT	NRMT
COMPLETE SET (40)	80.00	36.00
STATED ODDS 1:5		

*DIE CUT STARS: 4X TO 10X BASE CARD HI
*DIE CUT ROOKIES: 1.5X TO 4X BASE CARD HI
HOLO DC: STATED ODDS 1:75 ..

❑ 1	Joe Montana	8.00	3.60
❑ 2	Dan Marino	12.00	5.50
❑ 3	Drew Bledsoe	6.00	2.70
❑ 4	Ben Coates	1.25	.55
❑ 5	Curtis Martin	8.00	3.60
❑ 6	Kyle Brady	1.00	.45
❑ 7	Marshall Faulk	4.00	1.80
❑ 8	Ki-Jana Carter	1.25	.55
❑ 9	Leroy Hoard	.60	.25
❑ 10	James O. Stewart	6.00	2.70
❑ 11	Mark Bruener	.40	.18
❑ 12	Charles Johnson	1.25	.55
❑ 13	Rod Woodson	1.25	.55
❑ 14	John Elway	12.00	5.50
❑ 15	Tim Brown	2.50	1.10
❑ 16	Napoleon Kaufman	6.00	2.70
❑ 17	Natrone Means	2.50	1.10
❑ 18	Jimmy Oliver	.20	.09
❑ 19	Christian Fauria	.20	.09
❑ 20	Joey Galloway	8.00	3.60
❑ 21	Chris Warren	1.25	.55
❑ 22	Kerry Collins	3.00	1.35
❑ 23	Mario Bates	2.50	1.10
❑ 24	Jerome Bettis	2.50	1.10
❑ 25	William Floyd	2.50	1.10
❑ 26	Jerry Rice	6.00	2.70
❑ 27	J.J. Stokes	2.50	1.10
❑ 28	Steve Young	5.00	2.20
❑ 29	Troy Aikman	6.00	2.70
❑ 30	Michael Irvin	2.50	1.10
❑ 31	Emmitt Smith	10.00	4.50
❑ 32	Rodney Hampton	1.25	.55
❑ 33	Heath Shuler	2.50	1.10
❑ 34	Michael Westbrook	5.00	2.20
❑ 35	Barry Sanders	12.00	5.50
❑ 36	Brett Favre	12.00	5.50
❑ 37	Cris Carter	2.50	1.10
❑ 38	Warren Moon	1.25	.55
❑ 39	James A.Stewart	.20	.09
❑ 40	Errict Rhett	2.50	1.10

1995 SP Championship

	MINT	NRMT
COMPLETE SET (225)	60.00	27.00
COMMON CARD (1-225)	.15	.07
SEMISTARS	.30	.14

	MINT	NRMT
UNLISTED STARS	.50	.23
COMP.DIE CUT SET (225)	120.00	55.00
*DC STARS: 1.5X TO 3X HI COLUMN		
*DC RCs: .6X TO 1.5X HI		
DIE CUTS ONE PER PACK		

❑ 1 Frank Sanders RC .... 2.00 .90
❑ 2 Stoney Case RC .... .75 .35
❑ 3 Lorenzo Styles RC .... .15 .07
❑ 4 Todd Collins RC .... .50 .23
❑ 5 Darick Holmes RC .... .30 .14
❑ 6 Brian DeMarco .... .30 .14
❑ 7 Tyrone Poole RC .... .30 .14
❑ 8 Kerry Collins RC .... 2.00 .90
❑ 9 Rashaan Salaam RC .... .50 .23
❑ 10 Steve Stenstrom RC .... .15 .07
❑ 11 Ki-Jana Carter RC .... .50 .23
❑ 12 Eric Zeier RC .... .75 .35
❑ 13 Sherman Williams RC .... .15 .07
❑ 14 Terrell Davis RC 20.00 9.00
❑ 15 David Dunn .... .15 .07
❑ 16 Luther Elliss RC .... .15 .07
❑ 17 Craig Newsome RC .... .15 .07
❑ 18 Antonio Freeman RC 6.00 2.70
❑ 19 Steve McNair RC 6.00 2.70
❑ 20 Anthony Cook .... .15 .07
❑ 21 Rodney Thomas RC .... .50 .23
❑ 22 Ellis Johnson .... .15 .07
❑ 23 Ken Dilger RC .... .30 .14
❑ 24 James O. Stewart RC .. 5.00 2.20
❑ 25 Pete Mitchell RC .... .50 .23
❑ 26 Tamarick Vanover RC .... .50 .23
❑ 27 Orlando Thomas .... .15 .07
❑ 28 Corey Fuller RC .... .15 .07
❑ 29 Curtis Martin RC 6.00 2.70
❑ 30 Ty Law RC .... .30 .14
❑ 31 Roell Preston RC .... 1.00 .45
❑ 32 Mark Fields RC .... .15 .07
❑ 33 Tyrone Wheatley RC 2.50 1.10
❑ 34 Kyle Brady RC .... .50 .23
❑ 35 Napoleon Kaufman RC .. 5.00 2.20
❑ 36 Kordell Stewart RC 6.00 2.70
❑ 37 Mark Bruener RC .... .30 .14
❑ 38 Terrance Shaw RC .... .15 .07
❑ 39 Terrell Fletcher RC .... .15 .07
❑ 40 J.J. Stokes RC .... 1.25 .55
❑ 41 Christian Fauria RC .... .15 .07
❑ 42 Joey Galloway RC 6.00 2.70
❑ 43 Kevin Carter RC .... .50 .23
❑ 44 Warren Sapp RC .... .75 .35
❑ 45 Michael Westbrook RC .. 4.00 1.80
❑ 46 Clyde Simmons .... .15 .07
❑ 47 Rob Moore .... .15 .07
❑ 48 Seth Joyner .... .15 .07
❑ 49 Dave Krieg .... .15 .07
❑ 50 Garrison Hearst .... .50 .23
❑ 51 Aeneas Williams .... .15 .07
❑ 52 Terance Mathis .... .30 .14
❑ 53 Bert Emanuel UER .... .50 .23
Name spelled Emanual
❑ 54 Chris Doleman .... .15 .07
❑ 55 Craig Heyward .... .30 .14
❑ 56 Jeff George .... .30 .14
❑ 57 Eric Metcalf .... .30 .14
❑ 58 Jim Kelly .... .50 .23
❑ 59 Andre Reed .... .30 .14
❑ 60 Russell Copeland .... .15 .07
❑ 61 Bruce Smith .... .50 .23
❑ 62 Cornelius Bennett .... .30 .14
❑ 63 Jeff Burris .... .15 .07
❑ 64 Mark Carrier WR .... .30 .14
❑ 65 Pete Metzelaars .... .15 .07
❑ 66 Frank Reich .... .15 .07
❑ 67 Sam Mills .... .30 .14
❑ 68 John Kasay .... .15 .07
❑ 69 Willie Green .... .30 .14
❑ 70 Curtis Conway .... .50 .23
❑ 71 Erik Kramer .... .15 .07
❑ 72 Donnell Woolford .... .15 .07
❑ 73 Mark Carrier .... .15 .07
❑ 74 Jeff Graham .... .15 .07
❑ 75 Raymont Harris .... .15 .07
❑ 76 Carl Pickens .... .50 .23
❑ 77 Darnay Scott .... .50 .23
❑ 78 Jeff Blake RC .... 2.00 .90
❑ 79 Dan Wilkinson .... .30 .14
❑ 80 Tony McGee .... .15 .07
❑ 81 Eric Bieniemy .... .15 .07
❑ 82 Vinny Testaverde .... .30 .14
❑ 83 Eric Turner .... .15 .07
❑ 84 Leroy Hoard .... .15 .07
❑ 85 Lorenzo White .... .15 .07
❑ 86 Antonio Langham .... .15 .07
❑ 87 Andre Rison .... .30 .14
❑ 88 Troy Aikman .... 1.50 .70
❑ 89 Michael Irvin .... .50 .23
❑ 90 Charles Haley .... .30 .14
❑ 91 Daryl Johnston .... .30 .14
❑ 92 Jay Novacek .... .30 .14
❑ 93 Emmitt Smith 2.50 1.10
❑ 94 Shannon Sharpe .... .30 .14
❑ 95 Anthony Miller .... .30 .14
❑ 96 Mike Pritchard .... .15 .07
❑ 97 Glyn Milburn .... .15 .07
❑ 98 Simon Fletcher .... .15 .07
❑ 99 John Elway 3.00 1.35
❑ 100 Henry Thomas .... .15 .07
❑ 101 Herman Moore .... .50 .23
❑ 102 Scott Mitchell .... .30 .14
❑ 103 Bennie Blades .... .15 .07
❑ 104 Chris Spielman .... .30 .14
❑ 105 Barry Sanders 3.00 1.35
❑ 106 Mark Ingram .... .15 .07
❑ 107 Edgar Bennett .... .30 .14
❑ 108 Reggie White .... .50 .23
❑ 109 Sean Jones .... .15 .07
❑ 110 Robert Brooks .... .50 .23
❑ 111 Brett Favre 3.00 1.35
❑ 112 Chris Chandler .... .30 .14
❑ 113 Haywood Jeffires .... .15 .07
❑ 114 Gary Brown .... .15 .07
❑ 115 Al Smith .... .15 .07
❑ 116 Ray Childress .... .15 .07
❑ 117 Mel Gray .... .15 .07
❑ 118 Jim Harbaugh .... .30 .14
❑ 119 Sean Dawkins .... .30 .14
❑ 120 Roosevelt Potts .... .15 .07
❑ 121 Marshall Faulk .... .75 .35
❑ 122 Tony Bennett .... .15 .07
❑ 123 Quentin Coryatt .... .30 .14
❑ 124 Desmond Howard .... .30 .14
❑ 125 Tony Boselli .... .30 .14
❑ 126 Steve Beuerlein .... .15 .07
❑ 127 Jeff Lageman .... .15 .07
❑ 128 Rob Johnson RC 4.00 1.80
❑ 129 Ernest Givins .... .15 .07
❑ 130 Willie Davis .... .30 .14
❑ 131 Marcus Allen .... .50 .23
❑ 132 Neil Smith .... .30 .14
❑ 133 Greg Hill .... .30 .14
❑ 134 Steve Bono .... .30 .14
❑ 135 Lake Dawson .... .30 .14
❑ 136 Dan Marino 3.00 1.35
❑ 137 Terry Kirby .... .30 .14
❑ 138 Irving Fryar .... .30 .14
❑ 139 O.J. McDuffie .... .50 .23
❑ 140 Bryan Cox .... .15 .07
❑ 141 Eric Green .... .15 .07
❑ 142 Cris Carter .... .50 .23
❑ 143 Robert Smith .... .50 .23
❑ 144 John Randle .... .15 .07
❑ 145 Jake Reed .... .30 .14
❑ 146 Dewayne Washington .... .30 .14
❑ 147 Warren Moon .... .30 .14
❑ 148 Dave Meggett .... .15 .07
❑ 149 Ben Coates .... .30 .14
❑ 150 Vincent Brisby .... .15 .07
❑ 151 Willie McGinest .... .30 .14
❑ 152 Chris Slade .... .30 .14
❑ 153 Drew Bledsoe .... 1.50 .70
❑ 154 Eric Allen .... .15 .07
❑ 155 Mario Bates .... .50 .23
❑ 156 Jim Everett .... .15 .07
❑ 157 Renaldo Turnbull .... .15 .07
❑ 158 Tyrone Hughes .... .30 .14
❑ 159 Michael Haynes .... .30 .14
❑ 160 Mike Sherrard .... .15 .07
❑ 161 Dave Brown .... .30 .14
❑ 162 Chris Calloway .... .15 .07
❑ 163 Keith Hamilton .... .15 .07
❑ 164 Rodney Hampton .... .30 .14
❑ 165 Herschel Walker .... .30 .14
❑ 166 Adrian Murrell .... .30 .14
❑ 167 Johnny Mitchell .... .15 .07
❑ 168 Boomer Esiason .... .30 .14
❑ 169 Mo Lewis .... .15 .07
❑ 170 Brad Baxter .... .15 .07
❑ 171 Aaron Glenn .... .15 .07
❑ 172 Jeff Hostetler .... .30 .14
❑ 173 Harvey Williams .... .15 .07
❑ 174 Tim Brown .... .50 .23
❑ 175 Terry McDaniel .... .15 .07
❑ 176 Pat Swilling .... .15 .07
❑ 177 Rocket Ismail .... .30 .14
❑ 178 Randall Cunningham .... .50 .23
❑ 179 Calvin Williams .... .30 .14
❑ 180 Ricky Watters .... .50 .23
❑ 181 Charlie Garner .... .30 .14
❑ 182 Fred Barnett .... .30 .14
❑ 183 Rodney Peete .... .15 .07
❑ 184 Neil O'Donnell .... .30 .14
❑ 185 Charles Johnson .... .30 .14
❑ 186 Rod Woodson .... .30 .14
❑ 187 Byron Bam Morris .... .30 .14
❑ 188 Kevin Greene .... .30 .14
❑ 189 Greg Lloyd .... .30 .14
❑ 190 Chris Miller .... .15 .07
❑ 191 Isaac Bruce .... .75 .35
❑ 192 Roman Phifer .... .15 .07
❑ 193 Jerome Bettis .... .50 .23
❑ 194 Carlos Jenkins .... .15 .07
❑ 195 Troy Drayton .... .15 .07
❑ 196 Andre Coleman .... .15 .07
❑ 197 Natrone Means .... .50 .23
❑ 198 Leslie O'Neal .... .30 .14
❑ 199 Junior Seau .... .50 .23
❑ 200 Tony Martin .... .30 .14
❑ 201 Stan Humphries .... .30 .14
❑ 202 Steve Young .... 1.25 .55
❑ 203 Jerry Rice .... 1.50 .70
❑ 204 Brent Jones .... .15 .07
❑ 205 Dana Stubblefield .... .50 .23
❑ 206 Lee Woodall .... .15 .07
❑ 207 Merton Hanks .... .15 .07
❑ 208 Rick Mirer .... .50 .23
❑ 209 Brian Blades .... .30 .14
❑ 210 Chris Warren .... .30 .14
❑ 211 Sam Adams .... .15 .07
❑ 212 Cortez Kennedy .... .30 .14
❑ 213 Eugene Robinson .... .15 .07
❑ 214 Alvin Harper .... .15 .07
❑ 215 Trent Dilfer .... .50 .23
❑ 216 Hardy Nickerson .... .15 .07
❑ 217 Errict Rhett .... .50 .23
❑ 218 Eric Curry .... .15 .07
❑ 219 Jackie Harris .... .15 .07
❑ 220 Henry Ellard .... .30 .14
❑ 221 Terry Allen .... .30 .14
❑ 222 Brian Mitchell .... .15 .07
❑ 223 Ken Harvey .... .15 .07
❑ 224 Gus Frerotte .... .50 .23
❑ 225 Heath Shuler .... .50 .23
❑ P116 Joe Montana Promo .. 3.00 1.35
Numbered 116

1995 SP Championship Playoff Showcase

	MINT	NRMT
COMPLETE SET (20)	100.00	45.00

STATED ODDS 1:15 ....
*DIE CUT STARS: 5X TO 10X BASE CARD HI
*DIE CUT ROOKIES: 2.5X TO 5X BASE CARD HI
DIE CUTS: STATED ODDS 1:20 ..

Card	MINT	NRMT
❑ PS1 Troy Aikman	10.00	4.50
❑ PS2 Jerry Rice	10.00	4.50
❑ PS3 Isaac Bruce	5.00	2.20
❑ PS4 Rodney Peete	1.00	.45
❑ PS5 Rashaan Salaam	1.50	.70
❑ PS6 Brett Favre	20.00	9.00
❑ PS7 Alvin Harper	1.00	.45
❑ PS8 Cris Carter	3.00	1.35
❑ PS9 Michael Westbrook	12.00	5.50
❑ PS10 Jeff George	2.00	.90
❑ PS11 Natrone Means	3.00	1.35
❑ PS12 Dan Marino	20.00	9.00
❑ PS13 Steve Bono	2.00	.90
❑ PS14 Greg Lloyd	2.00	.90
❑ PS15 Jim Kelly	3.00	1.35
❑ PS16 Jeff Hostetler	2.00	.90
❑ PS17 Marshall Faulk	5.00	2.20
❑ PS18 John Elway	20.00	9.00
❑ PS19 Jeff Blake	6.00	2.70
❑ PS20 Andre Rison	2.00	.90

1996 SP

	MINT	NRMT
COMPLETE SET (188)	150.00	70.00
COMMON CARD (1-188)	.25	.11
SEMISTARS	.50	.23
UNLISTED STARS	1.00	.45
FOIL PROSPECTS (1-20)	.50	.23
FOIL SEMISTARS	1.00	.45
CONDITION SENSITIVE SET !		

Card	MINT	NRMT
❑ 1 Keyshawn Johnson PP RC	15.00	6.75
❑ 2 Kevin Hardy PP RC	1.00	.45
❑ 3 Simeon Rice PP RC	1.00	.45
❑ 4 Jonathan Ogden PP RC	.50	.23
❑ 5 Eddie George PP RC	25.00	11.00
❑ 6 Terry Glenn PP RC	8.00	3.60
❑ 7 Terrell Owens PP RC	15.00	6.75
❑ 8 Tim Biakabutuka PP RC	6.00	2.70
❑ 9 Lawrence Phillips PP RC	2.00	.90
❑ 10 Alex Molden PP RC	.50	.23
❑ 11 Regan Upshaw PP RC	.50	.23
❑ 12 Rickey Dudley PP RC	1.00	.45
❑ 13 Duane Clemons PP RC	.50	.23
❑ 14 John Mobley PP RC	.50	.23
❑ 15 Eddie Kennison RC	1.00	.45
❑ 16 Karim Abdul-Jabbar PP RC	3.00	1.35
❑ 17 Eric Moulds PP RC	10.00	4.50
❑ 18 Marvin Harrison PP RC	20.00	9.00
❑ 19 Stepfret Williams PP RC	.50	.23
❑ 20 Stephen Davis PP RC	25.00	11.00
❑ 21 Deion Sanders	1.25	.55
❑ 22 Emmitt Smith	3.00	1.35
❑ 23 Troy Aikman	2.00	.90
❑ 24 Michael Irvin	1.00	.45
❑ 25 Herschel Walker	.50	.23
❑ 26 Kavika Pittman RC	.25	.11
❑ 27 Andre Hastings	.25	.11
❑ 28 Jerome Bettis	1.00	.45
❑ 29 Mike Tomczak	.25	.11
❑ 30 Kordell Stewart	1.50	.70
❑ 31 Charles Johnson	.25	.11
❑ 32 Greg Lloyd	.50	.23
❑ 33 Brett Favre	4.00	1.80
❑ 34 Mark Chmura	.50	.23
❑ 35 Edgar Bennett	.50	.23
❑ 36 Robert Brooks	.50	.23
❑ 37 Craig Newsome	.25	.11
❑ 38 Reggie White	1.00	.45
❑ 39 Jim Harbaugh	.50	.23
❑ 40 Marshall Faulk	1.00	.45
❑ 41 Sean Dawkins	.25	.11
❑ 42 Quentin Coryatt	.25	.11
❑ 43 Ray Buchanan	.25	.11
❑ 44 Ken Dilger	.50	.23
❑ 45 Jerry Rice	2.00	.90
❑ 46 J.J. Stokes	1.00	.45
❑ 47 Steve Young	1.50	.70
❑ 48 Derek Loville	.25	.11
❑ 49 Terry Kirby	.50	.23
❑ 50 Ken Norton	.25	.11
❑ 51 Tamarick Vanover	.50	.23
❑ 52 Marcus Allen	1.00	.45
❑ 53 Steve Bono	.25	.11
❑ 54 Neil Smith	.25	.11
❑ 55 Derrick Thomas	.50	.23
❑ 56 Dale Carter	.25	.11
❑ 57 Terance Mathis	.25	.11
❑ 58 Eric Metcalf	.25	.11
❑ 59 Jamal Anderson RC	20.00	9.00
❑ 60 Bert Emanuel	.50	.23
❑ 61 Craig Heyward	.25	.11
❑ 62 Cornelius Bennett	.25	.11
❑ 63 Tony Martin	.50	.23
❑ 64 Stan Humphries	.50	.23
❑ 65 Andre Coleman	.25	.11
❑ 66 Junior Seau	.50	.23
❑ 67 Terrell Fletcher	.25	.11
❑ 68 John Carney	.25	.11
❑ 69 Charlie Jones RC	.50	.23
❑ 70 Ricky Watters	.50	.23
❑ 71 Charlie Garner	.25	.11
❑ 72 Bobby Hoying RC	2.00	.90
❑ 73 Jason Dunn RC	.50	.23
❑ 74 Bobby Taylor	.25	.11
❑ 75 Irving Fryar	.50	.23
❑ 76 Jim Kelly	1.00	.45
❑ 77 Thurman Thomas	1.00	.45
❑ 78 Bruce Smith	.50	.23
❑ 79 Bryce Paup	.25	.11
❑ 80 Darick Holmes	.25	.11
❑ 81 Andre Reed	.50	.23
❑ 82 Glyn Milburn	.25	.11
❑ 83 Brett Perriman	.25	.11
❑ 84 Herman Moore	1.00	.45
❑ 85 Scott Mitchell	.50	.23
❑ 86 Barry Sanders	4.00	1.80
❑ 87 Johnnie Morton	.50	.23
❑ 88 Dan Marino	4.00	1.80
❑ 89 O.J. McDuffie	.50	.23
❑ 90 Stanley Pritchett RC	.50	.23
❑ 91 Zach Thomas RC	2.50	1.10
❑ 92 Daryl Gardener RC	.25	.11
❑ 93 Rashaan Salaam	1.00	.45
❑ 94 Erik Kramer	.25	.11
❑ 95 Curtis Conway	1.00	.45
❑ 96 Bobby Engram RC	1.00	.45
❑ 97 Walt Harris RC	.25	.11
❑ 98 Bryan Cox	.25	.11
❑ 99 John Elway	4.00	1.80
❑ 100 Terrell Davis	4.00	1.80
❑ 101 Anthony Miller	.50	.23
❑ 102 Shannon Sharpe	.50	.23
❑ 103 Tory James	.25	.11
❑ 104 Jeff Lewis RC	2.50	1.10
❑ 105 Joey Galloway	1.50	.70
❑ 106 Chris Warren	.50	.23
❑ 107 Rick Mirer	.50	.23
❑ 108 Cortez Kennedy	.25	.11
❑ 109 Michael Sinclair	.25	.11
❑ 110 John Friesz	.25	.11
❑ 111 Warren Moon	.50	.23
❑ 112 Cris Carter	1.00	.45
❑ 113 Jake Reed	.50	.23
❑ 114 Robert Smith	.50	.23
❑ 115 John Randle	.25	.11
❑ 116 Orlando Thomas	.25	.11
❑ 117 Jeff Hostetler	.25	.11
❑ 118 Tim Brown	1.00	.45
❑ 119 Joe Aska	.25	.11
❑ 120 Napoleon Kaufman	1.25	.55
❑ 121 Terry McDaniel	.25	.11
❑ 122 Harvey Williams	.25	.11
❑ 123 Trent Dilfer	1.00	.45
❑ 124 Reggie Brooks	.25	.11
❑ 125 Alvin Harper	.25	.11
❑ 126 Mike Alstott RC	8.00	3.60
❑ 127 Hardy Nickerson	.25	.11
❑ 128 Mario Bates	.50	.23
❑ 129 Jim Everett	.25	.11
❑ 130 Tyrone Hughes	.25	.11
❑ 131 Michael Haynes	.25	.11
❑ 132 Eric Allen	.25	.11
❑ 133 Isaac Bruce	1.00	.45
❑ 134 Kevin Carter	.25	.11
❑ 135 Leslie O'Neal	.25	.11
❑ 136 Tony Banks RC	10.00	4.50
❑ 137 Chris Chandler	.50	.23
❑ 138 Steve McNair	1.50	.70
❑ 139 Chris Sanders	.50	.23
❑ 140 Ronnie Harmon	.25	.11
❑ 141 Willie Davis	.25	.11
❑ 142 Michael Westbrook	1.00	.45
❑ 143 Terry Allen	.50	.23
❑ 144 Brian Mitchell	.25	.11
❑ 145 Henry Ellard	.25	.11
❑ 146 Gus Frerotte	1.00	.45
❑ 147 Kerry Collins	1.00	.45
❑ 148 Sam Mills	.25	.11
❑ 149 Wesley Walls	.50	.23
❑ 150 Kevin Greene	.50	.23
❑ 151 Muhsin Muhammad RC	10.00	4.50
❑ 152 Winslow Oliver	.25	.11
❑ 153 Jeff Blake	1.00	.45
❑ 154 Carl Pickens	1.00	.45
❑ 155 Darnay Scott	.50	.23
❑ 156 Garrison Hearst	.50	.23
❑ 157 Marco Battaglia RC	.25	.11
❑ 158 Drew Bledsoe	2.00	.90
❑ 159 Curtis Martin	1.50	.70
❑ 160 Shawn Jefferson	.25	.11
❑ 161 Ben Coates	.50	.23
❑ 162 Lawyer Milloy	.25	.11
❑ 163 Tyrone Wheatley	.50	.23
❑ 164 Rodney Hampton	.50	.23
❑ 165 Chris Calloway	.25	.11
❑ 166 Dave Brown	.25	.11
❑ 167 Amani Toomer RC	1.00	.45
❑ 168 Vinny Testaverde	.50	.23
❑ 169 Michael Jackson	.50	.23
❑ 170 Eric Turner	.25	.11
❑ 171 DeRon Jenkins	.25	.11
❑ 172 Jermaine Lewis RC	2.50	1.10
❑ 173 Frank Sanders	.50	.23
❑ 174 Rob Moore	.50	.23
❑ 175 Kent Graham	.25	.11
❑ 176 Leeland McElroy RC	1.00	.45
❑ 177 Larry Centers	.50	.23
❑ 178 Eric Swann	.25	.11
❑ 179 Mark Brunell	2.00	.90
❑ 180 Willie Jackson	.25	.11
❑ 181 James O. Stewart	.50	.23
❑ 182 Natrone Means	1.00	.45
❑ 183 Tony Brackens RC	1.00	.45
❑ 184 Adrian Murrell	1.00	.45
❑ 185 Neil O'Donnell	.50	.23

❑ 186 Hugh Douglas	.25	.11
❑ 187 Wayne Chrebet	1.25	.55
❑ 188 Alex Van Dyke RC	.50	.23
❑ SP13 Dan Marino Promo	3.00	1.35

1996 SP Explosive

	MINT	NRMT
COMPLETE SET (20)	800.00	350.00
STATED ODDS 1:360		
❑ X1 Emmitt Smith	80.00	36.00
❑ X2 Jerry Rice	50.00	22.00
❑ X3 Rashaan Salaam	25.00	11.00
❑ X4 Brett Favre	100.00	45.00
❑ X5 Napoleon Kaufman	30.00	13.50
❑ X6 Tim Biakabutuka	20.00	9.00
❑ X7 John Elway	100.00	45.00
❑ X8 Steve Young	40.00	18.00
❑ X9 Isaac Bruce	25.00	11.00
❑ X10 Troy Aikman	50.00	22.00
❑ X11 Drew Bledsoe	50.00	22.00
❑ X12 Carl Pickens	25.00	11.00
❑ X13 Dan Marino	100.00	45.00
❑ X14 Eddie George	80.00	36.00
❑ X15 Joey Galloway	40.00	18.00
❑ X16 Deion Sanders	30.00	13.50
❑ X17 Curtis Martin	40.00	18.00
❑ X18 Marshall Faulk	25.00	11.00
❑ X19 Keyshawn Johnson	50.00	22.00
❑ X20 Barry Sanders	100.00	45.00

1996 SP Focus on the Future

	MINT	NRMT
COMPLETE SET (30)	200.00	90.00
STATED ODDS 1:30		
❑ F1 Leeland McElroy	2.00	.90
❑ F2 Frank Sanders	6.00	2.70
❑ F3 Darick Holmes	3.00	1.35
❑ F4 Eric Moulds	20.00	9.00
❑ F5 Kerry Collins	12.00	5.50
❑ F6 Tim Biakabutuka	12.00	5.50
❑ F7 Ki-Jana Carter	1.00	.45
❑ F8 Jeff Blake	12.00	5.50
❑ F9 John Mobley	1.00	.45
❑ F10 Johnnie Morton	6.00	2.70
❑ F11 Eddie George	50.00	22.00
❑ F12 Steve McNair	20.00	9.00
❑ F13 Marshall Faulk	12.00	5.50
❑ F14 Kevin Hardy	2.00	.90
❑ F15 Tamarick Vanover	6.00	2.70
❑ F16 Karim Abdul-Jabbar	6.00	2.70
❑ F17 Drew Bledsoe	25.00	11.00
❑ F18 Curtis Martin	20.00	9.00
❑ F19 Mario Bates	6.00	2.70
❑ F20 Danny Kanell	1.00	.45
❑ F21 Keyshawn Johnson	30.00	13.50
❑ F22 Napoleon Kaufman	15.00	6.75
❑ F23 Rickey Dudley	2.00	.90
❑ F24 Kordell Stewart	20.00	9.00
❑ F25 Lawrence Phillips	4.00	1.80
❑ F26 Isaac Bruce	12.00	5.50
❑ F27 J.J. Stokes	12.00	5.50
❑ F28 Joey Galloway	20.00	9.00
❑ F29 Errict Rhett	6.00	2.70
❑ F30 Mike Alstott	15.00	6.75

1996 SP Holoviews

	MINT	NRMT
COMPLETE SET (48)	150.00	70.00
STATED ODDS 1:7		
*DC STARS: 4X TO 8X BASE CARD HI		
*DIE CUT ROOKIES: 1X TO 2X BASE CARD HI		
DIE CUT STATED ODDS 1:74		
❑ 1 Jerry Rice	6.00	2.70
❑ 2 Herman Moore	3.00	1.35
❑ 3 Kerry Collins	3.00	1.35
❑ 4 Brett Favre	12.00	5.50
❑ 5 Junior Seau	1.50	.70
❑ 6 Troy Aikman	6.00	2.70
❑ 7 John Elway	12.00	5.50
❑ 8 Steve Young	5.00	2.20
❑ 9 Reggie White	3.00	1.35
❑ 10 Kordell Stewart	5.00	2.20
❑ 11 Drew Bledsoe	6.00	2.70
❑ 12 Jeff Blake	3.00	1.35
❑ 13 Dan Marino	12.00	5.50
❑ 14 Curtis Martin	5.00	2.20
❑ 15 Marshall Faulk	3.00	1.35
❑ 16 Greg Lloyd	1.50	.70
❑ 17 Cris Carter	3.00	1.35
❑ 18 Isaac Bruce	3.00	1.35
❑ 19 Joey Galloway	5.00	2.20
❑ 20 Barry Sanders	12.00	5.50
❑ 21 Emmitt Smith	10.00	4.50
❑ 22 Edgar Bennett	1.50	.70
❑ 23 Rashaan Salaam	3.00	1.35
❑ 24 Steve McNair	5.00	2.20
❑ 25 Tamarick Vanover	1.50	.70
❑ 26 Deion Sanders	4.00	1.80
❑ 27 Keyshawn Johnson	12.00	5.50
❑ 28 Kevin Hardy	.75	.35
❑ 29 Simeon Rice	.75	.35
❑ 30 Lawrence Phillips	1.50	.70
❑ 31 Tim Biakabutuka	5.00	2.20
❑ 32 Terry Glenn	6.00	2.70
❑ 33 Rickey Dudley	.75	.35
❑ 34 Regan Upshaw	.40	.18
❑ 35 Eddie George	20.00	9.00
❑ 36 John Mobley	.40	.18
❑ 37 Eddie Kennison	.75	.35
❑ 38 Marvin Harrison	15.00	6.75
❑ 39 Leeland McElroy	.75	.35
❑ 40 Eric Moulds	8.00	3.60
❑ 41 Alex Van Dyke	.40	.18
❑ 42 Mike Alstott	6.00	2.70
❑ 43 Jeff Lewis	2.00	.90
❑ 44 Bobby Engram	.75	.35
❑ 45 Derrick Mayes	.40	.18
❑ 46 Karim Abdul-Jabbar	2.50	1.10
❑ 47 Stepfret Williams	.40	.18
❑ 48 Stephen Davis	20.00	9.00

1996 SP SPx Force

	MINT	NRMT
COMPLETE SET (5)	400.00	180.00
COMMON CARD (FR1-FR5)	30.00	13.50
STATED ODDS 1:950		
SET PRICE INCLUDES CHEAPEST AUTO.		
AUTO STATED ODDS 1:8820		
❑ FR1 Keyshawn Johnson Lawrence Phillips Terry Glenn Tim Biakabutuka	30.00	13.50
❑ FR2 Barry Sanders Emmitt Smith Marshall Faulk Curtis Martin	60.00	27.00
❑ FR3 Dan Marino Brett Favre Drew Bledsoe Troy Aikman	60.00	27.00
❑ FR4 Jerry Rice Herman Moore Carl Pickens Isaac Bruce	40.00	18.00
❑ FR5A Keyshawn Johnson AUTO (signed card number 5)	300.00	135.00
❑ FR5B Dan Marino AUTO (signed card number 5)	600.00	275.00
❑ FR5C Jerry Rice AUTO (signed card number 5)	500.00	220.00
❑ FR5D Barry Sanders AUTO (signed card number 5 available via redemption)	600.00	275.00

1997 SP Authentic

	MINT	NRMT
COMPLETE SET (198)	135.00	60.00
COMMON CARD (31-198)	.30	.14
SEMISTARS	.50	.23
UNLISTED STARS	1.00	.45
COMMON ROOKIE (1-30)	.50	.23
ROOKIE SEMISTARS	1.00	.45
ROOKIE UNL.STARS	1.50	.70
AIKMAN AUDIO ODDS 1:22B,1:130PB		
❑ 1 Orlando Pace RC	.30	.14
❑ 2 Darrell Russell RC	.30	.14
❑ 3 Shawn Springs RC	.50	.23
❑ 4 Peter Boulware RC	.50	.23
❑ 5 Bryant Westbrook RC	.30	.14
❑ 6 Walter Jones RC	.30	.14
❑ 7 Ike Hilliard RC	5.00	2.20
❑ 8 James Farrior RC	.30	.14
❑ 9 Tom Knight RC	.30	.14
❑ 10 Warrick Dunn RC	15.00	6.75
❑ 11 Tony Gonzalez RC	20.00	9.00
❑ 12 Reinard Wilson RC	.30	.14
❑ 13 Yatil Green RC	.50	.23
❑ 14 Reidel Anthony RC	4.00	1.80

❑ 15 Kenny Holmes RC	.30	.14
❑ 16 Dwayne Rudd RC	.30	.14
❑ 17 Renaldo Wynn RC	.30	.14
❑ 18 David LaFleur RC	2.50	1.10
❑ 19 Antowain Smith RC	10.00	4.50
❑ 20 Jim Druckenmiller RC	2.50	1.10
❑ 21 Rae Carruth RC	.50	.23
❑ 22 Byron Hanspard RC	6.00	2.70
❑ 23 Jake Plummer RC	50.00	22.00
❑ 24 Joey Kent RC	1.00	.45
❑ 25 Corey Dillon RC	25.00	11.00
❑ 26 Danny Wuerffel RC	3.00	1.35
❑ 27 Will Blackwell RC	1.00	.45
❑ 28 Troy Davis RC	1.00	.45
❑ 29 Darnell Autry RC	1.00	.45
❑ 30 Pat Barnes RC	2.50	1.10
❑ 31 Kent Graham	.30	.14
❑ 32 Simeon Rice	.50	.23
❑ 33 Frank Sanders	.50	.23
❑ 34 Rob Moore	.50	.23
❑ 35 Eric Swann	.30	.14
❑ 36 Chris Chandler	.50	.23
❑ 37 Jamal Anderson	1.50	.70
❑ 38 Terance Mathis	.50	.23
❑ 39 Bert Emanuel	.50	.23
❑ 40 Michael Booker	.30	.14
❑ 41 Vinny Testaverde	.50	.23
❑ 42 Byron Bam Morris	.30	.14
❑ 43 Michael Jackson	.50	.23
❑ 44 Derrick Alexander WR	.50	.23
❑ 45 Jamie Sharper RC	.30	.14
❑ 46 Kim Herring RC	.30	.14
❑ 47 Todd Collins	.30	.14
❑ 48 Thurman Thomas	1.00	.45
❑ 49 Andre Reed	.50	.23
❑ 50 Quinn Early	.30	.14
❑ 51 Bryce Paup	.30	.14
❑ 52 Lonnie Johnson	.30	.14
❑ 53 Kerry Collins	.50	.23
❑ 54 Anthony Johnson	.30	.14
❑ 55 Tim Biakabutuka	.50	.23
❑ 56 Muhsin Muhammad	.50	.23
❑ 57 Sam Mills	.30	.14
❑ 58 Wesley Walls	.50	.23
❑ 59 Rick Mirer	.30	.14
❑ 60 Raymont Harris	.30	.14
❑ 61 Curtis Conway	.50	.23
❑ 62 Bobby Engram	.50	.23
❑ 63 Bryan Cox	.30	.14
❑ 64 John Allred RC	.30	.14
❑ 65 Jeff Blake	.50	.23
❑ 66 Ki-Jana Carter	.30	.14
❑ 67 Darnay Scott	.50	.23
❑ 68 Carl Pickens	1.00	.45
❑ 69 Dan Wilkinson	.30	.14
❑ 70 Troy Aikman	2.50	1.10
❑ 71 Emmitt Smith	4.00	1.80
❑ 72 Michael Irvin	1.00	.45
❑ 73 Deion Sanders	1.00	.45
❑ 74 Anthony Miller	.30	.14
❑ 75 Antonio Anderson RC	.30	.14
❑ 76 John Elway	5.00	2.20
❑ 77 Terrell Davis	4.00	1.80
❑ 78 Rod Smith WR	1.00	.45
❑ 79 Shannon Sharpe	.50	.23
❑ 80 Neil Smith	.50	.23
❑ 81 Trevor Pryce RC	.30	.14
❑ 82 Scott Mitchell	.50	.23
❑ 83 Barry Sanders	5.00	2.20
❑ 84 Herman Moore	1.00	.45
❑ 85 Johnnie Morton	.50	.23
❑ 86 Matt Russell RC	.30	.14
❑ 87 Brett Favre	5.00	2.20
❑ 88 Edgar Bennett	.50	.23
❑ 89 Robert Brooks	.50	.23
❑ 90 Antonio Freeman	1.50	.70
❑ 91 Reggie White	1.00	.45
❑ 92 Craig Newsome	.30	.14
❑ 93 Jim Harbaugh	.50	.23
❑ 94 Marshall Faulk	1.00	.45
❑ 95 Sean Dawkins	.30	.14
❑ 96 Marvin Harrison	1.00	.45
❑ 97 Quentin Coryatt	.30	.14
❑ 98 Tarik Glenn RC	.30	.14
❑ 99 Mark Brunell	2.50	1.10
❑ 100 Natrone Means	1.00	.45
❑ 101 Keenan McCardell	.50	.23
❑ 102 Jimmy Smith	.50	.23
❑ 103 Tony Brackens	.30	.14
❑ 104 Kevin Hardy	.30	.14
❑ 105 Elvis Grbac	.50	.23
❑ 106 Marcus Allen	1.00	.45
❑ 107 Greg Hill	.30	.14
❑ 108 Derrick Thomas	.50	.23
❑ 109 Dale Carter	.30	.14
❑ 110 Dan Marino	5.00	2.20
❑ 111 Karim Abdul-Jabbar	1.00	.45
❑ 112 Brian Manning RC	.30	.14
❑ 113 Daryl Gardener	.30	.14
❑ 114 Troy Drayton	.30	.14
❑ 115 Zach Thomas	.50	.23
❑ 116 Jason Taylor RC	.30	.14
❑ 117 Brad Johnson	1.25	.55
❑ 118 Robert Smith	.50	.23
❑ 119 John Randle	.30	.14
❑ 120 Cris Carter	1.00	.45
❑ 121 Jake Reed	.50	.23
❑ 122 Randall Cunningham	1.00	.45
❑ 123 Drew Bledsoe	2.50	1.10
❑ 124 Curtis Martin	1.50	.70
❑ 125 Terry Glenn	1.00	.45
❑ 126 Willie McGinest	.30	.14
❑ 127 Chris Canty RC	.30	.14
❑ 128 Sedrick Shaw RC	1.50	.70
❑ 129 Heath Shuler	.30	.14
❑ 130 Mario Bates	.30	.14
❑ 131 Ray Zellars	.30	.14
❑ 132 Andre Hastings	.30	.14
❑ 133 Dave Brown	.30	.14
❑ 134 Tyrone Wheatley	.50	.23
❑ 135 Rodney Hampton	.50	.23
❑ 136 Chris Calloway	.30	.14
❑ 137 Tiki Barber RC	2.00	.90
❑ 138 Neil O'Donnell	.50	.23
❑ 139 Adrian Murrell	.50	.23
❑ 140 Wayne Chrebet	1.00	.45
❑ 141 Keyshawn Johnson	1.00	.45
❑ 142 Hugh Douglas	.30	.14
❑ 143 Jeff George	.50	.23
❑ 144 Napoleon Kaufman	1.00	.45
❑ 145 Tim Brown	1.00	.45
❑ 146 Desmond Howard	.50	.23
❑ 147 Rickey Dudley	.50	.23
❑ 148 Terry McDaniel	.30	.14
❑ 149 Ty Detmer	.50	.23
❑ 150 Ricky Watters	.50	.23
❑ 151 Chris T. Jones	.30	.14
❑ 152 Irving Fryar	.50	.23
❑ 153 Mike Mamula	.30	.14
❑ 154 Jon Harris RC	.30	.14
❑ 155 Kordell Stewart	2.00	.90
❑ 156 Jerome Bettis	1.00	.45
❑ 157 Charles Johnson	.50	.23
❑ 158 Greg Lloyd	.30	.14
❑ 159 George Jones RC	.50	.23
❑ 160 Terrell Fletcher	.30	.14
❑ 161 Stan Humphries	.50	.23
❑ 162 Tony Martin	.50	.23
❑ 163 Eric Metcalf	.50	.23
❑ 164 Junior Seau	.50	.23
❑ 165 Rod Woodson	.50	.23
❑ 166 Steve Young	2.00	.90
❑ 167 Terry Kirby	.50	.23
❑ 168 Garrison Hearst	.50	.23
❑ 169 Jerry Rice	2.50	1.10
❑ 170 Ken Norton	.30	.14
❑ 171 Kevin Greene	.50	.23
❑ 172 Lamar Smith	.30	.14
❑ 173 Warren Moon	1.00	.45
❑ 174 Chris Warren	.50	.23
❑ 175 Cortez Kennedy	.30	.14
❑ 176 Joey Galloway	1.50	.70
❑ 177 Tony Banks	.50	.23
❑ 178 Isaac Bruce	1.00	.45
❑ 179 Eddie Kennison	.50	.23
❑ 180 Kevin Carter	.30	.14
❑ 181 Craig Heyward	.30	.14
❑ 182 Trent Dilfer	1.00	.45
❑ 183 Errict Rhett	.30	.14
❑ 184 Mike Alstott	1.00	.45
❑ 185 Hardy Nickerson	.30	.14
❑ 186 Ronde Barber RC	.30	.14
❑ 187 Steve McNair	1.50	.70
❑ 188 Eddie George	2.50	1.10
❑ 189 Chris Sanders	.30	.14
❑ 190 Blaine Bishop	.30	.14
❑ 191 Derrick Mason RC	.30	.14
❑ 192 Gus Frerotte	.30	.14
❑ 193 Terry Allen	1.00	.45
❑ 194 Brian Mitchell	.30	.14
❑ 195 Alvin Harper	.30	.14
❑ 196 Jeff Hostetler	.30	.14
❑ 197 Leslie Shepherd	.30	.14
❑ 198 Stephen Davis	2.50	1.10
❑ A1 Aikman Audio Blue	4.00	1.80
❑ A2 Aikman Audio Pro Bowl	10.00	4.50
❑ A3 Aikman Audio White (500 cards made)	30.00	13.50

1997 SP Authentic Mark of a Legend

	MINT	NRMT
COMPLETE SET (7)	500.00	220.00
COMMON CARD (ML1-ML7)	60.00	27.00

SOME ALSO ISSUED ON SILVER FOIL STOCK
STATED ODDS 1:168
REDEMPTION EXPIRATION: 10/30/98

❑ ML1 Bob Griese	60.00	27.00
❑ ML2 Roger Staubach	80.00	36.00
❑ ML3 Joe Montana	175.00	80.00
❑ ML4 Franco Harris (white stock)	60.00	27.00
❑ ML5 Gale Sayers (silver foil stock)	60.00	27.00
❑ ML6 Steve Largent	60.00	27.00
❑ ML7 Tony Dorsett	60.00	27.00

1997 SP Authentic ProFiles

	MINT	NRMT
COMPLETE SET (40)	150.00	70.00

STATED ODDS 1:5
*DIE CUT STARS: 2X TO 5X BASE CARD HI
*DIE CUT ROOKIES: .4X TO 1X BASE CARD HI
DIE CUT STATED ODDS 1:12
*DIE CUT 100s STARS: 12X TO 30X BASE CARD HI
*DIE CUT 100s ROOKIES: 2.5X TO 6X BASE CARD HI
STATED PRINT RUN 100 SERIAL #'d SETS

❑ P1 Dan Marino	12.00	5.50
❑ P2 Kordell Stewart	5.00	2.20
❑ P3 Emmitt Smith	10.00	4.50
❑ P4 Brett Favre	12.00	5.50
❑ P5 Marcus Allen	2.50	1.10
❑ P6 Jerry Rice	6.00	2.70
❑ P7 Jeff George	1.25	.55
❑ P8 Mark Brunell	6.00	2.70
❑ P9 Eddie George	6.00	2.70
❑ P10 Cris Carter	2.50	1.10
❑ P11 Tim Biakabutuka	1.25	.55
❑ P12 Ike Hilliard	2.50	1.10
❑ P13 Darrell Russell	.15	.07
❑ P14 Jim Druckenmiller	1.25	.55
❑ P15 Rae Carruth	.25	.11
❑ P16 Warrick Dunn	8.00	3.60

❑ P17 Herman Moore 2.50 1.10
❑ P18 Deion Sanders 2.50 1.10
❑ P19 Drew Bledsoe 6.00 2.70
❑ P20 Jeff Blake 1.25 .55
❑ P21 Keyshawn Johnson 2.50 1.10
❑ P22 Curtis Martin 4.00 1.80
❑ P23 Michael Irvin 2.50 1.10
❑ P24 Barry Sanders 12.00 5.50
❑ P25 Carl Pickens 2.50 1.10
❑ P26 Steve McNair 4.00 1.80
❑ P27 Terry Allen 2.50 1.10
❑ P28 Terrell Davis 10.00 4.50
❑ P29 Lawrence Phillips .75 .35
❑ P30 Marshall Faulk 2.50 1.10
❑ P31 Karim Abdul-Jabbar 2.50 1.10
❑ P32 Steve Young 5.00 2.20
❑ P33 Tim Brown 2.50 1.10
❑ P34 Antowain Smith 5.00 2.20
❑ P35 Kerry Collins 1.25 .55
❑ P36 Reggie White 2.50 1.10
❑ P37 John Elway 12.00 5.50
❑ P38 Jerome Bettis 2.50 1.10
❑ P39 Troy Aikman 6.00 2.70
❑ P40 Junior Seau 1.25 .55

1997 SP Authentic Sign of the Times

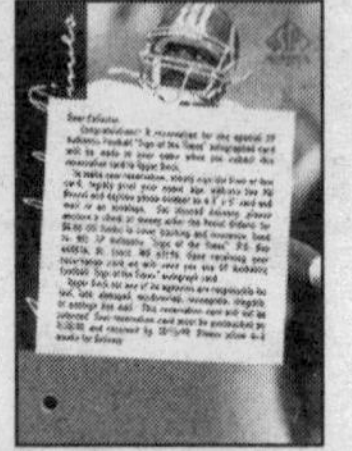

	MINT	NRMT
COMPLETE SET (27)	1200.00	550.00
COMMON CARD (1-27)	12.00	5.50
SEMISTARS	15.00	6.75
UNLISTED STARS	20.00	9.00

SOME ALSO ISSUED ON SILVER FOIL STOCK
STATED ODDS 1:24

❑ 1 Karim Abdul-Jabbar 20.00 9.00
(white stock)
❑ 2 Troy Aikman 100.00 45.00
❑ 3 Terry Allen 20.00 9.00
❑ 4 Reidel Anthony 15.00 6.75
❑ 5 Jerome Bettis 30.00 13.50
❑ 6 Will Blackwell 12.00 5.50
❑ 7 Jeff Blake 15.00 6.75
❑ 8 Robert Brooks 15.00 6.75
❑ 9 Tim Brown 20.00 9.00
❑ 10 Isaac Bruce 15.00 6.75
❑ 11 Rae Carruth 15.00 6.75
(white stock)
❑ 12 Kerry Collins 15.00 6.75
❑ 13 Terrell Davis 100.00 45.00
❑ 14 Jim Druckenmiller 20.00 9.00
❑ 15 Warrick Dunn 30.00 13.50
❑ 16 Marshall Faulk 20.00 9.00
❑ 17 Joey Galloway 20.00 9.00
❑ 18 Eddie George 60.00 27.00
(silver foil stock)
❑ 19 Tony Gonzalez 30.00 13.50
❑ 20 George Jones 12.00 5.50
❑ 21 Napoleon Kaufman 30.00 13.50
❑ 22A Dan Marino 250.00 110.00
(silver foil stock)
❑ 22B Dan Marino 200.00 90.00
(white stock)
❑ 23 Curtis Martin 50.00 22.00
❑ 24 Herman Moore 20.00 9.00
❑ 25A Jerry Rice 200.00 90.00
(silver foil stock)
❑ 25B Jerry Rice 200.00 90.00
(white stock)
❑ 26 Rashaan Salaam 12.00 5.50
❑ 27 Antowain Smith 20.00 9.00
❑ 28 Emmitt Smith 250.00 110.00
(silver foil stock)

1997 SP Authentic Traditions

	MINT	NRMT
COMPLETE SET (6)	2200.00	1000.00
COMMON CARD (TD1-TD6)	200.00	90.00

EXPIRATION DATE: 9/30/98
STATED ODDS 1:1440

❑ TD1 Dan Marino 500.00 220.00
Bob Griese
❑ TD2 Troy Aikman 350.00 160.00
Roger Staubach
❑ TD3 Jerry Rice 1000.00 450.00
Joe Montana
❑ TD4 Jerome Bettis 200.00 90.00
Franco Harris
❑ TD5 Emmitt Smith 350.00 160.00
Tony Dorsett
❑ TD6 Joey Galloway 200.00 90.00
Steve Largent

1998 SP Authentic

	MINT	NRMT
COMPLETE SET (126)	2000.00	900.00
COMP.SET w/o SP's (84)	40.00	18.00
COMMON CARD (43-126)	.20	.09
SEMISTARS	.40	.18
UNLISTED STARS	.75	.35
COMMON ROOKIE (1-30)	12.00	5.50
ROOKIE SEMISTARS	20.00	9.00
ROOKIE UNLISTED STARS	30.00	13.50

ROOKIE SUBSET PRINT RUN 2000 #'d SETS

COMMON TIME WARP (31-42)	4.00	1.80
SEMISTAR TIME WARPS	6.00	2.70

TIME WARP SUBSET PRINT RUN 2000 #'d SETS

COMP.DIE CUT SET (126)	2000.00	900.00

*DIE CUT TIME WARP 31-42: .6X TO 1.5X HI
*DIE CUT STARS 43-126: 3X TO 8X
*DIE CUT YOUNG STARS 43-126: 2.5X TO 6X
*DIE CUT RCs 1-30: .4X TO 1X
DIE CUT PRINT RUN 500 SERIAL #'d SETS

❑ 1 Andre Wadsworth RC 20.00 9.00
❑ 2 Corey Chavous RC 12.00 5.50
❑ 3 Keith Brooking RC 20.00 9.00
❑ 4 Duane Starks RC 12.00 5.50
❑ 5 Pat Johnson RC 20.00 9.00
❑ 6 Jason Peter RC 12.00 5.50
❑ 7 Curtis Enis RC 80.00 36.00
❑ 8 Takeo Spikes RC 20.00 9.00
❑ 9 Greg Ellis RC 12.00 5.50
❑ 10 Marcus Nash RC 35.00 16.00
❑ 11 Brian Griese RC 150.00 70.00
❑ 12 Germane Crowell RC 70.00 32.00
❑ 13 Vonnie Holliday RC 20.00 9.00
❑ 14 Peyton Manning RC 500.00 220.00
❑ 15 Jerome Pathon RC 20.00 9.00
❑ 16 Fred Taylor RC 250.00 110.00
❑ 17 John Avery RC 20.00 9.00
❑ 18 Randy Moss RC 450.00 200.00
❑ 19 Robert Edwards RC 30.00 13.50
❑ 20 Tony Simmons RC 30.00 13.50
❑ 21 Shaun Williams RC 12.00 5.50
❑ 22 Joe Jurevicius RC 20.00 9.00
❑ 23 Charles Woodson RC 60.00 27.00
❑ 24 Tra Thomas RC 12.00 5.50
❑ 25 Grant Wistrom RC 12.00 5.50
❑ 26 Ryan Leaf RC 60.00 27.00
❑ 27 Ahman Green RC 40.00 18.00
❑ 28 Jacquez Green RC 40.00 18.00
❑ 29 Kevin Dyson RC 60.00 27.00
❑ 30 Stephen Alexander RC 20.00 9.00
❑ 31 John Elway TW 20.00 9.00
❑ 32 Jerry Rice TW 12.00 5.50
❑ 33 Emmitt Smith TW 20.00 9.00
❑ 34 Steve Young TW 8.00 3.60
❑ 35 Jerome Bettis TW 6.00 2.70
❑ 36 Deion Sanders TW 6.00 2.70
❑ 37 Andre Rison TW 4.00 1.80
❑ 38 Warren Moon TW 6.00 2.70
❑ 39 Mark Brunell TW 10.00 4.50
❑ 40 Ricky Watters TW 4.00 1.80
❑ 41 Dan Marino TW 25.00 11.00
❑ 42 Brett Favre TW 25.00 11.00
❑ 43 Jake Plummer 2.50 1.10
❑ 44 Adrian Murrell .40 .18
❑ 45 Eric Swann .20 .09
❑ 46 Jamal Anderson .75 .35
❑ 47 Chris Chandler .40 .18
❑ 48 Jim Harbaugh .40 .18
❑ 49 Michael Jackson .20 .09
❑ 50 Jermaine Lewis .40 .18
❑ 51 Rob Johnson .40 .18
❑ 52 Antowain Smith .75 .35
❑ 53 Thurman Thomas .75 .35
❑ 54 Kerry Collins .40 .18
❑ 55 Fred Lane .40 .18
❑ 56 Rae Carruth .40 .18
❑ 57 Erik Kramer .20 .09
❑ 58 Curtis Conway .40 .18
❑ 59 Corey Dillon 1.25 .55
❑ 60 Neil O'Donnell .40 .18
❑ 61 Carl Pickens .75 .35
❑ 62 Troy Aikman 2.00 .90
❑ 63 Emmitt Smith 3.00 1.35
❑ 64 Deion Sanders .75 .35
❑ 65 Terrell Davis 3.00 1.35
❑ 66 John Elway 4.00 1.80
❑ 67 Rod Smith .40 .18
❑ 68 Scott Mitchell .40 .18
❑ 69 Barry Sanders 4.00 1.80
❑ 70 Herman Moore .75 .35
❑ 71 Brett Favre 4.00 1.80
❑ 72 Dorsey Levens .75 .35
❑ 73 Antonio Freeman .75 .35
❑ 74 Marshall Faulk .75 .35
❑ 75 Marvin Harrison .40 .18
❑ 76 Mark Brunell 1.50 .70
❑ 77 Keenan McCardell .40 .18
❑ 78 Jimmy Smith .40 .18
❑ 79 Andre Rison .40 .18
❑ 80 Elvis Grbac .40 .18
❑ 81 Derrick Alexander .40 .18
❑ 82 Dan Marino 4.00 1.80
❑ 83 Karim Abdul-Jabbar .75 .35
❑ 84 O.J. McDuffie .40 .18
❑ 85 Brad Johnson .75 .35
❑ 86 Cris Carter .75 .35

		MINT	NRMT
❑ 87	Robert Smith	.75	.35
❑ 88	Drew Bledsoe	1.50	.70
❑ 89	Terry Glenn	.75	.35
❑ 90	Ben Coates	.40	.18
❑ 91	Lamar Smith	.20	.09
❑ 92	Danny Wuerffel	.40	.18
❑ 93	Tiki Barber	.40	.18
❑ 94	Danny Kanell	.40	.18
❑ 95	Ike Hilliard	.40	.18
❑ 96	Curtis Martin	.75	.35
❑ 97	Keyshawn Johnson	.75	.35
❑ 98	Glenn Foley	.40	.18
❑ 99	Jeff George	.40	.18
❑ 100	Tim Brown	.75	.35
❑ 101	Napoleon Kaufman	.75	.35
❑ 102	Bobby Hoying	.40	.18
❑ 103	Charlie Garner	.20	.09
❑ 104	Irving Fryar	.40	.18
❑ 105	Kordell Stewart	.75	.35
❑ 106	Jerome Bettis	.75	.35
❑ 107	Charles Johnson	.20	.09
❑ 108	Tony Banks	.40	.18
❑ 109	Isaac Bruce	.75	.35
❑ 110	Natrone Means	.75	.35
❑ 111	Junior Seau	.40	.18
❑ 112	Steve Young	1.25	.55
❑ 113	Jerry Rice	2.00	.90
❑ 114	Garrison Hearst	.75	.35
❑ 115	Ricky Watters	.40	.18
❑ 116	Warren Moon	.75	.35
❑ 117	Joey Galloway	.75	.35
❑ 118	Trent Dilfer	.75	.35
❑ 119	Warrick Dunn	1.25	.55
❑ 120	Mike Alstott	.75	.35
❑ 121	Steve McNair	.75	.35
❑ 122	Eddie George	1.50	.70
❑ 123	Yancey Thigpen	.20	.09
❑ 124	Gus Frerotte	.20	.09
❑ 125	Terry Allen	.75	.35
❑ 126	Michael Westbrook	.40	.18
❑ AE13	Dan Marino SAMPLE	2.00	.90

1998 SP Authentic Maximum Impact

	MINT	NRMT
COMPLETE SET (30)	60.00	27.00
COMMON CARD (SE1-SE30)	.60	.25
SEMISTARS	1.00	.45
STATED ODDS 1:4		

		MINT	NRMT
❑ SE1	Brett Favre	5.00	2.20
❑ SE2	Warrick Dunn	1.50	.70
❑ SE3	Junior Seau	1.00	.45
❑ SE4	Steve Young	1.50	.70
❑ SE5	Herman Moore	1.25	.55
❑ SE6	Antowain Smith	1.25	.55
❑ SE7	John Elway	5.00	2.20
❑ SE8	Troy Aikman	2.50	1.10
❑ SE9	Dorsey Levens	1.25	.55
❑ SE10	Kordell Stewart	1.00	.45
❑ SE11	Peyton Manning	12.00	5.50
❑ SE12	Eddie George	2.00	.90
❑ SE13	Dan Marino	5.00	2.20
❑ SE14	Joey Galloway	1.25	.55
❑ SE15	Mark Brunell	2.00	.90
❑ SE16	Jake Plummer	2.50	1.10
❑ SE17	Curtis Enis	4.00	1.80
❑ SE18	Corey Dillon	1.25	.55
❑ SE19	Rob Johnson	.60	.25
❑ SE20	Barry Sanders	5.00	2.20
❑ SE21	Deion Sanders	1.25	.55
❑ SE22	Napoleon Kaufman	1.25	.55
❑ SE23	Ryan Leaf	3.00	1.35
❑ SE24	Jerry Rice	2.50	1.10
❑ SE25	Drew Bledsoe	2.00	.90
❑ SE26	Jerome Bettis	1.25	.55
❑ SE27	Emmitt Smith	4.00	1.80
❑ SE28	Tim Brown	1.25	.55
❑ SE29	Curtis Martin	1.25	.55
❑ SE30	Terrell Davis	4.00	1.80

1998 SP Authentic Memorabilia

	MINT	NRMT
COMMON CARD (M1-M24)	40.00	18.00
STATED ODDS 1:864 OVERALL		
TRADE CARD EXPIRATION: 12/10/99		

		MINT	NRMT
❑ M1	Curtis Enis (signed NFL ball)	100.00	45.00
❑ M2	Ryan Leaf (signed NFL ball)	120.00	55.00
❑ M3	Randy Moss (signed NFL ball)	300.00	135.00
❑ M4	Takeo Spikes (signed NFL ball)	80.00	36.00
❑ M5	Andre Wadsworth (signed NFL ball)	80.00	36.00
❑ M6	Marcus Nash (signed NFL ball)	60.00	27.00
❑ M7	Curtis Enis (signed mini-football)	60.00	27.00
❑ M8	Ryan Leaf (signed mini-football)	80.00	36.00
❑ M9	Randy Moss (signed mini-football)	200.00	90.00
❑ M10	Takeo Spikes (signed mini-football)	40.00	18.00
❑ M11	Andre Wadsworth (signed mini-football)	40.00	18.00
❑ M12	Marcus Nash (signed mini-football)	40.00	18.00
❑ M13	Curtis Enis (Signed Helmet)	150.00	70.00
❑ M14	Ryan Leaf (Signed Helmet)	200.00	90.00
❑ M15	Randy Moss (Signed Helmet)	400.00	180.00
❑ M16	Takeo Spikes (Signed Helmet)	120.00	55.00
❑ M17	Andre Wadsworth (Signed Helmet)	120.00	55.00
❑ M18	Marcus Nash (Signed Helmet)	100.00	45.00
❑ M19	Curtis Enis Mini Helmet	60.00	27.00
❑ M20	Ryan Leaf Mini Helmet	80.00	36.00
❑ M21	Randy Moss Mini Helmet	200.00	90.00
❑ M22	Takeo Spikes Mini Helmet	40.00	18.00
❑ M23	Andre Wadsworth Mini Helmet	40.00	18.00
❑ M24	Marcus Nash Mini Helmet	40.00	18.00
❑ M25	Player's Ink Set		
❑ M26	Brett Favre Game Jersey		
❑ M27	Terrell Davis Game Jersey		
❑ M28	Dan Marino Game Jersey		
❑ M29	Jerry Rice Game Jersey..		
❑ M30	Mark Brunell Game Jersey		

1998 SP Authentic Player's Ink

	MINT	NRMT
COMPLETE SET (30)	1500.00	700.00
COMMON CARD	12.00	5.50
SEMISTARS	20.00	9.00
UNLISTED STARS	25.00	11.00

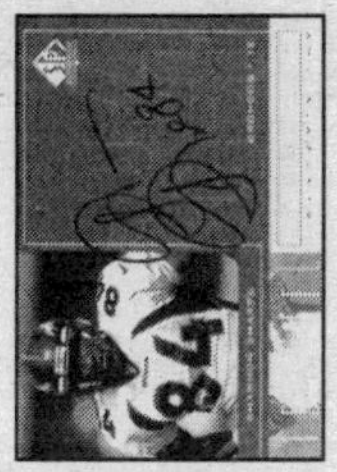

	MINT	NRMT
STATED ODDS 1:23 OVERALL ..		
COMMON SILVER	40.00	18.00
*SILVERS: 8X TO 2X GREENS....		
SILVER PRINT RUN 100 SERIAL #'d SETS		
SOME ISSUED AS TRADE REDEMPTIONS		
TRADE CARDS SAME PRICE......		
TRADE CARD EXPIRATION: 7/15/99		

		MINT	NRMT
❑ AW	Andre Wadsworth	20.00	9.00
❑ BG	Brian Griese	50.00	22.00
❑ BH	Bobby Hoying	20.00	9.00
❑ CD	Corey Dillon	25.00	11.00
❑ CE	Curtis Enis	40.00	18.00
❑ DL	Dorsey Levens	25.00	11.00
❑ DM	Dan Marino	200.00	90.00
❑ EG	Eddie George	40.00	18.00
❑ FL	Fred Lane	20.00	9.00
❑ FT	Fred Taylor	80.00	36.00
❑ GC	Germane Crowell	25.00	11.00
❑ JA	Jamal Anderson	25.00	11.00
❑ JM	Johnnie Morton	20.00	9.00
❑ JP	Jerome Pathon	12.00	5.50
❑ JP	Jake Plummer	50.00	22.00
❑ KJ	Keyshawn Johnson	40.00	18.00
❑ KM	Keenan McCardell	20.00	9.00
❑ KS	Kordell Stewart	50.00	22.00
❑ MA	Mike Alstott	25.00	11.00
❑ MJ	Michael Jackson	12.00	5.50
❑ MN	Marcus Nash	12.00	5.50
❑ RE	Robert Edwards	25.00	11.00
❑ RL	Ryan Leaf	40.00	18.00
❑ RM	Randy Moss	175.00	80.00
❑ SH	Skip Hicks	25.00	11.00
❑ SS	Shannon Sharpe	20.00	9.00
❑ TA	Troy Aikman	120.00	55.00
❑ TS	Takeo Spikes	20.00	9.00
❑ TV	Tamarick Vanover	12.00	5.50
❑ JRG	Jerry Rice/Green	250.00	110.00
❑ JRS	Jerry Rice/100 Silver	250.00	110.00

1998 SP Authentic Player's Ink Gold

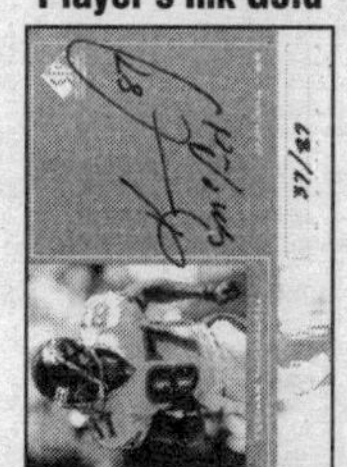

	MINT	NRMT
COMMON (#'d OF 81-90)	50.00	22.00
GOLDS SERIAL #'d TO PLAYER'S JERSEY NO.		
HOYING/KORDELL/AIKMAN NOT PRICED		

		MINT	NRMT
❑ AW	Andre Wadsworth/90..	50.00	22.00
❑ BG	Brian Griese/14	400.00	180.00
❑ BH	Bobby Hoying/7		

❑ CD Corey Dillon/28	100.00	45.00
❑ CE Curtis Enis/39	150.00	70.00
❑ DL Dorsey Levens/25	120.00	55.00
❑ DM Dan Marino/13	1500.00	700.00
❑ EG Eddie George/27	200.00	90.00
❑ FL Fred Lane/32	60.00	27.00
❑ FT Fred Taylor/28	300.00	135.00
❑ GC Germane Crowell/17	250.00	110.00
❑ JA Jamal Anderson/32	120.00	55.00
❑ JM Johnnie Morton/87	50.00	22.00
❑ JP Jerome Pathon/16	150.00	70.00
❑ JP Jake Plummer/16	400.00	180.00
❑ JR Jerry Rice/80	250.00	110.00
❑ KJ Keyshawn Johnson/19	120.00	55.00
❑ KM Keenan McCardell/87	50.00	22.00
❑ KS Kordell Stewart/10		
❑ MA Mike Alstott/40	100.00	45.00
❑ MJ Michael Jackson/81	50.00	22.00
❑ MN Marcus Nash/12	150.00	70.00
❑ RE Robert Edwards/47	80.00	36.00
❑ RL Ryan Leaf/16	250.00	110.00
❑ RM Randy Moss/18	1000.00	450.00
❑ SH Skip Hicks/20	200.00	90.00
❑ SS Shannon Sharpe/84	50.00	22.00
❑ TA Troy Aikman/8		
❑ TS Takeo Spikes/51	50.00	22.00
❑ TV Tamarick Vanover/87	50.00	22.00

1998 SP Authentic Special Forces

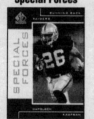

	MINT	NRMT
COMPLETE SET (30)	200.00	90.00
COMMON CARD (S1-S30)	2.50	1.10
SEMISTARS	4.00	1.80

STATED PRINT RUN 1000 SERIAL #'d SETS

❑ S1 Kordell Stewart	4.00	1.80
❑ S2 Charles Woodson	10.00	4.50
❑ S3 Terrell Davis	15.00	6.75
❑ S4 Brett Favre	20.00	9.00
❑ S5 Joey Galloway	6.00	2.70
❑ S6 Warrick Dunn	6.00	2.70
❑ S7 Ryan Leaf	8.00	3.60
❑ S8 Drew Bledsoe	8.00	3.60
❑ S9 Takeo Spikes	2.50	1.10
❑ S10 Barry Sanders	20.00	9.00
❑ S11 Troy Aikman	10.00	4.50
❑ S12 John Elway	20.00	9.00
❑ S13 Jerome Bettis	6.00	2.70
❑ S14 Karim Abdul-Jabbar	6.00	2.70
❑ S15 Tony Gonzalez	4.00	1.80
❑ S16 Steve Young	6.00	2.70
❑ S17 Napoleon Kaufman	6.00	2.70
❑ S18 Andre Wadsworth	2.50	1.10
❑ S19 Herman Moore	6.00	2.70
❑ S20 Fred Taylor	20.00	9.00
❑ S21 Deion Sanders	6.00	2.70
❑ S22 Peyton Manning	40.00	18.00
❑ S23 Jerry Rice	10.00	4.50
❑ S24 Dan Marino	20.00	9.00
❑ S25 Antonio Freeman	6.00	2.70
❑ S26 Curtis Enis	10.00	4.50
❑ S27 Jake Plummer	12.00	5.50
❑ S28 Steve McNair	6.00	2.70
❑ S29 Mark Brunell	8.00	3.60
❑ S30 Robert Edwards	4.00	1.80

1999 SP Authentic

	MINT	NRMT
COMPLETE SET (145)	1800.00	800.00
COMP.SET w/o SPs (90)	35.00	16.00
COMMON CARD (1-145)	.20	.09
SEMISTARS	.40	.18
UNLISTED STARS	.75	.35
COMMON ROOKIE (91-145)	15.00	6.75
ROOKIE SEMISTARS	20.00	9.00
ROOKIE UNL.STARS	30.00	13.50

ROOKIES PRINT RUN 1999 SER.#'d SET

❑ 1 Jake Plummer	1.50	.70
❑ 2 Adrian Murrell	.40	.18
❑ 3 Frank Sanders	.40	.18
❑ 4 Jamal Anderson	.75	.35
❑ 5 Chris Chandler	.40	.18
❑ 6 Terance Mathis	.40	.18
❑ 7 Priest Holmes	.75	.35
❑ 8 Jermaine Lewis	.40	.18
❑ 9 Antowain Smith	.75	.35
❑ 10 Doug Flutie	1.00	.45
❑ 11 Eric Moulds	.75	.35
❑ 12 Muhsin Muhammad	.40	.18
❑ 13 Tim Biakabutuka	.40	.18
❑ 14 Wesley Walls	.40	.18
❑ 15 Curtis Enis	.75	.35
❑ 16 Bobby Engram	.40	.18
❑ 17 Corey Dillon	.75	.35
❑ 18 Darnay Scott	.40	.18
❑ 19 Terry Kirby	.20	.09
❑ 20 Ty Detmer	.40	.18
❑ 21 Troy Aikman	2.00	.90
❑ 22 Michael Irvin	.40	.18
❑ 23 Emmitt Smith	2.00	.90
❑ 24 Terrell Davis	2.00	.90
❑ 25 Brian Griese	1.50	.70
❑ 26 Rod Smith	.40	.18
❑ 27 Shannon Sharpe	.40	.18
❑ 28 Barry Sanders	3.00	1.35
❑ 29 Charlie Batch	1.50	.70
❑ 30 Herman Moore	.75	.35
❑ 31 Johnnie Morton	.40	.18
❑ 32 Brett Favre	3.00	1.35
❑ 33 Antonio Freeman	.75	.35
❑ 34 Dorsey Levens	.75	.35
❑ 35 Mark Chmura	.40	.18
❑ 36 Peyton Manning	3.00	1.35
❑ 37 Marvin Harrison	.75	.35
❑ 38 Mark Brunell	1.25	.55
❑ 39 Fred Taylor	2.00	.90
❑ 40 Jimmy Smith	.40	.18
❑ 41 Elvis Grbac	.40	.18
❑ 42 Andre Rison	.40	.18
❑ 43 Dan Marino	3.00	1.35
❑ 44 O.J. McDuffie	.40	.18
❑ 45 Yatil Green	.20	.09
❑ 46 Randall Cunningham	.75	.35
❑ 47 Randy Moss	4.00	1.80
❑ 48 Robert Smith	.75	.35
❑ 49 Cris Carter	.75	.35
❑ 50 Drew Bledsoe	1.25	.55
❑ 51 Ben Coates	.20	.09
❑ 52 Terry Glenn	.75	.35
❑ 53 Eddie Kennison	.40	.18
❑ 54 Cam Cleeland	.20	.09
❑ 55 Ike Hilliard	.40	.18
❑ 56 Gary Brown	.20	.09
❑ 57 Kerry Collins	.40	.18
❑ 58 Vinny Testaverde	.40	.18
❑ 59 Keyshawn Johnson	.75	.35
❑ 60 Wayne Chrebet	.75	.35
❑ 61 Curtis Martin	.75	.35
❑ 62 Tim Brown	.75	.35
❑ 63 Napoleon Kaufman	.75	.35
❑ 64 Charles Woodson	.75	.35
❑ 65 Duce Staley	.75	.35
❑ 66 Charles Johnson	.40	.18
❑ 67 Kordell Stewart	.75	.35
❑ 68 Jerome Bettis	.75	.35
❑ 69 Marshall Faulk	.75	.35
❑ 70 Isaac Bruce	.75	.35
❑ 71 Trent Green	.40	.18
❑ 72 Jim Harbaugh	.40	.18
❑ 73 Junior Seau	.40	.18
❑ 74 Natrone Means	.40	.18
❑ 75 Steve Young	1.25	.55
❑ 76 Jerry Rice	2.00	.90
❑ 77 Terrell Owens	.75	.35
❑ 78 Lawrence Phillips	.40	.18
❑ 79 Joey Galloway	.75	.35
❑ 80 Ricky Watters	.40	.18
❑ 81 Jon Kitna	1.00	.45
❑ 82 Warrick Dunn	.75	.35
❑ 83 Trent Dilfer	.40	.18
❑ 84 Mike Alstott	.75	.35
❑ 85 Eddie George	1.00	.45
❑ 86 Steve McNair	.75	.35
❑ 87 Yancey Thigpen	.20	.09
❑ 88 Brad Johnson	.75	.35
❑ 89 Skip Hicks	.40	.18
❑ 90 Michael Westbrook	.40	.18
❑ 91 Ricky Williams RC	250.00	110.00
❑ 92 Tim Couch RC	300.00	135.00
❑ 93 Akili Smith RC	125.00	55.00
❑ 94 Edgerrin James RC	450.00	200.00
❑ 95 Donovan McNabb RC	135.00	60.00
❑ 96 Torry Holt RC	80.00	36.00
❑ 97 Cade McNown RC	150.00	70.00
❑ 98 Shaun King RC	135.00	60.00
❑ 99 Daunte Culpepper RC	150.00	70.00
❑ 100 Brock Huard RC	40.00	18.00
❑ 101 Chris Claiborne RC	20.00	9.00
❑ 102 James Johnson RC	40.00	18.00
❑ 103 Rob Konrad RC	30.00	13.50
❑ 104 Peerless Price RC	50.00	22.00
❑ 105 Kevin Faulk RC	40.00	18.00
❑ 106 Andy Katzenmoyer RC	30.00	13.50
❑ 107 Troy Edwards RC	50.00	22.00
❑ 108 Kevin Johnson RC	90.00	40.00
❑ 109 Mike Cloud RC	30.00	13.50
❑ 110 David Boston RC	50.00	22.00
❑ 111 Champ Bailey RC	40.00	18.00
❑ 112 D'Wayne Bates RC	20.00	9.00
❑ 113 Joe Germaine RC	30.00	13.50
❑ 114 Antoine Winfield RC	20.00	9.00
❑ 115 Fernando Bryant RC	20.00	9.00
❑ 116 Jevon Kearse RC	90.00	40.00
❑ 117 Chris McAlister RC	20.00	9.00
❑ 118 Brandon Stokley RC	20.00	9.00
❑ 119 Karsten Bailey RC	20.00	9.00
❑ 120 Daylon McCutcheon RC	20.00	9.00
❑ 121 Jermaine Fazande RC	30.00	13.50
❑ 122 Joel Makovicka RC	30.00	13.50
❑ 123 Ebenezer Ekuban RC	20.00	9.00
❑ 124 Joe Montgomery RC	30.00	13.50
❑ 125 Sean Bennett RC	30.00	13.50
❑ 126 Na Brown RC	30.00	13.50
❑ 127 De'Mond Parker RC	30.00	13.50
❑ 128 Sedrick Irvin RC	30.00	13.50
❑ 129 Terry Jackson RC	20.00	9.00
❑ 130 Jeff Paulk RC	20.00	9.00
❑ 131 Cecil Collins RC	30.00	13.50
❑ 132 Bobby Collins RC	20.00	9.00
❑ 133 Amos Zereoue RC	30.00	13.50
❑ 134 Travis McGriff RC	20.00	9.00
❑ 135 Larry Parker RC	20.00	9.00
❑ 136 Wane McGarity RC	20.00	9.00
❑ 137 Cecil Martin RC	20.00	9.00
❑ 138 Al Wilson RC	20.00	9.00
❑ 139 Jim Kleinsasser RC	30.00	13.50
❑ 140 Dat Nguyen RC	30.00	13.50
❑ 141 Marty Booker RC	30.00	13.50

		MINT	NRMT
❑ 142	Reginald Kelly RC	15.00	6.75
❑ 143	Scott Covington RC	20.00	9.00
❑ 144	Antuan Edwards RC	20.00	9.00
❑ 145	Craig Yeast RC	20.00	9.00
❑ WPA	W.Payton AUTO/100	400.00	180.00
❑ WPSP	Walter Payton (Game Jersey AUTO/34)	2000.00	900.00

1999 SP Authentic Excitement

	MINT	NRMT
COMMON CARD (1-90)	2.50	1.10
COMMON ROOKIE (91-145)	25.00	11.00
STATED PRINT RUN 250 SER.#'d SETS		

1999 SP Authentic Excitement Gold

	MINT	NRMT
COMMON CARD (1-90)	15.00	6.75
*STARS: 30X TO 80X HI COL.		
*YOUNG STARS: 25X TO 60X		
COMMON ROOKIE (91-145)	35.00	16.00
*RCs: 1.2X TO 2.5X		
STATED PRINT RUN 25 SER.#'d SETS		

1999 SP Authentic Athletic

	MINT	NRMT
COMPLETE SET (10)	30.00	13.50
COMMON CARD (A1-A10)	2.50	1.10
STATED ODDS 1:10		

		MINT	NRMT
❑ A1	Randy Moss	10.00	4.50
❑ A2	Steve McNair	2.50	1.10
❑ A3	Jamal Anderson	2.50	1.10
❑ A4	Curtis Martin	2.50	1.10
❑ A5	Kordell Stewart	2.50	1.10
❑ A6	Barry Sanders	10.00	4.50
❑ A7	Fred Taylor	5.00	2.20
❑ A8	Doug Flutie	3.00	1.35
❑ A9	Emmitt Smith	6.00	2.70
❑ A10	Steve Young	4.00	1.80

1999 SP Authentic Buy Back Autographs

	MINT	NRMT
COMMON CARD	40.00	18.00
SEMISTARS	50.00	22.00
STATED ODDS 1:576		
TRADE CARD EXPIRATION: 7/3/2000		
CARDS SERIAL #'d UNDER 9 NOT PRICED		

		MINT	NRMT
❑ 1	T.Aikman 93SP/12	250.00	110.00
❑ 2	T.Aikman 94SP/42	120.00	55.00
❑ 3	T.Aikman 95SP/94	80.00	36.00
❑ 4	T.Aikman 95SPC/24	200.00	90.00
❑ 5	T.Aikman 95SPH/4		
❑ 6	T.Aikman 96SP/28	250.00	110.00
❑ 7	T.Aikman 97SPA/8		
❑ 8	T.Aikman 98SPA/24	200.00	90.00
❑ 9	T.Aikman 98SPASF/2		
❑ 10	J.Anderson 96SP/15	150.00	70.00
❑ 11	J.Anderson 97SPA/5		
❑ 12	J.Anderson 98SPA/20	80.00	36.00
❑ 13	J.Bettis 93SP/25	100.00	45.00
❑ 14	J.Bettis 94SP/42	60.00	27.00
❑ 15	J.Bettis 95SP/93	40.00	18.00
❑ 16	J.Bettis 95SPC/25	80.00	36.00
❑ 17	J.Bettis 96SP/9	120.00	55.00
❑ 18	J.Bettis 97SPA/3		
❑ 19	J.Bettis 98SPA/63	50.00	22.00
❑ 20	D.Bledsoe 93SP/14	150.00	70.00
❑ 21	D.Bledsoe 94SP/28	150.00	70.00
❑ 22	D.Bledsoe 95SP/98	80.00	36.00
❑ 23	D.Bledsoe 95SPC/25	150.00	70.00
❑ 24	D.Bledsoe 95SPH/4		
❑ 25	D.Bledsoe 96SP/8		
❑ 26	D.Bledsoe 96SPH/1		
❑ 27	D.Bledsoe 97SPA/7		
❑ 28	D.Bledsoe 98SPA/117	60.00	27.00
❑ 29	D.Bledsoe 98SPASF/3		
❑ 30	T.Brown 93SP/19	80.00	36.00
❑ 31	T.Brown 94SP/36	50.00	22.00
❑ 32	T.Brown 95SPC/25	70.00	32.00
❑ 33	T.Brown 96SP/10	120.00	55.00
❑ 34	T.Brown 98SP/25	70.00	32.00
❑ 35	M.Brunell 93SP/8		
❑ 36	M.Brunell 96SP/7		
❑ 37	M.Brunell 97SPA/4		
❑ 38	M.Brunell 98SPA/21	150.00	70.00
❑ 39	W.Chrebet 95SP/43	40.00	18.00
❑ 40	W.Chrebet 96SP/14	100.00	45.00
❑ 41	T.Davis 95SP/14	350.00	160.00
❑ 42	T.Davis 97SPA/2		
❑ 43	T.Davis 98SPA/62	100.00	45.00
❑ 44	W.Dunn 98SPAMI/50	50.00	22.00
❑ 45	M.Faulk 94SP/28	300.00	135.00
❑ 46	M.Faulk 95SP/17	150.00	70.00
❑ 47	M.Faulk 95SPC/23	100.00	45.00
❑ 48	M.Faulk 97SPA/4		
❑ 49	M.Faulk 96SP/40	60.00	27.00
❑ 50	M.Faulk 98SPA/28	120.00	55.00
❑ 51	J.Galloway 95SP/30	80.00	36.00
❑ 52	J.Galloway 95SPC/48	60.00	27.00
❑ 53	J.Galloway 96SP/6		
❑ 54	J.Galloway 98SPA/68	50.00	22.00
❑ 55	E.George 96SP/17	300.00	135.00
❑ 56	E.George 97SPA/2		
❑ 57	E.George 98SPA/65	60.00	27.00
❑ 58	E.George 98SPAMI/48	70.00	32.00
❑ 59	B.Johnson 98SPA/70	50.00	22.00
❑ 60	Peyton Manning Trade	250.00	110.00
❑ 61	P.Manning 98UDEnc/60	250.00	110.00
❑ 62	P.Manning 98UDECT/16	350.00	160.00
❑ 63	Dan Marino Trade	200.00	90.00
❑ 64	D.Marino 95SP/100	120.00	55.00
❑ 65	D.Marino 95SPC/25	300.00	135.00
❑ 66	D.Marino 96SP/37	250.00	110.00
❑ 67	D.Marino 97SPA/7		
❑ 68	D.Marino 98SPA/44	250.00	110.00
❑ 69	N.Means Trade	40.00	18.00
❑ 70	H.Moore 93SP/18	100.00	45.00
❑ 71	H.Moore 94SP/45	50.00	22.00
❑ 72	H.Moore 95SP/84	40.00	18.00
❑ 73	H.Moore 95SPC/25	80.00	36.00
❑ 74	H.Moore 96SP/40	50.00	22.00
❑ 75	H.Moore 98SPA/30	60.00	27.00
❑ 76	Jake Plummer Trade	100.00	45.00
❑ 77	J.Plummer 98SPA/112	60.00	27.00
❑ 78	J.Rice 93SP/6		
❑ 79	J.Rice 94SP/8		
❑ 80	J.Rice 95SP/80	120.00	55.00
❑ 81	J.Rice 95SPC/28	200.00	90.00
❑ 82	J.Rice 95SPH/4		
❑ 83	J.Rice 96SPH/1	40.00	18.00
❑ 84	J.Rice 97SPA/3		
❑ 85	J.Rice 98SPA/61	150.00	70.00

1999 SP Authentic Maximum Impact

	MINT	NRMT
COMPLETE SET (10)	15.00	6.75
COMMON CARD (MI1-MI10)	1.25	.55
STATED ODDS 1:4		

		MINT	NRMT
❑ MI1	Jerry Rice	3.00	1.35
❑ MI2	Eddie George	1.50	.70
❑ MI3	Marshall Faulk	1.25	.55
❑ MI4	Keyshawn Johnson	1.25	.55
❑ MI5	Terrell Davis	3.00	1.35
❑ MI6	Warrick Dunn	1.25	.55
❑ MI7	Jerome Bettis	1.25	.55
❑ MI8	Drew Bledsoe	2.00	.90
❑ MI9	Curtis Martin	1.25	.55
❑ MI10	Brett Favre	5.00	2.20

1999 SP Authentic New Classics

	MINT	NRMT
COMPLETE SET (10)	40.00	18.00
COMMON CARD (NC1-NC10)	3.00	1.35

STATED ODDS 1:23

		MINT	NRMT
❑ NC1	Steve McNair	3.00	1.35
❑ NC2	Jon Kitna	4.00	1.80
❑ NC3	Curtis Enis	3.00	1.35
❑ NC4	Peyton Manning	10.00	4.50
❑ NC5	Fred Taylor	6.00	2.70
❑ NC6	Randy Moss	12.00	5.50
❑ NC7	Donovan McNabb	10.00	4.50
❑ NC8	Terrell Davis	8.00	3.60
❑ NC9	Keyshawn Johnson	3.00	1.35
❑ NC10	Ricky Williams	15.00	6.75

1999 SP Authentic NFL Headquarters

	MINT	NRMT
COMPLETE SET (10)	40.00	18.00
COMMON CARD (HQ1-HQ10)	3.00	1.35
STATED ODDS 1:10		

❑ HQ1	Brett Favre	10.00	4.50
❑ HQ2	Jake Plummer	5.00	2.20
❑ HQ3	Charlie Batch	4.00	1.80
❑ HQ4	Akili Smith	4.00	1.80
❑ HQ5	Troy Aikman	6.00	2.70
❑ HQ6	Drew Bledsoe	4.00	1.80
❑ HQ7	Dan Marino	10.00	4.50
❑ HQ8	Jon Kitna	3.00	1.35
❑ HQ9	Mark Brunell	4.00	1.80
❑ HQ10	Tim Couch	12.00	5.50

1999 SP Authentic Player's Ink

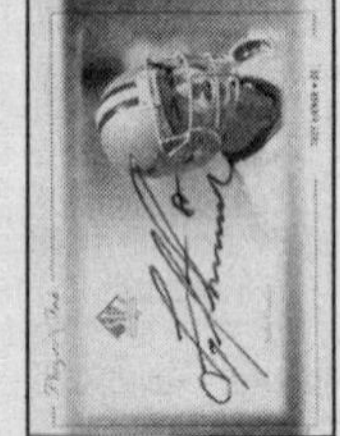

	MINT	NRMT
COMPLETE SET (40)	1800.00	800.00
COMMON CARD	20.00	9.00
SEMISTARS	25.00	11.00

STATED ODDS 1:23
*LEVEL 2 PARALLEL: .8X TO 2X HI COL.
LEVEL 2 PRINT RUN 100 SERIAL #'d SETS
TRADE CARD EXPIRATION: 7/10/2000
RICKY WILLIAMS SIGNED IN PURPLE ONLY

❑ AF-A	Antonio Freeman	25.00	11.00
❑ AS-A	Akili Smith	40.00	18.00
❑ BH-A	Brock Huard	25.00	11.00
❑ BJ-A	Brad Johnson	25.00	11.00
❑ BR-A	Mark Brunell	60.00	27.00
❑ CB-A	Champ Bailey	25.00	11.00
❑ CD-A	Corey Dillon	25.00	11.00
❑ CH-A	Charlie Batch	40.00	18.00
❑ CL-A	Mike Cloud	20.00	9.00
❑ CM-A	Cade McNown	50.00	22.00
❑ DB-A	David Boston	30.00	13.50
❑ DC-A	Daunte Culpepper	50.00	22.00
❑ DF-A	Doug Flutie	40.00	18.00
❑ DM-A	Dan Marino	175.00	80.00
❑ DR-A	Drew Bledsoe	60.00	27.00
❑ ED-A	Ed McCaffrey	20.00	9.00
❑ EG-A	Eddie George	40.00	18.00
❑ EJ-A	Edgerrin James	150.00	70.00
❑ EM-A	Eric Moulds	25.00	11.00
❑ HM-A	Herman Moore	25.00	11.00
❑ JA-A	Jamal Anderson	25.00	11.00
❑ JB-A	Jerome Bettis	25.00	11.00
❑ JG-A	Joey Galloway	25.00	11.00
❑ JP-A	Jake Plummer	60.00	27.00
❑ JR-A	Jerry Rice	120.00	55.00
❑ KF-A	Kevin Faulk	25.00	11.00
❑ MB-A	Michael Bishop	25.00	11.00
❑ MF-A	Marshall Faulk	50.00	22.00
❑ NM-A	Natrone Means	20.00	9.00
❑ PM-A	Peyton Manning	135.00	60.00
❑ RM-A	Randy Moss	150.00	70.00
❑ RW-A	R.Williams Purple	200.00	90.00
❑ SK-A	Shaun King	50.00	22.00
❑ SS-A	Shannon Sharpe	20.00	9.00
❑ TA-A	Troy Aikman	100.00	45.00
❑ TC-A	Tim Couch	100.00	45.00
❑ TD-A	Terrell Davis	80.00	36.00
❑ TE-A	Troy Edwards	30.00	13.50
❑ TH-A	Torry Holt	40.00	18.00
❑ TO-A	Terrell Owens	25.00	11.00
❑ WC-A	Wayne Chrebet	25.00	11.00

1999 SP Authentic Rookie Blitz

	MINT	NRMT
COMPLETE SET (19)	60.00	27.00
COMMON CARD (RB1-RB19)	2.00	.90
SEMISTARS	2.50	1.10
STATED ODDS 1:11		

❑ RB1	Edgerrin James	20.00	9.00
❑ RB2	Tim Couch	12.00	5.50
❑ RB3	Daunte Culpepper	8.00	3.60
❑ RB4	Champ Bailey	3.00	1.35
❑ RB5	Donovan McNabb	8.00	3.60
❑ RB6	Kevin Johnson	6.00	2.70
❑ RB7	Shaun King	8.00	3.60
❑ RB8	Peerless Price	4.00	1.80
❑ RB9	David Boston	4.00	1.80
❑ RB10	Ricky Williams	12.00	5.50
❑ RB11	Akili Smith	5.00	2.20
❑ RB12	Kevin Faulk	3.00	1.35
❑ RB13	D'Wayne Bates	2.00	.90
❑ RB14	Brock Huard	3.00	1.35
❑ RB15	Rob Konrad	2.00	.90
❑ RB16	Torry Holt	6.00	2.70
❑ RB17	Troy Edwards	4.00	1.80
❑ RB18	Cade McNown	8.00	3.60
❑ RB19	Cecil Collins	2.00	.90

1999 SP Authentic Supremacy

	MINT	NRMT
COMPLETE SET (12)	60.00	27.00
COMMON CARD (S1-S12)	3.00	1.35
STATED ODDS 1:23		

❑ S1	Terrell Davis	8.00	3.60
❑ S2	Joey Galloway	3.00	1.35
❑ S3	Dan Marino	12.00	5.50
❑ S4	Brett Favre	12.00	5.50
❑ S5	Emmitt Smith	8.00	3.60
❑ S6	Barry Sanders	12.00	5.50
❑ S7	Curtis Martin	3.00	1.35
❑ S8	Jamal Anderson	3.00	1.35
❑ S9	Jake Plummer	6.00	2.70
❑ S10	Randy Moss	12.00	5.50
❑ S11	Tim Couch	15.00	6.75
❑ S12	Peyton Manning	10.00	4.50

1999 SP Signature

	MINT	NRMT
COMPLETE SET (180)	400.00	180.00
COMP.SET w/o SP's (170)	100.00	45.00
COMMON CARD (1-170)	.50	.23
SEMISTARS	.75	.35
UNLISTED STARS	1.25	.55
COMMON ROOKIE (171-180)	20.00	9.00

UNPRICED LEGENDARY CUTS #'d TO 1

❑ 1	Jake Plummer	2.50	1.10
❑ 2	Mario Bates	.50	.23
❑ 3	Adrian Murrell	.75	.35
❑ 4	Jamal Anderson	1.25	.55
❑ 5	Chris Chandler	.75	.35
❑ 6	Bob Christian	.50	.23
❑ 7	O.J. Santiago	.50	.23
❑ 8	Jim Harbaugh	.75	.35
❑ 9	Priest Holmes	1.25	.55
❑ 10	Ray Lewis	.50	.23
❑ 11	Michael Jackson	.50	.23
❑ 12	Tony Siragusa	.50	.23
❑ 13	Doug Flutie	1.50	.70
❑ 14	Antowain Smith	1.25	.55
❑ 15	Eric Moulds	1.25	.55
❑ 16	William Floyd	.50	.23
❑ 17	Fred Lane	.50	.23
❑ 18	Muhsin Muhammad	.75	.35
❑ 19	Bobby Engram	.75	.35

❑ 20 Curtis Enis	1.25	.55
❑ 21 Curtis Conway	.75	.35
❑ 22 Corey Dillon	1.25	.55
❑ 23 Carl Pickens	.75	.35
❑ 24 Ashley Ambrose	.50	.23
❑ 25 Darnay Scott	.50	.23
❑ 26 Troy Aikman	3.00	1.35
❑ 27 Jason Garrett	.50	.23
❑ 28 Emmitt Smith	3.00	1.35
❑ 29 Deion Sanders	1.25	.55
❑ 30 John Elway	5.00	2.20
❑ 31 Terrell Davis	3.00	1.35
❑ 32 Ed McCaffrey	.75	.35
❑ 33 John Mobley	.50	.23
❑ 34 Maa Tanuvasa	.50	.23
❑ 35 Ray Crockett	.50	.23
❑ 36 Barry Sanders	5.00	2.20
❑ 37 Herman Moore	1.25	.55
❑ 38 Charlie Batch	2.50	1.10
❑ 39 Robert Porcher	.50	.23
❑ 40 Tommy Vardell	.50	.23
❑ 41 Brett Favre	5.00	2.20
❑ 42 Antonio Freeman	1.25	.55
❑ 43 Darick Holmes	.50	.23
❑ 44 Robert Brooks	.75	.35
❑ 45 Peyton Manning	6.00	2.70
❑ 46 Marshall Faulk	1.25	.55
❑ 47 Torrance Small	.50	.23
❑ 48 Lamont Warren	.50	.23
❑ 49 Zack Crockett	.50	.23
❑ 50 Mark Brunell	2.00	.90
❑ 51 Pete Mitchell	.50	.23
❑ 52 Fred Taylor	3.00	1.35
❑ 53 Jimmy Smith	.75	.35
❑ 54 Andre Rison	.75	.35
❑ 55 Rich Gannon	.75	.35
❑ 56 Donnell Bennett	.50	.23
❑ 57 Dan Marino	5.00	2.20
❑ 58 Karim Abdul-Jabbar	.75	.35
❑ 59 Troy Drayton	.50	.23
❑ 60 Jason Taylor	.50	.23
❑ 61 Cris Carter	1.25	.55
❑ 62 Randy Moss	6.00	2.70
❑ 63 Robert Smith	1.25	.55
❑ 64 Leroy Hoard	.50	.23
❑ 65 Randall Cunningham	1.25	.55
❑ 66 Derrick Alexander DE	.50	.23
❑ 67 Drew Bledsoe	2.00	.90
❑ 68 Robert Edwards	.75	.35
❑ 69 Willie McGinest	.50	.23
❑ 70 Chris Slade	.50	.23
❑ 71 Terry Glenn	1.25	.55
❑ 72 Ty Law	.50	.23
❑ 73 Kerry Collins	.75	.35
❑ 74 Sean Dawkins	.50	.23
❑ 75 Cam Cleeland	.50	.23
❑ 76 Sammy Knight	.50	.23
❑ 77 Danny Kanell	.50	.23
❑ 78 Gary Brown	.50	.23
❑ 79 Chris Calloway	.75	.35
❑ 80 Curtis Martin	1.25	.55
❑ 81 Keyshawn Johnson	1.25	.55
❑ 82 Vinny Testaverde	.75	.35
❑ 83 Leon Johnson	.50	.23
❑ 84 Kyle Brady	.50	.23
❑ 85 Tim Brown	1.25	.55
❑ 86 Jeff George	.75	.35
❑ 87 Rickey Dudley	.50	.23
❑ 88 Napoleon Kaufman	1.25	.55
❑ 89 James Jett	.75	.35
❑ 90 Harvey Williams	.50	.23
❑ 91 Koy Detmer	.50	.23
❑ 92 Duce Staley	1.25	.55
❑ 93 Charlie Garner	.75	.35
❑ 94 Jerome Bettis	1.25	.55
❑ 95 Kordell Stewart	1.25	.55
❑ 96 Courtney Hawkins	.50	.23
❑ 97 Hines Ward	.50	.23
❑ 98 Isaac Bruce	1.25	.55
❑ 99 Tony Banks	.75	.35
❑ 100 Greg Hill	.50	.23
❑ 101 Keith Lyle	.50	.23
❑ 102 Ryan Leaf	1.25	.55
❑ 103 Craig Whelihan	.50	.23
❑ 104 Charlie Jones	.50	.23
❑ 105 Junior Seau	.75	.35
❑ 106 Natrone Means	.75	.35
❑ 107 Rodney Harrison	.50	.23
❑ 108 Steve Young	2.00	.90
❑ 109 Garrison Hearst	.75	.35
❑ 110 Jerry Rice	3.00	1.35
❑ 111 Chris Doleman	.50	.23
❑ 112 Roy Barker	.50	.23
❑ 113 Ricky Watters	.75	.35
❑ 114 Jon Kitna	1.50	.70
❑ 115 Joey Galloway	1.25	.55
❑ 116 Chad Brown	.50	.23
❑ 117 Michael Sinclair	.50	.23
❑ 118 Warrick Dunn	1.25	.55
❑ 119 Mike Alstott	1.25	.55
❑ 120 Bert Emanuel	.75	.35
❑ 121 Hardy Nickerson	.50	.23
❑ 122 Eddie George	1.50	.70
❑ 123 Steve McNair	1.25	.55
❑ 124 Yancey Thigpen	.50	.23
❑ 125 Frank Wycheck	.50	.23
❑ 126 Jackie Harris	.50	.23
❑ 127 Terry Allen	.75	.35
❑ 128 Trent Green	.75	.35
❑ 129 Jamie Asher	.50	.23
❑ 130 Brian Mitchell	.50	.23
❑ 131 Lance Alworth	1.25	.55
❑ 132 Fred Biletnikoff	1.25	.55
❑ 133 Mel Blount	.50	.23
❑ 134 Cliff Branch	.50	.23
❑ 135 Harold Carmichael	.50	.23
❑ 136 Larry Csonka	1.25	.55
❑ 137 Eric Dickerson	.50	.23
❑ 138 Randy Gradishar	.50	.23
❑ 139 Joe Greene	.75	.35
❑ 140 Jack Ham	.75	.35
❑ 141 Ted Hendricks	.50	.23
❑ 142 Charlie Joiner	.50	.23
❑ 143 Ed Jones	.50	.23
❑ 144 Billy Kilmer	.50	.23
❑ 145 Paul Krause	.50	.23
❑ 146 James Lofton	.50	.23
❑ 147 Archie Manning	.75	.35
❑ 148 Don Maynard	.50	.23
❑ 149 Ozzie Newsome	.50	.23
❑ 150 Jim Otto	.50	.23
❑ 151 Lee Roy Selmon	.50	.23
❑ 152 Billy Sims	.50	.23
❑ 153 Mike Singletary	.75	.35
❑ 154 Ken Stabler	1.50	.70
❑ 155 John Stallworth	.75	.35
❑ 156 Roger Staubach	2.00	.90
❑ 157 Charley Taylor	.50	.23
❑ 158 Paul Warfield	1.25	.55
❑ 159 Kellen Winslow	.50	.23
❑ 160 Jack Youngblood	.50	.23
❑ 161 Bill Bergey	.50	.23
❑ 162 Raymond Berry	.75	.35
❑ 163 Chuck Howley	.50	.23
❑ 164 Rocky Bleier	.75	.35
❑ 165 Russ Francis	.50	.23
❑ 166 Drew Pearson	.50	.23
❑ 167 Mercury Morris	.50	.23
❑ 168 Dick Anderson	.50	.23
❑ 169 Earl Morrall	.50	.23
❑ 170 Jim Hart	.50	.23
❑ 171 Ricky Williams RC	50.00	22.00
❑ 172 Cade McNown RC	30.00	13.50
❑ 173 Tim Couch RC	50.00	22.00
❑ 174 Daunte Culpepper RC	30.00	13.50
❑ 175 Akili Smith RC	25.00	11.00
❑ 176 Brock Huard RC	20.00	9.00
❑ 177 Donovan McNabb RC	30.00	13.50
❑ 178 Michael Bishop RC	20.00	9.00
❑ 179 Shaun King RC	30.00	13.50
❑ 180 Torry Holt RC	25.00	11.00

1999 SP Signature Autographs

	MINT	NRMT
COMMON CARD	8.00	3.60
SEMISTARS	15.00	6.75
UNLISTED STARS	25.00	11.00
ONE AUTOGRAPH PER PACK		
*GOLD FOILS: .8X TO 2X		

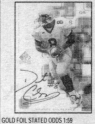

GOLD FOIL STATED ODDS 1:59

❑ AA Ashley Ambrose	8.00	3.60
❑ AF Antonio Freeman	75.00	34.00
❑ AK Akili Smith	120.00	55.00
❑ AM Adrian Murrell	15.00	6.75
❑ AN Dick Anderson	8.00	3.60
❑ AS Antowain Smith	25.00	11.00
❑ BB Bill Bergey	8.00	3.60
❑ BC Bob Christian	8.00	3.60
❑ BE Bobby Engram	15.00	6.75
❑ BH Brock Huard	80.00	36.00
❑ BT Bert Emanuel	15.00	6.75
❑ CB Charlie Batch	50.00	22.00
❑ CC Chris Chandler	15.00	6.75
❑ CD Corey Dillon	30.00	13.50
❑ CE Curtis Enis	40.00	18.00
❑ CG Charlie Garner	15.00	6.75
❑ CJ Charlie Joiner	15.00	6.75
❑ CK Ray Crockett	8.00	3.60
❑ CL Cameron Cleeland	15.00	6.75
❑ CP Mike Singletary	25.00	11.00
❑ CS Chris Slade	8.00	3.60
❑ CT Charley Taylor	15.00	6.75
❑ CW Curtis Conway	15.00	6.75
❑ CY Chris Calloway	8.00	3.60
❑ DA Derrick Alexander DE	8.00	3.60
❑ DB Donnell Bennett	8.00	3.60
❑ DC Daunte Culpepper	150.00	70.00
❑ DE Roy Barker	8.00	3.60
❑ DH Darick Holmes	8.00	3.60
❑ DM Dan Marino	400.00	180.00
❑ DP Drew Pearson	25.00	11.00
❑ EG Eddie George	90.00	40.00
❑ EJ Ed Too Tall Jones	15.00	6.75
❑ EM Eric Moulds	40.00	18.00
❑ ES Emmitt Smith	250.00	110.00
❑ FL Fred Lane	25.00	11.00
❑ FW Frank Wycheck	8.00	3.60
❑ GA Joey Galloway	75.00	34.00
❑ GB Gary Brown	8.00	3.60
❑ GE Jeff George	15.00	6.75
❑ GH Garrison Hearst	15.00	6.75
❑ GN Trent Green	15.00	6.75
❑ GR Randy Gradishar	8.00	3.60
❑ HC Harold Carmichael	15.00	6.75
❑ HL Greg Hill	8.00	3.60
❑ HM Herman Moore	50.00	22.00
❑ HN Hardy Nickerson	8.00	3.60
❑ HT Jim Hart	15.00	6.75
❑ HV Harvey Williams	8.00	3.60
❑ HW Hines Ward	15.00	6.75
❑ HY Chuck Howley	15.00	6.75
❑ IB Isaac Bruce	30.00	13.50
❑ JG Jason Garrett	15.00	6.75
❑ JH Jack Ham	15.00	6.75
❑ JJ James Jett	15.00	6.75
❑ JK Jackie Harris	8.00	3.60
❑ JL James Lofton	15.00	6.75
❑ JM John Mobley	8.00	3.60
❑ JP Jake Plummer	120.00	55.00
❑ JR Junior Seau	15.00	6.75
❑ JS Jimmy Smith	15.00	6.75
❑ JT Jason Taylor	8.00	3.60
❑ JY Jack Youngblood	15.00	6.75
❑ KA Karim Abdul-Jabbar	15.00	6.75
❑ KB Kyle Brady	8.00	3.60
❑ KD Koy Detmer	8.00	3.60
❑ KI Jon Kitna	25.00	11.00

❑ KJ Keyshawn Johnson	50.00	22.00
❑ KL Keith Lyle	8.00	3.60
❑ KR Brian Mitchell	8.00	3.60
❑ KS Ken Stabler	25.00	11.00
❑ KW Kellen Winslow	25.00	11.00
❑ LB Chad Brown	8.00	3.60
❑ LH Leroy Hoard	8.00	3.60
❑ LJ Leon Johnson	8.00	3.60
❑ LS Lee Roy Selmon	15.00	6.75
❑ LW Lamont Warren	8.00	3.60
❑ MA Mike Alstott	60.00	27.00
❑ MB Mario Bates	8.00	3.60
❑ MF Marshall Faulk	60.00	27.00
❑ MG Archie Manning	25.00	11.00
❑ MI Michael Bishop	80.00	36.00
❑ MJ Michael Jackson	15.00	6.75
❑ MK Mark Brunell	120.00	55.00
❑ ML Mel Blount	25.00	11.00
❑ MM Muhsin Muhammad	15.00	6.75
❑ MN Donovan McNabb	120.00	55.00
❑ MO Earl Morrall	15.00	6.75
❑ MS Michael Sinclair	8.00	3.60
❑ MT Maa Tanuvasa	8.00	3.60
❑ MY Mercury Morris	15.00	6.75
❑ ND Ricky Watters	40.00	18.00
❑ NM Natrone Means	30.00	13.50
❑ NO Sean Dawkins	8.00	3.60
❑ NY Don Maynard	15.00	6.75
❑ OJ O.J. Santiago	8.00	3.60
❑ OZ Ozzie Newsome	25.00	11.00
❑ PH Priest Holmes	25.00	11.00
❑ PK Paul Krause	15.00	6.75
❑ PT Pete Mitchell	8.00	3.60
❑ PW Paul Warfield	25.00	11.00
❑ QB Cade McNown	150.00	70.00
❑ RB Robert Brooks	60.00	27.00
❑ RD Rickey Dudley	8.00	3.60
❑ RE Robert Edwards	15.00	6.75
❑ RF Russ Francis	8.00	3.60
❑ RH Rodney Harrison	8.00	3.60
❑ RL Ray Lewis	8.00	3.60
❑ RM Randy Moss	300.00	135.00
❑ RP Robert Porcher	8.00	3.60
❑ RW Ricky Williams	250.00	110.00
❑ RY Raymond Berry	25.00	11.00
❑ SD Charlie Jones	15.00	6.75
❑ SH Shaun King	120.00	55.00
❑ SK Sammy Knight	15.00	6.75
❑ ST Duce Staley	25.00	11.00
❑ SW John Stallworth	25.00	11.00
❑ TA Troy Aikman	275.00	125.00
❑ TB Tim Brown	40.00	18.00
❑ TC Tim Couch	300.00	135.00
❑ TD Terrell Davis UDA	80.00	36.00
❑ TE Jamie Asher	8.00	3.60
❑ TH Ted Hendricks	15.00	6.75
❑ TL Ty Law	8.00	3.60
❑ TO Torrance Small	8.00	3.60
❑ TR Troy Drayton	8.00	3.60
❑ TS Tony Siragusa	8.00	3.60
❑ TV Tommy Vardell	8.00	3.60
❑ WF William Floyd	8.00	3.60
❑ WH Craig Whelihan	8.00	3.60
❑ WM Willie McGinest	8.00	3.60
❑ WP Torry Holt	120.00	55.00
❑ ZC Zack Crockett	8.00	3.60

1999 SP Signature Montana Great Performances

	MINT	NRMT
COMPLETE SET (10)	60.00	27.00
COMMON CARD (J1-J10)	8.00	3.60
RANDOM INSERTS IN PACKS		
COMMON SIGNATURE	120.00	55.00
SIGNATURE STATED ODDS 1:47		
COMMON GOLD SIGN.	500.00	220.00
GOLD SIGNATURE STATED ODDS 1:880		

❑ J1 Joe Montana	8.00	3.60
❑ J2 Joe Montana	8.00	3.60
❑ J3 Joe Montana	8.00	3.60
❑ J4 Joe Montana	8.00	3.60
❑ J5 Joe Montana	8.00	3.60

❑ J6 Joe Montana	8.00	3.60
❑ J7 Joe Montana	8.00	3.60
❑ J8 Joe Montana	8.00	3.60
❑ J9 Joe Montana	8.00	3.60
❑ J10 Joe Montana	8.00	3.60

1999 Sports Illustrated

	MINT	NRMT
COMPLETE SET (150)	75.00	34.00
COMMON CARD (1-150)	.15	.07
SEMISTARS	.30	.14
UNLISTED STARS	.60	.25
COMMON FRESH FACES	.60	.25
FRESH FACES SEMISTARS	1.00	.45
FRESH FACES UNL.STARS	2.00	.90

❑ 1 Bart Starr MVP	.60	.25
❑ 2 Bart Starr MVP	.60	.25
❑ 3 Joe Namath MVP	.60	.25
❑ 4 Len Dawson MVP	.15	.07
❑ 5 Chuck Howley MVP	.15	.07
❑ 6 Roger Staubach MVP	.60	.25
❑ 7 Jake Scott MVP	.15	.07
❑ 8 Larry Csonka MVP	.30	.14
❑ 9 Franco Harris MVP	.30	.14
❑ 10 Fred Biletnikoff MVP	.30	.14
❑ 11 Harvey Martin MVP Randy White MVP	.15	.07
❑ 12 Terry Bradshaw MVP	.60	.25
❑ 13 Terry Bradshaw MVP	.60	.25
❑ 14 Jim Plunkett MVP	.15	.07
❑ 15 Joe Montana MVP	.75	.35
❑ 16 Marcus Allen MVP	.30	.14
❑ 17 Joe Montana MVP	.75	.35
❑ 18 Richard Dent MVP	.30	.14
❑ 19 Phil Simms MVP	.15	.07
❑ 20 Doug Williams MVP	.15	.07
❑ 21 Jerry Rice MVP	.75	.35
❑ 22 Joe Montana MVP	.75	.35
❑ 23 Ottis Anderson MVP	.15	.07
❑ 24 Mark Rypien MVP	.15	.07
❑ 25 Troy Aikman MVP	.75	.35
❑ 26 Emmitt Smith MVP	1.25	.55
❑ 27 Steve Young MVP	.60	.25
❑ 28 Larry Brown MVP	.15	.07
❑ 29 Desmond Howard MVP	.30	.14
❑ 30 Terrell Davis MVP	1.25	.55
❑ 31 Y.A. Tittle	.30	.14
❑ 32 Paul Hornung	.30	.14
❑ 33 Gale Sayers	.30	.14
❑ 34 Garo Yepremian	.15	.07
❑ 35 Bert Jones	.15	.07
❑ 36 Joe Washington	.15	.07
❑ 37 Joe Theismann	.15	.07
❑ 38 Roger Craig	.15	.07
❑ 39 Mike Singletary	.15	.07
❑ 40 Bobby Bell	.15	.07
❑ 41 Ken Houston	.15	.07
❑ 42 Lenny Moore	.15	.07
❑ 43 Mark Moseley	.15	.07
❑ 44 Chuck Bednarik	.15	.07
❑ 45 Ted Hendricks	.15	.07
❑ 46 Steve Largent	.60	.25
❑ 47 Bob Lilly	.15	.07
❑ 48 Don Maynard	.15	.07
❑ 49 John Mackey	.15	.07
❑ 50 Anthony Munoz	.15	.07
❑ 51 Bobby Mitchell	.15	.07
❑ 52 Jim Brown	.60	.25
❑ 53 Otto Graham	.30	.14
❑ 54 Earl Morrall	.15	.07
❑ 55 Danny White	.15	.07
❑ 56 Karim Abdul-Jabbar	.30	.14
❑ 57 Charlie Garner	.30	.14
❑ 58 Jeff Blake	.30	.14
❑ 59 Reggie White	.60	.25
❑ 60 Derrick Thomas	.30	.14
❑ 61 Duce Staley	.60	.25
❑ 62 Tim Brown	.60	.25
❑ 63 Elvis Grbac	.30	.14
❑ 64 Tony Banks	.30	.14
❑ 65 Rob Johnson	.30	.14
❑ 66 Danny Kanell	.15	.07
❑ 67 Marshall Faulk	.60	.25
❑ 68 Warrick Dunn	.60	.25
❑ 69 Dan Marino	3.00	1.35
❑ 70 Jimmy Smith	.30	.14
❑ 71 John Elway	3.00	1.35
❑ 72 Charles Way	.15	.07
❑ 73 Ricky Watters	.30	.14
❑ 74 Terry Glenn	.60	.25
❑ 75 Bobby Hoying	.30	.14
❑ 76 Curtis Martin	.60	.25
❑ 77 Trent Dilfer	.30	.14
❑ 78 Emmitt Smith	2.50	1.10
❑ 79 Irving Fryar	.30	.14
❑ 80 Troy Aikman	1.50	.70
❑ 81 Barry Sanders	3.00	1.35
❑ 82 Brett Favre	3.00	1.35
❑ 83 Robert Smith	.60	.25
❑ 84 Dorsey Levens	.60	.25
❑ 85 Cris Carter	.60	.25
❑ 86 Jeff George	.30	.14
❑ 87 Jerome Bettis	.60	.25
❑ 88 Warren Moon	.60	.25
❑ 89 Steve Young	1.00	.45
❑ 90 Fred Lane	.15	.07
❑ 91 Jerry Rice	1.50	.70
❑ 92 Natrone Means	.30	.14
❑ 93 Mike Alstott	.60	.25
❑ 94 Kordell Stewart	.60	.25
❑ 95 Jake Plummer	2.00	.90
❑ 96 Jamal Anderson	.60	.25
❑ 97 Corey Dillon	1.00	.45
❑ 98 Deion Sanders	.60	.25
❑ 99 Mark Brunell	1.25	.55
❑ 100 Garrison Hearst	.30	.14
❑ 101 Andre Rison	.30	.14
❑ 102 Antowain Smith	.60	.25
❑ 103 Drew Bledsoe	1.25	.55
❑ 104 Eddie George	.75	.35
❑ 105 Keyshawn Johnson	.60	.25
❑ 106 Isaac Bruce	.60	.25
❑ 107 Rob Moore	.30	.14
❑ 108 Steve McNair	.60	.25
❑ 109 Terrell Davis	2.50	1.10
❑ 110 Carl Pickens	.30	.14
❑ 111 Wayne Chrebet	.30	.14
❑ 112 Kerry Collins	.30	.14
❑ 113 Eric Metcalf	.15	.07
❑ 114 Joey Galloway	.60	.25
❑ 115 Shannon Sharpe	.30	.14
❑ 116 Robert Brooks	.30	.14
❑ 117 Glenn Foley	.30	.14
❑ 118 Yancey Thigpen	.15	.07
❑ 119 Frank Sanders	.30	.14

	MINT	NRMT
❑ 120 Herman Moore	.60	.25
❑ 121 Antonio Freeman	.60	.25
❑ 122 Michael Irvin	.30	.14
❑ 123 Brad Johnson	.60	.25
❑ 124 James Stewart	.30	.14
❑ 125 Jim Harbaugh	.30	.14
❑ 126 Peyton Manning FF	10.00	4.50
❑ 127 Ryan Leaf FF	.30	.14
❑ 128 Curtis Enis FF	2.00	.90
❑ 129 Fred Taylor FF	6.00	2.70
❑ 130 Randy Moss FF	10.00	4.50
❑ 131 John Avery FF	2.00	.90
❑ 132 Charles Woodson FF	2.00	.90
❑ 133 Robert Edwards FF	2.00	.90
❑ 134 Charlie Batch FF	5.00	2.20
❑ 135 Brian Griese FF	5.00	2.20
❑ 136 Skip Hicks FF	.60	.25
❑ 137 Jacquez Green FF	2.00	.90
❑ 138 Robert Holcombe FF	2.00	.90
❑ 139 Kevin Dyson FF	2.00	.90
❑ 140 Rodney Williams FF	.60	.25
❑ 141 Ahman Green FF	1.00	.45
❑ 142 Tavian Banks FF	2.00	.90
❑ 143 Donald Hayes FF	1.00	.45
❑ 144 Tony Simmons FF	2.00	.90
❑ 145 Pat Johnson FF	2.00	.90
❑ 146 Marcus Nash FF	2.00	.90
❑ 147 Germane Crowell FF	2.00	.90
❑ 148 R.W. McQuarters FF	.60	.25
❑ 149 Jonathan Quinn FF	2.00	.90
❑ 150 Andre Wadsworth FF	.60	.25
❑ P35 Gale Sayers Promo	1.00	.45

1999 Sports Illustrated Autographs

	MINT	NRMT
COMPLETE SET (35)	3000.00	1350.00
COMMON CARD (1-35)	10.00	4.50
SEMISTARS	12.00	5.50
UNLISTED STARS	15.00	6.75
ONE PER PACK		

	MINT	NRMT
❑ 1 Ottis Anderson	12.00	5.50
❑ 2 Chuck Bednarik	12.00	5.50
❑ 3 Bobby Bell	12.00	5.50
❑ 4 Terry Bradshaw	350.00	160.00
❑ 5 Jim Brown	150.00	70.00
❑ 6 Roger Craig	20.00	9.00
❑ 7 Len Dawson	120.00	55.00
❑ 8 Otto Graham	20.00	9.00
❑ 9 Franco Harris	120.00	55.00
❑ 10 Ted Hendricks	12.00	5.50
❑ 11 Paul Hornung	150.00	70.00
❑ 12 Ken Houston	12.00	5.50
❑ 13 Bert Jones	12.00	5.50
❑ 14 Steve Largent	25.00	11.00
❑ 15 Bob Lilly	12.00	5.50
❑ 16 John Mackey	12.00	5.50
❑ 17 Don Maynard	15.00	6.75
❑ 18 Bobby Mitchell	12.00	5.50
❑ 19 Joe Montana	400.00	180.00
❑ 20 Lenny Moore	12.00	5.50
❑ 21 Earl Morrall	12.00	5.50
❑ 22 Mark Moseley	10.00	4.50
❑ 23 Anthony Munoz	12.00	5.50
❑ 24 Joe Namath	350.00	160.00
❑ 25 Jim Plunkett	15.00	6.75
❑ 26 Gale Sayers	25.00	11.00
❑ 27 Mike Singletary	80.00	36.00
❑ 28 Bart Starr	400.00	180.00
❑ 29 Roger Staubach	200.00	90.00
❑ 30 Joe Theismann	60.00	27.00
❑ 31 Y.A. Tittle	100.00	45.00
❑ 32 Joe Washington	12.00	5.50
❑ 33 Danny White	12.00	5.50
❑ 34 Doug Williams	120.00	55.00
❑ 35 Garo Yepremian	10.00	4.50

1999 Sports Illustrated Canton Calling

	MINT	NRMT
COMPLETE SET (8)	60.00	27.00
COMMON CARD (1-8)	4.00	1.80
STATED ODDS 1:12 HOBBY		
*GOLD CARDS: 1.5X TO 4X HI COL.		
GOLD STATED ODDS 1:120		

	MINT	NRMT
❑ 1 Warren Moon	4.00	1.80
❑ 2 Emmitt Smith	12.00	5.50
❑ 3 Jerry Rice	8.00	3.60
❑ 4 Brett Favre	15.00	6.75
❑ 5 Barry Sanders	15.00	6.75
❑ 6 Dan Marino	15.00	6.75
❑ 7 John Elway	15.00	6.75
❑ 8 Troy Aikman	8.00	3.60

1999 Sports Illustrated Covers

	MINT	NRMT
COMPLETE SET (60)	25.00	11.00
COMMON CARD (1-60)	.15	.07
SEMISTARS	.30	.14
UNLISTED STARS	.60	.25
ONE PER PACK		

	MINT	NRMT
❑ 1 Jim Brown	.60	.25
❑ 2 Y.A. Tittle	.30	.14
❑ 3 Dallas Cowboys	.15	.07
❑ 4 Joe Namath	.60	.25
❑ 5 Bart Starr	.60	.25
❑ 6 Earl Morrall	.15	.07
❑ 7 Minnesota Vikings	.15	.07
❑ 8 Kansas City Chiefs	.15	.07
❑ 9 Len Dawson	.30	.14
❑ 10 Monday Night Football	.15	.07
❑ 11 Jim Plunkett	.30	.14
❑ 12 Garo Yepremian	.15	.07
❑ 13 Larry Csonka	.30	.14
❑ 14 Terry Bradshaw	.60	.25
❑ 15 Franco Harris	.30	.14
❑ 16 Bert Jones	.15	.07
❑ 17 Harvey Martin Randy White	.15	.07
❑ 18 Roger Staubach	.60	.25
❑ 19 Marcus Allen	.60	.25
❑ 20 Joe Washington	.15	.07
❑ 21 Dan Marino	3.00	1.35
❑ 22 Joe Theismann	.30	.14
❑ 23 Roger Craig	.30	.14
❑ 24 Mike Singletary	.30	.14
❑ 25 Chicago Bears Dan Hampton	.15	.07
❑ 26 Phil Simms	.30	.14
❑ 27 Vinny Testaverde	.30	.14
❑ 28 Doug Williams	.15	.07
❑ 29 Jerry Rice	1.50	.70
❑ 30 Herschel Walker	.30	.14
❑ 31 Joe Montana	1.50	.70
❑ 32 Ottis Anderson	.15	.07
❑ 33 Rocket Ismail	.30	.14
❑ 34 Bruce Smith	.30	.14
❑ 35 Thurman Thomas	.30	.14
❑ 36 Mark Rypien	.15	.07
❑ 37 Jim Harbaugh	.30	.14
❑ 38 Randall Cunningham	.60	.25
❑ 39 Troy Aikman	1.50	.70
❑ 40 Reggie White	.60	.25
❑ 41 Junior Seau	.30	.14
❑ 42 Emmitt Smith	2.50	1.10
❑ 43 Natrone Means	.30	.14
❑ 44 Ricky Watters	.30	.14
❑ 45 Pittsburgh Steelers	.15	.07
❑ 46 Steve Young Troy Aikman	1.00	.45
❑ 47 Steve Young	1.00	.45
❑ 48 Deion Sanders	.60	.25
❑ 49 Elvis Grbac	.30	.14
❑ 50 Packers vs. Chiefs Brett Favre Reggie White Robert Brooks Marcus Allen Neil Smith Steve Bono	.15	.07
❑ 51 Brett Favre	3.00	1.35
❑ 52 Mark Brunell Kerry Collins	1.00	.45
❑ 53 Antonio Freeman	.60	.25
❑ 54 Desmond Howard	.30	.14
❑ 55 AFC Central QB's	.60	.25
❑ 56 Warrick Dunn	.60	.25
❑ 57 Jerome Bettis	.60	.25
❑ 58 John Elway	3.00	1.35
❑ 59 Brent Jones	.15	.07
❑ 60 Terrell Davis	2.50	1.10

1996 SPx

	MINT	NRMT
COMPLETE SET (50)	40.00	18.00
COMMON CARD (1-50)	.50	.23
SEMISTARS	1.00	.45
UNLISTED STARS	2.00	.90
COMP.GOLD SET (50)	100.00	45.00

*GOLD STARS: 1X TO 2.5X HI COLUMN
GOLD STATED ODDS 1:7
MONTANA TRIB.STATED ODDS 1:95
MONTANA AUTO STATED ODDS 1:433
MARINO RB STATED ODDS 1:81
MARINO AUTO STATED ODDS 1:433

Card	MINT	NRMT
❑ 1 Frank Sanders	1.00	.45
❑ 2 Terance Mathis	.50	.23
❑ 3 Todd Collins	1.00	.45
❑ 4 Kerry Collins	2.00	.90
❑ 5 Carl Pickens	2.00	.90
❑ 6 Darnay Scott	1.00	.45
❑ 7 Ki-Jana Carter	1.00	.45
❑ 8 Eric Zeier	.50	.23
❑ 9 Andre Rison	1.00	.45
❑ 10 Sherman Williams	.50	.23
❑ 11 Troy Aikman	4.00	1.80
❑ 12 Michael Irvin	2.00	.90
❑ 13 Emmitt Smith	6.00	2.70
❑ 14 Shannon Sharpe	1.00	.45
❑ 15 John Elway	8.00	3.60
❑ 16 Barry Sanders	8.00	3.60
❑ 17 Brett Favre	8.00	3.60
❑ 18 Rodney Thomas	.50	.23
❑ 19 Marshall Faulk	2.00	.90
❑ 20 James O.Stewart	1.00	.45
❑ 21 Greg Hill	1.00	.45
❑ 22 Tamarick Vanover	1.00	.45
❑ 23 Dan Marino	8.00	3.60
❑ 24 Cris Carter	2.00	.90
❑ 25 Warren Moon	1.00	.45
❑ 26 Drew Bledsoe	4.00	1.80
❑ 27 Ben Coates	1.00	.45
❑ 28 Curtis Martin	4.00	1.80
❑ 29 Mario Bates	1.00	.45
❑ 30 Tyrone Wheatley	1.00	.45
❑ 31 Rodney Hampton	1.00	.45
❑ 32 Kyle Brady	.50	.23
❑ 33 Jeff Hostetler	.50	.23
❑ 34 Napoleon Kaufman	3.00	1.35
❑ 35 Tim Brown	2.00	.90
❑ 36 Charles Johnson	.50	.23
❑ 37 Rod Woodson UER Incorrect birth year	1.00	.45
❑ 38 Natrone Means	2.00	.90
❑ 39 J.J. Stokes	2.00	.90
❑ 40 Steve Young	4.00	1.80
❑ 41 Brent Jones	.50	.23
❑ 42 Jerry Rice	4.00	1.80
❑ 43 Joe Montana	8.00	3.60
❑ 44 Rick Mirer	1.00	.45
❑ 45 Chris Warren	1.00	.45
❑ 46 Joey Galloway	4.00	1.80
❑ 47 Isaac Bruce	2.00	.90
❑ 48 Jerome Bettis	2.00	.90
❑ 49 Errict Rhett	1.00	.45
❑ 50 Michael Westbrook	2.00	.90
❑ UDT13 Dan Marino Record Breaker	15.00	6.75
❑ UDT13 Dan Marino AUTO Record Breaker signed	120.00	55.00
❑ UDT19 Joe Montana Tribute	15.00	6.75
❑ UDT19 Joe Montana AUTO Tribute card signed	120.00	55.00
❑ P1 Dan Marino Promo	6.00	2.70
❑ P2 Joe Montana Promo	4.00	1.80

1996 SPx HoloFame

	MINT	NRMT
COMPLETE SET (10)	80.00	36.00
STATED ODDS 1:24		
❑ HM1 Troy Aikman	12.00	5.50
❑ HM2 Emmitt Smith	30.00	13.50
❑ HM3 Barry Sanders	12.00	5.50
❑ HM4 Steve Young	10.00	4.50
❑ HM5 Jerry Rice	12.00	5.50
❑ HM6 John Elway	12.00	5.50
❑ HM7 Marshall Faulk	6.00	2.70
❑ HM8 Dan Marino	30.00	13.50
❑ HM9 Drew Bledsoe	12.00	5.50
❑ HM10 Natrone Means	6.00	2.70

1997 SPx

	MINT	NRMT
COMPLETE SET (50)	40.00	18.00
COMMON CARD (1-50)	.40	.18
SEMISTARS	.75	.35
UNLISTED STARS	1.50	.70
COMP.GOLD SET (50)	150.00	70.00
*GOLD STARS: 1.5X TO 3X HI COL.		
GOLD STATED ODDS 1:9		
❑ 1 Jerry Rice	4.00	1.80
❑ 2 Steve Young	3.00	1.35
❑ 3 Karim Abdul-Jabbar	1.50	.70
❑ 4 Dan Marino	8.00	3.60
❑ 5 Bobby Engram	.75	.35
❑ 6 Rashaan Salaam	.40	.18
❑ 7 Marvin Harrison	1.50	.70
❑ 8 Jim Harbaugh	.75	.35
❑ 9 Marshall Faulk	1.50	.70
❑ 10 Eric Moulds	1.50	.70
❑ 11 Thurman Thomas	1.50	.70
❑ 12 Tamarick Vanover	.75	.35
❑ 13 Steve Bono	.75	.35
❑ 14 Warren Moon	1.50	.70
❑ 15 Cris Carter	1.50	.70
❑ 16 Carl Pickens	1.50	.70
❑ 17 Ki-Jana Carter	.40	.18
❑ 18 Jeff Blake	.75	.35
❑ 19 Tim Biakabutuka	.75	.35
❑ 20 Kerry Collins	.75	.35
❑ 21 Leeland McElroy	.40	.18
❑ 22 Simeon Rice	.75	.35
❑ 23 John Elway	8.00	3.60
❑ 24 Terrell Davis	8.00	3.60
❑ 25 Jeff Lewis	.40	.18
❑ 26 Terry Glenn	1.50	.70
❑ 27 Curtis Martin	2.00	.90
❑ 28 Drew Bledsoe	4.00	1.80
❑ 29 Lawrence Phillips	.40	.18
❑ 30 Isaac Bruce	1.50	.70
❑ 31 Eddie Kennison	.75	.35
❑ 32 Keyshawn Johnson	1.50	.70
❑ 33 Stepfret Williams	.40	.18
❑ 34 Emmitt Smith	6.00	2.70
❑ 35 Troy Aikman	4.00	1.80
❑ 36 Deion Sanders	1.50	.70
❑ 37 Joey Galloway	2.00	.90
❑ 38 Rick Mirer	.40	.18
❑ 39 Rickey Dudley	.75	.35
❑ 40 Jeff Hostetler	.40	.18
❑ 41 Junior Seau	.75	.35
❑ 42 Derrick Mayes	.75	.35
❑ 43 Brett Favre	8.00	3.60
❑ 44 Edgar Bennett	.75	.35
❑ 45 Barry Sanders	8.00	3.60
❑ 46 Herman Moore	1.50	.70
❑ 47 Kordell Stewart	2.00	.90
❑ 48 Jerome Bettis	1.50	.70
❑ 49 Eddie George	4.00	1.80
❑ 50 Steve McNair	2.00	.90
❑ P80 Jerry Rice Promo numbered SPX80 (1996 on copyright line)	3.00	1.35

1997 SPx HoloFame

	MINT	NRMT
COMPLETE SET (20)	300.00	135.00
STATED ODDS 1:75		
❑ HX1 Jerry Rice	20.00	9.00
❑ HX2 Emmitt Smith	30.00	13.50
❑ HX3 Karim Abdul-Jabbar	8.00	3.60
❑ HX4 Brett Favre	40.00	18.00
❑ HX5 Curtis Martin	10.00	4.50
❑ HX6 Eddie Kennison	4.00	1.80
❑ HX7 Troy Aikman	20.00	9.00
❑ HX8 Steve Young	15.00	6.75
❑ HX9 Tim Biakabutuka	4.00	1.80
❑ HX10 Reggie White	8.00	3.60
❑ HX11 Terry Glenn	8.00	3.60
❑ HX12 Lawrence Phillips	2.00	.90
❑ HX13 Dan Marino	40.00	18.00
❑ HX14 Deion Sanders	8.00	3.60
❑ HX15 Terrell Davis	40.00	18.00
❑ HX16 Marvin Harrison	8.00	3.60
❑ HX17 Eddie George	20.00	9.00
❑ HX18 Marshall Faulk	8.00	3.60
❑ HX19 Keyshawn Johnson	8.00	3.60
❑ HX20 Barry Sanders	40.00	18.00

1997 SPx ProMotion

	MINT	NRMT
COMPLETE SET (6)	200.00	90.00
STATED ODDS 1:433		
❑ 1 Dan Marino	50.00	22.00
❑ 2 Joe Montana	50.00	22.00
❑ 3 Troy Aikman	25.00	11.00
❑ 4 Barry Sanders	50.00	22.00
❑ 5 Karim Abdul-Jabbar	10.00	4.50
❑ 6 Eddie George	25.00	11.00

1997 SPx ProMotion Autographs

	MINT	NRMT
COMPLETE SET (6)	2500.00	1100.00
COMMON CARD (1-6)	150.00	70.00
STATED ODDS 1:4331		
STATED PRINT RUN 100		
❑ 1 Dan Marino	600.00	275.00
❑ 2 Joe Montana	700.00	325.00

	MINT	NRMT
❑ 3 Troy Aikman	500.00	220.00
❑ 4 Barry Sanders	600.00	275.00
❑ 5 Karim Abdul-Jabbar	200.00	90.00
❑ 6 Eddie George	200.00	90.00

1998 SPx

	MINT	NRMT
COMPLETE SET (50)	80.00	36.00
COMMON CARD (1-50)	.50	.23
SEMISTARS	.75	.35
UNLISTED STARS	1.50	.70
OVERALL PARALLEL ODDS ONE PER PACK		
COMP.BRONZE SET (50)	160.00	70.00
*BRONZE STARS: .75X TO 2X HI COL.		
*BRONZE YOUNG STARS: .6X TO 1.5X		
BRONZE STATED ODDS 1:3		
COMP.GOLD SET (50)	500.00	220.00
*GOLD STARS: 2.5X TO 6X HI COL.		
*GOLD YOUNG STARS: 2X TO 5X		
GOLD STATED ODDS 1:17		
COMMON GRAND FINALE	20.00	9.00
*GRAND FINALE STARS: 12X TO 30X		
*GRAND FINALE YOUNG STARS: 10X TO 25X		
GRAND FINALE STATED PRINT RUN 50 SETS		
COMP.SILVER SET (50)	250.00	110.00
*SILVER STARS: 1.25X TO 3X HI COL.		
*SILVER YOUNG STARS: 1X TO 2.5X		
SILVER STATED ODDS 1:6		
COMP.STEEL SET (50)	100.00	45.00
*STEEL STARS: .6X TO 1.2X HI COL.		
*STEEL YOUNG STARS: .5X TO 1X		
STEEL STATED ODDS 1:1		

	MINT	NRMT
❑ 1 Jake Plummer	6.00	2.70
❑ 2 Byron Hanspard	.75	.35
❑ 3 Vinny Testaverde	.75	.35
❑ 4 Antowain Smith	1.50	.70
❑ 5 Kerry Collins	.75	.35
❑ 6 Rae Carruth	.75	.35
❑ 7 Darnell Autry	.50	.23
❑ 8 Rick Mirer	.50	.23
❑ 9 Jeff Blake	.75	.35
❑ 10 Carl Pickens	1.50	.70
❑ 11 Troy Aikman	4.00	1.80
❑ 12 Emmitt Smith	6.00	2.70
❑ 13 Deion Sanders	1.50	.70
❑ 14 John Elway	8.00	3.60
❑ 15 Terrell Davis	6.00	2.70
❑ 16 Herman Moore	1.50	.70
❑ 17 Barry Sanders	8.00	3.60
❑ 18 Brett Favre	8.00	3.60
❑ 19 Reggie White	1.50	.70
❑ 20 Marshall Faulk	1.50	.70
❑ 21 Mark Brunell	3.00	1.35
❑ 22 Elvis Grbac	.75	.35
❑ 23 Marcus Allen	1.50	.70
❑ 24 Karim Abdul-Jabbar	1.50	.70
❑ 25 Dan Marino	8.00	3.60
❑ 26 Cris Carter	1.50	.70
❑ 27 Drew Bledsoe	3.00	1.35
❑ 28 Curtis Martin	1.50	.70
❑ 29 Heath Shuler	.50	.23
❑ 30 Ike Hilliard	.75	.35
❑ 31 Keyshawn Johnson	1.50	.70
❑ 32 Jeff George	.75	.35
❑ 33 Napoleon Kaufman	1.50	.70
❑ 34 Darrell Russell	.50	.23
❑ 35 Ricky Watters	.75	.35
❑ 36 Kordell Stewart	1.50	.70
❑ 37 Jerome Bettis	1.50	.70
❑ 38 Junior Seau	.75	.35
❑ 39 Steve Young	2.50	1.10
❑ 40 Jerry Rice	4.00	1.80
❑ 41 Joey Galloway	1.50	.70
❑ 42 Chris Warren	.75	.35
❑ 43 Orlando Pace	.50	.23
❑ 44 Isaac Bruce	1.50	.70
❑ 45 Tony Banks	.75	.35
❑ 46 Trent Dilfer	1.50	.70
❑ 47 Warrick Dunn	2.50	1.10
❑ 48 Steve McNair	1.50	.70
❑ 49 Eddie George	3.00	1.35
❑ 50 Terry Allen	1.50	.70
❑ NNO Piece of History Trade	1.00	.45

1998 SPx HoloFame

	MINT	NRMT
COMPLETE SET (20)	300.00	135.00
COMMON CARD (HF1-HF20)	10.00	4.50
STATED ODDS 1:54		

	MINT	NRMT
❑ HF1 Troy Aikman	25.00	11.00
❑ HF2 Emmitt Smith	40.00	18.00
❑ HF3 John Elway	50.00	22.00
❑ HF4 Terrell Davis	40.00	18.00
❑ HF5 Herman Moore	10.00	4.50
❑ HF6 Reggie White	10.00	4.50
❑ HF7 Brett Favre	50.00	22.00
❑ HF8 Napoleon Kaufman	10.00	4.50
❑ HF9 Dan Marino	50.00	22.00
❑ HF10 Karim Abdul-Jabbar	10.00	4.50
❑ HF11 Cris Carter	10.00	4.50
❑ HF12 Drew Bledsoe	20.00	9.00
❑ HF13 Curtis Martin	10.00	4.50
❑ HF14 Kordell Stewart	12.00	5.50
❑ HF15 Junior Seau	10.00	4.50
❑ HF16 Steve Young	15.00	6.75
❑ HF17 Jerry Rice	25.00	11.00
❑ HF18 Marshall Faulk	10.00	4.50
❑ HF19 Eddie George	20.00	9.00
❑ HF20 Terry Allen	10.00	4.50

1998 SPx ProMotion

	MINT	NRMT
COMPLETE SET (10)	500.00	220.00
COMMON CARD (P1-P10)	25.00	11.00
STATED ODDS 1:252		

	MINT	NRMT
❑ P1 Troy Aikman	50.00	22.00
❑ P2 Emmitt Smith	80.00	36.00
❑ P3 Terrell Davis	70.00	32.00
❑ P4 Brett Favre	100.00	45.00
❑ P5 Marcus Allen	30.00	13.50
❑ P6 Dan Marino	100.00	45.00
❑ P7 Drew Bledsoe	40.00	18.00
❑ P8 Ike Hilliard	25.00	11.00
❑ P9 Warrick Dunn	30.00	13.50
❑ P10 Eddie George	40.00	18.00

1998 SPx Finite

	MINT	NRMT
COMPLETE SET (370)	2500.00	1100.00
COMP.SERIES 1 (190)	1200.00	550.00
COMP.SERIES 2 (180)	1400.00	650.00
COMMON CARD (1-90)	.75	.35
SEMISTARS 1-90	1.25	.55
UNLISTED STARS 1-90	2.00	.90
1-90 PRINT RUN 7600 SERIAL #'d SETS		
COMMON PM (91-120)	1.50	.70
SEMISTARS PM	2.50	1.10
91-120 PM PRINT RUN 5500 SERIAL #'d SETS		
COMMON YM (121-150)	1.50	.70
SEMISTARS YM	2.50	1.10
UNLISTED STARS YM	4.00	1.80
121-150 YM PRINT RUN 3000 SERIAL #'d SETS		
COMMON PE (151-170)	2.50	1.10
SEMISTARS PE	4.00	1.80
151-170 PE PRINT RUN 2500 SERIAL #'d SETS		
COMMON HG (171-180)	6.00	2.70
171-180 HG PRINT RUN 1250 SERIAL #'d SETS		
COMMON ROOKIE (181-190)	15.00	6.75
ROOKIE SEMISTARS 181-190	20.00	9.00
181-190 ROOK.PRINT RUN 1998 SER.#'d SETS		
COMMON CARD (191-280)	.40	.18
SEMISTARS 191-280	.75	.35
UNLISTED STARS 191-280	1.25	.55
COMMON ROOKIE (191-280)	1.25	.55
ROOKIE SEMISTARS 191-280	2.50	1.10
191-280 PRINT RUN 10,100 SERIAL #'d SETS		
218/221/239 PRINT RUN 1998 SER.#'d SETS		
COMMON ET (281-310)	1.00	.45
SEMISTARS ET	1.50	.70
281-310 ET PRINT RUN 7200 SERIAL #'d SETS		
COMMON NS (311-340)	1.50	.70
SEMISTARS NS	2.50	1.10
UNLISTED STARS NS	5.00	2.20
311-340 NS PRINT RUN 4000 SERIAL #'d SETS		
321/338/339 NS PRINT RUN 1700 #'d SETS		
COMMON SS (341-360)	1.50	.70
SEMISTARS SS	3.00	1.35
341-360 SS PRINT RUN 2700 SERIAL #'d SETS		
COMMON UV (361-370)	5.00	2.20
361-370 UV PRINT RUN 1620 SERIAL #'d SETS		

	MINT	NRMT
❑ 1 Jake Plummer	6.00	2.70
❑ 2 Eric Swann	.75	.35
❑ 3 Rob Moore	1.25	.55
❑ 4 Jamal Anderson	2.00	.90
❑ 5 Byron Hanspard	1.25	.55
❑ 6 Cornelius Bennett	.75	.35
❑ 7 Michael Jackson	.75	.35
❑ 8 Peter Boulware	.75	.35
❑ 9 Jermaine Lewis	1.25	.55
❑ 10 Antowain Smith	2.00	.90
❑ 11 Bruce Smith	1.25	.55
❑ 12 Bryce Paup	.75	.35
❑ 13 Rae Carruth	1.25	.55
❑ 14 Michael Bates	.75	.35
❑ 15 Fred Lane	1.25	.55
❑ 16 Darnell Autry	1.25	.55
❑ 17 Curtis Conway	1.25	.55
❑ 18 Erik Kramer	.75	.35
❑ 19 Corey Dillon	3.00	1.35
❑ 20 Darnay Scott	1.25	.55
❑ 21 Reinard Wilson	.75	.35
❑ 22 Troy Aikman	5.00	2.20
❑ 23 David LaFleur	.75	.35
❑ 24 Emmitt Smith	8.00	3.60
❑ 25 John Elway	10.00	4.50
❑ 26 John Mobley	.75	.35
❑ 27 Terrell Davis	8.00	3.60
❑ 28 Rod Smith	1.25	.55
❑ 29 Bryant Westbrook	.75	.35

No.	Card	Mint	NrMt
30	Scott Mitchell	1.25	.55
31	Barry Sanders	10.00	4.50
32	Dorsey Levens	2.00	.90
33	Antonio Freeman	2.00	.90
34	Reggie White	2.00	.90
35	Marshall Faulk	2.00	.90
36	Marvin Harrison	1.25	.55
37	Ken Dilger	.75	.35
38	Mark Brunell	4.00	1.80
39	Keenan McCardell	1.25	.55
40	Renaldo Wynn	.75	.35
41	Marcus Allen	2.00	.90
42	Elvis Grbac	1.25	.55
43	Andre Rison	1.25	.55
44	Yatil Green	.75	.35
45	Zach Thomas	.75	.35
46	Karim Abdul-Jabbar UER Karim Abdul front , back	2.00	.90
47	John Randle	1.25	.55
48	Brad Johnson	2.00	.90
49	Jake Reed	1.25	.55
50	Danny Wuerffel	1.25	.55
51	Andre Hastings	.75	.35
52	Drew Bledsoe	4.00	1.80
53	Terry Glenn	2.00	.90
54	Ty Law	.75	.35
55	Danny Kanell	1.25	.55
56	Tiki Barber	1.25	.55
57	Jessie Armstead	.75	.35
58	Glenn Foley	1.25	.55
59	James Farrior	.75	.35
60	Wayne Chrebet	2.00	.90
61	Tim Brown	2.00	.90
62	Napoleon Kaufman	2.00	.90
63	Darrell Russell	.75	.35
64	Bobby Hoying	1.25	.55
65	Irving Fryar	1.25	.55
66	Charlie Garner	.75	.35
67	Will Blackwell	.75	.35
68	Kordell Stewart	2.00	.90
69	Levon Kirkland	.75	.35
70	Tony Banks	1.25	.55
71	Ryan McNeil	.75	.35
72	Isaac Bruce	2.00	.90
73	Tony Martin	1.25	.55
74	Junior Seau	1.25	.55
75	Natrone Means	2.00	.90
76	Jerry Rice	5.00	2.20
77	Garrison Hearst	2.00	.90
78	Terrell Owens	2.00	.90
79	Warren Moon	2.00	.90
80	Joey Galloway	2.00	.90
81	Chad Brown	.75	.35
82	Warrick Dunn	2.00	.90
83	Mike Alstott	2.00	.90
84	Hardy Nickerson	.75	.35
85	Steve McNair	2.00	.90
86	Chris Sanders	.75	.35
87	Darryll Lewis	.75	.35
88	Gus Frerotte	.75	.35
89	Terry Allen	2.00	.90
90	Chris Dishman	.75	.35
91	Kordell Stewart PM	3.00	1.35
92	Jerry Rice PM	6.00	2.70
93	Michael Irvin PM	3.00	1.35
94	Brett Favre PM	12.00	5.50
95	Jeff George PM	2.50	1.10
96	Joey Galloway PM	3.00	1.35
97	John Elway PM	12.00	5.50
98	Troy Aikman PM	6.00	2.70
99	Steve Young PM	4.00	1.80
100	Andre Rison PM	2.50	1.10
101	Ben Coates PM	2.50	1.10
102	Robert Brooks PM	2.50	1.10
103	Dan Marino PM	12.00	5.50
104	Isaac Bruce PM	3.00	1.35
105	Junior Seau PM	2.50	1.10
106	Jake Plummer PM	8.00	3.60
107	Curtis Conway PM	2.50	1.10
108	Jeff Blake PM	2.50	1.10
109	Rod Smith PM	2.50	1.10
110	Barry Sanders PM	12.00	5.50
111	Deion Sanders PM	3.00	1.35
112	Drew Bledsoe PM	5.00	2.20
113	Emmitt Smith PM	10.00	4.50
114	Herman Moore PM	3.00	1.35
115	Dorsey Levens PM	3.00	1.35
116	Jimmy Smith PM	2.50	1.10
117	Tony Martin PM	1.50	.70
118	Carl Pickens PM	3.00	1.35
119	Keyshawn Johnson PM	3.00	1.35
120	Cris Carter PM	3.00	1.35
121	Warrick Dunn YM	4.00	1.80
122	Marshall Faulk YM	4.00	1.80
123	Trent Dilfer YM	4.00	1.80
124	Napoleon Kaufman YM	4.00	1.80
125	Corey Dillon YM	6.00	2.70
126	Darrell Russell YM	1.50	.70
127	Danny Kanell YM	2.50	1.10
128	Reidel Anthony YM	4.00	1.80
129	Steve McNair YM	4.00	1.80
130	Ike Hilliard YM	2.50	1.10
131	Tony Banks YM	2.50	1.10
132	Yatil Green YM	1.50	.70
133	J.J. Stokes YM	2.50	1.10
134	Fred Lane YM	2.50	1.10
135	Bryant Westbrook YM	1.50	.70
136	Jake Plummer YM	12.00	5.50
137	Byron Hanspard YM	2.50	1.10
138	Rae Carruth YM	2.50	1.10
139	Keyshawn Johnson YM	4.00	1.80
140	Jim Druckenmiller YM	2.50	1.10
141	Amani Toomer YM	2.50	1.10
142	Troy Davis YM	1.50	.70
143	Antowain Smith YM	4.00	1.80
144	Shawn Springs YM	1.50	.70
145	Rickey Dudley YM	1.50	.70
146	Terry Glenn YM	4.00	1.80
147	Johnnie Morton YM	2.50	1.10
148	David LaFleur YM	1.50	.70
149	Eddie Kennison YM	2.50	1.10
150	Bobby Hoying YM	2.50	1.10
151	Junior Seau PE	4.00	1.80
152	Shannon Sharpe PE	4.00	1.80
153	Bruce Smith PE	4.00	1.80
154	Brett Favre PE	20.00	9.00
155	Emmitt Smith PE	15.00	6.75
156	Keenan McCardell PE	2.50	1.10
157	Kordell Stewart PE	5.00	2.20
158	Troy Aikman PE	10.00	4.50
159	Steve Young PE	6.00	2.70
160	Tim Brown PE	5.00	2.20
161	Eddie George PE	8.00	3.60
162	Herman Moore PE	5.00	2.20
163	Dan Marino PE	20.00	9.00
164	Dorsey Levens PE	5.00	2.20
165	Jerry Rice PE	10.00	4.50
166	Warren Sapp PE	4.00	1.80
167	Robert Smith PE	5.00	2.20
168	Mark Brunell PE	8.00	3.60
169	Terrell Davis PE	15.00	6.75
170	Jerome Bettis PE	5.00	2.20
171	Dan Marino HG	30.00	13.50
172	Barry Sanders HG	30.00	13.50
173	Marcus Allen HG	8.00	3.60
174	Brett Favre HG	30.00	13.50
175	Warrick Dunn HG	8.00	3.60
176	Eddie George HG	12.00	5.50
177	John Elway HG	30.00	13.50
178	Troy Aikman HG	15.00	6.75
179	Cris Carter HG	8.00	3.60
180	Terrell Davis HG	25.00	11.00
181	Peyton Manning RC	250.00	110.00
182	Ryan Leaf RC	30.00	13.50
183	Andre Wadsworth RC	20.00	9.00
184	Charles Woodson RC	30.00	13.50
185	Curtis Enis RC	50.00	22.00
186	Grant Wistrom RC	15.00	6.75
187	Fred Taylor RC	135.00	60.00
188	Takeo Spikes RC	20.00	9.00
189	Kevin Dyson RC	30.00	13.50
190	Robert Edwards RC	20.00	9.00
191	Adrian Murrell	.75	.35
192	Simeon Rice	.75	.35
193	Frank Sanders	.75	.35
194	Chris Chandler	.75	.35
195	Terance Mathis	.75	.35
196	Keith Brooking RC	.75	.35
197	Jim Harbaugh	.75	.35
198	Errict Rhett	.75	.35
199	Pat Johnson RC	2.50	1.10
200	Rob Johnson	.75	.35
201	Andre Reed	.75	.35
202	Thurman Thomas	1.25	.55
203	Kerry Collins	.75	.35
204	William Floyd	.40	.18
205	Sean Gilbert	.40	.18
206	Bobby Engram	.75	.35
207	Edgar Bennett	.75	.35
208	Walt Harris	.75	.35
209	Carl Pickens	1.25	.55
210	Neil O'Donnell	.75	.35
211	Tony McGee	.40	.18
212	Deion Sanders	1.25	.55
213	Michael Irvin	1.25	.55
214	Greg Ellis RC	1.25	.55
215	Shannon Sharpe	.75	.35
216	Neil Smith	.75	.35
217	Marcus Nash RC	2.50	1.10
218	Brian Griese RC	70.00	32.00
219	Johnnie Morton	.75	.35
220	Herman Moore	1.25	.55
221	Charlie Batch RC	60.00	27.00
222	Robert Brooks	.75	.35
223	Mark Chmura	.75	.35
224	Brett Favre	6.00	2.70
225	Jerome Pathon RC	2.50	1.10
226	Zack Crockett	.40	.18
227	Dan Footman	.40	.18
228	Jimmy Smith	.75	.35
229	Bryce Paup	.40	.18
230	James Stewart	.75	.35
231	Derrick Thomas	.75	.35
232	Derrick Alexander	.75	.35
233	Tony Gonzalez	.40	.18
234	Dan Marino	6.00	2.70
235	O.J. McDuffie	.75	.35
236	Troy Drayton	.40	.18
237	Cris Carter	1.25	.55
238	Robert Smith	1.25	.55
239	Randy Moss RC	175.00	80.00
240	Lamar Smith	.40	.18
241	Sean Dawkins	.40	.18
242	Alex Molden	.40	.18
243	Ben Coates	.75	.35
244	Ted Johnson	.40	.18
245	Sedrick Shaw	.40	.18
246	Ike Hilliard	.75	.35
247	Jason Sehorn	.40	.18
248	Michael Strahan	.40	.18
249	Keyshawn Johnson	1.25	.55
250	Curtis Martin	1.25	.55
251	Jeff George	.75	.35
252	Rickey Dudley	.40	.18
253	James Jett	.75	.35
254	Bobby Taylor	.75	.35
255	Rodney Peete	.75	.35
256	William Thomas	.75	.35
257	Jerome Bettis	1.25	.55
258	Charles Johnson	.40	.18
259	Chris Fuamatu-Ma'afala RC	2.50	1.10
260	Eddie Kennison	.75	.35
261	Az-Zahir Hakim RC	6.00	2.70
262	Robert Holcombe RC	2.50	1.10
263	Bryan Still	.40	.18
264	Mikhael Ricks RC	2.50	1.10
265	Charlie Jones	.40	.18
266	J.J. Stokes	.75	.35
267	Marc Edwards	.40	.18
268	Steve Young	2.00	.90
269	Ricky Watters	.75	.35
270	Cortez Kennedy	.40	.18
271	Shawn Springs	.40	.18
272	Trent Dilfer	1.25	.55
273	Warren Sapp	.75	.35
274	Reidel Anthony	.75	.35
275	Yancey Thigpen	.40	.18
276	Chris Sanders	.40	.18
277	Eddie George	2.50	1.10
278	Leslie Shepherd	.40	.18
279	Skip Hicks RC	2.50	1.10
280	Dana Stubblefield	.40	.18
281	John Elway ET	8.00	3.60
282	Brett Favre ET	8.00	3.60
283	Junior Seau ET	1.50	.70
284	Barry Sanders ET	8.00	3.60
285	Jerry Rice ET	4.00	1.80
286	Antonio Freeman ET	2.00	.90

❑ 287 Peyton Manning ET 25.00 11.00
❑ 288 Warrick Dunn ET .... 2.00 .90
❑ 289 Steve Young ET 2.50 1.10
❑ 290 Dan Marino ET 8.00 3.60
❑ 291 Jerome Bettis ET .... 2.00 .90
❑ 292 Ryan Leaf ET 6.00 2.70
❑ 293 Deion Sanders ET .... 2.00 .90
❑ 294 Eddie George ET 3.00 1.35
❑ 295 Joey Galloway ET .... 2.00 .90
❑ 296 Troy Aikman ET 4.00 1.80
❑ 297 Andre Wadsworth ET .. 1.00 .45
❑ 298 Terrell Davis ET 6.00 2.70
❑ 299 Steve McNair ET .... 2.00 .90
❑ 300 Jake Plummer ET 4.00 1.80
❑ 301 Emmitt Smith ET 6.00 2.70
❑ 302 Isaac Bruce ET .... 2.00 .90
❑ 303 Kordell Stewart ET ...... 2.00 .90
❑ 304 Dorsey Levens ET .... 2.00 .90
❑ 305 Antowain Smith ET ...... 2.00 .90
❑ 306 Drew Bledsoe ET 3.00 1.35
❑ 307 Marshall Faulk ET .... 2.00 .90
❑ 308 Herman Moore ET .... 2.00 .90
❑ 309 Mark Brunell ET 3.00 1.35
❑ 310 Charles Woodson ET .. 6.00 2.70
❑ 311 Peyton Manning NS .. 30.00 13.50
❑ 312 Curtis Enis NS 10.00 4.50
❑ 313 Terry Fair NS RC 8.00 3.60
❑ 314 Andre Wadsworth NS .. 2.50 1.10
❑ 315 Anthony Simmons NS RC 1.50 .70
❑ 316 Jacquez Green NS RC 12.00 5.50
❑ 317 Takeo Spikes NS 2.50 1.10
❑ 318 Vonnie Holliday NS RC 8.00 3.60
❑ 319 Kyle Turley NS RC ...... 1.50 .70
❑ 320 Keith Brooking NS 2.50 1.10
❑ 321 Randy Moss NS 60.00 27.00
❑ 322 Shaun Williams NS RC 1.50 .70
❑ 323 Greg Ellis NS .... 1.50 .70
❑ 324 Mikhael Ricks NS 2.50 1.10
❑ 325 Charles Woodson NS 10.00 4.50
❑ 326 Corey Chavous NS RC 1.50 .70
❑ 327 Stephen Alexander NS RC 8.00 3.60
❑ 328 Marcus Nash NS 5.00 2.20
❑ 329 Tra Thomas NS RC .... 1.50 .70
❑ 330 Duane Starks NS RC .. 8.00 3.60
❑ 331 John Avery NS RC 8.00 3.60
❑ 332 Kevin Dyson NS 8.00 3.60
❑ 333 Fred Taylor NS 20.00 9.00
❑ 334 Grant Wistrom NS .... 1.50 .70
❑ 335 Ryan Leaf NS 10.00 4.50
❑ 336 Robert Edwards NS 5.00 2.20
❑ 337 Jason Peter NS RC .... 1.50 .70
❑ 338 Brian Griese NS 25.00 11.00
❑ 339 Charlie Batch NS 25.00 11.00
❑ 340 Pat Johnson NS 2.50 1.10
❑ 341 John Elway SS 15.00 6.75
❑ 342 Curtis Enis SS 10.00 4.50
❑ 343 Antonio Freeman SS 4.00 1.80
❑ 344 Mark Brunell SS 6.00 2.70
❑ 345 Robert Edwards SS 5.00 2.20
❑ 346 Ryan Leaf SS 10.00 4.50
❑ 347 Steve Young SS 5.00 2.20
❑ 348 Jerome Bettis SS 4.00 1.80
❑ 349 Antowain Smith SS 4.00 1.80
❑ 350 Tim Brown SS 4.00 1.80
❑ 351 Peyton Manning SS .. 30.00 13.50
❑ 352 Troy Aikman SS 8.00 3.60
❑ 353 Natrone Means SS 4.00 1.80
❑ 354 Dan Marino SS 15.00 6.75
❑ 355 Junior Seau SS .... 1.50 .70
❑ 356 Brad Johnson SS 4.00 1.80
❑ 357 Jerry Rice SS 8.00 3.60
❑ 358 Drew Bledsoe SS 6.00 2.70
❑ 359 Fred Taylor SS 20.00 9.00
❑ 360 Emmitt Smith SS 12.00 5.50
❑ 361 Terrell Davis UV 20.00 9.00
❑ 362 Kordell Stewart UV 5.00 2.20
❑ 363 Barry Sanders UV 25.00 11.00
❑ 364 Jake Plummer UV 12.00 5.50
❑ 365 Brett Favre UV 25.00 11.00
❑ 366 Curtis Enis UV 15.00 6.75
❑ 367 Eddie George UV 10.00 4.50
❑ 368 Napoleon Kaufman UV 5.00 2.20
❑ 369 Randy Moss UV 50.00 22.00
❑ 370 Warrick Dunn UV 5.00 2.20
❑ S8 Troy Aikman SAMPLE .. 1.00 .45
❑ S234 Dan Marino Sample .. 2.00 .90

1998 SPx Finite Radiance

	MINT	NRMT
COMMON CARD (1-90)	1.00	.45

*1-90 RADIANCE STARS: .6X TO 1.5X HI
1-90 PRINT RUN 3800 SERIAL #'d SETS
*91-120 RADIANCE STARS: .6X TO 1.5X HI
91-120 PM PRINT RUN 2750 SERIAL #'d SETS
*121-150 RADIANCE STARS: .6X TO 1.5X HI
121-150 YM PRINT RUN 1500 SERIAL #'d SETS
*151-170 RADIANCE STARS: .75X TO 2X HI
151-170 PE PRINT RUN 1000 SERIAL #'d SETS
*171-180 RADIANCE STARS: 2X TO 5X
171-180 HG PRINT RUN 100 SERIAL #'d SETS
COMMON ROOK.(181-190) 50.00 22.00
181-190 PRINT RUN 50 SERIAL #'d SETS
*191-280 RADIANCE STARS: .6X TO 1.5X HI
*191-280 RADIANCE RCs: .4X TO 1X
191-280 PRINT RUN 5050 SERIAL #'d SETS
218/221/239 PRINT RUN 1700 SER.#'d SETS
*281-310 RADIANCE STARS: .6X TO 1.5X
281-310 ET PRINT RUN 3600 SER.#'d SETS
*311-340 RADIANCE STARS: .6X TO 1.5X
311-340 NS PRINT RUN 2000 SER.#'d SETS
321/338/339 PRINT RUN 850 SER.#'d SETS
*341-360 RADIANCE STARS: .75X TO 2X
341-360 SS PRINT RUN 900 SER.#'d SETS
*361-370 RADIANCE STARS: .75X TO 2X
*361-370 RAD.ROOKIES: .6X TO 1.5X
361-370 UV PRINT RUN 540 SER.#'d SETS

❑ 181 Peyton Manning 400.00 180.00
❑ 182 Ryan Leaf 100.00 45.00
❑ 183 Andre Wadsworth 70.00 32.00
❑ 184 Charles Woodson 120.00 55.00
❑ 185 Curtis Enis 120.00 55.00
❑ 187 Fred Taylor 200.00 90.00
❑ 188 Takeo Spikes 70.00 32.00
❑ 189 Kevin Dyson 100.00 45.00

1998 SPx Finite Spectrum

	MINT	NRMT
COMMON CARD (1-90)	2.50	1.10

*1-90 SPECTRUM STARS: 1.25X TO 3X HI
1-90 PRINT RUN 1900 SERIAL #'d SETS
*91-120 SPECTRUM PM STARS: 1.25X TO 3X
91-120 PM PRINT RUN 1375 SERIAL #'d SETS
*121-150 SPECTRUM YM STARS: 1.25X TO 3X
121-150 YM PRINT RUN 750 SERIAL #'d SETS
*151-170 SPECTRUM PE STARS: 6X TO 15X
151-170 PE PRINT RUN 50 SERIAL #'d SETS
171-180 HG PRINT RUN 1 SERIAL #'d SET
181-190 PRINT RUN 1 SERIAL #'d SET
*191-280 SPECTRUM STARS: 3X TO 8X
*191-280 SPECTRUM RCs: 1.25X TO 3X
*218/221/239 SPECTRUM RCs: .5X TO 1.2X
191-280 PRINT RUN 325 SERIAL #'d SETS
*281-310 SPECTRUM ET STARS: 4X TO 10X
*281-310 SPECTRUM ROOKIES: 1.25X TO 3X
281-310 ET PRINT RUN 150 SERIAL #'d SETS
*311-340 SPECTRUM NS: 3X TO 8X
*321/338/339 SPECTRUM NS: 1.5X TO 4X
311-340 NS PRINT RUN 50 SERIAL #'d SETS
*341-360 SPECTRUM SS STARS: 10X TO 25X
*341-360 SPECTRUM SS ROOKIES: 4X TO 10X
341-360 SS PRINT RUN 25 SERIAL #'d SETS
361-370 UV PRINT RUN 1 #'d SET

1998 SPx Finite UD Authentics

	MINT	NRMT
COMP.BLUE INK SET (4)	350.00	160.00
COMMON BLUE INK	60.00	27.00
RANDOM INSERTS IN PACKS		

❑ DM1 Dan Marino/400 ...... 120.00 55.00
❑ JM1 Joe Montana/1984 .. 100.00 45.00
❑ RS1 Roger Staubach/463 80.00 36.00
❑ TA1 Troy Aikman/1992 .... 60.00 27.00

1999 SPx

	MINT	NRMT
COMPLETE SET (135)	2500.00	1100.00
COMP.SET w/o SP's (90)	25.00	11.00
COMMON CARD (1-90)	.30	.14
SEMISTARS	.60	.25
UNLISTED STARS	1.25	.55
COMMON ROOKIE (91-135) ..	12.00	5.50
ROOKIE SEMISTARS	15.00	6.75

UNLESS NOTED ROOKIES ARE #'d OF 1999
SOME RC AUTOS ISSUED VIA MAIL REDEMPT. ....

❑ 1 Jake Plummer 2.50 1.10
❑ 2 Adrian Murrell .... .60 .25
❑ 3 Frank Sanders .... .60 .25
❑ 4 Jamal Anderson .... 1.25 .55
❑ 5 Chris Chandler .... .60 .25
❑ 6 Terance Mathis .... .60 .25
❑ 7 Tony Banks .... .60 .25
❑ 8 Priest Holmes .... 1.25 .55
❑ 9 Jermaine Lewis .... .60 .25
❑ 10 Antowain Smith .... 1.25 .55
❑ 11 Doug Flutie .... 1.50 .70
❑ 12 Eric Moulds .... 1.25 .55
❑ 13 Tim Biakabutuka .... .60 .25
❑ 14 Steve Beuerlein .... .60 .25
❑ 15 Muhsin Muhammad .... .60 .25
❑ 16 Bobby Engram .... .60 .25
❑ 17 Curtis Conway .... .60 .25
❑ 18 Curtis Enis .... 1.25 .55
❑ 19 Corey Dillon .... 1.25 .55
❑ 20 Jeff Blake .... .60 .25

❑ 21 Carl Pickens .60 .25
❑ 22 Ty Detmer .60 .25
❑ 23 Terry Kirby .30 .14
❑ 24 Leslie Shepherd .30 .14
❑ 25 Troy Aikman 3.00 1.35
❑ 26 Emmitt Smith 3.00 1.35
❑ 27 Deion Sanders 1.25 .55
❑ 28 Terrell Davis 3.00 1.35
❑ 29 Rod Smith .60 .25
❑ 30 Bubby Brister .60 .25
❑ 31 Barry Sanders 5.00 2.20
❑ 32 Herman Moore 1.25 .55
❑ 33 Charlie Batch 2.50 1.10
❑ 34 Brett Favre 5.00 2.20
❑ 35 Antonio Freeman 1.25 .55
❑ 36 Dorsey Levens 1.25 .55
❑ 37 Peyton Manning 5.00 2.20
❑ 38 Marvin Harrison 1.25 .55
❑ 39 Jerome Pathon .30 .14
❑ 40 Mark Brunell 2.00 .90
❑ 41 Jimmy Smith .60 .25
❑ 42 Fred Taylor 3.00 1.35
❑ 43 Elvis Grbac .60 .25
❑ 44 Andre Rison .60 .25
❑ 45 Warren Moon 1.25 .55
❑ 46 Dan Marino 5.00 2.20
❑ 47 Karim Abdul-Jabbar .60 .25
❑ 48 O.J. McDuffie .60 .25
❑ 49 Randall Cunningham 1.25 .55
❑ 50 Robert Smith 1.25 .55
❑ 51 Randy Moss 5.00 2.20
❑ 52 Drew Bledsoe 2.00 .90
❑ 53 Terry Glenn 1.25 .55
❑ 54 Tony Simmons .30 .14
❑ 55 Danny Wuerffel .30 .14
❑ 56 Cam Cleeland .30 .14
❑ 57 Kerry Collins .60 .25
❑ 58 Gary Brown .30 .14
❑ 59 Ike Hilliard .30 .14
❑ 60 Vinny Testaverde .60 .25
❑ 61 Curtis Martin 1.25 .55
❑ 62 Keyshawn Johnson 1.25 .55
❑ 63 Rich Gannon .60 .25
❑ 64 Napoleon Kaufman 1.25 .55
❑ 65 Tim Brown 1.25 .55
❑ 66 Duce Staley 1.25 .55
❑ 67 Doug Pederson .30 .14
❑ 68 Charles Johnson .30 .14
❑ 69 Kordell Stewart 1.25 .55
❑ 70 Jerome Bettis 1.25 .55
❑ 71 Trent Green .60 .25
❑ 72 Marshall Faulk 1.25 .55
❑ 73 Ryan Leaf 1.25 .55
❑ 74 Natrone Means .60 .25
❑ 75 Jim Harbaugh .60 .25
❑ 76 Steve Young 2.00 .90
❑ 77 Garrison Hearst .60 .25
❑ 78 Jerry Rice 3.00 1.35
❑ 79 Terrell Owens 1.25 .55
❑ 80 Ricky Watters .60 .25
❑ 81 Joey Galloway 1.25 .55
❑ 82 Jon Kitna 1.50 .70
❑ 83 Warrick Dunn 1.25 .55
❑ 84 Trent Dilfer .60 .25
❑ 85 Mike Alstott 1.25 .55
❑ 86 Steve McNair 1.25 .55
❑ 87 Eddie George 1.50 .70
❑ 88 Yancey Thigpen .30 .14
❑ 89 Skip Hicks 1.25 .55
❑ 90 Michael Westbrook .60 .25
❑ 91 Amos Zereoue RC 12.00 5.50
❑ 92 Chris Claiborne AUTO RC 20.00 9.00
❑ 93 Scott Covington RC 12.00 5.50
❑ 94 Jeff Paulk RC 12.00 5.50
❑ 95 Brandon Stokley AUTO RC 20.00 9.00
❑ 96 Antoine Winfield RC 12.00 5.50
❑ 97 Reginald Kelly RC 12.00 5.50
❑ 98 Jermaine Fazande AUTO 25.00 11.00
❑ 99 Andy Katzenmoyer RC 12.00 5.50
❑ 100 Craig Yeast RC 12.00 5.50
❑ 101 Joe Montgomery RC 15.00 6.75
❑ 102 Darrin Chiaverini RC 15.00 6.75
❑ 103 Travis McGriff RC 12.00 5.50
❑ 104 Jevon Kearse RC 60.00 27.00
❑ 105 Joel Makovicka AUTO RC 20.00 9.00
❑ 106 Aaron Brooks RC 15.00 6.75
❑ 107 Chris McAlister RC 12.00 5.50
❑ 108 Jim Kleinsasser RC 12.00 5.50
❑ 109 Ebenezer Ekuban RC 15.00 6.75
❑ 110 Karsten Bailey RC 12.00 5.50
❑ 111 Sedrick Irvin AUTO RC 25.00 11.00
❑ 112 D'Wayne Bates AUTO RC 20.00 9.00
❑ 113 Joe Germaine AUTO RC 30.00 13.50
❑ 114 Cecil Collins AUTO RC 25.00 11.00
❑ 115 Mike Cloud RC 15.00 6.75
❑ 116 James Johnson RC 20.00 9.00
❑ 117 Champ Bailey AUTO RC 30.00 13.50
❑ 118 Rob Konrad RC 12.00 5.50
❑ 119 Peerless Price AUTO RC 50.00 22.00
❑ 120 Kevin Faulk AUTO RC 30.00 13.50
❑ 121 Dameane Douglas RC 12.00 5.50
❑ 122 Kevin Johnson AUTO RC 60.00 27.00
❑ 123 Troy Edwards AUTO RC 40.00 18.00
❑ 124 Edgerrin James AUTO RC 300.00 135.00
❑ 125 David Boston AUTO RC 40.00 18.00
❑ 126 Michael Bishop AUTO RC 30.00 13.50
❑ 127A Shaun King AUTO SP RC 425.00 190.00
❑ 127B Shaun King Trade 80.00 36.00
❑ 128 Brock Huard AUTO RC 35.00 16.00
❑ 129 Torry Holt AUTO RC 75.00 34.00
❑ 130 Cade McNown AU/500 RC 350.00 160.00
❑ 131 Tim Couch AU/500 RC 450.00 200.00
❑ 132 Donovan McNabb AUTO RC 80.00 36.00
❑ 133 Akili Smith AU/500 RC 300.00 135.00
❑ 134 D.Culpepper AU/500 RC 350.00 160.00
❑ 135 Ricky Williams AU/500 RC 450.00 200.00
❑ S8 Troy Aikman Sample 3.00 1.35

1999 SPx Radiance

	MINT	NRMT
COMPLETE SET (135)	2000.00	900.00
*RADIANCE STARS: 7X TO 20X HI COL.		
*RADIANCE YOUNG STARS: 6X TO 15X		
COMMON ROOKIE (91-135)	20.00	9.00
ROOKIE SEMISTARS	30.00	13.50
RADIANCE PRINT RUN 100 SER.#'d SETS		
UNPRICED SPECTRUMS #'d OF 1 SET MADE		

❑ 91 Amos Zereoue 30.00 13.50
❑ 92 Chris Claiborne 30.00 13.50
❑ 93 Scott Covington 30.00 13.50
❑ 94 Jeff Paulk 30.00 13.50
❑ 95 Brandon Stokley 30.00 13.50
❑ 96 Antoine Winfield 20.00 9.00
❑ 97 Reginald Kelly 20.00 9.00
❑ 98 Jermaine Fazande 30.00 13.50
❑ 99 Andy Katzenmoyer 30.00 13.50
❑ 100 Craig Yeast 30.00 13.50
❑ 101 Joe Montgomery 30.00 13.50
❑ 102 Darrin Chiaverini 30.00 13.50
❑ 103 Travis McGriff 30.00 13.50
❑ 104 Jevon Kearse 60.00 27.00
❑ 105 Joel Makovicka 30.00 13.50
❑ 106 Aaron Brooks 30.00 13.50
❑ 107 Chris McAlister 30.00 13.50
❑ 108 Jim Kleinsasser 30.00 13.50
❑ 109 Ebenezer Ekuban 30.00 13.50
❑ 110 Karsten Bailey 30.00 13.50
❑ 111 Sedrick Irvin 30.00 13.50
❑ 112 D'Wayne Bates 30.00 13.50
❑ 113 Joe Germaine 30.00 13.50
❑ 114 Cecil Collins 30.00 13.50
❑ 115 Mike Cloud 30.00 13.50
❑ 116 James Johnson 40.00 18.00
❑ 117 Champ Bailey 40.00 18.00
❑ 118 Rob Konrad 30.00 13.50
❑ 119 Peerless Price 50.00 22.00
❑ 120 Kevin Faulk 40.00 18.00
❑ 121 Dameane Douglas 20.00 9.00
❑ 122 Kevin Johnson 80.00 36.00
❑ 123 Troy Edwards 50.00 22.00
❑ 124 Edgerrin James 250.00 110.00
❑ 125 David Boston 50.00 22.00
❑ 126 Michael Bishop 40.00 18.00
❑ 127 Shaun King 100.00 45.00
❑ 128 Brock Huard 40.00 18.00
❑ 129 Torry Holt 80.00 36.00
❑ 130 Cade McNown 100.00 45.00
❑ 131 Tim Couch 150.00 70.00
❑ 132 Donovan McNabb 100.00 45.00
❑ 133 Akili Smith 60.00 27.00
❑ 134 Daunte Culpepper 100.00 45.00
❑ 135 Ricky Williams 150.00 70.00

1999 SPx Highlight Heroes

	MINT	NRMT
COMPLETE SET (10)	25.00	11.00
COMMON CARD (H1-H10)	2.50	1.10
STATED ODDS 1:9		

❑ H1 Jake Plummer 5.00 2.20
❑ H2 Doug Flutie 3.00 1.35
❑ H3 Garrison Hearst 2.50 1.10
❑ H4 Fred Taylor 5.00 2.20
❑ H5 Dorsey Levens 2.50 1.10
❑ H6 Kordell Stewart 2.50 1.10
❑ H7 Marshall Faulk 2.50 1.10
❑ H8 Steve Young 4.00 1.80
❑ H9 Troy Aikman 6.00 2.70
❑ H10 Jerome Bettis 2.50 1.10

1999 SPx Masters

	MINT	NRMT
COMPLETE SET (15)	80.00	36.00
COMMON CARD (M1-M15)	3.00	1.35
STATED ODDS 1:17		

❑ M1 Dan Marino 12.00 5.50
❑ M2 Barry Sanders 12.00 5.50
❑ M3 Peyton Manning 10.00 4.50
❑ M4 Joey Galloway 4.00 1.80

Card	Player	MINT	NRMT
❑ M5	Steve Young	5.00	2.20
❑ M6	Warrick Dunn	4.00	1.80
❑ M7	Deion Sanders	4.00	1.80
❑ M8	Fred Taylor	6.00	2.70
❑ M9	Charlie Batch	5.00	2.20
❑ M10	Jamal Anderson	4.00	1.80
❑ M11	Jake Plummer	6.00	2.70
❑ M12	Terrell Davis	8.00	3.60
❑ M13	Eddie George	4.00	1.80
❑ M14	Mark Brunell	5.00	2.20
❑ M15	Randy Moss	10.00	4.50

1999 SPx Prolifics

	MINT	NRMT
COMPLETE SET (15)	60.00	27.00
COMMON CARD (P1-P15)	2.00	.90
SEMISTARS	3.00	1.35
STATED ODDS 1:17		

Card	Player	MINT	NRMT
❑ P1	John Elway	12.00	5.50
❑ P2	Barry Sanders	12.00	5.50
❑ P3	Jamal Anderson	2.00	.90
❑ P4	Terrell Owens	2.00	.90
❑ P5	Marshall Faulk	2.00	.90
❑ P6	Napoleon Kaufman	2.00	.90
❑ P7	Antonio Freeman	2.00	.90
❑ P8	Doug Flutie	4.00	1.80
❑ P9	Vinny Testaverde	2.00	.90
❑ P10	Jerry Rice	8.00	3.60
❑ P11	Eric Moulds	2.00	.90
❑ P12	Emmitt Smith	8.00	3.60
❑ P13	Brett Favre	12.00	5.50
❑ P14	Randall Cunningham	2.00	.90
❑ P15	Keyshawn Johnson	2.00	.90

1999 SPx Spxcitement

	MINT	NRMT
COMPLETE SET (20)	30.00	13.50
COMMON CARD (S1-S20)	1.00	.45
SEMISTARS	1.25	.55
STATED ODDS 1:3		

Card	Player	MINT	NRMT
❑ S1	Troy Aikman	3.00	1.35
❑ S2	Edgerrin James	10.00	4.50
❑ S3	Jerry Rice	3.00	1.35
❑ S4	Daunte Culpepper	4.00	1.80
❑ S5	Antowain Smith	3.00	1.35
❑ S6	Kevin Faulk	1.50	.70
❑ S7	Steve McNair	1.50	.70
❑ S8	Antonio Freeman	1.50	.70
❑ S9	Torry Holt	3.00	1.35
❑ S10	Napoleon Kaufman	1.50	.70
❑ S11	Curtis Martin	1.50	.70
❑ S12	Randall Cunningham	1.50	.70
❑ S13	Eric Moulds	1.50	.70
❑ S14	Priest Holmes	1.50	.70
❑ S15	David Boston	2.00	.90
❑ S16	Herman Moore	1.50	.70
❑ S17	Champ Bailey	1.50	.70
❑ S18	Vinny Testaverde	1.00	.45
❑ S19	Garrison Hearst	1.00	.45
❑ S20	Jon Kitna	1.50	.70

1999 SPx Spxtreme

	MINT	NRMT
COMPLETE SET (20)	50.00	22.00
COMMON CARD (X1-X20)	1.25	.55
SEMISTARS	2.00	.90
STATED ODDS 1:6		

Card	Player	MINT	NRMT
❑ X1	Emmitt Smith	5.00	2.20
❑ X2	Brock Huard	2.00	.90
❑ X3	David Boston	2.50	1.10
❑ X4	Edgerrin James	15.00	6.75
❑ X5	Kevin Faulk	2.00	.90
❑ X6	Daunte Culpepper	5.00	2.20
❑ X7	Charlie Batch	2.50	1.10
❑ X8	Torry Holt	4.00	1.80
❑ X9	Andre Rison	1.25	.55
❑ X10	Karim Abdul-Jabbar	1.25	.55
❑ X11	Kordell Stewart	2.50	1.10
❑ X12	Curtis Enis	2.50	1.10
❑ X13	Terrell Owens	2.50	1.10
❑ X14	Curtis Martin	2.50	1.10
❑ X15	Ricky Watters	1.25	.55
❑ X16	Corey Dillon	2.50	1.10
❑ X17	Tim Brown	2.50	1.10
❑ X18	Warrick Dunn	2.50	1.10
❑ X19	Drew Bledsoe	3.00	1.35
❑ X20	Eddie George	2.50	1.10

1999 SPx Starscape

	MINT	NRMT
COMPLETE SET (10)	20.00	9.00
COMMON CARD (ST1-ST10)	2.00	.90
STATED ODDS 1:9		

Card	Player	MINT	NRMT
❑ ST1	Randy Moss	6.00	2.70
❑ ST2	Keyshawn Johnson	2.50	1.10
❑ ST3	Curtis Enis	2.50	1.10
❑ ST4	Jerome Bettis	2.50	1.10
❑ ST5	Mark Brunell	3.00	1.35
❑ ST6	Antowain Smith	2.50	1.10
❑ ST7	Joey Galloway	2.50	1.10
❑ ST8	Drew Bledsoe	3.00	1.35
❑ ST9	Corey Dillon	2.50	1.10
❑ ST10	Steve McNair	2.50	1.10

1999 SPx Winning Materials

	MINT	NRMT
COMPLETE SET (10)	1200.00	550.00
COMMON CARD	60.00	27.00
STATED ODDS 1:252		

Card	Player	MINT	NRMT
❑ BF-S	Brett Favre	150.00	70.00
❑ CM-S	Cade McNown	100.00	45.00
❑ DB-S	David Boston	60.00	27.00
❑ DC-S	Daunte Culpepper	100.00	45.00
❑ DM-S	Dan Marino	150.00	70.00
❑ JR-A	Jerry Rice AUTO/80	500.00	220.00
❑ JR-S	Jerry Rice	120.00	55.00
❑ MC-S	Donovan McNabb	100.00	45.00
❑ RW-S	Ricky Williams	150.00	70.00
❑ TC-A	Tim Couch AUTO/2		
❑ TC-S	Tim Couch	175.00	80.00
❑ TH-S	Torry Holt	60.00	27.00

1991 Stadium Club

	MINT	NRMT
COMPLETE SET (500)	70.00	32.00
COMMON CARD (1-500)	.20	.09
SEMISTARS	.40	.18
UNLISTED STARS	.75	.35

Card	Player	MINT	NRMT
❑ 1	Pepper Johnson	.20	.09
❑ 2	Emmitt Smith	6.00	2.70
❑ 3	Deion Sanders	1.50	.70
❑ 4	Andre Collins	.20	.09
❑ 5	Eric Metcalf	.40	.18
❑ 6	Richard Dent	.40	.18
❑ 7	Eric Martin	.20	.09
❑ 8	Marcus Allen	.75	.35
❑ 9	Gary Anderson K	.20	.09
❑ 10	Joey Browner	.20	.09
❑ 11	Lorenzo White	.20	.09
❑ 12	Bruce Smith	.75	.35
❑ 13	Mark Boyer	.20	.09
❑ 14	Mike Piel	.20	.09

❑ 15 Albert Bentley .20 .09
❑ 16 Bennie Blades .20 .09
❑ 17 Jason Staurovsky .20 .09
❑ 18 Anthony Toney .20 .09
❑ 19 Dave Krieg .40 .18
❑ 20 Harvey Williams RC .75 .35
❑ 21 Bubba Paris .20 .09
❑ 22 Tim McGee .20 .09
❑ 23 Brian Noble .20 .09
❑ 24 Vinny Testaverde .40 .18
❑ 25 Doug Widell .20 .09
❑ 26 John Jackson RC .20 .09
❑ 27 Marion Butts .40 .18
❑ 28 Deron Cherry .20 .09
❑ 29 Don Warren .20 .09
❑ 30 Rod Woodson .75 .35
❑ 31 Mike Baab .20 .09
❑ 32 Greg Jackson RC .20 .09
❑ 33 Jerry Robinson .20 .09
❑ 34 Dalton Hilliard .20 .09
❑ 35 Brian Jordan .40 .18
❑ 36 James Thornton UER .20 .09
(Misspelled Thorton
on card back)
❑ 37 Michael Irvin .75 .35
❑ 38 Billy Joe Tolliver .20 .09
❑ 39 Jeff Herrod .20 .09
❑ 40 Scott Norwood .20 .09
❑ 41 Ferrell Edmunds .20 .09
❑ 42 Andre Waters .20 .09
❑ 43 Kevin Glover .20 .09
❑ 44 Ray Berry .20 .09
❑ 45 Timm Rosenbach .20 .09
❑ 46 Reuben Davis .20 .09
❑ 47 Charles Wilson .20 .09
❑ 48 Todd Marinovich RC .20 .09
❑ 49 Harris Barton .20 .09
❑ 50 Jim Breech .20 .09
❑ 51 Ron Holmes .20 .09
❑ 52 Chris Singleton .20 .09
❑ 53 Pat Leahy .20 .09
❑ 54 Tom Newberry .20 .09
❑ 55 Greg Montgomery .20 .09
❑ 56 Robert Blackmon .20 .09
❑ 57 Jay Hilgenberg .20 .09
❑ 58 Rodney Hampton .75 .35
❑ 59 Brett Perriman .75 .35
❑ 60 Ricky Watters RC 6.00 2.70
❑ 61 Howie Long .40 .18
❑ 62 Frank Cornish .20 .09
❑ 63 Chris Miller .40 .18
❑ 64 Keith Taylor .20 .09
❑ 65 Tony Paige .20 .09
❑ 66 Gary Zimmerman .20 .09
❑ 67 Mark Royals RC .20 .09
❑ 68 Ernie Jones .20 .09
❑ 69 David Grant .20 .09
❑ 70 Shane Conlan .20 .09
❑ 71 Jerry Rice 3.00 1.35
❑ 72 Christian Okoye .20 .09
❑ 73 Eddie Murray .20 .09
❑ 74 Reggie White .75 .35
❑ 75 Jeff Graham RC 1.00 .45
❑ 76 Mark Jackson .20 .09
❑ 77 David Grayson .20 .09
❑ 78 Dan Stryzinski .20 .09
❑ 79 Sterling Sharpe .75 .35
❑ 80 Cleveland Gary .20 .09
❑ 81 Johnny Meads .20 .09
❑ 82 Howard Cross .20 .09
❑ 83 Ken O'Brien .20 .09
❑ 84 Brian Blades .40 .18
❑ 85 Ethan Horton .20 .09
❑ 86 Bruce Armstrong .20 .09
❑ 87 James Washington RC .20 .09
❑ 88 Eugene Daniel .20 .09
❑ 89 James Lofton .40 .18
❑ 90 Louis Oliver .20 .09
❑ 91 Boomer Esiason .40 .18
❑ 92 Seth Joyner .40 .18
❑ 93 Mark Carrier WR .75 .35
❑ 94 Brett Favre RC UER 50.00 22.00
(Favre misspelled
as Farve)
❑ 95 Lee Williams .20 .09
❑ 96 Neal Anderson .40 .18
❑ 97 Brent Jones .75 .35
❑ 98 John Alt .20 .09
❑ 99 Rodney Peete .40 .18
❑ 100 Steve Broussard .20 .09
❑ 101 Cedric Mack .20 .09
❑ 102 Pat Swilling .40 .18
❑ 103 Stan Humphries .75 .35
❑ 104 Darrell Thompson .20 .09
❑ 105 Reggie Langhorne .20 .09
❑ 106 Kenny Davidson .20 .09
❑ 107 Jim Everett .40 .18
❑ 108 Keith Millard .20 .09
❑ 109 Garry Lewis .20 .09
❑ 110 Jeff Hostetler .40 .18
❑ 111 Lamar Lathon .20 .09
❑ 112 Johnny Bailey .20 .09
❑ 113 Cornelius Bennett .40 .18
❑ 114 Travis McNeal .20 .09
❑ 115 Jeff Lageman .20 .09
❑ 116 Nick Bell RC .20 .09
❑ 117 Calvin Williams .40 .18
❑ 118 Shawn Lee RC .20 .09
❑ 119 Anthony Munoz .40 .18
❑ 120 Jay Novacek .75 .35
❑ 121 Kevin Fagan .20 .09
❑ 122 Leo Goeas .20 .09
❑ 123 Vance Johnson .20 .09
❑ 124 Brent Williams .20 .09
❑ 125 Clarence Verdin .20 .09
❑ 126 Luis Sharpe .20 .09
❑ 127 Darrell Green .20 .09
❑ 128 Barry Word .20 .09
❑ 129 Steve Walsh .20 .09
❑ 130 Bryan Hinkle .20 .09
❑ 131 Ed West .20 .09
❑ 132 Jeff Campbell .20 .09
❑ 133 Dennis Byrd .20 .09
❑ 134 Nate Odomes .20 .09
❑ 135 Trace Armstrong .20 .09
❑ 136 Jarvis Williams .20 .09
❑ 137 Warren Moon .75 .35
❑ 138 Eric Moten RC .20 .09
❑ 139 Tony Woods .20 .09
❑ 140 Phil Simms .40 .18
❑ 141 Ricky Reynolds .20 .09
❑ 142 Frank Stams .20 .09
❑ 143 Kevin Mack .20 .09
❑ 144 Wade Wilson .40 .18
❑ 145 Shawn Collins .20 .09
❑ 146 Roger Craig .40 .18
❑ 147 Jeff Feagles RC .20 .09
❑ 148 Norm Johnson .20 .09
❑ 149 Terance Mathis .40 .18
❑ 150 Reggie Cobb .20 .09
❑ 151 Chip Banks .20 .09
❑ 152 Darryl Pollard .20 .09
❑ 153 Karl Mecklenburg .20 .09
❑ 154 Ricky Proehl .20 .09
❑ 155 Pete Stoyanovich .20 .09
❑ 156 John Stephens .20 .09
❑ 157 Ron Morris .20 .09
❑ 158 Steve DeBerg .20 .09
❑ 159 Mike Munchak .20 .09
❑ 160 Brett Maxie .20 .09
❑ 161 Don Beebe .20 .09
❑ 162 Martin Mayhew .20 .09
❑ 163 Merril Hoge .20 .09
❑ 164 Kelvin Pritchett RC .40 .18
❑ 165 Jim Jeffcoat .20 .09
❑ 166 Myron Guyton .20 .09
❑ 167 Ickey Woods .20 .09
❑ 168 Andre Ware .40 .18
❑ 169 Gary Plummer .20 .09
❑ 170 Henry Ellard .40 .18
❑ 171 Scott Davis .20 .09
❑ 172 Randall McDaniel .20 .09
❑ 173 Randal Hill RC .40 .18
❑ 174 Anthony Bell .20 .09
❑ 175 Gary Anderson RB .20 .09
❑ 176 Byron Evans .20 .09
❑ 177 Tony Mandarich .20 .09
❑ 178 Jeff George 1.50 .70
❑ 179 Art Monk .40 .18
❑ 180 Mike Kenn .20 .09
❑ 181 Sean Landeta .20 .09
❑ 182 Shaun Gayle .20 .09
❑ 183 Michael Carter .20 .09
❑ 184 Robb Thomas .20 .09
❑ 185 Richmond Webb .20 .09
❑ 186 Carnell Lake .20 .09
❑ 187 Rueben Mayes .20 .09
❑ 188 Issiac Holt .20 .09
❑ 189 Leon Seals .20 .09
❑ 190 Al Smith .20 .09
❑ 191 Steve Atwater .20 .09
❑ 192 Greg McMurtry .20 .09
❑ 193 Al Toon .40 .18
❑ 194 Cortez Kennedy .75 .35
❑ 195 Gill Byrd .20 .09
❑ 196 Carl Zander .20 .09
❑ 197 Robert Brown .20 .09
❑ 198 Buford McGee .20 .09
❑ 199 Mervyn Fernandez .20 .09
❑ 200 Mike Dumas RC .20 .09
❑ 201 Rob Burnett RC .20 .09
❑ 202 Brian Mitchell .40 .18
❑ 203 Randall Cunningham .75 .35
❑ 204 Sammie Smith .20 .09
❑ 205 Ken Clarke .20 .09
❑ 206 Floyd Dixon .20 .09
❑ 207 Ken Norton .75 .35
❑ 208 Tony Siragusa RC .20 .09
❑ 209 Louis Lipps .20 .09
❑ 210 Chris Martin .20 .09
❑ 211 Jamie Mueller .20 .09
❑ 212 Dave Waymer .20 .09
❑ 213 Donnell Woolford .20 .09
❑ 214 Paul Gruber .20 .09
❑ 215 Ken Harvey .40 .18
❑ 216 Henry Jones RC .40 .18
❑ 217 Tommy Barnhardt RC .20 .09
❑ 218 Arthur Cox .20 .09
❑ 219 Pat Terrell .20 .09
❑ 220 Curtis Duncan .20 .09
❑ 221 Jeff Jaeger .20 .09
❑ 222 Scott Stephen RC .20 .09
❑ 223 Rob Moore 1.50 .70
❑ 224 Chris Hinton .20 .09
❑ 225 Marv Cook .20 .09
❑ 226 Patrick Hunter RC .20 .09
❑ 227 Earnest Byner .20 .09
❑ 228 Troy Aikman 3.00 1.35
❑ 229 Kevin Walker RC .20 .09
❑ 230 Keith Jackson .40 .18
❑ 231 Russell Maryland RC UER .75 .35
(Card back says
Dallas Cowboy)
❑ 232 Charles Haley .40 .18
❑ 233 Nick Lowery .20 .09
❑ 234 Erik Howard .20 .09
❑ 235 Leonard Smith .20 .09
❑ 236 Tim Irwin .20 .09
❑ 237 Simon Fletcher .20 .09
❑ 238 Thomas Everett .20 .09
❑ 239 Reggie Roby .20 .09
❑ 240 Leroy Hoard .40 .18
❑ 241 Wayne Haddix .20 .09
❑ 242 Gary Clark .75 .35
❑ 243 Eric Andolsek .20 .09
❑ 244 Jim Wahler RC .20 .09
❑ 245 Vaughan Johnson .20 .09
❑ 246 Kevin Butler .20 .09
❑ 247 Steve Tasker .40 .18
❑ 248 LeRoy Butler .40 .18
❑ 249 Darion Conner .20 .09
❑ 250 Eric Turner RC .40 .18
❑ 251 Kevin Ross .20 .09
❑ 252 Stephen Baker .20 .09
❑ 253 Harold Green .40 .18
❑ 254 Rohn Stark .20 .09
❑ 255 Joe Nash .20 .09
❑ 256 Jesse Sapolu .20 .09
❑ 257 Willie Gault .40 .18
❑ 258 Jerome Brown .20 .09
❑ 259 Ken Willis .20 .09
❑ 260 Courtney Hall .20 .09
❑ 261 Hart Lee Dykes .20 .09
❑ 262 William Fuller .40 .18
❑ 263 Stan Thomas .20 .09
❑ 264 Dan Marino 5.00 2.20
❑ 265 Ron Cox .20 .09
❑ 266 Eric Green .20 .09

❑ 267 Anthony Carter	.40	.18
❑ 268 Jerry Ball	.20	.09
❑ 269 Ron Hall	.20	.09
❑ 270 Dennis Smith	.20	.09
❑ 271 Eric Hill	.20	.09
❑ 272 Dan McGwire RC	.20	.09
❑ 273 Lewis Billups UER Louis on back	.20	.09
❑ 274 Rickey Jackson	.20	.09
❑ 275 Jim Sweeney	.20	.09
❑ 276 Pat Beach	.20	.09
❑ 277 Kevin Porter	.20	.09
❑ 278 Mike Sherrard	.20	.09
❑ 279 Andy Heck	.20	.09
❑ 280 Ron Brown	.20	.09
❑ 281 Lawrence Taylor	.75	.35
❑ 282 Anthony Pleasant	.20	.09
❑ 283 Wes Hopkins	.20	.09
❑ 284 Jim Lachey	.20	.09
❑ 285 Tim Harris	.20	.09
❑ 286 Tory Epps	.20	.09
❑ 287 Wendell Davis	.20	.09
❑ 288 Bubba McDowell	.20	.09
❑ 289 Bubby Brister	.20	.09
❑ 290 Chris Zorich RC	.75	.35
❑ 291 Mike Merriweather	.20	.09
❑ 292 Burt Grossman	.20	.09
❑ 293 Erik McMillan	.20	.09
❑ 294 John Elway	5.00	2.20
❑ 295 Toi Cook RC	.20	.09
❑ 296 Tom Rathman	.20	.09
❑ 297 Matt Bahr	.20	.09
❑ 298 Chris Spielman	.40	.18
❑ 299 Freddie Joe Nunn (Troy Aikman and Emmitt Smith shown in background)	.40	.18
❑ 300 Jim C. Jensen	.20	.09
❑ 301 David Fulcher UER (Rookie card should be '88, not '89)	.20	.09
❑ 302 Tommy Hodson	.20	.09
❑ 303 Stephone Paige	.20	.09
❑ 304 Greg Townsend	.20	.09
❑ 305 Dean Biasucci	.20	.09
❑ 306 Jimmie Jones	.20	.09
❑ 307 Eugene Marve	.20	.09
❑ 308 Flipper Anderson	.20	.09
❑ 309 Darryl Talley	.20	.09
❑ 310 Mike Croel RC	.20	.09
❑ 311 Thane Gash	.20	.09
❑ 312 Perry Kemp	.20	.09
❑ 313 Heath Sherman	.20	.09
❑ 314 Mike Singletary	.40	.18
❑ 315 Chip Lohmiller	.20	.09
❑ 316 Tunch Ilkin	.20	.09
❑ 317 Junior Seau	1.50	.70
❑ 318 Mike Gann	.20	.09
❑ 319 Tim McDonald	.20	.09
❑ 320 Kyle Clifton	.20	.09
❑ 321 Dan Owens	.20	.09
❑ 322 Tim Grunhard	.20	.09
❑ 323 Stan Brock	.20	.09
❑ 324 Rodney Holman	.20	.09
❑ 325 Mark Ingram	.40	.18
❑ 326 Browning Nagle RC	.20	.09
❑ 327 Joe Montana	5.00	2.20
❑ 328 Carl Lee	.20	.09
❑ 329 John L. Williams	.20	.09
❑ 330 David Griggs	.20	.09
❑ 331 Clarence Kay	.20	.09
❑ 332 Irving Fryar	.40	.18
❑ 333 Doug Smith RC**	.20	.09
❑ 334 Kent Hull	.20	.09
❑ 335 Mike Wilcher	.20	.09
❑ 336 Ray Donaldson	.20	.09
❑ 337 Mark Carrier DB UER (Rookie card should be '90, not '89)	.20	.09
❑ 338 Kelvin Martin	.20	.09
❑ 339 Keith Byars	.20	.09
❑ 340 Wilber Marshall	.20	.09
❑ 341 Ronnie Lott	.40	.18
❑ 342 Blair Thomas	.20	.09
❑ 343 Ronnie Harmon	.20	.09
❑ 344 Brian Brennan	.20	.09
❑ 345 Charles McRae RC	.20	.09
❑ 346 Michael Cofer	.20	.09
❑ 347 Keith Willis	.20	.09
❑ 348 Bruce Kozerski	.20	.09
❑ 349 Dave Meggett	.40	.18
❑ 350 John Taylor	.40	.18
❑ 351 Johnny Holland	.20	.09
❑ 352 Steve Christie	.20	.09
❑ 353 Ricky Ervins RC	.40	.18
❑ 354 Robert Massey	.20	.09
❑ 355 Derrick Thomas	.75	.35
❑ 356 Tommy Kane	.20	.09
❑ 357 Melvin Bratton	.20	.09
❑ 358 Bruce Matthews	.40	.18
❑ 359 Mark Duper	.40	.18
❑ 360 Jeff Wright RC	.20	.09
❑ 361 Barry Sanders	6.00	2.70
❑ 362 Chuck Webb RC	.20	.09
❑ 363 Darryl Grant	.20	.09
❑ 364 William Roberts	.20	.09
❑ 365 Reggie Rutland	.20	.09
❑ 366 Clay Matthews	.40	.18
❑ 367 Anthony Miller	.40	.18
❑ 368 Mike Prior	.20	.09
❑ 369 Jessie Tuggle	.20	.09
❑ 370 Brad Muster	.20	.09
❑ 371 Jay Schroeder	.20	.09
❑ 372 Greg Lloyd	.75	.35
❑ 373 Mike Cofer	.20	.09
❑ 374 James Brooks	.40	.18
❑ 375 Danny Noonan UER (Misspelled Noonen on card back)	.20	.09
❑ 376 Latin Berry RC	.20	.09
❑ 377 Brad Baxter	.20	.09
❑ 378 Godfrey Myles RC	.20	.09
❑ 379 Morten Andersen	.20	.09
❑ 380 Keith Woodside	.20	.09
❑ 381 Bobby Humphrey	.20	.09
❑ 382 Mike Golic	.20	.09
❑ 383 Keith McCants	.20	.09
❑ 384 Anthony Thompson	.20	.09
❑ 385 Mark Clayton	.40	.18
❑ 386 Neil Smith	.75	.35
❑ 387 Bryan Millard	.20	.09
❑ 388 Mel Gray UER (Wrong Mel Gray pictured on card back)	.40	.18
❑ 389 Ernest Givins	.40	.18
❑ 390 Reyna Thompson	.20	.09
❑ 391 Eric Bieniemy RC	.20	.09
❑ 392 Jon Hand	.20	.09
❑ 393 Mark Rypien	.40	.18
❑ 394 Bill Romanowski	.20	.09
❑ 395 Thurman Thomas	.75	.35
❑ 396 Jim Harbaugh	.75	.35
❑ 397 Don Mosebar	.20	.09
❑ 398 Andre Rison	.40	.18
❑ 399 Mike Johnson	.20	.09
❑ 400 Dermontti Dawson	.20	.09
❑ 401 Herschel Walker	.40	.18
❑ 402 Joe Prokop	.20	.09
❑ 403 Eddie Brown	.20	.09
❑ 404 Nate Newton	.40	.18
❑ 405 Damone Johnson RC	.20	.09
❑ 406 Jessie Hester	.20	.09
❑ 407 Jim Arnold	.20	.09
❑ 408 Ray Agnew	.20	.09
❑ 409 Michael Brooks	.20	.09
❑ 410 Keith Sims	.20	.09
❑ 411 Carl Banks	.20	.09
❑ 412 Jonathan Hayes	.20	.09
❑ 413 Richard Johnson RC	.20	.09
❑ 414 Darryll Lewis RC	.40	.18
❑ 415 Jeff Bryant	.20	.09
❑ 416 Leslie O'Neal	.40	.18
❑ 417 Andre Reed	.40	.18
❑ 418 Charles Mann	.20	.09
❑ 419 Keith DeLong	.20	.09
❑ 420 Bruce Hill	.20	.09
❑ 421 Matt Brock RC	.20	.09
❑ 422 Johnny Johnson	.20	.09
❑ 423 Mark Bortz	.20	.09
❑ 424 Ben Smith	.20	.09
❑ 425 Jeff Cross	.20	.09
❑ 426 Irv Pankey	.20	.09
❑ 427 Hassan Jones	.20	.09
❑ 428 Andre Tippett	.20	.09
❑ 429 Tim Worley	.20	.09
❑ 430 Daniel Stubbs	.20	.09
❑ 431 Max Montoya	.20	.09
❑ 432 Jumbo Elliott	.20	.09
❑ 433 Duane Bickett	.20	.09
❑ 434 Nate Lewis RC	.20	.09
❑ 435 Leonard Russell RC	.75	.35
❑ 436 Hoby Brenner	.20	.09
❑ 437 Ricky Sanders	.20	.09
❑ 438 Pierce Holt	.20	.09
❑ 439 Derrick Fenner	.20	.09
❑ 440 Drew Hill	.20	.09
❑ 441 Will Wolford	.20	.09
❑ 442 Albert Lewis	.20	.09
❑ 443 James Francis	.20	.09
❑ 444 Chris Jacke	.20	.09
❑ 445 Mike Farr	.20	.09
❑ 446 Stephen Braggs	.20	.09
❑ 447 Michael Haynes	.75	.35
❑ 448 Freeman McNeil UER 2,008 Pounds for weight	.20	.09
❑ 449 Kevin Donnalley	.20	.09
❑ 450 John Offerdahl	.20	.09
❑ 451 Eric Allen	.20	.09
❑ 452 Keith McKeller	.20	.09
❑ 453 Kevin Greene	.75	.35
❑ 454 Ronnie Lippett	.20	.09
❑ 455 Ray Childress	.20	.09
❑ 456 Mike Saxon	.20	.09
❑ 457 Mark Robinson	.20	.09
❑ 458 Greg Kragen	.20	.09
❑ 459 Steve Jordan	.20	.09
❑ 460 John Johnson RC	.20	.09
❑ 461 Sam Mills	.20	.09
❑ 462 Bo Jackson	.40	.18
❑ 463 Mark Collins	.20	.09
❑ 464 Percy Snow	.20	.09
❑ 465 Jeff Bostic	.20	.09
❑ 466 Jacob Green	.20	.09
❑ 467 Dexter Carter	.20	.09
❑ 468 Rich Camarillo	.20	.09
❑ 469 Bill Brooks	.20	.09
❑ 470 John Carney	.20	.09
❑ 471 Don Majkowski	.20	.09
❑ 472 Ralph Tamm RC	.20	.09
❑ 473 Fred Barnett	.75	.35
❑ 474 Jim Covert	.20	.09
❑ 475 Kenneth Davis	.20	.09
❑ 476 Jerry Gray	.20	.09
❑ 477 Broderick Thomas	.20	.09
❑ 478 Chris Doleman	.20	.09
❑ 479 Haywood Jeffires	.40	.18
❑ 480 Craig Heyward	.40	.18
❑ 481 Markus Koch	.20	.09
❑ 482 Tim Krumrie	.20	.09
❑ 483 Robert Clark	.20	.09
❑ 484 Mike Rozier	.20	.09
❑ 485 Danny Villa	.20	.09
❑ 486 Gerald Williams	.20	.09
❑ 487 Steve Wisniewski	.20	.09
❑ 488 J.B. Brown	.20	.09
❑ 489 Eugene Robinson	.20	.09
❑ 490 Ottis Anderson	.40	.18
❑ 491 Tony Stargell	.20	.09
❑ 492 Jack Del Rio	.20	.09
❑ 493 Lamar Rogers RC	.20	.09
❑ 494 Ricky Nattiel	.20	.09
❑ 495 Dan Saleaumua	.20	.09
❑ 496 Checklist 1-100	.20	.09
❑ 497 Checklist 101-200	.20	.09
❑ 498 Checklist 201-300	.20	.09
❑ 499 Checklist 301-400	.20	.09
❑ 500 Checklist 401-500	.20	.09

1992 Stadium Club

	MINT	NRMT
COMPLETE SET (700)	150.00	70.00
COMP.SERIES 1 (300)	15.00	6.75
COMP.SERIES 2 (300)	15.00	6.75
COMP.HIGH SER.(100)	120.00	55.00
COMMON CARD (1-600)	.08	.04
COMMON CARD (601-700)	.50	.23
SEMISTARS 1-600	.15	.07

SEMISTARS 601-700	.75	.35
UNLISTED STARS 1-600	.30	.14
UNLISTED STARS 601-700	1.50	.70
COMP.NO.1 DRAFT SET (4)	35.00	16.00
NO.1 DRAFT:INSERTS IN HIGH SERIES		
COMP.QB LEGENDS SET (6)	18.00	8.00
QB LEGENDS:INSERTS IN HIGH SERIES		

❑ 1	Mark Rypien	.08	.04
❑ 2	Carlton Bailey RC	.15	.07
❑ 3	Kevin Glover	.08	.04
❑ 4	Vance Johnson	.08	.04
❑ 5	Jim Jeffcoat	.08	.04
❑ 6	Dan Saleaumua	.08	.04
❑ 7	Darion Conner	.08	.04
❑ 8	Don Maggs	.08	.04
❑ 9	Richard Dent	.15	.07
❑ 10	Mark Murphy	.08	.04
❑ 11	Wesley Carroll	.08	.04
❑ 12	Chris Burkett	.08	.04
❑ 13	Steve Wallace	.08	.04
❑ 14	Jacob Green	.08	.04
❑ 15	Roger Ruzek	.08	.04
❑ 16	J.B. Brown	.08	.04
❑ 17	Dave Meggett	.15	.07
❑ 18	D.J. Johnson	.08	.04
❑ 19	Rich Gannon	.08	.04
❑ 20	Kevin Mack	.08	.04
❑ 21A	Reggie Cobb ERR (Buccaneers upside down on card front)	.08	.04
❑ 21B	Reggie Cobb COR	.08	.04
❑ 22	Nate Lewis	.08	.04
❑ 23	Doug Smith	.08	.04
❑ 24	Irving Fryar	.15	.07
❑ 25	Anthony Thompson	.08	.04
❑ 26	Duane Bickett	.08	.04
❑ 27	Don Majkowski	.08	.04
❑ 28	Mark Schlereth RC	.08	.04
❑ 29	Melvin Jenkins	.08	.04
❑ 30	Michael Haynes	.15	.07
❑ 31	Greg Lewis	.08	.04
❑ 32	Kenneth Davis	.08	.04
❑ 33	Derrick Thomas	.30	.14
❑ 34	David Williams	.08	.04
❑ 35	Neal Anderson	.08	.04
❑ 36	Andre Collins	.08	.04
❑ 37	Jesse Solomon	.08	.04
❑ 38	Barry Sanders	3.00	1.35
❑ 39	Jeff Gossett	.08	.04
❑ 40	Rickey Jackson	.08	.04
❑ 41	Ray Berry	.08	.04
❑ 42	Leroy Hoard	.15	.07
❑ 43	Eric Thomas	.08	.04
❑ 44	Brian Washington	.08	.04
❑ 45	Pat Terrell	.08	.04
❑ 46	Eugene Robinson	.08	.04
❑ 47	Luis Sharpe	.08	.04
❑ 48	Jerome Brown	.08	.04
❑ 49	Mark Collins	.08	.04
❑ 50	Johnny Holland	.08	.04
❑ 51	Tony Paige	.08	.04
❑ 52	Willie Green	.08	.04
❑ 53	Steve Atwater	.08	.04
❑ 54	Brad Muster	.08	.04
❑ 55	Cris Dishman	.08	.04
❑ 56	Eddie Anderson	.08	.04
❑ 57	Sam Mills	.08	.04
❑ 58	Donald Evans	.08	.04
❑ 59	Jon Vaughn	.08	.04
❑ 60	Marion Butts	.08	.04
❑ 61	Rodney Holman	.08	.04
❑ 62	Dwayne White RC	.08	.04
❑ 63	Martin Mayhew	.08	.04
❑ 64	Jonathan Hayes	.08	.04
❑ 65	Andre Rison	.15	.07
❑ 66	Calvin Williams	.15	.07
❑ 67	James Washington	.08	.04
❑ 68	Tim Harris	.08	.04
❑ 69	Jim Ritcher	.08	.04
❑ 70	Johnny Johnson	.08	.04
❑ 71	John Offerdahl	.08	.04
❑ 72	Herschel Walker	.15	.07
❑ 73	Perry Kemp	.08	.04
❑ 74	Erik Howard	.08	.04
❑ 75	Lamar Lathon	.08	.04
❑ 76	Greg Kragen	.08	.04
❑ 77	Jay Schroeder	.08	.04
❑ 78	Jim Arnold	.08	.04
❑ 79	Chris Miller	.15	.07
❑ 80	Deron Cherry	.08	.04
❑ 81	Jim Harbaugh	.30	.14
❑ 82	Gill Fenerty	.08	.04
❑ 83	Fred Stokes	.08	.04
❑ 84	Roman Phifer	.08	.04
❑ 85	Clyde Simmons	.08	.04
❑ 86	Vince Newsome	.08	.04
❑ 87	Lawrence Dawsey	.15	.07
❑ 88	Eddie Brown	.08	.04
❑ 89	Greg Montgomery	.08	.04
❑ 90	Jeff Lageman	.08	.04
❑ 91	Terry Wooden	.08	.04
❑ 92	Nate Newton	.15	.07
❑ 93	David Richards	.08	.04
❑ 94	Derek Russell	.08	.04
❑ 95	Steve Jordan	.08	.04
❑ 96	Hugh Millen	.08	.04
❑ 97	Mark Duper	.08	.04
❑ 98	Sean Landeta	.08	.04
❑ 99	James Thornton	.08	.04
❑ 100	Darrell Green	.08	.04
❑ 101	Harris Barton	.08	.04
❑ 102	John Alt	.08	.04
❑ 103	Mike Farr	.08	.04
❑ 104	Bob Golic	.08	.04
❑ 105	Gene Atkins	.08	.04
❑ 106	Gary Anderson K	.08	.04
❑ 107	Norm Johnson	.08	.04
❑ 108	Eugene Daniel	.08	.04
❑ 109	Kent Hull	.08	.04
❑ 110	John Elway	2.50	1.10
❑ 111	Rich Camarillo	.08	.04
❑ 112	Charles Wilson	.08	.04
❑ 113	Matt Bahr	.08	.04
❑ 114	Mark Carrier WR	.15	.07
❑ 115	Richmond Webb	.08	.04
❑ 116	Charles Mann	.08	.04
❑ 117	Tim McGee	.08	.04
❑ 118	Wes Hopkins	.08	.04
❑ 119	Mo Lewis	.08	.04
❑ 120	Warren Moon	.30	.14
❑ 121	Damone Johnson	.08	.04
❑ 122	Kevin Gogan	.08	.04
❑ 123	Joey Browner	.08	.04
❑ 124	Tommy Kane	.08	.04
❑ 125	Vincent Brown	.08	.04
❑ 126	Barry Word	.08	.04
❑ 127	Michael Brooks	.08	.04
❑ 128	Jumbo Elliott	.08	.04
❑ 129	Marcus Allen	.30	.14
❑ 130	Tom Waddle	.08	.04
❑ 131	Jim Dombrowski	.08	.04
❑ 132	Aeneas Williams	.15	.07
❑ 133	Clay Matthews	.15	.07
❑ 134	Thurman Thomas	.30	.14
❑ 135	Dean Biasucci	.08	.04
❑ 136	Moe Gardner	.08	.04
❑ 137	James Campen	.08	.04
❑ 138	Tim Johnson	.08	.04
❑ 139	Erik Kramer	.15	.07
❑ 140	Keith McCants	.08	.04
❑ 141	John Carney	.08	.04
❑ 142	Tunch Ilkin	.08	.04
❑ 143	Louis Oliver	.08	.04
❑ 144	Bill Maas	.08	.04
❑ 145	Wendell Davis	.08	.04
❑ 146	Pepper Johnson	.08	.04
❑ 147	Howie Long	.15	.07
❑ 148	Brett Maxie	.08	.04
❑ 149	Tony Casillas	.08	.04
❑ 150	Michael Carter	.08	.04
❑ 151	Byron Evans	.08	.04
❑ 152	Lorenzo White	.08	.04
❑ 153	Larry Kelm	.08	.04
❑ 154	Andy Heck	.08	.04
❑ 155	Harry Newsome	.08	.04
❑ 156	Chris Singleton	.08	.04
❑ 157	Mike Kenn	.08	.04
❑ 158	Jeff Faulkner	.08	.04
❑ 159	Ken Lanier	.08	.04
❑ 160	Darryl Talley	.08	.04
❑ 161	Louie Aguiar RC	.08	.04
❑ 162	Danny Copeland	.08	.04
❑ 163	Kevin Porter	.08	.04
❑ 164	Trace Armstrong	.08	.04
❑ 165	Dermontti Dawson	.08	.04
❑ 166	Fred McAfee RC	.08	.04
❑ 167	Ronnie Lott	.15	.07
❑ 168	Tony Mandarich	.08	.04
❑ 169	Howard Cross	.08	.04
❑ 170	Vestee Jackson	.08	.04
❑ 171	Jeff Herrod	.08	.04
❑ 172	Randy Hilliard RC	.08	.04
❑ 173	Robert Wilson	.08	.04
❑ 174	Joe Walter RC	.08	.04
❑ 175	Chris Spielman	.15	.07
❑ 176	Darryl Henley	.08	.04
❑ 177	Jay Hilgenberg	.08	.04
❑ 178	John Kidd	.08	.04
❑ 179	Doug Widell	.08	.04
❑ 180	Seth Joyner	.15	.07
❑ 181	Nick Bell	.08	.04
❑ 182	Don Griffin	.08	.04
❑ 183	Johnny Meads	.08	.04
❑ 184	Jeff Bostic	.08	.04
❑ 185	Johnny Hector	.08	.04
❑ 186	Jessie Tuggle	.08	.04
❑ 187	Robb Thomas	.08	.04
❑ 188	Shane Conlan	.08	.04
❑ 189	Michael Zordich RC	.08	.04
❑ 190	Emmitt Smith	3.00	1.35
❑ 191	Robert Blackmon	.08	.04
❑ 192	Carl Lee	.08	.04
❑ 193	Harry Galbreath	.08	.04
❑ 194	Ed King	.08	.04
❑ 195	Stan Thomas	.08	.04
❑ 196	Andre Waters	.08	.04
❑ 197	Pat Harlow	.08	.04
❑ 198	Zefross Moss	.08	.04
❑ 199	Bobby Hebert	.08	.04
❑ 200	Doug Riesenberg	.08	.04
❑ 201	Mike Croel	.08	.04
❑ 202	Jeff Jaeger	.08	.04
❑ 203	Gary Plummer	.08	.04
❑ 204	Chris Jacke	.08	.04
❑ 205	Neil O'Donnell	.30	.14
❑ 206	Mark Bortz	.08	.04
❑ 207	Tim Barnett	.08	.04
❑ 208	Jerry Ball	.08	.04
❑ 209	Chip Lohmiller	.08	.04
❑ 210	Jim Everett	.15	.07
❑ 211	Tim McKyer	.08	.04
❑ 212	Aaron Craver	.08	.04
❑ 213	John L. Williams	.08	.04
❑ 214	Simon Fletcher	.08	.04
❑ 215	Walter Reeves	.08	.04
❑ 216	Terance Mathis	.15	.07
❑ 217	Mike Pitts	.08	.04
❑ 218	Bruce Matthews	.08	.04
❑ 219	Howard Ballard	.08	.04
❑ 220	Leonard Russell	.15	.07
❑ 221	Michael Stewart	.08	.04
❑ 222	Mike Merriweather	.08	.04
❑ 223	Ricky Sanders	.08	.04
❑ 224	Ray Horton	.08	.04
❑ 225	Michael Jackson	.15	.07
❑ 226	Bill Romanowski	.08	.04
❑ 227	Steve McMichael UER (His wife is former Mrs. Illinois, not Miss Illinois)	.15	.07

❑ 228 Chris Martin .08 .04
❑ 229 Tim Green .08 .04
❑ 230 Karl Mecklenburg .08 .04
❑ 231 Felix Wright .08 .04
❑ 232 Charles McRae .08 .04
❑ 233 Pete Stoyanovich .08 .04
❑ 234 Stephen Baker .08 .04
❑ 235 Herman Moore 1.00 .45
❑ 236 Terry McDaniel .08 .04
❑ 237 Dalton Hilliard .08 .04
❑ 238 Gill Byrd .08 .04
❑ 239 Leon Seals .08 .04
❑ 240 Rod Woodson .30 .14
❑ 241 Curtis Duncan .08 .04
❑ 242 Keith Jackson .15 .07
❑ 243 Mark Stepnoski .15 .07
❑ 244 Art Monk .15 .07
❑ 245 Matt Stover .08 .04
❑ 246 John Roper .08 .04
❑ 247 Rodney Hampton .30 .14
❑ 248 Steve Wisniewski .08 .04
❑ 249 Bryan Millard .08 .04
❑ 250 Todd Lyght .08 .04
❑ 251 Marvin Washington .08 .04
❑ 252 Eric Swann .15 .07
❑ 253 Bruce Kozerski .08 .04
❑ 254 Jon Hand .08 .04
❑ 255 Scott Fulhage .08 .04
❑ 256 Chuck Cecil .08 .04
❑ 257 Eric Martin .08 .04
❑ 258 Eric Metcalf .15 .07
❑ 259 T.J. Turner .08 .04
❑ 260 Kirk Lowdermilk .08 .04
❑ 261 Keith McKeller .08 .04
❑ 262 Wymon Henderson .08 .04
❑ 263 David Alexander .08 .04
❑ 264 George Jamison .08 .04
❑ 265 Ken Norton Jr. .30 .14
❑ 266 Jim Lachey .08 .04
❑ 267 Bo Orlando RC .08 .04
❑ 268 Nick Lowery .08 .04
❑ 269 Keith Van Horne .08 .04
❑ 270 Dwight Stone .08 .04
❑ 271 Keith DeLong .08 .04
❑ 272 James Francis .08 .04
❑ 273 Greg McMurtry .08 .04
❑ 274 Ethan Horton .08 .04
❑ 275 Stan Brock .08 .04
❑ 276 Ken Harvey .08 .04
❑ 277 Ronnie Harmon .08 .04
❑ 278 Mike Pritchard .15 .07
❑ 279 Kyle Clifton .08 .04
❑ 280 Anthony Johnson .15 .07
❑ 281 Esera Tuaolo .08 .04
❑ 282 Vernon Turner .08 .04
❑ 283 David Griggs .08 .04
❑ 284 Dino Hackett .08 .04
❑ 285 Carwell Gardner .08 .04
❑ 286 Ron Hall .08 .04
❑ 287 Reggie White .30 .14
❑ 288 Checklist 1-100 .08 .04
❑ 289 Checklist 101-200 .08 .04
❑ 290 Checklist 201-300 .08 .04
❑ 291 Mark Clayton MC .08 .04
❑ 292 Pat Swilling MC .08 .04
❑ 293 Ernest Givins MC .08 .04
❑ 294 Broderick Thomas MC .08 .04
❑ 295 John Friesz MC .08 .04
❑ 296 Cornelius Bennett MC .08 .04
❑ 297 Anthony Carter MC .15 .07
❑ 298 Earnest Byner MC .08 .04
❑ 299 Michael Irvin MC .30 .14
❑ 300 Cortez Kennedy MC .08 .04
❑ 301 Barry Sanders MC 1.50 .70
❑ 302 Mike Croel MC .08 .04
❑ 303 Emmitt Smith MC 2.00 .90
❑ 304 Leonard Russell MC .08 .04
❑ 305 Neal Anderson MC .08 .04
❑ 306 Derrick Thomas MC .15 .07
❑ 307 Mark Rypien MC .08 .04
❑ 308 Reggie White MC .15 .07
❑ 309 Rod Woodson MC .15 .07
❑ 310 Rodney Hampton MC .15 .07
❑ 311 Carnell Lake .08 .04
❑ 312 Robert Delpino .08 .04
❑ 313 Brian Blades .15 .07
❑ 314 Marc Spindler .08 .04
❑ 315 Scott Norwood .08 .04
❑ 316 Frank Warren .08 .04
❑ 317 David Treadwell .08 .04
❑ 318 Steve Broussard .08 .04
❑ 319 Lorenzo Lynch .08 .04
❑ 320 Ray Agnew .08 .04
❑ 321 Derrick Walker .08 .04
❑ 322 Vinson Smith RC .08 .04
❑ 323 Gary Clark .30 .14
❑ 324 Charles Haley .15 .07
❑ 325 Keith Byars .08 .04
❑ 326 Winston Moss .08 .04
❑ 327 Paul McJulien RC UER .08 .04
(Has Brett Perriman card back; see also 453)
❑ 328 Tony Covington .08 .04
❑ 329 Mark Carrier DB .08 .04
❑ 330 Mark Tuinei .08 .04
❑ 331 Tracy Simien RC .08 .04
❑ 332 Jeff Wright .08 .04
❑ 333 Bryan Cox .15 .07
❑ 334 Lonnie Young .08 .04
❑ 335 Clarence Verdin .08 .04
❑ 336 Dan Fike .08 .04
❑ 337 Steve Sewell .08 .04
❑ 338 Gary Zimmerman .08 .04
❑ 339 Barney Bussey .08 .04
❑ 340 William Perry .15 .07
❑ 341 Jeff Hostetler .15 .07
❑ 342 Doug Smith .08 .04
❑ 343 Cleveland Gary .08 .04
❑ 344 Todd Marinovich .08 .04
❑ 345 Rich Moran .08 .04
❑ 346 Tony Woods .08 .04
❑ 347 Vaughan Johnson .08 .04
❑ 348 Marv Cook .08 .04
❑ 349 Pierce Holt .08 .04
❑ 350 Gerald Williams .08 .04
❑ 351 Kevin Butler .08 .04
❑ 352 William White .08 .04
❑ 353 Henry Rolling .08 .04
❑ 354 James Joseph .08 .04
❑ 355 Vinny Testaverde .15 .07
❑ 356 Scott Radecic .08 .04
❑ 357 Lee Johnson .08 .04
❑ 358 Steve Tasker .15 .07
❑ 359 David Lutz .08 .04
❑ 360 Audray McMillian UER .08 .04
(Name on back misspelled Audrey)
❑ 361 Brad Baxter .08 .04
❑ 362 Mark Dennis .08 .04
❑ 363 Erric Pegram .15 .07
❑ 364 Sean Jones .15 .07
❑ 365 William Roberts .08 .04
❑ 366 Steve Young 1.00 .45
❑ 367 Joe Jacoby .08 .04
❑ 368 Richard Brown RC .08 .04
❑ 369 Keith Kartz .08 .04
❑ 370 Freddie Joe Nunn .08 .04
❑ 371 Darren Comeaux .08 .04
❑ 372 Larry Brown DB .08 .04
❑ 373 Haywood Jeffires .15 .07
❑ 374 Tom Newberry .08 .04
❑ 375 Steve Bono RC .30 .14
❑ 376 Kevin Ross .08 .04
❑ 377 Kelvin Pritchett .08 .04
❑ 378 Jessie Hester .08 .04
❑ 379 Mitchell Price .08 .04
❑ 380 Barry Foster .15 .07
❑ 381 Reyna Thompson .08 .04
❑ 382 Cris Carter .75 .35
❑ 383 Lemuel Stinson .08 .04
❑ 384 Rod Bernstine .08 .04
❑ 385 James Lofton .15 .07
❑ 386 Kevin Murphy .08 .04
❑ 387 Greg Townsend .08 .04
❑ 388 Edgar Bennett RC .40 .18
❑ 389 Rob Moore .15 .07
❑ 390 Eugene Lockhart .08 .04
❑ 391 Bern Brostek .08 .04
❑ 392 Craig Heyward .15 .07
❑ 393 Ferrell Edmunds .08 .04
❑ 394 John Kasay .08 .04
❑ 395 Jesse Sapolu .08 .04
❑ 396 Jim Breech .08 .04
❑ 397 Neil Smith .30 .14
❑ 398 Bryce Paup .30 .14
❑ 399 Tony Tolbert .08 .04
❑ 400 Bubby Brister .08 .04
❑ 401 Dennis Smith .08 .04
❑ 402 Dan Owens .08 .04
❑ 403 Steve Beuerlein .08 .04
❑ 404 Rick Tuten .08 .04
❑ 405 Eric Allen .08 .04
❑ 406 Eric Hill .08 .04
❑ 407 Don Warren .08 .04
❑ 408 Greg Jackson .08 .04
❑ 409 Chris Doleman .08 .04
❑ 410 Anthony Munoz .15 .07
❑ 411 Michael Young .08 .04
❑ 412 Cornelius Bennett .15 .07
❑ 413 Ray Childress .08 .04
❑ 414 Kevin Call .08 .04
❑ 415 Burt Grossman .08 .04
❑ 416 Scott Miller .08 .04
❑ 417 Tim Newton .08 .04
❑ 418 Robert Young .08 .04
❑ 419 Tommy Vardell RC .15 .07
❑ 420 Michael Walter .08 .04
❑ 421 Chris Port RC .08 .04
❑ 422 Carlton Haselrig RC .08 .04
❑ 423 Rodney Peete .15 .07
❑ 424 Scott Stephen .08 .04
❑ 425 Chris Warren .30 .14
❑ 426 Scott Galbraith RC .08 .04
❑ 427 Fuad Reveiz UER .08 .04
(Born in Colombia, not Columbia)
❑ 428 Irv Eatman .08 .04
❑ 429 David Szott .08 .04
❑ 430 Brent Williams .08 .04
❑ 431 Mike Horan .08 .04
❑ 432 Brent Jones .15 .07
❑ 433 Paul Gruber .08 .04
❑ 434 Carlos Huerta .08 .04
❑ 435 Scott Case .08 .04
❑ 436 Greg Davis .08 .04
❑ 437 Ken Clarke .08 .04
❑ 438 Alfred Williams .08 .04
❑ 439 Jim C. Jensen .08 .04
❑ 440 Louis Lipps .08 .04
❑ 441 Larry Roberts .08 .04
❑ 442 James Jones .08 .04
❑ 443 Don Mosebar .08 .04
❑ 444 Quinn Early .15 .07
❑ 445 Robert Brown .08 .04
❑ 446 Tom Thayer .08 .04
❑ 447 Michael Irvin .30 .14
❑ 448 Jarrod Bunch .08 .04
❑ 449 Riki Ellison .08 .04
❑ 450 Joe Phillips .08 .04
❑ 451 Ernest Givins .15 .07
❑ 452 Glenn Parker .08 .04
❑ 453 Brett Perriman UER .30 .14
(Has Paul McJulien card back; see also 327)
❑ 454 Jayice Pearson RC .08 .04
❑ 455 Mark Jackson .08 .04
❑ 456 Siran Stacy RC .08 .04
❑ 457 Rufus Porter .08 .04
❑ 458 Michael Ball .08 .04
❑ 459 Craig Taylor .08 .04
❑ 460 George Thomas RC .08 .04
❑ 461 Alvin Wright .08 .04
❑ 462 Ron Hallstrom .08 .04
❑ 463 Mike Mooney RC .08 .04
❑ 464 Dexter Carter .08 .04
❑ 465 Marty Carter RC .08 .04
❑ 466 Pat Swilling .15 .07
❑ 467 Mike Golic .08 .04
❑ 468 Reggie Roby .08 .04
❑ 469 Randall McDaniel .08 .04
❑ 470 John Stephens .08 .04
❑ 471 Ricardo McDonald RC .08 .04
❑ 472 Wilber Marshall .08 .04
❑ 473 Jim Sweeney .08 .04
❑ 474 Ernie Jones .08 .04
❑ 475 Bennie Blades .08 .04
❑ 476 Don Beebe .08 .04
❑ 477 Grant Feasel .08 .04

❑ 478 Ernie Mills .08 .04
❑ 479 Tony Jones .08 .04
❑ 480 Jeff Uhlenhake .08 .04
❑ 481 Gaston Green .08 .04
❑ 482 John Taylor .15 .07
❑ 483 Anthony Smith .08 .04
❑ 484 Tony Bennett .08 .04
❑ 485 David Brandon RC .08 .04
❑ 486 Shawn Jefferson .08 .04
❑ 487 Christian Okoye .08 .04
❑ 488 Leonard Marshall .08 .04
❑ 489 Jay Novacek .15 .07
❑ 490 Harold Green .08 .04
❑ 491 Bubba McDowell .08 .04
❑ 492 Gary Anderson RB .08 .04
❑ 493 Terrell Buckley RC .08 .04
❑ 494 Jamie Dukes RC .08 .04
❑ 495 Morten Andersen .08 .04
❑ 496 Henry Thomas .08 .04
❑ 497 Bill Lewis .08 .04
❑ 498 Jeff Cross .08 .04
❑ 499 Hardy Nickerson .15 .07
❑ 500 Henry Ellard .15 .07
❑ 501 Joe Bowden RC .08 .04
❑ 502 Brian Noble .08 .04
❑ 503 Mike Cofer .08 .04
❑ 504 Jeff Bryant .08 .04
❑ 505 Lomas Brown .08 .04
❑ 506 Chip Banks .08 .04
❑ 507 Keith Traylor .08 .04
❑ 508 Mark Kelso .08 .04
❑ 509 Dexter McNabb RC .08 .04
❑ 510 Gene Chilton RC .08 .04
❑ 511 George Thornton .08 .04
❑ 512 Jeff Criswell .08 .04
❑ 513 Brad Edwards .08 .04
❑ 514 Ron Heller .08 .04
❑ 515 Tim Brown .30 .14
❑ 516 Keith Hamilton RC .08 .04
❑ 517 Mark Higgs .08 .04
❑ 518 Tommy Barnhardt .08 .04
❑ 519 Brian Jordan .15 .07
❑ 520 Ray Crockett .08 .04
❑ 521 Karl Wilson .08 .04
❑ 522 Ricky Reynolds .08 .04
❑ 523 Max Montoya .08 .04
❑ 524 David Little .08 .04
❑ 525 Alonzo Mitz RC .08 .04
❑ 526 Darryll Lewis .08 .04
❑ 527 Keith Henderson .08 .04
❑ 528 LeRoy Butler .08 .04
❑ 529 Rob Burnett .08 .04
❑ 530 Chris Chandler .30 .14
❑ 531 Maury Buford .08 .04
❑ 532 Mark Ingram .08 .04
❑ 533 Mike Saxon .08 .04
❑ 534 Bill Fralic .08 .04
❑ 535 Craig Patterson RC .08 .04
❑ 536 John Randle .15 .07
❑ 537 Dwayne Harper .08 .04
❑ 538 Chris Hakel RC .08 .04
❑ 539 Maurice Hurst .08 .04
❑ 540 Warren Powers UER .08 .04
(Front has photo
of Ron Holmes)
❑ 541 Will Wolford .08 .04
❑ 542 Dennis Gibson .08 .04
❑ 543 Jackie Slater .08 .04
❑ 544 Floyd Turner .08 .04
❑ 545 Guy McIntyre .08 .04
❑ 546 Eric Green .08 .04
❑ 547 Rohn Stark .08 .04
❑ 548 William Fuller .15 .07
❑ 549 Alvin Harper .15 .07
❑ 550 Mark Clayton .15 .07
❑ 551 Natu Tuatagaloa RC .08 .04
❑ 552 Fred Barnett .30 .14
❑ 553 Bob Whitfield RC .08 .04
❑ 554 Courtney Hall .08 .04
❑ 555 Brian Mitchell .15 .07
❑ 556 Patrick Hunter .08 .04
❑ 557 Rick Bryan .08 .04
❑ 558 Anthony Carter .15 .07
❑ 559 Jim Wahler .08 .04
❑ 560 Joe Morris .08 .04
❑ 561 Tony Zendejas .08 .04
❑ 562 Mervyn Fernandez .08 .04
❑ 563 Jamie Williams .08 .04
❑ 564 Darrell Thompson .08 .04
❑ 565 Adrian Cooper .08 .04
❑ 566 Chris Goode .08 .04
❑ 567 Jeff Davidson RC .08 .04
❑ 568 James Hasty .08 .04
❑ 569 Chris Mims RC .15 .07
❑ 570 Ray Seals RC .08 .04
❑ 571 Myron Guyton .08 .04
❑ 572 Todd McNair .08 .04
❑ 573 Andre Tippett .08 .04
❑ 574 Kirby Jackson .08 .04
❑ 575 Mel Gray .15 .07
❑ 576 Stephone Paige .08 .04
❑ 577 Scott Davis .08 .04
❑ 578 John Gesek .08 .04
❑ 579 Earnest Byner .08 .04
❑ 580 John Friesz .15 .07
❑ 581 Al Smith .08 .04
❑ 582 Flipper Anderson .08 .04
❑ 583 Amp Lee RC .08 .04
❑ 584 Greg Lloyd .30 .14
❑ 585 Cortez Kennedy .15 .07
❑ 586 Keith Sims .08 .04
❑ 587 Terry Allen .30 .14
❑ 588 David Fulcher .08 .04
❑ 589 Chris Hinton .08 .04
❑ 590 Tim McDonald .08 .04
❑ 591 Bruce Armstrong .08 .04
❑ 592 Sterling Sharpe .30 .14
❑ 593 Tom Rathman .08 .04
❑ 594 Bill Brooks .08 .04
❑ 595 Broderick Thomas .08 .04
❑ 596 Jim Wilks .08 .04
❑ 597 Tyrone Braxton UER .08 .04
(Bio for Melvin Braxton)
❑ 598 Checklist 301-400 UER .08 .04
(Audray McMillian is
misspelled Audrey)
❑ 599 Checklist 401-500 .08 .04
❑ 600 Checklist 501-600 .08 .04
❑ 601 Andre Reed MC .75 .35
❑ 602 Troy Aikman MC 4.00 1.80
❑ 603 Dan Marino MC 6.00 2.70
❑ 604 Randall Cunningham MC .75 .35
❑ 605 Jim Kelly MC 1.50 .70
❑ 606 Deion Sanders MC 2.00 .90
❑ 607 Junior Seau MC 1.50 .70
❑ 608 Jerry Rice MC 4.00 1.80
❑ 609 Bruce Smith MC .75 .35
❑ 610 Lawrence Taylor MC 1.50 .70
❑ 611 Todd Collins RC .50 .23
❑ 612 Ty Detmer 1.50 .70
❑ 613 Browning Nagle .50 .23
❑ 614 Tony Sacca RC UER .50 .23
(Reverse negative
photo on back)
❑ 615 Boomer Esiason .75 .35
❑ 616 Billy Joe Tolliver .50 .23
❑ 617 Leslie O'Neal .75 .35
❑ 618 Mark Wheeler RC .50 .23
❑ 619 Eric Dickerson .75 .35
❑ 620 Phil Simms .75 .35
❑ 621 Troy Vincent RC .75 .35
❑ 622 Jason Hanson RC .75 .35
❑ 623 Andre Reed .75 .35
❑ 624 Russell Maryland .75 .35
❑ 625 Steve Emtman RC .50 .23
❑ 626 Sean Gilbert RC 1.50 .70
❑ 627 Dana Hall RC .75 .35
❑ 628 Dan McGwire .50 .23
❑ 629 Lewis Billups .50 .23
❑ 630 Darryl Williams RC .50 .23
❑ 631 Dwayne Sabb RC .50 .23
❑ 632 Mark Royals .50 .23
❑ 633 Cary Conklin .50 .23
❑ 634 Al Toon .75 .35
❑ 635 Junior Seau 1.50 .70
❑ 636 Greg Skrepenak RC UER .50 .23
(Card misnumbered 686)
❑ 637 Deion Sanders 3.00 1.35
❑ 638 Steve DeOssie .50 .23
❑ 639 Randall Cunningham 1.50 .70
❑ 640 Jim Kelly 1.50 .70
❑ 641 Michael Brandon RC .50 .23
❑ 642 Clayton Holmes RC .50 .23
❑ 643 Webster Slaughter .50 .23
❑ 644 Ricky Proehl .50 .23
❑ 645 Jerry Rice 5.00 2.20
❑ 646 Carl Banks .50 .23
❑ 647 J.J.Birden .50 .23
❑ 648 Tracy Scroggins RC .50 .23
❑ 649 Alonzo Spellman RC .75 .35
❑ 650 Joe Montana 8.00 3.60
❑ 651 Courtney Hawkins RC .75 .35
❑ 652 Corey Widmer RC .50 .23
❑ 653 Robert Brooks RC 6.00 2.70
❑ 654 Darren Woodson RC 1.50 .70
❑ 655 Derrick Fenner .50 .23
❑ 656 Steve Christie .50 .23
❑ 657 Chester McGlockton RC 1.50 .70
❑ 658 Steve Israel RC .50 .23
❑ 659 Robert Harris RC .50 .23
❑ 660 Dan Marino 8.00 3.60
❑ 661 Ed McCaffrey 5.00 2.20
❑ 662 Johnny Mitchell RC .50 .23
❑ 663 Timm Rosenbach .50 .23
❑ 664 Anthony Miller .75 .35
❑ 665 Merril Hoge .50 .23
❑ 666 Eugene Chung RC .50 .23
❑ 667 Rueben Mayes .50 .23
❑ 668 Martin Bayless .50 .23
❑ 669 Ashley Ambrose RC .75 .35
❑ 670 Michael Cofer UER .50 .23
(Back shows card for
Mike Cofer, the kicker)
❑ 671 Shane Dronett RC .50 .23
❑ 672 Bernie Kosar .75 .35
❑ 673 Mike Singletary .75 .35
❑ 674 Mike Lodish RC .50 .23
❑ 675 Phillippi Sparks RC .50 .23
❑ 676 Joel Steed RC .50 .23
❑ 677 Kevin Fagan .50 .23
❑ 678 Randal Hill .50 .23
❑ 679 Ken O'Brien .50 .23
❑ 680 Lawrence Taylor 1.50 .70
❑ 681 Harvey Williams 1.50 .70
❑ 682 Quentin Coryatt RC 1.50 .70
❑ 683 Brett Favre 100.00 45.00
❑ 684 Robert Jones RC .50 .23
❑ 685 Michael Dean Perry .75 .35
❑ 686 Bruce Smith 1.50 .70
❑ 687 Troy Auzenne RC .50 .23
❑ 688 Thomas McLemore RC .50 .23
❑ 689 Dale Carter RC 1.50 .70
❑ 690 Marc Boutte RC .50 .23
❑ 691 Jeff George 1.50 .70
❑ 692 Dion Lambert RC UER .50 .23
(Birthdate is 2/12/19; should
be 2/12/69)
❑ 693 Vaughn Dunbar RC .50 .23
❑ 694 Derek Brown TE RC .50 .23
❑ 695 Troy Aikman 5.00 2.20
❑ 696 John Fina RC .50 .23
❑ 697 Kevin Smith RC 1.50 .70
❑ 698 Corey Miller RC .50 .23
❑ 699 Lance Olberding RC .50 .23
❑ 700 Checklist 601-700 UER .50 .23
(Numbering sequence
off from 616 to 636)
❑ P1 Promo Sheet blue 10.00 4.50
National July 10-12, 1992
Barry Sanders
Gene Atkins
Louis Oliver
Paul Gruber
Emmitt Smith
Steve Jordan
Warren Moon
Seth Joyner
Ronnie Lott
❑ P2 Promo Sheet red 12.00 5.50
National July 9, 1992
Barry Sanders
Gene Atkins
Louis Oliver
Paul Gruber
Emmitt Smith
Steve Jordan
Warren Moon
Seth Joyner
Ronnie Lott

1993 Stadium Club

	MINT	NRMT
COMPLETE SET (550)	50.00	22.00
COMP.SERIES 1 (250)	25.00	11.00
COMP.SERIES 2 (250)	18.00	8.00
COMP.HIGH SERIES (50)	8.00	3.60
COMP.HIGH FACT.SET (51)	12.00	5.50
COMMON CARD (1-550)	.10	.05
SEMISTARS	.20	.09
UNLISTED STARS	.40	.18
COMP.FIRST DAY (550)	1200.00	550.00
COMP.FIRST DAY SER.1	600.00	275.00
COMP.FIRST DAY SER.2	400.00	180.00
COMP.FIRST DAY HI SER.	250.00	110.00

*FIRST DAY STARS: 6X to 15X HI COL.
*FIRST DAY RCs: 3X to 8X HI COL.
SERIES 1/2 RANDOM INSERTS IN PACKS
HIGH SERIES: ONE PER FACTORY SET

❑ 1 Sterling Sharpe	.20	.09
❑ 2 Chris Burkett	.10	.05
❑ 3 Santana Dotson	.20	.09
❑ 4 Michael Jackson	.20	.09
❑ 5 Neal Anderson	.10	.05
❑ 6 Bryan Cox	.10	.05
❑ 7 Dennis Gibson	.10	.05
❑ 8 Jeff Graham	.20	.09
❑ 9 Roger Ruzek	.10	.05
❑ 10 Duane Bickett	.10	.05
❑ 11 Charles Mann	.10	.05
❑ 12 Tommy Maddox	.10	.05
❑ 13 Vaughn Dunbar	.10	.05
❑ 14 Gary Plummer	.10	.05
❑ 15 Chris Miller	.20	.09
❑ 16 Chris Warren	.20	.09
❑ 17 Alvin Harper	.20	.09
❑ 18 Eric Dickerson	.20	.09
❑ 19 Mike Jones	.10	.05
❑ 20 Ernest Givins	.20	.09
❑ 21 Natrone Means RC	2.00	.90
❑ 22 Doug Riesenberg	.10	.05
❑ 23 Barry Word	.10	.05
❑ 24 Sean Salisbury	.10	.05
❑ 25 Derrick Fenner	.10	.05
❑ 26 David Howard	.10	.05
❑ 27 Mark Kelso	.10	.05
❑ 28 Todd Lyght	.10	.05
❑ 29 Dana Hall	.10	.05
❑ 30 Eric Metcalf	.20	.09
❑ 31 Jason Hanson	.10	.05
❑ 32 Dwight Stone	.10	.05
❑ 33 Johnny Mitchell	.10	.05
❑ 34 Reggie Roby	.10	.05
❑ 35 Terrell Buckley	.10	.05
❑ 36 Steve McMichael	.20	.09
❑ 37 Marty Carter	.10	.05
❑ 38 Seth Joyner	.10	.05
❑ 39 Rohn Stark	.10	.05
❑ 40 Eric Curry RC	.10	.05
❑ 41 Tommy Barnhardt	.10	.05
❑ 42 Karl Mecklenburg	.10	.05
❑ 43 Darion Conner	.10	.05
❑ 44 Ronnie Harmon	.10	.05
❑ 45 Cortez Kennedy	.20	.09
❑ 46 Tim Brown	.40	.18
❑ 47 Bill Lewis	.10	.05
❑ 48 Randall McDaniel	.10	.05
❑ 49 Curtis Duncan	.10	.05
❑ 50 Troy Aikman	1.50	.70
❑ 51 David Klingler	.10	.05
❑ 52 Brent Jones	.20	.09
❑ 53 Dave Krieg	.20	.09
❑ 54 Bruce Smith	.40	.18
❑ 55 Vincent Brown	.10	.05
❑ 56 O.J. McDuffie RC	2.00	.90
❑ 57 Cleveland Gary	.10	.05
❑ 58 Larry Centers RC	.40	.18
❑ 59 Pepper Johnson	.10	.05
❑ 60 Dan Marino	3.00	1.35
❑ 61 Robert Porcher	.10	.05
❑ 62 Jim Harbaugh	.40	.18
❑ 63 Sam Mills	.10	.05
❑ 64 Gary Anderson RB	.10	.05
❑ 65 Neil O'Donnell	.20	.09
❑ 66 Keith Byars	.10	.05
❑ 67 Jeff Herrod	.10	.05
❑ 68 Marion Butts	.10	.05
❑ 69 Terry McDaniel	.10	.05
❑ 70 John Elway	3.00	1.35
❑ 71 Steve Broussard	.10	.05
❑ 72 Kelvin Martin	.10	.05
❑ 73 Tom Carter RC	.20	.09
❑ 74 Bryce Paup	.40	.18
❑ 75 Jim Kelly UER back shows 1992 Topps card as RC	.20	.09
❑ 76 Bill Romanowski	.10	.05
❑ 77 Andre Collins	.10	.05
❑ 78 Mike Farr	.10	.05
❑ 79 Henry Ellard	.20	.09
❑ 80 Dale Carter	.10	.05
❑ 81 Johnny Bailey	.10	.05
❑ 82 Garrison Hearst RC	2.50	1.10
❑ 83 Brent Williams	.10	.05
❑ 84 Ricardo McDonald	.10	.05
❑ 85 Emmitt Smith	3.00	1.35
❑ 86 Vai Sikahema	.10	.05
❑ 87 Jackie Harris	.10	.05
❑ 88 Alonzo Spellman	.10	.05
❑ 89 Mark Wheeler	.10	.05
❑ 90 Dalton Hilliard	.10	.05
❑ 91 Mark Higgs	.10	.05
❑ 92 Aaron Wallace	.10	.05
❑ 93 Earnest Byner	.10	.05
❑ 94 Stanley Richard	.10	.05
❑ 95 Cris Carter	.75	.35
❑ 96 Bobby Houston RC	.10	.05
❑ 97 Craig Heyward	.20	.09
❑ 98 Bernie Kosar	.20	.09
❑ 99 Mike Croel	.10	.05
❑ 100 Deion Sanders	1.00	.45
❑ 101 Warren Moon	.20	.09
❑ 102 Christian Okoye	.10	.05
❑ 103 Ricky Watters	.40	.18
❑ 104 Eric Swann	.20	.09
❑ 105 Rodney Hampton	.20	.09
❑ 106 Daryl Johnston	.20	.09
❑ 107 Andre Reed	.20	.09
❑ 108 Jerome Bettis RC	2.50	1.10
❑ 109 Eugene Daniel	.10	.05
❑ 110 Leonard Russell	.20	.09
❑ 111 Darryl Williams	.10	.05
❑ 112 Rod Woodson	.20	.09
❑ 113 Boomer Esiason	.20	.09
❑ 114 James Hasty	.10	.05
❑ 115 Marc Boutte	.10	.05
❑ 116 Tom Waddle	.10	.05
❑ 117 Lawrence Dawsey	.10	.05
❑ 118 Mark Collins	.10	.05
❑ 119 Willie Gault	.10	.05
❑ 120 Barry Sanders	3.00	1.35
❑ 121 Leroy Hoard	.20	.09
❑ 122 Anthony Munoz	.20	.09
❑ 123 Jesse Sapolu	.10	.05
❑ 124 Art Monk	.20	.09
❑ 125 Randal Hill	.10	.05
❑ 126 John Offerdahl	.10	.05
❑ 127 Carlos Jenkins	.10	.05
❑ 128 Al Smith	.10	.05
❑ 129 Michael Irvin	.40	.18
❑ 130 Kenneth Davis	.10	.05
❑ 131 Curtis Conway RC	1.50	.70
❑ 132 Steve Atwater	.10	.05
❑ 133 Neil Smith	.20	.09
❑ 134 Steve Everitt RC	.10	.05
❑ 135 Chris Mims	.10	.05
❑ 136 Rickey Jackson	.10	.05
❑ 137 Edgar Bennett	.40	.18
❑ 138 Mike Pritchard	.20	.09
❑ 139 Richard Dent	.20	.09
❑ 140 Barry Foster	.20	.09
❑ 141 Eugene Robinson	.10	.05
❑ 142 Jackie Slater	.10	.05
❑ 143 Paul Gruber	.10	.05
❑ 144 Rob Moore	.20	.09
❑ 145 Robert Smith RC	2.50	1.10
❑ 146 Lorenzo White	.10	.05
❑ 147 Tommy Vardell	.10	.05
❑ 148 Dave Meggett	.10	.05
❑ 149 Vince Workman	.10	.05
❑ 150 Terry Allen	.40	.18
❑ 151 Howie Long	.20	.09
❑ 152 Charles Haley	.20	.09
❑ 153 Pete Metzelaars	.10	.05
❑ 154 John Copeland RC	.20	.09
❑ 155 Aeneas Williams	.10	.05
❑ 156 Ricky Sanders	.10	.05
❑ 157 Andre Ware	.10	.05
❑ 158 Tony Paige	.10	.05
❑ 159 Jerome Henderson	.10	.05
❑ 160 Harold Green	.10	.05
❑ 161 Wymon Henderson	.10	.05
❑ 162 Andre Rison	.20	.09
❑ 163 Donald Evans	.10	.05
❑ 164 Todd Scott	.10	.05
❑ 165 Steve Emtman	.10	.05
❑ 166 William Fuller	.10	.05
❑ 167 Michael Dean Perry	.20	.09
❑ 168 Randall Cunningham	.40	.18
❑ 169 Toi Cook	.10	.05
❑ 170 Browning Nagle	.10	.05
❑ 171 Darryl Henley	.10	.05
❑ 172 George Teague RC	.20	.09
❑ 173 Derrick Thomas	.20	.09
❑ 174 Jay Novacek	.20	.09
❑ 175 Mark Carrier DB	.10	.05
❑ 176 Kevin Fagan	.10	.05
❑ 177 Nate Lewis	.10	.05
❑ 178 Courtney Hawkins	.10	.05
❑ 179 Robert Blackmon	.10	.05
❑ 180 Rick Mirer RC	.75	.35
❑ 181 Mike Lodish	.10	.05
❑ 182 Jarrod Bunch	.10	.05
❑ 183 Anthony Smith	.10	.05
❑ 184 Brian Noble	.10	.05
❑ 185 Eric Bieniemy	.10	.05
❑ 186 Keith Jackson	.20	.09
❑ 187 Eric Martin	.10	.05
❑ 188 Vance Johnson	.10	.05
❑ 189 Kevin Mack	.10	.05
❑ 190 Rich Camarillo	.10	.05
❑ 191 Ashley Ambrose	.10	.05
❑ 192 Ray Childress	.10	.05
❑ 193 Jim Arnold	.10	.05
❑ 194 Ricky Ervins	.10	.05
❑ 195 Gary Anderson K	.10	.05
❑ 196 Eric Allen	.10	.05
❑ 197 Roger Craig	.20	.09
❑ 198 Jon Vaughn	.10	.05
❑ 199 Tim McDonald	.10	.05
❑ 200 Broderick Thomas	.10	.05
❑ 201 Jessie Tuggle	.10	.05
❑ 202 Alonzo Mitz	.10	.05
❑ 203 Harvey Williams	.20	.09
❑ 204 Russell Maryland	.10	.05
❑ 205 Marvin Washington	.10	.05
❑ 206 Jim Everett	.20	.09
❑ 207 Trace Armstrong	.10	.05
❑ 208 Steve Young	1.50	.70
❑ 209 Tony Woods	.10	.05
❑ 210 Brett Favre	4.00	1.80
❑ 211 Nate Odomes	.10	.05
❑ 212 Ricky Proehl	.10	.05
❑ 213 Jim Dombrowski	.10	.05
❑ 214 Anthony Carter	.20	.09
❑ 215 Tracy Simien	.10	.05
❑ 216 Clay Matthews	.20	.09
❑ 217 Patrick Bates RC	.10	.05
❑ 218 Jeff George	.40	.18
❑ 219 David Fulcher	.10	.05

❑ 220 Phil Simms .20 .09
❑ 221 Eugene Chung .10 .05
❑ 222 Reggie Cobb .10 .05
❑ 223 Jim Sweeney .10 .05
❑ 224 Greg Lloyd .40 .18
❑ 225 Sean Jones .10 .05
❑ 226 Marvin Jones RC .10 .05
❑ 227 Bill Brooks .10 .05
❑ 228 Moe Gardner .10 .05
❑ 229 Louis Oliver .10 .05
❑ 230 Flipper Anderson .10 .05
❑ 231 Marc Spindler .10 .05
❑ 232 Jerry Rice 2.00 .90
❑ 233 Chip Lohmiller .10 .05
❑ 234 Nolan Harrison .10 .05
❑ 235 Heath Sherman .10 .05
❑ 236 Reyna Thompson .10 .05
❑ 237 Derrick Walker .10 .05
❑ 238 Rufus Porter .10 .05
❑ 239 Checklist 1-125 .10 .05
❑ 240 Checklist 126-250 .10 .05
❑ 241 John Elway MC 1.50 .70
❑ 242 Troy Aikman MC .75 .35
❑ 243 Steve Emtman MC .10 .05
❑ 244 Ricky Watters MC .20 .09
❑ 245 Barry Foster MC .10 .05
❑ 246 Dan Marino MC 1.50 .70
❑ 247 Reggie White MC .20 .09
❑ 248 Thurman Thomas MC .20 .09
❑ 249 Broderick Thomas MC .10 .05
❑ 250 Joe Montana MC 1.50 .70
❑ 251 Tim Goad .10 .05
❑ 252 Joe Nash .10 .05
❑ 253 Anthony Johnson .20 .09
❑ 254 Carl Pickens .40 .18
❑ 255 Steve Beuerlein .10 .05
❑ 256 Anthony Newman .10 .05
❑ 257 Corey Miller .10 .05
❑ 258 Steve DeBerg .10 .05
❑ 259 Johnny Holland .10 .05
❑ 260 Jerry Ball .10 .05
❑ 261 Siupeli Malamala RC .10 .05
❑ 262 Steve Wisniewski .10 .05
❑ 263 Kelvin Pritchett .10 .05
❑ 264 Chris Gardocki .10 .05
❑ 265 Henry Thomas .10 .05
❑ 266 Arthur Marshall RC .10 .05
❑ 267 Quinn Early .20 .09
❑ 268 Jonathan Hayes .10 .05
❑ 269 Erric Pegram .20 .09
❑ 270 Clyde Simmons .10 .05
❑ 271 Eric Moten .10 .05
❑ 272 Brian Mitchell .20 .09
❑ 273 Adrian Cooper .10 .05
❑ 274 Gaston Green .10 .05
❑ 275 John Taylor .20 .09
❑ 276 Jeff Uhlenhake .10 .05
❑ 277 Phil Hansen .10 .05
❑ 278A Kevin Williams RC WR .40 .18
(missing draft pick logo on front)
❑ 278B Kevin Williams RC WR COR .40 .18
(with draft pick logo)
❑ 279 Robert Massey .10 .05
❑ 280A Drew Bledsoe RC ERR 12.00 5.50
(missing draft pick logo on front)
❑ 280B Drew Bledsoe RC COR 6.00 2.70
(draft pick logo on front)
❑ 281 Walter Reeves .10 .05
❑ 282A Carlton Gray RC ERR .25 .11
(missing draft pick logo on front)
❑ 282B Carlton Gray COR .15 .07
(draft pick logo on front)
❑ 283 Derek Brown TE .10 .05
❑ 284 Martin Mayhew .10 .05
❑ 285 Sean Gilbert .20 .09
❑ 286 Jessie Hester .10 .05
❑ 287 Mark Clayton .10 .05
❑ 288 Blair Thomas .10 .05
❑ 289 J.J. Birden .10 .05
❑ 290 Shannon Sharpe .40 .18
❑ 291 Richard Fain RC .10 .05
❑ 292 Gene Atkins .10 .05
❑ 293 Burt Grossman .10 .05
❑ 294 Chris Doleman .10 .05
❑ 295 Pat Swilling .10 .05
❑ 296 Mike Kenn .10 .05
❑ 297 Merril Hoge .10 .05
❑ 298 Don Mosebar .10 .05
❑ 299 Kevin Smith .20 .09
❑ 300 Darrell Green .10 .05
❑ 301A Dan Footman RC ERR .25 .11
(missing draft pick logo on front)
❑ 301B Dan Footman RC COR .15 .07
draft pick logo on front)
❑ 302 Vestee Jackson .10 .05
❑ 303 Carwell Gardner .10 .05
❑ 304 Amp Lee .10 .05
❑ 305 Bruce Matthews .10 .05
❑ 306 Antone Davis .10 .05
❑ 307 Dean Biasucci .10 .05
❑ 308 Maurice Hurst .10 .05
❑ 309 John Kasay .10 .05
❑ 310 Lawrence Taylor .20 .09
❑ 311 Ken Harvey .10 .05
❑ 312 Willie Davis .20 .09
❑ 313 Tony Bennett .10 .05
❑ 314 Jay Schroeder .10 .05
❑ 315 Darren Perry .10 .05
❑ 316A Troy Drayton RC ERR .25 .11
(missing draft pick logo on front)
❑ 316B Troy Drayton RC COR .15 .07
(draft pick logo on front)
❑ 317A Dan Williams RC ERR .25 .11
(missing draft pick logo on front)
❑ 317B Dan Williams COR .15 .07
(draft pick logo on front)
❑ 318 Michael Haynes .20 .09
❑ 319 Renaldo Turnbull .10 .05
❑ 320 Junior Seau .20 .09
❑ 321 Ray Crockett .10 .05
❑ 322 Will Furrer .10 .05
❑ 323 Byron Evans .10 .05
❑ 324 Jim McMahon .10 .05
❑ 325 Robert Jones .10 .05
❑ 326 Eric Davis .10 .05
❑ 327 Jeff Cross .10 .05
❑ 328 Kyle Clifton .10 .05
❑ 329 Haywood Jeffires .20 .09
❑ 330 Jeff Hostetler .20 .09
❑ 331 Darryl Talley .10 .05
❑ 332 Keith McCants .10 .05
❑ 333 Mo Lewis .10 .05
❑ 334 Matt Stover .10 .05
❑ 335 Ferrell Edmunds .10 .05
❑ 336 Matt Brock .10 .05
❑ 337 Ernie Mills .10 .05
❑ 338 Shane Dronett .10 .05
❑ 339 Brad Muster .10 .05
❑ 340 Jesse Solomon .10 .05
❑ 341 John Randle .10 .05
❑ 342 Chris Spielman .20 .09
❑ 343 David Whitmore .10 .05
❑ 344 Glenn Parker .10 .05
❑ 345 Marco Coleman .10 .05
❑ 346 Kenneth Gant .10 .05
❑ 347 Cris Dishman .10 .05
❑ 348 Kenny Walker .10 .05
❑ 349A Roosevelt Potts RC ERR .25 .11
(missing draft pick logo on front)
❑ 349B Roosevelt Potts RC COR .15 .07
(draft pick logo on front)
❑ 350 Reggie White .40 .18
❑ 351 Gerald Robinson .10 .05
❑ 352 Mark Rypien .10 .05
❑ 353 Stan Humphries .20 .09
❑ 354 Chris Singleton .10 .05
❑ 355 Herschel Walker .20 .09
❑ 356 Ron Hall .10 .05
❑ 357 Ethan Horton .10 .05
❑ 358 Anthony Pleasant .10 .05
❑ 359A Thomas Smith RC ERR .25 .11
(missing draft pick logo on front)
❑ 359B Thomas Smith RC COR .15 .07
(draft pick logo on front)
❑ 360 Audray McMillian .10 .05
❑ 361 D.J. Johnson .10 .05
❑ 362 Ron Heller .10 .05
❑ 363 Bern Brostek .10 .05
❑ 364 Ronnie Lott .20 .09
❑ 365 Reggie Johnson .10 .05
❑ 366 Lin Elliott .10 .05
❑ 367 Lemuel Stinson .10 .05
❑ 368 William White .10 .05
❑ 369 Ernie Jones .10 .05
❑ 370 Tom Rathman .10 .05
❑ 371 Tommy Kane .10 .05
❑ 372 David Brandon .10 .05
❑ 373 Lee Johnson .10 .05
❑ 374 Wade Wilson .10 .05
❑ 375 Nick Lowery .10 .05
❑ 376 Bubba McDowell .10 .05
❑ 377A Wayne Simmons RC ERR .25 .11
(missing draft pick logo on front)
❑ 377B Wayne Simmons RC COR .15 .07
(draft pick logo on front)
❑ 378 Calvin Williams .20 .09
❑ 379 Courtney Hall .10 .05
❑ 380 Troy Vincent .10 .05
❑ 381 Tim McGee .10 .05
❑ 382 Russell Freeman RC .10 .05
❑ 383 Steve Tasker .20 .09
❑ 384A Michael Strahan RC ERR .25 .11
(missing draft pick logo on front)
❑ 384B Michael Strahan COR .15 .07
(draft pick logo on front)
❑ 385 Greg Skrepenak .10 .05
❑ 386 Jake Reed .20 .09
❑ 387 Pete Stoyanovich .10 .05
❑ 388 Levon Kirkland .10 .05
❑ 389 Mel Gray .20 .09
❑ 390 Brian Washington .10 .05
❑ 391 Don Griffin .10 .05
❑ 392 Desmond Howard .20 .09
❑ 393 Luis Sharpe .10 .05
❑ 394 Mike Johnson .10 .05
❑ 395 Andre Tippett .10 .05
❑ 396 Donnell Woolford .10 .05
❑ 397A Demetrius DuBose RC ERR .40 .18
(missing draft pick logo on front)
❑ 397B Demetrius DuBose RC COR .30 .14
(draft pick logo on front)
❑ 398 Pat Terrell .10 .05
❑ 399 Todd McNair .10 .05
❑ 400 Ken Norton .20 .09
❑ 401 Keith Hamilton .10 .05
❑ 402 Andy Heck .10 .05
❑ 403 Jeff Gossett .10 .05
❑ 404 Dexter McNabb .10 .05
❑ 405 Richmond Webb .10 .05
❑ 406 Irving Fryar .20 .09
❑ 407 Brian Hansen .10 .05
❑ 408 David Little .10 .05
❑ 409A Glyn Milburn RC ERR .40 .18
(missing draft pick logo on front)
❑ 409B Glyn Milburn RC COR .20 .09
(draft pick logo on front)
❑ 410 Doug Dawson .10 .05
❑ 411 Scott Mersereau .10 .05
❑ 412 Don Beebe .10 .05
❑ 413 Vaughan Johnson .10 .05
❑ 414 Jack Del Rio .10 .05
❑ 415A Darrien Gordon RC ERR .25 .11
(missing draft pick logo on front)
❑ 415B Darrien Gordon RC COR .15 .07
(draft pick logo on front)
❑ 416 Mark Schlereth .10 .05
❑ 417 Lomas Brown .10 .05
❑ 418 William Thomas .10 .05
❑ 419 James Francis .10 .05
❑ 420 Quentin Coryatt .20 .09
❑ 421 Tyji Armstrong .10 .05
❑ 422 Hugh Millen .10 .05
❑ 423 Adrian White RC .10 .05
❑ 424 Eddie Anderson .10 .05
❑ 425 Mark Ingram .10 .05
❑ 426 Ken O'Brien .10 .05
❑ 427 Simon Fletcher .10 .05
❑ 428 Tim McKyer .10 .05
❑ 429 Leonard Marshall .10 .05
❑ 430 Eric Green .10 .05
❑ 431 Leonard Harris .10 .05
❑ 432 Darin Jordan RC .10 .05
❑ 433 Erik Howard .10 .05
❑ 434 David Lang .10 .05
❑ 435 Eric Turner .10 .05
❑ 436 Michael Cofer .10 .05
❑ 437 Jeff Bryant .10 .05
❑ 438 Charles McRae .10 .05

Card	Mint	NRMT
❑ 439 Henry Jones	.10	.05
❑ 440 Joe Montana	3.00	1.35
❑ 441 Morten Andersen	.10	.05
❑ 442 Jeff Jaeger	.10	.05
❑ 443 Leslie O'Neal	.20	.09
❑ 444 LeRoy Butler	.10	.05
❑ 445 Steve Jordan	.10	.05
❑ 446 Brad Edwards	.10	.05
❑ 447 J.B. Brown	.10	.05
❑ 448 Kerry Cash	.10	.05
❑ 449 Mark Tuinei	.10	.05
❑ 450 Rodney Peete	.10	.05
❑ 451 Sheldon White	.10	.05
❑ 452 Wesley Carroll	.10	.05
❑ 453 Brad Baxter	.10	.05
❑ 454 Mike Pitts	.10	.05
❑ 455 Greg Montgomery	.10	.05
❑ 456 Kenny Davidson	.10	.05
❑ 457 Scott Fulhage	.10	.05
❑ 458 Greg Townsend	.10	.05
❑ 459 Rod Bernstine	.10	.05
❑ 460 Gary Clark	.20	.09
❑ 461 Hardy Nickerson	.20	.09
❑ 462 Sean Landeta	.10	.05
❑ 463 Rob Burnett	.10	.05
❑ 464 Fred Barnett	.20	.09
❑ 465 John L. Williams	.10	.05
❑ 466 Anthony Miller	.20	.09
❑ 467 Roman Phifer	.10	.05
❑ 468 Rich Moran	.10	.05
❑ 469A Willie Roaf RC ERR (missing draft pick logo on front)	.25	.11
❑ 469B Willie Roaf RC COR (draft pick logo on front)	.15	.07
❑ 470 William Perry	.20	.09
❑ 471 Marcus Allen	.40	.18
❑ 472 Carl Lee	.10	.05
❑ 473 Kurt Gouveia	.10	.05
❑ 474 Jarvis Williams	.10	.05
❑ 475 Alfred Williams	.10	.05
❑ 476 Mark Stepnoski	.10	.05
❑ 477 Steve Wallace	.10	.05
❑ 478 Pat Harlow	.10	.05
❑ 479 Chip Banks	.10	.05
❑ 480 Cornelius Bennett	.20	.09
❑ 481A Ryan McNeil RC ERR (missing draft pick logo on front)	.25	.11
❑ 481B Ryan McNeil RC COR (draft pick logo on front)	.20	.09
❑ 482 Norm Johnson	.10	.05
❑ 483 Dermontti Dawson	.10	.05
❑ 484 Dwayne White	.10	.05
❑ 485 Derek Russell	.10	.05
❑ 486 Lionel Washington	.10	.05
❑ 487 Eric Hill	.10	.05
❑ 488 Micheal Barrow	.10	.05
❑ 489 Checklist 251-375 UER (No. 277 Hansen misspelled Hanson)	.10	.05
❑ 490 Checklist 376-500 UER (No. 488 Micheal Barrow misspelled Michael)	.10	.05
❑ 491 Emmitt Smith MC	1.50	.70
❑ 492 Derrick Thomas MC	.20	.09
❑ 493 Deion Sanders MC	.40	.18
❑ 494 Randall Cunningham MC	.20	.09
❑ 495 Sterling Sharpe MC	.20	.09
❑ 496 Barry Sanders MC	1.50	.70
❑ 497 Thurman Thomas MC	.20	.09
❑ 498 Brett Favre MC	2.00	.90
❑ 499 Vaughan Johnson MC	.10	.05
❑ 500 Steve Young MC	.75	.35
❑ 501 Marvin Jones MC	.10	.05
❑ 502 Reggie Brooks RC MC	.20	.09
❑ 503 Eric Curry MC	.10	.05
❑ 504 Drew Bledsoe MC	2.50	1.10
❑ 505 Glyn Milburn MC	.20	.09
❑ 506 Jerome Bettis MC	1.00	.45
❑ 507 Robert Smith MC	1.00	.45
❑ 508 Dana Stubblefield RC MC	.20	.09
❑ 509 Tom Carter MC	.20	.09
❑ 510 Rick Mirer MC	.60	.25
❑ 511 Russell Copeland RC	.20	.09
❑ 512 Deon Figures RC	.10	.05
❑ 513 Tony McGee RC	.20	.09
❑ 514 Derrick Lassic RC	.10	.05
❑ 515 Everett Lindsay RC	.10	.05
❑ 516 Derek Brown RC RBK	.10	.05
❑ 517 Harold Alexander RC	.10	.05
❑ 518 Tom Scott RC	.10	.05
❑ 519 Elvis Grbac RC	2.00	.90
❑ 520 Terry Kirby RC	.40	.18
❑ 521 Doug Pelfrey RC	.10	.05
❑ 522 Horace Copeland RC	.20	.09
❑ 523 Irv Smith RC	.10	.05
❑ 524 Lincoln Kennedy RC	.10	.05
❑ 525 Jason Elam RC	.20	.09
❑ 526 Qadry Ismail RC	.40	.18
❑ 527 Artie Smith RC	.10	.05
❑ 528 Tyrone Hughes RC	.20	.09
❑ 529 Lance Gunn RC	.10	.05
❑ 530 Vincent Brisby RC	.40	.18
❑ 531 Patrick Robinson RC	.10	.05
❑ 532 Raghib Ismail	.20	.09
❑ 533 Willie Beamon RC	.10	.05
❑ 534 Vaughn Hebron RC	.10	.05
❑ 535 Darren Drozdov RC	.40	.18
❑ 536 James Jett RC	2.00	.90
❑ 537 Michael Bates RC	.10	.05
❑ 538 Tom Rouen RC	.10	.05
❑ 539 Michael Husted RC	.10	.05
❑ 540 Greg Robinson RC	.10	.05
❑ 541 Carl Banks	.10	.05
❑ 542 Kevin Greene	.40	.18
❑ 543 Scott Mitchell	.40	.18
❑ 544 Michael Brooks	.10	.05
❑ 545 Shane Conlan	.10	.05
❑ 546 Vinny Testaverde	.20	.09
❑ 547 Robert Delpino	.10	.05
❑ 548 Bill Fralic	.10	.05
❑ 549 Carlton Bailey	.10	.05
❑ 550 Johnny Johnson	.10	.05
❑ NNO Jerry Rice RB UER (Wrong date for record touchdown)	10.00	4.50
❑ P1 Promo Sheet (Johnny Bailey, Vai Sikahema, Richard Dent, Sterling Sharpe, Tommy Barnhardt, Cris Carter, Cortez Kennedy, Christian Okoye, Reggie Cobb)	6.00	2.70

1993 Stadium Club Master Photos I

	MINT	NRMT
COMPLETE SET (12)	15.00	6.75

ONE PER SERIES 1 HOBBY BOX
*TRADE CARDS: .4X to 1X BASE CARD HI
PRICES ARE PER SINGLE LARGE CARD

Card	Mint	NRMT
❑ 1 Barry Foster	.40	.18
❑ 2 Barry Sanders	6.00	2.70
❑ 3 Reggie Cobb	.20	.09
❑ 4 Cortez Kennedy	.40	.18
❑ 5 Steve Young	3.00	1.35
❑ 6 Ricky Watters	.75	.35
❑ 7 Rob Moore	.40	.18
❑ 8 Derrick Thomas	.40	.18
❑ 9 Jeff George	.75	.35
❑ 10 Sterling Sharpe	.40	.18
❑ 11 Bruce Smith	.75	.35
❑ 12 Deion Sanders	2.00	.90

1993 Stadium Club Master Photos II

	MINT	NRMT
COMPLETE SET (12)	8.00	3.60

ONE PER SERIES 2 HOBBY BOX
*TRADE CARDS: .4X to 1X BASE CARD HI
PRICES ARE PER SINGLE LARGE CARD

Card	Mint	NRMT
❑ 1 Morten Andersen	.20	.09
❑ 2 Ken Norton Jr.	.40	.18
❑ 3 Clyde Simmons	.20	.09
❑ 4 Roman Phifer	.20	.09
❑ 5 Greg Townsend	.20	.09
❑ 6 Darryl Talley	.20	.09
❑ 7 Herschel Walker	.40	.18
❑ 8 Reggie White	.75	.35
❑ 9 Jesse Solomon	.20	.09
❑ 10 Joe Montana	6.00	2.70
❑ 11 John Taylor	.40	.18
❑ 12 Cornelius Bennett	.40	.18

1993 Stadium Club Super Teams

	MINT	NRMT
COMPLETE SET (28)	75.00	34.00
COMMON TEAM (1-28)	1.50	.70
SEMISTARS	2.50	1.10

UNNUMBERED CARDS LISTED ALPHABET.
STATED ODDS 1:24 H/R, 1:15 JUM

Card	Mint	NRMT
❑ 1 Bears (Jim Harbaugh)	2.50	1.10
❑ 2 Bengals (David Klingler)	1.50	.70
❑ 3 Bills WIN (Jim Kelly)	4.00	1.80
❑ 4 Broncos (John Elway)	12.00	5.50
❑ 5 Browns (Bernie Kosar)	1.50	.70
❑ 6 Buccaneers (Reggie Cobb)	1.50	.70
❑ 7 Cardinals (Eric Swann)	1.50	.70
❑ 8 Chargers (Stan Humphries)	2.50	1.10
❑ 9 Chiefs WIN (Derrick Thomas)	4.00	1.80

	MINT	NRMT
❑ 10 Colts	1.50	.70
Steve Emtman		
❑ 11 Cowboys WIN	15.00	6.75
Emmitt Smith		
❑ 12 Dolphins	12.00	5.50
Dan Marino		
❑ 13 Eagles	2.50	1.10
Randall Cunningham		
❑ 14 Falcons	4.00	1.80
Deion Sanders		
❑ 15 49ers WIN	8.00	3.60
Steve Young		
❑ 16 Giants	2.50	1.10
Lawrence Taylor		
❑ 17 Jets	1.50	.70
Brad Baxter		
❑ 18 Lions WIN	12.00	5.50
Barry Sanders		
❑ 19 Oilers WIN	4.00	1.80
Warren Moon		
❑ 20 Packers	12.00	5.50
Brett Favre		
❑ 21 Patriots	1.50	.70
Brent Williams		
❑ 22 Raiders	2.50	1.10
Howie Long		
❑ 23 Rams	1.50	.70
Cleveland Gary		
❑ 24 Redskins	1.50	.70
Mark Rypien		
❑ 25 Saints	1.50	.70
Sam Mills		
❑ 26 Seahawks	1.50	.70
Cortez Kennedy		
❑ 27 Steelers	1.50	.70
Barry Foster		
❑ 28 Vikings	2.50	1.10
Terry Allen		

1994 Stadium Club

	MINT	NRMT
COMPLETE SET (630)	70.00	32.00
COMP.SERIES 1 (270)	30.00	13.50
COMP.SERIES 2 (270)	30.00	13.50
COMP.HIGH SERIES (90)	15.00	6.75
COMMON CARD (1-630)	.10	.05
SEMISTARS	.20	.09
UNLISTED STARS	.40	.18
COMP.FIRST DAY (630)	1200.00	550.00
COMP.FIRST DAY SER.1	500.00	220.00
COMP.FIRST DAY SER.2	500.00	220.00
COMP.FIRST DAY HIGH SER.	250.00	110.00

*FIRST DAY STARS: 4X to 10X HI COL.
*FIRST DAY RCS: 2.5X to 6X HI ..
STATED ODDS 1:24H/R,1:15J SER.1-2
STATED ODDS 1:12 SERIES 3....

	MINT	NRMT
❑ 1 Dan Wilkinson RC	.20	.09
❑ 2 Chip Lohmiller	.10	.05
❑ 3 Roosevelt Potts	.10	.05
❑ 4 Martin Mayhew	.10	.05
❑ 5 Shane Conlan	.10	.05
❑ 6 Sam Adams RC	.20	.09
❑ 7 Mike Kenn	.10	.05
❑ 8 Tim Goad	.10	.05
❑ 9 Tony Jones	.10	.05
❑ 10 Ronald Moore	.10	.05
❑ 11 Mark Bortz	.10	.05
❑ 12 Darren Carrington	.10	.05
❑ 13 Eric Martin	.10	.05
❑ 14 Eric Allen	.10	.05
❑ 15 Aaron Glenn RC	.20	.09
❑ 16 Bryan Cox	.10	.05
❑ 17 Levon Kirkland	.10	.05
❑ 18 Qadry Ismail	.40	.18
❑ 19 Shane Dronett	.10	.05
❑ 20 Chris Spielman	.20	.09
❑ 21 Rob Fredrickson RC	.20	.09
❑ 22 Wayne Simmons	.10	.05
❑ 23 Glenn Montgomery	.10	.05
❑ 24 Jason Sehorn RC	.10	.05
❑ 25 Nick Lowery	.10	.05
❑ 26 Dennis Brown	.10	.05
❑ 27 Kenneth Davis	.10	.05
❑ 28 Shante Carver RC	.10	.05
❑ 29 Ryan Yarborough RC	.10	.05
❑ 30 Cortez Kennedy	.20	.09
❑ 31 Anthony Pleasant	.10	.05
❑ 32 Jessie Tuggle	.10	.05
❑ 33 Herschel Walker	.20	.09
❑ 34 Andre Collins	.10	.05
❑ 35 William Floyd RC	.40	.18
❑ 36 Harold Green	.10	.05
❑ 37 Courtney Hawkins	.10	.05
❑ 38 Curtis Conway	.40	.18
❑ 39 Ben Coates	.40	.18
❑ 40 Natrone Means	.40	.18
❑ 41 Eric Hill	.10	.05
❑ 42 Keith Kartz	.10	.05
❑ 43 Alexander Wright	.10	.05
❑ 44 Willie Roaf	.10	.05
❑ 45 Vencie Glenn	.10	.05
❑ 46 Ronnie Lott	.20	.09
❑ 47 George Koonce	.10	.05
❑ 48 Rod Woodson	.40	.18
❑ 49 Tim Grunhard	.10	.05
❑ 50 Cody Carlson	.10	.05
❑ 51 Bryant Young RC	.40	.18
❑ 52 Jay Novacek	.20	.09
❑ 53 Darryl Talley	.10	.05
❑ 54 Harry Colon	.10	.05
❑ 55 Dave Meggett	.10	.05
❑ 56 Aubrey Beavers RC	.10	.05
❑ 57 James Folston	.10	.05
❑ 58 Willie Davis	.20	.09
❑ 59 Jason Elam	.10	.05
❑ 60 Eric Metcalf	.20	.09
❑ 61 Bruce Armstrong	.10	.05
❑ 62 Ron Heller	.10	.05
❑ 63 LeRoy Butler	.10	.05
❑ 64 Terry Obee	.10	.05
❑ 65 Kurt Gouveia	.10	.05
❑ 66 Pierce Holt	.10	.05
❑ 67 David Alexander	.10	.05
❑ 68 Deral Boykin	.10	.05
❑ 69 Carl Pickens	.40	.18
❑ 70 Broderick Thomas	.10	.05
❑ 71 Barry Sanders CT	1.50	.70
❑ 72 Qadry Ismail CT	.40	.18
❑ 73 Thurman Thomas CT	.40	.18
❑ 74 Junior Seau	.40	.18
❑ 75 Vinny Testaverde	.20	.09
❑ 76 Tyrone Hughes	.20	.09
❑ 77 Nate Newton	.10	.05
❑ 78 Eric Swann	.20	.09
❑ 79 Brad Baxter	.10	.05
❑ 80 Dana Stubblefield	.40	.18
❑ 81 Jumbo Elliott	.10	.05
❑ 82 Steve Wisniewski	.10	.05
❑ 83 Eddie Robinson	.10	.05
❑ 84 Isaac Davis	.10	.05
❑ 85 Cris Carter	.60	.25
❑ 86 Mel Gray	.10	.05
❑ 87 Cornelius Bennett	.20	.09
❑ 88 Neil O'Donnell	.40	.18
❑ 89 Jon Hand	.10	.05
❑ 90 John Elway	3.00	1.35
❑ 91 Bill Hitchcock	.10	.05
❑ 92 Neil Smith	.40	.18
❑ 93 Joe Johnson RC	.10	.05
❑ 94 Edgar Bennett	.40	.18
❑ 95 Vincent Brown	.10	.05
❑ 96 Tommy Vardell	.10	.05
❑ 97 Donnell Woolford	.10	.05
❑ 98 Lincoln Kennedy	.10	.05
❑ 99 O.J. McDuffie	.40	.18
❑ 100 Heath Shuler RC	.40	.18
❑ 101 Jerry Rice BO	.75	.35
❑ 102 Erik Williams BO	.10	.05
❑ 103 Randall McDaniel BO	.10	.05
❑ 104 Dermontti Dawson BO	.10	.05
❑ 105 Nate Newton BO	.10	.05
❑ 106 Harris Barton BO	.10	.05
❑ 107 Shannon Sharpe BO	.20	.09
❑ 108 Sterling Sharpe BO	.20	.09
❑ 109 Steve Young BO	.60	.25
❑ 110 Emmitt Smith BO	1.25	.55
❑ 111 Thurman Thomas BO	.40	.18
❑ 112 Kyle Clifton	.10	.05
❑ 113 Desmond Howard	.20	.09
❑ 114 Quinn Early	.20	.09
❑ 115 David Klingler	.10	.05
❑ 116 Bern Brostek	.10	.05
❑ 117 Gary Clark	.20	.09
❑ 118 Courtney Hall	.10	.05
❑ 119 Joe King	.10	.05
❑ 120 Quentin Coryatt	.10	.05
❑ 121 Johnnie Morton RC	1.50	.70
❑ 122 Andre Reed	.20	.09
❑ 123 Eric Davis	.10	.05
❑ 124 Jack Del Rio	.10	.05
❑ 125 Greg Lloyd	.40	.18
❑ 126 Bubba McDowell	.10	.05
❑ 127 Mark Jackson	.10	.05
❑ 128 Jeff Jaeger	.10	.05
❑ 129 Chris Warren	.20	.09
❑ 130 Tom Waddle	.10	.05
❑ 131 Tony Smith	.10	.05
❑ 132 Todd Collins	.10	.05
❑ 133 Mark Bavaro	.10	.05
❑ 134 Joe Phillips	.10	.05
❑ 135 Chris Jacke	.10	.05
❑ 136 Glyn Milburn	.20	.09
❑ 137 Keith Jackson	.10	.05
❑ 138 Steve Tovar	.10	.05
❑ 139 Tim Johnson	.10	.05
❑ 140 Brian Washington	.10	.05
❑ 141 Troy Drayton	.10	.05
❑ 142 Dewayne Washington RC	.20	.09
❑ 143 Erik Williams	.10	.05
❑ 144 Eric Turner	.10	.05
❑ 145 John Taylor	.20	.09
❑ 146 Richard Cooper	.10	.05
❑ 147 Van Malone	.10	.05
❑ 148 Tim Ruddy RC	.10	.05
❑ 149 Henry Jones	.10	.05
❑ 150 Tim Brown	.40	.18
❑ 151 Stan Humphries	.40	.18
❑ 152 Harry Newsome	.10	.05
❑ 153 Craig Erickson	.10	.05
❑ 154 Gary Anderson K	.10	.05
❑ 155 Ray Childress	.10	.05
❑ 156 Howard Cross	.10	.05
❑ 157 Heath Sherman	.10	.05
❑ 158 Terrell Buckley	.10	.05
❑ 159 J.B. Brown	.10	.05
❑ 160 Joe Montana	3.00	1.35
❑ 161 David Wyman	.10	.05
❑ 162 Norm Johnson	.10	.05
❑ 163 Rod Stephens	.10	.05
❑ 164 Willie McGinest RC	.40	.18
❑ 165 Barry Sanders	3.00	1.35
❑ 166 Marc Logan	.10	.05
❑ 167 Anthony Newman	.10	.05
❑ 168 Russell Maryland	.10	.05
❑ 169 Luis Sharpe	.10	.05
❑ 170 Jim Kelly	.40	.18
❑ 171 Tre Johnson RC	.10	.05
❑ 172 Johnny Mitchell	.10	.05
❑ 173 David Palmer RC	1.00	.45
❑ 174 Bob Dahl	.10	.05
❑ 175 Aaron Wallace	.10	.05
❑ 176 Chris Gardocki	.10	.05
❑ 177 Hardy Nickerson	.20	.09
❑ 178 Jeff Query	.10	.05
❑ 179 Leslie O'Neal	.10	.05
❑ 180 Kevin Greene	.40	.18
❑ 181 Alonzo Spellman	.10	.05
❑ 182 Reggie Brooks	.20	.09

No.	Player	Price	Price
183	Dana Stubblefield	.40	.18
184	Tyrone Hughes	.20	.09
185	Drew Bledsoe GE	1.00	.45
186	Ronald Moore GE	.10	.05
187	Jason Elam GE	.10	.05
188	Rick Mirer GE	.40	.18
189	Willie Roaf GE	.10	.05
190	Jerome Bettis GE	.40	.18
191	Brad Hopkins	.10	.05
192	Derek Brown RBK	.10	.05
193	Nolan Harrison	.10	.05
194	John Randle	.10	.05
195	Carlton Bailey	.10	.05
196	Kevin Williams	.20	.09
197	Greg Hill RC	1.00	.45
198	Mark McMillian	.10	.05
199	Brad Edwards	.10	.05
200	Dan Marino	3.00	1.35
201	Ricky Watters	.40	.18
202	George Teague	.10	.05
203	Steve Beuerlein	.10	.05
204	Jeff Burris RC	.20	.09
205	Steve Atwater	.10	.05
206	John Thierry RC	.10	.05
207	Patrick Hunter	.10	.05
208	Wayne Gandy	.10	.05
209	Derrick Moore	.10	.05
210	Phil Simms	.20	.09
211	Kirk Lowdermilk	.10	.05
212	Patrick Robinson	.10	.05
213	Kevin Mitchell	.10	.05
214	Jonathan Hayes	.10	.05
215	Michael Dean Perry	.20	.09
216	John Fina	.10	.05
217	Anthony Smith	.10	.05
218	Paul Gruber	.10	.05
219	Carnell Lake	.10	.05
220	Carl Lee	.10	.05
221	Steve Christie	.10	.05
222	Greg Montgomery	.10	.05
223	Reggie Brooks	.20	.09
224	Derrick Thomas	.40	.18
225	Eric Metcalf	.20	.09
226	Michael Haynes	.20	.09
227	Bobby Hebert	.10	.05
228	Tyrone Hughes	.20	.09
229	Donald Frank	.10	.05
230	Vaughan Johnson	.10	.05
231	Eric Thomas	.10	.05
232	Ernest Givins	.20	.09
233	Charles Haley	.20	.09
234	Darrell Green	.10	.05
235	Harold Alexander	.10	.05
236	Dwayne Sabb	.10	.05
237	Harris Barton	.10	.05
238	Randall Cunningham	.40	.18
239	Ray Buchanan	.10	.05
240	Sterling Sharpe	.20	.09
241	Chris Mims	.10	.05
242	Mark Carrier DB	.10	.05
243	Ricky Proehl	.10	.05
244	Michael Brooks	.10	.05
245	Sean Gilbert	.10	.05
246	David Lutz	.10	.05
247	Kelvin Martin	.10	.05
248	Scottie Graham RC	.20	.09
249	Irving Fryar	.20	.09
250	Ricardo McDonald	.10	.05
251	Marvcus Patton	.10	.05
252	Errict Rhett RC	2.00	.90
253	Winston Moss	.10	.05
254	Rod Bernstine	.10	.05
255	Terry Wooden	.10	.05
256	Antonio Langham RC	.20	.09
257	Tommy Barnhardt	.10	.05
258	Marvin Washington	.10	.05
259	Bo Orlando	.10	.05
260	Marcus Allen	.40	.18
261	Mario Bates RC	.40	.18
262	Marco Coleman	.10	.05
263	Doug Riesenberg	.10	.05
264	Jesse Sapolu	.10	.05
265	Dermontti Dawson	.10	.05
266	Fernando Smith RC	.10	.05
267	David Szott	.10	.05
268	Steve Christie	.10	.05
269	Bruce Matthews	.10	.05
270	Michael Irvin	.40	.18
271	Seth Joyner	.10	.05
272	Santana Dotson	.20	.09
273	Vincent Brisby	.40	.18
274	Rohn Stark	.10	.05
275	John Copeland	.10	.05
276	Toby Wright	.10	.05
277	David Griggs	.10	.05
278	Aaron Taylor	.10	.05
279	Chris Doleman	.10	.05
280	Reggie Brooks	.20	.09
281	Flipper Anderson	.10	.05
282	Alvin Harper	.20	.09
283	Chris Hinton	.10	.05
284	Kelvin Pritchett	.10	.05
285	Russell Copeland	.10	.05
286	Dwight Stone	.10	.05
287	Jeff Gossett	.10	.05
288	Larry Allen RC	.20	.09
289	Kevin Mawae	.10	.05
290	Mark Collins	.10	.05
291	Chris Zorich	.10	.05
292	Vince Buck	.10	.05
293	Gene Atkins	.10	.05
294	Webster Slaughter	.10	.05
295	Steve Young	1.25	.55
296	Dan Williams	.10	.05
297	Jessie Armstead	.10	.05
298	Victor Bailey	.10	.05
299	John Carney	.10	.05
300	Emmitt Smith	2.50	1.10
301	Bucky Brooks RC	.10	.05
302	Mo Lewis	.10	.05
303	Eugene Daniel	.10	.05
304	Tyji Armstrong	.10	.05
305	Eugene Chung	.10	.05
306	Rocket Ismail	.20	.09
307	Sean Jones	.10	.05
308	Rick Cunningham	.10	.05
309	Ken Harvey	.10	.05
310	Jeff George	.40	.18
311	Jon Vaughn	.10	.05
312	Roy Barker RC	.10	.05
313	Micheal Barrow	.10	.05
314	Ryan McNeil	.10	.05
315	Pete Stoyanovich	.10	.05
316	Darryl Williams	.10	.05
317	Renaldo Turnbull	.10	.05
318	Eric Green	.10	.05
319	Nate Lewis	.10	.05
320	Mike Flores	.10	.05
321	Derek Russell	.10	.05
322	Marcus Spears	.10	.05
323	Corey Miller	.10	.05
324	Derrick Thomas	.40	.18
325	Steve Everitt	.10	.05
326	Brent Jones	.20	.09
327	Marshall Faulk RC	5.00	2.20
328	Don Beebe	.10	.05
329	Harry Swayne	.10	.05
330	Boomer Esiason	.20	.09
331	Don Mosebar	.10	.05
332	Isaac Bruce RC	4.00	1.80
333	Rickey Jackson	.10	.05
334	Daryl Johnston	.20	.09
335	Lorenzo Lynch	.10	.05
336	Brian Blades	.20	.09
337	Michael Timpson	.10	.05
338	Reggie Cobb	.10	.05
339	Joe Walter	.10	.05
340	Barry Foster	.10	.05
341	Richmond Webb	.10	.05
342	Pat Swilling	.10	.05
343	Shaun Gayle	.10	.05
344	Reggie Roby	.10	.05
345	Chris Calloway	.10	.05
346	Doug Dawson	.10	.05
347	Rob Burnett	.10	.05
348	Dana Hall	.10	.05
349	Horace Copeland	.10	.05
350	Shannon Sharpe	.20	.09
351	Rich Miano	.10	.05
352	Henry Thomas	.10	.05
353	Dan Saleaumua	.10	.05
354	Kevin Ross	.10	.05
355	Morten Andersen	.10	.05
356	Anthony Blaylock	.10	.05
357	Stanley Richard	.10	.05
358	Albert Lewis	.10	.05
359	Darren Woodson	.20	.09
360	Drew Bledsoe	1.50	.70
361	Eric Mahlum	.10	.05
362	Trent Dilfer RC	2.00	.90
363	William Roberts	.10	.05
364	Robert Brooks	.40	.18
365	Jason Hanson	.10	.05
366	Troy Vincent	.10	.05
367	William Thomas	.10	.05
368	Lonnie Johnson RC	.10	.05
369	Jamir Miller RC	.10	.05
370	Michael Jackson	.20	.09
371	Charlie Ward CT RC	.40	.18
372	Shannon Sharpe CT	.20	.09
373	Jackie Slater CT	.10	.05
374	Steve Young CT	.60	.25
375	Bobby Wilson	.10	.05
376	Paul Frase	.10	.05
377	Dale Carter	.10	.05
378	Robert Delpino	.10	.05
379	Bert Emanuel RC	1.00	.45
380	Rick Mirer	.40	.18
381	Carlos Jenkins	.10	.05
382	Gary Brown	.10	.05
383	Doug Pelfrey	.10	.05
384	Dexter Carter	.10	.05
385	Chris Miller	.10	.05
386	Charles Johnson RC	.40	.18
387	James Joseph	.10	.05
388	Darrin Smith	.10	.05
389	James Jett	.10	.05
390	Junior Seau	.40	.18
391	Chris Slade	.10	.05
392	Jim Harbaugh	.40	.18
393	Herman Moore	.40	.18
394	Thomas Randolph RC	.10	.05
395	Lamar Thomas	.10	.05
396	Reggie Rivers	.10	.05
397	Larry Centers	.40	.18
398	Chad Brown	.10	.05
399	Terry Kirby	.40	.18
400	Bruce Smith	.40	.18
401	Keenan McCardell RC	2.00	.90
402	Tim McDonald	.10	.05
403	Robert Smith	.40	.18
404	Matt Brock	.10	.05
405	Tony McGee	.10	.05
406	Ethan Horton	.10	.05
407	Michael Haynes	.20	.09
408	Steve Jackson	.10	.05
409	Erik Kramer	.20	.09
410	Jerome Bettis	.40	.18
411	D.J. Johnson	.10	.05
412	John Alt	.10	.05
413	Jeff Lageman	.10	.05
414	Rick Tuten	.10	.05
415	Jeff Robinson	.10	.05
416	Kevin Lee RC	.10	.05
417	Thomas Lewis RC	.20	.09
418	Kerry Cash	.10	.05
419	Chuck Levy RC	.10	.05
420	Mark Ingram	.10	.05
421	Dennis Gibson	.10	.05
422	Tyronne Drakeford	.10	.05
423	James Washington	.10	.05
424	Dante Jones	.10	.05
425	Eugene Robinson	.10	.05
426	Johnny Johnson	.10	.05
427	Brian Mitchell	.10	.05
428	Charles Mincy	.10	.05
429	Mark Carrier WR	.20	.09
430	Vince Workman	.10	.05
431	James Francis	.10	.05
432	Clay Matthews	.10	.05
433	Randall McDaniel	.10	.05
434	Brad Ottis	.10	.05
435	Bruce Smith	.40	.18
436	Cortez Kennedy BD	.10	.05
437	John Randle BD	.10	.05
438	Neil Smith BD	.20	.09
439	Cornelius Bennett BD	.20	.09
440	Junior Seau BD	.20	.09

❑ 441 Derrick Thomas BD .20 .09
❑ 442 Rod Woodson BD .20 .09
❑ 443 Terry McDaniel BD .10 .05
❑ 444 Tim McDonald BD .10 .05
❑ 445 Mark Carrier DB BD .10 .05
❑ 446 Irv Smith .10 .05
❑ 447 Steve Wallace .10 .05
❑ 448 Cris Dishman .10 .05
❑ 449 Bill Brooks .10 .05
❑ 450 Jeff Hostetler .20 .09
❑ 451 Brenston Buckner RC .10 .05
❑ 452 Ken Ruettgers .10 .05
❑ 453 Marc Boutte .10 .05
❑ 454 John Offerdahl .10 .05
❑ 455 Allen Aldridge .10 .05
❑ 456 Steve Emtman .10 .05
❑ 457 Andre Rison .20 .09
❑ 458 Shawn Jefferson .10 .05
❑ 459 Todd Steussie RC .20 .09
❑ 460 Scott Mitchell .40 .18
❑ 461 Tom Carter .10 .05
❑ 462 Donnell Bennett RC .40 .18
❑ 463 James Jones .10 .05
❑ 464 Antone Davis .10 .05
❑ 465 Jim Everett .20 .09
❑ 466 Tony Tolbert .10 .05
❑ 467 Merril Hoge .10 .05
❑ 468 Michael Bates .10 .05
❑ 469 Phil Hansen .10 .05
❑ 470 Rodney Hampton .40 .18
❑ 471 Aeneas Williams .10 .05
❑ 472 Al Del Greco .10 .05
❑ 473 Todd Lyght .10 .05
❑ 474 Joel Steed .10 .05
❑ 475 Merton Hanks .20 .09
❑ 476 Tony Stargell .10 .05
❑ 477 Greg Robinson .10 .05
❑ 478 Roger Duffy .10 .05
❑ 479 Simon Fletcher .10 .05
❑ 480 Reggie White .40 .18
❑ 481 Lee Johnson .10 .05
❑ 482 Wayne Martin .10 .05
❑ 483 Thurman Thomas .40 .18
❑ 484 Warren Moon .40 .18
❑ 485 Sam Rogers RC .10 .05
❑ 486 Erric Pegram .10 .05
❑ 487 Will Wolford .10 .05
❑ 488 Duane Young .10 .05
❑ 489 Keith Hamilton .10 .05
❑ 490 Haywood Jeffires .20 .09
❑ 491 Trace Armstrong .10 .05
❑ 492 J.J. Birden .10 .05
❑ 493 Ricky Ervins .10 .05
❑ 494 Robert Blackmon .10 .05
❑ 495 William Perry .20 .09
❑ 496 Robert Massey .10 .05
❑ 497 Jim Jeffcoat .10 .05
❑ 498 Pat Harlow .10 .05
❑ 499 Jeff Cross .10 .05
❑ 500 Jerry Rice 1.50 .70
❑ 501 Darnay Scott RC 1.50 .70
❑ 502 Clyde Simmons .10 .05
❑ 503 Henry Rolling .10 .05
❑ 504 James Hasty .10 .05
❑ 505 Leroy Thompson .10 .05
❑ 506 Darrell Thompson .10 .05
❑ 507 Tim Bowens RC .20 .09
❑ 508 Gerald Perry .10 .05
❑ 509 Mike Croel .10 .05
❑ 510 Sam Mills .10 .05
❑ 511 Steve Young RZ .60 .25
❑ 512 Hardy Nickerson RZ .20 .09
❑ 513 Cris Carter RZ .20 .09
❑ 514 Boomer Esiason RZ .10 .05
❑ 515 Bruce Smith RZ .20 .09
❑ 516 Emmitt Smith RZ 1.25 .55
❑ 517 Eugene Robinson RZ .10 .05
❑ 518 Gary Brown RZ .10 .05
❑ 519 Jerry Rice RZ .75 .35
❑ 520 Troy Aikman RZ .75 .35
❑ 521 Marcus Allen RZ .20 .09
❑ 522 Junior Seau RZ .20 .09
❑ 523 Sterling Sharpe RZ .20 .09
❑ 524 Dana Stubblefield RZ .20 .09
❑ 525 Tom Carter RZ .10 .05
❑ 526 Pete Metzelaars .10 .05
❑ 527 Russell Freeman .10 .05
❑ 528 Keith Cash .10 .05
❑ 529 Willie Drewrey .10 .05
❑ 530 Randal Hill .10 .05
❑ 531 Pepper Johnson .10 .05
❑ 532 Rob Moore .20 .09
❑ 533 Todd Kelly .10 .05
❑ 534 Keith Byars .10 .05
❑ 535 Mike Fox .10 .05
❑ 536 Brett Favre 3.00 1.35
❑ 537 Terry McDaniel .10 .05
❑ 538 Darren Perry .10 .05
❑ 539 Maurice Hurst .10 .05
❑ 540 Troy Aikman 1.50 .70
❑ 541 Junior Seau .40 .18
❑ 542 Steve Broussard .10 .05
❑ 543 Lorenzo White .10 .05
❑ 544 Terry McDaniel .10 .05
❑ 545 Henry Thomas .10 .05
❑ 546 Tyrone Hughes .20 .09
❑ 547 Mark Collins .10 .05
❑ 548 Gary Anderson K .10 .05
❑ 549 Darrell Green .10 .05
❑ 550 Jerry Rice 1.25 .55
❑ 551 Cornelius Bennett .20 .09
❑ 552 Aeneas Williams .10 .05
❑ 553 Eric Metcalf .20 .09
❑ 554 Jumbo Elliott .10 .05
❑ 555 Mo Lewis .10 .05
❑ 556 Darren Carrington .10 .05
❑ 557 Kevin Greene .40 .18
❑ 558 John Elway 2.50 1.10
❑ 559 Eugene Robinson .10 .05
❑ 560 Drew Bledsoe 1.25 .55
❑ 561 Fred Barnett .20 .09
❑ 562 Bernie Parmalee RC .40 .18
❑ 563 Bryce Paup .40 .18
❑ 564 Donnell Woolford .10 .05
❑ 565 Terance Mathis .20 .09
❑ 566 Santana Dotson .20 .09
❑ 567 Randall McDaniel .10 .05
❑ 568 Stanley Richard .10 .05
❑ 569 Brian Blades .20 .09
❑ 570 Jerome Bettis .40 .18
❑ 571 Neil Smith .40 .18
❑ 572 Andre Reed .20 .09
❑ 573 Michael Bankston .10 .05
❑ 574 Dana Stubblefield .40 .18
❑ 575 Rod Woodson .40 .18
❑ 576 Ken Harvey .10 .05
❑ 577 Andre Rison .20 .09
❑ 578 Darion Conner .10 .05
❑ 579 Michael Strahan .10 .05
❑ 580 Barry Sanders 2.50 1.10
❑ 581 Pepper Johnson .10 .05
❑ 582 Lewis Tillman .10 .05
❑ 583 Jeff George .40 .18
❑ 584 Michael Haynes .20 .09
❑ 585 Herschel Walker .20 .09
❑ 586 Tim Brown .40 .18
❑ 587 Jim Kelly .40 .18
❑ 588 Ricky Watters .40 .18
❑ 589 Randall Cunningham .40 .18
❑ 590 Troy Aikman UER 1.25 .55
Threw for 56
TD's in 93 season
❑ 591 Ken Norton Jr. .20 .09
❑ 592 Cortez Kennedy .20 .09
❑ 593 Ricky Ervins .10 .05
❑ 594 Cris Carter .50 .23
❑ 595 Sterling Sharpe .20 .09
❑ 596 John Randle .10 .05
❑ 597 Shannon Sharpe .20 .09
❑ 598 Ray Crittenden RC .10 .05
❑ 599 Barry Foster .10 .05
❑ 600 Deion Sanders .60 .25
❑ 601 Seth Joyner .10 .05
❑ 602 Chris Warren .20 .09
❑ 603 Tom Rathman .10 .05
❑ 604 Brett Favre 2.50 1.10
❑ 605 Marshall Faulk 2.00 .90
❑ 606 Terry Allen .20 .09
❑ 607 Ben Coates .40 .18
❑ 608 Brian Washington .10 .05
❑ 609 Henry Ellard .20 .09
❑ 610 Dave Meggett .10 .05
❑ 611 Stan Humphries .40 .18
❑ 612 Warren Moon .40 .18
❑ 613 Marcus Allen .40 .18
❑ 614 Ed McDaniel .10 .05
❑ 615 Joe Montana 2.50 1.10
❑ 616 Jeff Hostetler .20 .09
❑ 617 Johnny Johnson .10 .05
❑ 618 Andre Coleman RC .10 .05
❑ 619 Willie Davis .20 .09
❑ 620 Rick Mirer .40 .18
❑ 621 Dan Marino 2.50 1.10
❑ 622 Rob Moore .20 .09
❑ 623 Byron Bam Morris RC .40 .18
❑ 624 Natrone Means .40 .18
❑ 625 Steve Young .75 .35
❑ 626 Jim Everett .20 .09
❑ 627 Michael Brooks .10 .05
❑ 628 Dermontti Dawson .10 .05
❑ 629 Reggie White .40 .18
❑ 630 Emmitt Smith 1.50 .70
❑ 0 Micheal Barrow TSC 4.00 1.80
❑ NNO Checklist Card 1 .10 .05
❑ NNO Checklist Card 2 .10 .05
❑ NNO Checklist Card 3 .10 .05

1994 Stadium Club Bowman's Best

	MINT	NRMT
COMPLETE SET (45)	50.00	22.00

TOPPS 1995 COPYRIGHT ON CARDBACK
STATED ODDS 1:3 SER.3
*REFRACT.STARS: 2X TO 5X BASIC CARDS
*REFRACT.ROOKIES: 1X TO 2.5X
REFRACTOR STATED ODDS 1:12 SER.3

❑ BK1 Jerry Rice 3.00 1.35
❑ BK2 Deion Sanders 1.25 .55
❑ BK3 Reggie White .75 .35
❑ BK4 Dan Marino 6.00 2.70
❑ BK5 Natrone Means .75 .35
❑ BK6 Rick Mirer .75 .35
❑ BK7 Michael Irvin .75 .35
❑ BK8 John Elway 6.00 2.70
❑ BK9 Junior Seau .75 .35
❑ BK10 Drew Bledsoe 3.00 1.35
❑ BK11 Sterling Sharpe .40 .18
❑ BK12 Brett Favre 6.00 2.70
❑ BK13 Troy Aikman 3.00 1.35
❑ BK14 Barry Sanders 6.00 2.70
❑ BK15 Steve Young 2.50 1.10
❑ BK16 Emmitt Smith 5.00 2.20
❑ BK17 Joe Montana 6.00 2.70
❑ BU1 Marshall Faulk 10.00 4.50
❑ BU2 Derrick Alexander WR 2.00 .90
❑ BU3 Darnay Scott 1.50 .70
❑ BU4 Gus Frerotte 1.00 .45
❑ BU5 Jeff Blake 5.00 2.20
❑ BU6 Charles Johnson .40 .18
❑ BU7 Thomas Lewis .20 .09
❑ BU8 Charlie Garner 2.00 .90
❑ BU9 Aaron Glenn .20 .09
❑ BU10 William Floyd .40 .18
❑ BU11 Antonio Langham .20 .09
❑ BU12 Errict Rhett 2.00 .90
❑ BU13 Heath Shuler .40 .18
❑ BU14 Jeff Burris .20 .09
❑ BU15 Dan Wilkinson .20 .09

❑ BU16 Rob Fredrickson .... .20 .09
❑ BU17 Tim Bowens .... .20 .09
❑ 18 Deion Sanders .... 2.00 .90
Aaron Glenn
❑ 19 Barry Sanders 6.00 2.70
Marshall Faulk
❑ 20 Daryl Johnston .... 1.00 .45
William Floyd
❑ 21 Reggie White .... 1.25 .55
Tim Bowens
❑ 22 Troy Aikman 3.00 1.35
Heath Shuler
❑ 23 Donnell Woolford .... .50 .23
Antonio Langham
❑ 24 Rodney Hampton .... 2.00 .90
Errict Rhett
❑ 25 Tyrone Hughes .... .50 .23
Jeff Burris
❑ 26 Henry Thomas .... .50 .23
Dan Wilkinson
❑ 27 Jerry Rice 3.00 1.35
Derrick Alexander WR
❑ 28 Emmitt Smith 4.00 1.80
Byron Bam Morris

1994 Stadium Club Dynasty and Destiny

	MINT	NRMT
COMPLETE SET (6)	20.00	9.00
COMP.SERIES 1 (3)	12.00	5.50
COMP.SERIES 2 (3)	8.00	3.60
COMMON CARD (1-6)	2.00	.90
SEMISTARS	3.00	1.35

STATED ODDS 1:24 HOB/RET, 1:15JUM

❑ 1 Emmitt Smith 6.00 2.70
Walter Payton
❑ 2 Steve Largent .... 2.00 .90
Tom Waddle
❑ 3 Randy White .... 2.00 .90
Cortez Kennedy
❑ 4 Troy Aikman 4.00 1.80
Dan Fouts
❑ 5 Junior Seau 3.00 1.35
Mike Singletary
❑ 6 Shannon Sharpe .... 2.00 .90
Ozzie Newsome

1994 Stadium Club Expansion Team Redemption

	MINT	NRMT
JAGUARS PRIZE SET (22)	20.00	9.00
PANTHERS PRIZE SET (22)	20.00	9.00
COMMON JAGUAR (J1-J22)	1.00	.45
COMMON PANTHER (P1-P22)	1.00	.45
SEMISTAR PRIZE CARDS	1.25	.55
STAR PRIZE CARDS	1.50	.70

PRIZES AVAILABLE VIA MAIL REDEMPTION
COMP.TRADE CARD SET (6).. 3.00 1.35
THREE DIFF.TRADE CARDS PER TEAM
TRADE CARD STATED ODDS 1:24 SER.3

❑ J1 James O. Stewart 8.00 3.60

❑ J2 Kelvin Pritchett .... 1.00 .45
❑ J3 Mike Dumas .... 1.00 .45
❑ J4 Brian DeMarco .... 1.00 .45
❑ J5 James Williams .... 1.00 .45
❑ J6 Ernest Givins .... 1.00 .45
❑ J7 Harry Colon .... 1.00 .45
❑ J8 Derek Brown .... 1.00 .45
❑ J9 Santo Stephens .... 1.00 .45
❑ J10 Jeff Lageman .... 1.00 .45
❑ J11 Bryan Barker .... 1.00 .45
❑ J12 Dave Widell .... 1.00 .45
❑ J13 Willie Jackson .... 1.25 .55
❑ J14 Vinnie Clark .... 1.00 .45
❑ J15 Mickey Washington .... 1.00 .45
❑ J16 Le'Shai Maston .... 1.00 .45
❑ J17 Darren Carrington .... 1.00 .45
❑ J18 Steve Beuerlein .... 1.25 .55
❑ J19 Mark Williams .... 1.00 .45
❑ J20 Keith Goganious .... 1.00 .45
❑ J21 Shawn Bouwens .... 1.00 .45
❑ J22 Chris Hudson .... 1.00 .45
❑ P1 Kerry Collins 4.00 1.80
❑ P2 Rod Smith .... 1.00 .45
❑ P3 Willie Green .... 1.00 .45
❑ P4 Greg Kragen .... 1.00 .45
❑ P5 Blake Brockermeyer .... 1.00 .45
❑ P6 Bob Christian .... 1.00 .45
❑ P7 Carlton Bailey .... 1.00 .45
❑ P8 Bubba McDowell .... 1.00 .45
❑ P9 Matt Elliott .... 1.00 .45
❑ P10 Tyrone Poole .... 1.25 .55
❑ P11 John Kasay .... 1.25 .55
❑ P12 Gerald Williams .... 1.00 .45
❑ P13 Derrick Moore .... 1.00 .45
❑ P14 Don Beebe .... 1.00 .45
❑ P15 Sam Mills .... 1.25 .55
❑ P16 Darion Conner .... 1.00 .45
❑ P17 Eric Guliford .... 1.00 .45
❑ P18 Mike Fox .... 1.00 .45
❑ P19 Pete Metzelaars .... 1.00 .45
❑ P20 Frank Reich .... 1.25 .55
❑ P21 Mark Carrier .... 1.50 .70
❑ P22 Vince Workman .... 1.00 .45
❑ NNO Jacksonville Jaguars .... .50 .23
Defense Redemption
❑ NNO Jacksonville Jaguars .... .50 .23
Offense Redemption
❑ NNO Jacksonville Jaguars .... .50 .23
Special Teams Redemption
❑ NNO Carolina Panthers .... .50 .23
Defense Redemption
❑ NNO Carolina Panthers .... .50 .23
Offense Redemption
❑ NNO Carolina Panthers .... .50 .23
Special Teams Redemption
❑ NNO Carolina Panthers .... .50 .23
Jacksonville Jaguars
Complete Set Redemption

1994 Stadium Club Frequent Scorer Points Upgrades

	MINT	NRMT
COMPLETE SET (10)	60.00	27.00

ONE CARD VIA MAIL PER 30 FS POINTS

❑ 55 Dave Meggett .... .75 .35
❑ 75 Vinny Testaverde .... 1.50 .70
❑ 129 Chris Warren .... 1.50 .70
❑ 151 Stan Humphries 3.00 1.35
❑ 200 Dan Marino 20.00 9.00
❑ 310 Jeff George 3.00 1.35
❑ 327 Marshall Faulk 12.00 5.50
❑ 360 Drew Bledsoe 10.00 4.50
❑ 374 Steve Young 8.00 3.60
❑ 380 Rick Mirer 3.00 1.35

1994 Stadium Club Ring Leaders

	MINT	NRMT
COMPLETE SET (12)	40.00	18.00

STATED ODDS 1:24 SERIES 2....

❑ 1 Emmitt Smith 12.00 5.50
❑ 2 Steve Young 6.00 2.70
❑ 3 Deion Sanders 3.00 1.35
❑ 4 Warren Moon .... 2.00 .90
❑ 5 Thurman Thomas .... 2.00 .90
❑ 6 Jerry Rice 8.00 3.60
❑ 7 Sterling Sharpe .... 1.00 .45
❑ 8 Barry Sanders 15.00 6.75
❑ 9 Reggie White .... 2.00 .90
❑ 10 Michael Irvin .... 2.00 .90
❑ 11 Ronnie Lott .... 1.00 .45
❑ 12 Herschel Walker .... 1.00 .45

1994 Stadium Club Super Teams

	MINT	NRMT
COMPLETE SET (28)	100.00	45.00
COMMON TEAM (1-28)	2.00	.90
SEMISTARS	3.00	1.35

STATED ODDS 1:24 HOB/RET, 1:15JUM

❑ 1 Cardinals .... 2.00 .90
Steve Beuerlein
❑ 2 Falcons .... 2.00 .90
Drew Hill
❑ 3 Bills 3.00 1.35
Jim Kelly
❑ 4 Bears .... 2.00 .90
Joe Cain
❑ 5 Bengals .... 2.00 .90
Derrick Fenner

❑ 6 Browns	2.00	.90
Tommy Vardell		
❑ 7 Cowboys WIN	10.00	4.50
Emmitt Smith		
❑ 8 Broncos	10.00	4.50
John Elway		
❑ 9 Lions	10.00	4.50
Barry Sanders		
❑ 10 Packers	10.00	4.50
Brent Favre		
❑ 11 Oilers	2.00	.90
Gary Brown		
❑ 12 Colts	2.00	.90
Zefross Moss		
❑ 13 Chiefs	6.00	2.70
Joe Montana		
❑ 14 Raiders	2.00	.90
Howie Long		
❑ 15 Rams	3.00	1.35
Jerome Bettis		
❑ 16 Dolphins WIN	4.00	1.80
Irving Fryar		
❑ 17 Vikings WIN	4.00	1.80
Cris Carter		
❑ 18 Patriots	6.00	2.70
Drew Bledsoe		
❑ 19 Saints	2.00	.90
Rickey Jackson		
❑ 20 Giants	2.00	.90
Phil Simms		
❑ 21 Jets	2.00	.90
Boomer Esiason		
❑ 22 Eagles	2.00	.90
Herschel Walker		
❑ 23 Steelers WIN	4.00	1.80
Neil O'Donnell		
❑ 24 Chargers WIN	4.00	1.80
Natrone Means		
❑ 25 49ers WIN	12.00	5.50
Jerry Rice		
Steve Young		
❑ 26 Seahawks	3.00	1.35
Rick Mirer		
❑ 27 Buccaneers	2.00	.90
Craig Erickson		
❑ 28 Redskins	2.00	.90
Reggie Brooks		

1995 Stadium Club

	MINT	NRMT
COMPLETE SET (450)	70.00	32.00
COMP.SERIES 1 (225)	35.00	16.00
COMP.SERIES 2 (225)	35.00	16.00
COMMON CARD (1-405)	.10	.05
SEMISTARS	.20	.09
UNLISTED STARS	.40	.18
COMMON SP (181-225/406-450)	.20	.09
SEMISTARS SP	.30	.14
UNLISTED STARS SP	.60	.25
ONE SP PER PACK		

*EXTREME CORPS DIFFRACT: .75X TO 1.25X
RANDOM INSERTS IN ALL PACKS

❑ 1 Steve Young	1.25	.55
❑ 2 Stan Humphries	.20	.09
❑ 3 Chris Boniol RC	.10	.05
❑ 4 Darren Perry	.10	.05
❑ 5 Vinny Testaverde	.20	.09
❑ 6 Aubrey Beavers	.10	.05
❑ 7 Dewayne Washington	.20	.09
❑ 8 Marion Butts	.10	.05
❑ 9 George Koonce	.10	.05
❑ 10 Joe Cain	.10	.05
❑ 11 Mike Johnson	.10	.05
❑ 12 Dale Carter	.20	.09
❑ 13 Greg Biekert	.10	.05
❑ 14 Aaron Pierce	.10	.05
❑ 15 Aeneas Williams	.10	.05
❑ 16 Stephen Grant RC	.10	.05
❑ 17 Henry Jones	.10	.05
❑ 18 James Williams	.10	.05
❑ 19 Andy Harmon	.10	.05
❑ 20 Anthony Miller	.20	.09
❑ 21 Kevin Ross	.10	.05
❑ 22 Erik Howard	.10	.05
❑ 23 Brian Blades	.20	.09
❑ 24 Trent Dilfer	.40	.18
❑ 25 Roman Phifer	.10	.05
❑ 26 Bruce Kozerski	.10	.05
❑ 27 Henry Ellard	.20	.09
❑ 28 Rich Camarillo	.10	.05
❑ 29 Richmond Webb	.10	.05
❑ 30 George Teague	.10	.05
❑ 31 Antonio Langham	.10	.05
❑ 32 Barry Foster	.20	.09
❑ 33 Bruce Armstrong	.10	.05
❑ 34 Tim McDonald	.10	.05
❑ 35 James Harris DE	.10	.05
❑ 36 Lomas Brown	.10	.05
❑ 37 Jay Novacek	.20	.09
❑ 38 John Thierry	.10	.05
❑ 39 John Elliott	.10	.05
❑ 40 Terry McDaniel	.10	.05
❑ 41 Shawn Lee	.10	.05
❑ 42 Shane Dronett	.10	.05
❑ 43 Cornelius Bennett	.20	.09
❑ 44 Steve Bono	.20	.09
❑ 45 Byron Evans	.10	.05
❑ 46 Eugene Robinson	.10	.05
❑ 47 Tony Bennett	.10	.05
❑ 48 Michael Bankston	.10	.05
❑ 49 Willie Roaf	.10	.05
❑ 50 Bobby Houston	.10	.05
❑ 51 Ken Harvey	.10	.05
❑ 52 Bruce Matthews	.10	.05
❑ 53 Lincoln Kennedy	.10	.05
❑ 54 Todd Lyght	.10	.05
❑ 55 Paul Gruber	.10	.05
❑ 56 Corey Sawyer	.10	.05
❑ 57 Myron Guyton	.10	.05
❑ 58 John Jackson	.10	.05
❑ 59 Sean Jones	.10	.05
❑ 60 Pepper Johnson	.10	.05
❑ 61 Steve Walsh	.10	.05
❑ 62 Corey Miller	.10	.05
❑ 63 Fuad Reveiz	.10	.05
❑ 64 Rickey Jackson	.10	.05
❑ 65 Scott Mitchell	.20	.09
❑ 66 Michael Irvin	.40	.18
❑ 67 Andre Reed	.20	.09
❑ 68 Mark Seay	.20	.09
❑ 69 Keith Byars	.10	.05
❑ 70 Marcus Allen	.40	.18
❑ 71 Shannon Sharpe	.20	.09
❑ 72 Eric Hill	.10	.05
❑ 73 James Washington	.10	.05
❑ 74 Greg Jackson	.10	.05
❑ 75 Chris Warren	.20	.09
❑ 76 Will Wolford	.10	.05
❑ 77 Anthony Smith	.10	.05
❑ 78 Cris Dishman	.10	.05
❑ 79 Carl Pickens	.40	.18
❑ 80 Tyrone Hughes	.20	.09
❑ 81 Chris Miller	.10	.05
❑ 82 Clay Matthews	.20	.09
❑ 83 Lonnie Marts	.10	.05
❑ 84 Jerome Henderson	.10	.05
❑ 85 Ben Coates	.20	.09
❑ 86 Deon Figures	.10	.05
❑ 87 Anthony Pleasant	.10	.05
❑ 88 Guy McIntyre	.10	.05
❑ 89 Jake Reed	.20	.09
❑ 90 Rodney Hampton	.20	.09
❑ 91 Santana Dotson	.10	.05
❑ 92 Jeff Blackshear	.10	.05
❑ 93 Willie Clay	.10	.05
❑ 94 Nate Newton	.20	.09
❑ 95 Bucky Brooks	.10	.05
❑ 96 Lamar Lathon	.10	.05
❑ 97 Tim Grunhard	.10	.05
❑ 98 Harris Barton	.10	.05
❑ 99 Brian Mitchell	.10	.05
❑ 100 Natrone Means	.40	.18
❑ 101 Sean Dawkins	.20	.09
❑ 102 Chris Slade	.20	.09
❑ 103 Tom Rathman	.10	.05
❑ 104 Fred Barnett	.20	.09
❑ 105 Gary Brown	.10	.05
❑ 106 Leonard Russell	.10	.05
❑ 107 Alfred Williams	.10	.05
❑ 108 Kelvin Martin	.10	.05
❑ 109 Alexander Wright	.10	.05
❑ 110 O.J. McDuffie	.40	.18
❑ 111 Mario Bates	.40	.18
❑ 112 Tony Casillas	.10	.05
❑ 113 Michael Timpson	.10	.05
❑ 114 Robert Brooks	.40	.18
❑ 115 Rob Burnett	.10	.05
❑ 116 Mark Collins	.10	.05
❑ 117 Chris Calloway	.10	.05
❑ 118 Courtney Hawkins	.10	.05
❑ 119 Marvcus Patton	.10	.05
❑ 120 Greg Lloyd	.20	.09
❑ 121 Ryan McNeil	.10	.05
❑ 122 Gary Plummer	.10	.05
❑ 123 Dwayne Sabb	.10	.05
❑ 124 Jessie Hester	.10	.05
❑ 125 Terance Mathis	.20	.09
❑ 126 Steve Atwater	.10	.05
❑ 127 Lorenzo Lynch	.10	.05
❑ 128 James Francis	.10	.05
❑ 129 John Fina	.10	.05
❑ 130 Emmitt Smith	2.50	1.10
❑ 131 Bryan Cox	.10	.05
❑ 132 Robert Blackmon	.10	.05
❑ 133 Kenny Davidson	.10	.05
❑ 134 Eugene Daniel	.10	.05
❑ 135 Vince Buck	.10	.05
❑ 136 Leslie O'Neal	.20	.09
❑ 137 James Jett	.20	.09
❑ 138 Johnny Johnson	.10	.05
❑ 139 Michael Zordich	.10	.05
❑ 140 Warren Moon	.20	.09
❑ 141 William White	.10	.05
❑ 142 Carl Banks	.10	.05
❑ 143 Marty Carter	.10	.05
❑ 144 Keith Hamilton	.10	.05
❑ 145 Alvin Harper	.10	.05
❑ 146 Corey Harris	.10	.05
❑ 147 Elijah Alexander RC	.10	.05
❑ 148 Darrell Green	.10	.05
❑ 149 Yancey Thigpen RC	.40	.18
❑ 150 Deion Sanders	1.00	.45
❑ 151 Burt Grossman	.10	.05
❑ 152 J.B. Brown	.10	.05
❑ 153 Johnny Bailey	.10	.05
❑ 154 Harvey Williams	.10	.05
❑ 155 Jeff Blake RC	1.25	.55
❑ 156 Al Smith	.10	.05
❑ 157 Chris Doleman	.10	.05
❑ 158 Garrison Hearst	.40	.18

❑ 159 Bryce Paup .40 .18
❑ 160 Herman Moore .40 .18
❑ 161 Cortez Kennedy .20 .09
❑ 162 Marquez Pope .10 .05
❑ 163 Quinn Early .20 .09
❑ 164 Broderick Thomas .10 .05
❑ 165 Jeff Herrod .10 .05
❑ 166 Robert Jones .10 .05
❑ 167 Mo Lewis .10 .05
❑ 168 Ray Crittenden .10 .05
❑ 169 Raymont Harris .10 .05
❑ 170 Bruce Smith .40 .18
❑ 171 Dana Stubblefield .40 .18
❑ 172 Charles Haley .20 .09
❑ 173 Charles Johnson .20 .09
❑ 174 Shawn Jefferson .10 .05
❑ 175 Leroy Hoard .10 .05
❑ 176 Bernie Parmalee .20 .09
❑ 177 Scottie Graham .20 .09
❑ 178 Edgar Bennett .20 .09
❑ 179 Aubrey Matthews .10 .05
❑ 180 Don Beebe .10 .05
❑ 181 Eric Swann EC SP .30 .14
❑ 182 Jeff George EC SP .30 .14
❑ 183 Jim Kelly EC SP .60 .25
❑ 184 Sam Mills EC SP .30 .14
❑ 185 Mark Carrier DB EC SP .20 .09
❑ 186 Dan Wilkinson EC SP .30 .14
❑ 187 Eric Turner EC SP .20 .09
❑ 188 Troy Aikman EC SP 2.00 .90
❑ 189 John Elway EC SP 4.00 1.80
❑ 190 Barry Sanders EC SP 4.00 1.80
❑ 191 Brett Favre EC SP 4.00 1.80
❑ 192 Micheal Barrow EC SP .20 .09
❑ 193 Marshall Faulk EC SP 1.25 .55
❑ 194 Steve Beuerlein EC SP .20 .09
❑ 195 Neil Smith EC SP .30 .14
❑ 196 Jeff Hostetler EC SP .30 .14
❑ 197 Jerome Bettis EC SP .60 .25
❑ 198 Dan Marino EC SP 4.00 1.80
❑ 199 Cris Carter EC SP .60 .25
❑ 200 Drew Bledsoe EC SP 2.00 .90
❑ 201 Jim Everett EC SP .20 .09
❑ 202 Dave Brown EC SP .30 .14
❑ 203 Boomer Esiason EC SP .30 .14
❑ 204 Randall Cunningham EC SP .30 .14
❑ 205 Rod Woodson EC SP .30 .14
❑ 206 Junior Seau EC SP .60 .25
❑ 207 Jerry Rice EC SP 2.00 .90
❑ 208 Rick Mirer EC SP .60 .25
❑ 209 Errict Rhett EC SP .60 .25
❑ 210 Heath Shuler EC SP .60 .25
❑ 211 Bobby Taylor DP SP RC .30 .14
❑ 212 Jesse James DP SP RC .20 .09
❑ 213 Devin Bush DP SP RC .20 .09
❑ 214 Luther Elliss DP SP RC .20 .09
❑ 215 Kerry Collins DP SP RC 1.25 .55
❑ 216 Derrick Alexander DE DP SP .20 .09
❑ 217 Rashaan Salaam DP SP .30 .14
❑ 218 J.J. Stokes DP SP RC 1.25 .55
❑ 219 Todd Collins DP SP RC .30 .14
❑ 220 Ki-Jana Carter DP SP RC .30 .14
❑ 221 Kyle Brady DP SP RC .30 .14
❑ 222 Kevin Carter DP SP RC .20 .09
❑ 223 Tony Boselli DP SP RC .30 .14
❑ 224 Scott Gragg DP SP RC .20 .09
❑ 225 Warren Sapp DP SP RC 1.00 .45
❑ 226 Ricky Reynolds .10 .05
❑ 227 Roosevelt Potts .10 .05
❑ 228 Jessie Tuggle .10 .05
❑ 229 Anthony Newman .10 .05
❑ 230 Randall Cunningham .40 .18
❑ 231 Jason Elam .10 .05
❑ 232 Darnay Scott .40 .18
❑ 233 Tom Carter .10 .05
❑ 234 Micheal Barrow .10 .05
❑ 235 Steve Tasker .20 .09
❑ 236 Howard Cross .10 .05
❑ 237 Charles Wilson .10 .05
❑ 238 Rob Fredrickson .10 .05
❑ 239 Russell Maryland .10 .05
❑ 240 Dan Marino 3.00 1.35
❑ 241 Rafael Robinson .10 .05
❑ 242 Ed McDaniel .10 .05
❑ 243 Brett Perriman .20 .09
❑ 244 Chuck Levy .10 .05
❑ 245 Errict Rhett .40 .18
❑ 246 Tracy Simien .10 .05
❑ 247 Steve Everitt .10 .05
❑ 248 John Jurkovic .10 .05
❑ 249 Johnny Mitchell .10 .05
❑ 250 Mark Carrier .10 .05
❑ 251 Merton Hanks .10 .05
❑ 252 Joe Johnson .10 .05
❑ 253 Andre Coleman .10 .05
❑ 254 Ray Buchanan .10 .05
❑ 255 Jeff George .20 .09
❑ 256 Shane Conlan .10 .05
❑ 257 Gus Frerotte .40 .18
❑ 258 Doug Pelfrey .10 .05
❑ 259 Glenn Montgomery .10 .05
❑ 260 John Elway 3.00 1.35
❑ 261 Larry Centers .20 .09
❑ 262 Calvin Williams .20 .09
❑ 263 Gene Atkins .10 .05
❑ 264 Tim Brown .40 .18
❑ 265 Leon Lett .10 .05
❑ 266 Martin Mayhew .10 .05
❑ 267 Arthur Marshall .10 .05
❑ 268 Maurice Hurst .10 .05
❑ 269 Greg Hill .20 .09
❑ 270 Junior Seau .40 .18
❑ 271 Rick Mirer .40 .18
❑ 272 Jack Del Rio .10 .05
❑ 273 Lewis Tillman .10 .05
❑ 274 Renaldo Turnbull .10 .05
❑ 275 Dan Footman .10 .05
❑ 276 John Taylor .10 .05
❑ 277 Russell Copeland .10 .05
❑ 278 Tracy Scroggins .10 .05
❑ 279 Lou Benfatti .10 .05
❑ 280 Rod Woodson .20 .09
❑ 281 Troy Drayton .10 .05
❑ 282 Quentin Coryatt .20 .09
❑ 283 Craig Heyward .20 .09
❑ 284 Jeff Cross .10 .05
❑ 285 Hardy Nickerson .10 .05
❑ 286 Dorsey Levens 1.25 .55
❑ 287 Derek Russell .10 .05
❑ 288 Seth Joyner .10 .05
❑ 289 Kimble Anders .20 .09
❑ 290 Drew Bledsoe 1.50 .70
❑ 291 Bryant Young .20 .09
❑ 292 Chris Zorich .10 .05
❑ 293 Michael Strahan .10 .05
❑ 294 Kevin Greene .20 .09
❑ 295 Aaron Glenn .10 .05
❑ 296 Jimmy Spencer RC .10 .05
❑ 297 Eric Turner .10 .05
❑ 298 William Thomas .10 .05
❑ 299 Dan Wilkinson .20 .09
❑ 300 Troy Aikman 1.50 .70
❑ 301 Terry Wooden .10 .05
❑ 302 Heath Shuler .40 .18
❑ 303 Jeff Burris .10 .05
❑ 304 Mark Stepnoski .10 .05
❑ 305 Chris Mims .10 .05
❑ 306 Todd Steussie .10 .05
❑ 307 Johnnie Morton .20 .09
❑ 308 Darryl Talley .10 .05
❑ 309 Nolan Harrison .10 .05
❑ 310 Dave Brown .20 .09
❑ 311 Brent Jones .10 .05
❑ 312 Curtis Conway .40 .18
❑ 313 Ronald Humphrey .10 .05
❑ 314 Richie Anderson RC .10 .05
❑ 315 Jim Everett .10 .05
❑ 316 Willie Davis .20 .09
❑ 317 Ed Cunningham .10 .05
❑ 318 Willie McGinest .20 .09
❑ 319 Sean Gilbert .20 .09
❑ 320 Brett Favre 3.00 1.35
❑ 321 Bennie Thompson .10 .05
❑ 322 Neil O'Donnell .20 .09
❑ 323 Vince Workman .10 .05
❑ 324 Terry Kirby .20 .09
❑ 325 Simon Fletcher .10 .05
❑ 326 Ricardo McDonald .10 .05
❑ 327 Duane Young .10 .05
❑ 328 Jim Harbaugh .20 .09
❑ 329 D.J. Johnson .10 .05
❑ 330 Boomer Esiason .20 .09
❑ 331 Donnell Woolford .10 .05
❑ 332 Mike Sherrard .10 .05
❑ 333 Tyrone Legette .10 .05
❑ 334 Larry Brown DB .10 .05
❑ 335 William Floyd .40 .18
❑ 336 Reggie Brooks .20 .09
❑ 337 Patrick Bates .10 .05
❑ 338 Jim Jeffcoat .10 .05
❑ 339 Ray Childress .10 .05
❑ 340 Cris Carter .40 .18
❑ 341 Charlie Garner .20 .09
❑ 342 Bill Hitchcock .10 .05
❑ 343 Levon Kirkland .10 .05
❑ 344 Robert Porcher .10 .05
❑ 345 Darryl Williams .10 .05
❑ 346 Vincent Brisby .10 .05
❑ 347 Kenyon Rasheed .10 .05
❑ 348 Floyd Turner .10 .05
❑ 349 Bob Whitfield .10 .05
❑ 350 Jerome Bettis .40 .18
❑ 351 Brad Baxter .10 .05
❑ 352 Darrin Smith .10 .05
❑ 353 Lamar Thomas .10 .05
❑ 354 Lorenzo Neal .10 .05
❑ 355 Erik Kramer .10 .05
❑ 356 Dwayne Harper .10 .05
❑ 357 Doug Evans .10 .05
❑ 358 Jeff Feagles .10 .05
❑ 359 Ray Crockett .10 .05
❑ 360 Neil Smith .20 .09
❑ 361 Troy Vincent .10 .05
❑ 362 Don Griffin .10 .05
❑ 363 Michael Brooks .10 .05
❑ 364 Carlton Gray .10 .05
❑ 365 Thomas Smith .10 .05
❑ 366 Ken Norton .20 .09
❑ 367 Tony McGee .10 .05
❑ 368 Eric Metcalf .20 .09
❑ 369 Mel Gray .10 .05
❑ 370 Barry Sanders 3.00 1.35
❑ 371 Rocket Ismail .20 .09
❑ 372 Chad Brown .20 .09
❑ 373 Qadry Ismail .20 .09
❑ 374 Anthony Prior .10 .05
❑ 375 Kevin Lee .10 .05
❑ 376 Robert Young .10 .05
❑ 377 Kevin Williams WR .20 .09
❑ 378 Tydus Winans .10 .05
❑ 379 Ricky Watters .40 .18
❑ 380 Jim Kelly .40 .18
❑ 381 Eric Swann .20 .09
❑ 382 Mike Pritchard .10 .05
❑ 383 Derek Brown RBK .10 .05
❑ 384 Dennis Gibson .10 .05
❑ 385 Byron Bam Morris .20 .09
❑ 386 Reggie White .40 .18
❑ 387 Jeff Graham .10 .05
❑ 388 Marshall Faulk .75 .35
❑ 389 Joe Phillips .10 .05
❑ 390 Jeff Hostetler .20 .09
❑ 391 Irving Fryar .20 .09
❑ 392 Stevon Moore .10 .05
❑ 393 Bert Emanuel .40 .18
❑ 394 Leon Searcy .10 .05
❑ 395 Robert Smith .40 .18
❑ 396 Michael Bates .10 .05
❑ 397 Thomas Lewis .20 .09
❑ 398 Joe Bowden .10 .05
❑ 399 Steve Tovar .10 .05
❑ 400 Jerry Rice 1.50 .70
❑ 401 Toby Wright .10 .05
❑ 402 Daryl Johnston .20 .09
❑ 403 Vincent Brown .10 .05
❑ 404 Marvin Washington .10 .05
❑ 405 Chris Spielman .20 .09
❑ 406 Willie Jackson ET SP .30 .14
❑ 407 Harry Boatswain ET SP .20 .09
❑ 408 Kelvin Pritchett ET SP .20 .09
❑ 409 Dave Widell ET SP .20 .09
❑ 410 Frank Reich ET SP .20 .09
❑ 411 Corey Mayfield ET SP .20 .09
❑ 412 Pete Metzelaars ET SP .20 .09
❑ 413 Keith Goganious ET SP .20 .09
❑ 414 John Kasay ET SP .20 .09
❑ 415 Ernest Givins ET SP .20 .09
❑ 416 Randy Baldwin ET SP .20 .09

❑ 417 Shawn Bouwens ET SP	.20	.09
❑ 418 Mike Fox ET SP	.20	.09
❑ 419 Mark Carrier WR ET SP	.30	.14
❑ 420 Steve Beuerlein ET SP	.20	.09
❑ 421 Steve Lofton ET SP	.20	.09
❑ 422 Jeff Lageman ET SP	.20	.09
❑ 423 Paul Butcher ET SP	.20	.09
❑ 424 Mark Brunell ET SP	2.00	.90
❑ 425 Vernon Turner ET SP	.20	.09
❑ 426 Tim McKyer ET SP	.20	.09
❑ 427 James Williams ET SP	.20	.09
❑ 428 Tommy Barnhardt ET SP	.20	.09
❑ 429 Rogerick Green ET SP	.20	.09
❑ 430 Desmond Howard ET SP	.30	.14
❑ 431 Darion Conner ET SP	.20	.09
❑ 432 Reggie Clark ET SP	.20	.09
❑ 433 Eric Guliford ET SP	.20	.09
❑ 434 Rob Johnson ET SP RC	2.50	1.10
❑ 435 Sam Mills ET SP	.30	.14
❑ 436 Kordell Stewart RC SP	5.00	2.20
❑ 437 James O. Stewart SP RC	3.00	1.35
❑ 438 Zach Wiegert SP	.20	.09
❑ 439 Ellis Johnson RC SP	.20	.09
❑ 440 Matt O'Dwyer RC SP	.20	.09
❑ 441 Anthony Cook RC SP	.20	.09
❑ 442 Ron Davis RC SP	.20	.09
❑ 443 Chris Hudson RC SP	.20	.09
❑ 444 Hugh Douglas RC SP	.30	.14
❑ 445 Tyrone Poole RC SP	.30	.14
❑ 446 Korey Stringer RC SP	.20	.09
❑ 447 Ruben Brown RC SP	.20	.09
❑ 448 Brian DeMarco RC SP	.20	.09
❑ 449 Michael Westbrook RC SP	2.50	1.10
❑ 450 Steve McNair RC SP	5.00	2.20

1995 Stadium Club Ground Attack

	MINT	NRMT
COMPLETE SET (15)	40.00	18.00
COMMON CARD (G1-G15)	1.50	.70
SEMISTARS	2.00	.90

STATED ODDS 1:18H,1:6J,1:12R SER.2
STATED ODDS 1:16 SPEC.RET SER.2

❑ G1 Emmitt Smith Daryl Johnston	8.00	3.60
❑ G2 Brett Favre Edgar Bennett	12.00	5.50
❑ G3 Bernie Parmalee Irving Spikes	1.50	.70
❑ G4 John Elway Glen Milburn	12.00	5.50
❑ G5 Rick Mirer Chris Warren	2.00	.90
❑ G6 Greg Hill Marcus Allen	2.00	.90
❑ G7 Errict Rhett Vince Workman	2.00	.90
❑ G8 Byron Bam Morris Eric Pegram	2.00	.90
❑ G9 Derek Brown RBK Mario Bates	1.50	.70
❑ G10 Steve Young William Floyd	5.00	2.20
❑ G11 Charlie Garner Randall Cunningham	1.50	.70
❑ G12 Lewis Tillman Raymont Harris	1.50	.70
❑ G13 Harvey Williams Jeff Hostetler	1.50	.70
❑ G14 Garrison Hearst Larry Centers	2.00	.90
❑ G15 Marshall Faulk Roosevelt Potts	2.00	.90

1995 Stadium Club Metalists

	MINT	NRMT
COMPLETE SET (8)	30.00	13.50

STATED ODDS 1:24H, 1:9J, 1:28R SER.1
STATED ODDS 1:21 SPEC.RET SER.1

❑ M1 Jerry Rice	5.00	2.20
❑ M2 Barry Sanders	10.00	4.50
❑ M3 John Elway	10.00	4.50
❑ M4 Dana Stubblefield	1.25	.55
❑ M5 Emmitt Smith	8.00	3.60
❑ M6 Deion Sanders	3.00	1.35
❑ M7 Marshall Faulk	2.50	1.10
❑ M8 Steve Young	4.00	1.80

1995 Stadium Club MVPs

	MINT	NRMT
COMPLETE SET (8)	25.00	11.00

STATED ODDS 1:24H, 1:9J, 1:24R SER.2
STATED ODDS 1:28 SPEC.RET SER.2

❑ MVP1 Jerry Rice	4.00	1.80
❑ MVP2 Boomer Esiason	.50	.23
❑ MVP3 Randall Cunningham	1.00	.45
❑ MVP4 Marcus Allen	1.00	.45
❑ MVP5 John Elway	8.00	3.60
❑ MVP6 Dan Marino	8.00	3.60
❑ MVP7 Emmitt Smith	6.00	2.70
❑ MVP8 Steve Young	3.00	1.35

1995 Stadium Club Nemeses

	MINT	NRMT
COMPLETE SET (15)	60.00	27.00
COMMON CARD (N1-N15)	2.50	1.10
SEMISTARS	4.00	1.80

STATED ODDS 1:24H, 1:9J, 1:16SP.RET SER.1

❑ N1 Barry Sanders Jack Del Rio	12.00	5.50
❑ N2 Reggie White Lomas Brown	6.00	2.70
❑ N3 Terry McDaniel Anthony Miller	2.50	1.10
❑ N4 Brett Favre Chris Spielman	12.00	5.50
❑ N5 Junior Seau Chris Warren	4.00	1.80
❑ N6 Cortez Kennedy Steve Wisniewski	2.50	1.10
❑ N7 Rod Woodson Tim Brown	4.00	1.80
❑ N8 Troy Aikman Michael Brooks	8.00	3.60
❑ N9 Bruce Smith Bruce Armstrong	4.00	1.80
❑ N10 Jerry Rice Donnell Woolford	8.00	3.60
❑ N11 Emmitt Smith Seth Joyner	10.00	4.50
❑ N12 Dan Marino Cornelius Bennett	12.00	5.50
❑ N13 Marshall Faulk Bryan Cox	6.00	2.70
❑ N14 Stan Humphries Greg Lloyd	4.00	1.80
❑ N15 Michael Irvin Deion Sanders	5.00	2.20

1995 Stadium Club Nightmares

	MINT	NRMT
COMPLETE SET (30)	100.00	45.00
COMP.SERIES 1 (15)	70.00	32.00
COMP.SERIES 2 (15)	30.00	13.50

NM1-NM15: STATED ODDS 1:24H, 1:9J SER.1
NM16-NM30: ODDS 1:18H, 1:6J SER.2

❑ NM1 Drew Bledsoe	10.00	4.50
❑ NM2 Barry Sanders	20.00	9.00
❑ NM3 Reggie White	3.00	1.35
❑ NM4 Michael Irvin	3.00	1.35
❑ NM5 Jerry Rice	10.00	4.50
❑ NM6 Jerome Bettis	3.00	1.35
❑ NM7 Dan Marino	20.00	9.00

❑ NM8 Bruce Smith 3.00 1.35
❑ NM9 Steve Young 8.00 3.60
❑ NM10 Junior Seau 3.00 1.35
❑ NM11 Emmitt Smith 20.00 9.00
❑ NM12 Deion Sanders 8.00 3.60
❑ NM13 Rod Woodson .... 1.50 .70
❑ NM14 Marshall Faulk 5.00 2.20
❑ NM15 Troy Aikman 10.00 4.50
❑ NM16 Stan Humphries .... 1.50 .70
❑ NM17 Chris Warren .... 1.50 .70
❑ NM18 Jack Del Rio .... .75 .35
❑ NM19 Randall Cunningham 3.00 1.35
❑ NM20 Natrone Means 3.00 1.35
❑ NM21 Dana Stubblefield 3.00 1.35
❑ NM22 Jim Kelly 3.00 1.35
❑ NM23 Cris Carter 3.00 1.35
❑ NM24 Cornelius Bennett .... 1.50 .70
❑ NM25 Errict Rhett 3.00 1.35
❑ NM26 Terry McDaniel .... .75 .35
❑ NM27 Rodney Hampton...... 1.50 .70
❑ NM28 Brett Favre 20.00 9.00
❑ NM29 Bryan Cox .... .75 .35
❑ NM30 John Elway 20.00 9.00

1995 Stadium Club Power Surge

	MINT	NRMT
COMPLETE SET (24)	80.00	36.00
COMP.SERIES 1 (12)	50.00	22.00
COMP.SERIES 2 (12)	30.00	13.50

P1-P12: STATED ODDS 1:18H, 1:28R SER.1
PS1-PS12:ODDS 1:36HOB/RET,1:32SR SER.2

❑ P1 Steve Young 8.00 3.60
❑ P2 Natrone Means 2.50 1.10
❑ P3 Cris Carter 2.50 1.10
❑ P4 Junior Seau 2.50 1.10
❑ P5 Barry Sanders 20.00 9.00
❑ P6 Michael Irvin 2.50 1.10
❑ P7 John Elway 20.00 9.00
❑ P8 Emmitt Smith 15.00 6.75
❑ P9 Greg Lloyd .... 1.25 .55
❑ P10 Jerry Rice 10.00 4.50
❑ P11 Marshall Faulk 5.00 2.20
❑ P12 Drew Bledsoe 10.00 4.50
❑ PS1 Dan Marino 20.00 9.00
❑ PS2 Ken Harvey .... .60 .25
❑ PS3 Chris Warren .... 1.25 .55
❑ PS4 Henry Ellard .... 1.25 .55
❑ PS5 Marshall Faulk 5.00 2.20
❑ PS6 Irving Fryar .... 1.25 .55
❑ PS7 Kevin Ross .... .60 .25
❑ PS8 Vince Workman .... .60 .25
❑ PS9 Ray Buchanan .... .60 .25
❑ PS10 Tony Martin .... 1.25 .55
❑ PS11 D.J.Johnson .... .60 .25
❑ PS12 Steve Young 8.00 3.60

1996 Stadium Club

	MINT	NRMT
COMPLETE SET (360)	60.00	27.00
COMP.SERIES 1 (180)	30.00	13.50
COMP.SERIES 2 (180)	30.00	13.50
COMMON CARD (1-360)	.10	.05
CL (NNO)	.05	.02
SEMISTARS	.25	.11
UNLISTED STARS	.50	.23

*DOT MATRIX FOILS: 4X TO 10X HI COL
DOT MAT.ODDS 1:12H/R, 1:4J SER.1
DOT MAT.ODDS 1:12H, 1:16R SER.2
*MATCH PROOF STARS: 15X TO 40X HI
MAT.PROOF STAT.ODDS 1:240 SER.1
MAT.PROOF ODDS 1:150H, 1:200R SER.2

❑ 1 Kyle Brady .... .10 .05
❑ 2 Mickey Washington .... .10 .05
❑ 3 Seth Joyner .... .10 .05
❑ 4 Vinny Testaverde .... .25 .11
❑ 5 Thomas Randolph .... .10 .05
❑ 6 Heath Shuler .... .25 .11
❑ 7 Ty Law .... .10 .05
❑ 8 Blake Brockermeyer .... .10 .05
❑ 9 Darryll Lewis .... .10 .05
❑ 10 Jeff Blake .... .50 .23
❑ 11 Tyrone Hughes .... .10 .05
❑ 12 Horace Copeland .... .10 .05
❑ 13 Roman Phifer .... .10 .05
❑ 14 Eugene Robinson .... .10 .05
❑ 15 Anthony Miller .... .25 .11
❑ 16 Robert Smith .... .25 .11
❑ 17 Chester McGlockton .... .10 .05
❑ 18 Marty Carter .... .10 .05
❑ 19 Scott Mitchell .... .25 .11
❑ 20 O.J. McDuffie .... .25 .11
❑ 21 Stan Humphries .... .25 .11
❑ 22 Eugene Daniel .... .10 .05
❑ 23 Devin Bush .... .10 .05
❑ 24 Darick Holmes .... .10 .05
❑ 25 Ricky Watters .... .25 .11
❑ 26 J.J. Stokes .... .50 .23
❑ 27 George Koonce .... .10 .05
❑ 28 Tamarick Vanover .... .25 .11
❑ 29 Yancey Thigpen .... .25 .11
❑ 30 Troy Aikman .... 1.25 .55
❑ 31 Rashaan Salaam .... .50 .23
❑ 32 Anthony Cook .... .10 .05
❑ 33 Tim McKyer .... .10 .05
❑ 34 Dale Carter .... .10 .05
❑ 35 Marvin Washington .... .10 .05
❑ 36 Terry Allen .... .25 .11
❑ 37 Keith Goganious .... .10 .05
❑ 38 Pepper Johnson .... .10 .05
❑ 39 Dave Brown .... .10 .05
❑ 40 Levon Kirkland .... .10 .05
❑ 41 Ken Dilger .... .25 .11
❑ 42 Harvey Williams .... .10 .05
❑ 43 Robert Blackmon .... .10 .05
❑ 44 Kevin Carter .... .10 .05
❑ 45 Warren Moon .... .25 .11
❑ 46 Allen Aldridge .... .10 .05
❑ 47 Terance Mathis .... .10 .05
❑ 48 Junior Seau .... .25 .11
❑ 49 William Fuller .... .10 .05
❑ 50 Lee Woodall .... .10 .05
❑ 51 Aeneas Williams .... .10 .05
❑ 52 Thomas Smith .... .10 .05
❑ 53 Chris Slade .... .10 .05
❑ 54 Eric Allen .... .10 .05
❑ 55 David Sloan .... .10 .05
❑ 56 Hardy Nickerson .... .10 .05
❑ 57 Michael Irvin .... .50 .23
❑ 58 Corey Sawyer .... .10 .05
❑ 59 Eric Green .... .10 .05
❑ 60 Reggie White .... .50 .23
❑ 61 Isaac Bruce .... .50 .23
❑ 62 Darrell Green .... .10 .05
❑ 63 Aaron Glenn .... .10 .05
❑ 64 Mark Brunell .... 1.25 .55
❑ 65 Mark Carrier WR .... .10 .05
❑ 66 Mel Gray .... .10 .05
❑ 67 Phillippi Sparks .... .10 .05
❑ 68 Ernie Mills .... .10 .05
❑ 69 Rick Mirer .... .25 .11
❑ 70 Neil Smith .... .10 .05
❑ 71 Terry McDaniel .... .10 .05
❑ 72 Terrell Davis 3.00 1.35
❑ 73 Alonzo Spellman .... .10 .05
❑ 74 Jessie Tuggle .... .10 .05
❑ 75 Terry Kirby .... .25 .11
❑ 76 David Palmer .... .10 .05
❑ 77 Calvin Williams .... .10 .05
❑ 78 Shaun Gayle .... .10 .05
❑ 79 Bryant Young .... .25 .11
❑ 80 Jim Harbaugh .... .25 .11
❑ 81 Michael Jackson .... .25 .11
❑ 82 Dave Meggett .... .10 .05
❑ 83 Henry Thomas .... .10 .05
❑ 84 Jim Kelly .... .50 .23
❑ 85 Frank Sanders .... .25 .11
❑ 86 Daryl Johnston .... .25 .11
❑ 87 Alvin Harper .... .10 .05
❑ 88 John Copeland .... .10 .05
❑ 89 Mark Chmura .... .25 .11
❑ 90 Jim Everett .... .10 .05
❑ 91 Bobby Houston .... .10 .05
❑ 92 Willie Jackson .... .10 .05
❑ 93 Carlton Bailey .... .10 .05
❑ 94 Todd Lyght .... .10 .05
❑ 95 Ken Harvey .... .10 .05
❑ 96 Erric Pegram .... .10 .05
❑ 97 Anthony Smith .... .10 .05
❑ 98 Kimble Anders .... .25 .11
❑ 99 Steve McNair .... 1.00 .45
❑ 100 Jeff George .... .25 .11
❑ 101 Michael Timpson .... .10 .05
❑ 102 Brent Jones .... .10 .05
❑ 103 Mike Mamula .... .10 .05
❑ 104 Jeff Cross .... .10 .05
❑ 105 Craig Newsome .... .10 .05
❑ 106 Howard Cross .... .10 .05
❑ 107 Terry Wooden .... .10 .05
❑ 108 Randall McDaniel .... .10 .05
❑ 109 Andre Reed .... .25 .11
❑ 110 Steve Atwater .... .10 .05
❑ 111 Larry Centers .... .25 .11
❑ 112 Tony Bennett .... .10 .05
❑ 113 Drew Bledsoe .... 1.25 .55
❑ 114 Terrell Fletcher .... .10 .05
❑ 115 Warren Sapp .... .10 .05
❑ 116 Deion Sanders .... .75 .35
❑ 117 Bryce Paup .... .10 .05
❑ 118 Mario Bates .... .25 .11
❑ 119 Steve Tovar .... .10 .05
❑ 120 Barry Sanders 2.50 1.10
❑ 121 Tony Boselli .... .10 .05
❑ 122 Micheal Barrow .... .10 .05
❑ 123 Sam Mills .... .10 .05
❑ 124 Tim Brown .... .50 .23
❑ 125 Darren Perry .... .10 .05
❑ 126 Brian Blades .... .10 .05
❑ 127 Tyrone Wheatley .... .25 .11
❑ 128 Derrick Thomas .... .25 .11
❑ 129 Edgar Bennett .... .25 .11
❑ 130 Cris Carter .... .50 .23
❑ 131 Stephen Grant .... .10 .05
❑ 132 Kevin Williams .... .10 .05
❑ 133 Darnay Scott .... .25 .11
❑ 134 Rod Stephens .... .10 .05
❑ 135 Ken Norton .... .10 .05
❑ 136 Tim Biakabutuka RC .... 1.00 .45
❑ 137 Willie Anderson RC .... .10 .05
❑ 138 Lawrence Phillips RC ..... .75 .35
❑ 139 Jonathan Ogden RC ...... .10 .05
❑ 140 Simeon Rice RC .... .50 .23
❑ 141 Alex Van Dyke RC .... .25 .11
❑ 142 Jerome Woods RC .... .10 .05
❑ 143 Eric Moulds RC .... 2.00 .90
❑ 144 Mike Alstott RC .... 1.50 .70
❑ 145 Marvin Harrison RC...... 3.00 1.35
❑ 146 Duane Clemons RC ...... .10 .05

❑ 147 Regan Upshaw RC .... .10 .05
❑ 148 Eddie Kennison RC........ .50 .23
❑ 149 John Mobley RC .... .10 .05
❑ 150 Keyshawn Johnson RC 3.00 1.35
❑ 151 Marco Battaglia RC......... .10 .05
❑ 152 Rickey Dudley RC.......... .50 .23
❑ 153 Kevin Hardy RC .... .50 .23
❑ 154 Curtis Martin SM .... 1.00 .45
❑ 155 Dan Marino SM............ 2.50 1.10
❑ 156 Rashaan Salaam SM ..... .25 .11
❑ 157 Joey Galloway SM ...... 1.00 .45
❑ 158 John Elway SM 2.50 1.10
❑ 159 Marshall Faulk SM .... .50 .23
❑ 160 Jerry Rice SM .... 1.25 .55
❑ 161 Darren Bennett SM .... .10 .05
❑ 162 Tamarick Vanover SM.... .25 .11
❑ 163 Orlando Thomas SM...... .10 .05
❑ 164 Jim Kelly SM .... .50 .23
❑ 165 Larry Brown SM .... .10 .05
❑ 166 Errict Rhett SM .... .25 .11
❑ 167 Warren Moon SM .... .10 .05
❑ 168 Hugh Douglas SM.......... .10 .05
❑ 169 Jim Everett SM .... .10 .05
❑ 170 AFC Championship Game.... .10 .05
Colts vs. Steelers
Hail Mary Pass
❑ 171 Larry Centers SM .... .25 .11
❑ 172 Marcus Allen GM........... .50 .23
❑ 173 Morten Andersen GM .... .10 .05
❑ 174 Brett Favre GM 2.50 1.10
❑ 175 Jerry Rice GM.............. 1.25 .55
❑ 176 Glyn Milburn GM............ .10 .05
❑ 177 Thurman Thomas GM.... .25 .11
❑ 178 Michael Irvin GM............ .25 .11
❑ 179 Barry Sanders GM 2.50 1.10
❑ 180 Dan Marino GM............ 2.50 1.10
❑ 181 Joey Galloway............. 1.00 .45
❑ 182 Dwayne Harper .... .10 .05
❑ 183 Antonio Langham .... .10 .05
❑ 184 Chris Zorich.................. .10 .05
❑ 185 Willie McGinest .... .10 .05
❑ 186 Wayne Chrebet .... .25 .11
❑ 187 Dermontti Dawson.......... .10 .05
❑ 188 Charlie Garner............... .10 .05
❑ 189 Quentin Coryatt.............. .10 .05
❑ 190 Rodney Hampton .... .25 .11
❑ 191 Kelvin Pritchett .... .10 .05
❑ 192 Willie Green.................... .10 .05
❑ 193 Garrison Hearst.............. .25 .11
❑ 194 Tracy Scroggins .... .10 .05
❑ 195 Rocket Ismail.................. .10 .05
❑ 196 Michael Westbrook .... .50 .23
❑ 197 Troy Drayton .... .10 .05
❑ 198 Rob Fredrickson .... .10 .05
❑ 199 Sean Lumpkin................ .10 .05
❑ 200 John Elway 2.50 1.10
❑ 201 Bernie Parmalee .... .10 .05
❑ 202 Chris Chandler .... .25 .11
❑ 203 Lake Dawson .... .10 .05
❑ 204 Orlando Thomas .... .10 .05
❑ 205 Carl Pickens .... .50 .23
❑ 206 Kurt Schulz .... .10 .05
❑ 207 Clay Matthews................ .10 .05
❑ 208 Winston Moss .... .10 .05
❑ 209 Sean Dawkins .... .10 .05
❑ 210 Emmitt Smith............... 2.00 .90
❑ 211 Mark Carrier DB .... .10 .05
❑ 212 Clyde Simmons.............. .10 .05
❑ 213 Derrick Brooks................ .10 .05
❑ 214 William Floyd.................. .25 .11
❑ 215 Aaron Hayden................ .10 .05
❑ 216 Brian DeMarco .... .10 .05
❑ 217 Ben Coates .... .25 .11
❑ 218 Renaldo Turnbull............ .10 .05
❑ 219 Adrian Murrell .... .50 .23
❑ 220 Marcus Allen.................. .50 .23
❑ 221 Brett Maxie .... .10 .05
❑ 222 Trev Alberts.................... .10 .05
❑ 223 Darren Woodson............ .25 .11
❑ 224 Brian Mitchell.................. .10 .05
❑ 225 Michael Haynes.............. .10 .05
❑ 226 Sean Jones .... .10 .05
❑ 227 Eric Zeier........................ .10 .05
❑ 228 Herman Moore .... .50 .23
❑ 229 Shane Conlan .... .10 .05
❑ 230 Chris Warren.................. .25 .11
❑ 231 Dana Stubblefield .... .25 .11
❑ 232 Andre Coleman.............. .10 .05
❑ 233 Kordell Stewart UER .... 1.00 .45
card actually numbered 223
❑ 234 Ray Crockett .... .10 .05
❑ 235 Craig Heyward .... .10 .05
❑ 236 Mike Fox .... .10 .05
❑ 237 Derek Brown RBK.......... .10 .05
❑ 238 Thomas Lewis................ .10 .05
❑ 239 Hugh Douglas................ .10 .05
❑ 240 Tom Carter .... .10 .05
❑ 241 Toby Wright.................... .10 .05
❑ 242 Jason Belser .... .10 .05
❑ 243 Rodney Peete .... .10 .05
❑ 244 Napoleon Kaufman .... .75 .35
❑ 245 Merton Hanks .... .10 .05
❑ 246 Harry Colon.................... .10 .05
❑ 247 Greg Hill .... .25 .11
❑ 248 Vincent Brisby................ .10 .05
❑ 249 Eric Hill .... .10 .05
❑ 250 Brett Favre 2.50 1.10
❑ 251 Leroy Hoard .... .10 .05
❑ 252 Eric Guliford .... .10 .05
❑ 253 Stanley Richard.............. .25 .11
❑ 254 Carlos Jenkins................ .10 .05
❑ 255 D'Marco Farr .... .10 .05
❑ 256 Carlton Gray .... .10 .05
❑ 257 Derek Loville .... .10 .05
❑ 258 Ray Buchanan................ .10 .05
❑ 259 Jake Reed...................... .25 .11
❑ 260 Dan Marino 2.50 1.10
❑ 261 Brad Baxter.................... .10 .05
❑ 262 Pat Swilling .... .10 .05
❑ 263 Andy Harmon .... .10 .05
❑ 264 Harold Green.................. .10 .05
❑ 265 Shannon Sharpe .... .25 .11
❑ 266 Erik Kramer .... .10 .05
❑ 267 Lamar Lathon .... .10 .05
❑ 268 Stevon Moore .... .10 .05
❑ 269 Tony Martin .... .25 .11
❑ 270 Bruce Smith.................... .25 .11
❑ 271 James Washington .... .10 .05
❑ 272 Tyrone Poole.................. .10 .05
❑ 273 Eric Swann .... .10 .05
❑ 274 Dexter Carter.................. .10 .05
❑ 275 Greg Lloyd...................... .25 .11
❑ 276 Michael Zordich.............. .10 .05
❑ 277 Steve Wisniewski .... .10 .05
❑ 278 Chris Calloway .... .10 .05
❑ 279 Irv Smith .... .10 .05
❑ 280 Steve Young .... 1.00 .45
❑ 281 James O.Stewart............ .25 .11
❑ 282 Blaine Bishop .... .10 .05
❑ 283 Rob Moore .... .25 .11
❑ 284 Eric Metcalf .... .10 .05
❑ 285 Kerry Collins .... .50 .23
❑ 286 Dan Wilkinson................ .10 .05
❑ 287 Curtis Conway................ .50 .23
❑ 288 Jay Novacek .... .10 .05
❑ 289 Henry Ellard .... .10 .05
❑ 290 Curtis Martin .... 1.00 .45
❑ 291 Brett Perriman................ .10 .05
❑ 292 Jeff Lageman .... .10 .05
❑ 293 Trent Dilfer .... .50 .23
❑ 294 Cortez Kennedy .... .10 .05
❑ 295 Jeff Hostetler.................. .10 .05
❑ 296 Mark Fields .... .10 .05
❑ 297 Qadry Ismail .... .10 .05
❑ 298 Steve Bono .... .10 .05
❑ 299 Tony Tolbert .... .10 .05
❑ 300 Jerry Rice .... 1.25 .55
❑ 301 Marvcus Patton.............. .10 .05
❑ 302 Robert Brooks................ .50 .23
❑ 303 Terry Ray .... .10 .05
❑ 304 John Thierry .... .10 .05
❑ 305 Errict Rhett .... .25 .11
❑ 306 Ricardo McDonald.......... .10 .05
❑ 307 Antonio London.............. .10 .05
❑ 308 Lonnie Johnson.............. .10 .05
❑ 309 Mark Collins .... .10 .05
❑ 310 Marshall Faulk................ .50 .23
❑ 311 Anthony Pleasant .... .10 .05
❑ 312 Howard Griffith .... .10 .05
❑ 313 Roosevelt Potts.............. .10 .05
❑ 314 Jim Flanigan .... .10 .05
❑ 315 'Omar Ellison RC .... .10 .05
❑ 316 Boomer Esiason SP ...... .25 .11
❑ 317 Leslie O'Neal SP............ .10 .05
❑ 318 Jerome Bettis SP .... .50 .23
❑ 319 Larry Brown SP.............. .10 .05
❑ 320 Neil O'Donnell SP .... .25 .11
❑ 321 Andre Rison SP.............. .25 .11
❑ 322 Cornelius Bennett SP .... .10 .05
❑ 323 Quinn Early SP .... .10 .05
❑ 324 Bryan Cox SP .... .10 .05
❑ 325 Irving Fryar SP .... .25 .11
❑ 326 Eddie Robinson SP........ .10 .05
❑ 327 Chris Doleman SP.......... .10 .05
❑ 328 Sean Gilbert SP .... .10 .05
❑ 329 Steve Walsh SP .... .10 .05
❑ 330 Kevin Greene SP .... .25 .11
❑ 331 Chris Spielman SP .... .10 .05
❑ 332 Jeff Graham SP.............. .10 .05
❑ 333 Anthony Dorsett RC SP .10 .05
❑ 334 Amani Toomer RC SP.... .50 .23
❑ 335 Walt Harris RC SP .... .10 .05
❑ 336 Ray Mickens RC SP ...... .10 .05
❑ 337 Danny Kanell RC SP...... .50 .23
❑ 338 Daryl Gardener RC SP .. .10 .05
❑ 339 Jonathan Ogden SP ...... .10 .05
❑ 340 Eddie George RC SP .. 4.00 1.80
❑ 341 Jeff Lewis RC SP .... .75 .35
❑ 342 Terrell Owens RC SP .. 3.00 1.35
❑ 343 Brian Dawkins RC SP.... .10 .05
❑ 344 Tim Biakabutuka SP ...... .50 .23
❑ 345 Marvin Harrison SP...... 1.25 .55
❑ 346 Lawyer Milloy RC SP .... .10 .05
❑ 347 Eric Moulds SP .... 1.00 .45
❑ 348 Alex Van Dyke SP.......... .25 .11
❑ 349 John Mobley SP .... .10 .05
❑ 350 Kevin Hardy SP.............. .50 .23
❑ 351 Ray Lewis RC SP .... .10 .05
❑ 352 Lawrence Phillips SP .... .50 .23
❑ 353 Stepfret Williams RC SP .25 .11
❑ 354 Bobby Engram RC SP .. .50 .23
❑ 355 Leeland McElroy RC SP .50 .23
❑ 356 Marco Battaglia SP .... .10 .05
❑ 357 Rickey Dudley SP .... .50 .23
❑ 358 Bobby Hoying RC SP ..... .75 .35
❑ 359 Cedric Jones RC SP...... .10 .05
❑ 360 Keyshawn Johnson SP 1.25 .55
❑ P19 Scott Mitchell Proto
team name on back .. .50 .23
not ghosted in white
❑ P31 R.Salaam Proto .... .75 .35
team name on back
not ghosted in white
❑ P56 H.Nickerson Proto.......... .50 .23
team name on back
not ghosted in white

1996 Stadium Club Brace Yourself

	MINT	NRMT
COMPLETE SET (10)	80.00	36.00

STATED ODDS 1:24 HOB, 1:32 RET SER.2

❑ BY1 Dan Marino............... 20.00 9.00
❑ BY2 Marshall Faulk 4.00 1.80
❑ BY3 Greg Lloyd .... 2.00 .90
❑ BY4 Steve Young............... 8.00 3.60
❑ BY5 Emmitt Smith 15.00 6.75
❑ BY6 Junior Seau .... 2.00 .90

		MINT	NRMT
❑ BY7	Chris Warren	2.00	.90
❑ BY8	Jerry Rice	10.00	4.50
❑ BY9	Troy Aikman	10.00	4.50
❑ BY10	Barry Sanders	20.00	9.00

1996 Stadium Club Contact Prints

	MINT	NRMT
COMPLETE SET (10)	20.00	9.00
COMMON CARD (CP1-CP10)	1.50	.70
SEMISTARS	2.00	.90

SER.1 STATED ODDS 1:12HOB/RET, 1:4 JUM

		MINT	NRMT
❑ CP1	Ken Norton vs. Drew Bledsoe	3.50	1.55
❑ CP2	Chris Zorich vs. Barry Sanders	4.00	1.80
❑ CP3	Corey Harris vs. Harvey Williams	1.50	.70
❑ CP4	Sam Mills vs. Thurman Thomas	2.00	.90
❑ CP5	Bryce Paup vs. Derrick Moore	1.50	.70
❑ CP6	Rob Fredrickson vs. Chris Warren	1.50	.70
❑ CP7	Darnell Walker vs. Bernie Parmalee	1.50	.70
❑ CP8	Derrick Thomas vs. Gus Frerotte	2.00	.90
❑ CP9	Hardy Nickerson vs. Robert Smith	1.50	.70
❑ CP10	Reggie White vs. Dave Brown	2.00	.90

1996 Stadium Club Cut Backs

	MINT	NRMT
COMPLETE SET (8)	60.00	27.00

STATED ODDS 1:36 HOB, 1:12 JUM SER.1

		MINT	NRMT
❑ C1	Emmitt Smith	20.00	9.00
❑ C2	Barry Sanders	25.00	11.00
❑ C3	Curtis Martin	10.00	4.50
❑ C4	Chris Warren	2.50	1.10
❑ C5	Errict Rhett	2.50	1.10
❑ C6	Rodney Hampton	2.50	1.10
❑ C7	Ricky Watters	2.50	1.10
❑ C8	Terry Allen	2.50	1.10

1996 Stadium Club Fusion

	MINT	NRMT
COMPLETE SET (16)	80.00	36.00

*SINGLES: 3X TO 8X BASE CARD HI
STATED ODDS 1:24 SER.2 HOBBY

		MINT	NRMT
❑ F1A	Steve Young	8.00	3.60
❑ F1B	Jerry Rice	10.00	4.50
❑ F2A	Drew Bledsoe	10.00	4.50
❑ F2B	Curtis Martin	8.00	3.60
❑ F3A	Trent Dilfer	4.00	1.80
❑ F3B	Errict Rhett	2.00	.90
❑ F4A	Jeff Hostetler	.75	.35
❑ F4B	Tim Brown	4.00	1.80
❑ F5A	Brett Favre	20.00	9.00
❑ F5B	Robert Brooks	4.00	1.80
❑ F6A	Jim Harbaugh	2.00	.90
❑ F6B	Marshall Faulk	4.00	1.80
❑ F7A	Rashaan Salaam	4.00	1.80
❑ F7B	Erik Kramer	.75	.35
❑ F8A	Scott Mitchell	2.00	.90
❑ F8B	Barry Sanders	20.00	9.00

1996 Stadium Club Laser Sites

	MINT	NRMT
COMPLETE SET (8)	80.00	36.00

STATED ODDS 1:36 HOB, 1:12 JUM SER.1

		MINT	NRMT
❑ LS1	Brett Favre	25.00	11.00
❑ LS2	Dan Marino	25.00	11.00
❑ LS3	Steve Young	10.00	4.50
❑ LS4	Troy Aikman	12.00	5.50
❑ LS5	Jim Harbaugh	2.50	1.10
❑ LS6	Scott Mitchell	2.50	1.10
❑ LS7	Erik Kramer	1.00	.45
❑ LS8	Warren Moon	2.50	1.10

1996 Stadium Club Namath Finest

	MINT	NRMT
COMPLETE SET (10)	80.00	36.00
COMMON CARD (1-10)	10.00	4.50
NAMATH 1965	12.00	5.50

STATED ODDS 1:24 HOB/RET, 1:8 JUM SER.1

	MINT	NRMT
REFRACTOR SET (10)	150.00	70.00

REFRACTORS: 1X TO 2X
REF.STAT.ODDS 1:96 H/R, 1:32 JUM SER.1

		MINT	NRMT
❑ 1	Joe Namath 1965	12.00	5.50
❑ 2	Joe Namath 1966	10.00	4.50
❑ 3	Joe Namath 1967	10.00	4.50
❑ 4	Joe Namath 1968	10.00	4.50
❑ 5	Joe Namath 1969	10.00	4.50
❑ 6	Joe Namath 1970	10.00	4.50
❑ 7	Joe Namath 1971	10.00	4.50
❑ 8	Joe Namath 1972	10.00	4.50
❑ 9	Joe Namath IA 1972	10.00	4.50
❑ 10	Joe Namath 1973	10.00	4.50

1996 Stadium Club New Age

	MINT	NRMT
COMPLETE SET (20)	100.00	45.00

STATED ODDS 1:24 HOB, 1:32 RET SER.2

		MINT	NRMT
❑ NA1	Alex Van Dyke	2.00	.90
❑ NA2	Lawrence Phillips	6.00	2.70
❑ NA3	Tim Biakabutuka	8.00	3.60
❑ NA4	Reggie Brown	.75	.35
❑ NA5	Duane Clemons	.75	.35
❑ NA6	Marco Battaglia	.75	.35
❑ NA7	Cedric Jones	.75	.35
❑ NA8	Jerome Woods	.75	.35
❑ NA9	Eric Moulds	15.00	6.75
❑ NA10	Kevin Hardy	4.00	1.80
❑ NA11	Rickey Dudley	4.00	1.80
❑ NA12	Regan Upshaw	.75	.35
❑ NA13	Eddie Kennison	4.00	1.80
❑ NA14	Jonathan Ogden	.75	.35
❑ NA15	John Mobley	.75	.35
❑ NA16	Mike Alstott	12.00	5.50
❑ NA17	Alex Molden	.75	.35
❑ NA18	Marvin Harrison	25.00	11.00
❑ NA19	Simeon Rice	4.00	1.80
❑ NA20	Keyshawn Johnson	25.00	11.00

1996 Stadium Club Photo Gallery

	MINT	NRMT
COMPLETE SET (21)	200.00	90.00

STATED ODDS 1:18 HOB, 1:24 RET SER.2

Card	Player	MINT	NRMT
❑ PG1	Emmitt Smith	20.00	9.00
❑ PG2	Jeff Blake	5.00	2.20
❑ PG3	Junior Seau	2.50	1.10
❑ PG4	Robert Brooks	5.00	2.20
❑ PG5	Barry Sanders	25.00	11.00
❑ PG6	Drew Bledsoe	12.00	5.50
❑ PG7	Joey Galloway	10.00	4.50
❑ PG8	Marshall Faulk	5.00	2.20
❑ PG9	Mark Brunell	12.00	5.50
❑ PG10	Jerry Rice	12.00	5.50
❑ PG11	Rashaan Salaam	5.00	2.20
❑ PG12	Troy Aikman	12.00	5.50
❑ PG13	Steve Young	10.00	4.50
❑ PG14	Tim Brown	5.00	2.20
❑ PG15	Brett Favre	25.00	11.00
❑ PG16	Kerry Collins	5.00	2.20
❑ PG17	John Elway	25.00	11.00
❑ PG18	Curtis Martin	10.00	4.50
❑ PG19	Deion Sanders	8.00	3.60
❑ PG20	Dan Marino	25.00	11.00
❑ PG21	Chris Warren	2.50	1.10

1996 Stadium Club Pro Bowl

	MINT	NRMT
COMPLETE SET (20)	150.00	70.00
COMMON CARD (PB1-PB20)	4.00	1.80
SEMISTARS	6.00	2.70

STATED ODDS 1:24 RET. SER.1

Card	Player	MINT	NRMT
❑ PB1	Brett Favre	30.00	13.50
❑ PB2	Bruce Smith	4.00	1.80
❑ PB3	Ricky Watters	6.00	2.70
❑ PB4	Yancey Thigpen	4.00	1.80
❑ PB5	Barry Sanders	30.00	13.50
❑ PB6	Jim Harbaugh	6.00	2.70
❑ PB7	Michael Irvin	6.00	2.70
❑ PB8	Chris Warren	4.00	1.80
❑ PB9	Dana Stubblefield	4.00	1.80
❑ PB10	Jeff Blake	4.00	1.80
❑ PB11	Emmitt Smith	25.00	11.00
❑ PB12	Bryce Paup	4.00	1.80
❑ PB13	Steve Young	12.00	5.50
❑ PB14	Kevin Greene	4.00	1.80
❑ PB15	Jerry Rice	15.00	6.75
❑ PB16	Curtis Martin	10.00	4.50
❑ PB17	Reggie White	6.00	2.70
❑ PB18	Derrick Thomas	4.00	1.80
❑ PB19	Cris Carter	4.00	1.80
❑ PB20	Greg Lloyd	4.00	1.80

1997 Stadium Club

	MINT	NRMT
COMPLETE SET (340)	70.00	32.00
COMP.SERIES 1 (170)	35.00	16.00
COMP.SERIES 2 (170)	35.00	16.00
COMMON CARD (1-340)	.15	.07
SEMISTARS	.25	.11
UNLISTED STARS	.50	.23
COMP.FIRST DAY (340)	2000.00	900.00

*FIRST DAY STARS: 10X TO 25X HI COL.
*FIRST DAY RCs: 5X TO 12X
FIRST DAY STATED ODDS 1:24 RETAIL

	MINT	NRMT
COMP.ONE OF KIND (340)	3000.00	1350.00

*ONE OF KIND STARS: 15X TO 40X HI
*ONE OF KIND RCs: 10X TO 25X

ONE OF KIND ODDS 1:48H/R, 1:30J

Card	Player	MINT	NRMT
❑ 1	Junior Seau	.25	.11
❑ 2	Michael Irvin	.50	.23
❑ 3	Marcus Allen	.50	.23
❑ 4	Dale Carter	.15	.07
❑ 5	Darnell Autry RC	.25	.11
❑ 6	Isaac Bruce	.50	.23
❑ 7	Darrell Green	.25	.11
❑ 8	Joey Galloway	.75	.35
❑ 9	Steve Atwater	.15	.07
❑ 10	Kordell Stewart	.75	.35
❑ 11	Tony Brackens	.15	.07
❑ 12	Gus Frerotte	.15	.07
❑ 13	Henry Ellard	.15	.07
❑ 14	Charles Way	.25	.11
❑ 15	Jim Druckenmiller RC	.75	.35
❑ 16	Orlando Thomas	.15	.07
❑ 17	Terrell Davis	2.50	1.10
❑ 18	Jim Schwantz	.15	.07
❑ 19	Derrick Thomas	.25	.11
❑ 20	Curtis Martin	.75	.35
❑ 21	Deion Sanders	.50	.23
❑ 22	Bruce Smith	.25	.11
❑ 23	Jake Reed	.25	.11
❑ 24	Leeland McElroy	.15	.07
❑ 25	Jerome Bettis	.50	.23
❑ 26	Neil Smith	.25	.11
❑ 27	Terry Allen	.50	.23
❑ 28	Gilbert Brown	.15	.07
❑ 29	Steve McNair	.75	.35
❑ 30	Kerry Collins	.25	.11
❑ 31	Thurman Thomas	.50	.23
❑ 32	Kenny Holmes RC	.15	.07
❑ 33	Karim Abdul-Jabbar	.50	.23
❑ 34	Steve Young	1.00	.45
❑ 35	Jerry Rice	1.50	.70
❑ 36	Jeff George	.25	.11
❑ 37	Errict Rhett	.15	.07
❑ 38	Mike Alstott	.50	.23
❑ 39	Tim Brown	.50	.23
❑ 40	Keyshawn Johnson	.50	.23
❑ 41	Jim Harbaugh	.25	.11
❑ 42	Kevin Hardy	.15	.07
❑ 43	Kevin Greene	.25	.11
❑ 44	Eric Metcalf	.25	.11
❑ 45	Troy Aikman	1.50	.70
❑ 46	Marshall Faulk	.50	.23
❑ 47	Shannon Sharpe	.25	.11
❑ 48	Warren Moon	.50	.23
❑ 49	Mark Brunell	1.50	.70
❑ 50	Dan Marino	3.00	1.35
❑ 51	Byron Hanspard RC	1.50	.70
❑ 52	Chris Chandler	.25	.11
❑ 53	Wayne Chrebet	.50	.23
❑ 54	Antonio Langham	.15	.07
❑ 55	Barry Sanders	3.00	1.35
❑ 56	Curtis Conway	.25	.11
❑ 57	Ricky Watters	.25	.11
❑ 58	William Thomas	.15	.07
❑ 59	Chris Warren	.25	.11
❑ 60	Terry Glenn	.50	.23
❑ 61	Peter Boulware RC	.25	.11
❑ 62	Chad Cota	.15	.07
❑ 63	Eddie Kennison	.25	.11
❑ 64	Lamar Smith	.15	.07
❑ 65	Brett Favre	3.00	1.35
❑ 66	Michael Westbrook	.25	.11
❑ 67	Larry Centers	.25	.11
❑ 68	Trent Dilfer	.50	.23
❑ 69	Stevon Moore	.15	.07
❑ 70	John Elway	3.00	1.35
❑ 71	Bryce Paup	.15	.07
❑ 72	Quentin Coryatt	.15	.07
❑ 73	Rashaan Salaam	.15	.07
❑ 74	Thomas Lewis	.15	.07
❑ 75	Drew Bledsoe	1.50	.70
❑ 76	Cris Carter	.50	.23
❑ 77	Joe Bowden	.15	.07
❑ 78	Allen Aldridge	.15	.07
❑ 79	Zach Thomas	.25	.11
❑ 80	Emmitt Smith	2.50	1.10
❑ 81	Daryl Johnston	.25	.11
❑ 82	Vinny Testaverde	.25	.11
❑ 83	James O.Stewart	.25	.11
❑ 84	Edgar Bennett	.25	.11
❑ 85	Shawn Springs RC	.25	.11
❑ 86	Elvis Grbac	.25	.11
❑ 87	Levon Kirkland	.15	.07
❑ 88	Jeff Graham	.15	.07
❑ 89	Terrell Fletcher	.15	.07
❑ 90	Eddie George	1.50	.70
❑ 91	Jessie Tuggle	.15	.07
❑ 92	Terrell Owens	.50	.23
❑ 93	Wayne Martin	.15	.07
❑ 94	Dwayne Harper	.15	.07
❑ 95	Mark Collins	.15	.07
❑ 96	Marvcus Patton	.15	.07
❑ 97	Napoleon Kaufman	.50	.23
❑ 98	Keenan McCardell	.25	.11
❑ 99	Ty Detmer	.25	.11
❑ 100	Reggie White	.50	.23
❑ 101	William Floyd	.25	.11
❑ 102	Scott Mitchell	.25	.11
❑ 103	Robert Blackmon	.15	.07
❑ 104	Dan Wilkinson	.15	.07
❑ 105	Warren Sapp	.25	.11
❑ 106	Dave Meggett	.15	.07
❑ 107	Brian Mitchell	.15	.07
❑ 108	Tyrone Poole	.15	.07
❑ 109	Derrick Alexander WR	.25	.11
❑ 110	David Palmer	.15	.07
❑ 111	James Farrior RC	.15	.07
❑ 112	Chad Brown	.15	.07
❑ 113	Marty Carter	.15	.07
❑ 114	Lawrence Phillips	.15	.07
❑ 115	Wesley Walls	.25	.11
❑ 116	John Friesz	.15	.07
❑ 117	Roman Phifer	.15	.07
❑ 118	Jason Sehorn	.25	.11
❑ 119	Henry Thomas	.15	.07
❑ 120	Natrone Means	.50	.23
❑ 121	Ty Law	.15	.07
❑ 122	Tony Gonzalez RC	2.50	1.10
❑ 123	Kevin Williams	.15	.07
❑ 124	Regan Upshaw	.15	.07
❑ 125	Antonio Freeman	.75	.35
❑ 126	Jessie Armstead	.15	.07
❑ 127	Pat Barnes RC	.50	.23
❑ 128	Charlie Garner	.15	.07
❑ 129	Irving Fryar	.25	.11
❑ 130	Rickey Dudley	.25	.11
❑ 131	Rodney Harrison	.15	.07
❑ 132	Brent Jones	.25	.11
❑ 133	Neil O'Donnell	.25	.11
❑ 134	Darryll Lewis	.15	.07
❑ 135	Jason Belser	.15	.07
❑ 136	Mark Chmura	.25	.11
❑ 137	Seth Joyner	.15	.07
❑ 138	Herschel Walker	.25	.11
❑ 139	Santana Dotson	.15	.07
❑ 140	Carl Pickens	.50	.23
❑ 141	Terance Mathis	.25	.11
❑ 142	Walt Harris	.15	.07
❑ 143	John Mobley	.15	.07
❑ 144	Gabe Northern	.15	.07
❑ 145	Herman Moore	.50	.23
❑ 146	Michael Jackson	.25	.11
❑ 147	Chris Sanders	.15	.07
❑ 148	LeShon Johnson	.15	.07
❑ 149	Darrell Russell RC	.15	.07
❑ 150	Winslow Oliver	.15	.07
❑ 151	Tamarick Vanover	.25	.11
❑ 152	Tony Martin	.25	.11

Card	MINT	NRMT
❑ 153 Lamar Lathon	.15	.07
❑ 154 Ray Mickens	.15	.07
❑ 155 Derrick Brooks	.15	.07
❑ 156 Warrick Dunn RC	2.50	1.10
❑ 157 Tim McDonald	.15	.07
❑ 158 Keith Lyle	.15	.07
❑ 159 Terry McDaniel	.15	.07
❑ 160 Andre Hastings	.15	.07
❑ 161 Phillippi Sparks	.15	.07
❑ 162 Tedy Bruschi	.15	.07
❑ 163 Bryant Westbrook RC	.15	.07
❑ 164 Victor Green	.15	.07
❑ 165 Jimmy Smith	.25	.11
❑ 166 Greg Biekert	.15	.07
❑ 167 Frank Sanders	.25	.11
❑ 168 Chris Doleman	.15	.07
❑ 169 Phil Hansen	.15	.07
❑ 170 Walter Jones RC	.15	.07
❑ 171 Mark Carrier WR	.15	.07
❑ 172 Greg Hill	.15	.07
❑ 173 Erik Kramer	.15	.07
❑ 174 Chris Spielman	.15	.07
❑ 175 Tom Knight RC	.15	.07
❑ 176 Sam Mills	.15	.07
❑ 177 Robert Smith	.25	.11
❑ 178 Dorsey Levens	.50	.23
❑ 179 Chris Slade	.15	.07
❑ 180 Troy Vincent	.15	.07
❑ 181 Mario Bates	.15	.07
❑ 182 Ed McCaffrey	.25	.11
❑ 183 Mike Mamula	.15	.07
❑ 184 Chad Hennings	.15	.07
❑ 185 Stan Humphries	.25	.11
❑ 186 Reinard Wilson	.15	.07
❑ 187 Kevin Carter	.15	.07
❑ 188 Qadry Ismail	.25	.11
❑ 189 Cortez Kennedy	.15	.07
❑ 190 Eric Swann	.15	.07
❑ 191 Corey Dillon RC	3.00	1.35
❑ 192 Renaldo Wynn	.15	.07
❑ 193 Bobby Hebert	.15	.07
❑ 194 Fred Barnett	.15	.07
❑ 195 Ray Lewis	.15	.07
❑ 196 Robert Jones	.15	.07
❑ 197 Brian Williams	.15	.07
❑ 198 Willie McGinest	.15	.07
❑ 199 Jake Plummer RC	6.00	2.70
❑ 200 Aeneas Williams	.15	.07
❑ 201 Ashley Ambrose	.15	.07
❑ 202 Cornelius Bennett	.15	.07
❑ 203 Mo Lewis	.15	.07
❑ 204 James Hasty	.15	.07
❑ 205 Carnell Lake	.15	.07
❑ 206 Heath Shuler	.15	.07
❑ 207 Dana Stubblefield	.15	.07
❑ 208 Corey Miller	.15	.07
❑ 209 Ike Hilliard RC	1.50	.70
❑ 210 Bryant Young	.15	.07
❑ 211 Hardy Nickerson	.15	.07
❑ 212 Blaine Bishop	.15	.07
❑ 213 Marcus Robertson	.15	.07
❑ 214 Tony Bennett	.15	.07
❑ 215 Kent Graham	.15	.07
❑ 216 Steve Bono	.25	.11
❑ 217 Will Blackwell RC	.50	.23
❑ 218 Tyrone Braxton	.15	.07
❑ 219 Eric Moulds	.50	.23
❑ 220 Rod Woodson	.25	.11
❑ 221 Anthony Johnson	.15	.07
❑ 222 Willie Davis	.15	.07
❑ 223 Darrin Smith	.15	.07
❑ 224 Rick Mirer	.15	.07
❑ 225 Marvin Harrison	.50	.23
❑ 226 Terrell Buckley	.15	.07
❑ 227 Joe Aska	.15	.07
❑ 228 Yatil Green RC	.25	.11
❑ 229 William Fuller	.15	.07
❑ 230 Eddie Robinson	.15	.07
❑ 231 Brian Blades	.15	.07
❑ 232 Michael Sinclair	.15	.07
❑ 233 Ken Harvey	.15	.07
❑ 234 Harvey Williams	.15	.07
❑ 235 Simeon Rice	.25	.11
❑ 236 Chris T. Jones	.15	.07
❑ 237 Bert Emanuel	.25	.11
❑ 238 Corey Sawyer	.15	.07
❑ 239 Chris Calloway	.15	.07
❑ 240 Jeff Blake	.25	.11
❑ 241 Alonzo Spellman	.15	.07
❑ 242 Bryan Cox	.15	.07
❑ 243 Antowain Smith RC	2.00	.90
❑ 244 Tim Biakabutuka	.25	.11
❑ 245 Ray Crockett	.15	.07
❑ 246 Dwayne Rudd	.15	.07
❑ 247 Glyn Milburn	.15	.07
❑ 248 Gary Plummer	.15	.07
❑ 249 O.J. McDuffie	.25	.11
❑ 250 Willie Clay	.15	.07
❑ 251 Jim Everett	.15	.07
❑ 252 Eugene Daniel	.15	.07
❑ 253 Corey Widmer	.15	.07
❑ 254 Mel Gray	.15	.07
❑ 255 Ken Norton	.15	.07
❑ 256 Johnnie Morton	.25	.11
❑ 257 Courtney Hawkins	.15	.07
❑ 258 Ricardo McDonald	.15	.07
❑ 259 Todd Lyght	.15	.07
❑ 260 Micheal Barrow	.15	.07
❑ 261 Aaron Glenn	.15	.07
❑ 262 Jeff Herrod	.15	.07
❑ 263 Troy Davis RC	.50	.23
❑ 264 Eric Hill	.15	.07
❑ 265 Darrien Gordon	.15	.07
❑ 266 Lake Dawson	.15	.07
❑ 267 John Randle	.15	.07
❑ 268 Henry Jones	.15	.07
❑ 269 Mickey Washington	.15	.07
❑ 270 Amani Toomer	.25	.11
❑ 271 Steve Grant	.15	.07
❑ 272 Adrian Murrell	.25	.11
❑ 273 Derrick Witherspoon	.15	.07
❑ 274 Albert Lewis	.15	.07
❑ 275 Ben Coates	.25	.11
❑ 276 Reidel Anthony RC	1.50	.70
❑ 277 Jim Schwantz	.15	.07
❑ 278 Aaron Hayden	.15	.07
❑ 279 Ryan McNeil	.15	.07
❑ 280 LeRoy Butler	.15	.07
❑ 281 Craig Newsome	.15	.07
❑ 282 Bill Romanowski	.15	.07
❑ 283 Michael Bankston	.15	.07
❑ 284 Kevin Smith	.15	.07
❑ 285 Byron Bam Morris	.15	.07
❑ 286 Darnay Scott	.25	.11
❑ 287 David LaFleur RC	.25	.11
❑ 288 Randall Cunningham	.50	.23
❑ 289 Eric Davis	.15	.07
❑ 290 Todd Collins	.15	.07
❑ 291 Steve Tovar	.15	.07
❑ 292 Jermaine Lewis	.50	.23
❑ 293 Alfred Williams	.15	.07
❑ 294 Brad Johnson	.60	.25
❑ 295 Charles Johnson	.25	.11
❑ 296 Ted Johnson	.15	.07
❑ 297 Merton Hanks	.15	.07
❑ 298 Andre Coleman	.15	.07
❑ 299 Keith Jackson	.15	.07
❑ 300 Terry Kirby	.25	.11
❑ 301 Tony Banks	.25	.11
❑ 302 Terrance Shaw	.15	.07
❑ 303 Bobby Engram	.25	.11
❑ 304 Hugh Douglas	.15	.07
❑ 305 Lawyer Milloy	.15	.07
❑ 306 James Jett	.25	.11
❑ 307 Joey Kent RC	.50	.23
❑ 308 Rodney Hampton	.25	.11
❑ 309 Dewayne Washington	.15	.07
❑ 310 Kevin Lockett RC	.25	.11
❑ 311 Ki-Jana Carter	.15	.07
❑ 312 Jeff Lageman	.15	.07
❑ 313 Don Beebe	.15	.07
❑ 314 Willie Williams	.15	.07
❑ 315 Tyrone Wheatley	.25	.11
❑ 316 Leslie O'Neal	.15	.07
❑ 317 Quinn Early	.15	.07
❑ 318 Sean Gilbert	.15	.07
❑ 319 Tim Bowens	.15	.07
❑ 320 Sean Dawkins	.15	.07
❑ 321 Ken Dilger	.15	.07
❑ 322 George Koonce	.15	.07
❑ 323 Jevon Langford	.15	.07
❑ 324 Mike Caldwell	.15	.07
❑ 325 Orlando Pace RC	.15	.07
❑ 326 Garrison Hearst	.25	.11
❑ 327 Mike Tomczak	.15	.07
❑ 328 Rob Moore	.25	.11
❑ 329 Andre Reed	.25	.11
❑ 330 Kimble Anders	.25	.11
❑ 331 Qadry Ismail	.25	.11
❑ 332 Eric Allen	.15	.07
❑ 333 Dave Brown	.15	.07
❑ 334 Bennie Blades	.15	.07
❑ 335 Jamal Anderson	1.00	.45
❑ 336 John Lynch	.15	.07
❑ 337 Tyrone Hughes	.15	.07
❑ 338 Ronnie Harmon	.15	.07
❑ 339 Rae Carruth RC	.50	.23
❑ 340 Robert Brooks	.25	.11
❑ P1 Junior Seau Prototype (line of text below copyrights)	.50	.23
❑ P20 Curtis Martin Prototype (line of text below copyrights)	1.00	.45
❑ P21 Deion Sanders Prototype (line of text below copyrights)	.50	.23
❑ P30 Kerry Collins Prototype (line of text below copyrights)	.75	.35
❑ P47 Sh.Sharpe Prototype line of text below copyrights	.50	.23
❑ P84 Edgar Bennett Prototype (line of text below copyrights)	.50	.23

1997 Stadium Club Aerial Assault

	MINT	NRMT
COMPLETE SET (10)	50.00	22.00

STATED ODDS 1:12 HOB/RET, 1:4 JUM

Card	MINT	NRMT
❑ AA1 Dan Marino	12.00	5.50
❑ AA2 Mark Brunell	6.00	2.70
❑ AA3 Troy Aikman	6.00	2.70
❑ AA4 Ty Detmer	1.00	.45
❑ AA5 John Elway	12.00	5.50
❑ AA6 Drew Bledsoe	6.00	2.70
❑ AA7 Steve Young	4.00	1.80
❑ AA8 Vinny Testaverde	1.00	.45
❑ AA9 Kerry Collins	1.00	.45
❑ AA10 Brett Favre	12.00	5.50

1997 Stadium Club Bowman's Best Previews

	MINT	NRMT
COMPLETE SET (15)	80.00	36.00

STATED ODDS 1:24 HOB/RET, 1:8 JUM
*REFRACTORS: 9X TO 18X BASE CARD HI
REFRACTOR STATED ODDS 1:96
*ATOMIC REFRACTORS: 17.5X TO 35X BASE CARD HI
ATOMIC REFRACTOR ODDS 1:192

Card	MINT	NRMT
❑ BBP1 Dan Marino	20.00	9.00
❑ BBP2 Terry Allen	4.00	1.80
❑ BBP3 Jerome Bettis	4.00	1.80
❑ BBP4 Kevin Greene	2.00	.90
❑ BBP5 Junior Seau	2.00	.90
❑ BBP6 Brett Favre	20.00	9.00
❑ BBP7 Isaac Bruce	4.00	1.80

❑ BBP8	Michael Irvin	4.00	1.80
❑ BBP9	Kerry Collins	2.00	.90
❑ BBP10	Karim Abdul-Jabbar	4.00	1.80
❑ BBP11	Keenan McCardell	2.00	.90
❑ BBP12	Ricky Watters	2.00	.90
❑ BBP13	Mark Brunell	10.00	4.50
❑ BBP14	Jerry Rice	10.00	4.50
❑ BBP15	Drew Bledsoe	10.00	4.50

1997 Stadium Club Bowman's Best Rookie Previews

	MINT	NRMT
COMPLETE SET (15)	40.00	18.00

STATED ODDS 1:24
*REFRACTORS: 6X TO 12X BASE CARD HI
REFRACTOR STATED ODDS 1:96
*ATOMIC REFRACTORS: 12.5X TO 25X BASE CARD HI
ATOMIC REFRACTOR ODDS 1:192

❑ BBP1	Orlando Pace	.75	.35
❑ BBP2	David LaFleur	1.25	.55
❑ BBP3	James Farrior	.75	.35
❑ BBP4	Tony Gonzalez	12.00	5.50
❑ BBP5	Ike Hilliard	8.00	3.60
❑ BBP6	Antowain Smith	10.00	4.50
❑ BBP7	Tom Knight	.75	.35
❑ BBP8	Troy Davis	2.50	1.10
❑ BBP9	Yatil Green	1.25	.55
❑ BBP10	Jim Druckenmiller	4.00	1.80
❑ BBP11	Bryant Westbrook	.75	.35
❑ BBP12	Darrell Russell	.75	.35
❑ BBP13	Rae Carruth	2.50	1.10
❑ BBP14	Shawn Springs	1.25	.55
❑ BBP15	Peter Boulware	1.25	.55

1997 Stadium Club Co-Signers

	MINT	NRMT
COMPLETE SET (105)	3500.00	1600.00
COMMON CARD (CO1-CO36)	40.00	18.00
SEMISTARS CO1-CO36	60.00	27.00
COMMON CARD (CO37-CO72)	30.00	13.50
SEMISTARS CO37-CO72	50.00	22.00
COMMON (CO73-CO108)	15.00	6.75
SEMISTARS CO73-CO108	25.00	11.00

SERIES 1 OVERALL STATED ODDS 1:63

SERIES 2 OVERALL STATED ODDS 1:68

❑ CO1	Karim Abdul-Jabbar / Eddie George	250.00	110.00
❑ CO2	Trace Armstrong / Alonzo Spellman	40.00	18.00
❑ CO3	Steve Atwater / Kevin Hardy	40.00	18.00
❑ CO4	Fred Barnett / Lake Dawson	60.00	27.00
❑ CO5	Blaine Bishop / Darrell Green	40.00	18.00
❑ CO6	Jeff Blake / Gus Frerotte	100.00	45.00
❑ CO7	Steve Bono / Cris Carter	100.00	45.00
❑ CO8	Tim Brown / Isaac Bruce	120.00	55.00
❑ CO9	Wayne Chrebet / Mickey Washington	40.00	18.00
❑ CO10	Curtis Conway / Eddie Kennison	40.00	18.00
❑ CO11	Eric Davis / Jason Sehorn	40.00	18.00
❑ CO12	Terrell Davis / Thurman Thomas	100.00	45.00
❑ CO13	Ken Dilger / Kent Graham	60.00	27.00
❑ CO14	Stephen Grant / Marvcus Patton	40.00	18.00
❑ CO16	Rodney Hampton / Dave Meggett	60.00	27.00
❑ CO17	Merton Hanks / Aeneas Williams	40.00	18.00
❑ CO19	Brent Jones / Wesley Walls	40.00	18.00
❑ CO20	Carnell Lake / Tim McDonald	40.00	18.00
❑ CO21	Thomas Lewis / Keith Lyle	40.00	18.00
❑ CO22	Leeland McElroy / Jeff Lageman	60.00	27.00
❑ CO24	Herman Moore / Desmond Howard	60.00	27.00
❑ CO25	Stevon Moore / William Thomas	40.00	18.00
❑ CO26	Adrian Murrell / Levon Kirkland	60.00	27.00
❑ CO27	Simeon Rice / Winslow Oliver	40.00	18.00
❑ CO28	Bill Romanowski / Gary Plummer	40.00	18.00
❑ CO30	Chris Slade / Kevin Greene	40.00	18.00
❑ CO31	Derrick Thomas / Chris T. Jones	80.00	36.00
❑ CO32	Orlando Thomas / Bobby Engram	60.00	27.00
❑ CO33	Amani Toomer / Thomas Randolph	60.00	27.00
❑ CO34	Steve Tovar / Ellis Johnson LB	40.00	18.00
❑ CO35	Herschel Walker / Anthony Johnson	40.00	18.00
❑ CO36	Darren Woodson / Aaron Glenn	40.00	18.00
❑ CO37	Karim Abdul-Jabbar / Thurman Thomas	80.00	36.00
❑ CO38	Blaine Bishop / Tim McDonald	30.00	13.50
❑ CO39	Jeff Blake / Derrick Thomas	80.00	36.00
❑ CO41	Cris Carter / Marvin Harrison	100.00	45.00
❑ CO42	Curtis Conway / Wesley Walls	50.00	22.00
❑ CO43	Willie Davis / Amani Toomer	50.00	22.00
❑ CO44	Lake Dawson / Ray Mickens	50.00	22.00
❑ CO45	Ken Dilger / Ellis Johnson LB	50.00	22.00
❑ CO46	Bobby Engram / Thomas Lewis	30.00	13.50
❑ CO47	Gus Frerotte / Chris T. Jones	80.00	36.00
❑ CO48	Eddie George / Terrell Davis	200.00	90.00
❑ CO49	Aaron Glenn / Eric Davis	30.00	13.50
❑ CO50	Kent Graham / Steve Tovar	30.00	13.50
❑ CO51	Darrell Green / Carnell Lake	30.00	13.50
❑ CO52	Kevin Greene / Steve Atwater	50.00	22.00
❑ CO53	Rodney Hampton / Anthony Johnson	50.00	22.00
❑ CO54	Kevin Hardy / Merton Hanks	30.00	13.50
❑ CO55	Desmond Howard / Tim Brown	80.00	36.00
❑ CO56	Eddie Kennison / Brent Jones	50.00	22.00
❑ CO57	Levon Kirkland / Simeon Rice	30.00	13.50
❑ CO58	Jeff Lageman / Adrian Murrell	50.00	22.00
❑ CO59	Keith Lyle / Wayne Chrebet	50.00	22.00
❑ CO60	Dave Meggett / Herschel Walker	50.00	22.00
❑ CO61	Herman Moore / Isaac Bruce	100.00	45.00
❑ CO62	Winslow Oliver / Leeland McElroy	30.00	13.50
❑ CO63	Marvcus Patton / Keith Hamilton	30.00	13.50
❑ CO65	Thomas Randolph / Fred Barnett	30.00	13.50
❑ CO66	Alonzo Spellman / Stephen Grant	30.00	13.50
❑ CO67	Chris Spielman / Stevon Moore	30.00	13.50
❑ CO68	William Thomas / Bill Romanowski	30.00	13.50
❑ CO69	Mike Tomczak / Trace Armstrong	30.00	13.50
❑ CO70	Mickey Washington / Orlando Thomas	30.00	13.50
❑ CO71	Aeneas Williams / Chris Slade	30.00	13.50
❑ CO72	Darren Woodson / Jason Sehorn	30.00	13.50
❑ CO73	Trace Armstrong / Keith Hamilton	15.00	6.75
❑ CO74	Steve Atwater / Chris Slade	15.00	6.75
❑ CO75	Fred Barnett / Amani Toomer	25.00	11.00
❑ CO76	Tim Brown / Herman Moore	80.00	36.00
❑ CO77	Isaac Bruce / Desmond Howard	60.00	27.00
❑ CO78	Wayne Chrebet / Thomas Lewis	25.00	11.00
❑ CO79	Eric Davis / Darren Woodson	15.00	6.75
❑ CO80	Terrell Davis / Karim Abdul-Jabbar	100.00	45.00
❑ CO81	Willie Davis / Lake Dawson	25.00	11.00
❑ CO82	Bobby Engram / Marvin Washington	15.00	6.75

Card	Player	MINT	NRMT
❑ CO83	Stephen Grant Mike Tomczak	15.00	6.75
❑ CO84	Merton Hanks Kevin Greene	15.00	6.75
❑ CO85	Marvin Harrison Steve Bono	50.00	22.00
❑ CO86	Anthony Johnson Dave Meggett	15.00	6.75
❑ CO87	Ellis Johnson LB Kent Graham	15.00	6.75
❑ CO88	Brent Jones Curtis Conway	25.00	11.00
❑ CO89	Chris T. Jones Jeff Blake	50.00	22.00
❑ CO90	Carnell Lake Blaine Bishop	15.00	6.75
❑ CO91	Tim McDonald Darrell Green	15.00	6.75
❑ CO92	Ray Mickens Thomas Randolph	15.00	6.75
❑ CO93	Stevon Moore Gary Plummer	15.00	6.75
❑ CO94	Adrian Murrell Leeland McElroy	25.00	11.00
❑ CO95	Winslow Oliver Levon Kirkland	15.00	6.75
❑ CO96	Marvcus Patton Alonzo Spellman	15.00	6.75
❑ CO98	Simeon Rice Jeff Lageman	15.00	6.75
❑ CO99	Junior Seau Bill Romanowski	25.00	11.00
❑ CO100	Jason Sehorn Aaron Glenn	15.00	6.75
❑ CO101	Derrick Thomas Gus Frerotte	40.00	18.00
❑ CO102	Orlando Thomas Keith Lyle	15.00	6.75
❑ CO103	Thurman Thomas Eddie George	100.00	45.00
❑ CO104	William Thomas Chris Spielman	15.00	6.75
❑ CO105	Steve Tovar Ken Dilger	15.00	6.75
❑ CO106	Herschel Walker Rodney Hampton	25.00	11.00
❑ CO107	Wesley Walls Eddie Kennison	40.00	18.00
❑ CO108	Aeneas Williams Kevin Hardy	15.00	6.75

1997 Stadium Club Grid Kids

	MINT	NRMT
COMPLETE SET (20)	80.00	36.00

STATED ODDS 1:36 HOB/RET, 1:12 JUM

Card	Player	MINT	NRMT
❑ GK1	Orlando Pace	.60	.25
❑ GK2	Darrell Russell	.60	.25
❑ GK3	Shawn Springs	1.00	.45
❑ GK4	Peter Boulware	1.00	.45
❑ GK5	Bryant Westbrook	.60	.25
❑ GK6	Darnell Autry	1.00	.45
❑ GK7	Ike Hilliard	6.00	2.70
❑ GK8	James Farrior	.60	.25
❑ GK9	Jake Plummer	25.00	11.00
❑ GK10	Tony Gonzalez	10.00	4.50
❑ GK11	Yatil Green	1.00	.45
❑ GK12	Corey Dillon	12.00	5.50
❑ GK13	Dwayne Rudd	.60	.25
❑ GK14	Renaldo Wynn	.60	.25
❑ GK15	David LaFleur	1.00	.45
❑ GK16	Antowain Smith	8.00	3.60
❑ GK17	Jim Druckenmiller	3.00	1.35
❑ GK18	Rae Carruth	2.00	.90
❑ GK19	Tom Knight	.60	.25
❑ GK20	Byron Hanspard	6.00	2.70

1997 Stadium Club Never Compromise

	MINT	NRMT
COMPLETE SET (40)	200.00	90.00

STATED ODDS 1:12 SERIES 2....

Card	Player	MINT	NRMT
❑ NC1	Orlando Pace	.75	.35
❑ NC2	Corey Dillon	15.00	6.75
❑ NC3	Tony Gonzalez	12.00	5.50
❑ NC4	Tom Knight	.75	.35
❑ NC5	Deion Sanders	4.00	1.80
❑ NC6	Dwayne Rudd	1.25	.55
❑ NC7	Warrick Dunn	12.00	5.50
❑ NC8	Kenny Holmes	.75	.35
❑ NC9	Will Blackwell	2.50	1.10
❑ NC10	Shawn Springs	1.25	.55
❑ NC11	Rae Carruth	2.50	1.10
❑ NC12	Edgar Bennett	2.00	.90
❑ NC13	Walter Jones	.75	.35
❑ NC14	Reidel Anthony	8.00	3.60
❑ NC15	Troy Davis	2.50	1.10
❑ NC16	Mark Brunell	12.00	5.50
❑ NC17	Pat Barnes	2.50	1.10
❑ NC18	Reggie White	4.00	1.80
❑ NC19	Darrell Russell	.75	.35
❑ NC20	Ike Hilliard	8.00	3.60
❑ NC21	Emmitt Smith	20.00	9.00
❑ NC22	David LaFleur	1.25	.55
❑ NC23	Yatil Green	1.25	.55
❑ NC24	Barry Sanders	25.00	11.00
❑ NC25	Bryant Westbrook	.75	.35
❑ NC26	Lawrence Phillips	1.25	.55
❑ NC27	Peter Boulware	1.25	.55
❑ NC28	Joey Kent	2.50	1.10
❑ NC29	Kevin Lockett	1.25	.55
❑ NC30	Derrick Thomas	2.00	.90
❑ NC31	Antowain Smith	10.00	4.50
❑ NC32	James Farrior	.75	.35
❑ NC33	Kordell Stewart	6.00	2.70
❑ NC34	Byron Hanspard	8.00	3.60
❑ NC35	Jim Druckenmiller	4.00	1.80
❑ NC36	Reinard Wilson	1.25	.55
❑ NC37	Darnell Autry	1.25	.55
❑ NC38	Steve Young	8.00	3.60
❑ NC39	Renaldo Wynn	.75	.35
❑ NC40	Jake Plummer	30.00	13.50

1997 Stadium Club Offensive Strikes

	MINT	NRMT
COMPLETE SET (10)	40.00	18.00

STATED ODDS 1:12 HOBY/RET, 1:4 JUM

Card	Player	MINT	NRMT
❑ AF1	Jerry Rice	5.00	2.20
❑ AF2	Carl Pickens UER (Perkins on back)	1.50	.70
❑ AF3	Shannon Sharpe	.75	.35
❑ AF4	Herman Moore	1.50	.70
❑ AF5	Terry Glenn	1.50	.70
❑ GC1	Barry Sanders	10.00	4.50
❑ GC2	Curtis Martin	2.50	1.10
❑ GC3	Emmitt Smith	8.00	3.60
❑ GC4	Terrell Davis	8.00	3.60
❑ GC5	Eddie George	5.00	2.20

1997 Stadium Club Triumvirate I

	MINT	NRMT
COMP.SERIES 1 SET (18)	120.00	55.00

STATED ODDS 1:36 SER.1 RETAIL
*REFRACTORS: 15X TO 30X BASE CARD HI
REFRACTOR STATED ODDS 1:144
*ATOMIC REF: 30X TO 60X BASE CARD HI
ATOMIC REF.STATED ODDS 1:288

Card	Player	MINT	NRMT
❑ T1A	Emmitt Smith	20.00	9.00
❑ T1B	Troy Aikman	12.00	5.50
❑ T1C	Michael Irvin	4.00	1.80
❑ T2A	Curtis Martin	6.00	2.70
❑ T2B	Drew Bledsoe	12.00	5.50
❑ T2C	Terry Glenn	4.00	1.80
❑ T3A	Barry Sanders	25.00	11.00
❑ T3B	Scott Mitchell	2.00	.90
❑ T3C	Herman Moore	4.00	1.80
❑ T4A	William Floyd	2.00	.90
❑ T4B	Steve Young	8.00	3.60
❑ T4C	Jerry Rice	12.00	5.50
❑ T5A	Terrell Davis	20.00	9.00
❑ T5B	John Elway	25.00	11.00
❑ T5C	Shannon Sharpe	2.00	.90
❑ T6A	Edgar Bennett	2.00	.90
❑ T6B	Brett Favre	25.00	11.00
❑ T6C	Antonio Freeman	6.00	2.70

1997 Stadium Club Triumvirate II

	MINT	NRMT
COMP.SERIES 2 SET (18)	150.00	70.00

STATED ODDS 1:36 SER.2 RETAIL
*REFRACTORS STARS: 15X TO 30X BASE CARD HI
*REFRACTOR ROOKIES: 3X TO 6X BASE CARD HI

REFRACTOR STATED ODDS 1:144
*ATOMIC REF STARS: 25X TO 60X BASE CARD HI
*ATOMIC REF. ROOKIES: 6X TO 12X BASE CARD HI
ATOMIC REF.STATED ODDS 1:288

❑ T1A	John Elway	25.00	11.00
❑ T1B	Drew Bledsoe	12.00	5.50
❑ T1C	Dan Marino	25.00	11.00
❑ T2A	Troy Aikman	12.00	5.50
❑ T2B	Brett Favre	25.00	11.00
❑ T2C	Steve Young	8.00	3.60
❑ T3A	Terrell Davis	20.00	9.00
❑ T3B	Eddie George	12.00	5.50
❑ T3C	Curtis Martin	6.00	2.70
❑ T4A	Emmitt Smith	20.00	9.00
❑ T4B	Ricky Watters	2.00	.90
❑ T4C	Barry Sanders	25.00	11.00
❑ T5A	Peter Boulware	.50	.23
❑ T5B	Shawn Springs	.50	.23
❑ T5C	Tony Gonzalez	5.00	2.20
❑ T6A	Jake Plummer	12.00	5.50
❑ T6B	Orlando Pace	.30	.14
❑ T6C	Jim Druckenmiller	1.50	.70

1998 Stadium Club

	MINT	NRMT
COMPLETE SET (195)	100.00	45.00
COMMON CARD (1-165)	.15	.07
SEMISTARS	.30	.14
UNLISTED STARS	.60	.25
COMMON ROOKIE (166-195)	2.00	.90
ROOKIE SEMISTARS	2.50	1.10
ROOKIE UNLISTED STARS	3.00	1.35

ROOKIE STATED ODDS 1:2 H/R, 1:1 JUM
COMP.ONE OF KIND (195) 1200.00 550.00
*ONE OF KIND STARS: 10X TO 25X HI COL.
*ONE OF KIND YOUNG STARS: 8X TO 20X
*ONE OF KIND RCs: 3X TO 6X....
ONE OF KIND ODDS 1:32 H, 1:19 JUM HOB
ONE OF KIND PRINT RUN 150 SETS
COMP.FIRST DAY (195) 1000.00 450.00
*FIRST DAY STARS: 10X TO 20X HI COL.
*FIRST DAY YOUNG STARS: 7.5X TO 15X
*FIRST DAY RCs: 1.5X TO 4X......
FIRST DAY STATED ODDS 1:47 RET
FIRST DAY STATED PRINT RUN 200 SETS

❑ 1	Barry Sanders	3.00	1.35
❑ 2	Tony Martin	.30	.14
❑ 3	Fred Lane	.30	.14
❑ 4	Darren Woodson	.15	.07
❑ 5	Andre Reed	.30	.14
❑ 6	Blaine Bishop	.15	.07
❑ 7	Robert Brooks	.30	.14
❑ 8	Tony Banks	.30	.14
❑ 9	Charles Way	.15	.07
❑ 10	Mark Brunell	1.25	.55
❑ 11	Darrell Green	.30	.14
❑ 12	Aeneas Williams	.15	.07
❑ 13	Rob Johnson	.30	.14
❑ 14	Deion Sanders	.60	.25
❑ 15	Marshall Faulk	.60	.25
❑ 16	Stephen Boyd	.15	.07
❑ 17	Adrian Murrell	.30	.14
❑ 18	Wayne Chrebet	.60	.25
❑ 19	Michael Sinclair	.15	.07
❑ 20	Dan Marino	3.00	1.35
❑ 21	Willie Davis	.15	.07
❑ 22	Chris Warren	.30	.14
❑ 23	John Mobley	.15	.07
❑ 24	Shannon Sharpe	.30	.14
❑ 25	Thurman Thomas	.60	.25
❑ 26	Corey Dillon	1.00	.45
❑ 27	Zach Thomas	.15	.07
❑ 28	James Jett	.30	.14
❑ 29	Eric Metcalf	.15	.07
❑ 30	Drew Bledsoe	1.25	.55
❑ 31	Scott Greene	.15	.07
❑ 32	Simeon Rice	.30	.14
❑ 33	Robert Smith	.60	.25
❑ 34	Keenan McCardell	.30	.14
❑ 35	Jessie Armstead	.15	.07
❑ 36	Jerry Rice	1.50	.70
❑ 37	Eric Green	.15	.07
❑ 38	Terrell Owens	.60	.25
❑ 39	Tim Brown	.60	.25
❑ 40	Vinny Testaverde	.30	.14
❑ 41	Brian Stablein	.15	.07
❑ 42	Bert Emanuel	.30	.14
❑ 43	Terry Glenn	.60	.25
❑ 44	Chad Cota	.15	.07
❑ 45	Jermaine Lewis	.30	.14
❑ 46	Derrick Thomas	.30	.14
❑ 47	O.J. McDuffie	.30	.14
❑ 48	Frank Wycheck	.15	.07
❑ 49	Steve Broussard	.15	.07
❑ 50	Terrell Davis	2.50	1.10
❑ 51	Eric Allen	.15	.07
❑ 52	Napoleon Kaufman	.60	.25
❑ 53	Dan Wilkinson	.15	.07
❑ 54	Kerry Collins	.30	.14
❑ 55	Frank Sanders	.30	.14
❑ 56	Jeff Burris	.15	.07
❑ 56	Ricky Proehl	.15	.07
❑ 57	Michael Westbrook	.30	.14
❑ 58	Michael McCrary	.15	.07
❑ 59	Bobby Hoying	.30	.14
❑ 60	Jerome Bettis	.60	.25
❑ 61	Amp Lee	.15	.07
❑ 62	Levon Kirkland	.15	.07
❑ 63	Dana Stubblefield	.15	.07
❑ 64	Terance Mathis	.30	.14
❑ 65	Mark Chmura	.30	.14
❑ 66	Bryant Westbrook	.15	.07
❑ 67	Rod Smith	.30	.14
❑ 68	Derrick Alexander	.30	.14
❑ 69	Jason Taylor	.15	.07
❑ 70	Eddie George	1.25	.55
❑ 71	Elvis Grbac	.30	.14
❑ 72	Junior Seau	.30	.14
❑ 73	Marvin Harrison	.30	.14
❑ 74	Neil O'Donnell	.30	.14
❑ 75	Johnnie Morton	.30	.14
❑ 76	John Randle	.30	.14
❑ 77	Danny Kanell	.30	.14
❑ 78	Charlie Garner	.15	.07
❑ 79	J.J. Stokes	.30	.14
❑ 80	Troy Aikman	1.50	.70
❑ 81	Gus Frerotte	.15	.07
❑ 82	Jake Plummer	2.00	.90
❑ 83	Andre Hastings	.15	.07
❑ 84	Steve Atwater	.15	.07
❑ 85	Larry Centers	.15	.07
❑ 86	Kevin Hardy	.15	.07
❑ 87	Willie McGinest	.15	.07
❑ 88	Joey Galloway	.60	.25
❑ 89	Charles Johnson	.15	.07
❑ 90	Warrick Dunn	1.00	.45
❑ 91	Derrick Rodgers	.15	.07
❑ 92	Aaron Glenn	.15	.07
❑ 93	Shawn Jefferson	.15	.07
❑ 94	Antonio Freeman	.60	.25
❑ 95	Jake Reed	.30	.14
❑ 96	Reidel Anthony	.30	.14
❑ 97	Cris Dishman	.15	.07
❑ 98	Jason Sehorn	.15	.07
❑ 99	Herman Moore	.60	.25
❑ 100	John Elway	3.00	1.35
❑ 101	Brad Johnson	.60	.25
❑ 102	Jeff George	.30	.14
❑ 103	Emmitt Smith	2.50	1.10
❑ 104	Steve McNair	.60	.25
❑ 105	Ed McCaffrey	.30	.14
❑ 107	Dorsey Levens	.60	.25
❑ 108	Michael Jackson	.15	.07
❑ 109	Carl Pickens	.60	.25
❑ 110	James Stewart	.30	.14
❑ 111	Karim Abdul-Jabbar	.60	.25
❑ 112	Jim Harbaugh	.30	.14
❑ 113	Yancey Thigpen	.15	.07
❑ 114	Chad Brown	.15	.07
❑ 115	Chris Sanders	.15	.07
❑ 116	Cris Carter	.60	.25
❑ 117	Glenn Foley	.30	.14
❑ 118	Ben Coates	.30	.14
❑ 119	Jamal Anderson	.60	.25
❑ 120	Steve Young	1.00	.45
❑ 121	Scott Mitchell	.30	.14
❑ 122	Rob Moore	.30	.14
❑ 123	Bobby Engram	.30	.14
❑ 124	Rod Woodson	.30	.14
❑ 125	Terry Allen	.60	.25
❑ 126	Warren Sapp	.30	.14
❑ 127	Irving Fryar	.30	.14
❑ 128	Isaac Bruce	.60	.25
❑ 129	Rae Carruth	.30	.14
❑ 130	Sean Dawkins	.15	.07
❑ 131	Andre Rison	.30	.14
❑ 132	Kevin Greene	.30	.14
❑ 133	Warren Moon	.60	.25
❑ 134	Keyshawn Johnson	.60	.25
❑ 135	Jay Graham	.15	.07
❑ 136	Mike Alstott	.60	.25
❑ 137	Peter Boulware	.15	.07
❑ 138	Doug Evans	.15	.07
❑ 139	Jimmy Smith	.30	.14
❑ 140	Kordell Stewart	.60	.25
❑ 141	Tamarick Vanover	.15	.07
❑ 142	Chris Slade	.15	.07
❑ 143	Freddie Jones	.15	.07
❑ 144	Erik Kramer	.15	.07
❑ 145	Ricky Watters	.30	.14
❑ 146	Chris Chandler	.30	.14
❑ 147	Garrison Hearst	.60	.25
❑ 148	Trent Dilfer	.60	.25
❑ 149	Bruce Smith	.30	.14
❑ 150	Brett Favre	3.00	1.35
❑ 151	Will Blackwell	.15	.07
❑ 152	Rickey Dudley	.15	.07
❑ 153	Natrone Means	.60	.25
❑ 154	Curtis Conway	.30	.14
❑ 155	Tony Gonzalez	.15	.07
❑ 156	Jeff Blake	.30	.14
❑ 157	Michael Irvin	.60	.25
❑ 158	Curtis Martin	.60	.25
❑ 159	Tim McDonald	.15	.07
❑ 160	Wesley Walls	.30	.14
❑ 161	Michael Strahan	.15	.07
❑ 162	Reggie White	.60	.25
❑ 163	Jeff Graham	.15	.07
❑ 164	Ray Lewis	.15	.07
❑ 165	Antowain Smith	.60	.25
❑ 166	Ryan Leaf RC	4.00	1.80
❑ 167	Jerome Pathon RC	2.50	1.10
❑ 168	Duane Starks RC	2.00	.90
❑ 169	Brian Simmons RC	2.00	.90
❑ 170	Pat Johnson RC	2.50	1.10
❑ 171	Keith Brooking RC	2.50	1.10
❑ 172	Kevin Dyson RC	4.00	1.80
❑ 173	Robert Edwards RC	3.00	1.35
❑ 174	Grant Wistrom RC	2.00	.90
❑ 175	Curtis Enis RC	5.00	2.20
❑ 176	John Avery RC	3.00	1.35
❑ 177	Jason Peter RC	2.00	.90
❑ 178	Brian Griese RC	8.00	3.60
❑ 179	Tavian Banks RC	2.50	1.10
❑ 180	Andre Wadsworth RC	2.50	1.10
❑ 181	Skip Hicks RC	4.00	1.80
❑ 182	Hines Ward RC	2.50	1.10
❑ 183	Greg Ellis RC	2.00	.90
❑ 184	Robert Holcombe RC	3.00	1.35
❑ 185	Joe Jurevicius RC	2.50	1.10
❑ 186	Takeo Spikes RC	2.50	1.10
❑ 187	Ahman Green RC	2.50	1.10
❑ 188	Jacquez Green RC	4.00	1.80
❑ 189	Randy Moss RC	20.00	9.00
❑ 190	Charles Woodson RC	5.00	2.20
❑ 191	Fred Taylor RC	12.00	5.50
❑ 192	Marcus Nash RC	4.00	1.80

		MINT	NRMT
❑ 193	Germane Crowell RC	5.00	2.20
❑ 194	Tim Dwight RC	4.00	1.80
❑ 195	Peyton Manning RC	20.00	9.00

1998 Stadium Club Chrome

	MINT	NRMT
COMPLETE SET (20)	120.00	55.00
COMMON CARD (SCC1-SCC20)	3.00	1.35
STATED ODDS 1:12 H/R, 1:6 JUM		
*REFRACTORS: 1X TO 2X HI COL.		
REFRACTOR ODDS 1:48 H/R, 1:24 JUM		
*JUMBOS: SAME PRICE		
JUMBO ODDS ONE PER BOX		

		MINT	NRMT
❑ SCC1	John Elway	15.00	6.75
❑ SCC2	Mark Brunell	8.00	3.60
❑ SCC3	Jerome Bettis	4.00	1.80
❑ SCC4	Steve Young	5.00	2.20
❑ SCC5	Herman Moore	4.00	1.80
❑ SCC6	Emmitt Smith	12.00	5.50
❑ SCC7	Warrick Dunn	4.00	1.80
❑ SCC8	Dan Marino	15.00	6.75
❑ SCC9	Kordell Stewart	3.00	1.35
❑ SCC10	Barry Sanders	15.00	6.75
❑ SCC11	Tim Brown	4.00	1.80
❑ SCC12	Dorsey Levens	4.00	1.80
❑ SCC13	Eddie George	6.00	2.70
❑ SCC14	Jerry Rice	8.00	3.60
❑ SCC15	Terrell Davis	12.00	5.50
❑ SCC16	Napoleon Kaufman	4.00	1.80
❑ SCC17	Troy Aikman	8.00	3.60
❑ SCC18	Drew Bledsoe	6.00	2.70
❑ SCC19	Antonio Freeman	4.00	1.80
❑ SCC20	Brett Favre	15.00	6.75

1998 Stadium Club Co-Signers

	MINT	NRMT
COMPLETE SET (12)	2200.00	1000.00
COMMON CARD (CO1-CO12)	40.00	18.00
CO1-CO4: STATED ODDS 1:9400H, 1:5640J		
CO5-CO8: STATED ODDS 1:3133H, 1:1880J		
CO9-CO12: STATED ODDS 1:261H, 1:157J		
OVERALL STATED ODDS 1:235H, 1:141J		

		MINT	NRMT
❑ CO1	Peyton Manning Ryan Leaf	500.00	220.00
❑ CO2	Dan Marino Kordell Stewart	500.00	220.00
❑ CO3	Eddie George Corey Dillon	120.00	55.00
❑ CO4	Dorsey Levens Mike Alstott	250.00	110.00
❑ CO5	Ryan Leaf Dan Marino	300.00	135.00
❑ CO6	Peyton Manning Kordell Stewart	300.00	135.00
❑ CO7	Eddie George Mike Alstott	120.00	55.00
❑ CO8	Dorsey Levens Corey Dillon	150.00	70.00
❑ CO9	Peyton Manning Dan Marino	200.00	90.00
❑ CO10	Ryan Leaf Kordell Stewart	50.00	22.00
❑ CO11	Eddie George Dorsey Levens	60.00	27.00
❑ CO12	Mike Alstott Corey Dillon	40.00	18.00

1998 Stadium Club Double Threat

	MINT	NRMT
COMPLETE SET (10)	50.00	22.00
COMMON CARD (DT1-DT10)	2.50	1.10
STATED ODDS 1:8 H/R, 1:4 JUM		

		MINT	NRMT
❑ DT1	Marshall Faulk Peyton Manning	12.00	5.50
❑ DT2	Curtis Conway Curtis Enis	4.00	1.80
❑ DT3	Drew Bledsoe Robert Edwards	5.00	2.20
❑ DT4	Warrick Dunn Jacquez Green	3.00	1.35
❑ DT5	John Elway Marcus Nash	10.00	4.50
❑ DT6	Mark Brunell Fred Taylor	6.00	2.70
❑ DT7	Eddie George Kevin Dyson	4.00	1.80
❑ DT8	Michael Jackson Pat Johnson	2.50	1.10
❑ DT9	Terry Glenn Tony Simmons	2.50	1.10
❑ DT10	Natrone Means Ryan Leaf	3.00	1.35

1998 Stadium Club Leading Legends

	MINT	NRMT
COMPLETE SET (10)	40.00	18.00
COMMON CARD (1-10)	2.00	.90
STATED ODDS 1:12 RETAIL		

		MINT	NRMT
❑ 1	John Elway	10.00	4.50
❑ 2	Brett Favre	10.00	4.50
❑ 3	Dan Marino	10.00	4.50
❑ 4	Warren Moon	3.00	1.35
❑ 5	Jerry Rice	5.00	2.20
❑ 6	Barry Sanders	10.00	4.50
❑ 7	Bruce Smith	2.00	.90
❑ 8	Emmitt Smith	8.00	3.60
❑ 9	Reggie White	3.00	1.35
❑ 10	Steve Young	3.00	1.35

1998 Stadium Club Prime Rookies

	MINT	NRMT
COMPLETE SET (10)	40.00	18.00
COMMON CARD (PR1-PR10)	2.00	.90
SEMISTARS	2.50	1.10
UNLISTED STARS	3.00	1.35
STATED ODDS 1:8 H/R, 1:4 JUM		

		MINT	NRMT
❑ PR1	Ryan Leaf	4.00	1.80
❑ PR2	Andre Wadsworth	2.50	1.10
❑ PR3	Fred Taylor	8.00	3.60
❑ PR4	Kevin Dyson	3.00	1.35
❑ PR5	Charles Woodson	4.00	1.80
❑ PR6	Robert Edwards	3.00	1.35
❑ PR7	Grant Wistrom	2.00	.90
❑ PR8	Curtis Enis	4.00	1.80
❑ PR9	Randy Moss	12.00	5.50
❑ PR10	Peyton Manning	12.00	5.50

1998 Stadium Club Triumvirate Luminous

	MINT	NRMT
COMPLETE SET (15)	80.00	36.00
COMMON CARD (T1A-T5C)	3.00	1.35
SEMISTARS	5.00	2.20
STATED ODDS 1:24 H, 1:12 JUM HOB		

*LUMINESCENT CARDS: 1X TO 2X HI
LUMINESCENT ODDS 1:96 H, 1:48 JUM HOB
*ILLUMINATOR CARDS: 1.5X TO 3X HI
ILLUMINATOR ODDS 1:192 H, 1:96 JUM HOB

❑ T1A Terrell Davis	15.00	6.75
❑ T1B John Elway	20.00	9.00
❑ T1C Shannon Sharpe	5.00	2.20
❑ T2A Barry Sanders	20.00	9.00
❑ T2B Scott Mitchell	3.00	1.35
❑ T2C Herman Moore	8.00	3.60
❑ T3A Dorsey Levens	8.00	3.60
❑ T3B Brett Favre	20.00	9.00
❑ T3C Antonio Freeman	8.00	3.60
❑ T4A Emmitt Smith	15.00	6.75
❑ T4B Troy Aikman	10.00	4.50
❑ T4C Michael Irvin	8.00	3.60
❑ T5A Napoleon Kaufman	8.00	3.60
❑ T5B Jeff George	5.00	2.20
❑ T5C Tim Brown	8.00	3.60

1999 Stadium Club

	MINT	NRMT
COMPLETE SET (200)	70.00	32.00
COMP.SET w/o SP's (150)	20.00	9.00
COMMON CARD (1-200)	.15	.07
SEMISTARS	.30	.14
UNLISTED STARS	.60	.25
COMMON ROOKIE (151-175)	1.50	.70
ROOKIE SEMISTARS	2.50	1.10

ROOKIE SUBSET STATED ODDS 1:3 H/R

❑ 1 Dan Marino	2.50	1.10
❑ 2 Andre Reed	.30	.14
❑ 3 Michael Westbrook	.30	.14
❑ 4 Isaac Bruce	.60	.25
❑ 5 Curtis Martin	.60	.25
❑ 6 Courtney Hawkins	.15	.07
❑ 7 Charles Way	.15	.07
❑ 8 Terrell Owens	.60	.25
❑ 9 Warrick Dunn	.60	.25
❑ 10 Jake Plummer	1.25	.55
❑ 11 Chad Brown	.15	.07
❑ 12 Yancey Thigpen	.15	.07
❑ 13 Lamar Thomas	.15	.07
❑ 14 Keenan McCardell	.30	.14
❑ 15 Shannon Sharpe	.30	.14
❑ 16 Robert Brooks	.30	.14
❑ 17 Cameron Cleeland	.15	.07
❑ 18 Derrick Thomas	.30	.14
❑ 19 Mark Brunell	1.00	.45
❑ 20 Jamal Anderson	.60	.25
❑ 21 Germane Crowell	.30	.14
❑ 22 Rod Smith	.30	.14
❑ 23 Ty Law	.15	.07
❑ 24 Cris Carter	.60	.25
❑ 25 Terrell Davis	1.50	.70
❑ 26 Takeo Spikes	.15	.07
❑ 27 Tim Biakabutuka	.30	.14
❑ 28 Jermaine Lewis	.30	.14
❑ 29 Adrian Murrell	.30	.14
❑ 30 Doug Flutie	.75	.35
❑ 31 Curtis Enis	.60	.25
❑ 32 Skip Hicks	.60	.25
❑ 33 Steve McNair	.60	.25
❑ 34 Charles Woodson	.60	.25
❑ 35 Jessie Armstead	.15	.07
❑ 36 Shawn Springs	.15	.07
❑ 37 Levon Kirkland	.15	.07
❑ 38 Freddie Jones	.15	.07
❑ 39 Warren Sapp	.15	.07
❑ 40 Emmitt Smith	1.50	.70
❑ 41 Reidel Anthony	.30	.14
❑ 42 Tony Simmons	.15	.07
❑ 43 Andre Hastings	.15	.07
❑ 44 Byron Bam Morris	.15	.07
❑ 45 Jimmy Smith	.30	.14
❑ 46 Antonio Freeman	.60	.25
❑ 47 Herman Moore	.60	.25
❑ 48 Muhsin Muhammad	.30	.14
❑ 49 Chris Chandler	.30	.14
❑ 50 John Elway	2.50	1.10
❑ 51 Aeneas Williams	.15	.07
❑ 52 Bobby Engram	.30	.14
❑ 53 Keith Poole	.15	.07
❑ 54 Zach Thomas	.30	.14
❑ 55 Mike Alstott	.60	.25
❑ 56 Junior Seau	.30	.14
❑ 57 Aaron Glenn	.15	.07
❑ 58 Darrell Green	.15	.07
❑ 59 Thurman Thomas	.30	.14
❑ 60 Troy Aikman	1.50	.70
❑ 61 Bill Romanowski	.15	.07
❑ 62 Wesley Walls	.30	.14
❑ 63 Andre Wadsworth	.15	.07
❑ 64 Robert Smith	.60	.25
❑ 65 Elvis Grbac	.30	.14
❑ 66 Terry Fair	.15	.07
❑ 67 Ben Coates	.30	.14
❑ 68 Bert Emanuel	.30	.14
❑ 69 Jacquez Green	.30	.14
❑ 70 Barry Sanders	2.50	1.10
❑ 71 James Jett	.30	.14
❑ 72 Gary Brown	.15	.07
❑ 73 Stephen Alexander	.15	.07
❑ 74 Wayne Chrebet	.30	.14
❑ 75 Drew Bledsoe	1.00	.45
❑ 76 John Lynch	.15	.07
❑ 77 Jake Reed	.30	.14
❑ 78 Marvin Harrison	.60	.25
❑ 79 Johnnie Morton	.30	.14
❑ 80 Brett Favre	2.50	1.10
❑ 81 Charlie Batch	1.25	.55
❑ 82 Antowain Smith	.60	.25
❑ 83 Mikhael Ricks	.15	.07
❑ 84 Derrick Mayes	.15	.07
❑ 85 John Mobley	.15	.07
❑ 86 Ernie Mills	.15	.07
❑ 87 Jeff Blake	.30	.14
❑ 88 Curtis Conway	.30	.14
❑ 89 Bruce Smith	.30	.14
❑ 90 Peyton Manning	2.50	1.10
❑ 91 Tyrone Davis	.15	.07
❑ 92 Ray Buchanan	.15	.07
❑ 93 Tim Dwight	.60	.25
❑ 94 O.J. McDuffie	.30	.14
❑ 95 Vonnie Holliday	.15	.07
❑ 96 Jon Kitna	.75	.35
❑ 97 Trent Dilfer	.30	.14
❑ 98 Jerome Bettis	.60	.25
❑ 99 Dedric Ward	.15	.07
❑ 100 Fred Taylor	1.50	.70
❑ 101 Ike Hilliard	.15	.07
❑ 102 Frank Wycheck	.15	.07
❑ 103 Eric Moulds	.60	.25
❑ 104 Rob Moore	.30	.14
❑ 105 Ed McCaffrey	.30	.14
❑ 106 Carl Pickens	.30	.14
❑ 107 Priest Holmes	.60	.25
❑ 108 Kevin Hardy	.15	.07
❑ 109 Terry Glenn	.60	.25
❑ 110 Keyshawn Johnson	.60	.25
❑ 111 Karim Abdul-Jabbar	.30	.14
❑ 112 Stephen Boyd	.15	.07
❑ 113 Ahman Green	.30	.14
❑ 114 Duce Staley	.60	.25
❑ 115 Vinny Testaverde	.30	.14
❑ 116 Napoleon Kaufman	.60	.25
❑ 117 Frank Sanders	.30	.14
❑ 118 Peter Boulware	.15	.07
❑ 119 Kevin Greene	.15	.07
❑ 120 Steve Young	1.00	.45
❑ 121 Darnay Scott	.15	.07
❑ 122 Deion Sanders	.60	.25
❑ 123 Corey Dillon	.60	.25
❑ 124 Randall Cunningham	.60	.25
❑ 125 Eddie George	.75	.35
❑ 126 Derrick Alexander	.15	.07
❑ 127 Mark Chmura	.15	.07
❑ 128 Michael Sinclair	.15	.07
❑ 129 Rickey Dudley	.15	.07
❑ 130 Joey Galloway	.60	.25
❑ 131 Michael Strahan	.15	.07
❑ 132 Ricky Proehl	.15	.07
❑ 133 Natrone Means	.30	.14
❑ 134 Dorsey Levens	.60	.25
❑ 135 Andre Rison	.30	.14
❑ 136 Alonzo Mayes	.15	.07
❑ 137 John Randle	.30	.14
❑ 138 Terance Mathis	.30	.14
❑ 139 Rae Carruth	.30	.14
❑ 140 Jerry Rice	1.50	.70
❑ 141 Michael Irvin	.30	.14
❑ 142 Oronde Gadsden	.15	.07
❑ 143 Jerome Pathon	.15	.07
❑ 144 Ricky Watters	.30	.14
❑ 145 J.J. Stokes	.30	.14
❑ 146 Kordell Stewart	.60	.25
❑ 147 Tim Brown	.60	.25
❑ 148 Garrison Hearst	.30	.14
❑ 149 Tony Gonzalez	.30	.14
❑ 150 Randy Moss	2.50	1.10
❑ 151 Daunte Culpepper RC	8.00	3.60
❑ 152 Amos Zereoue RC	2.50	1.10
❑ 153 Champ Bailey RC	3.00	1.35
❑ 154 Peerless Price RC	4.00	1.80
❑ 155 Edgerrin James RC	20.00	9.00
❑ 156 Joe Germaine RC	2.50	1.10
❑ 157 David Boston RC	4.00	1.80
❑ 158 Kevin Faulk RC	3.00	1.35
❑ 159 Troy Edwards RC	4.00	1.80
❑ 160 Akili Smith RC	5.00	2.20
❑ 161 Kevin Johnson RC	6.00	2.70
❑ 162 Rob Konrad RC	2.50	1.10
❑ 163 Shaun King RC	8.00	3.60
❑ 164 James Johnson RC	3.00	1.35
❑ 165 Donovan McNabb RC	8.00	3.60
❑ 166 Torry Holt RC	6.00	2.70
❑ 167 Mike Cloud RC	2.50	1.10
❑ 168 Sedrick Irvin RC	2.50	1.10
❑ 169 Cade McNown RC	8.00	3.60
❑ 170 Ricky Williams RC	12.00	5.50
❑ 171 Karsten Bailey RC	1.50	.70
❑ 172 Cecil Collins RC	2.50	1.10
❑ 173 Brock Huard RC	3.00	1.35
❑ 174 D'Wayne Bates RC	2.50	1.10
❑ 175 Tim Couch RC	12.00	5.50
❑ 176 Torrance Small	.15	.07
❑ 177 Warren Moon	.60	.25
❑ 178 Rocket Ismail	.30	.14
❑ 179 Marshall Faulk	.60	.25
❑ 180 Trent Green	.30	.14
❑ 181 Sean Dawkins	.15	.07
❑ 182 Pete Mitchell	.15	.07
❑ 183 Jeff Graham	.15	.07
❑ 184 Eddie Kennison	.30	.14
❑ 185 Kerry Collins	.30	.14
❑ 186 Eric Green	.15	.07
❑ 187 Kyle Brady	.15	.07
❑ 188 Tony Martin	.30	.14
❑ 189 Jim Harbaugh	.30	.14
❑ 190 Erik Kramer	.15	.07
❑ 191 Steve Atwater	.15	.07
❑ 192 Chad Bratzke	.15	.07
❑ 193 Charles Johnson	.15	.07
❑ 194 Damon Gibson	.15	.07
❑ 195 Jeff George	.30	.14
❑ 196 Scott Mitchell	.15	.07
❑ 197 Terry Kirby	.15	.07
❑ 198 Rich Gannon	.30	.14
❑ 199 Chris Spielman	.15	.07
❑ 200 Brad Johnson	.60	.25

1999 Stadium Club First Day

	MINT	NRMT
COMPLETE SET (200)	600.00	275.00

COMMON CARD (1-200) .... 2.00 .90
*STARS: 6X TO 15X HI COL. ......
*YOUNG STARS: 5X TO 12X ......
COMMON ROOKIE (151-175) .. 6.00 2.70
*RCs: 1.5X TO 4X ....
STATED PRINT RUN 150 SER.#'d SETS
STATED ODDS 1:38 RETAIL ......

1999 Stadium Club One of a Kind

	MINT	NRMT
COMPLETE SET (200)	600.00	275.00
COMMON CARD (1-200)	2.00	.90

*STARS: 6X TO 15X HI COL. ......
*YOUNG STARS: 5X TO 12X ......
COMMON ROOKIE (151-175) .. 6.00 2.70
*RCs: 1.5X TO 4X ....
STATED PRINT RUN 150 SER.#'d SETS
STATED ODDS 1:48 HOBBY ......

1999 Stadium Club 3X3 Luminous

	MINT	NRMT
COMPLETE SET (15)	80.00	36.00
COMMON CARD (T1A-T5C)	3.00	1.35

STATED ODDS 1:36 HOB/RET, 1:18 HTA
*LUMINESCENT: .8X TO 2X HI COL.
LUMINESCENT ODDS 1:144 H/R,1:72 HTA
*ILLUMINATOR: 1.2X TO 3X HI COL.
ILLUMINATOR ODDS 1:288 H/R,1:144 HTA

❑ T1A	Brett Favre	12.00	5.50
❑ T1B	Troy Aikman	8.00	3.60
❑ T1C	Jake Plummer	6.00	2.70
❑ T2A	Jamal Anderson	3.00	1.35
❑ T2B	Emmitt Smith	8.00	3.60
❑ T2C	Barry Sanders	12.00	5.50
❑ T3A	Antonio Freeman	3.00	1.35
❑ T3B	Randy Moss	10.00	4.50
❑ T3C	Jerry Rice	8.00	3.60
❑ T4A	Peyton Manning	10.00	4.50
❑ T4B	John Elway	12.00	5.50
❑ T4C	Dan Marino	12.00	5.50
❑ T5A	Fred Taylor	6.00	2.70
❑ T5B	Terrell Davis	8.00	3.60
❑ T5C	Curtis Martin	3.00	1.35

1999 Stadium Club Chrome Previews

	MINT	NRMT
COMPLETE SET (20)	100.00	45.00
COMMON CARD (C1-C20)	2.50	1.10

STATED ODDS 1:24 HOB/RET, 1:6 HTA
*REFRACTORS: .8X TO 2X HI COL.
REFRACTOR STATED ODDS 1:96H/R,1:24HTA ....
*JUMBOS: .3X TO .8X HI COL. ....
JUMBOS STATED ODDS 1:96H/R,1:24HTA
*JUMBO REFRACTORS: 1X TO 2.5X HI COL.
JUMBO REFRACTOR ODDS 1:12 HOBBY BOXES

❑ C1	Randy Moss	8.00	3.60
❑ C2	Terrell Davis	6.00	2.70
❑ C3	Peyton Manning	8.00	3.60
❑ C4	Fred Taylor	5.00	2.20
❑ C5	John Elway	10.00	4.50
❑ C6	Steve Young	4.00	1.80
❑ C7	Brett Favre	10.00	4.50
❑ C8	Jamal Anderson	2.50	1.10
❑ C9	Barry Sanders	10.00	4.50
❑ C10	Dan Marino	10.00	4.50
❑ C11	Jerry Rice	6.00	2.70
❑ C12	Emmitt Smith	6.00	2.70
❑ C13	Randall Cunningham	2.50	1.10
❑ C14	Troy Aikman	6.00	2.70
❑ C15	Akili Smith	4.00	1.80
❑ C16	Donovan McNabb	6.00	2.70
❑ C17	Edgerrin James	15.00	6.75
❑ C18	Torry Holt	4.00	1.80
❑ C19	Ricky Williams	10.00	4.50
❑ C20	Tim Couch	10.00	4.50

1999 Stadium Club Co-Signers

	MINT	NRMT
COMPLETE SET (6)	1500.00	700.00
COMMON CARD (CS1-CS6)	150.00	70.00

CS1/CS2 STATED ODDS 1:2854H,1:1142HTA
CS3-CS6 STATED ODDS 1:1189H,1:476HTA
OVERALL STATED ODDS 1:840H,1: HTA
TRADE CARD EXPIRATION: 4/30/2000

❑ CS1	Terrell Davis / Ricky Williams	175.00	80.00
❑ CS2	Terrell Davis / Edgerrin James	250.00	110.00
❑ CS3	Tim Couch / Dan Marino	300.00	135.00
❑ CS4	Tim Couch / Peyton Manning	350.00	160.00
❑ CS5	Randy Moss / Jerry Rice	300.00	135.00
❑ CS6	Dan Marino / Vinny Testaverde	150.00	70.00

1999 Stadium Club Emperors of the Zone

	MINT	NRMT
COMPLETE SET (10)	30.00	13.50
COMMON CARD (E1-E10)	1.25	.55

STATED ODDS 1:12 HOB/RET, 1:4 HTA

❑ E1	Ricky Williams	5.00	2.20
❑ E2	Brett Favre	5.00	2.20
❑ E3	Donovan McNabb	3.00	1.35
❑ E4	Peyton Manning	4.00	1.80
❑ E5	Terrell Davis	3.00	1.35
❑ E6	Jamal Anderson	1.25	.55
❑ E7	Edgerrin James	8.00	3.60
❑ E8	Fred Taylor	2.50	1.10
❑ E9	Tim Couch	5.00	2.20
❑ E10	Randy Moss	4.00	1.80

1999 Stadium Club Lone Star Autographs

	MINT	NRMT
COMPLETE SET (11)	1000.00	450.00
COMMON CARD (LS1-LS11)	25.00	11.00

OVERALL STATED ODDS 1:697

❑ LS1	Randy Moss	120.00	55.00
❑ LS2	Jerry Rice	150.00	70.00
❑ LS3	Peyton Manning	150.00	70.00
❑ LS4	Vinny Testaverde	25.00	11.00
❑ LS5	Tim Couch	120.00	55.00
❑ LS6	Dan Marino	150.00	70.00
❑ LS7	Edgerrin James	175.00	80.00
❑ LS8	Fred Taylor	60.00	27.00
❑ LS9	Garrison Hearst	25.00	11.00
❑ LS10	Antonio Freeman	40.00	18.00
❑ LS11	Torry Holt	50.00	22.00

1999 Stadium Club Never Compromise

	MINT	NRMT
COMPLETE SET (30)	80.00	36.00
COMMON CARD (NC1-NC30)..	1.50	.70

STATED ODDS 1:12 HOB/RET, 1:4 HTA

❑ NC1	Tim Couch	6.00	2.70
❑ NC2	David Boston	2.00	.90
❑ NC3	Daunte Culpepper	4.00	1.80
❑ NC4	Donovan McNabb	4.00	1.80
❑ NC5	Ricky Williams	6.00	2.70
❑ NC6	Troy Edwards	2.00	.90
❑ NC7	Akili Smith	2.50	1.10
❑ NC8	Torry Holt	3.00	1.35
❑ NC9	Cade McNown	4.00	1.80
❑ NC10	Edgerrin James	10.00	4.50
❑ NC11	Randy Moss	5.00	2.20
❑ NC12	Peyton Manning	5.00	2.20
❑ NC13	Eddie George	2.00	.90
❑ NC14	Fred Taylor	3.00	1.35
❑ NC15	Jamal Anderson	2.00	.90
❑ NC16	Joey Galloway	2.00	.90
❑ NC17	Terrell Davis	4.00	1.80
❑ NC18	Keyshawn Johnson	2.00	.90
❑ NC19	Antonio Freeman	2.00	.90
❑ NC20	Jake Plummer	3.00	1.35
❑ NC21	Steve Young	2.50	1.10
❑ NC22	Barry Sanders	6.00	2.70
❑ NC23	Dan Marino	6.00	2.70
❑ NC24	Emmitt Smith	4.00	1.80
❑ NC25	Brett Favre	6.00	2.70
❑ NC26	Randall Cunningham	2.00	.90
❑ NC27	John Elway	6.00	2.70
❑ NC28	Drew Bledsoe	2.50	1.10
❑ NC29	Jerry Rice	4.00	1.80
❑ NC30	Troy Aikman	4.00	1.80

1999 Stadium Club Chrome

	MINT	NRMT
COMPLETE SET (150)	90.00	40.00
COMMON CARD (1-150)	.25	.11
SEMISTARS	.50	.23
UNLISTED STARS	1.00	.45
COMMON ROOKIE (119-143)	3.00	1.35
ROOKIE SEMISTARS	4.00	1.80

Card	MINT	NRMT
❑ 1 Dan Marino	4.00	1.80
❑ 2 Andre Reed	.50	.23
❑ 3 Michael Westbrook	.50	.23
❑ 4 Isaac Bruce	1.00	.45
❑ 5 Curtis Martin	1.00	.45
❑ 6 Terrell Owens	1.00	.45
❑ 7 Warrick Dunn	1.00	.45
❑ 8 Jake Plummer	2.00	.90
❑ 9 Chad Brown	.25	.11
❑ 10 Yancey Thigpen	.50	.23
❑ 11 Keenan McCardell	.50	.23
❑ 12 Shannon Sharpe	.50	.23
❑ 13 Cameron Cleeland	.25	.11
❑ 14 Mark Brunell	1.50	.70
❑ 15 Jamal Anderson	1.00	.45
❑ 16 Germane Crowell	.50	.23
❑ 17 Rod Smith	.50	.23
❑ 18 Cris Carter	1.00	.45
❑ 19 Terrell Davis	2.50	1.10
❑ 20 Tim Biakabutuka	.50	.23
❑ 21 Jermaine Lewis	.50	.23
❑ 22 Adrian Murrell	.50	.23
❑ 23 Doug Flutie	1.25	.55
❑ 24 Curtis Enis	1.00	.45
❑ 25 Skip Hicks	.50	.23
❑ 26 Steve McNair	1.00	.45
❑ 27 Charles Woodson	1.00	.45
❑ 28 Freddie Jones	.25	.11
❑ 29 Warren Sapp	.50	.23
❑ 30 Emmitt Smith	2.50	1.10
❑ 31 Reidel Anthony	.25	.11
❑ 32 Tony Simmons	.25	.11
❑ 33 Andre Hastings	.25	.11
❑ 34 Byron Bam Morris	.25	.11
❑ 35 Jimmy Smith	.50	.23
❑ 36 Antonio Freeman	1.00	.45
❑ 37 Herman Moore	1.00	.45
❑ 38 Muhsin Muhammad	.50	.23
❑ 39 Chris Chandler	.50	.23
❑ 40 John Elway	4.00	1.80
❑ 41 Bobby Engram	.50	.23
❑ 42 Keith Poole	.25	.11
❑ 43 Mike Alstott	1.00	.45
❑ 44 Junior Seau	.50	.23
❑ 45 Thurman Thomas	.50	.23
❑ 46 Troy Aikman	2.50	1.10
❑ 47 Wesley Walls	.50	.23
❑ 48 Robert Smith	1.00	.45
❑ 49 Elvis Grbac	.50	.23
❑ 50 Ben Coates	.25	.11
❑ 51 Bert Emanuel	.50	.23
❑ 52 Jacquez Green	.25	.11
❑ 53 Barry Sanders	4.00	1.80
❑ 54 James Jett	.25	.11
❑ 55 Gary Brown	.25	.11
❑ 56 Stephen Alexander	.25	.11
❑ 57 Wayne Chrebet	1.00	.45
❑ 58 Drew Bledsoe	1.50	.70
❑ 59 Jake Reed	.50	.23
❑ 60 Marvin Harrison	1.00	.45
❑ 61 Johnnie Morton	.50	.23
❑ 62 Brett Favre	4.00	1.80
❑ 63 Charlie Batch	2.00	.90
❑ 64 Antowain Smith	1.00	.45
❑ 65 Ernie Mills	.25	.11
❑ 66 Jeff Blake	.50	.23
❑ 67 Curtis Conway	.50	.23
❑ 68 Bruce Smith	.50	.23
❑ 69 Peyton Manning	4.00	1.80
❑ 70 Tim Dwight	1.00	.45
❑ 71 O.J. McDuffie	.50	.23
❑ 72 Jon Kitna	1.25	.55
❑ 73 Trent Dilfer	.50	.23
❑ 74 Jerome Bettis	1.00	.45
❑ 75 Dedric Ward	.25	.11
❑ 76 Fred Taylor	2.50	1.10
❑ 77 Ike Hilliard	.50	.23
❑ 78 Frank Wycheck	.25	.11
❑ 79 Eric Moulds	1.00	.45
❑ 80 Rob Moore	.50	.23
❑ 81 Ed McCaffrey	.50	.23
❑ 82 Carl Pickens	.50	.23
❑ 83 Priest Holmes	1.00	.45
❑ 84 Terry Glenn	1.00	.45
❑ 85 Keyshawn Johnson	1.00	.45
❑ 86 Karim Abdul-Jabbar	.50	.23
❑ 87 Ahman Green	.50	.23
❑ 88 Duce Staley	1.00	.45
❑ 89 Vinny Testaverde	.50	.23
❑ 90 Napoleon Kaufman	1.00	.45
❑ 91 Frank Sanders	.50	.23
❑ 92 Steve Young	1.50	.70
❑ 93 Darnay Scott	.50	.23
❑ 94 Deion Sanders	1.00	.45
❑ 95 Corey Dillon	1.00	.45
❑ 96 Randall Cunningham	1.00	.45
❑ 97 Eddie George	1.25	.55
❑ 98 Derrick Alexander	.50	.23
❑ 99 Mark Chmura	.50	.23
❑ 100 Rickey Dudley	.25	.11
❑ 101 Joey Galloway	1.00	.45
❑ 102 Ricky Proehl	.25	.11
❑ 103 Natrone Means	.50	.23
❑ 104 Dorsey Levens	1.00	.45
❑ 105 Andre Rison	.50	.23
❑ 106 John Randle	.50	.23
❑ 107 Terance Mathis	.50	.23
❑ 108 Rae Carruth	.25	.11
❑ 109 Jerry Rice	2.50	1.10
❑ 110 Michael Irvin	.50	.23
❑ 111 Oronde Gadsden	.25	.11
❑ 112 Jerome Pathon	.25	.11
❑ 113 Ricky Watters	.50	.23
❑ 114 J.J. Stokes	.50	.23
❑ 115 Kordell Stewart	1.00	.45
❑ 116 Tim Brown	1.00	.45
❑ 117 Tony Gonzalez	.50	.23
❑ 118 Randy Moss	4.00	1.80
❑ 119 Daunte Culpepper RC	8.00	3.60
❑ 120 Amos Zereoue RC	4.00	1.80
❑ 121 Champ Bailey RC	5.00	2.20
❑ 122 Peerless Price RC	5.00	2.20
❑ 123 Edgerrin James RC	20.00	9.00
❑ 124 Joe Germaine RC		
❑ 125 David Boston RC	5.00	2.20
❑ 126 Kevin Faulk RC	5.00	2.20
❑ 127 Troy Edwards RC	5.00	2.20
❑ 128 Akili Smith RC	6.00	2.70
❑ 129 Kevin Johnson RC	6.00	2.70
❑ 130 Rob Konrad RC	4.00	1.80
❑ 131 Shaun King RC	8.00	3.60
❑ 132 James Johnson RC	5.00	2.20
❑ 133 Donovan McNabb RC	8.00	3.60
❑ 134 Torry Holt RC	6.00	2.70
❑ 135 Mike Cloud RC	4.00	1.80
❑ 136 Sedrick Irvin RC		
❑ 137 Cade McNown RC	8.00	3.60
❑ 138 Ricky Williams RC	12.00	5.50
❑ 139 Karsten Bailey RC	3.00	1.35
❑ 140 Cecil Collins RC	4.00	1.80
❑ 141 Brock Huard RC	5.00	2.20
❑ 142 D'Wayne Bates RC	3.00	1.35
❑ 143 Tim Couch RC	12.00	5.50
❑ 144 Rocket Ismail	.50	.23
❑ 145 Marshall Faulk	1.00	.45
❑ 146 Trent Green	.50	.23
❑ 147 Tony Martin	.50	.23
❑ 148 Jim Harbaugh	.50	.23
❑ 149 Rich Gannon	.50	.23
❑ 150 Brad Johnson	1.00	.45

1999 Stadium Club Chrome First Day

	MINT	NRMT
COMPLETE SET (150)	1000.00	450.00
COMMON CARD (1-150)	6.00	2.70
*STARS: 10X TO 25X HI COL.		
*YOUNG STARS: 8X TO 20X		
*RCs: 3X TO 8X		
STATED ODDS 1:59		
STATED PRINT RUN 100 SER.#'d SETS		

1999 Stadium Club Chrome First Day Refractors

	MINT	NRMT
COMMON CARD (1-150)	15.00	6.75
*STARS: 25X TO 60X HI COL.		
*YOUNG STARS: 20X TO 50X		
*RCs: 6X TO 15X		
STATED ODDS 1:235		
STATED PRINT RUN 25 SER.#'d SETS		

1999 Stadium Club Chrome Refractors

	MINT	NRMT
COMPLETE SET (150)	300.00	135.00
COMMON CARD (1-150)	1.50	.70
*STARS: 2.5X TO 6X HI COL.		
*YOUNG STARS: 2X TO 5X		
*RCs: .8X TO 2X		
STATED ODDS 1:12		

1999 Stadium Club Chrome Clear Shots

	MINT	NRMT
COMPLETE SET (9)	40.00	18.00

COMMON CARD (1-9)	1.50	.70
SEMISTARS	2.50	1.10
STATED ODDS 1:22		
*REFRACTORS: 1X TO 2.5X HI COL.		
REFRACTOR STATED ODDS 1:110		
CARD NUMBERS HAVE AN SCCE PREFIX		

❑ 1 David Boston	3.00	1.35
❑ 2 Edgerrin James	20.00	9.00
❑ 3 Chris Claiborne	1.50	.70
❑ 4 Torry Holt	5.00	2.20
❑ 5 Tim Couch	12.00	5.50
❑ 6 Donovan McNabb	6.00	2.70
❑ 7 Akili Smith	4.00	1.80
❑ 8 Champ Bailey	2.50	1.10
❑ 9 Troy Edwards	3.00	1.35

1999 Stadium Club Chrome Eyes of the Game

	MINT	NRMT
COMPLETE SET (7)	50.00	22.00
COMMON CARD (20-26)	6.00	2.70
STATED ODDS 1:20		
*REFRACTORS: 1X TO 2.5X HI COL.		
REFRACTOR STATED ODDS 1:100		
CARD NUMBERS HAVE AN SCCE PREFIX		

❑ 20 Tim Couch	8.00	3.60
❑ 21 Ricky Williams	8.00	3.60
❑ 22 Barry Sanders	10.00	4.50
❑ 23 Brett Favre	10.00	4.50
❑ 24 Terrell Davis	6.00	2.70
❑ 25 Peyton Manning	8.00	3.60
❑ 26 Randy Moss	8.00	3.60

1999 Stadium Club Chrome Never Compromise

	MINT	NRMT
COMPLETE SET (40)	150.00	70.00
COMMON CARD (NC1-NC40)	2.00	.90
SEMISTARS	2.50	1.10
UNLISTED STARS	3.00	1.35
STATED ODDS 1:6		
*REFRACTORS: 1X TO 2.5X HI COL.		

REFRACTOR STATED ODDS 1:30

❑ NC1 Tim Couch	10.00	4.50
❑ NC2 David Boston	3.00	1.35
❑ NC3 Daunte Culpepper	6.00	2.70
❑ NC4 Donovan McNabb	6.00	2.70
❑ NC5 Ricky Williams	10.00	4.50
❑ NC6 Troy Edwards	3.00	1.35
❑ NC7 Akili Smith	4.00	1.80
❑ NC8 Torry Holt	5.00	2.20
❑ NC9 Cade McNown	6.00	2.70
❑ NC10 Edgerrin James	15.00	6.75
❑ NC11 Cecil Collins	2.00	.90
❑ NC12 Peerless Price	3.00	1.35
❑ NC13 Kevin Johnson	5.00	2.20
❑ NC14 Champ Bailey	2.50	1.10
❑ NC15 Kevin Faulk	2.50	1.10
❑ NC16 D'Wayne Bates	2.00	.90
❑ NC17 Shaun King	6.00	2.70
❑ NC18 Sedrick Irvin	2.50	1.10
❑ NC19 James Johnson	2.50	1.10
❑ NC20 Rob Konrad	2.50	1.10
❑ NC21 Randy Moss	12.00	5.50
❑ NC22 Peyton Manning	10.00	4.50
❑ NC23 Eddie George	4.00	1.80
❑ NC24 Fred Taylor	6.00	2.70
❑ NC25 Jamal Anderson	3.00	1.35
❑ NC26 Joey Galloway	3.00	1.35
❑ NC27 Terrell Davis	8.00	3.60
❑ NC28 Keyshawn Johnson	3.00	1.35
❑ NC29 Antonio Freeman	3.00	1.35
❑ NC30 Jake Plummer	6.00	2.70
❑ NC31 Steve Young	5.00	2.20
❑ NC32 Barry Sanders	12.00	5.50
❑ NC33 Dan Marino	12.00	5.50
❑ NC34 Emmitt Smith	8.00	3.60
❑ NC35 Brett Favre	12.00	5.50
❑ NC36 Randall Cunningham	3.00	1.35
❑ NC37 John Elway	12.00	5.50
❑ NC38 Drew Bledsoe	5.00	2.20
❑ NC39 Jerry Rice	8.00	3.60
❑ NC40 Troy Aikman	8.00	3.60

1999 Stadium Club Chrome True Colors

	MINT	NRMT
COMPLETE SET (10)	60.00	27.00
COMMON CARD (10-19)	4.00	1.80
STATED ODDS 1:24		
*REFRACTORS: 1X TO 2.5X HI COL.		
REFRACTOR STATED ODDS 1:120		
CARD NUMBERS HAVE AN SCCE PREFIX		

❑ 10 Doug Flutie	4.00	1.80
❑ 11 Steve Young	5.00	2.20
❑ 12 Jake Plummer	6.00	2.70
❑ 13 Jerry Rice	8.00	3.60
❑ 14 Randy Moss	10.00	4.50
❑ 15 Fred Taylor	6.00	2.70
❑ 16 Peyton Manning	10.00	4.50
❑ 17 Dan Marino	12.00	5.50
❑ 18 Brett Favre	12.00	5.50
❑ 19 Emmitt Smith	8.00	3.60

1950 Topps Felt Backs

	NRMT	VG-E
COMPLETE SET (100)	5500.00	2500.00
COMMON CARD (1-100)	40.00	18.00
SEMISTARS	50.00	22.00
COMMON YEL. BOR.	60.00	27.00
SEMISTARS YELLOW	90.00	40.00
CARDS PRICED IN NM CONDITION		

❑ 1 Lou Allen	40.00	18.00
❑ 2 Morris Bailey	40.00	18.00
❑ 3 George Bell	40.00	18.00
❑ 4 Lindy Berry HOR	40.00	18.00
❑ 5A Mike Boldin	40.00	18.00
❑ 5B Mike Boldin	60.00	27.00
❑ 6A Bernie Botula	40.00	18.00
❑ 6B Bernie Botula	60.00	27.00
❑ 7 Bob Bowlby	40.00	18.00
❑ 8 Bob Bucher	40.00	18.00
❑ 9A Al Burnett	40.00	18.00
❑ 9B Al Burnett	60.00	27.00
❑ 10 Don Burson	40.00	18.00
❑ 11 Paul Campbell	40.00	18.00
❑ 12 Herb Carey	40.00	18.00
❑ 13A Bimbo Cecconi	40.00	18.00
❑ 13B Bimbo Cecconi	60.00	27.00
❑ 14 Bill Chauncey	40.00	18.00
❑ 15 Dick Clark	40.00	18.00
❑ 16 Tom Coleman	40.00	18.00
❑ 17 Billy Conn	40.00	18.00
❑ 18 John Cox	40.00	18.00
❑ 19 Lou Creekmur RC	90.00	40.00
❑ 20 Glen Davis RC	50.00	22.00
❑ 21 Warren Davis	40.00	18.00
❑ 22 Bob Deuber	40.00	18.00
❑ 23 Ray Dooney	40.00	18.00
❑ 24 Tom Dublinski	40.00	18.00
❑ 25 Jeff Fleischman	40.00	18.00
❑ 26 Jack Friedland	40.00	18.00
❑ 27 Bob Fuchs	40.00	18.00
❑ 28 Arnold Galiffa RC	50.00	22.00
❑ 29 Dick Gilman	40.00	18.00
❑ 30A Frank Gitschier	40.00	18.00
❑ 30B Frank Gitschier	60.00	27.00
❑ 31 Gene Glick	40.00	18.00
❑ 32 Bill Gregus	40.00	18.00
❑ 33 Harold Hagan	40.00	18.00
❑ 34 Charles Hall	40.00	18.00
❑ 35A Leon Hart	80.00	36.00
❑ 35B Leon Hart	120.00	55.00
❑ 36A Bob Hester	40.00	18.00
❑ 36B Bob Hester	60.00	27.00

Card	NRMT	VG-E
❑ 37 George Hughes	40.00	18.00
❑ 38 Levi Jackson	50.00	22.00
❑ 39A Jackie Jensen	140.00	65.00
❑ 39B Jackie Jensen	250.00	110.00
❑ 40 Charlie Justice	125.00	55.00
❑ 41 Gary Kerkorian	40.00	18.00
❑ 42 Bernie Krueger	40.00	18.00
❑ 43 Bill Kuhn	40.00	18.00
❑ 44 Dean Laun	40.00	18.00
❑ 45 Chet Leach	40.00	18.00
❑ 46A Bobby Lee	40.00	18.00
❑ 46B Bobby Lee	60.00	27.00
❑ 47 Roger Lehew	40.00	18.00
❑ 48 Glenn Lippman	40.00	18.00
❑ 49 Melvin Lyle	40.00	18.00
❑ 50 Len Makowski	40.00	18.00
❑ 51A Al Malekoff	40.00	18.00
❑ 51B Al Malekoff	60.00	27.00
❑ 52A Jim Martin	50.00	22.00
❑ 52B Jim Martin	90.00	40.00
❑ 53 Frank Mataya	40.00	18.00
❑ 54A Ray Mathews RC	50.00	22.00
❑ 54B Ray Mathews RC	90.00	40.00
❑ 55A Dick McKissack	40.00	18.00
❑ 55B Dick McKissack	60.00	27.00
❑ 56 Frank Miller	40.00	18.00
❑ 57A John Miller	40.00	18.00
❑ 57B John Miller	60.00	27.00
❑ 58 Ed Modzelewski RC	50.00	22.00
❑ 59 Don Mouser	40.00	18.00
❑ 60 James Murphy	40.00	18.00
❑ 61A Ray Nagle	40.00	18.00
❑ 61B Ray Nagle	60.00	27.00
❑ 62 Leo Nomellini	175.00	80.00
❑ 63 James O'Day	40.00	18.00
❑ 64 Joe Paterno RC	1250.00	550.00
❑ 65 Andy Pavich	40.00	18.00
❑ 66A Pete Perini	40.00	18.00
❑ 66B Pete Perini	60.00	27.00
❑ 67 Jim Powers	40.00	18.00
❑ 68 Dave Rakestraw	40.00	18.00
❑ 69 Herb Rich	40.00	18.00
❑ 70 Fran Rogel RC	40.00	18.00
❑ 71A Darrell Royal RC	125.00	55.00
❑ 71B Darrell Royal RC	200.00	90.00
❑ 72 Steve Sawle	40.00	18.00
❑ 73 Nick Sebek	40.00	18.00
❑ 74 Herb Seidell	40.00	18.00
❑ 75A Charles Shaw	40.00	18.00
❑ 75B Charles Shaw	60.00	27.00
❑ 76A Emil Sitko RC	50.00	22.00
❑ 76B Emil Sitko RC	90.00	40.00
❑ 77 Ed(Butch) Songin RC	50.00	22.00
❑ 78A Mariano Stalloni	40.00	18.00
❑ 78B Mariano Stalloni	60.00	27.00
❑ 79 Ernie Stautner RC	200.00	90.00
❑ 80 Don Stehley	40.00	18.00
❑ 81 Gil Stevenson	40.00	18.00
❑ 82 Bishop Strickland	40.00	18.00
❑ 83 Harry Szulborski	40.00	18.00
❑ 84A Wally Teninga	40.00	18.00
❑ 84B Wally Teninga	60.00	27.00
❑ 85 Clayton Tonnemaker	40.00	18.00
❑ 86A Deacon Dan Towler RC	80.00	36.00
❑ 86B Deacon Dan Towler RC	120.00	55.00
❑ 87A Bert Turek	40.00	18.00
❑ 87B Bert Turek	60.00	27.00
❑ 88 Harry Ulinski	40.00	18.00
❑ 89 Leon Van Billingham	40.00	18.00
❑ 90 Langdon Viracola	40.00	18.00
❑ 91 Leo Wagner	40.00	18.00
❑ 92A Doak Walker	200.00	90.00
❑ 92B Doak Walker	375.00	170.00
❑ 93 Jim Ward	40.00	18.00
❑ 94 Art Weiner	40.00	18.00
❑ 95 Dick Weiss	40.00	18.00
❑ 96 Froggie Williams	40.00	18.00
❑ 97 Robert Red Wilson	40.00	18.00
❑ 98 Roger Red Wilson	40.00	18.00
❑ 99 Carl Wren	40.00	18.00
❑ 100A Pete Zinaich	40.00	18.00
❑ 100B Pete Zinaich	60.00	27.00

1951 Topps Magic

	NRMT	VG-E
COMPLETE SET (75)	1100.00	500.00
COMMON CARD (1-75)	18.00	8.00
SEMISTARS	25.00	11.00

*BACK UNSCRATCHED: 1.5X TO 2.5X
CARDS PRICED IN NM CONDITION !

Card	NRMT	VG-E
❑ 1 Jimmy Monahan RC	30.00	13.50
❑ 2 Bill Wade RC	50.00	22.00
❑ 3 Bill Reichardt	18.00	8.00
❑ 4 Babe Parilli RC	50.00	22.00
❑ 5 Billie Burkhalter	18.00	8.00
❑ 6 Ed Weber	18.00	8.00
❑ 7 Tom Scott	25.00	11.00
❑ 8 Frank Guthridge	18.00	8.00
❑ 9 John Karras	18.00	8.00
❑ 10 Vic Janowicz RC	150.00	70.00
❑ 11 Lloyd Hill	18.00	8.00
❑ 12 Jim Weatherall RC	25.00	11.00
❑ 13 Howard Hansen	18.00	8.00
❑ 14 Lou D'Achille	18.00	8.00
❑ 15 Johnny Turco	18.00	8.00
❑ 16 Jerrell Price	18.00	8.00
❑ 17 John Coatta	18.00	8.00
❑ 18 Bruce Patton	18.00	8.00
❑ 19 Marion Campbell RC	35.00	16.00
❑ 20 Blaine Earon	18.00	8.00
❑ 21 Dewey McConnell	18.00	8.00
❑ 22 Ray Beck	18.00	8.00
❑ 23 Jim Prewett	18.00	8.00
❑ 24 Bob Steele	18.00	8.00
❑ 25 Art Betts	18.00	8.00
❑ 26 Walt Trillhaase	18.00	8.00
❑ 27 Gil Bartosh	18.00	8.00
❑ 28 Bob Bestwick	18.00	8.00
❑ 29 Tom Rushing	18.00	8.00
❑ 30 Bert Rechichar RC	35.00	16.00
❑ 31 Bill Owens	18.00	8.00
❑ 32 Mike Goggins	18.00	8.00
❑ 33 John Petitbon	18.00	8.00
❑ 34 Byron Townsend	18.00	8.00
❑ 35 Ed Rotticci	18.00	8.00
❑ 36 Steve Wadiak	18.00	8.00
❑ 37 Bobby Marlow RC	25.00	11.00
❑ 38 Bill Fuchs	18.00	8.00
❑ 39 Ralph Staub	18.00	8.00
❑ 40 Bill Vesprini	18.00	8.00
❑ 41 Zack Jordan	18.00	8.00
❑ 42 Bob Smith RC	25.00	11.00
❑ 43 Charles Hanson	18.00	8.00
❑ 44 Glenn Smith	18.00	8.00
❑ 45 Armand Kitto	18.00	8.00
❑ 46 Vinnie Drake	18.00	8.00
❑ 47 Bill Putich	18.00	8.00
❑ 48 George Young RC	40.00	18.00
❑ 49 Don McRae	18.00	8.00
❑ 50 Frank Smith	18.00	8.00
❑ 51 Dick Hightower	18.00	8.00
❑ 52 Clyde Pickard	18.00	8.00
❑ 53 Bob Reynolds	18.00	8.00
❑ 54 Dick Gregory	18.00	8.00
❑ 55 Dale Samuels	18.00	8.00
❑ 56 Gale Galloway	18.00	8.00
❑ 57 Vic Pujo	18.00	8.00
❑ 58 Dave Waters	18.00	8.00
❑ 59 Joe Ernest	18.00	8.00
❑ 60 Elmer Costa	18.00	8.00
❑ 61 Nick Liotta	18.00	8.00
❑ 62 John Dottley	18.00	8.00
❑ 63 Hi Faubion	18.00	8.00
❑ 64 David Harr	18.00	8.00
❑ 65 Bill Matthews	18.00	8.00
❑ 66 Carroll McDonald	18.00	8.00
❑ 67 Dick Dewing	18.00	8.00
❑ 68 Joe Johnson	18.00	8.00
❑ 69 Arnold Burwitz	18.00	8.00
❑ 70 Ed Dobrowolski	18.00	8.00
❑ 71 Joe Dudeck	18.00	8.00
❑ 72 Johnny Bright RC	25.00	11.00
❑ 73 Harold Loehlein	18.00	8.00
❑ 74 Lawrence Hairston	18.00	8.00
❑ 75 Bob Carey RC	25.00	11.00

1955 Topps All-American

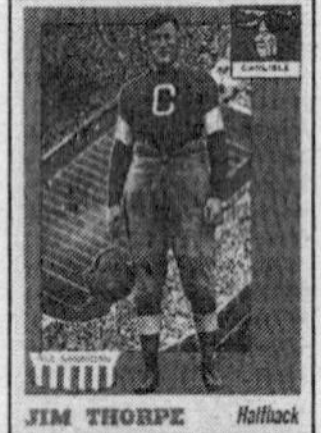

	NRMT	VG-E
COMPLETE SET (100)	3600.00	1600.00
COMMON CARD (1-92)	16.00	7.25
SEMISTARS 1-92	20.00	9.00
SP (9/11/15/25/41)	30.00	13.50
SP (51/54/55/57/61)	30.00	13.50
SP (65/77/83/86/87)	30.00	13.50
SEMISTARS SP (18/26/28)	40.00	18.00
SEMISTARS SP (36/42)	40.00	18.00
COMMON SP (93-100)	40.00	18.00

CARDS PRICED IN NM CONDITION !

Card	NRMT	VG-E
❑ 1 Herman Hickman RC !	125.00	31.00
❑ 2 John Kimbrough	16.00	7.25
❑ 3 Ed Weir	16.00	7.25
❑ 4 Erny Pinckert	16.00	7.25
❑ 5 Bobby Grayson	16.00	7.25
❑ 6 Nile Kinnick RC UER Spelled Niles	100.00	45.00
❑ 7 Andy Bershak	16.00	7.25
❑ 8 George Cafego RC	16.00	7.25
❑ 9 Tom Hamilton SP	30.00	13.50
❑ 10 Bill Dudley	40.00	18.00
❑ 11 Bobby Dodd SP	30.00	13.50
❑ 12 Otto Graham	200.00	90.00
❑ 13 Aaron Rosenberg	16.00	7.25
❑ 14A Gaynell Tinsley RC ERR (with Whizzer White bio)	100.00	45.00
❑ 14B Gaynell Tinsley RC COR (correct bio)	25.00	11.00
❑ 15 Ed Kaw SP	30.00	13.50
❑ 16 Knute Rockne	275.00	125.00
❑ 17 Bob Reynolds	16.00	7.25
❑ 18 Pudge Heffelfinger RC SP	40.00	18.00
❑ 19 Bruce Smith	35.00	16.00
❑ 20 Sammy Baugh	200.00	90.00
❑ 21A Whizzer White RC SP ERR (with Gaynell Tinsley bio)	150.00	70.00
❑ 21B Whizzer White RC SP COR (correct bio)	80.00	36.00
❑ 22 Brick Muller	16.00	7.25
❑ 23 Dick Kazmaier RC	16.00	7.25
❑ 24 Ken Strong	40.00	18.00
❑ 25 Casimir Myslinski SP	30.00	13.50
❑ 26 Larry Kelley RC SP	40.00	18.00
❑ 27 Red Grange UER Card says he was QB should say halfback	300.00	135.00

Card	NRMT	VG-E
❑ 28 Mel Hein RC SP	40.00	18.00
❑ 29 Leo Nomellini SP	70.00	32.00
❑ 30 Wes Fesler	16.00	7.25
❑ 31 George Sauer Sr. RC	20.00	9.00
❑ 32 Hank Foldberg	16.00	7.25
❑ 33 Bob Higgins	16.00	7.25
❑ 34 Davey O'Brien RC	40.00	18.00
❑ 35 Tom Harmon RC SP	60.00	27.00
❑ 36 Turk Edwards SP	40.00	18.00
❑ 37 Jim Thorpe	400.00	180.00
❑ 38A Amos Alonzo Stagg RC ERR	100.00	45.00
Wrong back 19		
❑ 38B Amos Alonzo Stagg COR RC	60.00	27.00
❑ 39 Jerome Holland RC	20.00	9.00
❑ 40 Donn Moomaw	16.00	7.25
❑ 41 Joseph Alexander SP	30.00	13.50
❑ 42 Eddie Tryon RC SP	40.00	18.00
❑ 43 George Savitsky	16.00	7.25
❑ 44 Ed Garbisch	16.00	7.25
❑ 45 Elmer Oliphant	16.00	7.25
❑ 46 Arnold Lassman	16.00	7.25
❑ 47 Bo McMillin RC	20.00	9.00
❑ 48 Ed Widseth	16.00	7.25
❑ 49 Don Zimmerman	16.00	7.25
❑ 50 Ken Kavanaugh	20.00	9.00
❑ 51 Duane Purvis SP	30.00	13.50
❑ 52 John Lujack	50.00	22.00
❑ 53 John F. Green	16.00	7.25
❑ 54 Edwin Dooley SP	30.00	13.50
❑ 55 Frank Merritt SP	30.00	13.50
❑ 56 Ernie Nevers RC	70.00	32.00
❑ 57 Vic Hanson SP	30.00	13.50
❑ 58 Ed Franco	16.00	7.25
❑ 59 Doc Blanchard RC	50.00	22.00
❑ 60 Dan Hill	16.00	7.25
❑ 61 Charles Brickley SP	30.00	13.50
❑ 62 Harry Newman	16.00	7.25
❑ 63 Charlie Justice	35.00	16.00
❑ 64 Benny Friedman RC	20.00	9.00
❑ 65 Joe Donchess SP	30.00	13.50
❑ 66 Bruiser Kinard RC	35.00	16.00
❑ 67 Frankie Albert	20.00	9.00
❑ 68 Four Horsemen RC SP	500.00	220.00
Jim Crowley		
Elmer Layden		
Creighton Miller		
Harry Stuhldreher		
❑ 69 Frank Sinkwich RC	20.00	9.00
❑ 70 Bill Daddio	16.00	7.25
❑ 71 Bobby Wilson	16.00	7.25
❑ 72 Chub Peabody	16.00	7.25
❑ 73 Paul Governali	20.00	9.00
❑ 74 Gene McEver	16.00	7.25
❑ 75 Hugh Gallarneau	16.00	7.25
❑ 76 Angelo Bertelli RC	20.00	9.00
❑ 77 Bowden Wyatt SP	30.00	13.50
❑ 78 Jay Berwanger RC	35.00	16.00
❑ 79 Pug Lund	16.00	7.25
❑ 80 Bennie Oosterbaan	16.00	7.25
❑ 81 Cotton Warburton	16.00	7.25
❑ 82 Alex Wojciechowicz	30.00	13.50
❑ 83 Ted Coy SP	30.00	13.50
❑ 84 Ace Parker RC SP	40.00	18.00
❑ 85 Sid Luckman	110.00	50.00
❑ 86 Albie Booth SP	30.00	13.50
❑ 87 Adolph Schultz SP	30.00	13.50
❑ 88 Ralph Kercheval	16.00	7.25
❑ 89 Marshall Goldberg	20.00	9.00
❑ 90 Charlie O'Rourke	16.00	7.25
❑ 91 Bob Odell UER	16.00	7.25
Photo actually		
Howard Odell		
❑ 92 Biggie Munn	16.00	7.25
❑ 93 Willie Heston SP	40.00	18.00
❑ 94 Joe Bernard SP	40.00	18.00
❑ 95 Chris(Red) Cagle SP	40.00	18.00
❑ 96 Bill Hollenback SP	40.00	18.00
❑ 97 Don Hutson RC SP	225.00	100.00
❑ 98 Beattie Feathers SP	70.00	32.00
❑ 99 Don Whitmire SP	40.00	18.00
❑ 100 Fats Henry SP RC	160.00	40.00

1956 Topps

	NRMT	VG-E
COMPLETE SET (120)	1400.00	650.00
COMMON CARD (1-120)	6.00	2.70
SEMISTARS	8.00	3.60
UNLISTED STARS	12.00	5.50
CARDS SP (10/34/46/70)	25.00	11.00
CARDS SP (82/94/106/118)	25.00	11.00
REDSKINS SP (25/37/73)	22.00	10.00
REDSKINS SP (85/97/109)	22.00	10.00
TEAM CARDS	18.00	8.00

CARDS PRICED IN NM CONDITION !

Card	NRMT	VG-E
❑ 1 Johnny Carson SP	80.00	20.00
❑ 2 Gordy Soltau	6.00	2.70
❑ 3 Frank Varrichione	6.00	2.70
❑ 4 Eddie Bell	6.00	2.70
❑ 5 Alex Webster RC	12.00	5.50
❑ 6 Norm Van Brocklin	30.00	13.50
❑ 7 Green Bay Packers	18.00	8.00
Team Card		
❑ 8 Lou Creekmur	12.00	5.50
❑ 9 Lou Groza	25.00	11.00
❑ 10 Tom Bienemann SP	25.00	11.00
❑ 11 George Blanda	50.00	22.00
❑ 12 Alan Ameche	12.00	5.50
❑ 13 Vic Janowicz SP	45.00	20.00
❑ 14 Dick Moegle	8.00	3.60
❑ 15 Fran Rogel	6.00	2.70
❑ 16 Harold Giancanelli	6.00	2.70
❑ 17 Emlen Tunnell	15.00	6.75
❑ 18 Tank Younger	12.00	5.50
❑ 19 Billy Howton	8.00	3.60
❑ 20 Jack Christiansen	15.00	6.75
❑ 21 Darrel Brewster	6.00	2.70
❑ 22 Chicago Cardinals SP	100.00	45.00
Team Card		
❑ 23 Ed Brown	8.00	3.60
❑ 24 Joe Campanella	6.00	2.70
❑ 25 Leon Heath SP	22.00	10.00
❑ 26 San Francisco 49ers	18.00	8.00
Team Card		
❑ 27 Dick Flanagan	6.00	2.70
❑ 28 Chuck Bednarik	25.00	11.00
❑ 29 Kyle Rote	12.00	5.50
❑ 30 Les Richter	8.00	3.60
❑ 31 Howard Ferguson	6.00	2.70
❑ 32 Dorne Dibble	6.00	2.70
❑ 33 Kenny Konz	6.00	2.70
❑ 34 Dave Mann SP	25.00	11.00
❑ 35 Rick Casares	12.00	5.50
❑ 36 Art Donovan	30.00	13.50
❑ 37 Chuck Drazenovich SP	22.00	10.00
❑ 38 Joe Arenas	6.00	2.70
❑ 39 Lynn Chandnois	6.00	2.70
❑ 40 Philadelphia Eagles	18.00	8.00
Team Card		
❑ 41 Roosevelt Brown RC	30.00	13.50
❑ 42 Tom Fears	25.00	11.00
❑ 43 Gary Knafelc	6.00	2.70
❑ 44 Joe Schmidt RC	45.00	20.00
❑ 45 Cleveland Browns	18.00	8.00
Team Card UER		
(Card back does not		
credit the Browns with		
being Champs in 1955)		
❑ 46 Len Teeuws RC SP	25.00	11.00
❑ 47 Bill George RC	30.00	13.50
❑ 48 Baltimore Colts	18.00	8.00
Team Card		
❑ 49 Eddie LeBaron SP	45.00	20.00
❑ 50 Hugh McElhenny	25.00	11.00
❑ 51 Ted Marchibroda	12.00	5.50
❑ 52 Adrian Burk	6.00	2.70
❑ 53 Frank Gifford	75.00	34.00
❑ 54 Charley Toogood	6.00	2.70
❑ 55 Tobin Rote	8.00	3.60
❑ 56 Bill Stits	6.00	2.70
❑ 57 Don Colo	6.00	2.70
❑ 58 Ollie Matson SP	75.00	34.00
❑ 59 Harlon Hill	8.00	3.60
❑ 60 Lenny Moore RC !	90.00	40.00
❑ 61 Washington Redskins SP	90.00	40.00
Team Card		
❑ 62 Billy Wilson	6.00	2.70
❑ 63 Pittsburgh Steelers	18.00	8.00
Team Card		
❑ 64 Bob Pellegrini	6.00	2.70
❑ 65 Ken MacAfee	6.00	2.70
❑ 66 Willard Sherman	6.00	2.70
❑ 67 Roger Zatkoff	6.00	2.70
❑ 68 Dave Middleton	6.00	2.70
❑ 69 Ray Renfro	8.00	3.60
❑ 70 Don Stonesifer SP	25.00	11.00
❑ 71 Stan Jones RC	30.00	13.50
❑ 72 Jim Mutscheller	6.00	2.70
❑ 73 Volney Peters SP	22.00	10.00
❑ 74 Leo Nomellini	20.00	9.00
❑ 75 Ray Mathews	6.00	2.70
❑ 76 Dick Bielski	6.00	2.70
❑ 77 Charley Conerly	25.00	11.00
❑ 78 Elroy Hirsch	25.00	11.00
❑ 79 Bill Forester RC	8.00	3.60
❑ 80 Jim Doran	6.00	2.70
❑ 81 Fred Morrison	6.00	2.70
❑ 82 Jack Simmons SP	25.00	11.00
❑ 83 Bill McColl	6.00	2.70
❑ 84 Bert Rechichar	6.00	2.70
❑ 85 Joe Scudero SP	22.00	10.00
❑ 86 Y.A. Tittle UER	50.00	22.00
(misspelled Yelverton on back)		
❑ 87 Ernie Stautner	20.00	9.00
❑ 88 Norm Willey	6.00	2.70
❑ 89 Bob Schnelker	6.00	2.70
❑ 90 Dan Towler	12.00	5.50
❑ 91 John Martinkovic	6.00	2.70
❑ 92 Detroit Lions	18.00	8.00
Team Card		
❑ 93 George Ratterman	8.00	3.60
❑ 94 Chuck Ulrich SP	25.00	11.00
❑ 95 Bobby Watkins	6.00	2.70
❑ 96 Buddy Young	12.00	5.50
❑ 97 Billy Wells SP	22.00	10.00
❑ 98 Bob Toneff	6.00	2.70
❑ 99 Bill McPeak	6.00	2.70
❑ 100 Bobby Thomason	6.00	2.70
❑ 101 Roosevelt Grier RC	40.00	18.00
❑ 102 Ron Waller	6.00	2.70
❑ 103 Bobby Dillon	6.00	2.70
❑ 104 Leon Hart	12.00	5.50
❑ 105 Mike McCormack	15.00	6.75
❑ 106 John Olszewski SP	25.00	11.00
❑ 107 Bill Wightkin	6.00	2.70
❑ 108 George Shaw RC	8.00	3.60
❑ 109 Dale Atkeson SP	22.00	10.00
❑ 110 Joe Perry	25.00	11.00
❑ 111 Dale Dodrill	6.00	2.70
❑ 112 Tom Scott	6.00	2.70
❑ 113 New York Giants	18.00	8.00
Team Card		
❑ 114 Los Angeles Rams	18.00	8.00
Team Card UER		
(back incorrect, Rams		
were not 1955 champs)		
❑ 115 Al Carmichael	6.00	2.70
❑ 116 Bobby Layne	50.00	22.00
❑ 117 Ed Modzelewski	6.00	2.70
❑ 118 Lamar McHan RC SP	25.00	11.00
❑ 119 Chicago Bears	18.00	8.00
Team Card		
❑ 120 Billy Vessels RC !	35.00	8.75
❑ AD1 Lou Groza	250.00	110.00
Don Colo		
Darrel Brewster		
(ad back panel)		
❑ NNO Checklist Card SP	400.00	100.00
(unnumbered)		
❑ C1 Contest Card	80.00	36.00

Sunday, October 14
Colts vs. Packers
Cards vs. Redskins
❑ C2 Contest Card 80.00 36.00
Sunday, October 14
Rams vs. Lions
Giants vs. Browns
❑ C3 Contest Card 80.00 36.00
Sunday, October 14
Eagles vs. Steelers
49ers vs. Bears
❑ CA Contest Card 90.00 40.00
Sunday, November 25
Bears vs. Giants
Rams vs. Colts
❑ CB Contest Card 110.00 50.00
Sunday, November 25
Steelers vs. Cards
49ers vs. Eagles

1957 Topps

	NRMT	VG-E
COMPLETE SET (154)	2200.00	1000.00
COMMON CARD (1-88)	4.00	1.80
SEMISTARS 1-88	6.00	2.70
UNLISTED STARS 1-88	10.00	4.50
COMMON CARD (89-154)	10.00	4.50
SEMISTARS 89-154	12.00	5.50
UNLISTED STARS 89-154	14.00	6.25
COMMON DP (91/93/98)	8.00	3.60
COM. DP (100/103/107)	8.00	3.60
COM. DP (110/111/113)	8.00	3.60
COM. DP (120/122/127)	8.00	3.60
COM. DP (139/140/143)	8.00	3.60
COM. DP (148/149/153)	8.00	3.60
SEMISTARS 89-154 DP	10.00	4.50

CARDS PRICED IN NM CONDITION

❑ 1 Eddie LeBaron 40.00 10.00
❑ 2 Pete Retzlaff RC 15.00 6.75
❑ 3 Mike McCormack 12.00 5.50
❑ 4 Lou Baldacci 4.00 1.80
❑ 5 Gino Marchetti 15.00 6.75
❑ 6 Leo Nomellini 20.00 9.00
❑ 7 Bobby Watkins 4.00 1.80
❑ 8 Dave Middleton 4.00 1.80
❑ 9 Bobby Dillon 4.00 1.80
❑ 10 Les Richter 6.00 2.70
❑ 11 Roosevelt Brown 15.00 6.75
❑ 12 Lavern Torgeson RC 4.00 1.80
❑ 13 Dick Bielski 4.00 1.80
❑ 14 Pat Summerall 20.00 9.00
❑ 15 Jack Butler RC 10.00 4.50
❑ 16 John Henry Johnson 15.00 6.75
❑ 17 Art Spinney 4.00 1.80
❑ 18 Bob St. Clair 12.00 5.50
❑ 19 Perry Jeter 4.00 1.80
❑ 20 Lou Creekmur 12.00 5.50
❑ 21 Dave Hanner 6.00 2.70
❑ 22 Norm Van Brocklin 30.00 13.50
❑ 23 Don Chandler RC 10.00 4.50
❑ 24 Al Dorow 4.00 1.80
❑ 25 Tom Scott 4.00 1.80
❑ 26 Ollie Matson 20.00 9.00
❑ 27 Fran Rogel 4.00 1.80
❑ 28 Lou Groza 25.00 11.00
❑ 29 Billy Vessels 6.00 2.70
❑ 30 Y.A. Tittle 40.00 18.00
❑ 31 George Blanda 40.00 18.00
❑ 32 Bobby Layne 40.00 18.00
❑ 33 Billy Howton 6.00 2.70
❑ 34 Bill Wade 10.00 4.50
❑ 35 Emlen Tunnell 15.00 6.75
❑ 36 Leo Elter 4.00 1.80
❑ 37 Clarence Peaks RC 6.00 2.70
❑ 38 Don Stonesifer 4.00 1.80
❑ 39 George Tarasovic 4.00 1.80
❑ 40 Darrel Brewster 4.00 1.80
❑ 41 Bert Rechichar 4.00 1.80
❑ 42 Billy Wilson 4.00 1.80
❑ 43 Ed Brown 6.00 2.70
❑ 44 Gene Gedman 4.00 1.80
❑ 45 Gary Knafelc 4.00 1.80
❑ 46 Elroy Hirsch 20.00 9.00
❑ 47 Don Heinrich 6.00 2.70
❑ 48 Gene Brito 4.00 1.80
❑ 49 Chuck Bednarik 25.00 11.00
❑ 50 Dave Mann 4.00 1.80
❑ 51 Bill McPeak 4.00 1.80
❑ 52 Kenny Konz 4.00 1.80
❑ 53 Alan Ameche 10.00 4.50
❑ 54 Gordy Soltau 4.00 1.80
❑ 55 Rick Casares 6.00 2.70
❑ 56 Charlie Ane 4.00 1.80
❑ 57 Al Carmichael 4.00 1.80
❑ 58A Willard Sherman ERR 300.00 135.00
(no team on front)
❑ 58B Willard Sherman COR 4.00 1.80
❑ 59 Kyle Rote 10.00 4.50
❑ 60 Chuck Drazenovich 4.00 1.80
❑ 61 Bobby Walston 4.00 1.80
❑ 62 John Olszewski 4.00 1.80
❑ 63 Ray Mathews 4.00 1.80
❑ 64 Maurice Bassett 4.00 1.80
❑ 65 Art Donovan 25.00 11.00
❑ 66 Joe Arenas 4.00 1.80
❑ 67 Harlon Hill 6.00 2.70
❑ 68 Yale Lary 12.00 5.50
❑ 69 Bill Forester 6.00 2.70
❑ 70 Bob Boyd 4.00 1.80
❑ 71 Andy Robustelli 20.00 9.00
❑ 72 Sam Baker RC 6.00 2.70
❑ 73 Bob Pellegrini 4.00 1.80
❑ 74 Leo Sanford 4.00 1.80
❑ 75 Sid Watson 4.00 1.80
❑ 76 Ray Renfro 6.00 2.70
❑ 77 Carl Taseff 4.00 1.80
❑ 78 Clyde Conner 4.00 1.80
❑ 79 J.C. Caroline 4.00 1.80
❑ 80 Howard Cassady RC 15.00 6.75
❑ 81 Tobin Rote 6.00 2.70
❑ 82 Ron Waller 4.00 1.80
❑ 83 Jim Patton RC 6.00 2.70
❑ 84 Volney Peters 4.00 1.80
❑ 85 Dick Lane RC 40.00 18.00
❑ 86 Royce Womble 4.00 1.80
❑ 87 Duane Putnam RC 6.00 2.70
❑ 88 Frank Gifford 75.00 34.00
❑ 89 Steve Meilinger 10.00 4.50
❑ 90 Buck Lansford 10.00 4.50
❑ 91 Lindon Crow DP 7.00 3.10
❑ 92 Ernie Stautner DP 20.00 9.00
❑ 93 Preston Carpenter DP RC 10.00 4.50
❑ 94 Raymond Berry RC 125.00 55.00
❑ 95 Hugh McElhenny 30.00 13.50
❑ 96 Stan Jones 20.00 9.00
❑ 97 Dorne Dibble 10.00 4.50
❑ 98 Joe Scudero DP 7.00 3.10
❑ 99 Eddie Bell 10.00 4.50
❑ 100 Joe Childress DP 7.00 3.10
❑ 101 Elbert Nickel 12.00 5.50
❑ 102 Walt Michaels 12.00 5.50
❑ 103 Jim Mutscheller DP 7.00 3.10
❑ 104 Earl Morrall RC 40.00 18.00
❑ 105 Larry Strickland 10.00 4.50
❑ 106 Jack Christiansen 15.00 6.75
❑ 107 Fred Cone DP 9.00 4.00
❑ 108 Bud McFadin RC 12.00 5.50
❑ 109 Charley Conerly 25.00 11.00
❑ 110 Tom Runnels DP 7.00 3.10
❑ 111 Ken Keller DP 7.00 3.10
❑ 112 James Root 10.00 4.50
❑ 113 Ted Marchibroda DP 10.00 4.50
❑ 114 Don Paul 10.00 4.50
❑ 115 George Shaw 12.00 5.50
❑ 116 Dick Moegle 12.00 5.50
❑ 117 Don Bingham 10.00 4.50
❑ 118 Leon Hart 14.00 6.25
❑ 119 Bart Starr RC 450.00 200.00
❑ 120 Paul Miller DP 7.00 3.10
❑ 121 Alex Webster 12.00 5.50
❑ 122 Ray Wietecha DP 7.00 3.10
❑ 123 Johnny Carson 10.00 4.50
❑ 124 Tommy McDonald DP RC 25.00 11.00
❑ 125 Jerry Tubbs RC 12.00 5.50
❑ 126 Jack Scarbath 10.00 4.50
❑ 127 Ed Modzelewski DP 9.00 4.00
❑ 128 Lenny Moore 50.00 22.00
❑ 129 Joe Perry DP 25.00 11.00
❑ 130 Bill Wightkin 10.00 4.50
❑ 131 Jim Doran 10.00 4.50
❑ 132 Howard Ferguson UER 10.00 4.50
(Name misspelled Furgeson on front)
❑ 133 Tom Wilson 10.00 4.50
❑ 134 Dick James 10.00 4.50
❑ 135 Jimmy Harris 10.00 4.50
❑ 136 Chuck Ulrich 10.00 4.50
❑ 137 Lynn Chandnois 10.00 4.50
❑ 138 John Unitas DP RC 450.00 200.00
❑ 139 Jim Ridlon DP 7.00 3.10
❑ 140 Zeke Bratkowski DP 10.00 4.50
❑ 141 Ray Krouse 10.00 4.50
❑ 142 John Martinkovic 10.00 4.50
❑ 143 Jim Cason DP 7.00 3.10
❑ 144 Ken MacAfee 10.00 4.50
❑ 145 Sid Youngelman RC 12.00 5.50
❑ 146 Paul Larson 10.00 4.50
❑ 147 Len Ford 30.00 13.50
❑ 148 Bob Toneff DP 7.00 3.10
❑ 149 Ronnie Knox DP 7.00 3.10
❑ 150 Jim David RC 12.00 5.50
❑ 151 Paul Hornung RC 400.00 180.00
❑ 152 Tank Younger 14.00 6.25
❑ 153 Bill Svoboda DP 7.00 3.10
❑ 154 Fred Morrison 70.00 17.50
❑ AD1 Al Dorow 175.00 80.00
Harlon Hill
Bert Rechichar
(Ollie Matson back)
(ad back panel)
❑ NNO Checklist Card SP 750.00 190.00

1958 Topps

	NRMT	VG-E
COMPLETE SET (132)	1250.00	550.00
COMMON CARD (1-132)	4.00	1.80
SEMISTARS	5.00	2.20
UNLISTED STARS	8.00	3.60
TEAM CARDS	6.00	2.70

CARDS PRICED IN NM CONDITION

❑ 1 Gene Filipski RC ! 15.00 3.70
❑ 2 Bobby Layne 30.00 13.50
❑ 3 Joe Schmidt 12.00 5.50
❑ 4 Bill Barnes 4.00 1.80
❑ 5 Milt Plum RC 8.00 3.60
❑ 6 Billy Howton UER 5.00 2.20
(Misspelled Billie
on card front)
❑ 7 Howard Cassady 5.00 2.20

❑ 8 Jim Dooley 4.00 1.80
❑ 9 Cleveland Browns 6.00 2.70
Team Card
❑ 10 Lenny Moore 20.00 9.00
❑ 11 Darrel Brewster 4.00 1.80
❑ 12 Alan Ameche.................. 8.00 3.60
❑ 13 Jim David 4.00 1.80
❑ 14 Jim Mutscheller 4.00 1.80
❑ 15 Andy Robustelli UER.... 10.00 4.50
(Never played for
San Francisco)
❑ 16 Gino Marchetti............. 12.00 5.50
❑ 17 Ray Renfro 5.00 2.20
❑ 18 Yale Lary....................... 8.00 3.60
❑ 19 Gary Glick 4.00 1.80
❑ 20 Jon Arnett RC 8.00 3.60
❑ 21 Bob Boyd....................... 4.00 1.80
❑ 22 John Unitas UER....... 125.00 55.00
(College: Pittsburgh
should be Louisville)
❑ 23 Zeke Bratkowski 5.00 2.20
❑ 24 Sid Youngelman UER 4.00 1.80
(Misspelled Youngleman
on card back)
❑ 25 Leo Elter 4.00 1.80
❑ 26 Kenny Konz.................. 4.00 1.80
❑ 27 Washington Redskins 6.00 2.70
Team Card
❑ 28 Carl Brettschneider UER 4.00 1.80
(Misspelled on back
as Brettschnieder)
❑ 29 Chicago Bears............... 6.00 2.70
Team Card
❑ 30 Alex Webster................. 5.00 2.20
❑ 31 Al Carmichael 4.00 1.80
❑ 32 Bobby Dillon 4.00 1.80
❑ 33 Steve Meilinger 4.00 1.80
❑ 34 Sam Baker 4.00 1.80
❑ 35 Chuck Bednarik UER .. 15.00 6.75
(Misspelled Bednarick
on card back)
❑ 36 Bert Vic Zucco.............. 4.00 1.80
❑ 37 George Tarasovic 4.00 1.80
❑ 38 Bill Wade...................... 8.00 3.60
❑ 39 Dick Stanfel.................. 5.00 2.20
❑ 40 Jerry Norton 4.00 1.80
❑ 41 San Francisco 49ers 6.00 2.70
Team Card
❑ 42 Emlen Tunnell 10.00 4.50
❑ 43 Jim Doran 4.00 1.80
❑ 44 Ted Marchibroda 8.00 3.60
❑ 45 Chet Hanulak 4.00 1.80
❑ 46 Dale Dodrill 4.00 1.80
❑ 47 Johnny Carson 4.00 1.80
❑ 48 Dick Deschaine 4.00 1.80
❑ 49 Billy Wells UER 4.00 1.80
(College should be
Michigan State)
❑ 50 Larry Morris.................. 4.00 1.80
❑ 51 Jack McClairen 4.00 1.80
❑ 52 Lou Groza 15.00 6.75
❑ 53 Rick Casares................. 5.00 2.20
❑ 54 Don Chandler 5.00 2.20
❑ 55 Duane Putnam 4.00 1.80
❑ 56 Gary Knafelc 4.00 1.80
❑ 57 Earl Morrall UER 10.00 4.50
(Misspelled Moral
on card back)
❑ 58 Ron Kramer RC............. 5.00 2.20
❑ 59 Mike McCormack 8.00 3.60
❑ 60 Gern Nagler.................. 4.00 1.80
❑ 61 New York Giants 6.00 2.70
Team Card
❑ 62 Jim Brown RC ! 450.00 200.00
❑ 63 Joe Marconi RC UER 4.00 1.80
(Avg. gain should be 4.4)
❑ 64 R.C. Owens RC UER 5.00 2.20
(Photo actually
Don Owens)
❑ 65 Jimmy Carr RC 5.00 2.20
❑ 66 Bart Starr UER 100.00 45.00
(Life and year
stats reversed)
❑ 67 Tom Wilson 4.00 1.80
❑ 68 Lamar McHan 4.00 1.80
❑ 69 Chicago Cardinals.......... 6.00 2.70
Team Card
❑ 70 Jack Christiansen 8.00 3.60
❑ 71 Don McIlhenny RC 4.00 1.80
❑ 72 Ron Waller 4.00 1.80
❑ 73 Frank Gifford 50.00 22.00
❑ 74 Bert Rechichar 4.00 1.80
❑ 75 John Henry Johnson 10.00 4.50
❑ 76 Jack Butler 5.00 2.20
❑ 77 Frank Varrichione 4.00 1.80
❑ 78 Ray Mathews 4.00 1.80
❑ 79 Marv Matuszak UER 4.00 1.80
(Misspelled Matuzsak
on card front)
❑ 80 Harlon Hill UER 4.00 1.80
(Lifetime yards and
Avg. gain incorrect)
❑ 81 Lou Creekmur 8.00 3.60
❑ 82 Woodley Lewis UER 4.00 1.80
(misspelled Woodly on
front; end on front
and halfback on back)
❑ 83 Don Heinrich 4.00 1.80
❑ 84 Charley Conerly UER .. 15.00 6.75
(Misspelled Charlie
on card back)
❑ 85 Los Angeles Rams 6.00 2.70
Team Card
❑ 86 Y.A. Tittle.................... 30.00 13.50
❑ 87 Bobby Walston 4.00 1.80
❑ 88 Earl Putman 4.00 1.80
❑ 89 Leo Nomellini 15.00 6.75
❑ 90 Sonny Jurgensen RC 100.00 45.00
❑ 91 Don Paul 4.00 1.80
❑ 92 Paige Cothren 4.00 1.80
❑ 93 Joe Perry..................... 15.00 6.75
❑ 94 Tobin Rote..................... 5.00 2.20
❑ 95 Billy Wilson 4.00 1.80
❑ 96 Green Bay Packers 6.00 2.70
Team Card
❑ 97 Lavern Torgeson........... 4.00 1.80
❑ 98 Milt Davis...................... 4.00 1.80
❑ 99 Larry Strickland 4.00 1.80
❑ 100 Matt Hazeltine RC 5.00 2.20
❑ 101 Walt Yowarsky 4.00 1.80
❑ 102 Roosevelt Brown......... 8.00 3.60
❑ 103 Jim Ringo 10.00 4.50
❑ 104 Joe Krupa 4.00 1.80
❑ 105 Les Richter 5.00 2.20
❑ 106 Art Donovan 18.00 8.00
❑ 107 John Olszewski 4.00 1.80
❑ 108 Ken Keller 4.00 1.80
❑ 109 Philadelphia Eagles...... 6.00 2.70
Team Card
❑ 110 Baltimore Colts 6.00 2.70
Team Card
❑ 111 Dick Bielski 4.00 1.80
❑ 112 Eddie LeBaron 8.00 3.60
❑ 113 Gene Brito................... 4.00 1.80
❑ 114 Willie Galimore RC 8.00 3.60
❑ 115 Detroit Lions 6.00 2.70
Team Card
❑ 116 Pittsburgh Steelers 6.00 2.70
Team Card
❑ 117 L.G. Dupre................... 5.00 2.20
❑ 118 Babe Parilli 5.00 2.20
❑ 119 Bill George 10.00 4.50
❑ 120 Raymond Berry 40.00 18.00
❑ 121 Jim Podoley UER 4.00 1.80
(Photo actually
Volney Peters;
Podoly in cartoon)
❑ 122 Hugh McElhenny....... 15.00 6.75
❑ 123 Ed Brown.................... 5.00 2.20
❑ 124 Dick Moegle 5.00 2.20
❑ 125 Tom Scott 4.00 1.80
❑ 126 Tommy McDonald...... 10.00 4.50
❑ 127 Ollie Matson 15.00 6.75
❑ 128 Preston Carpenter........ 4.00 1.80
❑ 129 George Blanda 30.00 13.50
❑ 130 Gordy Soltau 4.00 1.80
❑ 131 Dick Nolan RC.............. 5.00 2.20
❑ 132 Don Bosseler RC ! 20.00 5.00
❑ NNO Free Felt Initial Card 20.00 9.00

1959 Topps

ALEX KARRAS
DEF. TACKLE DETROIT LIONS

	NRMT	VG-E
COMPLETE SET (176)	900.00	400.00
COMMON CARD (1-88)...........	3.00	1.35
SEMISTARS 1-88.....................	4.00	1.80
UNLISTED STARS 1-88...........	6.00	2.70
COMMON CARD (89-176).........	2.00	.90
SEMISTARS 89-176.................	3.00	1.35
UNLISTED STARS 89-176.......	5.00	2.20
TEAM CARDS 1-88	6.00	2.70
TEAM CARDS 89-176	4.00	1.80

CARDS PRICED IN NM CONDITION

❑ 1 Johnny Unitas 100.00 25.00
❑ 2 Gene Brito....................... 3.00 1.35
❑ 3 Detroit Lions 6.00 2.70
Team Card
(checklist back)
❑ 4 Max McGee RC............. 15.00 6.75
❑ 5 Hugh McElhenny.......... 15.00 6.75
❑ 6 Joe Schmidt 8.00 3.60
❑ 7 Kyle Rote....................... 6.00 2.70
❑ 8 Clarence Peaks.............. 3.00 1.35
❑ 9 Pittsburgh Steelers 3.50 1.55
Pennant Card
❑ 10 Jim Brown 150.00 70.00
❑ 11 Ray Mathews 3.00 1.35
❑ 12 Bobby Dillon 3.00 1.35
❑ 13 Joe Childress 3.00 1.35
❑ 14 Terry Barr RC 3.00 1.35
❑ 15 Del Shofner RC............. 4.00 1.80
❑ 16 Bob Pellegrini UER 3.00 1.35
(Misspelled Pellagrini
on card back)
❑ 17 Baltimore Colts 6.00 2.70
Team Card
(checklist back)
❑ 18 Preston Carpenter.......... 3.00 1.35
❑ 19 Leo Nomellini 10.00 4.50
❑ 20 Frank Gifford 50.00 22.00
❑ 21 Charlie Ane 3.00 1.35
❑ 22 Jack Butler 3.00 1.35
❑ 23 Bart Starr.................... 60.00 27.00
❑ 24 Chicago Cardinals.......... 3.50 1.55
Pennant Card
❑ 25 Bill Barnes..................... 3.00 1.35
❑ 26 Walt Michaels 4.00 1.80
❑ 27 Clyde Conner UER 3.00 1.35
(Misspelled Connor
on card back)
❑ 28 Paige Cothren 3.00 1.35
❑ 29 Roosevelt Grier 6.00 2.70
❑ 30 Alan Ameche................. 6.00 2.70
❑ 31 Philadelphia Eagles........ 6.00 2.70
Team Card
(checklist back)
❑ 32 Dick Nolan.................... 4.00 1.80
❑ 33 R.C. Owens.................... 4.00 1.80
❑ 34 Dale Dodrill 3.00 1.35
❑ 35 Gene Gedman................ 3.00 1.35
❑ 36 Gene Lipscomb RC...... 10.00 4.50
❑ 37 Ray Renfro 4.00 1.80
❑ 38 Cleveland Browns 3.50 1.55
Pennant Card
❑ 39 Bill Forester.................... 4.00 1.80
❑ 40 Bobby Layne.............. 25.00 11.00
❑ 41 Pat Summerall............ 10.00 4.50

❑ 42 Jerry Mertens	3.00	1.35
❑ 43 Steve Myhra	3.00	1.35
❑ 44 John Henry Johnson	8.00	3.60
❑ 45 Woodley Lewis UER (misspelled Woody)	3.00	1.35
❑ 46 Green Bay Packers Team Card (checklist back)	8.00	3.60
❑ 47 Don Owens UER (Def.Tackle on front, Linebacker on back)	3.00	1.35
❑ 48 Ed Beatty	3.00	1.35
❑ 49 Don Chandler	3.00	1.35
❑ 50 Ollie Matson	12.00	5.50
❑ 51 Sam Huff RC	50.00	22.00
❑ 52 Tom Miner	3.00	1.35
❑ 53 New York Giants Pennant Card	3.50	1.55
❑ 54 Kenny Konz	3.00	1.35
❑ 55 Raymond Berry	20.00	9.00
❑ 56 Howard Ferguson UER (Misspelled Fergeson on card back)	3.00	1.35
❑ 57 Chuck Ulrich	3.00	1.35
❑ 58 Bob St. Clair	6.00	2.70
❑ 59 Don Burroughs RC	3.00	1.35
❑ 60 Lou Groza	12.00	5.50
❑ 61 San Francisco 49ers Team Card (checklist back)	6.00	2.70
❑ 62 Andy Nelson	3.00	1.35
❑ 63 Harold Bradley	3.00	1.35
❑ 64 Dave Hanner	4.00	1.80
❑ 65 Charley Conerly	10.00	4.50
❑ 66 Gene Cronin	3.00	1.35
❑ 67 Duane Putnam	3.00	1.35
❑ 68 Baltimore Colts Pennant Card	3.50	1.55
❑ 69 Ernie Stautner	8.00	3.60
❑ 70 Jon Arnett	4.00	1.80
❑ 71 Ken Panfil	3.00	1.35
❑ 72 Matt Hazeltine	3.00	1.35
❑ 73 Harley Sewell	3.00	1.35
❑ 74 Mike McCormack	6.00	2.70
❑ 75 Jim Ringo	8.00	3.60
❑ 76 Los Angeles Rams Team Card (checklist back)	6.00	2.70
❑ 77 Bob Gain RC	3.00	1.35
❑ 78 Buzz Nutter	3.00	1.35
❑ 79 Jerry Norton	3.00	1.35
❑ 80 Joe Perry	12.00	5.50
❑ 81 Carl Brettschneider	3.00	1.35
❑ 82 Paul Hornung	60.00	27.00
❑ 83 Philadelphia Eagles Pennant Card	3.50	1.55
❑ 84 Les Richter	4.00	1.80
❑ 85 Howard Cassady	4.00	1.80
❑ 86 Art Donovan	15.00	6.75
❑ 87 Jim Patton	4.00	1.80
❑ 88 Pete Retzlaff	4.00	1.80
❑ 89 Jim Mutscheller	2.00	.90
❑ 90 Zeke Bratkowski	3.00	1.35
❑ 91 Washington Redskins Team Card (Checklist back)	4.00	1.80
❑ 92 Art Hunter	2.00	.90
❑ 93 Gern Nagler	2.00	.90
❑ 94 Chuck Weber	2.00	.90
❑ 95 Lew Carpenter RC	3.00	1.35
❑ 96 Stan Jones	5.00	2.20
❑ 97 Ralph Guglielmi UER (Misspelled Gugliemi on card front)	3.00	1.35
❑ 98 Green Bay Packers Pennant Card	3.00	1.35
❑ 99 Ray Wietecha	2.00	.90
❑ 100 Lenny Moore	12.00	5.50
❑ 101 Jim Ray Smith RC UER (Lions logo on front)	3.00	1.35
❑ 102 Abe Woodson RC	3.00	1.35
❑ 103 Alex Karras RC	40.00	18.00
❑ 104 Chicago Bears Team Card (checklist back)	4.00	1.80
❑ 105 John David Crow RC	12.00	5.50
❑ 106 Joe Fortunato RC	2.00	.90
❑ 107 Babe Parilli	3.00	1.35
❑ 108 Proverb Jacobs	2.00	.90
❑ 109 Gino Marchetti	8.00	3.60
❑ 110 Bill Wade	3.00	1.35
❑ 111 San Francisco 49ers Pennant Card	3.00	1.35
❑ 112 Karl Rubke	2.00	.90
❑ 113 Dave Middleton UER (Browns logo in upper left corner)	2.00	.90
❑ 114 Roosevelt Brown	5.00	2.20
❑ 115 John Olszewski	2.00	.90
❑ 116 Jerry Kramer RC	30.00	13.50
❑ 117 King Hill RC	3.00	1.35
❑ 118 Chicago Cardinals Team Card (Checklist back)	4.00	1.80
❑ 119 Frank Varrichione	2.00	.90
❑ 120 Rick Casares	3.00	1.35
❑ 121 George Strugar	2.00	.90
❑ 122 Bill Glass RC UER (Center on front, tackle on back)	3.00	1.35
❑ 123 Don Bosseler	2.00	.90
❑ 124 John Reger	2.00	.90
❑ 125 Jim Ninowski RC	2.00	.90
❑ 126 Los Angeles Rams Pennant Card	3.00	1.35
❑ 127 Willard Sherman	2.00	.90
❑ 128 Bob Schnelker	2.00	.90
❑ 129 Ollie Spencer	2.00	.90
❑ 130 Y.A. Tittle	25.00	11.00
❑ 131 Yale Lary	5.00	2.20
❑ 132 Jim Parker RC	20.00	9.00
❑ 133 New York Giants Team Card (Checklist back)	4.00	1.80
❑ 134 Jim Schrader	2.00	.90
❑ 135 M.C. Reynolds	2.00	.90
❑ 136 Mike Sandusky	2.00	.90
❑ 137 Ed Brown	3.00	1.35
❑ 138 Al Barry	2.00	.90
❑ 139 Detroit Lions Pennant Card	3.00	1.35
❑ 140 Bobby Mitchell RC	35.00	16.00
❑ 141 Larry Morris	2.00	.90
❑ 142 Jim Phillips RC	3.00	1.35
❑ 143 Jim David	2.00	.90
❑ 144 Joe Krupa	2.00	.90
❑ 145 Willie Galimore	3.00	1.35
❑ 146 Pittsburgh Steelers Team Card (Checklist back)	4.00	1.80
❑ 147 Andy Robustelli	8.00	3.60
❑ 148 Billy Wilson	2.00	.90
❑ 149 Leo Sanford	2.00	.90
❑ 150 Eddie LeBaron	5.00	2.20
❑ 151 Bill McColl	2.00	.90
❑ 152 Buck Lansford UER (Tackle on front, guard on back)	2.00	.90
❑ 153 Chicago Bears Pennant Card	3.00	1.35
❑ 154 Leo Sugar	2.00	.90
❑ 155 Jim Taylor RC UER (Photo actually other Jim Taylor, Cardinal LB)	25.00	11.00
❑ 156 Lindon Crow	2.00	.90
❑ 157 Jack McClairen	2.00	.90
❑ 158 Vince Costello RC UER (Linebacker on front, Guard on back)	2.00	.90
❑ 159 Stan Wallace	2.00	.90
❑ 160 Mel Triplett RC	2.00	.90
❑ 161 Cleveland Browns Team Card (Checklist back)	4.00	1.80
❑ 162 Dan Currie	3.00	1.35
❑ 163 L.G. Dupre UER (Misspelled DuPre on back)	3.00	1.35
❑ 164 John Morrow UER (Center on front, Linebacker on back)	2.00	.90
❑ 165 Jim Podoley	2.00	.90
❑ 166 Bruce Bosley RC	2.00	.90
❑ 167 Harlon Hill	2.00	.90
❑ 168 Washington Redskins Pennant Card	3.00	1.35
❑ 169 Junior Wren	2.00	.90
❑ 170 Tobin Rote	3.00	1.35
❑ 171 Art Spinney	2.00	.90
❑ 172 Chuck Drazenovich UER (Linebacker on front, Defensive Back on back)	2.00	.90
❑ 173 Bobby Joe Conrad RC	3.00	1.35
❑ 174 Jesse Richardson	2.00	.90
❑ 175 Sam Baker	2.00	.90
❑ 176 Tom Tracy RC !	8.00	2.00

1960 Topps

	NRMT	VG-E
COMPLETE SET (132)	600.00	275.00
COMMON CARD (1-132)	2.50	1.10
SEMISTARS	3.00	1.35
UNLISTED STARS	4.00	1.80
TEAM CARDS	3.00	1.35

CARDS PRICED IN NM CONDITION

Card		
❑ 1 John Unitas	80.00	20.00
❑ 2 Alan Ameche	4.00	1.80
❑ 3 Lenny Moore	10.00	4.50
❑ 4 Raymond Berry	12.00	5.50
❑ 5 Jim Parker	8.00	3.60
❑ 6 George Preas	2.50	1.10
❑ 7 Art Spinney	2.50	1.10
❑ 8 Bill Pellington RC	3.00	1.35
❑ 9 John Sample RC	3.00	1.35
❑ 10 Gene Lipscomb UER (Def. Tackle on front, Tackle on back)	3.00	1.35
❑ 11 Baltimore Colts Team Card (Checklist 67-132)	3.00	1.35
❑ 12 Ed Brown	3.00	1.35
❑ 13 Rick Casares	3.00	1.35
❑ 14 Willie Galimore	3.00	1.35
❑ 15 Jim Dooley	2.50	1.10
❑ 16 Harlon Hill UER (Lifetime yards and Avg. gain incorrect)	2.50	1.10
❑ 17 Stan Jones UER (Defensive ... All-Star Team, should be Offensive)	4.00	1.80
❑ 18 Bill George	4.00	1.80
❑ 19 Erich Barnes RC	2.50	1.10
❑ 20 Doug Atkins UER (reversed negative)	6.00	2.70
❑ 21 Chicago Bears Team Card (Checklist 1-66)	3.00	1.35
❑ 22 Milt Plum	3.00	1.35
❑ 23 Jim Brown	100.00	45.00
❑ 24 Sam Baker	2.50	1.10
❑ 25 Bobby Mitchell	10.00	4.50
❑ 26 Ray Renfro	3.00	1.35
❑ 27 Billy Howton	3.00	1.35
❑ 28 Jim Ray Smith	2.50	1.10
❑ 29 Jim Shofner RC	3.00	1.35
❑ 30 Bob Gain	2.50	1.10

Card	NM	VG-E
❑ 31 Cleveland Browns Team Card (Checklist 1-66)	3.00	1.35
❑ 32 Don Heinrich	2.50	1.10
❑ 33 Ed Modzelewski UER (Lifetime yards and Avg. gain incorrect)	2.50	1.10
❑ 34 Fred Cone	2.50	1.10
❑ 35 L.G. Dupre	3.00	1.35
❑ 36 Dick Bielski	2.50	1.10
❑ 37 Charlie Ane UER (Misspelled Charley)	2.50	1.10
❑ 38 Jerry Tubbs	3.00	1.35
❑ 39 Doyle Nix	2.50	1.10
❑ 40 Ray Krouse	2.50	1.10
❑ 41 Earl Morrall	4.00	1.80
❑ 42 Howard Cassady	3.00	1.35
❑ 43 Dave Middleton	2.50	1.10
❑ 44 Jim Gibbons RC	3.00	1.35
❑ 45 Darris McCord	2.50	1.10
❑ 46 Joe Schmidt	6.00	2.70
❑ 47 Terry Barr	2.50	1.10
❑ 48 Yale Lary UER (Def.back on front, halfback on back)	4.00	1.80
❑ 49 Gil Mains	2.50	1.10
❑ 50 Detroit Lions Team Card (Checklist 1-66)	3.00	1.35
❑ 51 Bart Starr	45.00	20.00
❑ 52 Jim Taylor UER (photo actually Jim Taylor, Cardinal LB)	8.00	3.60
❑ 53 Lew Carpenter	3.00	1.35
❑ 54 Paul Hornung UER (Halfback on front, fullback on back)	40.00	18.00
❑ 55 Max McGee	4.00	1.80
❑ 56 Forrest Gregg RC	35.00	16.00
❑ 57 Jim Ringo	5.00	2.20
❑ 58 Bill Forester	3.00	1.35
❑ 59 Dave Hanner	3.00	1.35
❑ 60 Green Bay Packers Team Card (Checklist 67-132)	8.00	3.60
❑ 61 Bill Wade	3.00	1.35
❑ 62 Frank Ryan RC	4.00	1.80
❑ 63 Ollie Matson	10.00	4.50
❑ 64 Jon Arnett	3.00	1.35
❑ 65 Del Shofner	3.00	1.35
❑ 66 Jim Phillips	2.50	1.10
❑ 67 Art Hunter	2.50	1.10
❑ 68 Les Richter	3.00	1.35
❑ 69 Lou Michaels RC	3.00	1.35
❑ 70 John Baker	2.50	1.10
❑ 71 Los Angeles Rams Team Card (Checklist 1-66)	3.00	1.35
❑ 72 Charley Conerly	8.00	3.60
❑ 73 Mel Triplett	2.50	1.10
❑ 74 Frank Gifford	35.00	16.00
❑ 75 Alex Webster	3.00	1.35
❑ 76 Bob Schnelker	2.50	1.10
❑ 77 Pat Summerall	8.00	3.60
❑ 78 Roosevelt Brown	4.00	1.80
❑ 79 Jim Patton	2.50	1.10
❑ 80 Sam Huff UER (Def.tackle on front, linebacker on back)	15.00	6.75
❑ 81 Andy Robustelli	6.00	2.70
❑ 82 New York Giants Team Card (Checklist 1-66)	3.00	1.35
❑ 83 Clarence Peaks	2.50	1.10
❑ 84 Bill Barnes	2.50	1.10
❑ 85 Pete Retzlaff	3.00	1.35
❑ 86 Bobby Walston	2.50	1.10
❑ 87 Chuck Bednarik UER (Misspelled Bednarick on both sides of card)	8.00	3.60
❑ 88 Bob Pellegrini (Misspelled Pellagrini on both sides)	2.50	1.10
❑ 89 Tom Brookshier RC	3.00	1.35
❑ 90 Marion Campbell	3.00	1.35
❑ 91 Jesse Richardson	2.50	1.10
❑ 92 Philadelphia Eagles Team Card (Checklist 1-66)	3.00	1.35
❑ 93 Bobby Layne	25.00	11.00
❑ 94 John Henry Johnson	6.00	2.70
❑ 95 Tom Tracy UER (Halfback on front, fullback on back)	3.00	1.35
❑ 96 Preston Carpenter	2.50	1.10
❑ 97 Frank Varrichione UER (Reversed negative)	2.50	1.10
❑ 98 John Nisby	2.50	1.10
❑ 99 Dean Derby	2.50	1.10
❑ 100 George Tarasovic	2.50	1.10
❑ 101 Ernie Stautner	5.00	2.20
❑ 102 Pittsburgh Steelers Team Card (Checklist 67-132)	3.00	1.35
❑ 103 King Hill	2.50	1.10
❑ 104 Mal Hammack	2.50	1.10
❑ 105 John David Crow	3.00	1.35
❑ 106 Bobby Joe Conrad	3.00	1.35
❑ 107 Woodley Lewis	2.50	1.10
❑ 108 Don Gillis	2.50	1.10
❑ 109 Carl Brettschneider	2.50	1.10
❑ 110 Leo Sugar	2.50	1.10
❑ 111 Frank Fuller	2.50	1.10
❑ 112 St. Louis Cardinals Team Card (Checklist 67-132)	3.00	1.35
❑ 113 Y.A. Tittle	25.00	11.00
❑ 114 Joe Perry	8.00	3.60
❑ 115 J.D. Smith RC	3.00	1.35
❑ 116 Hugh McElhenny	8.00	3.60
❑ 117 Billy Wilson	2.50	1.10
❑ 118 Bob St. Clair	4.00	1.80
❑ 119 Matt Hazeltine	2.50	1.10
❑ 120 Abe Woodson	2.50	1.10
❑ 121 Leo Nomellini	5.00	2.20
❑ 122 San Francisco 49ers Team Card (Checklist 67-132)	3.00	1.35
❑ 123 Ralph Guglielmi UER (Misspelled Gugliemi on card front)	2.50	1.10
❑ 124 Don Bosseler	2.50	1.10
❑ 125 John Olszewski	2.50	1.10
❑ 126 Bill Anderson UER (Walt on back)	2.50	1.10
❑ 127 Joe Walton RC	3.00	1.35
❑ 128 Jim Schrader	2.50	1.10
❑ 129 Ralph Felton	2.50	1.10
❑ 130 Gary Glick	2.50	1.10
❑ 131 Bob Toneff	2.50	1.10
❑ 132 Washington Redskins Team Card (Checklist 67-132)	30.00	7.50
❑ AD1 Alan Ameche Paul Hornung Tom Tracy (Gene Cronin back)	125.00	55.00
❑ AD2 Del Shofner Milt Plum Jim Patton (Gene Cronin back)	90.00	40.00
❑ AD3 Bob St.Clair Jim Shofner Gil Mains (Gene Cronin back)	100.00	45.00
❑ AD4 Tom Brookshier Packers Team George Preas (Gene Cronin back)	100.00	45.00

1961 Topps

	NRMT	VG-E
COMPLETE SET (198)	1000.00	450.00
COMMON CARD (1-132)	2.50	1.10
SEMISTARS 1-132	3.00	1.35
UNLISTED STARS 1-132	4.00	1.80
COMMON CARD (133-198)	3.00	1.35
SEMISTARS 133-198	4.00	1.80
UNLISTED STARS 133-198	6.00	2.70
TEAM CARDS	3.00	1.35

CARDS PRICED IN NM CONDITION

Card	NM	VG-E
❑ 1 Johnny Unitas	100.00	25.00
❑ 2 Lenny Moore	12.00	5.50
❑ 3 Alan Ameche	4.00	1.80
❑ 4 Raymond Berry	12.00	5.50
❑ 5 Jim Mutscheller	2.50	1.10
❑ 6 Jim Parker	5.00	2.20
❑ 7 Gino Marchetti	6.00	2.70
❑ 8 Gene Lipscomb	4.00	1.80
❑ 9 Baltimore Colts Team Card	3.00	1.35
❑ 10 Bill Wade	3.00	1.35
❑ 11 Johnny Morris RC UER (Years pro and return averages wrong)	6.00	2.70
❑ 12 Rick Casares	3.00	1.35
❑ 13 Harlon Hill	2.50	1.10
❑ 14 Stan Jones	4.00	1.80
❑ 15 Doug Atkins	5.00	2.20
❑ 16 Bill George	4.00	1.80
❑ 17 J.C. Caroline	2.50	1.10
❑ 18 Chicago Bears Team Card	3.00	1.35
❑ 19 Big Time Football Comes to Texas (Eddie LeBaron)	3.00	1.35
❑ 20 Eddie LeBaron	3.00	1.35
❑ 21 Don McIlhenny	2.50	1.10
❑ 22 L.G. Dupre	3.00	1.35
❑ 23 Jim Doran	2.50	1.10
❑ 24 Billy Howton	3.00	1.35
❑ 25 Buzz Guy	2.50	1.10
❑ 26 Jack Patera RC	2.50	1.10
❑ 27 Tom Franckhauser UER (misspelled Frankhauser)	2.50	1.10
❑ 28 Dallas Cowboys Team Card	15.00	6.75
❑ 29 Jim Ninowski	2.50	1.10
❑ 30 Dan Lewis RC	2.50	1.10
❑ 31 Nick Pietrosante RC	3.00	1.35
❑ 32 Gail Cogdill RC	3.00	1.35
❑ 33 Jim Gibbons	2.50	1.10
❑ 34 Jim Martin	2.50	1.10
❑ 35 Alex Karras	15.00	6.75
❑ 36 Joe Schmidt	5.00	2.20
❑ 37 Detroit Lions Team Card	3.00	1.35
❑ 38 Packers' Hornung Sets NFL Scoring Record	18.00	8.00
❑ 39 Bart Starr	40.00	18.00
❑ 40 Paul Hornung	40.00	18.00
❑ 41 Jim Taylor	30.00	13.50
❑ 42 Max McGee	4.00	1.80
❑ 43 Boyd Dowler RC	8.00	3.60
❑ 44 Jim Ringo	5.00	2.20
❑ 45 Hank Jordan RC	20.00	9.00
❑ 46 Bill Forester	3.00	1.35
❑ 47 Green Bay Packers Team Card	8.00	3.60
❑ 48 Frank Ryan	3.00	1.35
❑ 49 Jon Arnett	3.00	1.35
❑ 50 Ollie Matson	8.00	3.60
❑ 51 Jim Phillips	2.50	1.10
❑ 52 Del Shofner	3.00	1.35
❑ 53 Art Hunter	2.50	1.10
❑ 54 Gene Brito	2.50	1.10

Card	NRMT	VG-E
❑ 55 Lindon Crow	2.50	1.10
❑ 56 Los Angeles Rams Team Card	3.00	1.35
❑ 57 Colts' Unitas 25 TD Passes	25.00	11.00
❑ 58 Y.A. Tittle	30.00	13.50
❑ 59 John Brodie RC	40.00	18.00
❑ 60 J.D. Smith	2.50	1.10
❑ 61 R.C. Owens	3.00	1.35
❑ 62 Clyde Conner	2.50	1.10
❑ 63 Bob St. Clair	4.00	1.80
❑ 64 Leo Nomellini	6.00	2.70
❑ 65 Abe Woodson	2.50	1.10
❑ 66 San Francisco 49ers Team Card	3.00	1.35
❑ 67 Checklist Card	40.00	10.00
❑ 68 Milt Plum	3.00	1.35
❑ 69 Ray Renfro	3.00	1.35
❑ 70 Bobby Mitchell	8.00	3.60
❑ 71 Jim Brown	100.00	45.00
❑ 72 Mike McCormack	4.00	1.80
❑ 73 Jim Ray Smith	2.50	1.10
❑ 74 Sam Baker	2.50	1.10
❑ 75 Walt Michaels	3.00	1.35
❑ 76 Cleveland Browns Team Card	3.00	1.35
❑ 77 Jimmy Brown Gains 1257 Yards	35.00	16.00
❑ 78 George Shaw	2.50	1.10
❑ 79 Hugh McElhenny	8.00	3.60
❑ 80 Clancy Osborne	2.50	1.10
❑ 81 Dave Middleton	2.50	1.10
❑ 82 Frank Youso	2.50	1.10
❑ 83 Don Joyce	2.50	1.10
❑ 84 Ed Culpepper	2.50	1.10
❑ 85 Charley Conerly	8.00	3.60
❑ 86 Mel Triplett	2.50	1.10
❑ 87 Kyle Rote	3.00	1.35
❑ 88 Roosevelt Brown	4.00	1.80
❑ 89 Ray Wietecha	2.50	1.10
❑ 90 Andy Robustelli	5.00	2.20
❑ 91 Sam Huff	8.00	3.60
❑ 92 Jim Patton	2.50	1.10
❑ 93 New York Giants Team Card	3.00	1.35
❑ 94 Charley Conerly UER Leads Giants for 13th Year (Misspelled Charlie on card)	6.00	2.70
❑ 95 Sonny Jurgensen	25.00	11.00
❑ 96 Tommy McDonald	4.00	1.80
❑ 97 Bill Barnes	2.50	1.10
❑ 98 Bobby Walston	2.50	1.10
❑ 99 Pete Retzlaff	3.00	1.35
❑ 100 Jim McCusker	2.50	1.10
❑ 101 Chuck Bednarik	8.00	3.60
❑ 102 Tom Brookshier	3.00	1.35
❑ 103 Philadelphia Eagles Team Card	3.00	1.35
❑ 104 Bobby Layne	30.00	13.50
❑ 105 John Henry Johnson	4.00	1.80
❑ 106 Tom Tracy	3.00	1.35
❑ 107 Buddy Dial RC	2.50	1.10
❑ 108 Jimmy Orr RC	5.00	2.20
❑ 109 Mike Sandusky	2.50	1.10
❑ 110 John Reger	2.50	1.10
❑ 111 Junior Wren	2.50	1.10
❑ 112 Pittsburgh Steelers Team Card	3.00	1.35
❑ 113 Bobby Layne Sets New Passing Record	10.00	4.50
❑ 114 John Roach	2.50	1.10
❑ 115 Sam Etcheverry RC**/C	3.00	1.35
❑ 116 John David Crow	3.00	1.35
❑ 117 Mal Hammack	2.50	1.10
❑ 118 Sonny Randle RC	3.00	1.35
❑ 119 Leo Sugar	2.50	1.10
❑ 120 Jerry Norton	2.50	1.10
❑ 121 St. Louis Cardinals Team Card	3.00	1.35
❑ 122 Checklist Card	50.00	12.50
❑ 123 Ralph Guglielmi	2.50	1.10
❑ 124 Dick James	2.50	1.10
❑ 125 Don Bosseler	2.50	1.10
❑ 126 Joe Walton	2.50	1.10
❑ 127 Bill Anderson	2.50	1.10
❑ 128 Vince Promuto RC	2.50	1.10
❑ 129 Bob Toneff	2.50	1.10
❑ 130 John Paluck	2.50	1.10
❑ 131 Washington Redskins Team Card	3.00	1.35
❑ 132 Browns' Plum Wins NFL Passing Title	2.50	1.10
❑ 133 Abner Haynes	8.00	3.60
❑ 134 Mel Branch UER (Def. Tackle on front, Def. End on back)	4.00	1.80
❑ 135 Jerry Cornelison UER (Misspelled Cornielson)	3.00	1.35
❑ 136 Bill Krisher	3.00	1.35
❑ 137 Paul Miller	3.00	1.35
❑ 138 Jack Spikes	4.00	1.80
❑ 139 Johnny Robinson RC	8.00	3.60
❑ 140 Cotton Davidson RC	4.00	1.80
❑ 141 Dave Smith	3.00	1.35
❑ 142 Bill Groman	3.00	1.35
❑ 143 Rich Michael	3.00	1.35
❑ 144 Mike Dukes	3.00	1.35
❑ 145 George Blanda	25.00	11.00
❑ 146 Billy Cannon	6.00	2.70
❑ 147 Dennit Morris	3.00	1.35
❑ 148 Jacky Lee UER (Misspelled Jackie on card back)	4.00	1.80
❑ 149 Al Dorow	3.00	1.35
❑ 150 Don Maynard RC	60.00	27.00
❑ 151 Art Powell RC	8.00	3.60
❑ 152 Sid Youngelman	3.00	1.35
❑ 153 Bob Mischak	3.00	1.35
❑ 154 Larry Grantham	3.00	1.35
❑ 155 Tom Saidock	3.00	1.35
❑ 156 Roger Donnahoo	3.00	1.35
❑ 157 Laverne Torczon	3.00	1.35
❑ 158 Archie Matsos RC	4.00	1.80
❑ 159 Elbert Dubenion	4.00	1.80
❑ 160 Wray Carlton RC	4.00	1.80
❑ 161 Rich McCabe	3.00	1.35
❑ 162 Ken Rice	3.00	1.35
❑ 163 Art Baker	3.00	1.35
❑ 164 Tom Rychlec	3.00	1.35
❑ 165 Mack Yoho	3.00	1.35
❑ 166 Jack Kemp	125.00	55.00
❑ 167 Paul Lowe	6.00	2.70
❑ 168 Ron Mix	10.00	4.50
❑ 169 Paul Maguire	6.00	2.70
❑ 170 Volney Peters	3.00	1.35
❑ 171 Ernie Wright RC	4.00	1.80
❑ 172 Ron Nery RC	3.00	1.35
❑ 173 Dave Kocourek RC	4.00	1.80
❑ 174 Jim Colclough	3.00	1.35
❑ 175 Babe Parilli	4.00	1.80
❑ 176 Billy Lott	3.00	1.35
❑ 177 Fred Bruney	3.00	1.35
❑ 178 Ross O'Hanley	3.00	1.35
❑ 179 Walt Cudzik	3.00	1.35
❑ 180 Charley Leo	3.00	1.35
❑ 181 Bob Dee	3.00	1.35
❑ 182 Jim Otto RC	40.00	18.00
❑ 183 Eddie Macon	3.00	1.35
❑ 184 Dick Christy	3.00	1.35
❑ 185 Alan Miller	3.00	1.35
❑ 186 Tom Flores RC	20.00	9.00
❑ 187 Joe Cannavino	3.00	1.35
❑ 188 Don Manoukian	3.00	1.35
❑ 189 Bob Coolbaugh	3.00	1.35
❑ 190 Lionel Taylor RC	8.00	3.60
❑ 191 Bud McFadin	3.00	1.35
❑ 192 Goose Gonsoulin RC	6.00	2.70
❑ 193 Frank Tripucka	4.00	1.80
❑ 194 Gene Mingo RC	4.00	1.80
❑ 195 Eldon Danenhauer	3.00	1.35
❑ 196 Bob McNamara	3.00	1.35
❑ 197 Dave Rolle UER (End on front, Fullback on back)	3.00	1.35
❑ 198 Checklist Card UER! (135 Cornielson)	100.00	25.00
❑ AD1 Jim Martin George Shaw Jim Ray Smith	100.00	45.00

1962 Topps

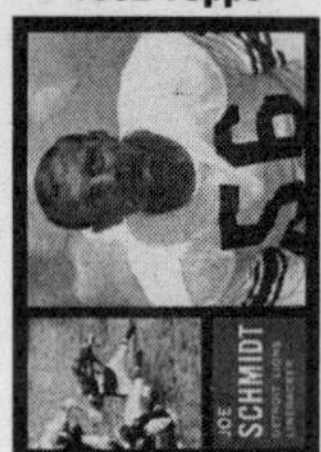

	NRMT	VG-E
COMPLETE SET (176)	1800.00	800.00
COMMON CARD (1-176)	4.00	1.80
SEMISTARS	5.00	2.20
UNLISTED STARS	6.00	2.70
SP (7/11/15/24/40/45/46)	8.00	3.60
SP (48/52/61/74/86/91/93)	8.00	3.60
SP (95-100/113/117/121)	8.00	3.60
SP (125/132/135/137/142)	8.00	3.60
SP (149/154/171/174)	8.00	3.60
SEMISTARS SP (3/13/27/73)	10.00	4.50
SEMISTARS SP (77/78/80)	10.00	4.50
SEMISTARS SP (120/130/133)	10.00	4.50
SEMISTARS SP (140/141)	10.00	4.50
TEAM CARDS	6.00	2.70
TEAMS SP (62/89/138)	18.00	8.00

CARDS PRICED IN NM CONDITION !

Card	NRMT	VG-E
❑ 1 John Unitas	150.00	38.00
❑ 2 Lenny Moore	12.00	5.50
❑ 3 Alex Hawkins RC SP	10.00	4.50
❑ 4 Joe Perry	8.00	3.60
❑ 5 Raymond Berry SP	40.00	18.00
❑ 6 Steve Myhra	4.00	1.80
❑ 7 Tom Gilburg SP	8.00	3.60
❑ 8 Gino Marchetti	8.00	3.60
❑ 9 Bill Pellington	4.00	1.80
❑ 10 Andy Nelson	4.00	1.80
❑ 11 Wendell Harris SP	8.00	3.60
❑ 12 Baltimore Colts Team Card	6.00	2.70
❑ 13 Bill Wade SP	10.00	4.50
❑ 14 Willie Galimore	5.00	2.20
❑ 15 Johnny Morris SP	8.00	3.60
❑ 16 Rick Casares	5.00	2.20
❑ 17 Mike Ditka RC	200.00	90.00
❑ 18 Stan Jones	6.00	2.70
❑ 19 Roger LeClerc	4.00	1.80
❑ 20 Angelo Coia	4.00	1.80
❑ 21 Doug Atkins	7.00	3.10
❑ 22 Bill George	6.00	2.70
❑ 23 Richie Petitbon RC	5.00	2.20
❑ 24 Ron Bull RC SP	8.00	3.60
❑ 25 Chicago Bears Team Card	6.00	2.70
❑ 26 Howard Cassady	5.00	2.20
❑ 27 Ray Renfro SP	10.00	4.50
❑ 28 Jim Brown	150.00	70.00
❑ 29 Rich Kreitling	4.00	1.80
❑ 30 Jim Ray Smith	4.00	1.80
❑ 31 John Morrow	4.00	1.80
❑ 32 Lou Groza	10.00	4.50
❑ 33 Bob Gain	4.00	1.80
❑ 34 Bernie Parrish	4.00	1.80
❑ 35 Jim Shofner	4.00	1.80
❑ 36 Ernie Davis RC SP	140.00	65.00
❑ 37 Cleveland Browns Team Card	6.00	2.70
❑ 38 Eddie LeBaron	5.00	2.20
❑ 39 Don Meredith SP	100.00	45.00
❑ 40 J.W. Lockett SP	8.00	3.60
❑ 41 Don Perkins RC	8.00	3.60
❑ 42 Billy Howton	5.00	2.20
❑ 43 Dick Bielski	4.00	1.80
❑ 44 Mike Connelly RC	4.00	1.80
❑ 45 Jerry Tubbs SP	8.00	3.60

❑ 46 Don Bishop SP	8.00	3.60
❑ 47 Dick Moegle	4.00	1.80
❑ 48 Bobby Plummer SP	8.00	3.60
❑ 49 Dallas Cowboys Team Card	20.00	9.00
❑ 50 Milt Plum	5.00	2.20
❑ 51 Dan Lewis	4.00	1.80
❑ 52 Nick Pietrosante SP	8.00	3.60
❑ 53 Gail Cogdill	4.00	1.80
❑ 54 Jim Gibbons	4.00	1.80
❑ 55 Jim Martin	4.00	1.80
❑ 56 Yale Lary	6.00	2.70
❑ 57 Darris McCord	4.00	1.80
❑ 58 Alex Karras	15.00	6.75
❑ 59 Joe Schmidt	7.00	3.10
❑ 60 Dick Lane	6.00	2.70
❑ 61 John Lomakoski SP	8.00	3.60
❑ 62 Detroit Lions SP Team Card	18.00	8.00
❑ 63 Bart Starr SP	100.00	45.00
❑ 64 Paul Hornung SP	75.00	34.00
❑ 65 Tom Moore SP	12.00	5.50
❑ 66 Jim Taylor SP	50.00	22.00
❑ 67 Max McGee SP	12.00	5.50
❑ 68 Jim Ringo SP	15.00	6.75
❑ 69 Fuzzy Thurston RC SP	20.00	9.00
❑ 70 Forrest Gregg	7.00	3.10
❑ 71 Boyd Dowler	6.00	2.70
❑ 72 Hank Jordan SP	15.00	6.75
❑ 73 Bill Forester SP	10.00	4.50
❑ 74 Earl Gros SP	8.00	3.60
❑ 75 Green Bay Packers SP Team Card	35.00	16.00
❑ 76 Checklist SP	80.00	20.00
❑ 77 Zeke Bratkowski SP (Inset photo is Johnny Unitas)	10.00	4.50
❑ 78 Jon Arnett SP	10.00	4.50
❑ 79 Ollie Matson SP	30.00	13.50
❑ 80 Dick Bass SP	10.00	4.50
❑ 81 Jim Phillips	4.00	1.80
❑ 82 Carroll Dale RC	5.00	2.20
❑ 83 Frank Varrichione	4.00	1.80
❑ 84 Art Hunter	4.00	1.80
❑ 85 Danny Villanueva RC	4.00	1.80
❑ 86 Les Richter SP	8.00	3.60
❑ 87 Lindon Crow	4.00	1.80
❑ 88 Roman Gabriel RC SP (Inset photo is Y.A. Tittle)	60.00	27.00
❑ 89 Los Angeles Rams SP Team Card	18.00	8.00
❑ 90 Fran Tarkenton SP RC UER (Small photo actually Jurgensen with air-brushed jersey)	175.00	80.00
❑ 91 Jerry Reichow SP	8.00	3.60
❑ 92 Hugh McElhenny SP	30.00	13.50
❑ 93 Mel Triplett SP	8.00	3.60
❑ 94 Tommy Mason RC SP	10.00	4.50
❑ 95 Dave Middleton SP	8.00	3.60
❑ 96 Frank Youso SP	8.00	3.60
❑ 97 Mike Mercer SP	8.00	3.60
❑ 98 Rip Hawkins SP	8.00	3.60
❑ 99 Cliff Livingston SP	8.00	3.60
❑ 100 Roy Winston RC SP	8.00	3.60
❑ 101 Minnesota Vikings SP Team Card	25.00	11.00
❑ 102 Y.A. Tittle	30.00	13.50
❑ 103 Joe Walton	4.00	1.80
❑ 104 Frank Gifford	40.00	18.00
❑ 105 Alex Webster	5.00	2.20
❑ 106 Del Shofner	5.00	2.20
❑ 107 Don Chandler	4.00	1.80
❑ 108 Andy Robustelli	7.00	3.10
❑ 109 Jim Katcavage RC	5.00	2.20
❑ 110 Sam Huff SP	40.00	18.00
❑ 111 Erich Barnes	4.00	1.80
❑ 112 Jim Patton	4.00	1.80
❑ 113 Jerry Hillebrand SP	8.00	3.60
❑ 114 New York Giants Team Card	6.00	2.70
❑ 115 Sonny Jurgensen	30.00	13.50
❑ 116 Tommy McDonald	6.00	2.70
❑ 117 Ted Dean SP	8.00	3.60
❑ 118 Clarence Peaks	4.00	1.80
❑ 119 Bobby Walston	4.00	1.80
❑ 120 Pete Retzlaff SP	10.00	4.50
❑ 121 Jim Schrader SP	8.00	3.60
❑ 122 J.D. Smith T	4.00	1.80
❑ 123 King Hill	4.00	1.80
❑ 124 Maxie Baughan	5.00	2.20
❑ 125 Pete Case SP	8.00	3.60
❑ 126 Philadelphia Eagles Team Card	6.00	2.70
❑ 127 Bobby Layne UER (Bears until 1958, should be Lions)	35.00	16.00
❑ 128 Tom Tracy	5.00	2.20
❑ 129 John Henry Johnson	6.00	2.70
❑ 130 Buddy Dial SP	10.00	4.50
❑ 131 Preston Carpenter	4.00	1.80
❑ 132 Lou Michaels SP	8.00	3.60
❑ 133 Gene Lipscomb SP	10.00	4.50
❑ 134 Ernie Stautner SP	20.00	9.00
❑ 135 John Reger SP	8.00	3.60
❑ 136 Myron Pottios RC	4.00	1.80
❑ 137 Bob Ferguson SP	8.00	3.60
❑ 138 Pittsburgh Steelers SP Team Card	18.00	8.00
❑ 139 Sam Etcheverry	5.00	2.20
❑ 140 John David Crow SP	10.00	4.50
❑ 141 Bobby Joe Conrad SP	10.00	4.50
❑ 142 Prentice Gautt RC SP	8.00	3.60
❑ 143 Frank Mestnick	4.00	1.80
❑ 144 Sonny Randle	5.00	2.20
❑ 145 Gerry Perry UER (T-K on both sides, but Def. End in bio)	4.00	1.80
❑ 146 Jerry Norton	4.00	1.80
❑ 147 Jimmy Hill	4.00	1.80
❑ 148 Bill Stacy	4.00	1.80
❑ 149 Fate Echols SP	8.00	3.60
❑ 150 St. Louis Cardinals Team Card	6.00	2.70
❑ 151 Bill Kilmer RC	25.00	11.00
❑ 152 John Brodie	18.00	8.00
❑ 153 J.D. Smith RB	5.00	2.20
❑ 154 C.R. Roberts SP	8.00	3.60
❑ 155 Monty Stickles	4.00	1.80
❑ 156 Clyde Conner UER (Misspelled Connor on card back)	4.00	1.80
❑ 157 Bob St. Clair	6.00	2.70
❑ 158 Tommy Davis RC	4.00	1.80
❑ 159 Leo Nomellini	8.00	3.60
❑ 160 Matt Hazeltine	4.00	1.80
❑ 161 Abe Woodson	4.00	1.80
❑ 162 Dave Baker	4.00	1.80
❑ 163 San Francisco 49ers Team Card	6.00	2.70
❑ 164 Norm Snead RC SP	25.00	11.00
❑ 165 Dick James (Inset photo is Don Bosseler)	5.00	2.20
❑ 166 Bobby Mitchell	8.00	3.60
❑ 167 Sam Horner	4.00	1.80
❑ 168 Bill Barnes	4.00	1.80
❑ 169 Bill Anderson	4.00	1.80
❑ 170 Fred Dugan	4.00	1.80
❑ 171 John Aveni SP	8.00	3.60
❑ 172 Bob Toneff	4.00	1.80
❑ 173 Jim Kerr	4.00	1.80
❑ 174 Leroy Jackson SP	8.00	3.60
❑ 175 Washington Redskins Team Card	6.00	2.70
❑ 176 Checklist !	100.00	25.00

1963 Topps

	NRMT	VG-E
COMPLETE SET (170)	1350.00	600.00
COMMON CARD (1-170)	2.50	1.10
SEMISTARS	3.00	1.35
UNLISTED STARS	5.00	2.20
SP (16/18/20/21/23/50)	6.00	2.70
SP (52-55/57/58/76)	6.00	2.70
SP (78-81/83/113/115-120)	6.00	2.70
SP (124-128/130-132)	6.00	2.70
SP (160-168)	6.00	2.70
SEMISTAR SP (13/15/22/51)	8.00	3.60
SEMISTAR SP (73/77/114/122)	8.00	3.60
UNL.STAR SP (17/56/75)	10.00	4.50
UNL.STAR SP (111/112/158)		
TEAM CARDS	4.00	1.80
TEAMS SP (12/24/36/72)	10.00	4.50
TEAMS SP (121/133/145)	10.00	4.50
TEAMS SP (157/169)	10.00	4.50

CARDS PRICED IN NM CONDITION !

❑ 1 John Unitas	100.00	25.00
❑ 2 Lenny Moore	8.00	3.60
❑ 3 Jimmy Orr	2.50	1.10
❑ 4 Raymond Berry	8.00	3.60
❑ 5 Jim Parker	5.00	2.20
❑ 6 Alex Sandusky	2.50	1.10
❑ 7 Dick Szymanski	2.50	1.10
❑ 8 Gino Marchetti	6.00	2.70
❑ 9 Billy Ray Smith RC	3.00	1.35
❑ 10 Bill Pellington	2.50	1.10
❑ 11 Bob Boyd RC	2.50	1.10
❑ 12 Baltimore Colts SP Team Card	10.00	4.50
❑ 13 Frank Ryan SP	8.00	3.60
❑ 14 Jim Brown SP	200.00	90.00
❑ 15 Ray Renfro SP	8.00	3.60
❑ 16 Rich Kreitling SP	6.00	2.70
❑ 17 Mike McCormack SP	10.00	4.50
❑ 18 Jim Ray Smith SP	6.00	2.70
❑ 19 Lou Groza SP	20.00	9.00
❑ 20 Bill Glass SP	6.00	2.70
❑ 21 Galen Fiss SP	6.00	2.70
❑ 22 Don Fleming RC SP	8.00	3.60
❑ 23 Bob Gain SP	6.00	2.70
❑ 24 Cleveland Browns SP Team Card	10.00	4.50
❑ 25 Milt Plum	3.00	1.35
❑ 26 Dan Lewis	2.50	1.10
❑ 27 Nick Pietrosante	2.50	1.10
❑ 28 Gail Cogdill	2.50	1.10
❑ 29 Harley Sewell	2.50	1.10
❑ 30 Jim Gibbons	2.50	1.10
❑ 31 Carl Brettschneider	2.50	1.10
❑ 32 Dick Lane	5.00	2.20
❑ 33 Yale Lary	5.00	2.20
❑ 34 Roger Brown RC	3.00	1.35
❑ 35 Joe Schmidt	6.00	2.70
❑ 36 Detroit Lions SP Team Card	10.00	4.50
❑ 37 Roman Gabriel	8.00	3.60
❑ 38 Zeke Bratkowski	3.00	1.35
❑ 39 Dick Bass	3.00	1.35
❑ 40 Jon Arnett	3.00	1.35
❑ 41 Jim Phillips	2.50	1.10
❑ 42 Frank Varrichione	2.50	1.10
❑ 43 Danny Villanueva	2.50	1.10
❑ 44 Deacon Jones RC	50.00	22.00
❑ 45 Lindon Crow	2.50	1.10
❑ 46 Marlin McKeever	2.50	1.10
❑ 47 Ed Meador RC	2.50	1.10
❑ 48 Los Angeles Rams Team Card	4.00	1.80
❑ 49 Y.A. Tittle SP	45.00	20.00
❑ 50 Del Shofner SP	6.00	2.70
❑ 51 Alex Webster SP	8.00	3.60
❑ 52 Phil King SP	6.00	2.70
❑ 53 Jack Stroud SP	6.00	2.70
❑ 54 Darrell Dess SP	6.00	2.70
❑ 55 Jim Katcavage SP	6.00	2.70

Card	NRMT	VG-E
❑ 56 Roosevelt Grier SP	10.00	4.50
❑ 57 Erich Barnes SP	6.00	2.70
❑ 58 Jim Patton SP	6.00	2.70
❑ 59 Sam Huff SP	18.00	8.00
❑ 60 New York Giants Team Card	4.00	1.80
❑ 61 Bill Wade	3.00	1.35
❑ 62 Mike Ditka	60.00	27.00
❑ 63 Johnny Morris	2.50	1.10
❑ 64 Roger LeClerc	2.50	1.10
❑ 65 Roger Davis	2.50	1.10
❑ 66 Joe Marconi	2.50	1.10
❑ 67 Herman Lee	2.50	1.10
❑ 68 Doug Atkins	6.00	2.70
❑ 69 Joe Fortunato	2.50	1.10
❑ 70 Bill George	5.00	2.20
❑ 71 Richie Petitbon	3.00	1.35
❑ 72 Chicago Bears SP Team Card	10.00	4.50
❑ 73 Eddie LeBaron SP	8.00	3.60
❑ 74 Don Meredith SP	60.00	27.00
❑ 75 Don Perkins SP	10.00	4.50
❑ 76 Amos Marsh SP	6.00	2.70
❑ 77 Billy Howton SP	8.00	3.60
❑ 78 Andy Cvercko SP	6.00	2.70
❑ 79 Sam Baker SP	6.00	2.70
❑ 80 Jerry Tubbs SP	6.00	2.70
❑ 81 Don Bishop SP	6.00	2.70
❑ 82 Bob Lilly RC SP	150.00	70.00
❑ 83 Jerry Norton SP	6.00	2.70
❑ 84 Dallas Cowboys SP Team Card	20.00	9.00
❑ 85 Checklist Card	25.00	6.25
❑ 86 Bart Starr	50.00	22.00
❑ 87 Jim Taylor	25.00	11.00
❑ 88 Boyd Dowler	5.00	2.20
❑ 89 Forrest Gregg	6.00	2.70
❑ 90 Fuzzy Thurston	6.00	2.70
❑ 91 Jim Ringo	6.00	2.70
❑ 92 Ron Kramer	3.00	1.35
❑ 93 Hank Jordan	6.00	2.70
❑ 94 Bill Forester	3.00	1.35
❑ 95 Willie Wood RC	30.00	13.50
❑ 96 Ray Nitschke RC	90.00	40.00
❑ 97 Green Bay Packers Team Card	8.00	3.60
❑ 98 Fran Tarkenton	60.00	27.00
❑ 99 Tommy Mason	3.00	1.35
❑ 100 Mel Triplett	2.50	1.10
❑ 101 Jerry Reichow	2.50	1.10
❑ 102 Frank Youso	2.50	1.10
❑ 103 Hugh McElhenny	8.00	3.60
❑ 104 Gerald Huth	2.50	1.10
❑ 105 Ed Sharockman	2.50	1.10
❑ 106 Rip Hawkins	2.50	1.10
❑ 107 Jim Marshall RC	30.00	13.50
❑ 108 Jim Prestel	2.50	1.10
❑ 109 Minnesota Vikings Team Card	4.00	1.80
❑ 110 Sonny Jurgensen SP	25.00	11.00
❑ 111 Tim Brown SP RC	10.00	4.50
❑ 112 Tommy McDonald SP	10.00	4.50
❑ 113 Clarence Peaks SP	6.00	2.70
❑ 114 Pete Retzlaff SP	8.00	3.60
❑ 115 Jim Schrader SP	6.00	2.70
❑ 116 Jim McCusker SP	6.00	2.70
❑ 117 Don Burroughs SP	6.00	2.70
❑ 118 Maxie Baughan SP	6.00	2.70
❑ 119 Riley Gunnels SP	6.00	2.70
❑ 120 Jimmy Carr SP	6.00	2.70
❑ 121 Philadelphia Eagles SP Team Card	10.00	4.50
❑ 122 Ed Brown SP	8.00	3.60
❑ 123 John Henry Johnson SP	15.00	6.75
❑ 124 Buddy Dial SP	6.00	2.70
❑ 125 Bill Red Mack SP	6.00	2.70
❑ 126 Preston Carpenter SP	6.00	2.70
❑ 127 Ray Lemek SP	6.00	2.70
❑ 128 Buzz Nutter SP	6.00	2.70
❑ 129 Ernie Stautner SP	15.00	6.75
❑ 130 Lou Michaels SP	6.00	2.70
❑ 131 Clendon Thomas RC SP	6.00	2.70
❑ 132 Tom Bettis SP	6.00	2.70
❑ 133 Pittsburgh Steelers SP Team Card	10.00	4.50
❑ 134 John Brodie	8.00	3.60
❑ 135 J.D. Smith	2.50	1.10
❑ 136 Bill Kilmer UER (College listed as San Francisco 49ers)	5.00	2.20
❑ 137 Bernie Casey RC	3.00	1.35
❑ 138 Tommy Davis	2.50	1.10
❑ 139 Ted Connolly	2.50	1.10
❑ 140 Bob St. Clair	5.00	2.20
❑ 141 Abe Woodson	2.50	1.10
❑ 142 Matt Hazeltine	2.50	1.10
❑ 143 Leo Nomellini	6.00	2.70
❑ 144 Dan Colchico	2.50	1.10
❑ 145 San Francisco 49ers SP Team Card	10.00	4.50
❑ 146 Charlie Johnson RC	8.00	3.60
❑ 147 John David Crow	3.00	1.35
❑ 148 Bobby Joe Conrad	3.00	1.35
❑ 149 Sonny Randle	2.50	1.10
❑ 150 Prentice Gautt	2.50	1.10
❑ 151 Taz Anderson	2.50	1.10
❑ 152 Ernie McMillan RC	3.00	1.35
❑ 153 Jimmy Hill	2.50	1.10
❑ 154 Bill Koman	2.50	1.10
❑ 155 Larry Wilson RC	20.00	9.00
❑ 156 Don Owens	2.50	1.10
❑ 157 St. Louis Cardinals SP Team Card	10.00	4.50
❑ 158 Norm Snead SP	10.00	4.50
❑ 159 Bobby Mitchell SP	15.00	6.75
❑ 160 Bill Barnes SP	6.00	2.70
❑ 161 Fred Dugan SP	6.00	2.70
❑ 162 Don Bosseler SP	6.00	2.70
❑ 163 John Nisby SP	6.00	2.70
❑ 164 Riley Mattson SP	6.00	2.70
❑ 165 Bob Toneff SP	6.00	2.70
❑ 166 Rod Breedlove SP	6.00	2.70
❑ 167 Dick James SP	6.00	2.70
❑ 168 Claude Crabb SP UER (Claud on front and back)	6.00	2.70
❑ 169 Washington Redskins SP Team Card	10.00	4.50
❑ 170 Checklist Card UER ! (108 Jim Prestal)	60.00	15.00
❑ AD1 Charlie Johnson John David Crow Bobby Joe Conrad (Y.A. Tittle/ad back panel)	100.00	45.00

1964 Topps

	NRMT	VG-E
COMPLETE SET (176)	1500.00	700.00
COMMON CARD (1-176)	4.00	1.80
SEMISTARS	5.00	2.20
UNLISTED STARS	6.00	2.70
SP(6/7/9/15/16/18/19)	6.00	2.70
SP(27/28/34/41/42)	6.00	2.70
SP(44-46/52-54/56/58)	6.00	2.70
SP(67/70-74/76/77/79/80)	6.00	2.70
SP(83-86/102/106/107/111)	6.00	2.70
SP(112/114/119/120/122)	6.00	2.70
SP(124/132/140/142/144)	6.00	2.70
SP(146/147/149/160-162)	6.00	2.70
SP(167/169/170/172)	6.00	2.70
SEMISTAR SP (4/17/26/47)	10.00	4.50
SEMISTAR SP (75/78/91/94)	10.00	4.50
SEMISTAR SP (99/104/105/127)	10.00	4.50
SEMISTAR SP (137/154/171/174)	10.00	4.50
UNL. STARS SP (38/64/150/165)	12.00	5.50
TEAM CARDS	6.00	2.70

CARDS PRICED IN NM CONDITION

Card	NRMT	VG-E
❑ 1 Tommy Addison SP	30.00	7.50
❑ 2 Houston Antwine RC	4.00	1.80
❑ 3 Nick Buoniconti	15.00	6.75
❑ 4 Ron Burton SP	10.00	4.50
❑ 5 Gino Cappelletti UER (Misspelled Cappalletti on card front)	5.00	2.20
❑ 6 Jim Colclough SP	6.00	2.70
❑ 7 Bob Dee SP	6.00	2.70
❑ 8 Larry Eisenhauer	4.00	1.80
❑ 9 Dick Felt SP	6.00	2.70
❑ 10 Larry Garron	4.00	1.80
❑ 11 Art Graham	4.00	1.80
❑ 12 Ron Hall	4.00	1.80
❑ 13 Charles Long	4.00	1.80
❑ 14 Don McKinnon	4.00	1.80
❑ 15 Don Oakes SP	6.00	2.70
❑ 16 Ross O'Hanley SP	6.00	2.70
❑ 17 Babe Parilli SP	10.00	4.50
❑ 18 Jesse Richardson SP	6.00	2.70
❑ 19 Jack Rudolph SP	6.00	2.70
❑ 20 Don Webb RC	4.00	1.80
❑ 21 Boston Patriots Team Card	6.00	2.70
❑ 22 Ray Abruzzese UER (photo is Ed Rutkowski)	4.00	1.80
❑ 23 Stew Barber RC	4.00	1.80
❑ 24 Dave Behrman	4.00	1.80
❑ 25 Al Bemiller	4.00	1.80
❑ 26 Elbert Dubenion SP	10.00	4.50
❑ 27 Jim Dunaway RC SP	6.00	2.70
❑ 28 Booker Edgerson SP	6.00	2.70
❑ 29 Cookie Gilchrist SP	20.00	9.00
❑ 30 Jack Kemp SP	175.00	80.00
❑ 31 Daryle Lamonica RC	75.00	34.00
❑ 32 Bill Miller	4.00	1.80
❑ 33 Herb Paterra RC	4.00	1.80
❑ 34 Ken Rice SP	6.00	2.70
❑ 35 Ed Rutkowski UER (photo is Ray Abruzzese)	4.00	1.80
❑ 36 George Saimes RC	4.00	1.80
❑ 37 Tom Sestak	4.00	1.80
❑ 38 Billy Shaw SP	12.00	5.50
❑ 39 Mike Stratton	5.00	2.20
❑ 40 Gene Sykes	4.00	1.80
❑ 41 John Tracey SP	6.00	2.70
❑ 42 Sid Youngelman SP	6.00	2.70
❑ 43 Buffalo Bills Team Card	6.00	2.70
❑ 44 Eldon Danenhauer SP	6.00	2.70
❑ 45 Jim Fraser SP	6.00	2.70
❑ 46 Chuck Gavin SP	6.00	2.70
❑ 47 Goose Gonsoulin SP	10.00	4.50
❑ 48 Ernie Barnes RC	4.00	1.80
❑ 49 Tom Janik	4.00	1.80
❑ 50 Billy Joe RC	5.00	2.20
❑ 51 Ike Lassiter RC	4.00	1.80
❑ 52 John McCormick SP	6.00	2.70
❑ 53 Bud McFadin SP	6.00	2.70
❑ 54 Gene Mingo SP	6.00	2.70
❑ 55 Charlie Mitchell	4.00	1.80
❑ 56 John Nocera SP	6.00	2.70
❑ 57 Tom Nomina	4.00	1.80
❑ 58 Harold Olson SP	6.00	2.70
❑ 59 Bob Scarpitto	4.00	1.80
❑ 60 John Sklopan	4.00	1.80
❑ 61 Mickey Slaughter	4.00	1.80
❑ 62 Don Stone	4.00	1.80
❑ 63 Jerry Sturm	4.00	1.80
❑ 64 Lionel Taylor SP	12.00	5.50
❑ 65 Denver Broncos SP Team Card	20.00	9.00
❑ 66 Scott Appleton RC	4.00	1.80
❑ 67 Tony Banfield SP	6.00	2.70
❑ 68 George Blanda SP	60.00	27.00
❑ 69 Billy Cannon	6.00	2.70
❑ 70 Doug Cline SP	6.00	2.70
❑ 71 Gary Cutsinger SP	6.00	2.70
❑ 72 Willard Dewveall SP	6.00	2.70
❑ 73 Don Floyd SP	6.00	2.70
❑ 74 Freddy Glick SP	6.00	2.70
❑ 75 Charlie Hennigan SP	10.00	4.50

- ❑ 76 Ed Husmann SP 6.00 2.70
- ❑ 77 Bobby Jancik SP 6.00 2.70
- ❑ 78 Jacky Lee SP 10.00 4.50
- ❑ 79 Bob McLeod SP 6.00 2.70
- ❑ 80 Rich Michael SP 6.00 2.70
- ❑ 81 Larry Onesti RC 4.00 1.80
- ❑ 82 Checklist Card UER 60.00 15.00 (16 Ross O'Hanldy)
- ❑ 83 Bob Schmidt SP 6.00 2.70
- ❑ 84 Walt Suggs SP 6.00 2.70
- ❑ 85 Bob Talamini SP 6.00 2.70
- ❑ 86 Charley Tolar SP 6.00 2.70
- ❑ 87 Don Trull RC 4.00 1.80
- ❑ 88 Houston Oilers Team Card 6.00 2.70
- ❑ 89 Fred Arbanas 4.00 1.80
- ❑ 90 Bobby Bell RC 40.00 18.00
- ❑ 91 Mel Branch SP 10.00 4.50
- ❑ 92 Buck Buchanan RC 40.00 18.00
- ❑ 93 Ed Budde RC 4.00 1.80
- ❑ 94 Chris Burford SP 10.00 4.50
- ❑ 95 Walt Corey RC 5.00 2.20
- ❑ 96 Len Dawson SP 75.00 34.00
- ❑ 97 Dave Grayson RC 4.00 1.80
- ❑ 98 Abner Haynes 6.00 2.70
- ❑ 99 Sherrill Headrick SP 10.00 4.50
- ❑ 100 E.J. Holub 4.00 1.80
- ❑ 101 Bobby Hunt 4.00 1.80
- ❑ 102 Frank Jackson SP 6.00 2.70
- ❑ 103 Curtis McClinton 5.00 2.20
- ❑ 104 Jerry Mays SP 10.00 4.50
- ❑ 105 Johnny Robinson SP 10.00 4.50
- ❑ 106 Jack Spikes SP 6.00 2.70
- ❑ 107 Smokey Stover SP 6.00 2.70
- ❑ 108 Jim Tyrer RC 8.00 3.60
- ❑ 109 Duane Wood SP 6.00 2.70
- ❑ 110 Kansas City Chiefs Team Card 6.00 2.70
- ❑ 111 Dick Christy SP 6.00 2.70
- ❑ 112 Dan Ficca SP 6.00 2.70
- ❑ 113 Larry Grantham 4.00 1.80
- ❑ 114 Curley Johnson SP 6.00 2.70
- ❑ 115 Gene Heeter 4.00 1.80
- ❑ 116 Jack Klotz 4.00 1.80
- ❑ 117 Pete Liske RC 5.00 2.20
- ❑ 118 Bob McAdam 4.00 1.80
- ❑ 119 Dee Mackey SP 6.00 2.70
- ❑ 120 Bill Mathis SP 10.00 4.50
- ❑ 121 Don Maynard 35.00 16.00
- ❑ 122 Dainard Paulson SP 6.00 2.70
- ❑ 123 Gerry Philbin RC 5.00 2.20
- ❑ 124 Mark Smolinski SP 6.00 2.70
- ❑ 125 Matt Snell RC 20.00 9.00
- ❑ 126 Mike Taliaferro 4.00 1.80
- ❑ 127 Bake Turner RC SP 10.00 4.50
- ❑ 128 Jeff Ware 4.00 1.80
- ❑ 129 Clyde Washington 4.00 1.80
- ❑ 130 Dick Wood RC 4.00 1.80
- ❑ 131 New York Jets Team Card 6.00 2.70
- ❑ 132 Dalva Allen SP 6.00 2.70
- ❑ 133 Dan Birdwell 4.00 1.80
- ❑ 134 Dave Costa RC 4.00 1.80
- ❑ 135 Dobie Craig 4.00 1.80
- ❑ 136 Clem Daniels 5.00 2.20
- ❑ 137 Cotton Davidson SP 10.00 4.50
- ❑ 138 Claude Gibson 4.00 1.80
- ❑ 139 Tom Flores SP 15.00 6.75
- ❑ 140 Wayne Hawkins SP 6.00 2.70
- ❑ 141 Ken Herock 4.00 1.80
- ❑ 142 Jon Jelacic SP 6.00 2.70
- ❑ 143 Joe Krakoski 4.00 1.80
- ❑ 144 Archie Matsos SP 6.00 2.70
- ❑ 145 Mike Mercer 4.00 1.80
- ❑ 146 Alan Miller SP 6.00 2.70
- ❑ 147 Bob Mischak SP 6.00 2.70
- ❑ 148 Jim Otto SP 30.00 13.50
- ❑ 149 Clancy Osborne SP 6.00 2.70
- ❑ 150 Art Powell SP 12.00 5.50
- ❑ 151 Bo Roberson 4.00 1.80 (Raider helmet placed over his foot)
- ❑ 152 Fred Williamson SP 15.00 6.75
- ❑ 153 Oakland Raiders Team Card 6.00 2.70
- ❑ 154 Chuck Allen RC SP 10.00 4.50
- ❑ 155 Lance Alworth 50.00 22.00
- ❑ 156 George Blair 4.00 1.80
- ❑ 157 Earl Faison 4.00 1.80
- ❑ 158 Sam Gruneisen 4.00 1.80
- ❑ 159 John Hadl RC 35.00 16.00
- ❑ 160 Dick Harris SP 6.00 2.70
- ❑ 161 Emil Karas SP 6.00 2.70
- ❑ 162 Dave Kocourek SP 6.00 2.70
- ❑ 163 Ernie Ladd 6.00 2.70
- ❑ 164 Keith Lincoln 6.00 2.70
- ❑ 165 Paul Lowe SP 12.00 5.50
- ❑ 166 Charley McNeil 4.00 1.80
- ❑ 167 Jacque MacKinnon SP 6.00 2.70
- ❑ 168 Ron Mix SP 18.00 8.00
- ❑ 169 Don Norton SP 6.00 2.70
- ❑ 170 Don Rogers SP 6.00 2.70
- ❑ 171 Tobin Rote SP 10.00 4.50
- ❑ 172 Henry Schmidt SP 6.00 2.70
- ❑ 173 Bud Whitehead 4.00 1.80
- ❑ 174 Ernie Wright SP 10.00 4.50
- ❑ 175 San Diego Chargers Team Card 6.00 2.70
- ❑ 176 Checklist SP UER ! 160.00 40.00 (155 Lance Allworth)

1965 Topps

	NRMT	VG-E
COMPLETE SET (176)	4000.00	1800.00
COMMON CARD (1-176)	7.00	3.10
SEMISTARS	10.00	4.50
SP (2/7/11/15/18/19/21)	12.00	5.50
SP (22/24-26/31/32/34)	12.00	5.50
SP (38-40/42/43/47-50)	12.00	5.50
SP (55/58/60-64/66-68)	12.00	5.50
SP (70-72/75/77)	12.00	5.50
SP (80-83/86/88/89)	12.00	5.50
SP (92/93/95/96/100)	12.00	5.50
SP (101-105/108/110-115)	12.00	5.50
SP (118/119/124/128/130)	12.00	5.50
SP (131/135/142-144)	12.00	5.50
SP (147-149/151/157)	12.00	5.50
SEMISTAR SP(28/33/52/56/107)	15.00	6.75
SEMISTAR SP(109/125/136/138)	15.00	6.75
UNL. STAR SP(4/5/17/65/78/116)	20.00	9.00
UNL.STAR SP(134,165,166,175)	20.00	9.00
SEMISTARS SP	15.00	6.75
UNLISTED STARS SP	20.00	9.00

CARDS PRICED IN NM CONDITION !

- ❑ 1 Tommy Addison SP 35.00 8.75
- ❑ 2 Houston Antwine SP 12.00 5.50
- ❑ 3 Nick Buoniconti SP 30.00 13.50
- ❑ 4 Ron Burton SP 20.00 9.00
- ❑ 5 Gino Cappelletti SP 20.00 9.00
- ❑ 6 Jim Colclough 7.00 3.10
- ❑ 7 Bob Dee SP 12.00 5.50
- ❑ 8 Larry Eisenhauer 7.00 3.10
- ❑ 9 J.D. Garrett 7.00 3.10
- ❑ 10 Larry Garron 7.00 3.10
- ❑ 11 Art Graham SP 12.00 5.50
- ❑ 12 Ron Hall 7.00 3.10
- ❑ 13 Charles Long 7.00 3.10
- ❑ 14 Jon Morris RC 10.00 4.50
- ❑ 15 Billy Neighbors SP 12.00 5.50
- ❑ 16 Ross O'Hanley 7.00 3.10
- ❑ 17 Babe Parilli SP 20.00 9.00
- ❑ 18 Tony Romeo SP 12.00 5.50
- ❑ 19 Jack Rudolph SP 12.00 5.50
- ❑ 20 Bob Schmidt 7.00 3.10
- ❑ 21 Don Webb SP 12.00 5.50
- ❑ 22 Jim Whalen SP 12.00 5.50
- ❑ 23 Stew Barber 7.00 3.10
- ❑ 24 Glenn Bass SP 12.00 5.50
- ❑ 25 Al Bemiller SP 12.00 5.50
- ❑ 26 Wray Carlton SP 12.00 5.50
- ❑ 27 Tom Day 7.00 3.10
- ❑ 28 Elbert Dubenion SP 15.00 6.75
- ❑ 29 Jim Dunaway 7.00 3.10
- ❑ 30 Pete Gogolak RC SP 20.00 9.00
- ❑ 31 Dick Hudson SP 12.00 5.50
- ❑ 32 Harry Jacobs SP 12.00 5.50
- ❑ 33 Billy Joe SP 15.00 6.75
- ❑ 34 Tom Keating RC SP 12.00 5.50
- ❑ 35 Jack Kemp SP 175.00 80.00
- ❑ 36 Daryle Lamonica SP 45.00 20.00
- ❑ 37 Paul Maguire SP 20.00 9.00
- ❑ 38 Ron McDole RC SP 12.00 5.50
- ❑ 39 George Saimes SP 12.00 5.50
- ❑ 40 Tom Sestak SP 12.00 5.50
- ❑ 41 Billy Shaw SP 20.00 9.00
- ❑ 42 Mike Stratton SP 12.00 5.50
- ❑ 43 John Tracey SP 12.00 5.50
- ❑ 44 Ernie Warlick 7.00 3.10
- ❑ 45 Odell Barry 7.00 3.10
- ❑ 46 Willie Brown RC SP 90.00 40.00
- ❑ 47 Gerry Bussell SP 12.00 5.50
- ❑ 48 Eldon Danenhauer SP 12.00 5.50
- ❑ 49 Al Denson SP 12.00 5.50
- ❑ 50 Hewritt Dixon RC SP 15.00 6.75
- ❑ 51 Cookie Gilchrist SP 30.00 13.50
- ❑ 52 Goose Gonsoulin SP 15.00 6.75
- ❑ 53 Abner Haynes SP 20.00 9.00
- ❑ 54 Jerry Hopkins 7.00 3.10
- ❑ 55 Ray Jacobs SP 12.00 5.50
- ❑ 56 Jacky Lee SP 15.00 6.75
- ❑ 57 John McCormick 7.00 3.10
- ❑ 58 Bob McCullough SP 12.00 5.50
- ❑ 59 John McGeever 7.00 3.10
- ❑ 60 Charlie Mitchell SP 12.00 5.50
- ❑ 61 Jim Perkins SP 12.00 5.50
- ❑ 62 Bob Scarpitto SP 12.00 5.50
- ❑ 63 Mickey Slaughter SP 12.00 5.50
- ❑ 64 Jerry Sturm SP 12.00 5.50
- ❑ 65 Lionel Taylor SP 20.00 9.00
- ❑ 66 Scott Appleton SP 12.00 5.50
- ❑ 67 Johnny Baker SP 12.00 5.50
- ❑ 68 Sonny Bishop SP 12.00 5.50
- ❑ 69 George Blanda SP 100.00 45.00
- ❑ 70 Sid Blanks SP 12.00 5.50
- ❑ 71 Ode Burrell SP 12.00 5.50
- ❑ 72 Doug Cline SP 12.00 5.50
- ❑ 73 Willard Dewveall 7.00 3.10
- ❑ 74 Larry Elkins RC 7.00 3.10
- ❑ 75 Don Floyd SP 12.00 5.50
- ❑ 76 Freddy Glick 7.00 3.10
- ❑ 77 Tom Goode SP 12.00 5.50
- ❑ 78 Charlie Hennigan SP 20.00 9.00
- ❑ 79 Ed Husmann 7.00 3.10
- ❑ 80 Bobby Jancik SP 12.00 5.50
- ❑ 81 Bud McFadin SP 12.00 5.50
- ❑ 82 Bob McLeod SP 12.00 5.50
- ❑ 83 Jim Norton SP 12.00 5.50
- ❑ 84 Walt Suggs 7.00 3.10
- ❑ 85 Bob Talamini 7.00 3.10
- ❑ 86 Charley Tolar SP 12.00 5.50
- ❑ 87 Checklist SP ! 150.00 38.00
- ❑ 88 Don Trull SP 12.00 5.50
- ❑ 89 Fred Arbanas SP 12.00 5.50
- ❑ 90 Pete Beathard RC SP 12.00 5.50
- ❑ 91 Bobby Bell SP 35.00 16.00
- ❑ 92 Mel Branch SP 12.00 5.50
- ❑ 93 Tommy Brooker SP 12.00 5.50
- ❑ 94 Buck Buchanan SP 35.00 16.00
- ❑ 95 Ed Budde SP 12.00 5.50
- ❑ 96 Chris Burford SP 12.00 5.50
- ❑ 97 Walt Corey 7.00 3.10
- ❑ 98 Jerry Cornelison 7.00 3.10
- ❑ 99 Len Dawson SP 100.00 45.00
- ❑ 100 Jon Gilliam SP 12.00 5.50
- ❑ 101 Sherrill Headrick SP UER 12.00 5.50 (Name spelled Sherill on front)
- ❑ 102 Dave Hill SP 12.00 5.50
- ❑ 103 E.J. Holub SP 12.00 5.50

❑ 104 Bobby Hunt SP	12.00	5.50
❑ 105 Frank Jackson SP	12.00	5.50
❑ 106 Jerry Mays	10.00	4.50
❑ 107 Curtis McClinton SP	15.00	6.75
❑ 108 Bobby Ply SP	12.00	5.50
❑ 109 Johnny Robinson SP	15.00	6.75
❑ 110 Jim Tyrer SP	12.00	5.50
❑ 111 Bill Baird SP	12.00	5.50
❑ 112 Ralph Baker RC SP	12.00	5.50
❑ 113 Sam DeLuca SP	12.00	5.50
❑ 114 Larry Grantham SP	15.00	6.75
❑ 115 Gene Heeter SP	12.00	5.50
❑ 116 Winston Hill RC SP	20.00	9.00
❑ 117 John Huarte RC SP	30.00	13.50
❑ 118 Cosmo Iacavazzi SP	12.00	5.50
❑ 119 Curley Johnson SP	12.00	5.50
❑ 120 Dee Mackey UER (College WVU, should be East Texas State)	7.00	3.10
❑ 121 Don Maynard	50.00	22.00
❑ 122 Joe Namath SP RC	1400.00	650.00
❑ 123 Dainard Paulson	7.00	3.10
❑ 124 Gerry Philbin SP	12.00	5.50
❑ 125 Sherman Plunkett RC SP	15.00	6.75
❑ 126 Mark Smolinski	7.00	3.10
❑ 127 Matt Snell SP	30.00	13.50
❑ 128 Mike Taliaferro SP	12.00	5.50
❑ 129 Bake Turner SP	12.00	5.50
❑ 130 Clyde Washington SP	12.00	5.50
❑ 131 Verlon Biggs RC SP	12.00	5.50
❑ 132 Dalva Allen	7.00	3.10
❑ 133 Fred Biletnikoff RC SP	225.00	100.00
❑ 134 Billy Cannon SP	20.00	9.00
❑ 135 Dave Costa SP	12.00	5.50
❑ 136 Clem Daniels SP	15.00	6.75
❑ 137 Ben Davidson RC SP	60.00	27.00
❑ 138 Cotton Davidson SP	15.00	6.75
❑ 139 Tom Flores SP	20.00	9.00
❑ 140 Claude Gibson	7.00	3.10
❑ 141 Wayne Hawkins	7.00	3.10
❑ 142 Archie Matsos SP	12.00	5.50
❑ 143 Mike Mercer SP	12.00	5.50
❑ 144 Bob Mischak SP	12.00	5.50
❑ 145 Jim Otto	30.00	13.50
❑ 146 Art Powell UER (Photo actually Clem Daniels)	10.00	4.50
❑ 147 Warren Powers SP	12.00	5.50
❑ 148 Ken Rice SP	12.00	5.50
❑ 149 Bo Roberson SP	12.00	5.50
❑ 150 Harry Schuh RC	7.00	3.10
❑ 151 Larry Todd SP	12.00	5.50
❑ 152 Fred Williamson SP	20.00	9.00
❑ 153 J.R. Williamson	7.00	3.10
❑ 154 Chuck Allen	10.00	4.50
❑ 155 Lance Alworth	75.00	34.00
❑ 156 Frank Buncom	7.00	3.10
❑ 157 Steve DeLong RC SP	12.00	5.50
❑ 158 Earl Faison SP	15.00	6.75
❑ 159 Kenny Graham SP	12.00	5.50
❑ 160 George Gross SP	12.00	5.50
❑ 161 John Hadl SP	30.00	13.50
❑ 162 Emil Karas SP	12.00	5.50
❑ 163 Dave Kocourek SP	12.00	5.50
❑ 164 Ernie Ladd SP	20.00	9.00
❑ 165 Keith Lincoln SP	20.00	9.00
❑ 166 Paul Lowe SP	20.00	9.00
❑ 167 Jacque MacKinnon	7.00	3.10
❑ 168 Ron Mix	20.00	9.00
❑ 169 Don Norton SP	12.00	5.50
❑ 170 Bob Petrich	7.00	3.10
❑ 171 Rick Redman SP	12.00	5.50
❑ 172 Pat Shea	7.00	3.10
❑ 173 Walt Sweeney RC SP	15.00	6.75
❑ 174 Dick Westmoreland RC	7.00	3.10
❑ 175 Ernie Wright SP	20.00	9.00
❑ 176 Checklist SP !	225.00	55.00

1966 Topps

	NRMT	VG-E
COMPLETE SET (132)	1500.00	700.00
COMMON CARD (1-132)	5.00	2.20
SEMISTARS	7.00	3.10
UNLISTED STARS	10.00	4.50

CARDS PRICED IN NM CONDITION !

❑ 1 Tommy Addison	20.00	5.00
❑ 2 Houston Antwine	5.00	2.20
❑ 3 Nick Buoniconti	10.00	4.50
❑ 4 Gino Cappelletti	7.00	3.10
❑ 5 Bob Dee	5.00	2.20
❑ 6 Larry Garron	5.00	2.20
❑ 7 Art Graham	5.00	2.20
❑ 8 Ron Hall	5.00	2.20
❑ 9 Charles Long	5.00	2.20
❑ 10 Jon Morris	5.00	2.20
❑ 11 Don Oakes	5.00	2.20
❑ 12 Babe Parilli	7.00	3.10
❑ 13 Don Webb	5.00	2.20
❑ 14 Jim Whalen	5.00	2.20
❑ 15 Funny Ring Checklist	300.00	75.00
❑ 16 Stew Barber	5.00	2.20
❑ 17 Glenn Bass	5.00	2.20
❑ 18 Dave Behrman	5.00	2.20
❑ 19 Al Bemiller	5.00	2.20
❑ 20 George Butch Byrd RC	7.00	3.10
❑ 21 Wray Carlton	5.00	2.20
❑ 22 Tom Day	5.00	2.20
❑ 23 Elbert Dubenion	7.00	3.10
❑ 24 Jim Dunaway	5.00	2.20
❑ 25 Dick Hudson	5.00	2.20
❑ 26 Jack Kemp	150.00	70.00
❑ 27 Daryle Lamonica	20.00	9.00
❑ 28 Tom Sestak	5.00	2.20
❑ 29 Billy Shaw	10.00	4.50
❑ 30 Mike Stratton	5.00	2.20
❑ 31 Eldon Danenhauer	5.00	2.20
❑ 32 Cookie Gilchrist	10.00	4.50
❑ 33 Goose Gonsoulin	7.00	3.10
❑ 34 Wendell Hayes RC	10.00	4.50
❑ 35 Abner Haynes	10.00	4.50
❑ 36 Jerry Hopkins	5.00	2.20
❑ 37 Ray Jacobs	5.00	2.20
❑ 38 Charlie Janerette	5.00	2.20
❑ 39 Ray Kubala	5.00	2.20
❑ 40 John McCormick	5.00	2.20
❑ 41 Leroy Moore	5.00	2.20
❑ 42 Bob Scarpitto	5.00	2.20
❑ 43 Mickey Slaughter	5.00	2.20
❑ 44 Jerry Sturm	5.00	2.20
❑ 45 Lionel Taylor	10.00	4.50
❑ 46 Scott Appleton	5.00	2.20
❑ 47 Johnny Baker	5.00	2.20
❑ 48 George Blanda	30.00	13.50
❑ 49 Sid Blanks	5.00	2.20
❑ 50 Danny Brabham	5.00	2.20
❑ 51 Ode Burrell	5.00	2.20
❑ 52 Gary Cutsinger	5.00	2.20
❑ 53 Larry Elkins	5.00	2.20
❑ 54 Don Floyd	5.00	2.20
❑ 55 Willie Frazier RC	7.00	3.10
❑ 56 Freddy Glick	5.00	2.20
❑ 57 Charlie Hennigan	7.00	3.10
❑ 58 Bobby Jancik	5.00	2.20
❑ 59 Rich Michael	5.00	2.20
❑ 60 Don Trull	5.00	2.20
❑ 61 Checklist Card	55.00	14.00
❑ 62 Fred Arbanas	5.00	2.20
❑ 63 Pete Beathard	5.00	2.20
❑ 64 Bobby Bell	10.00	4.50
❑ 65 Ed Budde	5.00	2.20
❑ 66 Chris Burford	5.00	2.20
❑ 67 Len Dawson	40.00	18.00
❑ 68 Jon Gilliam	5.00	2.20
❑ 69 Sherrill Headrick	5.00	2.20
❑ 70 E.J. Holub UER (College: TCU, should be Texas Tech)	5.00	2.20
❑ 71 Bobby Hunt	5.00	2.20
❑ 72 Curtis McClinton	7.00	3.10
❑ 73 Jerry Mays	5.00	2.20
❑ 74 Johnny Robinson	7.00	3.10
❑ 75 Otis Taylor RC	25.00	11.00
❑ 76 Tom Erlandson	7.00	3.10
❑ 77 Norm Evans RC UER (Flanker on front, tackle on back)	10.00	4.50
❑ 78 Tom Goode	7.00	3.10
❑ 79 Mike Hudock	7.00	3.10
❑ 80 Frank Jackson	7.00	3.10
❑ 81 Billy Joe	7.00	3.10
❑ 82 Dave Kocourek	7.00	3.10
❑ 83 Bo Roberson	7.00	3.10
❑ 84 Jack Spikes	7.00	3.10
❑ 85 Jim Warren RC	7.00	3.10
❑ 86 Willie West RC	7.00	3.10
❑ 87 Dick Westmoreland	7.00	3.10
❑ 88 Eddie Wilson	7.00	3.10
❑ 89 Dick Wood	7.00	3.10
❑ 90 Verlon Biggs	7.00	3.10
❑ 91 Sam DeLuca	5.00	2.20
❑ 92 Winston Hill	5.00	2.20
❑ 93 Dee Mackey	5.00	2.20
❑ 94 Bill Mathis	5.00	2.20
❑ 95 Don Maynard	30.00	13.50
❑ 96 Joe Namath	250.00	110.00
❑ 97 Dainard Paulson	5.00	2.20
❑ 98 Gerry Philbin	7.00	3.10
❑ 99 Sherman Plunkett	5.00	2.20
❑ 100 Paul Rochester	5.00	2.20
❑ 101 George Sauer Jr. RC	15.00	6.75
❑ 102 Matt Snell	10.00	4.50
❑ 103 Jim Turner RC	7.00	3.10
❑ 104 Fred Biletnikoff UER (Misspelled on back as Bilentnikoff)	50.00	22.00
❑ 105 Bill Budness	5.00	2.20
❑ 106 Billy Cannon	10.00	4.50
❑ 107 Clem Daniels	7.00	3.10
❑ 108 Ben Davidson	15.00	6.75
❑ 109 Cotton Davidson	7.00	3.10
❑ 110 Claude Gibson	5.00	2.20
❑ 111 Wayne Hawkins	5.00	2.20
❑ 112 Ken Herock	5.00	2.20
❑ 113 Bob Mischak	5.00	2.20
❑ 114 Gus Otto	5.00	2.20
❑ 115 Jim Otto	20.00	9.00
❑ 116 Art Powell	10.00	4.50
❑ 117 Harry Schuh	5.00	2.20
❑ 118 Chuck Allen	5.00	2.20
❑ 119 Lance Alworth	40.00	18.00
❑ 120 Frank Buncom	5.00	2.20
❑ 121 Steve DeLong	5.00	2.20
❑ 122 John Farris	5.00	2.20
❑ 123 Kenny Graham	5.00	2.20
❑ 124 Sam Gruneisen	5.00	2.20
❑ 125 John Hadl	10.00	4.50
❑ 126 Walt Sweeney	5.00	2.20
❑ 127 Keith Lincoln	10.00	4.50
❑ 128 Ron Mix	10.00	4.50
❑ 129 Don Norton	5.00	2.20
❑ 130 Pat Shea	5.00	2.20
❑ 131 Ernie Wright	10.00	4.50
❑ 132 Checklist Card	100.00	25.00

1967 Topps

	NRMT	VG-E
COMPLETE SET (132)	700.00	325.00
COMMON CARD (1-132)	3.00	1.35
SEMISTARS	4.00	1.80
UNLISTED STARS	6.00	2.70

CARDS PRICED IN NM CONDITION

❑ 1 John Huarte	18.00	4.50
❑ 2 Babe Parilli	4.00	1.80
❑ 3 Gino Cappelletti	4.00	1.80
❑ 4 Larry Garron	3.00	1.35
❑ 5 Tommy Addison	3.00	1.35
❑ 6 Jon Morris	3.00	1.35
❑ 7 Houston Antwine	3.00	1.35

❑ 8	Don Oakes	3.00	1.35
❑ 9	Larry Eisenhauer	3.00	1.35
❑ 10	Jim Hunt	3.00	1.35
❑ 11	Jim Whalen	3.00	1.35
❑ 12	Art Graham	3.00	1.35
❑ 13	Nick Buoniconti	6.00	2.70
❑ 14	Bob Dee	3.00	1.35
❑ 15	Keith Lincoln	6.00	2.70
❑ 16	Tom Flores	4.00	1.80
❑ 17	Art Powell	4.00	1.80
❑ 18	Stew Barber	3.00	1.35
❑ 19	Wray Carlton	3.00	1.35
❑ 20	Elbert Dubenion	4.00	1.80
❑ 21	Jim Dunaway	3.00	1.35
❑ 22	Dick Hudson	3.00	1.35
❑ 23	Harry Jacobs	3.00	1.35
❑ 24	Jack Kemp	90.00	40.00
❑ 25	Ron McDole	3.00	1.35
❑ 26	George Saimes	3.00	1.35
❑ 27	Tom Sestak	3.00	1.35
❑ 28	Billy Shaw	6.00	2.70
❑ 29	Mike Stratton	3.00	1.35
❑ 30	Nemiah Wilson RC	3.00	1.35
❑ 31	John McCormick	3.00	1.35
❑ 32	Rex Mirich	3.00	1.35
❑ 33	Dave Costa	3.00	1.35
❑ 34	Goose Gonsoulin	4.00	1.80
❑ 35	Abner Haynes	6.00	2.70
❑ 36	Wendell Hayes	4.00	1.80
❑ 37	Archie Matsos	3.00	1.35
❑ 38	John Bramlett	3.00	1.35
❑ 39	Jerry Sturm	3.00	1.35
❑ 40	Max Leetzow	3.00	1.35
❑ 41	Bob Scarpitto	3.00	1.35
❑ 42	Lionel Taylor	6.00	2.70
❑ 43	Al Denson	3.00	1.35
❑ 44	Miller Farr RC	3.00	1.35
❑ 45	Don Trull	3.00	1.35
❑ 46	Jacky Lee	4.00	1.80
❑ 47	Bobby Jancik	3.00	1.35
❑ 48	Ode Burrell	3.00	1.35
❑ 49	Larry Elkins	3.00	1.35
❑ 50	W.K. Hicks	3.00	1.35
❑ 51	Sid Blanks	3.00	1.35
❑ 52	Jim Norton	3.00	1.35
❑ 53	Bobby Maples RC	3.00	1.35
❑ 54	Bob Talamini	3.00	1.35
❑ 55	Walt Suggs	3.00	1.35
❑ 56	Gary Cutsinger	3.00	1.35
❑ 57	Danny Brabham	3.00	1.35
❑ 58	Ernie Ladd	6.00	2.70
❑ 59	Checklist Card	50.00	22.00
❑ 60	Pete Beathard	3.00	1.35
❑ 61	Len Dawson	30.00	13.50
❑ 62	Bobby Hunt	3.00	1.35
❑ 63	Bert Coan	3.00	1.35
❑ 64	Curtis McClinton	4.00	1.80
❑ 65	Johnny Robinson	4.00	1.80
❑ 66	E.J. Holub	3.00	1.35
❑ 67	Jerry Mays	3.00	1.35
❑ 68	Jim Tyrer	4.00	1.80
❑ 69	Bobby Bell	6.00	2.70
❑ 70	Fred Arbanas	3.00	1.35
❑ 71	Buck Buchanan	6.00	2.70
❑ 72	Chris Burford	3.00	1.35
❑ 73	Otis Taylor	6.00	2.70
❑ 74	Cookie Gilchrist	8.00	3.60
❑ 75	Earl Faison	3.00	1.35
❑ 76	George Wilson Jr.	4.00	1.80
❑ 77	Rick Norton	3.00	1.35
❑ 78	Frank Jackson	4.00	1.80
❑ 79	Joe Auer	3.00	1.35
❑ 80	Willie West	3.00	1.35
❑ 81	Jim Warren	3.00	1.35
❑ 82	Wahoo McDaniel RC	40.00	18.00
❑ 83	Ernie Park	3.00	1.35
❑ 84	Billy Neighbors	3.00	1.35
❑ 85	Norm Evans	4.00	1.80
❑ 86	Tom Nomina	3.00	1.35
❑ 87	Rich Zecher	3.00	1.35
❑ 88	Dave Kocourek	3.00	1.35
❑ 89	Bill Baird	3.00	1.35
❑ 90	Ralph Baker	3.00	1.35
❑ 91	Verlon Biggs	3.00	1.35
❑ 92	Sam DeLuca	3.00	1.35
❑ 93	Larry Grantham	4.00	1.80
❑ 94	Jim Harris	3.00	1.35
❑ 95	Winston Hill	3.00	1.35
❑ 96	Bill Mathis	3.00	1.35
❑ 97	Don Maynard	20.00	9.00
❑ 98	Joe Namath	150.00	70.00
❑ 99	Gerry Philbin	4.00	1.80
❑ 100	Paul Rochester	3.00	1.35
❑ 101	George Sauer Jr.	4.00	1.80
❑ 102	Matt Snell	6.00	2.70
❑ 103	Daryle Lamonica	10.00	4.50
❑ 104	Glenn Bass	3.00	1.35
❑ 105	Jim Otto	6.00	2.70
❑ 106	Fred Biletnikoff	30.00	13.50
❑ 107	Cotton Davidson	4.00	1.80
❑ 108	Larry Todd	3.00	1.35
❑ 109	Billy Cannon	6.00	2.70
❑ 110	Clem Daniels	4.00	1.80
❑ 111	Dave Grayson	3.00	1.35
❑ 112	Kent McCloughan RC	3.00	1.35
❑ 113	Bob Svihus	3.00	1.35
❑ 114	Ike Lassiter	3.00	1.35
❑ 115	Harry Schuh	3.00	1.35
❑ 116	Ben Davidson	8.00	3.60
❑ 117	Tom Day	3.00	1.35
❑ 118	Scott Appleton	3.00	1.35
❑ 119	Steve Tensi RC	3.00	1.35
❑ 120	John Hadl	6.00	2.70
❑ 121	Paul Lowe	4.00	1.80
❑ 122	Jim Allison	3.00	1.35
❑ 123	Lance Alworth	30.00	13.50
❑ 124	Jacque MacKinnon	3.00	1.35
❑ 125	Ron Mix	6.00	2.70
❑ 126	Bob Petrich	3.00	1.35
❑ 127	Howard Kindig	3.00	1.35
❑ 128	Steve DeLong	3.00	1.35
❑ 129	Chuck Allen	3.00	1.35
❑ 130	Frank Buncom	3.00	1.35
❑ 131	Speedy Duncan RC	4.00	1.80
❑ 132	Checklist Card	70.00	17.50

1968 Topps

	NRMT	VG-E
COMPLETE SET (219)	550.00	250.00
COMMON CARD (1-131)	1.50	.70
SEMISTARS 1-131	2.00	.90
UNLISTED STARS 1-131	3.00	1.35
COMMON CARD (132-219)	2.00	.90
SEMISTARS 132-219	2.50	1.10
UNLISTED STARS 132-219	4.00	1.80

CARDS PRICED IN NM CONDITION

❑ 1	Bart Starr	40.00	10.00
❑ 2	Dick Bass	2.00	.90
❑ 3	Grady Alderman	1.50	.70
❑ 4	Obert Logan	1.50	.70
❑ 5	Ernie Koy RC	2.00	.90
❑ 6	Don Hultz	1.50	.70
❑ 7	Earl Gros	1.50	.70
❑ 8	Jim Bakken	1.50	.70
❑ 9	George Mira	2.00	.90
❑ 10	Carl Kammerer	1.50	.70
❑ 11	Willie Frazier	1.50	.70
❑ 12	Kent McCloughan UER (McCloughlan on card back)	1.50	.70
❑ 13	George Sauer Jr.	2.00	.90
❑ 14	Jack Clancy	1.50	.70
❑ 15	Jim Tyrer	2.00	.90
❑ 16	Bobby Maples	1.50	.70
❑ 17	Bo Hickey	1.50	.70
❑ 18	Frank Buncom	1.50	.70
❑ 19	Keith Lincoln	2.00	.90
❑ 20	Jim Whalen	1.50	.70
❑ 21	Junior Coffey	1.50	.70
❑ 22	Billy Ray Smith	1.50	.70
❑ 23	Johnny Morris	1.50	.70
❑ 24	Ernie Green	1.50	.70
❑ 25	Don Meredith	25.00	11.00
❑ 26	Wayne Walker	1.50	.70
❑ 27	Carroll Dale	2.00	.90
❑ 28	Bernie Casey	2.00	.90
❑ 29	Dave Osborn RC	2.00	.90
❑ 30	Ray Poage	1.50	.70
❑ 31	Homer Jones	1.50	.70
❑ 32	Sam Baker	1.50	.70
❑ 33	Bill Saul	1.50	.70
❑ 34	Ken Willard	2.00	.90
❑ 35	Bobby Mitchell	4.00	1.80
❑ 36	Gary Garrison RC	2.00	.90
❑ 37	Billy Cannon	2.00	.90
❑ 38	Ralph Baker	1.50	.70
❑ 39	Howard Twilley RC	4.00	1.80
❑ 40	Wendell Hayes	2.00	.90
❑ 41	Jim Norton	1.50	.70
❑ 42	Tom Beer	1.50	.70
❑ 43	Chris Burford	1.50	.70
❑ 44	Stew Barber	1.50	.70
❑ 45	Leroy Mitchell UER (Lifetime Int. should be 3, not 2)	1.50	.70
❑ 46	Dan Grimm	1.50	.70
❑ 47	Jerry Logan	1.50	.70
❑ 48	Andy Livingston	1.50	.70
❑ 49	Paul Warfield	12.00	5.50
❑ 50	Don Perkins	2.00	.90
❑ 51	Ron Kramer	1.50	.70
❑ 52	Bob Jeter RC""/C	2.00	.90
❑ 53	Les Josephson RC	1.50	.70
❑ 54	Bobby Walden	1.50	.70
❑ 55	Checklist Card	15.00	3.70
❑ 56	Walter Roberts	1.50	.70
❑ 57	Henry Carr	1.50	.70
❑ 58	Gary Ballman	1.50	.70
❑ 59	J.R. Wilburn	1.50	.70
❑ 60	Jim Hart RC	10.00	4.50
❑ 61	Jim Johnson	3.00	1.35
❑ 62	Chris Hanburger	2.00	.90
❑ 63	John Hadl	3.00	1.35
❑ 64	Hewritt Dixon	2.00	.90
❑ 65	Joe Namath	75.00	34.00
❑ 66	Jim Warren	1.50	.70
❑ 67	Curtis McClinton	2.00	.90
❑ 68	Bob Talamini	1.50	.70
❑ 69	Steve Tensi	1.50	.70
❑ 70	Dick Van Raaphorst UER (Van Raap Horst on card back)	1.50	.70
❑ 71	Art Powell	2.00	.90
❑ 72	Jim Nance RC	4.00	1.80
❑ 73	Bob Riggle	1.50	.70
❑ 74	John Mackey	5.00	2.20
❑ 75	Gale Sayers	40.00	18.00
❑ 76	Gene Hickerson	1.50	.70
❑ 77	Dan Reeves	10.00	4.50
❑ 78	Tom Nowatzke	1.50	.70

Card	NRMT	VG-E
❑ 79 Elijah Pitts	3.00	1.35
❑ 80 Lamar Lundy	2.00	.90
❑ 81 Paul Flatley	1.50	.70
❑ 82 Dave Whitsell	1.50	.70
❑ 83 Spider Lockhart	2.00	.90
❑ 84 Dave Lloyd	1.50	.70
❑ 85 Roy Jefferson	2.00	.90
❑ 86 Jackie Smith	6.00	2.70
❑ 87 John David Crow	2.00	.90
❑ 88 Sonny Jurgensen	6.00	2.70
❑ 89 Ron Mix	3.00	1.35
❑ 90 Clem Daniels	2.00	.90
❑ 91 Cornell Gordon	1.50	.70
❑ 92 Tom Goode	1.50	.70
❑ 93 Bobby Bell	3.00	1.35
❑ 94 Walt Suggs	1.50	.70
❑ 95 Eric Crabtree	1.50	.70
❑ 96 Sherrill Headrick	1.50	.70
❑ 97 Wray Carlton	1.50	.70
❑ 98 Gino Cappelletti	2.00	.90
❑ 99 Tommy McDonald	3.00	1.35
❑ 100 John Unitas	25.00	11.00
❑ 101 Richie Petitbon	1.50	.70
❑ 102 Erich Barnes	1.50	.70
❑ 103 Bob Hayes	8.00	3.60
❑ 104 Milt Plum	2.00	.90
❑ 105 Boyd Dowler	2.00	.90
❑ 106 Ed Meador	1.50	.70
❑ 107 Fred Cox	1.50	.70
❑ 108 Steve Stonebreaker RC	1.50	.70
❑ 109 Aaron Thomas	1.50	.70
❑ 110 Norm Snead	2.00	.90
❑ 111 Paul Martha RC	1.50	.70
❑ 112 Jerry Stovall	1.50	.70
❑ 113 Kay McFarland	1.50	.70
❑ 114 Pat Richter	1.50	.70
❑ 115 Rick Redman	1.50	.70
❑ 116 Tom Keating	1.50	.70
❑ 117 Matt Snell	2.00	.90
❑ 118 Dick Westmoreland	1.50	.70
❑ 119 Jerry Mays	1.50	.70
❑ 120 Sid Blanks	1.50	.70
❑ 121 Al Denson	1.50	.70
❑ 122 Bobby Hunt	1.50	.70
❑ 123 Mike Mercer	1.50	.70
❑ 124 Nick Buoniconti	3.00	1.35
❑ 125 Ron Vanderkelen RC	1.50	.70
❑ 126 Ordell Braase	1.50	.70
❑ 127 Dick Butkus	45.00	20.00
❑ 128 Gary Collins	2.00	.90
❑ 129 Mel Renfro	6.00	2.70
❑ 130 Alex Karras	5.00	2.20
❑ 131 Herb Adderley	5.00	2.20
❑ 132 Roman Gabriel	4.00	1.80
❑ 133 Bill Brown	2.50	1.10
❑ 134 Kent Kramer	2.00	.90
❑ 135 Tucker Frederickson	2.50	1.10
❑ 136 Nate Ramsey	2.00	.90
❑ 137 Marv Woodson	2.00	.90
❑ 138 Ken Gray	2.00	.90
❑ 139 John Brodie	5.00	2.20
❑ 140 Jerry Smith	2.00	.90
❑ 141 Brad Hubbert	2.00	.90
❑ 142 George Blanda	20.00	9.00
❑ 143 Pete Lammons RC	2.00	.90
❑ 144 Doug Moreau	2.00	.90
❑ 145 E.J. Holub	2.00	.90
❑ 146 Ode Burrell	2.00	.90
❑ 147 Bob Scarpitto	2.00	.90
❑ 148 Andre White	2.00	.90
❑ 149 Jack Kemp	50.00	22.00
❑ 150 Art Graham	2.00	.90
❑ 151 Tommy Nobis	6.00	2.70
❑ 152 Willie Richardson RC	2.50	1.10
❑ 153 Jack Concannon	2.00	.90
❑ 154 Bill Glass	2.00	.90
❑ 155 Craig Morton RC	10.00	4.50
❑ 156 Pat Studstill	2.00	.90
❑ 157 Ray Nitschke	8.00	3.60
❑ 158 Roger Brown	2.00	.90
❑ 159 Joe Kapp RC**/C	5.00	2.20
❑ 160 Jim Taylor (Shown in uniform of Green Bay Packers)	12.00	5.50
❑ 161 Fran Tarkenton	15.00	6.75
❑ 162 Mike Ditka	25.00	11.00
❑ 163 Andy Russell RC	6.00	2.70
❑ 164 Larry Wilson	4.00	1.80
❑ 165 Tommy Davis	2.00	.90
❑ 166 Paul Krause	4.00	1.80
❑ 167 Speedy Duncan	2.00	.90
❑ 168 Fred Biletnikoff	12.00	5.50
❑ 169 Don Maynard	10.00	4.50
❑ 170 Frank Emanuel	2.00	.90
❑ 171 Len Dawson	15.00	6.75
❑ 172 Miller Farr	2.00	.90
❑ 173 Floyd Little RC	20.00	9.00
❑ 174 Lonnie Wright	2.00	.90
❑ 175 Paul Costa	2.00	.90
❑ 176 Don Trull	2.00	.90
❑ 177 Jerry Simmons	2.00	.90
❑ 178 Tom Matte	2.50	1.10
❑ 179 Bennie McRae	2.00	.90
❑ 180 Jim Kanicki	2.00	.90
❑ 181 Bob Lilly	12.00	5.50
❑ 182 Tom Watkins	2.00	.90
❑ 183 Jim Grabowski RC	4.00	1.80
❑ 184 Jack Snow RC	4.00	1.80
❑ 185 Gary Cuozzo RC	2.50	1.10
❑ 186 Bill Kilmer	4.00	1.80
❑ 187 Jim Katcavage	2.00	.90
❑ 188 Floyd Peters	2.00	.90
❑ 189 Bill Nelsen	2.50	1.10
❑ 190 Bobby Joe Conrad	2.50	1.10
❑ 191 Kermit Alexander	2.00	.90
❑ 192 Charley Taylor UER (Called Charley and Charlie on back)	6.00	2.70
❑ 193 Lance Alworth	20.00	9.00
❑ 194 Daryle Lamonica	5.00	2.20
❑ 195 Al Atkinson	2.00	.90
❑ 196 Bob Griese RC	80.00	36.00
❑ 197 Buck Buchanan	4.00	1.80
❑ 198 Pete Beathard	2.00	.90
❑ 199 Nemiah Wilson	2.00	.90
❑ 200 Ernie Wright	2.00	.90
❑ 201 George Saimes	2.00	.90
❑ 202 John Charles	2.00	.90
❑ 203 Randy Johnson	2.00	.90
❑ 204 Tony Lorick	2.00	.90
❑ 205 Dick Evey	2.00	.90
❑ 206 Leroy Kelly	10.00	4.50
❑ 207 Lee Roy Jordan	6.00	2.70
❑ 208 Jim Gibbons	2.00	.90
❑ 209 Donny Anderson RC	4.00	1.80
❑ 210 Maxie Baughan	2.00	.90
❑ 211 Joe Morrison	2.00	.90
❑ 212 Jim Snowden	2.00	.90
❑ 213 Lenny Lyles	2.00	.90
❑ 214 Bobby Joe Green	2.00	.90
❑ 215 Frank Ryan	2.50	1.10
❑ 216 Cornell Green	2.50	1.10
❑ 217 Karl Sweetan	2.00	.90
❑ 218 Dave Williams	2.00	.90
❑ 219A Checklist 132-218 (green print on back)	18.00	4.50
❑ 219B Checklist 132-218 (blue print on back)	20.00	5.00

1969 Topps

	NRMT	VG-E
COMPLETE SET (263)	550.00	250.00
COMMON CARD (1-132)	1.50	.70
SEMISTARS 1-132	2.00	.90
UNLISTED STARS 1-132	3.00	1.35
COMMON CARD (133-263)	2.00	.90
SEMISTARS 133-263	2.50	1.10
UNLISTED STARS 133-263	4.00	1.80

FIRST SERIES CONDITION SENSITIVE CARDS PRICED IN NM CONDITION

Card	NRMT	VG-E
❑ 1 Leroy Kelly	20.00	5.00
❑ 2 Paul Flatley	1.50	.70
❑ 3 Jim Cadile	1.50	.70
❑ 4 Erich Barnes	1.50	.70
❑ 5 Willie Richardson	1.50	.70
❑ 6 Bob Hayes	5.00	2.20
❑ 7 Bob Jeter	2.00	.90
❑ 8 Jim Colclough	1.50	.70
❑ 9 Sherrill Headrick	1.50	.70
❑ 10 Jim Dunaway	1.50	.70
❑ 11 Bill Munson	2.00	.90
❑ 12 Jack Pardee	2.00	.90
❑ 13 Jim Lindsey	1.50	.70
❑ 14 Dave Whitsell	1.50	.70
❑ 15 Tucker Frederickson	1.50	.70
❑ 16 Alvin Haymond	2.00	.90
❑ 17 Andy Russell	2.00	.90
❑ 18 Tom Beer	1.50	.70
❑ 19 Bobby Maples	1.50	.70
❑ 20 Len Dawson	8.00	3.60
❑ 21 Willis Crenshaw	1.50	.70
❑ 22 Tommy Davis	1.50	.70
❑ 23 Rickie Harris	1.50	.70
❑ 24 Jerry Simmons	1.50	.70
❑ 25 John Unitas	35.00	16.00
❑ 26 Brian Piccolo RC UER (Misspelled Bryon on front and Bryan on back)	80.00	36.00
❑ 27 Bob Matheson	1.50	.70
❑ 28 Howard Twilley	2.00	.90
❑ 29 Jim Turner	2.00	.90
❑ 30 Pete Banaszak RC	2.00	.90
❑ 31 Lance Rentzel RC	2.00	.90
❑ 32 Bill Triplett	1.50	.70
❑ 33 Boyd Dowler	2.00	.90
❑ 34 Merlin Olsen	5.00	2.20
❑ 35 Joe Kapp	3.00	1.35
❑ 36 Dan Abramowicz RC	4.00	1.80
❑ 37 Spider Lockhart	2.00	.90
❑ 38 Tom Day	1.50	.70
❑ 39 Art Graham	1.50	.70
❑ 40 Bob Cappadona	1.50	.70
❑ 41 Gary Ballman	1.50	.70
❑ 42 Clendon Thomas	1.50	.70
❑ 43 Jackie Smith	4.00	1.80
❑ 44 Dave Wilcox	3.00	1.35
❑ 45 Jerry Smith	1.50	.70
❑ 46 Dan Grimm	1.50	.70
❑ 47 Tom Matte	2.00	.90
❑ 48 John Stofa	1.50	.70
❑ 49 Rex Mirich	1.50	.70
❑ 50 Miller Farr	1.50	.70
❑ 51 Gale Sayers	40.00	18.00
❑ 52 Bill Nelsen	2.00	.90
❑ 53 Bob Lilly	6.00	2.70
❑ 54 Wayne Walker	1.50	.70
❑ 55 Ray Nitschke	5.00	2.20
❑ 56 Ed Meador	1.50	.70
❑ 57 Lonnie Warwick	1.50	.70
❑ 58 Wendell Hayes	1.50	.70
❑ 59 Dick Anderson RC	5.00	2.20
❑ 60 Don Maynard	6.00	2.70
❑ 61 Tony Lorick	1.50	.70
❑ 62 Pete Gogolak	1.50	.70
❑ 63 Nate Ramsey	1.50	.70
❑ 64 Dick Shiner	1.50	.70
❑ 65 Larry Wilson	3.00	1.35
❑ 66 Ken Willard	2.00	.90
❑ 67 Charley Taylor UER (Led Redskins in pass interceptions)	5.00	2.20
❑ 68 Billy Cannon	2.00	.90
❑ 69 Lance Alworth	8.00	3.60
❑ 70 Jim Nance	2.00	.90
❑ 71 Nick Rassas	1.50	.70
❑ 72 Lenny Lyles	1.50	.70
❑ 73 Bennie McRae	1.50	.70
❑ 74 Bill Glass	1.50	.70

Card	NRMT	VG-E
❑ 75 Don Meredith	25.00	11.00
❑ 76 Dick LeBeau	1.50	.70
❑ 77 Carroll Dale	2.00	.90
❑ 78 Ron McDole	1.50	.70
❑ 79 Charley King	1.50	.70
❑ 80 Checklist 1-132 UER (26 Bryon Piccolo)	15.00	3.70
❑ 81 Dick Bass	2.00	.90
❑ 82 Roy Winston	1.50	.70
❑ 83 Don McCall	1.50	.70
❑ 84 Jim Katcavage	2.00	.90
❑ 85 Norm Snead	2.00	.90
❑ 86 Earl Gros	1.50	.70
❑ 87 Don Brumm	1.50	.70
❑ 88 Sonny Bishop	1.50	.70
❑ 89 Fred Arbanas	1.50	.70
❑ 90 Karl Noonan	1.50	.70
❑ 91 Dick Witcher	1.50	.70
❑ 92 Vince Promuto	1.50	.70
❑ 93 Tommy Nobis	4.00	1.80
❑ 94 Jerry Hill	1.50	.70
❑ 95 Ed O'Bradovich RC	1.50	.70
❑ 96 Ernie Kellerman	1.50	.70
❑ 97 Chuck Howley	2.00	.90
❑ 98 Hewritt Dixon	1.50	.70
❑ 99 Ron Mix	3.00	1.35
❑ 100 Joe Namath	75.00	34.00
❑ 101 Billy Gambrell	1.50	.70
❑ 102 Elijah Pitts	2.00	.90
❑ 103 Billy Truax RC	2.00	.90
❑ 104 Ed Sharockman	1.50	.70
❑ 105 Doug Atkins	3.00	1.35
❑ 106 Greg Larson	1.50	.70
❑ 107 Israel Lang	1.50	.70
❑ 108 Houston Antwine	1.50	.70
❑ 109 Paul Guidry	1.50	.70
❑ 110 Al Denson	1.50	.70
❑ 111 Roy Jefferson	2.00	.90
❑ 112 Chuck Latourette	1.50	.70
❑ 113 Jim Johnson	3.00	1.35
❑ 114 Bobby Mitchell	4.00	1.80
❑ 115 Randy Johnson	1.50	.70
❑ 116 Lou Michaels	1.50	.70
❑ 117 Rudy Kuechenberg	1.50	.70
❑ 118 Walt Suggs	1.50	.70
❑ 119 Goldie Sellers	1.50	.70
❑ 120 Larry Csonka RC !	75.00	34.00
❑ 121 Jim Houston	1.50	.70
❑ 122 Craig Baynham	1.50	.70
❑ 123 Alex Karras	5.00	2.20
❑ 124 Jim Grabowski	2.00	.90
❑ 125 Roman Gabriel	3.00	1.35
❑ 126 Larry Bowie	1.50	.70
❑ 127 Dave Parks	2.00	.90
❑ 128 Ben Davidson	3.00	1.35
❑ 129 Steve DeLong	1.50	.70
❑ 130 Fred Hill	1.50	.70
❑ 131 Ernie Koy	2.00	.90
❑ 132A Checklist 133-263 (no border)	15.00	3.70
❑ 132B Checklist 133-263 (thin white border like second series)	20.00	5.00
❑ 133 Dick Hoak	2.00	.90
❑ 134 Larry Stallings RC	2.00	.90
❑ 135 Clifton McNeil RC	2.00	.90
❑ 136 Walter Rock	2.00	.90
❑ 137 Billy Lothridge	2.00	.90
❑ 138 Bob Vogel	2.00	.90
❑ 139 Dick Butkus	40.00	18.00
❑ 140 Frank Ryan	2.50	1.10
❑ 141 Larry Garron	2.00	.90
❑ 142 George Saimes	2.00	.90
❑ 143 Frank Buncom	2.00	.90
❑ 144 Don Perkins	2.50	1.10
❑ 145 Johnnie Robinson UER (Misspelled Johnny)	2.00	.90
❑ 146 Lee Roy Caffey	2.50	1.10
❑ 147 Bernie Casey	2.50	1.10
❑ 148 Billy Martin E	2.00	.90
❑ 149 Gene Howard	2.00	.90
❑ 150 Fran Tarkenton	15.00	6.75
❑ 151 Eric Crabtree	2.00	.90
❑ 152 W.K. Hicks	2.00	.90
❑ 153 Bobby Bell	4.00	1.80
❑ 154 Sam Baker	2.00	.90
❑ 155 Marv Woodson	2.00	.90
❑ 156 Dave Williams	2.00	.90
❑ 157 Bruce Bosley UER (Considered one of the three centers in all of pro football)	2.00	.90
❑ 158 Carl Kammerer	2.00	.90
❑ 159 Jim Burson	2.00	.90
❑ 160 Roy Hilton	2.00	.90
❑ 161 Bob Griese	25.00	11.00
❑ 162 Bob Talamini	2.00	.90
❑ 163 Jim Otto	4.00	1.80
❑ 164 Ron Bull	2.00	.90
❑ 165 Walter Johnson RC	2.00	.90
❑ 166 Lee Roy Jordan	4.00	1.80
❑ 167 Mike Lucci	2.50	1.10
❑ 168 Willie Wood	4.00	1.80
❑ 169 Maxie Baughan	2.00	.90
❑ 170 Bill Brown	2.50	1.10
❑ 171 John Hadl	4.00	1.80
❑ 172 Gino Cappelletti	2.50	1.10
❑ 173 George Butch Byrd	2.50	1.10
❑ 174 Steve Stonebreaker	2.00	.90
❑ 175 Joe Morrison	2.00	.90
❑ 176 Joe Scarpati	2.00	.90
❑ 177 Bobby Walden	2.00	.90
❑ 178 Roy Shivers	2.00	.90
❑ 179 Kermit Alexander	2.00	.90
❑ 180 Pat Richter	2.00	.90
❑ 181 Pete Perreault	2.00	.90
❑ 182 Pete Duranko	2.00	.90
❑ 183 Leroy Mitchell	2.00	.90
❑ 184 Jim Simon	2.00	.90
❑ 185 Billy Ray Smith	2.00	.90
❑ 186 Jack Concannon	2.00	.90
❑ 187 Ben Davis	2.00	.90
❑ 188 Mike Clark	2.00	.90
❑ 189 Jim Gibbons	2.00	.90
❑ 190 Dave Robinson	2.50	1.10
❑ 191 Otis Taylor	2.50	1.10
❑ 192 Nick Buoniconti	4.00	1.80
❑ 193 Matt Snell	2.50	1.10
❑ 194 Bruce Gossett	2.00	.90
❑ 195 Mick Tingelhoff	2.50	1.10
❑ 196 Earl Leggett	2.00	.90
❑ 197 Pete Case	2.00	.90
❑ 198 Tom Woodeshick RC	2.00	.90
❑ 199 Ken Kortas	2.00	.90
❑ 200 Jim Hart	4.00	1.80
❑ 201 Fred Biletnikoff	10.00	4.50
❑ 202 Jacque MacKinnon	2.00	.90
❑ 203 Jim Whalen	2.00	.90
❑ 204 Matt Hazeltine	2.00	.90
❑ 205 Charlie Gogolak	2.00	.90
❑ 206 Ray Ogden	2.00	.90
❑ 207 John Mackey	4.00	1.80
❑ 208 Roosevelt Taylor	2.00	.90
❑ 209 Gene Hickerson	2.00	.90
❑ 210 Dave Edwards RC	2.50	1.10
❑ 211 Tom Sestak	2.00	.90
❑ 212 Ernie Wright	2.00	.90
❑ 213 Dave Costa	2.00	.90
❑ 214 Tom Vaughn	2.00	.90
❑ 215 Bart Starr	25.00	11.00
❑ 216 Les Josephson	2.00	.90
❑ 217 Fred Cox	2.00	.90
❑ 218 Mike Tilleman	2.00	.90
❑ 219 Darrell Dess	2.00	.90
❑ 220 Dave Lloyd	2.00	.90
❑ 221 Pete Beathard	2.00	.90
❑ 222 Buck Buchanan	4.00	1.80
❑ 223 Frank Emanuel	2.00	.90
❑ 224 Paul Martha	2.00	.90
❑ 225 Johnny Roland	2.00	.90
❑ 226 Gary Lewis	2.00	.90
❑ 227 Sonny Jurgensen UER (Chiefs logo)	6.00	2.70
❑ 228 Jim Butler	2.00	.90
❑ 229 Mike Curtis RC	6.00	2.70
❑ 230 Richie Petitbon	2.00	.90
❑ 231 George Sauer Jr.	2.50	1.10
❑ 232 George Blanda	20.00	9.00
❑ 233 Gary Garrison	2.00	.90
❑ 234 Gary Collins	2.50	1.10
❑ 235 Craig Morton	4.00	1.80
❑ 236 Tom Nowatzke	2.00	.90
❑ 237 Donny Anderson	2.50	1.10
❑ 238 Deacon Jones	4.00	1.80
❑ 239 Grady Alderman	2.00	.90
❑ 240 Bill Kilmer	4.00	1.80
❑ 241 Mike Taliaferro	2.00	.90
❑ 242 Stew Barber	2.00	.90
❑ 243 Bobby Hunt	2.00	.90
❑ 244 Homer Jones	2.00	.90
❑ 245 Bob Brown OT	2.50	1.10
❑ 246 Bill Asbury	2.00	.90
❑ 247 Charlie Johnson UER (Misspelled Charley on both sides)	2.50	1.10
❑ 248 Chris Hanburger	2.50	1.10
❑ 249 John Brodie	6.00	2.70
❑ 250 Earl Morrall	2.50	1.10
❑ 251 Floyd Little	5.00	2.20
❑ 252 Jerrel Wilson RC	2.00	.90
❑ 253 Jim Keyes	2.00	.90
❑ 254 Mel Renfro	4.00	1.80
❑ 255 Herb Adderley	4.00	1.80
❑ 256 Jack Snow	2.50	1.10
❑ 257 Charlie Durkee	2.00	.90
❑ 258 Charlie Harper	2.00	.90
❑ 259 J.R. Wilburn	2.00	.90
❑ 260 Charlie Krueger	2.00	.90
❑ 261 Pete Jacques	2.00	.90
❑ 262 Gerry Philbin	2.00	.90
❑ 263 Daryle Lamonica	10.00	2.50

1970 Topps

	NRMT	VG-E
COMPLETE SET (263)	475.00	210.00
COMMON CARD (1-132)	1.00	.45
SEMISTARS 1-132	1.50	.70
UNLISTED STARS 1-132	2.50	1.10
COMMON CARD (133-263)	1.25	.55
SEMISTARS 133-263	2.00	.90
UNLISTED STARS 133-263	3.00	1.35

CARDS PRICED IN NM CONDITION

Card	NRMT	VG-E
❑ 1 Len Dawson UER (Cartoon caption says, "AFL AN NFL")	20.00	5.00
❑ 2 Doug Hart	1.00	.45
❑ 3 Verlon Biggs	1.00	.45
❑ 4 Ralph Neely RC	1.50	.70
❑ 5 Harmon Wages	1.00	.45
❑ 6 Dan Conners	1.00	.45
❑ 7 Gino Cappelletti	1.50	.70
❑ 8 Erich Barnes	1.00	.45
❑ 9 Checklist 1-132	10.00	2.50
❑ 10 Bob Griese	15.00	6.75
❑ 11 Ed Flanagan	1.00	.45
❑ 12 George Seals	1.00	.45
❑ 13 Harry Jacobs	1.00	.45
❑ 14 Mike Haffner	1.00	.45
❑ 15 Bob Vogel	1.00	.45
❑ 16 Bill Peterson	1.00	.45
❑ 17 Spider Lockhart	1.00	.45
❑ 18 Billy Truax	1.00	.45
❑ 19 Jim Beirne	1.00	.45
❑ 20 Leroy Kelly	6.00	2.70
❑ 21 Dave Lloyd	1.00	.45
❑ 22 Mike Tilleman	1.00	.45
❑ 23 Gary Garrison	1.00	.45
❑ 24 Larry Brown RC	8.00	3.60

No.	Card	NRMT	VG-E
❑ 25	Jan Stenerud RC	12.00	5.50
❑ 26	Rolf Krueger	1.00	.45
❑ 27	Roland Lakes	1.00	.45
❑ 28	Dick Hoak	1.00	.45
❑ 29	Gene Washington RC	2.50	1.10
❑ 30	Bart Starr	20.00	9.00
❑ 31	Dave Grayson	1.00	.45
❑ 32	Jerry Rush	1.00	.45
❑ 33	Len St. Jean	1.00	.45
❑ 34	Randy Edmunds	1.00	.45
❑ 35	Matt Snell	1.50	.70
❑ 36	Paul Costa	1.00	.45
❑ 37	Mike Pyle	1.00	.45
❑ 38	Roy Hilton	1.00	.45
❑ 39	Steve Tensi	1.00	.45
❑ 40	Tommy Nobis	2.50	1.10
❑ 41	Pete Case	1.00	.45
❑ 42	Andy Rice	1.00	.45
❑ 43	Elvin Bethea RC	2.50	1.10
❑ 44	Jack Snow	1.50	.70
❑ 45	Mel Renfro	2.50	1.10
❑ 46	Andy Livingston	1.00	.45
❑ 47	Gary Ballman	1.00	.45
❑ 48	Bob DeMarco	1.00	.45
❑ 49	Steve DeLong	1.00	.45
❑ 50	Daryle Lamonica	4.00	1.80
❑ 51	Jim Lynch RC	1.00	.45
❑ 52	Mel Farr RC	1.00	.45
❑ 53	Bob Long	1.00	.45
❑ 54	John Elliott	1.00	.45
❑ 55	Ray Nitschke	5.00	2.20
❑ 56	Jim Shorter	1.00	.45
❑ 57	Dave Wilcox	2.50	1.10
❑ 58	Eric Crabtree	1.00	.45
❑ 59	Alan Page RC	25.00	11.00
❑ 60	Jim Nance	1.50	.70
❑ 61	Glen Ray Hines	1.00	.45
❑ 62	John Mackey	2.50	1.10
❑ 63	Ron McDole	1.00	.45
❑ 64	Tom Beier	1.00	.45
❑ 65	Bill Nelsen	1.50	.70
❑ 66	Paul Flatley	1.00	.45
❑ 67	Sam Brunelli	1.00	.45
❑ 68	Jack Pardee	1.50	.70
❑ 69	Brig Owens	1.00	.45
❑ 70	Gale Sayers	25.00	11.00
❑ 71	Lee Roy Jordan	2.50	1.10
❑ 72	Harold Jackson RC	5.00	2.20
❑ 73	John Hadl	2.50	1.10
❑ 74	Dave Parks	1.00	.45
❑ 75	Lem Barney RC	14.00	6.25
❑ 76	Johnny Roland	1.00	.45
❑ 77	Ed Budde	1.00	.45
❑ 78	Ben McGee	1.00	.45
❑ 79	Ken Bowman	1.00	.45
❑ 80	Fran Tarkenton	15.00	6.75
❑ 81	Gene Washington RC	5.00	2.20
❑ 82	Larry Grantham	1.00	.45
❑ 83	Bill Brown	1.50	.70
❑ 84	John Charles	1.00	.45
❑ 85	Fred Biletnikoff	7.00	3.10
❑ 86	Royce Berry	1.00	.45
❑ 87	Bob Lilly	5.00	2.20
❑ 88	Earl Morrall	1.50	.70
❑ 89	Jerry LeVias RC	1.50	.70
❑ 90	O.J. Simpson RC !	70.00	32.00
❑ 91	Mike Howell	1.00	.45
❑ 92	Ken Gray	1.00	.45
❑ 93	Chris Hanburger	1.00	.45
❑ 94	Larry Seiple RC	1.00	.45
❑ 95	Rich Jackson RC	1.00	.45
❑ 96	Rockne Freitas	1.00	.45
❑ 97	Dick Post RC	1.50	.70
❑ 98	Ben Hawkins	1.00	.45
❑ 99	Ken Reaves	1.00	.45
❑ 100	Roman Gabriel	2.50	1.10
❑ 101	Dave Rowe	1.00	.45
❑ 102	Dave Robinson	1.00	.45
❑ 103	Otis Taylor	1.50	.70
❑ 104	Jim Turner	1.00	.45
❑ 105	Joe Morrison	1.00	.45
❑ 106	Dick Evey	1.00	.45
❑ 107	Ray Mansfield	1.00	.45
❑ 108	Grady Alderman	1.00	.45
❑ 109	Bruce Gossett	1.00	.45
❑ 110	Bob Trumpy RC	4.00	1.80
❑ 111	Jim Hunt	1.00	.45
❑ 112	Larry Stallings	1.00	.45
❑ 113A	Lance Rentzel (name in red)	1.50	.70
❑ 113B	Lance Rentzel (name in black)	1.50	.70
❑ 114	Bubba Smith RC	25.00	11.00
❑ 115	Norm Snead	1.50	.70
❑ 116	Jim Otto	2.50	1.10
❑ 117	Bo Scott RC**/C	1.00	.45
❑ 118	Rick Redman	1.00	.45
❑ 119	George Butch Byrd	1.00	.45
❑ 120	George Webster RC	1.50	.70
❑ 121	Chuck Walton	1.00	.45
❑ 122	Dave Costa	1.00	.45
❑ 123	Al Dodd	1.00	.45
❑ 124	Len Hauss	1.00	.45
❑ 125	Deacon Jones	2.50	1.10
❑ 126	Randy Johnson	1.00	.45
❑ 127	Ralph Heck	1.00	.45
❑ 128	Emerson Boozer RC	1.50	.70
❑ 129	Johnny Robinson	1.50	.70
❑ 130	John Brodie	5.00	2.20
❑ 131	Gale Gillingham RC	1.00	.45
❑ 132	Checklist 133-263 DP UER (145 Charley Taylor misspelled Charlie)	6.00	1.50
❑ 133	Chuck Walker	1.25	.55
❑ 134	Bennie McRae	1.25	.55
❑ 135	Paul Warfield	7.00	3.10
❑ 136	Dan Darragh	1.25	.55
❑ 137	Paul Robinson RC	1.25	.55
❑ 138	Ed Philpott	1.25	.55
❑ 139	Craig Morton	3.00	1.35
❑ 140	Tom Dempsey RC	2.00	.90
❑ 141	Al Nelson	1.25	.55
❑ 142	Tom Matte	2.00	.90
❑ 143	Dick Schafrath	1.25	.55
❑ 144	Willie Brown	4.00	1.80
❑ 145	Charley Taylor UER (Misspelled Charlie on both sides)	5.00	2.20
❑ 146	John Huard	1.25	.55
❑ 147	Dave Osborn	1.25	.55
❑ 148	Gene Mingo	1.25	.55
❑ 149	Larry Hand	1.25	.55
❑ 150	Joe Namath	50.00	22.00
❑ 151	Tom Mack RC	7.00	3.10
❑ 152	Kenny Graham	1.25	.55
❑ 153	Don Herrmann	1.25	.55
❑ 154	Bobby Bell	3.00	1.35
❑ 155	Hoyle Granger	1.25	.55
❑ 156	Claude Humphrey RC	2.00	.90
❑ 157	Clifton McNeil	1.25	.55
❑ 158	Mick Tingelhoff	2.00	.90
❑ 159	Don Horn RC	1.25	.55
❑ 160	Larry Wilson	3.00	1.35
❑ 161	Tom Neville	1.25	.55
❑ 162	Larry Csonka	20.00	9.00
❑ 163	Doug Buffone RC	1.25	.55
❑ 164	Cornell Green	2.00	.90
❑ 165	Haven Moses RC	2.00	.90
❑ 166	Bill Kilmer	3.00	1.35
❑ 167	Tim Rossovich RC	1.25	.55
❑ 168	Bill Bergey RC	4.00	1.80
❑ 169	Gary Collins	2.00	.90
❑ 170	Floyd Little	3.00	1.35
❑ 171	Tom Keating	1.25	.55
❑ 172	Pat Fischer	1.25	.55
❑ 173	Walt Sweeney	1.25	.55
❑ 174	Greg Larson	1.25	.55
❑ 175	Carl Eller	2.00	.90
❑ 176	George Sauer Jr.	2.00	.90
❑ 177	Jim Hart	3.00	1.35
❑ 178	Bob Brown OT	1.25	.55
❑ 179	Mike Garrett RC	2.00	.90
❑ 180	John Unitas	25.00	11.00
❑ 181	Tom Regner	1.25	.55
❑ 182	Bob Jeter	1.25	.55
❑ 183	Gail Cogdill	1.25	.55
❑ 184	Earl Gros	1.25	.55
❑ 185	Dennis Partee	1.25	.55
❑ 186	Charlie Krueger	1.25	.55
❑ 187	Martin Baccaglio	1.25	.55
❑ 188	Charles Long	1.25	.55
❑ 189	Bob Hayes	4.00	1.80
❑ 190	Dick Butkus	25.00	11.00
❑ 191	Al Bemiller	1.25	.55
❑ 192	Dick Westmoreland	1.25	.55
❑ 193	Joe Scarpati	1.25	.55
❑ 194	Ron Snidow	1.25	.55
❑ 195	Earl McCullouch RC	1.25	.55
❑ 196	Jake Kupp	1.25	.55
❑ 197	Bob Lurtsema	1.25	.55
❑ 198	Mike Current	1.25	.55
❑ 199	Charlie Smith	1.25	.55
❑ 200	Sonny Jurgensen	6.00	2.70
❑ 201	Mike Curtis	2.00	.90
❑ 202	Aaron Brown	1.25	.55
❑ 203	Richie Petitbon	1.25	.55
❑ 204	Walt Suggs	1.25	.55
❑ 205	Roy Jefferson	1.25	.55
❑ 206	Russ Washington RC	1.25	.55
❑ 207	Woody Peoples RC	1.25	.55
❑ 208	Dave Williams	1.25	.55
❑ 209	John Zook RC	1.25	.55
❑ 210	Tom Woodeshick	1.25	.55
❑ 211	Howard Fest	1.25	.55
❑ 212	Jack Concannon	1.25	.55
❑ 213	Jim Marshall	3.00	1.35
❑ 214	Jon Morris	1.25	.55
❑ 215	Dan Abramowicz	2.00	.90
❑ 216	Paul Martha	1.25	.55
❑ 217	Ken Willard	1.25	.55
❑ 218	Walter Rock	1.25	.55
❑ 219	Garland Boyette	1.25	.55
❑ 220	Buck Buchanan	3.00	1.35
❑ 221	Bill Munson	2.00	.90
❑ 222	David Lee RC	1.25	.55
❑ 223	Karl Noonan	1.25	.55
❑ 224	Harry Schuh	1.25	.55
❑ 225	Jackie Smith	3.00	1.35
❑ 226	Gerry Philbin	1.25	.55
❑ 227	Ernie Koy	1.25	.55
❑ 228	Chuck Howley	2.00	.90
❑ 229	Billy Shaw	3.00	1.35
❑ 230	Jerry Hillebrand	1.25	.55
❑ 231	Bill Thompson RC	2.00	.90
❑ 232	Carroll Dale	2.00	.90
❑ 233	Gene Hickerson	1.25	.55
❑ 234	Jim Butler	1.25	.55
❑ 235	Greg Cook RC	1.25	.55
❑ 236	Lee Roy Caffey	1.25	.55
❑ 237	Merlin Olsen	4.00	1.80
❑ 238	Fred Cox	1.25	.55
❑ 239	Nate Ramsey	1.25	.55
❑ 240	Lance Alworth	7.00	3.10
❑ 241	Chuck Hinton	1.25	.55
❑ 242	Jerry Smith	1.25	.55
❑ 243	Tony Baker	1.25	.55
❑ 244	Nick Buoniconti	2.00	.90
❑ 245	Jim Johnson	3.00	1.35
❑ 246	Willie Richardson	1.25	.55
❑ 247	Fred Dryer RC	10.00	4.50
❑ 248	Bobby Maples	1.25	.55
❑ 249	Alex Karras	4.00	1.80
❑ 250	Joe Kapp	2.00	.90
❑ 251	Ben Davidson	3.00	1.35
❑ 252	Mike Stratton	1.25	.55
❑ 253	Les Josephson	1.25	.55
❑ 254	Don Maynard	6.00	2.70
❑ 255	Houston Antwine	1.25	.55
❑ 256	Mac Percival RC	1.25	.55
❑ 257	George Goeddeke	1.25	.55
❑ 258	Homer Jones	1.25	.55
❑ 259	Bob Berry	1.25	.55
❑ 260A	Calvin Hill RC (Name in red)	15.00	6.75
❑ 260B	Calvin Hill RC (Name in black)	20.00	9.00
❑ 261	Willie Wood	3.00	1.35
❑ 262	Ed Weisacosky	1.25	.55
❑ 263	Jim Tyrer	3.00	.75

1971 Topps

	NRMT	VG-E
COMPLETE SET (263)	500.00	220.00
COMMON CARD (1-132)	.75	.35
SEMISTARS 1-132	1.25	.55
UNLISTED STARS 1-132	2.00	.90
COMMON CARD (133-263)	1.00	.45

SEMISTARS 133-263 .... 1.50 .70
UNLISTED STARS 133-263 ...... 2.50 1.10
CONDITION SENSITIVE SET ......
CARDS PRICED IN NM CONDITION

❑ 1 John Unitas 30.00 7.50
❑ 2 Jim Butler .... .75 .35
❑ 3 Marty Schottenheimer RC 12.00 5.50
❑ 4 Joe O'Donnell .... .75 .35
❑ 5 Tom Dempsey .... 1.25 .55
❑ 6 Chuck Allen .... .75 .35
❑ 7 Ernie Kellerman .... .75 .35
❑ 8 Walt Garrison RC .... 2.00 .90
❑ 9 Bill Van Heusen .... .75 .35
❑ 10 Lance Alworth 8.00 3.60
❑ 11 Greg Landry RC .... 2.00 .90
❑ 12 Larry Krause .... .75 .35
❑ 13 Buck Buchanan .... 2.00 .90
❑ 14 Roy Gerela RC .... 1.25 .55
❑ 15 Clifton McNeil .... .75 .35
❑ 16 Bob Brown OT .... .75 .35
❑ 17 Lloyd Mumphord .... .75 .35
❑ 18 Gary Cuozzo .... .75 .35
❑ 19 Don Maynard 5.00 2.20
❑ 20 Larry Wilson .... 2.00 .90
❑ 21 Charlie Smith .... .75 .35
❑ 22 Ken Avery .... .75 .35
❑ 23 Billy Walik .... .75 .35
❑ 24 Jim Johnson .... 2.00 .90
❑ 25 Dick Butkus 25.00 11.00
❑ 26 Charley Taylor UER 4.00 1.80
(Misspelled Charlie
on both sides)
❑ 27 Checklist 1-132 UER 8.00 2.00
(26 Charlie Taylor
should be Charley)
❑ 28 Lionel Aldridge RC .... .75 .35
❑ 29 Billy Lothridge .... .75 .35
❑ 30 Terry Hanratty RC .... 1.25 .55
❑ 31 Lee Roy Jordan .... 2.00 .90
❑ 32 Rick Volk RC .... .75 .35
❑ 33 Howard Kindig .... .75 .35
❑ 34 Carl Garrett RC .... .75 .35
❑ 35 Bobby Bell .... 2.00 .90
❑ 36 Gene Hickerson .... .75 .35
❑ 37 Dave Parks .... .75 .35
❑ 38 Paul Martha .... .75 .35
❑ 39 George Blanda 15.00 6.75
❑ 40 Tom Woodeshick .... .75 .35
❑ 41 Alex Karras 3.00 1.35
❑ 42 Rick Redman .... .75 .35
❑ 43 Zeke Moore .... .75 .35
❑ 44 Jack Snow .... 1.25 .55
❑ 45 Larry Csonka 15.00 6.75
❑ 46 Karl Kassulke .... .75 .35
❑ 47 Jim Hart .... 2.00 .90
❑ 48 Al Atkinson .... .75 .35
❑ 49 Horst Muhlmann RC .... .75 .35
❑ 50 Sonny Jurgensen 5.00 2.20
❑ 51 Ron Johnson RC .... 1.25 .55
❑ 52 Cas Banaszek .... .75 .35
❑ 53 Bubba Smith 8.00 3.60
❑ 54 Bobby Douglass RC ...... 1.25 .55
❑ 55 Willie Wood .... 2.00 .90
❑ 56 Bake Turner .... .75 .35
❑ 57 Mike Morgan .... .75 .35
❑ 58 George Butch Byrd .... 1.25 .55
❑ 59 Don Horn .... .75 .35
❑ 60 Tommy Nobis .... 2.00 .90
❑ 61 Jan Stenerud 4.00 1.80
❑ 62 Altie Taylor RC .... .75 .35
❑ 63 Gary Pettigrew .... .75 .35
❑ 64 Spike Jones .... .75 .35
❑ 65 Duane Thomas RC .... 2.00 .90
❑ 66 Marty Domres RC .... .75 .35
❑ 67 Dick Anderson .... 1.25 .55
❑ 68 Ken Iman .... .75 .35
❑ 69 Miller Farr .... .75 .35
❑ 70 Daryle Lamonica 3.00 1.35
❑ 71 Alan Page 12.00 5.50
❑ 72 Pat Matson .... .75 .35
❑ 73 Emerson Boozer .... .75 .35
❑ 74 Pat Fischer .... .75 .35
❑ 75 Gary Collins .... 1.25 .55
❑ 76 John Fuqua RC .... 1.25 .55
❑ 77 Bruce Gossett .... .75 .35
❑ 78 Ed O'Bradovich .... .75 .35
❑ 79 Bob Tucker RC .... 1.25 .55
❑ 80 Mike Curtis .... 1.25 .55
❑ 81 Rich Jackson .... .75 .35
❑ 82 Tom Janik .... .75 .35
❑ 83 Gale Gillingham .... .75 .35
❑ 84 Jim Mitchell .... .75 .35
❑ 85 Charlie Johnson .... 1.25 .55
❑ 86 Edgar Chandler .... .75 .35
❑ 87 Cyril Pinder .... .75 .35
❑ 88 Johnny Robinson .... 1.25 .55
❑ 89 Ralph Neely .... .75 .35
❑ 90 Dan Abramowicz .... .75 .35
❑ 91 Mercury Morris RC 5.00 2.20
❑ 92 Steve DeLong .... .75 .35
❑ 93 Larry Stallings .... .75 .35
❑ 94 Tom Mack .... 2.00 .90
❑ 95 Hewritt Dixon .... .75 .35
❑ 96 Fred Cox .... .75 .35
❑ 97 Chris Hanburger .... .75 .35
❑ 98 Gerry Philbin .... .75 .35
❑ 99 Ernie Wright .... .75 .35
❑ 100 John Brodie 4.00 1.80
❑ 101 Tucker Frederickson ...... .75 .35
❑ 102 Bobby Walden .... .75 .35
❑ 103 Dick Gordon .... .75 .35
❑ 104 Walter Johnson .... .75 .35
❑ 105 Mike Lucci .... 1.25 .55
❑ 106 Checklist 133-263 DP .. 6.00 1.50
❑ 107 Ron Berger .... .75 .35
❑ 108 Dan Sullivan .... .75 .35
❑ 109 George Kunz RC .... .75 .35
❑ 110 Floyd Little .... 2.00 .90
❑ 111 Zeke Bratkowski .... 1.25 .55
❑ 112 Haven Moses .... 1.25 .55
❑ 113 Ken Houston RC 15.00 6.75
❑ 114 Willie Lanier RC 15.00 6.75
❑ 115 Larry Brown .... 2.00 .90
❑ 116 Tim Rossovich .... .75 .35
❑ 117 Errol Linden .... .75 .35
❑ 118 Mel Renfro .... 2.00 .90
❑ 119 Mike Garrett .... .75 .35
❑ 120 Fran Tarkenton 15.00 6.75
❑ 121 Garo Yepremian RC .... 2.00 .90
❑ 122 Glen Condren .... .75 .35
❑ 123 Johnny Roland .... .75 .35
❑ 124 Dave Herman .... .75 .35
❑ 125 Merlin Olsen 3.00 1.35
❑ 126 Doug Buffone .... .75 .35
❑ 127 Earl McCullouch .... .75 .35
❑ 128 Spider Lockhart .... .75 .35
❑ 129 Ken Willard .... .75 .35
❑ 130 Gene Washington .... .75 .35
❑ 131 Mike Phipps RC .... 1.25 .55
❑ 132 Andy Russell .... 1.25 .55
❑ 133 Ray Nitschke 4.00 1.80
❑ 134 Jerry Logan .... 1.00 .45
❑ 135 MacArthur Lane RC .... 1.50 .70
❑ 136 Jim Turner .... 1.00 .45
❑ 137 Kent McCloughan .... 1.00 .45
❑ 138 Paul Guidry .... 1.00 .45
❑ 139 Otis Taylor .... 1.50 .70
❑ 140 Virgil Carter RC .... 1.00 .45
❑ 141 Joe Dawkins .... 1.00 .45
❑ 142 Steve Preece .... 1.00 .45
❑ 143 Mike Bragg RC .... 1.00 .45
❑ 144 Bob Lilly 5.00 2.20
❑ 145 Joe Kapp .... 1.50 .70
❑ 146 Al Dodd .... 1.00 .45
❑ 147 Nick Buoniconti 2.50 1.10
❑ 148 Speedy Duncan .... 1.00 .45
(Back mentions his
trade to Redskins)
❑ 149 Cedrick Hardman RC .. 1.00 .45
❑ 150 Gale Sayers 25.00 11.00
❑ 151 Jim Otto 2.50 1.10
❑ 152 Billy Truax .... 1.00 .45
❑ 153 John Elliott .... 1.00 .45
❑ 154 Dick LeBeau .... 1.00 .45
❑ 155 Bill Bergey .... 1.50 .70
❑ 156 Terry Bradshaw RC ! 150.00 70.00
❑ 157 Leroy Kelly 6.00 2.70
❑ 158 Paul Krause 2.50 1.10
❑ 159 Ted Vactor .... 1.00 .45
❑ 160 Bob Griese 15.00 6.75
❑ 161 Ernie McMillan .... 1.00 .45
❑ 162 Donny Anderson .... 1.50 .70
❑ 163 John Pitts .... 1.00 .45
❑ 164 Dave Costa .... 1.00 .45
❑ 165 Gene Washington .... 1.50 .70
❑ 166 John Zook .... 1.00 .45
❑ 167 Pete Gogolak .... 1.00 .45
❑ 168 Erich Barnes .... 1.00 .45
❑ 169 Alvin Reed .... 1.00 .45
❑ 170 Jim Nance .... 1.50 .70
❑ 171 Craig Morton 2.50 1.10
❑ 172 Gary Garrison .... 1.00 .45
❑ 173 Joe Scarpati .... 1.00 .45
❑ 174 Adrian Young UER ...... 1.00 .45
(Photo actually
Rick Duncan)
❑ 175 John Mackey 2.50 1.10
❑ 176 Mac Percival .... 1.00 .45
❑ 177 Preston Pearson RC 4.00 1.80
❑ 178 Fred Biletnikoff 8.00 3.60
❑ 179 Mike Battle RC .... 1.00 .45
❑ 180 Len Dawson 8.00 3.60
❑ 181 Les Josephson .... 1.00 .45
❑ 182 Royce Berry .... 1.00 .45
❑ 183 Herman Weaver .... 1.00 .45
❑ 184 Norm Snead .... 1.50 .70
❑ 185 Sam Brunelli .... 1.00 .45
❑ 186 Jim Kiick RC 5.00 2.20
❑ 187 Austin Denney .... 1.00 .45
❑ 188 Roger Wehrli RC .... 1.50 .70
❑ 189 Dave Wilcox 2.50 1.10
❑ 190 Bob Hayes 2.50 1.10
❑ 191 Joe Morrison .... 1.00 .45
❑ 192 Manny Sistrunk .... 1.00 .45
❑ 193 Don Cockroft RC .... 1.00 .45
❑ 194 Lee Bouggess .... 1.00 .45
❑ 195 Bob Berry .... 1.00 .45
❑ 196 Ron Sellers .... 1.00 .45
❑ 197 George Webster .... 1.00 .45
❑ 198 Hoyle Granger .... 1.00 .45
❑ 199 Bob Vogel .... 1.00 .45
❑ 200 Bart Starr 20.00 9.00
❑ 201 Mike Mercer .... 1.00 .45
❑ 202 Dave Smith .... 1.00 .45
❑ 203 Lee Roy Caffey .... 1.00 .45
❑ 204 Mick Tingelhoff .... 1.50 .70
❑ 205 Matt Snell .... 1.50 .70
❑ 206 Jim Tyrer .... 1.00 .45
❑ 207 Willie Brown 2.50 1.10
❑ 208 Bob Johnson RC .... 1.00 .45
❑ 209 Deacon Jones 2.50 1.10
❑ 210 Charlie Sanders RC .... 1.50 .70
❑ 211 Jake Scott RC 6.00 2.70
❑ 212 Bob Anderson RC .... 1.00 .45
❑ 213 Charlie Krueger .... 1.00 .45
❑ 214 Jim Bakken .... 1.00 .45
❑ 215 Harold Jackson .... 1.50 .70
❑ 216 Bill Brundige .... 1.00 .45
❑ 217 Calvin Hill 5.00 2.20
❑ 218 Claude Humphrey .... 1.00 .45
❑ 219 Glen Ray Hines .... 1.00 .45
❑ 220 Bill Nelsen .... 1.50 .70
❑ 221 Roy Hilton .... 1.00 .45
❑ 222 Don Herrmann .... 1.00 .45
❑ 223 John Bramlett .... 1.00 .45
❑ 224 Ken Ellis .... 1.00 .45
❑ 225 Dave Osborn .... 1.50 .70
❑ 226 Edd Hargett RC .... 1.00 .45
❑ 227 Gene Mingo .... 1.00 .45

❑ 228 Larry Grantham 1.00 .45
❑ 229 Dick Post 1.00 .45
❑ 230 Roman Gabriel 2.50 1.10
❑ 231 Mike Eischeid 1.00 .45
❑ 232 Jim Lynch 1.00 .45
❑ 233 Lemar Parrish RC 1.50 .70
❑ 234 Cecil Turner 1.00 .45
❑ 235 Dennis Shaw RC 1.00 .45
❑ 236 Mel Farr 1.00 .45
❑ 237 Curt Knight 1.00 .45
❑ 238 Chuck Howley 1.50 .70
❑ 239 Bruce Taylor RC 1.00 .45
❑ 240 Jerry LeVias 1.00 .45
❑ 241 Bob Lurtsema 1.00 .45
❑ 242 Earl Morrall 1.50 .70
❑ 243 Kermit Alexander 1.00 .45
❑ 244 Jackie Smith 2.50 1.10
❑ 245 Joe Greene RC 40.00 18.00
❑ 246 Harmon Wages 1.00 .45
❑ 247 Errol Mann 1.00 .45
❑ 248 Mike McCoy 1.00 .45
❑ 249 Milt Morin RC 1.00 .45
❑ 250 Joe Namath UER 60.00 27.00
In 9th line, Joe is
spelled in small letters
❑ 251 Jackie Burkett 1.00 .45
❑ 252 Steve Chomyszak 1.00 .45
❑ 253 Ed Sharockman 1.00 .45
❑ 254 Robert Holmes RC 1.00 .45
❑ 255 John Hadl 2.50 1.10
❑ 256 Cornell Gordon 1.00 .45
❑ 257 Mark Moseley RC 1.50 .70
❑ 258 Gus Otto 1.00 .45
❑ 259 Mike Taliaferro 1.00 .45
❑ 260 O.J. Simpson 25.00 11.00
❑ 261 Paul Warfield 8.00 3.60
❑ 262 Jack Concannon 1.00 .45
❑ 263 Tom Matte 2.50 .60

1972 Topps

	NRMT	VG-E
COMPLETE SET (351)	2200.00	1000.00
COMMON CARD (1-132)	.50	.23
COMMON CARD (133-263)	.60	.25
SEMISTARS 1-263	1.00	.45
UNLISTED STARS 1-263	2.00	.90
COMMON CARD (264-351)	18.00	8.00
SEMISTARS 264-351	25.00	11.00
UNLISTED STARS 264-351	30.00	13.50

THIRD SERIES CONDITION SENSITIVE
CARDS PRICED IN NM CONDITION

❑ 1 AFC Rushing Leaders 4.00 1.80
Floyd Little
Larry Csonka
Marv Hubbard
❑ 2 NFC Rushing Leaders .50 .23
John Brockington
Steve Owens
Willie Ellison
❑ 3 AFC Passing Leaders 2.00 .90
Bob Griese
Len Dawson
Virgil Carter
❑ 4 NFC Passing Leaders 5.00 2.20
Roger Staubach
Greg Landry
Bill Kilmer
❑ 5 AFC Receiving Leaders 1.00 .45
Fred Biletnikoff
Otis Taylor
Randy Vataha
❑ 6 NFC Receiving Leaders .50 .23
Bob Tucker
Ted Kwalick
Harold Jackson
Roy Jefferson
❑ 7 AFC Scoring Leaders .50 .23
Garo Yepremian
Jan Stenerud
Jim O'Brien
❑ 8 NFC Scoring Leaders .50 .23
Curt Knight
Errol Mann
Bruce Gossett
❑ 9 Jim Kiick 2.00 .90
❑ 10 Otis Taylor 1.00 .45
❑ 11 Bobby Joe Green .50 .23
❑ 12 Ken Ellis .50 .23
❑ 13 John Riggins RC 20.00 9.00
❑ 14 Dave Parks .50 .23
❑ 15 John Hadl 2.00 .90
❑ 16 Ron Hornsby .50 .23
❑ 17 Chip Myers RC .50 .23
❑ 18 Bill Kilmer 2.00 .90
❑ 19 Fred Hoaglin .50 .23
❑ 20 Carl Eller 2.00 .90
❑ 21 Steve Zabel .50 .23
❑ 22 Vic Washington RC .50 .23
❑ 23 Len St. Jean .50 .23
❑ 24 Bill Thompson .50 .23
❑ 25 Steve Owens RC 2.00 .90
❑ 26 Ken Burrough RC 1.00 .45
❑ 27 Mike Clark .50 .23
❑ 28 Willie Brown 2.00 .90
❑ 29 Checklist 1-132 6.00 1.50
❑ 30 Marlin Briscoe RC .50 .23
❑ 31 Jerry Logan .50 .23
❑ 32 Donny Anderson 1.00 .45
❑ 33 Rich McGeorge .50 .23
❑ 34 Charlie Durkee .50 .23
❑ 35 Willie Lanier 4.00 1.80
❑ 36 Chris Farasopoulos .50 .23
❑ 37 Ron Shanklin RC .50 .23
❑ 38 Forrest Blue RC .50 .23
❑ 39 Ken Reaves .50 .23
❑ 40 Roman Gabriel 2.00 .90
❑ 41 Mac Percival .50 .23
❑ 42 Lem Barney 3.00 1.35
❑ 43 Nick Buoniconti 2.00 .90
❑ 44 Charlie Gogolak .50 .23
❑ 45 Bill Bradley RC 1.00 .45
❑ 46 Joe Jones .50 .23
❑ 47 Dave Williams .50 .23
❑ 48 Pete Athas .50 .23
❑ 49 Virgil Carter .50 .23
❑ 50 Floyd Little 2.00 .90
❑ 51 Curt Knight .50 .23
❑ 52 Bobby Maples .50 .23
❑ 53 Charlie West .50 .23
❑ 54 Marv Hubbard RC 1.00 .45
❑ 55 Archie Manning RC 20.00 9.00
❑ 56 Jim O'Brien RC 1.00 .45
❑ 57 Wayne Patrick .50 .23
❑ 58 Ken Bowman .50 .23
❑ 59 Roger Wehrli .50 .23
❑ 60 Charlie Sanders UER .50 .23
(Front WR, back TE)
❑ 61 Jan Stenerud 2.00 .90
❑ 62 Willie Ellison .50 .23
❑ 63 Walt Sweeney .50 .23
❑ 64 Ron Smith .50 .23
❑ 65 Jim Plunkett RC 15.00 6.75
❑ 66 Herb Adderley UER 2.00 .90
(misspelled Adderly)
❑ 67 Mike Reid RC 2.00 .90
❑ 68 Richard Caster RC 1.00 .45
❑ 69 Dave Wilcox 2.00 .90
❑ 70 Leroy Kelly 3.00 1.35
❑ 71 Bob Lee RC .50 .23
❑ 72 Verlon Biggs .50 .23
❑ 73 Henry Allison .50 .23
❑ 74 Steve Ramsey .50 .23
❑ 75 Claude Humphrey 1.00 .45
❑ 76 Bob Grim RC .50 .23
❑ 77 John Fuqua 1.00 .45
❑ 78 Ken Houston 4.00 1.80
❑ 79 Checklist 133-263 DP 5.00 1.25
❑ 80 Bob Griese 8.00 3.60
❑ 81 Lance Rentzel 1.00 .45
❑ 82 Ed Podolak RC 1.00 .45
❑ 83 Ike Hill .50 .23
❑ 84 George Farmer .50 .23
❑ 85 John Brockington RC 2.00 .90
❑ 86 Jim Otto 2.00 .90
❑ 87 Richard Neal .50 .23
❑ 88 Jim Hart 2.00 .90
❑ 89 Bob Babich .50 .23
❑ 90 Gene Washington 1.00 .45
❑ 91 John Zook .50 .23
❑ 92 Bobby Duhon .50 .23
❑ 93 Ted Hendricks RC 15.00 6.75
❑ 94 Rockne Freitas .50 .23
❑ 95 Larry Brown 2.00 .90
❑ 96 Mike Phipps 1.00 .45
❑ 97 Julius Adams .50 .23
❑ 98 Dick Anderson 1.00 .45
❑ 99 Fred Willis .50 .23
❑ 100 Joe Namath 30.00 13.50
❑ 101 L.C. Greenwood RC 15.00 6.75
❑ 102 Mark Nordquist .50 .23
❑ 103 Robert Holmes .50 .23
❑ 104 Ron Yary RC 2.00 .90
❑ 105 Bob Hayes 2.00 .90
❑ 106 Lyle Alzado RC 15.00 6.75
❑ 107 Bob Berry .50 .23
❑ 108 Phil Villapiano RC 1.00 .45
❑ 109 Dave Elmendorf .50 .23
❑ 110 Gale Sayers 18.00 8.00
❑ 111 Jim Tyrer .50 .23
❑ 112 Mel Gray RC 2.00 .90
❑ 113 Gerry Philbin .50 .23
❑ 114 Bob James .50 .23
❑ 115 Garo Yepremian 1.00 .45
❑ 116 Dave Robinson 1.00 .45
❑ 117 Jeff Queen .50 .23
❑ 118 Norm Snead 1.00 .45
❑ 119 Jim Nance IA 1.00 .45
❑ 120 Terry Bradshaw IA 15.00 6.75
❑ 121 Jim Kiick IA 1.00 .45
❑ 122 Roger Staubach IA 20.00 9.00
❑ 123 Bo Scott IA .50 .23
❑ 124 John Brodie IA 2.00 .90
❑ 125 Rick Volk IA .50 .23
❑ 126 John Riggins IA 6.00 2.70
❑ 127 Bubba Smith IA 2.00 .90
❑ 128 Roman Gabriel IA 1.00 .45
❑ 129 Calvin Hill IA 1.00 .45
❑ 130 Bill Nelsen IA .50 .23
❑ 131 Tom Matte IA 1.00 .45
❑ 132 Bob Griese IA 4.00 1.80
❑ 133 AFC Semi-Final 1.00 .45
Dolphins 27,
Chiefs 24
❑ 134 NFC Semi-Final 1.00 .45
Cowboys 20,
Vikings 12
(Duane Thomas
getting tackled)
❑ 135 AFC Semi-Final 1.00 .45
Colts 20,
Browns 3
(Don Nottingham)
❑ 136 NFC Semi-Final 1.00 .45
49ers 24,
Redskins 20
❑ 137 AFC Title Game 3.00 1.35
Dolphins 21,
Colts 0
(Johnny Unitas
getting tackled)
❑ 138 NFC Title Game 2.00 .90
Cowboys 14,
49ers 3
(Bob Lilly
making tackle)
❑ 139 Super Bowl 5.00 2.20
Cowboys 24,
Dolphins 3

(Roger Staubach rolling out)
❑ 140 Larry Csonka 8.00 3.60
❑ 141 Rick Volk .60 .25
❑ 142 Roy Jefferson 1.00 .45
❑ 143 Raymond Chester RC 1.00 .45
❑ 144 Bobby Douglass .60 .25
❑ 145 Bob Lilly 4.00 1.80
❑ 146 Harold Jackson 1.00 .45
❑ 147 Pete Gogolak .60 .25
❑ 148 Art Malone .60 .25
❑ 149 Ed Flanagan .60 .25
❑ 150 Terry Bradshaw 40.00 18.00
❑ 151 MacArthur Lane 1.00 .45
❑ 152 Jack Snow 1.00 .45
❑ 153 Al Beauchamp .60 .25
❑ 154 Bob Anderson .60 .25
❑ 155 Ted Kwalick RC .60 .25
❑ 156 Dan Pastorini RC 2.00 .90
❑ 157 Emmitt Thomas RC .60 .25
❑ 158 Randy Vataha RC .60 .25
❑ 159 Al Atkinson .60 .25
❑ 160 O.J. Simpson 15.00 6.75
❑ 161 Jackie Smith 2.00 .90
❑ 162 Ernie Kellerman .60 .25
❑ 163 Dennis Partee .60 .25
❑ 164 Jake Kupp .60 .25
❑ 165 John Unitas 20.00 9.00
❑ 166 Clint Jones RC .60 .25
❑ 167 Paul Warfield 6.00 2.70
❑ 168 Roland McDole .60 .25
❑ 169 Daryle Lamonica 2.00 .90
❑ 170 Dick Butkus 15.00 6.75
❑ 171 Jim Butler .60 .25
❑ 172 Mike McCoy .60 .25
❑ 173 Dave Smith .60 .25
❑ 174 Greg Landry 1.00 .45
❑ 175 Tom Dempsey 1.00 .45
❑ 176 John Charles .60 .25
❑ 177 Bobby Bell 2.00 .90
❑ 178 Don Horn .60 .25
❑ 179 Bob Trumpy 2.00 .90
❑ 180 Duane Thomas 1.00 .45
❑ 181 Merlin Olsen 3.00 1.35
❑ 182 Dave Herman .60 .25
❑ 183 Jim Nance 1.00 .45
❑ 184 Pete Beathard .60 .25
❑ 185 Bob Tucker .60 .25
❑ 186 Gene Upshaw RC 15.00 6.75
❑ 187 Bo Scott .60 .25
❑ 188 J.D. Hill RC .60 .25
❑ 189 Bruce Gossett .60 .25
❑ 190 Bubba Smith 4.00 1.80
❑ 191 Edd Hargett .60 .25
❑ 192 Gary Garrison .60 .25
❑ 193 Jake Scott 1.00 .45
❑ 194 Fred Cox .60 .25
❑ 195 Sonny Jurgensen 4.00 1.80
❑ 196 Greg Brezina RC .60 .25
❑ 197 Ed O'Bradovich .60 .25
❑ 198 John Rowser .60 .25
❑ 199 Altie Taylor UER .60 .25
(Taylor misspelled as Tayor on front)
❑ 200 Roger Staubach RC ! 150.00 70.00
❑ 201 Leroy Keyes RC .60 .25
❑ 202 Garland Boyette .60 .25
❑ 203 Tom Beer .60 .25
❑ 204 Buck Buchanan 2.00 .90
❑ 205 Larry Wilson 2.00 .90
❑ 206 Scott Hunter RC .60 .25
❑ 207 Ron Johnson .60 .25
❑ 208 Sam Brunelli .60 .25
❑ 209 Deacon Jones 2.00 .90
❑ 210 Fred Biletnikoff 6.00 2.70
❑ 211 Bill Nelsen 1.00 .45
❑ 212 George Nock .60 .25
❑ 213 Dan Abramowicz 1.00 .45
❑ 214 Irv Goode .60 .25
❑ 215 Isiah Robertson RC 1.00 .45
❑ 216 Tom Matte 1.00 .45
❑ 217 Pat Fischer .60 .25
❑ 218 Gene Washington .60 .25
❑ 219 Paul Robinson .60 .25
❑ 220 John Brodie 4.00 1.80
❑ 221 Manny Fernandez RC 1.00 .45
❑ 222 Errol Mann .60 .25
❑ 223 Dick Gordon .60 .25
❑ 224 Calvin Hill 2.00 .90
❑ 225 Fran Tarkenton UER 12.00 5.50
(Plays in the Masters each spring)
❑ 226 Jim Turner .60 .25
❑ 227 Jim Mitchell .60 .25
❑ 228 Pete Liske .60 .25
❑ 229 Carl Garrett .60 .25
❑ 230 Joe Greene 20.00 9.00
❑ 231 Gale Gillingham .60 .25
❑ 232 Norm Bulaich RC 1.00 .45
❑ 233 Spider Lockhart .60 .25
❑ 234 Ken Willard .60 .25
❑ 235 George Blanda 12.00 5.50
❑ 236 Wayne Mulligan .60 .25
❑ 237 Dave Lewis .60 .25
❑ 238 Dennis Shaw .60 .25
❑ 239 Fair Hooker .60 .25
❑ 240 Larry Little RC 15.00 6.75
❑ 241 Mike Garrett .60 .25
❑ 242 Glen Ray Hines .60 .25
❑ 243 Myron Pottios .60 .25
❑ 244 Charlie Joiner RC 18.00 8.00
❑ 245 Len Dawson 6.00 2.70
❑ 246 W.K. Hicks .60 .25
❑ 247 Les Josephson .60 .25
❑ 248 Lance Alworth UER 6.00 2.70
(Front TE, back WR)
❑ 249 Frank Nunley .60 .25
❑ 250 Mel Farr IA .60 .25
❑ 251 Johnny Unitas IA 8.00 3.60
❑ 252 George Farmer IA .60 .25
❑ 253 Duane Thomas IA 1.00 .45
❑ 254 John Hadl IA 2.00 .90
❑ 255 Vic Washington IA .60 .25
❑ 256 Don Horn IA .60 .25
❑ 257 L.C. Greenwood IA 2.00 .90
❑ 258 Bob Lee IA .60 .25
❑ 259 Larry Csonka IA 4.00 1.80
❑ 260 Mike McCoy IA .60 .25
❑ 261 Greg Landry IA 1.00 .45
❑ 262 Ray May IA .60 .25
❑ 263 Bobby Douglass IA .60 .25
❑ 264 Charlie Sanders AP 30.00 13.50
❑ 265 Ron Yary AP 30.00 13.50
❑ 266 Rayfield Wright AP 30.00 13.50
❑ 267 Larry Little AP 35.00 16.00
❑ 268 John Niland AP 30.00 13.50
❑ 269 Forrest Blue AP 30.00 13.50
❑ 270 Otis Taylor AP 30.00 13.50
❑ 271 Paul Warfield AP 50.00 22.00
❑ 272 Bob Griese AP 70.00 32.00
❑ 273 John Brockington AP 30.00 13.50
❑ 274 Floyd Little AP 30.00 13.50
❑ 275 Garo Yepremian AP 30.00 13.50
❑ 276 Jerrel Wilson AP 18.00 8.00
❑ 277 Carl Eller AP 30.00 13.50
❑ 278 Bubba Smith AP 40.00 18.00
❑ 279 Alan Page AP 40.00 18.00
❑ 280 Bob Lilly AP 60.00 27.00
❑ 281 Ted Hendricks AP 50.00 22.00
❑ 282 Dave Wilcox AP 30.00 13.50
❑ 283 Willie Lanier AP 35.00 16.00
❑ 284 Jim Johnson AP 30.00 13.50
❑ 285 Willie Brown AP 35.00 16.00
❑ 286 Bill Bradley AP 30.00 13.50
❑ 287 Ken Houston AP 35.00 16.00
❑ 288 Mel Farr 18.00 8.00
❑ 289 Kermit Alexander 18.00 8.00
❑ 290 John Gilliam RC 25.00 11.00
❑ 291 Steve Spurrier RC 100.00 45.00
❑ 292 Walter Johnson 18.00 8.00
❑ 293 Jack Pardee 25.00 11.00
❑ 294 Checklist 264-351 UER 80.00 20.00
(334 Charlie Taylor should be Charley)
❑ 295 Winston Hill 18.00 8.00
❑ 296 Hugo Hollas 18.00 8.00
❑ 297 Ray May RC 18.00 8.00
❑ 298 Jim Bakken 18.00 8.00
❑ 299 Larry Carwell 18.00 8.00
❑ 300 Alan Page 50.00 22.00
❑ 301 Walt Garrison 25.00 11.00
❑ 302 Mike Lucci 25.00 11.00
❑ 303 Nemiah Wilson 18.00 8.00
❑ 304 Carroll Dale 25.00 11.00
❑ 305 Jim Kanicki 18.00 8.00
❑ 306 Preston Pearson 30.00 13.50
❑ 307 Lemar Parrish 25.00 11.00
❑ 308 Earl Morrall 25.00 11.00
❑ 309 Tommy Nobis 25.00 11.00
❑ 310 Rich Jackson 18.00 8.00
❑ 311 Doug Cunningham 18.00 8.00
❑ 312 Jim Marsalis 18.00 8.00
❑ 313 Jim Beirne 18.00 8.00
❑ 314 Tom McNeill 18.00 8.00
❑ 315 Milt Morin 18.00 8.00
❑ 316 Rayfield Wright RC 25.00 11.00
❑ 317 Jerry LeVias 25.00 11.00
❑ 318 Travis Williams RC 25.00 11.00
❑ 319 Edgar Chandler 18.00 8.00
❑ 320 Bob Wallace 18.00 8.00
❑ 321 Delles Howell 18.00 8.00
❑ 322 Emerson Boozer 25.00 11.00
❑ 323 George Atkinson RC 25.00 11.00
❑ 324 Mike Montler 18.00 8.00
❑ 325 Randy Johnson 18.00 8.00
❑ 326 Mike Curtis UER 25.00 11.00
(Text on back states he was named Super Bowl MVP in 1972. Chuck Howley won the award)
❑ 327 Miller Farr 18.00 8.00
❑ 328 Horst Muhlmann 18.00 8.00
❑ 329 John Niland RC 25.00 11.00
❑ 330 Andy Russell 25.00 11.00
❑ 331 Mercury Morris 35.00 16.00
❑ 332 Jim Johnson 30.00 13.50
❑ 333 Jerrel Wilson 18.00 8.00
❑ 334 Charley Taylor UER 40.00 18.00
(Misspelled Charlie on both sides)
❑ 335 Dick LeBeau 18.00 8.00
❑ 336 Jim Marshall 30.00 13.50
❑ 337 Tom Mack 25.00 11.00
❑ 338 Steve Spurrier IA 60.00 27.00
❑ 339 Floyd Little IA 25.00 11.00
❑ 340 Len Dawson IA 40.00 18.00
❑ 341 Dick Butkus IA 70.00 32.00
❑ 342 Larry Brown IA 25.00 11.00
❑ 343 Joe Namath IA 250.00 110.00
❑ 344 Jim Turner IA 18.00 8.00
❑ 345 Doug Cunningham IA 18.00 8.00
❑ 346 Edd Hargett IA 18.00 8.00
❑ 347 Steve Owens IA 18.00 8.00
❑ 348 George Blanda IA 50.00 22.00
❑ 349 Ed Podolak IA 18.00 8.00
❑ 350 Rich Jackson IA 18.00 8.00
❑ 351 Ken Willard IA 40.00 18.00

1973 Topps

	NRMT-MT	EXC
COMPLETE SET (528)	400.00	180.00
COMMON CARD (1-528)	.50	.23
SEMISTARS	1.00	.45
UNLISTED STARS	1.50	.70
CL (68/224/358/498)	5.00	2.20
TEAM CHECKLISTS	4.00	1.80

TEAM CHECKLISTS: ONE PER PACK
1973-86 PRICED IN NM-MT CONDITION

❑ 1 Rushing Leaders 6.00 1.50

Larry Brown
O.J. Simpson
- ❑ 2 Passing Leaders .... 1.00 .45
Norm Snead
Earl Morrall
- ❑ 3 Receiving Leaders UER .. 1.50 .70
Harold Jackson
Fred Biletnikoff
(Charley Taylor mis-
spelled as Charlie)
- ❑ 4 Scoring Leaders .... .50 .23
Chester Marcol
Bobby Howfield
- ❑ 5 Interception Leaders .... .50 .23
Bill Bradley
Mike Sensibaugh
- ❑ 6 Punting Leaders .... .50 .23
Dave Chapple
Jerrel Wilson
- ❑ 7 Bob Trumpy .... 1.50 .70
- ❑ 8 Mel Tom .... .50 .23
- ❑ 9 Clarence Ellis .... .50 .23
- ❑ 10 John Niland .... .50 .23
- ❑ 11 Randy Jackson .... .50 .23
- ❑ 12 Greg Landry .... 1.50 .70
- ❑ 13 Cid Edwards .... .50 .23
- ❑ 14 Phil Olsen .... .50 .23
- ❑ 15 Terry Bradshaw 25.00 11.00
- ❑ 16 Al Cowlings RC .... 1.50 .70
- ❑ 17 Walker Gillette .... .50 .23
- ❑ 18 Bob Atkins .... .50 .23
- ❑ 19 Diron Talbert RC .... .50 .23
- ❑ 20 Jim Johnson .... 1.50 .70
- ❑ 21 Howard Twilley .... 1.00 .45
- ❑ 22 Dick Enderle .... .50 .23
- ❑ 23 Wayne Colman .... .50 .23
- ❑ 24 John Schmitt .... .50 .23
- ❑ 25 George Blanda 10.00 4.50
- ❑ 26 Milt Morin .... .50 .23
- ❑ 27 Mike Current .... .50 .23
- ❑ 28 Rex Kern RC .... .50 .23
- ❑ 29 MacArthur Lane .... 1.00 .45
- ❑ 30 Alan Page 3.00 1.35
- ❑ 31 Randy Vataha .... .50 .23
- ❑ 32 Jim Kearney .... .50 .23
- ❑ 33 Steve Smith .... .50 .23
- ❑ 34 Ken Anderson RC 15.00 6.75
- ❑ 35 Calvin Hill .... 1.50 .70
- ❑ 36 Andy Maurer .... .50 .23
- ❑ 37 Joe Taylor .... .50 .23
- ❑ 38 Deacon Jones .... 1.50 .70
- ❑ 39 Mike Weger .... .50 .23
- ❑ 40 Roy Gerela .... 1.00 .45
- ❑ 41 Les Josephson .... .50 .23
- ❑ 42 Dave Washington .... .50 .23
- ❑ 43 Bill Curry RC .... 1.00 .45
- ❑ 44 Fred Heron .... .50 .23
- ❑ 45 John Brodie 3.00 1.35
- ❑ 46 Roy Winston .... .50 .23
- ❑ 47 Mike Bragg .... .50 .23
- ❑ 48 Mercury Morris .... 1.50 .70
- ❑ 49 Jim Files .... .50 .23
- ❑ 50 Gene Upshaw 3.00 1.35
- ❑ 51 Hugo Hollas .... .50 .23
- ❑ 52 Rod Sherman .... .50 .23
- ❑ 53 Ron Snidow .... .50 .23
- ❑ 54 Steve Tannen RC .... .50 .23
- ❑ 55 Jim Carter .... .50 .23
- ❑ 56 Lydell Mitchell RC .... 1.50 .70
- ❑ 57 Jack Rudnay RC .... .50 .23
- ❑ 58 Halvor Hagen .... .50 .23
- ❑ 59 Tom Dempsey .... 1.00 .45
- ❑ 60 Fran Tarkenton 10.00 4.50
- ❑ 61 Lance Alworth 5.00 2.20
- ❑ 62 Vern Holland .... .50 .23
- ❑ 63 Steve DeLong .... .50 .23
- ❑ 64 Art Malone .... .50 .23
- ❑ 65 Isiah Robertson .... 1.00 .45
- ❑ 66 Jerry Rush .... .50 .23
- ❑ 67 Bryant Salter .... .50 .23
- ❑ 68 Checklist 1-132 .... 5.00 1.25
- ❑ 69 J.D. Hill .... .50 .23
- ❑ 70 Forrest Blue .... .50 .23
- ❑ 71 Myron Pottios .... .50 .23
- ❑ 72 Norm Thompson RC .... .50 .23
- ❑ 73 Paul Robinson .... .50 .23
- ❑ 74 Larry Grantham .... .50 .23
- ❑ 75 Manny Fernandez .... 1.00 .45
- ❑ 76 Kent Nix .... .50 .23
- ❑ 77 Art Shell RC 15.00 6.75
- ❑ 78 George Saimes .... .50 .23
- ❑ 79 Don Cockroft .... .50 .23
- ❑ 80 Bob Tucker .... 1.00 .45
- ❑ 81 Don McCauley RC .... .50 .23
- ❑ 82 Bob Brown DT .... .50 .23
- ❑ 83 Larry Carwell .... .50 .23
- ❑ 84 Mo Moorman .... .50 .23
- ❑ 85 John Gilliam .... 1.00 .45
- ❑ 86 Wade Key .... .50 .23
- ❑ 87 Ross Brupbacher .... .50 .23
- ❑ 88 Dave Lewis .... .50 .23
- ❑ 89 Franco Harris RC 60.00 27.00
- ❑ 90 Tom Mack .... 1.50 .70
- ❑ 91 Mike Tilleman .... .50 .23
- ❑ 92 Carl Mauck .... .50 .23
- ❑ 93 Larry Hand .... .50 .23
- ❑ 94 Dave Foley .... .50 .23
- ❑ 95 Frank Nunley .... .50 .23
- ❑ 96 John Charles .... .50 .23
- ❑ 97 Jim Bakken .... .50 .23
- ❑ 98 Pat Fischer .... 1.00 .45
- ❑ 99 Randy Rasmussen .... .50 .23
- ❑ 100 Larry Csonka 6.00 2.70
- ❑ 101 Mike Siani RC .... .50 .23
- ❑ 102 Tom Roussel .... .50 .23
- ❑ 103 Clarence Scott RC ...... 1.00 .45
- ❑ 104 Charlie Johnson .... 1.00 .45
- ❑ 105 Rick Volk .... .50 .23
- ❑ 106 Willie Young .... .50 .23
- ❑ 107 Emmitt Thomas .... 1.00 .45
- ❑ 108 Jon Morris .... .50 .23
- ❑ 109 Clarence Williams .... .50 .23
- ❑ 110 Rayfield Wright .... 1.00 .45
- ❑ 111 Norm Bulaich .... .50 .23
- ❑ 112 Mike Eischeid .... .50 .23
- ❑ 113 Speedy Thomas .... .50 .23
- ❑ 114 Glen Holloway .... .50 .23
- ❑ 115 Jack Ham RC 30.00 13.50
- ❑ 116 Jim Nettles .... .50 .23
- ❑ 117 Errol Mann .... .50 .23
- ❑ 118 John Mackey .... 1.50 .70
- ❑ 119 George Kunz .... .50 .23
- ❑ 120 Bob James .... .50 .23
- ❑ 121 Garland Boyette .... .50 .23
- ❑ 122 Mel Phillips .... .50 .23
- ❑ 123 Johnny Roland .... .50 .23
- ❑ 124 Doug Swift .... .50 .23
- ❑ 125 Archie Manning 4.00 1.80
- ❑ 126 Dave Herman .... .50 .23
- ❑ 127 Carleton Oats .... .50 .23
- ❑ 128 Bill Van Heusen .... .50 .23
- ❑ 129 Rich Jackson .... .50 .23
- ❑ 130 Len Hauss .... 1.00 .45
- ❑ 131 Billy Parks RC .... .50 .23
- ❑ 132 Ray May .... .50 .23
- ❑ 133 NFC Semi-Final 5.00 2.20
(Cowboys 30, 49ers 28:
Roger Staubach dropping back)
- ❑ 134 AFC Semi-Final 2.50 1.10
(Steelers 13, Raiders 7:
Immaculate Reception Game)
- ❑ 135 NFC Semi-Final .... 1.00 .45
(Redskins 16, Packers 3:
Redskins defense)
- ❑ 136 AFC Semi-Final .... 2.00 .90
(Dolphins 20, Browns 14:
Bob Griese handing
off to Larry Csonka)
- ❑ 137 NFC Title Game .... 1.50 .70
(Redskins 26, Cowboys 3:
Billy Kilmer handing
off to Larry Brown)
- ❑ 138 AFC Title Game .... 1.00 .45
(Dolphins 21, Steelers 17:
Miami stops John Fuqua)
- ❑ 139 Super Bowl .... 1.50 .70
(Dolphins 14, Redskins 7:
Miami defense)
- ❑ 140 Dwight White RC UER 2.00 .90
(College North Texas
State, should be
East Texas State)
- ❑ 141 Jim Marsalis .... .50 .23
- ❑ 142 Doug Van Horn .... .50 .23
- ❑ 143 Al Matthews .... .50 .23
- ❑ 144 Bob Windsor .... .50 .23
- ❑ 145 Dave Hampton RC .... .50 .23
- ❑ 146 Horst Muhlmann .... .50 .23
- ❑ 147 Wally Hilgenberg RC ...... .50 .23
- ❑ 148 Ron Smith .... .50 .23
- ❑ 149 Coy Bacon RC .... 1.00 .45
- ❑ 150 Winston Hill .... .50 .23
- ❑ 151 Ron Jessie RC .... 1.00 .45
- ❑ 152 Ken Iman .... .50 .23
- ❑ 153 Ron Saul .... .50 .23
- ❑ 154 Jim Braxton RC .... 1.00 .45
- ❑ 155 Bubba Smith 2.50 1.10
- ❑ 156 Gary Cuozzo .... 1.00 .45
- ❑ 157 Charlie Krueger .... 1.00 .45
- ❑ 158 Tim Foley RC .... 1.00 .45
- ❑ 159 Lee Roy Jordan .... 1.50 .70
- ❑ 160 Bob Brown OT .... 1.00 .45
- ❑ 161 Margene Adkins .... .50 .23
- ❑ 162 Ron Widby .... .50 .23
- ❑ 163 Jim Houston .... .50 .23
- ❑ 164 Joe Dawkins .... .50 .23
- ❑ 165 L.C. Greenwood 4.00 1.80
- ❑ 166 Richmond Flowers RC .. .50 .23
- ❑ 167 Curley Culp RC .... 1.50 .70
- ❑ 168 Len St. Jean .... .50 .23
- ❑ 169 Walter Rock .... .50 .23
- ❑ 170 Bill Bradley .... 1.00 .45
- ❑ 171 Ken Riley RC .... 1.50 .70
- ❑ 172 Rich Coady .... .50 .23
- ❑ 173 Don Hansen .... .50 .23
- ❑ 174 Lionel Aldridge .... .50 .23
- ❑ 175 Don Maynard 4.00 1.80
- ❑ 176 Dave Osborn .... 1.00 .45
- ❑ 177 Jim Bailey .... .50 .23
- ❑ 178 John Pitts .... .50 .23
- ❑ 179 Dave Parks .... .50 .23
- ❑ 180 Chester Marcol RC .... .50 .23
- ❑ 181 Len Rohde .... .50 .23
- ❑ 182 Jeff Staggs .... .50 .23
- ❑ 183 Gene Hickerson .... .50 .23
- ❑ 184 Charlie Evans .... .50 .23
- ❑ 185 Mel Renfro .... 1.50 .70
- ❑ 186 Marvin Upshaw .... .50 .23
- ❑ 187 George Atkinson .... 1.00 .45
- ❑ 188 Norm Evans .... 1.00 .45
- ❑ 189 Steve Ramsey .... .50 .23
- ❑ 190 Dave Chapple .... .50 .23
- ❑ 191 Gerry Mullins .... .50 .23
- ❑ 192 John Didion .... .50 .23
- ❑ 193 Bob Gladieux .... .50 .23
- ❑ 194 Don Hultz .... .50 .23
- ❑ 195 Mike Lucci .... .50 .23
- ❑ 196 John Wilbur .... .50 .23
- ❑ 197 George Farmer .... .50 .23
- ❑ 198 Tommy Casanova RC .. 1.00 .45
- ❑ 199 Russ Washington .... .50 .23
- ❑ 200 Claude Humphrey .... 1.50 .70
Tackling Roger Staubach
- ❑ 201 Pat Hughes .... .50 .23
- ❑ 202 Zeke Moore .... .50 .23
- ❑ 203 Chip Glass .... .50 .23
- ❑ 204 Glenn Ressler .... .50 .23
- ❑ 205 Willie Ellison .... 1.00 .45
- ❑ 206 John Leypoldt .... .50 .23
- ❑ 207 Johnny Fuller .... .50 .23
- ❑ 208 Bill Hayhoe .... .50 .23
- ❑ 209 Ed Bell .... .50 .23
- ❑ 210 Willie Brown .... 1.50 .70
- ❑ 211 Carl Eller .... 1.50 .70
- ❑ 212 Mark Nordquist .... .50 .23
- ❑ 213 Larry Willingham .... .50 .23
- ❑ 214 Nick Buoniconti .... 1.50 .70
- ❑ 215 John Hadl .... 1.50 .70
- ❑ 216 Jethro Pugh RC .... 1.50 .70
- ❑ 217 Leroy Mitchell .... .50 .23
- ❑ 218 Billy Newsome .... .50 .23
- ❑ 219 John McMakin .... .50 .23
- ❑ 220 Larry Brown .... 1.50 .70
- ❑ 221 Clarence Scott .... .50 .23
- ❑ 222 Paul Naumoff .... .50 .23
- ❑ 223 Ted Fritsch Jr. .... .50 .23
- ❑ 224 Checklist 133-264 .... 5.00 1.25
- ❑ 225 Dan Pastorini .... 1.50 .70

❑ 226 Joe Beauchamp UER .... .50 .23
(Safety on front, Cornerback on back)
❑ 227 Pat Matson .50 .23
❑ 228 Tony McGee .50 .23
❑ 229 Mike Phipps 1.00 .45
❑ 230 Harold Jackson 1.50 .70
❑ 231 Willie Williams .50 .23
❑ 232 Spike Jones .50 .23
❑ 233 Jim Tyrer .50 .23
❑ 234 Roy Hilton .50 .23
❑ 235 Phil Villapiano 1.00 .45
❑ 236 Charley Taylor UER 3.00 1.35
(Misspelled Charlie on both sides)
❑ 237 Malcolm Snider .50 .23
❑ 238 Vic Washington .50 .23
❑ 239 Grady Alderman .50 .23
❑ 240 Dick Anderson 1.00 .45
❑ 241 Ron Yankowski .50 .23
❑ 242 Billy Masters .50 .23
❑ 243 Herb Adderley 1.50 .70
❑ 244 David Ray .50 .23
❑ 245 John Riggins 8.00 3.60
❑ 246 Mike Wagner RC 1.50 .70
❑ 247 Don Morrison .50 .23
❑ 248 Earl McCullouch .50 .23
❑ 249 Dennis Wirgowski .50 .23
❑ 250 Chris Hanburger 1.00 .45
❑ 251 Pat Sullivan RC 1.50 .70
❑ 252 Walt Sweeney .50 .23
❑ 253 Willie Alexander .50 .23
❑ 254 Doug Dressler .50 .23
❑ 255 Walter Johnson .50 .23
❑ 256 Ron Hornsby .50 .23
❑ 257 Ben Hawkins .50 .23
❑ 258 Donnie Green .50 .23
❑ 259 Fred Hoaglin .50 .23
❑ 260 Jerrel Wilson .50 .23
❑ 261 Horace Jones .50 .23
❑ 262 Woody Peoples .50 .23
❑ 263 Jim Hill RC .50 .23
❑ 264 John Fuqua .50 .23
❑ 265 Donny Anderson KP .... 1.00 .45
❑ 266 Roman Gabriel KP 1.50 .70
❑ 267 Mike Garrett KP 1.00 .45
❑ 268 Rufus Mayes RC .50 .23
❑ 269 Chip Myrtle .50 .23
❑ 270 Bill Stanfill RC 1.00 .45
❑ 271 Clint Jones .50 .23
❑ 272 Miller Farr .50 .23
❑ 273 Harry Schuh .50 .23
❑ 274 Bob Hayes 1.50 .70
❑ 275 Bobby Douglass 1.00 .45
❑ 276 Gus Hollomon .50 .23
❑ 277 Del Williams .50 .23
❑ 278 Julius Adams .50 .23
❑ 279 Herman Weaver .50 .23
❑ 280 Joe Greene 8.00 3.60
❑ 281 Wes Chesson .50 .23
❑ 282 Charlie Harraway .50 .23
❑ 283 Paul Guidry .50 .23
❑ 284 Terry Owens .50 .23
❑ 285 Jan Stenerud 1.50 .70
❑ 286 Pete Athas .50 .23
❑ 287 Dale Lindsey .50 .23
❑ 288 Jack Tatum RC 10.00 4.50
❑ 289 Floyd Little 1.50 .70
❑ 290 Bob Johnson .50 .23
❑ 291 Tommy Hart RC .50 .23
❑ 292 Tom Mitchell .50 .23
❑ 293 Walt Patulski RC .50 .23
❑ 294 Jim Skaggs .50 .23
❑ 295 Bob Griese 6.00 2.70
❑ 296 Mike McCoy .50 .23
❑ 297 Mel Gray 1.00 .45
❑ 298 Bobby Bryant .50 .23
❑ 299 Blaine Nye RC .50 .23
❑ 300 Dick Butkus 12.00 5.50
❑ 301 Charlie Cowan RC .50 .23
❑ 302 Mark Lomas .50 .23
❑ 303 Josh Ashton .50 .23
❑ 304 Happy Feller .50 .23
❑ 305 Ron Shanklin .50 .23
❑ 306 Wayne Rasmussen .50 .23
❑ 307 Jerry Smith .50 .23
❑ 308 Ken Reaves .50 .23
❑ 309 Ron East .50 .23
❑ 310 Otis Taylor 1.50 .70
❑ 311 John Garlington .50 .23
❑ 312 Lyle Alzado 4.00 1.80
❑ 313 Remi Prudhomme .50 .23
❑ 314 Cornelius Johnson .50 .23
❑ 315 Lemar Parrish 1.00 .45
❑ 316 Jim Kiick 1.50 .70
❑ 317 Steve Zabel .50 .23
❑ 318 Alden Roche .50 .23
❑ 319 Tom Blanchard .50 .23
❑ 320 Fred Biletnikoff 4.00 1.80
❑ 321 Ralph Neely 1.00 .45
❑ 322 Dan Dierdorf RC 20.00 9.00
❑ 323 Richard Caster 1.00 .45
❑ 324 Gene Howard .50 .23
❑ 325 Elvin Bethea 1.00 .45
❑ 326 Carl Garrett 1.00 .45
❑ 327 Ron Billingsley .50 .23
❑ 328 Charlie West .50 .23
❑ 329 Tom Neville .50 .23
❑ 330 Ted Kwalick 1.00 .45
❑ 331 Rudy Redmond .50 .23
❑ 332 Henry Davis .50 .23
❑ 333 John Zook .50 .23
❑ 334 Jim Turner .50 .23
❑ 335 Len Dawson 5.00 2.20
❑ 336 Bob Chandler RC 1.00 .45
❑ 337 Al Beauchamp .50 .23
❑ 338 Tom Matte 1.00 .45
❑ 339 Paul Laaveg .50 .23
❑ 340 Ken Ellis .50 .23
❑ 341 Jim Langer RC 10.00 4.50
❑ 342 Ron Porter .50 .23
❑ 343 Jack Youngblood RC 12.00 5.50
❑ 344 Cornell Green 1.50 .70
❑ 345 Marv Hubbard 1.00 .45
❑ 346 Bruce Taylor .50 .23
❑ 347 Sam Havrilak .50 .23
❑ 348 Walt Sumner .50 .23
❑ 349 Steve O'Neal .50 .23
❑ 350 Ron Johnson 1.00 .45
❑ 351 Rockne Freitas .50 .23
❑ 352 Larry Stallings .50 .23
❑ 353 Jim Cadile .50 .23
❑ 354 Ken Burrough 1.00 .45
❑ 355 Jim Plunkett 4.00 1.80
❑ 356 Dave Long .50 .23
❑ 357 Ralph Anderson .50 .23
❑ 358 Checklist 265-396 5.00 1.25
❑ 359 Gene Washington 1.00 .45
❑ 360 Dave Wilcox 1.00 .45
❑ 361 Paul Smith .50 .23
❑ 362 Alvin Wyatt .50 .23
❑ 363 Charlie Smith .50 .23
❑ 364 Royce Berry .50 .23
❑ 365 Dave Elmendorf .50 .23
❑ 366 Scott Hunter 1.00 .45
❑ 367 Bob Kuechenberg RC .. 3.00 1.35
❑ 368 Pete Gogolak .50 .23
❑ 369 Dave Edwards .50 .23
❑ 370 Lem Barney 2.50 1.10
❑ 371 Verlon Biggs .50 .23
❑ 372 John Reaves RC .50 .23
❑ 373 Ed Podolak 1.00 .45
❑ 374 Chris Farasopoulos .50 .23
❑ 375 Gary Garrison .50 .23
❑ 376 Tom Funchess .50 .23
❑ 377 Bobby Joe Green .50 .23
❑ 378 Don Brumm .50 .23
❑ 379 Jim O'Brien .50 .23
❑ 380 Paul Krause 1.50 .70
❑ 381 Leroy Kelly 2.50 1.10
❑ 382 Ray Mansfield .50 .23
❑ 383 Dan Abramowicz 1.00 .45
❑ 384 John Outlaw RC .50 .23
❑ 385 Tommy Nobis 1.50 .70
❑ 386 Tom Domres .50 .23
❑ 387 Ken Willard .50 .23
❑ 388 Mike Stratton .50 .23
❑ 389 Fred Dryer 2.50 1.10
❑ 390 Jake Scott 1.50 .70
❑ 391 Rich Houston .50 .23
❑ 392 Virgil Carter .50 .23
❑ 393 Tody Smith .50 .23
❑ 394 Ernie Calloway .50 .23
❑ 395 Charlie Sanders 1.00 .45
❑ 396 Fred Willis .50 .23
❑ 397 Curt Knight .50 .23
❑ 398 Nemiah Wilson .50 .23
❑ 399 Carroll Dale 1.00 .45
❑ 400 Joe Namath 30.00 13.50
❑ 401 Wayne Mulligan .50 .23
❑ 402 Jim Harrison .50 .23
❑ 403 Tim Rossovich .50 .23
❑ 404 David Lee .50 .23
❑ 405 Frank Pitts .50 .23
❑ 406 Jim Marshall 1.50 .70
❑ 407 Bob Brown TE .50 .23
❑ 408 John Rowser .50 .23
❑ 409 Mike Montler .50 .23
❑ 410 Willie Lanier 1.50 .70
❑ 411 Bill Bell .50 .23
❑ 412 Cedrick Hardman .50 .23
❑ 413 Bob Anderson .50 .23
❑ 414 Earl Morrall 1.50 .70
❑ 415 Ken Houston 1.50 .70
❑ 416 Jack Snow 1.00 .45
❑ 417 Dick Cunningham .50 .23
❑ 418 Greg Larson .50 .23
❑ 419 Mike Bass 1.00 .45
❑ 420 Mike Reid 1.50 .70
❑ 421 Walt Garrison 1.50 .70
❑ 422 Pete Liske .50 .23
❑ 423 Jim Yarbrough .50 .23
❑ 424 Rich McGeorge .50 .23
❑ 425 Bobby Howfield .50 .23
❑ 426 Pete Banaszak .50 .23
❑ 427 Willie Holman .50 .23
❑ 428 Dale Hackbart .50 .23
❑ 429 Fair Hooker .50 .23
❑ 430 Ted Hendricks 5.00 2.20
❑ 431 Mike Garrett 1.00 .45
❑ 432 Glen Ray Hines .50 .23
❑ 433 Fred Cox .50 .23
❑ 434 Bobby Walden .50 .23
❑ 435 Bobby Bell 1.50 .70
❑ 436 Dave Rowe .50 .23
❑ 437 Bob Berry .50 .23
❑ 438 Bill Thompson .50 .23
❑ 439 Jim Beirne .50 .23
❑ 440 Larry Little 3.00 1.35
❑ 441 Rocky Thompson .50 .23
❑ 442 Brig Owens .50 .23
❑ 443 Richard Neal .50 .23
❑ 444 Al Nelson .50 .23
❑ 445 Chip Myers .50 .23
❑ 446 Ken Bowman .50 .23
❑ 447 Jim Purnell .50 .23
❑ 448 Altie Taylor .50 .23
❑ 449 Linzy Cole .50 .23
❑ 450 Bob Lilly 4.00 1.80
❑ 451 Charlie Ford .50 .23
❑ 452 Milt Sunde .50 .23
❑ 453 Doug Wyatt .50 .23
❑ 454 Don Nottingham RC .... 1.00 .45
❑ 455 John Unitas 15.00 6.75
❑ 456 Frank Lewis RC 1.00 .45
❑ 457 Roger Wehrli 1.00 .45
❑ 458 Jim Cheyunski .50 .23
❑ 459 Jerry Sherk RC 1.00 .45
❑ 460 Gene Washington 1.00 .45
❑ 461 Jim Otto 1.50 .70
❑ 462 Ed Budde .50 .23
❑ 463 Jim Mitchell 1.00 .45
❑ 464 Emerson Boozer 1.00 .45
❑ 465 Garo Yepremian 1.50 .70
❑ 466 Pete Duranko .50 .23
❑ 467 Charlie Joiner 8.00 3.60
❑ 468 Spider Lockhart 1.00 .45
❑ 469 Marty Domres .50 .23
❑ 470 John Brockington 1.50 .70
❑ 471 Ed Flanagan .50 .23
❑ 472 Roy Jefferson 1.00 .45
❑ 473 Julian Fagan .50 .23
❑ 474 Bill Brown 1.00 .45
❑ 475 Roger Staubach 40.00 18.00
❑ 476 Jan White .50 .23
❑ 477 Pat Holmes .50 .23
❑ 478 Bob DeMarco .50 .23
❑ 479 Merlin Olsen 2.50 1.10

❑ 480 Andy Russell 1.50 .70
❑ 481 Steve Spurrier 20.00 9.00
❑ 482 Nate Ramsey .50 .23
❑ 483 Dennis Partee .50 .23
❑ 484 Jerry Simmons .50 .23
❑ 485 Donny Anderson 1.50 .70
❑ 486 Ralph Baker .50 .23
❑ 487 Ken Stabler RC ! 70.00 32.00
❑ 488 Ernie McMillan .50 .23
❑ 489 Ken Burrow .50 .23
❑ 490 Jack Gregory RC .50 .23
❑ 491 Larry Seiple 1.00 .45
❑ 492 Mick Tingelhoff 1.00 .45
❑ 493 Craig Morton 1.50 .70
❑ 494 Cecil Turner .50 .23
❑ 495 Steve Owens 1.50 .70
❑ 496 Rickie Harris .50 .23
❑ 497 Buck Buchanan 1.50 .70
❑ 498 Checklist 397-528 5.00 1.25
❑ 499 Billy Kilmer 1.50 .70
❑ 500 O.J. Simpson 15.00 6.75
❑ 501 Bruce Gossett .50 .23
❑ 502 Art Thoms .50 .23
❑ 503 Larry Kaminski .50 .23
❑ 504 Larry Smith .50 .23
❑ 505 Bruce Van Dyke .50 .23
❑ 506 Alvin Reed .50 .23
❑ 507 Delles Howell .50 .23
❑ 508 Leroy Keyes .50 .23
❑ 509 Bo Scott 1.00 .45
❑ 510 Ron Yary 1.00 .45
❑ 511 Paul Warfield 5.00 2.20
❑ 512 Mac Percival .50 .23
❑ 513 Essex Johnson .50 .23
❑ 514 Jackie Smith 1.50 .70
❑ 515 Norm Snead 1.50 .70
❑ 516 Charlie Stukes .50 .23
❑ 517 Reggie Rucker RC 1.00 .45
❑ 518 Bill Sandeman UER .50 .23
(Should be a period between run and he instead of a comma)
❑ 519 Mel Farr 1.00 .45
❑ 520 Raymond Chester 1.00 .45
❑ 521 Fred Carr RC 1.00 .45
❑ 522 Jerry LeVias 1.00 .45
❑ 523 Jim Strong .50 .23
❑ 524 Roland McDole .50 .23
❑ 525 Dennis Shaw .50 .23
❑ 526 Dave Manders .50 .23
❑ 527 Skip Vanderbundt .50 .23
❑ 528 Mike Sensibaugh RC ! 1.50 .35

1974 Topps

	NRMT-MT	EXC
COMPLETE SET (528)	300.00	135.00
COMMON CARD (1-528)	.40	.18
SEMISTARS	.75	.35
UNLISTED STARS	1.50	.70
VAR (23A/116A)	5.00	2.20
VAR (49A/124A/126A/127A)	3.00	1.35
CL (117/262/391/498)	4.00	1.80
CONDITION SENSITIVE SET!		
TEAM CHECKLISTS	3.00	1.35
TEAM CHECKLISTS: ONE PER PACK		

❑ 1 O.J. Simpson RB UER 20.00 5.00
(Text on back says 100 years, should say 100 yards)
❑ 2 Blaine Nye .40 .18
❑ 3 Don Hansen .40 .18
❑ 4 Ken Bowman .40 .18
❑ 5 Carl Eller 1.50 .70
❑ 6 Jerry Smith .40 .18
❑ 7 Ed Podolak .40 .18
❑ 8 Mel Gray 1.50 .70
❑ 9 Pat Matson .40 .18
❑ 10 Floyd Little 1.50 .70
❑ 11 Frank Pitts .40 .18
❑ 12 Vern Den Herder RC .75 .35
❑ 13 John Fuqua .75 .35
❑ 14 Jack Tatum 2.00 .90
❑ 15 Winston Hill .40 .18
❑ 16 John Beasley .40 .18
❑ 17 David Lee .40 .18
❑ 18 Rich Coady .40 .18
❑ 19 Ken Willard .40 .18
❑ 20 Coy Bacon .75 .35
❑ 21 Ben Hawkins .40 .18
❑ 22 Paul Guidry .40 .18
❑ 23A Norm Snead 5.00 2.20
(Vertical pose; 1973 stats; one asterisk before TCG on back)
❑ 23B Norm Snead HOR .75 .35
❑ 24 Jim Yarbrough .40 .18
❑ 25 Jack Reynolds RC 3.00 1.35
❑ 26 Josh Ashton .40 .18
❑ 27 Donnie Green .40 .18
❑ 28 Bob Hayes 1.50 .70
❑ 29 John Zook .40 .18
❑ 30 Bobby Bryant .40 .18
❑ 31 Scott Hunter .75 .35
❑ 32 Dan Dierdorf 6.00 2.70
❑ 33 Curt Knight .40 .18
❑ 34 Elmo Wright RC .40 .18
❑ 35 Essex Johnson .40 .18
❑ 36 Walt Sumner .40 .18
❑ 37 Marv Montgomery .40 .18
❑ 38 Tim Foley .75 .35
❑ 39 Mike Siani .40 .18
❑ 40 Joe Greene 6.00 2.70
❑ 41 Bobby Howfield .40 .18
❑ 42 Del Williams .40 .18
❑ 43 Don McCauley .40 .18
❑ 44 Randy Jackson .40 .18
❑ 45 Ron Smith .40 .18
❑ 46 Gene Washington .75 .35
❑ 47 Po James .40 .18
❑ 48 Solomon Freelon .40 .18
❑ 49A Bob Windsor 3.00 1.35
(Vertical pose; 1973 stats; one asterisk before TCG on back)
❑ 49B Bob Windsor HOR .40 .18
❑ 50 John Hadl 1.50 .70
❑ 51 Greg Larson .40 .18
❑ 52 Steve Owens .75 .35
❑ 53 Jim Cheyunski .40 .18
❑ 54 Rayfield Wright .75 .35
❑ 55 Dave Hampton .40 .18
❑ 56 Ron Widby .40 .18
❑ 57 Milt Sunde .40 .18
❑ 58 Billy Kilmer 1.50 .70
❑ 59 Bobby Bell 1.50 .70
❑ 60 Jim Bakken .40 .18
❑ 61 Rufus Mayes .40 .18
❑ 62 Vic Washington .40 .18
❑ 63 Gene Washington .75 .35
❑ 64 Clarence Scott .40 .18
❑ 65 Gene Upshaw 2.00 .90
❑ 66 Larry Seiple .75 .35
❑ 67 John McMakin .40 .18
❑ 68 Ralph Baker .40 .18
❑ 69 Lydell Mitchell .75 .35
❑ 70 Archie Manning 2.50 1.10
❑ 71 George Farmer .40 .18
❑ 72 Ron East .40 .18
❑ 73 Al Nelson .40 .18
❑ 74 Pat Hughes .40 .18
❑ 75 Fred Willis .40 .18
❑ 76 Larry Walton .40 .18
❑ 77 Tom Neville .40 .18
❑ 78 Ted Kwalick .40 .18
❑ 79 Walt Patulski .40 .18
❑ 80 John Niland .40 .18
❑ 81 Ted Fritsch Jr. .40 .18
❑ 82 Paul Krause 1.50 .70
❑ 83 Jack Snow .75 .35
❑ 84 Mike Bass .40 .18
❑ 85 Jim Tyrer .40 .18
❑ 86 Ron Yankowski .40 .18
❑ 87 Mike Phipps .75 .35
❑ 88 Al Beauchamp .40 .18
❑ 89 Riley Odoms RC 1.50 .70
❑ 90 MacArthur Lane .40 .18
❑ 91 Art Thoms .40 .18
❑ 92 Marlin Briscoe .40 .18
❑ 93 Bruce Van Dyke .40 .18
❑ 94 Tom Myers RC .40 .18
❑ 95 Calvin Hill 1.50 .70
❑ 96 Bruce Laird .40 .18
❑ 97 Tony McGee .40 .18
❑ 98 Len Rohde .40 .18
❑ 99 Tom McNeill .40 .18
❑ 100 Delles Howell .40 .18
❑ 101 Gary Garrison .40 .18
❑ 102 Dan Goich .40 .18
❑ 103 Len St. Jean .40 .18
❑ 104 Zeke Moore .40 .18
❑ 105 Ahmad Rashad RC 15.00 6.75
❑ 106 Mel Renfro 1.50 .70
❑ 107 Jim Mitchell .40 .18
❑ 108 Ed Budde .40 .18
❑ 109 Harry Schuh .40 .18
❑ 110 Greg Pruitt RC 4.00 1.80
❑ 111 Ed Flanagan .40 .18
❑ 112 Larry Stallings .40 .18
❑ 113 Chuck Foreman RC 4.00 1.80
❑ 114 Royce Berry .40 .18
❑ 115 Gale Gillingham .40 .18
❑ 116A Charlie Johnson 5.00 2.20
(Vertical pose; 1973 stats; one asterisk before TCG on back)
❑ 116B Charlie Johnson HOR 1.50 .70
❑ 117 Checklist 1-132 UER 4.00 1.00
(345 Hamburger)
❑ 118 Bill Butler .40 .18
❑ 119 Roy Jefferson .75 .35
❑ 120 Bobby Douglass .75 .35
❑ 121 Harold Carmichael AP RC 12.00
5.50
❑ 122 George Kunz AP .40 .18
❑ 123 Larry Little AP 2.00 .90
❑ 124A Forrest Blue AP 3.00 1.35
(Not All-Pro style; 1973 stats; one asterisk before TCG on back)
❑ 124B Forrest Blue AP .40 .18
❑ 125 Ron Yary AP .75 .35
❑ 126A Tom Mack 3.00 1.35
(Not All-Pro style; 1973 stats; one asterisk before TCG on back)
❑ 126B Tom Mack AP 1.50 .70
❑ 127A Bob Tucker 3.00 1.35
(Not All-Pro style; 1973 stats; one asterisk before TCG on back)
❑ 127B Bob Tucker AP .75 .35
❑ 128 Paul Warfield AP 4.00 1.80
❑ 129 Fran Tarkenton AP 10.00 4.50
❑ 130 O.J. Simpson AP 12.00 5.50
❑ 131 Larry Csonka AP 6.00 2.70
❑ 132 Bruce Gossett AP .40 .18
❑ 133 Bill Stanfill AP .75 .35
❑ 134 Alan Page AP 2.50 1.10
❑ 135 Paul Smith AP .40 .18
❑ 136 Claude Humphrey AP .75 .35
❑ 137 Jack Ham AP 10.00 4.50
❑ 138 Lee Roy Jordan AP 1.50 .70
❑ 139 Phil Villapiano AP .75 .35
❑ 140 Ken Ellis AP .40 .18
❑ 141 Willie Brown AP 1.50 .70
❑ 142 Dick Anderson AP .75 .35
❑ 143 Bill Bradley AP .75 .35
❑ 144 Jerrel Wilson AP .40 .18

❑ 145 Reggie Rucker .75 .35
❑ 146 Marty Domres .40 .18
❑ 147 Bob Kowalkowski .40 .18
❑ 148 John Matuszak RC 5.00 2.20
❑ 149 Mike Adamle RC .75 .35
❑ 150 John Unitas 15.00 6.75
❑ 151 Charlie Ford .40 .18
❑ 152 Bob Klein RC .40 .18
❑ 153 Jim Merlo .40 .18
❑ 154 Willie Young .40 .18
❑ 155 Donny Anderson .75 .35
❑ 156 Brig Owens .40 .18
❑ 157 Bruce Jarvis .40 .18
❑ 158 Ron Carpenter .40 .18
❑ 159 Don Cockroft .40 .18
❑ 160 Tommy Nobis 1.50 .70
❑ 161 Craig Morton 1.50 .70
❑ 162 Jon Staggers .40 .18
❑ 163 Mike Eischeid .40 .18
❑ 164 Jerry Sisemore RC .40 .18
❑ 165 Cedrick Hardman .40 .18
❑ 166 Bill Thompson .75 .35
❑ 167 Jim Lynch .75 .35
❑ 168 Bob Moore .40 .18
❑ 169 Glen Edwards .40 .18
❑ 170 Mercury Morris 1.50 .70
❑ 171 Julius Adams .40 .18
❑ 172 Cotton Speyrer .40 .18
❑ 173 Bill Munson .75 .35
❑ 174 Benny Johnson .40 .18
❑ 175 Burgess Owens RC .40 .18
❑ 176 Cid Edwards .40 .18
❑ 177 Doug Buffone .40 .18
❑ 178 Charlie Cowan .40 .18
❑ 179 Bob Newland .40 .18
❑ 180 Ron Johnson .75 .35
❑ 181 Bob Rowe .40 .18
❑ 182 Len Hauss .40 .18
❑ 183 Joe DeLamielleure RC 1.50 .70
❑ 184 Sherman White RC .40 .18
❑ 185 Fair Hooker .40 .18
❑ 186 Nick Mike-Mayer .40 .18
❑ 187 Ralph Neely .40 .18
❑ 188 Rich McGeorge .40 .18
❑ 189 Ed Marinaro RC 4.00 1.80
❑ 190 Dave Wilcox .75 .35
❑ 191 Joe Owens .40 .18
❑ 192 Bill Van Heusen .40 .18
❑ 193 Jim Kearney .40 .18
❑ 194 Otis Sistrunk RC 1.50 .70
❑ 195 Ron Shanklin .40 .18
❑ 196 Bill Lenkaitis .40 .18
❑ 197 Tom Drougas .40 .18
❑ 198 Larry Hand .40 .18
❑ 199 Mack Alston .40 .18
❑ 200 Bob Griese 6.00 2.70
❑ 201 Earlie Thomas .40 .18
❑ 202 Carl Gersbach .40 .18
❑ 203 Jim Harrison .40 .18
❑ 204 Jake Kupp .40 .18
❑ 205 Merlin Olsen 2.00 .90
❑ 206 Spider Lockhart .75 .35
❑ 207 Walker Gillette .40 .18
❑ 208 Verlon Biggs .40 .18
❑ 209 Bob James .40 .18
❑ 210 Bob Trumpy 1.50 .70
❑ 211 Jerry Sherk HOR .40 .18
❑ 212 Andy Maurer .40 .18
❑ 213 Fred Carr .40 .18
❑ 214 Mick Tingelhoff .75 .35
❑ 215 Steve Spurrier 15.00 6.75
❑ 216 Richard Harris .40 .18
❑ 217 Charlie Greer .40 .18
❑ 218 Buck Buchanan 1.50 .70
❑ 219 Ray Guy RC 10.00 4.50
❑ 220 Franco Harris 15.00 6.75
❑ 221 Darryl Stingley RC 1.50 .70
❑ 222 Rex Kern .40 .18
❑ 223 Toni Fritsch .75 .35
❑ 224 Levi Johnson .40 .18
❑ 225 Bob Kuechenberg .75 .35
❑ 226 Elvin Bethea .75 .35
❑ 227 Al Woodall RC .75 .35
❑ 228 Terry Owens .40 .18
❑ 229 Bivian Lee .40 .18
❑ 230 Dick Butkus 10.00 4.50
❑ 231 Jim Bertelsen RC .75 .35
❑ 232 John Mendenhall RC .40 .18
❑ 233 Conrad Dobler RC 1.50 .70
❑ 234 J.D. Hill .75 .35
❑ 235 Ken Houston 1.50 .70
❑ 236 Dave Lewis .40 .18
❑ 237 John Garlington .40 .18
❑ 238 Bill Sandeman .40 .18
❑ 239 Alden Roche .40 .18
❑ 240 John Gilliam .75 .35
❑ 241 Bruce Taylor .40 .18
❑ 242 Vern Winfield .40 .18
❑ 243 Bobby Maples .40 .18
❑ 244 Wendell Hayes .40 .18
❑ 245 George Blanda 8.00 3.60
❑ 246 Dwight White .75 .35
❑ 247 Sandy Durko .40 .18
❑ 248 Tom Mitchell .40 .18
❑ 249 Chuck Walton .40 .18
❑ 250 Bob Lilly 3.00 1.35
❑ 251 Doug Swift .40 .18
❑ 252 Lynn Dickey RC 1.50 .70
❑ 253 Jerome Barkum RC .40 .18
❑ 254 Clint Jones .40 .18
❑ 255 Billy Newsome .40 .18
❑ 256 Bob Asher .40 .18
❑ 257 Joe Scibelli .40 .18
❑ 258 Tom Blanchard .40 .18
❑ 259 Norm Thompson .40 .18
❑ 260 Larry Brown 1.50 .70
❑ 261 Paul Seymour .40 .18
❑ 262 Checklist 133-264 4.00 1.00
❑ 263 Doug Dieken RC .40 .18
❑ 264 Lemar Parrish .75 .35
❑ 265 Bob Lee UER .40 .18
(listed as Atlanta
Hawks on card back)
❑ 266 Bob Brown DT .40 .18
❑ 267 Roy Winston .40 .18
❑ 268 Randy Beisler .40 .18
❑ 269 Joe Dawkins .40 .18
❑ 270 Tom Dempsey .75 .35
❑ 271 Jack Rudnay .40 .18
❑ 272 Art Shell 5.00 2.20
❑ 273 Mike Wagner .75 .35
❑ 274 Rick Cash .40 .18
❑ 275 Greg Landry 1.50 .70
❑ 276 Glenn Ressler .40 .18
❑ 277 Billy Joe DuPree RC 3.00 1.35
❑ 278 Norm Evans .40 .18
❑ 279 Billy Parks .40 .18
❑ 280 John Riggins 6.00 2.70
❑ 281 Lionel Aldridge .40 .18
❑ 282 Steve O'Neal .40 .18
❑ 283 Craig Clemons .40 .18
❑ 284 Willie Williams .40 .18
❑ 285 Isiah Robertson .75 .35
❑ 286 Dennis Shaw .40 .18
❑ 287 Bill Brundige .40 .18
❑ 288 John Leypoldt .40 .18
❑ 289 John DeMarie .40 .18
❑ 290 Mike Reid 1.50 .70
❑ 291 Greg Brezina .40 .18
❑ 292 Willie Buchanon RC .40 .18
❑ 293 Dave Osborn .75 .35
❑ 294 Mel Phillips .40 .18
❑ 295 Haven Moses .75 .35
❑ 296 Wade Key .40 .18
❑ 297 Marvin Upshaw .40 .18
❑ 298 Ray Mansfield .40 .18
❑ 299 Edgar Chandler .40 .18
❑ 300 Marv Hubbard .75 .35
❑ 301 Herman Weaver .40 .18
❑ 302 Jim Bailey .40 .18
❑ 303 D.D. Lewis RC 1.50 .70
❑ 304 Ken Burrough .75 .35
❑ 305 Jake Scott 1.50 .70
❑ 306 Randy Rasmussen .40 .18
❑ 307 Pettis Norman .40 .18
❑ 308 Carl Johnson .40 .18
❑ 309 Joe Taylor .40 .18
❑ 310 Pete Gogolak .40 .18
❑ 311 Tony Baker .40 .18
❑ 312 John Richardson .40 .18
❑ 313 Dave Robinson .75 .35
❑ 314 Reggie McKenzie RC 1.50 .70
❑ 315 Isaac Curtis RC 1.50 .70
❑ 316 Thom Darden .40 .18
❑ 317 Ken Reaves .40 .18
❑ 318 Malcolm Snider .40 .18
❑ 319 Jeff Siemon RC .75 .35
❑ 320 Dan Abramowicz .75 .35
❑ 321 Lyle Alzado 2.00 .90
❑ 322 John Reaves .40 .18
❑ 323 Morris Stroud .40 .18
❑ 324 Bobby Walden .40 .18
❑ 325 Randy Vataha .40 .18
❑ 326 Nemiah Wilson .40 .18
❑ 327 Paul Naumoff .40 .18
❑ 328 Rushing Leaders 3.00 1.35
O.J. Simpson
John Brockington
❑ 329 Passing Leaders 5.00 2.20
Ken Stabler
Roger Staubach
❑ 330 Receiving Leaders 1.50 .70
Fred Willis
Harold Carmichael
❑ 331 Scoring Leaders .75 .35
Roy Gerela
David Ray
❑ 332 Interception Leaders .75 .35
Dick Anderson
Mike Wagner
Bobby Bryant
❑ 333 Punting Leaders .75 .35
Jerrel Wilson
Tom Wittum
❑ 334 Dennis Nelson .40 .18
❑ 335 Walt Garrison .75 .35
❑ 336 Tody Smith .40 .18
❑ 337 Ed Bell .40 .18
❑ 338 Bryant Salter .40 .18
❑ 339 Wayne Colman .40 .18
❑ 340 Garo Yepremian .75 .35
❑ 341 Bob Newton .40 .18
❑ 342 Vince Clements RC .40 .18
❑ 343 Ken Iman .40 .18
❑ 344 Jim Tolbert .40 .18
❑ 345 Chris Hanburger .75 .35
❑ 346 Dave Foley .40 .18
❑ 347 Tommy Casanova .75 .35
❑ 348 John James .40 .18
❑ 349 Clarence Williams .40 .18
❑ 350 Leroy Kelly 1.50 .70
❑ 351 Stu Voigt RC .75 .35
❑ 352 Skip Vanderbundt .40 .18
❑ 353 Pete Duranko .40 .18
❑ 354 John Outlaw .40 .18
❑ 355 Jan Stenerud 1.50 .70
❑ 356 Barry Pearson .40 .18
❑ 357 Brian Dowling RC .40 .18
❑ 358 Dan Conners .40 .18
❑ 359 Bob Bell .40 .18
❑ 360 Rick Volk .40 .18
❑ 361 Pat Toomay .75 .35
❑ 362 Bob Gresham .40 .18
❑ 363 John Schmitt .40 .18
❑ 364 Mel Rogers .40 .18
❑ 365 Manny Fernandez .75 .35
❑ 366 Ernie Jackson .40 .18
❑ 367 Gary Huff RC .75 .35
❑ 368 Bob Grim .40 .18
❑ 369 Ernie McMillan .40 .18
❑ 370 Dave Elmendorf .40 .18
❑ 371 Mike Bragg .40 .18
❑ 372 John Skorupan .40 .18
❑ 373 Howard Fest .40 .18
❑ 374 Jerry Tagge RC .75 .35
❑ 375 Art Malone .40 .18
❑ 376 Bob Babich .40 .18
❑ 377 Jim Marshall 1.50 .70
❑ 378 Bob Hoskins .40 .18
❑ 379 Don Zimmerman .40 .18
❑ 380 Ray May .40 .18
❑ 381 Emmitt Thomas .75 .35
❑ 382 Terry Hanratty .75 .35
❑ 383 John Hannah RC 15.00 6.75
❑ 384 George Atkinson .40 .18
❑ 385 Ted Hendricks 3.00 1.35
❑ 386 Jim O'Brien .40 .18
❑ 387 Jethro Pugh .75 .35

❑ 388 Elbert Drungo .40 .18
❑ 389 Richard Caster .75 .35
❑ 390 Deacon Jones 1.50 .70
❑ 391 Checklist 265-396 4.00 1.00
❑ 392 Jess Phillips .40 .18
❑ 393 Garry Lyle UER .40 .18
(Misspelled Gary
on card front)
❑ 394 Jim Files .40 .18
❑ 395 Jim Hart 1.50 .70
❑ 396 Dave Chapple .40 .18
❑ 397 Jim Langer 2.00 .90
❑ 398 John Wilbur .40 .18
❑ 399 Dwight Harrison .40 .18
❑ 400 John Brockington .75 .35
❑ 401 Ken Anderson 6.00 2.70
❑ 402 Mike Tilleman .40 .18
❑ 403 Charlie Hall .40 .18
❑ 404 Tommy Hart .40 .18
❑ 405 Norm Bulaich .75 .35
❑ 406 Jim Turner .40 .18
❑ 407 Mo Moorman .40 .18
❑ 408 Ralph Anderson .40 .18
❑ 409 Jim Otto 1.50 .70
❑ 410 Andy Russell 1.50 .70
❑ 411 Glenn Doughty .40 .18
❑ 412 Altie Taylor .40 .18
❑ 413 Marv Bateman .40 .18
❑ 414 Willie Alexander .40 .18
❑ 415 Bill Zapalac RC .40 .18
❑ 416 Russ Washington .40 .18
❑ 417 Joe Federspiel .40 .18
❑ 418 Craig Cotton .40 .18
❑ 419 Randy Johnson .40 .18
❑ 420 Harold Jackson 1.50 .70
❑ 421 Roger Wehrli .75 .35
❑ 422 Charlie Harraway .40 .18
❑ 423 Spike Jones .40 .18
❑ 424 Bob Johnson .40 .18
❑ 425 Mike McCoy .40 .18
❑ 426 Dennis Havig HOR .40 .18
❑ 427 Bob McKay .40 .18
❑ 428 Steve Zabel .40 .18
❑ 429 Horace Jones .40 .18
❑ 430 Jim Johnson 1.50 .70
❑ 431 Roy Gerela .75 .35
❑ 432 Tom Graham .40 .18
❑ 433 Curley Culp .75 .35
❑ 434 Ken Mendenhall .40 .18
❑ 435 Jim Plunkett 2.50 1.10
❑ 436 Julian Fagan .40 .18
❑ 437 Mike Garrett .75 .35
❑ 438 Bobby Joe Green .40 .18
❑ 439 Jack Gregory HOR .40 .18
❑ 440 Charlie Sanders .75 .35
❑ 441 Bill Curry .75 .35
❑ 442 Bob Pollard .40 .18
❑ 443 David Ray .40 .18
❑ 444 Terry Metcalf RC 3.00 1.35
❑ 445 Pat Fischer .75 .35
❑ 446 Bob Chandler .75 .35
❑ 447 Bill Bergey .75 .35
❑ 448 Walter Johnson .40 .18
❑ 449 Charlie Young RC 1.50 .70
❑ 450 Chester Marcol .40 .18
❑ 451 Ken Stabler 25.00 11.00
❑ 452 Preston Pearson 1.50 .70
❑ 453 Mike Current .40 .18
❑ 454 Ron Bolton .40 .18
❑ 455 Mark Lomas .40 .18
❑ 456 Raymond Chester .75 .35
❑ 457 Jerry LeVias .75 .35
❑ 458 Skip Butler .40 .18
❑ 459 Mike Livingston RC .40 .18
❑ 460 AFC Semi-Finals .75 .35
Raiders 33,
Steelers 14 and
Dolphins 34,
Bengals 16
❑ 461 NFC Semi-Finals 4.00 1.80
Vikings 27,
Redskins 20 and
Cowboys 27,
Rams 16
(Staubach)
❑ 462 Playoff Championship .. 3.00 1.35
Dolphins 27,
Raiders 10 and
Vikings 27,
Cowboys 10
(Ken Stabler and
Fran Tarkenton)
❑ 463 Super Bowl 2.00 .90
Dolphins 24,
Vikings 7
❑ 464 Wayne Mulligan .40 .18
❑ 465 Horst Muhlmann .40 .18
❑ 466 Milt Morin .40 .18
❑ 467 Don Parish .40 .18
❑ 468 Richard Neal .40 .18
❑ 469 Ron Jessie .75 .35
❑ 470 Terry Bradshaw 20.00 9.00
❑ 471 Fred Dryer 1.50 .70
❑ 472 Jim Carter .40 .18
❑ 473 Ken Burrow .40 .18
❑ 474 Wally Chambers RC .75 .35
❑ 475 Dan Pastorini 1.50 .70
❑ 476 Don Morrison .40 .18
❑ 477 Carl Mauck .40 .18
❑ 478 Larry Cole RC .75 .35
❑ 479 Jim Kiick 1.50 .70
❑ 480 Willie Lanier 1.50 .70
❑ 481 Don Herrmann .75 .35
❑ 482 George Hunt .40 .18
❑ 483 Bob Howard .40 .18
❑ 484 Myron Pottios .40 .18
❑ 485 Jackie Smith 1.50 .70
❑ 486 Vern Holland .40 .18
❑ 487 Jim Braxton .40 .18
❑ 488 Joe Reed .40 .18
❑ 489 Wally Hilgenberg .40 .18
❑ 490 Fred Biletnikoff 4.00 1.80
❑ 491 Bob DeMarco HOR .40 .18
❑ 492 Mark Nordquist .40 .18
❑ 493 Larry Brooks .40 .18
❑ 494 Pete Athas .40 .18
❑ 495 Emerson Boozer .75 .35
❑ 496 L.C. Greenwood 2.00 .90
❑ 497 Rockne Freitas .40 .18
❑ 498 Checklist 397-528 UER 4.00 1.00
(510 Charlie Taylor
should be Charley)
❑ 499 Joe Schmiesing .40 .18
❑ 500 Roger Staubach 25.00 11.00
❑ 501 Al Cowlings UER .75 .35
(Def. tackle on front,
Def. End on back)
❑ 502 Sam Cunningham RC .. 1.50 .70
❑ 503 Dennis Partee .40 .18
❑ 504 John Didion .40 .18
❑ 505 Nick Buoniconti 1.50 .70
❑ 506 Carl Garrett .75 .35
❑ 507 Doug Van Horn .40 .18
❑ 508 Jamie Rivers .40 .18
❑ 509 Jack Youngblood 4.00 1.80
❑ 510 Charley Taylor UER 2.50 1.10
(Misspelled Charlie
on both sides)
❑ 511 Ken Riley 1.50 .70
❑ 512 Joe Ferguson RC 2.00 .90
❑ 513 Bill Lueck .40 .18
❑ 514 Ray Brown .40 .18
❑ 515 Fred Cox .40 .18
❑ 516 Joe Jones .40 .18
❑ 517 Larry Schreiber .40 .18
❑ 518 Dennis Wirgowski .40 .18
❑ 519 Leroy Mitchell .40 .18
❑ 520 Otis Taylor 1.50 .70
❑ 521 Henry Davis .40 .18
❑ 522 Bruce Barnes .40 .18
❑ 523 Charlie Smith .40 .18
❑ 524 Bert Jones RC 5.00 2.20
❑ 525 Lem Barney 2.00 .90
❑ 526 John Fitzgerald RC .40 .18
❑ 527 Tom Funchess .40 .18
❑ 528 Steve Tannen 1.50 .70

1975 Topps

	NRMT-MT	EXC
COMPLETE SET (528)	300.00	135.00
COMMON CARD (1-528)	.30	.14
SEMISTARS	.75	.35
UNLISTED STARS	1.50	.70
CL (31/251/376/517)	4.00	1.80

❑ 1 Rushing Leaders 1.50 .35
Lawrence McCutcheon
Otis Armstrong
❑ 2 Passing Leaders 1.50 .70
Sonny Jurgensen
Ken Anderson
❑ 3 Receiving Leaders 1.50 .70
Charlie Young
Lydell Mitchell
❑ 4 Scoring Leaders .75 .35
Chester Marcol
Roy Gerela
❑ 5 Interception Leaders .75 .35
Ray Brown
Emmitt Thomas
❑ 6 Punting Leaders 1.50 .70
Tom Blanchard
Ray Guy
❑ 7 George Blanda 5.00 2.20
(Black jersey;
highlights on back)
❑ 8 George Blanda 5.00 2.20
(White jersey;
career record on back)
❑ 9 Ralph Baker .30 .14
❑ 10 Don Woods .30 .14
❑ 11 Bob Asher .30 .14
❑ 12 Mel Blount RC 20.00 9.00
❑ 13 Sam Cunningham .75 .35
❑ 14 Jackie Smith 1.50 .70
❑ 15 Greg Landry .75 .35
❑ 16 Buck Buchanan 1.50 .70
❑ 17 Haven Moses .75 .35
❑ 18 Clarence Ellis .30 .14
❑ 19 Jim Carter .30 .14
❑ 20 Charley Taylor UER 2.00 .90
(Misspelled Charlie
on card front)
❑ 21 Jess Phillips .30 .14
❑ 22 Larry Seiple .30 .14
❑ 23 Doug Dieken .30 .14
❑ 24 Ron Saul .30 .14
❑ 25 Isaac Curtis UER 1.50 .70
(Misspelled Issac
on card front)
❑ 26 Gary Larsen RC .30 .14
❑ 27 Bruce Jarvis .30 .14
❑ 28 Steve Zabel .30 .14
❑ 29 John Mendenhall .30 .14
❑ 30 Rick Volk .30 .14
❑ 31 Checklist 1-132 4.00 1.00
❑ 32 Dan Abramowicz .75 .35
❑ 33 Bubba Smith 1.50 .70
❑ 34 David Ray .30 .14
❑ 35 Dan Dierdorf 4.00 1.80
❑ 36 Randy Rasmussen .30 .14
❑ 37 Bob Howard .30 .14
❑ 38 Gary Huff .75 .35
❑ 39 Rocky Bleier RC 20.00 9.00
❑ 40 Mel Gray .75 .35
❑ 41 Tony McGee .30 .14
❑ 42 Larry Hand .30 .14
❑ 43 Wendell Hayes .30 .14
❑ 44 Doug Wilkerson RC .30 .14

❑	45	Paul Smith	.30	.14
❑	46	Dave Robinson	.75	.35
❑	47	Bivian Lee	.30	.14
❑	48	Jim Mandich RC	.75	.35
❑	49	Greg Pruitt	1.50	.70
❑	50	Dan Pastorini UER	1.50	.70
		(5/26/39 birthdate incorrect)		
❑	51	Ron Pritchard	.30	.14
❑	52	Dan Conners	.30	.14
❑	53	Fred Cox	.30	.14
❑	54	Tony Greene	.30	.14
❑	55	Craig Morton	1.50	.70
❑	56	Jerry Sisemore	.30	.14
❑	57	Glenn Doughty	.30	.14
❑	58	Larry Schreiber	.30	.14
❑	59	Charlie Waters RC	4.00	1.80
❑	60	Jack Youngblood	1.50	.70
❑	61	Bill Lenkaitis	.30	.14
❑	62	Greg Brezina	.30	.14
❑	63	Bob Pollard	.30	.14
❑	64	Mack Alston	.30	.14
❑	65	Drew Pearson RC	20.00	9.00
❑	66	Charlie Stukes	.30	.14
❑	67	Emerson Boozer	.75	.35
❑	68	Dennis Partee	.30	.14
❑	69	Bob Newton	.30	.14
❑	70	Jack Tatum	1.50	.70
❑	71	Frank Lewis	.30	.14
❑	72	Bob Young	.30	.14
❑	73	Julius Adams	.30	.14
❑	74	Paul Naumoff	.30	.14
❑	75	Otis Taylor	1.50	.70
❑	76	Dave Hampton	.30	.14
❑	77	Mike Current	.30	.14
❑	78	Brig Owens	.30	.14
❑	79	Bobby Scott	.30	.14
❑	80	Harold Carmichael	3.00	1.35
❑	81	Bill Stanfill	.30	.14
❑	82	Bob Babich	.30	.14
❑	83	Vic Washington	.30	.14
❑	84	Mick Tingelhoff	.75	.35
❑	85	Bob Trumpy	1.50	.70
❑	86	Earl Edwards	.30	.14
❑	87	Ron Hornsby	.30	.14
❑	88	Don McCauley	.30	.14
❑	89	Jim Johnson	1.50	.70
❑	90	Andy Russell	.75	.35
❑	91	Cornell Green	1.50	.70
❑	92	Charlie Cowan	.30	.14
❑	93	Jon Staggers	.30	.14
❑	94	Billy Newsome	.30	.14
❑	95	Willie Brown	1.50	.70
❑	96	Carl Mauck	.30	.14
❑	97	Doug Buffone	.30	.14
❑	98	Preston Pearson	.75	.35
❑	99	Jim Bakken	.30	.14
❑	100	Bob Griese	5.00	2.20
❑	101	Bob Windsor	.30	.14
❑	102	Rockne Freitas	.30	.14
❑	103	Jim Marsalis	.30	.14
❑	104	Bill Thompson	.75	.35
❑	105	Ken Burrow	.30	.14
❑	106	Diron Talbert	.30	.14
❑	107	Joe Federspiel	.30	.14
❑	108	Norm Bulaich	.75	.35
❑	109	Bob DeMarco	.30	.14
❑	110	Tom Wittum	.30	.14
❑	111	Larry Hefner	.30	.14
❑	112	Tody Smith	.30	.14
❑	113	Stu Voigt	.30	.14
❑	114	Horst Muhlmann	.30	.14
❑	115	Ahmad Rashad	6.00	2.70
❑	116	Joe Dawkins	.30	.14
❑	117	George Kunz	.30	.14
❑	118	D.D. Lewis	.75	.35
❑	119	Levi Johnson	.30	.14
❑	120	Len Dawson	4.00	1.80
❑	121	Jim Bertelsen	.30	.14
❑	122	Ed Bell	.30	.14
❑	123	Art Thoms	.30	.14
❑	124	Joe Beauchamp	.30	.14
❑	125	Jack Ham	6.00	2.70
❑	126	Carl Garrett	.30	.14
❑	127	Roger Finnie	.30	.14
❑	128	Howard Twilley	.75	.35
❑	129	Bruce Barnes	.30	.14
❑	130	Nate Wright	.30	.14
❑	131	Jerry Tagge	.30	.14
❑	132	Floyd Little	1.50	.70
❑	133	John Zook	.30	.14
❑	134	Len Hauss	.30	.14
❑	135	Archie Manning	1.50	.70
❑	136	Po James	.30	.14
❑	137	Walt Sumner	.30	.14
❑	138	Randy Beisler	.30	.14
❑	139	Willie Alexander	.30	.14
❑	140	Garo Yepremian	.75	.35
❑	141	Chip Myers	.30	.14
❑	142	Jim Braxton	.30	.14
❑	143	Doug Van Horn	.30	.14
❑	144	Stan White	.30	.14
❑	145	Roger Staubach	25.00	11.00
❑	146	Herman Weaver	.30	.14
❑	147	Marvin Upshaw	.30	.14
❑	148	Bob Klein	.30	.14
❑	149	Earlie Thomas	.30	.14
❑	150	John Brockington	.75	.35
❑	151	Mike Siani	.30	.14
❑	152	Sam Davis	.30	.14
❑	153	Mike Wagner	.75	.35
❑	154	Larry Stallings	.30	.14
❑	155	Wally Chambers	.30	.14
❑	156	Randy Vataha	.30	.14
❑	157	Jim Marshall	1.50	.70
❑	158	Jim Turner	.30	.14
❑	159	Walt Sweeney	.30	.14
❑	160	Ken Anderson	4.00	1.80
❑	161	Ray Brown	.30	.14
❑	162	John Didion	.30	.14
❑	163	Tom Dempsey	.30	.14
❑	164	Clarence Scott	.30	.14
❑	165	Gene Washington	.75	.35
❑	166	Willie Rogers	.30	.14
❑	167	Doug Swift	.30	.14
❑	168	Rufus Mayes	.30	.14
❑	169	Marv Bateman	.30	.14
❑	170	Lydell Mitchell	.75	.35
❑	171	Ron Smith	.30	.14
❑	172	Bill Munson	.75	.35
❑	173	Bob Grim	.30	.14
❑	174	Ed Budde	.30	.14
❑	175	Bob Lilly UER	3.00	1.35
		(Was first draft, not first player)		
❑	176	Jim Youngblood RC	1.50	.70
❑	177	Steve Tannen	.30	.14
❑	178	Rich McGeorge	.30	.14
❑	179	Jim Tyrer	.30	.14
❑	180	Forrest Blue	.30	.14
❑	181	Jerry LeVias	.75	.35
❑	182	Joe Gilliam RC	.30	.14
❑	183	Jim Otis RC	.75	.35
❑	184	Mel Tom	.30	.14
❑	185	Paul Seymour	.30	.14
❑	186	George Webster	.30	.14
❑	187	Pete Duranko	.30	.14
❑	188	Essex Johnson	.30	.14
❑	189	Bob Lee	.75	.35
❑	190	Gene Upshaw	1.50	.70
❑	191	Tom Myers	.30	.14
❑	192	Don Zimmerman	.30	.14
❑	193	John Garlington	.30	.14
❑	194	Skip Butler	.30	.14
❑	195	Tom Mitchell	.30	.14
❑	196	Jim Langer	1.50	.70
❑	197	Ron Carpenter	.30	.14
❑	198	Dave Foley	.30	.14
❑	199	Bert Jones	1.50	.70
❑	200	Larry Brown	.75	.35
❑	201	All Pro Receivers	2.00	.90
		Charley Taylor		
		Fred Biletnikoff		
❑	202	All Pro Tackles	.30	.14
		Rayfield Wright		
		Russ Washington		
❑	203	All Pro Guards	1.50	.70
		Tom Mack		
		Larry Little		
❑	204	All Pro Centers	.30	.14
		Jeff Van Note		
		Jack Rudnay		
❑	205	All Pro Guards	1.50	.70
		Gale Gillingham		
		John Hannah		
❑	206	All Pro Tackles	1.50	.70
		Dan Dierdorf		
		Winston Hill		
❑	207	All Pro Tight Ends	.75	.35
		Charlie Young		
		Riley Odoms		
❑	208	All Pro Quarterbacks	4.00	1.80
		Fran Tarkenton		
		Ken Stabler		
❑	209	All Pro Backs	3.00	1.35
		Lawrence McCutcheon		
		O.J. Simpson		
❑	210	All Pro Backs	.75	.35
		Terry Metcalf		
		Otis Armstrong		
❑	211	All Pro Receivers	.75	.35
		Mel Gray		
		Isaac Curtis		
❑	212	All Pro Kickers	.30	.14
		Chester Marcol		
		Roy Gerela		
❑	213	All Pro Ends	.75	.35
		Jack Youngblood		
		Elvin Bethea		
❑	214	All Pro Tackles	.75	.35
		Alan Page		
		Otis Sistrunk		
❑	215	All Pro Tackles	1.50	.70
		Merlin Olsen		
		Mike Reid		
❑	216	All Pro Ends	1.50	.70
		Carl Eller		
		Lyle Alzado		
❑	217	All Pro Linebackers	1.50	.70
		Ted Hendricks		
		Phil Villapiano		
❑	218	All Pro Linebackers	1.50	.70
		Lee Roy Jordan		
		Willie Lanier		
❑	219	All Pro Linebackers	.75	.35
		Isiah Robertson		
		Andy Russell		
❑	220	All Pro Cornerbacks	.30	.14
		Nate Wright		
		Emmitt Thomas		
❑	221	All Pro Cornerbacks	.30	.14
		Willie Buchanon		
		Lemar Parrish		
❑	222	All Pro Safeties	.75	.35
		Ken Houston		
		Dick Anderson		
❑	223	All Pro Safeties	1.50	.70
		Cliff Harris		
		Jack Tatum		
❑	224	All Pro Punters	.75	.35
		Tom Wittum		
		Ray Guy		
❑	225	All Pro Returners	.75	.35
		Terry Metcalf		
		Greg Pruitt		
❑	226	Ted Kwalick	.30	.14
❑	227	Spider Lockhart	.75	.35
❑	228	Mike Livingston	.30	.14
❑	229	Larry Cole	.30	.14
❑	230	Gary Garrison	.30	.14
❑	231	Larry Brooks	.30	.14
❑	232	Bobby Howfield	.30	.14
❑	233	Fred Carr	.30	.14
❑	234	Norm Evans	.30	.14
❑	235	Dwight White	.75	.35
❑	236	Conrad Dobler	.75	.35
❑	237	Garry Lyle	.30	.14
❑	238	Darryl Stingley	1.50	.70
❑	239	Tom Graham	.30	.14
❑	240	Chuck Foreman	1.50	.70
❑	241	Ken Riley	.75	.35
❑	242	Don Morrison	.30	.14
❑	243	Lynn Dickey	.75	.35
❑	244	Don Cockroft	.30	.14
❑	245	Claude Humphrey	.75	.35
❑	246	John Skorupan	.30	.14
❑	247	Raymond Chester	.75	.35
❑	248	Cas Banaszek	.30	.14

❑ 249 Art Malone .30 .14
❑ 250 Ed Flanagan .30 .14
❑ 251 Checklist 133-264 4.00 1.00
❑ 252 Nemiah Wilson .30 .14
❑ 253 Ron Jessie .30 .14
❑ 254 Jim Lynch .30 .14
❑ 255 Bob Tucker .75 .35
❑ 256 Terry Owens .30 .14
❑ 257 John Fitzgerald .30 .14
❑ 258 Jack Snow .75 .35
❑ 259 Garry Puetz .30 .14
❑ 260 Mike Phipps .75 .35
❑ 261 Al Matthews .30 .14
❑ 262 Bob Kuechenberg .30 .14
❑ 263 Ron Yankowski .30 .14
❑ 264 Ron Shanklin .30 .14
❑ 265 Bobby Douglass .75 .35
❑ 266 Josh Ashton .30 .14
❑ 267 Bill Van Heusen .30 .14
❑ 268 Jeff Siemon .30 .14
❑ 269 Bob Newland .30 .14
❑ 270 Gale Gillingham .30 .14
❑ 271 Zeke Moore .30 .14
❑ 272 Mike Tilleman .30 .14
❑ 273 John Leypoldt .30 .14
❑ 274 Ken Mendenhall .30 .14
❑ 275 Norm Snead .75 .35
❑ 276 Bill Bradley .75 .35
❑ 277 Jerry Smith .30 .14
❑ 278 Clarence Davis .30 .14
❑ 279 Jim Yarbrough .30 .14
❑ 280 Lemar Parrish .30 .14
❑ 281 Bobby Bell 1.50 .70
❑ 282 Lynn Swann RC UER 55.00 25.00
(Wide Reciever on front)
❑ 283 John Hicks .30 .14
❑ 284 Coy Bacon .75 .35
❑ 285 Lee Roy Jordan 1.50 .70
❑ 286 Willie Buchanon .30 .14
❑ 287 Al Woodall .30 .14
❑ 288 Reggie Rucker .75 .35
❑ 289 John Schmitt .30 .14
❑ 290 Carl Eller 1.50 .70
❑ 291 Jake Scott .75 .35
❑ 292 Donny Anderson .75 .35
❑ 293 Charley Wade .30 .14
❑ 294 John Tanner .30 .14
❑ 295 Charlie Johnson .75 .35
(Misspelled Charley
on both sides)
❑ 296 Tom Blanchard .30 .14
❑ 297 Curley Culp .75 .35
❑ 298 Jeff Van Note RC .75 .35
❑ 299 Bob James .30 .14
❑ 300 Franco Harris 8.00 3.60
❑ 301 Tim Berra .75 .35
❑ 302 Bruce Gossett .30 .14
❑ 303 Verlon Biggs .30 .14
❑ 304 Bob Kowalkowski .30 .14
❑ 305 Marv Hubbard .30 .14
❑ 306 Ken Avery .30 .14
❑ 307 Mike Adamle .30 .14
❑ 308 Don Herrmann .30 .14
❑ 309 Chris Fletcher .30 .14
❑ 310 Roman Gabriel 1.50 .70
❑ 311 Billy Joe DuPree 1.50 .70
❑ 312 Fred Dryer 1.50 .70
❑ 313 John Riggins 5.00 2.20
❑ 314 Bob McKay .30 .14
❑ 315 Ted Hendricks 1.50 .70
❑ 316 Bobby Bryant .30 .14
❑ 317 Don Nottingham .30 .14
❑ 318 John Hannah 4.00 1.80
❑ 319 Rich Coady .30 .14
❑ 320 Phil Villapiano .75 .35
❑ 321 Jim Plunkett 1.50 .70
❑ 322 Lyle Alzado 1.50 .70
❑ 323 Ernie Jackson .30 .14
❑ 324 Billy Parks .30 .14
❑ 325 Willie Lanier 1.50 .70
❑ 326 John James .30 .14
❑ 327 Joe Ferguson .75 .35
❑ 328 Ernie Holmes RC 1.50 .70
❑ 329 Bruce Laird .30 .14
❑ 330 Chester Marcol .30 .14
❑ 331 Dave Wilcox .75 .35
❑ 332 Pat Fischer .75 .35
❑ 333 Steve Owens .75 .35
❑ 334 Royce Berry .30 .14
❑ 335 Russ Washington .30 .14
❑ 336 Walker Gillette .30 .14
❑ 337 Mark Nordquist .30 .14
❑ 338 James Harris RC 1.50 .70
❑ 339 Warren Koegel .30 .14
❑ 340 Emmitt Thomas .75 .35
❑ 341 Walt Garrison .75 .35
❑ 342 Thom Darden .30 .14
❑ 343 Mike Eischeid .30 .14
❑ 344 Ernie McMillan .30 .14
❑ 345 Nick Buoniconti 1.50 .70
❑ 346 George Farmer .30 .14
❑ 347 Sam Adams .30 .14
❑ 348 Larry Cipa .30 .14
❑ 349 Bob Moore .30 .14
❑ 350 Otis Armstrong RC 1.50 .70
❑ 351 George Blanda RB 3.00 1.35
All Time Scoring
Leader
❑ 352 Fred Cox RB .75 .35
151 Straight PAT's
❑ 353 Tom Dempsey RB .75 .35
63 Yard FG
❑ 354 Ken Houston RB 1.50 .70
9th Int. for TD
(Shown as Oiler,
should be Redskin)
❑ 355 O.J. Simpson RB 5.00 2.20
2003 Yard Season
❑ 356 Ron Smith RB .75 .35
All Time Return
Yardage Mark
❑ 357 Bob Atkins .30 .14
❑ 358 Pat Sullivan .75 .35
❑ 359 Joe DeLamielleure .75 .35
❑ 360 Lawrence McCutcheon RC 1.50 .70
❑ 361 David Lee .30 .14
❑ 362 Mike McCoy .30 .14
❑ 363 Skip Vanderbundt .30 .14
❑ 364 Mark Moseley .75 .35
❑ 365 Lem Barney 1.50 .70
❑ 366 Doug Dressler .30 .14
❑ 367 Dan Fouts RC 45.00 20.00
❑ 368 Bob Hyland .30 .14
❑ 369 John Outlaw .30 .14
❑ 370 Roy Gerela .30 .14
❑ 371 Isiah Robertson .75 .35
❑ 372 Jerome Barkum .30 .14
❑ 373 Ed Podolak .30 .14
❑ 374 Milt Morin .30 .14
❑ 375 John Niland .30 .14
❑ 376 Checklist 265-396 UER 4.00 1.00
(295 Charlie Johnson
missppelled as Charley)
❑ 377 Ken Iman .30 .14
❑ 378 Manny Fernandez .75 .35
❑ 379 Dave Gallagher .30 .14
❑ 380 Ken Stabler 15.00 6.75
❑ 381 Mack Herron .30 .14
❑ 382 Bill McClard .30 .14
❑ 383 Ray May .30 .14
❑ 384 Don Hansen .30 .14
❑ 385 Elvin Bethea .75 .35
❑ 386 Joe Scibelli .30 .14
❑ 387 Neal Craig .30 .14
❑ 388 Marty Domres .30 .14
❑ 389 Ken Ellis .30 .14
❑ 390 Charlie Young .75 .35
❑ 391 Tommy Hart .30 .14
❑ 392 Moses Denson .30 .14
❑ 393 Larry Walton .30 .14
❑ 394 Dave Green .30 .14
❑ 395 Ron Johnson .75 .35
❑ 396 Ed Bradley .30 .14
❑ 397 J.T. Thomas .30 .14
❑ 398 Jim Bailey .30 .14
❑ 399 Barry Pearson .30 .14
❑ 400 Fran Tarkenton 8.00 3.60
❑ 401 Jack Rudnay .30 .14
❑ 402 Rayfield Wright .75 .35
❑ 403 Roger Wehrli .75 .35
❑ 404 Vern Den Herder .30 .14
❑ 405 Fred Biletnikoff 3.00 1.35
❑ 406 Ken Grandberry .30 .14
❑ 407 Bob Adams .30 .14
❑ 408 Jim Merlo .30 .14
❑ 409 John Pitts .30 .14
❑ 410 Dave Osborn .75 .35
❑ 411 Dennis Havig .30 .14
❑ 412 Bob Johnson .30 .14
❑ 413 Ken Burrough UER .75 .35
(Misspelled Burrow
on card front)
❑ 414 Jim Cheyunski .30 .14
❑ 415 MacArthur Lane .30 .14
❑ 416 Joe Theismann RC**/C 25.00 11.00
❑ 417 Mike Boryla RC .30 .14
❑ 418 Bruce Taylor .30 .14
❑ 419 Chris Hanburger .75 .35
❑ 420 Tom Mack .75 .35
❑ 421 Errol Mann .30 .14
❑ 422 Jack Gregory .30 .14
❑ 423 Harrison Davis .30 .14
❑ 424 Burgess Owens .30 .14
❑ 425 Joe Greene 5.00 2.20
❑ 426 Morris Stroud .30 .14
❑ 427 John DeMarie .30 .14
❑ 428 Mel Renfro 1.50 .70
❑ 429 Cid Edwards .30 .14
❑ 430 Mike Reid 1.50 .70
❑ 431 Jack Mildren .30 .14
❑ 432 Jerry Simmons .30 .14
❑ 433 Ron Yary .75 .35
❑ 434 Howard Stevens .30 .14
❑ 435 Ray Guy 2.00 .90
❑ 436 Tommy Nobis 1.50 .70
❑ 437 Solomon Freelon .30 .14
❑ 438 J.D. Hill .75 .35
❑ 439 Toni Linhart .30 .14
❑ 440 Dick Anderson .75 .35
❑ 441 Guy Morriss .30 .14
❑ 442 Bob Hoskins .30 .14
❑ 443 John Hadl 1.50 .70
❑ 444 Roy Jefferson .30 .14
❑ 445 Charlie Sanders .75 .35
❑ 446 Pat Curran .30 .14
❑ 447 David Knight .30 .14
❑ 448 Bob Brown DT .30 .14
❑ 449 Pete Gogolak .30 .14
❑ 450 Terry Metcalf 1.50 .70
❑ 451 Bill Bergey 1.50 .70
❑ 452 Dan Abramowicz HL .75 .35
105 Straight Games
❑ 453 Otis Armstrong HL .75 .35
183 Yard Game
❑ 454 Cliff Branch HL 1.50 .70
13 TD Passes
❑ 455 John James HL .30 .14
Record 96 Punts
❑ 456 Lydell Mitchell HL .75 .35
13 Passes in Game
❑ 457 Lemar Parrish HL .75 .35
3 TD Punt Returns
❑ 458 Ken Stabler HL 5.00 2.20
26 TD Passes
in One Season
❑ 459 Lynn Swann HL 8.00 3.60
577 Yards in
Punt Returns
❑ 460 Emmitt Thomas HL .30 .14
73 Yd. Interception
❑ 461 Terry Bradshaw 20.00 9.00
❑ 462 Jerrel Wilson .30 .14
❑ 463 Walter Johnson .30 .14
❑ 464 Golden Richards .75 .35
❑ 465 Tommy Casanova .75 .35
❑ 466 Randy Jackson .30 .14
❑ 467 Ron Bolton .30 .14
❑ 468 Joe Owens .30 .14
❑ 469 Wally Hilgenberg .30 .14
❑ 470 Riley Odoms .75 .35
❑ 471 Otis Sistrunk .75 .35
❑ 472 Eddie Ray .30 .14
❑ 473 Reggie McKenzie .75 .35
❑ 474 Elbert Drungo .30 .14
❑ 475 Mercury Morris 1.50 .70
❑ 476 Dan Dickel .30 .14
❑ 477 Merritt Kersey .30 .14

Card	NRMT-MT	EXC
❑ 478 Mike Holmes	.30	.14
❑ 479 Clarence Williams	.30	.14
❑ 480 Billy Kilmer	1.50	.70
❑ 481 Altie Taylor	.30	.14
❑ 482 Dave Elmendorf	.30	.14
❑ 483 Bob Rowe	.30	.14
❑ 484 Pete Athas	.30	.14
❑ 485 Winston Hill	.30	.14
❑ 486 Bo Matthews	.30	.14
❑ 487 Earl Thomas	.30	.14
❑ 488 Jan Stenerud	1.50	.70
❑ 489 Steve Holden	.30	.14
❑ 490 Cliff Harris RC	4.00	1.80
❑ 491 Boobie Clark RC	.75	.35
❑ 492 Joe Taylor	.30	.14
❑ 493 Tom Neville	.30	.14
❑ 494 Wayne Colman	.30	.14
❑ 495 Jim Mitchell	.30	.14
❑ 496 Paul Krause	1.50	.70
❑ 497 Jim Otto	1.50	.70
❑ 498 John Rowser	.30	.14
❑ 499 Larry Little	1.50	.70
❑ 500 O.J. Simpson	10.00	4.50
❑ 501 John Dutton RC	1.50	.70
❑ 502 Pat Hughes	.30	.14
❑ 503 Malcolm Snider	.30	.14
❑ 504 Fred Willis	.30	.14
❑ 505 Harold Jackson	1.50	.70
❑ 506 Mike Bragg	.30	.14
❑ 507 Jerry Sherk	.75	.35
❑ 508 Mirro Roder	.30	.14
❑ 509 Tom Sullivan	.30	.14
❑ 510 Jim Hart	1.50	.70
❑ 511 Cedrick Hardman	.30	.14
❑ 512 Blaine Nye	.30	.14
❑ 513 Elmo Wright	.30	.14
❑ 514 Herb Orvis	.30	.14
❑ 515 Richard Caster	.75	.35
❑ 516 Doug Kotar RC	.30	.14
❑ 517 Checklist 397-528	4.00	1.00
❑ 518 Jesse Freitas	.30	.14
❑ 519 Ken Houston	1.50	.70
❑ 520 Alan Page	1.50	.70
❑ 521 Tim Foley	.75	.35
❑ 522 Bill Olds	.30	.14
❑ 523 Bobby Maples	.30	.14
❑ 524 Cliff Branch RC	15.00	6.75
❑ 525 Merlin Olsen	1.50	.70
❑ 526 AFC Champs Pittsburgh 24, Oakland 13 (Bradshaw and Franco Harris)	4.00	1.80
❑ 527 NFC Champs Minnesota 14, Los Angeles 10 (C.Foreman tackled)	1.50	.70
❑ 528 Super Bowl IX Steelers 16, Vikings 6 (Bradshaw watching pass)	5.00	1.25

1976 Topps

	NRMT-MT	EXC
COMPLETE SET (528)	350.00	160.00
COMMON CARD (1-528)	.30	.14
SEMISTARS	.75	.35
UNLISTED STARS	1.50	.70
TC (451-478)	2.00	.90
CL (67/177/273/507)	3.00	1.35

Card	NRMT-MT	EXC
❑ 1 George Blanda RB First to Score 2000 Points	5.00	1.25
❑ 2 Neal Colzie RB Punt Returns	.75	.35
❑ 3 Chuck Foreman RB Catches 73 Passes	.75	.35
❑ 4 Jim Marshall RB 26th Fumble Recovery	.75	.35
❑ 5 Terry Metcalf RB Most all-purpose yards; season	.75	.35
❑ 6 O.J. Simpson RB 23 Touchdowns	3.00	1.35
❑ 7 Fran Tarkenton RB Most Attempts;Season	3.00	1.35
❑ 8 Charley Taylor RB Career Receptions	1.50	.70
❑ 9 Ernie Holmes	.75	.35
❑ 10 Ken Anderson AP	1.50	.70
❑ 11 Bobby Bryant	.30	.14
❑ 12 Jerry Smith	.75	.35
❑ 13 David Lee	.30	.14
❑ 14 Robert Newhouse RC	1.50	.70
❑ 15 Vern Den Herder	.30	.14
❑ 16 John Hannah	1.50	.70
❑ 17 J.D. Hill	.75	.35
❑ 18 James Harris	.75	.35
❑ 19 Willie Buchanon	.30	.14
❑ 20 Charlie Young AP	.75	.35
❑ 21 Jim Yarbrough	.30	.14
❑ 22 Ronnie Coleman	.30	.14
❑ 23 Don Cockroft	.30	.14
❑ 24 Willie Lanier	1.50	.70
❑ 25 Fred Biletnikoff	3.00	1.35
❑ 26 Ron Yankowski	.30	.14
❑ 27 Spider Lockhart	.30	.14
❑ 28 Bob Johnson	.30	.14
❑ 29 J.T. Thomas	.30	.14
❑ 30 Ron Yary AP	.75	.35
❑ 31 Brad Dusek RC	.30	.14
❑ 32 Raymond Chester	.75	.35
❑ 33 Larry Little	1.50	.70
❑ 34 Pat Leahy RC	1.50	.70
❑ 35 Steve Bartkowski RC	4.00	1.80
❑ 36 Tom Myers	.30	.14
❑ 37 Bill Van Heusen	.30	.14
❑ 38 Russ Washington	.30	.14
❑ 39 Tom Sullivan	.30	.14
❑ 40 Curley Culp AP	.75	.35
❑ 41 Johnnie Gray	.30	.14
❑ 42 Bob Klein	.30	.14
❑ 43 Lem Barney	1.50	.70
❑ 44 Harvey Martin RC	4.00	1.80
❑ 45 Reggie Rucker	.75	.35
❑ 46 Neil Clabo	.30	.14
❑ 47 Ray Hamilton	.30	.14
❑ 48 Joe Ferguson	.75	.35
❑ 49 Ed Podolak	.30	.14
❑ 50 Ray Guy AP	1.50	.70
❑ 51 Glen Edwards	.30	.14
❑ 52 Jim LeClair	.30	.14
❑ 53 Mike Barnes	.30	.14
❑ 54 Nat Moore RC	1.50	.70
❑ 55 Billy Kilmer	1.50	.70
❑ 56 Larry Stallings	.30	.14
❑ 57 Jack Gregory	.30	.14
❑ 58 Steve Mike-Mayer	.30	.14
❑ 59 Virgil Livers	.30	.14
❑ 60 Jerry Sherk AP	.75	.35
❑ 61 Guy Morriss	.30	.14
❑ 62 Barty Smith	.30	.14
❑ 63 Jerome Barkum	.30	.14
❑ 64 Ira Gordon	.30	.14
❑ 65 Paul Krause	1.50	.70
❑ 66 John McMakin	.30	.14
❑ 67 Checklist 1-132	3.00	.75
❑ 68 Charlie Johnson UER (Misspelled Charley on both sides)	.75	.35
❑ 69 Tommy Nobis	1.50	.70
❑ 70 Lydell Mitchell	.75	.35
❑ 71 Vern Holland	.30	.14
❑ 72 Tim Foley	.75	.35
❑ 73 Golden Richards	.75	.35
❑ 74 Bryant Salter	.30	.14
❑ 75 Terry Bradshaw	20.00	9.00
❑ 76 Ted Hendricks	1.50	.70
❑ 77 Rich Saul RC	.30	.14
❑ 78 John Smith	.30	.14
❑ 79 Altie Taylor	.30	.14
❑ 80 Cedrick Hardman AP	.30	.14
❑ 81 Ken Payne	.30	.14
❑ 82 Zeke Moore	.30	.14
❑ 83 Alvin Maxson	.30	.14
❑ 84 Wally Hilgenberg	.30	.14
❑ 85 John Niland	.30	.14
❑ 86 Mike Sensibaugh	.30	.14
❑ 87 Ron Johnson	.75	.35
❑ 88 Winston Hill	.30	.14
❑ 89 Charlie Joiner	4.00	1.80
❑ 90 Roger Wehrli AP	.75	.35
❑ 91 Mike Bragg	.30	.14
❑ 92 Dan Dickel	.30	.14
❑ 93 Earl Morrall	.75	.35
❑ 94 Pat Toomay	.30	.14
❑ 95 Gary Garrison	.30	.14
❑ 96 Ken Geddes	.30	.14
❑ 97 Mike Current	.30	.14
❑ 98 Bob Avellini RC	.75	.35
❑ 99 Dave Pureifory	.30	.14
❑ 100 Franco Harris AP	8.00	3.60
❑ 101 Randy Logan	.30	.14
❑ 102 John Fitzgerald	.30	.14
❑ 103 Gregg Bingham RC	.75	.35
❑ 104 Jim Plunkett	1.50	.70
❑ 105 Carl Eller	1.50	.70
❑ 106 Larry Walton	.30	.14
❑ 107 Clarence Scott	.30	.14
❑ 108 Skip Vanderbundt	.30	.14
❑ 109 Boobie Clark	.75	.35
❑ 110 Tom Mack AP	.75	.35
❑ 111 Bruce Laird	.30	.14
❑ 112 Dave Dalby RC	.30	.14
❑ 113 John Leypoldt	.30	.14
❑ 114 Barry Pearson	.30	.14
❑ 115 Larry Brown	.75	.35
❑ 116 Jackie Smith	1.50	.70
❑ 117 Pat Hughes	.30	.14
❑ 118 Al Woodall	.30	.14
❑ 119 John Zook	.30	.14
❑ 120 Jake Scott AP	.75	.35
❑ 121 Rich Glover	.30	.14
❑ 122 Ernie Jackson	.30	.14
❑ 123 Otis Armstrong	1.50	.70
❑ 124 Bob Grim	.30	.14
❑ 125 Jeff Siemon	.75	.35
❑ 126 Harold Hart	.30	.14
❑ 127 John DeMarie	.30	.14
❑ 128 Dan Fouts	12.00	5.50
❑ 129 Jim Kearney	.30	.14
❑ 130 John Dutton AP	.75	.35
❑ 131 Calvin Hill	1.50	.70
❑ 132 Toni Fritsch	.30	.14
❑ 133 Ron Jessie	.30	.14
❑ 134 Don Nottingham	.30	.14
❑ 135 Lemar Parrish	.30	.14
❑ 136 Russ Francis RC	1.50	.70
❑ 137 Joe Reed	.30	.14
❑ 138 C.L. Whittington	.30	.14
❑ 139 Otis Sistrunk	.75	.35
❑ 140 Lynn Swann AP	20.00	9.00
❑ 141 Jim Carter	.30	.14
❑ 142 Mike Montler	.30	.14
❑ 143 Walter Johnson	.30	.14
❑ 144 Doug Kotar	.30	.14
❑ 145 Roman Gabriel	1.50	.70
❑ 146 Billy Newsome	.30	.14
❑ 147 Ed Bradley	.30	.14
❑ 148 Walter Payton RC	225.00	100.00
❑ 149 Johnny Fuller	.30	.14
❑ 150 Alan Page AP	1.50	.70
❑ 151 Frank Grant	.30	.14
❑ 152 Dave Green	.30	.14
❑ 153 Nelson Munsey	.30	.14
❑ 154 Jim Mandich	.30	.14
❑ 155 Lawrence McCutcheon	1.50	.70

❑ 156 Steve Ramsey .30 .14
❑ 157 Ed Flanagan .30 .14
❑ 158 Randy White RC 25.00 11.00
❑ 159 Gerry Mullins .30 .14
❑ 160 Jan Stenerud AP 1.50 .70
❑ 161 Steve Odom .30 .14
❑ 162 Roger Finnie .30 .14
❑ 163 Norm Snead .75 .35
❑ 164 Jeff Van Note .75 .35
❑ 165 Bill Bergey 1.50 .70
❑ 166 Allen Carter .30 .14
❑ 167 Steve Holden .30 .14
❑ 168 Sherman White .30 .14
❑ 169 Bob Berry .30 .14
❑ 170 Ken Houston AP 1.50 .70
❑ 171 Bill Olds .30 .14
❑ 172 Larry Seiple .30 .14
❑ 173 Cliff Branch 4.00 1.80
❑ 174 Reggie McKenzie .75 .35
❑ 175 Dan Pastorini 1.50 .70
❑ 176 Paul Naumoff .30 .14
❑ 177 Checklist 133-264 3.00 .75
❑ 178 Durwood Keeton .30 .14
❑ 179 Earl Thomas .30 .14
❑ 180 L.C. Greenwood AP 1.50 .70
❑ 181 John Outlaw .30 .14
❑ 182 Frank Nunley .30 .14
❑ 183 Dave Jennings RC .75 .35
❑ 184 MacArthur Lane .30 .14
❑ 185 Chester Marcol .30 .14
❑ 186 J.J. Jones .30 .14
❑ 187 Tom DeLeone .30 .14
❑ 188 Steve Zabel .30 .14
❑ 189 Ken Johnson .30 .14
❑ 190 Rayfield Wright AP .75 .35
❑ 191 Brent McClanahan .30 .14
❑ 192 Pat Fischer .75 .35
❑ 193 Roger Carr RC .75 .35
❑ 194 Manny Fernandez .75 .35
❑ 195 Roy Gerela .30 .14
❑ 196 Dave Elmendorf .30 .14
❑ 197 Bob Kowalkowski .30 .14
❑ 198 Phil Villapiano .75 .35
❑ 199 Will Wynn .30 .14
❑ 200 Terry Metcalf 1.50 .70
❑ 201 Passing Leaders 2.00 .90
Ken Anderson
Fran Tarkenton
❑ 202 Receiving Leaders .75 .35
Reggie Rucker
Lydell Mitchell
Chuck Foreman
❑ 203 Rushing Leaders 2.50 1.10
O.J. Simpson
Jim Otis
❑ 204 Scoring Leaders 2.50 1.10
O.J. Simpson
Chuck Foreman
❑ 205 Interception Leaders 1.50 .70
Mel Blount
Paul Krause
❑ 206 Punting Leaders .75 .35
Ray Guy
Herman Weaver
❑ 207 Ken Ellis .30 .14
❑ 208 Ron Saul .30 .14
❑ 209 Toni Linhart .30 .14
❑ 210 Jim Langer AP 1.50 .70
❑ 211 Jeff Wright .30 .14
❑ 212 Moses Denson .30 .14
❑ 213 Earl Edwards .30 .14
❑ 214 Walker Gillette .30 .14
❑ 215 Bob Trumpy .75 .35
❑ 216 Emmitt Thomas .75 .35
❑ 217 Lyle Alzado 1.50 .70
❑ 218 Carl Garrett .75 .35
❑ 219 Van Green .30 .14
❑ 220 Jack Lambert AP RC 30.00 13.50
❑ 221 Spike Jones .30 .14
❑ 222 John Hadl 1.50 .70
❑ 223 Billy Johnson RC 1.50 .70
❑ 224 Tony McGee .30 .14
❑ 225 Preston Pearson .75 .35
❑ 226 Isiah Robertson .75 .35
❑ 227 Errol Mann .30 .14
❑ 228 Paul Seal .30 .14
❑ 229 Roland Harper RC .30 .14
❑ 230 Ed White AP RC .75 .35
❑ 231 Joe Theismann 6.00 2.70
❑ 232 Jim Cheyunski .30 .14
❑ 233 Bill Stanfill .75 .35
❑ 234 Marv Hubbard .30 .14
❑ 235 Tommy Casanova .75 .35
❑ 236 Bob Hyland .30 .14
❑ 237 Jesse Freitas .30 .14
❑ 238 Norm Thompson .30 .14
❑ 239 Charlie Smith .30 .14
❑ 240 John James AP .30 .14
❑ 241 Alden Roche .30 .14
❑ 242 Gordon Jolley .30 .14
❑ 243 Larry Ely .30 .14
❑ 244 Richard Caster .30 .14
❑ 245 Joe Greene 4.00 1.80
❑ 246 Larry Schreiber .30 .14
❑ 247 Terry Schmidt .30 .14
❑ 248 Jerrel Wilson .30 .14
❑ 249 Marty Domres .30 .14
❑ 250 Isaac Curtis AP .75 .35
❑ 251 Harold McLinton .30 .14
❑ 252 Fred Dryer 1.50 .70
❑ 253 Bill Lenkaitis .30 .14
❑ 254 Don Hardeman .30 .14
❑ 255 Bob Griese 4.00 1.80
❑ 256 Oscar Roan RC .30 .14
❑ 257 Randy Gradishar RC 2.50 1.10
❑ 258 Bob Thomas RC .30 .14
❑ 259 Joe Owens .30 .14
❑ 260 Cliff Harris AP 1.50 .70
❑ 261 Frank Lewis .30 .14
❑ 262 Mike McCoy .30 .14
❑ 263 Rickey Young RC .30 .14
❑ 264 Brian Kelley RC .30 .14
❑ 265 Charlie Sanders .75 .35
❑ 266 Jim Hart 1.50 .70
❑ 267 Greg Gantt .30 .14
❑ 268 John Ward .30 .14
❑ 269 Al Beauchamp .30 .14
❑ 270 Jack Tatum AP 1.50 .70
❑ 271 Jim Lash .30 .14
❑ 272 Diron Talbert .30 .14
❑ 273 Checklist 265-396 3.00 .75
❑ 274 Steve Spurrier 8.00 3.60
❑ 275 Greg Pruitt 1.50 .70
❑ 276 Jim Mitchell .30 .14
❑ 277 Jack Rudnay .30 .14
❑ 278 Freddie Solomon RC .75 .35
❑ 279 Frank LeMaster .30 .14
❑ 280 Wally Chambers AP .30 .14
❑ 281 Mike Collier .30 .14
❑ 282 Clarence Williams .30 .14
❑ 283 Mitch Hoopes .30 .14
❑ 284 Ron Bolton .30 .14
❑ 285 Harold Jackson 1.50 .70
❑ 286 Greg Landry .75 .35
❑ 287 Tony Greene .30 .14
❑ 288 Howard Stevens .30 .14
❑ 289 Roy Jefferson .30 .14
❑ 290 Jim Bakken AP .30 .14
❑ 291 Doug Sutherland .30 .14
❑ 292 Marvin Cobb .30 .14
❑ 293 Mack Alston .30 .14
❑ 294 Rod McNeill .30 .14
❑ 295 Gene Upshaw 1.50 .70
❑ 296 Dave Gallagher .30 .14
❑ 297 Larry Ball .30 .14
❑ 298 Ron Howard .30 .14
❑ 299 Don Strock RC 1.50 .70
❑ 300 O.J. Simpson AP 8.00 3.60
❑ 301 Ray Mansfield .30 .14
❑ 302 Larry Marshall .30 .14
❑ 303 Dick Himes .30 .14
❑ 304 Ray Wersching RC .30 .14
❑ 305 John Riggins 4.00 1.80
❑ 306 Bob Parsons .30 .14
❑ 307 Ray Brown .30 .14
❑ 308 Len Dawson 3.00 1.35
❑ 309 Andy Maurer .30 .14
❑ 310 Jack Youngblood AP 1.50 .70
❑ 311 Essex Johnson .30 .14
❑ 312 Stan White .30 .14
❑ 313 Drew Pearson 4.00 1.80
❑ 314 Rockne Freitas .30 .14
❑ 315 Mercury Morris 1.50 .70
❑ 316 Willie Alexander .30 .14
❑ 317 Paul Warfield 3.00 1.35
❑ 318 Bob Chandler .75 .35
❑ 319 Bobby Walden .30 .14
❑ 320 Riley Odoms AP .75 .35
❑ 321 Mike Boryla .30 .14
❑ 322 Bruce Van Dyke .30 .14
❑ 323 Pete Banaszak .30 .14
❑ 324 Darryl Stingley 1.50 .70
❑ 325 John Mendenhall .30 .14
❑ 326 Dan Dierdorf 2.00 .90
❑ 327 Bruce Taylor .30 .14
❑ 328 Don McCauley .30 .14
❑ 329 John Reaves UER .30 .14
(24 attempts in '72; should be 224)
❑ 330 Chris Hanburger AP .75 .35
❑ 331 NFC Champions 3.00 1.35
Cowboys 37,
Rams 7
(Roger Staubach)
❑ 332 AFC Champions 2.00 .90
Steelers 16,
Raiders 10
(Franco Harris)
❑ 333 Super Bowl X 2.50 1.10
Steelers 21,
Cowboys 17
(Terry Bradshaw)
❑ 334 Godwin Turk .30 .14
❑ 335 Dick Anderson .75 .35
❑ 336 Woody Green .30 .14
❑ 337 Pat Curran .30 .14
❑ 338 Council Rudolph .30 .14
❑ 339 Joe Lavender .30 .14
❑ 340 John Gilliam AP .75 .35
❑ 341 Steve Furness RC .75 .35
❑ 342 D.D. Lewis .75 .35
❑ 343 Duane Carrell .30 .14
❑ 344 Jon Morris .30 .14
❑ 345 John Brockington .75 .35
❑ 346 Mike Phipps .75 .35
❑ 347 Lyle Blackwood RC .30 .14
❑ 348 Julius Adams .30 .14
❑ 349 Terry Hermeling .30 .14
❑ 350 Rolland Lawrence AP RC .30 .14
❑ 351 Glenn Doughty .30 .14
❑ 352 Doug Swift .30 .14
❑ 353 Mike Strachan .30 .14
❑ 354 Craig Morton 1.50 .70
❑ 355 George Blanda 5.00 2.20
❑ 356 Garry Puetz .30 .14
❑ 357 Carl Mauck .30 .14
❑ 358 Walt Patulski .30 .14
❑ 359 Stu Voigt .30 .14
❑ 360 Fred Carr AP .30 .14
❑ 361 Po James .30 .14
❑ 362 Otis Taylor 1.50 .70
❑ 363 Jeff West .30 .14
❑ 364 Gary Huff .75 .35
❑ 365 Dwight White .75 .35
❑ 366 Dan Ryczek .30 .14
❑ 367 Jon Keyworth RC .30 .14
❑ 368 Mel Renfro 1.50 .70
❑ 369 Bruce Coslet RC 1.50 .70
❑ 370 Len Hauss AP .30 .14
❑ 371 Rick Volk .30 .14
❑ 372 Howard Twilley .75 .35
❑ 373 Cullen Bryant RC .75 .35
❑ 374 Bob Babich .30 .14
❑ 375 Herman Weaver .30 .14
❑ 376 Steve Grogan RC 3.00 1.35
❑ 377 Bubba Smith 1.50 .70
❑ 378 Burgess Owens .30 .14
❑ 379 Al Matthews .30 .14
❑ 380 Art Shell 1.50 .70
❑ 381 Larry Brown .30 .14
❑ 382 Horst Muhlmann .30 .14
❑ 383 Ahmad Rashad 2.50 1.10
❑ 384 Bobby Maples .30 .14
❑ 385 Jim Marshall 1.50 .70
❑ 386 Joe Dawkins .30 .14
❑ 387 Dennis Partee .30 .14
❑ 388 Eddie McMillan .30 .14
❑ 389 Randy Johnson .30 .14

❑ 390 Bob Kuechenberg AP .30 .14
❑ 391 Rufus Mayes .30 .14
❑ 392 Lloyd Mumphord .30 .14
❑ 393 Ike Harris .30 .14
❑ 394 Dave Hampton .30 .14
❑ 395 Roger Staubach 20.00 9.00
❑ 396 Doug Buffone .30 .14
❑ 397 Howard Fest .30 .14
❑ 398 Wayne Mulligan .30 .14
❑ 399 Bill Bradley .75 .35
❑ 400 Chuck Foreman AP 1.50 .70
❑ 401 Jack Snow .75 .35
❑ 402 Bob Howard .30 .14
❑ 403 John Matuszak 1.50 .70
❑ 404 Bill Munson .75 .35
❑ 405 Andy Russell .75 .35
❑ 406 Skip Butler .30 .14
❑ 407 Hugh McKinnis .30 .14
❑ 408 Bob Penchion .30 .14
❑ 409 Mike Bass .30 .14
❑ 410 George Kunz AP .30 .14
❑ 411 Ron Pritchard .30 .14
❑ 412 Barry Smith .30 .14
❑ 413 Norm Bulaich .30 .14
❑ 414 Marv Bateman .30 .14
❑ 415 Ken Stabler 12.00 5.50
❑ 416 Conrad Dobler .75 .35
❑ 417 Bob Tucker .75 .35
❑ 418 Gene Washington .75 .35
❑ 419 Ed Marinaro 1.50 .70
❑ 420 Jack Ham AP 4.00 1.80
❑ 421 Jim Turner .30 .14
❑ 422 Chris Fletcher .30 .14
❑ 423 Carl Barzilauskas .30 .14
❑ 424 Robert Brazile RC 1.50 .70
❑ 425 Harold Carmichael 2.00 .90
❑ 426 Ron Jaworski RC 5.00 2.20
❑ 427 Ed Too Tall Jones RC 20.00 9.00
❑ 428 Larry McCarren .30 .14
❑ 429 Mike Thomas RC .30 .14
❑ 430 Joe DeLamielleure AP .30 .14
❑ 431 Tom Blanchard .30 .14
❑ 432 Ron Carpenter .30 .14
❑ 433 Levi Johnson .30 .14
❑ 434 Sam Cunningham .75 .35
❑ 435 Garo Yepremian .75 .35
❑ 436 Mike Livingston .30 .14
❑ 437 Larry Csonka 4.00 1.80
❑ 438 Doug Dieken .75 .35
❑ 439 Bill Lueck .30 .14
❑ 440 Tom MacLeod AP .30 .14
❑ 441 Mick Tingelhoff .75 .35
❑ 442 Terry Hanratty .75 .35
❑ 443 Mike Siani .30 .14
❑ 444 Dwight Harrison .30 .14
❑ 445 Jim Otis .75 .35
❑ 446 Jack Reynolds .75 .35
❑ 447 Jean Fugett RC .75 .35
❑ 448 Dave Beverly .30 .14
❑ 449 Bernard Jackson RC .30 .14
❑ 450 Charley Taylor 2.00 .90
❑ 451 Atlanta Falcons 2.00 .50
Team Checklist
❑ 452 Baltimore Colts 2.00 .50
Team Checklist
❑ 453 Buffalo Bills 2.00 .50
Team Checklist
❑ 454 Chicago Bears 2.00 .50
Team Checklist
❑ 455 Cincinnati Bengals 2.00 .50
Team Checklist
❑ 456 Cleveland Browns 2.00 .50
Team Checklist
❑ 457 Dallas Cowboys 2.00 .50
Team Checklist
❑ 458 Denver Broncos UER 2.00 .50
Team Checklist
(Charlie Johnson
spelled Charley)
❑ 459 Detroit Lions 2.00 .50
Team Checklist
❑ 460 Green Bay Packers 2.00 .50
Team Checklist
❑ 461 Houston Oilers 2.00 .50
Team Checklist
❑ 462 Kansas City Chiefs 2.00 .50
Team Checklist
❑ 463 Los Angeles Rams 2.00 .50
Team Checklist
❑ 464 Miami Dolphins 2.00 .50
Team Checklist
❑ 465 Minnesota Vikings 2.00 .50
Team Checklist
❑ 466 New England Patriots 2.00 .50
Team Checklist
❑ 467 New Orleans Saints 2.00 .50
Team Checklist
❑ 468 New York Giants 2.00 .50
Team Checklist
❑ 469 New York Jets 2.00 .50
Team Checklist
❑ 470 Oakland Raiders 2.00 .50
Team Checklist
❑ 471 Philadelphia Eagles 2.00 .50
Team Checklist
❑ 472 Pittsburgh Steelers 2.00 .50
Team Checklist
❑ 473 St. Louis Cardinals 2.00 .50
Team Checklist
❑ 474 San Diego Chargers 2.00 .50
Team Checklist
❑ 475 San Francisco 49ers 2.00 .50
Team Checklist
❑ 476 Seattle Seahawks 2.00 .50
Team Checklist
❑ 477 Tampa Bay Buccaneers 2.00 .50
Team Checklist
❑ 478 Washington Redskins 2.00 .50
Team Checklist
❑ 479 Fred Cox .30 .14
❑ 480 Mel Blount AP 6.00 2.70
❑ 481 John Bunting .30 .14
❑ 482 Ken Mendenhall .30 .14
❑ 483 Will Harrell .30 .14
❑ 484 Marlin Briscoe .30 .14
❑ 485 Archie Manning 1.50 .70
❑ 486 Tody Smith .30 .14
❑ 487 George Hunt .30 .14
❑ 488 Roscoe Word .30 .14
❑ 489 Paul Seymour .30 .14
❑ 490 Lee Roy Jordan AP 1.50 .70
❑ 491 Chip Myers .30 .14
❑ 492 Norm Evans .30 .14
❑ 493 Jim Bertelsen .30 .14
❑ 494 Mark Moseley .75 .35
❑ 495 George Buehler .30 .14
❑ 496 Charlie Hall .30 .14
❑ 497 Marvin Upshaw .30 .14
❑ 498 Tom Banks RC .30 .14
❑ 499 Randy Vataha .30 .14
❑ 500 Fran Tarkenton AP 6.00 2.70
❑ 501 Mike Wagner .75 .35
❑ 502 Art Malone .30 .14
❑ 503 Fred Cook .30 .14
❑ 504 Rich McGeorge .30 .14
❑ 505 Ken Burrough .75 .35
❑ 506 Nick Mike-Mayer .30 .14
❑ 507 Checklist 397-528 3.00 .75
❑ 508 Steve Owens .75 .35
❑ 509 Brad Van Pelt RC .30 .14
❑ 510 Ken Riley AP .75 .35
❑ 511 Art Thoms .30 .14
❑ 512 Ed Bell .30 .14
❑ 513 Tom Wittum .30 .14
❑ 514 Jim Braxton .30 .14
❑ 515 Nick Buoniconti 1.50 .70
❑ 516 Brian Sipe RC 5.00 2.20
❑ 517 Jim Lynch .30 .14
❑ 518 Prentice McCray .30 .14
❑ 519 Tom Dempsey .30 .14
❑ 520 Mel Gray AP .75 .35
❑ 521 Nate Wright .30 .14
❑ 522 Rocky Bleier 6.00 2.70
❑ 523 Dennis Johnson .30 .14
❑ 524 Jerry Sisemore .30 .14
❑ 525 Bert Jones .30 .14
❑ 526 Perry Smith .30 .14
❑ 527 Blaine Nye .30 .14
❑ 528 Bob Moore 1.50 .35

1977 Topps

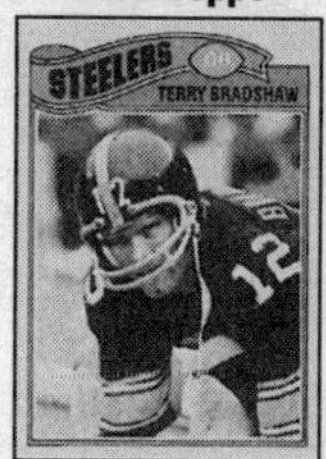

	NRMT-MT	EXC
COMPLETE SET (528)	200.00	90.00
COMMON CARD (1-528)	.25	.11
SEMISTARS	.50	.23
UNLISTED STARS	1.00	.45
CL (67/256/332/417)	2.00	.90

❑ 1 Passing Leaders 2.50 .60
James Harris
Ken Stabler
❑ 2 Receiving Leaders 1.00 .45
Drew Pearson
MacArthur Lane
❑ 3 Rushing Leaders 10.00 4.50
Walter Payton
O.J. Simpson
❑ 4 Scoring Leaders .50 .23
Mark Moseley
Toni Linhart
❑ 5 Interception Leaders .50 .23
Monte Jackson
Ken Riley
❑ 6 Punting Leaders .25 .11
John James
Marv Bateman
❑ 7 Mike Phipps .50 .23
❑ 8 Rick Volk .25 .11
❑ 9 Steve Furness .50 .23
❑ 10 Isaac Curtis .50 .23
❑ 11 Nate Wright .50 .23
❑ 12 Jean Fugett .25 .11
❑ 13 Ken Mendenhall .25 .11
❑ 14 Sam Adams .25 .11
❑ 15 Charlie Waters 1.00 .45
❑ 16 Bill Stanfill .25 .11
❑ 17 John Holland .25 .11
❑ 18 Pat Haden RC 2.00 .90
❑ 19 Bob Young .25 .11
❑ 20 Wally Chambers AP .25 .11
❑ 21 Lawrence Gaines .25 .11
❑ 22 Larry McCarren .25 .11
❑ 23 Horst Muhlmann .25 .11
❑ 24 Phil Villapiano .50 .23
❑ 25 Greg Pruitt .50 .23
❑ 26 Ron Howard .25 .11
❑ 27 Craig Morton 1.00 .45
❑ 28 Rufus Mayes .25 .11
❑ 29 Lee Roy Selmon RC UER 10.00 4.50
Misspelled Leroy
❑ 30 Ed White AP .50 .23
❑ 31 Harold McLinton .25 .11
❑ 32 Glenn Doughty .25 .11
❑ 33 Bob Kuechenberg 1.00 .45
❑ 34 Duane Carrell .25 .11
❑ 35 Riley Odoms .25 .11
❑ 36 Bobby Scott .25 .11
❑ 37 Nick Mike-Mayer .25 .11
❑ 38 Bill Lenkaitis .25 .11
❑ 39 Roland Harper .50 .23
❑ 40 Tommy Hart AP .25 .11
❑ 41 Mike Sensibaugh .25 .11
❑ 42 Rusty Jackson .25 .11
❑ 43 Levi Johnson .25 .11
❑ 44 Mike McCoy .25 .11
❑ 45 Roger Staubach 15.00 6.75

❑ 46 Fred Cox .25 .11
❑ 47 Bob Babich .25 .11
❑ 48 Reggie McKenzie .50 .23
❑ 49 Dave Jennings .25 .11
❑ 50 Mike Haynes AP RC 6.00 2.70
❑ 51 Larry Brown .50 .23
❑ 52 Marvin Cobb .25 .11
❑ 53 Fred Cook .25 .11
❑ 54 Freddie Solomon .50 .23
❑ 55 John Riggins 2.50 1.10
❑ 56 John Bunting .25 .11
❑ 57 Ray Wersching .50 .23
❑ 58 Mike Livingston .25 .11
❑ 59 Billy Johnson .50 .23
❑ 60 Mike Wagner AP .25 .11
❑ 61 Waymond Bryant .25 .11
❑ 62 Jim Otis .50 .23
❑ 63 Ed Galigher .25 .11
❑ 64 Randy Vataha .25 .11
❑ 65 Jim Zorn RC 3.00 1.35
❑ 66 Jon Keyworth .25 .11
❑ 67 Checklist 1-132 2.00 .50
❑ 68 Henry Childs .25 .11
❑ 69 Thom Darden .25 .11
❑ 70 George Kunz AP .25 .11
❑ 71 Lenvil Elliott .25 .11
❑ 72 Curtis Johnson .25 .11
❑ 73 Doug Van Horn .25 .11
❑ 74 Joe Theismann 4.00 1.80
❑ 75 Dwight White .50 .23
❑ 76 Scott Laidlaw .25 .11
❑ 77 Monte Johnson .25 .11
❑ 78 Dave Beverly .25 .11
❑ 79 Jim Mitchell .25 .11
❑ 80 Jack Youngblood AP 1.00 .45
❑ 81 Mel Gray .50 .23
❑ 82 Dwight Harrison .25 .11
❑ 83 John Hadl .50 .23
❑ 84 Matt Blair RC 1.00 .45
❑ 85 Charlie Sanders .25 .11
❑ 86 Noah Jackson .25 .11
❑ 87 Ed Marinaro .50 .23
❑ 88 Bob Howard .25 .11
❑ 89 John McDaniel .25 .11
❑ 90 Dan Dierdorf AP 1.50 .70
❑ 91 Mark Moseley .50 .23
❑ 92 Cleo Miller .25 .11
❑ 93 Andre Tillman .25 .11
❑ 94 Bruce Taylor .25 .11
❑ 95 Bert Jones 1.00 .45
❑ 96 Anthony Davis RC 1.00 .45
❑ 97 Don Goode .25 .11
❑ 98 Ray Rhodes RC 6.00 2.70
❑ 99 Mike Webster RC 10.00 4.50
❑ 100 O.J. Simpson AP 5.00 2.20
❑ 101 Doug Plank RC .25 .11
❑ 102 Efren Herrera .50 .23
❑ 103 Charlie Smith .25 .11
❑ 104 Carlos Brown .25 .11
❑ 105 Jim Marshall 1.00 .45
❑ 106 Paul Naumoff .25 .11
❑ 107 Walter White .25 .11
❑ 108 John Cappelletti RC 2.50 1.10
❑ 109 Chip Myers .25 .11
❑ 110 Ken Stabler AP 10.00 4.50
❑ 111 Joe Ehrmann .25 .11
❑ 112 Rick Engles .25 .11
❑ 113 Jack Dolbin RC .25 .11
❑ 114 Ron Bolton .25 .11
❑ 115 Mike Thomas .25 .11
❑ 116 Mike Fuller .25 .11
❑ 117 John Hill .25 .11
❑ 118 Richard Todd RC 1.00 .45
❑ 119 Duriel Harris RC .50 .23
❑ 120 John James AP .25 .11
❑ 121 Lionel Antoine .25 .11
❑ 122 John Skorupan .25 .11
❑ 123 Skip Butler .25 .11
❑ 124 Bob Tucker .25 .11
❑ 125 Paul Krause .50 .23
❑ 126 Dave Hampton .25 .11
❑ 127 Tom Wittum .25 .11
❑ 128 Gary Huff .50 .23
❑ 129 Emmitt Thomas .25 .11
❑ 130 Drew Pearson AP 2.00 .90
❑ 131 Ron Saul .25 .11
❑ 132 Steve Niehaus .25 .11
❑ 133 Fred Carr 1.00 .45
❑ 134 Norm Bulaich .25 .11
❑ 135 Bob Trumpy .50 .23
❑ 136 Greg Landry .50 .23
❑ 137 George Buehler .25 .11
❑ 138 Reggie Rucker .50 .23
❑ 139 Julius Adams .25 .11
❑ 140 Jack Ham AP 2.50 1.10
❑ 141 Wayne Morris RC .25 .11
❑ 142 Marv Bateman .25 .11
❑ 143 Bobby Maples .25 .11
❑ 144 Harold Carmichael 1.00 .45
❑ 145 Bob Avellini .50 .23
❑ 146 Harry Carson RC 3.00 1.35
❑ 147 Lawrence Pillers .25 .11
❑ 148 Ed Williams .25 .11
❑ 149 Dan Pastorini .50 .23
❑ 150 Ron Yary AP .50 .23
❑ 151 Joe Lavender .25 .11
❑ 152 Pat McInally RC .50 .23
❑ 153 Lloyd Mumphord .25 .11
❑ 154 Cullen Bryant .50 .23
❑ 155 Willie Lanier 1.00 .45
❑ 156 Gene Washington .50 .23
❑ 157 Scott Hunter .25 .11
❑ 158 Jim Merlo .25 .11
❑ 159 Randy Grossman .50 .23
❑ 160 Blaine Nye AP .25 .11
❑ 161 Ike Harris .25 .11
❑ 162 Doug Dieken .25 .11
❑ 163 Guy Morriss .25 .11
❑ 164 Bob Parsons .25 .11
❑ 165 Steve Grogan 1.00 .45
❑ 166 John Brockington .50 .23
❑ 167 Charlie Joiner 2.50 1.10
❑ 168 Ron Carpenter .25 .11
❑ 169 Jeff Wright .25 .11
❑ 170 Chris Hanburger AP .25 .11
❑ 171 Roosevelt Leaks RC .50 .23
❑ 172 Larry Little 1.00 .45
❑ 173 John Matuszak .50 .23
❑ 174 Joe Ferguson .50 .23
❑ 175 Brad Van Pelt .50 .23
❑ 176 Dexter Bussey RC .50 .23
❑ 177 Steve Largent RC 50.00 22.00
❑ 178 Dewey Selmon .50 .23
❑ 179 Randy Gradishar 1.00 .45
❑ 180 Mel Blount AP 3.00 1.35
❑ 181 Dan Neal .25 .11
❑ 182 Rich Szaro .25 .11
❑ 183 Mike Boryla .25 .11
❑ 184 Steve Jones .25 .11
❑ 185 Paul Warfield 2.50 1.10
❑ 186 Greg Buttle RC .25 .11
❑ 187 Rich McGeorge .25 .11
❑ 188 Leon Gray RC .50 .23
❑ 189 John Shinners .25 .11
❑ 190 Toni Linhart AP .25 .11
❑ 191 Robert Miller .25 .11
❑ 192 Jake Scott .25 .11
❑ 193 Jon Morris .25 .11
❑ 194 Randy Crowder .25 .11
❑ 195 Lynn Swann UER 15.00 6.75
(Interception Record
on card back)
❑ 196 Marsh White .25 .11
❑ 197 Rod Perry RC .25 .11
❑ 198 Willie Hall .25 .11
❑ 199 Mike Hartenstine .25 .11
❑ 200 Jim Bakken AP .25 .11
❑ 201 Atlanta Falcons UER 1.25 .30
Team Checklist
(79 Jim Mitchell
is not listed)
❑ 202 Baltimore Colts 1.25 .30
Team Checklist
❑ 203 Buffalo Bills 1.25 .30
Team Checklist
❑ 204 Chicago Bears 1.25 .30
Team Checklist
❑ 205 Cincinnati Bengals 1.25 .30
Team Checklist
❑ 206 Cleveland Browns 1.25 .30
Team Checklist
❑ 207 Dallas Cowboys 1.25 .30
Team Checklist
❑ 208 Denver Broncos 1.25 .30
Team Checklist
❑ 209 Detroit Lions 1.25 .30
Team Checklist
❑ 210 Green Bay Packers 1.25 .30
Team Checklist
❑ 211 Houston Oilers 1.25 .30
Team Checklist
❑ 212 Kansas City Chiefs 1.25 .30
Team Checklist
❑ 213 Los Angeles Rams 1.25 .30
Team Checklist
❑ 214 Miami Dolphins 1.25 .30
Team Checklist
❑ 215 Minnesota Vikings 1.25 .30
Team Checklist
❑ 216 New England Patriots 1.25 .30
Team Checklist
❑ 217 New Orleans Saints 1.25 .30
Team Checklist
❑ 218 New York Giants 1.25 .30
Team Checklist
❑ 219 New York Jets 1.25 .30
Team Checklist
❑ 220 Oakland Raiders 1.25 .30
Team Checklist
❑ 221 Philadelphia Eagles 1.25 .30
Team Checklist
❑ 222 Pittsburgh Steelers 1.25 .30
Team Checklist
❑ 223 St. Louis Cardinals 1.25 .30
Team Checklist
❑ 224 San Diego Chargers 1.25 .30
Team Checklist
❑ 225 San Francisco 49ers 1.25 .30
Team Checklist
❑ 226 Seattle Seahawks 1.25 .30
Team Checklist
❑ 227 Tampa Bay Buccaneers 1.25 .30
Team Checklist UER
(Lee Roy Selmon mis-
spelled as Leroy)
❑ 228 Washington Redskins 1.25 .30
Team Checklist
❑ 229 Sam Cunningham .50 .23
❑ 230 Alan Page AP 1.00 .45
❑ 231 Eddie Brown .25 .11
❑ 232 Stan White .25 .11
❑ 233 Vern Den Herder .25 .11
❑ 234 Clarence Davis .25 .11
❑ 235 Ken Anderson 1.00 .45
❑ 236 Karl Chandler .25 .11
❑ 237 Will Harrell .25 .11
❑ 238 Clarence Scott .25 .11
❑ 239 Bo Rather .25 .11
❑ 240 Robert Brazile AP .50 .23
❑ 241 Bob Bell .25 .11
❑ 242 Rolland Lawrence .25 .11
❑ 243 Tom Sullivan .25 .11
❑ 244 Larry Brunson .25 .11
❑ 245 Terry Bradshaw 12.00 5.50
❑ 246 Rich Saul .25 .11
❑ 247 Cleveland Elam .25 .11
❑ 248 Don Woods .25 .11
❑ 249 Bruce Laird .25 .11
❑ 250 Coy Bacon AP .50 .23
❑ 251 Russ Francis 1.00 .45
❑ 252 Jim Braxton .25 .11
❑ 253 Perry Smith .25 .11
❑ 254 Jerome Barkum .25 .11
❑ 255 Garo Yepremian .50 .23
❑ 256 Checklist 133-264 2.00 .50
❑ 257 Tony Galbreath RC .50 .23
❑ 258 Troy Archer .25 .11
❑ 259 Brian Sipe 1.00 .45
❑ 260 Billy Joe DuPree AP .50 .23
❑ 261 Bobby Walden .25 .11
❑ 262 Larry Marshall .25 .11
❑ 263 Ted Fritsch Jr. .25 .11
❑ 264 Larry Hand .25 .11
❑ 265 Tom Mack .50 .23
❑ 266 Ed Bradley .25 .11
❑ 267 Pat Leahy .50 .23
❑ 268 Louis Carter .25 .11
❑ 269 Archie Griffin RC 6.00 2.70

❑ 270	Art Shell AP	1.00	.45
❑ 271	Stu Voigt	.25	.11
❑ 272	Prentice McCray	.25	.11
❑ 273	MacArthur Lane	.25	.11
❑ 274	Dan Fouts	6.00	2.70
❑ 275	Charlie Young	.50	.23
❑ 276	Wilbur Jackson RC	.25	.11
❑ 277	John Hicks	.25	.11
❑ 278	Nat Moore	1.00	.45
❑ 279	Virgil Livers	.25	.11
❑ 280	Curley Culp AP	.50	.23
❑ 281	Rocky Bleier	2.50	1.10
❑ 282	John Zook	.25	.11
❑ 283	Tom DeLeone	.25	.11
❑ 284	Danny White RC	8.00	3.60
❑ 285	Otis Armstrong	.50	.23
❑ 286	Larry Walton	.25	.11
❑ 287	Jim Carter	.25	.11
❑ 288	Don McCauley	.25	.11
❑ 289	Frank Grant	.25	.11
❑ 290	Roger Wehrli AP	.50	.23
❑ 291	Mick Tingelhoff	.50	.23
❑ 292	Bernard Jackson	.25	.11
❑ 293	Tom Owen RC	.25	.11
❑ 294	Mike Esposito	.25	.11
❑ 295	Fred Biletnikoff	2.50	1.10
❑ 296	Revie Sorey RC	.25	.11
❑ 297	John McMakin	.25	.11
❑ 298	Dan Ryczek	.25	.11
❑ 299	Wayne Moore	.25	.11
❑ 300	Franco Harris AP	4.00	1.80
❑ 301	Rick Upchurch RC	1.00	.45
❑ 302	Jim Stienke	.25	.11
❑ 303	Charlie Davis	.25	.11
❑ 304	Don Cockroft	.25	.11
❑ 305	Ken Burrough	.50	.23
❑ 306	Clark Gaines	.25	.11
❑ 307	Bobby Douglass	.25	.11
❑ 308	Ralph Perretta	.25	.11
❑ 309	Wally Hilgenberg	.25	.11
❑ 310	Monte Jackson AP RC	.50	.23
❑ 311	Chris Bahr RC	.50	.23
❑ 312	Jim Cheyunski	.25	.11
❑ 313	Mike Patrick	.25	.11
❑ 314	Ed Too Tall Jones	5.00	2.20
❑ 315	Bill Bradley	.25	.11
❑ 316	Benny Malone	.25	.11
❑ 317	Paul Seymour	.25	.11
❑ 318	Jim Laslavic	.25	.11
❑ 319	Frank Lewis	.50	.23
❑ 320	Ray Guy AP	1.00	.45
❑ 321	Allan Ellis	.25	.11
❑ 322	Conrad Dobler	.50	.23
❑ 323	Chester Marcol	.25	.11
❑ 324	Doug Kotar	.25	.11
❑ 325	Lemar Parrish	.50	.23
❑ 326	Steve Holden	.25	.11
❑ 327	Jeff Van Note	.50	.23
❑ 328	Howard Stevens	.25	.11
❑ 329	Brad Dusek	.50	.23
❑ 330	Joe DeLamielleure AP	.25	.11
❑ 331	Jim Plunkett	1.00	.45
❑ 332	Checklist 265-396	2.00	.50
❑ 333	Lou Piccone	.25	.11
❑ 334	Ray Hamilton	.25	.11
❑ 335	Jan Stenerud	.50	.23
❑ 336	Jeris White	.25	.11
❑ 337	Sherman Smith RC	.25	.11
❑ 338	Dave Green	.25	.11
❑ 339	Terry Schmidt	.25	.11
❑ 340	Sammie White AP RC	1.00	.45
❑ 341	Jon Kolb RC	.25	.11
❑ 342	Randy White	8.00	3.60
❑ 343	Bob Klein	.25	.11
❑ 344	Bob Kowalkowski	.25	.11
❑ 345	Terry Metcalf	.50	.23
❑ 346	Joe Danelo	.25	.11
❑ 347	Ken Payne	.25	.11
❑ 348	Neal Craig	.25	.11
❑ 349	Dennis Johnson	.25	.11
❑ 350	Bill Bergey AP	.50	.23
❑ 351	Raymond Chester	.25	.11
❑ 352	Bob Matheson	.25	.11
❑ 353	Mike Kadish	.25	.11
❑ 354	Mark Van Eeghen RC	1.00	.45
❑ 355	L.C. Greenwood	1.00	.45
❑ 356	Sam Hunt	.25	.11
❑ 357	Darrell Austin	.25	.11
❑ 358	Jim Turner	.25	.11
❑ 359	Ahmad Rashad	2.00	.90
❑ 360	Walter Payton AP	40.00	18.00
❑ 361	Mark Arneson	.25	.11
❑ 362	Jerrel Wilson	.25	.11
❑ 363	Steve Bartkowski	1.00	.45
❑ 364	John Watson	.25	.11
❑ 365	Ken Riley	.50	.23
❑ 366	Gregg Bingham	.25	.11
❑ 367	Golden Richards	.50	.23
❑ 368	Clyde Powers	.25	.11
❑ 369	Diron Talbert	.25	.11
❑ 370	Lydell Mitchell	.50	.23
❑ 371	Bob Jackson	.25	.11
❑ 372	Jim Mandich	.25	.11
❑ 373	Frank LeMaster	.25	.11
❑ 374	Benny Ricardo	.25	.11
❑ 375	Lawrence McCutcheon	.50	.23
❑ 376	Lynn Dickey	.50	.23
❑ 377	Phil Wise	.25	.11
❑ 378	Tony McGee	.25	.11
❑ 379	Norm Thompson	.25	.11
❑ 380	Dave Casper AP RC	4.00	1.80
❑ 381	Glen Edwards	.25	.11
❑ 382	Bob Thomas	.25	.11
❑ 383	Bob Chandler	.50	.23
❑ 384	Rickey Young	.50	.23
❑ 385	Carl Eller	1.00	.45
❑ 386	Lyle Alzado	1.00	.45
❑ 387	John Leypoldt	.25	.11
❑ 388	Gordon Bell	.25	.11
❑ 389	Mike Bragg	.25	.11
❑ 390	Jim Langer AP	1.00	.45
❑ 391	Vern Holland	.25	.11
❑ 392	Nelson Munsey	.25	.11
❑ 393	Mack Mitchell	.25	.11
❑ 394	Tony Adams	.25	.11
❑ 395	Preston Pearson	.50	.23
❑ 396	Emanuel Zanders	.25	.11
❑ 397	Vince Papale	.25	.11
❑ 398	Joe Fields RC	.50	.23
❑ 399	Craig Clemons	.25	.11
❑ 400	Fran Tarkenton AP	5.00	2.20
❑ 401	Andy Johnson	.25	.11
❑ 402	Willie Buchanon	.25	.11
❑ 403	Pat Curran	.25	.11
❑ 404	Ray Jarvis	.25	.11
❑ 405	Joe Greene	2.50	1.10
❑ 406	Bill Simpson	.25	.11
❑ 407	Ronnie Coleman	.25	.11
❑ 408	J.K. McKay	.50	.23
❑ 409	Pat Fischer	.50	.23
❑ 410	John Dutton AP	.50	.23
❑ 411	Boobie Clark	.25	.11
❑ 412	Pat Tilley RC	1.00	.45
❑ 413	Don Strock	.50	.23
❑ 414	Brian Kelley	.25	.11
❑ 415	Gene Upshaw	1.00	.45
❑ 416	Mike Montler	.25	.11
❑ 417	Checklist 397-528	2.00	.50
❑ 418	John Gilliam	.25	.11
❑ 419	Brent McClanahan	.25	.11
❑ 420	Jerry Sherk AP	.25	.11
❑ 421	Roy Gerela	.25	.11
❑ 422	Tim Fox	.50	.23
❑ 423	John Ebersole	.25	.11
❑ 424	James Scott	.25	.11
❑ 425	Delvin Williams RC	.50	.23
❑ 426	Spike Jones	.25	.11
❑ 427	Harvey Martin	1.00	.45
❑ 428	Don Herrmann	.25	.11
❑ 429	Calvin Hill	.50	.23
❑ 430	Isiah Robertson AP	.25	.11
❑ 431	Tony Greene	.25	.11
❑ 432	Bob Johnson	.25	.11
❑ 433	Lem Barney	1.00	.45
❑ 434	Eric Torkelson	.25	.11
❑ 435	John Mendenhall	.25	.11
❑ 436	Larry Seiple	.50	.23
❑ 437	Art Kuehn	.25	.11
❑ 438	John Vella	.25	.11
❑ 439	Greg Latta	.25	.11
❑ 440	Roger Carr AP	.50	.23
❑ 441	Doug Sutherland	.25	.11
❑ 442	Mike Kruczek	.25	.11
❑ 443	Steve Zabel	.25	.11
❑ 444	Mike Pruitt RC	1.00	.45
❑ 445	Harold Jackson	.50	.23
❑ 446	George Jakowenko	.25	.11
❑ 447	John Fitzgerald	.25	.11
❑ 448	Carey Joyce	.25	.11
❑ 449	Jim LeClair	.25	.11
❑ 450	Ken Houston AP	1.00	.45
❑ 451	Steve Grogan RB Most Touchdowns Rushing by QB, Season	.50	.23
❑ 452	Jim Marshall RB Most Games Played, Lifetime	.50	.23
❑ 453	O.J. Simpson RB Most Yardage, Rushing, Game	2.50	1.10
❑ 454	Fran Tarkenton RB Most Yardage, Passing, Lifetime	3.00	1.35
❑ 455	Jim Zorn RB Most Passing Yards Season, Rookie	.50	.23
❑ 456	Robert Pratt	.25	.11
❑ 457	Walker Gillette	.25	.11
❑ 458	Charlie Hall	.25	.11
❑ 459	Robert Newhouse	.50	.23
❑ 460	John Hannah AP	1.00	.45
❑ 461	Ken Reaves	.25	.11
❑ 462	Herman Weaver	.25	.11
❑ 463	James Harris	.50	.23
❑ 464	Howard Twilley	.50	.23
❑ 465	Jeff Siemon	.50	.23
❑ 466	John Outlaw	.25	.11
❑ 467	Chuck Muncie RC	1.00	.45
❑ 468	Bob Moore	.25	.11
❑ 469	Robert Woods	.25	.11
❑ 470	Cliff Branch AP	2.00	.90
❑ 471	Johnnie Gray	.25	.11
❑ 472	Don Hardeman	.25	.11
❑ 473	Steve Ramsey	.25	.11
❑ 474	Steve Mike-Mayer	.25	.11
❑ 475	Gary Garrison	.25	.11
❑ 476	Walter Johnson	.25	.11
❑ 477	Neil Clabo	.25	.11
❑ 478	Len Hauss	.25	.11
❑ 479	Darryl Stingley	.50	.23
❑ 480	Jack Lambert AP	8.00	3.60
❑ 481	Mike Adamle	.50	.23
❑ 482	David Lee	.25	.11
❑ 483	Tom Mullen	.25	.11
❑ 484	Claude Humphrey	.25	.11
❑ 485	Jim Hart	1.00	.45
❑ 486	Bobby Thompson RB	.25	.11
❑ 487	Jack Rudnay	.25	.11
❑ 488	Rich Sowells	.25	.11
❑ 489	Reuben Gant	.25	.11
❑ 490	Cliff Harris AP	1.00	.45
❑ 491	Bob Brown DT	.25	.11
❑ 492	Don Nottingham	.25	.11
❑ 493	Ron Jessie	.25	.11
❑ 494	Otis Sistrunk	.50	.23
❑ 495	Billy Kilmer	.50	.23
❑ 496	Oscar Roan	.25	.11
❑ 497	Bill Van Heusen	.25	.11
❑ 498	Randy Logan	.25	.11
❑ 499	John Smith	.25	.11
❑ 500	Chuck Foreman AP	.50	.23
❑ 501	J.T. Thomas	.25	.11
❑ 502	Steve Schubert	.25	.11
❑ 503	Mike Barnes	.25	.11
❑ 504	J.V. Cain	.25	.11
❑ 505	Larry Csonka	3.00	1.35
❑ 506	Elvin Bethea	.50	.23
❑ 507	Ray Easterling	.25	.11
❑ 508	Joe Reed	.25	.11
❑ 509	Steve Odom	.25	.11
❑ 510	Tommy Casanova AP	.25	.11
❑ 511	Dave Dalby	.25	.11
❑ 512	Richard Caster	.25	.11
❑ 513	Fred Dryer	1.00	.45
❑ 514	Jeff Kinney	.25	.11
❑ 515	Bob Griese	3.00	1.35
❑ 516	Butch Johnson RC	1.00	.45
❑ 517	Gerald Irons	.25	.11

Card	NRMT-MT	EXC
❑ 518 Don Calhoun	.25	.11
❑ 519 Jack Gregory	.25	.11
❑ 520 Tom Banks AP	.25	.11
❑ 521 Bobby Bryant	.25	.11
❑ 522 Reggie Harrison	.25	.11
❑ 523 Terry Hermeling	.25	.11
❑ 524 David Taylor	.25	.11
❑ 525 Brian Baschnagel RC	.50	.23
❑ 526 AFC Championship Raiders 24, Steelers 7 (Stabler)	1.00	.45
❑ 527 NFC Championship Vikings 24, Rams 13	.50	.23
❑ 528 Super Bowl XI Raiders 32, Vikings 14 (line play)	1.00	.25

1978 Topps

	NRMT-MT	EXC
COMPLETE SET (528)	150.00	70.00
COMMON CARD (1-528)	.20	.09
SEMISTARS	.50	.23
UNLISTED STARS	1.00	.45
TL (501-528)	.60	.25
CL (107/257/388/488)	1.00	.45

Card	NRMT-MT	EXC
❑ 1 Gary Huff HL Huff Leads Bucs to First Win	1.00	.25
❑ 2 Craig Morton HL Morton Passes Broncos to Super Bowl	1.00	.45
❑ 3 Walter Payton HL Rushes for 275 Yards	8.00	3.60
❑ 4 O.J. Simpson HL Reaches 10,000 Yards	2.00	.90
❑ 5 Fran Tarkenton HL Completes 17 of 18	2.00	.90
❑ 6 Bob Thomas HL Thomas' FG Sends Bears to Playoffs	.20	.09
❑ 7 Joe Pisarcik	.50	.23
❑ 8 Skip Thomas	.20	.09
❑ 9 Roosevelt Leaks	.20	.09
❑ 10 Ken Houston AP	1.00	.45
❑ 11 Tom Blanchard	.20	.09
❑ 12 Jim Turner	.20	.09
❑ 13 Tom DeLeone	.20	.09
❑ 14 Jim LeClair	.20	.09
❑ 15 Bob Avellini	.50	.23
❑ 16 Tony McGee	.20	.09
❑ 17 James Harris	.50	.23
❑ 18 Terry Nelson	.20	.09
❑ 19 Rocky Bleier	2.00	.90
❑ 20 Joe DeLamielleure AP	.50	.23
❑ 21 Richard Caster	.20	.09
❑ 22 A.J. Duhe RC	1.00	.45
❑ 23 John Outlaw	.20	.09
❑ 24 Danny White	1.25	.55
❑ 25 Larry Csonka	2.50	1.10
❑ 26 David Hill	.50	.23
❑ 27 Mark Arneson	.20	.09
❑ 28 Jack Tatum	.50	.23
❑ 29 Norm Thompson	.20	.09
❑ 30 Sammie White	.50	.23
❑ 31 Dennis Johnson	.20	.09
❑ 32 Robin Earl	.20	.09
❑ 33 Don Cockroft	.20	.09
❑ 34 Bob Johnson	.20	.09
❑ 35 John Hannah	1.00	.45
❑ 36 Scott Hunter	.20	.09
❑ 37 Ken Burrough	.50	.23
❑ 38 Wilbur Jackson	.50	.23
❑ 39 Rich McGeorge	.20	.09
❑ 40 Lyle Alzado AP	1.00	.45
❑ 41 John Ebersole	.20	.09
❑ 42 Gary Green RC	.20	.09
❑ 43 Art Kuehn	.20	.09
❑ 44 Glen Edwards	.50	.23
❑ 45 Lawrence McCutcheon	.50	.23
❑ 46 Duriel Harris	.20	.09
❑ 47 Rich Szaro	.20	.09
❑ 48 Mike Washington	.20	.09
❑ 49 Stan White	.20	.09
❑ 50 Dave Casper AP	1.00	.45
❑ 51 Len Hauss	.20	.09
❑ 52 James Scott	.20	.09
❑ 53 Brian Sipe	1.00	.45
❑ 54 Gary Shirk	.20	.09
❑ 55 Archie Griffin	1.00	.45
❑ 56 Mike Patrick	.20	.09
❑ 57 Mario Clark	.20	.09
❑ 58 Jeff Siemon	.20	.09
❑ 59 Steve Mike-Mayer	.20	.09
❑ 60 Randy White AP	4.00	1.80
❑ 61 Darrell Austin	.20	.09
❑ 62 Tom Sullivan	.20	.09
❑ 63 Johnny Rodgers RC	1.00	.45
❑ 64 Ken Reaves	.20	.09
❑ 65 Terry Bradshaw	10.00	4.50
❑ 66 Fred Steinfort	.20	.09
❑ 67 Curley Culp	.50	.23
❑ 68 Ted Hendricks	1.00	.45
❑ 69 Raymond Chester	.20	.09
❑ 70 Jim Langer AP	1.00	.45
❑ 71 Calvin Hill	.50	.23
❑ 72 Mike Hartenstine	.20	.09
❑ 73 Gerald Irons	.20	.09
❑ 74 Billy Brooks	.50	.23
❑ 75 John Mendenhall	.20	.09
❑ 76 Andy Johnson	.20	.09
❑ 77 Tom Wittum	.20	.09
❑ 78 Lynn Dickey	.50	.23
❑ 79 Carl Eller	1.00	.45
❑ 80 Tom Mack	.50	.23
❑ 81 Clark Gaines	.20	.09
❑ 82 Lem Barney	1.00	.45
❑ 83 Mike Montler	.20	.09
❑ 84 Jon Kolb	.20	.09
❑ 85 Bob Chandler	.50	.23
❑ 86 Robert Newhouse	.50	.23
❑ 87 Frank LeMaster	.20	.09
❑ 88 Jeff West	.20	.09
❑ 89 Lyle Blackwood	.50	.23
❑ 90 Gene Upshaw AP	1.00	.45
❑ 91 Frank Grant	.20	.09
❑ 92 Tom Hicks	.20	.09
❑ 93 Mike Pruitt	.50	.23
❑ 94 Chris Bahr	.20	.09
❑ 95 Russ Francis	.50	.23
❑ 96 Norris Thomas	.20	.09
❑ 97 Gary Barbaro RC	.50	.23
❑ 98 Jim Merlo	.20	.09
❑ 99 Karl Chandler	.20	.09
❑ 100 Fran Tarkenton	4.00	1.80
❑ 101 Abdul Salaam	.20	.09
❑ 102 Marv Kellum	.20	.09
❑ 103 Herman Weaver	.20	.09
❑ 104 Roy Gerela	.20	.09
❑ 105 Harold Jackson	.50	.23
❑ 106 Dewey Selmon	.50	.23
❑ 107 Checklist 1-132	1.00	.25
❑ 108 Clarence Davis	.20	.09
❑ 109 Robert Pratt	.20	.09
❑ 110 Harvey Martin AP	1.00	.45
❑ 111 Brad Dusek	.20	.09
❑ 112 Greg Latta	.20	.09
❑ 113 Tony Peters	.20	.09
❑ 114 Jim Braxton	.20	.09
❑ 115 Ken Riley	.50	.23
❑ 116 Steve Nelson	.20	.09
❑ 117 Rick Upchurch	.50	.23
❑ 118 Spike Jones	.20	.09
❑ 119 Doug Kotar	.20	.09
❑ 120 Bob Griese AP	2.50	1.10
❑ 121 Burgess Owens	.20	.09
❑ 122 Rolf Benirschke RC	.50	.23
❑ 123 Haskel Stanback RC	.20	.09
❑ 124 J.T. Thomas	.20	.09
❑ 125 Ahmad Rashad	1.50	.70
❑ 126 Rick Kane	.20	.09
❑ 127 Elvin Bethea	.20	.09
❑ 128 Dave Dalby	.20	.09
❑ 129 Mike Barnes	.20	.09
❑ 130 Isiah Robertson	.20	.09
❑ 131 Jim Plunkett	1.00	.45
❑ 132 Allan Ellis	.20	.09
❑ 133 Mike Bragg	.20	.09
❑ 134 Bob Jackson	.20	.09
❑ 135 Coy Bacon	.20	.09
❑ 136 John Smith	.20	.09
❑ 137 Chuck Muncie	.50	.23
❑ 138 Johnnie Gray	.20	.09
❑ 139 Jimmy Robinson	.20	.09
❑ 140 Tom Banks	.20	.09
❑ 141 Marvin Powell RC	.20	.09
❑ 142 Jerrel Wilson	.20	.09
❑ 143 Ron Howard	.20	.09
❑ 144 Rob Lytle RC	.50	.23
❑ 145 L.C. Greenwood	1.00	.45
❑ 146 Morris Owens	.20	.09
❑ 147 Joe Reed	.20	.09
❑ 148 Mike Kadish	.20	.09
❑ 149 Phil Villapiano	.50	.23
❑ 150 Lydell Mitchell	.50	.23
❑ 151 Randy Logan	.20	.09
❑ 152 Mike Williams	.20	.09
❑ 153 Jeff Van Note	.50	.23
❑ 154 Steve Schubert	.20	.09
❑ 155 Billy Kilmer	.50	.23
❑ 156 Boobie Clark	.20	.09
❑ 157 Charlie Hall	.20	.09
❑ 158 Raymond Clayborn RC	1.00	.45
❑ 159 Jack Gregory	.20	.09
❑ 160 Cliff Harris AP	1.00	.45
❑ 161 Joe Fields	.20	.09
❑ 162 Don Nottingham	.20	.09
❑ 163 Ed White	.50	.23
❑ 164 Toni Fritsch	.20	.09
❑ 165 Jack Lambert	4.00	1.80
❑ 166 NFC Champions Cowboys 23, Vikings 6 (Roger Staubach)	1.50	.70
❑ 167 AFC Champions Broncos 20, Raiders 17 (Lytle running)	.50	.23
❑ 168 Super Bowl XII Cowboys 27, Broncos 10 (Tony Dorsett)	3.00	1.35
❑ 169 Neal Colzie RC	.20	.09
❑ 170 Cleveland Elam AP	.20	.09
❑ 171 David Lee	.20	.09
❑ 172 Jim Otis	.20	.09
❑ 173 Archie Manning	1.00	.45
❑ 174 Jim Carter	.20	.09
❑ 175 Jean Fugett	.20	.09
❑ 176 Willie Parker	.20	.09
❑ 177 Haven Moses	.50	.23
❑ 178 Horace King	.20	.09
❑ 179 Bob Thomas	.20	.09
❑ 180 Monte Jackson	.20	.09
❑ 181 Steve Zabel	.20	.09
❑ 182 John Fitzgerald	.20	.09
❑ 183 Mike Livingston	.20	.09
❑ 184 Larry Poole	.20	.09
❑ 185 Isaac Curtis	.50	.23
❑ 186 Chuck Ramsey	.20	.09
❑ 187 Bob Klein	.20	.09
❑ 188 Ray Rhodes	1.00	.45
❑ 189 Otis Sistrunk	.50	.23
❑ 190 Bill Bergey	.50	.23
❑ 191 Sherman Smith	.50	.23
❑ 192 Dave Green	.20	.09

❑ 193 Carl Mauck .20 .09
❑ 194 Reggie Harrison .20 .09
❑ 195 Roger Carr .50 .23
❑ 196 Steve Bartkowski 1.00 .45
❑ 197 Ray Wersching .20 .09
❑ 198 Willie Buchanon .20 .09
❑ 199 Neil Clabo .20 .09
❑ 200 Walter Payton AP 25.00 11.00
UER (Born 7/5/54,
should be 7/25/54)
❑ 201 Sam Adams .20 .09
❑ 202 Larry Gordon .20 .09
❑ 203 Pat Tilley .50 .23
❑ 204 Mack Mitchell .20 .09
❑ 205 Ken Anderson 1.00 .45
❑ 206 Scott Dierking .20 .09
❑ 207 Jack Rudnay .20 .09
❑ 208 Jim Stienke .20 .09
❑ 209 Bill Simpson .20 .09
❑ 210 Errol Mann .20 .09
❑ 211 Bucky Dilts .20 .09
❑ 212 Reuben Gant .20 .09
❑ 213 Thomas Henderson RC 1.50 .70
❑ 214 Steve Furness .50 .23
❑ 215 John Riggins 2.00 .90
❑ 216 Keith Krepfle RC .20 .09
❑ 217 Fred Dean RC .50 .23
❑ 218 Emanuel Zanders .20 .09
❑ 219 Don Testerman .20 .09
❑ 220 George Kunz .20 .09
❑ 221 Darryl Stingley .50 .23
❑ 222 Ken Sanders .20 .09
❑ 223 Gary Huff .20 .09
❑ 224 Gregg Bingham .20 .09
❑ 225 Jerry Sherk .20 .09
❑ 226 Doug Plank .20 .09
❑ 227 Ed Taylor .20 .09
❑ 228 Emery Moorehead .20 .09
❑ 229 Reggie Williams RC 1.00 .45
❑ 230 Claude Humphrey .20 .09
❑ 231 Randy Cross RC 2.00 .90
❑ 232 Jim Hart 1.00 .45
❑ 233 Bobby Bryant .20 .09
❑ 234 Larry Brown .20 .09
❑ 235 Mark Van Eeghen .50 .23
❑ 236 Terry Hermeling .20 .09
❑ 237 Steve Odom .20 .09
❑ 238 Jan Stenerud 1.00 .45
❑ 239 Andre Tillman .20 .09
❑ 240 Tom Jackson AP RC 4.00 1.80
❑ 241 Ken Mendenhall .20 .09
❑ 242 Tim Fox .20 .09
❑ 243 Don Herrmann .20 .09
❑ 244 Eddie McMillan .20 .09
❑ 245 Greg Pruitt .50 .23
❑ 246 J.K. McKay .20 .09
❑ 247 Larry Keller .20 .09
❑ 248 Dave Jennings .50 .23
❑ 249 Bo Harris .20 .09
❑ 250 Revie Sorey .20 .09
❑ 251 Tony Greene .20 .09
❑ 252 Butch Johnson .50 .23
❑ 253 Paul Naumoff .20 .09
❑ 254 Rickey Young .50 .23
❑ 255 Dwight White .50 .23
❑ 256 Joe Lavender .20 .09
❑ 257 Checklist 133-264 1.00 .25
❑ 258 Ronnie Coleman .20 .09
❑ 259 Charlie Smith .20 .09
❑ 260 Ray Guy AP 1.00 .45
❑ 261 David Taylor .20 .09
❑ 262 Bill Lenkaitis .20 .09
❑ 263 Jim Mitchell .20 .09
❑ 264 Delvin Williams .20 .09
❑ 265 Jack Youngblood 1.00 .45
❑ 266 Chuck Crist .20 .09
❑ 267 Richard Todd .50 .23
❑ 268 Dave Logan RC .50 .23
❑ 269 Rufus Mayes .20 .09
❑ 270 Brad Van Pelt .20 .09
❑ 271 Chester Marcol .20 .09
❑ 272 J.V. Cain .20 .09
❑ 273 Larry Seiple .20 .09
❑ 274 Brent McClanahan .20 .09
❑ 275 Mike Wagner .20 .09
❑ 276 Diron Talbert .20 .09
❑ 277 Brian Baschnagel .20 .09
❑ 278 Ed Podolak .20 .09
❑ 279 Don Goode .20 .09
❑ 280 John Dutton .50 .23
❑ 281 Don Calhoun .20 .09
❑ 282 Monte Johnson .20 .09
❑ 283 Ron Jessie .20 .09
❑ 284 Jon Morris .20 .09
❑ 285 Riley Odoms .20 .09
❑ 286 Marv Bateman .20 .09
❑ 287 Joe Klecko RC 1.00 .45
❑ 288 Oliver Davis .20 .09
❑ 289 John McDaniel .20 .09
❑ 290 Roger Staubach 12.00 5.50
❑ 291 Brian Kelley .20 .09
❑ 292 Mike Hogan .20 .09
❑ 293 John Leypoldt .20 .09
❑ 294 Jack Novak .20 .09
❑ 295 Joe Greene 2.00 .90
❑ 296 John Hill .20 .09
❑ 297 Danny Buggs .20 .09
❑ 298 Ted Albrecht .20 .09
❑ 299 Nelson Munsey .20 .09
❑ 300 Chuck Foreman .50 .23
❑ 301 Dan Pastorini .50 .23
❑ 302 Tommy Hart .20 .09
❑ 303 Dave Beverly .20 .09
❑ 304 Tony Reed RC .50 .23
❑ 305 Cliff Branch 1.50 .70
❑ 306 Clarence Duren .20 .09
❑ 307 Randy Rasmussen .20 .09
❑ 308 Oscar Roan .20 .09
❑ 309 Lenvil Elliott .20 .09
❑ 310 Dan Dierdorf AP 1.00 .45
❑ 311 Johnny Perkins .20 .09
❑ 312 Rafael Septien RC .50 .23
❑ 313 Terry Beeson .20 .09
❑ 314 Lee Roy Selmon 2.00 .90
❑ 315 Tony Dorsett RC ! 30.00 13.50
❑ 316 Greg Landry .50 .23
❑ 317 Jake Scott .20 .09
❑ 318 Dan Peiffer .20 .09
❑ 319 John Bunting .20 .09
❑ 320 John Stallworth RC 15.00 6.75
❑ 321 Bob Howard .20 .09
❑ 322 Larry Little 1.00 .45
❑ 323 Reggie McKenzie .50 .23
❑ 324 Duane Carrell .20 .09
❑ 325 Ed Simonini .20 .09
❑ 326 John Vella .20 .09
❑ 327 Wesley Walker RC 3.00 1.35
❑ 328 Jon Keyworth .20 .09
❑ 329 Ron Bolton .20 .09
❑ 330 Tommy Casanova .20 .09
❑ 331 Passing Leaders 4.00 1.80
Bob Griese
Roger Staubach
❑ 332 Receiving Leaders 1.00 .45
Lydell Mitchell
Ahmad Rashad
❑ 333 Rushing Leaders 3.00 1.35
Mark Van Eeghen
Walter Payton
❑ 334 Scoring Leaders 3.00 1.35
Errol Mann
Walter Payton
❑ 335 Interception Leaders .20 .09
Lyle Blackwood
Rolland Lawrence
❑ 336 Punting Leaders .50 .23
Ray Guy
Tom Blanchard
❑ 337 Robert Brazile .50 .23
❑ 338 Charlie Joiner 1.50 .70
❑ 339 Joe Ferguson .50 .23
❑ 340 Bill Thompson .20 .09
❑ 341 Sam Cunningham .50 .23
❑ 342 Curtis Johnson .20 .09
❑ 343 Jim Marshall 1.00 .45
❑ 344 Charlie Sanders .20 .09
❑ 345 Willie Hall .20 .09
❑ 346 Pat Haden 1.00 .45
❑ 347 Jim Bakken .20 .09
❑ 348 Bruce Taylor .20 .09
❑ 349 Barty Smith .20 .09
❑ 350 Drew Pearson AP 1.50 .70
❑ 351 Mike Webster 2.50 1.10
❑ 352 Bobby Hammond .20 .09
❑ 353 Dave Mays .20 .09
❑ 354 Pat McInally .20 .09
❑ 355 Toni Linhart .20 .09
❑ 356 Larry Hand .20 .09
❑ 357 Ted Fritsch Jr. .20 .09
❑ 358 Larry Marshall .20 .09
❑ 359 Waymond Bryant .20 .09
❑ 360 Louie Kelcher RC .50 .23
❑ 361 Stanley Morgan RC 2.00 .90
❑ 362 Bruce Harper RC .50 .23
❑ 363 Bernard Jackson .20 .09
❑ 364 Walter White .20 .09
❑ 365 Ken Stabler 8.00 3.60
❑ 366 Fred Dryer 1.00 .45
❑ 367 Ike Harris .20 .09
❑ 368 Norm Bulaich .20 .09
❑ 369 Merv Krakau .20 .09
❑ 370 John James .20 .09
❑ 371 Bennie Cunningham RC .20 .09
❑ 372 Doug Van Horn .20 .09
❑ 373 Thom Darden .20 .09
❑ 374 Eddie Edwards RC .20 .09
❑ 375 Mike Thomas .20 .09
❑ 376 Fred Cook .20 .09
❑ 377 Mike Phipps .50 .23
❑ 378 Paul Krause 1.00 .45
❑ 379 Harold Carmichael 1.00 .45
❑ 380 Mike Haynes AP 1.00 .45
❑ 381 Wayne Morris .20 .09
❑ 382 Greg Buttle .20 .09
❑ 383 Jim Zorn 1.00 .45
❑ 384 Jack Dolbin .20 .09
❑ 385 Charlie Waters 1.00 .45
❑ 386 Dan Ryczek .20 .09
❑ 387 Joe Washington RC 1.00 .45
❑ 388 Checklist 265-396 1.00 .25
❑ 389 James Hunter .20 .09
❑ 390 Billy Johnson .50 .23
❑ 391 Jim Allen .20 .09
❑ 392 George Buehler .20 .09
❑ 393 Harry Carson .20 .09
❑ 394 Cleo Miller .20 .09
❑ 395 Gary Burley .20 .09
❑ 396 Mark Moseley .50 .23
❑ 397 Virgil Livers .20 .09
❑ 398 Joe Ehrmann .20 .09
❑ 399 Freddie Solomon .20 .09
❑ 400 O.J. Simpson 4.00 1.80
❑ 401 Julius Adams .20 .09
❑ 402 Artimus Parker .20 .09
❑ 403 Gene Washington .50 .23
❑ 404 Herman Edwards .20 .09
❑ 405 Craig Morton 1.00 .45
❑ 406 Alan Page 1.00 .45
❑ 407 Larry McCarren .20 .09
❑ 408 Tony Galbreath .50 .23
❑ 409 Roman Gabriel 1.00 .45
❑ 410 Efren Herrera AP .20 .09
❑ 411 Jim Smith RC 1.00 .45
❑ 412 Bill Bryant .20 .09
❑ 413 Doug Dieken .20 .09
❑ 414 Marvin Cobb .20 .09
❑ 415 Fred Biletnikoff 2.00 .90
❑ 416 Joe Theismann 2.50 1.10
❑ 417 Roland Harper .20 .09
❑ 418 Derrel Luce .20 .09
❑ 419 Ralph Perretta .20 .09
❑ 420 Louis Wright RC 1.00 .45
❑ 421 Prentice McCray .20 .09
❑ 422 Garry Puetz .20 .09
❑ 423 Alfred Jenkins RC 1.00 .45
❑ 424 Paul Seymour .20 .09
❑ 425 Garo Yepremian .50 .23
❑ 426 Emmitt Thomas .20 .09
❑ 427 Dexter Bussey .20 .09
❑ 428 John Sanders .20 .09
❑ 429 Ed Too Tall Jones 2.00 .90
❑ 430 Ron Yary .50 .23
❑ 431 Frank Lewis .50 .23
❑ 432 Jerry Golsteyn .20 .09
❑ 433 Clarence Scott .20 .09
❑ 434 Pete Johnson RC 1.00 .45
❑ 435 Charlie Young .50 .23
❑ 436 Harold McLinton .20 .09

- ❑ 437 Noah Jackson .20 .09
- ❑ 438 Bruce Laird .20 .09
- ❑ 439 John Matuszak .50 .23
- ❑ 440 Nat Moore AP .50 .23
- ❑ 441 Leon Gray .20 .09
- ❑ 442 Jerome Barkum .20 .09
- ❑ 443 Steve Largent 12.00 5.50
- ❑ 444 John Zook .20 .09
- ❑ 445 Preston Pearson .50 .23
- ❑ 446 Conrad Dobler .50 .23
- ❑ 447 Wilbur Summers .20 .09
- ❑ 448 Lou Piccone .20 .09
- ❑ 449 Ron Jaworski 1.00 .45
- ❑ 450 Jack Ham AP 1.50 .70
- ❑ 451 Mick Tingelhoff .50 .23
- ❑ 452 Clyde Powers .20 .09
- ❑ 453 John Cappelletti 1.00 .45
- ❑ 454 Dick Ambrose .20 .09
- ❑ 455 Lemar Parrish .20 .09
- ❑ 456 Ron Saul .20 .09
- ❑ 457 Bob Parsons .20 .09
- ❑ 458 Glenn Doughty .20 .09
- ❑ 459 Don Woods .20 .09
- ❑ 460 Art Shell AP 1.00 .45
- ❑ 461 Sam Hunt .20 .09
- ❑ 462 Lawrence Pillers .20 .09
- ❑ 463 Henry Childs .20 .09
- ❑ 464 Roger Wehrli .20 .09
- ❑ 465 Otis Armstrong .50 .23
- ❑ 466 Bob Baumhower RC 1.00 .45
- ❑ 467 Ray Jarvis .20 .09
- ❑ 468 Guy Morriss .20 .09
- ❑ 469 Matt Blair .50 .23
- ❑ 470 Billy Joe DuPree .50 .23
- ❑ 471 Roland Hooks .20 .09
- ❑ 472 Joe Danelo .20 .09
- ❑ 473 Reggie Rucker .50 .23
- ❑ 474 Vern Holland .20 .09
- ❑ 475 Mel Blount 1.50 .70
- ❑ 476 Eddie Brown .20 .09
- ❑ 477 Bo Rather .20 .09
- ❑ 478 Don McCauley .20 .09
- ❑ 479 Glen Walker .20 .09
- ❑ 480 Randy Gradishar AP 1.00 .45
- ❑ 481 Dave Rowe .20 .09
- ❑ 482 Pat Leahy .50 .23
- ❑ 483 Mike Fuller .20 .09
- ❑ 484 David Lewis .20 .09
- ❑ 485 Steve Grogan 1.00 .45
- ❑ 486 Mel Gray .50 .23
- ❑ 487 Eddie Payton RC .50 .23
- ❑ 488 Checklist 397-528 1.00 .25
- ❑ 489 Stu Voigt .20 .09
- ❑ 490 Rolland Lawrence AP .20 .09
- ❑ 491 Nick Mike-Mayer .20 .09
- ❑ 492 Troy Archer .20 .09
- ❑ 493 Benny Malone .20 .09
- ❑ 494 Golden Richards .50 .23
- ❑ 495 Chris Hanburger .20 .09
- ❑ 496 Dwight Harrison .20 .09
- ❑ 497 Gary Fencik RC 1.00 .45
- ❑ 498 Rich Saul .20 .09
- ❑ 499 Dan Fouts 4.00 1.80
- ❑ 500 Franco Harris AP 4.00 1.80
- ❑ 501 Atlanta Falcons TL .60 .15
  - Haskel Stanback
  - Alfred Jenkins
  - Claude Humphrey
  - Jeff Merrow
  - Rolland Lawrence
  - (checklist back)
- ❑ 502 Baltimore Colts TL .60 .15
  - Lydell Mitchell
  - Lydell Mitchell
  - Lyle Blackwood
  - Fred Cook
  - (checklist back)
- ❑ 503 Buffalo Bills TL .60 .15
  - O.J. Simpson
  - Bob Chandler
  - Tony Greene
  - Sherman White
  - (checklist back)
- ❑ 504 Chicago Bears TL 2.00 .50
  - Walter Payton
  - James Scott
  - Allan Ellis
  - Ron Rydalch
  - (checklist back)
- ❑ 505 Cincinnati Bengals TL .60 .15
  - Pete Johnson
  - Billy Brooks
  - Lemar Parrish
  - Reggie Williams
  - Gary Burley
  - (checklist back)
- ❑ 506 Cleveland Browns TL .60 .15
  - Greg Pruitt
  - Reggie Rucker
  - Thom Darden
  - Mack Mitchell
  - (checklist back)
- ❑ 507 Dallas Cowboys TL 2.50 .60
  - Tony Dorsett
  - Drew Pearson
  - Cliff Harris
  - Harvey Martin
  - (checklist back)
- ❑ 508 Denver Broncos TL .60 .15
  - Otis Armstrong
  - Haven Moses
  - Bill Thompson
  - Rick Upchurch
  - (checklist back)
- ❑ 509 Detroit Lions TL .60 .15
  - Horace King
  - David Hill
  - James Hunter
  - Ken Sanders
  - (checklist back)
- ❑ 510 Green Bay Packers TL .60 .15
  - Barty Smith
  - Steve Odom
  - Steve Luke
  - Mike C. McCoy
  - Dave Pureifory
  - Dave Roller
  - (checklist back)
- ❑ 511 Houston Oilers TL .60 .15
  - Ronnie Coleman
  - Ken Burrough
  - Mike Reinfeldt
  - James Young
  - (checklist back)
- ❑ 512 Kansas City Chiefs TL .60 .15
  - Ed Podolak
  - Walter White
  - Gary Barbaro
  - Wilbur Young
  - (checklist back)
- ❑ 513 Los Angeles Rams TL .60 .15
  - Lawrence McCutcheon
  - Harold Jackson
  - Bill Simpson
  - Jack Youngblood
  - (checklist back)
- ❑ 514 Miami Dolphins TL .60 .15
  - Benny Malone
  - Nat Moore
  - Curtis Johnson
  - A.J. Duhe
  - (checklist back)
- ❑ 515 Minnesota Vikings TL .60 .15
  - Chuck Foreman
  - Sammie White
  - Bobby Bryant
  - Carl Eller
  - (checklist back)
- ❑ 516 New England Patriots TL .60 .15
  - Sam Cunningham
  - Darryl Stingley
  - Mike Haynes
  - Tony McGee
  - (checklist back)
- ❑ 517 New Orleans Saints TL .60 .15
  - Chuck Muncie
  - Don Herrmann
  - Chuck Crist
  - Elois Grooms
  - (checklist back)
- ❑ 518 New York Giants TL .60 .15
  - Bobby Hammond
  - Jimmy Robinson
  - Bill Bryant
  - John Mendenhall
  - (checklist back)
- ❑ 519 New York Jets TL .60 .15
  - Clark Gaines
  - Wesley Walker
  - Burgess Owens
  - Joe Klecko
  - (checklist back)
- ❑ 520 Oakland Raiders TL .60 .15
  - Mark Van Eeghen
  - Dave Casper
  - Jack Tatum
  - Neal Colzie
  - (checklist back)
- ❑ 521 Philadelphia Eagles TL .60 .15
  - Mike Hogan
  - Harold Carmichael
  - Herman Edwards
  - John Sanders
  - Lem Burnham
  - (checklist back)
- ❑ 522 Pittsburgh Steelers TL .60 .15
  - Franco Harris
  - Jim Smith
  - Mel Blount
  - Steve Furness
  - (checklist back)
- ❑ 523 St.Louis Cardinals TL .60 .15
  - Terry Metcalf
  - Mel Gray
  - Roger Wehrli
  - Mike Dawson
  - (checklist back)
- ❑ 524 San Diego Chargers TL .60 .15
  - Rickey Young
  - Charlie Joiner
  - Mike Fuller
  - Gary Johnson
  - (checklist back)
- ❑ 525 San Francisco 49ers TL .60 .15
  - Delvin Williams
  - Gene Washington
  - Mel Phillips
  - Dave Washington
  - Cleveland Elam
  - (checklist back)
- ❑ 526 Seattle Seahawks TL 1.50 .35
  - Sherman Smith
  - Steve Largent
  - Autry Beamon
  - Walter Packer
  - (checklist back)
- ❑ 527 Tampa Bay Bucs TL .20 .05
  - Morris Owens
  - Isaac Hagins
  - Mike Washington
  - Lee Roy Selmon
  - (checklist back)
- ❑ 528 Wash. Redskins TL .60 .15
  - Mike Thomas
  - Jean Fugett
  - Ken Houston
  - Dennis Johnson
  - (checklist back)

1979 Topps

	NRMT-MT	EXC
COMPLETE SET (528)	150.00	70.00
COMMON CARD (1-528)	.20	.09
SEMISTARS	.50	.23
UNLISTED STARS	1.00	.45
TEAM LEADERS	.75	.35
CL (114/232/368/486)	1.00	.45
❑ 1 Passing Leaders	8.00	2.00
Roger Staubach		
Terry Bradshaw		
❑ 2 Receiving Leaders	1.00	.45
Rickey Young		
Steve Largent		
❑ 3 Rushing Leaders	8.00	3.60
Walter Payton		
Earl Campbell		
❑ 4 Scoring Leaders	.20	.09
Frank Corral		
Pat Leahy		
❑ 5 Interception Leaders	.20	.09
Willie Buchanon		
Ken Stone		
Thom Darden		
❑ 6 Punting Leaders	.20	.09
Tom Skladany		
Pat McInally		
❑ 7 Johnny Perkins	.20	.09
❑ 8 Charles Phillips	.20	.09
❑ 9 Derrel Luce	.20	.09
❑ 10 John Riggins	1.25	.55
❑ 11 Chester Marcol	.20	.09
❑ 12 Bernard Jackson	.20	.09
❑ 13 Dave Logan	.20	.09
❑ 14 Bo Harris	.20	.09
❑ 15 Alan Page	1.00	.45
❑ 16 John Smith	.20	.09
❑ 17 Dwight McDonald	.20	.09
❑ 18 John Cappelletti	.50	.23
❑ 19 Pittsburgh Steelers TL	1.00	.45
Franco Harris		
Larry Anderson		
Tony Dungy		
L.C. Greenwood		
(checklist back)		
❑ 20 Bill Bergey AP	.50	.23
❑ 21 Jerome Barkum	.20	.09
❑ 22 Larry Csonka	2.50	1.10
❑ 23 Joe Ferguson	.50	.23
❑ 24 Ed Too Tall Jones	1.25	.55
❑ 25 Dave Jennings	.50	.23
❑ 26 Horace King	.20	.09
❑ 27 Steve Little	.50	.23
❑ 28 Morris Bradshaw	.20	.09
❑ 29 Joe Ehrmann	.20	.09
❑ 30 Ahmad Rashad AP	1.00	.45
❑ 31 Joe Lavender	.20	.09
❑ 32 Dan Neal	.20	.09
❑ 33 Johnny Evans	.20	.09
❑ 34 Pete Johnson	.50	.23
❑ 35 Mike Haynes AP	1.00	.45
❑ 36 Tim Mazzetti	.20	.09
❑ 37 Mike Barber RC	.20	.09
❑ 38 San Francisco 49ers TL	1.00	.45
O.J. Simpson		
Freddie Solomon		
Chuck Crist		
Cedrick Hardman		
(checklist back)		
❑ 39 Bill Gregory	.20	.09
❑ 40 Randy Gradishar AP	1.00	.45
❑ 41 Richard Todd	.50	.23
❑ 42 Henry Marshall	.20	.09
❑ 43 John Hill	.20	.09
❑ 44 Sidney Thornton	.20	.09
❑ 45 Ron Jessie	.20	.09
❑ 46 Bob Baumhower	.50	.23
❑ 47 Johnnie Gray	.20	.09
❑ 48 Doug Williams RC	6.00	2.70
❑ 49 Don McCauley	.20	.09
❑ 50 Ray Guy AP	.50	.23
❑ 51 Bob Klein	.20	.09
❑ 52 Golden Richards	.20	.09
❑ 53 Mark Miller	.20	.09
❑ 54 John Sanders	.20	.09
❑ 55 Gary Burley	.20	.09
❑ 56 Steve Nelson	.20	.09
❑ 57 Buffalo Bills TL	.75	.35
Terry Miller		
Frank Lewis		
Mario Clark		
Lucius Sanford		
(checklist back)		
❑ 58 Bobby Bryant	.20	.09
❑ 59 Rick Kane	.20	.09
❑ 60 Larry Little	1.00	.45
❑ 61 Ted Fritsch Jr.	.20	.09
❑ 62 Larry Mallory	.20	.09
❑ 63 Marvin Powell	.20	.09
❑ 64 Jim Hart	1.00	.45
❑ 65 Joe Greene AP	1.50	.70
❑ 66 Walter White	.20	.09
❑ 67 Gregg Bingham	.20	.09
❑ 68 Errol Mann	.20	.09
❑ 69 Bruce Laird	.20	.09
❑ 70 Drew Pearson	1.00	.45
❑ 71 Steve Bartkowski	1.00	.45
❑ 72 Ted Albrecht	.20	.09
❑ 73 Charlie Hall	.20	.09
❑ 74 Pat McInally	.20	.09
❑ 75 Al(Bubba) Baker AP RC	1.00	.45
❑ 76 New England Pats TL	.75	.35
Sam Cunningham		
Stanley Morgan		
Mike Haynes		
Tony McGee		
(checklist back)		
❑ 77 Steve DeBerg RC	2.00	.90
❑ 78 John Yarno	.20	.09
❑ 79 Stu Voigt	.20	.09
❑ 80 Frank Corral AP	.20	.09
❑ 81 Troy Archer	.20	.09
❑ 82 Bruce Harper	.20	.09
❑ 83 Tom Jackson	1.50	.70
❑ 84 Larry Brown	.50	.23
❑ 85 Wilbert Montgomery AP RC	1.00	.45
❑ 86 Butch Johnson	.50	.23
❑ 87 Mike Kadish	.20	.09
❑ 88 Ralph Perretta	.20	.09
❑ 89 David Lee	.20	.09
❑ 90 Mark Van Eeghen	.50	.23
❑ 91 John McDaniel	.20	.09
❑ 92 Gary Fencik	.50	.23
❑ 93 Mack Mitchell	.20	.09
❑ 94 Cincinnati Bengals TL	.75	.35
Pete Johnson		
Isaac Curtis		
Dick Jauron		
Ross Browner		
(checklist back)		
❑ 95 Steve Grogan	1.00	.45
❑ 96 Garo Yepremian	.50	.23
❑ 97 Barty Smith	.20	.09
❑ 98 Frank Reed	.20	.09
❑ 99 Jim Clack	.20	.09
❑ 100 Chuck Foreman	.50	.23
❑ 101 Joe Klecko	1.00	.45
❑ 102 Pat Tilley	.50	.23
❑ 103 Conrad Dobler	.50	.23
❑ 104 Craig Colquitt	.20	.09
❑ 105 Dan Pastorini	.50	.23
❑ 106 Rod Perry AP	.20	.09
❑ 107 Nick Mike-Mayer	.20	.09
❑ 108 John Matuszak	.50	.23
❑ 109 David Taylor	.20	.09
❑ 110 Billy Joe DuPree AP	.50	.23
❑ 111 Harold McLinton	.20	.09
❑ 112 Virgil Livers	.20	.09
❑ 113 Cleveland Browns TL	.75	.35
Greg Pruitt		
Reggie Rucker		
Thom Darden		
Mack Mitchell		
(checklist back)		
❑ 114 Checklist 1-132	1.00	.25
❑ 115 Ken Anderson	1.00	.45
❑ 116 Bill Lenkaitis	.20	.09
❑ 117 Bucky Dilts	.20	.09
❑ 118 Tony Greene	.20	.09
❑ 119 Bobby Hammond	.20	.09
❑ 120 Nat Moore	.50	.23
❑ 121 Pat Leahy AP	.50	.23
❑ 122 James Harris	.50	.23
❑ 123 Lee Roy Selmon	1.25	.55
❑ 124 Bennie Cunningham	.50	.23
❑ 125 Matt Blair AP	.50	.23
❑ 126 Jim Allen	.20	.09
❑ 127 Alfred Jenkins	.50	.23
❑ 128 Arthur Whittington	.20	.09
❑ 129 Norm Thompson	.20	.09
❑ 130 Pat Haden	1.00	.45
❑ 131 Freddie Solomon	.20	.09
❑ 132 Chicago Bears TL	2.00	.90
Walter Payton		
James Scott		
Gary Fencik		
Alan Page		
(checklist back)		
❑ 133 Mark Moseley	.20	.09
❑ 134 Cleo Miller	.20	.09
❑ 135 Ross Browner RC	.50	.23
❑ 136 Don Calhoun	.20	.09
❑ 137 David Whitehurst	.20	.09
❑ 138 Terry Beeson	.20	.09
❑ 139 Ken Stone	.20	.09
❑ 140 Brad Van Pelt AP	.20	.09
❑ 141 Wesley Walker AP	1.00	.45
❑ 142 Jan Stenerud	1.00	.45
❑ 143 Henry Childs	.20	.09
❑ 144 Otis Armstrong	1.00	.45
❑ 145 Dwight White	.50	.23
❑ 146 Steve Wilson	.20	.09
❑ 147 Tom Skladany AP RC	.20	.09
❑ 148 Lou Piccone	.20	.09
❑ 149 Monte Johnson	.20	.09
❑ 150 Joe Washington	.50	.23
❑ 151 Philadelphia Eagles TL	.75	.35
Wilbert Montgomery		
Harold Carmichael		
Herman Edwards		
Dennis Harrison		
(checklist back)		
❑ 152 Fred Dean	.20	.09
❑ 153 Rolland Lawrence	.20	.09
❑ 154 Brian Baschnagel	.20	.09
❑ 155 Joe Theismann	2.00	.90
❑ 156 Marvin Cobb	.20	.09
❑ 157 Dick Ambrose	.20	.09
❑ 158 Mike Patrick	.20	.09
❑ 159 Gary Shirk	.20	.09
❑ 160 Tony Dorsett	12.00	5.50
❑ 161 Greg Buttle	.20	.09
❑ 162 A.J. Duhe	.50	.23
❑ 163 Mick Tingelhoff	.50	.23
❑ 164 Ken Burrough	.50	.23
❑ 165 Mike Wagner	.20	.09
❑ 166 AFC Championship	1.00	.45
Steelers 34,		
Oilers 5		
(Franco Harris)		
❑ 167 NFC Championship	.50	.23
Cowboys 28,		
Rams 0		
(line of scrimmage)		
❑ 168 Super Bowl XIII	1.25	.55
Steelers 35,		
Cowboys 31		
(Franco Harris)		
❑ 169 Oakland Raiders TL	.75	.35
Mark Van Eeghen		
Dave Casper		
Charles Phillips		
Ted Hendricks		
(checklist back)		
❑ 170 O.J. Simpson	4.00	1.80
❑ 171 Doug Nettles	.20	.09
❑ 172 Dan Dierdorf AP	1.00	.45
❑ 173 Dave Beverly	.20	.09
❑ 174 Jim Zorn	1.00	.45
❑ 175 Mike Thomas	.20	.09
❑ 176 John Outlaw	.20	.09
❑ 177 Jim Turner	.20	.09
❑ 178 Freddie Scott	.20	.09
❑ 179 Mike Phipps	.50	.23
❑ 180 Jack Youngblood AP	1.00	.45
❑ 181 Sam Hunt	.20	.09
❑ 182 Tony Hill RC	1.00	.45

❑ 183 Gary Barbaro .20 .09
❑ 184 Archie Griffin .50 .23
❑ 185 Jerry Sherk .20 .09
❑ 186 Bobby Jackson .20 .09
❑ 187 Don Woods .20 .09
❑ 188 New York Giants TL .75 .35
Doug Kotar
Jimmy Robinson
Terry Jackson
George Martin
(checklist back)
❑ 189 Raymond Chester .20 .09
❑ 190 Joe DeLamielleure AP .20 .09
❑ 191 Tony Galbreath .50 .23
❑ 192 Robert Brazile AP .50 .23
❑ 193 Neil O'Donoghue .20 .09
❑ 194 Mike Webster AP 1.00 .45
❑ 195 Ed Simonini .20 .09
❑ 196 Benny Malone .20 .09
❑ 197 Tom Wittum .20 .09
❑ 198 Steve Largent AP 8.00 3.60
❑ 199 Tommy Hart .20 .09
❑ 200 Fran Tarkenton 3.00 1.35
❑ 201 Leon Gray AP .20 .09
❑ 202 Leroy Harris .20 .09
❑ 203 Eric Williams .20 .09
❑ 204 Thom Darden AP .20 .09
❑ 205 Ken Riley .50 .23
❑ 206 Clark Gaines .20 .09
❑ 207 Kansas City Chiefs TL .75 .35
Tony Reed
Tony Reed
Tim Gray
Art Still
(checklist back)
❑ 208 Joe Danelo .20 .09
❑ 209 Glen Walker .20 .09
❑ 210 Art Shell 1.00 .45
❑ 211 Jon Keyworth .20 .09
❑ 212 Herman Edwards .20 .09
❑ 213 John Fitzgerald .20 .09
❑ 214 Jim Smith .50 .23
❑ 215 Coy Bacon .50 .23
❑ 216 Dennis Johnson .20 .09
❑ 217 John Jefferson RC 3.00 1.35
(Charlie Joiner
in background)
❑ 218 Gary Weaver .20 .09
❑ 219 Tom Blanchard .20 .09
❑ 220 Bert Jones 1.00 .45
❑ 221 Stanley Morgan 1.00 .45
❑ 222 James Hunter .20 .09
❑ 223 Jim O'Bradovich .20 .09
❑ 224 Carl Mauck .20 .09
❑ 225 Chris Bahr .20 .09
❑ 226 New York Jets TL .75 .35
Kevin Long
Wesley Walker
Bobby Jackson
Burgess Owens
Joe Klecko
(checklist back)
❑ 227 Roland Harper .20 .09
❑ 228 Randy Dean .20 .09
❑ 229 Bob Jackson .20 .09
❑ 230 Sammie White .50 .23
❑ 231 Mike Dawson .20 .09
❑ 232 Checklist 133-264 1.00 .25
❑ 233 Ken MacAfee .20 .09
❑ 234 Jon Kolb AP .20 .09
❑ 235 Willie Hall .20 .09
❑ 236 Ron Saul AP .20 .09
❑ 237 Haskel Stanback .20 .09
❑ 238 Zenon Andrusyshyn .20 .09
❑ 239 Norris Thomas .20 .09
❑ 240 Rick Upchurch .50 .23
❑ 241 Robert Pratt .20 .09
❑ 242 Julius Adams .20 .09
❑ 243 Rich McGeorge .20 .09
❑ 244 Seattle Seahawks TL 1.25 .55
Sherman Smith
Steve Largent
Cornell Webster
Bill Gregory
(checklist back)
❑ 245 Blair Bush RC .20 .09
❑ 246 Billy Johnson .50 .23
❑ 247 Randy Rasmussen .20 .09
❑ 248 Brian Kelley .20 .09
❑ 249 Mike Pruitt .50 .23
❑ 250 Harold Carmichael AP 1.00 .45
❑ 251 Mike Hartenstine .20 .09
❑ 252 Robert Newhouse .50 .23
❑ 253 Gary Danielson RC 1.00 .45
❑ 254 Mike Fuller .20 .09
❑ 255 L.C. Greenwood AP 1.00 .45
❑ 256 Lemar Parrish .20 .09
❑ 257 Ike Harris .20 .09
❑ 258 Ricky Bell RC 1.00 .45
❑ 259 Willie Parker .20 .09
❑ 260 Gene Upshaw 1.00 .45
❑ 261 Glenn Doughty .20 .09
❑ 262 Steve Zabel .20 .09
❑ 263 Atlanta Falcons TL .75 .35
Bubba Bean
Wallace Francis
Rolland Lawrence
Greg Brezina
(checklist back)
❑ 264 Ray Wersching .20 .09
❑ 265 Lawrence McCutcheon .50 .23
❑ 266 Willie Buchanon AP .20 .09
❑ 267 Matt Robinson .20 .09
❑ 268 Reggie Rucker .50 .23
❑ 269 Doug Van Horn .20 .09
❑ 270 Lydell Mitchell .50 .23
❑ 271 Vern Holland .20 .09
❑ 272 Eason Ramson .20 .09
❑ 273 Steve Towle .20 .09
❑ 274 Jim Marshall 1.00 .45
❑ 275 Mel Blount 1.25 .55
❑ 276 Bob Kuziel .20 .09
❑ 277 James Scott .20 .09
❑ 278 Tony Reed .20 .09
❑ 279 Dave Green .20 .09
❑ 280 Toni Linhart .20 .09
❑ 281 Andy Johnson .20 .09
❑ 282 Los Angeles Rams TL .75 .35
Cullen Bryant
Willie Miller
Rod Perry
Pat Thomas
Larry Brooks
(checklist back)
❑ 283 Phil Villapiano .50 .23
❑ 284 Dexter Bussey .20 .09
❑ 285 Craig Morton 1.00 .45
❑ 286 Guy Morriss .20 .09
❑ 287 Lawrence Pillers .20 .09
❑ 288 Gerald Irons .20 .09
❑ 289 Scott Perry .20 .09
❑ 290 Randy White AP 2.00 .90
❑ 291 Jack Gregory .20 .09
❑ 292 Bob Chandler .20 .09
❑ 293 Rich Szaro .20 .09
❑ 294 Sherman Smith .20 .09
❑ 295 Tom Banks AP .20 .09
❑ 296 Revie Sorey AP .20 .09
❑ 297 Ricky Thompson .20 .09
❑ 298 Ron Yary .50 .23
❑ 299 Lyle Blackwood .20 .09
❑ 300 Franco Harris 2.50 1.10
❑ 301 Houston Oilers TL 3.00 1.35
Earl Campbell
Ken Burrough
Willie Alexander
Elvin Bethea
(checklist back)
❑ 302 Scott Bull .20 .09
❑ 303 Dewey Selmon .50 .23
❑ 304 Jack Rudnay .20 .09
❑ 305 Fred Biletnikoff 2.00 .90
❑ 306 Jeff West .20 .09
❑ 307 Shafer Suggs .20 .09
❑ 308 Ozzie Newsome RC 15.00 6.75
❑ 309 Boobie Clark .20 .09
❑ 310 James Lofton RC 15.00 6.75
❑ 311 Joe Pisarcik .20 .09
❑ 312 Bill Simpson AP .20 .09
❑ 313 Haven Moses .50 .23
❑ 314 Jim Merlo .20 .09
❑ 315 Preston Pearson .50 .23
❑ 316 Larry Tearry .20 .09
❑ 317 Tom Dempsey .20 .09
❑ 318 Greg Latta .20 .09
❑ 319 Wash. Redskins TL .75 .35
John Riggins
John McDaniel
Jake Scott
Coy Bacon
(checklist back)
❑ 320 Jack Ham AP 1.25 .55
❑ 321 Harold Jackson .50 .23
❑ 322 George Roberts .20 .09
❑ 323 Ron Jaworski 1.00 .45
❑ 324 Jim Otis .20 .09
❑ 325 Roger Carr .50 .23
❑ 326 Jack Tatum .50 .23
❑ 327 Derrick Gaffney .20 .09
❑ 328 Reggie Williams 1.00 .45
❑ 329 Doug Dieken .20 .09
❑ 330 Efren Herrera .20 .09
❑ 331 Earl Campbell RB 6.00 2.70
Most Yards
Rushing, Rookie
❑ 332 Tony Galbreath RB .20 .09
Most Receptions,
Running Back, Game
❑ 333 Bruce Harper RB .20 .09
Most Combined Kick
Return Yards, Season
❑ 334 John James RB .20 .09
Most Punts, Season
❑ 335 Walter Payton RB 4.00 1.80
Most Combined
Attempts, Season
❑ 336 Rickey Young RB .20 .09
Most Receptions,
Running Back, Season
❑ 337 Jeff Van Note .50 .23
❑ 338 San Diego Chargers TL .75 .35
Lydell Mitchell
John Jefferson
Mike Fuller
Fred Dean
(checklist back)
❑ 339 Stan Walters AP RC .20 .09
❑ 340 Louis Wright AP .50 .23
❑ 341 Horace Ivory .20 .09
❑ 342 Andre Tillman .20 .09
❑ 343 Greg Coleman RC .20 .09
❑ 344 Doug English AP RC 1.00 .45
❑ 345 Ted Hendricks 1.00 .45
❑ 346 Rich Saul .20 .09
❑ 347 Mel Gray .50 .23
❑ 348 Toni Fritsch .20 .09
❑ 349 Cornell Webster .20 .09
❑ 350 Ken Houston 1.00 .45
❑ 351 Ron Johnson .50 .23
❑ 352 Doug Kotar .20 .09
❑ 353 Brian Sipe 1.00 .45
❑ 354 Billy Brooks .20 .09
❑ 355 John Dutton .50 .23
❑ 356 Don Goode .20 .09
❑ 357 Detroit Lions TL .75 .35
Dexter Bussey
David Hill
Jim Allen
Al(Bubba) Baker
(checklist back)
❑ 358 Reuben Gant .20 .09
❑ 359 Bob Parsons .20 .09
❑ 360 Cliff Harris AP 1.00 .45
❑ 361 Raymond Clayborn .50 .23
❑ 362 Scott Dierking .20 .09
❑ 363 Bill Bryan .20 .09
❑ 364 Mike Livingston .20 .09
❑ 365 Otis Sistrunk .50 .23
❑ 366 Charlie Young .50 .23
❑ 367 Keith Wortman .20 .09
❑ 368 Checklist 265-396 1.00 .25
❑ 369 Mike Michel .20 .09
❑ 370 Delvin Williams AP .20 .09
❑ 371 Steve Furness .50 .23
❑ 372 Emery Moorehead .20 .09
❑ 373 Clarence Scott .20 .09
❑ 374 Rufus Mayes .20 .09
❑ 375 Chris Hanburger .20 .09

	Card	NRMT	EXC
❑ 376	Baltimore Colts TL	.75	.35
	Joe Washington		
	Roger Carr		
	Norm Thompson		
	John Dutton		
	(checklist back)		
❑ 377	Bob Avellini	.50	.23
❑ 378	Jeff Siemon	.20	.09
❑ 379	Roland Hooks	.20	.09
❑ 380	Russ Francis	.50	.23
❑ 381	Roger Wehrli	.20	.09
❑ 382	Joe Fields	.20	.09
❑ 383	Archie Manning	1.00	.45
❑ 384	Rob Lytle	.20	.09
❑ 385	Thomas Henderson	.50	.23
❑ 386	Morris Owens	.20	.09
❑ 387	Dan Fouts	3.00	1.35
❑ 388	Chuck Crist	.20	.09
❑ 389	Ed O'Neil	.20	.09
❑ 390	Earl Campbell AP RC	30.00	13.50
❑ 391	Randy Grossman	.20	.09
❑ 392	Monte Jackson	.20	.09
❑ 393	John Mendenhall	.20	.09
❑ 394	Miami Dolphins TL	.75	.35
	Delvin Williams		
	Duriel Harris		
	Tim Foley		
	Vern Den Herder		
	(checklist back)		
❑ 395	Isaac Curtis	.50	.23
❑ 396	Mike Bragg	.20	.09
❑ 397	Doug Plank	.20	.09
❑ 398	Mike Barnes	.20	.09
❑ 399	Calvin Hill	.50	.23
❑ 400	Roger Staubach AP	10.00	4.50
❑ 401	Doug Beaudoin	.20	.09
❑ 402	Chuck Ramsey	.20	.09
❑ 403	Mike Hogan	.20	.09
❑ 404	Mario Clark	.20	.09
❑ 405	Riley Odoms	.20	.09
❑ 406	Carl Eller	.50	.23
❑ 407	Green Bay Packers TL	2.00	.90
	Terdell Middleton		
	James Lofton		
	Willie Buchanon		
	Ezra Johnson		
	(checklist back)		
❑ 408	Mark Arneson	.20	.09
❑ 409	Vince Ferragamo RC	1.00	.45
❑ 410	Cleveland Elam	.20	.09
❑ 411	Donnie Shell RC	4.00	1.80
❑ 412	Ray Rhodes	1.00	.45
❑ 413	Don Cockroft	.20	.09
❑ 414	Don Bass	.50	.23
❑ 415	Cliff Branch	1.00	.45
❑ 416	Diron Talbert	.20	.09
❑ 417	Tom Hicks	.20	.09
❑ 418	Roosevelt Leaks	.20	.09
❑ 419	Charlie Joiner	1.00	.45
❑ 420	Lyle Alzado AP	1.00	.45
❑ 421	Sam Cunningham	.50	.23
❑ 422	Larry Keller	.20	.09
❑ 423	Jim Mitchell	.20	.09
❑ 424	Randy Logan	.20	.09
❑ 425	Jim Langer	1.00	.45
❑ 426	Gary Green	.20	.09
❑ 427	Luther Blue	.20	.09
❑ 428	Dennis Johnson	.20	.09
❑ 429	Danny White	1.00	.45
❑ 430	Roy Gerela	.20	.09
❑ 431	Jimmy Robinson	.20	.09
❑ 432	Minnesota Vikings TL	.75	.35
	Chuck Foreman		
	Ahmad Rashad		
	Bobby Bryant		
	Mark Mullaney		
	(checklist back)		
❑ 433	Oliver Davis	.20	.09
❑ 434	Lenvil Elliott	.20	.09
❑ 435	Willie Miller	.20	.09
❑ 436	Brad Dusek	.20	.09
❑ 437	Bob Thomas	.20	.09
❑ 438	Ken Mendenhall	.20	.09
❑ 439	Clarence Davis	.20	.09
❑ 440	Bob Griese	2.50	1.10
❑ 441	Tony McGee	.20	.09
❑ 442	Ed Taylor	.20	.09
❑ 443	Ron Howard	.20	.09
❑ 444	Wayne Morris	.20	.09
❑ 445	Charlie Waters	1.00	.45
❑ 446	Rick Danmeier	.20	.09
❑ 447	Paul Naumoff	.20	.09
❑ 448	Keith Krepfle	.20	.09
❑ 449	Rusty Jackson	.20	.09
❑ 450	John Stallworth	4.00	1.80
❑ 451	New Orleans Saints TL	.75	.35
	Tony Galbreath		
	Henry Childs		
	Tom Myers		
	Elex Price		
	(checklist back)		
❑ 452	Ron Mikolajczyk	.20	.09
❑ 453	Fred Dryer	1.00	.45
❑ 454	Jim LeClair	.20	.09
❑ 455	Greg Pruitt	.50	.23
❑ 456	Jake Scott	.20	.09
❑ 457	Steve Schubert	.20	.09
❑ 458	George Kunz	.20	.09
❑ 459	Mike Williams	.20	.09
❑ 460	Dave Casper AP	.50	.23
❑ 461	Sam Adams	.20	.09
❑ 462	Abdul Salaam	.20	.09
❑ 463	Terdell Middleton	.50	.23
❑ 464	Mike Wood	.20	.09
❑ 465	Bill Thompson AP	.20	.09
❑ 466	Larry Gordon	.20	.09
❑ 467	Benny Ricardo	.20	.09
❑ 468	Reggie McKenzie	.50	.23
❑ 469	Dallas Cowboys TL	1.25	.55
	Tony Dorsett		
	Tony Hill		
	Benny Barnes		
	Harvey Martin		
	Randy White		
	(checklist back)		
❑ 470	Rickey Young	.50	.23
❑ 471	Charlie Smith	.20	.09
❑ 472	Al Dixon	.20	.09
❑ 473	Tom DeLeone	.20	.09
❑ 474	Louis Breeden	.50	.23
❑ 475	Jack Lambert	2.00	.90
❑ 476	Terry Hermeling	.20	.09
❑ 477	J.K. McKay	.20	.09
❑ 478	Stan White	.20	.09
❑ 479	Terry Nelson	.20	.09
❑ 480	Walter Payton AP	20.00	9.00
❑ 481	Dave Dalby	.20	.09
❑ 482	Burgess Owens	.20	.09
❑ 483	Rolf Benirschke	.20	.09
❑ 484	Jack Dolbin	.20	.09
❑ 485	John Hannah AP	1.00	.45
❑ 486	Checklist 397-528	1.00	.25
❑ 487	Greg Landry	.50	.23
❑ 488	St. Louis Cardinals TL	.75	.35
	Jim Otis		
	Pat Tilley		
	Ken Stone		
	Mike Dawson		
	(checklist back)		
❑ 489	Paul Krause	.50	.23
❑ 490	John James	.20	.09
❑ 491	Merv Krakau	.20	.09
❑ 492	Dan Doornink	.20	.09
❑ 493	Curtis Johnson	.20	.09
❑ 494	Rafael Septien	.20	.09
❑ 495	Jean Fugett	.20	.09
❑ 496	Frank LeMaster	.20	.09
❑ 497	Allan Ellis	.20	.09
❑ 498	Billy Waddy RC	.50	.23
❑ 499	Hank Bauer	.20	.09
❑ 500	Terry Bradshaw AP UER	8.00	3.60
	(Stat headers on back are for a runner)		
❑ 501	Larry McCarren	.20	.09
❑ 502	Fred Cook	.20	.09
❑ 503	Chuck Muncie	.50	.23
❑ 504	Herman Weaver	.20	.09
❑ 505	Eddie Edwards	.20	.09
❑ 506	Tony Peters	.20	.09
❑ 507	Denver Broncos TL	.75	.35
	Lonnie Perrin		
	Riley Odoms		
	Steve Foley		
	Bernard Jackson		
	Lyle Alzado		
	(checklist back)		
❑ 508	Jimbo Elrod	.20	.09
❑ 509	David Hill	.20	.09
❑ 510	Harvey Martin	1.00	.45
❑ 511	Terry Miller	.50	.23
❑ 512	June Jones RC	.50	.23
❑ 513	Randy Cross	1.00	.45
❑ 514	Duriel Harris	.20	.09
❑ 515	Harry Carson	1.00	.45
❑ 516	Tim Fox	.20	.09
❑ 517	John Zook	.20	.09
❑ 518	Bob Tucker	.20	.09
❑ 519	Kevin Long	.20	.09
❑ 520	Ken Stabler	6.00	2.70
❑ 521	John Bunting	.20	.09
❑ 522	Rocky Bleier	1.25	.55
❑ 523	Noah Jackson	.20	.09
❑ 524	Cliff Parsley	.20	.09
❑ 525	Louie Kelcher AP	.50	.23
❑ 526	Tampa Bay Bucs TL	.75	.35
	Ricky Bell		
	Morris Owens		
	Cedric Brown		
	Lee Roy Selmon		
	(checklist back)		
❑ 527	Bob Brudzinski	.20	.09
❑ 528	Danny Buggs	.20	.09

1980 Topps

	NRMT-MT	EXC
COMPLETE SET (528)	60.00	27.00
COMMON CARD (1-528)	.15	.07
SEMISTARS	.50	.23
UNLISTED STARS	1.00	.45
CL (102/246/391/509)	.60	.25

	Card	NRMT-MT	EXC
❑ 1	Ottis Anderson RB	1.00	.45
	Most Yardage, Rushing, Rookie		
❑ 2	Harold Carmichael RB	1.00	.45
	Most Consec. Games, One or More Receptions		
❑ 3	Dan Fouts RB	1.00	.45
	Most Yardage, Passing, Season		
❑ 4	Paul Krause RB	.50	.23
	Most Interceptions, Lifetime		
❑ 5	Rick Upchurch RB	.50	.23
	Most Punt Return Yards, Lifetime		
❑ 6	Garo Yepremian RB	.15	.07
	Most Consecutive Field Goals		
❑ 7	Harold Jackson	.50	.23
❑ 8	Mike Williams	.15	.07
❑ 9	Calvin Hill	.50	.23
❑ 10	Jack Ham AP	1.00	.45
❑ 11	Dan Melville	.15	.07
❑ 12	Matt Robinson	.15	.07
❑ 13	Billy Campfield	.15	.07
❑ 14	Phil Tabor	.15	.07
❑ 15	Randy Hughes UER	.15	.07
	(Cowboys didn't play in SB VII)		

❑ 16 Andre Tillman .15 .07
❑ 17 Isaac Curtis .50 .23
❑ 18 Charley Hannah .15 .07
❑ 19 Wash. Redskins TL 1.00 .45
John Riggins
Danny Buggs
Joe Lavender
Coy Bacon
(checklist back)
❑ 20 Jim Zorn .50 .23
❑ 21 Brian Baschnagel .15 .07
❑ 22 Jon Keyworth .15 .07
❑ 23 Phil Villapiano .15 .07
❑ 24 Richard Osborne .15 .07
❑ 25 Rich Saul AP .15 .07
❑ 26 Doug Beaudoin .15 .07
❑ 27 Cleveland Elam .15 .07
❑ 28 Charlie Joiner 1.00 .45
❑ 29 Dick Ambrose .15 .07
❑ 30 Mike Reinfeldt AP RC .15 .07
❑ 31 Matt Bahr RC 1.00 .45
❑ 32 Keith Krepfle .15 .07
❑ 33 Herb Scott .15 .07
❑ 34 Doug Kotar .15 .07
❑ 35 Bob Griese 1.50 .70
❑ 36 Jerry Butler RC .15 .07
❑ 37 Rolland Lawrence .15 .07
❑ 38 Gary Weaver .15 .07
❑ 39 Kansas City Chiefs TL .50 .23
Ted McKnight
J.T. Smith
Gary Barbaro
Art Still
(checklist back)
❑ 40 Chuck Muncie .50 .23
❑ 41 Mike Hartenstine .15 .07
❑ 42 Sammie White .50 .23
❑ 43 Ken Clark .15 .07
❑ 44 Clarence Harmon .15 .07
❑ 45 Bert Jones 1.00 .45
❑ 46 Mike Washington .15 .07
❑ 47 Joe Fields .15 .07
❑ 48 Mike Wood .15 .07
❑ 49 Oliver Davis .15 .07
❑ 50 Stan Walters AP .15 .07
❑ 51 Riley Odoms .15 .07
❑ 52 Steve Pisarkiewicz .15 .07
❑ 53 Tony Hill 1.00 .45
❑ 54 Scott Perry .15 .07
❑ 55 George Martin RC .15 .07
❑ 56 George Roberts .15 .07
❑ 57 Seattle Seahawks TL 1.00 .45
Sherman Smith
Steve Largent
Dave Brown
Manu Tuiasosopo
(checklist back)
❑ 58 Billy Johnson .50 .23
❑ 59 Reuben Gant .15 .07
❑ 60 Dennis Harrah AP RC .15 .07
❑ 61 Rocky Bleier 1.00 .45
❑ 62 Sam Hunt .15 .07
❑ 63 Allan Ellis .15 .07
❑ 64 Ricky Thompson .15 .07
❑ 65 Ken Stabler 4.00 1.80
❑ 66 Dexter Bussey .15 .07
❑ 67 Ken Mendenhall .15 .07
❑ 68 Woodrow Lowe .15 .07
❑ 69 Thom Darden .15 .07
❑ 70 Randy White AP 1.50 .70
❑ 71 Ken MacAfee .15 .07
❑ 72 Ron Jaworski 1.00 .45
❑ 73 William Andrews RC 1.00 .45
❑ 74 Jimmy Robinson .15 .07
❑ 75 Roger Wehrli AP .15 .07
❑ 76 Miami Dolphins TL 1.00 .45
Larry Csonka
Nat Moore
Neal Colzie
Gerald Small
Vern Den Herder
(checklist back)
❑ 77 Jack Rudnay .15 .07
❑ 78 James Lofton 2.00 .90
❑ 79 Robert Brazile .50 .23
❑ 80 Russ Francis .50 .23
❑ 81 Ricky Bell 1.00 .45
❑ 82 Bob Avellini .50 .23
❑ 83 Bobby Jackson .15 .07
❑ 84 Mike Bragg .15 .07
❑ 85 Cliff Branch 1.00 .45
❑ 86 Blair Bush .15 .07
❑ 87 Sherman Smith .15 .07
❑ 88 Glen Edwards .15 .07
❑ 89 Don Cockroft .15 .07
❑ 90 Louis Wright AP .50 .23
❑ 91 Randy Grossman .15 .07
❑ 92 Carl Hairston RC 1.00 .45
❑ 93 Archie Manning 1.00 .45
❑ 94 New York Giants TL .50 .23
Billy Taylor
Earnest Gray
George Martin
(checklist back)
❑ 95 Preston Pearson .50 .23
❑ 96 Rusty Chambers .15 .07
❑ 97 Greg Coleman .15 .07
❑ 98 Charlie Young .15 .07
❑ 99 Matt Cavanaugh RC .50 .23
❑ 100 Jesse Baker .15 .07
❑ 101 Doug Plank .15 .07
❑ 102 Checklist 1-132 .60 .15
❑ 103 Luther Bradley RC .15 .07
❑ 104 Bob Kuziel .15 .07
❑ 105 Craig Morton .50 .23
❑ 106 Sherman White .15 .07
❑ 107 Jim Breech RC .50 .23
❑ 108 Hank Bauer .15 .07
❑ 109 Tom Blanchard .15 .07
❑ 110 Ozzie Newsome AP 2.00 .90
❑ 111 Steve Furness .15 .07
❑ 112 Frank LeMaster .15 .07
❑ 113 Dallas Cowboys TL 1.00 .45
Tony Dorsett
Tony Hill
Harvey Martin
(checklist back)
❑ 114 Doug Van Horn .15 .07
❑ 115 Delvin Williams .15 .07
❑ 116 Lyle Blackwood .15 .07
❑ 117 Derrick Gaffney .15 .07
❑ 118 Cornell Webster .15 .07
❑ 119 Sam Cunningham .50 .23
❑ 120 Jim Youngblood AP .50 .23
❑ 121 Bob Thomas .15 .07
❑ 122 Jack Thompson RC .50 .23
❑ 123 Randy Cross 1.00 .45
❑ 124 Karl Lorch .15 .07
❑ 125 Mel Gray .15 .07
❑ 126 John James .15 .07
❑ 127 Terdell Middleton .15 .07
❑ 128 Leroy Jones .15 .07
❑ 129 Tom DeLeone .15 .07
❑ 130 John Stallworth AP 1.50 .70
❑ 131 Jimmie Giles RC .50 .23
❑ 132 Philadelphia Eagles TL 1.00 .45
Wilbert Montgomery
Harold Carmichael
Brenard Wilson
Carl Hairston
(checklist back)
❑ 133 Gary Green .15 .07
❑ 134 John Dutton .50 .23
❑ 135 Harry Carson AP 1.00 .45
❑ 136 Bob Kuechenberg .50 .23
❑ 137 Ike Harris .15 .07
❑ 138 Tommy Kramer RC 1.00 .45
❑ 139 Sam Adams .15 .07
❑ 140 Doug English AP .50 .23
❑ 141 Steve Schubert .15 .07
❑ 142 Rusty Jackson .15 .07
❑ 143 Reese McCall .15 .07
❑ 144 Scott Dierking .15 .07
❑ 145 Ken Houston AP 1.00 .45
❑ 146 Bob Martin .15 .07
❑ 147 Sam McCullum .15 .07
❑ 148 Tom Banks .15 .07
❑ 149 Willie Buchanon .15 .07
❑ 150 Greg Pruitt .50 .23
❑ 151 Denver Broncos TL 1.00 .45
Otis Armstrong
Rick Upchurch
Steve Foley
Brison Manor
(checklist back)
❑ 152 Don Smith .15 .07
❑ 153 Pete Johnson .50 .23
❑ 154 Charlie Smith .15 .07
❑ 155 Mel Blount 1.00 .45
❑ 156 John Mendenhall .15 .07
❑ 157 Danny White 1.00 .45
❑ 158 Jimmy Cefalo RC .50 .23
❑ 159 Richard Bishop AP .15 .07
❑ 160 Walter Payton AP 10.00 4.50
❑ 161 Dave Dalby .15 .07
❑ 162 Preston Dennard .15 .07
❑ 163 Johnnie Gray .15 .07
❑ 164 Russell Erxleben .15 .07
❑ 165 Toni Fritsch AP .15 .07
❑ 166 Terry Hermeling .15 .07
❑ 167 Roland Hooks .15 .07
❑ 168 Roger Carr .15 .07
❑ 169 San Diego Chargers TL 1.00 .45
Clarence Williams
John Jefferson
Woodrow Lowe
Ray Preston
Wilbur Young
(checklist back)
❑ 170 Ottis Anderson AP RC 4.00 1.80
❑ 171 Brian Sipe 1.00 .45
❑ 172 Leonard Thompson .15 .07
❑ 173 Tony Reed .15 .07
❑ 174 Bob Tucker .15 .07
❑ 175 Joe Greene 1.00 .45
❑ 176 Jack Dolbin .15 .07
❑ 177 Chuck Ramsey .15 .07
❑ 178 Paul Hofer .15 .07
❑ 179 Randy Logan .15 .07
❑ 180 David Lewis AP .15 .07
❑ 181 Duriel Harris .15 .07
❑ 182 June Jones .50 .23
❑ 183 Larry McCarren .15 .07
❑ 184 Ken Johnson .15 .07
❑ 185 Charlie Waters 1.00 .45
❑ 186 Noah Jackson .15 .07
❑ 187 Reggie Williams .50 .23
❑ 188 New England Patriots TL .50 .23
Sam Cunningham
Harold Jackson
Raymond Clayborn
Tony McGee
(checklist back)
❑ 189 Carl Eller .50 .23
❑ 190 Ed White AP .15 .07
❑ 191 Mario Clark .15 .07
❑ 192 Roosevelt Leaks .15 .07
❑ 193 Ted McKnight .15 .07
❑ 194 Danny Buggs .15 .07
❑ 195 Lester Hayes RC 1.00 .45
❑ 196 Clarence Scott .15 .07
❑ 197 New Orleans Saints TL .50 .23
Chuck Muncie
Wes Chandler
Tom Myers
Elois Grooms
Don Reese
(checklist back)
❑ 198 Richard Caster .15 .07
❑ 199 Louie Giammona .15 .07
❑ 200 Terry Bradshaw 5.00 2.20
❑ 201 Ed Newman .15 .07
❑ 202 Fred Dryer 1.00 .45
❑ 203 Dennis Franks .15 .07
❑ 204 Bob Breunig RC .50 .23
❑ 205 Alan Page 1.00 .45
❑ 206 Earnest Gray RC .15 .07
❑ 207 Minnesota Vikings TL 1.00 .45
Rickey Young
Ahmad Rashad
Tom Hannon
Nate Wright
Mark Mullaney
(checklist back)
❑ 208 Horace Ivory .15 .07
❑ 209 Isaac Hagins .15 .07
❑ 210 Gary Johnson AP .15 .07
❑ 211 Kevin Long .15 .07

❑ 212 Bill Thompson .15 .07
❑ 213 Don Bass .15 .07
❑ 214 George Starke RC .15 .07
❑ 215 Efren Herrera .15 .07
❑ 216 Theo Bell .15 .07
❑ 217 Monte Jackson .15 .07
❑ 218 Reggie McKenzie .15 .07
❑ 219 Bucky Dilts .15 .07
❑ 220 Lyle Alzado 1.00 .45
❑ 221 Tim Foley .15 .07
❑ 222 Mark Arneson .15 .07
❑ 223 Fred Quillan .15 .07
❑ 224 Benny Ricardo .15 .07
❑ 225 Phil Simms RC 12.00 5.50
❑ 226 Chicago Bears TL 1.25 .55
Walter Payton
Brian Baschnagel
Gary Fencik
Terry Schmidt
Jim Osborne
(checklist back)
❑ 227 Max Runager .15 .07
❑ 228 Barty Smith .15 .07
❑ 229 Jay Saldi .50 .23
❑ 230 John Hannah AP 1.00 .45
❑ 231 Tim Wilson .15 .07
❑ 232 Jeff Van Note .15 .07
❑ 233 Henry Marshall .15 .07
❑ 234 Diron Talbert .15 .07
❑ 235 Garo Yepremian .50 .23
❑ 236 Larry Brown .15 .07
❑ 237 Clarence Williams .15 .07
❑ 238 Burgess Owens .15 .07
❑ 239 Vince Ferragamo .50 .23
❑ 240 Rickey Young .15 .07
❑ 241 Dave Logan .15 .07
❑ 242 Larry Gordon .15 .07
❑ 243 Terry Miller .15 .07
❑ 244 Baltimore Colts TL 1.00 .45
Joe Washington
Joe Washington
Fred Cook
(checklist back)
❑ 245 Steve DeBerg 1.00 .45
❑ 246 Checklist 133-264 .60 .15
❑ 247 Greg Latta .15 .07
❑ 248 Raymond Clayborn .50 .23
❑ 249 Jim Clack .15 .07
❑ 250 Drew Pearson 1.00 .45
❑ 251 John Bunting .15 .07
❑ 252 Rob Lytle .15 .07
❑ 253 Jim Hart 1.00 .45
❑ 254 John McDaniel .15 .07
❑ 255 Dave Pear AP .15 .07
❑ 256 Donnie Shell 1.00 .45
❑ 257 Dan Doornink .15 .07
❑ 258 Wallace Francis RC 1.00 .45
❑ 259 Dave Beverly .15 .07
❑ 260 Lee Roy Selmon AP 1.00 .45
❑ 261 Doug Dieken .15 .07
❑ 262 Gary Davis .15 .07
❑ 263 Bob Rush .15 .07
❑ 264 Buffalo Bills TL .50 .23
Curtis Brown
Frank Lewis
Keith Moody
Sherman White
(checklist back)
❑ 265 Greg Landry .50 .23
❑ 266 Jan Stenerud .50 .23
❑ 267 Tom Hicks .15 .07
❑ 268 Pat McInally .15 .07
❑ 269 Tim Fox .15 .07
❑ 270 Harvey Martin 1.00 .45
❑ 271 Dan Lloyd .15 .07
❑ 272 Mike Barber .15 .07
❑ 273 Wendell Tyler RC 1.00 .45
❑ 274 Jeff Komlo .15 .07
❑ 275 Wes Chandler RC 1.00 .45
❑ 276 Brad Dusek .15 .07
❑ 277 Charlie Johnson .15 .07
❑ 278 Dennis Swilley .15 .07
❑ 279 Johnny Evans .15 .07
❑ 280 Jack Lambert AP 1.50 .70
❑ 281 Vern Den Herder .15 .07
❑ 282 Tampa Bay Bucs TL 1.00 .45
Ricky Bell
Isaac Hagins
Lee Roy Selmon
(checklist back)
❑ 283 Bob Klein .15 .07
❑ 284 Jim Turner .15 .07
❑ 285 Marvin Powell AP .50 .23
❑ 286 Aaron Kyle .15 .07
❑ 287 Dan Neal .15 .07
❑ 288 Wayne Morris .15 .07
❑ 289 Steve Bartkowski .50 .23
❑ 290 Dave Jennings AP .50 .23
❑ 291 John Smith .15 .07
❑ 292 Bill Gregory .15 .07
❑ 293 Frank Lewis .15 .07
❑ 294 Fred Cook .15 .07
❑ 295 David Hill AP .15 .07
❑ 296 Wade Key .15 .07
❑ 297 Sidney Thornton .15 .07
❑ 298 Charlie Hall .15 .07
❑ 299 Joe Lavender .15 .07
❑ 300 Tom Rafferty RC .15 .07
❑ 301 Mike Renfro RC .50 .23
❑ 302 Wilbur Jackson .50 .23
❑ 303 Green Bay Packers TL 1.00 .45
Terdell Middleton
James Lofton
Johnnie Gray
Robert Barber
Ezra Johnson
(checklist back)
❑ 304 Henry Childs .15 .07
❑ 305 Russ Washington AP .15 .07
❑ 306 Jim LeClair .15 .07
❑ 307 Tommy Hart .15 .07
❑ 308 Gary Barbaro .15 .07
❑ 309 Billy Taylor .15 .07
❑ 310 Ray Guy .50 .23
❑ 311 Don Hasselbeck .15 .07
❑ 312 Doug Williams 1.00 .45
❑ 313 Nick Mike-Mayer .15 .07
❑ 314 Don McCauley .15 .07
❑ 315 Wesley Walker 1.00 .45
❑ 316 Dan Dierdorf 1.00 .45
❑ 317 Dave Brown RC .50 .23
❑ 318 Leroy Harris .15 .07
❑ 319 Pittsburgh Steelers TL 1.00 .45
Franco Harris
John Stallworth
Jack Lambert
Steve Furness
L.C. Greenwood
(checklist back)
❑ 320 Mark Moseley AP UER .15 .07
(Bio on back refers
to him as Mike)
❑ 321 Mark Dennard .15 .07
❑ 322 Terry Nelson .15 .07
❑ 323 Tom Jackson 1.00 .45
❑ 324 Rick Kane .15 .07
❑ 325 Jerry Sherk .15 .07
❑ 326 Ray Preston .15 .07
❑ 327 Golden Richards .15 .07
❑ 328 Randy Dean .15 .07
❑ 329 Rick Danmeier .15 .07
❑ 330 Tony Dorsett 6.00 2.70
❑ 331 Passing Leaders 3.00 1.35
Dan Fouts
Roger Staubach
❑ 332 Receiving Leaders .50 .23
Joe Washington
Ahmad Rashad
❑ 333 Sacks Leaders 1.00 .45
Jesse Baker
Al(Bubba) Baker
Jack Youngblood
❑ 334 Scoring Leaders 1.00 .45
John Smith
Mark Moseley
❑ 335 Interception Leaders 1.00 .45
Mike Reinfeldt
Lemar Parrish
❑ 336 Punting Leaders 1.00 .45
Bob Grupp
Dave Jennings
❑ 337 Freddie Solomon .15 .07
❑ 338 Cincinnati Bengals TL .50 .23
Pete Johnson
Don Bass
Dick Jauron
Gary Burley
(checklist back)
❑ 339 Ken Stone .15 .07
❑ 340 Greg Buttle AP .15 .07
❑ 341 Bob Baumhower .50 .23
❑ 342 Billy Waddy .15 .07
❑ 343 Cliff Parsley .15 .07
❑ 344 Walter White .15 .07
❑ 345 Mike Thomas .15 .07
❑ 346 Neil O'Donoghue .15 .07
❑ 347 Freddie Scott .15 .07
❑ 348 Joe Ferguson .50 .23
❑ 349 Doug Nettles .15 .07
❑ 350 Mike Webster AP 1.00 .45
❑ 351 Ron Saul .15 .07
❑ 352 Julius Adams .15 .07
❑ 353 Rafael Septien .15 .07
❑ 354 Cleo Miller .15 .07
❑ 355 Keith Simpson AP .15 .07
❑ 356 Johnny Perkins .15 .07
❑ 357 Jerry Sisemore .15 .07
❑ 358 Arthur Whittington .15 .07
❑ 359 St. Louis Cardinals TL 1.00 .45
Ottis Anderson
Pat Tilley
Ken Stone
Bob Pollard
(checklist back)
❑ 360 Rick Upchurch .50 .23
❑ 361 Kim Bokamper RC .15 .07
❑ 362 Roland Harper .15 .07
❑ 363 Pat Leahy .15 .07
❑ 364 Louis Breeden .15 .07
❑ 365 John Jefferson 1.00 .45
❑ 366 Jerry Eckwood .15 .07
❑ 367 David Whitehurst .15 .07
❑ 368 Willie Parker .15 .07
❑ 369 Ed Simonini .15 .07
❑ 370 Jack Youngblood AP 1.00 .45
❑ 371 Don Warren RC 1.00 .45
❑ 372 Andy Johnson .15 .07
❑ 373 D.D. Lewis .50 .23
❑ 374A Beasley Reece RC ERR 1.00 .45
(No S in position
on front of card)
❑ 374B Beasley Reece COR RC .50 .23
❑ 375 L.C. Greenwood 1.00 .45
❑ 376 Cleveland Browns TL .50 .23
Mike Pruitt
Dave Logan
Thom Darden
Jerry Sherk
(checklist back)
❑ 377 Herman Edwards .15 .07
❑ 378 Rob Carpenter RC .15 .07
❑ 379 Herman Weaver .15 .07
❑ 380 Gary Fencik AP .15 .07
❑ 381 Don Strock .50 .23
❑ 382 Art Shell 1.00 .45
❑ 383 Tim Mazzetti .15 .07
❑ 384 Bruce Harper .15 .07
❑ 385 Al(Bubba) Baker .50 .23
❑ 386 Conrad Dobler .15 .07
❑ 387 Stu Voigt .15 .07
❑ 388 Ken Anderson 1.00 .45
❑ 389 Pat Tilley .15 .07
❑ 390 John Riggins 1.00 .45
❑ 391 Checklist 265-396 .60 .15
❑ 392 Fred Dean AP .15 .07
❑ 393 Benny Barnes RC .15 .07
❑ 394 Los Angeles Rams TL .50 .23
Wendell Tyler
Preston Dennard
Nolan Cromwell
Jim Youngblood
Jack Youngblood
(checklist back)
❑ 395 Brad Van Pelt .15 .07
❑ 396 Eddie Hare .15 .07
❑ 397 John Sciarra RC .15 .07
❑ 398 Bob Jackson .15 .07

❑ 399 John Yarno .15 .07
❑ 400 Franco Harris AP 2.00 .90
❑ 401 Ray Wersching .15 .07
❑ 402 Virgil Livers .15 .07
❑ 403 Raymond Chester .15 .07
❑ 404 Leon Gray .15 .07
❑ 405 Richard Todd .50 .23
❑ 406 Larry Little 1.00 .45
❑ 407 Ted Fritsch Jr. .15 .07
❑ 408 Larry Mucker .15 .07
❑ 409 Jim Allen .15 .07
❑ 410 Randy Gradishar 1.00 .45
❑ 411 Atlanta Falcons TL 1.00 .45
William Andrews
Wallace Francis
Rolland Lawrence
Don Smith
(checklist back)
❑ 412 Louie Kelcher .50 .23
❑ 413 Robert Newhouse .50 .23
❑ 414 Gary Shirk .15 .07
❑ 415 Mike Haynes AP 1.00 .45
❑ 416 Craig Colquitt .15 .07
❑ 417 Lou Piccone .15 .07
❑ 418 Clay Matthews RC 2.00 .90
❑ 419 Marvin Cobb .15 .07
❑ 420 Harold Carmichael AP 1.00 .45
❑ 421 Uwe Von Schamann .50 .23
❑ 422 Mike Phipps .50 .23
❑ 423 Nolan Cromwell RC 1.00 .45
❑ 424 Glenn Doughty .15 .07
❑ 425 Bob Young AP .15 .07
❑ 426 Tony Galbreath .15 .07
❑ 427 Luke Prestridge .15 .07
❑ 428 Terry Beeson .15 .07
❑ 429 Jack Tatum .50 .23
❑ 430 Lemar Parrish AP .15 .07
❑ 431 Chester Marcol .15 .07
❑ 432 Houston Oilers TL 1.00 .45
Dan Pastorini
Ken Burrough
Mike Reinfeldt
Jesse Baker
(checklist back)
❑ 433 John Fitzgerald .15 .07
❑ 434 Gary Jeter RC .50 .23
❑ 435 Steve Grogan 1.00 .45
❑ 436 Jon Kolb UER .15 .07
John on front
❑ 437 Jim O'Bradovich UER .15 .07
(Neil O'Donoghue's bio)
❑ 438 Gerald Irons .15 .07
❑ 439 Jeff West .15 .07
❑ 440 Wilbert Montgomery .50 .23
❑ 441 Norris Thomas .15 .07
❑ 442 James Scott .15 .07
❑ 443 Curtis Brown .15 .07
❑ 444 Ken Fantetti .15 .07
❑ 445 Pat Haden 1.00 .45
❑ 446 Carl Mauck .15 .07
❑ 447 Bruce Laird .15 .07
❑ 448 Otis Armstrong .15 .07
❑ 449 Gene Upshaw 1.00 .45
❑ 450 Steve Largent AP 6.00 2.70
❑ 451 Benny Malone .15 .07
❑ 452 Steve Nelson .15 .07
❑ 453 Mark Cotney .15 .07
❑ 454 Joe Danelo .15 .07
❑ 455 Billy Joe DuPree .50 .23
❑ 456 Ron Johnson .15 .07
❑ 457 Archie Griffin .50 .23
❑ 458 Reggie Rucker .15 .07
❑ 459 Claude Humphrey .15 .07
❑ 460 Lydell Mitchell .50 .23
❑ 461 Steve Towle .15 .07
❑ 462 Revie Sorey .15 .07
❑ 463 Tom Skladany .15 .07
❑ 464 Clark Gaines .15 .07
❑ 465 Frank Corral .15 .07
❑ 466 Steve Fuller RC .50 .23
❑ 467 Ahmad Rashad AP 1.00 .45
❑ 468 Oakland Raiders TL 1.00 .45
Mark Van Eeghen
Cliff Branch
Lester Hayes
Willie Jones
(checklist back)
❑ 469 Brian Peets .15 .07
❑ 470 Pat Donovan AP RC .50 .23
❑ 471 Ken Burrough .15 .07
❑ 472 Don Calhoun .15 .07
❑ 473 Bill Bryan .15 .07
❑ 474 Terry Jackson .15 .07
❑ 475 Joe Theismann 1.25 .55
❑ 476 Jim Smith .50 .23
❑ 477 Joe DeLamielleure .15 .07
❑ 478 Mike Pruitt AP .50 .23
❑ 479 Steve Mike-Mayer .15 .07
❑ 480 Bill Bergey .50 .23
❑ 481 Mike Fuller .15 .07
❑ 482 Bob Parsons .15 .07
❑ 483 Billy Brooks .15 .07
❑ 484 Jerome Barkum .15 .07
❑ 485 Larry Csonka 1.50 .70
❑ 486 John Hill .15 .07
❑ 487 Mike Dawson .15 .07
❑ 488 Detroit Lions TL .50 .23
Dexter Bussey
Freddie Scott
Jim Allen
Luther Bradley
Al(Bubba) Baker
(checklist back)
❑ 489 Ted Hendricks 1.00 .45
❑ 490 Dan Pastorini .50 .23
❑ 491 Stanley Morgan 1.00 .45
❑ 492 AFC Championship 1.00 .45
Steelers 27,
Oilers 13
(Rocky Bleier running)
❑ 493 NFC Championship .50 .23
Rams 9,
Buccaneers 0
(Vince Ferragamo)
❑ 494 Super Bowl XIV 1.00 .45
Steelers 31,
Rams 19
(line play)
❑ 495 Dwight White .50 .23
❑ 496 Haven Moses .15 .07
❑ 497 Guy Morriss .15 .07
❑ 498 Dewey Selmon .50 .23
❑ 499 Dave Butz RC 1.00 .45
❑ 500 Chuck Foreman .50 .23
❑ 501 Chris Bahr .15 .07
❑ 502 Mark Miller .15 .07
❑ 503 Tony Greene .15 .07
❑ 504 Brian Kelley .15 .07
❑ 505 Joe Washington .50 .23
❑ 506 Butch Johnson .50 .23
❑ 507 New York Jets TL .50 .23
Clark Gaines
Wesley Walker
Burgess Owens
Joe Klecko
(checklist back0
❑ 508 Steve Little .15 .07
❑ 509 Checklist 397-528 .60 .15
❑ 510 Mark Van Eeghen .15 .07
❑ 511 Gary Danielson .50 .23
❑ 512 Manu Tuiasosopo .15 .07
❑ 513 Paul Coffman RC .50 .23
❑ 514 Cullen Bryant .15 .07
❑ 515 Nat Moore .50 .23
❑ 516 Bill Lenkaitis .15 .07
❑ 517 Lynn Cain RC .15 .07
❑ 518 Gregg Bingham .15 .07
❑ 519 Ted Albrecht .15 .07
❑ 520 Dan Fouts AP 2.00 .90
❑ 521 Bernard Jackson .15 .07
❑ 522 Coy Bacon .15 .07
❑ 523 Tony Franklin RC .50 .23
❑ 524 Bo Harris .15 .07
❑ 525 Bob Grupp AP .15 .07
❑ 526 San Francisco 49ers TL 1.00 .45
Paul Hofer
Freddie Solomon
James Owens
Dwaine Board
(checklist back)
❑ 527 Steve Wilson .15 .07
❑ 528 Bennie Cunningham .50 .23

1981 Topps

	NRMT-MT	EXC
COMPLETE SET (528)	225.00	100.00
COMMON CARD (1-528)	.15	.07
SEMISTARS	.40	.18
UNLISTED STARS	.75	.35
CL (127/259/389/517)	.50	.23

❑ 1 Passing Leaders .75 .35
Ron Jaworski
Brian Sipe
❑ 2 Receiving Leaders .75 .35
Earl Cooper
Kellen Winslow
❑ 3 Sack Leaders .40 .18
Al(Bubba) Baker
Gary Johnson
❑ 4 Scoring Leaders .15 .07
Eddie Murray
John Smith
❑ 5 Interception Leaders .40 .18
Nolan Cromwell
Lester Hayes
❑ 6 Punting Leaders .15 .07
Dave Jennings
Luke Prestridge
❑ 7 Don Calhoun .15 .07
❑ 8 Jack Tatum .40 .18
❑ 9 Reggie Rucker .15 .07
❑ 10 Mike Webster AP .75 .35
❑ 11 Vince Evans RC .75 .35
❑ 12 Ottis Anderson SA .75 .35
❑ 13 Leroy Harris .15 .07
❑ 14 Gordon King .15 .07
❑ 15 Harvey Martin .75 .35
❑ 16 Johnny Lam Jones RC .40 .18
❑ 17 Ken Greene .15 .07
❑ 18 Frank Lewis .15 .07
❑ 19 Seattle Seahawks TL .75 .35
Jim Jodat
Dave Brown
John Harris
Steve Largent
Jacob Green
(checklist back)
❑ 20 Lester Hayes AP .75 .35
❑ 21 Uwe Von Schamann .15 .07
❑ 22 Joe Washington .15 .07
❑ 23 Louie Kelcher .15 .07
❑ 24 Willie Miller .15 .07
❑ 25 Steve Grogan .75 .35
❑ 26 John Hill .15 .07
❑ 27 Stan White .15 .07
❑ 28 William Andrews SA .40 .18
❑ 29 Clarence Scott .15 .07
❑ 30 Leon Gray AP .15 .07
❑ 31 Craig Colquitt .15 .07
❑ 32 Doug Williams .75 .35
❑ 33 Bob Breunig .40 .18
❑ 34 Billy Taylor .15 .07
❑ 35 Harold Carmichael .75 .35
❑ 36 Ray Wersching .15 .07
❑ 37 Dennis Johnson .15 .07
❑ 38 Archie Griffin .40 .18
❑ 39 Los Angeles Rams TL .40 .18
Cullen Bryant
Billy Waddy

Nolan Cromwell
Jack Youngblood
(checklist back)
❑ 40 Gary Fencik AP .40 .18
❑ 41 Lynn Dickey .15 .07
❑ 42 Steve Bartkowski SA .40 .18
❑ 43 Art Shell .75 .35
❑ 44 Wilbur Jackson .15 .07
❑ 45 Frank Corral .15 .07
❑ 46 Ted McKnight .15 .07
❑ 47 Joe Klecko .40 .18
❑ 48 Dan Doornink .15 .07
❑ 49 Doug Dieken .15 .07
❑ 50 Jerry Robinson AP RC .40 .18
❑ 51 Wallace Francis .15 .07
❑ 52 Dave Preston RC .15 .07
❑ 53 Jay Saldi .15 .07
❑ 54 Rush Brown .15 .07
❑ 55 Phil Simms 3.00 1.35
❑ 56 Nick Mike-Mayer .15 .07
❑ 57 Wash. Redskins TL 2.00 .90
Wilbur Jackson
Art Monk
Lemar Parrish
Coy Bacon
(checklist back)
❑ 58 Mike Renfro .15 .07
❑ 59 Ted Brown SA .15 .07
❑ 60 Steve Nelson AP .15 .07
❑ 61 Sidney Thornton .15 .07
❑ 62 Kent Hill .15 .07
❑ 63 Don Bessillieu .15 .07
❑ 64 Fred Cook .15 .07
❑ 65 Raymond Chester .15 .07
❑ 66 Rick Kane .15 .07
❑ 67 Mike Fuller .15 .07
❑ 68 Dewey Selmon .40 .18
❑ 69 Charles White RC .75 .35
❑ 70 Jeff Van Note AP .15 .07
❑ 71 Robert Newhouse .40 .18
❑ 72 Roynell Young RC .15 .07
❑ 73 Lynn Cain SA .15 .07
❑ 74 Mike Friede .15 .07
❑ 75 Earl Cooper RC .15 .07
❑ 76 New Orleans Saints TL .40 .18
Jimmy Rogers
Wes Chandler
Tom Myers
Elois Grooms
Derland Moore
(checklist back)
❑ 77 Rick Danmeier .15 .07
❑ 78 Darrol Ray .15 .07
❑ 79 Gregg Bingham .15 .07
❑ 80 John Hannah AP .75 .35
❑ 81 Jack Thompson .40 .18
❑ 82 Rick Upchurch .40 .18
❑ 83 Mike Butler .15 .07
❑ 84 Don Warren .15 .07
❑ 85 Mark Van Eeghen .15 .07
❑ 86 J.T. Smith RC .75 .35
❑ 87 Herman Weaver .15 .07
❑ 88 Terry Bradshaw SA 2.00 .90
❑ 89 Charlie Hall .15 .07
❑ 90 Donnie Shell .75 .35
❑ 91 Ike Harris .15 .07
❑ 92 Charlie Johnson .15 .07
❑ 93 Rickey Watts .15 .07
❑ 94 New England Patriots TL .75 .35
Vagas Ferguson
Stanley Morgan
Raymond Clayborn
Julius Adams
(checklist back)
❑ 95 Drew Pearson .75 .35
❑ 96 Neil O'Donoghue .15 .07
❑ 97 Conrad Dobler .15 .07
❑ 98 Jewerl Thomas RC .15 .07
❑ 99 Mike Barber .15 .07
❑ 100 Billy Sims AP RC 2.00 .90
❑ 101 Vern Den Herder .15 .07
❑ 102 Greg Landry .40 .18
❑ 103 Joe Cribbs SA .40 .18
❑ 104 Mark Murphy RC .15 .07
❑ 105 Chuck Muncie .40 .18
❑ 106 Alfred Jackson .40 .18
❑ 107 Chris Bahr .15 .07
❑ 108 Gordon Jones .15 .07
❑ 109 Willie Harper RC .15 .07
❑ 110 Dave Jennings AP .15 .07
❑ 111 Bennie Cunningham .15 .07
❑ 112 Jerry Sisemore .15 .07
❑ 113 Cleveland Browns TL .75 .35
Mike Pruitt
Dave Logan
Ron Bolton
Lyle Alzado
(checklist back)
❑ 114 Rickey Young .15 .07
❑ 115 Ken Anderson .75 .35
❑ 116 Randy Gradishar .75 .35
❑ 117 Eddie Lee Ivery RC .15 .07
❑ 118 Wesley Walker .75 .35
❑ 119 Chuck Foreman .40 .18
❑ 120 Nolan Cromwell AP .40 .18
UER (Rushing TD's
added wrong)
❑ 121 Curtis Dickey SA .15 .07
❑ 122 Wayne Morris .15 .07
❑ 123 Greg Stemrick .15 .07
❑ 124 Coy Bacon .15 .07
❑ 125 Jim Zorn .40 .18
(Steve Largent
in background)
❑ 126 Henry Childs .15 .07
❑ 127 Checklist 1-132 .50 .23
❑ 128 Len Walterscheid .15 .07
❑ 129 Johnny Evans .15 .07
❑ 130 Gary Barbaro AP .15 .07
❑ 131 Jim Smith .15 .07
❑ 132 New York Jets TL .40 .18
Scott Dierking
Bruce Harper
Ken Schroy
Mark Gastineau
(checklist back)
❑ 133 Curtis Brown .15 .07
❑ 134 D.D. Lewis .15 .07
❑ 135 Jim Plunkett .75 .35
❑ 136 Nat Moore .40 .18
❑ 137 Don McCauley .15 .07
❑ 138 Tony Dorsett SA .75 .35
❑ 139 Julius Adams .15 .07
❑ 140 Ahmad Rashad AP .75 .35
❑ 141 Rich Saul .15 .07
❑ 142 Ken Fantetti .15 .07
❑ 143 Kenny Johnson .15 .07
❑ 144 Clark Gaines .15 .07
❑ 145 Mark Moseley .15 .07
❑ 146 Vernon Perry RC .15 .07
❑ 147 Jerry Eckwood .15 .07
❑ 148 Freddie Solomon .15 .07
❑ 149 Jerry Sherk .15 .07
❑ 150 Kellen Winslow AP RC 8.00 3.60
❑ 151 Green Bay Packers TL .75 .35
Eddie Lee Ivery
James Lofton
Johnnie Gray
Mike Butler
(checklist back)
❑ 152 Ross Browner .15 .07
❑ 153 Dan Fouts SA .75 .35
❑ 154 Woody Peoples .15 .07
❑ 155 Jack Lambert 1.00 .45
❑ 156 Mike Dennis .15 .07
❑ 157 Rafael Septien .15 .07
❑ 158 Archie Manning .75 .35
❑ 159 Don Hasselbeck .15 .07
❑ 160 Alan Page AP .75 .35
❑ 161 Arthur Whittington .15 .07
❑ 162 Billy Waddy .15 .07
❑ 163 Horace Belton .15 .07
❑ 164 Luke Prestridge .15 .07
❑ 165 Joe Theismann .75 .35
❑ 166 Morris Towns .15 .07
❑ 167 Dave Brown .15 .07
❑ 168 Ezra Johnson .15 .07
❑ 169 Tampa Bay Buccaneers TL .15
.07
Ricky Bell
Gordon Jones
Mike Washington
Lee Roy Selmon
(checklist back)
❑ 170 Joe DeLamielleure AP .15 .07
❑ 171 Earnest Gray SA .15 .07
❑ 172 Mike Thomas .15 .07
❑ 173 Jim Haslett RC 1.25 .55
❑ 174 David Woodley RC .40 .18
❑ 175 Al(Bubba) Baker .40 .18
❑ 176 Nesby Glasgow RC .15 .07
❑ 177 Pat Leahy .15 .07
❑ 178 Tom Brahaney .15 .07
❑ 179 Herman Edwards .15 .07
❑ 180 Junior Miller AP RC .15 .07
❑ 181 Richard Wood RC .15 .07
❑ 182 Lenvil Elliott .15 .07
❑ 183 Sammie White .40 .18
❑ 184 Russell Erxleben .15 .07
❑ 185 Ed Too Tall Jones .75 .35
❑ 186 Ray Guy SA .40 .18
❑ 187 Haven Moses .15 .07
❑ 188 New York Giants TL .40 .18
Billy Taylor
Earnest Gray
Mike Dennis
Gary Jeter
(checklist back)
❑ 189 David Whitehurst .15 .07
❑ 190 John Jefferson AP .75 .35
❑ 191 Terry Beeson .15 .07
❑ 192 Dan Ross RC .40 .18
❑ 193 Dave Williams .15 .07
❑ 194 Art Monk RC 12.00 5.50
❑ 195 Roger Wehrli .15 .07
❑ 196 Ricky Feacher .15 .07
❑ 197 Miami Dolphins TL .75 .35
Delvin Williams
Tony Nathan
Gerald Small
Kim Bokamper
A.J. Duhe
(checklist back)
❑ 198 Carl Roaches RC .15 .07
❑ 199 Billy Campfield .15 .07
❑ 200 Ted Hendricks AP .75 .35
❑ 201 Fred Smerlas RC .75 .35
❑ 202 Walter Payton SA 3.00 1.35
❑ 203 Luther Bradley .15 .07
❑ 204 Herb Scott .15 .07
❑ 205 Jack Youngblood .75 .35
❑ 206 Danny Pittman .15 .07
❑ 207 Houston Oilers TL .40 .18
Carl Roaches
Mike Barber
Jack Tatum
Jesse Baker
Robert Brazile
(checklist back)
❑ 208 Vagas Ferguson RC .40 .18
❑ 209 Mark Dennard .15 .07
❑ 210 Lemar Parrish AP .15 .07
❑ 211 Bruce Harper .15 .07
❑ 212 Ed Simonini .15 .07
❑ 213 Nick Lowery RC .75 .35
❑ 214 Kevin House RC .40 .18
❑ 215 Mike Kenn RC .75 .35
❑ 216 Joe Montana RC ! 225.00 100.00
❑ 217 Joe Senser .15 .07
❑ 218 Lester Hayes SA .40 .18
❑ 219 Gene Upshaw .75 .35
❑ 220 Franco Harris 1.25 .55
❑ 221 Ron Bolton .15 .07
❑ 222 Charles Alexander RC .40 .18
❑ 223 Matt Robinson .15 .07
❑ 224 Ray Oldham .15 .07
❑ 225 George Martin .15 .07
❑ 226 Buffalo Bills TL .75 .35
Joe Cribbs
Jerry Butler
Steve Freeman
Ben Williams
(checklist back)
❑ 227 Tony Franklin .15 .07
❑ 228 George Cumby .15 .07
❑ 229 Butch Johnson .40 .18
❑ 230 Mike Haynes AP .75 .35
❑ 231 Rob Carpenter .40 .18

❑ 232 Steve Fuller .40 .18
❑ 233 John Sawyer .15 .07
❑ 234 Kenny King SA .15 .07
❑ 235 Jack Ham .75 .35
❑ 236 Jimmy Rogers .15 .07
❑ 237 Bob Parsons .15 .07
❑ 238 Marty Lyons RC .75 .35
❑ 239 Pat Tilley .15 .07
❑ 240 Dennis Harrah AP .15 .07
❑ 241 Thom Darden .15 .07
❑ 242 Rolf Benirschke .15 .07
❑ 243 Gerald Small .15 .07
❑ 244 Atlanta Falcons TL .75 .35
William Andrews
Alfred Jenkins
Al Richardson
Joel Williams
(checklist back)
❑ 245 Roger Carr .15 .07
❑ 246 Sherman White .15 .07
❑ 247 Ted Brown .15 .07
❑ 248 Matt Cavanaugh .40 .18
❑ 249 John Dutton .15 .07
❑ 250 Bill Bergey AP .40 .18
❑ 251 Jim Allen .15 .07
❑ 252 Mike Nelms SA .15 .07
❑ 253 Tom Blanchard .15 .07
❑ 254 Ricky Thompson .15 .07
❑ 255 John Matuszak .40 .18
❑ 256 Randy Grossman .15 .07
❑ 257 Ray Griffin .15 .07
❑ 258 Lynn Cain .15 .07
❑ 259 Checklist 133-264 .50 .23
❑ 260 Mike Pruitt AP .40 .18
❑ 261 Chris Ward .15 .07
❑ 262 Fred Steinfort .15 .07
❑ 263 James Owens .15 .07
❑ 264 Chicago Bears TL 1.50 .70
Walter Payton
James Scott
Len Walterscheid
Dan Hampton
(checklist back)
❑ 265 Dan Fouts 1.50 .70
❑ 266 Arnold Morgado .15 .07
❑ 267 John Jefferson SA .75 .35
❑ 268 Bill Lenkaitis .15 .07
❑ 269 James Jones .15 .07
❑ 270 Brad Van Pelt .15 .07
❑ 271 Steve Largent 2.50 1.10
❑ 272 Elvin Bethea .15 .07
❑ 273 Cullen Bryant .15 .07
❑ 274 Gary Danielson .40 .18
❑ 275 Tony Galbreath .15 .07
❑ 276 Dave Butz .15 .07
❑ 277 Steve Mike-Mayer .15 .07
❑ 278 Ron Johnson .15 .07
❑ 279 Tom DeLeone .15 .07
❑ 280 Ron Jaworski .75 .35
❑ 281 Mel Gray .15 .07
❑ 282 San Diego Chargers TL .75 .35
Chuck Muncie
John Jefferson
Glen Edwards
Gary Johnson
(checklist back)
❑ 283 Mark Brammer .15 .07
❑ 284 Alfred Jenkins SA .40 .18
❑ 285 Greg Buttle .15 .07
❑ 286 Randy Hughes .15 .07
❑ 287 Delvin Williams .15 .07
❑ 288 Brian Baschnagel .15 .07
❑ 289 Gary Jeter .15 .07
❑ 290 Stanley Morgan AP .75 .35
❑ 291 Gerry Ellis .15 .07
❑ 292 Al Richardson .15 .07
❑ 293 Jimmie Giles .40 .18
❑ 294 Dave Jennings SA .15 .07
❑ 295 Wilbert Montgomery .40 .18
❑ 296 Dave Pureifory .15 .07
❑ 297 Greg Hawthorne .15 .07
❑ 298 Dick Ambrose .15 .07
❑ 299 Terry Hermeling .15 .07
❑ 300 Danny White .75 .35
❑ 301 Ken Burrough .15 .07
❑ 302 Paul Hofer .15 .07
❑ 303 Denver Broncos TL .75 .35
Jim Jensen
Haven Moses
Steve Foley
Rulon Jones
(checklist back)
❑ 304 Eddie Payton .40 .18
❑ 305 Isaac Curtis .40 .18
❑ 306 Benny Ricardo .15 .07
❑ 307 Riley Odoms .15 .07
❑ 308 Bob Chandler .15 .07
❑ 309 Larry Heater .15 .07
❑ 310 Art Still AP RC .75 .35
❑ 311 Harold Jackson .40 .18
❑ 312 Charlie Joiner SA .75 .35
❑ 313 Jeff Nixon .15 .07
❑ 314 Aundra Thompson .15 .07
❑ 315 Richard Todd .40 .18
❑ 316 Dan Hampton RC 2.50 1.10
❑ 317 Doug Marsh .15 .07
❑ 318 Louie Giammona .15 .07
❑ 319 San Francisco 49ers TL .75 .35
Earl Cooper
Dwight Clark
Ricky Churchman
Dwight Hicks
Jim Stuckey
(checklist back)
❑ 320 Manu Tuiasosopo .15 .07
❑ 321 Rich Milot .15 .07
❑ 322 Mike Guman .15 .07
❑ 323 Bob Kuechenberg .40 .18
❑ 324 Tom Skladany .15 .07
❑ 325 Dave Logan .15 .07
❑ 326 Bruce Laird .15 .07
❑ 327 James Jones SA .15 .07
❑ 328 Joe Danelo .15 .07
❑ 329 Kenny King RC .40 .18
❑ 330 Pat Donovan AP .15 .07
❑ 331 Earl Cooper RB .40 .18
Most Receptions,
Running Back,
Season, Rookie
❑ 332 John Jefferson RB .75 .35
Most Cons. Seasons,
1000 Yards Receiving,
Start of Career
❑ 333 Kenny King RB .40 .18
Longest Pass Caught,
Super Bowl History
❑ 334 Rod Martin RB .40 .18
Most Interceptions
Super Bowl Game
❑ 335 Jim Plunkett RB .75 .35
Longest Pass,
Super Bowl History
❑ 336 Bill Thompson RB .40 .18
Most Touchdowns,
Fumble Recoveries,
Lifetime
❑ 337 John Cappelletti .40 .18
❑ 338 Detroit Lions TL .75 .35
Billy Sims
Freddie Scott
Jim Allen
James Hunter
Al(Bubba) Baker
(checklist back)
❑ 339 Don Smith .15 .07
❑ 340 Rod Perry AP .15 .07
❑ 341 David Lewis .15 .07
❑ 342 Mark Gastineau RC .75 .35
❑ 343 Steve Largent SA .75 .35
❑ 344 Charlie Young .15 .07
❑ 345 Toni Fritsch .15 .07
❑ 346 Matt Blair .40 .18
❑ 347 Don Bass .15 .07
❑ 348 Jim Jensen RC .40 .18
❑ 349 Karl Lorch .15 .07
❑ 350 Brian Sipe AP .40 .18
❑ 351 Theo Bell .15 .07
❑ 352 Sam Adams .15 .07
❑ 353 Paul Coffman .15 .07
❑ 354 Eric Harris .15 .07
❑ 355 Tony Hill .40 .18
❑ 356 J.T. Turner .15 .07
❑ 357 Frank LeMaster .15 .07
❑ 358 Jim Jodat .15 .07
❑ 359 Oakland Raiders TL .75 .35
Mark Van Eeghen
Cliff Branch
Lester Hayes
Cedrick Hardman
Ted Hendricks
(checklist back)
❑ 360 Joe Cribbs AP RC .75 .35
❑ 361 James Lofton SA .75 .35
❑ 362 Dexter Bussey .15 .07
❑ 363 Bobby Jackson .15 .07
❑ 364 Steve DeBerg .75 .35
❑ 365 Ottis Anderson 1.00 .45
❑ 366 Tom Myers .15 .07
❑ 367 John James .15 .07
❑ 368 Reese McCall .15 .07
❑ 369 Jack Reynolds .40 .18
❑ 370 Gary Johnson AP .15 .07
❑ 371 Jimmy Cefalo .15 .07
❑ 372 Horace Ivory .15 .07
❑ 373 Garo Yepremian .15 .07
❑ 374 Brian Kelley .15 .07
❑ 375 Terry Bradshaw 4.00 1.80
❑ 376 Dallas Cowboys TL .75 .35
Tony Dorsett
Tony Hill
Dennis Thurman
Charlie Waters
Harvey Martin
(checklist back)
❑ 377 Randy Logan .15 .07
❑ 378 Tim Wilson .15 .07
❑ 379 Archie Manning SA .75 .35
❑ 380 Revie Sorey AP .15 .07
❑ 381 Randy Holloway .15 .07
❑ 382 Henry Lawrence .15 .07
❑ 383 Pat McInally .15 .07
❑ 384 Kevin Long .15 .07
❑ 385 Louis Wright .40 .18
❑ 386 Leonard Thompson .15 .07
❑ 387 Jan Stenerud .40 .18
❑ 388 Raymond Butler RC .15 .07
❑ 389 Checklist 265-396 .50 .23
❑ 390 Steve Bartkowski AP .40 .18
❑ 391 Clarence Harmon .15 .07
❑ 392 Wilbert Montgomery SA .40 .18
❑ 393 Billy Joe DuPree .40 .18
❑ 394 Kansas City Chiefs TL .40 .18
Ted McKnight
Henry Marshall
Gary Barbaro
Art Still
(checklist back)
❑ 395 Earnest Gray .15 .07
❑ 396 Ray Hamilton .15 .07
❑ 397 Brenard Wilson .15 .07
❑ 398 Calvin Hill .75 .35
❑ 399 Robin Cole .15 .07
❑ 400 Walter Payton AP 8.00 3.60
❑ 401 Jim Hart .75 .35
❑ 402 Ron Yary .40 .18
❑ 403 Cliff Branch .75 .35
❑ 404 Roland Hooks .15 .07
❑ 405 Ken Stabler 3.00 1.35
❑ 406 Chuck Ramsey .15 .07
❑ 407 Mike Nelms RC .15 .07
❑ 408 Ron Jaworski SA .40 .18
❑ 409 James Hunter .15 .07
❑ 410 Lee Roy Selmon AP .75 .35
❑ 411 Baltimore Colts TL .40 .18
Curtis Dickey
Roger Carr
Bruce Laird
Mike Barnes
(checklist back)
❑ 412 Henry Marshall .15 .07
❑ 413 Preston Pearson .40 .18
❑ 414 Richard Bishop .15 .07
❑ 415 Greg Pruitt .40 .18
❑ 416 Matt Bahr .40 .18
❑ 417 Tom Mullady .15 .07
❑ 418 Glen Edwards .15 .07
❑ 419 Sam McCullum .15 .07
❑ 420 Stan Walters AP .15 .07

- ❑ 421 George Roberts .15 .07
- ❑ 422 Dwight Clark RC 4.00 1.80
- ❑ 423 Pat Thomas RC .15 .07
- ❑ 424 Bruce Harper SA .15 .07
- ❑ 425 Craig Morton .40 .18
- ❑ 426 Derrick Gaffney .15 .07
- ❑ 427 Pete Johnson .15 .07
- ❑ 428 Wes Chandler .75 .35
- ❑ 429 Burgess Owens .15 .07
- ❑ 430 James Lofton AP 2.00 .90
- ❑ 431 Tony Reed .15 .07
- ❑ 432 Minnesota Vikings TL .75 .35
  Ted Brown
  Ahmad Rashad
  John Turner
  Doug Sutherland
  (checklist back)
- ❑ 433 Ron Springs RC .40 .18
- ❑ 434 Tim Fox .15 .07
- ❑ 435 Ozzie Newsome 2.00 .90
- ❑ 436 Steve Furness .15 .07
- ❑ 437 Will Lewis .15 .07
- ❑ 438 Mike Hartenstine .15 .07
- ❑ 439 John Bunting .15 .07
- ❑ 440 Eddie Murray RC .75 .35
- ❑ 441 Mike Pruitt SA .40 .18
- ❑ 442 Larry Swider .15 .07
- ❑ 443 Steve Freeman .15 .07
- ❑ 444 Bruce Hardy RC .15 .07
- ❑ 445 Pat Haden .40 .18
- ❑ 446 Curtis Dickey RC .15 .07
- ❑ 447 Doug Wilkerson .15 .07
- ❑ 448 Alfred Jenkins .40 .18
- ❑ 449 Dave Dalby .15 .07
- ❑ 450 Robert Brazile AP .15 .07
- ❑ 451 Bobby Hammond .15 .07
- ❑ 452 Raymond Clayborn .15 .07
- ❑ 453 Jim Miller .15 .07
- ❑ 454 Roy Simmons .15 .07
- ❑ 455 Charlie Waters .75 .35
- ❑ 456 Ricky Bell .75 .35
- ❑ 457 Ahmad Rashad SA .75 .35
- ❑ 458 Don Cockroft .15 .07
- ❑ 459 Keith Krepfle .15 .07
- ❑ 460 Marvin Powell AP .15 .07
- ❑ 461 Tommy Kramer .75 .35
- ❑ 462 Jim LeClair .15 .07
- ❑ 463 Freddie Scott .15 .07
- ❑ 464 Rob Lytle .15 .07
- ❑ 465 Johnnie Gray .15 .07
- ❑ 466 Doug France RC .15 .07
- ❑ 467 Carlos Carson RC .40 .18
- ❑ 468 St. Louis Cardinals TL .75 .35
  Ottis Anderson
  Pat Tilley
  Ken Stone
  Curtis Greer
  Steve Neils
  (checklist back)
- ❑ 469 Efren Herrera .15 .07
- ❑ 470 Randy White AP 1.00 .45
- ❑ 471 Richard Caster .15 .07
- ❑ 472 Andy Johnson .15 .07
- ❑ 473 Billy Sims SA .75 .35
- ❑ 474 Joe Lavender .15 .07
- ❑ 475 Harry Carson .40 .18
- ❑ 476 John Stallworth 1.00 .45
- ❑ 477 Bob Thomas .15 .07
- ❑ 478 Keith Wright .15 .07
- ❑ 479 Ken Stone .15 .07
- ❑ 480 Carl Hairston AP .40 .18
- ❑ 481 Reggie McKenzie .15 .07
- ❑ 482 Bob Griese 1.50 .70
- ❑ 483 Mike Bragg .15 .07
- ❑ 484 Scott Dierking .15 .07
- ❑ 485 David Hill .15 .07
- ❑ 486 Brian Sipe SA .40 .18
- ❑ 487 Rod Martin RC .40 .18
- ❑ 488 Cincinnati Bengals TL .40 .18
  Pete Johnson
  Dan Ross
  Louis Breeden
  Eddie Edwards
  (checklist back)
- ❑ 489 Preston Dennard .15 .07
- ❑ 490 John Smith AP .15 .07
- ❑ 491 Mike Reinfeldt .15 .07
- ❑ 492 1980 NFC Champions .75 .35
  Eagles 20,
  Cowboys 7
  (Ron Jaworski)
- ❑ 493 1980 AFC Champions .75 .35
  Raiders 34,
  Chargers 27
  (Jim Plunkett)
- ❑ 494 Super Bowl XV .75 .35
  Raiders 27,
  Eagles 10
  (Plunkett handing
  off to Kenny King)
- ❑ 495 Joe Greene .75 .35
- ❑ 496 Charlie Joiner .75 .35
- ❑ 497 Rolland Lawrence .15 .07
- ❑ 498 Al(Bubba) Baker SA .40 .18
- ❑ 499 Brad Dusek .15 .07
- ❑ 500 Tony Dorsett 4.00 1.80
- ❑ 501 Robin Earl .15 .07
- ❑ 502 Theotis Brown RC .15 .07
- ❑ 503 Joe Ferguson .40 .18
- ❑ 504 Beasley Reece .15 .07
- ❑ 505 Lyle Alzado .75 .35
- ❑ 506 Tony Nathan RC .75 .35
- ❑ 507 Philadelphia Eagles TL .40 .18
  Wilbert Montgomery
  Charlie Smith
  Brenard Wilson
  Claude Humphrey
  (checklist back)
- ❑ 508 Herb Orvis .15 .07
- ❑ 509 Clarence Williams .15 .07
- ❑ 510 Ray Guy AP .40 .18
- ❑ 511 Jeff Komlo .15 .07
- ❑ 512 Freddie Solomon SA .15 .07
- ❑ 513 Tim Mazzetti .15 .07
- ❑ 514 Elvis Peacock RC .15 .07
- ❑ 515 Russ Francis .40 .18
- ❑ 516 Roland Harper .15 .07
- ❑ 517 Checklist 397-528 .50 .23
- ❑ 518 Billy Johnson .40 .18
- ❑ 519 Dan Dierdorf .75 .35
- ❑ 520 Fred Dean AP .15 .07
- ❑ 521 Jerry Butler .15 .07
- ❑ 522 Ron Saul .15 .07
- ❑ 523 Charlie Smith .15 .07
- ❑ 524 Kellen Winslow SA 3.00 1.35
- ❑ 525 Bert Jones .75 .35
- ❑ 526 Pittsburgh Steelers TL .75 .35
  Franco Harris
  Theo Bell
  Donnie Shell
  L.C. Greenwood
  (checklist back)
- ❑ 527 Duriel Harris .15 .07
- ❑ 528 William Andrews .75 .35

1982 Topps

	NRMT-MT	EXC
COMPLETE SET (528)	80.00	36.00
COMMON CARD (1-528)	.15	.07
SEMISTARS	.40	.18
UNLISTED STARS	.75	.35
CL (525-528)	.40	.18

- ❑ 1 Ken Anderson RB .75 .35
  Most Completions,
  Super Bowl Game
- ❑ 2 Dan Fouts RB .75 .35
  Most Passing Yards,
  Playoff Game
- ❑ 3 LeRoy Irvin RB .15 .07
  Most Punt Return
  Yardage, Game
- ❑ 4 Stump Mitchell RB .15 .07
  Most Return
  Yardage, Season
- ❑ 5 George Rogers RB .75 .35
  Most Rushing Yards,
  Rookie Season
- ❑ 6 Dan Ross RB .15 .07
  Most Receptions,
  Super Bowl Game
- ❑ 7 AFC Championship .75 .35
  Bengals 27,
  Chargers 7
  (Ken Anderson
  handing off to
  Pete Johnson)
- ❑ 8 NFC Championship .75 .35
  49ers 28,
  Cowboys 27
  (Earl Cooper)
- ❑ 9 Super Bowl XVI .75 .35
  49ers 26,
  Bengals 7
  (Anthony Munoz
  blocking)
- ❑ 10 Baltimore Colts TL .15 .07
  Curtis Dickey
  Raymond Butler
  Larry Braziel
  Bruce Laird
- ❑ 11 Raymond Butler .15 .07
- ❑ 12 Roger Carr .15 .07
- ❑ 13 Curtis Dickey .40 .18
- ❑ 14 Zachary Dixon .15 .07
- ❑ 15 Nesby Glasgow .15 .07
- ❑ 16 Bert Jones .75 .35
- ❑ 17 Bruce Laird .15 .07
- ❑ 18 Reese McCall .15 .07
- ❑ 19 Randy McMillan .15 .07
- ❑ 20 Ed Simonini .15 .07
- ❑ 21 Buffalo Bills TL .40 .18
  Joe Cribbs
  Frank Lewis
  Mario Clark
  Fred Smerlas
- ❑ 22 Mark Brammer .15 .07
- ❑ 23 Curtis Brown .15 .07
- ❑ 24 Jerry Butler .15 .07
- ❑ 25 Mario Clark .15 .07
- ❑ 26 Joe Cribbs .40 .18
- ❑ 27 Joe Cribbs IA .40 .18
- ❑ 28 Joe Ferguson .40 .18
- ❑ 29 Jim Haslett .15 .07
- ❑ 30 Frank Lewis AP .15 .07
- ❑ 31 Frank Lewis IA .15 .07
- ❑ 32 Shane Nelson .15 .07
- ❑ 33 Charles Romes .15 .07
- ❑ 34 Bill Simpson .15 .07
- ❑ 35 Fred Smerlas .15 .07
- ❑ 36 Cincinnati Bengals TL .40 .18
  Pete Johnson
  Cris Collinsworth
  Ken Riley
  Reggie Williams
- ❑ 37 Charles Alexander .15 .07
- ❑ 38 Ken Anderson AP .75 .35
- ❑ 39 Ken Anderson IA .75 .35
- ❑ 40 Jim Breech .15 .07
- ❑ 41 Jim Breech IA .15 .07
- ❑ 42 Louis Breeden .15 .07
- ❑ 43 Ross Browner .15 .07
- ❑ 44 Cris Collinsworth RC 1.00 .45
- ❑ 45 Cris Collinsworth IA .75 .35
- ❑ 46 Isaac Curtis .15 .07
- ❑ 47 Pete Johnson .15 .07
- ❑ 48 Pete Johnson IA .15 .07
- ❑ 49 Steve Kreider .15 .07
- ❑ 50 Pat McInally AP .15 .07

❑ 51 Anthony Munoz AP RC 8.00 3.60
❑ 52 Dan Ross .15 .07
❑ 53 David Verser RC .15 .07
❑ 54 Reggie Williams .40 .18
❑ 55 Cleveland Browns TL .40 .18
Mike Pruitt
Ozzie Newsome
Clarence Scott
Lyle Alzado
❑ 56 Lyle Alzado .75 .35
❑ 57 Dick Ambrose .15 .07
❑ 58 Ron Bolton .15 .07
❑ 59 Steve Cox .15 .07
❑ 60 Joe DeLamielleure .15 .07
❑ 61 Tom DeLeone .15 .07
❑ 62 Doug Dieken .15 .07
❑ 63 Ricky Feacher .15 .07
❑ 64 Don Goode .15 .07
❑ 65 Robert L. Jackson RC .15 .07
❑ 66 Dave Logan .15 .07
❑ 67 Ozzie Newsome 1.00 .45
❑ 68 Ozzie Newsome IA .75 .35
❑ 69 Greg Pruitt .40 .18
❑ 70 Mike Pruitt .40 .18
❑ 71 Mike Pruitt IA .40 .18
❑ 72 Reggie Rucker .15 .07
❑ 73 Clarence Scott .15 .07
❑ 74 Brian Sipe .40 .18
❑ 75 Charles White .40 .18
❑ 76 Denver Broncos TL .40 .18
Rick Parros
Steve Watson
Steve Foley
Rulon Jones
❑ 77 Rubin Carter .15 .07
❑ 78 Steve Foley .15 .07
❑ 79 Randy Gradishar .40 .18
❑ 80 Tom Jackson .75 .35
❑ 81 Craig Morton .40 .18
❑ 82 Craig Morton IA .40 .18
❑ 83 Riley Odoms .15 .07
❑ 84 Rick Parros .15 .07
❑ 85 Dave Preston .15 .07
❑ 86 Tony Reed .15 .07
❑ 87 Bob Swenson RC .15 .07
❑ 88 Bill Thompson .15 .07
❑ 89 Rick Upchurch .40 .18
❑ 90 Steve Watson AP RC .40 .18
❑ 91 Steve Watson IA .15 .07
❑ 92 Houston Oilers TL .15 .07
Carl Roaches
Ken Burrough
Carter Hartwig
Greg Stemrick
Jesse Baker
❑ 93 Mike Barber .15 .07
❑ 94 Elvin Bethea .15 .07
❑ 95 Gregg Bingham .15 .07
❑ 96 Robert Brazile AP .15 .07
❑ 97 Ken Burrough .15 .07
❑ 98 Toni Fritsch .15 .07
❑ 99 Leon Gray .15 .07
❑ 100 Gifford Nielsen RC .40 .18
❑ 101 Vernon Perry .15 .07
❑ 102 Mike Reinfeldt .15 .07
❑ 103 Mike Renfro .15 .07
❑ 104 Carl Roaches AP .15 .07
❑ 105 Ken Stabler 2.00 .90
❑ 106 Greg Stemrick .15 .07
❑ 107 J.C. Wilson .15 .07
❑ 108 Tim Wilson .15 .07
❑ 109 Kansas City Chiefs TL .15 .07
Joe Delaney
J.T. Smith
Eric Harris
Ken Kremer
❑ 110 Gary Barbaro AP .15 .07
❑ 111 Brad Budde .15 .07
❑ 112 Joe Delaney AP RC .75 .35
❑ 113 Joe Delaney IA .40 .18
❑ 114 Steve Fuller .15 .07
❑ 115 Gary Green .15 .07
❑ 116 James Hadnot .15 .07
❑ 117 Eric Harris .15 .07
❑ 118 Billy Jackson .15 .07
❑ 119 Bill Kenney RC .15 .07
❑ 120 Nick Lowery AP .75 .35
❑ 121 Nick Lowery IA .40 .18
❑ 122 Henry Marshall .15 .07
❑ 123 J.T. Smith .40 .18
❑ 124 Art Still .15 .07
❑ 125 Miami Dolphins TL .40 .18
Tony Nathan
Duriel Harris
Glenn Blackwood
Bob Baumhower
❑ 126 Bob Baumhower AP .40 .18
❑ 127 Glenn Blackwood .15 .07
❑ 128 Jimmy Cefalo .15 .07
❑ 129 A.J. Duhe .40 .18
❑ 130 Andra Franklin RC .15 .07
❑ 131 Duriel Harris .15 .07
❑ 132 Nat Moore .40 .18
❑ 133 Tony Nathan .40 .18
❑ 134 Ed Newman .15 .07
❑ 135 Earnie Rhone .15 .07
❑ 136 Don Strock .15 .07
❑ 137 Tommy Vigorito .15 .07
❑ 138 Uwe Von Schamann .15 .07
❑ 139 Uwe Von Schamann IA .15 .07
❑ 140 David Woodley .40 .18
❑ 141 New England Pats TL .40 .18
Tony Collins
Stanley Morgan
Tim Fox
Rick Sanford
Tony McGee
❑ 142 Julius Adams .15 .07
❑ 143 Richard Bishop .15 .07
❑ 144 Matt Cavanaugh .15 .07
❑ 145 Raymond Clayborn .15 .07
❑ 146 Tony Collins RC .15 .07
❑ 147 Vagas Ferguson .15 .07
❑ 148 Tim Fox .15 .07
❑ 149 Steve Grogan .40 .18
❑ 150 John Hannah AP .75 .35
❑ 151 John Hannah IA .40 .18
❑ 152 Don Hasselbeck .15 .07
❑ 153 Mike Haynes .40 .18
❑ 154 Harold Jackson .40 .18
❑ 155 Andy Johnson .15 .07
❑ 156 Stanley Morgan .40 .18
❑ 157 Stanley Morgan IA .40 .18
❑ 158 Steve Nelson .15 .07
❑ 159 Rod Shoate .15 .07
❑ 160 New York Jets TL .40 .18
Freeman McNeil
Wesley Walker
Darrol Ray
Joe Klecko
❑ 161 Dan Alexander .15 .07
❑ 162 Mike Augustyniak .15 .07
❑ 163 Jerome Barkum .15 .07
❑ 164 Greg Buttle .15 .07
❑ 165 Scott Dierking .15 .07
❑ 166 Joe Fields .15 .07
❑ 167 Mark Gastineau AP .40 .18
❑ 168 Mark Gastineau IA .40 .18
❑ 169 Bruce Harper .15 .07
❑ 170 Johnny Lam Jones .15 .07
❑ 171 Joe Klecko AP .40 .18
❑ 172 Joe Klecko IA .40 .18
❑ 173 Pat Leahy .40 .18
❑ 174 Pat Leahy IA .15 .07
❑ 175 Marty Lyons .40 .18
❑ 176 Freeman McNeil RC .75 .35
❑ 177 Marvin Powell AP .15 .07
❑ 178 Chuck Ramsey .15 .07
❑ 179 Darrol Ray .15 .07
❑ 180 Abdul Salaam .15 .07
❑ 181 Richard Todd .40 .18
❑ 182 Richard Todd IA .40 .18
❑ 183 Wesley Walker .40 .18
❑ 184 Chris Ward .15 .07
❑ 185 Oakland Raiders TL .40 .18
Kenny King
Derrick Ramsey
Lester Hayes
Odis McKinney
Rod Martin
❑ 186 Cliff Branch .75 .35
❑ 187 Bob Chandler .15 .07
❑ 188 Ray Guy .40 .18
❑ 189 Lester Hayes AP .40 .18
❑ 190 Ted Hendricks AP .75 .35
❑ 191 Monte Jackson .15 .07
❑ 192 Derrick Jensen .15 .07
❑ 193 Kenny King .15 .07
❑ 194 Rod Martin .15 .07
❑ 195 John Matuszak .40 .18
❑ 196 Matt Millen RC 1.50 .70
❑ 197 Derrick Ramsey .15 .07
❑ 198 Art Shell .75 .35
❑ 199 Mark Van Eeghen .15 .07
❑ 200 Arthur Whittington .15 .07
❑ 201 Marc Wilson RC .40 .18
❑ 202 Pittsburgh Steelers TL .75 .35
Franco Harris
John Stallworth
Mel Blount
Jack Lambert
Gary Dunn
❑ 203 Mel Blount AP .75 .35
❑ 204 Terry Bradshaw 3.00 1.35
❑ 205 Terry Bradshaw IA 1.25 .55
❑ 206 Craig Colquitt .15 .07
❑ 207 Bennie Cunningham .15 .07
❑ 208 Russell Davis .15 .07
❑ 209 Gary Dunn .15 .07
❑ 210 Jack Ham .75 .35
❑ 211 Franco Harris 1.00 .45
❑ 212 Franco Harris IA .75 .35
❑ 213 Jack Lambert AP .75 .35
❑ 214 Jack Lambert IA .75 .35
❑ 215 Mark Malone RC .75 .35
❑ 216 Frank Pollard RC .15 .07
❑ 217 Donnie Shell AP .75 .35
❑ 218 Jim Smith .15 .07
❑ 219 John Stallworth .75 .35
❑ 220 John Stallworth IA .75 .35
❑ 221 David Trout .15 .07
❑ 222 Mike Webster AP .75 .35
❑ 223 San Diego Chargers TL .75 .35
Chuck Muncie
Charlie Joiner
Willie Buchanon
Gary Johnson
❑ 224 Rolf Benirschke .15 .07
❑ 225 Rolf Benirschke IA .15 .07
❑ 226 James Brooks RC .75 .35
❑ 227 Willie Buchanon .15 .07
❑ 228 Wes Chandler .75 .35
❑ 229 Wes Chandler IA .40 .18
❑ 230 Dan Fouts 1.00 .45
❑ 231 Dan Fouts IA .75 .35
❑ 232 Gary Johnson AP .15 .07
❑ 233 Charlie Joiner .75 .35
❑ 234 Charlie Joiner IA .75 .35
❑ 235 Louie Kelcher .15 .07
❑ 236 Chuck Muncie AP .40 .18
❑ 237 Chuck Muncie IA .15 .07
❑ 238 George Roberts .15 .07
❑ 239 Ed White .15 .07
❑ 240 Doug Wilkerson AP .15 .07
❑ 241 Kellen Winslow AP 2.00 .90
❑ 242 Kellen Winslow IA .75 .35
❑ 243 Seattle Seahawks TL .75 .35
Theotis Brown
Steve Largent
John Harris
Jacob Green
❑ 244 Theotis Brown .15 .07
❑ 245 Dan Doornink .15 .07
❑ 246 John Harris .15 .07
❑ 247 Efren Herrera .15 .07
❑ 248 David Hughes .15 .07
❑ 249 Steve Largent 2.00 .90
❑ 250 Steve Largent IA .75 .35
❑ 251 Sam McCullum .15 .07
❑ 252 Sherman Smith .15 .07
❑ 253 Manu Tuiasosopo .15 .07
❑ 254 John Yarno .15 .07
❑ 255 Jim Zorn .40 .18
(Sitting with Dave Krieg)
❑ 256 Jim Zorn IA .40 .18
❑ 257 Passing Leaders 4.00 1.80
Ken Anderson
Joe Montana

❑ 258 Receiving Leaders .75 .35
Kellen Winslow
Dwight Clark
❑ 259 QB Sack Leaders .15 .07
Joe Klecko
Curtis Greer
❑ 260 Scoring Leaders .40 .18
Jim Breech
Nick Lowery
Eddie Murray
Rafael Septien
❑ 261 Interception Leaders .40 .18
John Harris
Everson Walls
❑ 262 Punting Leaders .15 .07
Pat McInally
Tom Skladany
❑ 263 Brothers: Bahr .15 .07
Chris and Matt
❑ 264 Brothers: Blackwood .40 .18
Lyle and Glenn
❑ 265 Brothers: Brock .15 .07
Pete and Stan
❑ 266 Brothers: Griffin .40 .18
Archie and Ray
❑ 267 Brothers: Hannah .75 .35
John and Charley
❑ 268 Brothers: Jackson .15 .07
Monte and Terry
❑ 269 Brothers: Payton 1.00 .45
Eddie and Walter
❑ 270 Brothers: Selmon .75 .35
Dewey and Lee Roy
❑ 271 Atlanta Falcons TL .40 .18
William Andrews
Alfred Jenkins
Tom Pridemore
Al Richardson
❑ 272 William Andrews .40 .18
❑ 273 William Andrews IA .40 .18
❑ 274 Steve Bartkowski .40 .18
❑ 275 Steve Bartkowski IA .40 .18
❑ 276 Bobby Butler .15 .07
❑ 277 Lynn Cain .15 .07
❑ 278 Wallace Francis .15 .07
❑ 279 Alfred Jackson .15 .07
❑ 280 John James .15 .07
❑ 281 Alfred Jenkins AP .15 .07
❑ 282 Alfred Jenkins IA .15 .07
❑ 283 Kenny Johnson .15 .07
❑ 284 Mike Kenn AP .75 .35
❑ 285 Fulton Kuykendall .15 .07
❑ 286 Mick Luckhurst RC .15 .07
❑ 287 Mick Luckhurst IA .15 .07
❑ 288 Junior Miller .15 .07
❑ 289 Al Richardson .15 .07
❑ 290 R.C. Thielemann RC .15 .07
❑ 291 Jeff Van Note .15 .07
❑ 292 Chicago Bears TL .75 .35
Walter Payton
Ken Margerum
Gary Fencik
Dan Hampton
Alan Page
❑ 293 Brian Baschnagel .15 .07
❑ 294 Robin Earl .15 .07
❑ 295 Vince Evans .40 .18
❑ 296 Gary Fencik AP .15 .07
❑ 297 Dan Hampton .75 .35
❑ 298 Noah Jackson .15 .07
❑ 299 Ken Margerum .15 .07
❑ 300 Jim Osborne .15 .07
❑ 301 Bob Parsons .15 .07
❑ 302 Walter Payton 6.00 2.70
❑ 303 Walter Payton IA 2.50 1.10
❑ 304 Revie Sorey .15 .07
❑ 305 Matt Suhey RC .75 .35
(Walter Payton
in background)
❑ 306 Rickey Watts .15 .07
❑ 307 Dallas Cowboys TL .75 .35
Tony Dorsett
Tony Hill
Everson Walls
Harvey Martin
❑ 308 Bob Breunig .15 .07
❑ 309 Doug Cosbie RC .15 .07
❑ 310 Pat Donovan AP .15 .07
❑ 311 Tony Dorsett AP 1.50 .70
❑ 312 Tony Dorsett IA .75 .35
❑ 313 Michael Downs RC .15 .07
❑ 314 Billy Joe DuPree .40 .18
❑ 315 John Dutton .15 .07
❑ 316 Tony Hill .40 .18
❑ 317 Butch Johnson .40 .18
❑ 318 Ed Too Tall Jones AP .75 .35
❑ 319 James Jones .15 .07
❑ 320 Harvey Martin .75 .35
❑ 321 Drew Pearson .75 .35
❑ 322 Herb Scott AP .15 .07
❑ 323 Rafael Septien AP .15 .07
❑ 324 Rafael Septien IA .15 .07
❑ 325 Ron Springs .40 .18
❑ 326 Dennis Thurman RC .15 .07
❑ 327 Everson Walls RC .75 .35
❑ 328 Everson Walls IA .75 .35
❑ 329 Danny White .75 .35
❑ 330 Danny White IA .40 .18
❑ 331 Randy White AP .75 .35
❑ 332 Randy White IA .75 .35
❑ 333 Detroit Lions TL .40 .18
Billy Sims
Freddie Scott
Jim Allen
Dave Pureifory
❑ 334 Jim Allen .15 .07
❑ 335 Al(Bubba) Baker .40 .18
❑ 336 Dexter Bussey .15 .07
❑ 337 Doug English AP .40 .18
❑ 338 Ken Fantetti .15 .07
❑ 339 William Gay .15 .07
❑ 340 David Hill .15 .07
❑ 341 Eric Hipple RC .15 .07
❑ 342 Rick Kane .15 .07
❑ 343 Ed Murray .75 .35
❑ 344 Ed Murray IA .40 .18
❑ 345 Ray Oldham .15 .07
❑ 346 Dave Pureifory .15 .07
❑ 347 Freddie Scott .15 .07
❑ 348 Freddie Scott IA .15 .07
❑ 349 Billy Sims AP .75 .35
❑ 350 Billy Sims IA .75 .35
❑ 351 Tom Skladany AP .15 .07
❑ 352 Leonard Thompson .15 .07
❑ 353 Stan White .15 .07
❑ 354 Green Bay Packers TL .75 .35
Gerry Ellis
James Lofton
Maurice Harvey
Mark Lee
Mike Butler
❑ 355 Paul Coffman .15 .07
❑ 356 George Cumby .15 .07
❑ 357 Lynn Dickey .15 .07
❑ 358 Lynn Dickey IA .15 .07
❑ 359 Gerry Ellis .15 .07
❑ 360 Maurice Harvey .15 .07
❑ 361 Harlan Huckleby .15 .07
❑ 362 John Jefferson .75 .35
❑ 363 Mark Lee RC .15 .07
❑ 364 James Lofton AP 1.00 .45
❑ 365 James Lofton IA .75 .35
❑ 366 Jan Stenerud .40 .18
❑ 367 Jan Stenerud IA .40 .18
❑ 368 Rich Wingo .15 .07
❑ 369 Los Angeles Rams TL .40 .18
Wendell Tyler
Preston Dennard
Nolan Cromwell
Jack Youngblood
❑ 370 Frank Corral .15 .07
❑ 371 Nolan Cromwell AP .40 .18
❑ 372 Nolan Cromwell IA .40 .18
❑ 373 Preston Dennard .15 .07
❑ 374 Mike Fanning .15 .07
❑ 375 Doug France .15 .07
❑ 376 Mike Guman .15 .07
❑ 377 Pat Haden .40 .18
❑ 378 Dennis Harrah .15 .07
❑ 379 Drew Hill RC .75 .35
❑ 380 LeRoy Irvin RC .15 .07
❑ 381 Cody Jones .15 .07
❑ 382 Rod Perry .15 .07
❑ 383 Rich Saul AP .15 .07
❑ 384 Pat Thomas .15 .07
❑ 385 Wendell Tyler .40 .18
❑ 386 Wendell Tyler IA .40 .18
❑ 387 Billy Waddy .15 .07
❑ 388 Jack Youngblood .75 .35
❑ 389 Minnesota Vikings TL .15 .07
Ted Brown
Joe Senser
Tom Hannon
Willie Teal
Matt Blair
❑ 390 Matt Blair AP .15 .07
❑ 391 Ted Brown .15 .07
❑ 392 Ted Brown IA .15 .07
❑ 393 Rick Danmeier .15 .07
❑ 394 Tommy Kramer .40 .18
❑ 395 Mark Mullaney .15 .07
❑ 396 Eddie Payton .15 .07
❑ 397 Ahmad Rashad .75 .35
❑ 398 Joe Senser .15 .07
❑ 399 Joe Senser IA .15 .07
❑ 400 Sammie White .40 .18
❑ 401 Sammie White IA .15 .07
❑ 402 Ron Yary .15 .07
❑ 403 Rickey Young .15 .07
❑ 404 New Orleans Saints TL .40 .18
George Rogers
Guido Merkens
Dave Waymer
Rickey Jackson
❑ 405 Russell Erxleben .15 .07
❑ 406 Elois Grooms .15 .07
❑ 407 Jack Holmes .15 .07
❑ 408 Archie Manning .75 .35
❑ 409 Derland Moore .15 .07
❑ 410 George Rogers RC .75 .35
❑ 411 George Rogers IA .75 .35
❑ 412 Toussaint Tyler .15 .07
❑ 413 Dave Waymer RC .15 .07
❑ 414 Wayne Wilson .15 .07
❑ 415 New York Giants TL .15 .07
Rob Carpenter
Johnny Perkins
Beasley Reece
George Martin
❑ 416 Scott Brunner RC .15 .07
❑ 417 Rob Carpenter .15 .07
❑ 418 Harry Carson AP .40 .18
❑ 419 Bill Currier .15 .07
❑ 420 Joe Danelo .15 .07
❑ 421 Joe Danelo IA .15 .07
❑ 422 Mark Haynes RC .15 .07
❑ 423 Terry Jackson .15 .07
❑ 424 Dave Jennings .15 .07
❑ 425 Gary Jeter .15 .07
❑ 426 Brian Kelley .15 .07
❑ 427 George Martin .15 .07
❑ 428 Curtis McGriff .15 .07
❑ 429 Bill Neill .15 .07
❑ 430 Johnny Perkins .15 .07
❑ 431 Beasley Reece .15 .07
❑ 432 Gary Shirk .15 .07
❑ 433 Phil Simms 2.00 .90
❑ 434 Lawrence Taylor AP RC 20.00 9.00
❑ 435 Lawrence Taylor IA 10.00 4.50
❑ 436 Brad Van Pelt .15 .07
❑ 437 Philadelphia Eagles TL .40 .18
Wilbert Montgomery
Harold Carmichael
Brenard Wilson
Carl Hairston
❑ 438 John Bunting .15 .07
❑ 439 Billy Campfield .15 .07
❑ 440 Harold Carmichael .75 .35
❑ 441 Harold Carmichael IA .75 .35
❑ 442 Herman Edwards .15 .07
❑ 443 Tony Franklin .15 .07
❑ 444 Tony Franklin IA .15 .07
❑ 445 Carl Hairston .15 .07
❑ 446 Dennis Harrison .15 .07
❑ 447 Ron Jaworski .75 .35
❑ 448 Charlie Johnson .15 .07
❑ 449 Keith Krepfle .15 .07
❑ 450 Frank LeMaster .15 .07

❑ 451 Randy Logan	.15	.07
❑ 452 Wilbert Montgomery	.40	.18
❑ 453 Wilbert Montgomery IA	.40	.18
❑ 454 Hubie Oliver	.15	.07
❑ 455 Jerry Robinson	.15	.07
❑ 456 Jerry Robinson IA	.15	.07
❑ 457 Jerry Sisemore	.15	.07
❑ 458 Charlie Smith	.15	.07
❑ 459 Stan Walters	.15	.07
❑ 460 Brenard Wilson	.15	.07
❑ 461 Roynell Young AP	.15	.07
❑ 462 St. Louis Cardinals TL	.40	.18
Ottis Anderson		
Pat Tilley		
Ken Greene		
Curtis Greer		
❑ 463 Ottis Anderson	.75	.35
❑ 464 Ottis Anderson IA	.75	.35
❑ 465 Carl Birdsong	.15	.07
❑ 466 Rush Brown	.15	.07
❑ 467 Mel Gray	.40	.18
❑ 468 Ken Greene	.15	.07
❑ 469 Jim Hart	.75	.35
❑ 470 E.J. Junior RC	.40	.18
❑ 471 Neil Lomax RC	.75	.35
❑ 472 Stump Mitchell RC	.75	.35
❑ 473 Wayne Morris	.15	.07
❑ 474 Neil O'Donoghue	.15	.07
❑ 475 Pat Tilley	.15	.07
❑ 476 Pat Tilley IA	.15	.07
❑ 477 San Francisco 49ers TL	.40	.18
Ricky Patton		
Dwight Clark		
Dwight Hicks		
Fred Dean		
❑ 478 Dwight Clark	.75	.35
❑ 479 Dwight Clark IA	.75	.35
❑ 480 Earl Cooper	.15	.07
❑ 481 Randy Cross AP	.40	.18
❑ 482 Johnny Davis	.15	.07
❑ 483 Fred Dean	.15	.07
❑ 484 Fred Dean IA	.15	.07
❑ 485 Dwight Hicks RC	.75	.35
❑ 486 Ronnie Lott AP RC	20.00	9.00
❑ 487 Ronnie Lott IA	6.00	2.70
❑ 488 Joe Montana AP	25.00	11.00
❑ 489 Joe Montana IA	12.00	5.50
❑ 490 Ricky Patton	.15	.07
❑ 491 Jack Reynolds	.40	.18
❑ 492 Freddie Solomon	.15	.07
❑ 493 Ray Wersching	.15	.07
❑ 494 Charlie Young	.15	.07
❑ 495 Tampa Bay Bucs TL	.40	.18
Jerry Eckwood		
Kevin House		
Cedric Brown		
Lee Roy Selmon		
❑ 496 Cedric Brown	.15	.07
❑ 497 Neal Colzie	.15	.07
❑ 498 Jerry Eckwood	.15	.07
❑ 499 Jimmie Giles AP	.40	.18
❑ 500 Hugh Green RC	.75	.35
❑ 501 Kevin House	.15	.07
❑ 502 Kevin House IA	.15	.07
❑ 503 Cecil Johnson	.15	.07
❑ 504 James Owens	.15	.07
❑ 505 Lee Roy Selmon AP	.75	.35
❑ 506 Mike Washington	.15	.07
❑ 507 James Wilder RC	.40	.18
❑ 508 Doug Williams	.40	.18
❑ 509 Wash. Redskins TL	.75	.35
Joe Washington		
Art Monk		
Mark Murphy		
Perry Brooks		
❑ 510 Perry Brooks	.15	.07
❑ 511 Dave Butz	.40	.18
❑ 512 Wilbur Jackson	.15	.07
❑ 513 Joe Lavender	.15	.07
❑ 514 Terry Metcalf	.40	.18
❑ 515 Art Monk	3.00	1.35
❑ 516 Mark Moseley	.15	.07
❑ 517 Mark Murphy	.15	.07
❑ 518 Mike Nelms AP	.15	.07
❑ 519 Lemar Parrish	.15	.07
❑ 520 John Riggins	.75	.35
❑ 521 Joe Theismann	.75	.35
❑ 522 Ricky Thompson	.15	.07
❑ 523 Don Warren UER	.15	.07
(photo actually		
Ricky Thompson)		
❑ 524 Joe Washington	.40	.18
❑ 525 Checklist 1-132	.40	.18
❑ 526 Checklist 133-264	.40	.18
❑ 527 Checklist 265-396	.40	.18
❑ 528 Checklist 397-528	.40	.18

1983 Topps

	NRMT-MT	EXC
COMPLETE SET (396)	50.00	22.00
COMMON CARD (1-396)	.10	.05
SEMISTARS	.30	.14
UNLISTED STARS	.60	.25
CL (394-396)	.20	.09

❑ 1 Ken Anderson RB	.60	.25
20 Consecutive		
Pass Completions		
❑ 2 Tony Dorsett RB	.60	.25
99 Yard Run		
❑ 3 Dan Fouts RB	.60	.25
30 Games Over		
300 Yards Passing		
❑ 4 Joe Montana RB	3.00	1.35
Five Straight		
300 Yard Games		
❑ 5 Mark Moseley RB	.30	.14
21 Straight		
Field Goals		
❑ 6 Mike Nelms RB	.10	.05
Most Yards,		
Punt Returns,		
Super Bowl Game		
❑ 7 Darrol Ray RB	.10	.05
Longest Interception		
Return, Playoff Game		
❑ 8 John Riggins RB	.60	.25
Most Yards Rushing,		
Super Bowl Game		
❑ 9 Fulton Walker RB	.10	.05
Most Yards,		
Kickoff Returns,		
Super Bowl Game		
❑ 10 NFC Championship	.60	.25
Redskins 31,		
Cowboys 17		
(John Riggins tackled)		
❑ 11 AFC Championship	.30	.14
Dolphins 14,		
Jets 0		
❑ 12 Super Bowl XVII	.10	.05
Redskins 27,		
Dolphins 17		
(John Riggins running)		
❑ 13 Atlanta Falcons TL	.30	.14
William Andrews		
❑ 14 William Andrews DP PB	.30	.14
❑ 15 Steve Bartkowski	.30	.14
❑ 16 Bobby Butler	.10	.05
❑ 17 Buddy Curry	.10	.05
❑ 18 Alfred Jackson DP	.10	.05
❑ 19 Alfred Jenkins	.10	.05
❑ 20 Kenny Johnson	.10	.05
❑ 21 Mike Kenn PB	.10	.05
❑ 22 Mick Luckhurst	.10	.05
❑ 23 Junior Miller	.10	.05
❑ 24 Al Richardson	.10	.05
❑ 25 Gerald Riggs DP RC	.30	.14
❑ 26 R.C. Thielemann PB	.10	.05
❑ 27 Jeff Van Note PB	.10	.05
❑ 28 Chicago Bears TL	1.00	.45
Walter Payton		
❑ 29 Brian Baschnagel	.10	.05
❑ 30 Dan Hampton PB	.60	.25
❑ 31 Mike Hartenstine	.10	.05
❑ 32 Noah Jackson	.10	.05
❑ 33 Jim McMahon RC	6.00	2.70
❑ 34 Emery Moorehead DP	.10	.05
❑ 35 Bob Parsons	.10	.05
❑ 36 Walter Payton	6.00	2.70
❑ 37 Terry Schmidt	.10	.05
❑ 38 Mike Singletary RC	8.00	3.60
❑ 39 Matt Suhey DP	.30	.14
❑ 40 Rickey Watts DP	.10	.05
❑ 41 Otis Wilson DP RC	.30	.14
❑ 42 Dallas Cowboys TL	.60	.25
Tony Dorsett		
❑ 43 Bob Breunig PB	.30	.14
❑ 44 Doug Cosbie	.10	.05
❑ 45 Pat Donovan PB	.10	.05
❑ 46 Tony Dorsett DP PB	1.00	.45
❑ 47 Tony Hill	.30	.14
❑ 48 Butch Johnson DP	.30	.14
❑ 49 Ed Jones DP PB	.60	.25
❑ 50 Harvey Martin DP	.30	.14
❑ 51 Drew Pearson	.60	.25
❑ 52 Rafael Septien	.10	.05
❑ 53 Ron Springs DP	.10	.05
❑ 54 Dennis Thurman	.10	.05
❑ 55 Everson Walls PB	.30	.14
❑ 56 Danny White DP PB	.60	.25
❑ 57 Randy White PB	.60	.25
❑ 58 Detroit Lions TL	.30	.14
Billy Sims		
❑ 59 Al(Bubba) Baker DP	.30	.14
❑ 60 Dexter Bussey DP	.10	.05
❑ 61 Gary Danielson DP	.10	.05
❑ 62 Keith Dorney DP PB	.10	.05
❑ 63 Doug English PB	.10	.05
❑ 64 Ken Fantetti DP	.10	.05
❑ 65 Alvin Hall DP	.10	.05
❑ 66 David Hill DP	.10	.05
❑ 67 Eric Hipple	.10	.05
❑ 68 Ed Murray DP	.30	.14
❑ 69 Freddie Scott	.10	.05
❑ 70 Billy Sims DP PB	.30	.14
❑ 71 Tom Skladany DP	.10	.05
❑ 72 Leonard Thompson DP	.10	.05
❑ 73 Bobby Watkins	.10	.05
❑ 74 Green Bay Packers TL	.10	.05
Eddie Lee Ivery		
❑ 75 John Anderson	.10	.05
❑ 76 Paul Coffman PB	.10	.05
❑ 77 Lynn Dickey	.10	.05
❑ 78 Mike Douglass DP	.10	.05
❑ 79 Eddie Lee Ivery	.10	.05
❑ 80 John Jefferson DP PB	.60	.25
❑ 81 Ezra Johnson	.10	.05
❑ 82 Mark Lee	.10	.05
❑ 83 James Lofton PB	.60	.25
❑ 84 Larry McCarren PB	.10	.05
❑ 85 Jan Stenerud DP	.30	.14
❑ 86 Los Angeles Rams TL	.10	.05
Wendell Tyler		
❑ 87 Bill Bain DP	.10	.05
❑ 88 Nolan Cromwell PB	.30	.14
❑ 89 Preston Dennard	.10	.05
❑ 90 Vince Ferragamo DP	.30	.14
❑ 91 Mike Guman	.10	.05
❑ 92 Kent Hill PB	.10	.05
❑ 93 Mike Lansford DP RC	.10	.05
❑ 94 Rod Perry	.10	.05
❑ 95 Pat Thomas DP	.10	.05
❑ 96 Jack Youngblood	.60	.25
❑ 97 Minnesota Vikings TL	.10	.05
Ted Brown		
❑ 98 Matt Blair PB	.10	.05
❑ 99 Ted Brown	.10	.05
❑ 100 Greg Coleman	.10	.05

❑ 101 Randy Holloway .10 .05
❑ 102 Tommy Kramer .30 .14
❑ 103 Doug Martin DP .10 .05
❑ 104 Mark Mullaney .10 .05
❑ 105 Joe Senser .10 .05
❑ 106 Willie Teal DP .10 .05
❑ 107 Sammie White .30 .14
❑ 108 Rickey Young .10 .05
❑ 109 New Orleans Saints TL .. .30 .14
George Rogers
❑ 110 Stan Brock RC .10 .05
❑ 111 Bruce Clark RC .10 .05
❑ 112 Russell Erxleben DP .10 .05
❑ 113 Russell Gary .10 .05
❑ 114 Jeff Groth DP .10 .05
❑ 115 John Hill DP .10 .05
❑ 116 Derland Moore .10 .05
❑ 117 George Rogers PB .30 .14
❑ 118 Ken Stabler 1.50 .70
❑ 119 Wayne Wilson .10 .05
❑ 120 New York Giants TL .10 .05
Butch Woolfolk
❑ 121 Scott Brunner .10 .05
❑ 122 Rob Carpenter .10 .05
❑ 123 Harry Carson PB .30 .14
❑ 124 Joe Danelo DP .10 .05
❑ 125 Earnest Gray .10 .05
❑ 126 Mark Haynes DP PB .30 .14
❑ 127 Terry Jackson .10 .05
❑ 128 Dave Jennings PB .10 .05
❑ 129 Brian Kelley .10 .05
❑ 130 George Martin .10 .05
❑ 131 Tom Mullady .10 .05
❑ 132 Johnny Perkins .10 .05
❑ 133 Lawrence Taylor PB 5.00 2.20
❑ 134 Brad Van Pelt .10 .05
❑ 135 Butch Woolfolk DP .10 .05
❑ 136 Philadelphia Eagles TL .. .30 .14
Wilbert Montgomery
❑ 137 Harold Carmichael .60 .25
❑ 138 Herman Edwards .10 .05
❑ 139 Tony Franklin DP .10 .05
❑ 140 Carl Hairston DP .10 .05
❑ 141 Dennis Harrison DP PB .. .10 .05
❑ 142 Ron Jaworski DP .30 .14
❑ 143 Frank LeMaster .10 .05
❑ 144 Wilbert Montgomery DP .30 .14
❑ 145 Guy Morriss .10 .05
❑ 146 Jerry Robinson .10 .05
(TD stats don't match)
❑ 147 Max Runager .10 .05
❑ 148 Ron Smith DP .10 .05
❑ 149 John Spagnola .10 .05
❑ 150 Stan Walters DP .10 .05
❑ 151 Roynell Young DP .10 .05
❑ 152 St. Louis Cardinals TL .30 .14
Ottis Anderson
❑ 153 Ottis Anderson .60 .25
❑ 154 Carl Birdsong .10 .05
❑ 155 Dan Dierdorf DP .60 .25
❑ 156 Roy Green RC .60 .25
❑ 157 Elois Grooms .10 .05
❑ 158 Neil Lomax DP .30 .14
❑ 159 Wayne Morris .10 .05
❑ 160 Tootie Robbins RC .10 .05
❑ 161 Luis Sharpe RC .10 .05
❑ 162 Pat Tilley .10 .05
❑ 163 San Francisco 49ers TL .10 .05
Jeff Moore
❑ 164 Dwight Clark PB .60 .25
❑ 165 Randy Cross PB .30 .14
❑ 166 Russ Francis .30 .14
❑ 167 Dwight Hicks PB .10 .05
❑ 168 Ronnie Lott PB 2.50 1.10
❑ 169 Joe Montana DP 10.00 4.50
❑ 170 Jeff Moore .10 .05
❑ 171 Renaldo Nehemiah DP RC .60 .25
❑ 172 Freddie Solomon .10 .05
❑ 173 Ray Wersching DP .10 .05
❑ 174 Tampa Bay Bucs TL .10 .05
James Wilder
❑ 175 Cedric Brown .10 .05
❑ 176 Bill Capece .10 .05
❑ 177 Neal Colzie .10 .05
❑ 178 Jimmie Giles PB .10 .05
❑ 179 Hugh Green PB .30 .14
❑ 180 Kevin House DP .10 .05
❑ 181 James Owens .10 .05
❑ 182 Lee Roy Selmon PB .60 .25
❑ 183 Mike Washington .10 .05
❑ 184 James Wilder .10 .05
❑ 185 Doug Williams DP .30 .14
❑ 186 Wash. Redskins TL .60 .25
John Riggins
❑ 187 Jeff Bostic DP RC .60 .25
❑ 188 Charlie Brown PB RC .30 .14
❑ 189 Vernon Dean DP .10 .05
❑ 190 Joe Jacoby RC .60 .25
❑ 191 Dexter Manley RC .30 .14
❑ 192 Rich Milot .10 .05
❑ 193 Art Monk DP 1.00 .45
❑ 194 Mark Moseley DP PB .10 .05
❑ 195 Mike Nelms PB .10 .05
❑ 196 Neal Olkewicz DP .10 .05
❑ 197 Tony Peters PB .10 .05
❑ 198 John Riggins DP .60 .25
❑ 199 Joe Theismann PB .60 .25
❑ 200 Don Warren .10 .05
❑ 201 Jeris White DP .10 .05
❑ 202 Passing Leaders .60 .25
Joe Theismann
Ken Anderson
❑ 203 Receiving Leaders .30 .14
Dwight Clark
Kellen Winslow
❑ 204 Rushing Leaders .60 .25
Tony Dorsett
Freeman McNeil
❑ 205 Scoring Leaders 1.25 .55
Wendell Tyler
Marcus Allen
❑ 206 Interception Leaders .30 .14
Everson Walls
AFC Tie (Four)
❑ 207 Punting Leaders .10 .05
Carl Birdsong
Luke Prestridge
❑ 208 Baltimore Colts TL .10 .05
Randy McMillan
❑ 209 Matt Bouza .10 .05
❑ 210 Johnie Cooks DP RC .10 .05
❑ 211 Curtis Dickey .10 .05
❑ 212 Nesby Glasgow DP .10 .05
❑ 213 Derrick Hatchett .10 .05
❑ 214 Randy McMillan .10 .05
❑ 215 Mike Pagel RC .30 .14
❑ 216 Rohn Stark DP RC .30 .14
❑ 217 Donnell Thompson DP RC .10
.05
❑ 218 Leo Wisniewski DP .10 .05
❑ 219 Buffalo Bills TL .30 .14
Joe Cribbs
❑ 220 Curtis Brown .10 .05
❑ 221 Jerry Butler .10 .05
❑ 222 Greg Cater DP .10 .05
❑ 223 Joe Cribbs .30 .14
❑ 224 Joe Ferguson .30 .14
❑ 225 Roosevelt Leaks .10 .05
❑ 226 Frank Lewis .10 .05
❑ 227 Eugene Marve RC .10 .05
❑ 228 Fred Smerlas DP PB .10 .05
❑ 229 Ben Williams DP PB .10 .05
❑ 230 Cincinnati Bengals TL .10 .05
Pete Johnson
❑ 231 Charles Alexander .10 .05
❑ 232 Ken Anderson DP PB .60 .25
❑ 233 Jim Breech DP .10 .05
❑ 234 Ross Browner .10 .05
❑ 235 Cris Collinsworth .60 .25
DP PB
❑ 236 Isaac Curtis .10 .05
❑ 237 Pete Johnson .10 .05
❑ 238 Steve Kreider DP .10 .05
❑ 239 Max Montoya DP RC .10 .05
❑ 240 Anthony Munoz PB 1.00 .45
❑ 241 Ken Riley .10 .05
❑ 242 Dan Ross PB .10 .05
❑ 243 Reggie Williams .30 .14
❑ 244 Cleveland Browns TL .30 .14
Mike Pruitt
❑ 245 Chip Banks DP PB RC .. .30 .14
❑ 246 Tom Cousineau DP RC .. .30 .14
❑ 247 Joe DeLamielleure DP .. .10 .05
❑ 248 Doug Dieken DP .10 .05
❑ 249 Hanford Dixon RC .10 .05
❑ 250 Ricky Feacher DP .10 .05
❑ 251 Lawrence Johnson DP .. .10 .05
❑ 252 Dave Logan DP .10 .05
❑ 253 Paul McDonald DP .10 .05
❑ 254 Ozzie Newsome DP .60 .25
❑ 255 Mike Pruitt .30 .14
❑ 256 Clarence Scott DP .10 .05
❑ 257 Brian Sipe DP .30 .14
❑ 258 Dwight Walker DP .10 .05
❑ 259 Charles White .30 .14
❑ 260 Denver Broncos TL .10 .05
Gerald Willhite
❑ 261 Steve DeBerg DP .30 .14
❑ 262 Randy Gradishar DP PB .30 .14
❑ 263 Rulon Jones DP RC .10 .05
❑ 264 Rich Karlis DP .10 .05
❑ 265 Don Latimer .10 .05
❑ 266 Rick Parros DP .10 .05
❑ 267 Luke Prestridge PB .10 .05
❑ 268 Rick Upchurch PB .30 .14
❑ 269 Steve Watson DP .10 .05
❑ 270 Gerald Willhite DP .10 .05
❑ 271 Houston Oilers TL .10 .05
Gifford Nielsen
❑ 272 Harold Bailey .10 .05
❑ 273 Jesse Baker DP .10 .05
❑ 274 Gregg Bingham DP .10 .05
❑ 275 Robert Brazile DP PB .10 .05
❑ 276 Donnie Craft .10 .05
❑ 277 Daryl Hunt .10 .05
❑ 278 Archie Manning DP .30 .14
❑ 279 Gifford Nielsen .10 .05
❑ 280 Mike Renfro .10 .05
❑ 281 Carl Roaches DP .10 .05
❑ 282 Kansas City Chiefs TL .30 .14
Joe Delaney
❑ 283 Gary Barbaro PB .10 .05
❑ 284 Joe Delaney .10 .05
❑ 285 Jeff Gossett RC .60 .25
❑ 286 Gary Green DP PB .10 .05
❑ 287 Eric Harris DP .10 .05
❑ 288 Billy Jackson DP .10 .05
❑ 289 Bill Kenney DP .10 .05
❑ 290 Nick Lowery .60 .25
❑ 291 Henry Marshall .10 .05
❑ 292 Art Still DP PB .10 .05
❑ 293 Los Angeles Raiders TL 2.00 .90
Marcus Allen
❑ 294 Marcus Allen DP PB RC 20.00 9.00
❑ 295 Lyle Alzado .60 .25
❑ 296 Chris Bahr DP .10 .05
❑ 297 Cliff Branch .60 .25
❑ 298 Todd Christensen RC .75 .35
❑ 299 Ray Guy .30 .14
❑ 300 Frank Hawkins DP .10 .05
❑ 301 Lester Hayes DP PB .10 .05
❑ 302 Ted Hendricks DP PB .60 .25
❑ 303 Kenny King DP .10 .05
❑ 304 Rod Martin .10 .05
❑ 305 Matt Millen DP .60 .25
❑ 306 Burgess Owens .10 .05
❑ 307 Jim Plunkett .60 .25
❑ 308 Miami Dolphins TL .30 .14
Andra Franklin
❑ 309 Bob Baumhower PB .10 .05
❑ 310 Glenn Blackwood .10 .05
❑ 311 Lyle Blackwood DP .10 .05
❑ 312 A.J. Duhe .10 .05
❑ 313 Andra Franklin PB .10 .05
❑ 314 Duriel Harris .10 .05
❑ 315 Bob Kuechenberg DP PB .30 .14
❑ 316 Don McNeal .10 .05
❑ 317 Tony Nathan .30 .14
❑ 318 Ed Newman PB .10 .05
❑ 319 Earnie Rhone DP .10 .05
❑ 320 Joe Rose DP .10 .05
❑ 321 Don Strock DP .10 .05
❑ 322 Uwe Von Schamann .10 .05
❑ 323 David Woodley DP .30 .14
❑ 324 New England Pats TL .10 .05
Tony Collins
❑ 325 Julius Adams .10 .05

❑ 326	Pete Brock	.10	.05
❑ 327	Rich Camarillo DP RC	.10	.05
❑ 328	Tony Collins DP	.10	.05
❑ 329	Steve Grogan	.30	.14
❑ 330	John Hannah PB	.60	.25
❑ 331	Don Hasselbeck	.10	.05
❑ 332	Mike Haynes PB	.30	.14
❑ 333	Roland James RC	.10	.05
❑ 334A	Stanley Morgan ERR (%%Inside Linebacker~ printed upside down on card back)	.60	.25
❑ 334B	Stanley Morgan COR	.30	.14
❑ 335	Steve Nelson	.10	.05
❑ 336	Kenneth Sims DP	.10	.05
❑ 337	Mark Van Eeghen	.30	.14
❑ 338	New York Jets TL Freeman McNeil	.30	.14
❑ 339	Greg Buttle	.10	.05
❑ 340	Joe Fields PB	.10	.05
❑ 341	Mark Gastineau DP PB	.30	.14
❑ 342	Bruce Harper	.10	.05
❑ 343	Bobby Jackson	.10	.05
❑ 344	Bobby Jones	.10	.05
❑ 345	Johnny Lam Jones DP	.10	.05
❑ 346	Joe Klecko	.30	.14
❑ 347	Marty Lyons	.10	.05
❑ 348	Freeman McNeil PB	.60	.25
❑ 349	Lance Mehl RC	.10	.05
❑ 350	Marvin Powell DP PB	.10	.05
❑ 351	Darrol Ray DP	.10	.05
❑ 352	Abdul Salaam	.10	.05
❑ 353	Richard Todd	.30	.14
❑ 354	Wesley Walker PB	.30	.14
❑ 355	Pittsburgh Steelers TL Franco Harris	.60	.25
❑ 356	Gary Anderson K DP RC	1.00	.45
❑ 357	Mel Blount DP	.60	.25
❑ 358	Terry Bradshaw DP	1.25	.55
❑ 359	Larry Brown PB	.10	.05
❑ 360	Bennie Cunningham	.10	.05
❑ 361	Gary Dunn	.10	.05
❑ 362	Franco Harris	.75	.35
❑ 363	Jack Lambert PB	.60	.25
❑ 364	Frank Pollard	.10	.05
❑ 365	Donnie Shell PB	.30	.14
❑ 366	John Stallworth PB	.60	.25
❑ 367	Loren Toews	.10	.05
❑ 368	Mike Webster DP PB	.60	.25
❑ 369	Dwayne Woodruff RC	.10	.05
❑ 370	San Diego Chargers TL Chuck Muncie	.30	.14
❑ 371	Rolf Benirschke DP PB	.10	.05
❑ 372	James Brooks	.60	.25
❑ 373	Wes Chandler PB	.30	.14
❑ 374	Dan Fouts DP PB	.60	.25
❑ 375	Tim Fox	.10	.05
❑ 376	Gary Johnson PB	.10	.05
❑ 377	Charlie Joiner DP	.60	.25
❑ 378	Louie Kelcher	.10	.05
❑ 379	Chuck Muncie PB	.10	.05
❑ 380	Cliff Thrift	.10	.05
❑ 381	Doug Wilkerson PB	.10	.05
❑ 382	Kellen Winslow PB	.75	.35
❑ 383	Seattle Seahawks TL Sherman Smith	.10	.05
❑ 384	Kenny Easley PB RC	.60	.25
❑ 385	Jacob Green RC	.30	.14
❑ 386	John Harris	.10	.05
❑ 387	Michael Jackson	.10	.05
❑ 388	Norm Johnson RC	.10	.05
❑ 389	Steve Largent	1.25	.55
❑ 390	Keith Simpson	.10	.05
❑ 391	Sherman Smith	.10	.05
❑ 392	Jeff West DP	.10	.05
❑ 393	Jim Zorn DP	.30	.14
❑ 394	Checklist 1-132	.20	.09
❑ 395	Checklist 133-264	.20	.09
❑ 396	Checklist 265-396	.20	.09

1984 Topps

	NRMT-MT	EXC
COMPLETE SET (396)	250.00	110.00
COMP.FACT.SET (396)	250.00	110.00
COMMON CARD (1-396)	.10	.05
SEMISTARS	.25	.11
UNLISTED STARS	.50	.23
CL (394-396)	.20	.09

BEWARE MARINO COUNTERFEITS

❑ 1	Eric Dickerson RB Sets Rookie Mark With 1808 Yards	.50	.23
❑ 2	Ali Haji-Sheikh RB Sets Field Goal Mark as a Rookie	.25	.11
❑ 3	Franco Harris RB Records Eighth 1000 Yard Year	.50	.23
❑ 4	Mark Moseley RB 161 Points Sets Mark for Kickers	.25	.11
❑ 5	John Riggins RB 24 Rushing TD's	.50	.23
❑ 6	Jan Stenerud RB 338th Career FG	.25	.11
❑ 7	AFC Championship Raiders 30, Seahawks 14 (Marcus Allen running)	.50	.23
❑ 8	NFC Championship Redskins 24, 49ers 21 (John Riggins running)	.25	.11
❑ 9	Super Bowl XVIII UER Raiders 38, Redskins 9 (hand-off to Marcus Allen; score wrong, 28-9 on card front)	.50	.23
❑ 10	Indianapolis Colts TL Curtis Dickey	.10	.05
❑ 11	Raul Allegre RC	.10	.05
❑ 12	Curtis Dickey	.25	.11
❑ 13	Ray Donaldson RC	.25	.11
❑ 14	Nesby Glasgow	.10	.05
❑ 15	Chris Hinton PB RC	.50	.23
❑ 16	Vernon Maxwell RC	.10	.05
❑ 17	Randy McMillan	.10	.05
❑ 18	Mike Pagel	.25	.11
❑ 19	Rohn Stark	.25	.11
❑ 20	Leo Wisniewski	.10	.05
❑ 21	Buffalo Bills TL Joe Cribbs	.25	.11
❑ 22	Jerry Butler	.10	.05
❑ 23	Joe Danelo	.10	.05
❑ 24	Joe Ferguson	.25	.11
❑ 25	Steve Freeman	.10	.05
❑ 26	Roosevelt Leaks	.25	.11
❑ 27	Frank Lewis	.10	.05
❑ 28	Eugene Marve	.10	.05
❑ 29	Booker Moore	.10	.05
❑ 30	Fred Smerlas PB	.10	.05
❑ 31	Ben Williams	.25	.11
❑ 32	Cincinnati Bengals TL Cris Collinsworth	.25	.11
❑ 33	Charles Alexander	.10	.05
❑ 34	Ken Anderson	.50	.23
❑ 35	Ken Anderson IR	.50	.23
❑ 36	Jim Breech	.10	.05
❑ 37	Cris Collinsworth PB	.50	.23
❑ 38	Cris Collinsworth IR	.50	.23
❑ 39	Isaac Curtis	.25	.11
❑ 40	Eddie Edwards	.10	.05
❑ 41	Ray Horton RC	.10	.05
❑ 42	Pete Johnson	.25	.11
❑ 43	Steve Kreider	.10	.05
❑ 44	Max Montoya	.10	.05
❑ 45	Anthony Munoz PB	.50	.23
❑ 46	Reggie Williams	.25	.11
❑ 47	Cleveland Browns TL Mike Pruitt	.25	.11
❑ 48	Matt Bahr	.25	.11
❑ 49	Chip Banks PB	.10	.05
❑ 50	Tom Cousineau	.10	.05
❑ 51	Joe DeLamielleure	.10	.05
❑ 52	Doug Dieken	.10	.05
❑ 53	Bob Golic RC	.50	.23
❑ 54	Bobby Jones	.10	.05
❑ 55	Dave Logan	.10	.05
❑ 56	Clay Matthews	.50	.23
❑ 57	Paul McDonald	.10	.05
❑ 58	Ozzie Newsome	.50	.23
❑ 59	Ozzie Newsome IR	.50	.23
❑ 60	Mike Pruitt	.25	.11
❑ 61	Denver Broncos TL Steve Watson	.25	.11
❑ 62	Barney Chavous RC	.10	.05
❑ 63	John Elway RC !	120.00	55.00
❑ 64	Steve Foley	.10	.05
❑ 65	Tom Jackson	.50	.23
❑ 66	Rich Karlis	.10	.05
❑ 67	Luke Prestridge	.10	.05
❑ 68	Zach Thomas	.10	.05
❑ 69	Rick Upchurch	.25	.11
❑ 70	Steve Watson	.25	.11
❑ 71	Sammy Winder RC	.25	.11
❑ 72	Louis Wright PB	.25	.11
❑ 73	Houston Oilers TL Tim Smith	.10	.05
❑ 74	Jesse Baker	.10	.05
❑ 75	Gregg Bingham	.10	.05
❑ 76	Robert Brazile	.25	.11
❑ 77	Steve Brown	.10	.05
❑ 78	Chris Dressel	.10	.05
❑ 79	Doug France	.10	.05
❑ 80	Florian Kempf	.10	.05
❑ 81	Carl Roaches	.25	.11
❑ 82	Tim Smith RC	.25	.11
❑ 83	Willie Tullis	.10	.05
❑ 84	Kansas City Chiefs TL Carlos Carson	.10	.05
❑ 85	Mike Bell	.10	.05
❑ 86	Theotis Brown	.10	.05
❑ 87	Carlos Carson PB	.50	.23
❑ 88	Carlos Carson IR	.25	.11
❑ 89	Deron Cherry PB RC	.25	.11
❑ 90	Gary Green PB	.10	.05
❑ 91	Billy Jackson	.10	.05
❑ 92	Bill Kenney	.25	.11
❑ 93	Bill Kenney IR	.25	.11
❑ 94	Nick Lowery	.50	.23
❑ 95	Henry Marshall	.10	.05
❑ 96	Art Still	.10	.05
❑ 97	Los Angeles Raiders TL Todd Christensen	.25	.11
❑ 98	Marcus Allen	5.00	2.20
❑ 99	Marcus Allen IR	2.50	1.10
❑ 100	Lyle Alzado	.25	.11
❑ 101	Lyle Alzado IR	.25	.11
❑ 102	Chris Bahr	.10	.05
❑ 103	Malcolm Barnwell RC	.10	.05
❑ 104	Cliff Branch	.50	.23
❑ 105	Todd Christensen PB	.50	.23
❑ 106	Todd Christensen IR	.50	.23
❑ 107	Ray Guy	.50	.23
❑ 108	Frank Hawkins	.10	.05
❑ 109	Lester Hayes PB	.25	.11
❑ 110	Ted Hendricks PB	.50	.23
❑ 111	Howie Long PB RC	15.00	6.75
❑ 112	Rod Martin PB	.25	.11
❑ 113	Vann McElroy PB RC	.10	.05
❑ 114	Jim Plunkett	.50	.23
❑ 115	Greg Pruitt PB	.25	.11
❑ 116	Miami Dolphins TL Mark Duper	.50	.23
❑ 117	Bob Baumhower PB	.10	.05
❑ 118	Doug Betters PB RC	.10	.05
❑ 119	A.J. Duhe	.10	.05

❑ 120 Mark Duper PB RC ...... .50 .23
❑ 121 Andra Franklin................ .10 .05
❑ 122 William Judson .... .10 .05
❑ 123 Dan Marino PB RC UER 120.00 55.00
(Quaterback on back)
❑ 124 Dan Marino IR........... 15.00 6.75
❑ 125 Nat Moore .... .25 .11
❑ 126 Ed Newman PB.............. .10 .05
❑ 127 Reggie Roby RC .... .25 .11
❑ 128 Gerald Small .... .10 .05
❑ 129 Dwight Stephenson PB RC 1.25
.55
❑ 130 Uwe Von Schamann ...... .10 .05
❑ 131 New England Pats TL .... .10 .05
Tony Collins
❑ 132 Rich Camarillo PB.......... .25 .11
❑ 133 Tony Collins PB............ .25 .11
❑ 134 Tony Collins IR .... .10 .05
❑ 135 Bob Cryder .... .10 .05
❑ 136 Steve Grogan .... .25 .11
❑ 137 John Hannah PB............ .50 .23
❑ 138 Brian Holloway PB RC .. .10 .05
❑ 139 Roland James .... .10 .05
❑ 140 Stanley Morgan.............. .25 .11
❑ 141 Rick Sanford .... .10 .05
❑ 142 Mosi Tatupu RC .... .10 .05
❑ 143 Andre Tippett RC .... .50 .23
❑ 144 New York Jets TL .... .25 .11
Wesley Walker
❑ 145 Jerome Barkum.............. .10 .05
❑ 146 Mark Gastineau PB........ .25 .11
❑ 147 Mark Gastineau IR .... .25 .11
❑ 148 Bruce Harper.................. .10 .05
❑ 149 Johnny Lam Jones .... .10 .05
❑ 150 Joe Klecko PB................ .25 .11
❑ 151 Pat Leahy .... .10 .05
❑ 152 Freeman McNeil .... .25 .11
❑ 153 Lance Mehl .... .10 .05
❑ 154 Marvin Powell PB .... .25 .11
❑ 155 Darrol Ray...................... .10 .05
❑ 156 Pat Ryan RC .... .10 .05
❑ 157 Kirk Springs.................... .10 .05
❑ 158 Wesley Walker .... .25 .11
❑ 159 Pittsburgh Steelers TL.... .50 .23
Franco Harris
❑ 160 Walter Abercrombie RC .25 .11
❑ 161 Gary Anderson K PB...... .50 .23
❑ 162 Terry Bradshaw........... 1.50 .70
❑ 163 Craig Colquitt .... .10 .05
❑ 164 Bennie Cunningham ...... .10 .05
❑ 165 Franco Harris .... .50 .23
❑ 166 Franco Harris IR .... .50 .23
❑ 167 Jack Lambert PB............ .50 .23
❑ 168 Jack Lambert IR .... .50 .23
❑ 169 Frank Pollard.................. .10 .05
❑ 170 Donnie Shell .... .25 .11
❑ 171 Mike Webster PB .... .25 .11
❑ 172 Keith Willis RC .... .10 .05
❑ 173 Rick Woods.................... .10 .05
❑ 174 San Diego Chargers TL .50 .23
Kellen Winslow
❑ 175 Rolf Benirschke.............. .10 .05
❑ 176 James Brooks .... .25 .11
❑ 177 Maury Buford................. .10 .05
❑ 178 Wes Chandler PB .... .25 .11
❑ 179 Dan Fouts PB .... .60 .25
❑ 180 Dan Fouts IR.................. .50 .23
❑ 181 Charlie Joiner .... .50 .23
❑ 182 Linden King.................... .10 .05
❑ 183 Chuck Muncie .... .25 .11
❑ 184 Billy Ray Smith RC .... .50 .23
❑ 185 Danny Walters RC .... .10 .05
❑ 186 Kellen Winslow PB .... .60 .25
❑ 187 Kellen Winslow IR.......... .50 .23
❑ 188 Seattle Seahawks TL .... .50 .23
Curt Warner
❑ 189 Steve August................. .10 .05
❑ 190 Dave Brown.................... .10 .05
❑ 191 Zachary Dixon................ .10 .05
❑ 192 Kenny Easley .... .25 .11
❑ 193 Jacob Green .... .10 .05
❑ 194 Norm Johnson................ .25 .11
❑ 195 Dave Krieg RC .... 1.50 .70
❑ 196 Steve Largent .... 1.00 .45
❑ 197 Steve Largent IR........... .50 .23
❑ 198 Curt Warner PB RC ...... .50 .23
❑ 199 Curt Warner IR .... .50 .23
❑ 200 Jeff West .... .10 .05
❑ 201 Charlie Young .... .10 .05
❑ 202 Passing Leaders 6.00 2.70
Dan Marino
Steve Bartkowski
❑ 203 Receiving Leaders .... .25 .11
Todd Christensen
Charlie Brown
Earnest Gray
Roy Green
❑ 204 Rushing Leaders........... .50 .23
Curt Warner
Eric Dickerson
❑ 205 Scoring Leaders .... .10 .05
Gary Anderson K
Mark Moseley
❑ 206 Interception Leaders ...... .10 .05
Vann McElroy
Ken Riley
Mark Murphy
❑ 207 Punting Leaders .... .10 .05
Rich Camarillo
Greg Coleman
❑ 208 Atlanta Falcons TL .... .25 .11
William Andrews
❑ 209 William Andrews PB ...... .25 .11
❑ 210 William Andrews IR........ .25 .11
❑ 211 Stacey Bailey RC .... .10 .05
❑ 212 Steve Bartkowski........... .50 .23
❑ 213 Steve Bartkowski IR ...... .25 .11
❑ 214 Ralph Giacomarro.......... .10 .05
❑ 215 Billy Johnson PB .... .25 .11
❑ 216 Mike Kenn PB .... .25 .11
❑ 217 Mick Luckhurst .... .10 .05
❑ 218 Gerald Riggs .... .50 .23
❑ 219 R.C. Thielemann PB ...... .10 .05
❑ 220 Jeff Van Note .... .25 .11
❑ 221 Chicago Bears TL .... .75 .35
Walter Payton
❑ 222 Jim Covert RC............... .50 .23
❑ 223 Leslie Frazier................. .10 .05
❑ 224 Willie Gault RC .... .50 .23
❑ 225 Mike Hartenstine .... .10 .05
❑ 226 Noah Jackson UER........ .10 .05
(photo actually
Jim Osborne)
❑ 227 Jim McMahon .... 1.25 .55
❑ 228 Walter Payton PB 4.00 1.80
❑ 229 Walter Payton IR.......... 1.25 .55
❑ 230 Mike Richardson RC ...... .10 .05
❑ 231 Terry Schmidt .... .10 .05
❑ 232 Mike Singletary PB ...... 1.25 .55
❑ 233 Matt Suhey .... .25 .11
❑ 234 Bob Thomas .... .10 .05
❑ 235 Dallas Cowboys TL .... .50 .23
Tony Dorsett
❑ 236 Bob Breunig .... .10 .05
❑ 237 Doug Cosbie PB .... .25 .11
❑ 238 Tony Dorsett PB .... 1.00 .45
❑ 239 Tony Dorsett IR............. .50 .23
❑ 240 John Dutton................... .10 .05
❑ 241 Tony Hill .... .25 .11
❑ 242 Ed Jones PB .... .50 .23
❑ 243 Drew Pearson .... .50 .23
❑ 244 Rafael Septien............... .10 .05
❑ 245 Ron Springs .... .25 .11
❑ 246 Dennis Thurman .... .10 .05
❑ 247 Everson Walls PB .... .10 .05
❑ 248 Danny White .... .50 .23
❑ 249 Randy White PB .... .50 .23
❑ 250 Detroit Lions TL............. .25 .11
Billy Sims
❑ 251 Jeff Chadwick RC .... .25 .11
❑ 252 Garry Cobb .... .10 .05
❑ 253 Doug English PB............ .25 .11
❑ 254 William Gay.................... .10 .05
❑ 255 Eric Hipple..................... .25 .11
❑ 256 James Jones RC............ .25 .11
❑ 257 Bruce McNorton .... .10 .05
❑ 258 Eddie Murray................. .25 .11
❑ 259 Ulysses Norris .... .10 .05
❑ 260 Billy Sims...................... .50 .23
❑ 261 Billy Sims IR .... .25 .11
❑ 262 Leonard Thompson........ .10 .05
❑ 263 Green Bay Packers TL .. .50 .23
James Lofton
❑ 264 John Anderson .... .10 .05
❑ 265 Paul Coffman PB........... .25 .11
❑ 266 Lynn Dickey................... .25 .11
❑ 267 Gerry Ellis .... .10 .05
❑ 268 John Jefferson............... .50 .23
❑ 269 John Jefferson IR .... .50 .23
❑ 270 Ezra Johnson .... .10 .05
❑ 271 Tim Lewis .... .10 .05
❑ 272 James Lofton PB........... .50 .23
❑ 273 James Lofton IR .... .50 .23
❑ 274 Larry McCarren PB .... .10 .05
❑ 275 Jan Stenerud.................. .25 .11
❑ 276 Los Angeles Rams TL.... .50 .23
Eric Dickerson
❑ 277 Mike Barber................... .10 .05
❑ 278 Jim Collins..................... .10 .05
❑ 279 Nolan Cromwell PB........ .25 .11
❑ 280 Eric Dickerson PB RC 15.00 6.75
❑ 281 Eric Dickerson IR .... 2.00 .90
❑ 282 George Farmer .... .10 .05
❑ 283 Vince Ferragamo........... .25 .11
❑ 284 Kent Hill PB................... .10 .05
❑ 285 John Misko .... .10 .05
❑ 286 Jackie Slater PB RC...... .50 .23
❑ 287 Jack Youngblood........... .25 .11
❑ 288 Minnesota Vikings TL .... .10 .05
Darrin Nelson
❑ 289 Ted Brown..................... .25 .11
❑ 290 Greg Coleman............... .10 .05
❑ 291 Steve Dils .... .10 .05
❑ 292 Tony Galbreath .... .10 .05
❑ 293 Tommy Kramer .... .25 .11
❑ 294 Doug Martin................... .10 .05
❑ 295 Darrin Nelson RC .... .25 .11
❑ 296 Benny Ricardo............... .10 .05
❑ 297 John Swain .... .10 .05
❑ 298 John Turner................... .10 .05
❑ 299 New Orleans Saints TL .. .25 .11
George Rogers
❑ 300 Morten Andersen RC .. 1.50 .70
❑ 301 Russell Erxleben .... .10 .05
❑ 302 Jeff Groth .... .10 .05
❑ 303 Rickey Jackson PB RC .50 .23
❑ 304 Johnnie Poe .... .10 .05
❑ 305 George Rogers .... .25 .11
❑ 306 Richard Todd................. .25 .11
❑ 307 Jim Wilks RC................. .10 .05
❑ 308 Dave Wilson RC .... .10 .05
❑ 309 Wayne Wilson .... .10 .05
❑ 310 New York Giants TL ...... .10 .05
Earnest Gray
❑ 311 Leon Bright .... .10 .05
❑ 312 Scott Brunner .... .10 .05
❑ 313 Rob Carpenter............... .10 .05
❑ 314 Harry Carson PB........... .25 .11
❑ 315 Earnest Gray................. .10 .05
❑ 316 Ali Haji-Sheikh PB RC .. .10 .05
❑ 317 Mark Haynes PB .... .25 .11
❑ 318 Dave Jennings .... .10 .05
❑ 319 Brian Kelley................... .10 .05
❑ 320 Phil Simms .... .75 .35
❑ 321 Lawrence Taylor PB 3.00 1.35
❑ 322 Lawrence Taylor IR...... 1.50 .70
❑ 323 Brad Van Pelt .... .10 .05
❑ 324 Butch Woolfolk .... .10 .05
❑ 325 Philadelphia Eagles TL .. .25 .11
Mike Quick
❑ 326 Harold Carmichael .... .25 .11
❑ 327 Herman Edwards .... .10 .05
❑ 328 Michael Haddix RC .... .10 .05
❑ 329 Dennis Harrison .... .10 .05
❑ 330 Ron Jaworski................. .25 .11
❑ 331 Wilbert Montgomery ...... .25 .11
❑ 332 Hubie Oliver .... .10 .05
❑ 333 Mike Quick PB RC .... .50 .23
❑ 334 Jerry Robinson .... .10 .05
❑ 335 Max Runager................. .10 .05
❑ 336 Michael Williams .... .10 .05
❑ 337 St. Louis Cardinals TL.... .25 .11
Ottis Anderson
❑ 338 Ottis Anderson .... .50 .23
❑ 339 Al(Bubba) Baker .... .25 .11
❑ 340 Carl Birdsong PB........... .10 .05
❑ 341 David Galloway.............. .10 .05
❑ 342 Roy Green PB............... .25 .11

#	Card	NRMT-MT	EXC
343	Roy Green IR	.25	.11
344	Curtis Greer RC	.10	.05
345	Neil Lomax	.25	.11
346	Doug Marsh	.10	.05
347	Stump Mitchell	.25	.11
348	Lionel Washington RC ..	.25	.11
349	San Francisco 49ers TL	.25	.11
	Dwight Clark		
350	Dwaine Board	.10	.05
351	Dwight Clark	.50	.23
352	Dwight Clark IR	.25	.11
353	Roger Craig RC !	3.00	1.35
354	Fred Dean	.25	.11
355	Fred Dean IR	.50	.23
	Marino in background		
356	Dwight Hicks PB	.25	.11
357	Ronnie Lott PB	1.00	.45
358	Joe Montana PB	10.00	4.50
359	Joe Montana IR	3.00	1.35
360	Freddie Solomon	.10	.05
361	Wendell Tyler	.10	.05
362	Ray Wersching	.10	.05
363	Eric Wright RC	.25	.11
364	Tampa Bay Bucs TL	.10	.05
	Kevin House		
365	Gerald Carter	.10	.05
366	Hugh Green PB	.25	.11
367	Kevin House	.25	.11
368	Michael Morton RC	.10	.05
369	James Owens	.10	.05
370	Booker Reese	.10	.05
371	Lee Roy Selmon PB	.50	.23
372	Jack Thompson	.25	.11
373	James Wilder	.25	.11
374	Steve Wilson	.10	.05
375	Wash. Redskins TL	.50	.23
	John Riggins		
376	Jeff Bostic PB	.10	.05
377	Charlie Brown PB	.50	.23
378	Charlie Brown IR	.25	.11
379	Dave Butz PB	.25	.11
380	Darrell Green RC	6.00	2.70
381	Russ Grimm PB RC	.50	.23
382	Joe Jacoby PB	.25	.11
383	Dexter Manley	.25	.11
384	Art Monk	1.00	.45
385	Mark Moseley	.25	.11
386	Mark Murphy PB	.10	.05
387	Mike Nelms	.10	.05
388	John Riggins	.50	.23
389	John Riggins IR	.50	.23
390	Joe Theismann PB	.50	.23
391	Joe Theismann IR	.50	.23
392	Don Warren	.25	.11
393	Joe Washington	.25	.11
394	Checklist 1-132	.20	.09
395	Checklist 133-264	.20	.09
396	Checklist 265-396	.20	.09

1984 Topps USFL

	NRMT-MT	EXC
COMP.FACT.SET (132)	350.00	160.00
COMMON CARD (1-132)	1.50	.70
SEMISTARS	2.50	1.10
UNLISTED STARS	4.00	1.80

BEWARE KELLY COUNTERFEITS

#	Card	NRMT-MT	EXC
1	Luther Bradley	1.50	.70
2	Frank Corral	1.50	.70
3	Trumaine Johnson	1.50	.70
4	Greg Landry	2.50	1.10
5	Kit Lathrop	1.50	.70
6	Kevin Long	1.50	.70
7	Tim Spencer	1.50	.70
8	Stan White	1.50	.70
9	Buddy Aydelette	1.50	.70
10	Tom Banks	1.50	.70
11	Fred Bohannon	1.50	.70
12	Joe Cribbs	4.00	1.80
13	Joey Jones	1.50	.70
14	Scott Norwood XRC	2.50	1.10
15	Jim Smith	2.50	1.10
16	Cliff Stoudt	4.00	1.80
17	Vince Evans	4.00	1.80
18	Vagas Ferguson	1.50	.70
19	John Gillen	1.50	.70
20	Kris Haines	1.50	.70
21	Glenn Hyde	1.50	.70
22	Mark Keel	1.50	.70
23	Gary Lewis	1.50	.70
24	Doug Plank	1.50	.70
25	Neil Balholm	1.50	.70
26	David Dumars	1.50	.70
27	David Martin	1.50	.70
28	Craig Penrose	1.50	.70
29	Dave Stalls	1.50	.70
30	Harry Sydney XRC	1.50	.70
31	Vincent White	1.50	.70
32	George Yarno	1.50	.70
33	Kiki DeAyala	1.50	.70
34	Sam Harrell	1.50	.70
35	Mike Hawkins	1.50	.70
36	Jim Kelly XRC !	80.00	36.00
37	Mark Rush	1.50	.70
38	Ricky Sanders XRC	6.00	2.70
39	Paul Bergmann	1.50	.70
40	Tom Dinkel	1.50	.70
41	Wyatt Henderson	1.50	.70
42	Vaughan Johnson XRC	2.50	1.10
43	Willie McClendon	1.50	.70
44	Matt Robinson	1.50	.70
45	George Achica	1.50	.70
46	Mark Adickes	1.50	.70
47	Howard Carson	1.50	.70
48	Kevin Nelson	1.50	.70
49	Jeff Partridge	1.50	.70
50	Jo Jo Townsell	2.50	1.10
51	Eddie Weaver	1.50	.70
52	Steve Young XRC !	175.00	80.00
53	Derrick Crawford	1.50	.70
54	Walter Lewis	1.50	.70
55	Phil McKinnely	1.50	.70
56	Vic Minore	1.50	.70
57	Gary Shirk	1.50	.70
58	Reggie White XRC	70.00	32.00
59	Anthony Carter XRC UER	12.00	5.50
	College stats are wrong		
60	John Corker	1.50	.70
61	David Greenwood	1.50	.70
62	Bobby Hebert XRC	4.00	1.80
63	Derek Holloway	1.50	.70
64	Ken Lacy	1.50	.70
65	Tyrone McGriff	1.50	.70
66	Ray Pinney	1.50	.70
67	Gary Barbaro	1.50	.70
68	Sam Bowers	1.50	.70
69	Clarence Collins	1.50	.70
70	Willie Harper	1.50	.70
71	Jim LeClair	1.50	.70
72	Bobby Leopold	1.50	.70
73	Brian Sipe	4.00	1.80
74	Herschel Walker XRC	20.00	9.00
75	Junior Ah You	1.50	.70
76	Marcus Dupree XRC	4.00	1.80
77	Marcus Marek	1.50	.70
78	Tim Mazzetti	1.50	.70
79	Mike Robinson	1.50	.70
80	Dan Ross	4.00	1.80
81	Mark Schellen	1.50	.70
82	Johnnie Walton	1.50	.70
83	Gordon Banks	1.50	.70
84	Fred Besana	1.50	.70
85	Dave Browning	1.50	.70
86	Eric Jordan	1.50	.70
87	Frank Manumaleuga	1.50	.70
88	Gary Plummer XRC	6.00	2.70
89	Stan Talley	1.50	.70
90	Arthur Whittington	1.50	.70
91	Terry Beeson	1.50	.70
92	Mel Gray	4.00	1.80
93	Mike Katolin	1.50	.70
94	Dewey McClain	1.50	.70
95	Sidney Thornton	1.50	.70
96	Doug Williams	4.00	1.80
97	Kelvin Bryant XRC	4.00	1.80
98	John Bunting	1.50	.70
99	Irv Eatman XRC	2.50	1.10
100	Scott Fitzkee	1.50	.70
101	Chuck Fusina	1.50	.70
102	Sean Landeta XRC	2.50	1.10
103	David Trout	1.50	.70
104	Scott Woerner	1.50	.70
105	Glenn Carano	1.50	.70
106	Ron Crosby	1.50	.70
107	Jerry Holmes	1.50	.70
108	Bruce Huther	1.50	.70
109	Mike Rozier XRC	4.00	1.80
110	Larry Swider	1.50	.70
111	Danny Buggs	1.50	.70
112	Putt Choate	1.50	.70
113	Rich Garza	1.50	.70
114	Joey Hackett	1.50	.70
115	Rick Neuheisel XRC	4.00	1.80
116	Mike St. Clair	1.50	.70
117	Gary Anderson XRC	4.00	1.80
118	Zenon Andrusyshyn	1.50	.70
119	Doug Beaudoin	1.50	.70
120	Mike Butler	1.50	.70
121	Willie Gillespie	1.50	.70
122	Fred Nordgren	1.50	.70
123	John Reaves	1.50	.70
124	Eric Truvillion	1.50	.70
125	Reggie Collier	1.50	.70
126	Mike Guess	1.50	.70
127	Mike Hohensee	1.50	.70
128	Craig James XRC	6.00	2.70
129	Eric Robinson	1.50	.70
130	Billy Taylor	1.50	.70
131	Joey Walters	1.50	.70
132	Checklist 1-132	2.50	1.10

1985 Topps

	NRMT-MT	EXC
COMPLETE SET (396)	60.00	27.00
COMP.FACT.SET (396)	75.00	34.00
COMMON CARD (1-396)	.10	.05
SEMISTARS	.25	.11
UNLISTED STARS	.50	.23
CL (394-396)	.15	.07

CONDITION SENSITIVE SET
1973-85 PRICED IN NM-MT CONDITION

#	Card	NRMT-MT	EXC
1	Mark Clayton RB	.50	.23
	Most Touchdown Receptions, Season		
2	Eric Dickerson RB	.50	.23
	Most Yards Rushing, Season		
3	Charlie Joiner RB	.50	.23
	Most Receptions,		

Career
❑ 4 Dan Marino RB UER 6.00 2.70
Most Touchdown
Passes, Season
(Dolphins misspelled
as Dophins)
❑ 5 Art Monk RB .... .50 .23
Most Receptions,
Season
❑ 6 Walter Payton RB .... 1.00 .45
Most Yards
Rushing, Career
❑ 7 NFC Championship .... .25 .11
49ers 23, Bears 0
(Matt Suhey tackled)
❑ 8 AFC Championship .... .25 .11
Dolphins 45,
Steelers 28
(Woody Bennett over)
❑ 9 Super Bowl XIX .... .25 .11
49ers 38,
Dolphins 16
(Wendell Tyler)
❑ 10 Atlanta Falcons TL .... .10 .05
Stretching For The
First Down
(Gerald Riggs)
❑ 11 William Andrews .... .25 .11
❑ 12 Stacey Bailey .... .10 .05
❑ 13 Steve Bartkowski .... .50 .23
❑ 14 Rick Bryan RC .... .10 .05
❑ 15 Alfred Jackson .... .10 .05
❑ 16 Kenny Johnson .... .10 .05
❑ 17 Mike Kenn AP .... .10 .05
❑ 18 Mike Pitts RC .... .10 .05
❑ 19 Gerald Riggs .... .25 .11
❑ 20 Sylvester Stamps .... .10 .05
❑ 21 R.C. Thielemann .... .10 .05
❑ 22 Chicago Bears TL .... .75 .35
Sweetness Sets
Record Straight
(Walter Payton)
❑ 23 Todd Bell AP RC .... .10 .05
❑ 24 Richard Dent AP RC 3.00 1.35
❑ 25 Gary Fencik .... .25 .11
❑ 26 Dave Finzer .... .10 .05
❑ 27 Leslie Frazier .... .10 .05
❑ 28 Steve Fuller .... .25 .11
❑ 29 Willie Gault .... .50 .23
❑ 30 Dan Hampton AP .... .50 .23
❑ 31 Jim McMahon .... .75 .35
❑ 32 Steve McMichael RC .... .50 .23
❑ 33 Walter Payton AP 3.00 1.35
❑ 34 Mike Singletary .... .75 .35
❑ 35 Matt Suhey .... .10 .05
❑ 36 Bob Thomas .... .10 .05
❑ 37 Dallas Cowboys TL .... .50 .23
Busting Through
The Defense
(Tony Dorsett)
❑ 38 Bill Bates RC .... 1.00 .45
❑ 39 Doug Cosbie .... .25 .11
❑ 40 Tony Dorsett .... .75 .35
❑ 41 Michael Downs .... .10 .05
❑ 42 Mike Hegman RC UER .... .10 .05
(reference to SB VIII,
should be SB XIII)
❑ 43 Tony Hill .... .25 .11
❑ 44 Gary Hogeboom RC .... .10 .05
❑ 45 Jim Jeffcoat RC .... .50 .23
❑ 46 Ed Too Tall Jones .... .50 .23
❑ 47 Mike Renfro .... .10 .05
❑ 48 Rafael Septien .... .10 .05
❑ 49 Dennis Thurman .... .10 .05
❑ 50 Everson Walls .... .25 .11
❑ 51 Danny White .... .50 .23
❑ 52 Randy White .... .50 .23
❑ 53 Detroit Lions TL .... .10 .05
Popping One Loose
(Lions' Defense)
❑ 54 Jeff Chadwick .... .10 .05
❑ 55 Mike Cofer RC .... .10 .05
❑ 56 Gary Danielson .... .10 .05
❑ 57 Keith Dorney .... .10 .05
❑ 58 Doug English .... .25 .11
❑ 59 William Gay .... .10 .05
❑ 60 Ken Jenkins .... .10 .05
❑ 61 James Jones .... .25 .11
❑ 62 Eddie Murray .... .25 .11
❑ 63 Billy Sims .... .50 .23
❑ 64 Leonard Thompson .... .10 .05
❑ 65 Bobby Watkins .... .10 .05
❑ 66 Green Bay Packers TL .... .25 .11
Spotting His
Deep Receiver
(Lynn Dickey)
❑ 67 Paul Coffman .... .10 .05
❑ 68 Lynn Dickey .... .25 .11
❑ 69 Mike Douglass .... .10 .05
❑ 70 Tom Flynn RC .... .10 .05
❑ 71 Eddie Lee Ivery .... .10 .05
❑ 72 Ezra Johnson .... .10 .05
❑ 73 Mark Lee .... .10 .05
❑ 74 Tim Lewis .... .10 .05
❑ 75 James Lofton .... .50 .23
❑ 76 Bucky Scribner .... .10 .05
❑ 77 Los Angeles Rams TL .... .50 .23
Record-Setting
Ground Attack
(Eric Dickerson)
❑ 78 Nolan Cromwell .... .25 .11
❑ 79 Eric Dickerson AP .... 1.25 .55
❑ 80 Henry Ellard RC 3.00 1.35
❑ 81 Kent Hill .... .10 .05
❑ 82 LeRoy Irvin .... .25 .11
❑ 83 Jeff Kemp RC .... .25 .11
❑ 84 Mike Lansford .... .10 .05
❑ 85 Barry Redden .... .10 .05
❑ 86 Jackie Slater .... .50 .23
❑ 87 Doug Smith RC C .... .25 .11
❑ 88 Jack Youngblood .... .25 .11
❑ 89 Minnesota Vikings TL .... .10 .05
Smothering The
Opposition
(Vikings' Defense)
❑ 90 Alfred Anderson RC .... .10 .05
❑ 91 Ted Brown .... .25 .11
❑ 92 Greg Coleman .... .10 .05
❑ 93 Tommy Hannon .... .10 .05
❑ 94 Tommy Kramer .... .25 .11
❑ 95 Leo Lewis RC .... .25 .11
❑ 96 Doug Martin .... .10 .05
❑ 97 Darrin Nelson .... .25 .11
❑ 98 Jan Stenerud AP .... .25 .11
❑ 99 Sammie White .... .25 .11
❑ 100 New Orleans Saints TL .. .10 .05
Hurdling Over
Front Line
❑ 101 Morten Andersen .... .50 .23
❑ 102 Hoby Brenner RC .... .25 .11
❑ 103 Bruce Clark .... .10 .05
❑ 104 Hokie Gajan .... .10 .05
❑ 105 Brian Hansen RC .... .10 .05
❑ 106 Rickey Jackson .... .50 .23
❑ 107 George Rogers .... .25 .11
❑ 108 Dave Wilson .... .10 .05
❑ 109 Tyrone Young .... .10 .05
❑ 110 New York Giants TL .... .10 .05
Engulfing The
Quarterback
(Giants' Defense)
❑ 111 Carl Banks RC .... .50 .23
❑ 112 Jim Burt RC .... .25 .11
❑ 113 Rob Carpenter .... .10 .05
❑ 114 Harry Carson .... .25 .11
❑ 115 Earnest Gray .... .10 .05
❑ 116 Ali Haji-Sheikh .... .10 .05
❑ 117 Mark Haynes AP .... .25 .11
❑ 118 Bobby Johnson .... .10 .05
❑ 119 Lionel Manuel RC .... .25 .11
❑ 120 Joe Morris RC .... .50 .23
❑ 121 Zeke Mowatt RC .... .25 .11
❑ 122 Jeff Rutledge RC .... .10 .05
❑ 123 Phil Simms .... .50 .23
❑ 124 Lawrence Taylor AP .... 1.50 .70
❑ 125 Philadelphia Eagles TL .. .10 .05
Finding The Wide
Open Spaces
(Wilbert Montgomery)
❑ 126 Greg Brown .... .10 .05
❑ 127 Ray Ellis .... .10 .05
❑ 128 Dennis Harrison .... .10 .05
❑ 129 Wes Hopkins RC .... .25 .11
❑ 130 Mike Horan .... .10 .05
❑ 131 Kenny Jackson RC .... .10 .05
❑ 132 Ron Jaworski .... .25 .11
❑ 133 Paul McFadden .... .10 .05
❑ 134 Wilbert Montgomery .... .25 .11
❑ 135 Mike Quick .... .50 .23
❑ 136 John Spagnola .... .10 .05
❑ 137 St.Louis Cardinals TL .... .10 .05
Exploiting The
Air Route
(Neil Lomax)
❑ 138 Ottis Anderson .... .50 .23
❑ 139 Al(Bubba) Baker .... .25 .11
❑ 140 Roy Green .... .25 .11
❑ 141 Curtis Greer .... .10 .05
❑ 142 E.J. Junior AP .... .10 .05
❑ 143 Neil Lomax .... .25 .11
❑ 144 Stump Mitchell .... .25 .11
❑ 145 Neil O'Donoghue .... .10 .05
❑ 146 Pat Tilley .... .10 .05
❑ 147 Lionel Washington .... .10 .05
❑ 148 San Francisco 49ers TL 1.25 .55
The Road To
Super Bowl XIX
(Joe Montana)
❑ 149 Dwaine Board .... .10 .05
❑ 150 Dwight Clark .... .50 .23
❑ 151 Roger Craig .... 1.00 .45
❑ 152 Randy Cross AP .... .25 .11
❑ 153 Fred Dean .... .25 .11
❑ 154 Keith Fahnhorst RC .... .10 .05
❑ 155 Dwight Hicks .... .10 .05
❑ 156 Ronnie Lott .... .50 .23
❑ 157 Joe Montana 10.00 4.50
❑ 158 Renaldo Nehemiah .... .25 .11
❑ 159 Fred Quillan .... .10 .05
❑ 160 Jack Reynolds .... .10 .05
❑ 161 Freddie Solomon .... .10 .05
❑ 162 Keena Turner RC .... .10 .05
❑ 163 Wendell Tyler .... .10 .05
❑ 164 Ray Wersching .... .10 .05
❑ 165 Carlton Williamson .... .10 .05
❑ 166 Tampa Bay Bucs TL .... .25 .11
Protecting The
Quarterback
(Steve DeBerg)
❑ 167 Gerald Carter .... .10 .05
❑ 168 Mark Cotney .... .10 .05
❑ 169 Steve DeBerg .... .50 .23
❑ 170 Sean Farrell RC .... .10 .05
❑ 171 Hugh Green .... .25 .11
❑ 172 Kevin House .... .25 .11
❑ 173 David Logan .... .10 .05
❑ 174 Michael Morton .... .10 .05
❑ 175 Lee Roy Selmon .... .50 .23
❑ 176 James Wilder .... .10 .05
❑ 177 Wash. Redskins TL .... .50 .23
Diesel Named Desire
(John Riggins)
❑ 178 Charlie Brown .... .10 .05
❑ 179 Monte Coleman RC .... .25 .11
❑ 180 Vernon Dean .... .10 .05
❑ 181 Darrell Green .... .50 .23
❑ 182 Russ Grimm .... .25 .11
❑ 183 Joe Jacoby .... .25 .11
❑ 184 Dexter Manley .... .25 .11
❑ 185 Art Monk AP .... .50 .23
❑ 186 Mark Moseley .... .25 .11
❑ 187 Calvin Muhammad .... .10 .05
❑ 188 Mike Nelms .... .10 .05
❑ 189 John Riggins .... .50 .23
❑ 190 Joe Theismann .... .50 .23
❑ 191 Joe Washington .... .25 .11
❑ 192 Passing Leaders 10.00 4.50
Dan Marino
Joe Montana
❑ 193 Receiving Leaders .... .25 .11
Ozzie Newsome
Art Monk
❑ 194 Rushing Leaders .... .50 .23
Earnest Jackson
Eric Dickerson
❑ 195 Scoring Leaders .... .10 .05
Gary Anderson K
Ray Wersching

❑ 196 Interception Leaders .10 .05
Kenny Easley
Tom Flynn
❑ 197 Punting Leaders .10 .05
Jim Arnold
Brian Hansen
❑ 198 Buffalo Bills TL .10 .05
Rushing Toward
Rookie Stardom
(Greg Bell)
❑ 199 Greg Bell RC .25 .11
❑ 200 Preston Dennard .10 .05
❑ 201 Joe Ferguson .25 .11
❑ 202 Byron Franklin .10 .05
❑ 203 Steve Freeman .10 .05
❑ 204 Jim Haslett .10 .05
❑ 205 Charles Romes .10 .05
❑ 206 Fred Smerlas .10 .05
❑ 207 Darryl Talley RC .50 .23
❑ 208 Van Williams .10 .05
❑ 209 Cincinnati Bengals TL .25 .11
Advancing The
Ball Downfield
(Ken Anderson and
Larry Kinnebrew)
❑ 210 Ken Anderson .50 .23
❑ 211 Jim Breech .10 .05
❑ 212 Louis Breeden .10 .05
❑ 213 James Brooks .25 .11
❑ 214 Ross Browner .25 .11
❑ 215 Eddie Edwards .10 .05
❑ 216 M.L. Harris .10 .05
❑ 217 Bobby Kemp .10 .05
❑ 218 Larry Kinnebrew RC .10 .05
❑ 219 Anthony Munoz AP .50 .23
❑ 220 Reggie Williams .25 .11
❑ 221 Cleveland Browns TL .10 .05
Evading The
Defensive Pursuit
(Boyce Green)
❑ 222 Matt Bahr .25 .11
❑ 223 Chip Banks .10 .05
❑ 224 Reggie Camp .10 .05
❑ 225 Tom Cousineau .10 .05
❑ 226 Joe DeLamielleure .10 .05
❑ 227 Ricky Feacher .10 .05
❑ 228 Boyce Green RC .10 .05
❑ 229 Al Gross .10 .05
❑ 230 Clay Matthews .50 .23
❑ 231 Paul McDonald .10 .05
❑ 232 Ozzie Newsome AP .50 .23
❑ 233 Mike Pruitt .25 .11
❑ 234 Don Rogers .10 .05
❑ 235 Denver Broncos TL 2.50 1.10
Thousand Yarder
Gets The Ball
(Sammy Winder and
John Elway)
❑ 236 Rubin Carter .10 .05
❑ 237 Barney Chavous .10 .05
❑ 238 John Elway 15.00 6.75
❑ 239 Steve Foley .10 .05
❑ 240 Mike Harden RC .10 .05
❑ 241 Tom Jackson .50 .23
❑ 242 Butch Johnson .10 .05
❑ 243 Rulon Jones .10 .05
❑ 244 Rich Karlis .10 .05
❑ 245 Steve Watson .25 .11
❑ 246 Gerald Willhite .10 .05
❑ 247 Sammy Winder .25 .11
❑ 248 Houston Oilers TL .10 .05
Eluding A
Traffic Jam
(Larry Moriarty)
❑ 249 Jesse Baker .10 .05
❑ 250 Carter Hartwig .10 .05
❑ 251 Warren Moon RC**/C 15.00 6.75
❑ 252 Larry Moriarty RC .10 .05
❑ 253 Mike Munchak RC .50 .23
❑ 254 Carl Roaches .10 .05
❑ 255 Tim Smith .25 .11
❑ 256 Willie Tullis .10 .05
❑ 257 Jamie Williams RC .10 .05
❑ 258 Indianapolis Colts TL .10 .05
Start Of A
Long Gainer
(Art Schlichter)
❑ 259 Raymond Butler .10 .05
❑ 260 Johnie Cooks .10 .05
❑ 261 Eugene Daniel .10 .05
❑ 262 Curtis Dickey .25 .11
❑ 263 Chris Hinton .25 .11
❑ 264 Vernon Maxwell .10 .05
❑ 265 Randy McMillan .10 .05
❑ 266 Art Schlichter RC .25 .11
❑ 267 Rohn Stark .25 .11
❑ 268 Leo Wisniewski .10 .05
❑ 269 Kansas City Chiefs TL .10 .05
Pigskin About To
Soar Upward
(Bill Kenney)
❑ 270 Jim Arnold .10 .05
❑ 271 Mike Bell .10 .05
❑ 272 Todd Blackledge RC .25 .11
❑ 273 Carlos Carson .25 .11
❑ 274 Deron Cherry .25 .11
❑ 275 Herman Heard RC .10 .05
❑ 276 Bill Kenney .25 .11
❑ 277 Nick Lowery .50 .23
❑ 278 Bill Maas RC .10 .05
❑ 279 Henry Marshall .10 .05
❑ 280 Art Still .10 .05
❑ 281 Los Angeles Raiders TL .50 .23
Diving For The
Goal Line
(Marcus Allen)
❑ 282 Marcus Allen 2.50 1.10
❑ 283 Lyle Alzado .25 .11
❑ 284 Chris Bahr .10 .05
❑ 285 Malcolm Barnwell .10 .05
❑ 286 Cliff Branch .50 .23
❑ 287 Todd Christensen .50 .23
❑ 288 Ray Guy .50 .23
❑ 289 Lester Hayes .25 .11
❑ 290 Mike Haynes AP .25 .11
❑ 291 Henry Lawrence .10 .05
❑ 292 Howie Long 2.00 .90
❑ 293 Rod Martin AP .25 .11
❑ 294 Vann McElroy .10 .05
❑ 295 Matt Millen .25 .11
❑ 296 Bill Pickel RC .10 .05
❑ 297 Jim Plunkett .50 .23
❑ 298 Dokie Williams RC .10 .05
❑ 299 Marc Wilson .25 .11
❑ 300 Miami Dolphins TL .25 .11
Super Duper
Performance
(Mark Duper)
❑ 301 Bob Baumhower .10 .05
❑ 302 Doug Betters .10 .05
❑ 303 Glenn Blackwood .25 .11
❑ 304 Lyle Blackwood .25 .11
❑ 305 Kim Bokamper .10 .05
❑ 306 Charles Bowser .10 .05
❑ 307 Jimmy Cefalo .10 .05
❑ 308 Mark Clayton AP RC .75 .35
❑ 309 A.J. Duhe .10 .05
❑ 310 Mark Duper .50 .23
❑ 311 Andra Franklin .10 .05
❑ 312 Bruce Hardy .10 .05
❑ 313 Pete Johnson .25 .11
❑ 314 Dan Marino AP UER 15.00 6.75
(Fouts 4802 yards in
1981, should be 4082)
❑ 315 Tony Nathan .25 .11
❑ 316 Ed Newman .10 .05
❑ 317 Reggie Roby AP .50 .23
❑ 318 Dwight Stephenson AP .25 .11
❑ 319 Uwe Von Schamann .10 .05
❑ 320 New England Pats TL .10 .05
Refusing To
Be Denied
(Tony Collins)
❑ 321 Raymond Clayborn .25 .11
❑ 322 Tony Collins .25 .11
❑ 323 Tony Eason RC .50 .23
❑ 324 Tony Franklin .10 .05
❑ 325 Irving Fryar RC 5.00 2.20
❑ 326 John Hannah AP .50 .23
❑ 327 Brian Holloway .10 .05
❑ 328 Craig James RC* .75 .35
❑ 329 Stanley Morgan .25 .11
❑ 330 Steve Nelson AP .10 .05
❑ 331 Derrick Ramsey .10 .05
❑ 332 Stephen Starring .25 .11
❑ 333 Mosi Tatupu .10 .05
❑ 334 Andre Tippett .50 .23
❑ 335 New York Jets TL .25 .11
Thwarting The
Passing Game
(Mark Gastineau
and Joe Ferguson)
❑ 336 Russell Carter RC .10 .05
❑ 337 Mark Gastineau AP .25 .11
❑ 338 Bruce Harper .10 .05
❑ 339 Bobby Humphery RC .10 .05
❑ 340 Johnny Lam Jones .10 .05
❑ 341 Joe Klecko .25 .11
❑ 342 Pat Leahy .10 .05
❑ 343 Marty Lyons .25 .11
❑ 344 Freeman McNeil .25 .11
❑ 345 Lance Mehl .10 .05
❑ 346 Ken O'Brien RC .50 .23
❑ 347 Marvin Powell .10 .05
❑ 348 Pat Ryan .10 .05
❑ 349 Mickey Shuler RC .10 .05
❑ 350 Wesley Walker .25 .11
❑ 351 Pittsburgh Steelers TL .25 .11
Testing Defensive
Pass Coverage
(Mark Malone)
❑ 352 Walter Abercrombie .10 .05
❑ 353 Gary Anderson K .25 .11
❑ 354 Robin Cole .10 .05
❑ 355 Bennie Cunningham .10 .05
❑ 356 Rich Erenberg .10 .05
❑ 357 Jack Lambert .50 .23
❑ 358 Louis Lipps RC .50 .23
❑ 359 Mark Malone .25 .11
❑ 360 Mike Merriweather RC .10 .05
❑ 361 Frank Pollard .10 .05
❑ 362 Donnie Shell .25 .11
❑ 363 John Stallworth .50 .23
❑ 364 Sam Washington .10 .05
❑ 365 Mike Webster .25 .11
❑ 366 Dwayne Woodruff .10 .05
❑ 367 San Diego Chargers TL .10 .05
Jarring The
Ball Loose
(Chargers' Defense)
❑ 368 Rolf Benirschke .10 .05
❑ 369 Gill Byrd RC .50 .23
❑ 370 Wes Chandler .25 .11
❑ 371 Bobby Duckworth .10 .05
❑ 372 Dan Fouts .50 .23
❑ 373 Mike Green .10 .05
❑ 374 Pete Holohan RC .10 .05
❑ 375 Earnest Jackson RC .25 .11
❑ 376 Lionel James RC .25 .11
❑ 377 Charlie Joiner .50 .23
❑ 378 Billy Ray Smith .25 .11
❑ 379 Kellen Winslow .50 .23
❑ 380 Seattle Seahawks TL .25 .11
Setting Up For
The Air Attack
(Dave Krieg)
❑ 381 Dave Brown .10 .05
❑ 382 Jeff Bryant .10 .05
❑ 383 Dan Doornink .10 .05
❑ 384 Kenny Easley AP .25 .11
❑ 385 Jacob Green .25 .11
❑ 386 David Hughes .10 .05
❑ 387 Norm Johnson .10 .05
❑ 388 Dave Krieg .50 .23
❑ 389 Steve Largent 1.00 .45
❑ 390 Joe Nash RC .10 .05
❑ 391 Daryl Turner RC .10 .05
❑ 392 Curt Warner .50 .23
❑ 393 Fredd Young RC .25 .11
❑ 394 Checklist 1-132 .15 .07
❑ 395 Checklist 133-264 .15 .07
❑ 396 Checklist 265-396 .15 .07

1985 Topps USFL

	NRMT-MT	EXC
COMP.FACT.SET (132)	135.00	60.00
COMMON CARD (1-132)	.50	.23

Card	MINT	NRMT
SEMISTARS	1.00	.45
UNLISTED STARS	2.00	.90
❑ 1 Case DeBruijn	.50	.23
❑ 2 Mike Katolin	.50	.23
❑ 3 Bruce Laird	.50	.23
❑ 4 Kit Lathrop	.50	.23
❑ 5 Kevin Long	.50	.23
❑ 6 Karl Lorch	.50	.23
❑ 7 Dave Tipton	.50	.23
❑ 8 Doug Williams	2.00	.90
❑ 9 Luis Zendejas XRC	.50	.23
❑ 10 Kelvin Bryant	1.00	.45
❑ 11 Willie Collier	.50	.23
❑ 12 Irv Eatman	.50	.23
❑ 13 Scott Fitzkee	.50	.23
❑ 14 William Fuller XRC	4.00	1.80
❑ 15 Chuck Fusina	.50	.23
❑ 16 Pete Kugler	.50	.23
❑ 17 Garcia Lane	.50	.23
❑ 18 Mike Lush	.50	.23
❑ 19 Sam Mills XRC	5.00	2.20
❑ 20 Buddy Aydelette	.50	.23
❑ 21 Joe Cribbs	2.00	.90
❑ 22 David Dumars	.50	.23
❑ 23 Robin Earl	.50	.23
❑ 24 Joey Jones	.50	.23
❑ 25 Leon Perry	.50	.23
❑ 26 Dave Pureifory	.50	.23
❑ 27 Bill Roe	.50	.23
❑ 28 Doug Smith XRC ! DT	2.00	.90
❑ 29 Cliff Stoudt	1.00	.45
❑ 30 Jeff Delaney	.50	.23
❑ 31 Vince Evans	1.00	.45
❑ 32 Leonard Harris XRC	.50	.23
❑ 33 Bill Johnson	.50	.23
❑ 34 Marc Lewis	.50	.23
❑ 35 David Martin	.50	.23
❑ 36 Bruce Thornton	.50	.23
❑ 37 Craig Walls	.50	.23
❑ 38 Vincent White	.50	.23
❑ 39 Luther Bradley	.50	.23
❑ 40 Pete Catan	.50	.23
❑ 41 Kiki DeAyala	.50	.23
❑ 42 Toni Fritsch	.50	.23
❑ 43 Sam Harrell	.50	.23
❑ 44 Richard Johnson XRC	1.00	.45
❑ 45 Jim Kelly	20.00	9.00
❑ 46 Gerald McNeil XRC	.50	.23
❑ 47 Clarence Verdin XRC	2.00	.90
❑ 48 Dale Walters	.50	.23
❑ 49 Gary Clark XRC	10.00	4.50
❑ 50 Tom Dinkel	.50	.23
❑ 51 Mike Edwards	.50	.23
❑ 52 Brian Franco	.50	.23
❑ 53 Bob Gruber	.50	.23
❑ 54 Robbie Mahfouz	.50	.23
❑ 55 Mike Rozier	1.00	.45
❑ 56 Brian Sipe	1.00	.45
❑ 57 J.T. Turner	.50	.23
❑ 58 Howard Carson	.50	.23
❑ 59 Wymon Henderson XRC	.50	.23
❑ 60 Kevin Nelson	.50	.23
❑ 61 Jeff Partridge	.50	.23
❑ 62 Ben Rudolph	.50	.23
❑ 63 Jo Jo Townsell	1.00	.45
❑ 64 Eddie Weaver	.50	.23
❑ 65 Steve Young	60.00	27.00
❑ 66 Tony Zendejas XRC	1.00	.45
❑ 67 Mossy Cade	.50	.23
❑ 68 Leonard Coleman XRC	.50	.23
❑ 69 John Corker	.50	.23
❑ 70 Derrick Crawford	.50	.23
❑ 71 Art Kuehn	.50	.23
❑ 72 Walter Lewis	.50	.23
❑ 73 Tyrone McGriff	.50	.23
❑ 74 Tim Spencer	1.00	.45
❑ 75 Reggie White	20.00	9.00
❑ 76 Gizmo Williams XRC	2.00	.90
❑ 77 Sam Bowers	.50	.23
❑ 78 Maurice Carthon XRC	1.00	.45
❑ 79 Clarence Collins	.50	.23
❑ 80 Doug Flutie XRC	70.00	32.00
❑ 81 Freddie Gilbert	.50	.23
❑ 82 Kerry Justin	.50	.23
❑ 83 Dave Lapham	.50	.23
❑ 84 Rick Partridge	.50	.23
❑ 85 Roger Ruzek XRC	1.00	.45
❑ 86 Herschel Walker	10.00	4.50
❑ 87 Gordon Banks	.50	.23
❑ 88 Monte Bennett	.50	.23
❑ 89 Albert Bentley XRC	1.00	.45
❑ 90 Novo Bojovic	.50	.23
❑ 91 Dave Browning	.50	.23
❑ 92 Anthony Carter	2.00	.90
❑ 93 Bobby Hebert	2.00	.90
❑ 94 Ray Pinney	.50	.23
❑ 95 Stan Talley	.50	.23
❑ 96 Ruben Vaughan	.50	.23
❑ 97 Curtis Bledsoe	.50	.23
❑ 98 Reggie Collier	.50	.23
❑ 99 Jerry Doerger	.50	.23
❑ 100 Jerry Golsteyn	.50	.23
❑ 101 Bob Niziolek	.50	.23
❑ 102 Joel Patten	.50	.23
❑ 103 Ricky Simmons	.50	.23
❑ 104 Joey Walters	.50	.23
❑ 105 Marcus Dupree	1.00	.45
❑ 106 Jeff Gossett	1.00	.45
❑ 107 Frank Lockett	.50	.23
❑ 108 Marcus Marek	.50	.23
❑ 109 Kenny Neil	.50	.23
❑ 110 Robert Pennywell	.50	.23
❑ 111 Matt Robinson	.50	.23
❑ 112 Dan Ross	1.00	.45
❑ 113 Doug Woodward	.50	.23
❑ 114 Danny Buggs	.50	.23
❑ 115 Putt Choate	.50	.23
❑ 116 Greg Fields	.50	.23
❑ 117 Ken Hartley	.50	.23
❑ 118 Nick Mike-Mayer	.50	.23
❑ 119 Rick Neuheisel	2.00	.90
❑ 120 Peter Raeford	.50	.23
❑ 121 Gary Worthy	.50	.23
❑ 122 Gary Anderson RB	1.00	.45
❑ 123 Zenon Andrusyshyn	.50	.23
❑ 124 Greg Boone	.50	.23
❑ 125 Mike Butler	.50	.23
❑ 126 Mike Clark	.50	.23
❑ 127 Willie Gillespie	.50	.23
❑ 128 James Harrell	.50	.23
❑ 129 Marvin Harvey	.50	.23
❑ 130 John Reaves	1.00	.45
❑ 131 Eric Truvillion	.50	.23
❑ 132 Checklist 1-132	1.00	.45

1986 Topps

	MINT	NRMT
COMPLETE SET (396)	150.00	70.00
COMP.FACT.SET (396)	200.00	90.00
COMMON CARD (1-396)	.10	.05
SEMISTARS	.25	.11
UNLISTED STARS	.50	.23
CL (394-396)	.12	.05
COMP.1000 YARD SET	6.00	2.70
1000 YARD: ONE PER PACK		
❑ 1 Marcus Allen RB Most Yards From Scrimmage, Season	.75	.35
❑ 2 Eric Dickerson RB Most Yards Rushing, Playoff Game	.50	.23

Card	MINT	NRMT
❑ 3 Lionel James RB Most All-Purpose Yards, Season	.10	.05
❑ 4 Steve Largent RB Most Seasons, 50 or More Receptions	.50	.23
❑ 5 George Martin RB Most Touchdowns, Def. Lineman, Career	.10	.05
❑ 6 Stephone Paige RB Most Yards Receiving, Game	.10	.05
❑ 7 Walter Payton RB Most Consecutive Games, 100 or More Yards Rushing	.75	.35
❑ 8 Super Bowl XX Bears 46, Patriots 10 (Jim McMahon handing off)	.25	.11
❑ 9 Bears TL (Walter Payton in Motion)	.60	.25
❑ 10 Jim McMahon	.50	.23
❑ 11 Walter Payton AP	2.50	1.10
❑ 12 Matt Suhey	.10	.05
❑ 13 Willie Gault	.25	.11
❑ 14 Dennis McKinnon RC	.10	.05
❑ 15 Emery Moorehead	.10	.05
❑ 16 Jim Covert AP	.25	.11
❑ 17 Jay Hilgenberg AP RC	.50	.23
❑ 18 Kevin Butler RC	.25	.11
❑ 19 Richard Dent AP	.75	.35
❑ 20 William Perry RC	.50	.23
❑ 21 Steve McMichael	.50	.23
❑ 22 Dan Hampton	.50	.23
❑ 23 Otis Wilson	.10	.05
❑ 24 Mike Singletary	.60	.25
❑ 25 Wilber Marshall RC	.50	.23
❑ 26 Leslie Frazier	.10	.05
❑ 27 Dave Duerson RC	.10	.05
❑ 28 Gary Fencik	.10	.05
❑ 29 Patriots TL (Craig James on the Run)	.50	.23
❑ 30 Tony Eason	.10	.05
❑ 31 Steve Grogan	.25	.11
❑ 32 Craig James	.50	.23
❑ 33 Tony Collins	.10	.05
❑ 34 Irving Fryar	1.25	.55
❑ 35 Brian Holloway AP	.10	.05
❑ 36 John Hannah AP	.50	.23
❑ 37 Tony Franklin	.10	.05
❑ 38 Garin Veris RC	.10	.05
❑ 39 Andre Tippett AP	.25	.11
❑ 40 Steve Nelson	.10	.05
❑ 41 Raymond Clayborn	.10	.05
❑ 42 Fred Marion RC	.10	.05
❑ 43 Rich Camarillo	.10	.05
❑ 44 Dolphins TL (Dan Marino Sets Up)	2.00	.90
❑ 45 Dan Marino AP	10.00	4.50
❑ 46 Tony Nathan	.25	.11
❑ 47 Ron Davenport RC	.10	.05
❑ 48 Mark Duper	.50	.23
❑ 49 Mark Clayton	.50	.23
❑ 50 Nat Moore	.25	.11
❑ 51 Bruce Hardy	.10	.05
❑ 52 Roy Foster	.10	.05
❑ 53 Dwight Stephenson	.25	.11

❑ 54 Fuad Reveiz RC .25 .11
❑ 55 Bob Baumhower .10 .05
❑ 56 Mike Charles .10 .05
❑ 57 Hugh Green .25 .11
❑ 58 Glenn Blackwood .10 .05
❑ 59 Reggie Roby .25 .11
❑ 60 Raiders TL .50 .23
(Marcus Allen Cuts Upfield)
❑ 61 Marc Wilson .10 .05
❑ 62 Marcus Allen AP 1.50 .70
❑ 63 Dokie Williams .10 .05
❑ 64 Todd Christensen .50 .23
❑ 65 Chris Bahr .10 .05
❑ 66 Fulton Walker .10 .05
❑ 67 Howie Long 1.25 .55
❑ 68 Bill Pickel .10 .05
❑ 69 Ray Guy .50 .23
❑ 70 Greg Townsend RC .50 .23
❑ 71 Rod Martin .25 .11
❑ 72 Matt Millen .25 .11
❑ 73 Mike Haynes AP .25 .11
❑ 74 Lester Hayes .25 .11
❑ 75 Vann McElroy .10 .05
❑ 76 Rams TL .50 .23
(Eric Dickerson Stiff-Arm)
❑ 77 Dieter Brock RC**/C .25 .11
❑ 78 Eric Dickerson .75 .35
❑ 79 Henry Ellard 1.00 .45
❑ 80 Ron Brown RC .25 .11
❑ 81 Tony Hunter RC .10 .05
❑ 82 Kent Hill AP .10 .05
❑ 83 Doug Smith .10 .05
❑ 84 Dennis Harrah .10 .05
❑ 85 Jackie Slater .50 .23
❑ 86 Mike Lansford .10 .05
❑ 87 Gary Jeter .10 .05
❑ 88 Mike Wilcher .10 .05
❑ 89 Jim Collins .10 .05
❑ 90 LeRoy Irvin .25 .11
❑ 91 Gary Green .10 .05
❑ 92 Nolan Cromwell .25 .11
❑ 93 Dale Hatcher RC .10 .05
❑ 94 Jets TL .25 .11
(Freeman McNeil Powers)
❑ 95 Ken O'Brien .50 .23
❑ 96 Freeman McNeil .25 .11
❑ 97 Tony Paige RC .10 .05
❑ 98 Johnny Lam Jones .10 .05
❑ 99 Wesley Walker .25 .11
❑ 100 Kurt Sohn .10 .05
❑ 101 Al Toon RC .50 .23
❑ 102 Mickey Shuler .10 .05
❑ 103 Marvin Powell .10 .05
❑ 104 Pat Leahy .10 .05
❑ 105 Mark Gastineau .25 .11
❑ 106 Joe Klecko AP .25 .11
❑ 107 Marty Lyons .10 .05
❑ 108 Lance Mehl .10 .05
❑ 109 Bobby Jackson .10 .05
❑ 110 Dave Jennings .10 .05
❑ 111 Broncos TL .25 .11
(Sammy Winder Up Middle)
❑ 112 John Elway 10.00 4.50
❑ 113 Sammy Winder .25 .11
❑ 114 Gerald Willhite .10 .05
❑ 115 Steve Watson .10 .05
❑ 116 Vance Johnson RC .50 .23
❑ 117 Rich Karlis .10 .05
❑ 118 Rulon Jones .10 .05
❑ 119 Karl Mecklenburg AP RC .50 .23
❑ 120 Louis Wright .10 .05
❑ 121 Mike Harden .10 .05
❑ 122 Dennis Smith RC .50 .23
❑ 123 Steve Foley .10 .05
❑ 124 Cowboys TL .25 .11
(Tony Hill Evades Defender)
❑ 125 Danny White .50 .23
❑ 126 Tony Dorsett .60 .25
❑ 127 Timmy Newsome .10 .05
❑ 128 Mike Renfro .10 .05
❑ 129 Tony Hill .25 .11
❑ 130 Doug Cosbie AP .25 .11
❑ 131 Rafael Septien .10 .05
❑ 132 Ed Too Tall Jones .50 .23
❑ 133 Randy White .50 .23
❑ 134 Jim Jeffcoat .50 .23
❑ 135 Everson Walls AP .25 .11
❑ 136 Dennis Thurman .10 .05
❑ 137 Giants TL .25 .11
(Joe Morris Opening)
❑ 138 Phil Simms .50 .23
❑ 139 Joe Morris .50 .23
❑ 140 George Adams RC .10 .05
❑ 141 Lionel Manuel .25 .11
❑ 142 Bobby Johnson .10 .05
❑ 143 Phil McConkey RC .25 .11
❑ 144 Mark Bavaro RC .50 .23
❑ 145 Zeke Mowatt .10 .05
❑ 146 Brad Benson RC .10 .05
❑ 147 Bart Oates RC .25 .11
❑ 148 Leonard Marshall AP RC .50 .23
❑ 149 Jim Burt .25 .11
❑ 150 George Martin .10 .05
❑ 151 Lawrence Taylor AP 1.25 .55
❑ 152 Harry Carson AP .25 .11
❑ 153 Elvis Patterson RC .10 .05
❑ 154 Sean Landeta RC* .25 .11
❑ 155 49ers TL .50 .23
(Roger Craig Scampers)
❑ 156 Joe Montana 8.00 3.60
❑ 157 Roger Craig .50 .23
❑ 158 Wendell Tyler .10 .05
❑ 159 Carl Monroe .10 .05
❑ 160 Dwight Clark .25 .11
❑ 161 Jerry Rice RC ! 100.00 45.00
❑ 162 Randy Cross .25 .11
❑ 163 Keith Fahnhorst .10 .05
❑ 164 Jeff Stover .10 .05
❑ 165 Michael Carter RC .10 .05
❑ 166 Dwaine Board .10 .05
❑ 167 Eric Wright .25 .11
❑ 168 Ronnie Lott .75 .35
❑ 169 Carlton Williamson .10 .05
❑ 170 Redskins TL .25 .11
(Dave Butz Gets His Man)
❑ 171 Joe Theismann .50 .23
❑ 172 Jay Schroeder RC .50 .23
❑ 173 George Rogers .25 .11
❑ 174 Ken Jenkins .10 .05
❑ 175 Art Monk AP .50 .23
❑ 176 Gary Clark RC* 2.00 .90
❑ 177 Joe Jacoby .25 .11
❑ 178 Russ Grimm .25 .11
❑ 179 Mark Moseley .10 .05
❑ 180 Dexter Manley .25 .11
❑ 181 Charles Mann RC .50 .23
❑ 182 Vernon Dean .10 .05
❑ 183 Raphel Cherry RC .10 .05
❑ 184 Curtis Jordan .10 .05
❑ 185 Browns TL .50 .23
(Bernie Kosar Fakes Handoff)
❑ 186 Gary Danielson .25 .11
❑ 187 Bernie Kosar RC 3.00 1.35
❑ 188 Kevin Mack RC .50 .23
❑ 189 Earnest Byner RC .75 .35
❑ 190 Glen Young .10 .05
❑ 191 Ozzie Newsome .50 .23
❑ 192 Mike Baab .10 .05
❑ 193 Cody Risien .25 .11
❑ 194 Bob Golic .25 .11
❑ 195 Reggie Camp .10 .05
❑ 196 Chip Banks .25 .11
❑ 197 Tom Cousineau .10 .05
❑ 198 Frank Minnifield RC .10 .05
❑ 199 Al Gross .10 .05
❑ 200 Seahawks TL .25 .11
(Curt Warner Breaks Free)
❑ 201 Dave Krieg .50 .23
❑ 202 Curt Warner .25 .11
❑ 203 Steve Largent AP .60 .25
❑ 204 Norm Johnson .10 .05
❑ 205 Daryl Turner .10 .05
❑ 206 Jacob Green .10 .05
❑ 207 Joe Nash .10 .05
❑ 208 Jeff Bryant .10 .05
❑ 209 Randy Edwards .10 .05
❑ 210 Fredd Young .10 .05
❑ 211 Kenny Easley .10 .05
❑ 212 John Harris .10 .05
❑ 213 Packers TL .10 .05
(Paul Coffman Conquers)
❑ 214 Lynn Dickey .25 .11
❑ 215 Gerry Ellis .10 .05
❑ 216 Eddie Lee Ivery .10 .05
❑ 217 Jessie Clark .10 .05
❑ 218 James Lofton .50 .23
❑ 219 Paul Coffman .10 .05
❑ 220 Alphonso Carreker .10 .05
❑ 221 Ezra Johnson .10 .05
❑ 222 Mike Douglass .10 .05
❑ 223 Tim Lewis .10 .05
❑ 224 Mark Murphy RC .10 .05
❑ 225 Passing Leaders: 1.00 .45
Ken O'Brien AFC
Joe Montana NFC
❑ 226 Receiving Leaders: .25 .11
Lionel James AFC
Roger Craig NFC
❑ 227 Rushing Leaders: .50 .23
Marcus Allen AFC
Gerald Riggs NFC
❑ 228 Scoring Leaders: .25 .11
Gary Anderson K AFC
Kevin Butler NFC
❑ 229 Interception Leaders: .10 .05
Eugene Daniel AFC
Albert Lewis AFC
Everson Walls NFC
❑ 230 Chargers TL .50 .23
(Dan Fouts Over Top)
❑ 231 Dan Fouts .50 .23
❑ 232 Lionel James .10 .05
❑ 233 Gary Anderson RB RC .50 .23
❑ 234 Tim Spencer RC* .25 .11
❑ 235 Wes Chandler .25 .11
❑ 236 Charlie Joiner .50 .23
❑ 237 Kellen Winslow .50 .23
❑ 238 Jim Lachey RC .50 .23
❑ 239 Bob Thomas .10 .05
❑ 240 Jeffery Dale .10 .05
❑ 241 Ralf Mojsiejenko .10 .05
❑ 242 Lions TL .10 .05
(Eric Hipple Spots Receiver)
❑ 243 Eric Hipple .10 .05
❑ 244 Billy Sims .25 .11
❑ 245 James Jones .10 .05
❑ 246 Pete Mandley RC .10 .05
❑ 247 Leonard Thompson .10 .05
❑ 248 Lomas Brown RC .25 .11
❑ 249 Eddie Murray .25 .11
❑ 250 Curtis Green .10 .05
❑ 251 William Gay .10 .05
❑ 252 Jimmy Williams .10 .05
❑ 253 Bobby Watkins .10 .05
❑ 254 Bengals TL .50 .23
(Boomer Esiason Zeroes In)
❑ 255 Boomer Esiason RC 6.00 2.70
❑ 256 James Brooks .25 .11
❑ 257 Larry Kinnebrew .10 .05
❑ 258 Cris Collinsworth .25 .11
❑ 259 Mike Martin .10 .05
❑ 260 Eddie Brown RC .50 .23
❑ 261 Anthony Munoz .50 .23
❑ 262 Jim Breech .10 .05
❑ 263 Ross Browner .25 .11
❑ 264 Carl Zander .10 .05
❑ 265 James Griffin .10 .05
❑ 266 Robert Jackson .10 .05
❑ 267 Pat McInally .10 .05
❑ 268 Eagles TL .50 .23
(Ron Jaworski Surveys)
❑ 269 Ron Jaworski .25 .11
❑ 270 Earnest Jackson .25 .11
❑ 271 Mike Quick .25 .11
❑ 272 John Spagnola .10 .05
❑ 273 Mark Dennard .10 .05
❑ 274 Paul McFadden .10 .05
❑ 275 Reggie White RC* 10.00 4.50
❑ 276 Greg Brown .10 .05
❑ 277 Herman Edwards .10 .05
❑ 278 Roynell Young .10 .05
❑ 279 Wes Hopkins AP .10 .05
❑ 280 Steelers TL .25 .11
(Walter Abercrombie Inches)
❑ 281 Mark Malone .25 .11
❑ 282 Frank Pollard .10 .05
❑ 283 Walter Abercrombie .10 .05
❑ 284 Louis Lipps .50 .23

No.	Player	Mint	NrMt
285	John Stallworth	.50	.23
286	Mike Webster	.25	.11
287	Gary Anderson K AP	.25	.11
288	Keith Willis	.10	.05
289	Mike Merriweather	.10	.05
290	Dwayne Woodruff	.10	.05
291	Donnie Shell	.25	.11
292	Vikings TL	.25	.11
	(Tommy Kramer Audible)		
293	Tommy Kramer	.25	.11
294	Darrin Nelson	.10	.05
295	Ted Brown	.25	.11
296	Buster Rhymes	.10	.05
297	Anthony Carter RC*	1.00	.45
298	Steve Jordan RC	.50	.23
299	Keith Millard RC	.50	.23
300	Joey Browner RC	.50	.23
301	John Turner	.10	.05
302	Greg Coleman	.10	.05
303	Chiefs TL	.10	.05
	(Todd Blackledge)		
304	Bill Kenney	.10	.05
305	Herman Heard	.10	.05
306	Stephone Paige RC	.50	.23
307	Carlos Carson	.25	.11
308	Nick Lowery	.25	.11
309	Mike Bell	.10	.05
310	Bill Maas	.10	.05
311	Art Still	.10	.05
312	Albert Lewis RC	.50	.23
313	Deron Cherry AP	.25	.11
314	Colts TL	.10	.05
	(Rohn Stark Booms It)		
315	Mike Pagel	.10	.05
316	Randy McMillan	.10	.05
317	Albert Bentley RC*	.25	.11
318	George Wonsley RC	.10	.05
319	Robbie Martin	.10	.05
320	Pat Beach	.10	.05
321	Chris Hinton	.25	.11
322	Duane Bickett RC	.50	.23
323	Eugene Daniel	.10	.05
324	Cliff Odom RC	.10	.05
325	Rohn Stark AP	.25	.11
326	Cardinals TL	.10	.05
	(Stump Mitchell Outside)		
327	Neil Lomax	.25	.11
328	Stump Mitchell	.25	.11
329	Ottis Anderson	.50	.23
330	J.T. Smith	.25	.11
331	Pat Tilley	.10	.05
332	Roy Green	.25	.11
333	Lance Smith RC	.10	.05
334	Curtis Greer	.10	.05
335	Freddie Joe Nunn RC	.25	.11
336	E.J. Junior	.25	.11
337	Lonnie Young RC	.10	.05
338	Saints TL	.10	.05
	(Wayne Wilson running)		
339	Bobby Hebert RC*	.50	.23
340	Dave Wilson	.10	.05
341	Wayne Wilson	.10	.05
342	Hoby Brenner	.10	.05
343	Stan Brock	.25	.11
344	Morten Andersen	.50	.23
345	Bruce Clark	.10	.05
346	Rickey Jackson	.50	.23
347	Dave Waymer	.10	.05
348	Brian Hansen	.10	.05
349	Oilers TL	.50	.23
	(Warren Moon Throws Bomb)		
350	Warren Moon	3.00	1.35
351	Mike Rozier RC*	.50	.23
352	Butch Woolfolk	.10	.05
353	Drew Hill	.50	.23
354	Willie Drewrey RC	.10	.05
355	Tim Smith	.25	.11
356	Mike Munchak	.25	.11
357	Ray Childress RC	.50	.23
358	Frank Bush	.10	.05
359	Steve Brown	.10	.05
360	Falcons TL	.10	.05
	(Gerald Riggs Around End)		
361	David Archer RC	.50	.23
362	Gerald Riggs	.25	.11
363	William Andrews	.25	.11
364	Billy Johnson	.25	.11
365	Arthur Cox	.10	.05
366	Mike Kenn	.10	.05
367	Bill Fralic RC	.25	.11
368	Mick Luckhurst	.10	.05
369	Rick Bryan	.10	.05
370	Bobby Butler	.10	.05
371	Rick Donnelly RC	.10	.05
372	Buccaneers TL	.10	.05
	(James Wilder Sweeps Left)		
373	Steve DeBerg	.50	.23
374	Steve Young RC*	35.00	16.00
375	James Wilder	.10	.05
376	Kevin House	.10	.05
377	Gerald Carter	.10	.05
378	Jimmie Giles	.25	.11
379	Sean Farrell	.10	.05
380	Donald Igwebuike	.10	.05
381	David Logan	.10	.05
382	Jeremiah Castille RC	.10	.05
383	Bills TL	.10	.05
	(Greg Bell Sees Daylight)		
384	Bruce Mathison RC	.10	.05
385	Joe Cribbs	.25	.11
386	Greg Bell	.25	.11
387	Jerry Butler	.10	.05
388	Andre Reed RC	6.00	2.70
389	Bruce Smith RC	6.00	2.70
390	Fred Smerlas	.10	.05
391	Darryl Talley	.50	.23
392	Jim Haslett	.10	.05
393	Charles Romes	.10	.05
394	Checklist 1-132	.12	.05
395	Checklist 133-264	.12	.05
396	Checklist 265-396	.12	.05

1987 Topps

	MINT	NRMT
COMPLETE SET (396)	40.00	18.00
COMP.FACT.SET (396)	40.00	18.00
COMMON CARD (1-396)	.10	.05
SEMISTARS	.25	.11
UNLISTED STARS	.50	.23
COMP.1000 YARD SET (24)	6.00	2.70
1000 YARD: ONE PER PACK		

1987-PRESENT PRICED IN MINT CONDITION

No.	Player	Mint	NrMt
1	Super Bowl XXI	.50	.23
	Giants 39,		
	Broncos 20		
	(Line play shown)		
2	Todd Christensen RB	.25	.11
	Most Seasons,		
	80 or More Receptions		
3	Dave Jennings RB	.10	.05
	Most Punts, Career		
4	Charlie Joiner RB	.50	.23
	Most Receiving		
	Yards, Career		
5	Steve Largent RB	.50	.23
	Most Cons. Games		
	With a Reception		
6	Dan Marino RB	2.00	.90
	Most Cons. Seasons,		
	30 or More TD Passes		
7	Donnie Shell RB	.25	.11
	Most Interceptions,		
	Strong Safety, Career		
8	Phil Simms RB	.50	.23
	Highest Completion		
	Percentage, Super Bowl		
9	New York Giants TL	.25	.11
	(Mark Bavaro Pulls Free)		
10	Phil Simms	.50	.23
11	Joe Morris AP	.25	.11
12	Maurice Carthon RC**	.10	.05
13	Lee Rouson	.10	.05
14	Bobby Johnson	.10	.05
15	Lionel Manuel	.10	.05
16	Phil McConkey	.10	.05
17	Mark Bavaro AP	.50	.23
18	Zeke Mowatt	.10	.05
19	Raul Allegre	.10	.05
20	Sean Landeta	.10	.05
21	Brad Benson	.10	.05
22	Jim Burt	.10	.05
23	Leonard Marshall	.50	.23
24	Carl Banks	.50	.23
25	Harry Carson	.10	.05
26	Lawrence Taylor AP	.75	.35
27	Terry Kinard RC	.10	.05
28	Pepper Johnson RC	.50	.23
29	Erik Howard RC	.10	.05
30	Broncos TL	.10	.05
	(Gerald Willhite Dives)		
31	John Elway	6.00	2.70
32	Gerald Willhite	.10	.05
33	Sammy Winder	.25	.11
34	Ken Bell	.10	.05
35	Steve Watson	.10	.05
36	Rich Karlis	.10	.05
37	Keith Bishop	.10	.05
38	Rulon Jones	.10	.05
39	Karl Mecklenburg AP	.50	.23
40	Louis Wright	.10	.05
41	Mike Harden	.10	.05
42	Dennis Smith	.25	.11
43	Bears TL	.50	.23
	(Walter Payton Barrels)		
44	Jim McMahon	.50	.23
45	Doug Flutie RC**	12.00	5.50
46	Walter Payton	1.25	.55
47	Matt Suhey	.10	.05
48	Willie Gault	.25	.11
49	Dennis Gentry RC	.10	.05
50	Kevin Butler	.10	.05
51	Jim Covert AP	.10	.05
52	Jay Hilgenberg	.25	.11
53	Dan Hampton	.25	.11
54	Steve McMichael	.50	.23
55	William Perry	.50	.23
56	Richard Dent	.50	.23
57	Otis Wilson	.10	.05
58	Mike Singletary AP	.50	.23
59	Wilber Marshall	.50	.23
60	Mike Richardson	.10	.05
61	Dave Duerson	.10	.05
62	Gary Fencik	.10	.05
63	Redskins TL	.25	.11
	(George Rogers Plunges)		
64	Jay Schroeder	.25	.11
65	George Rogers	.25	.11
66	Kelvin Bryant RC**	.25	.11
67	Ken Jenkins	.10	.05
68	Gary Clark	.50	.23
69	Art Monk	.50	.23
70	Clint Didier RC	.10	.05
71	Steve Cox	.10	.05
72	Joe Jacoby	.10	.05
73	Russ Grimm	.10	.05
74	Charles Mann	.25	.11
75	Dave Butz	.10	.05
76	Dexter Manley AP	.25	.11
77	Darrell Green AP	.50	.23
78	Curtis Jordan	.10	.05
79	Browns TL	.10	.05
	(Harry Holt Sees Daylight)		
80	Bernie Kosar	.50	.23
81	Curtis Dickey	.10	.05
82	Kevin Mack	.25	.11
83	Herman Fontenot	.10	.05
84	Brian Brennan RC	.10	.05
85	Ozzie Newsome	.50	.23

❑ 86 Jeff Gossett .25 .11
❑ 87 Cody Risien AP .10 .05
❑ 88 Reggie Camp .10 .05
❑ 89 Bob Golic .10 .05
❑ 90 Carl Hairston .10 .05
❑ 91 Chip Banks .10 .05
❑ 92 Frank Minnifield .10 .05
❑ 93 Hanford Dixon AP .10 .05
❑ 94 Gerald McNeil RC** .10 .05
❑ 95 Dave Puzzuoli .10 .05
❑ 96 Patriots TL .10 .05
(Andre Tippett Gets
His Man (Marcus Allen))
❑ 97 Tony Eason .25 .11
❑ 98 Craig James .25 .11
❑ 99 Tony Collins .25 .11
❑ 100 Mosi Tatupu .10 .05
❑ 101 Stanley Morgan .25 .11
❑ 102 Irving Fryar .50 .23
❑ 103 Stephen Starring .10 .05
❑ 104 Tony Franklin AP .10 .05
❑ 105 Rich Camarillo .10 .05
❑ 106 Garin Veris .10 .05
❑ 107 Andre Tippett AP .25 .11
❑ 108 Don Blackmon .10 .05
❑ 109 Ronnie Lippett RC .10 .05
❑ 110 Raymond Clayborn .10 .05
❑ 111 49ers TL .25 .11
(Roger Craig Up the Middle)
❑ 112 Joe Montana 6.00 2.70
❑ 113 Roger Craig .50 .23
❑ 114 Joe Cribbs .25 .11
❑ 115 Jerry Rice AP 8.00 3.60
❑ 116 Dwight Clark .25 .11
❑ 117 Ray Wersching .10 .05
❑ 118 Max Runager .10 .05
❑ 119 Jeff Stover .10 .05
❑ 120 Dwaine Board .10 .05
❑ 121 Tim McKyer RC .25 .11
❑ 122 Don Griffin RC .25 .11
❑ 123 Ronnie Lott AP .50 .23
❑ 124 Tom Holmoe .10 .05
❑ 125 Charles Haley RC 1.25 .55
❑ 126 Jets TL .10 .05
(Mark Gastineau Seeks)
❑ 127 Ken O'Brien .25 .11
❑ 128 Pat Ryan .10 .05
❑ 129 Freeman McNeil .25 .11
❑ 130 Johnny Hector RC .10 .05
❑ 131 Al Toon AP .50 .23
❑ 132 Wesley Walker .25 .11
❑ 133 Mickey Shuler .10 .05
❑ 134 Pat Leahy .10 .05
❑ 135 Mark Gastineau .25 .11
❑ 136 Joe Klecko .25 .11
❑ 137 Marty Lyons .10 .05
❑ 138 Bob Crable .10 .05
❑ 139 Lance Mehl .10 .05
❑ 140 Dave Jennings .10 .05
❑ 141 Harry Hamilton RC .10 .05
❑ 142 Lester Lyles .10 .05
❑ 143 Bobby Humphery UER .. .10 .05
(Misspelled Humphrey
on card front)
❑ 144 Rams TL .50 .23
(Eric Dickerson
Through the Line)
❑ 145 Jim Everett RC 2.00 .90
❑ 146 Eric Dickerson AP .50 .23
❑ 147 Barry Redden .10 .05
❑ 148 Ron Brown .25 .11
❑ 149 Kevin House .10 .05
❑ 150 Henry Ellard .50 .23
❑ 151 Doug Smith .10 .05
❑ 152 Dennis Harrah AP .10 .05
❑ 153 Jackie Slater .25 .11
❑ 154 Gary Jeter .10 .05
❑ 155 Carl Ekern .10 .05
❑ 156 Mike Wilcher .10 .05
❑ 157 Jerry Gray RC .10 .05
❑ 158 LeRoy Irvin .10 .05
❑ 159 Nolan Cromwell .25 .11
❑ 160 Chiefs TL .10 .05
(Todd Blackledge Hands Off)
❑ 161 Bill Kenney .10 .05
❑ 162 Stephone Paige .25 .11
❑ 163 Henry Marshall .10 .05
❑ 164 Carlos Carson .10 .05
❑ 165 Nick Lowery .25 .11
❑ 166 Irv Eatman RC** .10 .05
❑ 167 Brad Budde .10 .05
❑ 168 Art Still .10 .05
❑ 169 Bill Maas AP .10 .05
❑ 170 Lloyd Burruss RC .10 .05
❑ 171 Deron Cherry AP .10 .05
❑ 172 Seahawks TL .25 .11
(Curt Warner Finds Opening)
❑ 173 Dave Krieg .50 .23
❑ 174 Curt Warner .25 .11
❑ 175 John L. Williams RC .50 .23
❑ 176 Bobby Joe Edmonds RC .25 .11
❑ 177 Steve Largent .60 .25
❑ 178 Bruce Scholtz .10 .05
❑ 179 Norm Johnson .10 .05
❑ 180 Jacob Green .10 .05
❑ 181 Fredd Young .10 .05
❑ 182 Dave Brown .10 .05
❑ 183 Kenny Easley .10 .05
❑ 184 Bengals TL .25 .11
(James Brooks Stiff-Arm)
❑ 185 Boomer Esiason .50 .23
❑ 186 James Brooks .25 .11
❑ 187 Larry Kinnebrew .10 .05
❑ 188 Cris Collinsworth .25 .11
❑ 189 Eddie Brown .50 .23
❑ 190 Tim McGee RC .50 .23
❑ 191 Jim Breech .10 .05
❑ 192 Anthony Munoz .50 .23
❑ 193 Max Montoya .10 .05
❑ 194 Eddie Edwards .10 .05
❑ 195 Ross Browner .25 .11
❑ 196 Emanuel King .10 .05
❑ 197 Louis Breeden .10 .05
❑ 198 Vikings TL .10 .05
(Darrin Nelson In Motion)
❑ 199 Tommy Kramer .25 .11
❑ 200 Darrin Nelson .10 .05
❑ 201 Allen Rice .10 .05
❑ 202 Anthony Carter .50 .23
❑ 203 Leo Lewis .10 .05
❑ 204 Steve Jordan .50 .23
❑ 205 Chuck Nelson RC .10 .05
❑ 206 Greg Coleman .10 .05
❑ 207 Gary Zimmerman RC .25 .11
❑ 208 Doug Martin .10 .05
❑ 209 Keith Millard .10 .05
❑ 210 Issiac Holt RC .10 .05
❑ 211 Joey Browner .25 .11
❑ 212 Rufus Bess .10 .05
❑ 213 Raiders TL .50 .23
(Marcus Allen Quick Feet)
❑ 214 Jim Plunkett .50 .23
❑ 215 Marcus Allen 1.00 .45
❑ 216 Napoleon McCallum RC .25 .11
❑ 217 Dokie Williams .10 .05
❑ 218 Todd Christensen .50 .23
❑ 219 Chris Bahr .10 .05
❑ 220 Howie Long .60 .25
❑ 221 Bill Pickel .10 .05
❑ 222 Sean Jones RC .75 .35
❑ 223 Lester Hayes .25 .11
❑ 224 Mike Haynes .25 .11
❑ 225 Vann McElroy .10 .05
❑ 226 Fulton Walker .10 .05
❑ 227 Passing Leaders 1.25 .55
Tommy Kramer,
Minnesota Vikings
Dan Marino,
❑ 228 Receiving Leaders 1.25 .55
Jerry Rice,
San Francisco 49ers
Todd Christensen,
❑ 229 Rushing Leaders .50 .23
Eric Dickerson,
Los Angeles Rams
Curt Warner,
❑ 230 Scoring Leaders .10 .05
Kevin Butler,
Chicago Bears
Tony Franklin,
❑ 231 Interception Leaders .50 .23
Ronnie Lott,
San Francisco 49ers
Deron Cherry,
❑ 232 Dolphins TL .25 .11
(Reggie Roby Booms It)
❑ 233 Dan Marino AP 6.00 2.70
❑ 234 Lorenzo Hampton RC .10 .05
❑ 235 Tony Nathan .25 .11
❑ 236 Mark Duper .50 .23
❑ 237 Mark Clayton .50 .23
❑ 238 Nat Moore .25 .11
❑ 239 Bruce Hardy .10 .05
❑ 240 Reggie Roby .25 .11
❑ 241 Roy Foster .10 .05
❑ 242 Dwight Stephenson AP .25 .11
❑ 243 Hugh Green .10 .05
❑ 244 John Offerdahl RC .50 .23
❑ 245 Mark Brown .10 .05
❑ 246 Doug Betters .10 .05
❑ 247 Bob Baumhower .10 .05
❑ 248 Falcons TL .10 .05
(Gerald Riggs Uses Blockers)
❑ 249 David Archer .50 .23
❑ 250 Gerald Riggs .25 .11
❑ 251 William Andrews .25 .11
❑ 252 Charlie Brown .10 .05
❑ 253 Arthur Cox .10 .05
❑ 254 Rick Donnelly .10 .05
❑ 255 Bill Fralic AP .10 .05
❑ 256 Mike Gann RC .10 .05
❑ 257 Rick Bryan .10 .05
❑ 258 Bret Clark .10 .05
❑ 259 Mike Pitts .10 .05
❑ 260 Cowboys TL .50 .23
(Tony Dorsett Cuts)
❑ 261 Danny White .50 .23
❑ 262 Steve Pelluer RC .10 .05
❑ 263 Tony Dorsett .50 .23
❑ 264 Herschel Walker RC UER 2.50 1.10
(Stats show 12 TD's
in '86, text says 14)
❑ 265 Timmy Newsome .10 .05
❑ 266 Tony Hill .25 .11
❑ 267 Mike Sherrard RC .50 .23
❑ 268 Jim Jeffcoat .50 .23
❑ 269 Ron Fellows .10 .05
❑ 270 Bill Bates .50 .23
❑ 271 Michael Downs .10 .05
❑ 272 Saints TL .25 .11
(Bobby Hebert Fakes)
❑ 273 Dave Wilson .10 .05
❑ 274 Rueben Mayes RC UER .10 .05
(Stats show 1353 comple-
tions, should be yards)
❑ 275 Hoby Brenner .10 .05
❑ 276 Eric Martin RC .50 .23
❑ 277 Morten Andersen .25 .11
❑ 278 Brian Hansen .10 .05
❑ 279 Rickey Jackson .50 .23
❑ 280 Dave Waymer .10 .05
❑ 281 Bruce Clark .10 .05
❑ 282 James Geathers RC .25 .11
❑ 283 Steelers TL .25 .11
(Walter Abercrombie Resists)
❑ 284 Mark Malone .25 .11
❑ 285 Earnest Jackson .10 .05
❑ 286 Walter Abercrombie .10 .05
❑ 287 Louis Lipps .25 .11
❑ 288 John Stallworth UER .50 .23
(Stats only go up
through 1981)
❑ 289 Gary Anderson K .10 .05
❑ 290 Keith Willis .10 .05
❑ 291 Mike Merriweather .10 .05
❑ 292 Lupe Sanchez .10 .05
❑ 293 Donnie Shell .25 .11
❑ 294 Eagles TL .50 .23
(Keith Byars Inches Ahead)
❑ 295 Mike Reichenbach .10 .05
❑ 296 Randall Cunningham RC ! 12.00 5.50
❑ 297 Keith Byars RC .75 .35
❑ 298 Mike Quick .25 .11
❑ 299 Kenny Jackson .10 .05
❑ 300 John Teltschik RC .10 .05
❑ 301 Reggie White AP 3.00 1.35
❑ 302 Ken Clarke .10 .05
❑ 303 Greg Brown .10 .05

❑ 304 Roynell Young .10 .05
❑ 305 Andre Waters RC .50 .23
❑ 306 Oilers TL .50 .23
(Warren Moon Plots Play)
❑ 307 Warren Moon 1.50 .70
❑ 308 Mike Rozier .25 .11
❑ 309 Drew Hill .25 .11
❑ 310 Ernest Givins RC .50 .23
❑ 311 Lee Johnson RC .10 .05
❑ 312 Kent Hill .10 .05
❑ 313 Dean Steinkuhler RC .25 .11
❑ 314 Ray Childress .50 .23
❑ 315 John Grimsley RC .10 .05
❑ 316 Jesse Baker .10 .05
❑ 317 Lions TL .10 .05
(Eric Hipple Surveys)
❑ 318 Chuck Long RC .25 .11
❑ 319 James Jones .10 .05
❑ 320 Garry James .10 .05
❑ 321 Jeff Chadwick .10 .05
❑ 322 Leonard Thompson .10 .05
❑ 323 Pete Mandley .10 .05
❑ 324 Jimmie Giles .25 .11
❑ 325 Herman Hunter .10 .05
❑ 326 Keith Ferguson .10 .05
❑ 327 Devon Mitchell .10 .05
❑ 328 Cardinals TL .10 .05
(Neil Lomax Audible)
❑ 329 Neil Lomax .25 .11
❑ 330 Stump Mitchell .10 .05
❑ 331 Earl Ferrell .10 .05
❑ 332 Vai Sikahema RC .25 .11
❑ 333 Ron Wolfley RC .10 .05
❑ 334 J.T. Smith .25 .11
❑ 335 Roy Green .25 .11
❑ 336 Al(Bubba) Baker .10 .05
❑ 337 Freddie Joe Nunn .10 .05
❑ 338 Cedric Mack .10 .05
❑ 339 Chargers TL .25 .11
(Gary Anderson Evades)
❑ 340 Dan Fouts .50 .23
❑ 341 Gary Anderson UER .50 .23
(Two Topps logos
on card front)
❑ 342 Wes Chandler .25 .11
❑ 343 Kellen Winslow .50 .23
❑ 344 Ralf Mojsiejenko .10 .05
❑ 345 Rolf Benirschke .10 .05
❑ 346 Lee Williams RC .25 .11
❑ 347 Leslie O'Neal RC 1.00 .45
❑ 348 Billy Ray Smith .25 .11
❑ 349 Gill Byrd .25 .11
❑ 350 Packers TL .10 .05
(Paul Ott Carruth Around End)
❑ 351 Randy Wright .10 .05
❑ 352 Kenneth Davis RC .50 .23
❑ 353 Gerry Ellis .10 .05
❑ 354 James Lofton .50 .23
❑ 355 Phillip Epps RC .10 .05
❑ 356 Walter Stanley RC .10 .05
❑ 357 Eddie Lee Ivery .10 .05
❑ 358 Tim Harris RC .50 .23
❑ 359 Mark Lee UER .10 .05
(Red flag, rest of
Packers have yellow)
❑ 360 Mossy Cade .10 .05
❑ 361 Bills TL 1.00 .45
(Jim Kelly Works Ground)
❑ 362 Jim Kelly RC** 8.00 3.60
❑ 363 Robb Riddick RC .10 .05
❑ 364 Greg Bell .10 .05
❑ 365 Andre Reed 1.25 .55
❑ 366 Pete Metzelaars RC .50 .23
❑ 367 Sean McNanie .10 .05
❑ 368 Fred Smerlas .10 .05
❑ 369 Bruce Smith 2.00 .90
❑ 370 Darryl Talley .25 .11
❑ 371 Charles Romes .10 .05
❑ 372 Colts TL .10 .05
(Rohn Stark High and Far)
❑ 373 Jack Trudeau RC .25 .11
❑ 374 Gary Hogeboom .10 .05
❑ 375 Randy McMillan .10 .05
❑ 376 Albert Bentley .10 .05
❑ 377 Matt Bouza .10 .05
❑ 378 Bill Brooks RC 1.00 .45
❑ 379 Rohn Stark AP .10 .05
❑ 380 Chris Hinton .10 .05
❑ 381 Ray Donaldson .10 .05
❑ 382 Jon Hand RC .10 .05
❑ 383 Buccaneers TL .10 .05
(James Wilder Braces)
❑ 384 Steve Young 6.00 2.70
❑ 385 James Wilder .10 .05
❑ 386 Frank Garcia .10 .05
❑ 387 Gerald Carter .10 .05
❑ 388 Phil Freeman .10 .05
❑ 389 Calvin Magee .10 .05
❑ 390 Donald Igwebuike .10 .05
❑ 391 David Logan .10 .05
❑ 392 Jeff Davis .10 .05
❑ 393 Chris Washington .10 .05
❑ 394 Checklist 1-132 .10 .05
❑ 395 Checklist 133-264 .10 .05
❑ 396 Checklist 265-396 .10 .05

1988 Topps

	MINT	NRMT
COMPLETE SET (396)	12.00	5.50
COMP.FACT.SET (396)	15.00	6.75
COMMON CARD (1-396)	.05	.02
SEMISTARS	.20	.09
UNLISTED STARS	.40	.18
COMP.1000 YARD SET (28)	4.00	1.80
1000 YARD: ONE PER PACK		

❑ 1 Super Bowl XXII .20 .09
Redskins 42,
Broncos 10
(Redskins celebrating)
❑ 2 Vencie Glenn RB .05 .02
Longest Interception
Return
❑ 3 Steve Largent RB .40 .18
Most Receptions,
Career
❑ 4 Joe Montana RB .75 .35
Most Consecutive
Pass Completions
❑ 5 Walter Payton RB .40 .18
Most Rushing
Touchdowns, Career
❑ 6 Jerry Rice RB .75 .35
Most Touchdown
Receptions, Season
❑ 7 Redskins TL .20 .09
(Kelvin Bryant Sees Daylight)
❑ 8 Doug Williams .20 .09
❑ 9 George Rogers .20 .09
❑ 10 Kelvin Bryant .20 .09
❑ 11 Timmy Smith SR .20 .09
❑ 12 Art Monk .40 .18
❑ 13 Gary Clark .40 .18
❑ 14 Ricky Sanders RC** .40 .18
❑ 15 Steve Cox .05 .02
❑ 16 Joe Jacoby .05 .02
❑ 17 Charles Mann .20 .09
❑ 18 Dave Butz .05 .02
❑ 19 Darrell Green AP .20 .09
❑ 20 Dexter Manley .05 .02
❑ 21 Barry Wilburn .05 .02
❑ 22 Broncos TL .05 .02
(Sammy Winder Winds
Through)
❑ 23 John Elway AP 2.00 .90
❑ 24 Sammy Winder .05 .02
❑ 25 Vance Johnson .20 .09
❑ 26 Mark Jackson RC .40 .18
❑ 27 Ricky Nattiel SR RC .05 .02
❑ 28 Clarence Kay .05 .02
❑ 29 Rich Karlis .05 .02
❑ 30 Keith Bishop .05 .02
❑ 31 Mike Horan .05 .02
❑ 32 Rulon Jones .05 .02
❑ 33 Karl Mecklenburg .20 .09
❑ 34 Jim Ryan .05 .02
❑ 35 Mark Haynes .20 .09
❑ 36 Mike Harden .05 .02
❑ 37 49ers TL .40 .18
(Roger Craig Gallops
For Yardage)
❑ 38 Joe Montana 2.00 .90
❑ 39 Steve Young 1.00 .45
❑ 40 Roger Craig .20 .09
❑ 41 Tom Rathman RC .40 .18
❑ 42 Joe Cribbs .20 .09
❑ 43 Jerry Rice AP 2.00 .90
❑ 44 Mike Wilson RC .05 .02
❑ 45 Ron Heller RC .05 .02
❑ 46 Ray Wersching .05 .02
❑ 47 Michael Carter .05 .02
❑ 48 Dwaine Board .05 .02
❑ 49 Michael Walter .05 .02
❑ 50 Don Griffin .05 .02
❑ 51 Ronnie Lott .40 .18
❑ 52 Charles Haley .40 .18
❑ 53 Dana McLemore .05 .02
❑ 54 Saints TL .20 .09
(Bobby Hebert Hands Off)
❑ 55 Bobby Hebert .20 .09
❑ 56 Rueben Mayes .05 .02
❑ 57 Dalton Hilliard RC .05 .02
❑ 58 Eric Martin .20 .09
❑ 59 John Tice RC .05 .02
❑ 60 Brad Edelman .05 .02
❑ 61 Morten Andersen AP .20 .09
❑ 62 Brian Hansen .05 .02
❑ 63 Mel Gray RC .40 .18
❑ 64 Rickey Jackson .20 .09
❑ 65 Sam Mills RC** .40 .18
❑ 66 Pat Swilling RC .40 .18
❑ 67 Dave Waymer .05 .02
❑ 68 Bears TL .20 .09
(Willie Gault Powers
Forward)
❑ 69 Jim McMahon .40 .18
❑ 70 Mike Tomczak RC .05 .02
❑ 71 Neal Anderson RC .40 .18
❑ 72 Willie Gault .20 .09
❑ 73 Dennis Gentry .05 .02
❑ 74 Dennis McKinnon .05 .02
❑ 75 Kevin Butler .05 .02
❑ 76 Jim Covert .05 .02
❑ 77 Jay Hilgenberg .05 .02
❑ 78 Steve McMichael .20 .09
❑ 79 William Perry .20 .09
❑ 80 Richard Dent .40 .18
❑ 81 Ron Rivera RC .05 .02
❑ 82 Mike Singletary AP .40 .18
❑ 83 Dan Hampton .20 .09
❑ 84 Dave Duerson .05 .02
❑ 85 Browns TL .20 .09
(Bernie Kosar Lets
It Go)
❑ 86 Bernie Kosar .40 .18
❑ 87 Earnest Byner .40 .18
❑ 88 Kevin Mack .20 .09
❑ 89 Webster Slaughter RC .40 .18
❑ 90 Gerald McNeil .05 .02
❑ 91 Brian Brennan .05 .02
❑ 92 Ozzie Newsome .40 .18
❑ 93 Cody Risien .05 .02
❑ 94 Bob Golic .05 .02
❑ 95 Carl Hairston .05 .02
❑ 96 Mike Johnson RC .05 .02
❑ 97 Clay Matthews .20 .09
❑ 98 Frank Minnifield .05 .02
❑ 99 Hanford Dixon AP .05 .02

- ❑ 100 Dave Puzzuoli .05 .02
- ❑ 101 Felix Wright RC**/C .05 .02
- ❑ 102 Oilers TL .40 .18
  (Warren Moon Over The Top)
- ❑ 103 Warren Moon .50 .23
- ❑ 104 Mike Rozier .05 .02
- ❑ 105 Alonzo Highsmith SR RC .20 .09
- ❑ 106 Drew Hill .20 .09
- ❑ 107 Ernest Givins .40 .18
- ❑ 108 Curtis Duncan RC .40 .18
- ❑ 109 Tony Zendejas RC** .05 .02
- ❑ 110 Mike Munchak AP .05 .02
- ❑ 111 Kent Hill .05 .02
- ❑ 112 Ray Childress .20 .09
- ❑ 113 Al Smith RC .20 .09
- ❑ 114 Keith Bostic RC .05 .02
- ❑ 115 Jeff Donaldson .05 .02
- ❑ 116 Colts TL .40 .18
  (Eric Dickerson Finds Opening)
- ❑ 117 Jack Trudeau .05 .02
- ❑ 118 Eric Dickerson AP .40 .18
- ❑ 119 Albert Bentley .05 .02
- ❑ 120 Matt Bouza .05 .02
- ❑ 121 Bill Brooks .40 .18
- ❑ 122 Dean Biasucci RC .05 .02
- ❑ 123 Chris Hinton .05 .02
- ❑ 124 Ray Donaldson .05 .02
- ❑ 125 Ron Solt RC .05 .02
- ❑ 126 Donnell Thompson .05 .02
- ❑ 127 Barry Krauss RC .05 .02
- ❑ 128 Duane Bickett .05 .02
- ❑ 129 Mike Prior RC .05 .02
- ❑ 130 Seahawks TL .20 .09
  (Curt Warner Follows Blocking)
- ❑ 131 Dave Krieg .20 .09
- ❑ 132 Curt Warner .20 .09
- ❑ 133 John L. Williams .40 .18
- ❑ 134 Bobby Joe Edmonds .05 .02
- ❑ 135 Steve Largent .40 .18
- ❑ 136 Raymond Butler .05 .02
- ❑ 137 Norm Johnson .05 .02
- ❑ 138 Ruben Rodriguez .05 .02
- ❑ 139 Blair Bush .05 .02
- ❑ 140 Jacob Green .05 .02
- ❑ 141 Joe Nash .05 .02
- ❑ 142 Jeff Bryant .05 .02
- ❑ 143 Fredd Young AP .05 .02
- ❑ 144 Brian Bosworth SR RC .40 .18
- ❑ 145 Kenny Easley AP .05 .02
- ❑ 146 Vikings TL .20 .09
  (Tommy Kramer Spots His Man)
- ❑ 147 Wade Wilson RC .40 .18
- ❑ 148 Tommy Kramer .20 .09
- ❑ 149 Darrin Nelson .05 .02
- ❑ 150 D.J. Dozier SR RC .20 .09
- ❑ 151 Anthony Carter .20 .09
- ❑ 152 Leo Lewis .05 .02
- ❑ 153 Steve Jordan .20 .09
- ❑ 154 Gary Zimmerman .05 .02
- ❑ 155 Chuck Nelson .05 .02
- ❑ 156 Henry Thomas SR RC .40 .18
- ❑ 157 Chris Doleman RC .40 .18
- ❑ 158 Scott Studwell RC .05 .02
- ❑ 159 Jesse Solomon RC .05 .02
- ❑ 160 Joey Browner AP .05 .02
- ❑ 161 Neal Guggemos .05 .02
- ❑ 162 Steelers TL .20 .09
  (Louis Lipps In a Crowd)
- ❑ 163 Mark Malone .05 .02
- ❑ 164 Walter Abercrombie .05 .02
- ❑ 165 Earnest Jackson .05 .02
- ❑ 166 Frank Pollard .05 .02
- ❑ 167 Dwight Stone RC .20 .09
- ❑ 168 Gary Anderson K .05 .02
- ❑ 169 Harry Newsome RC .05 .02
- ❑ 170 Keith Willis .05 .02
- ❑ 171 Keith Gary .05 .02
- ❑ 172 David Little RC .05 .02
- ❑ 173 Mike Merriweather .05 .02
- ❑ 174 Dwayne Woodruff .05 .02
- ❑ 175 Patriots TL .40 .18
  (Irving Fryar One on One)
- ❑ 176 Steve Grogan .20 .09
- ❑ 177 Tony Eason .20 .09
- ❑ 178 Tony Collins .20 .09
- ❑ 179 Mosi Tatupu .05 .02
- ❑ 180 Stanley Morgan .20 .09
- ❑ 181 Irving Fryar .40 .18
- ❑ 182 Stephen Starring .05 .02
- ❑ 183 Tony Franklin .05 .02
- ❑ 184 Rich Camarillo .05 .02
- ❑ 185 Garin Veris .05 .02
- ❑ 186 Andre Tippett AP .20 .09
- ❑ 187 Ronnie Lippett .05 .02
- ❑ 188 Fred Marion .05 .02
- ❑ 189 Dolphins TL .75 .35
  (Dan Marino Play-Action Pass)
- ❑ 190 Dan Marino 2.00 .90
- ❑ 191 Troy Stradford SR RC .05 .02
- ❑ 192 Lorenzo Hampton .05 .02
- ❑ 193 Mark Duper .20 .09
- ❑ 194 Mark Clayton .20 .09
- ❑ 195 Reggie Roby .20 .09
- ❑ 196 Dwight Stephenson AP .05 .02
- ❑ 197 T.J. Turner .05 .02
- ❑ 198 John Bosa SR .05 .02
- ❑ 199 Jackie Shipp .05 .02
- ❑ 200 John Offerdahl .20 .09
- ❑ 201 Mark Brown .05 .02
- ❑ 202 Paul Lankford .05 .02
- ❑ 203 Chargers TL .40 .18
  (Kellen Winslow Sure Hands)
- ❑ 204 Tim Spencer .05 .02
- ❑ 205 Gary Anderson RB .20 .09
- ❑ 206 Curtis Adams .05 .02
- ❑ 207 Lionel James .05 .02
- ❑ 208 Chip Banks .05 .02
- ❑ 209 Kellen Winslow .40 .18
- ❑ 210 Ralf Mojsiejenko .05 .02
- ❑ 211 Jim Lachey .20 .09
- ❑ 212 Lee Williams .05 .02
- ❑ 213 Billy Ray Smith .05 .02
- ❑ 214 Vencie Glenn RC .20 .09
- ❑ 215 Passing Leaders .50 .23
  Bernie Kosar
  Joe Montana
- ❑ 216 Receiving Leaders .20 .09
  Al Toon
  J.T. Smith
- ❑ 217 Rushing Leaders .20 .09
  Charles White
  Eric Dickerson
- ❑ 218 Scoring Leaders .40 .18
  Jim Breech
  Jerry Rice
- ❑ 219 Interception Leaders .05 .02
  Keith Bostic
  Mark Kelso
  Mike Prior
  Barry Wilburn
- ❑ 220 Bills TL .40 .18
  (Jim Kelly Plots His Course)
- ❑ 221 Jim Kelly .75 .35
- ❑ 222 Ronnie Harmon RC .40 .18
- ❑ 223 Robb Riddick .05 .02
- ❑ 224 Andre Reed .40 .18
- ❑ 225 Chris Burkett RC .05 .02
- ❑ 226 Pete Metzelaars .40 .18
- ❑ 227 Bruce Smith AP .50 .23
- ❑ 228 Darryl Talley .20 .09
- ❑ 229 Eugene Marve .05 .02
- ❑ 230 Cornelius Bennett SR RC .75 .35
- ❑ 231 Mark Kelso RC .05 .02
- ❑ 232 Shane Conlan SR RC .40 .18
- ❑ 233 Eagles TL .40 .18
  (Randall Cunningham QB Keeper)
- ❑ 234 Randall Cunningham 1.00 .45
- ❑ 235 Keith Byars .40 .18
- ❑ 236 Anthony Toney RC .05 .02
- ❑ 237 Mike Quick .20 .09
- ❑ 238 Kenny Jackson .05 .02
- ❑ 239 John Spagnola .05 .02
- ❑ 240 Paul McFadden .05 .02
- ❑ 241 Reggie White AP .60 .25
- ❑ 242 Ken Clarke .05 .02
- ❑ 243 Mike Pitts .05 .02
- ❑ 244 Clyde Simmons RC .40 .18
- ❑ 245 Seth Joyner RC .40 .18
- ❑ 246 Andre Waters .40 .18
- ❑ 247 Jerome Brown SR RC .40 .18
- ❑ 248 Cardinals TL .05 .02
  (Stump Mitchell On the Run)
- ❑ 249 Neil Lomax .20 .09
- ❑ 250 Stump Mitchell .05 .02
- ❑ 251 Earl Ferrell .05 .02
- ❑ 252 Vai Sikahema .05 .02
- ❑ 253 J.T. Smith AP .20 .09
- ❑ 254 Roy Green .20 .09
- ❑ 255 Robert Awalt SR .20 .09
- ❑ 256 Freddie Joe Nunn .05 .02
- ❑ 257 Leonard Smith RC .05 .02
- ❑ 258 Travis Curtis .05 .02
- ❑ 259 Cowboys TL .40 .18
  (Herschel Walker Around End)
- ❑ 260 Danny White .40 .18
- ❑ 261 Herschel Walker .40 .18
- ❑ 262 Tony Dorsett .40 .18
- ❑ 263 Doug Cosbie .05 .02
- ❑ 264 Roger Ruzek RC** .20 .09
- ❑ 265 Darryl Clack .05 .02
- ❑ 266 Ed Too Tall Jones .40 .18
- ❑ 267 Jim Jeffcoat .05 .02
- ❑ 268 Everson Walls .05 .02
- ❑ 269 Bill Bates .20 .09
- ❑ 270 Michael Downs .05 .02
- ❑ 271 Giants TL .20 .09
  (Mark Bavaro Drives Ahead)
- ❑ 272 Phil Simms .40 .18
- ❑ 273 Joe Morris .20 .09
- ❑ 274 Lee Rouson .05 .02
- ❑ 275 George Adams .05 .02
- ❑ 276 Lionel Manuel .05 .02
- ❑ 277 Mark Bavaro AP .20 .09
- ❑ 278 Raul Allegre .05 .02
- ❑ 279 Sean Landeta .05 .02
- ❑ 280 Erik Howard .05 .02
- ❑ 281 Leonard Marshall .20 .09
- ❑ 282 Carl Banks AP .20 .09
- ❑ 283 Pepper Johnson .20 .09
- ❑ 284 Harry Carson .20 .09
- ❑ 285 Lawrence Taylor .40 .18
- ❑ 286 Terry Kinard .05 .02
- ❑ 287 Rams TL .40 .18
  (Jim Everett Races Downfield)
- ❑ 288 Jim Everett .40 .18
- ❑ 289 Charles White AP .20 .09
- ❑ 290 Ron Brown .20 .09
- ❑ 291 Henry Ellard .40 .18
- ❑ 292 Mike Lansford .05 .02
- ❑ 293 Dale Hatcher .05 .02
- ❑ 294 Doug Smith .05 .02
- ❑ 295 Jackie Slater AP .20 .09
- ❑ 296 Jim Collins .05 .02
- ❑ 297 Jerry Gray .05 .02
- ❑ 298 LeRoy Irvin .05 .02
- ❑ 299 Nolan Cromwell .20 .09
- ❑ 300 Kevin Greene RC 1.25 .55
- ❑ 301 Jets TL .20 .09
  (Ken O'Brien Reads Defense)
- ❑ 302 Ken O'Brien .20 .09
- ❑ 303 Freeman McNeil .20 .09
- ❑ 304 Johnny Hector .05 .02
- ❑ 305 Al Toon .20 .09
- ❑ 306 Jo Jo Townsell RC .20 .09
- ❑ 307 Mickey Shuler .05 .02
- ❑ 308 Pat Leahy .05 .02
- ❑ 309 Roger Vick .05 .02
- ❑ 310 Alex Gordon RC .05 .02
- ❑ 311 Troy Benson .05 .02
- ❑ 312 Bob Crable .05 .02
- ❑ 313 Harry Hamilton .05 .02
- ❑ 314 Packers TL .05 .02
  (Phillip Epps Ready for Contact)
- ❑ 315 Randy Wright .05 .02
- ❑ 316 Kenneth Davis .20 .09
- ❑ 317 Phillip Epps .05 .02
- ❑ 318 Walter Stanley .05 .02
- ❑ 319 Frankie Neal .05 .02
- ❑ 320 Don Bracken .05 .02
- ❑ 321 Brian Noble RC .20 .09
- ❑ 322 Johnny Holland SR RC .20 .09
- ❑ 323 Tim Harris .20 .09
- ❑ 324 Mark Murphy .05 .02
- ❑ 325 Raiders TL .40 .18
  (Bo Jackson All Alone)

❑ 326 Marc Wilson .05 .02
❑ 327 Bo Jackson SR RC 2.50 1.10
❑ 328 Marcus Allen .40 .18
❑ 329 James Lofton .40 .18
❑ 330 Todd Christensen .20 .09
❑ 331 Chris Bahr .05 .02
❑ 332 Stan Talley .05 .02
❑ 333 Howie Long .40 .18
❑ 334 Sean Jones .40 .18
❑ 335 Matt Millen .20 .09
❑ 336 Stacey Toran .05 .02
❑ 337 Vann McElroy .05 .02
❑ 338 Greg Townsend .20 .09
❑ 339 Bengals TL .40 .18
(Boomer Esiason Calls Signals)
❑ 340 Boomer Esiason .40 .18
❑ 341 Larry Kinnebrew .05 .02
❑ 342 Stanford Jennings RC .05 .02
❑ 343 Eddie Brown .20 .09
❑ 344 Jim Breech .05 .02
❑ 345 Anthony Munoz AP .40 .18
❑ 346 Scott Fulhage RC .05 .02
❑ 347 Tim Krumrie RC .05 .02
❑ 348 Reggie Williams .20 .09
❑ 349 David Fulcher RC .05 .02
❑ 350 Buccaneers TL .05 .02
(James Wilder Free and Clear)
❑ 351 Frank Garcia .05 .02
❑ 352 Vinny Testaverde SR RC 4.00 1.80
❑ 353 James Wilder .05 .02
❑ 354 Jeff Smith .05 .02
❑ 355 Gerald Carter .05 .02
❑ 356 Calvin Magee .05 .02
❑ 357 Donald Igwebuike .05 .02
❑ 358 Ron Holmes RC .05 .02
❑ 359 Chris Washington .05 .02
❑ 360 Ervin Randle .05 .02
❑ 361 Chiefs TL .05 .02
(Bill Kenney Ground Attack)
❑ 362 Bill Kenney .05 .02
❑ 363 Christian Okoye SR RC .40 .18
❑ 364 Paul Palmer .05 .02
❑ 365 Stephone Paige .20 .09
❑ 366 Carlos Carson .05 .02
❑ 367 Kelly Goodburn RC .05 .02
❑ 368 Bill Maas AP .05 .02
❑ 369 Mike Bell .05 .02
❑ 370 Dino Hackett RC .05 .02
❑ 371 Deron Cherry .05 .02
❑ 372 Lions TL .05 .02
(James Jones Stretches For More)
❑ 373 Chuck Long .20 .09
❑ 374 Garry James .05 .02
❑ 375 James Jones .05 .02
❑ 376 Pete Mandley .05 .02
❑ 377 Gary Lee SR .05 .02
❑ 378 Eddie Murray .05 .02
❑ 379 Jim Arnold .05 .02
❑ 380 Dennis Gibson SR RC .05 .02
❑ 381 Mike Cofer .05 .02
❑ 382 James Griffin .05 .02
❑ 383 Falcons TL .05 .02
(Gerald Riggs Carries Heavy Load)
❑ 384 Scott Campbell .05 .02
❑ 385 Gerald Riggs .20 .09
❑ 386 Floyd Dixon RC .05 .02
❑ 387 Rick Donnelly AP .05 .02
❑ 388 Bill Fralic AP .20 .09
❑ 389 Major Everett .05 .02
❑ 390 Mike Gann .05 .02
❑ 391 Tony Casillas RC .20 .09
❑ 392 Rick Bryan .05 .02
❑ 393 John Rade RC .05 .02
❑ 394 Checklist 1-132 .05 .02
❑ 395 Checklist 133-264 .05 .02
❑ 396 Checklist 265-396 .05 .02

1989 Topps

	MINT	NRMT
COMPLETE SET (396)	12.00	5.50
COMP.FACT.SET (396)	20.00	9.00
COMMON CARD (1-396)	.05	.02
SEMISTARS	.10	.05
UNLISTED STARS	.25	.11
COMP.1000 YARD SET (24)	4.00	1.80
1000 YARD: ONE PER PACK		

❑ 1 Super Bowl XXIII .50 .23
(Joe Montana back to pass)
❑ 2 Tim Brown RB .50 .23
Most Combined Net Yards Gained, Rookie Season
❑ 3 Eric Dickerson RB .10 .05
Most Consecutive Seasons, Start of Career, 1000 or More Yards Rushing
❑ 4 Steve Largent RB .25 .11
Most Yards Receiving, Career
❑ 5 Dan Marino RB .75 .35
Most Seasons 4000 or More Yards Passing
❑ 6 49ers Team .50 .23
Joe Montana On The Run
❑ 7 Jerry Rice 1.50 .70
❑ 8 Roger Craig .25 .11
❑ 9 Ronnie Lott .10 .05
❑ 10 Michael Carter .05 .02
❑ 11 Charles Haley .25 .11
❑ 12 Joe Montana 2.00 .90
❑ 13 John Taylor RC .10 .05
❑ 14 Michael Walter .05 .02
❑ 15 Mike Cofer K RC .05 .02
❑ 16 Tom Rathman .05 .02
❑ 17 Daniel Stubbs RC .05 .02
❑ 18 Keena Turner .05 .02
❑ 19 Tim McKyer .05 .02
❑ 20 Larry Roberts .05 .02
❑ 21 Jeff Fuller .05 .02
❑ 22 Bubba Paris .05 .02
❑ 23 Bengals Team UER .10 .05
Boomer Esiason Measures Up (Should be versus Steelers in week three)
❑ 24 Eddie Brown .05 .02
❑ 25 Boomer Esiason .10 .05
❑ 26 Tim Krumrie .05 .02
❑ 27 Ickey Woods RC .10 .05
❑ 28 Anthony Munoz .10 .05
❑ 29 Tim McGee .05 .02
❑ 30 Max Montoya .05 .02
❑ 31 David Grant .05 .02
❑ 32 Rodney Holman RC .05 .02
(Cincinnati Bengals on card front is subject to various printing errors)
❑ 33 David Fulcher .10 .05
❑ 34 Jim Skow .05 .02
❑ 35 James Brooks .10 .05
❑ 36 Reggie Williams .05 .02
❑ 37 Eric Thomas RC .05 .02
❑ 38 Stanford Jennings .05 .02
❑ 39 Jim Breech .05 .02
❑ 40 Bills Team .25 .11
Jim Kelly Reads Defense
❑ 41 Shane Conlan .05 .02
❑ 42 Scott Norwood RC** .05 .02
❑ 43 Cornelius Bennett .10 .05
❑ 44 Bruce Smith .25 .11
❑ 45 Thurman Thomas RC 1.00 .45
❑ 46 Jim Kelly .50 .23
❑ 47 John Kidd .05 .02
❑ 48 Kent Hull RC .05 .02
❑ 49 Art Still .05 .02
❑ 50 Fred Smerlas .05 .02
❑ 51A Derrick Burroughs .05 .02
(White name plate)
❑ 51B Derrick Burroughs .05 .02
(Yellow name plate)
❑ 52 Andre Reed .25 .11
❑ 53 Robb Riddick .05 .02
❑ 54 Chris Burkett .05 .02
❑ 55 Ronnie Harmon .10 .05
❑ 56 Mark Kelso UER .05 .02
(team shown as %%Buffalo Bill~)
❑ 57 Bears Team .05 .02
Thomas Sanders Changes Pace
❑ 58 Mike Singletary .10 .05
❑ 59 Jay Hilgenberg UER .05 .02
(letter %%g~ is missing from Chicago)
❑ 60 Richard Dent .10 .05
❑ 61 Ron Rivera .05 .02
❑ 62 Jim McMahon .10 .05
❑ 63 Mike Tomczak .10 .05
❑ 64 Neal Anderson .10 .05
❑ 65 Dennis Gentry .05 .02
❑ 66 Dan Hampton .10 .05
❑ 67 David Tate .05 .02
❑ 68 Thomas Sanders RC .05 .02
❑ 69 Steve McMichael .10 .05
❑ 70 Dennis McKinnon .05 .02
❑ 71 Brad Muster RC .05 .02
❑ 72 Vestee Jackson RC .05 .02
❑ 73 Dave Duerson .05 .02
❑ 74 Vikings Team .05 .02
Millard Gets His Man
❑ 75 Joey Browner .05 .02
❑ 76 Carl Lee RC .05 .02
❑ 77 Gary Zimmerman .05 .02
❑ 78 Hassan Jones RC .05 .02
❑ 79 Anthony Carter .10 .05
❑ 80 Ray Berry .05 .02
❑ 81 Steve Jordan .05 .02
❑ 82 Issiac Holt .05 .02
❑ 83 Wade Wilson .10 .05
❑ 84 Chris Doleman .10 .05
❑ 85 Alfred Anderson .05 .02
❑ 86 Keith Millard .05 .02
❑ 87 Darrin Nelson .05 .02
❑ 88 D.J. Dozier .05 .02
❑ 89 Scott Studwell .05 .02
❑ 90 Oilers Team .05 .02
Tony Zendejas Big Boot
❑ 91 Bruce Matthews RC .25 .11
❑ 92 Curtis Duncan .05 .02
❑ 93 Warren Moon .25 .11
❑ 94 Johnny Meads RC .05 .02
❑ 95 Drew Hill .05 .02
❑ 96 Alonzo Highsmith .05 .02
❑ 97 Mike Munchak .05 .02
❑ 98 Mike Rozier .05 .02
❑ 99 Tony Zendejas .05 .02
❑ 100 Jeff Donaldson .05 .02
❑ 101 Ray Childress .05 .02
❑ 102 Sean Jones .10 .05
❑ 103 Ernest Givins .10 .05
❑ 104 William Fuller RC** .25 .11
❑ 105 Allen Pinkett RC .05 .02
❑ 106 Eagles Team .10 .05
Randall Cunningham Fakes Field
❑ 107 Keith Jackson RC .25 .11
❑ 108 Reggie White .25 .11
❑ 109 Clyde Simmons .10 .05
❑ 110 John Teltschik .05 .02
❑ 111 Wes Hopkins .05 .02
❑ 112 Keith Byars .10 .05
❑ 113 Jerome Brown .10 .05
❑ 114 Mike Quick .05 .02
❑ 115 Randall Cunningham .40 .18

❑ 116 Anthony Toney .05 .02
❑ 117 Ron Johnson .05 .02
❑ 118 Terry Hoage .05 .02
❑ 119 Seth Joyner .10 .05
❑ 120 Eric Allen RC .25 .11
❑ 121 Cris Carter RC 2.50 1.10
❑ 122 Rams Team .05 .02
Greg Bell Runs To Glory
❑ 123 Tom Newberry RC .05 .02
❑ 124 Pete Holohan .05 .02
❑ 125 Robert Delpino RC UER .05 .02
(Listed as Raider
on card back)
❑ 126 Carl Ekern .05 .02
❑ 127 Greg Bell .05 .02
❑ 128 Mike Lansford .05 .02
❑ 129 Jim Everett .10 .05
❑ 130 Mike Wilcher .05 .02
❑ 131 Jerry Gray .05 .02
❑ 132 Dale Hatcher .05 .02
❑ 133 Doug Smith .05 .02
❑ 134 Kevin Greene .25 .11
❑ 135 Jackie Slater .05 .02
❑ 136 Aaron Cox RC .05 .02
❑ 137 Henry Ellard .25 .11
❑ 138 Browns Team .10 .05
Bernie Kosar Quick
Release
❑ 139 Frank Minnifield .05 .02
❑ 140 Webster Slaughter .10 .05
❑ 141 Bernie Kosar .10 .05
❑ 142 Charles Buchanan .05 .02
❑ 143 Clay Matthews .10 .05
❑ 144 Reggie Langhorne RC .05 .02
❑ 145 Hanford Dixon .05 .02
❑ 146 Brian Brennan .05 .02
❑ 147 Earnest Byner .05 .02
❑ 148 Michael Dean Perry RC .10 .05
❑ 149 Kevin Mack .05 .02
❑ 150 Matt Bahr .05 .02
❑ 151 Ozzie Newsome .10 .05
❑ 152 Saints Team .10 .05
Craig Heyward Motors
Forward
❑ 153 Morten Andersen .05 .02
❑ 154 Pat Swilling .10 .05
❑ 155 Sam Mills .10 .05
❑ 156 Lonzell Hill .05 .02
❑ 157 Dalton Hilliard .05 .02
❑ 158 Craig Heyward RC .10 .05
❑ 159 Vaughan Johnson RC** .05 .02
❑ 160 Rueben Mayes .05 .02
❑ 161 Gene Atkins RC .05 .02
❑ 162 Bobby Hebert .10 .05
❑ 163 Rickey Jackson .10 .05
❑ 164 Eric Martin .05 .02
❑ 165 Giants Team .05 .02
Joe Morris Up
The Middle
❑ 166 Lawrence Taylor .25 .11
❑ 167 Bart Oates .05 .02
❑ 168 Carl Banks .05 .02
❑ 169 Eric Moore .05 .02
❑ 170 Sheldon White RC .05 .02
❑ 171 Mark Collins RC .05 .02
❑ 172 Phil Simms .10 .05
❑ 173 Jim Burt .05 .02
❑ 174 Stephen Baker RC .10 .05
❑ 175 Mark Bavaro .10 .05
❑ 176 Pepper Johnson .05 .02
❑ 177 Lionel Manuel .05 .02
❑ 178 Joe Morris .05 .02
❑ 179 John Elliott RC .05 .02
❑ 180 Gary Reasons RC .05 .02
❑ 181 Seahawks Team .10 .05
Dave Krieg Winds Up
❑ 182 Brian Blades RC .25 .11
❑ 183 Steve Largent .25 .11
❑ 184 Rufus Porter RC .05 .02
❑ 185 Ruben Rodriguez .05 .02
❑ 186 Curt Warner .05 .02
❑ 187 Paul Moyer .05 .02
❑ 188 Dave Krieg .10 .05
❑ 189 Jacob Green .05 .02
❑ 190 John L. Williams .05 .02
❑ 191 Eugene Robinson RC .05 .02
❑ 192 Brian Bosworth .10 .05
❑ 193 Patriots Team .05 .02
Tony Eason Behind
Blocking
❑ 194 John Stephens RC .05 .02
❑ 195 Robert Perryman RC .05 .02
❑ 196 Andre Tippett .05 .02
❑ 197 Fred Marion .05 .02
❑ 198 Doug Flutie .75 .35
❑ 199 Stanley Morgan .05 .02
❑ 200 Johnny Rembert RC .05 .02
❑ 201 Tony Eason .05 .02
❑ 202 Marvin Allen .05 .02
❑ 203 Raymond Clayborn .05 .02
❑ 204 Irving Fryar .25 .11
❑ 205 Colts Team .05 .02
Chris Chandler
All Alone
❑ 206 Eric Dickerson .10 .05
❑ 207 Chris Hinton .05 .02
❑ 208 Duane Bickett .05 .02
❑ 209 Chris Chandler RC .75 .35
❑ 210 Jon Hand .05 .02
❑ 211 Ray Donaldson .05 .02
❑ 212 Dean Biasucci .05 .02
❑ 213 Bill Brooks .10 .05
❑ 214 Chris Goode RC .05 .02
❑ 215 Clarence Verdin RC** .05 .02
❑ 216 Albert Bentley .05 .02
❑ 217 Passing Leaders .10 .05
Wade Wilson
Boomer Esiason
❑ 218 Receiving Leaders .10 .05
Henry Ellard
Al Toon
❑ 219 Rushing Leaders .10 .05
Herschel Walker
Eric Dickerson
❑ 220 Scoring Leaders .05 .02
Mike Cofer
Scott Norwood
❑ 221 Intercept Leaders .05 .02
Scott Case
Erik McMillan
❑ 222 Jets Team .05 .02
Ken O'Brien Surveys
Scene
❑ 223 Erik McMillan RC .05 .02
❑ 224 James Hasty RC .05 .02
❑ 225 Al Toon .10 .05
❑ 226 John Booty RC .05 .02
❑ 227 Johnny Hector .05 .02
❑ 228 Ken O'Brien .05 .02
❑ 229 Marty Lyons .05 .02
❑ 230 Mickey Shuler .05 .02
❑ 231 Robin Cole .05 .02
❑ 232 Freeman McNeil .05 .02
❑ 233 Marion Barber .05 .02
❑ 234 Jo Jo Townsell .05 .02
❑ 235 Wesley Walker .05 .02
❑ 236 Roger Vick .05 .02
❑ 237 Pat Leahy .05 .02
❑ 238 Broncos Team UER .50 .23
John Elway Ground Attack
(Score of week 15 says
42-21, should be 42-14)
❑ 239 Mike Horan .05 .02
❑ 240 Tony Dorsett .25 .11
❑ 241 John Elway 2.00 .90
❑ 242 Mark Jackson .05 .02
❑ 243 Sammy Winder .05 .02
❑ 244 Rich Karlis .05 .02
❑ 245 Vance Johnson .10 .05
❑ 246 Steve Sewell RC .05 .02
❑ 247 Karl Mecklenburg UER .05 .02
(Drafted 2, should be 12)
❑ 248 Rulon Jones .05 .02
❑ 249 Simon Fletcher RC .05 .02
❑ 250 Redskins Team .10 .05
Doug Williams Sets Up
❑ 251 Chip Lohmiller RC .05 .02
❑ 252 Jamie Morris .05 .02
❑ 253 Mark Rypien RC UER .10 .05
(14 1988 completions,
should be 114)
❑ 254 Barry Wilburn .05 .02
❑ 255 Mark May RC .05 .02
❑ 256 Wilber Marshall .05 .02
❑ 257 Charles Mann .05 .02
❑ 258 Gary Clark .25 .11
❑ 259 Doug Williams .10 .05
❑ 260 Art Monk .10 .05
❑ 261 Kelvin Bryant .05 .02
❑ 262 Dexter Manley .05 .02
❑ 263 Ricky Sanders .05 .02
❑ 264 Raiders Team .25 .11
Marcus Allen Through
the Line
❑ 265 Tim Brown RC 1.50 .70
❑ 266 Jay Schroeder .05 .02
❑ 267 Marcus Allen .25 .11
❑ 268 Mike Haynes .10 .05
❑ 269 Bo Jackson .25 .11
❑ 270 Steve Beuerlein RC .60 .25
❑ 271 Vann McElroy .05 .02
❑ 272 Willie Gault .10 .05
❑ 273 Howie Long .10 .05
❑ 274 Greg Townsend .05 .02
❑ 275 Mike Wise .05 .02
❑ 276 Cardinals Team .05 .02
Neil Lomax Looks Long
❑ 277 Luis Sharpe .05 .02
❑ 278 Scott Dill .05 .02
❑ 279 Vai Sikahema .05 .02
❑ 280 Ron Wolfley .05 .02
❑ 281 David Galloway .05 .02
❑ 282 Jay Novacek RC .25 .11
❑ 283 Neil Lomax .05 .02
❑ 284 Robert Awalt .05 .02
❑ 285 Cedric Mack .05 .02
❑ 286 Freddie Joe Nunn .05 .02
❑ 287 J.T. Smith .05 .02
❑ 288 Stump Mitchell .05 .02
❑ 289 Roy Green .10 .05
❑ 290 Dolphins Team .50 .23
Dan Marino High and Far
❑ 291 Jarvis Williams RC .05 .02
❑ 292 Troy Stradford .05 .02
❑ 293 Dan Marino 2.00 .90
❑ 294 T.J. Turner .05 .02
❑ 295 John Offerdahl .05 .02
❑ 296 Ferrell Edmunds RC .05 .02
❑ 297 Scott Schwedes .05 .02
❑ 298 Lorenzo Hampton .05 .02
❑ 299 Jim C.Jensen RC .05 .02
❑ 300 Brian Sochia .05 .02
❑ 301 Reggie Roby .05 .02
❑ 302 Mark Clayton .10 .05
❑ 303 Chargers Team .05 .02
Tim Spencer Leads
the Way
❑ 304 Lee Williams .05 .02
❑ 305 Gary Plummer RC** .05 .02
❑ 306 Gary Anderson RB .05 .02
❑ 307 Gill Byrd .05 .02
❑ 308 Jamie Holland RC .05 .02
❑ 309 Billy Ray Smith .05 .02
❑ 310 Lionel James .05 .02
❑ 311 Mark Vlasic RC .05 .02
❑ 312 Curtis Adams .05 .02
❑ 313 Anthony Miller RC .25 .11
❑ 314 Steelers Team .05 .02
Frank Pollard Set
for Action
❑ 315 Bubby Brister RC .50 .23
❑ 316 David Little .05 .02
❑ 317 Tunch Ilkin RC .05 .02
❑ 318 Louis Lipps .10 .05
❑ 319 Warren Williams RC .05 .02
❑ 320 Dwight Stone .10 .05
❑ 321 Merril Hoge RC .05 .02
❑ 322 Thomas Everett RC .05 .02
❑ 323 Rod Woodson RC .50 .23
❑ 324 Gary Anderson K .05 .02
❑ 325 Buccaneers Team .05 .02
Ron Hall in Pursuit
❑ 326 Donnie Elder .05 .02
❑ 327 Vinny Testaverde .30 .14
❑ 328 Harry Hamilton .05 .02
❑ 329 James Wilder .05 .02
❑ 330 Lars Tate .05 .02
❑ 331 Mark Carrier WR RC .25 .11

	Card		MINT	NRMT
❑	332	Bruce Hill RC	.05	.02
❑	333	Paul Gruber RC	.05	.02
❑	334	Ricky Reynolds	.05	.02
❑	335	Eugene Marve	.05	.02
❑	336	Falcons Team Joel Williams Holds On	.05	.02
❑	337	Aundray Bruce RC	.05	.02
❑	338	John Rade	.05	.02
❑	339	Scott Case RC	.05	.02
❑	340	Robert Moore	.05	.02
❑	341	Chris Miller RC	.25	.11
❑	342	Gerald Riggs	.10	.05
❑	343	Gene Lang	.05	.02
❑	344	Marcus Cotton	.05	.02
❑	345	Rick Donnelly	.05	.02
❑	346	John Settle RC	.05	.02
❑	347	Bill Fralic	.05	.02
❑	348	Chiefs Team Dino Hackett Zeros In	.05	.02
❑	349	Steve DeBerg	.05	.02
❑	350	Mike Stensrud	.05	.02
❑	351	Dino Hackett	.05	.02
❑	352	Deron Cherry	.10	.05
❑	353	Christian Okoye	.05	.02
❑	354	Bill Maas	.05	.02
❑	355	Carlos Carson	.05	.02
❑	356	Albert Lewis	.05	.02
❑	357	Paul Palmer	.05	.02
❑	358	Nick Lowery	.05	.02
❑	359	Stephone Paige	.05	.02
❑	360	Lions Team Chuck Long Gets the Snap	.05	.02
❑	361	Chris Spielman RC	.25	.11
❑	362	Jim Arnold	.05	.02
❑	363	Devon Mitchell	.05	.02
❑	364	Mike Cofer	.05	.02
❑	365	Bennie Blades RC	.05	.02
❑	366	James Jones	.05	.02
❑	367	Garry James	.05	.02
❑	368	Pete Mandley	.05	.02
❑	369	Keith Ferguson	.05	.02
❑	370	Dennis Gibson	.05	.02
❑	371	Packers Team UER Johnny Holland Over the Top (Week 16 has vs. Vikings, but they played Bears)	.05	.02
❑	372	Brent Fullwood RC	.05	.02
❑	373	Don Majkowski RC UER (3 TD's in 1987, should be 5)	.10	.05
❑	374	Tim Harris	.05	.02
❑	375	Keith Woodside RC	.05	.02
❑	376	Mark Murphy	.05	.02
❑	377	Dave Brown DB	.05	.02
❑	378	Perry Kemp RC	.05	.02
❑	379	Sterling Sharpe RC	.75	.35
❑	380	Chuck Cecil RC	.05	.02
❑	381	Walter Stanley	.05	.02
❑	382	Cowboys Team Steve Pelluer Lets It Go	.05	.02
❑	383	Michael Irvin RC	1.25	.55
❑	384	Bill Bates	.10	.05
❑	385	Herschel Walker	.25	.11
❑	386	Darryl Clack	.05	.02
❑	387	Danny Noonan	.05	.02
❑	388	Eugene Lockhart RC	.05	.02
❑	389	Ed Too Tall Jones	.10	.05
❑	390	Steve Pelluer	.05	.02
❑	391	Ray Alexander	.05	.02
❑	392	Nate Newton RC	.10	.05
❑	393	Garry Cobb	.05	.02
❑	394	Checklist 1-132	.05	.02
❑	395	Checklist 133-264	.05	.02
❑	396	Checklist 265-396	.05	.02

1989 Topps Traded

	MINT	NRMT
COMP.FACT.SET (132)	20.00	9.00
COMMON CARD (1T-132T)	.05	.02
SEMISTARS	.10	.05
UNLISTED STARS	.25	.11

	Card		MINT	NRMT
❑	1T	Eric Ball RC	.05	.02
❑	2T	Tony Mandarich RC	.05	.02
❑	3T	Shawn Collins RC	.05	.02
❑	4T	Ray Bentley RC	.05	.02
❑	5T	Tony Casillas	.05	.02
❑	6T	Al Del Greco RC	.05	.02
❑	7T	Dan Saleaumua RC	.10	.05
❑	8T	Keith Bishop	.05	.02
❑	9T	Rodney Peete RC	.25	.11
❑	10T	Lorenzo White RC	.25	.11
❑	11T	Steve Smith RC	.10	.05
❑	12T	Pete Mandley	.05	.02
❑	13T	Mervyn Fernandez RC**/C	.05	.02
❑	14T	Flipper Anderson RC	.25	.11
❑	15T	Louis Oliver RC	.10	.05
❑	16T	Rick Fenney	.05	.02
❑	17T	Gary Jeter	.05	.02
❑	18T	Greg Cox	.05	.02
❑	19T	Bubba McDowell RC	.10	.05
❑	20T	Ron Heller	.05	.02
❑	21T	Tim McDonald RC	.05	.02
❑	22T	Jerrol Williams RC	.05	.02
❑	23T	Marion Butts RC	.10	.05
❑	24T	Steve Young	.75	.35
❑	25T	Mike Merriweather	.05	.02
❑	26T	Richard Johnson	.05	.02
❑	27T	Gerald Riggs	.10	.05
❑	28T	Dave Waymer	.05	.02
❑	29T	Issiac Holt	.05	.02
❑	30T	Deion Sanders RC	1.50	.70
❑	31T	Todd Blackledge	.05	.02
❑	32T	Jeff Cross RC	.05	.02
❑	33T	Steve Wisniewski RC	.10	.05
❑	34T	Ron Brown	.10	.05
❑	35T	Rod Bernstine RC	.05	.02
❑	36T	Jeff Uhlenhake RC	.05	.02
❑	37T	Donnell Woolford RC	.25	.11
❑	38T	Bob Gagliano RC	.05	.02
❑	39T	Ezra Johnson	.05	.02
❑	40T	Ron Jaworski	.05	.02
❑	41T	Lawyer Tillman RC	.05	.02
❑	42T	Lorenzo Lynch RC	.05	.02
❑	43T	Mike Alexander	.05	.02
❑	44T	Tim Worley RC	.05	.02
❑	45T	Guy Bingham	.05	.02
❑	46T	Cleveland Gary RC	.05	.02
❑	47T	Danny Peebles	.05	.02
❑	48T	Clarence Weathers RC	.05	.02
❑	49T	Jeff Lageman RC	.25	.11
❑	50T	Eric Metcalf RC	.25	.11
❑	51T	Myron Guyton RC	.05	.02
❑	52T	Steve Atwater RC	.05	.02
❑	53T	John Fourcade RC	.05	.02
❑	54T	Randall McDaniel RC	.10	.05
❑	55T	Al Noga RC	.05	.02
❑	56T	Sammie Smith RC	.10	.05
❑	57T	Jesse Solomon	.05	.02
❑	58T	Greg Kragen RC	.05	.02
❑	59T	Don Beebe RC	.25	.11
❑	60T	Hart Lee Dykes RC	.10	.05
❑	61T	Trace Armstrong RC	.10	.05
❑	62T	Steve Pelluer	.05	.02
❑	63T	Barry Krauss	.05	.02
❑	64T	Kevin Murphy RC	.05	.02
❑	65T	Steve Tasker RC	.25	.11
❑	66T	Jessie Small RC	.05	.02
❑	67T	Dave Meggett RC	.25	.11
❑	68T	Dean Hamel	.05	.02
❑	69T	Jim Covert	.05	.02
❑	70T	Troy Aikman RC	6.00	2.70
❑	71T	Raul Allegre	.05	.02
❑	72T	Chris Jacke RC	.10	.05
❑	73T	Leslie O'Neal	.10	.05
❑	74T	Keith Taylor RC	.05	.02
❑	75T	Steve Walsh RC	.25	.11
❑	76T	Tracy Rocker	.05	.02
❑	77T	Robert Massey RC	.10	.05
❑	78T	Bryan Wagner	.05	.02
❑	79T	Steve DeOssie	.05	.02
❑	80T	Carnell Lake RC	.10	.05
❑	81T	Frank Reich RC	.25	.11
❑	82T	Tyrone Braxton RC	.05	.02
❑	83T	Barry Sanders RC	12.00	5.50
❑	84T	Pete Stoyanovich RC	.10	.05
❑	85T	Paul Palmer	.05	.02
❑	86T	Billy Joe Tolliver RC	.05	.02
❑	87T	Eric Hill RC	.10	.05
❑	88T	Gerald McNeil	.05	.02
❑	89T	Bill Hawkins RC	.05	.02
❑	90T	Derrick Thomas RC	1.25	.55
❑	91T	Jim Harbaugh RC	.75	.35
❑	92T	Brian Williams OL	.05	.02
❑	93T	Jack Trudeau	.05	.02
❑	94T	Leonard Smith	.05	.02
❑	95T	Gary Hogeboom	.05	.02
❑	96T	A.J. Johnson RC	.05	.02
❑	97T	Jim McMahon	.10	.05
❑	98T	David Williams RC	.05	.02
❑	99T	Rohn Stark	.05	.02
❑	100T	Sean Landeta	.05	.02
❑	101T	Tim Johnson RC	.05	.02
❑	102T	Andre Rison RC	.75	.35
❑	103T	Earnest Byner	.10	.05
❑	104T	Don McPherson RC	.05	.02
❑	105T	Zefross Moss RC	.05	.02
❑	106T	Frank Stams RC	.05	.02
❑	107T	Courtney Hall RC	.10	.05
❑	108T	Marc Logan RC	.05	.02
❑	109T	James Lofton	.25	.11
❑	110T	Lewis Tillman RC	.10	.05
❑	111T	Irv Pankey RC	.05	.02
❑	112T	Ralf Mojsiejenko	.05	.02
❑	113T	Bobby Humphrey RC	.05	.02
❑	114T	Chris Burkett	.05	.02
❑	115T	Greg Lloyd RC	.25	.11
❑	116T	Matt Millen	.10	.05
❑	117T	Carl Zander	.05	.02
❑	118T	Wayne Martin RC	.25	.11
❑	119T	Mike Saxon	.05	.02
❑	120T	Herschel Walker	.10	.05
❑	121T	Andy Heck RC	.05	.02
❑	122T	Mark Robinson	.05	.02
❑	123T	Keith Van Horne RC	.05	.02
❑	124T	Ricky Hunley	.05	.02
❑	125T	Timm Rosenbach RC	.10	.05
❑	126T	Steve Grogan	.10	.05
❑	127T	Stephen Braggs RC	.05	.02
❑	128T	Terry Long	.05	.02
❑	129T	Evan Cooper	.05	.02
❑	130T	Robert Lyles	.05	.02
❑	131T	Mike Webster	.10	.05
❑	132T	Checklist 1-132	.05	.02

1990 Topps

	MINT	NRMT
COMPLETE SET (528)	10.00	4.50
COMP.FACT.SET (528)	12.00	5.50
COMMON CARD (1-528)	.04	.02
SEMISTARS	.10	.05
UNLISTED STARS	.25	.11
COMP.TIFFANY SET (528)	200.00	90.00
*TIFFANY STARS: 6X TO 15X HI COL.		
*TIFFANY RCs: 3X TO 8X		
❑ 1 Joe Montana RB	.50	.23
Most TD Passes,		
Super Bowl		
❑ 2 Flipper Anderson RB	.04	.02
Most Receiving		
Yards, Game		
❑ 3 Troy Aikman RB	.40	.18
Most Passing Yards,		
Game, Rookie		
❑ 4 Kevin Butler RB	.04	.02
Most Consecutive		
Field Goals		
❑ 5 Super Bowl XXIV	.04	.02
49ers 55		
Broncos 10		
(line of scrimmage)		
❑ 6 Dexter Carter RC	.04	.02
❑ 7 Matt Millen	.10	.05
❑ 8 Jerry Rice	.75	.35
❑ 9 Ronnie Lott	.10	.05
❑ 10 John Taylor	.10	.05
❑ 11 Guy McIntyre	.04	.02
❑ 12 Roger Craig	.10	.05
❑ 13 Joe Montana	1.25	.55
❑ 14 Brent Jones RC	.25	.11
❑ 15 Tom Rathman	.04	.02
❑ 16 Harris Barton	.04	.02
❑ 17 Charles Haley	.10	.05
❑ 18 Pierce Holt RC	.04	.02
❑ 19 Michael Carter	.04	.02
❑ 20 Chet Brooks	.04	.02
❑ 21 Eric Wright	.04	.02
❑ 22 Mike Cofer	.04	.02
❑ 23 Jim Fahnhorst	.04	.02
❑ 24 Keena Turner	.04	.02
❑ 25 Don Griffin	.04	.02
❑ 26 Kevin Fagan RC	.04	.02
❑ 27 Bubba Paris	.04	.02
❑ 28 Rushing Leaders	.50	.23
Barry Sanders		
Christian Okoye		
❑ 29 Steve Atwater	.04	.02
❑ 30 Tyrone Braxton	.04	.02
❑ 31 Ron Holmes	.04	.02
❑ 32 Bobby Humphrey	.04	.02
❑ 33 Greg Kragen	.04	.02
❑ 34 David Treadwell	.04	.02
❑ 35 Karl Mecklenburg	.04	.02
❑ 36 Dennis Smith	.04	.02
❑ 37 John Elway	1.25	.55
❑ 38 Vance Johnson	.04	.02
❑ 39 Simon Fletcher UER	.04	.02
(Front DL, back LB)		
❑ 40 Jim Juriga	.04	.02
❑ 41 Mark Jackson	.04	.02
❑ 42 Melvin Bratton RC	.04	.02
❑ 43 Wymon Henderson RC**	.04	.02
❑ 44 Ken Bell	.04	.02
❑ 45 Sammy Winder	.04	.02
❑ 46 Alphonso Carreker	.04	.02
❑ 47 Orson Mobley RC	.04	.02
❑ 48 Rodney Hampton RC	.40	.18
❑ 49 Dave Meggett	.10	.05
❑ 50 Myron Guyton	.04	.02
❑ 51 Phil Simms	.10	.05
❑ 52 Lawrence Taylor	.25	.11
❑ 53 Carl Banks	.04	.02
❑ 54 Pepper Johnson	.04	.02
❑ 55 Leonard Marshall	.04	.02
❑ 56 Mark Collins	.04	.02
❑ 57 Erik Howard	.04	.02
❑ 58 Eric Dorsey RC	.04	.02
❑ 59 Ottis Anderson	.10	.05
❑ 60 Mark Bavaro	.04	.02
❑ 61 Odessa Turner RC	.04	.02
❑ 62 Gary Reasons	.04	.02
❑ 63 Maurice Carthon	.04	.02
❑ 64 Lionel Manuel	.04	.02
❑ 65 Sean Landeta	.04	.02
❑ 66 Perry Williams	.04	.02
❑ 67 Pat Terrell RC	.04	.02
❑ 68 Flipper Anderson	.04	.02
❑ 69 Jackie Slater	.04	.02
❑ 70 Tom Newberry	.04	.02
❑ 71 Jerry Gray	.04	.02
❑ 72 Henry Ellard	.10	.05
❑ 73 Doug Smith	.04	.02
❑ 74 Kevin Greene	.25	.11
❑ 75 Jim Everett	.10	.05
❑ 76 Mike Lansford	.04	.02
❑ 77 Greg Bell	.04	.02
❑ 78 Pete Holohan	.04	.02
❑ 79 Robert Delpino	.04	.02
❑ 80 Mike Wilcher	.04	.02
❑ 81 Mike Piel	.04	.02
❑ 82 Mel Owens	.04	.02
❑ 83 Michael Stewart RC	.04	.02
❑ 84 Ben Smith RC	.04	.02
❑ 85 Keith Jackson	.10	.05
❑ 86 Reggie White	.25	.11
❑ 87 Eric Allen	.04	.02
❑ 88 Jerome Brown	.04	.02
❑ 89 Robert Drummond	.04	.02
❑ 90 Anthony Toney	.04	.02
❑ 91 Keith Byars	.04	.02
❑ 92 Cris Carter	.50	.23
❑ 93 Randall Cunningham	.25	.11
❑ 94 Ron Johnson	.04	.02
❑ 95 Mike Quick	.04	.02
❑ 96 Clyde Simmons	.04	.02
❑ 97 Mike Pitts	.04	.02
❑ 98 Izel Jenkins RC	.04	.02
❑ 99 Seth Joyner	.10	.05
❑ 100 Mike Schad	.04	.02
❑ 101 Wes Hopkins	.04	.02
❑ 102 Kirk Lowdermilk	.04	.02
❑ 103 Rick Fenney	.04	.02
❑ 104 Randall McDaniel	.04	.02
❑ 105 Herschel Walker	.10	.05
❑ 106 Al Noga	.04	.02
❑ 107 Gary Zimmerman	.04	.02
❑ 108 Chris Doleman	.04	.02
❑ 109 Keith Millard	.04	.02
❑ 110 Carl Lee	.04	.02
❑ 111 Joey Browner	.04	.02
❑ 112 Steve Jordan	.04	.02
❑ 113 Reggie Rutland RC	.04	.02
❑ 114 Wade Wilson	.10	.05
❑ 115 Anthony Carter	.10	.05
❑ 116 Rich Karlis	.04	.02
❑ 117 Hassan Jones	.04	.02
❑ 118 Henry Thomas	.04	.02
❑ 119 Scott Studwell	.04	.02
❑ 120 Ralf Mojsiejenko	.04	.02
❑ 121 Earnest Byner	.04	.02
❑ 122 Gerald Riggs	.10	.05
❑ 123 Tracy Rocker	.04	.02
❑ 124 A.J. Johnson	.04	.02
❑ 125 Charles Mann	.04	.02
❑ 126 Art Monk	.10	.05
❑ 127 Ricky Sanders	.04	.02
❑ 128 Gary Clark	.25	.11
❑ 129 Jim Lachey	.04	.02
❑ 130 Martin Mayhew RC	.04	.02
❑ 131 Ravin Caldwell	.04	.02
❑ 132 Don Warren	.04	.02
❑ 133 Mark Rypien	.10	.05
❑ 134 Ed Simmons RC	.04	.02
❑ 135 Darryl Grant	.04	.02
❑ 136 Darrell Green	.10	.05
❑ 137 Chip Lohmiller	.04	.02
❑ 138 Tony Bennett RC	.25	.11
❑ 139 Tony Mandarich	.04	.02
❑ 140 Sterling Sharpe	.25	.11
❑ 141 Tim Harris	.04	.02
❑ 142 Don Majkowski	.04	.02
❑ 143 Rich Moran RC	.04	.02
❑ 144 Jeff Query	.04	.02
❑ 145 Brent Fullwood	.04	.02
❑ 146 Chris Jacke	.04	.02
❑ 147 Keith Woodside	.04	.02
❑ 148 Perry Kemp	.04	.02
❑ 149 Herman Fontenot	.04	.02
❑ 150 Dave Brown DB	.04	.02
❑ 151 Brian Noble	.04	.02
❑ 152 Johnny Holland	.04	.02
❑ 153 Mark Murphy	.04	.02
❑ 154 Bob Nelson	.04	.02
❑ 155 Darrell Thompson RC	.04	.02
❑ 156 Lawyer Tillman	.04	.02
❑ 157 Eric Metcalf	.25	.11
❑ 158 Webster Slaughter	.10	.05
❑ 159 Frank Minnifield	.04	.02
❑ 160 Brian Brennan	.04	.02
❑ 161 Thane Gash RC	.04	.02
❑ 162 Robert Banks DE	.04	.02
❑ 163 Bernie Kosar	.10	.05
❑ 164 David Grayson	.04	.02
❑ 165 Kevin Mack	.04	.02
❑ 166 Mike Johnson	.04	.02
❑ 167 Tim Manoa	.04	.02
❑ 168 Ozzie Newsome	.10	.05
❑ 169 Felix Wright	.04	.02
❑ 170 Al(Bubba) Baker	.10	.05
❑ 171 Reggie Langhorne	.04	.02
❑ 172 Clay Matthews	.10	.05
❑ 173 Andrew Stewart	.04	.02
❑ 174 Barry Foster RC	.25	.11
❑ 175 Tim Worley	.04	.02
❑ 176 Tim Johnson	.04	.02
❑ 177 Carnell Lake	.04	.02
❑ 178 Greg Lloyd	.25	.11
❑ 179 Rod Woodson	.25	.11
❑ 180 Tunch Ilkin	.04	.02
❑ 181 Dermontti Dawson	.10	.05
❑ 182 Gary Anderson K	.04	.02
❑ 183 Bubby Brister	.04	.02
❑ 184 Louis Lipps	.10	.05
❑ 185 Merril Hoge	.04	.02
❑ 186 Mike Mularkey	.04	.02
❑ 187 Derek Hill	.04	.02
❑ 188 Rodney Carter	.04	.02
❑ 189 Dwayne Woodruff	.04	.02
❑ 190 Keith Willis	.04	.02
❑ 191 Jerry Olsavsky	.04	.02
❑ 192 Mark Stock	.04	.02
❑ 193 Sacks Leaders	.04	.02
Chris Doleman		
Lee Williams		
❑ 194 Leonard Smith	.04	.02
❑ 195 Darryl Talley	.04	.02
❑ 196 Mark Kelso	.04	.02
❑ 197 Kent Hull	.04	.02
❑ 198 Nate Odomes RC	.10	.05
❑ 199 Pete Metzelaars	.04	.02
❑ 200 Don Beebe	.10	.05
❑ 201 Ray Bentley	.04	.02
❑ 202 Steve Tasker	.10	.05
❑ 203 Scott Norwood	.04	.02
❑ 204 Andre Reed	.25	.11
❑ 205 Bruce Smith	.25	.11
❑ 206 Thurman Thomas	.25	.11
❑ 207 Jim Kelly	.25	.11
❑ 208 Cornelius Bennett	.10	.05
❑ 209 Shane Conlan	.04	.02
❑ 210 Larry Kinnebrew	.04	.02
❑ 211 Jeff Alm RC	.04	.02
❑ 212 Robert Lyles	.04	.02
❑ 213 Bubba McDowell	.04	.02
❑ 214 Mike Munchak	.04	.02
❑ 215 Bruce Matthews	.10	.05
❑ 216 Warren Moon	.25	.11
❑ 217 Drew Hill	.04	.02
❑ 218 Ray Childress	.04	.02
❑ 219 Steve Brown	.04	.02
❑ 220 Alonzo Highsmith	.04	.02
❑ 221 Allen Pinkett	.04	.02
❑ 222 Sean Jones	.10	.05
❑ 223 Johnny Meads	.04	.02
❑ 224 John Grimsley	.04	.02
❑ 225 Haywood Jeffires RC	.25	.11
❑ 226 Curtis Duncan	.04	.02
❑ 227 Greg Montgomery RC	.04	.02
❑ 228 Ernest Givins	.10	.05
❑ 229 Passing Leaders	.30	.14
Joe Montana		
Boomer Esiason		
❑ 230 Robert Massey	.04	.02

❑ 231 John Fourcade .04 .02
❑ 232 Dalton Hilliard .04 .02
❑ 233 Vaughan Johnson .04 .02
❑ 234 Hoby Brenner .04 .02
❑ 235 Pat Swilling .10 .05
❑ 236 Kevin Haverdink .04 .02
❑ 237 Bobby Hebert .04 .02
❑ 238 Sam Mills .10 .05
❑ 239 Eric Martin .04 .02
❑ 240 Lonzell Hill .04 .02
❑ 241 Steve Trapilo .04 .02
❑ 242 Rickey Jackson .10 .05
❑ 243 Craig Heyward .10 .05
❑ 244 Rueben Mayes .04 .02
❑ 245 Morten Andersen .04 .02
❑ 246 Percy Snow RC .04 .02
❑ 247 Pete Mandley .04 .02
❑ 248 Derrick Thomas .25 .11
❑ 249 Dan Saleaumua .04 .02
❑ 250 Todd McNair RC .04 .02
❑ 251 Leonard Griffin .04 .02
❑ 252 Jonathan Hayes .04 .02
❑ 253 Christian Okoye .04 .02
❑ 254 Albert Lewis .04 .02
❑ 255 Nick Lowery .04 .02
❑ 256 Kevin Ross .04 .02
❑ 257 Steve DeBerg UER .04 .02
(Total 45,046,
should be 25,046)
❑ 258 Stephone Paige .04 .02
❑ 259 James Saxon RC .04 .02
❑ 260 Herman Heard .04 .02
❑ 261 Deron Cherry .04 .02
❑ 262 Dino Hackett .04 .02
❑ 263 Neil Smith .25 .11
❑ 264 Steve Pelluer .04 .02
❑ 265 Eric Thomas .04 .02
❑ 266 Eric Ball .04 .02
❑ 267 Leon White .04 .02
❑ 268 Tim Krumrie .04 .02
❑ 269 Jason Buck .04 .02
❑ 270 Boomer Esiason .10 .05
❑ 271 Carl Zander .04 .02
❑ 272 Eddie Brown .04 .02
❑ 273 David Fulcher .04 .02
❑ 274 Tim McGee .04 .02
❑ 275 James Brooks .10 .05
❑ 276 Rickey Dixon RC .04 .02
❑ 277 Ickey Woods .04 .02
❑ 278 Anthony Munoz .10 .05
❑ 279 Rodney Holman .04 .02
❑ 280 Mike Alexander .04 .02
❑ 281 Mervyn Fernandez .04 .02
❑ 282 Steve Wisniewski .10 .05
❑ 283 Steve Smith .04 .02
❑ 284 Howie Long .10 .05
❑ 285 Bo Jackson .25 .11
❑ 286 Mike Dyal .04 .02
❑ 287 Thomas Benson .04 .02
❑ 288 Willie Gault .10 .05
❑ 289 Marcus Allen .25 .11
❑ 290 Greg Townsend .04 .02
❑ 291 Steve Beuerlein .10 .05
❑ 292 Scott Davis .04 .02
❑ 293 Eddie Anderson RC .04 .02
❑ 294 Terry McDaniel .04 .02
❑ 295 Tim Brown .25 .11
❑ 296 Bob Golic .04 .02
❑ 297 Jeff Jaeger RC .04 .02
❑ 298 Jeff George RC 1.00 .45
❑ 299 Chip Banks .04 .02
❑ 300 Andre Rison UER .25 .11
(Photo actually
Clarence Weathers)
❑ 301 Rohn Stark .04 .02
❑ 302 Keith Taylor .04 .02
❑ 303 Jack Trudeau .04 .02
❑ 304 Chris Hinton .04 .02
❑ 305 Ray Donaldson .04 .02
❑ 306 Jeff Herrod RC .04 .02
❑ 307 Clarence Verdin .04 .02
❑ 308 Jon Hand .04 .02
❑ 309 Bill Brooks .04 .02
❑ 310 Albert Bentley .04 .02
❑ 311 Mike Prior .04 .02
❑ 312 Pat Beach .04 .02
❑ 313 Eugene Daniel .04 .02
❑ 314 Duane Bickett .04 .02
❑ 315 Dean Biasucci .04 .02
❑ 316 Richmond Webb RC .04 .02
❑ 317 Jeff Cross .04 .02
❑ 318 Louis Oliver .04 .02
❑ 319 Sammie Smith .04 .02
❑ 320 Pete Stoyanovich .04 .02
❑ 321 John Offerdahl .04 .02
❑ 322 Ferrell Edmunds .04 .02
❑ 323 Dan Marino 1.25 .55
❑ 324 Andre Brown .04 .02
❑ 325 Reggie Roby .04 .02
❑ 326 Jarvis Williams .04 .02
❑ 327 Roy Foster .04 .02
❑ 328 Mark Clayton .10 .05
❑ 329 Brian Sochia .04 .02
❑ 330 Mark Duper .10 .05
❑ 331 T.J. Turner .04 .02
❑ 332 Jeff Uhlenhake .04 .02
❑ 333 Jim C.Jensen .04 .02
❑ 334 Cortez Kennedy RC .25 .11
❑ 335 Andy Heck .04 .02
❑ 336 Rufus Porter .04 .02
❑ 337 Brian Blades .10 .05
❑ 338 Dave Krieg .10 .05
❑ 339 John L. Williams .04 .02
❑ 340 David Wyman .04 .02
❑ 341 Paul Skansi RC .04 .02
❑ 342 Eugene Robinson .04 .02
❑ 343 Joe Nash .04 .02
❑ 344 Jacob Green .04 .02
❑ 345 Jeff Bryant .04 .02
❑ 346 Ruben Rodriguez .04 .02
❑ 347 Norm Johnson .04 .02
❑ 348 Darren Comeaux .04 .02
❑ 349 Andre Ware RC .10 .05
❑ 350 Richard Johnson .04 .02
❑ 351 Rodney Peete .10 .05
❑ 352 Barry Sanders 2.50 1.10
❑ 353 Chris Spielman .25 .11
❑ 354 Eddie Murray .04 .02
❑ 355 Jerry Ball .04 .02
❑ 356 Mel Gray .10 .05
❑ 357 Eric Williams RC .04 .02
❑ 358 Robert Clark RC .04 .02
❑ 359 Jason Phillips .04 .02
❑ 360 Terry Taylor RC .04 .02
❑ 361 Bennie Blades .04 .02
❑ 362 Michael Cofer .04 .02
❑ 363 Jim Arnold .04 .02
❑ 364 Marc Spindler RC .04 .02
❑ 365 Jim Covert .04 .02
❑ 366 Jim Harbaugh .25 .11
❑ 367 Neal Anderson .10 .05
❑ 368 Mike Singletary .10 .05
❑ 369 John Roper .04 .02
❑ 370 Steve McMichael .10 .05
❑ 371 Dennis Gentry .04 .02
❑ 372 Brad Muster .04 .02
❑ 373 Ron Morris .04 .02
❑ 374 James Thornton .04 .02
❑ 375 Kevin Butler .04 .02
❑ 376 Richard Dent .10 .05
❑ 377 Dan Hampton .10 .05
❑ 378 Jay Hilgenberg .04 .02
❑ 379 Donnell Woolford .04 .02
❑ 380 Trace Armstrong .04 .02
❑ 381 Junior Seau RC 1.00 .45
❑ 382 Rod Bernstine .04 .02
❑ 383 Marion Butts .10 .05
❑ 384 Burt Grossman .04 .02
❑ 385 Darrin Nelson .04 .02
❑ 386 Leslie O'Neal .10 .05
❑ 387 Billy Joe Tolliver .04 .02
❑ 388 Courtney Hall .04 .02
❑ 389 Lee Williams .04 .02
❑ 390 Anthony Miller .25 .11
❑ 391 Gill Byrd .04 .02
❑ 392 Wayne Walker .04 .02
❑ 393 Billy Ray Smith .04 .02
❑ 394 Vencie Glenn .04 .02
❑ 395 Tim Spencer .04 .02
❑ 396 Gary Plummer .04 .02
❑ 397 Arthur Cox .04 .02
❑ 398 Jamie Holland .04 .02
❑ 399 Keith McCants RC .04 .02
❑ 400 Kevin Murphy .04 .02
❑ 401 Danny Peebles .04 .02
❑ 402 Mark Robinson .04 .02
❑ 403 Broderick Thomas .04 .02
❑ 404 Ron Hall .04 .02
❑ 405 Mark Carrier WR .25 .11
❑ 406 Paul Gruber .04 .02
❑ 407 Vinny Testaverde .10 .05
❑ 408 Bruce Hill .04 .02
❑ 409 Lars Tate .04 .02
❑ 410 Harry Hamilton .04 .02
❑ 411 Ricky Reynolds .04 .02
❑ 412 Donald Igwebuike .04 .02
❑ 413 Reuben Davis .04 .02
❑ 414 William Howard .04 .02
❑ 415 Winston Moss RC .04 .02
❑ 416 Chris Singleton RC .04 .02
❑ 417 Hart Lee Dykes .04 .02
❑ 418 Steve Grogan .10 .05
❑ 419 Bruce Armstrong .04 .02
❑ 420 Robert Perryman .04 .02
❑ 421 Andre Tippett .04 .02
❑ 422 Sammy Martin .04 .02
❑ 423 Stanley Morgan .04 .02
❑ 424 Cedric Jones .04 .02
❑ 425 Sean Farrell .04 .02
❑ 426 Marc Wilson .04 .02
❑ 427 John Stephens .04 .02
❑ 428 Eric Sievers RC .04 .02
❑ 429 Maurice Hurst RC .04 .02
❑ 430 Johnny Rembert .04 .02
❑ 431 Receiving Leaders .30 .14
Jerry Rice
Andre Reed
❑ 432 Eric Hill .04 .02
❑ 433 Gary Hogeboom .04 .02
❑ 434 Timm Rosenbach UER .. .04 .02
(Born 1967 in Everett,
Wa., should be 1966
in Missoula, Mont.)
❑ 435 Tim McDonald .04 .02
❑ 436 Rich Camarillo .04 .02
❑ 437 Luis Sharpe .04 .02
❑ 438 J.T. Smith .04 .02
❑ 439 Roy Green .10 .05
❑ 440 Ernie Jones RC .04 .02
❑ 441 Robert Awalt .04 .02
❑ 442 Vai Sikahema .04 .02
❑ 443 Joe Wolf .04 .02
❑ 444 Stump Mitchell .04 .02
❑ 445 David Galloway .04 .02
❑ 446 Ron Wolfley .04 .02
❑ 447 Freddie Joe Nunn .04 .02
❑ 448 Blair Thomas RC .10 .05
❑ 449 Jeff Lageman .04 .02
❑ 450 Tony Eason .04 .02
❑ 451 Erik McMillan .04 .02
❑ 452 Jim Sweeney .04 .02
❑ 453 Ken O'Brien .04 .02
❑ 454 Johnny Hector .04 .02
❑ 455 Jo Jo Townsell .04 .02
❑ 456 Roger Vick .04 .02
❑ 457 James Hasty .04 .02
❑ 458 Dennis Byrd RC .10 .05
❑ 459 Ron Stallworth .04 .02
❑ 460 Mickey Shuler .04 .02
❑ 461 Bobby Humphery .04 .02
❑ 462 Kyle Clifton .04 .02
❑ 463 Al Toon .10 .05
❑ 464 Freeman McNeil .04 .02
❑ 465 Pat Leahy .04 .02
❑ 466 Scott Case .04 .02
❑ 467 Shawn Collins .04 .02
❑ 468 Floyd Dixon .04 .02
❑ 469 Deion Sanders .50 .23
❑ 470 Tony Casillas .04 .02
❑ 471 Michael Haynes RC .25 .11
❑ 472 Chris Miller .25 .11
❑ 473 John Settle .04 .02
❑ 474 Aundray Bruce .04 .02
❑ 475 Gene Lang .04 .02
❑ 476 Tim Gordon RC .04 .02
❑ 477 Scott Fulhage .04 .02
❑ 478 Bill Fralic .04 .02
❑ 479 Jessie Tuggle RC .04 .02

		MINT	NRMT
❑ 480	Marcus Cotton	.04	.02
❑ 481	Steve Walsh	.10	.05
❑ 482	Troy Aikman	.75	.35
❑ 483	Ray Horton	.04	.02
❑ 484	Tony Tolbert RC	.10	.05
❑ 485	Steve Folsom	.04	.02
❑ 486	Ken Norton RC	.25	.11
❑ 487	Kelvin Martin RC	.04	.02
❑ 488	Jack Del Rio	.04	.02
❑ 489	Daryl Johnston RC	.75	.35
❑ 490	Bill Bates	.10	.05
❑ 491	Jim Jeffcoat	.04	.02
❑ 492	Vince Albritton	.04	.02
❑ 493	Eugene Lockhart	.04	.02
❑ 494	Mike Saxon	.04	.02
❑ 495	James Dixon	.04	.02
❑ 496	Willie Broughton	.04	.02
❑ 497	Checklist 1-132	.04	.02
❑ 498	Checklist 133-264	.04	.02
❑ 499	Checklist 265-396	.04	.02
❑ 500	Checklist 397-528	.04	.02
❑ 501	Bears Team (Jim) Harbaugh Eludes the Pursuit	.10	.05
❑ 502	Bengals Team Boomer (Esiason) Studies the Defense	.04	.02
❑ 503	Bills Team (Shane) Conlan Calls Defensive Scheme	.04	.02
❑ 504	Broncos Team (Melvin) Bratton Breaks Away	.04	.02
❑ 505	Browns Team (Bernie) Kosar Calls the Play	.04	.02
❑ 506	Buccaneers Team (Winston) Moss Assists in Squeeze Play	.04	.02
❑ 507	Cardinals Team (Michael) Zordich Saves the Day	.04	.02
❑ 508	Chargers Team (Lee) Williams Plugs the Hole	.04	.02
❑ 509	Chiefs Team (Deron) Cherry Applies The %%D~	.04	.02
❑ 510	Colts Team (Jack) Trudeau Begins a Reverse	.04	.02
❑ 511	Cowboys Team (Troy) Aikman Directs Ground Attack	.30	.14
❑ 512	Dolphins Team Double-Decker By (Louis) Oliver and (Jarvis) Williams	.04	.02
❑ 513	Eagles Team (Anthony) Toney Bangs into the Line	.04	.02
❑ 514	Falcons Team (Jessie) Tuggle Falls on Fumble	.04	.02
❑ 515	49ers Team (Joe) Montana To (Roger) Craig, A Winning Duo	.30	.14
❑ 516	Giants Team (Phil) Simms Likes His O.J. (Anderson)	.04	.02
❑ 517	Jets Team A (James) Hasty Return	.04	.02
❑ 518	Lions Team (Bob) Gagliano Orchestrates The Offense	.04	.02
❑ 519	Oilers Team (Warren) Moon Scrambles to Daylight	.10	.05
❑ 520	Packers Team A Bit Of Packer Majik	.04	.02
❑ 521	Patriots Team (John) Stephens Steams Ahead	.04	.02
❑ 522	Raiders Team Bo (Jackson) Knows Yardage	.10	.05
❑ 523	Rams Team (Jim) Everett Rolls Right	.04	.02
❑ 524	Redskins Team (Gerald) Riggs Rumbles Downfield	.04	.02
❑ 525	Saints Team (Sam) Mills Takes A Stand	.04	.02
❑ 526	Seahawks Team (Grant) Feasel Sets To Snap	.04	.02
❑ 527	Steelers Team (Bubby) Brister Has a Clear Lane	.04	.02
❑ 528	Vikings Team (Rick) Fenney Spots Opening	.04	.02

1990 Topps 1000 Yard Club

	MINT	NRMT
COMPLETE SET (30)	5.00	2.20
ONE PER PACK		

		MINT	NRMT
❑ 1	Jerry Rice	.75	.35
❑ 2	Christian Okoye	.05	.02
❑ 3	Barry Sanders	2.50	1.10
❑ 4	Sterling Sharpe	.25	.11
❑ 5	Mark Carrier WR	.25	.11
❑ 6	Henry Ellard	.10	.05
❑ 7	Andre Reed	.25	.11
❑ 8	Neal Anderson	.10	.05
❑ 9	Dalton Hilliard	.05	.02
❑ 10	Anthony Miller	.25	.11
❑ 11	Thurman Thomas	.25	.11
❑ 12	James Brooks	.10	.05
❑ 13	Webster Slaughter	.10	.05
❑ 14	Gary Clark	.25	.11
❑ 15	Tim McGee	.05	.02
❑ 16	Art Monk	.10	.05
❑ 17	Bobby Humphrey	.05	.02
❑ 18	Flipper Anderson	.05	.02
❑ 19	Ricky Sanders	.05	.02
❑ 20	Greg Bell	.05	.02
❑ 21	Vance Johnson	.05	.02
❑ 22	Richard Johnson UER (Topps logo in upper right corner)	.05	.02
❑ 23	Eric Martin	.05	.02
❑ 24	John Taylor	.10	.05
❑ 25	Mervyn Fernandez	.05	.02
❑ 26	Anthony Carter	.10	.05
❑ 27	Brian Blades	.10	.05
❑ 28	Roger Craig	.10	.05
❑ 29	Ottis Anderson	.10	.05
❑ 30	Mark Clayton	.10	.05

1990 Topps Traded

	MINT	NRMT
COMP.FACT.SET (132)	12.00	5.50
COMMON CARD (1T-132T)	.05	.02
SEMISTARS	.10	.05
UNLISTED STARS	.25	.11

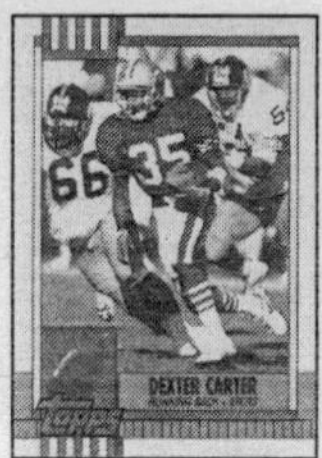

		MINT	NRMT
❑ 1T	Gerald McNeil	.05	.02
❑ 2T	Andre Rison	.25	.11
❑ 3T	Steve Walsh	.25	.11
❑ 4T	Lorenzo White	.10	.05
❑ 5T	Max Montoya	.05	.02
❑ 6T	William Roberts RC	.05	.02
❑ 7T	Alonzo Highsmith	.05	.02
❑ 8T	Chris Hinton	.10	.05
❑ 9T	Stanley Morgan	.10	.05
❑ 10T	Mickey Shuler	.05	.02
❑ 11T	Bobby Humphery	.05	.02
❑ 12T	Gary Anderson RB	.05	.02
❑ 13T	Mike Tomczak	.10	.05
❑ 14T	Anthony Pleasant RC	.10	.05
❑ 15T	Walter Stanley	.05	.02
❑ 16T	Greg Bell	.05	.02
❑ 17T	Tony Martin RC	1.50	.70
❑ 18T	Terry Kinard	.05	.02
❑ 19T	Cris Carter	.50	.23
❑ 20T	James Wilder	.05	.02
❑ 21T	Jerry Kauric	.05	.02
❑ 22T	Irving Fryar	.25	.11
❑ 23T	Ken Harvey RC	.25	.11
❑ 24T	James Williams RC	.05	.02
❑ 25T	Ron Cox RC	.05	.02
❑ 26T	Andre Ware	.25	.11
❑ 27T	Emmitt Smith RC	8.00	3.60
❑ 28T	Junior Seau	.60	.25
❑ 29T	Mark Carrier RC	.25	.11
❑ 30T	Rodney Hampton	.25	.11
❑ 31T	Rob Moore RC	1.25	.55
❑ 32T	Bern Brostek RC	.05	.02
❑ 33T	Dexter Carter	.10	.05
❑ 34T	Blair Thomas	.10	.05
❑ 35T	Harold Green RC	.25	.11
❑ 36T	Darrell Thompson	.05	.02
❑ 37T	Eric Green RC	.25	.11
❑ 38T	Renaldo Turnbull RC	.25	.11
❑ 39T	Leroy Hoard RC	.50	.23
❑ 40T	Anthony Thompson RC	.10	.05
❑ 41T	Jeff George	.60	.25
❑ 42T	Alexander Wright RC	.05	.02
❑ 43T	Richmond Webb	.05	.02
❑ 44T	Cortez Kennedy	.25	.11
❑ 45T	Ray Agnew RC	.05	.02
❑ 46T	Percy Snow	.05	.02
❑ 47T	Chris Singleton	.05	.02
❑ 48T	James Francis RC	.10	.05
❑ 49T	Tony Bennett	.10	.05
❑ 50T	Reggie Cobb RC	.10	.05
❑ 51T	Barry Foster	.25	.11
❑ 52T	Ben Smith	.05	.02
❑ 53T	Anthony Smith RC	.25	.11
❑ 54T	Steve Christie RC	.05	.02
❑ 55T	Johnny Bailey RC	.10	.05
❑ 56T	Alan Grant RC	.05	.02
❑ 57T	Eric Floyd RC	.05	.02
❑ 58T	Robert Blackmon RC	.05	.02
❑ 59T	Brent Williams	.05	.02
❑ 60T	Raymond Clayborn	.05	.02
❑ 61T	Dave Duerson	.05	.02
❑ 62T	Derrick Fenner RC	.10	.05
❑ 63T	Ken Willis	.05	.02
❑ 64T	Brad Baxter RC	.10	.05
❑ 65T	Tony Paige	.05	.02
❑ 66T	Jay Schroeder	.05	.02
❑ 67T	Jim Breech	.05	.02
❑ 68T	Barry Word RC	.10	.05

❑ 69T Anthony Dilweg	.05	.02
❑ 70T Rich Gannon RC	2.00	.90
❑ 71T Stan Humphries RC	.25	.11
❑ 72T Jay Novacek	.25	.11
❑ 73T Tommy Kane RC	.05	.02
❑ 74T Everson Walls	.05	.02
❑ 75T Mike Rozier	.10	.05
❑ 76T Robb Thomas	.05	.02
❑ 77T Terance Mathis RC	2.00	.90
❑ 78T LeRoy Irvin	.05	.02
❑ 79T Jeff Donaldson	.05	.02
❑ 80T Ethan Horton RC	.10	.05
❑ 81T J.B. Brown RC	.05	.02
❑ 82T Joe Kelly	.05	.02
❑ 83T John Carney RC	.05	.02
❑ 84T Dan Stryzinski RC	.05	.02
❑ 85T John Kidd	.05	.02
❑ 86T Al Smith	.10	.05
❑ 87T Travis McNeal	.05	.02
❑ 88T Reyna Thompson RC	.05	.02
❑ 89T Rick Donnelly	.05	.02
❑ 90T Marv Cook RC	.10	.05
❑ 91T Mike Farr RC	.05	.02
❑ 92T Daniel Stubbs	.05	.02
❑ 93T Jeff Campbell RC	.05	.02
❑ 94T Tim McKyer	.05	.02
❑ 95T Ian Beckles RC	.05	.02
❑ 96T Lemuel Stinson	.05	.02
❑ 97T Frank Cornish	.05	.02
❑ 98T Riki Ellison	.05	.02
❑ 99T Jamie Mueller RC	.05	.02
❑ 100T Brian Hansen	.05	.02
❑ 101T Warren Powers RC	.05	.02
❑ 102T Howard Cross RC	.05	.02
❑ 103T Tim Grunhard RC	.05	.02
❑ 104T Johnny Johnson RC	.25	.11
❑ 105T Calvin Williams RC	.25	.11
❑ 106T Keith McCants	.05	.02
❑ 107T Lamar Lathon RC	.10	.05
❑ 108T Steve Broussard RC	.10	.05
❑ 109T Glenn Parker RC	.05	.02
❑ 110T Alton Montgomery RC	.05	.02
❑ 111T Jim McMahon	.10	.05
❑ 112T Aaron Wallace RC	.05	.02
❑ 113T Keith Sims RC	.05	.02
❑ 114T Ervin Randle	.05	.02
❑ 115T Walter Wilson	.05	.02
❑ 116T Terry Wooden RC	.05	.02
❑ 117T Bernard Clark	.05	.02
❑ 118T Tony Stargell RC	.05	.02
❑ 119T Jimmie Jones RC	.05	.02
❑ 120T Andre Collins RC	.10	.05
❑ 121T Ricky Proehl RC	.10	.05
❑ 122T Darion Conner RC	.10	.05
❑ 123T Jeff Rutledge	.05	.02
❑ 124T Heath Sherman RC	.10	.05
❑ 125T Tommie Agee RC	.05	.02
❑ 126T Tory Epps RC	.05	.02
❑ 127T Tommy Hodson RC	.05	.02
❑ 128T Jessie Hester RC	.05	.02
❑ 129T Alfred Oglesby RC	.05	.02
❑ 130T Chris Chandler	.25	.11
❑ 131T Fred Barnett RC	.25	.11
❑ 132T Checklist 1-132	.05	.02

1991 Topps

	MINT	NRMT
COMPLETE SET (660)	15.00	6.75
COMP.FACT.SET (660)	15.00	6.75
COMMON CARD (1-660)	.04	.02
SEMISTARS	.10	.05
UNLISTED STARS	.25	.11

Card	MINT	NRMT
❑ 1 Super Bowl XXV	.04	.02
❑ 2 Roger Craig HL	.10	.05
❑ 3 Derrick Thomas HL	.10	.05
❑ 4 Pete Stoyanovich HL	.04	.02
❑ 5 Ottis Anderson HL	.10	.05
❑ 6 Jerry Rice HL	.50	.23
❑ 7 Warren Moon HL	.10	.05
❑ 8 Leaders Passing Yards	.10	.05
Warren Moon		
Jim Everett		
❑ 9 Leaders Rushing	.50	.23
Barry Sanders		
Thurman Thomas		
❑ 10 Leaders Receiving	.30	.14
Jerry Rice		
Haywood Jeffires		
❑ 11 Leaders Interceptions	.04	.02
Mark Carrier DB		
Richard Johnson		
❑ 12 Leaders Sacks	.10	.05
Derrick Thomas		
Charles Haley		
❑ 13 Jumbo Elliott	.04	.02
❑ 14 Leonard Marshall	.04	.02
❑ 15 William Roberts	.04	.02
❑ 16 Lawrence Taylor	.25	.11
❑ 17 Mark Ingram	.10	.05
❑ 18 Rodney Hampton	.25	.11
❑ 19 Carl Banks	.04	.02
❑ 20 Ottis Anderson	.10	.05
❑ 21 Mark Collins	.04	.02
❑ 22 Pepper Johnson	.04	.02
❑ 23 Dave Meggett	.10	.05
❑ 24 Reyna Thompson	.04	.02
❑ 25 Stephen Baker	.04	.02
❑ 26 Mike Fox	.04	.02
❑ 27 Maurice Carthon UER	.04	.02
(Herschel Walker misspelled as Herschell)		
❑ 28 Jeff Hostetler	.25	.11
❑ 29 Greg Jackson RC	.04	.02
❑ 30 Sean Landeta	.04	.02
❑ 31 Bart Oates	.04	.02
❑ 32 Phil Simms	.10	.05
❑ 33 Erik Howard	.04	.02
❑ 34 Myron Guyton	.04	.02
❑ 35 Mark Bavaro	.04	.02
❑ 36 Jarrod Bunch RC	.04	.02
❑ 37 Will Wolford	.04	.02
❑ 38 Ray Bentley	.04	.02
❑ 39 Nate Odomes	.04	.02
❑ 40 Scott Norwood	.04	.02
❑ 41 Darryl Talley	.04	.02
❑ 42 Carwell Gardner	.04	.02
❑ 43 James Lofton	.10	.05
❑ 44 Shane Conlan	.04	.02
❑ 45 Steve Tasker	.10	.05
❑ 46 James Williams	.04	.02
❑ 47 Kent Hull	.04	.02
❑ 48 Al Edwards	.04	.02
❑ 49 Frank Reich	.10	.05
❑ 50 Leon Seals	.04	.02
❑ 51 Keith McKeller	.04	.02
❑ 52 Thurman Thomas	.25	.11
❑ 53 Leonard Smith	.04	.02
❑ 54 Andre Reed	.10	.05
❑ 55 Kenneth Davis	.04	.02
❑ 56 Jeff Wright RC	.04	.02
❑ 57 Jamie Mueller	.04	.02
❑ 58 Jim Ritcher	.04	.02
❑ 59 Bruce Smith	.25	.11
❑ 60 Ted Washington RC	.04	.02
❑ 61 Guy McIntyre	.04	.02
❑ 62 Michael Carter	.04	.02
❑ 63 Pierce Holt	.04	.02
❑ 64 Darryl Pollard	.04	.02
❑ 65 Mike Sherrard	.04	.02
❑ 66 Dexter Carter	.04	.02
❑ 67 Bubba Paris	.04	.02
❑ 68 Harry Sydney	.04	.02
❑ 69 Tom Rathman	.04	.02
❑ 70 Jesse Sapolu	.04	.02
❑ 71 Mike Cofer	.04	.02
❑ 72 Keith DeLong	.04	.02
❑ 73 Joe Montana	1.25	.55
❑ 74 Bill Romanowski	.04	.02
❑ 75 John Taylor	.10	.05
❑ 76 Brent Jones	.25	.11
❑ 77 Harris Barton	.04	.02
❑ 78 Charles Haley	.10	.05
❑ 79 Eric Davis	.04	.02
❑ 80 Kevin Fagan	.04	.02
❑ 81 Jerry Rice	.75	.35
❑ 82 Dave Waymer	.04	.02
❑ 83 Todd Marinovich RC	.04	.02
❑ 84 Steve Smith	.04	.02
❑ 85 Tim Brown	.25	.11
❑ 86 Ethan Horton	.04	.02
❑ 87 Marcus Allen	.25	.11
❑ 88 Terry McDaniel	.04	.02
❑ 89 Thomas Benson	.04	.02
❑ 90 Roger Craig	.10	.05
❑ 91 Don Mosebar	.04	.02
❑ 92 Aaron Wallace	.04	.02
❑ 93 Eddie Anderson	.04	.02
❑ 94 Willie Gault	.10	.05
❑ 95 Howie Long	.10	.05
❑ 96 Jay Schroeder	.04	.02
❑ 97 Ronnie Lott	.10	.05
❑ 98 Bob Golic	.04	.02
❑ 99 Bo Jackson	.10	.05
❑ 100 Max Montoya	.04	.02
❑ 101 Scott Davis	.04	.02
❑ 102 Greg Townsend	.04	.02
❑ 103 Garry Lewis	.04	.02
❑ 104 Mervyn Fernandez	.04	.02
❑ 105 Steve Wisniewski UER	.04	.02
(Back has drafted, should be traded to)		
❑ 106 Jeff Jaeger	.04	.02
❑ 107 Nick Bell RC	.04	.02
❑ 108 Mark Dennis RC	.04	.02
❑ 109 Jarvis Williams	.04	.02
❑ 110 Mark Clayton	.10	.05
❑ 111 Harry Galbreath	.04	.02
❑ 112 Dan Marino	1.25	.55
❑ 113 Louis Oliver	.04	.02
❑ 114 Pete Stoyanovich	.04	.02
❑ 115 Ferrell Edmunds	.04	.02
❑ 116 Jeff Cross	.04	.02
❑ 117 Richmond Webb	.04	.02
❑ 118 Jim C. Jensen	.04	.02
❑ 119 Keith Sims	.04	.02
❑ 120 Mark Duper	.10	.05
❑ 121 Shawn Lee RC	.04	.02
❑ 122 Reggie Roby	.04	.02
❑ 123 Jeff Uhlenhake	.04	.02
❑ 124 Sammie Smith	.04	.02
❑ 125 John Offerdahl	.04	.02
❑ 126 Hugh Green	.04	.02
❑ 127 Tony Paige	.04	.02
❑ 128 David Griggs	.04	.02
❑ 129 J.B. Brown	.04	.02
❑ 130 Harvey Williams RC	.25	.11
❑ 131 John Alt	.04	.02
❑ 132 Albert Lewis	.04	.02
❑ 133 Robb Thomas	.04	.02
❑ 134 Neil Smith	.25	.11
❑ 135 Stephone Paige	.04	.02
❑ 136 Nick Lowery	.04	.02
❑ 137 Steve DeBerg	.04	.02
❑ 138 Rich Baldinger RC	.04	.02
❑ 139 Percy Snow	.04	.02
❑ 140 Kevin Porter	.04	.02
❑ 141 Chris Martin	.04	.02
❑ 142 Deron Cherry	.04	.02
❑ 143 Derrick Thomas	.25	.11
❑ 144 Tim Grunhard	.04	.02
❑ 145 Todd McNair	.04	.02
❑ 146 David Szott	.04	.02
❑ 147 Dan Saleaumua	.04	.02
❑ 148 Jonathan Hayes	.04	.02
❑ 149 Christian Okoye	.04	.02
❑ 150 Dino Hackett	.04	.02
❑ 151 Bryan Barker RC	.04	.02

❑ 152 Kevin Ross .04 .02
❑ 153 Barry Word .04 .02
❑ 154 Stan Thomas .04 .02
❑ 155 Brad Muster .04 .02
❑ 156 Donnell Woolford .04 .02
❑ 157 Neal Anderson .10 .05
❑ 158 Jim Covert .04 .02
❑ 159 Jim Harbaugh .25 .11
❑ 160 Shaun Gayle .04 .02
❑ 161 William Perry .10 .05
❑ 162 Ron Morris .04 .02
❑ 163 Mark Bortz .04 .02
❑ 164 James Thornton .04 .02
❑ 165 Ron Rivera .04 .02
❑ 166 Kevin Butler .04 .02
❑ 167 Jay Hilgenberg .04 .02
❑ 168 Peter Tom Willis .04 .02
❑ 169 Johnny Bailey .04 .02
❑ 170 Ron Cox .04 .02
❑ 171 Keith Van Horne .04 .02
❑ 172 Mark Carrier DB .10 .05
❑ 173 Richard Dent .10 .05
❑ 174 Wendell Davis .04 .02
❑ 175 Trace Armstrong .04 .02
❑ 176 Mike Singletary .10 .05
❑ 177 Chris Zorich RC .25 .11
❑ 178 Gerald Riggs .04 .02
❑ 179 Jeff Bostic .04 .02
❑ 180 Kurt Gouveia RC .04 .02
❑ 181 Stan Humphries .25 .11
❑ 182 Chip Lohmiller .04 .02
❑ 183 Raleigh McKenzie RC .04 .02
❑ 184 Alvin Walton .04 .02
❑ 185 Earnest Byner .04 .02
❑ 186 Markus Koch .04 .02
❑ 187 Art Monk .10 .05
❑ 188 Ed Simmons .04 .02
❑ 189 Bobby Wilson RC .04 .02
❑ 190 Charles Mann .04 .02
❑ 191 Darrell Green .04 .02
❑ 192 Mark Rypien .10 .05
❑ 193 Ricky Sanders .04 .02
❑ 194 Jim Lachey .04 .02
❑ 195 Martin Mayhew .04 .02
❑ 196 Gary Clark .25 .11
❑ 197 Wilber Marshall .04 .02
❑ 198 Darryl Grant .04 .02
❑ 199 Don Warren .04 .02
❑ 200 Ricky Ervins RC UER .10 .05
(Front has Chiefs, back has Redskins)
❑ 201 Eric Allen .04 .02
❑ 202 Anthony Toney .04 .02
❑ 203 Ben Smith UER .04 .02
(Front CB, back S)
❑ 204 David Alexander .04 .02
❑ 205 Jerome Brown .04 .02
❑ 206 Mike Golic .04 .02
❑ 207 Roger Ruzek .04 .02
❑ 208 Andre Waters .04 .02
❑ 209 Fred Barnett .25 .11
❑ 210 Randall Cunningham .25 .11
❑ 211 Mike Schad .04 .02
❑ 212 Reggie White .25 .11
❑ 213 Mike Bellamy .04 .02
❑ 214 Jeff Feagles RC .04 .02
❑ 215 Wes Hopkins .04 .02
❑ 216 Clyde Simmons .04 .02
❑ 217 Keith Byars .04 .02
❑ 218 Seth Joyner .10 .05
❑ 219 Byron Evans .04 .02
❑ 220 Keith Jackson .10 .05
❑ 221 Calvin Williams .10 .05
❑ 222 Mike Dumas RC .04 .02
❑ 223 Ray Childress .04 .02
❑ 224 Ernest Givins .10 .05
❑ 225 Lamar Lathon .04 .02
❑ 226 Greg Montgomery .04 .02
❑ 227 Mike Munchak .04 .02
❑ 228 Al Smith .04 .02
❑ 229 Bubba McDowell .04 .02
❑ 230 Haywood Jeffires .10 .05
❑ 231 Drew Hill .04 .02
❑ 232 William Fuller .10 .05
❑ 233 Warren Moon .25 .11
❑ 234 Doug Smith RC** .04 .02
❑ 235 Cris Dishman RC .04 .02
❑ 236 Teddy Garcia RC .04 .02
❑ 237 Richard Johnson RC .04 .02
❑ 238 Bruce Matthews .10 .05
❑ 239 Gerald McNeil .04 .02
❑ 240 Johnny Meads .04 .02
❑ 241 Curtis Duncan .04 .02
❑ 242 Sean Jones .10 .05
❑ 243 Lorenzo White .04 .02
❑ 244 Rob Carpenter RC .04 .02
❑ 245 Bruce Reimers .04 .02
❑ 246 Ickey Woods .04 .02
❑ 247 Lewis Billups .04 .02
❑ 248 Boomer Esiason .10 .05
❑ 249 Tim Krumrie .04 .02
❑ 250 David Fulcher .04 .02
❑ 251 Jim Breech .04 .02
❑ 252 Mitchell Price RC .04 .02
❑ 253 Carl Zander .04 .02
❑ 254 Barney Bussey RC .04 .02
❑ 255 Leon White .04 .02
❑ 256 Eddie Brown .04 .02
❑ 257 James Francis .04 .02
❑ 258 Harold Green .10 .05
❑ 259 Anthony Munoz .10 .05
❑ 260 James Brooks .10 .05
❑ 261 Kevin Walker RC UER .04 .02
(Hometown should be West Milford Township)
❑ 262 Bruce Kozerski .04 .02
❑ 263 David Grant .04 .02
❑ 264 Tim McGee .04 .02
❑ 265 Rodney Holman .04 .02
❑ 266 Dan McGwire RC .04 .02
❑ 267 Andy Heck .04 .02
❑ 268 Dave Krieg .10 .05
❑ 269 David Wyman .04 .02
❑ 270 Robert Blackmon .04 .02
❑ 271 Grant Feasel .04 .02
❑ 272 Patrick Hunter RC .04 .02
❑ 273 Travis McNeal .04 .02
❑ 274 John L. Williams .04 .02
❑ 275 Tony Woods .04 .02
❑ 276 Derrick Fenner .04 .02
❑ 277 Jacob Green .04 .02
❑ 278 Brian Blades .10 .05
❑ 279 Eugene Robinson .04 .02
❑ 280 Terry Wooden .04 .02
❑ 281 Jeff Bryant .04 .02
❑ 282 Norm Johnson .04 .02
❑ 283 Joe Nash UER .04 .02
Front DT, Back NT)
❑ 284 Rick Donnelly .04 .02
❑ 285 Chris Warren .25 .11
❑ 286 Tommy Kane .04 .02
❑ 287 Cortez Kennedy .25 .11
❑ 288 Ernie Mills RC .10 .05
❑ 289 Dermontti Dawson .04 .02
❑ 290 Tunch Ilkin .04 .02
❑ 291 Tim Worley .04 .02
❑ 292 David Little .04 .02
❑ 293 Gary Anderson K .04 .02
❑ 294 Chris Calloway .04 .02
❑ 295 Carnell Lake .04 .02
❑ 296 Dan Stryzinski .04 .02
❑ 297 Rod Woodson .25 .11
❑ 298 John Jackson RC .04 .02
❑ 299 Bubby Brister .04 .02
❑ 300 Thomas Everett .04 .02
❑ 301 Merril Hoge .04 .02
❑ 302 Eric Green .04 .02
❑ 303 Greg Lloyd .25 .11
❑ 304 Gerald Williams .04 .02
❑ 305 Bryan Hinkle .04 .02
❑ 306 Keith Willis .04 .02
❑ 307 Louis Lipps .04 .02
❑ 308 Donald Evans .04 .02
❑ 309 D.J. Johnson .04 .02
❑ 310 Wesley Carroll RC .04 .02
❑ 311 Eric Martin .04 .02
❑ 312 Brett Maxie .04 .02
❑ 313 Rickey Jackson .04 .02
❑ 314 Robert Massey .04 .02
❑ 315 Pat Swilling .10 .05
❑ 316 Morten Andersen .04 .02
❑ 317 Toi Cook RC .04 .02
❑ 318 Sam Mills .04 .02
❑ 319 Steve Walsh .04 .02
❑ 320 Tommy Barnhardt RC .04 .02
❑ 321 Vince Buck .04 .02
❑ 322 Joel Hilgenberg .04 .02
❑ 323 Rueben Mayes .04 .02
❑ 324 Renaldo Turnbull .04 .02
❑ 325 Brett Perriman .25 .11
❑ 326 Vaughan Johnson .04 .02
❑ 327 Gill Fenerty .04 .02
❑ 328 Stan Brock .04 .02
❑ 329 Dalton Hilliard .04 .02
❑ 330 Hoby Brenner .04 .02
❑ 331 Craig Heyward .10 .05
❑ 332 Jon Hand .04 .02
❑ 333 Duane Bickett .04 .02
❑ 334 Jessie Hester .04 .02
❑ 335 Rohn Stark .04 .02
❑ 336 Zefross Moss .04 .02
❑ 337 Bill Brooks .04 .02
❑ 338 Clarence Verdin .04 .02
❑ 339 Mike Prior .04 .02
❑ 340 Chip Banks .04 .02
❑ 341 Dean Biasucci .04 .02
❑ 342 Ray Donaldson .04 .02
❑ 343 Jeff Herrod .04 .02
❑ 344 Donnell Thompson .04 .02
❑ 345 Chris Goode .04 .02
❑ 346 Eugene Daniel .04 .02
❑ 347 Pat Beach .04 .02
❑ 348 Keith Taylor .04 .02
❑ 349 Jeff George .25 .11
❑ 350 Tony Siragusa RC .04 .02
❑ 351 Randy Dixon .04 .02
❑ 352 Albert Bentley .04 .02
❑ 353 Russell Maryland RC .25 .11
❑ 354 Mike Saxon .04 .02
❑ 355 Godfrey Myles RC UER .04 .02
(Misspelled Miles on card front)
❑ 356 Mark Stepnoski RC .10 .05
❑ 357 James Washington RC .04 .02
❑ 358 Jay Novacek .25 .11
❑ 359 Kelvin Martin .04 .02
❑ 360 Emmitt Smith UER 2.00 .90
(Played for Florida, not Florida State)
❑ 361 Jim Jeffcoat .04 .02
❑ 362 Alexander Wright .04 .02
❑ 363 James Dixon UER .04 .02
(Photo is not Dixon on card front)
❑ 364 Alonzo Highsmith .04 .02
❑ 365 Daniel Stubbs .04 .02
❑ 366 Jack Del Rio .04 .02
❑ 367 Mark Tuinei RC .04 .02
❑ 368 Michael Irvin .25 .11
❑ 369 John Gesek RC .04 .02
❑ 370 Ken Willis .04 .02
❑ 371 Troy Aikman .75 .35
❑ 372 Jimmie Jones .04 .02
❑ 373 Nate Newton .10 .05
❑ 374 Issiac Holt .04 .02
❑ 375 Alvin Harper RC .25 .11
❑ 376 Todd Kalis .04 .02
❑ 377 Wade Wilson .10 .05
❑ 378 Joey Browner .04 .02
❑ 379 Chris Doleman .04 .02
❑ 380 Hassan Jones .04 .02
❑ 381 Henry Thomas .04 .02
❑ 382 Darrell Fullington .04 .02
❑ 383 Steve Jordan .04 .02
❑ 384 Gary Zimmerman .04 .02
❑ 385 Ray Berry .04 .02
❑ 386 Cris Carter .50 .23
❑ 387 Mike Merriweather .04 .02
❑ 388 Carl Lee .04 .02
❑ 389 Keith Millard .04 .02
❑ 390 Reggie Rutland .04 .02
❑ 391 Anthony Carter .10 .05
❑ 392 Mark Dusbabek .04 .02
❑ 393 Kirk Lowdermilk .04 .02
❑ 394 Al Noga UER .04 .02
(Card says DT, should be DE)
❑ 395 Herschel Walker .10 .05

❑ 396 Randall McDaniel .04 .02
❑ 397 Herman Moore RC 2.00 .90
❑ 398 Eddie Murray .04 .02
❑ 399 Lomas Brown .04 .02
❑ 400 Marc Spindler .04 .02
❑ 401 Bennie Blades .04 .02
❑ 402 Kevin Glover .04 .02
❑ 403 Aubrey Matthews RC .04 .02
❑ 404 Michael Cofer .04 .02
❑ 405 Robert Clark .04 .02
❑ 406 Eric Andolsek .04 .02
❑ 407 William White .04 .02
❑ 408 Rodney Peete .10 .05
❑ 409 Mel Gray .10 .05
❑ 410 Jim Arnold .04 .02
❑ 411 Jeff Campbell .04 .02
❑ 412 Chris Spielman .10 .05
❑ 413 Jerry Ball .04 .02
❑ 414 Dan Owens .04 .02
❑ 415 Barry Sanders 1.50 .70
❑ 416 Andre Ware .10 .05
❑ 417 Stanley Richard RC .04 .02
❑ 418 Gill Byrd .04 .02
❑ 419 John Kidd .04 .02
❑ 420 Sam Seale .04 .02
❑ 421 Gary Plummer .04 .02
❑ 422 Anthony Miller .10 .05
❑ 423 Ronnie Harmon .04 .02
❑ 424 Frank Cornish .04 .02
❑ 425 Marion Butts .10 .05
❑ 426 Leo Goeas .04 .02
❑ 427 Junior Seau .25 .11
❑ 428 Courtney Hall .04 .02
❑ 429 Leslie O'Neal .10 .05
❑ 430 Martin Bayless .04 .02
❑ 431 John Carney .04 .02
❑ 432 Lee Williams .04 .02
❑ 433 Arthur Cox .04 .02
❑ 434 Burt Grossman .04 .02
❑ 435 Nate Lewis RC .04 .02
❑ 436 Rod Bernstine .04 .02
❑ 437 Henry Rolling RC .04 .02
❑ 438 Billy Joe Tolliver .04 .02
❑ 439 Vinnie Clark RC .04 .02
❑ 440 Brian Noble .04 .02
❑ 441 Charles Wilson .04 .02
❑ 442 Don Majkowski .04 .02
❑ 443 Tim Harris .04 .02
❑ 444 Scott Stephen RC .04 .02
❑ 445 Perry Kemp .04 .02
❑ 446 Darrell Thompson .04 .02
❑ 447 Chris Jacke .04 .02
❑ 448 Mark Murphy .04 .02
❑ 449 Ed West .04 .02
❑ 450 LeRoy Butler .10 .05
❑ 451 Keith Woodside .04 .02
❑ 452 Tony Bennett .10 .05
❑ 453 Mark Lee .04 .02
❑ 454 James Campen RC .04 .02
❑ 455 Robert Brown .04 .02
❑ 456 Sterling Sharpe .25 .11
❑ 457A Tony Mandarich ERR 2.50 1.10
Broncos listed as team
❑ 457B Tony Mandarich COR .04 .02
Packers listed as team
❑ 458 Johnny Holland .04 .02
❑ 459 Matt Brock RC .04 .02
❑ 460A Esera Tuaolo RC ERR .04 .02
(See also 462; no 1991 NFL Draft Pick logo)
❑ 460B Esera Tuaolo RC COR .04 .02
(See also 462; 1991 NFL Draft Pick logo on front)
❑ 461 Freeman McNeil .04 .02
❑ 462 Terance Mathis UER .25 .11
(Card numbered incorrectly as 460)
❑ 463 Rob Moore .25 .11
❑ 464 Darrell Davis RC .04 .02
❑ 465 Chris Burkett .04 .02
❑ 466 Jeff Criswell .04 .02
❑ 467 Tony Stargell .04 .02
❑ 468 Ken O'Brien .04 .02
❑ 469 Erik McMillan .04 .02
❑ 470 Jeff Lageman UER .04 .02
(Front DE, back LB)
❑ 471 Pat Leahy .04 .02
❑ 472 Dennis Byrd .04 .02
❑ 473 Jim Sweeney .04 .02
❑ 474 Brad Baxter .04 .02
❑ 475 Joe Kelly .04 .02
❑ 476 Al Toon .10 .05
❑ 477 Joe Prokop .04 .02
❑ 478 Mark Boyer .04 .02
❑ 479 Kyle Clifton .04 .02
❑ 480 James Hasty .04 .02
❑ 481 Browning Nagle RC .04 .02
❑ 482 Gary Anderson RB .04 .02
❑ 483 Mark Carrier WR .25 .11
❑ 484 Ricky Reynolds .04 .02
❑ 485 Bruce Hill .04 .02
❑ 486 Steve Christie .04 .02
❑ 487 Paul Gruber .04 .02
❑ 488 Jesse Anderson .04 .02
❑ 489 Reggie Cobb .04 .02
❑ 490 Harry Hamilton .04 .02
❑ 491 Vinny Testaverde .10 .05
❑ 492 Mark Royals RC .04 .02
❑ 493 Keith McCants .04 .02
❑ 494 Ron Hall .04 .02
❑ 495 Ian Beckles .04 .02
❑ 496 Mark Robinson .04 .02
❑ 497 Reuben Davis .04 .02
❑ 498 Wayne Haddix .04 .02
❑ 499 Kevin Murphy .04 .02
❑ 500 Eugene Marve .04 .02
❑ 501 Broderick Thomas .04 .02
❑ 502 Eric Swann RC UER .25 .11
(Draft pick logo missing from card front)
❑ 503 Ernie Jones .04 .02
❑ 504 Rich Camarillo .04 .02
❑ 505 Tim McDonald .04 .02
❑ 506 Freddie Joe Nunn .04 .02
❑ 507 Tim Jorden RC .04 .02
❑ 508 Johnny Johnson .04 .02
❑ 509 Eric Hill .04 .02
❑ 510 Derek Kennard .04 .02
❑ 511 Ricky Proehl .04 .02
❑ 512 Bill Lewis .04 .02
❑ 513 Roy Green .04 .02
❑ 514 Anthony Bell .04 .02
❑ 515 Timm Rosenbach .04 .02
❑ 516 Jim Wahler RC .04 .02
❑ 517 Anthony Thompson .04 .02
❑ 518 Ken Harvey .10 .05
❑ 519 Luis Sharpe .04 .02
❑ 520 Walter Reeves .04 .02
❑ 521 Lonnie Young .04 .02
❑ 522 Rod Saddler .04 .02
❑ 523 Todd Lyght RC .04 .02
❑ 524 Alvin Wright .04 .02
❑ 525 Flipper Anderson .04 .02
❑ 526 Jackie Slater .04 .02
❑ 527 Damone Johnson RC .04 .02
❑ 528 Cleveland Gary .04 .02
❑ 529 Mike Piel .04 .02
❑ 530 Buford McGee .04 .02
❑ 531 Michael Stewart .04 .02
❑ 532 Jim Everett .10 .05
❑ 533 Mike Wilcher .04 .02
❑ 534 Irv Pankey .04 .02
❑ 535 Bern Brostek .04 .02
❑ 536 Henry Ellard .10 .05
❑ 537 Doug Smith .04 .02
❑ 538 Larry Kelm .04 .02
❑ 539 Pat Terrell .04 .02
❑ 540 Tom Newberry .04 .02
❑ 541 Jerry Gray .04 .02
❑ 542 Kevin Greene .25 .11
❑ 543 Duval Love RC .04 .02
❑ 544 Frank Stams .04 .02
❑ 545 Mike Croel RC .04 .02
❑ 546 Mark Jackson .04 .02
❑ 547 Greg Kragen .04 .02
❑ 548 Karl Mecklenburg .04 .02
❑ 549 Simon Fletcher .04 .02
❑ 550 Bobby Humphrey .04 .02
❑ 551 Ken Lanier .04 .02
❑ 552 Vance Johnson .04 .02
❑ 553 Ron Holmes .04 .02
❑ 554 John Elway 1.25 .55
❑ 555 Melvin Bratton .04 .02
❑ 556 Dennis Smith .04 .02
❑ 557 Ricky Nattiel .04 .02
❑ 558 Clarence Kay .04 .02
❑ 559 Michael Brooks .04 .02
❑ 560 Mike Horan .04 .02
❑ 561 Warren Powers .04 .02
❑ 562 Keith Kartz .04 .02
❑ 563 Shannon Sharpe .50 .23
❑ 564 Wymon Henderson .04 .02
❑ 565 Steve Atwater .04 .02
❑ 566 David Treadwell .04 .02
❑ 567 Bruce Pickens RC .04 .02
❑ 568 Jessie Tuggle .04 .02
❑ 569 Chris Hinton .04 .02
❑ 570 Keith Jones .04 .02
❑ 571 Bill Fralic .04 .02
❑ 572 Mike Rozier .04 .02
❑ 573 Scott Fulhage .04 .02
❑ 574 Floyd Dixon .04 .02
❑ 575 Andre Rison .10 .05
❑ 576 Darion Conner .04 .02
❑ 577 Brian Jordan .10 .05
❑ 578 Michael Haynes .25 .11
❑ 579 Oliver Barnett .04 .02
❑ 580 Shawn Collins .04 .02
❑ 581 Tim Green .04 .02
❑ 582 Deion Sanders .40 .18
❑ 583 Mike Kenn .04 .02
❑ 584 Mike Gann .04 .02
❑ 585 Chris Miller .10 .05
❑ 586 Tory Epps .04 .02
❑ 587 Steve Broussard .04 .02
❑ 588 Gary Wilkins .04 .02
❑ 589 Eric Turner RC .10 .05
❑ 590 Thane Gash .04 .02
❑ 591 Clay Matthews .10 .05
❑ 592 Mike Johnson .04 .02
❑ 593 Raymond Clayborn .04 .02
❑ 594 Leroy Hoard .10 .05
❑ 595 Reggie Langhorne .04 .02
❑ 596 Mike Baab .04 .02
❑ 597 Anthony Pleasant .04 .02
❑ 598 David Grayson .04 .02
❑ 599 Rob Burnett RC .04 .02
❑ 600 Frank Minnifield .04 .02
❑ 601 Gregg Rakoczy .04 .02
❑ 602 Eric Metcalf UER .25 .11
(1989 stats given twice)
❑ 603 Paul Farren .04 .02
❑ 604 Brian Brennan .04 .02
❑ 605 Tony Jones .04 .02
❑ 606 Stephen Braggs .04 .02
❑ 607 Kevin Mack .04 .02
❑ 608 Pat Harlow RC .04 .02
❑ 609 Marv Cook .04 .02
❑ 610 John Stephens .04 .02
❑ 611 Ed Reynolds .04 .02
❑ 612 Tim Goad .04 .02
❑ 613 Chris Singleton .04 .02
❑ 614 Bruce Armstrong .04 .02
❑ 615 Tommy Hodson .04 .02
❑ 616 Sammy Martin .04 .02
❑ 617 Andre Tippett .04 .02
❑ 618 Johnny Rembert .04 .02
❑ 619 Maurice Hurst .04 .02
❑ 620 Vincent Brown .04 .02
❑ 621 Ray Agnew .04 .02
❑ 622 Ronnie Lippett .04 .02
❑ 623 Greg McMurtry .04 .02
❑ 624 Brent Williams .04 .02
❑ 625 Jason Staurovsky .04 .02
❑ 626 Marvin Allen .04 .02
❑ 627 Hart Lee Dykes .04 .02
❑ 628 Atlanta Falcons .04 .02
Team: (Keith) Jones Jumps for Yardage
❑ 629 Buffalo Bills .04 .02
Team: (Jeff) Wright Goes for a Block
❑ 630 Chicago Bears .10 .05
Team: (Jim) Harbaugh Makes Like a Halfback
❑ 631 Cincinnati Bengals .04 .02
Team: (Stanford) Jennings Cuts Through Hole

❑ 632 Cleveland Browns .04 .02
Team: (Eric) Metcalf
Makes a Return
❑ 633 Dallas Cowboys .04 .02
Team: (Kelvin) Martin
Makes a Move
❑ 634 Denver Broncos .04 .02
Team: (Shannon) Sharpe
Into the Wedge
❑ 635 Detroit Lions .04 .02
Team: (Rodney) Peete
Hunted by a Bear
(Mike Singletary)
❑ 636 Green Bay Packers .04 .02
Team: (Don) Majkowski
Orchestrates Some Magic
❑ 637 Houston Oilers .10 .05
Team: (Warren) Moon
Monitors the Action
❑ 638 Indianapolis Colts .04 .02
Team: (Jeff) George
Releases Just in Time
❑ 639 Kansas City Chiefs .04 .02
Team: (Christian) Okoye
Powers Ahead
❑ 640 Los Angeles Raiders .10 .05
Team: (Marcus) Allen
Crosses the Plane
❑ 641 Los Angeles Rams .04 .02
Team: (Jim) Everett
Connects With Soft Touch
❑ 642 Miami Dolphins .04 .02
Team: (Pete) Stoyanovich
Kicks It Through
❑ 643 Minnesota Vikings .04 .02
Team: (Rich) Gannon
Loads Cannon
❑ 644 New Eng. Patriots .04 .02
Team: (John) Stephens
Gets Stood Up
❑ 645 New Orleans Saints .04 .02
Team: (Gill) Fenerty
Finds Opening
❑ 646 New York Giants .04 .02
Team: (Maurice) Carthon
Inches Ahead
❑ 647 New York Jets .04 .02
Team: (Pat) Leahy
Perfect on Extra Point
❑ 648 Philadelphia Eagles .04 .02
Team: (Randall) Cunningham
Calls Own Play for TD
❑ 649 Phoenix Cardinals .04 .02
Team: (Bill) Lewis
Provides the Protection
❑ 650 Pittsburgh Steelers .04 .02
Team: (Bubby) Brister
Eyes Downfield Attack
❑ 651 San Diego Chargers .04 .02
Team: (John) Friesz
Finds the Passing Lane
❑ 652 San Francisco 49ers .04 .02
Team: (Dexter) Carter
Follows Rathman's Block
❑ 653 Seattle Seahawks .04 .02
Team: (Derrick) Fenner
With Fancy Footwork
❑ 654 Tampa Bay Buccaneers .04 .02
Team: (Reggie) Cobb
Hurdles His Way
to First Down
❑ 655 Washington Redskins .04 .02
Team: (Earnest) Byner
Cuts Back to
Follow Block
❑ 656 Checklist 1-132 .04 .02
❑ 657 Checklist 132-264 .04 .02
❑ 658 Checklist 265-396 .04 .02
❑ 659 Checklist 397-528 .04 .02
❑ 660 Checklist 529-660 .04 .02

1991 Topps 1000 Yard Club

	MINT	NRMT
COMPLETE SET (18)	5.00	2.20
ONE PER PACK		

	MINT	NRMT
❑ 1 Jerry Rice	1.00	.45
❑ 2 Barry Sanders	1.25	.55
❑ 3 Thurman Thomas	.35	.16
❑ 4 Henry Ellard	.25	.11
❑ 5 Marion Butts	.15	.07
❑ 6 Earnest Byner	.15	.07
❑ 7 Andre Rison	.35	.16
❑ 8 Bobby Humphrey	.15	.07
❑ 9 Gary Clark	.25	.11
❑ 10 Sterling Sharpe	.35	.16
❑ 11 Flipper Anderson	.15	.07
❑ 12 Neal Anderson	.15	.07
❑ 13 Haywood Jeffires	.25	.11
❑ 14 Stephone Paige	.15	.07
❑ 15 Drew Hill	.15	.07
❑ 16 Barry Word	.15	.07
❑ 17 Anthony Carter	.15	.07
❑ 18 James Brooks	.15	.07

1992 Topps

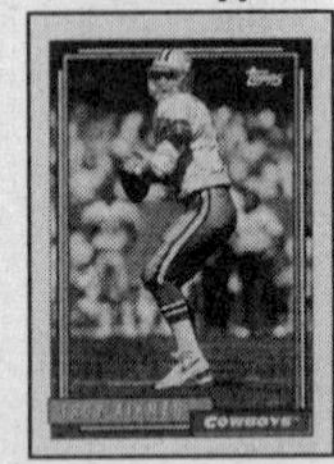

	MINT	NRMT
COMPLETE SET (759)	40.00	18.00
COMP.FACT.SET (680)	35.00	16.00
COMP.SERIES 1 (330)	15.00	6.75
COMP.SERIES 2 (330)	15.00	6.75
COMP.HIGH SER.(99)	10.00	4.50
COMP.FACT.HIGH SET (113)	10.00	4.50
COMMON CARD (1-759)	.05	.02
SEMISTARS	.10	.05
UNLISTED STARS	.25	.11
COMP.NO.1 DRAFT SET (4)	4.00	1.80
NO.1 DRAFT:INS.IN HIGH SER. PACKS		
COMP.GOLD SET (759)	150.00	70.00
COMP.GOLD SERIES 1 (330)	60.00	27.00
COMP.GOLD SERIES 2 (330)	60.00	27.00
COMP.GOLD HIGH SER.(99)	30.00	13.50
*GOLD STARS: 1.5X to 3X HI COLUMN		
*GOLD RCs: 1.25X to 2.5X HI		
ONE PER WAX PACK/THREE PER RACK		
TWENTY PER LO FACTORY SET		
TEN PER HIGH FACTORY SET		

	MINT	NRMT
❑ 1 Tim McGee	.05	.02
❑ 2 Rich Camarillo	.05	.02
❑ 3 Anthony Johnson	.10	.05
❑ 4 Larry Kelm	.05	.02
❑ 5 Irving Fryar	.10	.05
❑ 6 Joey Browner	.05	.02
❑ 7 Michael Walter	.05	.02
❑ 8 Cortez Kennedy	.10	.05
❑ 9 Reyna Thompson	.05	.02
❑ 10 John Friesz	.10	.05
❑ 11 Leroy Hoard	.10	.05
❑ 12 Steve McMichael	.10	.05
❑ 13 Marvin Washington	.05	.02
❑ 14 Clyde Simmons	.05	.02
❑ 15 Stephone Paige	.05	.02
❑ 16 Mike Utley	.10	.05
❑ 17 Tunch Ilkin	.05	.02
❑ 18 Lawrence Dawsey	.10	.05
❑ 19 Vance Johnson	.05	.02
❑ 20 Bryce Paup	.25	.11
❑ 21 Jeff Wright	.05	.02
❑ 22 Gill Fenerty	.05	.02
❑ 23 Lamar Lathon	.05	.02
❑ 24 Danny Copeland	.05	.02
❑ 25 Marcus Allen	.25	.11
❑ 26 Tim Green	.05	.02
❑ 27 Pete Stoyanovich	.05	.02
❑ 28 Alvin Harper	.10	.05
❑ 29 Roy Foster	.05	.02
❑ 30 Eugene Daniel	.05	.02
❑ 31 Luis Sharpe	.05	.02
❑ 32 Terry Wooden	.05	.02
❑ 33 Jim Breech	.05	.02
❑ 34 Randy Hilliard RC	.05	.02
❑ 35 Roman Phifer	.05	.02
❑ 36 Erik Howard	.05	.02
❑ 37 Chris Singleton	.05	.02
❑ 38 Matt Stover	.05	.02
❑ 39 Tim Irwin	.05	.02
❑ 40 Karl Mecklenburg	.05	.02
❑ 41 Joe Phillips	.05	.02
❑ 42 Bill Jones RC	.05	.02
❑ 43 Mark Carrier DB	.05	.02
❑ 44 George Jamison	.05	.02
❑ 45 Rob Taylor	.05	.02
❑ 46 Jeff Jaeger	.05	.02
❑ 47 Don Majkowski	.05	.02
❑ 48 Al Edwards	.05	.02
❑ 49 Curtis Duncan	.05	.02
❑ 50 Sam Mills	.05	.02
❑ 51 Terance Mathis	.10	.05
❑ 52 Brian Mitchell	.10	.05
❑ 53 Mike Pritchard	.10	.05
❑ 54 Calvin Williams	.10	.05
❑ 55 Hardy Nickerson	.10	.05
❑ 56 Nate Newton	.10	.05
❑ 57 Steve Wallace	.05	.02
❑ 58 John Offerdahl	.05	.02
❑ 59 Aeneas Williams	.10	.05
❑ 60 Lee Johnson	.05	.02
❑ 61 Ricardo McDonald RC	.05	.02
❑ 62 David Richards	.05	.02
❑ 63 Paul Gruber	.05	.02
❑ 64 Greg McMurtry	.05	.02
❑ 65 Jay Hilgenberg	.05	.02
❑ 66 Tim Grunhard	.05	.02
❑ 67 Dwayne White RC	.05	.02
❑ 68 Don Beebe	.05	.02
❑ 69 Simon Fletcher	.05	.02
❑ 70 Warren Moon	.25	.11
❑ 71 Chris Jacke	.05	.02
❑ 72 Steve Wisniewski UER (Traded to Raiders, not drafted by them)	.05	.02
❑ 73 Mike Cofer	.05	.02
❑ 74 Tim Johnson UER (No position listed on back)	.05	.02
❑ 75 T.J. Turner	.05	.02
❑ 76 Scott Case	.05	.02
❑ 77 Michael Jackson	.10	.05
❑ 78 Jon Hand	.05	.02
❑ 79 Stan Brock	.05	.02
❑ 80 Robert Blackmon	.05	.02
❑ 81 D.J. Johnson	.05	.02
❑ 82 Damone Johnson	.05	.02

❑ 83 Marc Spindler .05 .02
❑ 84 Larry Brown DB .05 .02
❑ 85 Ray Berry .05 .02
❑ 86 Andre Waters .05 .02
❑ 87 Carlos Huerta .05 .02
❑ 88 Brad Muster .05 .02
❑ 89 Chuck Cecil .05 .02
❑ 90 Nick Lowery .05 .02
❑ 91 Cornelius Bennett .10 .05
❑ 92 Jessie Tuggle .05 .02
❑ 93 Mark Schlereth RC .05 .02
❑ 94 Vestee Jackson .05 .02
❑ 95 Eric Bieniemy .05 .02
❑ 96 Jeff Hostetler .10 .05
❑ 97 Ken Lanier .05 .02
❑ 98 Wayne Haddix .05 .02
❑ 99 Lorenzo White .05 .02
❑ 100 Mervyn Fernandez .05 .02
❑ 101 Brent Williams .05 .02
❑ 102 Ian Beckles .05 .02
❑ 103 Harris Barton .05 .02
❑ 104 Edgar Bennett RC .25 .11
❑ 105 Mike Pitts .05 .02
❑ 106 Fuad Reveiz .05 .02
❑ 107 Vernon Turner .05 .02
❑ 108 Tracy Hayworth RC .05 .02
❑ 109 Checklist 1-110 .05 .02
❑ 110 Tom Waddle .05 .02
❑ 111 Fred Stokes .05 .02
❑ 112 Howard Ballard .05 .02
❑ 113 David Szott .05 .02
❑ 114 Tim McKyer .05 .02
❑ 115 Kyle Clifton .05 .02
❑ 116 Tony Bennett .05 .02
❑ 117 Joel Hilgenberg .05 .02
❑ 118 Dwayne Harper .05 .02
❑ 119 Mike Baab .05 .02
❑ 120 Mark Clayton .10 .05
❑ 121 Eric Swann .10 .05
❑ 122 Neil O'Donnell .25 .11
❑ 123 Mike Munchak .05 .02
❑ 124 Howie Long .10 .05
❑ 125 John Elway UER 1.25 .55
(Card says 6-year vet, should be 9)
❑ 126 Joe Prokop .05 .02
❑ 127 Pepper Johnson .05 .02
❑ 128 Richard Dent .10 .05
❑ 129 Robert Porcher RC .10 .05
❑ 130 Earnest Byner .05 .02
❑ 131 Kent Hull .05 .02
❑ 132 Mike Merriweather .05 .02
❑ 133 Scott Fulhage .05 .02
❑ 134 Kevin Porter .05 .02
❑ 135 Tony Casillas .05 .02
❑ 136 Dean Biasucci .05 .02
❑ 137 Ben Smith .05 .02
❑ 138 Bruce Kozerski .05 .02
❑ 139 Jeff Campbell .05 .02
❑ 140 Kevin Greene .25 .11
❑ 141 Gary Plummer .05 .02
❑ 142 Vincent Brown .05 .02
❑ 143 Ron Hall .05 .02
❑ 144 Louie Aguiar RC .05 .02
❑ 145 Mark Duper .05 .02
❑ 146 Jesse Sapolu .05 .02
❑ 147 Jeff Gossett .05 .02
❑ 148 Brian Noble .05 .02
❑ 149 Derek Russell .05 .02
❑ 150 Carlton Bailey RC .10 .05
❑ 151 Kelly Goodburn .05 .02
❑ 152 Audray McMillian UER .05 .02
(Misspelled Audrey)
❑ 153 Neal Anderson .05 .02
❑ 154 Bill Maas .05 .02
❑ 155 Rickey Jackson .05 .02
❑ 156 Chris Miller .10 .05
❑ 157 Darren Comeaux .05 .02
❑ 158 David Williams .05 .02
❑ 159 Rich Gannon .05 .02
❑ 160 Kevin Mack .05 .02
❑ 161 Jim Arnold .05 .02
❑ 162 Reggie White .25 .11
❑ 163 Leonard Russell .10 .05
❑ 164 Doug Smith .05 .02
❑ 165 Tony Mandarich .05 .02
❑ 166 Greg Lloyd .25 .11
❑ 167 Jumbo Elliott .05 .02
❑ 168 Jonathan Hayes .05 .02
❑ 169 Jim Ritcher .05 .02
❑ 170 Mike Kenn .05 .02
❑ 171 James Washington .05 .02
❑ 172 Tim Harris .05 .02
❑ 173 James Thornton .05 .02
❑ 174 John Brandes RC .05 .02
❑ 175 Fred McAfee RC .05 .02
❑ 176 Henry Rolling .05 .02
❑ 177 Tony Paige .05 .02
❑ 178 Jay Schroeder .05 .02
❑ 179 Jeff Herrod .05 .02
❑ 180 Emmitt Smith 1.50 .70
❑ 181 Wymon Henderson .05 .02
❑ 182 Rob Moore .10 .05
❑ 183 Robert Wilson .05 .02
❑ 184 Michael Zordich RC .05 .02
❑ 185 Jim Harbaugh .25 .11
❑ 186 Vince Workman .10 .05
❑ 187 Ernest Givins .10 .05
❑ 188 Herschel Walker .10 .05
❑ 189 Dan Fike .05 .02
❑ 190 Seth Joyner .10 .05
❑ 191 Steve Young .60 .25
❑ 192 Dennis Gibson .05 .02
❑ 193 Darryl Talley .05 .02
❑ 194 Emile Harry .05 .02
❑ 195 Bill Fralic .05 .02
❑ 196 Michael Stewart .05 .02
❑ 197 James Francis .05 .02
❑ 198 Jerome Henderson .05 .02
❑ 199 John L. Williams .05 .02
❑ 200 Rod Woodson .25 .11
❑ 201 Mike Farr .05 .02
❑ 202 Greg Montgomery .05 .02
❑ 203 Andre Collins .05 .02
❑ 204 Scott Miller .05 .02
❑ 205 Clay Matthews .10 .05
❑ 206 Ethan Horton .05 .02
❑ 207 Rich Miano .05 .02
❑ 208 Chris Mims RC .10 .05
❑ 209 Anthony Morgan .05 .02
❑ 210 Rodney Hampton .25 .11
❑ 211 Chris Hinton .05 .02
❑ 212 Esera Tuaolo .05 .02
❑ 213 Shane Conlan .05 .02
❑ 214 John Carney .05 .02
❑ 215 Kenny Walker .05 .02
❑ 216 Scott Radecic .05 .02
❑ 217 Chris Martin .05 .02
❑ 218 Checklist 111-220 UER .05 .02
(152 Audray McMillian misspelled Audrey)
❑ 219 Wesley Carroll UER .05 .02
(Stats say 1st round pick, bio correctly has 2nd)
❑ 220 Bill Romanowski .05 .02
❑ 221 Reggie Cobb .05 .02
❑ 222 Alfred Anderson .05 .02
❑ 223 Cleveland Gary .05 .02
❑ 224 Eddie Blake RC .05 .02
❑ 225 Chris Spielman .10 .05
❑ 226 John Roper .05 .02
❑ 227 George Thomas RC .05 .02
❑ 228 Jeff Faulkner .05 .02
❑ 229 Chip Lohmiller UER .05 .02
(RFK Stadium not identified on back)
❑ 230 Hugh Millen .05 .02
❑ 231 Ray Horton .05 .02
❑ 232 James Campen .05 .02
❑ 233 Howard Cross .05 .02
❑ 234 Keith McKeller .05 .02
❑ 235 Dino Hackett .05 .02
❑ 236 Jerome Brown .05 .02
❑ 237 Andy Heck .05 .02
❑ 238 Rodney Holman .05 .02
❑ 239 Bruce Matthews .05 .02
❑ 240 Jeff Lageman .05 .02
❑ 241 Bobby Hebert .05 .02
❑ 242 Gary Anderson K .05 .02
❑ 243 Mark Bortz .05 .02
❑ 244 Rich Moran .05 .02
❑ 245 Jeff Uhlenhake .05 .02
❑ 246 Ricky Sanders .05 .02
❑ 247 Clarence Kay .05 .02
❑ 248 Ed King .05 .02
❑ 249 Eddie Anderson .05 .02
❑ 250 Amp Lee RC .05 .02
❑ 251 Norm Johnson .05 .02
❑ 252 Michael Carter .05 .02
❑ 253 Felix Wright .05 .02
❑ 254 Leon Seals .05 .02
❑ 255 Nate Lewis .05 .02
❑ 256 Kevin Call .05 .02
❑ 257 Darryl Henley .05 .02
❑ 258 Jon Vaughn .05 .02
❑ 259 Matt Bahr .05 .02
❑ 260 Johnny Johnson .05 .02
❑ 261 Ken Norton .25 .11
❑ 262 Wendell Davis .05 .02
❑ 263 Eugene Robinson .05 .02
❑ 264 David Treadwell .05 .02
❑ 265 Michael Haynes .10 .05
❑ 266 Robb Thomas .05 .02
❑ 267 Nate Odomes .05 .02
❑ 268 Martin Mayhew .05 .02
❑ 269 Perry Kemp .05 .02
❑ 270 Jerry Ball .05 .02
❑ 271 Tommy Vardell RC .10 .05
❑ 272 Ernie Mills .05 .02
❑ 273 Mo Lewis .05 .02
❑ 274 Roger Ruzek .05 .02
❑ 275 Steve Smith .05 .02
❑ 276 Bo Orlando RC .05 .02
❑ 277 Louis Oliver .05 .02
❑ 278 Toi Cook .05 .02
❑ 279 Eddie Brown .05 .02
❑ 280 Keith McCants .05 .02
❑ 281 Rob Burnett .05 .02
❑ 282 Keith DeLong .05 .02
❑ 283 Stan Thomas UER .05 .02
(9th line bio notes, the word of is in caps)
❑ 284 Robert Brown .05 .02
❑ 285 John Alt .05 .02
❑ 286 Randy Dixon .05 .02
❑ 287 Siran Stacy RC .05 .02
❑ 288 Ray Agnew .05 .02
❑ 289 Darion Conner .05 .02
❑ 290 Kirk Lowdermilk .05 .02
❑ 291 Greg Jackson .05 .02
❑ 292 Ken Harvey .05 .02
❑ 293 Jacob Green .05 .02
❑ 294 Mark Tuinei .05 .02
❑ 295 Mark Rypien .05 .02
❑ 296 Gerald Robinson RC .05 .02
❑ 297 Broderick Thompson .05 .02
❑ 298 Doug Widell .05 .02
❑ 299 Carwell Gardner .05 .02
❑ 300 Barry Sanders 1.50 .70
❑ 301 Eric Metcalf .10 .05
❑ 302 Eric Thomas .05 .02
❑ 303 Terrell Buckley RC .05 .02
❑ 304 Byron Evans .05 .02
❑ 305 Johnny Hector .05 .02
❑ 306 Steve Broussard .05 .02
❑ 307 Gene Atkins .05 .02
❑ 308 Terry McDaniel .05 .02
❑ 309 Charles McRae .05 .02
❑ 310 Jim Lachey .05 .02
❑ 311 Pat Harlow .05 .02
❑ 312 Kevin Butler .05 .02
❑ 313 Scott Stephen .05 .02
❑ 314 Dermontti Dawson .05 .02
❑ 315 Johnny Meads .05 .02
❑ 316 Checklist 221-330 .05 .02
❑ 317 Aaron Craver .05 .02
❑ 318 Michael Brooks .05 .02
❑ 319 Guy McIntyre .05 .02
❑ 320 Thurman Thomas .25 .11
❑ 321 Courtney Hall .05 .02
❑ 322 Dan Saleaumua .05 .02
❑ 323 Vinson Smith RC .05 .02
❑ 324 Steve Jordan .05 .02
❑ 325 Walter Reeves .05 .02
❑ 326 Erik Kramer .10 .05
❑ 327 Duane Bickett .05 .02
❑ 328 Tom Newberry .05 .02

❑	329	John Kasay	.05	.02
❑	330	Dave Meggett	.10	.05
❑	331	Kevin Ross	.05	.02
❑	332	Keith Hamilton RC	.05	.02
❑	333	Dwight Stone	.05	.02
❑	334	Mel Gray	.10	.05
❑	335	Harry Galbreath	.05	.02
❑	336	William Perry	.10	.05
❑	337	Brian Blades	.10	.05
❑	338	Randall McDaniel	.05	.02
❑	339	Pat Coleman RC	.05	.02
❑	340	Michael Irvin	.25	.11
❑	341	Checklist 331-440	.05	.02
❑	342	Chris Mohr	.05	.02
❑	343	Greg Davis	.05	.02
❑	344	Dave Cadigan	.05	.02
❑	345	Art Monk	.10	.05
❑	346	Tim Goad	.05	.02
❑	347	Vinnie Clark	.05	.02
❑	348	David Fulcher	.05	.02
❑	349	Craig Heyward	.10	.05
❑	350	Ronnie Lott	.10	.05
❑	351	Dexter Carter	.05	.02
❑	352	Mark Jackson	.05	.02
❑	353	Brian Jordan	.10	.05
❑	354	Ray Donaldson	.05	.02
❑	355	Jim Price	.05	.02
❑	356	Rod Bernstine	.05	.02
❑	357	Tony Mayberry RC	.05	.02
❑	358	Richard Brown RC	.05	.02
❑	359	David Alexander	.05	.02
❑	360	Haywood Jeffires	.10	.05
❑	361	Henry Thomas	.05	.02
❑	362	Jeff Graham	.25	.11
❑	363	Don Warren	.05	.02
❑	364	Scott Davis	.05	.02
❑	365	Harlon Barnett	.05	.02
❑	366	Mark Collins	.05	.02
❑	367	Rick Tuten	.05	.02
❑	368	Lonnie Marts RC UER (Injured Reserved should be Reserve)	.05	.02
❑	369	Dennis Smith	.05	.02
❑	370	Steve Tasker	.10	.05
❑	371	Robert Massey	.05	.02
❑	372	Ricky Reynolds	.05	.02
❑	373	Alvin Wright	.05	.02
❑	374	Kelvin Martin	.05	.02
❑	375	Vince Buck	.05	.02
❑	376	John Kidd	.05	.02
❑	377	William White	.05	.02
❑	378	Bryan Cox	.10	.05
❑	379	Jamie Dukes RC	.05	.02
❑	380	Anthony Munoz	.10	.05
❑	381	Mark Gunn RC	.05	.02
❑	382	Keith Henderson	.05	.02
❑	383	Charles Wilson	.05	.02
❑	384	Shawn McCarthy RC	.05	.02
❑	385	Ernie Jones	.05	.02
❑	386	Nick Bell	.05	.02
❑	387	Derrick Walker	.05	.02
❑	388	Mark Stepnoski	.10	.05
❑	389	Broderick Thomas	.05	.02
❑	390	Reggie Roby	.05	.02
❑	391	Bubba McDowell	.05	.02
❑	392	Eric Martin	.05	.02
❑	393	Toby Caston RC	.05	.02
❑	394	Bern Brostek	.05	.02
❑	395	Christian Okoye	.05	.02
❑	396	Frank Minnifield	.05	.02
❑	397	Mike Golic	.05	.02
❑	398	Grant Feasel	.05	.02
❑	399	Michael Ball	.05	.02
❑	400	Mike Croel	.05	.02
❑	401	Maury Buford	.05	.02
❑	402	Jeff Bostic UER (Signed as free agent in 1980, not 1984)	.05	.02
❑	403	Sean Landeta	.05	.02
❑	404	Terry Allen	.25	.11
❑	405	Donald Evans	.05	.02
❑	406	Don Mosebar	.05	.02
❑	407	D.J. Dozier	.05	.02
❑	408	Bruce Pickens	.05	.02
❑	409	Jim Dombrowski	.05	.02
❑	410	Deron Cherry	.05	.02
❑	411	Richard Johnson	.05	.02
❑	412	Alexander Wright	.05	.02
❑	413	Tom Rathman	.05	.02
❑	414	Mark Dennis	.05	.02
❑	415	Phil Hansen	.05	.02
❑	416	Lonnie Young	.05	.02
❑	417	Burt Grossman	.05	.02
❑	418	Tony Covington	.05	.02
❑	419	John Stephens	.05	.02
❑	420	Jim Everett	.10	.05
❑	421	Johnny Holland	.05	.02
❑	422	Mike Barber RC	.05	.02
❑	423	Carl Lee	.05	.02
❑	424	Craig Patterson RC	.05	.02
❑	425	Greg Townsend	.05	.02
❑	426	Brett Perriman	.25	.11
❑	427	Morten Andersen	.05	.02
❑	428	John Gesek	.05	.02
❑	429	Bryan Barker	.05	.02
❑	430	John Taylor	.10	.05
❑	431	Donnell Woolford	.05	.02
❑	432	Ron Holmes	.05	.02
❑	433	Lee Williams	.05	.02
❑	434	Alfred Oglesby	.05	.02
❑	435	Jarrod Bunch	.05	.02
❑	436	Carlton Haselrig RC	.05	.02
❑	437	Rufus Porter	.05	.02
❑	438	Rohn Stark	.05	.02
❑	439	Tony Jones	.05	.02
❑	440	Andre Rison	.10	.05
❑	441	Eric Hill	.05	.02
❑	442	Jesse Solomon	.05	.02
❑	443	Jackie Slater	.05	.02
❑	444	Donnie Elder	.05	.02
❑	445	Brett Maxie	.05	.02
❑	446	Max Montoya	.05	.02
❑	447	Will Wolford	.05	.02
❑	448	Craig Taylor	.05	.02
❑	449	Jimmie Jones	.05	.02
❑	450	Anthony Carter	.10	.05
❑	451	Brian Bollinger RC	.05	.02
❑	452	Checklist 441-550	.05	.02
❑	453	Brad Edwards	.05	.02
❑	454	Gene Chilton RC	.05	.02
❑	455	Eric Allen	.05	.02
❑	456	William Roberts	.05	.02
❑	457	Eric Green	.05	.02
❑	458	Irv Eatman	.05	.02
❑	459	Derrick Thomas	.25	.11
❑	460	Tommy Kane	.05	.02
❑	461	LeRoy Butler	.05	.02
❑	462	Oliver Barnett	.05	.02
❑	463	Anthony Smith	.05	.02
❑	464	Cris Dishman	.05	.02
❑	465	Pat Terrell	.05	.02
❑	466	Greg Kragen	.05	.02
❑	467	Rodney Peete	.10	.05
❑	468	Willie Drewrey	.05	.02
❑	469	Jim Wilks	.05	.02
❑	470	Vince Newsome	.05	.02
❑	471	Chris Gardocki	.05	.02
❑	472	Chris Chandler	.25	.11
❑	473	George Thornton	.05	.02
❑	474	Albert Lewis	.05	.02
❑	475	Kevin Glover	.05	.02
❑	476	Joe Bowden RC	.05	.02
❑	477	Harry Sydney	.05	.02
❑	478	Bob Golic	.05	.02
❑	479	Tony Zendejas	.05	.02
❑	480	Brad Baxter	.05	.02
❑	481	Steve Beuerlein	.05	.02
❑	482	Mark Higgs	.05	.02
❑	483	Drew Hill	.05	.02
❑	484	Bryan Millard	.05	.02
❑	485	Mark Kelso	.05	.02
❑	486	David Grant	.05	.02
❑	487	Gary Zimmerman	.05	.02
❑	488	Leonard Marshall	.05	.02
❑	489	Keith Jackson	.10	.05
❑	490	Sterling Sharpe	.25	.11
❑	491	Ferrell Edmunds	.05	.02
❑	492	Wilber Marshall	.05	.02
❑	493	Charles Haley	.10	.05
❑	494	Riki Ellison	.05	.02
❑	495	Bill Brooks	.05	.02
❑	496	Bill Hawkins	.05	.02
❑	497	Erik Williams	.05	.02
❑	498	Leon Searcy RC	.10	.05
❑	499	Mike Horan	.05	.02
❑	500	Pat Swilling	.10	.05
❑	501	Maurice Hurst	.05	.02
❑	502	William Fuller	.10	.05
❑	503	Tim Newton	.05	.02
❑	504	Lorenzo Lynch	.05	.02
❑	505	Tim Barnett	.05	.02
❑	506	Tom Thayer	.05	.02
❑	507	Chris Burkett	.05	.02
❑	508	Ronnie Harmon	.05	.02
❑	509	James Brooks	.10	.05
❑	510	Bennie Blades	.05	.02
❑	511	Roger Craig	.10	.05
❑	512	Tony Woods	.05	.02
❑	513	Greg Lewis	.05	.02
❑	514	Erric Pegram	.10	.05
❑	515	Elvis Patterson	.05	.02
❑	516	Jeff Cross	.05	.02
❑	517	Myron Guyton	.05	.02
❑	518	Jay Novacek	.10	.05
❑	519	Leo Barker RC	.05	.02
❑	520	Keith Byars	.05	.02
❑	521	Dalton Hilliard	.05	.02
❑	522	Ted Washington	.05	.02
❑	523	Dexter McNabb RC	.05	.02
❑	524	Frank Reich	.10	.05
❑	525	Henry Ellard	.10	.05
❑	526	Barry Foster	.10	.05
❑	527	Barry Word	.05	.02
❑	528	Gary Anderson RB	.05	.02
❑	529	Reggie Rutland	.05	.02
❑	530	Stephen Baker	.05	.02
❑	531	John Flannery	.05	.02
❑	532	Steve Wright	.05	.02
❑	533	Eric Sanders	.05	.02
❑	534	Bob Whitfield RC	.05	.02
❑	535	Gaston Green	.05	.02
❑	536	Anthony Pleasant	.05	.02
❑	537	Jeff Bryant	.05	.02
❑	538	Jarvis Williams	.05	.02
❑	539	Jim Morrissey	.05	.02
❑	540	Andre Tippett	.05	.02
❑	541	Gill Byrd	.05	.02
❑	542	Raleigh McKenzie	.05	.02
❑	543	Jim Sweeney	.05	.02
❑	544	David Lutz	.05	.02
❑	545	Wayne Martin	.05	.02
❑	546	Karl Wilson	.05	.02
❑	547	Pierce Holt	.05	.02
❑	548	Doug Smith	.05	.02
❑	549	Nolan Harrison RC	.05	.02
❑	550	Freddie Joe Nunn	.05	.02
❑	551	Eric Moore	.05	.02
❑	552	Cris Carter	.50	.23
❑	553	Kevin Gogan	.05	.02
❑	554	Harold Green	.05	.02
❑	555	Kenneth Davis	.05	.02
❑	556	Travis McNeal	.05	.02
❑	557	Jim C. Jensen	.05	.02
❑	558	Willie Green	.05	.02
❑	559	Scott Galbraith RC UER (Drafted in 1990, not 1989)	.05	.02
❑	560	Louis Lipps	.05	.02
❑	561	Matt Brock	.05	.02
❑	562	Mike Prior	.05	.02
❑	563	Checklist 551-660	.05	.02
❑	564	Robert Delpino	.05	.02
❑	565	Vinny Testaverde	.10	.05
❑	566	Willie Gault	.10	.05
❑	567	Quinn Early	.10	.05
❑	568	Eric Moten	.05	.02
❑	569	Lance Smith	.05	.02
❑	570	Darrell Green	.05	.02
❑	571	Moe Gardner	.05	.02
❑	572	Steve Atwater	.05	.02
❑	573	Ray Childress	.05	.02
❑	574	Dave Krieg	.10	.05
❑	575	Bruce Armstrong	.05	.02
❑	576	Fred Barnett	.25	.11
❑	577	Don Griffin	.05	.02
❑	578	David Brandon RC	.05	.02
❑	579	Robert Young	.05	.02
❑	580	Keith Van Horne	.05	.02

#	Player	Mint	Nrmt
❑ 581	Jeff Criswell	.05	.02
❑ 582	Lewis Tillman	.05	.02
❑ 583	Bubby Brister	.05	.02
❑ 584	Aaron Wallace	.05	.02
❑ 585	Chris Doleman	.05	.02
❑ 586	Marty Carter RC	.05	.02
❑ 587	Chris Warren	.25	.11
❑ 588	David Griggs	.05	.02
❑ 589	Darrell Thompson	.05	.02
❑ 590	Marion Butts	.05	.02
❑ 591	Scott Norwood	.05	.02
❑ 592	Lomas Brown	.05	.02
❑ 593	Daryl Johnston	.25	.11
❑ 594	Alonzo Mitz RC	.05	.02
❑ 595	Tommy Barnhardt	.05	.02
❑ 596	Tim Jorden	.05	.02
❑ 597	Neil Smith	.25	.11
❑ 598	Todd Marinovich	.05	.02
❑ 599	Sean Jones	.10	.05
❑ 600	Clarence Verdin	.05	.02
❑ 601	Trace Armstrong	.05	.02
❑ 602	Steve Bono RC	.25	.11
❑ 603	Mark Ingram	.05	.02
❑ 604	Flipper Anderson	.05	.02
❑ 605	James Jones	.05	.02
❑ 606	Al Noga	.05	.02
❑ 607	Rick Bryan	.05	.02
❑ 608	Eugene Lockhart	.05	.02
❑ 609	Charles Mann	.05	.02
❑ 610	James Hasty	.05	.02
❑ 611	Jeff Feagles	.05	.02
❑ 612	Tim Brown	.25	.11
❑ 613	David Little	.05	.02
❑ 614	Keith Sims	.05	.02
❑ 615	Kevin Murphy	.05	.02
❑ 616	Ray Crockett	.05	.02
❑ 617	Jim Jeffcoat	.05	.02
❑ 618	Patrick Hunter	.05	.02
❑ 619	Keith Kartz	.05	.02
❑ 620	Peter Tom Willis	.05	.02
❑ 621	Vaughan Johnson	.05	.02
❑ 622	Shawn Jefferson	.05	.02
❑ 623	Anthony Thompson	.05	.02
❑ 624	John Rienstra	.05	.02
❑ 625	Don Maggs	.05	.02
❑ 626	Todd Lyght	.05	.02
❑ 627	Brent Jones	.10	.05
❑ 628	Todd McNair	.05	.02
❑ 629	Winston Moss	.05	.02
❑ 630	Mark Carrier WR	.10	.05
❑ 631	Dan Owens	.05	.02
❑ 632	Sammie Smith UER (Old team front, correct new team back; acquired via trade, not draft)	.05	.02
❑ 633	James Lofton	.10	.05
❑ 634	Paul McJulien RC	.05	.02
❑ 635	Tony Tolbert	.05	.02
❑ 636	Carnell Lake	.05	.02
❑ 637	Gary Clark	.25	.11
❑ 638	Brian Washington	.05	.02
❑ 639	Jessie Hester	.05	.02
❑ 640	Doug Riesenberg	.05	.02
❑ 641	Joe Walter RC	.05	.02
❑ 642	John Rade	.05	.02
❑ 643	Wes Hopkins	.05	.02
❑ 644	Kelly Stouffer	.05	.02
❑ 645	Marv Cook	.05	.02
❑ 646	Ken Clarke	.05	.02
❑ 647	Bobby Humphrey UER (Old team front, correct new team back; acquired via trade, not draft)	.05	.02
❑ 648	Tim McDonald	.05	.02
❑ 649	Donald Frank RC	.05	.02
❑ 650	Richmond Webb	.05	.02
❑ 651	Lemuel Stinson	.05	.02
❑ 652	Merton Hanks	.10	.05
❑ 653	Frank Warren	.05	.02
❑ 654	Thomas Benson	.05	.02
❑ 655	Al Smith	.05	.02
❑ 656	Steve DeBerg	.05	.02
❑ 657	Jayice Pearson RC	.05	.02
❑ 658	Joe Morris	.05	.02
❑ 659	Fred Strickland	.05	.02
❑ 660	Kelvin Pritchett	.05	.02
❑ 661	Lewis Billups	.05	.02
❑ 662	Todd Collins RC	.05	.02
❑ 663	Corey Miller RC	.05	.02
❑ 664	Levon Kirkland RC	.05	.02
❑ 665	Jerry Rice	.75	.35
❑ 666	Mike Lodish RC	.05	.02
❑ 667	Chuck Smith RC	.05	.02
❑ 668	Lance Olberding RC	.05	.02
❑ 669	Kevin Smith RC	.25	.11
❑ 670	Dale Carter RC	.25	.11
❑ 671	Sean Gilbert RC	.25	.11
❑ 672	Ken O'Brien	.05	.02
❑ 673	Ricky Proehl	.05	.02
❑ 674	Junior Seau	.25	.11
❑ 675	Courtney Hawkins RC	.10	.05
❑ 676	Eddie Robinson RC	.05	.02
❑ 677	Tom Jeter RC	.05	.02
❑ 678	Jeff George	.25	.11
❑ 679	Cary Conklin	.05	.02
❑ 680	Rueben Mayes	.05	.02
❑ 681	Sean Lumpkin RC	.05	.02
❑ 682	Dan Marino	1.25	.55
❑ 683	Ed McDaniel RC	.05	.02
❑ 684	Greg Skrepenak RC	.05	.02
❑ 685	Tracy Scroggins RC	.05	.02
❑ 686	Tommy Maddox RC	.05	.02
❑ 687	Mike Singletary	.10	.05
❑ 688	Patrick Rowe RC	.05	.02
❑ 689	Phillippi Sparks RC	.05	.02
❑ 690	Joel Steed RC	.05	.02
❑ 691	Kevin Fagan	.05	.02
❑ 692	Deion Sanders	.50	.23
❑ 693	Bruce Smith	.25	.11
❑ 694	David Klingler RC	.10	.05
❑ 695	Clayton Holmes RC	.05	.02
❑ 696	Brett Favre	2.50	1.10
❑ 697	Marc Boutte RC	.05	.02
❑ 698	Dwayne Sabb RC	.05	.02
❑ 699	Ed McCaffrey	.30	.14
❑ 700	Randall Cunningham	.25	.11
❑ 701	Quentin Coryatt RC	.25	.11
❑ 702	Bernie Kosar	.10	.05
❑ 703	Vaughn Dunbar RC	.05	.02
❑ 704	Browning Nagle	.05	.02
❑ 705	Mark Wheeler RC	.05	.02
❑ 706	Paul Siever RC	.05	.02
❑ 707	Anthony Miller	.10	.05
❑ 708	Corey Widmer RC	.05	.02
❑ 709	Eric Dickerson	.10	.05
❑ 710	Martin Bayless	.05	.02
❑ 711	Jason Hanson RC	.10	.05
❑ 712	Michael Dean Perry	.10	.05
❑ 713	Billy Joe Tolliver UER (Stats say 1991 Chargers, should be Falcons)	.05	.02
❑ 714	Chad Hennings RC	.10	.05
❑ 715	Bucky Richardson RC	.05	.02
❑ 716	Steve Israel RC	.05	.02
❑ 717	Robert Harris RC	.05	.02
❑ 718	Timm Rosenbach	.05	.02
❑ 719	Joe Montana	1.25	.55
❑ 720	Derek Brown TE RC	.05	.02
❑ 721	Robert Brooks RC	1.00	.45
❑ 722	Boomer Esiason	.10	.05
❑ 723	Troy Auzenne RC	.05	.02
❑ 724	John Fina RC	.05	.02
❑ 725	Chris Crooms RC	.05	.02
❑ 726	Eugene Chung RC	.05	.02
❑ 727	Darren Woodson RC	.25	.11
❑ 728	Leslie O'Neal	.10	.05
❑ 729	Dan McGwire	.05	.02
❑ 730	Al Toon	.10	.05
❑ 731	Michael Brandon RC	.05	.02
❑ 732	Steve DeOssie	.05	.02
❑ 733	Jim Kelly	.25	.11
❑ 734	Webster Slaughter	.05	.02
❑ 735	Tony Smith RC	.05	.02
❑ 736	Shane Collins RC	.05	.02
❑ 737	Randal Hill	.05	.02
❑ 738	Chris Holder RC	.05	.02
❑ 739	Russell Maryland	.10	.05
❑ 740	Carl Pickens RC	.60	.25
❑ 741	Andre Reed	.10	.05
❑ 742	Steve Emtman RC	.05	.02
❑ 743	Carl Banks	.05	.02
❑ 744	Troy Aikman	.75	.35
❑ 745	Mark Royals	.05	.02
❑ 746	J.J. Birden	.05	.02
❑ 747	Michael Cofer	.05	.02
❑ 748	Darryl Ashmore RC	.05	.02
❑ 749	Dion Lambert RC	.05	.02
❑ 750	Phil Simms	.10	.05
❑ 751	Reggie E. White RC	.05	.02
❑ 752	Harvey Williams	.25	.11
❑ 753	Ty Detmer	.25	.11
❑ 754	Tony Brooks RC	.05	.02
❑ 755	Steve Christie	.05	.02
❑ 756	Lawrence Taylor	.25	.11
❑ 757	Merril Hoge	.05	.02
❑ 758	Robert Jones RC	.05	.02
❑ 759	Checklist 661-759	.05	.02

1992 Topps 1000 Yard Club

	MINT	NRMT
COMPLETE SET (20)	15.00	6.75

THREE PER JUMBO PACK..........
*GOLDS: 4X TO 10X BASE CARD HI
GOLDS RANDOM INSERTS IN FACTORY SETS ....

#	Player	Mint	Nrmt
❑ 1	Emmitt Smith	4.00	1.80
❑ 2	Barry Sanders	4.00	1.80
❑ 3	Michael Irvin	.60	.25
❑ 4	Thurman Thomas	.60	.25
❑ 5	Gary Clark	.60	.25
❑ 6	Haywood Jeffires	.25	.11
❑ 7	Michael Haynes	.25	.11
❑ 8	Drew Hill	.15	.07
❑ 9	Mark Duper	.15	.07
❑ 10	James Lofton	.25	.11
❑ 11	Rodney Hampton	.60	.25
❑ 12	Mark Clayton	.25	.11
❑ 13	Henry Ellard	.25	.11
❑ 14	Art Monk	.25	.11
❑ 15	Earnest Byner	.15	.07
❑ 16	Gaston Green	.15	.07
❑ 17	Christian Okoye	.15	.07
❑ 18	Irving Fryar	.25	.11
❑ 19	John Taylor	.25	.11
❑ 20	Brian Blades	.25	.11

1993 Topps

	MINT	NRMT
COMPLETE SET (660)	25.00	11.00
COMP.FACT.SET (673)	50.00	22.00
COMP.SERIES 1 (330)	15.00	6.75
COMP.SERIES 2 (330)	10.00	4.50
COMMON CARD (1-660)	.05	.02
SEMISTARS	.10	.05
UNLISTED STARS	.25	.11
COMP.GOLD SET (660)	90.00	40.00
COMP.GOLD SER.1 (330)	50.00	22.00
COMP.GOLD SER.2 (330)	40.00	18.00
CL REPLACE (329G)	1.00	.45
CL REPLACE (330G/659G/660G)	.50	.23

*GOLD STARS: 1.5X to 3X HI COLUMN
*GOLD RCs: 1.25X to 2.5X HI ......
ONE PER FOIL PACK/THREE PER RACK PACK ......
FIVE PER JUMBO PACK/TEN PER FACT.SET

	MINT	NRMT
❑ 1 Art Monk RB	.05	.02
❑ 2 Jerry Rice RB	.50	.23
❑ 3 Stanley Richard	.05	.02
❑ 4 Ron Hall	.05	.02
❑ 5 Daryl Johnston	.25	.11
❑ 6 Wendell Davis	.05	.02
❑ 7 Vaughn Dunbar	.05	.02
❑ 8 Mike Jones	.05	.02
❑ 9 Anthony Johnson	.10	.05
❑ 10 Chris Miller	.10	.05
❑ 11 Kyle Clifton	.05	.02
❑ 12 Curtis Conway RC	.50	.23
❑ 13 Lionel Washington	.05	.02
❑ 14 Reggie Johnson	.05	.02
❑ 15 David Little	.05	.02
❑ 16 Nick Lowery	.05	.02
❑ 17 Darryl Williams	.05	.02
❑ 18 Brent Jones	.10	.05
❑ 19 Bruce Matthews	.05	.02
❑ 20 Heath Sherman	.05	.02
❑ 21 John Kasay UER (Text on back states he did not attempt any FG's over 50 yds. but made 8)	.05	.02
❑ 22 Troy Drayton RC	.10	.05
❑ 23 Eric Metcalf	.10	.05
❑ 24 Andre Tippett	.05	.02
❑ 25 Rodney Hampton	.25	.11
❑ 26 Henry Jones	.05	.02
❑ 27 Jim Everett	.10	.05
❑ 28 Steve Jordan	.05	.02
❑ 29 LeRoy Butler	.05	.02
❑ 30 Troy Vincent	.05	.02
❑ 31 Nate Lewis	.05	.02
❑ 32 Rickey Jackson	.05	.02
❑ 33 Darion Conner	.05	.02
❑ 34 Tom Carter RC	.10	.05
❑ 35 Jeff George	.25	.11
❑ 36 Larry Centers RC	.25	.11
❑ 37 Reggie Cobb	.05	.02
❑ 38 Mike Saxon	.05	.02
❑ 39 Brad Baxter	.05	.02
❑ 40 Reggie White	.25	.11
❑ 41 Haywood Jeffires	.10	.05
❑ 42 Alfred Williams	.05	.02
❑ 43 Aaron Wallace	.05	.02
❑ 44 Tracy Simien	.05	.02
❑ 45 Pat Harlow	.05	.02
❑ 46 D.J. Johnson	.05	.02
❑ 47 Don Griffin	.05	.02
❑ 48 Flipper Anderson	.05	.02
❑ 49 Keith Kartz	.05	.02
❑ 50 Bernie Kosar	.10	.05
❑ 51 Kent Hull	.05	.02
❑ 52 Erik Howard	.05	.02
❑ 53 Pierce Holt	.05	.02
❑ 54 Dwayne Harper	.05	.02
❑ 55 Bennie Blades	.05	.02
❑ 56 Mark Duper	.05	.02
❑ 57 Brian Noble	.05	.02
❑ 58 Jeff Feagles	.05	.02
❑ 59 Michael Haynes	.10	.05
❑ 60 Junior Seau	.25	.11
❑ 61 Gary Anderson RB	.05	.02
❑ 62 Jon Hand	.05	.02
❑ 63 Lin Elliott RC	.05	.02
❑ 64 Dana Stubblefield RC	.25	.11
❑ 65 Vaughan Johnson	.05	.02
❑ 66 Mo Lewis	.05	.02
❑ 67 Aeneas Williams	.05	.02
❑ 68 David Fulcher	.05	.02
❑ 69 Chip Lohmiller	.05	.02
❑ 70 Greg Townsend	.05	.02
❑ 71 Simon Fletcher	.05	.02
❑ 72 Sean Salisbury	.05	.02
❑ 73 Christian Okoye	.05	.02
❑ 74 Jim Arnold	.05	.02
❑ 75 Bruce Smith	.25	.11
❑ 76 Fred Barnett	.10	.05
❑ 77 Bill Romanowski	.05	.02
❑ 78 Dermontti Dawson	.05	.02
❑ 79 Bern Brostek	.05	.02
❑ 80 Warren Moon	.25	.11
❑ 81 Bill Fralic	.05	.02
❑ 82 Lomas Brown FP	.05	.02
❑ 83 Duane Bickett FP	.05	.02
❑ 84 Neil Smith FP	.10	.05
❑ 85 Reggie White FP	.10	.05
❑ 86 Tim McDonald FP	.05	.02
❑ 87 Leslie O'Neal FP	.05	.02
❑ 88 Steve Young FP	.40	.18
❑ 89 Paul Gruber FP	.05	.02
❑ 90 Wilber Marshall FP	.05	.02
❑ 91 Trace Armstrong	.05	.02
❑ 92 Bobby Houston RC	.05	.02
❑ 93 George Thornton	.05	.02
❑ 94 Keith McCants	.05	.02
❑ 95 Ricky Sanders	.05	.02
❑ 96 Jackie Harris	.05	.02
❑ 97 Todd Marinovich	.05	.02
❑ 98 Henry Thomas	.05	.02
❑ 99 Jeff Wright	.05	.02
❑ 100 John Elway	1.50	.70
❑ 101 Garrison Hearst RC	1.00	.45
❑ 102 Roy Foster	.05	.02
❑ 103 David Lang	.05	.02
❑ 104 Matt Stover	.05	.02
❑ 105 Lawrence Taylor	.25	.11
❑ 106 Pete Stoyanovich	.05	.02
❑ 107 Jessie Tuggle	.05	.02
❑ 108 William White	.05	.02
❑ 109 Andy Harmon RC	.10	.05
❑ 110 John L. Williams	.05	.02
❑ 111 Jon Vaughn	.05	.02
❑ 112 John Alt	.05	.02
❑ 113 Chris Jacke	.05	.02
❑ 114 Jim Breech	.05	.02
❑ 115 Eric Martin	.05	.02
❑ 116 Derrick Walker	.05	.02
❑ 117 Ricky Ervins	.05	.02
❑ 118 Roger Craig	.10	.05
❑ 119 Jeff Gossett	.05	.02
❑ 120 Emmitt Smith	1.50	.70
❑ 121 Bob Whitfield	.05	.02
❑ 122 Alonzo Spellman	.05	.02
❑ 123 David Klingler	.05	.02
❑ 124 Tommy Maddox	.05	.02
❑ 125 Robert Porcher	.05	.02
❑ 126 Edgar Bennett	.25	.11
❑ 127 Harvey Williams	.10	.05
❑ 128 Dave Brown RC	.25	.11
❑ 129 Johnny Mitchell	.05	.02
❑ 130 Drew Bledsoe RC	3.00	1.35
❑ 131 Zefross Moss	.05	.02
❑ 132 Nate Odomes	.05	.02
❑ 133 Rufus Porter	.05	.02
❑ 134 Jackie Slater	.05	.02
❑ 135 Steve Young	.75	.35
❑ 136 Chris Calloway	.05	.02
❑ 137 Steve Atwater	.05	.02
❑ 138 Mark Carrier DB	.05	.02
❑ 139 Marvin Washington	.05	.02
❑ 140 Barry Foster	.10	.05
❑ 141 Ricky Reynolds	.05	.02
❑ 142 Bubba McDowell	.05	.02
❑ 143 Dan Footman RC	.05	.02
❑ 144 Richmond Webb	.05	.02
❑ 145 Mike Pritchard	.10	.05
❑ 146 Chris Spielman	.10	.05
❑ 147 Dave Krieg	.10	.05
❑ 148 Nick Bell	.05	.02
❑ 149 Vincent Brown	.05	.02
❑ 150 Seth Joyner	.05	.02
❑ 151 Tommy Kane	.05	.02
❑ 152 Carlton Gray RC	.05	.02
❑ 153 Harry Newsome	.05	.02
❑ 154 Rohn Stark	.05	.02
❑ 155 Shannon Sharpe	.25	.11
❑ 156 Charles Haley	.10	.05
❑ 157 Cornelius Bennett	.10	.05
❑ 158 Doug Riesenberg	.05	.02
❑ 159 Amp Lee	.05	.02
❑ 160 Sterling Sharpe UER (Card front pictures Edgar Bennett)	.25	.11
❑ 161 Alonzo Mitz	.05	.02
❑ 162 Pat Terrell	.05	.02
❑ 163 Mark Schlereth	.05	.02
❑ 164 Gary Anderson K	.05	.02
❑ 165 Quinn Early	.10	.05
❑ 166 Jerome Bettis RC	1.00	.45
❑ 167 Lawrence Dawsey	.05	.02
❑ 168 Derrick Thomas	.25	.11
❑ 169 Rodney Peete	.05	.02
❑ 170 Jim Kelly	.25	.11
❑ 171 Deion Sanders TL	.25	.11
❑ 172 Richard Dent TL	.05	.02
❑ 173 Emmitt Smith TL	.75	.35
❑ 174 Barry Sanders TL	.75	.35
❑ 175 Sterling Sharpe TL	.05	.02
❑ 176 Cleveland Gary TL	.05	.02
❑ 177 Terry Allen TL	.10	.05
❑ 178 Vaughan Johnson TL	.05	.02
❑ 179 Rodney Hampton TL	.05	.02
❑ 180 Randall Cunningham TL	.10	.05
❑ 181 Ricky Proehl TL	.05	.02
❑ 182 Jerry Rice TL	.50	.23
❑ 183 Reggie Cobb TL	.05	.02
❑ 184 Earnest Byner TL	.05	.02
❑ 185 Jeff Lageman	.05	.02
❑ 186 Carlos Jenkins	.05	.02
❑ 187 Cardinals Draft Picks: Ernest Dye, Ronald Moore, Garrison Hearst, Ben Coleman	.40	.18
❑ 188 Todd Lyght	.05	.02
❑ 189 Carl Simpson RC	.05	.02
❑ 190 Barry Sanders	1.50	.70
❑ 191 Jim Harbaugh	.25	.11
❑ 192 Roger Ruzek	.05	.02
❑ 193 Brent Williams	.05	.02
❑ 194 Chip Banks	.05	.02
❑ 195 Mike Croel	.05	.02
❑ 196 Marion Butts	.05	.02
❑ 197 James Washington	.05	.02
❑ 198 John Offerdahl	.05	.02
❑ 199 Tom Rathman	.05	.02
❑ 200 Joe Montana	1.50	.70
❑ 201 Pepper Johnson	.05	.02
❑ 202 Cris Dishman	.05	.02
❑ 203 Adrian White RC	.05	.02
❑ 204 Reggie Brooks RC	.10	.05
❑ 205 Cortez Kennedy	.10	.05
❑ 206 Robert Massey	.05	.02
❑ 207 Toi Cook	.05	.02
❑ 208 Harry Sydney	.05	.02
❑ 209 Lincoln Kennedy RC	.05	.02
❑ 210 Randall McDaniel	.05	.02
❑ 211 Eugene Daniel	.05	.02
❑ 212 Rob Burnett	.05	.02
❑ 213 Steve Broussard	.05	.02
❑ 214 Brian Washington	.05	.02
❑ 215 Leonard Renfro RC	.05	.02
❑ 216 Audray McMillian LL, Henry Jones	.05	.02
❑ 217 Sterling Sharpe LL, Anthony Miller	.05	.02
❑ 218 Clyde Simmons LL, Leslie O'Neal	.05	.02
❑ 219 Emmitt Smith LL, Barry Foster	.40	.18
❑ 220 Steve Young LL, Warren Moon	.25	.11
❑ 221 Mel Gray	.10	.05
❑ 222 Luis Sharpe	.05	.02
❑ 223 Eric Moten	.05	.02
❑ 224 Albert Lewis	.05	.02
❑ 225 Alvin Harper	.10	.05

❑ 226 Steve Wallace .05 .02
❑ 227 Mark Higgs .05 .02
❑ 228 Eugene Lockhart .05 .02
❑ 229 Sean Jones .05 .02
❑ 230 Buccaneers Draft Picks .05 .02
Eric Curry
Lamar Thomas
Demetrious DuBose
John Lynch
❑ 231 Jimmy Williams .05 .02
(Text states drafted in 1992; he was drafted in 1982)
❑ 232 Demetrius DuBose RC .05 .02
❑ 233 John Roper .05 .02
❑ 234 Keith Hamilton .05 .02
❑ 235 Donald Evans .05 .02
❑ 236 Kenneth Davis .05 .02
❑ 237 John Copeland RC .10 .05
❑ 238 Leonard Russell .10 .05
❑ 239 Ken Harvey .05 .02
❑ 240 Dale Carter .05 .02
❑ 241 Anthony Pleasant .05 .02
❑ 242 Darrell Green .05 .02
❑ 243 Natrone Means RC .75 .35
❑ 244 Rob Moore .10 .05
❑ 245 Chris Doleman .05 .02
❑ 246 J.B. Brown .05 .02
❑ 247 Ray Crockett .05 .02
❑ 248 John Taylor .10 .05
❑ 249 Russell Maryland .05 .02
❑ 250 Brett Favre 2.00 .90
❑ 251 Carl Pickens .25 .11
❑ 252 Andy Heck .05 .02
❑ 253 Jerome Henderson .05 .02
❑ 254 Deion Sanders .50 .23
❑ 255 Steve Emtman .05 .02
❑ 256 Calvin Williams .10 .05
❑ 257 Sean Gilbert .10 .05
❑ 258 Don Beebe .05 .02
❑ 259 Robert Smith RC 1.00 .45
❑ 260 Robert Blackmon .05 .02
❑ 261 Jim Kelly TL .10 .05
❑ 262 Harold Green TL UER .05 .02
(Harold Green is identified as Gaston Green)
❑ 263 Clay Matthews TL .05 .02
❑ 264 John Elway TL .75 .35
❑ 265 Warren Moon TL .10 .05
❑ 266 Jeff George TL .10 .05
❑ 267 Derrick Thomas TL .05 .02
❑ 268 Howie Long TL .05 .02
❑ 269 Dan Marino TL .75 .35
❑ 270 Jon Vaughn TL .05 .02
❑ 271 Chris Burkett TL .05 .02
❑ 272 Barry Foster TL .05 .02
❑ 273 Marion Butts TL .05 .02
❑ 274 Chris Warren TL .05 .02
❑ 275 Michael Strahan and .05 .02
Marcus Buckley RC
Giants Draft Picks
❑ 276 Tony Casillas .05 .02
❑ 277 Jarrod Bunch .05 .02
❑ 278 Eric Green .05 .02
❑ 279 Stan Brock .05 .02
❑ 280 Chester McGlockton .10 .05
❑ 281 Ricky Watters .25 .11
❑ 282 Dan Saleaumua .05 .02
❑ 283 Rich Camarillo .05 .02
❑ 284 Cris Carter .50 .23
❑ 285 Rick Mirer RC .50 .23
❑ 286 Matt Brock .05 .02
❑ 287 Burt Grossman .05 .02
❑ 288 Andre Collins .05 .02
❑ 289 Mark Jackson .05 .02
❑ 290 Dan Marino 1.50 .70
❑ 291 Cornelius Bennett FG .05 .02
❑ 292 Steve Atwater FG .05 .02
❑ 293 Bryan Cox FG .05 .02
❑ 294 Sam Mills FG .05 .02
❑ 295 Pepper Johnson FG .05 .02
❑ 296 Seth Joyner FG .05 .02
❑ 297 Chris Spielman FG .05 .02
❑ 298 Junior Seau FG .10 .05
❑ 299 Cortez Kennedy FG .05 .02
❑ 300 Broderick Thomas FG .05 .02
❑ 301 Todd McNair .05 .02
❑ 302 Nate Newton .10 .05
❑ 303 Michael Walter .05 .02
❑ 304 Clyde Simmons .05 .02
❑ 305 Ernie Mills .05 .02
❑ 306 Steve Wisniewski .05 .02
❑ 307 Coleman Rudolph RC .05 .02
❑ 308 Thurman Thomas .25 .11
❑ 309 Reggie Roby .05 .02
❑ 310 Eric Swann .10 .05
❑ 311 Mark Wheeler .05 .02
❑ 312 Jeff Herrod .05 .02
❑ 313 Leroy Hoard .10 .05
❑ 314 Patrick Bates RC .05 .02
❑ 315 Earnest Byner .05 .02
❑ 316 Dave Meggett .05 .02
❑ 317 George Teague RC .10 .05
❑ 318 Ray Childress .05 .02
❑ 319 Mike Kenn .05 .02
❑ 320 Jason Hanson .05 .02
❑ 321 Gary Clark .10 .05
❑ 322 Chris Gardocki .05 .02
❑ 323 Ken Norton .10 .05
❑ 324 Eric Curry RC .05 .02
❑ 325 Byron Evans .05 .02
❑ 326 O.J. McDuffie RC .75 .35
❑ 327 Dwight Stone .05 .02
❑ 328 Tommy Barnhardt .05 .02
❑ 329 Checklist 1-165 .05 .02
❑ 330 Checklist 166-329 .05 .02
❑ 331 Erik Williams .05 .02
❑ 332 Phil Hansen .05 .02
❑ 333 Martin Harrison RC .05 .02
❑ 334 Mark Ingram .05 .02
❑ 335 Mark Rypien .05 .02
❑ 336 Anthony Miller .10 .05
❑ 337 Antone Davis .05 .02
❑ 338 Mike Munchak .05 .02
❑ 339 Wayne Martin .05 .02
❑ 340 Joe Montana 1.50 .70
❑ 341 Deon Figures RC .10 .05
❑ 342 Ed McDaniel .05 .02
❑ 343 Chris Burkett .05 .02
❑ 344 Tony Smith .05 .02
❑ 345 James Lofton .10 .05
❑ 346 Courtney Hawkins .05 .02
❑ 347 Dennis Smith .05 .02
❑ 348 Anthony Morgan .05 .02
❑ 349 Chris Goode .05 .02
❑ 350 Phil Simms .10 .05
❑ 351 Patrick Hunter .05 .02
❑ 352 Brett Perriman .25 .11
❑ 353 Corey Miller .05 .02
❑ 354 Harry Galbreath .05 .02
❑ 355 Mark Carrier WR .10 .05
❑ 356 Troy Drayton .10 .05
❑ 357 Greg Davis .05 .02
❑ 358 Tim Krumrie .05 .02
❑ 359 Tim McDonald .05 .02
❑ 360 Webster Slaughter .05 .02
❑ 361 Steve Christie .05 .02
❑ 362 Courtney Hall .05 .02
❑ 363 Charles Mann .05 .02
❑ 364 Vestee Jackson .05 .02
❑ 365 Robert Jones .05 .02
❑ 366 Rich Miano .05 .02
❑ 367 Morten Andersen .05 .02
❑ 368 Jeff Graham .10 .05
❑ 369 Martin Mayhew .05 .02
❑ 370 Anthony Carter .10 .05
❑ 371 Greg Kragen .05 .02
❑ 372 Ron Cox .05 .02
❑ 373 Perry Williams .05 .02
❑ 374 Willie Gault .05 .02
❑ 375 Chris Warren .10 .05
❑ 376 Reyna Thompson .05 .02
❑ 377 Bennie Thompson .05 .02
❑ 378 Kevin Mack .05 .02
❑ 379 Clarence Verdin .05 .02
❑ 380 Marc Boutte .05 .02
❑ 381 Marvin Jones RC .05 .02
❑ 382 Greg Jackson .05 .02
❑ 383 Steve Bono .25 .11
❑ 384 Terrell Buckley .05 .02
❑ 385 Garrison Hearst .50 .23
❑ 386 Mike Brim .05 .02
❑ 387 Jesse Sapolu .05 .02
❑ 388 Carl Lee .05 .02
❑ 389 Jeff Cross .05 .02
❑ 390 Karl Mecklenburg .05 .02
❑ 391 Chad Hennings .05 .02
❑ 392 Oliver Barnett .05 .02
❑ 393 Dalton Hilliard .05 .02
❑ 394 Broderick Thompson .05 .02
❑ 395 Raghib Ismail .10 .05
❑ 396 John Kidd .05 .02
❑ 397 Eddie Anderson .05 .02
❑ 398 Lamar Lathon .05 .02
❑ 399 Darren Perry .05 .02
❑ 400 Drew Bledsoe 1.50 .70
❑ 401 Ferrell Edmunds .05 .02
❑ 402 Lomas Brown .05 .02
❑ 403 Drew Hill .05 .02
❑ 404 David Whitmore .05 .02
❑ 405 Mike Johnson .05 .02
❑ 406 Paul Gruber .05 .02
❑ 407 Kirk Lowdermilk .05 .02
❑ 408 Curtis Conway .25 .11
❑ 409 Bryce Paup .25 .11
❑ 410 Boomer Esiason .10 .05
❑ 411 Jay Schroeder .05 .02
❑ 412 Anthony Newman .05 .02
❑ 413 Ernie Jones .05 .02
❑ 414 Carlton Bailey .05 .02
❑ 415 Kenneth Gant .05 .02
❑ 416 Todd Scott .05 .02
❑ 417 Anthony Smith .05 .02
❑ 418 Erik McMillan .05 .02
❑ 419 Ronnie Harmon .05 .02
❑ 420 Andre Reed .10 .05
❑ 421 Wymon Henderson .05 .02
❑ 422 Carnell Lake .05 .02
❑ 423 Al Noga .05 .02
❑ 424 Curtis Duncan .05 .02
❑ 425 Mike Gann .05 .02
❑ 426 Eugene Robinson .05 .02
❑ 427 Scott Mersereau .05 .02
❑ 428 Chris Singleton .05 .02
❑ 429 Gerald Robinson .05 .02
❑ 430 Pat Swilling .05 .02
❑ 431 Ed McCaffrey .10 .05
❑ 432 Neal Anderson .05 .02
❑ 433 Joe Phillips .05 .02
❑ 434 Jerry Ball .05 .02
❑ 435 Tyronne Stowe .05 .02
❑ 436 Dana Stubblefield .25 .11
❑ 437 Eric Curry .05 .02
❑ 438 Derrick Fenner .05 .02
❑ 439 Mark Clayton .05 .02
❑ 440 Quentin Coryatt .10 .05
❑ 441 Willie Roaf RC .10 .05
❑ 442 Ernest Dye .05 .02
❑ 443 Jeff Jaeger .05 .02
❑ 444 Stan Humphries .25 .11
❑ 445 Johnny Johnson .05 .02
❑ 446 Larry Brown DB .05 .02
❑ 447 Kurt Gouveia .05 .02
❑ 448 Qadry Ismail RC .25 .11
❑ 449 Dan Footman .05 .02
❑ 450 Tom Waddle .05 .02
❑ 451 Kelvin Martin .05 .02
❑ 452 Kanavis McGhee .05 .02
❑ 453 Herman Moore .50 .23
❑ 454 Jesse Solomon .05 .02
❑ 455 Shane Conlan .05 .02
❑ 456 Joel Steed .05 .02
❑ 457 Charles Arbuckle .05 .02
❑ 458 Shane Dronett .05 .02
❑ 459 Steve Tasker .10 .05
❑ 460 Herschel Walker .10 .05
❑ 461 Willie Davis .25 .11
❑ 462 Al Smith .05 .02
❑ 463 O.J. McDuffie .25 .11
❑ 464 Kevin Fagan .05 .02
❑ 465 Hardy Nickerson .10 .05
❑ 466 Leonard Marshall .05 .02
❑ 467 John Baylor .05 .02
❑ 468 Jay Novacek .10 .05
❑ 469 Wayne Simmons RC .05 .02
❑ 470 Tommy Vardell .05 .02
❑ 471 Cleveland Gary .05 .02
❑ 472 Mark Collins .05 .02
❑ 473 Craig Heyward .10 .05

❑ 474 John Copeland UER ...... .10 .05
(Bio states he was born 0-29-70 instead of 9-29-70)
❑ 475 Jeff Hostetler .... .10 .05
❑ 476 Brian Mitchell .... .10 .05
❑ 477 Natrone Means .... .40 .18
❑ 478 Brad Muster .... .05 .02
❑ 479 David Lutz .... .05 .02
❑ 480 Andre Rison .... .10 .05
❑ 481 Michael Zordich .... .05 .02
❑ 482 Jim McMahon .... .05 .02
❑ 483 Carlton Gray .... .05 .02
❑ 484 Chris Mohr .... .05 .02
❑ 485 Ernest Givins .... .10 .05
❑ 486 Tony Tolbert .... .05 .02
❑ 487 Vai Sikahema .... .05 .02
❑ 488 Larry Webster .... .05 .02
❑ 489 James Hasty .... .05 .02
❑ 490 Reggie White .... .25 .11
❑ 491 Reggie Rivers RC .... .05 .02
❑ 492 Roman Phifer .... .05 .02
❑ 493 Levon Kirkland .... .05 .02
❑ 494 Demetrius DuBose .... .05 .02
❑ 495 William Perry .... .10 .05
❑ 496 Clay Matthews .... .10 .05
❑ 497 Aaron Jones .... .05 .02
❑ 498 Jack Trudeau .... .05 .02
❑ 499 Michael Brooks .... .05 .02
❑ 500 Jerry Rice .... 1.00 .45
❑ 501 Lonnie Marts .... .05 .02
❑ 502 Tim McGee .... .05 .02
❑ 503 Kelvin Pritchett .... .05 .02
❑ 504 Bobby Hebert .... .05 .02
❑ 505 Audray McMillian .... .05 .02
❑ 506 Chuck Cecil .... .05 .02
❑ 507 Leonard Renfro .... .05 .02
❑ 508 Ethan Horton .... .05 .02
❑ 509 Kevin Smith .... .10 .05
❑ 510 Louis Oliver .... .05 .02
❑ 511 John Stephens .... .05 .02
❑ 512 Browning Nagle .... .05 .02
❑ 513 Ricardo McDonald .... .05 .02
❑ 514 Leslie O'Neal .... .10 .05
❑ 515 Lorenzo White .... .05 .02
❑ 516 Thomas Smith RC .... .10 .05
❑ 517 Tony Woods .... .05 .02
❑ 518 Darryl Henley .... .05 .02
❑ 519 Robert Delpino .... .05 .02
❑ 520 Rod Woodson .... .25 .11
❑ 521 Phillippi Sparks .... .05 .02
❑ 522 Jessie Hester .... .05 .02
❑ 523 Shaun Gayle .... .05 .02
❑ 524 Brad Edwards .... .05 .02
❑ 525 Randall Cunningham .... .25 .11
❑ 526 Marv Cook .... .05 .02
❑ 527 Dennis Gibson .... .05 .02
❑ 528 Erric Pegram .... .10 .05
❑ 529 Terry McDaniel .... .05 .02
❑ 530 Troy Aikman .... .75 .35
❑ 531 Irving Fryar .... .10 .05
❑ 532 Blair Thomas .... .05 .02
❑ 533 Jim Wilks .... .05 .02
❑ 534 Michael Jackson .... .10 .05
❑ 535 Eric Davis .... .05 .02
❑ 536 James Campen .... .05 .02
❑ 537 Steve Beuerlein .... .05 .02
❑ 538 Robert Smith .... .50 .23
❑ 539 J.J. Birden .... .05 .02
❑ 540 Broderick Thomas .... .05 .02
❑ 541 Darryl Talley .... .05 .02
❑ 542 Russell Freeman RC .... .05 .02
❑ 543 David Alexander .... .05 .02
❑ 544 Chris Mims .... .05 .02
❑ 545 Coleman Rudolph .... .05 .02
❑ 546 Steve McMichael .... .10 .05
❑ 547 David Williams .... .05 .02
❑ 548 Chris Hinton .... .05 .02
❑ 549 Jim Jeffcoat .... .05 .02
❑ 550 Howie Long .... .10 .05
❑ 551 Roosevelt Potts RC .... .05 .02
❑ 552 Bryan Cox .... .05 .02
❑ 553 David Richards UER .... .05 .02
(Photo on front is Stanley Richards)
❑ 554 Reggie Brooks .... .10 .05
❑ 555 Neil O'Donnell .... .25 .11
❑ 556 Irv Smith RC .... .05 .02
❑ 557 Henry Ellard .... .10 .05
❑ 558 Steve DeBerg .... .05 .02
❑ 559 Jim Sweeney .... .05 .02
❑ 560 Harold Green .... .05 .02
❑ 561 Darrell Thompson .... .05 .02
❑ 562 Vinny Testaverde .... .10 .05
❑ 563 Bubby Brister .... .05 .02
❑ 564 Sean Landeta .... .05 .02
❑ 565 Neil Smith .... .25 .11
❑ 566 Craig Erickson .... .10 .05
❑ 567 Jim Ritcher .... .05 .02
❑ 568 Don Mosebar .... .05 .02
❑ 569 John Gesek .... .05 .02
❑ 570 Gary Plummer .... .05 .02
❑ 571 Norm Johnson .... .05 .02
❑ 572 Ron Heller .... .05 .02
❑ 573 Carl Simpson .... .05 .02
❑ 574 Greg Montgomery .... .05 .02
❑ 575 Dana Hall .... .05 .02
❑ 576 Vencie Glenn .... .05 .02
❑ 577 Dean Biasucci .... .05 .02
❑ 578 Rod Bernstine UER .... .05 .02
(Name spelled Bemstein on front)
❑ 579 Randal Hill .... .05 .02
❑ 580 Sam Mills .... .05 .02
❑ 581 Santana Dotson .... .10 .05
❑ 582 Greg Lloyd .... .25 .11
❑ 583 Eric Thomas .... .05 .02
❑ 584 Henry Rolling .... .05 .02
❑ 585 Tony Bennett .... .05 .02
❑ 586 Sheldon White .... .05 .02
❑ 587 Mark Kelso .... .05 .02
❑ 588 Marc Spindler .... .05 .02
❑ 589 Greg McMurtry .... .05 .02
❑ 590 Art Monk .... .10 .05
❑ 591 Marco Coleman .... .05 .02
❑ 592 Tony Jones .... .05 .02
❑ 593 Melvin Jenkins .... .05 .02
❑ 594 Kevin Ross .... .05 .02
❑ 595 William Fuller .... .05 .02
❑ 596 James Joseph .... .05 .02
❑ 597 Lamar McGriggs RC .... .05 .02
❑ 598 Gill Byrd .... .05 .02
❑ 599 Alexander Wright .... .05 .02
❑ 600 Rick Mirer .... .25 .11
❑ 601 Richard Dent .... .10 .05
❑ 602 Thomas Everett .... .05 .02
❑ 603 Jack Del Rio .... .05 .02
❑ 604 Jerome Bettis .... .50 .23
❑ 605 Ronnie Lott .... .10 .05
❑ 606 Marty Carter .... .05 .02
❑ 607 Arthur Marshall RC .... .05 .02
❑ 608 Lee Johnson .... .05 .02
❑ 609 Bruce Armstrong .... .05 .02
❑ 610 Ricky Proehl .... .05 .02
❑ 611 Will Wolford .... .05 .02
❑ 612 Mike Prior .... .05 .02
❑ 613 George Jamison .... .05 .02
❑ 614 Gene Atkins .... .05 .02
❑ 615 Merril Hoge .... .05 .02
❑ 616 Desmond Howard UER .... .10 .05
(Stats indicate 8 TD's receiving; he had 0)
❑ 617 Jarvis Williams .... .05 .02
❑ 618 Marcus Allen .... .25 .11
❑ 619 Gary Brown .... .05 .02
❑ 620 Bill Brooks .... .05 .02
❑ 621 Eric Allen .... .05 .02
❑ 622 Todd Kelly .... .05 .02
❑ 623 Michael Dean Perry .... .10 .05
❑ 624 David Braxton .... .05 .02
❑ 625 Mike Sherrard .... .05 .02
❑ 626 Jeff Bryant .... .05 .02
❑ 627 Eric Bieniemy .... .05 .02
❑ 628 Tim Brown .... .25 .11
❑ 629 Troy Auzenne .... .05 .02
❑ 630 Michael Irvin .... .25 .11
❑ 631 Maurice Hurst .... .05 .02
❑ 632 Duane Bickett .... .05 .02
❑ 633 George Teague .... .10 .05
❑ 634 Vince Workman .... .05 .02
❑ 635 Renaldo Turnbull .... .05 .02
❑ 636 Johnny Bailey .... .05 .02
❑ 637 Dan Williams RC .... .05 .02
❑ 638 James Thornton .... .05 .02
❑ 639 Terry Allen .... .25 .11
❑ 640 Kevin Greene .... .25 .11
❑ 641 Tony Zendejas .... .05 .02
❑ 642 Scott Kowalkowski RC .. .05 .02
❑ 643 Jeff Query UER .... .05 .02
(Text states he played for Packers in '92; he played for Bengals)
❑ 644 Brian Blades .... .10 .05
❑ 645 Keith Jackson .... .10 .05
❑ 646 Monte Coleman .... .05 .02
❑ 647 Guy McIntyre .... .05 .02
❑ 648 Barry Word .... .05 .02
❑ 649 Steve Everitt RC .... .05 .02
❑ 650 Patrick Bates .... .05 .02
❑ 651 Marcus Robertson RC .... .05 .02
❑ 652 John Carney .... .05 .02
❑ 653 Derek Brown TE .... .05 .02
❑ 654 Carwell Gardner .... .05 .02
❑ 655 Moe Gardner .... .05 .02
❑ 656 Andre Ware .... .05 .02
❑ 657 Keith Van Horne .... .05 .02
❑ 658 Hugh Millen .... .05 .02
❑ 659 Checklist 330-495 .... .05 .02
❑ 660 Checklist 496-660 .... .05 .02

1993 Topps Black Gold

	MINT	NRMT
COMPLETE SET (44)	30.00	13.50
COMP.SERIES 1 SET (22)	12.00	5.50
COMP.SERIES 2 SET (22)	18.00	8.00
EXPIRED TRADE CARDS	.75	.35

STATED ODDS 1:72H/R, 1:14JUM, 1:24RAK
THREE PER FACTORY SET........

❑ 1 Kelvin Martin .... .15 .07
❑ 2 Audray McMillian .... .15 .07
❑ 3 Terry Allen .... .75 .35
❑ 4 Vai Sikahema .... .15 .07
❑ 5 Clyde Simmons .... .15 .07
❑ 6 Lorenzo White .... .15 .07
❑ 7 Michael Irvin .... .75 .35
❑ 8 Troy Aikman 2.50 1.10
❑ 9 Mark Kelso .... .15 .07
❑ 10 Cleveland Gary .... .15 .07
❑ 11 Greg Montgomery .... .15 .07
❑ 12 Jerry Rice 3.00 1.35
❑ 13 Rod Woodson .... .75 .35
❑ 14 Leslie O'Neal .... .30 .14
❑ 15 Harold Green .... .15 .07
❑ 16 Randall Cunningham .... .75 .35
❑ 17 Ricky Watters .... .75 .35
❑ 18 Andre Rison .... .30 .14
❑ 19 Eugene Robinson .... .15 .07
❑ 20 Wayne Martin .... .15 .07
❑ 21 Chris Warren .... .30 .14
❑ 22 Anthony Miller .... .30 .14
❑ 23 Steve Young 2.50 1.10
❑ 24 Tim Harris .... .15 .07
❑ 25 Emmitt Smith 5.00 2.20
❑ 26 Sterling Sharpe .... .75 .35
❑ 27 Henry Jones .... .15 .07
❑ 28 Warren Moon .... .75 .35
❑ 29 Barry Foster .... .30 .14
❑ 30 Dale Carter .... .15 .07
❑ 31 Mel Gray .... .30 .14
❑ 32 Barry Sanders 5.00 2.20
❑ 33 Dan Marino 5.00 2.20
❑ 34 Fred Barnett .... .30 .14

❑ 35 Deion Sanders 1.50 .70
❑ 36 Simon Fletcher .15 .07
❑ 37 Donnell Woolford .15 .07
❑ 38 Reggie Cobb .15 .07
❑ 39 Brett Favre 6.00 2.70
❑ 40 Thurman Thomas .75 .35
❑ 41 Rodney Hampton .75 .35
❑ 42 Eric Martin .15 .07
❑ 43 Pete Stoyanovich .15 .07
❑ 44 Herschel Walker .30 .14
❑ A Winner A 1-11 Expired .50 .23
❑ B Winner B 12-22 UER Exp. .50 .23
(Card No. 17 listed as Herschel Walker instead of Ricky Watters)
❑ C Winner C 23-33 Expired .50 .23
❑ D Winner D 34-44 Expired .50 .23
❑ AB Winner AB 1-22 Expired .50 .23
❑ CD Winner C/D 23-44 Exp. .50 .23

1994 Topps

	MINT	NRMT
COMPLETE SET (660)	50.00	22.00
COMP.FACT.SET	60.00	27.00
COMP.SERIES 1 (330)	25.00	11.00
COMP.SERIES 2 (330)	25.00	11.00
COMMON CARD (1-660)	.05	.02
SEMISTARS	.10	.05
UNLISTED STARS	.25	.11
COMP.SPEC.EFFECTS (660)	350.00	160.00
COMP.SPEC.EFF.SER.1 (330)	175.00	80.00
COMP.SPEC.EFF.SER.2 (330)	175.00	80.00

*SPEC.EFFECTS STARS: 3.5X to 7X HI COL.

*SPEC.EFFECTS RCs: 2X to 4X HI
SE STATED ODDS 1:2 H/R, 2:1 RACK

❑ 1 Emmitt Smith 1.50 .70
❑ 2 Russell Copeland .05 .02
❑ 3 Jesse Sapolu .05 .02
❑ 4 David Szott .05 .02
❑ 5 Rodney Hampton .25 .11
❑ 6 Bubba McDowell .05 .02
❑ 7 Bryce Paup .25 .11
❑ 8 Winston Moss .05 .02
❑ 9 Brett Perriman .10 .05
❑ 10 Rod Woodson .25 .11
❑ 11 John Randle .05 .02
❑ 12 David Wyman .05 .02
❑ 13 Jeff Cross .05 .02
❑ 14 Richard Cooper .05 .02
❑ 15 Johnny Mitchell .05 .02
❑ 16 David Alexander .05 .02
❑ 17 Ronnie Harmon .05 .02
❑ 18 Tyronne Stowe UER .05 .02
Tyrone on both sides
❑ 19 Chris Zorich .05 .02
❑ 20 Rob Burnett .05 .02
❑ 21 Harold Alexander .05 .02
❑ 22 Rod Stephens .05 .02
❑ 23 Mark Wheeler .05 .02
❑ 24 Dwayne Sabb .05 .02
❑ 25 Troy Drayton .05 .02
❑ 26 Kurt Gouveia .05 .02
❑ 27 Warren Moon .25 .11
❑ 28 Jeff Query .05 .02
❑ 29 Chuck Levy RC .05 .02
❑ 30 Bruce Smith .25 .11
❑ 31 Doug Riesenberg .05 .02
❑ 32 Willie Drewrey .05 .02
❑ 33 Nate Newton UER .05 .02
(Listed as Defensive End; should be guard)
❑ 34 James Jett .05 .02
❑ 35 George Teague .05 .02
❑ 36 Marc Spindler .05 .02
❑ 37 Jack Del Rio .05 .02
❑ 38 Dale Carter .05 .02
❑ 39 Steve Atwater .05 .02
❑ 40 Herschel Walker .10 .05
❑ 41 James Hasty .05 .02
❑ 42 Seth Joyner .05 .02
❑ 43 Keith Jackson .05 .02
❑ 44 Tommy Vardell .05 .02
❑ 45 Antonio Langham RC .10 .05
❑ 46 Derek Brown RBK .05 .02
❑ 47 John Wojciechowski .05 .02
❑ 48 Horace Copeland .05 .02
❑ 49 Luis Sharpe .05 .02
❑ 50 Pat Harlow .05 .02
❑ 51 David Palmer RC .50 .23
❑ 52 Tony Smith .05 .02
❑ 53 Tim Johnson .05 .02
❑ 54 Anthony Newman .05 .02
❑ 55 Terry Wooden .05 .02
❑ 56 Derrick Fenner .05 .02
❑ 57 Mike Fox .05 .02
❑ 58 Brad Hopkins .05 .02
❑ 59 Daryl Johnston UER .10 .05
(Johnson on front)
❑ 60 Steve Young .75 .35
❑ 61 Scottie Graham RC .10 .05
❑ 62 Nolan Harrison .05 .02
❑ 63 David Richards .05 .02
❑ 64 Chris Mohr .05 .02
❑ 65 Hardy Nickerson .10 .05
❑ 66 Heath Sherman .05 .02
❑ 67 Irving Fryar .10 .05
❑ 68 Ray Buchanan UER .05 .02
(Buchannan on front)
❑ 69 Jay Taylor .05 .02
❑ 70 Shannon Sharpe .10 .05
❑ 71 Vinny Testaverde .10 .05
❑ 72 Renaldo Turnbull .05 .02
❑ 73 Dwight Stone .05 .02
❑ 74 Willie McGinest RC .25 .11
❑ 75 Darrell Green .05 .02
❑ 76 Kyle Clifton .05 .02
❑ 77 Leo Goeas .05 .02
❑ 78 Ken Ruettgers .05 .02
❑ 79 Craig Heyward .10 .05
❑ 80 Andre Rison .10 .05
❑ 81 Chris Mims .05 .02
❑ 82 Gary Clark .10 .05
❑ 83 Ricardo McDonald .05 .02
❑ 84 Patrick Hunter .05 .02
❑ 85 Bruce Matthews .05 .02
❑ 86 Russell Maryland .05 .02
❑ 87 Gary Anderson K .05 .02
❑ 88 Brad Edwards .05 .02
❑ 89 Carlton Bailey .05 .02
❑ 90 Qadry Ismail .25 .11
❑ 91 Terry McDaniel .05 .02
❑ 92 Willie Green .05 .02
❑ 93 Cornelius Bennett .10 .05
❑ 94 Paul Gruber .05 .02
❑ 95 Pete Stoyanovich .05 .02
❑ 96 Merton Hanks .10 .05
❑ 97 Tre Johnson RC .05 .02
❑ 98 Jonathan Hayes .05 .02
❑ 99 Jason Elam .05 .02
❑ 100 Jerome Bettis .25 .11
❑ 101 Ronnie Lott .10 .05
❑ 102 Maurice Hurst .05 .02
❑ 103 Kirk Lowdermilk .05 .02
❑ 104 Tony Jones .05 .02
❑ 105 Steve Beuerlein .05 .02
❑ 106 Isaac Davis RC .05 .02
❑ 107 Vaughan Johnson .05 .02
❑ 108 Terrell Buckley .05 .02
❑ 109 Pierce Holt .05 .02
❑ 110 Alonzo Spellman .05 .02
❑ 111 Patrick Robinson .05 .02
❑ 112 Cortez Kennedy .10 .05
❑ 113 Kevin Williams .10 .05
❑ 114 Danny Copeland .05 .02
❑ 115 Chris Doleman .05 .02
❑ 116 Jerry Rice LL .50 .23
❑ 117 Neil Smith LL .10 .05
❑ 118 Emmitt Smith LL .75 .35
❑ 119 Eugene Robinson LL .05 .02
Nate Odomes
❑ 120 Steve Young LL .25 .11
❑ 121 Carnell Lake .05 .02
❑ 122 Ernest Givins UER .10 .05
(Givens on front)
❑ 123 Henry Jones .05 .02
❑ 124 Michael Brooks .05 .02
❑ 125 Jason Hanson .05 .02
❑ 126 Andy Harmon .05 .02
❑ 127 Errict Rhett RC 1.50 .70
❑ 128 Harris Barton .05 .02
❑ 129 Greg Robinson .05 .02
❑ 130 Derrick Thomas .25 .11
❑ 131 Keith Kartz .05 .02
❑ 132 Lincoln Kennedy .05 .02
❑ 133 Leslie O'Neal .05 .02
❑ 134 Tim Goad .05 .02
❑ 135 Rohn Stark .05 .02
❑ 136 O.J. McDuffie .25 .11
❑ 137 Donnell Woolford .05 .02
❑ 138 Jamir Miller RC .05 .02
❑ 139 Eric Thomas UER .05 .02
(Listed as tight end; he is a cornerback)
❑ 140 Willie Roaf .05 .02
❑ 141 Wayne Gandy RC .05 .02
❑ 142 Mike Brim .05 .02
❑ 143 Kelvin Martin .05 .02
❑ 144 Edgar Bennett .25 .11
❑ 145 Michael Dean Perry .10 .05
❑ 146 Shante Carver RC .05 .02
❑ 147 Jessie Armstead UER .05 .02
(Jesse on both sides)
❑ 148 Mo Elewonibi .05 .02
❑ 149 Dana Stubblefield .25 .11
❑ 150 Cody Carlson .05 .02
❑ 151 Vencie Glenn .05 .02
❑ 152 Levon Kirkland .05 .02
❑ 153 Derrick Moore .05 .02
❑ 154 John Fina .05 .02
❑ 155 Jeff Hostetler .10 .05
❑ 156 Courtney Hawkins .05 .02
❑ 157 Todd Collins .05 .02
❑ 158 Neil Smith .25 .11
❑ 159 Simon Fletcher .05 .02
❑ 160 Dan Marino 2.00 .90
❑ 161 Sam Adams RC .10 .05
❑ 162 Marvin Washington .05 .02
❑ 163 John Copeland .05 .02
❑ 164 Eugene Robinson .05 .02
❑ 165 Mark Carrier DB .05 .02
❑ 166 Mike Kenn .05 .02
❑ 167 Tyrone Hughes .10 .05
❑ 168 Darren Carrington .05 .02
❑ 169 Shane Conlan .05 .02
❑ 170 Ricky Proehl .05 .02
❑ 171 Jeff Herrod .05 .02
❑ 172 Mark Carrier WR .10 .05
❑ 173 George Koonce .05 .02
❑ 174 Desmond Howard .10 .05
❑ 175 Dave Meggett .05 .02
❑ 176 Charles Haley .10 .05
❑ 177 Steve Wisniewski .05 .02
❑ 178 Dermontti Dawson .05 .02
❑ 179 Tim McDonald .05 .02
❑ 180 Broderick Thomas .05 .02
❑ 181 Bernard Dafney .05 .02
❑ 182 Bo Orlando .05 .02
❑ 183 Andre Reed .10 .05
❑ 184 Randall Cunningham .25 .11
❑ 185 Chris Spielman .10 .05
❑ 186 Keith Byars .05 .02
❑ 187 Ben Coates .25 .11
❑ 188 Tracy Simien .05 .02
❑ 189 Carl Pickens .25 .11
❑ 190 Reggie White .25 .11
❑ 191 Norm Johnson .05 .02
❑ 192 Brian Washington .05 .02

No.	Player	Price 1	Price 2
193	Stan Humphries	.25	.11
194	Fred Stokes	.05	.02
195	Dan Williams	.05	.02
196	John Elway TOG	.75	.35
197	Eric Allen TOG	.05	.02
198	Hardy Nickerson TOG	.10	.05
199	Jerome Bettis TOG	.10	.05
200	Troy Aikman TOG	.50	.23
201	Thurman Thomas TOG	.10	.05
202	Cornelius Bennett TOG	.10	.05
203	Michael Irvin TOG	.10	.05
204	Jim Kelly TOG	.10	.05
205	Junior Seau TOG	.10	.05
206	Heath Shuler RC UER (Rifle spelled rife on back)	.25	.11
207	Howard Cross UER (Listed as linebacker; he he plays tight end)	.05	.02
208	Pat Swilling	.05	.02
209	Pete Metzelaars	.05	.02
210	Tony McGee	.05	.02
211	Neil O'Donnell	.25	.11
212	Eugene Chung	.05	.02
213	J.B. Brown	.05	.02
214	Marcus Allen	.25	.11
215	Harry Newsome	.05	.02
216	Greg Hill RC	.50	.23
217	Ryan Yarborough	.05	.02
218	Marty Carter	.05	.02
219	Bern Brostek	.05	.02
220	Boomer Esiason	.10	.05
221	Vince Buck	.05	.02
222	Jim Jeffcoat	.05	.02
223	Bob Dahl	.05	.02
224	Marion Butts	.05	.02
225	Ronald Moore	.05	.02
226	Robert Blackmon	.05	.02
227	Curtis Conway	.25	.11
228	Jon Hand	.05	.02
229	Shane Dronett	.05	.02
230	Erik Williams UER (Misspelled Eric on front)	.05	.02
231	Dennis Brown	.05	.02
232	Ray Childress	.05	.02
233	Johnnie Morton RC	.25	.11
234	Kent Hull	.05	.02
235	John Elliott	.05	.02
236	Ron Heller	.05	.02
237	J.J. Birden	.05	.02
238	Thomas Randolph RC	.05	.02
239	Chip Lohmiller	.05	.02
240	Tim Brown	.25	.11
241	Steve Tovar	.05	.02
242	Moe Gardner	.05	.02
243	Vincent Brown	.05	.02
244	Tony Zendejas	.05	.02
245	Eric Allen	.05	.02
246	Joe King RC	.05	.02
247	Mo Lewis	.05	.02
248	Rod Bernstine	.05	.02
249	Tom Waddle	.05	.02
250	Junior Seau	.25	.11
251	Eric Metcalf	.10	.05
252	Cris Carter	.50	.23
253	Bill Hitchcock	.05	.02
254	Zefross Moss	.05	.02
255	Morten Andersen	.05	.02
256	Keith Rucker RC	.05	.02
257	Chris Jacke	.05	.02
258	Richmond Webb	.05	.02
259	Herman Moore	.25	.11
260	Phil Simms	.10	.05
261	Mark Tuinei	.05	.02
262	Don Beebe	.05	.02
263	Marc Logan	.05	.02
264	Willie Davis	.10	.05
265	David Klingler	.05	.02
266	Martin Mayhew UER (Listed as wide receiver; he is a cornerback)	.05	.02
267	Mark Bavaro	.05	.02
268	Greg Lloyd	.25	.11
269	Al Del Greco	.05	.02
270	Reggie Brooks	.10	.05
271	Greg Townsend	.05	.02
272	Rohn Stark CAL	.05	.02
273	Marcus Allen CAL	.10	.05
274	Ronnie Lott CAL	.10	.05
275	Dan Marino CAL	.75	.35
276	Sean Gilbert	.05	.02
277	LeRoy Butler	.05	.02
278	Troy Auzenne	.05	.02
279	Eric Swann	.10	.05
280	Quentin Coryatt	.05	.02
281	Anthony Pleasant	.05	.02
282	Brad Baxter	.05	.02
283	Carl Lee	.05	.02
284	Courtney Hall	.05	.02
285	Quinn Early	.10	.05
286	Eddie Robinson	.05	.02
287	Marco Coleman	.05	.02
288	Harold Green	.05	.02
289	Santana Dotson	.10	.05
290	Robert Porcher	.05	.02
291	Joe Phillips	.05	.02
292	Mark McMillian	.05	.02
293	Eric Davis	.05	.02
294	Mark Jackson	.05	.02
295	Darryl Talley	.05	.02
296	Curtis Duncan	.05	.02
297	Bruce Armstrong	.05	.02
298	Eric Hill	.05	.02
299	Andre Collins	.05	.02
300	Jay Novacek	.10	.05
301	Roosevelt Potts	.05	.02
302	Eric Martin	.05	.02
303	Chris Warren	.10	.05
304	Deral Boykin RC	.05	.02
305	Jessie Tuggle	.05	.02
306	Glyn Milburn	.10	.05
307	Terry Obee	.05	.02
308	Eric Turner	.05	.02
309	Dewayne Washington RC	.10	.05
310	Sterling Sharpe	.10	.05
311	Jeff Gossett	.05	.02
312	John Carney	.05	.02
313	Aaron Glenn RC	.10	.05
314	Nick Lowery	.05	.02
315	Thurman Thomas	.25	.11
316	Troy Aikman MG	.50	.23
317	Thurman Thomas MG	.10	.05
318	Michael Irvin MG	.10	.05
319	Steve Beuerlein MG	.05	.02
320	Jerry Rice	1.00	.45
321	Alexander Wright	.05	.02
322	Michael Bates	.05	.02
323	Greg Davis	.05	.02
324	Mark Bortz	.05	.02
325	Kevin Greene	.25	.11
326	Wayne Simmons	.05	.02
327	Wayne Martin	.05	.02
328	Michael Irvin UER (Stats on back have three career touchdowns; should be 34)	.25	.11
329	Checklist 1-165	.05	.02
330	Checklist 166-330	.05	.02
331	Doug Pelfrey	.05	.02
332	Myron Guyton	.05	.02
333	Howard Ballard	.05	.02
334	Ricky Ervins	.05	.02
335	Steve Emtman	.05	.02
336	Eric Curry	.05	.02
337	Bert Emanuel RC	.50	.23
338	Darryl Ashmore	.05	.02
339	Stevon Moore	.05	.02
340	Garrison Hearst	.25	.11
341	Vance Johnson	.05	.02
342	Anthony Johnson	.10	.05
343	Merril Hoge	.05	.02
344	William Thomas	.05	.02
345	Scott Mitchell	.25	.11
346	Jim Everett	.10	.05
347	Ray Crockett	.05	.02
348	Bryan Cox	.05	.02
349	Charles Johnson RC	.25	.11
350	Randall McDaniel	.05	.02
351	Micheal Barrow	.05	.02
352	Darrell Thompson	.05	.02
353	Kevin Gogan	.05	.02
354	Brad Daluiso	.05	.02
355	Mark Collins	.05	.02
356	Bryant Young RC	.25	.11
357	Steve Christie	.05	.02
358	Derek Kennard	.05	.02
359	Jon Vaughn	.05	.02
360	Drew Bledsoe	1.25	.55
361	Randy Baldwin	.05	.02
362	Kevin Ross	.05	.02
363	Reuben Davis	.05	.02
364	Chris Miller	.05	.02
365	Tim McGee	.05	.02
366	Tony Woods	.05	.02
367	Dean Biasucci	.05	.02
368	George Jamison	.05	.02
369	Lorenzo Lynch	.05	.02
370	Johnny Johnson	.05	.02
371	Greg Kragen	.05	.02
372	Vinson Smith	.05	.02
373	Vince Workman	.05	.02
374	Allen Aldridge	.05	.02
375	Terry Kirby	.25	.11
376	Mario Bates RC	.25	.11
377	Dixon Edwards	.05	.02
378	Leon Searcy	.05	.02
379	Eric Guliford RC	.05	.02
380	Gary Brown	.05	.02
381	Phil Hansen	.05	.02
382	Keith Hamilton	.05	.02
383	John Alt	.05	.02
384	John Taylor	.10	.05
385	Reggie Cobb	.05	.02
386	Rob Fredrickson RC	.10	.05
387	Pepper Johnson	.05	.02
388	Kevin Lee RC	.05	.02
389	Stanley Richard	.05	.02
390	Jackie Slater	.05	.02
391	Darrick Brilz	.05	.02
392	John Gesek	.05	.02
393	Kelvin Pritchett	.05	.02
394	Aeneas Williams	.05	.02
395	Henry Ford	.05	.02
396	Eric Mahlum	.05	.02
397	Tom Rouen	.05	.02
398	Vinnie Clark	.05	.02
399	Jim Sweeney	.05	.02
400	Troy Aikman UER Threw for 56 TD's in 1993	1.00	.45
401	Toi Cook	.05	.02
402	Dan Saleaumua	.05	.02
403	Andy Heck	.05	.02
404	Deon Figures	.05	.02
405	Henry Thomas	.05	.02
406	Glenn Montgomery	.05	.02
407	Trent Dilfer RC	1.50	.70
408	Eddie Murray	.05	.02
409	Gene Atkins	.05	.02
410	Mike Sherrard	.05	.02
411	Don Mosebar	.05	.02
412	Thomas Smith	.05	.02
413	Ken Norton Jr.	.10	.05
414	Robert Brooks	.25	.11
415	Jeff Lageman	.05	.02
416	Tony Siragusa	.05	.02
417	Brian Blades	.10	.05
418	Matt Stover	.05	.02
419	Jesse Solomon	.05	.02
420	Reggie Roby	.05	.02
421	Shawn Jefferson	.05	.02
422	Marc Boutte	.05	.02
423	William White	.05	.02
424	Clyde Simmons	.05	.02
425	Anthony Miller	.10	.05
426	Brent Jones	.10	.05
427	Tim Grunhard	.05	.02
428	Alfred Williams	.05	.02
429	Roy Barker RC	.05	.02
430	Dante Jones	.05	.02
431	Leroy Thompson	.05	.02
432	Marcus Robertson	.05	.02
433	Thomas Lewis RC	.10	.05
434	Sean Jones	.05	.02
435	Michael Haynes	.10	.05
436	Albert Lewis	.05	.02
437	Tim Bowens RC	.10	.05
438	Marvcus Patton	.05	.02
439	Rich Miano	.05	.02
440	Craig Erickson	.05	.02
441	Larry Allen RC	.10	.05

- ❑ 442 Fernando Smith .05 .02
- ❑ 443 D.J. Johnson .05 .02
- ❑ 444 Leonard Russell .05 .02
- ❑ 445 Marshall Faulk RC 4.00 1.80
- ❑ 446 Najee Mustafaa .05 .02
- ❑ 447 Brian Hansen .05 .02
- ❑ 448 Isaac Bruce RC 4.00 1.80
- ❑ 449 Kevin Scott .05 .02
- ❑ 450 Natrone Means .25 .11
- ❑ 451 Tracy Rogers RC .05 .02
- ❑ 452 Mike Croel .05 .02
- ❑ 453 Anthony Edwards .05 .02
- ❑ 454 Brenston Buckner RC .05 .02
- ❑ 455 Tom Carter .05 .02
- ❑ 456 Burt Grossman .05 .02
- ❑ 457 Jimmy Spencer RC .05 .02
- ❑ 458 Rocket Ismail .10 .05
- ❑ 459 Fred Strickland .05 .02
- ❑ 460 Jeff Burris RC .10 .05
- ❑ 461 Adrian Hardy .05 .02
- ❑ 462 Lamar McGriggs .05 .02
- ❑ 463 Webster Slaughter .05 .02
- ❑ 464 Demetrius DuBose .05 .02
- ❑ 465 Dave Brown .10 .05
- ❑ 466 Kenneth Gant .05 .02
- ❑ 467 Erik Kramer .10 .05
- ❑ 468 Mark Ingram .05 .02
- ❑ 469 Roman Phifer .05 .02
- ❑ 470 Steve Young .50 .23
- ❑ 471 Nick Lowery .05 .02
- ❑ 472 Irving Fryar .10 .05
- ❑ 473 Art Monk .10 .05
- ❑ 474 Mel Gray .05 .02
- ❑ 475 Reggie White .25 .11
- ❑ 476 Eric Ball .05 .02
- ❑ 477 Dwayne Harper .05 .02
- ❑ 478 Will Shields .05 .02
- ❑ 479 Roger Harper .05 .02
- ❑ 480 Rick Mirer .25 .11
- ❑ 481 Vincent Brisby .25 .11
- ❑ 482 John Jurkovic RC .10 .05
- ❑ 483 Michael Jackson .10 .05
- ❑ 484 Ed Cunningham .05 .02
- ❑ 485 Brad Ottis .05 .02
- ❑ 486 Sterling Palmer RC .05 .02
- ❑ 487 Tony Bennett .05 .02
- ❑ 488 Mike Pritchard .05 .02
- ❑ 489 Bucky Brooks RC .05 .02
- ❑ 490 Troy Vincent .05 .02
- ❑ 491 Eric Green .05 .02
- ❑ 492 Van Malone .05 .02
- ❑ 493 Marcus Spears .05 .02
- ❑ 494 Brian Williams OL .05 .02
- ❑ 495 Robert Smith .25 .11
- ❑ 496 Haywood Jeffires .10 .05
- ❑ 497 Darrin Smith .05 .02
- ❑ 498 Tommy Barnhardt .05 .02
- ❑ 499 Anthony Smith .05 .02
- ❑ 500 Ricky Watters .25 .11
- ❑ 501 Antone Davis .05 .02
- ❑ 502 David Braxton .05 .02
- ❑ 503 Donnell Bennett RC .25 .11
- ❑ 504 Donald Evans .05 .02
- ❑ 505 Lewis Tillman .05 .02
- ❑ 506 Lance Smith .05 .02
- ❑ 507 Aaron Taylor .05 .02
- ❑ 508 Ricky Sanders .05 .02
- ❑ 509 Dennis Smith .05 .02
- ❑ 510 Barry Foster .05 .02
- ❑ 511 Stan Brock .05 .02
- ❑ 512 Henry Rolling .05 .02
- ❑ 513 Walter Reeves .05 .02
- ❑ 514 John Booty .05 .02
- ❑ 515 Kenneth Davis .05 .02
- ❑ 516 Cris Dishman .05 .02
- ❑ 517 Bill Lewis .05 .02
- ❑ 518 Jeff Bryant .05 .02
- ❑ 519 Brian Mitchell .05 .02
- ❑ 520 Joe Montana 2.00 .90
- ❑ 521 Keith Sims .05 .02
- ❑ 522 Harry Colon .05 .02
- ❑ 523 Leon Lett .05 .02
- ❑ 524 Carlos Jenkins .05 .02
- ❑ 525 Victor Bailey .05 .02
- ❑ 526 Harvey Williams .10 .05
- ❑ 527 Irv Smith .05 .02
- ❑ 528 Jason Sehorn RC .05 .02
- ❑ 529 John Thierry RC .05 .02
- ❑ 530 Brett Favre 2.00 .90
- ❑ 531 Sean Dawkins RC .25 .11
- ❑ 532 Erric Pegram .05 .02
- ❑ 533 Jimmy Williams .05 .02
- ❑ 534 Michael Timpson .05 .02
- ❑ 535 Flipper Anderson .05 .02
- ❑ 536 John Parrella .05 .02
- ❑ 537 Freddie Joe Nunn .05 .02
- ❑ 538 Doug Dawson .05 .02
- ❑ 539 Michael Stewart .05 .02
- ❑ 540 John Elway 2.00 .90
- ❑ 541 Ronnie Lott .10 .05
- ❑ 542 Barry Sanders .75 .35
- ❑ 543 Andre Reed .10 .05
- ❑ 544 Deion Sanders .25 .11
- ❑ 545 Dan Marino .75 .35
- ❑ 546 Carlton Bailey .05 .02
- ❑ 547 Emmitt Smith .75 .35
- ❑ 548 Alvin Harper .10 .05
- ❑ 549 Eric Metcalf .10 .05
- ❑ 550 Jerry Rice .50 .23
- ❑ 551 Derrick Thomas .25 .11
- ❑ 552 Mark Collins .05 .02
- ❑ 553 Eric Turner .05 .02
- ❑ 554 Sterling Sharpe .25 .11
- ❑ 555 Steve Young .40 .18
- ❑ 556 Darnay Scott RC .75 .35
- ❑ 557 Joel Steed .05 .02
- ❑ 558 Dennis Gibson .05 .02
- ❑ 559 Charles Mincy .05 .02
- ❑ 560 Rickey Jackson .05 .02
- ❑ 561 Dave Cadigan .05 .02
- ❑ 562 Rick Tuten .05 .02
- ❑ 563 Mike Caldwell .05 .02
- ❑ 564 Todd Steussie RC .10 .05
- ❑ 565 Kevin Smith .05 .02
- ❑ 566 Arthur Marshall .05 .02
- ❑ 567 Aaron Wallace .05 .02
- ❑ 568 Calvin Williams .10 .05
- ❑ 569 Todd Kelly .05 .02
- ❑ 570 Barry Sanders 2.00 .90
- ❑ 571 Shaun Gayle .05 .02
- ❑ 572 Will Wolford .05 .02
- ❑ 573 Ethan Horton .05 .02
- ❑ 574 Chris Slade .05 .02
- ❑ 575 Jeff Wright .05 .02
- ❑ 576 Toby Wright .05 .02
- ❑ 577 Lamar Thomas .05 .02
- ❑ 578 Chris Singleton .05 .02
- ❑ 579 Ed West .05 .02
- ❑ 580 Jeff George .25 .11
- ❑ 581 Kevin Mitchell .05 .02
- ❑ 582 Chad Brown .05 .02
- ❑ 583 Rich Camarillo .05 .02
- ❑ 584 Gary Zimmerman .05 .02
- ❑ 585 Randal Hill .05 .02
- ❑ 586 Keith Cash .05 .02
- ❑ 587 Sam Mills .05 .02
- ❑ 588 Shawn Lee .05 .02
- ❑ 589 Kent Graham .10 .05
- ❑ 590 Steve Everitt .05 .02
- ❑ 591 Rob Moore .10 .05
- ❑ 592 Kevin Mawae .05 .02
- ❑ 593 Jerry Ball .05 .02
- ❑ 594 Larry Brown DB .05 .02
- ❑ 595 Tim Krumrie .05 .02
- ❑ 596 Aubrey Beavers RC .05 .02
- ❑ 597 Chris Hinton .05 .02
- ❑ 598 Greg Montgomery .05 .02
- ❑ 599 Jimmie Jones .05 .02
- ❑ 600 Jim Kelly .25 .11
- ❑ 601 Joe Johnson RC .05 .02
- ❑ 602 Tim Irwin .05 .02
- ❑ 603 Steve Jackson .05 .02
- ❑ 604 James Williams RC .05 .02
- ❑ 605 Blair Thomas .05 .02
- ❑ 606 Danan Hughes .05 .02
- ❑ 607 Russell Freeman .05 .02
- ❑ 608 Andre Hastings .10 .05
- ❑ 609 Ken Harvey .05 .02
- ❑ 610 Jim Harbaugh .25 .11
- ❑ 611 Emmitt Smith MG .75 .35
- ❑ 612 Andre Rison MG .10 .05
- ❑ 613 Steve Young MG .40 .18
- ❑ 614 Anthony Miller MG .05 .02
- ❑ 615 Barry Sanders MG 1.00 .45
- ❑ 616 Bernie Kosar .10 .05
- ❑ 617 Chris Gardocki .05 .02
- ❑ 618 William Floyd RC .25 .11
- ❑ 619 Matt Brock .05 .02
- ❑ 620 Dan Wilkinson RC .10 .05
- ❑ 621 Tony Meola RC .10 .05
- ❑ 622 Tony Tolbert .05 .02
- ❑ 623 Mike Zandofsky .05 .02
- ❑ 624 William Fuller .05 .02
- ❑ 625 Steve Jordan .05 .02
- ❑ 626 Mike Johnson .05 .02
- ❑ 627 Ferrell Edmunds .05 .02
- ❑ 628 Gene Williams .05 .02
- ❑ 629 Willie Beamon .05 .02
- ❑ 630 Gerald Perry .05 .02
- ❑ 631 John Baylor .05 .02
- ❑ 632 Carwell Gardner .05 .02
- ❑ 633 Thomas Everett .05 .02
- ❑ 634 Lamar Lathon .05 .02
- ❑ 635 Michael Bankston .05 .02
- ❑ 636 Ray Crittenden RC .05 .02
- ❑ 637 Kimble Anders .10 .05
- ❑ 638 Robert Delpino .05 .02
- ❑ 639 Darren Perry .05 .02
- ❑ 640 Byron Evans .05 .02
- ❑ 641 Mark Higgs .05 .02
- ❑ 642 Lorenzo Neal .05 .02
- ❑ 643 Henry Ellard .10 .05
- ❑ 644 Trace Armstrong .05 .02
- ❑ 645 Greg McMurtry .05 .02
- ❑ 646 Steve McMichael .10 .05
- ❑ 647 Terance Mathis .10 .05
- ❑ 648 Eric Bieniemy .05 .02
- ❑ 649 Bobby Houston .05 .02
- ❑ 650 Alvin Harper .10 .05
- ❑ 651 James Folston .05 .02
- ❑ 652 Mel Gray .05 .02
- ❑ 653 Adrian Cooper .05 .02
- ❑ 654 Dexter Carter .05 .02
- ❑ 655 Don Griffin .05 .02
- ❑ 656 Corey Widmer .05 .02
- ❑ 657 Lee Johnson .05 .02
- ❑ 658 Nate Odomes .05 .02
- ❑ 659 Checklist .05 .02
- ❑ 660 Checklist .05 .02
- ❑ P1 Promo Sheet 5.00 2.20
  Stan Humphries
  Darryl Talley
  Rodney Hampton
  Jerome Bettis
  Chris Zorich
  Harry Newsome
  Tyrone Hughes
  Rod Woodson
  Chris Spielman
- ❑ P2 Promo Sheet Special Effects 4.00 1.80
  Jerome Bettis
  Chris Zorich
  Harry Newsome

1994 Topps All-Pros

	MINT	NRMT
COMPLETE SET (25)	40.00	18.00
STATED ODDS 1:36 SERIES 2		

Card	MINT	NRMT
1 Michael Irvin	2.50	1.10
2 Erik Williams	.50	.23
3 Steve Wisniewski	.50	.23
4 Dermontti Dawson	.50	.23
5 Nate Newton	.50	.23
6 Harris Barton	.50	.23
7 Shannon Sharpe	1.00	.45
8 Jerry Rice	10.00	4.50
9 Troy Aikman	10.00	4.50
10 Barry Sanders	20.00	9.00
11 Jerome Bettis	2.50	1.10
12 Jason Hanson	.50	.23
13 Eric Metcalf	1.00	.45
14 Reggie White	2.50	1.10
15 Cortez Kennedy	1.00	.45
16 Michael Dean Perry	1.00	.45
17 Bruce Smith	2.50	1.10
18 Darryl Talley	.50	.23
19 Hardy Nickerson	1.00	.45
20 Derrick Thomas	2.50	1.10
21 Mark Collins	.50	.23
22 Eric Allen	.50	.23
23 Tim McDonald	.50	.23
24 Marcus Robertson	.50	.23
25 Greg Montgomery	.50	.23

1994 Topps 1000/3000

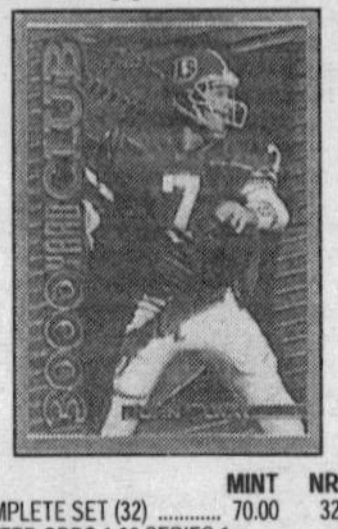

	MINT	NRMT
COMPLETE SET (32)	70.00	32.00
STATED ODDS 1:36 SERIES 1		

Card	MINT	NRMT
1 Jerry Rice	6.00	2.70
2 Chris Warren	.60	.25
3 Leonard Russell	.30	.14
4 Gary Brown	.30	.14
5 Tim Brown	1.50	.70
6 Erric Pegram	.30	.14
7 Irving Fryar	.60	.25
8 Anthony Miller	.60	.25
9 Reggie Langhorne	.30	.14
10 Thurman Thomas	1.50	.70
11 Reggie Brooks	.60	.25
12 Andre Rison	.60	.25
13 Ronald Moore	.30	.14
14 Michael Irvin	1.50	.70
15 Barry Sanders	12.00	5.50
16 Cris Carter	3.00	1.35
17 Rodney Hampton	1.50	.70
18 Jerome Bettis	1.50	.70
19 Sterling Sharpe	.60	.25
20 Emmitt Smith	10.00	4.50
21 John Elway	12.00	5.50
22 Brett Favre	12.00	5.50
23 Jim Kelly	1.50	.70
24 Warren Moon	1.50	.70
25 Phil Simms	.60	.25
26 Craig Erickson	.30	.14
27 Neil O'Donnell	1.50	.70
28 Steve Young	5.00	2.20
29 Steve Beuerlein	.30	.14
30 Troy Aikman	6.00	2.70
31 Jeff Hostetler	.60	.25
32 Boomer Esiason	.60	.25

1995 Topps

	MINT	NRMT
COMPLETE SET (468)	40.00	18.00
COMP.FACT.SET (478)	50.00	22.00
COMP.SERIES 1 (248)	20.00	9.00
COMP.SERIES 2 (220)	20.00	9.00
COMMON CARD (1-468)	.10	.05
STEVE YOUNG (421-425)	.50	.23
SEMISTARS	.20	.09
UNLISTED STARS	.30	.14
COMP.HIT LIST SET (20)	6.00	2.70
SER.1 STATED ODDS 1:4		

Card	MINT	NRMT
1 Barry Sanders	1.00	.45
2 Chris Warren	.20	.09
3 Jerry Rice	.50	.23
4 Emmitt Smith	.75	.35
5 Henry Ellard	.20	.09
6 Natrone Means TYC	.30	.14
7 Terance Mathis	.20	.09
8 Tim Brown TYC	.20	.09
9 Andre Reed	.20	.09
10 Marshall Faulk	.30	.14
11 Irving Fryar	.20	.09
12 Cris Carter	.30	.14
13 Michael Irvin	.30	.14
14 Jake Reed	.20	.09
15 Ben Coates	.20	.09
16 Herman Moore	.30	.14
17 Carl Pickens	.30	.14
18 Fred Barnett	.20	.09
19 Sterling Sharpe	.20	.09
20 Anthony Miller	.20	.09
21 Thurman Thomas	.30	.14
22 Andre Rison	.20	.09
23 Brian Blades	.20	.09
24 Rodney Hampton	.20	.09
25 Terry Allen	.20	.09
26 Jerome Bettis	.30	.14
27 Errict Rhett	.30	.14
28 Rob Moore	.10	.05
29 Shannon Sharpe	.20	.09
30 Drew Bledsoe	.50	.23
31 Dan Marino	1.00	.45
32 Warren Moon	.20	.09
33 Steve Young	.40	.18
34 Brett Favre	1.00	.45
35 Jim Everett	.10	.05
36 Jeff George	.20	.09
37 John Elway	1.00	.45
38 Jeff Hostetler	.20	.09
39 Randall Cunningham	.30	.14
40 Stan Humphries	.20	.09
41 Jim Kelly	.30	.14
42 Tommy Barnhardt	.10	.05
43 Bob Whitfield	.10	.05
44 William Thomas	.10	.05
45 Glyn Milburn	.10	.05
46 Steve Christie	.10	.05
47 Kevin Mawae	.10	.05
48 Vencie Glenn	.10	.05
49 Eric Curry	.10	.05
50 Jeff Hostetler	.20	.09
51 Tyronne Stowe	.10	.05
52 Steve Jackson	.10	.05
53 Ben Coleman	.10	.05
54 Brad Baxter	.10	.05
55 Darryl Williams	.10	.05
56 Troy Drayton	.10	.05
57 George Teague	.10	.05
58 Calvin Williams	.20	.09
59 Jeff Cross	.10	.05
60 Leroy Hoard	.10	.05
61 John Carney	.10	.05
62 Daryl Johnston	.20	.09
63 Jim Jeffcoat	.10	.05
64 Matt Stover	.10	.05
65 LeRoy Butler	.10	.05
66 Curtis Conway	.30	.14
67 O.J. McDuffie	.30	.14
68 Robert Massey	.10	.05
69 Ed McDaniel	.10	.05
70 William Floyd	.30	.14
71 Willie Davis	.20	.09
72 William Roberts	.10	.05
73 Chester McGlockton	.20	.09
74 D.J. Johnson	.10	.05
75 Rondell Jones	.10	.05
76 Morten Andersen	.10	.05
77 Glenn Parker	.10	.05
78 William Fuller	.10	.05
79 Ray Buchanan	.10	.05
80 Maurice Hurst	.10	.05
81 Wayne Gandy	.10	.05
82 Marcus Turner	.10	.05
83 Greg Davis	.10	.05
84 Terry Wooden	.10	.05
85 Thomas Everett	.10	.05
86 Steve Broussard	.10	.05
87 Tom Carter	.10	.05
88 Glenn Montgomery	.10	.05
89 Larry Allen	.20	.09
90 Donnell Woolford	.10	.05
91 John Alt	.10	.05
92 Phil Hansen	.10	.05
93 Seth Joyner	.10	.05
94 Michael Brooks	.10	.05
95 Randall McDaniel	.10	.05
96 Tydus Winans	.10	.05
97 Rob Fredrickson	.10	.05
98 Ray Crockett	.10	.05
99 Courtney Hall	.10	.05
100 Merton Hanks	.10	.05
101 Aaron Glenn	.10	.05
102 Roosevelt Potts	.10	.05
103 Leon Lett	.10	.05
104 Jessie Tuggle	.10	.05
105 Martin Mayhew	.10	.05
106 Willie Roaf	.10	.05
107 Todd Lyght	.10	.05
108 Ernest Givins	.10	.05
109 Tony McGee	.10	.05
110 Barry Sanders	2.00	.90
111 Dermontti Dawson	.20	.09
112 Rick Tuten	.10	.05
113 Vincent Brisby	.10	.05
114 Charlie Garner	.20	.09
115 Irving Fryar	.20	.09
116 Stevon Moore	.10	.05
117 Matt Darby	.10	.05
118 Howard Cross	.10	.05
119 John Gesek	.10	.05
120 Jack Del Rio	.10	.05
121 Marcus Allen	.30	.14
122 Torrance Small	.10	.05
123 Chris Mims	.10	.05
124 Don Mosebar	.10	.05
125 Carl Pickens	.30	.14
126 Tom Rouen	.10	.05
127 Garrison Hearst	.30	.14
128 Charles Johnson	.20	.09
129 Derek Brown RBK	.10	.05
130 Troy Aikman	1.00	.45
131 Troy Vincent	.10	.05
132 Ken Ruettgers	.10	.05
133 Michael Jackson	.20	.09
134 Dennis Gibson	.10	.05
135 Brett Perriman	.20	.09
136 Jeff Graham	.10	.05
137 Chad Brown	.20	.09
138 Ken Norton Jr.	.20	.09
139 Chris Slade	.20	.09
140 Dave Brown	.20	.09

❑	141	Bert Emanuel	.30	.14
❑	142	Renaldo Turnbull	.10	.05
❑	143	Jim Harbaugh	.20	.09
❑	144	Micheal Barrow	.10	.05
❑	145	Vincent Brown	.10	.05
❑	146	Bryant Young	.20	.09
❑	147	Boomer Esiason	.20	.09
❑	148	Sean Gilbert	.20	.09
❑	149	Greg Truitt	.10	.05
❑	150	Rod Woodson	.20	.09
❑	151	Robert Porcher	.10	.05
❑	152	Joe Phillips	.10	.05
❑	153	Gary Zimmerman	.10	.05
❑	154	Bruce Smith	.30	.14
❑	155	Randall Cunningham	.30	.14
❑	156	Fred Strickland	.10	.05
❑	157	Derrick Alexander WR	.30	.14
❑	158	James Williams	.10	.05
❑	159	Scott Dill	.10	.05
❑	160	Tim Bowens	.10	.05
❑	161	Floyd Turner	.10	.05
❑	162	Ronnie Harmon	.10	.05
❑	163	Wayne Martin	.10	.05
❑	164	John Randle	.10	.05
❑	165	Larry Centers	.20	.09
❑	166	Larry Brown DB	.10	.05
❑	167	Albert Lewis	.10	.05
❑	168	Michael Strahan	.10	.05
❑	169	Reggie Brooks	.20	.09
❑	170	Craig Heyward	.20	.09
❑	171	Pat Harlow	.10	.05
❑	172	Eugene Robinson	.10	.05
❑	173	Shane Conlan	.10	.05
❑	174	Bennie Blades	.10	.05
❑	175	Neil O'Donnell	.20	.09
❑	176	Steve Tovar	.10	.05
❑	177	Donald Evans	.10	.05
❑	178	Brent Jones	.10	.05
❑	179	Ray Childress	.10	.05
❑	180	Reggie White	.30	.14
❑	181	David Alexander	.10	.05
❑	182	Greg Hill	.20	.09
❑	183	Vinny Testaverde	.20	.09
❑	184	Jeff Burris	.10	.05
❑	185	Hardy Nickerson	.10	.05
❑	186	Terry Kirby	.20	.09
❑	187	Kirk Lowdermilk	.10	.05
❑	188	Eric Swann	.20	.09
❑	189	Chris Zorich	.10	.05
❑	190	Simon Fletcher	.10	.05
❑	191	Qadry Ismail	.20	.09
❑	192	Heath Shuler	.30	.14
❑	193	Michael Haynes	.20	.09
❑	194	Mike Sherrard	.10	.05
❑	195	Nolan Harrison	.10	.05
❑	196	Marcus Robertson	.10	.05
❑	197	Kevin Williams WR	.20	.09
❑	198	Moe Gardner	.10	.05
❑	199	Rick Mirer	.30	.14
❑	200	Junior Seau	.30	.14
❑	201	Byron Bam Morris	.20	.09
❑	202	Willie McGinest	.20	.09
❑	203	Chris Spielman	.20	.09
❑	204	Darnay Scott	.30	.14
❑	205	Jesse Sapolu	.10	.05
❑	206	Marvin Washington	.10	.05
❑	207	Anthony Newman	.10	.05
❑	208	Cortez Kennedy	.20	.09
❑	209	Quentin Coryatt	.20	.09
❑	210	Neil Smith	.20	.09
❑	211	Keith Sims	.10	.05
❑	212	Sean Jones	.10	.05
❑	213	Tony Jones	.10	.05
❑	214	Lewis Tillman	.10	.05
❑	215	Darren Woodson	.20	.09
❑	216	Jason Hanson	.10	.05
❑	217	John Taylor	.10	.05
❑	218	Shawn Lee	.10	.05
❑	219	Kevin Greene	.20	.09
❑	220	Jerry Rice	1.00	.45
❑	221	Ki-Jana Carter RC	.30	.14
❑	222	Tony Boselli RC	.20	.09
❑	223	Michael Westbrook RC	1.50	.70
❑	224	Kerry Collins RC	1.00	.45
❑	225	Kevin Carter RC	.30	.14
❑	226	Kyle Brady RC	.30	.14
❑	227	J.J. Stokes RC	.75	.35
❑	228	Derrick Alexander DE RC	.10	.05
❑	229	Warren Sapp RC	.50	.23
❑	230	Ruben Brown RC	.10	.05
❑	231	Hugh Douglas RC	.20	.09
❑	232	Luther Elliss RC	.10	.05
❑	233	Rashaan Salaam RC	.30	.14
❑	234	Tyrone Poole RC	.20	.09
❑	235	Korey Stringer	.10	.05
❑	236	Devin Bush RC	.10	.05
❑	237	Cory Raymer	.10	.05
❑	238	Zach Wiegert RC	.10	.05
❑	239	Ron Davis RC	.10	.05
❑	240	Todd Collins QB RC	.30	.14
❑	241	Bobby Taylor RC	.20	.09
❑	242	Patrick Riley RC	.10	.05
❑	243	Scott Gragg	.10	.05
❑	244	Marvcus Patton	.10	.05
❑	245	Alvin Harper	.10	.05
❑	246	Ricky Watters	.30	.14
❑	247	Checklist 1	.10	.05
❑	248	Checklist 2	.10	.05
❑	249	Terance Mathis	.20	.09
❑	250	Mark Carrier DB	.10	.05
❑	251	Elijah Alexander	.10	.05
❑	252	George Koonce	.10	.05
❑	253	Tony Bennett	.10	.05
❑	254	Steve Wisniewski	.10	.05
❑	255	Bernie Parmalee	.20	.09
❑	256	Dwayne Sabb	.10	.05
❑	257	Lorenzo Neal	.10	.05
❑	258	Corey Miller	.10	.05
❑	259	Fred Barnett	.20	.09
❑	260	Greg Lloyd	.20	.09
❑	261	Robert Blackmon	.10	.05
❑	262	Ken Harvey	.10	.05
❑	263	Eric Hill	.10	.05
❑	264	Russell Copeland	.10	.05
❑	265	Jeff Blake RC	1.00	.45
❑	266	Carl Banks	.10	.05
❑	267	Jay Novacek	.20	.09
❑	268	Mel Gray	.10	.05
❑	269	Kimble Anders	.20	.09
❑	270	Cris Carter	.30	.14
❑	271	Johnny Mitchell	.10	.05
❑	272	Shawn Jefferson	.10	.05
❑	273	Doug Brien	.10	.05
❑	274	Sean Landeta	.10	.05
❑	275	Scott Mitchell	.20	.09
❑	276	Charles Wilson	.10	.05
❑	277	Anthony Smith	.10	.05
❑	278	Anthony Miller	.20	.09
❑	279	Steve Walsh	.10	.05
❑	280	Drew Bledsoe	1.00	.45
❑	281	Jamir Miller	.10	.05
❑	282	Robert Brooks UER Rushing and receiving totals are reversed	.30	.14
❑	283	Sean Lumpkin	.10	.05
❑	284	Bryan Cox	.10	.05
❑	285	Byron Evans	.10	.05
❑	286	Chris Doleman	.10	.05
❑	287	Anthony Pleasant	.10	.05
❑	288	Stephen Grant RC	.10	.05
❑	289	Doug Riesenberg	.10	.05
❑	290	Natrone Means	.30	.14
❑	291	Henry Thomas	.10	.05
❑	292	Mike Pritchard	.10	.05
❑	293	Courtney Hawkins	.10	.05
❑	294	Bill Bates	.20	.09
❑	295	Jerome Bettis	.30	.14
❑	296	Russell Maryland	.10	.05
❑	297	Stanley Richard	.10	.05
❑	298	William White	.10	.05
❑	299	Dan Wilkinson	.20	.09
❑	300	Steve Young	.75	.35
❑	301	Gary Brown	.10	.05
❑	302	Jake Reed	.20	.09
❑	303	Carlton Gray	.10	.05
❑	304	Levon Kirkland	.10	.05
❑	305	Shannon Sharpe	.20	.09
❑	306	Luis Sharpe	.10	.05
❑	307	Marshall Faulk	.40	.18
❑	308	Stan Humphries	.20	.09
❑	309	Chris Calloway	.10	.05
❑	310	Tim Brown	.30	.14
❑	311	Steve Everitt	.10	.05
❑	312	Raymont Harris	.10	.05
❑	313	Tim McDonald	.10	.05
❑	314	Trent Dilfer	.30	.14
❑	315	Jim Everett	.10	.05
❑	316	Ray Crittenden	.10	.05
❑	317	Jim Kelly	.30	.14
❑	318	Andre Reed	.20	.09
❑	319	Chris Miller	.10	.05
❑	320	Bobby Houston	.10	.05
❑	321	Charles Haley	.20	.09
❑	322	James Francis	.10	.05
❑	323	Bernard Williams	.10	.05
❑	324	Michael Bates	.10	.05
❑	325	Brian Mitchell	.10	.05
❑	326	Mike Johnson	.10	.05
❑	327	Eric Bieniemy	.10	.05
❑	328	Aubrey Beavers	.10	.05
❑	329	Dale Carter	.20	.09
❑	330	Emmitt Smith	1.50	.70
❑	331	Darren Perry	.10	.05
❑	332	Marquez Pope	.10	.05
❑	333	Clyde Simmons	.10	.05
❑	334	Corey Croom	.10	.05
❑	335	Thomas Randolph	.10	.05
❑	336	Harvey Williams	.10	.05
❑	337	Michael Timpson	.10	.05
❑	338	Eugene Daniel	.10	.05
❑	339	Shane Dronett	.10	.05
❑	340	Eric Turner	.10	.05
❑	341	Eric Metcalf	.20	.09
❑	342	Leslie O'Neal	.20	.09
❑	343	Mark Wheeler	.10	.05
❑	344	Mark Pike	.10	.05
❑	345	Brett Favre	2.00	.90
❑	346	Johnny Bailey	.10	.05
❑	347	Henry Ellard	.20	.09
❑	348	Chris Gardocki	.10	.05
❑	349	Henry Jones	.10	.05
❑	350	Dan Marino	2.00	.90
❑	351	Lake Dawson	.20	.09
❑	352	Mark McMillian	.10	.05
❑	353	Deion Sanders	.60	.25
❑	354	Antonio London	.10	.05
❑	355	Cris Dishman	.10	.05
❑	356	Ricardo McDonald	.10	.05
❑	357	Dexter Carter	.10	.05
❑	358	Kevin Smith	.10	.05
❑	359	Yancey Thigpen RC	.30	.14
❑	360	Chris Warren	.20	.09
❑	361	Quinn Early	.20	.09
❑	362	John Mangum	.10	.05
❑	363	Santana Dotson	.10	.05
❑	364	Rocket Ismail	.20	.09
❑	365	Aeneas Williams	.10	.05
❑	366	Dan Williams	.10	.05
❑	367	Sean Dawkins	.20	.09
❑	368	Pepper Johnson	.10	.05
❑	369	Roman Phifer	.10	.05
❑	370	Rodney Hampton	.20	.09
❑	371	Darrell Green	.10	.05
❑	372	Michael Zordich	.10	.05
❑	373	Andre Coleman	.10	.05
❑	374	Wayne Simmons	.10	.05
❑	375	Michael Irvin	.30	.14
❑	376	Clay Matthews	.20	.09
❑	377	Dewayne Washington	.20	.09
❑	378	Keith Byars	.10	.05
❑	379	Todd Collins LB	.30	.14
❑	380	Mark Collins	.10	.05
❑	381	Joel Steed	.10	.05
❑	382	Bart Oates	.10	.05
❑	383	Al Smith	.10	.05
❑	384	Rafael Robinson	.10	.05
❑	385	Mo Lewis	.10	.05
❑	386	Aubrey Matthews	.10	.05
❑	387	Corey Sawyer	.10	.05
❑	388	Bucky Brooks	.10	.05
❑	389	Erik Kramer	.10	.05
❑	390	Tyrone Hughes	.20	.09
❑	391	Terry McDaniel	.10	.05
❑	392	Craig Erickson	.10	.05
❑	393	Mike Flores	.10	.05
❑	394	Harry Swayne	.10	.05
❑	395	Irving Spikes	.20	.09
❑	396	Lorenzo Lynch	.10	.05

		MINT	NRMT
❑ 397	Antonio Langham	.10	.05
❑ 398	Edgar Bennett	.20	.09
❑ 399	Thomas Lewis	.20	.09
❑ 400	John Elway	2.00	.90
❑ 401	Jeff George	.20	.09
❑ 402	Errict Rhett	.30	.14
❑ 403	Bill Romanowski	.10	.05
❑ 404	Alexander Wright	.10	.05
❑ 405	Warren Moon	.20	.09
❑ 406	Eddie Robinson	.10	.05
❑ 407	John Copeland	.10	.05
❑ 408	Robert Jones	.10	.05
❑ 409	Steve Bono	.20	.09
❑ 410	Cornelius Bennett	.20	.09
❑ 411	Ben Coates	.20	.09
❑ 412	Dana Stubblefield	.30	.14
❑ 413	Darryl Talley	.10	.05
❑ 414	Brian Blades	.20	.09
❑ 415	Herman Moore	.30	.14
❑ 416	Nick Lowery	.10	.05
❑ 417	Donnell Bennett	.20	.09
❑ 418	Van Malone	.10	.05
❑ 419	Pete Stoyanovich	.10	.05
❑ 420	Joe Montana	2.00	.90
❑ 421	Steve Young Super Bowl XXIX MVP	.50	.23
❑ 422	Steve Young Quarterback Rating Leaders	.50	.23
❑ 423	Steve Young Super Bowl Touchdown Record	.50	.23
❑ 424	Steve Young NFL League MVP	.50	.23
❑ 425	Steve Young Pro Bowl	.50	.23
❑ 426	Rod Stephens	.10	.05
❑ 427	Ellis Johnson RC UER Card is numbered 436	.10	.05
❑ 428	Kordell Stewart RC	2.50	1.10
❑ 429	James O. Stewart RC	2.00	.90
❑ 430	Steve McNair RC	2.50	1.10
❑ 431	Brian DeMarco	.20	.09
❑ 432	Matt O'Dwyer	.10	.05
❑ 433	Lorenzo Styles RC	.10	.05
❑ 434	Anthony Cook RC	.10	.05
❑ 435	Jesse James	.10	.05
❑ 436	Darryl Pounds	.10	.05
❑ 437	Derrick Graham	.10	.05
❑ 438	Vernon Turner	.10	.05
❑ 439	Carlton Bailey	.10	.05
❑ 440	Darion Conner	.10	.05
❑ 441	Randy Baldwin	.10	.05
❑ 442	Tim McKyer	.10	.05
❑ 443	Sam Mills	.20	.09
❑ 444	Bob Christian	.10	.05
❑ 445	Steve Lofton	.10	.05
❑ 446	Lamar Lathon	.10	.05
❑ 447	Tony Smith	.10	.05
❑ 448	Don Beebe	.10	.05
❑ 449	Barry Foster	.20	.09
❑ 450	Frank Reich	.10	.05
❑ 451	Pete Metzelaars	.10	.05
❑ 452	Reggie Cobb	.10	.05
❑ 453	Jeff Lageman	.10	.05
❑ 454	Derek Brown TE	.10	.05
❑ 455	Desmond Howard	.20	.09
❑ 456	Vinnie Clark	.10	.05
❑ 457	Keith Goganious	.10	.05
❑ 458	Shawn Bouwens	.10	.05
❑ 459	Rob Johnson RC	1.50	.70
❑ 460	Steve Beuerlein	.10	.05
❑ 461	Mark Brunell	1.00	.45
❑ 462	Harry Colon	.10	.05
❑ 463	Chris Hudson	.10	.05
❑ 464	Darren Carrington	.10	.05
❑ 465	Ernest Givins	.10	.05
❑ 466	Kelvin Pritchett	.10	.05
❑ 467	Checklist (249-358)	.10	.05
❑ 468	Checklist (358-468)	.10	.05

1995 Topps 1000/3000 Boosters

	MINT	NRMT
COMPLETE SET (41)	120.00	55.00
STATED ODDS 1:36H,1:18J,1:72 SR SER.1		

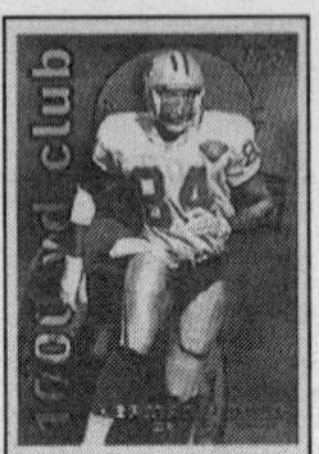

		MINT	NRMT
❑ 1	Barry Sanders	20.00	9.00
❑ 2	Chris Warren	2.00	.90
❑ 3	Jerry Rice	10.00	4.50
❑ 4	Emmitt Smith	15.00	6.75
❑ 5	Henry Ellard	2.00	.90
❑ 6	Natrone Means	3.00	1.35
❑ 7	Terance Mathis	2.00	.90
❑ 8	Tim Brown	3.00	1.35
❑ 9	Andre Reed	2.00	.90
❑ 10	Marshall Faulk	4.00	1.80
❑ 11	Irving Fryar	2.00	.90
❑ 12	Cris Carter	3.00	1.35
❑ 13	Michael Irvin	3.00	1.35
❑ 14	Jake Reed	2.00	.90
❑ 15	Ben Coates	2.00	.90
❑ 16	Herman Moore	3.00	1.35
❑ 17	Carl Pickens	3.00	1.35
❑ 18	Fred Barnett	2.00	.90
❑ 19	Sterling Sharpe	2.00	.90
❑ 20	Anthony Miller	2.00	.90
❑ 21	Thurman Thomas	3.00	1.35
❑ 22	Andre Rison	2.00	.90
❑ 23	Brian Blades	2.00	.90
❑ 24	Rodney Hampton	2.00	.90
❑ 25	Terry Allen	2.00	.90
❑ 26	Jerome Bettis	3.00	1.35
❑ 27	Errict Rhett	3.00	1.35
❑ 28	Rob Moore	1.00	.45
❑ 29	Shannon Sharpe	2.00	.90
❑ 30	Drew Bledsoe	10.00	4.50
❑ 31	Dan Marino	20.00	9.00
❑ 32	Warren Moon	2.00	.90
❑ 33	Steve Young	8.00	3.60
❑ 34	Brett Favre	20.00	9.00
❑ 35	Jim Everett	1.00	.45
❑ 36	Jeff George	2.00	.90
❑ 37	John Elway	20.00	9.00
❑ 38	Jeff Hostetler	2.00	.90
❑ 39	Randall Cunningham	3.00	1.35
❑ 40	Stan Humphries	2.00	.90
❑ 41	Jim Kelly	3.00	1.35

1995 Topps Air Raid

	MINT	NRMT
COMPLETE SET (10)	60.00	27.00
COMMON CARD (1-10)	3.00	1.35
SEMISTARS	5.00	2.20
SER.2 STATED ODDS 1:20J,1:24R,1:48SP.RET		

		MINT	NRMT
❑ 1	Steve Young Jerry Rice	10.00	4.50
❑ 2	Cris Carter Warren Moon	5.00	2.20
❑ 3	Terance Mathis Jeff George	3.00	1.35
❑ 4	Dave Brown Michael Sherrard	3.00	1.35
❑ 5	Drew Bledsoe Ben Coates	10.00	4.50
❑ 6	John Elway Shannon Sharpe	15.00	6.75
❑ 7	Jeff Blake Carl Pickens	5.00	2.20
❑ 8	Dan Marino Irving Fryar	15.00	6.75
❑ 9	Fred Barnett Randall Cunningham	3.00	1.35
❑ 10	Troy Aikman Michael Irvin	10.00	4.50

1995 Topps All-Pros

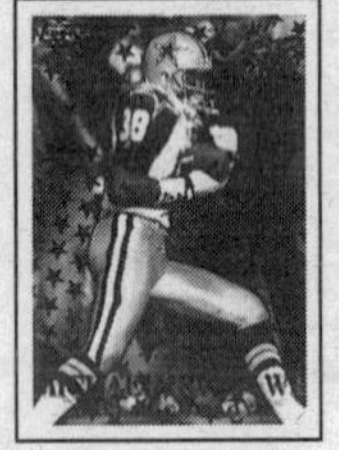

	MINT	NRMT
COMPLETE SET (22)	25.00	11.00
SER.2 STATED ODDS 1:8 HOBBY		

		MINT	NRMT
❑ 1	Jerry Rice	5.00	2.20
❑ 2	Lomas Brown	.50	.23
❑ 3	Nate Newton	.50	.23
❑ 4	Dermontti Dawson	1.00	.45
❑ 5	Keith Sims	.50	.23
❑ 6	Richmond Webb	.50	.23
❑ 7	Shannon Sharpe	1.00	.45
❑ 8	Michael Irvin	1.50	.70
❑ 9	Steve Young	4.00	1.80
❑ 10	Barry Sanders	10.00	4.50
❑ 11	Marshall Faulk	2.00	.90
❑ 12	Bruce Smith	1.50	.70
❑ 13	Dana Stubblefield	1.50	.70
❑ 14	John Randle	.50	.23
❑ 15	Reggie White	1.50	.70
❑ 16	Greg Lloyd	1.00	.45
❑ 17	Junior Seau	1.50	.70
❑ 18	Cornelius Bennett	1.00	.45
❑ 19	Rod Woodson	1.00	.45
❑ 20	Deion Sanders	3.00	1.35
❑ 21	Darren Woodson	1.00	.45
❑ 22	Merton Hanks	.50	.23

1995 Topps Expansion Team Boosters

	MINT	NRMT
COMPLETE SET (30)	80.00	36.00
COMMON CARD (437-466)	1.00	.45
SEMISTARS	1.50	.70
SER.2 STATED ODDS 1:36H/R, 1:18J		
SER.2 STATED ODDS 1:72 SPECIAL RET.		

		MINT	NRMT
❑ 437	Derrick Graham	1.00	.45
❑ 438	Vernon Turner	1.00	.45
❑ 439	Carlton Bailey	1.00	.45
❑ 440	Darion Conner	1.00	.45
❑ 441	Randy Baldwin	1.00	.45
❑ 442	Tim McKyer	1.00	.45
❑ 443	Sam Mills	1.00	.45
❑ 444	Bob Christian	1.00	.45

❑	445 Steve Lofton	1.00	.45
❑	446 Lamar Lathon	1.00	.45
❑	447 Tony Smith RB	1.00	.45
❑	448 Don Beebe	1.50	.70
❑	449 Barry Foster	1.50	.70
❑	450 Frank Reich	1.50	.70
❑	451 Pete Metzelaars	1.00	.45
❑	452 Reggie Cobb	1.00	.45
❑	453 Jeff Lageman	1.00	.45
❑	454 Derek Brown TE	1.00	.45
❑	455 Desmond Howard	1.50	.70
❑	456 Vinnie Clark	1.00	.45
❑	457 Keith Goganious	1.00	.45
❑	458 Shawn Bowens	1.00	.45
❑	459 Rob Johnson	10.00	4.50
❑	460 Steve Beuerlein	1.50	.70
❑	461 Mark Brunell	20.00	9.00
❑	462 Harry Colon	1.00	.45
❑	463 Chris Hudson	1.00	.45
❑	464 Darren Carrington	1.00	.45
❑	465 Ernest Givins	1.00	.45
❑	466 Kelvin Pritchett	1.00	.45

1995 Topps Finest Boosters

	MINT	NRMT
COMPLETE SET (22)	80.00	36.00

STATED ODDS 1:36H/R,1:18J,1:72SR.SER.2
*REFRACTORS: 6X to 15X BASE CARD HI
STATED ODDS 1:36H,1:216J,1:432R SER.2

❑	B166 Barry Sanders	15.00	6.75
❑	B167 Bryant Young	1.50	.70
❑	B168 Boomer Esiason	1.50	.70
❑	B169 Terance Mathis	1.50	.70
❑	B170 Troy Aikman	8.00	3.60
❑	B171 Junior Seau	2.00	.90
❑	B172 Rodney Hampton	1.50	.70
❑	B173 Jim Everett	.75	.35
❑	B174 Dan Marino	15.00	6.75
❑	B175 Steve Young	5.00	2.20
❑	B176 Cris Carter	2.00	.90
❑	B177 Eric Swann	1.50	.70
❑	B178 Rick Mirer	2.00	.90
❑	B179 Jerome Bettis	2.00	.90
❑	B180 Emmitt Smith	10.00	4.50
❑	B181 Jim Kelly	2.00	.90
❑	B182 John Elway	15.00	6.75
❑	B183 Dana Stubblefield	2.00	.90
❑	B184 Drew Bledsoe	8.00	3.60
❑	B185 Jerry Rice	8.00	3.60
❑	B186 Michael Irvin	2.00	.90
❑	B187 Bruce Smith	2.00	.90

1995 Topps Florida Hot Bed

	MINT	NRMT
COMPLETE SET (15)	12.00	5.50

ONE PER SPECIAL RETAIL PACK

❑	FH1 Deion Sanders	2.50	1.10
❑	FH2 Brian Blades	.75	.35
❑	FH3 Errict Rhett	1.25	.55
❑	FH4 Kevin Williams	.75	.35
❑	FH5 Cortez Kennedy	.75	.35
❑	FH6 Corey Sawyer	.40	.18
❑	FH7 Russell Maryland	.40	.18
❑	FH8 Emmitt Smith	6.00	2.70
❑	FH9 Vinny Testaverde	.75	.35
❑	FH10 William Floyd	1.25	.55
❑	FH11 Brett Perriman	.75	.35
❑	FH12 Nate Newton	.40	.18
❑	FH13 Jim Kelly	1.25	.55
❑	FH14 LeRoy Butler	.40	.18
❑	FH15 Michael Irvin	1.25	.55

1995 Topps Mystery Finest

	MINT	NRMT
COMPLETE SET (27)	40.00	18.00

STATED ODDS 1:36H,1:12J,1:72SP RET SER.1
*REFRACTORS: 4X to 10X BASIC CARDS
STATED ODDS 1:36H,1:216J,1:864R SER.1

❑	1 Troy Aikman	5.00	2.20
❑	2 Jerome Bettis	1.50	.70
❑	3 Drew Bledsoe	5.00	2.20
❑	4 Tim Brown	1.50	.70
❑	5 Cris Carter	1.50	.70
❑	6 Henry Ellard	1.00	.45
❑	7 John Elway	10.00	4.50
❑	8 Marshall Faulk	2.00	.90
❑	9 Brett Favre	10.00	4.50
❑	10 Irving Fryar	1.00	.45
❑	11 Rodney Hampton	1.00	.45
❑	12 Stan Humphries	1.00	.45
❑	13 Michael Irvin	1.50	.70
❑	14 Jim Kelly	1.50	.70
❑	15 Dan Marino	10.00	4.50
❑	16 Terance Mathis	1.00	.45
❑	17 Natrone Means	1.50	.70
❑	18 Warren Moon	1.00	.45
❑	19 Herman Moore	1.50	.70
❑	20 Andre Reed	1.00	.45
❑	21 Errict Rhett	1.50	.70
❑	22 Jerry Rice	5.00	2.20
❑	23 Barry Sanders	10.00	4.50
❑	24 Emmitt Smith	8.00	3.60
❑	25 Chris Warren	1.00	.45
❑	26 Ricky Watters	1.50	.70
❑	27 Steve Young	4.00	1.80
❑	NNO Set Redemption	100.00	45.00

1995 Topps Profiles

	MINT	NRMT
COMPLETE SET (15)	30.00	13.50

STATED ODDS 1:12H/R,1:6J,1:24SR SER.2

❑	1 Emmitt Smith	10.00	4.50
❑	2 Chris Spielman	1.25	.55
❑	3 Rod Woodson	1.25	.55
❑	4 Deion Sanders	4.00	1.80
❑	5 Junior Seau	2.00	.90
❑	6 Byron Evans	.60	.25
❑	7 Jerome Bettis	2.00	.90
❑	8 Charles Haley	1.25	.55
❑	9 Jerry Rice	6.00	2.70
❑	10 Barry Sanders	12.00	5.50
❑	11 Hardy Nickerson	.60	.25
❑	12 Natrone Means	2.00	.90
❑	13 Darren Woodson	1.25	.55
❑	14 Reggie White	2.00	.90
❑	15 Troy Aikman	6.00	2.70

1995 Topps Sensational Sophomores

	MINT	NRMT
COMPLETE SET (10)	15.00	6.75
COMMON CARD (1-10)	1.25	.55
SEMISTARS	2.50	1.10
UNLISTED STARS	4.00	1.80

STATED ODDS 1:9JUM, 1:48 SP RET SER.1

❑	1 Marshall Faulk	4.00	1.80
❑	2 Heath Shuler	2.50	1.10
❑	3 Tim Bowens	1.25	.55
❑	4 Bryant Young	1.25	.55
❑	5 Dan Wilkinson	1.25	.55
❑	6 Errict Rhett	1.25	.55
❑	7 Andre Coleman	1.25	.55
❑	8 Aaron Glenn	1.25	.55
❑	9 Trent Dilfer	2.50	1.10
❑	10 Byron Bam Morris	1.25	.55

1995 Topps Yesteryear

	MINT	NRMT
COMPLETE SET (15)	60.00	27.00

SER.1 STATED ODDS 1:72 HOBBY

❑	1 Stan Humphries	1.50	.70
❑	2 Dan Marino	15.00	6.75
❑	3 Irving Fryar	1.50	.70

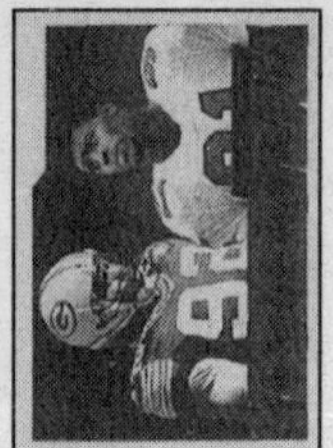

- ❑ 4 Warren Moon 1.50 .70
- ❑ 5 Steve Young 6.00 2.70
- ❑ 6 Kevin Greene 1.50 .70
- ❑ 7 Jeff Hostetler 1.50 .70
- ❑ 8 Jack Del Rio .75 .35
- ❑ 9 Reggie White 2.50 1.10
- ❑ 10 Jerry Rice 8.00 3.60
- ❑ 11 Bruce Smith 2.50 1.10
- ❑ 12 Rod Woodson 1.50 .70
- ❑ 13 Deion Sanders 5.00 2.20
- ❑ 14 Barry Sanders 15.00 6.75
- ❑ 15 Brett Favre 15.00 6.75

1996 Topps

	MINT	NRMT
COMPLETE SET (440)	35.00	16.00
COMP.FACT.SET (448)	50.00	22.00
COMP.CER.FACT.SET (445)	40.00	18.00
COMMON CARD (1-440)	.10	.05
SEMISTARS	.20	.09
UNLISTED STARS	.30	.14
FOUR PER CEREAL FACT.SET ..		

- ❑ 1 Troy Aikman 1.00 .45
- ❑ 2 Kevin Greene .20 .09
- ❑ 3 Robert Brooks .30 .14
- ❑ 4 Eugene Daniel .10 .05
- ❑ 5 Rodney Peete .10 .05
- ❑ 6 James Hasty .10 .05
- ❑ 7 Tim McDonald .10 .05
- ❑ 8 Darick Holmes .10 .05
- ❑ 9 Morten Andersen .10 .05
- ❑ 10 Junior Seau .20 .09
- ❑ 11 Brett Perriman .10 .05
- ❑ 12 Eric Green .10 .05
- ❑ 13 Jim Flanigan .10 .05
- ❑ 14 Cortez Kennedy .10 .05
- ❑ 15 Orlando Thomas .10 .05
- ❑ 16 Anthony Miller .20 .09
- ❑ 17 Sean Gilbert .10 .05
- ❑ 18 Rob Fredrickson .10 .05
- ❑ 19 Willie Green .10 .05
- ❑ 20 Jeff Blake .30 .14
- ❑ 21 Trent Dilfer .30 .14
- ❑ 22 Chris Chandler .20 .09
- ❑ 23 Renaldo Turnbull .10 .05
- ❑ 24 Dave Meggett .10 .05
- ❑ 25 Heath Shuler .20 .09
- ❑ 26 Michael Jackson .20 .09
- ❑ 27 Thomas Randolph .10 .05
- ❑ 28 Keith Goganious .10 .05
- ❑ 29 Seth Joyner .10 .05
- ❑ 30 Wayne Chrebet .30 .14
- ❑ 31 Craig Newsome .10 .05
- ❑ 32 William Fuller .10 .05
- ❑ 33 Merton Hanks .10 .05
- ❑ 34 Dale Carter .10 .05
- ❑ 35 Quentin Coryatt .10 .05
- ❑ 36 Robert Jones .10 .05
- ❑ 37 Eric Metcalf .10 .05
- ❑ 38 Byron Bam Morris .20 .09
- ❑ 39 Bill Brooks .10 .05
- ❑ 40 Barry Sanders 2.00 .90
- ❑ 41 Michael Haynes .10 .05
- ❑ 42 Joey Galloway .75 .35
- ❑ 43 Robert Smith .20 .09
- ❑ 44 John Thierry .10 .05
- ❑ 45 Bryan Cox .10 .05
- ❑ 46 Anthony Parker .10 .05
- ❑ 47 Harvey Williams .10 .05
- ❑ 48 Terrell Davis 2.50 1.10
- ❑ 49 Darnay Scott .20 .09
- ❑ 50 Kerry Collins .30 .14
- ❑ 51 Cris Dishman .10 .05
- ❑ 52 Dwayne Harper .10 .05
- ❑ 53 Warren Sapp .10 .05
- ❑ 54 Will Moore .10 .05
- ❑ 55 Earnest Byner .10 .05
- ❑ 56 Aaron Glenn .10 .05
- ❑ 57 Michael Westbrook .30 .14
- ❑ 58 Vencie Glenn .10 .05
- ❑ 59 Rob Moore .20 .09
- ❑ 60 Mark Brunell 1.00 .45
- ❑ 61 Craig Heyward .10 .05
- ❑ 62 Eric Allen .10 .05
- ❑ 63 Bill Romanowski .10 .05
- ❑ 64 Dana Stubblefield .20 .09
- ❑ 65 Steve Bono .10 .05
- ❑ 66 George Koonce .10 .05
- ❑ 67 Larry Brown .10 .05
- ❑ 68 Warren Moon .20 .09
- ❑ 69 Erric Pegram .10 .05
- ❑ 70 Jim Kelly .30 .14
- ❑ 71 Jason Belser .10 .05
- ❑ 72 Henry Thomas .10 .05
- ❑ 73 Mark Carrier DB .10 .05
- ❑ 74 Terry Wooden .10 .05
- ❑ 75 Terry McDaniel .10 .05
- ❑ 76 O.J. McDuffie .20 .09
- ❑ 77 Dan Wilkinson .10 .05
- ❑ 78 Blake Brockermeyer .10 .05
- ❑ 79 Micheal Barrow .10 .05
- ❑ 80 Dave Brown .10 .05
- ❑ 81 Todd Lyght .10 .05
- ❑ 82 Henry Ellard .10 .05
- ❑ 83 Jeff Lageman .10 .05
- ❑ 84 Anthony Pleasant .10 .05
- ❑ 85 Aeneas Williams .10 .05
- ❑ 86 Vincent Brisby .10 .05
- ❑ 87 Terrell Fletcher .10 .05
- ❑ 88 Brad Baxter .10 .05
- ❑ 89 Shannon Sharpe .20 .09
- ❑ 90 Errict Rhett .20 .09
- ❑ 91 Michael Zordich .10 .05
- ❑ 92 Dan Saleaumua .10 .05
- ❑ 93 Devin Bush .10 .05
- ❑ 94 Wayne Simmons .10 .05
- ❑ 95 Tyrone Hughes .10 .05
- ❑ 96 John Randle .10 .05
- ❑ 97 Tony Tolbert .10 .05
- ❑ 98 Yancey Thigpen .20 .09
- ❑ 99 J.J. Stokes .30 .14
- ❑ 100 Marshall Faulk .30 .14
- ❑ 101 Barry Minter .10 .05
- ❑ 102 Glenn Foley .20 .09
- ❑ 103 Chester McGlockton .10 .05
- ❑ 104 Carlton Gray .10 .05
- ❑ 105 Terry Kirby .20 .09
- ❑ 106 Darryll Lewis .10 .05
- ❑ 107 Thomas Smith .10 .05
- ❑ 108 Mike Fox .10 .05
- ❑ 109 Antonio Langham .10 .05
- ❑ 110 Drew Bledsoe 1.00 .45
- ❑ 111 Troy Drayton .10 .05
- ❑ 112 Marvcus Patton .10 .05
- ❑ 113 Tyrone Wheatley .20 .09
- ❑ 114 Desmond Howard .20 .09
- ❑ 115 Johnny Mitchell .10 .05
- ❑ 116 Dave Krieg .10 .05
- ❑ 117 Natrone Means .30 .14
- ❑ 118 Herman Moore .30 .14
- ❑ 119 Darren Woodson .20 .09
- ❑ 120 Ricky Watters .20 .09
- ❑ 121 Emmitt Smith TYC .75 .35
- ❑ 122 Barry Sanders TYC 1.00 .45
- ❑ 123 Curtis Martin TYC .30 .14
- ❑ 124 Chris Warren TYC .20 .09
- ❑ 125 Terry Allen TYC .20 .09
- ❑ 126 Ricky Watters TYC .20 .09
- ❑ 127 Errict Rhett TYC .20 .09
- ❑ 128 Rodney Hampton TYC .10 .05
- ❑ 129 Terrell Davis TYC 1.25 .55
- ❑ 130 Harvey Williams TYC .10 .05
- ❑ 131 Craig Heyward TYC .10 .05
- ❑ 132 Marshall Faulk TYC .20 .09
- ❑ 133 Rashaan Salaam TYC .20 .09
- ❑ 134 Garrison Hearst TYC .20 .09
- ❑ 135 Edgar Bennett TYC .20 .09
- ❑ 136 Thurman Thomas TYC .20 .09
- ❑ 137 Brian Washington .10 .05
- ❑ 138 Derek Loville .10 .05
- ❑ 139 Curtis Conway .30 .14
- ❑ 140 Isaac Bruce .30 .14
- ❑ 141 Ricardo McDonald .10 .05
- ❑ 142 Bruce Armstrong .10 .05
- ❑ 143 Will Wolford .10 .05
- ❑ 144 Thurman Thomas .30 .14
- ❑ 145 Mel Gray .10 .05
- ❑ 146 Napoleon Kaufman .50 .23
- ❑ 147 Terry Allen .20 .09
- ❑ 148 Chris Calloway .10 .05
- ❑ 149 Harry Colon .10 .05
- ❑ 150 Pepper Johnson .10 .05
- ❑ 151 Marco Coleman .10 .05
- ❑ 152 Shawn Jefferson .10 .05
- ❑ 153 Larry Centers .20 .09
- ❑ 154 Lamar Lathon .10 .05
- ❑ 155 Mark Chmura .20 .09
- ❑ 156 Dermontti Dawson .10 .05
- ❑ 157 Alvin Harper .10 .05
- ❑ 158 Randall McDaniel .10 .05
- ❑ 159 Allen Aldridge .10 .05
- ❑ 160 Chris Warren .20 .09
- ❑ 161 Jessie Tuggle .10 .05
- ❑ 162 Sean Lumpkin .10 .05
- ❑ 163 Bobby Houston .10 .05
- ❑ 164 Dexter Carter .10 .05
- ❑ 165 Erik Kramer .10 .05
- ❑ 166 Brock Marion .10 .05
- ❑ 167 Toby Wright .10 .05
- ❑ 168 John Copeland .10 .05
- ❑ 169 Sean Dawkins .10 .05
- ❑ 170 Tim Brown .30 .14
- ❑ 171 Darion Conner .10 .05
- ❑ 172 Aaron Hayden RC .10 .05
- ❑ 173 Charlie Garner .10 .05
- ❑ 174 Anthony Cook .10 .05
- ❑ 175 Derrick Thomas .20 .09
- ❑ 176 Willie McGinest .10 .05
- ❑ 177 Thomas Lewis .10 .05
- ❑ 178 Sherman Williams .10 .05
- ❑ 179 Cornelius Bennett .10 .05
- ❑ 180 Frank Sanders .30 .14
- ❑ 181 Leroy Hoard .10 .05
- ❑ 182 Bernie Parmalee .10 .05
- ❑ 183 Sterling Palmer .10 .05
- ❑ 184 Kelvin Pritchett .10 .05
- ❑ 185 Kordell Stewart .75 .35
- ❑ 186 Brent Jones .10 .05
- ❑ 187 Robert Blackmon .10 .05
- ❑ 188 Adrian Murrell .30 .14
- ❑ 189 Edgar Bennett .20 .09
- ❑ 190 Rashaan Salaam .30 .14
- ❑ 191 Ellis Johnson .10 .05
- ❑ 192 Andre Coleman .10 .05
- ❑ 193 Will Shields .10 .05
- ❑ 194 Derrick Brooks .10 .05
- ❑ 195 Carl Pickens .30 .14
- ❑ 196 Carlton Bailey .10 .05
- ❑ 197 Terance Mathis .20 .09
- ❑ 198 Carlos Jenkins .10 .05
- ❑ 199 Derrick Alexander DE .10 .05

❑ 200 Deion Sanders	.60	.25
❑ 201 Glyn Milburn	.10	.05
❑ 202 Chris Sanders	.20	.09
❑ 203 Rocket Ismail	.10	.05
❑ 204 Fred Barnett	.10	.05
❑ 205 Quinn Early	.10	.05
❑ 206 Henry Jones	.10	.05
❑ 207 Herschel Walker	.20	.09
❑ 208 James Washington	.10	.05
❑ 209 Lee Woodall	.10	.05
❑ 210 Neil Smith	.10	.05
❑ 211 Tony Bennett	.10	.05
❑ 212 Ernie Mills	.10	.05
❑ 213 Clyde Simmons	.10	.05
❑ 214 Chris Slade	.10	.05
❑ 215 Tony Boselli	.10	.05
❑ 216 Ryan McNeil	.10	.05
❑ 217 Rob Burnett	.10	.05
❑ 218 Stan Humphries	.20	.09
❑ 219 Rick Mirer	.20	.09
❑ 220 Troy Vincent	.10	.05
❑ 221 Sean Jones	.10	.05
❑ 222 Marty Carter	.10	.05
❑ 223 Boomer Esiason	.20	.09
❑ 224 Charles Haley	.20	.09
❑ 225 Sam Mills	.10	.05
❑ 226 Greg Biekert	.10	.05
❑ 227 Bryant Young	.20	.09
❑ 228 Ken Dilger	.20	.09
❑ 229 Levon Kirkland	.10	.05
❑ 230 Brian Mitchell	.10	.05
❑ 231 Hardy Nickerson	.10	.05
❑ 232 Elvis Grbac	.20	.09
❑ 233 Kurt Schulz	.10	.05
❑ 234 Chris Doleman	.10	.05
❑ 235 Tamarick Vanover	.20	.09
❑ 236 Jesse Campbell	.10	.05
❑ 237 William Thomas	.10	.05
❑ 238 Shane Conlan	.10	.05
❑ 239 Jason Elam	.10	.05
❑ 240 Steve McNair	.75	.35
❑ 241 Jerry Rice TYC	.50	.23
❑ 242 Isaac Bruce TYC	.30	.14
❑ 243 Herman Moore TYC	.30	.14
❑ 244 Michael Irvin TYC	.20	.09
❑ 245 Robert Brooks TYC	.30	.14
❑ 246 Brett Perriman TYC	.10	.05
❑ 247 Cris Carter TYC	.30	.14
❑ 248 Tim Brown TYC	.20	.09
❑ 249 Yancey Thigpen TYC	.20	.09
❑ 250 Jeff Graham TYC	.10	.05
❑ 251 Carl Pickens TYC	.30	.14
❑ 252 Tony Martin TYC	.10	.05
❑ 253 Eric Metcalf TYC	.10	.05
❑ 254 Jake Reed TYC	.20	.09
❑ 255 Quinn Early TYC	.10	.05
❑ 256 Anthony Miller TYC	.20	.09
❑ 257 Joey Galloway TYC	.30	.14
❑ 258 Bert Emanuel TYC	.20	.09
❑ 259 Terance Mathis TYC	.10	.05
❑ 260 Curtis Conway TYC	.20	.09
❑ 261 Henry Ellard TYC	.10	.05
❑ 262 Mark Carrier WR TYC	.10	.05
❑ 263 Brian Blades TYC	.10	.05
❑ 264 William Roaf	.10	.05
❑ 265 Ed McDaniel	.10	.05
❑ 266 Nate Newton	.10	.05
❑ 267 Brett Maxie	.10	.05
❑ 268 Anthony Smith	.10	.05
❑ 269 Mickey Washington	.10	.05
❑ 270 Jerry Rice	1.00	.45
❑ 271 Shaun Gayle	.10	.05
❑ 272 Gilbert Brown	.20	.09
❑ 273 Mark Bruener	.10	.05
❑ 274 Eugene Robinson	.10	.05
❑ 275 Marvin Washington	.10	.05
❑ 276 Keith Sims	.10	.05
❑ 277 Ashley Ambrose	.10	.05
❑ 278 Garrison Hearst	.20	.09
❑ 279 Donnell Woolford	.10	.05
❑ 280 Cris Carter	.30	.14
❑ 281 Curtis Martin	.75	.35
❑ 282 Scott Mitchell	.20	.09
❑ 283 Stevon Moore	.10	.05
❑ 284 Roman Phifer	.10	.05
❑ 285 Ken Harvey	.10	.05
❑ 286 Rodney Hampton	.20	.09
❑ 287 Willie Davis	.10	.05
❑ 288 Yonel Jourdain	.10	.05
❑ 289 Brian DeMarco	.10	.05
❑ 290 Reggie White	.30	.14
❑ 291 Kevin Williams	.10	.05
❑ 292 Gary Plummer	.10	.05
❑ 293 Terrance Shaw	.10	.05
❑ 294 Calvin Williams	.10	.05
❑ 295 Eddie Robinson	.10	.05
❑ 296 Tony McGee	.10	.05
❑ 297 Clay Matthews	.10	.05
❑ 298 Joe Cain	.10	.05
❑ 299 Tim McKyer	.10	.05
❑ 300 Greg Lloyd	.20	.09
❑ 301 Steve Wisniewski	.10	.05
❑ 302 Ray Buchanan	.10	.05
❑ 303 Lake Dawson	.10	.05
❑ 304 Kevin Carter	.10	.05
❑ 305 Phillippi Sparks	.10	.05
❑ 306 Emmitt Smith	1.50	.70
❑ 307 Ruben Brown	.10	.05
❑ 308 Tom Carter	.10	.05
❑ 309 William Floyd	.20	.09
❑ 310 Jim Everett	.10	.05
❑ 311 Vincent Brown	.10	.05
❑ 312 Dennis Gibson	.10	.05
❑ 313 Lorenzo Lynch	.10	.05
❑ 314 Corey Harris	.10	.05
❑ 315 James O.Stewart	.20	.09
❑ 316 Kyle Brady	.10	.05
❑ 317 Irving Fryar	.20	.09
❑ 318 Jake Reed	.20	.09
❑ 319 Vinny Testaverde	.20	.09
❑ 320 John Elway	2.00	.90
❑ 321 Tracy Scroggins	.10	.05
❑ 322 Chris Spielman	.10	.05
❑ 323 Horace Copeland	.10	.05
❑ 324 Chris Zorich	.10	.05
❑ 325 Mike Mamula	.10	.05
❑ 326 Henry Ford	.10	.05
❑ 327 Steve Walsh	.10	.05
❑ 328 Stanley Richard	.20	.09
❑ 329 Mike Jones	.10	.05
❑ 330 Jim Harbaugh	.20	.09
❑ 331 Darren Perry	.10	.05
❑ 332 Ken Norton	.10	.05
❑ 333 Kimble Anders	.20	.09
❑ 334 Harold Green	.10	.05
❑ 335 Tyrone Poole	.10	.05
❑ 336 Mark Fields	.10	.05
❑ 337 Darren Bennett	.10	.05
❑ 338 Mike Sherrard	.10	.05
❑ 339 Terry Ray	.10	.05
❑ 340 Bruce Smith	.20	.09
❑ 341 Daryl Johnston	.20	.09
❑ 342 Vinnie Clark	.10	.05
❑ 343 Mike Caldwell	.10	.05
❑ 344 Vinson Smith	.10	.05
❑ 345 Mo Lewis	.10	.05
❑ 346 Brian Blades	.10	.05
❑ 347 Rod Stephens	.10	.05
❑ 348 David Palmer	.10	.05
❑ 349 Blaine Bishop	.10	.05
❑ 350 Jeff George	.20	.09
❑ 351 George Teague	.10	.05
❑ 352 Jeff Hostetler	.10	.05
❑ 353 Michael Strahan	.10	.05
❑ 354 Eric Davis	.10	.05
❑ 355 Jerome Bettis	.30	.14
❑ 356 Irv Smith	.10	.05
❑ 357 Jeff Herrod	.10	.05
❑ 358 Jay Novacek	.10	.05
❑ 359 Bryce Paup	.10	.05
❑ 360 Neil O'Donnell	.20	.09
❑ 361 Eric Swann	.10	.05
❑ 362 Corey Sawyer	.10	.05
❑ 363 Ty Law	.10	.05
❑ 364 Bo Orlando	.10	.05
❑ 365 Marcus Allen	.30	.14
❑ 366 Mark McMillian	.10	.05
❑ 367 Mark Carrier WR	.10	.05
❑ 368 Jackie Harris	.10	.05
❑ 369 Steve Atwater	.10	.05
❑ 370 Steve Young	.75	.35
❑ 371 Brett Favre TYC	1.00	.45
❑ 372 Scott Mitchell TYC	.10	.05
❑ 373 Warren Moon TYC	.10	.05
❑ 374 Jeff George TYC	.20	.09
❑ 375 Jim Everett TYC	.10	.05
❑ 376 John Elway TYC	1.00	.45
❑ 377 Erik Kramer TYC	.10	.05
❑ 378 Jeff Blake TYC	.20	.09
❑ 379 Dan Marino TYC	1.00	.45
❑ 380 Dave Krieg TYC	.10	.05
❑ 381 Drew Bledsoe TYC	.50	.23
❑ 382 Stan Humphries TYC	.10	.05
❑ 383 Troy Aikman TYC	.50	.23
❑ 384 Steve Young TYC	.35	.16
❑ 385 Jim Kelly TYC	.30	.14
❑ 386 Steve Bono TYC	.10	.05
❑ 387 David Sloan	.10	.05
❑ 388 Jeff Graham	.10	.05
❑ 389 Hugh Douglas	.10	.05
❑ 390 Dan Marino	2.00	.90
❑ 391 Winston Moss	.10	.05
❑ 392 Darrell Green	.10	.05
❑ 393 Mark Stepnoski	.10	.05
❑ 394 Bert Emanuel	.20	.09
❑ 395 Eric Zeier	.10	.05
❑ 396 Willie Jackson	.10	.05
❑ 397 Qadry Ismail	.10	.05
❑ 398 Michael Brooks	.10	.05
❑ 399 D'Marco Farr	.10	.05
❑ 400 Brett Favre	2.00	.90
❑ 401 Carnell Lake	.10	.05
❑ 402 Pat Swilling	.10	.05
❑ 403 Stephen Grant	.10	.05
❑ 404 Steve Tasker	.10	.05
❑ 405 Ben Coates	.20	.09
❑ 406 Steve Tovar	.10	.05
❑ 407 Tony Martin	.20	.09
❑ 408 Greg Hill	.20	.09
❑ 409 Eric Guliford	.10	.05
❑ 410 Michael Irvin	.30	.14
❑ 411 Eric Hill	.10	.05
❑ 412 Mario Bates	.20	.09
❑ 413 Brian Stablein RC	.10	.05
❑ 414 Marcus Jones RC	.10	.05
❑ 415 Reggie Brown LB RC	.10	.05
❑ 416 Lawrence Phillips RC	.50	.23
❑ 417 Alex Van Dyke RC	.20	.09
❑ 418 Daryl Gardener RC	.10	.05
❑ 419 Mike Alstott RC	1.25	.55
❑ 420 Kevin Hardy RC	.30	.14
❑ 421 Rickey Dudley RC	.30	.14
❑ 422 Jerome Woods RC	.10	.05
❑ 423 Eric Moulds RC	1.50	.70
❑ 424 Cedric Jones RC	.10	.05
❑ 425 Simeon Rice RC	.30	.14
❑ 426 Marvin Harrison RC	2.00	.90
❑ 427 Tim Biakabutuka RC	.75	.35
❑ 428 Duane Clemons RC	.10	.05
❑ 429 Alex Molden RC	.10	.05
❑ 430 Keyshawn Johnson RC	2.00	.90
❑ 431 Willie Anderson RC	.10	.05
❑ 432 John Mobley RC	.10	.05
❑ 433 Leeland McElroy RC	.30	.14
❑ 434 Regan Upshaw RC	.10	.05
❑ 435 Eddie George RC	3.00	1.35
❑ 436 Jonathan Ogden RC	.10	.05
❑ 437 Eddie Kennison RC	.30	.14
❑ 438 Jermane Mayberry RC	.10	.05
❑ 439 Checklist 1 of 2	.10	.05
❑ 440 Checklist 2 of 2	.10	.05
❑ P1 Joe Namath Promo Steve Young	15.00	6.75
❑ P1R Joe Namath Promo Steve Young (Refractor version)	20.00	9.00

1996 Topps Broadway's Reviews

	MINT	NRMT
COMPLETE SET (10)	25.00	11.00
STATED ODDS 1:12H, 1:8R, 1:3J, 1:6 SP.RET		
❑ BR1 Kerry Collins	1.00	.45
❑ BR2 Drew Bledsoe	3.00	1.35
❑ BR3 Jeff Blake	1.00	.45

❑ BR4 Brett Favre	6.00	2.70
❑ BR5 Scott Mitchell	.60	.25
❑ BR6 Troy Aikman	3.00	1.35
❑ BR7 Steve Young	2.50	1.10
❑ BR8 Jim Harbaugh	.60	.25
❑ BR9 John Elway	6.00	2.70
❑ BR10 Dan Marino	6.00	2.70

1996 Topps 40th Anniversary Retros

	MINT	NRMT
COMPLETE SET (40)	75.00	34.00
STATED ODDS 1:6 HOB, 1:4 RET, 1:4 SP.RET		
❑ 1 Jim Harbaugh 1956	.75	.35
❑ 2 Greg Lloyd 1957	.75	.35
❑ 3 Barry Sanders 1958	8.00	3.60
❑ 4 Merton Hanks 1959	.75	.35
❑ 5 Herman Moore 1960	2.00	.90
❑ 6 Tim Brown 1961	1.25	.55
❑ 7 Brett Favre 1962	8.00	3.60
❑ 8 Cris Carter 1963	1.25	.55
❑ 9 Curtis Martin 1964	5.00	2.20
❑ 10 Bryce Paup 1965	.75	.35
❑ 11 Steve Bono 1966	.75	.35
❑ 12 Blaine Bishop 1967	.75	.35
❑ 13 Emmitt Smith 1968	6.00	2.70
❑ 14 Carnell Lake 1969	.75	.35
❑ 15 Marshall Faulk 1970	1.50	.70
❑ 16 Mike Morris 1971	.75	.35
❑ 17 Shannon Sharpe 1972	2.00	.90
❑ 18 Steve Young 1973	3.00	1.35
❑ 19 Jeff George 1974	1.25	.55
❑ 20 Junior Seau 1975	1.25	.55
❑ 21 Chris Warren 1976	.75	.35
❑ 22 Heath Shuler 1977	1.25	.55
❑ 23 Jeff Blake 1978	1.25	.55
❑ 24 Reggie White 1979	2.00	.90
❑ 25 Jeff Hostetler 1980	.75	.35
❑ 26 Errict Rhett 1981	1.25	.55
❑ 27 Rodney Hampton 1982	1.25	.55
❑ 28 Jerry Rice 1983	4.00	1.80
❑ 29 Jim Everett 1984	.75	.35
❑ 30 Isaac Bruce 1985	2.00	.90
❑ 31 Dan Marino 1986	8.00	3.60
❑ 32 Marcus Allen 1987	2.00	.90
❑ 33 Erik Kramer 1988	.75	.35
❑ 34 John Elway 1989	5.00	2.20
❑ 35 Ricky Watters 1990	1.25	.55
❑ 36 Troy Aikman 1991	4.00	1.80
❑ 37 Drew Bledsoe 1992	4.00	1.80
❑ 38 Scott Mitchell 1993	.75	.35
❑ 39 Rashaan Salaam 1994	.75	.35
❑ 40 Kerry Collins 1995	1.25	.55

1996 Topps Hobby Masters

	MINT	NRMT
COMPLETE SET (20)	150.00	70.00
STATED ODDS 1:10 JUMBO		
❑ HM1 Brett Favre	20.00	9.00
❑ HM2 Emmitt Smith	15.00	6.75
❑ HM3 Drew Bledsoe	10.00	4.50
❑ HM4 Marshall Faulk	3.00	1.35
❑ HM5 Steve Young	8.00	3.60
❑ HM6 Barry Sanders	20.00	9.00
❑ HM7 Troy Aikman	10.00	4.50
❑ HM8 Jerry Rice	10.00	4.50
❑ HM9 Michael Irvin	3.00	1.35
❑ HM10 Dan Marino	20.00	9.00
❑ HM11 Chris Warren	2.00	.90
❑ HM12 Reggie White	3.00	1.35
❑ HM13 Jeff Blake	3.00	1.35
❑ HM14 Greg Lloyd	2.00	.90
❑ HM15 Curtis Martin	8.00	3.60
❑ HM16 Junior Seau	2.00	.90
❑ HM17 Kerry Collins	3.00	1.35
❑ HM18 Deion Sanders	6.00	2.70
❑ HM19 Joey Galloway	8.00	3.60
❑ HM20 John Elway	20.00	9.00

1996 Topps Namath Reprint

	MINT	NRMT
COMPLETE SET (10)	50.00	22.00
COMMON NAMATH (1-10)	6.00	2.70
NAMATH 1965 (1)	8.00	3.60
NAM.ODDS 1:18H,1:12R,1:5J,1:12 SP.RET		
FOUR PER CEREAL FACT.SET		
❑ 1 Joe Namath 1965 (standard sized card)	8.00	3.60
❑ 2 Joe Namath 1966	6.00	2.70
❑ 3 Joe Namath 1967	6.00	2.70
❑ 4 Joe Namath 1968	6.00	2.70
❑ 5 Joe Namath 1969	6.00	2.70
❑ 6 Joe Namath 1970	6.00	2.70
❑ 7 Joe Namath 1971	6.00	2.70
❑ 8 Joe Namath 1972	6.00	2.70
❑ 9 Joe Namath 1972	6.00	2.70
❑ 10 Joe Namath 1973	6.00	2.70
❑ NNO Joe Namath 1965 (large 1965 Topps size)	4.00	1.80

1996 Topps Turf Warriors

	MINT	NRMT
COMPLETE SET (22)	125.00	55.00
STAT.ODDS 1:36 HOB, 1:24 RET, 1:18 SP.RET		
❑ TW1 Bryce Paup	1.00	.45
❑ TW2 Ben Coates	2.00	.90
❑ TW3 Jim Harbaugh	2.00	.90
❑ TW4 Brian Mitchell	1.00	.45
❑ TW5 Brett Favre	20.00	9.00
❑ TW6 Junior Seau	2.00	.90
❑ TW7 Michael Irvin	3.00	1.35
❑ TW8 Steve Young	8.00	3.60
❑ TW9 Terry McDaniel	1.00	.45
❑ TW10 Curtis Martin	8.00	3.60
❑ TW11 Greg Lloyd	2.00	.90
❑ TW12 Cris Carter	3.00	1.35
❑ TW13 Emmitt Smith	15.00	6.75
❑ TW14 Reggie White	3.00	1.35
❑ TW15 Marshall Faulk	3.00	1.35
❑ TW16 Jerry Rice	10.00	4.50
❑ TW17 Shannon Sharpe	2.00	.90
❑ TW18 Dan Marino	20.00	9.00
❑ TW19 Ken Norton	1.00	.45
❑ TW20 Barry Sanders	20.00	9.00
❑ TW21 Neil Smith	1.00	.45
❑ TW22 Troy Aikman	10.00	4.50

1997 Topps

	MINT	NRMT
COMPLETE SET (415)	40.00	18.00
COMP.FACT.SET (424)	60.00	27.00
COMMON CARD (1-385)	.10	.05
SEMISTARS	.20	.09
UNLISTED STARS	.40	.18
COMMON ROOKIE (386-415)	.30	.14
ROOKIE SEMISTARS	.50	.23
ROOKIE UNL.STARS	.75	.35
DRAFT PICK ODDS 1:3 HOB, 1:1 JUM		

COMP.MINT.CANTON (415) 700.00 325.00
*STARS: 6X TO 12X HI COLUMN
*RCs: 1.5X TO 3X HI
MINTED IN CANTON STATED ODDS 1:6

	No.	Player	Hi	Lo
❑	1	Brett Favre	2.00	.90
❑	2	Lawyer Milloy	.10	.05
❑	3	Tim Biakabutuka	.20	.09
❑	4	Clyde Simmons	.10	.05
❑	5	Deion Sanders	.40	.18
❑	6	Anthony Miller	.10	.05
❑	7	Marquez Pope	.10	.05
❑	8	Mike Tomczak	.10	.05
❑	9	William Thomas	.10	.05
❑	10	Marshall Faulk	.40	.18
❑	11	John Randle	.10	.05
❑	12	Jim Kelly	.40	.18
❑	13	Steve Bono	.20	.09
❑	14	Rod Stephens	.10	.05
❑	15	Stan Humphries	.20	.09
❑	16	Terrell Buckley	.10	.05
❑	17	Ki-Jana Carter	.10	.05
❑	18	Marcus Robertson	.10	.05
❑	19	Corey Harris	.10	.05
❑	20	Rashaan Salaam	.10	.05
❑	21	Rickey Dudley	.20	.09
❑	22	Jamir Miller	.10	.05
❑	23	Martin Mayhew	.10	.05
❑	24	Jason Sehorn	.20	.09
❑	25	Isaac Bruce	.40	.18
❑	26	Johnnie Morton	.20	.09
❑	27	Antonio Langham	.10	.05
❑	28	Cornelius Bennett	.10	.05
❑	29	Joe Johnson	.10	.05
❑	30	Keyshawn Johnson	.40	.18
❑	31	Willie Green	.10	.05
❑	32	Craig Newsome	.10	.05
❑	33	Brock Marion	.10	.05
❑	34	Corey Fuller	.10	.05
❑	35	Ben Coates	.20	.09
❑	36	Ty Detmer	.20	.09
❑	37	Charles Johnson	.20	.09
❑	38	Willie Jackson	.10	.05
❑	39	Tyronne Drakeford	.10	.05
❑	40	Gus Frerotte	.10	.05
❑	41	Robert Blackmon	.10	.05
❑	42	Andre Coleman	.10	.05
❑	43	Mario Bates	.10	.05
❑	44	Chris Calloway	.10	.05
❑	45	Terry McDaniel	.10	.05
❑	46	Anthony Davis	.10	.05
❑	47	Stanley Pritchett	.10	.05
❑	48	Ray Buchanan	.10	.05
❑	49	Chris Chandler	.20	.09
❑	50	Ashley Ambrose	.10	.05
❑	51	Tyrone Braxton	.10	.05
❑	52	Pepper Johnson	.10	.05
❑	53	Frank Sanders	.20	.09
❑	54	Clay Matthews	.10	.05
❑	55	Bruce Smith	.20	.09
❑	56	Jermaine Lewis	.40	.18
❑	57	Mark Carrier WR UER (features the cardback for Mark Carrier DB)	.10	.05
❑	58	Jeff Graham	.10	.05
❑	59	Keith Lyle	.10	.05
❑	60	Trent Dilfer	.40	.18
❑	61	Trace Armstrong	.10	.05
❑	62	Jeff Herrod	.10	.05
❑	63	Tyrone Wheatley	.20	.09
❑	64	Torrance Small	.10	.05
❑	65	Chris Warren	.20	.09
❑	66	Terry Kirby	.20	.09
❑	67	Erric Pegram	.10	.05
❑	68	Sean Gilbert	.10	.05
❑	69	Greg Biekert	.10	.05
❑	70	Ricky Watters	.20	.09
❑	71	Chris Hudson	.10	.05
❑	72	Tamarick Vanover	.20	.09
❑	73	Orlando Thomas	.10	.05
❑	74	Jimmy Spencer	.10	.05
❑	75	John Mobley	.10	.05
❑	76	Henry Thomas	.10	.05
❑	77	Santana Dotson	.10	.05
❑	78	Boomer Esiason	.20	.09
❑	79	Bobby Hebert	.10	.05
❑	80	Kerry Collins	.20	.09
❑	81	Bobby Engram	.20	.09
❑	82	Kevin Smith	.10	.05
❑	83	Rick Mirer	.10	.05
❑	84	Ted Johnson	.10	.05
❑	85	Derrick Alexander WR	.20	.09
❑	86	Hugh Douglas	.10	.05
❑	87	Rodney Harrison	.10	.05
❑	88	Roman Phifer	.10	.05
❑	89	Warren Moon	.40	.18
❑	90	Thurman Thomas	.40	.18
❑	91	Michael McCrary	.10	.05
❑	92	Dana Stubblefield	.10	.05
❑	93	Andre Hastings UER front reads Hasting	.10	.05
❑	94	William Fuller	.10	.05
❑	95	Jeff Hostetler	.10	.05
❑	96	Danny Kanell	.20	.09
❑	97	Mark Fields	.10	.05
❑	98	Eddie Robinson	.10	.05
❑	99	Daryl Gardener	.10	.05
❑	100	Drew Bledsoe	1.00	.45
❑	101	Winslow Oliver	.10	.05
❑	102	Raymont Harris	.10	.05
❑	103	LeShon Johnson	.10	.05
❑	104	Byron Bam Morris	.10	.05
❑	105	Herman Moore	.40	.18
❑	106	Keith Jackson	.10	.05
❑	107	Chris Penn	.10	.05
❑	108	Robert Griffith RC	.10	.05
❑	109	Jeff Burris	.10	.05
❑	110	Troy Aikman	1.00	.45
❑	111	Allen Aldridge	.10	.05
❑	112	Mel Gray	.10	.05
❑	113	Aaron Bailey	.10	.05
❑	114	Michael Strahan	.10	.05
❑	115	Adrian Murrell	.20	.09
❑	116	Chris Mims	.10	.05
❑	117	Robert Jones	.10	.05
❑	118	Derrick Brooks	.10	.05
❑	119	Tom Carter	.10	.05
❑	120	Carl Pickens	.40	.18
❑	121	Tony Brackens	.10	.05
❑	122	O.J. McDuffie	.20	.09
❑	123	Napoleon Kaufman	.40	.18
❑	124	Chris T. Jones	.10	.05
❑	125	Kordell Stewart	.50	.23
❑	126	Ray Zellars	.10	.05
❑	127	Jessie Tuggle	.10	.05
❑	128	Greg Kragen	.10	.05
❑	129	Brett Perriman	.10	.05
❑	130	Steve Young	.60	.25
❑	131	Willie Clay	.10	.05
❑	132	Kimble Anders	.20	.09
❑	133	Eugene Daniel	.10	.05
❑	134	Jevon Langford	.10	.05
❑	135	Shannon Sharpe	.20	.09
❑	136	Wayne Simmons	.10	.05
❑	137	Leeland McElroy	.10	.05
❑	138	Mike Caldwell	.10	.05
❑	139	Eric Moulds	.40	.18
❑	140	Eddie George	1.00	.45
❑	141	Jamal Anderson	.60	.25
❑	142	Michael Timpson	.10	.05
❑	143	Tony Tolbert	.10	.05
❑	144	Robert Smith	.20	.09
❑	145	Mike Alstott	.40	.18
❑	146	Gary Jones	.10	.05
❑	147	Terrance Shaw	.10	.05
❑	148	Carlton Gray	.10	.05
❑	149	Kevin Carter	.10	.05
❑	150	Darrell Green	.20	.09
❑	151	David Dunn	.10	.05
❑	152	Ken Norton	.10	.05
❑	153	Chad Brown	.10	.05
❑	154	Pat Swilling	.10	.05
❑	155	Irving Fryar	.20	.09
❑	156	Michael Haynes	.10	.05
❑	157	Shawn Jefferson	.10	.05
❑	158	Stephen Grant	.10	.05
❑	159	James O.Stewart	.20	.09
❑	160	Derrick Thomas	.20	.09
❑	161	Tim Bowens	.10	.05
❑	162	Dixon Edwards	.10	.05
❑	163	Micheal Barrow	.10	.05
❑	164	Antonio Freeman	.50	.23
❑	165	Terrell Davis	1.50	.70
❑	166	Henry Ellard	.10	.05
❑	167	Daryl Johnston	.20	.09
❑	168	Bryan Cox	.10	.05
❑	169	Chad Cota	.10	.05
❑	170	Vinny Testaverde	.20	.09
❑	171	Andre Reed	.20	.09
❑	172	Larry Centers	.20	.09
❑	173	Craig Heyward	.10	.05
❑	174	Glyn Milburn	.10	.05
❑	175	Hardy Nickerson	.10	.05
❑	176	Corey Miller	.10	.05
❑	177	Bobby Houston	.10	.05
❑	178	Marco Coleman	.10	.05
❑	179	Winston Moss	.10	.05
❑	180	Tony Banks	.20	.09
❑	181	Jeff Lageman	.10	.05
❑	182	Jason Belser	.10	.05
❑	183	James Jett	.20	.09
❑	184	Wayne Martin	.10	.05
❑	185	Dave Meggett	.10	.05
❑	186	Terrell Owens	.40	.18
❑	187	Willie Williams	.10	.05
❑	188	Eric Turner	.10	.05
❑	189	Chuck Smith	.10	.05
❑	190	Simeon Rice	.20	.09
❑	191	Kevin Greene	.20	.09
❑	192	Lance Johnstone	.10	.05
❑	193	Marty Carter	.10	.05
❑	194	Ricardo McDonald	.10	.05
❑	195	Michael Irvin	.40	.18
❑	196	George Koonce	.10	.05
❑	197	Robert Porcher	.10	.05
❑	198	Mark Collins	.10	.05
❑	199	Louis Oliver	.10	.05
❑	200	John Elway	2.00	.90
❑	201	Jake Reed	.20	.09
❑	202	Rodney Hampton	.20	.09
❑	203	Aaron Glenn	.10	.05
❑	204	Mike Mamula	.10	.05
❑	205	Terry Allen	.40	.18
❑	206	John Lynch	.10	.05
❑	207	Todd Lyght	.10	.05
❑	208	Dean Wells	.10	.05
❑	209	Aaron Hayden	.10	.05
❑	210	Blaine Bishop	.10	.05
❑	211	Bert Emanuel	.20	.09
❑	212	Mark Carrier DB UER (features the cardback for Mark Carrier WR)	.10	.05
❑	213	Dale Carter	.10	.05
❑	214	Jimmy Smith	.20	.09
❑	215	Jim Harbaugh	.20	.09
❑	216	Jeff George	.20	.09
❑	217	Anthony Newman	.10	.05
❑	218	Ty Law	.10	.05
❑	219	Brent Jones	.20	.09
❑	220	Emmitt Smith	1.50	.70
❑	221	Bennie Blades	.10	.05
❑	222	Alfred Williams	.10	.05
❑	223	Eugene Robinson	.10	.05
❑	224	Fred Barnett	.10	.05
❑	225	Errict Rhett	.10	.05
❑	226	Leslie O'Neal	.10	.05
❑	227	Michael Sinclair	.10	.05
❑	228	Marvcus Patton	.10	.05
❑	229	Darrien Gordon	.10	.05
❑	230	Jerome Bettis	.40	.18
❑	231	Troy Vincent	.10	.05
❑	232	Ray Mickens	.10	.05
❑	233	Lonnie Johnson	.10	.05
❑	234	Charles Way	.20	.09
❑	235	Chris Sanders	.10	.05
❑	236	Bracey Walker	.10	.05
❑	237	Dave Krieg UER front has Bears logo	.10	.05
❑	238	Kent Graham	.10	.05
❑	239	Ray Lewis	.10	.05
❑	240	Cris Carter	.40	.18
❑	241	Elvis Grbac	.20	.09
❑	242	Eric Davis	.10	.05
❑	243	Harvey Williams	.10	.05
❑	244	Eric Allen	.10	.05
❑	245	Bryant Young	.10	.05
❑	246	Terrell Fletcher	.10	.05
❑	247	Darren Perry	.10	.05

Card	Player	MINT	NRMT
❑ 248	Ken Harvey	.10	.05
❑ 249	Marvin Washington	.10	.05
❑ 250	Marcus Allen	.40	.18
❑ 251	Darrin Smith	.10	.05
❑ 252	James Francis	.10	.05
❑ 253	Michael Jackson	.20	.09
❑ 254	Ryan McNeil	.10	.05
❑ 255	Mark Chmura	.20	.09
❑ 256	Keenan McCardell	.20	.09
❑ 257	Tony Bennett	.10	.05
❑ 258	Irving Spikes	.10	.05
❑ 259	Jason Dunn	.10	.05
❑ 260	Joey Galloway	.50	.23
❑ 261	Eddie Kennison	.20	.09
❑ 262	Lonnie Marts	.10	.05
❑ 263	Thomas Lewis	.10	.05
❑ 264	Tedy Bruschi	.10	.05
❑ 265	Steve Atwater	.10	.05
❑ 266	Dorsey Levens	.40	.18
❑ 267	Kurt Schulz	.10	.05
❑ 268	Rob Moore	.20	.09
❑ 269	Walt Harris	.10	.05
❑ 270	Steve McNair	.50	.23
❑ 271	Bill Romanowski	.10	.05
❑ 272	Sean Dawkins	.10	.05
❑ 273	Don Beebe	.10	.05
❑ 274	Fernando Smith	.10	.05
❑ 275	Willie McGinest	.10	.05
❑ 276	Levon Kirkland	.10	.05
❑ 277	Tony Martin	.20	.09
❑ 278	Warren Sapp	.20	.09
❑ 279	Lamar Smith	.10	.05
❑ 280	Mark Brunell	1.00	.45
❑ 281	Jim Everett	.10	.05
❑ 282	Victor Green	.10	.05
❑ 283	Mike Jones	.10	.05
❑ 284	Charlie Garner	.10	.05
❑ 285	Karim Abdul-Jabbar	.40	.18
❑ 286	Michael Westbrook	.20	.09
❑ 287	Lawrence Phillips	.10	.05
❑ 288	Amani Toomer	.20	.09
❑ 289	Neil Smith	.20	.09
❑ 290	Barry Sanders	2.00	.90
❑ 291	Willie Davis	.10	.05
❑ 292	Bo Orlando	.10	.05
❑ 293	Alonzo Spellman	.10	.05
❑ 294	Eric Hill	.10	.05
❑ 295	Wesley Walls	.20	.09
❑ 296	Todd Collins	.10	.05
❑ 297	Stevon Moore	.10	.05
❑ 298	Eric Metcalf	.20	.09
❑ 299	Darren Woodson	.10	.05
❑ 300	Jerry Rice	1.00	.45
❑ 301	Scott Mitchell	.20	.09
❑ 302	Ray Crockett	.10	.05
❑ 303	Jim Schwantz RC UER back reads Schwartz	.10	.05
❑ 304	Steve Tovar	.10	.05
❑ 305	Terance Mathis	.20	.09
❑ 306	Earnest Byner	.10	.05
❑ 307	Chris Spielman	.10	.05
❑ 308	Curtis Conway	.20	.09
❑ 309	Cris Dishman	.10	.05
❑ 310	Marvin Harrison	.40	.18
❑ 311	Sam Mills	.10	.05
❑ 312	Brent Alexander RC	.10	.05
❑ 313	Shawn Wooden	.10	.05
❑ 314	Dewayne Washington	.10	.05
❑ 315	Terry Glenn	.40	.18
❑ 316	Winfred Tubbs	.10	.05
❑ 317	Dave Brown	.10	.05
❑ 318	Neil O'Donnell	.20	.09
❑ 319	Anthony Parker	.10	.05
❑ 320	Junior Seau	.20	.09
❑ 321	Brian Mitchell	.10	.05
❑ 322	Regan Upshaw	.10	.05
❑ 323	Darryl Williams	.10	.05
❑ 324	Chris Doleman	.10	.05
❑ 325	Rod Woodson	.20	.09
❑ 326	Derrick Witherspoon	.10	.05
❑ 327	Chester McGlockton	.10	.05
❑ 328	Mickey Washington	.10	.05
❑ 329	Greg Hill	.10	.05
❑ 330	Reggie White	.40	.18
❑ 331	John Copeland	.10	.05
❑ 332	Doug Evans	.10	.05
❑ 333	Lamar Lathon	.10	.05
❑ 334	Mark Maddox	.10	.05
❑ 335	Natrone Means	.40	.18
❑ 336	Corey Widmer	.10	.05
❑ 337	Terry Wooden	.10	.05
❑ 338	Merton Hanks	.10	.05
❑ 339	Cortez Kennedy	.10	.05
❑ 340	Tyrone Hughes	.10	.05
❑ 341	Tim Brown	.40	.18
❑ 342	John Jurkovic	.10	.05
❑ 343	Carnell Lake	.10	.05
❑ 344	Stanley Richard	.10	.05
❑ 345	Darryll Lewis	.10	.05
❑ 346	Dan Wilkinson	.10	.05
❑ 347	Broderick Thomas	.10	.05
❑ 348	Brian Williams	.10	.05
❑ 349	Eric Swann	.10	.05
❑ 350	Dan Marino	2.00	.90
❑ 351	Anthony Johnson	.10	.05
❑ 352	Joe Cain	.10	.05
❑ 353	Quinn Early	.10	.05
❑ 354	Seth Joyner	.10	.05
❑ 355	Garrison Hearst	.20	.09
❑ 356	Edgar Bennett	.20	.09
❑ 357	Brian Washington	.10	.05
❑ 358	Kevin Hardy	.10	.05
❑ 359	Quentin Coryatt	.10	.05
❑ 360	Tim McDonald	.10	.05
❑ 361	Brian Blades	.10	.05
❑ 362	Courtney Hawkins	.10	.05
❑ 363	Ray Farmer	.10	.05
❑ 364	Jessie Armstead	.10	.05
❑ 365	Curtis Martin	.50	.23
❑ 366	Zach Thomas	.20	.09
❑ 367	Frank Wycheck	.10	.05
❑ 368	Darnay Scott	.20	.09
❑ 369	Percy Ellsworth	.10	.05
❑ 370	Desmond Howard	.20	.09
❑ 371	Aeneas Williams	.10	.05
❑ 372	Bryce Paup	.10	.05
❑ 373	Michael Bates	.10	.05
❑ 374	Brad Johnson	.50	.23
❑ 375	Jeff Blake	.20	.09
❑ 376	Donnell Woolford UER front photo incorrect	.10	.05
❑ 377	Mo Lewis	.10	.05
❑ 378	Phillippi Sparks	.10	.05
❑ 379	Michael Bankston	.10	.05
❑ 380	LeRoy Butler	.10	.05
❑ 381	Tyrone Poole	.10	.05
❑ 382	Wayne Chrebet	.40	.18
❑ 383	Chris Slade	.10	.05
❑ 384	Checklist 1 (1-208)	.10	.05
❑ 385	Checklist 2 (209-415)	.10	.05
❑ 386	Will Blackwell RC SP	.40	.18
❑ 387	Tom Knight RC SP	.10	.05
❑ 388	Darnell Autry RC SP	.50	.23
❑ 389	Bryant Westbrook RC SP	.10	.05
❑ 390	David LaFleur RC SP	.50	.23
❑ 391	Antowain Smith RC SP	2.00	.90
❑ 392	Kevin Lockett RC SP	.50	.23
❑ 393	Rae Carruth RC SP	.75	.35
❑ 394	Renaldo Wynn RC SP	.30	.14
❑ 395	Jim Druckenmiller RC SP	1.00	.45
❑ 396	Kenny Holmes RC SP	.30	.14
❑ 397	Shawn Springs RC SP	.50	.23
❑ 398	Troy Davis RC SP	.75	.35
❑ 399	Dwayne Rudd RC SP	.30	.14
❑ 400	Orlando Pace RC SP	.30	.14
❑ 401	Byron Hanspard RC SP	1.50	.70
❑ 402	Corey Dillon RC SP	4.00	1.80
❑ 403	Walter Jones RC SP	.30	.14
❑ 404	Reidel Anthony RC SP	1.50	.70
❑ 405	Peter Boulware RC SP	.50	.23
❑ 406	Reinard Wilson RC SP	.30	.14
❑ 407	Pat Barnes RC SP	.75	.35
❑ 408	Yatil Green RC SP	.75	.35
❑ 409	Joey Kent RC SP	.75	.35
❑ 410	Ike Hilliard RC SP	1.50	.70
❑ 411	Jake Plummer RC SP	8.00	3.60
❑ 412	Darrell Russell RC SP	.30	.14
❑ 413	James Farrior RC SP	.30	.14
❑ 414	Tony Gonzalez RC SP	3.00	1.35
❑ 415	Warrick Dunn RC SP	3.00	1.35
❑ P40	Gus Frerotte Promo green border on back	.25	.11
❑ P170	V.Testaverde Promo green border on back	.25	.11
❑ P240	Cris Carter Promo green border on back	.40	.18
❑ P250	Marcus Allen Promo green border on back	.40	.18
❑ P285	Karim Abdul-Jabbar Promo green border on back	.40	.18
❑ P356	Edgar Bennett Promo green border on back	.25	.11

1997 Topps Career Best

	MINT	NRMT
COMPLETE SET (5)	50.00	22.00
RANDOM INSERTS IN PACKS		
❑ 1 Dan Marino	25.00	11.00
❑ 2 Marcus Allen	5.00	2.20
❑ 3 Marcus Allen	5.00	2.20
❑ 4 Reggie White	5.00	2.20
❑ 5 Jerry Rice	12.00	5.50

1997 Topps Hall Bound

	MINT	NRMT
COMPLETE SET (15)	100.00	45.00
STATED ODDS 1:36 HOB, 1:8 JUM		
❑ HB1 Jerry Rice	10.00	4.50
❑ HB2 Rod Woodson	2.00	.90
❑ HB3 Marcus Allen	4.00	1.80
❑ HB4 Reggie White	4.00	1.80
❑ HB5 Emmitt Smith	15.00	6.75
❑ HB6 Junior Seau	2.00	.90
❑ HB7 Troy Aikman	10.00	4.50
❑ HB8 Bruce Smith	2.00	.90
❑ HB9 John Elway	20.00	9.00
❑ HB10 Brett Favre	20.00	9.00
❑ HB11 Thurman Thomas	4.00	1.80
❑ HB12 Deion Sanders	4.00	1.80
❑ HB13 Dan Marino	20.00	9.00
❑ HB14 Steve Young	6.00	2.70
❑ HB15 Barry Sanders	20.00	9.00

1997 Topps Autographs

	MINT	NRMT
COMPLETE SET (12)	400.00	180.00
COMMON CARD	20.00	9.00
SEMISTARS	30.00	13.50

CURRENT PLAYER ODDS 1:218H,1:60J
SEAU ODDS 1:364 HOB, 1:100 JUM
HAYNES/WEBSTER ODDS 1:436H,1:120J
MARA ODDS 1:872 HOB,1:240 JUM
SHULA ODDS 1:290HOB,1:80 JUM

Card	MINT	NRMT
❑ 1 Karim Abdul-Jabbar	40.00	18.00
❑ 2 Terrell Davis	80.00	36.00
❑ 3 Eddie George	40.00	18.00
❑ 4 Jim Harbaugh	30.00	13.50
❑ 5 Desmond Howard	20.00	9.00
❑ 6 Herman Moore	40.00	18.00
❑ 7 Junior Seau	30.00	13.50
❑ 8 Chris Warren	30.00	13.50
❑ HF1 Mike Haynes (1989 Topps style)	30.00	13.50
❑ HF2 Don Shula (1972 Topps style)	60.00	27.00
❑ HF3 Wellington Mara (1986 Topps style)	80.00	36.00
❑ HF4 Mike Webster (1988 Topps style)	30.00	13.50

1997 Topps High Octane

	MINT	NRMT
COMPLETE SET (15)	100.00	45.00

STATED ODDS 1:36 HOB, 1:8 JUM

Card	MINT	NRMT
❑ HO1 Brett Favre	20.00	9.00
❑ HO2 Jerome Bettis	4.00	1.80
❑ HO3 Jerry Rice	10.00	4.50
❑ HO4 Junior Seau	2.00	.90
❑ HO5 Emmitt Smith	15.00	6.75
❑ HO6 Herman Moore	4.00	1.80
❑ HO7 Shannon Sharpe	2.00	.90
❑ HO8 Curtis Martin	5.00	2.20
❑ HO9 Eddie George	10.00	4.50
❑ HO10 Barry Sanders	20.00	9.00
❑ HO11 John Elway	20.00	9.00
❑ HO12 Steve Young	6.00	2.70
❑ HO13 Drew Bledsoe	10.00	4.50
❑ HO14 Troy Aikman	10.00	4.50
❑ HO15 Dan Marino	20.00	9.00

1997 Topps Mystery Finest Bronze

	MINT	NRMT
COMP.BRONZE SET (20)	80.00	36.00

BRONZE STATED ODDS 1:36 HOB, 1:8 JUM
*BRONZE REFRACTORS: 10X TO 25X BASE CARD HI
BRONZE REF.ODDS 1:144 HOB, 1:38 JUM
*GOLDS: 12X TO 30X BASE CARD HI
GOLD STATED ODDS 1:324 HOB, 1:88 JUM
*GOLD REFRACTORS: 50X TO 120 BASE CARD HI
GOLD REF.ODDS 1:1296 HOB, 1:354 JUM
*SILVERS: 5X TO 12X BASE CARD HI
SILVER STATED ODDS 1:108 HOB, 1:28 JUM
*SILVER REFRACT: 15X TO 40X BASE CARD HI
SILVER REF.ODDS 1:432 HOB, 1:116 JUM

Card	MINT	NRMT
❑ M1 Barry Sanders	12.00	5.50
❑ M2 Mark Brunell	6.00	2.70
❑ M3 Terrell Davis	10.00	4.50
❑ M4 Isaac Bruce	2.50	1.10
❑ M5 Jerry Rice	6.00	2.70
❑ M6 Drew Bledsoe	6.00	2.70
❑ M7 Carl Pickens	2.50	1.10
❑ M8 Steve Young	4.00	1.80
❑ M9 Cris Carter	2.50	1.10
❑ M10 John Elway	12.00	5.50
❑ M11 Junior Seau	1.25	.55
❑ M12 Herman Moore	2.50	1.10
❑ M13 Vinny Testaverde	1.25	.55
❑ M14 Jerome Bettis	2.50	1.10
❑ M15 Troy Aikman	6.00	2.70
❑ M16 Reggie White	2.50	1.10
❑ M17 Kerry Collins	1.25	.55
❑ M18 Curtis Martin	3.00	1.35
❑ M19 Shannon Sharpe	1.25	.55
❑ M20 Brett Favre	12.00	5.50

1997 Topps Season's Best

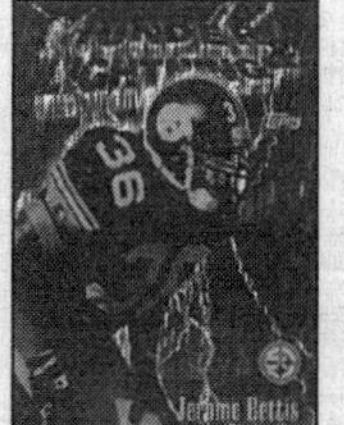

	MINT	NRMT
COMPLETE SET (25)	60.00	27.00

STATED ODDS: 1:16 HOB, 1:4 JUM

Card	MINT	NRMT
❑ 1 Mark Brunell	6.00	2.70
❑ 2 Vinny Testaverde	1.25	.55
❑ 3 Drew Bledsoe	6.00	2.70
❑ 4 Brett Favre	12.00	5.50
❑ 5 Jeff Blake	1.25	.55
❑ 6 Barry Sanders	12.00	5.50
❑ 7 Terrell Davis	10.00	4.50
❑ 8 Jerome Bettis	2.50	1.10
❑ 9 Ricky Watters	1.25	.55
❑ 10 Eddie George	6.00	2.70
❑ 11 Brian Mitchell	.60	.25
❑ 12 Tyrone Hughes	.60	.25
❑ 13 Eric Metcalf	1.25	.55
❑ 14 Glyn Milburn	.60	.25
❑ 15 Ricky Watters	1.25	.55
❑ 16 Kevin Greene	1.25	.55
❑ 17 Lamar Lathon	.60	.25
❑ 18 Bruce Smith	1.25	.55
❑ 19 Michael Sinclair UER (front reads Michael McCrary)	.60	.25
❑ 20 Derrick Thomas	1.25	.55
❑ 21 Jerry Rice	6.00	2.70
❑ 22 Herman Moore	2.50	1.10
❑ 23 Carl Pickens	2.50	1.10
❑ 24 Cris Carter	2.50	1.10
❑ 25 Brett Perriman	.60	.25

1997 Topps Underclassmen

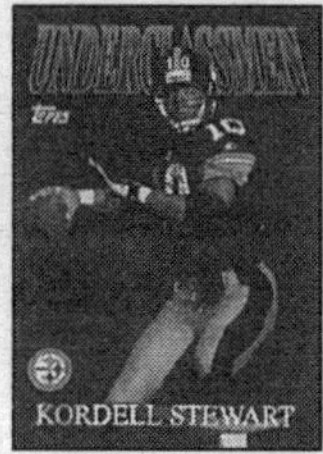

	MINT	NRMT
COMPLETE SET (10)	40.00	18.00

STATED ODDS: 1:24 RET

Card	MINT	NRMT
❑ U1 Kerry Collins	2.50	1.10
❑ U2 Karim Abdul-Jabbar	5.00	2.20
❑ U3 Simeon Rice	2.50	1.10
❑ U4 Keyshawn Johnson	5.00	2.20
❑ U5 Eddie George	12.00	5.50
❑ U6 Eddie Kennison	2.50	1.10
❑ U7 Terry Glenn	5.00	2.20
❑ U8 Kevin Hardy	1.25	.55
❑ U9 Steve McNair	6.00	2.70
❑ U10 Kordell Stewart	6.00	2.70

1998 Topps

	MINT	NRMT
COMPLETE SET (360)	60.00	27.00
COMP.FACT.SET (365)	70.00	32.00
COMMON CARD (1-330)	.10	.05
SEMISTARS	.20	.09
UNLISTED STARS	.40	.18
COMMON ROOKIE (331-360)	1.25	.55
ROOKIE SEMISTARS	2.00	.90
ROOKIE UNLISTED STARS	2.50	1.10

ROOKIE SUBSET ODDS 1:3

Card	MINT	NRMT
❑ 1 Barry Sanders	2.00	.90
❑ 2 Derrick Rodgers	.10	.05
❑ 3 Chris Calloway	.10	.05

❑	4	Bruce Armstrong	.10	.05
❑	5	Horace Copeland	.10	.05
❑	6	Chad Brown	.10	.05
❑	7	Ken Harvey	.10	.05
❑	8	Levon Kirkland	.10	.05
❑	9	Glenn Foley	.20	.09
❑	10	Corey Dillon	.50	.23
❑	11	Sean Dawkins	.10	.05
❑	12	Curtis Conway	.20	.09
❑	13	Chris Chandler	.20	.09
❑	14	Kerry Collins	.20	.09
❑	15	Jonathan Ogden	.10	.05
❑	16	Sam Shade	.10	.05
❑	17	Vaughn Hebron	.10	.05
❑	18	Quentin Coryatt	.10	.05
❑	19	Jerris McPhail	.10	.05
❑	20	Warrick Dunn	.50	.23
❑	21	Wayne Martin	.10	.05
❑	22	Chad Lewis	.10	.05
❑	23	Danny Kanell	.20	.09
❑	24	Shawn Springs	.10	.05
❑	25	Emmitt Smith	1.50	.70
❑	26	Todd Lyght	.10	.05
❑	27	Donnie Edwards	.10	.05
❑	28	Charlie Jones	.10	.05
❑	29	Willie McGinest	.10	.05
❑	30	Steve Young	.50	.23
❑	31	Darrell Russell	.10	.05
❑	32	Gary Anderson	.10	.05
❑	33	Stanley Richard	.10	.05
❑	34	Leslie O'Neal	.10	.05
❑	35	Dermontti Dawson	.10	.05
❑	36	Jeff Brady	.10	.05
❑	37	Kimble Anders	.20	.09
❑	38	Glyn Milburn	.10	.05
❑	39	Greg Hill	.10	.05
❑	40	Freddie Jones	.10	.05
❑	41	Bobby Engram	.20	.09
❑	42	Aeneas Williams	.10	.05
❑	43	Antowain Smith	.40	.18
❑	44	Reggie White	.40	.18
❑	45	Rae Carruth	.20	.09
❑	46	Leon Johnson	.10	.05
❑	47	Bryant Young	.10	.05
❑	48	Jamie Asher	.10	.05
❑	49	Hardy Nickerson	.10	.05
❑	50	Jerome Bettis	.40	.18
❑	51	Michael Strahan	.10	.05
❑	52	John Randle	.20	.09
❑	53	Kevin Hardy	.10	.05
❑	54	Eric Bjornson	.10	.05
❑	55	Morten Andersen UER (misspelled Anderson)	.10	.05
❑	56	Larry Centers	.10	.05
❑	57	Bryce Paup	.10	.05
❑	58	John Mobley	.10	.05
❑	59	Michael Bates	.10	.05
❑	60	Tim Brown	.40	.18
❑	61	Doug Evans	.10	.05
❑	62	Will Shields	.10	.05
❑	63	Jeff Graham	.10	.05
❑	64	Henry Jones	.10	.05
❑	65	Steve Broussard	.10	.05
❑	66	Blaine Bishop	.10	.05
❑	67	Ernie Conwell	.10	.05
❑	68	Heath Shuler	.10	.05
❑	69	Eric Metcalf	.10	.05
❑	70	Terry Glenn	.40	.18
❑	71	James Hasty	.10	.05
❑	72	Robert Porcher	.10	.05
❑	73	Keenan McCardell	.20	.09
❑	74	Tyrone Hughes	.10	.05
❑	75	Troy Aikman	1.00	.45
❑	76	Peter Boulware	.10	.05
❑	77	Rob Johnson	.20	.09
❑	78	Erik Kramer	.10	.05
❑	79	Kevin Smith	.10	.05
❑	80	Andre Rison	.20	.09
❑	81	Jim Harbaugh	.20	.09
❑	82	Chris Hudson	.10	.05
❑	83	Ray Zellars	.10	.05
❑	84	Jeff George	.20	.09
❑	85	Willie Davis	.10	.05
❑	86	Jason Gildon	.10	.05
❑	87	Robert Brooks	.20	.09
❑	88	Chad Cota	.10	.05
❑	89	Simeon Rice	.20	.09
❑	90	Mark Brunell	.75	.35
❑	91	Jay Graham	.10	.05
❑	92	Scott Greene	.10	.05
❑	93	Jeff Blake	.20	.09
❑	94	Jason Belser	.10	.05
❑	95	Derrick Alexander DE	.10	.05
❑	96	Ty Law	.10	.05
❑	97	Charles Johnson	.10	.05
❑	98	James Jett	.20	.09
❑	99	Darrell Green	.20	.09
❑	100	Brett Favre	2.00	.90
❑	101	George Jones	.10	.05
❑	102	Derrick Mason	.10	.05
❑	103	Sam Adams	.10	.05
❑	104	Lawrence Phillips	.10	.05
❑	105	Randal Hill	.10	.05
❑	106	John Mangum	.10	.05
❑	107	Natrone Means	.40	.18
❑	108	Bill Romanowski	.10	.05
❑	109	Terance Mathis	.20	.09
❑	110	Bruce Smith	.20	.09
❑	111	Pete Mitchell	.10	.05
❑	112	Duane Clemons	.10	.05
❑	113	Willie Clay	.10	.05
❑	114	Eric Allen	.10	.05
❑	115	Troy Drayton	.10	.05
❑	116	Derrick Thomas	.20	.09
❑	117	Charles Way	.10	.05
❑	118	Wayne Chrebet	.40	.18
❑	119	Bobby Hoying	.20	.09
❑	120	Michael Jackson	.10	.05
❑	121	Gary Zimmerman	.10	.05
❑	122	Yancey Thigpen	.10	.05
❑	123	Dana Stubblefield	.10	.05
❑	124	Keith Lyle	.10	.05
❑	125	Marco Coleman	.10	.05
❑	126	Karl Williams	.10	.05
❑	127	Stephen Davis	.10	.05
❑	128	Chris Sanders	.10	.05
❑	129	Cris Dishman	.10	.05
❑	130	Jake Plummer	1.00	.45
❑	131	Darryl Williams	.10	.05
❑	132	Merton Hanks	.10	.05
❑	133	Torrance Small	.10	.05
❑	134	Aaron Glenn	.10	.05
❑	135	Chester McGlockton	.10	.05
❑	136	William Thomas	.10	.05
❑	137	Kordell Stewart	.40	.18
❑	138	Jason Taylor	.10	.05
❑	139	Lake Dawson	.10	.05
❑	140	Carl Pickens	.40	.18
❑	141	Eugene Robinson	.10	.05
❑	142	Ed McCaffrey	.20	.09
❑	143	Lamar Lathon	.10	.05
❑	144	Ray Buchanan	.10	.05
❑	145	Thurman Thomas	.40	.18
❑	146	Andre Reed	.20	.09
❑	147	Wesley Walls	.20	.09
❑	148	Rob Moore	.20	.09
❑	149	Darren Woodson	.10	.05
❑	150	Eddie George	.75	.35
❑	151	Michael Irvin	.40	.18
❑	152	Johnnie Morton	.20	.09
❑	153	Ken Dilger	.10	.05
❑	154	Tony Boselli	.10	.05
❑	155	Randall McDaniel	.10	.05
❑	156	Mark Fields	.10	.05
❑	157	Phillippi Sparks	.10	.05
❑	158	Troy Davis	.10	.05
❑	159	Troy Vincent	.10	.05
❑	160	Cris Carter	.40	.18
❑	161	Amp Lee	.10	.05
❑	162	Will Blackwell	.10	.05
❑	163	Chad Scott	.10	.05
❑	164	Henry Ellard	.20	.09
❑	165	Robert Jones	.10	.05
❑	166	Garrison Hearst	.40	.18
❑	167	James McKnight	.10	.05
❑	168	Rodney Harrison	.20	.09
❑	169	Adrian Murrell	.20	.09
❑	170	Rod Smith WR	.20	.09
❑	171	Desmond Howard	.20	.09
❑	172	Ben Coates	.20	.09
❑	173	David Palmer	.10	.05
❑	174	Zach Thomas	.10	.05
❑	175	Dale Carter	.10	.05
❑	176	Mark Chmura	.20	.09
❑	177	Elvis Grbac	.20	.09
❑	178	Jason Hanson	.10	.05
❑	179	Walt Harris	.10	.05
❑	180	Ricky Watters	.20	.09
❑	181	Ray Lewis	.10	.05
❑	182	Lonnie Johnson	.10	.05
❑	183	Marvin Harrison	.20	.09
❑	184	Dorsey Levens	.40	.18
❑	185	Tony Gonzalez	.10	.05
❑	186	Andre Hastings	.10	.05
❑	187	Kevin Turner	.10	.05
❑	188	Mo Lewis	.10	.05
❑	189	Jason Sehorn	.10	.05
❑	190	Drew Bledsoe	.75	.35
❑	191	Michael Sinclair	.10	.05
❑	192	William Floyd	.10	.05
❑	193	Kenny Holmes	.10	.05
❑	194	Marvcus Patton	.10	.05
❑	195	Warren Sapp	.20	.09
❑	196	Junior Seau	.20	.09
❑	197	Ryan McNeil	.10	.05
❑	198	Tyrone Wheatley	.20	.09
❑	199	Robert Smith	.40	.18
❑	200	Terrell Davis	1.50	.70
❑	201	Brett Perriman	.10	.05
❑	202	Tamarick Vanover	.10	.05
❑	203	Stephen Boyd	.10	.05
❑	204	Zack Crockett	.10	.05
❑	205	Sherman Williams	.10	.05
❑	206	Neil Smith	.20	.09
❑	207	Jermaine Lewis	.20	.09
❑	208	Kevin Williams	.10	.05
❑	209	Byron Hanspard	.20	.09
❑	210	Warren Moon	.40	.18
❑	211	Tony McGee	.10	.05
❑	212	Raymont Harris	.10	.05
❑	213	Eric Davis	.10	.05
❑	214	Darrien Gordon	.10	.05
❑	215	James Stewart	.20	.09
❑	216	Derrick Mayes	.20	.09
❑	217	Brad Johnson	.40	.18
❑	218	Karim Abdul-Jabbar UER (Jabbar missing from name)	.40	.18
❑	219	Hugh Douglas	.10	.05
❑	220	Terry Allen	.40	.18
❑	221	Rhett Hall	.10	.05
❑	222	Terrell Fletcher	.10	.05
❑	223	Carnell Lake	.10	.05
❑	224	Darryll Lewis	.10	.05
❑	225	Chris Slade	.10	.05
❑	226	Michael Westbrook	.20	.09
❑	227	Willie Williams	.10	.05
❑	228	Tony Banks	.20	.09
❑	229	Keyshawn Johnson	.40	.18
❑	230	Mike Alstott	.40	.18
❑	231	Tiki Barber	.20	.09
❑	232	Jake Reed	.20	.09
❑	233	Eric Swann	.10	.05
❑	234	Eric Moulds	.40	.18
❑	235	Vinny Testaverde	.20	.09
❑	236	Jessie Tuggle	.10	.05
❑	237	Ryan Wetnight RC	.10	.05
❑	238	Tyrone Poole	.10	.05
❑	239	Bryant Westbrook	.10	.05
❑	240	Steve McNair	.40	.18
❑	241	Jimmy Smith	.20	.09
❑	242	Dewayne Washington	.10	.05
❑	243	Robert Harris	.10	.05
❑	244	Rod Woodson	.20	.09
❑	245	Reidel Anthony	.20	.09
❑	246	Jessie Armstead	.10	.05
❑	247	O.J. McDuffie	.20	.09
❑	248	Carlton Gray	.10	.05
❑	249	LeRoy Butler	.10	.05
❑	250	Jerry Rice	1.00	.45
❑	251	Frank Sanders	.20	.09
❑	252	Todd Collins	.10	.05
❑	253	Fred Lane	.20	.09
❑	254	David Dunn	.10	.05
❑	255	Micheal Barrow	.10	.05
❑	256	Luther Elliss	.10	.05
❑	257	Scott Mitchell	.20	.09
❑	258	Dave Meggett	.10	.05
❑	259	Rickey Dudley	.10	.05

	Card	MINT	NRMT
❑	260 Isaac Bruce	.40	.18
❑	261 Tony Martin	.20	.09
❑	262 Leslie Shepherd	.10	.05
❑	263 Derrick Brooks	.10	.05
❑	264 Greg Lloyd	.10	.05
❑	265 Terrell Buckley	.10	.05
❑	266 Antonio Freeman	.40	.18
❑	267 Tony Brackens	.10	.05
❑	268 Mark McMillian	.10	.05
❑	269 Dexter Coakley	.10	.05
❑	270 Dan Marino	2.00	.90
❑	271 Bryan Cox	.10	.05
❑	272 Leeland McElroy	.10	.05
❑	273 Jeff Burris	.10	.05
❑	274 Eric Green	.10	.05
❑	275 Darnay Scott	.20	.09
❑	276 Greg Clark	.10	.05
❑	277 Mario Bates	.20	.09
❑	278 Eric Turner	.10	.05
❑	279 Neil O'Donnell	.20	.09
❑	280 Herman Moore	.40	.18
❑	281 Gary Brown	.10	.05
❑	282 Terrell Owens	.40	.18
❑	283 Frank Wycheck	.10	.05
❑	284 Trent Dilfer	.40	.18
❑	285 Curtis Martin	.40	.18
❑	286 Ricky Proehl	.10	.05
❑	287 Steve Atwater	.10	.05
❑	288 Aaron Bailey	.10	.05
❑	289 William Henderson	.10	.05
❑	290 Marcus Allen	.40	.18
❑	291 Tom Knight	.10	.05
❑	292 Quinn Early	.10	.05
❑	293 Michael McCrary	.10	.05
❑	294 Bert Emanuel	.20	.09
❑	295 Tom Carter	.10	.05
❑	296 Kevin Glover	.10	.05
❑	297 Marshall Faulk	.40	.18
❑	298 Harvey Williams	.10	.05
❑	299 Chris Warren	.20	.09
❑	300 John Elway	2.00	.90
❑	301 Eddie Kennison	.20	.09
❑	302 Gus Frerotte	.10	.05
❑	303 Regan Upshaw	.10	.05
❑	304 Kevin Gogan	.10	.05
❑	305 Napoleon Kaufman	.40	.18
❑	306 Charlie Garner	.10	.05
❑	307 Shawn Jefferson	.10	.05
❑	308 Tommy Vardell	.10	.05
❑	309 Mike Hollis	.10	.05
❑	310 Irving Fryar	.20	.09
❑	311 Shannon Sharpe	.20	.09
❑	312 Byron Bam Morris	.10	.05
❑	313 Jamal Anderson	.40	.18
❑	314 Chris Gedney	.10	.05
❑	315 Chris Spielman	.10	.05
❑	316 Derrick Alexander WR	.20	.09
❑	317 O.J. Santiago	.10	.05
❑	318 Anthony Miller	.10	.05
❑	319 Ki-Jana Carter	.10	.05
❑	320 Deion Sanders	.40	.18
❑	321 Joey Galloway	.40	.18
❑	322 J.J. Stokes	.20	.09
❑	323 Rodney Thomas	.10	.05
❑	324 John Lynch	.10	.05
❑	325 Mike Pritchard	.10	.05
❑	326 Terrance Shaw	.10	.05
❑	327 Ted Johnson	.10	.05
❑	328 Ashley Ambrose	.10	.05
❑	329 Checklist 1	.10	.05
❑	330 Checklist 2	.10	.05
❑	331 Jerome Pathon RC	2.00	.90
❑	332 Ryan Leaf RC	3.00	1.35
❑	333 Duane Starks RC	1.25	.55
❑	334 Brian Simmons RC	1.25	.55
❑	335 Keith Brooking RC	2.00	.90
❑	336 Robert Edwards RC	2.50	1.10
❑	337 Curtis Enis RC	5.00	2.20
❑	338 John Avery RC	2.50	1.10
❑	339 Fred Taylor RC	10.00	4.50
❑	340 Germane Crowell RC	5.00	2.20
❑	341 Hines Ward RC	2.00	.90
❑	342 Marcus Nash RC	3.00	1.35
❑	343 Jacquez Green RC	3.00	1.35
❑	344 Joe Jurevicius RC	2.00	.90
❑	345 Greg Ellis RC	1.25	.55
❑	346 Brian Griese RC	6.00	2.70
❑	347 Tavian Banks RC	2.00	.90
❑	348 Robert Holcombe RC	2.50	1.10
❑	349 Skip Hicks RC	3.00	1.35
❑	350 Ahman Green RC	2.00	.90
❑	351 Takeo Spikes RC	2.00	.90
❑	352 Randy Moss RC	20.00	9.00
❑	353 Andre Wadsworth RC	2.00	.90
❑	354 Jason Peter RC	1.25	.55
❑	355 Grant Wistrom RC	1.25	.55
❑	356 Charles Woodson RC	5.00	2.20
❑	357 Kevin Dyson RC	3.00	1.35
❑	358 Pat Johnson RC	2.00	.90
❑	359 Tim Dwight RC	3.00	1.35
❑	360 Peyton Manning RC	20.00	9.00
❑	P1 Robert Tisch (Promo card of Giants' owner)	5.00	2.20

1998 Topps Autographs

	MINT	NRMT
COMPLETE SET (15)	600.00	275.00
COMMON CARD (A1-A15)	15.00	6.75
SEMISTARS	20.00	9.00
UNLISTED STARS	25.00	11.00
STATED ODDS 1:260 HOBBY		

	Card	MINT	NRMT
❑	A1 Randy Moss	200.00	90.00
❑	A2 Mike Alstott	25.00	11.00
❑	A3 Jake Plummer	60.00	27.00
❑	A4 Corey Dillon	40.00	18.00
❑	A5 Kordell Stewart	30.00	13.50
❑	A6 Eddie George	60.00	27.00
❑	A7 Jason Sehorn	15.00	6.75
❑	A8 Joey Galloway	25.00	11.00
❑	A9 Ryan Leaf	40.00	18.00
❑	A10 Peyton Manning	200.00	90.00
❑	A11 Dwight Stephenson	20.00	9.00
❑	A12 Anthony Munoz	40.00	18.00
❑	A13 Mike Singletary	40.00	18.00
❑	A14 Tommy McDonald	20.00	9.00
❑	A15 Paul Krause	25.00	11.00

1998 Topps Generation 2000

	MINT	NRMT
COMPLETE SET (15)	50.00	22.00
COMMON CARD (GE1-GE15)	1.50	.70
SEMISTARS	2.50	1.10
UNLISTED STARS	4.00	1.80
STATED ODDS 1:18H/R, 1:12RET.JUM.		

	Card	MINT	NRMT
❑	GE1 Warrick Dunn	5.00	2.20
❑	GE2 Tony Gonzalez	1.50	.70
❑	GE3 Corey Dillon	5.00	2.20
❑	GE4 Antowain Smith	4.00	1.80
❑	GE5 Mike Alstott	4.00	1.80
❑	GE6 Kordell Stewart	4.00	1.80
❑	GE7 Peter Boulware	1.50	.70
❑	GE8 Jake Plummer	8.00	3.60
❑	GE9 Tiki Barber	2.50	1.10
❑	GE10 Terrell Davis	12.00	5.50
❑	GE11 Steve McNair	4.00	1.80
❑	GE12 Curtis Martin	4.00	1.80
❑	GE13 Napoleon Kaufman	4.00	1.80
❑	GE14 Terrell Owens	4.00	1.80
❑	GE15 Eddie George	6.00	2.70

1998 Topps Gridiron Gods

	MINT	NRMT
COMPLETE SET (15)	80.00	36.00
COMMON CARD (G1-G15)	3.00	1.35
STATED ODDS 1:36 HOBBY		

	Card	MINT	NRMT
❑	G1 Barry Sanders	15.00	6.75
❑	G2 Jerry Rice	8.00	3.60
❑	G3 Herman Moore	3.00	1.35
❑	G4 Drew Bledsoe	6.00	2.70
❑	G5 Kordell Stewart	3.00	1.35
❑	G6 Tim Brown	3.00	1.35
❑	G7 Eddie George	6.00	2.70
❑	G8 Dorsey Levens	3.00	1.35
❑	G9 Warrick Dunn	5.00	2.20
❑	G10 Brett Favre	15.00	6.75
❑	G11 Terrell Davis	12.00	5.50
❑	G12 Steve Young	5.00	2.20
❑	G13 Jerome Bettis	3.00	1.35
❑	G14 Mark Brunell	6.00	2.70
❑	G15 John Elway	15.00	6.75

1998 Topps Hidden Gems

	MINT	NRMT
COMPLETE SET (15)	20.00	9.00
COMMON CARD (HG1-HG15)	.60	.25
SEMISTARS	1.00	.45

	MINT	NRMT
UNLISTED STARS	1.25	.55

STATED ODDS 1:12RET,1:8RET.JUMBO

Card	Player	MINT	NRMT
❑ HG1	Andre Reed	1.00	.45
❑ HG2	Kevin Greene	1.00	.45
❑ HG3	Tony Martin	1.00	.45
❑ HG4	Shannon Sharpe	1.00	.45
❑ HG5	Terry Allen	1.25	.55
❑ HG6	Brett Favre	6.00	2.70
❑ HG7	Ben Coates	1.00	.45
❑ HG8	Michael Sinclair	.60	.25
❑ HG9	Keenan McCardell	1.00	.45
❑ HG10	Brad Johnson	1.25	.55
❑ HG11	Mark Brunell	2.50	1.10
❑ HG12	Dorsey Levens	1.25	.55
❑ HG13	Terrell Davis	6.00	2.70
❑ HG14	Curtis Martin	1.25	.55
❑ HG15	Derrick Rodgers	.60	.25

1998 Topps Measures of Greatness

	MINT	NRMT
COMPLETE SET (15)	80.00	36.00
COMMON CARD (MG1-MG15)	3.00	1.35

STATED ODDS 1:36H/R, 1:24RET.JUM.

Card	Player	MINT	NRMT
❑ MG1	John Elway	15.00	6.75
❑ MG2	Marcus Allen	6.00	2.70
❑ MG3	Jerry Rice	8.00	3.60
❑ MG4	Tim Brown	6.00	2.70
❑ MG5	Warren Moon	6.00	2.70
❑ MG6	Bruce Smith	3.00	1.35
❑ MG7	Troy Aikman	8.00	3.60
❑ MG8	Reggie White	6.00	2.70
❑ MG9	Irving Fryar	3.00	1.35
❑ MG10	Barry Sanders	15.00	6.75
❑ MG11	Cris Carter	6.00	2.70
❑ MG12	Emmitt Smith	12.00	5.50
❑ MG13	Dan Marino	15.00	6.75
❑ MG14	Rod Woodson	3.00	1.35
❑ MG15	Brett Favre	15.00	6.75

1998 Topps Mystery Finest

	MINT	NRMT
COMPLETE SET (20)	150.00	70.00
COMMON CARD (M1-M20)	3.00	1.35
SEMISTARS	4.00	1.80
UNLISTED STARS	5.00	2.20

STATED ODDS 1:36H/R, 1:24 RET.JUM.
*REFRACTORS: 1X TO 2.5X HI COL.
REFRACTOR STATED ODDS 1:144

Card	Player	MINT	NRMT
❑ M1	Steve Young	6.00	2.70
❑ M2	Dan Marino	20.00	9.00
❑ M3	Brett Favre	20.00	9.00
❑ M4	Drew Bledsoe	8.00	3.60
❑ M5	Mark Brunell	8.00	3.60
❑ M6	Troy Aikman	10.00	4.50
❑ M7	Kordell Stewart	4.00	1.80
❑ M8	John Elway	20.00	9.00
❑ M9	Barry Sanders	20.00	9.00
❑ M10	Jerome Bettis	5.00	2.20
❑ M11	Eddie George	8.00	3.60
❑ M12	Emmitt Smith	15.00	6.75
❑ M13	Curtis Martin	4.00	1.80
❑ M14	Warrick Dunn	6.00	2.70
❑ M15	Dorsey Levens	5.00	2.20
❑ M16	Terrell Davis	15.00	6.75
❑ M17	Herman Moore	5.00	2.20
❑ M18	Jerry Rice	10.00	4.50
❑ M19	Tim Brown	5.00	2.20
❑ M20	Yancey Thigpen	3.00	1.35

1998 Topps Season's Best

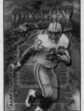

	MINT	NRMT
COMPLETE SET (30)	60.00	27.00
COMMON CARD (1-30)	.75	.35
SEMISTARS	1.25	.55
UNLISTED STARS	2.00	.90

STATED ODDS 1:12

Card	Player	MINT	NRMT
❑ 1	Terrell Davis	8.00	3.60
❑ 2	Barry Sanders	10.00	4.50
❑ 3	Jerome Bettis	2.00	.90
❑ 4	Dorsey Levens	2.00	.90
❑ 5	Eddie George	4.00	1.80
❑ 6	Brett Favre	10.00	4.50
❑ 7	Mark Brunell	4.00	1.80
❑ 8	Jeff George	1.25	.55
❑ 9	Steve Young	3.00	1.35
❑ 10	John Elway	10.00	4.50
❑ 11	Herman Moore	2.00	.90
❑ 12	Rob Moore	1.25	.55
❑ 13	Yancey Thigpen	.75	.35
❑ 14	Cris Carter	2.00	.90
❑ 15	Tim Brown	2.00	.90
❑ 16	Bruce Smith	1.25	.55
❑ 17	Michael Sinclair	.75	.35
❑ 18	John Randle	1.25	.55
❑ 19	Dana Stubblefield	.75	.35
❑ 20	Michael Strahan	.75	.35
❑ 21	Tamarick Vanover	.75	.35
❑ 22	Darrien Gordon	.75	.35
❑ 23	Michael Bates	.75	.35
❑ 24	David Meggett	.75	.35
❑ 25	Jermaine Lewis	1.25	.55
❑ 26	Terrell Davis	8.00	3.60
❑ 27	Jerry Rice	5.00	2.20
❑ 28	Barry Sanders	10.00	4.50
❑ 29	John Randle	1.25	.55
❑ 30	John Elway	10.00	4.50

1999 Topps

	MINT	NRMT
COMPLETE SET (357)	70.00	32.00
COMP.SET w/o SP's (330)	20.00	9.00
COMMON CARD (1-357)	.15	.07
SEMISTARS	.25	.11
UNLISTED STARS	.50	.23
COMMON ROOKIE (329-355)	2.00	.90
ROOKIE SEMISTARS	2.50	1.10

ROOKIE SUBSET ODDS 1:5H/R,1:3J,1:1HTA

Card	Player	MINT	NRMT
❑ 1	Terrell Davis	1.25	.55
❑ 2	Adrian Murrell	.25	.11
❑ 3	Ernie Mills	.15	.07
❑ 4	Jimmy Hitchcock	.15	.07
❑ 5	Charlie Garner	.25	.11
❑ 6	Blaine Bishop	.15	.07
❑ 7	Junior Seau	.25	.11
❑ 8	Andre Rison	.25	.11
❑ 9	Jake Reed	.25	.11
❑ 10	Cris Carter	.50	.23
❑ 11	Torrance Small	.15	.07
❑ 12	Ronald McKinnon	.15	.07
❑ 13	Tyrone Davis	.15	.07
❑ 14	Warren Moon	.50	.23
❑ 15	Joe Johnson	.15	.07
❑ 16	Bert Emanuel	.25	.11
❑ 17	Brad Culpepper	.15	.07
❑ 18	Henry Jones	.15	.07
❑ 19	Jonathan Ogden	.15	.07
❑ 20	Terrell Owens	.50	.23
❑ 21	Derrick Mason	.15	.07
❑ 22	Jon Ritchie	.15	.07
❑ 23	Eric Metcalf	.15	.07
❑ 24	Kevin Carter	.15	.07
❑ 25	Fred Taylor	1.25	.55
❑ 26	DeWayne Washington	.15	.07
❑ 27	William Thomas	.15	.07
❑ 28	Rocket Ismail	.25	.11
❑ 29	Jason Taylor	.15	.07
❑ 30	Doug Flutie	.60	.25
❑ 31	Michael Sinclair	.15	.07
❑ 32	Yancey Thigpen	.15	.07
❑ 33	Darnay Scott	.15	.07
❑ 34	Amani Toomer	.15	.07
❑ 35	Edgar Bennett	.15	.07
❑ 36	LeRoy Butler	.15	.07
❑ 37	Jessie Tuggle	.15	.07
❑ 38	Andrew Glover	.15	.07
❑ 39	Tim McDonald	.15	.07
❑ 40	Marshall Faulk	.50	.23
❑ 41	Ray Mickens	.15	.07
❑ 42	Kimble Anders	.25	.11
❑ 43	Trent Green	.25	.11
❑ 44	Dermontti Dawson	.15	.07
❑ 45	Greg Ellis	.15	.07
❑ 46	Hugh Douglas	.15	.07
❑ 47	Amp Lee	.15	.07
❑ 48	Lamar Thomas	.15	.07
❑ 49	Curtis Conway	.25	.11
❑ 50	Emmitt Smith	1.25	.55
❑ 51	Elvis Grbac	.25	.11
❑ 52	Tony Simmons	.15	.07
❑ 53	Darrin Smith	.15	.07
❑ 54	Donovin Darius	.15	.07
❑ 55	Corey Chavous	.15	.07
❑ 56	Phillippi Sparks	.15	.07

❑ 57	Luther Elliss	.15	.07
❑ 58	Tim Dwight	.50	.23
❑ 59	Andre Hastings	.15	.07
❑ 60	Dan Marino	2.00	.90
❑ 61	Micheal Barrow	.15	.07
❑ 62	Corey Fuller	.15	.07
❑ 63	Bill Romanowski	.15	.07
❑ 64	Derrick Rodgers	.25	.11
❑ 65	Natrone Means	.25	.11
❑ 66	Peter Boulware	.15	.07
❑ 67	Brian Mitchell	.15	.07
❑ 68	Cornelius Bennett	.15	.07
❑ 69	Dedric Ward	.15	.07
❑ 70	Drew Bledsoe	.75	.35
❑ 71	Freddie Jones	.15	.07
❑ 72	Derrick Thomas	.25	.11
❑ 73	Willie Davis	.15	.07
❑ 74	Larry Centers	.15	.07
❑ 75	Mark Brunell	.75	.35
❑ 76	Chuck Smith	.15	.07
❑ 77	Desmond Howard	.25	.11
❑ 78	Sedrick Shaw	.15	.07
❑ 79	Tiki Barber	.15	.07
❑ 80	Curtis Martin	.50	.23
❑ 81	Barry Minter	.15	.07
❑ 82	Skip Hicks	.50	.23
❑ 83	O.J. Santiago	.15	.07
❑ 84	Ed McCaffrey	.25	.11
❑ 85	Terrell Buckley	.15	.07
❑ 86	Charlie Jones	.15	.07
❑ 87	Pete Mitchell	.15	.07
❑ 88	La'Roi Glover	.15	.07
❑ 89	Eric Davis	.15	.07
❑ 90	John Elway	2.00	.90
❑ 91	Kavika Pittman	.15	.07
❑ 92	Fred Lane	.25	.11
❑ 93	Warren Sapp	.15	.07
❑ 94	Lorenzo Bromell	.15	.07
❑ 95	Lawyer Milloy	.15	.07
❑ 96	Aeneas Williams	.15	.07
❑ 97	Michael McCrary	.15	.07
❑ 98	Rickey Dudley	.15	.07
❑ 99	Bryce Paup	.15	.07
❑ 100	Jamal Anderson	.50	.23
❑ 101	D'Marco Farr	.15	.07
❑ 102	Johnnie Morton	.25	.11
❑ 103	Jeff Graham	.15	.07
❑ 104	Sam Cowart	.15	.07
❑ 105	Bryant Young	.15	.07
❑ 106	Jermaine Lewis	.25	.11
❑ 107	Chad Bratzke	.15	.07
❑ 108	Jeff Burris	.15	.07
❑ 109	Roell Preston	.15	.07
❑ 110	Vinny Testaverde	.25	.11
❑ 111	Ruben Brown	.15	.07
❑ 112	Darryll Lewis	.15	.07
❑ 113	Billy Davis	.15	.07
❑ 114	Bryant Westbrook	.15	.07
❑ 115	Stephen Alexander	.15	.07
❑ 116	Terrell Fletcher	.15	.07
❑ 117	Terry Glenn	.50	.23
❑ 118	Rod Smith	.25	.11
❑ 119	Carl Pickens	.25	.11
❑ 120	Tim Brown	.50	.23
❑ 121	Mikhael Ricks	.15	.07
❑ 122	Jason Gildon	.15	.07
❑ 123	Charles Way	.15	.07
❑ 124	Rob Moore	.25	.11
❑ 125	Jerome Bettis	.50	.23
❑ 126	Kerry Collins	.25	.11
❑ 127	Bruce Smith	.25	.11
❑ 128	James Hasty	.15	.07
❑ 129	Ken Norton Jr.	.15	.07
❑ 130	Charles Woodson	.50	.23
❑ 131	Tony McGee	.15	.07
❑ 132	Kevin Turner	.15	.07
❑ 133	Jerome Pathon	.15	.07
❑ 134	Garrison Hearst	.25	.11
❑ 135	Craig Newsome	.15	.07
❑ 136	Hardy Nickerson	.15	.07
❑ 137	Ray Lewis	.15	.07
❑ 138	Derrick Alexander	.15	.07
❑ 139	Phil Hansen	.15	.07
❑ 140	Joey Galloway	.50	.23
❑ 141	Oronde Gadsden	.15	.07
❑ 142	Herman Moore	.50	.23
❑ 143	Bobby Taylor	.15	.07
❑ 144	Mario Bates	.15	.07
❑ 145	Kevin Dyson	.25	.11
❑ 146	Aaron Glenn	.15	.07
❑ 147	Ed McDaniel	.15	.07
❑ 148	Terry Allen	.25	.11
❑ 149	Ike Hilliard	.15	.07
❑ 150	Steve Young	.75	.35
❑ 151	Eugene Robinson	.15	.07
❑ 152	John Mobley	.15	.07
❑ 153	Kevin Hardy	.15	.07
❑ 154	Lance Johnstone	.15	.07
❑ 155	Willie McGinest	.15	.07
❑ 156	Gary Anderson	.15	.07
❑ 157	Dexter Coakley	.15	.07
❑ 158	Mark Fields	.15	.07
❑ 159	Steve McNair	.50	.23
❑ 160	Corey Dillon	.50	.23
❑ 161	Zach Thomas	.25	.11
❑ 162	Kent Graham	.15	.07
❑ 163	Tony Parrish	.15	.07
❑ 164	Sam Gash	.15	.07
❑ 165	Kyle Brady	.15	.07
❑ 166	Donnell Bennett	.15	.07
❑ 167	Tony Martin	.25	.11
❑ 168	Michael Bates	.15	.07
❑ 169	Bobby Engram	.25	.11
❑ 170	Jimmy Smith	.25	.11
❑ 171	Vonnie Holliday	.15	.07
❑ 172	Simeon Rice	.15	.07
❑ 173	Kevin Greene	.15	.07
❑ 174	Mike Alstott	.50	.23
❑ 175	Eddie George	.60	.25
❑ 176	Michael Jackson	.15	.07
❑ 177	Neil O'Donnell	.25	.11
❑ 178	Sean Dawkins	.15	.07
❑ 179	Courtney Hawkins	.15	.07
❑ 180	Michael Irvin	.25	.11
❑ 181	Thurman Thomas	.25	.11
❑ 182	Cam Cleeland	.15	.07
❑ 183	Ellis Johnson	.15	.07
❑ 184	Will Blackwell	.15	.07
❑ 185	Ty Law	.15	.07
❑ 186	Merton Hanks	.15	.07
❑ 187	Dan Wilkinson	.15	.07
❑ 188	Andre Wadsworth	.15	.07
❑ 189	Troy Vincent	.15	.07
❑ 190	Frank Sanders	.25	.11
❑ 191	Stephen Boyd	.15	.07
❑ 192	Jason Elam	.15	.07
❑ 193	Kordell Stewart	.50	.23
❑ 194	Ted Johnson	.15	.07
❑ 195	Glyn Milburn	.15	.07
❑ 196	Gary Brown	.15	.07
❑ 197	Travis Hall	.15	.07
❑ 198	John Randle	.25	.11
❑ 199	Jay Riemersma	.15	.07
❑ 200	Barry Sanders	2.00	.90
❑ 201	Chris Spielman	.15	.07
❑ 202	Rod Woodson	.25	.11
❑ 203	Darrell Russell	.15	.07
❑ 204	Tony Boselli	.15	.07
❑ 205	Darren Woodson	.15	.07
❑ 206	Muhsin Muhammad	.25	.11
❑ 207	Jim Harbaugh	.25	.11
❑ 208	Isaac Bruce	.50	.23
❑ 209	Mo Lewis	.15	.07
❑ 210	Dorsey Levens	.50	.23
❑ 211	Frank Wycheck	.15	.07
❑ 212	Napoleon Kaufman	.50	.23
❑ 213	Walt Harris	.15	.07
❑ 214	Leon Lett	.15	.07
❑ 215	Karim Abdul-Jabbar	.25	.11
❑ 216	Carnell Lake	.15	.07
❑ 217	Byron Bam Morris	.15	.07
❑ 218	John Avery	.25	.11
❑ 219	Chris Slade	.15	.07
❑ 220	Robert Smith	.50	.23
❑ 221	Mike Pritchard	.15	.07
❑ 222	Ty Detmer	.25	.11
❑ 223	Randall Cunningham	.50	.23
❑ 224	Alonzo Mayes	.15	.07
❑ 225	Jake Plummer	1.00	.45
❑ 226	Derrick Mayes	.15	.07
❑ 227	Jeff Brady	.15	.07
❑ 228	John Lynch	.15	.07
❑ 229	Steve Atwater	.15	.07
❑ 230	Warrick Dunn	.50	.23
❑ 231	Shawn Jefferson	.15	.07
❑ 232	Erik Kramer	.15	.07
❑ 233	Ken Dilger	.15	.07
❑ 234	Ryan Leaf	.50	.23
❑ 235	Ray Buchanan	.15	.07
❑ 236	Kevin Williams	.15	.07
❑ 237	Ricky Watters	.25	.11
❑ 238	Dwayne Rudd	.15	.07
❑ 239	Duce Staley	.50	.23
❑ 240	Charlie Batch	1.00	.45
❑ 241	Tim Biakabutuka	.25	.11
❑ 242	Tony Gonzalez	.25	.11
❑ 243	Bryan Still	.15	.07
❑ 244	Donnie Edwards	.15	.07
❑ 245	Troy Aikman	1.25	.55
❑ 246	Tony Banks	.25	.11
❑ 247	Curtis Enis	.50	.23
❑ 248	Chris Chandler	.25	.11
❑ 249	James Jett	.25	.11
❑ 250	Brett Favre	2.00	.90
❑ 251	Keith Poole	.15	.07
❑ 252	Ricky Proehl	.15	.07
❑ 253	Shannon Sharpe	.25	.11
❑ 254	Robert Jones	.15	.07
❑ 255	Chad Brown	.15	.07
❑ 256	Ben Coates	.25	.11
❑ 257	Jacquez Green	.25	.11
❑ 258	Jessie Armstead	.15	.07
❑ 259	Dale Carter	.15	.07
❑ 260	Antowain Smith	.50	.23
❑ 261	Mark Chmura	.15	.07
❑ 262	Michael Westbrook	.25	.11
❑ 263	Marvin Harrison	.50	.23
❑ 264	Darrien Gordon	.15	.07
❑ 265	Rodney Harrison	.15	.07
❑ 266	Charles Johnson	.15	.07
❑ 267	Roman Phifer	.15	.07
❑ 268	Reidel Anthony	.25	.11
❑ 269	Jerry Rice	1.25	.55
❑ 270	Eric Moulds	.50	.23
❑ 271	Robert Porcher	.15	.07
❑ 272	Deion Sanders	.50	.23
❑ 273	Germane Crowell	.25	.11
❑ 274	Randy Moss	2.00	.90
❑ 275	Antonio Freeman	.50	.23
❑ 276	Trent Dilfer	.25	.11
❑ 277	Eric Turner	.15	.07
❑ 278	Jeff George	.25	.11
❑ 279	Levon Kirkland	.15	.07
❑ 280	O.J. McDuffie	.25	.11
❑ 281	Takeo Spikes	.15	.07
❑ 282	Jim Flanigan	.15	.07
❑ 283	Chris Warren	.15	.07
❑ 284	J.J. Stokes	.25	.11
❑ 285	Bryan Cox	.15	.07
❑ 286	Sam Madison	.15	.07
❑ 287	Priest Holmes	.50	.23
❑ 288	Keenan McCardell	.25	.11
❑ 289	Michael Strahan	.15	.07
❑ 290	Robert Edwards	.25	.11
❑ 291	Tommy Vardell	.15	.07
❑ 292	Wayne Chrebet	.25	.11
❑ 293	Chris Calloway	.15	.07
❑ 294	Wesley Walls	.25	.11
❑ 295	Derrick Brooks	.15	.07
❑ 296	Trace Armstrong	.15	.07
❑ 297	Brian Simmons	.15	.07
❑ 298	Darrell Green	.15	.07
❑ 299	Robert Brooks	.25	.11
❑ 300	Peyton Manning	2.00	.90
❑ 301	Dana Stubblefield	.15	.07
❑ 302	Shawn Springs	.15	.07
❑ 303	Leslie Shepherd	.15	.07
❑ 304	Ken Harvey	.15	.07
❑ 305	Jon Kitna	.60	.25
❑ 306	Terance Mathis	.25	.11
❑ 307	Andre Reed	.25	.11
❑ 308	Jackie Harris	.15	.07
❑ 309	Rich Gannon	.25	.11
❑ 310	Keyshawn Johnson	.50	.23
❑ 311	Victor Green	.15	.07
❑ 312	Eric Allen	.15	.07
❑ 313	Terry Fair	.15	.07
❑ 314	Jason Elam SH	.15	.07

❑ 315 Garrison Hearst SH	.25	.11
❑ 316 Jake Plummer SH	.60	.25
❑ 317 Randall Cunningham SH	.50	.23
❑ 318 Randy Moss SH	1.00	.45
❑ 319 Jamal Anderson SH	.50	.23
❑ 320 John Elway SH	1.00	.45
❑ 321 Doug Flutie SH	.50	.23
❑ 322 Emmitt Smith SH	.75	.35
❑ 323 Terrell Davis SH	.75	.35
❑ 324 Jerris McPhail	.15	.07
❑ 325 Damon Gibson	.15	.07
❑ 326 Jim Pyne	.15	.07
❑ 327 Antonio Langham	.15	.07
❑ 328 Freddie Solomon	.15	.07
❑ 329 Ricky Williams RC	12.00	5.50
❑ 330 Daunte Culpepper RC	8.00	3.60
❑ 331 Chris Claiborne RC	2.50	1.10
❑ 332 Amos Zereoue RC	2.50	1.10
❑ 333 Chris McAlister RC	2.00	.90
❑ 334 Kevin Faulk RC	3.00	1.35
❑ 335 James Johnson RC	3.00	1.35
❑ 336 Mike Cloud RC	2.50	1.10
❑ 337 Jevon Kearse RC	5.00	2.20
❑ 338 Akili Smith RC	5.00	2.20
❑ 339 Edgerrin James RC	20.00	9.00
❑ 340 Cecil Collins RC	2.50	1.10
❑ 341 Donovan McNabb RC	8.00	3.60
❑ 342 Kevin Johnson RC	6.00	2.70
❑ 343 Torry Holt RC	6.00	2.70
❑ 344 Rob Konrad RC	2.00	.90
❑ 345 Tim Couch RC	12.00	5.50
❑ 346 David Boston RC	4.00	1.80
❑ 347 Karsten Bailey RC	2.00	.90
❑ 348 Troy Edwards RC	4.00	1.80
❑ 349 Sedrick Irvin RC	2.50	1.10
❑ 350 Shaun King RC	8.00	3.60
❑ 351 Peerless Price RC	4.00	1.80
❑ 352 Brock Huard RC	3.00	1.35
❑ 353 Cade McNown RC	8.00	3.60
❑ 354 Champ Bailey RC	3.00	1.35
❑ 355 D'Wayne Bates RC	2.00	.90
❑ 356 Checklist Card	.15	.07
❑ 357 Checklist Card	.15	.07

1999 Topps Collection

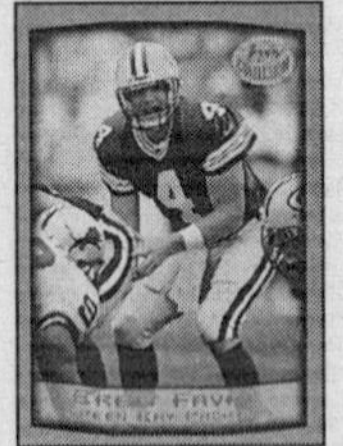

	MINT	NRMT
COMP.FACT.SET (357)	50.00	22.00
COMMON CARD (1-357)	.10	.05
COMMON ROOKIE (329-355)	1.50	.70

*COLLECTION CARDS: .3X TO 1X BASIC TOPPS

1999 Topps MVP Promotion

	MINT	NRMT
COMMON CARD (1-357)	6.00	2.70
COMMON ROOKIE (329-355)	10.00	4.50

*MVP STARS: 20X TO 50X HI COL.
*WINNER MVP STARS: 25X TO 60X HI COL.
*MVP YOUNG STARS: 15X TO 40X
*MVP RCs: 2.5X TO 6X
*WINNER MVP RCs: 3X TO 8X
MVP STATED ODDS 1:253 H/R, 1:69 HTA
MVP STATED PRINT RUN 100 SETS
17-CARDS WERE PRIZE WINNERS

Card		
❑ 34 Amani Toomer WIN	100.00	45.00
❑ 40 Marshall Faulk WIN	100.00	45.00
❑ 70 Drew Bledsoe WIN	100.00	45.00
❑ 117 Terry Glenn WIN	100.00	45.00
❑ 120 Tim Brown WIN	100.00	45.00
❑ 159 Steve McNair WIN	100.00	45.00
❑ 160 Corey Dillon WIN	100.00	45.00
❑ 170 Jimmy Smith WIN	100.00	45.00
❑ 208 Isaac Bruce WIN	100.00	45.00
❑ 210 Dorsey Levens WIN	100.00	45.00
❑ 245 Troy Aikman WIN	100.00	45.00
❑ 263 Marvin Harrison WIN	100.00	45.00
❑ 273 Germane Crowell WIN	100.00	45.00
❑ 278 Jeff George WIN	100.00	45.00
❑ 337 Jevon Kearse WIN	100.00	45.00
❑ 339 Edgerrin James WIN	100.00	45.00
❑ 353 Cade McNown WIN	100.00	45.00

1999 Topps MVP Promotion Prizes

	MINT	NRMT
COMPLETE SET (22)	120.00	55.00
COMMON CARD (MVP1-MVP22)	1.50	.70
SEMISTARS	3.00	1.35

SET WAS ISSUED VIA MAIL REDEMPTION

❑ MVP1 Troy Aikman	10.00	4.50
❑ MVP2 Drew Bledsoe	6.00	2.70
❑ MVP3 Marvin Harrison	3.00	1.35
❑ MVP4 Terry Glenn	3.00	1.35
❑ MVP5 Isaac Bruce	3.00	1.35
❑ MVP6 Marshall Faulk	3.00	1.35
❑ MVP7 Tim Brown	3.00	1.35
❑ MVP8 Edgerrin James	25.00	11.00
❑ MVP9 Germane Crowell	1.50	.70
❑ MVP10 Jevon Kearse	8.00	3.60
❑ MVP11 Jimmy Smith	1.50	.70
❑ MVP12 Jeff George	1.50	.70
❑ MVP13 Amani Toomer	1.50	.70
❑ MVP14 Corey Dillon	3.00	1.35
❑ MVP15 Cade McNown	10.00	4.50
❑ MVP16 Steve McNair	3.00	1.35
❑ MVP17 Dorsey Levens	3.00	1.35
❑ MVP18 Robert Smith	3.00	1.35
❑ MVP19 Eddie George	4.00	1.80
❑ MVP20 Ricky Proehl	1.50	.70
❑ MVP21 Kurt Warner	40.00	18.00
❑ MVP22 Kurt Warner MVP	40.00	18.00

1999 Topps All Matrix

	MINT	NRMT
COMPLETE SET (30)	60.00	27.00
COMMON CARD (AM1-AM30)	1.00	.45
SEMISTARS	2.00	.90

STATED ODDS 1:14 H/R, 1:9 JUM, 1:4 HTA

❑ AM1 Fred Taylor	4.00	1.80
❑ AM2 Ricky Watters	1.00	.45
❑ AM3 Curtis Martin	2.00	.90
❑ AM4 Eddie George	2.50	1.10
❑ AM5 Marshall Faulk	2.00	.90
❑ AM6 Emmitt Smith	5.00	2.20
❑ AM7 Barry Sanders	8.00	3.60
❑ AM8 Garrison Hearst	1.00	.45
❑ AM9 Jamal Anderson	2.00	.90
❑ AM10 Terrell Davis	5.00	2.20
❑ AM11 Chris Chandler	1.00	.45
❑ AM12 Steve McNair	2.00	.90
❑ AM13 Vinny Testaverde	1.00	.45
❑ AM14 Trent Green	1.00	.45
❑ AM15 Dan Marino	8.00	3.60
❑ AM16 Drew Bledsoe	3.00	1.35
❑ AM17 Randall Cunningham	2.00	.90
❑ AM18 Jake Plummer	4.00	1.80
❑ AM19 Peyton Manning	6.00	2.70
❑ AM20 Steve Young	3.00	1.35
❑ AM21 Brett Favre	8.00	3.60
❑ AM22 Tim Couch	8.00	3.60
❑ AM23 Edgerrin James	12.00	5.50
❑ AM24 David Boston	2.50	1.10
❑ AM25 Akili Smith	3.00	1.35
❑ AM26 Troy Edwards	2.50	1.10
❑ AM27 Torry Holt	4.00	1.80
❑ AM28 Donovan McNabb	5.00	2.20
❑ AM29 Daunte Culpepper	5.00	2.20
❑ AM30 Ricky Williams	8.00	3.60

1999 Topps Autographs

	MINT	NRMT
COMPLETE SET (10)	800.00	350.00
COMMON CARD (A1-A10)	30.00	13.50
SEMISTARS	40.00	18.00

STATED ODDS 1:509 HOB, 1:140 HTA
R.WILLIAMS AUTO ODDS 1:18,372H, 1:5057HTA

❑ A1 Randy Moss	120.00	55.00
❑ A2 Wayne Chrebet	30.00	13.50
❑ A3 Tim Couch	100.00	45.00
❑ A4 Joey Galloway	40.00	18.00
❑ A5 Ricky Williams	250.00	110.00
❑ A6 Doug Flutie	50.00	22.00
❑ A7 Terrell Owens	40.00	18.00
❑ A8 Marshall Faulk	40.00	18.00
❑ A9 Rod Smith	30.00	13.50
❑ A10 Dan Marino	120.00	55.00

1999 Topps Hall of Fame Autographs

	MINT	NRMT
COMPLETE SET (5)	250.00	110.00
COMMON CARD (HOF1-HOF5)	50.00	22.00
SEMISTARS	60.00	27.00

STATED ODDS 1:1832 HOB, 1:503 HTA

❑ HOF1 Eric Dickerson	60.00	27.00

		MINT	NRMT
❑ HOF2	Billy Shaw	50.00	22.00
❑ HOF3	Lawrence Taylor	80.00	36.00
❑ HOF4	Tom Mack	50.00	22.00
❑ HOF5	Ozzie Newsome	80.00	36.00

1999 Topps Jumbos

	MINT	NRMT
COMPLETE SET (8)	20.00	9.00
COMMON CARD (1-8)	2.50	1.10
ONE PER HOBBY BOX		

		MINT	NRMT
❑ 1	Barry Sanders	5.00	2.20
❑ 2	Randy Moss	4.00	1.80
❑ 3	Terrell Davis	3.00	1.35
❑ 4	Dan Marino	5.00	2.20
❑ 5	Fred Taylor	2.50	1.10
❑ 6	John Elway	5.00	2.20
❑ 7	Brett Favre	5.00	2.20
❑ 8	Peyton Manning	4.00	1.80

1999 Topps Mystery Chrome

	MINT	NRMT
COMPLETE SET (20)	80.00	36.00
COMMON CARD (M1-M20)	1.50	.70
SEMISTARS	3.00	1.35

STATED ODDS 1:36 H/R, 1:24 JUM, 1:8 HTA
*REFRACTORS: 1X TO 2.5X HI COL.
REFRACT.STATED ODDS 1:144H/R, 1:32 HTA

		MINT	NRMT
❑ M1	Terrell Davis	8.00	3.60
❑ M2	Steve Young	5.00	2.20
❑ M3	Fred Taylor	6.00	2.70
❑ M4	Chris Claiborne	1.50	.70
❑ M5	Terrell Davis	8.00	3.60
❑ M6	Randall Cunningham	3.00	1.35
❑ M7	Charlie Batch	5.00	2.20
❑ M8	Fred Taylor	6.00	2.70
❑ M9	Vinny Testaverde	1.50	.70
❑ M10	Jamal Anderson	3.00	1.35
❑ M11	Randy Moss	10.00	4.50
❑ M12	Keyshawn Johnson	3.00	1.35
❑ M13	Vinny Testaverde	1.50	.70
❑ M14	Chris Chandler	1.50	.70
❑ M15	Fred Taylor	6.00	2.70
❑ M16	Ricky Williams	12.00	5.50
❑ M17	Chris Chandler	1.50	.70
❑ M18	John Elway	12.00	5.50
❑ M19	Randy Moss	10.00	4.50
❑ M20	Troy Edwards	4.00	1.80

1999 Topps Picture Perfect

	MINT	NRMT
COMPLETE SET (10)	30.00	13.50
COMMON CARD (P1-P10)	2.00	.90

STATED ODDS 1:14 H/R, 1:9 JUM, 1:4 HTA

		MINT	NRMT
❑ P1	Steve Young	2.00	.90
❑ P2	Brett Favre	5.00	2.20
❑ P3	Terrell Davis	3.00	1.35
❑ P4	Peyton Manning	4.00	1.80
❑ P5	Jake Plummer	2.50	1.10
❑ P6	Fred Taylor	2.50	1.10
❑ P7	Barry Sanders	5.00	2.20
❑ P8	Dan Marino	5.00	2.20
❑ P9	John Elway	5.00	2.20
❑ P10	Randy Moss	4.00	1.80

1999 Topps Record Numbers Silver

	MINT	NRMT
COMPLETE SET (10)	30.00	13.50
COMMON CARD (RN1-RN10)	.50	.23

STATED ODDS 1:18 H/R, 1:8 JUM, 1:6 HTA

		MINT	NRMT
❑ RN1	Randy Moss	5.00	2.20
❑ RN2	Terrell Davis	4.00	1.80
❑ RN3	Emmitt Smith	4.00	1.80
❑ RN4	Barry Sanders	6.00	2.70
❑ RN5	Dan Marino	6.00	2.70
❑ RN6	Brett Favre	6.00	2.70
❑ RN7	Doug Flutie	2.00	.90
❑ RN8	Jerry Rice	4.00	1.80
❑ RN9	Peyton Manning	5.00	2.20
❑ RN10	Jason Elam	.50	.23

1999 Topps Record Numbers Gold

	MINT	NRMT
COMPLETE SET (10)	800.00	350.00
COMMON CARD (RN1-RN10)	10.00	4.50

RN1 STATED ODDS 1:255,682H, 1:82,176HTA
RN2 STATED ODDS 1:82,921H, 1:21,914HTA
RN3 STATED ODDS 1:36,965H, 1:9961HTA
RN4 STATED ODDS 1:4579H, 1:1259HTA
RN5 STATED ODDS 1:11,238H, 1:3072HTA
RN6 STATED ODDS 1:153,403H, 1:41,088HTA
RN7 STATED ODDS 1:1391H, 1:383HTA
RN8 STATED ODDS 1:28,147H, 1:7644HTA
RN9 STATED ODDS 1:1224H, 1:337HTA
RN10 STATED ODDS 1:73,049H, 1:20,544HTA

		MINT	NRMT
❑ RN1	Randy Moss/17	300.00	135.00
❑ RN2	Terrell Davis/56	120.00	55.00
❑ RN3	Emmitt Smith/125	60.00	27.00
❑ RN4	Barry Sanders/1000	40.00	18.00
❑ RN5	Dan Marino/408	40.00	18.00
❑ RN6	Brett Favre/30	300.00	135.00
❑ RN7	Doug Flutie/3291	10.00	4.50
❑ RN8	Jerry Rice/164	40.00	18.00
❑ RN9	Peyton Manning/3739	20.00	9.00
❑ RN10	Jason Elam/63	12.00	5.50

1999 Topps Season's Best

	MINT	NRMT
COMPLETE SET (30)	60.00	27.00
COMMON CARD (SB1-SB30)	.50	.23
SEMISTARS	1.00	.45
UNLISTED STARS	2.00	.90

STATED ODDS 1:18 H/R, 1:12 JUM, 1:6 HTA

		MINT	NRMT
❑ SB1	Terrell Davis	5.00	2.20
❑ SB2	Jamal Anderson	2.00	.90
❑ SB3	Garrison Hearst	1.00	.45
❑ SB4	Barry Sanders	8.00	3.60
❑ SB5	Emmitt Smith	5.00	2.20
❑ SB6	Randall Cunningham	2.00	.90
❑ SB7	Brett Favre	8.00	3.60
❑ SB8	Steve Young	3.00	1.35
❑ SB9	Jake Plummer	4.00	1.80
❑ SB10	Peyton Manning	6.00	2.70
❑ SB11	Antonio Freeman	2.00	.90
❑ SB12	Eric Moulds	2.00	.90
❑ SB13	Randy Moss	6.00	2.70
❑ SB14	Rod Smith	1.00	.45
❑ SB15	Jimmy Smith	1.00	.45
❑ SB16	Michael Sinclair	.50	.23
❑ SB17	Kevin Greene	.50	.23
❑ SB18	Michael Strahan	.50	.23
❑ SB19	Michael McCrary	.50	.23
❑ SB20	Hugh Douglas	.50	.23
❑ SB21	Deion Sanders	2.00	.90
❑ SB22	Terry Fair	.50	.23
❑ SB23	Jacquez Green	1.00	.45
❑ SB24	Corey Harris	.50	.23
❑ SB25	Tim Dwight	2.00	.90
❑ SB26	Dan Marino	8.00	3.60
❑ SB27	Barry Sanders	8.00	3.60
❑ SB28	Jerry Rice	5.00	2.20
❑ SB29	Bruce Smith	1.00	.45
❑ SB30	Darrien Gordon	.50	.23

2000 Topps

	MINT	NRMT
COMPLETE SET (400)	120.00	55.00
COMP.SET w/o SP's (360)	20.00	9.00
COMMON CARD (1-400)	.15	.07
SEMISTARS	.25	.11

UNLISTED STARS .50 .23
COMMON EUR.PROS (341-360) .75 .35
EUR.PROS SEMISTARS 1.00 .45
COMMON ROOKIE (361-400) 2.00 .90
ROOKIE SEMISTARS 2.50 1.10
ROOKIE SUBSET ODDS 1:5H/R,1:1HTA

❑ 1 Kurt Warner 2.50 1.10
❑ 2 Darrell Russell .15 .07
❑ 3 Courtney Hawkins .15 .07
❑ 4 Bryant Young .15 .07
❑ 5 Kent Graham .15 .07
❑ 6 Shawn Jefferson .15 .07
❑ 7 Wesley Walls .15 .07
❑ 8 Jessie Armstead .15 .07
❑ 9 Dedric Ward .15 .07
❑ 10 Emmitt Smith 1.25 .55
❑ 11 James Stewart .25 .11
❑ 12 Frank Sanders .15 .07
❑ 13 Ray Buchanan .15 .07
❑ 14 Olindo Mare .15 .07
❑ 15 Andre Reed .25 .11
❑ 16 Curtis Conway .25 .11
❑ 17 Patrick Jeffers .50 .23
❑ 18 Greg Hill .15 .07
❑ 19 John Unitas .50 .23
❑ 20 Brett Favre 2.00 .90
❑ 21 Jerome Pathon .15 .07
❑ 22 Jason Tucker .25 .11
❑ 23 Charles Johnson .15 .07
❑ 24 Brian Mitchell .15 .07
❑ 25 Billy Miller .15 .07
❑ 26 Jay Fiedler .50 .23
❑ 27 Marcus Pollard .15 .07
❑ 28 De'Mond Parker .15 .07
❑ 29 Leslie Shepherd .15 .07
❑ 30 Fred Taylor .75 .35
❑ 31 Michael Pittman .15 .07
❑ 32 Ricky Watters .15 .07
❑ 33 Derrick Brooks .15 .07
❑ 34 Junior Seau .25 .11
❑ 35 Troy Vincent .15 .07
❑ 36 Eric Allen .15 .07
❑ 37 Pete Mitchell .15 .07
❑ 38 Tony Simmons .15 .07
❑ 39 Az-Zahir Hakim .25 .11
❑ 40 Dan Marino 2.00 .90
❑ 41 Mac Cody .15 .07
❑ 42 Scott Dreisbach .15 .07
❑ 43 Al Wilson .15 .07
❑ 44 Luther Broughton RC .25 .11
❑ 45 Wane McGarity .15 .07
❑ 46 Stephen Boyd .15 .07
❑ 47 Michael Strahan .15 .07
❑ 48 Chris Chandler .25 .11
❑ 49 Tony Martin .25 .11
❑ 50 Edgerrin James 2.00 .90
❑ 51 John Randle .25 .11
❑ 52 Warrick Dunn .50 .23
❑ 53 Elvis Grbac .25 .11
❑ 54 Champ Bailey .25 .11
❑ 55 Kyle Brady .15 .07
❑ 56 John Lynch .15 .07
❑ 57 Kevin Carter .15 .07
❑ 58 Mike Pritchard .15 .07
❑ 59 Deon Mitchell .15 .07
❑ 60 Randy Moss 1.50 .70
❑ 61 Jermaine Fazande .15 .07
❑ 62 Donovan McNabb .75 .35
❑ 63 Richard Huntley .15 .07
❑ 64 Rich Gannon .25 .11
❑ 65 Aaron Glenn .15 .07
❑ 66 Amani Toomer .15 .07
❑ 67 Andre Hastings .15 .07
❑ 68 Ricky Williams 1.25 .55
❑ 69 Sam Madison .15 .07
❑ 70 Drew Bledsoe .75 .35
❑ 71 Eric Moulds .50 .23
❑ 72 Justin Armour .15 .07
❑ 73 Jamal Anderson .50 .23
❑ 74 Mario Bates .15 .07
❑ 75 Sam Gash .15 .07
❑ 76 Macey Brooks .15 .07
❑ 77 Tremain Mack .15 .07
❑ 78 David LaFleur .15 .07
❑ 79 Dexter Coakley .15 .07
❑ 80 Cris Carter .50 .23
❑ 81 Byron Chamberlain .15 .07
❑ 82 David Sloan .15 .07
❑ 83 Mike Devlin .15 .07
❑ 84 Jimmy Smith .25 .11
❑ 85 Derrick Alexander .25 .11
❑ 86 Damon Huard .50 .23
❑ 87 Jake Reed .25 .11
❑ 88 Darrell Green .15 .07
❑ 89 Derrick Mason .15 .07
❑ 90 Curtis Martin .50 .23
❑ 91 Donnie Abraham .15 .07
❑ 92 D'Marco Farr .15 .07
❑ 93 Ahman Green .25 .11
❑ 94 Shane Matthews .25 .11
❑ 95 Torrance Small .15 .07
❑ 96 Duce Staley .50 .23
❑ 97 Jon Ritchie .15 .07
❑ 98 Victor Green .15 .07
❑ 99 Kerry Collins .25 .11
❑ 100 Peyton Manning 1.50 .70
❑ 101 Ben Coates .15 .07
❑ 102 Thurman Thomas .25 .11
❑ 103 Cornelius Bennett .15 .07
❑ 104 Terance Mathis .15 .07
❑ 105 Adrian Murrell .25 .11
❑ 106 Donald Hayes .15 .07
❑ 107 Terry Kirby .15 .07
❑ 108 James Allen .15 .07
❑ 109 Ty Law .15 .07
❑ 110 Tim Brown .50 .23
❑ 111 Chad Bratzke .15 .07
❑ 112 Deion Sanders .50 .23
❑ 113 James Johnson .25 .11
❑ 114 Tony Richardson .15 .07
❑ 115 Tony Brackens .15 .07
❑ 116 Ken Dilger .15 .07
❑ 117 Albert Connell .15 .07
❑ 118 Neil O'Donnell .15 .07
❑ 119 Selucio Sanford EP RC .75 .35
❑ 120 Steve Young .75 .35
❑ 121 Tony Horne .15 .07
❑ 122 Charlie Rogers .15 .07
❑ 123 J.J. Stokes .25 .11
❑ 124 Kenny Bynum .15 .07
❑ 125 Jeff Graham .15 .07
❑ 126 Ike Hilliard .25 .11
❑ 127 Ray Lucas .50 .23
❑ 128 Terry Glenn .50 .23
❑ 129 Rickey Dudley .15 .07
❑ 130 Joey Galloway .50 .23
❑ 131 Brian Dawkins .15 .07
❑ 132 Rob Moore .25 .11
❑ 133 Bob Christian .15 .07
❑ 134 Anthony Wright RC .75 .35
❑ 135 Antowain Smith .50 .23
❑ 136 Kevin Johnson .50 .23
❑ 137 Scott Covington .15 .07
❑ 138 D'Wayne Bates .15 .07
❑ 139 Sam Cowart .15 .07
❑ 140 Isaac Bruce .50 .23
❑ 141 Tony McGee .15 .07
❑ 142 Dale Carter .15 .07
❑ 143 Matt Hasselbeck .25 .11
❑ 144 Torry Holt .50 .23
❑ 145 Daunte Culpepper .75 .35
❑ 146 Yatil Green .15 .07
❑ 147 Chris Howard .15 .07
❑ 148 Irving Fryar .15 .07
❑ 149 Derrick Mayes .25 .11
❑ 150 Warren Sapp .25 .11
❑ 151 Ricky Proehl .15 .07
❑ 152 Eric Kresser EP .75 .35
❑ 153 Jeff Garcia .50 .23
❑ 154 Freddie Jones .15 .07
❑ 155 Mike Cloud .15 .07
❑ 156 Wayne Chrebet .25 .11
❑ 157 Joe Montgomery .15 .07
❑ 158 Shannon Sharpe .25 .11
❑ 159 Eddie Kennison .15 .07
❑ 160 Eddie George .60 .25
❑ 161 Jay Riemersma .15 .07
❑ 162 Peter Boulware .15 .07
❑ 163 Aeneas Williams .15 .07
❑ 164 Jim Miller .15 .07
❑ 165 Jamir Miller .15 .07
❑ 166 Tim Biakabutuka .25 .11
❑ 167 Kordell Stewart .50 .23
❑ 168 Charlie Garner .25 .11
❑ 169 Germane Crowell .25 .11
❑ 170 Stephen Davis .50 .23
❑ 171 Jeff George .25 .11
❑ 172 Mark Brunell .75 .35
❑ 173 Stephen Alexander .15 .07
❑ 174 Mike Alstott .50 .23
❑ 175 Terry Allen .25 .11
❑ 176 Ed McCaffrey .15 .07
❑ 177 Bobby Engram .15 .07
❑ 178 Andre Cooper .15 .07
❑ 179 Kevin Faulk .15 .07
❑ 180 Errict Rhett .25 .11
❑ 181 Jammi German .15 .07
❑ 182 Oronde Gadsden .15 .07
❑ 183 Jevon Kearse .50 .23
❑ 184 Herman Moore .50 .23
❑ 185 Terrence Wilkins .50 .23
❑ 186 Rocket Ismail .25 .11
❑ 187 Patrick Johnson .15 .07
❑ 188 Simeon Rice .15 .07
❑ 189 Mo Lewis .15 .07
❑ 190 Qadry Ismail .15 .07
❑ 191 Terry Jackson .15 .07
❑ 192 Rashaan Shehee .15 .07
❑ 193 Charles Woodson .25 .11
❑ 194 Akili Smith .60 .25
❑ 195 Yancey Thigpen .15 .07
❑ 196 Michael Westbrook .25 .11
❑ 197 Donnell Bennett ,15 .07
❑ 198 Sedrick Irvin .15 .07
❑ 199 Keenan McCardell .25 .11
❑ 200 Marshall Faulk .50 .23
❑ 201 Jeff Blake .25 .11
❑ 202 Rob Johnson .25 .11
❑ 203 Vinny Testaverde .25 .11
❑ 204 Andy Katzenmoyer .15 .07
❑ 205 Michael Basnight .15 .07
❑ 206 Lance Schulters .15 .07
❑ 207 Shaun King .75 .35
❑ 208 Bill Schroeder .25 .11
❑ 209 Skip Hicks .25 .11
❑ 210 Jake Plummer .50 .23
❑ 211 Leroy Hoard .15 .07
❑ 212 Reggie Barlow .15 .07
❑ 213 E.G. Green .15 .07
❑ 214 Fred Lane .15 .07
❑ 215 Antonio Freeman .50 .23
❑ 216 Grant Wistrom .15 .07
❑ 217 Kevin Dyson .25 .11
❑ 218 Mikhael Ricks .15 .07
❑ 219 Rod Woodson .15 .07
❑ 220 Tim Dwight .50 .23
❑ 221 Darnay Scott .25 .11
❑ 222 Curtis Enis .50 .23
❑ 223 Sean Bennett .15 .07
❑ 224 Napoleon Kaufman .50 .23
❑ 225 Jonathan Linton .15 .07
❑ 226 Jim Harbaugh .25 .11
❑ 227 Hardy Nickerson .15 .07
❑ 228 Todd Lyght .15 .07
❑ 229 Dorsey Levens .50 .23
❑ 230 Steve Beuerlein .25 .11
❑ 231 Marty Booker .15 .07
❑ 232 Shawn Bryson .15 .07
❑ 233 James Hasty .15 .07
❑ 234 Brock Marion .15 .07
❑ 235 Larry Centers .15 .07
❑ 236 Charlie Batch .50 .23
❑ 237 Steve McNair .50 .23
❑ 238 Darrin Chiaverini .15 .07
❑ 239 Jerome Bettis .50 .23
❑ 240 Muhsin Muhammad .25 .11
❑ 241 Terrell Fletcher .15 .07
❑ 242 Jon Kitna .50 .23
❑ 243 Frank Wycheck .15 .07
❑ 244 Tony Gonzalez .25 .11
❑ 245 Ron Rivers .15 .07
❑ 246 Olandis Gary .60 .25
❑ 247 Jermaine Lewis .15 .07
❑ 248 Joe Jurevicius .15 .07
❑ 249 Richie Anderson .15 .07
❑ 250 Marcus Robinson .50 .23
❑ 251 Shawn Springs .15 .07

❑ 252 William Floyd	.15	.07
❑ 253 Bobby Shaw RC	.15	.07
❑ 254 Glyn Milburn	.15	.07
❑ 255 Brian Griese	.60	.25
❑ 256 Donnie Edwards	.15	.07
❑ 257 Joe Horn	.15	.07
❑ 258 Cameron Cleeland	.15	.07
❑ 259 Glenn Foley	.15	.07
❑ 260 Corey Dillon	.50	.23
❑ 261 Troy Brown	.15	.07
❑ 262 Stoney Case	.15	.07
❑ 263 Kevin Williams	.15	.07
❑ 264 London Fletcher RC	.25	.11
❑ 265 O.J. McDuffie	.25	.11
❑ 266 Jonathan Quinn	.15	.07
❑ 267 Trent Dilfer	.25	.11
❑ 268 Dameyune Craig	.15	.07
❑ 269 Terrell Owens	.50	.23
❑ 270 Tim Couch	1.25	.55
❑ 271 Dameane Douglas	.15	.07
❑ 272 Moses Moreno	.15	.07
❑ 273 Bruce Smith	.25	.11
❑ 274 Peerless Price	.50	.23
❑ 275 Sam Games	.15	.07
❑ 276 Natrone Means	.15	.07
❑ 277 Na Brown	.15	.07
❑ 278 Dave Moore	.15	.07
❑ 279 Chris Sanders	.15	.07
❑ 280 Troy Aikman	1.25	.55
❑ 281 Cecil Collins	.15	.07
❑ 282 Matthew Hatchette	.25	.11
❑ 283 Bill Romanowski	.15	.07
❑ 284 Basil Mitchell	.15	.07
❑ 285 Tony Banks	.25	.11
❑ 286 Jake Delhomme RC	2.00	.90
❑ 287 Keyshawn Johnson	.50	.23
❑ 288 Dexter McLeon	.15	.07
❑ 289 Corey Bradford	.25	.11
❑ 290 Terrell Davis	1.25	.55
❑ 291 Johnnie Morton	.25	.11
❑ 292 Kevin Lockett	.15	.07
❑ 293 Robert Smith	.50	.23
❑ 294 Jeff Lewis	.15	.07
❑ 295 Wali Rainer	.15	.07
❑ 296 Troy Edwards	.50	.23
❑ 297 Keith Poole	.15	.07
❑ 298 Priest Holmes	.25	.11
❑ 299 David Boston	.50	.23
❑ 300 Marvin Harrison	.50	.23
❑ 301 Levon Kirkland	.15	.07
❑ 302 Robert Holcombe	.15	.07
❑ 303 Autry Denson	.15	.07
❑ 304 Kevin Hardy	.15	.07
❑ 305 Rod Smith	.25	.11
❑ 306 Robert Porcher	.15	.07
❑ 307 Cade McNown	.75	.35
❑ 308 Craig Yeast	.15	.07
❑ 309 Doug Flutie	.60	.25
❑ 310 Jerry Rice	1.25	.55
❑ 311 Brad Johnson	.50	.23
❑ 312 Tiki Barber	.25	.11
❑ 313 Will Blackwell	.15	.07
❑ 314 Sean Dawkins	.15	.07
❑ 315 Jacquez Green	.25	.11
❑ 316 Zach Thomas	.25	.11
❑ 317 Gus Frerotte	.15	.07
❑ 318 Chris Warren	.15	.07
❑ 319 Carl Pickens	.25	.11
❑ 320 Tyrone Wheatley HL	.15	.07
❑ 321 Kurt Warner HL	1.25	.55
❑ 322 Dan Marino HL	1.00	.45
❑ 323 Cris Carter HL	.25	.11
❑ 324 Brett Favre HL	1.00	.45
❑ 325 Marshall Faulk HL	.25	.11
❑ 326 Jevon Kearse HL	.25	.11
❑ 327 Edgerrin James HL	1.00	.45
❑ 328 Emmitt Smith HL	.60	.25
❑ 329 Andre Reed HL	.15	.07
❑ 330 Kevin Dyson Frank Wycheck	.15	.07
❑ 331 Olindo Mare MM	.15	.07
❑ 332 Marcus Coleman MM	.15	.07
❑ 333 James Johnson MM	.15	.07
❑ 334 Ray Lucas MM	.25	.11
❑ 335 Dedric Ward MM	.15	.07
❑ 336 Richie Cunningham MM	.15	.07
❑ 337 James Hasty MM	.15	.07
❑ 338 Sedrick Shaw MM	.15	.07
❑ 339 Kurt Warner MM	1.25	.55
❑ 340 Marshall Faulk MM	.25	.11
❑ 341 Brian Shay EP	.75	.35
❑ 342 L.C. Stevens EP	.75	.35
❑ 343 Corey Thomas EP	.75	.35
❑ 344 Scott Milanovich EP	.75	.35
❑ 345 Pat Barnes EP	1.00	.45
❑ 346 Danny Wuerffel EP	1.00	.45
❑ 347 Kevin Daft EP	.75	.35
❑ 348 Ron Powlus EP RC	1.50	.70
❑ 349 Tony Graziani EP	1.00	.45
❑ 350 Norman Miller EP RC	.75	.35
❑ 351 Cory Sauter EP	.75	.35
❑ 352 Marcus Crandell EP RC	.75	.35
❑ 353 Sean Morey EP RC	.75	.35
❑ 354 Jeff Ogden EP	1.00	.45
❑ 355 Ted White EP	.75	.35
❑ 356 Jim Kubiak EP RC	.75	.35
❑ 357 Aaron Stecker EP RC	.75	.35
❑ 358 Ronnie Powell EP	.75	.35
❑ 359 Matt Lytle EP RC	.75	.35
❑ 360 Kendrick Nord EP RC	.75	.35
❑ 361 Tim Rattay RC	3.00	1.35
❑ 362 Rob Morris RC	2.00	.90
❑ 363 Chris Samuels RC	2.00	.90
❑ 364 Todd Husak RC	2.50	1.10
❑ 365 Ahmed Plummer RC	2.00	.90
❑ 366 Frank Murphy RC	2.50	1.10
❑ 367 Michael Wiley RC	3.00	1.35
❑ 368 Giovanni Carmazzi RC	5.00	2.20
❑ 369 Anthony Becht RC	2.50	1.10
❑ 370 John Abraham RC	2.00	.90
❑ 371 Shaun Alexander RC	8.00	3.60
❑ 372 Thomas Jones RC	8.00	3.60
❑ 373 Courtney Brown RC	5.00	2.20
❑ 374 Curtis Keaton RC	2.00	.90
❑ 375 Jerry Porter RC	3.00	1.35
❑ 376 Corey Simon RC	2.50	1.10
❑ 377 Dez White RC	3.00	1.35
❑ 378 Jamal Lewis RC	8.00	3.60
❑ 379 Ron Dayne RC	12.00	5.50
❑ 380 R.Jay Soward RC	3.00	1.35
❑ 381 Tee Martin RC	4.00	1.80
❑ 382 Shaun Ellis RC	2.00	.90
❑ 383 Brian Urlacher RC	3.00	1.35
❑ 384 Reuben Droughns RC	3.00	1.35
❑ 385 Travis Taylor RC	5.00	2.20
❑ 386 Plaxico Burress RC	6.00	2.70
❑ 387 Chad Pennington RC	10.00	4.50
❑ 388 Sylvester Morris RC	3.00	1.35
❑ 389 Ron Dugans RC	2.50	1.10
❑ 390 Joe Hamilton RC	2.50	1.10
❑ 391 Chris Redman RC	4.00	1.80
❑ 392 Trung Canidate RC	2.50	1.10
❑ 393 J.R. Redmond RC	4.00	1.80
❑ 394 Danny Farmer RC	2.50	1.10
❑ 395 Todd Pinkston RC	2.50	1.10
❑ 396 Dennis Northcutt RC	3.00	1.35
❑ 397 Laveranues Coles RC	2.50	1.10
❑ 398 Bubba Franks RC	3.00	1.35
❑ 399 Travis Prentice RC	3.00	1.35
❑ 400 Peter Warrick RC	12.00	5.50

2000 Topps MVP Promotion

	MINT	NRMT
COMMON CARD (1-319)	8.00	3.60
*STARS: 20X TO 50X HI COL.		
*YOUNG STARS: 15X TO 40X		
COMMON ROOKIE (361-400)	15.00	6.75
*RCs: 3X TO 8X		
STATED ODDS 1:234 HOB, 1:52 HTA		
REDEMPTION EXPIRATION DATE: 1/12/2001		

2000 Topps Pro Bowl Jerseys

	MINT	NRMT
COMPLETE SET (24)	1000.00	450.00
COMMON CARD	30.00	13.50
SEMISTARS	40.00	18.00
UNLISTED STARS	50.00	22.00
STATED ODDS 1:271 HOB, 1:60 HTA		

❑ BMOG Bruce Matthews	30.00	13.50
❑ CCWR Cris Carter	50.00	22.00
❑ CDRB Corey Dillon	50.00	22.00
❑ DRIL Darrell Russell	30.00	13.50
❑ EGRB Eddie George	60.00	27.00
❑ ESRB Emmitt Smith	100.00	45.00
❑ JAOL Jessie Armstead	30.00	13.50
❑ KCDE Kevin Carter	30.00	13.50
❑ KHOL Kevin Hardy	30.00	13.50
❑ KJWR Keyshawn Johnson	40.00	18.00
❑ KWQB Kurt Warner	120.00	55.00
❑ MAFB Mike Alstott	50.00	22.00
❑ MBQB Mark Brunell	80.00	36.00
❑ MHWR Marvin Harrison	50.00	22.00
❑ MMWR Muhsin Muhammad	30.00	13.50
❑ MSDE Michael Strahan	30.00	13.50
❑ OMPK Olindo Mare	30.00	13.50
❑ RGQB Rich Gannon	40.00	18.00
❑ RWFS Rod Woodson	40.00	18.00
❑ SBQB Steve Beuerlein	40.00	18.00
❑ TBDE Tony Brackens	30.00	13.50
❑ TGTE Tony Gonzalez	40.00	18.00
❑ WSIL Warren Sapp	40.00	18.00
❑ ZTIL Zach Thomas	40.00	18.00

2000 Topps Superbowl MVP Autograph Relic

	MINT	NRMT
COMMON CARD (SB1)	300.00	135.00
STATED ODDS 1:1287 HTA		
❑ SB1 Kurt Warner	300.00	135.00

2000 Topps Autographs

	MINT	NRMT
COMPLETE SET (15)	800.00	350.00
COMMON CARD	25.00	11.00
SEMISTARS	40.00	18.00
STATED ODDS 1:1015H/R, 1:226HTA		
REPORTED AUTO.PRINT RUNS 250-700		

❑ CP Chad Pennington	70.00	32.00
❑ EJ Edgerrin James	80.00	36.00
❑ JK Jon Kitna	25.00	11.00
❑ JS Jimmy Smith	25.00	11.00
❑ KW Kurt Warner	150.00	70.00
❑ MF Marshall Faulk	60.00	27.00
❑ MH Marvin Harrison	40.00	18.00
❑ PM Peyton Manning	120.00	55.00
❑ PW Peter Warrick SP		
❑ RD Ron Dayne	80.00	36.00
❑ SA Shaun Alexander	60.00	27.00
❑ SD Stephen Davis	40.00	18.00
❑ SM Sylvester Morris	25.00	11.00
❑ TJ Thomas Jones	60.00	27.00
❑ ZT Zach Thomas	25.00	11.00

2000 Topps Chrome Previews

	MINT	NRMT
COMPLETE SET (20)	40.00	18.00

COMMON CARD (CP1-CP20)	1.00	.45
SEMISTARS	1.50	.70
STATED ODDS 1:18 H/R, 1:5 HTA		

❑ CP1 Kurt Warner	6.00	2.70
❑ CP2 Shaun King	2.00	.90
❑ CP3 Brad Johnson	1.50	.70
❑ CP4 Daunte Culpepper	2.00	.90
❑ CP5 Brett Favre	6.00	2.70
❑ CP6 Eddie George	2.00	.90
❑ CP7 Dan Marino	6.00	2.70
❑ CP8 Randy Moss	5.00	2.20
❑ CP9 Troy Aikman	4.00	1.80
❑ CP10 Peyton Manning	5.00	2.20
❑ CP11 Fred Taylor	2.50	1.10
❑ CP12 Ricky Williams	3.00	1.35
❑ CP13 Jimmy Smith	1.00	.45
❑ CP14 Jerry Rice	4.00	1.80
❑ CP15 Marshall Faulk	1.50	.70
❑ CP16 Marvin Harrison	1.50	.70
❑ CP17 Stephen Davis	1.50	.70
❑ CP18 Isaac Bruce	1.50	.70
❑ CP19 Emmitt Smith	4.00	1.80
❑ CP20 Edgerrin James	5.00	2.20

2000 Topps Combos

	MINT	NRMT
COMPLETE SET (10)	15.00	6.75
COMMON CARD (CS1-CS10)	2.00	.90
STATED ODDS 1:12H/R 1:4HTA..		

❑ CS1 Johnny Unitas Peyton Manning	5.00	2.20
❑ CS2 Chris Carter Randy Moss	4.00	1.80
❑ CS3 Ricky Williams Edgerrin James	5.00	2.20
❑ CS4 Marvin Harrison Jimmy Smith	2.00	.90
❑ CS5 Isaac Bruce Joey Galloway	2.00	.90
❑ CS6 Donovan McNabb Tim Couch Shaun King Daunte Culpepper Akili Smith	5.00	2.20
❑ CS7 Stephen Davis Fred Taylor	2.50	1.10
❑ CS8 Marshall Faulk Eddie George	2.00	.90
❑ CS9 Emmitt Smith Troy Aikman	3.00	1.35
❑ CS10 Kurt Warner Dan Marino	6.00	2.70

2000 Topps Hall of Fame Autographs

	MINT	NRMT
COMPLETE SET (5)	500.00	220.00
COMMON CARD (HOF1-HOF5)	60.00	27.00
STATED ODDS 1:3551H/R, 1:790 HTA		

❑ HOF1 Joe Montana	300.00	135.00
❑ HOF2 Howie Long	100.00	45.00
❑ HOF3 Ronnie Lott	70.00	32.00
❑ HOF4 Dan Rooney	60.00	27.00
❑ HOF5 Dave Wilcox	60.00	27.00

2000 Topps Hobby Masters

	MINT	NRMT
COMPLETE SET (10)	25.00	11.00
COMMON CARD (HM1-HM10)	1.50	.70
STATED ODDS 1:5 HTA		

❑ HM1 Kurt Warner	6.00	2.70
❑ HM2 Ricky Williams	3.00	1.35
❑ HM3 Eddie George	2.00	.90
❑ HM4 Dan Marino	6.00	2.70
❑ HM5 Edgerrin James	5.00	2.20
❑ HM6 Marshall Faulk	1.50	.70
❑ HM7 Emmitt Smith	4.00	1.80
❑ HM8 Jerry Rice	4.00	1.80
❑ HM9 Brett Favre	6.00	2.70
❑ HM10 Randy Moss	5.00	2.20

2000 Topps Unitas Reprints

	MINT	NRMT
COMPLETE SET (18)	70.00	32.00
COMMON CARD (R1-R18)	5.00	2.20
STATED ODDS 1:19 HOB, 1:4 HTA		
*CHROME: .6X TO 1.5X HI COL.		
CHROME STATED ODDS 1:72 H, 1:20 HTA		
COMMON AUTO (R1-R18)	200.00	90.00
AUTO.STATED ODDS 1:13,678 H, 1:3048 HTA		

❑ R1 Johnny Unitas 1957	8.00	3.60
❑ R2 Johnny Unitas 1958	5.00	2.20
❑ R3 Johnny Unitas 1959	5.00	2.20
❑ R4 Johnny Unitas 1960	5.00	2.20
❑ R5 Johnny Unitas 1961	5.00	2.20
❑ R6 Johnny Unitas 1962	5.00	2.20
❑ R7 Johnny Unitas 1963	5.00	2.20
❑ R8 Johnny Unitas 1964	5.00	2.20
❑ R9 Johnny Unitas 1965	5.00	2.20
❑ R10 Johnny Unitas 1966	5.00	2.20
❑ R11 Johnny Unitas 1967	5.00	2.20
❑ R12 Johnny Unitas 1968	5.00	2.20
❑ R13 Johnny Unitas 1969	5.00	2.20
❑ R14 Johnny Unitas 1970	5.00	2.20
❑ R15 Johnny Unitas 1971	5.00	2.20
❑ R16 Johnny Unitas 1972	5.00	2.20
❑ R17 Johnny Unitas 1973		
❑ R18 Johnny Unitas 1974		

2000 Topps Jumbos

	MINT	NRMT
COMPLETE SET (8)	20.00	9.00
COMMON CARD (1-8)	1.25	.55
ONE PER HOBBY BOX		

❑ 1 Peyton Manning	4.00	1.80
❑ 2 Marshall Faulk	1.25	.55
❑ 3 Dan Marino	5.00	2.20
❑ 4 Randy Moss	4.00	1.80
❑ 5 Kurt Warner	5.00	2.20
❑ 6 Eddie George	1.50	.70
❑ 7 Brett Favre	5.00	2.20
❑ 8 Edgerrin James	4.00	1.80

2000 Topps Own the Game

	MINT	NRMT
COMPLETE SET (30)	50.00	22.00
COMMON CARD (OTG1-OTG30)	1.00	.45
SEMISTARS	1.50	.70
STATED ODDS 1:12H/R, 1:4 HTA		

❑ OTG1 Steve Beuerlein	1.00	.45
❑ OTG2 Kurt Warner	6.00	2.70
❑ OTG3 Peyton Manning	5.00	2.20
❑ OTG4 Brett Favre	6.00	2.70
❑ OTG5 Brad Johnson	1.50	.70
❑ OTG6 Edgerrin James	5.00	2.20
❑ OTG7 Curtis Martin	1.50	.70
❑ OTG8 Stephen Davis	1.50	.70
❑ OTG9 Emmitt Smith	4.00	1.80
❑ OTG10 Marshall Faulk	1.50	.70
❑ OTG11 Eddie George	2.00	.90
❑ OTG12 Duce Staley	1.50	.70
❑ OTG13 Charlie Garner	1.00	.45
❑ OTG14 Marvin Harrison	1.50	.70
❑ OTG15 Jimmy Smith	1.00	.45
❑ OTG16 Randy Moss	5.00	2.20
❑ OTG17 Marcus Robinson	1.50	.70
❑ OTG18 Tim Brown	1.50	.70
❑ OTG19 Germane Crowell	1.00	.45
❑ OTG20 Muhsin Muhammad	1.00	.45
❑ OTG21 Cris Carter	1.50	.70
❑ OTG22 Michael Westbrook	1.00	.45
❑ OTG23 Amani Toomer	1.00	.45
❑ OTG24 Keyshawn Johnson	1.50	.70
❑ OTG25 Isaac Bruce	1.50	.70
❑ OTG26 Kurt Warner	6.00	2.70
❑ OTG27 Stephen Davis	1.50	.70
❑ OTG28 Edgerrin James	5.00	2.20
❑ OTG29 Cris Carter	1.50	.70
❑ OTG30 Marvin Harrison	1.50	.70

2000 Topps Rookie Photo Shoot Autographs

	MINT	NRMT
COMMON CARD		
STATED ODDS 1:5761 H, 1:1276 HTA		

❑ AB Anthony Becht		

❑ BU Brian Urlacher
❑ CB Courtney Brown
❑ CK Curtis Keaton
❑ CP Chad Pennington
❑ CR Chris Redman
❑ CS Corey Simon
❑ DF Danny Farmer
❑ DN Dennis Northcutt
❑ DW Dez White
❑ JH Joe Hamilton
❑ JP Jerry Porter
❑ JR J.R. Redmond
❑ LC Laveranues Coles
❑ PB Plaxico Burress
❑ PW Peter Warrick
❑ RD Ron Dayne
❑ SA Shaun Alexander
❑ SM Sylvester Morris
❑ TC Trung Canidate
❑ TJ Thomas Jones
❑ TM Tee Martin
❑ TP Todd Pinkston
❑ TT Travis Taylor
❑ CSA Chris Samuels
❑ DFR Bubba Franks
❑ RDR Reuben Droughns
❑ RDU Ron Dugans
❑ TPR Travis Prentice

1996 Topps Chrome

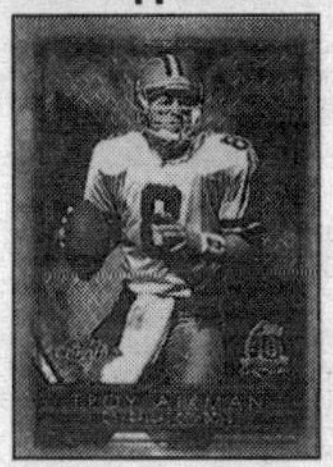

	MINT	NRMT
COMPLETE SET (165)	250.00	110.00
COMMON CARD (1-165)	.20	.09
SEMISTARS	.50	.23
UNLISTED STARS	1.00	.45
COMMON ROOKIES (150-164)	1.25	.55
ROOKIE SEMISTARS	2.00	.90
ALL ROOKIES CONDITION SENSITIVE !		
COMP.REFRACT.SET (165)	1200.00	550.00
*REFRACTOR STARS: 4X TO 10X HI COL.		
*REFRACTOR RCs: 1.2X TO 3X..		
REFRACTOR STATED ODDS 1:12		

❑ 1 Troy Aikman 2.50 1.10
❑ 2 Kevin Greene .50 .23
❑ 3 Robert Brooks 1.00 .45
❑ 4 Junior Seau .50 .23
❑ 5 Brett Perriman .20 .09
❑ 6 Cortez Kennedy .20 .09
❑ 7 Orlando Thomas .20 .09
❑ 8 Anthony Miller .50 .23
❑ 9 Jeff Blake 1.00 .45
❑ 10 Trent Dilfer 1.00 .45
❑ 11 Heath Shuler .50 .23
❑ 12 Michael Jackson .50 .23
❑ 13 Merton Hanks .20 .09
❑ 14 Dale Carter .20 .09
❑ 15 Eric Metcalf .20 .09
❑ 16 Barry Sanders 5.00 2.20
❑ 17 Joey Galloway 1.50 .70
❑ 18 Bryan Cox .20 .09
❑ 19 Harvey Williams .20 .09
❑ 20 Terrell Davis 5.00 2.20
❑ 21 Darnay Scott .50 .23
❑ 22 Kerry Collins 1.00 .45
❑ 23 Warren Sapp .20 .09
❑ 24 Michael Westbrook 1.00 .45
❑ 25 Mark Brunell 2.50 1.10
❑ 26 Craig Heyward .20 .09
❑ 27 Eric Allen .20 .09
❑ 28 Dana Stubblefield .50 .23
❑ 29 Steve Bono .20 .09
❑ 30 Larry Brown .20 .09
❑ 31 Warren Moon .50 .23
❑ 32 Jim Kelly 1.00 .45
❑ 33 Terry McDaniel .20 .09
❑ 34 Dan Wilkinson .20 .09
❑ 35 Dave Brown .20 .09
❑ 36 Todd Lyght .20 .09
❑ 37 Aeneas Williams .20 .09
❑ 38 Shannon Sharpe .50 .23
❑ 39 Errict Rhett .50 .23
❑ 40 Yancey Thigpen .50 .23
❑ 41 J.J. Stokes 1.00 .45
❑ 42 Marshall Faulk 1.00 .45
❑ 43 Chester McGlockton .20 .09
❑ 44 Darryll Lewis .20 .09
❑ 45 Drew Bledsoe 2.50 1.10
❑ 46 Tyrone Wheatley .50 .23
❑ 47 Herman Moore 1.00 .45
❑ 48 Darren Woodson .50 .23
❑ 49 Ricky Watters .50 .23
❑ 50 Emmitt Smith TYC 1.50 .70
❑ 51 Barry Sanders TYC 2.00 .90
❑ 52 Curtis Martin TYC 1.00 .45
❑ 53 Chris Warren TYC .50 .23
❑ 54 Errict Rhett TYC .50 .23
❑ 55 Rodney Hampton TYC .20 .09
❑ 56 Terrell Davis TYC 2.50 1.10
❑ 57 Marshall Faulk TYC .50 .23
❑ 58 Rashaan Salaam TYC .50 .23
❑ 59 Curtis Conway 1.00 .45
❑ 60 Isaac Bruce 1.00 .45
❑ 61 Thurman Thomas 1.00 .45
❑ 62 Terry Allen .50 .23
❑ 63 Lamar Lathon .20 .09
❑ 64 Mark Chmura .50 .23
❑ 65 Chris Warren .50 .23
❑ 66 Jessie Tuggle .20 .09
❑ 67 Erik Kramer .20 .09
❑ 68 Tim Brown 1.00 .45
❑ 69 Derrick Thomas .50 .23
❑ 70 Willie McGinest .20 .09
❑ 71 Frank Sanders .50 .23
❑ 72 Bernie Parmalee .20 .09
❑ 73 Kordell Stewart 1.50 .70
❑ 74 Brent Jones .20 .09
❑ 75 Edgar Bennett .50 .23
❑ 76 Rashaan Salaam 1.00 .45
❑ 77 Carl Pickens 1.00 .45
❑ 78 Terance Mathis .20 .09
❑ 79 Deion Sanders 1.25 .55
❑ 80 Glyn Milburn .20 .09
❑ 81 Lee Woodall .20 .09
❑ 82 Neil Smith .20 .09
❑ 83 Stan Humphries .50 .23
❑ 84 Rick Mirer .50 .23
❑ 85 Troy Vincent .20 .09
❑ 86 Sam Mills .20 .09
❑ 87 Brian Mitchell .20 .09
❑ 88 Hardy Nickerson .20 .09
❑ 89 Tamarick Vanover .50 .23
❑ 90 Steve McNair 1.50 .70
❑ 91 Jerry Rice TYC 1.00 .45
❑ 92 Isaac Bruce TYC 1.00 .45
❑ 93 Herman Moore TYC 1.00 .45
❑ 94 Cris Carter TYC 1.00 .45
❑ 95 Tim Brown TYC .50 .23
❑ 96 Carl Pickens TYC 1.00 .45
❑ 97 Joey Galloway TYC 1.00 .45
❑ 98 Jerry Rice 2.50 1.10
❑ 99 Cris Carter 1.00 .45
❑ 100 Curtis Martin 1.50 .70
❑ 101 Scott Mitchell .50 .23
❑ 102 Ken Harvey .20 .09
❑ 103 Rodney Hampton .50 .23
❑ 104 Reggie White 1.00 .45
❑ 105 Eddie Robinson .20 .09
❑ 106 Greg Lloyd .50 .23
❑ 107 Phillippi Sparks .20 .09
❑ 108 Emmitt Smith 4.00 1.80
❑ 109 Tom Carter .20 .09
❑ 110 Jim Everett .20 .09
❑ 111 James O.Stewart .50 .23
❑ 112 Kyle Brady .20 .09
❑ 113 Irving Fryar .50 .23
❑ 114 Vinny Testaverde .50 .23
❑ 115 John Elway 5.00 2.20
❑ 116 Chris Spielman .20 .09
❑ 117 Mike Mamula .20 .09
❑ 118 Jim Harbaugh .50 .23
❑ 119 Ken Norton .20 .09
❑ 120 Bruce Smith .50 .23
❑ 121 Daryl Johnston .50 .23
❑ 122 Blaine Bishop .20 .09
❑ 123 Jeff George .50 .23
❑ 124 Jeff Hostetler .20 .09
❑ 125 Jerome Bettis 1.00 .45
❑ 126 Jay Novacek .20 .09
❑ 127 Bryce Paup .20 .09
❑ 128 Neil O'Donnell .50 .23
❑ 129 Marcus Allen 1.00 .45
❑ 130 Steve Young 1.50 .70
❑ 131 Brett Favre TYC 2.00 .90
❑ 132 Scott Mitchell TYC .20 .09
❑ 133 John Elway TYC 2.00 .90
❑ 134 Jeff Blake TYC .50 .23
❑ 135 Dan Marino TYC 2.00 .90
❑ 136 Drew Bledsoe TYC 1.00 .45
❑ 137 Troy Aikman TYC 1.00 .45
❑ 138 Steve Young TYC 1.00 .45
❑ 139 Jim Kelly TYC 1.00 .45
❑ 140 Jeff Graham .20 .09
❑ 141 Hugh Douglas .20 .09
❑ 142 Dan Marino 5.00 2.20
❑ 143 Darrell Green .20 .09
❑ 144 Eric Zeier .20 .09
❑ 145 Brett Favre 5.00 2.20
❑ 146 Carnell Lake .20 .09
❑ 147 Ben Coates .50 .23
❑ 148 Tony Martin .50 .23
❑ 149 Michael Irvin 1.00 .45
❑ 150 Lawrence Phillips RC 12.00 5.50
❑ 151 Alex Van Dyke RC 2.00 .90
❑ 152 Kevin Hardy RC 2.00 .90
❑ 153 Rickey Dudley RC 6.00 2.70
❑ 154 Eric Moulds RC 30.00 13.50
❑ 155 Simeon Rice RC 2.50 1.10
❑ 156 Marvin Harrison RC 50.00 22.00
❑ 157 Tim Biakabutuka RC 20.00 9.00
❑ 158 Duane Clemons RC 1.25 .55
❑ 159 Keyshawn Johnson RC 50.00 22.00
❑ 160 John Mobley RC 2.00 .90
❑ 161 Leeland McElroy RC 2.00 .90
❑ 162 Eddie George RC 60.00 27.00
❑ 163 Jonathan Ogden RC 1.25 .55
❑ 164 Eddie Kennison RC 10.00 4.50
❑ 165 Checklist .20 .09

1996 Topps Chrome 40th Anniversary Retros

	MINT	NRMT
COMPLETE SET (40)	150.00	70.00
STATED ODDS 1:8		
REFRACTORS: 1.25X TO 3X BASE INSERT		
REF.STATED ODDS 1:24		

❑ 1 Jim Harbaugh 1956 1.50 .70
❑ 2 Greg Lloyd 1957 1.50 .70
❑ 3 Barry Sanders 1958 15.00 6.75

Card	Mint	Nrmt
4 Merton Hanks 1959	.60	.25
5 Herman Moore 1960	3.00	1.35
6 Tim Brown 1961	3.00	1.35
7 Brett Favre 1962	15.00	6.75
8 Cris Carter 1963	3.00	1.35
9 Curtis Martin 1964	5.00	2.20
10 Bryce Paup 1965	.60	.25
11 Steve Bono 1966	.60	.25
12 Blaine Bishop 1967	.60	.25
13 Emmitt Smith 1968	12.00	5.50
14 Carnell Lake 1969	.60	.25
15 Marshall Faulk 1970	3.00	1.35
16 Mike Morris 1971	.60	.25
17 Shannon Sharpe 1972	1.50	.70
18 Steve Young 1973	5.00	2.20
19 Jeff George 1974	1.50	.70
20 Junior Seau 1975	1.50	.70
21 Chris Warren 1976	1.50	.70
22 Heath Shuler 1977	1.50	.70
23 Jeff Blake 1978	3.00	1.35
24 Reggie White 1979	3.00	1.35
25 Jeff Hostetler 1980	.60	.25
26 Errict Rhett 1981	1.50	.70
27 Rodney Hampton 1982	1.50	.70
28 Jerry Rice 1983	8.00	3.60
29 Jim Everett 1984	.60	.25
30 Isaac Bruce 1985	3.00	1.35
31 Dan Marino 1986	15.00	6.75
32 Marcus Allen 1987	3.00	1.35
33 Erik Kramer 1988	.60	.25
34 John Elway 1989	15.00	6.75
35 Ricky Watters 1990	1.50	.70
36 Troy Aikman 1991	8.00	3.60
37 Drew Bledsoe 1992	8.00	3.60
38 Scott Mitchell 1993	1.50	.70
39 Rashaan Salaam 1994	3.00	1.35
40 Kerry Collins 1995	3.00	1.35

1996 Topps Chrome Tide Turners

	MINT	NRMT
COMPLETE SET (15)	70.00	32.00
STATED ODDS 1:12		
REFRACTORS: 1.25X TO 3X BASE INSERT		
REF.STATED ODDS 1:48		

Card	Mint	Nrmt
TT1 Rashaan Salaam	3.00	1.35
TT2 Warren Moon	1.50	.70
TT3 Marshall Faulk	3.00	1.35
TT4 Jeff Blake	3.00	1.35
TT5 Curtis Martin	5.00	2.20
TT6 Eric Metcalf	.60	.25
TT7 Errict Rhett	1.50	.70
TT8 Scott Mitchell	1.50	.70
TT9 Ricky Watters	1.50	.70
TT10 Jerry Rice	8.00	3.60
TT11 Emmitt Smith	12.00	5.50
TT12 Erik Kramer	.60	.25
TT13 Jim Harbaugh	1.50	.70
TT14 Barry Sanders	15.00	6.75
TT15 John Elway	15.00	6.75

1997 Topps Chrome

	MINT	NRMT
COMPLETE SET (165)	150.00	70.00
COMMON CARD (1-165)	.30	.14
SEMISTARS	.60	.25
UNLISTED STARS	1.25	.55
COMMON ROOKIES (143-163)	1.50	.70
ROOKIE SEMISTARS	2.50	1.10
ROOKIE UNL.STARS	3.00	1.35
COMP.REFRACT.SET (165)	2000.00	900.00
*REFRACT.STARS: 2.5X TO 6X HI COL.		
*REFRACTOR RCs: 1.2X TO 3X HI		
REFRACT.STATED ODDS 1:12		

Card	Mint	Nrmt
1 Brett Favre	6.00	2.70
2 Tim Biakabutuka	.60	.25
3 Deion Sanders	1.25	.55
4 Marshall Faulk	1.25	.55
5 John Randle	.30	.14
6 Stan Humphries	.60	.25
7 Ki-Jana Carter	.30	.14
8 Rashaan Salaam	.30	.14
9 Rickey Dudley	.60	.25
10 Isaac Bruce	1.25	.55
11 Keyshawn Johnson	1.25	.55
12 Ben Coates	.60	.25
13 Ty Detmer	.60	.25
14 Gus Frerotte	.30	.14
15 Mario Bates	.30	.14
16 Chris Calloway	.30	.14
17 Frank Sanders	.60	.25
18 Bruce Smith	.60	.25
19 Jeff Graham	.30	.14
20 Trent Dilfer	1.25	.55
21 Tyrone Wheatley	.60	.25
22 Chris Warren	.60	.25
23 Terry Kirby	.60	.25
24 Tony Gonzalez RC	15.00	6.75
25 Ricky Watters	.60	.25
26 Tamarick Vanover	.60	.25
27 Kerry Collins	.60	.25
28 Bobby Engram	.60	.25
29 Derrick Alexander WR	.60	.25
30 Hugh Douglas	.30	.14
31 Thurman Thomas	1.25	.55
32 Drew Bledsoe	3.00	1.35
33 LeShon Johnson	.30	.14
34 Byron Bam Morris	.30	.14
35 Herman Moore	1.25	.55
36 Troy Aikman	3.00	1.35
37 Mel Gray	.30	.14
38 Adrian Murrell	.60	.25
39 Carl Pickens	1.25	.55
40 Tony Brackens	.30	.14
41 O.J. McDuffie	.60	.25
42 Napoleon Kaufman	1.25	.55
43 Chris T. Jones	.30	.14
44 Kordell Stewart	1.50	.70
45 Steve Young	2.00	.90
46 Shannon Sharpe	.60	.25
47 Leeland McElroy	.30	.14
48 Eric Moulds	1.25	.55
49 Eddie George	3.00	1.35
50 Jamal Anderson	2.00	.90
51 Robert Smith	.60	.25
52 Mike Alstott	1.25	.55
53 Darrell Green	.60	.25
54 Irving Fryar	.60	.25
55 Derrick Thomas	.60	.25
56 Antonio Freeman	1.50	.70
57 Terrell Davis	5.00	2.20
58 Henry Ellard	.30	.14
59 Daryl Johnston	.60	.25
60 Bryan Cox	.30	.14
61 Vinny Testaverde	.60	.25
62 Andre Reed	.60	.25
63 Larry Centers	.60	.25
64 Hardy Nickerson	.30	.14
65 Tony Banks	.60	.25
66 Dave Meggett	.30	.14
67 Simeon Rice	.60	.25
68 Warrick Dunn RC	15.00	6.75
69 Michael Irvin	1.25	.55
70 John Elway	6.00	2.70
71 Jake Reed	.60	.25
72 Rodney Hampton	.60	.25
73 Aaron Glenn	.30	.14
74 Terry Allen	1.25	.55
75 Blaine Bishop	.30	.14
76 Bert Emanuel	.60	.25
77 Mark Carrier WR	.30	.14
78 Jimmy Smith	.60	.25
79 Jim Harbaugh	.60	.25
80 Brent Jones	.60	.25
81 Emmitt Smith	5.00	2.20
82 Fred Barnett	.30	.14
83 Errict Rhett	.30	.14
84 Michael Sinclair	.30	.14
85 Jerome Bettis	1.25	.55
86 Chris Sanders	.30	.14
87 Kent Graham	.30	.14
88 Cris Carter	1.25	.55
89 Harvey Williams	.30	.14
90 Eric Allen	.30	.14
91 Bryant Young	.30	.14
92 Marcus Allen	1.25	.55
93 Michael Jackson	.60	.25
94 Mark Chmura	.60	.25
95 Keenan McCardell	.60	.25
96 Joey Galloway	1.50	.70
97 Eddie Kennison	.60	.25
98 Steve Atwater	.30	.14
99 Dorsey Levens	1.25	.55
100 Rob Moore	.60	.25
101 Steve McNair	1.50	.70
102 Sean Dawkins	.30	.14
103 Don Beebe	.30	.14
104 Willie McGinest	.30	.14
105 Tony Martin	.60	.25
106 Mark Brunell	3.00	1.35
107 Karim Abdul-Jabbar	1.25	.55
108 Michael Westbrook	.60	.25
109 Lawrence Phillips	.30	.14
110 Barry Sanders	6.00	2.70
111 Willie Davis	.30	.14
112 Wesley Walls	.60	.25
113 Todd Collins	.30	.14
114 Jerry Rice	3.00	1.35
115 Scott Mitchell	.60	.25
116 Terance Mathis	.60	.25
117 Chris Spielman	.30	.14
118 Curtis Conway	.60	.25
119 Marvin Harrison	1.25	.55
120 Terry Glenn	1.25	.55
121 Dave Brown	.30	.14
122 Neil O'Donnell	.60	.25
123 Junior Seau	.60	.25
124 Reggie White	1.25	.55
125 Lamar Lathon	.30	.14
126 Natrone Means	1.25	.55
127 Tim Brown	1.25	.55
128 Eric Swann	.30	.14
129 Dan Marino	6.00	2.70
130 Anthony Johnson	.30	.14
131 Edgar Bennett	.60	.25
132 Kevin Hardy	.30	.14
133 Brian Blades	.30	.14
134 Curtis Martin	1.50	.70
135 Zach Thomas	.60	.25
136 Darnay Scott	.60	.25
137 Desmond Howard	.60	.25
138 Aeneas Williams	.30	.14
139 Bryce Paup	.30	.14
140 Brad Johnson	1.25	.55
141 Jeff Blake	.60	.25
142 Wayne Chrebet	1.25	.55
143 Will Blackwell RC	2.50	1.10
144 Tom Knight RC	.30	.14

	MINT	NRMT
❑ 145 Darnell Autry RC	.60	.25
❑ 146 Bryant Westbrook RC	.30	.14
❑ 147 David LaFleur RC	4.00	1.80
❑ 148 Antowain Smith RC	10.00	4.50
❑ 149 Rae Carruth RC	2.50	1.10
❑ 150 Jim Druckenmiller RC	4.00	1.80
❑ 151 Shawn Springs RC	1.50	.70
❑ 152 Troy Davis RC	3.00	1.35
❑ 153 Orlando Pace RC	1.50	.70
❑ 154 Byron Hanspard RC	8.00	3.60
❑ 155 Corey Dillon RC	20.00	9.00
❑ 156 Reidel Anthony RC	5.00	2.20
❑ 157 Peter Boulware RC	3.00	1.35
❑ 158 Reinard Wilson RC	1.50	.70
❑ 159 Pat Barnes RC	4.00	1.80
❑ 160 Joey Kent RC	3.00	1.35
❑ 161 Ike Hilliard RC	8.00	3.60
❑ 162 Jake Plummer RC	40.00	18.00
❑ 163 Darrell Russell RC	1.50	.70
❑ 164 Checklist Card	.30	.14
❑ 165 Checklist Card	.30	.14

1997 Topps Chrome Career Best

	MINT	NRMT
COMPLETE SET (5)	60.00	27.00
*REFRACTORS: 1X TO 2X HI COL.		
RANDOM INSERTS IN PACKS		

	MINT	NRMT
❑ 1 Dan Marino	30.00	13.50
❑ 2 Marcus Allen	6.00	2.70
❑ 3 Marcus Allen	6.00	2.70
❑ 4 Reggie White	6.00	2.70
❑ 5 Jerry Rice	15.00	6.75

1997 Topps Chrome Draft Year

	MINT	NRMT
COMPLETE SET (15)	200.00	90.00
COMMON CARD (DR1-DR15)	5.00	2.20
SEMISTARS	8.00	3.60
STATED ODDS 1:48		
*REFRACTORS: 1X TO 2X HI COL.		
REFRACTOR STATED ODDS 1:144		

	MINT	NRMT
❑ DR1 Dan Marino John Elway	30.00	13.50
❑ DR2 Reggie White Steve Young	12.00	5.50
❑ DR3 Bruce Smith Jerry Rice	15.00	6.75
❑ DR4 Ronnie Harmon Pat Swilling	5.00	2.20
❑ DR5 Jim Harbaugh Vinny Testaverde	5.00	2.20
❑ DR6 Micheal Irvin Tim Brown	8.00	3.60
❑ DR7 Troy Aikman Barry Sanders	30.00	13.50
❑ DR8 Emmitt Smith Junior Seau	25.00	11.00
❑ DR9 Brett Favre Ricky Watters	30.00	13.50
❑ DR10 Carl Pickens Jeff Blake	8.00	3.60
❑ DR11 Mark Brunell Drew Bledsoe	15.00	6.75
❑ DR12 Marshall Faulk Isaac Bruce	8.00	3.60
❑ DR13 Terrell Davis Curtis Martin	30.00	13.50
❑ DR14 Eddie George Terry Glenn	15.00	6.75
❑ DR15 Ike Hilliard Shawn Springs	8.00	3.60

1997 Topps Chrome Season's Best

	MINT	NRMT
COMPLETE SET (25)	100.00	45.00
COMMON CARD (1-25)	2.00	.90
SEMISTARS	3.00	1.35
UNLISTED STARS	5.00	2.20
STATED ODDS 1:12		
*REFRACTORS: 1X TO 2X HI COL.		
REFRACTOR STATED ODDS 1:36		

	MINT	NRMT
❑ 1 Mark Brunell	10.00	4.50
❑ 2 Vinny Testaverde	3.00	1.35
❑ 3 Drew Bledsoe	10.00	4.50
❑ 4 Brett Favre	20.00	9.00
❑ 5 Jeff Blake	3.00	1.35
❑ 6 Barry Sanders	20.00	9.00
❑ 7 Terrell Davis	15.00	6.75
❑ 8 Jerome Bettis	5.00	2.20
❑ 9 Ricky Watters	3.00	1.35
❑ 10 Eddie George	10.00	4.50
❑ 11 Brian Mitchell	2.00	.90
❑ 12 Tyrone Hughes	2.00	.90
❑ 13 Eric Metcalf	3.00	1.35
❑ 14 Glyn Milburn	2.00	.90
❑ 15 Ricky Watters	3.00	1.35
❑ 16 Kevin Greene	3.00	1.35
❑ 17 Lamar Lathon	2.00	.90
❑ 18 Bruce Smith	3.00	1.35
❑ 19 Michael Sinclair	2.00	.90
❑ 20 Derrick Thomas	3.00	1.35
❑ 21 Jerry Rice	10.00	4.50
❑ 22 Herman Moore	5.00	2.20
❑ 23 Carl Pickens	5.00	2.20
❑ 24 Cris Carter	5.00	2.20
❑ 25 Brett Perriman	2.00	.90

1997 Topps Chrome Underclassmen

	MINT	NRMT
COMPLETE SET (10)	30.00	13.50
STATED ODDS 1:16		
*REFRACTORS: 3X TO 6X BASE CARD HI		
REFRACTOR STATED ODDS 1:48		

	MINT	NRMT
❑ U1 Kerry Collins	2.00	.90
❑ U2 Karim Abdul-Jabbar	4.00	1.80
❑ U3 Simeon Rice	2.00	.90
❑ U4 Keyshawn Johnson	4.00	1.80
❑ U5 Eddie George	10.00	4.50
❑ U6 Eddie Kennison	2.00	.90
❑ U7 Terry Glenn	4.00	1.80
❑ U8 Kevin Hardy	1.00	.45
❑ U9 Steve McNair	5.00	2.20
❑ U10 Kordell Stewart	5.00	2.20

1998 Topps Chrome

	MINT	NRMT
COMPLETE SET (165)	250.00	110.00
COMMON CARD (1-165)	.25	.11
SEMISTARS	.50	.23
UNLISTED STARS	1.00	.45
COMMON ROOKIE	4.00	1.80
ROOKIE SEMISTARS	6.00	2.70
COMP.REFRACT. (165)	1200.00	550.00
*REFRACTOR STARS: 4X TO 10X HI COL.		
*REFRACTOR YOUNG STARS: 3X TO 8X		
*REFRACTOR RCs: 1X TO 2.5X		
REFRACTOR ODDS 1:12		

	MINT	NRMT
❑ 1 Barry Sanders	5.00	2.20
❑ 2 Duane Starks RC	4.00	1.80
❑ 3 J.J. Stokes	.50	.23
❑ 4 Joey Galloway	1.00	.45
❑ 5 Deion Sanders	1.00	.45
❑ 6 Anthony Miller	.25	.11
❑ 7 Jamal Anderson	1.00	.45
❑ 8 Shannon Sharpe	.50	.23
❑ 9 Irving Fryar	.50	.23
❑ 10 Curtis Martin	1.00	.45
❑ 11 Shawn Jefferson	.25	.11
❑ 12 Charlie Garner	.25	.11
❑ 13 Robert Edwards RC	6.00	2.70
❑ 14 Napoleon Kaufman	1.00	.45
❑ 15 Gus Frerotte	.25	.11

❑ 16 John Elway 5.00 2.20
❑ 17 Jerome Pathon RC 6.00 2.70
❑ 18 Marshall Faulk 1.00 .45
❑ 19 Michael McCrary .25 .11
❑ 20 Marcus Allen 1.00 .45
❑ 21 Trent Dilfer 1.00 .45
❑ 22 Frank Wycheck .25 .11
❑ 23 Terrell Owens 1.00 .45
❑ 24 Herman Moore 1.00 .45
❑ 25 Neil O'Donnell .50 .23
❑ 26 Darnay Scott .50 .23
❑ 27 Keith Brooking RC 6.00 2.70
❑ 28 Eric Green .25 .11
❑ 29 Dan Marino 5.00 2.20
❑ 30 Antonio Freeman 1.00 .45
❑ 31 Tony Martin .50 .23
❑ 32 Isaac Bruce 1.00 .45
❑ 33 Rickey Dudley .25 .11
❑ 34 Scott Mitchell .50 .23
❑ 35 Randy Moss RC 80.00 36.00
❑ 36 Fred Lane .50 .23
❑ 37 Frank Sanders .50 .23
❑ 38 Jerry Rice 2.50 1.10
❑ 39 O.J. McDuffie .50 .23
❑ 40 Jessie Armstead .25 .11
❑ 41 Reidel Anthony .50 .23
❑ 42 Steve McNair 1.00 .45
❑ 43 Jake Reed .50 .23
❑ 44 Charles Woodson RC .. 15.00 6.75
❑ 45 Tiki Barber .50 .23
❑ 46 Mike Alstott 1.00 .45
❑ 47 Keyshawn Johnson 1.00 .45
❑ 48 Tony Banks .50 .23
❑ 49 Michael Westbrook .50 .23
❑ 50 Chris Slade .25 .11
❑ 51 Terry Allen 1.00 .45
❑ 52 Karim Abdul-Jabbar 1.00 .45
❑ 53 Brad Johnson 1.00 .45
❑ 54 Tony McGee .25 .11
❑ 55 Kevin Dyson RC 12.00 5.50
❑ 56 Warren Moon 1.00 .45
❑ 57 Byron Hanspard .50 .23
❑ 58 Jermaine Lewis .50 .23
❑ 59 Neil Smith .50 .23
❑ 60 Tamarick Vanover .25 .11
❑ 61 Terrell Davis 4.00 1.80
❑ 62 Robert Smith 1.00 .45
❑ 63 Junior Seau .50 .23
❑ 64 Warren Sapp .50 .23
❑ 65 Michael Sinclair .25 .11
❑ 66 Ryan Leaf RC 15.00 6.75
❑ 67 Drew Bledsoe 2.00 .90
❑ 68 Jason Sehorn .25 .11
❑ 69 Andre Hastings .25 .11
❑ 70 Tony Gonzalez .25 .11
❑ 71 Dorsey Levens 1.00 .45
❑ 72 Ray Lewis .25 .11
❑ 73 Grant Wistrom RC 4.00 1.80
❑ 74 Elvis Grbac .50 .23
❑ 75 Mark Chmura .50 .23
❑ 76 Zach Thomas .25 .11
❑ 77 Ben Coates .50 .23
❑ 78 Rod Smith WR .50 .23
❑ 79 Andre Wadsworth RC 6.00 2.70
❑ 80 Garrison Hearst 1.00 .45
❑ 81 Will Blackwell .25 .11
❑ 82 Cris Carter 1.00 .45
❑ 83 Mark Fields .25 .11
❑ 84 Ken Dilger .25 .11
❑ 85 Johnnie Morton .50 .23
❑ 86 Michael Irvin 1.00 .45
❑ 87 Eddie George 2.00 .90
❑ 88 Rob Moore .50 .23
❑ 89 Takeo Spikes RC 6.00 2.70
❑ 90 Wesley Walls .50 .23
❑ 91 Andre Reed .50 .23
❑ 92 Thurman Thomas 1.00 .45
❑ 93 Ed McCaffrey .50 .23
❑ 94 Carl Pickens 1.00 .45
❑ 95 Jason Taylor .25 .11
❑ 96 Kordell Stewart 1.00 .45
❑ 97 Greg Ellis RC 4.00 1.80
❑ 98 Aaron Glenn .25 .11
❑ 99 Jake Plummer 3.00 1.35
❑ 100 Checklist .25 .11
❑ 101 Chris Sanders .25 .11
❑ 102 Michael Jackson .25 .11
❑ 103 Bobby Hoying .50 .23
❑ 104 Wayne Chrebet 1.00 .45
❑ 105 Charles Way .25 .11
❑ 106 Derrick Thomas .50 .23
❑ 107 Troy Drayton .25 .11
❑ 108 Robert Holcombe RC .. 6.00 2.70
❑ 109 Pete Mitchell .25 .11
❑ 110 Bruce Smith .50 .23
❑ 111 Terance Mathis .50 .23
❑ 112 Lawrence Phillips .25 .11
❑ 113 Brett Favre 5.00 2.20
❑ 114 Darrell Green .50 .23
❑ 115 Charles Johnson .25 .11
❑ 116 Jeff Blake .50 .23
❑ 117 Mark Brunell 2.00 .90
❑ 118 Simeon Rice .50 .23
❑ 119 Robert Brooks .50 .23
❑ 120 Jacquez Green RC 8.00 3.60
❑ 121 Willie Davis .25 .11
❑ 122 Jeff George .50 .23
❑ 123 Andre Rison .50 .23
❑ 124 Erik Kramer .25 .11
❑ 125 Peter Boulware .25 .11
❑ 126 Marcus Nash RC 10.00 4.50
❑ 127 Troy Aikman 2.50 1.10
❑ 128 Keenan McCardell .50 .23
❑ 129 Bryant Westbrook .25 .11
❑ 130 Terry Glenn 1.00 .45
❑ 131 Blaine Bishop .25 .11
❑ 132 Tim Brown 1.00 .45
❑ 133 Brian Griese RC 25.00 11.00
❑ 134 John Mobley .25 .11
❑ 135 Larry Centers .25 .11
❑ 136 Eric Bjornson .25 .11
❑ 137 Kevin Hardy .25 .11
❑ 138 John Randle .50 .23
❑ 139 Michael Strahan .25 .11
❑ 140 Jerome Bettis 1.00 .45
❑ 141 Rae Carruth .50 .23
❑ 142 Reggie White 1.00 .45
❑ 143 Antowain Smith 1.00 .45
❑ 144 Aeneas Williams .25 .11
❑ 145 Bobby Engram .50 .23
❑ 146 Germane Crowell RC 15.00 6.75
❑ 147 Freddie Jones .25 .11
❑ 148 Kimble Anders .50 .23
❑ 149 Steve Young 1.50 .70
❑ 150 Willie McGinest .25 .11
❑ 151 Emmitt Smith 4.00 1.80
❑ 152 Fred Taylor RC 40.00 18.00
❑ 153 Danny Kanell .50 .23
❑ 154 Warrick Dunn 1.50 .70
❑ 155 Kerry Collins .50 .23
❑ 156 Chris Chandler .50 .23
❑ 157 Curtis Conway .50 .23
❑ 158 Curtis Enis RC 15.00 6.75
❑ 159 Corey Dillon 1.50 .70
❑ 160 Glenn Foley .50 .23
❑ 161 Marvin Harrison .50 .23
❑ 162 Chad Brown .25 .11
❑ 163 Derrick Rodgers .25 .11
❑ 164 Levon Kirkland .25 .11
❑ 165 Peyton Manning RC .. 80.00 36.00

1998 Topps Chrome Hidden Gems

	MINT	NRMT
COMPLETE SET (15)	30.00	13.50
COMMON CARD (HG1-HG15)	1.00	.45
SEMISTARS	1.50	.70
UNLISTED STARS	2.50	1.10

STATED ODDS 1:12
*REFRACTORS: .75X TO 1.5X HI COL.
REFRACTOR ODDS 1:24

❑ HG1 Andre Reed 1.50 .70
❑ HG2 Kevin Greene 1.50 .70
❑ HG3 Tony Martin 1.50 .70
❑ HG4 Shannon Sharpe 1.50 .70
❑ HG5 Terry Allen 2.50 1.10
❑ HG6 Brett Favre 12.00 5.50
❑ HG7 Ben Coates 1.50 .70
❑ HG8 Michael Sinclair 1.00 .45
❑ HG9 Keenan McCardell 1.50 .70
❑ HG10 Brad Johnson 2.50 1.10
❑ HG11 Mark Brunell 5.00 2.20
❑ HG12 Dorsey Levens 2.50 1.10
❑ HG13 Terrell Davis 12.00 5.50
❑ HG14 Curtis Martin 2.50 1.10
❑ HG15 Derrick Rodgers 1.00 .45

1998 Topps Chrome Measures of Greatness

	MINT	NRMT
COMPLETE SET (15)	60.00	27.00
COMMON CARD (MG1-MG15)	1.50	.70
SEMISTARS	2.50	1.10

STATED ODDS 1:12
*REFRACTORS: 1X TO 2.5X HI COL.
REFRACTOR ODDS 1:48

❑ MG1 John Elway 12.00 5.50
❑ MG2 Marcus Allen 4.00 1.80
❑ MG3 Jerry Rice 6.00 2.70
❑ MG4 Tim Brown 4.00 1.80
❑ MG5 Warren Moon 4.00 1.80
❑ MG6 Bruce Smith 2.50 1.10
❑ MG7 Troy Aikman 6.00 2.70
❑ MG8 Reggie White 2.50 1.10
❑ MG9 Irving Fryar 1.50 .70
❑ MG10 Barry Sanders 12.00 5.50
❑ MG11 Cris Carter 4.00 1.80
❑ MG12 Emmitt Smith 10.00 4.50
❑ MG13 Dan Marino 12.00 5.50
❑ MG14 Rod Woodson 2.50 1.10
❑ MG15 Brett Favre 12.00 5.50

1998 Topps Chrome Season's Best

	MINT	NRMT
COMPLETE SET (30)	100.00	45.00
COMMON CARD (1-30)	1.25	.55
SEMISTARS	2.00	.90
UNLISTED STARS	3.00	1.35

STATED ODDS 1:8
*REFRACTOR STARS: .75X TO 1.5X HI COL.
REFRACTOR ODDS 1:24

❑ 1 Terrell Davis 12.00 5.50
❑ 2 Barry Sanders 15.00 6.75
❑ 3 Jerome Bettis 3.00 1.35

	MINT	NRMT
❑ 4 Dorsey Levens	3.00	1.35
❑ 5 Eddie George	6.00	2.70
❑ 6 Brett Favre	15.00	6.75
❑ 7 Mark Brunell	6.00	2.70
❑ 8 Jeff George	2.00	.90
❑ 9 Steve Young	5.00	2.20
❑ 10 John Elway	15.00	6.75
❑ 11 Herman Moore	3.00	1.35
❑ 12 Rob Moore	2.00	.90
❑ 13 Yancey Thigpen	1.25	.55
❑ 14 Cris Carter	3.00	1.35
❑ 15 Tim Brown	3.00	1.35
❑ 16 Bruce Smith	2.00	.90
❑ 17 Michael Sinclair	1.25	.55
❑ 18 John Randle	2.00	.90
❑ 19 Dana Stubblefield	1.25	.55
❑ 20 Michael Strahan	1.25	.55
❑ 21 Tamarick Vanover	1.25	.55
❑ 22 Darrien Gordon	1.25	.55
❑ 23 Michael Bates	1.25	.55
❑ 24 David Meggett	1.25	.55
❑ 25 Jermaine Lewis	2.00	.90
❑ 26 Terrell Davis	12.00	5.50
❑ 27 Jerry Rice	8.00	3.60
❑ 28 Barry Sanders	15.00	6.75
❑ 29 John Randle	2.00	.90
❑ 30 John Elway	15.00	6.75

1999 Topps Chrome

	MINT	NRMT
COMPLETE SET (165)	500.00	220.00
COMP.SET w/o SP's (135)	50.00	22.00
COMMON CARD (1-165)	.25	.11
SEMISTARS	.50	.23
UNLISTED STARS	1.00	.45
COMMON ROOKIE (135-164)	8.00	3.60
ROOKIE SEMISTARS	10.00	4.50

ROOKIE SUBSET STATED ODDS 1:8

	MINT	NRMT
❑ 1 Randy Moss	4.00	1.80
❑ 2 Keyshawn Johnson	1.00	.45
❑ 3 Priest Holmes	1.00	.45
❑ 4 Warren Moon	1.00	.45
❑ 5 Joey Galloway	1.00	.45
❑ 6 Zach Thomas	.50	.23
❑ 7 Cam Cleeland	.25	.11
❑ 8 Jim Harbaugh	.50	.23
❑ 9 Napoleon Kaufman	1.00	.45
❑ 10 Fred Taylor	2.50	1.10
❑ 11 Mark Brunell	1.50	.70
❑ 12 Shannon Sharpe	.50	.23
❑ 13 Jacquez Green	.50	.23
❑ 14 Adrian Murrell	.50	.23
❑ 15 Cris Carter	1.00	.45
❑ 16 Jerome Pathon	.25	.11
❑ 17 Drew Bledsoe	1.50	.70
❑ 18 Curtis Martin	1.00	.45
❑ 19 Johnnie Morton	.50	.23
❑ 20 Doug Flutie	1.25	.55
❑ 21 Carl Pickens	.50	.23
❑ 22 Jerome Bettis	1.00	.45
❑ 23 Derrick Alexander	.25	.11
❑ 24 Antowain Smith	1.00	.45
❑ 25 Barry Sanders	4.00	1.80
❑ 26 Reidel Anthony	.50	.23
❑ 27 Wayne Chrebet	.50	.23
❑ 28 Terance Mathis	.50	.23
❑ 29 Shawn Springs	.25	.11
❑ 30 Emmitt Smith	2.50	1.10
❑ 31 Robert Smith	1.00	.45
❑ 32 Charles Johnson	.25	.11
❑ 33 Mike Alstott	1.00	.45
❑ 34 Ike Hilliard	.25	.11
❑ 35 Ricky Watters	.50	.23
❑ 36 Charles Woodson	1.00	.45
❑ 37 Rod Smith	.50	.23
❑ 38 Pete Mitchell	.25	.11
❑ 39 Derrick Thomas	.50	.23
❑ 40 Dan Marino	4.00	1.80
❑ 41 Darnay Scott	.25	.11
❑ 42 Jake Reed	.50	.23
❑ 43 Chris Chandler	.50	.23
❑ 44 Dorsey Levens	1.00	.45
❑ 45 Kordell Stewart	1.00	.45
❑ 46 Eddie George	1.25	.55
❑ 47 Corey Dillon	1.00	.45
❑ 48 Rich Gannon	.50	.23
❑ 49 Chris Spielman	.25	.11
❑ 50 Jerry Rice	2.50	1.10
❑ 51 Trent Dilfer	.50	.23
❑ 52 Mark Chmura	.25	.11
❑ 53 Jimmy Smith	.50	.23
❑ 54 Isaac Bruce	1.00	.45
❑ 55 Karim Abdul-Jabbar	.50	.23
❑ 56 Sedrick Shaw	.25	.11
❑ 57 Jake Plummer	2.00	.90
❑ 58 Tony Gonzalez	.50	.23
❑ 59 Ben Coates	.50	.23
❑ 60 John Elway	4.00	1.80
❑ 61 Bruce Smith	.50	.23
❑ 62 Tim Brown	1.00	.45
❑ 63 Tim Dwight	1.00	.45
❑ 64 Yancey Thigpen	.25	.11
❑ 65 Terrell Owens	1.00	.45
❑ 66 Kyle Brady	.25	.11
❑ 67 Tony Martin	.50	.23
❑ 68 Michael Strahan	.25	.11
❑ 69 Deion Sanders	1.00	.45
❑ 70 Steve Young	1.50	.70
❑ 71 Dale Carter	.25	.11
❑ 72 Ty Law	.25	.11
❑ 73 Frank Wycheck	.25	.11
❑ 74 Marshall Faulk	1.00	.45
❑ 75 Vinny Testaverde	.50	.23
❑ 76 Chad Brown	.25	.11
❑ 77 Natrone Means	.50	.23
❑ 78 Bert Emanuel	.50	.23
❑ 79 Kerry Collins	.50	.23
❑ 80 Randall Cunningham	1.00	.45
❑ 81 Garrison Hearst	.50	.23
❑ 82 Curtis Enis	1.00	.45
❑ 83 Steve Atwater	.25	.11
❑ 84 Kevin Greene	.25	.11
❑ 85 Steve McNair	1.00	.45
❑ 86 Andre Reed	.50	.23
❑ 87 J.J. Stokes	.50	.23
❑ 88 Eric Moulds	1.00	.45
❑ 89 Marvin Harrison	1.00	.45
❑ 90 Troy Aikman	2.50	1.10
❑ 91 Herman Moore	1.00	.45
❑ 92 Michael Irvin	.50	.23
❑ 93 Frank Sanders	.50	.23
❑ 94 Duce Staley	1.00	.45
❑ 95 James Jett	.50	.23
❑ 96 Ricky Proehl	.25	.11
❑ 97 Andre Rison	.50	.23
❑ 98 Leslie Shepherd	.25	.11
❑ 99 Trent Green	.50	.23
❑ 100 Terrell Davis	2.50	1.10
❑ 101 Freddie Jones	.25	.11
❑ 102 Skip Hicks	1.00	.45
❑ 103 Jeff Graham	.25	.11
❑ 104 Rob Moore	.50	.23
❑ 105 Torrance Small	.25	.11
❑ 106 Antonio Freeman	1.00	.45
❑ 107 Robert Brooks	.50	.23
❑ 108 Jon Kitna	1.25	.55
❑ 109 Curtis Conway	.50	.23
❑ 110 Brett Favre	4.00	1.80
❑ 111 Warrick Dunn	1.00	.45
❑ 112 Elvis Grbac	.50	.23
❑ 113 Corey Fuller	.25	.11
❑ 114 Rickey Dudley	.25	.11
❑ 115 Jamal Anderson	1.00	.45
❑ 116 Terry Glenn	1.00	.45
❑ 117 Rocket Ismail	.50	.23
❑ 118 John Randle	.50	.23
❑ 119 Chris Calloway	.25	.11
❑ 120 Peyton Manning	4.00	1.80
❑ 121 Keenan McCardell	.50	.23
❑ 122 O.J. McDuffie	.50	.23
❑ 123 Ed McCaffrey	.50	.23
❑ 124 Charlie Batch	2.00	.90
❑ 125 Jason Elam SH	.25	.11
❑ 126 Randy Moss SH	2.00	.90
❑ 127 John Elway SH	2.00	.90
❑ 128 Emmitt Smith SH	1.25	.55
❑ 129 Terrell Davis SH	1.25	.55
❑ 130 Jerris McPhail	.25	.11
❑ 131 Damon Gibson	.25	.11
❑ 132 Jim Pyne	.25	.11
❑ 133 Antonio Langham	.25	.11
❑ 134 Freddie Solomon	.25	.11
❑ 135 Ricky Williams RC	60.00	27.00
❑ 136 Daunte Culpepper RC	40.00	18.00
❑ 137 Chris Claiborne RC	10.00	4.50
❑ 138 Amos Zereoue RC	10.00	4.50
❑ 139 Chris McAlister RC	8.00	3.60
❑ 140 Kevin Faulk RC	15.00	6.75
❑ 141 James Johnson RC	15.00	6.75
❑ 142 Mike Cloud RC	10.00	4.50
❑ 143 Jevon Kearse RC	25.00	11.00
❑ 144 Akili Smith RC	30.00	13.50
❑ 145 Edgerrin James RC	100.00	45.00
❑ 146 Cecil Collins RC	10.00	4.50
❑ 147 Donovan McNabb RC	40.00	18.00
❑ 148 Kevin Johnson RC	30.00	13.50
❑ 149 Torry Holt RC	30.00	13.50
❑ 150 Rob Konrad RC	10.00	4.50
❑ 151 Tim Couch RC	60.00	27.00
❑ 152 David Boston RC	20.00	9.00
❑ 153 Karsten Bailey RC	8.00	3.60
❑ 154 Troy Edwards RC	20.00	9.00
❑ 155 Sedrick Irvin RC	10.00	4.50
❑ 156 Shaun King RC	40.00	18.00
❑ 157 Peerless Price RC	20.00	9.00
❑ 158 Brock Huard RC	15.00	6.75
❑ 159 Cade McNown RC	40.00	18.00
❑ 160 Champ Bailey RC	15.00	6.75
❑ 161 D'Wayne Bates RC	8.00	3.60
❑ 162 Joe Germaine RC	10.00	4.50
❑ 163 Andy Katzenmoyer RC	10.00	4.50
❑ 164 Antoine Winfield RC	8.00	3.60
❑ 165 Checklist Card	.25	.11

1999 Topps Chrome Refractors

	MINT	NRMT
COMPLETE SET (165)	2500.00	1100.00
COMMON CARD (1-165)	2.00	.90
COMMON ROOKIE (135-164)	20.00	9.00

*REFRACTOR STARS: 3X TO 8X HI COL.
*REFRACTOR YOUNG STARS: 2.5X TO 6X
*REFRACTOR RCs: .8X TO 2X....
REFRACTOR VETERANS ODDS 1:12
REFRACTOR ROOKIES ODDS 1:32

1999 Topps Chrome All-Etch

	MINT	NRMT
COMPLETE SET (30)	200.00	90.00
COMMON CARD (AM1-AM30)	2.00	.90

SEMISTARS	4.00	1.80

STATED ODDS 1:24
*REFRACTOR STARS: 1.25X TO 3X HI COL.
*REFRACTOR ROOKIES: .75X TO 2X HI COL.
REFRACTOR STATED ODDS 1:120

Card	MINT	NRMT
❑ AM1 Fred Taylor	8.00	3.60
❑ AM2 Ricky Watters	2.00	.90
❑ AM3 Curtis Martin	4.00	1.80
❑ AM4 Eddie George	5.00	2.20
❑ AM5 Marshall Faulk	4.00	1.80
❑ AM6 Emmitt Smith	10.00	4.50
❑ AM7 Barry Sanders	15.00	6.75
❑ AM8 Garrison Hearst	2.00	.90
❑ AM9 Jamal Anderson	4.00	1.80
❑ AM10 Terrell Davis	10.00	4.50
❑ AM11 Chris Chandler	2.00	.90
❑ AM12 Steve McNair	4.00	1.80
❑ AM13 Vinny Testaverde	2.00	.90
❑ AM14 Trent Green	2.00	.90
❑ AM15 Dan Marino	15.00	6.75
❑ AM16 Drew Bledsoe	6.00	2.70
❑ AM17 Randall Cunningham	4.00	1.80
❑ AM18 Jake Plummer	8.00	3.60
❑ AM19 Peyton Manning	12.00	5.50
❑ AM20 Steve Young	6.00	2.70
❑ AM21 Brett Favre	15.00	6.75
❑ AM22 Tim Couch	15.00	6.75
❑ AM23 Edgerrin James	25.00	11.00
❑ AM24 David Boston	5.00	2.20
❑ AM25 Akili Smith	6.00	2.70
❑ AM26 Troy Edwards	5.00	2.20
❑ AM27 Torry Holt	8.00	3.60
❑ AM28 Donovan McNabb	10.00	4.50
❑ AM29 Daunte Culpepper	10.00	4.50
❑ AM30 Ricky Williams	15.00	6.75

1999 Topps Chrome Hall of Fame

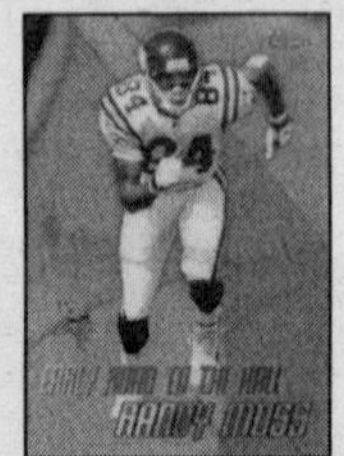

	MINT	NRMT
COMPLETE SET (30)	250.00	110.00
COMMON CARD (H1-H30)	4.00	1.80

STATED ODDS 1:29
*REFRACTOR STARS: 2.5X TO 6X HI COL.
*REFRACTOR ROOKIES: 2X TO 5X HI COL.
REFRACTOR PRINT RUN 100 SERIAL #'d SETS

Card	MINT	NRMT
❑ H1 Akili Smith	6.00	2.70
❑ H2 Troy Edwards	5.00	2.20
❑ H3 Donovan McNabb	10.00	4.50
❑ H4 Cade McNown	10.00	4.50
❑ H5 Ricky Williams	15.00	6.75
❑ H6 David Boston	5.00	2.20
❑ H7 Daunte Culpepper	10.00	4.50
❑ H8 Edgerrin James	25.00	11.00
❑ H9 Torry Holt	8.00	3.60
❑ H10 Tim Couch	15.00	6.75
❑ H11 Terrell Davis	10.00	4.50
❑ H12 Fred Taylor	8.00	3.60
❑ H13 Antonio Freeman	5.00	2.20
❑ H14 Jamal Anderson	5.00	2.20
❑ H15 Randy Moss	12.00	5.50
❑ H16 Joey Galloway	5.00	2.20
❑ H17 Eddie George	5.00	2.20
❑ H18 Jake Plummer	8.00	3.60
❑ H19 Curtis Martin	5.00	2.20
❑ H20 Peyton Manning	12.00	5.50
❑ H21 Barry Sanders	15.00	6.75
❑ H22 Steve Young	6.00	2.70
❑ H23 Cris Carter	5.00	2.20
❑ H24 Emmitt Smith	10.00	4.50
❑ H25 John Elway	15.00	6.75
❑ H26 Drew Bledsoe	6.00	2.70
❑ H27 Troy Aikman	10.00	4.50
❑ H28 Brett Favre	15.00	6.75
❑ H29 Jerry Rice	10.00	4.50
❑ H30 Dan Marino	15.00	6.75

1999 Topps Chrome Record Numbers

	MINT	NRMT
COMPLETE SET (10)	80.00	36.00
COMMON CARD (RN1-RN10)	2.00	.90

STATED ODDS 1:72
REFRACTORS: 1.25X TO 3X HI COL.
REFRACTOR STATED ODDS 1:360

Card	MINT	NRMT
❑ RN1 Randy Moss	12.00	5.50
❑ RN2 Terrell Davis	10.00	4.50
❑ RN3 Emmitt Smith	10.00	4.50
❑ RN4 Barry Sanders	15.00	6.75
❑ RN5 Dan Marino	15.00	6.75
❑ RN6 Brett Favre	15.00	6.75
❑ RN7 Doug Flutie	5.00	2.20
❑ RN8 Jerry Rice	10.00	4.50
❑ RN9 Peyton Manning	12.00	5.50
❑ RN10 Jason Elam	2.00	.90

1999 Topps Chrome Season's Best

	MINT	NRMT
COMPLETE SET (30)	100.00	45.00
COMMON CARD (SB1-SB30)	1.00	.45
SEMISTARS	2.00	.90
UNLISTED STARS	3.00	1.35

STATED ODDS: 1:24
*REFRACTORS: 1.25X TO 3X HI COL.
REFRACTOR STATED ODDS 1:120

Card	MINT	NRMT
❑ SB1 Terrell Davis	8.00	3.60
❑ SB2 Jamal Anderson	3.00	1.35
❑ SB3 Garrison Hearst	2.00	.90
❑ SB4 Barry Sanders	12.00	5.50
❑ SB5 Emmitt Smith	8.00	3.60
❑ SB6 Randall Cunningham	3.00	1.35
❑ SB7 Brett Favre	12.00	5.50
❑ SB8 Steve Young	5.00	2.20
❑ SB9 Jake Plummer	6.00	2.70
❑ SB10 Peyton Manning	10.00	4.50
❑ SB11 Antonio Freeman	3.00	1.35
❑ SB12 Eric Moulds	3.00	1.35
❑ SB13 Randy Moss	10.00	4.50
❑ SB14 Rod Smith	2.00	.90
❑ SB15 Jimmy Smith	2.00	.90
❑ SB16 Michael Sinclair	1.00	.45
❑ SB17 Kevin Greene	1.00	.45
❑ SB18 Michael Strahan	1.00	.45
❑ SB19 Michael McCrary	1.00	.45
❑ SB20 Hugh Douglas	1.00	.45
❑ SB21 Deion Sanders	3.00	1.35
❑ SB22 Terry Fair	1.00	.45
❑ SB23 Jacquez Green	2.00	.90
❑ SB24 Corey Harris	1.00	.45
❑ SB25 Tim Dwight	3.00	1.35
❑ SB26 Dan Marino	12.00	5.50
❑ SB27 Barry Sanders	12.00	5.50
❑ SB28 Jerry Rice	8.00	3.60
❑ SB29 Bruce Smith	2.00	.90
❑ SB30 Darrien Gordon	1.00	.45

1997 Topps Gallery

	MINT	NRMT
COMPLETE SET (135)	40.00	18.00
COMMON CARD (1-135)	.15	.07
SEMISTARS	.25	.11
UNLISTED STARS	.50	.23
COMP.PLAY.PRIV.ISSUE	2000.00	900.00

*PRIV.ISSUE STARS: 12.5X TO 30X HI COL.
*PRIV.ISSUE RCs: 5X TO 12X
PLAYER'S PRIVATE ISSUE ODDS 1:12

Card	MINT	NRMT
❑ 1 Orlando Pace RC	.15	.07
❑ 2 Darrell Russell RC	.15	.07
❑ 3 Shawn Springs RC	.25	.11
❑ 4 Peter Boulware RC	.25	.11
❑ 5 Bryant Westbrook RC	.15	.07
❑ 6 Walter Jones RC	.15	.07
❑ 7 Ike Hilliard RC	2.00	.90
❑ 8 James Farrior RC	.15	.07
❑ 9 Tom Knight RC	.15	.07
❑ 10 Warrick Dunn RC	4.00	1.80
❑ 11 Tony Gonzalez RC	4.00	1.80
❑ 12 Reinard Wilson RC	.15	.07
❑ 13 Yatil Green RC	.25	.11
❑ 14 Reidel Anthony RC	2.00	.90
❑ 15 Kenny Holmes RC	.15	.07
❑ 16 Dwayne Rudd RC	.15	.07
❑ 17 Renaldo Wynn RC	.15	.07
❑ 18 David LaFleur RC	1.00	.45
❑ 19 Antowain Smith RC	2.50	1.10
❑ 20 Jim Druckenmiller RC	.75	.35
❑ 21 Rae Carruth RC	.50	.23
❑ 22 Byron Hanspard RC	2.00	.90

❑ 23 Jake Plummer RC 10.00 4.50
❑ 24 Corey Dillon RC 5.00 2.20
❑ 25 Darnell Autry RC .25 .11
❑ 26 Kevin Lockett RC .50 .23
❑ 27 Troy Davis RC .50 .23
❑ 28 Mike Alstott .50 .23
❑ 29 Napoleon Kaufman .50 .23
❑ 30 Terrell Davis 2.00 .90
❑ 31 Byron Bam Morris .15 .07
❑ 32 Dana Stubblefield .15 .07
❑ 33 Ki-Jana Carter .15 .07
❑ 34 Hugh Douglas .15 .07
❑ 35 Natrone Means .50 .23
❑ 36 Marshall Faulk .50 .23
❑ 37 Tyrone Wheatley .25 .11
❑ 38 Tony Banks .25 .11
❑ 39 Marvin Harrison .50 .23
❑ 40 Eddie George 1.25 .55
❑ 41 Eddie Kennison .25 .11
❑ 42 Ray Mickens .15 .07
❑ 43 Mike Mamula .15 .07
❑ 44 Tamarick Vanover .25 .11
❑ 45 Rashaan Salaam .15 .07
❑ 46 Trent Dilfer .50 .23
❑ 47 John Mobley .15 .07
❑ 48 Gus Frerotte .15 .07
❑ 49 Isaac Bruce .50 .23
❑ 50 Mark Brunell 1.25 .55
❑ 51 Jamal Anderson .75 .35
❑ 52 Keyshawn Johnson .50 .23
❑ 53 Curtis Conway .25 .11
❑ 54 Zach Thomas .25 .11
❑ 55 Simeon Rice .25 .11
❑ 56 Lawrence Phillips .15 .07
❑ 57 Ty Detmer .25 .11
❑ 58 Bobby Engram .25 .11
❑ 59 Joey Galloway .60 .25
❑ 60 Curtis Martin .60 .25
❑ 61 Kevin Hardy .15 .07
❑ 62 Eric Moulds .50 .23
❑ 63 Michael Westbrook .25 .11
❑ 64 Robert Smith .25 .11
❑ 65 Karim Abdul-Jabbar .50 .23
❑ 66 Errict Rhett .15 .07
❑ 67 Ray Lewis .15 .07
❑ 68 Terry Glenn .50 .23
❑ 69 Leeland McElroy .15 .07
❑ 70 Kerry Collins .25 .11
❑ 71 Steve McNair .60 .25
❑ 72 Kordell Stewart .60 .25
❑ 73 Terry Allen .50 .23
❑ 74 Michael Irvin .50 .23
❑ 75 John Elway 2.50 1.10
❑ 76 Lamar Lathon .15 .07
❑ 77 Rob Moore .25 .11
❑ 78 Irving Fryar .25 .11
❑ 79 Jim Everett .15 .07
❑ 80 Steve Young .75 .35
❑ 81 Bryan Cox .15 .07
❑ 82 Dale Carter .15 .07
❑ 83 Chris Warren .25 .11
❑ 84 Shannon Sharpe .25 .11
❑ 85 Reggie White .50 .23
❑ 86 Deion Sanders .50 .23
❑ 87 Hardy Nickerson .15 .07
❑ 88 Edgar Bennett .25 .11
❑ 89 Kent Graham .15 .07
❑ 90 Dan Marino 2.50 1.10
❑ 91 Kevin Greene .25 .11
❑ 92 Derrick Thomas .25 .11
❑ 93 Carl Pickens .50 .23
❑ 94 Neil O'Donnell .25 .11
❑ 95 Drew Bledsoe 1.25 .55
❑ 96 Michael Haynes .15 .07
❑ 97 Tony Martin .25 .11
❑ 98 Scott Mitchell .25 .11
❑ 99 Rodney Hampton .25 .11
❑ 100 Brett Favre 2.50 1.10
❑ 101 Darrell Green .25 .11
❑ 102 Rod Woodson .25 .11
❑ 103 Chris Spielman .15 .07
❑ 104 Jake Reed .25 .11
❑ 105 Jerry Rice 1.25 .55
❑ 106 Jeff Hostetler .15 .07
❑ 107 Anthony Johnson .15 .07
❑ 108 Keenan McCardell .25 .11
❑ 109 Ben Coates .25 .11
❑ 110 Emmitt Smith 2.00 .90
❑ 111 LeRoy Butler .15 .07
❑ 112 Steve Atwater .15 .07
❑ 113 Ricky Watters .25 .11
❑ 114 Jim Harbaugh .25 .11
❑ 115 Marcus Allen .50 .23
❑ 116 Levon Kirkland .15 .07
❑ 117 Jessie Tuggle .15 .07
❑ 118 Ken Norton .15 .07
❑ 119 Thurman Thomas .50 .23
❑ 120 Junior Seau .25 .11
❑ 121 Tim Brown .50 .23
❑ 122 Michael Jackson .25 .11
❑ 123 Eric Metcalf .25 .11
❑ 124 Herman Moore .50 .23
❑ 125 Bruce Smith .25 .11
❑ 126 Cris Carter .50 .23
❑ 127 Dave Brown .15 .07
❑ 128 Jeff Blake .25 .11
❑ 129 Robert Blackmon .15 .07
❑ 130 Barry Sanders 2.50 1.10
❑ 131 Blaine Bishop .15 .07
❑ 132 Jerome Bettis .50 .23
❑ 133 Stan Humphries .25 .11
❑ 134 Vinny Testaverde .25 .11
❑ 135 Troy Aikman 1.25 .55
❑ P54 Zach Thomas Promo .. 1.00 .45
(on back HT/WT in yellow box instead of team name)

1997 Topps Gallery Critics Choice

	MINT	NRMT
COMPLETE SET (20)	150.00	70.00
STATED ODDS 1:24		

❑ CC1 Barry Sanders 25.00 11.00
❑ CC2 Jeff Blake 2.50 1.10
❑ CC3 Vinny Testaverde 2.50 1.10
❑ CC4 Ricky Watters 2.50 1.10
❑ CC5 John Elway 25.00 11.00
❑ CC6 Drew Bledsoe 12.00 5.50
❑ CC7 Kordell Stewart 6.00 2.70
❑ CC8 Mark Brunell 12.00 5.50
❑ CC9 Troy Aikman 12.00 5.50
❑ CC10 Brett Favre 25.00 11.00
❑ CC11 Kevin Hardy 1.50 .70
❑ CC12 Shannon Sharpe 2.50 1.10
❑ CC13 Emmitt Smith 20.00 9.00
❑ CC14 Rob Moore 2.50 1.10
❑ CC15 Eddie George 12.00 5.50
❑ CC16 Herman Moore 5.00 2.20
❑ CC17 Terry Glenn 5.00 2.20
❑ CC18 Jim Harbaugh 2.50 1.10
❑ CC19 Terrell Davis 20.00 9.00
❑ CC20 Junior Seau 2.50 1.10

1997 Topps Gallery Gallery of Heroes

	MINT	NRMT
COMPLETE SET (15)	200.00	90.00
STATED ODDS 1:36		

❑ GH1 Desmond Howard 8.00 3.60

❑ GH2 Marcus Allen 10.00 4.50
❑ GH3 Kerry Collins 5.00 2.20
❑ GH4 Troy Aikman 20.00 9.00
❑ GH5 Jerry Rice 20.00 9.00
❑ GH6 Drew Bledsoe 20.00 9.00
❑ GH7 John Elway 40.00 18.00
❑ GH8 Mark Brunell 20.00 9.00
❑ GH9 Junior Seau 8.00 3.60
❑ GH10 Brett Favre 40.00 18.00
❑ GH11 Dan Marino 40.00 18.00
❑ GH12 Barry Sanders 40.00 18.00
❑ GH13 Reggie White 10.00 4.50
❑ GH14 Emmitt Smith 30.00 13.50
❑ GH15 Steve Young 15.00 6.75

1997 Topps Gallery Peter Max Serigraphs

	MINT	NRMT
COMPLETE SET (10)	100.00	45.00
STATED ODDS 1:24		

*AUTOGRAPHS: 6X TO 12X HI COL.
AUTOGRAPH STATED ODDS 1:1200
AUTOGRAPH PRINT RUN 42 SERIAL #'d SETS

❑ PM1 Brett Favre 20.00 9.00
❑ PM2 Jerry Rice 10.00 4.50
❑ PM3 Emmitt Smith 15.00 6.75
❑ PM4 John Elway 20.00 9.00
❑ PM5 Barry Sanders 20.00 9.00
❑ PM6 Reggie White 4.00 1.80
❑ PM7 Steve Young 6.00 2.70
❑ PM8 Troy Aikman 10.00 4.50
❑ PM9 Drew Bledsoe 10.00 4.50
❑ PM10 Dan Marino 20.00 9.00

1997 Topps Gallery Photo Gallery

	MINT	NRMT
COMPLETE SET (15)	150.00	70.00
STATED ODDS 1:24		

❑ PG1 Eddie George 10.00 4.50
❑ PG2 Drew Bledsoe 10.00 4.50
❑ PG3 Brett Favre 20.00 9.00
❑ PG4 Emmitt Smith 15.00 6.75
❑ PG5 Dan Marino 20.00 9.00
❑ PG6 Terrell Davis 15.00 6.75

❑ PG7 Kevin Greene .... 2.00 .90
❑ PG8 Troy Aikman 10.00 4.50
❑ PG9 Curtis Martin 5.00 2.20
❑ PG10 Barry Sanders 20.00 9.00
❑ PG11 Junior Seau .... 2.00 .90
❑ PG12 Deion Sanders 4.00 1.80
❑ PG13 Steve Young 6.00 2.70
❑ PG14 Reggie White 4.00 1.80
❑ PG15 Jerry Rice 10.00 4.50

1998 Topps Gold Label Class 1

	MINT	NRMT
COMP.GOLD CLASS 1 (100)	80.00	36.00
COMMON GOLD CLASS 1	.25	.11
SEMISTARS	.50	.23
UNLISTED STARS	1.00	.45
COMMON ROOKIE	2.00	.90
ROOKIE SEMISTARS	4.00	1.80
COMP.BLACK CLASS 1 (100)	400.00	180.00

*BLACK CLASS 1 STARS: 2X TO 5X HI COL.
*BLACK CLASS 1 YOUNG STARS: 1.5X TO 4X
*BLACK CLASS 1 RCs: 1X TO 2X
BLACK CLASS 1 STATED ODDS 1:8
COMMON RED CLASS 1 ...... 10.00 4.50
*RED CLASS 1 STARS: 15X TO 40X HI COL.
*RED CLASS 1 YOUNG STARS: 12.5X TO 30X
*RED CLASS 1 RCs: 4X TO 10X..
RED CLASS 1 STATED ODDS 1:94
RED CLASS 1 PRINT RUN 100 SETS
CLASS 1 PLAYER NAMES IN FLAT GOLD FOIL ....

❑ 1 John Elway 5.00 2.20
❑ 2 Rob Moore .... .50 .23
❑ 3 Jamal Anderson .... 1.00 .45
❑ 4 Patrick Johnson .... .25 .11
❑ 5 Troy Aikman 2.50 1.10
❑ 6 Antowain Smith .... 1.00 .45
❑ 7 Wesley Walls .... .50 .23
❑ 8 Curtis Enis RC 6.00 2.70
❑ 9 Jimmy Smith .... .50 .23
❑ 10 Terrell Davis 4.00 1.80
❑ 11 Marshall Faulk .... 1.00 .45
❑ 12 Germane Crowell RC 6.00 2.70
❑ 13 Marcus Nash RC 4.00 1.80
❑ 14 Deion Sanders .... 1.00 .45
❑ 15 Dorsey Levens .... 1.00 .45
❑ 16 Corey Dillon .... 1.50 .70
❑ 17 Fred Taylor RC 15.00 6.75
❑ 18 Derrick Thomas .... .50 .23
❑ 19 Kevin Dyson RC 5.00 2.20
❑ 20 Peyton Manning RC 25.00 11.00
❑ 21 Warren Sapp .... .50 .23
❑ 22 Robert Holcombe RC 4.00 1.80
❑ 23 Joey Galloway .... 1.00 .45
❑ 24 Garrison Hearst .... 1.00 .45
❑ 25 Brett Favre 5.00 2.20
❑ 26 Aeneas Williams .... .25 .11
❑ 27 Danny Kanell .... .50 .23
❑ 28 Robert Smith .... 1.00 .45
❑ 29 Brad Johnson .... 1.00 .45
❑ 30 Dan Marino 5.00 2.20
❑ 31 Elvis Grbac .... .50 .23
❑ 32 Terry Allen .... 1.00 .45
❑ 33 Frank Sanders .... .50 .23
❑ 34 Peter Boulware .... .25 .11
❑ 35 Tim Brown .... 1.00 .45
❑ 36 Keyshawn Johnson .... 1.00 .45
❑ 37 Rae Carruth .... .50 .23
❑ 38 Michael Irvin .... 1.00 .45
❑ 39 Brian Griese RC 10.00 4.50
❑ 40 Kordell Stewart .... 1.00 .45
❑ 41 Johnnie Morton .... .50 .23
❑ 42 Robert Brooks .... .50 .23
❑ 43 Keenan McCardell .... .50 .23
❑ 44 Ben Coates .... .50 .23
❑ 45 Jerry Rice 2.50 1.10
❑ 46 Tony Simmons RC 4.00 1.80
❑ 47 Irving Fryar .... .50 .23
❑ 48 Jerome Pathon RC 4.00 1.80
❑ 49 Steve McNair .... 1.00 .45
❑ 50 Warrick Dunn .... 1.00 .45
❑ 51 Skip Hicks RC 4.00 1.80
❑ 52 Andre Wadsworth RC 4.00 1.80
❑ 53 Chris Chandler .... .50 .23
❑ 54 Curtis Conway .... .50 .23
❑ 55 Eddie George .... 2.00 .90
❑ 56 Jeff Blake .... .50 .23
❑ 57 Greg Ellis RC .... 2.00 .90
❑ 58 Scott Mitchell .... .50 .23
❑ 59 Antonio Freeman .... 1.00 .45
❑ 60 Drew Bledsoe .... 2.00 .90
❑ 61 Mark Brunell .... 2.00 .90
❑ 62 Andre Rison .... .50 .23
❑ 63 Cris Carter .... 1.00 .45
❑ 64 Jake Reed .... .50 .23
❑ 65 Napoleon Kaufman .... 1.00 .45
❑ 66 Terry Glenn .... 1.00 .45
❑ 67 Jason Sehorn .... .25 .11
❑ 68 Rickey Dudley .... .25 .11
❑ 69 Junior Seau .... .50 .23
❑ 70 Jerome Bettis .... 1.00 .45
❑ 71 Curtis Martin .... 1.00 .45
❑ 72 Warren Moon .... 1.00 .45
❑ 73 Isaac Bruce .... 1.00 .45
❑ 74 Mike Alstott .... 1.00 .45
❑ 75 Steve Young .... 1.50 .70
❑ 76 Jacquez Green RC 5.00 2.20
❑ 77 Gus Frerotte .... .25 .11
❑ 78 Michael Jackson .... .25 .11
❑ 79 Carl Pickens .... 1.00 .45
❑ 80 Bruce Smith .... .50 .23
❑ 81 Shannon Sharpe .... .50 .23
❑ 82 Herman Moore .... 1.00 .45
❑ 83 Reggie White .... 1.00 .45
❑ 84 Marvin Harrison .... .50 .23
❑ 85 Jake Plummer 2.50 1.10
❑ 86 Karim Abdul-Jabbar ...... 1.00 .45
❑ 87 John Randle .... .50 .23
❑ 88 Robert Edwards RC 4.00 1.80
❑ 89 Jeff George .... .50 .23
❑ 90 Emmitt Smith 4.00 1.80
❑ 91 Terrell Owens .... 1.00 .45
❑ 92 Trent Dilfer .... 1.00 .45
❑ 93 Darrell Green .... .50 .23
❑ 94 Andre Reed .... .50 .23
❑ 95 Ryan Leaf RC 5.00 2.20
❑ 96 Rod Smith WR .... .50 .23
❑ 97 O.J. McDuffie .... .50 .23
❑ 98 John Avery RC 4.00 1.80
❑ 99 Charles Way .... .25 .11
❑ 100 Barry Sanders 5.00 2.20

1998 Topps Gold Label Class 2

	MINT	NRMT
COMP.CLASS 2 GOLD (100)	150.00	70.00

*GOLD C2 STARS: .75X TO 2X GOLD CLASS 1
*GOLD CLASS 2 YOUNG STARS: .75X TO 1.5X
*GOLD CLASS 2 RCs: .6X TO 1.2X
GOLD CLASS 2 STATED ODDS 1:2
COMP.BLACK CLASS 2 (100) 600.00 275.00
*BLACK C2 STARS: 4X TO 10X GOLD CLASS 1
*BLACK CLASS 2 YOUNG STARS: 3X TO 8X
*BLACK CLASS 2 RCs: 1.25X TO 3X
BLACK CLASS 2 STATED ODDS 1:16
COMMON RED CLASS 2 ...... 12.00 5.50
*RED C2 STARS: 30X TO 60X GOLD CLASS 1
*RED CLASS 2 YOUNG STARS: 25X TO 50X
*RED CLASS 2 RCs: 6X TO 15X..
RED CLASS 2 STATED ODDS 1:87
RED CLASS 2 PRINT RUN 50 SETS
CLASS 2 PLAYER NAMES IN SILVER HOLOFOIL

1998 Topps Gold Label Class 3

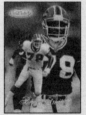

	MINT	NRMT
COMP.CLASS 3 GOLD (100)	250.00	110.00

*GOLD C3 STARS: 1.5X TO 3X GOLD CLASS 1
*GOLD CLASS 3 YOUNG STARS: 1X TO 2X
*GOLD CLASS 3 RCs: .75X TO 1.5X
GOLD CLASS 3 STATED ODDS 1:4
COMP.BLACK CLASS 3 (100) 1200.00 550.00
*BLACK C3 STARS: 6X TO 15X GOLD CLASS 1
*BLACK CLASS 3 YOUNG STARS: 5X TO 12X
*BLACK CLASS 3 RCs: 2X TO 5X
BLACK CLASS 3 STATED ODDS 1:32
COMMON RED CLASS 3 ...... 30.00 13.50
*RED C3 STARS: 50X TO 120X GOLD CLASS 1
*RED CLASS 3 YOUNG STARS: 40X TO 100X
*RED CLASS 3 RCs: 10X TO 25X
RED CLASS 3 STATED ODDS 1:375
RED CLASS 3 PRINT RUN 25 SETS
CLASS 3 PLAYER NAMES IN GOLD HOLOFOIL

1999 Topps Gold Label Class 1

	MINT	NRMT
COMPLETE SET (100)	80.00	36.00

COMMON CARD (1-100)	.25	.11
SEMISTARS	.50	.23
UNLISTED STARS	1.00	.45
COMMON ROOKIE	1.50	.70
ROOKIE SEMISTARS	2.50	1.10
COMP.BLACK CLASS 1 (100)	200.00	90.00

*BLACK CLASS 1 STARS: 1.5X TO 4X HI COL.
*BLACK CLASS 1 YOUNG STARS: 1.2X TO 3X
*BLACK CLASS 1 RCs: .6X TO 1.5X
BLACK CLASS 1 STATED ODDS 1:8
COMP.RED CLASS 1 (100) 1000.00 450.00
*RED CLASS 1 STARS: 8X TO 20X HI COL.
*RED CLASS 1 YOUNG STARS: 6X TO 15X
*RED CLASS 1 RCs: 3X TO 8X....
RED CLASS 1 STATED ODDS 1:79
RED CLASS 1 PRINT RUN 100 SER.#'d SETS

❑ 1 Terrell Davis	2.50	1.10
❑ 2 Jake Plummer	2.00	.90
❑ 3 Mike Cloud RC	2.50	1.10
❑ 4 D'Wayne Bates RC	2.50	1.10
❑ 5 Jamal Anderson	1.00	.45
❑ 6 Cecil Collins RC	3.00	1.35
❑ 7 Keyshawn Johnson	1.00	.45
❑ 8 Jerome Bettis	1.00	.45
❑ 9 Ricky Watters	.50	.23
❑ 10 Brett Favre	4.00	1.80
❑ 11 Joe Germaine RC	3.00	1.35
❑ 12 Eddie George	1.25	.55
❑ 13 Jevon Kearse RC	5.00	2.20
❑ 14 Skip Hicks	1.00	.45
❑ 15 James Johnson RC	3.00	1.35
❑ 16 Terry Glenn	1.00	.45
❑ 17 Troy Edwards RC	4.00	1.80
❑ 18 Karsten Bailey RC	1.50	.70
❑ 19 Trent Dilfer	.50	.23
❑ 20 Barry Sanders	4.00	1.80
❑ 21 Vinny Testaverde	.50	.23
❑ 22 Ed McCaffrey	.50	.23
❑ 23 Shannon Sharpe	.50	.23
❑ 24 Robert Smith	1.00	.45
❑ 25 Emmitt Smith	2.50	1.10
❑ 26 Rob Moore	.50	.23
❑ 27 J.J. Stokes	.50	.23
❑ 28 Champ Bailey RC	3.00	1.35
❑ 29 Napoleon Kaufman	1.00	.45
❑ 30 Fred Taylor	2.50	1.10
❑ 31 Corey Dillon	1.00	.45
❑ 32 Sedrick Irvin RC	3.00	1.35
❑ 33 Chris McAlister RC	1.50	.70
❑ 34 Warrick Dunn	1.00	.45
❑ 35 Isaac Bruce	1.00	.45
❑ 36 Peerless Price RC	4.00	1.80
❑ 37 Dorsey Levens	1.00	.45
❑ 38 Wayne Chrebet	.50	.23
❑ 39 Randall Cunningham	1.00	.45
❑ 40 Dan Marino	4.00	1.80
❑ 41 Chris Chandler	.50	.23
❑ 42 Mark Brunell	1.50	.70
❑ 43 Kevin Johnson RC	6.00	2.70
❑ 44 Natrone Means	.50	.23
❑ 45 Jerome Pathon	.25	.11
❑ 46 Daunte Culpepper RC	8.00	3.60
❑ 47 Akili Smith RC	5.00	2.20
❑ 48 Keenan McCardell	.50	.23
❑ 49 Steve McNair	1.00	.45
❑ 50 Randy Moss	4.00	1.80
❑ 51 Terance Mathis	.50	.23
❑ 52 Eric Moulds	1.00	.45
❑ 53 Rocket Ismail	.50	.23
❑ 54 Cade McNown RC	8.00	3.60
❑ 55 Kordell Stewart	1.00	.45
❑ 56 Rob Konrad RC	3.00	1.35
❑ 57 Andre Rison	.50	.23
❑ 58 Curtis Conway	.50	.23
❑ 59 Chris Claiborne RC	2.50	1.10
❑ 60 Jerry Rice	2.50	1.10
❑ 61 Peyton Manning	4.00	1.80
❑ 62 Jimmy Smith	.50	.23
❑ 63 Doug Flutie	1.25	.55
❑ 64 Frank Sanders	.50	.23
❑ 65 Antowain Smith	1.00	.45
❑ 66 Curtis Enis	1.00	.45
❑ 67 Charlie Batch	2.00	.90
❑ 68 Marvin Harrison	1.00	.45
❑ 69 Garrison Hearst	.50	.23
❑ 70 Ricky Williams RC	12.00	5.50
❑ 71 Torry Holt RC	6.00	2.70
❑ 72 Mike Alstott	1.00	.45
❑ 73 Drew Bledsoe	1.50	.70
❑ 74 O.J. McDuffie	.50	.23
❑ 75 Donovan McNabb RC	8.00	3.60
❑ 76 Curtis Martin	1.00	.45
❑ 77 Priest Holmes	1.00	.45
❑ 78 Antonio Freeman	1.00	.45
❑ 79 Herman Moore	1.00	.45
❑ 80 Tim Couch RC	12.00	5.50
❑ 81 Troy Aikman	2.50	1.10
❑ 82 David Boston RC	4.00	1.80
❑ 83 Tim Brown	1.00	.45
❑ 84 Kevin Faulk RC	3.00	1.35
❑ 85 Cris Carter	1.00	.45
❑ 86 Marshall Faulk	1.00	.45
❑ 87 Shaun King RC	8.00	3.60
❑ 88 Terrell Owens	1.00	.45
❑ 89 Carl Pickens	.50	.23
❑ 90 Steve Young	1.50	.70
❑ 91 Rod Smith	.50	.23
❑ 92 Michael Irvin	.50	.23
❑ 93 Ike Hilliard	.25	.11
❑ 94 Jon Kitna	1.25	.55
❑ 95 Brock Huard RC	3.00	1.35
❑ 96 Joey Galloway	1.00	.45
❑ 97 Amos Zereoue RC	3.00	1.35
❑ 98 Duce Staley	1.00	.45
❑ 99 John Elway	4.00	1.80
❑ 100 Edgerrin James RC	20.00	9.00

1999 Topps Gold Label Class 2

	MINT	NRMT
COMPLETE SET (100)	150.00	70.00

*CLASS 2 STARS: .75X TO 2X CLASS 1
*CLASS 2 YOUNG STARS: .6X TO 1.5X
*CLASS 2 RCs: .5X TO 1.2X ....
CLASS 2 STATED ODDS 1:2 ......
COMP.BLACK CLASS 2 (100) 400.00 180.00
*BLACK CLASS 2 STARS: 3X TO 8X HI COL.
*BLACK CLASS 2 YOUNG STARS: 2.5X TO 6X
*BLACK CLASS 2 RCs: 1.2X TO 3X
BLACK CLASS 2 STATED ODDS 1:16
COMP.RED CLASS 2 (100) 1500.00 700.00
*RED CLASS 2 STARS: 12X TO 30X HI COL.
*RED CLASS 2 YOUNG STARS: 10X TO 25X
*RED CLASS 2 RCs: 5X TO 12X..
RED CLASS 2 STATED ODDS 1:157
RED CLASS 2 PRINT RUN 50 SER.#'d SETS

1999 Topps Gold Label Class 3

	MINT	NRMT
COMPLETE SET (100)	250.00	110.00

*CLASS 3 STARS: 1.2X TO 3X CLASS 1
*CLASS 3 YOUNG STARS: .8X TO 2X
*CLASS 3 RCs: .6X TO 1.5X ....
CLASS 3 STATED ODDS 1:4 ......
COMP.BLACK CLASS 3 (100) 600.00 275.00
*BLACK CLASS 3 STARS: 5X TO 12X CLASS 1
*BLACK CLASS 3 YOUNG STARS: 4X TO 10X
*BLACK CLASS 3 RCs: 2X TO 5X
BLACK CLASS 3 STATED ODDS 1:32
COMMON RED CLASS 3 ...... 12.00 5.50
*RED CLASS 3 STARS: 20X TO 50X CLASS 1
*RED CLASS 3 YOUNG STARS: 15X TO 40X
*RED CLASS 3 RCs: 8X TO 20X..
RED CLASS 3 STATED ODDS 1:314
RED CLASS 3 PRINT RUN 25 SER.#'d SETS

1999 Topps Gold Label Race to Gold

	MINT	NRMT
COMP.GOLD SET (15)	60.00	27.00
COMMON GOLD LABEL (R1-R15)	1.50	.70
SEMISTARS	3.00	1.35

GOLD LABEL STATED ODDS 1:12
*BLACK LABEL: .8X TO 2X GOLD LABEL
BLACK LABEL STATED ODDS 1:48
R1-R5 RED LABELS: 15X TO 35X GOLDS
R1-R5 RED LABEL PRINT RUN 13 SER.#'d SETS
R1-R5 RED LABEL STATED ODDS 1:11,867
R6-R10 RED LABELS: 7X TO 20X GOLDS
R6-R10 RED LAB.PRINT RUN 34 SER.#'d SETS
R6-R10 RED LABEL STATED ODDS 1:4638
R11-R15 RED LABELS: 3X TO 8X GOLDS
R11-R15 RED LAB.PRINT RUN 80 SER.#'d SETS
R11-R15 RED LABEL STATED ODDS 1:1968

❑ R1 Brett Favre	12.00	5.50
❑ R2 Peyton Manning	10.00	4.50
❑ R3 Drew Bledsoe	5.00	2.20
❑ R4 Randall Cunningham	4.00	1.80
❑ R5 Jake Plummer	6.00	2.70
❑ R6 Emmitt Smith	8.00	3.60
❑ R7 Terrell Davis	8.00	3.60
❑ R8 Barry Sanders	12.00	5.50
❑ R9 Eddie George	4.00	1.80
❑ R10 Curtis Martin	4.00	1.80
❑ R11 Antonio Freeman	4.00	1.80
❑ R12 Eric Moulds	4.00	1.80
❑ R13 Joey Galloway	4.00	1.80
❑ R14 Rod Smith	1.50	.70
❑ R15 Randy Moss	10.00	4.50

1998 Topps Season Opener

	MINT	NRMT
COMPLETE SET (165)	150.00	70.00
COMMON CARD (1-165)	.10	.05

COMMON ROOKIE (1-30)	2.50	1.10
ROOKIE SEMISTARS	4.00	1.80
ROOKIE UNL.STARS	5.00	2.20

*SEAS.OPEN.STARS: SAME PRICE AS BASE SET
SEASON OPENER RETAIL ONLY PRODUCT

❑ 1 Peyton Manning RC	40.00	18.00
❑ 6 Robert Edwards RC	4.00	1.80
❑ 7 Curtis Enis RC	8.00	3.60
❑ 8 John Avery RC	4.00	1.80
❑ 9 Fred Taylor RC	25.00	11.00
❑ 10 Germane Crowell RC	8.00	3.60
❑ 12 Marcus Nash RC	5.00	2.20
❑ 13 Jacquez Green RC	6.00	2.70
❑ 16 Brian Griese RC	15.00	6.75
❑ 18 Robert Holcombe RC	4.00	1.80
❑ 19 Skip Hicks RC	5.00	2.20
❑ 20 Ahman Green RC	5.00	2.20
❑ 22 Randy Moss RC	40.00	18.00
❑ 26 Charles Woodson RC	8.00	3.60
❑ 27 Kevin Dyson RC	6.00	2.70
❑ 29 Tim Dwight RC	6.00	2.70
❑ 30 Ryan Leaf RC	6.00	2.70

1999 Topps Season Opener

	MINT	NRMT
COMPLETE SET (165)	40.00	18.00
COMMON CARD (1-165)	.10	.05
SEMISTARS	.20	.09
UNLISTED STARS	.40	.18
COMMON ROOKIE (145-164)	2.00	.90

❑ 1 Jerry Rice	1.00	.45
❑ 2 Emmitt Smith	1.00	.45
❑ 3 Curtis Martin	.40	.18
❑ 4 Ed McCaffrey	.20	.09
❑ 5 Oronde Gadsden	.10	.05
❑ 6 Byron Bam Morris	.10	.05
❑ 7 Michael Irvin	.20	.09
❑ 8 Shannon Sharpe	.20	.09
❑ 9 Levon Kirkland	.10	.05
❑ 10 Fred Taylor	1.00	.45
❑ 11 Andre Reed	.20	.09
❑ 12 Chad Brown	.10	.05
❑ 13 Skip Hicks	.40	.18
❑ 14 Tim Dwight	.40	.18
❑ 15 Michael Sinclair	.10	.05
❑ 16 Carl Pickens	.20	.09
❑ 17 Derrick Alexander WR	.20	.09
❑ 18 Kevin Greene	.10	.05
❑ 19 Duce Staley	.40	.18
❑ 20 Dan Marino	1.50	.70
❑ 21 Frank Sanders	.20	.09
❑ 22 Ricky Proehl	.10	.05
❑ 23 Frank Wycheck	.10	.05
❑ 24 Andre Rison	.20	.09
❑ 25 Natrone Means	.20	.09
❑ 26 Steve McNair	.40	.18
❑ 27 Vonnie Holliday	.10	.05
❑ 28 Charles Woodson	.40	.18
❑ 29 Rob Moore	.20	.09
❑ 30 John Elway	1.50	.70
❑ 31 Derrick Thomas	.20	.09
❑ 32 Jake Plummer	.75	.35
❑ 33 Mike Alstott	.40	.18
❑ 34 Keenan McCardell	.20	.09
❑ 35 Mark Chmura	.10	.05
❑ 36 Keyshawn Johnson	.40	.18
❑ 37 Priest Holmes	.40	.18
❑ 38 Antonio Freeman	.40	.18
❑ 39 Ty Law	.10	.05
❑ 40 Jamal Anderson	.40	.18
❑ 41 Courtney Hawkins	.10	.05
❑ 42 James Jett	.20	.09
❑ 43 Aaron Glenn	.10	.05
❑ 44 Jimmy Smith	.20	.09
❑ 45 Michael McCrary	.10	.05
❑ 46 Junior Seau	.20	.09
❑ 47 Bill Romanowski	.10	.05
❑ 48 Mark Brunell	.60	.25
❑ 49 Yancey Thigpen	.10	.05
❑ 50 Steve Young	.60	.25
❑ 51 Cris Carter	.40	.18
❑ 52 Vinny Testaverde	.20	.09
❑ 53 Zach Thomas	.20	.09
❑ 54 Kordell Stewart	.40	.18
❑ 55 Tim Biakabutuka	.20	.09
❑ 56 J.J. Stokes	.20	.09
❑ 57 Jon Kitna	.50	.23
❑ 58 Jacquez Green	.20	.09
❑ 59 Marvin Harrison	.40	.18
❑ 60 Barry Sanders	1.50	.70
❑ 61 Darrell Green	.10	.05
❑ 62 Terance Mathis	.20	.09
❑ 63 Ricky Watters	.20	.09
❑ 64 Chris Chandler	.20	.09
❑ 65 Cameron Cleeland	.10	.05
❑ 66 Rod Smith	.20	.09
❑ 67 Freddie Jones	.10	.05
❑ 68 Adrian Murrell	.20	.09
❑ 69 Terrell Owens	.40	.18
❑ 70 Troy Aikman	1.00	.45
❑ 71 John Mobley	.10	.05
❑ 72 Corey Dillon	.40	.18
❑ 73 Rickey Dudley	.10	.05
❑ 74 Randall Cunningham	.40	.18
❑ 75 Muhsin Muhammad	.20	.09
❑ 76 Stephen Boyd	.10	.05
❑ 77 Tony Gonzalez	.20	.09
❑ 78 Deion Sanders	.40	.18
❑ 79 Ben Coates	.20	.09
❑ 80 Brett Favre	1.50	.70
❑ 81 Shawn Springs	.10	.05
❑ 82 Dorsey Levens	.40	.18
❑ 83 Ray Buchanan	.10	.05
❑ 84 Charlie Batch	.75	.35
❑ 85 John Randle	.20	.09
❑ 86 Eddie George	.50	.23
❑ 87 Ray Lewis	.10	.05
❑ 88 Johnnie Morton	.20	.09
❑ 89 Kevin Hardy	.10	.05
❑ 90 O.J. McDuffie	.20	.09
❑ 91 Herman Moore	.40	.18
❑ 92 Tim Brown	.40	.18
❑ 93 Bert Emanuel	.20	.09
❑ 94 Elvis Grbac	.20	.09
❑ 95 Peter Boulware	.10	.05
❑ 96 Curtis Conway	.20	.09
❑ 97 Doug Flutie	.50	.23
❑ 98 Jake Reed	.20	.09
❑ 99 Ike Hilliard	.10	.05
❑ 100 Randy Moss	1.50	.70
❑ 101 Warren Sapp	.10	.05
❑ 102 Bruce Smith	.20	.09
❑ 103 Joey Galloway	.40	.18
❑ 104 Napoleon Kaufman	.40	.18
❑ 105 Warrick Dunn	.40	.18
❑ 106 Wayne Chrebet	.20	.09
❑ 107 Robert Brooks	.20	.09
❑ 108 Antowain Smith	.40	.18
❑ 109 Trent Dilfer	.20	.09
❑ 110 Peyton Manning	1.50	.70
❑ 111 Isaac Bruce	.40	.18
❑ 112 John Lynch	.10	.05
❑ 113 Terry Glenn	.40	.18
❑ 114 Garrison Hearst	.20	.09
❑ 115 Jerome Bettis	.40	.18
❑ 116 Darnay Scott	.10	.05
❑ 117 Lamar Thomas	.10	.05
❑ 118 Chris Spielman	.10	.05
❑ 119 Robert Smith	.40	.18
❑ 120 Drew Bledsoe	.60	.25
❑ 121 Reidel Anthony	.20	.09
❑ 122 Wesley Walls	.20	.09
❑ 123 Eric Moulds	.40	.18
❑ 124 Terrell Davis	1.00	.45
❑ 125 Dale Carter	.10	.05
❑ 126 Charles Johnson	.10	.05
❑ 127 Steve Atwater	.10	.05
❑ 128 Jim Harbaugh	.20	.09
❑ 129 Tony Martin	.20	.09
❑ 130 Kerry Collins	.20	.09
❑ 131 Trent Green	.20	.09
❑ 132 Marshall Faulk	.40	.18
❑ 133 Rocket Ismail	.20	.09
❑ 134 Warren Moon	.40	.18
❑ 135 Jerris McPhail	.10	.05
❑ 136 Damon Gibson	.10	.05
❑ 137 Jim Pyne	.10	.05
❑ 138 Antonio Langham	.10	.05
❑ 139 Freddie Solomon	.10	.05
❑ 140 Randy Moss SH	.75	.35
❑ 141 John Elway SH	.75	.35
❑ 142 Doug Flutie SH	.40	.18
❑ 143 Emmitt Smith SH	.50	.23
❑ 144 Terrell Davis SH	.50	.23
❑ 145 Troy Edwards RC	3.00	1.35
❑ 146 Torry Holt RC	5.00	2.20
❑ 147 Tim Couch RC	10.00	4.50
❑ 148 Sedrick Irvin RC	1.50	.70
❑ 149 Ricky Williams RC	10.00	4.50
❑ 150 Peerless Price RC	3.00	1.35
❑ 151 Mike Cloud RC	1.50	.70
❑ 152 Kevin Faulk RC	2.50	1.10
❑ 153 Kevin Johnson RC	5.00	2.20
❑ 154 James Johnson RC	2.50	1.10
❑ 155 Edgerrin James RC	15.00	6.75
❑ 156 D'Wayne Bates RC	2.00	.90
❑ 157 Donovan McNabb RC	6.00	2.70
❑ 158 David Boston RC	3.00	1.35
❑ 159 Daunte Culpepper RC	6.00	2.70
❑ 160 Champ Bailey RC	2.50	1.10
❑ 161 Cecil Collins RC	1.50	.70
❑ 162 Cade McNown RC	6.00	2.70
❑ 163 Brock Huard RC	2.50	1.10
❑ 164 Akili Smith RC	4.00	1.80
❑ 165 Checklist Card	.10	.05

1999 Topps Season Opener Autographs

	MINT	NRMT
COMPLETE SET (2)	400.00	180.00
COMMON CARD (A1-A2)	200.00	90.00
STATED ODDS 1:7126		

❑ A1 Tim Couch	250.00	110.00
❑ A2 Peyton Manning	200.00	90.00

1999 Topps Season Opener Football Fever

	MINT	NRMT
COMPLETE SET (55)	20.00	9.00
COMMON CARD (F1A-F15C)	.30	.14
ONE PER PACK		

❑ F1A Brett Favre 9/26 W	2.00	.90
❑ F1B Brett Favre 10/17	1.00	.45
❑ F1C Brett Favre 11/07	1.00	.45
❑ F1D Brett Favre 11/29	1.00	.45
❑ F2A Jake Plummer 9/27	.50	.23
❑ F2B Jake Plummer 10/03	.50	.23
❑ F2C Jake Plummer 10/31	.50	.23
❑ F2D Jake Plummer 12/05	.50	.23
❑ F3A Drew Bledsoe 9/19	.50	.23
❑ F3B Drew Bledsoe 10/03 W	.75	.35
❑ F3C Drew Bledsoe 10/24	.50	.23
❑ F3D Drew Bledsoe 12/05	.50	.23
❑ F4A Peyton Manning 9/12	.75	.35
❑ F4B Peyton Manning 10/17	.75	.35
❑ F4C Peyton Manning 10/24	.75	.35
❑ F4D Peyton Manning 12/12	.75	.35
❑ F5A Tim Couch 10/10	1.00	.45
❑ F5B Tim Couch 11/21	1.00	.45
❑ F5C Tim Couch 11/28	1.00	.45

❑ F5D Tim Couch 12/05	1.00	.45
❑ F6A Terrell Davis 9/13	.60	.25
❑ F6B Terrell Davis 10/03	.60	.25
❑ F6C Terrell Davis 10/31	.60	.25
❑ F6D Terrell Davis 12/19	.60	.25
❑ F7A Jamal Anderson 9/12	.30	.14
❑ F7B Jamal Anderson 10/17	.30	.14
❑ F7C Jamal Anderson 10/25	.30	.14
❑ F7D Jamal Anderson 12/05	.30	.14
❑ F8A Curtis Martin 9/12	.30	.14
❑ F8B Curtis Martin 10/17 W	.50	.23
❑ F8C Curtis Martin 10/24 W	.50	.23
❑ F8D Curtis Martin 11/21	.30	.14
❑ F9A Fred Taylor 9/26	.50	.23
❑ F9B Fred Taylor 10/17	.50	.23
❑ F9C Fred Taylor 10/31 W	1.00	.45
❑ F9D Fred Taylor 12/12	.50	.23
❑ F10A Ricky Williams 10/3	1.00	.45
❑ F10B Ricky Williams 10/10	1.00	.45
❑ F10C Ricky Williams 10/31 W	2.00	.90
❑ F10D Ricky Williams 12/12	1.00	.45
❑ F11A Antonio Freeman 9/26	.30	.14
❑ F11B Antonio Freeman 11/29	.30	.14
❑ F11C Antonio Freeman 12/12	.30	.14
❑ F12A Jerry Rice 9/19	.60	.25
❑ F12B Jerry Rice 10/24	.60	.25
❑ F12C Jerry Rice 11/29	.60	.25
❑ F13A Jimmy Smith 10/17	.30	.14
❑ F13B Jimmy Smith 10/31	.30	.14
❑ F13C Jimmy Smith 12/13	.30	.14
❑ F14A Randy Moss 10/24	.75	.35
❑ F14B Randy Moss 11/08	.75	.35
❑ F14C Randy Moss 12/20 W	1.50	.70
❑ F15A Torry Holt 10/03	.50	.23
❑ F15B Torry Holt 10/24	.50	.23
❑ F15C Torry Holt 12/05	.50	.23

1997 Topps Stars

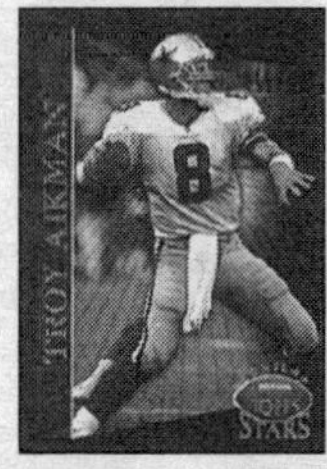

	MINT	NRMT
COMPLETE SET (125)	40.00	18.00
COMMON CARD (1-125)	.15	.07
SEMISTARS	.25	.11
UNLISTED STARS	.50	.23
CHECKLIST (NNO)	.10	.05
COMP.FOIL SET (125)	1000.00	450.00
*FOIL STARS: 12X TO 30X HI COL.		
*FOIL RCs: 4X TO 10X HI		
FOIL STATED ODDS 1:18		

❑ 1 Brett Favre	2.50	1.10
❑ 2 Michael Jackson	.25	.11
❑ 3 Simeon Rice	.25	.11
❑ 4 Thurman Thomas	.50	.23
❑ 5 Karim Abdul-Jabbar	.50	.23
❑ 6 Marvin Harrison	.50	.23
❑ 7 John Elway	2.50	1.10
❑ 8 Carl Pickens	.50	.23
❑ 9 Rod Woodson	.25	.11
❑ 10 Kerry Collins	.25	.11
❑ 11 Cortez Kennedy	.15	.07
❑ 12 William Fuller	.15	.07
❑ 13 Michael Irvin	.50	.23
❑ 14 Tyrone Braxton	.15	.07
❑ 15 Steve Young	.75	.35
❑ 16 Keith Lyle	.15	.07
❑ 17 Blaine Bishop	.15	.07
❑ 18 Jeff Hostetler	.15	.07
❑ 19 Levon Kirkland	.15	.07
❑ 20 Barry Sanders	2.50	1.10
❑ 21 Deion Sanders	.50	.23
❑ 22 Jamal Anderson	.75	.35
❑ 23 Eric Davis	.15	.07
❑ 24 Hardy Nickerson	.15	.07
❑ 25 LeRoy Butler	.15	.07
❑ 26 Mark Brunell	1.25	.55
❑ 27 Aeneas Williams	.15	.07
❑ 28 Curtis Martin	.60	.25
❑ 29 Wayne Chrebet	.50	.23
❑ 30 Jerry Rice	1.25	.55
❑ 31 Jake Reed	.25	.11
❑ 32 Wayne Martin	.15	.07
❑ 33 Derrick Alexander WR	.25	.11
❑ 34 Isaac Bruce	.50	.23
❑ 35 Terrell Davis	2.00	.90
❑ 36 Jerome Bettis	.50	.23
❑ 37 Keenan McCardell	.25	.11
❑ 38 Derrick Thomas	.25	.11
❑ 39 Jason Sehorn	.25	.11
❑ 40 Keyshawn Johnson	.50	.23
❑ 41 Jeff Blake	.25	.11
❑ 42 Terry Allen	.50	.23
❑ 43 Ben Coates	.25	.11
❑ 44 William Thomas	.15	.07
❑ 45 Bryce Paup	.15	.07
❑ 46 Bryant Young	.15	.07
❑ 47 Eric Swann	.15	.07
❑ 48 Tim Brown	.50	.23
❑ 49 Tony Martin	.25	.11
❑ 50 Eddie George	1.50	.70
❑ 51 Sam Mills	.15	.07
❑ 52 Terry McDaniel	.15	.07
❑ 53 Darren Woodson	.15	.07
❑ 54 Ashley Ambrose	.15	.07
❑ 55 Drew Bledsoe	1.25	.55
❑ 56 Larry Centers	.25	.11
❑ 57 Ty Detmer	.25	.11
❑ 58 Merton Hanks	.15	.07
❑ 59 Charles Johnson	.25	.11
❑ 60 Dan Marino	2.50	1.10
❑ 61 Joey Galloway	.60	.25
❑ 62 Junior Seau	.25	.11
❑ 63 Brett Perriman	.15	.07
❑ 64 Wesley Walls	.25	.11
❑ 65 Chad Brown	.15	.07
❑ 66 Henry Ellard	.15	.07
❑ 67 Keith Jackson	.15	.07
❑ 68 John Randle	.15	.07
❑ 69 Chester McGlockton	.15	.07
❑ 70 Emmitt Smith	2.00	.90
❑ 71 Vinny Testaverde	.25	.11
❑ 72 Steve Atwater	.15	.07
❑ 73 Irving Fryar	.25	.11
❑ 74 Gus Frerotte	.15	.07
❑ 75 Terry Glenn	.50	.23
❑ 76 Anthony Johnson	.15	.07
❑ 77 Jimmy Smith	.25	.11
❑ 78 Terrell Buckley	.15	.07
❑ 79 Kimble Anders	.25	.11
❑ 80 Cris Carter	.50	.23
❑ 81 Dave Meggett	.15	.07
❑ 82 Shannon Sharpe	.25	.11
❑ 83 Adrian Murrell	.25	.11
❑ 84 Herman Moore	.50	.23
❑ 85 Bruce Smith	.25	.11
❑ 86 Lamar Lathon	.15	.07
❑ 87 Ken Harvey	.15	.07
❑ 88 Curtis Conway	.25	.11
❑ 89 Alfred Williams	.15	.07
❑ 90 Troy Aikman	1.25	.55
❑ 91 Carnell Lake	.15	.07
❑ 92 Michael Sinclair	.15	.07
❑ 93 Ricky Watters	.25	.11
❑ 94 Kevin Greene	.25	.11
❑ 95 Reggie White	.50	.23
❑ 96 Tyrone Hughes	.15	.07
❑ 97 Dale Carter	.15	.07
❑ 98 Rob Moore	.25	.11
❑ 99 Tony Tolbert	.15	.07
❑ 100 Willie McGinest	.15	.07
❑ 101 Orlando Pace RC	.15	.07
❑ 102 Yatil Green RC	.25	.11
❑ 103 Antowain Smith RC	3.00	1.35
❑ 104 David LaFleur RC	.50	.23
❑ 105 Jake Plummer RC	15.00	6.75
❑ 106 Will Blackwell RC	.50	.23
❑ 107 Dwayne Rudd RC	.15	.07
❑ 108 Corey Dillon RC	8.00	3.60
❑ 109 Pat Barnes RC	.50	.23
❑ 110 Peter Boulware RC	.25	.11
❑ 111 Tony Gonzalez RC	5.00	2.20
❑ 112 Renaldo Wynn RC	.15	.07
❑ 113 Darrell Russell RC	.15	.07
❑ 114 Bryant Westbrook RC	.15	.07
❑ 115 James Farrior RC	.15	.07
❑ 116 Joey Kent RC	.50	.23
❑ 117 Rae Carruth RC	.50	.23
❑ 118 Jim Druckenmiller RC	1.00	.45
❑ 119 Byron Hanspard RC	2.50	1.10
❑ 120 Ike Hilliard RC	2.50	1.10
❑ 121 Kevin Lockett RC	.50	.23
❑ 122 Tom Knight RC	.15	.07
❑ 123 Shawn Springs RC	.25	.11
❑ 124 Troy Davis RC	.50	.23
❑ 125 Darnell Autry RC	.25	.11
❑ PP36 Jerome Bettis Promo	1.00	.45
❑ NNO Checklist Card	.15	.07

1997 Topps Stars Future Pro Bowlers

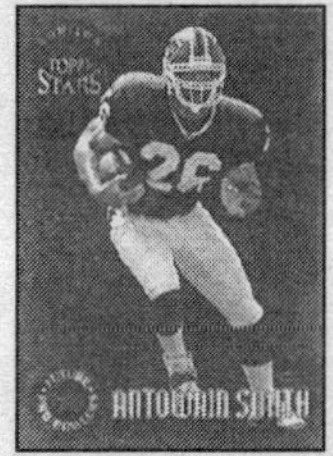

	MINT	NRMT
COMPLETE SET (15)	40.00	18.00
STATED ODDS 1:12 HOBBY		

❑ FPB1 Ike Hilliard	4.00	1.80
❑ FPB2 Tom Knight	2.00	.90
❑ FPB3 David LaFleur	3.00	1.35
❑ FPB4 Byron Hanspard	4.00	1.80
❑ FPB5 Kevin Lockett	3.00	1.35
❑ FPB6 Rae Carruth	3.00	1.35
❑ FPB7 Jim Druckenmiller	4.00	1.80
❑ FPB8 Darnell Autry	3.00	1.35
❑ FPB9 Joey Kent	4.00	1.80
❑ FPB10 Peter Boulware	3.00	1.35
❑ FPB11 Orlando Pace	2.00	.90
❑ FPB12 Troy Davis	4.00	1.80
❑ FPB13 Antowain Smith	8.00	3.60
❑ FPB14 Bryant Westbrook	2.00	.90
❑ FPB15 Yatil Green	3.00	1.35

1997 Topps Stars Rookie Reprints

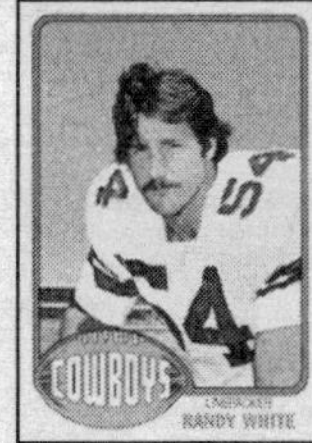

	MINT	NRMT
COMPLETE SET (10)	60.00	27.00
COMMON CARD (1-10)	5.00	2.20
SEMISTARS	6.00	2.70
STATED ODDS 1:64		
❑ 1 George Blanda	6.00	2.70
❑ 2 Dick Butkus	10.00	4.50
❑ 3 Len Dawson UER (Card numbered 4 of 10)	6.00	2.70
❑ 4 Jack Ham	5.00	2.20
❑ 5 Sam Huff	5.00	2.20
❑ 6 Deacon Jones	6.00	2.70
❑ 7 Ray Nitschke	7.00	3.10
❑ 8 Gale Sayers (1968 Topps card)	10.00	4.50
❑ 9 Randy White	5.00	2.20
❑ 10 Kellen Winslow	5.00	2.20

1997 Topps Stars Rookie Reprints Autographs

	MINT	NRMT
COMPLETE SET (10)	400.00	180.00
COMMON CARD (1-10)	40.00	18.00
SEMISTARS	50.00	22.00
RANDOM INSERTS IN HOBBY PACKS		
❑ 1 George Blanda	50.00	22.00
❑ 2 Dick Butkus	60.00	27.00
❑ 3 Len Dawson	50.00	22.00
❑ 4 Jack Ham	40.00	18.00
❑ 5 Sam Huff	40.00	18.00
❑ 6 Deacon Jones	50.00	22.00
❑ 7 Ray Nitschke	60.00	27.00
❑ 8 Gale Sayers	60.00	27.00
❑ 9 Randy White	40.00	18.00
❑ 10 Kellen Winslow	40.00	18.00

1997 Topps Stars Pro Bowl Memories

	MINT	NRMT
COMPLETE SET (10)	60.00	27.00
STATED ODDS 1:24		
❑ PBM1 Barry Sanders	20.00	9.00
❑ PBM2 Jeff Blake	2.00	.90
❑ PBM3 Ken Harvey	1.25	.55
❑ PBM4 Brett Favre	20.00	9.00
❑ PBM5 Jerry Rice	10.00	4.50
❑ PBM6 John Elway	20.00	9.00
❑ PBM7 Marshall Faulk	4.00	1.80
❑ PBM8 Steve Young	6.00	2.70
❑ PBM9 Mark Brunell	10.00	4.50
❑ PBM10 Troy Aikman	10.00	4.50

1997 Topps Stars Pro Bowl Stars

	MINT	NRMT
COMPLETE SET (30)	100.00	45.00
STATED ODDS 1:24		
❑ PB1 Brett Favre	25.00	11.00
❑ PB2 Mark Brunell	12.00	5.50
❑ PB3 Kerry Collins	2.50	1.10
❑ PB4 Drew Bledsoe	12.00	5.50
❑ PB5 Barry Sanders	25.00	11.00
❑ PB6 Terrell Davis	20.00	9.00
❑ PB7 Terry Allen	5.00	2.20
❑ PB8 Jerome Bettis	5.00	2.20
❑ PB9 Ricky Watters	2.50	1.10
❑ PB10 Curtis Martin	6.00	2.70
❑ PB11 Emmitt Smith	20.00	9.00
❑ PB12 Kimble Anders	2.50	1.10
❑ PB13 Jerry Rice	12.00	5.50
❑ PB14 Carl Pickens	5.00	2.20
❑ PB15 Herman Moore	5.00	2.20
❑ PB16 Tony Martin	2.50	1.10
❑ PB17 Isaac Bruce	5.00	2.20
❑ PB18 Tim Brown	5.00	2.20
❑ PB19 Wesley Walls	2.50	1.10
❑ PB20 Shannon Sharpe	2.50	1.10
❑ PB21 Dana Stubblefield	1.50	.70
❑ PB22 Reggie White	5.00	2.20
❑ PB23 Bruce Smith	2.50	1.10
❑ PB24 Bryant Young	1.50	.70
❑ PB25 Junior Seau	2.50	1.10
❑ PB26 Kevin Greene	2.50	1.10
❑ PB27 Derrick Thomas	2.50	1.10
❑ PB28 Chad Brown	1.50	.70
❑ PB29 Deion Sanders	5.00	2.20
❑ PB30 Rod Woodson	2.50	1.10

1998 Topps Stars

	MINT	NRMT
COMP.RED SET (150)	100.00	45.00
COMMON RED (1-150)	.25	.11
RED SEMISTARS	.50	.23
RED UNLISTED STARS	1.00	.45
COMMON ROOKIE	1.50	.70
ROOKIE SEMISTARS	2.50	1.10
ROOKIE UNLISTED STARS	3.00	1.35
RED PRINT RUN 8799 SERIAL #'d SETS		
COMP.BRONZE SET (150)	100.00	45.00
*BRONZE CARDS: SAME PRICE AS RED		
BRONZE PRINT RUN 8799 SERIAL #'d SETS		
COMP.SILVER SET (150)	150.00	70.00
*SILVER CARDS: .6X TO 1.5X HI COL.		
SILVER PRINT RUN 3999 SERIAL #'d SETS		
COMP.GOLD SET (150)	300.00	135.00
*GOLD STARS: 1.5X TO 3X HI COL.		
*GOLD RCs: 1X TO 2.5X		
GOLD STATED ODDS 1:2		
GOLD PRINT RUN 1999 SERIAL #'d SETS		
COMMON GOLD RBW.(1-150)	12.00	5.50
*GOLD RBW.STARS: 15X TO 30X HI COL.		
*GOLD RBW.YOUNG STARS: 12.5X TO 25X		
*GOLD RBW.RCs: 3X TO 8X		
GOLD RBW.STATED ODDS 1:41		
GOLD RBW.PRINT RUN 99 SERIAL #'d SETS		
RED CARDS PRICED BELOW		
❑ 1 John Elway	5.00	2.20
❑ 2 Duane Starks RC	1.50	.70
❑ 3 Bruce Smith	.50	.23
❑ 4 Jeff Blake	.50	.23
❑ 5 Carl Pickens	1.00	.45
❑ 6 Shannon Sharpe	.50	.23
❑ 7 Jerome Pathon RC	2.50	1.10
❑ 8 Jimmy Smith	.50	.23
❑ 9 Elvis Grbac	.50	.23
❑ 10 Mark Brunell	2.00	.90
❑ 11 Karim Abdul-Jabbar	1.00	.45
❑ 12 Terry Glenn	1.00	.45
❑ 13 Larry Centers	.25	.11
❑ 14 Jeff George	.50	.23
❑ 15 Terry Allen	1.00	.45
❑ 16 Charles Johnson	.25	.11
❑ 17 Chris Spielman	.25	.11
❑ 18 Ahman Green RC	.50	.23
❑ 19 Kevin Dyson RC	4.00	1.80
❑ 20 Dan Marino	5.00	2.20
❑ 21 Andre Wadsworth RC	2.50	1.10
❑ 22 Chris Chandler	.50	.23
❑ 23 Kerry Collins	.50	.23
❑ 24 Erik Kramer	.25	.11
❑ 25 Warrick Dunn	1.50	.70
❑ 26 Michael Irvin	1.00	.45
❑ 27 Herman Moore	1.00	.45
❑ 28 Dorsey Levens	1.00	.45
❑ 29 Cris Carter	1.00	.45
❑ 30 Drew Bledsoe	2.00	.90
❑ 31 Kevin Greene	.50	.23
❑ 32 Charles Way	.25	.11
❑ 33 Bobby Hoying	.50	.23
❑ 34 Tony Banks	.50	.23
❑ 35 Steve Young	1.50	.70
❑ 36 Trent Dilfer	1.00	.45
❑ 37 Warren Sapp	.50	.23
❑ 38 Skip Hicks RC	3.00	1.35
❑ 39 Michael Jackson	.25	.11
❑ 40 Curtis Martin	1.00	.45
❑ 41 Thurman Thomas	1.00	.45
❑ 42 Corey Dillon	1.50	.70
❑ 43 Brian Griese RC	8.00	3.60
❑ 44 Marshall Faulk	1.00	.45
❑ 45 Isaac Bruce	1.00	.45
❑ 46 Fred Taylor RC	12.00	5.50
❑ 47 Andre Rison	.50	.23
❑ 48 O.J. McDuffie	.50	.23
❑ 49 John Avery RC	3.00	1.35
❑ 50 Terrell Davis	4.00	1.80
❑ 51 Robert Edwards RC	3.00	1.35
❑ 52 Keyshawn Johnson	1.00	.45
❑ 53 Rickey Dudley	.25	.11
❑ 54 Hines Ward RC	2.50	1.10
❑ 55 Irving Fryar	.50	.23
❑ 56 Freddie Jones	.25	.11
❑ 57 Michael Sinclair	.25	.11
❑ 58 Darnay Scott	.50	.23

❑ 59 Tim Dwight RC	4.00	1.80
❑ 60 Tim Brown	1.00	.45
❑ 61 Ray Lewis	.25	.11
❑ 62 Curtis Enis RC	5.00	2.20
❑ 63 Emmitt Smith	4.00	1.80
❑ 64 Scott Mitchell	.50	.23
❑ 65 Antonio Freeman	1.00	.45
❑ 66 Randy Moss RC	20.00	9.00
❑ 67 Peyton Manning RC	20.00	9.00
❑ 68 Danny Kanell	.50	.23
❑ 69 Charlie Garner	.25	.11
❑ 70 Mike Alstott	1.00	.45
❑ 71 Grant Wistrom RC	1.50	.70
❑ 72 Jacquez Green RC	4.00	1.80
❑ 73 Gus Frerotte	.25	.11
❑ 74 Peter Boulware	.25	.11
❑ 75 Jerry Rice	2.50	1.10
❑ 76 Antowain Smith	1.00	.45
❑ 77 Brian Simmons RC	1.50	.70
❑ 78 Rod Smith	.50	.23
❑ 79 Marvin Harrison	.50	.23
❑ 80 Ryan Leaf RC	4.00	1.80
❑ 81 Keenan McCardell	.50	.23
❑ 82 Derrick Thomas	.50	.23
❑ 83 Zach Thomas	.25	.11
❑ 84 Ben Coates	.50	.23
❑ 85 Rob Moore	.50	.23
❑ 86 Wayne Chrebet	1.00	.45
❑ 87 Napoleon Kaufman	1.00	.45
❑ 88 Levon Kirkland	.25	.11
❑ 89 Junior Seau	.50	.23
❑ 90 Eddie George	2.00	.90
❑ 91 Warren Moon	1.00	.45
❑ 92 Anthony Simmons RC	1.50	.70
❑ 93 Steve McNair	1.00	.45
❑ 94 Frank Sanders	.50	.23
❑ 95 Joey Galloway	1.00	.45
❑ 96 Jamal Anderson	1.00	.45
❑ 97 Rae Carruth	.50	.23
❑ 98 Curtis Conway	.50	.23
❑ 99 Greg Ellis RC	1.50	.70
❑ 100 Kordell Stewart	1.00	.45
❑ 101 Germane Crowell RC	5.00	2.20
❑ 102 Mark Chmura	.50	.23
❑ 103 Robert Smith	1.00	.45
❑ 104 Andre Hastings	.25	.11
❑ 105 Reggie White	1.00	.45
❑ 106 Jessie Armstead	.25	.11
❑ 107 Kevin Hardy	.25	.11
❑ 108 Robert Holcombe RC	3.00	1.35
❑ 109 Garrison Hearst	1.00	.45
❑ 110 Jerome Bettis	1.00	.45
❑ 111 Reidel Anthony	.50	.23
❑ 112 Michael Westbrook	.50	.23
❑ 113 Pat Johnson RC	2.50	1.10
❑ 114 Andre Reed	.50	.23
❑ 115 Charles Woodson RC	5.00	2.20
❑ 116 Takeo Spikes RC	2.50	1.10
❑ 117 Marcus Nash RC	3.00	1.35
❑ 118 Tavian Banks RC	.50	.23
❑ 119 Tony Gonzalez	.25	.11
❑ 120 Jake Plummer	2.50	1.10
❑ 121 Tony Simmons RC	2.50	1.10
❑ 122 Aaron Glenn	.25	.11
❑ 123 Ricky Watters	.50	.23
❑ 124 Kimble Anders	.50	.23
❑ 125 Barry Sanders	5.00	2.20
❑ 126 Terance Mathis	.50	.23
❑ 127 Wesley Walls	.50	.23
❑ 128 Bobby Engram	.50	.23
❑ 129 Johnnie Morton	.50	.23
❑ 130 Brett Favre	5.00	2.20
❑ 131 Brad Johnson	1.00	.45
❑ 132 John Randle	.50	.23
❑ 133 Chris Sanders	.25	.11
❑ 134 Joe Jurevicius RC	2.50	1.10
❑ 135 Deion Sanders	1.00	.45
❑ 136 Terrell Owens	1.00	.45
❑ 137 Darrell Green	.50	.23
❑ 138 Jermaine Lewis	.50	.23
❑ 139 James Stewart	.50	.23
❑ 140 Troy Aikman	2.50	1.10
❑ 141 Hardy Nickerson	.25	.11
❑ 142 Blaine Bishop	.25	.11
❑ 143 Keith Brooking RC	3.00	1.35
❑ 144 Jason Peter RC	1.50	.70
❑ 145 Jake Reed	.50	.23
❑ 146 Jason Sehorn	.25	.11
❑ 147 Robert Brooks	.50	.23
❑ 148 J.J. Stokes	.50	.23
❑ 149 Michael Strahan	.25	.11
❑ 150 Glenn Foley	.50	.23
❑ NNO Checklist Card	.25	.11

1998 Topps Stars Galaxy

	MINT	NRMT
COMP.BRONZE SET (10)	600.00	275.00
COMMON BRONZE (G1-G10)	25.00	11.00

BRONZE STATED ODDS 1:611
BRONZE PRINT RUN 100 SERIAL #'d SETS
*SILVER CARDS: .5X TO 1.2X HI COL.
SILVER STATED ODDS 1:814
SILVER PRINT RUN 75 SERIAL #'d SETS
*GOLD CARDS: .6X TO 1.5X HI COL.
GOLD STATED ODDS 1:1222
GOLD PRINT RUN 50 SERIAL #'d SETS
GOLD RBW.STATED ODDS 1:12,215
GOLD RBW.PRINT RUN 5 SERIAL #'d SETS

Card	MINT	NRMT
❑ G1 Brett Favre	120.00	55.00
❑ G2 Barry Sanders	120.00	55.00
❑ G3 Jerry Rice	60.00	27.00
❑ G4 Herman Moore	40.00	18.00
❑ G5 Tim Brown	40.00	18.00
❑ G6 Steve Young	40.00	18.00
❑ G7 Cris Carter	40.00	18.00
❑ G8 John Elway	120.00	55.00
❑ G9 Mark Brunell	50.00	22.00
❑ G10 Terrell Davis	100.00	45.00

1998 Topps Stars Luminaries

	MINT	NRMT
COMP.BRONZE SET (15)	800.00	350.00
COMMON BRONZE (L1-L15)	20.00	9.00
BRONZE SEMISTARS	25.00	11.00

BRONZE STATED ODDS 1:407
BRONZE PRINT RUN 100 SERIAL #'d SETS
*SILVER CARDS: .5X TO 1.2X HI COL.
SILVER STATED ODDS 1:543
SILVER PRINT RUN 75 SERIAL #'d SETS
*GOLD CARDS: .6X TO 1.5X HI COL.
GOLD STATED ODDS 1:814
GOLD PRINT RUN 50 SERIAL #'d SETS
GOLD RBW.STATED ODDS 1:8144
GOLD RBW.PRINT RUN 5 SERIAL #'d SETS

Card	MINT	NRMT
❑ L1 Brett Favre	120.00	55.00
❑ L2 Steve Young	40.00	18.00
❑ L3 John Elway	120.00	55.00
❑ L4 Barry Sanders	120.00	55.00
❑ L5 Terrell Davis	100.00	45.00
❑ L6 Eddie George	50.00	22.00
❑ L7 Herman Moore	40.00	18.00
❑ L8 Tim Brown	40.00	18.00
❑ L9 Jerry Rice	60.00	27.00
❑ L10 Junior Seau	25.00	11.00
❑ L11 Bruce Smith	25.00	11.00
❑ L12 John Randle	20.00	9.00
❑ L13 Peyton Manning	120.00	55.00
❑ L14 Ryan Leaf	30.00	13.50
❑ L15 Curtis Enis	30.00	13.50

1998 Topps Stars Rookie Reprints

	MINT	NRMT
COMPLETE SET (8)	25.00	11.00
COMMON CARD (1-8)	2.00	.90
SEMISTARS	3.00	1.35
UNLISTED STARS	4.00	1.80

STATED ODDS 1:24

Card	MINT	NRMT
❑ 1 Walter Payton	10.00	4.50
❑ 2 Don Maynard	4.00	1.80
❑ 3 Charlie Joiner	3.00	1.35
❑ 4 Fred Biletnikoff	4.00	1.80
❑ 5 Paul Hornung	4.00	1.80
❑ 6 Gale Sayers	6.00	2.70
❑ 7 John Hannah	2.00	.90
❑ 8 Paul Warfield	4.00	1.80

1998 Topps Stars Rookie Reprints Autographs

	MINT	NRMT
COMPLETE SET (8)	500.00	220.00
COMMON CARD (1-8)	20.00	9.00
SEMISTARS	30.00	13.50

STATED ODDS 1:153

Card	MINT	NRMT
❑ 1 Walter Payton	300.00	135.00
❑ 2 Don Maynard	30.00	13.50
❑ 3 Charlie Joiner	30.00	13.50
❑ 4 Fred Biletnikoff	40.00	18.00
❑ 5 Paul Hornung	60.00	27.00
❑ 6 Gale Sayers	50.00	22.00
❑ 7 John Hannah	20.00	9.00
❑ 8 Paul Warfield	40.00	18.00

1998 Topps Stars Supernovas

	MINT	NRMT
COMP.BRONZE SET (10)	500.00	220.00
COMMON BRONZE (S1-S10)	15.00	6.75
BRONZE SEMISTARS	20.00	9.00
BRONZE UNLISTED STARS	25.00	11.00

BRONZE STATED ODDS 1:611
BRONZE PRINT RUN 100 SERIAL #'d SETS
*SILVER CARDS: .5X TO 1.2X HI COL.
SILVER STATED ODDS 1:814
SILVER PRINT RUN 75 SERIAL #'d SETS
*GOLD CARDS: .6X TO 1.5X HI COL.
GOLD STATED ODDS 1:1222
GOLD PRINT RUN 50 SERIAL #'d SETS
GOLD RBW.STATED ODDS 1:12,215
GOLD RBW.PRINT RUN 5 SERIAL #'d SETS

Card	MINT	NRMT
❑ S1 Ryan Leaf	30.00	13.50
❑ S2 Curtis Enis	30.00	13.50
❑ S3 Kevin Dyson	25.00	11.00
❑ S4 Randy Moss	120.00	55.00
❑ S5 Peyton Manning	120.00	55.00
❑ S6 Duane Starks	15.00	6.75
❑ S7 Grant Wistrom	15.00	6.75

Card	MINT	NRMT
❑ S8 Charles Woodson	30.00	13.50
❑ S9 Fred Taylor	60.00	27.00
❑ S10 Andre Wadsworth	20.00	9.00

1999 Topps Stars

	MINT	NRMT
COMPLETE SET (140)	50.00	22.00
COMMON CARD (1-140)	.20	.09
SEMISTARS	.40	.18
UNLISTED STARS	.75	.35
COMMON ROOKIE	1.00	.45
ROOKIE SEMISTARS	1.25	.55

PRO BOWL JERSEY REDEMPT.ODDS 1:36,942
PB JERSEY REDEMP.EXPIRATION 6/30/2000

Card	MINT	NRMT
❑ 1 Champ Bailey RC	1.50	.70
❑ 2 Akili Smith RC	2.50	1.10
❑ 3 Randy Moss	3.00	1.35
❑ 4 Cade McNown RC	4.00	1.80
❑ 5 Torry Holt RC	3.00	1.35
❑ 6 Troy Edwards RC	2.00	.90
❑ 7 David Boston RC	2.00	.90
❑ 8 Edgerrin James RC	10.00	4.50
❑ 9 Daunte Culpepper RC	4.00	1.80
❑ 10 Tim Couch RC	6.00	2.70
❑ 11 Ricky Williams RC	6.00	2.70
❑ 12 Fred Taylor	2.00	.90
❑ 13 Barry Sanders	3.00	1.35
❑ 14 Emmitt Smith	2.00	.90
❑ 15 Jerry Rice	2.00	.90
❑ 16 Jake Plummer	1.50	.70
❑ 17 Terrell Owens	.75	.35
❑ 18 Eric Moulds	.75	.35
❑ 19 Dan Marino	3.00	1.35
❑ 20 Steve McNair	.75	.35
❑ 21 Donovan McNabb RC	4.00	1.80
❑ 22 Curtis Martin	.75	.35
❑ 23 Peyton Manning	3.00	1.35
❑ 24 Garrison Hearst	.40	.18
❑ 25 Eddie George	1.00	.45
❑ 26 Antonio Freeman	.75	.35
❑ 27 Doug Flutie	1.00	.45
❑ 28 Kevin Faulk RC	1.50	.70
❑ 29 Brett Favre	3.00	1.35
❑ 30 Randall Cunningham	.75	.35
❑ 31 Mark Brunell	1.25	.55
❑ 32 Keyshawn Johnson	.75	.35
❑ 33 Terrell Davis	2.00	.90
❑ 34 Drew Bledsoe	1.25	.55
❑ 35 Jerome Bettis	.75	.35
❑ 36 Charlie Batch	1.50	.70
❑ 37 Steve Young	1.25	.55
❑ 38 Jamal Anderson	.75	.35
❑ 39 Troy Aikman	2.00	.90
❑ 40 John Elway	3.00	1.35
❑ 41 Amos Zereoue RC	1.25	.55
❑ 42 J.J. Stokes	.40	.18
❑ 43 Antowain Smith	.75	.35
❑ 44 Jimmy Smith	.40	.18
❑ 45 Shaun King RC	4.00	1.80
❑ 46 Jevon Kearse RC	2.50	1.10
❑ 47 Sedrick Irvin RC	1.25	.55
❑ 48 Rod Smith	.40	.18
❑ 49 Kevin Johnson RC	3.00	1.35
❑ 50 Joey Galloway	.75	.35
❑ 51 Mike Cloud RC	1.25	.55
❑ 52 D'Wayne Bates RC	1.00	.45
❑ 53 Peerless Price RC	2.00	.90
❑ 54 Herman Moore	.75	.35
❑ 55 Rob Konrad RC	1.25	.55
❑ 56 James Johnson RC	1.50	.70
❑ 57 Cecil Collins RC	1.00	.45
❑ 58 Wayne Chrebet	.75	.35
❑ 59 Cris Carter	.75	.35
❑ 60 Tim Brown	.75	.35
❑ 61 Frank Wycheck	.40	.18
❑ 62 Charles Woodson	.75	.35
❑ 63 Antoine Winfield RC	1.00	.45
❑ 64 Ryan Leaf	.75	.35
❑ 65 Ricky Watters	.40	.18
❑ 66 Yancey Thigpen	.20	.09
❑ 67 Michael Westbrook	.40	.18
❑ 68 Vinny Testaverde	.40	.18
❑ 69 Kordell Stewart	.75	.35
❑ 70 Duce Staley	.75	.35
❑ 71 Shannon Sharpe	.40	.18
❑ 72 Junior Seau	.40	.18
❑ 73 Bruce Smith	.40	.18
❑ 74 Frank Sanders	.40	.18
❑ 75 Lawrence Phillips	.40	.18
❑ 76 Robert Smith	.75	.35
❑ 77 Andre Reed	.40	.18
❑ 78 Darnay Scott	.40	.18
❑ 79 Adrian Murrell	.40	.18
❑ 80 Ricky Proehl	.20	.09
❑ 81 Zach Thomas	.40	.18
❑ 82 Deion Sanders	.75	.35
❑ 83 Andre Rison	.40	.18
❑ 84 Jake Reed	.40	.18
❑ 85 Carl Pickens	.40	.18
❑ 86 John Randle	.40	.18
❑ 87 Jerome Pathon	.20	.09
❑ 88 Brock Huard RC	1.50	.70
❑ 89 Elvis Grbac	.40	.18
❑ 90 Curtis Enis	.75	.35
❑ 91 Rickey Dudley	.20	.09
❑ 92 Amani Toomer	.20	.09
❑ 93 Robert Brooks	.20	.09
❑ 94 Derrick Alexander	.40	.18
❑ 95 Reidel Anthony	.20	.09
❑ 96 Mark Chmura	.20	.09
❑ 97 Trent Dilfer	.40	.18
❑ 98 Ebenezer Ekuban RC	1.00	.45
❑ 99 Tony Banks	.40	.18
❑ 100 Terry Glenn	.75	.35
❑ 101 Andre Hastings	.20	.09
❑ 102 Ike Hilliard	.40	.18
❑ 103 Michael Irvin	.40	.18
❑ 104 Napoleon Kaufman	.75	.35
❑ 105 Dorsey Levens	.75	.35
❑ 106 Ed McCaffrey	.40	.18
❑ 107 Natrone Means	.40	.18
❑ 108 Skip Hicks	.40	.18
❑ 109 James Jett	.20	.09
❑ 110 Priest Holmes	.75	.35
❑ 111 Tim Dwight	.75	.35
❑ 112 Curtis Conway	.40	.18
❑ 113 Jeff Blake	.40	.18
❑ 114 Karim Abdul-Jabbar	.40	.18
❑ 115 Karsten Bailey RC	1.00	.45
❑ 116 Chris Chandler	.40	.18
❑ 117 Germane Crowell	.40	.18
❑ 118 Warrick Dunn	.75	.35
❑ 119 Bert Emanuel	.40	.18
❑ 120 Jermaine Fazande RC	1.00	.45
❑ 121 Joe Germaine RC	1.25	.55
❑ 122 Tony Gonzalez	.40	.18
❑ 123 Jacquez Green	.20	.09
❑ 124 Marvin Harrison	.75	.35
❑ 125 Corey Dillon	.75	.35
❑ 126 Ben Coates	.20	.09
❑ 127 Chris Claiborne RC	1.25	.55
❑ 128 Isaac Bruce	.75	.35
❑ 129 Mike Alstott	.75	.35
❑ 130 Andy Katzenmoyer RC	1.25	.55
❑ 131 Jon Kitna	1.00	.45
❑ 132 Keenan McCardell	.40	.18
❑ 133 Johnnie Morton	.40	.18
❑ 134 O.J. McDuffie	.40	.18
❑ 135 Chris McAlister	1.00	.45
❑ 136 Terance Mathis	.40	.18
❑ 137 Thurman Thomas	.40	.18
❑ 138 Jermaine Lewis	.40	.18
❑ 139 Rob Moore	.40	.18
❑ 140 Brad Johnson	.75	.35
❑ P1 Pro Bowl Jersey Redemp.	800.00	350.00

1999 Topps Stars Parallel

	MINT	NRMT
COMPLETE SET (140)	500.00	220.00

*STARS: 3X TO 8X HI COL.
*YOUNG STARS: 2.5X TO 6X
*RCs: 1.2X TO 3X
CARDS SERIAL NUMBERED TO 299

1999 Topps Stars Two Star

	MINT	NRMT
COMPLETE SET (60)	40.00	18.00

*TWO STARS: SAME PRICE AS 1 STAR
ONE OR TWO CARDS PER PACK

1999 Topps Stars Two Star Parallel

	MINT	NRMT
COMPLETE SET (60)	500.00	220.00

*STARS: 4X TO 10X HI COL.
*YOUNG STARS: 3X TO 8X
*ROOKIES: 1.5X TO 4X
CARDS SERIAL NUMBERED TO 249

1999 Topps Stars Three Star

	MINT	NRMT
COMPLETE SET (40)	30.00	13.50

*THREE STARS: SAME PRICE AS 1 STAR
ONE PER PACK

1999 Topps Stars Three Star Parallel

	MINT	NRMT
COMPLETE SET (40)	500.00	220.00

*STARS: 5X TO 12X HI COL.
*YOUNG STARS: 4X TO 10X
*ROOKIES: 2X TO 5X
CARDS SERIAL NUMBERED TO 199

1999 Topps Stars Four Star

	MINT	NRMT
COMPLETE SET (10)	25.00	11.00

*FOUR STARS: SAME PRICE AS 1 STAR
STATED ODDS 1:4

1999 Topps Stars Four Star Parallel

	MINT	NRMT
COMPLETE SET (10)	150.00	70.00

*YOUNG STARS: 5X TO 12X
*ROOKIES: 2.5X TO 6X
CARDS SERIAL NUMBERED TO 99

1999 Topps Stars Autographs

	MINT	NRMT
COMPLETE SET (6)	350.00	160.00
COMMON CARD (A1-A6)	30.00	13.50

BLUE BACKGROUND STATED ODDS 1:419
GOLD BACKGROUND STATED ODDS 1:2528
RED BACKGROUND STATED ODDS 1:629

❑ A1 Tim Couch B	100.00	45.00
❑ A2 Torry Holt B	40.00	18.00
❑ A3 David Boston B	30.00	13.50
❑ A4 Fred Taylor R	50.00	22.00
❑ A5 Marshall Faulk R	50.00	22.00
❑ A6 Randy Moss G	120.00	55.00

1999 Topps Stars New Dawn

	MINT	NRMT
COMPLETE SET (20)	100.00	45.00
COMMON CARD (N1-N20)	2.50	1.10
SEMISTARS	3.00	1.35

STATED ODDS 1:31
STATED PRINT RUN 1000 SER.#'d SETS

❑ N1 Tim Couch	15.00	6.75
❑ N2 Kevin Faulk	4.00	1.80
❑ N3 Troy Edwards	5.00	2.20
❑ N4 Champ Bailey	4.00	1.80
❑ N5 Peerless Price	5.00	2.20
❑ N6 Kevin Johnson	8.00	3.60
❑ N7 Edgerrin James	25.00	11.00
❑ N8 Daunte Culpepper	10.00	4.50
❑ N9 Torry Holt	8.00	3.60
❑ N10 Donovan McNabb	10.00	4.50
❑ N11 Shaun King	10.00	4.50
❑ N12 Mike Cloud	3.00	1.35
❑ N13 Cade McNown	10.00	4.50
❑ N14 David Boston	5.00	2.20
❑ N15 James Johnson	4.00	1.80
❑ N16 Karsten Bailey	2.50	1.10
❑ N17 Sedrick Irvin	3.00	1.35
❑ N18 Akili Smith	6.00	2.70
❑ N19 D'Wayne Bates	2.50	1.10
❑ N20 Ricky Williams	15.00	6.75

1999 Topps Stars Rookie Relics

	MINT	NRMT
COMPLETE SET (3)	250.00	110.00
COMMON CARD (RR1-RR3)	50.00	22.00

STATED ODDS 1:209
TRADE CARD EXPIRATION: 6/30/2000

❑ RR1 Kurt Warner	150.00	70.00
❑ RR2 Torry Holt	50.00	22.00
❑ RR3 Donovan McNabb	50.00	22.00

1999 Topps Stars Rookie Reprints

	MINT	NRMT
COMPLETE SET (2)	10.00	4.50
COMMON CARD (1-2)	5.00	2.20

STATED ODDS 1:16

❑ 1 Roger Staubach	5.00	2.20
❑ 2 Terry Bradshaw	5.00	2.20

1999 Topps Stars Rookie Reprints Autographs

	MINT	NRMT
COMPLETE SET (2)	240.00	110.00
COMMON CARD (RA1-RA2)	120.00	55.00

STATED ODDS 1:629

1999 Topps Stars Stars of the Game

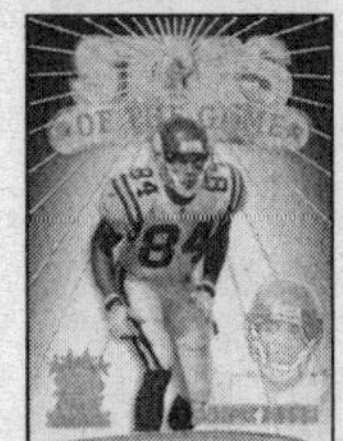

	MINT	NRMT
COMPLETE SET (10)	120.00	55.00
COMMON CARD (S1-S10)	3.00	1.35

STATED ODDS 1:31
STATED PRINT RUN 1999 SER.#'d SETS
WARNER TRADE EXPIRATION: 6/30/2000

❑ S1 Jamal Anderson	3.00	1.35
❑ S2 Dan Marino	12.00	5.50
❑ S3 Barry Sanders	12.00	5.50
❑ S4 Brett Favre	12.00	5.50
❑ S5 Emmitt Smith	8.00	3.60
❑ S6 Fred Taylor	6.00	2.70
❑ S7 Kurt Warner	40.00	18.00
❑ S8 Randy Moss	10.00	4.50
❑ S9 Peyton Manning	10.00	4.50
❑ S10 Terrell Davis	8.00	3.60

1999 Topps Stars Zone of Their Own

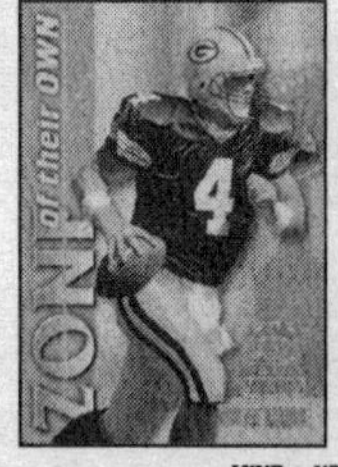

	MINT	NRMT
COMPLETE SET (10)	60.00	27.00
COMMON CARD (Z1-Z10)	3.00	1.35

STATED ODDS 1:31
STATED PRINT RUN 1999 SER.#'d SETS

❑ Z1 Randy Moss	10.00	4.50
❑ Z2 Eddie George	4.00	1.80
❑ Z3 Tim Brown	3.00	1.35
❑ Z4 Curtis Martin	3.00	1.35
❑ Z5 Brett Favre	12.00	5.50
❑ Z6 Barry Sanders	12.00	5.50
❑ Z7 Warrick Dunn	3.00	1.35
❑ Z8 Terrell Davis	8.00	3.60
❑ Z9 Ricky Williams	12.00	5.50
❑ Z10 Doug Flutie	4.00	1.80

1997 UD3

	MINT	NRMT
COMPLETE SET (90)	50.00	22.00
COMMON CARD (1-90)	.30	.14
SEMISTARS	.60	.25

UNLISTED STARS	1.00	.45
❑ 1 Orlando Pace RC	.30	.14
❑ 2 Walter Jones RC	.30	.14
❑ 3 Tony Gonzalez RC	3.00	1.35
❑ 4 David LaFleur RC	.60	.25
❑ 5 Jim Druckenmiller RC	1.25	.55
❑ 6 Jake Plummer RC	8.00	3.60
❑ 7 Pat Barnes RC	.60	.25
❑ 8 Ike Hilliard RC	1.50	.70
❑ 9 Reidel Anthony RC	1.50	.70
❑ 10 Rae Carruth RC	1.00	.45
❑ 11 Yatil Green RC	.60	.25
❑ 12 Joey Kent RC	1.00	.45
❑ 13 Will Blackwell RC	1.00	.45
❑ 14 Kevin Lockett RC	.60	.25
❑ 15 Warrick Dunn RC	3.00	1.35
❑ 16 Antowain Smith RC	2.00	.90
❑ 17 Troy Davis RC	1.00	.45
❑ 18 Byron Hanspard RC	1.50	.70
❑ 19 Corey Dillon RC	4.00	1.80
❑ 20 Darnell Autry RC	.60	.25
❑ 21 Peter Boulware RC	.60	.25
❑ 22 Darrell Russell RC	.30	.14
❑ 23 Kenny Holmes RC	.30	.14
❑ 24 Reinard Wilson RC	.30	.14
❑ 25 Renaldo Wynn RC	.30	.14
❑ 26 Dwayne Rudd RC	.30	.14
❑ 27 James Farrior RC	.30	.14
❑ 28 Shawn Springs RC	.60	.25
❑ 29 Bryant Westbrook RC	.30	.14
❑ 30 Tom Knight RC	.30	.14
❑ 31 Barry Sanders EC	5.00	2.20
❑ 32 Brett Favre EC	5.00	2.20
❑ 33 Brian Mitchell EC	.30	.14
❑ 34 Curtis Martin EC	1.50	.70
❑ 35 Dan Marino EC	5.00	2.20
❑ 36 Deion Sanders EC	1.00	.45
❑ 37 Drew Bledsoe EC	2.50	1.10
❑ 38 Eddie George EC	2.50	1.10
❑ 39 Edgar Bennett EC	.30	.14
❑ 40 Emmitt Smith EC	4.00	1.80
❑ 41 Isaac Bruce EC	1.00	.45
❑ 42 Jerome Bettis EC	1.00	.45
❑ 43 Jerry Rice EC	2.50	1.10
❑ 44 John Elway EC	5.00	2.20
❑ 45 Junior Seau EC	.60	.25
❑ 46 Karim Abdul-Jabbar EC	1.00	.45
❑ 47 Kerry Collins EC	.60	.25
❑ 48 Marshall Faulk EC	1.00	.45
❑ 49 Marvin Harrison EC	1.00	.45
❑ 50 Michael Irvin EC	1.00	.45
❑ 51 Natrone Means EC	1.00	.45
❑ 52 Reggie White EC	1.00	.45
❑ 53 Ricky Watters EC	.60	.25
❑ 54 Stan Humphries EC	.60	.25
❑ 55 Steve Young EC	1.50	.70
❑ 56 Terry Glenn EC	1.00	.45
❑ 57 Thurman Thomas EC	1.00	.45
❑ 58 Tony Martin EC	.60	.25
❑ 59 Troy Aikman EC	2.50	1.10
❑ 60 Vinny Testaverde EC	.60	.25
❑ 61 Anthony Johnson PH	.30	.14
❑ 62 Bobby Engram EC	.60	.25
❑ 63 Carl Pickens PH	.60	.25
❑ 64 Cris Carter PH	.60	.25
❑ 65 Derrick Witherspoon PH	.30	.14
❑ 66 Eddie Kennison PH	.60	.25
❑ 67 Eric Swann PH	.30	.14
❑ 68 Gus Frerotte PH	.60	.25
❑ 69 Herman Moore PH	1.00	.45
❑ 70 Irving Fryar PH	.60	.25
❑ 71 Jamal Anderson PH	1.50	.70
❑ 72 Jeff Blake PH	1.00	.45
❑ 73 Jim Harbaugh PH	.60	.25
❑ 74 Joey Galloway PH	1.50	.70
❑ 76 Kevin Greene PH	.60	.25
❑ 77 Keyshawn Johnson PH	1.00	.45
❑ 78 Kordell Stewart PH	1.50	.70
❑ 79 Marcus Allen PH	1.00	.45
❑ 80 Mario Bates PH	.30	.14
❑ 81 Mark Brunell PH	2.50	1.10
❑ 82 Michael Jackson PH	.60	.25
❑ 83 Mike Alstott PH	1.00	.45
❑ 84 Scott Mitchell PH	.60	.25
❑ 85 Shannon Sharpe PH	.60	.25
❑ 86 Steve McNair PH	1.50	.70
❑ 87 Terrell Davis PH	5.00	2.20
❑ 87 Keenan McCardell PH	.60	.25
❑ 88 Tim Brown PH	1.00	.45
❑ 89 Ty Detmer PH	.60	.25
❑ 90 Tyrone Wheatley PH	.60	.25

1997 UD3 Generation Excitement

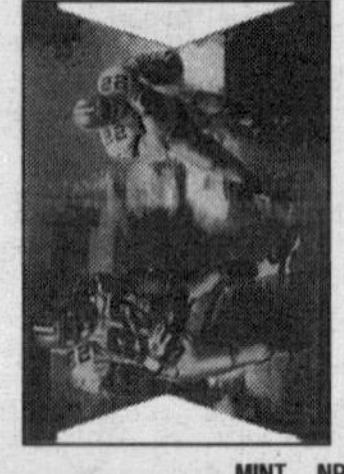

	MINT	NRMT
COMPLETE SET (15)	120.00	55.00
STATED ODDS 1:11		
❑ GE1 Jerry Rice	12.00	5.50
❑ GE2 Carl Pickens	3.00	1.35
❑ GE3 Curtis Conway	3.00	1.35
❑ GE4 John Elway	25.00	11.00
❑ GE5 Ike Hilliard	8.00	3.60
❑ GE6 Marvin Harrison	5.00	2.20
❑ GE7 Emmitt Smith	20.00	9.00
❑ GE8 Barry Sanders	25.00	11.00
❑ GE9 Deion Sanders	5.00	2.20
❑ GE10 Rae Carruth	1.50	.70
❑ GE11 Curtis Martin	8.00	3.60
❑ GE12 Terry Glenn	5.00	2.20
❑ GE13 Napoleon Kaufman	5.00	2.20
❑ GE14 Kordell Stewart	8.00	3.60
❑ GE15 Jake Plummer	12.00	5.50

1997 UD3 Marquee Attraction

	MINT	NRMT
COMPLETE SET (15)	350.00	160.00
STATED ODDS 1:144		
❑ MA1 Steve Young	20.00	9.00
❑ MA2 Troy Aikman	30.00	13.50
❑ MA3 Keyshawn Johnson	12.00	5.50
❑ MA4 Marcus Allen	12.00	5.50
❑ MA5 Dan Marino	60.00	27.00
❑ MA6 Mark Brunell	30.00	13.50
❑ MA7 Eddie George	30.00	13.50
❑ MA8 Brett Favre	60.00	27.00
❑ MA9 Drew Bledsoe	30.00	13.50
❑ MA10 Eddie Kennison	8.00	3.60
❑ MA11 Terrell Davis	60.00	27.00
❑ MA12 Warrick Dunn	20.00	9.00

❑ MA13 Yatil Green	4.00	1.80
❑ MA14 Troy Davis	6.00	2.70
❑ MA15 Shawn Springs	4.00	1.80

1997 UD3 Signature Performers

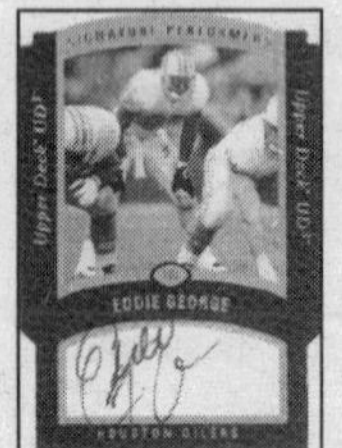

	MINT	NRMT
COMPLETE SET (4)	350.00	160.00
COMMON CARD (PF1-PF4)	60.00	27.00
STATED ODDS 1:1500		
❑ PF1 Curtis Martin (issued via redemption)	60.00	27.00
❑ PF2 Troy Aikman	150.00	70.00
❑ PF3 Marcus Allen	80.00	36.00
❑ PF4 Eddie George	80.00	36.00

1998 UD3

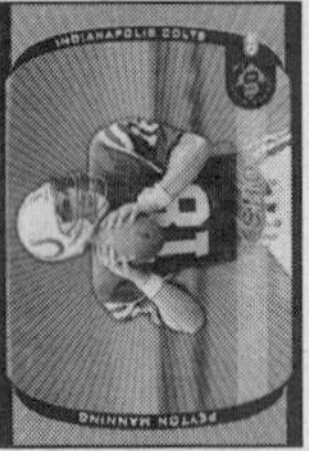

	MINT	NRMT
COMPLETE SET (270)	800.00	350.00
COMP.FS EMB.(30)	150.00	70.00
COMMON FS EMB.(1-30)	2.50	1.10
FS EMB.SEMISTARS	4.00	1.80
FS EMB.UNLISTED STARS	5.00	2.20
FUTURE SHOCK EMBOSSED ODDS 1:6		
COMP.NW EMB.(30)	30.00	13.50
COMMON NW EMB.(31-60)	1.50	.70
NW EMB.SEMISTARS	3.00	1.35
NEXT WAVE EMBOSSED ODDS 1:4		
COMP.UR EMB.(30)	40.00	18.00
COMMON UR EMB.(61-90)	.75	.35

UR EMB.SEMISTARS .... 1.50 .70
UPPER REALM EMBOSSED ODDS 1:1.25
COMP.FS FX (30) 250.00 110.00
COMMON FS FX (91-120)........ 4.00 1.80
FS FX SEMISTARS 5.00 2.20
FS FX UNLISTED STARS 6.00 2.70
FUTURE SHOCK FX ODDS 1:12
COMP.NW FX (30)................ 15.00 6.75
COMMON NW FX (121-150) ...... .75 .35
NW FX SEMISTARS .... 1.50 .70
NEXT WAVE FX ODDS 1:1.5 ......
COMP.UR FX (30) 100.00 45.00
COMMON UR FX (151-180) .... 2.00 .90
UR FX SEMISTARS.................. 4.00 1.80
UPPER REALM FX ODDS 1:6......
COMP.FS RBW.(30) 60.00 27.00
COMMON FS RBW.(181-210).. 1.00 .45
FS RBW.SEMISTARS .... 1.50 .70
FS RBW.UNLISTED STARS .... 2.00 .90
FUTURE SHOCK RBW.ODDS 1:1.33
COMP.NW RBW.(30).............. 60.00 27.00
COMMON NW RBW.(211-240) 3.00 1.35
NW RBW.SEMISTARS 6.00 2.70
NEXT WAVE RBW.ODDS 1:12 ....
COMP.UR RBW.(30) 200.00 90.00
COMMON UR RBW.(241-270).. 4.00 1.80
UR RBW.SEMISTARS 8.00 3.60
UPPER REALM RBW.ODDS 1:24
CARD #'S BELOW ARE SET # ON CARDBACK

❑ 1 Peyton Manning FE........ 25.00 11.00
❑ 2 Ryan Leaf FE 6.00 2.70
❑ 3 Andre Wadsworth FE 4.00 1.80
❑ 4 Charles Woodson FE 8.00 3.60
❑ 5 Curtis Enis FE 8.00 3.60
❑ 6 Grant Wistrom FE 4.00 1.80
❑ 7 Greg Ellis FE.................... 2.50 1.10
❑ 8 Fred Taylor FE 15.00 6.75
❑ 9 Duane Starks FE.............. 2.50 1.10
❑ 10 Keith Brooking FE 4.00 1.80
❑ 11 Takeo Spikes FE............ 4.00 1.80
❑ 12 Jason Peter FE 2.50 1.10
❑ 13 Anthony Simmons FE 2.50 1.10
❑ 14 Kevin Dyson FE 6.00 2.70
❑ 15 Brian Simmons FE 2.50 1.10
❑ 16 Robert Edwards FE........ 5.00 2.20
❑ 17 Randy Moss FE............ 25.00 11.00
❑ 18 John Avery FE............... 5.00 2.20
❑ 19 Marcus Nash FE 5.00 2.20
❑ 20 Jerome Pathon FE 4.00 1.80
❑ 21 Jacquez Green FE 6.00 2.70
❑ 22 Robert Holcombe FE...... 5.00 2.20
❑ 23 Pat Johnson FE.............. 4.00 1.80
❑ 24 Germane Crowell FE...... 8.00 3.60
❑ 25 Joe Jurevicius FE 4.00 1.80
❑ 26 Skip Hicks FE 4.00 1.80
❑ 27 Ahman Green FE 4.00 1.80
❑ 28 Brian Griese FE............ 10.00 4.50
❑ 29 Hines Ward FE 4.00 1.80
❑ 30 Tavian Banks FE............ 5.00 2.20
❑ 31 Warrick Dunn NE 3.00 1.35
❑ 32 Jake Plummer NE 12.00 5.50
❑ 33 Derrick Mayes NE 3.00 1.35
❑ 34 Napoleon Kaufman NE .. 3.00 1.35
❑ 35 Jamal Anderson NE 3.00 1.35
❑ 36 Marvin Harrison NE........ 3.00 1.35
❑ 37 Jermaine Lewis NE 3.00 1.35
❑ 38 Corey Dillon NE.............. 5.00 2.20
❑ 39 Keyshawn Johnson NE .. 3.00 1.35
❑ 40 Mike Alstott NE 3.00 1.35
❑ 41 Bobby Hoying NE 3.00 1.35
❑ 42 Keenan McCardell NE.... 3.00 1.35
❑ 43 Will Blackwell NE .... 1.50 .70
❑ 44 Peter Boulware NE .... 1.50 .70
❑ 45 Tony Banks NE 3.00 1.35
❑ 46 Rod Smith WR NE 3.00 1.35
❑ 47 Tony Gonzalez NE 3.00 1.35
❑ 48 Antowain Smith NE 3.00 1.35
❑ 49 Rae Carruth NE.............. 3.00 1.35
❑ 50 J.J. Stokes NE................ 3.00 1.35
❑ 51 Brad Johnson NE 3.00 1.35
❑ 52 Shawn Springs NE .... 1.50 .70
❑ 53 Elvis Grbac NE .... 1.50 .70
❑ 54 Jimmy Smith NE 3.00 1.35
❑ 55 Terry Glenn NE.............. 3.00 1.35
❑ 56 Tiki Barber NE................ 3.00 1.35
❑ 57 Gus Frerotte NE .... 1.50 .70
❑ 58 Danny Wuerffel NE 3.00 1.35
❑ 59 Fred Lane NE 3.00 1.35
❑ 60 Todd Collins NE .... 1.50 .70
❑ 61 Barry Sanders UE 8.00 3.60
❑ 62 Troy Aikman UE 4.00 1.80
❑ 63 Dan Marino UE 8.00 3.60
❑ 64 Drew Bledsoe UE 3.00 1.35
❑ 65 Dorsey Levens UE .... 1.50 .70
❑ 66 Jerome Bettis UE .... 1.50 .70
❑ 67 John Elway UE 8.00 3.60
❑ 68 Steve Young UE 2.50 1.10
❑ 69 Terrell Davis UE 6.00 2.70
❑ 70 Kordell Stewart UE .... 1.50 .70
❑ 71 Jeff George UE .... 1.50 .70
❑ 72 Emmitt Smith UE............ 6.00 2.70
❑ 73 Irving Fryar UE .... .75 .35
❑ 74 Brett Favre UE 8.00 3.60
❑ 75 Eddie George UE 3.00 1.35
❑ 76 Terry Allen UE................ 1.50 .70
❑ 77 Warren Moon UE .... 1.50 .70
❑ 78 Mark Brunell UE 3.00 1.35
❑ 79 Robert Smith UE............ 1.50 .70
❑ 80 Jerry Rice UE 4.00 1.80
❑ 81 Tim Brown UE................ 1.50 .70
❑ 82 Carl Pickens UE .... 1.50 .70
❑ 83 Joey Galloway UE.......... 1.50 .70
❑ 84 Herman Moore UE .... 1.50 .70
❑ 85 Adrian Murrell UE .... 1.50 .70
❑ 86 Thurman Thomas UE .... 1.50 .70
❑ 87 Robert Brooks UE .... 1.50 .70
❑ 88 Michael Irvin UE .... 1.50 .70
❑ 89 Andre Rison UE .... 1.50 .70
❑ 90 Marshall Faulk UE.......... 1.50 .70
❑ 91 Peyton Manning FF...... 40.00 18.00
❑ 92 Ryan Leaf FF 8.00 3.60
❑ 93 Andre Wadsworth FF 5.00 2.20
❑ 94 Charles Woodson FF .. 10.00 4.50
❑ 95 Curtis Enis FF 10.00 4.50
❑ 96 Grant Wistrom FF 4.00 1.80
❑ 97 Greg Ellis FF.................. 4.00 1.80
❑ 98 Fred Taylor FF 25.00 11.00
❑ 99 Duane Starks FF............ 4.00 1.80
❑ 100 Keith Brooking FF 5.00 2.20
❑ 101 Takeo Spikes FF.......... 5.00 2.20
❑ 102 Jason Peter FF 4.00 1.80
❑ 103 Anthony Simmons FF .. 4.00 1.80
❑ 104 Kevin Dyson FF............ 8.00 3.60
❑ 105 Brian Simmons FF 4.00 1.80
❑ 106 Robert Edwards FF...... 6.00 2.70
❑ 107 Randy Moss FF.......... 40.00 18.00
❑ 108 John Avery FF.............. 6.00 2.70
❑ 109 Marcus Nash FF 6.00 2.70
❑ 110 Jerome Pathon FF 5.00 2.20
❑ 111 Jacquez Green FF 8.00 3.60
❑ 112 Robert Holcombe FF.... 6.00 2.70
❑ 113 Pat Johnson FF............ 5.00 2.20
❑ 114 Germane Crowell FF.. 10.00 4.50
❑ 115 Joe Jurevicius FF 5.00 2.20
❑ 116 Skip Hicks FF 5.00 2.20
❑ 117 Ahman Green FF 5.00 2.20
❑ 118 Brian Griese FF.......... 15.00 6.75
❑ 119 Hines Ward FF 5.00 2.20
❑ 120 Tavian Banks FF.......... 5.00 2.20
❑ 121 Warrick Dunn NF.......... 1.50 .70
❑ 122 Jake Plummer NF 6.00 2.70
❑ 123 Derrick Mayes NF .... 1.50 .70
❑ 124 Napoleon Kaufman NF 1.50 .70
❑ 125 Jamal Anderson NF .... 1.50 .70
❑ 126 Marvin Harrison NF...... 1.50 .70
❑ 127 Jermaine Lewis NF ...... 1.50 .70
❑ 128 Corey Dillon NF............ 2.50 1.10
❑ 129 Keyshawn Johnson NF 1.50 .70
❑ 130 Mike Alstott NF .... 1.50 .70
❑ 131 Bobby Hoying NF .... 1.50 .70
❑ 132 Keenan McCardell NF.. 1.50 .70
❑ 133 Will Blackwell NF............ .75 .35
❑ 134 Peter Boulware NF .... .75 .35
❑ 135 Tony Banks NF .... 1.50 .70
❑ 136 Rod Smith NF .... 1.50 .70
❑ 137 Tony Gonzalez NF ...... 1.50 .70
❑ 138 Antowain Smith NF ...... 1.50 .70
❑ 139 Rae Carruth NF............ 1.50 .70
❑ 140 J.J. Stokes NF.............. 1.50 .70
❑ 141 Brad Johnson NF .... 1.50 .70
❑ 142 Shawn Springs NF .... .75 .35
❑ 143 Elvis Grbac NF .... .75 .35
❑ 144 Jimmy Smith NF .... 1.50 .70
❑ 145 Terry Glenn NF .... 1.50 .70
❑ 146 Tiki Barber NF.............. 1.50 .70
❑ 147 Gus Frerotte NF .... .75 .35
❑ 148 Danny Wuerffel NF ...... 1.50 .70
❑ 149 Fred Lane NF .... 1.50 .70
❑ 150 Todd Collins NF .... .75 .35
❑ 151 Barry Sanders UF 20.00 9.00
❑ 152 Troy Aikman UF 10.00 4.50
❑ 153 Dan Marino UF 20.00 9.00
❑ 154 Drew Bledsoe UF 8.00 3.60
❑ 155 Dorsey Levens UF 4.00 1.80
❑ 156 Jerome Bettis UF 4.00 1.80
❑ 157 John Elway UF 20.00 9.00
❑ 158 Steve Young UF 6.00 2.70
❑ 159 Terrell Davis UF 15.00 6.75
❑ 160 Kordell Stewart UF 4.00 1.80
❑ 161 Jeff George UF 4.00 1.80
❑ 162 Emmitt Smith UF........ 15.00 6.75
❑ 163 Irving Fryar UF .... 2.00 .90
❑ 164 Brett Favre UF............ 20.00 9.00
❑ 165 Eddie George UF 8.00 3.60
❑ 166 Terry Allen UF.............. 4.00 1.80
❑ 167 Warren Moon UF.......... 4.00 1.80
❑ 168 Mark Brunell UF 8.00 3.60
❑ 169 Robert Smith UF 4.00 1.80
❑ 170 Jerry Rice UF 10.00 4.50
❑ 171 Tim Brown UF.............. 4.00 1.80
❑ 172 Carl Pickens UF 4.00 1.80
❑ 173 Joey Galloway UF........ 4.00 1.80
❑ 174 Herman Moore UF 4.00 1.80
❑ 175 Adrian Murrell UF 4.00 1.80
❑ 176 Thurman Thomas UF .. 4.00 1.80
❑ 177 Robert Brooks UF 4.00 1.80
❑ 178 Michael Irvin UF 4.00 1.80
❑ 179 Andre Rison UF............ 4.00 1.80
❑ 180 Marshall Faulk UF........ 4.00 1.80
❑ 181 Peyton Manning FR RC 15.00 6.75
❑ 182 Ryan Leaf FR RC 3.00 1.35
❑ 183 Andre Wadsworth FR RC 1.50 .70
❑ 184 Charles Woodson FR RC 4.00 1.80
❑ 185 Curtis Enis FR RC........ 4.00 1.80
❑ 186 Grant Wistrom FR RC .. 1.00 .45
❑ 187 Greg Ellis FR RC.......... 1.00 .45
❑ 188 Fred Taylor FR RC 8.00 3.60
❑ 189 Duane Starks FR RC .. 1.00 .45
❑ 190 Keith Brooking FR RC .. 1.50 .70
❑ 191 Takeo Spikes FR RC .. 1.50 .70
❑ 192 Jason Peter FR RC ...... 1.00 .45
❑ 193 Anthony Simmons FR RC 1.00 .45
❑ 194 Kevin Dyson FR RC 3.00 1.35
❑ 195 Brian Simmons FR RC 1.00 .45
❑ 196 Robert Edwards FR RC 2.00 .90
❑ 197 Randy Moss FR RC .. 15.00 6.75
❑ 198 John Avery FR RC ...... 2.00 .90
❑ 199 Marcus Nash FR RC.... 2.00 .90
❑ 200 Jerome Pathon FR RC 1.50 .70
❑ 201 Jacquez Green FR RC 3.00 1.35
❑ 202 Robert Holcombe FR RC 2.00 .90
❑ 203 Pat Johnson FR RC .... 1.50 .70
❑ 204 Germane Crowell FR RC 5.00 2.20
❑ 205 Joe Jurevicius FR RC .. 1.50 .70
❑ 206 Skip Hicks FR RC .... 1.50 .70
❑ 207 Ahman Green FR RC .. 1.50 .70
❑ 208 Brian Griese FR RC 5.00 2.20
❑ 209 Hines Ward FR RC ...... 1.50 .70
❑ 210 Tavian Banks FR RC .. 1.50 .70
❑ 211 Warrick Dunn NR 6.00 2.70
❑ 212 Jake Plummer NR...... 25.00 11.00
❑ 213 Derrick Mayes NR........ 6.00 2.70
❑ 214 Napoleon Kaufman NR 6.00 2.70
❑ 215 Jamal Anderson NR 6.00 2.70
❑ 216 Marvin Harrison NR...... 6.00 2.70
❑ 217 Jermaine Lewis NR...... 6.00 2.70
❑ 218 Corey Dillon NR 10.00 4.50
❑ 219 Keyshawn Johnson NR 6.00 2.70
❑ 220 Mike Alstott NR 6.00 2.70
❑ 221 Bobby Hoying NR 6.00 2.70
❑ 222 Keenan McCardell NR 6.00 2.70
❑ 223 Will Blackwell NR 3.00 1.35
❑ 224 Peter Boulware NR 3.00 1.35
❑ 225 Tony Banks NR............ 6.00 2.70
❑ 226 Rod Smith NR.............. 6.00 2.70
❑ 227 Tony Gonzalez NR 6.00 2.70
❑ 228 Antowain Smith NR...... 3.00 1.35

❑ 229 Rae Carruth NR 6.00 2.70
❑ 230 J.J. Stokes NR 6.00 2.70
❑ 231 Brad Johnson NR 6.00 2.70
❑ 232 Shawn Springs NR 3.00 1.35
❑ 233 Elvis Grbac NR 3.00 1.35
❑ 234 Jimmy Smith NR 6.00 2.70
❑ 235 Terry Glenn NR............ 6.00 2.70
❑ 236 Tiki Barber NR.............. 6.00 2.70
❑ 237 Gus Frerotte NR 3.00 1.35
❑ 238 Danny Wuerffel NR 6.00 2.70
❑ 239 Fred Lane NR 6.00 2.70
❑ 240 Todd Collins NR 3.00 1.35
❑ 241 Barry Sanders UR...... 40.00 18.00
❑ 242 Troy Aikman UR 20.00 9.00
❑ 243 Dan Marino UR 40.00 18.00
❑ 244 Drew Bledsoe UR 15.00 6.75
❑ 245 Dorsey Levens UR 8.00 3.60
❑ 246 Jerome Bettis UR 8.00 3.60
❑ 247 John Elway UR 40.00 18.00
❑ 248 Steve Young UR 12.00 5.50
❑ 249 Terrell Davis UR 30.00 13.50
❑ 250 Kordell Stewart UR 8.00 3.60
❑ 251 Jeff George UR 8.00 3.60
❑ 252 Emmitt Smith UR........ 30.00 13.50
❑ 253 Irving Fryar UR 4.00 1.80
❑ 254 Brett Favre UR 40.00 18.00
❑ 255 Eddie George UR 15.00 6.75
❑ 256 Terry Allen UR.............. 8.00 3.60
❑ 257 Warren Moon UR 8.00 3.60
❑ 258 Mark Brunell UR 15.00 6.75
❑ 259 Robert Smith UR.......... 8.00 3.60
❑ 260 Jerry Rice UR 20.00 9.00
❑ 261 Tim Brown UR.............. 8.00 3.60
❑ 262 Carl Pickens UR 8.00 3.60
❑ 263 Joey Galloway UR........ 8.00 3.60
❑ 264 Herman Moore UR 8.00 3.60
❑ 265 Adrian Murrell UR 8.00 3.60
❑ 266 Thurman Thomas UR .. 8.00 3.60
❑ 267 Robert Brooks UR........ 8.00 3.60
❑ 268 Michael Irvin UR 8.00 3.60
❑ 269 Andre Rison UR 8.00 3.60
❑ 270 Marshall Faulk UR........ 8.00 3.60
❑ P243 Dan Marino UR Promo 1.50 .70

1998 UD3 Die Cuts

	MINT	NRMT
COMPLETE SET (270)	3500.00	1600.00

*EMB.DIE CUT 1-30: SAME PRICE
*EMB.DIE CUT 31-60: .5X TO 1.2X HI COL.
*EMB.DIE CUT 61-90: 1.2X TO 3X HI COL.
EMBOSSED PRINT RUN 2000 SERIAL #'d SETS
*FX DIE CUT 91-120: .5X TO 1.2X HI COL.
*FX DIE CUT 121-150: 2X TO 5X HI COL.
*FX DIE CUT 151-180: .5X TO 1.2X HI COL.
FX STATED PRINT RUN 1000 SETS
*RAINBOW DIE CUT 181-210: 6X TO 15X HI
*RAINBOW DIE CUT 211-240: 2X TO 5X HI
*RAINBOW DIE CUT 241-270: 1.5X TO 4X
RAINBOW PRINT RUN 100 SETS

1998 UD Choice

	MINT	NRMT
COMPLETE SET (438)	70.00	32.00
COMP.SERIES 1 (255)	35.00	16.00
COMP.SERIES 2 (183)	40.00	18.00
COMP.FACT.SER.1 (275)	40.00	18.00

COMMON CARD (1-438)............ .10 .05
SEMISTARS.............................. .20 .09
UNLISTED STARS...................... .40 .18
COMMON ROOKIE .... .40 .18
ROOKIE SEMISTARS .... .60 .25
ROOKIE UNLISTED STARS .... 1.00 .45
COMMON DOM.NEXT (256-285) 1.00 .45
DOM.NEXT SEMISTARS.......... 1.50 .70
DOM.NEXT UNL.STARS .... 2.00 .90
DOMIN.NEXT STATED ODDS 1:4 SER.2
DOMIN.NEXT SE CARDS: 1.5X TO 3X HI COL.
DOMIN.NEXT SE PRINT RUN 2000 SER.#'d SETS
COMP.CHOICE RES. (438).. 800.00 350.00
*CHOICE RESERVE STARS: 3X TO 8X HI COL.
*CHOICE RES.YOUNG STARS: 2.5X TO 6X
*CHOICE RESERVE RCs: 1.25X TO 3X
CHOICE RESERVE STATED ODDS 1:6
COMMON PRIME CHO.RES. 12.00 5.50
*PRIME CHOICE RES.STARS: 30X TO 80X
*PRIME CHO.RES.YOUNG STARS: 25X TO 60X
*PRIME CHOICE RESERVE RCs: 7.5X TO 20X
PRIME CHOICE RES. PRINT RUN 100 SETS

❑ 1 Jake Plummer .... 1.00 .45
❑ 2 Rob Moore .... .20 .09
❑ 3 Simeon Rice .... .20 .09
❑ 4 Larry Centers .... .10 .05
❑ 5 Aeneas Williams .... .10 .05
❑ 6 Chris Gedney .... .10 .05
❑ 7 Jamal Anderson .... .40 .18
❑ 8 Michael Booker .... .10 .05
❑ 9 Ronnie Bradford .... .10 .05
❑ 10 Cornelius Bennett .... .10 .05
❑ 11 Terance Mathis .... .20 .09
❑ 12 Byron Hanspard .... .20 .09
❑ 13 Peter Boulware .... .10 .05
❑ 14 Jonathan Ogden .... .10 .05
❑ 15 Jermaine Lewis................ .20 .09
❑ 16 Tony Siragusa .... .10 .05
❑ 17 Brian Kinchen .... .10 .05
❑ 18 Michael Jackson .... .10 .05
❑ 19 Doug Flutie .... .50 .23
❑ 20 Eric Moulds .... .40 .18
❑ 21 Antowain Smith .... .40 .18
❑ 22 Bruce Smith...................... .20 .09
❑ 23 Jay Riemersma .... .10 .05
❑ 24 Ruben Brown .... .10 .05
❑ 25 Fred Lane .... .20 .09
❑ 26 Rae Carruth....................... .20 .09
❑ 27 Wesley Walls..................... .20 .09
❑ 28 Winslow Oliver .... .10 .05
❑ 29 Tyrone Poole..................... .10 .05
❑ 30 Lamar Lathon .... .10 .05
❑ 31 Anthony Johnson .... .10 .05
❑ 32 Erik Kramer .... .10 .05
❑ 33 Darnell Autry .... .10 .05
❑ 34 Bobby Engram .... .20 .09
❑ 35 Curtis Conway................... .20 .09
❑ 36 Jeff Jaeger .... .10 .05
❑ 37 Chris Penn .... .10 .05
❑ 38 Corey Dillon...................... .50 .23
❑ 39 Jeff Blake .... .20 .09
❑ 40 Carl Pickens .... .40 .18
❑ 41 Ki-Jana Carter .... .10 .05
❑ 42 Reinard Wilson .... .10 .05
❑ 43 Tremain Mack .... .10 .05
❑ 44 Troy Aikman .... 1.00 .45
❑ 45 Larry Allen.......................... .10 .05
❑ 46 Darren Woodson .... .10 .05
❑ 47 Anthony Miller .... .10 .05
❑ 48 Erik Williams .... .10 .05
❑ 49 Deion Sanders .... .40 .18
❑ 50 Richie Cunningham........... .10 .05
❑ 51 John Elway .... 2.00 .90
❑ 52 Steve Atwater .... .10 .05
❑ 53 Ed McCaffrey .... .20 .09
❑ 54 Maa Tanuvasa .... .10 .05
❑ 55 John Mobley .... .10 .05
❑ 56 Bill Romanowski .... .10 .05
❑ 57 Shannon Sharpe .... .20 .09
❑ 58 Scott Mitchell..................... .20 .09
❑ 59 Jason Hanson .... .10 .05
❑ 60 Herman Moore .... .40 .18
❑ 61 Luther Elliss........................ .10 .05
❑ 62 Bryant Westbrook .... .10 .05
❑ 63 Kevin Abrams RC .... .20 .09
❑ 64 Brett Favre .... 2.00 .90
❑ 65 Gilbert Brown .... .10 .05
❑ 66 Antonio Freeman.............. .40 .18
❑ 67 Reggie White.................... .40 .18
❑ 68 Mark Chmura .... .20 .09
❑ 69 Seth Joyner....................... .10 .05
❑ 70 LeRoy Butler .... .10 .05
❑ 71 Marvin Harrison................. .20 .09
❑ 72 Marshall Faulk................... .40 .18
❑ 73 Ken Dilger .... .10 .05
❑ 74 Steve Morrison .... .10 .05
❑ 75 Zack Crockett .... .10 .05
❑ 76 Quentin Coryatt................. .10 .05
❑ 77 Keenan McCardell............. .20 .09
❑ 78 Mark Brunell .... .75 .35
❑ 79 Renaldo Wynn.................... .10 .05
❑ 80 Jimmy Smith .... .20 .09
❑ 81 James O. Stewart .... .20 .09
❑ 82 Kevin Hardy........................ .10 .05
❑ 83 Marcus Allen .... .40 .18
❑ 84 Andre Rison .... .20 .09
❑ 85 Pete Stoyanovich .... .10 .05
❑ 86 Tony Gonzalez .... .10 .05
❑ 87 Derrick Thomas................. .20 .09
❑ 88 Rich Gannon .... .10 .05
❑ 89 Elvis Grbac .... .20 .09
❑ 90 Dan Marino .... 2.00 .90
❑ 91 Lawrence Phillips .... .10 .05
❑ 92 Yatil Green .... .10 .05
❑ 93 Zach Thomas .... .10 .05
❑ 94 Olindo Mare RC .... .10 .05
❑ 95 Charles Jordan .... .10 .05
❑ 96 Brad Johnson .... .40 .18
❑ 97 Cris Carter.......................... .40 .18
❑ 98 Jake Reed........................... .20 .09
❑ 99 Ed McDaniel .... .10 .05
❑ 100 Dwayne Rudd .... .10 .05
❑ 101 Leroy Hoard .... .10 .05
❑ 102 Danny Wuerffel .... .20 .09
❑ 103 Troy Davis........................ .10 .05
❑ 104 Andre Hastings .... .10 .05
❑ 105 Nicky Savoie .... .10 .05
❑ 106 Willie Roaf........................ .10 .05
❑ 107 Ray Zellars .... .10 .05
❑ 108 Tedy Bruschi .... .10 .05
❑ 109 Drew Bledsoe .... .75 .35
❑ 110 Terry Glenn .... .40 .18
❑ 111 Ben Coates .... .20 .09
❑ 112 Willie Clay .... .10 .05
❑ 113 Chris Slade .... .10 .05
❑ 114 Larry Whigham .... .10 .05
❑ 115 Danny Kanell.................... .20 .09
❑ 116 Jessie Armstead .... .10 .05
❑ 117 Phillippi Sparks .... .10 .05
❑ 118 Michael Strahan .... .10 .05
❑ 119 Tiki Barber........................ .20 .09
❑ 120 Charles Way .... .10 .05
❑ 121 Chris Calloway .... .10 .05
❑ 122 Glenn Foley...................... .20 .09
❑ 123 Wayne Chrebet................ .40 .18
❑ 124 Kyle Brady........................ .10 .05
❑ 125 Keyshawn Johnson......... .40 .18
❑ 126 Aaron Glenn .... .10 .05
❑ 127 James Farrior .... .10 .05
❑ 128 Victor Green .... .10 .05
❑ 129 Jeff George .... .20 .09
❑ 130 Rickey Dudley .... .10 .05
❑ 131 Darrell Russell.................. .10 .05
❑ 132 Tim Brown .... .40 .18
❑ 133 James Trapp .... .10 .05
❑ 134 Napoleon Kaufman .... .40 .18
❑ 135 Bobby Hoying .... .20 .09
❑ 136 Irving Fryar .... .20 .09
❑ 137 Mike Mamula.................... .10 .05
❑ 138 Troy Vincent .... .10 .05
❑ 139 Bobby Taylor .... .10 .05
❑ 140 Chris Boniol...................... .10 .05
❑ 141 Jerome Bettis .... .40 .18
❑ 142 Charles Johnson .... .10 .05
❑ 143 Levon Kirkland .... .10 .05
❑ 144 Carnell Lake .... .10 .05
❑ 145 Will Blackwell .... .10 .05
❑ 146 Tim Lester .... .10 .05
❑ 147 Greg Lloyd........................ .10 .05
❑ 148 Tony Banks .... .20 .09
❑ 149 Ryan McNeil .... .10 .05

❑ 150 Orlando Pace .10 .05
❑ 151 Isaac Bruce .40 .18
❑ 152 Eddie Kennison .20 .09
❑ 153 Leslie O'Neal .10 .05
❑ 154 Darren Bennett .10 .05
❑ 155 Natrone Means .40 .18
❑ 156 Junior Seau .20 .09
❑ 157 Tony Martin .20 .09
❑ 158 Rodney Harrison .20 .09
❑ 159 Freddie Jones .10 .05
❑ 160 Terrell Owens .40 .18
❑ 161 Merton Hanks .10 .05
❑ 162 Chris Doleman .10 .05
❑ 163 Steve Young .50 .23
❑ 164 Chuck Levy .10 .05
❑ 165 J.J. Stokes .20 .09
❑ 166 Ken Norton .10 .05
❑ 167 Bennie Blades .10 .05
❑ 168 Chad Brown .10 .05
❑ 169 Warren Moon .40 .18
❑ 170 Cortez Kennedy .10 .05
❑ 171 Darryl Williams .10 .05
❑ 172 Michael Sinclair .10 .05
❑ 173 Trent Dilfer .40 .18
❑ 174 Mike Alstott .40 .18
❑ 175 Warren Sapp .20 .09
❑ 176 Reidel Anthony .20 .09
❑ 177 Derrick Brooks .10 .05
❑ 178 Horace Copeland .10 .05
❑ 179 Hardy Nickerson .10 .05
❑ 180 Steve McNair .40 .18
❑ 181 Anthony Dorsett .10 .05
❑ 182 Chris Sanders .10 .05
❑ 183 Derrick Mason .10 .05
❑ 184 Eddie George .75 .35
❑ 185 Blaine Bishop .10 .05
❑ 186 Gus Frerotte .10 .05
❑ 187 Terry Allen .40 .18
❑ 188 Darrell Green .20 .09
❑ 189 Ken Harvey .10 .05
❑ 190 Matt Turk .10 .05
❑ 191 Cris Dishman .10 .05
❑ 192 Keith Thibodeaux RC .10 .05
❑ 193 Peyton Manning RC 10.00 4.50
❑ 194 Ryan Leaf RC 1.50 .70
❑ 195 Charles Woodson RC 2.00 .90
❑ 196 Andre Wadsworth RC .60 .25
❑ 197 Keith Brooking RC 1.00 .45
❑ 198 Jason Peter RC .40 .18
❑ 199 Curtis Enis RC 2.00 .90
❑ 200 Randy Moss RC 10.00 4.50
❑ 201 Tra Thomas RC .40 .18
❑ 202 Robert Edwards RC 1.00 .45
❑ 203 Kevin Dyson RC 1.50 .70
❑ 204 Fred Taylor RC 4.00 1.80
❑ 205 Corey Chavous RC .40 .18
❑ 206 Grant Wistrom RC .40 .18
❑ 207 Vonnie Holliday RC .60 .25
❑ 208 Brian Simmons RC .40 .18
❑ 209 Jeremy Staat RC .40 .18
❑ 210 Alonzo Mayes RC .40 .18
❑ 211 Anthony Simmons RC .40 .18
❑ 212 Sam Cowart RC .40 .18
❑ 213 Flozell Adams RC .40 .18
❑ 214 Terry Fair RC .60 .25
❑ 215 Germane Crowell RC 2.00 .90
❑ 216 Robert Holcombe RC 1.00 .45
❑ 217 Jacquez Green RC 1.50 .70
❑ 218 Skip Hicks RC 1.00 .45
❑ 219 Takeo Spikes RC .60 .25
❑ 220 Az-Zahir Hakim RC 1.50 .70
❑ 221 Ahman Green RC 1.00 .45
❑ 222 Chris Fuamatu-Ma'afala RC .60 .25
❑ 223 Darnell Autry DYOC .10 .05
❑ 224 John Randle DYOC .10 .05
❑ 225 Scott Mitchell DYOC .10 .05
❑ 226 Troy Aikman DYOC .40 .18
❑ 227 Terrell Davis DYOC .40 .18
❑ 228 Kordell Stewart DYOC .40 .18
❑ 229 Warrick Dunn DYOC .40 .18
❑ 230 Craig Newsome DYOC .10 .05
❑ 231 Brett Favre DYOC .50 .23
❑ 232 Kordell Stewart DYOC .40 .18
❑ 233 Barry Sanders DYOC .50 .23
❑ 234 Dan Marino DYOC .50 .23
❑ 235 Dan Marino DYOC .50 .23
❑ 236 Tamarick Vanover DYOC .10 .05
❑ 237 Warrick Dunn DYOC .40 .18
❑ 238 Andre Rison DYOC .10 .05
❑ 239 Dan Marino DYOC .50 .23
❑ 240 Reggie White DYOC .40 .18
❑ 241 Tim Brown DYOC .40 .18
❑ 242 Joe Montana DYOC .50 .23
❑ 243 Robert Brooks DYOC .20 .09
❑ 244 Danny Kanell DYOC .10 .05
❑ 245 Emmitt Smith DYOC .60 .25
❑ 246 Barry Sanders DYOC .75 .35
❑ 247 Brett Favre DYOC .75 .35
❑ 248 Brett Favre DYOC .75 .35
❑ 249 Jerome Bettis DYOC .10 .05
❑ 250 Kordell Stewart DYOC .40 .18
❑ 251 Terrell Davis DYOC .75 .35
❑ 252 Drew Bledsoe DYOC .40 .18
❑ 253 Troy Aikman CL .40 .18
❑ 254 Dan Marino CL .75 .35
❑ 255 Warrick Dunn CL .40 .18
❑ 256 Peyton Manning DN 10.00 4.50
❑ 257 Ryan Leaf DN 2.00 .90
❑ 258 Andre Wadsworth DN 1.50 .70
❑ 259 Charles Woodson DN 2.50 1.10
❑ 260 Curtis Enis DN 2.50 1.10
❑ 261 Grant Wistrom DN 1.00 .45
❑ 262 Greg Ellis DN RC 1.00 .45
❑ 263 Fred Taylor DN 4.00 1.80
❑ 264 Duane Starks DN RC 1.00 .45
❑ 265 Keith Brooking DN 1.50 .70
❑ 266 Takeo Spikes DN 1.50 .70
❑ 267 Anthony Simmons DN 1.00 .45
❑ 268 Kevin Dyson DN 2.00 .90
❑ 269 Robert Edwards DN 2.00 .90
❑ 270 Randy Moss DN 10.00 4.50
❑ 271 John Avery DN RC 2.00 .90
❑ 272 Marcus Nash DN RC 2.00 .90
❑ 273 Jerome Pathon DN RC 1.50 .70
❑ 274 Jacquez Green DN 2.00 .90
❑ 275 Robert Holcombe DN 2.00 .90
❑ 276 Pat Johnson DN RC 1.50 .70
❑ 277 Germane Crowell DN 2.50 1.10
❑ 278 Tony Simmons DN RC 1.50 .70
❑ 279 Joe Jurevicius DN RC 1.50 .70
❑ 280 Skip Hicks DN 1.50 .70
❑ 281 Sam Cowart DN 1.00 .45
❑ 282 Rashaan Shehee DN RC 1.50 .70
❑ 283 Brian Griese DN RC 8.00 3.60
❑ 284 Tim Dwight DN RC 4.00 1.80
❑ 285 Ahman Green DN 1.50 .70
❑ 286 Adrian Murrell .20 .09
❑ 287 Corey Chavous .20 .09
❑ 288 Eric Swann .10 .05
❑ 289 Frank Sanders .20 .09
❑ 290 Eric Metcalf .10 .05
❑ 291 Jammi German RC .40 .18
❑ 292 Eugene Robinson .10 .05
❑ 293 Chris Chandler .20 .09
❑ 294 Tony Martin .20 .09
❑ 295 Jessie Tuggle .10 .05
❑ 296 Errict Rhett .20 .09
❑ 297 Jim Harbaugh .20 .09
❑ 298 Eric Green .20 .09
❑ 299 Ray Lewis .10 .05
❑ 300 Jamie Sharper .10 .05
❑ 301 Fred Coleman RC .40 .18
❑ 302 Rob Johnson .20 .09
❑ 303 Quinn Early .10 .05
❑ 304 Thurman Thomas .40 .18
❑ 305 Andre Reed .20 .09
❑ 306 Sean Gilbert .10 .05
❑ 307 Kerry Collins .20 .09
❑ 308 Jason Peter .10 .05
❑ 309 Michael Bates .10 .05
❑ 310 William Floyd .20 .09
❑ 311 Alonzo Mayes RC .40 .18
❑ 312 Tony Parrish RC .40 .18
❑ 313 Walt Harris .10 .05
❑ 314 Edgar Bennett .10 .05
❑ 315 Jeff Jaeger .10 .05
❑ 316 Brian Simmons .20 .09
❑ 317 David Dunn .10 .05
❑ 318 Ashley Ambrose .10 .05
❑ 319 Darnay Scott .20 .09
❑ 320 Neil O'Donnell .20 .09
❑ 321 Flozell Adams .20 .09
❑ 322 Stepfret Williams .10 .05
❑ 323 Emmitt Smith 1.50 .70
❑ 324 Michael Irvin .40 .18
❑ 325 Chris Warren .20 .09
❑ 326 Eric Brown RC .40 .18
❑ 327 Rod Smith WR .20 .09
❑ 328 Terrell Davis 1.50 .70
❑ 329 Neil Smith .20 .09
❑ 330 Darrien Gordon .10 .05
❑ 331 Curtis Alexander RC .40 .18
❑ 332 Barry Sanders 2.00 .90
❑ 333 David Sloan .10 .05
❑ 334 Johnnie Morton .20 .09
❑ 335 Robert Porcher .10 .05
❑ 336 Tommy Vardell .10 .05
❑ 337 Vonnie Holliday .20 .09
❑ 338 Dorsey Levens .40 .18
❑ 339 Derrick Mayes .20 .09
❑ 340 Robert Brooks .20 .09
❑ 341 Raymont Harris .10 .05
❑ 342 E.G. Green RC .60 .25
❑ 343 Carlton Gray .10 .05
❑ 344 Albert Fontenot .10 .05
❑ 345 Aaron Bailey .10 .05
❑ 346 Jeff Burris .10 .05
❑ 347 Donovin Darius RC .40 .18
❑ 348 Tavian Banks RC .20 .09
❑ 349 Aaron Beasley RC .40 .18
❑ 350 Tony Brackens .10 .05
❑ 351 Bryce Paup .10 .05
❑ 352 Chester McGlockton .10 .05
❑ 353 Leslie O'Neal .10 .05
❑ 354 Derrick Alexander WR .20 .09
❑ 355 Kimble Anders .20 .09
❑ 356 Tamarick Vanover .10 .05
❑ 357 Brock Marion .10 .05
❑ 358 Larry Shannon RC .40 .18
❑ 359 Karim Abdul-Jabbar .40 .18
❑ 360 Troy Drayton .10 .05
❑ 361 O.J. McDuffie .20 .09
❑ 362 John Randle .20 .09
❑ 363 David Palmer .10 .05
❑ 364 Robert Smith .40 .18
❑ 365 Kailee Wong RC .40 .18
❑ 366 Duane Clemons .10 .05
❑ 367 Kyle Turley RC .40 .18
❑ 368 Sean Dawkins .10 .05
❑ 369 Lamar Smith .10 .05
❑ 370 Cameron Cleeland RC .60 .25
❑ 371 Keith Poole .10 .05
❑ 372 Tebucky Jones RC .40 .18
❑ 373 Willie McGinest .10 .05
❑ 374 Ty Law .10 .05
❑ 375 Lawyer Milloy .10 .05
❑ 376 Tony Carter .10 .05
❑ 377 Shaun Williams RC .40 .18
❑ 378 Brian Alford RC .60 .25
❑ 379 Tyrone Wheatley .20 .09
❑ 380 Jason Sehorn .10 .05
❑ 381 David Patten RC 1.00 .45
❑ 382 Scott Frost RC .60 .25
❑ 383 Mo Lewis .10 .05
❑ 384 Kevin Williams DB RC .40 .18
❑ 385 Curtis Martin .40 .18
❑ 386 Vinny Testaverde .20 .09
❑ 387 Mo Collins RC .40 .18
❑ 388 James Jett .20 .09
❑ 389 Eric Allen .10 .05
❑ 390 Jon Ritchie RC UER .60 .25
(John on back)
❑ 391 Harvey Williams .10 .05
❑ 392 Tra Thomas .10 .05
❑ 393 Rodney Peete .10 .05
❑ 394 Hugh Douglas UER .10 .05
(card #395 on back)
❑ 395 Charlie Garner .10 .05
❑ 396 Karl Hankton RC .40 .18
❑ 397 Kordell Stewart .40 .18
❑ 398 George Jones .10 .05
❑ 399 Earl Holmes .10 .05
❑ 400 Hines Ward RC .60 .25
❑ 401 Jason Gildon .10 .05
❑ 402 Ricky Proehl .10 .05
❑ 403 Az-Zahir Hakim .10 .05
❑ 404 Amp Lee .10 .05
❑ 405 Eric Hill .10 .05

❑ 406 Leonard Little RC	.40	.18
❑ 407 Charlie Jones	.10	.05
❑ 408 Craig Whelihan RC	.10	.05
❑ 409 Terrell Fletcher	.10	.05
❑ 410 Kenny Bynum RC	.40	.18
❑ 411 Mikhael Ricks RC	.60	.25
❑ 412 R.W. McQuarters RC	.40	.18
❑ 413 Jerry Rice	1.00	.45
❑ 414 Garrison Hearst	.40	.18
❑ 415 Ty Detmer	.20	.09
❑ 416 Gabe Wilkins	.10	.05
❑ 417 Michael Black RC	1.00	.45
❑ 418 James McKnight	.10	.05
❑ 419 Darrin Smith	.10	.05
❑ 420 Joey Galloway	.40	.18
❑ 421 Ricky Watters	.20	.09
❑ 422 Warrick Dunn	.40	.18
❑ 423 Brian Kelly	.10	.05
❑ 424 Bert Emanuel	.20	.09
❑ 425 John Lynch	.10	.05
❑ 426 Regan Upshaw	.10	.05
❑ 427 Yancey Thigpen	.10	.05
❑ 428 Kenny Holmes	.10	.05
❑ 429 Frank Wycheck	.10	.05
❑ 430 Samari Rolle RC	.40	.18
❑ 431 Brian Mitchell	.10	.05
❑ 432 Stephen Alexander	.10	.05
❑ 433 Jamie Asher	.10	.05
❑ 434 Michael Westbrook	.20	.09
❑ 435 Dana Stubblefield	.10	.05
❑ 436 Dan Wilkinson	.10	.05
❑ 437 Dan Marino CL	.60	.25
❑ 438 Jerry Rice CL	.40	.18

1998 UD Choice Mini Bobbing Head

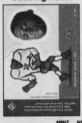

	MINT	NRMT
COMPLETE SET (30)	25.00	11.00
COMMON CARD (M1-M30)	.50	.23
SEMISTARS	.75	.35
UNLISTED STARS	1.00	.45
STATED ODDS 1:4		

❑ M1 Jake Plummer	2.50	1.10
❑ M2 Jamal Anderson	1.00	.45
❑ M3 Michael Jackson	.50	.23
❑ M4 Bruce Smith	.75	.35
❑ M5 Rae Carruth	.75	.35
❑ M6 Curtis Conway	.75	.35
❑ M7 Jeff Blake	.75	.35
❑ M8 Troy Aikman	2.50	1.10
❑ M9 Michael Irvin	1.00	.45
❑ M10 Terrell Davis	4.00	1.80
❑ M11 Barry Sanders	5.00	2.20
❑ M12 Herman Moore	1.00	.45
❑ M13 Reggie White	1.00	.45
❑ M14 Dorsey Levens	1.00	.45
❑ M15 Marvin Harrison	.75	.35
❑ M16 Keenan McCardell	.75	.35
❑ M17 Andre Rison	.75	.35
❑ M18 Dan Marino	5.00	2.20
❑ M19 Curtis Martin	1.00	.45
❑ M20 Keyshawn Johnson	1.00	.45
❑ M21 Tim Brown	1.00	.45
❑ M22 Kordell Stewart	1.00	.45
❑ M23 Greg Lloyd	.75	.35
❑ M24 Junior Seau	.75	.35
❑ M25 Jerry Rice	2.50	1.10
❑ M26 Merton Hanks	.50	.23
❑ M27 Joey Galloway	1.00	.45
❑ M28 Warrick Dunn	1.50	.70
❑ M29 Warren Sapp	.75	.35
❑ M30 Darrell Green	.75	.35

1998 UD Choice Starquest Blue

	MINT	NRMT
COMP.BLUE SET (30)	15.00	6.75
COMMON CARD (1-30)	.25	.11
SEMISTARS	.50	.23

BLUE STATED ODDS 1:1H, 20 PER FACT.SET
*GREENS: 1.5X TO 3X HI COL. ..
GREEN STATED ODDS 1:7 ....
*REDS: 3.5X TO 7X HI COL. ....
RED STATED ODDS 1:23 ....
*GOLDS: 25X TO 50X HI COL. ....
GOLD STATED PRINT RUN 100 SETS

❑ 1 Warren Moon	.50	.23
❑ 2 Jerry Rice	1.25	.55
❑ 3 Jeff George	.25	.11
❑ 4 Brett Favre	2.50	1.10
❑ 5 Junior Seau	.50	.23
❑ 6 Cris Carter	.50	.23
❑ 7 John Elway	2.50	1.10
❑ 8 Troy Aikman	1.25	.55
❑ 9 Steve Young	.75	.35
❑ 10 Kordell Stewart	.50	.23
❑ 11 Drew Bledsoe	1.00	.45
❑ 12 Dorsey Levens	.50	.23
❑ 13 Dan Marino	2.50	1.10
❑ 14 Joey Galloway	.50	.23
❑ 15 Antonio Freeman	.50	.23
❑ 16 Jake Plummer	1.25	.55
❑ 17 Corey Dillon	.50	.23
❑ 18 Mark Brunell	1.00	.45
❑ 19 Andre Rison	.25	.11
❑ 20 Barry Sanders	2.50	1.10
❑ 21 Deion Sanders	.50	.23
❑ 22 Emmitt Smith	2.00	.90
❑ 23 Antowain Smith	.50	.23
❑ 24 Herman Moore	.50	.23
❑ 25 Napoleon Kaufman	.50	.23
❑ 26 Jerome Bettis	.50	.23
❑ 27 Eddie George	1.00	.45
❑ 28 Warrick Dunn	.75	.35
❑ 29 Adrian Murrell	.50	.23
❑ 30 Terrell Davis	2.00	.90

1998 UD Choice Starquest/Rookquest Blue

	MINT	NRMT
COMPLETE SET (30)	30.00	13.50
COMMON CARD (SR1-SR30)	.25	.11
SEMISTARS	.50	.23
UNLISTED STARS	.75	.35

BLUE STATED ODDS ONE PER PACK
*GREENS: 1.5X TO 3X HI COL. ..
GREEN STATED ODDS 1:7 ....
*REDS: 3.5X TO 7X HI COL. ....

RED STATED ODDS 1:23 ....
*GOLDS: 20X TO 40X HI COL. ....
GOLD STATED PRINT RUN 100 SETS

❑ SR1 John Elway / Peyton Manning	5.00	2.20
❑ SR2 Drew Bledsoe / Ryan Leaf	1.50	.70
❑ SR3 Barry Sanders / Tavian Banks	2.50	1.10
❑ SR4 Brett Favre / Vonnie Holliday	2.50	1.10
❑ SR5 Junior Seau / Takeo Spikes	.50	.23
❑ SR6 Deion Sanders / Charles Woodson	1.00	.45
❑ SR7 Jerry Rice / Randy Moss	5.00	2.20
❑ SR8 Reggie White / Andre Wadsworth	.50	.23
❑ SR9 Emmitt Smith / Fred Taylor	2.50	1.10
❑ SR10 Michael Irvin / Kevin Dyson	.75	.35
❑ SR11 Troy Aikman / Shaun Williams	1.25	.55
❑ SR12 Jerome Bettis / Curtis Enis	1.25	.55
❑ SR13 Dan Marino / Brian Griese	3.00	1.35
❑ SR14 Steve Young / R.W.McQuarters	1.00	.45
❑ SR15 Dana Stubblefield / Greg Ellis	.25	.11
❑ SR16 Jake Plummer / Pat Johnson	1.25	.55
❑ SR17 Corey Dillon / Rashaan Shehee	.75	.35
❑ SR18 Mark Brunell / Jerome Pathon	1.00	.45
❑ SR19 Andre Rison / Jacquez Green	.75	.35
❑ SR20 Mike Alstott / Jon Ritchie	.50	.23
❑ SR21 Dorsey Levens / Ahman Green	.75	.35
❑ SR22 Kordell Stewart / Hines Ward	.75	.35
❑ SR23 Antowain Smith / Skip Hicks	.50	.23
❑ SR24 Herman Moore / Germane Crowell	1.00	.45
❑ SR25 Kevin Greene / Jason Peter	.50	.23
❑ SR26 Keyshawn Johnson / Marcus Nash	.75	.35
❑ SR27 Eddie George / Robert Holcombe	1.25	.55
❑ SR28 Warrick Dunn / John Avery	.25	.11
❑ SR29 Tamarick Vanover / Tim Dwight	.75	.35
❑ SR30 Terrell Davis / Robert Edwards	2.50	1.10

1999 UD Ionix

	MINT	NRMT
COMPLETE SET (90)	120.00	55.00
COMP.SET w/o SP's (60)	25.00	11.00
COMMON CARD (1-90)	.25	.11
SEMISTARS	.50	.23
UNLISTED STARS	1.00	.45
COMMON ROOKIE (61-90)	2.00	.90
ROOKIE SEMISTARS	2.50	1.10
ROOKIE SUBSET ODDS 1:4		

	MINT	NRMT
❑ 1 Jake Plummer	2.00	.90
❑ 2 Adrian Murrell	.50	.23
❑ 3 Jamal Anderson	1.00	.45
❑ 4 Chris Chandler	.50	.23
❑ 5 Priest Holmes	1.00	.45
❑ 6 Michael Jackson	.25	.11
❑ 7 Antowain Smith	1.00	.45
❑ 8 Doug Flutie	1.25	.55
❑ 9 Tim Biakabutuka	.50	.23
❑ 10 Muhsin Muhammad	.50	.23
❑ 11 Erik Kramer	.25	.11
❑ 12 Curtis Enis	1.00	.45
❑ 13 Corey Dillon	1.00	.45
❑ 14 Ty Detmer	.50	.23
❑ 15 Justin Armour	.25	.11
❑ 16 Troy Aikman	2.50	1.10
❑ 17 Emmitt Smith	2.50	1.10
❑ 18 John Elway	4.00	1.80
❑ 19 Terrell Davis	2.50	1.10
❑ 20 Barry Sanders	4.00	1.80
❑ 21 Charlie Batch	2.00	.90
❑ 22 Brett Favre	4.00	1.80
❑ 23 Dorsey Levens	1.00	.45
❑ 24 Marshall Faulk	1.00	.45
❑ 25 Peyton Manning	4.00	1.80
❑ 26 Mark Brunell	1.50	.70
❑ 27 Fred Taylor	2.50	1.10
❑ 28 Elvis Grbac	.50	.23
❑ 29 Andre Rison	.50	.23
❑ 30 Dan Marino	4.00	1.80
❑ 31 Karim Abdul-Jabbar	.50	.23
❑ 32 Randall Cunningham	1.00	.45
❑ 33 Randy Moss	4.00	1.80
❑ 34 Drew Bledsoe	1.50	.70
❑ 35 Terry Glenn	1.00	.45
❑ 36 Danny Wuerffel	.25	.11
❑ 37 Kent Graham	.25	.11
❑ 38 Gary Brown	.25	.11
❑ 39 Vinny Testaverde	.50	.23
❑ 40 Keyshawn Johnson	1.00	.45
❑ 41 Napoleon Kaufman	1.00	.45
❑ 42 Tim Brown	1.00	.45
❑ 43 Koy Detmer	.25	.11
❑ 44 Duce Staley	1.00	.45
❑ 45 Kordell Stewart	1.00	.45
❑ 46 Jerome Bettis	1.00	.45
❑ 47 Isaac Bruce	1.00	.45
❑ 48 Robert Holcombe	.50	.23
❑ 49 Jim Harbaugh	.50	.23
❑ 50 Natrone Means	.50	.23
❑ 51 Steve Young	1.50	.70
❑ 52 Jerry Rice	2.50	1.10
❑ 53 Jon Kitna	1.25	.55
❑ 54 Joey Galloway	1.00	.45
❑ 55 Warrick Dunn	1.00	.45
❑ 56 Trent Dilfer	.50	.23
❑ 57 Steve McNair	1.00	.45
❑ 58 Eddie George	1.25	.55
❑ 59 Skip Hicks	1.00	.45
❑ 60 Michael Westbrook	.50	.23
❑ 61 Tim Couch RC	15.00	6.75
❑ 62 Ricky Williams RC	15.00	6.75
❑ 63 Daunte Culpepper RC	8.00	3.60
❑ 64 Akili Smith RC	5.00	2.20
❑ 65 Donovan McNabb RC	8.00	3.60
❑ 66 Michael Bishop RC	3.00	1.35
❑ 67 Brock Huard RC	3.00	1.35
❑ 68 Torry Holt RC	6.00	2.70
❑ 69 Cade McNown RC	8.00	3.60
❑ 70 Shaun King RC	8.00	3.60
❑ 71 Champ Bailey RC	3.00	1.35
❑ 72 Chris Claiborne RC	2.50	1.10
❑ 73 Jevon Kearse RC	5.00	2.20
❑ 74 D'Wayne Bates RC	2.00	.90
❑ 75 David Boston RC	4.00	1.80
❑ 76 Edgerrin James RC	25.00	11.00
❑ 77 Sedrick Irvin RC	4.00	1.80
❑ 78 Dameane Douglas RC	2.00	.90
❑ 79 Troy Edwards RC	4.00	1.80
❑ 80 Ebenezer Ekuban RC	2.00	.90
❑ 81 Kevin Faulk RC	3.00	1.35
❑ 82 Joe Germaine RC	4.00	1.80
❑ 83 Kevin Johnson RC	6.00	2.70
❑ 84 Andy Katzenmoyer RC	4.00	1.80
❑ 85 Rob Konrad RC	4.00	1.80
❑ 86 Chris McAlister RC	2.00	.90
❑ 87 Peerless Price RC	4.00	1.80
❑ 88 Tai Streets RC	2.00	.90
❑ 89 Autry Denson RC	4.00	1.80
❑ 90 Amos Zereoue RC	4.00	1.80

1999 UD Ionix Reciprocal

	MINT	NRMT
COMPLETE SET (90)	400.00	180.00
COMMON CARD (1-60)	1.00	.45
*RECIP.STARS 1-60: 1.5X TO 4X HI COL.		
*RECIP.YOUNG STARS 1-60: 1.25X TO 3X		
RECIP.1-60 STATED ODDS 1:6		
COMMON ROOKIE (61-90)	6.00	2.70
*RECIPROCAL 61-90: .75X TO 2X HI COL.		
RECIP.61-90 STATED ODDS 1:19		

1999 UD Ionix Astronomix

	MINT	NRMT
COMPLETE SET (25)	200.00	90.00
COMMON CARD (A1-A25)	5.00	2.20
STATED ODDS 1:23		

	MINT	NRMT
❑ A1 Keyshawn Johnson	5.00	2.20
❑ A2 Emmitt Smith	12.00	5.50
❑ A3 Eddie George	6.00	2.70
❑ A4 Fred Taylor	10.00	4.50
❑ A5 Peyton Manning	15.00	6.75
❑ A6 John Elway	20.00	9.00
❑ A7 Brett Favre	20.00	9.00
❑ A8 Terrell Davis	12.00	5.50
❑ A9 Mark Brunell	8.00	3.60
❑ A10 Dan Marino	20.00	9.00
❑ A11 Randall Cunningham	5.00	2.20
❑ A12 Steve McNair	5.00	2.20
❑ A13 Jamal Anderson	5.00	2.20
❑ A14 Barry Sanders	20.00	9.00
❑ A15 Jake Plummer	10.00	4.50
❑ A16 Drew Bledsoe	8.00	3.60
❑ A17 Jerome Bettis	5.00	2.20
❑ A18 Jerry Rice	12.00	5.50
❑ A19 Warrick Dunn	5.00	2.20
❑ A20 Steve Young	8.00	3.60
❑ A21 Terrell Owens	5.00	2.20
❑ A22 Ricky Williams	15.00	6.75
❑ A23 Akili Smith	6.00	2.70
❑ A24 Cade McNown	10.00	4.50
❑ A25 David Boston	6.00	2.70

1999 UD Ionix Electric Forces

	MINT	NRMT
COMPLETE SET (20)	60.00	27.00
COMMON CARD (EF1-EF20)	1.50	.70
STATED ODDS 1:6		

	MINT	NRMT
❑ EF1 Ricky Williams	8.00	3.60
❑ EF2 Tim Couch	8.00	3.60
❑ EF3 Daunte Culpepper	4.00	1.80
❑ EF4 Akili Smith	2.50	1.10
❑ EF5 Cade McNown	4.00	1.80
❑ EF6 Donovan McNabb	4.00	1.80
❑ EF7 Brock Huard	2.00	.90
❑ EF8 Michael Bishop	2.50	1.10
❑ EF9 Torry Holt	3.00	1.35
❑ EF10 Peerless Price	2.00	.90
❑ EF11 Peyton Manning	5.00	2.20
❑ EF12 Jake Plummer	3.00	1.35
❑ EF13 John Elway	6.00	2.70
❑ EF14 Mark Brunell	2.50	1.10
❑ EF15 Steve Young	2.50	1.10
❑ EF16 Jamal Anderson	2.00	.90
❑ EF17 Kordell Stewart	2.00	.90
❑ EF18 Eddie George	2.00	.90
❑ EF19 Fred Taylor	3.00	1.35
❑ EF20 Brett Favre	6.00	2.70

1999 UD Ionix HoloGrFX

	MINT	NRMT
COMPLETE SET (10)	800.00	350.00
COMMON CARD (H1-H10)	30.00	13.50
STATED ODDS 1:1500		

	MINT	NRMT
❑ H1 Ricky Williams	80.00	36.00

❑ H2 Tim Couch	80.00	36.00
❑ H3 Cade McNown	50.00	22.00
❑ H4 Peyton Manning	100.00	45.00
❑ H5 Jake Plummer	60.00	27.00
❑ H6 Randy Moss	100.00	45.00
❑ H7 Barry Sanders	100.00	45.00
❑ H8 Jamal Anderson	50.00	22.00
❑ H9 Terrell Davis	80.00	36.00
❑ H10 Brett Favre	100.00	45.00

1999 UD Ionix Power F/X

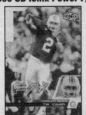

	MINT	NRMT
COMPLETE SET (9)	40.00	18.00
COMMON CARD (P1-P9)	2.00	.90
STATED ODDS 1:11		

Card		
❑ P1 Peyton Manning	6.00	2.70
❑ P2 Randy Moss	6.00	2.70
❑ P3 Terrell Davis	5.00	2.20
❑ P4 Steve Young	3.00	1.35
❑ P5 Dan Marino	8.00	3.60
❑ P6 Warrick Dunn	1.50	.70
❑ P7 Keyshawn Johnson	1.50	.70
❑ P8 Barry Sanders	8.00	3.60
❑ P9 Tim Couch	8.00	3.60

1999 UD Ionix UD Authentics

	MINT	NRMT
COMPLETE SET (10)	1400.00	650.00
COMMON CARD	50.00	22.00

NINE PLAYERS SIGNED 100 CARDS
RICKY WILLIAMS SIGNED 50 CARDS
RANDOM INSERTS IN PACKS
TRADE CARD EXPIRATION 7/15/2000

Card		
❑ AS Akili Smith	80.00	36.00
❑ BH Brock Huard	50.00	22.00
❑ CM Cade McNown	120.00	55.00
❑ DC Daunte Culpepper	100.00	45.00
❑ DM Donovan McNabb	100.00	45.00
❑ MB Michael Bishop	50.00	22.00
❑ RW Ricky Williams	300.00	135.00
❑ SK Shaun King	120.00	55.00
❑ TC Tim Couch	250.00	110.00
❑ TH Torry Holt	100.00	45.00

1999 UD Ionix Warp Zone

	MINT	NRMT
COMPLETE SET (15)	300.00	135.00
COMMON CARD (W1-W15)	10.00	4.50
STATED ODDS 1:108		

Card		
❑ W1 Ricky Williams	40.00	18.00
❑ W2 Tim Couch	40.00	18.00
❑ W3 Cade McNown	20.00	9.00
❑ W4 Daunte Culpepper	20.00	9.00
❑ W5 Akili Smith	12.00	5.50
❑ W6 Brock Huard	10.00	4.50
❑ W7 Donovan McNabb	20.00	9.00
❑ W8 Jake Plummer	20.00	9.00
❑ W9 Jamal Anderson	10.00	4.50
❑ W10 John Elway	40.00	18.00
❑ W11 Randy Moss	30.00	13.50
❑ W12 Terrell Davis	25.00	11.00
❑ W13 Troy Aikman	25.00	11.00
❑ W14 Barry Sanders	40.00	18.00
❑ W15 Fred Taylor	20.00	9.00

1991 Ultra

	MINT	NRMT
COMPLETE SET (300)	12.00	5.50
COMMON CARD (1-300)	.05	.02
SEMISTARS	.10	.05
UNLISTED STARS	.25	.11

❑ 1 Don Beebe	.05	.02
❑ 2 Shane Conlan	.05	.02
❑ 3 Pete Metzelaars	.05	.02
❑ 4 Jamie Mueller	.05	.02
❑ 5 Scott Norwood	.05	.02
❑ 6 Andre Reed	.10	.05
❑ 7 Leon Seals	.05	.02
❑ 8 Bruce Smith	.25	.11
❑ 9 Leonard Smith	.05	.02
❑ 10 Thurman Thomas	.25	.11
❑ 11 Lewis Billups	.05	.02
❑ 12 Jim Breech	.05	.02
❑ 13 James Brooks	.10	.05
❑ 14 Eddie Brown	.05	.02
❑ 15 Boomer Esiason	.10	.05
❑ 16 David Fulcher	.05	.02
❑ 17 Rodney Holman	.05	.02
❑ 18 Bruce Kozerski	.05	.02
❑ 19 Tim Krumrie	.05	.02
❑ 20 Tim McGee	.05	.02
❑ 21 Anthony Munoz	.10	.05
❑ 22 Leon White	.05	.02
❑ 23 Ickey Woods	.05	.02
❑ 24 Carl Zander	.05	.02
❑ 25 Brian Brennan	.05	.02
❑ 26 Thane Gash	.05	.02
❑ 27 Leroy Hoard	.10	.05
❑ 28 Mike Johnson	.05	.02
❑ 29 Reggie Langhorne	.05	.02
❑ 30 Kevin Mack	.05	.02
❑ 31 Clay Matthews	.10	.05
❑ 32 Eric Metcalf	.10	.05
❑ 33 Steve Atwater	.05	.02
❑ 34 Melvin Bratton	.05	.02
❑ 35 John Elway	1.25	.55
❑ 36 Bobby Humphrey	.05	.02
❑ 37 Mark Jackson	.05	.02
❑ 38 Vance Johnson	.05	.02
❑ 39 Ricky Nattiel	.05	.02
❑ 40 Steve Sewell	.05	.02
❑ 41 Dennis Smith	.05	.02
❑ 42 David Treadwell	.05	.02
❑ 43 Michael Young	.05	.02
❑ 44 Ray Childress	.05	.02
❑ 45 Cris Dishman RC	.05	.02
❑ 46 William Fuller	.10	.05
❑ 47 Ernest Givins	.10	.05
❑ 48 John Grimsley UER (Acquired line should be Trade '91, not Draft 6-'84)	.05	.02
❑ 49 Drew Hill	.05	.02
❑ 50 Haywood Jeffires	.10	.05
❑ 51 Sean Jones	.10	.05
❑ 52 Johnny Meads	.05	.02
❑ 53 Warren Moon	.25	.11
❑ 54 Al Smith	.05	.02
❑ 55 Lorenzo White	.05	.02
❑ 56 Albert Bentley	.05	.02
❑ 57 Duane Bickett	.05	.02
❑ 58 Bill Brooks	.05	.02
❑ 59 Jeff George	.25	.11
❑ 60 Mike Prior	.05	.02
❑ 61 Rohn Stark	.05	.02
❑ 62 Jack Trudeau	.05	.02
❑ 63 Clarence Verdin	.05	.02
❑ 64 Steve DeBerg	.05	.02
❑ 65 Emile Harry	.05	.02
❑ 66 Albert Lewis	.05	.02
❑ 67 Nick Lowery UER (NFL Exp. has 12 years, should be 13)	.05	.02
❑ 68 Todd McNair	.05	.02
❑ 69 Christian Okoye	.05	.02
❑ 70 Stephone Paige	.05	.02
❑ 71 Kevin Porter UER (Front has traded logo, but he has been a Chief all career)	.05	.02
❑ 72 Derrick Thomas	.25	.11
❑ 73 Robb Thomas	.05	.02
❑ 74 Barry Word	.05	.02
❑ 75 Marcus Allen	.25	.11
❑ 76 Eddie Anderson	.05	.02
❑ 77 Tim Brown	.25	.11
❑ 78 Mervyn Fernandez	.05	.02
❑ 79 Willie Gault	.10	.05
❑ 80 Ethan Horton	.05	.02
❑ 81 Howie Long	.10	.05
❑ 82 Vance Mueller	.05	.02
❑ 83 Jay Schroeder	.05	.02
❑ 84 Steve Smith	.05	.02
❑ 85 Greg Townsend	.05	.02
❑ 86 Mark Clayton	.10	.05
❑ 87 Jim C. Jensen	.05	.02
❑ 88 Dan Marino	1.25	.55
❑ 89 Tim McKyer UER (Acquired line should be Trade '91, not Trade '90)	.05	.02
❑ 90 John Offerdahl	.05	.02
❑ 91 Louis Oliver	.05	.02
❑ 92 Reggie Roby	.05	.02
❑ 93 Sammie Smith	.05	.02
❑ 94 Hart Lee Dykes	.05	.02
❑ 95 Irving Fryar	.10	.05
❑ 96 Tommy Hodson	.05	.02
❑ 97 Maurice Hurst	.05	.02
❑ 98 John Stephens	.05	.02
❑ 99 Andre Tippett	.05	.02
❑ 100 Mark Boyer	.05	.02
❑ 101 Kyle Clifton	.05	.02
❑ 102 James Hasty	.05	.02
❑ 103 Erik McMillan	.05	.02
❑ 104 Rob Moore	.25	.11
❑ 105 Joe Mott	.05	.02
❑ 106 Ken O'Brien	.05	.02
❑ 107 Ron Stallworth UER (Acquired line should be Trade '91, not Draft 4-'89)	.05	.02
❑ 108 Al Toon	.10	.05
❑ 109 Gary Anderson K	.05	.02
❑ 110 Bubby Brister	.05	.02
❑ 111 Thomas Everett	.05	.02
❑ 112 Merril Hoge	.05	.02
❑ 113 Louis Lipps	.05	.02
❑ 114 Greg Lloyd	.25	.11
❑ 115 Hardy Nickerson	.10	.05
❑ 116 Dwight Stone	.05	.02
❑ 117 Rod Woodson	.25	.11
❑ 118 Tim Worley	.05	.02
❑ 119 Rod Bernstine	.05	.02
❑ 120 Marion Butts	.10	.05
❑ 121 Gill Byrd	.05	.02
❑ 122 Arthur Cox	.05	.02
❑ 123 Burt Grossman	.05	.02
❑ 124 Ronnie Harmon	.05	.02
❑ 125 Anthony Miller	.10	.05
❑ 126 Leslie O'Neal	.10	.05
❑ 127 Gary Plummer	.05	.02

❑ 128 Sam Seale .05 .02
❑ 129 Junior Seau .25 .11
❑ 130 Broderick Thompson .05 .02
❑ 131 Billy Joe Tolliver .05 .02
❑ 132 Brian Blades .10 .05
❑ 133 Jeff Bryant .05 .02
❑ 134 Derrick Fenner .05 .02
❑ 135 Jacob Green .05 .02
❑ 136 Andy Heck .05 .02
❑ 137 Patrick Hunter RC UER .05 .02
(Photos on back
show 23 and 27)
❑ 138 Norm Johnson .05 .02
❑ 139 Tommy Kane .05 .02
❑ 140 Dave Krieg .10 .05
❑ 141 John L. Williams .05 .02
❑ 142 Terry Wooden .05 .02
❑ 143 Steve Broussard .05 .02
❑ 144 Keith Jones .05 .02
❑ 145 Brian Jordan .10 .05
❑ 146 Chris Miller .10 .05
❑ 147 John Rade .05 .02
❑ 148 Andre Rison .10 .05
❑ 149 Mike Rozier .05 .02
❑ 150 Deion Sanders .40 .18
❑ 151 Neal Anderson .10 .05
❑ 152 Trace Armstrong .05 .02
❑ 153 Kevin Butler .05 .02
❑ 154 Mark Carrier DB .10 .05
❑ 155 Richard Dent .10 .05
❑ 156 Dennis Gentry .05 .02
❑ 157 Jim Harbaugh .25 .11
❑ 158 Brad Muster .05 .02
❑ 159 William Perry .10 .05
❑ 160 Mike Singletary .10 .05
❑ 161 Lemuel Stinson .05 .02
❑ 162 Troy Aikman .75 .35
❑ 163 Michael Irvin .25 .11
❑ 164 Mike Saxon .05 .02
❑ 165 Emmitt Smith 2.00 .90
❑ 166 Jerry Ball .05 .02
❑ 167 Michael Cofer .05 .02
❑ 168 Rodney Peete .10 .05
❑ 169 Barry Sanders 1.50 .70
❑ 170 Robert Brown .05 .02
❑ 171 Anthony Dilweg .05 .02
❑ 172 Tim Harris .05 .02
❑ 173 Johnny Holland .05 .02
❑ 174 Perry Kemp .05 .02
❑ 175 Don Majkowski .05 .02
❑ 176 Brian Noble .05 .02
❑ 177 Jeff Query .05 .02
❑ 178 Sterling Sharpe .25 .11
❑ 179 Charles Wilson .05 .02
❑ 180 Keith Woodside .05 .02
❑ 181 Flipper Anderson UER .05 .02
(Back photo not him)
❑ 182 Bern Brostek .05 .02
❑ 183 Pat Carter RC .05 .02
❑ 184 Aaron Cox .05 .02
❑ 185 Henry Ellard .10 .05
❑ 186 Jim Everett .10 .05
❑ 187 Cleveland Gary .05 .02
❑ 188 Jerry Gray .05 .02
❑ 189 Kevin Greene .25 .11
❑ 190 Mike Wilcher .05 .02
❑ 191 Alfred Anderson .05 .02
❑ 192 Joey Browner .05 .02
❑ 193 Anthony Carter .10 .05
❑ 194 Chris Doleman .05 .02
❑ 195 Rick Fenney .05 .02
❑ 196 Darrell Fullington .05 .02
❑ 197 Rich Gannon .05 .02
❑ 198 Hassan Jones .05 .02
❑ 199 Steve Jordan .05 .02
❑ 200 Mike Merriweather .05 .02
❑ 201 Al Noga .05 .02
❑ 202 Herschel Walker .10 .05
❑ 203 Wade Wilson .10 .05
❑ 204 Morten Andersen .05 .02
❑ 205 Gene Atkins .05 .02
❑ 206 Toi Cook RC .05 .02
❑ 207 Craig Heyward .10 .05
❑ 208 Dalton Hilliard .05 .02
❑ 209 Vaughan Johnson .05 .02
❑ 210 Eric Martin .05 .02
❑ 211 Brett Perriman .25 .11
❑ 212 Pat Swilling .10 .05
❑ 213 Steve Walsh .05 .02
❑ 214 Ottis Anderson .10 .05
❑ 215 Carl Banks .05 .02
❑ 216 Maurice Carthon .05 .02
❑ 217 Mark Collins .05 .02
❑ 218 Rodney Hampton .25 .11
❑ 219 Erik Howard .05 .02
❑ 220 Mark Ingram .10 .05
❑ 221 Pepper Johnson .05 .02
❑ 222 Dave Meggett .10 .05
❑ 223 Phil Simms .10 .05
❑ 224 Lawrence Taylor .25 .11
❑ 225 Lewis Tillman .05 .02
❑ 226 Everson Walls .05 .02
❑ 227 Fred Barnett .25 .11
❑ 228 Jerome Brown .05 .02
❑ 229 Keith Byars .05 .02
❑ 230 Randall Cunningham .25 .11
❑ 231 Byron Evans .05 .02
❑ 232 Wes Hopkins .05 .02
❑ 233 Keith Jackson .10 .05
❑ 234 Heath Sherman .05 .02
❑ 235 Anthony Toney .05 .02
❑ 236 Reggie White .25 .11
❑ 237 Rich Camarillo .05 .02
❑ 238 Ken Harvey .10 .05
❑ 239 Eric Hill .05 .02
❑ 240 Johnny Johnson .05 .02
❑ 241 Ernie Jones .05 .02
❑ 242 Tim McDonald .05 .02
❑ 243 Timm Rosenbach .05 .02
❑ 244 Jay Taylor .05 .02
❑ 245 Dexter Carter .05 .02
❑ 246 Mike Cofer .05 .02
❑ 247 Kevin Fagan .05 .02
❑ 248 Don Griffin .05 .02
❑ 249 Charles Haley .10 .05
❑ 250 Brent Jones .25 .11
❑ 251 Joe Montana UER 1.25 .55
(Born: Monongahela,
not New Eagle)
❑ 252 Darryl Pollard .05 .02
❑ 253 Tom Rathman .05 .02
❑ 254 Jerry Rice .75 .35
❑ 255 John Taylor .10 .05
❑ 256 Steve Young .75 .35
❑ 257 Gary Anderson RB .05 .02
❑ 258 Mark Carrier WR .25 .11
❑ 259 Chris Chandler .25 .11
❑ 260 Reggie Cobb .05 .02
❑ 261 Reuben Davis .05 .02
❑ 262 Willie Drewrey .05 .02
❑ 263 Ron Hall .05 .02
❑ 264 Eugene Marve .05 .02
❑ 265 Winston Moss UER .05 .02
(Acquired line should
be Trade '91, not
Draft 2-'87)
❑ 266 Vinny Testaverde .10 .05
❑ 267 Broderick Thomas .05 .02
❑ 268 Jeff Bostic .05 .02
❑ 269 Earnest Byner .05 .02
❑ 270 Gary Clark .25 .11
❑ 271 Darrell Green .05 .02
❑ 272 Jim Lachey .05 .02
❑ 273 Wilber Marshall .05 .02
❑ 274 Art Monk .10 .05
❑ 275 Gerald Riggs .05 .02
❑ 276 Mark Rypien .10 .05
❑ 277 Ricky Sanders .05 .02
❑ 278 Alvin Walton .05 .02
❑ 279 Nick Bell RC .05 .02
❑ 280 Eric Bieniemy RC .05 .02
❑ 281 Jarrod Bunch RC .05 .02
❑ 282 Mike Croel RC .05 .02
❑ 283 Brett Favre RC 5.00 2.20
❑ 284 Moe Gardner RC .05 .02
❑ 285 Pat Harlow RC .05 .02
❑ 286 Randal Hill RC .10 .05
❑ 287 Todd Marinovich RC .05 .02
❑ 288 Russell Maryland RC .25 .11
❑ 289 Dan McGwire RC .05 .02
❑ 290 Ernie Mills RC UER .10 .05
(Patterns misspelled
as pattersn in
first sentence)
❑ 291 Herman Moore RC 2.00 .90
❑ 292 Godfrey Myles RC .05 .02
❑ 293 Browning Nagle RC .05 .02
❑ 294 Mike Pritchard RC .25 .11
❑ 295 Esera Tuaolo RC .05 .02
❑ 296 Mark Vander Poel RC .05 .02
❑ 297 Ricky Watters RC UER 1.50 .70
(Photo on back act-
ually Ray Griggs)
❑ 298 Chris Zorich RC .25 .11
❑ 299 Checklist Card .10 .05
(Randall Cunningham
and Emmitt Smith)
❑ 300 Checklist Card .10 .05
(Randall Cunningham
and Emmitt Smith)

1991 Ultra All-Stars

	MINT	NRMT
COMPLETE SET (10)	12.00	5.50

RANDOM INSERTS IN HOBBY PACKS

❑ 1 Barry Sanders 6.00 2.70
❑ 2 Keith Jackson .40 .18
❑ 3 Bruce Smith 1.00 .45
❑ 4 Randall Cunningham 1.00 .45
❑ 5 Dan Marino 5.00 2.20
❑ 6 Charles Haley .40 .18
❑ 7 John L. Williams .20 .09
❑ 8 Darrell Green .20 .09
❑ 9 Stephone Paige .20 .09
❑ 10 Kevin Greene 1.00 .45

1991 Ultra Performances

	MINT	NRMT
COMPLETE SET (10)	20.00	9.00

RANDOM INSERTS IN RETAIL PACKS

❑ 1 Emmitt Smith 10.00 4.50
❑ 2 Andre Rison .50 .23
❑ 3 Derrick Thomas 1.25 .55
❑ 4 Joe Montana 6.00 2.70
❑ 5 Warren Moon 1.25 .55
❑ 6 Mike Singletary .50 .23
❑ 7 Thurman Thomas 1.25 .55

❑ 8 Rod Woodson	1.25	.55
❑ 9 Jerry Rice	4.00	1.80
❑ 10 Reggie White	1.25	.55

1991 Ultra Update

	MINT	NRMT
COMP.FACT.SET (100)	25.00	11.00
COMMON CARD (U1-U100)	.10	.05
SEMISTARS	.20	.09
UNLISTED STARS	.40	.18

❑ U1 Brett Favre	15.00	6.75
❑ U2 Moe Gardner	.10	.05
❑ U3 Tim McKyer	.10	.05
❑ U4 Bruce Pickens RC	.10	.05
❑ U5 Mike Pritchard	.40	.18
❑ U6 Cornelius Bennett	.20	.09
❑ U7 Phil Hansen RC	.10	.05
❑ U8 Henry Jones RC	.20	.09
❑ U9 Mark Kelso	.10	.05
❑ U10 James Lofton	.20	.09
❑ U11 Anthony Morgan RC	.10	.05
❑ U12 Stan Thomas	.10	.05
❑ U13 Chris Zorich	.20	.09
❑ U14 Reggie Rembert	.10	.05
❑ U15 Alfred Williams RC	.10	.05
❑ U16 Michael Jackson RC	.75	.35
❑ U17 Ed King RC	.10	.05
❑ U18 Joe Morris	.10	.05
❑ U19 Vince Newsome	.10	.05
❑ U20 Tony Casillas	.10	.05
❑ U21 Russell Maryland	.40	.18
❑ U22 Jay Novacek	.40	.18
❑ U23 Mike Croel	.10	.05
❑ U24 Gaston Green	.10	.05
❑ U25 Kenny Walker RC	.10	.05
❑ U26 Melvin Jenkins RC	.10	.05
❑ U27 Herman Moore	4.00	1.80
❑ U28 Kelvin Pritchett RC	.20	.09
❑ U29 Chris Spielman	.20	.09
❑ U30 Vinnie Clark RC	.10	.05
❑ U31 Allen Rice	.10	.05
❑ U32 Vai Sikahema	.10	.05
❑ U33 Esera Tuaolo	.10	.05
❑ U34 Mike Dumas RC	.10	.05
❑ U35 John Flannery RC	.10	.05
❑ U36 Allen Pinkett	.10	.05
❑ U37 Tim Barnett RC	.10	.05
❑ U38 Dan Saleaumua	.10	.05
❑ U39 Harvey Williams RC	.40	.18
❑ U40 Nick Bell	.10	.05
❑ U41 Roger Craig	.20	.09
❑ U42 Ronnie Lott	.20	.09
❑ U43 Todd Marinovich	.10	.05
❑ U44 Robert Delpino	.10	.05
❑ U45 Todd Lyght RC	.10	.05
❑ U46 Robert Young RC	.20	.09
❑ U47 Aaron Craver RC	.10	.05
❑ U48 Mark Higgs RC	.10	.05
❑ U49 Vestee Jackson	.10	.05
❑ U50 Carl Lee	.10	.05
❑ U51 Felix Wright	.10	.05
❑ U52 Darrell Fullington	.10	.05
❑ U53 Pat Harlow	.10	.05
❑ U54 Eugene Lockhart	.10	.05
❑ U55 Hugh Millen RC	.10	.05
❑ U56 Leonard Russell RC	.40	.18
❑ U57 Jon Vaughn RC	.10	.05
❑ U58 Quinn Early	.20	.09
❑ U59 Bobby Hebert	.10	.05
❑ U60 Rickey Jackson	.10	.05
❑ U61 Sam Mills	.20	.09
❑ U62 Jarrod Bunch	.10	.05
❑ U63 John Elliott	.10	.05
❑ U64 Jeff Hostetler	.20	.09
❑ U65 Ed McCaffrey RC	10.00	4.50
❑ U66 Kanavis McGhee RC	.10	.05
❑ U67 Mo Lewis RC	.20	.09
❑ U68 Browning Nagle	.10	.05
❑ U69 Blair Thomas	.10	.05
❑ U70 Antone Davis RC	.10	.05
❑ U71 Brad Goebel RC (See card U74)	.10	.05
❑ U72 Jim McMahon	.20	.09
❑ U73 Clyde Simmons	.10	.05
❑ U74 Randal Hill UER (Card number on back U71 instead of U74)	.20	.09
❑ U75 Eric Swann RC	.40	.18
❑ U76 Tom Tupa	.10	.05
❑ U77 Jeff Graham RC	.40	.18
❑ U78 Eric Green	.10	.05
❑ U79 Neil O'Donnell RC	2.00	.90
❑ U80 Huey Richardson RC	.10	.05
❑ U81 Eric Bieniemy	.10	.05
❑ U82 John Friesz	.40	.18
❑ U83 Eric Moten RC	.10	.05
❑ U84 Stanley Richard RC	.10	.05
❑ U85 Todd Bowles	.10	.05
❑ U86 Merton Hanks RC	.40	.18
❑ U87 Tim Harris	.10	.05
❑ U88 Pierce Holt	.10	.05
❑ U89 Ted Washington RC	.10	.05
❑ U90 John Kasay RC	.20	.09
❑ U91 Dan McGwire	.10	.05
❑ U92 Lawrence Dawsey RC	.20	.09
❑ U93 Charles McRae RC	.10	.05
❑ U94 Jesse Solomon	.10	.05
❑ U95 Robert Wilson RC	.10	.05
❑ U96 Ricky Ervins RC	.20	.09
❑ U97 Charles Mann	.10	.05
❑ U98 Bobby Wilson RC	.10	.05
❑ U99 Jerry Rice Pro-Visions	1.50	.70
❑ U100 Checklist 1-100 (Nick Bell and Jim McMahon)	.10	.05

1992 Ultra

	MINT	NRMT
COMPLETE SET (450)	15.00	6.75
COMMON CARD (1-450)	.10	.05
SEMISTARS	.20	.09
UNLISTED STARS	.40	.18
COMP.C.MILLER SET (10)	6.00	2.70
C.MILLER CERT.AUTOGRAPH	40.00	18.00
MILLER:RAND.INSERTS IN FOIL PACKS		
MILLER SEND-OFF (11-12)	2.00	.90
COMP.REGGIE WHITE SET (10)	10.00	4.50
R.WHITE CERT. AUTOGRAPH	60.00	27.00
R.WHITE:RAND.INS.IN FOIL PACKS		
WHITE SEND-OFF (11-12)	2.50	1.10

❑ 1 Steve Broussard	.10	.05
❑ 2 Rick Bryan	.10	.05
❑ 3 Scott Case	.10	.05
❑ 4 Darion Conner	.10	.05
❑ 5 Bill Fralic	.10	.05
❑ 6 Moe Gardner	.10	.05
❑ 7 Tim Green	.10	.05
❑ 8 Michael Haynes	.20	.09
❑ 9 Chris Hinton	.10	.05
❑ 10 Mike Kenn	.10	.05
❑ 11 Tim McKyer	.10	.05
❑ 12 Chris Miller	.20	.09
❑ 13 Erric Pegram	.20	.09
❑ 14 Mike Pritchard	.20	.09
❑ 15 Andre Rison	.20	.09
❑ 16 Jessie Tuggle	.10	.05
❑ 17 Carlton Bailey RC	.20	.09
❑ 18 Howard Ballard	.10	.05
❑ 19 Cornelius Bennett	.20	.09
❑ 20 Shane Conlan	.10	.05
❑ 21 Kenneth Davis	.10	.05
❑ 22 Kent Hull	.10	.05
❑ 23 Mark Kelso	.10	.05
❑ 24 James Lofton	.20	.09
❑ 25 Keith McKeller	.10	.05
❑ 26 Nate Odomes	.10	.05
❑ 27 Jim Ritcher	.10	.05
❑ 28 Leon Seals	.10	.05
❑ 29 Darryl Talley	.10	.05
❑ 30 Steve Tasker	.20	.09
❑ 31 Thurman Thomas	.40	.18
❑ 32 Will Wolford	.10	.05
❑ 33 Jeff Wright	.10	.05
❑ 34 Neal Anderson	.10	.05
❑ 35 Trace Armstrong	.10	.05
❑ 36 Mark Carrier DB	.10	.05
❑ 37 Wendell Davis	.10	.05
❑ 38 Richard Dent	.20	.09
❑ 39 Shaun Gayle	.10	.05
❑ 40 Jim Harbaugh	.40	.18
❑ 41 Jay Hilgenberg	.10	.05
❑ 42 Darren Lewis	.10	.05
❑ 43 Steve McMichael	.20	.09
❑ 44 Anthony Morgan	.10	.05
❑ 45 Brad Muster	.10	.05
❑ 46 William Perry	.20	.09
❑ 47 John Roper	.10	.05
❑ 48 Lemuel Stinson	.10	.05
❑ 49 Tom Waddle	.10	.05
❑ 50 Donnell Woolford	.10	.05
❑ 51 Leo Barker RC	.10	.05
❑ 52 Eddie Brown	.10	.05
❑ 53 James Francis	.10	.05
❑ 54 David Fulcher UER (Photo on back actually Eddie Brown)	.10	.05
❑ 55 David Grant	.10	.05
❑ 56 Harold Green	.10	.05
❑ 57 Rodney Holman	.10	.05
❑ 58 Lee Johnson	.10	.05
❑ 59 Tim Krumrie	.10	.05
❑ 60 Tim McGee	.10	.05
❑ 61 Alonzo Mitz RC	.10	.05
❑ 62 Anthony Munoz	.20	.09
❑ 63 Alfred Williams	.10	.05
❑ 64 Stephen Braggs	.10	.05
❑ 65 Richard Brown RC	.10	.05
❑ 66 Randy Hilliard RC	.10	.05
❑ 67 Leroy Hoard	.20	.09
❑ 68 Michael Jackson	.20	.09
❑ 69 Mike Johnson	.10	.05
❑ 70 James Jones	.10	.05
❑ 71 Tony Jones	.10	.05
❑ 72 Ed King	.10	.05
❑ 73 Kevin Mack	.10	.05
❑ 74 Clay Matthews	.20	.09
❑ 75 Eric Metcalf	.20	.09
❑ 76 Vince Newsome	.10	.05
❑ 77 Steve Beuerlein	.10	.05
❑ 78 Larry Brown DB	.10	.05
❑ 79 Tony Casillas	.10	.05
❑ 80 Alvin Harper	.20	.09
❑ 81 Issiac Holt	.10	.05
❑ 82 Ray Horton	.10	.05
❑ 83 Michael Irvin	.40	.18
❑ 84 Daryl Johnston	.40	.18
❑ 85 Kelvin Martin	.10	.05

❑ 86	Ken Norton	.40	.18
❑ 87	Jay Novacek	.20	.09
❑ 88	Emmitt Smith	3.00	1.35
❑ 89	Vinson Smith RC	.10	.05
❑ 90	Mark Stepnoski	.20	.09
❑ 91	Tony Tolbert	.10	.05
❑ 92	Alexander Wright	.10	.05
❑ 93	Steve Atwater	.10	.05
❑ 94	Tyrone Braxton	.10	.05
❑ 95	Michael Brooks	.10	.05
❑ 96	Mike Croel	.10	.05
❑ 97	John Elway	2.50	1.10
❑ 98	Simon Fletcher	.10	.05
❑ 99	Gaston Green	.10	.05
❑ 100	Mark Jackson	.10	.05
❑ 101	Keith Kartz	.10	.05
❑ 102	Greg Kragen	.10	.05
❑ 103	Greg Lewis	.10	.05
❑ 104	Karl Mecklenburg	.10	.05
❑ 105	Derek Russell	.10	.05
❑ 106	Steve Sewell	.10	.05
❑ 107	Dennis Smith	.10	.05
❑ 108	David Treadwell	.10	.05
❑ 109	Kenny Walker	.10	.05
❑ 110	Michael Young	.10	.05
❑ 111	Jerry Ball	.10	.05
❑ 112	Bennie Blades	.10	.05
❑ 113	Lomas Brown	.10	.05
❑ 114	Scott Conover RC	.10	.05
❑ 115	Ray Crockett	.10	.05
❑ 116	Mel Gray	.20	.09
❑ 117	Willie Green	.10	.05
❑ 118	Erik Kramer	.20	.09
❑ 119	Dan Owens	.10	.05
❑ 120	Rodney Peete	.20	.09
❑ 121	Brett Perriman	.40	.18
❑ 122	Barry Sanders	3.00	1.35
❑ 123	Chris Spielman	.20	.09
❑ 124	Marc Spindler	.10	.05
❑ 125	William White	.10	.05
❑ 126	Tony Bennett	.10	.05
❑ 127	Matt Brock	.10	.05
❑ 128	LeRoy Butler	.10	.05
❑ 129	Chuck Cecil	.10	.05
❑ 130	Johnny Holland	.10	.05
❑ 131	Perry Kemp	.10	.05
❑ 132	Don Majkowski	.10	.05
❑ 133	Tony Mandarich	.10	.05
❑ 134	Brian Noble	.10	.05
❑ 135	Bryce Paup	.40	.18
❑ 136	Sterling Sharpe	.40	.18
❑ 137	Darrell Thompson	.10	.05
❑ 138	Mike Tomczak	.10	.05
❑ 139	Vince Workman	.20	.09
❑ 140	Ray Childress	.10	.05
❑ 141	Cris Dishman	.10	.05
❑ 142	Curtis Duncan	.10	.05
❑ 143	William Fuller	.20	.09
❑ 144	Ernest Givins	.20	.09
❑ 145	Haywood Jeffires	.20	.09
❑ 146	Sean Jones	.20	.09
❑ 147	Lamar Lathon	.10	.05
❑ 148	Bruce Matthews	.10	.05
❑ 149	Bubba McDowell	.10	.05
❑ 150	Johnny Meads	.10	.05
❑ 151	Warren Moon	.40	.18
❑ 152	Mike Munchak	.10	.05
❑ 153	Bo Orlando RC	.10	.05
❑ 154	Al Smith	.10	.05
❑ 155	Doug Smith	.10	.05
❑ 156	Lorenzo White	.10	.05
❑ 157	Chip Banks	.10	.05
❑ 158	Duane Bickett	.10	.05
❑ 159	Bill Brooks	.10	.05
❑ 160	Eugene Daniel	.10	.05
❑ 161	Jon Hand	.10	.05
❑ 162	Jeff Herrod	.10	.05
❑ 163	Jessie Hester	.10	.05
❑ 164	Scott Radecic	.10	.05
❑ 165	Rohn Stark	.10	.05
❑ 166	Clarence Verdin	.10	.05
❑ 167	John Alt	.10	.05
❑ 168	Tim Barnett	.10	.05
❑ 169	Tim Grunhard	.10	.05
❑ 170	Dino Hackett	.10	.05
❑ 171	Jonathan Hayes	.10	.05
❑ 172	Bill Maas	.10	.05
❑ 173	Chris Martin	.10	.05
❑ 174	Christian Okoye	.10	.05
❑ 175	Stephone Paige	.10	.05
❑ 176	Jayice Pearson RC	.10	.05
❑ 177	Kevin Porter	.10	.05
❑ 178	Kevin Ross	.10	.05
❑ 179	Dan Saleaumua	.10	.05
❑ 180	Tracy Simien RC	.10	.05
❑ 181	Neil Smith	.40	.18
❑ 182	Derrick Thomas	.40	.18
❑ 183	Robb Thomas	.10	.05
❑ 184	Barry Word	.10	.05
❑ 185	Marcus Allen	.40	.18
❑ 186	Eddie Anderson	.10	.05
❑ 187	Nick Bell	.10	.05
❑ 188	Tim Brown	.40	.18
❑ 189	Mervyn Fernandez	.10	.05
❑ 190	Willie Gault	.20	.09
❑ 191	Jeff Gossett	.10	.05
❑ 192	Ethan Horton	.10	.05
❑ 193	Jeff Jaeger	.10	.05
❑ 194	Howie Long	.20	.09
❑ 195	Ronnie Lott	.20	.09
❑ 196	Todd Marinovich	.10	.05
❑ 197	Don Mosebar	.10	.05
❑ 198	Jay Schroeder	.10	.05
❑ 199	Anthony Smith	.10	.05
❑ 200	Greg Townsend	.10	.05
❑ 201	Lionel Washington	.10	.05
❑ 202	Steve Wisniewski	.10	.05
❑ 203	Flipper Anderson	.10	.05
❑ 204	Robert Delpino	.10	.05
❑ 205	Henry Ellard	.20	.09
❑ 206	Jim Everett	.20	.09
❑ 207	Kevin Greene	.40	.18
❑ 208	Darryl Henley	.10	.05
❑ 209	Damone Johnson	.10	.05
❑ 210	Larry Kelm	.10	.05
❑ 211	Todd Lyght	.10	.05
❑ 212	Jackie Slater	.10	.05
❑ 213	Michael Stewart	.10	.05
❑ 214	Pat Terrell	.10	.05
❑ 215	Robert Young	.10	.05
❑ 216	Mark Clayton	.20	.09
❑ 217	Bryan Cox	.20	.09
❑ 218	Jeff Cross	.10	.05
❑ 219	Mark Duper	.10	.05
❑ 220	Harry Galbreath	.10	.05
❑ 221	David Griggs	.10	.05
❑ 222	Mark Higgs	.10	.05
❑ 223	Vestee Jackson	.10	.05
❑ 224	John Offerdahl	.10	.05
❑ 225	Louis Oliver	.10	.05
❑ 226	Tony Paige	.10	.05
❑ 227	Reggie Roby	.10	.05
❑ 228	Pete Stoyanovich	.10	.05
❑ 229	Richmond Webb	.10	.05
❑ 230	Terry Allen	.40	.18
❑ 231	Ray Berry	.10	.05
❑ 232	Anthony Carter	.20	.09
❑ 233	Cris Carter	.75	.35
❑ 234	Chris Doleman	.10	.05
❑ 235	Rich Gannon	.10	.05
❑ 236	Steve Jordan	.10	.05
❑ 237	Carl Lee	.10	.05
❑ 238	Randall McDaniel	.10	.05
❑ 239	Mike Merriweather	.10	.05
❑ 240	Harry Newsome	.10	.05
❑ 241	John Randle	.20	.09
❑ 242	Henry Thomas	.10	.05
❑ 243	Bruce Armstrong	.10	.05
❑ 244	Vincent Brown	.10	.05
❑ 245	Marv Cook	.10	.05
❑ 246	Irving Fryar	.20	.09
❑ 247	Pat Harlow	.10	.05
❑ 248	Maurice Hurst	.10	.05
❑ 249	Eugene Lockhart	.10	.05
❑ 250	Greg McMurtry	.10	.05
❑ 251	Hugh Millen	.10	.05
❑ 252	Leonard Russell	.20	.09
❑ 253	Chris Singleton	.10	.05
❑ 254	Andre Tippett	.10	.05
❑ 255	Jon Vaughn	.10	.05
❑ 256	Morten Andersen	.10	.05
❑ 257	Gene Atkins	.10	.05
❑ 258	Wesley Caroll	.10	.05
❑ 259	Jim Dombrowski	.10	.05
❑ 260	Quinn Early	.20	.09
❑ 261	Bobby Hebert	.10	.05
❑ 262	Joel Hilgenberg	.10	.05
❑ 263	Rickey Jackson	.10	.05
❑ 264	Vaughan Johnson	.10	.05
❑ 265	Eric Martin	.10	.05
❑ 266	Brett Maxie	.10	.05
❑ 267	Fred McAfee RC	.10	.05
❑ 268	Sam Mills	.10	.05
❑ 269	Pat Swilling	.20	.09
❑ 270	Floyd Turner	.10	.05
❑ 271	Steve Walsh	.10	.05
❑ 272	Stephen Baker	.10	.05
❑ 273	Jarrod Bunch	.10	.05
❑ 274	Mark Collins	.10	.05
❑ 275	John Elliott	.10	.05
❑ 276	Myron Guyton	.10	.05
❑ 277	Rodney Hampton	.40	.18
❑ 278	Jeff Hostetler	.20	.09
❑ 279	Mark Ingram	.10	.05
❑ 280	Pepper Johnson	.10	.05
❑ 281	Sean Landeta	.10	.05
❑ 282	Leonard Marshall	.10	.05
❑ 283	Kanavis McGhee	.10	.05
❑ 284	Dave Meggett	.20	.09
❑ 285	Bart Oates	.10	.05
❑ 286	Phil Simms	.20	.09
❑ 287	Reyna Thompson	.10	.05
❑ 288	Lewis Tillman	.10	.05
❑ 289	Brad Baxter	.10	.05
❑ 290	Mike Brim RC	.10	.05
❑ 291	Chris Burkett	.10	.05
❑ 292	Kyle Clifton	.10	.05
❑ 293	James Hasty	.10	.05
❑ 294	Joe Kelly	.10	.05
❑ 295	Jeff Lageman	.10	.05
❑ 296	Mo Lewis	.10	.05
❑ 297	Erik McMillan	.10	.05
❑ 298	Scott Mersereau	.10	.05
❑ 299	Rob Moore	.20	.09
❑ 300	Tony Stargell	.10	.05
❑ 301	Jim Sweeney	.10	.05
❑ 302	Marvin Washington	.10	.05
❑ 303	Lonnie Young	.10	.05
❑ 304	Eric Allen	.10	.05
❑ 305	Fred Barnett	.40	.18
❑ 306	Keith Byars	.10	.05
❑ 307	Byron Evans	.10	.05
❑ 308	Wes Hopkins	.10	.05
❑ 309	Keith Jackson	.20	.09
❑ 310	James Joseph	.10	.05
❑ 311	Seth Joyner	.20	.09
❑ 312	Roger Ruzek	.10	.05
❑ 313	Clyde Simmons	.10	.05
❑ 314	William Thomas	.10	.05
❑ 315	Reggie White	.40	.18
❑ 316	Calvin Williams	.20	.09
❑ 317	Rich Camarillo	.10	.05
❑ 318	Jeff Faulkner	.10	.05
❑ 319	Ken Harvey	.10	.05
❑ 320	Eric Hill	.10	.05
❑ 321	Johnny Johnson	.10	.05
❑ 322	Ernie Jones	.10	.05
❑ 323	Tim McDonald	.10	.05
❑ 324	Freddie Joe Nunn	.10	.05
❑ 325	Luis Sharpe	.10	.05
❑ 326	Eric Swann	.20	.09
❑ 327	Aeneas Williams	.20	.09
❑ 328	Michael Zordich RC	.10	.05
❑ 329	Gary Anderson K	.10	.05
❑ 330	Bubby Brister	.10	.05
❑ 331	Barry Foster	.20	.09
❑ 332	Eric Green	.10	.05
❑ 333	Bryan Hinkle	.10	.05
❑ 334	Tunch Ilkin	.10	.05
❑ 335	Carnell Lake	.10	.05
❑ 336	Louis Lipps	.10	.05
❑ 337	David Little	.10	.05
❑ 338	Greg Lloyd	.40	.18
❑ 339	Neil O'Donnell	.40	.18
❑ 340	Rod Woodson	.40	.18
❑ 341	Rod Bernstine	.10	.05
❑ 342	Marion Butts	.10	.05
❑ 343	Gill Byrd	.10	.05

❑ 344 John Friesz	.20	.09
❑ 345 Burt Grossman	.10	.05
❑ 346 Courtney Hall	.10	.05
❑ 347 Ronnie Harmon	.10	.05
❑ 348 Shawn Jefferson	.10	.05
❑ 349 Nate Lewis	.10	.05
❑ 350 Craig McEwen RC	.10	.05
❑ 351 Eric Moten	.10	.05
❑ 352 Gary Plummer	.10	.05
❑ 353 Henry Rolling	.10	.05
❑ 354 Broderick Thompson	.10	.05
❑ 355 Derrick Walker	.10	.05
❑ 356 Harris Barton	.10	.05
❑ 357 Steve Bono RC	.40	.18
❑ 358 Todd Bowles	.10	.05
❑ 359 Dexter Carter	.10	.05
❑ 360 Michael Carter	.10	.05
❑ 361 Keith DeLong	.10	.05
❑ 362 Charles Haley	.20	.09
❑ 363 Merton Hanks	.20	.09
❑ 364 Tim Harris	.10	.05
❑ 365 Brent Jones	.20	.09
❑ 366 Guy McIntyre	.10	.05
❑ 367 Tom Rathman	.10	.05
❑ 368 Bill Romanowski	.10	.05
❑ 369 Jesse Sapolu	.10	.05
❑ 370 John Taylor	.20	.09
❑ 371 Steve Young	1.50	.70
❑ 372 Robert Blackmon	.10	.05
❑ 373 Brian Blades	.20	.09
❑ 374 Jacob Green	.10	.05
❑ 375 Dwayne Harper	.10	.05
❑ 376 Andy Heck	.10	.05
❑ 377 Tommy Kane	.10	.05
❑ 378 John Kasay	.10	.05
❑ 379 Cortez Kennedy	.20	.09
❑ 380 Bryan Millard	.10	.05
❑ 381 Rufus Porter	.10	.05
❑ 382 Eugene Robinson	.10	.05
❑ 383 John L. Williams	.10	.05
❑ 384 Terry Wooden	.10	.05
❑ 385 Gary Anderson RB	.10	.05
❑ 386 Ian Beckles	.10	.05
❑ 387 Mark Carrier WR	.20	.09
❑ 388 Reggie Cobb	.10	.05
❑ 389 Tony Covington	.10	.05
❑ 390 Lawrence Dawsey	.20	.09
❑ 391 Ron Hall	.10	.05
❑ 392 Keith McCants	.10	.05
❑ 393 Charles McRae	.10	.05
❑ 394 Tim Newton	.10	.05
❑ 395 Jesse Solomon	.10	.05
❑ 396 Vinny Testaverde	.20	.09
❑ 397 Broderick Thomas	.10	.05
❑ 398 Robert Wilson	.10	.05
❑ 399 Earnest Byner	.10	.05
❑ 400 Gary Clark	.40	.18
❑ 401 Andre Collins	.10	.05
❑ 402 Brad Edwards	.10	.05
❑ 403 Kurt Gouveia	.10	.05
❑ 404 Darrell Green	.10	.05
❑ 405 Joe Jacoby	.10	.05
❑ 406 Jim Lachey	.10	.05
❑ 407 Chip Lohmiller	.10	.05
❑ 408 Charles Mann	.10	.05
❑ 409 Wilber Marshall	.10	.05
❑ 410 Brian Mitchell	.20	.09
❑ 411 Art Monk	.20	.09
❑ 412 Mark Rypien	.10	.05
❑ 413 Ricky Sanders	.10	.05
❑ 414 Mark Schlereth RC	.10	.05
❑ 415 Fred Stokes	.10	.05
❑ 416 Bobby Wilson	.10	.05
❑ 417 Corey Barlow RC	.10	.05
❑ 418 Edgar Bennett RC	.50	.23
❑ 419 Eddie Blake RC	.10	.05
❑ 420 Terrell Buckley RC	.10	.05
❑ 421 Willie Clay RC	.10	.05
❑ 422 Rodney Culver RC	.10	.05
❑ 423 Ed Cunningham RC	.10	.05
❑ 424 Mark D'Onofrio RC	.10	.05
❑ 425 Matt Darby RC	.10	.05
❑ 426 Charles Davenport RC	.10	.05
❑ 427 Will Furrer RC	.10	.05
❑ 428 Keith Goganious RC	.10	.05
❑ 429 Mario Bailey RC	.10	.05
❑ 430 Chris Hakel RC	.10	.05
❑ 431 Keith Hamilton RC	.10	.05
❑ 432 Aaron Pierce RC	.10	.05
❑ 433 Amp Lee RC	.10	.05
❑ 434 Scott Lockwood RC	.10	.05
❑ 435 Ricardo McDonald RC	.10	.05
❑ 436 Dexter McNabb RC	.10	.05
❑ 437 Chris Mims RC	.20	.09
❑ 438 Mike Mooney RC	.10	.05
❑ 439 Ray Roberts RC	.10	.05
❑ 440 Patrick Rowe RC	.10	.05
❑ 441 Leon Searcy RC	.20	.09
❑ 442 Siran Stacy RC	.10	.05
❑ 443 Kevin Turner RC	.10	.05
❑ 444 Tommy Vardell RC	.20	.09
❑ 445 Bob Whitfield RC	.10	.05
❑ 446 Darryl Williams RC	.10	.05
❑ 447 Checklist 1-110	.10	.05
❑ 448 Checklist 111-224	.10	.05
❑ 449 Checklist 230-340 UER (Missing 225-229)	.10	.05
❑ 450 Checklist 341-450	.10	.05

1992 Ultra Award Winners

	MINT	NRMT
COMPLETE SET (10)	10.00	4.50
RANDOM INSERTS IN FOIL PACKS		
❑ 1 Mark Rypien	.30	.14
❑ 2 Cornelius Bennett UPI AFC Defensive POY	.60	.25
❑ 3 Anthony Munoz NFL Man of the Year	.60	.25
❑ 4 Lawrence Dawsey UPI NFC ROY	.60	.25
❑ 5 Thurman Thomas Pro Football Weekly NFL Offensive POY	1.25	.55
❑ 6 Michael Irvin Pro Bowl MVP	1.25	.55
❑ 7 Mike Croel UPI AFC ROY	.30	.14
❑ 8 Barry Sanders Maxwell Club POY	10.00	4.50
❑ 9 Pat Swilling AP Defensive POY	.60	.25
❑ 10 Leonard Russell Pro Football Weekly NFL Offensive ROY	.60	.25

1993 Ultra

	MINT	NRMT
COMPLETE SET (500)	25.00	11.00
COMMON CARD (1-500)	.10	.05
SEMISTARS	.20	.09
UNLISTED STARS	.40	.18
COMPLETE M.IRVIN SET (10)	8.00	3.60
CERT.IRVIN AUTOGRAPH	70.00	32.00
IRVIN: RANDOM INS.IN PACKS		
COMM.IRVIN SEND-OFF 11-12	2.00	.90
❑ 1 Vinnie Clark	.10	.05
❑ 2 Darion Conner	.10	.05
❑ 3 Eric Dickerson	.20	.09
❑ 4 Moe Gardner	.10	.05
❑ 5 Tim Green	.10	.05

❑ 6 Roger Harper RC	.10	.05
❑ 7 Michael Haynes	.20	.09
❑ 8 Bobby Hebert	.10	.05
❑ 9 Chris Hinton	.10	.05
❑ 10 Pierce Holt	.10	.05
❑ 11 Mike Kenn	.10	.05
❑ 12 Lincoln Kennedy RC	.10	.05
❑ 13 Chris Miller	.20	.09
❑ 14 Mike Pritchard	.20	.09
❑ 15 Andre Rison	.20	.09
❑ 16 Deion Sanders	.75	.35
❑ 17 Tony Smith	.10	.05
❑ 18 Jessie Tuggle	.10	.05
❑ 19 Howard Ballard	.10	.05
❑ 20 Don Beebe	.10	.05
❑ 21 Cornelius Bennett	.20	.09
❑ 22 Bill Brooks	.10	.05
❑ 23 Kenneth Davis	.10	.05
❑ 24 Phil Hansen	.10	.05
❑ 25 Henry Jones	.10	.05
❑ 26 Jim Kelly	.40	.18
❑ 27 Nate Odomes	.10	.05
❑ 28 John Parrella RC	.10	.05
❑ 29 Andre Reed	.20	.09
❑ 30 Frank Reich	.20	.09
❑ 31 Jim Ritcher	.10	.05
❑ 32 Bruce Smith	.40	.18
❑ 33 Thomas Smith RC	.20	.09
❑ 34 Darryl Talley	.10	.05
❑ 35 Steve Tasker	.20	.09
❑ 36 Thurman Thomas	.40	.18
❑ 37 Jeff Wright	.10	.05
❑ 38 Neal Anderson	.10	.05
❑ 39 Trace Armstrong	.10	.05
❑ 40 Mark Carrier DB	.10	.05
❑ 41 Curtis Conway RC	1.00	.45
❑ 42 Wendell Davis	.10	.05
❑ 43 Richard Dent	.20	.09
❑ 44 Shaun Gayle	.10	.05
❑ 45 Jim Harbaugh	.40	.18
❑ 46 Craig Heyward	.20	.09
❑ 47 Darren Lewis	.10	.05
❑ 48 Steve McMichael	.20	.09
❑ 49 William Perry	.20	.09
❑ 50 Carl Simpson RC	.10	.05
❑ 51 Alonzo Spellman	.10	.05
❑ 52 Keith Van Horne	.10	.05
❑ 53 Tom Waddle	.10	.05
❑ 54 Donnell Woolford	.10	.05
❑ 55 John Copeland RC	.20	.09
❑ 56 Derrick Fenner	.10	.05
❑ 57 James Francis	.10	.05
❑ 58 Harold Green	.10	.05
❑ 59 David Klingler	.10	.05
❑ 60 Tim Krumrie	.10	.05
❑ 61 Ricardo McDonald	.10	.05
❑ 62 Tony McGee RC	.20	.09
❑ 63 Carl Pickens	.40	.18
❑ 64 Lamar Rogers	.10	.05
❑ 65 Jay Schroeder	.10	.05
❑ 66 Daniel Stubbs	.10	.05
❑ 67 Steve Tovar RC	.10	.05
❑ 68 Alfred Williams	.10	.05
❑ 69 Darryl Williams	.10	.05
❑ 70 Jerry Ball	.10	.05
❑ 71 David Brandon	.10	.05
❑ 72 Rob Burnett	.10	.05
❑ 73 Mark Carrier WR	.20	.09

❑	74	Steve Everitt RC	.10	.05
❑	75	Dan Footman RC	.10	.05
❑	76	Leroy Hoard	.20	.09
❑	77	Michael Jackson	.20	.09
❑	78	Mike Johnson	.10	.05
❑	79	Bernie Kosar	.20	.09
❑	80	Clay Matthews	.20	.09
❑	81	Eric Metcalf	.20	.09
❑	82	Michael Dean Perry	.20	.09
❑	83	Vinny Testaverde	.20	.09
❑	84	Tommy Vardell	.10	.05
❑	85	Troy Aikman	1.50	.70
❑	86	Larry Brown DB	.10	.05
❑	87	Tony Casillas	.10	.05
❑	88	Thomas Everett	.10	.05
❑	89	Charles Haley	.20	.09
❑	90	Alvin Harper	.20	.09
❑	91	Michael Irvin	.40	.18
❑	92	Jim Jeffcoat	.10	.05
❑	93	Daryl Johnston	.40	.18
❑	94	Robert Jones	.10	.05
❑	95	Leon Lett RC	.20	.09
❑	96	Russell Maryland	.10	.05
❑	97	Nate Newton	.20	.09
❑	98	Ken Norton	.20	.09
❑	99	Jay Novacek	.20	.09
❑	100	Darrin Smith RC	.20	.09
❑	101	Emmitt Smith	3.00	1.35
❑	102	Kevin Smith	.20	.09
❑	103	Mark Stepnoski	.10	.05
❑	104	Tony Tolbert	.10	.05
❑	105	Kevin Williams RC	.40	.18
❑	106	Steve Atwater	.10	.05
❑	107	Rod Bernstine	.10	.05
❑	108	Mike Croel	.10	.05
❑	109	Robert Delpino	.10	.05
❑	110	Shane Dronett	.10	.05
❑	111	John Elway	3.00	1.35
❑	112	Simon Fletcher	.10	.05
❑	113	Greg Kragen	.10	.05
❑	114	Tommy Maddox	.10	.05
❑	115	Arthur Marshall RC	.10	.05
❑	116	Karl Mecklenburg	.10	.05
❑	117	Glyn Milburn RC	.40	.18
❑	118	Reggie Rivers RC	.10	.05
❑	119	Shannon Sharpe	.40	.18
❑	120	Dennis Smith	.10	.05
❑	121	Kenny Walker	.10	.05
❑	122	Dan Williams RC	.10	.05
❑	123	Bennie Blades	.10	.05
❑	124	Lomas Brown	.10	.05
❑	125	Bill Fralic	.10	.05
❑	126	Mel Gray	.20	.09
❑	127	Willie Green	.10	.05
❑	128	Jason Hanson	.10	.05
❑	129	Antonio London RC	.10	.05
❑	130	Ryan McNeil RC	.10	.05
❑	131	Herman Moore	1.00	.45
❑	132	Rodney Peete	.10	.05
❑	133	Brett Perriman	.40	.18
❑	134	Kelvin Pritchett	.10	.05
❑	135	Barry Sanders	3.00	1.35
❑	136	Tracy Scroggins	.10	.05
❑	137	Chris Spielman	.20	.09
❑	138	Pat Swilling	.10	.05
❑	139	Andre Ware	.10	.05
❑	140	Edgar Bennett	.40	.18
❑	141	Tony Bennett	.10	.05
❑	142	Matt Brock	.10	.05
❑	143	Terrell Buckley	.10	.05
❑	144	LeRoy Butler	.10	.05
❑	145	Mark Clayton	.10	.05
❑	146	Brett Favre	4.00	1.80
❑	147	Jackie Harris	.10	.05
❑	148	Johnny Holland	.10	.05
❑	149	Bill Maas	.10	.05
❑	150	Brian Noble	.10	.05
❑	151	Bryce Paup	.40	.18
❑	152	Ken Ruettgers	.10	.05
❑	153	Sterling Sharpe	.40	.18
❑	154	Wayne Simmons RC	.10	.05
❑	155	John Stephens	.10	.05
❑	156	George Teague RC	.20	.09
❑	157	Reggie White	.40	.18
❑	158	Micheal Barrow	.10	.05
❑	159	Cody Carlson	.10	.05
❑	160	Ray Childress	.10	.05
❑	161	Cris Dishman	.10	.05
❑	162	Curtis Duncan	.10	.05
❑	163	William Fuller	.10	.05
❑	164	Ernest Givins	.20	.09
❑	165	Brad Hopkins RC	.10	.05
❑	166	Haywood Jeffires	.20	.09
❑	167	Lamar Lathon	.10	.05
❑	168	Wilber Marshall	.10	.05
❑	169	Bruce Matthews	.10	.05
❑	170	Bubba McDowell	.10	.05
❑	171	Warren Moon	.40	.18
❑	172	Mike Munchak	.10	.05
❑	173	Eddie Robinson	.10	.05
❑	174	Al Smith	.10	.05
❑	175	Lorenzo White	.10	.05
❑	176	Lee Williams	.10	.05
❑	177	Chip Banks	.10	.05
❑	178	John Baylor	.10	.05
❑	179	Duane Bickett	.10	.05
❑	180	Kerry Cash	.10	.05
❑	181	Quentin Coryatt	.20	.09
❑	182	Rodney Culver	.10	.05
❑	183	Steve Emtman	.10	.05
❑	184	Jeff George	.40	.18
❑	185	Jeff Herrod	.10	.05
❑	186	Jessie Hester	.10	.05
❑	187	Anthony Johnson	.20	.09
❑	188	Reggie Langhorne	.10	.05
❑	189	Roosevelt Potts RC	.10	.05
❑	190	Rohn Stark	.10	.05
❑	191	Clarence Verdin	.10	.05
❑	192	Will Wolford	.10	.05
❑	193	Marcus Allen	.40	.18
❑	194	John Alt	.10	.05
❑	195	Tim Barnett	.10	.05
❑	196	J.J.Birden	.10	.05
❑	197	Dale Carter	.10	.05
❑	198	Willie Davis	.40	.18
❑	199	Jaime Fields RC	.10	.05
❑	200	Dave Krieg	.20	.09
❑	201	Nick Lowery	.10	.05
❑	202	Charles Mincy RC	.10	.05
❑	203	Joe Montana	3.00	1.35
❑	204	Christian Okoye	.10	.05
❑	205	Dan Saleaumua	.10	.05
❑	206	Will Shields RC	.10	.05
❑	207	Tracy Simien	.10	.05
❑	208	Neil Smith	.40	.18
❑	209	Derrick Thomas	.40	.18
❑	210	Harvey Williams	.20	.09
❑	211	Barry Word	.10	.05
❑	212	Eddie Anderson	.10	.05
❑	213	Patrick Bates RC	.10	.05
❑	214	Nick Bell	.10	.05
❑	215	Tim Brown	.40	.18
❑	216	Willie Gault	.10	.05
❑	217	Gaston Green	.10	.05
❑	218	Billy Joe Hobert RC	.40	.18
❑	219	Ethan Horton	.10	.05
❑	220	Jeff Hostetler	.20	.09
❑	221	James Lofton	.20	.09
❑	222	Howie Long	.20	.09
❑	223	Todd Marinovich	.10	.05
❑	224	Terry McDaniel	.10	.05
❑	225	Winston Moss	.10	.05
❑	226	Anthony Smith	.10	.05
❑	227	Greg Townsend	.10	.05
❑	228	Aaron Wallace	.10	.05
❑	229	Lionel Washington	.10	.05
❑	230	Steve Wisniewski	.10	.05
❑	231	Flipper Anderson	.10	.05
❑	232	Jerome Bettis RC	2.00	.90
❑	233	Marc Boutte	.10	.05
❑	234	Shane Conlan	.10	.05
❑	235	Troy Drayton RC	.20	.09
❑	236	Henry Ellard	.20	.09
❑	237	Jim Everett	.20	.09
❑	238	Cleveland Gary	.10	.05
❑	239	Sean Gilbert	.20	.09
❑	240	Darryl Henley	.10	.05
❑	241	David Lang	.10	.05
❑	242	Todd Lyght	.10	.05
❑	243	Anthony Newman	.10	.05
❑	244	Roman Phifer	.10	.05
❑	245	Gerald Robinson	.10	.05
❑	246	Henry Rolling	.10	.05
❑	247	Jackie Slater	.10	.05
❑	248	Keith Byars	.10	.05
❑	249	Marco Coleman	.10	.05
❑	250	Bryan Cox	.10	.05
❑	251	Jeff Cross	.10	.05
❑	252	Irving Fryar	.20	.09
❑	253	Mark Higgs	.10	.05
❑	254	Dwight Hollier RC	.10	.05
❑	255	Mark Ingram	.10	.05
❑	256	Keith Jackson	.20	.09
❑	257	Terry Kirby RC	.40	.18
❑	258	Dan Marino	3.00	1.35
❑	259	O.J.McDuffie RC	1.50	.70
❑	260	John Offerdahl	.10	.05
❑	261	Louis Oliver	.10	.05
❑	262	Pete Stoyanovich	.10	.05
❑	263	Troy Vincent	.10	.05
❑	264	Richmond Webb	.10	.05
❑	265	Jarvis Williams	.10	.05
❑	266	Terry Allen	.40	.18
❑	267	Anthony Carter	.20	.09
❑	268	Cris Carter	.75	.35
❑	269	Roger Craig	.20	.09
❑	270	Jack Del Rio	.10	.05
❑	271	Chris Doleman	.10	.05
❑	272	Qadry Ismail RC	.40	.18
❑	273	Steve Jordan	.10	.05
❑	274	Randall McDaniel	.10	.05
❑	275	Audray McMillian	.10	.05
❑	276	John Randle	.10	.05
❑	277	Sean Salisbury	.10	.05
❑	278	Todd Scott	.10	.05
❑	279	Robert Smith RC	2.00	.90
❑	280	Henry Thomas	.10	.05
❑	281	Ray Agnew	.10	.05
❑	282	Bruce Armstrong	.10	.05
❑	283	Drew Bledsoe RC	6.00	2.70
❑	284	Vincent Brisby RC	.40	.18
❑	285	Vincent Brown	.10	.05
❑	286	Eugene Chung	.10	.05
❑	287	Marv Cook	.10	.05
❑	288	Pat Harlow	.10	.05
❑	289	Jerome Henderson	.10	.05
❑	290	Greg McMurtry	.10	.05
❑	291	Leonard Russell	.20	.09
❑	292	Chris Singleton	.10	.05
❑	293	Chris Slade RC	.20	.09
❑	294	Andre Tippett	.10	.05
❑	295	Brent Williams	.10	.05
❑	296	Scott Zolak	.10	.05
❑	297	Morten Andersen	.10	.05
❑	298	Gene Atkins	.10	.05
❑	299	Mike Buck	.10	.05
❑	300	Toi Cook	.10	.05
❑	301	Jim Dombrowski	.10	.05
❑	302	Vaughn Dunbar	.10	.05
❑	303	Quinn Early	.20	.09
❑	304	Joel Hilgenberg	.10	.05
❑	305	Dalton Hilliard	.10	.05
❑	306	Rickey Jackson	.10	.05
❑	307	Vaughan Johnson	.10	.05
❑	308	Reginald Jones	.10	.05
❑	309	Eric Martin	.10	.05
❑	310	Wayne Martin	.10	.05
❑	311	Sam Mills	.10	.05
❑	312	Brad Muster	.10	.05
❑	313	Willie Roaf RC	.20	.09
❑	314	Irv Smith RC	.10	.05
❑	315	Wade Wilson	.10	.05
❑	316	Carlton Bailey	.10	.05
❑	317	Michael Brooks	.10	.05
❑	318	Derek Brown TE	.10	.05
❑	319	Marcus Buckley RC	.10	.05
❑	320	Jarrod Bunch	.10	.05
❑	321	Mark Collins	.10	.05
❑	322	Eric Dorsey	.10	.05
❑	323	Rodney Hampton	.40	.18
❑	324	Mark Jackson	.10	.05
❑	325	Pepper Johnson	.10	.05
❑	326	Ed McCaffrey	.20	.09
❑	327	Dave Meggett	.10	.05
❑	328	Bart Oates	.10	.05
❑	329	Mike Sherrard	.10	.05
❑	330	Phil Simms	.20	.09
❑	331	Michael Strahan RC	.10	.05

❑ 332 Lawrence Taylor .40 .18
❑ 333 Brad Baxter .10 .05
❑ 334 Chris Burkett .10 .05
❑ 335 Kyle Clifton .10 .05
❑ 336 Boomer Esiason .20 .09
❑ 337 James Hasty .10 .05
❑ 338 Johnny Johnson .10 .05
❑ 339 Marvin Jones RC .10 .05
❑ 340 Jeff Lageman .10 .05
❑ 341 Mo Lewis .10 .05
❑ 342 Ronnie Lott .20 .09
❑ 343 Leonard Marshall .10 .05
❑ 344 Johnny Mitchell .10 .05
❑ 345 Rob Moore .20 .09
❑ 346 Browning Nagle .10 .05
❑ 347 Coleman Rudolph RC .10 .05
❑ 348 Blair Thomas .10 .05
❑ 349 Eric Thomas .10 .05
❑ 350 Brian Washington .10 .05
❑ 351 Marvin Washington .10 .05
❑ 352 Eric Allen .10 .05
❑ 353 Victor Bailey RC .10 .05
❑ 354 Fred Barnett .20 .09
❑ 355 Mark Bavaro .10 .05
❑ 356 Randall Cunningham .40 .18
❑ 357 Byron Evans .10 .05
❑ 358 Andy Harmon .20 .09
❑ 359 Tim Harris .10 .05
❑ 360 Lester Holmes .10 .05
❑ 361 Seth Joyner .10 .05
❑ 362 Keith Millard .10 .05
❑ 363 Leonard Renfro RC .10 .05
❑ 364 Heath Sherman .10 .05
❑ 365 Vai Sikahema .10 .05
❑ 366 Clyde Simmons .10 .05
❑ 367 William Thomas .10 .05
❑ 368 Herschel Walker .20 .09
❑ 369 Andre Waters .10 .05
❑ 370 Calvin Williams .20 .09
❑ 371 Johnny Bailey .10 .05
❑ 372 Steve Beuerlein .10 .05
❑ 373 Rich Camarillo .10 .05
❑ 374 Chuck Cecil .10 .05
❑ 375 Chris Chandler .20 .09
❑ 376 Gary Clark .20 .09
❑ 377 Ben Coleman RC .10 .05
❑ 378 Ernest Dye RC .10 .05
❑ 379 Ken Harvey .10 .05
❑ 380 Garrison Hearst RC 2.00 .90
❑ 381 Randal Hill .10 .05
❑ 382 Robert Massey .10 .05
❑ 383 Freddie Joe Nunn .10 .05
❑ 384 Ricky Proehl .10 .05
❑ 385 Luis Sharpe .10 .05
❑ 386 Tyronne Stowe .10 .05
❑ 387 Eric Swann .20 .09
❑ 388 Aeneas Williams .10 .05
❑ 389 Chad Brown RC .20 .09
❑ 390 Dermontti Dawson .10 .05
❑ 391 Donald Evans .10 .05
❑ 392 Deon Figures RC .20 .09
❑ 393 Barry Foster .20 .09
❑ 394 Jeff Graham .20 .09
❑ 395 Eric Green .10 .05
❑ 396 Kevin Greene .40 .18
❑ 397 Carlton Haselrig .10 .05
❑ 398 Andre Hastings RC .40 .18
❑ 399 D.J. Johnson .10 .05
❑ 400 Carnell Lake .10 .05
❑ 401 Greg Lloyd .40 .18
❑ 402 Neil O'Donnell .40 .18
❑ 403 Darren Perry .10 .05
❑ 404 Mike Tomczak .10 .05
❑ 405 Rod Woodson .40 .18
❑ 406 Eric Bieniemy .10 .05
❑ 407 Marion Butts .10 .05
❑ 408 Gill Byrd .10 .05
❑ 409 Darren Carrington RC .10 .05
❑ 410 Darrien Gordon RC .10 .05
❑ 411 Burt Grossman .10 .05
❑ 412 Courtney Hall .10 .05
❑ 413 Ronnie Harmon .10 .05
❑ 414 Stan Humphries .40 .18
❑ 415 Nate Lewis .10 .05
❑ 416 Natrone Means RC 1.50 .70
❑ 417 Anthony Miller .20 .09
❑ 418 Chris Mims .10 .05
❑ 419 Leslie O'Neal .20 .09
❑ 420 Gary Plummer .10 .05
❑ 421 Stanley Richard .10 .05
❑ 422 Junior Seau .40 .18
❑ 423 Harry Swayne .10 .05
❑ 424 Jerrol Williams .10 .05
❑ 425 Harris Barton .10 .05
❑ 426 Steve Bono .40 .18
❑ 427 Kevin Fagan .10 .05
❑ 428 Don Griffin .10 .05
❑ 429 Dana Hall .10 .05
❑ 430 Adrian Hardy .10 .05
❑ 431 Brent Jones .20 .09
❑ 432 Todd Kelly RC .10 .05
❑ 433 Amp Lee .10 .05
❑ 434 Tim McDonald .10 .05
❑ 435 Guy McIntyre .10 .05
❑ 436 Tom Rathman .10 .05
❑ 437 Jerry Rice 2.00 .90
❑ 438 Bill Romanowski .10 .05
❑ 439 Dana Stubblefield RC .40 .18
❑ 440 John Taylor .20 .09
❑ 441 Steve Wallace .10 .05
❑ 442 Michael Walter .10 .05
❑ 443 Ricky Watters .40 .18
❑ 444 Steve Young 1.50 .70
❑ 445 Robert Blackmon .10 .05
❑ 446 Brian Blades .20 .09
❑ 447 Jeff Bryant .10 .05
❑ 448 Ferrell Edmunds .10 .05
❑ 449 Carlton Gray RC .10 .05
❑ 450 Dwayne Harper .10 .05
❑ 451 Andy Heck .10 .05
❑ 452 Tommy Kane .10 .05
❑ 453 Cortez Kennedy .20 .09
❑ 454 Kelvin Martin .10 .05
❑ 455 Dan McGwire .10 .05
❑ 456 Rick Mirer RC .75 .35
❑ 457 Rufus Porter .10 .05
❑ 458 Ray Roberts .10 .05
❑ 459 Eugene Robinson .10 .05
❑ 460 Chris Warren .20 .09
❑ 461 John L. Williams .10 .05
❑ 462 Gary Anderson RB .10 .05
❑ 463 Tyji Armstrong .10 .05
❑ 464 Reggie Cobb .10 .05
❑ 465 Eric Curry RC .10 .05
❑ 466 Lawrence Dawsey .10 .05
❑ 467 Steve DeBerg .10 .05
❑ 468 Santana Dotson .20 .09
❑ 469 Demetrius DuBose RC .10 .05
❑ 470 Paul Gruber .10 .05
❑ 471 Ron Hall .10 .05
❑ 472 Courtney Hawkins .10 .05
❑ 473 Hardy Nickerson .20 .09
❑ 474 Ricky Reynolds .10 .05
❑ 475 Broderick Thomas .10 .05
❑ 476 Mark Wheeler .10 .05
❑ 477 Jimmy Williams .10 .05
❑ 478 Carl Banks .10 .05
❑ 479 Reggie Brooks RC .20 .09
❑ 480 Earnest Byner .10 .05
❑ 481 Tom Carter RC .20 .09
❑ 482 Andre Collins .10 .05
❑ 483 Brad Edwards .10 .05
❑ 484 Ricky Ervins .10 .05
❑ 485 Kurt Gouveia .10 .05
❑ 486 Darrell Green .10 .05
❑ 487 Desmond Howard .20 .09
❑ 488 Jim Lachey .10 .05
❑ 489 Chip Lohmiller .10 .05
❑ 490 Charles Mann .10 .05
❑ 491 Tim McGee .10 .05
❑ 492 Brian Mitchell .20 .09
❑ 493 Art Monk .20 .09
❑ 494 Mark Rypien .10 .05
❑ 495 Ricky Sanders .10 .05
❑ 496 Checklist 1-126 .10 .05
Chip Lohmiller
❑ 497 Checklist 127-254 .10 .05
Ricky Proehl
❑ 498 Checklist 255-382 .10 .05
Randall Cunningham
❑ 499 Checklist 383-500 .10 .05
Dave Meggett
❑ 500 Inserts Checklist .10 .05
William Perry

1993 Ultra All-Rookies

	MINT	NRMT
COMPLETE SET (10)	50.00	22.00
RANDOM INSERTS IN PACKS		

❑ 1 Patrick Bates .40 .18
❑ 2 Jerome Bettis 8.00 3.60
❑ 3 Drew Bledsoe 25.00 11.00
❑ 4 Curtis Conway 4.00 1.80
❑ 5 Garrison Hearst 8.00 3.60
❑ 6 Qadry Ismail 1.50 .70
❑ 7 Marvin Jones .40 .18
❑ 8 Glyn Milburn 1.50 .70
❑ 9 Rick Mirer 3.00 1.35
❑ 10 Kevin Williams 1.50 .70

1993 Ultra Award Winners

	MINT	NRMT
COMPLETE SET (10)	50.00	22.00
RANDOM INSERTS IN PACKS		

❑ 1 Troy Aikman 20.00 9.00
❑ 2 Dale Carter 1.25 .55
❑ 3 Chris Doleman 1.25 .55
❑ 4 Santana Dotson 2.50 1.10
❑ 5 Barry Foster 2.50 1.10
❑ 6 Jason Hanson 1.25 .55
❑ 7 Cortez Kennedy 2.50 1.10
❑ 8 Carl Pickens 5.00 2.20
❑ 9 Steve Tasker 2.50 1.10
❑ 10 Steve Young 20.00 9.00

1993 Ultra League Leaders

	MINT	NRMT
COMPLETE SET (10)	50.00	22.00
RANDOM INSERTS IN PACKS		

❑ 1 Haywood Jeffires 2.00 .90
❑ 2 Henry Jones 1.00 .45
❑ 3 Audray McMillian 1.00 .45
❑ 4 Warren Moon 4.00 1.80
❑ 5 Leslie O'Neal 2.00 .90

❑ 6 Deion Sanders	8.00	3.60
❑ 7 Sterling Sharpe	4.00	1.80
❑ 8 Clyde Simmons	1.00	.45
❑ 9 Emmitt Smith	30.00	13.50
❑ 10 Thurman Thomas	4.00	1.80

1993 Ultra Stars

	MINT	NRMT
COMPLETE SET (10)	60.00	27.00
RANDOM INSERTS IN JUMBO PACKS		

❑ 1 Brett Favre	40.00	18.00
❑ 2 Barry Foster	2.00	.90
❑ 3 Michael Irvin	4.00	1.80
❑ 4 Cortez Kennedy	2.00	.90
❑ 5 Deion Sanders	8.00	3.60
❑ 6 Junior Seau	4.00	1.80
❑ 7 Derrick Thomas	4.00	1.80
❑ 8 Ricky Watters	4.00	1.80
❑ 9 Reggie White	4.00	1.80
❑ 10 Steve Young	15.00	6.75

1993 Ultra Touchdown Kings

	MINT	NRMT
COMPLETE SET (10)	70.00	32.00
RANDOM INSERTS IN PACKS....		

❑ 1 Rodney Hampton	2.00	.90
❑ 2 Dan Marino	15.00	6.75
❑ 3 Art Monk	1.00	.45
❑ 4 Joe Montana	15.00	6.75
❑ 5 Jerry Rice	10.00	4.50
❑ 6 Andre Rison	1.00	.45
❑ 7 Barry Sanders	15.00	6.75
❑ 8 Sterling Sharpe	2.00	.90
❑ 9 Emmitt Smith	15.00	6.75
❑ 10 Thurman Thomas	2.00	.90

1994 Ultra

	MINT	NRMT
COMPLETE SET (525)	35.00	16.00
COMP.SERIES 1 (325)	20.00	9.00
COMP.SERIES 2 (200)	15.00	6.75
COMMON CARD (1-525)	.10	.05
SEMISTARS	.20	.09
UNLISTED STARS	.40	.18
ONE INSERT PER PACK, TWO PER JUMBO		
COMPLETE R.MIRER SET (10)	4.00	1.80
CERT.MIRER AUTOGRAPH	60.00	27.00
MIRER: RANDOM INS.IN PACKS		
MIRER SEND-OFF 11-12	1.50	.70

❑ 1 Steve Beuerlein	.10	.05
❑ 2 Gary Clark	.20	.09
❑ 3 Randal Hill	.10	.05
❑ 4 Seth Joyner	.10	.05
❑ 5 Jamir Miller RC	.10	.05
❑ 6 Ronald Moore	.10	.05
❑ 7 Luis Sharpe	.10	.05
❑ 8 Clyde Simmons	.10	.05
❑ 9 Eric Swann	.20	.09
❑ 10 Aeneas Williams	.10	.05
❑ 11 Chris Doleman	.10	.05
❑ 12 Bert Emanuel RC	1.00	.45
❑ 13 Moe Gardner	.10	.05
❑ 14 Jeff George	.40	.18
❑ 15 Roger Harper	.10	.05
❑ 16 Pierce Holt	.10	.05
❑ 17 Lincoln Kennedy	.10	.05
❑ 18 Erric Pegram	.10	.05
❑ 19 Andre Rison	.20	.09
❑ 20 Deion Sanders	.75	.35
❑ 21 Jessie Tuggle	.10	.05
❑ 22 Cornelius Bennett	.20	.09
❑ 23 Bill Brooks	.10	.05
❑ 24 Jeff Burris RC	.20	.09
❑ 25 Kent Hull	.10	.05
❑ 26 Henry Jones	.10	.05
❑ 27 Jim Kelly	.40	.18
❑ 28 Marvcus Patton	.10	.05
❑ 29 Andre Reed	.20	.09
❑ 30 Bruce Smith	.40	.18
❑ 31 Thomas Smith	.10	.05
❑ 32 Thurman Thomas	.40	.18
❑ 33 Jeff Wright	.10	.05
❑ 34 Trace Armstrong	.10	.05
❑ 35 Mark Carrier DB	.10	.05
❑ 36 Dante Jones	.10	.05
❑ 37 Erik Kramer	.20	.09
❑ 38 Terry Obee	.10	.05
❑ 39 Alonzo Spellman	.10	.05
❑ 40 John Thierry RC	.10	.05
❑ 41 Tom Waddle	.10	.05
❑ 42 Donnell Woolford	.10	.05
❑ 43 Tim Worley	.10	.05
❑ 44 Chris Zorich	.10	.05
❑ 45 John Copeland	.10	.05
❑ 46 Harold Green	.10	.05
❑ 47 David Klingler	.10	.05
❑ 48 Ricardo McDonald	.10	.05
❑ 49 Tony McGee	.10	.05
❑ 50 Louis Oliver	.10	.05
❑ 51 Carl Pickens	.40	.18
❑ 52 Darnay Scott RC	1.25	.55
❑ 53 Steve Tovar	.10	.05
❑ 54 Dan Wilkinson RC	.20	.09
❑ 55 Darryl Williams	.10	.05
❑ 56 Derrick Alexander WR RC	1.00	.45
❑ 57 Michael Jackson	.20	.09
❑ 58 Tony Jones	.10	.05
❑ 59 Antonio Langham RC	.20	.09
❑ 60 Eric Metcalf	.20	.09
❑ 61 Stevon Moore	.10	.05
❑ 62 Michael Dean Perry	.20	.09
❑ 63 Anthony Pleasant	.10	.05
❑ 64 Vinny Testaverde	.20	.09
❑ 65 Eric Turner	.10	.05
❑ 66 Tommy Vardell	.10	.05
❑ 67 Troy Aikman	1.50	.70
❑ 68 Larry Brown DB	.10	.05
❑ 69 Shante Carver RC	.10	.05
❑ 70 Charles Haley	.20	.09
❑ 71 Michael Irvin	.40	.18
❑ 72 Leon Lett	.10	.05
❑ 73 Nate Newton	.10	.05
❑ 74 Jay Novacek	.20	.09
❑ 75 Darrin Smith	.10	.05
❑ 76 Emmitt Smith	2.50	1.10
❑ 77 Tony Tolbert	.10	.05
❑ 78 Erik Williams	.10	.05
❑ 79 Kevin Williams WR	.20	.09
❑ 80 Steve Atwater	.10	.05
❑ 81 Rod Bernstine	.10	.05
❑ 82 Ray Crockett	.10	.05
❑ 83 Mike Croel	.10	.05
❑ 84 Shane Dronett	.10	.05
❑ 85 Jason Elam	.10	.05
❑ 86 John Elway	3.00	1.35
❑ 87 Simon Fletcher	.10	.05
❑ 88 Glyn Milburn	.20	.09
❑ 89 Anthony Miller	.20	.09
❑ 90 Shannon Sharpe	.20	.09
❑ 91 Gary Zimmerman	.10	.05
❑ 92 Bennie Blades	.10	.05
❑ 93 Lomas Brown	.10	.05
❑ 94 Mel Gray	.10	.05
❑ 95 Jason Hanson	.10	.05
❑ 96 Ryan McNeil	.10	.05
❑ 97 Scott Mitchell	.40	.18
❑ 98 Herman Moore	.40	.18
❑ 99 Johnnie Morton RC	1.25	.55
❑ 100 Robert Porcher	.10	.05
❑ 101 Barry Sanders	3.00	1.35
❑ 102 Chris Spielman	.20	.09
❑ 103 Pat Swilling	.10	.05
❑ 104 Edgar Bennett	.40	.18
❑ 105 Terrell Buckley	.10	.05
❑ 106 Reggie Cobb	.10	.05
❑ 107 Brett Favre	3.00	1.35
❑ 108 Sean Jones	.10	.05
❑ 109 Ken Ruettgers	.10	.05
❑ 110 Sterling Sharpe	.20	.09
❑ 111 Wayne Simmons	.10	.05
❑ 112 Aaron Taylor RC	.10	.05
❑ 113 George Teague	.10	.05
❑ 114 Reggie White	.40	.18
❑ 115 Micheal Barrow	.10	.05
❑ 116 Gary Brown	.10	.05
❑ 117 Cody Carlson	.10	.05
❑ 118 Ray Childress	.10	.05
❑ 119 Cris Dishman	.10	.05
❑ 120 Henry Ford RC	.10	.05
❑ 121 Haywood Jeffires	.20	.09
❑ 122 Bruce Matthews	.10	.05
❑ 123 Bubba McDowell	.10	.05
❑ 124 Marcus Robertson	.10	.05
❑ 125 Eddie Robinson	.10	.05
❑ 126 Webster Slaughter	.10	.05
❑ 127 Trev Alberts RC	.20	.09
❑ 128 Tony Bennett	.10	.05
❑ 129 Ray Buchanan	.10	.05
❑ 130 Quentin Coryatt	.10	.05
❑ 131 Eugene Daniel	.10	.05

Card	Player	Price	Price
❑ 132	Steve Emtman	.10	.05
❑ 133	Marshall Faulk RC	4.00	1.80
❑ 134	Jim Harbaugh	.40	.18
❑ 135	Roosevelt Potts	.10	.05
❑ 136	Rohn Stark	.10	.05
❑ 137	Marcus Allen	.40	.18
❑ 138	Donnell Bennett RC	.40	.18
❑ 139	Dale Carter	.10	.05
❑ 140	Tony Casillas	.10	.05
❑ 141	Mark Collins	.10	.05
❑ 142	Willie Davis	.20	.09
❑ 143	Tim Grunhard	.10	.05
❑ 144	Greg Hill RC	1.00	.45
❑ 145	Joe Montana	3.00	1.35
❑ 146	Tracy Simien	.10	.05
❑ 147	Neil Smith	.40	.18
❑ 148	Derrick Thomas	.40	.18
❑ 149	Tim Brown	.40	.18
❑ 150	James Folston RC	.10	.05
❑ 151	Rob Fredrickson RC	.20	.09
❑ 152	Jeff Hostetler	.20	.09
❑ 153	Rocket Ismail	.20	.09
❑ 154	James Jett	.10	.05
❑ 155	Terry McDaniel	.10	.05
❑ 156	Winston Moss	.10	.05
❑ 157	Greg Robinson	.10	.05
❑ 158	Anthony Smith	.10	.05
❑ 159	Steve Wisniewski	.10	.05
❑ 160	Flipper Anderson	.10	.05
❑ 161	Jerome Bettis	.40	.18
❑ 162	Isaac Bruce RC	4.00	1.80
❑ 163	Shane Conlan	.10	.05
❑ 164	Wayne Gandy RC	.10	.05
❑ 165	Sean Gilbert	.10	.05
❑ 166	Todd Lyght	.10	.05
❑ 167	Chris Miller	.10	.05
❑ 168	Anthony Newman	.10	.05
❑ 169	Roman Phifer	.10	.05
❑ 170	Jackie Slater	.10	.05
❑ 171	Gene Atkins	.10	.05
❑ 172	Aubrey Beavers RC	.10	.05
❑ 173	Tim Bowens RC	.20	.09
❑ 174	J.B. Brown	.10	.05
❑ 175	Marco Coleman	.10	.05
❑ 176	Bryan Cox	.10	.05
❑ 177	Irving Fryar	.20	.09
❑ 178	Terry Kirby	.40	.18
❑ 179	Dan Marino	3.00	1.35
❑ 180	Troy Vincent	.10	.05
❑ 181	Richmond Webb	.10	.05
❑ 182	Terry Allen	.20	.09
❑ 183	Cris Carter	.75	.35
❑ 184	Jack Del Rio	.10	.05
❑ 185	Vencie Glenn	.10	.05
❑ 186	Randall McDaniel	.10	.05
❑ 187	Warren Moon	.40	.18
❑ 188	David Palmer RC	1.00	.45
❑ 189	John Randle	.10	.05
❑ 190	Todd Scott	.10	.05
❑ 191	Todd Steussie RC	.20	.09
❑ 192	Henry Thomas	.10	.05
❑ 193	Dewayne Washington RC	.20	.09
❑ 194	Bruce Armstrong	.10	.05
❑ 195	Harlon Barnett	.10	.05
❑ 196	Drew Bledsoe	1.50	.70
❑ 197	Vincent Brisby	.40	.18
❑ 198	Vincent Brown	.10	.05
❑ 199	Marion Butts	.10	.05
❑ 200	Ben Coates	.40	.18
❑ 201	Todd Collins	.10	.05
❑ 202	Maurice Hurst	.10	.05
❑ 203	Willie McGinest RC	.40	.18
❑ 204	Ricky Reynolds	.10	.05
❑ 205	Chris Slade	.10	.05
❑ 206	Mario Bates RC	.40	.18
❑ 207	Derek Brown RBK	.10	.05
❑ 208	Vince Buck	.10	.05
❑ 209	Quinn Early	.20	.09
❑ 210	Jim Everett	.20	.09
❑ 211	Michael Haynes	.20	.09
❑ 212	Tyrone Hughes	.20	.09
❑ 213	Joe Johnson RC	.10	.05
❑ 214	Vaughan Johnson	.10	.05
❑ 215	Willie Roaf	.10	.05
❑ 216	Renaldo Turnbull	.10	.05
❑ 217	Michael Brooks	.10	.05
❑ 218	Dave Brown	.20	.09
❑ 219	Howard Cross	.10	.05
❑ 220	Stacey Dillard	.10	.05
❑ 221	Jumbo Elliott	.10	.05
❑ 222	Keith Hamilton	.10	.05
❑ 223	Rodney Hampton	.40	.18
❑ 224	Thomas Lewis RC	.20	.09
❑ 225	Dave Meggett	.10	.05
❑ 226	Corey Miller	.10	.05
❑ 227	Thomas Randolph RC	.10	.05
❑ 228	Mike Sherrard	.10	.05
❑ 229	Kyle Clifton	.10	.05
❑ 230	Boomer Esiason	.20	.09
❑ 231	Aaron Glenn RC	.20	.09
❑ 232	James Hasty	.10	.05
❑ 233	Bobby Houston	.10	.05
❑ 234	Johnny Johnson	.10	.05
❑ 235	Mo Lewis	.10	.05
❑ 236	Ronnie Lott	.20	.09
❑ 237	Rob Moore	.20	.09
❑ 238	Marvin Washington	.10	.05
❑ 239	Ryan Yarborough RC	.10	.05
❑ 240	Eric Allen	.10	.05
❑ 241	Victor Bailey	.10	.05
❑ 242	Fred Barnett	.20	.09
❑ 243	Mark Bavaro	.10	.05
❑ 244	Randall Cunningham	.40	.18
❑ 245	Byron Evans	.10	.05
❑ 246	William Fuller	.10	.05
❑ 247	Andy Harmon	.10	.05
❑ 248	William Perry	.20	.09
❑ 249	Herschel Walker	.20	.09
❑ 250	Bernard Williams RC	.10	.05
❑ 251	Dermontti Dawson	.10	.05
❑ 252	Deon Figures	.10	.05
❑ 253	Barry Foster	.10	.05
❑ 254	Kevin Greene	.40	.18
❑ 255	Charles Johnson RC	.40	.18
❑ 256	Levon Kirkland	.10	.05
❑ 257	Greg Lloyd	.40	.18
❑ 258	Neil O'Donnell	.40	.18
❑ 259	Darren Perry	.10	.05
❑ 260	Dwight Stone	.10	.05
❑ 261	Rod Woodson	.40	.18
❑ 262	John Carney	.10	.05
❑ 263	Issac Davis RC	.10	.05
❑ 264	Courtney Hall	.10	.05
❑ 265	Ronnie Harmon	.10	.05
❑ 266	Stan Humphries	.40	.18
❑ 267	Vance Johnson	.10	.05
❑ 268	Natrone Means	.40	.18
❑ 269	Chris Mims	.10	.05
❑ 270	Leslie O'Neal	.10	.05
❑ 271	Stanley Richard	.10	.05
❑ 272	Junior Seau	.40	.18
❑ 273	Harris Barton	.10	.05
❑ 274	Dennis Brown	.10	.05
❑ 275	Eric Davis	.10	.05
❑ 276	William Floyd RC	.40	.18
❑ 277	John Johnson	.10	.05
❑ 278	Tim McDonald	.10	.05
❑ 279	Ken Norton Jr.	.20	.09
❑ 280	Jerry Rice	1.50	.70
❑ 281	Jesse Sapolu	.10	.05
❑ 282	Dana Stubblefield	.40	.18
❑ 283	Ricky Watters	.40	.18
❑ 284	Bryant Young RC	.40	.18
❑ 285	Steve Young	1.00	.45
❑ 286	Sam Adams RC	.20	.09
❑ 287	Brian Blades	.20	.09
❑ 288	Ferrell Edmunds	.10	.05
❑ 289	Patrick Hunter	.10	.05
❑ 290	Cortez Kennedy	.20	.09
❑ 291	Rick Mirer	.40	.18
❑ 292	Nate Odomes	.10	.05
❑ 293	Ray Roberts	.10	.05
❑ 294	Eugene Robinson	.10	.05
❑ 295	Rod Stephens	.10	.05
❑ 296	Chris Warren	.20	.09
❑ 297	Marty Carter	.10	.05
❑ 298	Horace Copeland	.10	.05
❑ 299	Eric Curry	.10	.05
❑ 300	Santana Dotson	.20	.09
❑ 301	Craig Erickson	.10	.05
❑ 302	Paul Gruber	.10	.05
❑ 303	Courtney Hawkins	.10	.05
❑ 304	Martin Mayhew	.10	.05
❑ 305	Hardy Nickerson	.20	.09
❑ 306	Errict Rhett RC	1.50	.70
❑ 307	Vince Workman	.10	.05
❑ 308	Reggie Brooks	.20	.09
❑ 309	Tom Carter	.10	.05
❑ 310	Andre Collins	.10	.05
❑ 311	Brad Edwards	.10	.05
❑ 312	Kurt Gouveia	.10	.05
❑ 313	Darrell Green	.10	.05
❑ 314	Ethan Horton	.10	.05
❑ 315	Desmond Howard	.20	.09
❑ 316	Tre Johnson RC	.10	.05
❑ 317	Sterling Palmer RC	.10	.05
❑ 318	Heath Shuler RC	.40	.18
❑ 319	Tyronne Stowe	.10	.05
❑ 320	NFL 75th Anniversary	.10	.05
❑ 321	Checklist	.10	.05
❑ 322	Checklist	.10	.05
❑ 323	Checklist	.10	.05
❑ 324	Checklist	.10	.05
❑ 325	Checklist	.10	.05
❑ 326	Garrison Hearst	.40	.18
❑ 327	Eric Hill	.10	.05
❑ 328	Seth Joyner	.10	.05
❑ 329	Jim McMahon	.10	.05
❑ 330	Jamir Miller	.10	.05
❑ 331	Ricky Proehl	.10	.05
❑ 332	Clyde Simmons	.10	.05
❑ 333	Chris Doleman	.10	.05
❑ 334	Bert Emanuel	.40	.18
❑ 335	Jeff George	.40	.18
❑ 336	D.J. Johnson	.10	.05
❑ 337	Terance Mathis	.20	.09
❑ 338	Clay Matthews	.10	.05
❑ 339	Tony Smith	.10	.05
❑ 340	Don Beebe	.10	.05
❑ 341	Bucky Brooks RC	.10	.05
❑ 342	Jeff Burris	.20	.09
❑ 343	Kenneth Davis	.10	.05
❑ 344	Phil Hansen	.10	.05
❑ 345	Pete Metzelaars	.10	.05
❑ 346	Darryl Talley	.10	.05
❑ 347	Joe Cain	.10	.05
❑ 348	Curtis Conway	.40	.18
❑ 349	Shaun Gayle	.10	.05
❑ 350	Chris Gedney	.10	.05
❑ 351	Erik Kramer	.20	.09
❑ 352	Vinson Smith	.10	.05
❑ 353	John Thierry	.10	.05
❑ 354	Lewis Tillman	.10	.05
❑ 355	Mike Brim	.10	.05
❑ 356	Derrick Fenner	.10	.05
❑ 357	James Francis	.10	.05
❑ 358	Louis Oliver	.10	.05
❑ 359	Darnay Scott	.50	.23
❑ 360	Dan Wilkinson	.20	.09
❑ 361	Alfred Williams	.10	.05
❑ 362	Derrick Alexander WR	.40	.18
❑ 363	Rob Burnett	.10	.05
❑ 364	Mark Carrier WR	.20	.09
❑ 365	Steve Everitt	.10	.05
❑ 366	Leroy Hoard	.10	.05
❑ 367	Pepper Johnson	.10	.05
❑ 368	Antonio Langham	.20	.09
❑ 369	Shante Carver	.10	.05
❑ 370	Alvin Harper	.20	.09
❑ 371	Daryl Johnston	.20	.09
❑ 372	Russell Maryland	.10	.05
❑ 373	Kevin Smith	.10	.05
❑ 374	Mark Stepnoski	.10	.05
❑ 375	Darren Woodson	.20	.09
❑ 376	Allen Aldridge RC	.10	.05
❑ 377	Ray Crockett	.10	.05
❑ 378	Karl Mecklenburg	.10	.05
❑ 379	Anthony Miller	.20	.09
❑ 380	Mike Pritchard	.10	.05
❑ 381	Leonard Russell	.10	.05
❑ 382	Dennis Smith	.10	.05
❑ 383	Anthony Carter	.20	.09
❑ 384	Van Malone RC	.10	.05
❑ 385	Robert Massey	.10	.05
❑ 386	Scott Mitchell	.40	.18
❑ 387	Johnnie Morton	.40	.18
❑ 388	Brett Perriman	.20	.09
❑ 389	Tracy Scroggins	.10	.05

Card	Mint	NrMt
❑ 390 Robert Brooks	.40	.18
❑ 391 LeRoy Butler	.10	.05
❑ 392 Reggie Cobb	.10	.05
❑ 393 Sean Jones	.10	.05
❑ 394 George Koonce	.10	.05
❑ 395 Steve McMichael	.20	.09
❑ 396 Bryce Paup	.40	.18
❑ 397 Aaron Taylor	.10	.05
❑ 398 Henry Ford	.10	.05
❑ 399 Ernest Givins	.20	.09
❑ 400 Jeremy Nunley RC	.10	.05
❑ 401 Bo Orlando	.10	.05
❑ 402 Al Smith	.10	.05
❑ 403 Barron Wortham RC	.10	.05
❑ 404 Trev Alberts	.20	.09
❑ 405 Tony Bennett	.10	.05
❑ 406 Kerry Cash	.10	.05
❑ 407 Sean Dawkins RC	.40	.18
❑ 408 Marshall Faulk	2.00	.90
❑ 409 Jim Harbaugh	.40	.18
❑ 410 Jeff Herrod	.10	.05
❑ 411 Kimble Anders	.20	.09
❑ 412 Donnell Bennett	.20	.09
❑ 413 J.J. Birden	.10	.05
❑ 414 Mark Collins	.10	.05
❑ 415 Lake Dawson RC	.40	.18
❑ 416 Greg Hill	.40	.18
❑ 417 Charles Mincy	.10	.05
❑ 418 Greg Biekert	.10	.05
❑ 419 Rob Fredrickson	.20	.09
❑ 420 Nolan Harrison	.10	.05
❑ 421 Jeff Jaeger	.10	.05
❑ 422 Albert Lewis	.10	.05
❑ 423 Chester McGlockton	.10	.05
❑ 424 Tom Rathman	.10	.05
❑ 425 Harvey Williams	.20	.09
❑ 426 Isaac Bruce	1.50	.70
❑ 427 Troy Drayton	.10	.05
❑ 428 Wayne Gandy	.10	.05
❑ 429 Fred Stokes	.10	.05
❑ 430 Robert Young	.10	.05
❑ 431 Gene Atkins	.10	.05
❑ 432 Aubrey Beavers	.10	.05
❑ 433 Tim Bowens	.20	.09
❑ 434 Keith Byars	.10	.05
❑ 435 Jeff Cross	.10	.05
❑ 436 Mark Ingram	.10	.05
❑ 437 Keith Jackson	.10	.05
❑ 438 Michael Stewart	.10	.05
❑ 439 Chris Hinton	.10	.05
❑ 440 Qadry Ismail	.40	.18
❑ 441 Carlos Jenkins	.10	.05
❑ 442 Warren Moon	.40	.18
❑ 443 David Palmer	.20	.09
❑ 444 Jake Reed	.20	.09
❑ 445 Robert Smith	.40	.18
❑ 446 Todd Steussie	.20	.09
❑ 447 Dewayne Washington	.20	.09
❑ 448 Marion Butts	.10	.05
❑ 449 Tim Goad	.10	.05
❑ 450 Myron Guyton	.10	.05
❑ 451 Kevin Lee RC	.10	.05
❑ 452 Willie McGinest	.40	.18
❑ 453 Ricky Reynolds	.10	.05
❑ 454 Michael Timpson	.10	.05
❑ 455 Morten Andersen	.10	.05
❑ 456 Jim Everett	.20	.09
❑ 457 Michael Haynes	.20	.09
❑ 458 Joe Johnson	.10	.05
❑ 459 Wayne Martin	.10	.05
❑ 460 Sam Mills	.10	.05
❑ 461 Irv Smith	.10	.05
❑ 462 Carlton Bailey	.10	.05
❑ 463 Chris Calloway	.10	.05
❑ 464 Mark Jackson	.10	.05
❑ 465 Thomas Lewis	.20	.09
❑ 466 Thomas Randolph	.10	.05
❑ 467 Stevie Anderson RC	.10	.05
❑ 468 Brad Baxter	.10	.05
❑ 469 Aaron Glenn	.20	.09
❑ 470 Jeff Lageman	.10	.05
❑ 471 Johnny Mitchell	.10	.05
❑ 472 Art Monk	.20	.09
❑ 473 William Fuller	.10	.05
❑ 474 Charlie Garner RC	1.50	.70
❑ 475 Vaughn Hebron	.10	.05
❑ 476 Bill Romanowski	.10	.05
❑ 477 William Thomas	.10	.05
❑ 478 Greg Townsend	.10	.05
❑ 479 Bernard Williams	.10	.05
❑ 480 Calvin Williams	.20	.09
❑ 481 Eric Green	.10	.05
❑ 482 Charles Johnson	.40	.18
❑ 483 Carnell Lake	.10	.05
❑ 484 Byron Bam Morris RC	.40	.18
❑ 485 John L. Williams	.10	.05
❑ 486 Darren Carrington	.10	.05
❑ 487 Andre Coleman RC	.10	.05
❑ 488 Isaac Davis	.10	.05
❑ 489 Dwayne Harper	.10	.05
❑ 490 Tony Martin	.40	.18
❑ 491 Mark Seay RC	.40	.18
❑ 492 Richard Dent	.20	.09
❑ 493 William Floyd	.40	.18
❑ 494 Rickey Jackson	.10	.05
❑ 495 Brent Jones	.20	.09
❑ 496 Ken Norton Jr.	.20	.09
❑ 497 Gary Plummer	.10	.05
❑ 498 Deion Sanders	.75	.35
❑ 499 John Taylor	.20	.09
❑ 500 Lee Woodall RC	.10	.05
❑ 501 Bryant Young	.40	.18
❑ 502 Sam Adams	.20	.09
❑ 503 Howard Ballard	.10	.05
❑ 504 Michael Bates	.10	.05
❑ 505 Robert Blackmon	.10	.05
❑ 506 John Kasay	.10	.05
❑ 507 Kelvin Martin	.10	.05
❑ 508 Kevin Mawae RC	.10	.05
❑ 509 Rufus Porter	.10	.05
❑ 510 Lawrence Dawsey	.10	.05
❑ 511 Trent Dilfer RC	1.50	.70
❑ 512 Thomas Everett	.10	.05
❑ 513 Jackie Harris	.10	.05
❑ 514 Errict Rhett	.75	.35
❑ 515 Henry Ellard	.20	.09
❑ 516 John Friesz	.20	.09
❑ 517 Ken Harvey	.10	.05
❑ 518 Ethan Horton	.10	.05
❑ 519 Tre Johnson	.10	.05
❑ 520 Jim Lachey	.10	.05
❑ 521 Heath Shuler	.40	.18
❑ 522 Tony Woods	.10	.05
❑ 523 Checklist	.10	.05
❑ 524 Checklist	.10	.05
❑ 525 Checklist	.10	.05

1994 Ultra Achievement Awards

	MINT	NRMT
COMPLETE SET (10)	10.00	4.50
RANDOM INSERTS IN PACKS		
COMPLETE JUMBO SET (10)	25.00	11.00
*JUMBO CARDS: 1.25X to 2.5X BASE INSERT		
ONE JUMBO SET PER HOBBY CASE		
❑ 1 Marcus Allen	.40	.18
❑ 2 John Elway	3.00	1.35
❑ 3 Dan Marino	3.00	1.35
❑ 4 Joe Montana	3.00	1.35
❑ 5 Jerry Rice	1.50	.70
❑ 6 Barry Sanders	3.00	1.35
❑ 7 Sterling Sharpe	.20	.09
❑ 8 Emmitt Smith	2.50	1.10
❑ 9 Thurman Thomas	.40	.18
❑ 10 Reggie White	.40	.18

1994 Ultra Award Winners

	MINT	NRMT
COMPLETE SET (5)	4.00	1.80
RANDOM INSERTS IN PACKS		
❑ 1 Jerome Bettis	.50	.23
❑ 2 Rick Mirer	.50	.23
❑ 3 Emmitt Smith	3.00	1.35
❑ 4 Dana Stubblefield	.50	.23
❑ 5 Rod Woodson	.50	.23

1994 Ultra First Rounders

	MINT	NRMT
COMPLETE SET (20)	6.00	2.70
RANDOM INSERTS IN PACKS		
❑ 1 Sam Adams	.15	.07
❑ 2 Trev Alberts	.15	.07
❑ 3 Shante Carver	.10	.05
❑ 4 Marshall Faulk	3.00	1.35
❑ 5 William Floyd	.30	.14
❑ 6 Rob Fredrickson	.15	.07
❑ 7 Wayne Gandy	.10	.05
❑ 8 Aaron Glenn	.15	.07
❑ 9 Charles Johnson	.30	.14
❑ 10 Joe Johnson	.10	.05
❑ 11 Antonio Langham	.15	.07
❑ 12 Willie McGinest	.30	.14
❑ 13 Jamir Miller	.10	.05
❑ 14 Johnnie Morton	1.00	.45
❑ 15 Heath Shuler	.30	.14
❑ 16 John Thierry	.10	.05
❑ 17 Dewayne Washington	.15	.07
❑ 18 Dan Wilkinson	.15	.07
❑ 19 Bernard Williams	.10	.05
❑ 20 Bryant Young	.30	.14

1994 Ultra Flair Hot Numbers

	MINT	NRMT
COMPLETE SET (15)	20.00	9.00
RANDOM INSERTS IN SER.2 PACKS		
❑ 1 Troy Aikman	2.00	.90
❑ 2 Jerome Bettis	.50	.23
❑ 3 Tim Brown	.50	.23
❑ 4 John Elway	4.00	1.80
❑ 5 Rodney Hampton	.50	.23
❑ 6 Michael Irvin	.50	.23
❑ 7 Dan Marino	4.00	1.80
❑ 8 Joe Montana	4.00	1.80
❑ 9 Jerry Rice	2.00	.90
❑ 10 Andre Rison	.25	.11
❑ 11 Barry Sanders	4.00	1.80
❑ 12 Sterling Sharpe	.25	.11
❑ 13 Emmitt Smith	3.00	1.35
❑ 14 Thurman Thomas	.50	.23
❑ 15 Steve Young	1.25	.55

1994 Ultra Flair Scoring Power

	MINT	NRMT
COMPLETE SET (6)	10.00	4.50
RANDOM INSERTS IN SER.2 PACKS		
❑ 1 Marcus Allen	.75	.35
❑ 2 Natrone Means	.75	.35
❑ 3 Jerry Rice	3.00	1.35
❑ 4 Andre Rison	.40	.18
❑ 5 Emmitt Smith	5.00	2.20
❑ 6 Ricky Watters	.75	.35

1994 Ultra Flair Wave of the Future

	MINT	NRMT
COMPLETE SET (6)	5.00	2.20
RANDOM INSERTS IN SER.2 PACKS		
❑ 1 Trent Dilfer	1.25	.55
❑ 2 Marshall Faulk	3.00	1.35
❑ 3 Greg Hill	.75	.35
❑ 4 Charles Johnson	.30	.14

❑ 5 Heath Shuler	.30	.14
❑ 6 Dan Wilkinson	.15	.07

1994 Ultra Second Year Standouts

	MINT	NRMT
COMPLETE SET (15)	8.00	3.60
RANDOM INSERTS IN PACKS		
❑ 1 Jerome Bettis	.75	.35
❑ 2 Drew Bledsoe	3.00	1.35
❑ 3 Reggie Brooks	.40	.18
❑ 4 Tom Carter	.20	.09
❑ 5 Eric Curry	.20	.09
❑ 6 Jason Elam	.20	.09
❑ 7 Tyrone Hughes	.40	.18
❑ 8 James Jett	.20	.09
❑ 9 Terry Kirby	.75	.35
❑ 10 Natrone Means	.75	.35
❑ 11 Rick Mirer	.75	.35
❑ 12 Ronald Moore	.20	.09
❑ 13 Willie Roaf	.20	.09
❑ 14 Chris Slade	.20	.09
❑ 15 Dana Stubblefield	.75	.35

1994 Ultra Stars

	MINT	NRMT
COMPLETE SET (9)	100.00	45.00
RANDOM INSERTS IN 17-CARD PACKS		
❑ 1 Troy Aikman	15.00	6.75
❑ 2 Jerome Bettis	4.00	1.80
❑ 3 Tim Brown	4.00	1.80
❑ 4 Michael Irvin	4.00	1.80
❑ 5 Rick Mirer	4.00	1.80
❑ 6 Jerry Rice	15.00	6.75
❑ 7 Barry Sanders	30.00	13.50
❑ 8 Emmitt Smith	25.00	11.00
❑ 9 Rod Woodson	4.00	1.80

1994 Ultra Touchdown Kings

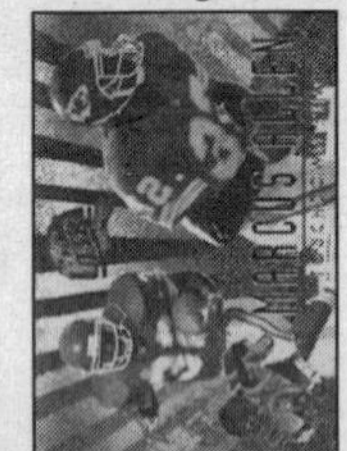

	MINT	NRMT
COMPLETE SET (9)	50.00	22.00
RANDOM INSERTS IN PACKS		
❑ 1 Marcus Allen	2.00	.90
❑ 2 Dan Marino	15.00	6.75
❑ 3 Joe Montana	15.00	6.75
❑ 4 Jerry Rice	8.00	3.60
❑ 5 Andre Rison	1.00	.45
❑ 6 Sterling Sharpe	1.00	.45
❑ 7 Emmitt Smith	12.00	5.50
❑ 8 Ricky Watters	2.00	.90
❑ 9 Steve Young	5.00	2.20

1995 Ultra

	MINT	NRMT
COMPLETE SET (550)	60.00	27.00
COMP.SERIES 1 (350)	30.00	13.50
COMP.SERIES 2 (200)	30.00	13.50
COMMON CARD (1-550)	.10	.05
SEMISTARS	.20	.09
UNLISTED STARS	.40	.18
COMP.GOLD MED.SET (550)	300.00	135.00
COMP.GOLD MED.1 (350)	180.00	80.00
COMP.GOLD MED.2 (200)	125.00	55.00
*GOLD MED. STARS: 3X TO 6X HI COLUMN		
*GOLD MED. RCs: 1.2X TO 3X HI		
ONE GOLD MEDALLION PER PACK		
❑ 1 Michael Bankston	.10	.05
❑ 2 Larry Centers	.20	.09
❑ 3 Garrison Hearst	.40	.18
❑ 4 Eric Hill	.10	.05
❑ 5 Seth Joyner	.10	.05
❑ 6 Lorenzo Lynch	.10	.05
❑ 7 Jamir Miller	.10	.05
❑ 8 Clyde Simmons	.10	.05

❑ 9 Eric Swann .20 .09
❑ 10 Aeneas Williams .10 .05
❑ 11 Devin Bush RC .10 .05
❑ 12 Ron Davis RC .10 .05
❑ 13 Chris Doleman .10 .05
❑ 14 Bert Emanuel .40 .18
❑ 15 Jeff George .20 .09
❑ 16 Roger Harper .10 .05
❑ 17 Craig Heyward .20 .09
❑ 18 Pierce Holt .10 .05
❑ 19 D.J. Johnson .10 .05
❑ 20 Terance Mathis .20 .09
❑ 21 Chuck Smith .10 .05
❑ 22 Jessie Tuggle .10 .05
❑ 23 Cornelius Bennett .20 .09
❑ 24 Ruben Brown RC .10 .05
❑ 25 Jeff Burris .10 .05
❑ 26 Matt Darby .10 .05
❑ 27 Phil Hansen .10 .05
❑ 28 Henry Jones .10 .05
❑ 29 Jim Kelly .40 .18
❑ 30 Mark Maddox RC .10 .05
❑ 31 Andre Reed .20 .09
❑ 32 Bruce Smith .40 .18
❑ 33 Don Beebe .10 .05
❑ 34 Kerry Collins RC 1.25 .55
❑ 35 Darion Conner .10 .05
❑ 36 Pete Metzelaars .10 .05
❑ 37 Sam Mills .20 .09
❑ 38 Tyrone Poole RC .20 .09
❑ 39 Joe Cain .10 .05
❑ 40 Mark Carrier DB .10 .05
❑ 41 Curtis Conway .40 .18
❑ 42 Jeff Graham .10 .05
❑ 43 Raymont Harris .10 .05
❑ 44 Erik Kramer .10 .05
❑ 45 Rashaan Salaam RC .40 .18
❑ 46 Lewis Tillman .10 .05
❑ 47 Donnell Woolford .10 .05
❑ 48 Chris Zorich .10 .05
❑ 49 Jeff Blake RC 1.25 .55
❑ 50 Mike Brim .10 .05
❑ 51 Ki-Jana Carter RC .40 .18
❑ 52 James Francis .10 .05
❑ 53 Carl Pickens .40 .18
❑ 54 Darnay Scott .40 .18
❑ 55 Steve Tovar .10 .05
❑ 56 Dan Wilkinson .20 .09
❑ 57 Alfred Williams .10 .05
❑ 58 Darryl Williams .10 .05
❑ 59 Derrick Alexander WR .40 .18
❑ 60 Rob Burnett .10 .05
❑ 61 Steve Everitt .10 .05
❑ 62 Leroy Hoard .10 .05
❑ 63 Michael Jackson .20 .09
❑ 64 Pepper Johnson .10 .05
❑ 65 Tony Jones .10 .05
❑ 66 Antonio Langham .10 .05
❑ 67 Anthony Pleasant .10 .05
❑ 68 Craig Powell RC .10 .05
❑ 69 Vinny Testaverde .20 .09
❑ 70 Eric Turner .10 .05
❑ 71 Troy Aikman 1.50 .70
❑ 72 Charles Haley .20 .09
❑ 73 Michael Irvin .40 .18
❑ 74 Daryl Johnston .20 .09
❑ 75 Robert Jones .10 .05
❑ 76 Leon Lett .10 .05
❑ 77 Russell Maryland .10 .05
❑ 78 Jay Novacek .20 .09
❑ 79 Darrin Smith .10 .05
❑ 80 Emmitt Smith 2.50 1.10
❑ 81 Kevin Smith .10 .05
❑ 82 Erik Williams .10 .05
❑ 83 Kevin Williams WR .20 .09
❑ 84 Sherman Williams RC .10 .05
❑ 85 Darren Woodson .20 .09
❑ 86 Elijah Alexander RC .10 .05
❑ 87 Steve Atwater .10 .05
❑ 88 Ray Crockett .10 .05
❑ 89 Shane Dronett .10 .05
❑ 90 Jason Elam .10 .05
❑ 91 John Elway 3.00 1.35
❑ 92 Simon Fletcher .10 .05
❑ 93 Glyn Milburn .10 .05
❑ 94 Anthony Miller .20 .09
❑ 95 Leonard Russell .10 .05
❑ 96 Shannon Sharpe .20 .09
❑ 97 Bennie Blades .10 .05
❑ 98 Lomas Brown .10 .05
❑ 99 Willie Clay .10 .05
❑ 100 Luther Elliss RC .10 .05
❑ 101 Mike Johnson .10 .05
❑ 102 Robert Massey .10 .05
❑ 103 Scott Mitchell .20 .09
❑ 104 Herman Moore .40 .18
❑ 105 Brett Perriman .20 .09
❑ 106 Robert Porcher .10 .05
❑ 107 Barry Sanders 3.00 1.35
❑ 108 Chris Spielman .20 .09
❑ 109 Edgar Bennett .20 .09
❑ 110 Robert Brooks .40 .18
❑ 111 LeRoy Butler .10 .05
❑ 112 Brett Favre 3.00 1.35
❑ 113 Sean Jones .10 .05
❑ 114 John Jurkovic .10 .05
❑ 115 George Koonce .10 .05
❑ 116 Wayne Simmons .10 .05
❑ 117 George Teague .10 .05
❑ 118 Reggie White .40 .18
❑ 119 Micheal Barrow .10 .05
❑ 120 Gary Brown .10 .05
❑ 121 Cody Carlson .10 .05
❑ 122 Ray Childress .10 .05
❑ 123 Cris Dishman .10 .05
❑ 124 Bruce Matthews .10 .05
❑ 125 Steve McNair RC 3.00 1.35
❑ 126 Marcus Robertson .10 .05
❑ 127 Webster Slaughter .10 .05
❑ 128 Al Smith .10 .05
❑ 129 Tony Bennett .10 .05
❑ 130 Ray Buchanan .10 .05
❑ 131 Quentin Coryatt .20 .09
❑ 132 Sean Dawkins .20 .09
❑ 133 Marshall Faulk .75 .35
❑ 134 Stephen Grant RC .10 .05
❑ 135 Jim Harbaugh .20 .09
❑ 136 Jeff Herrod .10 .05
❑ 137 Ellis Johnson RC .10 .05
❑ 138 Tony Siragusa .10 .05
❑ 139 Steve Beuerlein .10 .05
❑ 140 Tony Boselli RC .20 .09
❑ 141 Darren Carrington .10 .05
❑ 142 Reggie Cobb .10 .05
❑ 143 Kelvin Martin .10 .05
❑ 144 Kelvin Pritchett .10 .05
❑ 145 Joel Smeenge .10 .05
❑ 146 James O. Stewart RC 2.50 1.10
❑ 147 Marcus Allen .40 .18
❑ 148 Kimble Anders .20 .09
❑ 149 Dale Carter .20 .09
❑ 150 Mark Collins .10 .05
❑ 151 Willie Davis .20 .09
❑ 152 Lake Dawson .20 .09
❑ 153 Greg Hill .20 .09
❑ 154 Trezelle Jenkins RC .10 .05
❑ 155 Darren Mickell .10 .05
❑ 156 Tracy Simien .10 .05
❑ 157 Neil Smith .20 .09
❑ 158 William White .10 .05
❑ 159 Joe Aska RC .20 .09
❑ 160 Greg Biekert .10 .05
❑ 161 Tim Brown .40 .18
❑ 162 Rob Fredrickson .10 .05
❑ 163 Andrew Glover RC .10 .05
❑ 164 Jeff Hostetler .20 .09
❑ 165 Rocket Ismail .20 .09
❑ 166 Napoleon Kaufman RC 2.50 1.10
❑ 167 Terry McDaniel .10 .05
❑ 168 Chester McGlockton .20 .09
❑ 169 Anthony Smith .10 .05
❑ 170 Harvey Williams .10 .05
❑ 171 Steve Wisniewski .10 .05
❑ 172 Gene Atkins .10 .05
❑ 173 Aubrey Beavers .10 .05
❑ 174 Tim Bowens .10 .05
❑ 175 Bryan Cox .10 .05
❑ 176 Jeff Cross .10 .05
❑ 177 Irving Fryar .20 .09
❑ 178 Dan Marino 3.00 1.35
❑ 179 O.J. McDuffie .40 .18
❑ 180 Billy Milner .10 .05
❑ 181 Bernie Parmalee .20 .09
❑ 182 Troy Vincent .10 .05
❑ 183 Richmond Webb .10 .05
❑ 184 Derrick Alexander DE RC .10 .05
❑ 185 Cris Carter .40 .18
❑ 186 Jack Del Rio .10 .05
❑ 187 Qadry Ismail .20 .09
❑ 188 Ed McDaniel .10 .05
❑ 189 Randall McDaniel .10 .05
❑ 190 Warren Moon .20 .09
❑ 191 John Randle .10 .05
❑ 192 Jake Reed .20 .09
❑ 193 Fuad Reveiz .10 .05
❑ 194 Korey Stringer RC .10 .05
❑ 195 Dewayne Washington .20 .09
❑ 196 Bruce Armstrong .10 .05
❑ 197 Drew Bledsoe 1.50 .70
❑ 198 Vincent Brisby .10 .05
❑ 199 Vincent Brown .10 .05
❑ 200 Marion Butts .10 .05
❑ 201 Ben Coates .20 .09
❑ 202 Myron Guyton .10 .05
❑ 203 Maurice Hurst .10 .05
❑ 204 Mike Jones .10 .05
❑ 205 Ty Law RC .20 .09
❑ 206 Willie McGinest .20 .09
❑ 207 Chris Slade .20 .09
❑ 208 Mario Bates .40 .18
❑ 209 Quinn Early .20 .09
❑ 210 Jim Everett .10 .05
❑ 211 Mark Fields RC .10 .05
❑ 212 Michael Haynes .20 .09
❑ 213 Tyrone Hughes .20 .09
❑ 214 Joe Johnson .10 .05
❑ 215 Wayne Martin .10 .05
❑ 216 Willie Roaf .10 .05
❑ 217 Irv Smith .10 .05
❑ 218 Jimmy Spencer .10 .05
❑ 219 Winfred Tubbs .10 .05
❑ 220 Renaldo Turnbull .10 .05
❑ 221 Michael Brooks .10 .05
❑ 222 Dave Brown .20 .09
❑ 223 Chris Calloway .10 .05
❑ 224 Howard Cross .10 .05
❑ 225 John Elliott .10 .05
❑ 226 Keith Hamilton .10 .05
❑ 227 Rodney Hampton .20 .09
❑ 228 Thomas Lewis .20 .09
❑ 229 Thomas Randolph .10 .05
❑ 230 Mike Sherrard .10 .05
❑ 231 Michael Strahan .10 .05
❑ 232 Tyrone Wheatley RC 1.50 .70
❑ 233 Brad Baxter .10 .05
❑ 234 Kyle Brady RC .40 .18
❑ 235 Kyle Clifton .10 .05
❑ 236 Hugh Douglas RC .20 .09
❑ 237 Boomer Esiason .20 .09
❑ 238 Aaron Glenn .10 .05
❑ 239 Bobby Houston .10 .05
❑ 240 Johnny Johnson .10 .05
❑ 241 Mo Lewis .10 .05
❑ 242 Johnny Mitchell .10 .05
❑ 243 Marvin Washington .10 .05
❑ 244 Fred Barnett .20 .09
❑ 245 Randall Cunningham .40 .18
❑ 246 William Fuller .10 .05
❑ 247 Charlie Garner .20 .09
❑ 248 Andy Harmon .10 .05
❑ 249 Greg Jackson .10 .05
❑ 250 Mike Mamula RC .20 .09
❑ 251 Bill Romanowski .10 .05
❑ 252 Bobby Taylor RC .20 .09
❑ 253 William Thomas .10 .05
❑ 254 Calvin Williams .20 .09
❑ 255 Michael Zordich .10 .05
❑ 256 Chad Brown .20 .09
❑ 257 Mark Bruener RC .20 .09
❑ 258 Dermontti Dawson .20 .09
❑ 259 Barry Foster .20 .09
❑ 260 Kevin Greene .20 .09
❑ 261 Charles Johnson .20 .09
❑ 262 Carnell Lake .10 .05
❑ 263 Greg Lloyd .20 .09
❑ 264 Byron Bam Morris .20 .09
❑ 265 Neil O'Donnell .20 .09
❑ 266 Darren Perry .10 .05

❑ 267 Ray Seals .10 .05
❑ 268 Kordell Stewart RC 3.00 1.35
❑ 269 John L. Williams .10 .05
❑ 270 Rod Woodson .20 .09
❑ 271 Jerome Bettis .40 .18
❑ 272 Isaac Bruce .75 .35
❑ 273 Kevin Carter RC .40 .18
❑ 274 Shane Conlan .10 .05
❑ 275 Troy Drayton .10 .05
❑ 276 Sean Gilbert .20 .09
❑ 277 Todd Lyght .10 .05
❑ 278 Chris Miller .10 .05
❑ 279 Anthony Newman .10 .05
❑ 280 Roman Phifer .10 .05
❑ 281 Robert Young .10 .05
❑ 282 John Carney .10 .05
❑ 283 Andre Coleman .10 .05
❑ 284 Courtney Hall .10 .05
❑ 285 Ronnie Harmon .10 .05
❑ 286 Dwayne Harper .10 .05
❑ 287 Stan Humphries .20 .09
❑ 288 Shawn Jefferson .10 .05
❑ 289 Tony Martin .20 .09
❑ 290 Natrone Means .40 .18
❑ 291 Chris Mims .10 .05
❑ 292 Leslie O'Neal .20 .09
❑ 293 Junior Seau .40 .18
❑ 294 Mark Seay .20 .09
❑ 295 Eric Davis .10 .05
❑ 296 William Floyd .40 .18
❑ 297 Merton Hanks .10 .05
❑ 298 Brent Jones .10 .05
❑ 299 Ken Norton Jr. .20 .09
❑ 300 Gary Plummer .10 .05
❑ 301 Jerry Rice 1.50 .70
❑ 302 Deion Sanders 1.00 .45
❑ 303 Jesse Sapolu .10 .05
❑ 304 J.J. Stokes RC 1.00 .45
❑ 305 Dana Stubblefield .40 .18
❑ 306 John Taylor .10 .05
❑ 307 Steve Wallace .10 .05
❑ 308 Lee Woodall .10 .05
❑ 309 Bryant Young .20 .09
❑ 310 Steve Young 1.25 .55
❑ 311 Sam Adams .10 .05
❑ 312 Howard Ballard .10 .05
❑ 313 Robert Blackmon .10 .05
❑ 314 Brian Blades .20 .09
❑ 315 Joey Galloway RC 3.00 1.35
❑ 316 Carlton Gray .10 .05
❑ 317 Cortez Kennedy .20 .09
❑ 318 Rick Mirer .40 .18
❑ 319 Eugene Robinson .10 .05
❑ 320 Chris Warren .20 .09
❑ 321 Terry Wooden .10 .05
❑ 322 Derrick Brooks RC .10 .05
❑ 323 Lawrence Dawsey .10 .05
❑ 324 Trent Dilfer .40 .18
❑ 325 Santana Dotson .10 .05
❑ 326 Thomas Everett .10 .05
❑ 327 Paul Gruber .10 .05
❑ 328 Jackie Harris .10 .05
❑ 329 Courtney Hawkins .10 .05
❑ 330 Martin Mayhew .10 .05
❑ 331 Hardy Nickerson .10 .05
❑ 332 Errict Rhett .40 .18
❑ 333 Warren Sapp RC .60 .25
❑ 334 Charles Wilson .10 .05
❑ 335 Reggie Brooks .20 .09
❑ 336 Tom Carter .10 .05
❑ 337 Henry Ellard .20 .09
❑ 338 Ricky Ervins .10 .05
❑ 339 Darrell Green .10 .05
❑ 340 Ken Harvey .10 .05
❑ 341 Brian Mitchell .10 .05
❑ 342 Cory Raymer RC .10 .05
❑ 343 Heath Shuler .40 .18
❑ 344 Michael Westbrook RC 2.00 .90
❑ 345 Tony Woods .10 .05
❑ 346 Checklist .10 .05
❑ 347 Checklist .10 .05
❑ 348 Checklist .10 .05
❑ 349 Checklist .10 .05
❑ 350 Checklist .10 .05
❑ 351 Checklist .10 .05
❑ 352 Checklist .10 .05
❑ 353 Dave Krieg .10 .05
❑ 354 Rob Moore .10 .05
❑ 355 J.J. Birden .10 .05
❑ 356 Eric Metcalf .20 .09
❑ 357 Bryce Paup .40 .18
❑ 358 Willie Green .20 .09
❑ 359 Derrick Moore .10 .05
❑ 360 Michael Timpson .10 .05
❑ 361 Eric Bieniemy .10 .05
❑ 362 Keenan McCardell .40 .18
❑ 363 Andre Rison .20 .09
❑ 364 Lorenzo White .10 .05
❑ 365 Deion Sanders 1.00 .45
❑ 366 Wade Wilson .10 .05
❑ 367 Aaron Craver .10 .05
❑ 368 Michael Dean Perry .10 .05
❑ 369 Rod Smith WR RC 10.00 4.50
❑ 370 Henry Thomas .10 .05
❑ 371 Mark Ingram .10 .05
❑ 372 Chris Chandler .20 .09
❑ 373 Mel Gray .10 .05
❑ 374 Flipper Anderson .10 .05
❑ 375 Craig Erickson .10 .05
❑ 376 Mark Brunell 1.50 .70
❑ 377 Ernest Givins .10 .05
❑ 378 Randy Jordan .10 .05
❑ 379 Webster Slaughter .10 .05
❑ 380 Tamarick Vanover RC .40 .18
❑ 381 Gary Clark .10 .05
❑ 382 Steve Emtman .10 .05
❑ 383 Eric Green .10 .05
❑ 384 Louis Oliver .10 .05
❑ 385 Robert Smith .40 .18
❑ 386 Dave Meggett .10 .05
❑ 387 Eric Allen .10 .05
❑ 388 Wesley Walls .20 .09
❑ 389 Herschel Walker .20 .09
❑ 390 Ronald Moore .10 .05
❑ 391 Adrian Murrell .20 .09
❑ 392 Charles Wilson .10 .05
❑ 393 Derrick Fenner .10 .05
❑ 394 Pat Swilling .10 .05
❑ 395 Kelvin Martin .10 .05
❑ 396 Rodney Peete .10 .05
❑ 397 Ricky Watters .40 .18
❑ 398 Erric Pegram .20 .09
❑ 399 Leonard Russell .10 .05
❑ 400 Alexander Wright .10 .05
❑ 401 Darrien Gordon .10 .05
❑ 402 Alfred Pupunu .10 .05
❑ 403 Elvis Grbac .40 .18
❑ 404 Derek Loville .10 .05
❑ 405 Steve Broussard .10 .05
❑ 406 Ricky Proehl .10 .05
❑ 407 Bobby Joe Edmonds .10 .05
❑ 408 Alvin Harper .10 .05
❑ 409 Dave Moore .10 .05
❑ 410 Terry Allen .20 .09
❑ 411 Gus Frerotte .40 .18
❑ 412 Leslie Shepherd RC .20 .09
❑ 413 Stoney Case RC .60 .25
❑ 414 Frank Sanders RC 1.25 .55
❑ 415 Roell Preston RC .10 .05
❑ 416 Lorenzo Styles RC .10 .05
❑ 417 Justin Armour RC .10 .05
❑ 418 Todd Collins RC .40 .18
❑ 419 Darick Holmes RC .20 .09
❑ 420 Kerry Collins .60 .25
❑ 421 Tyrone Poole .10 .05
❑ 422 Rashaan Salaam .20 .09
❑ 423 Todd Sauerbrun RC .10 .05
❑ 424 Ki-Jana Carter .40 .18
❑ 425 David Dunn RC .10 .05
❑ 426 Ernest Hunter RC .10 .05
❑ 427 Eric Zeier RC .60 .25
❑ 428 Eric Bjornson RC .20 .09
❑ 429 Sherman Williams .10 .05
❑ 430 Terrell Davis RC 12.00 5.50
❑ 431 Luther Elliss .10 .05
❑ 432 Kez McCorvey RC .10 .05
❑ 433 Antonio Freeman RC 3.00 1.35
❑ 434 Craig Newsome RC .10 .05
❑ 435 Steve McNair 1.50 .70
❑ 436 Chris Sanders RC .40 .18
❑ 437 Zack Crockett RC .10 .05
❑ 438 Ellis Johnson .10 .05
❑ 439 Tony Boselli .20 .09
❑ 440 James O. Stewart 1.25 .55
❑ 441 Trezelle Jenkins .10 .05
❑ 442 Tamarick Vanover .40 .18
❑ 443 Derrick Alexander DE .10 .05
❑ 444 Chad May RC .10 .05
❑ 445 James A.Stewart RC .10 .05
❑ 446 Ty Law .10 .05
❑ 447 Curtis Martin RC 3.00 1.35
❑ 448 Will Moore RC .10 .05
❑ 449 Mark Fields .10 .05
❑ 450 Ray Zellars RC .20 .09
❑ 451 Charles Way RC .10 .05
❑ 452 Tyrone Wheatley .40 .18
❑ 453 Kyle Brady .40 .18
❑ 454 Wayne Chrebet RC 2.00 .90
❑ 455 Hugh Douglas .20 .09
❑ 456 Chris T.Jones RC .40 .18
❑ 457 Mike Mamula .10 .05
❑ 458 Fred McCrary RC .10 .05
❑ 459 Bobby Taylor .20 .09
❑ 460 Mark Bruener .20 .09
❑ 461 Kordell Stewart 1.50 .70
❑ 462 Kevin Carter .40 .18
❑ 463 Lovell Pinkney RC .10 .05
❑ 464 Johnny Thomas RC .10 .05
❑ 465 Terrell Fletcher RC .10 .05
❑ 466 Jimmy Oliver RC .10 .05
❑ 467 J.J. Stokes .40 .18
❑ 468 Christian Fauria RC .10 .05
❑ 469 Joey Galloway 1.50 .70
❑ 470 Derrick Brooks .10 .05
❑ 471 Warren Sapp .20 .09
❑ 472 Michael Westbrook 1.00 .45
❑ 473 Garrison Hearst .40 .18
❑ 474 Jeff George .20 .09
❑ 475 Terance Mathis .20 .09
❑ 476 Andre Reed .20 .09
❑ 477 Bruce Smith .40 .18
❑ 478 Lamar Lathon .10 .05
❑ 479 Curtis Conway .40 .18
❑ 480 Jeff Blake .40 .18
❑ 481 Carl Pickens .40 .18
❑ 482 Eric Turner .10 .05
❑ 483 Troy Aikman .75 .35
❑ 484 Michael Irvin .40 .18
❑ 485 Emmitt Smith 1.25 .55
❑ 486 John Elway 1.50 .70
❑ 487 Shannon Sharpe .20 .09
❑ 488 Herman Moore .40 .18
❑ 489 Barry Sanders 1.50 .70
❑ 490 Brett Favre 1.50 .70
❑ 491 Reggie White .40 .18
❑ 492 Haywood Jeffires .10 .05
❑ 493 Sean Dawkins .10 .05
❑ 494 Marshall Faulk .40 .18
❑ 495 Desmond Howard .20 .09
❑ 496 Steve Bono .20 .09
❑ 497 Derrick Thomas .20 .09
❑ 498 Irving Fryar .20 .09
❑ 499 Terry Kirby .20 .09
❑ 500 Dan Marino 1.50 .70
❑ 501 O.J. McDuffie .40 .18
❑ 502 Cris Carter .40 .18
❑ 503 Warren Moon .20 .09
❑ 504 Jake Reed .20 .09
❑ 505 Drew Bledsoe .75 .35
❑ 506 Ben Coates .20 .09
❑ 507 Jim Everett .10 .05
❑ 508 Rodney Hampton .20 .09
❑ 509 Mo Lewis .10 .05
❑ 510 Tim Brown .40 .18
❑ 511 Jeff Hostetler .20 .09
❑ 512 Rocket Ismail .20 .09
❑ 513 Chester McGlockton .20 .09
❑ 514 Fred Barnett .20 .09
❑ 515 Greg Lloyd .20 .09
❑ 516 Byron Bam Morris .20 .09
❑ 517 Rod Woodson .20 .09
❑ 518 Jerome Bettis .40 .18
❑ 519 Isaac Bruce .40 .18
❑ 520 Stan Humphries .20 .09
❑ 521 Natrone Means .40 .18
❑ 522 Junior Seau .40 .18
❑ 523 William Floyd .20 .09
❑ 524 Jerry Rice .75 .35

		MINT	NRMT
❑	525 Steve Young	.60	.25
❑	526 Cortez Kennedy	.20	.09
❑	527 Rick Mirer	.40	.18
❑	528 Chris Warren	.20	.09
❑	529 Trent Dilfer	.40	.18
❑	530 Errict Rhett	.40	.18
❑	531 Darrell Green	.10	.05
❑	532 Heath Shuler	.40	.18
❑	533 Stoney Case RO	.10	.05
❑	534 Eric Zeier RO	.40	.18
❑	535 Kerry Collins RO	.40	.18
❑	536 Steve McNair RO	1.00	.45
❑	537 Kordell Stewart RO	1.50	.70
❑	538 Rob Johnson RO RC	2.00	.90
❑	539 Eric Ball EE	.10	.05
❑	540 Darrick Brownlow EE	.10	.05
❑	541 Paul Butcher EE	.10	.05
❑	542 Carlester Crumpler EE	.10	.05
❑	543 Maurice Douglas EE	.10	.05
❑	544 Keith Elias EE	.10	.05
❑	545 Kenneth Gant EE	.10	.05
❑	546 Corey Harris EE	.10	.05
❑	547 Andre Hastings EE	.20	.09
❑	548 Thomas Homco EE	.10	.05
❑	549 Lenny McGill EE	.10	.05
❑	550 Mark Pike EE	.10	.05
❑	P1 Promo Sheet Dave Meggett Justin Armour Brett Favre William Floyd	2.00	.90
❑	P264 Byron Bam Morris Prototype Card back includes "1994 Steelers" in stat information	1.00	.45

1995 Ultra Achievements

	MINT	NRMT
COMPLETE SET (10)	10.00	4.50
STATED ODDS 1:7		
*GOLD MEDAL.: 1.5X TO 3X BASE CARD HI		

		MINT	NRMT
❑	1 Drew Bledsoe	2.50	1.10
❑	2 Cris Carter	.60	.25
❑	3 Ben Coates	.30	.14
❑	4 Mel Gray	.15	.07
❑	5 Jerry Rice	2.50	1.10
❑	6 Barry Sanders	5.00	2.20
❑	7 Deion Sanders	1.50	.70
❑	8 Herschel Walker	.30	.14
❑	9 Dewayne Washington	.30	.14
❑	10 Steve Young	2.00	.90

1995 Ultra All-Rookie Team

	MINT	NRMT
COMPLETE SET (10)	80.00	36.00
SER.2 STATED ODDS 1:55		
*HOT PACK: 1X TO 2.5X BASE CARD HI		
HP SET: SER.2 STATED ODDS 1:360		

		MINT	NRMT
❑	1 Michael Westbrook	10.00	4.50
❑	2 Terrell Davis	25.00	11.00
❑	3 Curtis Martin	15.00	6.75

		MINT	NRMT
❑	4 Joey Galloway	15.00	6.75
❑	5 Rashaan Salaam	2.00	.90
❑	6 J.J. Stokes	5.00	2.20
❑	7 Napoleon Kaufman	12.00	5.50
❑	8 Mike Mamula	1.00	.45
❑	9 Kyle Brady	2.00	.90
❑	10 Hugh Douglas	1.00	.45

1995 Ultra Award Winners

	MINT	NRMT
COMPLETE SET (6)	7.00	3.10
SER.1 STATED ODDS 1:5		
*GOLD MEDAL.: 1X TO 2X BASE CARD HI		

		MINT	NRMT
❑	1 Tim Bowens	.10	.05
❑	2 Marshall Faulk	.75	.35
❑	3 Dan Marino	3.00	1.35
❑	4 Barry Sanders	3.00	1.35
❑	5 Deion Sanders	1.00	.45
❑	6 Steve Young	1.25	.55

1995 Ultra First Rounders

	MINT	NRMT
COMPLETE SET (20)	25.00	11.00
SER.1 STATED ODDS 1:7		
*GOLD MEDAL.: 1.5X TO 3X BASE CARD HI		

		MINT	NRMT
❑	1 Derrick Alexander DE	.15	.07
❑	2 Tony Boselli	.30	.14
❑	3 Kyle Brady	.60	.25
❑	4 Mark Bruener	.30	.14
❑	5 Devin Bush	.15	.07
❑	6 Kevin Carter	.60	.25
❑	7 Ki-Jana Carter	.60	.25
❑	8 Kerry Collins	2.00	.90
❑	9 Mark Fields	.15	.07
❑	10 Joey Galloway	5.00	2.20
❑	11 Napoleon Kaufman	4.00	1.80
❑	12 Ty Law	.30	.14
❑	13 Mike Mamula	.30	.14
❑	14 Steve McNair	5.00	2.20
❑	15 Rashaan Salaam	.60	.25
❑	16 Warren Sapp	1.00	.45
❑	17 James O. Stewart	4.00	1.80
❑	18 J.J.Stokes	1.50	.70
❑	19 Michael Westbrook	3.00	1.35
❑	20 Tyrone Wheatley	2.50	1.10

1995 Ultra Magna Force

	MINT	NRMT
COMPLETE SET (20)	110.00	50.00
SER.2 STATED ODDS 1:20 HOBBY		

		MINT	NRMT
❑	1 Emmitt Smith	20.00	9.00
❑	2 Jerry Rice	10.00	4.50
❑	3 Drew Bledsoe	10.00	4.50
❑	4 Marshall Faulk	5.00	2.20
❑	5 Heath Shuler	3.00	1.35
❑	6 Carl Pickens	3.00	1.35
❑	7 Ben Coates	1.50	.70
❑	8 Terry Allen	1.50	.70
❑	9 Terance Mathis	1.50	.70
❑	10 Fred Barnett	1.50	.70
❑	11 O.J. McDuffie	3.00	1.35
❑	12 Garrison Hearst	3.00	1.35
❑	13 Deion Sanders	8.00	3.60
❑	14 Reggie White	3.00	1.35
❑	15 Herman Moore	3.00	1.35
❑	16 Brett Favre	20.00	9.00
❑	17 William Floyd	3.00	1.35
❑	18 Curtis Martin	12.00	5.50
❑	19 Joey Galloway	12.00	5.50
❑	20 Tyrone Wheatley	6.00	2.70

1995 Ultra Overdrive

	MINT	NRMT
COMPLETE SET (20)	60.00	27.00

SER.2 STATED ODDS 1:20 RETAIL

		MINT	NRMT
❑ 1	Barry Sanders	15.00	6.75
❑ 2	Troy Aikman	8.00	3.60
❑ 3	Natrone Means	2.00	.90
❑ 4	Steve Young	6.00	2.70
❑ 5	Errict Rhett	2.00	.90
❑ 6	Terrell Davis	25.00	11.00
❑ 7	Michael Westbrook	4.00	1.80
❑ 8	Michael Irvin	2.00	.90
❑ 9	Chris Warren	1.00	.45
❑ 10	Tim Brown	2.00	.90
❑ 11	Jerome Bettis	2.00	.90
❑ 12	Ricky Watters	2.00	.90
❑ 13	Derrick Thomas	1.50	.70
❑ 14	Bruce Smith	2.00	.90
❑ 15	Rashaan Salaam	.75	.35
❑ 16	Jeff Blake	2.50	1.10
❑ 17	Alvin Harper	.50	.23
❑ 18	Shannon Sharpe	1.00	.45
❑ 19	Eric Swann	1.00	.45
❑ 20	Andre Rison	1.00	.45

1995 Ultra Rising Stars

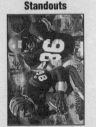

	MINT	NRMT
COMPLETE SET (9)	50.00	22.00

SER.1 STATED ODDS 1:37

*GOLD MED.STARS: 8X TO 16X BASE CARD HI

*GOLD MEDAL.: 3X TO 6X BASE CARD HI

		MINT	NRMT
❑ 1	Jerome Bettis	3.00	1.35
❑ 2	Jeff Blake	4.00	1.80
❑ 3	Drew Bledsoe	12.00	5.50
❑ 4	Ben Coates	1.50	.70
❑ 5	Marshall Faulk	6.00	2.70
❑ 6	Brett Favre	25.00	11.00
❑ 7	Natrone Means	3.00	1.35
❑ 8	Byron Bam Morris	1.50	.70
❑ 9	Eric Turner	.75	.35

1995 Ultra Second Year Standouts

	MINT	NRMT
COMPLETE SET (15)	8.00	3.60

SER.1 STATED ODDS 1:5

*GOLD MEDAL.: 5X TO 10X BASE CARD HI

		MINT	NRMT
❑ 1	Derrick Alexander WR	2.00	.90
❑ 2	Mario Bates	2.00	.90
❑ 3	Tim Bowens	.50	.23
❑ 4	Bert Emanuel	2.00	.90
❑ 5	Marshall Faulk	4.00	1.80
❑ 6	William Floyd	2.00	.90
❑ 7	Rob Fredrickson	.50	.23
❑ 8	Antonio Langham	.50	.23
❑ 9	Byron Bam Morris	1.00	.45
❑ 10	Errict Rhett	2.00	.90
❑ 11	Darnay Scott	2.00	.90
❑ 12	Heath Shuler	2.00	.90
❑ 13	Dewayne Washington	1.00	.45
❑ 14	Dan Wilkinson	1.00	.45
❑ 15	Bryant Young	1.00	.45

1995 Ultra Stars

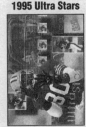

	MINT	NRMT
COMPLETE SET (10)	15.00	6.75

SER.1 STATED ODDS 1:7 JUMBO

*GOLD MEDAL.: 1.5X TO 3X BASE CARD HI

		MINT	NRMT
❑ 1	Tim Brown	.60	.25
❑ 2	Marshall Faulk	1.25	.55
❑ 3	Irving Fryar	.30	.14
❑ 4	Dan Marino	5.00	2.20
❑ 5	Natrone Means	.60	.25
❑ 6	Jerry Rice	2.50	1.10
❑ 7	Barry Sanders	5.00	2.20
❑ 8	Deion Sanders	1.50	.70
❑ 9	Emmitt Smith	4.00	1.80
❑ 10	Rod Woodson	.30	.14

1995 Ultra Touchdown Kings

	MINT	NRMT
COMPLETE SET (10)	10.00	4.50

SER.1 STATED ODDS 1:7

*GOLD MEDAL.: 1.5X TO 3X BASE CARD HI

		MINT	NRMT
❑ 1	Marshall Faulk	1.25	.55
❑ 2	Terance Mathis	.30	.14
❑ 3	Natrone Means	.60	.25
❑ 4	Herman Moore	.60	.25
❑ 5	Carl Pickens	.60	.25
❑ 6	Jerry Rice	2.50	1.10
❑ 7	Andre Rison	.30	.14
❑ 8	Emmitt Smith	4.00	1.80
❑ 9	Chris Warren	.30	.14
❑ 10	Steve Young	2.00	.90

1995 Ultra Ultrabilities

	MINT	NRMT
COMPLETE SET (30)	50.00	22.00

SER.2 STATED ODDS 1:5

		MINT	NRMT
❑ 1	Dan Marino	8.00	3.60
❑ 2	Steve Young	3.00	1.35
❑ 3	Drew Bledsoe	4.00	1.80
❑ 4	Jeff Blake	2.00	.90
❑ 5	Troy Aikman	4.00	1.80
❑ 6	John Elway	8.00	3.60
❑ 7	Trent Dilfer	1.00	.45
❑ 8	Steve Bono	.50	.23
❑ 9	Brett Favre	8.00	3.60
❑ 10	Kerry Collins	2.00	.90
❑ 11	Barry Sanders	8.00	3.60
❑ 12	Errict Rhett	1.00	.45
❑ 13	Emmitt Smith	6.00	2.70
❑ 14	Chris Warren	.50	.23
❑ 15	Irving Fryar	.50	.23
❑ 16	Charlie Garner	.50	.23
❑ 17	Tim Brown	1.00	.45
❑ 18	Eric Metcalf	.50	.23
❑ 19	Herman Moore	1.00	.45
❑ 20	Robert Smith	1.00	.45
❑ 21	Natrone Means	1.00	.45
❑ 22	Derrick Thomas	.50	.23
❑ 23	Bruce Smith	1.00	.45
❑ 24	Hugh Douglas	.30	.14
❑ 25	Mike Mamula	.30	.14
❑ 26	Jerome Bettis	1.00	.45
❑ 27	Byron Bam Morris UER Rams helmet on back	.50	.23
❑ 28	Tim Bowens	.25	.11
❑ 29	William Floyd	1.00	.45
❑ 30	Daryl Johnston	.50	.23

1996 Ultra

	MINT	NRMT
COMPLETE SET (200)	25.00	11.00
COMMON CARD (1-200)	.10	.05
SEMISTARS	.25	.11
UNLISTED STARS	.50	.23

		MINT	NRMT
❑ 1	Larry Centers	.25	.11

Card	Mint	NRMT
❑ 2 Garrison Hearst	.25	.11
❑ 3 Rob Moore	.25	.11
❑ 4 Eric Swann	.10	.05
❑ 5 Aeneas Williams	.10	.05
❑ 6 Bert Emanuel	.25	.11
❑ 7 Jeff George	.25	.11
❑ 8 Craig Heyward	.10	.05
❑ 9 Terance Mathis	.10	.05
❑ 10 Eric Metcalf	.10	.05
❑ 11 Cornelius Bennett	.10	.05
❑ 12 Darick Holmes	.10	.05
❑ 13 Jim Kelly	.50	.23
❑ 14 Bryce Paup	.10	.05
❑ 15 Bruce Smith	.25	.11
❑ 16 Mark Carrier WR	.10	.05
❑ 17 Kerry Collins	.50	.23
❑ 18 Lamar Lathon	.10	.05
❑ 19 Derrick Moore	.10	.05
❑ 20 Tyrone Poole	.10	.05
❑ 21 Curtis Conway	.50	.23
❑ 22 Jeff Graham	.10	.05
❑ 23 Raymont Harris	.25	.11
❑ 24 Erik Kramer	.10	.05
❑ 25 Rashaan Salaam	.50	.23
❑ 26 Jeff Blake	.50	.23
❑ 27 Ki-Jana Carter	.25	.11
❑ 28 Carl Pickens	.50	.23
❑ 29 Darnay Scott	.25	.11
❑ 30 Dan Wilkinson	.10	.05
❑ 31 Leroy Hoard	.10	.05
❑ 32 Michael Jackson	.25	.11
❑ 33 Andre Rison	.25	.11
❑ 34 Vinny Testaverde	.25	.11
❑ 35 Eric Turner	.10	.05
❑ 36 Troy Aikman	1.25	.55
❑ 37 Charles Haley	.25	.11
❑ 38 Michael Irvin	.50	.23
❑ 39 Daryl Johnston	.25	.11
❑ 40 Jay Novacek	.10	.05
❑ 41 Deion Sanders	.75	.35
❑ 42 Emmitt Smith	2.00	.90
❑ 43 Steve Atwater	.10	.05
❑ 44 Terrell Davis	3.00	1.35
❑ 45 John Elway	2.50	1.10
❑ 46 Anthony Miller	.25	.11
❑ 47 Shannon Sharpe	.25	.11
❑ 48 Scott Mitchell	.25	.11
❑ 49 Herman Moore	.50	.23
❑ 50 Johnnie Morton	.25	.11
❑ 51 Brett Perriman	.10	.05
❑ 52 Barry Sanders	2.50	1.10
❑ 53 Chris Spielman	.10	.05
❑ 54 Edgar Bennett	.25	.11
❑ 55 Robert Brooks	.50	.23
❑ 56 Mark Chmura	.25	.11
❑ 57 Brett Favre	2.50	1.10
❑ 58 Reggie White	.50	.23
❑ 59 Mel Gray	.10	.05
❑ 60 Haywood Jeffires	.10	.05
❑ 61 Steve McNair	1.00	.45
❑ 62 Chris Sanders	.25	.11
❑ 63 Rodney Thomas	.10	.05
❑ 64 Quentin Coryatt	.10	.05
❑ 65 Sean Dawkins	.10	.05
❑ 66 Ken Dilger	.25	.11
❑ 67 Marshall Faulk	.50	.23
❑ 68 Jim Harbaugh	.25	.11
❑ 69 Tony Boselli	.10	.05
❑ 70 Mark Brunell	1.25	.55
❑ 71 Desmond Howard	.25	.11
❑ 72 Jimmy Smith	.25	.11
❑ 73 James O. Stewart	.25	.11
❑ 74 Marcus Allen	.50	.23
❑ 75 Steve Bono	.10	.05
❑ 76 Lake Dawson	.10	.05
❑ 77 Neil Smith	.10	.05
❑ 78 Derrick Thomas	.25	.11
❑ 79 Tamarick Vanover	.25	.11
❑ 80 Bryan Cox	.10	.05
❑ 81 Irving Fryar	.25	.11
❑ 82 Eric Green	.10	.05
❑ 83 Dan Marino	2.50	1.10
❑ 84 O.J. McDuffie	.25	.11
❑ 85 Bernie Parmalee	.10	.05
❑ 86 Cris Carter	.50	.23
❑ 87 Qadry Ismail	.10	.05
❑ 88 Warren Moon	.25	.11
❑ 89 Jake Reed	.25	.11
❑ 90 Robert Smith	.25	.11
❑ 91 Drew Bledsoe	1.25	.55
❑ 92 Vincent Brisby	.10	.05
❑ 93 Ben Coates	.25	.11
❑ 94 Curtis Martin	1.00	.45
❑ 95 Willie McGinest	.10	.05
❑ 96 Dave Meggett	.10	.05
❑ 97 Mario Bates	.25	.11
❑ 98 Quinn Early	.10	.05
❑ 99 Jim Everett	.10	.05
❑ 100 Michael Haynes	.10	.05
❑ 101 Renaldo Turnbull	.10	.05
❑ 102 Dave Brown	.10	.05
❑ 103 Rodney Hampton	.25	.11
❑ 104 Mike Sherrard	.10	.05
❑ 105 Phillippi Sparks	.10	.05
❑ 106 Tyrone Wheatley	.25	.11
❑ 107 Hugh Douglas	.10	.05
❑ 108 Boomer Esiason	.25	.11
❑ 109 Aaron Glenn	.10	.05
❑ 110 Mo Lewis	.10	.05
❑ 111 Johnny Mitchell	.10	.05
❑ 112 Tim Brown	.50	.23
❑ 113 Jeff Hostetler	.10	.05
❑ 114 Rocket Ismail	.10	.05
❑ 115 Chester McGlockton	.10	.05
❑ 116 Harvey Williams	.10	.05
❑ 117 Fred Barnett	.10	.05
❑ 118 William Fuller	.10	.05
❑ 119 Charlie Garner	.10	.05
❑ 120 Ricky Watters	.25	.11
❑ 121 Calvin Williams	.10	.05
❑ 122 Kevin Greene	.25	.11
❑ 123 Greg Lloyd	.25	.11
❑ 124 Byron Bam Morris	.25	.11
❑ 125 Neil O'Donnell	.25	.11
❑ 126 Erric Pegram	.10	.05
❑ 127 Kordell Stewart	1.00	.45
❑ 128 Yancey Thigpen	.25	.11
❑ 129 Rod Woodson	.25	.11
❑ 130 Jerome Bettis	.50	.23
❑ 131 Isaac Bruce	.50	.23
❑ 132 Troy Drayton	.10	.05
❑ 133 Sean Gilbert	.10	.05
❑ 134 Chris Miller	.10	.05
❑ 135 Andre Coleman	.10	.05
❑ 136 Ronnie Harmon	.10	.05
❑ 137 Aaron Hayden RC	.10	.05
❑ 138 Stan Humphries	.25	.11
❑ 139 Natrone Means	.50	.23
❑ 140 Junior Seau	.25	.11
❑ 141 William Floyd	.25	.11
❑ 142 Merton Hanks	.10	.05
❑ 143 Brent Jones	.10	.05
❑ 144 Derek Loville	.10	.05
❑ 145 Jerry Rice	1.25	.55
❑ 146 J.J. Stokes	.50	.23
❑ 147 Steve Young	1.00	.45
❑ 148 Brian Blades	.10	.05
❑ 149 Joey Galloway	1.00	.45
❑ 150 Cortez Kennedy	.10	.05
❑ 151 Rick Mirer	.25	.11
❑ 152 Chris Warren	.25	.11
❑ 153 Derrick Brooks	.10	.05
❑ 154 Trent Dilfer	.50	.23
❑ 155 Alvin Harper	.10	.05
❑ 156 Jackie Harris	.10	.05
❑ 157 Hardy Nickerson	.10	.05
❑ 158 Errict Rhett	.25	.11
❑ 159 Terry Allen	.25	.11
❑ 160 Henry Ellard	.10	.05
❑ 161 Brian Mitchell	.10	.05
❑ 162 Heath Shuler	.25	.11
❑ 163 Michael Westbrook	.50	.23
❑ 164 Tim Biakabutuka RC	1.00	.45
❑ 165 Tony Brackens RC	.25	.11
❑ 166 Rickey Dudley RC	.50	.23
❑ 167 Bobby Engram RC	.50	.23
❑ 168 Daryl Gardener RC	.10	.05
❑ 169 Eddie George RC	4.00	1.80
❑ 170 Terry Glenn RC	1.50	.70
❑ 171 Kevin Hardy RC	.50	.23
❑ 172 Keyshawn Johnson RC	2.50	1.10
❑ 173 Cedric Jones RC	.10	.05
❑ 174 Leeland McElroy RC	.50	.23
❑ 175 Jonathan Ogden RC	.10	.05
❑ 176 Lawrence Phillips RC	.60	.25
❑ 177 Simeon Rice RC	.50	.23
❑ 178 Regan Upshaw RC	.10	.05
❑ 179 Justin Armour FI	.10	.05
❑ 180 Kyle Brady FI	.10	.05
❑ 181 Devin Bush FI	.10	.05
❑ 182 Kevin Carter FI	.10	.05
❑ 183 Wayne Chrebet FI	.25	.11
❑ 184 Napoleon Kaufman FI	.75	.35
❑ 185 Frank Sanders FI	.25	.11
❑ 186 Warren Sapp FI	.10	.05
❑ 187 Eric Zeier FI	.10	.05
❑ 188 Ray Zellars FI	.10	.05
❑ 189 Bill Brooks SW	.10	.05
❑ 190 Chris Calloway SW	.10	.05
❑ 191 Zack Crockett SW	.10	.05
❑ 192 Antonio Freeman SW	1.00	.45
❑ 193 Tyrone Hughes SW	.10	.05
❑ 194 Daryl Johnston SW	.25	.11
❑ 195 Tony Martin SW	.10	.05
❑ 196 Keenan McCardell SW	.50	.23
❑ 197 Glyn Milburn SW	.10	.05
❑ 198 David Palmer SW	.10	.05
❑ 199 Checklist	.10	.05
❑ 200 Checklist	.10	.05
❑ P1 Promo Sheet Trent Dilfer Brett Favre Mr.Momentum Daryl Johnston Secret Weapon	2.00	.90

1996 Ultra All-Rookie Die Cuts

	MINT	NRMT
COMPLETE SET (10)	120.00	55.00
COMMON CARD (1-10)	8.00	3.60
SEMISTARS	10.00	4.50
STATED ODDS 1:180		
❑ 1 Bobby Engram	10.00	4.50
❑ 2 Daryl Gardener	8.00	3.60
❑ 3 Eddie George	40.00	18.00
❑ 4 Terry Glenn	12.00	5.50
❑ 5 Kevin Hardy	8.00	3.60
❑ 6 Keyshawn Johnson	20.00	9.00
❑ 7 Cedric Jones	8.00	3.60
❑ 8 Leeland McElroy	10.00	4.50
❑ 9 Jonathan Ogden	8.00	3.60
❑ 10 Simeon Rice	10.00	4.50

1996 Ultra Mr. Momentum

	MINT	NRMT
COMPLETE SET (20)	40.00	18.00
STATED ODDS 1:10		
❑ 1 Robert Brooks	1.50	.70
❑ 2 Isaac Bruce	1.50	.70
❑ 3 Terrell Davis	10.00	4.50
❑ 4 John Elway	8.00	3.60
❑ 5 Marshall Faulk	1.50	.70
❑ 6 Brett Favre	8.00	3.60
❑ 7 Joey Galloway	3.00	1.35
❑ 8 Dan Marino	8.00	3.60

	MINT	NRMT
❑ 9 Curtis Martin	3.00	1.35
❑ 10 Herman Moore	1.50	.70
❑ 11 Carl Pickens	1.50	.70
❑ 12 Jerry Rice	4.00	1.80
❑ 13 Barry Sanders	8.00	3.60
❑ 14 Chris Sanders	.75	.35
❑ 15 Deion Sanders	2.50	1.10
❑ 16 Kordell Stewart	3.00	1.35
❑ 17 Tamarick Vanover	.75	.35
❑ 18 Chris Warren	.75	.35
❑ 19 Ricky Watters	.75	.35
❑ 20 Steve Young	3.00	1.35

1996 Ultra Pulsating

	MINT	NRMT
COMPLETE SET (10)	35.00	16.00
STATED ODDS 1:20		
❑ 1 Isaac Bruce	1.50	.70
❑ 2 Brett Favre	8.00	3.60
❑ 3 Joey Galloway	3.00	1.35
❑ 4 Curtis Martin	3.00	1.35
❑ 5 Rashaan Salaam	1.50	.70
❑ 6 Barry Sanders	8.00	3.60
❑ 7 Deion Sanders	2.50	1.10
❑ 8 Emmitt Smith	6.00	2.70
❑ 9 Kordell Stewart	3.00	1.35
❑ 10 Chris Warren	.75	.35

1996 Ultra Rookies

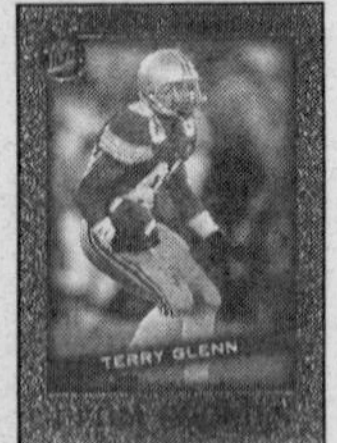

	MINT	NRMT
COMPLETE SET (30)	40.00	18.00
COMMON CARD (1-30)	.75	.35
SEMISTARS	1.25	.55
UNLISTED STARS	2.50	1.10
STATED ODDS 1:3		
❑ 1 Karim Abdul-Jabbar	2.50	1.10
❑ 2 Mike Alstott	4.00	1.80
❑ 3 Marco Battaglia	.75	.35
❑ 4 Tim Biakabutuka	3.00	1.35
❑ 5 Sean Boyd	.75	.35
❑ 6 Tony Brackens	1.25	.55
❑ 7 Duane Clemons	.75	.35
❑ 8 Bobby Engram	1.25	.55
❑ 9 Daryl Gardener	.75	.35
❑ 10 Eddie George	8.00	3.60
❑ 11 Terry Glenn	4.00	1.80
❑ 12 Kevin Hardy	.75	.35
❑ 13 Marvin Harrison	6.00	2.70
❑ 14 Dietrich Jells	.75	.35
❑ 15 Keyshawn Johnson	6.00	2.70
❑ 16 Lance Johnstone	.75	.35
❑ 17 Cedric Jones	.75	.35
❑ 18 Marcus Jones	.75	.35
❑ 19 Danny Kanell	1.25	.55
❑ 20 Markco Maddox RC	.75	.35
❑ 21 Derrick Mayes	1.25	.55
❑ 22 Leeland McElroy	1.25	.55
❑ 23 Dell McGee	.75	.35
❑ 24 Alex Molden	.75	.35
❑ 25 Eric Moulds	5.00	2.20
❑ 26 Jonathan Ogden	.75	.35
❑ 27 Lawrence Phillips	2.50	1.10
❑ 28 Simeon Rice	1.25	.55
❑ 29 Regan Upshaw	.75	.35
❑ 30 Jerome Woods	.75	.35

1996 Ultra Sledgehammer

	MINT	NRMT
COMPLETE SET (10)	40.00	18.00
STATED ODDS 1:15 HOBBY		
❑ 1 Jeff Blake	2.50	1.10
❑ 2 Terrell Davis	15.00	6.75
❑ 3 Hugh Douglas	.50	.23
❑ 4 Marshall Faulk	2.50	1.10
❑ 5 Michael Irvin	2.50	1.10
❑ 6 Steve McNair	5.00	2.20
❑ 7 Natrone Means	2.50	1.10
❑ 8 Errict Rhett	1.25	.55
❑ 9 Emmitt Smith	10.00	4.50
❑ 10 Rodney Thomas	.50	.23

1997 Ultra

	MINT	NRMT
COMPLETE SET (350)	80.00	36.00
COMP.SERIES 1 (200)	30.00	13.50
COMP.SERIES 2 (150)	50.00	22.00
COMMON CARD (1-350)	.15	.07
SEMISTARS	.25	.11
UNLISTED STARS	.50	.23
COMP.GOLD MED.SET (346)	400.00	180.00
COMP.GOLD MED.1 (198)	150.00	70.00
COMP.GOLD MED.2 (148)	250.00	110.00
*STARS: 1.5X TO 3X HI COL.		
*RCs: 1X TO 2X HI		
GOLD MEDALLION: ONE PER PACK		
COMP.PLAT.MED.SET (346)	4000.00	1800.00
COMP.PLAT.MEDAL.1 (198)	1800.00	800.00
COMP.PLAT.MEDAL.2 (148)	2200.00	1000.00
*PLAT.MED.STARS: 25X TO 50X HI COL.		
*PLAT.MED.RCs: 12.5X TO 25X		
PLAT.MEDALLION ODDS 1:100		
STATED PRINT RUN LESS THAN 150 SETS		
❑ 1 Brett Favre	2.50	1.10
❑ 2 Ricky Watters	.25	.11
❑ 3 Dan Marino	2.50	1.10
❑ 4 Bryan Still	.15	.07
❑ 5 Chester McGlockton	.15	.07
❑ 6 Tim Biakabutuka	.25	.11
❑ 7 Dave Brown	.15	.07
❑ 8 Mike Alstott	.50	.23
❑ 9 O.J. McDuffie	.25	.11
❑ 10 Mark Brunell	1.25	.55
❑ 11 Michael Bates	.15	.07
❑ 12 Tyrone Wheatley	.25	.11
❑ 13 Eddie George	1.25	.55
❑ 14 Kevin Greene	.25	.11
❑ 15 Jerris McPhail	.15	.07
❑ 16 Harvey Williams	.15	.07
❑ 17 Eric Swann	.15	.07
❑ 18 Carl Pickens	.50	.23
❑ 19 Terrell Davis	2.00	.90
❑ 20 Charles Way	.25	.11
❑ 21 Jamie Asher	.15	.07
❑ 22 Qadry Ismail	.25	.11
❑ 23 Lawrence Phillips	.15	.07
❑ 24 John Friesz	.15	.07
❑ 25 Dorsey Levens	.50	.23
❑ 26 Willie McGinest	.15	.07
❑ 27 Chris T. Jones	.15	.07
❑ 28 Cortez Kennedy	.15	.07
❑ 29 Raymont Harris	.15	.07
❑ 30 William Roaf	.15	.07
❑ 31 Ted Johnson	.15	.07
❑ 32 Tony Martin	.25	.11
❑ 33 Jim Everett	.15	.07
❑ 34 Ray Zellars	.15	.07
❑ 35 Derrick Alexander WR	.25	.11
❑ 36 Leonard Russell	.15	.07
❑ 37 William Thomas	.15	.07
❑ 38 Karim Abdul-Jabbar	.50	.23
❑ 39 Kevin Turner	.15	.07
❑ 40 Robert Brooks	.25	.11
❑ 41 Kent Graham	.15	.07
❑ 42 Tony Brackens	.15	.07
❑ 43 Rodney Hampton	.25	.11
❑ 44 Drew Bledsoe	1.25	.55
❑ 45 Barry Sanders	2.50	1.10
❑ 46 Tim Brown	.50	.23
❑ 47 Reggie White	.50	.23
❑ 48 Terry Allen	.50	.23
❑ 49 Jim Harbaugh	.25	.11
❑ 50 John Elway	2.50	1.10
❑ 51 William Floyd	.25	.11
❑ 52 Michael Jackson	.25	.11
❑ 53 Larry Centers	.25	.11
❑ 54 Emmitt Smith	2.00	.90
❑ 55 Bruce Smith	.25	.11
❑ 56 Terrell Owens	.50	.23
❑ 57 Deion Sanders	.50	.23
❑ 58 Neil O'Donnell	.25	.11

❑ 59 Kordell Stewart .75 .35
❑ 60 Bobby Engram .25 .11
❑ 61 Keenan McCardell .25 .11
❑ 62 Ben Coates .25 .11
❑ 63 Curtis Martin .75 .35
❑ 64 Hugh Douglas .15 .07
❑ 65 Eric Moulds .50 .23
❑ 66 Derrick Thomas .25 .11
❑ 67 Byron Bam Morris .15 .07
❑ 68 Bryan Cox .15 .07
❑ 69 Rob Moore .25 .11
❑ 70 Michael Haynes .15 .07
❑ 71 Brian Mitchell .15 .07
❑ 72 Alex Molden .15 .07
❑ 73 Steve Young .75 .35
❑ 74 Andre Reed .25 .11
❑ 75 Michael Westbrook .25 .11
❑ 76 Eric Metcalf .25 .11
❑ 77 Tony Banks .25 .11
❑ 78 Ken Dilger .15 .07
❑ 79 John Henry Mills RC .15 .07
❑ 80 Ashley Ambrose .15 .07
❑ 81 Jason Dunn .15 .07
❑ 82 Trent Dilfer .50 .23
❑ 83 Wayne Chrebet .50 .23
❑ 84 Ty Detmer .25 .11
❑ 85 Aeneas Williams .15 .07
❑ 86 Frank Wycheck .15 .07
❑ 87 Jessie Tuggle .15 .07
❑ 88 Steve McNair .75 .35
❑ 89 Chris Slade .15 .07
❑ 90 Anthony Johnson .15 .07
❑ 91 Simeon Rice .25 .11
❑ 92 Mike Tomczak .15 .07
❑ 93 Sean Jones .15 .07
❑ 94 Wesley Walls .25 .11
❑ 95 Thurman Thomas .50 .23
❑ 96 Scott Mitchell .25 .11
❑ 97 Desmond Howard .25 .11
❑ 98 Chris Warren .25 .11
❑ 99 Glyn Milburn .15 .07
❑ 100 Vinny Testaverde .25 .11
❑ 101 James O.Stewart .25 .11
❑ 102 Iheanyi Uwaezuoke .25 .11
❑ 103 Stan Humphries .25 .11
❑ 104 Terance Mathis .25 .11
❑ 105 Thomas Lewis .15 .07
❑ 106 Eddie Kennison .25 .11
❑ 107 Rashaan Salaam .15 .07
❑ 108 Curtis Conway .25 .11
❑ 109 Chris Sanders .15 .07
❑ 110 Marcus Allen .50 .23
❑ 111 Gilbert Brown .15 .07
❑ 112 Jason Sehorn .25 .11
❑ 113 Zach Thomas .25 .11
❑ 114 Bobby Hebert .15 .07
❑ 115 Herman Moore .50 .23
❑ 116 Ray Lewis .15 .07
❑ 117 Darnay Scott .25 .11
❑ 118 Jamal Anderson .75 .35
❑ 119 Keyshawn Johnson .50 .23
❑ 120 Adrian Murrell .25 .11
❑ 121 Sam Mills .15 .07
❑ 122 Irving Fryar .25 .11
❑ 123 Ki-Jana Carter .15 .07
❑ 124 Gus Frerotte .15 .07
❑ 125 Terry Glenn .50 .23
❑ 126 Quentin Coryatt .15 .07
❑ 127 Robert Smith .25 .11
❑ 128 Jeff Blake .25 .11
❑ 129 Natrone Means .50 .23
❑ 130 Isaac Bruce .50 .23
❑ 131 Lamar Lathon .15 .07
❑ 132 Johnnie Morton .25 .11
❑ 133 Jerry Rice 1.25 .55
❑ 134 Errict Rhett .15 .07
❑ 135 Junior Seau .25 .11
❑ 136 Joey Galloway .75 .35
❑ 137 Napoleon Kaufman .50 .23
❑ 138 Troy Aikman 1.25 .55
❑ 139 Kevin Hardy .15 .07
❑ 140 Jimmy Smith .25 .11
❑ 141 Edgar Bennett .25 .11
❑ 142 Hardy Nickerson .15 .07
❑ 143 Greg Lloyd .15 .07
❑ 144 Dale Carter .15 .07
❑ 145 Jake Reed .25 .11
❑ 146 Cris Carter .50 .23
❑ 147 Todd Collins .15 .07
❑ 148 Mel Gray .15 .07
❑ 149 Lawyer Milloy .15 .07
❑ 150 Kimble Anders .25 .11
❑ 151 Darick Holmes .15 .07
❑ 152 Bert Emanuel .25 .11
❑ 153 Marshall Faulk .50 .23
❑ 154 Frank Sanders .25 .11
❑ 155 Leeland McElroy .15 .07
❑ 156 Rickey Dudley .25 .11
❑ 157 Tamarick Vanover .25 .11
❑ 158 Kerry Collins .25 .11
❑ 159 Jeff Graham .15 .07
❑ 160 Jerome Bettis .50 .23
❑ 161 Greg Hill .15 .07
❑ 162 John Mobley .15 .07
❑ 163 Michael Irvin .50 .23
❑ 164 Marvin Harrison .50 .23
❑ 165 Jim Schwantz RC .15 .07
❑ 166 Jermaine Lewis .50 .23
❑ 167 Levon Kirkland .15 .07
❑ 168 Nilo Silvan .15 .07
❑ 169 Ken Norton .15 .07
❑ 170 Yancey Thigpen .25 .11
❑ 171 Antonio Freeman .75 .35
❑ 172 Terry Kirby .25 .11
❑ 173 Brad Johnson .60 .25
❑ 174 Reidel Anthony RC 1.25 .55
❑ 175 Tiki Barber RC .75 .35
❑ 176 Pat Barnes RC .50 .23
❑ 177 Michael Booker RC .15 .07
❑ 178 Peter Boulware RC .25 .11
❑ 179 Rae Carruth RC .50 .23
❑ 180 Troy Davis RC .50 .23
❑ 181 Corey Dillon RC 2.50 1.10
❑ 182 Jim Druckenmiller RC .75 .35
❑ 183 Warrick Dunn RC 2.00 .90
❑ 184 James Farrior RC .15 .07
❑ 185 Yatil Green RC .25 .11
❑ 186 Walter Jones RC .15 .07
❑ 187 Tom Knight RC .15 .07
❑ 188 Sam Madison RC .15 .07
❑ 189 Tyrus McCloud RC .15 .07
❑ 190 Orlando Pace RC .15 .07
❑ 191 Jake Plummer RC 5.00 2.20
❑ 192 Dwayne Rudd RC .15 .07
❑ 193 Darrell Russell RC .15 .07
❑ 194 Sedrick Shaw RC .50 .23
❑ 195 Shawn Springs RC .25 .11
❑ 196 Bryant Westbrook RC .15 .07
❑ 197 Danny Wuerffel RC 1.00 .45
❑ 198 Reinard Wilson RC .15 .07
❑ 199 Checklist .15 .07
Rodney Hampton
❑ 200 Checklist .50 .23
John Elway
❑ 201 Rick Mirer .15 .07
❑ 202 Torrance Small .15 .07
❑ 203 Ricky Proehl .15 .07
❑ 204 Will Blackwell RC .50 .23
❑ 205 Warrick Dunn 1.00 .45
❑ 206 Rob Johnson .50 .23
❑ 207 Jim Schwantz .15 .07
❑ 208 Ike Hilliard RC 1.25 .55
❑ 209 Chris Canty RC .15 .07
❑ 210 Chris Boniol .15 .07
❑ 211 Jim Druckenmiller .50 .23
❑ 212 Tony Gonzalez RC 2.00 .90
❑ 213 Scottie Graham .15 .07
❑ 214 Byron Hanspard RC 1.25 .55
❑ 215 Gary Brown .15 .07
❑ 216 Darrell Russell .15 .07
❑ 217 Sedrick Shaw .50 .23
❑ 218 Boomer Esiason .25 .11
❑ 219 Peter Boulware .25 .11
❑ 220 Willie Green .15 .07
❑ 221 Dietrich Jells .15 .07
❑ 222 Freddie Jones RC .25 .11
❑ 223 Eric Metcalf .25 .11
❑ 224 John Henry Mills .15 .07
❑ 225 Michael Timpson .15 .07
❑ 226 Danny Wuerffel .25 .11
❑ 227 Daimon Shelton RC .15 .07
❑ 228 Henry Ellard .15 .07
❑ 229 Flipper Anderson .15 .07
❑ 230 Hunter Goodwin RC .15 .07
❑ 231 Jay Graham RC .50 .23
❑ 232 Duce Staley RC 12.00 5.50
❑ 233 Lamar Thomas .15 .07
❑ 234 Rod Woodson .25 .11
❑ 235 Zack Crockett .15 .07
❑ 236 Ernie Mills .15 .07
❑ 237 Kyle Brady .15 .07
❑ 238 Jesse Campbell .15 .07
❑ 239 Anthony Miller .15 .07
❑ 240 Michael Haynes .15 .07
❑ 241 Qadry Ismail .25 .11
❑ 242 Tom Knight .15 .07
❑ 243 Brian Manning RC .15 .07
❑ 244 Derrick Mayes .25 .11
❑ 245 Jamie Sharper RC .15 .07
❑ 246 Sherman Williams .15 .07
❑ 247 Yatil Green .25 .11
❑ 248 Howard Griffith .15 .07
❑ 249 Brian Blades .15 .07
❑ 250 Mark Chmura .25 .11
❑ 251 Chris Darkins .15 .07
❑ 252 Willie Davis .15 .07
❑ 253 Quinn Early .15 .07
❑ 254 Marc Edwards RC .15 .07
❑ 255 Charlie Jones .25 .11
❑ 256 Jake Plummer 2.50 1.10
❑ 257 Heath Shuler .15 .07
❑ 258 Fred Barnett .15 .07
❑ 259 William Henderson .25 .11
❑ 260 Michael Booker .15 .07
❑ 261 Chad Brown .15 .07
❑ 262 Garrison Hearst .25 .11
❑ 263 Leon Johnson RC .15 .07
❑ 264 Antowain Smith RC 1.50 .70
❑ 265 Darnell Autry RC .25 .11
❑ 266 Craig Heyward .15 .07
❑ 267 Walter Jones .15 .07
❑ 268 Dexter Coakley RC .15 .07
❑ 269 Mercury Hayes .15 .07
❑ 270 Brett Perriman .15 .07
❑ 271 Chris Spielman .15 .07
❑ 272 Kevin Greene .25 .11
❑ 273 Kevin Lockett RC .25 .11
❑ 274 Troy Davis .50 .23
❑ 275 Brent Jones .25 .11
❑ 276 Chris Chandler .25 .11
❑ 277 Bryant Westbrook .15 .07
❑ 278 Desmond Howard .25 .11
❑ 279 Tyrone Hughes .15 .07
❑ 280 Kez McCorvey .15 .07
❑ 281 Stephen Davis 1.25 .55
❑ 282 Steve Everitt .15 .07
❑ 283 Andre Hastings .15 .07
❑ 284 Marcus Robinson RC 30.00 13.50
❑ 285 Donnell Woolford .15 .07
❑ 286 Mario Bates .15 .07
❑ 287 Corey Dillon 1.25 .55
❑ 288 Jackie Harris .15 .07
❑ 289 Lorenzo Neal .15 .07
❑ 290 Anthony Pleasant .15 .07
❑ 291 Andre Rison .25 .11
❑ 292 Amani Toomer .25 .11
❑ 293 Eric Turner .15 .07
❑ 294 Elvis Grbac .25 .11
❑ 295 Cris Dishman .15 .07
❑ 296 Tom Carter .15 .07
❑ 297 Mark Carrier DB .15 .07
❑ 298 Orlando Pace .15 .07
❑ 299 Jay Riemersma RC .15 .07
❑ 300 Daryl Johnston .25 .11
❑ 301 Joey Kent RC .50 .23
❑ 302 Ronnie Harmon .15 .07
❑ 303 Rocket Ismail .25 .11
❑ 304 Terrell Davis 2.00 .90
❑ 305 Sean Dawkins .15 .07
❑ 306 Jeff George .25 .11
❑ 307 David Palmer .15 .07
❑ 308 Dwayne Rudd .15 .07
❑ 309 J.J. Stokes .25 .11
❑ 310 James Farrior .15 .07
❑ 311 William Fuller .15 .07
❑ 312 George Jones RC .25 .11
❑ 313 John Allred RC .15 .07
❑ 314 Tony Graziani RC .50 .23

❑ 315 Jeff Hostetler .... .15 .07
❑ 316 Keith Poole RC .... .50 .23
❑ 317 Neil Smith .... .25 .11
❑ 318 Steve Tasker .... .15 .07
❑ 319 Mike Vrabel RC .... .15 .07
❑ 320 Pat Barnes .... .50 .23
❑ 321 James Hundon RC .... .15 .07
❑ 322 O.J. Santiago RC .... .50 .23
❑ 323 Billy Davis RC .... .15 .07
❑ 324 Shawn Springs .... .25 .11
❑ 325 Reinard Wilson RC .... .15 .07
❑ 326 Charles Johnson .... .25 .11
❑ 327 Micheal Barrow .... .15 .07
❑ 328 Derrick Mason RC........... .15 .07
❑ 329 Muhsin Muhammad........ .25 .11
❑ 330 David LaFleur RC .... .25 .11
❑ 331 Reidel Anthony .... .50 .23
❑ 332 Tiki Barber...................... .50 .23
❑ 333 Ray Buchanan................ .15 .07
❑ 334 John Elway 2.50 1.10
❑ 335 Alvin Harper .... .15 .07
❑ 336 Damon Jones RC .... .15 .07
❑ 337 Dedric Ward RC 2.50 1.10
❑ 338 Jim Everett .... .15 .07
❑ 339 Jon Harris .... .15 .07
❑ 340 Warren Moon .... .50 .23
❑ 341 Rae Carruth.................... .25 .11
❑ 342 John Mobley .... .15 .07
❑ 343 Tyrone Poole.................. .15 .07
❑ 344 Mike Cherry RC.............. .15 .07
❑ 345 Horace Copeland .... .15 .07
❑ 346 Deon Figures.................. .15 .07
❑ 347 Antwuan Wyatt RC .... .15 .07
❑ 348 Tommy Vardell .... .15 .07
❑ 349 Checklist (201-324)........ .15 .07
❑ 350 Checklist (325-350/inserts) .. .15 .07
❑ S1A Terrell Davis 150.00 70.00
(Sample Auto)
❑ AU3 Dan Marino AUTO .. 300.00 135.00
(reportedly 100 were signed)
❑ S1 Terrell Davis Sample .... 2.00 .90

1997 Ultra All-Rookie Team

	MINT	NRMT
COMPLETE SET (12)	50.00	22.00
STATED ODDS 1:18 SER.2.........		

❑ 1 Antowain Smith 6.00 2.70
❑ 2 Jay Graham...................... 2.00 .90
❑ 3 Ike Hilliard 5.00 2.20
❑ 4 Warrick Dunn 8.00 3.60
❑ 5 Tony Gonzalez 8.00 3.60
❑ 6 David LaFleur .... 1.00 .45
❑ 7 Reidel Anthony 5.00 2.20
❑ 8 Rae Carruth...................... 1.00 .45
❑ 9 Byron Hanspard 5.00 2.20
❑ 10 Joey Kent .... 2.00 .90
❑ 11 Kevin Lockett.................. 1.00 .45
❑ 12 Jake Plummer 20.00 9.00

1997 Ultra Blitzkrieg

	MINT	NRMT
COMPLETE SET (18)	60.00	27.00
STATED ODDS 1:6 SER.1...........		

*DIE CUTS: 1X TO 2.5X BASE INSERT
DIE CUT ODDS 1:36 SER.1 ....

❑ 1 Eddie George 4.00 1.80
❑ 2 Terry Glenn...................... 1.50 .70
❑ 3 Karim Abdul-Jabbar .... 1.50 .70
❑ 4 Emmitt Smith.................... 6.00 2.70
❑ 5 Dan Marino 8.00 3.60
❑ 6 Brett Favre 8.00 3.60
❑ 7 Keyshawn Johnson.......... 1.50 .70
❑ 8 Curtis Martin 2.50 1.10
❑ 9 Marvin Harrison............... 1.50 .70
❑ 10 Barry Sanders 8.00 3.60
❑ 11 Jerry Rice 4.00 1.80
❑ 12 Terrell Davis 6.00 2.70
❑ 13 Troy Aikman 4.00 1.80
❑ 14 Drew Bledsoe 4.00 1.80
❑ 15 John Elway 8.00 3.60
❑ 16 Kordell Stewart 2.50 1.10
❑ 17 Kerry Collins .... .75 .35
❑ 18 Steve Young 2.50 1.10

1997 Ultra Comeback Kids

	MINT	NRMT
COMPLETE SET (10)	30.00	13.50
STATED ODDS 1:8 SER.2...........		

❑ 1 Dan Marino 8.00 3.60
❑ 2 Barry Sanders 8.00 3.60
❑ 3 Jerry Rice 4.00 1.80
❑ 4 John Elway 8.00 3.60
❑ 5 Steve Young 2.50 1.10
❑ 6 Deion Sanders .... 1.50 .70
❑ 7 Mark Brunell 4.00 1.80
❑ 8 Tim Biakabutuka .... .75 .35
❑ 9 Tony Banks .... .75 .35
❑ 10 Terry Allen...................... 1.50 .70

1997 Ultra First Rounders

	MINT	NRMT
COMPLETE SET (12)	10.00	4.50
STATED ODDS 1:4 SER.2...........		

❑ 1 Antowain Smith .... 2.00 .90
❑ 2 Rae Carruth....................... .60 .25
❑ 3 Peter Boulware .... .30 .14
❑ 4 Shawn Springs .... .30 .14
❑ 5 Bryant Westbrook .... .20 .09
❑ 6 Orlando Pace .... .20 .09
❑ 7 Jim Druckenmiller .... 1.00 .45
❑ 8 Yatil Green .... .30 .14
❑ 9 Reidel Anthony .... 1.50 .70
❑ 10 Ike Hilliard .... 1.50 .70
❑ 11 Darrell Russell.................. .20 .09
❑ 12 Warrick Dunn 2.50 1.10

1997 Ultra Main Event

	MINT	NRMT
COMPLETE SET (10)	30.00	13.50
STATED ODDS 1:8 SER.2...........		

❑ 1 Dan Marino 8.00 3.60
❑ 2 Barry Sanders 8.00 3.60
❑ 3 Jerry Rice 4.00 1.80
❑ 4 Drew Bledsoe 4.00 1.80
❑ 5 John Elway 8.00 3.60
❑ 6 Troy Aikman 4.00 1.80
❑ 7 Deion Sanders .... 1.50 .70
❑ 8 Joey Galloway.................. 2.50 1.10
❑ 9 Steve McNair.................... 2.50 1.10
❑ 10 Marshall Faulk................ 1.50 .70

1997 Ultra Play of the Game

	MINT	NRMT
COMPLETE SET (10)	20.00	9.00
STATED ODDS 1:8 SER.1...........		

❑ 1 Deion Sanders .... 1.50 .70
❑ 2 Jerry Rice 4.00 1.80
❑ 3 Michael Westbrook .... .75 .35
❑ 4 Steve McNair.................... 2.50 1.10
❑ 5 Marshall Faulk.................. 1.50 .70
❑ 6 Terrell Davis 6.00 2.70
❑ 7 Mark Brunell 4.00 1.80
❑ 8 Isaac Bruce .... 1.50 .70
❑ 9 Tony Banks .... .75 .35
❑ 10 Jamal Anderson 2.50 1.10

1997 Ultra Reebok

	MINT	NRMT
COMP.REEBOK BRONZE (15)	4.00	1.80
SEMISTARS BRONZE...............	.30	.14
UNLISTED STARS BRONZE......	.40	.18

*REEBOK GOLDS: 2X TO 5X BRONZES
*REEBOK GREENS: 25X TO 50X BRONZES
*REEBOK REDS: 12.5X TO 25X BRONZES
*REEBOK SILVERS: .75X TO 2X BRONZES
OVERALL REEBOK ODDS ONE PER PACK

❑ 202 Torrance Small	.20	.09
❑ 207 Jim Schwantz	.20	.09
❑ 210 Chris Boniol	.20	.09
❑ 223 Eric Metcalf	.30	.14
❑ 238 Jesse Campbell	.20	.09
❑ 241 Qadry Ismail	.30	.14
❑ 270 Brett Perriman	.20	.09
❑ 271 Chris Spielman	.20	.09
❑ 278 Desmond Howard	.30	.14
❑ 282 Steve Everitt	.20	.09
❑ 289 Lorenzo Neal	.20	.09
❑ 317 Neil Smith	.30	.14
❑ 318 Steve Tasker	.30	.14
❑ 334 John Elway	1.25	.55
❑ 343 Tyrone Poole	.20	.09

1997 Ultra Rising Stars

	MINT	NRMT
COMPLETE SET (10)	12.00	5.50
STATED ODDS 1:4 SER.2		
❑ 1 Keyshawn Johnson	1.25	.55
❑ 2 Terrell Davis	5.00	2.20
❑ 3 Kordell Stewart	2.00	.90
❑ 4 Kerry Collins	.60	.25
❑ 5 Joey Galloway	2.00	.90
❑ 6 Steve McNair	2.00	.90
❑ 7 Jamal Anderson	2.00	.90
❑ 8 Michael Westbrook	.60	.25
❑ 9 Marshall Faulk	1.25	.55
❑ 10 Isaac Bruce	1.25	.55

1997 Ultra Rookies

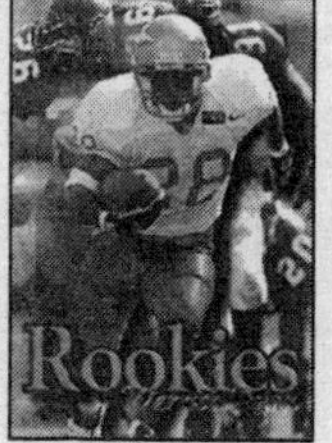

	MINT	NRMT
COMPLETE SET (12)	12.00	5.50
STATED ODDS 1:4 SER.1		
*GOLD EMBOSSED: 2X TO 4X BASE CARD HI		
GOLD EMBOSSED ODDS 1:18 SER.1		
❑ 1 Darnell Autry	.75	.35
❑ 2 Orlando Pace	.50	.23
❑ 3 Peter Boulware	.75	.35
❑ 4 Shawn Springs	.75	.35
❑ 5 Bryant Westbrook	.50	.23
❑ 6 Rae Carruth	1.00	.45
❑ 7 Jim Druckenmiller	1.50	.70
❑ 8 Yatil Green	.75	.35
❑ 9 James Farrior	.50	.23
❑ 10 Dwayne Rudd	.50	.23
❑ 11 Darrell Russell	.50	.23
❑ 12 Warrick Dunn	4.00	1.80

1997 Ultra Specialists

	MINT	NRMT
COMPLETE SET (18)	80.00	36.00
STATED ODDS 1:6 SER.2		
*ULTRA PARALLELS: 5X TO 10X BASE CARD HI		
ULTRA PARALLEL STATED ODDS 1:36 SER.2		
❑ 1 Eddie George	6.00	2.70
❑ 2 Terry Glenn	2.50	1.10
❑ 3 Karim Abdul-Jabbar	2.50	1.10
❑ 4 Emmitt Smith	10.00	4.50
❑ 5 Brett Favre	12.00	5.50
❑ 6 Mark Brunell	6.00	2.70
❑ 7 Curtis Martin	4.00	1.80
❑ 8 Kerry Collins	1.25	.55
❑ 9 Marvin Harrison	2.50	1.10
❑ 10 Jerry Rice	6.00	2.70
❑ 11 Tony Martin	1.25	.55
❑ 12 Terrell Davis	10.00	4.50
❑ 13 Troy Aikman	6.00	2.70
❑ 14 Drew Bledsoe	6.00	2.70
❑ 15 John Elway	12.00	5.50
❑ 16 Kordell Stewart	4.00	1.80
❑ 17 Keyshawn Johnson	2.50	1.10
❑ 18 Steve Young	4.00	1.80

1997 Ultra Starring Role

	MINT	NRMT
COMPLETE SET (10)	250.00	110.00
STATED ODDS 1:288 SER.1		
❑ 1 Emmitt Smith	40.00	18.00
❑ 2 Barry Sanders	50.00	22.00
❑ 3 Curtis Martin	15.00	6.75
❑ 4 Dan Marino	50.00	22.00
❑ 5 Keyshawn Johnson	10.00	4.50
❑ 6 Marvin Harrison	10.00	4.50
❑ 7 Terry Glenn	10.00	4.50
❑ 8 Eddie George	25.00	11.00
❑ 9 Brett Favre	50.00	22.00
❑ 10 Karim Abdul-Jabbar	10.00	4.50

1997 Ultra Stars

	MINT	NRMT
COMPLETE SET (10)	250.00	110.00
STATED ODDS 1:288 SER.1		
❑ 1 Emmitt Smith	50.00	22.00
❑ 2 Barry Sanders	60.00	27.00
❑ 3 Curtis Martin	20.00	9.00
❑ 4 Dan Marino	60.00	27.00
❑ 5 Mark Brunell	30.00	13.50
❑ 6 Marvin Harrison	12.00	5.50
❑ 7 Terry Glenn	12.00	5.50
❑ 8 Eddie George	30.00	13.50
❑ 9 Brett Favre	60.00	27.00
❑ 10 Karim Abdul-Jabbar	12.00	5.50

1997 Ultra Sunday School

	MINT	NRMT
COMPLETE SET (10)	25.00	11.00
STATED ODDS 1:8 SER.1		
❑ 1 Marvin Harrison	2.00	.90
❑ 2 Barry Sanders	10.00	4.50
❑ 3 Troy Aikman	5.00	2.20
❑ 4 Drew Bledsoe	5.00	2.20
❑ 5 John Elway	10.00	4.50
❑ 6 Kordell Stewart	3.00	1.35
❑ 7 Kerry Collins	1.00	.45
❑ 8 Steve Young	3.00	1.35
❑ 9 Deion Sanders	2.00	.90
❑ 10 Joey Galloway	3.00	1.35

1997 Ultra Talent Show

	MINT	NRMT
COMPLETE SET (10)	8.00	3.60
STATED ODDS 1:4 SER.1		
❑ 1 Joey Galloway	2.50	1.10
❑ 2 Steve McNair	2.50	1.10
❑ 3 Marshall Faulk	1.50	.70
❑ 4 Isaac Bruce	1.50	.70
❑ 5 Michael Westbrook	.75	.35
❑ 6 Zach Thomas	.75	.35
❑ 7 Jamal Anderson	2.50	1.10
❑ 8 Mike Alstott	1.50	.70
❑ 9 Mark Brunell	4.00	1.80
❑ 10 Eddie Kennison	.75	.35

1998 Ultra

	MINT	NRMT
COMPLETE SET (425)	250.00	110.00
COMP.SERIES 1 (225)	150.00	70.00
COMP.SERIES 2 (200)	100.00	45.00
COMMON CARD (1-200/226-385)	.15	.07
SEMISTARS	.30	.14
UNLISTED STARS	.60	.25
COMMON ROOKIE (201-225)	2.50	1.10
ROOKIE SEMISTARS 201-225	4.00	1.80
COMMON ROOKIE (386-425)	1.50	.70
ROOKIE SEMISTARS (386-425)	2.50	1.10
ROOKIE UNL.STARS (386-425)	4.00	1.80

ROOKIE SUBSET ODDS 1:3........

COMP.GOLD MED.SET (425)	900.00	400.00
COMP.GOLD MED.1 (225) ..	500.00	220.00
COMP.GOLD MED.2 (200) ..	400.00	180.00

*GOLD MED.STARS: 1.25X TO 3X HI COL.
*GOLD MED.YOUNG STARS: .75X TO 2X
*GOLD MED.SERIES 1 RCs: .75X TO 2X
*GOLD MED.SER.2 DRAFT PICKS: 1.5X TO 3X
VETERAN GOLD MED.ODDS 1:1 HOBBY
ROOKIE GOLD MEDALLION ODDS 1:24 HOB.

❑ 1 Barry Sanders	3.00	1.35
❑ 2 Brett Favre	3.00	1.35
❑ 3 Napoleon Kaufman	.60	.25
❑ 4 Robert Smith	.60	.25
❑ 5 Terry Allen	.60	.25
❑ 6 Vinny Testaverde	.30	.14
❑ 7 William Floyd	.15	.07
❑ 8 Carl Pickens	.60	.25
❑ 9 Antonio Freeman	.60	.25
❑ 10 Ben Coates	.30	.14
❑ 11 Elvis Grbac	.30	.14
❑ 12 Kerry Collins	.30	.14
❑ 13 Orlando Pace	.15	.07
❑ 14 Steve Broussard	.15	.07
❑ 15 Terance Mathis	.30	.14
❑ 16 Tiki Barber	.30	.14
❑ 17 Cris Carter	.60	.25
❑ 18 Eric Green	.15	.07
❑ 19 Eric Metcalf	.15	.07
❑ 20 Jeff George	.30	.14
❑ 21 Leslie Shepherd	.15	.07
❑ 22 Natrone Means	.60	.25
❑ 23 Scott Mitchell	.30	.14
❑ 24 Adrian Murrell	.30	.14
❑ 25 Gilbert Brown	.15	.07
❑ 26 Jimmy Smith	.30	.14
❑ 27 Mark Bruener	.15	.07
❑ 28 Troy Aikman	1.50	.70
❑ 29 Warrick Dunn	.60	.25
❑ 30 Jay Graham	.15	.07
❑ 31 Craig Whelihan RC	.15	.07
❑ 32 Ed McCaffrey	.30	.14
❑ 33 Jamie Asher	.15	.07
❑ 34 John Randle	.30	.14
❑ 35 Michael Jackson	.15	.07
❑ 36 Rickey Dudley	.15	.07
❑ 37 Sean Dawkins	.15	.07
❑ 38 Andre Rison	.30	.14
❑ 39 Bert Emanuel	.30	.14
❑ 40 Jeff Blake	.30	.14
❑ 41 Curtis Conway	.30	.14
❑ 42 Eddie Kennison	.30	.14
❑ 43 James McKnight	.15	.07
❑ 44 Rae Carruth	.30	.14
❑ 45 Tito Wooten RC	.15	.07
❑ 46 Cris Dishman	.15	.07
❑ 47 Ernie Conwell	.15	.07
❑ 48 Fred Lane	.30	.14
❑ 49 Jamal Anderson	.60	.25
❑ 50 Lake Dawson	.15	.07
❑ 51 Michael Strahan	.15	.07
❑ 52 Reggie White	.60	.25
❑ 53 Trent Dilfer	.60	.25
❑ 54 Troy Brown	.15	.07
❑ 55 Wesley Walls	.30	.14
❑ 56 Chidi Ahanotu	.15	.07
❑ 57 Dwayne Rudd	.15	.07
❑ 58 Jerry Rice	1.50	.70
❑ 59 Johnnie Morton	.30	.14
❑ 60 Sherman Williams	.15	.07
❑ 61 Steve McNair	.60	.25
❑ 62 Will Blackwell	.15	.07
❑ 63 Chris Chandler	.30	.14
❑ 64 Dexter Coakley	.15	.07
❑ 65 Horace Copeland	.15	.07
❑ 66 Jerald Moore	.15	.07
❑ 67 Leon Johnson	.15	.07
❑ 68 Mark Chmura	.30	.14
❑ 69 Micheal Barrow	.15	.07
❑ 70 Muhsin Muhammad	.30	.14
❑ 71 Terry Glenn	.60	.25
❑ 72 Tony Brackens	.15	.07
❑ 73 Chad Scott	.15	.07
❑ 74 Glenn Foley	.30	.14
❑ 75 Keenan McCardell	.30	.14
❑ 76 Peter Boulware	.15	.07
❑ 77 Reidel Anthony	.30	.14
❑ 78 William Henderson	.15	.07
❑ 79 Tony Martin	.30	.14
❑ 80 Tony Gonzalez	.15	.07
❑ 81 Charlie Jones	.15	.07
❑ 82 Chris Gedney	.15	.07
❑ 83 Chris Calloway	.15	.07
❑ 84 Dale Carter	.15	.07
❑ 85 Ki-Jana Carter	.15	.07
❑ 86 Shawn Springs	.15	.07
❑ 87 Antowain Smith	.60	.25
❑ 88 Eric Turner	.15	.07
❑ 89 John Mobley	.15	.07
❑ 90 Ken Dilger	.15	.07
❑ 91 Bobby Hoying	.30	.14
❑ 92 Curtis Martin	.60	.25
❑ 93 Drew Bledsoe	1.25	.55
❑ 94 Gary Brown	.15	.07
❑ 95 Marvin Harrison	.30	.14
❑ 96 Todd Collins	.15	.07
❑ 97 Chris Warren	.30	.14
❑ 98 Danny Kanell	.30	.14
❑ 99 Tony McGee	.15	.07
❑ 100 Rod Smith	.30	.14
❑ 101 Frank Sanders	.30	.14
❑ 102 Irving Fryar	.30	.14
❑ 103 Marcus Allen	.60	.25
❑ 104 Marshall Faulk	.60	.25
❑ 105 Bruce Smith	.30	.14
❑ 106 Charlie Garner	.15	.07
❑ 107 Paul Justin	.15	.07
❑ 108 Randal Hill	.15	.07
❑ 109 Erik Kramer	.15	.07
❑ 110 Rob Moore	.30	.14
❑ 111 Shannon Sharpe	.30	.14
❑ 112 Warren Moon	.60	.25
❑ 113 Zach Thomas	.15	.07
❑ 114 Dan Marino	3.00	1.35
❑ 115 Duce Staley	1.00	.45
❑ 116 Eric Swann	.15	.07
❑ 117 Kenny Holmes	.15	.07
❑ 118 Merton Hanks	.15	.07
❑ 119 Raymont Harris	.15	.07
❑ 120 Terrell Davis	2.50	1.10
❑ 121 Thurman Thomas	.60	.25
❑ 122 Wayne Martin	.15	.07
❑ 123 Charles Way	.15	.07
❑ 124 Chuck Smith	.15	.07
❑ 125 Corey Dillon	1.00	.45
❑ 126 Darnell Autry	.15	.07
❑ 127 Isaac Bruce	.60	.25
❑ 128 Joey Galloway	.60	.25
❑ 129 Kimble Anders	.30	.14
❑ 130 Aeneas Williams	.15	.07
❑ 131 Andre Hastings	.15	.07
❑ 132 Chad Lewis	.15	.07
❑ 133 J.J. Stokes	.30	.14
❑ 134 John Elway	3.00	1.35
❑ 135 Karim Abdul-Jabbar	.60	.25
❑ 136 Ken Harvey	.15	.07
❑ 137 Robert Brooks	.30	.14
❑ 138 Rodney Thomas	.15	.07
❑ 139 James Stewart	.30	.14
❑ 140 Billy Joe Hobert	.15	.07
❑ 141 Frank Wycheck	.15	.07
❑ 142 Jake Plummer	2.00	.90
❑ 143 Jerris McPhail	.15	.07
❑ 144 Kordell Stewart	.60	.25
❑ 145 Terrell Owens	.60	.25
❑ 146 Willie Green	.15	.07
❑ 147 Anthony Miller	.15	.07
❑ 148 Courtney Hawkins	.15	.07
❑ 149 Larry Centers	.15	.07
❑ 150 Gus Frerotte	.15	.07
❑ 151 O.J. McDuffie	.30	.14
❑ 152 Ray Zellars	.15	.07
❑ 153 Terry Kirby	.15	.07
❑ 154 Tommy Vardell	.15	.07
❑ 155 Willie Davis	.15	.07
❑ 156 Chris Canty	.15	.07
❑ 157 Byron Hanspard	.30	.14
❑ 158 Chris Penn	.15	.07
❑ 159 Damon Jones	.15	.07
❑ 160 Derrick Mayes	.30	.14
❑ 161 Emmitt Smith	2.50	1.10
❑ 162 Keyshawn Johnson	.60	.25
❑ 163 Mike Alstott	.60	.25
❑ 164 Tom Carter	.15	.07
❑ 165 Tony Banks	.30	.14
❑ 166 Bryant Westbrook	.15	.07
❑ 167 Chris Sanders	.15	.07
❑ 168 Deion Sanders	.60	.25
❑ 169 Garrison Hearst	.60	.25
❑ 170 Jason Taylor	.15	.07
❑ 171 Jerome Bettis	.60	.25
❑ 172 John Lynch	.15	.07
❑ 173 Troy Davis	.15	.07
❑ 174 Freddie Jones	.15	.07
❑ 175 Herman Moore	.60	.25
❑ 176 Jake Reed	.30	.14
❑ 177 Mark Brunell	1.25	.55
❑ 178 Ray Lewis	.15	.07
❑ 179 Stephen Davis	.15	.07
❑ 180 Tim Brown	.60	.25
❑ 181 Willie McGinest	.15	.07
❑ 182 Andre Reed	.30	.14
❑ 183 Darrien Gordon	.15	.07
❑ 184 David Palmer	.15	.07
❑ 185 James Jett	.30	.14
❑ 186 Junior Seau	.30	.14
❑ 187 Zack Crockett	.15	.07
❑ 188 Brad Johnson	.60	.25
❑ 189 Charles Johnson	.15	.07
❑ 190 Eddie George	1.25	.55
❑ 191 Jermaine Lewis	.30	.14
❑ 192 Michael Irvin	.60	.25
❑ 193 Reggie Brown LB	.15	.07
❑ 194 Steve Young	1.00	.45
❑ 195 Warren Sapp	.30	.14
❑ 196 Wayne Chrebet	.60	.25
❑ 197 David Dunn	.15	.07
❑ 198 Dorsey Levens CL	.30	.14
❑ 199 Troy Aikman CL	.60	.25
❑ 200 John Elway CL	.75	.35
❑ 201 Peyton Manning RC ..	40.00	18.00
❑ 202 Ryan Leaf RC	8.00	3.60
❑ 203 Charles Woodson RC	10.00	4.50
❑ 204 Andre Wadsworth RC ..	4.00	1.80
❑ 205 Brian Simmons RC	2.50	1.10
❑ 206 Curtis Enis RC	10.00	4.50
❑ 207 Randy Moss RC	40.00	18.00
❑ 208 Germane Crowell RC ..	8.00	3.60
❑ 209 Greg Ellis RC	2.50	1.10
❑ 210 Kevin Dyson RC	8.00	3.60
❑ 211 Skip Hicks RC	4.00	1.80
❑ 212 Alonzo Mayes RC	2.50	1.10
❑ 213 Robert Edwards RC	4.00	1.80
❑ 214 Fred Taylor RC	20.00	9.00
❑ 215 Robert Holcombe RC ..	4.00	1.80
❑ 216 John Dutton RC	2.50	1.10
❑ 217 Vonnie Holliday RC	4.00	1.80
❑ 218 Tim Dwight RC	6.00	2.70
❑ 219 Tavian Banks RC	4.00	1.80
❑ 220 Marcus Nash RC	4.00	1.80
❑ 221 Jason Peter RC	2.50	1.10
❑ 222 Michael Myers RC	2.50	1.10
❑ 223 Takeo Spikes RC	4.00	1.80
❑ 224 Kivuusama Mays RC	2.50	1.10
❑ 225 Jacquez Green RC	6.00	2.70
❑ 226 Doug Flutie	.60	.25
❑ 227 Ike Hilliard	.30	.14
❑ 228 Craig Heyward	.15	.07
❑ 229 Kevin Hardy	.15	.07

❑ 230 Jason Dunn .15 .07
❑ 231 Billy Davis .15 .07
❑ 232 Chester McGlockton .15 .07
❑ 233 Sean Gilbert .15 .07
❑ 234 Bert Emanuel .30 .14
❑ 235 Keith Byars .15 .07
❑ 236 Tyrone Wheatley .30 .14
❑ 237 Ricky Proehl .15 .07
❑ 238 Michael Bates .15 .07
❑ 239 Derrick Alexander .30 .14
❑ 240 Harvey Williams .15 .07
❑ 241 Mike Pritchard .15 .07
❑ 242 Paul Justin .15 .07
❑ 243 Jeff Hostetler .15 .07
❑ 244 Eric Moulds .60 .25
❑ 245 Jeff Burris .15 .07
❑ 246 Gary Brown .15 .07
❑ 247 Anthony Johnson .15 .07
❑ 248 Dan Wilkinson .15 .07
❑ 249 Chris Warren .30 .14
❑ 250 Chris Darkins .15 .07
❑ 251 Eric Metcalf .15 .07
❑ 252 Pat Swilling .15 .07
❑ 253 Lamar Smith .15 .07
❑ 254 Quinn Early .15 .07
❑ 255 Carlester Crumpler .15 .07
❑ 256 Eric Bieniemy .15 .07
❑ 257 Aaron Bailey .15 .07
❑ 258 Neil O'Donnell .30 .14
❑ 259 Rod Woodson .30 .14
❑ 260 Ricky Whittle .15 .07
❑ 261 Iheanyi Uwaezuoke .15 .07
❑ 262 Heath Shuler .15 .07
❑ 263 Darren Sharper .15 .07
❑ 264 John Henry Mills .15 .07
❑ 265 Marco Battaglia .15 .07
❑ 266 Yancey Thigpen .15 .07
❑ 267 Irv Smith .15 .07
❑ 268 Jamie Sharper .15 .07
❑ 269 Marcus Robinson 5.00 2.20
❑ 270 Dorsey Levens .60 .25
❑ 271 Qadry Ismail .15 .07
❑ 272 Desmond Howard .30 .14
❑ 273 Webster Slaughter .15 .07
❑ 274 Eugene Robinson .15 .07
❑ 275 Bill Romanowski .15 .07
❑ 276 Vincent Brisby .15 .07
❑ 277 Errict Rhett .30 .14
❑ 278 Albert Connell .15 .07
❑ 279 Thomas Lewis .15 .07
❑ 280 John Farquhar RC .15 .07
❑ 281 Marc Edwards .15 .07
❑ 282 Tyrone Davis .15 .07
❑ 283 Eric Allen .15 .07
❑ 284 Aaron Glenn .15 .07
❑ 285 Roosevelt Potts .15 .07
❑ 286 Kez McCorvey .15 .07
❑ 287 Joey Kent .30 .14
❑ 288 Jim Druckenmiller .30 .14
❑ 289 Sean Dawkins .15 .07
❑ 290 Edgar Bennett .15 .07
❑ 291 Vinny Testaverde .30 .14
❑ 292 Chris Slade .15 .07
❑ 293 Lamar Lathon .15 .07
❑ 294 Jackie Harris .15 .07
❑ 295 Jim Harbaugh .30 .14
❑ 296 Rob Fredrickson .15 .07
❑ 297 Ty Detmer .30 .14
❑ 298 Karl Williams .15 .07
❑ 299 Troy Drayton .15 .07
❑ 300 Curtis Martin .60 .25
❑ 301 Tamarick Vanover .15 .07
❑ 302 Lorenzo Neal .15 .07
❑ 303 John Hall .15 .07
❑ 304 Kevin Greene .30 .14
❑ 305 Bryan Still .15 .07
❑ 306 Neil Smith .30 .14
❑ 307 Greg Lloyd .15 .07
❑ 308 Shawn Jefferson .15 .07
❑ 309 Aaron Taylor .15 .07
❑ 310 Sedrick Shaw .15 .07
❑ 311 O.J. Santiago .15 .07
❑ 312 Kevin Abrams .15 .07
❑ 313 Dana Stubblefield .15 .07
❑ 314 Daryl Johnston .30 .14
❑ 315 Bryan Cox .15 .07
❑ 316 Jeff Graham .15 .07
❑ 317 Mario Bates .30 .14
❑ 318 Adrian Murrell .30 .14
❑ 319 Greg Hill .15 .07
❑ 320 Jahine Arnold .15 .07
❑ 321 Justin Armour .15 .07
❑ 322 Ricky Watters .30 .14
❑ 323 Lamont Warren .15 .07
❑ 324 Mack Strong .15 .07
❑ 325 Darnay Scott .30 .14
❑ 326 Brian Mitchell .15 .07
❑ 327 Rob Johnson .30 .14
❑ 328 Kent Graham .15 .07
❑ 329 Hugh Douglas .15 .07
❑ 330 Simeon Rice .30 .14
❑ 331 Rick Mirer .15 .07
❑ 332 Randall Cunningham .60 .25
❑ 333 Steve Atwater .15 .07
❑ 334 Latario Rachal .15 .07
❑ 335 Tony Martin .30 .14
❑ 336 Leroy Hoard .15 .07
❑ 337 Howard Griffith .15 .07
❑ 338 Kevin Lockett .15 .07
❑ 339 William Floyd .15 .07
❑ 340 Jerry Ellison .15 .07
❑ 341 Kyle Brady .15 .07
❑ 342 Michael Westbrook .30 .14
❑ 343 Kevin Turner .15 .07
❑ 344 David LaFleur .15 .07
❑ 345 Robert Jones .15 .07
❑ 346 Dave Brown .15 .07
❑ 347 Kevin Williams .15 .07
❑ 348 Amani Toomer .30 .14
❑ 349 Amp Lee .15 .07
❑ 350 Bryce Paup .15 .07
❑ 351 Dewayne Washington .15 .07
❑ 352 Mercury Hayes .15 .07
❑ 353 Tim Biakabutuka .30 .14
❑ 354 Ray Crockett .15 .07
❑ 355 Ted Washington .15 .07
❑ 356 Pete Mitchell .15 .07
❑ 357 Billy Jenkins RC .15 .07
❑ 358 Troy Aikman CL .60 .25
❑ 359 Drew Bledsoe CL .60 .25
❑ 360 Steve Young CL .60 .25
❑ 361 Antonio Freeman NG .30 .14
❑ 362 Antowain Smith NG .30 .14
❑ 363 Barry Sanders NG 2.00 .90
❑ 364 Bobby Hoying NG .15 .07
❑ 365 Brett Favre NG 2.00 .90
❑ 366 Corey Dillon NG .30 .14
❑ 367 Dan Marino NG 2.00 .90
❑ 368 Drew Bledsoe NG .75 .35
❑ 369 Eddie George NG .75 .35
❑ 370 Emmitt Smith NG 1.50 .70
❑ 371 Herman Moore NG .30 .14
❑ 372 Jake Plummer NG 1.00 .45
❑ 373 Jerome Bettis NG .30 .14
❑ 374 Jerry Rice NG 1.00 .45
❑ 375 Joey Galloway NG .30 .14
❑ 376 John Elway NG 2.00 .90
❑ 377 Kordell Stewart NG .30 .14
❑ 378 Mark Brunell NG .75 .35
❑ 379 Keyshawn Johnson NG .30 .14
❑ 380 Steve Young NG .60 .25
❑ 381 Steve McNair NG .30 .14
❑ 382 Terrell Davis NG 1.50 .70
❑ 383 Tim Brown NG .30 .14
❑ 384 Troy Aikman NG 1.00 .45
❑ 385 Warrick Dunn NG .60 .25
❑ 386 Ryan Leaf 5.00 2.20
❑ 387 Tony Simmons RC 2.50 1.10
❑ 388 Rodney Williams RC 1.50 .70
❑ 389 John Avery RC 4.00 1.80
❑ 390 Shaun Williams RC 1.50 .70
❑ 391 Anthony Simmons RC 1.50 .70
❑ 392 Rashaan Shehee RC 2.50 1.10
❑ 393 Robert Holcombe 1.50 .70
❑ 394 Larry Shannon RC 1.50 .70
❑ 395 Skip Hicks 4.00 1.80
❑ 396 Rod Rutledge RC 1.50 .70
❑ 397 Donald Hayes RC 2.50 1.10
❑ 398 Curtis Enis 6.00 2.70
❑ 399 Mikhael Ricks RC 2.50 1.10
❑ 400 Brian Griese RC 20.00 9.00
❑ 401 Michael Pittman RC 2.50 1.10
❑ 402 Jacquez Green 4.00 1.80
❑ 403 Jerome Pathon RC 2.50 1.10
❑ 404 Ahman Green RC 2.50 1.10
❑ 405 Marcus Nash 4.00 1.80
❑ 406 Randy Moss 25.00 11.00
❑ 407 Terry Fair RC 2.50 1.10
❑ 408 Jammi German RC 1.50 .70
❑ 409 Stephen Alexander RC 2.50 1.10
❑ 410 Grant Wistrom RC 1.50 .70
❑ 411 Charlie Batch RC 20.00 9.00
❑ 412 Fred Taylor 15.00 6.75
❑ 413 Pat Johnson RC 2.50 1.10
❑ 414 Robert Edwards 4.00 1.80
❑ 415 Keith Brooking RC 2.50 1.10
❑ 416 Peyton Manning 25.00 11.00
❑ 417 Duane Starks RC 1.50 .70
❑ 418 Andre Wadsworth 2.50 1.10
❑ 419 Brian Alford RC 4.00 1.80
❑ 420 Brian Kelly RC 1.50 .70
❑ 421 Joe Jurevicius RC 2.50 1.10
❑ 422 Tebucky Jones RC 1.50 .70
❑ 423 R.W. McQuarters RC 1.50 .70
❑ 424 Kevin Dyson 4.00 1.80
❑ 425 Charles Woodson 6.00 2.70
❑ R1 Reggie White COMM .60 .25
❑ P20 Jeff George Promo 1.00 .45

1998 Ultra Platinum Medallion

	MINT	NRMT
COMMON (1P-200P/226P-385P)	12.00	5.50
COMMON ROOKIE (201P-225P)	15.00	6.75
COMMON ROOKIE (386P-425P)	10.00	4.50

*PLAT.MED.STARS: 25X TO 60X HI COL.
*PLAT.MED.YOUNG STARS: 20X TO 50X
*PLAT.MED.RCs: 2X TO 5X
1-200/226-385 PRINT RUN 98 SER.#'d SETS
201-225/386-425 PRINT RUN 66 SER.#'d SETS
HOBBY ONLY INSERTS

1998 Ultra Sensational Sixty

	MINT	NRMT
COMPLETE SET (60)	40.00	18.00
COMMON CARD (1-60)	.40	.18
SEMISTARS	.75	.35
UNLISTED STARS	1.00	.45

ONE PER RETAIL PACK

❑ 1 Karim Abdul-Jabbar 1.00 .45
❑ 2 Troy Aikman 2.00 .90
❑ 3 Terry Allen 1.00 .45
❑ 4 Mike Alstott 1.00 .45
❑ 5 Tony Banks .75 .35
❑ 6 Jerome Bettis 1.00 .45
❑ 7 Drew Bledsoe 1.50 .70
❑ 8 Peter Boulware .40 .18
❑ 9 Robert Brooks .75 .35
❑ 10 Tim Brown 1.00 .45
❑ 11 Isaac Bruce 1.00 .45
❑ 12 Mark Brunell 1.50 .70
❑ 13 Cris Carter 1.00 .45
❑ 14 Kerry Collins .75 .35
❑ 15 Curtis Conway .75 .35
❑ 16 Terrell Davis 3.00 1.35
❑ 17 Troy Davis .40 .18

Card	MINT	NRMT
❑ 18 Trent Dilfer	1.00	.45
❑ 19 Corey Dillon	1.25	.55
❑ 20 Warrick Dunn	1.25	.55
❑ 21 John Elway	4.00	1.80
❑ 22 Bert Emanuel	.75	.35
❑ 23 Brett Favre	4.00	1.80
❑ 24 Antonio Freeman	1.00	.45
❑ 25 Gus Frerotte	.40	.18
❑ 26 Joey Galloway	1.00	.45
❑ 27 Eddie George	1.50	.70
❑ 28 Jeff George	.75	.35
❑ 29 Elvis Grbac	.75	.35
❑ 30 Marvin Harrison	.75	.35
❑ 31 Bobby Hoying	.75	.35
❑ 32 Michael Irvin	1.00	.45
❑ 33 Brad Johnson	1.00	.45
❑ 34 Keyshawn Johnson	1.00	.45
❑ 35 Dan Marino	4.00	1.80
❑ 36 Curtis Martin	1.00	.45
❑ 37 Tony Martin	.75	.35
❑ 38 Keenan McCardell	.75	.35
❑ 39 Steve McNair	1.00	.45
❑ 40 Warren Moon	1.00	.45
❑ 41 Herman Moore	1.00	.45
❑ 42 Johnnie Morton	.75	.35
❑ 43 Terrell Owens	1.00	.45
❑ 44 Carl Pickens	1.00	.45
❑ 45 Jake Plummer	2.50	1.10
❑ 46 Jerry Rice	2.00	.90
❑ 47 Andre Rison	.75	.35
❑ 48 Barry Sanders	4.00	1.80
❑ 49 Deion Sanders	1.00	.45
❑ 50 Junior Seau	.75	.35
❑ 51 Shannon Sharpe	.75	.35
❑ 52 Antowain Smith	1.00	.45
❑ 53 Emmitt Smith	3.00	1.35
❑ 54 Jimmy Smith	.75	.35
❑ 55 Robert Smith	1.00	.45
❑ 56 Kordell Stewart	1.00	.45
❑ 57 Jeff Blake	.75	.35
❑ 58 Charles Way	.40	.18
❑ 59 Reggie White	1.00	.45
❑ 60 Steve Young	1.25	.55

1998 Ultra Canton Classics

	MINT	NRMT
COMPLETE SET (10)	120.00	55.00
COMMON CARD (1-10)	6.00	2.70
STATED ODDS 1:288		
❑ 1 Terrell Davis	20.00	9.00
❑ 2 Brett Favre	25.00	11.00
❑ 3 John Elway	25.00	11.00
❑ 4 Barry Sanders	25.00	11.00
❑ 5 Eddie George	10.00	4.50
❑ 6 Jerry Rice	12.00	5.50
❑ 7 Emmitt Smith	20.00	9.00
❑ 8 Dan Marino	25.00	11.00
❑ 9 Troy Aikman	12.00	5.50
❑ 10 Marcus Allen	15.00	6.75

1998 Ultra Caught in the Draft

	MINT	NRMT
COMPLETE SET (15)	80.00	36.00
COMMON CARD (1-15)	3.00	1.35
SEMISTARS	4.00	1.80
STATED ODDS 1:24		
❑ 1 Andre Wadsworth	4.00	1.80
❑ 2 Curtis Enis	5.00	2.20
❑ 3 Germane Crowell	5.00	2.20
❑ 4 Peyton Manning	20.00	9.00
❑ 5 Tavian Banks	4.00	1.80
❑ 6 Fred Taylor	10.00	4.50
❑ 7 John Avery	4.00	1.80
❑ 8 Randy Moss	20.00	9.00
❑ 9 Robert Edwards	4.00	1.80
❑ 10 Charles Woodson	5.00	2.20
❑ 11 Ryan Leaf	4.00	1.80
❑ 12 Ahman Green	4.00	1.80
❑ 13 Robert Holcombe	4.00	1.80
❑ 14 Jacquez Green	4.00	1.80
❑ 15 Skip Hicks	3.00	1.35

1998 Ultra Damage, Inc.

	MINT	NRMT
COMPLETE SET (15)	100.00	45.00
COMMON CARD (1-15)	5.00	2.20
STATED ODDS 1:72		
❑ 1 Terrell Davis	15.00	6.75
❑ 2 Joey Galloway	6.00	2.70
❑ 3 Kordell Stewart	5.00	2.20
❑ 4 Troy Aikman	10.00	4.50
❑ 5 Barry Sanders	20.00	9.00
❑ 6 Ryan Leaf	6.00	2.70
❑ 7 Antonio Freeman	6.00	2.70
❑ 8 Keyshawn Johnson	6.00	2.70
❑ 9 Eddie George	8.00	3.60
❑ 10 Warrick Dunn	6.00	2.70
❑ 11 Drew Bledsoe	8.00	3.60
❑ 12 Peyton Manning	20.00	9.00
❑ 13 Antowain Smith	6.00	2.70
❑ 14 Brett Favre	20.00	9.00
❑ 15 Emmitt Smith	15.00	6.75

1998 Ultra Exclamation Points

	MINT	NRMT
COMPLETE SET (15)	400.00	180.00
COMMON CARD (1-15)	10.00	4.50
STATED ODDS 1:288		
❑ 1 Terrell Davis	40.00	18.00
❑ 2 Brett Favre	50.00	22.00
❑ 3 John Elway	50.00	22.00
❑ 4 Barry Sanders	50.00	22.00
❑ 5 Peyton Manning	50.00	22.00
❑ 6 Jerry Rice	25.00	11.00
❑ 7 Emmitt Smith	40.00	18.00
❑ 8 Dan Marino	50.00	22.00
❑ 9 Kordell Stewart	10.00	4.50
❑ 10 Mark Brunell	20.00	9.00
❑ 11 Ryan Leaf	12.00	5.50
❑ 12 Corey Dillon	12.00	5.50
❑ 13 Antowain Smith	12.00	5.50
❑ 14 Curtis Martin	12.00	5.50
❑ 15 Deion Sanders	12.00	5.50

1998 Ultra Flair Showcase Preview

	MINT	NRMT
COMPLETE SET (10)	150.00	70.00
COMMON CARD (1-10)	10.00	4.50
STATED ODDS 1:144		
❑ 1 Kordell Stewart	10.00	4.50
❑ 2 Mark Brunell	15.00	6.75
❑ 3 Terrell Davis	30.00	13.50
❑ 4 Brett Favre	40.00	18.00
❑ 5 Steve McNair	12.00	5.50
❑ 6 Curtis Martin	12.00	5.50
❑ 7 Warrick Dunn	15.00	6.75
❑ 8 Emmitt Smith	30.00	13.50
❑ 9 Dan Marino	40.00	18.00
❑ 10 Corey Dillon	12.00	5.50

1998 Ultra Indefensible

	MINT	NRMT
COMPLETE SET (10)	100.00	45.00
COMMON CARD (1-10)	6.00	2.70
SEMISTARS	8.00	3.60
STATED ODDS 1:144		
❑ 1 Jake Plummer	12.00	5.50
❑ 2 Mark Brunell	10.00	4.50
❑ 3 Terrell Davis	20.00	9.00
❑ 4 Jerry Rice	12.00	5.50
❑ 5 Barry Sanders	25.00	11.00
❑ 6 Curtis Martin	10.00	4.50

	MINT	NRMT
❑ 7 Warrick Dunn	12.00	5.50
❑ 8 Emmitt Smith	20.00	9.00
❑ 9 Dan Marino	25.00	11.00
❑ 10 Corey Dillon	6.00	2.70

1998 Ultra Next Century

	MINT	NRMT
COMPLETE SET (15)	150.00	70.00
COMMON CARD (1-15)	6.00	2.70
SEMISTARS	8.00	3.60
STATED ODDS 1:72		

	MINT	NRMT
❑ 1 Ryan Leaf	10.00	4.50
❑ 2 Peyton Manning	30.00	13.50
❑ 3 Charles Woodson	12.00	5.50
❑ 4 Randy Moss	30.00	13.50
❑ 5 Curtis Enis	12.00	5.50
❑ 6 Ahman Green	8.00	3.60
❑ 7 Skip Hicks	8.00	3.60
❑ 8 Andre Wadsworth	8.00	3.60
❑ 9 Germane Crowell	12.00	5.50
❑ 10 Robert Edwards	10.00	4.50
❑ 11 Tavian Banks	8.00	3.60
❑ 12 Takeo Spikes	8.00	3.60
❑ 13 Jacquez Green	10.00	4.50
❑ 14 Brian Simmons	6.00	2.70
❑ 15 Alonzo Mayes	6.00	2.70

1998 Ultra Rush Hour

	MINT	NRMT
COMPLETE SET (20)	40.00	18.00
COMMON CARD (1-20)	1.00	.45
SEMISTARS	1.50	.70
UNLISTED STARS	2.00	.90
STATED ODDS 1:6		

	MINT	NRMT
❑ 1 Robert Edwards	2.00	.90
❑ 2 John Elway	8.00	3.60
❑ 3 Mike Alstott	2.00	.90
❑ 4 Robert Holcombe	2.00	.90
❑ 5 Mark Brunell	3.00	1.35
❑ 6 Deion Sanders	2.00	.90
❑ 7 Curtis Martin	2.00	.90
❑ 8 Curtis Enis	4.00	1.80
❑ 9 Dorsey Levens	2.00	.90
❑ 10 Fred Taylor	10.00	4.50
❑ 11 John Avery	2.00	.90
❑ 12 Eddie George	3.00	1.35
❑ 13 Jake Plummer	4.00	1.80
❑ 14 Andre Wadsworth	1.50	.70
❑ 15 Fred Lane	1.00	.45
❑ 16 Corey Dillon	2.00	.90
❑ 17 Brett Favre	8.00	3.60
❑ 18 Kordell Stewart	2.00	.90
❑ 19 Steve McNair	2.00	.90
❑ 20 Warrick Dunn	2.50	1.10

1998 Ultra Shots

	MINT	NRMT
COMPLETE SET (20)	35.00	16.00
COMMON CARD (1-20)	1.50	.70
SEMISTARS	2.00	.90
STATED ODDS 1:6		

	MINT	NRMT
❑ 1 Deion Sanders	2.50	1.10
❑ 2 Corey Dillon	2.50	1.10
❑ 3 Mike Alstott	2.50	1.10
❑ 4 Jake Plummer	4.00	1.80
❑ 5 Antowain Smith	2.50	1.10
❑ 6 Kordell Stewart	2.00	.90
❑ 7 Curtis Martin	2.50	1.10
❑ 8 Bobby Hoying	2.00	.90
❑ 9 Kerry Collins	1.50	.70
❑ 10 Herman Moore	2.50	1.10
❑ 11 Terry Glenn	2.50	1.10
❑ 12 Eddie George	3.00	1.35
❑ 13 Drew Bledsoe	3.00	1.35
❑ 14 Steve McNair	2.50	1.10
❑ 15 Jerry Rice	4.00	1.80
❑ 16 Trent Dilfer	2.50	1.10
❑ 17 Joey Galloway	2.50	1.10
❑ 18 Dan Marino	8.00	3.60
❑ 19 Barry Sanders	8.00	3.60
❑ 20 Warrick Dunn	2.50	1.10

1998 Ultra Top 30

	MINT	NRMT
COMPLETE SET (30)	25.00	11.00
STATED ODDS: 1 PER RETAIL PACK		

	MINT	NRMT
❑ 1 Warrick Dunn	1.25	.55
❑ 2 Troy Aikman	1.50	.70
❑ 3 Trent Dilfer	.30	.14
❑ 4 Tony Banks	.30	.14
❑ 5 Tim Brown	.60	.25
❑ 6 Terrell Davis	2.50	1.10
❑ 7 Steve McNair	.60	.25
❑ 8 Steve Young	1.00	.45
❑ 9 Mark Brunell	1.25	.55
❑ 10 Kordell Stewart	1.00	.45
❑ 11 Keyshawn Johnson	.60	.25
❑ 12 John Elway	3.00	1.35
❑ 13 Joey Galloway	.60	.25
❑ 14 Jerry Rice	1.50	.70
❑ 15 Jerome Bettis	.60	.25
❑ 16 Jake Plummer	2.00	.90
❑ 17 Emmitt Smith	2.50	1.10
❑ 18 Eddie George	1.25	.55
❑ 19 Drew Bledsoe	1.25	.55
❑ 20 Dan Marino	3.00	1.35
❑ 21 Curtis Martin	.60	.25
❑ 22 Curtis Conway	.30	.14
❑ 23 Cris Carter	.60	.25
❑ 24 Corey Dillon	1.00	.45
❑ 25 Carl Pickens	.30	.14
❑ 26 Brett Favre	3.00	1.35
❑ 27 Bobby Hoying	.30	.14
❑ 28 Barry Sanders	3.00	1.35
❑ 29 Antowain Smith	.60	.25
❑ 30 Antonio Freeman	.60	.25

1998 Ultra Touchdown Kings

	MINT	NRMT
COMPLETE SET (15)	100.00	45.00
COMMON CARD (1-15)	4.00	1.80
SEMISTARS	6.00	2.70
STATED ODDS 1:24		

	MINT	NRMT
❑ 1 Terrell Davis	15.00	6.75
❑ 2 Joey Galloway	6.00	2.70
❑ 3 Kordell Stewart	6.00	2.70
❑ 4 Corey Dillon	6.00	2.70
❑ 5 Barry Sanders	20.00	9.00
❑ 6 Cris Carter	6.00	2.70
❑ 7 Antonio Freeman	6.00	2.70
❑ 8 Mike Alstott	6.00	2.70
❑ 9 Eddie George	8.00	3.60
❑ 10 Warrick Dunn	6.00	2.70
❑ 11 Drew Bledsoe	8.00	3.60
❑ 12 Karim Abdul-Jabbar	4.00	1.80
❑ 13 Mark Brunell	8.00	3.60
❑ 14 Brett Favre	20.00	9.00
❑ 15 Emmitt Smith	15.00	6.75

1999 Ultra

	MINT	NRMT
COMPLETE SET (300)	200.00	90.00
COMP.SET w/o SP's (250)	20.00	9.00
COMMON CARD (1-300)	.15	.07
SEMISTARS	.30	.14
UNLISTED STARS	.60	.25
COMMON BB (251-260)	.30	.14
BACK TO BACK SUBSET ODDS 1:8		
COMMON ROOKIE (261-300)	2.00	.90
ROOKIE SEMISTARS	3.00	1.35
ROOKIE UNL.STARS	4.00	1.80
ROOKIE SUBSET ODDS 1:4		
❑ 1 Terrell Davis	1.50	.70
❑ 2 Courtney Hawkins	.15	.07
❑ 3 Cris Carter	.60	.25
❑ 4 Darnay Scott	.15	.07
❑ 5 Darrell Green	.30	.14
❑ 6 Jimmy Smith	.30	.14
❑ 7 Doug Flutie	.75	.35
❑ 8 Michael Jackson	.15	.07
❑ 9 Warren Sapp	.30	.14
❑ 10 Greg Hill	.15	.07
❑ 11 Karim Abdul-Jabbar	.30	.14
❑ 12 Greg Ellis	.15	.07
❑ 13 Dan Marino	2.50	1.10
❑ 14 Napoleon Kaufman	.60	.25
❑ 15 Peyton Manning	2.50	1.10
❑ 16 Simeon Rice	.30	.14
❑ 17 Tony Simmons	.15	.07
❑ 18 Carlester Crumpler	.15	.07
❑ 19 Charles Johnson	.15	.07
❑ 20 Derrick Alexander	.15	.07
❑ 21 Kent Graham	.15	.07
❑ 22 Randall Cunningham	.60	.25
❑ 23 Trent Green	.30	.14
❑ 24 Chris Spielman	.15	.07
❑ 25 Carl Pickens	.30	.14
❑ 26 Bill Romanowski	.15	.07
❑ 27 Jermaine Lewis	.30	.14
❑ 28 Ahman Green	.30	.14
❑ 29 Bryan Still	.15	.07
❑ 30 Dorsey Levens	.60	.25
❑ 31 Frank Wycheck	.15	.07
❑ 32 Jerome Bettis	.60	.25
❑ 33 Reidel Anthony	.30	.14
❑ 34 Robert Jones	.15	.07
❑ 35 Terry Glenn	.60	.25
❑ 36 Tim Brown	.60	.25
❑ 37 Eric Metcalf	.15	.07
❑ 38 Kevin Greene	.30	.14
❑ 39 Takeo Spikes	.15	.07
❑ 40 Brian Mitchell	.15	.07
❑ 41 Duane Starks	.15	.07
❑ 42 Eddie George	.75	.35
❑ 43 Joe Jurevicius	.15	.07
❑ 44 Kimble Anders	.30	.14
❑ 45 Kordell Stewart	.60	.25
❑ 46 Leroy Hoard	.15	.07
❑ 47 Rod Smith	.30	.14
❑ 48 Terrell Owens	.60	.25
❑ 49 Ty Detmer	.30	.14
❑ 50 Charles Woodson	.60	.25
❑ 51 Andre Rison	.30	.14
❑ 52 Chris Slade	.15	.07
❑ 53 Frank Sanders	.30	.14
❑ 54 Michael Irvin	.30	.14
❑ 55 Jerome Pathon	.15	.07
❑ 56 Desmond Howard	.30	.14
❑ 57 Billy Davis	.15	.07
❑ 58 Anthony Simmons	.15	.07
❑ 59 James Jett	.30	.14
❑ 60 Jake Plummer	1.25	.55
❑ 61 John Avery	.30	.14
❑ 62 Marvin Harrison	.60	.25
❑ 63 Merton Hanks	.15	.07
❑ 64 Ricky Proehl	.15	.07
❑ 65 Steve Beuerlein	.15	.07
❑ 66 Willie McGinest	.15	.07
❑ 67 Bryce Paup	.15	.07
❑ 68 Brett Favre	2.50	1.10
❑ 69 Brian Griese	1.25	.55
❑ 70 Curtis Martin	.60	.25
❑ 71 Drew Bledsoe	1.00	.45
❑ 72 Jim Harbaugh	.30	.14
❑ 73 Joey Galloway	.60	.25
❑ 74 Natrone Means	.30	.14
❑ 75 O.J. McDuffie	.30	.14
❑ 76 Tiki Barber	.30	.14
❑ 77 Wesley Walls	.30	.14
❑ 78 Will Blackwell	.15	.07
❑ 79 Bert Emanuel	.30	.14
❑ 80 J.J. Stokes	.30	.14
❑ 81 Steve McNair	.60	.25
❑ 82 Adrian Murrell	.30	.14
❑ 83 Dexter Coakley	.15	.07
❑ 84 Jeff George	.30	.14
❑ 85 Marshall Faulk	.60	.25
❑ 86 Tim Biakabutuka	.30	.14
❑ 87 Troy Drayton	.15	.07
❑ 88 Ty Law	.15	.07
❑ 89 Brian Simmons	.15	.07
❑ 90 Eric Allen	.15	.07
❑ 91 Jon Kitna	.75	.35
❑ 92 Junior Seau	.30	.14
❑ 93 Kevin Turner	.15	.07
❑ 94 Larry Centers	.15	.07
❑ 95 Robert Edwards	.30	.14
❑ 96 Rocket Ismail	.30	.14
❑ 97 Sam Madison	.15	.07
❑ 98 Stephen Alexander	.15	.07
❑ 99 Trent Dilfer	.30	.14
❑ 100 Vonnie Holliday	.15	.07
❑ 101 Charlie Garner	.30	.14
❑ 102 Deion Sanders	.60	.25
❑ 103 Jamal Anderson	.60	.25
❑ 104 Mike Vanderjagt	.15	.07
❑ 105 Aeneas Williams	.15	.07
❑ 106 Daryl Johnston	.30	.14
❑ 107 Hugh Douglas	.15	.07
❑ 108 Torrance Small	.15	.07
❑ 109 Amani Toomer	.15	.07
❑ 110 Amp Lee	.15	.07
❑ 111 Germane Crowell	.30	.14
❑ 112 Marco Battaglia	.15	.07
❑ 113 Michael Westbrook	.30	.14
❑ 114 Randy Moss	2.50	1.10
❑ 115 Ricky Watters	.30	.14
❑ 116 Rob Johnson	.30	.14
❑ 117 Tony Gonzalez	.30	.14
❑ 118 Charles Way	.15	.07
❑ 119 Chris Penn	.15	.07
❑ 120 Eddie Kennison	.30	.14
❑ 121 Elvis Grbac	.30	.14
❑ 122 Eric Moulds	.60	.25
❑ 123 Terry Fair	.15	.07
❑ 124 Tony Banks	.30	.14
❑ 125 Chris Chandler	.30	.14
❑ 126 Emmitt Smith	1.50	.70
❑ 127 Herman Moore	.60	.25
❑ 128 Irv Smith	.15	.07
❑ 129 Kyle Brady	.15	.07
❑ 130 Lamont Warren	.15	.07
❑ 131 Troy Davis	.15	.07
❑ 132 Andre Reed	.30	.14
❑ 133 Justin Armour	.15	.07
❑ 134 James Hasty	.15	.07
❑ 135 Johnnie Morton	.30	.14
❑ 136 Reggie Barlow	.15	.07
❑ 137 Robert Holcombe	.30	.14
❑ 138 Sean Dawkins	.15	.07
❑ 139 Steve Atwater	.15	.07
❑ 140 Tim Dwight	.60	.25
❑ 141 Wayne Chrebet	.30	.14
❑ 142 Alonzo Mayes	.15	.07
❑ 143 Mark Brunell	1.00	.45
❑ 144 Antowain Smith	.60	.25
❑ 145 Byron Bam Morris	.15	.07
❑ 146 Isaac Bruce	.60	.25
❑ 147 Bryan Cox	.15	.07
❑ 148 Bryant Westbrook	.15	.07
❑ 149 Duce Staley	.60	.25
❑ 150 Barry Sanders	2.50	1.10
❑ 151 La'Roi Glover RC	.15	.07
❑ 152 Ray Crockett	.15	.07
❑ 153 Tony Brackens	.15	.07
❑ 154 Roy Barker	.15	.07
❑ 155 Kerry Collins	.30	.14
❑ 156 Andre Wadsworth	.15	.07
❑ 157 Cameron Cleeland	.15	.07
❑ 158 Koy Detmer	.15	.07
❑ 159 Marcus Pollard	.15	.07
❑ 160 Patrick Jeffers RC	8.00	3.60
❑ 161 Aaron Glenn	.15	.07
❑ 162 Andre Hastings	.15	.07
❑ 163 Bruce Smith	.30	.14
❑ 164 David Palmer	.15	.07
❑ 165 Erik Kramer	.30	.14
❑ 166 Orlando Pace	.15	.07
❑ 167 Robert Brooks	.30	.14
❑ 168 Shawn Springs	.15	.07
❑ 169 Terance Mathis	.30	.14
❑ 170 Chris Calloway	.15	.07
❑ 171 Gilbert Brown	.15	.07
❑ 172 Charlie Jones	.15	.07
❑ 173 Curtis Enis	.60	.25
❑ 174 Eugene Robinson	.15	.07
❑ 175 Garrison Hearst	.30	.14
❑ 176 Jason Elam	.15	.07
❑ 177 John Randle	.30	.14
❑ 178 Keith Poole	.15	.07
❑ 179 Kevin Hardy	.15	.07
❑ 180 Keyshawn Johnson	.60	.25
❑ 181 O.J. Santiago	.15	.07
❑ 182 Jacquez Green	.30	.14
❑ 183 Bobby Engram	.30	.14
❑ 184 Damon Jones	.15	.07
❑ 185 Freddie Jones	.15	.07
❑ 186 Jake Reed	.30	.14
❑ 187 Jerry Rice	1.50	.70
❑ 188 Joey Kent	.15	.07
❑ 189 Lamar Smith	.15	.07
❑ 190 John Elway	2.50	1.10
❑ 191 Leon Johnson	.15	.07
❑ 192 Mark Chmura	.30	.14
❑ 193 Peter Boulware	.15	.07
❑ 194 Zach Thomas	.30	.14
❑ 195 Marc Edwards	.15	.07
❑ 196 Mike Alstott	.60	.25
❑ 197 Yancey Thigpen	.15	.07
❑ 198 Oronde Gadsden	.15	.07
❑ 199 Rae Carruth	.30	.14
❑ 200 Troy Aikman	1.50	.70
❑ 201 Shawn Jefferson	.15	.07
❑ 202 Rob Moore	.30	.14
❑ 203 Rickey Dudley	.15	.07
❑ 204 Jason Taylor	.15	.07
❑ 205 Curtis Conway	.30	.14
❑ 206 Darrien Gordon	.15	.07
❑ 207 Eric Green	.15	.07
❑ 208 Jessie Armstead	.15	.07
❑ 209 Keenan McCardell	.30	.14
❑ 210 Robert Smith	.60	.25
❑ 211 Mo Lewis	.15	.07
❑ 212 Ryan Leaf	.60	.25
❑ 213 Steve Young	1.00	.45
❑ 214 Tyrone Davis	.15	.07
❑ 215 Chad Brown	.15	.07
❑ 216 Ike Hilliard	.15	.07
❑ 217 Jimmy Hitchcock	.15	.07
❑ 218 Kevin Dyson	.30	.14
❑ 219 Levon Kirkland	.15	.07
❑ 220 Neil O'Donnell	.30	.14
❑ 221 Ray Lewis	.15	.07
❑ 222 Shannon Sharpe	.30	.14
❑ 223 Skip Hicks	.60	.25
❑ 224 Brad Johnson	.60	.25
❑ 225 Charlie Batch	1.25	.55
❑ 226 Corey Dillon	.60	.25
❑ 227 Dale Carter	.15	.07
❑ 228 John Mobley	.15	.07
❑ 229 Hines Ward	.15	.07
❑ 230 Leslie Shepherd	.15	.07
❑ 231 Michael Strahan	.15	.07
❑ 232 R.W. McQuarters	.15	.07
❑ 233 Mike Pritchard	.15	.07
❑ 234 Antonio Freeman	.60	.25
❑ 235 Ben Coates	.30	.14
❑ 236 Michael Bates	.15	.07
❑ 237 Ed McCaffrey	.30	.14
❑ 238 Gary Brown	.15	.07
❑ 239 Mark Bruener	.15	.07
❑ 240 Mikhael Ricks	.15	.07
❑ 241 Muhsin Muhammad	.15	.07
❑ 242 Priest Holmes	.60	.25
❑ 243 Stephen Davis	.60	.25
❑ 244 Vinny Testaverde	.30	.14
❑ 245 Warrick Dunn	.60	.25

		MINT	NRMT
❑ 246	Derrick Mayes	.15	.07
❑ 247	Fred Taylor	1.50	.70
❑ 248	Drew Bledsoe CL	.30	.14
❑ 249	Eddie George CL	.30	.14
❑ 250	Steve Young CL	.30	.14
❑ 251	Jamal Anderson BB	1.25	.55
❑ 252	Darrien Gordon BB Bill Romanowski BB	.30	.14
❑ 253	Shannon Sharpe BB	.30	.14
❑ 254	Terrell Davis BB	3.00	1.35
❑ 255	Rod Smith BB	.30	.14
❑ 256	Rod Smith BB	.30	.14
❑ 257	John Elway BB	5.00	2.20
❑ 258	Tim Dwight BB	1.25	.55
❑ 259	John Elway BB Ed McCaffrey BB Howard Griffith BB Terrell Davis BB	4.00	1.80
❑ 260	John Elway BB	5.00	2.20
❑ 261	Ricky Williams RC	20.00	9.00
❑ 262	Tim Couch RC	20.00	9.00
❑ 263	Chris Claiborne RC	3.00	1.35
❑ 264	Champ Bailey RC	6.00	2.70
❑ 265	Torry Holt RC	10.00	4.50
❑ 266	Donovan McNabb RC	12.00	5.50
❑ 267	David Boston RC	8.00	3.60
❑ 268	Chris McAlister RC	3.00	1.35
❑ 269	Brock Huard RC	6.00	2.70
❑ 270	Daunte Culpepper RC	12.00	5.50
❑ 271	Matt Stinchcomb RC	2.00	.90
❑ 272	Edgerrin James RC	30.00	13.50
❑ 273	Jevon Kearse RC	10.00	4.50
❑ 274	Ebenezer Ekuban RC	3.00	1.35
❑ 275	Kris Farris RC	2.00	.90
❑ 276	Chris Terry RC	2.00	.90
❑ 277	Jerame Tuman RC	3.00	1.35
❑ 278	Akili Smith RC	10.00	4.50
❑ 279	Aaron Gibson RC	2.00	.90
❑ 280	Rahim Abdullah RC	3.00	1.35
❑ 281	Peerless Price RC	8.00	3.60
❑ 282	Antoine Winfield RC	3.00	1.35
❑ 283	Antuan Edwards RC	2.00	.90
❑ 284	Rob Konrad RC	4.00	1.80
❑ 285	Troy Edwards RC	8.00	3.60
❑ 286	John Thornton RC	2.00	.90
❑ 287	James Johnson RC	6.00	2.70
❑ 288	Gary Stills RC	2.00	.90
❑ 289	Mike Peterson RC	3.00	1.35
❑ 290	Kevin Faulk RC	6.00	2.70
❑ 291	Jared DeVries RC	2.00	.90
❑ 292	Martin Gramatica RC	2.00	.90
❑ 293	Montae Reagor RC	2.00	.90
❑ 294	Andy Katzenmoyer RC	4.00	1.80
❑ 295	Sedrick Irvin RC	4.00	1.80
❑ 296	D'Wayne Bates RC	3.00	1.35
❑ 297	Amos Zereoue RC	4.00	1.80
❑ 298	Dre' Bly RC	3.00	1.35
❑ 299	Kevin Johnson RC	10.00	4.50
❑ 300	Cade McNown RC	12.00	5.50
❑ P247	Fred Taylor Promo	1.50	.70

1999 Ultra Gold Medallion

	MINT	NRMT
COMPLETE SET (300)	400.00	180.00
COMMON CARD (1-300)	.50	.23

*GOLD MED.STARS: 1.25X TO 3X HI COL.
*GOLD MED.YOUNG STARS: 1X TO 2.5X
*GOLD MED.RCs: .6X TO 1.5X
GOLD MED.VETERAN ODDS ONE PER PACK
GOLD MED.DRAFT PICK ODDS 1:25 PACKS
GOLD MED.BACK TO BACK ODDS 1:50

1999 Ultra Platinum Medallion

	MINT	NRMT
COMMON CARD (1-300)	8.00	3.60

*PLAT.MED.STARS: 20X TO 50X HI COL.
*PLAT.MED.YOUNG STARS: 15X TO 40X
*PLAT.MED.RCs: 2.5X TO 6X
PM VETS PRINT RUN 99 SER.#'d SETS
PM DRAFT PICK PRINT RUN 65 SER.#'d SETS
PM BACK/BACK PRINT RUN 40 SER.#'d SETS

1999 Ultra As Good As It Gets

	MINT	NRMT
COMPLETE SET (15)	200.00	90.00
COMMON CARD (1-15)	6.00	2.70
SEMISTARS	10.00	4.50

STATED ODDS 1:288

		MINT	NRMT
❑ 1	Warrick Dunn	15.00	6.75
❑ 2	Terrell Davis	20.00	9.00
❑ 3	Robert Edwards	6.00	2.70
❑ 4	Randy Moss	25.00	11.00
❑ 5	Peyton Manning	25.00	11.00
❑ 6	Mark Brunell	12.00	5.50
❑ 7	John Elway	30.00	13.50
❑ 8	Jerry Rice	20.00	9.00
❑ 9	Jake Plummer	15.00	6.75
❑ 10	Fred Taylor	15.00	6.75
❑ 11	Emmitt Smith	20.00	9.00
❑ 12	Dan Marino	30.00	13.50
❑ 13	Charlie Batch	10.00	4.50
❑ 14	Brett Favre	30.00	13.50
❑ 15	Barry Sanders	30.00	13.50

1999 Ultra Caught In The Draft

	MINT	NRMT
COMPLETE SET (15)	50.00	22.00
COMMON CARD (1-15)	3.00	1.35

STATED ODDS 1:18

		MINT	NRMT
❑ 1	Ricky Williams	12.00	5.50
❑ 2	Tim Couch	12.00	5.50
❑ 3	Chris Claiborne	3.00	1.35
❑ 4	Champ Bailey	5.00	2.20
❑ 5	Torry Holt	6.00	2.70
❑ 6	Donovan McNabb	8.00	3.60
❑ 7	David Boston	4.00	1.80
❑ 8	Andy Katzenmoyer	5.00	2.20
❑ 9	Daunte Culpepper	8.00	3.60
❑ 10	Edgerrin James	20.00	9.00
❑ 11	Cade McNown	8.00	3.60
❑ 12	Troy Edwards	4.00	1.80
❑ 13	Akili Smith	5.00	2.20
❑ 14	Peerless Price	4.00	1.80
❑ 15	Amos Zereoue	5.00	2.20

1999 Ultra Counterparts

	MINT	NRMT
COMPLETE SET (15)	80.00	36.00
COMMON CARD (1-15)	4.00	1.80
SEMISTARS	5.00	2.20

STATED ODDS 1:36

		MINT	NRMT
❑ 1	Troy Aikman Michael Irvin	10.00	4.50
❑ 2	Drew Bledsoe Ben Coates	6.00	2.70
❑ 3	Terrell Davis Howard Griffith	10.00	4.50
❑ 4	Warrick Dunn Mike Alstott	5.00	2.20
❑ 5	Brett Favre Antonio Freeman	15.00	6.75
❑ 6	Jake Plummer Frank Sanders	8.00	3.60
❑ 7	Randy Moss Randall Cunningham	12.00	5.50
❑ 8	Eddie George Steve McNair	6.00	2.70
❑ 9	Keyshawn Johnson Wayne Chrebet	5.00	2.20
❑ 10	Ryan Leaf Mikhael Ricks	4.00	1.80
❑ 11	Peyton Manning Marshall Faulk	12.00	5.50
❑ 12	Barry Sanders Tommy Vardell	15.00	6.75
❑ 13	Charlie Batch Herman Moore	5.00	2.20
❑ 14	Emmitt Smith Daryl Johnston	10.00	4.50
❑ 15	Kordell Stewart Jerome Bettis	5.00	2.20

1999 Ultra Damage, Inc.

	MINT	NRMT
COMPLETE CARD (15)	150.00	70.00
COMMON CARD (1-15)	6.00	2.70

STATED ODDS 1:72

		MINT	NRMT
❑ 1	Brett Favre	20.00	9.00
❑ 2	Dan Marino	20.00	9.00
❑ 3	John Elway	20.00	9.00
❑ 4	Mark Brunell	10.00	4.50

Card	MINT	NRMT
❑ 5 Peyton Manning	20.00	9.00
❑ 6 Robert Edwards	6.00	2.70
❑ 7 Terrell Davis	12.00	5.50
❑ 8 Troy Aikman	12.00	5.50
❑ 9 Randy Moss	20.00	9.00
❑ 10 Kordell Stewart	8.00	3.60
❑ 11 Jerry Rice	12.00	5.50
❑ 12 Fred Taylor	12.00	5.50
❑ 13 Emmitt Smith	12.00	5.50
❑ 14 Charlie Batch	10.00	4.50
❑ 15 Barry Sanders	20.00	9.00

1999 Ultra Over The Top

	MINT	NRMT
COMPLETE SET (20)	20.00	9.00
COMMON CARD (1-20)	1.00	.45
STATED ODDS 1:6		

Card	MINT	NRMT
❑ 1 Troy Aikman	2.50	1.10
❑ 2 Drew Bledsoe	1.50	.70
❑ 3 Mark Brunell	1.50	.70
❑ 4 Randall Cunningham	1.00	.45
❑ 5 Jamal Anderson	1.00	.45
❑ 6 Warrick Dunn	1.00	.45
❑ 7 Robert Edwards	1.00	.45
❑ 8 John Elway	4.00	1.80
❑ 9 Eddie George	1.25	.55
❑ 10 Eric Moulds	1.00	.45
❑ 11 Keyshawn Johnson	1.00	.45
❑ 12 Ryan Leaf	1.00	.45
❑ 13 Dan Marino	4.00	1.80
❑ 14 Steve McNair	1.00	.45
❑ 15 Jake Plummer	2.00	.90
❑ 16 Jerry Rice	2.50	1.10
❑ 17 Deion Sanders	1.00	.45
❑ 18 Kordell Stewart	1.00	.45
❑ 19 Fred Taylor	2.00	.90
❑ 20 Steve Young	1.50	.70

2000 Ultra

	MINT	NRMT
COMPLETE SET (249)	150.00	70.00
COMP.SET w/o SP's (220)	20.00	9.00
COMMON CARD (1-220)	.15	.07
SEMISTARS	.30	.14
UNLISTED STARS	.60	.25
COMMON ROOKIE (220-250)	2.00	.90
ROOKIE SEMISTARS	3.00	1.35
ROOKIE SUBSET ODDS 1:4		

Card	MINT	NRMT
❑ 1 Kurt Warner	3.00	1.35
❑ 2 Derrick Alexander	.30	.14
❑ 3 Aaron Craver	.15	.07
❑ 4 Kevin Faulk	.30	.14
❑ 5 Marcus Robinson	.60	.25
❑ 6 Tony Banks	.30	.14
❑ 7 Jon Ritchie	.15	.07
❑ 8 Torry Holt	.60	.25
❑ 9 Joe Horn	.15	.07
❑ 10 Eddie George	.75	.35
❑ 11 Michael Westbrook	.30	.14
❑ 12 Gus Frerotte	.15	.07
❑ 13 Tim Brown	.60	.25
❑ 14 Tamarick Vanover	.15	.07
❑ 15 David Sloan	.15	.07
❑ 16 Darnay Scott	.15	.07
❑ 17 Junior Seau	.30	.14
❑ 18 Warren Sapp	.30	.14
❑ 19 Priest Holmes	.30	.14
❑ 20 Jerry Rice	1.50	.70
❑ 21 Cade McNown	1.00	.45
❑ 22 Johnnie Morton	.30	.14
❑ 23 Vinny Testaverde	.30	.14
❑ 24 James Jett	.15	.07
❑ 25 Tony Gonzalez	.30	.14
❑ 26 Charlie Batch	.60	.25
❑ 27 Tony Simmons	.15	.07
❑ 28 James Stewart	.30	.14
❑ 29 Corey Dillon	.60	.25
❑ 30 Ricky Williams	1.50	.70
❑ 31 Ryan Leaf	.60	.25
❑ 32 Terry Allen	.30	.14
❑ 33 Freddie Jones	.15	.07
❑ 34 Terry Kirby	.15	.07
❑ 35 Charles Johnson	.15	.07
❑ 36 William Henderson	.15	.07
❑ 37 Stephen Alexander	.15	.07
❑ 38 Moe Williams	.15	.07
❑ 39 David Boston	.60	.25
❑ 40 Emmitt Smith	1.50	.70
❑ 41 Ken Oxendine	.15	.07
❑ 42 Byron Hanspard	.15	.07
❑ 43 Dwight Stone	.15	.07
❑ 44 Jim Harbaugh	.30	.14
❑ 45 Curtis Enis	.60	.25
❑ 46 Peerless Price	.60	.25
❑ 47 Terance Mathis	.15	.07
❑ 48 Mike Alstott	.60	.25
❑ 49 Rod Smith	.30	.14
❑ 50 Marshall Faulk	.60	.25
❑ 51 Derrick Mayes	.30	.14
❑ 52 Keenan McCardell	.30	.14
❑ 53 Curtis Martin	.60	.25
❑ 54 Bobby Engram	.15	.07
❑ 55 Carl Pickens	.30	.14
❑ 56 Robert Smith	.60	.25
❑ 57 Ike Hilliard	.30	.14
❑ 58 Reidel Anthony	.30	.14
❑ 59 Jeff Graham	.15	.07
❑ 60 Mark Brunell	1.00	.45
❑ 61 Joe Montgomery	.15	.07
❑ 62 Ed McCaffrey	.15	.07
❑ 63 Kenny Bynum	.15	.07
❑ 64 Curtis Conway	.30	.14
❑ 65 Trent Dilfer	.30	.14
❑ 66 Jake Reed	.30	.14
❑ 67 Jake Plummer	.60	.25
❑ 68 Tony Martin	.30	.14
❑ 69 Yatil Green	.15	.07
❑ 70 Keyshawn Johnson	.60	.25
❑ 71 Leroy Hoard	.15	.07
❑ 72 Skip Hicks	.30	.14
❑ 73 Marvin Harrison	.60	.25
❑ 74 Steve Beuerlein	.30	.14
❑ 75 Will Blackwell	.15	.07
❑ 76 Derek Loville	.15	.07
❑ 77 Warrick Dunn	.60	.25
❑ 78 Amos Zereoue	.15	.07
❑ 79 Ray Lucas	.60	.25
❑ 80 Randy Moss	2.00	.90
❑ 81 Wesley Walls	.15	.07
❑ 82 Jimmy Smith	.30	.14
❑ 83 Kordell Stewart	.60	.25
❑ 84 Brian Griese	.75	.35
❑ 85 Martin Gramatica	.15	.07
❑ 86 Chris Chandler	.30	.14
❑ 87 Reggie Barlow	.15	.07
❑ 88 Jeff George	.30	.14
❑ 89 Tavian Banks	.15	.07
❑ 90 Mushin Muhammad	.30	.14
❑ 91 Steve McNair	.60	.25
❑ 92 Hines Ward	.15	.07
❑ 93 Brian Mitchell	.15	.07
❑ 94 Daunte Culpepper	1.00	.45
❑ 95 Tim Dwight	.60	.25
❑ 96 Terrence Wilkins	.60	.25
❑ 97 Fred Lane	.15	.07
❑ 98 Brett Favre	2.50	1.10
❑ 99 Richie Anderson	.15	.07
❑ 100 Jamal Anderson	.60	.25
❑ 101 Doug Flutie	.75	.35
❑ 102 Charles Woodson	.30	.14
❑ 103 Jacquez Green	.30	.14
❑ 104 Olandis Gary	.75	.35
❑ 105 Steve Young	1.00	.45
❑ 106 Wayne Chrebet	.30	.14
❑ 107 Karim Abdul-Jabbar	.30	.14
❑ 108 Andre Rison	.30	.14
❑ 109 Eddie Kennison	.15	.07
❑ 110 Jevon Kearse	.60	.25
❑ 111 Tony Richardson	.15	.07
❑ 112 Jake Delhomme RC	2.50	1.10
❑ 113 Errict Rhett	.30	.14
❑ 114 Akili Smith	.75	.35
❑ 115 Tyrone Wheatley	.30	.14
❑ 116 Corey Bradford	.30	.14
❑ 117 J.J. Stokes	.30	.14
❑ 118 Simeon Rice	.15	.07
❑ 119 Brad Johnson	.60	.25
❑ 120 Edgerrin James	2.50	1.10
❑ 121 Amani Toomer	.15	.07
❑ 122 O.J. McDuffie	.30	.14
❑ 123 Az-Zahir Hakim	.30	.14
❑ 124 Troy Edwards	.60	.25
❑ 125 Tim Biakabutuka	.30	.14
❑ 126 Jason Tucker	.30	.14
❑ 127 Charles Way	.15	.07
❑ 128 Terrell Davis	1.50	.70
❑ 129 Garrison Hearst	.30	.14
❑ 130 Fred Taylor	1.00	.45
❑ 131 Robert Holcombe	.15	.07
❑ 132 Frank Sanders	.30	.14
❑ 133 Morten Andersen	.15	.07
❑ 134 Cris Carter	.60	.25
❑ 135 Patrick Jeffers	.60	.25
❑ 136 Antonio Freeman	.60	.25
❑ 137 Jonathan Linton	.15	.07
❑ 138 Rashaan Shehee	.15	.07
❑ 139 Luther Broughton RC	.30	.14
❑ 140 Tim Couch	1.50	.70
❑ 141 Keith Poole	.15	.07
❑ 142 Champ Bailey	.30	.14
❑ 143 Yancey Thigpen	.15	.07
❑ 144 Joey Galloway	.60	.25
❑ 145 Mac Cody	.15	.07
❑ 146 Damon Huard	.60	.25
❑ 147 Dorsey Levens	.60	.25
❑ 148 Donovan McNabb	1.00	.45
❑ 149 Jamie Asher	.15	.07
❑ 150 Peyton Manning	2.00	.90
❑ 151 Leslie Shepherd	.15	.07
❑ 152 Charlie Rogers	.15	.07
❑ 153 Tony Horne	.15	.07
❑ 154 Jim Miller	.15	.07
❑ 155 Richard Huntley	.15	.07
❑ 156 Germane Crowell	.30	.14
❑ 157 Natrone Means	.15	.07
❑ 158 Justin Armour	.15	.07
❑ 159 Drew Bledsoe	1.00	.45
❑ 160 Dedric Ward	.15	.07
❑ 161 Allen Rossum	.15	.07
❑ 162 Ricky Watters	.30	.14
❑ 163 Kerry Collins	.30	.14
❑ 164 James Johnson	.30	.14
❑ 165 Elvis Grbac	.30	.14
❑ 166 Larry Centers	.15	.07
❑ 167 Rob Moore	.30	.14
❑ 168 Jay Riemersma	.15	.07
❑ 169 Bill Schroeder	.30	.14
❑ 170 Deion Sanders	.60	.25
❑ 171 Jerome Bettis	.60	.25
❑ 172 Dan Marino	2.50	1.10

	MINT	NRMT
❑ 173 Terrell Owens	.60	.25
❑ 174 Kevin Carter	.15	.07
❑ 175 Lamar Smith	.15	.07
❑ 176 Ken Dilger	.15	.07
❑ 177 Napoleon Kaufman	.60	.25
❑ 178 Kevin Williams	.15	.07
❑ 179 Tremain Mack	.15	.07
❑ 180 Troy Aikman	1.50	.70
❑ 181 Glyn Milburn	.15	.07
❑ 182 Pete Mitchell	.15	.07
❑ 183 Cameron Cleeland	.15	.07
❑ 184 Qadry Ismail	.15	.07
❑ 185 Michael Pittman	.15	.07
❑ 186 Kevin Dyson	.30	.14
❑ 187 Matt Hasselbeck	.30	.14
❑ 188 Kevin Johnson	.60	.25
❑ 189 Rich Gannon	.30	.14
❑ 190 Stephen Davis	.60	.25
❑ 191 Frank Wycheck	.15	.07
❑ 192 Eric Moulds	.60	.25
❑ 193 Jon Kitna	.60	.25
❑ 194 Mario Bates	.15	.07
❑ 195 Na Brown	.15	.07
❑ 196 Jeff Blake	.30	.14
❑ 197 Charles Evans	.15	.07
❑ 198 Oronde Gadsden	.15	.07
❑ 199 Donnell Bennett	.15	.07
❑ 200 Isaac Bruce	.60	.25
❑ 201 Olindo Mare	.15	.07
❑ 202 Darnell McDonald	.15	.07
❑ 203 Charlie Garner	.30	.14
❑ 204 Shawn Jefferson	.15	.07
❑ 205 Adrian Murrell	.30	.14
❑ 206 Peter Boulware	.15	.07
❑ 207 LeShon Johnson	.15	.07
❑ 208 Herman Moore	.60	.25
❑ 209 Duce Staley	.60	.25
❑ 210 Sean Dawkins	.15	.07
❑ 211 Antowain Smith	.60	.25
❑ 212 Albert Connell	.15	.07
❑ 213 Jeff Garcia	.60	.25
❑ 214 Kimble Anders	.15	.07
❑ 215 Shaun King	1.00	.45
❑ 216 Rocket Ismail	.30	.14
❑ 217 Andrew Glover	.15	.07
❑ 218 Rickey Dudley	.15	.07
❑ 219 Michael Basnight	.15	.07
❑ 220 Terry Glenn	.60	.25
❑ 221 Peter Warrick RC	15.00	6.75
❑ 222 Ron Dayne RC	15.00	6.75
❑ 223 Thomas Jones RC	10.00	4.50
❑ 224 Joe Hamilton RC	3.00	1.35
❑ 225 Tim Rattay RC	4.00	1.80
❑ 226 Chad Pennington RC	12.00	5.50
❑ 227 Dennis Northcutt RC	4.00	1.80
❑ 228 Troy Walters RC	3.00	1.35
❑ 229 Travis Prentice RC	4.00	1.80
❑ 230 Shaun Alexander RC	10.00	4.50
❑ 231 J.R. Redmond RC	5.00	2.20
❑ 232 Chris Redman RC	5.00	2.20
❑ 233 Tee Martin RC	5.00	2.20
❑ 234 Tom Brady RC	3.00	1.35
❑ 235 Travis Taylor RC	6.00	2.70
❑ 236 R.Jay Soward RC	4.00	1.80
❑ 237 Jamal Lewis RC	10.00	4.50
❑ 238 Giovanni Carmazzi RC	6.00	2.70
❑ 239 Dez White RC	4.00	1.80
❑ 240 LaVar Arrington RC SP	225.00	100.00
❑ 241 Laveranues Coles RC	3.00	1.35
❑ 242 Sherrod Gideon RC	2.00	.90
❑ 243 Trung Canidate RC	3.00	1.35
❑ 244 Michael Wiley RC	4.00	1.80
❑ 245 Anthony Lucas RC	3.00	1.35
❑ 246 Darrell Jackson RC	3.00	1.35
❑ 247 Plaxico Burress RC	8.00	3.60
❑ 248 Reuben Droughns RC	4.00	1.80
❑ 249 Marc Bulger RC	3.00	1.35
❑ 250 Danny Farmer RC	3.00	1.35

2000 Ultra Gold Medallion

	MINT	NRMT
COMPLETE SET (249)	300.00	135.00
COMMON CARD (1-220)	.50	.23

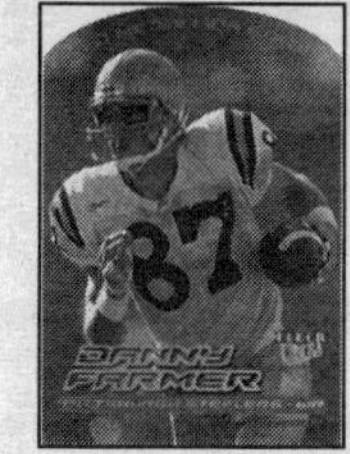

*GOLD MED.STARS: 1.2X TO 3X HI COL
*GOLD MED YOUNG STARS: 1X TO 2.5X

	MINT	NRMT
COMMON ROOKIE (220-250)	3.00	1.35

*GOLD MED.RC's: .6X TO 1.5X

	MINT	NRMT
❑ 240 LaVar Arrington SP	300.00	135.00

2000 Ultra Platinum Medallion

	MINT	NRMT
COMMON CARD (1-220)	15.00	6.75

*PLAT.STARS: 50X TO 120X HI COL
*PLAT.YOUNG STARS: 40X TO 100X
1-220 STATED PRINT RUN 50 SERIAL #'d SETS

	MINT	NRMT
COMMON ROOKIE (220-250)	40.00	18.00

*PLAT.RC's: 8X TO 20X
ROOKIE STATED PRINT RUN 25 SERIAL #'d SETS
CARD #240 ARRINGTON NOT RELEASED

2000 Ultra Autographics

	MINT	NRMT
COMMON CARD	10.00	4.50
SEMISTARS	15.00	6.75
UNLISTED STARS	20.00	9.00

*SILVER: .5X TO 1.2X HI COL
SILVER STATED PRINT RUN 250 SERIAL #'d SETS

	MINT	NRMT
❑ 2 Jamal Anderson	20.00	9.00
❑ 3 Jerome Bettis	20.00	9.00
❑ 4 Tim Biakabutuka	15.00	6.75
❑ 5 David Boston	20.00	9.00
❑ 6 Peter Boulware	10.00	4.50
❑ 7 Tom Brady	15.00	6.75
❑ 8 Isaac Bruce	25.00	11.00
❑ 9 Mark Brunell	40.00	18.00
❑ 10 Cris Carter	30.00	13.50
❑ 11 Germane Crowell	15.00	6.75
❑ 12 Terrell Davis	60.00	27.00
❑ 13 Ron Dayne	80.00	36.00
❑ 14 Tim Dwight	20.00	9.00
❑ 15 Deon Dyer	10.00	4.50
❑ 16 Kevin Dyson	15.00	6.75
❑ 17 Troy Edwards	20.00	9.00
❑ 18 Marshall Faulk	30.00	13.50
❑ 19 Christian Fauria	10.00	4.50
❑ 20 Jermaine Fazande	10.00	4.50
❑ 21 Rich Gannon	15.00	6.75
❑ 22 Jeff Garcia	25.00	11.00
❑ 23 Charlie Garner	15.00	6.75
❑ 24 Jeff Graham	10.00	4.50
❑ 25 Damon Griffin	10.00	4.50
❑ 26 Marvin Harrison/250	30.00	13.50
❑ 27 Tony Horne	15.00	6.75
❑ 28 Damon Huard	20.00	9.00
❑ 29 Darrell Jackson	15.00	6.75
❑ 30 Edgerrin James	80.00	36.00
❑ 31 Patrick Jeffers	15.00	6.75
❑ 32 Brad Johnson	20.00	9.00
❑ 33 Kevin Johnson	25.00	11.00
❑ 34 Rob Johnson	15.00	6.75
❑ 35 Terry Kirby	10.00	4.50
❑ 36 Jon Kitna	15.00	6.75
❑ 37 O.J. McDuffie	15.00	6.75
❑ 38 Rondell Mealey	10.00	4.50
❑ 39 Joe Montgomery	10.00	4.50
❑ 40 Herman Moore	20.00	9.00
❑ 41 Sylvester Morris	20.00	9.00
❑ 42 Eric Moulds	20.00	9.00
❑ 43 Muhsin Muhammad	20.00	9.00
❑ 44 Chad Pennington	60.00	27.00
❑ 45 Travis Prentice	20.00	9.00
❑ 46 Tim Rattay	20.00	9.00
❑ 47 Jon Ritchie	15.00	6.75
❑ 48 Antowain Smith	25.00	11.00
❑ 49 Kurt Warner	100.00	45.00
❑ 50 Chris Watson	10.00	4.50

2000 Ultra Dream Team

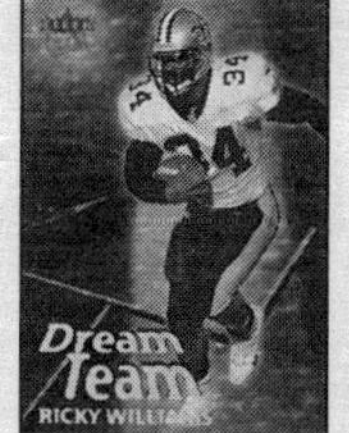

	MINT	NRMT
COMPLETE SET (10)	25.00	11.00
COMMON CARD (1-10)	1.50	.70

STATED ODDS 1:24

	MINT	NRMT
❑ 1 Terrell Davis	4.00	1.80
❑ 2 Brett Favre	6.00	2.70
❑ 3 Troy Aikman	4.00	1.80
❑ 4 Keyshawn Johnson	1.50	.70
❑ 5 Edgerrin James	5.00	2.20
❑ 6 Randy Moss	5.00	2.20
❑ 7 Marvin Harrison	1.50	.70
❑ 8 Kurt Warner	6.00	2.70
❑ 9 Fred Taylor	2.50	1.10
❑ 10 Ricky Williams	3.00	1.35

2000 Ultra Fast Lane

	MINT	NRMT
COMPLETE SET (15)	8.00	3.60

COMMON CARD (1-15) .50 .23
SEMISTARS .75 .35
STATED ODDS 1:3

❑ 1 Jimmy Smith .50 .23
❑ 2 Cris Carter .75 .35
❑ 3 Marvin Harrison .75 .35
❑ 4 Tim Brown .75 .35
❑ 5 Mushin Muhammad .50 .23
❑ 6 Isaac Bruce .75 .35
❑ 7 Bobby Engram .50 .23
❑ 8 Terance Mathis .50 .23
❑ 9 Randy Moss 2.50 1.10
❑ 10 Rocket Ismail .50 .23
❑ 11 Keyshawn Johnson .75 .35
❑ 12 Terry Glenn .75 .35
❑ 13 Jerry Rice 2.00 .90
❑ 14 Marcus Robinson .75 .35
❑ 15 Antonio Freeman .75 .35

2000 Ultra Feel the Game

	MINT	NRMT
COMPLETE SET (27)	700.00	325.00
COMMON CARD	20.00	9.00
SEMISTARS	25.00	11.00
STATED ODDS 1:144		
*GOLDS: 1X TO 2X HI COL.		
GOLD PRINT RUN 50 SERIAL #'d SETS		
❑ 1 Karim Abdul-Jabbar	20.00	9.00
❑ 2 Jamal Anderson	25.00	11.00
❑ 3 David Boston	25.00	11.00
❑ 4 Mark Brunell	50.00	22.00
❑ 5 Chris Chandler	20.00	9.00
❑ 6 Tim Couch	70.00	32.00
❑ 7 Tim Dwight Pants	35.00	16.00
❑ 8 Curtis Enis	30.00	13.50
❑ 9 Doug Flutie	40.00	18.00
❑ 10 Terry Glenn	20.00	9.00
❑ 11 Trent Green	20.00	9.00
❑ 12 Brian Griese	35.00	16.00
❑ 13 Az-Zahir Hakim Pants	25.00	11.00
❑ 14 Kevin Johnson	25.00	11.00
❑ 15 Terry Kirby	20.00	9.00
❑ 16 Dorsey Levens	25.00	11.00
❑ 17 Rob Moore	20.00	9.00
❑ 18 Johnnie Morton	25.00	11.00
❑ 19 Jake Plummer	30.00	13.50
❑ 20 Frank Sanders	20.00	9.00
❑ 21 Junior Seau	25.00	11.00
❑ 22 Emmitt Smith	70.00	32.00
❑ 23 Jimmy Smith	25.00	11.00
❑ 24 J.J. Stokes	20.00	9.00
❑ 25 Amani Toomer	20.00	9.00
❑ 26 Kurt Warner Pants	120.00	55.00
❑ 27 Charles Woodson	25.00	11.00

2000 Ultra Head of the Class

	MINT	NRMT
COMPLETE SET (10)	12.00	5.50
COMMON CARD (1-10)	.75	.35
SEMISTARS	1.00	.45
STATED ODDS 1:6		
❑ 1 Peter Warrick	4.00	1.80
❑ 2 Ron Dayne	4.00	1.80
❑ 3 Thomas Jones	2.50	1.10
❑ 4 Chad Pennington	3.00	1.35
❑ 5 Joe Hamilton	.75	.35
❑ 6 Shaun Alexander	2.50	1.10
❑ 7 J.R. Redmond	1.25	.55
❑ 8 Troy Walters	.75	.35
❑ 9 Travis Prentice	1.00	.45
❑ 10 Chris Redman	1.25	.55

2000 Ultra Instant Three Play

	MINT	NRMT
COMPLETE SET (15)	8.00	3.60
COMMON CARD (1-15)	.25	.11
SEMISTARS	.50	.23
UNLISTED STARS	.75	.35
STATED ODDS 1:3		
❑ 1 Peyton Manning	2.50	1.10
❑ 2 Curtis Enis	.75	.35
❑ 3 Charlie Batch	.75	.35
❑ 4 Fred Taylor	1.25	.55
❑ 5 Az-Zahir Hakim	.25	.11
❑ 6 Randy Moss	2.50	1.10

	MINT	NRMT
❑ 7 Jacquez Green	.50	.23
❑ 8 Kevin Dyson	.50	.23
❑ 9 Brian Griese	.75	.35
❑ 10 Rashaan Shehee	.25	.11
❑ 11 Tony Simmons	.25	.11
❑ 12 Charles Woodson	.50	.23
❑ 13 Hines Ward	.25	.11
❑ 14 Skip Hicks	.50	.23
❑ 15 Tim Dwight	.75	.35

2000 Ultra Millennium Monsters

	MINT	NRMT
COMPLETE SET (10)	15.00	6.75
COMMON CARD (1-10)	1.00	.45
STATED ODDS 1:12		
❑ 1 Tim Couch	2.00	.90
❑ 2 Eddie George	1.25	.55
❑ 3 Brian Griese	1.00	.45
❑ 4 Keyshawn Johnson	1.00	.45
❑ 5 Peyton Manning	3.00	1.35
❑ 6 Randy Moss	3.00	1.35
❑ 7 Ricky Williams	2.00	.90
❑ 8 Edgerrin James	3.00	1.35
❑ 9 Cade McNown	1.25	.55
❑ 10 Donovan McNabb	1.25	.55

2000 Ultra Won by One

	MINT	NRMT
COMPLETE SET (10)	60.00	27.00
COMMON CARD (1-10)	3.00	1.35
STATED ODDS 1:72		
❑ 1 Peyton Manning	10.00	4.50
❑ 2 Randy Moss	10.00	4.50
❑ 3 Brett Favre	12.00	5.50
❑ 4 Terrell Davis	8.00	3.60
❑ 5 Dan Marino	12.00	5.50
❑ 6 Jake Plummer	3.00	1.35
❑ 7 Tim Couch	6.00	2.70
❑ 8 Eddie George	4.00	1.80
❑ 9 Brian Griese	3.00	1.35
❑ 10 Kurt Warner	12.00	5.50

1991 Upper Deck

	MINT	NRMT
COMPLETE SET (700)	12.00	5.50
COMP.FACT.SET (700)	15.00	6.75
COMP.SERIES 1 SET (500)	8.00	3.60
COMP.SERIES 2 SET (200)	4.00	1.80
COMP.FACT.SERIES 2 (200)	4.00	1.80
COMMON CARD (1-700)	.04	.02
SEMISTARS	.10	.05
UNLISTED STARS	.25	.11
COMP.MONTANA HERO.(10)	12.00	5.50
MONTANA HEADER SP (NNO)	8.00	3.60
CERTIFIED AUTO/2500 (AU)	150.00	70.00
MONTANA: RANDOM INS.IN LO SERIES		
COMP.NAMATH HERO.(10)	12.00	5.50
NAMATH HEADER SP (NNO)	8.00	3.60
CERTIFIED AUTO/2500 (AU)	150.00	70.00
NAMATH: RANDOM INS.IN HI SERIES		
❑ 1 Star Rookie Checklist Dan McGwire	.04	.02
❑ 2 Eric Bieniemy RC	.04	.02
❑ 3 Mike Dumas RC	.04	.02
❑ 4 Mike Croel RC	.04	.02
❑ 5 Russell Maryland RC	.25	.11
❑ 6 Charles McRae RC	.04	.02

	Card	Price	Price
❑	7 Dan McGwire RC	.04	.02
❑	8 Mike Pritchard RC	.25	.11
❑	9 Ricky Watters RC	1.50	.70
❑	10 Chris Zorich RC	.25	.11
❑	11 Browning Nagle RC	.04	.02
❑	12 Wesley Carroll RC	.04	.02
❑	13 Brett Favre RC	6.00	2.70
❑	14 Rob Carpenter RC	.04	.02
❑	15 Eric Swann RC	.25	.11
❑	16 Stanley Richard RC	.04	.02
❑	17 Herman Moore RC	2.00	.90
❑	18 Todd Marinovich RC	.04	.02
❑	19 Aaron Craver RC	.04	.02
❑	20 Chuck Webb RC	.04	.02
❑	21 Todd Lyght RC	.04	.02
❑	22 Greg Lewis RC	.04	.02
❑	23 Eric Turner RC	.10	.05
❑	24 Alvin Harper RC	.25	.11
❑	25 Jarrod Bunch RC	.04	.02
❑	26 Bruce Pickens RC	.04	.02
❑	27 Harvey Williams RC	.25	.11
❑	28 Randal Hill RC	.10	.05
❑	29 Nick Bell RC	.04	.02
❑	30 Jim Everett AT	.10	.05
	Henry Ellard		
❑	31 Randall Cunningham AT	.04	.02
	Keith Jackson		
❑	32 Steve DeBerg AT	.04	.02
	Stephone Paige		
❑	33 Warren Moon AT	.10	.05
	Drew Hill		
❑	34 Dan Marino AT	.50	.23
	Mark Clayton		
❑	35 Joe Montana AT	.50	.23
	Jerry Rice		
❑	36 Percy Snow	.04	.02
❑	37 Kelvin Martin	.04	.02
❑	38 Scott Case	.04	.02
❑	39 John Gesek RC	.04	.02
❑	40 Barry Word	.04	.02
❑	41 Cornelius Bennett	.10	.05
❑	42 Mike Kenn	.04	.02
❑	43 Andre Reed	.10	.05
❑	44 Bobby Hebert	.04	.02
❑	45 William Perry	.10	.05
❑	46 Dennis Byrd	.04	.02
❑	47 Martin Mayhew	.04	.02
❑	48 Issiac Holt	.04	.02
❑	49 William White	.04	.02
❑	50 JoJo Townsell	.04	.02
❑	51 Jarvis Williams	.04	.02
❑	52 Joey Browner	.04	.02
❑	53 Pat Terrell	.04	.02
❑	54 Joe Montana UER	1.25	.55
	(Born Monongahela, not New Eagle)		
❑	55 Jeff Herrod	.04	.02
❑	56 Cris Carter	.50	.23
❑	57 Jerry Rice	.75	.35
❑	58 Brett Perriman	.25	.11
❑	59 Kevin Fagan	.04	.02
❑	60 Wayne Haddix	.04	.02
❑	61 Tommy Kane	.04	.02
❑	62 Pat Beach	.04	.02
❑	63 Jeff Lageman	.04	.02
❑	64 Hassan Jones	.04	.02
❑	65 Bennie Blades	.04	.02
❑	66 Tim McGee	.04	.02
❑	67 Robert Blackmon	.04	.02
❑	68 Fred Stokes RC	.04	.02
❑	69 Barney Bussey RC	.04	.02
❑	70 Eric Metcalf	.10	.05
❑	71 Mark Kelso	.04	.02
❑	72 Neal Anderson TC	.04	.02
❑	73 Boomer Esiason TC	.04	.02
❑	74 Thurman Thomas TC	.25	.11
❑	75 John Elway TC	.50	.23
❑	76 Eric Metcalf TC	.10	.05
❑	77 Vinny Testaverde TC	.10	.05
❑	78 Johnny Johnson TC	.04	.02
❑	79 Anthony Miller TC	.10	.05
❑	80 Derrick Thomas TC	.10	.05
❑	81 Jeff George TC	.10	.05
❑	82 Troy Aikman TC	.40	.18
❑	83 Dan Marino TC	.50	.23
❑	84 Randall Cunningham TC	.10	.05
❑	85 Deion Sanders TC	.04	.02
❑	86 Jerry Rice TC	.40	.18
❑	87 Lawrence Taylor TC	.10	.05
❑	88 Al Toon TC	.04	.02
❑	89 Barry Sanders TC	.60	.25
❑	90 Warren Moon TC	.10	.05
❑	91 Don Majkowski TC	.04	.02
❑	92 Andre Tippett TC	.04	.02
❑	93 Bo Jackson TC	.10	.05
❑	94 Jim Everett TC	.10	.05
❑	95 Art Monk TC	.10	.05
❑	96 Morten Andersen TC	.04	.02
❑	97 John L. Williams TC	.04	.02
❑	98 Rod Woodson TC	.10	.05
❑	99 Herschel Walker TC	.10	.05
❑	100 Checklist 1-100	.04	.02
❑	101 Steve Young	.75	.35
❑	102 Jim Lachey	.04	.02
❑	103 Tom Rathman	.04	.02
❑	104 Earnest Byner	.04	.02
❑	105 Karl Mecklenburg	.04	.02
❑	106 Wes Hopkins	.04	.02
❑	107 Michael Irvin	.25	.11
❑	108 Burt Grossman	.04	.02
❑	109 Jay Novacek UER	.25	.11
	(Wearing 82, but card says he wears 84)		
❑	110 Ben Smith	.04	.02
❑	111 Rod Woodson	.25	.11
❑	112 Ernie Jones	.04	.02
❑	113 Bryan Hinkle	.04	.02
❑	114 Vai Sikahema	.04	.02
❑	115 Bubby Brister	.04	.02
❑	116 Brian Blades	.10	.05
❑	117 Don Majkowski	.04	.02
❑	118 Rod Bernstine	.04	.02
❑	119 Brian Noble	.04	.02
❑	120 Eugene Robinson	.04	.02
❑	121 John Taylor	.10	.05
❑	122 Vance Johnson	.04	.02
❑	123 Art Monk	.10	.05
❑	124 John Elway	1.25	.55
❑	125 Dexter Carter	.04	.02
❑	126 Anthony Miller	.10	.05
❑	127 Keith Jackson	.10	.05
❑	128 Albert Lewis	.04	.02
❑	129 Billy Ray Smith	.04	.02
❑	130 Clyde Simmons	.04	.02
❑	131 Merril Hoge	.04	.02
❑	132 Ricky Proehl	.04	.02
❑	133 Tim McDonald	.04	.02
❑	134 Louis Lipps	.04	.02
❑	135 Ken Harvey	.10	.05
❑	136 Sterling Sharpe	.10	.05
❑	137 Gill Byrd	.04	.02
❑	138 Tim Harris	.04	.02
❑	139 Derrick Fenner	.04	.02
❑	140 Johnny Holland	.04	.02
❑	141 Ricky Sanders	.04	.02
❑	142 Bobby Humphrey	.04	.02
❑	143 Roger Craig	.10	.05
❑	144 Steve Atwater	.04	.02
❑	145 Ickey Woods	.04	.02
❑	146 Randall Cunningham	.25	.11
❑	147 Marion Butts	.10	.05
❑	148 Reggie White	.25	.11
❑	149 Ronnie Harmon	.04	.02
❑	150 Mike Saxon	.04	.02
❑	151 Greg Townsend	.04	.02
❑	152 Troy Aikman	.75	.35
❑	153 Shane Conlan	.04	.02
❑	154 Deion Sanders	.40	.18
❑	155 Bo Jackson	.10	.05
❑	156 Jeff Hostetler	.10	.05
❑	157 Albert Bentley	.04	.02
❑	158 James Williams	.04	.02
❑	159 Bill Brooks	.04	.02
❑	160 Nick Lowery	.04	.02
❑	161 Ottis Anderson	.10	.05
❑	162 Kevin Greene	.25	.11
❑	163 Neil Smith	.25	.11
❑	164 Jim Everett	.10	.05
❑	165 Derrick Thomas	.25	.11
❑	166 John L. Williams	.04	.02
❑	167 Timm Rosenbach	.04	.02
❑	168 Leslie O'Neal	.10	.05
❑	169 Clarence Verdin	.04	.02
❑	170 Dave Krieg	.10	.05
❑	171 Steve Broussard	.04	.02
❑	172 Emmitt Smith	2.00	.90
❑	173 Andre Rison	.10	.05
❑	174 Bruce Smith	.25	.11
❑	175 Mark Clayton	.10	.05
❑	176 Christian Okoye	.04	.02
❑	177 Duane Bickett	.04	.02
❑	178 Stephone Paige	.04	.02
❑	179 Fredd Young	.04	.02
❑	180 Mervyn Fernandez	.04	.02
❑	181 Phil Simms	.10	.05
❑	182 Pete Holohan	.04	.02
❑	183 Pepper Johnson	.04	.02
❑	184 Jackie Slater	.04	.02
❑	185 Stephen Baker	.04	.02
❑	186 Frank Cornish	.04	.02
❑	187 Dave Waymer	.04	.02
❑	188 Terance Mathis	.10	.05
❑	189 Darryl Talley	.04	.02
❑	190 James Hasty	.04	.02
❑	191 Jay Schroeder	.04	.02
❑	192 Kenneth Davis	.04	.02
❑	193 Chris Miller	.10	.05
❑	194 Scott Davis	.04	.02
❑	195 Tim Green	.04	.02
❑	196 Dan Saleaumua	.04	.02
❑	197 Rohn Stark	.04	.02
❑	198 John Alt	.04	.02
❑	199 Steve Tasker	.10	.05
❑	200 Checklist 101-200	.04	.02
❑	201 Freddie Joe Nunn	.04	.02
❑	202 Jim Breech	.04	.02
❑	203 Roy Green	.04	.02
❑	204 Gary Anderson RB	.04	.02
❑	205 Rich Camarillo	.04	.02
❑	206 Mark Bortz	.04	.02
❑	207 Eddie Brown	.04	.02
❑	208 Brad Muster	.04	.02
❑	209 Anthony Munoz	.10	.05
❑	210 Dalton Hilliard	.04	.02
❑	211 Erik McMillan	.04	.02
❑	212 Perry Kemp	.04	.02
❑	213 Jim Thornton	.04	.02
❑	214 Anthony Dilweg	.04	.02
❑	215 Cleveland Gary	.04	.02
❑	216 Leo Goeas	.04	.02
❑	217 Mike Merriweather	.04	.02
❑	218 Courtney Hall	.04	.02
❑	219 Wade Wilson	.10	.05
❑	220 Billy Joe Tolliver	.04	.02
❑	221 Harold Green	.10	.05
❑	222 Al(Bubba) Baker	.10	.05
❑	223 Carl Zander	.04	.02
❑	224 Thane Gash	.04	.02
❑	225 Kevin Mack	.04	.02
❑	226 Morten Andersen	.04	.02
❑	227 Dennis Gentry	.04	.02
❑	228 Vince Buck	.04	.02
❑	229 Mike Singletary	.10	.05
❑	230 Rueben Mayes	.04	.02
❑	231 Mark Carrier WR	.25	.11
❑	232 Tony Mandarich	.04	.02
❑	233 Al Toon	.10	.05
❑	234 Renaldo Turnbull	.04	.02
❑	235 Broderick Thomas	.04	.02
❑	236 Anthony Carter	.10	.05
❑	237 Flipper Anderson	.04	.02
❑	238 Jerry Robinson	.04	.02
❑	239 Vince Newsome	.04	.02
❑	240 Keith Millard	.04	.02
❑	241 Reggie Langhorne	.04	.02
❑	242 James Francis	.04	.02
❑	243 Felix Wright	.04	.02
❑	244 Neal Anderson	.10	.05
❑	245 Boomer Esiason	.10	.05
❑	246 Pat Swilling	.10	.05
❑	247 Richard Dent	.10	.05
❑	248 Craig Heyward	.10	.05
❑	249 Ron Morris	.04	.02
❑	250 Eric Martin	.04	.02
❑	251 Jim C. Jensen	.04	.02
❑	252 Anthony Toney	.04	.02
❑	253 Sammie Smith	.04	.02
❑	254 Calvin Williams	.10	.05

❑ 255	Dan Marino	1.25	.55
❑ 256	Warren Moon	.25	.11
❑ 257	Tommie Agee	.04	.02
❑ 258	Haywood Jeffires	.10	.05
❑ 259	Eugene Lockhart	.04	.02
❑ 260	Drew Hill	.04	.02
❑ 261	Vinny Testaverde	.10	.05
❑ 262	Jim Arnold	.04	.02
❑ 263	Steve Christie	.04	.02
❑ 264	Chris Spielman	.10	.05
❑ 265	Reggie Cobb	.04	.02
❑ 266	John Stephens	.04	.02
❑ 267	Jay Hilgenberg	.04	.02
❑ 268	Brent Williams	.04	.02
❑ 269	Rodney Hampton	.25	.11
❑ 270	Irving Fryar	.10	.05
❑ 271	Terry McDaniel	.04	.02
❑ 272	Reggie Roby	.04	.02
❑ 273	Allen Pinkett	.04	.02
❑ 274	Tim McKyer	.04	.02
❑ 275	Bob Golic	.04	.02
❑ 276	Wilber Marshall	.04	.02
❑ 277	Ray Childress	.04	.02
❑ 278	Charles Mann	.04	.02
❑ 279	Cris Dishman RC	.04	.02
❑ 280	Mark Rypien	.10	.05
❑ 281	Michael Cofer	.04	.02
❑ 282	Keith Byars	.04	.02
❑ 283	Mike Rozier	.04	.02
❑ 284	Seth Joyner	.10	.05
❑ 285	Jessie Tuggle	.04	.02
❑ 286	Mark Bavaro	.04	.02
❑ 287	Eddie Anderson	.04	.02
❑ 288	Sean Landeta	.04	.02
❑ 289	Howie Long (With George Brett)	.10	.05
❑ 290	Reyna Thompson	.04	.02
❑ 291	Ferrell Edmunds	.04	.02
❑ 292	Willie Gault	.10	.05
❑ 293	John Offerdahl	.04	.02
❑ 294	Tim Brown	.25	.11
❑ 295	Bruce Matthews	.10	.05
❑ 296	Kevin Ross	.04	.02
❑ 297	Lorenzo White	.04	.02
❑ 298	Dino Hackett	.04	.02
❑ 299	Curtis Duncan	.04	.02
❑ 300	Checklist 201-300	.04	.02
❑ 301	Andre Ware	.10	.05
❑ 302	David Little	.04	.02
❑ 303	Jerry Ball	.04	.02
❑ 304	Dwight Stone UER (He's a WR, not RB)	.04	.02
❑ 305	Rodney Peete	.10	.05
❑ 306	Mike Baab	.04	.02
❑ 307	Tim Worley	.04	.02
❑ 308	Paul Farren	.04	.02
❑ 309	Carnell Lake	.04	.02
❑ 310	Clay Matthews	.10	.05
❑ 311	Alton Montgomery	.04	.02
❑ 312	Ernest Givins	.10	.05
❑ 313	Mike Horan	.04	.02
❑ 314	Sean Jones	.10	.05
❑ 315	Leonard Smith	.04	.02
❑ 316	Carl Banks	.04	.02
❑ 317	Jerome Brown	.04	.02
❑ 318	Everson Walls	.04	.02
❑ 319	Ron Heller	.04	.02
❑ 320	Mark Collins	.04	.02
❑ 321	Eddie Murray	.04	.02
❑ 322	Jim Harbaugh	.25	.11
❑ 323	Mel Gray	.10	.05
❑ 324	Keith Van Horne	.04	.02
❑ 325	Lomas Brown	.04	.02
❑ 326	Carl Lee	.04	.02
❑ 327	Ken O'Brien	.04	.02
❑ 328	Dermontti Dawson	.04	.02
❑ 329	Brad Baxter	.04	.02
❑ 330	Chris Doleman	.04	.02
❑ 331	Louis Oliver	.04	.02
❑ 332	Frank Stams	.04	.02
❑ 333	Mike Munchak	.04	.02
❑ 334	Fred Strickland	.04	.02
❑ 335	Mark Duper	.10	.05
❑ 336	Jacob Green	.04	.02
❑ 337	Tony Paige	.04	.02
❑ 338	Jeff Bryant	.04	.02
❑ 339	Lemuel Stinson	.04	.02
❑ 340	David Wyman	.04	.02
❑ 341	Lee Williams	.04	.02
❑ 342	Trace Armstrong	.04	.02
❑ 343	Junior Seau	.25	.11
❑ 344	John Roper	.04	.02
❑ 345	Jeff George	.25	.11
❑ 346	Herschel Walker	.10	.05
❑ 347	Sam Clancy	.04	.02
❑ 348	Steve Jordan	.04	.02
❑ 349	Nate Odomes	.04	.02
❑ 350	Martin Bayless	.04	.02
❑ 351	Brent Jones	.25	.11
❑ 352	Ray Agnew	.04	.02
❑ 353	Charles Haley	.10	.05
❑ 354	Andre Tippett	.04	.02
❑ 355	Ronnie Lott	.10	.05
❑ 356	Thurman Thomas	.25	.11
❑ 357	Fred Barnett	.25	.11
❑ 358	James Lofton	.10	.05
❑ 359	William Frizzell RC	.04	.02
❑ 360	Keith McKeller	.04	.02
❑ 361	Rodney Holman	.04	.02
❑ 362	Henry Ellard	.10	.05
❑ 363	David Fulcher	.04	.02
❑ 364	Jerry Gray	.04	.02
❑ 365	James Brooks	.10	.05
❑ 366	Tony Stargell	.04	.02
❑ 367	Keith McCants	.04	.02
❑ 368	Lewis Billups	.04	.02
❑ 369	Ervin Randle	.04	.02
❑ 370	Pat Leahy	.04	.02
❑ 371	Bruce Armstrong	.04	.02
❑ 372	Steve DeBerg	.04	.02
❑ 373	Guy McIntyre	.04	.02
❑ 374	Deron Cherry	.04	.02
❑ 375	Fred Marion	.04	.02
❑ 376	Michael Haddix	.04	.02
❑ 377	Kent Hull	.04	.02
❑ 378	Jerry Holmes	.04	.02
❑ 379	Jim Ritcher	.04	.02
❑ 380	Ed West	.04	.02
❑ 381	Richmond Webb	.04	.02
❑ 382	Mark Jackson	.04	.02
❑ 383	Tom Newberry	.04	.02
❑ 384	Ricky Nattiel	.04	.02
❑ 385	Keith Sims	.04	.02
❑ 386	Ron Hall	.04	.02
❑ 387	Ken Norton	.25	.11
❑ 388	Paul Gruber	.04	.02
❑ 389	Daniel Stubbs	.04	.02
❑ 390	Ian Beckles	.04	.02
❑ 391	Hoby Brenner	.04	.02
❑ 392	Tory Epps	.04	.02
❑ 393	Sam Mills	.04	.02
❑ 394	Chris Hinton	.04	.02
❑ 395	Steve Walsh	.04	.02
❑ 396	Simon Fletcher	.04	.02
❑ 397	Tony Bennett	.10	.05
❑ 398	Aundray Bruce	.04	.02
❑ 399	Mark Murphy	.04	.02
❑ 400	Checklist 301-400	.04	.02
❑ 401	Barry Sanders LL	.60	.25
❑ 402	Jerry Rice LL	.40	.18
❑ 403	Warren Moon LL	.10	.05
❑ 404	Derrick Thomas LL	.10	.05
❑ 405	Nick Lowery LL	.04	.02
❑ 406	Mark Carrier DB LL	.10	.05
❑ 407	Michael Carter	.04	.02
❑ 408	Chris Singleton	.04	.02
❑ 409	Matt Millen	.10	.05
❑ 410	Ronnie Lippett	.04	.02
❑ 411	E.J. Junior	.04	.02
❑ 412	Ray Donaldson	.04	.02
❑ 413	Keith Willis	.04	.02
❑ 414	Jessie Hester	.04	.02
❑ 415	Jeff Cross	.04	.02
❑ 416	Greg Jackson RC	.04	.02
❑ 417	Alvin Walton	.04	.02
❑ 418	Bart Oates	.04	.02
❑ 419	Chip Lohmiller	.04	.02
❑ 420	John Elliott	.04	.02
❑ 421	Randall McDaniel	.04	.02
❑ 422	Richard Johnson RC	.04	.02
❑ 423	Al Noga	.04	.02
❑ 424	Lamar Lathon	.04	.02
❑ 425	Rick Fenney	.04	.02
❑ 426	Jack Del Rio	.04	.02
❑ 427	Don Mosebar	.04	.02
❑ 428	Luis Sharpe	.04	.02
❑ 429	Steve Wisniewski	.04	.02
❑ 430	Jimmie Jones	.04	.02
❑ 431	Freeman McNeil	.04	.02
❑ 432	Ron Rivera	.04	.02
❑ 433	Hart Lee Dykes	.04	.02
❑ 434	Mark Carrier DB	.10	.05
❑ 435	Rob Moore	.25	.11
❑ 436	Gary Clark	.25	.11
❑ 437	Heath Sherman	.04	.02
❑ 438	Darrell Green	.04	.02
❑ 439	Jessie Small	.04	.02
❑ 440	Monte Coleman	.04	.02
❑ 441	Leonard Marshall	.04	.02
❑ 442	Richard Johnson	.04	.02
❑ 443	Dave Meggett	.10	.05
❑ 444	Barry Sanders	1.50	.70
❑ 445	Lawrence Taylor	.25	.11
❑ 446	Marcus Allen	.25	.11
❑ 447	Johnny Johnson	.04	.02
❑ 448	Aaron Wallace	.04	.02
❑ 449	Anthony Thompson	.04	.02
❑ 450	Steve DeBerg Dan Marino Team MVP CL 453-473	.40	.18
❑ 451	Andre Rison MVP	.10	.05
❑ 452	Thurman Thomas MVP	.10	.05
❑ 453	Neal Anderson MVP	.04	.02
❑ 454	Boomer Esiason MVP	.04	.02
❑ 455	Eric Metcalf MVP	.10	.05
❑ 456	Emmitt Smith MVP	1.00	.45
❑ 457	Bobby Humphrey MVP	.04	.02
❑ 458	Barry Sanders MVP	.60	.25
❑ 459	Sterling Sharpe MVP	.10	.05
❑ 460	Warren Moon MVP	.10	.05
❑ 461	Albert Bentley MVP	.04	.02
❑ 462	Steve DeBerg MVP	.04	.02
❑ 463	Greg Townsend MVP	.04	.02
❑ 464	Henry Ellard MVP	.10	.05
❑ 465	Dan Marino MVP	.50	.23
❑ 466	Anthony Carter MVP	.10	.05
❑ 467	John Stephens MVP	.04	.02
❑ 468	Pat Swilling MVP	.04	.02
❑ 469	Ottis Anderson MVP	.10	.05
❑ 470	Dennis Byrd MVP	.04	.02
❑ 471	Randall Cunningham MVP	.10	.05
❑ 472	Johnny Johnson MVP	.04	.02
❑ 473	Rod Woodson MVP	.10	.05
❑ 474	Anthony Miller MVP	.10	.05
❑ 475	Jerry Rice MVP	.40	.18
❑ 476	John L.Williams MVP	.04	.02
❑ 477	Wayne Haddix MVP	.04	.02
❑ 478	Earnest Byner MVP	.04	.02
❑ 479	Doug Widell	.04	.02
❑ 480	Tommy Hodson	.04	.02
❑ 481	Shawn Collins	.04	.02
❑ 482	Rickey Jackson	.04	.02
❑ 483	Tony Casillas	.04	.02
❑ 484	Vaughan Johnson	.04	.02
❑ 485	Floyd Dixon	.04	.02
❑ 486	Eric Green	.04	.02
❑ 487	Harry Hamilton	.04	.02
❑ 488	Gary Anderson K	.04	.02
❑ 489	Bruce Hill	.04	.02
❑ 490	Gerald Williams	.04	.02
❑ 491	Cortez Kennedy	.25	.11
❑ 492	Chet Brooks	.04	.02
❑ 493	Dwayne Harper RC	.04	.02
❑ 494	Don Griffin	.04	.02
❑ 495	Andy Heck	.04	.02
❑ 496	David Treadwell	.04	.02
❑ 497	Irv Pankey	.04	.02
❑ 498	Dennis Smith	.04	.02
❑ 499	Marcus Dupree	.04	.02
❑ 500	Checklist 401-500	.04	.02
❑ 501	Wendell Davis	.04	.02
❑ 502	Matt Bahr	.04	.02
❑ 503	Rob Burnett RC	.04	.02
❑ 504	Maurice Carthon	.04	.02
❑ 505	Donnell Woolford	.04	.02
❑ 506	Howard Ballard	.04	.02
❑ 507	Mark Boyer	.04	.02
❑ 508	Eugene Marve	.04	.02

❑ 509 Joe Kelly .04 .02
❑ 510 Will Wolford .04 .02
❑ 511 Robert Clark .04 .02
❑ 512 Matt Brock RC .04 .02
❑ 513 Chris Warren .25 .11
❑ 514 Ken Willis .04 .02
❑ 515 George Jamison RC .04 .02
❑ 516 Rufus Porter .04 .02
❑ 517 Mark Higgs RC .04 .02
❑ 518 Thomas Everett .04 .02
❑ 519 Robert Brown .04 .02
❑ 520 Gene Atkins .04 .02
❑ 521 Hardy Nickerson .10 .05
❑ 522 Johnny Bailey .04 .02
❑ 523 William Frizzell .04 .02
❑ 524 Steve McMichael .10 .05
❑ 525 Kevin Porter .04 .02
❑ 526 Carwell Gardner .04 .02
❑ 527 Eugene Daniel .04 .02
❑ 528 Vestee Jackson .04 .02
❑ 529 Chris Goode .04 .02
❑ 530 Leon Seals .04 .02
❑ 531 Darion Conner .04 .02
❑ 532 Stan Brock .04 .02
❑ 533 Kirby Jackson RC .04 .02
❑ 534 Marv Cook .04 .02
❑ 535 Bill Fralic .04 .02
❑ 536 Keith Woodside .04 .02
❑ 537 Hugh Green .04 .02
❑ 538 Grant Feasel .04 .02
❑ 539 Bubba McDowell .04 .02
❑ 540 Vai Sikahema .04 .02
❑ 541 Aaron Cox .04 .02
❑ 542 Roger Craig .10 .05
❑ 543 Robb Thomas .04 .02
❑ 544 Ronnie Lott .10 .05
❑ 545 Robert Delpino .04 .02
❑ 546 Greg McMurtry .04 .02
❑ 547 Jim Morrissey RC .04 .02
❑ 548 Johnny Rembert .04 .02
❑ 549 Markus Paul RC .04 .02
❑ 550 Karl Wilson RC .04 .02
❑ 551 Gaston Green .04 .02
❑ 552 Willie Drewrey .04 .02
❑ 553 Michael Young .04 .02
❑ 554 Tom Tupa .04 .02
❑ 555 John Friesz .25 .11
❑ 556 Cody Carlson RC .04 .02
❑ 557 Eric Allen .04 .02
❑ 558 Thomas Benson .04 .02
❑ 559 Scott Mersereau RC .04 .02
❑ 560 Lionel Washington .04 .02
❑ 561 Brian Brennan .04 .02
❑ 562 Jim Jeffcoat .04 .02
❑ 563 Jeff Jaeger .04 .02
❑ 564 D.J. Johnson .04 .02
❑ 565 Danny Villa .04 .02
❑ 566 Don Beebe .04 .02
❑ 567 Michael Haynes .25 .11
❑ 568 Brett Faryniarz RC .04 .02
❑ 569 Mike Prior .04 .02
❑ 570 John Davis RC .04 .02
❑ 571 Vernon Turner RC .04 .02
❑ 572 Michael Brooks .04 .02
❑ 573 Mike Gann .04 .02
❑ 574 Ron Holmes .04 .02
❑ 575 Gary Plummer .04 .02
❑ 576 Bill Romanowski .04 .02
❑ 577 Chris Jacke .04 .02
❑ 578 Gary Reasons .04 .02
❑ 579 Tim Jorden RC .04 .02
❑ 580 Tim McKyer .04 .02
❑ 581 Johnnie Jackson RC .04 .02
❑ 582 Ethan Horton .04 .02
❑ 583 Pete Stoyanovich .04 .02
❑ 584 Jeff Query .04 .02
❑ 585 Frank Reich .10 .05
❑ 586 Riki Ellison .04 .02
❑ 587 Eric Hill .04 .02
❑ 588 Anthony Shelton RC .04 .02
❑ 589 Steve Smith .04 .02
❑ 590 Garth Jax RC .04 .02
❑ 591 Greg Davis RC .04 .02
❑ 592 Bill Maas .04 .02
❑ 593 Henry Rolling RC .04 .02
❑ 594 Keith Jones .04 .02
❑ 595 Tootie Robbins .04 .02
❑ 596 Brian Jordan .10 .05
❑ 597 Derrick Walker RC .04 .02
❑ 598 Jonathan Hayes .04 .02
❑ 599 Nate Lewis RC .04 .02
❑ 600 Checklist 501-600 .04 .02
❑ 601 AFC Checklist RF .04 .02
Mike Croel
Greg Lewis
Keith Traylor
Kenny Walker
❑ 602 James Jones RF RC .04 .02
❑ 603 Tim Barnett RF RC .04 .02
❑ 604 Ed King RF RC .04 .02
❑ 605 Shane Curry RF .04 .02
❑ 606 Mike Croel RF .04 .02
❑ 607 Bryan Cox RF RC .25 .11
❑ 608 Shawn Jefferson RF RC .10 .05
❑ 609 Kenny Walker RF RC .04 .02
❑ 610 Michael Jackson RF RC .25 .11
❑ 611 Jon Vaughn RF RC .04 .02
❑ 612 Greg Lewis RF .04 .02
❑ 613 Joe Valerio RF .04 .02
❑ 614 Pat Harlow RF RC .04 .02
❑ 615 Henry Jones RF RC .10 .05
❑ 616 Jeff Graham RF RC .25 .11
❑ 617 Darryll Lewis RF RC .10 .05
❑ 618 Keith Traylor RF RC UER .04 .02
(Bronchos on back)
❑ 619 Scott Miller RF .04 .02
❑ 620 Nick Bell RF .04 .02
❑ 621 John Flannery RF RC .04 .02
❑ 622 Leonard Russell RF RC .10 .05
❑ 623 Alfred Williams RF RC .04 .02
❑ 624 Browning Nagle RF .04 .02
❑ 625 Harvey Williams RF .10 .05
❑ 626 Dan McGwire RF .04 .02
❑ 627 NFC Checklist RF .50 .23
Brett Favre
Moe Gardner
Erric Pegram
Bruce Pickens
Mike Pritchard
❑ 628 William Thomas RF RC .04 .02
❑ 629 Lawrence Dawsey RF RC .10 .05
❑ 630 Aeneas Williams RF RC .10 .05
❑ 631 Stan Thomas RF .04 .02
❑ 632 Randal Hill RF .04 .02
❑ 633 Moe Gardner RF RC .04 .02
❑ 634 Alvin Harper RF .10 .05
❑ 635 Esera Tuaolo RF RC .04 .02
❑ 636 Russell Maryland RF .10 .05
❑ 637 Anthony Morgan RF RC .04 .02
❑ 638 Erric Pegram RF RC .25 .11
❑ 639 Herman Moore RF 1.00 .45
❑ 640 Ricky Ervins RF RC .10 .05
❑ 641 Kelvin Pritchett RF RC .10 .05
❑ 642 Roman Phifer RF RC .04 .02
❑ 643 Antone Davis RF RC .04 .02
❑ 644 Mike Pritchard RF .10 .05
❑ 645 Vinnie Clark RF RC .04 .02
❑ 646 Jake Reed RF RC .75 .35
❑ 647 Brett Favre RF 2.50 1.10
❑ 648 Todd Lyght RF .04 .02
❑ 649 Bruce Pickens RF .04 .02
❑ 650 Darren Lewis RF RC .04 .02
❑ 651 Wesley Carroll RF .04 .02
❑ 652 James Joseph RF RC .10 .05
❑ 653 Robert Delpino AR .04 .02
Tim McDonald
❑ 654 Vencie Glenn AR .04 .02
Deion Sanders
❑ 655 Jerry Rice AR .30 .14
Terry McDaniel
❑ 656 Barry Sanders AR .50 .23
Derrick Thomas
❑ 657 Ken Tippins AR .04 .02
Lorenzo White
❑ 658 Christian Okoye AR .04 .02
Jacob Green
❑ 659 Rich Gannon .04 .02
❑ 660 Johnny Meads .04 .02
❑ 661 J.J. Birden RC .10 .05
❑ 662 Bruce Kozerski .04 .02
❑ 663 Felix Wright .04 .02
❑ 664 Al Smith .04 .02
❑ 665 Stan Humphries .25 .11
❑ 666 Alfred Anderson .04 .02
❑ 667 Nate Newton .10 .05
❑ 668 Vince Workman RC .10 .05
❑ 669 Ricky Reynolds .04 .02
❑ 670 Bryce Paup RC .25 .11
❑ 671 Gill Fenerty .04 .02
❑ 672 Darrell Thompson .04 .02
❑ 673 Anthony Smith .04 .02
❑ 674 Darryl Henley RC .04 .02
❑ 675 Brett Maxie .04 .02
❑ 676 Craig Taylor RC .04 .02
❑ 677 Steve Wallace .10 .05
❑ 678 Jeff Feagles RC .04 .02
❑ 679 James Washington RC .04 .02
❑ 680 Tim Harris .04 .02
❑ 681 Dennis Gibson .04 .02
❑ 682 Toi Cook RC .04 .02
❑ 683 Lorenzo Lynch .04 .02
❑ 684 Brad Edwards RC .04 .02
❑ 685 Ray Crockett RC .04 .02
❑ 686 Harris Barton .04 .02
❑ 687 Byron Evans .04 .02
❑ 688 Eric Thomas .04 .02
❑ 689 Jeff Criswell .04 .02
❑ 690 Eric Ball .04 .02
❑ 691 Brian Mitchell .10 .05
❑ 692 Quinn Early .10 .05
❑ 693 Aaron Jones .04 .02
❑ 694 Jim Dombrowski .04 .02
❑ 695 Jeff Bostic .04 .02
❑ 696 Tony Casillas .04 .02
❑ 697 Ken Lanier .04 .02
❑ 698 Henry Thomas .04 .02
❑ 699 Steve Beuerlein .04 .02
❑ 700 Checklist 601-700 .04 .02
❑ P1 Joe Montana Promo 3.00 1.35
Numbered 1
❑ P2 Barry Sanders Promo 2.00 .90
Numbered 500
❑ SP1 Darrell Green .50 .23
NFL's Fastest Man
❑ SP2 Don Shula CO 2.00 .90
300th Victory

1991 Upper Deck Game Breaker Holograms

	MINT	NRMT
COMPLETE SET (9)	8.00	3.60
RANDOM INSERTS IN PACKS		

❑ GB1 Barry Sanders 3.00 1.35
❑ GB2 Thurman Thomas .50 .23
❑ GB3 Bobby Humphrey .10 .05
❑ GB4 Earnest Byner .10 .05
❑ GB5 Emmitt Smith 4.00 1.80
❑ GB6 Neal Anderson .20 .09
❑ GB7 Marion Butts .20 .09
❑ GB8 James Brooks .20 .09
❑ GB9 Marcus Allen .50 .23

1992 Upper Deck

	MINT	NRMT
COMPLETE SET (620)	15.00	6.75
COMP.SERIES 1 (400)	10.00	4.50

COMP.SERIES 2 (220)	5.00	2.20
COMMON CARD (1-620)	.05	.02
SEMISTARS	.10	.05
UNLISTED STARS	.25	.11
COMP.MARINO HERO (10)	30.00	13.50
MARINO HEADER (NNO)	5.00	2.20
MARINO HEADER AUTO/2800	100.00	45.00
RANDOM INSERTS IN SER.2 PACKS		
COMP.PAYTON HERO (10)	25.00	11.00
PAYTON HEADER (NNO)	5.00	2.20
PAYTON HEADER AUTO/2800	100.00	45.00
RANDOM INSERTS IN SER.1 PACKS		
SP3/SP4 STATED ODDS 1:54 PACKS		

- ❑ 1 Star Rookie Checklist .10 .05
  Edgar Bennett
  Terrell Buckley
  Dexter McNabb
- ❑ 2 Edgar Bennett RC .25 .11
- ❑ 3 Eddie Blake RC .05 .02
- ❑ 4 Brian Bollinger RC .05 .02
- ❑ 5 Joe Bowden RC .05 .02
- ❑ 6 Terrell Buckley RC .05 .02
- ❑ 7 Willie Clay RC .05 .02
- ❑ 8 Ed Cunningham RC .05 .02
- ❑ 9 Matt Darby RC .05 .02
- ❑ 10 Will Furrer RC .05 .02
- ❑ 11 Chris Hakel RC .05 .02
- ❑ 12 Carlos Huerta .05 .02
- ❑ 13 Amp Lee RC .05 .02
- ❑ 14 Ricardo McDonald RC .05 .02
- ❑ 15 Dexter McNabb RC .05 .02
- ❑ 16 Chris Mims RC .10 .05
- ❑ 17 Derrick Moore RC .10 .05
- ❑ 18 Mark D'Onofrio RC .05 .02
- ❑ 19 Patrick Rowe RC .05 .02
- ❑ 20 Leon Searcy RC .10 .05
- ❑ 21 Torrance Small RC .25 .11
- ❑ 22 Jimmy Smith RC 2.50 1.10
- ❑ 23 Tony Smith RC .05 .02
- ❑ 24 Siran Stacy RC .05 .02
- ❑ 25 Kevin Turner RC .05 .02
- ❑ 26 Tommy Vardell RC .10 .05
- ❑ 27 Bob Whitfield RC .05 .02
- ❑ 28 Darryl Williams RC .05 .02
- ❑ 29 Jeff Sydner RC .05 .02
- ❑ 30 All-Rookie Checklist .05 .02
  Mike Croel
  Leonard Russell
- ❑ 31 Todd Marinovich AR .05 .02
- ❑ 32 Leonard Russell AR .05 .02
- ❑ 33 Nick Bell AR .05 .02
- ❑ 34 Alvin Harper AR .05 .02
- ❑ 35 Mike Pritchard AR .05 .02
- ❑ 36 Lawrence Dawsey AR .05 .02
- ❑ 37 Tim Barnett AR .05 .02
- ❑ 38 John Flannery AR .05 .02
- ❑ 39 Stan Thomas AR .05 .02
- ❑ 40 Ed King AR .05 .02
- ❑ 41 Charles McRae AR .05 .02
- ❑ 42 Eric Moten AR .05 .02
- ❑ 43 Moe Gardner AR .05 .02
- ❑ 44 Kenny Walker AR .05 .02
- ❑ 45 Esera Tuaolo AR .05 .02
- ❑ 46 Alfred Williams AR .05 .02
- ❑ 47 Bryan Cox AR .05 .02
- ❑ 48 Mo Lewis AR .05 .02
- ❑ 49 Mike Croel AR .05 .02
- ❑ 50 Stanley Richard AR .05 .02
- ❑ 51 Tony Covington AR .05 .02
- ❑ 52 Larry Brown DB AR .05 .02
- ❑ 53 Aeneas Williams AR .05 .02
- ❑ 54 John Kasay AR .05 .02
- ❑ 55 Jon Vaughn AR .05 .02
- ❑ 56 David Fulcher .05 .02
- ❑ 57 Barry Foster .10 .05
- ❑ 58 Terry Wooden .05 .02
- ❑ 59 Gary Anderson K .05 .02
- ❑ 60 Alfred Williams .05 .02
- ❑ 61 Robert Blackmon .05 .02
- ❑ 62 Brian Noble .05 .02
- ❑ 63 Terry Allen .25 .11
- ❑ 64 Darrell Green .05 .02
- ❑ 65 Darren Comeaux .05 .02
- ❑ 66 Rob Burnett .05 .02
- ❑ 67 Jarrod Bunch .05 .02
- ❑ 68 Michael Jackson .10 .05
- ❑ 69 Greg Lloyd .25 .11
- ❑ 70 Richard Brown RC .05 .02
- ❑ 71 Harold Green .05 .02
- ❑ 72 William Fuller .10 .05
- ❑ 73 Mark Carrier DB TC .05 .02
- ❑ 74 David Fulcher TC .05 .02
- ❑ 75 Cornelius Bennett TC .05 .02
- ❑ 76 Steve Atwater TC .05 .02
- ❑ 77 Kevin Mack TC .05 .02
- ❑ 78 Mark Carrier WR TC .05 .02
- ❑ 79 Tim McDonald TC .05 .02
- ❑ 80 Marion Butts TC .05 .02
- ❑ 81 Christian Okoye TC .05 .02
- ❑ 82 Jeff Herrod TC .05 .02
- ❑ 83 Emmitt Smith TC .60 .25
- ❑ 84 Mark Duper TC .05 .02
- ❑ 85 Keith Jackson TC .05 .02
- ❑ 86 Andre Rison TC .10 .05
- ❑ 87 John Taylor TC .05 .02
- ❑ 88 Rodney Hampton TC .10 .05
- ❑ 89 Rob Moore TC .05 .02
- ❑ 90 Chris Spielman TC .05 .02
- ❑ 91 Haywood Jeffires TC .05 .02
- ❑ 92 Sterling Sharpe TC .10 .05
- ❑ 93 Irving Fryar TC .10 .05
- ❑ 94 Marcus Allen TC .10 .05
- ❑ 95 Henry Ellard TC .05 .02
- ❑ 96 Mark Rypien TC .05 .02
- ❑ 97 Pat Swilling TC .05 .02
- ❑ 98 Brian Blades TC .05 .02
- ❑ 99 Eric Green TC .05 .02
- ❑ 100 Anthony Carter TC .05 .02
- ❑ 101 Burt Grossman .05 .02
- ❑ 102 Gary Anderson RB .05 .02
- ❑ 103 Neil Smith .25 .11
- ❑ 104 Jeff Feagles .05 .02
- ❑ 105 Shane Conlan .05 .02
- ❑ 106 Jay Novacek .10 .05
- ❑ 107 Bill Brooks .05 .02
- ❑ 108 Mark Ingram .05 .02
- ❑ 109 Anthony Munoz .10 .05
- ❑ 110 Wendell Davis .05 .02
- ❑ 111 Jim Everett .10 .05
- ❑ 112 Bruce Matthews .05 .02
- ❑ 113 Mark Higgs .05 .02
- ❑ 114 Chris Warren .25 .11
- ❑ 115 Brad Baxter .05 .02
- ❑ 116 Greg Townsend .05 .02
- ❑ 117 Al Smith .05 .02
- ❑ 118 Jeff Cross .05 .02
- ❑ 119 Terry McDaniel .05 .02
- ❑ 120 Ernest Givins .10 .05
- ❑ 121 Fred Barnett .25 .11
- ❑ 122 Flipper Anderson .05 .02
- ❑ 123 Floyd Turner .05 .02
- ❑ 124 Stephen Baker .05 .02
- ❑ 125 Tim Johnson .05 .02
- ❑ 126 Brent Jones .10 .05
- ❑ 127 Leonard Marshall .05 .02
- ❑ 128 Jim Price .05 .02
- ❑ 129 Jessie Hester .05 .02
- ❑ 130 Mark Carrier WR .10 .05
- ❑ 131 Bubba McDowell .05 .02
- ❑ 132 Andre Tippett .05 .02
- ❑ 133 James Hasty .05 .02
- ❑ 134 Mel Gray .10 .05
- ❑ 135 Christian Okoye .05 .02
- ❑ 136 Earnest Byner .05 .02
- ❑ 137 Ferrell Edmunds .05 .02
- ❑ 138 Henry Ellard .10 .05
- ❑ 139 Rob Moore .10 .05
- ❑ 140 Brian Jordan .10 .05
- ❑ 141 Clarence Verdin .05 .02
- ❑ 142 Cornelius Bennett .10 .05
- ❑ 143 John Taylor .10 .05
- ❑ 144 Derrick Thomas .25 .11
- ❑ 145 Thurman Thomas .25 .11
- ❑ 146 Warren Moon .25 .11
- ❑ 147 Vinny Testaverde .10 .05
- ❑ 148 Steve Bono RC .25 .11
- ❑ 149 Robb Thomas .05 .02
- ❑ 150 John Friesz .10 .05
- ❑ 151 Richard Dent .10 .05
- ❑ 152 Eddie Anderson .05 .02
- ❑ 153 Kevin Greene .25 .11
- ❑ 154 Marion Butts .05 .02
- ❑ 155 Barry Sanders 1.50 .70
- ❑ 156 Andre Rison .10 .05
- ❑ 157 Ronnie Lott .10 .05
- ❑ 158 Eric Allen .05 .02
- ❑ 159 Mark Clayton .10 .05
- ❑ 160 Terance Mathis .10 .05
- ❑ 161 Darryl Talley .05 .02
- ❑ 162 Eric Metcalf .10 .05
- ❑ 163 Reggie Cobb .05 .02
- ❑ 164 Ernie Jones .05 .02
- ❑ 165 David Griggs .05 .02
- ❑ 166 Tom Rathman .05 .02
- ❑ 167 Bubby Brister .05 .02
- ❑ 168 Broderick Thomas .05 .02
- ❑ 169 Chris Doleman .05 .02
- ❑ 170 Charles Haley .10 .05
- ❑ 171 Michael Haynes .10 .05
- ❑ 172 Rodney Hampton .25 .11
- ❑ 173 Nick Bell .05 .02
- ❑ 174 Gene Atkins .05 .02
- ❑ 175 Mike Merriweather .05 .02
- ❑ 176 Reggie Roby .05 .02
- ❑ 177 Bennie Blades .05 .02
- ❑ 178 John L. Williams .05 .02
- ❑ 179 Rodney Peete .10 .05
- ❑ 180 Greg Montgomery .05 .02
- ❑ 181 Vince Newsome .05 .02
- ❑ 182 Andre Collins .05 .02
- ❑ 183 Erik Kramer .10 .05
- ❑ 184 Bryan Hinkle .05 .02
- ❑ 185 Reggie White .25 .11
- ❑ 186 Bruce Armstrong .05 .02
- ❑ 187 Anthony Carter .10 .05
- ❑ 188 Pat Swilling .10 .05
- ❑ 189 Robert Delpino .05 .02
- ❑ 190 Brent Williams .05 .02
- ❑ 191 Johnny Johnson .05 .02
- ❑ 192 Aaron Craver .05 .02
- ❑ 193 Vincent Brown .05 .02
- ❑ 194 Herschel Walker .10 .05
- ❑ 195 Tim McDonald .05 .02
- ❑ 196 Gaston Green .05 .02
- ❑ 197 Brian Blades .10 .05
- ❑ 198 Rod Bernstine .05 .02
- ❑ 199 Brett Perriman .25 .11
- ❑ 200 John Elway 1.25 .55
- ❑ 201 Michael Carter .05 .02
- ❑ 202 Mark Carrier DB .05 .02
- ❑ 203 Cris Carter .50 .23
- ❑ 204 Kyle Clifton .05 .02
- ❑ 205 Alvin Wright .05 .02
- ❑ 206 Andre Ware .05 .02
- ❑ 207 Dave Waymer .05 .02
- ❑ 208 Darren Lewis .05 .02
- ❑ 209 Joey Browner .05 .02
- ❑ 210 Rich Miano .05 .02
- ❑ 211 Marcus Allen .25 .11
- ❑ 212 Steve Broussard .05 .02
- ❑ 213 Joel Hilgenberg .05 .02
- ❑ 214 Bo Orlando RC .05 .02
- ❑ 215 Clay Matthews .10 .05
- ❑ 216 Chris Hinton .05 .02
- ❑ 217 Al Edwards .05 .02
- ❑ 218 Tim Brown .25 .11
- ❑ 219 Sam Mills .05 .02
- ❑ 220 Don Majkowski .05 .02
- ❑ 221 James Francis .05 .02

222 Steve Hendrickson RC .05 .02
223 James Thornton .05 .02
224 Byron Evans .05 .02
225 Pepper Johnson .05 .02
226 Darryl Henley .05 .02
227 Simon Fletcher .05 .02
228 Hugh Millen .05 .02
229 Tim McGee .05 .02
230 Richmond Webb .05 .02
231 Tony Bennett .05 .02
232 Nate Odomes .05 .02
233 Scott Case .05 .02
234 Dalton Hilliard .05 .02
235 Paul Gruber .05 .02
236 Jeff Lageman .05 .02
237 Tony Mandarich .05 .02
238 Cris Dishman .05 .02
239 Steve Walsh .05 .02
240 Moe Gardner .05 .02
241 Bill Romanowski .05 .02
242 Chris Zorich .10 .05
243 Stephone Paige .05 .02
244 Mike Croel .05 .02
245 Leonard Russell .10 .05
246 Mark Rypien .05 .02
247 Aeneas Williams .10 .05
248 Steve Atwater .05 .02
249 Michael Stewart .05 .02
250 Pierce Holt .05 .02
251 Kevin Mack .05 .02
252 Sterling Sharpe .25 .11
253 Lawrence Dawsey .10 .05
254 Emmitt Smith 1.50 .70
255 Todd Marinovich .05 .02
256 Neal Anderson .05 .02
257 Mo Lewis .05 .02
258 Vance Johnson .05 .02
259 Rickey Jackson .05 .02
260 Esera Tuaolo .05 .02
261 Wilber Marshall .05 .02
262 Keith Henderson .05 .02
263 William Thomas .05 .02
264 Rickey Dixon .05 .02
265 Dave Meggett .10 .05
266 Gerald Riggs .05 .02
267 Tim Harris .05 .02
268 Ken Harvey .05 .02
269 Clyde Simmons .05 .02
270 Irving Fryar .10 .05
271 Darion Conner .05 .02
272 Vince Workman .10 .05
273 Jim Harbaugh .25 .11
274 Lorenzo White .05 .02
275 Bobby Hebert .05 .02
276 Duane Bickett .05 .02
277 Jeff Bryant .05 .02
278 Scott Stephen .05 .02
279 Bob Golic .05 .02
280 Steve McMichael .10 .05
281 Jeff Graham .25 .11
282 Keith Jackson .10 .05
283 Howard Ballard .05 .02
284 Michael Brooks .05 .02
285 Freeman McNeil .05 .02
286 Rodney Holman .05 .02
287 Eric Bieniemy .05 .02
288 Seth Joyner .10 .05
289 Carwell Gardner .05 .02
290 Brian Mitchell .10 .05
291 Chris Miller .10 .05
292 Ray Berry .05 .02
293 Matt Brock .05 .02
294 Eric Thomas .05 .02
295 John Kasay .05 .02
296 Jay Hilgenberg .05 .02
297 Darrell Thompson .05 .02
298 Rich Gannon .05 .02
299 Steve Young .60 .25
300 Mike Kenn .05 .02
301 Emmitt Smith SL .60 .25
302 Haywood Jeffires SL .05 .02
303 Michael Irvin SL .25 .11
304 Warren Moon SL .10 .05
305 Chip Lohmiller SL .05 .02
306 Barry Sanders SL .60 .25
307 Ronnie Lott SL .10 .05
308 Pat Swilling SL .05 .02
309 Thurman Thomas SL .10 .05
310 Reggie Roby SL .05 .02
311 Season Leader CL .10 .05
Warren Moon
Michael Irvin
Thurman Thomas
312 Jacob Green .05 .02
313 Stephen Braggs .05 .02
314 Haywood Jeffires .10 .05
315 Freddie Joe Nunn .05 .02
316 Gary Clark .25 .11
317 Tim Barnett .05 .02
318 Mark Duper .05 .02
319 Eric Green .05 .02
320 Robert Wilson .05 .02
321 Michael Ball .05 .02
322 Eric Martin .05 .02
323 Alexander Wright .05 .02
324 Jessie Tuggle .05 .02
325 Ronnie Harmon .05 .02
326 Jeff Hostetler .10 .05
327 Eugene Daniel .05 .02
328 Ken Norton Jr. .25 .11
329 Reyna Thompson .05 .02
330 Jerry Ball .05 .02
331 Leroy Hoard .10 .05
332 Chris Martin .05 .02
333 Keith McKeller .05 .02
334 Brian Washington .05 .02
335 Eugene Robinson .05 .02
336 Maurice Hurst .05 .02
337 Dan Saleaumua .05 .02
338 Neil O'Donnell .25 .11
339 Dexter Davis .05 .02
340 Keith McCants .05 .02
341 Steve Beuerlein .05 .02
342 Roman Phifer .05 .02
343 Bryan Cox .10 .05
344 Art Monk .10 .05
345 Michael Irvin .25 .11
346 Vaughan Johnson .05 .02
347 Jeff Herrod .05 .02
348 Stanley Richard .05 .02
349 Michael Young .05 .02
350 Team MVP Checklist .10 .05
Rodney Hampton
Reggie Cobb
351 Jim Harbaugh MVP .10 .05
352 David Fulcher MVP .05 .02
353 Thurman Thomas MVP .10 .05
354 Gaston Green MVP .05 .02
355 Leroy Hoard MVP .05 .02
356 Reggie Cobb MVP .05 .02
357 Tim McDonald MVP .05 .02
358 R.Harmon MVP UER .05 .02
Bernstine misspelled
as Bernstein
359 Derrick Thomas MVP .10 .05
360 Jeff Herrod MVP .05 .02
361 Michael Irvin MVP .25 .11
362 Mark Higgs MVP .05 .02
363 Reggie White MVP .10 .05
364 Chris Miller MVP .05 .02
365 Steve Young MVP .30 .14
366 Rodney Hampton MVP .10 .05
367 Jeff Lageman MVP .05 .02
368 Barry Sanders MVP .60 .25
369 Haywood Jeffires MVP .05 .02
370 Tony Bennett MVP .05 .02
371 Leonard Russell MVP .05 .02
372 Jeff Jaeger MVP .05 .02
373 Robert Delpino MVP .05 .02
374 Mark Rypien MVP .05 .02
375 Pat Swilling MVP .05 .02
376 Cortez Kennedy MVP .10 .05
377 Eric Green MVP .05 .02
378 Cris Carter MVP .10 .05
379 John Roper .05 .02
380 Barry Word .05 .02
381 Shawn Jefferson .05 .02
382 Tony Casillas .05 .02
383 John Baylor RC .05 .02
384 Al Noga .05 .02
385 Charles Mann .05 .02
386 Gill Byrd .05 .02
387 Chris Singleton .05 .02
388 James Joseph .05 .02
389 Larry Brown DB .05 .02
390 Chris Spielman .10 .05
391 Anthony Thompson .05 .02
392 Karl Mecklenburg .05 .02
393 Joe Kelly .05 .02
394 Kanavis McGhee .05 .02
395 Bill Maas .05 .02
396 Marv Cook .05 .02
397 Louis Lipps .05 .02
398 Marty Carter RC .05 .02
399 Louis Oliver .05 .02
400 Eric Swann .10 .05
401 Troy Auzenne RC .05 .02
402 Kurt Barber .05 .02
403 Marc Boutte RC .05 .02
404 Dale Carter .10 .05
405 Marco Coleman .10 .05
406 Quentin Coryatt .25 .11
407 Shane Dronett RC .05 .02
408 Vaughn Dunbar .05 .02
409 Steve Emtman .05 .02
410 Dana Hall RC .10 .05
411 Jason Hansen RC .10 .05
412 Courtney Hawkins RC .10 .05
413 Terrell Buckley .05 .02
414 Robert Jones RC .05 .02
415 David Klingler .05 .02
416 Tommy Maddox .05 .02
417 Johnny Mitchell RC .05 .02
418 Carl Pickens .25 .11
419 Tracy Scroggins .05 .02
420 Tony Sacca RC .05 .02
421 Kevin Smith .25 .11
422 Alonzo Spellman .10 .05
423 Troy Vincent RC .10 .05
424 Sean Gilbert RC .25 .11
425 Larry Webster RC .05 .02
426 Rookie Force Checklist .25 .11
Carl Pickens
David Klingler
427 Bill Fralic .05 .02
428 Kevin Murphy .05 .02
429 Lemuel Stinson .05 .02
430 Harris Barton .05 .02
431 Dino Hackett .05 .02
432 John Stephens .05 .02
433 Keith Jennings RC .05 .02
434 Derrick Fenner .05 .02
435 Kenneth Gant RC .05 .02
436 Willie Gault .10 .05
437 Steve Jordan .05 .02
438 Charles Haley .10 .05
439 Keith Kartz .05 .02
440 Nate Lewis .05 .02
441 Doug Widell .05 .02
442 William White .05 .02
443 Eric Hill .05 .02
444 Melvin Jenkins .05 .02
445 David Wyman .05 .02
446 Ed West .05 .02
447 Brad Muster .05 .02
448 Ray Childress .05 .02
449 Kevin Ross .05 .02
450 Johnnie Jackson .05 .02
451 Tracy Simien RC .05 .02
452 Don Mosebar .05 .02
453 Jay Hilgenberg .05 .02
454 Wes Hopkins .05 .02
455 Jay Schroeder .05 .02
456 Jeff Bostic .05 .02
457 Bryce Paup .25 .11
458 Dave Waymer .05 .02
459 Toi Cook .05 .02
460 Anthony Smith .05 .02
461 Don Griffin .05 .02
462 Bill Hawkins .05 .02
463 Courtney Hall .05 .02
464 Jeff Uhlenhake .05 .02
465 Mike Sherrard .05 .02
466 James Jones .05 .02
467 Jerrol Williams .05 .02
468 Eric Ball .05 .02
469 Randall McDaniel .05 .02
470 Alvin Harper .10 .05

- ❑ 471 Tom Waddle .05 .02
- ❑ 472 Tony Woods .05 .02
- ❑ 473 Kelvin Martin .05 .02
- ❑ 474 Jon Vaughn .05 .02
- ❑ 475 Gill Fenerty .05 .02
- ❑ 476 Aundray Bruce .05 .02
- ❑ 477 Morten Andersen .05 .02
- ❑ 478 Lamar Lathon .05 .02
- ❑ 479 Steve DeOssie .05 .02
- ❑ 480 Marvin Washington .05 .02
- ❑ 481 Herschel Walker .10 .05
- ❑ 482 Howie Long .10 .05
- ❑ 483 Calvin Williams .10 .05
- ❑ 484 Brett Favre 2.50 1.10
- ❑ 485 Johnny Bailey .05 .02
- ❑ 486 Jeff Gossett .05 .02
- ❑ 487 Carnell Lake .05 .02
- ❑ 488 Michael Zordich RC .05 .02
- ❑ 489 Henry Rolling .05 .02
- ❑ 490 Steve Smith .05 .02
- ❑ 491 Vestee Jackson .05 .02
- ❑ 492 Ray Crockett .05 .02
- ❑ 493 Dexter Carter .05 .02
- ❑ 494 Nick Lowery .05 .02
- ❑ 495 Cortez Kennedy .10 .05
- ❑ 496 Cleveland Gary .05 .02
- ❑ 497 Kelly Stouffer .05 .02
- ❑ 498 Carl Carter .05 .02
- ❑ 499 Shannon Sharpe .25 .11
- ❑ 500 Roger Craig .10 .05
- ❑ 501 Willie Drewrey .05 .02
- ❑ 502 Mark Schlereth RC .05 .02
- ❑ 503 Tony Martin .25 .11
- ❑ 504 Tom Newberry .05 .02
- ❑ 505 Ron Hall .05 .02
- ❑ 506 Scott Miller .05 .02
- ❑ 507 Donnell Woolford .05 .02
- ❑ 508 Dave Krieg .10 .05
- ❑ 509 Eric Pegram .10 .05
- ❑ 510 Checklist 401-510 .05 .02
- ❑ 511 Barry Sanders SBK .60 .25
- ❑ 512 Thurman Thomas SBK .10 .05
- ❑ 513 Warren Moon SBK .10 .05
- ❑ 514 John Elway SBK .50 .23
- ❑ 515 Ronnie Lott SBK .10 .05
- ❑ 516 Emmitt Smith SBK .60 .25
- ❑ 517 Andre Rison SBK .10 .05
- ❑ 518 Steve Atwater SBK .05 .02
- ❑ 519 Steve Young SBK .30 .14
- ❑ 520 Mark Rypien SBK .05 .02
- ❑ 521 Rich Camarillo .05 .02
- ❑ 522 Mark Bavaro .05 .02
- ❑ 523 Brad Edwards .05 .02
- ❑ 524 Chad Hennings RC .10 .05
- ❑ 525 Tony Paige .05 .02
- ❑ 526 Shawn Moore .05 .02
- ❑ 527 Sidney Johnson RC .05 .02
- ❑ 528 Sanjay Beach RC .05 .02
- ❑ 529 Kelvin Pritchett .05 .02
- ❑ 530 Jerry Holmes .05 .02
- ❑ 531 Al Del Greco .05 .02
- ❑ 532 Bob Gagliano .05 .02
- ❑ 533 Drew Hill .05 .02
- ❑ 534 Donald Frank RC .05 .02
- ❑ 535 Pio Sagapolutele RC .05 .02
- ❑ 536 Jackie Slater .05 .02
- ❑ 537 Vernon Turner .05 .02
- ❑ 538 Bobby Humphrey .05 .02
- ❑ 539 Audray McMillian .05 .02
- ❑ 540 Gary Brown RC .25 .11
- ❑ 541 Wesley Carroll .05 .02
- ❑ 542 Nate Newton .10 .05
- ❑ 543 Vai Sikahema .05 .02
- ❑ 544 Chris Chandler .25 .11
- ❑ 545 Nolan Harrison RC .05 .02
- ❑ 546 Mark Green .05 .02
- ❑ 547 Ricky Watters .25 .11
- ❑ 548 J.J. Birden .05 .02
- ❑ 549 Cody Carlson .05 .02
- ❑ 550 Tim Green .05 .02
- ❑ 551 Mark Jackson .05 .02
- ❑ 552 Vince Buck .05 .02
- ❑ 553 George Jamison .05 .02
- ❑ 554 Anthony Pleasant .05 .02
- ❑ 555 Reggie Johnson .05 .02
- ❑ 556 John Jackson .05 .02
- ❑ 557 Ian Beckles .05 .02
- ❑ 558 Buford McGee .05 .02
- ❑ 559 Fuad Reveiz UER .05 .02
  (Born in Colombia, not Columbia)
- ❑ 560 Joe Montana 1.25 .55
- ❑ 561 Phil Simms .10 .05
- ❑ 562 Greg McMurtry .05 .02
- ❑ 563 Gerald Williams .05 .02
- ❑ 564 Dave Cadigan .05 .02
- ❑ 565 Rufus Porter .05 .02
- ❑ 566 Jim Kelly .25 .11
- ❑ 567 Deion Sanders .50 .23
- ❑ 568 Mike Singletary .10 .05
- ❑ 569 Boomer Esiason .10 .05
- ❑ 570 Andre Reed .10 .05
- ❑ 571 James Washington .05 .02
- ❑ 572 Jack Del Rio .05 .02
- ❑ 573 Gerald Perry .05 .02
- ❑ 574 Vinnie Clark .05 .02
- ❑ 575 Mike Piel .05 .02
- ❑ 576 Michael Dean Perry .10 .05
- ❑ 577 Ricky Proehl .05 .02
- ❑ 578 Leslie O'Neal .10 .05
- ❑ 579 Russell Maryland .10 .05
- ❑ 580 Eric Dickerson .10 .05
- ❑ 581 Fred Strickland .05 .02
- ❑ 582 Nick Lowery .05 .02
- ❑ 583 Joe Milinichik RC .05 .02
- ❑ 584 Mark Vlasic .05 .02
- ❑ 585 James Lofton .10 .05
- ❑ 586 Bruce Smith .25 .11
- ❑ 587 Harvey Williams .25 .11
- ❑ 588 Bernie Kosar .10 .05
- ❑ 589 Carl Banks .05 .02
- ❑ 590 Jeff George .25 .11
- ❑ 591 Fred Jones RC .05 .02
- ❑ 592 Todd Scott .05 .02
- ❑ 593 Keith Jones .05 .02
- ❑ 594A Tootie Robbins ERR .05 .02
  (Card has him as a Denver Bronco)
- ❑ 594B Tootie Robbins COR .05 .02
- ❑ 595 Todd Philcox RC .05 .02
- ❑ 596 Browning Nagle .05 .02
- ❑ 597 Troy Aikman .75 .35
- ❑ 598 Dan Marino 1.25 .55
- ❑ 599 Lawrence Taylor .25 .11
- ❑ 600 Webster Slaughter .05 .02
- ❑ 601 Aaron Cox .05 .02
- ❑ 602 Matt Stover .05 .02
- ❑ 603 Keith Sims .05 .02
- ❑ 604 Dennis Smith .05 .02
- ❑ 605 Kevin Porter .05 .02
- ❑ 606 Anthony Miller .10 .05
- ❑ 607 Ken O'Brien .05 .02
- ❑ 608 Randall Cunningham .25 .11
- ❑ 609 Timm Rosenbach .05 .02
- ❑ 610 Junior Seau .25 .11
- ❑ 611 Johnny Rembert .05 .02
- ❑ 612 Rick Tuten .05 .02
- ❑ 613 Willie Green .05 .02
- ❑ 614 Sean Salisbury RC UER .05 .02
  (He is listed with Lions in 1990 and Chargers in 1991; he was with Vikings both years)
- ❑ 615 Martin Bayless .05 .02
- ❑ 616 Jerry Rice .75 .35
- ❑ 617 Randal Hill .05 .02
- ❑ 618 Dan McGwire .05 .02
- ❑ 619 Merril Hoge .05 .02
- ❑ 620 Checklist 571-620 .05 .02
- ❑ SP3 James Lofton Yardage .75 .35
- ❑ SP4 Art Monk Catches .50 .23

1992 Upper Deck Gold

	MINT	NRMT
COMPLETE SET (50)	12.00	5.50
COMMON CARD (G1-G50)	.10	.05
SEMISTARS	.15	.07
UNLISTED STARS	.30	.14

PACKS FOUND IN SER.1 BOXES

- ❑ G1 Steve Emtman RC .10 .05
- ❑ G2 Carl Pickens RC .60 .25

- ❑ G3 Dale Carter RC .30 .14
- ❑ G4 Greg Skrepenak RC .10 .05
- ❑ G5 Kevin Smith RC .30 .14
- ❑ G6 Marco Coleman RC .15 .07
- ❑ G7 David Klingler RC .15 .07
- ❑ G8 Phillippi Sparks RC .10 .05
- ❑ G9 Tommy Maddox RC .10 .05
- ❑ G10 Quentin Coryatt RC .15 .07
- ❑ G11 Ty Detmer .30 .14
- ❑ G12 Vaughn Dunbar RC .10 .05
- ❑ G13 Ashley Ambrose RC .15 .07
- ❑ G14 Kurt Barber RC .10 .05
- ❑ G15 Chester McGlockton RC .30 .14
- ❑ G16 Todd Collins RC .10 .05
- ❑ G17 Steve Israel RC .10 .05
- ❑ G18 Marquez Pope RC .10 .05
- ❑ G19 Alonzo Spellman RC .15 .07
- ❑ G20 Tracy Scroggins RC .10 .05
- ❑ G21 Jim Kelly QC .30 .14
- ❑ G22 Troy Aikman QC .60 .25
- ❑ G23 Randall Cunningham QC .30 .14
- ❑ G24 Bernie Kosar QC .15 .07
- ❑ G25 Dan Marino QC 1.00 .45
- ❑ G26 Andre Reed .15 .07
- ❑ G27 Deion Sanders .50 .23
- ❑ G28 Randal Hill .10 .05
- ❑ G29 Eric Dickerson .15 .07
- ❑ G30 Jim Kelly .30 .14
- ❑ G31 Bernie Kosar .15 .07
- ❑ G32 Mike Singletary .15 .07
- ❑ G33 Anthony Miller .15 .07
- ❑ G34 Harvey Williams .30 .14
- ❑ G35 Randall Cunningham .30 .14
- ❑ G36 Joe Montana 1.25 .55
- ❑ G37 Dan McGwire .10 .05
- ❑ G38 Al Toon .15 .07
- ❑ G39 Carl Banks .10 .05
- ❑ G40 Troy Aikman .75 .35
- ❑ G41 Junior Seau .30 .14
- ❑ G42 Jeff George .30 .14
- ❑ G43 Michael Dean Perry .15 .07
- ❑ G44 Lawrence Taylor .30 .14
- ❑ G45 Dan Marino 1.25 .55
- ❑ G46 Jerry Rice .75 .35
- ❑ G47 Boomer Esiason .15 .07
- ❑ G48 Bruce Smith .30 .14
- ❑ G49 Leslie O'Neal .15 .07
- ❑ G50 Checklist Card .10 .05

1992 Upper Deck Coach's Report

	MINT	NRMT
COMPLETE SET (20)	16.00	7.25
COMMON CARD (CR1-CR20)	.40	.18
SEMISTARS	.75	.35

RANDOM INSERTS IN SER.2 HOBBY PACKS

- ❑ CR1 Mike Pritchard .75 .35
- ❑ CR2 Will Furrer .40 .18
- ❑ CR3 Alfred Williams .40 .18
- ❑ CR4 Tommy Vardell .40 .18
- ❑ CR5 Brett Favre 8.00 3.60
- ❑ CR6 Alvin Harper .75 .35
- ❑ CR7 Mike Croel .40 .18
- ❑ CR8 Herman Moore 3.50 1.55
- ❑ CR9 Edgar Bennett 1.00 .45
- ❑ CR10 Todd Marinovich .40 .18

- ❑ CR11 Aeneas Williams .... .75 .35
- ❑ CR12 Ricky Watters........... 2.00 .90
- ❑ CR13 Amp Lee.................... .40 .18
- ❑ CR14 Terrell Buckley............ .40 .18
- ❑ CR15 Tim Barnett .... .40 .18
- ❑ CR16 Nick Bell..................... .40 .18
- ❑ CR17 Leonard Russell........... .40 .18
- ❑ CR18 Lawrence Dawsey ...... .75 .35
- ❑ CR19 Robert Porcher............ .40 .18
- ❑ CR20 Checklist .... 1.00 .45 (Ricky Watters)

1992 Upper Deck Fanimation

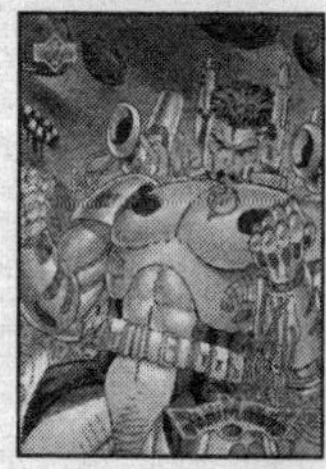

	MINT	NRMT
COMPLETE SET (10)	25.00	11.00
RANDOM INSERTS IN SER.2 RETAIL PACKS		

- ❑ F1 Jim Kelly .... 2.00 .90 (Shotgun Kelly)
- ❑ F2 Dan Marino .... 8.00 3.60 (Machine Gun)
- ❑ F3 Lawrence Taylor .... 2.00 .90 (The Giant)
- ❑ F4 Deion Sanders .... 4.00 1.80 (Neon Deion)
- ❑ F5 Troy Aikman .... 6.00 2.70 (The Marshall)
- ❑ F6 Junior Seau.................... 2.00 .90 (The Warrior)
- ❑ F7 Mike Singletary .... 1.25 .55 (Samurai)
- ❑ F8 Eric Dickerson................ 1.25 .55 (The Raider)
- ❑ F9 Jerry Rice .... 6.00 2.70 (Goldfinger)
- ❑ F10 Checklist Card............. 4.00 1.80 Jim Kelly, Dan Marino

1992 Upper Deck Game Breaker Holograms

	MINT	NRMT
COMPLETE SET (9)	6.00	2.70
STATED ODDS 1:30 PACKS........		
GB2/GB5/GB7 ISSUED WITH SER.2		

- ❑ GB1 Art Monk........................ .40 .18

- ❑ GB2 Drew Hill....................... .20 .09
- ❑ GB3 Haywood Jeffires .... .40 .18
- ❑ GB4 Andre Rison .... .40 .18
- ❑ GB5 Mark Clayton .... .40 .18
- ❑ GB6 Jerry Rice.................... 3.00 1.35
- ❑ GB7 Michael Haynes .... .40 .18
- ❑ GB8 Andre Reed .... .40 .18
- ❑ GB9 Michael Irvin............... 1.00 .45

1992 Upper Deck Pro Bowl

	MINT	NRMT
COMPLETE SET (16)	25.00	11.00
COMMON PAIR (PB1-PB16)....	1.25	.55
CL (PB16)...........................	2.00	.90
SEMISTARS..........................	1.50	.70
STATED ODDS 1:30 SER.1 PACKS		

- ❑ PB1 Haywood Jeffires .... 2.00 .90 Michael Irvin
- ❑ PB2 Mark Clayton .... 1.25 .55 Gary Clark
- ❑ PB3 Anthony Munoz .... 1.50 .70 Jim Lachey
- ❑ PB4 Warren Moon .... 1.50 .70 Mark Rypien
- ❑ PB5 Thurman Thomas........ 7.00 3.10 Barry Sanders
- ❑ PB6 Marion Butts .... 7.00 3.10 Emmitt Smith
- ❑ PB7 Greg Townsend .... 2.00 .90 Reggie White
- ❑ PB8 Cornelius Bennett........ 1.25 .55 Seth Joyner
- ❑ PB9 Derrick Thomas .... 1.50 .70 Pat Swilling
- ❑ PB10 Darryl Talley .... 1.25 .55 Chris Spielman
- ❑ PB11 Ronnie Lott............... 1.50 .70 Mark Carrier DB
- ❑ PB12 Steve Atwater........... 1.25 .55 Shaun Gayle
- ❑ PB13 Rod Woodson........... 1.50 .70 Darrell Green
- ❑ PB14 Jeff Gossett .... 1.25 .55 Chip Lohmiller
- ❑ PB15 Tim Brown .... 2.00 .90 Mel Gray
- ❑ PB16 Checklist Card .... 2.00 .90

1993 Upper Deck

	MINT	NRMT
COMPLETE SET (530)	30.00	13.50
COMMON CARD (1-530)...........	.05	.02
SEMISTARS..............................	.10	.05
UNLISTED STARS......................	.25	.11

- ❑ 1 Star Rookie Checklist .... .25 .11 Rick Mirer, Garrison Hearst, Curtis Conway, Lincoln Kennedy
- ❑ 2 Eric Curry SR RC .... .05 .02
- ❑ 3 Rick Mirer SR RC .... .50 .23
- ❑ 4 Dan Williams SR RC.......... .05 .02
- ❑ 5 Marvin Jones SR RC.......... .05 .02
- ❑ 6 Willie Roaf SR RC.............. .05 .02
- ❑ 7 Reggie Brooks SR RC .... .10 .05
- ❑ 8 Horace Copeland SR RC .. .10 .05
- ❑ 9 Lincoln Kennedy SR RC .... .05 .02
- ❑ 10 Curtis Conway SR RC...... .50 .23
- ❑ 11 Drew Bledsoe SR RC 3.00 1.35
- ❑ 12 Patrick Bates SR RC......... .05 .02
- ❑ 13 Wayne Simmons SR RC.. .05 .02
- ❑ 14 Irv Smith SR RC .... .05 .02
- ❑ 15 Robert Smith SR RC...... 1.00 .45
- ❑ 16 O.J. McDuffie SR RC ...... .75 .35
- ❑ 17 Darrien Gordon SR RC .... .05 .02
- ❑ 18 John Copeland SR RC .... .10 .05
- ❑ 19 Derek Brown RBK SR RC .05 .02
- ❑ 20 Jerome Bettis SR RC .... 1.00 .45
- ❑ 21 Deon Figures SR RC ...... .05 .02
- ❑ 22 Glyn Milburn SR RC .... .25 .11
- ❑ 23 Garrison Hearst SR RC.. 1.00 .45
- ❑ 24 Qadry Ismail SR RC .... .25 .11
- ❑ 25 Terry Kirby SR RC .... .25 .11
- ❑ 26 Lamar Thomas SR RC .... .05 .02
- ❑ 27 Tom Carter SR RC .... .10 .05
- ❑ 28 Andre Hastings SR RC .... .25 .11
- ❑ 29 George Teague SR RC.... .10 .05
- ❑ 30 All-Rookie Team CL .... .25 .11 Tommy Maddox
- ❑ 31 David Klingler ART .... .05 .02
- ❑ 32 Tommy Maddox ART ...... .05 .02
- ❑ 33 Vaughn Dunbar ART......... .05 .02
- ❑ 34 Rodney Culver ART .... .05 .02
- ❑ 35 Carl Pickens ART .... .25 .11
- ❑ 36 Courtney Hawkins ART.... .05 .02
- ❑ 37 Tyji Armstrong ART.......... .05 .02
- ❑ 38 Ray Roberts ART .... .05 .02
- ❑ 39 Troy Auzenne ART .... .05 .02
- ❑ 40 Shane Dronett ART.......... .05 .02
- ❑ 41 Chris Mims ART .... .05 .02
- ❑ 42 Sean Gilbert ART .... .05 .02
- ❑ 43 Steve Emtman ART .... .05 .02
- ❑ 44 Robert Jones ART............ .05 .02
- ❑ 45 Marco Coleman ART........ .05 .02
- ❑ 46 Ricardo McDonald ART .. .05 .02
- ❑ 47 Quentin Coryatt ART........ .10 .05
- ❑ 48 Dana Hall ART .... .05 .02
- ❑ 49 Darren Perry ART .... .05 .02
- ❑ 50 Darryl Williams ART .... .05 .02
- ❑ 51 Kevin Smith ART.............. .05 .02
- ❑ 52 Terrell Buckley ART .... .05 .02
- ❑ 53 Troy Vincent ART .... .05 .02
- ❑ 54 Lin Elliott ART .... .05 .02
- ❑ 55 Dale Carter ART .... .05 .02

☐ 56 Steve Atwater HIT	.05	.02
☐ 57 Junior Seau HIT	.10	.05
☐ 58 Ronnie Lott HIT	.05	.02
☐ 59 Louis Oliver HIT	.05	.02
☐ 60 Cortez Kennedy HIT	.05	.02
☐ 61 Pat Swilling HIT	.05	.02
☐ 62 Hitmen Checklist	.05	.02
☐ 63 Curtis Conway TC	.25	.11
☐ 64 Alfred Williams TC	.05	.02
☐ 65 Jim Kelly TC	.10	.05
☐ 66 Simon Fletcher TC	.05	.02
☐ 67 Eric Metcalf TC	.05	.02
☐ 68 Lawrence Dawsey TC	.05	.02
☐ 69 Garrison Hearst TC	.50	.23
☐ 70 Anthony Miller TC	.05	.02
☐ 71 Neil Smith TC	.05	.02
☐ 72 Jeff George TC	.10	.05
☐ 73 Emmitt Smith TC	.75	.35
☐ 74 Dan Marino TC	.75	.35
☐ 75 Clyde Simmons TC	.05	.02
☐ 76 Deion Sanders TC	.25	.11
☐ 77 Ricky Watters TC	.10	.05
☐ 78 Rodney Hampton TC	.10	.05
☐ 79 Brad Baxter TC	.05	.02
☐ 80 Barry Sanders TC	.75	.35
☐ 81 Warren Moon TC	.10	.05
☐ 82 Brett Favre TC	1.00	.45
☐ 83 Drew Bledsoe TC	1.25	.55
☐ 84 Eric Dickerson TC	.10	.05
☐ 85 Cleveland Gary TC	.05	.02
☐ 86 Earnest Byner TC	.05	.02
☐ 87 Wayne Martin TC	.05	.02
☐ 88 Rick Mirer TC	.25	.11
☐ 89 Barry Foster TC	.05	.02
☐ 90 Terry Allen TC	.10	.05
☐ 91 Vinnie Clark	.05	.02
☐ 92 Howard Ballard	.05	.02
☐ 93 Eric Ball	.05	.02
☐ 94 Marc Boutte	.05	.02
☐ 95 Larry Centers RC	.25	.11
☐ 96 Gary Brown	.05	.02
☐ 97 Hugh Millen	.05	.02
☐ 98 Anthony Newman RC	.05	.02
☐ 99 Darrell Thompson	.05	.02
☐ 100 George Jamison	.05	.02
☐ 101 James Francis	.05	.02
☐ 102 Leonard Harris	.05	.02
☐ 103 Lomas Brown	.05	.02
☐ 104 James Lofton	.10	.05
☐ 105 Jamie Dukes	.05	.02
☐ 106 Quinn Early	.10	.05
☐ 107 Ernie Jones	.05	.02
☐ 108 Torrance Small	.05	.02
☐ 109 Michael Carter	.05	.02
☐ 110 Aeneas Williams	.05	.02
☐ 111 Renaldo Turnbull	.05	.02
☐ 112 Al Smith	.05	.02
☐ 113 Troy Auzenne	.05	.02
☐ 114 Stephen Baker	.05	.02
☐ 115 Daniel Stubbs	.05	.02
☐ 116 Dana Hall	.05	.02
☐ 117 Lawrence Taylor	.25	.11
☐ 118 Ron Hall	.05	.02
☐ 119 Derrick Fenner	.05	.02
☐ 120 Martin Mayhew	.05	.02
☐ 121 Jay Schroeder	.05	.02
☐ 122 Michael Zordich	.05	.02
☐ 123 Ed McCaffrey	.10	.05
☐ 124 John Stephens	.05	.02
☐ 125 Brad Edwards	.05	.02
☐ 126 Don Griffin	.05	.02
☐ 127 Broderick Thomas	.05	.02
☐ 128 Ted Washington	.05	.02
☐ 129 Haywood Jeffires	.10	.05
☐ 130 Gary Plummer	.05	.02
☐ 131 Mark Wheeler	.05	.02
☐ 132 Ty Detmer	.25	.11
☐ 133 Derrick Walker	.05	.02
☐ 134 Henry Ellard	.10	.05
☐ 135 Neal Anderson	.05	.02
☐ 136 Bruce Smith	.25	.11
☐ 137 Cris Carter	.50	.23
☐ 138 Vaughn Dunbar	.05	.02
☐ 139 Dan Marino	1.50	.70
☐ 140 Troy Aikman	.75	.35
☐ 141 Randall Cunningham	.25	.11
☐ 142 Daryl Johnston	.25	.11
☐ 143 Mark Clayton	.05	.02
☐ 144 Rich Gannon	.05	.02
☐ 145 Nate Newton	.10	.05
☐ 146 Willie Gault	.05	.02
☐ 147 Brian Washington	.05	.02
☐ 148 Fred Barnett	.10	.05
☐ 149 Gill Byrd	.05	.02
☐ 150 Art Monk	.10	.05
☐ 151 Stan Humphries	.25	.11
☐ 152 Charles Mann	.05	.02
☐ 153 Greg Lloyd	.25	.11
☐ 154 Marvin Washington	.05	.02
☐ 155 Bernie Kosar	.10	.05
☐ 156 Pete Metzelaars	.05	.02
☐ 157 Chris Hinton	.05	.02
☐ 158 Jim Harbaugh	.25	.11
☐ 159 Willie Davis	.25	.11
☐ 160 Leroy Thompson	.05	.02
☐ 161 Scott Miller	.05	.02
☐ 162 Eugene Robinson	.05	.02
☐ 163 David Little	.05	.02
☐ 164 Pierce Holt	.05	.02
☐ 165 James Hasty	.05	.02
☐ 166 Dave Krieg	.10	.05
☐ 167 Gerald Williams	.05	.02
☐ 168 Kyle Clifton	.05	.02
☐ 169 Bill Brooks	.05	.02
☐ 170 Vance Johnson	.05	.02
☐ 171 Greg Townsend	.05	.02
☐ 172 Jason Belser	.05	.02
☐ 173 Brett Perriman	.25	.11
☐ 174 Steve Jordan	.05	.02
☐ 175 Kelvin Martin	.05	.02
☐ 176 Greg Kragen	.05	.02
☐ 177 Kerry Cash	.05	.02
☐ 178 Chester McGlockton	.10	.05
☐ 179 Jim Kelly	.25	.11
☐ 180 Todd McNair	.05	.02
☐ 181 Leroy Hoard	.10	.05
☐ 182 Seth Joyner	.05	.02
☐ 183 Sam Gash RC	.05	.02
☐ 184 Joe Nash	.05	.02
☐ 185 Lin Elliott RC	.05	.02
☐ 186 Robert Porcher	.05	.02
☐ 187 Tommy Hodson	.05	.02
☐ 188 Greg Lewis	.05	.02
☐ 189 Dan Saleaumua	.05	.02
☐ 190 Chris Goode	.05	.02
☐ 191 Henry Thomas	.05	.02
☐ 192 Bobby Hebert	.05	.02
☐ 193 Clay Matthews	.10	.05
☐ 194 Mark Carrier WR	.10	.05
☐ 195 Anthony Pleasant	.05	.02
☐ 196 Eric Dorsey	.05	.02
☐ 197 Clarence Verdin	.05	.02
☐ 198 Marc Spindler	.05	.02
☐ 199 Tommy Maddox	.05	.02
☐ 200 Wendell Davis	.05	.02
☐ 201 John Fina	.05	.02
☐ 202 Alonzo Spellman	.05	.02
☐ 203 Darryl Williams	.05	.02
☐ 204 Mike Croel	.05	.02
☐ 205 Ken Norton Jr.	.10	.05
☐ 206 Mel Gray	.10	.05
☐ 207 Chuck Cecil	.05	.02
☐ 208 John Flannery	.05	.02
☐ 209 Chip Banks	.05	.02
☐ 210 Chris Martin	.05	.02
☐ 211 Dennis Brown	.05	.02
☐ 212 Vinny Testaverde	.10	.05
☐ 213 Nick Bell	.05	.02
☐ 214 Robert Delpino	.05	.02
☐ 215 Mark Higgs	.05	.02
☐ 216 Al Noga	.05	.02
☐ 217 Andre Tippett	.05	.02
☐ 218 Pat Swilling	.05	.02
☐ 219 Phil Simms	.10	.05
☐ 220 Ricky Proehl	.05	.02
☐ 221 William Thomas	.05	.02
☐ 222 Jeff Graham	.10	.05
☐ 223 Darion Conner	.05	.02
☐ 224 Mark Carrier DB	.05	.02
☐ 225 Willie Green	.05	.02
☐ 226 Reggie Rivers RC	.05	.02
☐ 227 Andre Reed	.10	.05
☐ 228 Deion Sanders	.50	.23
☐ 229 Chris Doleman	.05	.02
☐ 230 Jerry Ball	.05	.02
☐ 231 Eric Dickerson	.10	.05
☐ 232 Carlos Jenkins	.05	.02
☐ 233 Mike Johnson	.05	.02
☐ 234 Marco Coleman	.05	.02
☐ 235 Leslie O'Neal	.10	.05
☐ 236 Browning Nagle	.05	.02
☐ 237 Carl Pickens	.25	.11
☐ 238 Steve Emtman	.05	.02
☐ 239 Alvin Harper	.10	.05
☐ 240 Keith Jackson	.10	.05
☐ 241 Jerry Rice	1.00	.45
☐ 242 Cortez Kennedy	.10	.05
☐ 243 Tyji Armstrong	.05	.02
☐ 244 Troy Vincent	.05	.02
☐ 245 Randal Hill	.05	.02
☐ 246 Robert Blackmon	.05	.02
☐ 247 Junior Seau	.25	.11
☐ 248 Sterling Sharpe	.25	.11
☐ 249 Thurman Thomas	.25	.11
☐ 250 David Klingler	.05	.02
☐ 251 Jeff George	.25	.11
☐ 252 Anthony Miller	.10	.05
☐ 253 Earnest Byner	.05	.02
☐ 254 Eric Swann	.10	.05
☐ 255 Jeff Herrod	.05	.02
☐ 256 Eddie Robinson	.05	.02
☐ 257 Eric Allen	.05	.02
☐ 258 John Taylor	.10	.05
☐ 259 Sean Gilbert	.10	.05
☐ 260 Ray Childress	.05	.02
☐ 261 Michael Haynes	.10	.05
☐ 262 Greg McMurtry	.05	.02
☐ 263 Bill Romanowski	.05	.02
☐ 264 Todd Lyght	.05	.02
☐ 265 Clyde Simmons	.05	.02
☐ 266 Webster Slaughter	.05	.02
☐ 267 J.J. Birden	.05	.02
☐ 268 Aaron Wallace	.05	.02
☐ 269 Carl Banks	.05	.02
☐ 270 Ricardo McDonald	.05	.02
☐ 271 Michael Brooks	.05	.02
☐ 272 Dale Carter	.05	.02
☐ 273 Mike Pritchard	.10	.05
☐ 274 Derek Brown TE	.05	.02
☐ 275 Burt Grossman	.05	.02
☐ 276 Mark Schlereth	.05	.02
☐ 277 Karl Mecklenburg	.05	.02
☐ 278 Rickey Jackson	.05	.02
☐ 279 Ricky Ervins	.05	.02
☐ 280 Jeff Bryant	.05	.02
☐ 281 Eric Martin	.05	.02
☐ 282 Carlton Haselrig	.05	.02
☐ 283 Kevin Mack	.05	.02
☐ 284 Brad Muster	.05	.02
☐ 285 Kelvin Pritchett	.05	.02
☐ 286 Courtney Hawkins	.05	.02
☐ 287 Levon Kirkland	.05	.02
☐ 288 Steve DeBerg	.05	.02
☐ 289 Edgar Bennett	.25	.11
☐ 290 Michael Dean Perry	.10	.05
☐ 291 Richard Dent	.10	.05
☐ 292 Howie Long	.10	.05
☐ 293 Chris Mims	.05	.02
☐ 294 Kurt Barber	.05	.02
☐ 295 Wilber Marshall	.05	.02
☐ 296 Ethan Horton	.05	.02
☐ 297 Tony Bennett	.05	.02
☐ 298 Johnny Johnson	.05	.02
☐ 299 Craig Heyward	.10	.05
☐ 300 Steve Israel	.05	.02
☐ 301 Kenneth Gant	.05	.02
☐ 302 Eugene Chung	.05	.02
☐ 303 Harvey Williams	.10	.05
☐ 304 Jarrod Bunch	.05	.02
☐ 305 Darren Perry	.05	.02
☐ 306 Steve Christie	.05	.02
☐ 307 John Randle	.05	.02
☐ 308 Warren Moon	.25	.11
☐ 309 Charles Haley	.10	.05
☐ 310 Tony Smith	.05	.02
☐ 311 Steve Broussard	.05	.02
☐ 312 Alfred Williams	.05	.02
☐ 313 Terrell Buckley	.05	.02

❑ 314 Trace Armstrong .05 .02
❑ 315 Brian Mitchell .10 .05
❑ 316 Steve Atwater .05 .02
❑ 317 Nate Lewis .05 .02
❑ 318 Richard Brown .05 .02
❑ 319 Rufus Porter .05 .02
❑ 320 Pat Harlow .05 .02
❑ 321 Anthony Smith .05 .02
❑ 322 Jack Del Rio .05 .02
❑ 323 Darryl Talley .05 .02
❑ 324 Sam Mills .05 .02
❑ 325 Chris Miller .10 .05
❑ 326 Ken Harvey .05 .02
❑ 327 Rod Woodson .25 .11
❑ 328 Tony Tolbert .05 .02
❑ 329 Todd Kinchen .05 .02
❑ 330 Brian Noble .05 .02
❑ 331 Dave Meggett .05 .02
❑ 332 Chris Spielman .10 .05
❑ 333 Barry Word .05 .02
❑ 334 Jessie Hester .05 .02
❑ 335 Michael Jackson .10 .05
❑ 336 Mitchell Price .05 .02
❑ 337 Michael Irvin .25 .11
❑ 338 Simon Fletcher .05 .02
❑ 339 Keith Jennings .05 .02
❑ 340 Vai Sikahema .05 .02
❑ 341 Roger Craig .10 .05
❑ 342 Ricky Watters .25 .11
❑ 343 Reggie Cobb .05 .02
❑ 344 Kanavis McGhee .05 .02
❑ 345 Barry Foster .10 .05
❑ 346 Marion Butts .05 .02
❑ 347 Bryan Cox .05 .02
❑ 348 Wayne Martin .05 .02
❑ 349 Jim Everett .10 .05
❑ 350 Nate Odomes .05 .02
❑ 351 Anthony Johnson .10 .05
❑ 352 Rodney Hampton .25 .11
❑ 353 Terry Allen .25 .11
❑ 354 Derrick Thomas .25 .11
❑ 355 Calvin Williams .10 .05
❑ 356 Pepper Johnson .05 .02
❑ 357 John Elway 1.50 .70
❑ 358 Steve Young .75 .35
❑ 359 Emmitt Smith 1.50 .70
❑ 360 Brett Favre 2.00 .90
❑ 361 Cody Carlson .05 .02
❑ 362 Vincent Brown .05 .02
❑ 363 Gary Anderson RB .05 .02
❑ 364 Jon Vaughn .05 .02
❑ 365 Todd Marinovich .05 .02
❑ 366 Carnell Lake .05 .02
❑ 367 Kurt Gouveia .05 .02
❑ 368 Lawrence Dawsey .05 .02
❑ 369 Neil O'Donnell .25 .11
❑ 370 Duane Bickett .05 .02
❑ 371 Ronnie Harmon .05 .02
❑ 372 Rodney Peete .05 .02
❑ 373 Cornelius Bennett .10 .05
❑ 374 Brad Baxter .05 .02
❑ 375 Ernest Givins .10 .05
❑ 376 Keith Byars .05 .02
❑ 377 Eric Bieniemy .05 .02
❑ 378 Mike Brim .05 .02
❑ 379 Darren Lewis .05 .02
❑ 380 Heath Sherman .05 .02
❑ 381 Leonard Russell .10 .05
❑ 382 Brent Jones .10 .05
❑ 383 David Whitmore .05 .02
❑ 384 Ray Roberts .05 .02
❑ 385 John Offerdahl .05 .02
❑ 386 Keith McCants .05 .02
❑ 387 John Baylor .05 .02
❑ 388 Amp Lee .05 .02
❑ 389 Chris Warren .10 .05
❑ 390 Herman Moore .50 .23
❑ 391 Johnny Bailey .05 .02
❑ 392 Tim Johnson .05 .02
❑ 393 Eric Metcalf .10 .05
❑ 394 Chris Chandler .10 .05
❑ 395 Mark Rypien .05 .02
❑ 396 Christian Okoye .05 .02
❑ 397 Shannon Sharpe .25 .11
❑ 398 Eric Hill .05 .02
❑ 399 David Lang .05 .02
❑ 400 Bruce Matthews .05 .02
❑ 401 Harold Green .05 .02
❑ 402 Mo Lewis .05 .02
❑ 403 Terry McDaniel .05 .02
❑ 404 Wesley Carroll .05 .02
❑ 405 Richmond Webb .05 .02
❑ 406 Andre Rison .10 .05
❑ 407 Lonnie Young .05 .02
❑ 408 Tommy Vardell .05 .02
❑ 409 Gene Atkins .05 .02
❑ 410 Sean Salisbury .05 .02
❑ 411 Kenneth Davis .05 .02
❑ 412 John L. Williams .05 .02
❑ 413 Roman Phifer .05 .02
❑ 414 Bennie Blades .05 .02
❑ 415 Tim Brown .25 .11
❑ 416 Lorenzo White .05 .02
❑ 417 Tony Casillas .05 .02
❑ 418 Tom Waddle .05 .02
❑ 419 David Fulcher .05 .02
❑ 420 Jessie Tuggle .05 .02
❑ 421 Emmitt Smith SL .75 .35
❑ 422 Clyde Simmons SL .05 .02
❑ 423 Sterling Sharpe SL .10 .05
❑ 424 Sterling Sharpe SL .10 .05
❑ 425 Emmitt Smith SL .75 .35
❑ 426 Dan Marino SL .75 .35
❑ 427 Henry Jones SL .05 .02
Audray McMillian
❑ 428 Thurman Thomas SL .10 .05
❑ 429 Greg Montgomery SL .05 .02
❑ 430 Pete Stoyanovich SL .05 .02
❑ 431 Season Leaders CL .40 .18
Emmitt Smith
❑ 432 Steve Young BB .40 .18
❑ 433 Jerry Rice BB .50 .23
❑ 434 Ricky Watters BB .10 .05
❑ 435 Barry Foster BB .05 .02
❑ 436 Cortez Kennedy BB .05 .02
❑ 437 Warren Moon BB .10 .05
❑ 438 Thurman Thomas BB .10 .05
❑ 439 Brett Favre BB 1.00 .45
❑ 440 Andre Rison BB .10 .05
❑ 441 Barry Sanders BB .75 .35
❑ 442 Berman's Best RC CL .05 .02
Chris Berman
❑ 443 Moe Gardner .05 .02
❑ 444 Robert Jones .05 .02
❑ 445 Reggie Langhorne .05 .02
❑ 446 Flipper Anderson .05 .02
❑ 447 James Washington .05 .02
❑ 448 Aaron Craver .05 .02
❑ 449 Jack Trudeau .05 .02
❑ 450 Neil Smith .25 .11
❑ 451 Chris Burkett .05 .02
❑ 452 Russell Maryland .05 .02
❑ 453 Drew Hill .05 .02
❑ 454 Barry Sanders 1.50 .70
❑ 455 Jeff Cross .05 .02
❑ 456 Bennie Thompson .05 .02
❑ 457 Marcus Allen .25 .11
❑ 458 Tracy Scroggins .05 .02
❑ 459 LeRoy Butler .05 .02
❑ 460 Joe Montana 1.50 .70
❑ 461 Eddie Anderson .05 .02
❑ 462 Tim McDonald .05 .02
❑ 463 Ronnie Lott .10 .05
❑ 464 Gaston Green .05 .02
❑ 465 Shane Conlan .05 .02
❑ 466 Leonard Marshall .05 .02
❑ 467 Melvin Jenkins .05 .02
❑ 468 Don Beebe .05 .02
❑ 469 Johnny Mitchell .05 .02
❑ 470 Darryl Henley .05 .02
❑ 471 Boomer Esiason .10 .05
❑ 472 Mark Kelso .05 .02
❑ 473 John Booty .05 .02
❑ 474 Pete Stoyanovich .05 .02
❑ 475 Thomas Smith RC .10 .05
❑ 476 Carlton Gray RC .05 .02
❑ 477 Dana Stubblefield RC .25 .11
❑ 478 Ryan McNeil RC .05 .02
❑ 479 Natrone Means RC .75 .35
❑ 480 Carl Simpson RC .05 .02
❑ 481 Robert O'Neal RC .05 .02
❑ 482 Demetrius DuBose RC .05 .02
❑ 483 Darrin Smith RC .10 .05
❑ 484 Micheal Barrow RC .05 .02
❑ 485 Chris Slade RC .10 .05
❑ 486 Steve Tovar RC .05 .02
❑ 487 Ron George RC .05 .02
❑ 488 Steve Tasker .10 .05
❑ 489 Will Furrer .05 .02
❑ 490 Reggie White .25 .11
❑ 491 Sean Jones .05 .02
❑ 492 Gary Clark .10 .05
❑ 493 Donnell Woolford .05 .02
❑ 494 Steve Beuerlein .05 .02
❑ 495 Anthony Carter .10 .05
❑ 496 Louis Oliver .05 .02
❑ 497 Chris Zorich .05 .02
❑ 498 David Brandon .05 .02
❑ 499 Bubba McDowell .05 .02
❑ 500 Adrian Cooper .05 .02
❑ 501 Bill Johnson .05 .02
❑ 502 Shawn Jefferson .05 .02
❑ 503 Siran Stacy .05 .02
❑ 504 James Jones .05 .02
❑ 505 Tom Rathman .05 .02
❑ 506 Vince Buck .05 .02
❑ 507 Kent Graham RC .25 .11
❑ 508 Darren Carrington RC .05 .02
❑ 509 Rickey Dixon .05 .02
❑ 510 Toi Cook .05 .02
❑ 511 Steve Smith .05 .02
❑ 512 Eric Green .05 .02
❑ 513 Phillippi Sparks .05 .02
❑ 514 Lee Williams .05 .02
❑ 515 Gary Reasons .05 .02
❑ 516 Shane Dronett .05 .02
❑ 517 Jay Novacek .10 .05
❑ 518 Kevin Greene .25 .11
❑ 519 Derek Russell .05 .02
❑ 520 Quentin Coryatt .10 .05
❑ 521 Santana Dotson .10 .05
❑ 522 Donald Frank .05 .02
❑ 523 Mike Prior .05 .02
❑ 524 Dwight Hollier RC .05 .02
❑ 525 Eric Davis .05 .02
❑ 526 Dalton Hilliard .05 .02
❑ 527 Rodney Culver .05 .02
❑ 528 Jeff Hostetler .10 .05
❑ 529 Ernie Mills .05 .02
❑ 530 Craig Erickson .10 .05
❑ P1 Eric Dickerson Promo 2.00 .90
Numbered 231

1993 Upper Deck America's Team

	MINT	NRMT
COMPLETE SET (15)	50.00	22.00
COMMON CARD (AT1-AT14)	2.00	.90
EMM.SMITH HEADER (NNO)	10.00	4.50
SEMISTARS	3.00	1.35
UNLISTED STARS	5.00	2.20

STATED ODDS 1:25 HOBBY
JUMBO CARDS: .15X TO .3X HI COLUMN
JUMBOS:ONE PER SPEC.RETAIL BLISTER

❑ AT1 Roger Staubach 10.00 4.50
❑ AT2 Chuck Howley 2.00 .90
❑ AT3 Harvey Martin 2.00 .90
❑ AT4 Randy White 3.00 1.35

Card	MINT	NRMT
❑ AT5 Bob Lilly	3.00	1.35
❑ AT6 Drew Pearson	3.00	1.35
❑ AT7 Emmitt Smith	15.00	6.75
❑ AT8 Troy Aikman	10.00	4.50
❑ AT9 Ken Norton Jr.	3.00	1.35
❑ AT10 Robert Jones	2.00	.90
❑ AT11 Russell Maryland	2.00	.90
❑ AT12 Jay Novacek	3.00	1.35
❑ AT13 Michael Irvin	5.00	2.20
❑ AT14 Troy Aikman CL	6.00	2.70
❑ NNO Header Card Emmitt Smith	10.00	4.50

1993 Upper Deck Future Heroes

	MINT	NRMT
COMPLETE SET (10)	15.00	6.75
STATED ODDS 1:20 HOB/JUM....		
ONE PER SPECIAL RETAIL PACK	1.25	.55

Card	MINT	NRMT
❑ 37 Barry Foster	.30	.14
❑ 38 Junior Seau	.75	.35
❑ 39 Emmitt Smith	5.00	2.20
❑ 40 Troy Aikman	2.50	1.10
❑ 41 David Klingler	.15	.07
❑ 42 Ricky Watters	.75	.35
❑ 43 Barry Sanders	5.00	2.20
❑ 44 Brett Favre	6.00	2.70
❑ 45 Emmitt Smith Checklist	1.25	.55
❑ NNO Ricky Watters Header	.50	.23

1993 Upper Deck Pro Bowl

	MINT	NRMT
COMPLETE SET (20)	100.00	45.00
STATED ODDS 1:25 RETAIL		

Card	MINT	NRMT
❑ PB1 Andre Reed	1.00	.45
❑ PB2 Dan Marino	15.00	6.75
❑ PB3 Warren Moon	2.50	1.10
❑ PB4 Anthony Miller	1.00	.45
❑ PB5 Barry Foster	1.00	.45
❑ PB6 Steve Atwater	.50	.23
❑ PB7 Cortez Kennedy	1.00	.45
❑ PB8 Junior Seau	2.50	1.10
❑ PB9 Jerry Rice	10.00	4.50
❑ PB10 Michael Irvin	2.50	1.10
❑ PB11 Sterling Sharpe	2.50	1.10
❑ PB12 Steve Young	8.00	3.60
❑ PB13 Troy Aikman	8.00	3.60
❑ PB14 Brett Favre	20.00	9.00
❑ PB15 Emmitt Smith	15.00	6.75
❑ PB16 Rodney Hampton	2.50	1.10
❑ PB17 Barry Sanders	15.00	6.75
❑ PB18 Ricky Watters	2.50	1.10
❑ PB19 Pat Swilling	.50	.23
❑ PB20 Checklist Card	4.00	1.80

1993 Upper Deck Rookie Exchange

	MINT	NRMT
COMPLETE SET (6)	12.00	5.50
TRADE CARD STATED ODDS 1:72		
ONE SET PER TRADE CARD BY MAIL	1.50	.70

Card	MINT	NRMT
❑ RE1 Trade Upper Deck Card Expired	.50	.23
❑ RE1X Trade Upper Deck Card Punched	.50	.23
❑ RE2 Drew Bledsoe	6.00	2.70
❑ RE3 Rick Mirer	1.00	.45
❑ RE4 Garrison Hearst	2.00	.90
❑ RE5 Marvin Jones	.10	.05
❑ RE6 Curtis Conway	1.00	.45
❑ RE7 Jerome Bettis	2.00	.90

1993 Upper Deck Team MVPs

	MINT	NRMT
COMPLETE SET (29)	25.00	11.00
ONE PER JUMBO PACK..............		

Card	MINT	NRMT
❑ TM1 Neal Anderson	.20	.09
❑ TM2 Harold Green	.20	.09
❑ TM3 Thurman Thomas	1.00	.45
❑ TM4 John Elway	6.00	2.70
❑ TM5 Eric Metcalf	.40	.18
❑ TM6 Reggie Cobb	.20	.09
❑ TM7 Johnny Bailey	.20	.09
❑ TM8 Junior Seau	1.00	.45
❑ TM9 Derrick Thomas	1.00	.45
❑ TM10 Steve Emtman	.20	.09
❑ TM11 Troy Aikman	3.00	1.35
❑ TM12 Dan Marino	6.00	2.70
❑ TM13 Clyde Simmons	.20	.09
❑ TM14 Andre Rison	.40	.18
❑ TM15 Steve Young	3.00	1.35
❑ TM16 Rodney Hampton	1.00	.45
❑ TM17 Rob Moore	.40	.18
❑ TM18 Barry Sanders	6.00	2.70
❑ TM19 Warren Moon	1.00	.45
❑ TM20 Sterling Sharpe	1.00	.45
❑ TM21 Jon Vaughn	.20	.09
❑ TM22 Tim Brown	1.00	.45
❑ TM23 Jim Everett	.40	.18
❑ TM24 Gary Clark	.40	.18
❑ TM25 Wayne Martin	.20	.09
❑ TM26 Cortez Kennedy	.40	.18
❑ TM27 Barry Foster	.40	.18
❑ TM28 Terry Allen	1.00	.45
❑ TM29 Checklist Card	.50	.23

1994 Upper Deck

	MINT	NRMT
COMPLETE SET (330)	25.00	11.00
COMMON CARD (1-330)	.10	.05
SEMISTARS	.20	.09
UNLISTED STARS	.40	.18
COMP.ELEC.GOLD (330)	800.00	350.00
*GOLD STARS: 6X to 15X HI COL.		
*GOLD RCs: 3X to 8X HI		
GOLD STATED ODDS 1:35.........		
COMP.ELEC.SILVER (330)	120.00	55.00
*SILVER STARS: 1.25X to 3X HI COLUMN		
*SILVER RCS: .75X to 2X HI		
ONE GOLD OR SILVER PER HOBBY PACK		
TWO GOLD OR SILVER PER SPEC.RET.PACK		

Card	MINT	NRMT
❑ 1 Dan Wilkinson RC	.20	.09
❑ 2 Antonio Langham RC	.20	.09
❑ 3 Derrick Alexander WR RC	1.00	.45
❑ 4 Charles Johnson RC	.40	.18
❑ 5 Bucky Brooks RC	.10	.05
❑ 6 Trev Alberts RC	.20	.09
❑ 7 Marshall Faulk RC	4.00	1.80
❑ 8 Willie McGinest RC	.40	.18
❑ 9 Aaron Glenn RC	.20	.09
❑ 10 Ryan Yarborough RC	.10	.05
❑ 11 Greg Hill RC	1.00	.45
❑ 12 Sam Adams RC	.20	.09
❑ 13 John Thierry RC	.10	.05
❑ 14 Johnnie Morton RC	1.25	.55
❑ 15 LeShon Johnson RC	.20	.09
❑ 16 David Palmer RC	1.00	.45
❑ 17 Trent Dilfer RC	1.50	.70
❑ 18 Jamir Miller RC	.10	.05
❑ 19 Thomas Lewis RC	.20	.09
❑ 20 Heath Shuler RC	.40	.18
❑ 21 Wayne Gandy	.10	.05
❑ 22 Isaac Bruce RC	4.00	1.80
❑ 23 Joe Johnson RC	.10	.05
❑ 24 Mario Bates RC	.40	.18
❑ 25 Bryant Young RC	.40	.18
❑ 26 William Floyd RC	.40	.18
❑ 27 Errict Rhett RC	1.50	.70
❑ 28 Chuck Levy RC	.10	.05
❑ 29 Darnay Scott RC	1.25	.55
❑ 30 Rob Fredrickson RC	.20	.09
❑ 31 Jamir Miller HW	.10	.05
❑ 32 Thomas Lewis HW	.10	.05
❑ 33 John Thierry HW	.10	.05
❑ 34 Sam Adams HW	.10	.05
❑ 35 Joe Johnson HW	.10	.05
❑ 36 Bryant Young HW	.20	.09
❑ 37 Wayne Gandy HW	.10	.05
❑ 38 LeShon Johnson HW	.10	.05
❑ 39 Mario Bates HW	.20	.09
❑ 40 Greg Hill HW	.20	.09
❑ 41 Andy Heck	.10	.05
❑ 42 Warren Moon	.40	.18
❑ 43 Jim Everett	.20	.09
❑ 44 Bill Romanowski	.10	.05
❑ 45 Michael Haynes	.20	.09
❑ 46 Chris Doleman	.10	.05
❑ 47 Merril Hoge	.10	.05
❑ 48 Chris Miller	.10	.05
❑ 49 Clyde Simmons	.10	.05
❑ 50 Jeff George	.40	.18
❑ 51 Jeff Burris RC	.20	.09
❑ 52 Ethan Horton	.10	.05

	No.	Player	Price	Price
❑	53	Scott Mitchell	.40	.18
❑	54	Howard Ballard	.10	.05
❑	55	Lewis Tillman	.10	.05
❑	56	Marion Butts	.10	.05
❑	57	Erik Kramer	.20	.09
❑	58	Ken Norton Jr.	.20	.09
❑	59	Anthony Miller	.20	.09
❑	60	Chris Hinton	.10	.05
❑	61	Ricky Proehl	.10	.05
❑	62	Craig Heyward	.20	.09
❑	63	Darryl Talley	.10	.05
❑	64	Tim Worley	.10	.05
❑	65	Derrick Fenner	.10	.05
❑	66	Jerry Ball	.10	.05
❑	67	Darrin Smith	.10	.05
❑	68	Mike Croel	.10	.05
❑	69	Ray Crockett	.10	.05
❑	70	Tony Bennett	.10	.05
❑	71	Webster Slaughter	.10	.05
❑	72	Anthony Johnson	.20	.09
❑	73	Charles Mincy	.10	.05
❑	74	Calvin Jones RC	.10	.05
❑	75	Henry Ellard	.20	.09
❑	76	Troy Vincent	.10	.05
❑	77	Sean Salisbury	.10	.05
❑	78	Pat Harlow	.10	.05
❑	79	James Williams RC	.10	.05
❑	80	Dave Brown	.20	.09
❑	81	Kent Graham	.20	.09
❑	82	Seth Joyner	.10	.05
❑	83	Deon Figures	.10	.05
❑	84	Stanley Richard	.10	.05
❑	85	Tom Rathman	.10	.05
❑	86	Rod Stephens	.10	.05
❑	87	Ray Seals	.10	.05
❑	88	Andre Collins	.10	.05
❑	89	Cornelius Bennett	.20	.09
❑	90	Richard Dent	.20	.09
❑	91	Louis Oliver	.10	.05
❑	92	Rodney Peete	.10	.05
❑	93	Jackie Harris	.10	.05
❑	94	Tracy Simien	.10	.05
❑	95	Greg Townsend	.10	.05
❑	96	Michael Stewart	.10	.05
❑	97	Irving Fryar	.20	.09
❑	98	Todd Collins	.10	.05
❑	99	Irv Smith	.10	.05
❑	100	Chris Calloway	.10	.05
❑	101	Kevin Greene	.40	.18
❑	102	John Friesz	.20	.09
❑	103	Steve Bono	.20	.09
❑	104	Brian Blades	.20	.09
❑	105	Reggie Cobb	.10	.05
❑	106	Eric Swann	.20	.09
❑	107	Mike Pritchard	.10	.05
❑	108	Bill Brooks	.10	.05
❑	109	Jim Harbaugh	.40	.18
❑	110	David Whitmore	.10	.05
❑	111	Eddie Anderson	.10	.05
❑	112	Ray Crittenden RC	.10	.05
❑	113	Mark Collins	.10	.05
❑	114	Brian Washington	.10	.05
❑	115	Barry Foster	.10	.05
❑	116	Gary Plummer	.10	.05
❑	117	Marc Logan	.10	.05
❑	118	John L. Williams	.10	.05
❑	119	Marty Carter	.10	.05
❑	120	Kurt Gouveia	.10	.05
❑	121	Ronald Moore	.10	.05
❑	122	Pierce Holt	.10	.05
❑	123	Henry Jones	.10	.05
❑	124	Donnell Woolford	.10	.05
❑	125	Steve Tovar	.10	.05
❑	126	Anthony Pleasant	.10	.05
❑	127	Jay Novacek	.20	.09
❑	128	Dan Williams	.10	.05
❑	129	Barry Sanders	3.00	1.35
❑	130	Robert Brooks	.40	.18
❑	131	Lorenzo White	.10	.05
❑	132	Kerry Cash	.10	.05
❑	133	Joe Montana	3.00	1.35
❑	134	Jeff Hostetler	.20	.09
❑	135	Jerome Bettis	.40	.18
❑	136	Dan Marino	3.00	1.35
❑	137	Vencie Glenn	.10	.05
❑	138	Vincent Brown	.10	.05
❑	139	Rickey Jackson	.10	.05
❑	140	Carlton Bailey	.10	.05
❑	141	Jeff Lageman	.10	.05
❑	142	William Thomas	.10	.05
❑	143	Neil O'Donnell	.40	.18
❑	144	Shawn Jefferson	.10	.05
❑	145	Steve Young	1.00	.45
❑	146	Chris Warren	.20	.09
❑	147	Courtney Hawkins	.10	.05
❑	148	Brad Edwards	.10	.05
❑	149	O.J. McDuffie	.40	.18
❑	150	David Lang	.10	.05
❑	151	Chuck Cecil	.10	.05
❑	152	Norm Johnson	.10	.05
❑	153	Pete Metzelaars	.10	.05
❑	154	Shaun Gayle	.10	.05
❑	155	Alfred Williams	.10	.05
❑	156	Eric Turner	.10	.05
❑	157A	Emmitt Smith ERR incorrect stat totals	2.50	1.10
❑	157B	Emmitt Smith COR corrected stats	2.50	1.10
❑	158	Steve Atwater	.10	.05
❑	159	Robert Porcher	.10	.05
❑	160	Edgar Bennett	.40	.18
❑	161	Bubba McDowell	.10	.05
❑	162	Jeff Herrod	.10	.05
❑	163	Keith Cash	.10	.05
❑	164	Patrick Bates	.10	.05
❑	165	Todd Lyght	.10	.05
❑	166	Mark Higgs	.10	.05
❑	167	Carlos Jenkins	.10	.05
❑	168	Drew Bledsoe	1.50	.70
❑	169	Wayne Martin	.10	.05
❑	170	Mike Sherrard	.10	.05
❑	171	Ronnie Lott	.20	.09
❑	172	Fred Barnett	.20	.09
❑	173	Eric Green	.10	.05
❑	174	Leslie O'Neal	.10	.05
❑	175	Brent Jones	.20	.09
❑	176	Jon Vaughn	.10	.05
❑	177	Vince Workman	.10	.05
❑	178	Ron Middleton	.10	.05
❑	179	Terry McDaniel	.10	.05
❑	180	Willie Davis	.20	.09
❑	181	Gary Clark	.20	.09
❑	182	Bobby Hebert	.10	.05
❑	183	Russell Copeland	.10	.05
❑	184	Chris Gedney	.10	.05
❑	185	Tony McGee	.10	.05
❑	186	Rob Burnett	.10	.05
❑	187	Charles Haley	.20	.09
❑	188	Shannon Sharpe	.20	.09
❑	189	Mel Gray	.10	.05
❑	190	George Teague	.10	.05
❑	191	Ernest Givins	.20	.09
❑	192	Ray Buchanan	.10	.05
❑	193	J.J. Birden	.10	.05
❑	194	Tim Brown	.40	.18
❑	195	Tim Lester	.10	.05
❑	196	Marco Coleman	.10	.05
❑	197	Randall McDaniel	.10	.05
❑	198	Bruce Armstrong	.10	.05
❑	199	Willie Roaf	.10	.05
❑	200	Greg Jackson	.10	.05
❑	201	Johnny Mitchell	.10	.05
❑	202	Calvin Williams	.20	.09
❑	203	Jeff Graham	.10	.05
❑	204	Darren Carrington	.10	.05
❑	205	Jerry Rice	1.50	.70
❑	206	Cortez Kennedy	.20	.09
❑	207	Charles Wilson	.10	.05
❑	208	James Jenkins RC	.10	.05
❑	209	Ray Childress	.10	.05
❑	210	LeRoy Butler	.10	.05
❑	211	Randal Hill	.10	.05
❑	212	Lincoln Kennedy	.10	.05
❑	213	Kenneth Davis	.10	.05
❑	214	Terry Obee	.10	.05
❑	215	Ricardo McDonald	.10	.05
❑	216	Pepper Johnson	.10	.05
❑	217	Alvin Harper	.20	.09
❑	218	John Elway	3.00	1.35
❑	219	Derrick Moore	.10	.05
❑	220	Terrell Buckley	.10	.05
❑	221	Haywood Jeffires	.20	.09
❑	222	Jessie Hester	.10	.05
❑	223	Kimble Anders	.20	.09
❑	224	Rocket Ismail	.20	.09
❑	225	Roman Phifer	.10	.05
❑	226	Bryan Cox	.10	.05
❑	227	Cris Carter	.75	.35
❑	228	Sam Gash	.10	.05
❑	229	Renaldo Turnbull	.10	.05
❑	230	Rodney Hampton	.40	.18
❑	231	Johnny Johnson	.10	.05
❑	232	Tim Harris	.10	.05
❑	233	Leroy Thompson	.10	.05
❑	234	Junior Seau	.40	.18
❑	235	Tim McDonald	.10	.05
❑	236	Eugene Robinson	.10	.05
❑	237	Lawrence Dawsey	.10	.05
❑	238	Tim Johnson	.10	.05
❑	239	Jason Elam	.10	.05
❑	240	Willie Green	.10	.05
❑	241	Larry Centers	.40	.18
❑	242	Erric Pegram	.10	.05
❑	243	Bruce Smith	.40	.18
❑	244	Alonzo Spellman	.10	.05
❑	245	Carl Pickens	.40	.18
❑	246	Michael Jackson	.20	.09
❑	247	Kevin Williams	.20	.09
❑	248	Glyn Milburn	.20	.09
❑	249	Herman Moore	.40	.18
❑	250	Brett Favre	3.00	1.35
❑	251	Al Smith	.10	.05
❑	252	Roosevelt Potts	.10	.05
❑	253	Marcus Allen	.40	.18
❑	254	Anthony Smith	.10	.05
❑	255	Sean Gilbert	.10	.05
❑	256	Keith Byars	.10	.05
❑	257	Scottie Graham RC	.20	.09
❑	258	Leonard Russell	.10	.05
❑	259	Eric Martin	.10	.05
❑	260	Jarrod Bunch	.10	.05
❑	261	Rob Moore	.20	.09
❑	262	Herschel Walker	.20	.09
❑	263	Levon Kirkland	.10	.05
❑	264	Chris Mims	.10	.05
❑	265	Ricky Watters	.40	.18
❑	266	Rick Mirer	.40	.18
❑	267	Santana Dotson	.20	.09
❑	268	Reggie Brooks	.20	.09
❑	269	Garrison Hearst	.40	.18
❑	270	Thurman Thomas	.40	.18
❑	271	Johnny Bailey	.10	.05
❑	272	Andre Rison	.20	.09
❑	273	Jim Kelly	.40	.18
❑	274	Mark Carrier DB	.10	.05
❑	275	David Klingler	.10	.05
❑	276	Eric Metcalf	.20	.09
❑	277	Troy Aikman	1.50	.70
❑	278	Simon Fletcher	.10	.05
❑	279	Pat Swilling	.10	.05
❑	280	Sterling Sharpe	.20	.09
❑	281	Cody Carlson	.10	.05
❑	282	Steve Emtman	.10	.05
❑	283	Neil Smith	.20	.09
❑	284	James Jett	.10	.05
❑	285	Shane Conlan	.10	.05
❑	286	Keith Jackson	.10	.05
❑	287	Qadry Ismail	.40	.18
❑	288	Chris Slade	.10	.05
❑	289	Derek Brown RBK	.10	.05
❑	290	Phil Simms	.20	.09
❑	291	Boomer Esiason	.20	.09
❑	292	Eric Allen	.10	.05
❑	293	Rod Woodson	.40	.18
❑	294	Ronnie Harmon	.10	.05
❑	295	John Taylor	.20	.09
❑	296	Ferrell Edmunds	.10	.05
❑	297	Craig Erickson	.10	.05
❑	298	Brian Mitchell	.10	.05
❑	299	Dante Jones	.10	.05
❑	300	John Copeland	.10	.05
❑	301	Steve Beuerlein	.10	.05
❑	302	Deion Sanders	.75	.35
❑	303	Andre Reed	.20	.09
❑	304	Curtis Conway	.40	.18
❑	305	Harold Green	.10	.05
❑	306	Vinny Testaverde	.20	.09
❑	307	Michael Irvin	.40	.18

Card	MINT	NRMT
❑ 308 Rod Bernstine	.10	.05
❑ 309 Chris Spielman	.20	.09
❑ 310 Reggie White	.40	.18
❑ 311 Gary Brown	.10	.05
❑ 312 Quentin Coryatt	.10	.05
❑ 313 Derrick Thomas	.40	.18
❑ 314 Greg Robinson	.10	.05
❑ 315 Troy Drayton	.10	.05
❑ 316 Terry Kirby	.40	.18
❑ 317 John Randle	.10	.05
❑ 318 Ben Coates	.40	.18
❑ 319 Tyrone Hughes	.20	.09
❑ 320 Corey Miller	.10	.05
❑ 321 Brad Baxter	.10	.05
❑ 322 Randall Cunningham	.40	.18
❑ 323 Greg Lloyd	.40	.18
❑ 324 Stan Humphries	.40	.18
❑ 325 Dana Stubblefield	.40	.18
❑ 326 Kelvin Martin	.10	.05
❑ 327 Hardy Nickerson	.20	.09
❑ 328 Desmond Howard	.20	.09
❑ 329 Mark Carrier WR	.20	.09
❑ 330 Daryl Johnston	.20	.09
❑ P19 Joe Montana Promo	2.00	.90

1994 Upper Deck Predictor Award Winners

	MINT	NRMT
COMPLETE SET (20)	50.00	22.00
STATED ODDS 1:20 HOBBY		
H PREFIX PRIZE SET (20)	30.00	13.50

*PRIZE STARS: .6X TO 1.2X BASE CARD HI
*PRIZE ROOKIES: .3X TO .6X BASE CARD HI
PRIZES FOR PREDICTOR WINNERS

Card	MINT	NRMT
❑ HP1 Emmitt Smith	8.00	3.60
❑ HP2 Barry Sanders W2	10.00	4.50
❑ HP3 Jerome Bettis	1.25	.55
❑ HP4 Joe Montana	10.00	4.50
❑ HP5 Dan Marino	10.00	4.50
❑ HP6 Marshall Faulk	6.00	2.70
❑ HP7 Dan Wilkinson	.30	.14
❑ HP8 Sterling Sharpe	.60	.25
❑ HP9 Thurman Thomas	1.25	.55
❑ HP10 The Longshot W1	.30	.14
❑ HP11 Marshall Faulk W1	6.00	2.70
❑ HP12 Trent Dilfer	2.50	1.10
❑ HP13 Heath Shuler	.60	.25
❑ HP14 David Palmer	1.50	.70
❑ HP15 Charles Johnson	.60	.25
❑ HP16 Greg Hill	1.50	.70
❑ HP17 Johnnie Morton	2.00	.90
❑ HP18 Errict Rhett	2.50	1.10
❑ HP19 Darnay Scott	2.00	.90
❑ HP20 The Longshot W2	.30	.14

1994 Upper Deck Predictor League Leaders

	MINT	NRMT
COMPLETE SET (30)	50.00	22.00
STATED ODDS 1:20 RETAIL		
R PREFIX PRIZE SET (30)	30.00	13.50

*PRIZE STARS: .6X to 1.2X BASE CARD HI
*PRIZE ROOKIES: .25X to .6X BASE CARD HI
PRIZES FOR PREDICTOR WINNERS

Card	MINT	NRMT
❑ RP1 Troy Aikman	5.00	2.20
❑ RP2 Steve Young	3.00	1.35
❑ RP3 John Elway	10.00	4.50
❑ RP4 Joe Montana	10.00	4.50
❑ RP5 Brett Favre	10.00	4.50
❑ RP6 Heath Shuler	.60	.25
❑ RP7 Dan Marino W2	10.00	4.50
❑ RP8 Rick Mirer	1.25	.55
❑ RP9 Drew Bledsoe W1	5.00	2.20
❑ RP10 The Longshot	.30	.14
❑ RP11 Emmitt Smith	8.00	3.60
❑ RP12 Barry Sanders W1	10.00	4.50
❑ RP13 Jerome Bettis	1.25	.55
❑ RP14 Rodney Hampton	1.25	.55
❑ RP15 Thurman Thomas	1.25	.55
❑ RP16 Marshall Faulk	6.00	2.70
❑ RP17 Barry Foster	.30	.14
❑ RP18 Reggie Brooks	.60	.25
❑ RP19 Ricky Watters	1.25	.55
❑ RP20 The Longshot W2	.30	.14
❑ RP21 Jerry Rice	5.00	2.20
❑ RP22 Sterling Sharpe	.60	.25
❑ RP23 Andre Rison	.60	.25
❑ RP24 Michael Irvin	1.25	.55
❑ RP25 Tim Brown	1.25	.55
❑ RP26 Shannon Sharpe	.60	.25
❑ RP27 Andre Reed	.60	.25
❑ RP28 Irving Fryar	.60	.25
❑ RP29 Charles Johnson	.60	.25
❑ RP30 The Longshot W2	.30	.14

1994 Upper Deck Pro Bowl

	MINT	NRMT
COMPLETE SET (20)	100.00	45.00
STATED ODDS 1:20		4.00

Card	MINT	NRMT
❑ PB1 Jerome Bettis	3.00	1.35
❑ PB2 Jay Novacek	1.50	.70
❑ PB3 Shannon Sharpe	1.50	.70
❑ PB4 Brent Jones	1.50	.70
❑ PB5 Andre Rison	1.50	.70
❑ PB6 Tim Brown	3.00	1.35
❑ PB7 Anthony Miller	1.50	.70
❑ PB8 Jerry Rice	12.00	5.50
❑ PB9 Brett Favre	25.00	11.00
❑ PB10 Emmitt Smith	20.00	9.00
❑ PB11 Steve Young	8.00	3.60
❑ PB12 John Elway	25.00	11.00
❑ PB13 Warren Moon	3.00	1.35
❑ PB14 Thurman Thomas	3.00	1.35
❑ PB15 Ricky Watters	3.00	1.35
❑ PB16 Rod Woodson	3.00	1.35
❑ PB17 Reggie White	3.00	1.35
❑ PB18 Tyrone Hughes	1.50	.70
❑ PB19 Derrick Thomas	3.00	1.35
❑ PB20 Checklist	1.50	.70

1995 Upper Deck

	MINT	NRMT
COMPLETE SET (300)	30.00	13.50
COMMON CARD (1-300)	.10	.05
SEMISTARS	.20	.09
UNLISTED STARS	.40	.18
COMP.ELEC.GOLD (300)	600.00	275.00
*GOLD STARS: 5X TO 12X HI COL.		
*GOLD RCs: 2.5X TO 6X HI		
GOLD STATED ODDS 1:35 RETAIL		
COMP.ELEC.SILVER (300)	125.00	55.00
*SILVER STARS: 1X TO 2.5X HI COL.		
*SILVER RCs: .6X TO 1.5X HI		
ONE GOLD OR SILVER PER RETAIL PACK		
TWO GOLD OR SILV.PER SPEC.RET.PACK		

Card	MINT	NRMT
❑ 1 Ki-Jana Carter RC	.40	.18
❑ 2 Tony Boselli RC	.20	.09
❑ 3 Steve McNair RC	4.00	1.80
❑ 4 Michael Westbrook RC	2.50	1.10
❑ 5 Kerry Collins RC	1.25	.55
❑ 6 Kevin Carter RC	.40	.18
❑ 7 James A.Stewart RC	.10	.05
❑ 8 Joey Galloway RC	4.00	1.80
❑ 9 Kyle Brady RC	.40	.18
❑ 10 J.J. Stokes RC	1.00	.45
❑ 11 Derrick Alexander DE RC	.10	.05
❑ 12 Warren Sapp RC	.60	.25
❑ 13 Mark Fields RC UER Linebacker on front, running back on back	.10	.05
❑ 14 Tyrone Wheatley RC	2.00	.90
❑ 15 Napoleon Kaufman RC	3.00	1.35
❑ 16 James O. Stewart RC	3.00	1.35
❑ 17 Luther Elliss RC	.10	.05
❑ 18 Rashaan Salaam RC	.40	.18
❑ 19 Jimmy Oliver RC	.10	.05
❑ 20 Mark Bruener RC	.20	.09
❑ 21 Derrick Brooks RC	.10	.05
❑ 22 Christian Fauria RC	.10	.05
❑ 23 Ray Zellars RC	.20	.09
❑ 24 Todd Collins RC	.40	.18
❑ 25 Sherman Williams RC	.10	.05
❑ 26 Frank Sanders RC	1.25	.55
❑ 27 Rodney Thomas RC	.40	.18
❑ 28 Rob Johnson RC	2.50	1.10
❑ 29 Steve Stenstrom RC	.10	.05
❑ 30 Curtis Martin RC	4.00	1.80
❑ 31 Gary Clark	.10	.05
❑ 32 Troy Aikman	1.50	.70
❑ 33 Mike Sherrard	.10	.05
❑ 34 Fred Barnett	.20	.09
❑ 35 Henry Ellard	.20	.09
❑ 36 Terry Allen	.20	.09

No.	Player	Price	Price
❑ 37	Jeff Graham	.10	.05
❑ 38	Herman Moore	.40	.18
❑ 39	Brett Favre	3.00	1.35
❑ 40	Trent Dilfer	.40	.18
❑ 41	Derek Brown RBK	.10	.05
❑ 42	Andre Rison	.20	.09
❑ 43	Flipper Anderson	.10	.05
❑ 44	Jerry Rice	1.50	.70
❑ 45	Andre Reed	.20	.09
❑ 46	Sean Dawkins	.20	.09
❑ 47	Irving Fryar	.20	.09
❑ 48	Vincent Brisby	.10	.05
❑ 49	Rob Moore	.10	.05
❑ 50	Carl Pickens	.40	.18
❑ 51	Vinny Testaverde	.20	.09
❑ 52	Ray Childress	.10	.05
❑ 53	Eric Green	.10	.05
❑ 54	Anthony Miller	.20	.09
❑ 55	Lake Dawson	.20	.09
❑ 56	Tim Brown	.40	.18
❑ 57	Stan Humphries	.20	.09
❑ 58	Rick Mirer	.40	.18
❑ 59	Randal Hill	.10	.05
❑ 60	Charles Haley	.20	.09
❑ 61	Chris Calloway	.10	.05
❑ 62	Calvin Williams	.20	.09
❑ 63	Ethan Horton	.10	.05
❑ 64	Cris Carter	.40	.18
❑ 65	Curtis Conway	.40	.18
❑ 66	Scott Mitchell	.20	.09
❑ 67	Edgar Bennett	.20	.09
❑ 68	Craig Erickson	.10	.05
❑ 69	Jim Everett	.10	.05
❑ 70	Terance Mathis	.20	.09
❑ 71	Robert Young	.10	.05
❑ 72	Brent Jones	.10	.05
❑ 73	Thurman Thomas	.40	.18
❑ 74	Marshall Faulk	.75	.35
❑ 75	O.J. McDuffie	.40	.18
❑ 76	Ben Coates	.20	.09
❑ 77	Johnny Mitchell	.10	.05
❑ 78	Darnay Scott	.40	.18
❑ 79	Derrick Alexander WR	.40	.18
❑ 80	Lorenzo White	.10	.05
❑ 81	Charles Johnson	.20	.09
❑ 82	John Elway	3.00	1.35
❑ 83	Willie Davis	.20	.09
❑ 84	James Jett	.20	.09
❑ 85	Mark Seay	.20	.09
❑ 86	Brian Blades	.20	.09
❑ 87	Ronald Moore	.10	.05
❑ 88	Alvin Harper	.10	.05
❑ 89	Dave Brown	.20	.09
❑ 90	Randall Cunningham	.40	.18
❑ 91	Heath Shuler	.40	.18
❑ 92	Jake Reed	.20	.09
❑ 93	Donnell Woolford	.10	.05
❑ 94	Barry Sanders	3.00	1.35
❑ 95	Reggie White	.40	.18
❑ 96	Lawrence Dawsey	.10	.05
❑ 97	Michael Haynes	.20	.09
❑ 98	Bert Emanuel	.40	.18
❑ 99	Troy Drayton	.10	.05
❑ 100	Steve Young	1.25	.55
❑ 101	Bruce Smith	.40	.18
❑ 102	Roosevelt Potts	.10	.05
❑ 103	Dan Marino	3.00	1.35
❑ 104	Michael Timpson	.10	.05
❑ 105	Boomer Esiason	.20	.09
❑ 106	David Klingler	.20	.09
❑ 107	Eric Metcalf	.20	.09
❑ 108	Gary Brown	.10	.05
❑ 109	Neil O'Donnell	.20	.09
❑ 110	Shannon Sharpe	.20	.09
❑ 111	Joe Montana	3.00	1.35
❑ 112	Jeff Hostetler	.20	.09
❑ 113	Ronnie Harmon	.10	.05
❑ 114	Chris Warren	.20	.09
❑ 115	Larry Centers	.20	.09
❑ 116	Michael Irvin	.40	.18
❑ 117	Rodney Hampton	.20	.09
❑ 118	Herschel Walker	.20	.09
❑ 119	Reggie Brooks	.20	.09
❑ 120	Qadry Ismail	.20	.09
❑ 121	Chris Zorich	.10	.05
❑ 122	Chris Spielman	.20	.09
❑ 123	Sean Jones	.10	.05
❑ 124	Errict Rhett	.40	.18
❑ 125	Tyrone Hughes	.20	.09
❑ 126	Jeff George	.20	.09
❑ 127	Chris Miller	.10	.05
❑ 128	Ricky Watters	.40	.18
❑ 129	Jim Kelly	.40	.18
❑ 130	Tony Bennett	.10	.05
❑ 131	Terry Kirby	.20	.09
❑ 132	Drew Bledsoe	1.50	.70
❑ 133	Johnny Johnson	.10	.05
❑ 134	Dan Wilkinson	.20	.09
❑ 135	Leroy Hoard	.10	.05
❑ 136	Darryl Lewis	.10	.05
❑ 137	Barry Foster	.20	.09
❑ 138	Shane Dronett	.10	.05
❑ 139	Marcus Allen	.40	.18
❑ 140	Harvey Williams	.10	.05
❑ 141	Tony Martin	.20	.09
❑ 142	Rod Stephens	.10	.05
❑ 143	Eric Swann	.20	.09
❑ 144	Daryl Johnston	.20	.09
❑ 145	Dave Meggett	.10	.05
❑ 146	Charlie Garner	.20	.09
❑ 147	Ken Harvey	.10	.05
❑ 148	Warren Moon	.20	.09
❑ 149	Steve Walsh	.10	.05
❑ 150	Pat Swilling	.10	.05
❑ 151	Terrell Buckley	.10	.05
❑ 152	Courtney Hawkins	.10	.05
❑ 153	Willie Roaf	.10	.05
❑ 154	Chris Doleman	.10	.05
❑ 155	Jerome Bettis	.40	.18
❑ 156	Dana Stubblefield	.40	.18
❑ 157	Cornelius Bennett	.20	.09
❑ 158	Quentin Coryatt	.20	.09
❑ 159	Bryan Cox	.10	.05
❑ 160	Marion Butts	.10	.05
❑ 161	Aaron Glenn	.10	.05
❑ 162	Louis Oliver	.10	.05
❑ 163	Eric Turner	.10	.05
❑ 164	Cris Dishman	.10	.05
❑ 165	John L. Williams	.10	.05
❑ 166	Simon Fletcher	.10	.05
❑ 167	Neil Smith	.20	.09
❑ 168	Chester McGlockton	.20	.09
❑ 169	Natrone Means	.40	.18
❑ 170	Sam Adams	.10	.05
❑ 171	Clyde Simmons	.10	.05
❑ 172	Jay Novacek	.20	.09
❑ 173	Keith Hamilton	.10	.05
❑ 174	William Fuller	.10	.05
❑ 175	Tom Carter	.10	.05
❑ 176	John Randle	.10	.05
❑ 177	Lewis Tillman	.10	.05
❑ 178	Mel Gray	.10	.05
❑ 179	George Teague	.10	.05
❑ 180	Hardy Nickerson	.10	.05
❑ 181	Mario Bates	.40	.18
❑ 182	D.J. Johnson	.10	.05
❑ 183	Sean Gilbert	.20	.09
❑ 184	Bryant Young	.20	.09
❑ 185	Jeff Burris	.10	.05
❑ 186	Floyd Turner	.10	.05
❑ 187	Troy Vincent	.10	.05
❑ 188	Willie McGinest	.20	.09
❑ 189	James Hasty	.10	.05
❑ 190	Jeff Blake RC	1.25	.55
❑ 191	Stevon Moore	.10	.05
❑ 192	Ernest Givins	.10	.05
❑ 193	Byron Bam Morris	.20	.09
❑ 194	Ray Crockett	.10	.05
❑ 195	Dale Carter	.20	.09
❑ 196	Terry McDaniel	.10	.05
❑ 197	Leslie O'Neal	.20	.09
❑ 198	Cortez Kennedy	.20	.09
❑ 199	Seth Joyner	.10	.05
❑ 200	Emmitt Smith	2.50	1.10
❑ 201	Thomas Lewis	.20	.09
❑ 202	Andy Harmon	.10	.05
❑ 203	Ricky Ervins	.10	.05
❑ 204	Fuad Reveiz	.10	.05
❑ 205	John Thierry	.10	.05
❑ 206	Bennie Blades	.10	.05
❑ 207	LeShon Johnson	.20	.09
❑ 208	Charles Wilson	.10	.05
❑ 209	Joe Johnson	.10	.05
❑ 210	Chuck Smith	.10	.05
❑ 211	Roman Phifer	.10	.05
❑ 212	Ken Norton Jr.	.20	.09
❑ 213	Bucky Brooks	.10	.05
❑ 214	Ray Buchanan	.10	.05
❑ 215	Tim Bowens	.10	.05
❑ 216	Vincent Brown	.10	.05
❑ 217	Marcus Turner	.10	.05
❑ 218	Derrick Fenner	.10	.05
❑ 219	Antonio Langham	.10	.05
❑ 220	Cody Carlson	.10	.05
❑ 221	Greg Lloyd	.20	.09
❑ 222	Steve Atwater	.10	.05
❑ 223	Donnell Bennett	.20	.09
❑ 224	Rocket Ismail	.20	.09
❑ 225	John Carney	.10	.05
❑ 226	Eugene Robinson	.10	.05
❑ 227	Aeneas Williams	.10	.05
❑ 228	Darrin Smith	.10	.05
❑ 229	Phillippi Sparks	.10	.05
❑ 230	Eric Allen	.10	.05
❑ 231	Brian Mitchell	.10	.05
❑ 232	David Palmer	.20	.09
❑ 233	Mark Carrier DB	.10	.05
❑ 234	Dave Krieg	.10	.05
❑ 235	Robert Brooks	.40	.18
❑ 236	Eric Curry	.10	.05
❑ 237	Wayne Martin	.10	.05
❑ 238	Craig Heyward	.20	.09
❑ 239	Isaac Bruce	.75	.35
❑ 240	Deion Sanders	1.00	.45
❑ 241	Steve Tasker	.20	.09
❑ 242	Jim Harbaugh	.20	.09
❑ 243	Aubrey Beavers	.10	.05
❑ 244	Chris Slade	.20	.09
❑ 245	Mo Lewis	.10	.05
❑ 246	Alfred Williams	.10	.05
❑ 247	Michael Dean Perry	.10	.05
❑ 248	Marcus Robertson	.10	.05
❑ 249	Kevin Greene	.20	.09
❑ 250	Leonard Russell	.10	.05
❑ 251	Greg Hill	.20	.09
❑ 252	Rob Fredrickson	.10	.05
❑ 253	Junior Seau	.40	.18
❑ 254	Rick Tuten	.10	.05
❑ 255	Garrison Hearst	.40	.18
❑ 256	Russell Maryland	.10	.05
❑ 257	Michael Brooks	.10	.05
❑ 258	Bernard Williams	.10	.05
❑ 259	Reggie Roby	.10	.05
❑ 260	Dewayne Washington	.20	.09
❑ 261	Raymont Harris	.10	.05
❑ 262	Brett Perriman	.20	.09
❑ 263	LeRoy Butler	.10	.05
❑ 264	Santana Dotson	.10	.05
❑ 265	Irv Smith	.10	.05
❑ 266	Ron George	.10	.05
❑ 267	Marquez Pope	.10	.05
❑ 268	William Floyd	.40	.18
❑ 269	Matt Darby	.10	.05
❑ 270	Jeff Herrod	.10	.05
❑ 271	Bernie Parmalee	.20	.09
❑ 272	Leroy Thompson	.10	.05
❑ 273	Ronnie Lott	.20	.09
❑ 274	Steve Tovar	.10	.05
❑ 275	Michael Jackson	.20	.09
❑ 276	Al Smith	.10	.05
❑ 277	Rod Woodson	.20	.09
❑ 278	Glyn Milburn	.10	.05
❑ 279	Kimble Anders	.20	.09
❑ 280	Anthony Smith	.10	.05
❑ 281	Andre Coleman	.10	.05
❑ 282	Terry Wooden	.10	.05
❑ 283	Mickey Washington	.10	.05
❑ 284	Steve Beuerlein	.10	.05
❑ 285	Mark Brunell	1.50	.70
❑ 286	Keith Goganious	.10	.05
❑ 287	Desmond Howard	.20	.09
❑ 288	Darren Carrington	.10	.05
❑ 289	Derek Brown TE	.10	.05
❑ 290	Reggie Cobb	.10	.05
❑ 291	Jeff Lageman	.10	.05
❑ 292	Lamar Lathon	.10	.05
❑ 293	Sam Mills	.20	.09
❑ 294	Carlton Bailey	.10	.05

❑ 295 Mark Carrier WR .20 .09
❑ 296 Willie Green .20 .09
❑ 297 Frank Reich .10 .05
❑ 298 Don Beebe .10 .05
❑ 299 Tim McKyer .10 .05
❑ 300 Pete Metzelaars .10 .05
❑ P1 Joe Montana Promo 2.00 .90
base brand card
Numbered 19
❑ P2 Joe Montana Promo 2.00 .90
Predictor card
Numbered 19
❑ P3 Marshall Faulk Promo 1.50 .70
Pro Bowl hologram card
Numbered PB95

1995 Upper Deck Joe Montana Trilogy

	MINT	NRMT
COMPLETE SET (23)	60.00	27.00
COMP.CC SERIES 1 (9)	20.00	9.00
COMP.UD SERIES 2 (9)	25.00	11.00
COMP.SP SERIES 3 (5)	20.00	9.00
COMMON CC	3.00	1.35
COMMON UD	4.00	1.80
COMMON SP	5.00	2.20

MT1-MT8: COL. CHOICE STATED ODDS 1:12
MT9-MT16: UP. DECK STATED ODDS 1:12
MT17-MT21: SP STATED ODDS 1:29

❑ MT1 Joe Montana 3.00 1.35
1977-NCAA Champs
❑ MT2 Joe Montana 3.00 1.35
1978-Cotton Bowl
❑ MT3 Joe Montana 3.00 1.35
The 1978 NFL Draft
❑ MT4 Joe Montana 3.00 1.35
The Catch
❑ MT5 Joe Montana 3.00 1.35
Super Bowl XVI
❑ MT6 Joe Montana 3.00 1.35
Super Bowl XVI MVP
❑ MT7 Joe Montana 3.00 1.35
Super Bowl XIX
❑ MT8 Joe Montana 3.00 1.35
Super Bowl XIX MVP
❑ MT9 Joe Montana 4.00 1.80
The Drive
❑ MT10 Joe Montana 4.00 1.80
Super Bowl XXIII
❑ MT11 Joe Montana 4.00 1.80
1989-Dream Season
❑ MT12 Joe Montana 4.00 1.80
NFL MVP
Back-To-Back
❑ MT13 Joe Montana 4.00 1.80
Super Bowl XXIV
❑ MT14 Joe Montana 4.00 1.80
Super Bowl XXIV
MVP
❑ MT15 Joe Montana 4.00 1.80
Back-To-Back
Super Bowls
❑ MT16 Joe Montana 4.00 1.80
The Comeback
❑ MT17 Joe Montana 5.00 2.20
❑ MT18 Joe Montana 5.00 2.20
❑ MT19 Joe Montana 5.00 2.20
❑ MT20 Joe Montana 5.00 2.20
❑ CCH Collector's Choice Header 3.00 1.35
❑ SPH SP Header 4.00 1.80
❑ UDH Upper Deck Header 5.00 2.20

1995 Upper Deck Predictor Award Winners

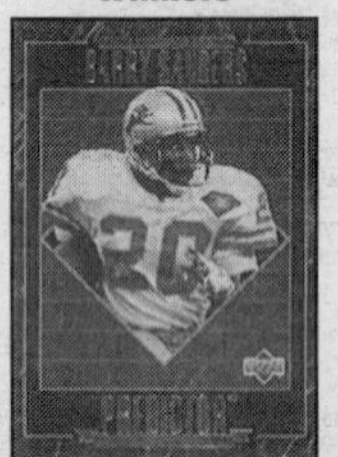

	MINT	NRMT
COMPLETE SET (20)	60.00	27.00

STATED ODDS 1:35 HOBBY
*PRIZE STARS: .6X TO 1.5X BASE CARD HI
*PRIZE ROOKIES: .3X TO .8X BASE CARD HI
REDEEMED PRIZES FOR PREDICT.WINNERS

❑ HP1 Dan Marino 10.00 4.50
❑ HP2 Steve Young 4.00 1.80
❑ HP3 Drew Bledsoe 5.00 2.20
❑ HP4 Troy Aikman 5.00 2.20
❑ HP5 Barry Sanders 10.00 4.50
❑ HP6 Emmitt Smith 8.00 3.60
❑ HP7 Jerry Rice W2 5.00 2.20
❑ HP8 Steve McNair 6.00 2.70
❑ HP9 Natrone Means 1.50 .70
❑ HP10 The Longshot W1 .30 .14
❑ HP11 Ki-Jana Carter .60 .25
❑ HP12 Steve McNair 6.00 2.70
❑ HP13 Michael Westbrook 4.00 1.80
❑ HP14 Kerry Collins 2.00 .90
❑ HP15 Joey Galloway 6.00 2.70
❑ HP16 Kyle Brady .60 .25
❑ HP17 Napoleon Kaufman 5.00 2.20
❑ HP18 Tyrone Wheatley 3.00 1.35
❑ HP19 Rashaan Salaam .60 .25
❑ HP20 The Longshot W1 .30 .14

1995 Upper Deck Predictor League Leaders

	MINT	NRMT
COMPLETE SET (30)	80.00	36.00

STATED ODDS 1:30 RET,1:17 SPEC.RET
*PRIZE STARS: .6X TO 1.5X BASE CARD HI
*PRIZE ROOKIES: .3X TO .8X BASE CARD HI
REDEEMED PRIZES FOR PREDICT.WINNERS

❑ RP1 Dan Marino 10.00 4.50
❑ RP2 Steve Young 4.00 1.80
❑ RP3 Drew Bledsoe 5.00 2.20
❑ RP4 Troy Aikman 5.00 2.20
❑ RP5 John Elway 10.00 4.50
❑ RP6 Brett Favre W2 10.00 4.50
❑ RP7 Stan Humphries .75 .35
❑ RP8 Jeff George .75 .35
❑ RP9 Kerry Collins 2.00 .90
❑ RP10 The Longshot W1 .30 .14
❑ RP11 Barry Sanders W2 10.00 4.50
❑ RP12 Chris Warren .75 .35
❑ RP13 Emmitt Smith W1 8.00 3.60
❑ RP14 Natrone Means 1.50 .70
❑ RP15 Rodney Hampton .75 .35
❑ RP16 Marshall Faulk 2.50 1.10
❑ RP17 Errict Rhett 1.50 .70
❑ RP18 Napoleon Kaufman 5.00 2.20
❑ RP19 Ki-Jana Carter .60 .25
❑ RP20 The Longshot .30 .14
❑ RP21 Jerry Rice W1 5.00 2.20
❑ RP22 Ben Coates .75 .35
❑ RP23 Cris Carter 1.50 .70
❑ RP24 Andre Reed .75 .35
❑ RP25 Andre Rison .75 .35
❑ RP26 Tim Brown 1.50 .70
❑ RP27 Michael Irvin 1.50 .70
❑ RP28 Irving Fryar .75 .35
❑ RP29 Michael Westbrook 4.00 1.80
❑ RP30 The Longshot W2 .30 .14

1995 Upper Deck Pro Bowl

	MINT	NRMT
COMPLETE SET (25)	100.00	45.00

STATED ODDS 1:25

❑ PB1 Barry Sanders 25.00 11.00
❑ PB2 Brent Jones .75 .35
❑ PB3 Cris Carter 3.00 1.35
❑ PB4 Emmitt Smith 20.00 9.00
❑ PB5 Jay Novacek 1.50 .70
❑ PB6 Jerome Bettis 3.00 1.35
❑ PB7 Jerry Rice 12.00 5.50
❑ PB8 Michael Irvin 3.00 1.35
❑ PB9 Ricky Watters 3.00 1.35
❑ PB10 Steve Young 10.00 4.50
❑ PB11 Troy Aikman 12.00 5.50
❑ PB12 Warren Moon 1.50 .70
❑ PB13 Terance Mathis 1.50 .70
❑ PB14 Ben Coates 1.50 .70
❑ PB15 Chris Warren 1.50 .70
❑ PB16 Dan Marino 25.00 11.00
❑ PB17 Drew Bledsoe 12.00 5.50
❑ PB18 Irving Fryar 1.50 .70
❑ PB19 Jeff Hostetler 1.50 .70
❑ PB20 John Elway 25.00 11.00
❑ PB21 Leroy Hoard .75 .35
❑ PB22 Marshall Faulk 6.00 2.70
❑ PB23 Natrone Means 3.00 1.35
❑ PB24 Tim Brown 3.00 1.35
❑ PB25 Checklist 1.50 .70

1995 Upper Deck Special Edition

	MINT	NRMT
COMPLETE SET (90)	30.00	13.50
ONE SILVER PER HOBBY PACK		
*GOLD SE STARS: 5X TO 10X BASE CARD HI		
*GOLD SE ROOKIES: 2.5X TO 5X BASE CARD HI		
GOLD STATED ODDS 1:35 HOBBY		

Card	MINT	NRMT
❑ SE1 Terry Kirby	.30	.14
❑ SE2 Marcus Allen	.60	.25
❑ SE3 Bernie Parmalee	.30	.14
❑ SE4 Vernon Turner	.15	.07
❑ SE5 Dolphins Defense	.15	.07
❑ SE6 Kevin Turner	.15	.07
❑ SE7 Henry Thomas	.15	.07
❑ SE8 Barry Sanders	5.00	2.20
❑ SE9 Marshall Faulk	1.25	.55
❑ SE10 Bill Bates	.30	.14
❑ SE11 Stan Humphries	.30	.14
❑ SE12 Barry Foster	.30	.14
❑ SE13 Shannon Sharpe	.30	.14
❑ SE14 Joe Montana	5.00	2.20
❑ SE15 Bryan Cox	.15	.07
❑ SE16 Dale Carter	.30	.14
❑ SE17 Drew Bledsoe	2.50	1.10
❑ SE18 Dan Marino	5.00	2.20
❑ SE19 Ricky Watters	.60	.25
❑ SE20 Alvin Harper	.15	.07
❑ SE21 Harris Barton	.15	.07
❑ SE22 Dan Marino	5.00	2.20
❑ SE23 Ronnie Harmon	.15	.07
❑ SE24 Michael Irvin	.60	.25
❑ SE25 Emmitt Smith	4.00	1.80
❑ SE26 Jeff Christy	.15	.07
❑ SE27 Terry Allen	.30	.14
❑ SE28 Randall Cunningham	.60	.25
❑ SE29 Todd Steussie	.15	.07
❑ SE30 Warren Moon	.30	.14
❑ SE31 Robert Griffith	.15	.07
❑ SE32 Tony Tolbert	.15	.07
❑ SE33 William Fuller	.15	.07
❑ SE34 Bernard Williams	.15	.07
❑ SE35 Charlie Garner	.30	.14
❑ SE36 Troy Aikman	2.50	1.10
❑ SE37 Alvin Harper	.15	.07
❑ SE38 Kenneth Gant	.15	.07
❑ SE39 Daryl Johnston	.30	.14
❑ SE40 Ben Coates	.30	.14
❑ SE41 Rickey Jackson	.15	.07
❑ SE42 O.J. McDuffie	.60	.25
❑ SE43 Marion Butts	.15	.07
❑ SE44 The Snap	.15	.07
❑ SE45 Kimble Anders	.30	.14
❑ SE46 Chiefs Defense	.30	.14
❑ SE47 Richmond Webb	.15	.07
❑ SE48 Carlos Jenkins	.15	.07
❑ SE49 James Harris DE	.15	.07
❑ SE50 Dexter Carter	.15	.07
❑ SE51 Qadry Ismail	.30	.14
❑ SE52 Jeff Herrod	.15	.07
❑ SE53 Sean Jones	.15	.07
❑ SE54 Keith Sims	.15	.07
❑ SE55 William Floyd	.60	.25
❑ SE56 Don Majkowski	.15	.07
❑ SE57 Chargers Defense	.15	.07
❑ SE58 Byron Evans	.15	.07
❑ SE59 Chad Hennings	.15	.07
❑ SE60 Eric Allen	.15	.07
❑ SE61 Curtis Martin	3.00	1.35
❑ SE62 Napoleon Kaufman	2.50	1.10
❑ SE63 Kevin Carter	.30	.14
❑ SE64 Luther Elliss	.10	.05
❑ SE65 Frank Sanders	1.00	.45
❑ SE66 Rob Johnson	2.00	.90
❑ SE67 Christian Fauria	.10	.05
❑ SE68 Kyle Brady	.30	.14
❑ SE69 Ray Zellars	.15	.07
❑ SE70 James A.Stewart	.10	.05
❑ SE71 Ty Law	.15	.07
❑ SE72 Rodney Thomas	.30	.14
❑ SE73 Jimmy Oliver	.10	.05
❑ SE74 James O. Stewart	2.50	1.10
❑ SE75 Dave Barr	.15	.07
❑ SE76 Kordell Stewart	4.00	1.80
❑ SE77 Michael Westbrook	2.00	.90
❑ SE78 Bobby Taylor	.15	.07
❑ SE79 Mark Fields	.10	.05
❑ SE80 Kerry Collins	1.00	.45
❑ SE81 Natrone Means	.60	.25
❑ SE82 Mark Seay	.30	.14
❑ SE83 Deion Sanders	1.50	.70
❑ SE84 Dana Stubblefield	.60	.25
❑ SE85 49ers Defense	.30	.14
❑ SE86 Alfred Pupunu	.15	.07
❑ SE87 Tim Harris	.15	.07
❑ SE88 Jerry Rice	2.50	1.10
❑ SE89 Steve Young	2.00	.90
❑ SE90 Steve Young Jerry Rice	2.50	1.10

1996 Upper Deck

	MINT	NRMT
COMPLETE SET (300)	30.00	13.50
COMMON CARD (1-300)	.10	.05
SEMISTARS	.25	.11
UNLISTED STARS	.50	.23

Card	MINT	NRMT
❑ 1 Keyshawn Johnson RC	2.50	1.10
❑ 2 Kevin Hardy RC	.50	.23
❑ 3 Simeon Rice RC	.50	.23
❑ 4 Jonathan Ogden RC	.10	.05
❑ 5 Cedric Jones RC	.10	.05
❑ 6 Lawrence Phillips RC	.60	.25
❑ 7 Tim Biakabutuka RC	1.00	.45
❑ 8 Terry Glenn RC	1.50	.70
❑ 9 Rickey Dudley RC	.50	.23
❑ 10 Willie Anderson RC	.10	.05
❑ 11 Alex Molden RC	.10	.05
❑ 12 Regan Upshaw RC	.10	.05
❑ 13 Walt Harris RC	.10	.05
❑ 14 Eddie George RC	4.00	1.80
❑ 15 John Mobley RC	.10	.05
❑ 16 Duane Clemons RC	.10	.05
❑ 17 Eddie Kennison RC	.50	.23
❑ 18 Marvin Harrison RC	2.50	1.10
❑ 19 Daryl Gardener RC	.10	.05
❑ 20 Leeland McElroy RC	.50	.23
❑ 21 Eric Moulds RC	2.00	.90
❑ 22 Alex Van Dyke RC	.25	.11
❑ 23 Mike Alstott RC	1.50	.70
❑ 24 Jeff Lewis RC	.60	.25
❑ 25 Bobby Engram RC	.50	.23
❑ 26 Derrick Mayes RC	1.00	.45
❑ 27 Karim Abdul-Jabbar RC	1.00	.45
❑ 28 Bobby Hoying RC	.60	.25
❑ 29 Stepfret Williams RC	.25	.11
❑ 30 Chris Darkins RC	.10	.05
❑ 31 Stephen Davis RC	4.00	1.80
❑ 32 Danny Kanell RC	.50	.23
❑ 33 Tony Brackens RC	.25	.11
❑ 34 Leslie O'Neal	.10	.05
❑ 35 Chris Doleman	.10	.05
❑ 36 Larry Brown	.10	.05
❑ 37 Ronnie Harmon	.10	.05
❑ 38 Chris Spielman	.10	.05
❑ 39 John Jurkovic	.10	.05
❑ 40 Shawn Jefferson	.10	.05
❑ 41 William Floyd	.25	.11
❑ 42 Eric Davis	.10	.05
❑ 43 Willie Clay	.10	.05
❑ 44 Marco Coleman	.10	.05
❑ 45 Lorenzo White	.10	.05
❑ 46 Neil O'Donnell	.25	.11
❑ 47 Natrone Means	.50	.23
❑ 48 Cornelius Bennett	.10	.05
❑ 49 Steve Walsh	.10	.05
❑ 50 Jerome Bettis	.50	.23
❑ 51 Boomer Esiason	.25	.11
❑ 52 Glyn Milburn	.10	.05
❑ 53 Kevin Greene	.25	.11
❑ 54 Seth Joyner	.10	.05
❑ 55 Jeff Graham	.10	.05
❑ 56 Darren Woodson	.25	.11
❑ 57 Dale Carter	.10	.05
❑ 58 Lorenzo Lynch	.10	.05
❑ 59 Tim Brown	.50	.23
❑ 60 Jerry Rice	1.25	.55
❑ 61 Garrison Hearst	.25	.11
❑ 62 Eric Metcalf	.10	.05
❑ 63 Leroy Hoard	.10	.05
❑ 64 Thurman Thomas	.50	.23
❑ 65 Sam Mills	.10	.05
❑ 66 Curtis Conway	.50	.23
❑ 67 Carl Pickens	.50	.23
❑ 68 Deion Sanders	.75	.35
❑ 69 Shannon Sharpe	.25	.11
❑ 70 Herman Moore	.50	.23
❑ 71 Robert Brooks	.50	.23
❑ 72 Rodney Thomas	.10	.05
❑ 73 Ken Dilger	.25	.11
❑ 74 Mark Brunell	1.25	.55
❑ 75 Marcus Allen	.50	.23
❑ 76 Dan Marino	2.50	1.10
❑ 77 Robert Smith	.25	.11
❑ 78 Drew Bledsoe	1.25	.55
❑ 79 Jim Everett	.10	.05
❑ 80 Rodney Hampton	.25	.11
❑ 81 Adrian Murrell	.50	.23
❑ 82 Daryl Hobbs	.10	.05
❑ 83 Ricky Watters	.25	.11
❑ 84 Yancey Thigpen	.25	.11
❑ 85 Roman Phifer	.10	.05
❑ 86 Tony Martin	.25	.11
❑ 87 Dana Stubblefield	.25	.11
❑ 88 Joey Galloway	1.00	.45
❑ 89 Errict Rhett	.25	.11
❑ 90 Terry Allen	.25	.11
❑ 91 Aeneas Williams	.10	.05
❑ 92 Craig Heyward	.10	.05
❑ 93 Vinny Testaverde	.25	.11
❑ 94 Bryce Paup	.10	.05
❑ 95 Kerry Collins	.50	.23
❑ 96 Rashaan Salaam	.50	.23
❑ 97 Dan Wilkinson	.10	.05
❑ 98 Jay Novacek	.10	.05
❑ 99 John Elway	2.50	1.10
❑ 100 Bennie Blades	.10	.05
❑ 101 Edgar Bennett	.25	.11
❑ 102 Darryll Lewis	.10	.05
❑ 103 Marshall Faulk	.50	.23
❑ 104 Bryan Schwartz	.10	.05
❑ 105 Tamarick Vanover	.25	.11
❑ 106 Terry Kirby	.25	.11
❑ 107 John Randle	.10	.05
❑ 108 Ted Johnson RC	.10	.05
❑ 109 Mario Bates	.25	.11
❑ 110 Phillippi Sparks	.10	.05
❑ 111 Marvin Washington	.10	.05
❑ 112 Terry McDaniel	.10	.05
❑ 113 Bobby Taylor	.10	.05
❑ 114 Carnell Lake	.10	.05
❑ 115 Troy Drayton	.10	.05
❑ 116 Darren Bennett	.10	.05
❑ 117 J.J. Stokes	.50	.23
❑ 118 Rick Mirer	.25	.11
❑ 119 Jackie Harris	.10	.05
❑ 120 Ken Harvey	.10	.05
❑ 121 Rob Moore	.25	.11
❑ 122 Jeff George	.25	.11
❑ 123 Andre Rison	.25	.11
❑ 124 Darick Holmes	.10	.05
❑ 125 Tim McKyer	.10	.05
❑ 126 Alonzo Spellman	.10	.05
❑ 127 Jeff Blake	.50	.23
❑ 128 Kevin Williams	.10	.05
❑ 129 Anthony Miller	.25	.11
❑ 130 Barry Sanders	2.50	1.10
❑ 131 Brett Favre	2.50	1.10
❑ 132 Steve McNair	1.00	.45
❑ 133 Jim Harbaugh	.25	.11

❑ 134 Desmond Howard .25 .11
❑ 135 Steve Bono .10 .05
❑ 136 Bernie Parmalee .10 .05
❑ 137 Warren Moon .25 .11
❑ 138 Curtis Martin 1.00 .45
❑ 139 Irv Smith .10 .05
❑ 140 Thomas Lewis .10 .05
❑ 141 Kyle Brady .10 .05
❑ 142 Napoleon Kaufman .75 .35
❑ 143 Mike Mamula .10 .05
❑ 144 Erric Pegram .10 .05
❑ 145 Isaac Bruce .50 .23
❑ 146 Andre Coleman .10 .05
❑ 147 Merton Hanks .10 .05
❑ 148 Brian Blades .10 .05
❑ 149 Hardy Nickerson .10 .05
❑ 150 Michael Westbrook .50 .23
❑ 151 Larry Centers .25 .11
❑ 152 Morten Andersen .10 .05
❑ 153 Michael Jackson .25 .11
❑ 154 Bruce Smith .25 .11
❑ 155 Derrick Moore .10 .05
❑ 156 Mark Carrier DB .10 .05
❑ 157 John Copeland .10 .05
❑ 158 Emmitt Smith 2.00 .90
❑ 159 Jason Elam .10 .05
❑ 160 Scott Mitchell .25 .11
❑ 161 Mark Chmura .25 .11
❑ 162 Blaine Bishop .10 .05
❑ 163 Tony Bennett .10 .05
❑ 164 Pete Mitchell .25 .11
❑ 165 Dan Saleaumua .10 .05
❑ 166 Pete Stoyanovich .10 .05
❑ 167 Cris Carter .50 .23
❑ 168 Vince Brisby .10 .05
❑ 169 Wayne Martin .10 .05
❑ 170 Tyrone Wheatley .25 .11
❑ 171 Mo Lewis .10 .05
❑ 172 Harvey Williams .10 .05
❑ 173 Calvin Williams .10 .05
❑ 174 Norm Johnson .10 .05
❑ 175 Mark Rypien .10 .05
❑ 176 Stan Humphries .25 .11
❑ 177 Derek Loville .10 .05
❑ 178 Christian Fauria .10 .05
❑ 179 Warren Sapp .10 .05
❑ 180 Henry Ellard .10 .05
❑ 181 Jamir Miller .10 .05
❑ 182 Jessie Tuggle .10 .05
❑ 183 Stevon Moore .10 .05
❑ 184 Jim Kelly .50 .23
❑ 185 Mark Carrier WR .10 .05
❑ 186 Chris Zorich .10 .05
❑ 187 Harold Green .10 .05
❑ 188 Chris Boniol .10 .05
❑ 189 Allen Aldridge .10 .05
❑ 190 Brett Perriman .10 .05
❑ 191 Chris Jacke .10 .05
❑ 192 Todd McNair .10 .05
❑ 193 Floyd Turner .10 .05
❑ 194 Jeff Lageman .10 .05
❑ 195 Derrick Thomas .25 .11
❑ 196 Eric Green .10 .05
❑ 197 Orlando Thomas .10 .05
❑ 198 Ben Coates .25 .11
❑ 199 Tyrone Hughes .10 .05
❑ 200 Dave Brown .10 .05
❑ 201 Brad Baxter .10 .05
❑ 202 Chester McGlockton .10 .05
❑ 203 Rodney Peete .10 .05
❑ 204 Willie Williams .10 .05
❑ 205 Kevin Carter .10 .05
❑ 206 Aaron Hayden RC .10 .05
❑ 207 Steve Young 1.00 .45
❑ 208 Chris Warren .25 .11
❑ 209 Eric Curry .10 .05
❑ 210 Brian Mitchell .10 .05
❑ 211 Frank Sanders .25 .11
❑ 212 Terance Mathis UER .10 .05
name misspelled Terence
❑ 213 Eric Turner .10 .05
❑ 214 Bill Brooks .10 .05
❑ 215 John Kasay .10 .05
❑ 216 Erik Kramer .10 .05
❑ 217 Darnay Scott .25 .11
❑ 218 Charles Haley .25 .11
❑ 219 Steve Atwater .10 .05
❑ 220 Jason Hanson .10 .05
❑ 221 LeRoy Butler .10 .05
❑ 222 Cris Dishman .10 .05
❑ 223 Sean Dawkins .10 .05
❑ 224 James O. Stewart .25 .11
❑ 225 Greg Hill .25 .11
❑ 226 Jeff Cross .10 .05
❑ 227 Qadry Ismail .10 .05
❑ 228 Dave Meggett .10 .05
❑ 229 Eric Allen .10 .05
❑ 230 Chris Calloway .10 .05
❑ 231 Wayne Chrebet .25 .11
❑ 232 Jeff Hostetler .10 .05
❑ 233 Andy Harmon .10 .05
❑ 234 Greg Lloyd .25 .11
❑ 235 Toby Wright .10 .05
❑ 236 Junior Seau .25 .11
❑ 237 Bryant Young .25 .11
❑ 238 Robert Blackmon .10 .05
❑ 239 Trent Dilfer .50 .23
❑ 240 Leslie Shepherd .10 .05
❑ 241 Eric Swann .10 .05
❑ 242 Bert Emanuel .25 .11
❑ 243 Antonio Langham .10 .05
❑ 244 Steve Christie .10 .05
❑ 245 Tyrone Poole .10 .05
❑ 246 Jim Flanigan .10 .05
❑ 247 Tony McGee .10 .05
❑ 248 Michael Irvin .50 .23
❑ 249 Byron Bam Morris .25 .11
❑ 250 Terrell Davis 3.00 1.35
❑ 251 Johnnie Morton .25 .11
❑ 252 Sean Jones .10 .05
❑ 253 Chris Sanders .25 .11
❑ 254 Quentin Coryatt .10 .05
❑ 255 Willie Jackson .10 .05
❑ 256 Mark Collins .10 .05
❑ 257 Randal Hill .10 .05
❑ 258 David Palmer .10 .05
❑ 259 Will Moore .10 .05
❑ 260 Michael Haynes .10 .05
❑ 261 Mike Sherrard .10 .05
❑ 262 William Thomas .10 .05
❑ 263 Kordell Stewart 1.00 .45
❑ 264 D'Marco Farr .10 .05
❑ 265 Terrell Fletcher .10 .05
❑ 266 Lee Woodall .10 .05
❑ 267 Eugene Robinson .10 .05
❑ 268 Alvin Harper .10 .05
❑ 269 Gus Frerotte .50 .23
❑ 270 Antonio Freeman 1.00 .45
❑ 271 Clyde Simmons .10 .05
❑ 272 Chuck Smith .10 .05
❑ 273 Steve Tasker .10 .05
❑ 274 Kevin Butler .10 .05
❑ 275 Steve Tovar .10 .05
❑ 276 Troy Aikman 1.25 .55
❑ 277 Aaron Craver .10 .05
❑ 278 Henry Thomas .10 .05
❑ 279 Craig Newsome .10 .05
❑ 280 Brent Jones .10 .05
❑ 281 Micheal Barrow .10 .05
❑ 282 Ray Buchanan .10 .05
❑ 283 Jimmy Smith .25 .11
❑ 284 Neil Smith .10 .05
❑ 285 O.J. McDuffie .25 .11
❑ 286 Jake Reed .25 .11
❑ 287 Ty Law .10 .05
❑ 288 Torrance Small .10 .05
❑ 289 Hugh Douglas .10 .05
❑ 290 Pat Swilling .10 .05
❑ 291 Charlie Garner .10 .05
❑ 292 Ernie Mills .10 .05
❑ 293 John Carney .10 .05
❑ 294 Ken Norton .10 .05
❑ 295 Cortez Kennedy .10 .05
❑ 296 Derrick Brooks .10 .05
❑ 297 Heath Shuler .25 .11
❑ 298 Reggie White .50 .23
❑ 299 Kimble Anders .25 .11
❑ 300 Willie McGinest .10 .05
❑ P96 Dan Marino Promo 2.00 .90
(Predictor Promo Card)
❑ MS1 Dan Marino 5.00 2.20
Dynamic Debut
Meet the Stars Prize
❑ MS2 Dan Marino 5.00 2.20
Magic Memories
Meet the Stars Prize

1996 Upper Deck Game Face

	MINT	NRMT
COMPLETE SET (10)	10.00	4.50
ONE PER SPECIAL RETAIL PACK		

❑ GF1 Dan Marino 4.00 1.80
❑ GF2 Barry Sanders 4.00 1.80
❑ GF3 Jerry Rice 2.00 .90
❑ GF4 Stan Humphries .40 .18
❑ GF5 Drew Bledsoe 2.00 .90
❑ GF6 Greg Lloyd .40 .18
❑ GF7 Jim Harbaugh .40 .18
❑ GF8 Rashaan Salaam .75 .35
❑ GF9 Jeff Blake .75 .35
❑ GF10 Reggie White .75 .35

1996 Upper Deck Game Jersey

	MINT	NRMT
COMPLETE SET (10)	4000.00	1800.00
COMMON CARD (GJ1-GJ10)	80.00	36.00
STATED ODDS 1:2500		
CONDITION SENSITIVE SET!		

❑ GJ1 Dan Marino Teal 500.00 220.00
❑ GJ2 Jerry Rice Red 350.00 160.00
❑ GJ3 Joe Montana 600.00 275.00
❑ GJ4 Jerry Rice White 350.00 160.00
❑ GJ5 Rashaan Salaam 80.00 36.00
❑ GJ6 Marshall Faulk 250.00 110.00
❑ GJ7 Dan Marino White 500.00 220.00
❑ GJ8 Steve Young 250.00 110.00
❑ GJ9 Barry Sanders 500.00 220.00
❑ GJ10 Mark Brunell 250.00 110.00

1996 Upper Deck Hot Properties

	MINT	NRMT
COMPLETE SET (20)	120.00	55.00
COMMON CARD (HT1-HT20)	2.50	1.10

	MINT	NRMT
SEMISTARS	4.00	1.80
UNLISTED STARS	6.00	2.70
STATED ODDS 1:11		
*GOLD CARDS: 1X TO 2X REDS		
GOLD STATED ODDS 1:71		

Card	Players	MINT	NRMT
❑ HT1	Dan Marino / Drew Bledsoe	12.00	5.50
❑ HT2	Jerry Rice / J.J. Stokes	8.00	3.60
❑ HT3	Kordell Stewart / Deion Sanders	8.00	3.60
❑ HT4	Brett Favre / Rick Mirer	15.00	6.75
❑ HT5	Jeff Blake / Steve McNair	6.00	2.70
❑ HT6	Emmitt Smith / Errict Rhett	12.00	5.50
❑ HT7	John Elway / Warren Moon	12.00	5.50
❑ HT8	Steve Young / Mark Brunell	8.00	3.60
❑ HT9	Troy Aikman / Kerry Collins	8.00	3.60
❑ HT10	Joey Galloway / Chris Sanders	6.00	2.70
❑ HT11	Herman Moore / Cris Carter	6.00	2.70
❑ HT12	Rodney Hampton / Terrell Davis	15.00	6.75
❑ HT13	Carl Pickens / Isaac Bruce	4.00	1.80
❑ HT14	Rashaan Salaam / Michael Westbrook	4.00	1.80
❑ HT15	Marshall Faulk / Curtis Martin	6.00	2.70
❑ HT16	Tamarick Vanover / Eric Metcalf	2.50	1.10
❑ HT17	Keyshwan Johnson / Terry Glenn	12.00	5.50
❑ HT18	Lawrence Phillips / Tim Biakabutuka	6.00	2.70
❑ HT19	Kevin Hardy / Simeon Rice	2.50	1.10
❑ HT20	Barry Sanders / Thurman Thomas	15.00	6.75

1996 Upper Deck Predictors

	MINT	NRMT
COMP.HOBBY SET (20)	60.00	27.00
COMP.RETAIL SET (20)	60.00	27.00
PH1-PH20: STATED ODDS 1:23 HOBBY		
PR1-PR20: ODDS 1:23 RET, 1:14 SPEC.RET		

Card	Player	MINT	NRMT
❑ PH1	Dan Marino / 450 Yards Passing L	8.00	3.60
❑ PH2	Steve Young / 35 Completions L	3.00	1.35
❑ PH3	Brett Favre / 375 Yards Passing W	8.00	3.60
❑ PH4	Drew Bledsoe / 35 Completions W	4.00	1.80
❑ PH5	Jeff George / 380 Yards Passing L	.75	.35
❑ PH6	John Elway / 30 Completions W	8.00	3.60
❑ PH7	Barry Sanders / 190 Total Yards W	8.00	3.60
❑ PH8	Curtis Martin / 58 Yard Play L	3.00	1.35
❑ PH9	Marshall Faulk / 195 Total Yards L	1.50	.70
❑ PH10	Emmitt Smith / 75 Yard Play L	6.00	2.70
❑ PH11	Terrell Davis / 150 Yards Rushing W	10.00	4.50
❑ PH12	Errict Rhett / 50 Yard Play L	.75	.35
❑ PH13	Lawrence Phillips / 55 Yard Play L	.75	.35
❑ PH14	Jerry Rice / 14 Receptions L	4.00	1.80
❑ PH15	Michael Irvin / 130 Yards Receiving W	1.50	.70
❑ PH16	Joey Galloway / 10 Receptions L	3.00	1.35
❑ PH17	Herman Moore / 190 Yards Receiving L	1.50	.70
❑ PH18	Isaac Bruce / 12 Receptions L	1.50	.70
❑ PH19	Carl Pickens / 150 Yards Receiving W	1.50	.70
❑ PH20	Keyshawn Johnson / 11 Receptions L	3.00	1.35
❑ PR1	Dan Marino / 35 Completions L	8.00	3.60
❑ PR2	Steve Young / 435 Total Yards W	3.00	1.35
❑ PR3	Brett Favre / 30 Completions L	8.00	3.60
❑ PR4	Drew Bledsoe / 350 Yards Passing W	4.00	1.80
❑ PR5	Jeff George / 35 Completions L	.75	.35
❑ PR6	John Elway / 350 Yards Passing W	8.00	3.60
❑ PR7	Barry Sanders / 70 Yard Play L	8.00	3.60
❑ PR8	Curtis Martin / 160 Yards Rushing W	3.00	1.35
❑ PR9	Marshall Faulk / 75 Yard Play L	1.50	.70
❑ PR10	Emmitt Smith / 195 Total Yards L	6.00	2.70
❑ PR11	Terrell Davis / 59 Yard Play W	10.00	4.50
❑ PR12	Errict Rhett / 150 Yards Rushing L	.75	.35
❑ PR13	Lawrence Phillips / 130 Yards Rushing L	.75	.35
❑ PR14	Jerry Rice / 200 Yards Receiving L	4.00	1.80
❑ PR15	Michael Irvin / 12 Receptions W	1.50	.70
❑ PR16	Joey Galloway / 250 Total Yards L	3.00	1.35
❑ PR17	Herman Moore / 12 Receptions W	1.50	.70
❑ PR18	Isaac Bruce / 200 Yards Receiving W	1.50	.70
❑ PR19	Carl Pickens / 10 Receptions W	1.50	.70
❑ PR20	Keyshawn Johnson / 140 Yards Receiving L	3.00	1.35

1996 Upper Deck Pro Bowl

	MINT	NRMT
COMPLETE SET (20)	100.00	45.00
STATED ODDS 1:33		

Card	Player	MINT	NRMT
❑ PB1	Warren Moon	2.00	.90
❑ PB2	Brett Favre	20.00	9.00
❑ PB3	Steve Young	8.00	3.60
❑ PB4	Barry Sanders	20.00	9.00
❑ PB5	Emmitt Smith	15.00	6.75
❑ PB6	Jerry Rice	10.00	4.50
❑ PB7	Herman Moore	4.00	1.80
❑ PB8	Michael Irvin	4.00	1.80
❑ PB9	Mark Chmura	2.00	.90
❑ PB10	Reggie White	4.00	1.80
❑ PB11	Jim Harbaugh	2.00	.90
❑ PB12	Jeff Blake	4.00	1.80
❑ PB13	Curtis Martin	8.00	3.60
❑ PB14	Marshall Faulk	4.00	1.80
❑ PB15	Chris Warren	2.00	.90
❑ PB16	Bryan Cox	.75	.35
❑ PB17	Junior Seau	2.00	.90
❑ PB18	Carl Pickens	4.00	1.80
❑ PB19	Yancey Thigpen	2.00	.90
❑ PB20	Ben Coates	2.00	.90

1996 Upper Deck Proview

	MINT	NRMT
COMPLETE SET (40)	100.00	45.00
COMMON CARD (PV1-PV40)	.30	.14
ONE PER UD TECH RETAIL PACK		
*SILVER STARS: 5X TO 10X BASE CARD HI		
*SILVER YOUNG STARS: 4X TO 8X BASE CARD HI		
*SILVER ROOKIES: 1.75X TO 3.5X BASE CARD HI		
SILVER ODDS 1:35 UD TECH PACKS		
*GOLD STARS: 10X TO 25X BASE CARD HI		
*GOLD YOUNG STARS: 8X TO 20X BASE CARD HI		
*GOLD ROOKIES: 4X TO 10X BASE CARD HI		
GOLD ODDS 1:143 UD TECH PACKS		

Card	Player	MINT	NRMT
❑ PV1	Warren Moon	.75	.35
❑ PV2	Jerry Rice	4.00	1.80
❑ PV3	Brett Favre	8.00	3.60
❑ PV4	Jim Harbaugh	.75	.35
❑ PV5	Junior Seau	.75	.35
❑ PV6	Jeff Blake	1.50	.70

❑ PV7 John Elway 8.00 3.60
❑ PV8 Troy Aikman 4.00 1.80
❑ PV9 Steve Young 3.00 1.35
❑ PV10 Kordell Stewart 2.50 1.10
❑ PV11 Drew Bledsoe 4.00 1.80
❑ PV12 Jim Kelly 1.50 .70
❑ PV13 Dan Marino 8.00 3.60
❑ PV14 Kerry Collins 1.25 .55
❑ PV15 Jeff Hostetler .30 .14
❑ PV16 Terry Allen .75 .35
❑ PV17 Carl Pickens 1.50 .70
❑ PV18 Mark Brunell 4.00 1.80
❑ PV19 Keyshawn Johnson 3.00 1.35
❑ PV20 Barry Sanders 8.00 3.60
❑ PV21 Deion Sanders 2.50 1.10
❑ PV22 Emmitt Smith 6.00 2.70
❑ PV23 Curtis Conway 1.50 .70
❑ PV24 Herman Moore 1.50 .70
❑ PV25 Joey Galloway 2.50 1.10
❑ PV26 Robert Smith .75 .35
❑ PV27 Eddie George 5.00 2.20
❑ PV28 Curtis Martin 2.50 1.10
❑ PV29 Marshall Faulk 1.25 .55
❑ PV30 Terrell Davis 8.00 3.60
❑ PV31 Rashaan Salaam 1.25 .55
❑ PV32 Jamal Anderson 6.00 2.70
❑ PV33 Karim Abdul-Jabbar 1.25 .55
❑ PV34 Edgar Bennett .75 .35
❑ PV35 Thurman Thomas 1.50 .70
❑ PV36 Jerome Bettis 1.50 .70
❑ PV37 Tim Brown 1.50 .70
❑ PV38 Chris Sanders .60 .25
❑ PV39 Eddie Kennison .60 .25
❑ PV40 Shannon Sharpe .75 .35

1996 Upper Deck Team Trio

	MINT	NRMT
COMPLETE SET (90)	80.00	36.00

STATED ODDS 1:4 HOB/RET, 1:2 SPEC.RET

❑ TT1 Curtis Conway 1.25 .55
❑ TT2 Darnay Scott .60 .25
❑ TT3 Bryce Paup .25 .11
❑ TT4 Terrell Davis 8.00 3.60
❑ TT5 Hardy Nickerson .25 .11
❑ TT6 Frank Sanders .60 .25
❑ TT7 Stan Humphries .60 .25
❑ TT8 Tamarick Vanover .60 .25
❑ TT9 Sean Dawkins .25 .11
❑ TT10 Deion Sanders 2.00 .90
❑ TT11 Dan Marino 6.00 2.70
❑ TT12 Charlie Garner .25 .11
❑ TT13 Eric Metcalf .25 .11
❑ TT14 J.J. Stokes 1.25 .55
❑ TT15 Chris Calloway .25 .11
❑ TT16 Pete Mitchell .60 .25
❑ TT17 Wayne Chrebet .60 .25
❑ TT18 Herman Moore 1.25 .55
❑ TT19 Steve McNair 2.50 1.10
❑ TT20 Edgar Bennett .60 .25
❑ TT21 Kerry Collins 1.25 .55
❑ TT22 Vincent Brisby .25 .11
❑ TT23 Jeff Hostetler .25 .11
❑ TT24 Kevin Carter .25 .11
❑ TT25 Michael Jackson .60 .25
❑ TT26 Michael Westbrook 1.25 .55
❑ TT27 Tyrone Hughes .25 .11
❑ TT28 Joey Galloway 2.50 1.10
❑ TT29 Byron Bam Morris .60 .25
❑ TT30 Warren Moon .60 .25
❑ TT31 Rashaan Salaam 1.25 .55
❑ TT32 Jeff Blake 1.25 .55
❑ TT33 Thurman Thomas 1.25 .55
❑ TT34 John Elway 6.00 2.70
❑ TT35 Errict Rhett .60 .25
❑ TT36 Garrison Hearst .60 .25
❑ TT37 Andre Coleman .25 .11
❑ TT38 Steve Bono .25 .11
❑ TT39 Marshall Faulk 1.25 .55
❑ TT40 Troy Aikman 3.00 1.35
❑ TT41 Terry Kirby .60 .25
❑ TT42 Rodney Peete .25 .11
❑ TT43 Craig Heyward .25 .11
❑ TT44 Steve Young 2.50 1.10
❑ TT45 Rodney Hampton .60 .25
❑ TT46 Mark Brunell 3.00 1.35
❑ TT47 Kyle Brady .25 .11
❑ TT48 Scott Mitchell .60 .25
❑ TT49 Chris Sanders .60 .25
❑ TT50 Brett Favre 6.00 2.70
❑ TT51 Mark Carrier WR .25 .11
❑ TT52 Drew Bledsoe 3.00 1.35
❑ TT53 Napoleon Kaufman 2.00 .90
❑ TT54 Mark Rypien .25 .11
❑ TT55 Andre Rison .60 .25
❑ TT56 Terry Allen .60 .25
❑ TT57 Jim Everett .25 .11
❑ TT58 Chris Warren .60 .25
❑ TT59 Kordell Stewart 2.50 1.10
❑ TT60 Jake Reed .60 .25
❑ TT61 Erik Kramer .25 .11
❑ TT62 Carl Pickens 1.25 .55
❑ TT63 Jim Kelly 1.25 .55
❑ TT64 Anthony Miller .60 .25
❑ TT65 Trent Dilfer 1.25 .55
❑ TT66 Larry Centers .60 .25
❑ TT67 Junior Seau .60 .25
❑ TT68 Marcus Allen 1.25 .55
❑ TT69 Jim Harbaugh .60 .25
❑ TT70 Emmitt Smith 5.00 2.20
❑ TT71 O.J.McDuffie .60 .25
❑ TT72 Ricky Watters .60 .25
❑ TT73 Jeff George .60 .25
❑ TT74 Jerry Rice 3.00 1.35
❑ TT75 Dave Brown .25 .11
❑ TT76 James O. Stewart .60 .25
❑ TT77 Adrian Murrell 1.25 .55
❑ TT78 Barry Sanders 6.00 2.70
❑ TT79 Rodney Thomas .25 .11
❑ TT80 Robert Brooks 1.25 .55
❑ TT81 Derrick Moore .25 .11
❑ TT82 Curtis Martin 2.50 1.10
❑ TT83 Tim Brown 1.25 .55
❑ TT84 Isaac Bruce 1.25 .55
❑ TT85 Vinny Testaverde .60 .25
❑ TT86 Henry Ellard .25 .11
❑ TT87 Mario Bates .60 .25
❑ TT88 Rick Mirer .60 .25
❑ TT89 Yancey Thigpen .60 .25
❑ TT90 Cris Carter 1.25 .55

1996 Upper Deck TV-Cels

	MINT	NRMT
COMPLETE SET (20)	400.00	180.00
COMMON CARD (1-20)	10.00	4.50
COMMON WIN (15/17-19)	8.00	3.60
SEMISTARS	15.00	6.75

RANDOM INSERTS IN PACKS
PRIZES FOR PREDICTOR WINNERS

❑ 1 Dan Marino 100.00 45.00
❑ 2 Steve Young 1W 10.00 4.50
❑ 3 Brett Favre 1W 20.00 9.00
❑ 4 Drew Bledsoe 2W 10.00 4.50
❑ 5 Jeff George 2W 10.00 4.50
❑ 6 John Elway 2W 20.00 9.00
❑ 7 Barry Sanders 1W 20.00 9.00
❑ 8 Curtis Martin 1W 10.00 4.50
❑ 9 Marshall Faulk 15.00 6.75
❑ 10 Emmitt Smith 80.00 36.00
❑ 11 Terrell Davis 1W 25.00 11.00
❑ 12 Errict Rhett 10.00 4.50
❑ 13 Lawrence Phillips 15.00 6.75
❑ 14 Jerry Rice 50.00 22.00
❑ 15 Michael Irvin W 15.00 6.75
❑ 16 Joey Galloway 15.00 6.75
❑ 17 Herman Moore W 15.00 6.75
❑ 18 Isaac Bruce W 8.00 3.60
❑ 19 Carl Pickens W 15.00 6.75
❑ 20 Keyshawn Johnson 30.00 13.50

1997 Upper Deck

	MINT	NRMT
COMPLETE SET (300)	50.00	22.00
COMMON CARD (1-300)	.15	.07
SEMISTARS	.25	.11
UNLISTED STARS	.50	.23

*GAME DATED FOILS: 15X TO 40X
PARALLELS FEATURE ALL-FOIL FRONTS
GAME DATED FOIL ODDS 1:1500

❑ 1 Orlando Pace RC .15 .07
❑ 2 Darrell Russell RC .15 .07
❑ 3 Shawn Springs RC .25 .11
❑ 4 Bryant Westbrook RC .15 .07
❑ 5 Ike Hilliard RC 1.25 .55
❑ 6 Peter Boulware RC .25 .11
❑ 7 Tom Knight RC .15 .07
❑ 8 Yatil Green RC .25 .11
❑ 9 Tony Gonzalez RC 2.00 .90
❑ 10 Reidel Anthony RC 1.25 .55
❑ 11 Warrick Dunn RC 2.00 .90
❑ 12 Kenny Holmes RC .15 .07
❑ 13 Jim Druckenmiller RC .75 .35
❑ 14 James Farrior RC .15 .07
❑ 15 David LaFleur RC .25 .11
❑ 16 Antowain Smith RC 1.50 .70
❑ 17 Rae Carruth RC .50 .23
❑ 18 Dwayne Rudd RC .15 .07
❑ 19 Jake Plummer RC 5.00 2.20
❑ 20 Reinard Wilson RC .15 .07
❑ 21 Byron Hanspard RC 1.25 .55
❑ 22 Will Blackwell RC .50 .23
❑ 23 Troy Davis RC .50 .23
❑ 24 Corey Dillon RC 2.50 1.10
❑ 25 Joey Kent RC .50 .23
❑ 26 Renaldo Wynn RC .15 .07
❑ 27 Pat Barnes RC .50 .23
❑ 28 Kevin Lockett RC .25 .11

❑ 29 Darnell Autry RC .25 .11
❑ 30 Walter Jones RC .15 .07
❑ 31 Trevor Pryce RC .15 .07
❑ 32 Dan Marino SRF 1.25 .55
❑ 33 Steve Young SRF .50 .23
❑ 34 John Elway SRF 1.25 .55
❑ 35 Jerry Rice SRF .60 .25
❑ 36 Tim Brown SRF .50 .23
❑ 37 Deion Sanders SRF .50 .23
❑ 38 Troy Aikman SRF .60 .25
❑ 39 Barry Sanders SRF 1.25 .55
❑ 40 Emmitt Smith SRF 1.00 .45
❑ 41 Junior Seau SRF .25 .11
❑ 42 Neil Smith .25 .11
❑ 43 Brett Perriman .15 .07
❑ 44 Jim Everett .15 .07
❑ 45 Qadry Ismail .25 .11
❑ 46 Dana Stubblefield .15 .07
❑ 47 Bryant Young .15 .07
❑ 48 Ken Norton Jr. .15 .07
❑ 49 Terrell Owens .50 .23
❑ 50 Jerry Rice 1.25 .55
❑ 51 Steve Young .75 .35
❑ 52 Terry Kirby .25 .11
❑ 53 Chris Doleman .15 .07
❑ 54 Lee Woodall .15 .07
❑ 55 Merton Hanks .15 .07
❑ 56 Garrison Hearst .25 .11
❑ 57 Rashaan Salaam .15 .07
❑ 58 Raymont Harris .15 .07
❑ 59 Curtis Conway .25 .11
❑ 60 Bobby Engram .25 .11
❑ 61 Bryan Cox .15 .07
❑ 62 Walt Harris .15 .07
❑ 63 Tyrone Hughes .15 .07
❑ 64 Rick Mirer .15 .07
❑ 65 Jeff Blake .25 .11
❑ 66 Carl Pickens .50 .23
❑ 67 Darnay Scott .25 .11
❑ 68 Tony McGee .15 .07
❑ 69 Ki-Jana Carter .15 .07
❑ 70 Ashley Ambrose .15 .07
❑ 71 Dan Wilkinson .15 .07
❑ 72 Chris Spielman .15 .07
❑ 73 Todd Collins .15 .07
❑ 74 Andre Reed .25 .11
❑ 75 Quinn Early .15 .07
❑ 76 Eric Moulds .50 .23
❑ 77 Darick Holmes .15 .07
❑ 78 Thurman Thomas .50 .23
❑ 79 Bruce Smith .25 .11
❑ 80 Bryce Paup .15 .07
❑ 81 John Elway 2.50 1.10
❑ 82 Terrell Davis 2.00 .90
❑ 83 Anthony Miller .15 .07
❑ 84 Shannon Sharpe .25 .11
❑ 85 Alfred Williams .15 .07
❑ 86 John Mobley .15 .07
❑ 87 Tory James .15 .07
❑ 88 Steve Atwater .15 .07
❑ 89 Darrien Gordon .15 .07
❑ 90 Mike Alstott .50 .23
❑ 91 Errict Rhett .15 .07
❑ 92 Trent Dilfer .50 .23
❑ 93 Courtney Hawkins .15 .07
❑ 94 Warren Sapp .25 .11
❑ 95 Regan Upshaw .15 .07
❑ 96 Hardy Nickerson .15 .07
❑ 97 Donnie Abraham RC .15 .07
❑ 98 Larry Centers .25 .11
❑ 99 Aeneas Williams .15 .07
❑ 100 Kent Graham .15 .07
❑ 101 Rob Moore .25 .11
❑ 102 Frank Sanders .25 .11
❑ 103 Leeland McElroy .15 .07
❑ 104 Eric Swann .15 .07
❑ 105 Simeon Rice .25 .11
❑ 106 Seth Joyner .15 .07
❑ 107 Stan Humphries .25 .11
❑ 108 Tony Martin .25 .11
❑ 109 Charlie Jones .25 .11
❑ 110 Andre Coleman UER .15 .07
(card mistakenly #103)
❑ 111 Terrell Fletcher .15 .07
❑ 112 Junior Seau .25 .11
❑ 113 Eric Metcalf .25 .11
❑ 114 Chris Penn .15 .07
❑ 115 Marcus Allen .50 .23
❑ 116 Greg Hill .15 .07
❑ 117 Tamarick Vanover .25 .11
❑ 118 Lake Dawson .15 .07
❑ 119 Derrick Thomas .25 .11
❑ 120 Dale Carter .15 .07
❑ 121 Elvis Grbac .25 .11
❑ 122 Aaron Bailey .15 .07
❑ 123 Jim Harbaugh .25 .11
❑ 124 Marshall Faulk .50 .23
❑ 125 Sean Dawkins .15 .07
❑ 126 Marvin Harrison .50 .23
❑ 127 Ken Dilger .15 .07
❑ 128 Tony Bennett .15 .07
❑ 129 Jeff Herrod .15 .07
❑ 130 Chris Gardocki .15 .07
❑ 131 Cary Blanchard .15 .07
❑ 132 Troy Aikman 1.25 .55
❑ 133 Emmitt Smith 2.00 .90
❑ 134 Sherman Williams .15 .07
❑ 135 Michael Irvin .50 .23
❑ 136 Eric Bjornson .15 .07
❑ 137 Herschel Walker .25 .11
❑ 138 Tony Tolbert .15 .07
❑ 139 Deion Sanders .50 .23
❑ 140 Daryl Johnston .25 .11
❑ 141 Dan Marino 2.50 1.10
❑ 142 O.J. McDuffie .25 .11
❑ 143 Troy Drayton .15 .07
❑ 144 Karim Abdul-Jabbar .50 .23
❑ 145 Stanley Pritchett .15 .07
❑ 146 Fred Barnett .15 .07
❑ 147 Zach Thomas .25 .11
❑ 148 Shawn Wooden .15 .07
❑ 149 Ty Detmer .25 .11
❑ 150 Derrick Witherspoon .15 .07
❑ 151 Ricky Watters .25 .11
❑ 152 Charlie Garner .15 .07
❑ 153 Chris T. Jones .15 .07
❑ 154 Irving Fryar .25 .11
❑ 155 Mike Mamula .15 .07
❑ 156 Troy Vincent .15 .07
❑ 157 Bobby Taylor .15 .07
❑ 158 Chris Boniol .15 .07
❑ 159 Devin Bush .15 .07
❑ 160 Bert Emanuel .25 .11
❑ 161 Jamal Anderson .75 .35
❑ 162 Terance Mathis .25 .11
❑ 163 Cornelius Bennett .15 .07
❑ 164 Ray Buchanan .15 .07
❑ 165 Chris Chandler .25 .11
❑ 166 Dave Brown .15 .07
❑ 167 Danny Kanell .25 .11
❑ 168 Rodney Hampton .25 .11
❑ 169 Tyrone Wheatley .25 .11
❑ 170 Amani Toomer .25 .11
❑ 171 Chris Calloway .15 .07
❑ 172 Thomas Lewis .15 .07
❑ 173 Phillippi Sparks .15 .07
❑ 174 Mark Brunell 1.25 .55
❑ 175 Keenan McCardell .25 .11
❑ 176 Willie Jackson .15 .07
❑ 177 Jimmy Smith .25 .11
❑ 178 Pete Mitchell .15 .07
❑ 179 Natrone Means .50 .23
❑ 180 Kevin Hardy .15 .07
❑ 181 Tony Brackens .15 .07
❑ 182 James O. Stewart .25 .11
❑ 183 Wayne Chrebet .50 .23
❑ 184 Keyshawn Johnson .50 .23
❑ 185 Adrian Murrell .25 .11
❑ 186 Neil O'Donnell .25 .11
❑ 187 Hugh Douglas .15 .07
❑ 188 Mo Lewis .15 .07
❑ 189 Marvin Washington .15 .07
❑ 190 Aaron Glenn .15 .07
❑ 191 Barry Sanders 2.50 1.10
❑ 192 Scott Mitchell .25 .11
❑ 193 Herman Moore .50 .23
❑ 194 Johnnie Morton .25 .11
❑ 195 Glyn Milburn .15 .07
❑ 196 Reggie Brown LB .25 .11
❑ 197 Jason Hanson .15 .07
❑ 198 Steve McNair .60 .25
❑ 199 Eddie George 1.25 .55
❑ 200 Ronnie Harmon .15 .07
❑ 201 Chris Sanders .15 .07
❑ 202 Willie Davis .15 .07
❑ 203 Frank Wycheck .15 .07
❑ 204 Darryll Lewis .15 .07
❑ 205 Blaine Bishop .15 .07
❑ 206 Robert Brooks .25 .11
❑ 207 Brett Favre 2.50 1.10
❑ 208 Edgar Bennett .25 .11
❑ 209 Dorsey Levens .50 .23
❑ 210 Derrick Mayes .25 .11
❑ 211 Antonio Freeman .60 .25
❑ 212 Mark Chmura .25 .11
❑ 213 Reggie White .50 .23
❑ 214 Gilbert Brown .15 .07
❑ 215 LeRoy Butler .15 .07
❑ 216 Craig Newsome .15 .07
❑ 217 Kerry Collins .25 .11
❑ 218 Wesley Walls .25 .11
❑ 219 Muhsin Muhammad .25 .11
❑ 220 Anthony Johnson .15 .07
❑ 221 Tim Biakabutuka .25 .11
❑ 222 Kevin Greene .25 .11
❑ 223 Sam Mills .15 .07
❑ 224 John Kasay .15 .07
❑ 225 Micheal Barrow .15 .07
❑ 226 Drew Bledsoe 1.25 .55
❑ 227 Curtis Martin .60 .25
❑ 228 Terry Glenn .50 .23
❑ 229 Ben Coates .25 .11
❑ 230 Shawn Jefferson .15 .07
❑ 231 Willie McGinest .15 .07
❑ 232 Ted Johnson .15 .07
❑ 233 Lawyer Milloy .15 .07
❑ 234 Ty Law .15 .07
❑ 235 Willie Clay .15 .07
❑ 236 Tim Brown .50 .23
❑ 237 Rickey Dudley .25 .11
❑ 238 Napoleon Kaufman .50 .23
❑ 239 Chester McGlockton .15 .07
❑ 240 Rob Fredrickson .15 .07
❑ 241 Terry McDaniel .15 .07
❑ 242 Desmond Howard .25 .11
❑ 243 Jeff George .25 .11
❑ 244 Isaac Bruce .50 .23
❑ 245 Tony Banks .25 .11
❑ 246 Lawrence Phillips UER .15 .07
(card mistakenly #247)
❑ 247 Kevin Carter .15 .07
❑ 248 Roman Phifer .15 .07
❑ 249 Keith Lyle .15 .07
❑ 250 Eddie Kennison .25 .11
❑ 251 Craig Heyward .15 .07
❑ 252 Vinny Testaverde .25 .11
❑ 253 Derrick Alexander WR .25 .11
❑ 254 Michael Jackson .25 .11
❑ 255 Byron Bam Morris .15 .07
❑ 256 Eric Green .15 .07
❑ 257 Ray Lewis .15 .07
❑ 258 Antonio Langham .15 .07
❑ 259 Michael McCrary .15 .07
❑ 260 Gus Frerotte .15 .07
❑ 261 Terry Allen .50 .23
❑ 262 Brian Mitchell .15 .07
❑ 263 Michael Westbrook .25 .11
❑ 264 Sean Gilbert .15 .07
❑ 265 Rich Owens .15 .07
❑ 266 Ken Harvey .15 .07
❑ 267 Jeff Hostetler .15 .07
❑ 268 Michael Haynes .15 .07
❑ 269 Mario Bates .15 .07
❑ 270 Renaldo Turnbull UER .15 .07
(card mistakenly #273)
❑ 271 Ray Zellars .15 .07
❑ 272 Joe Johnson .15 .07
❑ 273 Eric Allen .15 .07
❑ 274 Heath Shuler .15 .07
❑ 275 Daryl Hobbs .15 .07
❑ 276 John Friesz .15 .07
❑ 277 Brian Blades .15 .07
❑ 278 Joey Galloway .60 .25
❑ 279 Chris Warren .25 .11
❑ 280 Lamar Smith .15 .07
❑ 281 Cortez Kennedy .15 .07
❑ 282 Chad Brown .15 .07
❑ 283 Warren Moon .50 .23

❑ 284 Jerome Bettis	.50	.23
❑ 285 Charles Johnson	.25	.11
❑ 286 Kordell Stewart	.60	.25
❑ 287 Erric Pegram	.15	.07
❑ 288 Norm Johnson	.15	.07
❑ 289 Levon Kirkland	.15	.07
❑ 290 Greg Lloyd	.15	.07
❑ 291 Carnell Lake	.15	.07
❑ 292 Brad Johnson	.60	.25
❑ 293 Cris Carter	.50	.23
❑ 294 Jake Reed	.25	.11
❑ 295 Robert Smith	.25	.11
❑ 296 Derrick Alexander DE	.15	.07
❑ 297 John Randle	.15	.07
❑ 298 Dixon Edwards	.15	.07
❑ 299 Orlanda Thomas	.15	.07
❑ 300 Dewayne Washington	.15	.07

1997 Upper Deck Game Jersey

	MINT	NRMT
COMPLETE SET (10)	2000.00	900.00
COMMON CARD (GJ1-GJ10)	100.00	45.00
SEMISTARS	150.00	70.00

MULTI-COLORED PATCHES CARRY PREMIUMS
STATED ODDS 1:2600

❑ GJ1 Warren Moon	150.00	70.00
❑ GJ2 Joey Galloway	200.00	90.00
❑ GJ3 Terrell Davis	300.00	135.00
❑ GJ4 Brett Favre (green jersey)	300.00	135.00
❑ GJ5 Brett Favre (white jersey)	300.00	135.00
❑ GJ6 Reggie White	150.00	70.00
❑ GJ7 John Elway	400.00	180.00
❑ GJ8 Troy Aikman	300.00	135.00
❑ GJ9 Carl Pickens	100.00	45.00
❑ GJ10 Herman Moore	100.00	45.00

1997 Upper Deck Memorable Moments

	MINT	NRMT
COMPLETE SET (10)	12.00	5.50

ONE PER SPECIAL RETAIL COLL.CHOICE

❑ 1 Steve Young	.75	.35
❑ 2 Dan Marino	2.50	1.10
❑ 3 Terrell Davis	2.00	.90
❑ 4 Brett Favre	2.50	1.10
❑ 5 Ricky Watters	.25	.11
❑ 6 Terry Glenn	.50	.23
❑ 7 John Elway	2.50	1.10
❑ 8 Troy Aikman	1.25	.55
❑ 9 Terry Allen	.50	.23
❑ 10 Joey Galloway	.60	.25

1997 Upper Deck MVPs

	MINT	NRMT
COMPLETE SET (20)	800.00	350.00

STATED PRINT RUN 100 SERIAL #'d SETS

❑ 1 Jerry Rice	60.00	27.00
❑ 2 Carl Pickens	25.00	11.00
❑ 3 Terrell Davis	100.00	45.00
❑ 4 Mike Alstott	25.00	11.00
❑ 5 Simeon Rice	12.00	5.50
❑ 6 Junior Seau	12.00	5.50
❑ 7 Marcus Allen	25.00	11.00
❑ 8 Troy Aikman	60.00	27.00
❑ 9 Dan Marino	120.00	55.00
❑ 10 Ricky Watters	12.00	5.50
❑ 11 Mark Brunell	60.00	27.00
❑ 12 Barry Sanders	120.00	55.00
❑ 13 Eddie George	60.00	27.00
❑ 14 Brett Favre	120.00	55.00
❑ 15 Kerry Collins	12.00	5.50
❑ 16 Drew Bledsoe	60.00	27.00
❑ 17 Napoleon Kaufman	25.00	11.00
❑ 18 Isaac Bruce	25.00	11.00
❑ 19 Terry Allen	25.00	11.00
❑ 20 Jerome Bettis	25.00	11.00

1997 Upper Deck Star Crossed

	MINT	NRMT
COMPLETE SET (30)	40.00	18.00

SC1-SC9 STATED ODDS 1:23 HOBBY
SC10-SC18 STATED ODDS 1:27 SPEC.RETAIL
SC19-SC27 STATED ODDS 1:27 RETAIL
TRADE CARD STATED ODDS 1:270

❑ SC1 Dan Marino	5.00	2.20
❑ SC2 Mark Brunell	2.50	1.10
❑ SC3 Kerry Collins	.50	.23
❑ SC4 Jerry Rice	2.50	1.10
❑ SC5 Curtis Martin	1.25	.55
❑ SC6 Isaac Bruce	1.00	.45
❑ SC7 Eddie George	2.50	1.10
❑ SC8 Kevin Greene	.50	.23
❑ SC9 Deion Sanders	1.00	.45
❑ SC10 Troy Aikman	2.50	1.10
❑ SC11 John Elway	5.00	2.20
❑ SC12 Steve Young	1.50	.70
❑ SC13 Barry Sanders	5.00	2.20
❑ SC14 Jerome Bettis	1.00	.45
❑ SC15 Herman Moore	1.00	.45
❑ SC16 Keyshawn Johnson	1.00	.45
❑ SC17 Simeon Rice	.50	.23
❑ SC18 Bruce Smith	.50	.23
❑ SC19 Drew Bledsoe	2.50	1.10
❑ SC20 Kordell Stewart	1.25	.55
❑ SC21 Brett Favre	5.00	2.20
❑ SC22 Emmitt Smith	4.00	1.80
❑ SC23 Terrell Davis	4.00	1.80
❑ SC24 Carl Pickens	1.00	.45
❑ SC25 Terry Glenn	1.00	.45
❑ SC26 Reggie White	1.00	.45
❑ SC27 Rod Woodson	1.00	.45
❑ SC28 Trade Card	.30	.14
❑ SC29 Trade Card	.30	.14
❑ SC30 Trade Card	.30	.14

1997 Upper Deck Team Mates

	MINT	NRMT
COMPLETE SET (60)	40.00	18.00

STATED ODDS 1:4 HOBBY, 1:2 RETAIL

❑ TM1 Simeon Rice	.40	.18
❑ TM2 Eric Swann	.25	.11
❑ TM3 Terance Mathis	.40	.18
❑ TM4 Jamal Anderson	1.25	.55
❑ TM5 Vinny Testaverde	.40	.18
❑ TM6 Michael Jackson	.40	.18
❑ TM7 Thurman Thomas	.75	.35
❑ TM8 Bruce Smith	.40	.18
❑ TM9 Kerry Collins	.40	.18
❑ TM10 Anthony Johnson	.25	.11
❑ TM11 Bobby Engram	.40	.18
❑ TM12 Bryan Cox	.25	.11
❑ TM13 Carl Pickens	.75	.35
❑ TM14 Jeff Blake	.40	.18
❑ TM15 Troy Aikman	2.00	.90
❑ TM16 Emmitt Smith	3.00	1.35
❑ TM17 John Elway	4.00	1.80
❑ TM18 Terrell Davis	3.00	1.35
❑ TM19 Herman Moore	.75	.35
❑ TM20 Barry Sanders	4.00	1.80
❑ TM21 Brett Favre	4.00	1.80
❑ TM22 Reggie White	.75	.35
❑ TM23 Eddie George	2.00	.90
❑ TM24 Steve McNair	1.00	.45
❑ TM25 Marshall Faulk	.75	.35
❑ TM26 Jim Harbaugh	.40	.18
❑ TM27 Mark Brunell	2.00	.90
❑ TM28 Keenan McCardell	.40	.18
❑ TM29 Marcus Allen	.75	.35
❑ TM30 Derrick Thomas	.40	.18
❑ TM31 Dan Marino	4.00	1.80
❑ TM32 Karim Abdul-Jabbar	.75	.35
❑ TM33 Cris Carter	.75	.35
❑ TM34 Jake Reed	.40	.18
❑ TM35 Curtis Martin	1.00	.45
❑ TM36 Drew Bledsoe	2.00	.90
❑ TM37 Mario Bates	.25	.11
❑ TM38 Ray Zellars	.25	.11
❑ TM39 Keyshawn Johnson	.75	.35
❑ TM40 Adrian Murrell	.40	.18
❑ TM41 Tyrone Wheatley	.40	.18
❑ TM42 Rodney Hampton	.40	.18
❑ TM43 Napoleon Kaufman	.75	.35
❑ TM44 Tim Brown	.75	.35
❑ TM45 Ricky Watters	.40	.18
❑ TM46 Chris T. Jones	.25	.11
❑ TM47 Kordell Stewart	1.00	.45
❑ TM48 Jerome Bettis	.75	.35
❑ TM49 Junior Seau	.40	.18
❑ TM50 Tony Martin	.40	.18
❑ TM51 Steve Young	1.25	.55
❑ TM52 Jerry Rice	2.00	.90

❑ TM53 Joey Galloway .... 1.00 .45
❑ TM54 Chris Warren .... .40 .18
❑ TM55 Tony Banks .... .40 .18
❑ TM56 Eddie Kennison .... .40 .18
❑ TM57 Mike Alstott .... .75 .35
❑ TM58 Erict Rhett.................. .25 .11
❑ TM59 Terry Allen .... .75 .35
❑ TM60 Gus Frerotte............... .25 .11

1998 Upper Deck

	MINT	NRMT
COMPLETE SET (255)	250.00	110.00
COMP.SET w/o SP's (213)......	25.00	11.00
COMMON CARD (1-252/CL)	.15	.07
SEMISTARS..........................	.25	.11
UNLISTED STARS......................	.50	.23
COMMON ROOKIE (1-42)	2.50	1.10
ROOKIE SEMISTARS	3.00	1.35
ROOKIE UNLISTED STARS	4.00	1.80
ROOKIE SUBSET ODDS 1:4.......		
COMMON BRONZE................	15.00	6.75
*BRONZE STARS: 40X TO 80X ..		
*BRONZE YOUNG STARS: 30X TO 60X		
*BRONZE RC'S: 2X TO 4X		
BRONZE PRINT RUN 100 SERIAL #'d SETS		

❑ 1 Peyton Manning RC 50.00 22.00
❑ 2 Ryan Leaf RC 10.00 4.50
❑ 3 Andre Wadsworth RC 3.00 1.35
❑ 4 Charles Woodson RC 12.00 5.50
❑ 5 Curtis Enis RC............... 12.00 5.50
❑ 6 Grant Wistrom RC........... 2.50 1.10
❑ 7 Greg Ellis RC 2.50 1.10
❑ 8 Fred Taylor RC 25.00 11.00
❑ 9 Duane Starks RC 2.50 1.10
❑ 10 Keith Brooking RC........... 3.00 1.35
❑ 11 Takeo Spikes RC 3.00 1.35
❑ 12 Jason Peter RC............. 2.50 1.10
❑ 13 Anthony Simmons RC.... 2.50 1.10
❑ 14 Kevin Dyson RC 10.00 4.50
❑ 15 Brian Simmons RC 2.50 1.10
❑ 16 Robert Edwards RC 4.00 1.80
❑ 17 Randy Moss RC 50.00 22.00
❑ 18 John Avery RC 4.00 1.80
❑ 19 Marcus Nash RC........... 4.00 1.80
❑ 20 Jerome Pathon RC 3.00 1.35
❑ 21 Jacquez Green RC 8.00 3.60
❑ 22 Robert Holcombe RC 4.00 1.80
❑ 23 Pat Johnson RC 3.00 1.35
❑ 24 Germane Crowell RC .. 12.00 5.50
❑ 25 Joe Jurevicius RC 3.00 1.35
❑ 26 Skip Hicks RC 4.00 1.80
❑ 27 Ahman Green RC 4.00 1.80
❑ 28 Brian Griese RC 20.00 9.00
❑ 29 Hines Ward RC 3.00 1.35
❑ 30 Tavian Banks RC 3.00 1.35
❑ 31 Tony Simmons RC 3.00 1.35
❑ 32 Victor Riley RC 2.50 1.10
❑ 33 Rashaan Shehee RC 3.00 1.35
❑ 34 R.W. McQuarters RC 2.50 1.10
❑ 35 Flozell Adams RC 2.50 1.10
❑ 36 Tra Thomas RC.............. 2.50 1.10
❑ 37 Greg Favors RC 2.50 1.10
❑ 38 Jon Ritchie RC 3.00 1.35
❑ 39 Jesse Haynes RC 2.50 1.10
❑ 40 Ryan Sutter RC.............. 2.50 1.10
❑ 41 Mo Collins RC 2.50 1.10
❑ 42 Tim Dwight RC 10.00 4.50
❑ 43 Chris Chandler .... .25 .11
❑ 44 Byron Hanspard .... .25 .11
❑ 45 Jessie Tuggle .... .15 .07
❑ 46 Jamal Anderson .... .50 .23
❑ 47 Terance Mathis .... .25 .11
❑ 48 Morten Andersen............. .15 .07
❑ 49 Jake Plummer .... 1.50 .70
❑ 50 Mario Bates .... .25 .11
❑ 51 Frank Sanders.................. .25 .11
❑ 52 Adrian Murrell .... .25 .11
❑ 53 Simeon Rice .... .25 .11
❑ 54 Aeneas Williams .... .15 .07
❑ 55 Eric Swann UER .... .15 .07
(number on back 98)
❑ 56 Jim Harbaugh .... .25 .11
❑ 57 Michael Jackson .... .15 .07
❑ 58 Peter Boulware .... .15 .07
❑ 59 Errict Rhett .... .25 .11
❑ 60 Jermaine Lewis .... .25 .11
❑ 61 Eric Zeier......................... .25 .11
❑ 62 Rod Woodson .... .25 .11
❑ 63 Rob Johnson.................... .50 .23
❑ 64 Antowain Smith .... .50 .23
❑ 65 Bruce Smith...................... .25 .11
❑ 66 Eric Moulds .... .50 .23
❑ 67 Andre Reed .... .25 .11
❑ 68 Thurman Thomas .... .50 .23
❑ 69 Lonnie Johnson................ .15 .07
❑ 70 Kerry Collins .... .25 .11
❑ 71 Kevin Greene .... .25 .11
❑ 72 Fred Lane .... .25 .11
❑ 73 Rae Carruth...................... .25 .11
❑ 74 Michael Bates .... .15 .07
❑ 75 William Floyd................... .15 .07
❑ 76 Sean Gilbert .... .15 .07
❑ 77 Erik Kramer .... .15 .07
❑ 78 Edgar Bennett .... .15 .07
❑ 79 Curtis Conway.................. .25 .11
❑ 80 Darnell Autry .... .15 .07
❑ 81 Ryan Wetnight RC .... .15 .07
❑ 82 Walt Harris .... .15 .07
❑ 83 Bobby Engram .... .25 .11
❑ 84 Jeff Blake .... .25 .11
❑ 85 Carl Pickens .... .50 .23
❑ 86 Darnay Scott .... .25 .11
❑ 87 Corey Dillon..................... .75 .35
❑ 88 Reinard Wilson .... .15 .07
❑ 89 Ashley Ambrose .... .15 .07
❑ 90 Troy Aikman .... 1.25 .55
❑ 91 Michael Irvin .... .50 .23
❑ 92 Emmitt Smith................. 2.00 .90
❑ 93 Deion Sanders .... .50 .23
❑ 94 David LaFleur .... .15 .07
❑ 95 Chris Warren .... .25 .11
❑ 96 Darren Woodson.............. .15 .07
❑ 97 John Elway 2.50 1.10
❑ 98 Terrell Davis .... 2.00 .90
❑ 99 Rod Smith .... .25 .11
❑ 100 Shannon Sharpe .... .25 .11
❑ 101 Ed McCaffrey .... .25 .11
❑ 102 Steve Atwater .... .15 .07
❑ 103 John Mobley .... .15 .07
❑ 104 Darrien Gordon .... .15 .07
❑ 105 Barry Sanders 2.50 1.10
❑ 106 Scott Mitchell.................. .25 .11
❑ 107 Herman Moore .... .50 .23
❑ 108 Johnnie Morton .... .25 .11
❑ 109 Robert Porcher .... .15 .07
❑ 110 Bryant Westbrook .... .15 .07
❑ 111 Tommy Vardell .... .15 .07
❑ 112 Brett Favre 2.50 1.10
❑ 113 Dorsey Levens .... .50 .23
❑ 114 Reggie White.................. .50 .23
❑ 115 Antonio Freeman............ .50 .23
❑ 116 Robert Brooks .... .25 .11
❑ 117 Mark Chmura .... .25 .11
❑ 118 Derrick Mayes .... .25 .11
❑ 119 Gilbert Brown .... .15 .07
❑ 120 Marshall Faulk................ .50 .23
❑ 121 Jeff Burris .... .15 .07
❑ 122 Marvin Harrison.............. .25 .11
❑ 123 Quentin Coryatt.............. .15 .07
❑ 124 Ken Dilger .... .15 .07
❑ 125 Zack Crockett .... .15 .07
❑ 126 Mark Brunell .... 1.00 .45
❑ 127 Bryce Paup .... .15 .07
❑ 128 Tony Brackens .... .15 .07
❑ 129 Renaldo Wynn................ .15 .07
❑ 130 Keenan McCardell.......... .25 .11
❑ 131 Jimmy Smith .... .25 .11
❑ 132 Kevin Hardy.................... .15 .07
❑ 133 Elvis Grbac .... .25 .11
❑ 134 Tamarick Vanover .... .15 .07
❑ 135 Chester McGlockton ...... .15 .07
❑ 136 Andre Rison .... .25 .11
❑ 137 Derrick Alexander .... .25 .11
❑ 138 Tony Gonzalez .... .15 .07
❑ 139 Derrick Thomas.............. .25 .11
❑ 140 Dan Marino 2.50 1.10
❑ 141 Karim Abdul-Jabbar ...... .50 .23
❑ 142 O.J. McDuffie .... .25 .11
❑ 143 Yatil Green .... .15 .07
❑ 144 Charles Jordan .... .15 .07
❑ 145 Brock Marion................... .15 .07
❑ 146 Zach Thomas .... .15 .07
❑ 147 Brad Johnson .... .50 .23
❑ 148 Cris Carter...................... .50 .23
❑ 149 Jake Reed....................... .25 .11
❑ 150 Robert Smith .... .50 .23
❑ 151 John Randle .... .25 .11
❑ 152 Dwayne Rudd .... .15 .07
❑ 153 Randall Cunningham...... .50 .23
❑ 154 Drew Bledsoe .... 1.00 .45
❑ 155 Terry Glenn .... .50 .23
❑ 156 Ben Coates .... .25 .11
❑ 157 Willie Clay .... .15 .07
❑ 158 Chris Slade .... .15 .07
❑ 159 Derrick Cullors RC .... .25 .11
❑ 160 Ty Law............................ .15 .07
❑ 161 Danny Wuerffel .... .25 .11
❑ 162 Andre Hastings .... .15 .07
❑ 163 Troy Davis....................... .15 .07
❑ 164 Billy Joe Hobert.............. .15 .07
❑ 165 Eric Guliford .... .15 .07
❑ 166 Mark Fields .... .15 .07
❑ 167 Alex Molden .... .15 .07
❑ 168 Danny Kanell .... .25 .11
❑ 169 Tiki Barber...................... .25 .11
❑ 170 Charles Way .... .15 .07
❑ 171 Amani Toomer................ .25 .11
❑ 172 Michael Strahan .... .15 .07
❑ 173 Jessie Armstead .... .15 .07
❑ 174 Jason Sehorn .... .15 .07
❑ 175 Glenn Foley.................... .25 .11
❑ 176 Curtis Martin .... .50 .23
❑ 177 Aaron Glenn .... .15 .07
❑ 178 Keyshawn Johnson......... .50 .23
❑ 179 James Farrior .... .15 .07
❑ 180 Wayne Chrebet .... .50 .23
❑ 181 Keith Byars .... .15 .07
❑ 182 Jeff George .... .25 .11
❑ 183 Napoleon Kaufman .... .50 .23
❑ 184 Tim Brown...................... .50 .23
❑ 185 Darrell Russell................ .15 .07
❑ 186 Rickey Dudley .... .15 .07
❑ 187 James Jett...................... .25 .11
❑ 188 Desmond Howard .... .25 .11
❑ 189 Bobby Hoying .... .25 .11
❑ 190 Charlie Garner................ .15 .07
❑ 191 Irving Fryar .... .25 .11
❑ 192 Chris T. Jones................. .15 .07
❑ 193 Mike Mamula.................. .15 .07
❑ 194 Troy Vincent .... .15 .07
❑ 195 Kordell Stewart .... .50 .23
❑ 196 Jerome Bettis .... .50 .23
❑ 197 Will Blackwell .... .15 .07
❑ 198 Levon Kirkland .... .15 .07
❑ 199 Carnell Lake .... .15 .07
❑ 200 Charles Johnson .... .15 .07
❑ 201 Greg Lloyd...................... .15 .07
❑ 202 Donnell Woolford............ .15 .07
❑ 203 Tony Banks .... .25 .11
❑ 204 Amp Lee .... .15 .07
❑ 205 Isaac Bruce .... .50 .23
❑ 206 Eddie Kennison .... .25 .11
❑ 207 Ryan McNeil .... .15 .07
❑ 208 Mike Jones .... .15 .07
❑ 209 Ernie Conwell .... .15 .07
❑ 210 Natrone Means .... .50 .23
❑ 211 Junior Seau .... .25 .11
❑ 212 Tony Martin..................... .25 .11

Card	Player	MINT	NRMT
213	Freddie Jones	.15	.07
214	Bryan Still	.15	.07
215	Rodney Harrison	.25	.11
216	Steve Young	.75	.35
217	Jerry Rice	1.25	.55
218	Garrison Hearst	.50	.23
219	J.J. Stokes	.25	.11
220	Ken Norton	.15	.07
221	Greg Clark	.15	.07
222	Terrell Owens	.50	.23
223	Bryant Young	.15	.07
224	Warren Moon	.50	.23
225	Jon Kitna	1.50	.70
226	Ricky Watters	.25	.11
227	Chad Brown	.15	.07
228	Joey Galloway	.50	.23
229	Shawn Springs	.15	.07
230	Cortez Kennedy	.15	.07
231	Trent Dilfer	.50	.23
232	Warrick Dunn	.50	.23
233	Mike Alstott	.50	.23
234	Warren Sapp	.25	.11
235	Bert Emanuel	.25	.11
236	Reidel Anthony	.25	.11
237	Hardy Nickerson	.15	.07
238	Derrick Brooks	.15	.07
239	Steve McNair	.50	.23
240	Yancey Thigpen	.15	.07
241	Anthony Dorsett	.15	.07
242	Blaine Bishop	.15	.07
243	Kenny Holmes	.15	.07
244	Eddie George	1.00	.45
245	Chris Sanders	.15	.07
246	Gus Frerotte	.15	.07
247	Terry Allen	.50	.23
248	Dana Stubblefield	.15	.07
249	Michael Westbrook	.25	.11
250	Darrell Green	.25	.11
251	Brian Mitchell	.15	.07
252	Ken Harvey	.15	.07
CL1	Troy Aikman CL	.50	.23
CL2	Dan Marino CL	.75	.35
CL3	Herman Moore CL	.25	.11

1998 Upper Deck Constant Threat

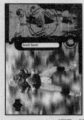

	MINT	NRMT
COMPLETE SET (30)	100.00	45.00
COMMON CARD (CT1-CT30)	1.00	.45
SEMISTARS	1.50	.70
UNLISTED STARS	2.50	1.10

STATED ODDS 1:12
*BRONZE DIE CUT STARS: 12X TO 30X
*BRONZE DIE CUT ROOKIES: 8X TO 20X
BRONZE DIE CUT PRINT RUN 25 SETS
*SILVER DIE CUTS: .75X TO 2X..
SILVER DIE CUT PRINT RUN 1000 SETS

Card	Player	MINT	NRMT
CT1	Dan Marino	10.00	4.50
CT2	Peyton Manning	15.00	6.75
CT3	Randy Moss	15.00	6.75
CT4	Brett Favre	10.00	4.50
CT5	Mark Brunell	4.00	1.80
CT6	Keyshawn Johnson	2.50	1.10
CT7	John Elway	10.00	4.50
CT8	Troy Aikman	5.00	2.20
CT9	Steve Young	3.00	1.35
CT10	Kordell Stewart	2.50	1.10
CT11	Drew Bledsoe	4.00	1.80
CT12	Joey Galloway	2.50	1.10
CT13	Elvis Grbac	1.50	.70
CT14	Marvin Harrison	1.00	.45
CT15	Napoleon Kaufman	2.50	1.10
CT16	Ryan Leaf	3.00	1.35
CT17	Jake Plummer	5.00	2.20
CT18	Terrell Davis	8.00	3.60
CT19	Steve McNair	2.50	1.10
CT20	Barry Sanders	10.00	4.50
CT21	Deion Sanders	2.50	1.10
CT22	Emmitt Smith	8.00	3.60
CT23	Antowain Smith	2.50	1.10
CT24	Herman Moore	2.50	1.10
CT25	Curtis Martin	2.50	1.10
CT26	Jerry Rice	5.00	2.20
CT27	Eddie George	4.00	1.80
CT28	Warrick Dunn	2.50	1.10
CT29	Curtis Enis	4.00	1.80
CT30	Michael Irvin	2.50	1.10

1998 Upper Deck Define the Game

	MINT	NRMT
COMPLETE SET (30)	80.00	36.00
COMMON CARD (DG1-DG30)	1.00	.45
SEMISTARS	2.00	.90

STATED ODDS 1:8
*BRONZE DIE CUT STARS: 15X TO 30X
*BRONZE DIE CUT ROOKIES: 10X TO 20X
BRONZE DIE CUT PRINT RUN 50 SETS
*SILVER DIE CUTS: .75X TO 2X..
SILVER DIE CUT PRINT RUN 1500 SETS

Card	Player	MINT	NRMT
DG1	Dan Marino	10.00	4.50
DG2	Curtis Enis	3.00	1.35
DG3	Dorsey Levens	2.00	.90
DG4	Charles Woodson	3.00	1.35
DG5	Junior Seau	2.00	.90
DG6	Tiki Barber	2.00	.90
DG7	Randy Moss	15.00	6.75
DG8	Troy Aikman	5.00	2.20
DG9	Jake Plummer	5.00	2.20
DG10	Corey Dillon	2.50	1.10
DG11	Jerry Rice	5.00	2.20
DG12	Emmitt Smith	8.00	3.60
DG13	Herman Moore	2.50	1.10
DG14	Brad Johnson	2.50	1.10
DG15	Gus Frerotte	1.00	.45
DG16	Ryan Leaf	3.00	1.35
DG17	Shannon Sharpe	2.00	.90
DG18	Jermaine Lewis	2.00	.90
DG19	Jerome Bettis	2.50	1.10
DG20	Barry Sanders	10.00	4.50
DG21	Terry Allen	2.50	1.10
DG22	Reidel Anthony	2.00	.90
DG23	Isaac Bruce	2.50	1.10
DG24	Mike Alstott	2.50	1.10
DG25	Rae Carruth	2.00	.90
DG26	Tamarick Vanover	1.00	.45
DG27	Eddie George	4.00	1.80
DG28	Warrick Dunn	2.50	1.10
DG29	Tony Gonzalez	1.00	.45
DG30	Keenan McCardell	2.00	.90

1998 Upper Deck Game Jersey

	MINT	NRMT
COMPLETE SET (20)	2500.00	1100.00
COMMON CARD (GJ1-GJ20)	50.00	22.00
SEMISTARS	80.00	36.00

1-10 STATED ODDS 1:2500
11-20 STATED ODDS 1:288 HOBBY

Card	Player	MINT	NRMT
GJ1	Brett Favre	200.00	90.00
GJ2	Reggie White	100.00	45.00
GJ3	Barry Sanders	200.00	90.00
GJ4	John Elway	200.00	90.00
GJ5	Mark Brunell	150.00	70.00
GJ6	Mike Alstott	120.00	55.00
GJ7	Ryan Leaf	120.00	55.00
GJ8	Andre Wadsworth	50.00	22.00
GJ9	Robert Edwards	50.00	22.00
GJ10	Kevin Dyson	80.00	36.00
GJ11	Dan Marino	250.00	110.00
GJ11S	Dan Marino AUTO/13	5000.00	2200.00
GJ12	Deion Sanders	100.00	45.00
GJ13	Steve Young	120.00	55.00
GJ14	Terrell Davis	120.00	55.00
GJ15	Tim Brown	80.00	36.00
GJ16	Peyton Manning	350.00	160.00
GJ17	Takeo Spikes	50.00	22.00
GJ18	Curtis Enis	80.00	36.00
GJ19	Fred Taylor	175.00	80.00
GJ20	John Avery	50.00	22.00

1998 Upper Deck Super Powers

	MINT	NRMT
COMPLETE SET (30)	50.00	22.00
COMMON CARD (S1-S30)	1.00	.45
SEMISTARS	1.50	.70

STATED ODDS 1:4 HOB, 1:2 RET
*BRONZE DIE CUTS: 7.5X TO 20X
BRONZE DIE CUT PRINT RUN 100 SETS
*SILVER DIE CUTS: .75X TO 2X..
SILVER DIE CUT PRINT RUN 2000 SETS

Card	Player	MINT	NRMT
S1	Dan Marino	6.00	2.70
S2	Jerry Rice	3.00	1.35
S3	Napoleon Kaufman	1.50	.70
S4	Brett Favre	6.00	2.70
S5	Andre Rison	1.00	.45
S6	Jerome Bettis	1.50	.70
S7	John Elway	6.00	2.70
S8	Troy Aikman	3.00	1.35
S9	Steve Young	2.00	.90
S10	Kordell Stewart	1.50	.70
S11	Drew Bledsoe	2.50	1.10
S12	Antonio Freeman	1.50	.70
S13	Mark Brunell	2.50	1.10
S14	Shannon Sharpe	1.50	.70
S15	Trent Dilfer	1.50	.70
S16	Peyton Manning	10.00	4.50
S17	Cris Carter	1.50	.70
S18	Michael Irvin	1.50	.70
S19	Terry Glenn	1.50	.70
S20	Keyshawn Johnson	1.50	.70
S21	Deion Sanders	1.50	.70

❑ S22 Emmitt Smith	5.00	2.20
❑ S23 Marcus Allen	1.50	.70
❑ S24 Dorsey Levens	1.50	.70
❑ S25 Jake Plummer	3.00	1.35
❑ S26 Eddie George	2.50	1.10
❑ S27 Tim Brown	1.50	.70
❑ S28 Warrick Dunn	1.50	.70
❑ S29 Reggie White	1.50	.70
❑ S30 Terrell Davis	5.00	2.20

1999 Upper Deck

	MINT	NRMT
COMPLETE SET (270)	200.00	90.00
COMP.SET w/o SP's (225)	25.00	11.00
COMMON CARD (1-270)	.15	.07
SEMISTARS	.30	.14
UNLISTED STARS	.60	.25
COMMON ROOKIE (226-270)	2.00	.90
ROOKIE SEMISTARS	3.00	1.35
ROOKIE UNL.STARS	4.00	1.80

ROOKIE SUBSET STATED ODDS 1:4

Card	MINT	NRMT
❑ 1 Jake Plummer	1.25	.55
❑ 2 Adrian Murrell	.30	.14
❑ 3 Rob Moore	.30	.14
❑ 4 Larry Centers	.15	.07
❑ 5 Simeon Rice	.15	.07
❑ 6 Andre Wadsworth	.15	.07
❑ 7 Frank Sanders	.30	.14
❑ 8 Tim Dwight	.60	.25
❑ 9 Ray Buchanan	.15	.07
❑ 10 Chris Chandler	.30	.14
❑ 11 Jamal Anderson	.60	.25
❑ 12 O.J. Santiago	.15	.07
❑ 13 Danny Kanell	.15	.07
❑ 14 Terance Mathis	.30	.14
❑ 15 Priest Holmes	.60	.25
❑ 16 Tony Banks	.30	.14
❑ 17 Ray Lewis	.15	.07
❑ 18 Patrick Johnson	.15	.07
❑ 19 Michael Jackson	.15	.07
❑ 20 Michael McCrary	.15	.07
❑ 21 Jermaine Lewis	.30	.14
❑ 22 Eric Moulds	.60	.25
❑ 23 Doug Flutie	.75	.35
❑ 24 Antowain Smith	.60	.25
❑ 25 Rob Johnson	.30	.14
❑ 26 Bruce Smith	.30	.14
❑ 27 Andre Reed	.30	.14
❑ 28 Thurman Thomas	.30	.14
❑ 29 Fred Lane	.30	.14
❑ 30 Wesley Walls	.30	.14
❑ 31 Tim Biakabutuka	.30	.14
❑ 32 Kevin Greene	.15	.07
❑ 33 Steve Beuerlein	.15	.07
❑ 34 Muhsin Muhammad	.30	.14
❑ 35 Rae Carruth	.30	.14
❑ 36 Bobby Engram	.30	.14
❑ 37 Curtis Enis	.60	.25
❑ 38 Edgar Bennett	.15	.07
❑ 39 Erik Kramer	.15	.07
❑ 40 Steve Stenstrom	.15	.07
❑ 41 Alonzo Mayes	.15	.07
❑ 42 Curtis Conway	.30	.14
❑ 43 Tony McGee	.15	.07
❑ 44 Darnay Scott	.15	.07
❑ 45 Jeff Blake	.30	.14
❑ 46 Corey Dillon	.60	.25
❑ 47 Ki-Jana Carter	.15	.07
❑ 48 Takeo Spikes	.15	.07
❑ 49 Carl Pickens	.30	.14
❑ 50 Ty Detmer	.30	.14
❑ 51 Leslie Shepherd	.15	.07
❑ 52 Terry Kirby	.15	.07
❑ 53 Marquez Pope	.15	.07
❑ 54 Antonio Langham	.15	.07
❑ 55 Jamir Miller	.15	.07
❑ 56 Derrick Alexander DT	.15	.07
❑ 57 Troy Aikman	1.50	.70
❑ 58 Rocket Ismail	.30	.14
❑ 59 Emmitt Smith	1.50	.70
❑ 60 Michael Irvin	.30	.14
❑ 61 David LaFleur	.15	.07
❑ 62 Chris Warren	.15	.07
❑ 63 Deion Sanders	.60	.25
❑ 64 Greg Ellis	.15	.07
❑ 65 John Elway	2.50	1.10
❑ 66 Bubby Brister	.15	.07
❑ 67 Terrell Davis	1.50	.70
❑ 68 Ed McCaffrey	.30	.14
❑ 69 John Mobley	.15	.07
❑ 70 Bill Romanowski	.15	.07
❑ 71 Rod Smith	.30	.14
❑ 72 Shannon Sharpe	.30	.14
❑ 73 Charlie Batch	1.25	.55
❑ 74 Germane Crowell	.30	.14
❑ 75 Johnnie Morton	.15	.07
❑ 76 Barry Sanders	2.50	1.10
❑ 77 Robert Porcher	.15	.07
❑ 78 Stephen Boyd	.15	.07
❑ 79 Herman Moore	.60	.25
❑ 80 Brett Favre	2.50	1.10
❑ 81 Mark Chmura	.15	.07
❑ 82 Antonio Freeman	.60	.25
❑ 83 Robert Brooks	.30	.14
❑ 84 Vonnie Holliday	.15	.07
❑ 85 Bill Schroeder	.60	.25
❑ 86 Dorsey Levens	.60	.25
❑ 87 Santana Dotson	.15	.07
❑ 88 Peyton Manning	2.50	1.10
❑ 89 Jerome Pathon	.15	.07
❑ 90 Marvin Harrison	.60	.25
❑ 91 Ellis Johnson	.15	.07
❑ 92 Ken Dilger	.15	.07
❑ 93 E.G. Green	.15	.07
❑ 94 Jeff Burris	.15	.07
❑ 95 Mark Brunell	1.00	.45
❑ 96 Fred Taylor	1.50	.70
❑ 97 Jimmy Smith	.30	.14
❑ 98 James Stewart	.30	.14
❑ 99 Kyle Brady	.15	.07
❑ 100 Dave Thomas RC	.15	.07
❑ 101 Keenan McCardell	.30	.14
❑ 102 Elvis Grbac	.30	.14
❑ 103 Tony Gonzalez	.30	.14
❑ 104 Andre Rison	.30	.14
❑ 105 Donnell Bennett	.15	.07
❑ 106 Derrick Thomas	.30	.14
❑ 107 Warren Moon	.60	.25
❑ 108 Derrick Alexander WR	.30	.14
❑ 109 Dan Marino	2.50	1.10
❑ 110 O.J. McDuffie	.30	.14
❑ 111 Karim Abdul-Jabbar	.30	.14
❑ 112 John Avery	.30	.14
❑ 113 Sam Madison	.15	.07
❑ 114 Jason Taylor	.15	.07
❑ 115 Zach Thomas	.30	.14
❑ 116 Randall Cunningham	.60	.25
❑ 117 Randy Moss	2.50	1.10
❑ 118 Cris Carter	.60	.25
❑ 119 Jake Reed	.30	.14
❑ 120 Matthew Hatchette	.15	.07
❑ 121 John Randle	.30	.14
❑ 122 Robert Smith	.60	.25
❑ 123 Drew Bledsoe	1.00	.45
❑ 124 Ben Coates	.30	.14
❑ 125 Terry Glenn	.60	.25
❑ 126 Ty Law	.15	.07
❑ 127 Tony Simmons	.15	.07
❑ 128 Ted Johnson	.15	.07
❑ 129 Tony Carter	.15	.07
❑ 130 Willie McGinest	.15	.07
❑ 131 Danny Wuerffel	.15	.07
❑ 132 Cameron Cleeland	.15	.07
❑ 133 Eddie Kennison	.30	.14
❑ 134 Joe Johnson	.15	.07
❑ 135 Andre Hastings	.15	.07
❑ 136 La'Roi Glover	.15	.07
❑ 137 Kent Graham	.15	.07
❑ 138 Tiki Barber	.15	.07
❑ 139 Gary Brown	.15	.07
❑ 140 Ike Hilliard	.15	.07
❑ 141 Jason Sehorn	.15	.07
❑ 142 Michael Strahan	.15	.07
❑ 143 Amani Toomer	.15	.07
❑ 144 Kerry Collins	.30	.14
❑ 145 Vinny Testaverde	.30	.14
❑ 146 Wayne Chrebet	.30	.14
❑ 147 Curtis Martin	.60	.25
❑ 148 Mo Lewis	.15	.07
❑ 149 Aaron Glenn	.15	.07
❑ 150 Steve Atwater	.15	.07
❑ 151 Keyshawn Johnson	.60	.25
❑ 152 James Farrior	.15	.07
❑ 153 Rich Gannon	.30	.14
❑ 154 Tim Brown	.60	.25
❑ 155 Darrell Russell	.15	.07
❑ 156 Rickey Dudley	.15	.07
❑ 157 Charles Woodson	.60	.25
❑ 158 James Jett	.30	.14
❑ 159 Napoleon Kaufman	.60	.25
❑ 160 Duce Staley	.60	.25
❑ 161 Doug Pederson	.15	.07
❑ 162 Bobby Hoying	.30	.14
❑ 163 Koy Detmer	.15	.07
❑ 164 Kevin Turner	.15	.07
❑ 165 Charles Johnson	.15	.07
❑ 166 Mike Mamula	.15	.07
❑ 167 Jerome Bettis	.60	.25
❑ 168 Courtney Hawkins	.15	.07
❑ 169 Will Blackwell	.15	.07
❑ 170 Kordell Stewart	.60	.25
❑ 171 Richard Huntley	.30	.14
❑ 172 Levon Kirkland	.15	.07
❑ 173 Hines Ward	.15	.07
❑ 174 Trent Green	.30	.14
❑ 175 Marshall Faulk	.60	.25
❑ 176 Az-Zahir Hakim	.15	.07
❑ 177 Amp Lee	.15	.07
❑ 178 Robert Holcombe	.30	.14
❑ 179 Isaac Bruce	.60	.25
❑ 180 Kevin Carter	.15	.07
❑ 181 Jim Harbaugh	.30	.14
❑ 182 Junior Seau	.30	.14
❑ 183 Natrone Means	.30	.14
❑ 184 Ryan Leaf	.60	.25
❑ 185 Charlie Jones	.15	.07
❑ 186 Rodney Harrison	.15	.07
❑ 187 Mikhael Ricks	.15	.07
❑ 188 Steve Young	1.00	.45
❑ 189 Terrell Owens	.60	.25
❑ 190 Jerry Rice	1.50	.70
❑ 191 J.J. Stokes	.30	.14
❑ 192 Irv Smith	.15	.07
❑ 193 Bryant Young	.15	.07
❑ 194 Garrison Hearst	.30	.14
❑ 195 Jon Kitna	.75	.35
❑ 196 Ahman Green	.30	.14
❑ 197 Joey Galloway	.60	.25
❑ 198 Ricky Watters	.30	.14
❑ 199 Chad Brown	.15	.07
❑ 200 Shawn Springs	.15	.07
❑ 201 Mike Pritchard	.15	.07
❑ 202 Trent Dilfer	.30	.14
❑ 203 Reidel Anthony	.30	.14
❑ 204 Bert Emanuel	.30	.14
❑ 205 Warrick Dunn	.60	.25
❑ 206 Jacquez Green	.30	.14
❑ 207 Hardy Nickerson	.15	.07
❑ 208 Mike Alstott	.60	.25
❑ 209 Eddie George	.75	.35
❑ 210 Steve McNair	.60	.25
❑ 211 Kevin Dyson	.30	.14
❑ 212 Frank Wycheck	.15	.07
❑ 213 Jackie Harris	.15	.07
❑ 214 Blaine Bishop	.15	.07
❑ 215 Yancey Thigpen	.15	.07
❑ 216 Brad Johnson	.60	.25
❑ 217 Rodney Peete	.15	.07

❑ 218 Michael Westbrook	.30	.14
❑ 219 Skip Hicks	.60	.25
❑ 220 Brian Mitchell	.15	.07
❑ 221 Dan Wilkinson	.15	.07
❑ 222 Dana Stubblefield	.15	.07
❑ 223 Kordell Stewart CL	.30	.14
❑ 224 Fred Taylor CL	.60	.25
❑ 225 Warrick Dunn CL	.30	.14
❑ 226 Champ Bailey RC	6.00	2.70
❑ 227 Chris McAlister RC	3.00	1.35
❑ 228 Jevon Kearse RC	10.00	4.50
❑ 229 Ebenezer Ekuban RC	3.00	1.35
❑ 230 Chris Claiborne RC	3.00	1.35
❑ 231 Andy Katzenmoyer RC	4.00	1.80
❑ 232 Tim Couch RC	25.00	11.00
❑ 233 Daunte Culpepper RC	15.00	6.75
❑ 234 Akili Smith RC	10.00	4.50
❑ 235 Donovan McNabb RC	15.00	6.75
❑ 236 Sean Bennett RC	4.00	1.80
❑ 237 Brock Huard RC	6.00	2.70
❑ 238 Cade McNown RC	15.00	6.75
❑ 239 Shaun King RC	15.00	6.75
❑ 240 Joe Germaine RC	4.00	1.80
❑ 241 Ricky Williams RC	25.00	11.00
❑ 242 Edgerrin James RC	40.00	18.00
❑ 243 Sedrick Irvin RC	4.00	1.80
❑ 244 Kevin Faulk RC	6.00	2.70
❑ 245 Rob Konrad RC	4.00	1.80
❑ 246 James Johnson RC	6.00	2.70
❑ 247 Amos Zereoue RC	4.00	1.80
❑ 248 Torry Holt RC	12.00	5.50
❑ 249 D'Wayne Bates RC	4.00	1.80
❑ 250 David Boston RC	8.00	3.60
❑ 251 Dameane Douglas RC	4.00	1.80
❑ 252 Troy Edwards RC	8.00	3.60
❑ 253 Kevin Johnson RC	12.00	5.50
❑ 254 Peerless Price RC	8.00	3.60
❑ 255 Antoine Winfield RC	3.00	1.35
❑ 256 Mike Cloud RC	4.00	1.80
❑ 257 Joe Montgomery RC	4.00	1.80
❑ 258 Jermaine Fazande RC	3.00	1.35
❑ 259 Scott Covington RC	4.00	1.80
❑ 260 Aaron Brooks RC	4.00	1.80
❑ 261 Patrick Kerney RC	2.00	.90
❑ 262 Cecil Collins RC	4.00	1.80
❑ 263 Chris Greisen RC	6.00	2.70
❑ 264 Craig Yeast RC	3.00	1.35
❑ 265 Karsten Bailey RC	3.00	1.35
❑ 266 Reginald Kelly RC	2.00	.90
❑ 267 Al Wilson RC	3.00	1.35
❑ 268 Jeff Paulk RC	4.00	1.80
❑ 269 Jim Kleinsasser RC	4.00	1.80
❑ 270 Darrin Chiaverini RC	3.00	1.35

1999 Upper Deck Exclusives Silver

	MINT	NRMT
COMMON CARD (1-270)	8.00	3.60

*EXC.SILVER STARS: 20X TO 50X HI COL.
*EXC.SILVER YOUNG STARS: 15X TO 40X
*EXC.SILVER RCs: 1.5X TO 4X ..
EXC.SILVER PRINT RUN 100 SER.#'d SETS
UNPRICED GOLD PARALLEL SER.#'d TO 1

1999 Upper Deck 21 TD Salute

	MINT	NRMT
COMPLETE SET (10)	40.00	18.00
COMMON CARD (TD1-TD10)	5.00	2.20

STATED ODDS 1:23
*SILVERS: 3X TO 8X HI COL.
SILVER STATED PRINT RUN 100 SER.#'d SETS
UNPRICED GOLD PARALLEL SER.#'d TO 1

❑ TD1 Terrell Davis	5.00	2.20
❑ TD2 Terrell Davis	5.00	2.20
❑ TD3 Terrell Davis	5.00	2.20
❑ TD4 Terrell Davis	5.00	2.20
❑ TD5 Terrell Davis	5.00	2.20
❑ TD6 Terrell Davis	5.00	2.20
❑ TD7 Terrell Davis	5.00	2.20
❑ TD8 Terrell Davis	5.00	2.20
❑ TD9 Terrell Davis	5.00	2.20
❑ TD10 Terrell Davis	5.00	2.20

1999 Upper Deck Game Jersey

	MINT	NRMT
COMPLETE SET (21)	3500.00	1600.00
COMMON CARD	60.00	27.00

HOBBY PACK (H) STATED ODDS 1:288
HOBBY/RETAIL ODDS 1:2500

❑ BH Brock Huard H	60.00	27.00
❑ BS Barry Sanders H	150.00	70.00
❑ CM Cade McNown H	120.00	55.00
❑ DB Drew Bledsoe H/R	150.00	70.00
❑ DC Daunte Culpepper H	100.00	45.00
❑ DF Doug Flutie H/R	100.00	45.00
❑ DM Dan Marino H/R	250.00	110.00
❑ DV David Boston H	60.00	27.00
❑ EJ Edgerrin James H/R	400.00	180.00
❑ EM Eric Moulds H	60.00	27.00
❑ JA Jamal Anderson H/R	80.00	36.00
❑ JE John Elway H	150.00	70.00
❑ JR Jerry Rice H	120.00	55.00
❑ KJ Keyshawn Johnson H/R	80.00	36.00
❑ MC Donovan McNabb H	100.00	45.00
❑ PM Peyton Manning H	200.00	90.00
❑ RM Randy Moss H/R	400.00	180.00
❑ SY Steve Young H/R	120.00	55.00
❑ TA Troy Aikman H	120.00	55.00
❑ TC Tim Couch H	300.00	135.00
❑ TD Terrell Davis H/R	200.00	90.00
❑ BH-A Brock Huard AUTO/5 H		
❑ CM-A Cade McNown AUTO/8 H		
❑ TC-A Tim Couch AUTO/2 H/R		
❑ TD-A T.Davis AUTO/30 H/R	1500.00	700.00

1999 Upper Deck Game Jersey Patch

	MINT	NRMT
COMPLETE SET (19)	8000.00	3600.00
COMMON CARD	200.00	90.00

STATED ODDS 1:7500

❑ BH-P Brock Huard	200.00	90.00
❑ BS-P Barry Sanders	800.00	350.00
❑ CM-P Cade McNown	400.00	180.00
❑ DB-P Drew Bledsoe	400.00	180.00
❑ DC-P Daunte Culpepper	400.00	180.00
❑ DF-P Doug Flutie	400.00	180.00
❑ DM-P Dan Marino	800.00	350.00
❑ DV-P David Boston	250.00	110.00
❑ EJ-P Edgerrin James	800.00	350.00
❑ JA-P Jamal Anderson	300.00	135.00
❑ JE-P John Elway	800.00	350.00
❑ JR-P Jerry Rice	500.00	220.00
❑ MC-P Donovan McNabb	400.00	180.00
❑ PM-P Peyton Manning	600.00	275.00
❑ RM-P Randy Moss	800.00	350.00
❑ SY-P Steve Young	400.00	180.00
❑ TA-P Troy Aikman	500.00	220.00
❑ TC-P Tim Couch	600.00	275.00
❑ TD-P Terrell Davis	500.00	220.00

1999 Upper Deck Highlight Zone

	MINT	NRMT
COMPLETE SET (20)	120.00	55.00
COMMON CARD (Z1-Z20)	3.00	1.35

STATED ODDS 1:23
*SILVERS: 2.5X TO 6X HI COL.
SILVER STATED PRINT RUN 100 SER.#'d SETS
UNPRICED GOLD PARALLEL SER.#'d TO 1

❑ Z1 Terrell Davis	8.00	3.60
❑ Z2 Ricky Williams	10.00	4.50
❑ Z3 Akili Smith	5.00	2.20
❑ Z4 Charlie Batch	5.00	2.20
❑ Z5 Jake Plummer	6.00	2.70
❑ Z6 Emmitt Smith	8.00	3.60
❑ Z7 Dan Marino	12.00	5.50
❑ Z8 Tim Couch	10.00	4.50
❑ Z9 Randy Moss	10.00	4.50
❑ Z10 Troy Aikman	8.00	3.60
❑ Z11 Barry Sanders	12.00	5.50
❑ Z12 Jerry Rice	8.00	3.60
❑ Z13 Mark Brunell	5.00	2.20
❑ Z14 Jamal Anderson	3.00	1.35
❑ Z15 Peyton Manning	10.00	4.50
❑ Z16 Jerome Bettis	3.00	1.35
❑ Z17 Donovan McNabb	6.00	2.70
❑ Z18 Steve Young	5.00	2.20
❑ Z19 Keyshawn Johnson	3.00	1.35
❑ Z20 Brett Favre	12.00	5.50

1999 Upper Deck Livewires

	MINT	NRMT
COMPLETE SET (15)	25.00	11.00
COMMON CARD (L1-L15)	1.25	.55

STATED ODDS 1:10
*SILVERS: 6X TO 15X HI COL.
SILVER STATED PRINT RUN 100 SER.#'d SETS
UNPRICED GOLD PARALLEL SER.#'d TO 1

❑ L1 Jake Plummer	2.50	1.10
❑ L2 Jamal Anderson	1.25	.55
❑ L3 Emmitt Smith	3.00	1.35
❑ L4 John Elway	5.00	2.20
❑ L5 Barry Sanders	5.00	2.20
❑ L6 Brett Favre	5.00	2.20
❑ L7 Mark Brunell	2.00	.90

❑ L8 Fred Taylor	2.50	1.10
❑ L9 Randy Moss	4.00	1.80
❑ L10 Drew Bledsoe	2.00	.90
❑ L11 Keyshawn Johnson	1.25	.55
❑ L12 Jerome Bettis	1.25	.55
❑ L13 Kordell Stewart	1.25	.55
❑ L14 Terrell Owens	1.25	.55
❑ L15 Eddie George	1.50	.70

1999 Upper Deck PowerDeck Inserts

	MINT	NRMT
COMPLETE SET (16)	300.00	135.00
COMMON CARD (1-16)	3.00	1.35
STATED ODDS 1:24		
SP STATED ODDS 1:288		

❑ 1 Troy Aikman	8.00	3.60
❑ 2 Tim Couch SP	60.00	27.00
❑ 3 Daunte Culpepper SP	30.00	13.50
❑ 4 Terrell Davis	8.00	3.60
❑ 5 John Elway SP	40.00	18.00
❑ 6 Joe Germaine	3.00	1.35
❑ 7 Brock Huard	3.00	1.35
❑ 8 Shaun King	8.00	3.60
❑ 9 Dan Marino SP	40.00	18.00
❑ 10 Peyton Manning SP	40.00	18.00
❑ 11 Donovan McNabb	8.00	3.60
❑ 12 Cade McNown SP	30.00	13.50
❑ 13 Joe Montana	12.00	5.50
❑ 14 Randy Moss	12.00	5.50
❑ 15 Barry Sanders SP	40.00	18.00
❑ 16 Akili Smith SP	20.00	9.00

1999 Upper Deck Quarterback Class

	MINT	NRMT
COMPLETE SET (15)	30.00	13.50
COMMON CARD (QC1-QC15)	1.50	.70
STATED ODDS 1:10		
*SILVERS: 6X TO 15X HI COL.		
SILVER STATED PRINT RUN 100 SER.#'d SETS		
UNPRICED GOLD PARALLEL SER.#'d TO 1		

❑ QC1 Tim Couch	6.00	2.70
❑ QC2 Akili Smith	2.50	1.10
❑ QC3 Daunte Culpepper	4.00	1.80
❑ QC4 Cade McNown	4.00	1.80
❑ QC5 Donovan McNabb	4.00	1.80
❑ QC6 Brock Huard	1.50	.70
❑ QC7 John Elway	5.00	2.20
❑ QC8 Dan Marino	5.00	2.20
❑ QC9 Brett Favre	5.00	2.20
❑ QC10 Charlie Batch	2.00	.90
❑ QC11 Steve Young	2.00	.90
❑ QC12 Jake Plummer	2.50	1.10
❑ QC13 Peyton Manning	4.00	1.80
❑ QC14 Mark Brunell	2.00	.90
❑ QC15 Troy Aikman	3.00	1.35

1999 Upper Deck Strike Force

	MINT	NRMT
COMPLETE SET (30)	40.00	18.00
COMMON CARD (SF1-SF30)	.50	.23
SEMISTARS	1.00	.45
STATED ODDS 1:4		
*SILVERS: 8X TO 20X HI COL.		
SILVER STATED PRINT RUN 100 SER.#'d SETS		
UNPRICED GOLD PARALLEL SER.#'d TO 1		

❑ SF1 Jamal Anderson	1.00	.45
❑ SF2 Keyshawn Johnson	1.00	.45
❑ SF3 Eddie George	1.25	.55
❑ SF4 Steve Young	1.50	.70
❑ SF5 Emmitt Smith	2.50	1.10
❑ SF6 Karim Abdul-Jabbar	.50	.23
❑ SF7 Kordell Stewart	1.00	.45
❑ SF8 Cade McNown	3.00	1.35
❑ SF9 Tim Couch	5.00	2.20
❑ SF10 Corey Dillon	1.00	.45
❑ SF11 Peyton Manning	3.00	1.35
❑ SF12 Curtis Martin	1.00	.45
❑ SF13 Jerome Bettis	1.00	.45
❑ SF14 Jon Kitna	1.25	.55
❑ SF15 Dan Marino	4.00	1.80
❑ SF16 Eric Moulds	1.00	.45
❑ SF17 Charlie Batch	1.50	.70
❑ SF18 Ricky Williams	5.00	2.20
❑ SF19 Terrell Owens	1.00	.45
❑ SF20 Ty Detmer	1.00	.45
❑ SF21 Curtis Enis	1.00	.45
❑ SF22 Doug Flutie	1.25	.55
❑ SF23 Randall Cunningham	1.00	.45
❑ SF24 Donovan McNabb	3.00	1.35
❑ SF25 Steve McNair	1.00	.45
❑ SF26 Terrell Davis	2.50	1.10
❑ SF27 Daunte Culpepper	3.00	1.35
❑ SF28 Warrick Dunn	1.00	.45
❑ SF29 Akili Smith	2.00	.90
❑ SF30 Barry Sanders	4.00	1.80

1999 Upper Deck Century Legends

	MINT	NRMT
COMPLETE SET (173)	50.00	22.00
COMMON CARD (1-180)	.15	.07
SEMISTARS	.30	.14
UNLISTED STARS	.50	.23
COMMON ROOKIE (131-160)	.75	.35
ROOKIE SEMISTARS	1.25	.55
CARDS 4/6/14/26/31/38/43 NOT RELEASED		

❑ 1 Jim Brown	2.00	.90
❑ 2 Jerry Rice	1.25	.55
❑ 3 Joe Montana	3.00	1.35
❑ 5 Johnny Unitas	1.25	.55
❑ 7 Otto Graham	.50	.23
❑ 8 Walter Payton	3.00	1.35
❑ 9 Dick Butkus	1.00	.45
❑ 10 Bob Lilly	.30	.14
❑ 11 Sammy Baugh	.50	.23
❑ 12 Barry Sanders	2.00	.90
❑ 13 Deacon Jones	.30	.14
❑ 15 Gino Marchetti	.15	.07
❑ 16 John Elway	2.00	.90
❑ 17 Anthony Munoz	.15	.07
❑ 18 Ray Nitschke	.30	.14
❑ 19 Dick Lane	.15	.07
❑ 20 John Hannah	.15	.07
❑ 21 Gale Sayers	1.00	.45
❑ 22 Reggie White	.30	.14
❑ 23 Ronnie Lott	.30	.14
❑ 24 Jim Parker	.15	.07
❑ 25 Merlin Olsen	.30	.14
❑ 27 Dan Marino	2.00	.90
❑ 28 Forrest Gregg	.30	.14
❑ 29 Roger Staubach	1.50	.70
❑ 30 Jack Lambert	.30	.14
❑ 32 Marion Motley	.15	.07
❑ 33 Earl Campbell	.50	.23
❑ 34 Alan Page	.15	.07
❑ 35 Bronko Nagurski	.30	.14
❑ 36 Mel Blount	.15	.07
❑ 37 Deion Sanders	.50	.23
❑ 39 Sid Luckman	.30	.14
❑ 40 Raymond Berry	.30	.14
❑ 41 Bart Starr	1.25	.55
❑ 42 Willie Lanier	.15	.07
❑ 44 Terry Bradshaw	1.50	.70
❑ 45 Herb Adderley	.30	.14
❑ 46 Steve Largent	.30	.14
❑ 47 Jack Ham	.30	.14
❑ 48 John Mackey	.15	.07
❑ 49 Bill George	.15	.07
❑ 50 Willie Brown	.15	.07
❑ 51 Jerry Rice	1.25	.55
❑ 52 Barry Sanders	2.00	.90
❑ 53 John Elway	2.00	.90
❑ 54 Reggie White	.30	.14
❑ 55 Dan Marino	2.00	.90
❑ 56 Deion Sanders	.50	.23
❑ 57 Bruce Smith	.30	.14
❑ 58 Steve Young	.75	.35
❑ 59 Emmitt Smith	1.25	.55
❑ 60 Brett Favre	2.00	.90
❑ 61 Rod Woodson	.30	.14
❑ 62 Troy Aikman	1.25	.55
❑ 63 Terrell Davis	1.25	.55
❑ 64 Michael Irvin	.30	.14
❑ 65 Andre Rison	.30	.14
❑ 66 Warren Moon	.50	.23
❑ 67 Thurman Thomas	.30	.14
❑ 68 Randall Cunningham	.50	.23
❑ 69 Jerome Bettis	.50	.23
❑ 70 Junior Seau	.30	.14
❑ 71 Drew Bledsoe	.75	.35
❑ 72 Andre Reed	.30	.14
❑ 73 Tim Brown	.50	.23
❑ 74 Derrick Thomas	.30	.14
❑ 75 Jake Plummer	1.00	.45

❑ 76 Kordell Stewart .... .50 .23
❑ 77 Herman Moore .... .50 .23
❑ 78 Shannon Sharpe .... .30 .14
❑ 79 Antonio Freeman.............. .50 .23
❑ 80 Ricky Watters .... .30 .14
❑ 81 Warrick Dunn .... .50 .23
❑ 82 Mark Brunell .... .75 .35
❑ 83 Randy Moss .... 2.00 .90
❑ 84 Fred Taylor .... 1.25 .55
❑ 85 Curtis Martin .... .50 .23
❑ 86 Keyshawn Johnson .... .50 .23
❑ 87 Eddie George .... .60 .25
❑ 88 Marshall Faulk.................. .50 .23
❑ 89 Joey Galloway.................. .50 .23
❑ 90 Vinny Testaverde .... .30 .14
❑ 91 Garrison Hearst................ .30 .14
❑ 92 Jimmy Smith .... .30 .14
❑ 93 Doug Flutie .... .60 .25
❑ 94 Napoleon Kaufman .... .50 .23
❑ 95 Natrone Means .... .30 .14
❑ 96 Peyton Manning .... 2.00 .90
❑ 97 Steve McNair.................... .50 .23
❑ 98 Corey Dillon...................... .50 .23
❑ 99 Terrell Owens .... .50 .23
❑ 100 Charlie Batch................ 1.00 .45
❑ 101 Brett Favre APR .... 1.50 .70
❑ 102 Terrell Davis APR .... 1.00 .45
❑ 103 Roger Staubach APR .. 1.25 .55
❑ 104 Terry Bradshaw APR .. 1.25 .55
❑ 105 Fran Tarkenton APR ...... .60 .25
❑ 106 Walter Payton APR 2.50 1.10
❑ 107 Mark Brunell APR .... .60 .25
❑ 108 Jim Brown APR............ 1.50 .70
❑ 109 Kordell Stewart APR ...... .50 .23
❑ 110 Bart Starr APR .... 1.00 .45
❑ 111 Steve Largent APR .... .30 .14
❑ 112 Raymond Berry APR...... .15 .07
❑ 113 Emmitt Smith APR ...... 1.00 .45
❑ 114 Forrest Gregg APR .... .15 .07
❑ 115 Drew Bledsoe APR .... .60 .25
❑ 116 Dick Butkus APR............ .60 .25
❑ 117 Johnny Unitas APR...... 1.00 .45
❑ 118 Joe Montana APR........ 2.50 1.10
❑ 119 Deacon Jones APR........ .15 .07
❑ 120 Steve Young APR.......... .60 .25
❑ 121 Bob Lilly APR .... .15 .07
❑ 122 Troy Aikman APR .... 1.00 .45
❑ 123 Alan Page APR .... .15 .07
❑ 124 Earl Campbell APR........ .60 .25
❑ 125 Deion Sanders APR ...... .50 .23
❑ 126 Ronnie Lott APR .... .30 .14
❑ 127 Reggie White APR .... .30 .14
❑ 128 Marshall Faulk APR ...... .50 .23
❑ 129 Gale Sayers APR .... .75 .35
❑ 130 Dick Lane APR .... .15 .07
❑ 131 Ricky Williams RC........ 6.00 2.70
❑ 132 Tim Couch RC.............. 6.00 2.70
❑ 133 Donovan McNabb RC .. 4.00 1.80
❑ 134 Daunte Culpepper RC .. 4.00 1.80
❑ 135 Edgerrin James RC.... 12.00 5.50
❑ 136 Cade McNown RC 4.00 1.80
❑ 137 Torry Holt RC 3.00 1.35
❑ 138 David Boston RC.......... 2.00 .90
❑ 139 Champ Bailey RC .... 2.00 .90
❑ 140 Peerless Price RC........ 2.00 .90
❑ 141 D'Wayne Bates RC .... .75 .35
❑ 142 Joe Germaine RC .... 1.25 .55
❑ 143 Brock Huard RC .... 1.50 .70
❑ 144 Chris Claiborne RC........ .75 .35
❑ 145 Jevon Kearse RC 2.50 1.10
❑ 146 Troy Edwards RC .... 2.00 .90
❑ 147 Amos Zereoue RC ...... 1.25 .55
❑ 148 Aaron Brooks RC .... 1.25 .55
❑ 149 Andy Katzenmoyer RC 1.25 .55
❑ 150 Kevin Faulk RC............ 1.50 .70
❑ 151 Shaun King RC............ 4.00 1.80
❑ 152 Kevin Johnson RC 3.00 1.35
❑ 153 Dameane Douglas RC .. .75 .35
❑ 154 Mike Cloud RC .... 1.25 .55
❑ 155 Sedrick Irvin RC .... 1.25 .55
❑ 156 Akili Smith RC.............. 2.50 1.10
❑ 157 Rob Konrad RC............ 1.25 .55
❑ 158 Scott Covington RC...... 1.25 .55
❑ 159 Jeff Paulk RC .... .75 .35
❑ 160 Shawn Bryson RC.......... .75 .35
❑ 161 Joe Montana CM.......... 2.50 1.10
❑ 162 John Elway CM .... 1.50 .70
❑ 163 Joe Namath CM .... 1.50 .70
❑ 164 Jerry Rice CM .... 1.00 .45
❑ 165 Terry Bradshaw CM .... 1.25 .55
❑ 166 Jim Brown CM.............. 1.50 .70
❑ 167 Paul Warfield CM .... .30 .14
❑ 168 Herman Moore CM .... .50 .23
❑ 169 Walter Payton CM........ 2.50 1.10
❑ 170 Roger Staubach CM .... 1.25 .55
❑ 171 Ken Stabler CM............ 1.00 .45
❑ 172A Steve Young CM.......... .60 .25
❑ 172B John Riggins CM ERR 80.00 36.00
(card is partially embossed)
❑ 173 Troy Aikman CM .... 1.00 .45
❑ 174 Fran Tarkenton CM........ .60 .25
❑ 175 Doug Williams CM.......... .15 .07
❑ 176 Steve Largent CM .... .30 .14
❑ 177 Marcus Allen CM............ .30 .14
❑ 178 Mike Singletary CM........ .15 .07
❑ 179 Earl Campbell CM.......... .30 .14
❑ 180 Dan Fouts CM................ .30 .14
❑ WPAC W.Payton AUTO/50 700.00 325.00
❑ WPCL W.Payton AUTO/34 2000.00 900.00
signed Jersey card

1999 Upper Deck Century Legends Century Collection

	MINT	NRMT
COMMON CARD (1-180)..........	4.00	1.80
*STARS: 10X TO 25X HI COL.		
*YOUNG STARS: 8X TO 20X		
*RCs: 3X TO 8X HI COL.		
STATED PRINT RUN 100 SER.#'d SETS		

1999 Upper Deck Century Legends 20th Century Superstars

	MINT	NRMT
COMPLETE SET (10)	30.00	13.50
COMMON CARD (S1-S10)	1.50	.70
STATED ODDS 1:11		

❑ S1 Tim Couch 6.00 2.70
❑ S2 Ricky Williams............... 6.00 2.70
❑ S3 Akili Smith 2.50 1.10
❑ S4 Donovan McNabb 4.00 1.80
❑ S5 Jake Plummer 3.00 1.35
❑ S6 Brett Favre 6.00 2.70
❑ S7 Steve Young 2.50 1.10
❑ S8 Randy Moss 5.00 2.20
❑ S9 Kordell Stewart .... 1.50 .70
❑ S10 Peyton Manning 5.00 2.20

1999 Upper Deck Century Legends Epic Milestones

	MINT	NRMT
COMPLETE SET (10)	40.00	18.00
COMMON CARD (EM1-EM10)	1.50	.70
STATED ODDS 1:11		

❑ EM1 John Elway 6.00 2.70
❑ EM2 Joe Montana 8.00 3.60
❑ EM3 Randy Moss................ 5.00 2.20
❑ EM4 Terrell Davis................ 4.00 1.80
❑ EM5 Dan Marino 6.00 2.70
❑ EM6 Jamal Anderson.......... 1.50 .70
❑ EM8 Barry Sanders 6.00 2.70
❑ EM9 Emmitt Smith 4.00 1.80
❑ EM10 Walter Payton 8.00 3.60

1999 Upper Deck Century Legends Epic Signatures

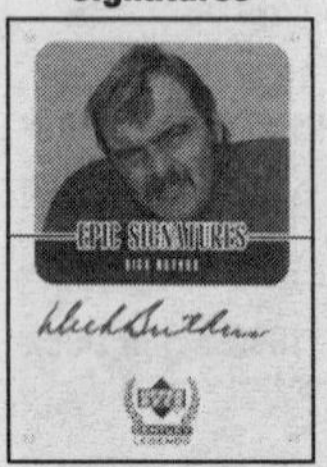

	MINT	NRMT
COMPLETE SET (30)	1800.00	800.00
COMMON CARD	12.00	5.50
SEMISTARS..........................	20.00	9.00
STATED ODDS 1:23		
*CENTURY GOLDS: .8X TO 2X BASIC AUTOS		
UNITAS NOT PART OF CENTURY PARALLEL		
CENTURY GOLD PRINT RUN 100 SER.#'d SETS		

❑ AM Art Monk 20.00 9.00
❑ CC Cris Carter 30.00 13.50
❑ CJ Charlie Joiner 20.00 9.00
❑ DB Dick Butkus 60.00 27.00
❑ DF Dan Fouts..................... 20.00 9.00
❑ DM Dan Marino 200.00 90.00
❑ DR Dan Reeves 20.00 9.00
❑ DW Doug Williams 25.00 11.00

		MINT	NRMT
❑ EC	Earl Campbell	50.00	22.00
❑ FL	Floyd Little	12.00	5.50
❑ FT	Fran Tarkenton	60.00	27.00
❑ GS	Gale Sayers	30.00	13.50
❑ HC	Harold Carmichael	12.00	5.50
❑ JM	Joe Montana	250.00	110.00
❑ JN	Joe Namath	250.00	110.00
❑ JR1	Jerry Rice	300.00	135.00
❑ JR2	Jerry Rice/100	200.00	90.00
❑ JU	Johnny Unitas	120.00	55.00
❑ JY	Jack Youngblood	12.00	5.50
❑ LD	Len Dawson	20.00	9.00
❑ MS	Mike Singletary	20.00	9.00
❑ MY	Don Maynard	12.00	5.50
❑ ON	Ozzie Newsome	12.00	5.50
❑ PW	Paul Warfield	20.00	9.00
❑ RB	Raymond Berry	20.00	9.00
❑ RM	Randy Moss	150.00	70.00
❑ RS	Roger Staubach	80.00	36.00
❑ SL	Steve Largent	25.00	11.00
❑ TA	Troy Aikman	80.00	36.00
❑ TB	Terry Bradshaw	100.00	45.00
❑ TD	Terrell Davis	80.00	36.00

1999 Upper Deck Century Legends Jerseys of the Century

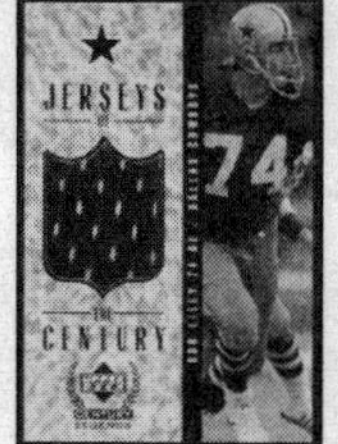

	MINT	NRMT
COMPLETE SET (9)	1500.00	700.00
COMMON CARD (GJ1-GJ10)	80.00	36.00

CARD #GJ9 NEVER RELEASED
STATED ODDS 1:418
*MULTI-COLORED SWATCHES: .6X TO 1.2X

		MINT	NRMT
❑ GJ1	Jerry Rice	200.00	90.00
❑ GJ2	Roger Staubach	200.00	90.00
❑ GJ3	Warren Moon	80.00	36.00
❑ GJ4	Ken Stabler	100.00	45.00
❑ GJ5	Reggie White	80.00	36.00
❑ GJ6	Dan Marino	300.00	135.00
❑ GJ7	Doug Flutie	80.00	36.00
❑ GJ8	Bob Lilly	80.00	36.00

1999 Upper Deck Century Legends Tour de Force

	MINT	NRMT
COMPLETE SET (10)	50.00	22.00
COMMON CARD (A1-A10)	2.50	1.10

STATED ODDS 1:23

		MINT	NRMT
❑ A1	Tim Couch	10.00	4.50
❑ A2	Ricky Williams	10.00	4.50
❑ A3	Peyton Manning	8.00	3.60
❑ A4	Troy Aikman	6.00	2.70
❑ A5	Jake Plummer	5.00	2.20
❑ A6	Jamal Anderson	2.50	1.10
❑ A7	Terrell Davis	6.00	2.70
❑ A8	Barry Sanders	10.00	4.50
❑ A9	Fred Taylor	5.00	2.20
❑ A10	Keyshawn Johnson	2.50	1.10

1998 Upper Deck Encore

	MINT	NRMT
COMPLETE SET (150)	250.00	110.00
COMMON CARD (1-150)	.25	.11
SEMISTARS	.40	.18
UNLISTED STARS	.75	.35
COMMON ROOKIE (1-30)	2.50	1.10
ROOKIE SEMISTARS	4.00	1.80
COMMON F/X GOLD	4.00	1.80

*F/X GOLD STARS: 10X TO 25X HI COL.
*F/X GOLD YOUNG STARS: 8X TO 20X
*F/X GOLD RCs: 1X TO 2.5X
F/X GOLD PRINT RUN 125 SERIAL #'d SETS

		MINT	NRMT
❑ 1	Peyton Manning RC	30.00	13.50
❑ 2	Ryan Leaf RC	10.00	4.50
❑ 3	Andre Wadsworth RC	4.00	1.80
❑ 4	Charles Woodson RC	12.00	5.50
❑ 5	Curtis Enis RC	12.00	5.50
❑ 6	Fred Taylor RC	20.00	9.00
❑ 7	Duane Starks RC	2.50	1.10
❑ 8	Keith Brooking RC	4.00	1.80
❑ 9	Takeo Spikes RC	4.00	1.80
❑ 10	Kevin Dyson RC	10.00	4.50
❑ 11	Robert Edwards RC	4.00	1.80
❑ 12	Randy Moss RC	30.00	13.50
❑ 13	John Avery RC	4.00	1.80
❑ 14	Marcus Nash RC	6.00	2.70
❑ 15	Jerome Pathon RC	4.00	1.80
❑ 16	Jacquez Green RC	8.00	3.60
❑ 17	Robert Holcombe RC	4.00	1.80
❑ 18	Pat Johnson RC	4.00	1.80
❑ 19	Skip Hicks RC	6.00	2.70
❑ 20	Ahman Green RC	6.00	2.70
❑ 21	Brian Griese RC	15.00	6.75
❑ 22	Hines Ward RC	4.00	1.80
❑ 23	Tavian Banks RC	4.00	1.80
❑ 24	Tony Simmons RC	4.00	1.80
❑ 25	Rashaan Shehee RC	4.00	1.80
❑ 26	R.W. McQuarters RC	2.50	1.10
❑ 27	Jon Ritchie RC	4.00	1.80
❑ 28	Ryan Sutter RC	2.50	1.10
❑ 29	Tim Dwight RC	10.00	4.50
❑ 30	Charlie Batch RC	15.00	6.75
❑ 31	Chris Chandler	.40	.18
❑ 32	Jamal Anderson	.75	.35
❑ 33	Terance Mathis	.40	.18
❑ 34	Jake Plummer	2.50	1.10
❑ 35	Mario Bates	.40	.18
❑ 36	Frank Sanders	.40	.18
❑ 37	Adrian Murrell	.40	.18
❑ 38	Jim Harbaugh	.40	.18
❑ 39	Michael Jackson	.25	.11
❑ 40	Jermaine Lewis	.40	.18
❑ 41	Doug Flutie	1.00	.45
❑ 42	Rob Johnson	.40	.18
❑ 43	Antowain Smith	.75	.35
❑ 44	Eric Moulds	.75	.35
❑ 45	Thurman Thomas	.75	.35
❑ 46	Kevin Greene	.25	.11
❑ 47	Fred Lane	.40	.18
❑ 48	Rae Carruth	.40	.18
❑ 49	William Floyd	.25	.11
❑ 50	Erik Kramer	.25	.11
❑ 51	Edgar Bennett	.25	.11
❑ 52	Curtis Conway	.40	.18
❑ 53	Bobby Engram	.40	.18
❑ 54	Jeff Blake	.40	.18
❑ 55	Carl Pickens	.75	.35
❑ 56	Darnay Scott	.25	.11
❑ 57	Corey Dillon	1.00	.45
❑ 58	Troy Aikman	2.00	.90
❑ 59	Michael Irvin	.75	.35
❑ 60	Emmitt Smith	3.00	1.35
❑ 61	Deion Sanders	.75	.35
❑ 62	John Elway	4.00	1.80
❑ 63	Terrell Davis	3.00	1.35
❑ 64	Rod Smith WR	.40	.18
❑ 65	Shannon Sharpe	.40	.18
❑ 66	Ed McCaffrey	.40	.18
❑ 67	Barry Sanders	4.00	1.80
❑ 68	Scott Mitchell	.25	.11
❑ 69	Herman Moore	.75	.35
❑ 70	Johnnie Morton	.40	.18
❑ 71	Brett Favre	4.00	1.80
❑ 72	Dorsey Levens	.75	.35
❑ 73	Reggie White	.75	.35
❑ 74	Antonio Freeman	.75	.35
❑ 75	Robert Brooks	.40	.18
❑ 76	Marshall Faulk	.75	.35
❑ 77	Marvin Harrison	.40	.18
❑ 78	Mark Brunell	1.50	.70
❑ 79	Keenan McCardell	.40	.18
❑ 80	Jimmy Smith	.40	.18
❑ 81	Elvis Grbac	.40	.18
❑ 82	Andre Rison	.40	.18
❑ 83	Tony Gonzalez	.25	.11
❑ 84	Derrick Thomas	.40	.18
❑ 85	Dan Marino	4.00	1.80
❑ 86	Karim Abdul-Jabbar	.75	.35
❑ 87	O.J. McDuffie	.40	.18
❑ 88	Zach Thomas	.25	.11
❑ 89	Brad Johnson	.75	.35
❑ 90	Cris Carter	.75	.35
❑ 91	Jake Reed	.40	.18
❑ 92	Robert Smith	.75	.35
❑ 93	John Randle	.40	.18
❑ 94	Randall Cunningham	.75	.35
❑ 95	Drew Bledsoe	1.50	.70
❑ 96	Terry Glenn	.75	.35
❑ 97	Ben Coates	.40	.18
❑ 98	Danny Wuerffel	.40	.18
❑ 99	Andre Hastings	.25	.11
❑ 100	Troy Davis	.25	.11
❑ 101	Danny Kanell	.40	.18
❑ 102	Tiki Barber	.40	.18
❑ 103	Amani Toomer	.40	.18
❑ 104	Vinny Testaverde	.40	.18
❑ 105	Glenn Foley	.40	.18
❑ 106	Curtis Martin	.75	.35
❑ 107	Keyshawn Johnson	.75	.35
❑ 108	Wayne Chrebet	.75	.35
❑ 109	Jeff George	.40	.18
❑ 110	Napoleon Kaufman	.75	.35
❑ 111	Tim Brown	.75	.35
❑ 112	James Jett	.25	.11
❑ 113	Bobby Hoying	.40	.18
❑ 114	Charlie Garner	.25	.11
❑ 115	Irving Fryar	.40	.18
❑ 116	Kordell Stewart	.75	.35
❑ 117	Jerome Bettis	.75	.35
❑ 118	Will Blackwell	.25	.11
❑ 119	Charles Johnson	.25	.11
❑ 120	Tony Banks	.40	.18
❑ 121	Amp Lee	.25	.11
❑ 122	Isaac Bruce	.75	.35

❑ 123 Eddie Kennison	.40	.18
❑ 124 Natrone Means	.75	.35
❑ 125 Junior Seau	.40	.18
❑ 126 Bryan Still	.25	.11
❑ 127 Steve Young	1.00	.45
❑ 128 Jerry Rice	2.00	.90
❑ 129 Garrison Hearst	.75	.35
❑ 130 J.J. Stokes	.40	.18
❑ 131 Terrell Owens	.75	.35
❑ 132 Warren Moon	.25	.11
❑ 133 Jon Kitna	2.00	.90
❑ 134 Ricky Watters	.40	.18
❑ 135 Joey Galloway	.75	.35
❑ 136 Trent Dilfer	.75	.35
❑ 137 Warrick Dunn	.75	.35
❑ 138 Mike Alstott	.75	.35
❑ 139 Bert Emanuel	.40	.18
❑ 140 Reidel Anthony	.40	.18
❑ 141 Steve McNair	.75	.35
❑ 142 Yancey Thigpen	.25	.11
❑ 143 Eddie George	1.50	.70
❑ 144 Chris Sanders	.25	.11
❑ 145 Gus Frerotte	.25	.11
❑ 146 Terry Allen	.75	.35
❑ 147 Michael Westbrook	.40	.18
❑ 148 Troy Aikman CL	.75	.35
❑ 149 Dan Marino CL	1.00	.45
❑ 150 Randy Moss CL	8.00	3.60

1998 Upper Deck Encore UD Authentics

	MINT	NRMT
COMPLETE SET (5)	600.00	275.00
COMMON CARD	60.00	27.00
STATED ODDS 1:288		
TRADE EXPIRATION: 1/8/2000....		
❑ DM2 Dan Marino	150.00	70.00
❑ JM2 Joe Montana (49ers photo)	120.00	55.00
❑ MB2 Mark Brunell	60.00	27.00
❑ RM Randy Moss	175.00	80.00
❑ TD Terrell Davis	100.00	45.00

1998 Upper Deck Encore Constant Threat

	MINT	NRMT
COMPLETE SET (15)	80.00	36.00
COMMON CARD (CT1-CT15)	2.00	.90
STATED ODDS 1:11		
❑ CT1 Dan Marino	10.00	4.50
❑ CT2 Peyton Manning	15.00	6.75
❑ CT3 Randy Moss	15.00	6.75
❑ CT4 Brett Favre	10.00	4.50
❑ CT5 Mark Brunell	4.00	1.80
❑ CT6 John Elway	10.00	4.50
❑ CT7 Ryan Leaf	3.00	1.35
❑ CT8 Jake Plummer	5.00	2.20
❑ CT9 Terrell Davis	8.00	3.60
❑ CT10 Barry Sanders	10.00	4.50
❑ CT11 Emmitt Smith	8.00	3.60
❑ CT12 Curtis Martin	2.00	.90
❑ CT13 Eddie George	4.00	1.80
❑ CT14 Warrick Dunn	2.00	.90
❑ CT15 Curtis Enis	4.00	1.80

1998 Upper Deck Encore Driving Forces

	MINT	NRMT
COMPLETE SET (14)	60.00	27.00
COMMON CARD (F1-F14)	3.00	1.35
STATED ODDS 1:23		
*F/X GOLDS: .75X TO 2X HI COL.		
F/X STATED PRINT RUN 1500 SER.#'d SETS		
❑ F1 Terrell Davis	12.00	5.50
❑ F2 Barry Sanders	15.00	6.75
❑ F3 Doug Flutie	4.00	1.80
❑ F4 Mark Brunell	6.00	2.70
❑ F5 Garrison Hearst	3.00	1.35
❑ F6 Jamal Anderson	3.00	1.35
❑ F7 Jerry Rice	8.00	3.60
❑ F8 John Elway	15.00	6.75
❑ F9 Robert Smith	3.00	1.35
❑ F10 Kordell Stewart	3.00	1.35
❑ F11 Eddie George	6.00	2.70
❑ F12 Antonio Freeman	3.00	1.35
❑ F13 Dan Marino	15.00	6.75
❑ F14 Steve Young	5.00	2.20

1998 Upper Deck Encore Milestones

	MINT	NRMT
COMPLETE SET (8)	1600.00	700.00
COMMON CARD	40.00	18.00
RANDOM INSERTS IN PACKS....		
❑ 1 Peyton Manning/26	300.00	135.00
❑ 12 Randy Moss/17	500.00	220.00
❑ 60 Emmitt Smith/124	60.00	27.00
❑ 62 John Elway/50	150.00	70.00
❑ 63 Terrell Davis/30	200.00	90.00
❑ 67 Barry Sanders/100	120.00	55.00
❑ 85 Dan Marino/400	50.00	22.00
❑ 128 Jerry Rice/184	40.00	18.00

1998 Upper Deck Encore Rookie Encore

	MINT	NRMT
COMPLETE SET (10)	80.00	36.00
COMMON CARD (RE1-RE10)	4.00	1.80
STATED ODDS 1:23		
*F/X GOLDS: 1.25X TO 3X HI COL.		
F/X STATED PRINT RUN 500 SER.#'d SETS		
❑ RE1 Randy Moss	25.00	11.00
❑ RE2 Peyton Manning	25.00	11.00
❑ RE3 Charlie Batch	10.00	4.50
❑ RE4 Fred Taylor	15.00	6.75
❑ RE5 Robert Edwards	4.00	1.80
❑ RE6 Curtis Enis	6.00	2.70
❑ RE7 Robert Holcombe	4.00	1.80
❑ RE8 Ryan Leaf	5.00	2.20
❑ RE9 John Avery	4.00	1.80
❑ RE10 Tim Dwight	5.00	2.20

1998 Upper Deck Encore Super Powers

	MINT	NRMT
COMPLETE SET (15)	80.00	36.00
COMMON CARD (S1-S15)	2.00	.90
STATED ODDS 1:11		
❑ S1 Dan Marino	10.00	4.50
❑ S2 Napoleon Kaufman	2.00	.90
❑ S3 Brett Favre	10.00	4.50
❑ S4 John Elway	10.00	4.50
❑ S5 Randy Moss	15.00	6.75
❑ S6 Kordell Stewart	2.00	.90
❑ S7 Mark Brunell	4.00	1.80
❑ S8 Peyton Manning	15.00	6.75
❑ S9 Emmitt Smith	8.00	3.60
❑ S10 Jake Plummer	5.00	2.20

Card	Mint	Nrmt
❑ S11 Eddie George	4.00	1.80
❑ S12 Warrick Dunn	2.00	.90
❑ S13 Jerome Bettis	2.00	.90
❑ S14 Terrell Davis	8.00	3.60
❑ S15 Fred Taylor	10.00	4.50

1998 Upper Deck Encore Superstar Encore

	MINT	NRMT
COMPLETE SET (6)	50.00	22.00
COMMON CARD (RR1-RR6)	4.00	1.80
STATED ODDS 1:23		

*F/X GOLD STARS: 12X TO 30X HI COL.
*F/X GOLD ROOKIE: 8X TO 20X HI COL.
F/X STATED PRINT RUN 25 SER.#'d SETS

Card	Mint	Nrmt
❑ RR1 Brett Favre	10.00	4.50
❑ RR2 Barry Sanders	10.00	4.50
❑ RR3 Mark Brunell	4.00	1.80
❑ RR4 Emmitt Smith	8.00	3.60
❑ RR5 Randy Moss	25.00	11.00
❑ RR6 Terrell Davis	8.00	3.60

1999 Upper Deck Encore

	MINT	NRMT
COMPLETE SET (225)	250.00	110.00
COMP.SET w/o SP's (180)	50.00	22.00
COMMON CARD (1-180)	.20	.09
SEMISTARS	.40	.18
UNLISTED STARS	.75	.35
COMMON ROOKIE (181-225)	4.00	1.80
ROOKIE SEMISTARS	5.00	2.20
ROOKIE SUBSET STATED ODDS 1:8		

Card	Mint	Nrmt
❑ 1 Jake Plummer	1.25	.55
❑ 2 Adrian Murrell	.40	.18
❑ 3 Rob Moore	.40	.18
❑ 4 Simeon Rice	.20	.09
❑ 5 Andre Wadsworth	.20	.09
❑ 6 Frank Sanders	.40	.18
❑ 7 Tim Dwight	.75	.35
❑ 8 Chris Chandler	.40	.18
❑ 9 Jamal Anderson	.75	.35
❑ 10 O.J. Santiago	.40	.18
❑ 11 Tony Graziani	.20	.09
❑ 12 Terance Mathis	.40	.18
❑ 13 Priest Holmes	.75	.35
❑ 14 Stoney Case	.20	.09
❑ 15 Ray Lewis	.20	.09
❑ 16 Peter Boulware	.20	.09
❑ 17 Errict Rhett	.40	.18
❑ 18 Jermaine Lewis	.40	.18
❑ 19 Eric Moulds	.75	.35
❑ 20 Doug Flutie	1.00	.45
❑ 21 Antowain Smith	.75	.35
❑ 22 Rob Johnson	.40	.18
❑ 23 Bruce Smith	.40	.18
❑ 24 Andre Reed	.40	.18
❑ 25 Wesley Walls	.40	.18
❑ 26 Tim Biakabutuka	.40	.18
❑ 27 Fred Lane	.40	.18
❑ 28 Steve Beuerlein	.40	.18
❑ 29 Muhsin Muhammad	.40	.18
❑ 30 Rae Carruth	.20	.09
❑ 31 Bobby Engram	.40	.18
❑ 32 Curtis Enis	.75	.35
❑ 33 Edgar Bennett	.20	.09
❑ 34 Curtis Conway	.40	.18
❑ 35 Shane Matthews	.75	.35
❑ 36 Tony McGee	.20	.09
❑ 37 Darnay Scott	.40	.18
❑ 38 Jeff Blake	.40	.18
❑ 39 Corey Dillon	.75	.35
❑ 40 Ki-Jana Carter	.20	.09
❑ 41 Ty Detmer	.40	.18
❑ 42 Leslie Shepherd	.20	.09
❑ 43 Terry Kirby	.40	.18
❑ 44 Antonio Langham	.20	.09
❑ 45 Jamir Miller	.20	.09
❑ 46 Marc Edwards	.20	.09
❑ 47 Troy Aikman	2.00	.90
❑ 48 Rocket Ismail	.40	.18
❑ 49 Emmitt Smith	2.00	.90
❑ 50 Michael Irvin	.40	.18
❑ 51 Deion Sanders	.75	.35
❑ 52 Greg Ellis	.20	.09
❑ 53 Bubby Brister	.40	.18
❑ 54 Terrell Davis	2.00	.90
❑ 55 Ed McCaffrey	.40	.18
❑ 56 Rod Smith	.40	.18
❑ 57 Shannon Sharpe	.40	.18
❑ 58 Brian Griese	1.50	.70
❑ 59 Charlie Batch	1.50	.70
❑ 60 Germane Crowell	.40	.18
❑ 61 Johnnie Morton	.40	.18
❑ 62 Robert Porcher	.20	.09
❑ 63 Ron Rivers	.20	.09
❑ 64 Herman Moore	.75	.35
❑ 65 Brett Favre	3.00	1.35
❑ 66 Bill Schroeder	.75	.35
❑ 67 Antonio Freeman	.75	.35
❑ 68 Dorsey Levens	.75	.35
❑ 69 Desmond Howard	.40	.18
❑ 70 Vonnie Holliday	.40	.18
❑ 71 Peyton Manning	2.50	1.10
❑ 72 Jerome Pathon	.40	.18
❑ 73 Marvin Harrison	.75	.35
❑ 74 Ken Dilger	.40	.18
❑ 75 E.G. Green	.20	.09
❑ 76 Cornelius Bennett	.20	.09
❑ 77 Mark Brunell	1.25	.55
❑ 78 Fred Taylor	2.00	.90
❑ 79 Jimmy Smith	.40	.18
❑ 80 James Stewart	.40	.18
❑ 81 Keenan McCardell	.40	.18
❑ 82 Carnell Lake	.20	.09
❑ 83 Elvis Grbac	.40	.18
❑ 84 Tony Gonzalez	.40	.18
❑ 85 Andre Rison	.40	.18
❑ 86 Derrick Thomas	.40	.18
❑ 87 Warren Moon	.75	.35
❑ 88 Derrick Alexander WR	.40	.18
❑ 89 Dan Marino	3.00	1.35
❑ 90 O.J. McDuffie	.40	.18
❑ 91 Karim Abdul-Jabbar	.40	.18
❑ 92 Sam Madison	.20	.09
❑ 93 Zach Thomas	.40	.18
❑ 94 Tony Martin	.40	.18
❑ 95 Randall Cunningham	.75	.35
❑ 96 Randy Moss	2.50	1.10
❑ 97 Cris Carter	.75	.35
❑ 98 Jake Reed	.40	.18
❑ 99 John Randle	.20	.09
❑ 100 Robert Smith	.75	.35
❑ 101 Drew Bledsoe	1.25	.55
❑ 102 Ben Coates	.40	.18
❑ 103 Terry Glenn	.40	.18
❑ 104 Tony Simmons	.20	.09
❑ 105 Terry Allen	.40	.18
❑ 106 Danny Wuerffel	.20	.09
❑ 107 Cameron Cleeland	.20	.09
❑ 108 Eddie Kennison	.40	.18
❑ 109 Billy Joe Hobert	.20	.09
❑ 110 Andre Hastings	.20	.09
❑ 111 Kent Graham	.20	.09
❑ 112 Tiki Barber	.40	.18
❑ 113 Gary Brown	.20	.09
❑ 114 Ike Hilliard	.40	.18
❑ 115 Jason Sehorn	.20	.09
❑ 116 Kerry Collins	.40	.18
❑ 117 Vinny Testaverde	.40	.18
❑ 118 Wayne Chrebet	.75	.35
❑ 119 Curtis Martin	.75	.35
❑ 120 Rick Mirer	.40	.18
❑ 121 Aaron Glenn	.20	.09
❑ 122 Keyshawn Johnson	.75	.35
❑ 123 Rich Gannon	.40	.18
❑ 124 Tim Brown	.75	.35
❑ 125 Darrell Russell	.20	.09
❑ 126 Tyrone Wheatley	.75	.35
❑ 127 Charles Woodson	.75	.35
❑ 128 Napoleon Kaufman	.75	.35
❑ 129 Duce Staley	.75	.35
❑ 130 Doug Pederson	.20	.09
❑ 131 Kevin Turner	.20	.09
❑ 132 Charles Johnson	.20	.09
❑ 133 Jerome Bettis	.75	.35
❑ 134 Courtney Hawkins	.20	.09
❑ 135 Kordell Stewart	.75	.35
❑ 136 Richard Huntley	.20	.09
❑ 137 Levon Kirkland	.20	.09
❑ 138 Hines Ward	.20	.09
❑ 139 Kurt Warner RC	25.00	11.00
❑ 140 Marshall Faulk	.75	.35
❑ 141 Az-Zahir Hakim	.40	.18
❑ 142 Amp Lee	.20	.09
❑ 143 Isaac Bruce	.75	.35
❑ 144 Kevin Carter	.20	.09
❑ 145 Jim Harbaugh	.40	.18
❑ 146 Junior Seau	.20	.09
❑ 147 Natrone Means	.40	.18
❑ 148 Rodney Harrison	.20	.09
❑ 149 Mikhael Ricks	.20	.09
❑ 150 Erik Kramer	.20	.09
❑ 151 Steve Young	1.25	.55
❑ 152 Terrell Owens	.75	.35
❑ 153 Jerry Rice	2.00	.90
❑ 154 J.J. Stokes	.40	.18
❑ 155 Jeff Garcia RC	10.00	4.50
❑ 156 Lawrence Phillips	.40	.18
❑ 157 Jon Kitna	1.00	.45
❑ 158 Derrick Mayes	.40	.18
❑ 159 Ricky Watters	.40	.18
❑ 160 Chad Brown	.20	.09
❑ 161 Shawn Springs	.20	.09
❑ 162 Sean Dawkins	.20	.09
❑ 163 Trent Dilfer	.40	.18
❑ 164 Reidel Anthony	.40	.18
❑ 165 Bert Emanuel	.40	.18
❑ 166 Warrick Dunn	.75	.35
❑ 167 Jacquez Green	.20	.09
❑ 168 Mike Alstott	.75	.35
❑ 169 Eddie George	1.00	.45
❑ 170 Steve McNair	.75	.35
❑ 171 Kevin Dyson	.40	.18
❑ 172 Frank Wycheck	.20	.09
❑ 173 Blaine Bishop	.20	.09
❑ 174 Yancey Thigpen	.40	.18
❑ 175 Brad Johnson	.75	.35
❑ 176 Michael Westbrook	.40	.18
❑ 177 Skip Hicks	.40	.18
❑ 178 Brian Mitchell	.20	.09
❑ 179 Dana Stubblefield	.20	.09
❑ 180 Stephen Davis	.75	.35
❑ 181 Champ Bailey RC	6.00	2.70
❑ 182 Chris McAlister RC	5.00	2.20
❑ 183 Jevon Kearse RC	10.00	4.50

❑ 184 Ebenezer Ekuban RC .. 5.00 2.20
❑ 185 Chris Claiborne RC 5.00 2.20
❑ 186 Andy Katzenmoyer RC 5.00 2.20
❑ 187 Tim Couch RC........... 25.00 11.00
❑ 188 Daunte Culpepper RC 15.00 6.75
❑ 189 Akili Smith RC 10.00 4.50
❑ 190 Donovan McNabb RC 15.00 6.75
❑ 191 Sean Bennett RC 5.00 2.20
❑ 192 Brock Huard RC 6.00 2.70
❑ 193 Cade McNown RC 15.00 6.75
❑ 194 Shaun King RC 15.00 6.75
❑ 195 Joe Germaine RC 5.00 2.20
❑ 196 Ricky Williams RC...... 25.00 11.00
❑ 197 Edgerrin James RC.... 40.00 18.00
❑ 198 Sedrick Irvin RC 5.00 2.20
❑ 199 Kevin Faulk RC 6.00 2.70
❑ 200 Rob Konrad RC............ 5.00 2.20
❑ 201 James Johnson RC...... 6.00 2.70
❑ 202 Amos Zereoue RC 5.00 2.20
❑ 203 Torry Holt RC 12.00 5.50
❑ 204 D'Wayne Bates RC 5.00 2.20
❑ 205 David Boston RC.......... 8.00 3.60
❑ 206 Dameane Douglas RC 5.00 2.20
❑ 207 Troy Edwards RC 8.00 3.60
❑ 208 Kevin Johnson RC 12.00 5.50
❑ 209 Peerless Price RC........ 8.00 3.60
❑ 210 Antoine Winfield RC 5.00 2.20
❑ 211 Mike Cloud RC 5.00 2.20
❑ 212 Joe Montgomery RC 5.00 2.20
❑ 213 Jermaine Fazande RC 5.00 2.20
❑ 214 Scott Covington RC...... 5.00 2.20
❑ 215 Aaron Brooks RC 5.00 2.20
❑ 216 Terry Jackson RC 5.00 2.20
❑ 217 Cecil Collins RC 5.00 2.20
❑ 218 Olandis Gary RC 15.00 6.75
❑ 219 Craig Yeast RC 5.00 2.20
❑ 220 Karsten Bailey RC........ 5.00 2.20
❑ 221 Reginald Kelly RC........ 4.00 1.80
❑ 222 Travis McGriff RC 5.00 2.20
❑ 223 Jeff Paulk RC 5.00 2.20
❑ 224 Jim Kleinsasser RC...... 5.00 2.20
❑ 225 Jason Tucker RC 12.00 5.50
❑ WPE W.Payton Jer.AUTO/34 2000.00 900.00

1999 Upper Deck Encore F/X

	MINT	NRMT
COMPLETE SET (225)	2000.00	900.00
COMMON CARD (1-180)..........	6.00	2.70
*STARS: 12X TO 30X HI COL.		
*YOUNG STARS: 10X TO 25X		
COMMON ROOKIE (181-225)	12.00	5.50
*RCs: 1.2X TO 3X		
STATED PRINT RUN 100 SER.#'d SETS		
UNPRICED F/X GOLD SERIAL #'d OF 1 SET		

❑ 139 Kurt Warner.............. 150.00 70.00

1999 Upper Deck Encore Electric Currents

	MINT	NRMT
COMPLETE SET (20)	20.00	9.00

COMMON CARD (EC1-EC20)....	.75	.35
SEMISTARS............................	1.50	.70
STATED ODDS 1:6		

❑ EC1 Steve Young............... 2.50 1.10
❑ EC2 Doug Flutie................. 2.00 .90
❑ EC3 Jon Kitna .... 2.00 .90
❑ EC4 Randall Cunningham ......
❑ EC5 Curtis Enis ....
❑ EC6 Jerry Rice.................... 4.00 1.80
❑ EC7 Antonio Freeman ....
❑ EC8 Keyshawn Johnson ....
❑ EC9 Steve McNair ....
❑ EC10 Kordell Stewart..............
❑ EC11 Drew Bledsoe........... 2.50 1.10
❑ EC12 Corey Dillon ....
❑ EC13 Vinny Testaverde .... .75 .35
❑ EC14 Tim Brown ....
❑ EC15 Antowain Smith ....
❑ EC16 Charlie Batch 2.50 1.10
❑ EC17 Stephen Davis ....
❑ EC18 Isaac Bruce ....
❑ EC19 Curtis Martin..................
❑ EC20 Ricky Watters............. .75 .35

1999 Upper Deck Encore Game Used Helmets

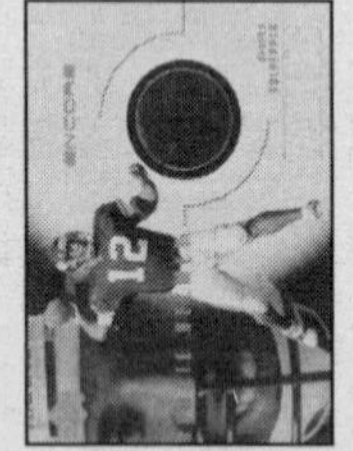

	MINT	NRMT
COMPLETE SET (20)	1500.00	700.00
COMMON CARD	40.00	18.00
STATED ODDS 1:575		

❑ H-AS Akili Smith................ 80.00 36.00
❑ H-BF Brett Favre 150.00 70.00
❑ H-BH Brock Huard 50.00 22.00
❑ H-CB Champ Bailey......... 60.00 27.00
❑ H-CC Cecil Collins 50.00 22.00
❑ H-CM Cade McNown 120.00 55.00
❑ H-DB David Boston 60.00 27.00
❑ H-DC Daunte Culpepper 100.00 45.00
❑ H-DM Dan Marino 150.00 70.00
❑ H-DW D'Wayne Bates 40.00 18.00
❑ H-EJ Edgerrin James 200.00 90.00
❑ H-JR Jerry Rice 100.00 45.00
❑ H-KF Kevin Faulk 50.00 22.00
❑ H-KJ Kevin Johnson.......... 80.00 36.00
❑ H-MB Mark Brunell........... 60.00 27.00
❑ H-MC Donovan McNabb .. 80.00 36.00
❑ H-TC Tim Couch 150.00 70.00
❑ H-TD Terrell Davis 80.00 36.00
❑ H-TE Troy Edwards 60.00 27.00
❑ H-TH Torry Holt 100.00 45.00

1999 Upper Deck Encore Live Wires

	MINT	NRMT
COMPLETE SET (15)	40.00	18.00
COMMON CARD (L1-L15)........	2.00	.90
STATED ODDS 1:11		

❑ L1 Jake Plummer 3.00 1.35
❑ L2 Jamal Anderson .... 2.00 .90
❑ L3 Emmitt Smith.................. 5.00 2.20
❑ L4 John Elway 8.00 3.60
❑ L5 Barry Sanders 8.00 3.60
❑ L6 Brett Favre 8.00 3.60
❑ L7 Mark Brunell 3.00 1.35
❑ L8 Fred Taylor 4.00 1.80
❑ L9 Randy Moss 6.00 2.70
❑ L10 Drew Bledsoe 3.00 1.35
❑ L11 Keyshawn Johnson...... 2.00 .90
❑ L12 Jerome Bettis .... 2.00 .90
❑ L13 Kordell Stewart .... 2.00 .90
❑ L14 Terrell Owens .... 2.00 .90
❑ L15 Eddie George 2.50 1.10

1999 Upper Deck Encore Seize the Game

	MINT	NRMT
COMPLETE SET (30)	100.00	45.00
COMMON CARD (SG1-SG20)..	3.00	1.35
SG1-SG20 STATED ODDS 1:20 ..		
COMMON CARD (SG21-SG30)	4.00	1.80
SG21-SG30 STATED ODDS 1:23		
*SG1-SG20 F/X GOLD: 1X TO 2.5X HI COL.		
*SG21-SG30 F/X GOLD: 1.2X TO 3X HI COL.		
PARALLEL PRINT RUN 250 SER.#'d SETS		

❑ SG1 Donovan McNabb 5.00 2.20
❑ SG2 Keyshawn Johnson 3.00 1.35
❑ SG3 Eddie George............. 4.00 1.80
❑ SG4 Randall Cunningham .. 3.00 1.35
❑ SG5 Charlie Batch 5.00 2.20
❑ SG6 Curtis Martin............... 3.00 1.35
❑ SG7 Edgerrin James 15.00 6.75
❑ SG8 Jake Plummer 5.00 2.20

		MINT	NRMT
❑ SG9	Drew Bledsoe	5.00	2.20
❑ SG10	Marshall Faulk	3.00	1.35
❑ SG11	Fred Taylor	6.00	2.70
❑ SG12	Terrell Owens	3.00	1.35
❑ SG13	Jerome Bettis	3.00	1.35
❑ SG14	Antonio Freeman	3.00	1.35
❑ SG15	Corey Dillon	3.00	1.35
❑ SG16	Jerry Rice	8.00	3.60
❑ SG17	Curtis Enis	3.00	1.35
❑ SG18	Warrick Dunn	3.00	1.35
❑ SG19	Kordell Stewart	3.00	1.35
❑ SG20	Jamal Anderson	3.00	1.35
❑ SG21	Terrell Davis	6.00	2.70
❑ SG22	Randy Moss	8.00	3.60
❑ SG23	Troy Aikman	6.00	2.70
❑ SG24	Dan Marino	10.00	4.50
❑ SG25	Ricky Williams	10.00	4.50
❑ SG26	Peyton Manning	8.00	3.60
❑ SG27	Steve Young	4.00	1.80
❑ SG28	Tim Couch	10.00	4.50
❑ SG29	Emmitt Smith	6.00	2.70
❑ SG30	Brett Favre	10.00	4.50

1999 Upper Deck Encore UD Authentics

	MINT	NRMT
COMPLETE SET (15)	1500.00	700.00
COMMON CARD	30.00	13.50
STATED ODDS 1:144		
SHAUN KING TRADE EXPIRATION: 8/7/2000		

		MINT	NRMT
❑ BH	Brock Huard	30.00	13.50
❑ CM	Cade McNown	60.00	27.00
❑ DB	David Boston	30.00	13.50
❑ EJ	Edgerrin James	175.00	80.00
❑ JN	Joe Namath	150.00	70.00
❑ KF	Kevin Faulk	30.00	13.50
❑ KW	Kurt Warner	175.00	80.00
❑ MB	Mark Brunell	60.00	27.00
❑ PM	Peyton Manning	150.00	70.00
❑ RM	Randy Moss	120.00	55.00
❑ SK	Shaun King	60.00	27.00
❑ TA	Troy Aikman	100.00	45.00
❑ TC	Tim Couch	120.00	55.00
❑ TE	Troy Edwards	40.00	18.00
❑ TH	Torry Holt	40.00	18.00

1999 Upper Deck Encore Upper Realm

	MINT	NRMT
COMPLETE SET (10)	30.00	13.50
COMMON CARD (UR1-UR10)	.75	.35
SEMISTARS	1.50	.70
STATED ODDS 1:12		

		MINT	NRMT
❑ UR1	Randy Moss	5.00	2.20
❑ UR2	Warrick Dunn		
❑ UR3	Stephen Davis		
❑ UR4	Peyton Manning	5.00	2.20
❑ UR5	Tim Biakabutuka	.75	.35
❑ UR6	Steve Young	2.50	1.10
❑ UR7	Kurt Warner	20.00	9.00
❑ UR8	Steve McNair		
❑ UR9	Dan Marino	6.00	2.70
❑ UR10	Jake Plummer	2.50	1.10

1999 Upper Deck HoloGrFX

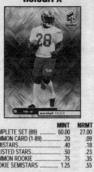

	MINT	NRMT
COMPLETE SET (89)	60.00	27.00
COMMON CARD (1-89)	.20	.09
SEMISTARS	.40	.18
UNLISTED STARS	.50	.23
COMMON ROOKIE	.75	.35
ROOKIE SEMISTARS	1.25	.55

		MINT	NRMT
❑ 1	Jake Plummer	1.50	.70
❑ 2	Jamal Anderson	.50	.23
❑ 3	Priest Holmes	.50	.23
❑ 4	Antowain Smith	.50	.23
❑ 5	Doug Flutie	.75	.35
❑ 6	Tim Biakabutuka	.40	.18
❑ 7	Curtis Enis	.50	.23
❑ 8	Corey Dillon	.50	.23
❑ 9	Darnay Scott	.20	.09
❑ 10	Leslie Shepherd	.20	.09
❑ 11	Troy Aikman	2.00	.90
❑ 12	Emmitt Smith	2.00	.90
❑ 13	Michael Irvin	.40	.18
❑ 14	Terrell Davis	2.00	.90
❑ 15	Shannon Sharpe	.40	.18
❑ 16	Rod Smith	.40	.18
❑ 17	Barry Sanders	3.00	1.35
❑ 18	Charlie Batch	1.50	.70
❑ 19	Herman Moore	.50	.23
❑ 20	Brett Favre	3.00	1.35
❑ 21	Dorsey Levens	.50	.23
❑ 22	Antonio Freeman	.50	.23
❑ 23	Peyton Manning	3.00	1.35
❑ 24	Mark Brunell	1.25	.55
❑ 25	Fred Taylor	2.00	.90
❑ 26	Jimmy Smith	.40	.18
❑ 27	Andre Rison	.40	.18
❑ 28	Tony Gonzalez	.40	.18
❑ 29	Dan Marino	3.00	1.35
❑ 30	Karim Abdul-Jabbar	.40	.18
❑ 31	Randy Moss	3.00	1.35
❑ 32	Randall Cunningham	.50	.23
❑ 33	Drew Bledsoe	1.25	.55
❑ 34	Terry Glenn	.50	.23
❑ 35	Cameron Cleeland	.20	.09
❑ 36	Andre Hastings	.20	.09
❑ 37	Amani Toomer	.20	.09
❑ 38	Kent Graham	.20	.09
❑ 39	Curtis Martin	.50	.23
❑ 40	Keyshawn Johnson	.50	.23
❑ 41	Vinny Testaverde	.40	.18
❑ 42	Napoleon Kaufman	.50	.23
❑ 43	Tim Brown	.50	.23
❑ 44	Duce Staley	.50	.23
❑ 45	Kordell Stewart	.50	.23
❑ 46	Jerome Bettis	.50	.23
❑ 47	Marshall Faulk	.50	.23
❑ 48	Natrone Means	.40	.18
❑ 49	Ryan Leaf	.20	.09
❑ 50	Steve Young	1.25	.55
❑ 51	Jerry Rice	2.00	.90
❑ 52	Terrell Owens	.50	.23
❑ 53	Joey Galloway	.50	.23
❑ 54	Ricky Watters	.40	.18
❑ 55	Jon Kitna	1.00	.45
❑ 56	Warrick Dunn	.50	.23
❑ 57	Trent Dilfer	.40	.18
❑ 58	Steve McNair	.50	.23
❑ 59	Eddie George	.75	.35
❑ 60	Brad Johnson	.50	.23
❑ 61	Tim Couch RC	8.00	3.60
❑ 62	Donovan McNabb RC	4.00	1.80
❑ 63	Akili Smith RC	2.50	1.10
❑ 64	Edgerrin James RC	12.00	5.50
❑ 65	Ricky Williams RC	8.00	3.60
❑ 66	Torry Holt RC	3.00	1.35
❑ 67	Champ Bailey RC	1.50	.70
❑ 68	David Boston RC	2.00	.90
❑ 69	Daunte Culpepper RC	4.00	1.80
❑ 70	Cade McNown RC	4.00	1.80
❑ 71	Troy Edwards RC	2.00	.90
❑ 72	Kevin Johnson RC	3.00	1.35
❑ 73	James Johnson RC	1.50	.70
❑ 74	Rob Konrad RC	3.00	1.35
❑ 75	Kevin Faulk RC	1.50	.70
❑ 76	Shaun King RC	4.00	1.80
❑ 77	Peerless Price RC	2.00	.90
❑ 78	Mike Cloud RC	3.00	1.35
❑ 79	Jermaine Fazande RC	.75	.35
❑ 80	D'Wayne Bates RC	.75	.35
❑ 81	Brock Huard RC	1.50	.70
❑ 82	Marty Booker RC	.75	.35
❑ 83	Karsten Bailey RC	.75	.35
❑ 84	Al Wilson RC	3.00	1.35
❑ 85	Joe Germaine RC	3.00	1.35
❑ 86	Dameane Douglas RC	.75	.35
❑ 87	Sedrick Irvin RC	3.00	1.35
❑ 88	Aaron Brooks RC	1.25	.55
❑ 89	Cecil Collins RC	3.00	1.35

1999 Upper Deck HoloGrFX Ausome

	MINT	NRMT
COMPLETE SET (90)	150.00	70.00
COMMON CARD (1-90)	.75	.35

*AUSOME STARS: 1.5X TO 4X HI COL.
*AUSOME YOUNG STARS: 1.2X TO 3X
AUSOME VETERAN STATED ODDS 1:8
*AUSOME RCs: .6X TO 1.5X
AUSOME DRAFT PICK STATED ODDS 1:17

1999 Upper Deck HoloGrFX 24/7

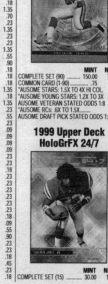

	MINT	NRMT
COMPLETE SET (15)	30.00	13.50

COMMON CARD (N1-N15) ...... 1.00 .45
STATED ODDS 1:3 ....
*GOLD CARDS: 3X TO 8X HI COL.
GOLD STATED ODDS 1:105........

❑ N1 Jake Plummer	2.50	1.10
❑ N2 Emmitt Smith	3.00	1.35
❑ N3 Terrell Davis	3.00	1.35
❑ N4 Peyton Manning	4.00	1.80
❑ N5 Drew Bledsoe	2.00	.90
❑ N6 Troy Aikman	3.00	1.35
❑ N7 Ricky Williams	5.00	2.20
❑ N8 Keyshawn Johnson	1.00	.45
❑ N9 Akili Smith	2.00	.90
❑ N10 Eddie George	1.25	.55
❑ N11 Edgerrin James	10.00	4.50
❑ N12 David Boston	1.50	.70
❑ N13 Cade McNown	3.00	1.35
❑ N14 Jerome Bettis	1.00	.45
❑ N15 Herman Moore	1.00	.45

1999 Upper Deck HoloGrFX Future Fame

	MINT	NRMT
COMPLETE SET (6)	40.00	18.00
COMMON CARD (FF1-FF6)	2.50	1.10

STATED ODDS 1:34 ....
*GOLD CARDS: 1.2X TO 3X HI COL.
GOLD STATED ODDS 1:431........

❑ FF1 John Elway	10.00	4.50
❑ FF2 Dan Marino	10.00	4.50
❑ FF3 Emmitt Smith	6.00	2.70
❑ FF4 Randy Moss	8.00	3.60
❑ FF5 Tim Brown	2.50	1.10
❑ FF6 Barry Sanders	10.00	4.50

1999 Upper Deck HoloGrFX Star View

	MINT	NRMT
COMPLETE SET (9)	30.00	13.50
COMMON CARD (S1-S9)	2.50	1.10

STATED ODDS 1:17 ....
*GOLD CARDS: 1.2X TO 3X HI COL.
GOLD STATED ODDS 1:210........

❑ S1 Dan Marino	6.00	2.70
❑ S2 Brett Favre	6.00	2.70
❑ S3 Barry Sanders	6.00	2.70
❑ S4 Terrell Davis	4.00	1.80
❑ S5 Mark Brunell	2.50	1.10
❑ S6 Eddie George	2.50	1.10
❑ S7 Fred Taylor	3.00	1.35
❑ S8 Tim Couch	6.00	2.70
❑ S9 Randy Moss	5.00	2.20

1999 Upper Deck HoloGrFX UD Authentics

	MINT	NRMT
COMMON CARD (1-19)	25.00	11.00

STATED ODDS 1:432 ....

❑ AS Akili Smith	50.00	22.00
❑ BH Brock Huard	25.00	11.00
❑ CM Cade McNown	70.00	32.00
❑ DC Daunte Culpepper	60.00	27.00
❑ DM Donovan McNabb	60.00	27.00
❑ EG Eddie George	70.00	32.00
❑ EJ Edgerrin James	200.00	90.00
❑ EM Eric Moulds	25.00	11.00
❑ JA Jamal Anderson	25.00	11.00
❑ JP Jake Plummer	120.00	55.00
❑ JR Jerry Rice	120.00	55.00
❑ PM Peyton Manning	175.00	80.00
❑ RW Ricky Williams	150.00	70.00
❑ SK Shaun King	60.00	27.00
❑ SY Steve Young	80.00	36.00
❑ TA Troy Aikman	100.00	45.00
❑ TC Tim Couch	120.00	55.00
❑ TH Torry Holt	50.00	22.00

1997 Upper Deck Legends Autographs

	MINT	NRMT
COMPLETE SET (162)	9000.00	4000.00
COMMON CARD (AL1-AL178)	10.00	4.50
SEMISTARS	20.00	9.00
UNLISTED STARS	25.00	11.00
COMMON NEVER SIGNED	3.00	1.35

STATED ODDS 1:5H, 1:7 SPEC.RET,1:10R

❑ AL1 Bart Starr	800.00	350.00
❑ AL2 Jim Brown	750.00	350.00
❑ AL3 Joe Namath	800.00	350.00
❑ AL4 Walter Payton	800.00	350.00
❑ AL5 Terry Bradshaw	650.00	300.00
❑ AL6 Franco Harris	700.00	325.00
❑ AL7 Dan Fouts	30.00	13.50
❑ AL8 Steve Largent	40.00	18.00
❑ AL9 Johnny Unitas	550.00	250.00
❑ AL10 Gale Sayers	50.00	22.00
❑ AL11 Roger Staubach	200.00	90.00
❑ AL12 Tony Dorsett	400.00	180.00
❑ AL13 Fran Tarkenton	60.00	27.00
❑ AL14 Charley Taylor	10.00	4.50
❑ AL15 Ray Nitschke	70.00	32.00
❑ AL16 Jim Ringo	30.00	13.50
❑ AL17 Dick Butkus	700.00	325.00
❑ AL18 Fred Biletnikoff	40.00	18.00
❑ AL19 Lenny Moore	20.00	9.00
❑ AL20 Len Dawson	60.00	27.00
❑ AL21 Lance Alworth	50.00	22.00
❑ AL22 Chuck Bednarik	20.00	9.00
❑ AL23 Raymond Berry	20.00	9.00
❑ AL24 Donnie Shell	25.00	11.00
❑ AL25 Mel Blount	20.00	9.00
❑ AL26 Willie Brown	10.00	4.50
❑ AL27 Ken Houston	10.00	4.50
❑ AL28 Larry Csonka	200.00	90.00
❑ AL29 Mike Ditka	40.00	18.00
❑ AL30 Art Donovan	10.00	4.50
❑ AL31 Sam Huff	20.00	9.00
❑ AL32 Lem Barney	10.00	4.50
❑ AL33 Hugh McElhenny	10.00	4.50
❑ AL34 Otto Graham	50.00	22.00
❑ AL35 Joe Greene	200.00	90.00
❑ AL36 Mike Rozier	50.00	22.00
❑ AL37 Lou Groza	20.00	9.00
❑ AL38 Ted Hendricks	10.00	4.50
❑ AL39 Elroy Hirsch	20.00	9.00
❑ AL40 Paul Hornung	40.00	18.00
❑ AL41 Charlie Joiner	20.00	9.00
❑ AL42 Deacon Jones	25.00	11.00
❑ AL43 Bill Bradley	10.00	4.50
❑ AL44 Floyd Little	10.00	4.50
❑ AL45 Willie Lanier	10.00	4.50
❑ AL46 Bob Lilly	20.00	9.00
❑ AL47 Sid Luckman trade never signed	3.00	1.35
❑ AL48 John Mackey	10.00	4.50
❑ AL49 Don Maynard	20.00	9.00
❑ AL50 Mike McCormack	30.00	13.50
❑ AL51 Bobby Mitchell	10.00	4.50
❑ AL52 Ron Mix	10.00	4.50
❑ AL53 Marion Motley	10.00	4.50
❑ AL54 Leo Nomellini	20.00	9.00
❑ AL55 Mark Duper	40.00	18.00
❑ AL56 Mel Renfro	20.00	9.00
❑ AL57 Jim Otto	20.00	9.00
❑ AL58 Alan Page	20.00	9.00
❑ AL59 Joe Perry	10.00	4.50
❑ AL60 Andy Robustelli	10.00	4.50
❑ AL61 Lee Roy Selmon	10.00	4.50
❑ AL62 Jackie Smith	10.00	4.50
❑ AL63 Art Shell	50.00	22.00
❑ AL64 Jan Stenerud	10.00	4.50
❑ AL65 Gene Upshaw	10.00	4.50
❑ AL66 Y.A. Tittle	40.00	18.00
❑ AL67 Paul Warfield	30.00	13.50
❑ AL68 Kellen Winslow	50.00	22.00
❑ AL69 Randy White	20.00	9.00
❑ AL70 Larry Wilson	10.00	4.50
❑ AL71 Willie Wood trade never signed	3.00	1.35
❑ AL72 Jack Ham	20.00	9.00
❑ AL73 Jack Youngblood	10.00	4.50
❑ AL74 Danny Abramowicz	10.00	4.50
❑ AL75 Dick Anderson	10.00	4.50
❑ AL76 Ken Anderson	10.00	4.50
❑ AL77 Steve Bartkowski	10.00	4.50
❑ AL78 Bill Bergey	10.00	4.50
❑ AL79 Rocky Bleier	20.00	9.00
❑ AL80 Cliff Branch	20.00	9.00
❑ AL81 John Brodie	20.00	9.00
❑ AL82 Bobby Bell	10.00	4.50
❑ AL83 Billy Cannon	50.00	22.00
❑ AL84 Gino Cappelletti	10.00	4.50
❑ AL85 Harold Carmichael	10.00	4.50
❑ AL86 Dave Casper	10.00	4.50
❑ AL87 Wes Chandler	20.00	9.00
❑ AL88 Todd Christensen	10.00	4.50
❑ AL89 Dwight Clark	20.00	9.00
❑ AL90 Mark Clayton	25.00	11.00
❑ AL91 Cris Collinsworth	10.00	4.50
❑ AL92 Roger Craig	20.00	9.00
❑ AL93 Randy Cross	20.00	9.00
❑ AL94 Isaac Curtis	10.00	4.50
❑ AL95 Mike Curtis	10.00	4.50
❑ AL96 Ben Davidson	10.00	4.50
❑ AL97 Fred Dean trade never signed	3.00	1.35
❑ AL98 Tom Dempsey	10.00	4.50
❑ AL99 Eric Dickerson	30.00	13.50
❑ AL100 Lynn Dickey	20.00	9.00
❑ AL102 Carl Eller	40.00	18.00
❑ AL103 Chuck Foreman	10.00	4.50
❑ AL104 Russ Francis trade never signed	3.00	1.35
❑ AL106 Gary Garrison	10.00	4.50

Card	Player	Mint	NRMT
❑ AL107	Randy Gradishar	10.00	4.50
❑ AL108	L.C. Greenwood	30.00	13.50
❑ AL109	Rosey Grier	20.00	9.00
❑ AL110	Steve Grogan	10.00	4.50
❑ AL111	Ray Guy	10.00	4.50
❑ AL112	John Hadl	10.00	4.50
❑ AL113	Jim Hart	10.00	4.50
❑ AL115	Mike Haynes	25.00	11.00
❑ AL116	Charlie Hennigan	10.00	4.50
❑ AL117	Chuck Howley	10.00	4.50
❑ AL118	Harold Jackson	10.00	4.50
❑ AL119	Tom Jackson	10.00	4.50
❑ AL120	Ron Jaworski	10.00	4.50
❑ AL121	John Jefferson	10.00	4.50
❑ AL122	Billy Johnson trade never signed	3.00	1.35
❑ AL123	Ed Too Tall Jones	30.00	13.50
❑ AL124	Jack Kemp	80.00	36.00
❑ AL125	Jim Kiick	10.00	4.50
❑ AL126	Billy Kilmer	10.00	4.50
❑ AL127	Jerry Kramer	20.00	9.00
❑ AL128	Paul Krause	10.00	4.50
❑ AL129	Daryle Lamonica	20.00	9.00
❑ AL131	James Lofton	10.00	4.50
❑ AL133	Archie Manning	40.00	18.00
❑ AL134	Jim Marshall	40.00	18.00
❑ AL135	Harvey Martin	30.00	13.50
❑ AL136	Tommy McDonald	10.00	4.50
❑ AL137	Max McGee	20.00	9.00
❑ AL138	Reggie McKenzie	10.00	4.50
❑ AL139	Karl Mecklenburg	10.00	4.50
❑ AL141	Terry Metcalf	10.00	4.50
❑ AL142	Matt Millen	50.00	22.00
❑ AL143	Earl Morrall	20.00	9.00
❑ AL144	Mercury Morris	30.00	13.50
❑ AL146	Joe Morris	10.00	4.50
❑ AL147	Mark Moseley	10.00	4.50
❑ AL148	Haven Moses	10.00	4.50
❑ AL149	Chuck Muncie	10.00	4.50
❑ AL150	Anthony Munoz	30.00	13.50
❑ AL151	Tommy Nobis	10.00	4.50
❑ AL152	Babe Parilli	10.00	4.50
❑ AL153	Drew Pearson	30.00	13.50
❑ AL154	Ozzie Newsome	20.00	9.00
❑ AL155	Jim Plunkett	40.00	18.00
❑ AL156	William Perry	10.00	4.50
❑ AL157	Johnny Robinson	10.00	4.50
❑ AL158	Ahmad Rashad	30.00	13.50
❑ AL159	George Rogers	20.00	9.00
❑ AL160	Sterling Sharpe	40.00	18.00
❑ AL161	Billy Sims	10.00	4.50
❑ AL163	Mike Singletary	25.00	11.00
❑ AL164	Charlie Sanders	10.00	4.50
❑ AL165	Bubba Smith	125.00	55.00
❑ AL166	Ken Stabler	100.00	45.00
❑ AL167	Freddie Solomon	10.00	4.50
❑ AL168	John Stallworth	20.00	9.00
❑ AL169	Dwight Stephenson	10.00	4.50
❑ AL172	Lionel Taylor	10.00	4.50
❑ AL173	Otis Taylor	100.00	45.00
❑ AL174	Joe Theismann	40.00	18.00
❑ AL175	Bob Trumpy trade never signed	3.00	1.35
❑ AL176	Mike Webster	50.00	22.00
❑ AL177	Jim Zorn	10.00	4.50
❑ AL178	Joe Montana	500.00	220.00

1997 Upper Deck Legends Sign of the Times

	MINT	NRMT
COMPLETE SET (10)	2500.00	1100.00
COMMON CARD (ST1-ST10)	150.00	70.00
STATED PRINT RUN 100 SETS		

Card	Player	Mint	NRMT
❑ ST1	Joe Montana	400.00	180.00
❑ ST2	Fran Tarkenton	200.00	90.00
❑ ST3	Johnny Unitas	250.00	110.00
❑ ST4	Joe Namath	350.00	160.00
❑ ST5	Terry Bradshaw	250.00	110.00
❑ ST6	Jim Brown	300.00	135.00
❑ ST7	Franco Harris	150.00	70.00
❑ ST8	Walter Payton	400.00	180.00

Card	Player	Mint	NRMT
❑ ST9	Steve Largent	150.00	70.00
❑ ST10	Bart Starr	300.00	135.00

1999 Upper Deck MVP

	MINT	NRMT
COMPLETE SET (220)	30.00	13.50
COMMON CARD (1-200)	.10	.05
SEMISTARS	.20	.09
UNLISTED STARS	.40	.18
COMMON ROOKIE (201-220)	.75	.35
ROOKIE SEMISTARS	1.00	.45

Card	Player	Mint	NRMT
❑ 1	Jake Plummer	.75	.35
❑ 2	Adrian Murrell	.20	.09
❑ 3	Larry Centers	.10	.05
❑ 4	Frank Sanders	.20	.09
❑ 5	Andre Wadsworth	.10	.05
❑ 6	Rob Moore	.20	.09
❑ 7	Simeon Rice	.10	.05
❑ 8	Jamal Anderson	.40	.18
❑ 9	Chris Chandler	.20	.09
❑ 10	Chuck Smith	.10	.05
❑ 11	Terance Mathis	.20	.09
❑ 12	Tim Dwight	.40	.18
❑ 13	Ray Buchanan	.10	.05
❑ 14	O.J. Santiago	.10	.05
❑ 15	Eric Zeier	.20	.09
❑ 16	Priest Holmes	.40	.18
❑ 17	Michael Jackson	.10	.05
❑ 18	Jermaine Lewis	.20	.09
❑ 19	Michael McCrary	.10	.05
❑ 20	Rob Johnson	.20	.09
❑ 21	Antowain Smith	.40	.18
❑ 22	Thurman Thomas	.20	.09
❑ 23	Doug Flutie	.50	.23
❑ 24	Eric Moulds	.40	.18
❑ 25	Bruce Smith	.20	.09
❑ 26	Andre Reed	.20	.09
❑ 27	Fred Lane	.10	.05
❑ 28	Tim Biakabutuka	.20	.09
❑ 29	Rae Carruth	.20	.09
❑ 30	Wesley Walls	.20	.09
❑ 31	Steve Beuerlein	.10	.05
❑ 32	Muhsin Muhammad	.20	.09
❑ 33	Erik Kramer	.10	.05
❑ 34	Edgar Bennett	.10	.05
❑ 35	Curtis Conway	.20	.09
❑ 36	Curtis Enis	.40	.18
❑ 37	Bobby Engram	.20	.09
❑ 38	Alonzo Mayes	.10	.05
❑ 39	Corey Dillon	.40	.18
❑ 40	Jeff Blake	.20	.09
❑ 41	Carl Pickens	.20	.09
❑ 42	Darnay Scott	.10	.05
❑ 43	Tony McGee	.10	.05
❑ 44	Ki-Jana Carter	.10	.05
❑ 45	Ty Detmer	.20	.09
❑ 46	Terry Kirby	.10	.05
❑ 47	Justin Armour	.10	.05
❑ 48	Freddie Solomon	.10	.05
❑ 49	Marquez Pope	.10	.05
❑ 50	Antonio Langham	.10	.05
❑ 51	Troy Aikman	1.00	.45
❑ 52	Emmitt Smith	1.00	.45
❑ 53	Deion Sanders	.40	.18
❑ 54	Rocket Ismail	.20	.09
❑ 55	Michael Irvin	.20	.09
❑ 56	Chris Warren	.10	.05
❑ 57	Greg Ellis	.10	.05
❑ 58	John Elway	1.50	.70
❑ 59	Terrell Davis	1.00	.45
❑ 60	Rod Smith	.20	.09
❑ 61	Shannon Sharpe	.20	.09
❑ 62	Ed McCaffrey	.20	.09
❑ 63	John Mobley	.10	.05
❑ 64	Bill Romanowski	.10	.05
❑ 65	Barry Sanders	1.50	.70
❑ 66	Johnnie Morton	.20	.09
❑ 67	Herman Moore	.40	.18
❑ 68	Charlie Batch	.75	.35
❑ 69	Germane Crowell	.20	.09
❑ 70	Robert Porcher	.10	.05
❑ 71	Brett Favre	1.50	.70
❑ 72	Antonio Freeman	.40	.18
❑ 73	Dorsey Levens	.40	.18
❑ 74	Mark Chmura	.20	.09
❑ 75	Vonnie Holliday	.10	.05
❑ 76	Bill Schroeder	.40	.18
❑ 77	Marshall Faulk	.40	.18
❑ 78	Marvin Harrison	.40	.18
❑ 79	Peyton Manning	1.50	.70
❑ 80	Jerome Pathon	.10	.05
❑ 81	E.G. Green	.10	.05
❑ 82	Ellis Johnson	.10	.05
❑ 83	Mark Brunell	.60	.25
❑ 84	Jimmy Smith	.20	.09
❑ 85	Keenan McCardell	.20	.09
❑ 86	Fred Taylor	1.00	.45
❑ 87	James Stewart	.20	.09
❑ 88	Kevin Hardy	.10	.05
❑ 89	Elvis Grbac	.20	.09
❑ 90	Andre Rison	.20	.09
❑ 91	Derrick Alexander WR	.20	.09
❑ 92	Tony Gonzalez	.20	.09
❑ 93	Donnell Bennett	.10	.05
❑ 94	Derrick Thomas	.20	.09
❑ 95	Tamarick Vanover	.10	.05
❑ 96	Dan Marino	1.50	.70
❑ 97	Karim Abdul-Jabbar	.20	.09
❑ 98	Zach Thomas	.20	.09
❑ 99	O.J. McDuffie	.20	.09
❑ 100	John Avery	.20	.09
❑ 101	Sam Madison	.10	.05
❑ 102	Randall Cunningham	.40	.18
❑ 103	Cris Carter	.40	.18
❑ 104	Robert Smith	.40	.18
❑ 105	Randy Moss	1.50	.70
❑ 106	Jake Reed	.20	.09
❑ 107	Matthew Hatchette	.10	.05
❑ 108	John Randle	.20	.09
❑ 109	Drew Bledsoe	.60	.25
❑ 110	Terry Glenn	.40	.18
❑ 111	Ben Coates	.20	.09
❑ 112	Ty Law	.10	.05
❑ 113	Tony Simmons	.10	.05
❑ 114	Ted Johnson	.10	.05
❑ 115	Danny Wuerffel	.10	.05
❑ 116	Lamar Smith	.10	.05
❑ 117	Sean Dawkins	.10	.05
❑ 118	Cameron Cleeland	.10	.05
❑ 119	Joe Johnson	.10	.05
❑ 120	Andre Hastings	.10	.05
❑ 121	Kent Graham	.10	.05
❑ 122	Gary Brown	.10	.05
❑ 123	Amani Toomer	.10	.05
❑ 124	Tiki Barber	.10	.05

❑ 125 Ike Hilliard .10 .05
❑ 126 Jason Sehorn .10 .05
❑ 127 Vinny Testaverde .20 .09
❑ 128 Curtis Martin .40 .18
❑ 129 Keyshawn Johnson .40 .18
❑ 130 Wayne Chrebet .20 .09
❑ 131 Mo Lewis .10 .05
❑ 132 Steve Atwater .10 .05
❑ 133 Donald Hollas .10 .05
❑ 134 Napoleon Kaufman .40 .18
❑ 135 Tim Brown .40 .18
❑ 137 Rickey Dudley .10 .05
❑ 138 Charles Woodson .40 .18
❑ 139 Koy Detmer .10 .05
❑ 140 Duce Staley .40 .18
❑ 141 Charlie Garner .20 .09
❑ 142 Doug Pederson .10 .05
❑ 143 Jeff Graham .10 .05
❑ 144 Charles Johnson .10 .05
❑ 145 Kordell Stewart .40 .18
❑ 146 Jerome Bettis .40 .18
❑ 147 Hines Ward .10 .05
❑ 148 Courtney Hawkins .10 .05
❑ 149 Will Blackwell .10 .05
❑ 150 Richard Huntley .20 .09
❑ 151 Levon Kirkland .10 .05
❑ 152 Trent Green .20 .09
❑ 153 Tony Banks .20 .09
❑ 154 Isaac Bruce .40 .18
❑ 155 Eddie Kennison .20 .09
❑ 156 Az-Zahir Hakim .10 .05
❑ 157 Amp Lee .10 .05
❑ 158 Robert Holcombe .20 .09
❑ 159 Ryan Leaf .40 .18
❑ 160 Natrone Means .20 .09
❑ 161 Jim Harbaugh .20 .09
❑ 162 Junior Seau .20 .09
❑ 163 Charlie Jones .10 .05
❑ 164 Rodney Harrison .10 .05
❑ 165 Steve Young .60 .25
❑ 166 Jerry Rice 1.00 .45
❑ 167 Garrison Hearst .20 .09
❑ 168 Terrell Owens .40 .18
❑ 169 J.J. Stokes .20 .09
❑ 170 Bryant Young .10 .05
❑ 171 Ricky Watters .20 .09
❑ 172 Joey Galloway .40 .18
❑ 173 Jon Kitna .50 .23
❑ 174 Ahman Green .20 .09
❑ 175 Mike Pritchard .10 .05
❑ 176 Chad Brown .10 .05
❑ 177 Warrick Dunn .40 .18
❑ 178 Trent Dilfer .20 .09
❑ 179 Mike Alstott .40 .18
❑ 180 Reidel Anthony .20 .09
❑ 181 Bert Emanuel .20 .09
❑ 182 Jacquez Green .20 .09
❑ 183 Hardy Nickerson .10 .05
❑ 184 Steve McNair .40 .18
❑ 185 Eddie George .50 .23
❑ 186 Yancey Thigpen .10 .05
❑ 187 Frank Wycheck .10 .05
❑ 188 Kevin Dyson .20 .09
❑ 189 Jackie Harris .10 .05
❑ 190 Blaine Bishop .10 .05
❑ 191 Skip Hicks .40 .18
❑ 192 Michael Westbrook .20 .09
❑ 193 Stephen Alexander .10 .05
❑ 194 Leslie Shepherd .10 .05
❑ 195 Casey Weldon .10 .05
❑ 196 Brian Mitchell .10 .05
❑ 197 Dan Wilkinson .10 .05
❑ 198 Terrell Davis CL .50 .23
❑ 199 Troy Aikman CL .40 .18
❑ 200 Tim Couch CL 2.50 1.10
❑ 201 Ricky Williams RC 5.00 2.20
❑ 202 Tim Couch RC 5.00 2.20
❑ 203 Akili Smith RC 2.00 .90
❑ 204 Daunte Culpepper RC 3.00 1.35
❑ 205 Torry Holt RC 2.50 1.10
❑ 206 Edgerrin James RC 10.00 4.50
❑ 207 David Boston RC 1.50 .70
❑ 208 Peerless Price RC 1.50 .70
❑ 209 Chris Claiborne RC .75 .35
❑ 210 Champ Bailey RC 1.25 .55
❑ 211 Cade McNown RC 3.00 1.35
❑ 212 Jevon Kearse RC 2.00 .90
❑ 213 Joe Germaine RC 1.00 .45
❑ 214 D'Wayne Bates RC .75 .35
❑ 215 Dameane Douglas RC .75 .35
❑ 216 Troy Edwards RC 1.50 .70
❑ 217 Sedrick Irvin RC 1.00 .45
❑ 218 Brock Huard RC 1.25 .55
❑ 219 Amos Zereoue RC 1.00 .45
❑ 220 Donovan McNabb RC 3.00 1.35

1999 Upper Deck MVP Gold Script

	MINT	NRMT
COMMON CARD (1-220)	6.00	2.70
*GOLD STARS: 25X TO 60X HI COL.		
*GOLD YOUNG STARS: 20X TO 50X		
*GOLD RCs: 12X TO 25X		
GOLD SCRIPT PRINT RUN 100 SER.#'d SETS		

1999 Upper Deck MVP Silver Script

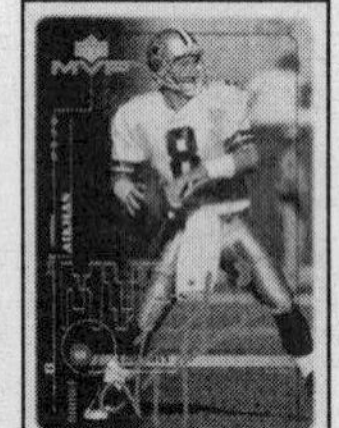

	MINT	NRMT
COMPLETE SET (217)	120.00	55.00
*SILVER STARS: 1.5X TO 4X HI COL.		
*SILVER YOUNG STARS: 1.25X TO 3X		
*SILVER RCs: .6X TO 1.5X		
STATED ODDS 1:2		

1999 Upper Deck MVP Super Script

	MINT	NRMT
COMMON CARD (1-220)	15.00	6.75
*STARS: 60X TO 150X HI COL.		
*YOUNG STARS: 50X TO 120X		
*RCs: 20X TO 50X		
STATED PRINT RUN 25 SERIAL #'d SETS		

1999 Upper Deck MVP Draw Your Own Card

	MINT	NRMT
COMPLETE SET (30)	20.00	9.00
COMMON CARD (W1-W30)	.20	.09
SEMISTARS	.40	.18
UNLISTED STARS	.75	.35

STATED ODDS 1:6

❑ W1 Brett Favre 2.00 .90
❑ W2 Emmitt Smith 1.25 .55
❑ W3 John Elway 2.00 .90
❑ W4 Emmitt Smith 1.25 .55
❑ W5 Randy Moss 1.50 .70
❑ W6 Terrell Davis 1.25 .55
❑ W7 Steve Young .75 .35
❑ W8 Drew Bledsoe .75 .35
❑ W9 Troy Aikman 1.25 .55
❑ W10 Terry Allen .40 .18
❑ W11 Warrick Dunn .75 .35
❑ W12 Kimble Anders .40 .18
❑ W13 Joey Galloway .75 .35
❑ W14 Barry Sanders 3.00 1.35
❑ W15 Mark Brunell 1.25 .55
❑ W16 Bruce Smith .40 .18
❑ W17 Randy Moss 2.50 1.10
❑ W18 Jerome Bettis .75 .35
❑ W19 John Elway 3.00 1.35
❑ W20 Jerome Bettis .75 .35
❑ W21 Brett Favre 3.00 1.35
❑ W22 Troy Aikman 2.00 .90
❑ W23 Cris Carter .75 .35
❑ W24 Jason Gildon .20 .09
❑ W25 Randall Cunningham .75 .35
❑ W26 Thurman Thomas .40 .18
❑ W27 Jerry Rice 2.00 .90
❑ W28 Jerome Bettis .75 .35
❑ W29 Steve Young 1.25 .55
❑ W30 Reggie White .75 .35

1999 Upper Deck MVP Drive Time

	MINT	NRMT
COMPLETE SET (14)	8.00	3.60
COMMON CARD (DT1-DT14)	.75	.35
STATED ODDS 1:6		

❑ DT1 Steve Young 1.25 .55
❑ DT2 Kordell Stewart 1.00 .45
❑ DT3 Eric Moulds 1.00 .45
❑ DT4 Corey Dillon 1.00 .45
❑ DT5 Doug Flutie 1.00 .45
❑ DT6 Charlie Batch 1.25 .55
❑ DT7 Curtis Martin 1.00 .45
❑ DT8 Marshall Faulk 1.00 .45
❑ DT9 Terrell Owens 1.00 .45

❑ DT10 Antowain Smith	1.00	.45
❑ DT11 Troy Aikman	2.00	.90
❑ DT12 Drew Bledsoe	1.25	.55
❑ DT13 Keyshawn Johnson	1.00	.45
❑ DT14 Steve McNair	1.00	.45

1999 Upper Deck MVP Dynamics

	MINT	NRMT
COMPLETE SET (15)	60.00	27.00
COMMON CARD (D1-D15)	3.00	1.35
STATED ODDS 1:28		

❑ D1 John Elway	12.00	5.50
❑ D2 Steve Young	5.00	2.20
❑ D3 Jake Plummer	6.00	2.70
❑ D4 Fred Taylor	6.00	2.70
❑ D5 Mark Brunell	5.00	2.20
❑ D6 Joey Galloway	4.00	1.80
❑ D7 Terrell Davis	8.00	3.60
❑ D8 Randy Moss	10.00	4.50
❑ D9 Charlie Batch	5.00	2.20
❑ D10 Peyton Manning	10.00	4.50
❑ D11 Barry Sanders	12.00	5.50
❑ D12 Eddie George	4.00	1.80
❑ D13 Warrick Dunn	4.00	1.80
❑ D14 Jamal Anderson	4.00	1.80
❑ D15 Brett Favre	12.00	5.50

1999 Upper Deck MVP Game Used Souvenirs

	MINT	NRMT
COMPLETE SET (22)	1000.00	450.00
COMMON CARD	40.00	18.00
STATED ODDS 1:130		

❑ AS-S Akili Smith	40.00	18.00
❑ BF-S Brett Favre	100.00	45.00
❑ BH-S Brock Huard	40.00	18.00
❑ BS-S Barry Sanders	100.00	45.00
❑ CB-S Champ Bailey	40.00	18.00
❑ CM-S Cade McNown	60.00	27.00
❑ DB-S David Boston	40.00	18.00
❑ DC-S Daunte Culpepper	60.00	27.00
❑ DF-S Doug Flutie	50.00	22.00
❑ DM-S Dan Marino	100.00	45.00
❑ EJ-S Edgerrin James	120.00	55.00
❑ ES-S Emmitt Smith	80.00	36.00
❑ JA-S Jamal Anderson	40.00	18.00
❑ JE-S John Elway	100.00	45.00
❑ JP-S Jake Plummer	50.00	22.00
❑ KJ-S Keyshawn Johnson	40.00	18.00
❑ MC-S Donovan McNabb	60.00	27.00
❑ PM-S Peyton Manning	100.00	45.00
❑ RM-A Randy Moss AUTO/84	400.00	180.00
❑ RM-S Randy Moss	100.00	45.00
❑ TC-S Tim Couch	80.00	36.00
❑ TD-A Terrell Davis AUTO/30	500.00	220.00
❑ TD-S Terrell Davis	60.00	27.00
❑ TH-S Torry Holt	50.00	22.00

1999 Upper Deck MVP Jumbos

	MINT	NRMT
COMPLETE SET (10)	40.00	18.00
COMMON CARD (201-220)	2.00	.90

❑ 201 Ricky Williams	6.00	2.70
❑ 202 Tim Couch	6.00	2.70
❑ 203 Akili Smith	2.50	1.10
❑ 204 Daunte Culpepper	4.00	1.80
❑ 205 Torry Holt	3.00	1.35
❑ 206 Edgerrin James	10.00	4.50
❑ 207 David Boston	2.50	1.10
❑ 211 Cade McNown	4.00	1.80
❑ 218 Brock Huard		
❑ 220 Donovan McNabb	4.00	1.80

1999 Upper Deck MVP Power Surge

	MINT	NRMT
COMPLETE SET (15)	20.00	9.00
COMMON CARD (PS1-PS15)	.75	.35
SEMISTARS	1.50	.70
STATED ODDS 1:9		

❑ PS1 Jerome Bettis	1.50	.70
❑ PS2 Eddie George	2.00	.90
❑ PS3 Karim Abdul-Jabbar	.75	.35
❑ PS4 Curtis Martin	1.50	.70
❑ PS5 Antowain Smith	1.50	.70
❑ PS6 Kordell Stewart	1.50	.70
❑ PS7 Curtis Enis	1.50	.70
❑ PS8 Joey Galloway	1.50	.70
❑ PS9 Mark Brunell	2.50	1.10
❑ PS10 Peyton Manning	5.00	2.20
❑ PS11 Antonio Freeman	1.50	.70
❑ PS12 Jerry Rice	4.00	1.80
❑ PS13 Eric Moulds	1.50	.70
❑ PS14 Drew Bledsoe	2.50	1.10
❑ PS15 Fred Taylor	3.00	1.35

1999 Upper Deck MVP ProSign

	MINT	NRMT
COMPLETE SET (34)		
COMMON CARD	12.00	5.50
SEMISTARS	20.00	9.00
UNLISTED STARS	30.00	13.50
STATED ODDS 1:216 RETAIL		
SOME CARDS ISSUED VIA MAIL REDEMPTION		

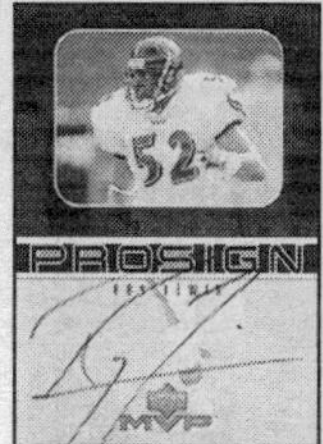

❑ AG Ahman Green	20.00	9.00
❑ AM Adrian Murrell	20.00	9.00
❑ AS Antowain Smith	30.00	13.50
❑ BH Brock Huard	30.00	13.50
❑ CB Charlie Batch	60.00	27.00
❑ CC Curtis Conway	20.00	9.00
❑ CM Cade McNown SP		
❑ DC Daunte Culpepper Trade	60.00	27.00
❑ DM Donovan McNabb	70.00	32.00
❑ EM Eric Moulds	30.00	13.50
❑ EM Ed McCaffrey	20.00	9.00
❑ FT Fred Taylor	60.00	27.00
❑ GH Greg Hill	12.00	5.50
❑ JA Jamal Anderson	40.00	18.00
❑ JM John Mobley	12.00	5.50
❑ JS Jimmy Smith	20.00	9.00
❑ MB Michael Bishop	40.00	18.00
❑ MF Marshall Faulk	40.00	18.00
❑ MM Muhsin Muhammad	20.00	9.00
❑ PH Priest Holmes	30.00	13.50
❑ RE Robert Edwards	20.00	9.00
❑ RL Ray Lewis	12.00	5.50
❑ RM Randy Moss SP		
❑ RW Ricky Williams Trade	300.00	135.00
❑ RW Ricky Watters	20.00	9.00
❑ SK Shaun King	70.00	32.00
❑ SS Shannon Sharpe	20.00	9.00
❑ TD Terrell Davis	80.00	36.00
❑ TG Trent Green	20.00	9.00
❑ TH Torry Holt SP		
❑ TR Troy Drayton	12.00	5.50
❑ KAJ Karim Abdul-Jabbar	20.00	9.00

1999 Upper Deck MVP Strictly Business

	MINT	NRMT
COMPLETE SET (13)	40.00	18.00
COMMON CARD (SB1-SB13)	2.00	.90
STATED ODDS 1:14		

❑ SB1 Eddie George	2.50	1.10
❑ SB2 Curtis Martin	2.50	1.10
❑ SB3 Fred Taylor	4.00	1.80
❑ SB4 Steve Young	3.00	1.35
❑ SB5 Kordell Stewart	2.50	1.10
❑ SB6 Corey Dillon	2.50	1.10
❑ SB7 Dan Marino	8.00	3.60
❑ SB8 Jake Plummer	4.00	1.80
❑ SB9 Jerry Rice	5.00	2.20

❑ SB10 Warrick Dunn 2.50 1.10
❑ SB11 Jerome Bettis 2.50 1.10
❑ SB12 John Elway............... 8.00 3.60
❑ SB13 Randy Moss 6.00 2.70

1999 Upper Deck MVP Theatre

	MINT	NRMT
COMPLETE SET (15)	25.00	11.00
COMMON CARD (M1-M15)......	1.25	.55
STATED ODDS 1:9		

❑ M1 Terrell Davis.................. 3.00 1.35
❑ M2 Corey Dillon .... 2.00 .90
❑ M3 Brett Favre 5.00 2.20
❑ M4 Jerry Rice....................... 3.00 1.35
❑ M5 Emmitt Smith 3.00 1.35
❑ M6 Dan Marino..................... 5.00 2.20
❑ M7 Jerome Bettis .... 2.00 .90
❑ M8 Napoleon Kaufman ...... 2.00 .90
❑ M9 Keyshawn Johnson ...... 2.00 .90
❑ M10 Warrick Dunn .... 2.00 .90
❑ M11 Barry Sanders 5.00 2.20
❑ M12 Troy Aikman................ 3.00 1.35
❑ M13 Jamal Anderson.......... 2.00 .90
❑ M14 Randall Cunningham .. 2.00 .90
❑ M15 Doug Flutie.................. 1.50 .70

2000 Upper Deck MVP

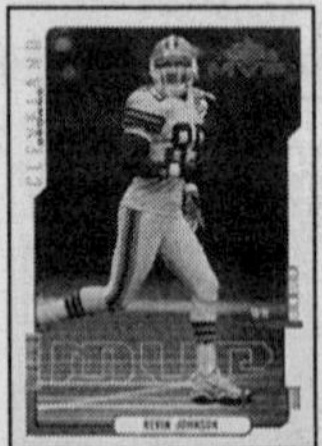

	MINT	NRMT
COMPLETE SET (218)	25.00	11.00
COMMON CARD (1-187)...........	.10	.05
SEMISTARS...............................	.20	.09
UNLISTED STARS......................	.40	.18
COMMON ROOKIE (188-220)....	.40	.18
ROOKIE SEMISTARS	.60	.25

❑ 1 Jake Plummer.................... .40 .18
❑ 2 Michael Pittman.................. .10 .05
❑ 3 Rob Moore .... .20 .09
❑ 4 David Boston........................ .40 .18
❑ 5 Frank Sanders...................... .20 .09
❑ 6 Aeneas Williams .... .10 .05
❑ 7 Kwamie Lassiter .... .10 .05
❑ 8 Tim Dwight .... .40 .18
❑ 9 Chris Chandler .... .20 .09
❑ 10 Jamal Anderson .... .40 .18
❑ 11 Shawn Jefferson .... .10 .05
❑ 12 Qadry Ismail .... .10 .05
❑ 13 Jermaine Lewis................ .10 .05
❑ 14 Rod Woodson .... .10 .05
❑ 15 Michael McCrary .... .10 .05
❑ 16 Tony Banks .... .20 .09
❑ 17 Peter Boulware .... .10 .05
❑ 18 Shannon Sharpe .... .20 .09
❑ 19 Peerless Price.................. .40 .18
❑ 20 Rob Johnson.................... .20 .09
❑ 21 Eric Moulds .... .40 .18
❑ 22 Doug Flutie .... .50 .23
❑ 23 Muhsin Muhammad.......... .20 .09
❑ 24 Patrick Jeffers .... .40 .18
❑ 25 Steve Beuerlein................ .20 .09
❑ 26 Tim Biakabutuka .... .20 .09
❑ 27 Michael Bates .... .10 .05
❑ 28 Cade McNown.................. .60 .25
❑ 29 Curtis Enis......................... .40 .18
❑ 30 Marcus Robinson .... .40 .18
❑ 31 Shane Matthews .... .20 .09
❑ 32 Bobby Engram .... .20 .09
❑ 33 Glyn Milburn .... .10 .05
❑ 34 Akili Smith .... .50 .23
❑ 35 Corey Dillon...................... .40 .18
❑ 36 Darnay Scott .... .20 .09
❑ 37 Tremain Mack .... .10 .05
❑ 38 Tim Couch...................... 1.00 .45
❑ 39 Kevin Johnson.................. .40 .18
❑ 40 Darrin Chiaverini .... .10 .05
❑ 41 Jamir Miller .... .10 .05
❑ 42 Errict Rhett .... .20 .09
❑ 43 Troy Aikman .... 1.00 .45
❑ 44 Emmitt Smith................. 1.00 .45
❑ 45 Rocket Ismail.................... .20 .09
❑ 46 Jason Tucker..................... .20 .09
❑ 47 Dexter Coakley .... .10 .05
❑ 48 Joey Galloway.................. .40 .18
❑ 49 Greg Ellis........................... .10 .05
❑ 50 Terrell Davis .... 1.00 .45
❑ 51 Olandis Gary .... .50 .23
❑ 52 Brian Griese .... .50 .23
❑ 53 Ed McCaffrey .... .20 .09
❑ 54 Rod Smith .... .20 .09
❑ 55 Trevor Pryce .... .10 .05
❑ 56 Charlie Batch.................... .40 .18
❑ 57 Germane Crowell .... .20 .09
❑ 58 Johnnie Morton .... .20 .09
❑ 59 Robert Porcher .... .10 .05
❑ 60 Luther Elliss...................... .10 .05
❑ 61 James Stewart .... .20 .09
❑ 62 Brett Favre .... 1.50 .70
❑ 63 Antonio Freeman............. .40 .18
❑ 64 Bill Schroeder .... .20 .09
❑ 65 Dorsey Levens .... .40 .18
❑ 66 Peyton Manning .... 1.25 .55
❑ 67 Edgerrin James............ 1.50 .70
❑ 68 Marvin Harrison............... .40 .18
❑ 69 Ken Dilger .... .10 .05
❑ 70 Terrence Wilkins .... .40 .18
❑ 71 Mark Brunell .... .60 .25
❑ 72 Fred Taylor .... .60 .25
❑ 73 Jimmy Smith .... .20 .09
❑ 74 Keenan McCardell........... .20 .09
❑ 75 Carnell Lake .... .10 .05
❑ 76 Tony Brackens .... .10 .05
❑ 77 Kevin Hardy...................... .10 .05
❑ 78 Hardy Nickerson .... .10 .05
❑ 79 Elvis Grbac .... .20 .09
❑ 80 Tony Gonzalez .... .20 .09
❑ 81 Derrick Alexander .... .20 .09
❑ 82 Donnell Bennett................ .10 .05
❑ 83 James Hasty .... .10 .05
❑ 84 Jay Fiedler........................ .40 .18
❑ 85 James Johnson................ .20 .09
❑ 86 Tony Martin .... .20 .09
❑ 87 Damon Huard .... .40 .18
❑ 88 O.J. McDuffie .... .20 .09
❑ 89 Oronde Gadsden.............. .10 .05
❑ 90 Zach Thomas .... .20 .09
❑ 91 Sam Madison .... .10 .05
❑ 92 Jeff George .... .20 .09
❑ 93 Randy Moss .... 1.25 .55
❑ 94 Robert Smith .... .40 .18
❑ 95 Cris Carter......................... .40 .18
❑ 96 Matthew Hatchette .... .20 .09
❑ 97 Drew Bledsoe .... .60 .25
❑ 98 Terry Glenn....................... .40 .18
❑ 99 Troy Brown .... .10 .05
❑ 100 Kevin Faulk .... .20 .09
❑ 101 Lawyer Milloy .... .10 .05
❑ 102 Ricky Williams............. 1.00 .45
❑ 103 Keith Poole .... .10 .05
❑ 104 Jake Reed....................... .20 .09
❑ 105 Cam Cleeland .... .10 .05
❑ 106 Jeff Blake .... .20 .09
❑ 107 Andrew Glover .... .10 .05
❑ 108 Kerry Collins .... .20 .09
❑ 109 Amani Toomer................ .10 .05
❑ 110 Joe Montgomery .... .10 .05
❑ 111 Ike Hilliard .... .20 .09
❑ 112 Michael Strahan .... .10 .05
❑ 113 Jessie Armstead .... .10 .05
❑ 114 Ray Lucas .... .40 .18
❑ 115 Keyshawn Johnson........ .40 .18
❑ 116 Curtis Martin .... .40 .18
❑ 117 Vinny Testaverde .... .20 .09
❑ 118 Wayne Chrebet .... .20 .09
❑ 119 Dedric Ward .... .10 .05
❑ 120 Tim Brown....................... .40 .18
❑ 121 Rich Gannon .... .20 .09
❑ 122 Tyrone Wheatley............ .20 .09
❑ 123 Napoleon Kaufman .... .40 .18
❑ 124 Charles Woodson .... .20 .09
❑ 125 Darrell Russell................ .10 .05
❑ 126 Duce Staley.................... .40 .18
❑ 127 Donovan McNabb .... .60 .25
❑ 128 Torrance Small .... .10 .05
❑ 129 Allen Rossum .... .10 .05
❑ 130 Brian Dawkins .... .10 .05
❑ 131 Troy Vincent .... .10 .05
❑ 132 Troy Edwards .... .40 .18
❑ 133 Jerome Bettis .... .40 .18
❑ 134 Hines Ward .... .10 .05
❑ 135 Kordell Stewart .... .40 .18
❑ 136 Levon Kirkland .... .10 .05
❑ 137 Kent Graham................... .10 .05
❑ 138 Marshall Faulk................ .40 .18
❑ 139 Kurt Warner................. 2.00 .90
❑ 140 Torry Holt .... .40 .18
❑ 141 Isaac Bruce .... .40 .18
❑ 142 Kevin Carter .... .10 .05
❑ 143 Az-Zahir Hakim .... .20 .09
❑ 144 Todd Lyght .... .10 .05
❑ 145 Jermaine Fazande .... .10 .05
❑ 146 Curtis Conway................ .20 .09
❑ 147 Freddie Jones .... .10 .05
❑ 148 Junior Seau..................... .20 .09
❑ 149 Jeff Graham .... .10 .05
❑ 150 Ryan Leaf .... .40 .18
❑ 151 Rodney Harrison............ .10 .05
❑ 152 Steve Young .... .60 .25
❑ 153 Jerry Rice .... 1.00 .45
❑ 154 Charlie Garner................ .20 .09
❑ 155 Terrell Owens .... .40 .18
❑ 156 Jeff Garcia...................... .40 .18
❑ 157 Bryant Young .... .10 .05
❑ 158 Lance Schulters .... .10 .05
❑ 159 Ricky Watters .... .10 .05
❑ 160 Jon Kitna .... .40 .18
❑ 161 Derrick Mayes .... .20 .09
❑ 162 Sean Dawkins .... .10 .05
❑ 163 Cortez Kennedy .... .10 .05
❑ 164 Chad Brown .... .10 .05
❑ 165 Warrick Dunn .... .40 .18
❑ 166 Shaun King .... .60 .25
❑ 167 Mike Alstott .... .40 .18
❑ 168 Warren Sapp.................. .20 .09
❑ 169 Jacquez Green .... .20 .09
❑ 170 Derrick Brooks................ .10 .05
❑ 171 John Lynch .... .10 .05
❑ 172 Donnie Abraham .... .10 .05
❑ 173 Eddie George .... .50 .23
❑ 174 Steve McNair.................. .40 .18
❑ 175 Kevin Dyson .... .20 .09
❑ 176 Jevon Kearse .... .40 .18
❑ 177 Yancey Thigpen .... .10 .05
❑ 178 Frank Wycheck .... .10 .05
❑ 179 Eddie Robinson.............. .10 .05
❑ 180 Samari Rolle .... .10 .05
❑ 181 Brad Johnson .... .40 .18
❑ 182 Stephen Davis................ .40 .18
❑ 183 Michael Westbrook .... .20 .09

❑ 184 Albert Connell .... .10 .05
❑ 185 Brian Mitchell................. .10 .05
❑ 186 Bruce Smith.................... .20 .09
❑ 187 Stephen Alexander .... .10 .05
❑ 188 Peter Warrick RC 3.00 1.35
❑ 189 Cutout Card/Arrington 25.00 11.00
❑ 190 Chris Redman RC........ 1.00 .45
❑ 191 Courtney Brown RC .... 1.25 .55
❑ 192 Brian Urlacher RC.......... .75 .35
❑ 193 Plaxico Burress RC...... 1.50 .70
❑ 194 Corey Simon RC .... .60 .25
❑ 195 Bubba Franks RC .... .75 .35
❑ 196 Deon Grant RC .... .40 .18
❑ 197 Michael Wiley RC .... .75 .35
❑ 198 Tim Rattay RC................ .75 .35
❑ 199 Ron Dayne RC 3.00 1.35
❑ 200 Sylvester Morris RC ...... .75 .35
❑ 201 Shaun Alexander RC .. 2.00 .90
❑ 202 Dez White RC .... .75 .35
❑ 203 Thomas Jones RC ...... 2.00 .90
❑ 204 Reuben Droughns RC.... .75 .35
❑ 205 Travis Taylor RC .... 1.25 .55
❑ 206 Trevor Gaylor RC .... .40 .18
❑ 207 Jamal Lewis RC .... 2.00 .90
❑ 208 Chad Pennington RC .. 2.50 1.10
❑ 209 J.R. Redmond RC........ 1.00 .45
❑ 210 Laveranues Coles RC.... .60 .25
❑ 211 Travis Prentice RC .... .75 .35
❑ 212 R.Jay Soward RC .... .75 .35
❑ 213 Todd Pinkston RC.......... .60 .25
❑ 214 Dennis Northcutt RC ...... .75 .35
❑ 215 Shyrone Stith RC .... .40 .18
❑ 216 Tee Martin RC............. 1.00 .45
❑ 217 Giovanni Carmazzi RC 1.25 .55
❑ 218 Drew Bledsoe CL .... .20 .09
❑ 219 Steve Young CL .... .20 .09
❑ 220 Donovan McNabb CL SP 25.00 11.00
❑ GJGM Joe Montana Jersey 400.00 180.00

2000 Upper Deck MVP Gold Script

	MINT	NRMT
COMMON CARD (1-220)..........	3.00	1.35

*GOLD SCRIPT STARS: 12X TO 30X HI COL.
*GOLD SCRIPT YOUNG STARS: 10X TO 25X

COMMON ROOKIE (188-217)	10.00	4.50

*GOLD SCRIPT RCs: 10X TO 25X
STATED PRINT RUN 100 SER.#'d SETS

2000 Upper Deck MVP Silver Script

	MINT	NRMT
COMPLETE SET (220)	100.00	45.00

*SILVER SCRIPT STARS: 1.2X TO 3X HI COL.
*SILVER SCRIPT YOUNG STARS: 1X TO 2.5X
*SILVER SCRIPT RCs: .8X TO 2X
STATED ODDS 1:2 ....

2000 Upper Deck MVP Super Script

	MINT	NRMT
COMMON CARD (1-220)........	10.00	4.50

*SUPER SCRIPT STARS: 40X TO 100X HI COL.
*SUPER SCRIPT YNG.STARS: 30X TO 80X

COMMON ROOKIE	25.00	11.00

*SUPER SCRIPT RCs: 25X TO 60X
STATED PRINT RUN 25 SERIAL #'d SETS

2000 Upper Deck MVP Air Show

	MINT	NRMT
COMPLETE SET (10)	12.00	5.50
COMMON CARD (AS1-AS10) ..	1.00	.45
SEMISTARS............................	1.50	.70

STATED ODDS 1:14 ....

❑ AS1 Brian Griese .... 2.00 .90
❑ AS2 Drew Bledsoe.............. 2.50 1.10
❑ AS3 Rob Johnson .... 1.00 .45

❑ AS4 Jeff Garcia .... 1.50 .70
❑ AS5 Ray Lucas .... 1.50 .70
❑ AS6 Jon Kitna .... 1.50 .70
❑ AS7 Jeff George.................. 1.00 .45
❑ AS8 Shaun King.................. 2.50 1.10
❑ AS9 Troy Aikman 4.00 1.80
❑ AS10 Steve Beuerlein .... 1.00 .45

2000 Upper Deck MVP Game Used Souvenirs

	MINT	NRMT
COMMON CARD	20.00	9.00
SEMISTARS............................	25.00	11.00

STATED ODDS 1:229 HOBBY ....

❑ AS Akili Smith.................. 25.00 11.00
❑ BF Brett Favre 60.00 27.00
❑ BG Brian Griese 25.00 11.00
❑ BJ Brad Johnson 20.00 9.00
❑ CB Charlie Batch 20.00 9.00
❑ CC Cris Carter 30.00 13.50
❑ CM Cade McNown........... 30.00 13.50
❑ DF Doug Flutie................. 25.00 11.00
❑ DM Dan Marino 80.00 36.00
❑ DM Donovan McNabb 30.00 13.50
❑ EG Eddie George SB/40 100.00 45.00
❑ EJ Edgerrin James........... 50.00 22.00
❑ ES Emmitt Smith 50.00 22.00
❑ FT Fred Taylor 30.00 13.50
❑ JK Jon Kitna..................... 20.00 9.00
❑ JP Jake Plummer 25.00 11.00
❑ JR Jerry Rice 50.00 22.00
❑ KE Keyshawn Johnson 25.00 11.00
❑ KJ Kevin Johnson 25.00 11.00
❑ KW Kurt Warner SB/40 .. 250.00 110.00
❑ MA Mike Alstott 25.00 11.00
❑ MB Mark Brunell............... 30.00 13.50
❑ MF Marshall Faulk 30.00 13.50
❑ PM Peyton Manning.......... 60.00 27.00
❑ RM Randy Moss.............. 60.00 27.00
❑ RW Ricky Williams 40.00 18.00
❑ SD Stephen Davis 25.00 11.00
❑ SK Shaun King................. 30.00 13.50
❑ TA Troy Aikman 40.00 18.00
❑ TC Tim Couch 40.00 18.00
❑ TD Terrell Davis............... 40.00 18.00

2000 Upper Deck MVP Game Used Souvenirs Autographs

	MINT	NRMT
COMMON CARD	100.00	45.00

AUTO STATED PRINT RUN 25 SERIAL #'d SETS

❑ ASA Akili Smith ....
❑ BGA Brian Griese........... 100.00 45.00
❑ BJA Brad Johnson 100.00 45.00
❑ CBA Charlie Batch 100.00 45.00
❑ CCA Cris Carter 100.00 45.00
❑ DFA Doug Flutie......................
❑ DMA Dan Marino 400.00 180.00
❑ EJA Edgerrin James 300.00 135.00
❑ JKA Jon Kitna................. 100.00 45.00
❑ JPA Jake Plummer.......... 120.00 55.00
❑ KEA Keyshawn Johnson 120.00 55.00
❑ KJA Kevin Johnson ....
❑ KWA Kurt Warner........... 500.00 220.00
❑ MBA Mark Brunell 150.00 70.00
❑ MFA Marshall Faulk...............
❑ PMA Peyton Manning 300.00 135.00
❑ RMA Randy Moss 300.00 135.00
❑ RWA Ricky Williams...............
❑ SDA Stephen Davis ....
❑ TAA Troy Aikman........... 250.00 110.00
❑ TCA Tim Couch 300.00 135.00
❑ TDA Terrell Davis........... 250.00 110.00

2000 Upper Deck MVP Headliners

	MINT	NRMT
COMPLETE SET (10)	6.00	2.70
COMMON CARD (H1-H10)	.75	.35
SEMISTARS............................	1.00	.45

STATED ODDS 1:6 ....

❑ H1 Isaac Bruce.................. 1.00 .45
❑ H2 Michael Westbrook.......... .75 .35
❑ H3 James Stewart .... .75 .35
❑ H4 Keyshawn Johnson ...... 1.00 .45
❑ H5 Marcus Robinson .... 1.00 .45
❑ H6 Charlie Batch .... 1.00 .45
❑ H7 Marvin Harrison .... 1.00 .45
❑ H8 Olandis Gary................. 1.00 .45
❑ H9 Curtis Martin.................. 1.00 .45
❑ H10 Jevon Kearse .... 1.00 .45

2000 Upper Deck MVP Highlight Reel

	MINT	NRMT
COMPLETE SET (7)	12.00	5.50
COMMON CARD (HR1-HR7)....	1.25	.55
SEMISTARS............................	2.00	.90

STATED ODDS 1:28 ....

❑ HR1 Marvin Harrison .... 2.00 .90
❑ HR2 Isaac Bruce .... 2.00 .90
❑ HR3 Cris Carter .... 2.00 .90
❑ HR4 Ray Lucas .... 2.00 .90
❑ HR5 Muhsin Muhammad .... 1.25 .55
❑ HR6 Eddie George............. 2.50 1.10
❑ HR7 Ricky Williams 4.00 1.80

2000 Upper Deck MVP Prolifics

	MINT	NRMT
COMPLETE SET (7)	25.00	11.00
COMMON CARD (P1-P7)	2.00	.90
STATED ODDS 1:28		
❑ P1 Brett Favre	8.00	3.60
❑ P2 Marshall Faulk	2.00	.90
❑ P3 Edgerrin James	6.00	2.70
❑ P4 Peyton Manning	6.00	2.70
❑ P5 Tim Couch	4.00	1.80
❑ P6 Dan Marino	8.00	3.60
❑ P7 Kurt Warner	8.00	3.60

2000 Upper Deck MVP ProSign

	MINT	NRMT
COMMON CARD	25.00	11.00
STATED ODDS 1:215 RETAIL		
*GOLD CARDS: X TO X HI COL.		
GOLD PRINT RUN 25 SER.#'d SETS		
DAN MARINO IN GOLD FOIL ONLY		
❑ BG Brian Griese	35.00	16.00
❑ CB Charlie Batch	30.00	13.50
❑ CP Chad Pennington		
❑ CR Chris Redman	30.00	13.50
❑ DM Dan Marino Gold		
❑ DW Dez White		
❑ EJ Edgerrin James		
❑ HT Ron Dayne		
❑ IB Isaac Bruce	30.00	13.50
❑ JK Jon Kitna	30.00	13.50
❑ JL Jamal Lewis	60.00	27.00
❑ JP Jake Plummer	30.00	13.50
❑ KC Kwame Cavil	25.00	11.00
❑ KJ Keyshawn Johnson		
❑ KW Kurt Warner	135.00	60.00
❑ MB Mark Brunell	40.00	18.00
❑ MF Marshall Faulk		
❑ PM Peyton Manning	80.00	36.00
❑ PW Peter Warrick		
❑ RD Ron Dugans		
❑ RM Randy Moss		
❑ RW Ricky Williams		
❑ SA Shaun Alexander	60.00	27.00
❑ TC Tim Couch	60.00	27.00
❑ TH Torry Holt	35.00	16.00
❑ TJ Thomas Jones	60.00	27.00
❑ TM Tee Martin		
❑ TT Travis Taylor		

2000 Upper Deck MVP Theatre

	MINT	NRMT
COMPLETE SET (10)	8.00	3.60
COMMON CARD (M1-M10)	.50	.23
SEMISTARS	1.00	.45
STATED ODDS 1:6		
❑ M1 Troy Edwards	1.00	.45
❑ M2 Ed McCaffrey	.50	.23

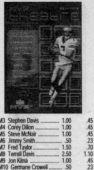

	MINT	NRMT
❑ M3 Stephen Davis	1.00	.45
❑ M4 Corey Dillon	1.00	.45
❑ M5 Steve McNair	1.00	.45
❑ M6 Jimmy Smith	.50	.23
❑ M7 Fred Taylor	1.50	.70
❑ M8 Terrell Davis	2.50	1.10
❑ M9 Jon Kitna	1.00	.45
❑ M10 Germane Crowell	.50	.23

1999 Upper Deck Ovation

	MINT	NRMT
COMPLETE SET (90)	120.00	55.00
COMP.SET w/o SP's (60)	20.00	9.00
COMMON CARD (1-60)	.20	.09
SEMISTARS	.40	.18
UNLISTED STARS	.75	.35
COMMON ROOKIE (61-90)	2.00	.90
ROOKIE SEMISTARS	3.00	1.35
ROOKIE SUBSET ODDS 1:4		
❑ 1 Jake Plummer	1.50	.70
❑ 2 Adrian Murrell	.40	.18
❑ 3 Jamal Anderson	.75	.35
❑ 4 Chris Chandler	.40	.18
❑ 5 Tony Banks	.40	.18
❑ 6 Antowain Smith	.75	.35
❑ 7 Doug Flutie	1.00	.45
❑ 8 Tim Biakabutuka	.40	.18
❑ 9 Steve Beuerlein	.20	.09
❑ 10 Curtis Conway	.40	.18
❑ 11 Curtis Enis	.75	.35
❑ 12 Corey Dillon	.75	.35
❑ 13 Jeff Blake	.40	.18
❑ 14 Ty Detmer	.40	.18
❑ 15 Troy Aikman	2.00	.90
❑ 16 Emmitt Smith	2.00	.90
❑ 17 Terrell Davis	2.00	.90
❑ 18 Bubby Brister	.20	.09
❑ 19 Barry Sanders	3.00	1.35
❑ 20 Charlie Batch	1.50	.70
❑ 21 Brett Favre	3.00	1.35
❑ 22 Dorsey Levens	.75	.35
❑ 23 Peyton Manning	3.00	1.35
❑ 24 Marvin Harrison	.75	.35
❑ 25 Mark Brunell	1.25	.55
❑ 26 Fred Taylor	2.00	.90
❑ 27 Elvis Grbac	.40	.18
❑ 28 Andre Rison	.40	.18
❑ 29 Dan Marino	3.00	1.35
❑ 30 Karim Abdul-Jabbar	.40	.18
❑ 31 Randall Cunningham	.75	.35
❑ 32 Randy Moss	3.00	1.35
❑ 33 Drew Bledsoe	1.25	.55
❑ 34 Terry Glenn	.75	.35
❑ 35 Danny Wuerffel	.20	.09
❑ 36 Cam Cleeland	.20	.09
❑ 37 Kerry Collins	.40	.18
❑ 38 Amani Toomer	.20	.09
❑ 39 Curtis Martin	.75	.35
❑ 40 Keyshawn Johnson	.75	.35
❑ 41 Napoleon Kaufman	.75	.35
❑ 42 Tim Brown	.75	.35
❑ 43 Doug Pederson	.20	.09
❑ 44 Charles Johnson	.20	.09
❑ 45 Kordell Stewart	.75	.35
❑ 46 Jerome Bettis	.75	.35
❑ 47 Trent Green	.40	.18
❑ 48 Marshall Faulk	.75	.35
❑ 49 Natrone Means	.40	.18
❑ 50 Jim Harbaugh	.40	.18
❑ 51 Steve Young	1.25	.55
❑ 52 Jerry Rice	2.00	.90
❑ 53 Joey Galloway	.75	.35
❑ 54 Jon Kitna	1.00	.45
❑ 55 Warrick Dunn	.75	.35
❑ 56 Trent Dilfer	.40	.18
❑ 57 Steve McNair	.75	.35
❑ 58 Eddie George	1.00	.45
❑ 59 Brad Johnson	.75	.35
❑ 60 Skip Hicks	.75	.35
❑ 61 Tim Couch RC	15.00	6.75
❑ 62 Donovan McNabb RC	10.00	4.50
❑ 63 Akili Smith RC	6.00	2.70
❑ 64 Edgerrin James RC	25.00	11.00
❑ 65 Ricky Williams RC	15.00	6.75
❑ 66 Torry Holt RC	8.00	3.60
❑ 67 Champ Bailey RC	4.00	1.80
❑ 68 David Boston RC	5.00	2.20
❑ 69 Daunte Culpepper RC	10.00	4.50
❑ 70 Cade McNown RC	10.00	4.50
❑ 71 Troy Edwards RC	5.00	2.20
❑ 72 Kevin Johnson RC	8.00	3.60
❑ 73 James Johnson RC	4.00	1.80
❑ 74 Rob Konrad RC	3.00	1.35
❑ 75 Kevin Faulk RC	4.00	1.80
❑ 76 Shaun King RC	10.00	4.50
❑ 77 Peerless Price RC	5.00	2.20
❑ 78 Mike Cloud RC	3.00	1.35
❑ 79 Jermaine Fazande RC	2.00	.90
❑ 80 D'Wayne Bates RC	2.00	.90
❑ 81 Brock Huard RC	4.00	1.80
❑ 82 Marty Booker RC	3.00	1.35
❑ 83 Karsten Bailey RC	2.00	.90
❑ 84 Al Wilson RC	3.00	1.35
❑ 85 Joe Germaine RC	2.50	1.10
❑ 86 Dameane Douglas RC	2.00	.90
❑ 87 Sedrick Irvin RC	2.50	1.10
❑ 88 Amos Zereoue RC	3.00	1.35
❑ 89 Cecil Collins RC	3.00	1.35
❑ 90 Ebenezer Ekuban RC	2.00	.90
❑ WPO W.Payton AUTO/34 signed game jersey card	2000.00	900.00

1999 Upper Deck Ovation Standing Ovation

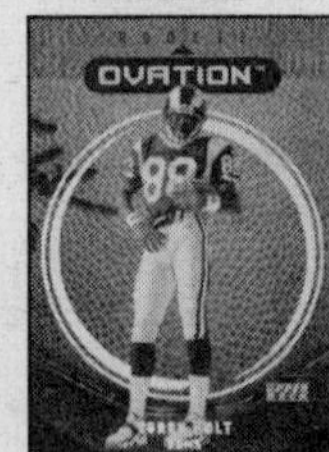

	MINT	NRMT
COMMON CARD (1-90)	12.00	5.50
*STARS: 25X TO 60X HI COL.		
*YOUNG STARS: 20X TO 50X HI COL.		
*RCs: 5X TO 12X HI COL.		
STATED PRINT RUN 50 SER.#'d SETS		

1999 Upper Deck Ovation A Piece of History

	MINT	NRMT
COMPLETE SET (13)	1000.00	450.00
COMMON CARD	30.00	13.50
STATED PRINT RUN 4560 TOTAL CARDS		
❑ AS-H Akili Smith	40.00	18.00
❑ BF-H Brett Favre	120.00	55.00
❑ BH-H Brock Huard	30.00	13.50
❑ CM-H Cade McNown	60.00	27.00
❑ DC-H Daunte Culpepper	60.00	27.00
❑ DM-H Dan Marino	120.00	55.00
❑ EJ-H Edgerrin James	175.00	80.00
❑ JG-H Joe Germaine	30.00	13.50
❑ JR-H Jerry Rice	100.00	45.00
❑ MC-H Donovan McNabb	60.00	27.00
❑ RW-H Ricky Williams	120.00	55.00
❑ SY-H Steve Young	60.00	27.00
❑ TH-H Torry Holt	50.00	22.00
❑ AS-A Akili Smith AUTO/11		
❑ CM-A Cade McNown AUTO/8		
❑ RW-A R.Williams AUTO/34	500.00	220.00
❑ TC-A Tim Couch AUTO/2		

1999 Upper Deck Ovation Center Stage

	MINT	NRMT
COMPLETE SET (24)	200.00	90.00
COMMON CARD (CS1-CS8)	1.25	.55
CS1-CS8 STATED ODDS 1:9		
COMMON CARD (CS9-CS16)	2.50	1.10
CS9-CS16 STATED ODDS 1:25		
COMMON CARD (CS17-CS24)	6.00	2.70
CS17-CS24 STATED ODDS 1:99		
❑ CS1 Walter Payton	4.00	1.80
❑ CS2 Barry Sanders	5.00	2.20
❑ CS3 Emmitt Smith	3.00	1.35
❑ CS4 Terrell Davis	3.00	1.35
❑ CS5 Jamal Anderson	1.25	.55
❑ CS6 Fred Taylor	2.50	1.10
❑ CS7 Ricky Williams	6.00	2.70
❑ CS8 Edgerrin James	12.00	5.50
❑ CS9 Walter Payton	8.00	3.60
❑ CS10 Barry Sanders	10.00	4.50
❑ CS11 Emmitt Smith	6.00	2.70
❑ CS12 Terrell Davis	6.00	2.70
❑ CS13 Jamal Anderson	2.50	1.10
❑ CS14 Fred Taylor	5.00	2.20
❑ CS15 Ricky Williams	12.00	5.50
❑ CS16 Edgerrin James	20.00	9.00
❑ CS17 Walter Payton	20.00	9.00
❑ CS18 Barry Sanders	25.00	11.00
❑ CS19 Emmitt Smith	15.00	6.75
❑ CS20 Terrell Davis	15.00	6.75
❑ CS21 Jamal Anderson	6.00	2.70
❑ CS22 Fred Taylor	12.00	5.50
❑ CS23 Ricky Williams	30.00	13.50
❑ CS24 Edgerrin James	50.00	22.00

1999 Upper Deck Ovation Curtain Calls

	MINT	NRMT
COMPLETE SET (30)	80.00	36.00
COMMON CARD (CC1-CC30)	2.00	.90
STATED ODDS 1:4		
❑ CC1 Peyton Manning	6.00	2.70
❑ CC2 Fred Taylor	4.00	1.80
❑ CC3 Randy Moss	6.00	2.70
❑ CC4 Cris Carter	3.00	1.35
❑ CC5 Troy Aikman	5.00	2.20
❑ CC6 Randall Cunningham	3.00	1.35
❑ CC7 Mark Brunell	3.00	1.35
❑ CC8 Jon Kitna	2.50	1.10
❑ CC9 Steve McNair	3.00	1.35
❑ CC10 Jake Plummer	4.00	1.80
❑ CC11 Jerry Rice	5.00	2.20
❑ CC12 Kordell Stewart	3.00	1.35
❑ CC13 Warrick Dunn	3.00	1.35
❑ CC14 Emmitt Smith	5.00	2.20
❑ CC15 Jerome Bettis	3.00	1.35
❑ CC16 Terrell Owens	3.00	1.35
❑ CC17 Antonio Freeman	3.00	1.35
❑ CC18 Joey Galloway	3.00	1.35
❑ CC19 Curtis Martin	3.00	1.35
❑ CC20 Tim Brown	3.00	1.35
❑ CC21 Charlie Batch	3.00	1.35
❑ CC22 Doug Flutie	2.50	1.10
❑ CC23 Barry Sanders	8.00	3.60
❑ CC24 Drew Bledsoe	3.00	1.35
❑ CC25 Corey Dillon	3.00	1.35
❑ CC26 Eddie George	2.50	1.10
❑ CC27 Keyshawn Johnson	3.00	1.35
❑ CC28 Steve Young	3.00	1.35
❑ CC29 Brett Favre	8.00	3.60
❑ CC30 Terrell Davis	5.00	2.20

1999 Upper Deck Ovation Spotlight

	MINT	NRMT
COMPLETE SET (15)	80.00	36.00
COMMON CARD (OS1-OS15)	3.00	1.35
STATED ODDS 1:9		
❑ OS1 Tim Couch	12.00	5.50
❑ OS2 Donovan McNabb	8.00	3.60
❑ OS3 Akili Smith	5.00	2.20
❑ OS4 Edgerrin James	20.00	9.00
❑ OS5 Ricky Williams	12.00	5.50
❑ OS6 Torry Holt	6.00	2.70
❑ OS7 Champ Bailey	3.00	1.35
❑ OS8 David Boston	4.00	1.80
❑ OS9 Daunte Culpepper	8.00	3.60
❑ OS10 Cade McNown	8.00	3.60
❑ OS11 Troy Edwards	4.00	1.80
❑ OS12 Kevin Johnson	6.00	2.70
❑ OS13 Joe Germaine	3.00	1.35
❑ OS14 Brock Huard	3.00	1.35
❑ OS15 Kevin Faulk	3.00	1.35

1999 Upper Deck Ovation Star Performers

	MINT	NRMT
COMPLETE SET (15)	120.00	55.00
COMMON CARD (SP1-SP15)	5.00	2.20
STATED ODDS 1:39		
❑ SP1 Terrell Davis	12.00	5.50
❑ SP2 Peyton Manning	15.00	6.75
❑ SP3 Brett Favre	20.00	9.00
❑ SP4 Dan Marino	20.00	9.00
❑ SP5 Barry Sanders	20.00	9.00
❑ SP6 Jamal Anderson	8.00	3.60
❑ SP7 Mark Brunell	8.00	3.60
❑ SP8 Jerome Bettis	8.00	3.60
❑ SP9 Charlie Batch	8.00	3.60
❑ SP10 Antowain Smith	8.00	3.60
❑ SP11 Jake Plummer	10.00	4.50
❑ SP12 Joey Galloway	8.00	3.60
❑ SP13 Randy Moss	15.00	6.75
❑ SP14 Steve Young	8.00	3.60
❑ SP15 Warrick Dunn	8.00	3.60

1999 Upper Deck Ovation Super Signatures Silver

	MINT	NRMT
COMP. SILVER SET (3)	700.00	325.00
COMMON SILVER	200.00	90.00
SILVER PRINT RUN 300 SER.#'d SETS		
*GOLDS: .75X TO 1.5X HI COL.		
GOLD STATED PRINT RUN 150 SER.#'d SETS		
UNPRICED RAINBOWS #'d OF 10 SETS MADE		
❑ JM Joe Montana	200.00	90.00
❑ JN Joe Namath	200.00	90.00
❑ WP Walter Payton	300.00	135.00

1999 Upper Deck PowerDeck

	MINT	NRMT
COMPLETE SET (30)	120.00	55.00
COMMON CARD (PD1-PD30)	3.00	1.35
ONE CD ROM PER PACK		

		MINT	NRMT
❑ PD1	Troy Aikman	8.00	3.60
❑ PD2	Drew Bledsoe	5.00	2.20
❑ PD3	Randy Moss	12.00	5.50
❑ PD4	Barry Sanders	12.00	5.50
❑ PD5	Brett Favre	12.00	5.50
❑ PD6	Terrell Davis	8.00	3.60
❑ PD7	Peyton Manning	12.00	5.50
❑ PD8	Emmitt Smith	8.00	3.60
❑ PD9	Dan Marino	12.00	5.50
❑ PD10	Jake Plummer	5.00	2.20
❑ PD11	Eddie George	4.00	1.80
❑ PD12	Jerry Rice	8.00	3.60
❑ PD13	Steve Young	5.00	2.20
❑ PD14	Mark Brunell	5.00	2.20
❑ PD15	Kordell Stewart	3.00	1.35
❑ PD16	Keyshawn Johnson	3.00	1.35
❑ PD17	Fred Taylor	8.00	3.60
❑ PD18	Jamal Anderson	3.00	1.35
❑ PD19	Cecil Collins	3.00	1.35
❑ PD20	Ricky Williams	12.00	5.50
❑ PD21	Tim Couch	12.00	5.50
❑ PD22	Donovan McNabb	8.00	3.60
❑ PD23	Akili Smith	6.00	2.70
❑ PD24	Edgerrin James	20.00	9.00
❑ PD25	Daunte Culpepper	10.00	4.50
❑ PD26	Brock Huard	4.00	1.80
❑ PD27	Torry Holt	6.00	2.70
❑ PD28	David Boston	5.00	2.20
❑ PD29	Cade McNown	10.00	4.50
❑ PD30	Champ Bailey	4.00	1.80
❑ WPPD	W.Payton Jer.AUTO/34	2000.00	900.00

1999 Upper Deck PowerDeck Auxiliary

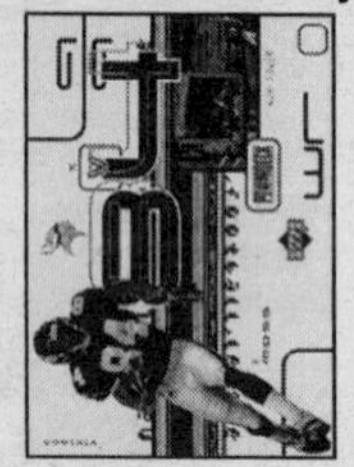

	MINT	NRMT
COMPLETE SET (30)	25.00	11.00
COMMON CARD (AUX1-AUX30)	.50	.23

APPROXIMATELY TWO PER PACK
UNPRICED GOLD CARDS SERIAL #'d OF 1

		MINT	NRMT
❑ AUX1	Troy Aikman	1.25	.55
❑ AUX2	Drew Bledsoe	.75	.35
❑ AUX3	Randy Moss	2.00	.90
❑ AUX4	Barry Sanders	2.00	.90
❑ AUX5	Brett Favre	2.00	.90
❑ AUX6	Terrell Davis	1.25	.55
❑ AUX7	Peyton Manning	2.00	.90
❑ AUX8	Emmitt Smith	1.25	.55
❑ AUX9	Dan Marino	2.00	.90
❑ AUX10	Jake Plummer	.75	.35
❑ AUX11	Eddie George	.60	.25
❑ AUX12	Jerry Rice	1.25	.55
❑ AUX13	Steve Young	.75	.35
❑ AUX14	Mark Brunell	.75	.35
❑ AUX15	Kordell Stewart	.50	.23
❑ AUX16	Keyshawn Johnson	.50	.23
❑ AUX17	Fred Taylor	1.25	.55
❑ AUX18	Jamal Anderson	.50	.23
❑ AUX19	Cecil Collins	1.00	.45
❑ AUX20	Ricky Williams	6.00	2.70
❑ AUX21	Tim Couch	6.00	2.70
❑ AUX22	Donovan McNabb	4.00	1.80
❑ AUX23	Akili Smith	2.50	1.10
❑ AUX24	Edgerrin James	10.00	4.50
❑ AUX25	Daunte Culpepper	4.00	1.80
❑ AUX26	Brock Huard	1.50	.70
❑ AUX27	Torry Holt	2.00	.90
❑ AUX28	David Boston	2.00	.90
❑ AUX29	Cade McNown	4.00	1.80
❑ AUX30	Champ Bailey	1.50	.70

1999 Upper Deck PowerDeck Autographs

	MINT	NRMT
COMMON CARD (1-13)	80.00	36.00

STATED PRINT RUN 50 SERIAL #'d SETS

		MINT	NRMT
❑ AS	Akili Smith	80.00	36.00
❑ BH	Brock Huard		
❑ CB	Champ Bailey	80.00	36.00
❑ CM	Cade McNown	100.00	45.00
❑ DB	David Boston		
❑ DC	Daunte Culpepper	100.00	45.00
❑ DM	Dan Marino	250.00	110.00
❑ EJ	Edgerrin James	300.00	135.00
❑ JP	Jake Plummer	100.00	45.00
❑ MC	Donovan McNabb		
❑ TA	Troy Aikman	150.00	70.00
❑ TC	Tim Couch	175.00	80.00
❑ TH	Torry Holt	80.00	36.00

1999 Upper Deck PowerDeck Most Valuable Performances

	MINT	NRMT
COMPLETE SET (7)	250.00	110.00
COMMON CARD (M1-M7)	12.00	5.50

STATED ODDS 1:287
*AUXILIARY CARDS: .25X TO .6X CD-ROMS
AUXILIARY STATED ODDS 1:287

		MINT	NRMT
❑ M1	Terrell Davis	30.00	13.50
❑ M2	Joe Montana	60.00	27.00
❑ M3	John Elway	50.00	22.00
❑ M4	Emmitt Smith	30.00	13.50
❑ M5	Jamal Anderson	12.00	5.50
❑ M6	Randy Moss	50.00	22.00
❑ M7	Brett Favre	50.00	22.00

1999 Upper Deck PowerDeck Powerful Moments

	MINT	NRMT
COMPLETE SET (6)	60.00	27.00
COMMON CARD (P1-P6)	10.00	4.50

STATED ODDS 1:23
*AUXILIARY CARDS: .25X TO .6X CD-ROMS
AUXILIARY STATED ODDS 1:23

		MINT	NRMT
❑ P1	Joe Montana	20.00	9.00
❑ P2	Terrell Davis	10.00	4.50
❑ P3	John Elway	15.00	6.75
❑ P4	Randy Moss	15.00	6.75
❑ P5	Dan Marino	15.00	6.75
❑ P6	Emmitt Smith	10.00	4.50

1999 Upper Deck PowerDeck Time Capsule

	MINT	NRMT
COMPLETE SET (6)	40.00	18.00
COMMON CARD (T1-T6)	8.00	3.60

STATED ODDS 1:7
*AUXILIARY CARDS: .25X TO .6X CD-ROMS
AUXILIARY STATED ODDS 1:7

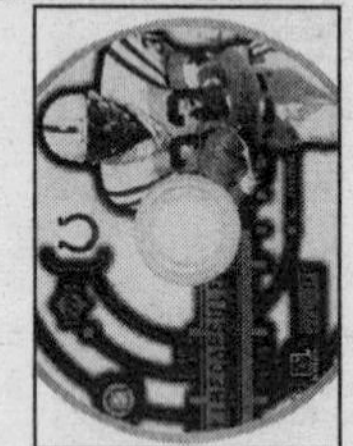

		MINT	NRMT
❑ T1	Edgerrin James	15.00	6.75
❑ T2	Barry Sanders	12.00	5.50
❑ T3	Terrell Davis	8.00	3.60
❑ T4	Emmitt Smith	8.00	3.60
❑ T5	Dan Marino	12.00	5.50
❑ T6	Tim Couch	10.00	4.50

2000 Upper Deck Pros and Prospects

	MINT	NRMT
COMPLETE SET (126)	1500.00	700.00
COMP.SET w/o SP's (84)	12.00	5.50
COMMON CARD (1-84)	.10	.05
SEMISTARS	.20	.09
UNLISTED STARS	.40	.18
COMMON ROOKIE (85-126)	15.00	6.75
ROOKIE SEMISTARS	20.00	9.00
ROOKIE UNLISTED STARS	25.00	11.00

ROOKIE STAT.PRINT RUN 1000 SERIAL #'d SETS

JOHN ELWAY AU CARRIES "GJG" PREFIX
JOHN ELWAY AU STATED PRINT RUN 350

❑ 1 Jake Plummer .40 .18
❑ 2 Michael Pittman .10 .05
❑ 3 Tim Dwight .40 .18
❑ 4 Chris Chandler .20 .09
❑ 5 Qadry Ismail .10 .05
❑ 6 Shannon Sharpe .20 .09
❑ 7 Peerless Price .40 .18
❑ 8 Rob Johnson .20 .09
❑ 9 Eric Moulds .40 .18
❑ 10 Muhsin Muhammad .20 .09
❑ 11 Patrick Jeffers .40 .18
❑ 12 Steve Beuerlein .20 .09
❑ 13 Cade McNown .60 .25
❑ 14 Curtis Enis .40 .18
❑ 15 Marcus Robinson .40 .18
❑ 16 Akili Smith .50 .23
❑ 17 Corey Dillon .40 .18
❑ 18 Tim Couch 1.00 .45
❑ 19 Kevin Johnson .40 .18
❑ 20 Errict Rhett .20 .09
❑ 21 Troy Aikman 1.00 .45
❑ 22 Emmitt Smith 1.00 .45
❑ 23 Rocket Ismail .20 .09
❑ 24 Terrell Davis 1.00 .45
❑ 25 Olandis Gary .50 .23
❑ 26 Brian Griese .50 .23
❑ 27 Ed McCaffrey .20 .09
❑ 28 Charlie Batch .40 .18
❑ 29 Germane Crowell .20 .09
❑ 30 James O. Stewart .20 .09
❑ 31 Brett Favre 1.50 .70
❑ 32 Antonio Freeman .40 .18
❑ 33 Dorsey Levens .40 .18
❑ 34 Peyton Manning 1.25 .55
❑ 35 Edgerrin James 1.50 .70
❑ 36 Marvin Harrison .40 .18
❑ 37 Mark Brunell .60 .25
❑ 38 Fred Taylor .60 .25
❑ 39 Jimmy Smith .20 .09
❑ 40 Elvis Grbac .20 .09
❑ 41 Tony Gonzalez .20 .09
❑ 42 Damon Huard .40 .18
❑ 43 James Johnson .20 .09
❑ 44 Jay Fiedler .40 .18
❑ 45 Randy Moss 1.25 .55
❑ 46 Robert Smith .40 .18
❑ 47 Cris Carter .40 .18
❑ 48 Drew Bledsoe .60 .25
❑ 49 Terry Glenn .40 .18
❑ 50 Ricky Williams 1.00 .45
❑ 51 Jeff Blake .20 .09
❑ 52 Keith Poole .10 .05
❑ 53 Kerry Collins .20 .09
❑ 54 Amani Toomer .10 .05
❑ 55 Vinny Testaverde .20 .09
❑ 56 Keyshawn Johnson .40 .18
❑ 57 Curtis Martin .40 .18
❑ 58 Tim Brown .40 .18
❑ 59 Rich Gannon .20 .09
❑ 60 Tyrone Wheatley .20 .09
❑ 61 Duce Staley .40 .18
❑ 62 Donovan McNabb .60 .25
❑ 63 Troy Edwards .40 .18
❑ 64 Jerome Bettis .40 .18
❑ 65 Marshall Faulk .40 .18
❑ 66 Kurt Warner 2.00 .90
❑ 67 Torry Holt .40 .18
❑ 68 Isaac Bruce .40 .18
❑ 69 Junior Seau .20 .09
❑ 70 Jeff Graham .10 .05
❑ 71 Steve Young .60 .25
❑ 72 Jerry Rice 1.00 .45
❑ 73 Charlie Garner .20 .09
❑ 74 Ricky Watters .20 .09
❑ 75 Jon Kitna .40 .18
❑ 76 Warrick Dunn .40 .18
❑ 77 Shaun King .60 .25
❑ 78 Mike Alstott .40 .18
❑ 79 Eddie George .50 .23
❑ 80 Steve McNair .40 .18
❑ 81 Kevin Dyson .20 .09
❑ 82 Brad Johnson .40 .18
❑ 83 Stephen Davis .40 .18
❑ 84 Michael Westbrook .20 .09
❑ 85 Peter Warrick RC 250.00 110.00
❑ 86 LaVar Arrington RC 100.00 45.00
❑ 87 Chris Redman RC 60.00 27.00
❑ 88 Courtney Brown RC 60.00 27.00
❑ 89 Plaxico Burress RC 100.00 45.00
❑ 90 Corey Simon RC 25.00 11.00
❑ 91 Bubba Franks RC 35.00 16.00
❑ 92 Deon Grant RC 20.00 9.00
❑ 93 Brian Urlacher RC 35.00 16.00
❑ 94 Ron Dayne RC 250.00 110.00
❑ 95 Sylvester Morris RC 35.00 16.00
❑ 96 Shaun Alexander RC 120.00 55.00
❑ 97 Dez White RC 35.00 16.00
❑ 98 Thomas Jones RC 120.00 55.00
❑ 99 Travis Taylor RC 60.00 27.00
❑ 100 Kwame Cavil RC 20.00 9.00
❑ 101 Jamal Lewis RC 120.00 55.00
❑ 102 Chad Pennington RC 150.00 70.00
❑ 103 J.R. Redmond RC 50.00 22.00
❑ 104 Sebastian Janikowski RC 20.00 9.00
❑ 105 Anthony Lucas RC 25.00 11.00
❑ 106 Travis Prentice RC 35.00 16.00
❑ 107 Danny Farmer RC 25.00 11.00
❑ 108 Sherrod Gideon RC 20.00 9.00
❑ 109 Todd Pinkston RC 25.00 11.00
❑ 110 Dennis Northcutt RC 35.00 16.00
❑ 111 Tim Rattay RC 35.00 16.00
❑ 112 Troy Walters RC 25.00 11.00
❑ 113 Michael Wiley RC 35.00 16.00
❑ 114 R.Jay Soward RC 35.00 16.00
❑ 115 Trung Canidate RC 25.00 11.00
❑ 116 Reuben Droughns RC 35.00 16.00
❑ 117 Rondell Mealey RC 20.00 9.00
❑ 118 Chris Coleman RC 15.00 6.75
❑ 119 Giovanni Carmazzi RC 60.00 27.00
❑ 120 Trevor Insley RC 15.00 6.75
❑ 121 Shyrone Stith RC 20.00 9.00
❑ 122 Gari Scott RC 25.00 11.00
❑ 123 Tee Martin RC 50.00 22.00
❑ 124 Tom Brady RC 25.00 11.00
❑ 125 Marcus Knight RC 15.00 6.75
❑ 126 Jerry Porter RC 35.00 16.00
❑ JE John Elway AU Jersey 300.00 135.00

2000 Upper Deck Pros and Prospects Future Fame

	MINT	NRMT
COMPLETE SET (10)	25.00	11.00
COMMON CARD (FF1-FF10)	2.50	1.10
STATED ODDS 1:6		

❑ FF1 Peter Warrick 8.00 3.60
❑ FF2 LaVar Arrington 5.00 2.20
❑ FF3 Courtney Brown 3.00 1.35
❑ FF4 Travis Taylor 3.00 1.35
❑ FF5 Plaxico Burress 4.00 1.80
❑ FF6 Ron Dayne 8.00 3.60
❑ FF7 Jamal Lewis 5.00 2.20
❑ FF8 Thomas Jones 5.00 2.20
❑ FF9 Chad Pennington 6.00 2.70
❑ FF10 Chris Redman 2.50 1.10

2000 Upper Deck Pros and Prospects Mirror Image

	MINT	NRMT
COMPLETE SET (10)	20.00	9.00
COMMON CARD (M1-M10)	1.50	.70
STATED ODDS 1:12		

❑ M1 Thomas Jones 3.00 1.35
Fred Taylor
❑ M2 Ron Dayne 5.00 2.20
Jerome Bettis
❑ M3 Plaxico Burress 4.00 1.80
Randy Moss
❑ M4 Peter Warrick 5.00 2.20
Marvin Harrison
❑ M5 Tee Martin 3.00 1.35
Peyton Manning
❑ M6 Chris Redman 3.00 1.35
Brett Favre
❑ M7 Lavar Arrington 2.50 1.10
Junior Seau
❑ M8 Dez White 1.50 .70
Jimmy Smith
❑ M9 Chad Pennington 5.00 2.20
Kurt Warner
❑ M10 Shaun Alexander 3.00 1.35
Marshall Faulk

2000 Upper Deck Pros and Prospects ProMotion

	MINT	NRMT
COMPLETE SET (10)	12.00	5.50
COMMON CARD (P1-P10)	1.00	.45
STATED ODDS 1:6		

❑ P1 Kurt Warner 5.00 2.20
❑ P2 Eddie George 1.25 .55
❑ P3 Marshall Faulk 1.00 .45
❑ P4 Keyshawn Johnson 1.00 .45
❑ P5 Emmitt Smith 2.50 1.10
❑ P6 Randy Moss 3.00 1.35
❑ P7 Marvin Harrison 1.00 .45
❑ P8 Mark Brunell 1.50 .70
❑ P9 Curtis Martin 1.00 .45
❑ P10 Brett Favre 4.00 1.80

2000 Upper Deck Pros and Prospects Report Card

	MINT	NRMT
COMPLETE SET (12)	20.00	9.00
COMMON CARD (RC1-RC12)	1.25	.55
SEMISTARS	1.50	.70
STATED ODDS 1:12		

❑ RC1 Edgerrin James 6.00 2.70
❑ RC2 Tim Couch 4.00 1.80
❑ RC3 Cade McNown 2.50 1.10
❑ RC4 Champ Bailey 1.25 .55
❑ RC5 Donovan McNabb 2.50 1.10
❑ RC6 Kevin Johnson 2.00 .90

Card	MINT	NRMT
❑ RC7 Shaun King	2.50	1.10
❑ RC8 Peerless Price	1.50	.70
❑ RC9 David Boston	1.50	.70
❑ RC10 Ricky Williams	4.00	1.80
❑ RC11 Akili Smith	2.00	.90
❑ RC12 Jevon Kearse	1.50	.70

2000 Upper Deck Pros and Prospects Signature Piece 1

	MINT	NRMT
COMPLETE SET (23)	2500.00	1100.00
COMMON CARD	40.00	18.00
SEMISTARS	50.00	22.00
UNLISTED STARS	60.00	27.00
STATED ODDS 1:96		

Card	MINT	NRMT
❑ SPBG Brian Griese	80.00	36.00
❑ SPCB Champ Bailey Trade	50.00	22.00
❑ SPCC Chris Claiborne	40.00	18.00
❑ SPDB Drew Bledsoe	120.00	55.00
❑ SPDF Danny Farmer	60.00	27.00
❑ SPDL Dorsey Levens	60.00	27.00
❑ SPDM Dan Marino	300.00	135.00
❑ SPEG Edgerrin James	250.00	110.00
❑ SPIB Isaac Bruce	60.00	27.00
❑ SPKJ Kevin Johnson	60.00	27.00
❑ SPKW Kurt Warner	350.00	160.00
❑ SPMB Mark Brunell	100.00	45.00
❑ SPMF Marshall Faulk	100.00	45.00
❑ SPMH Marvin Harrison	60.00	27.00
❑ SPOG Olandis Gary	80.00	36.00
❑ SPPM Peyton Manning	250.00	110.00
❑ SPRD Ron Dayne	250.00	110.00
❑ SPRL Ray Lucas	60.00	27.00
❑ SPRM Randy Moss	250.00	110.00
❑ SPTA Troy Aikman Trade	150.00	70.00
❑ SPTH Torry Holt	60.00	27.00
❑ SPTO Terrell Owens Trade	60.00	27.00
❑ SPWR Keyshawn Johnson Trade	60.00	27.00

2000 Upper Deck Pros and Prospects Signature Piece 2

	MINT	NRMT
COMMON CARD	120.00	55.00
CARDS SERIAL #'d TO PLAYER JERSEY		

Card	MINT	NRMT
❑ SPBG Brian Griese/14		
❑ SPCB Champ Bailey/24 Trade		
❑ SPCC Chris Claiborne/50	120.00	55.00
❑ SPDB Drew Bledsoe/11	300.00	135.00
❑ SPDF Danny Farmer/87	120.00	55.00
❑ SPDL Dorsey Levens/25	150.00	70.00
❑ SPDM Dan Marino/13	500.00	220.00
❑ SPED Edgerrin James/32	500.00	220.00
❑ SPIB Isaac Bruce/80	120.00	55.00
❑ SPKJ Kevin Johnson/86	120.00	55.00
❑ SPKW Kurt Warner/13	600.00	275.00
❑ SPMB Mark Brunell/8		
❑ SPMF Marshall Faulk/28	250.00	110.00
❑ SPMH Marvin Harrison/88	120.00	55.00
❑ SPOG Olandis Gary/22	175.00	80.00
❑ SPPM Peyton Manning/18		
❑ SPRD Ron Dayne/33	500.00	220.00
❑ SPRL Ray Lucas/6		
❑ SPRM Randy Moss/84	350.00	160.00
❑ SPTA Troy Aikman/8 Trade		
❑ SPTH Torry Holt/88	120.00	55.00
❑ SPTO Terrell Owens/81 Trade	120.00	55.00
❑ SPWR Keyshawn Johnson/19 Trade		

1999 Upper Deck Retro

	MINT	NRMT
COMPLETE SET (165)	50.00	22.00
COMMON CARD (1-165)	.15	.07
SEMISTARS	.30	.14
UNLISTED STARS	.60	.25
COMMON ROOKIE	1.00	.45

Card	MINT	NRMT
❑ 1 Jake Plummer	1.25	.55
❑ 2 Adrian Murrell	.30	.14
❑ 3 Rob Moore	.30	.14
❑ 4 Frank Sanders	.30	.14
❑ 5 David Boston RC	2.00	.90
❑ 6 Tim Dwight	.60	.25
❑ 7 Chris Chandler	.30	.14
❑ 8 Jamal Anderson	.60	.25
❑ 9 O.J. Santiago	.15	.07
❑ 10 Terance Mathis	.30	.14
❑ 11 Priest Holmes	.60	.25
❑ 12 Tony Banks	.30	.14
❑ 13 Patrick Johnson	.15	.07
❑ 14 Scott Mitchell	.15	.07
❑ 15 Jermaine Lewis	.30	.14
❑ 16 Eric Moulds	.60	.25
❑ 17 Doug Flutie	.75	.35
❑ 18 Antowain Smith	.60	.25
❑ 19 Thurman Thomas	.30	.14
❑ 20 Peerless Price RC	2.00	.90
❑ 21 Fred Lane	.30	.14
❑ 22 Tim Biakabutuka	.30	.14
❑ 23 Steve Beuerlein	.15	.07
❑ 24 Muhsin Muhammad	.30	.14
❑ 25 Rae Carruth	.30	.14
❑ 26 Curtis Enis	.60	.25
❑ 27 Walter Payton	5.00	2.20
❑ 28 Bobby Engram	.30	.14
❑ 29 Cade McNown RC	4.00	1.80
❑ 30 Curtis Conway	.30	.14
❑ 31 Darnay Scott	.15	.07
❑ 32 Jeff Blake	.30	.14
❑ 33 Corey Dillon	.60	.25
❑ 34 Akili Smith RC	2.50	1.10
❑ 35 Carl Pickens	.30	.14
❑ 36 Tim Couch RC	6.00	2.70
❑ 37 Ty Detmer	.30	.14
❑ 38 Jim Brown UER (photo is Terry Kirby)	2.50	1.10
❑ 39 Kevin Johnson RC	3.00	1.35
❑ 40 Ozzie Newsome	.15	.07
❑ 41 Troy Aikman	1.50	.70
❑ 42 Rocket Ismail	.30	.14
❑ 43 Emmitt Smith	1.50	.70
❑ 44 Michael Irvin	.30	.14
❑ 45 Deion Sanders	.60	.25
❑ 46 Roger Staubach	2.00	.90
❑ 47 John Elway	2.50	1.10
❑ 48 Bubby Brister	.15	.07
❑ 49 Terrell Davis	1.50	.70
❑ 50 Ed McCaffrey	.30	.14
❑ 51 Rod Smith	.30	.14
❑ 52 Shannon Sharpe	.30	.14
❑ 53 Charlie Batch	1.25	.55
❑ 54 Johnnie Morton	.30	.14
❑ 55 Barry Sanders	2.50	1.10
❑ 56 Sedrick Irvin RC	2.00	.90
❑ 57 Herman Moore	.60	.25
❑ 58 Brett Favre	2.50	1.10
❑ 59 Mark Chmura	.15	.07
❑ 60 Antonio Freeman	.60	.25
❑ 61 Robert Brooks	.30	.14
❑ 62 Dorsey Levens	.60	.25
❑ 63 Peyton Manning	2.50	1.10
❑ 64 Jerome Pathon	.15	.07
❑ 65 Marvin Harrison	.60	.25
❑ 66 Edgerrin James RC	10.00	4.50
❑ 67 Ken Dilger	.15	.07
❑ 68 Mark Brunell	1.00	.45
❑ 69 Fred Taylor	1.50	.70
❑ 70 Jimmy Smith	.30	.14
❑ 71 James Stewart	.30	.14
❑ 72 Keenan McCardell	.30	.14
❑ 73 Elvis Grbac	.30	.14
❑ 74 Mike Cloud RC	2.00	.90
❑ 75 Andre Rison	.30	.14
❑ 76 Tony Gonzalez	.30	.14
❑ 77 Warren Moon	.60	.25
❑ 78 Derrick Alexander WR	.30	.14
❑ 79 Dan Marino	2.50	1.10
❑ 80 O.J. McDuffie	.30	.14
❑ 81 James Johnson RC	1.50	.70
❑ 82 Paul Warfield	.15	.07
❑ 83 Cecil Collins RC	2.00	.90
❑ 84 Randall Cunningham	.60	.25
❑ 85 Randy Moss	2.50	1.10
❑ 86 Cris Carter	.60	.25
❑ 87 Fran Tarkenton	1.00	.45
❑ 88 Daunte Culpepper RC	4.00	1.80
❑ 89 Robert Smith	.60	.25
❑ 90 Drew Bledsoe	1.00	.45
❑ 91 Terry Glenn	.60	.25
❑ 92 Kevin Faulk RC	1.50	.70
❑ 93 Tony Simmons	.15	.07
❑ 94 Ben Coates	.30	.14
❑ 95 Billy Joe Hobert	.15	.07
❑ 96 Cameron Cleeland	.15	.07
❑ 97 Eddie Kennison	.30	.14
❑ 98 Andre Hastings	.15	.07
❑ 99 Ricky Williams RC	6.00	2.70
❑ 100 Kerry Collins	.30	.14
❑ 101 Joe Montgomery RC	2.00	.90
❑ 102 Gary Brown	.15	.07
❑ 103 Ike Hilliard	.15	.07
❑ 104 Amani Toomer	.15	.07
❑ 105 Vinny Testaverde	.30	.14
❑ 106 Wayne Chrebet	.30	.14
❑ 107 Curtis Martin	.60	.25
❑ 108 Joe Namath	2.50	1.10
❑ 109 Keyshawn Johnson	.60	.25
❑ 110 Don Maynard	.15	.07
❑ 111 Rich Gannon	.30	.14
❑ 112 Tim Brown	.60	.25
❑ 113 Charles Woodson	.60	.25
❑ 114 Rickey Dudley	.15	.07
❑ 115 Darrell Russell	.15	.07
❑ 116 Napoleon Kaufman	.60	.25
❑ 117 Donovan McNabb RC	4.00	1.80
❑ 118 Doug Pederson	.15	.07
❑ 119 Duce Staley	.60	.25
❑ 120 Torrance Small	.15	.07
❑ 121 Charles Johnson	.15	.07
❑ 122 Jerome Bettis	.60	.25
❑ 123 Courtney Hawkins	.15	.07
❑ 124 Kordell Stewart	.60	.25
❑ 125 Troy Edwards RC	2.00	.90
❑ 126 Amos Zereoue RC	2.00	.90
❑ 127 Trent Green	.30	.14
❑ 128 Marshall Faulk	.60	.25
❑ 129 Az-Zahir Hakim	.15	.07
❑ 130 Joe Germaine RC	2.00	.90
❑ 131 Torry Holt RC	3.00	1.35
❑ 132 Isaac Bruce	.60	.25
❑ 133 Jim Harbaugh	.30	.14
❑ 134 Junior Seau	.30	.14
❑ 135 Natrone Means	.30	.14
❑ 136 Ryan Leaf	.60	.25

		MINT	NRMT
❑ 137	Dan Fouts	.60	.25
❑ 138	Mikhael Ricks	.15	.07
❑ 139	Steve Young	1.00	.45
❑ 140	Terrell Owens	.60	.25
❑ 141	Jerry Rice	1.50	.70
❑ 142	J.J. Stokes	.30	.14
❑ 143	Lawrence Phillips	.30	.14
❑ 144	Joe Montana	4.00	1.80
❑ 145	Jon Kitna	.75	.35
❑ 146	Ahman Green	.30	.14
❑ 147	Joey Galloway	.60	.25
❑ 148	Ricky Watters	.30	.14
❑ 149	Brock Huard RC	1.50	.70
❑ 150	Steve Largent	.60	.25
❑ 151	Trent Dilfer	.30	.14
❑ 152	Reidel Anthony	.30	.14
❑ 153	Warrick Dunn	.60	.25
❑ 154	Mike Alstott	.60	.25
❑ 155	Shaun King RC	4.00	1.80
❑ 156	Eddie George	.75	.35
❑ 157	Steve McNair	.60	.25
❑ 158	Kevin Dyson	.30	.14
❑ 159	Frank Wycheck	.15	.07
❑ 160	Yancey Thigpen	.15	.07
❑ 161	Brad Johnson	.60	.25
❑ 162	Rodney Peete	.15	.07
❑ 163	Michael Westbrook	.30	.14
❑ 164	Skip Hicks	.60	.25
❑ 165	Champ Bailey RC	1.50	.70
❑ WP1	Walter Payton AUTO	300.00	135.00
❑ WPR	W.Payton Jer.AUTO/34	2000.00	900.00

1999 Upper Deck Retro Gold

	MINT	NRMT
COMPLETE SET (165)	600.00	275.00

*GOLD STARS: 5X TO 12X HI COL.
*GOLD YOUNG STARS: 4X TO 10X
*GOLD RCs: 2.5X TO 6X
GOLD STATED PRINT RUN 175 SER.#'d SETS

1999 Upper Deck Retro Inkredible

	MINT	NRMT
COMPLETE SET (30)	1600.00	700.00
COMMON CARD (1-30)	12.00	5.50
SEMISTARS	15.00	6.75
UNLISTED STARS	25.00	11.00

ONE PER BOX
SOME CARDS ISSUED VIA MAIL REDEMPTION
TRADE CARD EXPIRATION: 8/4/2000

		MINT	NRMT
❑ AK	Akili Smith	40.00	18.00
❑ AM	Adrian Murrell	12.00	5.50
❑ AS	Antowain Smith	15.00	6.75
❑ BH	Brock Huard	25.00	11.00
❑ CC	Cris Carter	30.00	13.50
❑ CM	Cade McNown	50.00	22.00
❑ DB	David Boston	30.00	13.50
❑ DC	Daunte Culpepper	50.00	22.00
❑ DF	Dan Fouts	25.00	11.00
❑ DL	Dorsey Levens	25.00	11.00
❑ FT	Fran Tarkenton	50.00	22.00
❑ GH	Garrison Hearst	12.00	5.50
❑ JK	Jon Kitna	25.00	11.00
❑ JM	Joe Montana	200.00	90.00
❑ JN	Joe Namath	200.00	90.00
❑ MC	Donovan McNabb	50.00	22.00
❑ OZ	Ozzie Newsome	12.00	5.50
❑ PW	Paul Warfield	25.00	11.00
❑ RG	Roger Staubach	80.00	36.00
❑ RM	Randy Moss	120.00	55.00
❑ RS	Rod Smith	15.00	6.75
❑ RW	Ricky Williams	150.00	70.00
❑ SK	Shaun King	50.00	22.00
❑ SL	Steve Largent	30.00	13.50
❑ TC	Tim Couch	120.00	55.00
❑ TD	Terrell Davis	80.00	36.00
❑ TH	Torry Holt	40.00	18.00
❑ TO	Terrell Owens	25.00	11.00
❑ WC	Wayne Chrebet	15.00	6.75
❑ WP	Walter Payton	300.00	135.00

1999 Upper Deck Retro Inkredible Gold

	MINT	NRMT
COMMON CARD (1-30)	30.00	13.50

SERIAL #'d TO PLAYER'S JERSEY
CARDS SER.#'d UNDER 20 NOT PRICED

		MINT	NRMT
❑ AK	Akili Smith/11		
❑ AM	Adrian Murrell/29	100.00	45.00
❑ AS	Antowain Smith/23	100.00	45.00
❑ BH	Brock Huard/5		
❑ CC	Cris Carter/80	60.00	27.00
❑ CM	Cade McNown/8		
❑ DB	David Boston/89	70.00	32.00
❑ DC	Daunte Culpepper/12		
❑ DF	Dan Fouts/14		
❑ DL	Dorsey Levens/25	120.00	55.00
❑ FT	Fran Tarkenton/10		
❑ GH	Garrison Hearst/20	60.00	27.00
❑ JK	Jon Kitna/7		
❑ JM	Joe Montana/16		
❑ JN	Joe Namath/12		
❑ MC	Donovan McNabb/5		
❑ OZ	Ozzie Newsome/82	30.00	13.50
❑ PW	Paul Warfield/42	80.00	36.00
❑ RG	Roger Staubach/12		
❑ RM	Randy Moss/84	250.00	110.00
❑ RS	Rod Smith/80	30.00	13.50
❑ RW	Ricky Williams/34	600.00	275.00
❑ SK	Shaun King/10		
❑ SL	Steve Largent/80	80.00	36.00
❑ TC	Tim Couch/2		
❑ TD	Terrell Davis/30	250.00	110.00
❑ TH	Torry Holt/88	80.00	36.00
❑ TO	Terrell Owens/81	60.00	27.00
❑ WC	Wayne Chrebet/80	30.00	13.50
❑ WP	Walter Payton/34	1000.00	450.00

1999 Upper Deck Retro Legends of the Fall

	MINT	NRMT
COMPLETE SET (30)	40.00	18.00
COMMON CARD (L1-L30)	.75	.35
SEMISTARS	1.25	.55

STATED ODDS 1:11
*SILVER CARDS: 7X TO 20X HI COL.
SILVER PRINT RUN 75 SER.#'d SETS

		MINT	NRMT
❑ L1	Jake Plummer	2.50	1.10
❑ L2	Corey Dillon	2.50	1.10
❑ L3	Curtis Martin	2.50	1.10
❑ L4	Vinny Testaverde	.75	.35
❑ L5	Brett Favre	5.00	2.20
❑ L6	Randy Moss	4.00	1.80
❑ L7	John Elway	5.00	2.20
❑ L8	Jerry Rice	3.00	1.35
❑ L9	Troy Aikman	3.00	1.35
❑ L10	Ricky Watters	.75	.35
❑ L11	Keyshawn Johnson	2.50	1.10
❑ L12	Mark Brunell	2.00	.90
❑ L13	Dorsey Levens	2.50	1.10
❑ L14	Steve McNair	2.50	1.10
❑ L15	Emmitt Smith	3.00	1.35
❑ L16	Marshall Faulk	2.50	1.10
❑ L17	Priest Holmes	2.50	1.10
❑ L18	Steve Young	2.00	.90
❑ L19	Skip Hicks	2.50	1.10
❑ L20	Eddie George	1.50	.70
❑ L21	Garrison Hearst	.75	.35
❑ L22	Drew Bledsoe	3.00	1.35
❑ L23	Warrick Dunn	2.50	1.10
❑ L24	Eric Moulds	2.50	1.10
❑ L25	Joey Galloway	2.50	1.10
❑ L26	Tim Brown	2.50	1.10
❑ L27	Chris Chandler	.75	.35
❑ L28	Peyton Manning	4.00	1.80
❑ L29	Antonio Freeman	2.50	1.10
❑ L30	Deion Sanders	2.50	1.10

1999 Upper Deck Retro Lunchboxes

	MINT	NRMT
COMPLETE SET (16)	250.00	110.00
COMMON CARD (1-16)	10.00	4.50

ONE DUAL PLAYER BOX PER CASE

		MINT	NRMT
❑ 1	Joe Montana	25.00	11.00
❑ 2	Ricky Williams	20.00	9.00
❑ 3	Randy Moss	15.00	6.75
❑ 4	Barry Sanders	15.00	6.75
❑ 5	John Elway	15.00	6.75
❑ 6	Terrell Davis	10.00	4.50
❑ 7	Dan Marino	15.00	6.75
❑ 8	Joe Namath	15.00	6.75
❑ 9	Joe Montana John Elway	25.00	11.00
❑ 10	Joe Montana Dan Marino	25.00	11.00
❑ 11	John Elway Dan Marino	25.00	11.00
❑ 12	Joe Montana Joe Namath	25.00	11.00
❑ 13	Ricky Williams Tim Couch	20.00	9.00
❑ 14	Joe Namath Dan Marino	25.00	11.00
❑ 15	Tim Couch Dan Marino	25.00	11.00
❑ 16	Barry Sanders Terrell Davis	20.00	9.00

1999 Upper Deck Retro Old School/New School

	MINT	NRMT
COMPLETE SET (30)	200.00	90.00
COMMON CARD (ON1-ON30)	2.50	1.10
SEMISTARS..............................	4.00	1.80

STATED PRINT RUN 1000 SER.#'d SETS
*LEVEL 2 CARDS: 3X TO 8X HI COL.
LEVEL 2 PRINT RUN 50 SER.#'d SETS

		MINT	NRMT
❑ ON1	Terrell Davis............. / Ricky Williams	12.00	5.50
❑ ON2	Joe Montana .... / Jake Plummer	20.00	9.00
❑ ON3	Cris Carter .... / Randy Moss	12.00	5.50
❑ ON4	Randall Cunningham .. / Daunte Culpepper	6.00	2.70
❑ ON5	Brett Favre .... / Jon Kitna	15.00	6.75
❑ ON6	Emmitt Smith .... / Fred Taylor	10.00	4.50
❑ ON7	Mark Brunell............... / Brock Huard	6.00	2.70
❑ ON8	John Elway .... / Peyton Manning	15.00	6.75
❑ ON9	Steve Young .... / Cade McNown	8.00	3.60
❑ ON10	Don Maynard .... / Kevin Johnson	4.00	1.80
❑ ON11	Dan Marino .... / Tim Couch	20.00	9.00
❑ ON12	Jerry Rice............... / Terrell Owens	10.00	4.50
❑ ON13	Marshall Faulk .... / Edgerrin James	20.00	9.00
❑ ON14	Dan Fouts .... / Akili Smith	5.00	2.20
❑ ON15	Barry Sanders .... / Jamal Anderson	15.00	6.75
❑ ON16	Terry Glenn .... / David Boston	4.00	1.80
❑ ON17	Deion Sanders......... / Champ Bailey	4.00	1.80
❑ ON18	Andre Reed .... / Eric Moulds	2.50	1.10
❑ ON19	Junior Seau .... / Chris Claiborne	2.50	1.10
❑ ON20	Steve Largent .... / Joey Galloway	4.00	1.80
❑ ON21	Kordell Stewart .... / Shaun King	4.00	1.80
❑ ON22	Ricky Watters........... / Kevin Faulk	4.00	1.80
❑ ON23	Thurman Thomas .... / Warrick Dunn	4.00	1.80
❑ ON24	Tim Brown .... / Troy Edwards	4.00	1.80
❑ ON25	Jerome Bettis........... / Cecil Collins	4.00	1.80
❑ ON26	Isaac Bruce .... / Torry Holt	6.00	2.70
❑ ON27	Fran Tarkenton .... / Donovan McNabb	8.00	3.60
❑ ON28	Warren Moon........... / Charlie Batch	6.00	2.70
❑ ON29	Herman Moore.......... / D'Wayne Bates	4.00	1.80
❑ ON30	Roger Staubach...... / Troy Aikman	12.00	5.50

1999 Upper Deck Retro Smashmouth

	MINT	NRMT
COMPLETE SET (15)	20.00	9.00
COMMON CARD (S1-S15)	.75	.35
SEMISTARS............................	1.25	.55

STATED ODDS 1:8 ....
*LEVEL 2 CARDS: 5X TO 12X HI COL.
LEVEL 2 PRINT RUN 100 SER.#'d SETS

		MINT	NRMT
❑ S3	John Elway	5.00	2.20
❑ S4	Brock Huard	1.50	.70
❑ S5	Daunte Culpepper.........	4.00	1.80
❑ S6	Charlie Batch	1.50	.70
❑ S7	Steve McNair	2.50	1.10
❑ S8	Corey Dillon	2.50	1.10
❑ S9	Natrone Means	.75	.35
❑ S10	Randall Cunningham ..	2.50	1.10
❑ S11	Drew Bledsoe	2.00	.90
❑ S12	Jerome Bettis	2.50	1.10
❑ S13	Antowain Smith...........	2.50	1.10
❑ S14	Steve Young	2.00	.90
❑ S15	Eddie George	1.50	.70

1999 Upper Deck Retro Throwback Attack

	MINT	NRMT
COMPLETE SET (15)	25.00	11.00
COMMON CARD (T1-T15)........	1.00	.45

STATED ODDS 1:5 ....
*GOLD CARDS: 2X TO 5X HI COL.
GOLD PRINT RUN 500 SER.#'d SETS

		MINT	NRMT
❑ T3	Troy Aikman	2.50	1.10
❑ T4	Eric Moulds	1.50	.70
❑ T5	Tim Couch.....................	4.00	1.80
❑ T6	Terrell Owens	1.50	.70
❑ T7	Champ Bailey	1.50	.70
❑ T8	Kordell Stewart	1.50	.70
❑ T9	Mark Brunell	1.50	.70
❑ T10	Curtis Martin	1.50	.70
❑ T11	Torry Holt	2.00	.90
❑ T12	David Boston...............	1.25	.55
❑ T13	Doug Flutie	1.25	.55
❑ T14	Edgerrin James...........	6.00	2.70
❑ T15	Akili Smith	1.50	.70

1999 Upper Deck Victory

	MINT	NRMT
COMPLETE SET (440)	60.00	27.00
COMP. SET w/o SP's (380)	10.00	4.50
COMMON CARD (1-380)............	.10	.05
SEMISTARS............................	.20	.09
UNLISTED STARS....................	.40	.18
COMMON ROOKIE (381-440)....	.50	.23
ROOKIE SEMISTARS	1.00	.45
ROOKIE UNL.STARS	1.50	.70

ROOKIE SUBSET CARDS ONE PER PACK

		MINT	NRMT
❑ 1	Checklist Card	.10	.05
❑ 2	Jake Plummer	.75	.35
❑ 3	Adrian Murrell	.20	.09
❑ 4	Michael Pittman..................	.10	.05
❑ 5	Frank Sanders....................	.20	.09
❑ 6	Andre Wadsworth	.10	.05
❑ 7	Rob Moore	.20	.09
❑ 8	Simeon Rice	.10	.05
❑ 9	Kwamie Lassiter RC	.10	.05
❑ 10	Mario Bates	.10	.05
❑ 11	Checklist Card..................	.10	.05
❑ 12	Jamal Anderson	.40	.18
❑ 13	Chris Chandler	.20	.09
❑ 14	Chuck Smith	.10	.05
❑ 15	Terance Mathis	.20	.09
❑ 16	Tim Dwight	.40	.18
❑ 17	Ray Buchanan..................	.10	.05
❑ 18	O.J. Santiago	.10	.05
❑ 19	Lester Archambeau.........	.10	.05
❑ 20	Checklist Card..................	.10	.05
❑ 21	Tony Banks	.20	.09
❑ 22	Priest Holmes	.40	.18
❑ 23	Michael Jackson	.10	.05
❑ 24	Jermaine Lewis	.20	.09
❑ 25	Michael McCrary	.10	.05
❑ 26	Rod Woodson	.20	.09
❑ 27	Checklist Card..................	.10	.05
❑ 28	Rob Johnson	.20	.09
❑ 29	Antowain Smith	.40	.18
❑ 30	Thurman Thomas	.20	.09
❑ 31	Doug Flutie	.50	.23
❑ 32	Eric Moulds	.40	.18
❑ 33	Bruce Smith......................	.20	.09
❑ 34	Andre Reed	.20	.09
❑ 35	Phil Hansen.......................	.10	.05
❑ 36	Checklist Card..................	.10	.05
❑ 37	Fred Lane	.20	.09
❑ 38	Tim Biakabutuka	.20	.09
❑ 39	Rae Carruth.......................	.20	.09
❑ 40	Wesley Walls.....................	.20	.09
❑ 41	Steve Beuerlein................	.10	.05
❑ 42	Muhsin Muhammad..........	.20	.09
❑ 43	Kevin Greene	.10	.05
❑ 44	Checklist Card..................	.10	.05
❑ 45	Erik Kramer	.10	.05
❑ 46	Edgar Bennett	.10	.05
❑ 47	Curtis Conway..................	.20	.09
❑ 48	Curtis Enis.........................	.40	.18
❑ 49	Bobby Engram	.20	.09
❑ 50	Alonzo Mayes	.10	.05
❑ 51	Tony Parrish	.10	.05
❑ 52	Glyn Milburn	.10	.05
❑ 53	Checklist Card..................	.10	.05
❑ 54	Corey Dillon......................	.40	.18
❑ 55	Jeff Blake	.20	.09
❑ 56	Carl Pickens	.20	.09
❑ 57	Darnay Scott	.10	.05
❑ 58	Tony McGee	.10	.05
❑ 59	Ki-Jana Carter...................	.10	.05
❑ 60	Takeo Spikes	.10	.05
❑ 61	Checklist Card..................	.10	.05
❑ 62	Ty Detmer	.20	.09
❑ 63	Terry Kirby.........................	.10	.05
❑ 64	Derrick Alexander DT	.10	.05
❑ 65	Leslie Shepherd	.10	.05
❑ 66	Marquez Pope...................	.10	.05
❑ 67	Antonio Langham	.10	.05
❑ 68	Marc Edwards...................	.10	.05
❑ 69	Checklist Card..................	.10	.05
❑ 70	Troy Aikman	1.00	.45
❑ 71	Emmitt Smith..................	1.00	.45

❑	72 Deion Sanders	.40	.18
❑	73 Rocket Ismail	.20	.09
❑	74 Michael Irvin	.20	.09
❑	75 Chris Warren	.10	.05
❑	76 Greg Ellis	.10	.05
❑	77 Kavika Pittman	.10	.05
❑	78 David LaFleur	.10	.05
❑	79 Checklist Card	.10	.05
❑	80 John Elway	1.50	.70
❑	81 Terrell Davis	1.00	.45
❑	82 Rod Smith	.20	.09
❑	83 Shannon Sharpe	.20	.09
❑	84 Ed McCaffrey	.20	.09
❑	85 John Mobley	.10	.05
❑	86 Bill Romanowski	.10	.05
❑	87 Jason Elam	.10	.05
❑	88 Howard Griffith	.10	.05
❑	89 Checklist Card	.10	.05
❑	90 Barry Sanders	1.50	.70
❑	91 Johnnie Morton	.20	.09
❑	92 Herman Moore	.40	.18
❑	93 Charlie Batch	.75	.35
❑	94 Germane Crowell	.20	.09
❑	95 Robert Porcher	.10	.05
❑	96 Stephen Boyd	.10	.05
❑	97 Checklist Card	.10	.05
❑	98 Brett Favre	1.50	.70
❑	99 Antonio Freeman	.40	.18
❑	100 Dorsey Levens	.40	.18
❑	101 Mark Chmura	.10	.05
❑	102 Vonnie Holliday	.10	.05
❑	103 Bill Schroeder	.40	.18
❑	104 LeRoy Butler	.10	.05
❑	105 William Henderson	.10	.05
❑	106 Checklist Card	.10	.05
❑	107 Peyton Manning	1.50	.70
❑	108 Marvin Harrison	.40	.18
❑	109 Ken Dilger	.10	.05
❑	110 Jerome Pathon	.10	.05
❑	111 E.G. Green	.10	.05
❑	112 Ellis Johnson	.10	.05
❑	113 Jeff Burris	.10	.05
❑	114 Checklist Card	.10	.05
❑	115 Mark Brunell	.60	.25
❑	116 Jimmy Smith	.20	.09
❑	117 Keenan McCardell	.20	.09
❑	118 Fred Taylor	1.00	.45
❑	119 James Stewart	.20	.09
❑	120 Dave Thomas	.10	.05
❑	121 Kyle Brady	.10	.05
❑	122 Bryce Paup	.10	.05
❑	123 Checklist Card	.10	.05
❑	124 Elvis Grbac	.20	.09
❑	125 Andre Rison	.20	.09
❑	126 Derrick Alexander WR	.20	.09
❑	127 Tony Gonzalez	.20	.09
❑	128 Donnell Bennett	.10	.05
❑	129 Derrick Thomas	.20	.09
❑	130 Tamarick Vanover	.10	.05
❑	131 Donnie Edwards	.10	.05
❑	132 Checklist Card	.10	.05
❑	133 Dan Marino	1.50	.70
❑	134 Karim Abdul-Jabbar	.20	.09
❑	135 Zach Thomas	.20	.09
❑	136 O.J. McDuffie	.20	.09
❑	137 John Avery	.20	.09
❑	138 Sam Madison	.10	.05
❑	139 Terrell Buckley	.10	.05
❑	140 Jason Taylor	.10	.05
❑	141 Oronde Gadsden	.10	.05
❑	142 Checklist Card	.10	.05
❑	143 Randall Cunningham	.40	.18
❑	144 Cris Carter	.40	.18
❑	145 Robert Smith	.40	.18
❑	146 Randy Moss	1.50	.70
❑	147 Jake Reed	.20	.09
❑	148 Leroy Hoard	.10	.05
❑	149 Matthew Hatchette	.10	.05
❑	150 John Randle	.20	.09
❑	151 Gary Anderson	.10	.05
❑	152 Checklist Card	.10	.05
❑	153 Drew Bledsoe	.60	.25
❑	154 Terry Glenn	.40	.18
❑	155 Ben Coates	.20	.09
❑	156 Ty Law	.10	.05
❑	157 Tony Simmons	.10	.05
❑	158 Ted Johnson	.10	.05
❑	159 Willie McGinest	.10	.05
❑	160 Tony Carter	.10	.05
❑	161 Shawn Jefferson	.10	.05
❑	162 Checklist Card	.10	.05
❑	163 Danny Wuerffel	.10	.05
❑	164 Lamar Smith	.10	.05
❑	165 Keith Poole	.10	.05
❑	166 Cameron Cleeland	.10	.05
❑	167 Joe Johnson	.10	.05
❑	168 Andre Hastings	.10	.05
❑	169 La'Roi Glover	.10	.05
❑	170 Aaron Craver	.10	.05
❑	171 Checklist Card	.10	.05
❑	172 Kent Graham	.10	.05
❑	173 Gary Brown	.10	.05
❑	174 Amani Toomer	.10	.05
❑	175 Tiki Barber	.10	.05
❑	176 Ike Hilliard	.10	.05
❑	177 Jason Sehorn	.10	.05
❑	178 Michael Strahan	.10	.05
❑	179 Charles Way	.10	.05
❑	180 Checklist Card	.10	.05
❑	181 Vinny Testaverde	.20	.09
❑	182 Curtis Martin	.40	.18
❑	183 Keyshawn Johnson	.40	.18
❑	184 Wayne Chrebet	.20	.09
❑	185 Mo Lewis	.10	.05
❑	186 Steve Atwater	.10	.05
❑	187 Leon Johnson	.10	.05
❑	188 Bryan Cox	.10	.05
❑	189 Checklist Card	.10	.05
❑	190 Rich Gannon	.20	.09
❑	191 Napoleon Kaufman	.40	.18
❑	192 Tim Brown	.40	.18
❑	193 Darrell Russell	.10	.05
❑	194 Rickey Dudley	.10	.05
❑	195 Charles Woodson	.40	.18
❑	196 Harvey Williams	.10	.05
❑	197 James Jett	.20	.09
❑	198 Checklist Card	.10	.05
❑	199 Koy Detmer	.10	.05
❑	200 Duce Staley	.40	.18
❑	201 Bobby Taylor	.10	.05
❑	202 Doug Pederson	.10	.05
❑	203 Karl Hankton	.10	.05
❑	204 Charles Johnson	.10	.05
❑	205 Kevin Turner	.10	.05
❑	206 Hugh Douglas	.10	.05
❑	207 Checklist Card	.10	.05
❑	208 Kordell Stewart	.40	.18
❑	209 Jerome Bettis	.40	.18
❑	210 Hines Ward	.10	.05
❑	211 Courtney Hawkins	.10	.05
❑	212 Will Blackwell	.10	.05
❑	213 Richard Huntley	.20	.09
❑	214 Levon Kirkland	.10	.05
❑	215 Jason Gildon	.10	.05
❑	216 Checklist Card	.10	.05
❑	217 Trent Green	.20	.09
❑	218 Isaac Bruce	.40	.18
❑	219 Az-Zahir Hakim	.10	.05
❑	220 Amp Lee	.10	.05
❑	221 Robert Holcombe	.20	.09
❑	222 Ricky Proehl	.10	.05
❑	223 Kevin Carter	.10	.05
❑	224 Marshall Faulk	.40	.18
❑	225 Checklist Card	.10	.05
❑	226 Ryan Leaf	.40	.18
❑	227 Natrone Means	.20	.09
❑	228 Jim Harbaugh	.20	.09
❑	229 Junior Seau	.20	.09
❑	230 Charlie Jones	.10	.05
❑	231 Rodney Harrison	.10	.05
❑	232 Terrell Fletcher	.10	.05
❑	233 Tremayne Stephens	.10	.05
❑	234 Checklist Card	.10	.05
❑	235 Steve Young	.60	.25
❑	236 Jerry Rice	1.00	.45
❑	237 Garrison Hearst	.20	.09
❑	238 Terrell Owens	.40	.18
❑	239 J.J. Stokes	.20	.09
❑	240 Bryant Young	.10	.05
❑	241 Tim McDonald	.10	.05
❑	242 Merton Hanks	.10	.05
❑	243 Travis Jervey	.10	.05
❑	244 Checklist Card	.10	.05
❑	245 Ricky Watters	.20	.09
❑	246 Joey Galloway	.40	.18
❑	247 Jon Kitna	.50	.23
❑	248 Ahman Green	.20	.09
❑	249 Mike Pritchard	.10	.05
❑	250 Chad Brown	.10	.05
❑	251 Christian Fauria	.10	.05
❑	252 Michael Sinclair	.10	.05
❑	253 Checklist Card	.10	.05
❑	254 Warrick Dunn	.40	.18
❑	255 Trent Dilfer	.20	.09
❑	256 Mike Alstott	.40	.18
❑	257 Reidel Anthony	.20	.09
❑	258 Bert Emanuel	.20	.09
❑	259 Jacquez Green	.20	.09
❑	260 Hardy Nickerson	.10	.05
❑	261 Derrick Brooks	.10	.05
❑	262 Dave Moore	.10	.05
❑	263 Checklist Card	.10	.05
❑	264 Steve McNair	.40	.18
❑	265 Eddie George	.50	.23
❑	266 Yancey Thigpen	.10	.05
❑	267 Frank Wycheck	.10	.05
❑	268 Kevin Dyson	.20	.09
❑	269 Jackie Harris	.10	.05
❑	270 Blaine Bishop	.10	.05
❑	271 Willie Davis	.10	.05
❑	272 Checklist Card	.10	.05
❑	273 Skip Hicks	.40	.18
❑	274 Michael Westbrook	.20	.09
❑	275 Stephen Alexander	.10	.05
❑	276 Dana Stubblefield	.10	.05
❑	277 Brad Johnson	.40	.18
❑	278 Brian Mitchell	.10	.05
❑	279 Dan Wilkinson	.10	.05
❑	280 Stephen Davis	.40	.18
❑	281 John Elway AV	.60	.25
❑	282 Dan Marino AV	.60	.25
❑	283 Troy Aikman AV	.40	.18
❑	284 Vinny Testaverde AV	.20	.09
❑	285 Corey Dillon AV	.40	.18
❑	286 Steve Young AV	.20	.09
❑	287 Randy Moss AV	.60	.25
❑	288 Drew Bledsoe AV	.20	.09
❑	289 Jerome Bettis AV	.40	.18
❑	290 Antonio Freeman AV	.40	.18
❑	291 Fred Taylor AV	.40	.18
❑	292 Doug Flutie AV	.40	.18
❑	293 Jerry Rice AV	.40	.18
❑	294 Peyton Manning AV	.60	.25
❑	295 Brett Favre AV	.60	.25
❑	296 Barry Sanders AV	.60	.25
❑	297 Keyshawn Johnson AV	.40	.18
❑	298 Mark Brunell AV	.20	.09
❑	299 Jamal Anderson AV	.40	.18
❑	300 Terrell Davis AV	.40	.18
❑	301 Randall Cunningham AV	.40	.18
❑	302 Kordell Stewart AV	.40	.18
❑	303 Warrick Dunn AV	.40	.18
❑	304 Jake Plummer AV	.20	.09
❑	305 Junior Seau AV	.20	.09
❑	306 Antowain Smith AV	.40	.18
❑	307 Charlie Batch AV	.20	.09
❑	308 Eddie George AV	.20	.09
❑	309 Michael Irvin AV	.20	.09
❑	310 Joey Galloway AV	.40	.18
❑	311 Randall Cunningham SL	.40	.18
❑	312 Vinny Testaverde SL	.20	.09
❑	313 Steve Young SL	.20	.09
❑	314 Chris Chandler SL	.20	.09
❑	315 John Elway SL	.60	.25
❑	316 Steve Young SL	.20	.09
❑	317 Randall Cunningham SL	.40	.18
❑	318 Brett Favre SL	.60	.25
❑	319 Vinny Testaverde SL	.20	.09
❑	320 Peyton Manning SL	.50	.23
❑	321 Terrell Davis SL	.40	.18
❑	322 Jamal Anderson SL	.40	.18
❑	323 Garrison Hearst SL	.20	.09
❑	324 Barry Sanders SL	.60	.25
❑	325 Emmitt Smith SL	.40	.18
❑	326 Terrell Davis SL	.40	.18
❑	327 Fred Taylor SL	.40	.18
❑	328 Jamal Anderson SL	.40	.18
❑	329 Emmitt Smith SL	.40	.18

- ❑ 330 Ricky Watters SL .20 .09
- ❑ 331 O.J. McDuffie SL .20 .09
- ❑ 332 Frank Sanders SL .20 .09
- ❑ 333 Rod Smith SL .20 .09
- ❑ 334 Marshall Faulk SL .40 .18
- ❑ 335 Antonio Freeman SL .40 .18
- ❑ 336 Randy Moss SL .60 .25
- ❑ 337 Antonio Freeman SL .40 .18
- ❑ 338 Terrell Owens SL .40 .18
- ❑ 339 Cris Carter SL .40 .18
- ❑ 340 Terance Mathis SL .20 .09
- ❑ 341 Jake Plummer VP .20 .09
- ❑ 342 Steve McNair VP .40 .18
- ❑ 343 Randy Moss VP .60 .25
- ❑ 344 Peyton Manning VP .60 .25
- ❑ 345 Mark Brunell VP .20 .09
- ❑ 346 Terrell Owens VP .40 .18
- ❑ 347 Antowain Smith VP .40 .18
- ❑ 348 Jerry Rice VP .40 .18
- ❑ 349 Troy Aikman VP .40 .18
- ❑ 350 Fred Taylor VP .40 .18
- ❑ 351 Charlie Batch VP .20 .09
- ❑ 352 Dan Marino VP .60 .25
- ❑ 353 Eddie George VP .20 .09
- ❑ 354 Drew Bledsoe VP .20 .09
- ❑ 355 Kordell Stewart VP .40 .18
- ❑ 356 Doug Flutie VP .40 .18
- ❑ 357 Deion Sanders VP .40 .18
- ❑ 358 Keyshawn Johnson VP .40 .18
- ❑ 359 Jerome Bettis VP .40 .18
- ❑ 360 Warrick Dunn VP .40 .18
- ❑ 361 John Elway RF .60 .25
- ❑ 362 Dan Marino RF .60 .25
- ❑ 363 Brett Favre RF .60 .25
- ❑ 364 Andre Rison RF .20 .09
- ❑ 365 Rod Woodson RF .20 .09
- ❑ 366 Jerry Rice RF .40 .18
- ❑ 367 Barry Sanders RF .60 .25
- ❑ 368 Thurman Thomas RF .20 .09
- ❑ 369 Troy Aikman RF .40 .18
- ❑ 370 Ricky Watters RF .20 .09
- ❑ 371 Jerome Bettis RF .40 .18
- ❑ 372 Reggie White RF .10 .05
- ❑ 373 Junior Seau RF .20 .09
- ❑ 374 Deion Sanders RF .40 .18
- ❑ 375 Chris Chandler RF .20 .09
- ❑ 376 Curtis Martin RF .40 .18
- ❑ 377 Kordell Stewart RF .40 .18
- ❑ 378 Mark Brunell RF .20 .09
- ❑ 379 Cris Carter RF .40 .18
- ❑ 380 Emmitt Smith RF .40 .18
- ❑ 381 Tim Couch RC 8.00 3.60
- ❑ 382 Donovan McNabb RC 5.00 2.20
- ❑ 383 Akili Smith RC 3.00 1.35
- ❑ 384 Edgerrin James RC 12.00 5.50
- ❑ 385 Ricky Williams RC 8.00 3.60
- ❑ 386 Torry Holt RC 4.00 1.80
- ❑ 387 Champ Bailey RC 2.00 .90
- ❑ 388 David Boston RC 2.50 1.10
- ❑ 389 Chris Claiborne RC 1.00 .45
- ❑ 390 Chris McAlister RC 1.00 .45
- ❑ 391 Daunte Culpepper RC 5.00 2.20
- ❑ 392 Cade McNown RC 5.00 2.20
- ❑ 393 Troy Edwards RC 2.50 1.10
- ❑ 394 John Tait RC .50 .23
- ❑ 395 Anthony McFarland RC 1.50 .70
- ❑ 396 Jevon Kearse RC 3.00 1.35
- ❑ 397 Damien Woody RC .50 .23
- ❑ 398 Matt Stinchcomb RC .50 .23
- ❑ 399 Luke Petitgout RC .50 .23
- ❑ 400 Ebenezer Ekuban RC 1.00 .45
- ❑ 401 L.J. Shelton RC .50 .23
- ❑ 402 Daylon McCutcheon RC .50 .23
- ❑ 403 Antoine Winfield RC 1.00 .45
- ❑ 404 Scott Covington RC 1.50 .70
- ❑ 405 Antuan Edwards RC .50 .23
- ❑ 406 Fernando Bryant RC 1.00 .45
- ❑ 407 Aaron Gibson RC .50 .23
- ❑ 408 Andy Katzenmoyer RC 1.50 .70
- ❑ 409 Dimitrius Underwood RC 1.00 .45
- ❑ 410 Patrick Kerney RC 1.00 .45
- ❑ 411 Al Wilson RC 1.50 .70
- ❑ 412 Kevin Johnson RC 3.00 1.35
- ❑ 413 Joel Makovicka RC 1.50 .70
- ❑ 414 Reginald Kelly RC .50 .23
- ❑ 415 Jeff Paulk RC 1.00 .45
- ❑ 416 Brandon Stokley RC 1.00 .45
- ❑ 417 Peerless Price RC 2.50 1.10
- ❑ 418 D'Wayne Bates RC 1.00 .45
- ❑ 419 Travis McGriff RC 1.50 .70
- ❑ 420 Sedrick Irvin RC 1.50 .70
- ❑ 421 Aaron Brooks RC 1.50 .70
- ❑ 422 Mike Cloud RC 1.50 .70
- ❑ 423 Joe Montgomery RC 1.50 .70
- ❑ 424 Shaun King RC 4.00 1.80
- ❑ 425 Dameane Douglas RC 1.50 .70
- ❑ 426 Joe Germaine RC 1.50 .70
- ❑ 427 James Johnson RC 2.00 .90
- ❑ 428 Michael Bishop RC 2.00 .90
- ❑ 429 Karsten Bailey RC 1.00 .45
- ❑ 430 Craig Yeast RC 1.00 .45
- ❑ 431 Jim Kleinsasser RC 1.50 .70
- ❑ 432 Martin Gramatica RC .50 .23
- ❑ 433 Jermaine Fazande RC 1.00 .45
- ❑ 434 Dre'Bly RC 1.00 .45
- ❑ 435 Brock Huard RC 2.00 .90
- ❑ 436 Rob Konrad RC 1.50 .70
- ❑ 437 Tony Bryant RC 1.00 .45
- ❑ 438 Sean Bennett RC 1.50 .70
- ❑ 439 Kevin Faulk RC 2.00 .90
- ❑ 440 Amos Zereoue RC 1.50 .70

Acknowledgments

A great deal of diligence, hard work, and dedicated effort went into this First Edition. The high standards to which we hold ourselves, however, could not have been met without the expert input and generous amount of time contributed by many people. Our sincere thanks are extended to each and every one of you.

Each year we refine the process of developing the most accurate and up-to-date information for this book. Thanks again to all of the contributors nationwide (listed below) as well as our staff here in Dallas.

Those who have worked closely with us on this and many other books have again proven themselves invaluable — Action Sports Cards, Mike Aronstein, Jerry Bell, Bubba Bennett, Chuck Bennett (Clubhouse), Mike Blaisdell, Bill Bossert (Mid-Atlantic Sports Cards), John Bradley (JOGO), Ralph Ciarlo, Mike Caffey, Don Chubey, Joe Colabella, Alan Custer, Flickball, Robert Der, Bill and Diane Dodge, Rick Donohoo, John Douglas, John Durkos, Fleer/SkyBox (Rich Bradley), Gervise Ford, Steve Freedman, Larry and Jeff Fritsch, Mike Gallella, Steven Galletta, Dick Gilkeson, Steve Gold (AU Sports), Mike and Howard Gordon, George Grauer, Jerry and Etta Hersh, Mike Hersh, Gary Hlady, Ed Kabala, Wayne Kleman, Lew Lipset, Michael McDonald, Pat Mills, Michael Moretto, Jeff Morris (Collector's Edge) Mike Mosier, Playoff, NFL Properties (Bill Barron), Don Niemi, Lawrence Nyeste, Mike O'Brien, Richard Ochoa, Oldies and Goodies (Nigel Spill), Pacific Trading Cards (Mike Cramer and Mike Monson), Michael Perrotta, Jack Pollard, Gavin Riley, Greg Rosen, Rotman Productions, John Rumierz, San Diego Sport Collectibles, Barry Sanders, Kevin Savage, Mike Schechter (MSA), Rick Smith, Gerry Sobie, John Spalding, Pat Quinn, Murvin Sterling (Reno Sports Cards), Richard Tattoli, Paul S. Taylor, Lee Temanson, Topps (Clay Luraschi), Upper Deck (Justin Kanoya), U-Trading Cards (Mike Livingston), Rob Veres (Burbank Sportscards), Brian Wentz, Dale Wesolewski, Bill Wesslund, Kit Young and Bob Ivanjack (Kit Young Cards), Robert Zanze, Steve Zeller, Dean Zindler, and Tim Zwick.

Many people have provided checklist verifications, errata, and/or background information. At the risk of inadvertently overlooking or omitting these many contributors, we would like to individually thank A & J Cards, Jerry Adamic, Aliso Hills Stamp and Coin, Rich Altman, Neil Armstrong (World Series Cards), Tom Barborich, Red Barnes, Bob Bawiel, William E. Baxendale, Dean Bedell, Patrick Benes, Carl Berg, Eric Berger, Kevin Bergson, Skip Bertman, Beulah Sports (Jeff Blatt), Brian L. Bigelow, David Bitar, Virgil Burns, Danny Cariseo, Dale Carlson, Bud Carter, Sally Carves, Dwight Chapin, Howard Churchill, Ralph H. Ciarlo, Orr Cihlar, Craig Coddling, Jon Cohen, Matt Collett, Taylor Crane, Jim Curie, Paul Czuchna, Samuel Davis, Tony Wayne Davis,Cliff Dolgins, Joseph Drelich, E and R Galleries, Ed Emmitt, The End Zone, Darrell Ereth, Doak Ewing, Rodney Faciane, Bob Farmer, Terry Faulkner, Fleischman and Walsh, Craig Frank, Mark Franke, Richard Freiburghouse, Brian Froehlich, Gallagher Archives, Tony Galovich, Tom Giacchino, Michael R. Gionet, David Giove, Todd Goldenberg, Jeff Goldstein, Gregg Gornes, Joseph Griffin, Robert G. Gross, Hall's Nostalgia, Steve Hart, Michael Hattley, Rod Heffern, Kevin Heffner, Dennis Heitland, Clay Hill, Russ Hoover, Nelson Hu, Don Hurry, Jeff Issler, Bob Ivanjack, Robert R. Jackson, Dan Jaskula, Terry Johnson, Craig Jones, Stewart Jones, Larry Jordon, Chuck Juliana, Loyd Jungling, Jay and Mary Kasper, Frank Katen, Jack Kemps (Triple Play), Rick Keplinger, John Kilian, Ron Klassnik, Don Knutsen, Bob and Bryan Kornfield, Terry Kreider, George Kruk, Thomas Kunnecke, Dan Lavin, Walter Ledzki, Marc Lefkowitz (Baseball Card Baron), Tom Leon (Unisource Collectibles), Irv Lerner, Ed Lim, Frank Lopez, Neil Lopez, Frank Lucito, Kevin

Lynch, Bud Lyle, Jim Macie, Gary Madrack, Paul Marchant, Adam Martin, Alex McCollum, Bob McDonald, Steve McHenry, Carlos Medina, Fernando Mercado, Chris Merrill, Blake Meyer, Lee Milazzo, Dick Millerd, Ron Moermond, Morgan Moore, John Morales, Brian Morris, Rusty Morse, Dick Mueller, Bob Nappe, Roger Neufeldt, Raymond Ng, John O'Hara, Glenn Olsen, Mike Orth, Andrew Pak, Clay Pasternack, Paul and Judy's, John Peavy, Mark Perna, Steve Peters, Ira Petsrillo, Tom Pfirrmann, Chris Pomerleau, Jeff Porter, Jeff Prillaman, Jonathan Pullano, Loran Pulver, Phil Regli, Tom Reid, Owen Ricker, Evelyn Roberts, Jim Roberts, Mark Rose, Chip Rosenberg, Blake and Sheldon Rudman, George Rusnak, Terry Ryan, Terry Sack, Joe Sak, Nathan Schank, R.J. Schulhof, Perry Schwartzberg, Patrick W. Scoggin, Dan Scolman, Rick Scruggs, Charlie Seaver, Burns Searfoss, Eric Shillito, Shinder's Cards, Bob Singer, John Smith, Keith Smith, Carl Specht, Don Spagnolo, Sportcards Etc., Vic Stanley, Bill Steinberg, Cary Stephenson, Dan Stickney, Jack Stowe, Del Stracke, Richard Strobino, Kevin Struss, Bob Swick, George Tahinos, Jeff Thomas (Koinz and Kardz), D. Tisdale, Bud Tompkins, Greg Tranter, John Tumazos, Eric Valkys, Wayne Varner, Kevin M. VanderKelen, Bill Vizas, Tom Wall, Mike Wasserman, Keith Watson, Mark Watson, Rick Wilson, Jay Wolt (Cavalcade of Sports), Paul Wright, Darryl Yee, Sheraton Yee, and Eugene Zalewski.

Every year we make active solicitations for expert input. We are particularly appreciative of the help (however extensive or cursory) provided for this volume. We receive many inquiries, comments and questions regarding material within this book. In fact, each and every one is read and digested. Time constraints, however, prevent us from personally replying. But keep sharing your knowledge. Even though we cannot respond to each letter, you are making significant contributions to the hobby through your interest and comments.

The effort to continually refine and improve our books also involves a growing number of people and types of expertise on our home team. Our company boasts a substantial Sports Data Publishing team, which strengthens our ability to provide comprehensive analysis of the marketplace.

Our football analysts played a major part in compiling this year's book, traveling thousands of miles during the past year to attend sports card shows and visit card shops around the United States and Canada. The Beckett Football specialists are Jim Churilla, Dan Hitt (Manager of SDP as well as Football Price Guide Editor), David Porter, Bill Sutherland and Joe White.

Dan Hitt's coordination of input as BFCM editor helped immeasurably; Rich Klein as research analyst and primary proofer also added many hours of painstaking work.

The effort was able assisted by the rest of the Price Guide analysts: Wayne Grove, Clint Hall, Denny Parsons, Scott Prusha, Grant Sandground (Senior Price Guide Editor) and Rob Springs (Assistant Manger of Sports Data Publishing). Also contributing to publishing functions were Brad Grmela and Keith Hower.

The price-gathering and analytical talents of this fine group of hobbyists have helped make our Beckett team stronger, while making this guide and its companion monthly Price Guide more widely recognized as the hobby's most reliable and relied-upon source of pricing information.

In addition, Regina McGill contributed many programming improvements to make this process smoother while Gean Paul Figari is responsible for the typesetting and general preparation of this volume.

NOTES

NOTES